Praise for Kenne [barcode: D1043882]

ENGLISH-RUSSIAN
RUSSIAN-ENGLISH
DICTIONARY

"Definitive."—*Washington Post*

"A book that bridges nations."—*Philadelphia Inquirer*

"A notable lexicographic achievement . . . concise and clearly presented. Impressive and beautifully published. I recommend it emphatically to all who have not yet arrived at that unattainable level where one can do without a dictionary."
—Sophia Lubensky, *The Modern Language Journal*

"Impressive. Far outshines its closest analog. For my money, one of the top five nonspecialized bilingual reference aids."
—James F. Shipp,
Chronicle of the American Translators Association

"[Katzner] has performed a great service to the world in compiling the first full-sized Russian-English, English-Russian dictionary ever published in the United States and the first one anywhere based on the American idiom."
—Daryl Frazell, *St. Petersburg Times*

OTHER BOOKS BY KENNETH KATZNER

A Russian Review Text (1962)
The Languages of the World (1975)

ENGLISH-RUSSIAN
RUSSIAN-ENGLISH
DICTIONARY

Revised and Expanded Edition

KENNETH KATZNER

John Wiley & Sons, Inc.

New York • Chichester • Brisbane • Toronto • Singapore

This publication is designed to provide accurate and authoritative information in regard to the subject matter covered. It is sold with the understanding that the publisher is not engaged in rendering professional services. If legal, accounting, medical, psychological, or any other expert assistance is required, the services of a competent professional person should be sought.
ADAPTED FROM A DECLARATION OF PRINCIPLES OF A JOINT COMMITTEE OF THE AMERICAN BAR ASSOCIATION AND PUBLISHERS.

Library of Congress Cataloging-in-Publication Data:

Katzner, Kenneth.
    English-Russian, Russian-English dictionary / Kenneth Katzner. —
Rev. and expanded ed.
        ISBN 0-471-05677-4 (alk. paper). —ISBN 0-471-01707-8 (pbk.)
        1. English language—Dictionaries—Russian.   2. Russian language—
Dictionaries—English.   I. Title.
PG2640.K34   1994
491.73'21—dc20   94-16915

Printed in the United States of America

14 15 16 17 18

Contents

Preface

This is the first full-size English-Russian Russian-English dictionary compiled and published in the United States. It is thus the only one of its size to be based on American, rather than British, English. It was written primarily with the English speaker in mind, although Russian speakers should also find much in it that is useful. It is a single, consistent, and fully integrated volume, with each half a mirror of the other.

All languages are in a constant state of evolution, but nowhere is this more true than in today's Russia, where new political, social, and economic institutions are continually being created as old ones are swept away. As a result, a tremendous number of new words— most of them foreign, and mostly from English—are coming into popular use. This creates a difficult problem for the lexicographer, as it is impossible to say precisely whether or when a certain new word has formally entered the language. With no official authority or source to fall back on, a dictionary's word list thus rests on many arbitrary decisions.

But a bilingual dictionary's major purpose is not to record new words, or to list as many words as possible, but rather to treat as comprehensively as possible the words that are included, especially those with many different meanings. Since each meaning of a word is usually rendered differently in a foreign language, a dictionary must treat each one as a separate translation problem. To distinguish between one meaning of an English word and another, this dictionary always gives a synonym or explanation of each meaning prior to giving the Russian equivalent.

This revised edition represents an expansion of the first edition of the dictionary by more than 10 percent. The greater part of the new material is found in the English-Russian section. It consists not so much of new entries, but rather of more detailed treatment of the already existing entries. Virtually every entry of more than a few lines in the English-Russian section has been revised or expanded in some way. In fact, the longer an entry was in the first edition, the more it has generally been expanded in the second.

The English-Russian section contains about 26,000 words, the Russian-English about 40,000. The entries in the English-Russian section are, on average, considerably longer, containing numerous everyday English phrases and full sentences together with the Russian translation. These have been chosen not simply as examples of usage, but rather because in most cases a word-for-word rendering will not do, and the best Russian rendition is not at all obvious to one who is not a native speaker of Russian.

The revised edition also reflects the vocabulary of the new "post-Soviet" period. Much of the obsolete terminology of the Soviet era has been removed, while new terms reflecting new institutions in the new Russia have been added. The Proper Nouns section lists new countries and new city names, as well as the new republics of the Russian Federation.

While the dictionary is based on American English, British usage and spellings have not been overlooked. Where the British spelling of a word differs from the American, the British spelling is both cross-referenced to the American spelling and listed as an alternate spelling under the American spelling.

The initial planning of this dictionary was done by the late Albert H. More-head, with important contributions from the late Waldemar von Zedtwitz and Salvatore Ramondino. The native Russian speakers who read over the manuscript for accuracy are Sima Ficks, Olga Postnikova, and Tori Loginov.

The typesetting of the revised edition was done by the author, using a Macintosh computer and the Microsoft Word word processing program. Pages were formatted using Quark XPress. The Russian font is a product of Linguist's Software Inc.

KENNETH KATZNER
Washington, D.C.
August 1994

On Using
the Dictionary

ALPHABETIZATION

All main entries are listed in strict alphabetical order. Derivative words may be run in under a main entry only if they immediately follow or precede the main entry word—that is, no other entry occurs alphabetically in between.

The numerous two-word lexical items that occur in English, such as *blank verse, light year, maiden name,* and *stumbling block,* are most often listed as separate entries in their regular alphabetical position, not run in under either of the two words which compromise them. For example, *light year* is not run in under either "light" or "year," but occurs as a separate entry after the word "lightweight." In the Russian-English section, however, such Russian items are run in under one of their two components.

LABELING OF MEANINGS

If an English word has more than one meaning, each meaning is identified by a label (usually a synonym) inserted in parentheses just before the Russian equivalent that follows. This label (the "contextual gist" label) should make clear which meaning is about to be rendered into Russian. A simple example might be the word "trunk," which is treated as follows: 1, (of a tree) ствол. 2, (of an elephant) хо́бот. 3, (torso) ту́ловище. 4, (large box or case) сунду́к. 5, (of an automobile) бага́жник. 6, *pl.* (for swimming) пла́вки. In some cases the label may be a special field label, such as *physics* or *finance.*

GENDER OF NOUNS

The gender of most Russian nouns is self-evident from their ending. For those ending in а ь, the designation *n.m.* indicates masculine and *n.f.* indicates feminine. The *n.m.* designation is also used with nouns such as дя́дя and слуга́, which are masculine despite their -a or -я ending, as well as with many masculine nouns denoting people where the feminine form immediately follows.

The designation *n.m. & f.* is used with a large group of nouns denoting people, which are masculine or feminine depending on the person. The designation *n.m. or f.* is used with a small group of nouns (e.g., колибри) that are both masculine and feminine.

Indeclinable nouns ending in -o may be assumed to be neuter unless otherwise indicated. For those with other endings the gender is always given (e.g., ко́фе, *n.m. indecl.*).

VERBS

If a Russian verb has both a perfective and imperfective aspect, it is always listed under the imperfective, with the perfective form following immediately in brackets. The perfective verb is also listed separately and cross-referenced to the imperfective verb unless it is alphabetically adjacent to the imperfective verb—that is, no other words occur between. (Even if adjacent it is sometimes included, in order to show an irregularity in its conjugation.)

Reflexive verbs are usually run in under the nonreflexive verb, with only the imperfective aspect given. Unless otherwise indicated, it may be assumed that the perfective of the reflexive verb is formed with the same prefix or ending as the perfective of the nonreflexive verb.

If a prefixed perfective verb is cross-referenced to its nonprefixed imperfective counterpart, it may be assumed that the perfective verb is conjugated like the imperfective verb.

In the treatment of English verbs, intransitive meanings have been set completely apart from transitive meanings, a practice followed by all large dictionaries of English but not, for some reason, by English-Russian dictionaries produced in Russia.

Abbreviations
Used in the Dictionary

abbr.	abbreviation	geog.	geography
acc.	accusative	geol.	geology
adj.	adjective	geom.	geometry
aero.	aeronautics	gram.	grammar
agric.	agriculture	hist.	history
anat.	anatomy	impers.	impersonal
approx.	approximately	impfv.	imperfective
archit.	architecture	indecl.	indeclinable
art.	article	indeterm.	indeterminate
astron.	astronomy	indir.	indirect
attrib.	attributive	inf.	infinitive
Bib.	Bible, Biblical	infl.	inflected
biol.	biology	instr.	instrumental
bot.	botany	interj.	interjection
Brit.	British	interr.	interrogative
cap.	capital, capitalized	intrans.	intransitive
chem.	chemistry	l.c.	lower case
colloq.	colloquial	ling.	linguistics
comm.	commerce	lit.	literature; literal
comp.	comparative	loc.	locative
conj.	conjunction	masc.	masculine
contr.	contraction	math.	mathematics
dat.	dative	mech.	mechanics
def.	definite	med.	medicine
dem.	demonstrative	metall.	metallurgy
dent.	dentistry	meteorol.	meteorology
dim.	dimunitive	mil.	military
dipl.	diplomacy	myth.	mythology
dir.	direct	n.	noun
eccles.	ecclesiastic	naut.	nautical
econ.	economics	neg.	negative
esp.	especially	neut.	neuter
fem.	feminine	n.f.	feminine noun
fig.	figurative	n.m.	masculine noun
fol.	followed	nom.	nominative
gen.	genitive	obj.	object

obs.	obsolete	rel.	relative
opp.	opposite	relig.	religion
Orth. Ch.	Orthodox Church	R.R.	railroads
part.	participle	sing.	singular
pers.	personal	superl.	superlative
pert.	pertaining	theat.	theater
pfv.	perfective	topog.	topography
philos.	philosophy	trans.	transitive
phonet.	phonetics	trig.	trigonometry
photog.	photography	U.S.	United States
physiol.	physiology	usu.	usually
pl.	plural	v.	verb
polit.	politics, political	var.	variant
poss.	possessive	v. aux.	auxiliary verb
prep.	preposition	v.i.	intransitive verb
prepl.	prepositional	v. impfv.	imperfective verb
pre-rev.	prerevolutionary	v. pfv.	perfective verb
pres.	present	v.r.	reflexive verb
pron.	pronoun	v.t.	transitive verb
pros.	prosody	vulg.	vulgar
psychol	psychology	zool.	zoology
refl.	reflexive		

Regular Russian Declension Patterns

NOUNS

Masculine

Nouns ending in a hard consonant

	Sing.	Pl.
Nom.	билет	билет-ы
Gen.	билет-а	билет-ов
Dat.	билет-у	билет-ам
Acc.	N. or G.	N. or G.
Instr.	билет-ом	билет-ами
Prepl.	билет-е	биет-ах

Nouns ending in ь

	Sing.	Pl
Nom.	роял-ь	роял-и
Gen.	роял-я	роял-ей
Dat.	роял-ю	роял-ям
Acc.	N. or G.	N. or G.
Instr.	роял-ем	роял-ями
Prepl.	роял-е	роял-ях

Nouns ending in й

	Sing.	Pl.
Nom.	музе-й	музе-и
Gen.	музе-я	музе-ев
Dat.	музе-ю	музе-ям
Acc.	N. or G.	N. or G.
Instr.	музе-ем	музе-ями
Prepl.	музе-е	музе-ях

Feminine

Nouns ending in a

	Sing.	Pl.
Nom.	картин-а	картин-ы
Gen.	картин-ы	картин
Dat.	картин-е	картин-ам
Acc.	картин-у	N. or G.
Instr.	картин-ой	картин-ами
Prepl.	картин-е	картин-ах

Nouns ending in я

	Sing.	Pl.
Nom.	недел-я	недел-и
Gen.	недел-и	недел-ь
Dat.	недел-е	недел-ям
Acc.	недел-ю	N or G.
Instr.	недел-ей	недел-ямн
Prepl.	недел-е	недел-ях

Nouns ending in ь

	Sing.	Pl.
Nom.	цел-ь	цел-и
Gen.	цел-и	цел-ей
Dat.	цел-и	цел-ям
Acc.	цел-ь	N. or G.
Instr.	цел-ью	цел-ями
Prepl.	цел-и	цел-ях

Neuter

Nouns ending in о

	Sing.	Pl.
Nom.	блюд-о	блюд-а
Gen.	блюд-а	блюд
Dat.	блюд-у	блюд-ам
Acc.	блюд-о	блюд-а
Instr.	блюд-ом	блюд-ами
Prepl.	блюд-е	блюд-ах

Nouns ending in ле, ре

	Sing.	Pl.
Nom.	пол-е	пол-я
Gen.	пол-я	пол-ей
Dat.,	пол-ю	пол-ям
Acc.	пол-е	пол-я
Instr.	пол-ем	пол-ями
Prepl.	пол-е	пол-ях

Nouns ending in це, ще, же

	Sing.	Pl.
Nom.	чудовищ-е	чудовищ-а
Gen.	чудовищ-а	чудовищ
Dat.	чудовищ-у	чудовищ-ам
Acc.	чудовищ-е	N. or G.
Instr.	чудовищ-ем	чудовищ-ами
Prepl.	чудовищ-е	чудовищ-ах

Nouns ending in ие

	Sing.	Pl.
Nom.	здан-ие	здан-ия
Gen.	здан-ия	здан-ий
Dat.	здан-ию	здан-иям
Acc.	здан-ие	здан-ия
Instr.	здан-ием	здан-иями
Prepl.	здан-ии	здан-иях

Nouns ending in ье, ьё

	Sing.	Pl.
Nom.	ущел-ье	ущел-ья
Gen.	ущел-ья	ущел-ий
Dat.	ущел-ью	ущел-ьям
Acc.	ущел-ье	ущел-ья
Instr.	ущел-ьем	ущел-ьями
Prepl.	ущел-ье	ущел-ьях

The accusative singular of all masculine nouns and the accusative plural of all nouns is the same as the nominative when the noun is inanimate, and the same as the genitive when the noun is animate. Animate nouns include people, animals, birds, fish, insects, and so on.

Special Rules

1. After the consonants г, к, х, ж, ч, ш, щ, the vowel ы is replaced by и (e.g., кни́ги, уро́ки, ножи́, све́чи), and я is replaced by а (e.g., ноча́м, веща́ми).
2. After the consonants ж, ч, ш, щ, ц, the instrumental case endings -ом and -ой become -ем and -ей when unstressed (e.g. му́жем, ты́сячей, ме́сяцем, пти́цей).
3. When stressed, the instrumental case endings -ем and -ей become -ём and -ёй (e.g., рулём, бельём, землёй, статьёй).
4. The prepositional singular ending for nouns ending in -ия is -ии (e.g. а́рмия-а́рмии).
5. The genitive plural of nouns ending in -ая, -ея, -ия, -уя is formed by replacing the я with й (e.g., ста́я-стай, ли́ния-ли́ний).
6. The genitive plural ending for nouns ending in ж, ч, ш, щ is -ей (e.g. ножей, ключей).
7. The genitive plural ending for nouns ending in ц is -ев when unstressed (e.g. ме́сяцев).

Note. All individual exceptions to the above tables and rules are indicated in the body of the dictionary under the entry for the given word. If only the genitive singular is indicated (e.g., рот — *gen.* рта; лед — *gen.* льда; за́яц — *gen.* за́йца; ручей — *gen.* ручья́) the irregularity occurs throughout the singular and plural declension of the noun. This also applies to shifts of stress — e.g., щит — *gen.* щита́; язы́к — *gen.* языка́; руль — *gen.* руля́ mean that the stress shifts to the ending throughout the singular and plural declension. If only the nominative plural is indicated (e.g., дуб — *pl.* дубы́; дом — *pl.* дома́; страна́ — *pl.* стра́ны; лицо́ — *pl.* ли́ца; колесо́ — *pl.* колёса) the irregularity or shift of stress occurs throughout the plural (but not the singular) declension of the noun.

ADJECTIVES

Adjectives ending in -о́й

	Masc.	Fem.	Neut.	Pl.
Nom.	прям-о́й	-а́я	-о́е	-ы́е
Gen.	прям-о́го	-о́й	-о́го	-ы́х
Dat.	прям-о́му	-о́й	-о́му	-ы́м
Acc.	N. or G.	-у́ю	-о́е	N. or G.
Instr.	прям-ы́м	-о́й	-ы́м	-ы́ми
Prepl.	прям-о́м	-о́й	-о́м	-ы́х

Adjectives ending in -ый

	Masc.	Fem.	Neut.	Pl.
Nom.	но́в-ый	-ая	-ое	-ые
Gen.	но́в-ого	-ой	-ого	-ых
Dat.	но́в-ому	-ой	-ому	-ым
Acc.	N. or G.	-ую	-ое	N. or G.
Instr.	но́вым	-ой	-ым	-ыми
Prepl.	но́в-ом	-ой	-ом	-ых

Adjectives ending in -го́й, -ко́й, -хо́й

	Masc.	Fem.	Neut.	Pl.
Nom.	плох-о́й	-а́я	-о́е	-и́е
Gen.	плох-о́го	-о́й	-о́го	-и́х
Dat.	плох-о́му	-о́й	-о́му	-и́м
Acc.	N. or G.	-у́ю	-о́е	N. or G.
Instr.	плох-и́м	-о́й	-и́м	-и́ми
Prepl.	плох-ом	-о́й	-о́м	-и́х

Adjectives ending in -гий, -кий, -хий

	Masc.	Fem.	Neut.	Pl.
Nom.	ти́х-ий	-ая	-ое	-ие
Gen.	ти́х-ого	-ой	-ого	-их
Dat.	ти́х-ому	-ой	-ому	-им
Acc.	N. or G.	-ую	-ое	N. or G.
Instr.	ти́х-им	-ой	-им	-ими
Prepl.	ти́х-ом	-ой	-ом	-их

Adjectives ending in -жо́й, -шо́й

	Masc.	Fem.	Neut.	Pl.
Nom.	больш-о́й	-а́я	-о́е	-и́е
Gen.	больш-о́го	-о́и	-о́го	-и́х
Dat.	больш-о́му	-о́й	-о́му	-и́м
Acc.	N. or G.	-у́ю	-о́е	N. or G.
Instr.	больш-и́м	-о́й	-и́м	-и́ми
Prepl.	больш-о́м	-о́й	-о́м	-их

Adjectives ending in -жий, -чий, -ший, -щий

	Masc.	Fem.	Neut.	Pl.
Nom.	све́ж-ий	-ая	-ее	-ие
Gen.	све́ж-его	-ей	-его	-их
Dat.	све́ж-ему	-ей	-ему	-им
Acc.	N. or G.	-ую	-ее	N. or G.
Instr.	све́ж-им	-ей	-им	-ими
Prepl.	све́ж-ем	-ей	-ем	-их

Adjectives ending in -ний

	Masc.	Fem.	Neut.	Pl.
Nom.	си́н-ий	-яя	-ее	-ие
Gen.	си́н-его	-ей	-его	-их
Dat.	си́н-ему	-ей	-ему	-им
Acc.	N. or G.	-юю	-ее	N. or G.
Instr.	си́н-им	-ей	-им	-ими
Prepl.	си́н-ем	-ей	-ем	-их

Adjectives ending in -бий, -вий, -зий, -лий, -сий*

	Masc.	Fem.	Neut.	Pl.
Nom.	ры́б-ий	-ья	-ье	-ьи
Gen.	ры́б-ьего	-ьей	-ьего	-ьих
Dat.	ры́б-ьему	-ьей	-ьему	-ьим
Acc.	N. or G.	-ью	-ье	N. or G.
Instr.	ры́б-ьим	-ьей	-ьим	-ьими
Prepl.	ры́б-ьем	-ьей	-ьем	-ьих

*Adjectives with these endings are derived mainly from the words for animals and other living creatures (e.g., коро́вий from коро́ва, ко́зий from коза́, собо́лий from со́боль, ли́сий from лиса́), and include some ending in -ний (оле́ний), -жий (медве́жий), -чий (пти́чий), and -ший (пету́ший).

Regular Verb Conjugation Patterns

I. Verbs ending in -ать

желáть: желáю, желáешь, желáет, желáем, желáете, желáют
дéлать: дéлаю, дéлаешь, дéлает, дéлаем, дéлаете, дéлают

II. Verbs ending in -ять

менять: меняю, меняешь, меняет, меняем, меняете, меняют

III. Verbs ending in -еть

имéть: имéю, имéешь, имéет, имéем, имéете, имéют

IV. Verbs ending in -ить

говори́ть: говорю́, говори́шь, говори́т, говори́м, говори́те, говоря́т
вéрить: вéрю, вéришь, вéрит, вéрим, вéрите, вéрят

V. Verbs ending in -уть

верну́ть: верну́, вернёшь, вернёт, вернём, вернёте, верну́т
трóнуть: трóну, трóнешь, трóнет, трóнем, трóнете, трóнут

After the letters ж, ч, ш, щ, the endings -ю and -ят are replaced by -у and -ат.

реши́ть: решу́, реши́шь, реши́т, реши́м, реши́те, реша́т

The conjugation of verbs with the infinitive endings -оть, -ыть, -сть, -сти, -зти, -зть, -чь, as well as all irregular verbs and those with shifts of stress, is given in the body of the dictionary under the entry for the given word.

Past Tense

Verbs ending in -ть

	Masculine	Feminine	Neuter	Plural
петь:	пел	пéла	пéло	пéли
мыть:	мыл	мы́ла	мы́ло	мы́ли

In the case of reflexive verbs -ся is added to those forms ending in consonant or ь, and -сь to those forms ending in a vowel.

одевáться: одевáюсь, одевáешься, одевáется, одевáемся, одевáетесь, одевáются
верну́ться: верну́сь, вернёшься, вернётся, вернёмся, вернётесь, верну́тся

Past tense: одевáлся, одевáлась, одевáлось, одевáлись

English-Russian
Section

A

A, a пе́рвая бу́ква англи́йского алфави́та. —*n.* **1,** (musical note) ля. **2,** (school grade) пятёрка. *Get an A,* получи́ть пятёрку; получи́ть «отли́чно». *Get straight A's,* учи́ться на кру́глые пятёрки. —**from A to Z,** от А до Я.

a *indef. art. Generally not rendered in Russian: a young man,* молодо́й челове́к; *a box of matches,* коро́бка спи́чек; *a story about a little girl,* расска́з о ма́ленькой де́вочке. ♦*Special uses:* **1,** (one) оди́н: *in a word,* одни́м сло́вом; *just a minute,* одну́ мину́тку. *He didn't say a word,* он ни сло́ва не сказа́л. *I didn't hear a thing,* я ничего́ не слы́шал(а). **2,** (a certain) оди́н; *an old friend of mine,* оди́н мой ста́рый друг. **3,** (of someone unknown) не́кий: *A Mr. Smith called,* вас спра́шивал не́кий ми́стер Смит. **4,** (such a) тако́й: *We live at a time when...,* мы живём в тако́е вре́мя, когда́... **5,** (per) в: *twice a week,* два ра́за в неде́лю. **6,** (for the amount specified) за (+ *acc.*): *two dollars a dozen,* два до́ллара за дю́жину.

aardvark *n.* трубкозу́б.

aback *adv., in* **take aback,** озада́чить; огоро́шить. *I was taken aback,* я был озада́чен.

abacus *n.* счёты.

abandon *v.t.* **1,** (leave; desert) покида́ть; оставля́ть; броса́ть. *Abandon a sinking ship,* поки́нуть то́нущий кора́бль. *Abandon a child,* подбра́сывать ребёнка. **2,** (give up) отка́зываться от: *abandon an attempt,* отказа́ться от попы́тки. *Abandon hope,* оставля́ть наде́жду. —*n.* беззабо́тность. *With abandon,* беззабо́тно. —**abandoned,** *adj.* поки́нутый.

abase *v.t.* унижа́ть. —**abasement,** *n.* униже́ние.

abash *v.t.* смуща́ть; конфу́зить. *Be abashed,* смуща́ться; конфу́зиться.

abate *v.t.* уменьша́ть; снижа́ть; ослабля́ть. —*v.i.* затиха́ть; утиха́ть; стиха́ть; спада́ть. *The storm has abated,* бу́ря зати́хла.

abatement *n.* уменьше́ние; сниже́ние; ослабле́ние. *Noise abatement,* сниже́ние у́ровня шу́ма. *Without abatement,* неосла́бно.

abbess *n.* аббати́са; игу́менья.

abbey *n.* абба́тство: *Westminster Abbey,* Вестми́нстерское абба́тство.

abbot *n.* абба́т; игу́мен; настоя́тель.

abbreviate *v.t.* сокраща́ть. —**abbreviation,** *n.* сокраще́ние.

ABC *n., usu. pl.* алфави́т; а́збука. *Learn the ABC's,* вы́учиться алфави́ту. *The ABC's of chemistry,* а́збука хи́мии. —**as simple as ABC,** как два́жды два четы́ре.

abdicate *v.t.* отрека́ться от. —*v.i.* отрека́ться от престо́ла. —**abdication,** *n.* отрече́ние от престо́ла.

abdomen *n.* живо́т.

abdominal *adj.* брюшно́й. *Abdominal pains,* боль в животе́.

abduct *v.t.* похища́ть. —**abduction,** *n.* похище́ние. —**abductor,** *n.* похити́тель.

aberrant *adj.* ненорма́льный.

aberration *n.* аберра́ция.

abet *v.t.* подстрека́ть. *Abet a crime,* подстрека́ть преступле́ние; соде́йствовать преступле́нию. —**abetment,** *n.* подстрека́тельство. —**abetter; abettor,** *n.* подстрека́тель.

abeyance *n.* (вре́менное) прекраще́ние. *Hold in abeyance,* откла́дывать.

abhor *v.t.* ненави́деть. *Nature abhors a vacuum,* приро́да не те́рпит пустоты́. —**abhorrence,** *n.* отвраще́ние. —**abhorrent,** *adj.* ненави́стный; отврати́тельный.

abide *v.t.* **1,** (await) ждать. **2,** (tolerate) терпе́ть. —*v.i.* **1,** (remain) остава́ться. **2,** (dwell) жить; прожива́ть. —**abide by, 1,** (live up to; keep) приде́рживаться: *abide by an agreement,* приде́рживаться догово́ра. **2,** (acquiesce in) подчиня́ться (+ *dat.*): *abide by the decision of the court,* подчиня́ться реше́нию суда́.

abiding *adj.* постоя́нный; неизме́нный.

ability *n.* спосо́бность; уме́ние. *The ability to speak,* спосо́бность говори́ть. *Reading ability,* уме́ние чита́ть. *Outstanding ability,* выдаю́щиеся спосо́бности. *A man of great ability,* челове́к больши́х спосо́бностей. *To the best of my ability,* по ме́ре сил; по ме́ре спосо́бностей.

abject *adj.* **1,** (wretched) уни́женный. *Abject poverty,* кра́йняя нищета́. **2,** (despicable) презре́нный.

ablaze *adj.* в огне́. *Set ablaze,* поджига́ть.

able *adj.* уме́лый; спосо́бный. *Able leader,* спосо́бный руководи́тель. —**be able,** мочь; уме́ть: *be able to predict the future,* мочь/уме́ть предска́зывать бу́дущее.

able-bodied *adj.* трудоспосо́бный; работоспосо́бный.

abloom *adj.* в цвету́.

ablution *n.* омове́ние.

ably *adv.* уме́ло.

abnormal *adj.* ненорма́льный. —**abnormality**, *n.* ненорма́льность. —**abnormally**, *adv.* ненорма́льно.

aboard *adv.* **1**, (position) на борту́; на корабле́. **2**, (motion) на́ борт; на кора́бль. *Go aboard*, сесть на кора́бль. *Take aboard*, брать на́ борт. —*prep.* на борту́ (+ *gen.*): *No smoking aboard the aircraft!*, нельзя́ кури́ть на борту́ самолёта. —**all aboard!**, **1**, (a train) по ваго́нам! **2**, (a ship) все на борт!

abode *n.* жили́ще.

abolish *v.t.* отменя́ть; упраздня́ть. —**abolition**, *n.* отме́на; упраздне́ние.

abominable *adj.* отврати́тельный; проти́вный; гну́сный.

abominate *v.t.* ненави́деть; пита́ть отвраще́ние к.

abomination *n.* **1**, (loathing) омерзе́ние. **2**, (loathsome thing) ме́рзость.

aboriginal *adj.* коренно́й; тузе́мный. —**aborigine**, *n.* абориге́н; тузе́мец.

abort *v.t.* **1**, (terminate the pregnancy of) сде́лать або́рт (+ *dat.*). **2**, *fig.* (terminate prematurely) прекраща́ть.

abortion *n.* або́рт. *Have an abortion*, сде́лать або́рт. *Perform an abortion upon*, сде́лать або́рт (+ *dat.*).

abortive *adj.* неуда́чный; неуда́вшийся; безрезульта́тный; беспло́дный. *Abortive attempt*, неуда́чная попы́тка. *Abortive coup*, неуда́вшийся переворо́т.

abound *v.i.* **1**, (exist in great numbers) име́ться в изоби́лии. **2**, *fol. by* **in** *or* **with** (have in great abundance) изоби́ловать (*instr.*).

about *adv.* **1**, (approximately) о́коло: *about an hour*, о́коло ча́са. *In about two weeks*, приме́рно че́рез две неде́ли. **2**, (nearly) почти́: *about ready*, почти́ гото́в. **3**, (at hand) круго́м; вокру́г: *There was no one about*, круго́м/вокру́г никого́ не́ было. —*prep.* **1**, (here and there in) по: *walk about town*, ходи́ть по го́роду. *Her things lay all about the room*, её ве́щи валя́лись по всей ко́мнате. **2**, (concerning) о: *I don't know anything about it*, я ничего́ не зна́ю об э́том. *I'm calling about the money*, я звоню́ по по́воду де́нег. *I've thought a lot about this question*, я мно́го ду́мал(а) над э́тим вопро́сом. *What is all the noise about?*, почему́ тако́й шум? *There is nothing you can do about it*, ничего́ не поде́лаешь. *I don't know about you, but I'm tired*, я не зна́ю как вы, а я уста́л(а). —**be about to**, собира́ться (+ *inf.*): *I was just about to call you*, я как раз собира́лся вам звони́ть. *The train is about to leave*, по́езд вот-во́т отойдёт. *I was about to ask, but...*, я спроси́л(а) бы́ло, но... —**how about...?**, *see* **how.** —**up and about**, на нога́х. —**what about...?**, *see* **what.**

about-face *n.* **1**, *mil.* поворо́т круго́м. *About face!*, круго́м! **2**, *fig.* (reversal) поворо́т на сто во́семьдесят гра́дусов.

above *prep.* **1**, (over) над; вы́ше. *Above sea level*, над у́ровнем мо́ря. *The water was above our knees*, вода́ была́ нам вы́ше коле́н. **2**, (in excess of) вы́ше: *above average*, вы́ше сре́днего. *Five degrees above*

zero, пять гра́дусов вы́ше нуля́. **3**, (superior to) вы́ше: *head and shoulders above the others*, на́ голову вы́ше други́х. *A major ranks above a captain*, майо́р вы́ше капита́на (по зва́нию). **4**, (beyond the reach of) вне: *above suspicion*, вне подозре́ний. **5**, (too honorable to engage in) вы́ше: *be above prejudice*, быть вы́ше предрассу́дков. —*adv.* вы́ше; наверху́. *From above*, све́рху; свы́ше. *As stated above*, как ска́зано вы́ше. *We live on the floor above*, мы живём этажо́м вы́ше. *Noise from the apartment above*, шум из кварти́ры наверху́. —*n., preceded by* **the**, вышеупомя́нутое. —**above all**, **1**, (most of all) бо́льше всего́. **2**, (most importantly) пре́жде всего́.

aboveboard *adj.* откры́тый; открове́нный. —*adv.* откры́то; открове́нно.

above-mentioned *adj.* вышеупомя́нутый.

abracadabra *n.* абракада́бра.

abrade *v.t.* сдира́ть (ко́жу).

abrasion *n.* сса́дина.

abrasive *n.* абрази́в. —*adj.* **1**, (causing abrasion) абрази́вный. **2**, *fig.* (causing friction or resentment) раздража́ющий.

abreast *adv.* в ряду́; в ряд. *Sit three abreast*, сиде́ть по́ трое в ряду́. *March three abreast*, маршир́ова́ть по́ трое в ряд/ряду́. *Draw abreast of*, поравня́ться с. —**keep abreast of**, **1**, (keep up with) идти́ в но́гу с. *Keep abreast of the times*, идти́ в но́гу с жи́знью *or* со вре́менем. **2**, (keep well posted on) следи́ть за.

abridge *v.t.* **1**, (shorten) сокраща́ть. **2**, (curtail, as rights) уре́зывать; ущемля́ть.

abridgment *also,* **abridgement** *n.* **1**, (act of abridging) сокраще́ние. **2**, (abridged edition) сокращённое изда́ние.

abroad *adv.* **1**, (location) за грани́цей; за рубежо́м. **2**, (direction) за грани́цу. *Trip abroad*, пое́здка за грани́цу. *Sell goods abroad*, продава́ть това́ры за грани́цу. *From abroad*, из-за грани́цы.

abrogate *v.t.* отменя́ть; аннули́ровать; расторга́ть. —**abrogation**, *n.* отме́на; аннули́рование; расторже́ние.

abrupt *adj.* **1**, (sudden) внеза́пный; ре́зкий; круто́й. *Abrupt departure*, внеза́пный отъе́зд. **2**, (steep) круто́й; обры́вистый. **3**, (brusque) ре́зкий. —**abruptly**, *adv.* внеза́пно. —**abruptness**, *n.* ре́зкость.

abscess *n.* абсце́сс; нары́в; гнойни́к.

abscissa *n.* абсци́сса.

abscond *v.i.* скрыва́ться; бежа́ть.

absence *n.* отсу́тствие. *Absence from class*, про́пуск заня́тий *or* уро́ков. *Absence from work*, нея́вка на рабо́ту. *Unexcused absence*, прогу́л. *In the absence of*, в отсу́тствие *or* за отсу́тствием (+ *gen.*). *In my absence*, в моё отсу́тствие. *During his absence from Moscow*, за вре́мя его́ отсу́тствия в Москве́. —**absence without leave**, самово́льная отлу́чка.

absent *adj.* отсу́тствующий. *Be absent from class/ meeting/*, отсу́тствовать на заня́тиях/ на собра́нии/. *Absent look*, отсу́тствующий взгляд. —*v.t.* [*usu.* **absent oneself**] отлуча́ться.

absentee *n.* отсу́тствующий. —**absentee vote**, голосова́ние по по́чте.

absenteeism *n.* (системати́ческие) прогу́лы.

absentia *see* **in absentia.**

absently *adv.* отсу́тствующим взгля́дом; рассе́янно.

absent-minded *adj.* рассе́янный. —**absent-mindedly,** *adv.* рассе́янно; по рассе́янности. —**absent-mindedness,** *n.* рассе́янность.

absinthe *n.* абсе́нт; полы́нная во́дка.

absolute *adj.* **1,** (complete; total) абсолю́тный; соверше́нный; по́лный. **2,** (unlimited; unqualified) абсолю́тный; безусло́вный. **3,** (sheer; utter) сплошно́й; су́щий. —*n.* абсолю́т. —**absolute majority,** абсолю́тное большинство́ голосо́в. —**absolute monarchy,** абсолю́тная мона́рхия. —**absolute pitch,** абсолю́тный слух. —**absolute zero,** абсолю́тный ноль.

absolutely *adv.* **1,** (perfectly; entirely; utterly) соверше́нно: *absolutely correct/certain,* соверше́нно пра́вильно/уве́рен(а). *Absolutely impossible,* соверше́нно *or* абсолю́тно невозмо́жно. **2,** (positively) абсолю́тно; реши́тельно. *Absolutely everything,* реши́тельно всё. *Absolutely nothing,* соверше́нно/абсолю́тно/реши́тельно/положи́тельно ничего́. **3,** *as an exclamation,* безусло́вно!

absolution *n.* **1,** (forgiveness) проще́ние. **2,** (remission of sin) отпуще́ние грехо́в.

absolutism *n.* абсолюти́зм. —**absolutist,** *n.* абсолюти́ст. —*adj.* абсолюти́стский.

absolve *v.t.* **1,** (acquit) опра́вдывать. **2,** (release) освобожда́ть. *Absolve of blame/responsibility,* снима́ть вину́/отве́тственность с (+ *gen.*). **3,** (remit, as a sin) проща́ть; отпуска́ть.

absorb *v.t.* **1,** (take in; suck up) вса́сывать; впи́тывать; вбира́ть; поглоща́ть. **2,** (engross) поглоща́ть. *Absorbed in one's work,* поглощён свое́й рабо́той; погружён в свою́ рабо́ту. *Become absorbed in,* погружа́ться *or* углубля́ться в (+ *acc.*). **3,** (incorporate) вбира́ть в себя́. **4,** (mentally assimilate) усва́ивать; воспринима́ть. *Absorb the material,* усво́ить материа́л.

absorbent *adj.* вса́сывающий; поглоща́ющий. —**absorbent cotton,** ва́та.

absorbing *adj.* увлека́тельный; захва́тывающий.

absorption *n.* вса́сывание; поглоще́ние; абсо́рбция.

abstain *v.i.* возде́рживаться: *abstain from eating meat,* возде́рживаться от мя́са. *Abstain from the voting,* возде́рживаться от голосова́ния.

abstemious *adj.* возде́ржанный.

abstention *n.* **1,** (act of abstaining) воздержа́ние. **2,** (failure to vote) воздержа́вшийся: *ten in favor, six against, five abstentions,* де́сять за, шесть про́тив, пять воздержа́вшихся.

abstinence *n.* воздержа́ние.

abstract *adj.* отвлечённый; абстра́ктный. *Abstract art,* абстракциони́зм; абстра́ктное иску́сство. —*n.* **1,** (synopsis) рефера́т; конспе́кт. **2,** (something abstract) абстра́кция. —*v.t.* **1,** (consider separately) абстраги́ровать. **2,** (make an abstract of) рефери́ровать; конспекти́ровать. —**in the abstract,** абстра́ктно; отвлечённо.

abstraction *n.* **1,** (abstract idea or concept)

абстра́кция; отвлече́ние. **2,** (absent-mindedness) рассе́янность.

abstruse *adj.* мудрёный; замыслова́тый; зау́мный.

absurd *adj.* неле́пый; абсу́рдный. —**absurdity,** *n.* неле́пость; абсу́рд; абсу́рдность.

abundance *n.* оби́лие; изоби́лие. *In abundance,* в изоби́лии; в избы́тке.

abundant *adj.* оби́льный: *abundant harvest,* оби́льный урожа́й.

abundantly *adv.* **1,** (in abundance) оби́льно. **2,** (extremely) преде́льно: *abundantly clear,* преде́льно я́сно.

abuse *v.t.* **1,** (misuse) злоупотребля́ть: *abuse power,* злоупотребля́ть вла́стью. **2,** (revile) руга́ть; обруга́ть. —*n.* **1,** (misuse; corrupt practice) злоупотребле́ние: *abuse of power,* злоупотребле́ние вла́стью. *Child abuse,* издева́тельство над ребёнком. **2,** (abusive language) ру́гань; брань.

abusive *adj.* руга́тельный; бра́нный; оскорби́тельный.

abut *v.t.* & *i.* примыка́ть (к).

abutment *n.* **1,** (point of contact) стык. **2,** (support for an arch) пята́. **3,** (support for a bridge) усто́й.

abysmal *adj.* жа́лкий. *Abysmal ignorance,* кра́йнее неве́жество. *Abysmal failure,* по́лный прова́л.

abyss *n.* про́пасть; бе́здна.

acacia *n.* ака́ция.

academic *adj.* академи́ческий. *Academic year,* уче́бный год.

academician *n.* акаде́мик.

academy *n.* **1,** (learned institution) акаде́мия: *academy of sciences,* акаде́мия нау́к. **2,** (specialized school) шко́ла; учи́лище; акаде́мия: *academy of music,* музыка́льная шко́ла; *military academy,* вое́нное учи́лище; вое́нная акаде́мия; *riding academy,* шко́ла верхово́й езды́.

acanthus *n.* ака́нт.

accede *v.i.* [*usu.* **accede to**] **1,** (consent to) соглаша́ться (на). *Accede to a request,* удовлетворя́ть про́сьбу. **2,** (assume, as an office) вступа́ть (в). *Accede to the throne,* вступи́ть на престо́л.

accelerate *v.t.* ускоря́ть. *Accelerated course,* ускоренный курс. —*v.i.* **1,** (pick up speed) ускоря́ться: *The pace accelerated,* темп уско́рился. *Accelerate before takeoff,* разогна́ться *or* набра́ть ско́рость пе́ред взлётом. **2,** (step on the accelerator) дава́ть газ. —**acceleration,** *n.* ускоре́ние.

accelerator *n.* **1,** (gas pedal) акселера́тор. **2,** *physics* ускори́тель: *linear accelerator,* лине́йный ускори́тель.

accent *n.* **1,** (stress) ударе́ние. **2,** (regional or national manner of speech) акце́нт: *speak with an accent,* говори́ть с акце́нтом. **3,** (accent mark) ударе́ние. —*v.t.* = **accentuate.**

accentuate *v.t.* **1,** (pronounce with heavy stress) акценти́ровать; де́лать ударе́ние на. **2,** (emphasize) акценти́ровать; де́лать акце́нт на.

accept *v.t.* **1,** (say yes to) принима́ть: *accept an offer/invitation,* принима́ть предложе́ние/приглаше́ние. **2,** (reconcile oneself to) мири́ться с; смиря́ться с:

accept one's fate, примири́ться *or* смири́ться со свое́й судьбо́й. **3,** (admit formally) принима́ть: *He was accepted at X college,* он был при́нят в университе́т икс.

acceptable *adj.* прие́млемый.

acceptance *n.* **1,** (act of accepting) приня́тие. **2,** (condition of being accepted) призна́ние: *gain acceptance,* получи́ть призна́ние.

access *n.* до́ступ: *gain access to,* получи́ть до́ступ к. —**access road,** подъездна́я доро́га.

accessible *adj.* досту́пный. —**accessibility,** *n.* досту́пность.

accession *n.* **1,** (to the throne) вступле́ние; восше́ствие (на престо́л); (to office) вступле́ние (в до́лжность). **2,** (something newly acquired) приобрете́ние. **3,** (agreement; assent) согла́сие.

accessory *n.* **1,** (extra piece of equipment) приста́вка. **2,** *pl.* (items of equipment) принадле́жности. **3,** *pl.* (extra items of dress) принадле́жности костю́ма. **4,** *law* соуча́стник: *accessory to a crime,* соуча́стник преступле́ния. —*adj.* подсо́бный.

accident *n.* **1,** (mishap) несча́стный слу́чай; катастро́фа; ава́рия. *Automobile accident,* автомоби́льная ава́рия. **2,** (chance occurrence) случа́йность. *It is no accident that...,* не случа́йно, что... **3,** (chance) слу́чай. *By accident,* случа́йно.

accidental *adj.* случа́йный; неча́янный. —**accidentally,** *adv.* случа́йно; неча́янно.

acclaim *v.t.* **1,** (welcome with applause) приве́тствовать. **2,** (praise; extol) расхва́ливать. **3,** (proclaim approvingly) провозглаша́ть. —*n.* **1,** (welcoming) шу́мное приве́тствие. **2,** (praise) восхвале́ние.

acclamation *n.* шу́мное одобре́ние. —**by acclamation,** единоду́шно; без голосова́ния.

acclimate *also,* **acclimatize** *v.t.* акклиматизи́ровать. *Become acclimated,* прижи́ться; акклиматизи́роваться. —**acclimation; acclimatization,** *n.* акклиматиза́ция.

accommodate *v.t.* **1,** (oblige; help) услу́живать; идти́ навстре́чу (+ *dat.*). **2,** (lodge) помеща́ть. **3,** (have space for) вмеща́ть. **4,** (adapt) приспоса́бливать. —**accommodating,** *adj.* услу́жливый; сгово́рчивый.

accommodation *n.* **1,** (a favor) услу́га. **2,** (convenience) удо́бство: *for the accommodation of,* для удо́бства (+ *gen.*). **3,** (adaptation; adjustment) приспособле́ние. **4,** (agreement; reconciliation) соглаше́ние; примире́ние. *Reach an accommodation,* дости́гнуть соглаше́ния. *An accommodation between the superpowers,* примире́ние сверхдержа́в. **5,** *pl.* (lodgings) помеще́ние; жильё. **6,** *pl.* (traveling space) ме́сто.

accompaniment *n.* **1,** (something added) добавле́ние. **2,** *music* аккомпанеме́нт; сопровожде́ние. —**accompanist,** *n.* аккомпаниа́тор.

accompany *v.t.* **1,** (go along with) сопровожда́ть. *Accompanied by,* в сопровожде́нии (+ *gen.*). **2,** (escort up to a point) провожа́ть. **3,** *music* аккомпани́ровать.

accomplice *n.* сообщник; соуча́стник.

accomplish *v.t.* соверша́ть; осуществля́ть; выполня́ть. *Accomplish a feat/miracle,* соверша́ть по́двиг/чу́до. *Accomplish a task,* вы́полнить *or* реши́ть зада́чу. *Accomplish one's purpose,* осуществи́ть свою́ цель; доби́ться свое́й це́ли. *Accomplish a great deal,* доби́ться мно́гого.

accomplished *adj.* **1,** (done) совершённый. *Accomplished fact,* соверши́вшийся факт. **2,** (proficient) зако́нченный.

accomplishment *n.* **1,** (completion) выполне́ние; осуществле́ние. **2,** (an achievement) достиже́ние.

accord *v.t.* **1,** (give; extend) ока́зывать: *the honor you have accorded me,* честь, кото́рую вы мне оказа́ли. **2,** (grant; bestow) предоставля́ть. —*v.i.* [*usu.* **accord with**] совпада́ть (с); сходи́ться (с); вяза́ться (с). —*n.* **1,** (an agreement) соглаше́ние. **2,** (harmony) согла́сие. —**be in accord with, 1,** (agree with) быть согла́сным с. **2,** (tally with) соотве́тствовать (+ *dat.*); согласова́ться с. —**of one's own accord,** по до́брой во́ле.

accordance *n.* соотве́тствие. *In accordance with,* в соотве́тствии с; согла́сно.

accordingly *adv.* **1,** (correspondingly) соотве́тственно; соотве́тствующим о́бразом. **2,** (consequently) таки́м о́бразом; исходя́ из э́того.

according to по; согла́сно; по слова́м (+ *gen.*). *According to legend,* по преда́нию; согла́сно леге́нде. *According to this theory,* по *or* согла́сно э́той тео́рии. *According to an official spokesman,* по слова́м официа́льного представи́теля. *Play according to the rules,* игра́ть по пра́вилам. *Everything went according to plan,* всё пошло́ по пла́ну. *Each according to his ability,* ка́ждый по его́ спосо́бностям.

accordion *n.* гармо́ника; аккордео́н. —**accordion pleats,** плиссе́.

accordionist *n.* гармони́ст; аккордеони́ст.

accost *v.t.* подходи́ть к; пристава́ть к; привя́зываться к.

account *n.* **1,** (business record) счёт: *open an account,* открыва́ть счёт. **2,** (report; description) отчёт; расска́з: *an account of events,* отчёт/расска́з о собы́тиях. **3,** (importance; worth) ва́жность. *Of no account,* не име́ющий значе́ния. **4,** (reason; basis) основа́ние; причи́на: *on that account,* на э́том основа́нии; по э́той причи́не. —*v.i.* [*usu.* **account for**] **1,** (explain) объясня́ть: *How do you account for the fact that...?,* чем вы объясня́ете то, что...? *This accounts for his strange behavior,* э́тим объясня́ется его́ стра́нное поведе́ние. **2,** (represent numerically) *inverted in Russian: Copper accounts for a third of all exports,* треть всего́ э́кспорта прихо́дится на медь. **3,** (give a statement of) отчи́тываться в: *account for one's expenses,* отчи́тываться в расхо́дах. *Account for every cent,* отчи́тываться за ка́ждую копе́йку (*or* в ка́ждой копе́йке). **4,** *All present and accounted for,* все налицо́. —**bring to account,** привлека́ть к отве́тственности. —**by all accounts,** по о́бщему мне́нию; по слова́м всех. —**call to account,** призыва́ть к отве́ту. —**give a good account of one-**

self, хорошо себя зарекомендовать. —**on account of**, из-за; вследствие (+ *gen.*). —**on no account**, ни в коем случае. —**on** (someone's) **account**, ради: *on my account*, ради меня. —**take into account**; **take account of**, принимать во внимание/ к сведению/ в расчёт; учитывать.

accountability *n.* ответственность; подотчётность.

accountable *adj.* ответственный; подотчётный. *Accountable for one's actions*, ответственный за свои поступки. *He is accountable to no one*, он никому не подотчётен; он ни перед кем не отчитывается. *You will be held accountable for this*, вы будете (*or* вам придётся) отвечать за это; с вас за это спросят.

accountant *n.* бухгалтер; счетовод.

accounting *n.* бухгалтерия; счетоводство. *Accounting department*, бухгалтерия.

accouterment *also*, **accoutrement** *n., usu. pl.* снаряжение.

accredit *v.t., dipl.* аккредитовать. —**accredited**, *adj.* аккредитованный.

accretion *n.* **1,** (growth in size) прирост. **2,** (accumulated matter) нарост.

accrue *v.i.* **1,** *fol. by* **to** (fall to) доставаться (+ *dat.*). **2,** (accumulate, as of interest) нарастать.

accumulate *v.t.* накоплять; копить. *Accumulate wealth*, накоплять богатство. —*v.i.* накопляться; скапливаться; копиться. *Dust accumulated on the shelf*, на полке накопилась пыль.

accumulation *n.* **1,** (act of accumulating) накопление. **2,** (that which has accumulated) скопление.

accuracy *n.* **1,** (freedom from error) точность. **2,** (precision, as with a weapon) меткость.

accurate *adj.* **1,** (free from error; correct) точный. **2,** (always hitting one's target) меткий. —**accurately**, *adv.* точно.

accursed *adj.* проклятый.

accusation *n.* обвинение: *an accusation of fraud*, обвинение в обмане.

accusative *adj.* винительный: *accusative case*, винительный падеж.

accusatory *adj.* обвинительный.

accuse *v.t.* обвинять: *accuse someone of lying*, обвинять кого-нибудь во лжи. —**accused**, *n., law* обвиняемый. —**accuser**, *n.* обвинитель.

accustom *v.t.* [*usu.* **accustom oneself**] приспосабливаться (к).

accustomed *adj.* **1,** (habitual) привычный. **2,** *fol. by* **to** (used to) привыкший (к): *I am not accustomed to this*, я к этому не привык(ла).

ace *n.* **1,** *cards* туз. **2,** (pilot) ас. —*adj., colloq.* первоклассный.

acerbic *adj.* **1,** (astringent) терпкий. **2,** *fig.* (caustic) едкий. —**acerbity**, *n.* терпкость; едкость.

acetate *n.* соль уксусной кислоты; уксуснокислая соль; ацетат.

acetic *adj.* уксусный. —**acetic acid**, уксусная кислота.

acetone *n.* ацетон.

acetylene *n.* ацетилен. —*adj.* ацетиленовый.

ache *n.* боль. —*v.i.* болеть; ныть. *An aching back*, больная спина. *My whole body aches*, у меня всё тело болит. *My heart aches*, у меня болит сердце; боль отдаётся в сердце. *I was aching to tell him*, меня так и подмывало сказать ему.

achieve *v.t.* достигать; добиться: *achieve one's goal*, достигнуть/добиться своей цели.

achievement *n.* достижение.

Achilles' heel ахиллесова пята.

Achilles' tendon ахиллесово сухожилие.

acid *n.* кислота: *sulfuric acid*, серная кислота. —*adj.* **1,** (containing acid) кислый; кислотный. **2,** (sour) кислый. **3,** (caustic, as of a remark) едкий.

acidity *n.* кислота; кислотность.

acknowledge *v.t.* **1,** (admit) признавать: *acknowledge one's mistakes*, признавать свои ошибки. **2,** (recognize and reply to) отвечать на: *acknowledge a letter*, отвечать на письмо. *Acknowledge receipt of*, подтверждать получение (+ *gen.*).

acknowledgment *also*, **acknowledgement** *n.* **1,** (act of admitting or recognizing) признание. *In acknowledgment of...*, в знак признания (+ *gen.*). **2,** (document confirming receipt) расписка.

acme *n.* высшая точка; верх; вершина. *The acme of perfection*, верх совершенства.

acne *n.* угри.

aconite *n.* аконит.

acorn *n.* жёлудь.

acoustic *also*, **acoustical** *adj.* акустический. —**acoustics**, *n.* акустика.

acquaint *v.t.* знакомить; ознакомлять. *Acquaint oneself with*, ознакомляться с.

acquaintance *n.* **1,** (state of being acquainted) знакомство. *Make someone's acquaintance*, (по)знакомиться с кем-нибудь. **2,** (person known to one) знакомый.

acquainted *adj.* знакомый. *Get acquainted*, знакомиться.

acquiesce *v.i.* неохотно соглашаться (*e.g.* на предложение). *Acquiesce to someone's demands*, уступить чьим-нибудь требованиям. —**acquiescence**, *n.* согласие. —**acquiescent**, *adj.* уступчивый.

acquire *v.t.* приобретать: *acquire knowledge/experience*, приобретать знания/опыт.

acquisition *n.* **1,** (act of acquiring; something acquired) приобретение. **2,** *library science* комплектование.

acquisitive *adj.* собственнический.

acquit *v.t.* оправдывать: *He was acquitted*, он был оправдан. —**acquit oneself**, вести себя; держаться. *Acquit oneself well*, хорошо себя зарекомендовать.

acquittal *n.* оправдание; оправдательный приговор.

acre *n.* акр.

acrid *adj.* едкий; терпкий.

acrimonious *adj.* едкий; злобный. —**acrimony**, *n.* едкость; злоба.

acrobat *n.* акробат. —**acrobatic**, *adj.* акробатический. —**acrobatics**, *n.* акробатика.

acronym *n.* аббревиатура.

acropolis *n.* акрополь.

across *prep.* **1,** (from one side to the other) через: *a* *bridge across the Danube*, мост че́рез Дуна́й. *Walk across the street*, перейти́ че́рез у́лицу. *Reach across the table*, тяну́ться че́рез стол. **2,** (on the other side of) че́рез: *be sitting across the aisle from*, сиде́ть че́рез прохо́д от. *They live across the street*, они́ живу́т че́рез у́лицу напро́тив. *The village is just across the border*, дере́вушка по ту сто́рону грани́цы. *His office is across the hall from mine*, его́ кабине́т напро́тив моего́. **3,** (along; through) по: *The clouds moved across the sky*, облака́ плы́ли по не́бу. **4,** (athwart) попере́к: *lie across the bed/road*, лежа́ть попере́к крова́ти/доро́ги. **5,** (crosswise upon): *with his hands across his chest*, со скрещёнными на груди́ рука́ми. —*adv.* **1,** (from one side to the other) *usu.* rendered by the prefix пере-: *Can you swim across?*, мо́жете переплы́ть? *The river is so wide you can't see across*, река́ така́я широ́кая, что неви́дно противополо́жного бе́рега. **2,** (in width): *The river is two miles across*, ширина́ реки́ две ми́ли. —**across from,** напро́тив.

acrostic *n.* акрости́х.

act *v.i.* **1,** (take action) де́йствовать; поступа́ть: *act decisively*, де́йствовать/поступа́ть реши́тельно. *We must act at once*, мы должны́ де́йствовать неме́дленно. *Act on someone's advice*, сле́довать чьему́-нибудь сове́ту. **2,** (behave) вести́ себя́: *act foolishly*, вести́ себя́ глу́по; *act like a child*, вести́ себя́ как ребёнок. **3,** *fol. by* **as** (serve as) выступа́ть в ро́ли *or* в ка́честве (+ *gen.*). *Act as a mediator*, выступа́ть в ка́честве посре́дника. **4,** (be an actor) игра́ть (на сце́не). —*v.t.* игра́ть. *The play was well acted*, актёры игра́ли хорошо́. —*n.* **1,** (deed) посту́пок; акт. *Act of courage*, му́жественный посту́пок. *Catch in the act*, пойма́ть с поли́чным. **2,** (law) акт. **3,** (part of a play or opera) де́йствие; акт. **4,** (item on a variety program) но́мер: *circus act*, цирково́й но́мер. **5,** (false show) коме́дия: *put on an act*, разы́грывать коме́дию. —**act out,** разы́грывать. —**act up,** *colloq.* шали́ть: *My back is beginning to act up*, спина́ начина́ет шали́ть.

acting *n.* **1,** (performance) игра́. *The acting was superb*, актёры игра́ли превосхо́дно. **2,** (profession) актёрство. —*adj.* исполня́ющий обя́занности (+ *gen.*): *acting manager*, исполня́ющий обя́занности заве́дующего.

actinium *n.* акти́ний.

action *n.* **1,** (doing something) де́йствие; де́йствия. *Quick action*, бы́стрые де́йствия. *Plan of action*, план де́йствий. *Freedom of action*, свобо́да де́йствий. *Man of action*, челове́к де́йствия *or* де́ла. *Take action*, де́йствовать; предпринима́ть де́йствия. *Put out of action*, выводи́ть из стро́я. **2,** *pl.* (acts; deeds) де́йствия; дела́. *Judge someone by his actions*, суди́ть о ком-нибудь по его́ дела́м. *Be responsible for one's actions*, отвеча́ть за свои́ посту́пки. **3,** (of a play or narrative) де́йствие. **4,** *mil.* (combat) бой: *be killed in action*, пасть в бою́. *See action*, воева́ть. **5,** *law* иск; проце́сс. *Take legal action*, начина́ть суде́бный проце́сс; подава́ть в суд.

activate *v.t.* **1,** (set in motion) приводи́ть в де́йствие.

2, *mil.* (place on active duty) призыва́ть на де́йствительную слу́жбу.

active *adj.* **1,** (energetic; busy) акти́вный; де́ятельный. *Take an active part in*, принима́ть де́ятельное уча́стие в (+ *prepl.*). **2,** (lively; agile) живо́й. **3,** (functioning; in operation) де́йствующий. *Active volcano*, де́йствующий вулка́н. **4,** *gram.* действи́тельный: *active voice*, действи́тельный зало́г. **5,** *mil.* действи́тельный: *active duty*, действи́тельная слу́жба. —**actively,** *adv.* акти́вно.

activist *n.* активи́ст.

activity *n.* **1,** *often pl.* (action; pursuits) де́ятельность: *political/subversive activities*, полити́ческая/подрывна́я де́ятельность. *Extracurricular activities*, внекла́ссная рабо́та; внекла́ссные мероприя́тия. **2,** (vigorous action) акти́вность. **3,** (action of the forces of nature) де́ятельность: *volcanic activity*, вулкани́ческая де́ятельность.

actor *n.* актёр. —**actress,** *n.* актри́са.

actual *adj.* действи́тельный; факти́ческий. *The actual state of affairs*, действи́тельное положе́ние дел. *In actual fact*, в действи́тельности; на са́мом де́ле.

actuality *n.* действи́тельность.

actually *adv.* действи́тельно; факти́чески; на са́мом де́ле.

actuate *v.t.* **1,** (put into action) приводи́ть в де́йствие. **2,** (impel) побужда́ть.

acuity *n.* острота́.

acumen *n.* проница́тельность; прозорли́вость.

acupuncture *n.* акупункту́ра; иглотерапи́я; иглоука́лывание.

acute *adj.* о́стрый: *acute shortage*, о́страя нехва́тка. —**acute accent,** о́строе ударе́ние. —**acute angle,** о́стрый у́гол.

ad *n.* объявле́ние; рекла́ма.

A.D. на́шей э́ры: *in 200 A.D.*, в двухсо́том году́ на́шей э́ры.

adage *n.* изрече́ние.

adagio *adv. & n.* ада́жио.

adamant *adj.* непрекло́нный.

Adam's apple ада́мово я́блоко; кады́к.

adapt *v.t.* **1,** (adjust) приспоса́бливать. **2,** (convert to a new medium) переде́лывать. *Adapt for the stage*, инсцени́ровать. —*v.i.* приспоса́бливаться: *adapt to a new situation*, приспосо́биться к но́вой обстано́вке.

adaptability *n.* приспособля́емость. —**adaptable,** *adj.* легко́ приспоса́бливающийся.

adaptation *n.* **1,** (act of adapting) приспособле́ние. **2,** (of a story, play, etc.) переде́лка. **3,** *biol.* адапта́ция.

adapter *n.* ада́птер.

add *v.t.* **1,** (put additionally) прибавля́ть; добавля́ть: *add salt to the soup*, прибавля́ть/добавля́ть соль в суп. *Add a line to a letter*, прибавля́ть стро́чку к письму́. *Add wood to the fire*, подкла́дывать дров в ого́нь. **2,** (state additionally) добавля́ть: *He added that...*, он доба́вил, что... **3,** (impart) придава́ть: *add zest to*, придава́ть пика́нтность (+ *dat.*). **4,** *math.* скла́дывать: *add two and two*, скла́дывать два и два. **5,** (join) присоединя́ть: *add one's voice to*, присоединя́ть свой го́лос к. —*v.i.* **1,** (do addition) скла́дывать чи́сла. **2,** *fol. by* **to** (augment) увели́чивать; уси́ливать. —**add on, 1,** (add additionally) прибавля́ть: *add on the interest,* прибавля́ть проце́нты. **2,** (build on) пристра́ивать. —**add up, 1,** (figure the total of) сумми́ровать; подыто́живать. **2,** *usu. neg.* (seem consistent) (не) сходи́ться; (не) выде́рживать кри́тики. —**add up to, 1,** (amount to) составля́ть; равня́ться (+ *dat.*). **2,** (signify; come down to) своди́ться (к).

added *adj.* дополни́тельный; доба́вочный.

addendum *n.* приложе́ние; дополне́ние.

adder *n.* (snake) гадю́ка.

addict *n.* **1,** (drug addict) наркома́н. **2,** (enthusiast) люби́тель. *Chess addict,* стра́стный шахмати́ст. —**addicted,** *adj.* пристрасти́вшийся.

addiction *n.* влече́ние. *Drug addiction,* наркома́ния.

adding machine счётная маши́на.

addition *n.* **1,** (act of adding; something added) прибавле́ние; добавле́ние; дополне́ние. *Addition to the family,* прибавле́ние семе́йства. *A welcome addition to our group,* жела́нное пополне́ние на́шей гру́ппы. **2,** *math.* сложе́ние. —**in addition,** вдоба́вок; кро́ме того́; к тому́ же. —**in addition to,** кро́ме; в дополне́ние к; в добавле́ние к.

additional *adj.* дополни́тельный; доба́вочный. *I need three additional helpers,* мне нужны́ ещё три помо́щника. *Pay an additional ten dollars,* доплати́ть де́сять до́лларов.

additionally *adv.* к тому́ же.

additive *n.* доба́вка; приса́дка.

addle *v.t.* **1,** (spoil) по́ртить. **2,** (confuse) пу́тать.

addled *adj.* **1,** (rotten, as of an egg) ту́хлый. **2,** (confused; mixed up) пу́таный.

address *n.* **1,** (dwelling or mailing place) а́дрес: *What is your address?,* како́й ваш а́дрес? **2,** (formal speech) выступле́ние: *in his address to the conference/delegates,* в своём выступле́нии на конфере́нции/ пе́ред делега́тами/. —*adj.* а́дресный. *Address book,* записна́я кни́жка. —*v.t.* **1,** (write the address on) писа́ть а́дрес на: *address envelopes,* писа́ть адреса́ на конве́ртах. **2,** (dispatch) адресова́ть: *address a letter to someone,* адресова́ть письмо́ кому́-нибудь. **3,** (apply to; appeal to) обраща́ться к; адресова́ться к. **4,** (call by a certain name or title) обраща́ться к: *address someone as "your honor",* обраща́ться к кому́-нибудь «ва́ша честь». **5,** (deliver a speech to) выступа́ть на *or* пе́ред. **6,** (direct, as a remark or question) адресова́ть. **7,** (begin to deal with, as a problem) бра́ться за; принима́ться за.

addressee *n.* адреса́т.

adduce *v.t.* приводи́ть.

adenoid *n.* адено́ид.

adept *adj.* иску́сный. *Be adept at,* иску́сно (+ *verb*).

adequacy *n.* доста́точность.

adequate *adj.* доста́точный: *Our supplies are adequate,* у нас доста́точно запа́сов. —**adequately,** *adv.* доста́точно.

adhere *v.i.* **1,** (stick fast) прилипа́ть; пристава́ть. **2,** *fol. by* **to** (follow consistently) приде́рживаться (+ *gen.*); держа́ться (+ *gen.*).

adherence *n.* приве́рженность.

adherent *n.* приве́рженец.

adhesion *n.* прилипа́ние.

adhesive *adj.* ли́пкий. —*n.* ли́пкое вещество́. —**adhesive tape,** ли́пкая ле́нта.

ad hoc специа́льный: *ad hoc committee,* специа́льный комите́т.

adieu *interj.* проща́й! —*n.* проща́ние.

ad infinitum до бесконе́чности.

adipose *adj.* жи́рный.

adjacent *adj.* сме́жный; сосе́дний. *Lie adjacent to,* прилега́ть к. —**adjacent angles,** сме́жные углы́.

adjective *n.* и́мя прилага́тельное. —**adjectival,** *adj. Adjectival endings,* оконча́ния имён прилага́тельных.

adjoin *v.t.* прилега́ть к; примыка́ть к. —**adjoining,** *adj.* сме́жный; прилега́ющий.

adjourn *v.t.* откла́дывать; закрыва́ть: *adjourn the talks,* отложи́ть перегово́ры; *adjourn the meeting,* закры́ть собра́ние. *Adjourn a game,* отложи́ть па́ртию. *Declare the meeting adjourned,* объяви́ть заседа́ние закры́тым. —*v.i.* **1,** (suspend or end proceedings) закрыва́ться; закрыва́ть заседа́ние; объявля́ть переры́в. **2,** *colloq.* (move) переходи́ть.

adjournment *n.* переры́в; *chess* откла́дывание.

adjudge *v.t.* признава́ть: *He was adjudged insane,* его́ призна́ли душевнобольны́м.

adjudicate *v.t.* выноси́ть реше́ние по.

adjunct *n.* прида́ток.

adjure *v.t.* **1,** (command solemnly) повелева́ть. **2,** (entreat) заклина́ть.

adjust *v.t.* **1,** (make accurate; set right) регули́ровать; нала́живать; настра́ивать. *Adjust a clock,* подводи́ть часы́. **2,** (move into the proper position) поправля́ть. **3,** (alter so as to make fit) подгоня́ть. **4,** (compose, as differences) ула́живать. —*v.i.* приспоса́бливаться: *adjust to city life,* приспосо́биться к городско́й жи́зни. *I'll adjust to your schedule,* я подстро́юсь под ва́ше расписа́ние.

adjustable *adj. Adjustable wrench,* разводно́й (га́ечный) ключ. *Adjustable shelves,* раздвижны́е по́лки. *Adjustable rate,* переме́нная ста́вка.

adjuster *n.* нала́дчик.

adjustment *n.* **1,** (adaptation) приспособле́ние. **2,** (regulating; setting) устано́вка; регулиро́вка. **3,** (fixing; setting right) попра́вка: *a slight adjustment,* небольша́я попра́вка. **4,** (composing, as differences) ула́живание.

adjutant *n.* адъюта́нт.

ad-lib *v.t. & i., colloq.* импровизи́ровать.

administer *v.t.* **1,** (manage) управля́ть. **2,** (inflict, as a beating, defeat, etc.) наноси́ть. **3,** (give remedially) дава́ть. *Administer first aid,* ока́зывать пе́рвую по́мощь. *Administer an injection,* сде́лать уко́л. **4,** (give; conduct, as a test) проводи́ть (экза́мен). **5,** (tender, as an oath): *administer the oath to someone,* приводи́ть кого́-нибудь к прися́ге. **6,** (dispense, as justice) отправля́ть (правосу́дие). —*v.i.* [*usu.* **administer to**] ока́зывать по́мощь (кому́-нибудь); удовлетворя́ть (чьи́-нибудь) ну́жды.

administration *n.* **1,** (managing) управле́ние. **2,** (managing officials) администра́ция. **3,** (government) администра́ция. **4,** (government bureau) управле́ние.

administrative *adj.* администрати́вный.

administrator *n.* администра́тор.

admirable *adj.* похва́льный; отли́чный.

admiral *n.* адмира́л. —**Admiral of the Fleet,** адмира́л фло́та.

admiralty *n.* адмиралте́йство.

admiration *n.* преклоне́ние; восхище́ние. *Admiration for,* преклоне́ние пе́ред; восхище́ние (+ *instr.*).

admire *v.t.* **1,** (esteem highly) преклоня́ться пе́ред. *I admire a man like that,* я преклоня́юсь пе́ред таки́м челове́ком. **2,** (watch with pleasure) любова́ться; *admire the landscape,* любова́ться пейза́жем.

admirer *n.* покло́нник; почита́тель. *I'm a big admirer of yours,* я ваш большо́й покло́нник.

admissible *adj.* допусти́мый; прие́млемый.

admission *n.* **1,** (act of admitting or letting in) впуск; до́пуск; прие́м; приня́тие. **2,** (entry) вход; до́ступ. *Gain admission to,* получи́ть до́ступ в *or* на. *Admission is free,* вход беспла́тный. **3,** (acknowledgment) призна́ние: *admission of guilt,* призна́ние вины́. —**admission charge,** входна́я пла́та.

admit *v.t.* **1,** (allow to enter) впуска́ть; допуска́ть; пропуска́ть. **2,** (allow to join) принима́ть: *admit to membership,* принима́ть в чле́ны. **3,** (acknowledge; confess) признава́ть: *admit defeat,* призна́ть себя́ побеждённым. *Admit one's mistake,* признава́ть свою́ оши́бку; признава́ться в свое́й оши́бке. *I admit (that) I was wrong,* я признаю́, что был непра́в. **4,** (concede; grant) допуска́ть. *Not a bad idea, you must admit!,* согласи́тесь, неплоха́я иде́я!

admittance *n.* **1,** (act of admitting) впуск; до́пуск; прие́м. **2,** (entry) вход: *no admittance!,* вход воспрещён!

admittedly *adv.* пра́вда; призна́ться.

admix *v.t.* переме́шивать.

admixture *n.* при́месь.

admonish *v.t.* **1,** (chide) де́лать замеча́ние (+ *dat.*). **2,** (advise; urge) увещева́ть.

admonition *n.* **1,** (mild rebuke) замеча́ние. **2,** (advice; warning) наставле́ние; нравоуче́ние; увеща́ние.

ad nauseam до тошноты́.

ado *n.* суета́. *Without further ado,* без дальне́йших церемо́ний; без да́льних слов. —**much ado about nothing,** мно́го шу́ма из ничего́.

adobe *n.* кирпи́ч-сыре́ц; сама́н. —*adj.* сама́нный; глиноби́тный.

adolescence *n.* о́трочество.

adolescent *n.* подро́сток. —*adj.* подро́стковый; о́троческий.

adopt *v.t.* **1,** (take into one's family) усыновля́ть; удочеря́ть. **2,** (vote to accept) принима́ть: *adopt a resolution,* принима́ть резолю́цию. **3,** (take up and follow) принима́ть; усва́ивать; перенима́ть; заи́мствовать. *Adopt a name/religion,* принима́ть фами́лию/рели́гию. *Adopt a plan,* принима́ть план. *Adopt a custom,* усво́ить обы́чай. *Adopt a wait-and-see attitude,* занима́ть выжида́тельную пози́цию.

adopted *adj.* прие́мный.

adoption *n.* **1,** (taking into one's family) усыновле́ние. *Give a child up for adoption,* отда́ть ребёнка на усыновле́ние. **2,** (acceptance and use; vote to accept) приня́тие.

adoptive *adj.* прие́мный.

adorable *adj.* преле́стный; восхити́тельный.

adore *v.t.* обожа́ть. —**adoration,** *n.* обожа́ние.

adorn *v.t.* украша́ть. —**adornment,** *n.* украше́ние.

adrenal *adj.* надпо́чечный. —**adrenal gland,** надпо́чечная железа́; надпо́чечник.

adrenalin *also,* **adrenaline** *n.* адренали́н.

adrift *adv.* по тече́нию: *set adrift,* пуска́ть по тече́нию. *Be adrift,* дрейфова́ть.

adroit *adj.* ло́вкий; прово́рный. —**adroitly,** *adv.* ло́вко. —**adroitness,** *n.* ло́вкость; прово́рство.

adsorb *v.t.* адсорби́ровать. —**adsorption,** *n.* адсо́рбция.

adulation *n.* **1,** (excessive praise) восхвале́ние. **2,** (intense admiration) преклоне́ние.

adult *n. & adj.* взро́слый. *Adult education,* обуче́ние взро́слых.

adulterate *v.t.* фальсифици́ровать; разбавля́ть. —**adulteration,** *n.* фальсифика́ция.

adulterer *n.* прелюбоде́й. —**adulteress,** *n.* прелюбоде́йка. —**adulterous,** *adj.* прелюбоде́йский.

adultery *n.* прелюбодея́ние. *Commit adultery,* соверша́ть прелюбодея́ние; прелюбоде́йствовать.

adulthood *n.* зре́лость; возмужа́лость.

adumbrate *v.t.* **1,** (outline sketchily) набра́сывать (*pfv.* наброса́ть). **2,** (foreshadow) предвеща́ть. **3,** (overshadow) затмева́ть.

advance *v.t.* **1,** (move forward) продвига́ть. *Advance a pawn,* дви́нуть *or* передви́нуть пе́шку вперёд. **2,** (put forward; offer) выдвига́ть: *advance a hypothesis,* выдвига́ть гипо́тезу. **3,** (lend) ссужа́ть: *advance money to someone,* ссужа́ть кого́-нибудь деньга́ми. —*v.i.* продвига́ться; выдвига́ться. *Troops are advancing on the capital,* войска́ продвига́ются к столи́це. *Advance to the semifinals,* вы́йти в полуфина́л. *Stock prices advanced,* курс а́кций повы́сился. —*n.* **1,** (move forward) продвиже́ние. **2,** *fig.* (important step forward) достиже́ние: *the latest advances in medicine,* после́дние достиже́ния медици́ны. **3,** (loan) ава́нс; ссу́да. **4,** *pl.* (overtures) домога́тельства; заи́грывания; уха́живания. —*adj.* **1,** (prior) предвари́тельный: *advance notice,* предвари́тельное уведомле́ние. *Advance copy,* сигна́льный экземпля́р. **2,** (going ahead) передово́й: *advance guard,* передово́й отря́д. —**in advance,** зара́нее; предвари́тельно; вперёд; ава́нсом. *Pay in advance,* плати́ть ава́нсом *or* вперёд.

advanced *adj.* **1,** (far along) продви́нутый: *advanced student,* продви́нутый учени́к *or* студе́нт. *Advanced course,* курс повы́шенной тру́дности. **2,** (modern; progressive) передово́й: *advanced methods,* передовы́е ме́тоды. **3,** (old) прекло́нный: *advanced age,* прекло́нный во́зраст. *Advanced in years,* прекло́нного во́зраста.

advancement *n.* продвиже́ние.

advantage *n.* **1,** (edge; superiority) преиму́щество: *enjoy a clear advantage over*, по́льзоваться я́вным преиму́ществом пе́ред. *Numerical advantage*, чи́сленное превосхо́дство. **2,** (factor giving an edge) преиму́щество; досто́инство. *Advantages and disadvantages*, досто́инства и недоста́тки. *Have a number of advantages over*, име́ть ряд преиму́ществ пе́ред. **3,** (benefit; profit) вы́года; по́льза. *Turn to one's advantage*, обраща́ть в свою́ по́льзу. —**take advantage of, 1,** (avail oneself of) по́льзоваться (+ *instr.*). **2,** (abuse; exploit) злоупотребля́ть; эксплуати́ровать. —**to advantage,** вы́годно; с по́льзой; в вы́годном све́те. —**to the best advantage, 1,** (in the best way) наилу́чшим о́бразом. **2,** (in the best light) в са́мом вы́годном све́те.

advantageous *adj.* вы́годный. *Advantageous position*, вы́годное *or* вы́игрышное положе́ние.

advent *n.* наступле́ние; прише́ствие.

adventure *n.* приключе́ние; авантю́ра. *Thirst for adventure*, жа́жда приключе́ний. —*adj.* приключе́нческий; авантю́рный: *adventure story*, приключе́нческий/авантю́рный рома́н.

adventurer *n.* иска́тель приключе́ний.

adventuresome *adj.* сме́лый; предприи́мчивый.

adventurism *n.* авантюри́зм. —**adventurist,** *n.* авантюри́ст. —**adventuristic,** *adj.* авантюристи́ческий.

adventurous *adj.* сме́лый; предприи́мчивый.

adverb *n.* наре́чие. —**adverbial,** *adj.* наре́чный.

adversary *n.* проти́вник.

adverse *adj.* неблагоприя́тный. *Adverse wind*, встре́чный ве́тер. *Adverse balance of trade*, пасси́вный торго́вый бала́нс. —**adversely,** *adv.* отрица́тельно.

adversity *n.* несча́стье; невзго́да.

advertise *v.t. & i.* реклами́ровать.

advertisement *n.* объявле́ние; рекла́ма.

advertiser *n.* реклáмодáтель.

advertising *n.* рекла́ма. —*adj.* рекла́мный.

advice *n.* сове́т.

advisable *adj.* целесообра́зный. —**advisability,** *n.* целесообра́зность.

advise *v.t.* **1,** (give advice to) сове́товать: *What do you advise me to do?*, что вы мне сове́туете де́лать? *He advised against it*, он сове́товал не де́лать э́того. *She advised me not to go*, она́ сове́товала мне не ходи́ть. **2,** (notify) сообща́ть; извеща́ть; уведомля́ть; дать знать.

advised *adj.* осведомлённый. *Keep someone advised*, держа́ть кого́-нибудь в ку́рсе дел. —**advisedly,** *adv.* наме́ренно; обду́манно. *I say this advisedly*, я наме́ренно э́то говорю́.

advisement *n.* рассмотре́ние. —**take under advisement,** рассма́тривать.

adviser *also,* **advisor** *n.* сове́тник.

advisory *adj.* консультати́вный. *In an advisory capacity*, в ка́честве сове́тника.

advocacy *n.* защи́та; подде́ржка.

advocate *v.t.* стоя́ть за; выступа́ть за. —*n.* **1,** (one who favors a cause) сторо́нник: *an advocate of reform*, сторо́нник рефо́рмы. **2,** *law* адвока́т; защи́тник.

adz *also,* **adze** *n.* тесло́.

aegis *n.* эги́да: *under the aegis of*, под эги́дой (+ *gen.*).

aeon *n.* = **eon**.

aerate *v.t.* прове́тривать. —**aeration,** *n.* аэра́ция.

aerial *adj.* возду́шный. *Aerial photograph*, аэросни́мок. *Aerial view of...*, вид (+ *gen.*) с самолёта. —*n.* анте́нна.

aerobics *n.* аэро́бика.

aerodrome *n.* = **airdrome**.

aerodynamics *n.* аэродина́мика. —**aerodynamic,** *adj.* аэродинами́ческий.

aeronaut *n.* воздухопла́ватель; аэрона́вт. —**aeronautical,** *adj.* авиацио́нный; воздухопла́вательный. *Aeronautical engineer*, авиацио́нный инжене́р. —**aeronautics,** *n.* воздухопла́вание; аэрона́втика.

aerosol *n.* аэрозо́ль. —*adj.* аэрозо́льный.

aerospace *n.* возду́шно-косми́ческое простра́нство. —*adj.* возду́шно-косми́ческий; авиакосми́ческий.

aerostat *n.* аэроста́т. —**aerostatics,** *n.* аэроста́тика.

aesthete *n.* = **esthete**. —**aesthetic,** *adj.* = **esthetic**. —**aesthetics,** *n.* = **esthetics**.

afar *adv., in* **from afar,** издалека́.

affable *adj.* приве́тливый. —**affability,** *n.* приве́тливость.

affair *n.* **1,** (event; matter; business) де́ло. *Foreign affairs*, иностра́нные дела́. *State of affairs*, положе́ние дел *or* веще́й. *It's none of your affair*, э́то не ва́ше де́ло. **2,** (amorous relationship) связь; рома́н.

affect *v.t.* **1,** (have an effect upon) влия́ть на (+ *acc.*); отража́ться на (+ *prepl.*). *Affect the outcome*, влия́ть на коне́чный результа́т. *Affect one's health*, отража́ться на (чьём-нибудь) здоро́вье. **2,** (touch; concern) затра́гивать: *The decision affects everyone*, реше́ние затра́гивает всех. **3,** (touch emotionally) тро́гать. **4,** (feign) притворя́ться; прики́дываться.

affectation *n.* де́ланность; жема́нство; аффекта́ция.

affected *adj.* **1,** (feigned) наи́гранный; напускно́й; аффекти́рованный. **2,** (artificial in manner) жема́нный; мане́рный. **3,** (moved by emotion) тро́нут; растро́ганный.

affection *n.* привя́занность. —**affectionate,** *adj.* ла́сковый.

affiance *v.t.* обруча́ть.

affidavit *n.* пи́сьменное показа́ние под прися́гой.

affiliate *v.t., usu. passive:* *be affiliated with*, име́ть связь с. —*v.i.* присоединя́ться. —*n.* филиа́л. —**affiliation,** *n.* принадле́жность.

affinity *n.* **1,** (natural attraction; liking) влече́ние. **2,** (similarity implying common origin) родство́; сро́дство.

affirm *v.t.* **1,** (assert positively) заявля́ть о: *affirm one's loyalty*, заяви́ть о свое́й лоя́льности. **2,** (confirm) подтвержда́ть; утвержда́ть.

affirmation *n.* **1,** (firm statement) заявле́ние. **2,** (confirmation) подтвержде́ние.

affirmative *adj.* утверди́тельный. *Answer in the affirmative*, отвеча́ть утверди́тельно. —**affirmatively,** *adv.* утверди́тельно.

affix *v.t.* **1,** (attach) прикрепля́ть. **2,** (stick on) накле́ивать; прикле́ивать. **3,** (write; stamp; imprint) накла́дывать; ста́вить: *affix a seal,* накла́дывать/ста́вить печа́ть. *Affix one's signature to,* ста́вить свою́ по́дпись под (+ *instr.*).

afflict *v.t.* поража́ть. *Be afflicted with,* страда́ть (+ *instr.*).

affliction *n.* **1,** (distress) несча́стье. **2,** (ailment) боле́знь.

affluence *n.* оби́лие; бога́тство.

affluent *adj.* бога́тый; состоя́тельный. *Affluent society,* о́бщество изоби́лия.

afford *v.t.* **1,** (have the means for) позво́лить себе́: *I can't afford it,* не могу́ э́того себе́ позво́лить; э́то мне не по сре́дствам (*or* не по карма́ну). *I can't afford the time,* у меня́ нет на э́то вре́мени. **2,** (give; provide) доставля́ть; предоставля́ть: *afford pleasure,* доставля́ть удово́льствие; *afford an opportunity,* предоставля́ть возмо́жность. *The balcony affords an excellent view of the lake,* с балко́на открыва́ется прекра́сный вид на о́зеро.

affront *v.t.* оскорбля́ть. —*n.* оскорбле́ние.

Afghan *adj.* [*also,* **Afghanistani**] афга́нский. —*n.* **1,** (native of Afghanistan) афга́нец; афга́нка. **2,** *l.c.* (woolen blanket) шерстяно́е одея́ло.

afield *adv.* от те́мы: *go rather far afield,* отклоня́ться от те́мы. *That would take us far afield,* э́то завело́ бы нас сли́шком далеко́.

afire *adj.* в огне́. *Set afire,* поджига́ть.

aflame *adj.* в огне́. *Be aflame,* быть в огне́; пыла́ть. *Set aflame,* поджига́ть.

afloat *adj. & adv.* на воде́; на плаву́. *Keep/remain afloat,* держа́ться на воде́/ на плаву́/ на пове́рхности/. *Set afloat,* спуска́ть на́ воду. *Rumors are afloat,* хо́дят слу́хи.

afoot *adv. & adj., obs.* пешко́м. —**be afoot,** гото́виться; затева́ться.

aforementioned *adj.* вышеупомя́нутый.

aforesaid *adj.* вышеска́занный; вышеука́занный.

aforethought *adj.* преднаме́ренный; предумы́шленный. —**with malice aforethought,** с зара́нее обду́манным (престу́пным) наме́рением; со злым у́мыслом.

afraid *adj., used predicatively: I am afraid,* мне стра́шно. *Be afraid of,* боя́ться (+ *gen.*). *Be afraid to,* боя́ться (+ *inf.*). *Be afraid that...,* боя́ться, что...

afresh *adv.* сно́ва: *start afresh,* начина́ть сно́ва.

African *adj.* африка́нский. —*n.* африка́нец.

Afrikaans *n.* африка́анс.

Afrikaner *n.* африка́нер.

aft *adv.* на корме́; на корму́.

after *prep.* **1,** (subsequent to) по́сле: *after dinner,* по́сле обе́да. ♦*With expressions of time,* че́рез: *after a year,* че́рез год; *after a while,* че́рез не́которое вре́мя. *Ten years after the war,* че́рез де́сять лет по́сле войны́. **2,** (following; behind; in pursuit of) за (+ *instr.*): *Summer comes after spring,* за весно́й идёт ле́то. *Time after time,* раз за ра́зом. *Repeat after me!,* повторя́йте за мной! *Run/look/clean up/after someone,* бежа́ть/присма́тривать/убира́ть за ке́м-

нибудь. *Call after someone,* кри́кнуть вдого́нку (+ *dat.*). *Make one mistake after another,* де́лать оши́бку за оши́бкой. **3,** (in telling time): *ten after two,* де́сять мину́т тре́тьего. *It is already after six,* уже́ седьмо́й час. **4,** (in honor of) в честь: *He was named after his grandfather,* его́ назва́ли в честь де́да. *The city was named after him,* го́род был на́зван его́ и́менем. **5,** (in view of) по́сле: *after what went on yesterday,* по́сле того́, что произошло́ вчера́. *After all she has been through,* по́сле всего́, что она́ пережила́. **6,** (in spite of) несмотря́ на: *after all he has done for you,* несмотря́ на всё, что он сде́лал для вас. —*adv.* **1,** (behind) сза́ди; позади́. **2,** (subsequently) поздне́е; пото́м. —*conj.* по́сле того́, как: *after he left,* по́сле того́, как он ушёл. *After you have read the book,* по́сле того́, как вы прочтёте кни́гу. *After learning about what happened,* узна́в о случи́вшемся. —**after all, 1,** (despite all; in the end) в конце́ концо́в; всё-таки. *Not so bad after all,* в конце́ концо́в не так уж пло́хо. *I was right after all,* я всё-таки был прав. **2,** (when all is said and done) же; ведь: *After all, she is your sister!,* она́ же твоя́ сестра́; ведь она́ твоя́ сестра́. —**after that,** вслед за тем. —**after the fact,** за́дним число́м. —**after you!,** по́сле вас!; прошу́ вас!

afterbirth *n.* послед.

after-dinner *adj.* послеобе́денный.

aftereffect *n.* после́дствие; отголо́сок.

afterglow *n.* вече́рняя заря́.

afterlife *n.* загро́бная жизнь.

aftermath *n.* отголо́ски.

afternoon *n.* вре́мя по́сле полу́дня; втора́я полови́на дня. —**in the afternoon,** днём; по́сле обе́да; во второ́й полови́не дня. *At three o'clock in the afternoon,* в три часа́ дня.

aftertaste *n.* при́вкус; оса́док.

afterward *also,* **afterwards** *adv.* по́сле; пото́м; впосле́дствии. *Soon afterward,* вско́ре.

afterword *n.* послесло́вие.

again *adv.* опя́ть; сно́ва; ещё раз. *What, again?,* что, опя́ть? *Try again,* попро́бовать ещё раз. *Meet again,* сно́ва встре́титься. *Happen again,* повторя́ться. *You are not to do that again!,* вы не должны́ бо́льше э́того де́лать. —**again and again,** сно́ва и сно́ва. —**but then again,** впро́чем. —**now and again,** вре́мя от вре́мени. —**time and again,** то и де́ло; неоднокра́тно. *I've told you time and again,* я тебе́ сто́лько раз говори́л(а).

against *prep.* **1,** (in opposition to) про́тив: *swim against the current,* плыть про́тив тече́ния. *Compete/struggle/rebel against,* состяза́ться/боро́ться/ восстава́ть про́тив. *Six in favor, three against,* шесть за, три про́тив. *He is against our marriage,* он про́тив на́шего бра́ка. *What have you got against him?,* что вы име́ете про́тив него́? *His age is against him,* его́ во́зраст рабо́тает про́тив него́. **2,** (contrary to) про́тив; вопреки́: *against one's will,* про́тив во́ли; *against someone's advice,* вопреки́ чьему́-нибудь сове́ту. *It's against the law,* э́то противозако́нно. **3,** (so as to strike) о (+ *acc.*): *The waves are* *beating against the shore,* во́лны бью́тся о бе́рег. *The rain was beating against the windowpanes,* дождь стуча́л в о́кна. **4,** (so as to touch) к: *lean against a wall,* прислоня́ться к стене́. *Place the table up against the wall,* поста́вить стол вплотну́ю к стене́. **5,** (in contrast to the background of) на фо́не (+ *gen.*): *stand out against the sky,* выделя́ться на фо́не не́ба. **6,** (in anticipation of) на: *money saved against a rainy day,* де́ньги, сбережённые на чёрный день. **7,** (compared to) про́тив: *$1,000 (as) against $500 last year,* ты́сяча до́лларов про́тив пятисо́т в про́шлом году́. **8,** (relative to) по отноше́нию к: *the value of the dollar against the German mark,* курс до́ллара по отноше́нию к неме́цкой ма́рке. **9,** (as a protection from) от: *insurance against breakage,* страхова́ние от поло́мки. *Protection against the cold,* защи́та от хо́лода. **10,** (as a debit on) под: *borrow money against an insurance policy,* занима́ть де́ньги под страхово́й по́лис.

agape *adj. & adv.* рази́нув рот.

agate *n.* ага́т. —*adj.* ага́товый.

agave *n.* ага́ва.

age *n.* **1,** (years since birth) во́зраст. *At my age,* в моём во́зрасте; в мои́ го́ды. *People of all ages,* лю́ди всех во́зрастов. *They are the same age,* они́ одни́х лет. *When I was your age,* когда́ я был (была́) в ва́шем во́зрасте. *Improve with age,* улучша́ться с во́зрастом. *Look young for one's age; not look one's age,* вы́глядеть мо́лодо для своего́ во́зраста; вы́глядеть моло́же свои́х лет. *She married a man twice her age,* она́ вы́шла за́муж за челове́ка, вдво́е ста́рше её. **2,** (old age) ста́рость: *live to a ripe old age,* дожи́ть до ста́рости. *Age has dimmed her memory,* ста́рость осла́била её па́мять. **3,** (adulthood) совершенноле́тие: *come of age,* дости́гнуть совершенноле́тия. *Be of age,* быть совершенноле́тним. **4,** (period in history) век; эпо́ха. *The Stone Age,* ка́менный век. *The Middle Ages,* сре́дние века́. *The ice age,* ледни́ко́вый пери́од. *The space age,* косми́ческий век. **5,** *often pl., colloq.* (a long time) це́лую ве́чность: *I haven't seen you for ages,* не ви́дел(а) вас це́лую ве́чность. *Ages ago,* о́чень давно́; давны́м давно́. —*adj.* возрастно́й: *age group,* возрастна́я гру́ппа. —*v.t.* **1,** (make old) ста́рить. **2,** (mature, as wine) выде́рживать. —*v.i.* **1,** (grow old) старе́ть. **2,** (mature, as of wine) созрева́ть. —**at the age of,** в во́зрасте (+ *gen.*): *at the age of twenty-five,* в во́зрасте двадцати́ пяти́ лет; в двадцатипяти́ле́тнем во́зрасте; в два́дцать пять лет.

aged *adj.* **1,** (old) ста́рый; престаре́лый. **2,** (of a certain age): *a girl aged five,* де́вочка пяти́ лет. **3,** (mature, as of wine) вы́держанный. —**the aged,** старики́.

ageing *adj. & n.* = **aging**.

ageless *adj.* **1,** (seeming not to grow old) ве́чно молодо́й. **2,** (eternal) ве́чный.

agency *n.* **1,** (bureau; department) аге́нтство; бюро́; управле́ние; учрежде́ние: *telegraph agency,* телегра́фное аге́нтство; *travel agency,* бюро́ путеше́ствий; *specialized agency,* специализи́рованное

учрежде́ние. *Central Intelligence Agency,* Центра́льное разве́дывательное управле́ние. **2,** (means; instrumentality) сре́дство. *Through the agency of,* посре́дством (+ *gen.*); че́рез посре́дство (+ *gen.*).

agenda *n.* пове́стка дня.

agent *n.* **1,** (person) аге́нт: *insurance agent,* страхово́й аге́нт; *intelligence agent,* аге́нт разве́дки. **2,** (substance) вещество́; сре́дство; аге́нт. *Toxic agent,* отравля́ющее вещество́. —**agent provocateur,** провока́тор.

age-old *adj.* веково́й; изве́чный. *Age-old argument,* изве́чный спор.

agglutination *n.* агглютина́ция. —**agglutinative,** *adj.* агглютинати́вный.

aggrandize *v.t.* увели́чивать; расширя́ть. —**aggrandizement,** *n.* увеличе́ние; расшире́ние.

aggravate *v.t.* **1,** (make worse) ухудша́ть; обостря́ть. **2,** *colloq.* (vex) раздража́ть; досажда́ть.

aggravating *adj.* доса́дный. —**aggravating circumstances,** отягча́ющие вину́ обстоя́тельства.

aggravation *n.* **1,** (making worse) ухудше́ние; обостре́ние. **2,** (vexation) раздраже́ние; доса́да.

aggregate *adj.* о́бщий: *the aggregate number of...,* о́бщее число́ (+ *gen.*). —*n.* совоку́пность: *in the aggregate,* в совоку́пности.

aggression *n.* агре́ссия. *Act of aggression,* акт агре́ссии.

aggressive *adj.* **1,** (militant; hostile) агресси́вный. **2,** (assertive; pushy) напо́ристый.

aggressiveness *n.* **1,** (militancy) агресси́вность. **2,** (assertiveness) напо́ристость.

aggressor *n.* агре́ссор.

aggrieve *v.t.* **1,** (distress) огорча́ть. **2,** (wrong) обижа́ть. *The aggrieved party,* потерпе́вшая сторона́.

aghast *adj.* в у́жасе.

agile *adj.* прово́рный. —**agility,** *n.* прово́рство.

aging *also,* **ageing** *n.* старе́ние: *the aging process,* проце́сс старе́ния. —*adj.* старе́ющий.

agitate *v.t.* **1,** (disturb, as the sea) волнова́ть. **2,** (shake briskly) взба́лтывать. **3,** (perturb) волнова́ть. —*v.i.* агити́ровать: *agitate for reform,* агити́ровать за рефо́рму. —**agitated,** *adj.* взволно́ванный.

agitation *n.* **1,** (agitated state) волне́ние. **2,** *polit.* агита́ция.

agitator *n.* агита́тор.

aglet *n.* **1,** (tip at the end of a lace) наконе́чник. **2,** (braid on a uniform) аксельба́нт.

aglow *adj., used predicatively:* *be aglow,* сия́ть; свети́ться. *She is all aglow,* она́ вся све́тится.

agnostic *n.* агно́стик. —*adj.* агности́ческий. —**agnosticism,** *n.* агностици́зм.

ago *adj.* тому́ наза́д: *two years ago,* два го́да тому́ наза́д. *He was here a little while ago,* он то́лько что был здесь. —*adv., in long ago,* давно́; **not long ago,** неда́вно. *As long ago as 1913,* ещё в ты́сяча девятьсо́т трина́дцатом году́.

agonize *v.i.* му́читься. —**agonizing,** *adj.* мучи́тельный.

agony *n.* **1,** (intense suffering) му́ка; муче́ние. *Be in agony,* ужа́сно страда́ть; му́читься. *Writhe in agony,* ко́рчиться в му́ках. **2,** (throes of death) (предсме́ртная) аго́ния.

agrarian *adj.* агра́рный.

agree *v.i.* **1,** (be of the same opinion) быть согла́сным; соглаша́ться: *I agree with you,* я с ва́ми согла́сен (согла́сна). **2,** *fol. by* **to** (consent to) соглаша́ться (+ *inf.*) *or with* на (+ *acc.*): *agree to a draw,* согласи́ться на ничью́. **3,** (reach agreement; make arrangements) договори́ться. *Agree on the price,* договори́ться о цене́; сходи́ться в цене́. **4,** (be in harmony; coincide) сходи́ться: *The figures don't agree,* ци́фры не схо́дятся. **5,** *fol. by* **with** (be suitable or good for): *Married life agrees with him,* супру́жеская жизнь ему́ по душе́. *Turnips don't agree with me,* мой желу́док не выно́сит ре́пы. **6,** *gram.* согласова́ться: *The adjective agrees with the noun in gender, number and case,* прилага́тельное согласу́ется с существи́тельным в ро́де, числе́ и падеже́.

agreeable *adj.* **1,** (pleasing) прия́тный. **2,** (ready to consent) согла́сный. *I am agreeable to going there,* я гото́в(а) пойти́ туда́; я не про́тив того́, что́бы пойти́ туда́. **3,** (amenable) сгово́рчивый. **4,** (acceptable; convenient) удо́бный. *Is that agreeable to you?,* э́то вам удо́бно?; э́то вас устра́ивает? *Find a date agreeable to all,* найти́ день удо́бный ка́ждому.

agreed *adj.* устано́вленный; поло́женный; усло́вный; усло́вленный. *Also,* **agreed-upon.**

agreement *n.* **1,** (harmony of opinion) согла́сие: *complete agreement,* по́лное согла́сие. *We are in agreement,* мы согла́сны друг с дру́гом. *Nod in agreement,* кива́ть голово́й в знак согла́сия. **2,** (arrangement; understanding) соглаше́ние: *cease-fire agreement,* соглаше́ние о прекраще́нии огня́. *Come to an agreement,* приходи́ть к соглаше́нию. **3,** *gram.* согласова́ние.

agriculture *n.* се́льское хозя́йство. —**agricultural,** *adj.* сельскохозя́йственный.

agronomy *n.* агроно́мия. —**agronomic,** *adj.* агроно́мический. —**agronomist,** *n.* агроно́м.

aground *adj.* на мели́. —*adv.* на мель: *run aground,* сесть на мель.

ah *interj.* а!; ах!

aha *interj.* ага́!

ahead *adv.* **1,** (forward) вперёд: *Full speed ahead!,* по́лный ход вперёд! *Set a clock ahead,* поста́вить *or* перевести́ часы́ вперёд. **2,** (in front of one) впереди́: *Ahead lay a river,* впереди́ была́ река́. *There is danger ahead,* впереди́ опа́сность. **3,** (into or for the future) вперёд: *look ahead,* загляну́ть вперёд. *Plan ahead,* плани́ровать зара́нее. *What lies ahead for him?,* что его́ ждёт впереди́? —**ahead of, 1,** (in front of) впереди́ (+ *gen.*): *walk ahead of the others,* идти́ впереди́ остальны́х. *They are way ahead of us,* они́ намно́го опереди́ли нас. *You have your whole life ahead of you,* у вас це́лая жизнь впереди́. **2,** (in advance of) ра́ньше (+ *gen.*); пре́жде (+ *gen.*). *Ahead of time,* ра́ньше вре́мени; ра́ньше сро́ка. *Be ahead of one's time,* опереди́ть своё вре́мя (*or* свой век). —**get ahead,** продвига́ться (вперёд). —**get ahead**

of, опережа́ть. —**go ahead!,** дава́йте! —**straight ahead,** пря́мо.

ahem *interj.* гм!

aid *v.t.* помога́ть: *aid the victims of the disaster,* помога́ть же́ртвам катастро́фы. —*n.* **1,** (assistance) по́мощь: *first aid,* ско́рая по́мощь; *foreign aid,* иностра́нная по́мощь. *Come to the aid of,* прийти́ на по́мощь (+ *dat.*). *With the aid of a microscope,* с по́мощью микроско́па. **2,** (helpful device) аппара́т: *hearing aid,* слухово́й аппара́т. **3,** *pl.* (teaching devices) посо́бия: *visual aids,* нагля́дные посо́бия.

aide *n.* **1,** *mil.* адъюта́нт. **2,** (assistant) помо́щник.

aide-de-camp *n.* адъюта́нт.

aide-mémoire *n.* па́мятная запи́ска.

AIDS *n.* СПИД.

aiguillette *n.* аксельба́нт.

ail *v.i.* недомога́ть; хвора́ть. —*v.t. What ails you?,* что вас беспоко́ит?

aileron *n.* элеро́н.

ailment *n.* боле́знь; недомога́ние; неду́г.

aim *n.* **1,** (objective) цель: *the aim of the experiment,* цель экспериме́нта. **2,** (act of aiming) прице́ливание. *Take aim at,* прице́ливаться в. *Do you have good aim?,* вы хорошо́ стреля́ете? —*v.t.* направля́ть; наводи́ть; наце́ливать: *aim a gun at,* направля́ть/наводи́ть/наце́ливать ору́жие на (+ *acc.*). *Aim a blow at,* направля́ть уда́р про́тив. —*v.i.* **1,** (take aim) це́литься; прице́ливаться; ме́тить. **2,** (aspire) стреми́ться (к); ме́тить. *Aim higher,* ме́тить вы́ше. **3,** *fol. by* **to** (have as one's goal) име́ть це́лью (+ *inf.*).

aimless *adj.* бесце́льный. —**aimlessly,** *adv.* бесце́льно.

air *n.* **1,** (atmosphere) во́здух. *Out in the open air,* на откры́том во́здухе. *Get some fresh air,* подыша́ть све́жим во́здухом. *Fire into the air,* вы́стрелить в во́здух. *Music filled the air,* во́здух напо́лнила му́зыка. **2,** *radio; TV* эфи́р: *on the air,* в эфи́ре. *Go on the air,* выходи́ть в эфи́р. **3,** (appearance) вид: *air of indifference,* равноду́шный вид. *Assume an air of importance,* принима́ть ва́жный вид; напуска́ть на себя́ ва́жность. **4,** (affected manners) *usu.* **in put on airs; give oneself airs,** ва́жничать; кривля́ться; лома́ться; задава́ться; зазнава́ться. **5,** (tune; melody) пе́сня; напе́в. —*adj.* возду́шный: *air filter,* возду́шный фильтр. *Air temperature,* температу́ра во́здуха. *Air travel,* пое́здки на самолёте. *Air pollution,* загрязне́ние во́здуха. —*v.t.* **1,** [*usu.* **air out**] (ventilate) прове́тривать. **2,** (express publicly; bring out into the open) разглаша́ть. **3,** (broadcast or televise) выпуска́ть в эфи́р. —*v.i.* [*usu.* **air out**] прове́триваться. —**be in the air,** ве́ять; па́хнуть: *Spring is in the air,* ве́ет/па́хнет весно́й. —**be up in the air,** висе́ть *or* повиса́ть в во́здухе. —**be walking on air,** ног под собо́й не чу́ять. —**by air,** на самолёте; самолётом. *Ship by air,* перевози́ть по во́здуху. —**clear the air,** разряди́ть атмосфе́ру. —**vanish into thin air,** раствори́ться *or* раста́ять в во́здухе; как сквозь зе́млю провали́ться; как в во́ду ка́нуть.

air base авиаба́за.

airborne *adj.* **1,** (aloft) в во́здухе. **2,** *mil.* (transported by air) возду́шно-деса́нтный. *Airborne landing,* вы́садка возду́шного деса́нта.

airbrush *n.* краскопу́льт.

air-condition *v.t.* кондициони́ровать. —**air-conditioned,** *adj.* кондициони́рованный; с кондиционе́ром. —**air conditioner,** кондиционе́р. —**air conditioning,** кондициони́рование во́здуха.

air-cooled *adj.* с возду́шным охлажде́нием.

aircraft *n.* **1,** (airplane) самолёт. **2,** (airplanes collectively) авиа́ция. —*adj.* авиацио́нный: *aircraft factory,* авиацио́нный заво́д. —**aircraft carrier,** авиано́сец.

air defense противовозду́шная оборо́на.

airdrome *also,* **aerodrome** *n.* аэродро́м.

airfield *n.* лётное по́ле; аэродро́м.

air force вое́нно-возду́шные си́лы.

air gun духово́е ружьё.

air hole отду́шина.

airily *adv.* ве́село; беззабо́тно.

airing *n.* прове́тривание.

airless *adj.* безвозду́шный.

airlift *n.* возду́шная перево́зка; «возду́шный мост». —*v.t.* перевози́ть *or* перебра́сывать по во́здуху.

airline *n.* авиакомпа́ния.

airliner *n.* возду́шный ла́йнер.

air mail авиапо́чта. "(*By*) *air mail*", а́виа; авиапо́чтой.

airman *n.* лётчик.

airplane *n.* самолёт.

air pocket возду́шная я́ма.

airport *n.* аэропо́рт.

air pressure давле́ние во́здуха.

air raid возду́шный налёт. —**air-raid shelter,** бомбоубе́жище. —**air-raid siren,** сире́на возду́шной трево́ги.

air route авиали́ния; авиатра́сса.

airship *n.* дирижа́бль.

air show авиацио́нная вы́ставка.

airsick *adj.* страда́ющий возду́шной боле́знью. *I became airsick,* меня́ укача́ло в самолёте. —**air-sickness,** *n.* возду́шная боле́знь.

airspace *n.* возду́шное простра́нство.

airspeed *n.* возду́шная ско́рость.

airstrip *n.* взлётно-поса́дочная полоса́.

airtight *adj.* гермети́ческий.

air time *radio; TV* эфи́рное вре́мя.

airwaves *n.pl.* эфи́р.

airway *n.* авиатра́сса.

airworthy *adj.* го́дный к полёту.

airy *adj.* **1,** (with plenty of air) по́лный во́здуха. **2,** (light; thin) возду́шный.

aisle *n.* прохо́д.

ajar *adj. & adv.* приоткры́тый; полуоткры́тый; полуотво́ренный. *Leave the door ajar,* оставля́ть дверь приоткры́той.

akimbo *adj. & adv.* подбоче́нившись. *Stand with arms akimbo,* подбоче́ниться.

akin *adj.* ро́дственный. *Be akin to,* быть сродни́ (+ *dat.*). *Something akin to,* не́что подо́бное (+ *dat.*).

alabaster *n.* алеба́стр. —*adj.* алеба́стровый.

à la carte **1,** *used adjectivally,* порцио́нный. **2,** *used adverbially,* по по́рциям.

alacrity *n.* быстрота́. *With alacrity,* бы́стро; жи́во.

alarm *n.* **1,** (sudden fear) трево́га: *sense of alarm,* чу́вство трево́ги. *Watch in/with alarm,* смотре́ть с трево́гой. **2,** (signal of danger) трево́га; наба́т. *Fire alarm,* пожа́рная трево́га. *Sound the alarm,* бить/забить/ударя́ть трево́гу; бить/забить/ударя́ть (в) наба́т. —*adj.* трево́жный; наба́тный: *alarm signal,* трево́жный сигна́л; *alarm bell,* наба́тный ко́локол. *Alarm system,* сигнализа́ция. —*v.t.* трево́жить: *alarm the passengers,* трево́жить пассажи́ров. —**alarm clock,** буди́льник.

alarmed *adj.* встрево́женный.

alarming *adj.* трево́жный.

alarmist *n.* паникёр.

alas *interj.* увы́!

Alaskan *adj.* аля́скинский.

Albanian *adj.* алба́нский. —*n.* **1,** (person) алба́нец; алба́нка. **2,** (language) алба́нский язы́к.

albatross *n.* альбатро́с.

albeit *conj.* хотя́ и; пусть. *Albeit for somewhat different reasons,* хотя́ и по не́сколько други́м причи́нам.

albino *n.* альбино́с. —**albinism,** *n.* альбини́зм.

album *n.* альбо́м.

albumen *n.* бело́к.

albumin *n.* альбуми́н.

alburnum *n.* за́болонь.

alchemy *n.* алхи́мия. —**alchemist,** *n.* алхи́мик.

alcohol *n.* **1,** (liquid) спирт; алкого́ль. **2,** (intoxicating beverages) алкого́ль; спиртны́е напи́тки.

alcoholic *adj.* спиртно́й; алкого́льный. —*n.* алкого́лик. —**alcoholism,** *n.* алкоголи́зм.

alcove *n.* алько́в; ни́ша.

alder *n.* ольха́.

alderman *n.* член городско́го сове́та.

ale *n.* эль.

alert *adj.* **1,** (watchful) насторо́женный; бди́тельный. *Be alert for pickpockets,* остерега́ться карма́нников. **2,** (mentally quick) бо́йкий. *At eighty she is still mentally alert,* в во́семьдесят лет она́ сохраня́ет я́сность ума́. —*n., mil.* трево́га. *Combat alert,* боево́е дежу́рство. *Place on alert,* поднима́ть по трево́ге. *In a state of alert,* в состоя́нии боево́й гото́вности. —*v.t.* настора́живать. *Alert the population to the danger,* предупреди́ть населе́ние об опа́сности. —**on the alert,** насторо́же; начеку́.

alertness *n.* я́сность ума́; жи́вость ума́.

alexandrite *n.* александри́т.

alfalfa *n.* люце́рна.

algae *n.pl.* во́доросль.

algebra *n.* а́лгебра. —**algebraic,** *adj.* алгебраи́ческий.

Algerian *adj.* алжи́рский. —*n.* алжи́рец; алжи́рка.

algorithm *n.* алгори́тм.

alias *n.* вы́мышленное и́мя. —*adv.* и́наче называ́емый; он же.

alibi *n.* **1,** *law* а́либи. **2,** *colloq.* (excuse) отгово́рка.

alien *n.* иностра́нец. —*adj.* **1,** (foreign; strange) чужо́й: *alien customs,* чужи́е обы́чаи. **2,** (adverse; hostile) чу́ждый: *alien ideology,* чу́ждая идеоло́гия. *It is alien to his nature,* э́то ему́ чу́ждо по ду́ху.

alienate *v.t.* отчужда́ть; отдаля́ть; отта́лкивать; разобща́ть. —**alienation,** *n.* отчужде́ние; отдале́ние.

alight *v.i.* **1,** (dismount) сходи́ть. **2,** (settle) сади́ться.

align *v.t.* **1,** (arrange in a straight line) выра́внивать. **2,** *fol. by* **oneself** (ally oneself) присоединя́ться.

alignment *n.* **1,** (act of aligning; arrtangement in a straight line) центро́вка. **2,** *mil.* выра́внивание; равне́ние. **3,** (political make-up or balance) расстано́вка сил.

alike *adj.* **1,** (similar) похо́жий. *They look alike,* (вне́шне) они́ похо́жи (друг на дру́га). **2,** (identical) одина́ковый. *Politicians are all alike,* все поли́тики одина́ковы; все поли́тики на одно́ лицо́. —*adv.* одина́ково: *dressed alike,* одина́ково оде́ты; *think alike,* мы́слить одина́ково. *Boys and girls alike,* как ма́льчики, так и де́вочки.

alimentary canal пищевари́тельный кана́л; желу́дочно-кише́чный тракт.

alimony *n.* алиме́нты.

alive *adj.* **1,** (living) живо́й: *He is still alive,* он ещё жив. *Get out alive,* вы́йти живы́м. *Take alive,* брать живы́м *or* живьём. *Buried alive,* за́живо погребённый. *Keep alive,* подде́рживать жизнь (+ *gen.*). *See someone alive,* ви́деть кого́-нибудь живы́м. *Find one's child alive,* заста́ть ребёнка в живы́х. *None of them is still alive,* никого́ из них бо́льше нет в живы́х. **2,** (lively; animated) живо́й. *Come alive,* ожива́ть; оживля́ться. *Look alive!,* жи́во!; живе́е! **3,** *fol. by* **to** (aware of; responsive to) чувстви́тельный (к). *Be alive to the danger,* сознава́ть опа́сность. **4,** *fol. by* **with** (swarming) киша́щий: *be alive with bees,* кише́ть пчёлами. —**more dead than alive,** скоре́е мёртвый чем живо́й; полумёртвый.

alkali *n.* щёлочь. —**alkaline,** *adj.* щелочно́й. —**alkalinity,** *n.* щёлочность.

alkaloid *n.* алкало́ид.

all *adj.* весь (вся, всё, все): *all day,* весь день; *all the time,* всё вре́мя; *all nations,* все стра́ны. —*pron.* **1,** (everything) всё: *That's all,* э́то всё. *All is well,* всё хорошо́. *All that is left of the house,* всё, что оста́лось от до́ма. *All he talked about was his work,* он то́лько и говори́л, что о свое́й рабо́те. **2,** (everyone) все: *All agree,* все согла́сны. *I saw all of them,* я ви́дел их всех. —*n.* [*usu.* **one's all**] *Give one's all,* отдава́ть все си́лы. *Stake one's all,* поста́вить всё на ка́рту. —*adv.* **1,** (completely) весь; соверше́нно; совсе́м. *Dressed all in white,* оде́т(а) весь/вся в бе́лое. *I got all wet,* я весь промо́к; я вся промо́кла. *All alone,* соверше́нно *or* совсе́м оди́н/одна́. **2,** *sports: The score was two-all,* счёт был два-два. —**all along,** *see* **along.** —**all at once,** *see* **once.** —**all but,** *see* **but.** —**all for,** целико́м за то, что́бы (+ *inf.*). —**all in,** *colloq.* без ног. —**all in all, 1,** (in general) в о́бщем и це́лом. **2,** (altogether) всего́. —**all over,** *see* **over.** —**all the same,** *see* **same.** —**all told,** в о́бщей сло́жности. —**all too** (+ *adj. or adv.*), сли́шком уж:

The summer passed all too quickly, ле́то прошло́ сли́шком уж бы́стро. —**at all, 1,** (whatsoever) никако́й: *no difference at all,* никако́й ра́зницы. *For no reason at all,* без вся́кой причи́ны. **2,** (in no way) ника́к: *That won't help at all,* э́то ника́к не помо́жет. **3,** (in any event) вообще́: *if that's at all possible,* е́сли э́то вообще́ возмо́жно. *I doubt whether he'll come at all,* я сомнева́юсь, придёт ли он вообще́. *Very rarely, if at all,* о́чень ре́дко, практи́чески никогда́. *See also* **not at all.** —**in all,** всего́; в о́бщей сло́жности. —**not all there,** *colloq.* не в своём уме́; не все до́ма. —**not at all,** *see* **not.** —**of all,** всего́: *most of all,* бо́льше всего́.

Allah *n.* алла́х.

all-around *adj.* всесторо́нний.

allay *v.t.* **1,** (lessen; relieve) смягча́ть; облегча́ть. **2,** (set to rest) успока́ивать. *Allay suspicion,* успока́ивать *or* усыпля́ть подозре́ние. *Allay fears,* развеивать *or* умеря́ть опасе́ния.

all clear отбо́й. *The all-clear signal,* отбо́й; сигна́л отбо́я.

all-conquering *adj.* всепобежда́ющий.

all-consuming *adj.* всепоглоща́ющий.

allegation *n.* (голосло́вное) утвержде́ние.

allege *v.t.* **1,** (assert) утвержда́ть. **2,** (offer as an excuse) ссыла́ться на.

alleged *adj.* предполага́емый: *the alleged murderer,* предполага́емый уби́йца. *For alleged improprieties,* я́кобы за наруше́ние прили́чий. —**allegedly,** *adv.* я́кобы.

allegiance *n.* ве́рность. *Oath of allegiance,* прися́га на ве́рность. *Pledge/swear allegiance,* кля́сться *or* присяга́ть в ве́рности.

allegory *n.* аллего́рия; иносказа́ние. —**allegorical,** *adj.* аллегори́ческий; иносказа́тельный.

allegretto *adv.* & *n.* аллегре́тто.

allegro *adv.* & *n.* алле́гро.

all-embracing *adj.* всеобъе́млющий.

allergen *n.* аллерге́н.

allergic *adj.* аллерги́ческий: *allergic reaction,* аллерги́ческая реа́кция. *Be allergic to,* име́ть аллерги́ю к; не выноси́ть. *He is allergic to penicillin,* у него́ аллерги́я к пеницилли́ну.

allergist *n.* аллерго́лог.

allergy *n.* аллерги́я.

alleviate *v.t.* облегча́ть; смягча́ть: *alleviate pain,* облегча́ть/смягча́ть боль. *Alleviate suffering,* облегча́ть страда́ние. —**alleviation,** *n.* облегче́ние; смягче́ние.

alley *n.* у́зкий переу́лок; у́зкий прохо́д. —**up one's alley,** *slang* как раз по чье́й-нибудь ча́сти.

alley cat бродя́чий кот.

alliance *n.* сою́з. *Form an alliance with,* заключи́ть сою́з с; блоки́роваться с.

allied *adj.* **1,** (united) сою́зный. *Be allied with,* быть сою́зником (+ *gen.*). **2,** (similar; related) сме́жный; ро́дственный.

alligator *n.* аллига́тор.

alliteration *n.* аллитера́ция.

allocate *v.t.* выделя́ть; ассигнова́ть; отводи́ть. *Allo-*

cate funds, выделя́ть/ассигнова́ть сре́дства. *Allocate time*, отводи́ть вре́мя.

allocation *n.* ассигнова́ние: *allocation of funds*, ассигнова́ние средств. *Budget allocations*, бюдже́тные ассигнова́ния.

allopath *n.* аллопа́т. —**allopathic**, *adj.* аллопати́ческий. —**allopathy**, *n.* аллопа́тия.

allot *v.t.* **1,** (parcel out) выделя́ть; распределя́ть. **2,** (allocate) выделя́ть; отводи́ть. *Within the allotted time*, в устано́вленный срок.

allotment *n.* **1,** (parceling out; allocating) выделе́ние; распределе́ние. **2,** (portion allotted) до́ля.

all-out *adj.* развёрнутый; тота́льный. —**go all out,** напряга́ть все си́лы; пусти́ться во все тя́жкие; лезть из ко́жи вон.

allow *v.t.* **1,** (permit) позволя́ть; разреша́ть. *He is not allowed to...*, ему́ не разреша́ется (+ *inf.*). *I will not allow him to insult my wife*, я не позво́лю ему́ оскорбля́ть мою́ жену́; я не позво́лю (*or* допущу́), что́бы он оскорбля́л мою́ жену́. *He was not allowed to see her*, его́ не допусти́ли к ней. **2,** (permit to happen) допуска́ть. *Allow a goal*, пропусти́ть гол. *Not allow the crisis to spread*, не допусти́ть того́, что́бы кри́зис распространя́лся. **3,** *fol. by* (permit to enter) допуска́ть; впуска́ть; пропуска́ть. **4,** (concede) допуска́ть. **5,** (acknowledge as valid) признава́ть пра́вильность (+ *gen.*): *allow a claim*, признава́ть пра́вильность прете́нзии. **6,** (provide; allot, as time) отводи́ть. **7,** *comm.* де́лать ски́дку (+ *dat.*): *allow someone 10%*, де́лать кому́-нибудь ски́дку на де́сять проце́нтов. —*v.i.* [*usu.* **allow for**] учи́тывать: *allow for all the possibilities*, учи́тывать все возмо́жности.

allowance *n.* **1,** (deduction) ски́дка. **2,** (money paid or given out) посо́бие. **3,** *mil.* (де́нежное) дово́льствие. *Housing allowance*, кварти́рное дово́льствие; кварти́рные де́ньги. *Travel allowance*, командиро́вочные де́ньги. **4,** (consideration) ски́дка: *make allowance for*, де́лать ски́дку на.

alloy *n.* сплав. —*v.t.* сплавля́ть.

all-powerful *adj.* всемогу́щий; всеси́льный.

all-purpose *adj.* универса́льный.

all right 1, (expression of assent) ла́дно; хорошо́. **2,** (O.K.) хорошо́. *It's all right with me*, я согла́сен; я не возража́ю. **3,** (so-so) так себе́. **4,** (unhurt) невреди́м. *Are you all right?*, вы не уши́блись? **5,** (recovered) здоро́в. **6,** *preceded by* it's *or* that's (it doesn't matter) ничего́. **7,** (without a doubt) бу́дьте уве́рены: *That's him, all right!*, бу́дьте уве́рены, э́то он!

all-round *adj.* всесторо́нний; универса́льный. *All-round education*, разносторо́ннее образова́ние.

allspice *n.* души́стый пе́рец; гвозди́чный пе́рец.

all-star *adj.* сбо́рный: *all-star team*, сбо́рная кома́нда.

all-time *adj.* непревзойдённый: *all-time record*, непревзойдённый реко́рд. *Prices reached an all-time high*, це́ны дости́гли небыва́ло высо́кого у́ровня.

allude *v.i.* [*usu.* **allude to**] ссыла́ться на; упомина́ть; намека́ть на.

allure *v.t.* зама́нивать; завлека́ть. —*n.* [*also*, **allure-**

ment] прима́нка; обольще́ние. —**alluring,** *adj.* зама́нчивый; маня́щий.

allusion *n.* ссы́лка; намёк; недомо́лвка.

alluvium *n.* нано́с; аллю́вий. —**alluvial,** *adj.* нано́сный; аллювиа́льный.

ally *n.* сою́зник. —*v.t.* *Ally oneself with*, вступа́ть в сою́з с. *Be allied with*, быть сою́зником (+ *gen.*).

almanac *n.* ежего́дник.

almighty *adj.* всемогу́щий. —**the Almighty,** Всевы́шний.

almond *n.* **1,** (tree) минда́ль. **2,** (nut) минда́льный оре́х; (*collectively*) минда́ль. —*adj.* минда́льный: *almond oil*, минда́льное ма́сло.

almost *adv.* почти́: *almost never*, почти́ никогда́. ♦*Of something that nearly happened, but did not*, едва́ не; чуть не: *I almost fell*, я едва́ не/ чуть не/ упа́л.

alms *n.* ми́лостыня: *give alms*, подава́ть ми́лостыню. —**almshouse,** *n.* богаде́льня.

aloe *n.* ало́э. —**aloes,** *n.* ало́э.

aloft *adj. & adv.* **1,** (on high) наверху́; в высоте́. **2,** (airborne) в во́здухе.

alone *adj. & adv.* **1,** (without company) оди́н: *Are you alone?*, вы оди́н (одна́)? *Be alone with*, быть наедине́ с. *He is not alone in this*, в э́том он не одино́к. *He is not alone in this opinion*, не он оди́н име́ет тако́е мне́ние. *The killer acted alone*, уби́йца де́йствовал в одино́чку. **2,** (only) оди́н: *God alone knows*, одному́ бо́гу изве́стно. *Words alone are not enough*, одни́х слов недоста́точно. *Man does not live by bread alone*, не хле́бом еди́ным жив челове́к. **3,** (with nothing else added) (оди́н) то́лько: *this year alone*, то́лько в э́том году́. *Moscow alone has a population of...*, в одно́й то́лько Москве́ живёт... *The head alone of the statue weighs...*, одна́ то́лько голова́ ста́туи ве́сит... —**go it alone,** *colloq.* де́йствовать в одино́чку. —**leave alone, 1,** *literally* оставля́ть одного́ (одну́, одни́х). **2,** (not bother) оставля́ть в поко́е. —**let alone, 1,** (leave alone) оставля́ть в поко́е. **2,** (not to mention) не говоря́ уже́ о.

along *prep.* **1,** (over the length of) по: *walk along the street*, идти́ по у́лице. *Stop along the way*, останови́ться по пути́. **2,** (along the side of) вдоль: *along the border*, вдоль грани́цы; *houses along the road*, дома́ вдоль доро́ги. —*adv.* **1,** (onward) да́льше; вперёд. *Move along!*, проходи́те вперёд! **2,** (with one) с собо́й: *take along*, взять с собо́й. *Bring a friend along*, привести́ с собо́й дру́га. —**all along, 1,** (all the time) всё вре́мя; с са́мого нача́ла. **2,** (along the entire) на всём протяже́нии (+ *gen.*). *All along the border*, вдоль всей грани́цы. *All along the way*, всю доро́гу; на протяже́нии всего́ пути́. —**along with,** вме́сте с. —**get along,** *see* get.

alongside *adv.* ря́дом. *Draw* (up) *alongside*, поравня́ться с. —*prep.* ря́дом с; во́зле.

aloof *adv.* в стороне́; особняко́м: *remain aloof*, держа́ться в стороне́/особняко́м/. —*adj.* отрешённый. —**aloofness,** *n.* отрешённость; отчуждённость.

aloud *adv.* вслух.

alpaca *n.* альпака́.

alpha *n.* áльфа. —**alpha particle,** áльфа-части́ца. —**alpha rays,** áльфа-лучи́.

alphabet *n.* áзбука; алфави́т. —**alphabetic; alphabetical,** *adj.* алфави́тный. —**alphabetize,** *v.t.* располага́ть в алфави́тном поря́дке.

Alpine *adj.* альпи́йский.

already *adv.* **1,** (by this time) уже́: *It is late already,* уже́ по́здно. *I have already eaten,* я уже́ пое́л(а). **2,** (without this) и без того́: *Things are tough enough already,* тяжело́ и без того́. *This complicates an already tense situation,* э́то усложня́ет и без того́ напряжённое положе́ние.

also *adv.* то́же; та́кже. *That is also true,* э́то то́же пра́вда. *I wish also to emphasize that...,* я то́же/ та́кже хочу́ подчеркну́ть, что...,

Altaic *adj.* алта́йский.

altar *n.* алта́рь; же́ртвенник.

alter *v.t.* **1,** (modify) изменя́ть. **2,** (adjust, as a garment) переде́лывать; перешива́ть. *Have a dress altered,* отда́ть пла́тье в переде́лку. —*v.i.* изменя́ться.

alteration *n.* **1,** (change) измене́ние. **2,** (adjustment, as of a garment) переде́лка. *Do you do alterations?,* вы переде́лываете *or* перешива́ете оде́жду?

altercation *n.* переба́нка.

alternate *v.t.* чередова́ть; перемежа́ть. —*v.i.* чередова́ться; перемежа́ться. —*n.* замести́тель. —*adj.* **1,** (alternating) череду́ющийся. **2,** (every other) ка́ждый второ́й. *On alternate days,* че́рез день. **3,** (alternative; substitute) запасно́й; альтернати́вный. **4,** *math.* (of an angle) противолежа́щий.

alternately *adv.* попереме́нно; вперемѐжку.

alternating current переме́нный ток.

alternation *n.* чередова́ние. *Alternation of the seasons,* сме́на времён го́да.

alternative *n.* вы́бор; альтернати́ва. *We have no alternative,* у нас нет вы́бора. —*adj.* альтернати́вный.

alternatively *adv.* и́ли же; в ка́честве альтернати́вы.

alternator *n.* альтерна́тор.

although *conj.* хотя́: *Although it was already dark, we decided to push on,* хотя́ бы́ло уже́ темно́, мы реши́ли идти́ да́льше.

altimeter *n.* альтиме́тр; высотоме́р.

altitude *n.* высота́. *At an altitude of,* на высоте́ (+ *gen.*).

alto *n.* альт. —*adj.* альто́вый.

altogether *adv.* **1,** (completely) совсе́м; вполне́. *I'm not altogether sure,* я не совсе́м уве́рен(а). **2,** (in all; all told) всего́; в о́бщей сло́жности. *How many are there altogether?,* ско́лько всего́ есть?

altruism *n.* альтруи́зм. —**altruist,** *n.* альтруи́ст. —**altruistic,** *adj.* альтруисти́ческий.

alum *n.* квасцы́.

aluminum *also, Brit.,* **aluminium** *n.* алюми́ний. —*adj.* алюми́ниевый.

alumnus *n.* пито́мец; воспи́танник.

alveolus *n.* лу́нка; альвео́ла. —**alveolar,** *adj.* альвеоля́рный.

always *adv.* всегда́: *He is always in a hurry,* он всегда́ спеши́т.

a.m. *abbr.* утра́: *at 9 a.m.,* в де́вять часо́в утра́. *At 2 a.m.,* в два часа́ но́чи.

amalgam *n.* амальга́ма.

amalgamate *v.t.* **1,** *chem.* амальгами́ровать. **2,** (merge) объединя́ть; слива́ть. —*v.i.* объединя́ться; слива́ться.

amalgamation *n.* **1,** *chem.* амальгама́ция. **2,** (mixture; blend) амальга́ма. **3,** (merger) слия́ние; объедине́ние.

amaranth *n.* амара́нт.

amaryllis *n.* амари́ллис.

amass *v.t.* накопля́ть: *amass wealth/knowledge,* накопля́ть бога́тство/зна́ния. *Amass a fortune,* нажива́ть состоя́ние.

amateur *n.* люби́тель; дилета́нт. —*adj.* люби́тельский; самодея́тельный. *Amateur photographer,* фото́граф-люби́тель. *Amateur status,* ста́тус люби́теля. —**amateurish,** *adj.* дилета́нтский.

amaze *v.t.* изумля́ть. *Be amazed,* изумля́ться.

amazement *n.* изумле́ние: *to my amazement,* к моему́ изумле́нию. *Stare in amazement,* смотре́ть изумлённо *or* в изумле́нии *or* с изумле́нием.

amazing *adj.* изуми́тельный. —**amazingly,** *adv.* изуми́тельно.

Amazon *n., myth.* амазо́нка.

ambassador *n.* посо́л. *Ambassador-at-large,* посо́л по осо́бым поруче́ниям.

ambassadorial *adj.* посо́льский. *At the ambassadorial level,* на у́ровне посло́в.

amber *n.* янта́рь. —*adj.* янта́рный.

ambergris *n.* а́мбра.

ambiance *n.* = ambience.

ambidextrous *adj.* владе́ющий одина́ково свобо́дно обе́ими рука́ми.

ambience *also,* **ambiance** *n.* среда́.

ambiguous *adj.* двусмы́сленный. —**ambiguity,** *n.* двусмы́сленность.

ambition *n.* **1,** (strong desire to succeed) честолю́бие. **2,** (object of one's aspirations) стремле́ние; мечта́. *One's great ambition in life,* мечта́ всей жи́зни; заве́тная мечта́. **3,** *pl.* (hopes of gaining or attaining something) амби́ции: *political ambitions,* полити́ческие амби́ции.

ambitious *adj.* **1,** (full of ambition) честолюби́вый. **2,** (requiring great effort) сме́лый: *ambitious undertaking,* сме́лое предприя́тие.

ambivalent *adj.* дво́йственный: *ambivalent feelings,* дво́йственное чу́вство. —**ambivalence,** *n.* дво́йственность.

amble *n.* и́ноходь. —*v.i.* **1,** (of a horse) идти́ и́ноходью. **2,** (of a person) идти́ нога́ за́ ногу.

ambrosia *n.* амбро́зия.

ambulance *n.* маши́на ско́рой по́мощи. *Call an ambulance,* вы́звать ско́рую по́мощь.

ambulatory *adj.* ходя́чий: *ambulatory patient,* ходя́чий больно́й. *He is ambulatory,* он мо́жет ходи́ть.

ambush *n.* заса́да. *Lie in ambush,* быть в заса́де. —*v.t.* напада́ть на (кого́-нибудь) из заса́ды. *Be ambushed,* попа́сть в заса́ду.

ameba *also,* **amoeba** *n.* амёба.

ameliorate *v.t.* улучша́ть. —*v.i.* улучша́ться. —**amelioration,** *n.* улучше́ние.

amen *interj.* ами́нь.

amenable *adj.* сгово́рчивый; покла́дистый; усту́пчивый; податливый.

amend *v.t.* **1,** (change; revise) изменя́ть: *amend a bill,* изменя́ть законопрое́кт. **2,** (add amendments to) вноси́ть попра́вки в.

amendment *n.* попра́вка: *amendment to a bill,* попра́вка к законопрое́кту.

amends *n.pl.* компенса́ция; возмеще́ние. —**make amends for,** искупа́ть; загла́живать.

amenity *n., usu. pl.* **1,** (conveniences) удо́бства. **2,** (social courtesies) прили́чия.

American *adj.* америка́нский. —*n.* америка́нец; америка́нка.

americium *n.* амери́ций.

amethyst *n.* амети́ст. —*adj.* амети́стовый.

amiable *adj.* приве́тливый. —**amiability,** *n.* приве́тливость.

amicability *n.* дружелю́бие.

amicable *adj.* **1,** (of personal relations) дру́жеский; дру́жественный; дружелю́бный. **2,** (of an agreement, settlement, etc.) полюбо́вный. —**amicably,** *adv.* полюбо́вно.

amid *prep.* среди́; посреди́. *Also,* **amidst.**

amidships *adv.* в середи́не корабля́.

amidst *prep.* = **amid.**

amino acid аминокислота́.

amiss *adj.* нела́дный: *Something is amiss,* что́-то нела́дно. —**take amiss,** обижа́ться на; толкова́ть в дурну́ю сто́рону.

amity *n.* дру́жба; согла́сие; дру́жеские отноше́ния.

ammeter *n.* ампермéтр.

ammonia *n.* аммиа́к. *Liquid ammonia,* нашаты́рный спирт.

ammonium *n.* аммо́ний. —**ammonium chloride,** нашаты́рь; хло́ристый аммо́ний. —**ammonium nitrate,** аммиа́чная *or* аммо́ниевая сели́тра. —**ammonium sulfate,** серноки́слый аммо́ний.

ammunition *n.* боеприпа́сы. —**ammunition belt,** патро́нная ле́нта; патронта́ш. —**ammunition dump,** склад боеприпа́сов.

amnesia *n.* поте́ря па́мяти; амнези́я.

amnesty *n.* амни́стия. *Grant amnesty to,* амнисти́ровать.

amoeba *n.* = **ameba.**

amok *adv.* = **amuck.**

among *prep.* **1,** (in between; surrounded by) среди́: *be among friends,* быть среди́ друзе́й. **2,** (in the group of) среди́; в числе́ (+ *gen.*). *First among equals,* пе́рвый среди́ ра́вных. *Among other things,* среди́ *or* в числе́ про́чего. *We were among the first to...,* мы бы́ли в числе́ пе́рвых, кто... *The U.S. is not among them,* США не в их числе́. **3,** (with one another) ме́жду (собо́й): *They quarreled among themselves,* они́ поссо́рились ме́жду собо́й. **4,** (in the opinion of many) у: *very popular among young people,* о́чень популя́рен у молодёжи. *Also,* **amongst.**

amoral *adj.* амора́льный. —**amorality,** *n.* амора́льность.

amorous *adj.* любо́вный; влюб́чивый. —**amorousness,** *n.* влюб́чивость.

amorphous *adj.* бесфо́рменный; амо́рфный.

amortize *v.t.* амортизи́ровать. —**amortization,** *n.* амортиза́ция.

amount *n.* **1,** (sum) су́мма: *the total amount,* о́бщая су́мма. *There is still a small amount to be paid,* ещё ну́жно заплати́ть небольшу́ю су́мму. **2,** (quantity) коли́чество: *a huge amount,* огро́мное коли́чество. *An enormous amount of work,* ма́сса рабо́ты. —*v.i.* [*usu.* **amount to**] **1,** (equal in total) составля́ть; выража́ться в су́мме (+ *gen.*). **2,** (be equivalent to) равня́ться (+ *dat.*); быть равноси́льным (+ *dat.*). *It amounts to the same thing,* всё равно́; э́то то же са́мое. **3,** *fol. by* **something, anything,** *etc.* (achieve success): *He'll never amount to anything,* из него́ никогда́ ничего́ не вы́йдет; из него́ ничего́ пу́тного не вы́йдет.

ampere *n.* ампе́р.

ampersand *n.* знак &.

amphibian *n.* земново́дное живо́тное; амфи́бия.

amphibious *adj.* **1,** (of an animal) земново́дный. **2,** (of a vehicle) пла́вающий. **3,** *mil.* морско́й деса́нтный. *Amphibious landing,* вы́садка морско́го деса́нта.

amphitheater *also,* **amphitheatre** *n.* амфитеа́тр.

ample *adj.* **1,** (abundant) оби́льный. **2,** (sufficient) доста́точный. **3,** (spacious) просто́рный.

amplification *n.* **1,** (enlargement) расшире́ние. **2,** (fuller statement) уточне́ние. **3,** *electronics* усиле́ние; звукоусиле́ние. *Amplification system,* систе́ма звукоусиле́ния.

amplifier *n.* усили́тель.

amplify *v.t.* **1,** (enlarge) расширя́ть. **2,** (enlarge upon, as a statement) дополня́ть. **3,** *electronics* уси́ливать.

amplitude *n.* **1,** (extent) широта́. **2,** *physics* амплиту́да.

amply *adv.* ще́дро: *amply rewarded,* ще́дро награжде́н.

ampule *also,* **ampoule** *n.* а́мпула.

amputate *v.t.* ампути́ровать; отнима́ть. —**amputation,** *n.* ампута́ция.

amuck *also,* **amok** *adv., in* **run amuck,** бу́йствовать; бу́йнить.

amulet *n.* амуле́т; ла́данка.

amuse *v.t.* развлека́ть; забавля́ть: *amuse the children with toys,* развлека́ть/забавля́ть дете́й игру́шками. *He is not amused,* ему́ не смешно́. —**amuse oneself,** развлека́ться; забавля́ться.

amusement *n.* **1,** (entertainment) развлече́ние; заба́ва. **2,** (enjoyment) удово́льствие. —**amusement park,** парк с аттракцио́нами; увесели́тельный парк; лу́на-парк.

amusing *adj.* смешно́й; заба́вный; занима́тельный. *I find it amusing that..,* мне заба́вно, что...

an *indef. art., var. of* **a.**

anachronism *n.* анахрони́зм. —**anachronistic,** *adj.* анахрони́ческий.

anaconda *n.* анако́нда.

anaemia *n.* = **anemia.** —**anaemic,** *adj.* = **anemic.**

anaerobe *n.* анаэро́б. —**anaerobic,** *adj.* анаэро́бный.

anaesthesia *n.* = **anesthesia.** —**anaesthetic,** *adj. & n.* = **anesthetic.** —**anaesthetize,** *v.t.* = **anesthetize.**

anagram *n.* анагра́мма.

anal *adj.* заднепрохо́дный; ана́льный.

analgesic *adj.* болеутоля́ющий. —*n.* болеутоля́ющее сре́дство.

analogous *adj.* аналоги́чный.

analogue *n.* ана́лог.

analogy *n.* анало́гия. *By analogy with,* по анало́гии с.

analyse *v.* = **analyze.**

analysis *n.* ана́лиз; разбо́р. —**in the final analysis,** в коне́чном ито́ге; в коне́чном счёте.

analyst *n.* анали́тик.

analytic *also,* **analytical** *adj.* аналити́ческий. —**analytic geometry,** аналити́ческая геоме́трия.

analyze *also,* **analyse** *v.t.* разбира́ть; анализи́ровать.

anapest *also,* **anapaest** *n.* ана́пест.

anarchism *n.* анархи́зм. —**anarchist,** *n.* анархи́ст. —**anarchistic,** *adj.* анархи́ческий.

anarchy *n.* ана́рхия; безвла́стие.

anathema *n.* ана́фема. —**anathematize,** *v.t.* предава́ть ана́феме.

anatomy *n.* анато́мия. —**anatomical,** *adj.* анатоми́ческий. —**anatomist,** *n.* ана́том. —**anatomize,** *v.t.* анатоми́ровать.

ancestor *n.* пре́док. —**ancestral,** *adj.* родово́й.

ancestry *n.* происхожде́ние. *Trace one's ancestry back to...,* A, (date back as far as) вести́ свой род от... B, (investigate as far back as) проследи́ть свой род до...

anchor *n.* я́корь. *At anchor,* на я́коре. —*v.t.* ста́вить на я́корь. —*v.i.* станови́ться на я́корь.

anchorage *n.* я́корная стоя́нка.

anchorite *n.* отше́льник; затво́рник.

anchorman *n.* веду́щий.

anchovy *n.* анчо́ус.

ancient *adj.* дре́вний; стари́нный; анти́чный. *Ancient Greece/history,* дре́вняя Гре́ция/исто́рия. *The ancient world,* дре́вний *or* анти́чный мир. *Ancient city,* дре́вний *or* стари́нный го́род. *Date back to ancient times,* восходи́ть к дре́вности. —**the ancients,** дре́вние.

ancillary *adj.* вспомога́тельный; подсо́бный.

and *conj.* и: *cause and effect,* причи́на и сле́дствие. ♦*Sometimes rendered by* с: *you and I,* мы с ва́ми; *bread and butter,* хлеб с ма́слом. ♦*When in contrast,* а: *He is Russian and she is French,* он ру́сский, а она́ францу́женка.

andante *adv. & n.* анда́нте.

andiron *n.* подста́вка для дров.

anecdote *n.* анекдо́т. —**anecdotal,** *adj.* анекдоти́ческий.

anemia *also,* **anaemia** *n.* малокро́вие; анеми́я. —**anemic;** **anaemic,** *adj.* малокро́вный; анеми́чный.

anemometer *n.* анемо́метр; ветроме́р.

anemone *n.* анемо́н; ве́треница. —**sea anemone,** акти́ния.

anent *prep., archaic* относи́тельно.

aneroid barometer анеро́ид.

anesthesia *also,* **anaesthesia** *n.* анестези́я; нарко́з. —**anesthesiologist,** *n.* анестезио́лог.

anesthetic *also,* **anaesthetic** *adj.* анестези́рующий; обезбо́ливающий. —*n.* анестези́рующее/обезбо́ливающее сре́дство; нарко́з.

anesthetize *also,* **anaesthetize** *v.t.* анестези́ровать; обезбо́ливать. —**anesthetization,** *n.* обезбо́ливание.

aneurysm *also,* **aneurism** *n.* аневри́зма.

anew *adv.* сно́ва; за́ново.

angel *n.* а́нгел. —**angelic,** *adj.* а́нгельский.

angelica *n.* дя́гиль; ду́дник.

anger *n.* гнев. *In anger,* в гне́ве. —*v.t.* серди́ть.

angina *n.* анги́на. —**angina pectoris,** грудна́я жа́ба; стенокарди́я.

angle *n.* **1,** *geom.* у́гол: *right angle,* прямо́й у́гол. *At a 45° angle,* под угло́м в со́рок пять гра́дусов. *At right angles to each other,* под прямы́м угло́м друг к дру́гу. *Hold something at an angle,* держа́ть что́-нибудь под угло́м. *Place the table at an angle to the wall,* поста́вить стол под угло́м к стене́. **2,** (aspect; point of view) то́чка зре́ния; у́гол зре́ния. *Consider a question from all angles,* рассма́тривать вопро́с со всех сторо́н. —*v.i.* **1,** (turn sharply) повора́чивать: *The road angles to the right,* доро́га повора́чивает напра́во. **2,** (fish) уди́ть ры́бу. **3,** *fol. by* **for** (slyly try to obtain) напра́шиваться на.

angler *n.* рыболо́в; уди́льщик.

Anglican *adj.* англика́нский.

Anglicism *n.* англици́зм.

Anglicize *v.t.* англизи́ровать.

angling *n.* уже́ние.

Anglophile *n.* англофи́л.

Anglo-Saxon *adj.* англосаксо́нский.

angrily *adv.* серди́то.

angry *adj.* серди́тый. *Be angry,* серди́ться. *He is very angry,* он о́чень серди́т. *I am not angry,* я не сержу́сь. *Don't be angry with him,* не серди́тесь на него́. *Why are you angry with me?,* почему́ вы се́рдитесь на меня́? *Become/get angry,* рассерди́ться. *Make someone angry,* рассерди́ть кого́-нибудь.

anguish *n.* му́ка; муче́ние. —**anguished,** *adj.* мучи́тельный: *anguished cry,* мучи́тельный крик.

angular *adj.* **1,** (having many angles) углова́тый: *angular features,* углова́тые черты́. **2,** (measured by an angle) углово́й: *angular velocity,* углова́я ско́рость. **3,** (gaunt) костля́вый. **4,** (lacking grace; stiff) углова́тый.

aniline *n.* анили́н. —**aniline dye,** анили́новая кра́ска.

animal *n.* живо́тное. *Wild animal,* ди́кое живо́тное; зверь. —*adj.* живо́тный: *animal fat,* живо́тный жир. —**animal husbandry,** животново́дство.

animate *v.t.* оживля́ть. —*adj.* одушевлённый: *animate being,* одушевлённое существо́.

animated *adj.* оживлённый. —**animated cartoon,** мультипликацио́нный фильм.

animation *n.* оживле́ние. *With (great) animation,* оживлённо; жи́во.

animism *n.* аними́зм. —**animist,** *n.* аними́ст. —**animistic,** *adj.* анимисти́ческий.

animosity *n.* вражде́бность; вражда́.

anise *n.* ани́с. —*adj.* ани́совый.

anisette *n.* анисовка.

ankle *n.* лодыжка; щиколотка. *Sprain one's ankle,* подвернуть себе ногу.

annals *n.pl.* анналы.

anneal *v.t.* **1,** (heat) отжигать. **2,** *fig.* (temper) закалять.

annex *v.t.* присоединять; отторгать; аннексировать. —*n.* **1,** (subsidiary building) пристройка. **2,** (supplement) приложение (к договору). —**annexation,** *n.* присоединение; отторжение; аннексия.

annihilate *v.t.* уничтожать; истреблять. —**annihilation,** *n.* уничтожение; истребление.

anniversary *n.* годовщина; юбилей. *On the anniversary of,* в годовщину (+ *gen.*). *On the second anniversary of,* во вторую годовщину (+ *gen.*). ♦*Specific anniversaries are usually rendered with the suffix* -летие: *tenth anniversary,* десятилетие. *The fiftieth anniversary of his death,* пятидесятилетие со дня его смерти. —*adj.* юбилейный: *anniversary year,* юбилейный год.

annotate *v.t.* комментировать. —**annotation,** *n.* комментарий; аннотация.

announce *v.t.* **1,** (declare publicly) заявлять; объявлять; сообщать. *Announce one's decision,* объявить *or* сообщить решение; объявить *or* заявить *or* сообщить о своём решении. *Announce the results over the radio,* объявить *or* сообщить результаты по радио. *We regret to announce that...,* с сожалением мы сообщаем, что... **2,** (state the arrival or presence of) докладывать о: *announce a visitor,* докладывать о посетителе.

announcement *n.* **1,** (statement) заявление: *make an announcement,* сделать заявление. **2,** (public notice) объявление.

announcer *n.* диктор.

annoy *v.t.* досаждать; раздражать: *His endless chatter annoys me,* меня раздражает *or* мне досаждает его бесконечная болтовня.

annoyance *n.* досада.

annoyed *adj.* раздражён. *Are you annoyed with me?,* вы сердиты на меня?

annoying *adj.* досадный. *How annoying!,* какая досада!

annual *adj.* **1,** (occurring once a year) ежегодный. **2,** (pertaining to a given year) годовой. **3,** *bot.* однолетний. —*n.* **1,** (publication) ежегодник. **2,** (plant) однолетнее растение. —**annually,** *adv.* ежегодно.

annuity *n.* ежегодная рента.

annul *v.t.* аннулировать; отменять; расторгать. —**annulment,** *n.* аннулирование; отмена; расторжение.

Annunciation *n., relig.* благовещение.

anode *n.* анод.

anoint *v.t.* помазывать. —**anointment,** *n.* помазание.

anomaly *n.* аномалия. —**anomalous,** *adj.* аномальный.

anonymity *n.* анонимность.

anonymous *adj.* анонимный. —**anonymously,** *adv.* анонимно.

anopheles *n.* анофелес.

another *adj. & pron.* **1,** (one more; an additional) ещё: *another glass of milk,* ещё стакан молока. *Give me another two weeks,* дайте мне ещё две недели. *Not another word!,* ни слова больше! *He won't be back for another month,* он не вернётся ещё месяц. *There is not another book like it,* второй такой книги как эта не существует. *What's another 100 dollars to him?,* что ему ещё сто долларов? **2,** (a different) другой: *another time,* в другой раз. *That's quite another matter,* это совсем другое дело. *From one place to another,* с одного места на другое. *Let's do it another way,* давайте сделаем это иначе. —**one another,** друг друга: *love one another,* любить друг друга. *Shake one another's hand,* пожать друг другу руку. —**one way or another,** так или иначе.

answer *v.t. & i.* отвечать: *answer someone,* отвечать кому-нибудь; *answer a question/letter,* отвечать на вопрос/письмо. *Answer the door,* открывать дверь. *Answer the telephone,* подходить к телефону. *Answer telephone calls,* отвечать на телефонные звонки. *Answer one's readers,* отвечать своим читателям. *Answer the purpose,* отвечать цели. *Answer the description,* соответствовать описанию. *Answer for one's actions,* отвечать за свои поступки. *Answer to the name of...,* откликаться *or* отзываться на имя (+ *nom.*). —*n.* **1,** (reply) ответ: *the answer to your question,* ответ на ваш вопрос. *In answer to your comment,* в ответ на ваше замечание. **2,** (solution) решение: *answer to a problem,* решение задачи. —**answer back,** грубить; дерзить.

answerable *adj.* ответственный. *Be answerable for,* отвечать за. *Be answerable to no one,* ни перед кем не отчитываться.

ant *n.* муравей.

antagonism *n.* антагонизм; вражда. —**antagonist,** *n.* антагонист. —**antagonistic,** *adj.* антагонистический; враждебный.

antagonize *v.t.* настраивать против себя; восстанавливать против себя; отталкивать.

antarctic *adj.* антарктический. —**Antarctic Circle,** Южный полярный круг.

ante *n.* ставка. *Raise the ante,* повысить ставку.

anteater *n.* муравьед. —**spiny anteater,** ехидна.

antecedent *n.* **1,** (something that goes before) предшествующее событие. **2,** *pl.* (ancestors) предки.

antechamber *n.* передняя; прихожая.

antedate *v.t.* **1,** (come before) предшествовать. **2,** (put an earlier date on) пометить *or* датировать задним числом.

antediluvian *adj.* допотопный.

antelope *n.* антилопа.

antenna *n.* антенна.

anterior *adj.* **1,** (forward; front) передний. **2,** (coming earlier) предшествующий.

anteroom *n.* передняя; прихожая.

anthem *n.* гимн: *national anthem,* государственный гимн.

anther *n.* пыльник.

anthill *n.* муравейник.
anthology *n.* антология; сборник.
anthracite *n.* антрацит. —*adj.* антрацитный; антрацитовый.
anthrax *n.* сибирская язва.
anthropoid *n.* антропоид. —*adj.* человекообразный.
anthropology *n.* антропология. —**anthropological,** *adj.* антропологический. —**anthropologist,** *n.* антрополог.
anthropomorphism *n.* антропоморфизм. —**anthropomorphic,** *adj.* антропоморфический. —**anthropomorphous,** *adj.* человекообразный.
antiaircraft *adj.* зенитный.
anti-American *adj.* антиамериканский. —**anti-Americanism,** *n.* антиамериканизм.
anti-ballistic missile антиракета.
antibiotic *n.* антибиотик.
antibody *n.* антитело.
antic *n., usu. pl.* шалости; выходки.
Antichrist *n.* антихрист.
anticipate *v.t.* **1,** (foresee) предвидеть. **2,** (expect) ожидать. **3,** (foresee and deal with in advance) предупреждать; предвосхищать.
anticipation *n.* **1,** (expectation) ожидание; предвидение; предвкушение: *in anticipation of,* в ожидании/ предвидении/предвкушении (+ *gen.*). **2,** (dealing with in advance) предвосхищение. **3,** (eagerness) нетерпение: *await with anticipation,* ждать с нетерпением.
anticoagulant *n.* антикоагулянт.
anticommunism *n.* антикоммунизм.
anticommunist *n.* антикоммунист. —*adj.* антикоммунистический.
anti-depressant *n.* антидепрессант.
antidote *n.* противоядие.
antifreeze *n.* антифриз.
antigen *n.* антиген.
antigovernment *adj.* антиправительственный.
antimatter *n.* антивещество.
anti-missile *adj.* противоракетный.
antimony *n.* сурьма.
antipathetic *adj.* **1,** *fol. by* **to** (averse) настроен против. **2,** (causing antipathy) антипатичный.
antipathy *n.* антипатия.
anti-personnel *adj., mil.* осколочный; противопехотный.
antipodes *n.pl.* антиподы.
antiquary *n.* антиквар. *Also,* **antiquarian.**
antiquated *adj.* устарелый; устаревший.
antique *adj.* старинный; антикварный. —*n.* антикварная вещь. *Antique dealer,* антиквар. *Antique shop,* антикварный магазин.
antiquity *n.* **1,** (ancient times; great age) древность; античность. **2,** *pl.* (ancient relics) древности.
antireligious *adj.* антирелигиозный.
anti-satellite *adj.* противоспутниковый.
anti-Semite *n.* антисемит. —**anti-Semitic,** *adj.* антисемитский. —**anti-Semitism,** *n.* антисемитизм.
antisepsis *n.* антисептика.
antiseptic *adj.* антисептический. —*n.* антисептик; *pl.* антисептика.

antisocial *adj.* **1,** (harmful to society) антиобщественный. **2,** (unsociable) необщительный.
anti-submarine *adj.* противолодочный.
antitank *adj.* противотанковый.
antithesis *n.* **1,** (opposite) антитеза. **2,** *logic* антитезис. —**antithetical,** *adj.* антитетический.
antitoxin *n.* антитоксин. —**antitoxic,** *adj.* антитоксический.
antiwar *adj.* антивоенный.
antler *n.* (олений) рог.
antonym *n.* антоним.
anus *n.* задний проход; заднепроходное отверстие.
anvil *n.* наковальня.
anxiety *n.* беспокойство; озабоченность.
anxious *adj.* **1,** (worried) озабоченный; беспокойный; неспокойный; тревожный. *Anxious moment,* тревожный момент. **2,** (eager) *be anxious to,* очень хотеться (+ *dat.*). *We are very anxious to see you,* мы вас очень ждём.
anxiously *adv.* с нетерпением: *anxiously await,* ждать с нетерпением.
any *adj. & pron.* **1,** (no matter which; every) любой; всякий: *any time,* в любое время; *any minute,* в любую минуту; с минуты на минуту; *in any case,* во всяком случае; *at any price,* любой ценой; *any day* (now), со дня на день. *Any of these will do,* любой из этих подойдёт. *Are any of you interested in going?,* кто-нибудь из вас хочет пойти? **2,** (some) какой-нибудь: *Have you any questions?,* у вас есть какие-нибудь вопросы? *Have you any money?,* у вас есть деньги? *If there are any left,* если что-нибудь осталось. *Before taking any action,* прежде чем предпринимать какие-нибудь действия. ♦*In neg. sentences,* никакой; ни один: *I didn't buy any books,* я не купил(а) никаких книг. *Your sweater is not in any of these drawers,* вашего свитера нет ни в одном из этих ящиков. *We haven't any flour today,* у нас сегодня нет муки. *I don't see any,* не вижу ни одного. —*adv. Not rendered in Russian: Is he any better today?,* ему лучше сегодня? ♦ *In neg. sentences,* нисколько: *He is not any better today,* ему сегодня нисколько не лучше. *It doesn't worry me any,* это меня (нисколько) не беспокоит. *I can't wait any longer,* я больше не могу ждать. *I can't go any farther,* я дальше не могу идти. —**any more, 1,** (some more) ещё: *Have you any more questions?,* у вас есть ещё вопросы? **2,** (no more) больше: *I haven't any more money,* у меня нет больше денег. *I don't want any more,* я больше не хочу. *See also* **anymore.**
anybody *pron.* = **anyone.**
anyhow *adv.* **1,** (in any case) во всяком случае. **2,** (just the same) всё-таки; всё же.
anymore *adv.* больше: *I don't go there anymore,* я больше не хожу туда. *I don't remember anymore,* я уже не помню. *Nothing surprises me anymore,* больше ничему не удивляюсь.
anyone *pron.* **1,** *in affirmative sentences,* любой; всякий; каждый; кто угодно: *Anyone can do it,* любой/ всякий/каждый может это сделать. *Anyone*

wishing to go, всякий, кто хочет идти. *Anyone who has witnessed...,* любой, кто был свидетелем (+ gen.). *That is anyone's right,* это право любого. *Ask anyone,* спросите кого угодно. *Anyone but him,* кто угодно, только не он. **2,** *in interr. and hypothetical sentences,* кто-нибудь: *Does anyone wish to speak?,* кто-нибудь хочет говорить? *Did you see anyone?,* вы видели кого-нибудь? **3,** *in neg. sentences,* никого: *I didn't see anyone,* я никого не видел(а). *Neither he nor anyone else,* ни он, никто другой.

anyplace *adv., colloq.* = **anywhere.**

anything *pron.* **1,** *in affirmative sentences,* всё; всякое; всё, что угодно. *Anything is possible,* всё возможно; всякое бывает. *I would give anything to...,* всё отдам, чтобы... *More than anything in the world,* больше всего на свете. *You can expect anything from him,* от него можно ожидать чего угодно. **2,** *in interr. and hypothetical sentences,* что-нибудь: *Do you want anything to drink?,* вы хотите что-нибудь выпить? *Have you anything to say?,* вам есть что сказать? *If anything should happen to me,* если что-нибудь со мной случится. **3,** *in neg. sentences,* ничего: *I don't know anything,* я ничего не знаю. *I've never seen anything like it,* я никогда не видел(а) ничего подобного. —**anything but,** совсем не: *anything but cheap,* совсем не дешёвый.

anytime *adv.* **1,** (at any time) в любое время; когда угодно. **2,** (whenever) когда бы ни; всякий раз, когда.

anyway *adv.* = **anyhow.**

anywhere *adv.* **1,** *in affirmative sentences,* где *or* куда угодно; где *or* куда бы то ни было. *Sit anywhere you like,* садитесь куда угодно. *Anywhere in the world,* где бы то ни было в мире. **2,** *in interr. and hypothetical sentences,* где-нибудь; когда-нибудь. *Have you seen him anywhere?,* вы видели его где-нибудь? **3,** *in neg. sentences,* нигде; никуда. *I can't find her anywhere,* я нигде не могу найти её.

aorta *n.* аорта.

apace *adv.* полным ходом: *proceed apace,* идти полным ходом.

apart *adv.* **1,** (separately) врозь; порознь; отдельно. *Live apart,* жить врозь/порознь. *Stand apart from the others,* стоять отдельно от других; *fig.* выделяться среди других. *With one's feet apart,* расставив ноги. **2,** (into pieces) на части. *Take apart,* разбирать. **3,** (at a stated interval): *live thousands of miles apart,* жить за тысячи миль друг от друга. *Our birthdays are three days apart,* наши дни рождения разделяют три дня. *They were born two years apart,* они родились с разрывом в два года. —**apart from,** помимо. *Apart from the bad weather, it was a nice trip,* если не считать плохую погоду, поездка удалась. —**tell apart,** различать.

apartheid *n.* апартеид.

apartment *n.* квартира. —**apartment house,** жилой дом; многоквартирный дом.

apathetic *adj.* апатичный.

apathy *n.* апатия.

ape *n.* обезьяна. —*v.t.* обезьянничать. —**ape-like,**

adj. обезьяний; обезьяноподобный. —**ape-man,** *n.* обезьяночеловек.

aperitif *n.* аперитив.

aperture *n.* отверстие; апертура.

apex *n.* вершина.

aphasia *n.* афазия.

aphelion *n.* афелий.

aphorism *n.* афоризм. —**aphoristic,** *adj.* афористический; афористичный.

apiary *n.* пасека; пчельник.

apiece *adv.* **1,** (per item) штука; за штуку: *cost six dollars apiece,* стоить по шесть долларов штука *or* за штуку. *Cost one dollar apiece,* стоить по доллару. **2,** (per person) каждый ... по: *They contributed $10 apiece,* каждый внёс по десять долларов.

aplomb *n.* апломб.

apocalypse *n.* апокалипсис. —**apocalyptic,** *adj.* апокалиптический; апокалипсический.

Apocrypha *n.pl.* апокрифы.

Apocryphal *adj.* **1,** (pertaining to the Apocrypha) апокрифический. **2,** *l.c.* (of doubtful authenticity) недостоверный.

apogee *n.* апогей.

apolitical *adj.* аполитичный.

Apollo *n.* Аполлон.

apologetic *adj.* извиняющийся. *He was very apologetic,* он очень извинялся. —**apologetically,** *adv.* извиняющимся тоном.

apologetics *n.* апологетика.

apologia *n.* апология.

apologist *n.* апологет.

apologize *v.i.* извиняться: *apologize to someone for something,* извиняться перед кем-нибудь за что-нибудь. *You have nothing to apologize for,* вам не за что извиняться; какие могут быть извинения?

apology *n.* извинение. *Letter of apology,* извинительное письмо. *You owe him an apology,* вы должны извиниться перед ним. *Vera sends her apologies,* Вера извиняется; Вера просит её извинить; Вера приносит *or* передаёт свои извинения.

apoplexy *n.* апоплексия. —**apoplectic,** *adj.* апоплексический.

apostasy *n.* отступничество; ренегатство.

apostate *n.* отступник. —*adj.* отступнический

a posteriori **1,** *used adverbially,* апостериори. **2,** *used adjectivally,* апостериорный.

apostle *n.* апостол. —**apostolic,** *adj.* апостольский.

apostrophe *n.* апостроф.

apothecary *n.* аптекарь.

apotheosis *n.* апофеоз.

appall *also,* **appal** *v.t.* ужасать; приводить в ужас. *Be appalled,* ужасаться; быть в ужасе; приходить в ужас. —**appalling,** *adj.* ужасный; вопиющий.

apparatus *n.* **1,** (device) аппарат; прибор. **2,** (group of instruments) аппаратура. **3,** *sports* гимнастические снаряды. **4,** (system of organization) аппарат: *spy apparatus,* шпионский аппарат.

apparel *n.* одежда; наряд. *Apparel shop,* магазин готового платья.

apparent *adj.* ви́димый: *for no apparent reason*, без ви́димой причи́ны. *It is apparent that...*, ви́дно, что... *It is apparent to all that...*, всем я́сно, что...

apparently *adv.* ви́димо; по-ви́димому.

apparition *n.* виде́ние; при́зрак; привиде́ние.

appeal *v.i.* **1,** (earnestly request) обраща́ться; призыва́ть. *Appeal to someone for help*, обраща́ться к кому́-нибудь за по́мощью. *Appeal for unity*, призыва́ть к еди́нству. **2,** *fol. by* to (strike favorably) нра́виться. *It doesn't appeal to me*, мне э́то не нра́вится; меня́ э́то не привлека́ет. **3,** *law* апелли́ровать; подава́ть апелля́цию; подава́ть кассацио́нную жа́лобу. —*v.t.* обжа́ловать: *appeal a verdict*, обжа́ловать пригово́р. —*n.* **1,** (call for aid or support) обраще́ние; призы́в; воззва́ние. *An appeal for help/unity*, призы́в на по́мощь/ к еди́нству/. *Make an appeal for aid*, обраща́ться с про́сьбой о соде́йствии. **2,** (attractiveness) привлека́тельность. **3,** *law* (general procedure) обжа́лование: *right of appeal*, пра́во обжа́лования; (request so made) апелля́ция; кассацио́нная жа́лоба. —**appealing,** *adj.* привлека́тельный.

appear *v.i.* **1,** (come into view) появля́ться: *appear in the distance*, появля́ться вдали́. **2,** (present oneself; show up) явля́ться; предста́ть: *appear in/ before the/ court*, яви́ться в суд; предста́ть пе́ред судо́м. **3,** (perform) выступа́ть (на сце́не); снима́ться (в кино́). **4,** (be published) выходи́ть (в свет). **5,** (seem) каза́ться; представля́ться. *Appear invincible*, каза́ться непобеди́мым. *More difficult than it appears at first*, бо́лее тру́дный, чем представля́ется на пе́рвый взгляд. *The rain appears to have stopped*, дождь как бу́дто ко́нчился.

appearance *n.* **1,** (coming into sight) появле́ние. *Put in an appearance*, появля́ться. **2,** (coming into public view) выступле́ние: *television appearance*, выступле́ние по телеви́дению. **3,** (outward aspect) вид; о́блик. *External appearance*, вне́шность; нару́жность. *For appearance's sake*, для ви́да. *Appearances are deceiving*, вне́шность обма́нчива. **4,** (semblance) ви́димость: *create the appearance of*, создава́ть ви́димость (+ *gen.*). *He gives the appearance of being very busy*, он де́лает вид, что о́чень за́нят. —**from all appearances,** по всей ви́димости.

appease *v.t.* **1,** (placate) умиротворя́ть. **2,** (assuage, as hunger) утоля́ть.

appeasement *n.* умиротворе́ние; соглаша́тельство. *Policy of appeasement*, соглаша́тельская поли́тика.

appeaser *n.* соглаша́тель.

appellate *adj.* апелляцио́нный: *appellate court*, апелляцио́нный суд.

appellation *n.* назва́ние; наименова́ние.

append *v.t.* прилага́ть; приобща́ть: *append something to a letter*, прилага́ть/приобща́ть что́-нибудь к письму́.

appendage *n.* прида́ток.

appendectomy *n.* удале́ние аппе́ндикса.

appendicitis *n.* аппендици́т.

appendix *n.* **1,** (of a document or book) приложе́ние. **2,** *anat.* аппе́ндикс.

apperception *n.* апперце́пция.

appertain *v.i.* [*usu.* **appertain to**] относи́ться (к).

appetite *n.* **1,** (desire for food) аппети́т. **2,** (craving) жа́жда; влече́ние. *Sexual appetite*, полово́е влече́ние.

appetizer *n.* заку́ска.

appetizing *adj.* аппети́тный; вку́сный.

applaud *v.i.* аплоди́ровать; рукоплеска́. —*v.t.* **1,** (clap to show approval of) аплоди́ровать (+ *dat.*). **2,** (approve of; commend) приве́тствовать.

applause *n.* аплодисме́нты; рукоплеска́ния.

apple *n.* я́блоко. —*adj.* **1,** (made of apples) я́блочный: *apple pie*, я́блочный пиро́г. **2,** (of an apple tree) я́блоневый: *apple blossom/orchard*, я́блоневый цвет/сад. —**apple of discord**, я́блоко раздо́ра.

applecart *n.* теле́жка с я́блоками. —**upset the applecart,** спу́тать все ка́рты; испо́ртить всю му́зыку.

applesauce *n.* я́блочное пюре́.

apple tree я́блоня.

appliance *n.* прибо́р; приспособле́ние.

applicable *adj.* примени́мый. *Not applicable to this case*, непримени́м к э́тому слу́чаю (*or* для да́нного слу́чая). —**applicability,** *n.* примени́мость.

applicant *n.* претенде́нт; кандида́т.

application *n.* **1,** (applying; putting on) наложе́ние. **2,** (putting to use) примене́ние; приложе́ние. **3,** (formal request) заявле́ние: *submit an application*, подава́ть заявле́ние. **4,** (diligence) прилежа́ние; стара́тельность.

applied *adj.* прикладно́й: *applied sciences*, прикладны́е нау́ки.

appliqué *n.* апплика́ция.

apply *v.t.* **1,** (lay on) накла́дывать; прикла́дывать; ста́вить. *Apply cream to one's face*, накла́дывать крем на лицо́. *Apply hot compresses*, ста́вить *or* прикла́дывать горя́чие компре́ссы. *Apply make-up*, кра́ситься. *Apply a coat of paint*, наноси́ть слой кра́ски. **2,** (put to use) применя́ть: *apply one's knowledge to*, применя́ть свои́ зна́ния к. *Apply the brakes*, тормози́ть. *Apply pressure to*, ока́зывать давле́ние на. **3,** (credit, as to an account) зачи́тывать. —*v.i.* **1,** (submit an application) обраща́ться; подава́ть заявле́ние. *Apply to the personnel department*, обраща́ться в отде́л ка́дров. *Apply for a loan*, подава́ть заявле́ние на получе́ние (*or* о предоставле́нии) ссу́ды. *Apply for a job as a typist*, подава́ть заявле́ние на до́лжность машини́стки. **2,** *fol. by* to (be applicable to) относи́ться (к): *This applies to all*, э́то отно́сится ко всем. *The rule does not apply in this case*, пра́вило непримени́мо в да́нном слу́чае. —**apply oneself to,** налега́ть на; принале́чь на.

appoint *v.t.* **1,** (designate) назнача́ть: *appoint someone to a position*, назнача́ть кого́-нибудь на до́лжность. *He was appointed plant manager*, он был назна́чен дире́ктором заво́да. **2,** *usu. passive* (furnish) обставля́ть: *well-appointed rooms*, хорошо́ обста́вленные ко́мнаты.

appointment *n.* **1,** (act of appointing or being appointed) назначе́ние. **2,** (scheduled meeting) свида́ние; (делова́я) встре́ча. *I have an appointment,* мне назна́чена делова́я встре́ча. *Make an appointment with the doctor,* записа́ться (на приём) к врачу́. *I have a doctor's appointment,* мне назна́чено прийти́ к врачу́. **3,** *pl.* (furnishings) обстано́вка.

apportion *v.t.* распределя́ть; выделя́ть. *Apportion seats in Congress,* распределя́ть места́ в конгре́ссе.

apportionment *n.* распределе́ние; выделе́ние; развёрстка; раскла́дка.

apposite *adj.* уме́стный; подходя́щий.

apposition *n.,* gram. приложе́ние.

appraisal *n.* оце́нка.

appraise *v.t.* оце́нивать: *The property was appraised at 100,000 dollars,* со́бственность была́ оценена́ в сто ты́сяч до́лларов.

appraiser *n.* оце́нщик.

appreciable *adj.* заме́тный; ощути́мый.

appreciate *v.t.* **1,** (see the value of) цени́ть: *appreciate good food,* цени́ть хоро́шую еду́. *No one appreciates me,* никто́ меня́ не це́нит. **2,** (recognize gratefully) быть благода́рным *or* призна́тельным: *I appreciate your help,* я благода́рен/призна́телен за по́мощь. *I would appreciate it if...,* бу́ду благода́рен/призна́телен е́сли... *I appreciate your calling,* спаси́бо, что позвони́ли. **3,** (realize; be aware of) понима́ть; отдава́ть себе́ отчёт в: *I appreciate the fact that...,* я понима́ю, что...; я отдаю́ себе́ отчёт в том, что... —*v.i.* повыша́ться в цене́.

appreciation *n.* **1,** (gratitude) призна́тельность. **2,** (sensitive awareness) понима́ние. **3,** (rise in value) повыше́ние сто́имости.

appreciative *adj.* призна́тельный.

apprehend *v.t.* **1,** (take into custody) аресто́вывать; брать под стра́жу. **2,** (comprehend; grasp) постига́ть.

apprehension *n.* **1,** (arrest) задержа́ние; аре́ст. **2,** (fear; concern) опасе́ние: *dispel someone's apprehensions,* развея́ть чьи́-нибудь опасе́ния.

apprehensive *adj.* озабо́ченный; беспоко́йный. —**apprehensiveness,** *n.* озабо́ченность; беспоко́йство.

apprentice *n.* учени́к; подмасте́рье. —*v.t.* отдава́ть в уче́ние. —**apprenticeship,** *n.* уче́ние; учени́чество.

apprise *v.t.* извеща́ть; осведомля́ть; уведомля́ть; информи́ровать.

approach *v.i.* подходи́ть; приближа́ться. *Someone was approaching from behind,* кто́-то подходи́л сза́ди. *Spring is fast approaching,* весна́ бы́стро приближа́ется. *The sound of approaching footsteps,* звук приближа́ющихся шаго́в. —*v.t.* **1,** (walk up to) подходи́ть к: *approach someone on the street,* подходи́ть к кому́-нибудь на у́лице. **2,** (draw near to) приближа́ться к: *approach the finish line,* приближа́ться к фи́нишу. **3,** (make an appeal or proposal to) обраща́ться к: *I decided to approach the boss,* я реши́л(а) обрати́ться к нача́льнику. **4,** (begin to deal with) подходи́ть к: *approach a matter differently,* подходи́ть к де́лу ина́че. —*n.* **1,** (coming up to) подхо́д; приближе́ние. **2,** (coming near in time) приближе́ние. **3,** (way by which a place is reached)

подхо́д; по́дступ. *The approach to a house,* подхо́д к до́му. *The approaches to a city,* по́дступы к го́роду. **4,** (method of approach, as to a problem) подхо́д: *try a new approach,* про́бовать но́вый подхо́д.

approachable *adj.* досту́пный.

approbation *n.* одобре́ние; апроба́ция.

appropriate *v.t.* **1,** (allot; allocate) ассигнова́ть. **2,** (take possession of) присва́ивать. —*adj.* **1,** (what is suitable or needed) подходя́щий; соотве́тствующий; надлежа́щий. *An appropriate time,* подходя́щее вре́мя. *Appropriate measures,* соотве́тствующие *or* надлежа́щие ме́ры. *Draw the appropriate conclusions,* сде́лать соотве́тствующие вы́воды. **2,** (apt) уме́стный: *appropriate remark,* уме́стное замеча́ние. —**appropriately,** *adv.* уме́стно.

appropriation *n.* **1,** (allotment of funds; funds so allotted) ассигнова́ние. **2,** (taking over; seizure) присвое́ние.

approval *n.* одобре́ние. *Shouts of approval,* одобри́тельные во́згласы. *Require Senate approval,* тре́бовать утвержде́ния сена́том.

approve *v.i.* [*usu.* **approve of**] одобря́ть. —*v.t.* утвержда́ть; одобря́ть: *approve a plan,* утвержда́ть/ одобря́ть план.

approving *adj.* одобри́тельный. —**approvingly,** *adv.* одобри́тельно.

approximate *adj.* приблизи́тельный. —*v.t.* приближа́ться к. —**approximately,** *adv.* приблизи́тельно; приме́рно. —**approximation,** *n.* приблизи́тельный подсчёт.

appurtenance *n.* **1,** (adjunct) прида́ток. **2,** *pl.* (accessories) принадле́жности.

apricot *n.* абрико́с. *Dried apricots,* курага́; урю́к. —*adj.* абрико́совый.

April *n.* апре́ль. —*adj.* апре́льский.

a priori 1, *used adverbially,* априо́ри. **2,** *used adjectivally,* априо́рный.

apron *n.* пере́дник; фа́ртук. —**be tied to someone's apron strings,** быть под башмако́м у кого́-нибудь.

apropos *adv.* кста́ти. —*adj.* уме́стный; кста́ти. *Be apropos,* быть кста́ти. —**apropos of,** относи́тельно; в связи́ с.

apse *n.* апси́да. *Also,* **apsis.**

apt *adj.* **1,** (pertinent) уда́чный; ме́ткий: *apt phrase,* уда́чная фра́за; *apt remark,* ме́ткое замеча́ние. **2,** (quick to learn) спосо́бный. **3,** *fol. by* **to** (inclined; likely) скло́нный (к): *People are apt to forget that...,* лю́ди скло́нны забыва́ть, что... *In such weather one is apt to catch cold,* в таку́ю пого́ду мо́жно легко́ простуди́ться.

aptitude *n.* спосо́бности: *an aptitude for languages,* спосо́бности к языка́м. —**aptitude test,** прове́рка спосо́бностей.

aptly *adv.* уме́стно; уда́чно.

aqualung *n.* аквала́нг.

aquamarine *n.* аквамари́н. —*adj.* аквамари́новый.

aquarium *n.* аква́риум.

Aquarius *n.* Водоле́й.

aquatic *adj.* водяно́й. *Aquatic mammal,* морско́е млекопита́ющее. *Aquatic sports,* во́дный спорт.

aquatint *n.* акватѝнта.

aqueduct *n.* акведук.

aquiline *adj.* орлѝный: *aquiline nose,* орлѝный нос.

Arab *n.* арѝб. —*adj.* арѝбский: *Arab countries,* арѝбские стрѝны.

arabesque *n.* арабѝска.

Arabian *adj.* аравѝйский.

Arabic *adj.* арѝбский. —*n.* арѝбский языќ. *Speak Arabic,* говорѝть по-арѝбски. —**Arabic numerals,** арѝбские цѝфры.

arable *adj.* пѝхотный: *arable land,* пѝхотная земля́.

Aramaic *adj.* арамѝйский. —*n.* арамѝйский языќ.

arbiter *n.* **1,** *law* арбѝтр; третѝйский судья́. **2,** (one who decides) законодѝтель: *arbiter of fashion,* законодѝтель мод.

arbitrary *adj.* произвѝльный; самоупрѝвный; самочѝнный. —**arbitrarily,** *adv.* произвѝльно. —**arbitrariness,** *n.* произвѝл; самоупрѝвство.

arbitrate *v.t.* решѝть в арбитрѝжном порядке.

arbitration *n.* арбитрѝж. *Court of arbitration,* третѝйский суд.

arbitrator *n.* арбѝтр; третѝйский судья́.

arbor *also,* **arbour** *n.* бесѝдка.

arboretum *n.* дендрѝрий.

arbour, *n.* = **arbor.**

arc *n.* дугѝ.

arcade *n.* **1,** *archit.* аркѝда. **2,** (covered passageway with shops) пассѝж.

arcane *adj.* заѝмный.

arch *n.* **1,** (curved structure) ѝрка; свод. **2,** (curve of the foot) свод стопы́. *Fallen arches,* плоскостѝпие. —*adj.* **1,** (sly) лукѝвый. **2,** (notorious) архи-: *arch liar,* архилгѝн. —*v.t.* выгибѝть: *arch one's back,* выгибѝть спѝну.

archaeology *n.* = **archeology.** —**archaeological,** *adj.* = **archeological.** —**archaeologist,** *n.* = **archeologist.**

archaic *adj.* архаѝчный; устарѝвший. —**archaism,** *n.* архаѝзм.

archangel *n.* архѝнгел.

archbishop *n.* архиепѝскоп.

archdeacon *n.* архидьяќон; *Orth. Ch.* протодьяќон.

archdiocese *n.* епѝрхия архиепѝскопа.

archduke *n.* эрцгѝрцог. —**archduchess,** *n.* эрцгерцогѝня. —**archduchy,** *n.* эрцгѝрцогство.

arched *adj.* ѝрочный; свѝдчатый; дугообрѝзный.

archenemy *n.* закля́тый враг.

archeology *also,* **archaeology** *n.* археолѝгия. —**archeological,** *adj.* археологѝческий. —**archeologist,** *n.* архѝолог.

archer *n.* стрелѝк из лѝка; лѝчник. —**archery,** *n.* стрельбѝ из лѝка.

archetype *n.* прототѝп; образѝц.

archimandrite *n.* архимандрѝт.

archipelago *n.* архипелѝг.

architect *n.* архитѝктор.

architecture *n.* архитектѝра. —**architectural,** *adj.* архитектѝрный.

archives *n.pl.* архѝв. —**archival,** *adj.* архѝвный. —**archivist,** *n.* архивѝст.

arch support супинѝтор.

archway *n.* свѝдчатый прохѝд.

arctic *adj.* арктѝческий; полярный. —**Arctic Circle,** Сѝверный полярный круг. —**Arctic Ocean,** Сѝверный Ледовѝтый океѝн.

ardent *adj.* страстный; я́рый; рѝвностный; пылкий; горячий. *Ardent admirer,* страстный *or* я́рый поклѝнник. *Ardent desire,* страстное *or* горячее желѝние. *Ardent Catholic,* рѝвностный катѝлик. —**ardently,** *adv.* страстно; горячѝ.

ardor *also,* **ardour** *n.* пыл; жар; рвѝние; задѝр.

arduous *adj.* трѝдный; тяжѝлый.

are *n.* (unit of area) ар.

area *n.* **1,** (two-dimensional extent) площадь: *the area of a circle,* площадь крѝга. **2,** (district) райѝн: *residential area,* жилѝй райѝн. **3,** (place; ground; site) площѝдка: *loading area,* погрѝзочная площѝдка. **4,** (field, as of study or interest) ѝбласть. *Area studies,* страновѝдение.

arena *n.* арѝна.

Argentinean *adj.* [*also,* **Argentine**] аргентѝнский. —*n.* аргентѝнец; аргентѝнка.

argon *n.* аргѝн.

argot *n.* арго; жаргѝн.

argue *v.i.* спѝрить: *argue about politics,* спѝрить о полѝтике; *argue over money,* спѝрить из-за дѝнег. *Let's not argue about it,* давѝйте не бѝдем спѝрить об ѝтом. —*v.t.* **1,** (plead, as a case) вестѝ (дѝло). **2,** (contend) утверждѝть; докѝзывать. **3,** (dispute): *I won't argue the point,* я не бѝду спѝрить об ѝтом; я и не спѝрю.

argument *n.* **1,** (quarrel) спор. *Have an argument,* спѝрить. **2,** (objection) возражѝние. *And no argument!,* без возражѝний!; без разговѝров!; и никакѝх разговѝров! **3,** (reason for or against) дѝвод; аргумѝнт: *strong argument,* сѝльный дѝвод/ аргумѝнт. *The arguments for and against,* дѝводы за и прѝтив. —**argumentation,** *n.* аргументѝция. —**argumentative,** *adj.* люѝбящий спѝрить.

aria *n.* ѝрия.

arid *adj.* сухѝй; засѝшливый; безвѝдный. —**aridity,** *n.* сѝхость.

Aries *n.* Овѝн.

arise *v.i.* **1,** (get up) вставѝть. **2,** (come about) возникѝть; вставѝть; создавѝться. *New problems arise every day,* нѝвые проблѝмы возникѝют кѝждый день. *Should the need/opportunity arise,* ѝсли вознѝкнет необходѝмость/ѝсли предстѝвится возмѝжность.

aristocracy *n.* аристокрѝтия. —**aristocrat,** *n.* аристокрѝт. —**aristocratic,** *adj.* аристократѝческий; аристократѝчный.

arithmetic *n.* арифмѝтика. —*adj.* [*also,* **arithmetical**] арифметѝческий.

ark *n.* **1,** (boat) ковчѝг: *Noah's ark,* Нѝев ковчѝг. **2,** (receptacle in the synagogue) ковчѝг. *Ark of the covenant,* ковчѝг завѝта.

arm *n.* **1,** (part of the body) рукѝ: *carry in one's arms,* нестѝ на рукѝх. *Under one's arm,* под мѝшкой. *Take my arm!,* возьмѝте моѝ рѝку. *Take someone by the arm,* взять когѝ-нибудь под руку. *Take in one's* *arms,* взять (ребёнка) нá руки; обнимáть (жéнщину). *He put his arm around her waist,* он обнял её за тáлию. **2,** (of a chair, sofa, etc.) рýчка. **3,** (of a dress, river, etc.) рукáв. **4,** *pl.* (weapons) *see* **arms.** —*v.t.* вооружáть. —*v.i.* вооружáться. —**arm in arm,** пóд руку. —**at arm's length,** на почтúтельном расстоянии. —**with open arms,** с распростёртыми объятиями.

armada *n.* армáда.

armadillo *n.* броненóсец.

armament *n.* **1,** (act of arming) вооружéние. **2,** *pl.* (arms) вооружéния. *The armaments industry,* воéнная промы́шленность.

armature *n.* я́корь; арматýра.

armband *n.* (нарукáвная) повя́зка; повя́зка на рукé *or* на рукавé.

armchair *n.* крéсло. —*adj.* кабинéтный: *armchair strategist,* кабинéтный стратéг.

armed *adj.* вооружённый: *armed conflict,* вооружённый конфлúкт; *armed robbery,* вооружённое ограблéние. *Heavily armed policemen,* сúльно вооружённая милúция. —**armed forces,** вооружённые сúлы.

Armenian *adj.* армя́нский. —*n.* **1,** (person) армяни́н; армя́нка. **2,** (language) армя́нский язы́к.

armful *n.* охáпка.

armhole *n.* прóйма.

armistice *n.* перемúрие.

armor *also,* **armour** *n.* **1,** (worn by medieval knights) доспéхи; лáты; броня́; пáнцирь. *Knight in armor,* ры́царь в доспéхах. *Suit of armor,* лáтные доспéхи. **2,** (for warships, tanks, etc.) броня́. **3,** *mil.* (armored vehicles) бронирóванные маши́ны. —*v.t.* бронировáть.

armored *adj.* **1,** (protected by armor) броневóй; бронирóванный; броненóсный. *Armored car,* бронемаши́на; бронеавтомобúль. *Armored cruiser,* бронирóванный *or* броненóсный крéйсер. *Armored personnel carrier,* бронетранспортёр. **2,** (equipped with armored vehicles) бронетáнковый: *armored division,* бронетáнковая диви́зия. *Armored column,* колóнна тáнков.

armor plate броневáя плита́; броневóй лист. *Also,* **armour plating.**

armory *also,* **armoury** *n.* арсенáл; склад орýжия.

armour *n.* = **armor.** —**armoury,** *n.* = **armory.**

armpit *n.* подмы́шка.

armrest *n.* подлокóтник.

arms *n.pl.* орýжие; вооружéния. *Arms race,* гóнка вооружéний. *Arms control,* контрóль над вооружéниями. *Take up arms,* брáться за орýжие. *Lay down one's arms,* сложи́ть орýжие. —**be up in arms over,** встрéтить в штыки́. —**under arms,** под ружьём.

army *n.* áрмия. —*adj.* армéйский: *army corps,* армéйский кóрпус; *army life,* армéйская жизнь.

arnica *n.* áрника.

aroma *n.* аромáт. —**aromatic,** *adj.* аромáтный; души́стый.

around *prep.* **1,** (encircling) вокрýг: *travel around*

the world, путешéствовать вокрýг свéта. *Build a fence around the garden,* обноси́ть сад забóром. **2,** (so as to avoid or get past) *rendered by the prefix* об-: *walk around the puddle,* обходи́ть лýжу. **3,** (by turning) за: *around the corner,* за углóм. **4,** (from place to place in; about) по: *walk around town,* ходи́ть по гóроду. *Show someone around town,* покáзывать комý-нибудь гóрод. **5,** *colloq.* (approximately) óколо: *around six dollars,* óколо шести́ дóлларов. —*adv.* кругóм; вокрýг. *Turn around,* повора́чиваться (кругóм); обора́чиваться. *There is no one around,* никогó нет кругóм. *For hundreds of miles around,* за сóтни миль.

arouse *v.t.* **1,** (awaken) буди́ть. **2,** (stir to action) возбуждáть. **3,** (evoke, as a feeling) возбуждáть; вызывáть; внушáть.

arpeggio *n.* арпéджио.

arquebus *n.* пища́ль.

arraign *v.t.* привлекáть к судý. —**arraignment,** *n.* привлечéние к судý.

arrange *v.t.* **1,** (put in correct order) располагáть; расставля́ть: *arrange the furniture,* располагáть/расставля́ть мéбель. *Arrange in alphabetical order,* располагáть в алфави́тном поря́дке. *Arrange the chess pieces on the board,* расставля́ть ша́хматы на доскé. **2,** (organize) устрáивать: *arrange a meeting between them,* устрóить их встрéчу. **3,** *music* аранжи́ровать. —*v.i.* **1,** *fol. by inf.* (agree) договáриваться; усла́вливаться; сговáриваться. **2,** *fol. by* **for** (see to it that) договáриваться так, чтóбы: *I'll arrange for you to be admitted,* я договорю́сь так, чтóбы вас впусти́ли *or* пропусти́ли.

arrangement *n.* **1,** (act of arranging; order) расположéние; расстанóвка; устрóйство. *Arrangement of furniture,* расстанóвка мéбели. *A flower arrangement,* компози́ция цветóв; букéт. *Table arrangement,* сервирóвка столá. **2,** (way something is to be done) план; вариáнт: *I suggest a different arrangement,* я предлагáю другóй план/вариáнт. **3,** *pl.* (plans; preparations) мéры; приготовлéния. *Make arrangements to leave,* готóвиться к отъéзду. *I've made arrangements for you to stay with my friends,* я устрóил так, чтóбы вы гости́ли у мои́х друзéй. **4,** *music* аранжирóвка; переложéние.

arrant *adj.* **1,** (notorious) отъя́вленный. **2,** (downright) сýщий.

array *n.* **1,** (arrangement) расположéние. **2,** *mil.* боевóй поря́док. **3,** (imposing collection or display) коллéкция; вы́ставка. —*v.t.* **1,** (deck out) одевáть. **2,** *mil.* выстрáивать.

arrears *n.pl.* задóлженность; недоúмка. *Be in arrears,* имéть задóлженность.

arrest *v.t.* **1,** (take into custody) арестóвывать; задéрживать. **2,** (check, as growth, a disease, etc.) задéрживать; останáвливать. **3,** (capture, as one's attention) прикóвывать. —*n.* **1,** (detention) арéст. *Under house arrest,* под дома́шним арéстом. *Place under arrest,* посади́ть под арéст; взять *or* заключи́ть под стрáжу. *You are under arrest!,* вы арестóваны! **2,** *med.* останóвка: *cardiac arrest,* останóвка сéрдца.

arresting *adj.* поража́ющий; захва́тывающий.

arrhythmia *n.* аритми́я.

arrival *n.* **1,** (act of arriving) прибы́тие; прихо́д; прие́зд. **2,** (one who has just arrived) новоприбы́вший.

arrive *v.i.* **1,** (come to or reach a place) приходи́ть; приезжа́ть; прибыва́ть. *Arrive home from work,* прийти́ домо́й с рабо́ты. *Arrive in time for the meeting,* прийти́ во́время на собра́ние. *He arrives from Paris on Sunday,* он приезжа́ет из Пари́жа в воскресе́нье. *The plane arrives at six,* самолёт прибыва́ет в шесть. *The train arrived late,* по́езд опозда́л. **2,** (come, as of a time or season) наступа́ть. **3,** *fol. by at* (reach, as a conclusion) приходи́ть (к).

arrogance *n.* высокоме́рие; надме́нность; зано́счивость.

arrogant *adj.* высокоме́рный; надме́нный; зано́счивый.

arrogate *v.t.* присва́ивать себе́.

arrow *n.* **1,** (projectile fired from a bow) стрела́. **2,** (pointer; indicator) стре́лка.

arrowhead *n.* наконе́чник стрелы́.

arsenal *n.* арсена́л.

arsenic *n.* мышья́к. —*adj.* мышьяко́вый.

arson *n.* поджо́г. —**arsonist,** *n.* поджига́тель.

art *n.* **1,** (creative work or skill) иску́сство. *Work of art,* произведе́ние иску́сства. *The art of embroidery,* иску́сство вышива́ния. *Study art,* изуча́ть иску́сство. **2,** *pl.* (liberal arts) гуманита́рные нау́ки. —*adj.* худо́жественный. *Art exhibit,* вы́ставка жи́вописи; худо́жественная вы́ставка. *Art museum,* музе́й иску́сства. *Art gallery, see* **gallery.** *Art collector,* коллекционе́р жи́вописи.

artefact *n.* = **artifact.**

artel *n.* арте́ль.

arterial *adj.* **1,** *anat.* артериа́льный. **2,** (of a highway) магистра́льный.

arteriosclerosis *n.* артериосклеро́з.

artery *n.* арте́рия.

artesian well артезиа́нский коло́дец.

artful *adj.* **1,** (wily) хи́трый. **2,** (skillful) ло́вкий.

arthritis *n.* артри́т.

artichoke *n.* артишо́к. *Jerusalem artichoke,* земляна́я гру́ша.

article *n.* **1,** (item) предме́т: *article of clothing,* предме́т оде́жды. *Toilet articles,* туале́тные принадле́жности. **2,** (composition written for publication) статья́. **3,** (paragraph of a treaty, constitution, etc.) статья́. **4,** *gram.* арти́кль; член.

articulate *v.t.* **1,** (enunciate) выгова́ривать. **2,** (express in words) выража́ть. —*v.i.* артикули́ровать. —*adj.* членоразде́льный. *He is very articulate,* он хорошо́ выража́ет свои́ мы́сли. —**articulation,** *n.* артикуля́ция.

artifact *also,* **artefact** *n.* предме́т челове́ческого труда́.

artifice *n.* уло́вка.

artificial *adj.* иску́сственный: *artificial flowers,* иску́сственные цветы́; *an artificial smile,* иску́сственная улы́бка. —**artificial limb,** проте́з. —**artifi-**

cial respiration, иску́сственное дыха́ние. *Give artificial respiration to,* отка́чивать.

artificiality *n.* иску́сственность.

artificially *adv.* иску́сственно.

artillery *n.* артилле́рия. —*adj.* артиллери́йский: *artillery fire,* артиллери́йский ого́нь. —**artilleryman,** *n.* артиллери́ст.

artisan *n.* реме́сленник.

artist *n.* **1,** (one who draws or paints) худо́жник. **2,** (performer) арти́ст.

artistic *adj.* **1,** (of or pert. to art) худо́жественный. **2,** (showing good taste or a talent for art) артисти́ческий.

artistry *n.* артисти́чность; артисти́зм; худо́жественность.

artless *adj.* **1,** (ingenuous) простоду́шный; бесхи́тростный. **2,** (done without skill; crude) безда́рный.

Aryan *adj.* ари́йский. —*n.* ари́ец; *pl.* ари́йцы.

as *conj.* **1,** (to the same degree that; in the same manner that) как: *thin as a rail,* худо́й как ще́пка. *Regard something as temporary,* рассма́тривать что́-нибудь как вре́менное. **2,** (according to what) как: *as is known,* как изве́стно; *as you can see,* как ви́дно. *As often happens,* как э́то ча́сто быва́ет. *Do as you are told,* де́лайте, как вам ве́лено. **3,** (at the same time that) когда́: *as I write these lines,* когда́ я пишу́ э́ти стро́ки. *As he was crossing the street, a car...,* когда́ он переходи́л че́рез у́лицу, маши́на... *As he was crossing the street, he...,* переходя́ че́рез у́лицу, он... *As a hurricane nears the mainland,* при приближе́нии урага́на к материку́. **4,** (because; since) так как: *We must be leaving, as it is already late,* на́до уйти́, так как уже́ по́здно. **5,** (to the degree that) по ме́ре того́, как: *as it became warmer,* по ме́ре того́, как станови́лось тепле́е. —*adv.* **1,** (equally) так же; тако́й же: *Our house is just as large,* наш дом тако́й же большо́й. **2,** (for example) как; как приме́р. *Such important people as...,* таки́е ва́жные ли́ца, как... *African languages, as Swahili,* африка́нские языки́, как наприме́р суахи́ли. —*prep.* как; в ка́честве (+ *gen.*). *As an example,* в ка́честве приме́ра. *I give you this advice as a friend,* сове́тую э́то вам, как друг. *The film stars as Gandhi,* в фи́льме ... игра́ет гла́вную роль Га́нди. ♦*Also rendered by the instr. case: work as a salesman,* рабо́тать продавцо́м; *dressed as a Cossack,* переоде́тый казако́м; *serve as a pretext,* служи́ть предло́гом. *Choose as one's successor,* выбира́ть (кого́-нибудь) свои́м прее́мником. *I was often ill as a child,* ребёнком (*or* в де́тстве) я ча́сто боле́л(а). *He learned the language as an adult,* он вы́учил язы́к взро́слым. —**as...as, 1,** (equally) тако́й (*or* так) же...как (и). *He is as tall as you,* он тако́й же высо́кий, как вы. *The rain stopped as suddenly as it began,* дождь прекрати́лся так же внеза́пно, как нача́лся. *The number of victims could be as high as 10,000,* число́ жертв мо́жет доходи́ть до десяти́ ты́сяч. **2,** (to the maximum) как мо́жно: *as soon as possible,* как мо́жно скоре́е. *Run as fast as you can,* бегите как мо́жно скоре́е. **3,** (no matter how) как ни: *as unbelievable as it seems,* как э́то ни ка́жется невероя́тным. *As smart as he is, he could not solve the problem,* как он ни умён, он не мог реши́ть зада́чу. **—as for,** что каса́ется (+ *gen.*). **—as if,** (как) бу́дто; как бы; сло́вно. *As if by magic,* как бу́дто по волшебству́. *As if you didn't know!,* как бу́дто вы не зна́ете. *You look as if you want to leave,* у вас тако́й вид, бу́дто вы хоти́те уйти́. *I remember it as if it were yesterday,* по́мню, сло́вно э́то бы́ло вчера́. **—as it is,** и без того́: *It's expensive enough as it is,* э́то и без того́ о́чень до́рого. **—as it were,** так сказа́ть. **—as of,** на: *as of June 1,* на пе́рвое ию́ня. *As of this moment,* в да́нный моме́нт. **—as though,** *see* **though. —as to** = **as for. —as well,** *see* **well. —as you were!,** *mil.* отста́вить!

asbestos *n.* асбе́ст. **—***adj.* асбе́стовый.

ascend *v.i.* поднима́ться; всходи́ть. **—***v.t.* поднима́ться по; всходи́ть на. *Ascend the throne,* взойти́ *or* вступи́ть на престо́л.

ascendancy *n.* госпо́дство: *gain ascendancy,* дости́гнуть госпо́дства.

ascendant *adj.* **1,** (rising) восходя́щий. **2,** (dominant) госпо́дствующий.

ascension *n.* **1,** (ascent) восхожде́ние. **2,** *cap., relig.* вознесе́ние.

ascent *n.* **1,** (upward movement) восхожде́ние; подъём. **2,** (slope) крутизна́; подъём.

ascertain *v.t.* выясня́ть; устана́вливать. *Ascertain the cause of the fire,* вы́яснить причи́ну пожа́ра. *Ascertain the truth,* установи́ть пра́вду.

ascetic *n.* аске́т; подви́жник. **—***adj.* аскети́ческий. **—asceticism,** *n.* аскети́зм.

ascorbic acid аскорби́новая кислота́.

ascribe *v.t.* припи́сывать: *The play is sometimes ascribed to Shakespeare,* пье́су иногда́ припи́сывают Шекспи́ру.

asepsis *n.* асе́птика. **—aseptic,** *adj.* асепти́ческий.

asexual *adj.* беспо́лый.

ash *n.* **1,** (tree) я́сень. *Mountain ash,* ряби́на. **2,** *usu. pl.* (residue after burning) пе́пел; зола́. **3,** (fine lava) пе́пел: *volcanic ash,* вулкани́ческий пе́пел. **4,** *pl.* (ruins) пе́пел: *rise from the ashes,* поднима́ться из пе́пла. **5,** *pl.* (human remains) прах.

ashamed *adj., used predicatively:* be ashamed, стыди́ться. *I am ashamed,* мне сты́дно. *Aren't you ashamed!,* как вам не сты́дно! *You ought to be ashamed of yourself!,* вам должно́ быть сты́дно!

ash can му́сорный я́щик.

ashen *adj.* **1,** (of the color of ashes) пе́пельного цве́та. **2,** (extremely pale) помертве́лый.

ashore *adv.* на бе́рег; к бе́регу. *Go ashore,* сходи́ть на бе́рег. *Swim ashore,* плыть к бе́регу. *Put ashore,* выса́живать на бе́рег. *Wash ashore,* выноси́ть *or* выбра́сывать на бе́рег. *The body was washed ashore,* труп был вы́несен на бе́рег; труп приби́ло к бе́регу.

ashtray *n.* пе́пельница.

Asian *also,* **Asiatic** *adj.* азиа́тский. **—***n.* азиа́т.

aside *adv.* в сто́рону; в стороне́. *Leave aside,* оставля́ть в стороне́. *Put/set aside,* откла́дывать (в сто́рону); сберега́ть. *Stand aside,* держа́ться в стороне́. *Stand aside!,* отойди́те в сто́рону! *Take someone aside,* отводи́ть кого́-нибудь в сто́рону. *Joking aside,* шу́тки в сто́рону. **—all else aside,** поми́мо всего́ про́чего. **—aside from,** поми́мо.

asinine *adj.* дура́цкий; идио́тский.

ask *v.t.* **1,** (put a question to; inquire about) спра́шивать: *I'll ask her,* я её спрошу́. *Ask a passer-by,* спроси́ть у прохо́жего. *Ask the way,* спроси́ть доро́гу. *Ask someone's opinion,* спроси́ть чьё-нибудь мне́ние. *Ask a question,* задава́ть вопро́с. **2,** (request) проси́ть: *ask someone to do the dishes,* проси́ть кого́-нибудь помы́ть посу́ду. *Ask him to come in,* попроси́те его́ войти́. *I have a favor to ask of you,* у меня́ к вам про́сьба. **3,** (invite) приглаша́ть; звать. *Ask someone to dance/ for a date/,* пригласи́ть кого́-нибудь на та́нец/ на свида́ние/. **4,** (charge, as an amount of money) проси́ть; спра́шивать. *Ask a high price,* запра́шивать высо́кую це́ну. **5,** (demand; expect) тре́бовать. **—***v.i.* спра́шивать: *If you don't know, ask,* е́сли не зна́ешь, спроси́. *She asked about you,* она́ о вас спра́шивала. **—ask for,** **1,** (request) проси́ть; спра́шивать: *ask for a book,* проси́ть/спра́шивать кни́гу; *ask for permission,* проси́ть/спра́шивать разреше́ния. *Ask for time off,* проси́ться в о́тпуск. *Ask someone for advice/ help,* проси́ть/спра́шивать у кого́-нибудь сове́та/ по́мощи; проси́ть кого́-нибудь о по́мощи. *Ask for one's money back,* проси́ть де́нег обра́тно. **2,** (ask to see) спра́шивать: *Someone was asking for you,* вас спра́шивал како́й-то челове́к. **3,** (invite, as trouble) напра́шиваться на (неприя́тности). *See also* **asking.**

askance *adv.* ко́со: *look askance,* смотре́ть ко́со.

askew *adv.* ко́со; кри́во.

asking *n. It's yours for the asking,* сто́ит то́лько попроси́ть. **—asking price,** запра́шиваемая цена́.

aslant *adv.* ко́со; на́искось.

asleep *adj., used predicatively* **1,** (sleeping): be asleep, спать. *Fall asleep,* засыпа́ть. **2,** (numb): *My foot is asleep,* я отсиде́л *or* отлежа́л (себе́) но́гу.

asp *n.* а́спид.

asparagus *n.* спа́ржа. **—***adj.* спа́ржевый: *asparagus soup,* спа́ржевый суп.

aspect *n.* **1,** (appearance) вид. **2,** (part; feature) сторона́; моме́нт; аспе́кт. *Consider a question in all its aspects,* рассма́тривать вопро́с со всех сторо́н. *Negative aspects,* отрица́тельные моме́нты. **3,** *gram.* вид: *imperfective aspect,* несоверше́нный вид.

aspectual *adj., gram.* видово́й.

aspen *n.* оси́на. **—***adj.* оси́новый.

asperity *n.* ре́зкость; гру́бость.

asperse *v.t.* клевета́ть на.

aspersion *n.* клевета́. *Cast aspersions on,* броса́ть тень на.

asphalt *n.* асфа́льт. **—***adj.* асфа́льтовый. **—***v.t.* асфальти́ровать.

asphyxia *n.* асфи́кция.

asphyxiate *v.t.* удуша́ть. *Be asphyxiated,* задыха́ться. **—asphyxiation,** *n.* удуше́ние; асфи́кция.

aspic *n.* заливно́е; сту́день.

aspirant *n.* претенде́нт.

aspirate *n. & adj.* придыха́тельный. —*v.t.* произноси́ть с придыха́нием.

aspiration *n.* **1,** (ambition) стремле́ние; устремле́ние. **2,** *phonet.* придыха́ние.

aspire *v.i.* [*usu.* **aspire to**] стреми́ться (к); претендова́ть (на). *Aspire to the role of...,* претендова́ть на роль (+ *gen.*).

aspirin *n.* аспири́н. *Aspirin tablet,* табле́тка аспири́на.

ass *n.* **1,** (donkey) осёл. **2,** *slang* (dope; jerk) болва́н. *Make an ass of oneself,* опростоволо́ситься. **3,** *slang* (buttocks) зад.

assail *v.t.* **1,** (assault) напада́ть на. **2,** (denounce) обру́шиваться на. **3,** *fig.* (beset) му́чить: *be assailed by doubts,* му́читься сомне́ниями.

assailant *n.* напада́ющий; налётчик.

assassin *n.* уби́йца.

assassinate *v.t.* убива́ть. *Attempt to assassinate,* покуша́ться на.

assassination *n.* уби́йство. *Assassination attempt,* покуше́ние (на).

assault *n.* **1,** (violent physical attack) нападе́ние. **2,** *mil.* штурм; ата́ка. —*adj., mil.* деса́нтный; штурмово́й. —*v.t.* напада́ть на; атакова́ть. —**assault and battery,** избие́ние; оскорбле́ние де́йствием.

assay *v.t.* **1,** (attempt) пыта́ться. **2,** (estimate) оце́нивать.

assemblage *n.* **1,** (gathering of persons) собра́ние. **2,** *mech.* сбо́рка; монта́ж.

assemble *v.t.* **1,** (bring together; put together) собира́ть: *assemble the players,* собира́ть игроко́в; *assemble a collection,* собира́ть колле́кцию. **2,** (organize, as a team) набира́ть. —*v.i.* собира́ться; сходи́ться; съезжа́ться. —**assembler,** *n.* сбо́рщик.

assembly *n.* **1,** (act of meeting or assembling) собра́ние: *freedom of assembly,* свобо́да собра́ний. **2,** (deliberative body) собра́ние; ассамбле́я. *Constituent assembly,* учреди́тельное собра́ние. *General Assembly (of the U.N.),* Генера́льная Ассамбле́я. **3,** (fitting together of parts) сбо́рка; монта́ж. **4,** (parts so assembled) у́зел; агрега́т. *Tail assembly, aero.* хвостово́е опере́ние. —**assembly hall,** а́ктовый зал. —**assembly line,** сбо́рочный конве́йер.

assent *v.i.* соглаша́ться. —*n.* согла́сие. *Nod in assent,* кива́ть голово́й в знак согла́сия.

assert *v.t.* **1,** (aver) утвержда́ть. **2,** (claim and forcefully defend) отста́ивать; предъявля́ть: *assert one's rights,* отста́ивать/предъявля́ть свои́ права́.

assertion *n.* утвержде́ние.

assertive *adj.* напо́ристый. —**assertiveness,** *n.* напо́ристость.

assess *v.t.* **1,** (evaluate) оце́нивать. **2,** (levy, as a fine) налага́ть; взы́скивать. **3,** (levy a payment upon) облага́ть. *Each member was assessed $200,* с ка́ждого чле́на собра́ли две́сти до́лларов.

assessment *n.* **1,** (evaluation) оце́нка. **2,** (payment assessed) обложе́ние.

asset *n.* **1,** (something advantageous) преиму́щество; це́нное ка́чество. **2,** *usu. pl., comm.* акти́в.

assiduous *adj.* приле́жный; стара́тельный; уси́дчивый. —**assiduousness; assiduity,** *n.* прилежа́ние; стара́тельность; уси́дчивость.

assign *v.t.* **1,** (appoint; designate) назнача́ть: *He was assigned to the embassy in London,* он был назна́чен в посо́льство в Ло́ндоне. **2,** *mil.* прикомандирова́ть. **3,** (give out, as a task, lesson, etc.) ста́вить (зада́чу); назнача́ть (рабо́ту); задава́ть (уро́к). *Assign someone the task of...,* ста́вить пе́ред ке́м-нибудь зада́чу (+ *gen.*). **4,** (allocate) отводи́ть: *assign rooms/ a role/,* отводи́ть ко́мнаты/роль.

assignment *n.* **1,** (appointment) назначе́ние. **2,** (task) поруче́ние; зада́ние. *Homework assignment,* дома́шнее зада́ние. **3,** (official trip) командиро́вка.

assimilate *v.t.* **1,** *physiol.* ассимили́ровать; усва́ивать. **2,** (absorb mentally) усва́ивать; воспринима́ть. —*v.i.* ассимили́роваться. —**assimilation,** *n.* ассимиля́ция; усвое́ние.

assist *v.t. & i.* помога́ть; соде́йствовать. *Assist someone in getting up,* помо́чь кому́-нибудь встать.

assistance *n.* по́мощь; соде́йствие. *Need assistance,* нужда́ться в по́мощи. *How may I be of assistance?,* чем я могу́ помо́чь?; чем могу́ быть поле́зен?

assistant *n. & adj.* помо́щник. *Assistant director,* помо́щник дире́ктора. —**assistant professor,** ассисте́нт.

associate *n.* сотру́дник; колле́га. —*v.t.* соединя́ть; свя́зывать; ассоции́ровать. *The problems associated with it,* свя́занные с э́тим пробле́мы. —*v.i.* обща́ться: *associate with foreigners,* обща́ться с иностра́нцами. —**associate member,** ассоции́рованный член. —**associate professor,** доце́нт.

association *n.* **1,** (act of associating) обще́ние. *The right of association,* пра́во на объедине́ние. **2,** (an organization) о́бщество; объедине́ние; ассоциа́ция. **3,** (connection in the mind) ассоциа́ция.

assonance *n.* созву́чие; ассона́нс. —**assonant,** *adj.* созву́чный.

assort *v.t.* сортирова́ть. —**assorted,** *adj.* ра́зные; ра́зного ро́да.

assortment *n.* вы́бор; подбо́р; ассортиме́нт.

assuage *v.t.* **1,** (allay) смягча́ть; облегча́ть. **2,** (calm) успока́ивать. **3,** (appease, as hunger) утоля́ть.

assume *v.t.* **1,** (suppose) предполага́ть; допуска́ть: *Let us assume that...,* предположи́м/допу́стим, что... **2,** (take on; take over) принима́ть: *assume a pose,* принима́ть по́зу; *assume command,* принима́ть кома́ндование. *Assume responsibility,* принима́ть *or* брать на себя́ отве́тственность. *Assume the offensive,* переходи́ть в наступле́ние. *Assume office,* вступи́ть в до́лжность. *Assume an injured look,* принима́ть оби́женный вид. *Assume a threatening character,* принима́ть *or* приобрета́ть угрожа́ющий хара́ктер.

assumed *adj.* **1,** (supposed; presumed) предполага́емый. **2,** (fictitious) вы́мышленный. *Under an assumed name,* под чужи́м и́менем.

assumption *n.* **1,** (supposition) предположе́ние. *Proceed on the assumption that...,* исходи́ть из предположе́ния (*or* из того́), что... **2,** (taking on; taking over) приня́тие (на себя́). **3,** (accession, as to a position) вступле́ние. **4,** *cap., relig.* успе́ние. *Cathedral of the Assumption,* Успе́нский собо́р.

assurance *n.* **1,** (positive statement) увере́ние; завере́ние. *Give assurances,* дава́ть завере́ния. **2,** (certainty) уве́ренность. **3,** (confidence) уве́ренность в себе́.

assure *v.t.* **1,** (promise confidently) уверя́ть; заверя́ть. *I assure you,* уверя́ю вас. **2,** (make certain) обеспе́чивать: *Success is assured,* успе́х обеспе́чен. —**you may rest assured,** мо́жете быть уве́рены.

assuredly *adv.* несомне́нно.

Assyrian *adj.* ассири́йский. —*n.* ассири́ец.

astatine *n.* аста́т.

aster *n.* а́стра.

asterisk *n.* звёздочка.

astern *adv.* **1,** (behind a ship) за кормо́й. **2,** (at the rear of a ship) на корме́.

asteroid *n.* астеро́ид.

asthma *n.* а́стма. —**asthmatic,** *adj.* астмати́ческий. —*n.* астма́тик.

astigmatism *n.* астигмати́зм. —**astigmatic,** *adj.* астигмати́ческий.

astir *adv.* **1,** (in motion) в движе́нии. **2,** (out of bed) на нога́х. **3,** (excited) взволно́ванный.

astonish *v.t.* изумля́ть; поража́ть. *I was astonished at...,* я изуми́лся (+ *dat.*); я был изумлён *or* поражён (+ *instr.*); меня́ порази́л (+ *nom.*). —**astonishing,** *adj.* изуми́тельный. —**astonishment,** *n.* изумле́ние.

astound *v.t.* изумля́ть; поража́ть. —**astounding,** *adj.* изуми́тельный; порази́тельный.

astrakhan *n.* кара́куль. —*adj.* кара́кулевый.

astray *adv.* с пути́. *Go astray,* сбива́ться с пути́; заблуди́ться. *Lead astray,* сбива́ть с пути́; вводи́ть в заблужде́ние.

astride *prep.* верхо́м на (+ *prepl.*).

astringent *adj.* **1,** (tending to constrict) вя́жущий. **2,** (harsh) те́рпкий. —*n.* вя́жущее сре́дство. —**astringency,** *n.* те́рпкость.

astrolabe *n.* астроля́бия.

astrology *n.* астроло́гия. —**astrologer,** *n.* астро́лог; звездочёт. —**astrological,** *adj.* астрологи́ческий.

astronaut *n.* космона́вт.

astronomy *n.* астроно́мия. —**astronomer,** *n.* астроно́м. —**astronomic(al),** *adj.* астрономи́ческий.

astrophysics *n.* астрофи́зика. —**astrophysical,** *adj.* астрофизи́ческий. —**astrophysicist,** *n.* астрофи́зик.

astute *adj.* проница́тельный; то́нкий. —**astuteness,** *n.* проница́тельность.

asunder *adv.* на ча́сти.

asylum *n.* **1,** (refuge) убе́жище: *political asylum,* полити́ческое убе́жище. **2,** (institution) сумасше́дший дом.

asymmetric *also,* **asymmetrical** *adj.* асимметри́чный; несимметри́чный. —**asymmetry,** *n.* асимметри́я; несимметри́чность.

at *prep.* **1,** (in; attending) в; на (+ *prepl.*): *at the theater,* в теа́тре; *at an intersection,* на перекрёстке; *at work,* на рабо́те; *at the meeting,* на собра́нии; *at the wedding,* на сва́дьбе. *At home,* до́ма. **2,** (near; by) у: *at the window,* у окна́. *At the gates of the city,* у воро́т го́рода. **3,** (indicating arrival) в; на (+ *acc.*): *arrive at school/work,* прийти́ в шко́лу/ на рабо́ту/. **4,** (at the home of) у: *at my uncle's,* у моего́ дя́ди. **5,** (with verbs of sitting) за: *be seated at the table,* сиде́ть за столо́м. **6,** (indicating the target or object of something) в; на (+ *acc.*). *Look at one's watch,* посмотре́ть на часы́. *Fire at a target,* стреля́ть в мише́нь *or* по мише́ни. *Angry at/ shout at/ someone,* серди́т на/ крича́ть на/ кого́-нибудь. **7,** (indicating rate, speed, degree, etc.): *at an altitude of,* на высоте́ (+ *gen.*). *At reduced prices,* по сни́женным це́нам. *At a snail's pace,* черепа́шьим ша́гом. *Drive at high speed,* е́хать с большо́й ско́ростью *or* на большо́й ско́рости. **8,** (indicating a certain time) в (+ *acc.*): *at noon,* в по́лдень; *at three o'clock,* в три часа́; *at that time,* в то вре́мя. ♦*But notice: at night,* но́чью; *at dawn,* на рассве́те; *at what time?,* в кото́ром часу́? *At 3:20,* два́дцать мину́т четвёртого; *at 3:30,* в полови́не четвёртого; в полчетвёртого; *at 3:50,* без десяти́ четы́ре. *At exactly 3:20,* ро́вно в два́дцать мину́т четвёртого. **9,** (indicating a state or condition) в; на (+ *prepl.*): *at peace,* в ми́ре; *at rest,* в поко́е; *at liberty,* на свобо́де; *at anchor,* на я́коре; *at one's leisure,* на досу́ге. **10,** (in accordance with) по: *at the request of,* по про́сьбе (+ *gen.*); *at one's discretion,* по своему́ усмотре́нию. **11,** (in reaction to) при: *at the sight of,* при ви́де (+ *gen.*); *shudder at the thought of,* содрога́ться при мы́сли о. **12,** *in various miscellaneous expressions: at fault,* винова́т; *at large,* на свобо́де. —**at all,** *see* **all.** —**at last,** наконе́ц. —**at once,** *see* **once.** —**at that, 1,** (after all) в конце́ концо́в: *not so bad at that,* в конце́ концо́в не так уж пло́хо. **2,** (besides) причём: *He solved all the problems, and rather quickly at that,* он реши́л все зада́чи, причём дово́льно бы́стро. *Only one tie, and a frayed one at that,* то́лько оди́н га́лстук, да и то поно́шенный.

ataman *n.* атама́н.

atavism *n.* атави́зм. —**atavistic,** *adj.* атависти́ческий.

ataxia *n.* атакси́я.

atheism *n.* атеи́зм; безбо́жие. —**atheist,** *n.* атеи́ст; безбо́жник. —**atheistic,** *adj.* атеисти́ческий.

Athenian *adj.* афи́нский.

athlete *n.* спортсме́н; атле́т.

athletic *adj.* атлети́ческий; спорти́вный. *Athletic field,* спорти́вная площа́дка; спорти́вное по́ле. *Athletic build,* атлети́ческое телосложе́ние. —**athletics,** *n.pl.* атле́тика.

athwart *prep.* поперёк.

Atlantic *adj.* атланти́ческий. —**Atlantic Ocean,** Атланти́ческий океа́н.

atlas *n.* а́тлас.

atmosphere *n.* **1,** (air) атмосфе́ра. **2,** *fig.* (setting; surroundings) обстано́вка; атмосфе́ра. —**atmospheric,** *adj.* атмосфе́рный.

atoll *n.* ато́лл.

atom *n.* а́том. *Atom-free zone,* беза́томная зо́на.

atomic *adj.* а́томный. —**atomic bomb,** а́томная бо́мба.

atomize *v.t.* распыля́ть. —**atomizer,** *n.* распыли́тель; пульвериза́тор.

atonal *adj.* атона́льный. —**atonality,** *n.* атона́льность.

atone *v.i.* [*usu.* **atone for**] искупа́ть. —**atonement,** *n.* искупле́ние.

atop *prep.* на верху́ (+ *gen.*).

atrocious *adj.* **1,** (cruel; brutal) зве́рский. **2,** *colloq.* (abominable) отврати́тельный.

atrocity *n.* зве́рство.

atrophy *n.* атрофи́я. —*v.i.* атрофи́роваться. —**atrophied,** *adj.* атрофи́рованный.

atropine *n.* атропи́н.

attach *v.t.* **1,** (fasten) прикрепля́ть: *attach an antenna to the roof,* прикрепля́ть анте́нну к кры́ше. **2,** (append) прилага́ть: *attached hereto,* при сём прилага́ется. **3,** (ascribe) придава́ть: *attach great importance to,* придава́ть большо́е значе́ние (+ *dat.*). **4,** *mil.* (assign) придава́ть. *See also* **attached.**

attaché *n.* атташе́.

attached *adj.* **1,** (fastened) прикреплённый. **2,** (affiliated): *He is attached to the university,* он рабо́тает при университе́те. **3,** *fol. by* **to** (devoted) привя́занный (к): *She is attached to her sister,* она́ привя́зана к свое́й сестре́.

attachment *n.* **1,** (attaching) прикрепле́ние. **2,** (affection) привя́занность. **3,** (accessory) приста́вка; наса́дка.

attack *v.t.* **1,** (assault; invade) напада́ть на. **2,** (criticize sharply) обру́шиваться на. **3,** (begin working on) бра́ться за. **4,** *med.* (strike) поража́ть. —*v.i.* наступа́ть; атакова́ть. —*n.* **1,** (assault; offensive) нападе́ние; ата́ка. *Surprise attack,* внеза́пное нападе́ние. **2,** (denunciaton) вы́пад; *pl.* напа́дки. *Attack(s) on/ against,* вы́пад про́тив; напа́дки на. **3,** *med.* (seizure) припа́док; при́ступ. *Heart attack,* серде́чный припа́док; инфа́ркт.

attacker *n.* напада́ющий: *fight off one's attackers,* отбива́ться от напада́ющих.

attain *v.t.* достига́ть; доби́ться. —**attainable,** *adj.* достижи́мый. —**attainment,** *n.* достиже́ние.

attempt *v.t.* пыта́ться: *attempt to land,* пыта́ться де́лать поса́дку. *Attempt a difficult task,* бра́ться за тру́дную зада́чу. *Attempt suicide,* покуша́ться на самоуби́йство. *Attempted murder,* покуше́ние на уби́йство. *Attempted coup,* попы́тка переворо́та. *He was killed attempting to...,* он поги́б при попы́тке (+ *inf.*). —*n.* **1,** (endeavor) попы́тка. *On the second attempt,* со второ́й попы́тки. **2,** (attack) покуше́ние: *attempt on someone's life,* покуше́ние на чью́-нибудь жизнь. *Make an attempt on someone's life,* покуша́ться на чью́-нибудь жизнь.

attend *v.t.* **1,** (be present at) прису́тствовать на. *Attend a meeting,* прису́тствовать *or* быть на собра́нии. *Attend a lecture,* прису́тствовать на ле́кции; слу́шать ле́кцию. *Attend a funeral,* быть на похорона́х; пойти́ на по́хороны. **2,** (go to regularly) посеща́ть: *attend classes/lectures,* посеща́ть заня́тия/ле́кции. **3,** (take care of; minister to) уха́живать за. —*v.i.* **1,** (be present) прису́тствовать. **2,** *fol. by* **to** (take care of)

де́лать; занима́ться; позабо́титься о. *Attend to a customer,* занима́ться покупа́телем; обслу́живать покупа́теля. *I have some things to attend to,* у меня́ есть ко́е-каки́е дела́.

attendance *n.* **1,** (act of attending) посеще́ние. *Attendance is compulsory,* посеще́ние обяза́тельно; я́вка обяза́тельна. **2,** (regularity of or number attending) посеща́емость: *poor attendance,* плоха́я посеща́емость. —**dance attendance on,** *see* **dance.**

attendant *n.* обслу́живающее лицо́; служи́тель. *Cloakroom attendant,* гардеро́бщик; гардеро́бщица. —*adj.* сопу́тствующий; привходя́щий: *attendant circumstances,* сопу́тствующие/привходя́щие обстоя́тельства.

attention *n.* **1,** (heed; care) внима́ние: *pay attention to,* обраща́ть внима́ние на. *Bring/come to someone's attention,* доводи́ть/доходи́ть до чьего́-нибудь све́дения. *He was given medical attention,* ему́ была́ ока́зана медици́нская по́мощь. **2,** *mil.* сто́йка «сми́рно»; строева́я сто́йка. *Attention!,* сми́рно! *Stand at attention,* стоя́ть по сто́йке «сми́рно»; стоя́ть *or* стать сми́рно; стоя́ть навы́тяжку; стать во фронт; принима́ть строеву́ю сто́йку; вы́тянуться в стру́нку.

attentive *adj.* внима́тельный. —**attentively,** *adv.* внима́тельно. —**attentiveness,** *n.* внима́тельность.

attest *v.t.* удостоверя́ть. —*v.i.* [*usu.* **attest to**] свиде́тельствовать о. —**attestation,** *n.* удостовере́ние.

attic *n.* черда́к. *In the attic,* на чердаке́.

attire *n.* наря́д; пла́тье. —*v.t., usu. passive* одева́ть: *smartly attired,* шика́рно оде́тый.

attitude *n.* **1,** (feeling; disposition) отноше́ние: *his attitude toward me,* его́ отноше́ние ко мне. **2,** (position; posture) по́за: *strike an attitude,* принима́ть по́зу.

attorney *n.* адвока́т; пове́ренный. —**power of attorney,** дове́ренность.

attorney general мини́стр юсти́ции.

attract *v.t.* привлека́ть. *Attract attention,* привлека́ть к себе́ внима́ние; обраща́ть на себя́ внима́ние. *Feel attracted to someone,* чу́вствовать влече́ние к кому́-нибудь.

attraction *n.* **1,** (power to attract; pull) притяже́ние; тяготе́ние. *Hold no attraction for,* не привлека́ть (кого́-нибудь). **2,** (feeling of being drawn) влече́ние: *feel an attraction toward someone,* чу́вствовать влече́ние к кому́-нибудь. **3,** (something that attracts) прима́нка. *Tourist attraction,* достопримеча́тельность. *The attractions of city life,* собла́зны городско́й жи́зни. **4,** (public entertainment) аттракцио́н.

attractive *adj.* **1,** (pretty; good-looking) привлека́тельный. **2,** (appealing; tempting) зама́нчивый: *attractive offer,* зама́нчивое предложе́ние. —**attractiveness,** *n.* привлека́тельность.

attribute *v.t.* припи́сывать: *To what do you attribute...?,* чему́ вы припи́сываете...? —*n.* **1,** (characteristic) сво́йство; атрибу́т. **2,** *gram.* определе́ние; атрибу́т.

attribution *n.* ссы́лка: *not for attribution,* без ссы́лки на исто́чник.

attributive *n.* атрибу́т. —*adj.* атрибути́вный.

attrition *n.* у́быль персона́ла. —**war of attrition,** война́ на истоще́ние.

attune *v.t.* **1,** (tune) настра́ивать. **2,** (bring into accord) согласо́вывать.

atypical *adj.* атипи́чный.

auburn *adj.* ру́сый; кашта́новый.

auction *n.* аукцио́н; торги́. —*v.t.* [*usu.* **auction off**] продава́ть с аукцио́на/ с торго́в/ с молотка́/. —**auctioneer,** *n.* аукциони́ст; аукционе́р.

audacious *adj.* **1,** (bold) сме́лый. **2,** (brazen) де́рзкий; на́глый.

audacity *n.* **1,** (boldness; daring) сме́лость. **2,** (effrontery) на́глость; де́рзость; бессты́дство. *Have the audacity to...,* име́ть на́глость *or* бессты́дство (+ *inf.*).

audibility *n.* слы́шимость.

audible *adj.* слы́шный. —**audibly,** *adv.* слы́шно. *Speak audibly,* говори́ть вслух; говори́ть гро́мко.

audience *n.* **1,** (spectators; listeners) аудито́рия; зри́тели; слу́шатели; пу́блика. **2,** (formal interview) аудие́нция.

audio *adj.* звуково́й. —*n.* звук.

audit *n.* прове́рка отчётности; реви́зия. —*v.t.* **1,** (conduct an audit of) ревизова́ть. **2,** (attend, as a course) слу́шать.

audition *n.* **1,** (hearing) слу́шание. **2,** (test performance) про́ба (на роль).

auditor *n.* реви́зор; фина́нсовый контролёр.

auditorium *n.* аудито́рия; зри́тельный зал; а́ктовый зал.

auditory *adj.* слухово́й.

Augean stables а́вгиевы коню́шни.

auger *n.* бура́в.

augment *v.t.* увели́чивать; прибавля́ть. —**augmentation,** *n.* увеличе́ние.

augur *n.* авгу́р. —*v.t.* предвеща́ть. —*v.i.* [*usu.* **augur well**] предвеща́ть хоро́шее.

augury *n.* предзнаменова́ние.

august *adj.* вели́чественный; внуши́тельный.

August *n.* а́вгуст. —*adj.* а́вгустовский.

auk *n.* гага́рка.

aunt *n.* тётя; тётка. —**aunty,** *n., colloq.* тётенька.

aura *n.* орео́л: *aura of mystery,* орео́л таи́нственности.

aureole *n.* орео́л.

auricle *n.* **1,** (chamber of the heart) предсе́рдие. **2,** (external part of the ear) ушна́я ра́ковина.

aurochs *n.* **1,** (extinct wild ox) тур. **2,** (European bison) зубр.

aurora *n.* **1,** (atmospheric phenomenon) сия́ние: *aurora borealis,* се́верное сия́ние. **2,** *poetic* (dawn) авро́ра.

auscultate *v.t.* выслу́шивать. —**auscultation,** *n.* выслу́шивание.

auspice *n., usu. pl.* покрови́тельство: *under the auspices of,* под покрови́тельством (+ *gen.*). *Under U.N. auspices,* под эги́дой ООН.

auspicious *adj.* благоприя́тный.

austere *adj.* стро́гий; суро́вый.

austerity *n.* стро́гая эконо́мия. *Austerity program,* режи́м эконо́мии.

Australian *adj.* австрали́йский. —*n.* австрали́ец; австрали́йка.

Austrian *adj.* австри́йский. —*n.* австри́ец; австри́йка.

authentic *adj.* по́длинный. —**authenticate,** *v.t.* устана́вливать по́длинность (+ *gen.*). —**authenticity,** *n.* по́длинность.

author *n.* а́втор.

authoritarian *adj.* авторита́рный. —**authoritarianism,** *n.* авторитари́зм.

authoritative *adj.* авторите́тный.

authority *n.* **1,** (power; jurisdiction) полномо́чие. *Exceed one's authority,* превыша́ть свои́ полномо́чия. **2,** *pl.* (those in charge) вла́сти: *wanted by the authorities,* разы́скивается властя́ми. **3,** (expert) авторите́т: *A/the leading authority on...,* веду́щий/гла́вный авторите́т по (+ *dat.*). **4,** (source of information) исто́чник: *on good authority,* из достове́рных исто́чников. **5,** (persuasive force): *speak with authority,* говори́ть авторите́тно.

authorization *n.* разреше́ние. *By authorization of,* по уполномо́чию (+ *gen.*).

authorize *v.t.* **1,** (empower) уполномо́чивать. **2,** (give permission to publish) авторизова́ть.

authorized *adj.* уполномо́ченный; авторизо́ванный. *Authorized representative,* полномо́чный представи́тель. *Authorized translation,* авторизо́ванный перево́д.

authorship *n.* а́вторство.

auto *n., colloq.* маши́на.

autobiography *n.* автобиогра́фия. —**autobiographical,** *adj.* автобиографи́ческий.

autocracy *n.* самодержа́вие; автокра́тия; единовла́стие. —**autocrat,** *n.* самоде́ржец; автокра́т. —**autocratic,** *adj.* самодержа́вный; автократи́ческий; единовла́стный.

autogiro *n.* автожи́р.

autograph *n.* авто́граф. —*v.t.* надпи́сывать. *Autographed copy,* именно́й экземпля́р.

automat *n.* рестора́н-автома́т.

automate *v.t.* автоматизи́ровать.

automatic *adj.* автомати́ческий. —**automatically,** *adv.* автомати́чески.

automation *n.* **1,** (science) автома́тика: *the age of automation,* век автома́тики. **2,** (act) автоматиза́ция: *automation of production,* автоматиза́ция произво́дства.

automaton *n.* автома́т.

automobile *n.* автомоби́ль. —*adj.* автомоби́льный.

automotive *adj.* автомоби́льный.

autonomous *adj.* автоно́мный. —**autonomy,** *n.* автоно́мия.

autopsy *n.* вскры́тие. *Perform an autopsy on,* проводи́ть вскры́тие те́ла (+ *gen.*).

autosuggestion *n.* самовнуше́ние.

autumn *n.* о́сень. *In autumn,* о́сенью. —*adj.* [*also,* **autumnal**] осе́нний: *autumn sky,* осе́ннее не́бо.

auxiliary *adj.* вспомога́тельный. —**auxiliary verb,** вспомога́тельный глаго́л.

avail *v.t.* приноси́ть по́льзу (+ *dat.*). *His efforts* *availed him nothing*, его́ уси́лия не принесли́ ему́ по́льзы; его́ усилия пропа́ли да́ром. —*n.* по́льза; вы́года. *To no avail*, напра́сно. *Be of little avail*, приноси́ть немно́го (*or* ма́ло) по́льзы. —**avail oneself of,** воспо́льзоваться (+ *instr.*).

availability *n.* нали́чие; досту́пность.

available *adj.* име́ющийся; досту́пный. *Be available*, име́ться; быть в нали́чии. *All available personnel*, весь име́ющийся персона́л. *He is not available right now*, он не мо́жет подойти́. *Make available to*, предоставля́ть в распоряже́ние (+ *gen.*). *As soon as it becomes available*, как то́лько э́то к нам посту́пит.

avalanche *n.* лави́на.

avant-garde *n.* авангарди́сты. —*adj.* авангарди́стский.

avarice *n.* жа́дность. —**avaricious,** *adj.* жа́дный.

avenge *v.t.* мстить за; брать рева́нш за. —**avenger,** *n.* мсти́тель.

avenue *n.* **1,** (wide street) проспе́кт; авеню́. *Fifth Avenue*, Пя́тая авеню́. **2,** *fig.* (means of achieving something) путь: *avenue to success*, путь к успе́ху. *Explore every avenue*, иссле́довать все возмо́жности.

aver *v.t.* утвержда́ть.

average *adj.* сре́дний: *a man of average height*, челове́к сре́днего ро́ста. *The average American*, сре́дний *or* рядово́й америка́нец. —*n.* сре́днее число́. *Above/below average*, вы́ше/ни́же сре́днего. —*v.t* **1,** (find the average of): *average figures together*, выводи́ть о́бщее число́. **2,** (amount to as an average) составля́ть в сре́днем: *average five percent*, составля́ть в сре́днем пять проце́нтов. —**on the average,** в сре́днем.

averse *adj., used predicatively*, не располо́жен. *Not be averse to*, быть не прочь (+ *inf.*).

aversion *n.* отвраще́ние; антипа́тия. *Have an aversion to*, пита́ть отвраще́ние к; испы́тывать антипа́тию к; бре́згать (+ *instr.*).

avert *v.t.* **1,** (turn away) отводи́ть: *avert one's eyes*, отводи́ть глаза́. **2,** (prevent) предотвраща́ть.

aviary *n.* вольё́р.

aviation *n.* авиа́ция. —*adj.* авиацио́нный.

aviator *n.* лё́тчик; авиа́тор.

avid *adj.* **1,** (greatly desirous) жа́дный. *Avid for power*, жа́ждущий вла́сти. **2,** (ardent) стра́стный; зая́длый: *avid hunter*, стра́стный/зая́длый охо́тник. *He is an avid reader*, он чита́ет запо́ем; он глота́ет кни́ги. —**avidity,** *n.* жа́дность. —**avidly,** *adv.* жа́дно; с жа́дностью.

avionics *n.* авио́ника.

avocado *n.* авока́до.

avocation *n.* побо́чное заня́тие.

avocet *n.* шилоклю́вка.

avoid *v.t.* **1,** (keep away from; refrain from) избега́ть: *avoid a friend / a trap / errors / publicity*, избега́ть дру́га/лову́шки/оши́бок/огла́ски. *In order to avoid*, во избежа́ние (+ *gen.*). *Avoid using a certain word*, избега́ть употребля́ть како́е-нибудь сло́во. *Avoid a puddle/crowd*, обходи́ть лу́жу/толпу́. **2,** (get out of the way of) уклоня́ться от: *avoid a blow/collision*, уклоня́ться от уда́ра/столкнове́ния. *Avoid hitting a pedestrian*, объе́хать пешехо́да.

avoidance *n.* уклоне́ние. *Avoidance of military service*, уклоне́ние от вое́нной слу́жбы.

avow *v.t.* откры́то признава́ть. —**avowal,** *n.* призна́ние.

avowed *adj.* неприкры́тый: *avowed racist*, неприкры́тый раси́ст.

await *v.t.* ждать; ожида́ть. *Await orders*, ждать приказа́ний. *Await the outcome*, ждать исхо́да де́ла. *He is awaiting trial*, он ждёт *or* ожида́ет суда́. *A big surprise awaits him*, его́ ждёт/ожида́ет большо́й сюрпри́з.

awake *v.t.* **1,** (wake up) буди́ть. **2,** (stir; arouse, as a feeling) пробужда́ть. —*v.i.* **1,** (wake up) просыпа́ться. **2,** *fol. by* to (become aware of) осознава́ть. —*adj.* бо́дрый: *wide-awake*, совсе́м бо́дрый. *Be awake*, не спать; бо́дрствовать. *Are you awake already?*, ты уже́ просну́лся? *Lie awake all night*, провести́ всю ночь без сна; бо́дрствовать всю ночь.

awaken *v.t. & i.* = **awake.** —**awakening,** *n.* пробужде́ние.

award *n.* награ́да: *award for bravery*, награ́да за му́жество. —*v.t.* награжда́ть; присужда́ть; присва́ивать; удоста́ивать. *Award a medal to*, награжда́ть (+ *acc.*) меда́лью. *Award a prize to*, присужда́ть пре́мию (+ *dat.*); удоста́ивать (+ *acc.*) пре́мии. *Award a degree to*, присужда́ть *or* присва́ивать сте́пень (+ *dat.*). *Award a pension to*, назнача́ть пе́нсию (+ *dat.*). *He was awarded $1,000 damages*, ему́ возмести́ли ты́сячу до́лларов за убы́тки. *He was awarded the Nobel Prize*, он удосто́ился Но́белевской пре́мии.

aware *adj., used predicatively*: *be aware (of)*, знать; сознава́ть; отдава́ть себе́ отчёт в (+ *prepl.*).

awareness *n.* понима́ние; созна́ние; осозна́ние.

away *adv.* прочь; вон. *Away with you!*, вон отсю́да! ♦ *Usu. rendered by a prefixed verb*: *go away*, уходи́ть; уезжа́ть; *run away*, убега́ть; *carry away*, уноси́ть; *throw away*, выбра́сывать; *sing away*, распе́ться; *waste away*, ча́хнуть. —*adj.* **1,** (absent; gone) в отъе́зде; в отлу́чке. *Be away*, уе́хать; отсу́тствовать; быть в отъе́зде/отлу́чке. *How long will you be away?*, как до́лго вас не бу́дет? **2,** (distant) на расстоя́нии (+ *gen.*): *ten miles away*, на расстоя́нии десяти́ миль. *The noise could be heard a mile away*, шум был слы́шен за ми́лю. *Christmas is three months away*, до Рождества́ оста́лось три ме́сяца.

awe *n.* страх; благогове́ние. *Be in awe of*, преклоня́ться пе́ред. —*v.t.* внуша́ть страх (+ *dat.*).

awesome *adj.* стра́шный; гро́зный.

awful *adj.* **1,** (very bad) ужа́сный; отврати́тельный. *How awful!*, како́й у́жас! **2,** (inspiring awe) гро́зный. *An awful stillness*, гробова́я тишина́. —**an awful lot of,** ма́сса (+ *gen.*).

awfully *adv.* **1,** (very badly) ужа́сно; отврати́тельно. **2,** (very; extremely) ужа́сно; о́чень: *awfully tired*, ужа́сно уста́л; *awfully kind of you*, о́чень любе́зно с ва́шей стороны́.

awhile *adv.* немно́го; не́которое вре́мя. *Wait awhile!*, подожди́те немно́го!

awkward *adj.* **1,** (clumsy) неуклю́жий; нело́вкий. *Awkward sentence,* неуклю́жая фра́за. **2,** (embarrassing; embarrassed) нело́вкий: *awkward situation/silence,* нело́вкое положе́ние/молча́ние. *Feel awkward,* чу́вствовать себя́ нело́вко. **3,** (inconvenient) неудо́бный: *come at an awkward time,* приходи́ть в неудо́бное вре́мя. —**awkwardly,** *adv.* неуклю́же; нело́вко. —**awkwardness,** *n.* неуклю́жесть; нело́вкость.

awl *n.* ши́ло.

awning *n.* наве́с; тент; зонт.

awry *adv.* **1,** (askew) ко́со; на́бок. **2,** (amiss) насма́рку: *go awry,* идти́/пойти́ насма́рку.

ax *also,* **axe** *n.* топо́р. —**get the ax,** *colloq.* вы́лететь (со слу́жбы).

axial *adj.* осево́й.

axil *n., bot.* па́зуха.

axiom *n.* аксио́ма. —**axiomatic,** *adj.* аксиомати́ческий.

axis *n.* ось. *The earth rotates on its axis,* Земля́ враща́ется вокру́г свое́й о́си.

axle *n.* ось. *Axle grease,* колёсная мазь; таво́т.

ayatollah *n.* аятолла́.

aye *adv.* да. —*n.* за: *three ayes, two nays,* три за, два про́тив. *The ayes have it,* большинство́ за. —**aye aye, sir!,** есть!

azalea *n.* аза́лия.

Azerbaijani *adj.* азербайджа́нский. —*n.* **1,** (person) азербайджа́нец; азербайджа́нка. **2,** (language) азербайджа́нский язы́к.

azimuth *n.* а́зимут.

Aztec *n.* ацте́к. —*adj.* ацте́кский.

azure *n.* лазу́рь. —*adj.* лазу́рный.

B

B, b втора́я бу́ква англи́йского алфави́та. —*n.* **1,** (musical note) си. **2,** (school grade) четвёрка.

baba au rhum ро́мовая ба́ба.

babble *v.i.* **1,** (prattle) лепета́ть. **2,** (of a brook) журча́ть. —*n.* **1,** (prattle) ле́пет. **2,** (of a brook) журча́ние.

babe *n.* **1,** (baby) младе́нец. **2,** *slang* (girl) девчо́нка.

babel *n.* смеше́ние языко́в; вавило́нское столпотворе́ние. —**Tower of Babel,** вавило́нская ба́шня.

baboon *n.* павиа́н.

babushka *n.* плато́к.

baby *n.* **1,** (infant) ребёнок. *Have a baby,* име́ть ребёнка. **2,** (young or newborn animal, bird, etc.) детёныш. *Baby elephant,* детёныш слона́; слонёнок. *Baby bird,* птене́ц. —*adj.* де́тский: *baby talk,* де́тский ле́пет. *Baby food,* де́тское пита́ние. *Baby brother,* брати́шка. *Baby sister,* сестрёнка. —*v.t.* балова́ть. —**baby carriage,** де́тская коля́ска. —**baby grand piano,** кабине́тный роя́ль. —**baby tooth,** моло́чный зуб.

babyish *adj.* ребя́ческий.

Babylonian *adj.* вавило́нский.

baby sitter приходя́щая ня́ня.

baccalaureate *n.* сте́пень бакала́вра.

baccarat *n.* баккара́.

bachelor *n.* **1,** (unmarried man) холостя́к. **2,** (holder of a bachelor's degree) бакала́вр. *Bachelor's degree,* сте́пень бакала́вра. —*adj.* холосто́й; холостя́цкий.

Bachelor apartment, холостя́цкая кварти́ра. —**bachelorhood,** *n.* холостя́цкая жизнь.

bacillus *n.* баци́лла; па́лочка.

back *n.* **1,** (part of the body) спина́. *With one's back to the sun,* спино́й к со́лнцу. **2,** (part of a chair, garment, etc.) спи́нка. *The dress is short in the back,* пла́тье коро́че сза́ди. **3,** (rear) зад; за́дняя часть; за́дняя сторона́. *Stand in the back,* стоя́ть сза́ди. *In the back of the hall,* в глубине́ за́ла. *In the back of the book,* в конце́ кни́ги. *Tie in back with a bow,* завяза́ть сза́ди ба́нтом. **4,** (reverse side) оборо́т; обра́тная *or* оборо́тная сторона́. *Back of a card,* руба́шка. *Back of the hand,* ты́льная сторона́ руки́. **5,** *sports* (defenseman) защи́тник. —*adj.* **1,** (dorsal) спинно́й. **2,** (rear) за́дний: *back seat,* за́днее сиде́нье. *Back door,* чёрный ход. **3,** (remote) глухо́й. *Back street,* закоу́лок. *Back country,* глушь. **4,** (of a past date) ста́рый: *back issue,* ста́рый но́мер. *Back taxes,* неопла́ченные нало́ги. —*adv.* **1,** (backward) наза́д: *step back,* шагну́ть наза́д. **2,** (of or toward where one began) обра́тно. *On the way back,* на обра́тном пути́. *When will he be back?,* когда́ он вернётся? **3,** (to the original possessor) наза́д; обра́тно: *give back,* отда́ть наза́д; *get back,* получи́ть обра́тно. **4,** (ago) тому́ наза́д: *a while back,* не́которое вре́мя тому́ наза́д. *Way back in 1940,* ещё в ты́сяча девятьсо́т сороково́м году́. ♦ *Often rendered by a prefixed verb: come back,* возвраща́ться; *hold back,* уде́рживать; *pay back,* отпла́чивать. —*v.t.* **1,** (move backward):

back the car out of the garage, выводи́ть маши́ну за́дним хо́дом из гаража́. *Back someone into a corner,* загоня́ть кого́-нибудь в у́гол. **2,** (support) подде́рживать. **3,** *fol. by* **up** (substantiate) подкрепля́ть. **4,** (put money on) финанси́ровать; субсиди́ровать. **5,** (bet on) ста́вить на. *Back the wrong horse,* ста́вить не на ту ло́шадь. —*v.i.* [*usu.* **back up**] **1,** (move backward) отходи́ть *or* подвига́ться *or* отодвига́ться наза́д; пя́титься. **2,** (go into reverse) отъезжа́ть наза́д; дава́ть за́дний ход. *As I was backing out into the street,* когда́ я выезжа́л(а) за́дним хо́дом на у́лицу. —**back and forth,** взад и впере́д. —**back down,** отступа́ть; бить отбо́й. —**back off,** отступа́ть. —**back out (of),** уклоня́ться (от). —**back to back,** спина́ (*or* спино́й) к спине́. —**behind someone's back,** за чьей-нибудь спино́й; за глаза́. —**break one's back,** *fig.* гнуть *or* лома́ть спи́ну. —**in back of, 1,** (position) за (+ *instr.*). **2,** (motion) за (+ *acc.*). —**know like the back of one's hand,** знать как свои́ пять па́льцев. —**there and back,** туда́ и обра́тно. —**turn one's back on,** поверну́ться спино́й к; отвора́чиваться от.

backache *n.* боль в спине́.

backboard *n.* **1,** (board supporting the back) доска́. **2,** *basketball* щит.

backbone *n.* **1,** (spine) позвоно́чник; спинно́й хребе́т. **2,** (fortitude) твёрдость хара́ктера. **3,** (mainstay) станово́й хребе́т; станова́я жи́ла; костя́к.

backbreaking *adj.* непоси́льный; ка́торжный.

backdate *v.t.* поме́тить за́дним число́м.

backdrop *n.* **1,** *theat.* за́дник. **2,** *fig.* (background) фон.

backer *n.* **1,** (supporter) сторо́нник. **2,** (patron) покрови́тель.

backfire *v.i.* дать осе́чку; возыме́ть обра́тное де́йствие; оберну́ться про́тив самого́ себя́.

backgammon *n.* трикра́к.

background *n.* **1,** (of a painting) фон; за́дний план. *Against a dark background,* на тёмном фо́не. *Appear in the background,* видне́ться на за́днем пла́не. *Melt into the background,* слива́ться с фо́ном. **2,** *fig.* (secondary place or position) за́дний план: *remain in the background,* остава́ться на за́днем пла́не. **3,** (underlying setting) фон: *against the background of these events,* на фо́не э́тих собы́тий. **4,** (events leading up to something) предысто́рия. **5,** (training; experience) подгото́вка.

backhand *n., tennis* уда́р сле́ва. —*adj. & adv.* сле́ва.

backhanded *adj.* **1,** = **backhand. 2,** (equivocal) сомни́тельный: *backhanded compliment,* сомни́тельный комплиме́нт.

backing *n.* **1,** (supporting material) подкла́дка. **2,** (support; endorsement) подде́ржка.

backlog *n.* **1,** (accumulation) скопле́ние. **2,** (reserve supply) запа́с.

backrest *n.* опо́ра для спины́.

backside *n., colloq.* зад; я́годицы.

backstage *adv.* **1,** (location) за кули́сами. **2,** (motion) за кули́сы. —*adj.* закули́сный.

backstroke *n.* пла́вание на спине́.

back talk возраже́ния. *No back talk!,* без возра-

же́ний!; без разгово́ров!; никаки́х разгово́ров!; не возража́ть!

backtrack *v.i.* **1,** (return over the same route) возвраща́ться по свои́м следа́м (*or* стопа́м). **2,** *fig.* (reverse oneself) дава́ть за́дний ход.

backup *adj. Backup man,* дублёр. *Backup driver,* води́тель-дублёр. *Backup light,* фона́рь за́днего хо́да.

backward *adv.* [*also,* **backwards**] **1,** (opp. of forward) наза́д: *a step backward,* шаг наза́д. **2,** (in the direction opp. to that which one is facing) за́дом. *Walk backwards,* пя́титься. *Put one's hat on backwards,* наде́ть ша́пку за́дом наперёд. **3,** (in reverse order) наоборо́т; в обра́тном поря́дке. —*adj.* **1,** (rearward) обра́тный; за́дний. *Backward glance,* взгляд наза́д. **2,** (lagging behind) отста́лый: *backward country,* отста́лая страна́. —**bend/lean over backwards,** вся́чески стара́ться; лезть из ко́жи вон. —**know backwards and forwards,** знать (что́-нибудь) вдоль и поперёк.

backwardness *n.* отста́лость.

backwards *adv.* = **backward.**

backwater *n.* за́водь; зато́н. *Quiet backwater,* ти́хая за́водь.

backwoods *n.pl.* глушь. —*adj.* глухо́й.

bacon *n.* беко́н; копчёная груди́нка.

bacteria *n., pl. of* **bacterium.** —**bacterial,** *adj.* бактериа́льный.

bacteriology *n.* бактериоло́гия. —**bacteriological,** *adj.* бактериологи́ческий. —**bacteriologist,** *n.* бактерио́лог.

bacterium *n.* бакте́рия.

bad *adj.* **1,** (not good) плохо́й; дурно́й. *Bad weather,* плоха́я пого́да. *Bad habits,* дурны́е привы́чки. *That's bad,* э́то пло́хо. *Smell bad,* пло́хо па́хнуть. **2,** (wicked) злой: *the bad fairy,* зла́я фе́я. **3,** (naughty) озорно́й; непослу́шный. **4,** (harmful) вре́дный: *bad for one's health,* вре́дно для здоро́вья. **5,** (sore; defective) больно́й: *a bad heart,* больно́е се́рдце. **6,** (severe) си́льный: *a bad cold,* си́льный на́сморк. —**get in bad,** *colloq.* впада́ть в неми́лость. —**go bad, 1,** (degenerate) вырожда́ться. **2,** (become tainted) по́ртиться. —**go from bad to worse,** станови́ться всё ху́же и ху́же. —**not a bad** (+ *noun*), неплохо́й. —**not bad,** непло́хо; ничего́. —**too bad,** о́чень жаль. *It's too bad that...,* жаль, что...

badge *n.* значо́к; бля́ха.

badger *n.* (animal) барсу́к. —*v.t.* (pester) пристава́ть к; трави́ть.

badly *adv.* **1,** (poorly) пло́хо; ду́рно; скве́рно. *Don't think badly of me!,* не ду́майте обо мне пло́хо; не помина́йте ли́хом. **2,** (very much; greatly) о́чень; си́льно. **3,** (severely) си́льно; тяжело́: *badly damaged,* си́льно повреждён; *badly wounded,* тяжело́ ра́нен. *Cut oneself badly,* си́льно поре́заться.

badminton *n.* бадминто́н.

baffle *v.t.* озада́чивать. —**baffled,** *adj.* озада́ченный. —**bafflement,** *n.* озада́ченность. —**baffling,** *adj.* недоуме́нный.

bag *n.* **1,** (for carrying something) су́мка. **2,** (sack) мешо́к. **3,** (paper bag) паке́т; паке́тик. **4,** (suitcase) чемода́н. **5,** (handbag) су́мка; су́мочка. **6,** (game killed in hunting) добы́ча. **7,** *pl.* (pouchlike folds of skin) мешки́ (под глаза́ми). —*v.t.* **1,** (put in a bag) класть в мешо́к. **2,** (capture) схва́тывать. **3,** (kill; capture, as game) добыва́ть. —**bag and baggage,** *colloq.* со все́ми пожи́тками. —**be left holding the bag,** *colloq.* оста́ться с но́сом; оста́ться при пи́ковом интере́се. —**it's in the bag,** *colloq.* де́ло в шля́пе.

bagel *n.* бара́нка; бу́блик.

baggage *n.* бага́ж. —*adj.* бага́жный: *baggage car,* бага́жный ваго́н; *baggage receipt/check,* бага́жная квита́нция. —**baggage compartment,** бага́жное отделе́ние; бага́жный отсе́к. —**baggage room,** ка́мера хране́ния (багажа́).

baggy *adj.* мешкова́тый.

bagpipe *n.* волы́нка. *Also,* **bagpipes.**

bah *interj.* тьфу!

bail *n.* поручи́тельство; пору́ка; зало́г. *Put up bail,* вноси́ть зало́г. *Put up bail for,* брать на пору́ки. *Release on bail,* отпуска́ть *or* выпуска́ть под зало́г; отпуска́ть на пору́ки. —*v.t.* [*usu.* **bail out**] **1,** (remove, as water; remove the water from) выче́рпывать. **2,** (put up bail for) брать на пору́ки. **3,** (help out of difficulty) выруча́ть. —*v.i.* [*usu.* **bail out**] выбра́сываться с парашю́том.

bailiff *n.* суде́бный исполни́тель; *pre-rev.* суде́бный при́став.

bailiwick *n.* часть: *not in my bailiwick,* не по мое́й ча́сти.

bait *n.* нажи́вка; прима́нка; наса́дка. *Swallow the bait,* попа́сться на у́дочку; попа́сться на крючо́к. —*v.t.* **1,** (apply bait to) наживля́ть. **2,** (entice) зама́нивать; прима́нивать. **3,** (torment; harass) трави́ть.

baize *n.* ба́йка. —*adj.* ба́йковый.

bake *v.t.* **1,** (cook in an oven) печь. **2,** (treat with heat, as bricks) обжига́ть. —*v.i.* **1,** (do baking) печь. **2,** (become baked) пе́чься. *Bake in the sun,* пе́чься *or* жа́риться на со́лнце.

baked *adj.* печёный.

bakelite *n.* бакели́т.

baker *n.* пе́карь; бу́лочник. —**baker's dozen,** чёртова дю́жина.

bakery *n.* **1,** (store) бу́лочная; хле́бный магази́н. **2,** (baking establishment) пека́рня.

baking *n.* пече́ние; вы́печка. —*adj.* пека́рный: *baking powder,* пека́рный порошо́к. —**baking sheet,** про́тивень. —**baking soda,** питьева́я со́да.

balalaika *n.* балала́йка.

balance *n.* **1,** (equilibrium) равнове́сие: *lose one's balance,* потеря́ть равнове́сие. *Throw/knock someone off balance,* выводи́ть *or* выбива́ть из равнове́сия. **2,** *bookkeeping* бала́нс; са́льдо. **3,** (remainder) оста́ток. **4,** (scale) весы́. —*v.t.* **1,** (keep in a state of equilibrium) уравнове́шивать. *Balance oneself,* баланси́ровать. *Balance a basket on one's head,* баланси́ровать корзи́ной на голове́. **2,** *bookkeeping* баланси́ровать. *Balance the books,* подводи́ть

бала́нс. **3,** (make commensurate) соразмеря́ть: *balance one's income and expenditures,* соразмеря́ть дохо́д с расхо́дами. —*v.i.* **1,** (be in equilibrium) баланси́ровать. **2,** (tally) сходи́ться: *The books don't balance,* счета́ не схо́дятся. —**balance of payments,** платёжный бала́нс. —**balance of power,** равнове́сие сил. —**balance of trade,** торго́вый бала́нс. —**hang in the balance,** зави́сеть от исхо́да де́ла. —**on balance,** в о́бщем и це́лом.

balanced *adj.* сбаланси́рованный. *Balanced budget,* сбаланси́рованный бюдже́т. *Balanced diet,* сбаланси́рованная дие́та.

balancer *n.* **1,** (acrobat) эквилибри́ст; балансёр. **2,** *mech.* стабилиза́тор.

balance sheet бала́нсовый отчёт.

balance wheel ма́ятник; баланси́р.

balcony *n.* балко́н. *Sit on/in the balcony,* сиде́ть на балко́не.

bald *adj.* лы́сый; плеши́вый. *Become bald,* лысе́ть; плеши́веть.

bald eagle орла́н.

balderdash *n.* белиберда́; галиматья́.

baldheaded *adj.* лы́сый; плеши́вый.

baldness *n.* плеши́вость.

bald spot лы́сина; плешь.

bale *n.* **1,** (bundle) тюк. **2,** (amount) ки́па: *bale of cotton,* ки́па хло́пка. —*v.t.* укла́дывать в тюки́.

baleful *adj.* **1,** (maleficent) па́губный. **2,** (sinister; ominous) злове́щий.

balk *also,* **baulk** *v.i.* (refuse) арта́читься; упря́миться. —*v.t.* (thwart) расстра́ивать; срыва́ть.

Balkan *adj.* балка́нский.

balky *adj.* упря́мый; с но́ровом.

ball *n.* **1,** (sphere) шар. *Ball of fire,* о́гненный шар. **2,** (used in games) мяч. *Play ball,* игра́ть в мяч. *Billiard ball,* билья́рдный шар. **3,** (of thread, yarn, etc.) клубо́к. *Curl up into a ball,* сверну́ться клубко́м. **4,** (projectile) ядро́: *cannon ball,* пу́шечное ядро́. **5,** (formal dance) бал. —*v.t.* [*usu.* **ball up**] *colloq.* перепу́тывать. —**have a ball,** *colloq.* весели́ться. —**on the ball,** *colloq.* расторо́пный. —**start the ball rolling,** положи́ть нача́ло.

ballad *n.* балла́да.

ballade *n.* балла́да.

ball-and-socket joint шарово́й шарни́р.

ballast *n.* балла́ст.

ball bearing шарикоподши́пник; ша́риковый подши́пник.

ballerina *n.* балери́на.

ballet *n.* бале́т. —*adj.* бале́тный: *ballet company,* бале́тная тру́ппа. *Ballet dancer,* арти́ст(ка) бале́та. —**ballet master,** балетме́йстер.

ballistic *adj.* баллисти́ческий: *ballistic missile,* баллисти́ческая раке́та. —**ballistics,** *n.* балли́стика.

balloon *n.* возду́шный шар. *Weather balloon,* зонд. —*v.i.* раздува́ться. —**balloonist,** *n.* аэрона́вт; воздухопла́ватель.

ballot *n.* **1,** (voting ticket) (избира́тельный) бюллете́нь. **2,** (vote; voting) голосова́ние; баллоти́ро́вка. *Secret ballot,* та́йное *or* закры́тое голосова́-

ние. *On the third ballot*, после тре́тьего ту́ра голосова́ния. —**ballot box,** избира́тельный я́щик; избира́тельная у́рна.

ball park стадио́н.

ball-point pen ша́риковая ру́чка.

ballroom *n.* танцева́льный зал. *Ballroom dancing,* ба́льные та́нцы.

ballyhoo *n., colloq.* шуми́ха. —*v.t., colloq.* разрекла́ми́ровать; труби́ть о.

balm *n.* **1,** (balsam) бальза́м. **2,** *fig.* (something that comforts) бальза́м; еле́й.

balmy *adj.* **1,** (mild) мя́гкий. **2,** *slang* (daft) сумасбро́дный.

baloney *n.* **1, = bologna. 2,** *slang* (nonsense) чушь; вздор.

balsa *n.* ба́льза.

balsam *n.* бальза́м.

Baltic *adj.* балти́йский; прибалти́йский.

baluster *n.* баля́сина.

balustrade *n.* балюстра́да.

bamboo *n.* бамбу́к. —*adj.* бамбу́ковый.

ban *v.t.* запреща́ть; налага́ть запре́т на. *Rallies are banned,* ми́тинги — под запре́том. —*n.* запре́т; запреще́ние. *Travel ban,* запре́т на пое́здки. *Nuclear test ban,* запреще́ние испыта́ний я́дерного ору́жия.

banal *adj.* бана́льный; изби́тый. —**banality,** *n.* бана́льность.

banana *n.* бана́н. —*adj.* бана́новый: *banana peel,* бана́новая кожура́.

band *n.* **1,** (strip for binding) ле́нта. *Armband,* повя́зка. *Hatband,* око́лыш. *Rubber band,* рези́нка. **2,** (stripe) полоса́. **3,** (group) гру́ппа. **4,** (gang) ба́нда; ша́йка. **5,** (orchestra) орке́стр. **6,** *radio* диапазо́н. —*v.t.* свя́зывать. —*v.i.* [*usu.* **band together**] объединя́ться.

bandage *n.* повя́зка; бинт. —*v.t.* перевя́зывать; бинтова́ть.

band-aid *n.* лейкопла́стырь.

bandanna *also,* **bandana** *n.* цветно́й плато́к.

bandbox *n.* карто́нка для шля́пы.

bandit *n.* разбо́йник; банди́т. —**banditry,** *n.* разбо́й; бандити́зм.

bandmaster *n.* капельме́йстер.

band saw ле́нточная пила́.

bandstand *n.* эстра́да для орке́стра; (оркестро́вая) ра́ковина.

bandy *v.t.* **1,** (toss back and forth) перебра́сываться (+ *instr.*). **2,** (circulate; spread) распространя́ть. *Rumors are being bandied about,* хо́дят слу́хи.

bandy-legged *adj.* кривоно́гий.

bane *n.* отра́ва. *The bane of one's existence,* отра́ва *or* прокля́тие чье́й-нибудь жи́зни.

baneful *adj.* па́губный; губи́тельный; ги́бельный.

bang *n.* **1,** (blow) уда́р. **2,** (sound) хлопо́к. **3,** *pl.* (of hair) чёлка. —*v.t.* **1,** (strike; pound) ударя́ть; сту́кать; хло́пать: *bang one's fist on the table,* ударя́ть/сту́кать/хло́пать кулако́м по́ столу. **2,** (strike repeatedly) би́ться: *bang one's head against the wall,* би́ться голово́й об сте́ну. **3,** (bump accidentally) ударя́ться; сту́каться: *bang one's head on the door,*

уда́риться/сту́кнуться голово́й о дверь. —*v.i.* **1,** (make a loud noise) хло́пать. **2,** *fol. by* **on** (pound) бить; ударя́ть; колоти́ть (*e.g.* в дверь *or* по́ столу). **3,** *fol. by* **into** *or* **against** (bump) ударя́ться о. —*interj.* бах!; бац! *Bang bang!*, бах-бах! —*adv., colloq.* пря́мо: *bang on the mark,* пря́мо в цель.

bangle *n.* брасле́т.

banish *v.t.* **1,** (exile) изгоня́ть; высыла́ть; ссыла́ть. **2,** (expel) выгоня́ть; прогоня́ть. **3,** *fig.* (dismiss, as a thought) отгоня́ть. —**banishment,** *n.* изгна́ние; вы́сылка; ссы́лка.

banister *also,* **bannister** *n.* пери́ла.

banjo *n.* ба́нджо.

bank *n.* **1,** (financial institution) банк. **2,** (river edge) бе́рег: *the left/west bank,* ле́вый/за́падный бе́рег. **3,** (long mound) вал. *Sandbank,* песча́ная мель. **4,** (of snow) зано́с. **5,** (of clouds) гряда́. **6,** (row; set) ряд. **7,** *aero.* крен. **8,** *games* банк: *break the bank,* сорва́ть банк. —*adj.* ба́нковый; ба́нковский. *Bank loan,* ба́нковская ссу́да. —*v.t.* **1,** (deposit in a bank) класть в банк. **2,** (heap up into a bank) сва́ливать в ку́чу; нава́ливать. **3,** (tilt, as an aircraft) накреня́ть. —*v.i.* **1,** (maintain a bank account) держа́ть де́ньги (в ба́нке). **2,** *fol. by* **on** (count on) рассчи́тывать (на); де́лать ста́вку (на).

bank account счёт в ба́нке; ба́нковский счёт.

bankbook *n.* ба́нковская кни́жка; сберега́тельная кни́жка.

banker *n.* **1,** (bank executive) банки́р. **2,** (in a game) банкомёт.

banking *n.* ба́нковое *or* ба́нковское де́ло. *Banking system,* ба́нковская систе́ма.

bank note банкно́т; де́нежный знак; креди́тный биле́т.

bankroll *n.* де́нежные сре́дства; фина́нсовые ресу́рсы.

bankrupt *adj.* обанкро́тившийся. *Go bankrupt,* потерпе́ть банкро́тство; обанкро́титься. —*v.t.* привести́ к банкро́тству.

bankruptcy *n.* банкро́тство. *Declare bankruptcy,* объяви́ть банкро́тство; объяви́ть себя́ банкро́том.

bank shot *billiards* дупле́т.

banner *n.* зна́мя. —*adj.* реко́рдный: *banner year,* реко́рдный год. *Banner headlines,* арши́нные заголо́вки.

bannister *n.* = **banister.**

banquet *n.* банке́т; пир. —*adj.* банке́тный: *banquet table,* банке́тный стол.

banter *n.* болтовня́.

banyan *n.* банья́н; бенга́льский фи́кус.

baobab *n.* баоба́б.

baptism *n.* креще́ние. —**baptism of fire,** боево́е креще́ние.

baptismal *adj.* крести́льный.

Baptist *n.* бапти́ст. —*adj.* бапти́стский. —**John the Baptist,** Иоа́нн Предте́ча.

baptistery *also,* **baptistry** *n.* **1,** (place for baptism) баптисте́рий. **2,** (baptismal font) купе́ль.

baptize *v.t.* крести́ть. *Be baptized,* крести́ться. *Were you baptized?*, вы крещёный; вы крещёная?

I was baptized, я был крещён; я была́ крещена́.
bar *n.* **1,** (of wood, metal, etc.) брусо́к. **2,** (of soap) кусо́к (мы́ла); (of chocolate) пли́тка (шокола́да); (of gold) сли́ток (зо́лота). **3,** *pl.* (of a cage or prison; on a window) решётка. *Behind bars,* за решёткой. **4,** (bolt) засо́в. **5,** (obstacle; barrier) прегра́да; барье́р. **6,** *sports* перекла́дина; *pl.* бру́сья; (*in high jumping*) пла́нка. **7,** (tavern) бар. **8,** (counter) сто́йка. **9,** (legal profession) адвокату́ра. *Admit to the bar,* принима́ть в колле́гию адвока́тов. **10,** *fig.* (place of judgment) суд. **11,** *music* такт. **12,** (unit of pressure) бар. —*v.t.* **1,** (bolt) запира́ть на засо́в. **2,** (block; obstruct) перекрыва́ть; прегражда́ть; загражда́ть; загора́живать. **3,** (exclude) исключа́ть. **4,** (forbid) запреща́ть. —*prep. in* **bar none,** без исключе́ния.
barb *n.* **1,** (of an arrow, fishhook, etc.) зубе́ц. **2,** (caustic remark) ко́лкость.
barbarian *n.* ва́рвар. —*adj.* ва́рварский.
barbaric *adj.* ва́рварский.
barbarism *n.* **1,** (barbarity) ва́рварство. **2,** *ling.* варвари́зм.
barbarity *n.* ва́рварство.
barbarous *adj.* ва́рварский.
barbecue *n.* **1,** (grill) ра́шпер. **2,** (roasted meat) зажа́ренное мя́со. —*v.t.* жа́рить.
barbed *adj.* **1,** (containing barbs) колю́чий. **2,** *fig.* (cutting) ко́лкий. —**barbed wire,** колю́чая про́волока. *Barbed wire fence,* забо́р из колю́чей про́волоки.
barbell *n.* шта́нга.
barber *n.* парикма́хер.
barberry *n.* барбари́с.
barbershop *n.* парикма́херская.
barbiturate *n.* барбитура́т.
barcarole *n.* баркаро́ла.
bard *n.* бард.
bare *adj.* **1,** (naked; uncovered) го́лый; наго́й. *With one's bare hands,* го́лыми рука́ми. *Bare feet,* босы́е но́ги. *In one's bare feet,* босико́м. *Sleep on the bare floor,* спать на го́лом полу́. **2,** (empty) пусто́й: *bare shelves,* пусты́е по́лки. **3,** (just sufficient): *the bare/ barest necessities,* са́мое необходи́мое. *Bare majority,* незначи́тельное большинство́. —*v.t.* **1,** (uncover) обнажа́ть; оголя́ть; раскрыва́ть. *Bare one's teeth,* ска́лить зу́бы. **2,** (reveal) обнажа́ть; раскрыва́ть. *Bare one's soul to,* откры́ть *or* раскры́ть ду́шу пе́ред. —**lay bare,** обнажа́ть; выкла́дывать.
bareback *adv.* без седла́.
barefaced *adj.* бессты́дный; неприкры́тый. *Barefaced lie,* на́глая ложь.
barefoot *adj.* босо́й; босоно́гий; разу́тый. —*adv.* босико́м.
barehanded *adj. & adv.* го́лыми рука́ми.
bareheaded *adj. & adv.* с непокры́той голово́й; простоволо́сый.
barely *adv.* едва́; е́ле; чуть; с трудо́м. *Barely noticeable,* едва́ заме́тный. *I can barely hear you,* я с трудо́м вас слы́шу.
bargain *n.* **1,** (deal) сде́лка. *It's a bargain!,* договори́лись!; по рука́м! **2,** (advantageous purchase) вы́годная поку́пка. —*adj. Bargain prices,*

сни́женные це́ны. —*v.i.* торгова́ться. —**bargain for,** ожида́ть. —**into the bargain,** в прида́чу.
bargaining *n.* перегово́ры; торг. —**bargaining chip,** предме́т то́рга. —**bargaining table,** стол перегово́ров.
barge *n.* ба́ржа. —*v.i.* [*usu.* **barge into**] ворва́ться в.
bargeman *n.* бурла́к.
barite *n.* бари́т.
baritone *n.* барито́н. —*adj.* барито́нный; баритона́льный.
barium *n.* ба́рий. —**barium sulfate,** сернокислый ба́рий.
bark *n.* **1,** (cry of a dog) лай. **2,** (covering of a tree) кора́. **3,** (sailing vessel) барк. —*v.i.* **1,** (of a dog) ла́ять. **2,** (of a person) га́ркать. —*v.t.* выкри́кивать: *bark* (*out*) *a command,* вы́крикнуть кома́нду. —**bark up the wrong tree,** быть на ло́жном пути́.
barley *n.* ячме́нь. —*adj.* ячме́нный.
barman *n.* ба́рмен.
barn *n.* **1,** (for storing crops) амба́р. **2,** (for stabling livestock) хлев; коро́вник.
barnacle *n.* усоно́гий рак. *Acorn barnacle,* морско́й жёлудь. *Goose barnacle,* морска́я у́точка. —**barnacle goose,** белощёкая каза́рка.
barn owl сипу́ха.
barnstorm *v.i.* гастроли́ровать (в прови́нции).
barn swallow дереве́нская ла́сточка; каса́тка.
barnyard *n.* пти́чий двор.
barometer *n.* баро́метр. —**barometric,** *adj.* барометри́ческий.
baron *n.* **1,** (nobleman) баро́н. **2,** (magnate) магна́т. —**baroness,** *n.* бароне́сса.
baronet *n.* бароне́т.
baronial *adj.* баро́нский.
barony *n.* баро́нство.
baroque *n.* баро́кко. —*adj.* в сти́ле баро́кко; баро́чный.
barracks *n.pl.* каза́рмы.
barracuda *n.* барраку́да.
barrage *n.* **1,** *mil.* загради́тельный ого́нь; огнево́й вал. *Artillery barrage,* артиллери́йский обстре́л. **2,** (torrent) пото́к; град.
barrel *n.* **1,** (cask) бо́чка. **2,** (unit of measure, esp. of oil) ба́ррель. **3,** (of a firearm) ствол. —**cash on the barrel,** де́ньги на бо́чку.
barrel organ шарма́нка.
barren *adj.* **1,** (of land) беспло́дный; неплодоро́дный. **2,** (of a woman) беспло́дная. —**barrenness,** *n.* беспло́дие; неплодоро́дность.
barricade *n.* баррика́да. —*v.t.* баррикади́ровать.
barrier *n.* **1,** (obstruction) барье́р. *Police barriers,* полице́йские рога́тки. **2,** (gate at a railroad crossing) шлагба́ум. **3,** *fig.* (obstacle) барье́р: *racial/trade barriers,* ра́совые/торго́вые барье́ры. —**language barrier,** языково́й барье́р. —**sound barrier,** звуково́й барье́р.
barring *prep.* исключа́я.
barrister *n., Brit.* адвока́т.
barroom *n.* бар.
barrow *n.* **1,** (wheelbarrow) та́чка. **2,** (burial mound) курга́н.

bartender *n.* бармен.

barter *n.* товарообмен; меновая торговля; бартер. —*v.t.* обменивать; променивать.

basal metabolism основной обмен.

basalt *n.* базальт. —*adj.* базальтовый.

base *n.* **1,** (foundation) основание; основа; база. *Base of a monument,* основание памятника. **2,** (installation) база: *naval base,* военно-морская база. *Base of operations,* операционная база. **3,** *chem.; math.* основание. —*adj.* **1,** (low; mean) низкий; низменный; подлый. *Base motives,* низменные побуждения. **2,** (of a base) базовый: *base hospital,* базовый госпиталь. **3,** (used as a starting point) базисный: *base period,* базисный период. *Base pay,* основной заработок. **4,** *in* **base metal,** неблагородный металл. —*v.t.* основывать; строить; базировать. *Based on facts,* основанный на фактах. *The movie is based on the novel by...,* фильм создан *or* поставлен по роману (+ *gen.*). —**be off base,** *colloq.* заблуждаться. —**not** (*or* **never**) **get to first base,** *colloq.* ничего не достигнуть; не сдвинуться с места.

baseball *n.* бейсбол.

baseless *adj.* необоснованный; неосновательный; безосновательный.

basement *n.* подвал. —*adj.* подвальный: *basement window,* подвальное окно.

baseness *n.* низость; подлость.

bash *v.t., colloq.* хлопать; шлёпать.

bashful *adj.* застенчивый; робкий. —**bashfulness,** *n.* застенчивость; робость.

basic *adj.* основной. —*n., usu. pl.* основы. —**basic training,** основная *or* первоначальная подготовка.

basically *adv.* в основном; по существу.

basil *n.* базилик.

basilica *n.* базилика.

basin *n.* **1,** (container) таз. **2,** (lowland) бассейн.

basis *n.* основа; основание; базис; база. *On the basis of,* на основании (+ *gen.*); на основе (+ *gen.*). *On a voluntary basis,* на добровольных началах. *On an individual basis,* в индивидуальном порядке. *These rumors have no basis,* эти слухи не имеют под собой основания.

bask *v.i.* **1,** (enjoy warmth) греться; нежиться (на солнце). **2,** *fig.* (revel) купаться: *bask in the glow of...,* купаться в лучах (+ *gen.*).

basket *n.* корзина; корзинка.

basketball *n.* баскетбол. *Basketball player,* баскетболист. —*adj.* баскетбольный.

Basque *adj.* баскский. —*n.* **1,** (person) баск; басконка. **2,** (language) баскский язык.

bas-relief *n.* барельеф. —*adj.* барельефный.

bass[1] (beis) *n., music* бас. —*adj.* басовый: *bass clef,* басовый ключ.

bass[2] (bas) *n.* (fish) окунь.

bass baritone баритональный бас.

bass drum турецкий барабан.

basso *n.* бас.

bassoon *n.* фагот. —**bassoonist,** *n.* фаготист.

bass viol контрабас.

bast *n.* лыко; луб; мочало. —*adj.* лыковый; лубяной.

bastard *n.* **1,** (illegitimate child) внебрачный ребёнок. **2,** *slang* (scoundrel) сволочь. —*adj.* внебрачный; незаконнорождённый.

baste *v.t.* **1,** (sew) метать; смётывать; намётывать; заметывать. **2,** (moisten) поливать.

bastion *n.* **1,** (fortification) бастион. **2,** *fig.* (bulwark) оплот.

bat *n.* **1,** (cudgel) дубина; дубинка. **2,** *sports* бита; лапта. **3,** (flying mammal) летучая мышь. —*v.t.* **1,** (hit) бить. **2,** (wink) моргать: *without batting an eye,* глазом не моргнув. *He didn't bat an eye,* он и бровью не повёл. —**go to bat for,** *colloq.* заступаться за; хлопотать за; распинаться за. —**right off the bat,** *colloq.* с места в карьер.

batch *n.* **1,** (of bread) выпечка. **2,** (of letters, papers, etc.) пачка. **3,** (lot, as of merchandise) партия.

bated *adj., in* **with bated breath,** не дыша; затаив дыхание; с затаённым дыханием.

bath *n.* **1,** (bathing) ванна: *take a bath,* принимать ванну. **2,** (bathtub) ванна. **3,** (bathroom) ванная комната. **4,** (public bath) баня.

bathe *v.t.* **1,** (place in liquid; give a bath to) купать. **2,** (apply liquid to for healing) обмывать; промывать. **3,** *fig.* (cover; flood) заливать: *bathed in sunlight,* залитый солнцем. —*v.i.* купаться.

bather *n.* купальщик.

bathhouse *n.* купальня.

bathing *n.* купание. —**bathing cap,** купальная шапочка. —**bathing suit,** купальный костюм; купальник.

bathrobe *n.* халат.

bathroom *n.* **1,** (for bathing) ванная; ванная комната. **2,** (lavatory) туалет; уборная.

bath towel банное полотенце.

bathtub *n.* ванна.

batiste *n.* батист.

baton *n.* **1,** (symbolic staff) жезл. **2,** (rod used by a conductor) (дирижёрская) палочка. **3,** *sports* эстафета; эстафетная палочка.

battalion *n.* батальон; дивизион. —*adj.* батальонный.

batten *v.t.* [*usu.* **batten down**] задраивать: *batten down the hatches,* задраивать люки.

batter *v.t.* **1,** (pound) биться о; колотить. *The waves battered the ship,* волны разбивались о борт корабля. *The storm battered the coast,* шторм обрушился на побережье. **2,** (damage by repeated blows) измять. *His battered face,* его разбитое лицо. **3,** *fol. by* **in** (bash in) вдавливать. —*n.* взбитое тесто.

battering ram таран.

battery *n.* **1,** (storage battery) батарея; аккумулятор. **2,** (small, as for a flashlight) батарейка. **3,** *mil.* батарея: *missile battery,* ракетная батарея. —**assault and battery,** *see* **assault.** —**battery-operated,** *adj.* батарейный.

batting *n.* ватин.

battle *n.* бой; битва; сражение. *The battle of Stalingrad,* битва под Сталинградом. *The battle of*

Borodino, би́тва при Бородине́. *He died in battle,* он поги́б в бою́. —*adj.* боево́й: *battle cry,* боево́й клич. —*v.t. & i.* сража́ться (с); боро́ться (с): *battle the enemy,* сража́ться/боро́ться с враго́м. *Battle the elements,* боро́ться со стихи́ей. —**do battle,** боро́ться; лома́ть ко́пья. *Do battle with,* дать бой (+ *dat.*).

battlefield *n.* по́ле бо́я; по́ле би́твы; по́ле сраже́ния. *Also,* **battleground.**

battle-hardened *adj.* закалённый в боя́х; обстре́лянный.

battlement *n.* зубча́тая крепостна́я стена́.

battleship *n.* лине́йный кора́бль; линко́р.

batty *adj., slang* сумасше́дший. *Drive batty,* своди́ть с ума́.

bauble *n.* безделу́шка.

baulk *v.* = **balk.**

bauxite *n.* бокси́т. —*adj.* бокси́товый.

Bavarian *adj.* бава́рский.

bawdy *adj.* са́льный; поха́бный.

bawl *v.i.* вопи́ть; ора́ть; реве́ть. —**bawl out,** *colloq.* брани́ть; разноси́ть.

bay *n.* **1,** (body of water) зали́в; бу́хта. **2,** *archit.* проле́т. **3,** (compartment in an aircraft) отсе́к: *bomb bay,* бо́мбовый отсе́к; *cargo bay,* грузово́й отсе́к. **4,** (bark) лай. **5,** (tree) лавр. —*adj.* (color of a horse) гнедо́й. —*v.i.* (bark) ла́ять. —**at bay,** за́гнанный; затра́вленный. *Hold at bay,* сде́рживать. —**bring to bay,** загоня́ть; (за)трави́ть.

bay leaf лавро́вый лист.

bayonet *n.* штык. —*v.t.* коло́ть штыко́м.

bay window фона́рь.

bazaar *n.* база́р.

bazooka *n.* противота́нковый гранатомёт.

B.C. до на́шей э́ры: *in 200 B.C.,* в двухсо́том году́ до на́шей э́ры.

be *v.i.* **1,** (expressing condition, location, etc.) быть: *I was home,* я был (была́) до́ма. *I will be home,* я бу́ду до́ма. ♦*Generally omitted in the present tense: He is ill,* он бо́лен; *she is not here,* её нет. ♦*When involving frequency or regularity,* быва́ть: *He is often over at our house,* Он ча́сто быва́ет у нас. *Have you ever been there?,* Вы когда́-нибудь быва́ли там? ♦*Also rendered by* есть, бу́дет *and various other verbs: An order is an order,* прика́з есть прика́з. *Leave everything as it is,* оста́вьте все как есть. *If nothing is done,* éсли ничего́ не бу́дет сде́лано. *Where is the nearest post office?,* где нахо́дится ближа́йшая по́чта? *Be in the majority,* оказа́ться в большинстве́. *How long will you be here?,* ско́лько вре́мени вы пробу́дете здесь? *He has been everywhere,* он побыва́л повсю́ду. **2,** (constitute; represent) явля́ться; составля́ть; представля́ть собо́й. *Be an exception,* составля́ть исключе́ние. —**be that as it may,** как бы то ни́ было. —**it was not to be,** не ту́т-то бы́ло. —**so be it,** так и быть; пусть бу́дет так. —**there is; there are,** *see* there. *See also* **were.**

beach *n.* пляж. —*adj.* пля́жный: *beach umbrella,* пля́жный зонт.

beachhead *n.* (примо́рский) плацда́рм.

beacon *n.* **1,** (signal light) сигна́льный ого́нь. **2,** (radio beacon) радиомая́к.

bead *n.* **1,** (single bead) бу́сина; би́серина. **2,** *pl.* (string of beads) бу́сы; би́сер. **3,** *pl.* (rosary) чётки. **4,** (drop, as of perspiration) ка́пля. —**draw a bead on,** взять на прице́л; взять на му́шку.

beaded *adj.* би́серный.

beagle *n.* го́нчая.

beak *n.* клюв.

beaker *n.* **1,** (laboratory container) мензу́рка. **2,** (goblet) ку́бок.

beam *n.* **1,** (of wood, metal, etc.) ба́лка; брус. **2,** (of light) луч. *Turn up/down the high beams,* включи́ть/притуши́ть да́льний свет. *Turn on the low beams,* переключи́ть фа́ры на бли́жний свет. **3,** (group of particles or waves traveling in parallel paths) пучо́к: *particle beam,* пучо́к части́ц. —*v.t.* **1,** (radiate) излуча́ть. **2,** (transmit) передава́ть; направля́ть. —*v.i.* сия́ть; *fig.* сия́ть от ра́дости.

bean *n.* боб. *Kidney bean,* фасо́ль. *String beans,* стручко́вая фасо́ль. *Coffee beans,* зёрна ко́фе. —*adj.* бобо́вый; фасо́левый. *Bean soup,* фасо́левый суп. —**not worth a hill of beans,** вы́еденного яйца́ не сто́ит. —**spill the beans,** *colloq.* проговори́ться; проболта́ться; вы́болтать секре́т.

beanpole *n., colloq.* каланча́.

bear *n.* медве́дь. —*adj.* [*also,* **bear's**] медве́жий: *bear hunt,* медве́жья охо́та. —*v.t.* **1,** (carry) нести́; носи́ть. *Bear arms,* носи́ть ору́жие. **2,** (bring and tell) приноси́ть: *bear glad tidings,* приноси́ть ра́достное изве́стие. **3,** (bring forth; produce) приноси́ть: *bear fruit,* приноси́ть плоды́. *Bear interest,* приноси́ть проце́нты. **4,** (give birth to) рожа́ть; рожда́ть. *She bore him two sons,* она́ родила́ ему́ двух сынове́й. **5,** (have; show) носи́ть: *bear traces,* носи́ть следы́; *bear one's name,* носи́ть чье-нибудь и́мя. *Bear a resemblance,* име́ть схо́дство. *Bear no relation to,* не име́ть никако́го отноше́ния к. **6,** (hold; harbor) (за)таи́ть: *bear a grudge,* (за)таи́ть оби́ду *or* зло́бу. **7,** (support, as weight) выде́рживать. **8,** (shoulder, as expense or responsibility) нести́. **9,** (endure; withstand) выноси́ть; терпе́ть; переноси́ть. *Bear the pain,* терпе́ть *or* переноси́ть боль. *I can't bear to look,* не могу́ (заста́вить себя́) посмотре́ть. *I can't bear the sight of him,* я его́ ви́деть не могу́. **10,** (merit) сто́ить: *The warning bears repeating,* предупрежде́ние сто́ит повторя́ть. **11,** *fol. by* **oneself** (conduct) вести́ себя́: *bear oneself with dignity,* вести́ себя́ с досто́инством. —*v.i.* забира́ть: *bear right,* забира́ть впра́во. —**bear down,** натужива́ться. —**bear down on,** нажима́ть на. —**bear in mind,** име́ть в виду́. —**bear on** *or* **upon,** име́ть отноше́ние к. —**bear out,** подтвержда́ть. —**bear up,** крепи́ться. —**bring to bear,** ока́зывать (давле́ние); напряга́ть (все си́лы).

bearable *adj.* сно́сный; терпи́мый.

beard *n.* борода́.

bearded *adj.* борода́тый. —**bearded vulture,** борода́ч; ягня́тник.

beardless *adj.* **1,** (having no beard) безборо́дый. **2,** *fig.* (callow) безу́сый.

bearer *n.* **1,** (of news) ве́стник. **2,** (of a check, document, etc.) пода́тель; предъяви́тель.

bearing *n.* **1,** (carrying) ноше́ние: *the bearing of arms,* ноше́ние ору́жия. **2,** (way of carrying oneself) вы́правка; оса́нка: *military bearing,* вое́нная вы́правка; *regal bearing,* ца́рственная оса́нка. **3,** *mech.* подши́пник: *ball bearing,* ша́риковый подши́пник. **4,** (relevance) отноше́ние: *have no bearing on,* не име́ть никако́го отноше́ния к. **5,** *pl.* (sense of direction) ориента́ция: *lose one's bearings,* потеря́ть ориента́цию. *Get one's bearings,* ориенти́роваться. **6,** *navigation* пе́ленг. *Take a bearing on,* пеленгова́ть.

bearskin *n.* медве́жья шку́ра. —*adj.* медве́жий: *bearskin coat,* медве́жья шу́ба.

beast *n.* зверь; живо́тное. —**beast of burden,** вью́чное живо́тное. —**beast of prey,** хи́щный зверь.

beastly *adj.* **1,** (bestial) зве́рский. **2,** *colloq.* (nasty; awful) скве́рный; зве́рский.

beat *v.t.* **1,** (strike repeatedly) бить в: *beat a drum,* бить в бараба́н. *Beat one's breast/chest,* бить себя́ в грудь. *Beat a carpet,* выбива́ть ковёр. **2,** (thrash; whip) бить; избива́ть. *Beat a horse,* бить ло́шадь. *Beat to death,* заби́ть до́ смерти. *He was severely beaten,* его́ жесто́ко избива́ли. **3,** (whip; churn) взбива́ть: *beat egg whites,* взбива́ть белки́. **4,** (clear, as a path) пробива́ть (тропу́). **5,** (mark, as time) отбива́ть (такт). **6,** (defeat) (по)би́ть; побежда́ть; выи́грывать у; обы́грывать. **7,** (get ahead of; reach a goal ahead of) опережа́ть. *He beat me to it,* он опереди́л меня́. **8,** *in* **beat a retreat,** бить отбо́й. **9,** *colloq.* (baffle): *It beats me!,* ума́ не приложу́. —*v.i.* **1,** (pulsate, as of the heart) би́ться. **2,** (sound when struck, as of drums) бить. **3,** *fol. by* **against** (dash; strike) бить (о *or* по); би́ться (о); стуча́ть (в); хлеста́ть (в *or* о). *The rain is beating against the windowpanes,* дождь бьёт в окно́ *or* по стёклам; дождь стучи́т *or* хле́щет в окно́. *The waves are beating against the shore,* во́лны бью́тся о бе́рег. —*n.* **1,** (beating) бие́ние; бой. *The beat of hoofs,* стук *or* цо́кот копы́т. **2,** (rounds; patrol) обхо́д; дозо́р. **3,** *music* ритм; такт. —*adj., slang* (exhausted) без ног. —**beat back,** отбива́ть. —**beat down, 1,** (flatten) прибива́ть. **2,** (of the sun) пали́ть; печь; припека́ть. —**beat it!,** *slang* вон отсю́да!; пошёл вон! —**beat off,** отбива́ть. —**beat up,** избива́ть.

beaten *adj.* **1,** (whipped up, as of eggs) взби́тый. **2,** (defeated) разби́тый; побеждённый. **3,** (crushed in spirit) уби́тый. **4,** (well-worn; familiar) изби́тый; проторённый: *the beaten track,* изби́тая/проторённая доро́га.

beatific *adj.* блаже́нный.

beatify *v.t.* причисля́ть к ли́ку блаже́нных. —**beatification,** *n.* причисле́ние к ли́ку блаже́нных.

beating *n.* **1,** (pulsation, as of the heart) бие́ние. **2,** (sound; beat) бой: *the beating of drums,* бараба́нный бой. **3,** (act of whipping or thrashing) избие́ние: *the beating of demonstrators,* избие́ние демонстра́нтов. **4,** (a whipping or thrashing) побо́и: *severe beating,* жесто́кие побо́и. *Administer a beating to someone,* нанести́ кому́-нибудь побо́и. **5,** (defeat) разгро́м. *Take a bad beating,* потерпе́ть жесто́кое пораже́ние.

beatitude *n.* блаже́нство. —**the Beatitudes,** за́поведи блаже́нства.

beat-up *adj., colloq.* **1,** (threadbare) поно́шенный. **2,** (dilapidated) полуразру́шенный.

beau *n.* покло́нник; кавале́р.

beautician *n.* **1,** (one who gives cosmetic treatments) космето́лог; космети́чка. **2,** (hairdresser) парикма́хер.

beautification *n.* украше́ние.

beautiful *adj.* краси́вый; прекра́сный. —**beautifully,** *adv.* краси́во.

beautify *v.t.* украша́ть.

beauty *n.* **1,** (beautifulness) красота́. **2,** (beautiful woman) краса́вица.

beauty parlor космети́ческий кабине́т.

beauty spot 1, (cosmetic patch) му́шка. **2,** (birthmark) ро́динка.

beaver *n.* **1,** (animal) бобр. **2,** (fur) бобёр; бобро́вый мех.

becalm *v.t.* успока́ивать.

because *conj.* потому́ что: *The baby is crying because he's hungry,* ребёнок пла́чет, потому́ что хо́чет есть. —**because of,** из-за. *It's all because of...,* э́то всё из-за...; всему́ вино́й (+ *nom.*).

beck *n.* киво́к. —**be at someone's beck and call,** быть у кого́-нибудь на побегу́шках.

beckon *v.t. & i.* мани́ть; подзыва́ть: *beckon to someone to come near,* помани́ть *or* подозва́ть кого́-нибудь к себе́.

becloud *v.t.* завола́кивать; затума́нивать.

become *v.i.* станови́ться (*pfv.* стать); де́латься. *Become a celebrity,* стать знамени́тостью. *Become necessary,* стать необходи́мым. *Become ill,* заболе́ть. *Become angry,* рассерди́ться. —*v.t.* **1,** (look attractive on) идти́ (+ *dat.*); быть к лицу́ (+ *dat.*). **2,** (befit) подоба́ть (+ *dat.*); быть к лицу́ (+ *dat.*). —**become of,** стать с; ста́ться с: *What's become of him?,* что с ним ста́ло/ста́лось? *What will become of me?,* что со мной бу́дет? *What's become of my matches?,* куда́ де́лись мои́ спи́чки?

becoming *adj.* **1,** (suitable; fitting) подоба́ющий; к лицу́. **2,** (attractive) к лицу́. *The dress is very becoming,* пла́тье вам идёт; пла́тье вам к лицу́.

bed *n.* **1,** (for sleeping) посте́ль; крова́ть. *Hospital bed,* (больни́чная) ко́йка. *Bed of straw,* соло́менная подсти́лка. *Be in bed,* быть в посте́ли. *Go to bed,* ложи́ться спать. *Put to bed,* укла́дывать. **2,** (quarters): *bed and board,* кварти́ра и стол; (accommodations): *bed and breakfast,* ночле́г и за́втрак. **3,** (flower bed) клу́мба; гряда́; гря́дка. **4,** (of a river) ру́сло. **5,** *geol.* пласт: *lava bed,* пласт ла́вы. **6,** *Oyster bed,* у́стричная ба́нка. —*adj.* посте́льный: *bed linen,* посте́льное бельё. —**get up on the wrong side of the bed,** встать с ле́вой ноги́. —**take to one's bed,** слечь в посте́ль.

bedazzle *v.t.* ослепля́ть.

bedbug *n.* клоп.

bedclothes *n.pl.* постéльное бельё.

bedding *n.* **1,** (items for a bed) постéльные принадлéжности. **2,** (material for an animal to sleep on) подстúлка. **3,** *geol.* напластовáние.

bedeck *v.t.* украшáть. *His chest was bedecked with medals,* его грудь былá увéшена медáлями.

bedevil *v.t.* мýчить; терзáть.

bedlam *n.* бедлáм; хáос.

Bedouin *n.* бедуúн.

bedpan *n.* подкладнóе сýдно.

bedpost *n.* стóлбик кровáти.

bedraggled *adj.* растрёпанный; взъерóшенный.

bed rest постéльный режúм.

bedridden *adj.* прикóванный к постéли.

bedrock *n.* **1,** *geol.* материкóвая порóда. **2,** *fig.* (fundamental principles) суть: *get down to bedrock,* добрáться до сýти дéла.

bedroom *n.* спáльня. —**bedroom slippers,** домáшние тýфли; тáпочки; шлёпанцы.

bedside *n. At someone's bedside,* у постéли (+ *gen.*).

bedsore *n.* прóлежень.

bedspread *n.* покрывáло.

bedstead *n.* кровáть.

bedtime *n.* врéмя ложúться спать. *It is bedtime,* порá спать.

bee *n.* пчелá. —*adj.* пчелúный. *Bee sting,* пчелúный укýс; укýс пчелы́.

beech *n.* бук. —*adj.* бýковый.

beechnut *n.* бýковый орéшек.

beechwood *n.* бук. —*adj.* бýковый.

beef *n.* **1,** (meat) говя́дина. *Roast beef,* рóстбиф. **2,** *slang* (complaint) жáлоба. —*adj.* говя́жий; мяснóй. *Beef cattle,* мяснóй скот. —*v.t.* [*usu.* **beef up**] пополня́ть. —*v.i., slang* (complain) ныть.

beefsteak *n.* бифштéкс.

beef stroganoff бефстрóганов.

beefy *adj.* мясúстый; мýскулистый.

beehive *n.* ýлей. *The place was a beehive of activity,* там кипéла бýрная дéятельность.

beekeeper *n.* пчеловóд; пáсечник. —**beekeeping,** *n.* пчеловóдство.

beep *n.* **1,** (sound of a horn) гудóк. **2,** (short high-pitched note) высóкий звук.

beeper *n.* зýммер.

beer *n.* пúво. —*adj.* пивнóй: *beer mug,* пивнáя крýжка. *Beer bottle/can,* буты́лка/бáнка из-под пúва.

beeswax *n.* пчелúный воск.

beet *n.* свёкла. —*adj.* свекóльный: *beet soup,* свекóльный суп. —**red as a beet,** крáсный как рак.

beetle *n.* жук.

beetle-browed *adj.* с навúсшими бровя́ми.

beet sugar свеклови́чный сáхар.

befall *v.t.* постигáть; выпадáть (+ *dat.*); обрýшиваться на.

befit *v.t.* подобáть: *befit the occasion,* подобáть слýчаю. *With all the honors befitting a man of his rank,* со всéми полагáющимися егó рáнгу пóчестями. —**befitting,** *adj.* подобáющий.

before *prep.* **1,** (prior to) до; пéред: *before the war,* до войны́; *before dinner,* пéред обéдом. *The day before his departure,* наканýне егó отъéзда. *Two years before his death,* за два гóда до егó смéрти. *That was before my time,* э́то бы́ло ещё до меня́. **2,** (ahead of; sooner than) рáньше (+ *gen.*); прéжде (+ *gen.*). *He got there before me,* он пришёл рáньше меня́. *A comes before B,* А предшéствует Б. **3,** (in front of) пéред: *before a large audience,* пéред большóй аудитóрией. *Appear before the court,* предстáть пéред судóм. —*conj.* **1,** (prior to the time that) прéжде чем; пéред тем, как; до тогó, как. *Before leaving the house,* прéжде чем (*or* пéред тем, как) вы́йти úз дому. *Before I came to America,* до тогó, как я приéхал в Амéрику. **2,** (lest) покá не: *before I forget,* покá (я) не забы́л. *Before it is too late,* покá не пóздно. **3,** (rather than) скорée чем: *They would die before surrendering,* онú скорée умрýт, чем сдадýтся. —*adv.* рáньше; прéжде. *I have never been here before,* я никогдá рáньше здесь не бывáл(а). *You should have thought of that before!,* нáдо бы́ло дýмать об э́том рáньше! —**as before,** по-прéжнему; по-стáрому. —**before last,** позапрóшлый: *the year before last,* позапрóшлый год. *The night before last,* позавчерá вéчером. —**before long,** в скóром врéмени. —**long before,** задóлго до. —**never before,** *see* **never.** —**shortly before,** незадóлго до.

beforehand *adv.* зарáнее; предварúтельно.

befoul *v.t.* загрязня́ть; загáживать.

befriend *v.t.* подружúться с.

befuddle *v.t.* **1,** (cloud, as the mind) дурмáнить. **2,** (confuse) озадáчивать.

beg *v.t.* **1,** (ask earnestly; plead with) умоля́ть; упрáшивать: *beg someone to come,* умоля́ть/упрáшивать когó-нибудь прийтú. **2,** (ask for earnestly) просúть: *beg permission,* просúть разрешéния. **3,** (evade; sidestep) обходúть (вопрóс). —*v.i.* **1,** (solicit alms) нúщенствовать; просúть мúлостыню. *Live by begging,* жить нúщенством. *Go begging to,* идтú на поклóн к. **2,** *fol. by* of (ask earnestly) óчень просúть; умоля́ть: *I beg of you,* я вас óчень прошý; умоля́ю вас. **3,** *fol. by* for (plead for) просúть; молúть о: *beg for mercy,* просúть пощáды; молúть о пощáде. **4,** *fol. by inf., used in certain forms of politeness: I beg to differ,* позвóлю себé не согласúться. **5,** (of a dog) служúть. —**beg off,** отговáриваться. —**go begging,** не имéть спрóса. —**I beg your pardon!, 1,** (please excuse me) извинúте!; простúте!; прошý прощéния! **2,** (what did you say?) простúте, что вы сказáли? **3,** (I disagree) извинúте!

beget *v.t.* **1,** (father; sire) родúть. **2,** *fig.* (generate) порождáть.

beggar *n.* нúщий. —*v.t.* не поддавáться: *beggar description,* не поддавáться описáнию. —**beggarly,** *adj.* нúщенский. —**beggary,** *n.* нúщенство.

begin *v.t.* **1,** *fol. by a noun,* начинáть: *begin work,* начинáть рабóту. **2,** *fol. by inf.* начинáть; стать: *He began to write,* он начáл/стал писáть. *It began to rain,* пошёл дождь. *Strange things were beginning to happen,* стáли происходúть стрáнные вéщи. ♦*Also with the prefix* за: *begin to cry,* заплáкать; *begin to* *sing,* запе́ть. —*v.i.* **1,** (start) начина́ть: *Let us begin,* начнём. **2,** (commence) начина́ться: *The meeting is beginning,* собра́ние начина́ется. **3,** *preceded by* **can't** (do in the slightest degree): *I can't begin to tell you,* не могу́ да́же сказа́ть. *It can't begin to compare with...,* э́то не идёт ни в како́е сравне́ние с... —**to begin with,** во-пе́рвых.

beginner *n.* начина́ющий.

beginning *n.* нача́ло. *In the beginning,* снача́ла; внача́ле. *From beginning to end,* с нача́ла до конца́. —*adj.* начина́ющий. —*prep.* начина́я с: *beginning July 1,* начина́я с пе́рвого ию́ля.

begone *interj.* убира́йся!; прочь!

begonia *n.* бего́ния.

begrudge *v.t.* **1,** (envy) зави́довать. **2,** (give reluctantly) жале́ть. *He begrudges every penny,* ему́ жаль ка́ждой копе́йки; он дрожи́т над ка́ждой копе́йкой.

beguile *v.t.* **1,** (trick) обольща́ть. **2,** (charm) очаро́вывать.

behalf *n.,* in **on/in behalf of, 1,** (speaking for; representing) от и́мени (+ *gen.*). **2,** (in the interest of; in support of; for the benefit of) в по́льзу (+ *gen.*): *speak on behalf of,* вы́сказаться в по́льзу (+ *gen.*).

behave *v.i.* **1,** (conduct oneself) вести́ себя́; держа́ть себя́. **2,** (comport oneself properly) вести́ себя́ хорошо́ *or* прили́чно.

behavior *also,* **behaviour** *n.* поведе́ние. *Be on one's best behavior,* вести́ себя́ идеа́льно.

behaviorism *n.* бихевиори́зм.

behead *v.t.* обезгла́вливать. —**beheading,** *n.* обезгла́вливание.

behemoth *n.* бегемо́т.

behest *n. At the behest of,* под дикто́вку (+ *gen.*).

behind *prep.* **1,** (on the far side of) за (+ *instr.*): *behind one's back,* за спино́й; *behind the wheel,* за рулём; *behind the scenes,* за кули́сами. *He closed the door behind her,* он закры́л за ней дверь. **2,** (to the far side of) за (+ *acc.*): *go behind the house,* зайти́ за дом; *fall behind the couch,* упа́сть за дива́н. **3,** (supporting) за (+ *instr.*): *The army is/stands behind him,* за ним стои́т а́рмия. **4,** (lagging behind): *be behind schedule,* отстава́ть. *Be behind the times,* отстава́ть от жи́зни *or* от вре́мени; не идти́ в но́гу с ве́ком. **5,** (underlying) за (+ *instr.*): *What's behind all this?,* что за э́тим кро́ется? **6,** (gone by; ended for) позади́: *The hardest part is behind us,* са́мая тру́дная часть позади́. —*adv.* позади́; сза́ди. *Follow closely behind,* идти́ сле́дом (за). *Be behind in one's work,* отстава́ть в рабо́те. *Be behind in one's payments/rent,* просро́чивать платежи́/квартпла́ту. —*n., colloq.* (buttocks) зад. —**from behind,** из-за (+ *gen.*): *dart out from behind a tree,* вы́лететь из-за де́рева. *Sneak up on someone from behind,* подкра́дываться к кому́-нибудь сза́ди. —**leave behind, 1,** (get way ahead of) оставля́ть позади́. **2,** (leave after death or departure) оставля́ть по́сле себя́.

behind-the-scenes *adj.* закули́сный.

behold *v.t.* смотре́ть; созерца́ть; зреть. —*interj.* смотри́(те)!

beholden *adj.* обя́занный.

behoove *v.t.* сле́довать (+ *dat.*); надлежа́ть (+ *dat.*). *It behooves you to...,* вам сле́дует (+ *inf.*).

beige *n.* цвет беж. —*adj.* бе́жевый.

being *n.* **1,** (existence) бытие́. **2,** (creature) существо́. *Human being,* челове́к. —**being as/that,** *colloq.* так как. —**come into being,** возника́ть; зарожда́ться. —**for the time being,** пока́; до поры́ до вре́мени.

belabor *also,* **belabour** *v.t.* **1,** (pummel) колоти́ть. **2,** (assail verbally) обру́шиваться на. **3,** (harp upon) пережёвывать.

belated *adj.* запозда́лый: *belated recognition,* запозда́лое призна́ние.

belch *v.i.* рыга́ть. —*v.t.* **1,** *fol. by* **up** (cough up) отры́гивать. **2,** *fol. by* **forth** (eject violently) изрыга́ть. —*n.* отры́жка.

beleaguer *v.t.* осажда́ть.

belfry *n.* колоко́льня.

Belgian *adj.* бельги́йский. —*n.* бельги́ец; бельги́йка.

belie *v.t.* опроверга́ть; противоре́чить.

belief *n.* **1,** (faith; trust) ве́ра: *belief in God,* ве́ра в бо́га. **2,** (opinion; conviction) убежде́ние: *suffer for one's beliefs,* страда́ть за свои́ убежде́ния. *It is my belief that...,* я счита́ю, что... —**beyond belief,** невероя́тно.

believable *adj.* правдоподо́бный.

believe *v.t.* **1,** (trust the word of; accept as true) ве́рить: *I believe you,* я вам ве́рю. *I can't believe it,* я не могу́ э́тому (*or* в э́то) пове́рить. *I don't believe a word he says,* я не ве́рю ни одному́ его́ сло́ву. *I couldn't believe my eyes,* я не ве́рил(а) свои́м глаза́м. *Believe it or not,* хоти́те ве́рьте, хоти́те нет. **2,** (be of a certain opinion) счита́ть: *I believe that he is mistaken,* я счита́ю, что он ошиба́ется. **3,** (think; be more or less sure) ду́мать: *I believe he left,* ду́маю, что он ушёл. —*v.i.* **1,** (have religious faith) ве́рить. **2,** *fol. by* **in** (have faith in) ве́рить (в): *believe in God,* ве́рить в бо́га. —**make believe,** притворя́ться.

believer *n.* ве́рующий.

belittle *v.t.* умаля́ть; принижа́ть.

bell *n.* **1,** (device to be rung) ко́локол; колоко́льчик. **2,** (electrical device, as a doorbell) звоно́к. **3,** (small sphere, as in sleigh bells) бубене́ц; бубе́нчик. **4,** *pl.* (musical instrument) колокола́. **5,** (flare of a wind instrument) раструб. **6,** *naut.* (ship's bell) ры́нда; (30-minute period) скля́нка: *four bells,* четы́ре скля́нки. —**ring a bell,** *colloq.* быть знако́мым: *The name rings a bell,* и́мя мне знако́мо. *The name doesn't ring a bell,* э́то и́мя мне ничего́ не говори́т.

belladonna *n.* беллодо́нна.

bell-bottom *adj.,* in **bell-bottom trousers,** брю́ки клёш.

bellboy *n.* коридо́рный.

belle *n.* краса́вица. —**belle of the ball,** цари́ца ба́ла.

bellflower *n.* колоко́льчик.

bellhop *n.* коридо́рный.

bellicose *adj.* вои́нственный. —**bellicosity,** *n.* вои́нственность.

belligerence *n.* вои́нственность.

belligerency *n.* состоя́ние войны́.

belligerent *adj.* **1,** (waging war) вою́ющий. **2,** (bellicose) войнственный. —*n.* вою́ющая сторона́.

bellow *v.i.* мыча́ть; реве́ть. —*n.* мыча́ние.

bellows *n.* мехи́.

bell ringer звона́рь.

bell tower колоко́льня.

belly *n.* **1,** (abdomen) живо́т; брю́хо. **2,** *colloq.* (paunch) брюшко́; пу́зо.

bellyache *n.* боль в животе́. —*v.i.*, *slang* (gripe) ныть.

bellyband *n.* подпру́га.

bellybutton *n.*, *colloq.* пуп; пупо́к.

belong *v.i.* до́лжен быть: *Where do these things belong?*, где должны́ быть э́ти ве́щи? *They belong in the attic*, они́ должны́ быть на чердаке́. *I belong here*, моё ме́сто здесь. —**belong to, 1,** (be the property of) принадлежа́ть (+ *dat.*). **2,** (be a member of) принадлежа́ть к; состоя́ть в. **3,** (be one of; be a part of) принадлежа́ть к; относи́ться к.

belongings *n.pl.* пожи́тки.

Belorussian *adj.* белору́сский. —*n.* **1,** (person) белору́с; белору́ска. **2,** (language) белору́сский язы́к.

beloved *adj.* возлю́бленный; люби́мый. *My beloved husband*, мой люби́мый муж.

below *adv.* **1,** (at a lower place or level) ни́же; внизу́. *From below*, сни́зу. *They live on the floor below*, они́ живу́т этажо́м ни́же. **2,** (to a lower place or level) вниз. —*prep.* ни́же; под. *Below zero*, ни́же нуля́. *Below average*, ни́же сре́днего. *Sink below the horizon*, сесть за горизо́нт.

belt *n.* **1,** (waistband) по́яс; реме́нь. **2,** (zone) по́яс; полоса́. **3,** *mech.* реме́нь: *fan belt*, реме́нь вентиля́тора. —*adj.* ремённый: *belt buckle*, ремённая пря́жка. *Belt drive*, ремённый приво́д; ремённая переда́ча.

beltway *n.* кольцева́я доро́га.

beluga *n.* **1,** (white whale) белу́ха. **2,** (white sturgeon) белу́га.

bemoan *v.t.* опла́кивать: *bemoan one's fate*, опла́кивать свою́ судьбу́.

bemused *adj.* **1,** (dazed; bewildered) ошеломлённый; расте́рянный. **2,** (lost in thought) в разду́мье.

bench *n.* **1,** (long seat) скамья́; скаме́йка; ла́вка. **2,** (work table) верста́к.

bench mark репе́р; пике́т.

bend *v.t.* **1,** (curve) гнуть; сгиба́ть; изгиба́ть. *Bend one's knees*, сгиба́ть коле́ни. *Bend out of shape*, искривля́ть. *Bend down a page in a book*, загиба́ть страни́цу в кни́ге. **2,** (incline; lean; bow) наклоня́ть: *bend one's head to one side*, наклоня́ть го́лову на́ бок. **3,** (exert, as efforts) прилага́ть; направля́ть; напряга́ть. **4,** (force to submit) подчиня́ть: *bend to one's will*, подчиня́ть свое́й во́ле. —*v.i.* **1,** (yield to force or pressure; sag) гну́ться; сгиба́ться. *Bend easily*, легко́ гну́ться. *Bend in the wind*, гну́ться от ве́тра. **2,** (curve, as of a road) повора́чивать. **3,** *fol. by* **over** *or* **down** (stoop) наклоня́ться; склоня́ться; нагиба́ться; сгиба́ться. **4,** (yield) гну́ться. —*n.* **1,** (in a road) поворо́т; изги́б; изви́лина. *Just around the bend*, сра́зу за поворо́том. **2,** (in a river) изги́б; изви́лина;

излу́чина; изви́в. **3,** (joint; crook) сгиб: *bend in one's elbow*, сгиб в ло́кте. *See also* **bent.**

bends *n.* кессо́нная боле́знь.

beneath *prep.* **1,** (below) под: *beneath the surface*, под пове́рхностью. **2,** (unworthy of) ни́же: *beneath one's dignity*, ни́же чьего́-нибудь досто́инства. *It is beneath him to lie*, лгать недосто́йно его́. —*adv.* внизу́; ни́же.

benediction *n.* заключи́тельная моли́тва.

benefactor *n.* благоде́тель.

beneficence *n.* **1,** (generosity; kindness) великоду́шие. **2,** (beneficent act) благодея́ние.

beneficent *adj.* **1,** (kind; generous) великоду́шный. **2,** (beneficial) благотво́рный; благоде́тельный.

beneficial *adj.* благотво́рный; поле́зный. *The beneficial effects of...*, благотво́рное влия́ние (+ *gen.*). *Beneficial to mankind/ one's health/*, поле́зен для челове́чества/здоро́вья.

beneficiary *n.* насле́дник.

benefit *n.* **1,** (advantage; good) вы́года; по́льза. *For the benefit of*, ра́ди. *Reap the benefits of*, пожина́ть плоды́ (+ *gen.*). *For the benefit of those who came late*, для тех, кто опозда́л. **2,** *pl.* (payments) льго́ты; посо́бие. *Fringe benefits*, дополни́тельные льго́ты. *Unemployment benefits*, посо́бие по безрабо́тице. **3,** *theat.* бенефи́с. *Benefit concert*, благотвори́тельный конце́рт. —*v.t.* приноси́ть по́льзу (+ *dat.*). —*v.i.* извлека́ть по́льзу. *Both sides benefit*, о́бе сто́роны вы́игрывают.

benevolent *adj.* доброжела́тельный; благожела́тельный. —**benevolence,** *n.* доброжела́тельность; благожела́тельность.

Bengali *adj.* бенга́льский. —*n.* **1,** (person) бенга́лец; бенга́лка. **2,** (language) бенга́льский язы́к.

benign *adj.* **1,** (kind; gracious) ми́лостивый. **2,** (mild; favorable) благотво́рный. **3,** *med.* (not malignant) доброка́чественный.

bent *adj.* **1,** (twisted out of shape) изо́гнутый; согну́вшийся: *bent axle*, изо́гнутая ось; *bent nail*, согну́вшийся гвоздь. *This spoon is slightly bent*, э́та ло́жка чуть изо́гнута. **2,** *fol. by* **on** (determined) реши́вшийся (на); по́лный реши́мости (+ *gen.*). —*n.* скло́нность; накло́нность; влече́ние; тя́га. *Literary bent*, влече́ние к литерату́ре.

benzene *n.* бензо́л.

benzine *n.* бензи́н.

benzoin *n.* ро́сный ла́дан; бензои́н.

benzol *n.* бензо́л.

bequeath *v.t.* завеща́ть: *bequeath one's property to one's son*, завеща́ть иму́щество сы́ну.

bequest *n.* посме́ртный дар.

berate *v.t.* руга́ть; брани́ть.

bereave *v.t.* лиша́ть. —**bereaved,** *adj.* скорбя́щий: *bereaved parents*, скорбя́щие роди́тели. —**bereavement,** *n.* тяжёлая утра́та.

bereft *adj.* лишённый: *bereft of hope*, лишён наде́жды.

beret *n.* бере́т.

beriberi *n.* бе́ри-бе́ри.

berkelium *n.* берке́лий.

berry *n.* я́года.

berserk *adj.* бе́шеный; обезу́мевший; исступлённый. *Go berserk,* взбеси́ться; обезу́меть; приходи́ть в исступле́ние.

berth *n.* **1,** (on a train) (спа́льное) ме́сто; по́лка. *Upper berth,* ве́рхнее ме́сто; ве́рхняя по́лка. *Lower berth,* ни́жнее ме́сто; ни́жняя по́лка. **2,** (on a ship) ме́сто; ко́йка. **3,** (place of moorage) я́корная стоя́нка; прича́л.

beryl *n.* бери́лл.

beryllium *n.* бери́ллий.

beseech *v.t.* умоля́ть; упра́шивать.

beset *v.t.* **1,** (attack) обру́шиваться на. **2,** (hem in) сти́скивать. **3,** (plague) му́чить: *be beset with doubts,* му́читься сомне́ниями. **4,** (stud) усыпа́ть.

beside *prep.* **1,** (alongside) ря́дом с; во́зле; по́дле. **2,** (other than) кро́ме; поми́мо. —**beside oneself,** вне себя́: *beside oneself with joy,* вне себя́ от ра́дости. —**beside the point,** не по де́лу; некста́ти; не по существу́. *That is beside the point,* э́то к де́лу не отно́сится.

besides *prep.* кро́ме; поми́мо. —*adv.* кро́ме того́; к тому́ же.

besiege *v.t.* **1,** (lay siege to) осажда́ть. **2,** (overwhelm, as with offers) засы́пать; осажда́ть.

besmirch *v.t.* **1,** (soil) па́чкать. **2,** (tarnish; dishonor) черни́ть; пятна́ть; поро́чить.

besom *n.* ве́ник.

bespatter *v.t.* забры́згивать.

bespeak *v.t.* **1,** (be indicative of) говори́ть о. **2,** (presage) предвеща́ть.

bespectacled *adj.* в очка́х.

bespoke *adj., Brit.* сде́ланный на зака́з.

besprinkle *v.t.* обры́згивать; окропля́ть; опры́скивать.

best *adj.* лу́чший; са́мый лу́чший; наилу́чший. *My best friend,* мой лу́чший друг. *Best wishes,* наилу́чшие пожела́ния. *The best man for the job,* са́мый подходя́щий челове́к для э́той до́лжности. —*adv.* лу́чше всего́; бо́льше всего́. *I like this one best,* э́тот мне нра́вится бо́льше всего́. *Do as you think best,* де́лайте, как вы счита́ете ну́жным. —*n.* **1,** [*usu.* **the best**] (those who are or that which is best) лу́чший; лу́чшее: *one of the best,* оди́н из лу́чших. *It's all for the best,* всё к лу́чшему. *Hope for the best,* наде́яться на лу́чшее. *Turn out for the best,* оберну́ться к лу́чшему. *The best we can hope for,* са́мое лу́чшее, что мы мо́жем ожида́ть. **2,** [*usu.* **one's best**] (the most one can do): *do one's best,* сде́лать всё возмо́жное; *try one's best,* стара́ться изо всех сил. —*v.t.* побежда́ть: *best one's rival,* победи́ть сопе́рника. —**all the best!,** всего́ хоро́шего!; всего́ до́брого!; всего́ лу́чшего! —**at best,** в лу́чшем слу́чае. —**be at one's best,** быть в уда́ре; быть на высоте́. —**get the best of,** брать верх над. —**had best,** бы лу́чше (+ *dat.*): *You had best go right away,* вам бы лу́чше пойти́ сейча́с же. —**make the best of, 1,** (exploit to the fullest) испо́льзовать наилу́чшим о́бразом. **2,** (deal with as best as possible) мири́ться с. —**think it best to...,** счита́ть

(счесть) за лу́чшее *or* за бла́го (+ *inf.*). —**to the best of my ability,** по ме́ре сил; по ме́ре спосо́бностей. —**to the best of my knowledge/belief,** насто́лько мне изве́стно.

bestial *adj.* зве́рский; живо́тный. —**bestiality,** *n.* зве́рство.

bestir *v.t.* [*usu.* **bestir oneself**] шевели́ться; раска́чиваться.

best man ша́фер.

bestow *v.t.* **1,** (give as a gift) дари́ть; дарова́ть; жа́ловать. **2,** (confer; award) присужда́ть; присва́ивать; награжда́ть. —**bestowal,** *n.* присужде́ние; присвое́ние; награжде́ние.

bestrew *v.t.* **1,** (scatter about) разбра́сывать. **2,** (cover with things scattered) усыпа́ть.

best seller бестсе́ллер.

bet *n.* пари́. —*v.i.* держа́ть пари́: *Do you want to bet?,* хоти́те держа́ть пари́? *Bet on a horse,* де́лать ста́вку (*or* ста́вить) на ло́шадь. —*v.t.* ста́вить; спо́рить на: *bet ten dollars,* ста́вить (*or* спо́рить на) де́сять до́лларов. *I'll bet you that...,* держу́ пари́, что... *I bet him ten dollars that...,* я поспо́рил с ним на де́сять до́лларов, что... —**you bet!,** коне́чно!; бу́дьте уве́рены!

beta *n.* бе́та. —**beta particle,** бе́та-части́ца. —**beta rays,** бе́та-лучи́.

betake *v.t.* [*usu.* **betake oneself**] отправля́ться.

betel *n.* бе́тель.

betide *v.t.* случа́ться с; постига́ть. *Woe betide...!,* го́ре (+ *dat.*)!

betray *v.t.* **1,** (be a traitor to; be disloyal to) изменя́ть (+ *dat.*); предава́ть (+ *acc.*). **2,** (disappoint, as someone's trust) обма́нывать. **3,** (reveal; give away) выдава́ть.

betrayal *n.* преда́тельство; изме́на. *Betrayal of principles,* изме́на при́нципам.

betroth *v.t.* обруча́ть; помо́лвить. —**betrothal,** *n.* обруче́ние; помо́лвка. —**betrothed,** *adj.* обручённый; помо́лвленный.

better *adj.* **1,** *modifier,* лу́чший: *find a better way,* найти́ лу́чший спо́соб. *This car has seen better days,* э́та маши́на знава́ла лу́чшие времена́. **2,** *predicate,* лу́чше: *He is better today,* ему́ лу́чше сего́дня. *She is feeling better,* ей ста́ло лу́чше *or* ле́гче. *Get better,* стать лу́чше; улучша́ться. —*adv.* лу́чше: *play better when it's warm,* игра́ть лу́чше, когда́ тепло́. *Better known,* бо́лее изве́стный. *I like this one better,* э́тот (э́та, э́то) мне бо́льше нра́вится. —*n.* **1,** (something better) лу́чшее: *a change for the better,* переме́на к лу́чшему. *To change for the better,* измени́ться в лу́чшую сто́рону. **2,** *pl.* (one's superiors) ста́ршие. —*v.t.* **1,** (improve) улучша́ть: *better the lives of the workers,* улучша́ть жизнь рабо́чих. **2,** (surpass) улучша́ть: *better the world record,* улучша́ть мирово́й реко́рд. —**be better off,** в лу́чшем состоя́нии. *You'd be better off...,* вы бы лу́чше (+ *past tense of verb*). —**get the better of,** брать верх над. *Get the better of the argument,* одержа́ть верх в спо́ре. —**never better,** как нельзя́ лу́чше; как никогда́. —**so much the better,** тем лу́чше. —**think better of**

it, оду́маться. —**you had better**..., вам бы лу́чше (+ *inf.*).

betterment *n.* улучше́ние.

bettor *n.* держа́щий пари́.

between *prep.* ме́жду: *between two lakes,* ме́жду двумя́ озёрами. *Between five and six o'clock,* ме́жду пятью́ и шестью́ часа́ми. *What's the difference between...?,* кака́я ра́зница ме́жду...? *A meeting between ... and ...,* встре́ча (кого́) с (кем). *We have only $10 between us,* у нас на двои́х то́лько де́сять до́лларов. —*adv.* [*usu.* **in between**] посреди́. —**between you and me,** ме́жду на́ми.

betwixt *prep., archaic* ме́жду. —**betwixt and between,** ни то ни сё.

bevel *n.* **1,** (tool) науго́льник. **2,** (sloping part) скос. —*v.t.* ска́шивать.

beverage *n.* напи́ток.

bevy *n.* **1,** (group) гру́ппа. **2,** (flock) ста́я.

bewail *v.t.* опла́кивать: *bewail one's misfortune,* опла́кивать свою́ судьбу́.

beware *v.i.* [*usu.* **beware of**] бере́чься; остерега́ться.

bewilder *v.t.* озада́чивать; сбива́ть с то́лку. —**bewildered,** *adj.* озада́ченный; недоуме́нный; недоумева́ющий. —**bewildering,** *adj.* недоумева́ющий. —**bewilderment,** *n.* недоуме́ние; растё́рянность.

bewitch *v.t.* **1,** (cast a spell over) заколдо́вывать; околдо́вывать; завора́живать. **2,** (captivate) очаро́вывать; зачаро́вывать; обвора́живать; завора́живать. —**bewitched,** *adj.* заколдо́ванный; зачаро́ванный. —**bewitching,** *adj.* очарова́тельный; обая́тельный; обворожи́тельный.

beyond *prep.* **1,** (past) да́льше. *The town lies beyond the river,* го́род лежи́т за реко́й. *Beyond the city limits,* за преде́лами го́рода. *Beyond the bounds of,* за преде́лами (+ *gen.*). *The matter never got beyond the talking stage,* да́льше разгово́ров де́ло не шло. **2,** (after) по́зже (+ *gen.*). *Our supplies won't last beyond next week,* на́ших запа́сов не хва́тит бо́льше чем на одну́ неде́лю. **3,** (in addition to; over and above) кро́ме. *Nothing beyond what I said yesterday,* ничего́ бо́льше того́, что я сказа́л(а) вчера́. **4,** (surpassing; exceeding) вне; вы́ше; свы́ше; сверх. *Beyond compare,* вне сравне́ния. *Beyond any doubt,* вне вся́кого сомне́ния. *Beyond belief,* невероя́тно. *Beyond all expectations,* сверх вся́кого ожида́ния. *Beyond my comprehension,* вы́ше моего́ понима́ния. *Live beyond one's means,* жить не по сре́дствам.

bias *n.* **1,** (oblique line) коса́я ли́ния. **2,** (partiality) пристра́стие. **3,** (prejudice) предубежде́ние; предрассу́док.

biased *also,* **biassed** *adj.* **1,** (partial; prejudiced) пристра́стный; предвзя́тый; предубеждённый. *Biased judge,* пристра́стный *or* предубеждённый судья́. *Biased opinion/attitude,* пристра́стное *or* предвзя́тое мне́ние/отноше́ние. *Be biased in favor of,* име́ть предрасположе́ние к. *Be biased against,* име́ть предубежде́ние про́тив. **2,** (slanted; one-sided) тенденцио́зный.

bib *n.* нагру́дник.

Bible *n.* би́блия. —**Biblical,** *adj.* библе́йский.

bibliography *n.* библиогра́фия. —**bibliographer,** *n.* библио́граф. —**bibliographic,** *adj.* библиографи́ческий.

bibliophile *n.* библиофи́л; книголю́б.

bicameral *adj.* двухпала́тный.

bicarbonate of soda двууглеки́слая со́да; питьева́я со́да.

bicentennial *adj.* двухсотле́тний. —*n.* двухсотле́тие. *Also,* **bicentenary.**

biceps *n.* двугла́вая мы́шца; би́цепс.

bicker *v.i.* спо́рить; вздо́рить; пререка́ться. —**bickering,** *n.* пререка́ния; грызня́.

bicuspid *n.* ма́лый коренно́й зуб.

bicycle *n.* велосипе́д. —*adj.* велосипе́дный: *bicycle racing,* велосипе́дные го́нки. —*v.i.* е́здить на велосипе́де. —**bicyclist,** *n.* велосипеди́ст.

bid *v.t.* **1,** (order) веле́ть. **2,** (ask) проси́ть. **3,** (say) *bid farewell to,* проща́ться с; *bid welcome,* приве́тствовать. **4,** (offer, as a certain sum) предлага́ть. **5,** *cards* объявля́ть. —*v.i.* **1,** (make a bid) де́лать предложе́ние; предлага́ть це́ну. **2,** *fol. by inf.* (seek; strive) добива́ться того́, чтобы (+ *inf.*). —*n.* **1,** (offer) предложе́ние. **2,** (attempt) попы́тка. **3,** *cards* объявле́ние. —**bid fair,** обеща́ть.

bidding *n.* **1,** (making of bids) предложе́ние цен. *Start the bidding,* сде́лать пе́рвое предложе́ние. **2,** (ordering; directing) дикто́вка: *at someone's bidding,* под чью́-нибудь дикто́вку. *Do someone's bidding,* выполня́ть чью́-нибудь во́лю.

bide *v.t., in* **bide one's time,** выжида́ть удо́бный слу́чай.

biennial *adj.* двухле́тний. —*n.* двухле́тнее расте́ние.

bier *n.* катафа́лк.

bifocal *adj.* бифока́льный; двухфо́кусный. —**bifocals,** *n.pl.* бифока́льные очки́.

bifurcate *v.i.* разветвля́ться. —**bifurcation,** *n.* разветвле́ние.

big *adj.* **1,** (large) большо́й: *big house,* большо́й дом. **2,** (too large, as of clothes) вели́к: *The dress is big on me,* пла́тье мне велико́. **3,** (elder) ста́рший: *my big sister,* моя́ ста́ршая сестра́. **4,** (important; prominent) кру́пный. **5,** (outstanding in its way) большо́й: *big secret/risk/liar,* большо́й секре́т/риск/лгун. —*adv., colloq.* кру́пно: *write big,* писа́ть кру́пно. *Go over big,* име́ть большо́й успе́х.

bigamist *n.* двоеже́нец.

bigamy *n.* двоебра́чие; двоежё́нство.

Big Dipper Больша́я Медве́дица.

big game кру́пный зверь; кру́пная дичь. *Big-game hunting,* охо́та на кру́пного зве́ря.

big-hearted *adj.* великоду́шный.

bighorn *n.* снежный бара́н.

bigmouth *n.* пустозво́н.

bigot *n.* фана́тик; изуве́р. —**bigoted,** *adj.* фанати́ческий; нетерпи́мый. —**bigotry,** *n.* фанати́зм.

big shot *slang* (больша́я) ши́шка.

bigwig *n., colloq.* туз; вороти́ла.

bike *n. & v., colloq.* = **bicycle.**

bilateral *adj.* двусторо́нний.

bile *n.* жёлчь. —**bile duct,** жёлчный прото́к.

bilingual *adj.* двуязы́чный. —**bilingualism,** *n.* двуязы́чие.

bilious *adj.* жёлчный.

bilk *v.t.* надува́ть; обжу́ливать.

bill *n.* **1,** (statement of charges) счёт: *water bill,* счёт за во́ду. **2,** (bank note) бума́жка; купю́ра: *ten-dollar bill,* десятидо́лларовая бума́жка/купю́ра. **3,** (draft of a proposed law) законопрое́кт; билль. **4,** (poster; announcement) афи́ша. *Theater bill,* театра́льная рекла́ма. **5,** (beak) клюв. —*v.t.* **1,** (present with a bill) подава́ть счёт (+ *dat.*). **2,** (advertise) анонси́ровать. —**bill and coo,** воркова́ть. —**fill the bill,** годи́ться; отвеча́ть тре́бованиям.

billboard *n.* рекла́мный щит.

billet *n.* помеще́ние; кварти́ра. —*v.t.* расквартирова́ть; ста́вить на посто́й. —**billeting,** *n.* расквартирова́ние; посто́й.

billfold *n.* бума́жник.

billiard *adj.* билья́рдный: *billiard ball,* билья́рдный шар.

billiards *n.* билья́рд. *Play billiards,* игра́ть в билья́рд.

billion *n.* миллиа́рд. —**billionth,** *adj.* миллиа́рдный.

bill of exchange ве́ксель.

bill of fare меню́.

bill of lading накладна́я; коносаме́нт.

Bill of Rights билль о права́х.

billow *n.* вал. —*v.i.* вздыма́ться; волнова́ться. —**billowy,** *adj.* вздыма́ющий.

billy club дуби́нка.

billy goat козёл; ко́злик.

bimetallic *adj.* биметалли́ческий. —**bimetallism,** *n.* биметалли́зм.

bimonthly *adj.* двухме́сячный. —*adv.* раз в два ме́сяца. —*n.* двухме́сячник.

bin *n.* **1,** (for grain) ларь; за́кром. **2,** (for coal) бу́нкер (для угля́).

binary *adj.* **1,** (having two components) двойно́й. **2,** *chem.; math.; astron.* бина́рный.

bind *v.t.* **1,** (tie up) вяза́ть; свя́зывать: *bind sheaves,* вяза́ть снопы́; *bind (someone) hand and foot,* связа́ть по рука́м и нога́м. **2,** *usu. fol. by* **up** (bandage) перевя́зывать. **3,** (fasten together, as a book) переплета́ть. **4,** (link closely) свя́зывать. **5,** (obligate) обя́зывать: *This does not bind you to anything,* э́то вас ни к чему́ не обя́зывает. *See also* **bound.**

binder *n.* **1,** (bookbinder) переплётчик. **2,** (holder of loose-leaf sheets) скоросшива́тель.

bindery *n.* переплётная.

binding *n.* **1,** (tying) вяза́ние. **2,** (covering of a book) переплёт. —*adj.* **1,** (obligatory) обя́зывающий; обяза́тельный. *The resolution is not binding (on)...,* резолю́ция не име́ет обяза́тельной си́лы (*or* не обяза́тельна) для... **2,** *physiol.* крепи́тельный. *Rice is binding,* рис крепи́т.

bindweed *n.* вьюно́к.

binge *n., colloq.* кутёж; вы́пивка. *Go on a binge,* прокути́ть.

bingo *n.* лото́.

binoculars *n.pl.* бино́кль.

binomial *n.* бино́м; двучле́н. —*adj.* двучле́нный. —**binomial theorum,** бино́м Нью́тона.

biochemistry *n.* биохи́мия. —**biochemical,** *adj.* биохими́ческий. —**biochemist,** *n.* биохи́мик.

biography *n.* биогра́фия. —**biographer,** *n.* био́граф. —**biographical,** *adj.* биографи́ческий.

biology *n.* биоло́гия. —**biological,** *adj.* биологи́ческий. —**biologist,** *n.* био́лог.

bionics *n.* био́ника.

biophysics *n.* биофи́зика.

biopsy *n.* биопси́я.

bipartisan *adj.* двухпарти́йный.

bipartite *adj.* двусторо́нний.

biped *adj.* двуно́гий. —*n.* двуно́гое живо́тное.

biplane *n.* бипла́н.

birch *n.* берёза. —*adj.* берёзовый. *Birch bark,* берёста. *Birch forest,* березня́к.

bird *n.* пти́ца. —*adj.* [*also,* **bird's**] пти́чий: *bird's nest,* пти́чье гнездо́. —**a bird in the hand is worth two in the bush,** не сули́ журавля́ в не́бе, а дай сини́цу в ру́ки. —**birds of a feather,** *see* **feather.** —**kill two birds with one stone,** уби́ть двух за́йцев одни́м уда́ром.

birdcage *n.* пти́чья кле́тка.

birdie *n.* пти́чка.

birdlime *n.* пти́чий клей.

bird of paradise ра́йская пти́ца.

birdseed *n.* пти́чий корм.

bird's-eye view вид с пти́чьего полёта.

birth *n.* **1,** (being born) рожде́ние. *Blind from birth,* слепо́й от рожде́ния *or* от приро́ды. *He weighed four pounds at birth,* при рожде́нии он ве́сил четы́ре фу́нта. **2,** (giving birth) ро́ды: *difficult birth,* тру́дные ро́ды. **3,** (lineage; descent) происхожде́ние. *He is Italian by birth,* он ро́дом из Ита́лии. —**give birth to,** рожа́ть. *She gave birth to a son,* у неё роди́лся сын.

birth certificate свиде́тельство о рожде́нии; ме́трика.

birth control контро́ль над рожда́емостью. *Practice birth control,* применя́ть противозача́точные сре́дства.

birthday *n.* день рожде́ния. *Birthday present,* пода́рок ко дню рожде́ния.

birth defect врождённый дефе́кт.

birthmark *n.* роди́мое пятно́; ро́динка.

birthplace *n.* ме́сто рожде́ния.

birth rate рожда́емость.

birthright *n.* пра́во перворо́дства.

biscuit *n.* пече́нье; суха́рь; гале́та.

bisect *v.t.* разреза́ть.

bisexual *adj.* двупо́лый.

bishop *n.* **1,** (prelate) епи́скоп. **2,** *chess* слон. —**bishopric,** *n.* сан епи́скопа.

bismuth *n.* ви́смут.

bison *n.* **1,** (American) бизо́н. **2,** (European) зубр.

bit *n.* **1,** (small piece) кусо́чек: *tear a letter to bits,* разорва́ть письмо́ на кусо́чки. *Smash to bits,* разби́ть вдре́безги. *He/ the house /was blown to bits,* его́ разорва́ло на ча́сти; дом взры́вом разнесло́ в ще́пки.

The wolf tore the sheep to bits, волк растерза́л овцу́. **2,** (small amount) чу́точка. *I'll have a bit of wine,* мне, пожа́луйста, немно́го вина́. *He needs a bit of encouragement,* его́ на́до немно́го подба́дривать. **3,** (mouthpiece of a bridle) удила́. **4,** (boring device) пёрка. **—a bit,** немно́го; немно́жко: *a bit larger,* немно́го бо́льше; побо́льше. *He is a bit of a coward,* он трусова́т. **—bit by bit,** ка́пля за ка́плей; ка́пля по ка́пле. **—bit part,** выходна́я роль. **—do one's bit,** внести́ свою́ ле́пту. **—every bit,** всё без оста́тка. **—not a bit,** ниско́лько; ничу́ть; ни ка́пли; ни чу́точки; ни на йо́ту. *You haven't changed a bit!,* вы совсе́м не измени́лись! **—take the bit in one's teeth,** закуси́ть удила́.

bitch *n.* су́ка. **—son of a bitch,** *vulg.* су́кин сын.

bite *v.t.* **1,** (grip or cut with the teeth) куса́ть. *Bite one's nails,* грызть *or* куса́ть но́гти. *Bite someone on the arm,* укуси́ть кого́-нибудь за́ руку (*or* в ру́ку). **2,** (of an insect, snake, etc.) куса́ть; жа́лить. —*v.i.* **1,** (grip something with the teeth) куса́ть. **2,** (tend to bite, as of a dog) куса́ться. **3,** (take the bait, as of a fish) клева́ть. **4,** *fig.* (take the bait; be tricked) попа́сться на у́дочку. —*n.* **1,** (piece bitten off): *take a bite out of something,* надкуси́ть что́-нибудь. **2,** (wound inflicted by biting) уку́с: *mosquito bite,* комари́ный уку́с. **3,** (snack; morsel) заку́ска. *Have a bite to eat,* закуси́ть. **4,** *dent.* прику́с. **—bite off,** отку́сывать. **—bite off more than one can chew,** сли́шком мно́го взять на себя́. **—bite one's lip,** закуси́ть губу́ *or* гу́бы. **—bite one's tongue,** прикуси́ть язы́к. **—once bitten twice shy,** пу́ганая воро́на куста́ бои́тся; обжёгшись на молоке́, на во́ду ду́ешь.

biting *adj.* **1,** (sharp, as of a wind) ре́зкий; хлёсткий. **2,** (caustic; mordant) е́дкий; ко́лкий; хлёсткий.

bitter *adj.* **1,** (acrid) го́рький: *bitter lemon/taste,* го́рький лимо́н/вкус. **2,** (intense) жесто́кий; лю́тый; ожесточённый. *Bitter cold,* лю́тый хо́лод. *Bitter enemy,* зле́йший враг. *Bitter hatred,* лю́тая не́нависть. *Bitter struggle,* ожесточённая борьба́. *Bitter disappointment,* го́рькое *or* жесто́кое разочарова́ние. **3,** (hard to accept) го́рький: *the bitter truth,* го́рькая пра́вда. *A bitter lesson,* жесто́кий уро́к. **4,** (embittered) озло́бленный. —*adv.* о́чень; ужа́сно. *Bitter cold,* ужа́сно хо́лодно. **—to the bitter end,** до са́мого конца́; до после́днего.

bitterly *adv.* го́рько: *cry/complain bitterly,* го́рько пла́кать/жа́ловаться. *Be bitterly disappointed,* жесто́ко разочарова́ться.

bittern *n.* выпь.

bitterness *n.* **1,** (bitter taste) го́речь. **2,** (bitter feelings) го́речь; озлобле́ние; ожесточе́ние.

bitters *n.pl.* го́рькая.

bitumen *n.* биту́м. **—bituminous,** *adj.* битумино́зный; биту́мный.

bivalent *adj.* двухвале́нтный.

bivalve *adj.* двуство́рчатый. —*n.* двуство́рчатый моллю́ск.

bivouac *n.* бива́к. —*v.i.* стоя́ть *or* располага́ться бива́ком.

biweekly *adj.* двухнеде́льный. —*adv.* раз в две неде́ли. —*n.* двухнеде́льник.

bizarre *adj.* стра́нный; дико́винный; экстравага́нтный.

blab *v.i.* (chatter) болта́ть. —*v.t.* (give away, as a secret) разба́лтывать; выба́лтывать.

blabbermouth *n., colloq.* болту́н.

black *adj.* чёрный. *Turn black,* черне́ть. *Paint the door black,* кра́сить дверь в чёрный цвет. —*n.* **1,** (color) чёрный цвет. *Dressed in black,* оде́т(а) в чёрное. **2,** (negro) негр; чёрный. **3,** *chess* чёрные: *black wins,* чёрные выи́грывают. **—black out, 1,** (extinguish all the lights in) затемня́ть. **2,** (lose consciousness) потеря́ть созна́ние.

black-and-blue *adj.* в синяка́х. *Beat (someone) black-and-blue,* избива́ть до синяко́в.

black-and-white *adj.* чёрно-бе́лый. *In black-and-white,* чёрным по бе́лому.

blackball *v.t.* забаллоти́ровать.

blackberry *n.* ежеви́ка. —*adj.* ежеви́чный.

blackbird *n.* чёрный дрозд.

blackboard *n.* доска́.

blacken *v.t.* черни́ть. —*v.i* черне́ть.

black eye подби́тый глаз. *Give someone a black eye,* подби́ть глаз кому́-нибудь.

black grouse те́терев.

blackguard *n.* подле́ц; негодя́й; мерза́вец.

blackhead *n.* у́горь.

black hole чёрная дыра́.

blacking *n.* ва́кса.

blackjack *n.* **1,** (weapon) дуби́на; дуби́нка. **2,** (card game) два́дцать одно́; очко́.

blacklist *n.* чёрный спи́сок. —*v.t.* вноси́ть в чёрный спи́сок.

black magic чёрная ма́гия.

blackmail *n.* шанта́ж. —*v.t.* шантажи́ровать. **—blackmailer,** *n.* шантажи́ст.

black market чёрный ры́нок: *on the black market,* на чёрном ры́нке.

blackness *n.* чернота́.

blackout *n.* **1,** (extinguishing of lights) затемне́ние; светомаскиро́вка. **2,** (fainting spell) поте́ря созна́ния; о́бморок.

black sheep парши́вая овца́ (в семье́).

blacksmith *n.* кузне́ц.

blackthorn *n.* тёрн; терно́вник.

bladder *n.* пузы́рь. *Bladder cancer,* рак мочево́го пузыря́.

blade *n.* **1,** (of a tool) ле́звие. **2,** (of a weapon, esp. a sword) клино́к. **3,** (of an oar, propeller, etc.) ло́пасть; лопа́тка. **4,** (of a saw) полотно́. **5,** (of a fan, windmill, etc.) крыло́. **6,** (of an ice skate) по́лоз. **7,** (of a leaf) пласти́нка. **8,** (of grass) трави́нка; были́нка. **9,** *colloq.* (dashing young man) у́харь; хват. **—razor blade,** ле́звие бри́твы. **—shoulder blade,** лопа́тка.

blame *v.t.* вини́ть: *Don't blame me!,* не вини́те меня́! *I don't blame you,* я вас не виню́ *or* не обвиня́ю. *Blame everything on,* вали́ть *or* сва́ливать всё на (+ *acc.*); вини́ть во всём (+ *acc.*). *Blame all one's troubles on,* вини́ть во всех бе́дах (+ *acc.*). *You can't blame him for* *this,* нельзя́ вини́ть его́ в э́том. *You have only yourself to blame,* вы мо́жете (*or* должны́) вини́ть то́лько себя́; вам не́кого вини́ть, кро́ме самого́ себя́. —*n.* **1,** (responsibility) вина́: *place the blame on,* возлага́ть вину́ на. **2,** (censure) порица́ние: *deserve blame,* заслу́живать порица́ния. —**be to blame,** быть винова́тым: *I am to blame,* я винова́т(а).

blameless *adj.* невино́вный; неви́нный.

blameworthy *adj.* предосуди́тельный.

blanch *v.t.* (bleach) бели́ть. —*v.i.* (turn pale) бледне́ть.

bland *adj.* **1,** (mild; not irritating) мя́гкий. *Bland diet,* уме́ренная дие́та. **2,** (flavorless; dull) пре́сный; бесцве́тный.

blandishment *n.* угово́р.

blank *adj.* **1,** (not written on) пусто́й; чи́стый. *Blank space,* пусто́е ме́сто; пробе́л. *Blank page,* чи́стая страни́ца. *Blank sheet of paper,* пусто́й лист бума́ги. **2,** (of a cartridge, shot, etc.) холосто́й. **3,** (solid, as of a wall) глухо́й. **4,** (vacant, as of a look) отсу́тствующий; неви́дящий. —*n.* **1,** (space) пусто́е ме́сто; про́пуск. *Fill in the blanks,* запо́лнить про́пуски. **2,** (form) бланк; анке́та. **3,** (blank cartridge) холосто́й патро́н. **4,** (loss of memory) прова́л па́мяти: *My mind is a complete blank,* у меня́ по́лный прова́л па́мяти. —**draw a blank,** ничего́ не доби́ться. —**go blank, 1,** *My mind went blank,* у меня́ отши́бло па́мять. **2,** *The screen went blank,* с экра́на пропа́ло изображе́ние.

blanket *n.* **1,** (bed covering) одея́ло. **2,** *fig.* (mantle) покро́в: *blanket of snow,* сне́жный покро́в. —*adj.* огу́льный: *blanket assertion,* огу́льное утвержде́ние. —*v.t.* оку́тывать: *blanketed in fog,* оку́танный тума́ном. *Fog blanketed the valley,* тума́н лёг на доли́ну. *Snow blanketed the city,* го́род был покры́т сне́гом.

blankly *adv.* отсу́тствующим взгля́дом.

blank verse бе́лые стихи́.

blare *v.t. & i.* труби́ть. —*n.* тру́бный звук.

blarney *n.* лесть.

blasé *adj.* пресы́щенный.

blaspheme *v.i.* богоху́льствовать; кощу́нствовать. —*v.t.* поноси́ть; хули́ть.

blasphemous *adj.* богоху́льный; кощу́нственный. —**blasphemy,** *n.* богоху́льство; кощу́нство.

blast *n.* **1,** (gust of air) поры́в (ве́тра); струя́ (во́здуха). **2,** (loud sound, as of a trumpet) (тру́бный) звук. **3,** (explosion) взрыв. **4,** *colloq.* (verbal attack) вы́пад. —*v.t.* **1,** (blow up) взрыва́ть: *blast rock,* взрыва́ть скалу́. **2,** *colloq.* (assail) обру́шиваться на. —*v.i.* [*usu.* **blast off**] стартова́ть; отрыва́ться от земли́. —**(at) full blast,** по́лным хо́дом; на всю мощь. *The radio was on full blast,* ра́дио бы́ло включено́ на всю мощь.

blasted *adj., colloq.* прокля́тый.

blast furnace до́мна; до́менная печь.

blasting *n.* взрывны́е рабо́ты. —**blasting powder,** ми́нный по́рох.

blast-off *n.* старт.

blatant *adj.* **1,** (noisy) крикли́вый. **2,** (obvious) я́вный: *a blatant lie,* я́вная ложь.

blather *n.* пустосло́вие.

blaze *n.* **1,** (flame) пла́мя. **2,** (fire) ого́нь; пожа́р: *fight the blaze,* боро́ться с огнём/пожа́ром. —*v.i.* **1,** (burn) горе́ть; пыла́ть. **2,** (give off great heat) пали́ть: *the blazing sun,* паля́щее со́лнце. **3,** *fol. by* **away** (fire rapidly) открыва́ть ого́нь. —*v.t., in* **blaze a trail,** прокла́дывать путь. —**like blazes,** *colloq.* со всех ног; сломя́ го́лову.

blazer *n.* спорти́вная ку́ртка; бле́йзер.

bleach *v.t.* бели́ть; отбе́ливать. —*n.* бели́льное сре́дство. —**bleached,** *adj.* отбе́ленный; белёный.

bleaching *n.* беле́ние. —*adj.* бели́льный. —**bleaching powder,** хло́рная и́звесть.

bleak *adj.* **1,** (desolate) пусты́нный: *bleak landscape,* пусты́нный ландша́фт. **2,** (dismal; unpromising) мра́чный: *a bleak future,* мра́чное бу́дущее.

bleary-eyed *adj.* осолове́лый; посолове́лый.

bleat *v.i.* бле́ять. —*n.* бле́яние.

bleed *v.i.* кровоточи́ть. *His nose is bleeding,* у него́ кровь течёт и́з носу. *Bleed profusely,* истека́ть кро́вью. *Bleed to death,* умере́ть от поте́ри кро́ви. *My heart bleeds for you,* моё се́рдце за вас кро́вью облива́ется. —*v.t.* **1,** (take blood from) пуска́ть кровь (+ *dat.*). **2,** *colloq.* (extort money from) обира́ть; обдира́ть. —**bleed white,** обобра́ть до ни́тки.

bleeding *n.* кровотече́ние. —*adj.* кровоточа́щий. *Bleeding gums,* кровоточи́вость дёсен.

blemish *n.* пятно́. —*v.t.* пятна́ть.

blend *v.t.* сме́шивать. —*v.i.* **1,** (merge; unite) сме́шиваться; слива́ться. **2,** (go well together) гармони́ровать; сочета́ться. *Blend in with,* впи́сываться в (+ *acc.*). —*n.* смесь; смеше́ние.

blender *n.* сме́ситель.

bless *v.t.* **1,** (ask divine favor for) благословля́ть: *God bless you!,* да благослови́т тебя́ Бог. ♦*After a sneeze,* будь здоро́в(а)!; бу́дьте здоро́вы! **2,** (endow) наделя́ть: *blessed with outstanding ability,* наделён исключи́тельными спосо́бностями. *Be blessed with good health,* по́льзоваться хоро́шим здоро́вьем.

blessed *adj.* **1,** (holy) свяще́нный. **2,** (blissful) блаже́нный. *Of blessed memory,* блаже́нной *or* све́тлой па́мяти.

blessing *n.* **1,** (benediction) благослове́ние. **2,** (that which gives happiness) бла́го. **3,** (approval) благослове́ние: *with the blessing of,* с благослове́ния (+ *gen.*).

blight *n.* **1,** (plant disease) ожо́ги расте́ний. **2,** *fig.* (plague) бич. —*v.t.* вреди́ть; губи́ть.

blind *adj.* слепо́й. *Blind man,* слепо́й; слепе́ц. *Go blind,* (о)слепну́ть. *Blind in one eye,* слепо́й на оди́н глаз. —*adv.* вслепу́ю. —*v.t.* ослепля́ть. —*n.* што́ра. *Venetian blinds,* подъёмные жалюзи́. —**rob (someone) blind,** *colloq.* ободра́ть кого́-нибудь как ли́пку. —**turn a blind eye to,** закрыва́ть глаза́ на; смотре́ть сквозь па́льцы на.

blind alley тупи́к.

blinders *n.pl.* шо́ры; нагла́зники.

blindfold *n.* повя́зка (на глаза́х). —*v.t.* завя́зывать глаза́ (+ *dat.*).

blindfolded *adj.* с завя́занными глаза́ми. —*adv.* вслепу́ю.

blinding *adj.* ослепи́тельный.

blindly *adv.* слéпо; вслепу́ю.

blindman's bluff жму́рки.

blindness *n.* слепота́.

blink *v.i.* **1,** (wink; flash) мига́ть; морга́ть. **2,** *fol. by* **at** (pretend not to see) смотрéть сквозь па́льцы (на). —*v.t.* мига́ть; морга́ть (глаза́ми). *Without blinking an eye,* гла́зом не моргну́в. —*on the blink, colloq.* не рабо́тает.

blinker *n.* **1,** (flashing light) мига́лка. **2,** *pl.* (shades for a horse's eyes) шо́ры; нагла́зники.

bliss *n.* блажéнство. —**blissful,** *adj.* блажéнный.

blister *n.* волды́рь; пузы́рь.

blistering *adj.* **1,** (of heat) паля́щий. **2,** (scathing, as of criticism) разно́сный.

blithe *adj.* весёлый; беспéчный; жизнера́достный.

blitzkrieg *n.* молниено́сная война́.

blizzard *n.* метéль; вью́га; пурга́; бура́н.

bloat *v.t.* вздува́ть; раздува́ть. —**bloated,** *adj.* взду́тый; разду́тый.

blob *n.* ка́пля; ша́рик.

bloc *n.* блок.

block *n.* **1,** (solid piece) глы́ба: *block of ice,* глы́ба льда. **2,** (of wood) чурба́н. **3,** (chopping block) коло́да; (execution block) пла́ха. **4,** *usu. pl.* (children's building blocks) ку́бики. **5,** (city block) кварта́л. **6,** (mold for shaping hats) болва́н; болва́нка. **7,** (large building brick) блок. **8,** (pulley) блок. **9,** (in an engine) блок: *cylinder block,* блок цили́ндров. **10,** (obstruction) прегра́да; зато́р. **11,** *sports* (body block) блок. **12,** *philately* блок. **13,** *slang* (head) башка́. *Knock one's block off,* всы́пать по пéрвое число́. —*v.t.* **1,** (obstruct) прегражда́ть; загражда́ть; загора́живать; перекрыва́ть. *Block someone's way,* прегражда́ть путь (+ *dat.*). *Block an entrance,* загора́живать вход. *Block traffic,* меша́ть движéнию. *The road is blocked by snow,* доро́гу занесло́ снéгом. *Block someone's view of the stage,* загора́живать кому́-нибудь сцéну. *You're blocking my view,* я за ва́ми не ви́жу. *He completely blocked my view,* он закры́л мне весь вид. **2,** (clog) забива́ть. *Blocked artery,* заку́поренная артéрия. **3,** (thwart) блоки́ровать: *block an attempt by...,* блоки́ровать попы́тку (+ *gen.*). **4,** *sports* блоки́ровать. **5,** *fol. by* **out** (outline) намеча́ть; набра́сывать.

blockade *n.* блока́да. —*v.t.* блоки́ровать.

blockage *n.* **1,** (act of blocking) прегражде́ние. **2,** (obstruction; jam) прегра́да; зато́р. **3,** *med.* непроходи́мость; заку́порка.

blockhead *n.* болва́н; тупи́ца.

blockhouse *n.* блокга́уз.

block letters печа́тные бу́квы.

blond *n.* [*fem.* **blonde**] блонди́н; блонди́нка. —*adj.* белоку́рый.

blood *n.* кровь. *It's in his blood,* э́то у него́ в крови́. —*adj.* **1,** (pert. to blood) кровяно́й. **2,** (related by blood) кро́вный. —**bad blood,** вражда́: *There is bad*

blood between them, они́ пита́ют вражду́ друг к дру́гу. —**in cold blood,** хладнокро́вно.

blood bank банк кро́ви.

blood bath крова́вая ба́ня.

blood clot сгу́сток кро́ви.

bloodcurdling *adj.* душераздира́ющий; исто́шный.

bloodhound *n.* ищéйка.

bloodless *adj.* бескро́вный.

bloodletting *n.* **1,** (drawing of blood) кровопуска́ние. **2,** (bloodshed) кровопроли́тие.

blood orange королёк.

blood poisoning зараже́ние кро́ви.

blood pressure кровяно́е давлéние.

bloodshed *n.* кровопроли́тие.

bloodshot *adj.* на́литый кро́вью. *Become bloodshot,* нали́ться кро́вью.

bloodstain *n.* кровяно́е *or* крова́вое пятно́. —**bloodstained,** *adj.* окрова́вленный.

bloodstream *n.* ток кро́ви.

bloodsucker *n.* **1,** (leech) пия́вка. **2,** (extortionist) кровопи́йца.

blood test ана́лиз *or* исслéдование кро́ви.

bloodthirsty *adj.* кровожа́дный.

blood transfusion перелива́ние кро́ви.

blood type гру́ппа кро́ви.

blood vessel кровено́сный сосу́д.

bloody *adj.* крова́вый. *Bloody battle,* крова́вый *or* кровопроли́тный бой. —*v.t.* окрова́вить. *Bloody someone's nose,* разби́ть кому́-нибудь нос.

bloom *v.i.* цвести́. —*n.* цвет: *in full bloom,* в по́лном цвету́. *Burst into bloom,* расцвета́ть; зацвести́. *Lose its bloom,* отцвета́ть.

bloomers *n.pl.* пантало́ны.

blossom *n.* цвет: *apple blossom,* я́блоневый цвет. —*v.i.* цвести́; расцвета́ть.

blot *n.* пятно́. *Inkblot,* кля́кса. —*v.t.* **1,** (stain) пятна́ть. **2,** (dry; soak up) промока́ть. —**blot out, 1,** (hide; cover; obscure) затмева́ть. **2,** (efface; erase) изгла́живать. **3,** (destroy) уничтожа́ть.

blotch *n.* **1,** (spot) пятно́. **2,** (blemish on the skin) прыщ.

blotter *n.* промока́шка.

blotting paper промока́тельная бума́га.

blouse *n.* блу́зка; ко́фточка.

blow *n.* **1,** (hard stroke; shock) уда́р: *with one blow,* одни́м уда́ром. *They came to blows,* у них дошло́ до дра́ки. *A blow to the family,* уда́р для семьи́. **2,** (blast of air) дуновéние. *Blow the candles out with one blow,* заду́ть свéчи одни́м дуновéнием (*or* одни́м вы́дохом). —*v.i.* **1,** (of the wind) дуть. **2,** (of a car horn, whistle, etc.) гудéть. **3,** (puff) дуть: *blow on one's fingers,* дуть на па́льцы. **4,** (be carried by the wind) летéть. *The paper blew away,* бума́жка улетéла. *Her hair was blowing in the wind,* её во́лосы развева́лись на ветру́ *or* по вéтру. *The door blew open/shut,* двéрь распахну́лась/захло́пнулась от вéтра. *The hurricane blew out to sea,* урага́н ушёл/отошёл/отодви́нулся в мо́ре. **5,** (of a fuse) перегорéть. —*v.t.* **1,** (drive by blowing) гнать (ли́стья); развева́ть (фла́ги). *Blow dust from the* *shelf,* сдува́ть пыль с по́лки. *Blow smoke in someone's face,* пуска́ть дым в лицо́ (+ *dat.*). *The ship was blown off course,* кора́бль снесло́ с ку́рса. **2,** (make, as glass, bubbles, etc.) выдува́ть (стекло́); пуска́ть (мы́льные пузыри́). **3,** (cause to sound, as a horn) труби́ть (в рог); (a whistle) дать (свисто́к); (a car horn) дать (гудо́к); гуде́ть. **4,** (clear, as one's nose) сморка́ть (нос); сморка́ться. **5,** *slang* (squander) транжи́рить; спуска́ть. **6,** *Blow a kiss,* посла́ть возду́шный поцелу́й. **7,** *in* **blow a fuse; blow one's top; blow one's stack,** *colloq.* взорва́ться. —**blow away,** сдува́ть. —**blow down,** сва́ливать. —**blow off, 1,** (blow away) сдува́ть; срыва́ть; сноси́ть. *The wind blew my hat off,* ве́тер сорва́л с меня́ шля́пу. *The hurricane blew off the roof,* урага́ном снесло́ кры́шу. *Also intrans.: My hat blew off,* у меня́ сду́ло шля́пу. **2,** (give off, as steam) выпуска́ть. **3,** *Blow off steam, fig., colloq.* дать вы́ход свои́м чу́вствам. —**blow out, 1,** (extinguish by blowing) задува́ть; туши́ть. **2,** (remove by blowing) выдува́ть. **3,** (clean out by blowing) продува́ть. **4,** (burst, as of a tire) ло́пнуть. **5,** (fail, as of a bulb) перегоре́ть. **6,** *Blow one's brains out,* пусти́ть себе́ пу́лю в лоб. —**blow over, 1,** (topple) сва́ливать. **2,** (end; pass, as of a storm or incident) проходи́ть; минова́ть; конча́ться. —**blow up, 1,** (inflate) надува́ть. **2,** (destroy) взрыва́ть; подрыва́ть. **3,** *photog.* (enlarge) увели́чивать. **4,** (exaggerate) раздува́ть. **5,** (explode) взорва́ться. **6,** *colloq.* (lose one's temper) взорва́ться. **7,** (of a storm) налета́ть.

blower *n.* вентиля́тор.

blowgun *n.* духово́е ружьё.

blowout *n.* разры́в (ши́ны). *I had a blowout,* у меня́ ло́пнула ши́на.

blowpipe *n.* пая́льная тру́бка.

blowtorch *n.* пая́льная ла́мпа.

blubber *n.* во́рвань.

bludgeon *n.* дуби́на; дуби́нка. —*v.t.* бить дуби́ной; дуба́сить.

blue *adj.* **1,** (color) си́ний (*dark*); голубо́й (*light*). *Turn blue from the cold,* посине́ть от хо́лода. **2,** (depressed) уны́лый; пода́вленный. —*n.* си́ний цвет; синева́. —*v.t.* подси́нивать. —**appear out of the blue,** с не́ба свали́ться. —**from out of the blue,** отку́да ни возьми́сь. —**once in a blue moon,** в ко́и-то ве́ки. *See also* **blues.**

bluebell *n.* колоко́льчик.

blueberry *n.* черни́ка. —*adj.* черни́чный: *blueberry pie,* черни́чный пиро́г.

blue-eyed *adj.* синегла́зый.

bluefish *n.* луфа́рь.

blue-gray *adj.* си́зый.

blueprint *n.* си́нька.

blues *n.pl.* **1,** (melancholy) хандра́. *Have the blues,* хандри́ть. **2,** *music* блюз.

bluff *v.t.* обма́нывать; вводи́ть в заблужде́ние. —*v.i.* блефова́ть. —*n.* **1,** (deception) блеф. **2,** (cliff) обры́в; утёс. —**call someone's bluff,** заста́вить кого́-нибудь раскры́ть свои́ ка́рты.

bluing *n.* си́нька.

bluish *adj.* синева́тый; голубова́тый.

blunder *n.* про́мах; опло́шность. —*v.i.* гру́бо ошиба́ться; оплоша́ть; промахну́ться.

blunt *adj.* **1,** (not sharp) тупо́й. **2,** (frank; straightforward) прямо́й. —*v.t.* притупля́ть. —**bluntly,** *adv.* пря́мо; начистоту́.

bluntness *n.* **1,** (dullness) ту́пость. **2,** (frankness) прямота́.

blur *v.t.* **1,** (obscure) затума́нивать. **2,** (make fuzzy, as a photograph) сма́зывать. *Come out blurred,* сма́зываться. —**blurry,** *adj.* расплы́вчатый.

blurt *v.t.* [*usu.* **blurt out**] сболтну́ть; вы́палить.

blush *v.i.* красне́ть. *Make someone blush,* вгоня́ть кого́-нибудь в кра́ску. —*n.* кра́ска стыда́. —**at first blush,** на пе́рвый взгля́д.

bluster *v.i.* **1,** (blow stormily) бушева́ть. **2,** (speak noisily or threateningly) куражи́ться. —*n.* пусты́е слова́; пусты́е угро́зы.

boa *n.* **1,** (snake) уда́в. **2,** (scarf) боа́. —**boa constrictor,** боа́.

boar *n.* **1,** (male hog) хряк. **2,** (wild boar) каба́н.

board *n.* **1,** (wooden strip; flat surface) доска́. *Bulletin board,* доска́ объявле́ний. *Ironing board,* глади́льная доска́. **2,** (meals) стол: *room and board,* кварти́ра и стол; пансио́н. **3,** (group of officials) правле́ние; управле́ние; сове́т; коми́ссия; колле́гия. *Board of directors,* сове́т директоро́в. *Board of inquiry,* сле́дственная коми́ссия. *Editorial board,* редакцио́нная колле́гия. *Be on the board,* быть чле́ном правле́ния. —*v.t.* **1,** *fol. by* **up** (cover with boards) забива́ть; заколоти́ть. **2,** (get on) сади́ться в *or* на: *board the aircraft/train,* сесть в *or* на самолёт/по́езд. *Board the ship,* сесть на парохо́д. **3,** (come alongside, as an enemy ship) брать на аборда́ж. —*v.i.* сесть в *or* на самолёт. —**on board,** на борту́; на борт; на́ борт. *Take on board (the aircraft),* брать *or* принима́ть на борт *or* на́ борт (самолёта).

boarder *n.* пансионе́р.

boarding *n.* поса́дка. —**boarding pass,** поса́дочный тало́н.

boarding house пансио́н.

boarding school шко́ла-интерна́т.

boardwalk *n.* доща́тый насти́л (на пля́же).

boast *v.i.* хвали́ться; хва́статься: *boast to someone about one's children,* хвали́ться/хва́статься пе́ред кем-нибудь свои́ми детьми́. —*v.t.* (proudly possess) горди́ться (+ *instr.*); мочь похва́статься (+ *instr.*); быть счастли́вым облада́телем (+ *gen.*). —*n.* хвастовство́. —**boastful,** *adj.* хвастли́вый.

boat *n.* **1,** (small vessel) ло́дка: *motor boat,* мото́рная ло́дка. **2,** (ship) парохо́д. —*adj.* ло́дочный: *boat races,* ло́дочные го́нки. —**in the same boat,** в тако́м же положе́нии. —**miss the boat,** *colloq.* прозева́ть удо́бный слу́чай.

boathouse *n.* ло́дочный сара́й.

boating *n.* ло́дочный спорт; ката́ние на ло́дке. *Go boating,* ката́ться на ло́дке.

boatman *n.* ло́дочник.

boatswain *n.* бо́цман.

bob *n.* **1,** (quick jerking motion) рыво́к. **2,** (knoblike weight) груз отве́са. **3,** (fishing float) поплаво́к. **4,** (short curl or knob of hair) завито́к. —*v.i. Bob up and down,* подпры́гивать. *Bob on the waves,* пока́чиваться на волна́х. —*v.t.* (cut short) ко́ротко стричь.

bobbin *n.* кату́шка; шпу́лька.

bobby *n., Brit., colloq.* полисме́н.

bobby pin зако́лка.

bobcat *n.* америка́нская рысь.

bobsled *n.* бо́бслей. *Also,* **bobsleigh.**

bode *v.t. & i.* предвеща́ть: *bode well,* предвеща́ть хоро́шее.

bodice *n.* лиф; корса́ж.

bodily *adj.* теле́сный: *bodily injuries,* теле́сные повреждéния. —*adv.* со́бственной персо́ной. *Throw someone bodily out of the room,* вы́швырнуть кого́-нибудь из ко́мнаты.

body *n.* **1,** (human form) те́ло: *the human body,* челове́ческое те́ло. **2,** (one's system) органи́зм: *the body's immune system,* имму́нная систе́ма органи́зма. **3,** (corpse) труп: *an unidentified body,* неопо́знанный труп. *Over my dead body!,* то́лько че́рез мой труп! **4,** (substance) те́ло: *foreign body,* иноро́дное *or* посторо́ннее те́ло. **5,** (object in space) те́ло: *celestial body,* небе́сное те́ло. **6,** *Body of water,* во́дное простра́нство; водоём. **7,** (of various devices) ко́рпус; (of a car) ку́зов; (of an airplane) фюзеля́ж. **8,** (central part, as of a book) основна́я часть. **9,** (group of persons) о́рган; коллекти́в: *legislative body,* законода́тельный о́рган; *student body,* студе́нческий коллекти́в. **10,** (amount; collection) коли́чество: *a large body of opinion,* большо́е коли́чество мне́ний. *A whole body of evidence,* це́лый ряд свиде́тельств. **11,** (density) пло́тность; про́чность. **12,** (consistency; strength, as of wine) кре́пость. —*adj. Body temperature,* температу́ра те́ла. —**body and soul,** душо́й и те́лом. —**keep body and soul together,** подде́рживать существова́ние; перебива́ться.

body check *sports* силово́й приём.

bodyguard *n.* телохрани́тель.

Boer *n.* бур. —*adj.* бу́рский. *Boer War,* а́нгло-бу́рская война́.

bog *n.* боло́то; тряси́на; топь. —*v.t. Become bogged down (in),* увяза́ть (в); погряза́ть (в). —*v.i. [usu.* **bog down**] (peter out) захлёбываться.

bogeyman *n.* бу́ка.

boggle *v.t.* потряса́ть: *boggle the mind,* потряса́ть ум.

boggy *adj.* боло́тистый.

bogus *adj.* подде́льный; фальши́вый.

Bohemian *adj.* **1,** (of or from Bohemia) боге́мский. **2,** (unconventional) боге́мный.

boil *v.t.* **1,** (bring to a boiling point, as water) кипяти́ть. **2,** (cook, as eggs) вари́ть. —*v.i.* кипе́ть: *The water/kettle is boiling,* вода́/ча́йник кипи́т. —*n.* **1,** (boiling state) кипе́ние: *bring to a boil,* доводи́ть до кипе́ния. **2,** (skin sore) нары́в; фуру́нкул. —**boil down,** своди́ть(ся): *boil (something) down to a few basic points,* своди́ть к не́скольким основны́м пу́нктам. *The whole thing*

boils down to this, всё де́ло сво́дится к э́тому. —**boil over,** убега́ть.

boiled *adj.* варёный; кипячёный; отварно́й.

boiler *n.* (парово́й) котёл; куб. —**boiler plate,** коте́льное желе́зо; коте́льный лист. —**boiler room,** коте́льная; коте́льное отделе́ние.

boilerman *n.* истопни́к.

boiling *adj.* кипя́щий. *Boiling water,* кипято́к. —**boiling hot,** горя́чий как кипято́к. —**boiling point,** то́чка кипе́ния.

boisterous *adj.* шумли́вый; бу́йный.

bold *adj.* **1,** (daring) сме́лый. **2,** (brazen) де́рзкий. **3,** (distinct to the eye) чёткий. **4,** *printing* жи́рный. —**make bold (to),** осме́ливаться (+ *inf.*).

boldface *n.* жи́рный шрифт. —*adj.* жи́рный.

bold-faced *adj.* **1,** (brazen) на́глый. **2,** *printing* жи́рный.

boldly *adv.* сме́ло.

boldness *n.* сме́лость.

boll *n., bot.* коро́бочка. —**boll weevil,** хло́пковый долгоно́сик.

bologna *n.* копчёная колбаса́.

Bolshevik *n.* большеви́к. —*adj.* большеви́стский.

bolster *n.* ва́лик. —*v.t.* подде́рживать; подкрепля́ть. *Bolster someone's spirits,* поднима́ть чьё-нибудь настрое́ние.

bolt *n.* **1,** (metal pin) болт. **2,** (sliding bar that locks) засо́в; задви́жка; шпингале́т. **3,** (sliding mechanism for a rifle) затво́р. **4,** (roll of material) руло́н. **5,** (of thunder or lightning) уда́р (гро́ма/мо́лнии). —*v.t.* **1,** (fasten with bolts) скрепля́ть болта́ми. **2,** (lock) закрыва́ть на засо́в *or* на задви́жку; задвига́ть. **3,** (break away from, as a political party) порва́ть с. —*v.i.* **1,** (dash; dart) бро́ситься: *bolt from the room,* бро́ситься вон из ко́мнаты. **2,** (of a horse) понести́. —**like a bolt from the blue,** (свали́ться) как снег на́ голову; как гром среди́ я́сного не́ба.

bomb *n.* бо́мба. —*adj.* бо́мбовый: *bomb load,* бо́мбовая нагру́зка. —*v.t.* бомбардирова́ть; бомби́ть. —**bomb out,** разбомби́ть: *bombed-out buildings,* разбомблённые зда́ния.

bombard *v.t.* **1,** (bomb) бомбардирова́ть. **2,** (shower, as with questions) забра́сывать (+ *instr.*); засы́пать (+ *instr.*).

bombardier *n.* бомбарди́р.

bombardment *n.* бомбардиро́вка. *Artillery bombardment,* артиллери́йский обстре́л.

bombast *n.* напы́щенность; высокопа́рность. —**bombastic,** *adj.* напы́щенный; высокопа́рный.

bomb bay бо́мбовый отсе́к.

bomber *n.* бомбардиро́вщик.

bombing *n.* бомбардиро́вка; бомбомета́ние.

bombshell *n.* бо́мба. *Political bombshell,* полити́ческая бо́мба.

bomb shelter бомбоубе́жище.

bombsight *n.* бомбардиро́вочный прице́л.

bona fide 1, (made in good faith) доброcо́вестный. **2,** (genuine) по́длинный.

bond *n.* **1,** (tie) связь. *Bonds of friendship,* у́зы дру́жбы. **2,** *pl.* (shackles) пу́ты; око́вы. **3,** *finance* облига́ция. **4,** (bail) пору́ка: *post bond for,* брать на пору́ки.

bondage *n.* ра́бство.

bondsman *n.* **1,** (guarantor) поручи́тель. **2,** (slave) раб. **—bondswoman,** *n.* раба́; рабы́ня.

bone *n.* кость. **—***adj.* ко́стный: *bone tissue/disease,* ко́стная ткань/боле́знь. **—***v.t.* вынима́ть ко́сти из. **—***v.i.* [*usu.* **bone up**] *slang* зубри́ть. **—bag of bones,** ко́жа да ко́сти. **—bone of contention,** я́блоко раздо́ра. **—chilled to the bone,** продро́гший до мо́зга косте́й. **—feel in one's bones,** чу́вствовать всем свои́м существо́м, (что...). **—have a bone to pick with,** име́ть счёты с. **—make no bones about,** не де́лать секре́та из.

bonehead *n., slang* болва́н; остоло́п.

boneless *adj.* беско́стный.

bone meal костяна́я мука́.

boner *n., slang* про́мах; опло́шность.

bonfire *n.* костёр.

bonnet *n.* **1,** (lady's hat) ка́пор; (child's hat) че́пчик. **2,** *Brit.* (hood of a car) капо́т.

bonus *n.* пре́мия; премиа́льные.

bon vivant жуи́р.

bon voyage счастли́вого пути́!

bony *adj.* **1,** (having many bones) кости́стый; костля́вый. **2,** (skinny) костля́вый.

boo *v.t. & i.* освИ́стывать.

booby *n.* болва́н; балбе́с.

booby trap ми́на-лову́шка.

book *n.* кни́га. **—***adj.* кни́жный: *book learning,* кни́жные зна́ния. **—***v.t.* (reserve) зака́зывать; брони́ровать. *We're all booked up,* все места́ за́няты; свобо́дных мест нет. **—be on the books,** быть на учёте. **—go by the book,** поступа́ть по пра́вилам. **—in my book,** на мой взгляд. **—keep the books,** вести́ кни́ги. **—know like a book,** знать как свои́ пять па́льцев.

bookbinder *n.* переплётчик. **—bookbinding,** *n.* переплётное де́ло.

bookcase *n.* кни́жный шкаф; этаже́рка.

bookend *n.* подста́вка для книг.

bookish *adj.* кни́жный.

bookkeeper *n.* бухга́лтер; счетово́д. **—bookkeeping,** *n.* бухгалте́рия; бухга́лтерский учёт; счетово́дство.

booklet *n.* кни́жечка; брошю́ра; букле́т.

bookmaker *n.* букме́кер.

bookmark *n.* закла́дка.

bookmobile *n.* библиоте́ка-передви́жка.

bookplate *n.* экслИ́брис; кни́жный знак.

book review реце́нзия на кни́гу.

bookseller *n.* продаве́ц книг. *Secondhand bookseller,* букинИ́ст.

bookshelf *n.* кни́жная по́лка; *pl.* стелла́ж для книг.

bookstore *n.* кни́жный магази́н.

bookworm *n.* кни́жный червь.

boom *n.* **1,** (deep rumbling sound) гул; гро́хот. **2,** (rapid rise) бум. **3,** (arm of a derrick) стрела́. **—***v.i.* **1,** (make a deep rumbling sound) греме́ть; грохота́ть. *Booming voice,* гу́лкий *or* громово́й го́лос. **2,** (flourish) процвета́ть. **—***interj.* бум!

boomerang *n.* бумера́нг. **—***v.i.* возыме́ть обра́тное де́йствие.

boon *n.* бла́го: *a boon to the city,* бла́го для го́рода. *A boon to progress,* толчо́к к прогре́ссу.

boondocks *n.pl., slang* глушь; захолу́стье.

boor *n.* хам; неве́жа; грубия́н. **—boorish,** *adj.* ха́мский. **—boorishness,** *n.* ха́мство.

boost *v.t.* **1,** (lift) поднима́ть. **2,** (raise, as prices) повыша́ть. **3,** (increase) увели́чивать. **—***n.* **1,** (lift) подъём. **2,** (help) соде́йствие. **3,** (raise) повыше́ние.

booster *n.* **1,** *electricity* усили́тель. **2,** *rocketry* ускори́тель. **3,** (enthusiastic supporter) патрио́т. **—booster rocket,** раке́та-носи́тель; раке́тный ускори́тель; ста́ртовый раке́тный дви́гатель.

boot *n.* **1,** (shoe) боти́нок; сапо́г. **2,** (kick) пино́к. **3,** *Brit.* (trunk of a car) бага́жник. **—***v.t.* **1,** (kick) пина́ть. **2,** *usu. fol. by* **out,** *slang* (expel) вы́гнать; вы́швырнуть. **—give the boot to,** выгоня́ть с рабо́ты. *He got the boot,* он был вы́гнан; он вы́летел. **—lick someone's boots,** лиза́ть пя́тки (+ *dat.*). **—to boot,** вдоба́вок; в прида́чу.

bootblack *n.* чи́стильщик сапо́г.

booth *n.* **1,** (small compartment) бу́дка; каби́на. *Telephone booth,* телефо́нная бу́дка. *Voting/polling booth,* каби́на для голосова́ния. **2,** (stall; stand) кио́ск; ларёк; пала́тка. *Change booth,* разме́нная ка́сса.

bootlicker *n.* лизоблю́д; подли́за.

booty *n.* добы́ча; трофе́и.

booze *n., colloq.* хмельно́е.

borax *n.* бура́.

border *n.* **1,** (boundary) грани́ца. **2,** (trim) кайма́; каёмка; бордю́р. **—***adj.* пограни́чный: *border post,* пограни́чный пост; пограни́чная заста́ва. **—***v.t.* **1,** (lie adjacent to) грани́чить с. **2,** (put a border or edging on) окаймля́ть; обшива́ть. **—***v.i.* [*usu.* **border on**] грани́чить с: *border on treason,* грани́чить с преда́тельством. **—border guard,** грани́чник.

bore *n.* **1,** (of a firearm) кана́л; (diameter of same) кали́бр. *Small-bore rifle,* малокали́берная винто́вка. **2,** (tiresome person) ску́чный *or* ну́дный челове́к. **—***v.t.* **1,** (drill) сверли́ть; бури́ть. *Bore a hole,* просве́рливать отве́рстие. **2,** (tire) надоеда́ть.

bored *adj.* ску́чный. *I am bored,* мне ску́чно; мне надое́ло. *Bored look,* скуча́ющий вид.

boredom *n.* ску́ка; тоска́.

boric *adj.* бо́рный. **—boric acid,** бо́рная кислота́.

boring *adj.* **1,** (used for drilling) бурово́й; бури́льный; сверли́льный. **2,** (tiresome) ску́чный; надое́дливый.

born *adj.* **1,** (brought forth by birth) рождённый: *born out of wedlock,* рождённый вне бра́ка. *I was born in France,* я роди́лся (родила́сь) во Фра́нции. *He was born to fly,* он рождён лета́ть. **2,** (having the natural talent of) прирождённый: *a born poet,* прирождё́нный поэ́т. **—in all one's born days,** за всю свою́ жизнь.

boron *n.* (element) бор.

borough *n.* городо́к.

borrow *v.t.* **1,** (take temporarily) брать: *borrow a book from the library,* брать кни́гу в библиоте́ке *or* из библиоте́ки. *May I borrow your pen for a moment?*, мо́жно попроси́ть на мину́ту ва́шу ру́чку? **2,** (receive as a loan) занима́ть; брать в долг; брать взаймы́. *Borrow money from someone,* занима́ть де́ньги у кого́-нибудь. **3,** (adopt; take over) заи́мствовать: *The word пейза́ж is borrowed from the French,* сло́во «пейза́ж» заи́мствовано из францу́зского языка́. —*v.i.* брать взаймы́: *borrow against future income,* брать взаймы́ под бу́дущие дохо́ды. —**borrower,** *n.* заёмщик.

borrowing *n.* **1,** *finance* за́ймы: *government borrowing,* за́ймы прави́тельства. **2,** (borrowed word) заи́мствование: *foreign borrowing,* иностра́нное *or* иноязы́чное заи́мствование.

borscht *also,* **borsch** *n.* борщ.

borzoi *n.* борза́я.

Bosnian *adj.* босни́йский.

bosom *n.* **1,** (breast) грудь. **2,** (space between the breast and covering garment) па́зуха: *remove from one's bosom,* вынима́ть из-за па́зухи. **3,** *fig.* (source of feelings) душа́. —**bosom friend,** закады́чный друг.

boss *n.* **1,** (employer; superior) нача́льник. **2,** (political chief) босс. —*v.t.* **1,** (manage) управля́ть. **2,** *fol. by* **around** (order about) кома́ндовать над.

bossy *adj.* вла́стный.

botany *n.* бота́ника. —**botanical,** *adj.* ботани́ческий. —**botanist,** *n.* бота́ник.

botch *v.t.* напу́тать.

both *adj.* о́ба; о́бе: *both boys,* о́ба ма́льчика; *with both hands,* обе́ими рука́ми. *On both sides of the street,* по обе́им сторона́м у́лицы. *People of both sexes,* ли́ца обо́его по́ла. —*pron.* о́ба; о́бе; и тот и друго́й. *Both of them are here,* они́ о́ба здесь. —*conj.* и... и; как..., так и: *He speaks both English and Russian,* он говори́т и по-англи́йски и по-ру́сски. *Both in London and Paris,* как в Ло́ндоне, так и в Пари́же.

bother *v.t.* **1,** (disturb) меша́ть: *No one will bother us here,* здесь нам никто́ не бу́дет меша́ть. **2,** (worry; trouble; cause discomfort to) беспоко́ить. —*v.i.* (take the trouble) беспоко́иться; (по)труди́ться: *Don't bother!,* не беспоко́йтесь!; не труди́тесь! *He didn't even bother to ask permission,* он да́же не потруди́лся попроси́ть разреше́ния. —*n.* **1,** (trouble) беспоко́йство. **2,** (nuisance; annoyance) доса́да.

bothersome *adj.* надое́дливый.

bottle *n.* буты́лка: *bottle of milk,* буты́лка молока́. *Milk bottle,* буты́лка из-под молока́. *Beer bottle,* буты́лка из-под пи́ва. *Ink bottle,* пузырёк для черни́л. *Medicine bottle,* скля́нка для лека́рств. *Perfume bottle,* флако́н для духо́в. *Infant's bottle,* рожо́к. —*v.t.* **1,** (put in bottles) разлива́ть по буты́лкам. **2,** *fol. by* **up** (stifle) сде́рживать. —**hit the bottle,** *slang* выпива́ть.

bottled *adj.* буты́лочный: *bottled beer,* буты́лочное пи́во.

bottleneck *n.* у́зкое ме́сто.

bottom *n.* дно: *bottom of a river/canyon,* дно реки́/каньо́на. *Bottom of a ship/barrel,* дно *or* дни́ще су́дна/бо́чки. *Bottom of a hill,* подно́жие холма́. *At the bottom of the stairs/page/list,* внизу́ ле́стницы/

страни́цы; в конце́ спи́ска. *Send a ship to the bottom,* пусти́ть *or* отпра́вить су́дно ко дну *or* на дно. *The ship sank to the bottom,* су́дно пошло́ ко дну. —*adj.* ни́жний: *the bottom step,* ни́жняя ступе́нька. —**at bottom,** в су́щности; по существу́. —**bottoms up!,** до дна! —**from the bottom of one's heart,** от всего́ се́рдца; от всей души́. —**from top to bottom,** све́рху до́низу. —**get to the bottom of,** добра́ться до су́ти (+ *gen.*).

bottomless *adj.* бездо́нный.

boudoir *n.* будуа́р.

bough *n.* сук.

bouillon *n.* бульо́н.

boulder *n.* валу́н.

boulevard *n.* проспе́кт.

bounce *v.i.* **1,** (rebound) пры́гать. *Bounce off,* отска́кивать от. **2,** (leap; spring) вска́кивать: *bounce out of bed,* вска́кивать с посте́ли. —*v.t.* **1,** (a ball) бить (мячо́м) о зе́млю. **2,** *slang* (dismiss; kick out) выгоня́ть. —*n.* **1,** (rebound) отско́к. *Catch the ball on the first bounce,* пойма́ть мяч с пе́рвого отско́ка. **2,** (resiliency) упру́гость. —**bounce back,** (recover quickly) оправля́ться.

bouncer *n., colloq.* вышиба́ла.

bouncy *adj.* **1,** (resilient) упру́гий: *bouncy cushions,* упру́гие поду́шки. **2,** (brisk; lively) задо́рный: *bouncy tune,* задо́рный моти́в.

bound *n.* **1,** (leap) прыжо́к; скачо́к. **2,** *pl.* (limits) грани́цы; преде́лы. *Exceed the bounds of...,* вы́йти за преде́лы (+ *gen.*). *Know no bounds,* не знать грани́ц. —*adj.* **1,** (tied) свя́занный: *bound hand and foot,* свя́занный по рука́м и нога́м. **2,** (of a book) в переплёте. **3,** (obligated) обя́занный. *You are not bound by this agreement,* э́то соглаше́ние вас ни к чему́ не обя́зывает. **4,** (headed for): *The train is bound for Moscow,* по́езд направля́ется в Москву́; по́езд сле́дует до Москвы́. **5,** (certain; sure): *It was bound to happen,* э́то и должно́ бы́ло случи́ться. *He is bound to find out about it,* он непреме́нно узна́ет об э́том. —*v.i.* **1,** (leap) пры́гать. *Bound over the fence,* перескочи́ть че́рез забо́р. *Bound out of bed,* вскочи́ть *or* соскочи́ть с посте́ли. **2,** *fol. by* **back** *or* **off** (rebound) отска́кивать (от). —*v.t.* [*usu. passive*] (border) грани́чить с: *Sweden is bounded on the west by Norway,* на за́паде Шве́ция грани́чит с Норве́гией. —**out of bounds,** *sports* вне игры́.

boundary *n.* грани́ца. —*adj.* пограни́чный. *Boundary marker,* пограни́чный *or* межево́й знак; пограни́чная ве́ха.

boundless *adj.* безграни́чный; беспреде́льный; безбре́жный; необозри́мый.

bounteous *adj.* = **bountiful.**

bountiful *adj.* **1,** (generous) ще́дрый. **2,** (abundant) оби́льный.

bounty *n.* **1,** (generosity) ще́дрость. **2,** (gift) дар. **3,** (reward) награ́да.

bouquet *n.* буке́т.

bourgeois *n.* буржуа́. —*adj.* буржуа́зный. —**bourgeoisie,** *n.* буржуази́я.

bout *n.* **1,** (contest) встре́ча; бой. **2,** (siege, as of illness) при́ступ. —**drinking bout,** запо́й; попо́йка.

boutonniere *n.* бутонье́рка.

bovine *adj.* бы́чий.

bow[1] (bau) *v.i.* **1,** (bend one's head or body) кла́няться. **2,** *fol. by* **down** (kneel) преклоня́ться. **3,** (yield) уступа́ть; поддава́ться; склоня́ться. *Bow to pressure,* уступа́ть/поддава́ться давле́нию. *Bow to the will of,* подчиня́ться во́ле (+ *gen.*). *Bow to the inevitable,* склоня́ться пе́ред неизбе́жным. —*v.t.* склоня́ть; наклоня́ть: *bow one's head,* склоня́ть/ наклоня́ть го́лову. —*n.* **1,** (bending of the head or body) покло́н. *Take a bow,* раскла́ниваться. **2,** (of a ship) нос. —**bow and scrape,** низкопокло́нничать. —**bow out,** выходи́ть; выбыва́ть.

bow[2] (bo) *n.* **1,** (for shooting arrows) лук. **2,** (for playing the violin) смычо́к. **3,** (knot) бант: *tied with a bow,* завя́занный ба́нтом.

bowel *n.* **1,** (intestine) кишка́; *pl.* кишки́; кише́чник. *Bowel movement,* стул. *Move one's bowels,* испражня́ться. **2,** *pl.* (innermost part) не́дра: *bowels of the earth,* не́дра земли́.

bower *n.* бесе́дка.

bowl *n.* **1,** (deep dish) ми́ска; глубо́кая таре́лка. **2,** (vase) ва́за. **3,** (of a toilet) унита́з. —*v.i.* (go bowling) игра́ть в ке́гли. —**bowl over, 1,** (knock down) свали́ть с ног. **2,** (stun) ошеломля́ть.

bowlegged *adj.* кривоно́гий.

bowler *n.* **1,** (one who bowls) игро́к в ке́гли. **2,** (hat) котело́к.

bowling *n.* (игра́ в) ке́гли. —**bowling alley,** кегельба́н.

bowls *n.* игра́ в шары́.

bowman *n.* стрело́к из лу́ка.

bowsprit *n.* бу́шприт.

bowstring *n.* тетива́.

bow tie ба́бочка; га́лстук-ба́бочка.

box *n.* **1,** (large, for storing or carrying things) я́щик; (small) коро́бка: *box of matches/candy,* коро́бка спи́чек/конфе́т. *Cardboard box,* карто́нка. **2,** *theat.* ло́жа. **3,** (booth) бу́дка: *sentry box,* карау́льная бу́дка. **4,** (blow) пощёчина. **5,** (species of tree) самши́т. —*v.t.* **1,** (put in a box) укла́дывать в я́щик. **2,** (strike) дать пощёчину (+ *dat.*). **3,** *fol. by* **in** (crowd; squeeze) втискивать. —*v.i.* бокси́ровать.

boxcar *n.* кры́тый ваго́н.

boxer *n.* **1,** (pugilist) боксёр. **2,** (dog) боксёр.

boxing *n.* бокс. —**boxing glove,** боксёрская перча́тка.

box office (театра́льная *or* биле́тная) ка́сса. *Be doing well at the box office,* де́лать хоро́шие сбо́ры; име́ть большо́й ка́ссовый успе́х. —**box-office receipts,** сбо́ры.

box seat ме́сто в ло́же.

boy *n.* ма́льчик.

boyar *n.* боя́рин.

boycott *n.* бойко́т. —*v.t.* бойкоти́ровать.

boyfriend *n.* прия́тель.

boyhood *n.* де́тство.

boyish *adj.* мальчи́шеский.

boy scout ска́ут.

bra *n.* бюстга́льтер.

brace *n.* **1,** (clamp) скоба́; скре́па. **2,** (tool holding a bit) коловоро́т. **3,** (pair; couple) па́ра. **4,** *pl., Brit.* (suspenders) подтя́жки. —*v.t.* **1,** (fasten) скрепля́ть. **2,** (invigorate) бодри́ть. —**brace oneself,** напряга́ться; собира́ться с си́лами.

bracelet *n.* брасле́т.

bracing *adj.* бодря́щий. *The air is bracing,* во́здух бодри́т.

bracket *n.* **1,** (shelf support) кронште́йн. **2,** *pl.* ([ ]) (квадра́тные) ско́бки. —*v.t.* **1,** (enclose in brackets) заключа́ть в ско́бки. **2,** (group together) ста́вить на одну́ до́ску.

brackish *adj.* солонова́тый.

brad *n.* гво́здик; шпи́лька.

brag *v.i.* хва́статься. *It is nothing to brag about,* похва́статься не́чем.

braggart *n.* хвасту́н; бахва́л; фанфаро́н.

Brahman *also,* **Brahmin** *n.* брахма́н. —**Brahmanism,** *n.* брахмани́зм.

braid *n.* **1,** (ornamental band) тесьма́. **2,** (of hair) коса́. —*v.t.* **1,** (plait) заплета́ть. **2,** (weave) плести́.

brain *n.* **1,** *anat.* мозг. *Use one's brains,* шевели́ть мозга́ми. *Rack one's brains,* лома́ть себе́ го́лову. **2,** *pl.* (culinary dish) мозги́. —*adj.* мозгово́й. —**brain drain,** уте́чка мозго́в.

brainchild *n., colloq.* де́тище.

brainless *adj., colloq.* безмо́зглый; безголо́вый.

brainstorm *n.* блестя́щая мысль.

brain trust мозгово́й трест.

brain-twister *n.* головоло́мка.

brainwash *v.t.* промыва́ть мозги́ (+ *dat.*).

brainwork *n.* мозгова́я рабо́та; у́мственный труд.

brainy *adj., colloq.* мозгови́тый; башкови́тый.

braise *v.t.* туши́ть.

brake *n.* то́рмоз. —*adj.* тормозно́й: *brake fluid,* тормозна́я жи́дкость. —*v.t. & i.* тормози́ть.

brakeman *n.* тормозно́й конду́ктор.

bramble *n.* кумани́ка.

brambling *n.* вьюро́к; юро́к.

bran *n.* о́труби.

branch *n.* **1,** (limb) ветвь; ве́тка. **2,** (offshoot) ответвле́ние. *Branch of a river,* ответвле́ние *or* рука́в реки́. *A branch of the Vasilyev family,* ветвь Васи́льевского ро́да; ветвь ро́да Васи́льевых. **3,** (commercial subdivision) филиа́л; отделе́ние. **4,** (field; division) о́трасль; разде́л; отде́л. *Branch of science/medicine,* о́трасль нау́ки; разде́л медици́ны. **5,** (division of government) ветвь: *the three branches of government,* три ве́тви вла́сти. *The executive branch,* исполни́тельная власть. **6,** *mil.* род войск; слу́жба; отде́л. —*adj.* филиа́льный: *branch office,* филиа́льное отделе́ние. *Branch line,* железнодоро́жная ве́тка. —*v.i.* **1,** (divide into branches) разветвля́ться. **2,** *fol. by* **off** (go off in a different direction) ответвля́ться. **3,** *fol. by* **out** (expand one's operations) расширя́ться; расширя́ть свою́ де́ятельность.

brand *n.* **1,** (make; kind) сорт; ма́рка. *Brand of to-*

bacco/coffee/soap, сорт ко́фе/табака́/мы́ла. *Brand of cigarettes,* ма́рка сигаре́т. *What brand do you smoke?,* каки́е сигаре́ты вы ку́рите?; что вы ку́рите? **2,** (burning piece of wood) головня́; голове́шка. **3,** (mark made on cattle) клеймо́; тавро́. —*v.t.* клейми́ть. —**branding iron,** клеймо́.

brandish *v.t.* разма́хивать; потряса́ть.

brand-new *adj.* совсе́м но́вый; но́венький. *Brand-new suit,* костю́м с иго́лочки.

brandy *n.* конья́к.

brant *n.* (goose) каза́рка.

brash *adj.* на́глый; де́рзкий.

brass *n.* **1,** (alloy) лату́нь. **2,** *slang* (top officials) верху́шка; голо́вка. —*adj.* лату́нный. —**brass band,** духово́й орке́стр. —**brass knuckles,** касте́т.

brassiere *n.* бюстга́льтер.

brat *n.* озорни́к; постре́л.

bravado *n.* брава́да.

brave *adj.* хра́брый: *brave man/act,* хра́брый челове́к/посту́пок. —*v.t.* брави́ровать: *brave danger,* брави́ровать опа́сностью. —**bravely,** *adv.* хра́бро. —**bravery,** *n.* хра́брость.

bravissimo *interj.* брави́ссимо!

bravo *interj.* бра́во!

bravura *n.* браву́рная му́зыка.

brawl *n.* сва́лка; дебо́ш; потасо́вка; сканда́л. —*v.i.* сканда́лить; дебоши́рить. —**brawler,** *n.* драчу́н; задира; забия́ка.

brawn *n.* му́скулы; му́скульная си́ла. —**brawny,** *adj.* му́скулистый.

bray *v.i.* крича́ть; реве́ть.

brazen *adj.* **1,** (resembling brass) ме́дный. **2,** (shameless) бессты́дный; беззасте́нчивый. —**brazenly,** *adv.* бессты́дно; нахра́пом.

brazier *n.* **1,** (worker in brass) ме́дник. **2,** (roasting pan) жаро́вня.

Brazilian *adj.* брази́льский. —*n.* брази́лец; бразилья́нка.

breach *n.* **1,** (break) брешь; проло́м. **2,** (violation; infringement) наруше́ние: *breach of contract,* наруше́ние догово́ра. *Breach of trust,* злоупотребле́ние дове́рием. —*v.t.* пробива́ть; прола́мывать.

bread *n.* хлеб. —*adj.* хле́бный: *bread crumbs,* хле́бные кро́шки. *Bread knife,* нож для хле́ба. —**take the bread out of someone's mouth,** отбива́ть хлеб у кого́-нибудь.

breadbasket *n.* **1,** (basket for carrying bread) хле́бница. **2,** (region that supplies much grain) жи́тница.

breadth *n.* **1,** (width) ширина́. **2,** (wide extent; scope) широта́.

breadwinner *n.* корми́лец.

break *v.t.* **1.** (split; fracture; put out of working order) лома́ть. *Break one's.watch/ one's leg/,* слома́ть часы́/но́гу. *Break one's neck,* слома́ть *or* сверну́ть себе́ ше́ю. *Break the ice,* слома́ть *or* разби́ть лёд. *Break the seal,* взлома́ть печа́ть. **2,** (smash; shatter) разбива́ть. *Break a window,* разби́ть окно́. **3,** (fail to keep; violate) наруша́ть: *break a promise/ one's word/ the law/,* наруша́ть обеща́ние/сло́во/зако́н. **4,** (inter-

rupt; disturb) наруша́ть; прерыва́ть: *break the silence,* наруша́ть/прерыва́ть молча́ние. **5,** (sever, as relations) разрыва́ть; рвать; порыва́ть. **6,** (wear down, as resistance) сломи́ть. *Break a strike,* сорва́ть забасто́вку. **7,** (divide into smaller units) разро́знивать: *break a set of something,* разро́знивать компле́кт чего́-нибудь. *Break a dollar,* разме́нивать до́ллар. **8,** (surpass, as a record) поби́ть. **9,** (get rid of, as a habit) отучи́ться от; изба́виться от. *Break someone of a habit,* отуча́ть кого́-нибудь от привы́чки. **10,** (convey, as bad news) сообща́ть. **11,** *colloq.* (bankrupt) разоря́ть. *Break the bank,* сорва́ть банк. **12,** *electricity* размыка́ть: *break a circuit,* размыка́ть цепь. **13,** *in various miscellaneous expressions: break a code,* разга́дывать код; *break camp,* снима́ться с ла́геря; *break ranks,* расходи́ться; *break someone's heart,* разби́ть чьё-нибудь се́рдце. *It breaks my heart,* у меня́ се́рдце разрыва́ется. —*v.i.* **1,** (become smashed, cracked, or useless) лома́ться; разбива́ться. **2,** (snap, as of a rope) рва́ться; обрыва́ться; разрыва́ться. **3,** (stop suddenly, as of one's voice) лома́ться; срыва́ться; прерыва́ться. **4,** (recess) де́лать переры́в: *break for lunch,* де́лать переры́в на обе́д. **5,** (make a sudden dash) бро́ситься: *break for the door,* бро́ситься к две́ри. **6,** (dawn): *Day is breaking,* (рас)света́ет. **7,** *fol. by* **with** (sever ties with) пор(ы)ва́ть с. *Break with tradition,* порва́ть с тради́цией. —*n.* **1,** (burst; rupture) разры́в; проры́в; проло́м. *Water-main break,* разры́в водопрово́дной магистра́ли. **2,** *fig.* (severing) разры́в: *break in diplomatic relations,* разры́в дипломати́ческих отноше́ний. **3,** (interruption; recess) переры́в: *without a break,* без переры́ва; бесперебо́йно. **4,** *Break of day,* рассве́т. **5,** (sudden dash) бросо́к. **6,** (escape, as from prison) бе́гство; побе́г (из тюрьмы́). **7,** *colloq.* (stroke of luck) счастли́вый слу́чай. *He gets all the breaks,* ему́ всегда́ везёт. *The breaks were against us,* нам не везло́. —**break apart,** разла́мываться. —**break away,** вырыва́ться. —**break down, 1,** (smash down, as a door) выла́мывать. **2,** (do away with, as barriers) сломи́ть. **3,** (divide) разбива́ть (на гру́ппы, катего́рии, *etc.*). **4,** (go out of working order) слома́ться; вы́йти из стро́я. *The car broke down,* маши́на слома́лась. *Communications broke down,* связь прервала́сь. **5,** (fail) прова́ливаться: *All efforts have broken down,* все попы́тки провали́лись. *Negotiations broke down,* перегово́ры зашли́ в тупи́к. **6,** (lose one's composure) не вы́держать: *She broke down and cried,* она́ не вы́держала и запла́кала. —**break even,** остава́ться при свои́х. —**break in, 1,** (enter by force) вла́мываться. **2,** (interrupt) вме́шиваться. **3,** (a car, motor, etc.) обка́тывать; (a horse) объезжа́ть; выезжа́ть; (shoes) разна́шивать. —**break into, 1,** (enter by force) врыва́ться в; вла́мываться в. **2,** (interrupt, as a conversation) вме́шиваться в. **3,** (give way to, as laughter) разрази́ться (+ *instr.*). *Break into song,* запе́ть (пе́сню). —**break off, 1,** (sever by breaking) отла́мывать; отбива́ть; отка́лывать. **2,** (come off) отла́мываться; отка́лываться. **3,** (halt abruptly) прекраща́ть; прерыва́ть. *Break off* *one's engagement*, расто́ргнуть помо́лвку; расстро́ить сва́дьбу. **4,** (sever, as relations) порыва́ть; разрыва́ть. **5,** *fol. by* **from** (split off from, as a group) отка́лываться (от). —**break open,** взла́мывать. —**break out, 1,** (start unexpectedly) вспы́хнуть; разрази́ться. **2,** (appear, as of a rash) выступа́ть; появля́ться; пока́зываться. *His face is broken out,* у него́ вы́ступила сыпь на лице́. *He broke out in a sweat,* его́ бро́сило в пот. **3,** (escape) вы́рваться. *Break out of prison,* бежа́ть из тюрьмы́. —**break through,** прорыва́ть; прорыва́ться сквозь; пробива́ть; пробива́ться сквозь. *The sun broke through the clouds,* со́лнце проби́лось сквозь ту́чи. —**break up, 1,** (force to disperse) разгоня́ть. **2,** (disperse; split up) расходи́ться. *He broke up with his wife,* он разошёлся с жено́й. **3,** (divide into smaller parts) разбива́ть. **4,** (be divided up) разбива́ться. **5,** (end with everyone dispersing) ко́нчиться. **6,** (cease to exist or function) распада́ться. *See also* **broken.**

breakable *adj.* ло́мкий; хру́пкий.

breakage *n.* поло́мка; бой.

breakdown *n.* **1,** (failure to function) ава́рия; поло́мка. **2,** (total failure) разва́л; срыв. *Breakdown in the negotiations,* срыв перегово́ров. **3,** (mental collapse) надры́в; надло́м. *Nervous breakdown,* неврасте́ния. **4,** (analysis; classification) разбо́р.

breaker *n.* (wave) буру́н.

breakfast *n.* за́втрак. *Have breakfast,* за́втракать.

breaking point моме́нт разры́ва. *Be at the breaking point* (*fig.*), быть на преде́ле. *Reach the breaking point,* дойти́ до то́чки; дойти́ до преде́ла.

breakneck *adj., in* **at breakneck speed,** сломя́ го́лову.

breakthrough *n.* прорыв.

breakup *n.* **1,** (breaking up into parts) распа́д; разва́л; разло́м; ло́мка. *The breakup of the Soviet Union,* распа́д/разва́л Сове́тского Сою́за. **2,** (split between people) разры́в.

breakwater *n.* мол; волноло́м; волноре́з.

bream *n.* (fish) лещ.

breast *n.* **1,** (human) грудь. **2,** (of a coat) борт: *double-breasted,* двубо́ртный. —*adj.* грудно́й; нагру́дный. *Breast pocket,* нагру́дный карма́н. *Breast feeding,* кормле́ние гру́дью. *Breast cancer,* рак моло́чной железы́. —**make a clean breast of it,** всё вы́ложить; облегчи́ть ду́шу.

breastbone *n.* груди́на.

breastplate *n.* нагру́дник.

breast stroke брасс.

breastwork *n.* бру́ствер.

breath *n.* **1,** (act of breathing) дыха́ние. *Hold one's breath,* затаи́ть дыха́ние. *Catch one's breath,* перевести́ дух; отдыша́ться. *Bad breath,* дурно́й за́пах изо рта. **2,** (a single breath) вдох. *Take a deep breath,* сде́лать глубо́кий вдох; глубоко́ вдохну́ть. —**be out of breath,** запыха́ться. —**it took my breath away,** у меня́ захвати́ло дух. —**like a breath of fresh air,** как глото́к све́жего во́здуха. —**under one's breath,** вполго́лоса; по́д нос. *Mumble something under one's breath,*

(про)бормота́ть что́-нибудь себе́ по́д нос.

breathe *v.i.* дыша́ть. *Breathe in,* вдыха́ть. *Breathe out,* выдыха́ть. —*v.t.* **1,** (inhale and exhale) дыша́ть (+ *instr.*): *breathe oxygen,* дыша́ть кислоро́дом. *Breathe new life into,* вдохну́ть но́вую жизнь в. **2,** (utter; whisper) пророни́ть; обмо́лвиться. *Not breathe a word,* не пророни́ть ни сло́ва; не обмо́лвиться ни сло́вом. —**breathe down someone's neck,** стоя́ть над чье́й-нибудь душо́й. —**breathe one's last,** испусти́ть дух; испусти́ть после́дний вздох.

breather *n.* (respite) переды́шка.

breathing *n.* дыха́ние. —**breathing space/spell,** переды́шка.

breathless *adj.* запыха́вшийся.

breathtaking *adj.* захва́тывающий.

breech *n.* **1,** (of a gun) казённая часть. **2,** (buttocks) я́годицы.

breeches *n.pl.* бри́джи. *Riding breeches,* рейту́зы; галифе́. *Also,* **britches.**

breed *v.t.* **1,** (mate; raise) разводи́ть. **2,** *fig.* (produce; generate; give rise to) порожда́ть. —*v.i.* плоди́ться; разводи́ться; размножа́ться. —*n.* поро́да.

breeder *n.* (of cattle) скотово́д; (of horses) конево́д. —**breeder reactor,** размножа́ющий реа́ктор.

breeding *n.* **1,** (producing of offspring) размноже́ние. **2,** (raising of animals) разведе́ние. ♦ *Usu. rendered by the suffix* -во́дство: *cattle breeding,* скотово́дство. **3,** (improving of strains) селе́кция. **4,** (good manners) воспи́танность. —**breeding ground, 1,** (of animals) ме́сто размноже́ния; (of sea mammals) ле́жбище; (of fish) нерести́лище. **2,** *fig.* (conducive place) оча́г; расса́дник.

breeze *n.* (лёгкий) ветеро́к. *Sea breeze,* бриз.

breezy *adj.* **1,** (brisk; windy) све́жий; ве́треный. **2,** (lively; sprightly) живо́й; лихо́й.

brethren *n.pl.* бра́тья; собра́тья.

brevity *n.* кра́ткость.

brew *v.t.* **1,** (make, as beer) вари́ть. **2,** (prepare, as tea) зава́ривать. —*v.i.* **1,** (be boiling) зава́риваться. **2,** *fig.* (begin to form) собира́ться; надвига́ться: *A storm is brewing,* собира́ется/надвига́ется гроза́.

brewer *n.* пивова́р. —**brewery,** *n.* пивова́ренный заво́д. —**brewing,** *n.* пивоваре́ние.

briar *n.* = **brier.**

bribe *n.* взя́тка. —*v.t.* подкупа́ть. —**bribery,** *n.* взя́точничество; по́дкуп.

bric-a-brac *n.* вещи́цы; безделу́шки.

brick *n.* кирпи́ч. —*adj.* кирпи́чный.

bricklayer *n.* ка́менщик.

brick-red *adj.* кирпи́чный; кирпи́чного цве́та.

brickwork *n.* кирпи́чная кла́дка.

bridal *adj.* сва́дебный; подвене́чный.

bride *n.* неве́ста.

bridegroom *n.* жени́х.

bridesmaid *n.* подру́жка неве́сты.

bridge *n.* **1,** (structure) мост. **2,** (on a ship) мо́стик. **3,** (of the nose) перено́сица. **4,** (of a stringed instrument) кобы́лка. **5,** (mounting for false teeth) мост. **6,** (card game) бридж. —*v.t.* **1,** (build a bridge across) наводи́ть мост че́рез. **2,** *fig.* (overcome) преодолевать. *Bridge the gap,* восполня́ть пробе́л; ликви-ди́ровать разры́в. —**burn one's bridges,** сжига́ть мосты́ *or* корабли́.

bridgehead *n.* плацда́рм; предмо́стное укрепле́ние.

bridle *n.* узда́; узде́чка. —*v.t.* взну́здывать; обу́здывать. —*v.i.* разозли́ться; вскипе́ть. —**bridle path,** вью́чная тропа́.

brief *adj.* **1,** (short in time) коро́ткий: *brief period,* коро́ткий пери́од. *Brief interruption,* небольшо́й переры́в. **2,** (concise) кра́ткий: *brief survey,* кра́ткий обзо́р. —*n.* сво́дка; резюме́. —*v.t.* инструкти́ровать. —**in brief,** вкра́тце; кра́тко; коро́че говоря́.

briefcase *n.* портфе́ль.

briefing *n.* инструкта́ж; бри́финг.

briefly *adv.* коро́тко; кра́тко; вкра́тце.

brier *also,* **briar** *n.* **1,** (thorny bush) шипо́вник. **2,** (heath) э́рика.

brig *n.* **1,** (ship) бриг. **2,** (place of confinement) гауптва́хта.

brigade *n.* **1,** *mil.* брига́да. **2,** (organized group) кома́нда; брига́да; дружи́на. *Fire brigade,* пожа́рная кома́нда; пожа́рная дружи́на.

brigadier general брига́дный генера́л; генера́л-майо́р.

brigand *n.* разбо́йник. —**brigandage,** *n.* разбо́й.

bright *adj.* **1,** (shining; luminous) я́ркий; све́тлый. *Bright light,* я́ркий свет. *Bright colors,* я́ркие цвета́. *Bright sun,* я́ркое со́лнце. *Bright red,* я́рко-кра́сный; я́рко-кра́сного цве́та. *Bright day,* све́тлый день. *Bright future,* све́тлое бу́дущее. **2,** (clever) смышлё́ный; сообрази́тельный.

brighten *v.t.* **1,** (make bright) озаря́ть. **2,** (bring color or life to) оживля́ть. —*v.i.* **1,** (become bright) светле́ть; проясня́ться. **2,** (become more cheerful) оживля́ться. **3,** (improve) улучша́ться.

brightly *adv.* я́рко.

brightness *n.* я́ркость; све́тлость.

brilliance *n.* блеск.

brilliant *adj.* **1,** (sparkling) я́ркий. **2,** (outstanding) блестя́щий. —**brilliantly,** *adv.* я́рко; блестя́ще.

brim *n.* **1,** (edge) край. *Filled to the brim,* по́лный до краё́в. **2,** (of a hat) поля́. —*v.i.* [*usu.* **brim with**] наполня́ться (+ *instr.*).

brine *n.* рассо́л.

bring *v.t.* **1,** (by carrying) приноси́ть: *Bring me my shoes,* принеси́ мне боти́нки. **2,** (on foot) приводи́ть: *bring someone to dinner,* приводи́ть кого́-нибудь к обе́ду. **3,** (by conveyance) привози́ть: *bring something from abroad,* привози́ть чтó-нибудь из-за грани́цы. *What brings you to Washington?,* что привело́ вас в Вашингто́н? **4,** (take along) брать; захва́тывать (с собо́й): *bring an umbrella,* брать/захва́тывать (с собо́й) зо́нтик. **5,** (cause to happen) приноси́ть: *bring results,* приноси́ть результа́ты. *Bring someone luck,* приноси́ть кому́-нибудь уда́чу. *Bring joy to,* доставля́ть ра́дость (+ *dat.*). *War brings suffering,* война́ прино́сит страда́ния. *It brought tears to my eyes,* э́то вы́звало у меня́ слё́зы. **6,** *in various miscellaneous expressions: bring to an end,*

положи́ть коне́ц (+ *dat.*); *bring to mind,* воскреша́ть в па́мяти; напомина́ть; *bring to one's senses,* наводи́ть на ум; вразумля́ть; *bring charges against,* предъявля́ть обвине́ние (+ *dat.*); *bring suit against,* подава́ть в суд на (+ *acc.*); предъявля́ть иск к; *bring home to,* внуша́ть; втолкова́ть. —**bring about,** вызыва́ть; осуществля́ть. —**bring around, 1,** (persuade) уговори́ть. **2,** (revive) приводи́ть в себя́. —**bring back,** верну́ть: *bring back the book/past,* верну́ть кни́гу/про́шлое. *Bring back to life,* воскреша́ть. *Bring back old memories,* вызыва́ть далё́кие воспомина́ния. *Bring back memories of childhood,* напомина́ть де́тство; напомина́ть о де́тстве. —**bring down, 1,** (carry down) сноси́ть; приноси́ть вниз. **2,** (cause to fall) обру́шивать. **3,** (succeed in lowering) сбива́ть: *bring down someone's temperature,* сбива́ть высо́кую температу́ру. **4,** (reduce, as swelling) уменьша́ть; сгоня́ть. **5,** (overthrow) сверга́ть. —**bring forth,** производи́ть на свет. —**bring in, 1,** (carry in) вноси́ть. **2,** (import) ввози́ть. **3,** (produce, as revenue) приноси́ть. **4,** (hire) привлека́ть. **5,** (render, as a verdict) выноси́ть. —**bring off,** осуществля́ть. —**bring on,** навлека́ть; вызыва́ть. —**bring oneself,** реша́ться. *I can't bring myself to do it,* не могу́ реши́ться на э́то; не могу́ заста́вить себя́ э́то сде́лать; у меня́ рука́ не поднима́ется сде́лать э́то. *I couldn't bring myself to tell him,* у меня́ язы́к не поверну́лся сказа́ть ему́. —**bring out, 1,** (carry out) выноси́ть. **2,** (produce) выпуска́ть. **3,** (make more apparent) обознача́ть; оттеня́ть. **4,** *Bring out into the open,* выводи́ть на чи́стую во́ду. —**bring together, 1,** (assemble in one place) собира́ть. **2,** (cause to meet) своди́ть; соединя́ть. **3,** (cause to become closer) сближа́ть. —**bring up, 1,** (raise; rear) воспи́тывать; расти́ть. **2,** (raise, as a subject) поднима́ть. **3,** *mil.* подводи́ть; подтя́гивать: *bring up the reserves,* подводи́ть/подтя́гивать резе́рвы. **4,** *Bring up the rear,* замыка́ть ше́ствие; *mil.* быть в обо́зе.

brink *n.* край; грань.

briny *adj.* солё́ный.

briquette *n.* брике́т.

brisk *adj.* **1,** (quick) бы́стрый: *at a brisk pace,* бы́стрым ша́гом. **2,** (lively) бо́йкий; оживлё́нный: *brisk business,* бо́йкая/оживлё́нная торго́вля. **3,** (fresh and invigorating) све́жий; бодря́щий.

brisket *n.* груди́нка; коре́йка.

bristle *n.* щети́на. —*v.i.* **1,** (become stiff and erect) щети́ниться. **2,** (show sudden anger) (вс)кипе́ть гне́вом. —**bristly,** *adj.* щети́нистый.

britches *n.pl.* = **breeches.**

British *adj.* англи́йский; брита́нский. —*n., preceded by* **the,** англича́не. —**British thermal unit,** брита́нская теплова́я едини́ца.

brittle *adj.* хру́пкий; ло́мкий.

broach *n.* **1,** (spit) ве́ртел. **2,** = **brooch.** —*v.t.* затра́гивать: *broach a subject,* затра́гивать вопро́с.

broad *adj.* широ́кий: *broad street/river/smile,* широ́кая у́лица/река́/улы́бка. *Broad hint,* прозра́чный намё́к. *In the broad sense of the word,* в широ́ком смы́сле э́того сло́ва. —**it's as broad as it is long,** что в лоб, что по́ лбу.

broadcast *n.* переда́ча; радиопереда́ча; трансля́ция. —*v.t.* передава́ть по ра́дио *or* в эфи́р; трансли́ровать. —*v.i.* вести́ радиопереда́чу; веща́ть.

broadcasting *n.* веща́ние; радиовеща́ние. —*adj.* радиовеща́тельный.

broadcloth *n.* сукно́.

broaden *v.t.* расширя́ть. —*v.i.* расширя́ться.

broad-gauge *adj.* ширококоле́йный.

broad jump прыжо́к в длину́. —**running broad jump,** прыжо́к с разбе́га. —**standing broad jump,** прыжо́к с ме́ста.

broadly *adv.* широко́: *interpret broadly,* широко́ толкова́ть. —**broadly speaking,** вообще́ говоря́.

broad-minded *adj.* терпи́мый; свободомы́слящий; с широ́кими взгля́дами.

broad-shouldered *adj.* широкопле́чий; плечи́стый.

broadside *n.* **1,** (firing of a ship's guns) залп. **2,** (verbal attack) град упрёков.

broadsword *n.* пала́ш.

broadtail *n.* каракульча́.

brocade *n.* парча́. —**brocaded,** *adj.* парчо́вый.

broccoli *n.* спа́ржевая капу́ста; бро́кколи.

brochure *n.* брошю́ра.

broil *v.t.* жа́рить. —*v.i.* жа́риться.

broiled *adj.* жа́реный.

broiler *n.* жаро́вня.

broiling *adj.* паля́щий: *broiling sun,* паля́щее со́лнце.

broke *adj., colloq.* без гроша́. —**go broke,** прогора́ть. —**go for broke,** идти́ ва-ба́нк.

broken *adj.* **1,** (fractured) сло́манный. **2,** (shattered) разби́тый; би́тый. *Broken glass,* би́тое стекло́. **3,** (not functioning) сло́манный. *The television set is broken,* телеви́зор слома́лся. **4,** (crushed in spirit) сло́мленный; надло́мленный. *Broken man,* сло́мленный челове́к. **5,** (imperfectly spoken) ло́маный: *in broken English,* на ло́маном англи́йском языке́. **6,** (violated, as of promises) несде́ржанный. **7,** (rugged, as of terrain) пересечённый. **8,** *Broken line* (---), преры́вистая ли́ния. **9,** *Broken heart,* разби́тое се́рдце.

broken-down *adj.* ве́тхий; обветша́лый; полуразру́шенный.

broken-hearted *adj.* с разби́тым се́рдцем; уби́тый го́рем.

broker *n.* **1,** (agent) комиссионе́р. **2,** (stockbroker) ма́клер.

brokerage *n.* **1,** (business of a broker) ма́клерство. **2,** (broker's fee) комиссио́нные. —**brokerage house,** ма́клерская фи́рма.

bromide *n.* **1,** *chem.* броми́д. ♦*In compounds, with* бро́мистый: *sodium bromide,* бро́мистый на́трий. **2,** *med.* бром. **3,** *colloq.* (cliché) бана́льность.

bromine *n.* бром.

bronchi *n.pl.* бро́нхи.

bronchial *adj.* бронхиа́льный. —**bronchial tubes,** бро́нхи.

bronchitis *n.* бронхи́т.

brontosaurus *n.* бронтоза́вр.

bronze *n.* бро́нза. —*adj.* бро́нзовый. —*v.t.* бронзирова́ть. —**Bronze Age,** бро́нзовый век.

brooch *n.* брошь; бро́шка.

brood *n.* вы́водок. —*v.i.* **1,** (sit on eggs) сиде́ть на я́йцах; выси́живать. **2,** (think long and moodily) заду́мываться (о).

brood hen насе́дка.

brood mare племенна́я кобы́ла.

brook *n.* руче́й. —*v.t.* терпе́ть: *brook no delay,* не терпе́ть отлага́тельства. —**brook trout,** ручьева́я форе́ль.

broom *n.* метла́.

broomstick *n.* па́лка (для) метлы́.

broth *n.* бульо́н.

brothel *n.* публи́чный дом; дом терпи́мости.

brother *n.* брат.

brotherhood *n.* бра́тство.

brother-in-law *n.* **1,** (husband's brother) де́верь. **2,** (wife's brother) шу́рин. **3,** (sister's husband; husband's sister's husband) зять. **4,** (wife's sister's husband) своя́к.

brotherly *adj.* бра́тский.

brow *n.* **1,** (eyebrow) бровь. **2,** (forehead) лоб.

browbeat *v.t.* запу́гивать.

brown *adj.* кори́чневый. *Brown eyes,* ка́рие глаза́. *Brown hair,* кашта́новые во́лосы. —*n.* кори́чневый цвет. —*v.t.* подрумя́нивать. —*v.i.* **1,** (become sunburned) загора́ть. **2,** *cooking* подрумя́ниваться.

brown bear бу́рый медве́дь.

brownie *n.* (goblin) домово́й.

browse *v.i.* смотре́ть; осма́триваться; огля́дываться.

bruise *n.* синя́к; уши́б; кровоподтёк; подтёк. —*v.t.* ушиба́ть.

brunet *n.* брюне́т. —**brunette,** *n.* брюне́тка.

brunt *n.* основна́я тя́жесть: *bear the brunt of,* вы́нести основну́ю тя́жесть (+ *gen.*).

brush *n.* **1,** (implement) щётка: *hairbrush,* щётка для воло́с. **2,** (paintbrush) кисть. **3,** (encounter; run-in) сты́чка. **4,** (underbrush) за́росль. **5,** *electricity* щётка. —*v.t.* **1,** (clean with a brush) чи́стить щёткой. *Brush one's teeth,* чи́стить зу́бы. **2,** (groom with a brush) причёсывать (во́лосы) щёткой. —*v.i.* [*usu.* **brush against**] задева́ть. —**brush aside,** отмета́ть; отма́хиваться от. —**brush away,** сма́хивать; отма́хивать: *brush away crumbs/flies,* сма́хивать кро́шки; отма́хивать мух. —**brush off, 1,** (remove with a brush) счища́ть; сма́хивать. **2,** (remove dirt, snow, etc. from) (по)чи́стить. **3,** (dismiss abruptly) отма́хиваться от. —**brush up,** освежа́ть: *brush up one's Russian,* освежи́ть свой ру́сский язы́к.

brushwood *n.* **1,** (tree branches) хво́рост. **2,** (underbrush) за́росль.

brushwork *n.* кисть.

brusque *adj.* гру́бый; ре́зкий; бесцеремо́нный. —**brusquely,** *adv.* гру́бо; ре́зко; бесцеремо́нно. —**brusqueness,** *n.* гру́бость; ре́зкость.

Brussels sprouts брюссе́льская капу́ста.

brutal *adj.* жесто́кий; зве́рский. —**brutality,** *n.* жесто́кость; зве́рство. —**brutally,** *adv.* жесто́ко; зве́рски.

brute *n.* **1,** (animal) живо́тное; зверь. **2,** (crude person) скоти́на. —*adj.* гру́бый: *brute force,* гру́бая си́ла.

bubble *n.* пузы́рь. —*v.i.* **1,** (give off bubbles) пузы́риться. **2,** (make a bubbling sound) клокота́ть.

bubo *n.* бубо́н.

bubonic *adj.* бубо́нный. —**bubonic plague,** бубо́нная чума́.

buccaneer *n.* пира́т.

buck *n.* **1,** (male deer) оле́нь. **2,** (male of various animals) саме́ц. **3,** *slang* (dollar) до́ллар. —*v.t., colloq.* (go against) проти́виться. —**buck up,** *colloq.* не па́дать ду́хом. —**pass the buck,** свали́ть отве́тственность на друго́го.

bucket *n.* ведро́. *The rain is coming down in buckets,* дождь льёт как из ведра́. —**drop in the bucket,** ка́пля в мо́ре. —**kick the bucket,** *slang* сыгра́ть в я́щик.

buckle *n.* пря́жка. —*v.t.* застёгивать (пря́жкой). *Buckle one's belt,* застёгивать пря́жку на по́ясе. —*v.i.* **1,** (warp; curl) коро́биться. **2,** (give way, as of one's legs) подка́шиваться; подла́мываться. —**buckle down,** запряга́ться.

buckram *n.* коленко́р.

buckshot *n.* кру́пная дробь; карте́чь.

buckskin *n.* оле́нья шку́ра.

buckthorn *n.* круши́на.

bucktooth *n.* торча́щий зуб.

buckwheat *n.* гречи́ха; гре́чневая крупа́. —*adj.* гре́чневый.

bucolic *adj.* дереве́нский.

bud *n.* по́чка; буто́н. —*v.i.* дава́ть по́чки. —**nip in the bud,** *see* **nip.**

Buddhism *n.* будди́зм. —**Buddhist,** *n.* будди́ст. —*adj.* будди́стский.

buddy *n., colloq.* това́рищ.

budge *v.t.* сдви́нуть с ме́ста. —*v.i.* шевели́ться.

budget *n.* бюдже́т. —*adj.* бюдже́тный: *budget deficit,* бюдже́тный дефици́т. —*v.t.* предусма́тривать в бюдже́те. *Budget one's time,* распределя́ть своё вре́мя. —**budgetary,** *adj.* бюдже́тный.

buff *n.* **1,** (leather) бу́йволовая ко́жа. **2,** (tan color) беж. **3,** *colloq.* (enthusiast) люби́тель. —*v.t.* лощи́ть; полирова́ть. —**in the buff,** нагишо́м.

buffalo *n.* **1,** (Old World animal) бу́йвол. **2,** (bison) бизо́н.

buffer *n.* бу́фер. —**buffer state,** бу́ферное госуда́рство. —**buffer zone,** бу́ферная зо́на.

buffet[1] (buf-it) *v.t.* **1,** (hit; club) ударя́ть; колоти́ть. **2,** (knock about) броса́ть (*impers.*): *The waves buffeted the ship,* парохо́д броса́ло по волна́м.

buffet[2] (bu-fay) *n.* буфе́т.

buffoon *n.* шут горо́ховый; скоморо́х; пая́ц; буффо́н. —**buffoonery,** *n.* шутовство́; скоморо́шество; буффона́да.

bug *n.* **1,** (insect) козя́вка; бука́шка. **2,** *colloq.* (defect) непола́дка. —*v.t., slang* **1,** (install a hidden microphone in) прослу́шивать: *This apartment is bugged,* э́та кварти́ра прослу́шивается. *Bugging device,* подслу́шивающее устро́йство. **2,** (nag) пили́ть: *Don't bug me!,* не пили́те меня́!

bugaboo *n.* пу́гало; жу́пел. *Also,* **bugbear.**

buggy *n.* кабриоле́т.

bugle *n.* **1,** (horn) горн. *Bugle call,* сигна́л го́рна. **2,** *pl.* (beads) стекля́рус. —**bugler,** *n.* горни́ст.

build *v.t.* стро́ить: *build a house,* стро́ить дом. *Build a road,* стро́ить *or* прокла́дывать доро́гу. *Build a fire,* разводи́ть *or* раскла́дывать костёр. *Build a nest,* вить гнездо́. *Build a collection,* составля́ть колле́кцию. *Build a fence around the yard,* обноси́ть двор забо́ром. —*v.i.* **1,** (construct something) стро́ить. **2,** (increase) уси́ливаться: *Pressure is building,* уси́ливается давле́ние. —*n.* сложе́ние: *of sturdy build,* кре́пкого сложе́ния. —**build in,** встра́ивать. —**build on,** пристра́ивать. —**build up, 1,** (create and add to) создава́ть. **2,** (increase; make larger) увели́чивать; нара́щивать. **3,** (develop, as an urban area) застра́ивать. **4,** (develop, as endurance or immunity) выраба́тывать. **5,** (increase, as strength or confidence) укрепля́ть. *Build up someone's hopes,* подава́ть наде́жду (+ *dat.*). **6,** (make better known) реклами́ровать. *Build oneself up,* набива́ть себе́ це́ну. **7,** (gradually become greater) расти́. *The crisis was building up for a long time,* кри́зис назрева́л давно́.

builder *n.* строи́тель.

building *n.* **1,** (structure) зда́ние; дом. **2,** (construction) строи́тельство; построе́ние. —*adj.* строи́тельный: *building materials,* строи́тельные материа́лы.

build-up *n.* **1,** (publicity; praise) рекла́ма. **2,** *mil.* нара́щивание (сил).

built *adj. A well-built house,* соли́дный дом. *He is well-built,* он хорошо́ сложён; он хоро́шего сложе́ния.

built-in *adj. built-in exposure meter,* встро́енный экспози́метр. *Built-in closet,* встро́енный *or* стенно́й шкаф.

bulb *n.* **1,** (light bulb) ла́мпочка. **2,** (of a plant) лу́ковица.

bulbous *adj.* лу́ковичный.

Bulgarian *adj.* болга́рский. —*n.* **1,** (person) болга́рин; болга́рка. **2,** (language) болга́рский язы́к.

bulge *v.i.* раздува́ться; распуха́ть; оттопы́риваться. —*n.* вы́пуклость; утолще́ние.

bulk *n.* **1,** (mass) объём. **2,** (the major part) основна́я часть *or* ма́сса. —**in bulk,** гурто́м.

bulkhead *n.* **1,** (on a ship) перебо́рка. **2,** (wall to hold back water) перемы́чка.

bulky *adj.* громо́здкий; объёмистый.

bull *n.* **1,** (animal) бык. **2,** (papal edict) бу́лла. —**bull in a china shop,** слон в посу́дной ла́вке. —**take the bull by the horns,** взять быка́ за рога́.

bulldog *n.* бульдо́г.

bulldoze *v.t.* сноси́ть бульдо́зером.

bulldozer *n.* бульдо́зер.

bullet *n.* пу́ля. —*adj.* пулево́й: *bullet wound,* пулева́я ра́на; *bullet hole,* пулева́я пробо́ина.

bulletin *n.* бюллете́нь. —**bulletin board,** доска́ объявле́ний.

bulletproof *adj.* пулесто́йкий; пуленепробива́емый; пуленепроница́емый. *Bulletproof vest,* бронежиле́т.

bullfight *n.* бой быко́в.

bullfinch *n.* снеги́рь.

bullion *n.* слитки: *gold bullion*, зо́лото в сли́тках.

bullock *n.* вол.

bull's-eye *n.* я́блоко мише́ни. *Hit the bull's-eye*, попа́сть в цель.

bully *n.* задира; забияка. —*v.t.* запу́гивать.

bulrush *n.* камы́ш.

bulwark *n.* **1,** (rampart) вал. **2,** *fig.* (bastion) оплот.

bum *n., colloq.* ло́дырь; бродя́га. —*adj., slang* плохо́й: *bum advice*, плохо́й сове́т. *Bum leg*, больна́я нога́. —*v.i.* [*usu.* **bum around**] слоня́ться. —*v.t., slang* (mooch) выкля́нчивать; стреля́ть.

bumblebee *n.* шмель.

bumbling *adj.* неуме́лый.

bump *n.* **1,** (swelling) ши́шка: *bump on one's head*, ши́шка на голове́. **2,** (in a road) уха́б. **3,** (jolt) толчо́к. —*v.t.* уда́риться (+ *instr.*); сту́кнуться (+ *instr.*). *Bump heads*, сту́кнуться голова́ми. *Bump one's head on the door*, уда́риться/сту́кнуться голово́й о дверь. —**bump into, 1,** (collide with) ната́лкиваться на; ста́лкиваться с. **2,** (meet by chance) ната́лкиваться на; натыка́ться на; набрести́ на. —**bump off,** *slang* уложи́ть.

bumper *n.* бу́фер; ба́мпер. —*adj., in* **bumper crop**; **bumper harvest,** небыва́лый *or* неви́данный урожа́й.

bumpiness *n.* тря́ска; *aero.* болта́нка.

bumpkin *n.* дереве́нщина.

bumpy *adj.* **1,** (covered with bumps) уха́бистый: *bumpy road*, уха́бистая доро́га. **2,** (full of jolts) тря́ский: *bumpy ride*, тря́ская езда́.

bun *n.* **1,** (pastry) сдо́бная бу́лка *or* бу́лочка; пы́шка; плю́шка. **2,** (hair worn in a roll) пучо́к: *wear one's hair in a bun*, носи́ть во́лосы пучко́м.

bunch *n.* **1,** (collection of similar things fastened together) свя́зка; пучо́к. **2,** (cluster, as of grapes) кисть; гроздь. **3,** *colloq.* (group of people) гру́ппа.

bundle *n.* **1,** (number of things bound together) свя́зка; у́зел; свёрток; па́чка; вяза́нка. **2,** (package) паке́т. —*v.t.* **1,** (wrap or tie together) свя́зывать в у́зел. **2,** (wrap snugly) заку́тывать. **3,** *fol. by* **off** (send away) спрова́живать. —*v.i.* [*usu.* **bundle up**] ку́таться; заку́тываться; уку́тываться. —**bundle of energy,** сгу́сток эне́ргии. —**bundle of nerves,** комо́к не́рвов.

bungalow *n.* до́мик.

bungle *v.t.* напу́тать.

bunion *n.* мозо́ль.

bunk *n.* **1,** (bed) ко́йка. **2,** *slang* (nonsense) вздор; чушь.

bunker *n.* **1,** (storage bin) бу́нкер. **2,** (fortified earthwork) блинда́ж. **3,** (underground shelter) бу́нкер.

bunny *n.* за́йчик.

Bunsen burner горе́лка Бу́нзена.

bunting *n.* **1,** (fabric) мате́рия (для фла́гов). **2,** (bird) овся́нка. *Snow bunting*, пу́ночка.

buoy *n.* буй; ба́кен. —*v.t.* поднима́ть: *buoy someone's spirits*, поднима́ть дух (+ *gen.*). *Buoyed by the success of the operation*, ободрённый успе́хом опера́ции.

buoyancy *n.* **1,** (ability to keep afloat) плаву́честь. **2,** *fig.* (exuberance) бо́дрость.

buoyant *adj.* **1,** (floating) плаву́чий. **2,** *fig.* (light-hearted) бо́дрый; жизнера́достный.

bur *n.* репе́йник.

burbot *n.* нали́м.

burden *n.* **1,** (load) но́ша. **2,** *fig.* (something borne with difficulty) бре́мя: *the burden of military expenditures*, бре́мя вое́нных расхо́дов. *Be a burden to*, быть в тя́гость (+ *dat.*). —*v.t.* обременя́ть. —**burden of proof,** обя́занность дока́зывать.

burdensome *adj.* обремени́тельный.

burdock *n.* лопу́х; репе́йник.

bureau *n.* **1,** (dresser) комо́д. **2,** (agency) бюро́: *Federal Bureau of Investigation*, Федера́льное бюро́ рассле́дований.

bureaucracy *n.* **1,** (bureaucratic methods) бюрократи́зм. **2,** (bureaucrats) бюрокра́тия. —**bureaucrat,** *n.* бюрокра́т. —**bureaucratic,** *adj.* бюрократи́ческий.

burgeon *v.i.* **1,** (bud) дава́ть по́чки. **2,** (expand rapidly) разраста́ться.

burgher *n.* бю́ргер.

burglar *n.* взло́мщик. —**burglarize,** *v.t.* взла́мывать. —**burglary,** *n.* кра́жа со взло́мом.

burgomaster *n.* бургоми́стр.

burial *n.* погребе́ние; захороне́ние. —**burial ground,** кла́дбище. —**burial mound,** курга́н; моги́льный холм. —**burial place,** ме́сто погребе́ния; ме́сто захороне́ния. —**burial vault,** склеп; усыпа́льница.

burlap *n.* холст; дерю́га. —*adj.* холщо́вый; дерю́жный.

burlesque *n.* бурле́ск.

burly *adj.* доро́дный; ро́слый.

bur marigold (plant) череда́.

Burmese *adj.* бирма́нский. *He is Burmese*, он бирма́нец. —*n.* **1,** (language) бирма́нский язы́к. **2,** *preceded by* **the** (people) бирма́нцы.

burn *v.t.* **1,** (deliberately set on fire) жечь: *burn garbage*, жечь му́сор. **2,** (accidentally singe) обжига́ть: *burn one's finger*, обжига́ть себе́ па́лец. *Burn oneself*, обжига́ться. *Burn a hole in*, прожига́ть дыру́ в (+ *prepl.*). **3,** (overcook) сжига́ть; поджига́ть. **4,** (cause a burning sensation in) жечь; щипа́ть. **5,** (consume, as fuel or electricity) потребля́ть; жечь. —*v.i.* **1,** (be on fire) горе́ть. *Burn to the ground*, сгоре́ть дотла́. *There is a smell of something burning*, что́-то гори́т; что́-то сгоре́ло; па́хнет горе́лым. **2,** (of food) горе́ть; подгора́ть. **3,** (of light, a lamp, etc.) горе́ть. *Leave the lights burning*, оставля́ть (горе́ть) свет. **4,** (cause a burning sensation; sting) жечь. **5,** (feel hot; smart) горе́ть. **6,** *fig.* (be consumed with, as an emotion) горе́ть: *burn with desire*, горе́ть жела́нием. —*n.* **1,** (injury) ожо́г: *suffer burns*, получи́ть ожо́ги. **2,** (sunburn) зага́р. *I got quite a burn*, я си́льно загоре́л(а). —**burn down, 1,** (raze) жечь. **2,** (be burned to the ground) сгоре́ть. —**burn one's fingers** (*fig.*), обжига́ться. —**burn out, 1,** (destroy by heat) выжига́ть. **2,** (go out, as of a bulb) перегоре́ть. **3,** (cause to go out) пережига́ть. —**burn up, 1,** (burn completely) сгора́ть. **2,** *colloq.* (infuriate) приводи́ть в я́рость. —**he has money to**

burn, де́нег у него́ —хоть пруд пруди́; у него́ де́нег ку́ры не клюю́т.

burner *n.* горе́лка; конфо́рка: *gas burner*, га́зовая горе́лка/конфо́рка.

burning *n.* сжига́ние; сожже́ние: *burning of trash/ books*, сжига́ние му́сора; сожже́ние книг. —*adj.* **1**, (on fire) горя́щий; пыла́ющий. **2**, (extremely hot) жгу́чий; паля́щий. *The burning sun*, паля́щее со́лнце. *Burning sensation*, жже́ние. *Burning question*, жгу́чий вопро́с.

burnish *v.t.* полирова́ть; ворони́ть.

burnt *adj.* жжёный; горе́лый. —**burnt offering**, жертвоприноше́ние.

burp *n., colloq.* отры́жка. —*v.i., colloq.* рыга́ть.

burr *n.* **1**, (rough edge on metal) заусе́ница. **2**, (guttural pronunciation of the letter R) карта́вость.

burro *n.* о́слик.

burrow *n.* нора́. —*v.i.* рыть нору́. *Burrowing rodent*, ро́ющий грызу́н.

bursa *n.* су́мка.

bursitis *n.* воспале́ние су́мки.

burst *v.i.* **1**, (break open) ло́паться; прорыва́ться. *The bubble burst*, пузы́рь ло́пнул. *The pipes burst*, тру́бы ло́пнули. *The dam burst*, плоти́ну прорва́ло. *The boiler burst*, котёл разорва́ло. *I am ready to burst*, я нае́лся (нае́лась) до отва́ла. **2**, (go off; explode) рва́ться: *Bombs were bursting in the sky*, бо́мбы рвали́сь на не́бе. **3**, *fol. by* with (be filled to overflowing) ломи́ться (от): *The shelves are bursting with books*, по́лки ло́мятся от книг. *He is bursting with energy*, эне́ргия в нём бьёт ключо́м. *She is bursting with envy*, она́ ло́пается от за́висти. **4**, *fol. by* into (come rushing into) врыва́ться (в); вломи́ться (в). **5**, *fol. by* into *or* out (give sudden expression to) разрази́ться (+ *instr.*): *burst into tears; burst out crying*, разрази́ться слеза́ми; распла́каться. *Burst out laughing*, разрази́ться сме́хом; рассмея́ться; расхохота́ться. *Burst into applause*, разрази́ться аплодисме́нтами. **6**, *Burst into flame*, вспы́хнуть пла́менем. —*v.t.* прорыва́ть: *burst the pipes*, прорыва́ть тру́бы. —*n.* **1**, (explosion) взрыв. *Burst of flame*, вспы́шка огня́. *Burst of thunder*, уда́р гро́ма. *Burst of machine-gun fire*, пулемётная о́чередь. **2**, *fig.* (outburst, as of laughter or applause) взрыв. *Burst of anger*, вспы́шка *or* поры́в гне́ва. *Burst of energy*, вспы́шка *or* прили́в эне́ргии. **3**, (spurt) бросо́к.

bury *v.t.* **1**, (place in a grave) хорони́ть: *bury the dead*, хорони́ть уме́рших. **2**, (conceal in the ground) зака́пывать; зарыва́ть. *Buried treasure*, клад. **3**, (submerge) погреба́ть: *Three people were buried in the rubble*, три челове́ка бы́ли погребены́ под разва́линами. **4**, (cover; hide) закрыва́ть: *bury one's face in one's hands*, закрыва́ть лицо́ рука́ми. *Bury one's head in a pillow*, зарыва́ться *or* уткну́ться голово́й в поду́шку. —**bury oneself in**, зарыва́ться в; уткну́ться в. *Bury oneself in a book*, уткну́ться (*or* уткну́ть нос) в кни́гу.

bus *n.* авто́бус. —*adj.* авто́бусный: *bus line*, авто́бусная ли́ния. *Bus driver*, води́тель авто́буса. *Bus stop*, остано́вка авто́буса. —*v.t.* перевози́ть на авто́бусе.

bush *n.* куст. —**beat around the bush**, ходи́ть вокру́г да о́коло; говори́ть обиняка́ми.

bushed *adj., colloq.* без ног.

bushel *n.* бу́шель.

bushing *n.* вту́лка.

bushy *adj.* густо́й: *bushy eyebrows*, густы́е бро́ви. *Bushy tail*, пуши́стый хвост.

business *n.* **1**, (commercial dealings) де́ло: *on business*, по де́лу; по дела́м. *Business is business*, де́ло есть де́ло. *Business is improving*, дела́ поправля́ются. *Do business with*, име́ть де́ло с. *Get down to business*, приступи́ть к де́лу. *Talk business*, говори́ть по де́лу. **2**, (establishment) предприя́тие; би́знес. **3**, (one's own affairs) де́ло: *It's none of your business*, э́то не ва́ше де́ло. *Mind your own business!*, не су́йся не в своё де́ло! *What business is it of yours?*, а вам како́е де́ло? —*adj.* делово́й: *business letter*, делово́е письмо́. *Business card*, визи́тная ка́рточка. *Business address*, служе́бный а́дрес. *Business trip*, командиро́вка. —**go about one's business**, занима́ться свои́ми дела́ми. —**go out of business**, ликвиди́роваться; прикрыва́ться. —**have no business** (+ *verb*), не име́ть пра́ва (+ *inf.*). —**make it one's business to...**, ста́вить себе́ це́лью (+ *inf.*). *I'll make it my business to be there*, я бу́ду там обяза́тельно. —**mean business**, не шути́ть. —**mix business with pleasure**, сочета́ть прия́тное с поле́зным.

businesslike *adj.* делово́й; делови́тый.

businessman *n.* предпринима́тель; бизнесме́н.

bust *n.* **1**, (bosom; sculpture) бюст. **2**, *slang* (flop) прова́л; неуда́ча. —*v.t., slang* **1**, (break) разбива́ть. **2**, (bankrupt) разоря́ть.

bustard *n.* дрофа́. —**little bustard**, стре́пет.

bustle *n.* суета́; суматоха; су́толока. —*v.i.* суети́ться; хлопота́ть. —**bustling**, *adj.* суетли́вый.

busy *adj.* **1**, (occupied) за́нятый: *I am very busy*, я о́чень за́нят (занята́). *He is busy packing*, он занима́ется упако́вкой веще́й. *The line is busy*, ли́ния занята́. **2**, (full of activity) *rendered variously in Russian*: *busy street*, оживлённая у́лица; *busy season*, горя́чее вре́мя; *busy schedule*, насы́щенное расписа́ние. —*v.t.* [*usu.* **busy oneself with**] занима́ться (+ *instr.*).

busybody *n.* хлопоту́н.

but *conj.* но: *slowly but surely*, ме́дленно, но ве́рно. *But on the other hand...*, но с друго́й стороны́... ♦*Also rendered by* a *and* да: *not he, but his brother*, не он, а его́ брат. *She would like to go, but she can't*, она́ и пошла́ бы, да не мо́жет. —*prep.* кро́ме: *everyone but me*, все, кро́ме меня́. *Anyone but him*, кто уго́дно, то́лько не он. *The whole truth and nothing but the truth*, вся пра́вда и ниче́го, кро́ме пра́вды. *We found nothing but ruins*, мы заста́ли одни́ разва́лины. *It caused us nothing but trouble*, э́то нам доставля́ло одни́ неприя́тности; э́то нам ничего́ не принесло́, кро́ме неприя́тностей. —*adv.* то́лько; лишь; про́сто. *He is but a child*, он лишь ребёнок. *Had I but known!*, е́сли бы я то́лько знал! *What could I do but agree?*, что мне остава́лось, как не согласи́ться? —*n.* «но»: *a slight "but"*, ма́ленькое «но». —**all but**, почти́: *all but certain,* почти́ уве́рен. —**but for,** е́сли бы не. —**but then,** зато́; впро́чем.

butane *n.* бута́н.

butcher *n.* **1,** (seller of meat) мясни́к. **2,** *fig.* (murderer) пала́ч. —*v.t.* **1,** (slaughter) ре́зать; зака́лывать. **2,** *fig.* (murder, as a language) кове́ркать (язы́к). —**butcher shop,** мясна́я ла́вка; мясно́й магази́н.

butchery *n.* бо́йня; резня́.

butler *n.* дворе́цкий.

butt *n.* **1,** (thick end) торе́ц; (*of an ax*) о́бух; обу́х. **2,** (rifle butt) прикла́д. **3,** (of a cigarette) оку́рок. **4,** *fig.* (target) мише́нь: *butt of jokes,* мише́нь для остро́т. —*v.t.* (ram) бода́ть. —*v.i.* бода́ться. —**butt in,** *colloq.* сова́ться.

butter *n.* ма́сло. *Butter knife,* нож для ма́сла. *Butter dish,* масле́нка. —*v.t.* **1,** (put butter on) нама́зывать ма́слом. **2,** *fol. by* **up,** *colloq.* (flatter) ума́сливать; зама́сливать; подма́зываться к.

buttercup *n.* лю́тик; куросле́п.

butterfly *n.* ба́бочка.

buttermilk *n.* па́хта.

buttocks *n.* я́годицы.

button *n.* **1,** (for a garment) пу́говица. **2,** (push button) кно́пка. —*v.t.* застёгивать. —*v.i.* застёгиваться. —**on the button,** *colloq.* ро́вно; то́чно.

buttonhole *n.* **1,** (for a button) пе́тля. **2,** (for a flower, ribbon, etc.) петли́ца.

buttress *n.* **1,** *archit.* контрофо́рс. **2,** *fig.* (prop) подпо́ра. —*v.t.* подде́рживать; подпира́ть; подкрепля́ть.

butyl *n.* бути́л.

butylene *n.* бутиле́н.

buxom *adj.* полногру́дый.

buy *v.t.* покупа́ть (*pfv.* купи́ть). *Buy one's wife a present,* купи́ть пода́рок жене́. —*n.* **1,** (purchase) поку́пка. *You got a good buy,* вы сде́лали уда́чную поку́пку. **2,** *colloq.* (bargain) вы́годная поку́пка. —**buy out,** выкупа́ть у (кого́-нибудь) его́ до́лю. —**buy up,** скупа́ть; раскупа́ть; закупа́ть; разбира́ть.

buyer *n.* **1,** (purchaser) покупа́тель. **2,** *comm.* (purchasing agent) заку́пщик.

buzz *v.i.* жужжа́ть. —*n.* **1,** (buzzing) жужжа́ние. **2,** (hum; rumble) гул. —**give someone a buzz,** *colloq.* позвони́ть кому́-нибудь.

buzzard *n.* каню́к; сары́ч.

buzzer *n.* зу́ммер.

by *prep.* **1,** (near) у; о́коло. *Stand by the window,* стоя́ть у окна́. *Sit by the fire,* сиде́ть у огня́. **2,** (beside) по́дле; во́зле; ря́дом с. **3,** (past; beyond) ми́мо: *pass by someone's house,* проходи́ть ми́мо чье́го-нибудь до́ма. **4,** (by way of) че́рез: *leave by the front door,* уходи́ть че́рез пара́дную дверь. **5,** (through the action or agency of) *rendered by the instr. case: done by me,* сде́ланный мно́ю; *by force of arms,* си́лой ору́жия. *He was killed by lightning,* его́ уби́ло мо́лнией. *What do you mean by that?,* что вы хоти́те э́тим сказа́ть? *The situation is complicated by the fact that...,* ситуа́ция усложня́ется тем, что... ◆*Also with the gen.: a novel by Turgenev,* рома́н Турге́нева; *a statement by the President,* заявле́ние президе́нта. ◆*With the -ing form of the verb,*

rendered by the verbal adv.: learn English by watching television, вы́учить англи́йский, смотря́ телеви́зор. **6,** (mode of travel or delivery) на (+ *prepl.*). ◆*Also rendered by the instr. case: go by train,* е́хать на по́езде *or* по́ездом. *Deliver by taxi,* доставля́ть на такси́. *Ship by air/rail,* перевози́ть по во́здуху/ по желе́зной доро́ге/. **7,** (with verbs of holding, seizing, etc.) за (+ *acc.*): *hold/lead (someone) by the hand,* держа́ть/вести́ (кого́-нибудь) за́ руку; *seize by the collar,* схвати́ть за ши́ворот. **8,** (means of communication) по: *by telephone,* по телефо́ну. **9,** *expressing various relationships,* по: *by mistake,* по оши́бке; *by nature,* по приро́де; *by profession,* по профе́ссии; *call by name,* называ́ть по и́мени; *judging by this,* судя́ по э́тому. **10,** (according to) по: *by my watch,* по мои́м часа́м. *By the expression on your face,* по выраже́нию ва́шего лица́. *The books are arranged by subject,* кни́ги расста́влены по предме́там. **11,** (before; no later than) к: *by two o'clock,* к двум часа́м. *By the end of the century,* к концу́ ве́ка. *By the time I get/got there,* когда́ я приду́/пришёл туда́. *By the time the police arrived,* к тому́ вре́мени, когда́ прибыла́ мили́ция. **12,** (born of) от: *a child by her first husband,* ребёнок от пе́рвого му́жа. **13,** (in units of) на: *sell by the pound,* продава́ть на фу́нты. **14,** (at intervals of) *rendered by the prefix* по-: *by the day/month,* подённо/поме́сячно. *He is paid by the day/hour,* ему́ пла́тят подённо; он на почасово́й опла́те. **15,** (in groups of) по: *one by one,* по одному́; оди́н за други́м; *two by two,* по́ двое. **16,** (in succession) за: *step by step,* шаг за ша́гом. *Day by day,* день ото дня. *Little by little,* ма́ло-пома́лу. **17,** (in or to the amount or degree specified) на: *older than you by two years,* ста́рше вас на два го́да. *Ahead by one point,* впереди́ на одно́ очко́. *Miss by a millimeter,* промахну́ться на миллиме́тр. **18,** *in multiplication and division,* на: *multiply/divide ten by five,* умно́жить/ раздели́ть де́сять на пять. **19,** *with dimensions,* на: *six meters by five,* шесть ме́тров на пять. **20,** *in various miscellaneous expressions: by day,* днём; *by night,* но́чью; *by heart,* наизу́сть; *by chance,* случа́йно; *by sight,* в лицо́; *by degrees,* постепе́нно; *by candlelight,* при свеча́х. —*adv.* **1,** (near) бли́зко; ря́дом. *Be standing by,* стоя́ть ря́дом. **2,** (past) ми́мо: *pass by,* пройти́ ми́мо. —**by and by,** со вре́менем. —**by and large,** в це́лом; в основно́м. —**by the way,** ме́жду про́чим; кста́ти.

bye *n., sports: He has/drew a bye,* он (был) свобо́ден от игры́.

bye-bye *interj.* до свида́нья!

Byelorussian *adj. & n.* = **Belorussian.**

bygone *adj.* мину́вший; было́й. —**let bygones be bygones,** что бы́ло, то прошло́.

bylaw *n.* пра́вило; *pl.* уста́в.

bypass *n.* обхо́д. —*v.t.* обходи́ть (стороно́й).

by-product *n.* побо́чный проду́кт.

byroad *n.* просёлок; просёлочная доро́га.

bystander *n.* свиде́тель; очеви́дец.

byword *n.* посло́вица; погово́рка. *Become a byword,* войти́ в посло́вицу.

Byzantine *adj.* византи́йский.

C

C, c тре́тья бу́ква англи́йского алфави́та. —*n.* **1,** (musical note) до. **2,** (school grade) тро́йка.

cab *n.* **1,** (taxi) такси́. *Cab driver,* шофёр такси́. **2,** (driver's compartment) каби́на.

cabal *n.* **1,** (group of plotters) кли́ка. **2,** (plot) за́говор.

cabana *n.* купа́льная каби́на.

cabaret *n.* кабаре́.

cabbage *n.* капу́ста. *Stuffed cabbage,* голубцы́. —*adj.* капу́стный: *cabbage field,* капу́стное по́ле. *Cabbage soup,* щи. —**cabbage butterfly,** капу́стница.

cabin *n.* **1,** (hut; cottage) хи́жина; до́мик. *Log cabin,* бреве́нчатый до́мик. **2,** (stateroom on a ship) каю́та. **3,** (of an airplane) каби́на. —**cabin boy,** ю́нга.

cabinet *n.* **1,** (cupboard; case) шкаф. *Medicine cabinet,* апте́чка. **2,** (of a radio, television set, etc.) ко́рпус. **3,** (advisory body of a chief executive) кабине́т. *Cabinet position,* министе́рский пост.

cabinetmaker *n.* столя́р.

cable *n.* **1,** (rope or wire) кана́т; трос. **2,** (underwater telegraph line) ка́бель. **3,** (cablegram) телегра́мма; каблогра́мма. —*v.t. & i.* телеграфи́ровать.

cable car подвесна́я вагоне́тка; фуникулёр.

cablegram *n.* каблогра́мма; телегра́мма.

cable television ка́бельное телеви́дение.

cabriolet *n.* кабриоле́т.

cacao *n.* кака́о.

cache *n.* тайни́к. *Cache of weapons,* та́йный склад ору́жия.

cackle *v.i.* (of a hen) куда́хтать; (of a goose) гогота́ть. —*n.* куда́хтанье; го́гот.

cacophonous *adj.* неблагозву́чный; какофони́ческий. —**cacophony,** *n.* неблагозву́чие; какофо́ния.

cactus *n.* ка́ктус.

cad *n.* хам.

cadaver *n.* труп. —**cadaverous,** *adj.* ме́ртвенный; помертве́лый.

caddish *adj.* ха́мский.

caddy *n.* ча́йница.

cadence *n.* **1,** (rhythm; beat) ритм; такт. **2,** *music* каде́нция.

cadenza *n.* каде́нция.

cadet *n.* **1,** *mil.* (student) курса́нт. **2,** *cap., hist.* (member of the Russian Constitutional Democrat party) каде́т.

cadge *v.t.* выпра́шивать; выкля́нчивать; стреля́ть.

cadmium *n.* ка́дмий.

cadre *n.* ка́дровый соста́в. —**cadres,** *n.pl.* ка́дры.

caecum *n.* = cecum.

Caesarean section ке́сарево сече́ние.

caesium *n.* = cesium.

café *n.* кафе́.

cafeteria *n.* кафете́рий.

caffeine *n.* кофеи́н.

caftan *n.* кафта́н.

cage *n.* кле́тка. —*v.t.* сажа́ть в кле́тку. *Feel caged in,* чу́вствовать себя́ как в кле́тке.

cagey *also,* **cagy** *adj.* осторо́жный; себе́ на уме́.

cahoots *n.pl., slang, in* **in cahoots with,** в сго́воре с.

caisson *n.* **1,** (watertight chamber) кессо́н. **2,** (ammunition wagon) заря́дный я́щик.

cajole *v.t.* угова́ривать; зада́бривать. —**cajolery,** *n.* угово́ры.

cake *n.* **1,** (pastry) торт; кекс. *Sponge cake,* бискви́т. **2,** (patty of meat or fish) котле́та: *fish cakes,* ры́бные котле́ты. **3,** (bar, as of soap) кусо́к; брусо́к. —*v.i.* ссыха́ться.

calabash *n.* горля́нка.

calamity *n.* бе́дствие. —**calamitous,** *adj.* бе́дственный.

calcify *v.t. & i.* превраща́ть(ся) в и́звесть.

calcium *n.* ка́льций. —*adj.* ка́льциевый. —**calcium carbide,** углеро́дистый ка́льций. —**calcium carbonate,** углеки́слый ка́льций. —**calcium chloride,** хлори́стый ка́льций. —**calcium oxide,** о́кись ка́льция.

calculate *v.t.* **1,** (compute) рассчи́тывать; подсчи́тывать; вычисля́ть; исчисля́ть. **2,** (intend; design) рассчи́тывать: *calculated for effect,* рассчи́танный на эффе́кт. —*v.i.* рассчи́тывать. *I had not calculated on that,* э́то не входи́ло в мои́ расчёты.

calculated *adj.* рассчи́танный: *calculated rudeness,* рассчи́танная гру́бость. —**calculated risk,** риск с то́чным расчётом; обду́манный риск.

calculating *adj.* **1,** (designed to calculate) счётный: *calculating machine,* счётная маши́на. **2,** (shrewd; cautious) расчётливый; себе́ на уме́.

calculation *n.* расчёт; подсчёт; вычисле́ние; исчисле́ние.

calculator *n.* калькуля́тор; арифмо́метр.

calculus *n.* исчисле́ние.

caldron *also,* **cauldron** *n.* котёл.
calendar *n.* календа́рь. —*adj.* календа́рный: *calendar year,* календа́рный год.
calender *n.* кала́ндр.
calf *n.* **1,** (young of the cow) телёнок. **2,** (young of other animals) детёныш. **3,** (rear part of the leg below the knee) икра́. —*adj.* [*also,* **calf's**] теля́чий: *calf's liver,* теля́чья печёнка.
calfskin *n.* теля́чья ко́жа; опо́ек.
caliber *also,* **calibre** *n.* **1,** (diameter) кали́бр. **2,** *fig.* (ability) ка́чества: *person of high caliber,* челове́к высо́ких ка́честв.
calibrate *v.t.* калиброва́ть. —**calibration,** *n.* калибро́вка.
calibre *n.* = **caliber.**
calico *n.* **1,** *U.S.* (printed cloth) си́тец. **2,** *Brit.* (unprinted) митка́ль. —*adj.* си́тцевый; митка́левый.
californium *n.* калифо́рний.
caliper *also,* **calliper** *n., usu. pl.* кронци́ркуль.
caliph *n.* хали́ф; кали́ф. —**caliphate,** *n.* халифа́т.
calisthenics *also,* **callisthenics** *n.* гимна́стика; заря́дка.
calk *v.t.* = **caulk.**
call *v.t.* **1,** (shout to) звать: *Your mother is calling you,* тебя́ зовёт ма́ма. **2,** (utter in a loud voice) называ́ть: *Who called my name?,* кто назва́л моё и́мя? **3,** (summon) вызыва́ть: *call a taxi/doctor,* вы́звать такси́/врача́. *Call a pupil to the blackboard,* вы́звать ученика́ к доске́. **4,** (telephone) звони́ть; вызыва́ть. *I'll call you at six,* я позвоню́ вам в шесть часо́в. *He called to say he would be late,* он позвони́л сказа́ть, что опа́здывает (*or* опозда́ет). *What number are you calling?,* по како́му но́меру вы звони́те? **5,** (name) называ́ть: *What is this called?,* как э́то называ́ется? *Call it what you will,* называ́йте, как хоти́те. *Call me by my first name,* зови́те *or* называ́йте меня́ про́сто по и́мени. *His friends call him Jack,* его́ друзья́ зову́т его́ Джек. **6,** (describe as specified) называ́ть: *call someone a liar,* назва́ть кого́-нибудь лжецо́м. *You could hardly call her beautiful,* её нельзя́ назва́ть краса́вицей. **7,** (declare) признава́ть: *call the game a draw,* призна́ть па́ртию ничье́й. *Let's call it a day,* на сего́дня хва́тит. **8,** (convene) созыва́ть: *call a meeting,* созыва́ть собра́ние. **9,** *with various nouns: call a strike,* объяви́ть забасто́вку; *call (someone) names,* обруга́ть; *call the roll,* де́лать перекли́чку; *call attention to,* обраща́ть (чьё-нибудь) внима́ние на. **10,** *in various expressions: call to mind,* воскреша́ть в па́мяти; напомина́ть; *call to order,* призыва́ть к поря́дку; *call to arms,* призыва́ть к ору́жию; *call into question,* ста́вить под вопро́с (*or* под сомне́ние). —*v.i.* **1,** (shout) звать: *call for help,* звать на по́мощь. *I heard someone calling,* я слы́шал, как кто́-то позва́л. *He called to me from across the street,* он позва́л меня́ с той стороны́ у́лицы. **2,** (phone) звони́ть: *No one called,* никто́ не звони́л. *Who is calling?,* кто его́ (её) спра́шивает? **3,** (of a ship) захо́дить: *call at a port,* заходи́ть в порт. —*n.* **1,** (cry; shout) крик: *call for help,* крик о по́мощи. **2,** (phone communication) вы́зов; звоно́к. *Receive many calls,*

получи́ть мно́го вы́зовов. *Were there any calls for me?,* мне никто́ не звони́л? *I'm expecting a phone call,* я жду телефо́нного звонка́. *I'll await your call,* я бу́ду ждать ва́шего звонка́. *Make a phone call,* звони́ть по телефо́ну. *May I make a call from your telephone?,* мо́жно позвони́ть от вас? **3,** (appeal) призы́в: *a call to action,* призы́в к де́йствию. **4,** (cry of a bird or animal) крик. *Mating call,* токова́ние. **5,** (sound of a horn) сигна́л: *bugle call,* сигна́л го́рна. **6,** (visit) визи́т: *courtesy call,* визи́т ве́жливости. *Pay a call on,* заходи́ть к; приходи́ть с визи́том к. —**call aside,** отводи́ть в сто́рону. —**call back, 1,** (summon back; recall) отзыва́ть. **2,** (telephone again) звони́ть ещё раз; перезвони́ть. —**call down,** *colloq.* отчита́ть. —**call for, 1,** (come and pick up) заходи́ть за; заезжа́ть за. **2,** (appeal for; advocate) призыва́ть к *or* на. **3,** (require) тре́бовать. —**call forth,** вызыва́ть. —**call in, 1,** (summon) вызыва́ть. **2,** (phone in) сообща́ть по телефо́ну. **3,** (retire from circulation) изыма́ть из обраще́ния. —**call off, 1,** (summon away) отзыва́ть. **2,** (read aloud) называ́ть. **3,** (cancel) отменя́ть. **4,** (halt before completing) прекраща́ть: *call off the search,* прекраща́ть по́иски. —**call on, 1,** (ask to recite, as in class) спра́шивать; вызыва́ть. **2,** (allow to speak) дава́ть *or* предоставля́ть сло́во (+ *dat.*). **3,** (visit briefly) посеща́ть; заходи́ть к. **4,** (urge) призыва́ть. **5,** (appeal to, as for help) обраща́ться к. —**call out, 1,** (shout) крича́ть; выкри́кивать. *Call out someone's name,* вы́крикнуть чьё-нибудь и́мя. **2,** (summon) вызыва́ть. —**call up, 1,** (call on the telephone) вызыва́ть; звони́ть. **2,** (summon for military service) призыва́ть; мобилизова́ть.
caller *n.* **1,** (on the telephone) звоня́щий. **2,** (visitor) посети́тель.
calligraphy *n.* каллигра́фия. —**calligraphic,** *adj.* каллиграфи́ческий.
calling *n.* призва́ние: *follow one's calling,* сле́довать своему́ призва́нию. —**calling card,** визи́тная ка́рточка.
calliper *n.* = **caliper.**
callisthenics *n.* = **calisthenics.**
call number шифр.
callous *adj.* **1,** [*also,* **calloused**] (hardened) огрубе́лый; загрубе́лый; мозо́листый. **2,** *fig.* (unfeeling) чёрствый; безду́шный. —**callousness,** *n.* чёрствость; безду́шие.
callow *adj.* зелёный; безу́сый; неопери́вшийся.
call sign позывно́й сигна́л; позывны́е.
callus *n.* мозо́ль.
calm *adj.* споко́йный: *calm sea,* споко́йное мо́ре; *calm voice,* споко́йный го́лос. *Everyone remained calm,* все сохраня́ли споко́йствие. —*n.* **1,** (tranquillity) споко́йствие. **2,** (absence of wind) зати́шье. *The calm before the storm,* зати́шье пе́ред грозо́й. —*v.t.* успока́ивать: *calm the children,* успоко́ить дете́й. *Calm fears,* уня́ть стра́сти; разве́ять опасе́ния. —*v.i.* [*usu.* **calm down**] успока́иваться. —**calmly,** *adv.* споко́йно.

caloric *adj.* тепловóй. *Caloric content,* калорийность.

calorie *n.* калóрия.

calorimeter *n.* калориметр; тепломéр.

calque *n.* кáлька.

calumniate *v.t.* клеветáть на. —**calumnious,** *adj.* клеветнический. —**calumny,** *n.* клеветá.

Calvary *n.* Голгóфа.

calve *v.i.* телиться.

calyx *n.* чáшечка.

cam *n.* кулáк; кулачóк; эксцéнтрик.

camaraderie *n.* товáрищество.

cambium *n.* кáмбий.

Cambodian *adj.* камбоджийский.

cambric *n.* батист.

camel *n.* верблюд.

camellia *n.* камéлия.

camel's hair 1, (hair) верблюжья шерсть. **2,** (cloth) верблюжье сукнó. —**camel's-hair,** *adj.* верблюжий.

cameo *n.* камéя.

camera *n.* фотографический аппарáт; фотоаппарáт. *Camera crew,* съёмочная грýппа. —**movie camera,** киноаппарáт; кинокáмера. —**television camera,** телевизиóнная кáмера; телекáмера.

cameraman *n.* кинооперáтор. *TV cameraman,* оперáтор телевидения.

camomile *also,* **chamomile** *n.* ромáшка; пупáвка.

camouflage *n.* маскирóвка; камуфляж. —*v.t.* маскировáть.

camp *n.* лáгерь: *prisoner-of-war camp,* лáгерь военноплéнных. *Split into two camps,* расколóться на два лáгеря. —*v.i.* **1,** (set up camp) располагáться лáгерем. **2,** *fol. by* **out** (sleep outdoors) жить в палáтках.

campaign *n.* кампáния; похóд. *Election campaign,* избирáтельная *or* предвыборная кампáния. *Fund-raising campaign,* кампáния по сбóру средств. *Economy campaign,* кампáния бережливости; похóд за эконóмию. —*v.i.* проводить кампáнию.

campanula *n.* колокóльчик.

campfire *n.* костёр.

camphor *n.* камфарá.

campsite *n.* кéмпинг.

campus *n.* университéтский городóк.

camshaft *n.* распределительный вал; кулачкóвый вал.

can¹ *v.aux.* **1,** (be able) мочь: *I cannot come today,* я не могý прийти сегóдня. *What can I do for you?,* чем могý быть вам полéзен? *Can you see the blackboard?,* вам видна доскá? *Run as fast as you can,* бегите как мóжно быстрéе. **2,** (know how) умéть: *Can you drive a car?,* вы умéете водить машину? *See also* **could.**

can² *n.* **1,** (small container) бáнка. *Tin can,* жестянка; консéрвная бáнка. *Beer can,* жестянка из-под пива. **2,** (large container) бидóн: *milk can,* бидóн для молокá. *Garbage can,* мýсорный ящик. *Watering can,* лéйка. —*v.t.* (preserve) консервировáть. —**can opener,** консéрвный нож; открывáлка для консéрвов. *See also* **canned.**

Canadian *adj.* канáдский. —*n.* канáдец; канáдка.

canal *n.* канáл.

canard *n.* ýтка.

canary *n.* канарéйка. —**canary-yellow,** *adj.* канарéечный; канарéечного цвéта.

cancan *n.* канкáн.

cancel *v.t.* **1,** (call off) отменять. **2,** (void) отменять; аннулировáть. **3,** (mark, as a postage stamp) погашáть. **4,** *fol. by* **out** (negate) сводить на нет. **5,** *math.* сокращáть.

cancellation *n.* **1,** (calling off) отмéна. **2,** (voiding) отмéна; аннулировáние. **3,** (marking of postage stamps) погашéние; (mark so made) гашéние. **4,** *math.* сокращéние.

cancer *n.* **1,** (disease) рак: *skin cancer,* рак кóжи. **2,** *cap., astron.* Рак. —*adj.* рáковый: *cancer cell,* рáковая клéтка. *Cancer patient,* рáковый больнóй. *Cancer research,* исслéдования в óбласти рáка.

cancerous *adj.* рáковый.

candelabrum *n.* канделябр.

candid *adj.* откровéнный; чистосердéчный.

candidacy *n.* кандидатýра.

candidate *n.* кандидáт. *Candidate for president,* кандидáт в президéнты; кандидáт на пост президéнта.

candied *adj.* засáхаренный.

candle *n.* свечá. —**burn the candle at both ends,** жечь свечý с двух концóв. —**not hold a candle to,** в подмётки не годиться (+ *dat.*). —**the game is not worth the candle,** игрá не стóит свеч.

candlelight *n.* свет свечи: *by candlelight,* при свéте свечи; при свечáх. —**candle-lit,** *adj.* освещённый свечáми.

candlepower *n.* сила свéта в свечáх. *Bulb of forty candlepower,* лáмпочка в сóрок свечéй.

candlestick *n.* подсвéчник.

candor *also,* **candour** *n.* откровéнность; чистосердéчие. —**in all candor,** со всей откровéнностью.

candy *n.* конфéты. *Piece of candy,* конфéта. —*adj.* конфéтный: *candy wrapper,* конфéтная обёртка.

cane *n.* **1,** (walking stick) пáлка; трость. *He walks with a cane,* он хóдит с пáлкой. **2,** (plant) тростник; камыш. *Sugar cane,* сáхарный тростник. —*v.t.* бить пáлкой. —**cane sugar,** тростникóвый сáхар.

canine *adj.* собáчий. —**canine tooth,** клык.

canister *n.* **1,** (container for tea or spices) корóбка; бáнка. **2,** (part of a gas mask; device for dispensing tear gas) корóбка. —**canister shot,** картéчь.

canker *n.* язва.

canned *adj.* консервированный. *Canned food,* консéрвы. *Canned meat,* мясные консéрвы. *Canned vegetables,* овощные консéрвы. *Canned fruit,* консервированные фрýкты.

cannery *n.* консéрвная фáбрика.

cannibal *n.* людоéд. —**cannibalism,** *n.* людоéдство. —**cannibalistic,** *adj.* людоéдский.

cannon *n.* **1,** (weapon) пýшка. **2,** *Brit.* (carom) карамбóль. —**cannon ball,** пýшечное ядрó. —**cannon fodder,** пýшечное мясо.

cannonade *n.* пýшечная пальбá; канонáда.

cannot = can not.

canny *adj.* **1,** (cautious) осмотрительный. **2,** (shrewd) себé на умé.

canoe *n.* каноэ; чёлн; челнок; байдарка. —**canoeist,** *n.* каноист.

canon *n.* **1,** (religious law; principle; rule) канон. **2,** (clergyman) каноник. **3,** *music* канон. —**canon law,** каноническое право.

canonical *adj.* канонический.

canonize *v.t.* канонизировать; причислять к лику святых.

canopy *n.* балдахин; полог.

cant *n.* жаргон; арго. *Thieves' cant,* воровской жаргон; блат.

cantaloupe *also,* **cantaloup** *n.* канталупа.

cantankerous *adj.* сварливый; вздорный.

cantata *n.* кантата.

canteen *n.* **1,** (flask) фляга; фляжка. **2,** *mil.* военный магазин; клуб-столовая.

canter *n.* лёгкий галоп. —*v.i.* идти лёгким галопом.

cantilever *n.* консоль. —**cantilever bridge,** консольный мост.

canto *n.* песнь.

canton *n.* кантон. —**cantonal,** *adj.* кантональный.

cantor *n.* кантор.

canvas *n.* **1,** (cloth) парусина. **2,** (a piece of such material on which to paint) холст. **3,** (painting on canvas) полотно. **4,** (loosely woven cloth for needlework) канва. —*adj.* парусиновый.

canvass *v.t.* **1,** (travel through) объездить. **2,** (poll; survey) опрашивать.

canyon *n.* каньон; ущелье.

cap *n.* **1,** (fur) шапка; (small) кепка; (part of a uniform) фуражка; (fool's, chef's, etc.) колпак. **2,** (covering, as for a bottle) колпачок. *Lens cap,* крышка объектива. **3,** (of a mushroom) шляпка. **4,** (percussion cap) капсюль. —*v.t.* **1,** (put a lid on, as a bottle) закрывать. **2,** (complete; top off) довершать. —**to cap all,** в довершение всего.

capability *n.* **1,** (ability) способность. **2,** *usu. pl.* (potential ability) возможности.

capable *adj.* способный: *capable worker,* способный работник. *Capable of anything,* способен на всё. —**capably,** *adv.* умело.

capacious *adj.* ёмкий; вместительный.

capacitor *n.* конденсатор.

capacity *n.* **1,** (ability to hold; volume) вместимость; ёмкость. *Filled to capacity,* полный до отказа; битком набитый. **2,** (ability) способность: *capacity for learning,* способность к учёбе; *carrying capacity,* пропускная способность. **3,** (maximum level of production) мощность: *operate at full/half capacity,* работать на полную мощность; работать в половину мощности. **4,** (position; function) качество: *in the capacity of...,* в качестве (+ *gen.*). —*adj.* полный: *play to capacity crowds,* делать полные сборы; идти с аншлагом.

cape *n.* **1,** (point of land) мыс: *Cape of Good Hope,* Мыс Доброй Надежды. **2,** (sleeveless outer garment) накидка; пелерина.

caper *n.* **1,** (playful leap) прыжок. **2,** (prank) выходка; проказа. **3,** *pl.* (condiment) каперсы.

capillary *n.* капилляр.

capital *n.* **1,** (capital city) столица. **2,** *econ.* капитал. —*adj.* **1,** (containing the seat of government) столичный: *capital city,* столичный город. **2,** *econ.* капитальный. *Capital investment,* капиталовложения. **3,** (punishable by death) наказуемый смертью. *Capital punishment,* смертная казнь; высшая мера наказания. **4,** (of a letter) прописной; заглавный; большой. *This word is spelled with a capital letter,* это слово пишется с большой буквы. **5,** *colloq.* (excellent; first-rate) превосходный; первоклассный. —**make capital of,** спекулировать на; выезжать на.

capitalism *n.* капитализм.

capitalist *n.* капиталист. —*adj.* [*also,* **capitalistic**] капиталистический.

capitalization *n.* **1,** *gram.* употребление прописных букв: *the rules for capitalization,* правила употребления прописных букв. **2,** *econ.* капитализация.

capitalize *v.t.* **1,** (write with a capital letter) писать с большой буквы. **2,** (convert into capital) капитализировать. —*v.i.* [*usu.* **capitalize on**] использовать; пользоваться.

capitol *n.* капитолий.

capitulate *v.i.* капитулировать. —**capitulation,** *n.* капитуляция.

capon *n.* каплун.

caprice *n.* каприз; причуда; прихоть.

capricious *adj.* капризный; прихотливый.

Capricorn *n.* Козерог. —**Tropic of Capricorn,** тропик Козерога.

capsize *v.t.* опрокидывать. —*v.i.* опрокидываться.

capstan *n.* кабестан; шпиль.

capsule *n.* **1,** (for enclosing a dose of medicine) капсула. **2,** (detachable part of a rocket) капсула; кабина. —*adj.* краткий: *capsule summary,* краткое изложение.

captain *n.* **1,** (military rank) капитан; (naval rank) капитан первого ранга. **2,** (ship's commander) капитан; командир. **3,** *sports* капитан.

caption *n.* **1,** (heading) заголовок. **2,** (of an illustration or cartoon) подпись. **3,** *motion pictures* субтитр.

captious *adj.* придирчивый.

captivate *v.t.* пленять; очаровывать; восхищать. —**captivating,** *adj.* пленительный; очаровательный; восхитительный.

captive *n.* пленник; пленный. —*adj.* взятый в плен; пленный. —**be taken captive,** попасть в плен. —**hold captive,** держать в плену. —**take captive,** взять в плен.

captivity *n.* **1,** (of people) плен; неволя. **2,** (of animals) неволя: *breed in captivity,* размножаться в неволе.

capture *v.t.* **1,** (take or seize by force) захватывать: *capture a town,* захватить город. *Capture a criminal,* схватить преступника. *Capture a bear,* поймать медведя. *Captured weapons,* трофейное оружие. **2,** (win in a contest) завоёвывать. **3,** *chess* брать. **4,** *fig.* (arrest, as one's imagination) захватывать; пленять; поражать. **5,** (record for posterity) запечатлевать; схватывать: *capture on film,* запечатлевать/схватывать на плёнке. **6,** *Capture the heart of,* покоря́ть се́рдце (+ *gen.*). —*n.* захва́т; пои́мка.

capuchin *n.* **1,** *cap.* (monk) капуци́н. **2,** (cloak) плащ с капюшо́ном. **3,** (monkey) капуци́н.

capybara *n.* водосви́нка.

car *n.* **1,** (automobile) маши́на; автомоби́ль. **2,** (of a train) ваго́н: *passenger car,* пассажи́рский ваго́н. —*adj.* *Car repairs,* ремо́нт автомоби́лей; авторемо́нт. *Car loan,* ссу́да на поку́пку маши́ны. *Car insurance,* страхова́ние автомоби́ля; страхо́вка на маши́ну.

caracul *also,* **karakul** *n.* **1,** (sheep) кораку́льская овца́. **2,** (fur) кара́куль.

carafe *n.* графи́н.

caramel *n.* караме́ль. —*adj.* караме́льный.

carat *n.* **1,** (unit of weight for gems) кара́т. **2,** = **karat.**

caravan *n.* карава́н.

caravel *n.* караве́лла.

caraway *n.* тмин. —*adj.* тми́нный.

carbide *n.* карби́д.

carbine *n.* караби́н.

carbohydrate *n.* углево́д.

carbolic *adj.* карбо́ловый. —**carbolic acid,** карбо́ловая кислота́; карбо́лка.

carbon *n.* углеро́д.

carbonate *n.* карбона́т; углеки́слая соль. —*v.t.* гази́ровать: *carbonated beverages,* газиро́ванные напи́тки.

carbon copy 1, (copy made with carbon paper) ко́пия. *Make carbon copies of,* писа́ть под копи́рку. **2,** *colloq.* (perfect likeness) то́чная ко́пия.

carbon dioxide углеки́слый газ.

carbonic acid углекислота́; у́гольная кислота́.

carbon monoxide уга́рный газ.

carbon paper копирова́льная бума́га; копи́рка.

carborundum *n.* карбору́нд.

carbuncle *n.* карбу́нкул.

carburetor *also,* **carburettor** *n.* карбюра́тор.

carcass *n.* ту́ша.

carcinogen *n.* канцероге́н; карциноге́н. —**carcinogenic,** *adj.* канцероге́нный.

card *n.* **1,** (piece of stiff paper used for various purposes) ка́рточка: *business card,* визи́тная ка́рточка. **2,** (playing card) ка́рта: *play cards,* игра́ть в ка́рты. **3,** (certificate of membership) биле́т: *membership card,* чле́нский биле́т. —*adj.* ка́рточный: *card trick/catalogue,* ка́рточный фо́кус/катало́г. —*v.t.* чеса́ть: *card wool,* чеса́ть шерсть. —**house of cards,** ка́рточный до́мик. —**it was not in the cards,** ви́дно, не судьба́! —**lay one's cards on the table,** вы́ложить ка́рты на стол.

cardboard *n.* карто́н. —*adj.* карто́нный; картона́жный.

card file картоте́ка.

cardiac *adj.* серде́чный. —**cardiac arrest,** остано́вка се́рдца.

cardigan *n.* шерстяна́я ко́фточка.

cardinal *adj.* основно́й; кардина́льный. *Cardinal principle,* основно́й при́нцип. —*n.* **1,** (prelate) кардина́л. **2,** (bird) кардина́л. —**cardinal number,**

коли́чественное числи́тельное. —**cardinal point,** страна́ све́та.

cardiogram *n.* кардиогра́мма.

cardiograph *n.* кардио́граф.

cardiology *n.* кардиоло́гия. —**cardiologist,** *n.* кардио́лог.

cardiovascular *adj.* серде́чно-сосу́дистый.

cardplayer *n.* игро́к в ка́рты. *Avid cardplayer,* зая́длый картёжник. —**cardplaying,** *n.* игра́ в ка́рты.

cardsharp *n.* шу́лер.

card table ка́рточный стол; ло́мберный стол.

care *n.* **1,** (concern; source of concern) забо́та: *my chief care,* гла́вная моя́ забо́та. *She hasn't a care in the world,* она́ не име́ет никаки́х забо́т. **2,** (close attention) ухо́д: *care of the sick,* ухо́д за больны́ми; *care of one's car,* ухо́д за маши́ной. *Free medical care,* беспла́тное медици́нское обслу́живание *or* обеспе́чение. *System of health care,* систе́ма здравоохране́ния. *Require constant care,* тре́бовать постоя́нного ухо́да. *He received excellent care,* за ним был прекра́сный ухо́д. **3,** (charge; supervision) попече́ние: *He was left in the care of his grandmother,* он оста́лся на попече́нии ба́бушки. *Under the care of a physician,* под наблюде́нием врача́. **4,** (painstaking application) тща́тельность. *With the greatest of care,* са́мым тща́тельным о́бразом. **5,** (caution) осторо́жность: *handle with care,* обраща́ться с осторо́жностью. —*v.i.* забо́титься: *care about one's future,* забо́титься о своём бу́дущем. *I don't care,* мне всё равно́. *I don't care what happens,* мне безразли́чно, что бу́дет. *I couldn't care less,* мне э́то соверше́нно безразли́чно. *What do I care?,* како́е мне де́ло? *What does he care about...!,* что ему́ до...? *He doesn't care about that,* ему́ нет де́ла до э́того. —*v.t.* хоте́ть: *I don't care to go,* мне не хо́чется идти́. —**care for, 1,** (tend) уха́живать за: *care for the wounded,* уха́живать за ра́неными. **2,** (enjoy; be fond of) люби́ть: *I don't care for opera,* я не люблю́ о́перы. **3,** (like; wish) хоте́ть: *Would you care for another cup of tea?,* хоти́те ещё ча́шку ча́ю? —**care of,** для переда́чи че́рез. —**take care,** быть осторо́жным. —**take care of, 1,** (care for) забо́титься о; уха́живать за; бере́чь; побере́чь. *Take care of the children,* забо́титься о де́тях; уха́живать за детьми́. *Take care of oneself,* бере́чь себя́; побере́чься. *Take care of one's skin,* хо́лить свою́ ко́жу. *She is able to take care of herself,* она́ в состоя́нии уха́живать за собо́й. **2,** (attend to) занима́ться (+ *instr.*); позабо́титься о. *Take care of personal matters,* занима́ться ли́чными дела́ми. *I'll take care of that,* я позабо́чусь об э́том. —**take care not to,** смотри́те, не (+ *imperative*).

careen *v.i.* крени́ться. *The car careened from side to side,* маши́ну броса́ло из стороны́ в сто́рону.

career *n.* карье́ра. —*adj.* ка́дровый: *career officer/diplomat,* ка́дровый офице́р/диплома́т. —**careerist,** *n.* карьери́ст.

carefree *adj.* беззабо́тный; беспе́чный.

careful *adj.* **1,** (cautious) осторо́жный. *Be careful!,* осторо́жно!; бу́дьте осторо́жны! **2,** (painstaking) тща́тельный.

carefully *adv.* **1,** (with caution) осторо́жно. **2,** (with great care) тща́тельно. **3,** (with close attention) внима́тельно.

careless *adj.* **1,** (slipshod) небре́жный. *Make a careless mistake,* допусти́ть оши́бку по небре́жности. **2,** (incautious) неосторо́жный: *careless handling/ remark,* неосторо́жное обраще́ние/замеча́ние. **3,** (inattentive) невнима́тельный: *careless driving,* невнима́тельная езда́. *Be careless about one's appearance,* не забо́титься о свое́й вне́шности *or* о своём вне́шнем ви́де. *How careless of me!,* како́й я нело́вкий! —**carelessly,** *adv.* небре́жно; неосторо́жно. —**carelessness,** *n.* небре́жность; неосторо́жность.

caress *n.* ла́ска. —*v.t.* ласка́ть.

caretaker *n.* дво́рник.

carfare *n.* проездна́я пла́та.

cargo *n.* груз. —*adj.* грузово́й: *cargo ship,* грузово́е су́дно.

Caribbean *adj.* кари́бский.

caricature *n.* карикату́ра.

caries *n.* костое́да; ка́риес.

carillon *n.* карильо́н.

carious *adj.* карио́зный.

carload *n.* ваго́н: *carload of coal,* ваго́н у́гля.

carmine *n.* карми́н. —*adj.* карми́нный; карми́новый.

carnage *n.* резня́; бо́йня.

carnal *adj.* **1,** (of the flesh) пло́тский. **2,** (sexual) полово́й.

carnation *n.* гвозди́ка.

carnival *n.* карнава́л.

carnivore *n.* плотоя́дное живо́тное. —**carnivorous,** *adj.* плотоя́дный.

carol *n.* рожде́ственская пе́сня; коля́дка.

carom *n.* карамбо́ль. —*v.i.* отска́кивать.

carotid artery со́нная арте́рия.

carousal *n.* кутёж; попо́йка.

carouse *v.i.* кути́ть; гуля́ть.

carousel *also,* **carrousel** *n.* карусе́ль.

carouser *n.* кути́ла; гуля́ка.

carp *n.* карп; саза́н; кара́сь. —*v.i.* придира́ться.

carpenter *n.* пло́тник. *Carpenter's tool,* пло́тничий инструме́нт.

carpentry *n.* пло́тничье *or* пло́тничное де́ло; пло́тничество.

carpet *n.* ковёр. —*v.t.* устила́ть ковро́м. —**call on the carpet,** *colloq.* вы́звать на ковёр.

carpet sweeper щётка для ковра́.

carping *adj.* приди́рчивый.

carriage *n.* **1,** (vehicle) коля́ска; экипа́ж; каре́та. *Baby carriage,* де́тская коля́ска. *Gun carriage,* лафе́т. **2,** *Brit.* (railroad passenger car) ваго́н. **3,** (moving part, as of a typewriter) каре́тка. **4,** (manner of carrying oneself; bearing) оса́нка; вы́правка.

carrier *n.* **1,** (one who carries something) перено́счик. **2,** (person transmitting a disease) носи́тель; (insect doing same) перено́счик. **3,** *mil.* транспортёр. **4,** (aircraft carrier) авиано́сец. —**carrier pigeon,** почто́вый го́лубь.

carrion *n.* па́даль; мертвечи́на.

carrot *n.* морко́вь. —*adj.* морко́вный: *carrot juice,* морко́вный сок. —**carrot and stick,** поли́тика кнута́ и пря́ника.

carrousel *n.* = **carousel**.

carry *v.t.* **1,** (bear) нести́: *carry a child in one's arms,* нести́ ребёнка на рука́х; *carry a pack on one's back,* нести́ ра́нец на спине́. **2,** (have or keep on one's person) носи́ть; держа́ть при себе́. *Carry money in one's pocket,* носи́ть де́ньги в карма́не. **3,** (transport) нести́; переноси́ть; (*by vehicle*) везти́; перевози́ть. *Carry the suitcases upstairs,* нести́ *or* переноси́ть чемода́ны наве́рх. *Carry the wounded from the battlefield,* выноси́ть ра́неных с по́ля бо́я. *Carry passengers and freight,* перевози́ть пассажи́ров и гру́зы. **4,** (cause to drift or float) уноси́ть: *carry out to sea,* уноси́ть в мо́ре. *The current carried the boat downstream,* тече́нием унесло́ ло́дку. **5,** (have in stock) держа́ть; торгова́ть. **6,** (be pregnant with) вына́шивать. **7,** (print, as an article or information) помеща́ть; печа́тать; публикова́ть. **8,** (extend) доводи́ть: *carry to an extreme,* доводи́ть до кра́йности. **9,** *in various miscellaneous expressions: carry weight,* име́ть вес; *carry insurance,* быть застрахо́ванным. —*v.i.* **1,** (travel, as of sound) доноси́ться. *His voice doesn't carry,* его́ го́лос пло́хо слы́шен. **2,** (be approved) проходи́ть. *The motion carried,* предложе́ние прошло́; предложе́ние бы́ло при́нято. —**carry away,** уноси́ть. *Be/get carried away, fig.* увлека́ться. —**carry forward,** bookkeeping транспорти́ровать. —**carry in,** вноси́ть. —**carry off.** *He was carried off on a stretcher,* его́ вы́несли на носи́лках. —**carry on, 1,** (engage in; conduct) вести́. **2,** (continue; keep up) продолжа́ть. **3,** *colloq.* (behave wildly) устра́ивать сце́ну; рвать и мета́ть. —**carry oneself,** держа́ться. —**carry out, 1,** *literally* выноси́ть. **2,** (fulfill, as an order, promise, etc.) выполня́ть; исполня́ть. **3,** (conduct, as an investigation, experiment, etc.) проводи́ть; производи́ть. **4,** (execute, as a mission, raid, coup, etc.) соверша́ть. **5,** (put into practice, as a plan or program) осуществля́ть. **6,** (implement, as a threat or sentence) приводи́ть в исполне́ние.

cart *n.* **1,** (vehicle pulled by an animal) теле́га; подво́да; двуко́лка. **2,** (handcart) (ручна́я) теле́жка. —*v.t.* **1,** (transport) везти́; перевози́ть. *Cart away,* увози́ть. **2,** (carry with great effort) тащи́ть. —**put the cart before the horse,** ста́вить теле́гу пе́ред ло́шадью.

cartel *n.* карте́ль.

carter *n.* во́зчик; ломово́й; ломово́й изво́зчик.

cartilage *n.* хрящ. —**cartilaginous,** *adj.* хрящева́тый.

cartography *n.* картогра́фия. —**cartographer,** *n.* карто́граф. —**cartographic,** *adj.* картографи́ческий.

carton *n.* карто́нка. *Carton of cigarettes,* блок сигаре́т.

cartoon *n.* **1,** (drawing) карикату́ра. **2,** (film) мультипликацио́нный фильм; мультфи́льм. —**cartoonist,** *n.* карикатури́ст.

cartridge *n.* патро́н. —**cartridge case,** ги́льза. —**cartridge clip,** обо́йма. —**cartridge pouch,** подсу́мок.

carve *v.t.* **1,** (make by cutting) ре́зать; (*specifically in wood*) выреза́ть; (*specifically in stone*) высека́ть. **2,** (slice, as meat) нареза́ть. **3,** *fol. by* **up** (divide up) разделя́ть; разбива́ть. **4,** *fol. by* **out** (achieve) кова́ть: *carve out a victory,* кова́ть побе́ду. *Carve out a career,* сде́лать карье́ру. —**carved,** *adj.* резно́й; вы́резной. —**carver,** *n.* ре́зчик. —**carving,** *n.* резьба́; резна́я рабо́та.

caryatid *n.* кариати́да.

cascade *n.* каска́д. —*v.i.* низверга́ться.

case *n.* **1,** (instance) слу́чай: *in most cases,* в большинстве́ слу́чаев. *In any case,* во вся́ком слу́чае. *In case...,* в том слу́чае, е́сли...; на слу́чай, е́сли... *In case of,* в слу́чае (+ *gen.*). *Just in case,* на вся́кий слу́чай. *Make an exception in someone's case,* сде́лать исключе́ние для кого́-нибудь. **2,** *preceded by* **the** (the actual state of affairs): *That is not the case,* э́то не так; э́то не ве́рно. *If that's the case; that being the case,* в тако́м слу́чае; е́сли де́ло обстои́т так. *As the case may be,* в зави́симости от обстоя́тельств. *As is often the case,* как э́то ча́сто быва́ет. *That does not alter the case,* э́то не меня́ет су́ти де́ла. **3,** *law* де́ло: *hear a case,* слу́шать де́ло. **4,** (argument in support of) до́воды: *the case for capital punishment,* до́воды в по́льзу сме́ртной ка́зни. **5,** (instance of disease) слу́чай: *a mild case of the flu,* лёгкий слу́чай гри́ппа. *Three cases of the mumps,* три слу́чая заболева́ния сви́нкой. **6,** (person being treated) больно́й: *a mental case,* психи́чески больно́й. *It's a hopeless case,* больно́й безнадёжен. **7,** *gram.* паде́ж: *accusative case,* вини́тельный паде́ж. **8,** (large box) я́щик: *packing case,* упако́вочный я́щик. **9,** (small box) футля́р: *eyeglass case,* футля́р для очко́в. *Cigarette case,* портсига́р. **10,** (cover) чехо́л: *case for a camera,* чехо́л для фотоаппара́та. **11,** (showcase) витри́на. **12,** (tray for storing type) ка́сса.

caseharden *v.t.* цементи́ровать.

case history исто́рия боле́зни.

casein *n.* казеи́н.

case law прецеде́нтное пра́во.

casemate *n.* казема́т.

casement *n.* ство́рка. —**casement window,** ство́рчатое окно́.

cash *n.* нали́чные (де́ньги): *pay cash,* плати́ть нали́чными. *Short of cash,* не при деньга́х. *Large amount(s) of cash,* кру́пная нали́чность. —*adj.* нали́чный: *cash payment,* нали́чный расчёт. —*v.t. Cash a check,* **1,** (of a person) предъяви́ть чек к опла́те. **2,** (of a bank) вы́дать де́ньги по че́ку.

cashbook *n.* ка́ссовая кни́га.

cash box ка́сса.

cashier *n.* касси́р. —*v.t.* увольня́ть со слу́жбы.

cashmere *n.* кашеми́р. —*adj.* кашеми́ровый.

cash register ка́сса.

casing *n.* кожу́х; ко́рпус.

casino *n.* казино́.

cask *n.* бо́чка; бочо́нок.

casket *n.* **1,** (small box) шкату́лка. **2,** (coffin) гроб.

cassava *n.* манио́ка.

cassette *n.* кассе́та.

Cassiopeia *n.* Кассиопе́я.

cassock *n.* ря́са.

cast *v.t.* **1,** (throw) броса́ть; кида́ть; мета́ть. *Cast overboard,* выбра́сывать за́ борт. *Cast a (fishing) line,* заки́дывать у́дочку. **2,** (cause to fall, drop, or occur) броса́ть: *cast anchor,* бро́сить я́корь; *cast a glance,* бро́сить взгляд. *Cast a shadow,* отбра́сывать тень. *Cast doubt upon,* ста́вить под сомне́ние. *Cast a spell over,* заколдо́вывать; околдо́вывать. *Cast one's lot with,* связа́ть свою́ судьбу́ с. **3,** (give, as a vote) подава́ть; отдава́ть (го́лос). **4,** (draw, as lots) броса́ть (жре́бий). *The die is cast,* жре́бий бро́шен. **5,** (shape; mold) лить; отлива́ть. —*n.* **1,** (mold) сле́пок. **2,** *med.* гипс: *put someone's arm in a cast,* накла́дывать гипс на́ руку. **3,** (actors in a play) соста́в исполни́телей. **4,** (tinge; shade) отте́нок. **5,** *Cast of mind,* склад ума́. —**cast about for,** изы́скивать. —**cast aside,** отбра́сывать. —**cast off, 1,** (throw off) сбра́сывать. **2,** (sail off, as of a boat) отва́ливать; отча́ливать.

castanets *n.pl.* кастанье́ты.

caste *n.* ка́ста. —*adj.* ка́стовый: *caste system,* ка́стовая систе́ма.

caster *n.* **1,** (founder) лите́йщик. **2,** [*also,* **castor**] (small wheel) колёсико; ро́лик.

castigate *v.t.* подверга́ть суро́вой кри́тике; бичева́ть.

Castilian *adj.* касти́льский.

casting *n.* **1,** (founding) литьё; отли́вка. **2,** (object cast in a mold) отли́вка; *pl.* литьё. **3,** *theat.* распределе́ние роле́й.

cast iron чугу́н. —**cast-iron,** *adj.* чугу́нный.

castle *n.* **1,** (fortress) за́мок. **2,** (chess piece) ладья́; тура́. —*v.i. chess* рокирова́ть(ся); де́лать рокиро́вку. —**castles in the air,** возду́шные за́мки.

castor *n.* **1,** (cloth) касто́р; бо́брик. **2,** = **caster.** —**castor oil,** касто́ровое ма́сло.

castrate *v.t.* кастри́ровать; холости́ть; оскопля́ть. —**castration,** *n.* кастра́ция.

casual *adj.* **1,** (chance) случа́йный. **2,** (informal; relaxed) непринуждённый; небре́жный. *Casual clothes,* повседне́вное пла́тье. **3,** (not serious) беспе́чный; беззабо́тный. **4,** (cursory) бе́глый. —**casually,** *adv.* случа́йно; небре́жно; мимохо́дом; попу́тно.

casualty *n.* **1,** (person injured or killed) же́ртва: *There were no casualties,* жертв не́ было. **2,** *pl., mil.* ра́неные; поте́ри. *Heavy casualties,* тяжёлые поте́ри.

casuist *n.* казуи́ст. —**casuistic,** *adj.* казуисти́ческий. —**casuistry,** *n.* казуи́стика.

cat *n.* ко́шка. *Male cat,* кот. —**let the cat out of the bag,** прогова́риваться; проба́лтываться; вы́болтать секре́т.

cataclysm *n.* катакли́зм. —**cataclysmic,** *adj.* катастрофи́ческий.

catacombs *n.pl.* катако́мбы.

catafalque *n.* катафа́лк.

Catalan *adj.* катало́нский; катала́нский.

catalepsy *n.* катале́псия. **—cataleptic,** *adj.* каталепти́ческий; каталепси́ческий.

catalogue *also,* **catalog** *n.* **1,** (source of information) катало́г: *card catalogue,* ка́рточный катало́г. **2,** (list of items for sale) прейскура́нт. **—***v.t.* каталогизи́ровать. **—cataloguer,** *n.* каталогиза́тор.

catalysis *n.* ката́лиз. **—catalyst,** *n.* катализа́тор. **—catalytic,** *adj.* каталити́ческий.

cat-and-mouse game игра́ в ко́шки-мы́шки.

catapult *n.* катапу́льта. **—***v.t.* подбра́сывать в во́здух. **—***v.i.* взлета́ть; вска́кивать; подска́кивать.

cataract *n.* **1,** (waterfall) водопа́д; катара́кт. **2,** (opacity of the eye) катара́кта.

catarrh *n.* ката́р.

catastrophe *n.* катастро́фа. **—catastrophic,** *adj.* катастрофи́ческий.

catch *v.t.* **1,** (grab; trap; capture) лови́ть (*pfv.* пойма́ть): *catch a ball/fish/thief,* пойма́ть мяч/ры́бу/во́ра. **2,** (take by surprise) застава́ть: *catch unawares,* заста́ть враспло́х. *Get caught in the rain/ a snowstorm/,* попа́сть под дождь/ в мете́ль/. *Be caught stealing,* попа́сться на кра́же. **3,** (catch up to; overtake) догоня́ть. **4,** (snag) зацепля́ть: *catch one's sleeve on a nail,* зацепи́ть рукаво́м за гвоздь. **5,** (jam, as one's fingers in a door) защемля́ть; прищемля́ть (па́льцы две́рью). **6,** (be in time for, as a train) успе́ть на; попа́сть на. **7,** (contract, as an illness) заража́ться (+ *instr.*); получа́ть; нажива́ть; схва́тывать. *Catch cold,* простужа́ться. **8,** (understand; grasp) ула́вливать. **9,** *colloq.* (hear) рассслы́шать. **10,** *in various miscellaneous expressions: catch fire,* загоре́ться; *catch sight of,* уви́деть; зави́деть; *catch one's breath,* перевести́ дух; отдыша́ться. **—***v.i.* **1,** (become snagged) зацепля́ться; задева́ть. **2,** (ignite) разжига́ться. **—***n.* **1,** (act of catching) пои́мка. **2,** (quantity caught) уло́в. **3,** (fastener) защёлка; язычо́к. **4,** (bolt; latch) задви́жка; шпингале́т. **5,** (game) игра́ в мяч: *play catch,* игра́ть в мяч. **6,** *colloq.* (hitch; rub) заце́пка; загво́здка. **7,** *colloq.* (trick) подво́х. *There must be a catch,* здесь что́-то нечи́сто. **—catch it,** *colloq.* доста́ться (+ *dat.*); попа́сть (+ *dat.*): *I'll catch it,* мне доста́нется; мне попадёт. **—catch on, 1,** (become popular) привива́ться. **2,** (get the knack) принора́вливаться. **3,** *colloq.* (grasp the meaning) понима́ть; смека́ть. **—catch oneself,** лови́ть себя́ (*with* на + *prepl.*). **—catch someone's eye, 1,** (get the attention of) лови́ть чей-нибудь взгляд. **2,** (happen to be seen by) привлека́ть чьё-нибудь внима́ние; попада́ться на глаза́ (+ *dat.*). **—catch up** (**with** *or* **to**), догоня́ть. *Catch up on one's sleep,* отсыпа́ться.

catching *adj.* зара́зный; зарази́тельный.

catchy *adj.* навя́зчивый; прили́пчивый.

catechism *n.* катехи́зис.

categorical *adj.* категори́ческий; реши́тельный. **—categorically,** *adv.* категори́чески; реши́тельно.

categorize *v.t.* **1,** (place in a category) подводи́ть под (каку́ю-нибудь) катего́рию. **2,** (characterize) характеризова́ть.

category *n.* катего́рия; разря́д.

cater *v.i.* [*usu.* **cater to**] **1,** (serve) обслу́живать. **2,** (satisfy) удовлетворя́ть. **3,** (indulge) потво́рствовать. **—***v.t.* обслу́живать.

cater-corner *also,* **cater-cornered** *adj. & adv.* = **catty-corner(ed).**

caterpillar *n.* гу́сеница. **—caterpillar tractor,** гу́сеничный тра́ктор. **—caterpillar tread,** гу́сеничная ле́нта.

catgut *n.* кетгу́т.

catharsis *n.* очище́ние желу́дка.

cathartic *adj.* слаби́тельный. **—***n.* слаби́тельное.

cathedral *n.* собо́р.

catheter *n.* кате́тер.

cathode *n.* като́д. **—cathode rays,** като́дные лучи́. **—cathode-ray tube,** като́дная тру́бка.

Catholic *adj.* католи́ческий. **—***n.* като́лик; католи́чка. **—Catholicism,** *n.* католици́зм; католи́чество.

catkin *n.* серёжка.

cat-o'-nine-tails *n.* ко́шки.

cattail *n.* рого́з.

cattle *n.* скот. *Herd of cattle,* ста́до коро́в. **—cattleman,** *n.* скотово́д.

catty-corner *also,* **catty-cornered** *adj. & adv.* на́искось.

Caucasian *adj.* **1,** (of the Caucasus) кавка́зский. **2,** (Caucasoid) европео́идный. **—***n.* европео́ид.

cauldron *n.* = **caldron.**

cauliflower *n.* цветна́я капу́ста.

caulk *also,* **calk** *v.t.* конопа́тить.

causal *adj.* причи́нный. **—causality,** *n.* причи́нность. **—causative,** *adj.* причи́нный.

cause *n.* **1,** (that which produces an effect) причи́на: *cause and effect,* причи́на и сле́дствие. *The cause of the fire,* причи́на пожа́ра. *What is the cause of it?,* чем э́то вы́звано? **2,** (grounds; occasion) основа́ние; по́вод; причи́на. *There is no cause for alarm,* нет основа́ний (*or* нет по́вода *or* нет причи́н) для трево́г. **3,** (principle; movement) де́ло: *the cause of peace,* де́ло ми́ра. *Make common cause with,* солидаризи́роваться с. **—***v.t.* **1,** (be the cause of; bring about) вызыва́ть; причиня́ть. *Cause an argument/ accident,* вы́звать спор/катастро́фу. *Cause trouble/ anxiety/grief,* причиня́ть неприя́тности/беспоко́йство/го́ре. *Cause harm/damage,* причиня́ть *or* наноси́ть *or* приноси́ть вред. *Cause a sensation,* вы́звать *or* произвести́ сенса́цию. **2,** (prompt; induce) побужда́ть; заставля́ть: *What caused him to...?,* что побуди́ло/заста́вило его́ (+ *inf.*).

caustic *adj.* **1,** (corrosive) е́дкий; каусти́ческий. **2,** (biting; sarcastic) е́дкий; ко́лкий; язви́тельный.

causticity *n.* е́дкость.

caustic soda *n.* е́дкий натр.

cauterize *v.t.* прижига́ть; выжига́ть. **—cauterization,** *n.* прижига́ние; выжига́ние.

caution *n.* **1,** (wariness) осторо́жность. **2,** (warning) предостереже́ние. **—***v.t.* предостерега́ть.

cautious *adj.* осторо́жный. **—cautiously,** *adv.* осторо́жно.

cavalcade *n.* кавалька́да.

cavalier *n.* ры́царь. —*adj.* **1,** (haughty) надме́нный. **2,** (offhand) бесцеремо́нный.

cavalry *n.* кавале́рия; ко́нница. —*adj.* кавалери́йский. —**cavalryman,** *n.* кавалери́ст; ко́нник.

cave *n.* пеще́ра. —*v.i.* [*usu.* **cave in**] обва́ливаться; обру́шиваться; ру́хнуть.

caveat *n.* огово́рка.

cave-in *n.* обва́л.

cave man пеще́рный челове́к.

cavern *n.* пеще́ра. —**cavernous,** *adj.* похо́жий на пеще́ру.

caviar *also,* **caviare** *n.* икра́.

cavil *v.i.* придира́ться. —*n.* приди́ра.

cavity *n.* **1,** (hole; depression) впа́дина. **2,** (natural hollow in the body) по́лость: *abdominal cavity,* брюшна́я по́лость. **3,** (in a tooth) дупло́; (in the lungs) каве́рна.

cavort *v.i.* **1,** (leap about) де́лать прыжки́. **2,** (romp; frolic) резви́ться.

caw *v.i.* ка́ркать. —*n.* ка́рканье.

cease *v.t.* **1,** (stop doing an action) перестава́ть. *Cease to exist,* переста́ть существова́ть; прекрати́ть своё существова́ние. *I never cease to be amazed* (*by*), не перестаю́ удивля́ться (+ *dat.*). **2,** (terminate) прекраща́ть: *cease hostilities,* прекрати́ть вое́нные де́йствия. —*v.i.* прекраща́ться: *The noise ceased,* шум прекрати́лся.

cease-fire *n.* прекраще́ние огня́.

ceaseless *adj.* непреста́нный; беспреста́нный.

cecum *also,* **caecum** *n.* слепа́я кишка́.

cedar *n.* кедр. —*adj.* кедро́вый.

cede *v.t.* сдава́ть; уступа́ть: *cede territory,* сдава́ть/ уступа́ть террито́рию.

cedilla *n.* седи́ль.

ceiling *n.* потоло́к. —**hit the ceiling,** *colloq.* прийти́ в я́рость; лезть (поле́зть) на́ стену.

celebrate *v.t.* **1,** (observe; commemorate) пра́здновать; справля́ть: *celebrate one's birthday,* пра́здновать/ справля́ть день рожде́ния. *Celebrate a victory,* пра́здновать побе́ду. *Celebrate New Year's Eve,* встреча́ть Но́вый год. **2,** (perform, as a mass) служи́ть (обе́дню). **3,** (extol) прославля́ть. —*v.i.* пра́здновать: *We should celebrate!,* ну́жно отпра́здновать!

celebrated *adj.* знамени́тый; просла́вленный.

celebration *n.* пра́здник; пра́зднование; пра́зднество; торжество́. *Let's have a celebration!,* дава́йте отпра́зднуем!

celebrity *n.* знамени́тость.

celerity *n.* быстрота́.

celery *n.* сельдере́й. —*adj.* сельдере́йный.

celesta *n.* челе́ста.

celestial *adj.* небе́сный. —**celestial navigation,** астронавига́ция.

celibacy *n.* безбра́чие.

celibate *adj.* безбра́чный; холосто́й. —*n.* холостя́к.

cell *n.* **1,** (in a prison) ка́мера; (in a monastery) ке́лья. **2,** *biol.* кле́тка. *Red blood cells,* кра́сные кровяны́е тельца́. **3,** (small tightly-knit group) яче́йка. **4,** *electricity* элеме́нт.

cellar *n.* по́греб. *Wine cellar,* ви́нный по́греб.

cellist *n.* виолончели́ст.

cellmate *n.* сосе́д по ка́мере; сока́мерник.

cello *n.* виолонче́ль.

cellophane *n.* целлофа́н. —*adj.* целлофа́новый.

cellular *adj.* кле́точный.

celluloid *n.* целлуло́ид.

cellulose *n.* клетча́тка; целлюло́за.

Celsius *adj.* Це́льсий: *ten degrees Celsius,* де́сять гра́дусов по Це́льсию.

Celt *n.* кельт. —**Celtic,** *adj.* ке́льтский.

cement *n.* цеме́нт. —*adj.* цеме́нтный. —*v.t.* **1,** (cover with cement) цементи́ровать. **2,** *fig.* (solidify) скрепля́ть.

cemetery *n.* кла́дбище.

censer *n.* кади́ло; кури́льница.

censor *n.* це́нзор. —*v.t.* подверга́ть цензу́ре. —**censorship,** *n.* цензу́ра.

censure *v.t.* порица́ть; осужда́ть. —*n.* порица́ние; осужде́ние.

census *n.* пе́репись.

cent *n.* цент. *Not have a cent to one's name,* не име́ть ни гроша́ за душо́й.

centaur *n.* кента́вр.

centenary *adj.* столе́тний. —*n.* столе́тие.

centennial *adj. & n.* = **centenary.**

center *also,* **centre** *n.* **1,** (middle) центр; середи́на. **2,** (focal point) центр: *shopping center,* торго́вый центр. *Be the center of attention,* быть в це́нтре внима́ния. **3,** *basketball* центрово́й. —*adj.* сре́дний: *center aisle,* сре́дний прохо́д. *Center line* (*in a road*), осева́я ли́ния. —*v.t.* **1,** (place in the center) помеща́ть в це́нтре. **2,** (direct toward one place; concentrate) сосредото́чивать. —*v.i.* сосредото́чиваться. *The conversation centered around one subject,* разгово́р шёл (*or* верте́лся) о́коло одного́ предме́та. —**center of gravity,** центр тя́жести.

centerfold *also,* **centrefold** *n.* разворо́т.

Centigrade *adj.* Це́льсий: *ten degrees Centigrade,* де́сять гра́дусов по Це́льсию.

centigram *n.* сантигра́мм.

centime *n.* санти́м.

centimeter *also,* **centimetre** *n.* сантиме́тр.

centipede *n.* многоно́жка; сороконо́жка.

centner *n.* це́нтнер.

central *adj.* центра́льный. *Central heating,* центра́льное отопле́ние. *The central idea of the book,* центра́льная мысль кни́ги. —**Central America,** Центра́льная Аме́рика. —**Central Asia,** Сре́дняя А́зия. —**Central Intelligence Agency,** Центра́льное разве́дывательное управле́ние.

centralization *n.* централиза́ция.

centralize *v.t.* централизова́ть. —**centralized,** *adj.* централизо́ванный.

centre *see* **center.**

centrifugal *adj.* центробе́жный: *centrifugal force,* центробе́жная си́ла.

centrifuge *n.* центрифу́га.

centripetal *adj.* центростреми́тельный.

centrist *n.* центри́ст. —*adj.* центри́стский.

century *n.* век; столе́тие. *In the 19th century,* в девятна́дцатом ве́ке.

century plant столе́тник.

ceramic *adj.* керами́ческий. —**ceramics,** *n.* кера́мика.

cereal *n.* **1,** (grain) (хле́бные) зла́ки. **2,** (breakfast food) блю́до из хле́бных зла́ков. —*adj.* хле́бный; зла́ковый.

cerebellum *n.* мозжечо́к.

cerebral *adj.* мозгово́й. —**cerebral hemorrhage,** кровоизлия́ние в мозг. —**cerebral palsy,** церебра́льный парали́ч.

cerebrum *n.* головно́й мозг.

ceremonial *adj.* церемониа́льный. —*n.* **1,** (ritual) церемониа́л. **2,** (rite) обря́д.

ceremonious *adj.* церемо́нный.

ceremony *n.* **1,** (formal event or ritual) церемо́ния: *wedding ceremony,* сва́дебная церемо́ния; *welcoming ceremony,* церемо́ния приве́тствия. *Ceremonies to mark the dedication of a monument,* торжества́ в честь откры́тия па́мятника. **2,** (formality) церемо́нии. *Without ceremony,* без церемо́ний; бесцеремо́нно. —**stand on ceremony,** церемо́ниться.

cerise *adj.* вишнёвый.

cerium *n.* це́рий.

certain *adj.* **1,** (sure; positive) уве́ренный: *I am certain,* я уве́рен(а). **2,** (sure to happen) ве́рный: *certain death,* ве́рная смерть. **3,** (sure; indisputable) несомне́нный: *One thing is certain,* одно́ несомне́нно. *He is certain to be late,* он несомне́нно опозда́ет. *It is by no means certain that...,* совсе́м не я́сно, что... **4,** (known but not specified) определённый: *in certain cases,* в определённых слу́чаях. **5,** (some but not others) не́который: *certain people,* не́которые лю́ди. **6,** (some but not all) не́который; изве́стный: *to a certain extent,* до не́которой/изве́стной сте́пени. **7,** *preceded by* **a** (unidentified) не́кий; не́кто: *a certain Mr. Smith,* не́кий/не́кто ми́стер Смит. *There is a certain irony in the fact that...,* есть не́кая иро́ния в том, что... —**for certain,** достове́рно; наверняка́: *know for certain,* знать достове́рно/наверняка́. —**make certain = make sure** (*see* **sure**).

certainly *adv.* **1,** (of course) коне́чно. **2,** (without a doubt) несомне́нно. —**certainly not,** ни в ко́ем слу́чае.

certainty *n.* **1,** (assuredness) уве́ренность. **2,** (anything certain) несомне́нный факт. —**know for a certainty,** знать наверняка́.

certificate *n.* удостовере́ние; свиде́тельство; спра́вка; аттеста́т; сертифика́т. *Birth certificate,* свиде́тельство о рожде́нии; ме́трика.

certification *n.* удостовере́ние.

certify *v.t.* удостоверя́ть; заверя́ть: *certified check,* удостове́ренный чек; *certified copy,* заве́ренная ко́пия. *This is to certify that...,* сим удостоверя́ется, что...

certitude *n.* уве́ренность.

ceruse *n.* **1,** (white lead) свинцо́вые бели́ла. **2,** (cosmetic) бели́ла.

cervical *adj.* ше́йный; заты́лочный. *Cervical cancer,* рак ше́йки ма́тки.

cervix *n.* **1,** (neck) ше́я. **2,** (necklike part of the uterus) ше́йка ма́тки.

cesium *also,* **caesium** *n.* це́зий.

cessation *n.* прекраще́ние.

cession *n.* сда́ча; усту́пка.

cesspool *n.* выгребна́я я́ма; помо́йная я́ма.

chafe *v.t.* тере́ть; натира́ть; стира́ть. —*v.i.* **1,** (rub) тере́ть. **2,** (be irritated or impatient) горе́ть от нетерпе́ния; горячи́ться.

chaff *n.* **1,** (husks) мяки́на; поло́ва. **2,** (fine-cut straw) се́чка.

chaffinch *n.* за́блик.

chagrin *n.* огорче́ние. —**chagrined,** *adj.* огорчённый.

chain *n.* **1,** (connected links) цепь; цепо́чка. *Put/keep the chain on the door,* запере́ть дверь на цепо́чку; держа́ть дверь на цепо́чке. **2,** (for a watch, pendant, etc.) цепо́чка: *watch chain,* цепо́чка для часо́в. **3,** *pl.* (shackles) це́пи; око́вы. *Put* (*someone*) *in chains,* закова́ть (кого́-нибудь) в це́пи. **4,** (range of mountains) (го́рная) цепь. **5,** (series) цепь: *chain of events,* цепь собы́тий. **6,** (network, as of stores) сеть. —*adj.* цепно́й: *chain link,* цепно́е звено́. —*v.t.* [*often* **chain up**] сажа́ть на цепь. *Chain a dog to a post,* прико́вывать соба́ку це́пью к столбу́. —**chain of command,** кома́ндные инста́нции. —**chain mail,** кольчу́га. —**chain reaction,** цепна́я реа́кция. —**chain saw,** цепна́я пила́. —**chain stitch,** та́мбур; та́мбурный шов; та́мбурная стро́чка; цепно́й стежо́к.

chain-smoke *v.i.* непреры́вно кури́ть.

chair *n.* **1,** (piece of furniture) стул. *Armchair,* кре́сло. *Be sitting in a chair,* сиде́ть на сту́ле; сиде́ть в кре́сле. **2,** (presiding officer) председа́тель. **3,** (professorship) ка́федра. —*v.t.* председа́тельствовать на (собра́нии).

chairman *n.* председа́тель. —**chairmanship,** *n.* председа́тельство.

chaise longue шезло́нг.

chalcedony *n.* халцедо́н.

chalet *n.* шале́.

chalice *n.* ча́ша.

chalk *n.* мел. —*v.t.* натира́ть ме́лом. —**chalk up, 1,** (earn; score) одержа́ть (побе́ду); набира́ть (очки́). **2,** *fol. by* **to** (attribute to) относи́ть на счёт (+ *gen.*).

chalky *adj.* мелово́й.

challenge *v.t.* **1,** (summon to a contest) вызыва́ть: *challenge to a duel,* вызыва́ть на дуэ́ль. **2,** (defy) броса́ть вы́зов (+ *dat.*). **3,** (call into question; dispute) оспа́ривать; подверга́ть сомне́нию. **4,** (demand identification from) оклика́ть. —*n.* **1,** (summons to a contest) вы́зов. **2,** (demand for identification) о́клик. **3,** *law* отво́д. —**challenge cup,** *sports* переходя́щий ку́бок.

challenger *n.* претенде́нт.

challenging *adj.* отве́тственный: *challenging assignment,* отве́тственное поруче́ние. *The work is not very challenging,* рабо́та не тре́бует больши́х уси́лий.

chamber *n.* **1,** (large room for a certain purpose) ка́мера: *compression chamber,* ка́мера сжа́тия. *Tor-*

ture chamber, застéнок. **2,** (bedroom) спáльня. **3,** (unit of a legislature) палáта: *chamber of deputies,* палáта депутáтов. **4,** (of a firearm) патрóнник.

chamberlain *n.* камергéр.

chambermaid *n.* гóрничная.

chamber music кáмерная мýзыка.

chamber of commerce торгóвая палáта.

chamber pot ночнóй горшóк.

chameleon *n.* хамелеóн.

chamois *n.* **1,** (antelope) сéрна. **2,** (soft leather) зáмша.

chamomile *n.* = **camomile.**

champ *n., colloq.* = **champion.** —*v.i.* чáвкать. —**champ at the bit,** грызть удилá.

champagne *n.* шампáнское.

champion *n.* **1,** (one who is ranked first) чемпиóн: *boxing champion,* чемпиóн по бóксу. **2,** (defender, as of a cause) побóрник. —*v.t.* борóться за. —*adj. Champion swimmer,* чемпиóн по плáванию.

championship *n.* **1,** (title) пéрвенство; чемпиóнство. *World championship,* мировóе пéрвенство. **2,** (competition) чемпионáт; пéрвенство. *World championship* (*e.g. chess*) *match,* матч на пéрвенство мúра; матч на звáние чемпиóна мúра. *World soccer championship,* чемпионáт мúра по футбóлу. **3,** (advocasу) борьбá; защúта.

chance *n.* **1,** (fortune; luck) слýчай; случáйность. *Game of chance,* азáртная игрá. *Leave to chance,* оставлять на вóлю слýчая. **2,** (opportunity) слýчай; возмóжность. *Have the chance to travel,* имéть возмóжность путешéствовать. *If you have the chance,* éсли вам предстáвится возмóжность (*or* удóбный слýчай). **3,** (probability) шанс: *one chance in ten,* одúн шанс из десятú. *Stand a chance,* имéть шáнсы. **4,** (risk) риск: *take a chance,* идтú на риск; рисковáть. —*adj.* случáйный: *a chance encounter,* случáйная встрéча. —*v.t.* рисковáть: *Let's chance it!,* рискнём! —*v.i. I chanced to be there,* я случáйно был (былá) там. —**by chance,** случáйно. —**by chance,** случáйно. —**chances are,** скорéе всегó.

chancellery *n.* канцелярия.

chancellor *n.* кáнцлер.

chancre *n.* шанкр. —**chancroid,** *n.* мягкий шанкр.

chancy *adj., colloq.* рискóванный.

chandelier *n.* люстра.

change *v.t.* **1,** (switch to other or another) менять: *change jobs,* менять рабóту. *Change clothes,* переодевáться; *change shoes,* переодевáть тýфли. *Change planes, trains, etc.,* пересáживаться; дéлать пересáдку. *Change sides,* перейтú на другýю стóрону. *Change hands,* перейтú в другúе рýки. **2,** (exchange; switch) меняться (+ *instr.*): *change places,* меняться местáми. **3,** (make different; alter) изменять; менять. *Change tactics,* изменять тáктику. *Change color,* менять свою окрáску. *Change one's name to,* менять úмя *or* фамúлию на... **4,** (replace) сменять: *change a tire,* сменúть шúну. **5,** (convert, as money) размéнивать: *change ten dollars,* разменять дéсять дóлларов. **6,** (diaper) перепеленáть (ребёнка). —*v.i.* **1,** (become different) меняться; изменяться; переменяться. *The situation*

changes practically every day, положéние меняется едвá ли не кáждый день. *You haven't changed a bit,* вы совсéм не изменúлись. **2,** (of a young man's voice) ломáться. **3,** (change clothes) переодевáться. *Change into a dress,* переодéться в плáтье. **4,** (change planes) пересáживаться. **5,** *fol. by off* (alternate) чередовáться. —*n.* **1,** (alteration; transformation) изменéние; перемéна: *change in the weather,* изменéние/перемéна погóды. *Change for the better,* перемéна к лýчшему. **2,** (replacement) смéна: *oil change,* смéна мáсла. **3,** (of planes, trains, etc.) пересáдка. **4,** (variety) разнообрáзие: *for a change,* для разнообрáзия. *It's a nice day, for a change,* наконéц-то хорóшая погóда! **5,** (set) смéна: *two changes of linen,* две смéны белья. **6,** (small money; coins) мéлочь. *Small change,* размéнная монéта. **7,** (money given back) сдáча: *change of a dollar,* сдáча с дóллара. *Keep the change!,* остáвьте себé сдáчу! —**change of life,** клúмакс.

changeability *n.* измéнчивость.

changeable *adj.* измéнчивый; непостоянный.

change booth размéнная кáсса.

changeover *n.* перехóд; переключéние.

change purse кошелёк.

channel *n.* **1,** (body of water) пролúв. *The English Channel,* Ла-Мáнш. **2,** (river bed) рýсло. **3,** (deep navigable passage) фарвáтер. **4,** *pl.* (means of communication) канáлы. **5,** *television* канáл. —*v.t.* направлять: *channel one's energies into,* направлять свою энéргию на (+ *acc.*).

chant *v.t. & i.* **1,** (sing) петь. **2,** (call out rhythmically) скандúровать. —*n.* песнопéние: *Gregorian chant,* григориáнское песнопéние.

chaos *n.* хáос. —**chaotic,** *adj.* хаотúческий; хаотúчный.

chap *v.t.* обвéтрить. *Chapped lips,* обвéтренные *or* потрéскавшиеся гýбы. —*v.i.* трéскаться. —*n., colloq.* (fellow) пáрень; мáлый.

chapel *n.* часóвня; капéлла. *The Sistine Chapel,* Сикстúнская капéлла.

chaperon *also,* **chaperone** *n.* сопровождáющий; руководúтель (грýппы).

chaplain *n.* капеллáн.

chapter *n.* **1,** (division of a book) главá. **2,** (branch of a society) отделéние.

char *v.t.* обýгливать.

character *n.* **1,** (individual nature) харáктер. *Character trait,* чертá харáктера. *Have a character of its own,* имéть свой сóбственный харáктер. *Out of character for him,* не харáктерно для негó; не в егó харáктере. **2,** (moral excellence) харáктер: *show character,* показáть харáктер. *Man of character,* человéк с сúльным харáктером. **3,** (person; personage) лúчность. **4,** (person in a play or novel) дéйствующее лицó; персонáж. **5,** *colloq.* (an eccentric) оригинáл; чудáк. **6,** *pl.* (symbols used in writing) письменá; иерóглифы. —**character actor,** харáктерный актёр. —**character reference,** характерúстика.

characteristic *n.* свóйство; осóбенность; чертá.

—*adj.* характе́рный; сво́йственный; прису́щий. *With his characteristic enthusiasm,* со сво́йственным *or* с прису́щим ему́ энтузиа́змом.

characterization *n.* характери́стика.

characterize *v.t.* характеризова́ть; квалифици́ровать.

charade *n.* шара́да.

charcoal *n.* дре́весный у́голь.

charge *v.t.* **1,** (ask as a price) брать; проси́ть: *How much do you charge for this?,* ско́лько вы берёте/про́сите за э́то? *Charge a fee,* взима́ть пла́ту. *Charge a high price,* запра́шивать высо́кую це́ну. *Charge a lot for...,* брать до́рого за (+ *acc.*). *They charged me ten dollars,* с меня́ взя́ли де́сять до́лларов. **2,** (record as a debt to be paid) запи́сывать: *Charge it to my account,* запиши́те э́то на мой счёт. *Do you wish to charge it?,* вам присла́ть счёт? **3,** (replenish, as a battery) заряжа́ть. **4,** (indict) предъявля́ть обвине́ние (+ *dat.*): *He has been charged with murder,* ему́ предъя́влено обвине́ние в уби́йстве. **5,** (attack) бро́ситься на. **6,** (entrust, as with an assignment) поруча́ть. —*v.i.* **1,** (ask payment) брать де́ньги; взима́ть пла́ту. **2,** (rush forward violently) бро́ситься. **3,** (attack vigorously) бро́ситься в ата́ку. —*n.* **1,** (money to be paid) пла́та: *admission charge,* входна́я пла́та. *Free of charge,* беспла́тно. *There is an extra charge for that,* за э́то взима́ется отде́льная пла́та; за э́то на́до заплати́ть отде́льно. **2,** (quantity of explosives or electricity) заря́д: *positive charge,* положи́тельный заря́д. **3,** (accusation) обвине́ние: *arrested on charges of...,* аресто́ван по обвине́нию в (+ *prepl.*). *Press charges against,* предъяви́ть обвине́ние (+ *dat.*). **4,** (attack) ата́ка: *cavalry charge,* кавалери́йская ата́ка. **5,** (custody) попече́ние: *I leave them in your charge,* оставля́ю их на ва́ше попече́ние. **6,** (ward) подопе́чный; пито́мец. —**be in charge,** распоряжа́ться. —**be in charge of,** ве́дать; заве́довать. —**put in charge of,** поста́вить во главе́ (+ *gen.*). —**take charge of,** взять в свои́ ру́ки.

charged *adj.* **1,** *physics* заря́женный: *charged particles,* заря́женные части́цы. **2,** *fig.* (tense) накалённый: *charged atmosphere,* накалённая атмосфе́ра.

chargé d'affaires пове́ренный в дела́х.

charger *n.* **1,** (for batteries) заря́дный агрега́т. **2,** (warhorse) строева́я ло́шадь; боево́й конь.

chariot *n.* колесни́ца. —**charioteer,** *n.* возни́ца.

charisma *n.* хари́зма. —**charismatic,** *adj.* харизмати́ческий.

charitable *adj.* **1,** (kind; generous) милосе́рдный. **2,** (philanthropic) благотвори́тельный. **3,** (lenient in judging) снисходи́тельный.

charity *n.***1,** (benevolence) милосе́рдие; ми́лость. **2,** (philanthropy) благотвори́тельность. *Raise money for charity,* собира́ть де́ньги на благотвори́тельные це́ли. **3,** (alms) ми́лостыня: *accept charity,* принима́ть ми́лостыню. **4,** (charitable institution) благотвори́тельное учрежде́ние.

charlatan *n.* шарлата́н. —**charlatanism,** *n.* шарлата́нство.

charm *n.* **1,** (delightful quality) пре́лесть: *lose its charm,* теря́ть свою́ пре́лесть. *The charm of country life,* пре́лести жи́зни в дере́вне. **2,** (ability to captivate) очарова́ние; обая́ние; ча́ры. *I succumbed to her charm,* я подда́лся её очарова́нию. **3,** (ornament) брело́к. —*v.t.* **1,** (captivate) очаро́вывать. **2,** (cast a spell over) заколдо́вывать.

charmed *adj.* очаро́ванный; заколдо́ванный. *Charmed!,* о́чень прия́тно! *He leads a charmed life,* он как бы заколдо́ван.

charmer *n.* (man) чароде́й; (woman) чароде́йка; чаровни́ца. —**snake charmer,** заклина́тель змей.

charming *adj.* очарова́тельный; обая́тельный; преле́стный.

charred *adj.* обгоре́лый; обу́гленный.

chart *n.* гра́фик; схе́ма; диагра́мма. —*v.t.* намеча́ть: *chart a course of action,* намеча́ть план де́йствий.

charter *n.* **1,** (grant of rights) ха́ртия. **2,** (constitution) уста́в: *the U.N. Charter,* уста́в ООН. —*v.t.* фрахтова́ть.

chartreuse *adj.* жёлто-зелёный.

charwoman *n.* домрабо́тница.

chary *adj.* **1,** (cautious) осторо́жный; осмотри́тельный. **2,** (sparing) скупо́й.

chase *v.t.* **1,** (pursue) гна́ться за: *chase a thief,* гна́ться за во́ром. *Chase up a tree,* загоня́ть на де́рево. **2,** *fol. by* **away** (drive away) отгоня́ть: *chase away a fly,* отгна́ть му́ху. **3,** *fol. by* **out** (drive out) выгоня́ть; прогоня́ть: *chase the children out of the room,* вы́гнать/прогна́ть дете́й из ко́мнаты. —*v.i.* **1,** *fol. by* **after** (run after) гна́ться за; бе́гать за. *Chase after women,* бе́гать за же́нщинами. **2,** *colloq.* (rush) бе́гать. *Chase all over town,* обега́ть весь го́род. —*n.* **1,** (pursuit) пого́ня. *Give chase,* погна́ться; пусти́ться вдого́нку. **2,** *preceded by* **the** (hunting) охо́та.

chasm *n.* про́пасть.

chassis *n.* шасси́.

chaste *adj.* целому́дренный.

chasten *v.t.* **1,** (punish; discipline) нака́зывать; кара́ть. **2,** (restrain; temper) сде́рживать; обу́здывать. *Have a chastening effect on,* де́йствовать на (+ *acc.*) отрезвля́юще.

chastise *v.t.* **1,** (punish; discipline) нака́зывать; кара́ть; бичева́ть. **2,** (rebuke; censure) порица́ть.

chastity *n.* целому́дрие.

chasuble *n.* ри́за.

chat *v.i.* бесе́довать. —*n.* бесе́да.

chattel *n.* дви́жимое иму́щество.

chatter *v.i.* **1,** (click, as of the teeth) стуча́ть. **2,** (jabber; prate) болта́ть; треща́ть. **3,** (utter rapid sounds, as of birds) щебета́ть. —*n.* **1,** (idle talk) болтовня́. **2,** (utterance of birds) щебет.

chatterbox *n.* болту́н; говору́н; балабо́лка; трещо́тка.

chatty *adj.* болтли́вый.

chauffeur *n.* шофёр; води́тель.

chauvinism *n.* шовини́зм. —**chauvinist,** *n.* шовини́ст. —**chauvinistic,** *adj.* шовинисти́ческий.

cheap *adj.* **1,** (inexpensive) дешёвый. **2,** (niggardly) скупо́й. —*adv.* дёшево: *buy/sell something cheap,* дёшево купи́ть/прода́ть что́-нибудь. *Get off cheap,* дёшево отде́латься.

cheapen *v.t.* **1,** (lessen the value of) обесце́нивать. **2,** (debase) опошля́ть.

cheaply *adv.* дёшево.

cheapskate *n., colloq.* скря́га; скопидо́м; сквалы́га.

cheat *v.t.* обма́нывать; надува́ть: *cheat someone out of two dollars,* обману́ть/наду́ть кого́-нибудь на два до́ллара. —*v.i.* **1,** (in a game) плутова́ть; жу́льничать. **2,** (on a test) спи́сывать (на экза́мене). **3,** *fol. by on* (be unfaithful to) изменя́ть (+ *dat.*). —*n.* [*also,* **cheater**] обма́нщик; плут; жу́лик.

check *n.* **1,** (restraint): *hold/keep in check,* сде́рживать; держа́ть в узде́. **2,** (test for accuracy) прове́рка. **3,** (check mark [√]) га́лочка; пти́чка. **4,** [*also,* **cheque**] (written order to pay money) чек. **5,** (ticket; slip) номеро́к. *Claim check,* квита́нция. **6,** (bill, as in a restaurant) счёт. **7,** (square in a checkered pattern) кле́тка. **8,** *chess* шах. —*v.t.* **1,** (halt) остана́вливать; заде́рживать. **2,** (hold back) сде́рживать; обу́здывать. **3,** (examine for accuracy or satisfactory condition) проверя́ть. *Check the oil,* прове́рить у́ровень ма́сла. **4,** [*often* **check off**] (mark with a check) отмеча́ть га́лочкой. **5,** (deposit for safekeeping) сдава́ть. *Check one's coat,* сдать пальто́ в гардеро́б. *Check one's luggage,* сдать бага́ж на хране́ние. *Check one's luggage through,* сдать ве́щи в бага́ж. —*v.i.* **1,** (make an inquiry) спра́шивать. *Check with the boss,* спра́шивать у нача́льника. **2,** (tally) сходи́ться; совпада́ть. —**check in,** регистри́роваться; пропи́сываться. —**check out, 1,** (settle up and leave) выпи́сываться (из гости́ницы). *Are you checking out today?,* вы сего́дня уезжа́ете? **2,** (investigate further) разузнава́ть. **3,** (agree; tally) сходи́ться. —**check (up) on,** проверя́ть.

checkbook *also,* **chequebook** *n.* че́ковая кни́жка.

checked *adj.* кле́тчатый; в кле́тку.

checker *n.* **1,** (one who checks) контролёр. **2,** (piece used in the game of checkers) ша́шка.

checkerboard *n.* ша́хматная *or* ша́шечная доска́.

checkered *also,* **chequered** *adj.* **1,** (having a pattern of squares) кле́тчатый; в кле́тку. **2,** *fig.* (full of ups and downs) бу́рный: *checkered career,* бу́рная жизнь.

checkers *n.* ша́шки.

checkmate *n.* мат. —*v.t.* сде́лать мат (+ *dat.*).

checkpoint *n.* контро́льный пункт; проходна́я бу́дка; проходна́я.

checkroom *n.* **1,** (for apparel) гардеро́б; раздева́лка. **2,** (for baggage) ка́мера хране́ния (багажа́).

checkup *n.* осмо́тр; обсле́дование. *Go into the hospital for a checkup,* лечь в больни́цу на обсле́дование.

cheek *n.* **1,** (side of the face) щека́. **2,** *colloq.* (effrontery) на́глость. —**turn the other cheek,** подставля́ть другу́ю щёку. —**with tongue in cheek,** в шу́тку.

cheekbone *n.* скула́.

cheep *v.i.* пища́ть. —*n.* писк.

cheer *n.* **1,** (shout of approval) во́зглас; ура́. **2,** (encouragement; comfort) ободре́ние. *Words of cheer,* ободря́ющие слова́. **3,** *Be of good cheer,* быть весёлым; не уныва́ть. —*v.t.* **1,** (acclaim with cheers) приве́тствовать (гро́мкими во́згласами); крича́ть ура́ в честь (+ *gen.*). **2,** *fol. by up* (gladden) ободря́ть; подба́дривать; (раз)весели́ть. —*v.i.* **1,** (shout cheers) крича́ть ура́. **2,** *fol. by up* (feel encouraged) ободря́ться; подба́дриваться; веселе́ть; развесели́ться; воспря́нуть ду́хом.

cheerful *adj.* бо́дрый; весёлый. —**cheerfulness,** *n.* бо́дрость; весёлость.

cheerio *interj., colloq.* до встре́чи!; пока́!

cheerless *adj.* мра́чный; безра́достный; безотра́дный.

cheery *adj.* бо́дрый. *A cheery smile,* ра́достная улы́бка.

cheese *n.* сыр. —*adj.* сы́рный: *cheese omelet,* сы́рный омле́т.

cheesecloth *n.* ма́рля.

cheetah *n.* гепа́рд.

chef *n.* шеф-по́вар.

chemical *adj.* хими́ческий. —*n.* хими́ческий препара́т; хими́ческий проду́кт; *pl.* химика́лии; химика́ты. —**chemical engineer,** инжене́р-хи́мик. —**chemical warfare,** хими́ческая война́.

chemise *n.* (же́нская) соро́чка.

chemist *n.* **1,** (specialist in chemistry) хи́мик. **2,** *Brit.* (druggist) апте́карь.

chemistry *n.* хи́мия. *Chemistry teacher,* учи́тель хи́мии.

chemotherapy *n.* химиотерапи́я.

chenille *n.* сине́ль.

cheque *n., Brit.* = **check** (*in sense #4*). —**chequebook,** *n.* = **checkbook.** —**chequered,** *adj.* = **checkered.**

cherish *v.t.* **1,** (hold dear) дорожи́ть. **2,** (nurture, as hopes) леле́ять.

cherry *n.* ви́шня. —*adj.* вишнёвый: *cherry jam,* вишнёвое варе́нье. —**cherry tree,** ви́шня.

cherub *n.* херуви́м. —**cherubic,** *adj.* херуви́мский.

chess *n.* ша́хматы: *play chess,* игра́ть в ша́хматы. —*adj.* ша́хматный: *chess tournament,* ша́хматный турни́р. —**chessboard,** *n.* ша́хматная доска́. —**chessman,** *n.* ша́хматная фигу́ра. —**chess player,** шахмати́ст.

chest *n.* **1,** (part of the body) грудь. **2,** (box) я́щик; сунду́к. *Medicine chest,* апте́чка. *Chest of drawers,* комо́д. —*adj.* грудно́й: *chest cavity,* грудна́я по́лость. *Chest pain,* боль в груди́. *Chest X-ray,* рентге́н грудно́й кле́тки.

chestnut *n.* кашта́н. —*adj.* кашта́новый. *Chestnut horse,* ры́жая ло́шадь.

cheviot *n.* шевио́т. —*adj.* шевио́товый.

chevron *n.* шевро́н; наши́вка.

chew *v.t. & i.* жева́ть: *chew one's food/cud,* жева́ть пи́щу/жва́чку. —**chew out,** *slang* вы́бранить; разруга́ть. —**chew the fat** *or* **rag,** *slang* бесе́довать.

chewing *n.* жева́ние; пережёвывание. *Inadequate chewing of food,* недоста́точное *or* непра́вильное пережёвывание пи́щи. —**chewing gum,** жева́тельная рези́нка; жва́чка. —**chewing tobacco,** жева́тельный таба́к.

chic *adj.* шика́рный; сти́льный.

chicanery *n.* интри́га; ко́зни; ка́верза.

chick *n.* **1,** (small chicken) цыплёнок. **2,** (young bird) птене́ц. **3,** *slang* (girl) девчо́нка.

chickadee *n.* га́ичка.

chicken *n.* **1,** (hen or rooster or its flesh) ку́рица. **2,** (young hen or rooster) цыплёнок. —*adj.* кури́ный: *chicken soup,* кури́ный бульо́н; *chicken livers,* кури́ная печёнка. —**chicken coop,** куря́тник. —**chicken pox,** ве́тряная о́спа; ветря́нка.

chickpea *n.* нут; туре́цкий горо́х.

chicory *n.* цико́рий.

chide *v.t.* побрани́ть; жури́ть.

chief *n.* глава́; нача́льник. *Chief of staff,* нача́льник шта́ба. *Chief of state,* глава́ госуда́рства. —*adj.* гла́вный: *chief question,* гла́вный вопро́с; *chief engineer,* гла́вный инжене́р. —**chiefly,** *adv.* гла́вным о́бразом.

chieftain *n.* вождь.

chiffon *n.* шифо́н. —*adj.* шифо́новый.

chiffonier *n.* шифонье́рка.

chignon *n.* шиньо́н.

child *n.* ребёнок. —*adj.* [*also,* **child's**] де́тский: *child labor,* де́тский труд. *Child psychology,* де́тская психоло́гия. —**child's play,** пустяко́вое де́ло; па́ра пустяко́в. *See also* **children**.

childbearing *n.* деторожде́ние. *Childbearing age,* деторо́дный во́зраст.

childbirth *n.* ро́ды. *Die in childbirth,* умере́ть от ро́дов.

childhood *n.* де́тство. *Since childhood,* с де́тства; с ма́лых лет. *One's childhood years,* де́тские го́ды.

childish *adj.* де́тский; ребя́ческий. —**childishly,** *adv.* как ребёнок. —**childishness,** *n.* ребя́чество.

childless *adj.* безде́тный. —**childlessness,** *n.* безде́тность.

childlike *adj.* де́тский; неви́нный.

children *n.pl.* де́ти. —**children's,** *adj.* де́тский.

Chilean *adj.* чили́йский. —*n.* чили́ец; чили́йка.

chill *n.* **1,** (sensation of cold) просту́да; озно́б. *Catch a chill,* схвати́ть просту́ду. *He has a chill,* его́ зноби́т. **2,** (coldness in the air) холодо́к. *There is a chill in the air,* свежо́. **3,** (feeling of sudden fear) хо́лод: *A chill ran down my spine,* хо́лод пробежа́л по мое́й спине́. **4,** (coolness, as in relations) холодо́к (в отноше́ниях). —*v.t.* охлажда́ть. *Chilled to the bone,* продро́гший до косте́й.

chilling *adj.* **1,** (freezing) леденя́щий: *chilling wind,* леденя́щий ве́тер. **2,** *fig.* (shocking; harrowing) леденя́щий кровь (+ *noun*).

chilly *adj.* прохла́дный; све́жий: *It is chilly in here,* здесь прохла́дно/свежо́. *It is getting chilly,* свеже́ет. *I am chilly,* мне прохла́дно.

chime *n.*, *usu. pl.* кура́нты. —*v.i.* бить; звуча́ть; звони́ть. —**chime in,** вверну́ть слове́чко; вступи́ть в разгово́р.

chimera *n.* химе́ра. —**chimerical,** *adj.* химери́ческий.

chimney *n.* (дымова́я) труба́. —**chimney sweep,** трубочи́ст.

chimpanzee *n.* шимпанзе́.

chin *n.* подборо́док. —**keep one's chin up,** не па́дать ду́хом.

china *n.* **1,** (porcelain) фарфо́р. **2,** (dishes) посу́да. —*adj.* **1,** (made of china) фарфо́ровый. **2,** (for china) посу́дный: *china closet,* посу́дный шкаф.

chinchilla *n.* шиншилла.

Chinese *adj.* кита́йский. *He* (*she*) *is Chinese,* он кита́ец; она́ китая́нка. —*n.* **1,** (language) кита́йский язы́к. *Speak Chinese,* говори́ть по-кита́йски. **2,** *preceded by* **the** (people) кита́йцы.

chink *n.* **1,** (slit) щель; расще́лина; сква́жина. **2,** (sound) звон; звя́канье.

chintz *n.* си́тец. —*adj.* си́тцевый.

chip *n.* **1,** (fragment) ще́пка. **2,** (imperfection caused by chipping) щерби́на. **3,** (counter used in gambling games) фи́шка; ма́рка. *Bargaining chip,* предме́т то́рга. —*v.t.* **1,** (damage slightly) надбива́ть. **2,** *fol. by* **away** (cut away, as ice) ска́лывать. —*v.i.* **1,** (lose a chip) би́ться. **2,** *fol. by* **off** (break off) отбива́ться: *A piece of the cup chipped off,* у ча́шки отби́лся край. —**chip in,** внести́ свою́ ле́пту. —**chip off the old block,** сын своего́ отца́. —**in the chips,** при деньга́х. —**when the chips are down,** в реша́ющий моме́нт.

chipmunk *n.* бурунду́к.

chipper *adj.*, *colloq.* бо́дрый; живо́й.

chiropody *n.* педикю́р. —**chiropodist,** *n.* педикю́рша.

chirp *v.i.* чири́кать; щебета́ть; стрекота́ть. —*n.* ще́бет.

chisel *n.* долото́. —*v.t.* **1,** (cut) выреза́ть; высека́ть. **2,** *slang* (swindle) надува́ть; обжу́ливать. —**chiseled,** *adj.* (of features) точёный. —**chiseler,** *n.*, *slang* рвач.

chit *n.* тало́н.

chitchat *n.* болтовня́; пересу́ды.

chivalry *n.* ры́царство. —**chivalrous,** *adj.* ры́царский; гала́нтный.

chive *n.* шнитт-лу́к.

chloric *adj.* хло́рный.

chloride *n.* хлори́д. ♦*In compounds,* хло́ристый: *hydrogen chloride,* хло́ристый водоро́д. —**chloride of lime,** хло́рная и́звесть.

chlorinate *v.t.* хлори́ровать. —**chlorination,** *n.* хлори́рование.

chlorine *n.* хлор.

chloroform *n.* хлорофо́рм. —*v.t.* хлороформи́ровать.

chlorophyll *n.* хлорофи́лл.

chlorous *adj.* хло́ристый.

chock-full *adj.* битко́м наби́тый; наби́тый до отка́за.

chocolate *n.* шокола́д. *Hot chocolate,* горя́чий шокола́д. *Box of chocolates,* шокола́дный набо́р. —*adj.* шокола́дный: *chocolate cake,* шокола́дный торт.

choice *n.* вы́бор: *freedom of choice,* свобо́да вы́бора. *Take your choice!,* выбира́й! *He was offered a book of his choice,* ему́ предложи́ли кни́гу на вы́бор. *We have no choice but to...,* нам не остаётся ничего́ ино́го (*or* друго́го вы́бора), как... —*adj.* отбо́рный; как на подбо́р: *choice apples,* отбо́рные я́блоки; я́блоки как на подбо́р.

choir *n.* **1,** (group of singers) хор. **2,** (part of a church) кли́рос. —**choirboy,** *n.* пе́вчий. —**choirmaster,** *n.* хорме́йстер.

choke *v.t.* **1,** (prevent from breathing) души́ть. **2,** (clog) забива́ть; засоря́ть. *The streets are choked with traffic,* у́лицы заби́ты маши́нами. **3,** (of weeds) заглуша́ть; засоря́ть. *The garden is becoming choked with weeds,* сад гло́хнет. **4,** *fol. by* **off** (suppress) души́ть; подавля́ть. **5,** *Choke back one's tears,* глота́ть слёзы. —*v.i.* **1,** (on something caught in one's throat) дави́ться; поперхну́ться: *choke on a bone,* (по)дави́ться/поперхну́ться ко́стью. **2,** (with tears, anger, etc.) задыха́ться (от). —*n., mech.* дро́ссель.

cholera *n.* холе́ра. *Cholera epidemic,* эпиде́мия холе́ры. —**choleric,** *adj.* холери́ческий.

cholesterol *n.* холестери́н.

choose *v.t.* **1,** (select) выбира́ть: *choose a profession,* выбира́ть профе́ссию. *Choose a gift for one's wife,* вы́брать пода́рок жене́ *or* для жены́. *There is little to choose between them,* ме́жду ни́ми нет большо́й ра́зницы. **2,** *fol. by inf.* (elect) реша́ть; реша́ться; предпочита́ть. *He chose to remain in Russia,* он реши́л оста́ться в Росси́и. —*v.i.* выбира́ть; де́лать вы́бор: *It is up to you to choose,* вам выбира́ть; вам де́лать вы́бор. *Choose from among these,* выбира́йте оди́н из э́тих. *There were plenty to choose from,* выбира́ть бы́ло из чего́. *We have nothing to choose from,* нам не́ из чего выбира́ть.

choosy *adj.* разбо́рчивый; привере́дливый.

chop *v.t.* **1,** (hew) руби́ть; коло́ть: *chop wood,* руби́ть/коло́ть дрова́. **2,** (mince) руби́ть: *chop meat/onions,* руби́ть мя́со/лук. —*n.* (отбивна́я) котле́та. *Lamb chop,* бара́нья котле́та. *Pork chop,* свина́я котле́та; свина́я отбивна́я. —**chop down,** руби́ть; сруба́ть; выруба́ть. —**chop off,** отруби́ть. —**chop up,** руби́ть; кроши́ть.

chopped *adj.* ру́бленый: *chopped meat,* ру́бленое мя́со.

chopper *n.* **1,** (tool) коса́рь; сека́ч. **2,** *colloq.* (helicopter) вертолёт.

choppy *adj.* **1,** (rough, as of the sea) взволно́ванный; неспоко́йный. **2,** (jerky) ре́зкий; поры́вистый.

chopsticks *n.pl.* па́лочки для еды́.

choral *adj.* хорово́й.

chorale *n.* хора́л.

chord *n.* **1,** *math.* хо́рда. **2,** *music* акко́рд. **3,** *anat. See* **cord. 4,** *fig.* (emotional response) струна́: *strike a sensitive chord,* заде́ть чувстви́тельную струну́.

chore *n., usu. pl.* хло́поты. *Household chores,* хло́поты *or* дела́ по хозя́йству. *I have some household chores to do,* мне ну́жно сде́лать не́сколько дел по хозя́йству.

chorea *n.* хоре́я.

choreography *n.* хореогра́фия. —**choreographer,** *n.* хорео́граф. —**choreographic,** *adj.* хореографи́ческий.

chorister *n.* пе́вчий; хори́ст.

chorus *n.* **1,** (singing group) хор. **2,** (refrain) припе́в. **3,** *fig.* (simultaneous utterance): *chorus of cheers,* дру́жные во́згласы. —**in a chorus,** хо́ром.

chosen *adj.* и́збранный.

Christ *n.* Христо́с.

christen *v.t.* **1,** (baptize) крести́ть. **2,** (name) нарека́ть.

christening *n.* **1,** (act) креще́ние. **2,** (ceremony) крести́ны.

Christian *adj.* христиа́нский. —*n.* христиани́н; христиа́нка. —**Christian name,** и́мя.

Christianity *n.* христиа́нство.

Christmas *n.* рождество́. *Merry Christmas!,* с рождество́м! —*adj.* рожде́ственский: *Christmas tree,* рожде́ственская ёлка. —**Christmas Eve,** сочéльник.

chromatic *adj.* хромати́ческий.

chrome *n.* хром. —**chrome alum,** хро́мовые квасцы́. —**chrome leather,** хром. —**chrome plating,** хроми́рование; хро́мовое покры́тие. —**chrome steel,** хро́мистая сталь.

chromic acid хро́мовая кислота́.

chromite *n.* хро́мистый железня́к; хроми́т.

chromium *n.* хром.

chromosome *n.* хромосо́ма.

chronic *adj.* **1,** *med.* хрони́ческий; застаре́лый: *chronic illness,* хрони́ческая/застаре́лая боле́знь. **2,** (of a person) хрони́ческий; закоренéлый: *chronic alcoholic,* хрони́ческий/закоренéлый алкого́лик. *Chronic gambler,* зая́длый игро́к. **3,** (long-standing) хрони́ческий: *chronic unemployment,* хрони́ческая безрабо́тица. **4,** (constant) ве́чный: *chronic complaints,* ве́чные жа́лобы.

chronicle *n.* ле́топись; хро́ника. —*v.t.* заноси́ть в дневни́к, ле́топись, *etc.* —**chronicler,** *n.* летопи́сец.

chronology *n.* хроноло́гия. —**chronological,** *adj.* хронологи́ческий.

chronometer *n.* хроно́метр.

chrysalis *n.* ку́колка.

chrysanthemum *n.* хризанте́ма.

chubby *adj.* пу́хлый.

chuck *n.* **1,** (cut of beef) лопа́тка. **2,** (clamp; wedge) патро́н. —*v.t.* **1,** (toss) швыря́ть. **2,** *colloq.* (toss out) вышвы́ривать.

chuckle *n.* смешо́к. —*v.i.* посме́иваться.

chum *n.* това́рищ; прия́тель.

chunk *n.* ломо́ть.

chunky *adj.* пло́тный; корена́стый.

church *n.* це́рковь. —*adj.* церко́вный: *church bells,* церко́вные колокола́.

churchwarden *n.* церко́вный ста́роста.

churl *n.* грубия́н.

churlish *adj.* гру́бый; злой.

churn *n.* маслобо́йка. —*v.t.* **1,** (stir) сбива́ть; па́хтать. **2,** *fol. by* **up** (dig up; tear up) изрыва́ть. **3,** *fol. by* **up** (cause to swirl, as water) взбива́ть.

chute *n.* жёлоб; лото́к. *Garbage/refuse chute,* мусоропро́вод.

cicada *n.* цика́да.

cider *n.* сидр.

cigar *n.* сига́ра. —*adj.* сига́рный: *cigar smoke,* сига́рный дым.

cigarette *n.* папиро́са; сигаре́та. —*adj.* папиро́сный: сигаре́тный: *cigarette smoke,* папиро́сный/сигаре́тный дым. *Cigarette smoker,* куря́щий сигаре́ты. *Cigarette butt,* оку́рок папиро́сы. —**cigarette case,** портсига́р. —**cigarette holder,** мундшту́к. —**cigarette lighter,** зажига́лка.

cinch *n., colloq.* (easy thing to do) пустяки́.

cinchona *n.* хи́нное де́рево.

cinder *n.* пе́пел; *pl.* зола́; гарь. —*adj.* гарево́й; га́ревый. *Cinder path,* га́ревая доро́жка.

Cinderella *n.* Зо́лушка.

cinema *n.* **1,** *preceded by* **the** (motion pictures collectively) кино́. **2,** (motion-picture theater) кино́; кинотеа́тр.

cinematography *n.* кинематогра́фия.

cinnabar *n.* ки́новарь.

cinnamon *n.* кори́ца.

cipher *n.* **1,** (zero) нуль. **2,** (code) шифр.

Circassian *adj.* черке́сский. —*n.* черке́с.

circle *n.* **1,** (round figure; circular movement) круг: *form a circle,* образова́ть круг; *stand in a circle,* стать в круг. **2,** *geog.* круг: *Arctic Circle,* Се́верный поля́рный круг. **3,** (small group) круг: *circle of acquaintances,* круг знако́мых. *Within the family circle,* в семе́йном кругу́. *Ruling/official circles,* пра́вящие/ официа́льные круги́. **4,** (social group) кружо́к: *drama circle,* драмати́ческий кружо́к. —*v.t.* **1,** (draw a circle around) обводи́ть. **2,** (go around) обходи́ть; объезжа́ть; облета́ть; враща́ться (*all with* вокру́г). **3,** (fly repeatedly over) кружи́ть над. *The plane circled the airfield three times before landing,* самолёт сде́лал три кру́га над (лётным) по́лем, пре́жде чем приземли́ться. —*v.i.* кружи́ть; опи́сывать круги́. —**go around in circles,** топта́ться на ме́сте.

circuit *n.* **1,** (regular journey) обхо́д; объе́зд. **2,** *aerospace* вито́к: *three circuits of the earth,* три витка́ вокру́г Земли́. **3,** *electricity* цепь; ко́нтур. *Short circuit,* коро́ткое замыка́ние. **4,** *electronics* схе́ма: *integrated circuit,* интегра́льная схе́ма. —**circuit breaker,** прерыва́тель. —**circuit court,** окружно́й суд.

circuitous *adj.* око́льный; обхо́дный; кру́жный.

circular *adj.* **1,** (round) кру́глый. **2,** (moving in a circle) кругово́й; кругообра́зный. —*n.* циркуля́р.

circulate *v.i.* **1,** (of blood) обраща́ться; циркули́ровать; (of air) циркули́ровать. **2,** *econ.* (of money) обраща́ться. **3,** (go around, as of rumors) ходи́ть; циркули́ровать; распространя́ться. —*v.t.* рассыла́ть; распространя́ть. *Circulate a petition,* распространя́ть пети́цию.

circulation *n.* **1,** (of blood) обраще́ние (кро́ви); кровообраще́ние. *Poor circulation,* плохо́е кровообраще́ние. **2,** (of air) циркуля́ция. **3,** (use) оборо́т; обраще́ние: *put into circulation,* пусти́ть в оборо́т/ в обраще́ние/. **4,** *econ.* обраще́ние: *withdraw from circulation,* изыма́ть из обраще́ния. **5,** (average number of copies sold) тира́ж: *The newspaper has a circulation of 500,000,* газе́та выхо́дит тиражо́м в пятьсо́т ты́сяч экземпля́ров; тира́ж газе́ты — пятьсо́т ты́сяч экземпля́ров. —**be out of circulation,** не появля́ться на лю́дях.

circulatory *adj.* кровено́сный: *circulatory system,* кровено́сная систе́ма.

circumcise *v.t.* обреза́ть. —**circumcision,** *n.* обре́зание.

circumference *n.* окру́жность.

circumlocution *n.* околи́чности.

circumnavigate *v.t. Circumnavigate the globe,* соверша́ть кругосве́тное пла́вание.

circumscribe *v.t.* **1,** (limit) ограни́чивать. **2,** *math.* опи́сывать. —**circumscription,** *n.* ограниче́ние.

circumspect *adj.* осмотри́тельный. —**circumspection,** *n.* осмотри́тельность.

circumstance *n.* **1,** (fact; event) обстоя́тельство: *He died under mysterious circumstances,* он поги́б при зага́дочных обстоя́тельствах. **2,** *pl.* (financial condition) обстоя́тельства: *in straitened circumstances,* в стеснённых обстоя́тельствах. —**under no circumstances,** ни в ко́ем слу́чае; ни под каки́м ви́дом; ни при каки́х обстоя́тельствах; ни при каки́х усло́виях.

circumstantial evidence ко́свенныеули́ки.

circumvent *v.t.* **1,** (surround; encircle) окружа́ть. **2,** (get around; evade) обходи́ть.

circus *n.* цирк. —*adj.* цирково́й: *circus performer,* цирково́й арти́ст.

cirrhosis *n.* цирро́з: *cirrhosis of the liver,* цирро́з пе́чени.

cistern *n.* цисте́рна.

citadel *n.* цитаде́ль.

citation *n.* **1,** (act of quoting) цити́рование. **2,** (quote) цита́та; ссы́лка. **3,** (commendation) благода́рность. **4,** (summons) вы́зов.

cite *v.t.* **1,** (quote) ссыла́ться на; цити́ровать. **2,** (refer to, as an example) приводи́ть. **3,** (commend, as for bravery) отлича́ть. **4,** *law* привлека́ть к отве́тственности.

citizen *n.* граждани́н.

citizenship *n.* гражда́нство.

citrate *n.* цитра́т.

citric acid лимо́нная кислота́.

citrus *n.* ци́трус. —*adj.* ци́трусовый.

city *n.* го́род. —*adj.* городско́й: *city council,* городско́й сове́т. —**city hall,** ра́туша.

civet *n.* виве́рра.

civic *adj.* гражда́нский: *civic duty,* гражда́нский долг.

civil *adj.* **1,** (pert. to citizens) гражда́нский. **2,** (polite) ве́жливый. —**civil defense,** гражда́нская оборо́на. —**civil engineer,** инжене́р-строи́тель. —**civil engineering,** строи́тельная те́хника. —**civil marriage,** гражда́нский брак. —**civil rights,** гражда́нские права́. —**civil servant,** госуда́рственный служа́щий. —**civil service,** гражда́нская слу́жба. —**civil war,** гражда́нская война́.

civilian *n.* шта́тский (челове́к); гражда́нское лицо́. —*adj.* гражда́нский; шта́тский. *The civilian population,* гражда́нское населе́ние. *Civilian clothes,* гражда́нская *or* шта́тская оде́жда.

civility *n.* **1,** (courtesy) ве́жливость. **2,** *pl.* (proprieties) прили́чия.

civilization *n.* цивилизация.

civilize *v.t.* цивилизовать. —**civilized,** *adj.* цивилизованный.

clabber *n.* простокваша.

clack *v.i.* цокать. —*n.* цокот.

clad *adj.* одётый. *Snow-clad,* заснёженный.

claim *v.t.* **1,** (assert one's right to) трёбовать; претендовать на. *Claim damages,* трёбовать возмещёния убытков. *Claim territory,* претендовать на территорию. *Claim the throne,* претендовать на престол. **2,** (call for; pick up) вострёбовать. *"Baggage claim",* «выдача багажа». **3,** (maintain; assert) утверждать: *He claims that...,* он утверждает, что... *Claim responsibility for a terrorist act,* взять на себя отвётственность за террористический акт. —*n.* **1,** (request; demand) претёнзия; притязание; трёбование. **2,** (assertion; contention) утверждёние. —**lay claim to,** претендовать на; предъявить трёбование *or* право на.

claimant *n.* претендёнт.

claim check квитанция.

clairvoyance *n.* ясновидение.

clairvoyant *adj.* ясновидящий. —*n.* ясновидец.

clam *n.* моллюск. —*v.i.* [*usu.* **clam up**] *colloq.* замолчать.

clamber *v.i.* карабкаться.

clamor *also,* **clamour** *n.* **1,** (din) шум; гам. **2,** (public outcry) шум. —*v.i.* кричать; шумёть.

clamp *n.* зажим; скрёпа. —*v.t.* скреплять. —**clamp down on,** подтягивать; приструнивать.

clan *n.* клан.

clandestine *adj.* тайный; скрытый.

clang *n.* лязг. —*v.t. & i.* лязгать.

clank *n.* лязг; цокот. —*v.t. & i.* лязгать; бряцать; цокать.

clannish *adj.* замкнутый; обособленный.

clap *v.t.* **1,** (strike together, as one's hands) бить; ударять; хлопать (в ладоши). **2,** (toss, as into jail) упрятывать; упекать. —*v.i.* хлопать. —*n.* **1,** (act of clapping) хлопанье. **2,** (sound, as of thunder) удар; раскат. *There was a clap of thunder,* ударил гром.

clapper *n.* язык (колокола).

claque *n.* клака. —**claqueur,** *n.* клакёр.

claret *n.* (wine) бордо. —*adj.* (color) бордо; цвёта бордо; бордовый.

clarification *n.* разъяснёние.

clarify *v.t.* разъяснять; прояснять; выяснять.

clarinet *n.* кларнёт. —**clarinetist,** *n.* кларнетист.

clarion *n.* фанфара. —*adj.* громкий; звучный.

clarity *n.* ясность.

clash *v.i.* **1,** (come into conflict) сталкиваться. **2,** (not go well together) дисгармонировать. —*n.* столкновёние.

clasp *n.* **1,** (hook) застёжка. **2,** (grip) объятие; пожатие. —*v.t.* **1,** (fasten) застёгивать. **2,** (grasp) обнимать; обхватывать. **3,** *Clasp one's hands (in despair),* ломать руки (в отчаянии).

class *n.* **1,** (social stratum) класс: *the working class,* рабочий класс. **2,** (group of pupils) класс: *How many pupils are there in your class?,* сколько ученико́в в

вашем классе? *Upper classes,* старшие классы. **3,** (instructional period) класс; *pl.* занятия. *Go to class,* идти в класс. *Evening classes,* вечёрние занятия. *Classes begin at 9:00,* занятия начинаются в дёвять часов. *Be late for class,* опоздать на урок. **4,** (alumni graduated in one year) выпуск: *the class of 1980,* выпуск тысяча девятьсот восьмидесятого года. **5,** (quality of accommodations on a plane, ship, etc.) класс: *travel first-class,* ёхать пёрвым классом. **6,** (category) класс. *He is in a class by himself,* он единственный в своём роде. *He is not in her class,* ему далеко до неё. —*adj.* **1,** (pertaining to social classes) классовый: *class consciousness,* классовое сознание. **2,** (pert. to a class in school) классный. —*v.t.* классифицировать.

classic *n.* классическое произведёние; *pl.* классика. —*adj.* классический.

classical *adj.* классический. —**classical music,** классическая музыка.

classicism *n.* классицизм. —**classicist,** *n.* классик.

classification *n.* **1,** (act of classifying) классификация. **2,** *mil.* гриф секрётности.

classified *adj.* **1,** (grouped) классифицированный. **2,** *mil.* секрётный; засекрёченный. —**classified ad,** объявлёние (в газёте).

classify *v.t.* **1,** (arrange by class) классифицировать. **2,** (declare to be secret) засекрёчивать.

classless *adj.* бесклассовый.

classmate *n.* одноклассник.

classroom *n.* класс; классная комната.

classy *adj., colloq.* шикарный; первоклассный.

clatter *n.* стук; топот; цокот. *The clatter of hoofs,* стук/топот/цокот копыт; конский топот. —*v.i.* гремёть; громыхать; цокать; тарабанить.

clause *n.* **1,** (part of a sentence) предложёние. **2,** (article; provision) статья; пункт.

claustrophobia *n.* боязнь оставаться в закрытом помещёнии; клаустрофобия.

clavichord *n.* клавикорды.

clavicle *n.* ключица.

claw *n.* **1,** (of a bird or animal) коготь. **2,** (of a lobster or crab) клешня. **3,** (of a hammer) лапа. —*v.t.* терзать когтями.

clay *n.* глина. —*adj.* глиняный: *clay tablets,* глиняные таблички. —**clayey,** *adj.* глинистый.

clay pigeon тарёлочка.

clean *adj.* чистый: *clean shirt/plate,* чистая рубашка/тарёлка. —*adv.* **1,** (so as to be clean) начисто: *sweep the floor clean,* начисто вымести пол. *Lick the plate clean,* облизывать тарёлку. **2,** *colloq.* (completely) совершённо: *I clean forgot,* я совершённо забыл(а). —*v.t.* чистить: *clean a carpet,* чистить ковёр; *clean one's rifle,* чистить винтовку. *Clean one's pipe,* прочищать трубку. —**clean out, 1,** (clear of rubbish) очищать. **2,** *colloq.* (of a robber) очистить; обокрасть *or* ограбить дочиста; (in gambling) обчищать; обыграть дочиста. —**clean up, 1,** (tidy up) убирать; прибирать. **2,** *colloq.* (finish up) закончить. **3,** *slang* (make a lot of money) сорвать куш. —**come clean,** *colloq.* признаться во всём.

clean-cut *adj.* опря́тный; хо́леный.

cleaner *n.* **1,** (person) чи́стильщик; убо́рщик. **2,** (establishment) химчи́стка: *take to the cleaners,* отдава́ть в химчи́стку. —**take to the cleaners,** *slang* (clean out in gambling) обища́ть; обыгра́ть до́чиста.

cleaning *n.* чи́стка. —**cleaning woman,** убо́рщица.

cleanliness *n.* чистота́.

cleanly *adj.* чистопло́тный. —*adv.* чи́сто.

cleanse *v.t.* чи́стить; очища́ть.

cleanser *n.* мо́ющее сре́дство.

clean-shaven *adj.* бри́тый; гла́дко вы́бритый.

cleanup *n.* очи́стка; убо́рка. *Cleanup operations,* очистны́е рабо́ты.

clear *adj.* **1,** (bright) я́сный: *clear day,* я́сный день. *Clear sky,* я́сное *or* чи́стое не́бо. **2,** (easily understood) я́сный: *clear answer,* я́сный отве́т. *Clear handwriting,* разбо́рчивый по́черк. *As clear as day,* я́сный как бо́жий день. *Make it clear that...,* дать я́сно поня́ть, что... *It is gradually becoming clear that...,* постепе́нно выясня́ется, что... **3,** (pure; unblemished) чи́стый: *clear water/skin/conscience,* чи́стая вода́/ко́жа/со́весть. **4,** (unobstructed) свобо́дный: *The way is clear,* путь свобо́ден. —*adv.* **1,** (distinctly) я́сно: *loud and clear,* гро́мко и я́сно. **2,** (all the way): *clear to the top,* до са́мой верши́ны. —*v.t.* **1,** (rid of dirt, unwanted objects, etc.) очища́ть: *clear the windshield,* очища́ть пере́днее стекло́; *clear the desk of papers,* очища́ть пи́сьменный стол от бума́г. *Clear the table,* убира́ть со стола́. *Clear the air,* очища́ть во́здух; *fig.* разряди́ть атмосфе́ру. *Clear one's throat,* отка́шливаться. *Clear the land,* расчища́ть зе́млю. *Clear a forest,* очища́ть лес. *Clear a path,* расчища́ть доро́жку. *Clear the way for,* открыва́ть *or* прокла́дывать доро́гу (+ *dat.*). **2,** (remove) убира́ть; счища́ть. *Clear the dishes from the table,* убира́ть посу́ду со стола́. *Clear the snow off the sidewalk,* счища́ть снег с тротуа́ра. **3,** (empty; vacate) освобожда́ть; очища́ть: *clear the premises,* освобожда́ть/очища́ть помеще́ние. **4,** (pass through) проходи́ть: *clear customs,* проходи́ть тамо́женный осмо́тр *or* досмо́тр. *The truck just cleared the tunnel,* грузови́к едва́ прошёл в тунне́ль. **5,** (jump over) брать: *clear a hurdle,* брать барье́р. **6,** (coordinate with a higher authority) согласо́вывать: *clear the plan with management,* согласова́ть план с дире́кцией. **7,** (authorize to see classified information) засекре́чивать. **8,** (acquit) очища́ть: *He was cleared of all charges,* он был очи́щен от всех обвине́ний. **9,** (earn; net) выруча́ть. **10,** *Clear one's name,* восстанови́ть своё до́брое и́мя. —*v.i.* **1,** (become clear; become free of clouds) проясня́ться. **2,** (dissipate, as of smoke) рассе́иваться. —**clear away,** убира́ть; счища́ть. —**clear out, 1,** (empty; clean up) очища́ть. **2,** *colloq.* (depart) убира́ться. —**clear up, 1,** (pick up and remove) убира́ть. **2,** (resolve) выясня́ть: *clear up a matter,* вы́яснить обстоя́тельства де́ла. *Clear up a misunderstanding,* вы́яснить *or* разреши́ть недоразуме́ние. *Clear up a mystery,* разга́дывать та́йну. **3,** (grow fair, as of the weather)

проясня́ться; разгу́ливаться. **4,** (disappear, as of a cold, rash, etc.) проходи́ть.

clearance *n.* **1,** (space) зазо́р. **2,** (sale) распрода́жа. **3,** = security clearance.

clear-cut *adj.* чёткий.

clearing *n.* **1,** (act of making clear) очи́стка; очище́ние; расчи́стка. **2,** (place cleared of trees) вы́рубка; поля́на. —**clearing house,** расчётная пала́та.

clearly *adv.* **1,** (in a clear manner) я́сно. *I see clearly now that...,* тепе́рь я я́сно ви́жу, что... **2,** (without a doubt) безусло́вно: *clearly the best,* безусло́вно са́мый лу́чший.

cleat *n.* шип; шипо́вка: *shoes with cleats,* кроссо́вки на шипа́х *or* на шипо́вках.

cleavage *n.* раско́л.

cleave *v.t.* раска́лывать; рассека́ть.

cleaver *n.* тя́пка; се́чка.

clef *n.* ключ.

cleft *n.* рассе́лина; расще́лина; тре́щина. —*adj.* раздвое́нный. —**cleft palate,** во́лчья пасть.

clematis *n.* ломоно́с.

clemency *n.* милосе́рдие; поща́да; поми́лование.

clench *v.t.* сжима́ть. *Clenched fists,* сжа́тые кулаки́.

clergy *n.* духове́нство. —**clergyman,** *n.* свяще́нник; духо́вное лицо́.

cleric *n.* духо́вное лицо́.

clerical *adj.* **1,** (pert. to the clergy) духо́вный. **2,** (pert. to office work) канцеля́рский.

clerk *n.* **1,** (office worker) конто́рский служа́щий; клерк. **2,** (salesperson) продаве́ц; прика́зчик. **3,** (record keeper) регистра́тор.

clever *adj.* **1,** (bright; intelligent) у́мный; сообрази́тельный; смышлёный. **2,** (showing skill or wit) ло́вкий; остроу́мный. —**cleverly,** *adv.* ло́вко; остроу́мно. —**cleverness,** *n.* ло́вкость; сообрази́тельность.

cliché *n.* клише́; штамп.

click *n.* щелчо́к: *a click of the camera,* щелчо́к фотоаппара́та. —*v.t.* щёлкать (+ *instr.*). *Click one's heels,* щёлкать *or* присту́кивать каблука́ми. —*v.i.* щёлкать: *The camera clicked,* фотоаппара́т щёлкнул.

client *n.* **1,** (customer) клие́нт. **2,** (of a lawyer) подзащи́тный.

clientele *n.* клиенту́ра.

cliff *n.* обры́в; утёс; (отве́сная) скала́. *Fall over a cliff,* упа́сть со скалы́; сорва́ться с обры́ва *or* со скалы́.

climactic *adj.* кульминацио́нный.

climate *n.* **1,** (type of weather) кли́мат. **2,** *fig.* (prevailing conditions) кли́мат; атмосфе́ра: *political climate,* полити́ческий кли́мат; полити́ческая атмосфе́ра. —**climatic,** *adj.* климати́ческий.

climax *n.* развя́зка; кульминацио́нный пункт; кульминацио́нный моме́нт. *Matters are approaching a climax,* де́ло идёт к развя́зке.

climb *v.i.* **1,** (clamber) лезть. *Climb up on the roof,* лезть *or* залеза́ть *or* забира́ться на кры́шу. *Climb like a monkey,* ла́зить как обезья́на. **2,** (walk upstairs) поднима́ться: *climb to the second floor,* поднима́ться на второ́й эта́ж. **3,** (increase; rise) расти́. **4,** (gain altitude) набира́ть высоту́. —*v.t.* лезть на; влеза́ть на; залеза́ть на; взбира́ться на. *Climb a tree*, лезть *or* влеза́ть на де́рево. *Climb (the) stairs*, поднима́ться по ле́стнице. *Climb a ladder*, лезть по ле́стнице. *Climb a hill/mountain*, лезть *or* взбира́ться на́ гору. —*n.* **1,** (act of climbing) подъём; восхожде́ние. **2,** *aero.* подъём; набо́р высоты́. —**climb down,** слеза́ть. —**climb in,** влеза́ть. —**climb into,** влеза́ть в (+ *acc.*). —**climb out,** вылеза́ть. —**climb over,** перелеза́ть (че́рез); лезть че́рез.

climber *n.* **1,** (mountain climber) альпини́ст. **2,** (plant) вью́щееся расте́ние.

climbing *n.* ла́занье. *Mountain climbing*, альпини́зм. —*adj.* (of a plant) вью́щийся. —**climbing irons,** ко́шки.

clinch *v.t.* **1,** (secure; fasten) заклёпывать. **2,** *fig.* (settle for good) реша́ть. *Clinch a deal*, заключи́ть сде́лку.

cling *v.i.* [*usu.* **cling to**] **1,** (adhere to) прилипа́ть (к). **2,** (hang on to) цепля́ться (за); льнуть (к). *Cling to a ledge*, цепля́ться за вы́ступ. *Cling to one's mother*, льнуть к ма́тери. *Cling to life*, цепля́ться за жизнь. *Cling to a hope*, цепля́ться за наде́жду.

clinic *n.* кли́ника. —**clinical,** *adj.* клини́ческий.

clink *n.* **1,** (sound) звон. **2,** *slang* (jail) куту́зка. —*v.t.* звене́ть (+ *instr.*). *Clink glasses*, чо́каться. *Clinking of glasses*, звон бока́лов.

clip *n.* **1,** (metal fastener) скре́пка. **2,** (piece of jewelry) брошь. **3,** (cartridge clip) (патро́нная) обо́йма. **4,** *colloq.* (pace) ход: *at a fast clip*, бы́стрым хо́дом. —*v.t.* **1,** (fasten with a clip) скрепля́ть. **2,** (trim) стричь; подстрига́ть; обреза́ть; подреза́ть. **3,** *fol. by* **out** (cut out) выреза́ть. **4,** *colloq.* (strike) дать: *clip someone on the ear*, дать кому́-нибудь по́ уху. —**clip someone's wings,** подреза́ть кры́лья (+ *dat.*).

clipper *n.* **1,** *usu. pl.* (shears) но́жницы. **2,** *usu. pl.* (device for cutting hair) маши́нка для стри́жки. **3,** (ship) кли́пер.

clipping *n.* вы́резка.

clique *n.* кли́ка.

clitoris *n.* кли́тор; похотни́к.

cloak *n.* **1,** (garment) плащ; ма́нтия. **2,** *fig.* (guise; cover) покро́в; ши́рма; ма́ска. —*v.t.* прикрыва́ть; маскирова́ть.

cloakroom *n.* гардеро́б; раздева́лка. *Cloakroom attendant*, гардеро́бщик.

clock *n.* часы́. *Alarm clock*, буди́льник. —*v.t.* хронометри́ровать. —**round the clock,** кру́глые су́тки.

clockwise *adv.* по часово́й стре́лке.

clockwork *n.* часово́й механи́зм. —**work like clockwork,** рабо́тать как часы́.

clod *n.* **1,** (lump) ком; глы́ба. **2,** (dolt) о́лух; недотёпа.

clog *v.t.* засоря́ть; забива́ть. *Become clogged*, засоря́ться. *The streets are clogged with bicycles*, у́лицы заби́ты велосипе́дами.

cloister *n.* **1,** (monastery) монасты́рь. **2,** (covered walk) (кры́тая) арка́да. —*v.t.* **1,** (confine to a monastery) заточа́ть в монасты́рь. **2,** (seclude) уединя́ть.

close[1] (klos) *adj.* **1,** (near) бли́зкий. *Close relative*, бли́зкий ро́дственник. *Close resemblance*, большо́е

сходство. *Close translation*, бли́зкий перево́д. *Close combat*, бли́жний бой. *Fire at close range*, стреля́ть с бли́зкого расстоя́ния. **2,** (intimate) бли́зкий; те́сный. *Close friend*, бли́зкий друг. *Close connection*, те́сная связь. **3,** (tight; compact) пло́тный; ча́стый. *Close weave*, пло́тное плете́ние. *Close print*, убо́ристый шрифт. *Close order, mil.* со́мкнутый строй. **4,** (keenly contested) напряжённый. *Close match*, напряжённый матч; упо́рная борьба́. *Close vote*, почти́ ра́вное деле́ние голосо́в. **5,** (rigorous; searching) внима́тельный. *Keep a close watch on*, внима́тельно следи́ть за. **6,** (stuffy) ду́шный: *It is close in here*, здесь ду́шно. —*adv.* бли́зко: *Don't get too close!*, не подходи́те сли́шком бли́зко! *Stand closer together!*, ста́ньте побли́же! *Follow close behind*, идти́ сле́дом (за). —**close by,** бли́зко; ря́дом. —**close to,** о́коло; бли́зко от *or* к. *The hotel is close to the station*, гости́ница бли́зко (*or* недалеко́) от вокза́ла. *He is close to the truth*, он бли́зок к и́стине. *She was close to tears/despair*, она́ была́ на гра́ни слёз; она́ была́ близка́ к отча́янию. *She was not close to her mother*, она́ не была́ близка́ к ма́тери. *He is close to sixty*, ему́ под шестьдеся́т. —**up close,** вблизи́: *The house looks different up close*, вблизи́ дом вы́глядит ина́че.

close[2] (kloz) *v.t.* **1,** (shut) закрыва́ть: *close the door*, закрыва́ть дверь; *close one's eyes*, закрыва́ть глаза́. **2,** (fill up; stop up) заде́лывать: *close a hole with putty*, заде́лывать дыру́ зама́зкой. **3,** (bring together; join) смыка́ть; спла́чивать: *close ranks*, смыка́ть/ спла́чивать ряды́. **4,** (end) зака́нчивать; заключа́ть: *close one's speech with an appeal*, зако́нчить/ заключи́ть свою́ речь призы́вом. **5,** (conclude successfully) заключа́ть: *close a deal*, заключи́ть сде́лку. —*v.i.* **1,** (shut; cease operations) закрыва́ться: *The window won't close*, окно́ не закрыва́ется. *Many factories are closing*, мно́гие заво́ды закрыва́ются. **2,** (conclude) зака́нчивать: *I shall close with the following observation*, зако́нчу сле́дующим замеча́нием. *In closing*, в заключе́ние. —*n.* закры́тие; коне́ц. *Draw to a close*, подходи́ть *or* идти́ *or* бли́зиться *or* приближа́ться к концу́. —**close down,** закрыва́ть; прикрыва́ть. —**close in,** смыка́ть кольцо́ окруже́ния. —**close out,** распродава́ть.

closed *adj.* закры́тый: *behind closed doors*, при закры́тых дверя́х. *The city is closed to foreigners*, го́род закры́т для иностра́нцев. *The subject is closed*, те́ма исче́рпана.

closed circuit за́мкнутая цепь.

close-fisted *adj.* прижи́мистый.

close-fitting *adj.* те́сный; в обтя́жку. *Close-fitting dress*, пла́тье, пло́тно облега́ющее фигу́ру.

close-knit *adj.* спа́янный.

closely *adv.* **1,** (intimately) те́сно: *closely connected*, те́сно свя́занный. *He closely resembles...*, он о́чень похо́ж на (+ *acc.*). **2,** (attentively) внима́тельно; чу́тко. *Closely guarded secret*, стро́го храни́мый секре́т.

close-mouthed *adj.* за́мкнутый.

closeness n. 1, (nearness) бли́зость. 2, (tightness) теснота́. 3, (stuffiness) духота́.

close-out n. распрода́жа.

closet n. шкаф. —v.t. [usu. **closet oneself**] уединя́ться.

close-up n. кру́пный план. Take a close-up of, снима́ть (кого́-нибудь) кру́пным пла́ном.

closing n. 1, (act of shutting) закры́тие. Closing time, вре́мя закры́тия. 2, (end; conclusion) заключе́ние. —adj. заключи́тельный.

closure n. закры́тие.

clot n. сгу́сток: blood clot, сгу́сток кро́ви. —v.t. сгуща́ть. —v.i. сгуща́ться; запека́ться.

cloth n. 1, (fabric) ткань; сукно́; мате́рия. 2, (small piece for wiping or dusting) суко́нка; тря́пка. —adj. суко́нный: cloth coat, суко́нное пальто́.

clothe v.t. одева́ть.

clothes n.pl. оде́жда; пла́тье. Comfortable clothes, удо́бная оде́жда. Dirty clothes, гря́зное бельё. —adj. платяно́й: clothes brush, платяна́я щётка.

clothesline n. верёвка для белья́.

clothespin n. прище́пка.

clothier n. торго́вец гото́вой оде́жды.

clothing n. оде́жда; пла́тье. —adj. вещево́й: clothing allowance, вещево́е дово́льствие. Clothing store, магази́н оде́жды; магази́н гото́вого пла́тья.

cloture n. прекраще́ние пре́ний.

cloud n. 1, (in the sky) о́блако: fly over the clouds, лете́ть над облака́ми. Storm cloud, ту́ча. 2, (mass of something in the air) о́блако; pl. клубы́. Cloud of dust, о́блако пы́ли. Thick clouds of smoke, густы́е клубы́ ды́ма. —adj. о́блачный: cloud cover, о́блачный покро́в. —v.t. затемня́ть; омрача́ть; затума́нивать. —v.i. [usu. **cloud up**] затума́ниваться. The sky is clouding up, не́бо затя́гивается ту́чами. —**be up in the clouds**, вита́ть в облака́х.

cloudberry n. моро́шка.

cloudburst n. ли́вень.

cloudiness n. о́блачность.

cloudless adj. безо́блачный.

cloudy adj. 1, (covered with or marked by clouds) о́блачный: cloudy sky/day, о́блачное не́бо; о́блачный день. 2, (murky, as of a liquid) му́тный.

clout n. 1, (blow) тума́к. 2, colloq. (influence) вес.

clove n. гвозди́ка.

cloven adj. раздво́енный. —**cloven hoof**, раздво́енное копы́то.

clover n. кле́вер. —**be in clover**, ката́ться как сыр в ма́сле; жить припева́ючи.

clown n. кло́ун. —v.i. пая́сничать; дура́читься. —**clownish**, adj. кло́унский; шутовско́й.

cloy v.t. пресыща́ть. —**cloying**, adj. при́торный; слаща́вый.

club n. 1, (cudgel) дуби́на; дуби́нка. 2, (golf club) клю́шка. 3, (association; group) клуб; кружо́к; (headquarters of same) клуб. 4, pl., cards тре́фы: king of clubs, коро́ль треф. —v.t. избива́ть; дуба́сить.

clubfoot n. изуро́дованная ступня́.

club soda со́довая вода́.

cluck v.i. клохта́ть. —n. клохта́нье.

clue n. путево́дная нить. Leave no clues, не оставля́ть никаки́х следо́в. Give someone a clue, наводи́ть кого́-нибудь на след. I haven't a clue, поня́тия не име́ю.

clump n. 1, (cluster) гру́ппа: clump of trees, гру́ппа дере́вьев. 2, (lump) комо́к. 3, (sound of heavy footsteps) то́пот.

clumsy adj. неуклю́жий. —**clumsily**, adv. неуклю́же. —**clumsiness**, n. неуклю́жесть.

cluster n. 1, (bunch, as of grapes) кисть; гроздь. 2, (small group) гру́ппа; ку́чка. Star cluster, звёздное скопле́ние. —v.i. спла́чиваться. Cluster around, окружа́ть; обступа́ть.

clutch v.t. хвата́ть; схва́тывать. —v.i. [usu. **clutch at**] хвата́ться за. —n. 1, (grip) хва́тка. 2, (of a car) сцепле́ние; му́фта. —**fall into the clutches of**, попа́сть в ко́гти or в ла́пы (+ gen., dat. or к).

clutter v.t. загроможда́ть; заставля́ть: The room was cluttered with furniture, ко́мната была́ загромождена́ or заста́влена ме́белью. Clutter one's mind with useless facts, засоря́ть ум беспо́лезными фа́ктами.

coach n. 1, (carriage) каре́та. 2, (railway car) ваго́н. 3, (tutor) репети́тор. 4, sports тре́нер. —v.t. 1, (tutor) репети́ровать; ната́скивать. 2, sports тренирова́ть. 3, (prompt) подска́зывать: No coaching!, не подска́зывать!

coach house каре́тный сара́й.

coachman n. ку́чер; вози́ца; изво́зчик.

coagulant n. сгуща́ющее сре́дство; коагуля́нт.

coagulate v.t. сгуща́ть; свёртывать. —v.i. сгуща́ться; свёртываться; запека́ться. —**coagulation**, n. свёртывание; коагуля́ция.

coal n. 1, (mineral) у́голь. 2, pl. (embers) у́гли. —adj. у́гольный; каменноу́гольный. Coal mine, у́гольная ша́хта. Coal gas/tar, каменноу́гольный газ/дёготь. —**rake over the coals**, зада́ть жа́ру (+ dat.); взять под обстре́л; разде́лывать под оре́х.

coalesce v.i. 1, (grow together) сраста́ться. 2, (unite; merge) объединя́ться; слива́ться. —**coalescence**, n. сраще́ние; соедине́ние.

coalition n. коали́ция.

coarse adj. 1, (rough; crude; unrefined) гру́бый. 2, (not fine, as of sand) кру́пный.

coarsen v.t. де́лать гру́бым. —v.i. грубе́ть.

coarseness n. гру́бость.

coast n. 1, (edge of the land facing the sea) бе́рег: along the coast, вдоль бе́рега; rocky coast, скали́стый бе́рег. An island off the coast of Maine, о́стров недалеко́ от (or вблизи́) бе́рега Мэ́на. 2, (region next to the sea) побере́жье: the West Coast, за́падное побере́жье. —v.i. кати́ться по ине́рции. —**the coast is clear**, путь свобо́ден.

coastal adj. берегово́й; прибре́жный. Coastal waters, прибре́жные во́ды.

coast guard 1, (unit guarding a coast) берегова́я охра́на. 2, cap. (U.S. branch of service) морска́я пограни́чная слу́жба.

coastline n. берегова́я ли́ния.

coat n. 1, (overcoat) пальто́. Fur coat, шу́ба. 2, (suit jacket) пиджа́к. **3,** (skin; fur) мех; шку́ра. **4,** (layer, as of paint) слой. *The door needs a coat of paint,* дверь на́до покра́сить. —*v.t.* покрыва́ть; залива́ть.

coated *adj. My tongue is coated,* у меня́ обложи́ло язы́к. —**coated lens,** просветлённый объекти́в. —**coated paper,** мелова́я бума́га.

coati *n.* носу́ха.

coating *n.* покры́тие; налёт.

coat of arms герб.

coat of mail па́нцирь; кольчу́га.

coatroom *n.* гардеро́б; раздева́лка.

coattail *n.* фа́лда.

coauthor *n.* соа́втор. —**coauthorship,** *n.* соа́вторство.

coax *v.t.* **1,** (try to persuade) угова́ривать; убежда́ть: *He coaxed me into going,* он уговори́л/убеди́л меня́ пойти́. **2,** (obtain by persuasion) выпра́шивать: *coax money out of someone,* вы́просить де́нег у кого́-нибудь.

coaxial cable коаксиа́льный ка́бель.

cob *n.* поча́ток кукуру́зы.

cobalt *n.* ко́бальт. —*adj.* ко́бальтовый.

cobbled *adj.* булы́жный.

cobbler *n.* сапо́жник.

cobblestone *n.* булы́жник. —*adj.* булы́жный.

cobra *n.* очко́вая змея́; ко́бра.

cobweb *n.* паути́на.

coca *n.* ко́ка.

cocaine *n.* кока́ин.

coccus *n.* кокк.

coccyx *n.* ко́пчик.

co-chairman *n.* сопредседа́тель.

cochineal *n.* кошени́ль.

cock *n.* **1,** (rooster) пету́х. **2,** (faucet) кран. **3,** (hammer of a firearm) куро́к. —*v.t.* **1,** (tilt) зала́мывать: *cock one's hat,* зала́мывать ша́пку. *Cock one's eye,* скоси́ть глаз. *Cock one's head to one side,* склони́ть го́лову на́бок. **2,** (set, as a firearm) взводи́ть куро́к (пистоле́та). *The gun is cocked,* куро́к на боево́м взво́де.

cockade *n.* кока́рда.

cock-and-bull story небыли́ца; ро́ссказни.

cockatoo *n.* какаду́.

cockchafer *n.* ма́йский жук; хрущ.

cocked hat треуго́лка.

cockerel *n.* петушо́к.

cockeyed *adj.* **1,** (cross-eyed) косогла́зый. **2,** *colloq.* (askew) косо́й. **3,** *colloq.* (absurd) глу́пый; дура́цкий.

cockfight *n.* петуши́ный бой.

cockiness *n.* самоуве́ренность.

cockle *n.* **1,** (weed) ку́коль; пле́вел. **2,** (mollusk) сердцеви́дка. —**cockles of one's heart,** тайники́ се́рдца.

cockpit *n.* каби́на (самолёта).

cockroach *n.* тарака́н.

cockscomb *n.* **1,** (comb of a cock) петуши́ный гре́бень. **2,** (plant) пету́ший гребешо́к.

cocksure *adj.* **1,** (absolutely sure) вполне́ уве́ренный. **2,** (too sure of oneself) самоуве́ренный.

cocktail *n.* кокте́йль.

cocky *adj., colloq.* самоуве́ренный; чванли́вый.

coco *n.* коко́совая па́льма; коко́с. *Also,* **coco palm; coconut palm.**

cocoa *n.* кака́о.

coconut *n.* коко́совый оре́х; коко́с. —*adj.* коко́совый.

cocoon *n.* ко́кон.

cod *n.* треска́.

C.O.D. нало́женным платежо́м.

coddle *v.t.* не́жить; изне́живать.

code *n.* **1,** (body of laws) ко́декс; свод зако́нов. *Criminal code,* уголо́вный ко́декс. **2,** (system of secret communication) код: *send a message in code,* переда́ть сообще́ние ко́дом. —*adj.* ко́довый: *code name,* ко́довое и́мя. —*v.t., usu. passive,* коди́ровать; шифрова́ть: *coded message,* коди́рованное/шифро́ванное сообще́ние; шифро́вка.

codeine *n.* кодеи́н.

codfish *n.* треска́.

codicil *n.* припи́ска.

codify *v.t.* кодифици́ровать. —**codification,** *n.* кодифика́ция.

cod-liver oil ры́бий жир.

coeducation *n.* совме́стное обуче́ние. —**coeducational,** *adj.* совме́стного обуче́ния.

coefficient *n.* коэффицие́нт.

coerce *v.t.* принужда́ть; заставля́ть. —**coercion,** *n.* принужде́ние. —**coercive,** *adj.* принуди́тельный.

coexist *v.i.* сосуществова́ть. —**coexistence,** *n.* сосуществова́ние.

coffee *n.* ко́фе. —*adj.* кофе́йный: *coffee beans,* кофе́йные бобы́. —**coffee-colored,** *adj.* кофе́йный; кофе́йного цве́та. —**coffee house,** кофе́йня. —**coffee mill,** кофе́йная ме́льница; кофе́йница. —**coffeepot,** *n.* кофе́йник.

coffer *n.* **1,** (strongbox) (де́нежный) я́щик. **2,** *pl.* (treasury) казна́.

coffin *n.* гроб.

cog *n.* зубе́ц.

cogent *adj.* убеди́тельный. —**cogency,** *n.* убеди́тельность.

cogitate *v.i.* размышля́ть; разду́мывать. —**cogitation,** *n.* размышле́ние.

cognac *n.* конья́к.

cognate *adj.* ро́дственный. —*n.* ро́дственное сло́во.

cognition *n.* позна́ние. —**cognitive,** *adj.* позна́вательный.

cognizance *n.* зна́ние. —**take cognizance of,** обраща́ть внима́ние на.

cognizant *adj. Be cognizant of,* осознава́ть; отдава́ть себе́ отчёт в.

cogwheel *n.* зубча́тое колесо́; шестерня́.

cohabit *v.i.* сожи́тельствовать. —**cohabitation,** *n.* сожи́тельство.

cohere *v.i.* слипа́ться; слепля́ться.

coherent *adj.* свя́зный; стро́йный. —**coherence,** *n.* свя́зность.

cohesion *n.* сплочённость; спа́янность.

cohesive *adj.* сплочённый.

cohort *n.* **1,** (band) отря́д. **2,** (associate) посо́бник.

coil *n.* **1,** (series of rings) вито́к. **2,** *electricity* кату́шка.

—*v.t.* нама́тывать; обма́тывать. —*v.i.* ви́ться; об-ви́ва́ться.

coin *n.* моне́та. —*v.t.* **1,** (mint) чека́нить. **2,** (invent, as a word or expression) создава́ть. —**the other side of the coin,** оборо́тная сторона́ меда́ли.

coinage *n.* **1,** (making of coins) чека́нка. **2,** (newly coined word) новообразова́ние.

coincide *v.i.* совпада́ть: *coincide with my arrival,* совпада́ть с мои́м прие́здом.

coincidence *n.* совпаде́ние: *by a curious coincidence,* по заба́вному совпаде́нию.

coincidental *adj.* случа́йный. *It's purely coincidental,* э́то чи́стая случа́йность.

coition *n.* совокупле́ние. *Also,* **coitus.**

coke *n.* кокс. —*adj.* ко́ксовый; коксова́льный: *coke oven,* ко́ксовая/коксова́льная печь. —**coking coal,** коксу́ющийся у́голь.

colander *n.* дуршла́г.

cold *adj.* холо́дный. *It is cold,* хо́лодно. *It is getting cold,* холода́ет; стано́вится хо́лодно. *I am cold,* мне хо́лодно. *My feet are cold,* у меня́ но́ги замёрзли. *Get cold (of food),* стыть; сты́нуть; остыва́ть. *Grow cold toward someone,* охладе́ть к кому́-нибудь. —*adv., colloq.* соверше́нно: *cold sober,* соверше́нно трезв. *Know something cold,* знать что́-нибудь до то́чки. *Turn someone down cold,* отказа́ть кому́-нибудь наотре́з. —*n.* **1,** (low temperature) хо́лод. *Stand (out) in the cold,* стоя́ть на хо́лоде. *Come in out of the cold,* зайти́ в дом от хо́лода. **2,** (ailment) просту́да; на́сморк. *Catch cold,* простуди́ться. —**be left out in the cold,** оста́ться за бо́ртом. —**leave someone cold,** не волнова́ть; не тро́гать. —**throw cold water on,** окати́ть холо́дной водо́й.

cold-blooded *adj.* **1,** *zool.* холоднокро́вный. **2,** (sensitive to cold) зя́бкий. **3,** (callous; heartless) хладнокро́вный.

cold cream кольдкре́м.

coldly *adv.* хо́лодно.

coldness *n.* хо́лодность.

cold war холо́дная война́.

coleslaw *n.* сала́т из шинко́ванной капу́сты.

colic *n.* ко́лики.

coliseum *also,* **colosseum** *n.* колизе́й.

colitis *n.* воспале́ние то́лстой кишки́; коли́т.

collaborate *v.i.* сотру́дничать. *Collaborate on a book,* сотру́дничать в кни́ге; совме́стно писа́ть кни́гу. *Collaborate with the enemy,* сотру́дничать с враго́м.

collaboration *n.* **1,** (on writing something) сотру́дничество. **2,** (with an enemy) посо́бничество (+ *dat.*).

collaborator *n.* **1,** (associate) сотру́дник. **2,** (one who collaborates with the enemy) коллаборациони́ст.

collapse *v.i.* **1,** (cave in) ру́шиться; ру́хнуть; обру́шиваться; обва́ливаться; прова́ливаться; разва́ливаться. **2,** (break down physically) вали́ться: *collapse from exhaustion,* свали́ться от уста́лости. *Collapse from the heat,* упа́сть в о́бморок от жары́. **3,** (break down completely) ру́хнуть; разва́ливаться; потерпе́ть крах. —*n.* **1,** (caving in) обва́л; разва́л. **2,** (extreme prostration): *in a state of collapse,* в о́бморочном состоя́нии. **3,** (failure) распа́д; разва́л;

круше́ние; крах. *Collapse of the government/economy,* паде́ние прави́тельства; разва́л эконо́мики.

collapsible *adj.* складно́й; раскладно́й; разбо́рный; откидно́й.

collar *n.* **1,** (of a coat) воротни́к; (of a shirt, blouse, etc.) воротничо́к. **2,** (for a dog) оше́йник; (for a horse) хому́т. —*v.t., colloq.* схва́тывать. —**get hot under the collar,** (раз)горячи́ться. —**seize by the collar,** схвати́ть за́ ворот; взять за ши́ворот.

collarbone *n.* ключи́ца.

collateral *n.* гара́нтия; обеспе́чение. —*adj.* **1,** (secondary; additional) побо́чный; второстепе́нный; дополни́тельный. **2,** (guaranteed by something pledged) обеспе́ченный.

colleague *n.* колле́га; сослужи́вец.

collect *v.t.* **1,** (gather) собира́ть: *collect evidence,* собира́ть доказа́тельства. *Collect one's thoughts,* собира́ться с мы́слями. *Collect dust,* пыли́ться. **2,** (save as a hobby) собира́ть; коллекциони́ровать. **3,** (pick up and take with one) брать; забира́ть. *Collect one's mail,* брать по́чту. *Collect the garbage,* брать *or* увози́ть му́сор. **4,** *chiefly Brit.* (pick up; call for) заезжа́ть за: *collect the children,* заезжа́ть за детьми́. **5,** (receive in payment) получа́ть: *collect a pension,* получа́ть пе́нсию. *Collect taxes,* собира́ть нало́ги. —*v.i.* собира́ться; набира́ться; ска́пливаться; накопля́ться. *Dust collected on the shelf,* пыль собрала́сь на по́лке. *Water collected in the basement,* вода́ собрала́сь в подва́ле. —**collect oneself,** овладе́ть собо́й.

collected *adj.* **1,** (gathered together) со́бранный. *Collected works,* собра́ние сочине́ний. **2,** (cool; calm; composed) хладнокро́вный.

collection *n.* **1,** (act of collecting) сбор; собира́ние. **2,** (assemblage, as of books, stamps, etc.) колле́кция; собра́ние. **3,** (anthology) сбо́рник. **4,** (soliciting of money) де́нежный сбор. **5,** (pickup of mail) вы́емка.

collective *adj.* **1,** (joint; common) коллекти́вный. **2,** *gram.* собира́тельный. —*n.* коллекти́в. —**collective farm,** колхо́з.

collectively *adv.* **1,** (through joint efforts) совме́стно; сообща́. **2,** (taken as a whole) в о́бщем; в совоку́пности.

collectivism *n.* коллективи́зм.

collectivize *v.t.* коллективизи́ровать. —**collectivization,** *n.* коллективиза́ция.

collector *n.* **1,** (one who collects for a hobby) коллекционе́р; собира́тель. **2,** (one who collects money due) сбо́рщик; *tax collector,* сбо́рщик нало́гов. **3,** *Ticket collector,* билетёр; контролёр; *garbage collector,* му́сорщик.

college *n.* **1,** (school of higher learning) университе́т; колле́дж; вуз. **2,** (body) колле́гия: *college of cardinals,* колле́гия кардина́лов. —*adj.* университе́тский: a *college education,* университе́тское образова́ние.

collegium *n.* колле́гия.

collide *v.i.* ста́лкиваться: *collide with an oncoming car,* столкну́ться со встре́чной маши́ной.

collie *n.* ко́лли; шотла́ндская овча́рка.

collision *n.* столкнове́ние.

collodion *n.* коллóдий.

colloid *n.* коллóид. —**colloidal**, *adj.* коллóидный.

colloquial *adj.* разговóрный. —**colloquialism**, *n.* разговóрное слóво *or* выраже́ние.

colloquium *n.* коллóквиум.

collusion *n.* сгóвор: *be in collusion with*, быть в сгóворе с.

Colombian *adj.* колумби́йский.

colon *n.* **1**, (punctuation mark) двоетóчие. **2**, *anat.* ободóчная кишка́. —**colon-rectal cancer**, рак прямóй и тóлстой кишóк.

colonel *n.* полкóвник.

colonial *adj.* колониа́льный. —**colonialism**, *n.* колониали́зм. —**colonialist**, *n.* колониза́тор.

colonist *n.* колони́ст.

colonize *v.t.* колонизи́ровать. —**colonization**, *n.* колониза́ция. —**colonizer**, *n.* колониза́тор.

colonnade *n.* колонна́да.

colony *n.* колóния.

color *also*, **colour** *n.* **1**, (hue) цвет; кра́ска. *What color is your car?*, какóго цве́та ва́ша маши́на? *Dress in bright colors*, одева́ться в я́ркие цвета́. *Paint in bright colors*, писа́ть я́ркими кра́сками. *Color in one's cheeks*, румя́нец. *Local color*, ме́стный колори́т. **2**, *pl.* (flag; banner) зна́мя. *Trooping of the colors*, вы́нос зна́мени. *Call to the colors*, призыва́ть на вое́нную слу́жбу. —*adj.* цветнóй: *color film*, цветна́я плёнка; *color television*, цветнóе телеви́дение. —*v.t.* **1**, (give color to) окра́шивать; раскра́шивать. *Brightly colored bird*, я́рко окра́шенная пти́ца. **2**, (influence to some degree) окра́шивать. —**show one's true colors**, показа́ть своё настоя́щее лицó. —**with flying colors**, с бле́ском.

coloration *n.* окра́ска; раскра́ска.

coloratura *n.* колорату́ра.

colorblind *also*, **colourblind** *adj.* страда́ющий цветовóй слепотóй. *I am colorblind*, я дальтóник.

colorblindness *also*, **colourblindness** *n.* цветова́я слепота́; дальтони́зм.

colored *also*, **coloured** *adj.* цветнóй.

colorful *also*, **colourful** *adj.* кра́сочный; колори́тный.

coloring *also*, **colouring** *n.* окра́ска; раскра́ска; раскра́шивание. —**coloring book**, альбóм для раскра́шивания.

colorless *also*, **colourless** *adj.* бесцве́тный.

colossal *adj.* колосса́льный.

colosseum *n.* = **coliseum**.

colossus *n.* колóсс.

colour *see* **color**. —**colourblind**, *adj.* = **colorblind**. —**coloured**, *adj.* = **colored**. —**colourful**, *adj.* = **colorful**. —**colouring**, *n.* = **coloring**. —**colourless**, *adj.* = **colorless**.

colt *n.* жеребёнок.

column *n.* **1**, (pillar) колóнна: *Corinthian columns*, кори́нфские колóнны. **2**, (of smoke) столб (ды́ма); (of mercury) стóлбик (ртýти). **3**, (in a book, newspaper, etc.) столбе́ц; колóнка. *Editor's column*, колóнка реда́ктора. **4**, (in a chart or table) графа́. **5**, (of

figures) колóнка; столбе́ц. **6**, *mil.* колóнна: *column of fours*, колóнна по четы́ре.

columnar *adj.* напеча́танный столбца́ми.

columned *adj.* колóнный.

columnist *n.* обозрева́тель; публици́ст.

colza *n.* суре́пица.

coma *n.* кóма. —**comatose**, *adj.* коматóзный.

comb *n.* **1**, (for the hair) гре́бень; гребёнка; расчёска. **2**, (crest of certain fowl) гре́бень; гребешóк. —*v.t.* **1**, (someone's hair) причёсывать; расчёсывать. *Comb one's hair*, причёсываться. *Comb one's hair back*, зачёсывать вóлосы наза́д. **2**, (card, as flax) чеса́ть. **3**, (search thoroughly) прочёсывать.

combat *n.* бой. *See combat*, уча́ствовать в бою́. —*adj.* боевóй: *combat vehicle*, боева́я маши́на. —*v.t.* боро́ться с *or* прóтив. *Combat crime*, боро́ться с престýпностью.

combatant *n.* деру́щийся.

combative *adj.* вои́нственный; драчли́вый.

combination *n.* сочета́ние; комбина́ция. *Combination of circumstances*, стече́ние *or* совпаде́ние обстоя́тельств. —**combination lock**, замóк с секре́том.

combine *v.t.* **1**, (join; amalgamate) объединя́ть; совмеща́ть: *combine two positions* (*into one*), объединя́ть/совмеща́ть две дóлжности. *Combine efforts*, объединя́ть *or* соединя́ть уси́лия. **2**, (mix) сочета́ть; совмеща́ть; соединя́ть; комбини́ровать. *Combine colors*, сочета́ть/комбини́ровать кра́ски. *Combine business with pleasure*, сочета́ть/совмеща́ть прия́тное с поле́зным. —*n.* (harvesting machine) комба́йн.

combined *adj.* **1**, (joint) совме́стный: *combined efforts*, совме́стные уси́лия. **2**, (consisting of several elements) свóдный.

combings *n.pl.* очи́стки.

combustible *adj.* горю́чий. —*n.* горю́чий материа́л. —**combustibility**, *n.* горю́честь.

combustion *n.* сгора́ние; воспламене́ние.

come *v.i.* **1**, (approach) идти́: *Come here!*, иди́ сюда́! *I'm coming!*, идý! *Here he comes*, вот он идёт. **2**, (arrive) приходи́ть; приезжа́ть: *He did not come*, он не пришёл; он не прие́хал. **3**, (of a time or season) наступа́ть; наста́ть; приходи́ть. **4**, *fol. by* **to** (reach) подходи́ть (к); подъезжа́ть (к): *come to an intersection*, подходи́ть/подъезжа́ть к перекрёстку. **5**, (progress) идти́: *How is your work coming?*, как идёт ва́ша рабóта? **6**, (occur; fall) приходи́ться: *come at a time when...*, приходи́ться на вре́мя когда́... *New Year's Day comes on a Thursday*, Нóвый год прихóдится (*or* выпада́ет) на четве́рг. *B comes after A*, бýква Б сле́дует за бýквой А. *The climax is yet to come*, развя́зка ещё впереди́. **7**, (be available): *This dress comes in five colors/sizes*, э́то пла́тье (мóжете найти́) в пяти́ цвета́х/разме́рах. **8**, (be due) причита́ться: *You have five dollars coming to you*, вам причита́ется пять дóлларов. *He got what was coming to him*, он получи́л всё, что емý причита́лось; *fig.* он получи́л по заслýгам. **9**, *fol. by inf.* (gradually have happen) стать: *I have come to regard* *him as...*, я стал счита́ть его́ (+ *instr.*). *I have come to know him well*, я узна́л его́ хорошо́. —**come about,** происходи́ть; случа́ться. —**come across, 1,** (encounter) натыка́ться на; ната́лкиваться на. *I came across an interesting article*, мне попа́лась *or* встре́тилась интере́сная статья́. **2,** (be effectively communicated) доходи́ть: *come across to the audience*, доходи́ть до аудито́рии. —**come along,** идти́; приходи́ть. *He came along with us*, он пришёл вме́сте с на́ми. *How are things coming along?*, как иду́т дела́? —**come apart,** распада́ться. —**come around, 1,** (revive) приходи́ть в себя́. **2,** (recover) оправля́ться. **3,** (agree in the end) соглаша́ться. **4,** *colloq.* (come and visit) заходи́ть. —**come away with,** выноси́ть. —**come back, 1,** (return) возвраща́ться. **2,** *fol. by* **to** (return to one's memory) вспомина́ться (+ *dat.*). —**come between,** разъединя́ть: *Nothing can come between us*, ничто́ нас не разъедини́т. —**come by, 1,** (drop by) заходи́ть. **2,** (obtain) достава́ть. —**come down, 1,** (descend) сходи́ть. **2,** (of rain) лить; сы́пать; (of snow) вали́ть; сы́пать. **3,** *fol. by* **to** (reach) доходи́ть (до): *Her hair came down to her waist*, у неё во́лосы доходи́ли до по́яса. **4,** (fall; decline) па́дать. *Come down in price*, па́дать в цене́. **5,** *fol. by* **to** (be handed down to, as of a custom or legend) доходи́ть (до). **6,** *fol. by* **with** (develop, as an illness) заболе́ть (+ *instr.*): *come down with pneumonia*, заболе́ть воспале́нием лёгких. *Come down with a cold*, получи́ть на́сморк. *I think I'm coming down with the flu*, ду́маю, что у меня́ начина́ется грипп. **7,** *fol. by* **to** (boil down to) своди́ться (к): *It comes down to this*, всё де́ло сво́дится к э́тому. —**come for,** приходи́ть за; приезжа́ть за; заходи́ть за; заезжа́ть за. —**come from, 1,** *literally* приходи́ть из. **2,** (originate from) *Wine comes from grapes*, вино́ де́лают из виногра́да. *He comes from California*, он ро́дом из Калифо́рнии. *She comes from a good family*, она́ из хоро́шей семьи́. *Where did this thing come from?*, отку́да взяла́сь э́та шту́ка? —**come in, 1,** (enter) входи́ть: *Please come in!*, входи́те, пожа́луйста! *Come in out of the rain*, зайти́ в дом от дождя́. **2,** (be received, as of letters, complaints, etc.) поступа́ть. **3,** (finish) приходи́ть: *come in last*, прийти́ после́дним (в бе́ге); прийти́ *or* оказа́ться после́дним (на вы́борах). **4,** *colloq.* (begin to play a role): *Where do I come in?*, в чём заключа́ется моя́ роль? **5,** *fol. by* **for** (be subjected to, as criticism) подверга́ться (+ *dat.*). **6,** *Come in for a landing*, идти́ *or* заходи́ть на поса́дку. —**come into, 1,** *literally* входи́ть в. **2,** (inherit) получи́ть (что) в насле́дство; достава́ться (+ *dat.*). **3,** *with various nouns*, входи́ть в: *come into use*, входи́ть в употребле́ние; *come into fashion*, входи́ть в мо́ду. *Come into being*, возника́ть. *Come into view*, показа́ться. *Come into one's head*, взбрести́ кому́-нибудь в го́лову. *Come into this world*, появи́ться на свет. *Come into play*, пойти́ в ход. —**come of,** выходи́ть из: *Nothing will come of it*, из э́того ничего́ не вы́йдет. *That's what comes of...*, вот к чему́ приво́дит... —**come off, 1,** (roll off; slide off) сходи́ть: *come off the assembly line*, сходи́ть с

конве́йера. *The door came off its hinges*, дверь соскочи́ла с пе́тель. *Come off the press*, выходи́ть из печа́ти. **2,** (come loose; peel off) сходи́ть; отходи́ть; отстава́ть; отска́кивать; отделя́ться; отрыва́ться; срыва́ться; отва́ливаться. **3,** *colloq.* (be successful) удава́ться: *The play did not come off*, пье́са не удала́сь. —**come on!, 1,** (hurry up) живе́й! **2,** (don't be silly) ну что вы!; да бро́сьте вы! —**come out, 1,** (emerge; be issued or released) выходи́ть. *The sun came out*, со́лнце вы́шло *or* вы́глянуло. *The stars are coming out*, звёзды появля́ются на не́бе. *Smoke is coming out of the chimney*, из трубы́ идёт дым. *The book came out only recently*, кни́га вы́шла совсе́м неда́вно. **2,** (turn out; end up) сойти́; вы́йти; ко́нчиться: *Everything came out all right*, всё сошло́ (*or* ко́нчилось) хорошо́. *Come out well in a picture*, вы́йти хорошо́ на сни́мке. *The picture came out well*, сни́мок получи́лся хоро́ший. **3,** (of a stain) выводи́ться. *Come out in the wash*, отсти́рываться. **4,** (take a position) выступа́ть: *come out in favor of/against*, вы́ступить за/про́тив. **5,** *fol. by* **with** (utter) выпа́ливать. —**come over, 1,** (visit) заходи́ть. **2,** (seize, as of an emotion) овладева́ть; завладева́ть. *What's come over you?*, что э́то на вас нашло́?; что э́то вы? —**come through, 1,** (seep through) проса́чиваться че́рез. **2,** (endure successfully) переноси́ть: *She came through the operation well*, она́ хорошо́ перенесла́ опера́цию. —**come to, 1,** (reach, as an end, agreement, etc.) приходи́ть к. **2,** (amount to) составля́ть: *The bill came to $50*, счёт соста́вил пятьдеся́т до́лларов. *It comes to the same thing*, всё равно́; э́то то же са́мое. **3,** (result in) своди́ться к: *come to naught*, своди́ться к нулю́. **4,** (reach, as a certain point) доходи́ть до: *if it comes to that*, е́сли де́ло дохо́дит до э́того; е́сли уж на то пошло́. *What things are coming to!*, до чего́ мы дошли́! *When it comes to...*, когда́ де́ло дохо́дит до...; по ча́сти (+ *gen.*). **5,** (regain consciousness) приходи́ть в себя́. **6,** (suddenly return to mind): *It'll come to me*, сейча́с вспо́мню. *It just came to me*, вспо́мнил! **7,** (be learned by) дава́ться: *Languages come easily to her*, языки́ даю́тся ей легко́. —**come true,** осуществля́ться; сбыва́ться; опра́вдываться. —**come under, 1,** (fit into, as a category) подпада́ть под. **2,** (be subjected to) подверга́ться (+ *dat.*); попада́ть под. *Come under severe criticism*, подверга́ться о́строй кри́тике. *Come under suspicion*, попа́сть под подозре́ние. *Come under enemy fire*, попа́сть под ого́нь проти́вника. —**come up, 1,** (rise) поднима́ться; всходи́ть. *Come up for air*, всплыть, что́бы подыша́ть (*or* набра́ть во́здуха). **2,** (sprout) всходи́ть. **3,** (arise, as in discussion) возника́ть. —**come up to, 1,** (approach) подходи́ть к. **2,** (reach on one's body) доходи́ть до: *The water came up to our knees*, вода́ доходи́ла нам до коле́н. *He comes up to my shoulder*, он мне достаёт до плеча́. —**come up with,** находи́ть. *Come up with an idea*, напа́сть на мысль. —**come upon,** набрести́ на; напада́ть на; находи́ть на. —**come what may,** будь, что бу́дет. —**how come?,** *see* **how.**

comedian *n.* ко́мик; сати́рик.

comedy *n.* коме́дия.
comely *adj.* хоро́шенький; милови́дный.
comet *n.* коме́та. *Halley's Comet*, коме́та Галле́я.
comfort *v.t.* утеша́ть: *comfort the bereaved parents*, утеша́ть скорбя́щих роди́телей. —*n.* **1**, (solace) утеше́ние: *words of comfort*, слова́ утеше́ния. *Take comfort in the fact that...*, утеша́ться тем, что... **2**, (physical ease) комфо́рт; ую́т. **3**, *pl.* (conveniences) удо́бства.
comfortable *adj.* **1**, (providing comfort) удо́бный; комфорта́бельный: *comfortable chair/shoes/apartment*, удо́бный стул; удо́бные ту́фли; комфорта́бельная кварти́ра. **2**, (in a state of comfort; at ease) *rendered by* удо́бно: *Are you comfortable*, вам удо́бно? *Make yourself comfortable!*, устра́ивайтесь *or* располага́йтесь (по)удо́бнее! **3**, (fairly well-to-do) безбе́дный: *comfortable existence*, безбе́дное существова́ние.
comfortably *adv.* удо́бно. *Seat five people comfortably*, свобо́дно вмеща́ть пять челове́к. *Live comfortably*, жить безбе́дно *or* в доста́тке.
comforter *n.* **1**, (one who comforts) утеши́тель. **2**, (quilted bedcover) стёганое одея́ло.
comforting *adj.* утеши́тельный.
comic *adj.* коми́ческий; шу́точный. —*n.* **1**, (entertainer) ко́мик. **2**, *pl.* (cartoon strips) ко́миксы. —**comic opera**, коми́ческая о́пера.
comical *adj.* коми́чный; коми́ческий; смешно́й.
coming *n.* **1**, (arrival) прихо́д; прие́зд. *The Second Coming*, второ́е прише́ствие. **2**, (advent, as of a season) наступле́ние. —*adj.* сле́дующий; бу́дущий; наступа́ющий; гряду́щий.
comma *n.* запята́я.
command *v.t.* **1**, (order) прика́зывать. **2**, *mil.* (be in command of) кома́ндовать: *command an army*, кома́ндовать а́рмией. **3**, (inspire, as respect) внуша́ть. **4**, (bring, as a high price) идти́; продава́ться (по высо́кой цене́). **5**, (afford, as a view): *The room commands a beautiful view of the ocean*, из ко́мнаты открыва́ется прекра́сный вид на океа́н. —*v.i.* **1**, (issue an order) прика́зывать. **2**, (exercise authority) кома́ндовать. —*n.* **1**, (an order) прика́з; кома́нда. **2**, (authority to command) кома́ндование. *Under the command of*, под кома́ндованием *or* под кома́ндой (+ *gen.*). *Be in command of*, кома́ндовать (+ *instr.*). *Take command of*, приня́ть кома́ндование *or* кома́нду над. **3**, (mastery) владе́ние. *Have an excellent command of English*, отли́чно *or* свобо́дно владе́ть англи́йским языко́м. —*adj.* кома́ндный: *command post*, кома́ндный пункт.
commandant *n.* коменда́нт.
commandeer *v.t.* реквизи́ровать.
commander *n.* **1**, *mil.* команди́р; кома́ндующий. **2**, *naval* капита́н второ́го ра́нга. —**commander in chief**, главнокома́ндующий.
commanding *adj.* **1**, (in command): *commanding officer*, кома́ндующий; команди́р. **2**, (authoritative) вла́стный. **3**, (high up; overlooking) госпо́дствующий; домини́рующий. *Commanding heights*, кома́ндная высота́.

commandment *n.* за́поведь. *The Ten Commandments*, де́сять за́поведей.
commando *n.* деса́нтник.
commemorate *v.t.* пра́здновать; ознаменова́ть. —**commemoration**, *n.* пра́зднование; ознаменова́ние.
commemorative *adj.* па́мятный; мемориа́льный. *Commemorative stamp*, юбиле́йная *or* па́мятная ма́рка.
commence *v.t.* начина́ть. —*v.i.* начина́ться.
commencement *n.* **1**, (beginning) нача́ло. **2**, (graduation exercises) выпускно́й акт.
commend *v.t.* **1**, (praise) хвали́ть. **2**, (recommend) рекомендова́ть.
commendable *adj.* похва́льный.
commendation *n.* **1**, (praise) похвала́. **2**, (award; citation) благода́рность.
commensurable *adj.* соизмери́мый.
commensurate *adj.* соразме́рный: *an income commensurate with one's needs*, дохо́д, соразме́рный со свои́ми ну́ждами. *The punishment is not commensurate with the crime*, наказа́ние не соотве́тствует преступле́нию.
comment *n.* замеча́ние: *a critical comment*, крити́ческое замеча́ние. *No comment*, никаки́х *or* без коммента́риев. —*v.i.* де́лать замеча́ние. *Comment on something*, комменти́ровать что́-нибудь. *Comment favorably on*, хорошо́ отзыва́ться о.
commentary *n.* коммента́рий; толкова́ние.
commentator *n.* обозрева́тель; коммента́тор.
commerce *n.* торго́вля; комме́рция.
commercial *adj.* комме́рческий; торго́вый. *Commercial bank/credit*, комме́рческий банк/креди́т. —*n.* рекла́ма.
commingle *v.t.* сме́шивать. —*v.i.* сме́шиваться.
commiserate *v.i.* [*usu.* **commiserate with**] соболе́зновать (+ *dat.*). —**commiseration**, *n.* соболе́знование.
commissar *n.* комисса́р.
commissariat *n.* **1**, (former Soviet ministry) комиссариа́т. **2**, *mil.* интенда́нтство.
commissary *n.* вое́нный магази́н.
commission *n.* **1**, (specially appointed body) коми́ссия. **2**, (fee) комиссио́нные; комиссио́нность. *Charge a commission*, взима́ть коми́ссию. **3**, (perpetration, as of a crime) соверше́ние. **4**, *mil.* офице́рское зва́ние. —*v.t.* поруча́ть; назнача́ть; уполномо́чивать. —**out of commission**, в неиспра́вности. *Go out of commission*, выходи́ть из стро́я. *Put out of commission*, выводи́ть из стро́я; приводи́ть в него́дность.
commissioned officer офице́р.
commissioner *n.* комисса́р. *High commissioner*, верхо́вный комисса́р.
commit *v.t.* **1**, (perpetrate) соверша́ть: *commit a crime*, соверша́ть преступле́ние. *Commit an error*, допусти́ть оши́бку. *Commit perjury*, лжесвиде́тельствовать. *Commit adultery*, соверша́ть прелюбодея́ние. *Commit atrocities*, твори́ть зве́рства. **2**, (obligate) обя́зывать: *This does not commit you to anything*, э́то вас ни к чему́ не обя́зывает. **3**, (consign, as to a mental institution) помеща́ть. **4**, (give over) пре-

дава́ть: *commit to the flames,* предава́ть огню́. —**commit oneself, 1,** (pledge oneself) обя́зываться. **2,** (take a firm position) связывать себя́ сло́вом. —**commit suicide,** поко́нчить жизнь самоуби́йством; поко́нчить с собо́й. —**commit to battle,** вводи́ть в бой. —**commit to memory,** зау́чивать.

commitment *n.* **1,** (confinement, as to an institution) помеще́ние. **2,** (pledge; obligation) обяза́тельство. **3,** (engagement) свида́ние. *I have a previous commitment,* у меня́ други́е пла́ны; я уже́ приглашён.

committee *n.* комите́т; коми́ссия.

commode *n.* **1,** (chest of drawers) комо́д. **2,** (movable washstand) умыва́льник. **3,** (chair enclosing a chamber pot) унита́з.

commodious *adj.* вмести́тельный; просто́рный.

commodity *n.* това́р; проду́кт; предме́т потребле́ния. —**commodity exchange,** това́рная би́ржа.

common *adj.* **1,** (mutual; joint; shared) о́бщий: *common interests,* о́бщие интере́сы. *Have a common goal,* име́ть о́бщую цель. **2,** (ordinary) обы́чный: *a common occurrence,* обы́чное явле́ние. *Common criminal,* уголо́вник; уголо́вный престу́пник. **3,** (widespread) распространённый: *a common name,* распространённое и́мя; *a common error,* распространённая оши́бка. *In common use,* употреби́тельный. *It is common knowledge that...,* общеизве́стно, что... **4,** (of the masses) рядово́й; просто́й: *the common man,* рядово́й челове́к; *the common people,* просто́й наро́д. **5,** (vulgar; coarse) по́шлый. —**in common,** о́бщий: *friends in common,* о́бщие знако́мые. *Have much in common,* име́ть мно́го о́бщего. *Have nothing in common,* не име́ть ничего́ о́бщего. *They have one thing in common,* их объединя́ет одно́; их объединя́ет одна́ о́бщая черта́.

commonality *n.* о́бщность.

common denominator о́бщий знамена́тель.

commoner *n.* челове́к из наро́да; просто́й челове́к.

common law обы́чное пра́во. —**common-law marriage,** факти́ческий брак.

commonly *adv.* обы́чно.

Common Market О́бщий ры́нок.

common noun и́мя нарица́тельное.

commonplace *adj.* бана́льный; изби́тый. —*n.* бана́льность; общее ме́сто.

common sense здра́вый смысл.

common stock обыкнове́нные а́кции.

commonwealth *n.* содру́жество: *the British Commonwealth,* Брита́нское содру́жество. —**Commonwealth of Independent States,** Содру́жество незави́симых госуда́рств.

commotion *n.* сумато́ха; переполо́х.

communal *adj.* общи́нный. *Communal apartment,* коммуна́льная кварти́ра.

commune *n.* общи́на; комму́на.

communicable *adj.* зара́зный: *communicable disease,* зара́зная боле́знь.

communicate *v.i.* **1,** (express oneself) объясня́ться. **2,** *fol. by* **with** (get in touch with) сообща́ться (с);

свя́зываться (с); сноси́ться (с). —*v.t.* сообща́ть; передава́ть.

communication *n.* **1,** *often pl.* (act or means of communicating) связь; сообще́ние: *telephone communications,* телефо́нная связь; телефо́нное сообще́ние. *Ministry of Communications,* министе́рство свя́зи. *Communications officer, mil.* офице́р свя́зи. *Be in constant communication with,* подде́рживать постоя́нную связь с. **2,** *often pl.* (transportation routes) сообще́ние; пути́ сообще́ния; *mil.* коммуника́ции. *Railway communications,* железнодоро́жное сообще́ние. **3,** (message) сообще́ние: *an urgent communication,* сро́чное сообще́ние. —**communications satellite,** спу́тник свя́зи.

communicative *adj.* открове́нный; разгово́рчивый.

communion *n.* **1,** (communication; association) обще́ние. **2,** *cap.* (Eucharist) прича́стие. *Receive Communion,* причаща́ться.

communiqué *n.* коммюнике́.

communism *n.* коммуни́зм.

communist *n.* коммуни́ст. —*adj.* коммунисти́ческий: *communist party,* коммунисти́ческая па́ртия.

community *n.* **1,** (neighborhood) райо́н. **2,** (group of people with common ties) общи́на; соо́бщество. **3,** (group of nations) соо́бщество. **4,** (identity; likeness) о́бщность. —**community property,** о́бщее иму́щество супру́гов.

commutation *n.* смягче́ние (наказа́ния *or* пригово́ра). —**commutation ticket,** сезо́нный биле́т.

commute *v.t.* смягча́ть (наказа́ние *or* пригово́р). —*v.i.* е́здить (ежедне́вно). —*n.* (ежедне́вная езда́. —**commuter,** *n.* ежедне́вный пассажи́р.

compact *adj.* пло́тный; компа́ктный; сжа́тый. —*n.* **1,** (cosmetics container) пу́дреница. **2,** (covenant) соглаше́ние; догово́р; конве́нция.

companion *n.* **1,** (comrade) това́рищ. **2,** (paid female attendant) компаньо́нка. **3,** (other of a pair) па́ра.

companionable *adj.* компане́йский.

companionship *n.* компа́ния.

company *n.* **1,** (business firm) компа́ния. **2,** (companionship; association) компа́ния; о́бщество. *In the company of,* в о́бществе (+ *gen.*). *Male company,* мужско́е о́бщество. *Keep company with,* води́ть компа́нию с; води́ться с. *Keep someone company,* составля́ть компа́нию (+ *dat.*). *Part company,* расходи́ться. **3,** (visitors; guests) го́сти. **4,** (troupe) тру́ппа: *touring company,* гастро́льная тру́ппа. **5,** *mil.* ро́та. —*adj.* фи́рменный: *company label,* фи́рменная этике́тка.

comparable *adj.* сравни́мый; сопостави́мый. *It is in no way comparable to...,* э́то не идёт ни в како́е сравне́ние с (+ *instr.*).

comparative *adj.* сравни́тельный. —**comparative degree,** *gram.* сравни́тельная сте́пень.

comparatively *adv.* сравни́тельно: *comparatively inexpensive,* сравни́тельно дёшево.

compare *v.t.* сра́внивать. *Compared to,* по сравне́нию с. *Compare notes,* обме́ниваться впечатле́ниями. —*v.i.* [*usu.* **compare to** *or* **with**] сравни́ться (с): *No one can compare to her,* никто́ не мо́жет сравни́ться с ней. *Compare favorably with,* вы́годно отлича́ться от; отлича́ться в лу́чшую сто́рону от; выи́грывать при сравне́нии с. —*n., in* **beyond compare,** вне сравне́ния.

comparison *n.* сравне́ние. *There is no comparison between them,* их нельзя́ сра́внивать.

compartment *n.* **1,** (space; section) отделе́ние; отсе́к. **2,** (on a train) купе́.

compass *n.* **1,** (instrument for determining direction) ко́мпас. *Surveyor's compass,* буссо́ль. **2,** *often pl.* (instrument for describing circles) ци́ркуль. —**compass point,** страна́ све́та.

compassion *n.* сострада́ние. —**compassionate,** *adj.* сострада́тельный.

compatible *adj.* совмести́мый. —**compatibility,** *n.* совмести́мость.

compatriot *n.* соотéчественник; земля́к.

compel *v.t.* заставля́ть; принужда́ть; вынужда́ть. *I feel compelled to warn you,* я чу́вствую себя́ обя́занным предупреди́ть вас.

compelling *adj.* **1,** (convincing) убеди́тельный: *compelling evidence,* убеди́тельное доказа́тельство. **2,** (holding one's attention) захва́тывающий.

compendium *n.* конспе́кт; компе́ндиум.

compensate *v.t.* **1,** (recompense; remunerate) вознагражда́ть. **2,** (indemnify) возмеща́ть: *compensate someone for damages,* возмеща́ть кому́-нибудь убы́тки. —*v.i.* [*usu.* **compensate for**] (make up for; offset) компенси́ровать.

compensation *n.* **1,** (restitution) компенса́ция; возмеще́ние: *compensation for damage,* компенса́ция/возмеще́ние убы́тков; компенса́ция за ущéрб. *Pay compensation for damage,* возмеща́ть убы́тки *or* ущéрб. **2,** (payment for services) вознагражде́ние.

compensatory *adj.* компенсацио́нный. —**compensatory leave,** отгу́л.

compete *v.i.* состяза́ться; соревнова́ться: *compete in a race/ for a prize/,* состяза́ться/соревнова́ться в бе́ге/ за приз/. *Compete for the championship,* соревнова́ться за чемпио́нский ти́тул; оспа́ривать пе́рвенство.

competence *n.* **1,** (ability) спосо́бность; компете́нтность. **2,** (jurisdiction) компете́нция.

competent *adj.* **1,** (qualified; capable) компете́нтный. **2,** (legally qualified) правомо́чный. **3,** (responsible for one's actions) дееспосо́бный.

competition *n.* **1,** (contest) состяза́ние; соревнова́ние; ко́нкурс. **2,** (business rivalry) конкуре́нция.

competitive *adj.* **1,** (involving competition) ко́нкурсный: *on a competitive basis,* на ко́нкурсной осно́ве. **2,** (able to compete) конкурентоспосо́бный. *Competitive prices,* конкурентоспосо́бные цéны. —**competitiveness,** *n.* конкурентоспосо́бность.

competitor *n.* конкуре́нт.

compilation *n.* **1,** (act of compiling) собира́ние; составле́ние; компиля́ция. **2,** (something compiled) компиля́ция.

compile *v.t.* **1,** (gather) собира́ть. **2,** (make up; write, as a list or dictionary) составля́ть.

compiler *n.* состави́тель; компиля́тор.

complacent *adj.* самодово́льный. —**complacency,** *n.* самодово́льство.

complain *v.i.* жа́ловаться. *Complain about the weather,* жа́ловаться на пого́ду. *Complain of a headache,* жа́ловаться на головну́ю боль. *Complain to the director,* жа́ловаться дире́ктору. *I can't complain,* я не могу́ пожа́ловаться.

complaint *n.* **1,** (grievance) жа́лоба. **2,** (ailment) недомога́ние.

complaisant *adj.* услу́жливый; любе́зный.

complement *n.* **1,** (that which completes) дополне́ние. **2,** (full quota) компле́кт. **3,** *gram.* дополне́ние. —*v.t.* дополня́ть.

complementary *adj.* дополня́ющий друг дру́га. *Complementary colors,* дополни́тельные цвета́.

complete *adj.* **1,** (entire) по́лный: *complete set,* по́лный набо́р. **2,** (finished) зако́нченный: *The job is complete,* рабо́та зако́нчена. **3,** (absolute; total) по́лный: *complete freedom,* по́лная свобо́да; *a complete surprise,* по́лная неожи́данность. —*v.t.* **1,** (finish) зака́нчивать; заверша́ть; доверша́ть. **2,** (make whole) (у)комплектова́ть: *complete a collection,* (у)комплектова́ть колле́кцию. *To complete the picture,* для полноты́ карти́ны. **3,** (fill out) заполня́ть.

completely *adv.* совсе́м; соверше́нно; вполне́; по́лностью. *I completely forgot,* я совсе́м/соверше́нно забы́л(а). *Completely by accident,* соверше́нно случа́йно. *Completely satisfied,* вполне́ удовлетворён. *Completely revised,* по́лностью перерабо́тан.

completeness *n.* полнота́; зако́нченность.

completion *n.* оконча́ние; заверше́ние.

complex *adj.* сло́жный: *a complex matter,* сло́жное де́ло. —*n.* **1,** (large system or unit) ко́мплекс. **2,** *psychoanalysis* ко́мплекс; ма́ния: *inferiority complex,* ко́мплекс неполноце́нности; *persecution complex,* ма́ния пресле́дования. —**complex sentence,** сложноподчинённое предложе́ние.

complexion *n.* **1,** (skin color) цвет лица́: *dark complexion,* сму́глый цвет лица́. **2,** *fig.* (aspect) свет; окра́ска. *Put a different complexion on something,* придава́ть чему́-нибудь другу́ю окра́ску.

complexity *n.* сло́жность.

compliance *n.* **1,** (act of complying) подчине́ние: *compliance with the law,* подчине́ние зако́ну. **2,** (acquiescence) согла́сие. **3,** (disposition to comply) усту́пчивость.

compliant *adj.* усту́пчивый.

complicate *v.t.* усложня́ть; осложня́ть. —**complicated,** *adj.* сло́жный.

complication *n.* **1,** (something that complicates) осложне́ние; усложне́ние. **2,** *med.* осложне́ние.

complicity *n.* соуча́стие: *complicity in a crime,* соуча́стие в преступле́нии.

compliment *n.* **1,** (expression of praise) комплиме́нт. **2,** *pl.* (greetings) приве́т; покло́н. —*v.t.* похвали́ть; сде́лать комплиме́нт (+ *dat.*).

complimentary *adj.* **1,** (containing a compliment) ле́стный. **2,** (given free) беспла́тный; дарово́й. *Complimentary ticket,* контрама́рка.

comply *v.i.* подчиня́ться. *Comply with the rules,* подчиня́ться пра́вилам. *Comply with a treaty,* соблюда́ть догово́р. *Comply with a request,* удовлетвори́ть *or* испо́лнить про́сьбу.

component *n.* составна́я часть; дета́ль; компоне́нт. —*adj.* составно́й: *component part,* составна́я часть.

comport *v.t.* [*usu.* **comport oneself**] вести́ себя́; держа́ть себя́.

comportment *n.* поведе́ние; мане́ра держа́ть себя́.

compose *v.t.* **1,** (write; draft) составля́ть. **2,** (create, as a poem or work of music) сочиня́ть. **3,** (reconcile, as differences) ула́живать. **4,** *printing* (set in type) набира́ть. —**be composed of,** состоя́ть из. —**compose oneself,** овладе́ть собо́й.

composed *adj.* споко́йный; хладнокро́вный.

composer *n.* компози́тор. *The composer of the song,* а́втор пе́сни.

composite *adj.* составно́й; сво́дный; ко́мплексный. —*n.* смесь; соста́в; соедине́ние.

composition *n.* **1,** (musical or literary work; essay for school) сочине́ние. **2,** (make-up; structure) соста́в. **3,** (artistic arrangement, as of a photograph) компози́ция. **4,** *printing* набо́р.

compositor *n.* набо́рщик.

compost *n.* компо́ст.

composure *n.* споко́йствие; самооблада́ние; хладнокро́вие. *Regain one's composure,* овладе́ть собо́й.

compote *n.* компо́т.

compound *n.* **1,** *chem.* соедине́ние. **2,** (enclosed area) огоро́женное ме́сто. —*adj.* составно́й; сло́жный. —*v.t.* **1,** (mix; combine) сме́шивать; соединя́ть. **2,** (add to; intensify) усугубля́ть; осложня́ть. —**compound fracture,** сло́жный перело́м. —**compound interest,** сло́жные проце́нты. —**compound sentence,** сложносочинённое предложе́ние.

comprehend *v.t.* **1,** (understand) понима́ть; постига́ть. **2,** (include) охва́тывать.

comprehensible *adj.* поня́тный; постижи́мый; вразуми́тельный.

comprehension *n.* понима́ние.

comprehensive *adj.* всесторо́нний; развёрнутый; всеобъе́млющий; ко́мплексный.

compress *v.t.* сжима́ть. —*n.* компре́сс: *hot compress,* согрева́ющий компре́сс. —**compressed air,** сжа́тый во́здух.

compression *n.* сжа́тие. —**compression chamber,** ка́мера сжа́тия. —**compression ratio,** сте́пень сжа́тия.

compressor *n.* компре́ссор.

comprise *v.t.* **1,** (consist of) состоя́ть из; заключа́ть в себе́. **2,** (constitute) составля́ть.

compromise *n.* компроми́сс. —*adj.* компроми́ссный: *compromise decision,* компроми́ссное реше́ние. —*v.i.* идти́ на компроми́сс. —*v.t.* **1,** (adjust by concessions) ула́живать: *compromise differences,* ула́живать разногла́сия. **2,** (weaken; go back on) поступа́ться: *compromise one's principles,* поступа́ться при́нципами. **3,** (place in a compromising position) компромети́ровать. —**compromiser,** *n.* согла́шатель. —**compromising,** *adj.* компромети́рующий.

comptroller *n.* контролёр.

compulsion *n.* принужде́ние: *under compulsion,* по принужде́нию. *Feel no compulsion to act immediately,* не счита́ть ну́жным де́йствовать неме́дленно.

compulsive *adj.* застаре́лый; неисправи́мый. *Compulsive desire,* неудержи́мое жела́ние.

compulsory *adj.* обяза́тельный. *Attendance is compulsory,* посеще́ние обяза́тельно; я́вка обяза́тельна.

compunction *n.* угрызе́ния со́вести. *Without compunction,* без зазре́ния со́вести.

computation *n.* вычисле́ние; подсчёт.

compute *v.t.* вычисля́ть; подсчи́тывать.

computer *n.* вычисли́тельная маши́на; вычисли́тель; компью́тер.

comrade *n.* това́рищ. —**comrade in arms,** това́рищ по ору́жию; сора́тник; сподви́жник.

comradeship *n.* това́рищество.

con *n., in* **the pros and cons,** до́воды за и про́тив.

concave *adj.* во́гнутый. —**concavity,** *n.* во́гнутость.

conceal *v.t.* скрыва́ть; ута́ивать. —**concealment,** *n.* скры́тие.

concede *v.t.* допуска́ть: *I'll concede that..,* допуска́ю, что... *Concede a point,* уступа́ть в спо́ре. —*v.i.* призна́ть своё пораже́ние (на вы́борах).

conceit *n.* самомне́ние. —**conceited,** *adj.* большо́го мне́ния о себе́; самовлюблённый.

conceivable *adj.* мы́слимый; возмо́жный; допусти́мый. *It is quite conceivable that...,* вполне́ возмо́жно/допусти́мо, что... *Every conceivable precaution,* всевозмо́жные ме́ры предосторо́жности.

conceivably *adv.* возмо́жно; допусти́мо: *There might conceivably be others,* возмо́жно/допусти́мо, что существу́ют и други́е.

conceive *v.t.* **1,** (form in the mind) заду́мывать. **2,** (become pregnant with) зача́ть. —*v.i.* **1,** *fol. by* **of** (form a mental image of) представля́ть себе́. **2,** (become pregnant) забере́менеть.

concentrate *v.t.* сосредото́чивать; концентри́ровать. —*v.i.* сосредото́чиваться; концентри́роваться. —*n.* концентра́т.

concentration *n.* **1,** (act of concentrating) сосредото́чение; концентра́ция. **2,** (complete attention) сосредото́ченность. *Powers of concentration,* спо́собность сосредото́чиваться (*or* к сосредото́чению). **3,** (dense grouping) сосредото́чение; скопле́ние. —**concentration camp,** концентрацио́нный ла́герь; концла́герь.

concentric *adj.* концентри́ческий.

concept *n.* поня́тие.

conception *n.* **1,** (mental picture; idea) поня́тие; представле́ние; конце́пция. **2,** (conceiving in the womb) зача́тие.

concern *n.* **1,** (matter of interest) де́ло: *That is not my concern; that is no concern of mine,* э́то не моё де́ло; э́то меня́ не каса́ется. **2,** (solicitude) забо́та; уча́стие: *show concern about,* проявля́ть забо́ту о; проявля́ть уча́стие к *or* в. *Concern for the safety of the passengers,* забо́та о безопа́сности пассажи́ров. **3,** (anxiety) беспоко́йство; обеспоко́енность; озабóченность. *A matter of great concern,* дéло большóй вáжности. **4,** (business enterprise) предприя́тие; концéрн. —*v.t.* **1,** (relate to; affect) касáться. *As far as I am concerned,* что касáется меня́. **2,** (trouble; worry) беспокóить; тревóжить. —**concern oneself, 1,** (worry) беспокóиться. **2,** *fol. by* with (busy oneself) занимáться (+ *instr.*).

concerned *adj.* **1,** (interested; involved) заинтересóванный: *the parties concerned,* заинтересóванные стóроны. **2,** (uneasy; troubled) озабóченный; обеспокóенный. *Don't be concerned,* не беспокóйтесь; не волну́йтесь.

concerning *prep.* относи́тельно; касáющийся; по пóводу.

concert *n.* концéрт: *go to a concert,* идти́ на концéрт. —*adj.* концéртный: *concert hall,* концéртный зал. —**in concert,** совмéстно; сообщá; дру́жно; заоднó.

concerted *adj.* согласóванный; дру́жный.

concertina *n.* концерти́но.

concertmaster *n.* концертмéйстер.

concerto *n.* концéрт.

concession *n.* **1,** (something conceded) усту́пка: *make concéssions,* идти́ на усту́пки. **2,** (commercial privilege) концéссия.

concessionaire *n.* концессионéр.

concessive *adj., gram.* уступи́тельный.

conciliate *v.t.* мири́ть; примиря́ть. —**conciliation,** *n.* примирéние. —**conciliator,** *n.* примири́тель. —**conciliatory,** *adj.* примири́тельный.

concise *adj.* сжáтый; крáткий. —**conciseness,** *n.* сжáтость; крáткость.

conclave *n.* **1,** (meeting) совещáние. **2,** *relig.* конклáв.

conclude *v.t.* заключáть: *conclude a deal,* заключи́ть сдéлку. *Conclude one's speech with a toast,* заключи́ть речь тóстом. *This leads me to conclude that...,* из э́того я заключáю, что... —*v.i.* закáнчиваться: *The article concludes with...,* статья́ закáнчивается (+ *instr.*).

concluding *adj.* заключи́тельный.

conclusion *n.* **1,** (close; closing part) заключéние. **2,** (final judgment or decision) заключéние; вы́вод: *come to a conclusion,* приходи́ть к заключéнию/вы́воду. —**in conclusion,** в заключéние.

conclusive *adj.* решáющий. *Conclusive evidence,* неопровержи́мые доказáтельства. —**conclusively,** *adv.* неопровержи́мо: *prove conclusively,* неопровержи́мо доказáть.

concoct *v.t.* **1,** (cook) стряпать. **2,** (devise) приду́мывать. **3,** (make up) выду́мывать; стряпать. —**concoction,** *n.* стряпня́.

concomitant *adj.* сопу́тствующий.

concord *n.* соглáсие.

concordat *n.* конкордáт.

concourse *n.* **1,** (large open space, as in a station) зал. **2,** (thoroughfare) проспéкт.

concrete *n.* бетóн. —*adj.* **1,** (made of concrete) бетóнный. **2,** (real; specific) конкрéтный. —**concrete number,** именóванное число́.

concubine *n.* налóжница.

concur *v.i.* **1,** (agree) быть соглáсным: *I concur with*

the decision, я соглáсен (соглáсна) с э́тим решéнием. **2,** (occur simultaneously) совпадáть.

concurrence *n.* **1,** (agreement) соглáсие. **2,** (coincidence) совпадéние.

concurrent *adj.* совпадáющий; одноврéменный. —**concurrently,** *adv.* одноврéменно.

concussion *n.* сотрясéние.

condemn *v.t.* **1,** (denounce) осуждáть. **2,** (sentence) осуждáть; пригова́ривать: *condemn to death,* осуждáть на смерть; пригова́ривать к смéртной кáзни. **3,** (doom to an unhappy fate) осуждáть; обрекáть. **4,** (declare unfit for use) признавáть негóдным (для жилья́).

condemnation *n.* осуждéние.

condensation *n.* **1,** (reduction of gas to liquid) конденсáция. **2,** (abridgment) сокращéние. **3,** (something abridged) сокращённое издáние.

condense *v.t.* **1,** (change from gas to liquid) конденси́ровать. **2,** (make thicker or more concentrated) сгущáть: *condensed milk,* сгущённое молокó. **3,** (abridge) сокращáть; сжимáть. —*v.i.* сгущáться.

condenser *n.* конденсáтор.

condescend *v.i.* снисходи́ть: *condescend to reply,* снисходи́ть до отвéта. —**condescending,** *adj.* снисходи́тельный. —**condescension,** *n.* снисхождéние; снисходи́тельность.

condiment *n.* припрáва.

condition *n.* **1,** (state) состоя́ние: *in good condition,* в хорóшем состоя́нии. **2,** (provision; stipulation) усло́вие: *on condition that...,* при усло́вии, что... *Lay down conditions,* стáвить усло́вия. **3,** *pl.* (circumstances) усло́вия: *working conditions,* усло́вия труда́. *Under such conditions,* при таки́х усло́виях. **4,** (state of fitness) фóрма: *out of condition,* не в фóрме. **5,** (ailment) болéзнь: *a heart condition,* болéзнь сéрдца. —*v.t.* **1,** (limit by a condition) обусло́вливать. **2,** (train) приучáть.

conditional *adj.* усло́вный. *Make something conditional upon,* постáвить усло́вием, что... —**conditional mood,** *gram.* усло́вное наклонéние.

conditionally *adv.* усло́вно.

conditioned reflex усло́вный рефлéкс.

condole *v.i.* [*usu.* **condole with**] соболéзновать (+ *dat.*).

condolence *n.* соболéзнование. *Letter of condolence,* письмó соболéзнования.

condom *n.* презервати́в.

condominium *n.* кондоми́ниум.

condone *v.t.* прощáть: *Such behavior cannot be condoned,* такóе поведéние нельзя́ прости́ть.

condor *n.* кóндор.

conducive *adj.* *Be conducive to,* располагáть к: *The atmosphere is conducive to work,* атмосфéра располагáет к рабóте.

conduct *v.t.* **1,** (guide; lead) води́ть; проводи́ть; сопровождáть. **2,** (carry out; perform; hold) вести́; проводи́ть; производи́ть. *Conduct (i.e. hold) a meeting/religious service/,* проводи́ть собрáние/слу́жбу. *Conduct negotiations,* вести́ перегово́ры. *Conduct an experiment,* проводи́ть *or* производи́ть *or* стáвить о́пыт. *Conduct an investigation,* вести́ *or* проводи́ть рассле́дование. **3,** (direct; run) вести́: *conduct (i.e. run) a meeting,* вести́ собра́ние; *conduct a lesson,* вести́ уро́к. *Conduct (i.e. lead) a religious service,* вести́ *or* (от)служи́ть слу́жбу; соверши́ть богослуже́ние. *Conduct mass,* (от)служи́ть ме́ссу. **4,** (direct, as an orchestra) дирижи́ровать. **5,** (convey, as electricity) проводи́ть. —*n.* **1,** (behavior) поведе́ние. **2,** (management) веде́ние. —**conduct oneself,** вести́ себя́; держа́ть себя́.

conductivity *n.* проводи́мость.

conductor *n.* **1,** (leader; guide) проводни́к. *Tour conductor,* экскурсово́д. **2,** (on a train) проводни́к; кондỳктор; (on a bus or streetcar) кондỳктор. **3,** (of an orchestra) дирижёр. **4,** *physics* проводни́к.

conduit *n.* трубопрово́д.

cone *n.* **1,** (geometric figure) ко́нус. **2,** (fruit, as of the pine) ши́шка.

confection *n.* конфе́та. —**confectioner,** *n.* конди́тер. —**confectionery,** *n.* конди́терская.

confederacy *n.* конфедера́ция.

confederate *n.* соо́бщник; соуча́стник. —*adj.* конфедерати́вный. —*v.i.* объединя́ться в сою́з. —**confederation,** *n.* конфедера́ция; федера́ция.

confer *v.t.* присва́ивать; присужда́ть; удоста́ивать. *Confer an award on,* удоста́ивать (+ *acc.*) награ́ды. *Confer a degree on,* присужда́ть *or* присва́ивать сте́пень (+ *dat.*). *Confer a title on,* присва́ивать зва́ние (+ *dat.*). —*v.i.* [*usu.* **confer with**] совеща́ться (с).

conferee *n.* уча́стник конфере́нции.

conference *n.* совеща́ние; конфере́нция. *Disarmament conference,* конфере́нция по разоруже́нию. *Conference hall,* конфере́нц-за́л. *Conference table,* стол перегово́ров. *Be in conference,* быть на совеща́нии.

confess *v.t.* **1,** (admit) признава́ть: *confess one's error,* признава́ть свою́ оши́бку. **2,** (acknowledge; concede) признава́ться: *I must confess I never heard of him,* признаю́сь, о нём не слы́шал. **3,** *relig.* испове́довать. *Confess one's sins,* испове́довать свои́ грехи́; испове́доваться. —*v.i.* **1,** (admit one's guilt) сознава́ться: *The suspect confessed,* подозрева́емый созна́лся. **2,** *fol. by* **to** (admit) признава́ться в; сознава́ться в: *confess to a crime,* призна́ться/ созна́ться в преступле́нии. **3,** *relig.* испове́доваться.

confession *n.* **1,** (admission of guilt) призна́ние. *Make a full confession,* по́лностью призна́ться. *Sign a confession,* подписа́ть обвини́тельное заключе́ние. *I have a confession to make — I forgot,* до́лжен призна́ться, я забы́л. **2,** *relig.* и́споведь.

confessional *n.* испове́да́льня.

confessor *n.* **1,** (priest who hears confessions) духовни́к; испове́дник. **2,** (person who confesses) испове́дник. *Edward the Confessor,* Эдуа́рд Испове́дник.

confetti *n.* конфетти́.

confidant *n.* пове́ренный.

confide *v.t.* доверя́ть; вверя́ть; поверя́ть. —*v.i.* [*usu.* **confide in**] дели́ться с: *She has no one she can confide in,* ей не́ с кем подели́ться.

confidence *n.* **1,** (trust) дове́рие. *My confidence in him,* моё дове́рие к нему́. *Have confidence in,* доверя́ть (+ *dat.*). *Vote of confidence,* во́тум дове́рия. **2,** (assurance; certainty) уве́ренность: *say with confidence,* сказа́ть с уве́ренностью. **3,** (self-assurance) уве́ренность в себе́: *He lacks confidence,* у него́ нет (*or* не хвата́ет) уве́ренности в себе́. —**in confidence,** по секре́ту. —**take into one's confidence,** доверя́ть свои́ та́йны (+ *dat.*).

confident *adj.* **1,** (sure) уве́ренный: *confident of victory,* уве́рен в побе́де. **2,** (self-assured) самоуве́ренный: *confident tone of voice,* самоуве́ренный тон го́лоса.

confidential *adj.* секре́тный; конфиденциа́льный.

confidentially *adv.* **1,** (in confidence) конфиденциа́льно; по секре́ту. **2,** *as an introductory word,* ме́жду на́ми.

confidently *adv.* уве́ренно; с уве́ренностью.

configuration *n.* конфигура́ция; очерта́ние.

confine *v.t.* **1,** (limit; restrict) ограни́чивать. *Confine oneself to...,* ограни́чиваться (+ *instr.*). **2,** (shut in) заключа́ть; содержа́ть: *confine to prison,* заключа́ть в тюрьму́; содержа́ть в тюрьме́. *Confined to bed,* прико́ванный к посте́ли.

confinement *n.* **1,** (being confined to a place) заключе́ние: *solitary confinement,* одино́чное заключе́ние. *Confinement to barracks,* каза́рменный аре́ст. **2,** (lying-in) ро́ды.

confines *n.pl.* преде́лы: *within the confines of,* в преде́лах (+ *gen.*).

confirm *v.t.* **1,** (corroborate) подтвержда́ть: *confirm a hypothesis,* подтверди́ть гипо́тезу; *confirm someone's suspicions,* подтверди́ть чьи-нибудь подозре́ния. **2,** (approve) утвержда́ть: *confirm someone for the post of...,* утверди́ть кого́-нибудь в до́лжности (+ *gen.*). **3,** *relig.* конфирмова́ть.

confirmation *n.* **1,** (corroboration) подтвержде́ние. **2,** (approval) утвержде́ние. **3,** *relig.* конфирма́ция.

confirmed *adj.* **1,** (deeply committed) убеждённый. **2,** (inveterate) закорене́лый: *confirmed bachelor,* закорене́лый холостя́к.

confiscate *v.t.* конфискова́ть. —**confiscation,** *n.* конфиска́ция.

conflagration *n.* пожа́р.

conflict *n.* **1,** (battle; war) конфли́кт. **2,** *fig.* (clash) столкнове́ние. —*v.i.* противоре́чить друг дру́гу. *Conflict with,* противоре́чить (+ *dat.*). —**conflicting,** *adj.* противоречи́вый; разноречи́вый.

confluence *n.* слия́ние; впаде́ние.

conform *v.i.* [*usu.* **conform to**] согласова́ться (с); соотве́тствовать (+ *dat.*); сообразова́ться (с); *Conform to a standard,* соотве́тствовать станда́рту. *Conform to a custom,* соблюда́ть обы́чай. *Make something conform to something,* согласова́ть что-нибудь с чём-нибудь.

conformance *n.* = **conformity.**

conformism *n.* конформи́зм.

conformity *n.* соотве́тствие; сообра́зность. *Be in conformity with,* согласова́ться с.

confound *v.t.* **1,** (bewilder) озада́чивать; ста́вить в тупи́к. **2,** (mistake for another) пу́тать.

confounded *adj.* **1,** (taken aback) озада́ченный. **2,** *colloq.* (damned) прокля́тый.

confront *v.t.* **1,** (face) стоя́ть пе́ред; стоя́ть лицо́м к. *The task confronting us,* зада́ча, стоя́щая пе́ред на́ми. **2,** (meet boldly) смотре́ть (+ *dat.*) в лицо́. **3,** *fol. by* with (bring face to face) ста́вить (пе́ред): *confront someone with a choice,* поста́вить кого́-нибудь пе́ред вы́бором. *When confronted with the evidence,* пе́ред лицо́м ули́к.

confrontation *n.* конфронта́ция.

confuse *v.t.* **1,** (mix up; perplex; throw off) сбива́ть с то́лку; пу́тать. **2,** (mistake; mix up) пу́тать; сме́шивать. **3,** (make unclear) запу́тывать: *confuse the issue,* запу́тывать де́ло.

confused *adj.* **1,** (perplexed) недоуме́нный: *confused look* (*on one's face*), недоуме́нное выраже́ние лица́. *Become confused,* сби́ться с то́лку; спу́таться; запу́таться. **2,** (muddled) спу́танный: *confused thoughts,* спу́танные мы́сли.

confusing *adj.* сби́вчивый; пу́таный: *confusing explanation,* сби́вчивое/пу́таное объясне́ние. *Confusing street pattern,* запу́танное расположе́ние у́лиц. *It's all very confusing!,* э́то всё непоня́тно!

confusion *n.* смяте́ние; замеша́тельство; расте́рянность. *Throw into confusion,* приводи́ть в замеша́тельство. *Retreat in confusion,* отступа́ть в беспоря́дке. *There is some confusion about what happened,* име́ются не́которые нея́сности относи́тельно того́, что случи́лось. *In the confusion no one remembered to...,* в сумато́хе все забы́ли (+ *inf.*). *All is confusion,* всё запу́тано.

congeal *v.t.* замора́живать. —*v.i.* **1,** (harden) застыва́ть. **2,** (coagulate) свёртываться.

congenial *adj.* **1,** (suited to each other) дру́жный: *congenial couple,* дру́жная па́ра. *Congenial tastes,* схо́дные вку́сы. **2,** (friendly; pleasant) дру́жеский; тёплый: *congenial atmosphere,* дру́жеская/тёплая атмосфе́ра. *Congenial host,* приве́тливый хозя́ин.

congeniality *n.* **1,** (likeness) схо́дство. **2,** (affability) дружелю́бие.

congenital *adj.* врождённый.

congest *v.t.* переполня́ть. —**congested,** *adj.* те́сный; перепо́лненный; ску́ченный.

congestion *n.* **1,** (overcrowding) ску́ченность; переполне́ние. **2,** (heavy traffic) зато́р; про́бка. **3,** *med.* засто́й кро́ви.

conglomerate *n.* конгломера́т. —**conglomeration,** *n.* нагроможде́ние; конгломера́т.

Congolese *adj.* конголе́зский.

congratulate *v.t.* поздравля́ть: *congratulate someone on his victory,* поздравля́ть кого́-нибудь с побе́дой.

congratulation *n.* поздравле́ние. *Congratulations!,* поздравля́ю вас! *Hearty congratulations,* серде́чные поздравле́ния.

congratulatory *adj.* поздрави́тельный.

congregate *v.i.* собира́ться; сходи́ться.

congregation *n.* **1,** (assemblage) собра́ние. **2,** *relig.* прихо́д.

congress *n.* **1,** (assembly) съезд; конгре́сс. *Party congress,* съезд па́ртии. *Congress of People's Deputies,*

Съезд наро́дных депута́тов. *Congress of Vienna,* Ве́нский конгре́сс. **2,** *cap.* (U.S. legislative body) конгре́сс.

congressional *adj.* относя́щийся к конгре́ссу. *Congressional committee,* коми́ссия конгре́сса.

congressman *n.* конгрессме́н.

congruent *adj., math.* конгруэ́нтный. —**congruence,** *n., math.* конгруэ́нция.

conic *adj.* кони́ческий. *Also,* **conical.**

conifer *n.* хво́йное де́рево. —**coniferous,** *adj.* хво́йный.

conjectural *adj.* предположи́тельный; гада́тельный.

conjecture *n.* дога́дка; предположе́ние; до́мысел. *That is a matter of pure conjecture,* об э́том мо́жно то́лько гада́ть. —*v.t. & i.* гада́ть; стро́ить дога́дки; предполага́ть.

conjugal *adj.* супру́жеский; бра́чный. *Conjugal bed,* бра́чное ло́же.

conjugate *v.t.* спряга́ть. —**conjugation,** *n.* спряже́ние.

conjunction *n.* **1,** (combination) сочета́ние. **2,** (simultaneous occurrence) совпаде́ние. **3,** (part of speech) сою́з. —**in conjunction with,** в связи́ с; в сочета́нии с.

conjunctivitis *n.* конъюнктиви́т.

conjure *v.t.* **1,** (summon by oath or magic spell) заклина́ть. **2,** *fol. by* up (evoke) вызыва́ть в воображе́нии. —*v.i.* (practice magic) колдова́ть.

conjurer *also,* **conjuror** *n.* **1,** (sorcerer) заклина́тель. **2,** (magician) волше́бник; фо́кусник.

conk *v.t., slang* (bash) сту́кнуть. —*v.i.* [*usu.* **conk out**] *slang* отказа́ться рабо́тать; загло́хнуть.

connect *v.t.* **1,** (link; join) соединя́ть; свя́зывать. *Connect wires,* соединя́ть провода́. *The cities are connected by a new highway,* города́ соединены́ но́вым шоссе́. *Please connect me with...,* пожа́луйста, соедини́те меня́ с (+ *instr.*). *The events are in no way connected,* э́ти собы́тия ника́к не свя́заны ме́жду собо́й. **2,** (hook up) подключа́ть: *connect a television set,* подключи́ть телеви́зор. —*v.i.* соединя́ться; сообща́ться. *The roads connect near Boston,* доро́ги соединя́ются о́коло Бо́стона. *The rooms connect,* ко́мнаты сообща́ются; ко́мнаты соединены́ ме́жду собо́й.

connecting *adj.* соедини́тельный; связу́ющий. *Connecting link,* связу́ющее звено́. *Connecting rooms,* сме́жные ко́мнаты. *Connecting tunnel,* перехо́дный тунне́ль. —**connecting rod,** шату́н; соедини́тельная тя́га.

connection *also,* **connexion** *n.* **1,** (act of connecting) соедине́ние. **2,** (link) связь: *There is no connection between the two events,* ме́жду двумя́ собы́тиями нет никако́й свя́зи. **3,** (context) отноше́ние; связь: *in this connection,* в э́том отноше́нии; в э́той связи́. **4,** (change of planes, trains, etc.) переса́дка: *make a connection in Paris,* де́лать переса́дку в Пари́же. **5,** (on the telephone) слы́шимость: *We have a bad connection,* слы́шимость плоха́я. **6,** *electricity* соедине́ние: *loose connection,* плохо́е соедине́ние. **7,** *pl.* (influential associates) свя́зи.

connective *adj.* соедини́тельный. —**connective tissue,** соедини́тельная ткань.

connexion *n.* = **connection.**

conning tower боева́я ру́бка.

connivance *n.* попусти́тельство.

connive *v.i.* **1,** *fol. by* **at** (tolerate) попусти́тельствовать (+ *dat.*). **2,** *fol. by* **with** (conspire with) интригова́ть (с).

connoisseur *n.* знато́к; цени́тель: *connoisseur of the arts,* знато́к/цени́тель иску́сств. *Connoisseur of wine,* знато́к вин. *He is a connoisseur of wine,* он зна́ет толк в ви́нах; он разбира́ется в ви́нах.

connotation *n.* дополни́тельное значе́ние; отте́нок.

connote *v.t.* означа́ть; говори́ть о; подразумева́ть.

connubial *adj.* супру́жеский; бра́чный.

conquer *v.t.* **1,** (defeat; vanquish) завоёвывать; побежда́ть; покоря́ть. *Conquer the enemy,* победи́ть врага́. *Conquer territory,* покоря́ть *or* завоёвывать террито́рию. **2,** *fig.* (overcome) преодолева́ть; побежда́ть. *Conquer one's fear of flying,* преодоле́ть страх пе́ред полётами. *Conquer a disease,* поборо́ть боле́знь. —**conqueror,** *n.* завоева́тель.

conquest *n.* **1,** (act of conquering) завоева́ние; покоре́ние. **2,** *pl.* (territory conquered) завоева́ния.

consanguineous *adj.* единокро́вный; ро́дственный. —**consanguinity,** *n.* родство́.

conscience *n.* со́весть. *Have on one's conscience,* име́ть на со́вести. —**in all conscience,** по со́вести говоря́.

conscientious *adj.* **1,** (scrupulous; honest) со́вестливый. **2,** (careful; painstaking) доброссо́вестный; испра́вный. —**conscientiousness,** *n.* доброссо́вестность.

conscious *adj.* **1,** (capable of thought) созна́тельный: *Man is a conscious being,* челове́к — созна́тельное существо́. **2,** (mentally awake) в созна́нии: *The patient is conscious,* больно́й — в созна́нии. **3,** *fol. by* **of** (aware of) сознаю́щий: *be conscious of the danger,* сознава́ть опа́сность. **4,** (deliberate) созна́тельный. —**consciously,** *adv.* созна́тельно.

consciousness *n.* **1,** (state of being conscious) созна́ние. *Lose consciousness,* потеря́ть созна́ние; лиши́ться чувств. *Regain consciousness,* приходи́ть в созна́ние; приходи́ть в себя́; очну́ться. **2,** (awareness) (само)созна́ние; созна́тельность: *class consciousness,* кла́ссовое (само)созна́ние; кла́ссовая созна́тельность.

conscript *n.* призывни́к. —*v.t.* призыва́ть.

conscription *n.* во́инская пови́нность.

consecrate *v.t.* освяща́ть. —**consecration,** *n.* освяще́ние.

consecutive *adj.* после́довательный. *Four consecutive days,* четы́ре дня подря́д. —**consecutively,** *adv.* после́довательно.

consensus *n.* **1,** (agreement) консе́нсус. **2,** (opinion of most) о́бщее мне́ние: *by common consensus,* по о́бщему мне́нию.

consent *v.i.* соглаша́ться: *consent to an offer,* согласи́ться на предложе́ние. *She consented to meet with him,* она́ согласи́лась встре́титься с ним. —*n.*

согла́сие: *give one's consent,* дать своё согла́сие. *By mutual/common consent,* по взаи́мному согла́сию; с о́бщего согла́сия.

consequence *n.* **1,** (effect) после́дствие; сле́дствие. *Take the consequences,* отвеча́ть за после́дствия. **2,** (importance) значе́ние: *of no consequence,* не име́ющий значе́ния.

consequent *adj.* вытека́ющий.

consequently *adv.* сле́довательно.

conservation *n.* **1,** (act of conserving) сохране́ние: *energy conservation,* сохране́ние эне́ргии. **2,** (protection of natural resources) охра́на приро́ды. —**conservationist,** *n.* сторо́нник охра́ны приро́ды.

conservatism *n.* консервати́зм.

conservative *adj.* **1,** (tending to oppose change) консервати́вный. **2,** (moderate; cautious) скро́мный: *conservative estimate,* скро́мный подсчёт. —*n.* консерва́тор.

conservatory *n.* **1,** (greenhouse) оранжере́я. **2,** (school of music) консервато́рия.

conserve *v.t.* сохраня́ть; бере́чь; сберега́ть: *conserve one's strength,* сохраня́ть/бере́чь/сберега́ть свои́ си́лы. *Conserve one's energy,* сохраня́ть эне́ргию.

consider *v.t.* **1,** (examine; take up) рассма́тривать. **2,** (think over) обду́мывать. **3,** (look upon; regard) счита́ть; рассма́тривать. *I consider him my friend,* я его́ счита́ю свои́м дру́гом. *I consider it an honor,* счита́ю за честь. *He considers himself a...,* он счита́ет *or* полага́ет себя́ (+ *instr.*). *I consider it madness,* я рассма́триваю э́то как безу́мие. **4,** (take into account) учи́тывать; счита́ться с; принима́ть во внима́ние. *All things considered,* принима́я всё во внима́ние. **5,** (show consideration for) счита́ться с. **6,** (weigh as a possibility) поду́мывать: *consider moving to Florida,* поду́мывать перее́хать (*or* о перее́зде) во Флори́ду. **7,** (believe; feel) счита́ть.

considerable *adj.* значи́тельный; нема́лый. —**considerably,** *adv.* значи́тельно.

considerate *adj.* внима́тельный; предупреди́тельный.

consideration *n.* **1,** (careful thought) рассмотре́ние. *The matter is under consideration,* де́ло сейча́с рассма́тривается. *We shall give the matter careful consideration,* мы тща́тельно рассмо́трим э́то де́ло. **2,** (factor to be considered) соображе́ние: *tactical considerations,* такти́ческие соображе́ния. **3,** (thoughtfulness toward others) внима́ние. *Lack of consideration,* невнима́тельность. *Have no consideration for others,* не счита́ться с други́ми. **4,** (payment) вознагражде́ние: *for a small consideration,* за небольшо́е вознагражде́ние. —**in consideration of, 1,** (in view of) принима́я во внима́ние; с учётом (+ *gen.*) **2,** (in return for) в благода́рность за. —**take into consideration,** принима́ть во внима́ние/ в соображе́ние/ к све́дению/ в расчёт; учи́тывать.

considered *adj.* обду́манный; проду́манный.

considering *prep.* принима́я во внима́ние; учи́тывая; ввиду́.

consign *v.t.* **1,** (entrust to someone's care) отдава́ть на попече́ние (+ *gen.*). **2,** (assign to an undesirable position; relegate) переводи́ть. *Consign to oblivion,* предавáть забвéнию. **3,** *comm.* (deliver for sale) отправля́ть.

consignment *n.* **1,** (delivery for sale) отпрáвка. **2,** (something consigned) пáртия (товáров); трáнспорт.

consist *v.i.* [*usu.* **consist of**] **1,** (be made up of) состоя́ть из: *The book consists of ten chapters,* кни́га состои́т из десяти́ глав. **2,** (be; involve) состоя́ть в: *What will my work consist of?,* в чём бу́дет состоя́ть моя́ рабóта?

consistency *n.* **1,** (adherence to pattern) послéдовательность. **2,** (firmness) плóтность; твёрдость; консистéнция.

consistent *adj.* **1,** (not varying) послéдовательный. **2,** *fol. by* **with** (not contradicting): *be consistent with,* соотвéтствовать (+ *dat.*); согласовáться с.

consistently *adv.* **1,** (in a consistent manner) послéдовательно. **2,** (unfailingly) постоя́нно: *He has been consistently wrong,* он постоя́нно ошибáлся.

consolation *n.* утешéние. *Take consolation in the fact that...,* утешáться тем, что... —**consolation prize,** утеши́тельный приз.

console[1] (kun-sol) *v.t.* утешáть.

console[2] (kan-sol) *n.* **1,** (bracket) консóль. **2,** (cabinet) кóрпус. **3,** (control panel) пульт.

consolidate *v.t.* **1,** (make secure) укрепля́ть; закрепля́ть; упрóчивать. *Consolidate power,* укрепля́ть власть. *Consolidate one's position,* упрóчивать своё положéние. **2,** (combine; merge) объединя́ть; сливáть: *consolidate three companies into one,* объединя́ть/сливáть три компáнии в одну́.

consolidation *n.* **1,** (making secure) укреплéние; закреплéние; консолидáция. **2,** (combining; merging) слия́ние; объединéние.

consommé *n.* бульóн.

consonance *n.* созву́чие; консонáнс.

consonant *n.* **1,** (sound) соглáсный звук. **2,** (letter) соглáсная бу́ква. —*adj.* **1,** (consonantal) соглáсный. **2,** (harmonious in sound) созву́чный. **3,** *fol. by* **with** (in keeping with) соглáсный (с). —**consonantal,** *adj.* соглáсный.

consort *n.* супру́г; супру́га. —*v.i.* [*usu.* **consort with**] общáться с; води́ться (с).

consortium *n.* консóрциум.

conspicuous *adj.* ви́дный; замéтный; бросáющийся в глазá. *Be conspicuous by one's absence,* блистáть свои́м отсу́тствием.

conspiracy *n.* зáговор. —**conspirator,** *n.* заговóрщик; конспирáтор. —**conspiratorial,** *adj.* заговóрщический.

conspire *v.i.* (тáйно) сговáриваться. *Conspire against,* устрáивать зáговор прóтив. *Conspire to overthrow the government,* устрáивать зáговор с цéлью свержéния прави́тельства.

constable *n.* констéбль.

constancy *n.* постоя́нство.

constant *adj.* постоя́нный. —*n.* постоя́нная величинá; констáнта. —**constantly,** *adv.* постоя́нно.

constellation *n.* созвéздие.

consternation *n.* у́жас; замешáтельство; растéрянность.

constipate *v.t.* крепи́ть. *He is constipated,* егó крепи́т. —**constipation,** *n.* запóр.

constituency *n.* избирáтельный óкруг.

constituent *adj.* **1,** (component) составнóй. **2,** (authorized to draw up a constitution) учреди́тельный. —*n.* **1,** (constituent part) составнáя часть. **2,** (voter) избирáтель.

constitute *v.t.* **1,** (make up; form) составля́ть: *constitute a quorum,* составля́ть квóрум. **2,** (be; represent) представля́ть (собóй): *constitute a threat,* представля́ть угрóзу; *constitute a violation of the law,* представля́ть собóй нарушéние закóна.

constitution *n.* **1,** (charter) конститу́ция. **2,** (physical make-up) (тéло)сложéние. *Strong constitution,* крéпкий органи́зм. *Iron constitution,* желéзное здорóвье.

constitutional *adj.* **1,** (of or in accordance with a constitution) конституциóнный. *Constitutional law,* госудáрственное прáво. **2,** (inherent in one's make-up) органи́ческий. —*n.* (walk; exercise) моциóн; прогу́лка для моциóна. —**constitutionality,** *n.* конституциóнность.

constrain *v.t.* **1,** (force) принуждáть; вынуждáть. **2,** (inhibit) скóвывать; стесня́ть.

constraint *n.* **1,** (something that holds back) стеснéние. **2,** (lack of ease) скóванность; стеснéние; принуждённость. **3,** (compulsion) принуждéние.

constrict *v.t.* **1,** (make smaller or narrower) су́живать. **2,** (produce a tight feeling in) стесня́ть; сжимáть; сдáвливать; сти́скивать.

constriction *n.* **1,** (act of constricting) сужéние. **2,** (feeling of pressure or tightness) стеснéние; сжáтие. *I feel a constriction in my chest,* мне тесни́т грудь.

construct *v.t.* стрóить; констру́ировать. *Construct a triangle,* стрóить треугóльник. *Construct a sentence,* стрóить предложéние.

construction *n.* **1,** (act of building) строи́тельство. *Be under construction,* стрóиться. **2,** (design) констру́кция. **3,** (interpretation) истолковáние. **4,** *gram.* констру́кция. —*adj.* строи́тельный. *Construction site,* строи́тельная площáдка; стрóйка.

constructive *adj.* конструкти́вный.

construe *v.t.* толковáть; истолкóвывать.

consul *n.* кóнсул. —**consular,** *adj.* кóнсульский. —**consulate,** *n.* кóнсульство.

consult *v.t.* **1,** (ask the advice of) совéтоваться с; консульти́роваться с. **2,** (refer to, as a dictionary) справля́ться в; обращáться к.

consultant *n.* консультáнт.

consultation *n.* **1,** (act of consulting) консультáция. **2,** (meeting between doctors) конси́лиум.

consultative *adj.* совещáтельный; консультати́вный.

consulting *adj. Rendered by* -консультáнт: *consulting engineer,* инженéр-консультáнт.

consume *v.t.* **1,** (use, as food, fuel, etc.) потребля́ть. **2,** (eat or drink up) съесть; вы́пить. **3,** (destroy, as of fire) пожирáть. **4,** (use up, as time, money, etc.) поглощáть. **5,** *fol. by* **with** (fill with, as an emotion) пожирáть; глодáть. *Be consumed with rage,* пылáть гнéвом. *He is consumed with envy,* егó глóжет зáвисть.

consumer *n.* потреби́тель. —**consumer goods,** потреби́тельские това́ры; това́ры широ́кого потребле́ния.

consummate *v.t.* заверша́ть; доводи́ть до конца́. —*adj.* зако́нченный: *a consummate artist,* зако́нченный арти́ст. —**consummation,** *n.* заверше́ние.

consumption *n.* **1,** (using up) потребле́ние. **2,** (amount consumed) расхо́д: *Energy consumption is down,* расхо́д эне́ргии сни́зился. **3,** (disease) чахо́тка. —**consumptive,** *adj.* чахо́точный.

contact *n.* **1,** (touching) конта́кт; соприкоснове́ние. **2,** (being in touch) конта́кт; связь. *Be in contact with,* быть в конта́кте с. *Come into contact with,* ста́лкиваться с. **3,** *usu. pl.* (helpful acquaintances) конта́кты; свя́зи. —*v.t.* **1,** (touch) соприкаса́ться с. **2,** (get in touch with) свя́зываться с.

contact lens конта́ктная ли́нза.

contagion *n.* зара́за.

contagious *adj.* **1,** *med.* зара́зный. **2,** *fig.* (of a smile, laughter, etc.) зарази́тельный.

contain *v.t.* **1,** (hold; include) содержа́ть: *Meat contains protein,* мя́со соде́ржит бело́к. *The proposal contains nothing new,* предложе́ние не соде́ржит ничего́ но́вого. **2,** (suppress; check; hold back) сде́рживать. —**contain oneself,** сде́рживаться; выде́рживать.

container *n.* **1,** (receptacle) сосу́д; вмести́лище. **2,** (for shipping goods) конте́йнер; та́ра. —*adj.* конте́йнерный: *container ship,* конте́йнерное су́дно.

containment *n.* сде́рживание.

contaminate *v.t.* загрязня́ть; заража́ть. —**contamination,** *n.* загрязне́ние; зараже́ние.

contemplate *v.t.* **1,** (gaze at) созерца́ть. **2,** (think about intently) разду́мывать о *or* над: *contemplate the future/ a problem/,* разду́мывать о бу́дущем/ над пробле́мой/. **3,** (think about doing) замышля́ть; поду́мывать. **4,** (expect) ожида́ть. —*v.i.* размышля́ть.

contemplation *n.* созерца́ние. *Be lost in contemplation of,* засма́триваться на; загля́дываться на.

contemplative *adj.* созерца́тельный.

contemporaneous *adj.* происходя́щий одновреме́нно (с).

contemporary *adj.* совреме́нный. —*n.* **1,** (person one's own age) све́рстник; рове́сник. **2,** (person living at the same time) совреме́нник.

contempt *n.* презре́ние. *Have contempt for; hold in contempt,* презира́ть. —**contempt of court,** оскорбле́ние суда́.

contemptible *adj.* презре́нный.

contemptuous *adj.* презри́тельный.

contend *v.i.* **1,** (compete) состяза́ться. *Contend for,* оспа́ривать. **2,** *fol. by* **with** (cope with) справля́ться с. —*v.t.* (assert) утвержда́ть: *He contends that...,* он утвержда́ет, что...,

contender *n.* претенде́нт.

content[1] (kan-tent) *n.* **1,** *pl.* (what is in a receptacle) содержи́мое. **2,** *pl.* (subject matter) содержа́ние: *the contents of a book,* содержа́ние кни́ги. **3,** (substance) содержа́ние: *form and content,* фо́рма и содер-

жа́ние. **4,** (amount of a substance contained) содержа́ние. *The fat content of milk,* содержа́ние жи́ра в молоке́; жи́рность молока́.

content[2] (kun-tent) *adj.* дово́льный. —*v.t.* удовлетворя́ть. *There's no contenting him,* на него́ не угоди́шь. *Content oneself with,* удовлетворя́ться (+ *instr.*); дово́льствоваться (+ *instr.*). —**to one's heart's content,** вдо́воль; вво́лю; ско́лько душе́ уго́дно; в своё удово́льствие.

contented *adj.* дово́льный. —**contentedly,** *adv.* дово́льно.

contention *n.* **1,** (competition) соревнова́ние. *Be in contention,* име́ть ша́нсы. **2,** (strife) раздо́р. **3,** (assertion) утвержде́ние. —**bone of contention,** я́блоко раздо́ра.

contentious *adj.* **1,** (argumentative) сварли́вый; вздо́рный. **2,** (causing contention) спо́рный.

contentment *n.* дово́льство.

contest *n.* **1,** (struggle; battle) борьба́. **2,** (competition) состяза́ние; соревнова́ние; ко́нкурс. *Beauty contest,* ко́нкурс красоты́. —*v.t.* оспа́ривать: *contest a will,* оспа́ривать завеща́ние.

contestant *n.* уча́стник состяза́ния.

context *n.* конте́кст. *Take out of context,* вырыва́ть из конте́кста.

contiguity *n.* сме́жность; соприкоснове́ние.

contiguous *adj.* сме́жный; соприкаса́ющийся; прилега́ющий; сопреде́льный.

continence *n.* воздержа́ние.

continent *n.* матери́к; контине́нт.

continental *adj.* материко́вый; континента́льный. —**continental shelf,** шельф.

contingency *n.* (возмо́жный) слу́чай.

contingent *adj.* **1,** (possible) возмо́жный. **2,** (chance) случа́йный. **3,** (dependent): *be contingent on,* зави́сеть от. —*n.* континге́нт.

continual *adj.* непреста́нный; беспреста́нный. —**continually,** *adv.* непреста́нно; беспреста́нно.

continuation *n.* продолже́ние.

continue *v.t.* продолжа́ть: *continue one's education,* продолжа́ть образова́ние; *continue working,* продолжа́ть рабо́тать. —*v.i.* продолжа́ть(ся): *Continue!* продолжа́йте! *Continue to negotiate,* продолжа́ть вести́ перегово́ры. *The struggle continues,* борьба́ продолжа́ется. *If the good weather continues,* е́сли проде́ржится хоро́шая пого́да. *The patient continues to improve,* состоя́ние больно́го продолжа́ет улучша́ться. —**to be continued,** продолже́ние сле́дует.

continuer *n.* продолжа́тель.

continuity *n.* непреры́вность; прее́мственность.

continuous *adj.* **1,** (uninterrupted) непреры́вный; беспреры́вный. **2,** (unbroken) сплошно́й. —**continuously,** *adv.* непреры́вно; беспреры́вно.

contort *v.t.* искривля́ть. —**contortion,** *n.* искривле́ние. —**contortionist,** *n.* челове́к-змея́.

contour *n.* ко́нтур; очерта́ние. —**contour map,** ко́нтурная ка́рта.

contraband *n.* контраба́нда. —*adj.* контраба́ндный.

contrabass *n.* контраба́с.

contrabassoon *n.* контрафагóт.
contraception *n.* предотвращéние зачáтия.
contraceptive *adj.* противозачáточный. —*n.* противозачáточное срéдство.
contract *n.* договóр; контрáкт; подрáд. —*v.t.* **1,** (incur, as debts) дéлать (долги). **2,** (catch, as a disease) получáть; подхвáтывать; наживáть. —*v.i.* **1,** (draw together) сокращáться; сжимáться. **2,** *fol. by* **for** *or* *inf.* (enter into a contract) заключи́ть договóр (на); контрактовáть.
contraction *n.* **1,** (act of contracting) сокращéние; сужéние. **2,** (condensed form of two words) сокращённое слóво.
contractor *n.* **1,** (one who contracts for anything) подрáдчик; контрагéнт. **2,** (builder) подрáдчик-строи́тель.
contractual *adj.* договóрный.
contradict *v.t.* противорéчить. *Contradict oneself,* противорéчить самомý (самóй) себé; впадáть в противорéчие. —**contradiction,** *n.* противорéчие. —**contradictory,** *adj.* противоречи́вый; разноречи́вый.
contradistinction *n., in* **in contradistinction to,** в отли́чие от; в противополóжность (+ *dat.*).
contralto *n.* контрáльто. —*adj.* контрáльтовый.
contraption *n., colloq.* приспособлéние.
contrapuntal *adj.* контрапункти́ческий.
contrary *adj.* **1,** (opposite) противополóжный: *contrary views,* противополóжные взглáды. **2,** *fol. by* **to** (in contradiction with) проти́вный (+ *dat.*). *Be contrary to,* противорéчить (+ *dat.*). **3,** (obstinate) упрáмый; сварли́вый. —*n. Quite the contrary,* совсéм наоборóт; как раз наоборóт. *Unless I hear to the contrary,* éсли я не услы́шу чегó-нибудь инóго. —**contrary to,** вопреки́; наперекóр. *Contrary to all expectations,* вопреки́ всем ожидáниям. *Contrary to what was written in the press,* вопреки́ томý, что писáла прéсса. —**on the contrary,** наоборóт; напрóтив.
contrast *n.* контрáст. *In contrast to,* в отли́чие от. —*v.t.* сопоставлáть; противопоставлáть. —*v.i.* контрасти́ровать.
contravene *v.t.* **1,** (violate) нарушáть. **2,** (go against; conflict with) идти́ вразрéз с; противорéчить. —**contravention,** *n.* нарушéние.
contribute *v.t.* **1,** (donate) жéртвовать. *Contribute one's share,* вноси́ть свою́ дóлю. **2,** (offer, as an idea, suggestion, etc.) вноси́ть; выдвигáть. **3,** (furnish for publication) писáть. —*v.i.* **1,** (give money) жéртвовать. **2,** (write articles) сотрýдничать (в газéте, в журнáле, *etc.*). **3,** *fol. by* **to** (help bring about) содéйствовать; спосóбствовать.
contribution *n.* **1,** (monetary donation) пожéртвование. *Make a contribution,* дéлать пожéртвование; пожéртвовать чтó-нибудь. **2,** (that which advances something) вклад: *make a contribution to science,* дéлать *or* вноси́ть вклад в наýку.
contributor *n.* **1,** (donor) жéртвователь. **2,** (writer of articles) сотрýдник (газéты, журнáла, *etc.*).
contrite *adj.* кáющийся. —**contrition,** *n.* раскáяние; покаáние.

contrivance *n.* **1,** (device) приспособлéние. **2,** (scheme) ухищрéние.
contrive *v.t.* **1,** (plan; devise) измышлáть. **2,** *fol. by inf.* (manage) ухитрáться; умудрáться; изловчи́ться; (succeed through trickery) ухищрáться.
control *v.t.* **1,** (regulate the operation of) управлáть; регули́ровать. *This button controls the heat,* э́то — кнóпка отоплéния. *Control prices,* регули́ровать цéны. **2,** (hold sway over; dominate) контроли́ровать; держáть под свои́м контрóлем. *Control the straits,* контроли́ровать проли́вы. *Controlling interest,* контрóльный пакéт (áкций). **3,** (keep under control) справлáться c: *control a child/horse/class,* справлáться с ребёнком/лóшадью/клáссом. **4,** (keep in check) сдéрживать; обýздывать. *Control one's emotions,* сдéрживать свои́ чýвства. *Control oneself,* владéть собóй; обуздáть себá. —*n.* **1,** (operation) управлéние. *Remote control,* дистанциóнное управлéние. **2,** (domination) контрóль: *control of the sea lanes,* контрóль над морски́ми путáми. *Gain control of,* взять под свой контрóль. **3,** (check) контрóль: *price controls,* контрóль над цéнами; *birth control,* контрóль над рождáемостью. **4,** *pl.* (instruments) рычаги́ управлéния. *Be at the controls,* стоáть за штурвáлом. —*adj.* контрóльный. *Control experiment,* контрóльный óпыт. *Control post,* контрóльный пост. *Control panel,* щит управлéния; пульт. —**be in control of,** владéть. —**due to circumstances beyond our control,** по не зави́сящим от нас обстоáтельствам. —**get control of oneself,** овладéть собóй. —**get out of control,** вы́йти из-под контрóля. —**go out of control,** потерáть управлéние. —**lose control of, 1,** (a vehicle or aircraft) потерáть управлéние (+ *instr.*). **2,** (a group, place, situation, etc.) терáть контрóль над. —**take control of,** взять под свой контрóль. —**under control,** в порáдке; нормáльно: *Everything is under control,* всё в порáдке; всё нормáльно. *The fire has been brought under control,* пожáр останóвлен.
controller *n.* **1,** *finance* контролёр. **2,** *aero.* диспéтчер: *air traffic controller,* диспéтчер воздýшного трáнспорта.
control tower диспéтчерская вы́шка; диспéтчерская.
controversial *adj.* спóрный; дискуссиóнный; полеми́ческий.
controversy *n.* спор; дискýссия; полéмика.
contuse *v.t.* контýзить. —**contusion,** *n.* контýзия; уши́б.
conundrum *n.* головолóмка.
convalesce *v.i.* выздорáвливать. —**convalescence,** *n.* выздоровлéние. —**convalescent,** *n. & adj.* выздорáвливающий.
convene *v.t.* созывáть; собирáть. —*v.i.* собирáться.
convenience *n.* удóбство. *For the convenience of,* для удóбства (+ *gen.*). *At your convenience,* когдá вам бýдет удóбно. *At your earliest convenience,* возмóжно скорéе. *With all the conveniences,* со всéми удóбствами. —**marriage of convenience,** брак по расчёту.

convenient *adj.* удо́бный: *Is that convenient for you?,* э́то вам удо́бно? *At any time convenient to you,* в любо́е удо́бное для вас вре́мя.

convent *n.* (же́нский) монасты́рь.

convention *n.* **1,** (assembly) съезд; *hist.* конве́нт. **2,** (agreement between nations) конве́нция: *consular convention,* ко́нсульская конве́нция. **3,** (custom) усло́вность.

conventional *adj.* **1,** (established by general agreement) усло́вный; общепри́нятый. **2,** *mil.* (non-nuclear) обы́чный: *conventional weapons,* обы́чное ору́жие.

conventionality *n.* усло́вность.

converge *v.i.* сходи́ться; стека́ться; слива́ться. *Thousands of demonstrators converged on the city,* ты́сячи демонстра́нтов съе́хались в го́род. **—convergence,** *n.* стече́ние; слия́ние.

conversant *adj.* осведомлённый; све́дущий. *Are you conversant with this matter?,* вы све́дущи в э́том де́ле?

conversation *n.* разгово́р; бесе́да. **—conversational,** *adj.* разгово́рный.

converse[1] (kun-**vurs**) *v.i.* разгова́ривать.

converse[2] (**kan**-vurs) *adj.* противополо́жный; обра́тный. **—**n.*, preceded by* **the** противополо́жное; обра́тное.

conversely *adv.* наоборо́т.

conversion *n.* **1,** (changing to something else) превраще́ние; обраще́ние. **2,** *relig.* обраще́ние; перехо́д: *conversion to Christianity,* обраще́ние/ перехо́д в христиа́нство. **3,** *econ.* конве́рсия.

convert *v.t.* **1,** (transform) превраща́ть: *convert starch to sugar,* превраща́ть крахма́л в са́хар; *convert a bedroom into a study,* превраща́ть спа́льню в кабине́т. *Convert a plant to coal,* переводи́ть заво́д на у́голь. **2,** (cause to change to another religion) обраща́ть (в другу́ю ве́ру). **3,** (change to a different unit of measurement) переводи́ть. **4,** *finance* конверти́ровать. **—**v.i.* переходи́ть; обраща́ться (в другу́ю ве́ру). *Convert to Christianity,* переходи́ть/ обраща́ться в христиа́нство. **—**n.* новообращённый; прозели́т.

converter *n.* конве́ртер.

convertibility *n.* обрати́мость.

convertible *adj.* **1,** *finance* обрати́мый; конверти́руемый. **2,** (of an automobile) откры́тый. **—**n.* откры́тый автомоби́ль.

convex *adj.* вы́пуклый. **—convexity,** *n.* вы́пуклость.

convey *v.t.* **1,** (carry; transport) везти́; перевози́ть. **2,** (communicate) передава́ть; сообща́ть; доводи́ть.

conveyance *n.* **1,** (act of conveying) перево́зка. **2,** (vehicle) перево́зочное сре́дство.

conveyor *also,* **conveyer** *n.* конве́йер; транспортёр. **—conveyor belt,** конве́йерная ле́нта; ле́нточный транспортёр.

convict *v.t.* осужда́ть. *A man convicted of murder,* челове́к, осуждённый за уби́йство. **—**n.* осуждённый; заключённый; ка́торжник.

conviction *n.* **1,** (finding guilty) осужде́ние. **2,** (one of a number of times convicted) суди́мость. **3,** (strong belief) убежде́ние. **4,** (air of certainty) убеждён-

ность. *With conviction,* убеждённо. *Carry conviction,* быть (о́чень) убеди́тельным.

convince *v.t.* убежда́ть: *I am convinced of it,* я убеждён (убеждена́) в э́том. *He convinced me to stay,* он убеди́л меня́ оста́ться..

convincing *adj.* убеди́тельный. **—convincingly,** *adv.* убеди́тельно.

convivial *adj.* **1,** (jovial) весёлый. **2,** (festive) пра́здничный. **3,** (friendly) дружелю́бный. **—conviviality,** *n.* весёлость.

convocation *n.* **1,** (summoning) созы́в. **2,** (ecclesiastic assembly) собо́р.

convoke *v.t.* созыва́ть.

convoluted *adj.* **1,** (twisted) изо́гнутый; изви́листый. **2,** (complicated; intricate) замыслова́тый.

convoy *n.* карава́н; коло́нна.

convulse *v.t.* вызыва́ть су́дорогу *or* конву́льсии у. *Be convulsed with laughter,* надрыва́ть живо́т со́ смеху.

convulsion *n.* су́дорога; конву́льсия. **—convulsive,** *adj.* су́дорожный; конвульси́вный.

coo *v.i.* воркова́ть.

cook *v.t.* гото́вить; вари́ть: *cook dinner,* гото́вить/ вари́ть обе́д. *Cook the food thoroughly,* хорошо́ *or* тща́тельно провари́ть пи́щу. **—**v.i.* **1,** (prepare food) гото́вить; стря́пать. *Do you know how to cook?,* вы уме́ете гото́вить? **2,** (of food) вари́ться. **—**n.* (man or woman) по́вар; (woman servant) куха́рка. *She is an excellent cook,* она́ прекра́сно гото́вит. **—cook up,** *colloq.* стря́пать. **—What's cooking?,** *colloq.* что происхо́дит?

cookbook *n.* пова́ренная кни́га.

cookery *n.* кулина́рия.

cookie *n.* пече́нье.

cooking *n.* ку́хня: *French cooking,* францу́зская ку́хня; *home cooking,* дома́шняя ку́хня. **—**adj.* ку́хонный: *cooking utensils,* ку́хонная посу́да *or* у́тварь.

cool *adj.* **1,** (moderately cold) прохла́дный: *cool weather/night/water,* прохла́дная пого́да/ночь/вода́. *How do you manage to keep cool in this weather?,* как вам удаётся не перегрева́ться при э́той пого́де? **2,** (calm; collected) споко́йный; хладнокро́вный. **3,** (not cordial) холо́дный: *cool reception,* холо́дный приём. **4,** *fol. by* **to** (unenthusiastic) прохла́дный: *He was cool to the idea,* он отнёсся прохла́дно к э́той иде́е. **—**v.t.* охлажда́ть; остужа́ть. **—**v.i.* **1,** (of soup, an engine, etc.) остыва́ть. **2,** *fol. by* **off** (of a person) освежа́ться; (of the weather) стать прохла́днее. **3,** (moderate; wane, as of feelings) остыва́ть. *Passions have cooled,* стра́сти улегли́сь. **4,** *fol. by* **to** (become less enthusiastic about) охладева́ть (к); остыва́ть (к). **—**n.* прохла́да: *the cool of the evening,* вече́рняя прохла́да. **—keep one's cool,** *colloq.* сохраня́ть споко́йствие. **—lose one's cool,** *colloq.* вы́йти из себя́; потеря́ть самооблада́ние.

cooler *n.* холоди́льник.

cool-headed *adj.* невозмути́мый. **—cool-headedness,** *n.* невозмути́мость.

coolie *n.* ку́ли.

cooling n. охлажде́ние. —adj. прохлади́тельный.

coolly adv. прохла́дно: react coolly, отнести́сь (к чему́-нибудь) прохла́дно.

coolness n. **1,** (relatively low temperature) прохла́да. **2,** (calmness) хладнокро́вие. **3,** (distance, as between people) холодо́к; охлажде́ние.

coop n. куря́тник. —v.t. [usu. **coop up**] заключа́ть. Be cooped up, юти́ться; жить в тесноте́. —**fly the coop,** colloq. удра́ть; смы́ться.

cooper n. бо́ндарь; боча́р.

cooperate v.i. сотру́дничать. —**cooperation,** n. сотру́дничество.

cooperative adj. **1,** (joint) совме́стный. **2,** (collectively owned and operated) кооперати́вный. **3,** (helpful) услу́жливый. —n. кооперати́в.

coordinate v.t. согласо́вывать; координи́ровать. —n., math. координа́та. —adj., gram.: coordinate clause, сочинённое предложе́ние; coordinate conjunction, сочини́тельный сою́з. —**coordinating committee,** координацио́нный комите́т.

coordination n. **1,** (act of coordinating) согласова́ние; координа́ция. **2,** (harmony of action) согласо́ванность; координа́ция. Lack of coordination, несогласо́ванность; разла́д. **3,** physiol. координа́ция.

coordinator n. координа́тор.

coot n. лысу́ха.

co-owner n. совладе́лец.

cop n., colloq. полице́йский; полисме́н.

copal n. копа́л.

cope v.i. [usu. **cope with**] справля́ться с: cope with an assignment, справля́ться с зада́нием.

copier n. **1,** (person) перепи́счик; копиро́вщик. **2,** (machine) копирова́льная маши́на.

copilot n. второ́й пило́т.

copious adj. оби́льный; бога́тый.

copper n. **1,** (metal) медь. **2,** (coin) медя́к. —adj. ме́дный.

copperhead n. щитомо́рдник.

coppersmith n. ме́дник.

copper sulfate ме́дный купоро́с.

coppice n. = copse.

copra n. ко́пра.

copse n. перелесо́к. Also, **coppice.**

Coptic adj. ко́птский.

copulate v.i. совокупля́ться. —**copulation,** n. совокупле́ние.

copulative adj., gram. соедини́тельный.

copy n. **1,** (duplicate; facsimile) ко́пия. Makes copies of, размножа́ть. Rough copy, чернови́к. **2,** (any of a number of something printed or written) экземпля́р. **3,** (written matter to be printed) материа́л. —v.t. **1,** (transcribe) перепи́сывать; спи́сывать. **2,** (reproduce) копи́ровать; снима́ть ко́пию с. **3,** (imitate) копи́ровать; подража́ть. —v.i. спи́сывать: copy off someone during an examination, спи́сывать у кого́-нибудь на экза́мене. —**copy out,** выпи́сывать.

copyholder n. корре́ктор-подчи́тчик.

copying n. копи́рование; копиро́вка. —**copying machine,** копирова́льная маши́на.

copyist n. перепи́счик; копиро́вщик.

copyright n. а́вторское пра́во.

coquetry n. коке́тство.

coquette n. коке́тка. —**coquettish,** adj. коке́тливый.

coral n. кора́лл. —adj. кора́лловый. —**coral reef,** кора́лловый риф.

cord n. **1,** (string) верёвка. **2,** (electrical wire) шнур. **3,** anat.: vocal cords, голосовы́е свя́зки; spinal cord, спинно́й мозг; umbilical cord, пупови́на. **4,** (rib in fabric) ру́бчик.

cordial adj. серде́чный; раду́шный. —n. ликёр. —**cordiality,** n. серде́чность; раду́шие. —**cordially,** adv. серде́чно; раду́шно.

cordon n. оцепле́ние; кордо́н. —v.t. [usu. **cordon off**] оцепля́ть.

corduroy n. ру́бчатый вельве́т.

core n. **1,** (central part of a fruit) сердцеви́на. **2,** (central portion of the earth) ядро́ (Земли́). **3,** (part of a nuclear reactor) серде́чник. **4,** fig. (essence) суть; ядро́: the core of the matter, суть/ядро́ де́ла. —**to the core,** до конца́ ногте́й; до мо́зга косте́й. Rotten to the core, наскво́зь прогни́вший.

coreligionist n. единове́рец.

coriander n. кориа́ндр. —adj. кориа́ндровый.

Corinthian adj. кори́нфский. Corinthian columns, кори́нфские коло́нны.

cork n. про́бка. —adj. про́бковый. —v.t. заку́поривать. —**cork oak,** про́бковый дуб.

corkscrew n. што́пор.

cormorant n. бакла́н.

corn n. **1,** (cereal grain or its kernels) кукуру́за. **2,** Brit. (grain) зерно́. **3,** (callus) мозо́ль. —adj. кукуру́зный.

corn crake коросте́ль; дерга́ч.

cornea n. рогова́я оболо́чка; рогови́ца.

corned beef солони́на.

corner n. **1,** (of a room) у́гол: in the corner, в углу́. **2,** (street corner) у́гол: on the corner, на углу́. Around the corner, за угло́м. Turn the corner, заверну́ть or поверну́ть за́ угол. The third house from the corner, тре́тий дом от угла́. **3,** (remote region) уголо́к: from all corners of the world, со всех уголко́в ми́ра. —adj. углово́й: corner room, углова́я ко́мната. —v.t. **1,** (force into a corner) загоня́ть в у́гол. **2,** comm. монополизи́ровать. —**cut corners,** уре́зывать расхо́ды; эконо́мить. —**just around the corner,** на носу́: Spring is just around the corner, весна́ на носу́. —**watch someone out of the corner of one's eye,** смотре́ть на кого́-нибудь и́скоса. —**see something out of the corner of one's eye,** ви́деть что́-нибудь кра́ем гла́за.

cornerstone n. краеуго́льный ка́мень.

cornet n. корне́т.

cornfield n. кукуру́зное по́ле.

corn flakes кукуру́зные хло́пья.

cornflower n. василёк.

cornice n. карни́з.

cornmeal n. кукуру́зная мука́.

corn oil кукуру́зное ма́сло.

cornstalk n. кукуру́зный сте́бель.

cornucopia n. рог изоби́лия.

corny *adj., colloq.* бана́льный; изби́тый.

corolla *n.* ве́нчик.

corollary *n.* вы́вод.

corona *n.* коро́на; вене́ц.

coronary *adj.* вене́чный: *coronary artery,* вене́чная арте́рия. —*n.* [*also,* **coronary thrombosis**] заку́порка арте́рий.

coronation *n.* венча́ние (на ца́рство); корона́ция.

coroner *n.* ме́дик суде́бной эксперти́зы.

coronet *n.* **1,** (small crown) коро́на. **2,** (jeweled headband) диаде́ма.

corporal *n.* капра́л. —*adj.* теле́сный: *corporal punishment,* теле́сное наказа́ние.

corporate *adj.* **1,** (pert. to a corporation) корпорати́вный. **2,** (joint; common) совме́стный.

corporation *n.* **1,** (company) корпора́ция. **2,** *colloq.* (paunch) брюшко́; пу́зо.

corporative *adj.* корпорати́вный.

corporeal *adj.* теле́сный.

corps *n.* **1,** (large army unit) ко́рпус. **2,** (specialized branch of the armed forces) слу́жба: *signal corps,* слу́жба свя́зи. *Marine Corps,* морска́я пехо́та. **3,** (body of people) ко́рпус: *diplomatic corps,* дипломати́ческий ко́рпус. —**corps de ballet,** кордебале́т.

corpse *n.* труп.

corpsman *n.* санита́р.

corpulent *adj.* доро́дный; ту́чный; гру́зный. —**corpulence,** *n.* полнота́; доро́дность; ту́чность.

corpuscle *n., usu. pl.* кровяны́е тельца́; кровяны́е ша́рики.

corpus delicti соста́в преступле́ния.

corral *n.* заго́н. —*v.t.* загоня́ть; вгоня́ть; сгоня́ть.

correct *v.t.* исправля́ть; поправля́ть: *correct an error,* исправля́ть/поправля́ть оши́бку. *Correct a pupil,* поправля́ть ученика́. *Correct an examination,* проверя́ть экзаменацио́нные рабо́ты. —*adj.* **1,** (right; accurate) пра́вильный; ве́рный: *the correct answer,* пра́вильный/ве́рный отве́т. *You are correct,* вы пра́вы. **2,** (proper, as of behavior) корре́ктный.

correction *n.* попра́вка; исправле́ние: *make corrections,* вноси́ть попра́вки/исправле́ния. *Course correction,* попра́вка к ку́рсу. —**house of correction,** исправи́тельный дом.

corrective *adj.* исправи́тельный.

correctly *adv.* пра́вильно; ве́рно. —**correctness,** *n.* пра́вильность; правота́.

correlate *v.t.* соотноси́ть. —*v.i.* соотноси́ться. —**correlation,** *n.* соотноше́ние.

correlative *adj.* соотноси́тельный.

correspond *v.i.* **1,** *fol. by* **to** (match; conform) соотве́тствовать (+ *dat.*). **2,** (write letters) перепи́сываться: *correspond with an old friend,* перепи́сываться со ста́рым дру́гом.

correspondence *n.* **1,** (agreement; similarity) соотве́тствие. **2,** (communication by letters) перепи́ска; корреспонде́нция. *Maintain a correspondence with,* подде́рживать перепи́ску с. —**correspondence course,** курс зао́чного обуче́ния; *pl.* зао́чные ку́рсы.

correspondent *n.* корреспонде́нт.

corresponding *adj.* соотве́тствующий.

corridor *n.* коридо́р. *In the corridors,* в кулуа́рах. *The corridors of power,* коридо́ры вла́сти.

corroborate *v.t.* подтвержда́ть. —**corroboration,** *n.* подтвержде́ние.

corrode *v.t.* разъеда́ть; выеда́ть. —*v.i.* ржа́веть.

corrosion *n.* корро́зия.

corrosive *adj.* е́дкий. —*n.* е́дкое вещество́. —**corrosive sublimate,** сулема́.

corrosiveness *n.* е́дкость.

corrugate *v.t.* гофрирова́ть. —**corrugated,** *adj.* гофриро́ванный; рифлёный.

corrupt *adj.* прода́жный; коррумпи́рованный. —*v.t.* развраща́ть; разлага́ть: *corrupt young people,* развраща́ть/разлага́ть молодёжь. *Corrupt the language with foreign words,* засоря́ть язы́к иностра́нными слова́ми.

corruption *n.* **1,** (act of perverting) развраще́ние. **2,** (graft) корру́пция.

corsage *n.* буке́т.

corsair *n.* корса́р.

corset *n.* корсе́т.

Corsican *adj.* корсика́нский.

cortege *n.* **1,** (procession) корте́ж. **2,** (retinue) сви́та.

cortex *n.* **1,** (bark) кора́. **2,** (of the brain) кора́ головно́го мо́зга.

cortisone *n.* кортизо́н.

corundum *n.* кору́нд; алма́зный шпат.

coruscate *v.i.* сверка́ть; блиста́ть.

corvette *n.* корве́т.

cosecant *n.* косе́канс.

cosine *n.* ко́синус.

cosmetic *n., usu. pl.* косме́тика. —*adj.* космети́ческий.

cosmetology *n.* косме́тика.

cosmic *adj.* косми́ческий. —**cosmic dust,** косми́ческая пыль. —**cosmic rays,** косми́ческие лучи́.

cosmogony *n.* космого́ния.

cosmology *n.* космоло́гия.

cosmonaut *n.* космона́вт.

cosmopolitan *adj.* космополити́ческий. —*n.* [*also,* **cosmopolite**] космополи́т. —**cosmopolitanism,** *n.* космополити́зм.

cosmos *n.* ко́смос.

Cossack *n.* каза́к. —*adj.* каза́цкий.

cost *n.* **1,** (amount paid; price) сто́имость: *cost of living,* сто́имость жи́зни. *The high/low cost of housing,* дорогови́зна/дешеви́зна жилья́. *Whatever the cost,* чего́ бы э́то ни сто́ило. *At the cost of,* цено́й (+ *gen.*). **2,** *usu. pl.* (amount spent in manufacturing or operating something) изде́ржки; расхо́ды. *Production costs,* изде́ржки произво́дства. *Fuel costs,* изде́ржки на то́пливо. *Overhead costs,* накладны́е расхо́ды. *Sell something at cost,* прода́ть что́-нибудь по себесто́имости. —*v.t. & i.* сто́ить; обходи́ться: *How much does it cost?,* ско́лько э́то сто́ит? *Cost someone dearly,* до́рого обходи́ться (+ *dat.*). *It cost him his life,* э́то сто́ило ему́ жи́зни. —**at all costs,** во что бы то ни ста́ло. —**to one's cost,** на свою́ беду́; на своё го́ре; на свою́ го́лову.

costly *adj.* дорого́й; дорогосто́ящий.

costume *n.* костю́м. —**costume designer,** костюме́р. —**costume jewelry,** бижуте́рия. —**costume party,** костюми́рованный бал.

cosy *adj.* = **cozy.**

cot *n.* расклаȩу́шка.

cotangent *n.* кота́нгенс.

coterie *n.* кружо́к.

cotillion *n.* котильо́н.

cottage *n.* котте́дж; до́мик; да́ча.

cottage cheese творо́г.

cottage industry куста́рный про́мысел; куста́рное произво́дство.

cotton *n.* **1,** (cloth) бума́жная ткань; хлопчато-бума́жная ткань. **2,** (plant from which it comes) хлопча́тник; хло́пок. **3,** (fibers of this plant) хло́пок. *Pick cotton,* собира́ть хло́пок. **4,** (absorbent cotton) ва́та. —*adj.* **1,** (pert. to the plant) хло́пковый: *cotton fiber,* хло́пковое волокно́. **2,** (made of cotton) бума́жный; хлопчатобума́жный; си́тцевый. —**cotton gin,** хлопкоочисти́тельная маши́на. —**cotton picker,** сбо́рщик хло́пка.

cottonseed *n.* хло́пковое се́мя. —**cottonseed oil,** хло́пковое ма́сло.

cotyledon *n.* семядо́ля.

couch *n.* куше́тка; дива́н. —*v.t.* (word) облека́ть: *couch in diplomatic language,* облека́ть в дипломати́ческие выраже́ния.

cougar *n.* кугуа́р.

cough *n.* ка́шель. *Cough medicine,* лека́рство *or* микст́ра от ка́шля. —*v.i.* ка́шлять. —**cough up,** отха́ркивать: *cough up phlegm,* отха́ркивать мокро́ту. *Cough up the money,* раскоше́литься.

could *v.aux.* **1,** *past tense of* **can:** *I couldn't have done it without you,* без тебя́ я не мог (могла́) бы э́того сде́лать. **2,** *used in polite requests: Could you tell me the time?,* вы не ска́жете кото́рый час? *Could you lend me a dollar?,* не мо́жете ли вы (*or* не могли́ бы вы) одолжи́ть мне до́ллар?

coulomb *n.* куло́н.

council *n.* **1,** (assembly) сове́т: *city council,* городско́й сове́т. *Council of ministers,* сове́т мини́стров. **2,** *relig.* собо́р: *the Council of Trent,* Триде́нтский собо́р. —**councilman,** *n.* член сове́та.

counsel *n.* **1,** (advice) сове́т. **2,** (lawyer) адвока́т. —*v.t.* сове́товать. —**keep one's own counsel,** храни́ть молча́ние. —**take counsel with,** совеща́ться с.

counselor *also,* **counsellor** *n.* **1,** (adviser) сове́тник. **2,** (lawyer) адвока́т.

count *v.t.* **1,** (add up; total) счита́ть (*pfv.* сосчита́ть): *count the money/votes,* (со)счита́ть де́ньги/голоса́. *Count the days,* счита́ть дни. *Count your change!,* прове́рьте сда́чу! **2,** (regard as; consider) счита́ть (*pfv.* счесть): *I count him among my friends,* я счита́ю его́ одни́м из мои́х друзе́й. —*v.i.* **1,** (name numbers in sequence) счита́ть: *count to ten,* счита́ть до десяти́. **2,** (be of significance) име́ть значе́ние; зна́чить: *count for little,* име́ть ма́ло значе́ния; ма́ло зна́чить. *Count for nothing,* не име́ть никако́го значе́ния. *That does not count,* э́то не

счита́ется; э́то не в счёт. *That will count against you,* э́то бу́дет говори́ть не в ва́шу по́льзу. *Every minute counts,* ка́ждая мину́та на счету́. **3,** (be valid; be official) засчи́тываться: *The goal did not count,* гол не засчи́тывался. **4,** *fol. by* **on** (rely on) рассчи́тывать (на); де́лать ста́вку (на). —*n.* **1,** (act of counting) счёт: *by my count,* по моему́ счёту. *Lose count of,* потеря́ть счёт (+ *dat.*). **2,** *law* пункт обвине́ния: *guilty on all counts,* вино́вный по всем пу́нктам обвине́ния. **3,** (nobleman) граф. —**count in,** включа́ть. —**count off,** отсчи́тывать. —**count out, 1,** (count while handing over) отсчи́тывать. **2,** (disregard; exclude) сбра́сывать со счето́в. —**not counting,** не счита́я; е́сли не счита́ть.

countdown *n.* обра́тный отсчёт вре́мени.

countenance *n.* **1,** (facial expression) выраже́ние лица́; ми́на. **2,** (composure) самооблада́ние. **3,** (approval) одобре́ние. —*v.t.* **1,** (approve) одобря́ть. **2,** (tolerate) терпе́ть.

counter *n.* **1,** (one who counts; device that records) счётчик. **2,** (flat surface for selling goods) прила́вок; (for serving food) сто́йка. **3,** (token) фи́шка; жето́н. —*adv. Run counter to,* идти́ вразре́з с. —*v.t.* пари́ровать. —**under the counter,** из-под прила́вка; из-под полы́.

counteract *v.t.* противоде́йствовать (+ *dat.*). —**counteraction,** *n.* противоде́йствие.

counterattack *n.* контрата́ка. —*v.t. & i.* контратакова́ть.

counterbalance *n.* противове́с. —*v.t.* уравнове́шивать.

counterblow *n.* встре́чный уда́р; контруда́р.

countercharge *n.* встре́чное обвине́ние.

counterclockwise *adv.* про́тив часово́й стре́лки.

counterespionage *n.* контрразве́дка.

counterfeit *adj.* подде́льный; подло́жный; фальши́вый. —*v.t.* подде́лывать. —*n.* подде́лка. —**counterfeiter,** *n.* подде́лыватель; фальшивомоне́тчик.

counterfoil *n.* корешо́к.

counterintelligence *n.* контрразве́дка.

counterman *n.* буфе́тчик.

countermand *v.t.* отменя́ть (прика́з).

countermeasure *n.* контрме́ра.

counteroffensive *n.* контрнаступле́ние.

counteroffer *n.* контрпредложе́ние.

counterpane *n.* покрыва́ло.

counterpart *n.* колле́га; собра́т. *The Trade Minister conferred with his Japanese counterpart,* мини́стр торго́вли совеща́лся со свои́м япо́нским колле́гой. *The African elephant is larger than its Asian counterpart,* африка́нский слон крупне́е своего́ азиа́тского собра́та.

counterpoint *n.* контрапу́нкт.

counterpoise *n.* противове́с.

counterproposal *n.* контрпредложе́ние.

counterrevolution *n.* контрреволю́ция.

counterrevolutionary *adj.* контрреволюцио́нный. —*n.* контрреволюционе́р.

countersign *v.t.* скрепля́ть. —*n.* паро́ль; про́пуск.

countersignature *n.* скре́па.

counterstroke *n.* контруда́р.

countersuit *n.* встре́чный иск.

counterweight *n.* противове́с.

countess *n.* графи́ня.

countless *adj.* бесчи́сленный; несчётный; неисчисли́мый.

country *n.* **1,** (nation) страна́. **2,** (land of one's birth or allegiance) ро́дина: *love one's country,* люби́ть свою́ ро́дину. **3,** (rural area) дере́вня: *live in the country,* жить в дере́вне. **4,** (region of a specified character) ме́стность: *hilly country,* холми́стая ме́стность. —*adj.* дереве́нский: *country life,* дереве́нская жизнь.

countryman *n.* сооте́чественник; земля́к.

countryside *n.* дере́вня; се́льская ме́стность.

county *n.* (in the U.S.) о́круг; (in Great Britain) гра́фство.

coup *n.* **1,** (brilliant stroke) ло́вкий *or* блестя́щий уда́р. **2,** (seizure of power) переворо́т: *palace coup,* дворцо́вый переворо́т. —**coup d'état,** госуда́рственный переворо́т.

couple *n.* **1,** (pair) па́ра. **2,** (man and woman) па́ра; па́рочка. *Married couple,* чета́. **3,** *colloq.* (a few; several) *rendered by* не́сколько: *in a couple of days,* че́рез не́сколько дней. —*v.t.* **1,** (hitch together) сцепля́ть. **2,** *fig.* (link) свя́зывать.

coupling *n.* му́фта; сцепле́ние; связь.

coupon *n.* тало́н; купо́н.

courage *n.* хра́брость; му́жество; отва́га. *Summon (up) the courage,* собра́ться с ду́хом.

courageous *adj.* хра́брый; му́жественный; отва́жный. —**courageously,** *adv.* хра́бро; му́жественно; отва́жно.

courier *n.* курье́р; на́рочный.

course *n.* **1,** (direction) курс: *follow a northerly course,* держа́ть курс на се́вер. *Stray off course,* отклоня́ться от ку́рса. *Throw someone off course,* сбить кого́-нибудь с пра́вильного ку́рса. **2,** (series of classes) курс: *history course,* курс исто́рии. *Take a typing course,* пройти́ *or* прослу́шать курс маши́нописи. **3,** (way of proceeding) курс: *course of treatment,* курс лече́ния. *Course of action,* о́браз де́йствий. **4,** (progression) тече́ние; ход: *in the course of,* в тече́ние (+ *gen.*); в хо́де (+ *gen.*). *Course of events,* ход *or* разви́тие собы́тий. *In the course of time,* с тече́нием вре́мени. *Take/run its course,* идти́ свои́м чередо́м. *Change the course of history,* измени́ть тече́ние исто́рии. **5,** (part of a meal) блю́до: *three-course dinner,* обе́д из трёх блюд. **6,** *sports* площа́дка: *golf course,* площа́дка для го́льфа. *Racecourse,* скакова́я доро́жка. —**as a matter of course,** как не́что само́ собо́й разуме́ющееся. *Take as a matter of course,* принима́ть как до́лжное. —**in due course,** в своё вре́мя. —**of course,** коне́чно.

court *n.* **1,** (tribunal) суд: *appear before the court,* предста́ть пе́ред судо́м. *Take to court,* привлека́ть к суду́. *Settle a case out of court,* реши́ть де́ло без суда́. **2,** (courtyard) двор. **3,** (sovereign and his council) двор. **4,** *sports* площа́дка. *Tennis court,* те́ннисный корт. —*adj.* **1,** (pert. to a court of law) суде́бный. **2,** (pert. to the court of a sovereign) придво́рный: *court jester,* придво́рный шут. —*v.t.* **1,** (seek the favor of) зайски́вать пе́ред. **2,** (woo) уха́живать за. **3,** (invite, as trouble) наклика́ть (беду́). —**pay court to,** уха́живать за.

courteous *adj.* ве́жливый; учти́вый; обходи́тельный. —**courteously,** *adv.* ве́жливо.

courtesan *n.* куртиза́нка.

courtesy *n.* **1,** (courteous behavior) ве́жливость; учти́вость. **2,** (helpful act) любе́зность. —**courtesy call,** визи́т ве́жливости.

courthouse *n.* зда́ние суда́.

courtier *n.* придво́рный.

courtly *adj.* ве́жливый; изы́сканный; гала́нтный.

court-martial *n.* вое́нный суд. —*v.t.* суди́ть вое́нным судо́м.

courtroom *n.* зал суда́; зал заседа́ний суда́.

courtship *n.* уха́живание.

courtyard *n.* двор.

cousin *n.* двою́родный брат; двою́родная сестра́. —**second cousin,** трою́родный брат; трою́родная сестра́.

cove *n.* бу́хточка.

covenant *n.* **1,** (agreement) соглаше́ние. **2,** *relig.* заве́т.

cover *v.t.* **1,** (place something over) покрыва́ть; закрыва́ть. *Cover a child with a blanket,* покрыва́ть/закрыва́ть/укрыва́ть ребёнка одея́лом. *Cover one's face with one's hands,* закрыва́ть лицо́ рука́ми. *Cover a pot with a lid,* накрыва́ть *or* прикрыва́ть кастрю́лю кры́шкой. **2,** (lie over) покрыва́ть: *Everything was covered with dust,* всё покры́лось (*or* бы́ло покры́то) пы́лью. **3,** (obscure) затя́гивать: *The sky is covered with clouds,* не́бо затяну́ло (*impers.*). **4,** *fol. by* **up** (conceal) покрыва́ть; скрыва́ть. *Cover up one's tracks,* замета́ть следы́; пря́тать концы́ в во́ду. **5,** (upholster) обива́ть; обтя́гивать. **6,** *mil.* прикрыва́ть: *cover a landing/retreat,* прикрыва́ть вы́садку/отступле́ние. **7,** (report on, as a newspaper story) освеща́ть. **8,** (include; take in) охва́тывать. **9,** (provide for, as a law, contract, etc.) предусма́тривать. **10,** (defray, as expenses) покрыва́ть; окупа́ть (расхо́ды). **11,** (insure) застрахо́вывать: *covered against fire,* застрахо́ван от огня́. **12,** (traverse, as a distance) проходи́ть; проезжа́ть; покрыва́ть. **13,** *cards* покрыва́ть. **14,** *Cover oneself with glory,* покрыва́ть себя́ сла́вой. —*n.* **1,** (lid) кры́шка. **2,** (something that covers) чехо́л: *couch cover,* чехо́л для дива́на. **3,** (blanket) одея́ло. **4,** (hard cover of a book) переплёт. *Read from cover to cover,* проче́сть от ко́рки до ко́рки *or* от доски́ до доски́. **5,** (soft cover of a book or magazine) обло́жка. **6,** (paper cover to protect a book) обёртка. **7,** (envelope) конве́рт: *under separate cover,* в отде́льном конве́рте. **8,** (shelter) укры́тие; прикры́тие. *Take cover,* укрыва́ться. **9,** (something that provides concealment) покро́в; прикры́тие: *under cover of night,* под покро́вом *or* под прикры́тием но́чи. **10,** (guise; front) прикры́тие. **11,** *mil.* прикры́тие: *air cover,* прикры́тие авиа́цией.

coverage *n.* **1,** (treatment in the media) освеще́ние: *extensive coverage in the press,* широ́кое освеще́ние в печа́ти. **2,** (insurance) (страхово́е) покры́тие.

covered *adj.* кры́тый; закры́тый. —**covered wagon,** кры́тая пово́зка; кры́тый фурго́н; киби́тка.

covering *n.* покры́тие; покро́в. —**covering letter,** сопроводи́тельное письмо́.

coverlet *n.* покрыва́ло.

covert *adj.* скры́тый.

covet *v.t.* жа́ждать; за́риться на. —**coveted,** *adj.* вожделе́нный. —**covetous,** *adj.* жа́дный.

covey *n.* **1,** (flock) ста́я. **2,** (bevy) гру́ппа.

cow *n.* **1,** (farm animal) коро́ва. **2,** (female of certain other animals) са́мка. —*adj.* [*also,* **cow's**] коро́вий: *cow's milk,* коро́вье молоко́. —*v.t.* (intimidate) запу́гивать.

coward *n.* трус. —**cowardice,** *n.* тру́сость. —**cowardly,** *adj.* трусли́вый.

cowberry *n.* брусни́ка.

cowboy *n.* ковбо́й. —*adj.* ковбо́йский: *cowboy hat,* ковбо́йская шля́па.

cower *v.i.* приседа́ть (от стра́ха).

cowhide *n.* **1,** (hide of a cow) коро́вья шку́ра. **2,** (leather) воло́вья ко́жа.

cowl *n.* **1,** (monk's hood) капюшо́н. **2,** *mech.* (cover; hood) колпа́к; капо́т.

cowling *n.* капо́т.

cowpox *n.* коро́вья о́спа.

cowshed *n.* коро́вник.

coy *adj.* **1,** (shy) засте́нчивый. **2,** (feigning shyness) жема́нный.

coyote *n.* лугово́й волк; койо́т.

coypu *n.* ну́трия.

cozy *also,* **cosy** *adj.* ую́тный.

crab *n.* **1,** (shellfish) краб. **2,** *colloq.* (grouch) брюзга́. —*v.i., colloq.* (complain) ворча́ть; ныть.

crab apple ди́кое я́блоко.

crabby *adj., colloq.* злой; брюзгли́вый.

crack *v.i.* **1,** (split) дать тре́щину; тре́снуть; тре́скаться. **2,** (make a sharp, snapping sound) треща́ть; тре́снуть. **3,** (break, as of one's voice) лома́ться. **4,** (break down) не вы́держать: *crack under the strain,* не вы́держать напряже́ния. —*v.t.* **1,** (break open) коло́ть; раска́лывать; щёлкать (оре́хи); разбива́ть (я́йца). **2,** (make a crack in) де́лать тре́щину в; надла́мывать. **3,** (snap, as a whip) щёлкать (кнуто́м). **4,** *colloq.* (utter, as a joke) отпуска́ть. **5,** (break into, as a safe) взла́мывать. **6,** (break, as a code) разга́дывать. —*n.* **1,** (fissure) тре́щина: *crack in the wall,* тре́щина в стене́. **2,** (slight opening) щель; щёлка. *Watch something through a crack in the fence,* смотре́ть на что́-нибудь че́рез щель в забо́ре. *Open the window a crack,* приоткрыва́ть окно́. **3,** (sound) щелчо́к; треск. *Crack of a whip,* щелчо́к кнута́. **4,** *colloq.* (attempt) попы́тка. *Take a crack at,* попыта́ться (+ *inf.*); про́бовать свои́ си́лы в *or* на. **5,** *colloq.* (remark) остро́та. **6,** *At the crack of dawn,* чуть свет. —*adj., colloq.* отбо́рный: *crack regiment,* отбо́рный полк. —**crack down on,** принима́ть круты́е ме́ры про́тив; приструнивать.

—**crack up, 1,** (have a breakdown) надла́мываться. **2,** *colloq.* (become convulsed with laughter) ло́паться от сме́ха; надрыва́ть живо́т (со смеху).

cracked *adj.* **1,** (split) надтре́снутый. **2,** *colloq.* (nutty) тро́нутый.

cracker *n.* **1,** (biscuit) гале́та; суха́рь. **2,** (party favor) хлопу́шка.

crackerjack *adj., colloq.* отли́чный; блестя́щий.

crackle *v.i.* треща́ть; тре́снуть; потре́скивать. —*n.* треск; трескотня́; треща́ние.

crackling *n.* **1,** (sound) треск; трескотня́; треща́ние. **2,** *pl.* (crisp remains of fat after rendering) шква́рки.

crackpot *n., slang* сумасбро́д.

cradle *n.* колыбе́ль.

craft *n.* **1,** (trade) ремесло́. **2,** (boat) су́дно. —**craft union,** цехово́й профсою́з.

craftsman *n.* **1,** (one engaged in a craft) реме́сленник. **2,** (skilled artisan) ма́стер. —**craftsmanship,** *n.* мастерство́.

crafty *adj.* хи́трый; лука́вый.

crag *n.* скала́; утёс. —**craggy,** *adj.* скали́стый; утёсистый.

crake *n.* ку́рочка.

cram *v.t.* **1,** (stuff into insufficient space) вти́скивать; впи́хивать; запи́хивать. **2,** (fill beyond normal capacity) набива́ть. —*v.i., colloq.* (study) зубри́ть. —**crammer,** *n.* зубри́ла.

cramp *n.* **1,** (muscle spasm) су́дорога. *I have a cramp in my leg,* у меня́ свело́ но́гу. **2,** *pl.* (sharp abdominal pains) схва́тки. *Stomach cramps,* схва́тки *or* ре́зи в животе́. —*v.t.* **1,** (cause a cramp in) своди́ть. **2,** (confine; restrain) стесня́ть.

cramped *adj.* те́сный. *We're rather cramped in here,* нам здесь теснова́то.

cranberry *n.* клю́ква. —*adj.* клю́квенный: *cranberry juice,* клю́квенный сок.

crane *n.* **1,** (bird) жура́вль. **2,** (derrick) подъёмный кран. —*v.t., in* **crane one's neck,** вытя́гивать ше́ю.

crane fly долгоно́жка.

cranium *n.* че́реп; черепна́я коро́бка. —**cranial,** *adj.* черепно́й.

crank *n.* **1,** (device) кривоши́п; (*for starting a car*) заводна́я рукоя́тка. **2,** *colloq.* (eccentric) чуда́к. **3,** *colloq.* (grouch) брюзга́. —*v.t.* **1,** *usu. fol. by* **up** (start with a crank) заводи́ть. **2,** *fol. by* **out** (produce mechanically) фабрикова́ть; штампова́ть.

crankcase *n.* ка́ртер.

crankshaft *n.* коле́нчатый вал.

cranky *adj.* брюзгли́вый.

cranny *n.* закоу́лок: *every nook and cranny,* все закоу́лки.

craps *n.* игра́ в ко́сти.

crash *v.i.* **1,** *fol. by* **into** (smash into) вре́заться (в). *Crash into each other,* ста́лкиваться. **2,** (fall with great noise) ру́шиться; ру́хнуть. *Come crashing down,* обвали́ться с гро́хотом. **3,** (of an airplane) разби́ться; упа́сть; потерпе́ть ава́рию. *Crash during takeoff,* разби́ться при взлёте. *Crash into a mountain,* вре́заться в го́ру. **4,** (of the stock market) потерпе́ть крах. —*v.t.* **1,** (smash) разбива́ть.

2, *colloq.* (come uninvited to) напроси́ться на. —*n.* **1,** (sound) гро́хот. *Fall with a crash,* упа́сть с гро́хотом. **2,** (collision; wreck) ава́рия; круше́ние; катастро́фа; ги́бель. *Plane crash,* авиацио́нная катастро́фа. **3,** (financial collapse) крах. —*adj.* уда́рный: *crash program,* уда́рная програ́мма. *Crash course,* уско́ренный *or* интенси́вный курс. —**crash helmet,** защи́тный шлем. —**crash landing,** авари́йная поса́дка.

crass *adj.* гру́бый.

crate *n.* я́щик. —*v.t.* упако́вывать в я́щик.

crater *n.* **1,** (of a volcano or on the moon) кра́тер. **2,** (resulting from a bomb) воро́нка.

crave *v.t.* жа́ждать.

craven *adj.* трусли́вый; малоду́шный.

craving *n.* жа́жда; стра́стное жела́ние.

craw *n.* зоб.

crawfish *n.* рак. *Also,* **crayfish.**

crawl *v.i.* **1,** (creep) ползти́. *Crawl in,* вполза́ть. *Crawl into,* вполза́ть в (+ *acc.*). *Crawl out,* выполза́ть. **2,** *fol. by* **with** (swarm; teem) кише́ть (+ *instr.*). —*n.,* swimming кроль. —**at a crawl,** черепа́шьим ша́гом.

crawler *n.* **1,** (one who crawls, esp. a baby) ползу́н; ползуно́к. **2,** (baby's garment) ползунки́.

crayfish *n.* = **crawfish.**

crayon *n.* цветно́й каранда́ш.

craze *n.* ма́ния. —*v.t.* доводи́ть до бе́шенства. —**crazed,** *adj.* бе́шеный; озвере́лый.

crazily *adv.* как сумасше́дший.

craziness *n.* глу́пость; безу́мие.

crazy *adj.* сумасше́дший; безу́мный. *Crazy about,* без ума́ от. *Drive crazy,* своди́ть с ума́; выводи́ть из себя́; доводи́ть до безу́мия. *Crazy prices,* сумасше́дшие це́ны. —**like crazy,** *colloq.* ужа́сно; безу́мно. *Run like crazy,* бежа́ть во все лопа́тки.

creak *v.i.* скрипе́ть. —*n.* скрип. —**creaky,** *adj.* скрипу́чий.

cream *n.* **1,** (part of milk) сли́вки. *Sour cream,* смета́на. *Whipped cream,* взби́тые сли́вки. **2,** (substance, as for a cake, for the face, etc.) крем. *Shaving cream,* крем для бритья́. *Cold cream,* кольдкре́м. **3,** *fig.* (best part) сли́вки: *the cream of society,* сли́вки о́бщества. —*adj.* **1,** (of or for cream) сли́вочный. **2,** (cream-colored) кре́мовый.

cream cheese сли́вочный сыр.

creamer *n.* сли́вочник.

creamery *n.* маслобо́йня; маслозаво́д.

cream of tartar ви́нный ка́мень.

creamy *adj.* сли́вочный.

crease *n.* скла́дка. —*v.t.* **1,** (wrinkle) мять. **2,** (graze) задева́ть: *The bullet creased his shoulder,* пу́ля заде́ла его́ в плечо́. —*v.i.* мя́ться: *crease easily,* легко́ мя́ться.

create *v.t.* создава́ть; твори́ть. *Create a work of art,* создава́ть произведе́ние иску́сства. *Create difficulties,* создава́ть тру́дности. *Create an impression,* создава́ть впечатле́ние. *Create doubts,* вызыва́ть сомне́ния. *God created the world,* Бог сотвори́л мир.

creation *n.* **1,** (act of creating) сотворе́ние; созда́ние. *Creation of the world,* сотворе́ние ми́ра. *Creation of*

capital, созда́ние капита́ла. **2,** (something created) творе́ние; созда́ние.

creative *adj.* тво́рческий; созида́тельный. —**creativity,** *n.* тво́рческая си́ла.

creator *n.* творе́ц; созда́тель.

creature *n.* существо́; созда́ние.

credence *n.* ве́ра. *Give/lend credence to; put/place credence in,* ве́рить; дава́ть ве́ру (+ *dat.*).

credentials *n.pl.* вери́тельные гра́моты. —**credentials committee,** манда́тная коми́ссия.

credibility *n.* **1,** (of a story or account) вероя́тность; правдоподо́бие. **2,** (of a person) надёжность; дове́рие к себе́.

credible *adj.* **1,** (plausible) вероя́тный; правдоподо́бный. **2,** (who can be believed) заслу́живающий дове́рия.

credit *n.* **1,** (credence) ве́ра. *Place credit in,* ве́рить. **2,** (praise; commendation) похвала́: *He deserves a lot of credit,* он о́чень досто́ин похвалы́. *Give credit to,* отдава́ть до́лжное *or* справедли́вость (+ *dat.*). *Give someone credit for something,* отдава́ть (+ *dat.*) до́лжное за (+ *acc.*); ста́вить что́-нибудь в заслу́гу (+ *dat.*). *Take credit for,* припи́сывать себе́. *Chief credit goes to...,* гла́вная заслу́га принадлежи́т (+ *dat.*). **3,** (favor; honor; reputation) честь: *To his credit it must be said that...,* к его́ че́сти на́до сказа́ть, что... *He is a credit to his profession,* он де́лает честь свое́й профе́ссии. *Have to one's credit,* име́ть на своём счету́. **4,** *comm.* креди́т: *buy on credit,* купи́ть в креди́т. *Grant credit(s) to,* предоставля́ть креди́т(ы) (+ *dat.*). *Millions of dollars in credits,* креди́ты на миллио́ны до́лларов. **5,** *bookkeeping* кре́дит. —*adj.* креди́тный. —*v.t.* **1,** (believe) ве́рить; доверя́ть. **2,** (attribute): *credit one's success to hard work,* объясня́ть свой успе́х упо́рным трудо́м. *He is credited with having invented the telescope,* ему́ принадлежи́т приорите́т в изобрете́нии телеско́па. **3,** (apply, as to an account) запи́сывать в креди́т (на чей-нибудь счёт). **4,** *bookkeeping* (enter on the credit side) прихо́довать.

creditable *adj.* похва́льный.

credit card креди́тная ка́рточка.

creditor *n.* кредито́р.

creditworthy *adj.* кредитоспосо́бный.

credo *n.* кре́до.

credulity *n.* легкове́рие. —**credulous,** *adj.* легкове́рный.

creed *n.* **1,** (credo) си́мвол ве́ры; кре́до. *The Apostles' Creed,* апо́стольский си́мвол ве́ры. **2,** (one's religion) вероиспове́дание.

creek *n.* **1,** (brook) руче́й. **2,** (inlet) за́водь; зато́н.

creel *n.* ве́рша.

creep *v.i.* **1,** (crawl) ползти́. **2,** (sneak) кра́сться. **3,** (of plants) ползти́; стла́ться. —**creep in, 1,** (sneak in) вкра́дываться; залеза́ть. **2,** *fig.* (of doubts, errors, etc.) вкра́дываться; закра́дываться. —**creep up** подкра́дываться. —**make one's flesh creep,** приводи́ть в содрога́ние.

creeper *n.* **1,** (plant) ползу́чее расте́ние. **2,** (bird) пищу́ха.

creeps *n.pl., colloq.* содрога́ние. *It gives me the creeps,* у меня́ мура́шки бе́гают по спине́; у меня́ моро́з по ко́же подира́ет.

cremate *v.t.* креми́ровать. —**cremation,** *n.* крема́ция. —**crematorium,** *n.* кремато́рий.

crenelated *also,* **crenellated** *adj.* зубча́тый.

Creole *n.* крео́л. —*adj.* крео́льский.

creosote *n.* креозо́т.

crepe *n.* креп; флёр. —*adj.* кре́повый.

crescendo *n.* креще́ндо.

crescent *n.* полуме́сяц; серп луны́.

cress *n.* кресс.

crest *n.* **1,** (comb of a bird) гре́бень; (feathered tuft) хохо́л. **2,** (top, as of a wave or hill) гре́бень. —**crested,** *adj.* хохла́тый.

crestfallen *adj.* уби́тый; приши́бленный; как в во́ду опу́щенный.

cretaceous *adj.* мелово́й.

cretin *n.* крети́н. —**cretinism,** *n.* кретини́зм.

cretonne *n.* крето́н. —*adj.* крето́новый; крето́нный.

crevice *n.* расще́лина.

crew *n.* **1,** (of a ship, plane, etc.) экипа́ж; кома́нда. *Train crew,* поездна́я брига́да. **2,** (group of workers) брига́да: *construction crew,* строи́тельная брига́да. *Film crew,* съёмочная гру́ппа. **3,** *mil.* расчёт: *gun crew,* оруди́йный расчёт.

crew cut ёжик: *in a crew cut,* ёжиком.

crib *n.* **1,** (child's bed) де́тская крова́ть. **2,** (feeding trough) я́сли. **3,** (bin for storing grain) ларь; за́кром. **4,** *colloq.* (concealed student's notes) шпарга́лка. —*v.i.* спи́сывать (у кого́-нибудь).

crick *n.* спазм; су́дорога.

cricket *n.* **1,** (insect) сверчо́к. **2,** (game) кри́кет.

crier *n.* [*usu.* **town crier**] глаша́тай.

crime *n.* **1,** (criminal act) преступле́ние. **2,** (criminality) престу́пность: *the increase in crime,* рост престу́пности.

Crimean *adj.* кры́мский. —**Crimean War,** Кры́мская война́.

criminal *n.* престу́пник. —*adj.* **1,** (constituting a crime) престу́пный: *criminal negligence,* престу́пная небре́жность. **2,** (pert. to the administration of penal law) уголо́вный: *criminal law,* уголо́вное пра́во.

criminology *n.* криминоло́гия. —**criminologist,** *n.* кримино́лог.

crimp *v.t.* **1,** (press into small folds) гофрирова́ть. **2,** (curl, as hair) завива́ть. —*n., in* **put a crimp in,** *colloq.* расстра́ивать (*e.g.* пла́ны).

crimson *adj.* мали́новый; багро́вый. —*n.* мали́новый цвет; багря́нец.

cringe *v.i.* **1,** (cower) съёживаться. **2,** (fawn) лебези́ть; раболе́пствовать.

crinkle *v.t.* мо́рщить.

cripple *n.* кале́ка. —*v.t.* **1,** (make a cripple of) кале́чить. **2,** (deal a crippling blow to) разруша́ть. *Cripple the economy,* расша́тывать хозя́йство. *Crippling blow,* сокруши́тельный уда́р.

crisis *n.* **1,** (general term) кри́зис: *energy crisis,* энерге́тический кри́зис. **2,** *med.* криз: *hypertension crisis,* гипертони́ческий криз.

crisp *adj.* **1,** (firm and fresh) хрустя́щий. *Crisp bill,* хрустя́щая купю́ра. **2,** (invigorating) бодря́щий; живи́тельный. **3,** (terse; pithy) чека́нный. —**burn to a crisp,** сгоре́ть дотла́.

crisscross *v.t.* перекре́щивать. —*v.i.* перекре́щиваться. —*adv.* крест-на́крест.

criterion *n.* крите́рий; мери́ло.

critic *n.* кри́тик. *Film critic,* кинокри́тик.

critical *adj.* **1,** (containing criticism) крити́ческий. **2,** (crucial) крити́ческий; отве́тственный; перело́мный. **3,** (extremely serious) крити́ческий.

critically *adv.* **1,** (gravely) тяжело́: *critically ill/wounded,* тяжело́ бо́лен/ра́нен. **2,** (vitally) жи́зненно: *critically important,* жи́зненно ва́жный.

criticism *n.* кри́тика: *criticism of his policies,* кри́тика его́ поли́тики. *Criticism of the government/president,* кри́тика в а́дрес (*or* по а́дресу) прави́тельства/президе́нта.

criticize *v.t.* критикова́ть; подверга́ть кри́тике.

critique *n.* реце́нзия; крити́ческий разбо́р.

croak *v.i.* ква́кать. —*n.* ква́канье.

Croat *n.* хорва́т. —**Croatian,** *adj.* хорва́тский.

crochet *v.t. & i.* вяза́ть (крючко́м).

crock *n.* гли́няный сосу́д.

crockery *n.* гли́няная посу́да.

crocodile *n.* крокоди́л. —*adj.* крокоди́ловый. —**crocodile tears,** крокоди́ловы слёзы.

crocus *n.* кро́кус.

crony *n.* дружо́к; ко́реш. —**cronyism,** *n.* протекциони́зм.

crook *n.* **1,** (bend) сгиб: *the crook of one's arm,* сгиб ло́ктя. **2,** (staff) по́сох: *shepherd's crook,* пасту́ший по́сох. **3,** *colloq.* (swindler) плут.

crooked *adj.* **1,** (not straight) криво́й. **2,** *colloq.* (dishonest) нечи́стый. —**crookedness,** *n.* кривизна́.

croon *v.t. & i.* напева́ть.

crop *n.* **1,** (farm product) культу́ра; посе́в. *Winter crops,* ози́мые культу́ры. *The crops are coming up,* посе́вы всхо́дят. *Crop rotation,* севооборо́т. **2,** (yield) урожа́й: *the corn crop,* урожа́й кукуру́зы. *Crop failure,* неурожа́й. **3,** (whip handle) кнутови́ще. **4,** (craw of a bird) зоб. —*v.t.* стричь: *closely cropped hair,* ко́ротко остри́женные во́лосы. —**crop up,** возника́ть.

croquet *n.* кроке́т.

crosier *also,* **crozier** *n.* по́сох.

cross *n.* **1,** (emblem or representation of same) крест. *Sign of the cross,* кре́стное знаме́ние; крест. *A heavy cross to bear,* тяжёлый крест. **2,** (hybrid) по́месь: *A mule is a cross between a donkey and a female horse,* мул — по́месь осла́ с кобы́лой. —*adj.* **1,** (transverse) попере́чный: *crossbeam,* попере́чная ба́лка. *Cross ventilation,* сквозна́я вентиля́ция. **2,** *in combinations* (involving interchange) перекрёстный: *cross-pollination,* перекрёстное опыле́ние. **3,** (ill-tempered) злой: *He is cross with me,* он зол на меня́. —*v.t.* **1,** (traverse) переходи́ть; переезжа́ть; пересека́ть. *Cross the street,* переходи́ть (че́рез) у́лицу. *Cross the border,* переезжа́ть (че́рез) грани́цу; пересека́ть грани́цу. *Cross a river,* переправля́ться че́рез ре́ку. **2,** (intersect) пересека́ть. **3,** (place cross-wise) скре́щивать: *cross swords*, скре́щивать шпа́ги *or* мечи́. *Cross one's legs*, класть *or* заки́дывать но́гу на́ ногу. **4,** (crossbreed) скре́щивать: *cross a horse with a donkey*, скрести́ть ло́шадь с осло́м. **5,** (double-cross) обма́нывать: *He does not like to be crossed*, он не лю́бит, что́бы его́ обма́нывали. **6,** *Cross one's mind*, приходи́ть в го́лову (+ *dat.*). —*v.i.* **1,** (go to the other side) переходи́ть. **2,** (intersect) пересека́ться. *Our paths did not cross*, на́ши пути́ не пересека́лись. **3,** *Cross in the mail*, размину́ться. —**cross off**, вычёркивать: *cross off the list*, вычёркивать из спи́ска. —**cross oneself**, крести́ться. —**cross out**, зачёркивать. —**cross up**, подводи́ть.

crossbar *n.* **1,** (crossbeam) попере́чина; перекла́дина. **2,** *sports* (for high jumping) пла́нка; (between goal posts) шта́нга.

crossbeam *n.* попере́чная ба́лка; попере́чина; перекла́дина.

crossbill *n.* клёст.

crossbow *n.* самостре́л.

crossbreed *v.t.* скре́щивать. —*n.* по́месь. —**cross-breeding,** *n.* скре́щивание; метиза́ция.

cross-country *adj.* **1,** (across a country) че́рез страну́: *a cross-country flight*, перелёт че́рез страну́. **2,** (across open country): *cross-country race*, кросс. **3,** (able to operate on any terrain) вездехо́дный. *Cross-country vehicle*, вездехо́д.

crosscurrent *n.* попере́чное тече́ние.

cross-cut saw попере́чная пила́.

cross-examination *n.* перекрёстный допро́с. —**cross-examine,** *v.t.* подверга́ть перекрёстному допро́су; допра́шивать.

cross-eye *n.* косогла́зие. —**cross-eyed,** *adj.* косогла́зый; косо́й. *He is slightly cross-eyed*, он слегка́ коси́т.

cross-fertilization *n.* перекрёстное оплодотворе́ние.

crossfire *n.* перекрёстный ого́нь.

crossing *n.* **1,** (act of crossing) перехо́д; перее́зд; перепра́ва. **2,** (place to cross) перехо́д; перее́зд. **3,** (intersection) перекрёсток; скреще́ние. **4,** (railroad crossing) перее́зд.

crosspiece *n.* попере́чина; крестови́на; перемы́чка.

cross-pollination *n.* перекрёстное опыле́ние.

cross-purposes *n.pl., in* **at cross-purposes,** напереко́р друг дру́гу.

cross-reference *n.* перекрёстная ссы́лка.

crossroad *n.* **1,** (road that crosses) попере́чная доро́га. **2,** *pl.* (place of intersection) распу́тье; перепу́тье. —**at the crossroads,** на распу́тье; на перепу́тье.

cross section попере́чное сече́ние; попере́чный разре́з.

crosswalk *n.* перехо́д.

crosswind *n.* боково́й ве́тер.

crosswise *adv.* крестообра́зно; крест-на́крест.

crossword puzzle кроссво́рд.

crotch *n.* проме́жность. *The trousers are tight in the crotch*, брю́ки узки́ в шагу́.

crotchety *adj.* причу́дливый; сварли́вый.

Croton bug пруса́к.

crouch *v.i.* приседа́ть.

croup *n.* круп.

croupier *n.* крупье́.

crouton *n.* грено́к.

crow *n.* воро́на. —*adj.* [*usu.* **crow's**] воро́ний: *crow's nest*, воро́нье гнездо́. —*v.i.* **1,** (cry, as of a rooster) кукаре́кать. **2,** *colloq.* (boast) труби́ть; прокрича́ть. —**as the crow flies,** по прямо́й.

crowbar *n.* лом.

crowd *n.* **1,** (throng; mob) толпа́: *a crowd of people*, толпа́ наро́да. *Avoid crowds*, избега́ть толпы́. **2,** (audience) зри́тели: *The crowd cheered*, зри́тели крича́ли «ура́». *Play to large crowds*, де́лать хоро́шие сбо́ры. **3,** (clique; set) компа́ния: *fall in with a bad crowd*, попа́сть в плоху́ю компа́нию. —*v.t.* **1,** (make uncomfortable) тесни́ть; стесня́ть. *Crowd one's neighbor*, тесни́ть сосе́да. **2,** (fill to excess) заполня́ть: *People crowded the stores*, пу́блика запо́лнила магази́ны. *Crowd a room with furniture*, загроможда́ть *or* заставля́ть ко́мнату ме́белью. **3,** (squeeze; cram) вти́скивать. *Crowd six people into a car*, помеща́ть шесть челове́к в маши́не. **4,** *fol. by* **out** (displace) вытесня́ть. —*v.i.* **1,** *fol. by* **into** (squeeze into) набива́ться в; вти́скиваться в. **2,** *fol. by* **around** (cluster around) обступа́ть; тесни́ться *or* толпи́ться вокру́г. **3,** *fol. by* **together** (gather closely together) толпи́ться; столпи́ться; тесни́ться; стесня́ться.

crowded *adj.* те́сный; лю́дный; перепо́лненный. *It is crowded in here*, здесь те́сно. *The bus was crowded*, авто́бус был перепо́лнен; в авто́бусе бы́ло те́сно. *The stores were crowded*, в магази́нах бы́ло мно́го наро́ду.

crown *n.* **1,** (of a sovereign) коро́на; вене́ц. **2,** (garland; wreath) вено́к. **3,** (of the head) те́мя; маку́шка; (of or for a tooth) коро́нка; (of a hat) тулья́; (of a tree) кро́на. **4,** (monetary unit) кро́на. —*v.t.* **1,** (enthrone) короно́вать; венча́ть на ца́рство. **2,** (be at the top of; climax) венча́ть. *Be crowned with success*, увенча́ться успе́хом. **3,** *dentistry* ста́вить коро́нку на (зуб). **4,** *checkers* проводи́ть (ша́шку) в да́мки. **5,** *colloq.* (hit on the head) дать по голове́.

crown colony коро́нная коло́ния.

crowning *adj.* *His crowning achievement*, его́ велича́йшее достиже́ние; верши́на его́ достиже́ний. *The crowning blow*, заверша́ющий уда́р.

crown prince насле́дный принц.

crow's-feet *n.pl.* гуси́ные ла́пки.

crozier *n.* = **crosier.**

crucial *adj.* реша́ющий; крити́ческий; отве́тственный; перело́мный.

crucible *n.* **1,** (vessel) ти́гель. **2,** *fig.* (ordeal) горни́ло.

crucifix *n.* распя́тие.

crucifixion *n.* распя́тие (на кресте́).

cruciform *adj.* крестообра́зный.

crucify *v.t.* распина́ть.

crude *adj.* **1,** (raw; unrefined) сыро́й. *Crude oil*, сыра́я нефть; нефть-сыре́ц. **2,** (coarse; unpolished) гру́бый: *crude person*, гру́бый челове́к; *crude remark*, гру́бое замеча́ние. **3,** (poorly made or done) грубый; аляпова́тый. *Crude attempt/workmanship,* грубая попы́тка/рабо́та. *Crude painting,* аляпова́тая карти́на. *Crude dwelling,* убо́гое жили́ще.

crudely *adv.* гру́бо. *To put it rather crudely,* гру́бо говоря́.

crudeness *n.* гру́бость. *Also,* **crudity.**

cruel *adj.* жесто́кий: *cruel person,* жесто́кий челове́к; *cruel treatment,* жесто́кое обраще́ние. —**cruelly,** *adv.* жесто́ко. —**cruelty,** *n.* жесто́кость.

cruet *n.* у́ксусница. *Cruet stand,* судо́к.

cruise *n.* морско́е путеше́ствие; круи́з. —*v.i.* крейси́ровать. *Cruising speed,* кре́йсерская ско́рость.

cruise missile крыла́тая раке́та.

cruiser *n.* кре́йсер.

crumb *n.* кро́шка.

crumble *v.t.* кроши́ть. —*v.i.* **1,** (fall into small pieces) кроши́ться; рассыпа́ться. **2,** (decay; disintegrate) распада́ться; разруша́ться.

crumbly *adj.* ры́хлый; рассы́пчатый.

crummy *adj., slang* дрянно́й; парши́вый.

crumpet *n.* сдо́бная пы́шка; лепёшка.

crumple *v.t.* мять; ко́мкать. —*v.i.* мя́ться.

crunch *v.t. & i.* хрусте́ть. —*n.* хруст.

crusade *n.* **1,** *hist.* кресто́вый похо́д. **2,** (campaign) похо́д; кампа́ния. —*v.i.* вести́ кампа́нию; боро́ться.

crusader *n.* **1,** *hist.* крестоно́сец. **2,** (strong advocate) боре́ц: *crusader for freedom,* боре́ц за свобо́ду.

crush *v.t.* **1,** (run over; trample) дави́ть; смять. *Crush to death,* задави́ть на́смерть. **2,** (grind into small particles) дроби́ть; размельча́ть. **3,** (crease; rumple) мять. **4,** (put down; suppress) подавля́ть; раздави́ть. **5,** (defeat; overwhelm) разбива́ть; (раз)громи́ть; раздави́ть. —*v.i.* мя́ться: *crush easily,* легко́ мя́ться. —*n.* **1,** (pressure from a crowd) да́вка; толчея́; толкотня́. **2,** *colloq.* (infatuation) увлече́ние. *Have a crush on,* увлека́ться (+ *instr.*).

crushed *adj.* **1,** (in small bits) дроблёный: *crushed ice,* дроблёный лёд. **2,** (creased; wrinkled) мя́тый. **3,** (crestfallen) уби́тый.

crusher *n.* дроби́лка. *Rock crusher,* камнедроби́лка.

crushing *adj.* сокруши́тельный: *crushing blow,* сокруши́тельный уда́р. *Crushing defeat,* сокруши́тельное *or* жесто́кое пораже́ние.

crust *n.* **1,** (of bread or a pie) ко́рка. **2,** (hard surface) кора́: *the earth's crust,* земна́я кора́.

crustacean *n.* ракообра́зное.

crutch *n.* косты́ль: *walk on crutches,* ходи́ть на костыля́х.

crux *n.* суть: *the crux of the matter,* суть де́ла.

cry *v.i.* **1,** (weep) пла́кать: *Don't cry!,* не плачь!; не пла́чьте! *Burst out crying,* распла́каться. **2,** (shout) (за)крича́ть. **3,** *fol. by* **out** (shriek) крича́ть; вскри́кивать. *Cry out in pain,* крича́ть от бо́ли. —*v.t.* **1,** *Cry one's eyes out,* вы́плакать все глаза́. **2,** *Cry oneself to sleep,* пла́кать пока́ (он) не засну́л. —*n.* **1,** (shout) крик: *a cry of joy,* крик ра́дости; *a cry for help,* крик о по́мощи. **2,** (spell of weeping) плач. *Have a good cry,* вы́плакаться; напла́каться. **3,** (call of an animal or bird) крик. **4,** (rallying cry) клич: *battle cry,* боево́й клич.

crybaby *n.* пла́кса.

crying *n.* плач. —*adj.* вопию́щий: *crying injustice,* вопию́щая несправедли́вость. *A crying need,* о́страя необходи́мость. *It's a crying shame!,* стыд и срам!

crypt *n.* склеп.

cryptic *adj.* зага́дочный; немногосло́вный; двусмы́сленный.

cryptogram *n.* криптогра́мма.

cryptographer *n.* шифрова́льщик.

cryptography *n.* криптогра́фия. —**cryptographic,** *adj.* криптографи́ческий.

crystal *n.* **1,** (clear glass) хруста́ль. **2,** (solid body) криста́лл. **3,** (of a watch) (часово́е) стекло́. —*adj.* хруста́льный.

crystal-clear *adj.* **1,** (of water) криста́льный; криста́льно чи́стый. **2,** *fig.* (obvious) преде́льно я́сный.

crystalline *adj.* кристалли́ческий.

crystallize *v.t.* кристаллизова́ть. —*v.i.* кристаллизова́ться. —**crystallization,** *n.* кристаллиза́ция.

cub *n.* детёныш. ♦*Compounds are rendered by the suffix* -ёнок *or* -о́нок: *lion cub,* львёнок; *bear cub,* медвежо́нок.

Cuban *adj.* куби́нский. —*n.* куби́нец; куби́нка.

cube *n.* **1,** (six-sided figure) куб. **2,** (small piece so shaped) ку́бик: *ice cube,* ку́бик льда. **3,** *math.* (third power) куб: *The cube of two is eight,* два в ку́бе — во́семь; куб двух ра́вен восьми́. —*v.t.* возводи́ть в куб. —**cube root,** куби́ческий ко́рень.

cubic *adj.* куби́ческий.

cubicle *n.* клету́шка.

cubism *n.* куби́зм.

cubit *n.* ло́коть.

cuckold *n.* рогоно́сец. —*v.t.* наставля́ть рога́ (+ *dat.*).

cuckoo *n.* куку́шка. —*v.i.* кукова́ть. —**cuckoo clock,** часы́ с куку́шкой.

cucumber *n.* огуре́ц. —*adj.* огуре́чный.

cud *n.* жва́чка: *chew the cud,* жева́ть жва́чку.

cuddle *v.t.* обнима́ть; прижима́ть к себе́. —*v.i.* [*usu.* **cuddle up**] прижима́ться.

cudgel *n.* дуби́на. —*v.t.* дуба́сить.

cue *n.* **1,** (signal on stage) ре́плика. **2,** *billiards* кий.

cuff *n.* **1,** (of a sleeve) манже́та; обшла́г. **2,** (of trousers) отворо́т. **3,** (slap) пощёчина. —**off the cuff,** экспро́мтом.

cuff link запо́нка.

cuirass *n.* кира́са.

cuisine *n.* ку́хня.

culinary *adj.* кулина́рный: *culinary art,* кулина́рное иску́сство.

cull *v.t.* **1,** (select) че́рпать; почерпну́ть. **2,** (pick; gather, as flowers) собира́ть.

culminate *v.i.* [*usu.* **culminate in**] конча́ться (+ *instr.*); вылива́ться в. —**culmination,** *n.* кульмина́ция; кульминацио́нный пункт.

culpable *adj.* вино́вный. —**culpability,** *n.* вино́вность.

culprit *n.* вино́вник.

cult *n.* культ.

cultivate *v.t.* **1,** (till) обраба́тывать; возде́лывать. **2,** (grow, as plants) выра́щивать; разводи́ть. **3,** *fig.*

(develop) развива́ть: *cultivate one's mind*, развива́ть ум. **4,** *fig.* (foster) воспи́тывать: *cultivate in someone a taste for literature*, воспи́тывать у кого́-нибудь вкус к литерату́ре. **5,** (seek the good will of) обха́живать; заи́скивать пе́ред; льнуть к.

cultivated *adj.* **1,** (tilled) обрабо́танный. **2,** (cultured) культу́рный; образо́ванный. **3,** (refined) утончённый.

cultivation *n.* **1,** (tillage) обрабо́тка. **2,** (development; fostering) разви́тие; воспита́ние.

cultural *adj.* культу́рный.

culture *n.* культу́ра.

cultured *adj.* культу́рный. —**cultured pearls,** иску́сственный *or* культиви́рованный же́мчуг.

culture medium пита́тельная среда́.

cumbersome *adj.* громо́здкий.

cummerbund *n.* куша́к.

cumulative *adj.* кумуляти́вный.

cumulous *adj.* кучево́й. —**cumulus,** *n.* кучевы́е облака́.

cuneiform *n.* кли́нопись.

cunning *adj.* хи́трый. —*n.* хи́трость.

cup *n.* **1,** (vessel) ча́шка: *a cup of tea,* ча́шка ча́ю. *Paper cup,* бума́жный стака́нчик. **2,** *sports* (trophy) ку́бок. —*v.t.,* in **cup one's hand,** держа́ть ру́ку го́рстью.

cupboard *n.* шкаф.

Cupid *n.* Купидо́н.

cupidity *n.* жа́дность; а́лчность.

cupola *n.* ку́пол.

cupping glass ба́нка.

cur *n.* ублю́док.

curable *adj.* излечи́мый.

curative *adj.* лече́бный; целе́бный; цели́тельный.

curator *n.* храни́тель.

curb *n.* **1,** (edge of a sidewalk) обо́чина. **2,** (restraint) узда́. *A curb on spending,* ограниче́ние расхо́дов. —*v.t.* **1,** (restrain) сде́рживать; укроща́ть: *curb an impulse,* сде́рживать/укроща́ть поры́в. **2,** (bring under control) обу́здывать: *curb inflation/ the arms race/,* обузда́ть инфля́цию/ го́нку вооруже́ний/. **3,** (reduce; cut back) ограни́чивать: *curb expenses,* ограни́чивать расхо́ды. *Curb production,* сокраща́ть произво́дство.

curd *n., often pl.* творо́г.

curdle *v.t.* свора́живать. —*v.i.* свёртываться; свора́живаться.

cure *v.t.* **1,** (heal; remedy) выле́чивать; изле́чивать: *cure an illness,* выле́чивать/изле́чивать боле́знь. *Cure someone of an illness,* выле́чивать/изле́чивать кого́-нибудь от боле́зни. *Be cured of,* вы́лечиться/ излечи́ться от. *I'm cured,* меня́ вы́лечили. **2,** (preserve, as meat) вя́лить; соли́ть; копти́ть. —*n.* **1,** (treatment) курс лече́ния; излече́ние. **2,** (recovery of one's health) излече́ние. **3,** (remedy) сре́дство: *a cure for cancer,* сре́дство от ра́ка.

cure-all *n.* панаце́я.

curfew *n.* коменда́нтский час.

curia *n.* ку́рия.

curiosity *n.* **1,** (inquisitiveness) любопы́тство. **2,**

(thirst for knowledge) любозна́тельность. **3,** (something that arouses interest) ре́дкость; дико́вина.

curious *adj.* **1,** (eager to find out; inquisitive) любопы́тный. *I am curious to know,* мне любопы́тно знать. *A curious look,* любопы́тный взгляд. **2,** (eager to learn; inquiring) любозна́тельный. **3,** (odd; strange) курьёзный.

curiously *adv.* любопы́тно. *Curiously enough...,* как ни стра́нно...

curium *n.* кю́рий.

curl *n.* ло́кон; завито́к; *pl.* ку́дри. —*v.t.* **1,** (form into ringlets, as hair) завива́ть. **2,** (cause to curve, as paper) коро́бить. **3,** *Curl one's lip,* криви́ть гу́бы. —*v.i.* **1,** (of hair) завива́ться; ви́ться. **2,** (of paper) коро́биться. **3,** (of smoke) клуби́ться. **4,** *fol. by* **up** (sit or lie cozily) свёртываться.

curler *n.* бигуди́; папильо́тка.

curlew *n.* кро́ншнеп.

curlicue *n.* завиту́шка; закорю́чка; крючо́к.

curling irons щипцы́ для зави́вки.

curly *adj.* кудря́вый; курча́вый; вью́щийся.

currant *n.* **1,** (fruit or berry) сморо́дина. **2,** (seedless raisin) кори́нка.

currency *n.* **1,** (money) валю́та; де́ньги. *Foreign currency,* иностра́нная валю́та. **2,** (prevalence; vogue) хожде́ние: *enjoy wide currency,* име́ть широ́кое хожде́ние. —*adj.* валю́тный: *currency reform,* валю́тная рефо́рма. *Hard currency reserves,* валю́тные резе́рвы.

current *n.* **1,** (flow) тече́ние: *against the current,* про́тив тече́ния. *Ocean currents,* океа́нские тече́ния. *Air current,* возду́шное тече́ние. *A current of air,* струя́ во́здуха. **2,** *electricity* ток. —*adj.* теку́щий; ны́нешний; тепе́решний. *Current events,* теку́щие собы́тия. *In the current issue,* в теку́щем но́мере.

currently *adv.* ны́не; в настоя́щее вре́мя.

curriculum *n.* курс обуче́ния; уче́бный план.

currier *n.* коже́вник.

curry *v.t.* выде́лывать (ко́жу). —**curry favor,** заи́скивать.

currycomb *n.* скребни́ца.

curse *n.* **1,** (imprecation) прокля́тие. *Heap curses upon,* осыпа́ть (+ *acc.*) прокля́тиями. *He seems to be under a curse,* он как бу́дто про́клят; на нём как бу́дто лежи́т прокля́тие. **2,** (bane) бич; прокля́тие. *The curse of mankind,* бич челове́чества. *The curse of my life,* прокля́тие мое́й жи́зни. —*v.t.* **1,** (damn) проклина́ть: *curse one's fate,* проклина́ть свою́ судьбу́. **2,** *fol. by* **out** (berate) руга́ть; обруга́ть. —*v.i.* (swear) руга́ться. —**curse word,** бра́нное сло́во; руга́тельство.

cursed *adj.* прокля́тый.

cursive *adj.* скоропи́сный.

cursory *adj.* бе́глый. —**cursorily,** *adv.* бе́гло.

curt *adj.* ре́зкий; отры́вистый.

curtail *v.t.* сокраща́ть; свёртывать; уре́зывать. —**curtailment,** *n.* сокраще́ние; свёртывание.

curtain *n.* **1,** (for a window) занаве́ска; што́ра. **2,** (on stage) за́навес. —*v.t.* заве́шивать; занаве́шивать.

Curtain off, отделя́ть занаве́ской. —**curtain call,** вы́зов (на сце́ну). —**curtain rod,** па́лка для штор.

curtsy *also,* **curtsey** *n.* revера́нс; приседа́ние; кни́ксен. —*v.i.* де́лать реверáнс; приседа́ть.

curvature *n.* кривизна́; искривле́ние.

curve *n.* **1,** (arc) крива́я. **2,** (bend) изги́б; изви́лина. **3,** (draftsman's instrument) лека́ло. —*v.i.* изгиба́ться: *The road curves,* доро́га изгиба́ется.

curved *adj.* криво́й; изо́гнутый.

curvilinear *adj.* криволине́йный.

cushion *n.* **1,** (pillow) поду́шка. **2,** (rim of a billiard table) борт. —*v.t.* смягча́ть (уда́р).

cuspid *n.* клык.

cuss *v.i., colloq.* руга́ться. —*v.t.* [*usu.* **cuss out**] *colloq.* разруга́ть. —*n., colloq.* ма́лый: *a queer old cuss,* стра́нный ма́лый.

custard *n.* заварно́й крем.

custodian *n.* **1,** (caretaker) храни́тель. **2,** (janitor) дво́рник.

custody *n.* **1,** (guardianship) опе́ка; опеку́нство; попече́ние. *Child custody,* опе́ка *or* опеку́нство над детьми́. *She was given/awarded custody of the children,* она́ получи́ла опеку́нство над детьми́; дете́й о́тдали на её попече́ние. **2,** (detention) аре́ст; содержа́ние под аре́стом. *In custody,* под аре́стом; под стра́жей. *Take into custody,* брать под аре́ст; брать под стра́жу. *Release from custody,* освобожда́ть из-под стра́жи.

custom *n.* обы́чай: *ancient custom,* стари́нный обы́чай. *It is not our custom to...,* у нас не при́нято (+ *inf.*). *See also* **customs.**

customarily *adv.* обы́чно.

customary *adj.* обы́чный; привы́чный. *In one's customary place,* на своём обы́чном ме́сте. *It is customary to...,* при́нято (+ *inf.*). *It is customary first to ask permission,* при́нято снача́ла спроси́ть разреше́ния.

customer *n.* зака́зчик; покупа́тель; клие́нт. *Two pairs per customer,* две па́ры в одни́ ру́ки.

customhouse *also,* **customshouse** *n.* тамо́жня.

custom-made *adj.* сде́ланный на зака́з.

customs *n.pl.* **1,** (agency) тамо́жня. *Pass through customs,* проходи́ть тамо́женный осмо́тр. **2,** (duty) по́шлина. —*adj.* тамо́женный. *Customs inspector,* тамо́женник.

customshouse *n.* = **customhouse.**

cut *v.t.* **1,** (divide into parts; slice; carve) ре́зать: *cut the meat,* ре́зать мя́со. *Cut something in half/two,* разреза́ть что́-нибудь попола́м/на́двое. **2,** (hurt; gash) поре́зать: *cut one's finger,* поре́зать себе́ па́лец. *Cut oneself,* поре́заться. *Cut someone's throat,* перере́зать го́рло (+ *dat.*). **3,** (sever) перереза́ть: *The wires have been cut,* провода́ перере́заны. *Cut communications,* перереза́ть *or* ре́зать коммуника́ции. **4,** (trim) подреза́ть (но́гти); стричь (во́лосы); среза́ть (цветы́). **5,** (mow) коси́ть. **6,** (cut out, as cloth) крои́ть. **7,** (shape, as gems) грани́ть. **8,** (divide in two, as of a road or river) рассека́ть. **9,** (have grown in, as a tooth): *He is cutting a tooth,* у него́ прореза́ется зуб. **10,** (reduce) сокраща́ть; снижа́ть. **11,** (shorten, as a book, article, etc.) сокраща́ть;

уре́зывать. **12,** *cards* снима́ть (коло́ду). **13,** *colloq.* (fail to attend, as classes) пропуска́ть; прогу́ливать (уро́ки). —*v.i.* **1,** (act as a sharp edge) ре́зать: *The knife does not cut,* нож не ре́жет. **2,** (be able to be cut) ре́заться: *The meat cuts easily,* мя́со легко́ ре́жется. **3,** *cards* снима́ть коло́ду. —*n.* **1,** (gash) поре́з. **2,** (of meat) кусо́к. **3,** (style of a garment) покро́й; фасо́н. **4,** (deletion) купю́ра. **5,** (reduction) сниже́ние; сокраще́ние. *Pay/tax cut,* сниже́ние зарпла́ты/нало́гов. —*adj.* **1,** (gashed) поре́занный. **2,** (trimmed, as of flowers) сре́занный. **3,** (of gems, glass, etc.) гранёный. **4,** (reduced) сни́женный; льго́тный. —**cut across,** пересека́ть. —**cut away,** среза́ть. —**cut back (on),** уре́зывать. —**cut down, 1,** (fell) руби́ть; сруба́ть; выруба́ть. **2,** (kill) среза́ть; сража́ть. **3,** (reduce) уре́зывать. *Cut down on one's smoking,* ме́ньше кури́ть. **4,** (shorten; abridge) сокраща́ть. —**cut off, 1,** (sever) отреза́ть. **2,** (isolate) отреза́ть; отрыва́ть; разобща́ть. **3,** (block, as a road) отреза́ть; перереза́ть. **4,** (halt) прекраща́ть: *cut off aid,* прекрати́ть по́мощь. **5,** (rudely interrupt) обрыва́ть; среза́ть. **6,** (shut off; disconnect) прерыва́ть; отключа́ть. *Cut off communications,* прерва́ть связь. **7,** (on the telephone) прерыва́ть; разъединя́ть: *We've been cut off,* нас прерва́ли/разъедини́ли. **8,** (stop the supply of, as water) перекрыва́ть. **9,** (cut in front of, when driving) подреза́ть. —**cut open,** разреза́ть; вскрыва́ть. —**cut out, 1,** (remove by cutting) выреза́ть. **2,** (shape by cutting, as material) выкра́ивать; раскра́ивать. **3,** (remove; delete) вычёркивать. **4,** *colloq.* (discontinue; give up) бро́сить (кури́ть); отказа́ться от (мя́са). **5,** *slang* (cease) переста́ть; бро́сить; прекрати́ть. *Cut it out!,* прекрати́! —**cut out for; cut out to be,** со́здан для: *He is not cut out for it,* он не со́здан для э́того. *He is not cut out to be a soldier,* он не годи́тся в солда́ты. —**cut short,** оборва́ть; прерва́ть. *Cut short a vacation,* прерва́ть о́тпуск. —**cut through, 1,** (cut across) пересека́ть. **2,** (penetrate) рассека́ть. —**cut up,** разреза́ть; ре́зать.

cutaway *n.* визи́тка. *Also,* **cutaway coat.**

cutback *n.* сокраще́ние.

cute *adj., colloq.* **1,** (pretty) хоро́шенький; ми́ленький. **2,** (appealing; quaint) причу́дливый.

cutlass *n.* теса́к.

cutlery *n.* ножево́й това́р.

cutlet *n.* (отбивна́я) котле́та. *Veal cutlet,* теля́чья отбивна́я.

cut-rate *adj.* льго́тный.

cutter *n.* **1,** (one who cuts) ре́зальщик. *Diamond cutter,* грани́льщик. *Woodcutter,* лесору́б. **2,** (of cloth) закро́йщик. **3,** (tool) резе́ц; реза́к. **4,** (boat) ка́тер; те́ндер.

cutthroat *n.* головоре́з. —*adj.* жесто́кий; ожесточённый.

cutting *n.* **1,** (act of cutting) ре́зание; ре́зка. **2,** (work of cutting material) кро́йка. **3,** (plant shoot used for grafting) черено́к. —*adj.* **1,** (that cuts) ре́жущий. *Cutting edge,* остриё. **2,** (chilling or piercing) ре́зкий. **3,** (sarcastic) ко́лкий; язви́тельный.

cuttlefish *n.* карака́тица; се́пия.

cyanic *adj.* циа́новый; циа́нистый.

cyanide *n.* циани́д. —**potassium cyanide,** циа́нистый ка́лий.

cyanogen *n.* циа́н.

cyanosis *n.* циано́з; синю́ха.

cybernetics *n.* киберне́тика.

cyclamen *n.* циклами́н.

cycle *n.* цикл. —*v.i.* е́здить на велосипе́де. —**cyclical,** *adj.* цикли́ческий.

cyclist *n.* **1,** (rider) велосипеди́ст. **2,** (racer) велого́нщик.

cyclone *n.* цикло́н. —**cyclonic,** *adj.* циклони́ческий.

cyclotron *n.* циклотро́н.

cylinder *n.* **1,** (geometric figure) цили́ндр. **2,** (rotating part of a revolver) бараба́н. **3,** (of an engine) цили́ндр. —**cylindrical,** *adj.* цилиндри́ческий.

cymbals *n.pl.* таре́лки.

cynic *n.* ци́ник. —**cynical,** *adj.* цини́чный. —**cynicism,** *n.* цини́зм; цини́чность.

cypress *n.* кипари́с.

Cyrillic alphabet кири́ллица.

cyst *n.* киста́.

cytology *n.* цитоло́гия. —**cytological,** *adj.* цитологи́ческий.

czar *n.* = tsar.

Czech *adj.* че́шский. —*n.* **1,** (person) чех; че́шка. **2,** (language) че́шский язы́к.

D

D, d четвёртая бу́ква англи́йского алфави́та. —*n.* **1,** (musical note) ре. **2,** (school grade) дво́йка.

dab *v.t.* **1,** (pat gently): *dab one's eyes with a handkerchief,* прикла́дывать плато́к к глаза́м. **2,** (pat with something moist; apply with light strokes) накла́дывать (с по́мощью тампо́на, салфе́тки, *etc.*). —*n.* (of paint) мазо́к; (of rouge) ка́пелька.

dabble *v.i.* [*usu.* **dabble in**] игра́ть в (+ *acc.*); балова́ться (+ *instr.*). —**dabbler,** *n.* люби́тель; дилета́нт.

dacha *n.* да́ча.

dachshund *n.* та́кса.

dactyl *n.* да́ктиль. —**dactylic,** *adj.* дактили́ческий.

dad *n., colloq.* па́па. *Also,* **daddy.**

daffodil *n.* нарци́сс.

daffy *adj., slang* сумасбро́дный.

daft *adj.* сумасше́дший.

dagger *n.* **1,** (knife) кинжа́л. **2,** *printing* (†) кре́стик.

dahlia *n.* георги́н.

daily *adj.* ежедне́вный. —*adv.* ежедне́вно. —*n.* ежедне́вная газе́та.

dainty *adj.* **1,** (delicately pretty or graceful) изя́щный; утончённый. **2,** (delicious and choice) ла́комый.

dairy *n.* моло́чная. —*adj.* моло́чный: *dairy products,* моло́чные проду́кты. —**dairy farm,** моло́чная фе́рма; моло́чное хозя́йство. —**dairymaid,** *n.* моло́чница. —**dairyman,** *n.* моло́чник.

dais *n.* помо́ст; возвыше́ние.

daisy *n.* **1,** (English daisy) маргари́тка. **2,** (oxeye daisy) нивя́ник; попо́вник.

dale *n.* доли́на; дол.

dally *v.i.* **1,** (dawdle) ме́шкать. **2,** *fol. by* with (trifle with; toy with) игра́ть (+ *instr.*).

dam *n.* **1,** (barrier) плоти́на. **2,** (female parent of an animal) ма́тка. —*v.t.* запру́живать; перекрыва́ть.

damage *n.* **1,** (harm; injury) вред; поврежде́ние; уще́рб; по́рча. **2,** *pl.* (compensation for losses): *suit for damages,* иск о возмеще́нии убы́тков. *Pay damages,* возмеща́ть убы́тки *or* уще́рб. —*v.t.* поврежда́ть. *Be damaged,* пострада́ть; получи́ть поврежде́ния. —**damaging,** *adj.* нанося́щий вред; разруши́тельный.

damask *n.* штоф. —*adj.* што́фный.

dame *n.* **1,** (lady) да́ма. **2,** *slang* (woman) ба́ба.

damn *v.t.* проклина́ть. —*adj., colloq.* прокля́тый. *Damn fool,* наби́тый дура́к. —*adv., colloq.* черто́вски. *You're damn right!,* вы соверше́нно пра́вы. —*interj.* [*also,* **damn it!**] чёрт (возьми́)!; прокля́тие! —**not give a damn,** (на)плева́ть: *He doesn't give a damn,* ему́ (на)плева́ть на э́то. —**not be worth a damn,** ни черта́ не сто́ить.

damnable *adj.* **1,** (meriting damnation) предосуди́тельный. **2,** *colloq.* (accursed) прокля́тый.

damnation *n.* **1,** (act of damning) прокля́тие. **2,** (eternal punishment) ве́чные му́ки.

damned *adj.* прокля́тый. *I'll be damned if...,* будь я про́клят, е́сли... *Well I'll be damned!,* ну и ну!

damning *adj.* изоблича́тельный.

damp *adj.* сыро́й; вла́жный. —*v.t.* [*usu.* **damp down**] туши́ть.

dampen *v.t.* **1,** (moisten) сма́чивать. **2,** (depress; cast a pall over) омрача́ть. **3,** (cool, as ardor or enthusiasm) охлажда́ть.

damper *n.* засло́нка; вью́шка. —**put a damper on,** расхола́живать; омрача́ть.

dampness *n.* сы́рость; вла́жность.

damsel *n.* деви́ца.

dance *v.t. & i.* танцева́ть. *Ask someone to dance,* пригласи́ть кого́-нибудь на та́нец. —*n.* **1,** (dancing; kind of dance) та́нец: *folk dance,* наро́дный та́нец; *modern dance,* та́нец моде́рн. **2,** (gathering of people for dancing) та́нцы; танцева́льный ве́чер; бал. *Invite someone to a dance,* пригласи́ть кого́-нибудь на та́нцы. —*adj.* танцева́льный: *dance hall,* танцева́льный зал. —**dance attendance on,** ходи́ть на за́дних ла́пках пе́ред. —**dance to someone's tune,** пляса́ть под чью́-нибудь ду́дку.

dancer *n.* **1,** (one who dances) танцо́р. **2,** (professional dancer) танцо́вщик; танцо́вщица.

dancing *n.* та́нцы: *folk dancing,* наро́дные та́нцы. —*adj.* танцева́льный. *Dancing lessons,* уро́ки та́нцев.

dandelion *n.* одува́нчик.

dander *n., usu. in* **get one's dander up,** разозли́ться.

dandle *v.t.* кача́ть: *dandle a child on one's knees,* кача́ть ребёнка на коле́нях.

dandruff *n.* пе́рхоть.

dandy *n.* **1,** (fop) щёголь; франт; де́нди. **2,** *colloq.* (excellent thing) пре́лесть. —*adj., colloq.* преле́стный.

Dane *n.* датча́нин; датча́нка. —**Great Dane,** да́тский дог.

danger *n.* опа́сность. *Be in danger,* быть в опа́сности; быть под угро́зой. *The danger of infection,* опа́сность зараже́ния. *A danger to society,* опа́сность для о́бщества. *Danger zone,* опа́сная зо́на. *Danger signal,* сигна́л опа́сности.

dangerous *adj.* опа́сный. —**dangerously,** *adv.* опа́сно. *Dangerously ill,* опа́сно *or* тяжело́ бо́лен. *Dangerously close to,* опа́сно бли́зок к.

dangle *v.t.* болта́ть: *dangle one's feet in the water,* болта́ть нога́ми в воде́. —*v.i.* болта́ться: *dangle on a string,* болта́ться на верёвке.

Danish *adj.* да́тский. —*n.* да́тский язы́к.

dank *adj.* сыро́й; промо́зглый.

dapper *adj.* хо́леный; щеголева́тый.

dapple *v.t.* испещря́ть. —*adj.* = **dappled.** —*n.* подпа́лина.

dappled *adj.* **1,** (spotted) пятни́стый. **2,** (of a horse) в я́блоках; чуба́рый.

dapple-gray *also,* **dapple-grey** *adj.* се́рый в я́блоках.

dare *v.t. & i.* сметь; осме́ливаться. *How dare you...!,* как ты сме́ешь (+ *inf.*)! *He wouldn't dare to do it,* он не посме́ет э́то сде́лать. —*v.t.* вызыва́ть. *I dare you to...,* а ну (+ *imperative*). —*n.* вы́зов. —**dare say,** сметь *or* осме́ливаться сказа́ть.

daredevil *n.* смельча́к; лиха́ч; удале́ц; головоре́з; сорвиголова́. —*adj.* опроме́тчивый; безрассу́дный.

daring *adj.* сме́лый. —*n.* сме́лость.

dark *adj.* тёмный: *dark night/street,* тёмная ночь/у́лица. *Dark hair/colors/glasses,* тёмные во́лосы/цвета́/очки́. *Dark suit,* тёмный костю́м. *Dark blue,* тёмно-си́ний. *Dark complexion,* сму́глое лицо́. *The dark side of the moon,* теневáя *or* обра́тная сторонá Луны́. *Get dark,* темне́ть. *It is dark already,* уже́ темно́. —*n.* темнота́; тьма; мрак. *See in the dark,* ви́деть в темноте́. *Before dark,* за́светло. *After dark,*

за́темно; по́сле наступле́ния темноты́. —**be/keep in the dark,** быть/держа́ть в неве́дении.

darken *v.t.* затемня́ть. —*v.i.* темне́ть.

dark-haired *adj.* темноволо́сый.

darkness *n.* темнота́; тьма; мрак.

darkroom *n.* тёмная ко́мната.

dark-skinned *adj.* темноко́жий.

darling *n.* **1,** (beloved person) ми́лый (ми́лая); дорого́й (дорога́я); ду́шенька; голу́бка. **2,** (someone in great favor) люби́мец; ба́ловень. —*adj.* **1,** (beloved) дорого́й; ми́лый. **2,** *colloq.* (cute; lovely) чуде́сный.

darn *v.t.* што́пать. —*adj., colloq.* [*also,* **darned**] прокля́тый.

darnel *n.* плёвел.

darning needle 1, (needle used in darning) што́пальная игла́. **2,** (dragonfly) стрекоза́.

dart *n.* **1,** (missile) стрела́. **2,** (dash; rush) бросо́к. —*v.i.* бро́ситься; ри́нуться; помча́ться. *Dart out from behind a bush,* вы́лететь из-за куста́.

dash *v.i.* **1,** (dart; rush) бро́ситься; ри́нуться; помча́ться. *Dash out of the room,* вы́бежать из ко́мнаты. **2,** (land with great force) би́ться; ударя́ться: *The waves dashed against the shore,* во́лны би́лись/ударя́лись о бе́рег. —*v.t.* **1,** (throw violently) бро́сить (изо всех сил): *dash to the ground,* бро́сить о зе́млю. **2,** (shatter, as hopes) разбива́ть. **3,** *fol. by* **off** (write hastily) набра́сывать; черкну́ть. —*n.* **1,** (rush) бросо́к. *Make a dash for the door,* бро́ситься к двери́. **2,** *sports* забе́г: *100-meter dash,* забе́г на сто ме́тров. **3,** (punctuation mark) (—) тире́. **4,** (bit; touch) при́месь.

dashboard *n.* прибо́рная доска́; щито́к.

dashing *adj.* лихо́й; бра́вый; удало́й; молодцева́тый.

dastard *n.* трус; подле́ц. —**dastardly,** *adj.* трусли́вый; подлый.

data *n.pl.* да́нные. —**data bank,** банк да́нных. —**data base,** ба́за да́нных. —**data processing,** обрабо́тка да́нных.

date *n.* **1,** (day of the month) число́: *What is today's date?,* како́е сего́дня число́? **2,** (statement of calendar time) да́та: *date of birth,* да́та рожде́ния. *Put the date on a letter,* проставля́ть да́ту на письме́. **3,** (day when something is to happen) срок: *by a certain date,* к определённому сро́ку. *Set the date,* назнача́ть срок. *Date of departure,* срок *or* день отъе́зда. **4,** (social engagement) свида́ние: *go out on dates,* ходи́ть на свида́ния. **5,** (fruit) фи́ник. —*v.t.* **1,** (put the date on) дати́ровать; помеча́ть: *The letter was dated May 6th,* письмо́ бы́ло дати́ровано/поме́чено шесты́м ма́я. **2,** (see socially) встреча́ться с. —*v.i.* восходи́ть; относи́ться. *Date from the time of...,* восходи́ть ко вре́мени (+ *gen.*). *This building dates from the 15th century,* э́то зда́ние отно́сится к пятна́дцатому ве́ку. —**to date,** до сих пор; на сего́дня; на да́нный моме́нт. —**up to date,** в ку́рсе де́ла. *Bring up to date,* вводи́ть в курс де́ла. *See also* **out-of-date** *and* **up-to-date.**

dated *adj.* **1,** (marked with a date) дати́рованный. **2,** (outdated) устаре́вший.

date line Ли́ния переме́ны да́ты. *Also,* **International Date Line.**

date palm фи́никовая па́льма.

dative *adj.* да́тельный: *dative case,* да́тельный паде́ж.

daub *v.t. & i.* ма́зать. —*n.* мазня́; пачкотня́.

daughter *n.* дочь. —**daughter-in-law,** *n.* неве́стка; сноха́.

daunt *v.t.* **1,** (make afraid) запу́гивать; устраша́ть. **2,** (dishearten) обескура́живать. —**dauntless,** *adj.* неустраши́мый; бесстра́шный.

dauphin *n.* дофи́н.

davenport *n.* дива́н-крова́ть.

dawdle *v.i.* ме́шкать; ло́дырничать; каните́литься.

dawn *n.* **1,** (daybreak) рассве́т; у́тренняя заря́. *At dawn,* на рассве́те. *It was already dawn when...,* уже́ рассвело́, когда́... **2,** *fig.* (beginning) заря́: *the dawn of a new era,* заря́ но́вой эпо́хи. —*v.i.* **1,** (begin to grow light) света́ть; рассвета́ть: *Day is dawning,* света́ет; рассвета́ет. **2,** (begin, as of an era) наступа́ть. **3,** *fol. by* **on** *or* **upon** (begin to be understood) осеня́ть; озаря́ть: *It dawned on me,* меня́ осени́ло/озари́ло; меня́ осени́ла/озари́ла мысль.

day *n.* день: *all day,* весь день. *Sunny day,* со́лнечный день. *Four times a day,* четы́ре ра́за в день. *Three days and three nights,* тро́е су́ток. *At any hour of the day or night,* в любо́е вре́мя су́ток. —*adj.* дневно́й: *the day shift,* дневна́я сме́на. —**any day (now),** со дня на́ день. —**day after day,** изо дня в день. —**day and night,** день и ночь; дни и но́чи. —**day by day,** день ото дня. —**day off,** выходно́й день. *Take a day off,* взять выходно́й. —**from day to day,** со дня на́ день. —**in one's day,** в своё вре́мя. —**in the old days,** в ста́рые времена́. —**in those days,** в те времена́. —**one day, 1,** *literally* оди́н день. **2,** (once in the past) одна́жды. **3,** (sometime in the future) когда́-нибудь. —**one of these days,** на днях. —**the day before,** накану́не. —**the other day,** на днях. —**these days,** в на́ше вре́мя; в на́ши дни. —**to this day,** по сей день.

daybed *n.* дива́н-крова́ть.

daybreak *n.* рассве́т.

daydream *n.* мечта́; грёза. —*v.i.* мечта́ть; гре́зить. —**daydreaming,** *n.* мечта́ние.

daylight *n.* **1,** (light of day) дневно́й свет. *In broad daylight,* средь бе́ла дня. **2,** (dawn) рассве́т: *before daylight,* до рассве́та; зате́мно. **3,** (daytime) вре́мя: *two hours of daylight,* два часа́ дневно́го вре́мени. —**beat the daylights out of,** *colloq.* не оста́вить живо́го ме́ста на (+ *prepl.*). —**scare the daylights out of,** *colloq.* напуга́ть до́ сме́рти. —**see daylight,** ви́деть просве́т.

daytime *n.* дневно́е вре́мя. *In the daytime,* днём. —*adj.* дневно́й: *daytime activities,* дневны́е заня́тия.

day-to-day *adj.* повседне́вный.

daywork *n.* подённая рабо́та; подёнщина. —**dayworker,** *n.* подёнщик; подённый.

daze *n.* отупе́ние. *Be in a daze,* быть (как) в чаду́. —*v.t.* ошеломля́ть. —**dazed,** *adj.* обалде́лый.

dazzle *v.t.* ослепля́ть. *One is dazzled by...,* в глаза́х ряби́т от...

dazzling *adj.* **1,** (blinding) ослепи́тельный. **2,** *fig.* (outstanding; breathtaking) блестя́щий.

deacon *n.* дья́кон.

deactivate *v.t.* **1,** (disband) распуска́ть. **2,** (render inoperative) обезвре́живать.

dead *adj.* **1,** (of a person) мёртвый. *He is dead,* он у́мер. *Dead body,* труп. *Play dead,* притворя́ться мёртвым. **2,** (of an animal) до́хлый. **3,** (of trees, leaves, etc.) сухо́й; (of flowers) увя́дший. **4,** (failing to operate): *The motor/radio/battery/telephone went dead,* мото́р загло́х; ра́дио умо́лкло; аккумуля́тор сел; связь оборвала́сь. *Dead battery,* се́вший аккумуля́тор. **5,** *with certain nouns,* мёртвый: *dead languages,* мёртвые языки́; *dead season,* мёртвый сезо́н; *dead silence,* мёртвая тишина́. —*adv.* соверше́нно: *dead right,* соверше́нно прав. *Dead against,* реши́тельно про́тив. *Dead tired,* до́ смерти уста́лый. *Dead drunk,* мертве́цки пьян. *Stop dead in one's tracks,* останови́ться как вко́панный. —*n.* **1,** *preceded by* **the** (those who have died) мёртвые; уме́ршие. *Rise from the dead,* воскреса́ть. *The number of dead and wounded,* число́ уби́тых и ра́неных. **2,** (coldest or darkest point) *rendered by* глубо́кий: *in the dead of night/winter,* глубо́кой но́чью/зимо́й.

dead center *also,* **dead centre** мёртвая то́чка: *move off dead center,* сдви́нуть(ся) с мёртвой то́чки.

deaden *v.t.* **1,** (make less intense) заглуша́ть: *deaden the sound/pain,* заглуша́ть звук/боль. **2,** (make numb) умерщвля́ть: *deaden a tooth,* умерщвля́ть нерв зу́ба.

dead end тупи́к. —**dead-end,** *adj.* тупико́вый.

dead heat одновре́менный фи́ниш. *Finish in a dead heat,* финиши́ровать одновре́менно.

dead letter 1, (undelivered letter) недоста́вленное письмо́. **2,** (something no longer valid or enforced) мёртвая бу́ква.

deadline *n.* срок; после́дний срок; кра́йний срок; преде́льный срок. *The deadline for payment,* срок платежа́.

deadlock *n.* мёртвая то́чка; тупи́к. —*v.t.* заводи́ть в тупи́к. *Be deadlocked,* заходи́ть в тупи́к.

deadly *adj.* смерте́льный; смертоно́сный. —*adv., colloq.* смерте́льно: *deadly dull,* смерте́льно ску́чно.

dead reckoning счисле́ние пути́.

dead weight мёртвый груз.

deaf *adj.* глухо́й. *Deaf in one ear,* глухо́й на одно́ у́хо. *Become deaf,* (о)гло́хнуть. *Be deaf to,* быть глухи́м к. —**fall on deaf ears,** оста́ться без внима́ния. —**turn a deaf ear to,** пропуска́ть ми́мо уше́й.

deaf-and-dumb *adj.* глухонемо́й.

deafen *v.t.* оглуша́ть. —**deafening,** *adj.* оглуши́тельный.

deaf-mute *n.* глухонемо́й.

deafness *n.* глухота́.

deal *n.* **1,** (transaction) сде́лка. *It's a deal!,* по рука́м! **2,** *cards* сда́ча: *It's your deal,* ва́ша сда́ча; вам сдава́ть. **3,** *in* **a great** (*or* **good**) **deal,** мно́го: *a great deal of money,* мно́го де́нег. *I learned a great deal,* я мно́гому научи́лся. *She is a good deal better today,* ей сего́дня значи́тельно лу́чше. —*v.t.* **1,** *usu. fol. by* **out** (apportion; distribute) раздава́ть; распределя́ть. **2,** *cards* сдава́ть (ка́рты). **3,** (administer, as a blow) наноси́ть. —*v.i.* **1,** *cards* сдава́ть ка́рты. *Who deals?,* кто сдаёт? **2,** *fol. by* **in** (sell; trade) торгова́ть (+ *instr.*). —**deal with, 1,** (have dealings with) име́ть де́ло с. **2,** (behave toward) поступа́ть с. **3,** (handle; take care of) справля́ться с. **4,** (take up; treat) рассма́тривать.

dealer *n.* **1,** (merchant; seller) торго́вец. *Drug dealer,* торго́вец нарко́тиками; деле́ц наркоби́знеса. **2,** *cards* тот, кто сдаёт ка́рты: *Who is the dealer?,* кто сдаёт?

dealing *n.* **1,** (conduct toward others) веде́ние дел: *honest dealing,* че́стное веде́ние дел. **2,** *usu. pl.* (transactions) сде́лки: *commercial dealings,* торго́вые сде́лки.

dean *n.* **1,** (university official) дека́н. **2,** (of a cathedral) настоя́тель. **3,** (senior member) старшина́: *dean of the diplomatic corps,* старшина́ дипломати́ческого ко́рпуса.

dear *adj.* дорого́й: *a dear friend,* дорого́й друг. *Dear Sasha!,* дорого́й Са́ша! *Dear to us all,* до́рог для всех нас. —*n., used in direct address,* дорого́й (дорога́я); ми́лый (ми́лая). —**oh dear!; dear me!,** бо́же мой!; о бо́же!; го́споди!

dearly *adv.* до́рого: *pay dearly for,* до́рого заплати́ть за. *It cost us dearly,* э́то нам до́рого обошло́сь. *Love someone dearly,* горячо́ люби́ть кого́-нибудь.

dearth *n.* недоста́ток; нехва́тка.

death *n.* смерть. *Be near death,* быть при́ смерти. *Sentence to death,* пригова́ривать к сме́ртной ка́зни. *Put to death,* казни́ть; предава́ть сме́рти. —*adj.* сме́ртный: *death penalty,* сме́ртная казнь; *death sentence,* сме́ртный пригово́р. *Death rate,* сме́ртность. *Death certificate,* свиде́тельство о сме́рти. —**at death's door,** при́ смерти. —**be the death of,** своди́ть в моги́лу; сжива́ть со све́та. —**to death,** на́смерть; *fig.* до́ смерти. *Beat to death,* забива́ть на́смерть. *Crush/trample to death,* задави́ть/затопта́ть на́смерть. *Be burned to death,* сгоре́ть за́живо. *Frighten to death,* напуга́ть до́ смерти. *Be bored to death,* смерте́льно скуча́ть. *He bled to death,* он истёк кро́вью. *He drank himself to death,* он допи́лся до́ смерти. —**to the death,** на́смерть: *fight to the death,* сража́ться на́смерть; боро́ться (*or* борьба́) не на жизнь, а на́ смерть.

deathbed *n.* сме́ртное ло́же. *On one's deathbed,* на сме́ртном одре́.

deathblow *n.* смерте́льный уда́р.

deathly *adj.* мёртвенный: *deathly pallor,* мёртвенная бле́дность. *Deathly silence,* гробово́е молча́ние; мёртвая тишина́. —*adv.* смерте́льно; пани́чески: *be deathly afraid of,* смерте́льно/пани́чески боя́ться (+ *gen.*).

death mask посме́ртная ма́ска.

debacle *n.* катастро́фа.

debar *v.t.* **1,** (shut out) не допуска́ть. **2,** (prevent) лиша́ть пра́ва: *debar from voting,* лиша́ть пра́ва го́лоса.

debark *v.t.* выса́живать. —*v.i.* выса́живаться. —**debarkation,** *n.* вы́садка.

debase *v.t.* **1,** (cheapen) обесце́нивать: *debase the currency,* обесце́нивать валю́ту. **2,** (lower in dignity) унижа́ть. *Debase oneself,* унижа́ться.

debatable *adj.* спо́рный; оспори́мый; дискусси́онный. *That's debatable,* э́то спо́рный вопро́с.

debate *v.i.* дебати́ровать. —*v.t.* **1,** (discuss) обсужда́ть; дебати́ровать; дискути́ровать. **2,** (consider; weigh) сообража́ть; взве́шивать. *I'm debating whether to invite him,* я пока́ не зна́ю, приглаша́ть ли мне его́ и́ли нет. —*n.* **1,** (discussion) деба́ты; пре́ния; диску́ссия. **2,** (formal contest) ди́спут. —**debating society,** дискусси́онный клуб.

debauch *v.t.* развраща́ть; совраща́ть. —**debauchery,** *n.* развра́т; разгу́л.

debenture *n.* облига́ция.

debilitate *v.t.* ослабля́ть; расслабля́ть. —**debilitation,** *n.* ослабле́ние; расслабле́ние.

debility *n.* сла́бость; бесси́лие.

debit *n.* де́бет. —*v.t.* дебетова́ть.

debonair *adj.* **1,** (affable; gracious) любе́зный. **2,** (carefree; gay) весёлый; жизнера́достный.

debris *n.* обло́мки.

debt *n.* долг. *He is deeply/heavily in debt,* у него́ больши́е долги́; он си́льно задолжа́л; он круго́м в долга́х. *I am in your debt,* я у вас в долгу́. *The debt crisis,* долгово́й кри́зис.

debtor *n.* должни́к. *Debtor's prison,* долгова́я тюрьма́; долгова́я я́ма.

debunk *v.t.* развенчивать.

debut *n.* дебю́т. *Make one's debut,* дебюти́ровать.

debutante *n.* дебюта́нтка.

decade *n.* десятиле́тие.

decadence *n.* упа́дочничество; декаде́нство.

decadent *adj.* упа́дочный; упа́дочнический; декаде́нтский. —*n.* декаде́нт.

decagon *n.* десятиуго́льник.

decahedron *n.* десятигра́нник. —**decahedral,** *adj.* десятигра́нный.

decal *n.* переводна́я карти́нка.

decamp *v.i.* **1,** (break camp) снима́ться с ла́геря. **2,** (depart suddenly or secretly) удира́ть; смыва́ться.

decanter *n.* графи́н.

decapitate *v.t.* обезгла́вливать. —**decapitation,** *n.* обезгла́вливание.

decathlon *n.* десятибо́рье.

decay *v.i.* **1,** (rot; decompose) гнить; разлага́ться; (*of teeth*) гнить; по́ртиться. **2,** (deteriorate physically) ветша́ть. *Decaying building,* обветша́лое зда́ние. **3,** *fig.* (go into a decline) приходи́ть в упа́док. —*n.* **1,** (decomposition) гние́ние; разложе́ние. *Tooth decay,* ка́риес зубо́в. **2,** (decline) упа́док. **3,** *chem.; physics* распа́д.

deceased *adj.* поко́йный. —*n., preceded by* **the** поко́йник; поко́йный; уме́рший.

deceit *n.* обма́н. —**deceitful,** *adj.* обма́нный; лжи́вый.

deceive *v.t.* обма́нывать: *deceive one's parents,* обма́нывать роди́телей. *My eyes must be deceiving me,* я не ве́рю глаза́м свои́м.

decelerate *v.t.* замедля́ть. —*v.i.* замедля́ть ход. —**deceleration,** *n.* замедле́ние.

December *n.* дека́брь. —*adj.* дека́брьский. —**Decembrist,** *n.* декабри́ст.

decency *n.* прили́чие. *A man without decency,* бессо́вестный челове́к. *He didn't have the decency to apologize,* у него́ хвати́ло со́вести не извиня́ться.

decent *adj.* 1, (proper) прили́чный. 2, (respectable) поря́дочный. 3, (adequate; passable) прили́чный. 4, (kind; thoughtful) любе́зный. —**decently,** *adv.* прили́чно.

decentralize *v.t.* децентрализова́ть. —**decentralization,** *n.* децентрализа́ция.

deception *n.* обма́н. —**deceptive,** *adj.* обма́нчивый.

decibel *n.* дециб́ел.

decide *v.t. & i.* реша́ть. *I decided to ask him,* я реши́л(а) спроси́ть его́. *I decided that...,* я реши́л(а), что... *Decide a question in someone's favor,* реши́ть вопро́с в чью́-нибудь по́льзу. *Decide the outcome of,* реша́ть исхо́д (+ *gen.*). *Decide on a course of action,* реши́ться на (како́й-нибудь) посту́пок.

decided *adj.* я́вный; беспо́рный; реши́тельный. *A decided advantage,* я́вное преиму́щество. —**decidedly,** *adv.* реши́тельно.

deciduous *adj.* листопа́дный.

decigram *also,* **decigramme** *n.* дециѓрамм.

deciliter *also,* **decilitre** *n.* децили́тр.

decimal *adj.* десяти́чный. *The decimal system,* десяти́чная систе́ма. —*n.* десяти́чная дробь.

decimate *v.t.* разоря́ть; коси́ть.

decimeter *also,* **decimetre** *n.* дециме́тр.

decipher *v.t.* 1, (decode) расшифро́вывать; дешифри́ровать. 2, (read; make out) разбира́ть. —**decipherment,** *n.* расшифро́вка; дешифро́вка.

decision *n.* реше́ние: *unanimous decision,* единоду́шное реше́ние.

decisive *adj.* 1, (forceful; conclusive) реши́тельный: *decisive person,* реши́тельный челове́к; *decisive victory,* реши́тельная побе́да. 2, (determining the final outcome) реша́ющий: *decisive factor,* реша́ющий фа́ктор. —**decisively,** *adv.* реши́тельно. —**decisiveness,** *n.* реши́тельность.

deck *n.* 1, (of a ship) па́луба. 2, (of a bridge) я́рус. 3, (pack of cards) коло́да. —*v.t.* украша́ть. *The city is decked with flags,* го́род уве́шан фла́гами. *Decked out in a new suit,* принаряже́н в но́вый костю́м.

deck chair шезло́нг.

deckhouse *n.* ру́бка.

declaim *v.t. & i.* деклами́ровать. —**declaimer,** *n.* деклама́тор.

declamation *n.* деклама́ция. —**declamatory,** *adj.* декламацио́нный.

declaration *n.* объявле́ние; деклара́ция. *Declaration of war,* объявле́ние войны́. *Declaration of love,* объясне́ние в любви́. *Customs declaration,* тамо́женная деклара́ция.

declarative *adj.* 1, (making a statement or assertion) декларати́вный. 2, *gram.* повествова́тельный.

declare *v.t.* 1, (announce formally; proclaim) объявля́ть: *declare war on,* объяви́ть войну́ (+ *dat.*). 2, (assert; avow) заявля́ть. 3, (pronounce) признава́ть: *declare someone insane,* признава́ть кого́-нибудь душевнобольны́м. 4, (make a statement of) деклари́ровать: *declare income,* деклари́ровать дохо́д. *Have you anything to declare?,* вы что́-нибудь деклари́руете?; вы что́-нибудь бу́дете деклари́ровать?

declassify *v.t.* рассекре́чивать.

declension *n., gram.* склоне́ние.

declinable *adj., gram.* склоня́емый.

declination *n.* 1, *astron.* склоне́ние. 2, (magnetic declination) магни́тное отклоне́ние.

decline *v.t.* 1, (turn down) отклоня́ть; отка́зываться от. *Decline the invitation,* отклони́ть приглаше́ние. *Decline the nomination,* отка́зывать в выдвиже́нии кандида́том. 2, *fol. by inf.* (refuse) отка́зываться. 3, *gram.* склоня́ть. —*v.i.* 1, (refuse to accept something) отка́зываться. 2, (decrease; go down) уменьша́ться; па́дать. 3, (deteriorate) приходи́ть в упа́док. —*n.* 1, (downward slope) склон. 2, (drop; reduction) паде́ние; сниже́ние. 3, (deterioration) упа́док.

declivity *n.* склон; спуск; отко́с.

decoction *n.* отва́р.

decode *v.t.* расшифро́вывать. —**decoding,** *n.* расшифро́вка.

décolleté *adj.* декольте́; декольтиро́ванный. —**décolletage,** *n.* декольте́.

decolonization *n.* деколониза́ция.

decompose *v.t.* разлага́ть. —*v.i.* разлага́ться. —**decomposition,** *n.* разложе́ние.

decompression *n.* декомпре́ссия.

decontaminate *v.t.* 1, (rid of germs) обеззара́живать. 2, (rid of poisonous or radioactive substances) дегази́ровать. —**decontamination,** *n.* обеззара́живание; дегаза́ция; дезактива́ция.

decontrol *v.t.* освобожда́ть от контро́ля.

décor *n.* обстано́вка.

decorate *v.t.* 1, (adorn) украша́ть; декори́ровать. *Decorate a Christmas tree,* украша́ть рожде́ственскую ёлку. 2, (furnish) обставля́ть; отде́лывать. 3, (award a medal to) награжда́ть.

decoration *n.* 1, (act of decorating) украше́ние. 2, (ornament) украше́ние. 3, (award) награ́да; знак отли́чия.

decorative *adj.* декорати́вный.

decorator *n.* декора́тор.

decorous *adj.* прили́чный; присто́йный; чи́нный.

decorum *n.* прили́чие; деко́рум.

decoy *n.* прима́нка. —*v.t.* зама́нивать; прима́нивать.

decrease *v.t.* уменьша́ть: *decrease the dose,* уменьша́ть до́зу. —*v.i.* уменьша́ться: *Their numbers are steadily decreasing,* их число́ неукло́нно уменьша́ется. —*n.* уменьше́ние: *decrease in the population,* уменьше́ние чи́сленности населе́ния.

decree *n.* ука́з; декре́т; постановле́ние. —*v.t. & i.* постановля́ть.

decrepit *adj.* дря́хлый. —**decrepitude,** *n.* дря́хлость.

decry *v.t.* осужда́ть; порица́ть.

dedicate *v.t.* 1, (devote; inscribe) посвяща́ть. *Dedicate a book to,* посвяща́ть кни́гу (+ *dat.*). 2, (open formally) открыва́ть.

dedicated adj. пре́данный.

dedication n. **1,** (act of dedicating) посвяще́ние. **2,** (formal opening) откры́тие. **3,** (devotion) пре́данность.

deduce v.t. выводи́ть: *From this I deduced that...*, из э́того я вы́вел, что...

deduct v.t. **1,** (subtract) вычита́ть. **2,** (withhold) уде́рживать; отчисля́ть.

deduction n. **1,** (subtraction; withholding; amount withheld) вы́чет; удержа́ние; отчисле́ние. **2,** (reasoning) деду́кция. **3,** (conclusion) вы́вод. —**deductive,** adj. дедукти́вный.

deed n. **1,** (act) посту́пок; де́ло. *Good deed,* до́брое де́ло. **2,** (exploit) по́двиг. **3,** pl. (action, as opposed to words) дела́. **4,** (legal document) акт; гра́мота.

deem v.t. счита́ть: *deem something necessary,* счита́ть что́-нибудь необходи́мым.

de-emphasize v.t. преуменьша́ть.

deep adj. **1,** (extending far down, back or into) глубо́кий: *deep hole/river,* глубо́кая я́ма/река́. *Deep cut,* глубо́кий поре́з. **2,** (having a specified depth): глубины́; глубино́й; в глубину́. *A well five meters deep,* коло́дец пятиметро́вой глубины́. *This lake is ten meters deep,* э́то о́зеро де́сять ме́тров глубино́й or в глубину́. **3,** (profound; intense) глубо́кий: *deep feelings,* глубо́кие чу́вства. **4,** (of sleep) глубо́кий; беспро́будный. **5,** (absorbed, as in thought) погружённый (в мы́сли). **6,** (low-pitched) ни́зкий; густо́й. **7,** (dark, as of a color) тёмный: *deep blue,* тёмно-си́ний. —adv. глубоко́: *dig deep,* рыть глубоко́. —**deep into,** вглубь (+ gen.).

deepen v.t. углубля́ть. —v.i. углубля́ться.

deeply adv. глубоко́: *breathe deeply,* дыша́ть глубоко́. *Deeply in debt,* круго́м в долга́х. *Deeply disappointed,* жесто́ко разочаро́ван.

deep-rooted adj. укорени́вшийся; закорене́лый.

deep-sea adj. глубоково́дный. *Deep-sea fishing,* ло́вля ры́бы в глубо́ких во́дах. *Deep-sea diving,* водола́зное де́ло.

deep-seated adj. укорени́вшийся.

deer n. оле́нь. —adj. [also, **deer's**] оле́ний: *deer hide,* оле́нья шку́ра.

deerskin n. оле́нья шку́ра. —adj. оле́ний: *deerskin coat,* оле́нья шу́ба.

deface v.t. **1,** (mar; disfigure) уро́довать; обезобра́живать. **2,** (efface; obliterate) стира́ть; изгла́живать.

de facto 1, *used adverbially,* де-фа́кто. **2,** *used adjectivally,* факти́ческий: *de facto recognition,* факти́ческое призна́ние.

defamation n. диффама́ция; поноше́ние; клевета́. —**defamatory,** adj. клеветни́ческий.

defame v.t. поноси́ть; клевета́ть.

default n. **1,** (failure to pay money due) неплатёж. **2,** (failure to appear) нея́вка. *The winner by default,* победи́тель за нея́вкой проти́вника. —v.i. не выполня́ть обяза́тельств.

defeat n. пораже́ние: *suffer a defeat,* потерпе́ть пораже́ние. *Admit defeat,* призна́ть себя́ побеждённым. —v.t. **1,** (vanquish) побежда́ть. **2,** (beat in a game) побежда́ть; (по)би́ть; выи́грывать у; обы́грывать. **3,** (thwart; frustrate) расстра́ивать; срыва́ть. *Defeat a bill,* провали́ть законопрое́кт.

defeatism n. пораже́нчество.

defeatist n. пораже́нец. —adj. пораже́нческий.

defecate v.i. испражня́ться. —**defecation,** n. испражне́ние.

defect n. поро́к; недоста́ток; дефе́кт; брак; изъя́н. *Speech defect,* дефе́кт ре́чи. —v.i. стать невозвраще́нцем; перебега́ть; переметну́ться.

defection n. перебе́жка.

defective adj. **1,** (imperfect; faulty) неиспра́вный; дефе́ктный; брако́ванный. **2,** (subnormal in intelligence) дефекти́вный. *Mentally defective,* у́мственно неполноце́нный; у́мственно отста́лый.

defector n. невозвраще́нец; перебе́жчик.

defence n. = **defense.** —**defenceless,** adj. = **defenseless.** —**defenceman,** n. = **defenseman.**

defend v.t. **1,** (protect) защища́ть; обороня́ть. *Defend the motherland,* защища́ть ро́дину. *Defend oneself,* защища́ться; отбива́ться. **2,** (uphold; stand up for) защища́ть; отста́ивать: *defend one's viewpoint,* защища́ть/отста́ивать свою́ то́чку зре́ния. *Defend someone against accusations,* защища́ть кого́-нибудь от обвине́ний. *Defend a dissertation,* защища́ть диссерта́цию.

defendant n., law подсуди́мый; обвиня́емый; отве́тчик.

defender n. защи́тник.

defense also, **defence** n. **1,** (protection) защи́та. *Self-defense,* самооборо́на; самозащи́та. *Come/rise to the defense of,* встать or подня́ться на защи́ту (+ gen.). *Speak in defense of,* выступа́ть в защи́ту (+ gen.). **2,** mil. оборо́на: *minister of defense,* мини́стр оборо́ны. *Defense expenditures,* затра́ты на оборо́ну. *Break through the enemy's defenses,* прорва́ть оборо́ну проти́вника. **3,** law; sports защи́та: *witness for the defense,* свиде́тель защи́ты. —**defense attorney,** защи́тник.

defenseless also, **defenceless** adj. беззащи́тный.

defenseman also, **defenceman** n. защи́тник.

defensive adj. обори́тельный. —n. оборо́на: *on the defensive,* в оборо́не.

defer v.t. (put off) откла́дывать; отсро́чивать. —v.i. [usu. **defer to**] **1,** (show deference to) относи́ться с почте́нием к. **2,** (yield to; rely on) полага́ться на. *I defer to your judgment,* я полага́юсь на ва́ше мне́ние.

deference n. уваже́ние; почте́ние; почти́тельность. *In deference to,* из уваже́ния к.

deferential adj. почти́тельный.

deferment n. отсро́чка. *Also,* **deferral.**

defiance n. неповинове́ние. *In defiance of,* вопреки́; напереко́р. *With defiance in his voice,* вызыва́ющим то́ном.

defiant adj. вызыва́ющий.

deficiency n. **1,** (shortage) недоста́ток; недоста́точность: *vitamin deficiency,* недоста́ток витами́нов; витами́нная недоста́точность. **2,** (shortcoming) недоста́ток.

deficient *adj.* имéющий недостáтки; недостáточный. *Be seriously deficient,* имéть серьёзные недостáтки.

deficit *n.* дефици́т.

defile *v.t.* оскверня́ть; развращáть. —*n.* (narrow passage) тесни́на. —**defilement,** *n.* осквернéние; развращéние.

define *v.t.* **1,** (give the definition of) определя́ть. **2,** (specify) определя́ть; устанáвливать; характеризовáть.

definite *adj.* определённый; тóчный. *Make it definite,* договори́ться определённо. *Nothing is definite yet,* покá ещё нет ничегó определённого. —**definite article,** *gram.* определённый арти́кль *or* член.

definitely *adv.* **1,** (for sure) определённо: *I can't say definitely,* не могý сказáть определённо. **2,** (absolutely) безуслóвно: *This is definitely the last time,* э́то безуслóвно послéдний раз. **3,** (without fail) обязáтельно.

definition *n.* **1,** (of a word) определéние. **2,** (clarity; sharpness) рéзкость.

definitive *adj.* окончáтельный. —**definitively,** *adv.* окончáтельно.

deflate *v.t.* **1,** (release the air from) спускáть. **2,** (puncture the pride of) сбивáть спесь с.

deflation *n., econ.* дефля́ция.

deflect *v.t.* отводи́ть; отклоня́ть; отбивáть. —*v.i.* отклоня́ться. —**deflection,** *n.* отклонéние.

deforest *v.t.* обезлéсить. —**deforestation,** *n.* обезлéсение.

deform *v.t.* урóдовать. —**deformation,** *n.* деформáция. —**deformed,** *adj.* урóдливый. —**deformity,** *n.* урóдство.

defraud *v.t.* обмáнывать.

defray *v.t.* покрывáть (расхóды). —**defrayal,** *n.* покры́тие (расхóдов).

defrock *v.t.* расстригáть; лишáть духóвного сáна.

defrost *v.t.* разморáживать. —*v.i.* разморáживаться. —**defroster,** *n.* обогревáтель.

deft *adj.* лóвкий; провóрный.

defunct *adj.* бóльше не существу́ющий.

defuse *v.t.* **1,** (deactivate, as a bomb) обезврéживать. **2,** *fig.* (calm; relax) разряжáть: *defuse tension/ the situation/,* разряжáть напряжéние/атмосфéру.

defy *v.t.* **1,** (openly challenge) брóсить вы́зов (+ *dat.*): *defy world opinion,* брóсить вы́зов мировóй общéственности. **2,** (ignore): *defy an order,* пренебрегáть прикáзом; ослу́шаться прикáза. *Defy death/danger,* презирáть смерть/опáсность. **3,** (dare): *I defy you to do it,* ручáюсь, что вам э́того не сдéлать. **4,** (be beyond) не поддавáться (+ *dat.*): *defy description,* не поддавáться описáнию. *His actions defy logic,* егó поступ́ки противорéчат лóгике (*or* лишены́ лóгики). *An act like that defies rational explanation,* такóй посту́пок не поддаётся рационáльному объяснéнию.

degeneracy *n.* вырождéние.

degenerate *v.i.* вырождáться; разлагáться; деградирóвать. —*n.* дегенерáт. —*adj.* вы́родившийся. — **degeneration,** *n.* вырождéние; дегенерáция; разложéние; деградáция. —**degenerative,** *adj.* вырождéнческий; дегенерати́вный.

degradation *n.* унижéние.

degrade *v.t.* унижáть. —**degrading,** *adj.* унизи́тельный.

degree *n.* **1,** (extent) стéпень: *to a certain degree,* до извéстной стéпени. *With varying degrees of success,* с рáзной стéпенью успéха. *First-degree burns,* ожóги пéрвой стéпени. **2,** (unit of measure for angles; unit of temperature) грáдус: *ten degrees below zero,* дéсять грáдусов ни́же нуля́. **3,** *gram.* стéпень: *comparative degree,* сравни́тельная стéпень. **4,** (academic title) (учёная) стéпень: *master's degree,* стéпень маги́стра. *Receive a law degree,* получи́ть диплóм юри́ста. —**by degrees,** постепéнно.

dehydrate *v.t.* обезвóживать. —**dehydration,** *n.* обезвóживание.

deice *v.t.* удаля́ть лёд от; устраня́ть обледенéние от. —**deicer,** *n.* антиобледени́тель.

deify *v.t.* обожествля́ть; обоготворя́ть. —**deification,** *n.* обожествлéние; обоготворéние.

deign *v.i.* снисходи́ть; соизволя́ть; соблаговоли́ть. *Deign to answer,* снисходи́ть до отвéта; соизвóлить/соблаговоли́ть отвéтить; удостóить (когó-нибудь) отвéтом.

deism *n.* деи́зм. —**deist,** *n.* дейст. —**deistic,** *adj.* деисти́ческий.

deity *n.* божествó.

dejected *adj.* уны́лый; подáвленный; удручённый; угнетённый. —**dejection,** *n.* уны́ние.

de jure де-ю́ре.

delay *v.t.* **1,** (cause to be late) задéрживать; замедля́ть. *Be delayed,* задержáться. **2,** (postpone) отклáдывать; отсрóчивать. —*v.i.* мéдлить. *Delay in answering,* мéдлить *or* тяну́ть с отвéтом. —*n.* **1,** (holdup) задéржка; замедлéние; промедлéние; проволóчка. *Without delay,* немéдленно; без промедлéния; без проволóчек. **2,** (short postponement) отсрóчка.

delayed-action *adj.* замéдленного дéйствия.

delectable *adj.* прелéстный.

delegate *n.* делегáт. —*v.t.* **1,** (assign) поручáть. **2,** (turn over to a subordinate) передавáть.

delegation *n.* **1,** (group of persons) делегáция. **2,** (turning over) передáча.

delete *v.t.* вычёркивать; убирáть; исключáть.

deleterious *adj.* врéдный; пáгубный; тлетвóрный.

deletion *n.* **1,** (act of deleting) вычёркивание. **2,** (something deleted) купю́ра.

delftware *n.* фая́нс.

deliberate *adj.* **1,** (intentional) нарочи́тый; намéренный; умы́шленный. **2,** (careful) осторóжный; осмотри́тельный. **3,** (unhurried) нетороли́вый. —*v.i.* **1,** (think carefully) соображáть. **2,** (consult; confer) совещáться.

deliberately *adv.* нарóчно; умы́шленно.

deliberation *n.* **1,** (careful thought) размышлéние. **2,** (slowness and care) осторóжность; осмотри́тельность. **3,** *pl.* (discussion and debate) рабóта: *conclude its deliberations,* закóнчить свою́ рабóту.

deliberative *adj.* совещáтельный: *deliberative body,* совещáтельный óрган.

delicacy *n.* **1,** (need of tactful treatment) делика́тность; щекотли́вость. **2,** (tact) делика́тность. **3,** (choice item of food) деликате́с; ла́комство.

delicate *adj.* **1,** (frail; tenuous) хру́пкий; делика́тный. *Delicate child,* хру́пкий ребёнок; *delicate health,* хру́пкое здоро́вье. *Upset the delicate balance,* нару́шить хру́пкое равнове́сие. **2,** (keen; fine; subtle; sensitive) то́нкий: *delicate work/operation,* то́нкая рабо́та/опера́ция; *delicate instrument,* то́нкий прибо́р; *delicate sense of smell,* то́нкое чу́вство обоня́ния. **3,** (needing tactful handling) щекотли́вый; делика́тный; *delicate subject,* щекотли́вый/делика́тный вопро́с.

delicatessen *n.* **1,** (store) гастрономи́ческий магази́н; магази́н кулина́рии; гастроно́м. **2,** (food) кулина́рия.

delicious *adj.* о́чень вку́сный.

delight *n.* **1,** (great pleasure) (большо́е) удово́льствие; наслажде́ние; отра́да. *To my delight,* к моему́ удово́льствию. *Take delight in,* получа́ть удово́льствие от. **2,** (something that gives great pleasure) пре́лесть. —*v.t.* восхища́ть. —*v.i.* [*usu.* **delight in**] наслажда́ться (+ *instr.*).

delighted *adj.* о́чень рад; восхищённый.

delightful *adj.* преле́стный; восхити́тельный.

delimit *v.t.* разграни́чивать; размежёвывать; отмежёвывать. —**delimitation,** *n.* разграниче́ние.

delineate *v.t.* **1,** (outline) оче́рчивать. **2,** (describe in detail) обрисо́вывать.

delinquency *n.* правонаруше́ние. *Juvenile delinquency,* де́тская престу́пность.

delinquent *adj.* **1,** (having done wrong) вино́вный. **2,** (overdue) просро́ченный. *Be delinquent in one's payments,* просро́чивать платежи́. —*n.* несовершенноле́тний *or* малоле́тний престу́пник; правонаруши́тель.

delirious *adj.* бредо́вый. *Be delirious,* быть в бреду́; бре́дить.

delirium *n.* бред.

deliver *v.t.* **1,** (take to a place) доставля́ть: *deliver a package/telegram,* доставля́ть посы́лку/телегра́мму. *Deliver a message,* передава́ть сообще́ние. *Deliver grain to the state,* сдава́ть хлеб госуда́рству. **2,** (distribute, as mail) разноси́ть. **3,** (present formally) вруча́ть: *deliver a protest,* вручи́ть проте́ст. **4,** (save; set free) избавля́ть. **5,** (deal, as a blow) наноси́ть. **6,** (give, as a speech, lecture, etc.) выступа́ть (с ре́чью); чита́ть (ле́кцию); де́лать (докла́д). **7,** (assist at the birth of) принима́ть. *Deliver babies,* принима́ть ро́ды.

deliverance *n.* избавле́ние. —**deliverer,** *n.* избави́тель.

delivery *n.* **1,** (delivering; transporting) доста́вка: *home delivery,* доста́вка на́ дом. *Grain deliveries,* поста́вки зерна́. **2,** (giving birth) ро́ды. **3,** (rescue) избавле́ние. **4,** (manner of speaking) ди́кция. **5,** *sports* пода́ча. —**delivery boy; deliveryman,** *n.* рассы́льный. —**delivery room,** роди́льное отделе́ние. —**delivery system,** *mil.* сре́дство доста́вки.

dell *n.* доли́на; (лесна́я) лощи́на.

delphinium *n.* живо́кость; шпо́рник.

delta *n.* де́льта. —**deltoid,** *adj.* дельтови́дный.

delude *v.t.* вводи́ть в заблужде́ние. *Delude oneself,* обма́нывать себя́; обольща́ться.

deluge *n.* **1,** (downpour) ли́вень. **2,** (flood) пото́п. **3,** (overwhelming influx) пото́к; град. —*v.t.* **1,** (flood) затопля́ть. **2,** *fig.* (swamp) засы́пать: *We've been deluged with requests,* нас засы́пали про́сьбами.

delusion *n.* заблужде́ние: *be under a delusion,* быть в заблужде́нии. —**delusions of grandeur,** ма́ния вели́чия.

de luxe роско́шный; люкс: *de luxe hotel,* гости́ница-люкс.

delve *v.i.* [*usu.* **delve into**] углубля́ться (в); вника́ть (в); проника́ть (в).

demagnetize *v.t.* размагни́чивать.

demagogue *n.* демаго́г. —**demagoguery; demagogy,** *n.* демаго́гия. —**demagogic,** *adj.* демагоги́ческий.

demand *v.t.* тре́бовать: *demand an apology,* тре́бовать извине́ния. *He demanded to be allowed to see her,* он потре́бовал, чтобы его́ допусти́ли к ней. —*n.* **1,** (insistent request) тре́бование: *demands for reform,* тре́бования рефо́рмы. **2,** *econ.* спрос: *supply and demand,* спрос и предложе́ние. *The demand for cars,* спрос на автомоби́ли. *Be in great demand,* име́ть большо́й спрос; быть в большо́м ходу́. —**on demand,** по тре́бованию.

demanding *adj.* тре́бовательный; взыска́тельный.

demarcate *v.t.* разграни́чивать.

demarcation *n.* демарка́ция. *Line of demarcation,* демаркацио́нная ли́ния.

démarche *n.* дема́рш.

demean *v.t.* унижа́ть; роня́ть. *Demean oneself,* унижа́ться; роня́ть себя́; роня́ть своё досто́инство.

demeanor *also,* **demeanour** *n.* поведе́ние; мане́ра держа́ть себя́.

demented *adj.* сумасше́дший; поме́шанный. —**dementia,** *n.* сумасше́ствие; помеша́тельство.

demerit *n.* **1,** (fault; defect) недоста́ток. **2,** (mark for bad conduct) взыска́ние.

demigod *n.* полубо́г.

demilitarization *n.* демилитариза́ция.

demilitarize *v.t.* демилитаризова́ть. *Demilitarized zone,* демилитаризо́ванная зо́на.

demise *n.* кончи́на.

demitasse *n.* ма́ленькая ча́шка.

demobilize *v.t.* демобилизова́ть. —**demobilization,** *n.* демобилиза́ция.

democracy *n.* демокра́тия.

democrat *n.* демокра́т. —**democratic,** *adj.* демократи́ческий.

democratize *v.t.* демократизи́ровать. —**democratization,** *n.* демократиза́ция.

demography *n.* демогра́фия. —**demographer,** *n.* демо́граф. —**demographic,** *adj.* демографи́ческий.

demolish *v.t.* **1,** (tear down) сноси́ть. **2,** (destroy) разруша́ть. **3,** *fig.* (refute, as a theory) разбива́ть.

demolition *n.* **1,** (tearing down) снос. **2,** (destruction) разруше́ние. —*adj.* подрывно́й: *demolition work,* подрывны́е рабо́ты. —**demolition bomb,** фуга́сная бо́мба.

demon *n.* де́мон; бес. —**demoniac; demonic,** *adj.* демони́ческий.

demonstrable *adj.* доказу́емый. —**demonstrably,** *adv.* я́вно.

demonstrate *v.t.* **1,** (show) демонстри́ровать: *demonstrate a new device,* демонстри́ровать но́вый прибо́р. **2,** (show clearly) пока́зывать: *The war demonstrated the superiority of...,* война́ показа́ла превосхо́дство (+ *gen.*). **3,** (prove) доказа́ть. **4,** (reveal, as a quality) проявля́ть: *demonstrate courage,* проявля́ть му́жество. —*v.i.* демонстри́ровать: *demonstrate against something,* демонстри́ровать про́тив чего-нибудь.

demonstration *n.* **1,** (show; display) демонстра́ция: *demonstration of merchandise,* демонстра́ция това́ров. **2,** (manifestation) проявле́ние: *demonstration of good will,* проявле́ние до́брой во́ли. **3,** (parade; march) демонстра́ция; манифеста́ция.

demonstrative *adj.* **1,** (given to showing one's feelings) экспанси́вный. **2,** (showing clearly; convincing) нагля́дный; доказа́тельный. **3,** *gram.* указа́тельный: *demonstrative pronoun,* указа́тельное местоиме́ние.

demonstrator *n.* **1,** (one who demonstrates something) демонстра́тор. **2,** (one who participates in a demonstration) демонстра́нт.

demoralize *v.t.* деморализова́ть; разлага́ть. —**demoralization,** *n.* деморализа́ция.

demote *v.t.* понижа́ть (в до́лжности, по слу́жбе, в чи́не, *etc.*); *mil.* разжа́ловать. —**demotion,** *n.* пониже́ние.

demur *v.i.* возража́ть.

demure *adj.* **1,** (sedate) степе́нный. **2,** (retiring; shy) засте́нчивый.

demurral *n.* возраже́ние.

den *n.* **1,** (lair) ло́говище; ло́гово; берло́га. *Lion's den,* ло́гово льва. **2,** (hideout for illegal activity) прито́н: *thieves'/gambling den,* воровско́й/иго́рный прито́н. *Opium den,* кури́льня о́пиума. *Den of iniquity,* прито́н развра́та. **3,** (study) кабине́т.

denature *v.t.* денатури́ровать. —**denatured alcohol,** денатури́рованный спирт; денатура́т.

dendrite *n.* дендри́т.

denial *n.* **1,** (act of denying) отрица́ние: *denial of one's guilt,* отрица́ние свое́й вины́. **2,** (statement denying something) опроверже́ние: *print a denial,* напеча́тать опроверже́ние. **3,** (refusal to grant something) отка́з; отклоне́ние: *denial of a request,* отка́з в про́сьбе; отклоне́ние про́сьбы. **4,** (repudiation) отрече́ние.

denigrate *v.t.* поро́чить; черни́ть; поноси́ть. —**denigration,** *n.* поноше́ние.

denizen *n.* жи́тель; обита́тель.

denomination *n.* **1,** (name) наименова́ние. **2,** (religious group) вероиспове́дание. **3,** (value of a coin or bill) досто́инство: *large denomination bills,* купю́ры кру́пного досто́инства.

denominator *n.* знамена́тель. *Least common denominator,* наиме́ньший о́бщий знамена́тель.

denotation *n.* **1,** (act of denoting) обозначе́ние. **2,** (explicit meaning) значе́ние.

denote *v.t.* **1,** (mean) зна́чить; означа́ть; обознача́ть. **2,** (indicate) обознача́ть: *On a map blue denotes water,* си́ний цвет на ка́рте обознача́ет мо́ре.

dénouement *n.* развя́зка.

denounce *v.t.* **1,** (condemn) осужда́ть. **2,** (inform against) доноси́ть на.

dense *adj.* **1,** (thick) густо́й; пло́тный: *dense forest,* густо́й лес; *dense fog,* густо́й *or* пло́тный тума́н. **2,** (thickheaded) тупо́й; тупоу́мный.

densely *adv.* гу́сто; пло́тно. *Densely populated,* густонаселённый; пло́тно населённый.

density *n.* **1,** (denseness) густота́; пло́тность. *Population density,* пло́тность населе́ния. **2,** *physics* пло́тность. **3,** (stupidity) тупоу́мие.

dent *n.* вмя́тина; вы́боина. *Dent in a fender,* вмя́тина в крыле́. —*v.t.* мять; вда́вливать; вмина́ть. *Dent someone's fender,* помя́ть чьё-нибудь крыло́.

dental *adj.* зубоврачебный; зубно́й. *Dental school/ practice,* зубоврачебная шко́ла/пра́ктика. *Dental technician,* зубно́й те́хник.

dentifrice *n.* зубно́й порошо́к; зубна́я па́ста.

dentine *also,* **dentin** *n.* денти́н.

dentist *n.* зубно́й врач; стомато́лог. —**dentistry,** *n.* стоматоло́гия.

denture *n.* зубно́й проте́з; че́люсть.

denude *v.t.* обнажа́ть; оголя́ть.

denunciation *n.* **1,** (condemnation) осужде́ние. **2,** (informing against) доно́с.

denunciatory *adj.* осужда́ющий.

deny *v.t.* **1,** (refuse to acknowledge) отрица́ть: *deny one's guilt,* отрица́ть свою́ вину́. *He denied that...,* он отрица́л, что... *Deny responsibility for,* не брать на себя́ отве́тственности за. *There is no denying that...,* нельзя́ не отрица́ть, что...; слов нет. **2,** (declare to be untrue) опроверга́ть: *deny a rumor/charge,* опрове́ргнуть слух/обвине́ние. **3,** (refuse to grant) отка́зывать в: *deny someone's request,* отка́зывать кому́-нибудь в про́сьбе. *He was denied permission,* ему́ не да́ли разреше́ния. **4,** (deprive) лиша́ть: *denied the right to vote,* лишён пра́ва го́лоса. —**deny oneself something,** отка́зывать себе́ в (+ *prepl.*).

deodorant *n.* дезодора́нт.

depart *v.i.* **1,** (leave) уходи́ть; уезжа́ть; отходи́ть; отправля́ться; отбыва́ть. **2,** *fol. by* **from** (deviate) отклоня́ться (от); отходи́ть (от); отступа́ть (от). *Depart from one's prepared text,* отступа́ть от подгото́вленного те́кста. —*v.t. Depart this world,* поки́нуть э́тот свет (*or* э́тот мир).

departed *adj.* уме́рший. —*n.* поко́йник.

department *n.* **1,** (section) отде́л; отделе́ние. *Personnel department,* отде́л ка́дров. *Shoe department,* обувно́й отде́л. *Order department,* отде́л зака́зов; стол зака́зов. *Children's department,* де́тское отделе́ние. **2,** (government bureau) ве́домство; министе́рство; департа́мент. *The State Department,* госуда́рственный департа́мент. *The Department of Defense,* министе́рство оборо́ны. **3,** (subdivision of a college) факульте́т; ка́федра.

departmental *adj.* ве́домственный.

department store универса́льный магази́н; универма́г.

departure *n.* **1,** (leaving) отъе́зд; ухо́д; отхо́д; отправле́ние; отбы́тие. **2,** (deviation) отклоне́ние; отступле́ние; отхо́д. —**point of departure,** то́чка отправле́ния.

depend *v.i.* [*usu.* **depend on**] **1,** (be contingent on) зави́сеть (от). *It (all) depends,* смотря́ по обстоя́тельствам. **2,** (rely on; count on) полага́ться (на); рассчи́тывать (на). —**depending on,** в зави́симости от; смотря́ по.

dependable *adj.* надёжный. —**dependability,** *n.* надёжность.

dependant *n.* = **dependent.**

dependence *n.* зави́симость. *Dependence on someone,* зави́симость от кого́-нибудь.

dependency *n.* **1,** = **dependence. 2,** (dependent territory) зави́симая страна́.

dependent *adj.* зави́симый: *dependent countries,* зави́симые стра́ны. *He is not dependent on anyone,* он ни от кого́ не зави́сит. *Be dependent on someone for something,* быть на иждиве́нии кого́-нибудь. —*n.* [*also,* **dependant**] иждиве́нец. *How many dependents have you?,* ско́лько у вас на иждиве́нии? —**dependent clause,** прида́точное предложе́ние.

depersonalize *v.t.* обезли́чивать.

depict *v.t.* изобража́ть.

deplete *v.t.* истоща́ть. *Become depleted,* истоща́ться; скуде́ть. —**depletion,** *n.* истоще́ние.

deplore *v.t.* сожале́ть о. —**deplorable,** *adj.* приско́рбный; плаче́вный.

deploy *v.t.* развёртывать; размеща́ть; дислоци́ровать. —**deployment,** *n.* развёртывание; размеще́ние; дислока́ция.

depopulate *v.t.* обезлю́дить. *Become depopulated,* обезлю́деть.

deport *v.t.* высыла́ть; депорти́ровать. —**deport oneself,** вести́ себя́; держа́ть себя́.

deportation *n.* вы́сылка; депорта́ция.

deportment *n.* поведе́ние; мане́ры.

depose *v.t.* сверга́ть; низлага́ть.

deposit *n.* **1,** (money placed in a bank) вклад; депози́т. **2,** (anything given as security) зало́г; зада́ток. **3,** (accumulation of minerals in the ground) за́лежь; месторожде́ние; ро́ссыпь. **4,** (natural accumulation) отложе́ние: *calcium/lime deposits,* ка́льциевые/известко́вые отложе́ния. —*v.t.* **1,** (place in a bank) класть в банк; депони́ровать. **2,** (place; drop) класть; опуска́ть. *Deposit a coin in a machine,* опуска́ть моне́ту в автома́т.

deposition *n.* **1,** (act of deposing) низложе́ние. **2,** (written statement used as evidence) показа́ние.

depositor *n.* вкла́дчик; депози́тор; депоне́нт.

depository *n.* храни́лище.

depot *n.* **1,** (warehouse) склад. **2,** (train or bus station) вокза́л; ста́нция.

deprave *v.t.* развраща́ть. —**depraved,** *adj.* развращённый; поро́чный. —**depravity,** *n.* развращённость; развра́т; поро́чность.

deprecate *v.t.* **1,** (express disapproval of) осужда́ть. **2,** (belittle) умаля́ть.

depreciate *v.i.* обесце́ниваться. —*v.t.* **1,** (lessen the value of) обесце́нивать. **2,** (belittle) умаля́ть.

depreciation *n.* **1,** (decline in value) обесце́нение; обесце́нивание. **2,** (allowance made for this in accounting) амортиза́ция.

depredation *n.* грабёж; ограбле́ние.

depress *v.t.* **1,** (dispirit) угнета́ть; удруча́ть; приводи́ть в мра́чное состоя́ние. **2,** (press down on) нажима́ть на. —**depressed,** *adj.* пода́вленный; удручённый; угнетённый. —**depressing,** *adj.* подавля́ющий; удруча́ющий.

depression *n.* **1,** (sunken place; hollow) впа́дина; углубле́ние. **2,** (low spirits) депре́ссия. **3,** (economic crisis) депре́ссия; кри́зис.

deprivation *n.* лише́ние: *deprivation of freedom,* лише́ние свобо́ды. *Suffer deprivations,* терпе́ть лише́ния.

deprive *v.t.* лиша́ть: *deprive someone of his rights,* лиша́ть кого́-нибудь прав.

depth *n.* **1,** (distance downward) глубина́: *at a depth of 200 meters,* на глубине́ двухсо́т ме́тров. **2,** *pl.* (deepest part) глубины́; глубь: *the ocean depths,* морски́е глуби́ны; морска́я глубь. *In the depths of despair,* в глубо́ком (*or* в по́лном) отча́янии. **3,** (intellectual capacity or profundity) глубина́; глубокомы́слие. —**in depth,** глубоко́.

depth charge глуби́нная бо́мба.

deputation *n.* депута́ция.

deputize *v.t.* назнача́ть замести́телем. —*v.i.* замеща́ть.

deputy *n.* **1,** (one appointed to act for another) замести́тель. **2,** (member of a legislature in certain countries) депута́т. —*adj. Deputy director,* замести́тель дире́ктора.

derail *v.t.* пуска́ть (по́езд) под отко́с. *Be derailed,* сходи́ть с ре́льсов. —**derailment,** *n.* сход с ре́льсов.

derange *v.t.* своди́ть с ума́. —**deranged,** *adj.* сумасше́дший; поме́шанный. *Become deranged,* сойти́ с ума́. —**derangement,** *n.* сумасше́ствие; умопомеша́тельство.

derby *n.* **1,** (hat) котело́к. **2,** *cap.* (race) де́рби.

derelict *n.* бродя́га; бося́к. —*adj. Be derelict in one's duty,* изменя́ть своему́ до́лгу.

dereliction *n.* наруше́ние: *dereliction of duty,* наруше́ние до́лга.

deride *v.t.* насмеха́ться над; осме́ивать; высме́ивать.

derision *n.* насме́шка; осмея́ние; издева́тельство. *Object of derision,* предме́т насме́шек.

derisive *adj.* насме́шливый; издева́тельский.

derivation *n.* **1,** (obtaining) получе́ние. *Derivation of a formula,* вы́вод фо́рмулы. **2,** (origin, as of a word) происхожде́ние.

derivative *adj.* произво́дный. —*n.* **1,** *chem.* произво́дное; дерива́т. **2,** *ling.* произво́дное сло́во. **3,** *math.* произво́дная.

derive *v.t.* **1,** (receive, as pleasure, benefit, etc.) получа́ть; извлека́ть. **2,** (deduce, as a formula) выводи́ть. —*v.i.* (originate) происходи́ть.

dermatology *n.* дерматоло́гия. —**dermatologist,** *n.* дермато́лог.

derogate *v.i.* [*usu.* derogate from] умаля́ть. —derogation, *n.* умале́ние.

derogatory *adj.* оскорби́тельный; оби́дный: *derogatory remarks*, оскорби́тельные/оби́дные замеча́ния.

derrick *n.* 1, (crane) де́ррик; де́ррик-кра́н. 2, (oil derrick) нефтяна́я вы́шка.

dervish *n.* де́рвиш.

desalinize *also*, desalinate *v.t.* опресня́ть. —desalinization; desalination, *n.* опресне́ние.

descend *v.i.* 1, (go down) сходи́ть; спуска́ться. *The plane descended to 2,000 meters*, самолёт сни́зился до двух ты́сяч ме́тров. *The road descends to the river*, доро́га сбега́ет к реке́. *In descending order*, в нисходя́щем поря́дке. 2, *fol. by* on (visit without warning) нагря́нуть (к). 3, *fol. by* to (stoop to) унижа́ться (до). 4, *fol. by from* [*also*, be descended from] (be a descendant of) происходи́ть (из). —*v.t.* сходи́ть с *or* по; спуска́ться с *or* по: *descend the staircase*, сходи́ть *or* спуска́ться по ле́стнице (*or* с ле́стницы).

descendant *n.* пото́мок.

descent *n.* 1, (downward motion) спуск: *descent from a mountain*, спуск с горы́. *Descent of an aircraft*, сниже́ние самолёта. *The plane is beginning its descent*, самолёт идёт на сниже́ние. 2, (downward slope) спуск; склон; скат. 3, (ancestry) происхожде́ние: *of Russian descent*, ру́сский по происхожде́нию. *Of noble descent*, благоро́дного происхожде́ния.

describe *v.t.* 1, (give a description of) опи́сывать. 2, (depict in a certain way) характеризова́ть.

description *n.* описа́ние. *Of every description*, вся́кого ро́да.

descriptive *adj.* описа́тельный. —descriptive geometry, начерта́тельная геоме́трия.

descry *v.t.* рассмотре́ть; разгляде́ть.

desecrate *v.t.* оскверня́ть. —desecration, *n.* оскверне́ние.

desegregate *v.t.* десегреги́ровать. —desegregation, *n.* десегрега́ция.

desert[1] (dez-ert) *n.* пусты́ня. —*adj.* пусты́нный. *Desert island*, необита́емый о́стров.

desert[2] (di-zurt) *v.t.* броса́ть; покида́ть; оставля́ть. —*v.i.*, *mil.* дезерти́ровать. —*n.*, *often pl.* заслу́га: *get one's just deserts*, получи́ть по заслу́гам.

deserted *adj.* безлю́дный; пусты́нный; опусте́лый. *The streets were deserted*, у́лицы бы́ли пусты́нны; на у́лицах бы́ло пу́сто.

deserter *n.* дезерти́р.

desertion *n.* 1, (abandonment) ухо́д (от семьи́). *Sue for divorce on grounds of desertion*, возбужда́ть де́ло о разво́де на основа́нии ухо́да от семьи́. 2, *mil.* дезерти́рство.

deserve *v.t.* заслу́живать: *deserve an award*, заслу́живать награ́ды. *He didn't deserve to win*, он не заслужи́л побе́ды. *He got what he deserved*, он получи́л по заслу́гам. —deserved, *adj.* заслу́женный; досто́йный. —deservedly, *adv.* заслу́женно; по заслу́гам; по пра́ву. —deserving, *adj.* досто́йный.

design *v.t.* 1, (plan, as a building) проекти́ровать. *A building designed by...*, зда́ние, постро́енное по прое́кту (+ *gen.*). 2, (same for an aircraft, machine, etc.) конструи́ровать; (clothes) модели́ровать; (a book or stage set) оформля́ть. 3, (intend; mean) предназнача́ть: *The dictionary is designed for children*, слова́рь предназна́чен для дете́й. *A law designed to protect consumers*, зако́н, напра́вленный на защи́ту потреби́телей. —*n.* 1, (pattern) узо́р. 2, (of a building) прое́кт; (of a machine) констру́кция; (of a book) оформле́ние. 3, (sketch) чертёж. 4, (purpose; intention) за́мысел; у́мысел. *By design*, с у́мыслом. *Have designs on*, име́ть ви́ды на.

designate *v.t.* 1, (indicate; mark) обознача́ть. 2, (appoint) назнача́ть. 3, (earmark) отводи́ть.

designation *n.* 1, (name; title) назва́ние. 2, (appointment) назначе́ние. 3, (mark; sign) обозначе́ние.

designedly *adv.* умы́шленно; с у́мыслом.

designer *n.* проектиро́вщик; констру́ктор; оформи́тель. *Aircraft designer*, авиаконстру́ктор. *Dress designer*, модельер. *Stage designer*, декора́тор; оформи́тель.

designing *adj.* интригу́ющий.

desirable *adj.* жела́тельный. —desirability, *n.* жела́тельность.

desire *v.t.* жела́ть: *desire happiness*, жела́ть сча́стья. *Leave much to be desired*, оставля́ть жела́ть мно́го лу́чшего. —*n.* жела́ние: *a great desire*, большо́е жела́ние. *Burn with desire*, горе́ть жела́нием. *I have no desire to go there*, у меня́ нет никако́го жела́ния пое́хать туда́.

desired *adj.* жела́нный; жела́емый. *Achieve the desired effect*, дать жела́емый результа́т; име́ть до́лжный эффе́кт; ока́зывать жела́емое де́йствие.

desirous *adj.* жела́ющий.

desist *v.i.* перестава́ть: *desist from smoking/arguing*, переста́ть кури́ть/спо́рить. *Desist in one's efforts to...*, отказа́ться от попы́ток (+ *inf.*).

desk *n.* (пи́сьменный) стол; рабо́чий стол. *School desk*, па́рта. *Information desk*, спра́вочный стол. *Hide/find something in the desk*, спря́тать что́-нибудь в стол; найти́ что́-нибудь в столе́. *At one's desk* (*i.e. at work*), за рабо́чим столо́м. —*adj.* насто́льный: *desk lamp*, насто́льная ла́мпа. *Desk drawer*, я́щик стола́. *Desk clerk*, портье́.

desman *n.* вы́хухоль.

desolate *adj.* 1, (barren) забро́шенный. 2, (deserted) пусты́нный; безлю́дный. —*v.t.* 1, (depopulate) обезлю́дить. 2, (devastate) опустоша́ть.

desolation *n.* 1, (laying waste) опустоше́ние. 2, (emptiness; waste) запусте́ние.

despair *n.* отча́яние. —*v.i.* отча́иваться.

desperado *n.* головоре́з.

desperate *adj.* отча́янный: *desperate attempt*, отча́янная попы́тка. *I am desperate*, я в отча́янном положе́нии.

desperately *adv.* 1, (with desperation) отча́янно: *fight desperately*, боро́ться отча́янно. *Try desperately*, все́ми си́лами стара́ться. 2, (extremely; frightfully) кра́йне; ужа́сно. *Desperately ill*, тяжело́ бо́лен. 3, (urgently) до заре́зу: *He needs money desperately*, ему́ нужны́ де́ньги до заре́зу.

desperation *n.* отча́яние.

despicable *adj.* презре́нный; ни́зкий; по́длый. —**despicably**, *adv.* ни́зко; по́дло.

despise *v.t.* презира́ть.

despite *prep.* несмотря́ на. *Despite the fact that...*, несмотря́ на то, что... *Despite all*, несмотря́ ни на что.

despoil *v.t.* гра́бить; разоря́ть.

despondent *adj.* уны́лый; пода́вленный. —**despondency**, *n.* уны́ние; пода́вленность.

despot *n.* де́спот. —**despotic**, *adj.* деспоти́ческий. —**despotism**, *n.* деспоти́зм; деспоти́я.

dessert *n.* десе́рт. *For dessert*, на сла́дкое; на десе́рт. —*adj.* десе́ртный: *dessert spoon*, десе́ртная ло́жка.

destabilize *v.t.* дестабилизи́ровать. —**destabilization**, *n.* дестабилиза́ция.

destination *n.* ме́сто назначе́ния.

destine *v.t.* предназнача́ть. *We were not destined to...*, нам не суждено́ (*or* нам не судьба́) бы́ло (+ *inf.*).

destiny *n.* судьба́.

destitute *adj.* обездо́ленный; обнища́лый. *Be left destitute*, оста́ться ни с чем *or* без средств. —**destitution** *n.* нищета́; обнища́ние.

destroy *v.t.* разруша́ть; уничтожа́ть. *The house was destroyed by fire*, дом был разру́шен пожа́ром. *The hurricane destroyed the crops*, урага́н уничто́жил посе́вы. *Destroy documents*, уничтожа́ть докуме́нты.

destroyer *n.* **1,** (one who or that which destroys) разруши́тель. **2,** (ship) эска́дренный миноно́сец; эсми́нец.

destruction *n.* **1,** (act of destroying) разруше́ние. **2,** (heavy damage) разруше́ния.

destructive *adj.* разруши́тельный.

desultory *adj.* несвя́зный; бессвя́зный; отры́вочный.

detach *v.t.* отделя́ть; снима́ть. —**detachable**, *adj.* съёмный; отрезно́й.

detached *adj.* **1,** (separate) отде́льный. **2,** (impartial) беспристра́стный.

detachment *n.* **1,** (removal) отделе́ние. **2,** (impartiality) беспристра́стие. **3,** *mil.* отря́д.

detail *n.* **1,** (minute element) подро́бность; дета́ль. *In detail*, дета́льно; подро́бно. *In greater detail*, подро́бнее. *Go into detail*, вдава́ться в подро́бности. **2,** *mil.* (small detachment) наря́д. —*v.t.* **1,** (describe minutely) подро́бно намеча́ть. **2,** *mil.* (assign) наряжа́ть; отряжа́ть.

detailed *adj.* подро́бный; дета́льный.

detain *v.t.* заде́рживать: *Don't let me detain you!*, не хочу́ вас заде́рживать. *He was detained by the police*, его́ задержа́ла поли́ция.

detect *v.t.* обнару́живать; ула́вливать. *Detect a flaw in the diamond*, обнару́жить изъя́н в бриллиа́нте. *Detect a note of sarcasm in someone's words*, улови́ть язви́тельную но́тку в чьи́х-нибудь слова́х.

detection *n.* обнаруже́ние. *Early detection of cancer*, ра́ннее распознава́ние ра́ка; ра́нняя диагно́стика ра́ка.

detective *n.* сы́щик; детекти́в. —**detective story**, детекти́в.

detector *n.* дете́ктор. *Lie detector*, дете́ктор лжи. *Metal detector*, дете́ктор мета́лла; металлоиска́тель. *Smoke detector*, пожа́рная сигнализа́ция. *Mine detector*, миноиска́тель.

détente *n.* разря́дка.

detention *n.* задержа́ние; содержа́ние под аре́стом. *Be in detention*, быть под стра́жей.

deter *v.t.* сде́рживать; уде́рживать. *Deter aggression*, сде́рживать агре́ссию. *Deter aggressors*, уде́рживать агре́ссоров. *A mean dog deters burglars*, зла́я соба́ка отпу́гивает взло́мщиков. *We will not be deterred in our efforts to...*, никто́ не собьёт нас с пути́ (+ *gen.*).

detergent *n.* мо́ющее сре́дство; стира́льный порошо́к.

deteriorate *v.i.* ухудша́ться; по́ртиться. —**deterioration**, *n.* ухудше́ние.

determinant *n.* определи́тель.

determinate *adj.* определённый; устано́вленный.

determination *n.* **1,** (act of determining) определе́ние; выясне́ние. **2,** (conclusion; decision) заключе́ние; реше́ние. **3,** (firm resolve) реши́мость; реши́тельность.

determine *v.t.* **1,** (ascertain) определя́ть; выясня́ть; устана́вливать. *Determine the distance between...*, определя́ть расстоя́ние ме́жду... *Determine the cause of the crash*, вы́яснить причи́ну катастро́фы. *Determine whether any others exist*, установи́ть, не существу́ют ли и други́е. **2,** (decide) определя́ть; реша́ть: *determine the outcome of*, определя́ть/реша́ть исхо́д (+ *gen.*). *Genes determine heredity*, ге́ны определя́ют насле́дственность.

determined *adj.* **1,** (forceful; resolute) реши́тельный. *Make a determined effort*, прилага́ть осо́бые уси́лия. **2,** (full of determination) по́лный реши́мости: *I am determined to...*, я по́лон (полна́) реши́мости (+ *inf.*).

determinism *n.* детермини́зм.

deterrence *n.* сде́рживание.

deterrent *adj.* сде́рживающий; уде́рживающий. —*n.* сде́рживающий фа́ктор.

detest *v.t.* ненави́деть. —**detestable,** *adj.* отврати́тельный; ме́рзкий. —**detestation**, *n.* не́нависть.

dethrone *v.t.* сверга́ть с престо́ла.

detonate *v.t.* взрыва́ть. —*v.i.* взрыва́ться; детони́ровать. —**detonation,** *n.* детона́ция. —**detonator,** *n.* детона́тор.

detour *n.* объе́зд; крюк. *Make a detour*, сде́лать крюк.

detract *v.i.* [*usu.* **detract from**] умаля́ть. —**detraction,** *n.* умале́ние. —**detractor,** *n.* хули́тель.

detriment *n.* вред; уще́рб: *to the detriment of*, во вред *or* в уще́рб (+ *dat.*).

detrimental *adj.* вре́дный: *detrimental to one's health*, вре́дно для здоро́вья.

deuce *n.* **1,** (two) дво́йка. **2,** *tennis* ра́вный счёт. **3,** *colloq.* (devil; dickens) чёрт: *What the deuce is he doing there!*, како́го чёрта он там де́лает!

deuterium *n.* дейте́рий.

Deuteronomy *n.* Второзако́ние.

devalue *v.t.* девальви́ровать. —**devaluation,** *n.* девальва́ция.

devastate *v.t.* **1,** (lay waste) опустоша́ть. **2,** *fig.* (shatter; demoralize) потряса́ть.

devastating *adj.* **1,** (extremely destructive) опустоши́тельный. *Devastating blow,* сокруши́тельный уда́р. **2,** *fig.* (withering; scathing) уничтожа́ющий; уби́йственный.

devastation *n.* опустоше́ние.

develop *v.t.* **1,** (expand; improve) развива́ть: *develop one's muscles,* развива́ть мускулату́ру. *Develop new sources of energy,* развива́ть но́вые исто́чники эне́ргии. **2,** (work out; perfect) разраба́тывать: *develop a method,* разраба́тывать ме́тод; *develop a new aircraft,* разраба́тывать но́вый самолёт. **3,** (acquire gradually) развива́ть; приобрета́ть; выраба́тывать. *Develop an interest in,* развива́ть интере́с к. *Develop a taste for,* приобрета́ть вкус к. *Develop pneumonia,* получи́ть воспале́ние лёгких. *Develop an immunity to,* вы́работать иммуните́т к. *He has developed the habit of...,* у него́ вы́работалась привы́чка (+ *inf.*). **4,** (build up) осва́ивать; застра́ивать: *develop new lands,* осва́ивать но́вые зе́мли; *develop the outskirts of a city,* застра́ивать окра́ину го́рода. **5,** *photog.* проявля́ть. —*v.i.* **1,** (increase in maturity, scope, etc.) развива́ться. *Developing countries,* развива́ющиеся стра́ны. **2,** (gradually come into being) создава́ться; скла́дываться: *A new situation has developed,* созда́ла́сь *or* сложи́лась но́вая ситуа́ция. **3,** *fol. by* **into** (gradually become) выраста́ть в; вылива́ться в. *Develop into an excellent pianist,* вы́расти в отли́чного пиани́ста. **4,** (turn out) выясня́ться: *It developed that...,* вы́яснилось, что...

developed *adj.* развито́й: *developed countries,* разви́тые стра́ны.

developer *n.* **1,** (builder) застро́йщик. **2,** *photog.* прояви́тель.

development *n.* **1,** (act or process of developing) разви́тие. **2,** (working out; designing) разрабо́тка. **3,** (building up) освое́ние; застро́йка. **4,** (event; occurrence) собы́тие. **5,** (group of dwellings) жило́й *or* жили́щный масси́в.

deviant *adj.* ненорма́льный; противоесте́ственный.

deviate *v.i.* [*usu.* **deviate from**] отклоня́ться (от); уклоня́ться (от); отступа́ть (от). —**deviation,** *n.* отклоне́ние; уклоне́ние; отступле́ние.

device *n.* **1,** (apparatus) прибо́р; устро́йство; приспособле́ние. **2,** (something used to achieve an effect) приём. **3,** (scheme) ухищре́ние. —**leave to one's own devices,** предоставля́ть самому́ себе́.

devil *n.* **1,** (spirit of evil) чёрт; дья́вол. *What the devil are you doing here?,* како́го чёрта ты тут де́лаешь? **2,** (person; fellow): *poor devil,* бедня́га; *lucky devil,* счастли́вец. —*adj.* [*usu.* **devil's**] чёртов. —**between the devil and the deep blue sea,** ме́жду двух огне́й; ме́жду мо́лотом и накова́льней. —**give someone the devil,** дать нагоня́й (+ *dat.*). —**talk of the devil!,** лёгок на поми́не!

devilish *adj.* чёрто́вский; дья́вольский. —**devilishly,** *adv.* черто́вски.

devil-may-care *adj.* бесшаба́шный; залихва́тский.

devious *adj.* **1,** (circuitous) око́льный. **2,** (shifty) увёртливый.

devise *v.t.* приду́мывать.

devoid *adj.* [*usu.* **devoid of**] лишённый (+ *gen.*).

devolve *v.i.* [*usu.* **devolve upon**] переходи́ть (к).

devote *v.t.* посвяща́ть: *devote all one's energies to,* посвяща́ть все си́лы (+ *dat.*). *Devote oneself to,* посвяща́ть себя́ (+ *dat.*); отдава́ться (+ *dat.*). *Devote time to,* посвяща́ть *or* уделя́ть вре́мя (+ *dat.*). *Devote attention to,* уделя́ть внима́ние (+ *dat.*).

devoted *adj.* пре́данный.

devotee *n.* покло́нник.

devotion *n.* пре́данность.

devour *v.t.* **1,** (consume) пожира́ть. **2,** *fig.* (read or listen to avidly) поглоща́ть. *Devour books,* поглоща́ть *or* глота́ть кни́ги. *Devour every word (when listening),* лови́ть ка́ждое сло́во.

devout *adj.* **1,** (pious) на́божный; благочести́вый. **2,** (earnest) и́скренний: *devout wish,* и́скреннее жела́ние.

dew *n.* роса́. —**dewdrop,** *n.* роси́нка; ка́пля росы́.

dewlap *n.* подгру́док.

dewy *adj.* роси́стый.

dexterity *n.* ло́вкость; прово́рство. —**dexterous,** *adj.* ло́вкий; прово́рный.

dextrose *n.* декстро́за.

diabetes *n.* диабе́т; са́харная боле́знь. —**diabetic,** *adj.* диабети́ческий. —*n.* диабе́тик.

diabolic *adj.* дья́вольский. *Also,* **diabolical.**

diacritical *adj.* диакрити́ческий. —**diacritical mark,** диакрити́ческий знак.

diadem *n.* диаде́ма.

diaeresis *n.* = **dieresis.**

diagnose *v.t.* распознава́ть; определя́ть (боле́знь).

diagnosis *n.* диа́гноз. *Make a diagnosis,* ста́вить диа́гноз.

diagnostic *adj.* диагности́ческий. —**diagnostician,** *n.* диагно́ст. —**diagnostics,** *n.* диагно́стика.

diagonal *adj.* диагона́льный. —*n.* диагона́ль. —**diagonally,** *adv.* по диагона́ли; на́искось.

diagram *n.* схе́ма; диагра́мма. —**diagrammatic,** *adj.* схемати́ческий.

dial *n.* **1,** (of a radio, gauge, etc.) шкала́; цифербла́т. **2,** (tuning knob) ру́чка (настро́йки). **3,** (of a telephone) диск. —*v.t.* **1,** (a telephone number) набира́ть (но́мер). **2,** (a radio station) настра́ивать.

dialect *n.* диале́кт; наре́чие; го́вор. —**dialectal,** *adj.* диале́ктный.

dialectical *adj.* диалекти́ческий. —**dialectics,** *n.* диале́ктика.

dialogue *n.* диало́г.

diameter *n.* диа́метр. *Six inches in diameter,* шесть дю́ймов в диа́метре.

diametrical *adj.* диаметра́льный.

diametrically *adv.* диаметра́льно: *diametrically opposite,* диаметра́льно противополо́жный.

diamond *n.* **1,** (stone) алма́з. **2,** (gem) бриллиа́нт. **3,** (figure) ромб. **4,** *pl., cards* бу́бны: *queen of diamonds,* да́ма бубён. —*adj.* бриллиа́нтовый; алма́зный. *Diamond ring,* бриллиа́нтовый пе́рстень.

diaper *n.* пелёнка. —*v.t.* пеленáть.

diaphragm *n.* **1**, *anat.* грудобрю́шная прегрáда; диафрáгма. **2**, *physics; mech.* мембрáна. **3**, *optics; photog.* диафрáгма.

diarchy *n.* двоевлáстие.

diarrhea *also,* **diarrhoea** *n.* понóс. *He has diarrhea*, его́ слáбит.

diary *n.* дневни́к.

diathermy *n.* диатерми́я.

diatonic *adj.* диатони́ческий.

diatribe *n.* брáнная речь.

dice *n.pl.* игрáльные кóсти. *Play dice*, игрáть в кóсти.

dichotomy *n.* деле́ние.

dickens *n., slang* чёрт: *What the dickens do you want?*, какóго чёрта вам ну́жно? —**give someone the dickens,** дать комý-нибудь нагоня́й.

dicker *v.i.* торговáться.

dickey *also,* **dicky** *n.* **1**, (shirt front) мани́шка . **2**, (bib) нагрýдник.

dicotyledon *n.* двудóльное расте́ние. —**dicotyledonous,** *adj.* двудóльный.

dictaphone *n.* диктофóн.

dictate *v.t. & i.* диктовáть: *dictate a letter/ the terms of a treaty/*, диктовáть письмó/ усло́вия договóра/. *He is used to dictating to everyone*, он привы́к диктовáть всем. —*n.* веле́ние: *the dictates of one's conscience*, веле́ния сóвести.

dictation *n.* **1**, (act of dictating, as a letter) диктóвка: *take dictation*, писáть под диктóвку. **2**, (classroom exercise) диктáнт.

dictator *n.* диктáтор. —**dictatorial,** *adj.* диктáторский. —**dictatorship,** *n.* диктатýра.

diction *n.* ди́кция.

dictionary *n.* словáрь.

dictum *n.* **1**, (authoritative pronouncement) постановле́ние. **2**, (saying) изрече́ние.

didactic *adj.* наставительный; назидáтельный; дидакти́ческий. —**didactics,** *n.* дидáктика.

die *v.i.* **1**, (of humans) умирáть: *die of cancer*, умирáть от рáка; *die in childbirth*, умирáть от рóдов. *Die of hunger, see* **hunger**. *Die laughing*, умирáть сó смеху. *Be dying of curiosity*, умирáть от любопы́тства. **2**, (of animals) дóхнуть; (of plants) ги́бнуть. —*v.t.* умирáть: *He died a natural death*, он ýмер есте́ственной (*or* своéй) сме́ртью. *He died a slow death*, он умирáл ме́дленно. —*n.* **1**, (engraving stamp) штамп. **2**, *sing. of* dice. *The die is cast*, жрéбий брóшен. —**be dying to,** жáждать; рвáться: *I am dying to see you*, я жáжду/рвусь уви́деть вас. *I am dying to tell her*, меня́ так и подмывáет сказáть ей. —**die away,** замолкáть; умолкáть. —**die down,** замирáть; затихáть; утихáть; стихáть; глóхнуть. —**die out, 1,** (of a fire) угасáть. **2**, (go out of use) отмирáть. **3**, (become extinct) вымирáть.

diehard *adj.* твердолóбый.

dieresis *also,* **diaeresis** *n.* две тóчки.

diesel *adj.* ди́зельный. *Diesel engine*, ди́зель. *Diesel locomotive*, тепловóз.

diet *n.* дие́та. *Go on a diet*, сесть на дие́ту. *Put on a*

diet, посади́ть на дие́ту. —*v.i.* быть на дие́те. —**dietary,** *adj.* диети́ческий.

dietetic *adj.* диети́ческий. —**dietetics,** *n.* диетолóгия; диете́тика.

dietitian *also,* **dietician** *n.* диетóлог.

differ *v.i.* **1**, (be dissimilar) отличáться; различáться. *Differ from the rest*, отличáться от остальны́х. *Differ in size*, различáться по разме́ру. **2**, (disagree) расходи́ться. *We differ on this issue*, нáши мне́ния по э́тому вопрóсу расхóдятся. *I beg to differ*, позвóлю себе́ не согласи́ться.

difference *n.* **1**, (dissimilarity; variation) рáзница: *the enormous difference between them*, огрóмная рáзница ме́жду ни́ми. *Age difference*, рáзница в вóзрасте. *Difference in time*, рáзница во вре́мени. *A difference of ten dollars*, рáзница в десяти́ дóлларах. *What's the difference?*, какáя рáзница? **2**, (disagreement) разноглáсие; расхожде́ние. *Difference of opinion*, разноглáсие/разли́чие/расхожде́ние во мне́ниях. *Settle our differences*, улáживать нáши разноглáсия *or* расхожде́ния. **3**, *math.* рáзность. —**make a difference**: *It makes a great difference*, большáя рáзница. *It makes no difference (to me)*, (мне) всё равнó.

different *adj.* **1**, (dissimilar) рáзный; разли́чный. *Our goals are different*, нáши це́ли разли́чные. *Speak different languages*, говори́ть на рáзных языкáх. *Here everything is different*, здесь всё по-другóму. *Be different from*, отличáться от. *That's different*, э́то другóе де́ло. *The next one will be completely different*, сле́дующий бýдет совсе́м ины́м. **2**, (another) другóй: *try a different method*, прóбовать другóй ме́тод. **3**, (various) рáзные: *try different remedies*, прóбовать рáзные срéдства. *In different ways*, по-рáзному.

differential *n.* **1**, (difference) разли́чие; рáзница: *price differential*, разли́чие/рáзница в цене́. **2**, *math; mech.* дифференциáл. —*adj.* дифференциáльный: *differential calculus/equation*, дифференциáльное исчисле́ние/уравне́ние.

differentiate *v.t. & i.* различáть; разграни́чивать.

differentiation *n.* разграниче́ние; дифференциáция.

differently *adv.* **1**, (in a different way) инáче; по-другóму. **2**, (in various ways) по-рáзному; разли́чно. *Interpret the law differently*, толковáть закóн разли́чно.

difficult *adj.* **1**, (hard to do, solve, or handle) трýдный: *difficult work*, трýдная рабóта; *a difficult problem*, трýдная задáча; *a difficult child*, трýдный ребёнок. **2**, (hard to deal or cope with; complex) слóжный: *a difficult matter*, слóжное де́ло. **3**, (unpleasant; trying; awkward) трýдный; затрудни́тельный; тяжёлый. *Difficult times*, тяжёлые временá. *Under difficult conditions*, в трýдных усло́виях. *In a difficult situation*, в затрудни́тельном положе́нии.

difficulty *n.* **1**, (quality of being difficult) трýдность. *With difficulty*, с трудóм. *Without difficulty*, без трудá. *He had no difficulty proving that...*, ему́ не состáвило никакóго трудá доказáть, что... **2**, (difficult situation) затрудне́ние: *be in difficulty*, быть в затрудне́нии. **3,** (complication; obstacle) затрудне́ние; тру́дность. *Present difficulties,* представля́ть тру́дности.

diffidence *n.* засте́нчивость; стесни́тельность. —**diffident,** *adj.* засте́нчивый; стесни́тельный.

diffuse *v.t.* **1,** (scatter) рассе́ивать. **2,** (disseminate, as knowledge) распространя́ть. —*adj.* **1,** (scattered) рассе́янный. **2,** (verbose) многосло́вный.

diffusion *n.* **1,** (dissemination) рассе́ивание; распростране́ние. **2,** *physics* диффу́зия. *Diffusion of light,* рассе́яние све́та.

dig *v.t. & i.* копа́ть; рыть: dig a hole/ditch/well, копа́ть *or* рыть я́му/кана́ву/коло́дец. *Dig a grave,* рыть моги́лу. *Dig a tunnel/canal,* рыть *or* проры́ть тунне́ль/кана́л. *Dig a moat around a fortress,* окружа́ть кре́пость рвом. *Dig deep,* копа́ть/рыть глубоко́. *Dig in the sand,* копа́ться/ры́ться в песке́. *Dig for gold,* иска́ть зо́лото. *Dig one's heels into the ground,* упира́ться нога́ми в зе́млю. —*n., colloq.* **1,** (poke) тычо́к. **2,** (gibe) шпи́лька. —**dig in,** ока́пываться. —**dig up, 1,** (tear up; churn up) иска́лывать; изрыва́ть. **2,** (unearth) выка́пывать; вырыва́ть (*pfv.* вы́рыть); отка́пывать; отрыва́ть (*pfv.* отры́ть). **3,** *colloq.* (find; discover) выка́пывать; отка́пывать; раска́пывать.

digest *v.t.* усва́ивать; перева́ривать. —*n.* **1,** (synopsis) резюме́. **2,** (collection) сбо́рник.

digestible *adj.* удобовари́мый. —**digestibility,** *n.* удобовари́мость.

digestion *n.* пищеваре́ние. —**digestive,** *adj.* пищевари́тельный.

digger *n.* копа́тель; землеко́п.

digging *n.* копа́ние; рытьё.

digit *n.* **1,** (finger; toe) па́лец. **2,** (number from 0 to 9) знак: two-digit number, двузна́чное число́.

digital computer цифрова́я вычисли́тельная маши́на.

digitalis *n.* наперстя́нка.

dignified *adj.* велича́вый; степе́нный.

dignify *v.t.* придава́ть досто́инство (+ *dat.*).

dignitary *n.* сано́вник; высокопоста́вленное лицо́.

dignity *n.* досто́инство. *Beneath one's dignity,* ни́же чьего́-нибудь досто́инства.

digress *v.i.* отклоня́ться; уклоня́ться; отступа́ть; отходи́ть; отвлека́ться. —**digression,** *n.* отклоне́ние; уклоне́ние; отступле́ние; экскурс.

dihedral *adj.* двугра́нный.

dike *also,* **dyke** *n.* да́мба.

diktat *n.* дикта́т.

dilapidated *adj.* ве́тхий; обветша́лый; обша́рпанный; полуразру́шенный.

dilate *v.t.* расширя́ть. —**dilation,** *n.* расшире́ние.

dilatory *adj.* ме́дленный; медли́тельный.

dilemma *n.* диле́мма. *Be in a dilemma,* стоя́ть пе́ред диле́ммой.

dilettante *n.* дилета́нт; люби́тель. —**dilettantism,** *n.* дилетанти́зм; дилета́нтство.

diligence *n.* прилежа́ние; стара́тельность; усе́рдие.

diligent *adj.* приле́жный; стара́тельный; усе́рдный. —**diligently,** *adv.* приле́жно; стара́тельно; усе́рдно.

dill *n.* укро́п.

dillydally *v.i.* ме́шкать; ло́дырничать.

dilute *v.t.* разбавля́ть; разжижа́ть; разводи́ть. —**dilution,** *n.* разжиже́ние.

dim *adj.* **1,** (not bright) ту́склый. *Dim light,* ту́склый *or* сла́бый свет. **2,** (nor clear; hazy; vague) сму́тный: *dim recollection,* сму́тное воспомина́ние. —*v.t.* притуши́ть. *Dim one's headlights,* притуши́ть фа́ры; включи́ть бли́жний свет. —*v.i.* тускне́ть. —**take a dim view of,** относи́ться скепти́чески к.

dime *n.* моне́та в де́сять це́нтов.

dimension *n.* **1,** (measurable extent) измере́ние. *Three-dimensional,* трёхме́рный. **2,** (extent; scope) разме́ры.

diminish *v.t.* уменьша́ть. —*v.i.* уменьша́ться.

diminuendo *n.* диминуэ́ндо.

diminution *n.* уменьше́ние.

diminutive *adj.* **1,** (small) ма́ленький; миниатю́рный. **2,** *gram.* уменьши́тельный. —*n.* уменьши́тельное существи́тельное.

dimly *adv.* **1,** (not brightly) ту́скло. *Dimly lit room,* сла́бо освещённая ко́мната. **2,** (vaguely) сму́тно.

dimness *n.* ту́склость.

dimple *n.* я́мочка.

dimwit *n., colloq.* тупоу́мный челове́к; тупи́ца; тугоду́м. —**dimwitted,** *adj., colloq.* тупоу́мный; тупоголо́вый.

din *n.* гро́хот; гвалт. —*v.t.* [*usu.* **din into**] вда́лбливать (что́-нибудь + *dat.*).

dine *v.i.* обе́дать.

diner *n.* **1,** (person dining) обе́дающий. **2,** (dining car) ваго́н-рестора́н. **3,** (small restaurant) заку́сочная.

dinghy *n.* я́лик.

dingy *adj.* ту́склый; мра́чный; убо́гий.

dining car ваго́н-рестора́н.

dining room столо́вая. *Dining room furniture,* ме́бель для столо́вой.

dinner *n.* обе́д; у́жин. *Have dinner,* обе́дать; у́жинать. *Give/get someone his/her dinner,* (на)корми́ть кого́-нибудь обе́дом/у́жином. *Make something for dinner,* (при)гото́вить что́-нибудь к обе́ду/у́жину. —*adj.* обе́денный: dinner table, обе́денный стол. —**dinner jacket,** смо́кинг. —**dinner party,** зва́ный обе́д.

dinnertime *n.* обе́денное вре́мя.

dinosaur *n.* диноза́вр.

dint *n., in* **by dint of,** посре́дством (+ *gen.*); путём (+ *gen.*).

diocese *n.* епа́рхия.

diode *n.* дио́д.

dioxide *n.* двуо́кись.

dip *v.t.* погружа́ть; окуна́ть; мака́ть; обма́кивать. *Dip a pen in ink,* погружа́ть/окуна́ть/мака́ть/обма́кивать перо́ в черни́ла. *Dip meat in sauce,* мака́ть/ обма́кивать мя́со в со́ус. —*v.i.* **1,** (descend; drop) спуска́ться; опуска́ться. *The sun dipped below the horizon,* со́лнце скры́лось за горизо́нтом. **2,** (decline; go down) па́дать; снижа́ться; пойти́ вниз. *Stock prices dipped,* курс а́кций сни́зился. **3,** *fol. by* **into** (have recourse to; fall back on) залеза́ть (в). —*n.*

1, (brief swim): *go for a dip,* пойти́ попла́вать. **2,** (depression, as in a road) впа́дина; углубле́ние. **3,** (drop; decline) паде́ние; сниже́ние.

diphtheria *n.* дифтери́я; дифтери́т. —**diphtherial,** *adj.* дифтери́йный.

diphthong *n.* дифто́нг; двугла́сный звук.

diploma *n.* дипло́м.

diplomacy *n.* **1,** (dealings between nations) дипло-ма́тия. **2,** (tact) дипломати́чность.

diplomat *n.* диплома́т.

diplomatic *adj.* **1,** (pert. to diplomacy) дипломати́ческий. **2,** (tactful) дипломати́ческий; дипломати́чный.

dipper *n.* **1,** (ladle) ковш; черпа́к. **2,** *cap., astron.* Медве́дица. **3,** (bird) оля́пка.

dipstick *n.* щуп.

dire *adj.* **1,** (grave; extreme) кра́йний: *dire need,* кра́йняя нужда́. *In dire straits,* в бе́дственном *or* в отча́янном положе́нии. **2,** (ominous) злове́щий: *dire predictions/warnings,* злове́щие предсказа́ния/ предупрежде́ния.

direct *adj.* **1,** (by the shortest way) прямо́й: *direct route,* прямо́й путь. **2,** (with nothing in between; immediate) прямо́й; непосре́дственный. *Direct hit/ connection/descendant,* прямо́е попада́ние; пряма́я связь; прямо́й пото́мок. *Direct result,* прямо́й *or* непосре́дственный результа́т. *Direct threat,* пряма́я *or* непосре́дственная угро́за. **3,** (straightforward) прямо́й: *direct answer,* прямо́й отве́т. —*adv.* пря́мо: *direct from the factory,* пря́мо с заво́да. —*v.t.* **1,** (aim; channel) направля́ть; обраща́ть. *Direct one's ener-gies/gaze toward,* направля́ть свои́ си́лы/ обраща́ть взгляд/ на (+ *acc.*). **2,** (show the way to) указа́ть доро́гу (+ *dat.*). **3,** (manage; run) руководи́ть: *direct an organization,* руководи́ть организа́цией. *Direct traffic,* регули́ровать движе́ние. **4,** (order) прика́зы-вать; предпи́сывать. **5,** *music* дирижи́ровать. **6,** *theat.* режисси́ровать. —**direct current,** постоя́н-ный ток. —**direct object,** *gram.* прямо́е допол-не́ние.

direction *n.* **1,** (course) направле́ние; сторона́: *in the direction of,* по направле́нию к; в сто́рону (+ *gen.*). *In all directions,* во всех направле́ниях; врассып-ну́ю. *Have a good/poor sense of direction,* хорошо́/ пло́хо ориенти́роваться. **2,** (management) руково́д-ство. **3,** *pl.* (instructions) указа́ния; инстру́кция. **4,** *theat.* режиссу́ра.

directional *adj.* напра́вленный: *directional antenna,* напра́вленная анте́нна. —**directional signal,** указа́тель поворо́та.

direction finder (ра́дио)пеленга́тор.

directive *n.* директи́ва; распоряже́ние; устано́вка.

directly *adv.* **1,** (without deviating) пря́мо: *sit directly in the sun,* сиде́ть пря́мо на со́лнце. *Come directly to the point,* приступи́ть пря́мо к де́лу. *Directly over-head,* над са́мой голово́й. **2,** (immediately) сра́зу; неме́дленно.

directness *n.* прямота́; прямоду́шие.

director *n.* **1,** (manager) дире́ктор. **2,** *theat.* режиссёр; постано́вщик.

directorate *n.* **1,** (board of directors) директора́т. **2,** (governmental department) управле́ние.

directorial *adj.* дире́кторский.

directory *n.* спра́вочник; указа́тель; а́дресная кни́га. *Telephone directory,* телефо́нная кни́га; телефо́н-ный спра́вочник.

dirge *n.* погреба́льное пе́ние.

dirigible *n.* дирижа́бль.

dirt *n.* **1,** (unclean matter) грязь: *covered with dirt,* покры́тый гря́зью. **2,** (loose earth) земля́: *a handful of dirt,* горсть земли́. —*adj.* грунтово́й: *dirt road,* грунто́вая доро́га.

dirt-cheap *adj.* деше́вле па́реной ре́пы. —*adv.* по дешёвке.

dirty *adj.* **1,** (unclean) гря́зный: *dirty hands,* гря́зные ру́ки; *dirty dishes,* гря́зная посу́да; *dirty clothes,* гря́зное бельё. **2,** (off-color; lewd) са́льный; скабрёзный. **3,** (mean; despicable) по́длый. —*v.t.* па́чкать; загрязня́ть. —**dirty look,** укори́зненный взгляд. *Give someone a dirty look,* посмотре́ть на кого́-нибудь укори́зненно. —**dirty trick,** зла́я шу́тка; по́длость; га́дость. *Play a dirty trick on,* сыгра́ть с (+ *instr.*) злу́ю шу́тку; подложи́ть свинью́ (+ *dat.*).

disability *n.* нетрудоспосо́бность; инвали́дность. *Disability pension,* пе́нсия по инвали́дности.

disable *v.t.* де́лать нетрудоспосо́бным; выводи́ть из стро́я.

disabled *adj.* **1,** (incapacitated) нетрудоспосо́бный; нерабо́тоспосо́бный; *mil.* небоеспосо́бный. *Dis-abled person,* инвали́д. **2,** (broken down, as of a vehi-cle) испо́ртившийся.

disabuse *v.t.* [*usu.* **disabuse of**] разубежда́ть (в); разуверя́ть (в).

disadvantage *n.* **1,** (unfavorable position) невы́года. *Be at a disadvantage,* быть в невы́годном поло-же́нии. **2,** (drawback) недоста́ток: *advantages and disadvantages,* досто́инства и недоста́тки. **3,** (detri-ment) вред: *work to the disadvantage of,* де́йствовать во вред (+ *dat.*).

disadvantageous *adj.* невы́годный.

disaffect *v.t.* отчужда́ть. —**disaffection,** *n.* отчужде́ние.

disagree *v.i.* **1,** (have different opinions) не согла-ша́ться; расходи́ться во мне́ниях. *I disagree with you,* я с ва́ми не согла́сен (согла́сна). **2,** (fail to coin-cide, as of versions of a story) расходи́ться; не сов-пада́ть; не сходи́ться. **3,** *fol. by* **with** (upset, as of food) пло́хо де́йствовать (на).

disagreeable *adj.* неприя́тный.

disagreement *n.* **1,** (difference of opinion) раз-ногла́сие; несогла́сие. **2,** (dispute; quarrel) ссо́ра.

disallow *v.t.* **1,** (reject as invalid) отклоня́ть. **2,** *sports* аннули́ровать: *disallow a goal,* аннули́ровать гол.

disappear *v.i.* **1,** (pass out of sight) исчеза́ть. *Disap-pear from view,* скры́ться и́з виду. **2,** (be missing; be lost) пропада́ть: *My watch has disappeared,* у меня́ пропа́ли часы́.

disappearance *n.* исчезнове́ние.

disappoint *v.t.* разочаро́вывать. —**disappointed,** *adj.* разочаро́ванный.

disappointing *adj.* разочаро́вывающий. *The exhibit is disappointing,* вы́ставка разочаро́вывает.

disappointment *n.* разочарова́ние.

disapproval *n.* **1,** (unfavorable attitude) неодобре́ние. *In disapproval,* неодобри́тельно. **2,** (rejection) отклоне́ние.

disapprove *v.i.* [*usu.* **disapprove of**] не одобря́ть. —*v.t.* (reject) отверга́ть; отклоня́ть. —**disapproving,** *adj.* неодобри́тельный.

disarm *v.t.* **1,** (seize a weapon from) обезору́живать; разоружа́ть. **2,** (reduce the armed forces or weapons of) разоружа́ть. **3,** (win over) обезору́живать. —*v.i.* разоружа́ться.

disarmament *n.* разоруже́ние.

disarming *adj.* обезору́живающий.

disarrange *v.t.* расстра́ивать; (пере)пу́тать; приводи́ть в беспоря́док.

disarray *n.* беспоря́док; расстро́йство.

disassemble *v.t.* разбира́ть (на ча́сти).

disassociate *v.* = **dissociate**.

disaster *n.* бе́дствие; катастро́фа. *On the brink of disaster,* на гра́ни катастро́фы.

disastrous *adj.* бе́дственный; катастрофи́ческий; ги́бельный.

disavow *v.t.* отрека́ться от; отка́зываться от; открещиваться от.

disavowal *n.* отрече́ние; отка́з.

disband *v.t.* распуска́ть; расформиро́вывать. —*v.i.* расходи́ться; рассе́иваться.

disbar *v.t.* лиша́ть пра́ва адвока́тской пра́ктики.

disbelief *n.* неве́рие. *In disbelief,* не ве́ря свои́м глаза́м *or* уша́м.

disbelieve *v.t.* не ве́рить.

disburse *v.t.* выпла́чивать. —**disbursement,** *n.* вы́плата.

disc *n.* = **disk.**

discard *v.t.* **1,** (throw away) выбра́сывать. **2,** (give up, as an idea or theory) отбра́сывать. **3,** *cards* сбра́сывать; ски́дывать; сноси́ть.

discern *v.t.* различа́ть; рассмотре́ть; разгляде́ть; распознава́ть. —**discernible,** *adj.* различи́мый. —**discerning,** *adj.* проница́тельный. —**discernment,** *n.* проница́тельность.

discharge *v.t.* **1,** (unload) выгружа́ть (груз); выса́живать (пассажи́ров). **2,** (release) освобожда́ть; (*from military service*) увольня́ть; демобилизова́ть; (*from a hospital*) выпи́сывать. **3,** (dismiss from a job) увольня́ть; рассчи́тывать. **4,** (perform, as duties) исполня́ть; выполня́ть. **5,** (pay off, as a debt) выпла́чивать. **6,** (pour forth; emit) выделя́ть; выбра́сывать. *Discharge into the atmosphere,* выбра́сывать в атмосфе́ру. **7,** (fire; shoot) выпуска́ть; пуска́ть. **8,** *electricity* разряжа́ть. —*v.i.* **1,** (go off, as of a gun) вы́стрелить. **2,** *electricity* разряжа́ться. —*n.* **1,** (from military service) увольне́ние; (from a hospital) вы́писка; (from a job) увольне́ние; расчёт. **2,** (fulfillment; performance) исполне́ние; выполне́ние. **3,** (payment, as of a debt) упла́та; покры́тие. **4,** (firing off) вы́стрел. **5,** (secretion) выделе́ние. *Vaginal discharge,* влага́лищные выделе́ния. **6,** *electricity* разря́д.

disciple *n.* **1,** *relig.* апо́стол. **2,** (pupil; follower) учени́к; после́дователь.

discipline *n.* дисципли́на. —*v.t.* дисциплини́ровать. —**disciplinary,** *adj.* дисциплина́рный.

disclaim *v.t.* отрица́ть: *He disclaimed any knowledge of the incident,* он отрица́л, что знал о происше́дшем. *Disclaim responsibility for,* не брать на себя́ отве́тственности за.

disclaimer *n.* опроверже́ние.

disclose *v.t.* раскрыва́ть; разглаша́ть. *Disclose the details,* раскры́ть подро́бности. *Disclose information,* разглаша́ть све́дения.

disclosure *n.* **1,** (act of disclosing) раскры́тие; разглаше́ние. **2,** (revelation) разоблаче́ние: *new disclosures about his finances,* но́вые разоблаче́ния его́ фина́нсовых дел.

discolor *also,* **discolour** *v.t.* обесцве́чивать. —**discoloration,** *n.* обесцве́чивание.

discomfit *v.t.* **1,** (frustrate; thwart) расстра́ивать. **2,** (disconcert) смуща́ть. —**discomfiture,** *n.* смуще́ние; замеша́тельство.

discomfort *n.* **1,** (lack of comfort) неудо́бство. **2,** (distress; embarrassment) неудо́бство; смуще́ние. **3,** (pain): *She is in great discomfort,* ей тяжело́; ей о́чень бо́льно.

discommode *v.t.* затрудня́ть; причиня́ть неудо́бство (+ *dat.*).

disconcert *v.t.* смуща́ть; сбива́ть; выводи́ть из равнове́сия.

disconnect *v.t.* отключа́ть; отсоединя́ть; разъединя́ть. *Disconnect a telephone,* отключи́ть телефо́н. *Disconnect a wire,* отсоедини́ть про́вод. *We've been disconnected,* нас разъедини́ли.

disconnected *adj.* несвя́зный; бессвя́зный.

disconsolate *adj.* неуте́шный.

discontent *n.* [*also,* **discontentment**] недово́льство. —*adj.* [*also,* **discontented**] недово́льный.

discontinue *v.t.* прекраща́ть. —**discontinuation,** *n.* прекраще́ние.

discord *n.* **1,** (dissension) раздо́р; разла́д. **2,** *music* диссона́нс.

discordant *adj.* **1,** (not in accord) противоречи́вый. **2,** (not harmonious in sound) нестро́йный; несогла́сный; неблагозву́чный.

discount *n.* ски́дка: *at a 10% discount,* со ски́дкой в *or* на де́сять проце́нтов. —*v.t.* **1,** *comm.* учи́тывать (ве́ксель). **2,** (take no account of) не счита́ться с; сбра́сывать со счето́в. *This threat cannot be discounted,* э́ту угро́зу нельзя́ сбра́сывать со счето́в. —**discount rate,** учётная ста́вка; учётный проце́нт.

discourage *v.t.* **1,** (dishearten) обескура́живать. **2,** *fol. by* **from** (dissuade) отгова́ривать (от). —**discouraged,** *adj.* обескура́женный. —**discouragement,** *n.* обескура́женность. —**discouraging,** *adj.* обескура́живающий.

discourse *n.* **1,** (conversation) разгово́р. **2,** (lengthy discussion) рассужде́ние. **3,** (treatise) тракта́т. —*v.i.* рассужда́ть.

discourteous *adj.* неве́жливый. —**discourtesy,** *n.* неве́жливость.

discover v.t. **1,** (be the first to see) открыва́ть. **2,** (find; detect; realize) обнару́живать. —**discoverer,** n. открыва́тель; первооткрыва́тель.

discovery n. откры́тие.

discredit v.t. **1,** (damage in reputation) поро́чить; дискредити́ровать. **2,** (not believe; discount) не ве́рить; не доверя́ть. **3,** (show to be untrue) разве́нчивать. —n. Bring discredit upon, дискредити́ровать.

discreet adj. благоразу́мный; такти́чный; осторо́жный. Discreet distance, почти́тельное расстоя́ние.

discrepancy n. несоотве́тствие; разногла́сие.

discretion n. **1,** (prudence) благоразу́мие; рассуди́тельность. **2,** (power to decide) усмотре́ние: at (someone's) discretion, по (чьему́-нибудь) усмотре́нию. Leave to someone's discretion, предоставля́ть на чьё-нибудь усмотре́ние. Use one's discretion, де́йствовать по своему́ усмотре́нию.

discretionary adj. дискрецио́нный.

discriminate v.i. **1,** (act with prejudice) дискримини́ровать. Discriminate against women, дискримини́ровать же́нщин. **2,** fol. by **between** (distinguish between) де́лать разли́чие (ме́жду).

discriminating adj. разбо́рчивый. Discriminating taste, то́нкий вкус.

discrimination n. **1,** (actions directed against minority groups) дискримина́ция: discrimination against Asians, дискримина́ция азиа́тов. **2,** (critical evaluation or judgment) разбо́рчивость.

discriminatory adj. дискриминацио́нный.

discus n. диск. Discus throw, мета́ние ди́ска.

discuss v.t. обсужда́ть: discuss a proposal, обсужда́ть предложе́ние. I do not wish to discuss the matter further, мне бы не хоте́лось бо́льше обсужда́ть э́тот вопро́с. This subject is discussed in Chapter 3, э́тот предме́т бу́дет обсужда́ться в главе́ тре́тьей.

discussion n. обсужде́ние; диску́ссия. Be under discussion, обсужда́ться.

disdain v.t. **1,** (scorn) презира́ть; гнуша́ться. **2,** fol. by inf. (refuse scornfully) бре́згать; гнуша́ться. —n. презре́ние. —**disdainful,** adj. презри́тельный.

disease n. боле́знь; заболева́ние: rare disease, ре́дкая боле́знь; ре́дкое заболева́ние. Parkinson's disease, боле́знь Паркинсо́на.

diseased adj. больно́й; заболе́вший.

disembark v.t. выса́живать. —v.i. выса́живаться; выгружа́ться. —**disembarkation,** n. вы́садка.

disembowel v.t. потроши́ть.

disenchant v.t. разочаро́вывать. —**disenchantment,** n. разочарова́ние.

disenfranchise v. = disfranchise.

disengage v.i. разъединя́ть. —v.i. разъединя́ться. —**disengagement,** n. разъедине́ние.

disentangle v.t. распу́тывать; вы́путывать.

disestablish v.t. отделя́ть (це́рковь) от госуда́рства.

disfavor also, **disfavour** n. неми́лость; опа́ла. Fall into disfavor, впасть в неми́лость.

disfigure v.t. обезобра́живать; уро́довать. —**disfigured,** adj. изуро́дованный. —**disfigurement,** n. уро́дство.

disfranchise v.t. лиша́ть гражда́нских or избира́тельных прав.

disgorge v.t. изверга́ть; изрыга́ть.

disgrace n. **1,** (shame; dishonor) позо́р; бесче́стье. Bring disgrace upon, (о)позо́рить. He is a disgrace to his profession, он позо́рит свою́ профе́ссию. **2,** (disfavor) неми́лость; опа́ла. —v.t. позо́рить; бесче́стить. —**disgrace oneself,** позо́риться; покры́ть себя́ позо́ром. He did not disgrace himself, он не уда́рил лицо́м в грязь.

disgraceful adj. позо́рный. It's simply disgraceful!, э́то про́сто безобра́зие!

disgruntle v.t. вызыва́ть (чьё-нибудь) недово́льство. —**disgruntled,** adj. недово́льный; в дурно́м настрое́нии.

disguise v.t. маскирова́ть; переодева́ть. Disguise one's voice, меня́ть or изменя́ть го́лос. Disguise oneself as, переодева́ться (+ instr.). —n. маскиро́вка. In disguise, замаскиро́ванный; переоде́тый.

disgust n. отвраще́ние. —v.t. внуша́ть отвраще́ние (+ dat.).

disgusted adj. I am/got disgusted, мне надое́ло; мне опроти́вело; мне осточерте́ло.

disgusting adj. отврати́тельный; проти́вный. It is disgusting to watch, проти́вно смотре́ть.

dish n. **1,** (small plate) таре́лка. **2,** pl. (table utensils) посу́да: do the dishes, мыть посу́ду. **3,** (particular food) блю́до: my favorite dish, моё люби́мое блю́до. —v.t. [usu. **dish out** or **dish up**] подава́ть; серви́рова́ть. —**dish antenna,** дискообра́зная анте́нна; блю́дце.

disharmony n. **1,** (dissonance) дисгармо́ния; неблагозву́чие. **2,** (discord) дисгармо́ния; разногла́сие.

dishcloth n. посу́дная тря́пка.

dishearten v.t. обескура́живать. Become disheartened, па́дать ду́хом. Don't become disheartened!, не уныва́йте!

disheveled also, **dishevelled** adj. растрёпанный; взъеро́шенный; взлохма́ченный.

dishonest adj. нече́стный. —**dishonestly,** adv. нече́стно. —**dishonesty,** n. нече́стность.

dishonor also, **dishonour** n. бесче́стье. —v.t. бесче́стить. —**dishonorable,** adj. бесче́стный.

dishpan n. таз (для мытья́ посу́ды).

dishrag n. посу́дная тря́пка.

dishtowel n. посу́дное полоте́нце.

dishwasher n. **1,** (person) судомо́йка. **2,** (machine) посудомо́ечная маши́на; посудомо́йка.

dishwater n. помо́и.

disillusion v.t. разочаро́вывать. —**disillusioned,** adj. разочаро́ванный. Become disillusioned, разочаро́вываться. —**disillusionment,** n. разочарова́ние.

disinclination n. нежела́ние; неохо́та.

disinclined adj. не скло́нен (к); не располо́жен (к).

disinfect v.t. дезинфици́ровать; обеззара́живать.

disinfectant adj. дезинфици́рующий. —n. дезинфици́рующее сре́дство. —**disinfection,** n. дезинфе́кция; обеззара́живание.

disinformation n. дезинформа́ция.

disingenuous *adj.* нейскренний; непрямо́й.

disinherit *v.t.* лиша́ть насле́дства. —**disinheritance,** *n.* лише́ние насле́дства.

disintegrate *v.i.* распада́ться. —**disintegration,** *n.* распа́д.

disinter *v.t.* выка́пывать; отка́пывать.

disinterest *n.* **1,** (impartiality) беспристра́стие. **2,** (indifference) равноду́шие. —**disinterested,** *adj.* незаинтересо́ванный; бескоры́стный.

disjoint *v.t.* **1,** (dislocate) вы́вихнуть. **2,** (take apart at the joints) разде́лывать.

disjointed *adj.* бессвя́зный; несвя́зный; отры́вистый; отры́вочный; обры́вочный.

disjunctive *adj.* раздели́тельный.

disk *also,* **disc** *n.* диск. —**disk brake,** ди́сковый то́рмоз. —**disk harrow,** ди́сковая борона́.

dislikable *adj.* неприя́тный.

dislike *v.t.* не люби́ть: *dislike each other,* не люби́ть друг дру́га. —*n.* [*also,* **disliking**] нелюбо́вь; нерасположе́ние; антипа́тия. *Take a disliking to,* невзлюби́ть; настро́иться про́тив.

dislocate *v.t., med.* вы́вихнуть.

dislocation *n.* **1,** (displacement) перемеще́ние. **2,** *med.* вы́вих.

dislodge *v.t.* выбива́ть; вышиба́ть.

disloyal *adj.* нелоя́льный. —**disloyalty,** *n.* нелоя́льность.

dismal *adj.* мра́чный; тоскли́вый; па́смурный.

dismantle *v.t.* разбира́ть; демонти́ровать.

dismay *v.t.* **1,** (distress) смуща́ть. **2,** (dishearten) обескура́живать. —*n.* **1,** (consternation) смуще́ние. **2,** (alarm) трево́га.

dismember *v.t.* расчленя́ть. —**dismemberment,** *n.* расчлене́ние.

dismiss *v.t.* **1,** (tell to go or disperse) отпуска́ть; распуска́ть: *dismiss the class,* отпуска́ть/распуска́ть класс. *Class dismissed!,* уро́к зако́нчен! **2,** (remove from office) смеща́ть; освобожда́ть; (from a job) увольня́ть; рассчи́тывать; (from a college or university) отчисля́ть. **3,** (put out of one's mind; reject as unworthy of consideration) отбра́сывать; отма́хиваться от; отмета́ть. **4,** *law* прекраща́ть (де́ло); отклоня́ть (иск). *Dismiss charges against,* снима́ть обвине́ния с (+ *gen.*).

dismissal *n.* **1,** (ordering or allowing to disperse) ро́спуск. **2,** (discharge; removal) увольне́ние; расчёт. —**dismissal notice,** уведомле́ние об увольне́нии.

dismount *v.i.* сходи́ть *or* слеза́ть с ло́шади; спе́шиваться.

disobedience *n.* непослуша́ние; неповинове́ние. —**civil disobedience,** гражда́нское неповинове́ние.

disobedient *adj.* непослу́шный.

disobey *v.t. & i.* не слу́шаться; ослу́шаться; не подчиня́ться. *Disobey an order/ the law/,* не подчиня́ться прика́зу/зако́ну; наруша́ть прика́з/зако́н.

disorder *n.* **1,** (disarray) беспоря́док. **2,** *often pl.* (public disturbances) беспоря́дки. **3,** (ailment) расстро́йство: *nervous disorder,* не́рвное расстро́йство. —*v.t.* (пере)пу́тать; приводи́ть в беспоря́док.

disorderly *adj.* **1,** (unsystematic) беспоря́дочный. **2,**

(unruly) бу́йный. —**disorderly conduct,** хулига́нство.

disorganize *v.t.* дезорганизова́ть. —**disorganization,** *n.* дезорганиза́ция; неорганизо́ванность. —**disorganized,** *adj.* дезорганизо́ванный; неорганизо́ванный; беспоря́дочный.

disorient *v.t.* дезориенти́ровать. —**disorientation,** *n.* дезориента́ция.

disown *v.t.* отрека́ться от; отка́зываться от.

disparage *v.t.* принижа́ть; поро́чить; хули́ть. —**disparagement,** *n.* приниже́ние. —**disparaging,** *adj.* оскорби́тельный; оби́дный.

disparate *adj.* разли́чный: *disparate elements,* разли́чные элеме́нты. —**disparity,** *n.* ра́зница; несоотве́тствие.

dispassionate *adj.* беспристра́стный.

dispatch *v.t.* **1,** (send off) отправля́ть. **2,** (kill) добива́ть; прика́нчивать. —*n.* **1,** (sending) отправле́ние; отпра́вка. **2,** (message) донесе́ние; депе́ша. **3,** (alacrity) быстрота́.

dispatcher *n.* диспе́тчер.

dispel *v.t.* рассе́ивать; разве́ивать; разгоня́ть. *Dispel doubts,* рассе́ивать *or* разве́ивать сомне́ния. *Dispel boredom,* разве́ивать *or* разгоня́ть тоску́.

dispensable *adj.* необяза́тельный; без чего мо́жно обойти́сь.

dispensary *n.* амбулато́рия.

dispensation *n.* **1,** (distribution) разда́ча. **2,** (release from an obligation) освобожде́ние (от обяза́тельства).

dispense *v.t.* **1,** (distribute) раздава́ть. **2,** (administer, as justice) отправля́ть (правосу́дие). —*v.i.* [*usu.* **dispense with**] обходи́ться без.

dispenser *n.* автома́т.

dispersal *n.* рассе́ивание; разго́н.

disperse *v.t.* рассе́ивать; разгоня́ть. *Disperse the demonstrators,* разогна́ть демонстра́нтов. —*v.i.* рассе́иваться; расходи́ться; разбега́ться. *The crowd dispersed,* толпа́ рассе́ялась *or* разошла́сь.

dispersion *n.* рассе́ивание; рассе́яние; *physics* диспе́рсия.

dispirit *v.t.* удруча́ть; угнета́ть. —**dispirited,** *adj.* удручённый; угнетённый.

displace *v.t.* **1,** (force out; supersede) вытесня́ть. **2,** (remove) смеща́ть. —**displaced person,** перемещённое лицо́.

displacement *n.* **1,** (superseding) вытесне́ние. **2,** (removal) смеще́ние. **3,** (tonnage) водоизмеще́ние. **4,** (of an engine) рабо́чий объём (дви́гателя).

display *v.t.* **1,** (exhibit) выставля́ть. **2,** (reveal; manifest) проявля́ть; обнару́живать. —*n.* **1,** (showing) пока́з. *Put on display,* выставля́ть напока́з. **2,** (exhibit) вы́ставка. **3,** (manifestation) проявле́ние.

displease *v.t.* не нра́виться: *displease the audience,* не нра́виться зри́телям. —**displeased,** *adj.* недово́льный. —**displeasure,** *n.* неудово́льствие; недово́льство.

disposable *adj.* однора́зовый; однора́зового употребле́ния *or* примене́ния; бро́совый.

disposal *n.* **1,** (arrangement) расположе́ние. **2,** (getting rid of) удале́ние: *waste disposal,* удале́ние отхо́дов. —**at one's disposal,** в чьём-нибудь распоряже́нии. *Have at one's disposal,* располага́ть (+ *instr.*); име́ть в своём распоряже́нии. *Place at one's disposal,* предоста́вить в чьё-нибудь распоряже́ние. *My room is at your disposal,* моя́ ко́мната к ва́шим услу́гам.

dispose *v.t.* **1,** (place; arrange) располага́ть. **2,** (incline in a certain way) настра́ивать; склоня́ть. —**dispose of, 1,** (get rid of; remove) удаля́ть; убира́ть. **2,** (take care of; finish off) поко́нчить с; разде́латься с; распра́виться с.

disposed *adj.* располо́женный. *Kindly disposed toward,* располо́жен к. *Be favorably disposed toward,* относи́ться благоскло́нно к.

disposition *n.* **1,** (arrangement) расположе́ние. **2,** (temperament) нрав; хара́ктер. **3,** (tendency) расположе́ние; скло́нность. **4,** (handling; distribution) распоряже́ние. **5,** *mil.* дислока́ция.

dispossess *v.t.* лиша́ть со́бственности.

disproportion *n.* несоразме́рность; непропорциона́льность; диспропо́рция.

disproportionate *adj.* несоразме́рный; непропорциона́льный. —**disproportionately,** *adv.* несоразме́рно; непропорциона́льно.

disprove *v.t.* опроверга́ть.

disputation *n.* деба́ты; ди́спут. —**disputatious,** *adj.* лю́бящий спо́рить.

dispute *n.* спор: *border dispute,* пограни́чный спор. *Be in dispute,* быть предме́том спо́ра. *Be beyond dispute,* не подлежа́ть сомне́нию. —*v.t.* оспа́ривать: *dispute a claim,* оспа́ривать притяза́ние. *Disputed territory,* спо́рная террито́рия. *No one disputes the fact that...,* никто́ не спо́рит с тем, что...

disqualify *v.t.* дисквалифици́ровать. —**disqualification,** *n.* дисквалифика́ция.

disquiet *v.t.* беспоко́ить; трево́жить. —*n.* [*also,* **disquietude**] беспоко́йство; трево́га. —**disquieting,** *adj.* беспоко́йный; трево́жный.

disquisition *n.* тракта́т.

disregard *v.t.* пренебрега́ть: *disregard advice/warnings,* пренебрега́ть сове́том/предупрежде́ниями. —*n.* пренебреже́ние. *Disregard of the rules of behavior,* пренебреже́ние пра́вилами поведе́ния. *Disregard for human rights,* пренебреже́ние к права́м челове́ка.

disrepair *n.* неиспра́вность. *Fall into disrepair,* приходи́ть в ве́тхость *or* в него́дность.

disreputable *adj.* по́льзующийся дурно́й сла́вой.

disrepute *n.* дурна́я сла́ва. *Fall into disrepute,* приобрести́ дурну́ю сла́ву.

disrespect *n.* неуваже́ние; непочте́ние; непочти́тельность. —**disrespectful,** *adj.* непочти́тельный.

disrobe *v.i.* раздева́ться; обнажа́ться.

disrupt *v.t.* срыва́ть; наруша́ть; дезорганизова́ть. *Disrupt a meeting,* сорва́ть собра́ние. *Disrupt telephone service,* наруша́ть телефо́нную связь. —**disruption,** *n.* наруше́ние; дезорганиза́ция.

disruptive *adj.* **1,** (tending to disrupt) подрывно́й. **2,** (unruly) непоко́рный.

dissatisfaction *n.* недово́льство; неудовлетворённость. *Dissatisfaction with the state of affairs,* недово́льство положе́нием дел. —**dissatisfied,** *adj.* недово́льный; неудовлетворённый.

dissect *v.t.* **1,** (cut apart) вскрыва́ть; анатоми́ровать. **2,** (analyze closely) разбира́ть.

dissection *n.* **1,** (cutting apart) вскры́тие. **2,** (analysis) разбо́р.

dissemble *v.t.* **1,** (conceal the real nature of) скрыва́ть; маскирова́ть. **2,** (feign) притворя́ться (+ *instr.*). —*v.i.* лука́вить; лицеме́рить; криви́ть душо́й.

disseminate *v.t.* распространя́ть. —**dissemination,** *n.* распростране́ние.

dissension *n.* разла́д; раздо́р.

dissent *v.i.* не соглаша́ться; возража́ть. *Dissenting vote,* го́лос про́тив. —*n.* инакомы́слие. —**dissenter,** *n.* инакомы́слящий.

dissertation *n.* диссерта́ция.

disservice *n.* плоха́я услу́га. *Do someone a disservice,* оказа́ть кому́-нибудь плоху́ю (*or* медве́жью) услу́гу; сослужи́ть кому́-нибудь плоху́ю слу́жбу.

dissidence *n.* инакомы́слие.

dissident *n.* инакомы́слящий; диссиде́нт. —*adj.* инакомы́слящий.

dissimilar *adj.* несхо́дный. —**dissimilarity,** *n.* несхо́дство.

dissipate *v.t.* **1,** (dispel) рассе́ивать; разве́ивать; разгоня́ть. **2,** (squander) растра́чивать; расточа́ть; прома́тывать. —*v.i.* рассе́иваться: *The fog dissipated,* тума́н рассе́ялся.

dissipated *adj.* распу́тный; развра́тный.

dissipation *n.* **1,** (dispelling) рассе́ивание. **2,** (squandering) расточи́тельство. **3,** (dissoluteness) распу́тство.

dissociate *v.t.* разобща́ть. *Dissociate oneself from,* отмежёвываться от.

dissolute *adj.* распу́тный; распу́щенный; развра́тный; беспу́тный. —**dissoluteness,** *n.* распу́тство; распу́щенность; беспу́тство.

dissolution *n.* **1,** (melting) растворе́ние. **2,** (termination) расторже́ние; ликвида́ция. **3,** (dismissal) ро́спуск. **4,** (breaking up) распа́д.

dissolve *v.t.* **1,** (cause to melt) растворя́ть: *dissolve the powder in water,* растворя́ть порошо́к в воде́. **2,** (terminate) расторга́ть (брак); ликвиди́ровать (компа́нию). **3,** (disband, as a union; dismiss, as an assembly) распуска́ть. —*v.i.* растворя́ться.

dissonance *n.* диссона́нс; неблагозву́чие. —**dissonant,** *adj.* неблагозву́чный; нестро́йный.

dissuade *v.t.* отгова́ривать; отсове́товать.

distaff *n.* пря́лка. —**distaff side,** же́нская ли́ния.

distance *n.* расстоя́ние; диста́нция. *At a distance,* на не́котором расстоя́нии. *In the distance,* в отдале́нии; вдали́; вдалеке́. *Into the distance,* вдаль. *From a distance,* и́здали; издалека́. *Quite a distance from here,* дово́льно далеко́ отсю́да. *Because of the great distance,* за да́льностью расстоя́ния. *It is within walking distance,* туда́ мо́жно дойти́ пешко́м. —*v.t.* [*usu.* **distance oneself**] отмежёвываться (от). —**keep one's distance,** держа́ться вдалеке́; держа́ться на расстоя́нии.

distant *adj.* **1,** (far away) далёкий; да́льний. *Distant star,* далёкая звезда́. *Distant lands,* далёкие стра́ны; далёкие *or* да́льние края́. **2,** *fig.* (remote) далёкий; да́льний; отдалённый. *Distant relative,* да́льний ро́дственник. *Distant friend,* далёкий друг. *Distant resemblance,* отдалённое схо́дство. *In the distant past,* в далёком про́шлом. **3,** *fig.* (cold; indifferent) холо́дный; сухо́й.

distantly *adv. They are distantly related,* они́ да́льние ро́дственники. *English and Sanskrit are distantly related,* англи́йский и санскри́тсткий языки́ име́ют отдалённое родство́.

distaste *n.* отвраще́ние; антипа́тия. —**distasteful,** *adj.* неприя́тный.

distemper *n.* **1,** (ill humor) плохо́е настрое́ние. **2,** (disease of dogs) соба́чья чума́. **3,** *painting* те́мпера.

distend *v.t.* вздува́ть. —*v.i.* вздува́ться. —**distended,** *adj.* взду́тый. *His stomach is distended,* у него́ живо́т взду́ло *or* вспу́чило.

distill *also,* **distil** *v.t.* **1,** (purify) дистилли́ровать: *distilled water,* дистилли́рованная вода́. **2,** (make, as whiskey) перегоня́ть; гнать.

distillation *n.* дистилля́ция; перего́нка; винокуре́ние.

distiller *n.* винокур. —**distillery,** *n.* перего́нный *or* винокуренный заво́д.

distinct *adj.* **1,** (clear; plain) отчётливый; чёткий. **2,** (evident; marked) я́вный; заме́тный. *Distinct improvement,* заме́тное улучше́ние. *Distinct advantage,* я́вное преиму́щество. **3,** (different) разли́чный: *distinct dialects,* разли́чные диале́кты. —**as distinct from,** в отли́чие от.

distinction *n.* **1,** (differentiation) разли́чие: *draw a distinction between,* проводи́ть разли́чие ме́жду. **2,** (eminence) изве́стность. *Man of distinction,* выдаю́щийся челове́к. **3,** (honor) честь: *dubious distinction,* сомни́тельная честь. *He has the distinction of being...,* у него́ вы́пала честь быть... **4,** (special recognition) отли́чие: *serve/graduate with distinction,* служи́ть/ око́нчить шко́лу/ с отли́чием.

distinctive *adj.* **1,** (distinguishing) отличи́тельный: *distinctive feature,* отличи́тельная черта́. **2,** (characteristic; peculiar) характе́рный; своеобра́зный. *Distinctive appearance,* характе́рная вне́шность. *Have a distinctive taste,* име́ть своеобра́зный вкус.

distinctly *adv.* отчётливо; чётко.

distinguish *v.t.* **1,** (tell apart) различа́ть; отлича́ть. *Distinguish colors,* различа́ть цвета́. *Distinguish good from evil,* отлича́ть добро́ от зла. **2,** (make different; set apart) отлича́ть. *Distinguishing characteristic,* отличи́тельная черта́. **3,** (discern) различа́ть: *distinguish an object in the dark,* различа́ть предме́т в темноте́. —*v.i.* [*usu.* **distinguish between**] де́лать разли́чие (ме́жду). —**distinguish oneself,** отлича́ться.

distinguishable *adj.* различи́мый.

distinguished *adj.* **1,** (eminent) выдаю́щийся. **2,** *in direct address,* уважа́емый: *distinguished guests,* уважа́емые го́сти. **3,** (dignified in appearance) импоза́нтный.

distort *v.t.* **1,** (contort) искажа́ть; искривля́ть. **2,** (misrepresent) искажа́ть; извраща́ть. —**distortion,** *n.* искаже́ние; извраще́ние.

distract *v.t.* отвлека́ть: *distract someone from his/her work,* отвлека́ть кого́-нибудь от рабо́ты.

distraction *n.* **1,** (act of distracting) отвлече́ние. **2,** (something that distracts) поме́ха. **3,** (madness) безу́мие: *love someone to distraction,* люби́ть кого́-нибудь до безу́мия.

distraught *adj.* обезу́мевший (от го́ря).

distress *n.* **1,** (pain; suffering) огорче́ние. **2,** (trouble; danger) бе́дствие. *Distress signal,* сигна́л бе́дствия. *A ship in distress,* су́дно, те́рпящее бе́дствие. —*v.t.* огорча́ть. —**distressed,** *adj.* огорчённый. —**distressing,** *adj.* огорчи́тельный; тя́гостный.

distribute *v.t.* **1,** (allot; parcel out) распределя́ть. **2,** (hand out) раздава́ть.

distribution *n.* **1,** (parceling out) распределе́ние; (handing out) разда́ча. **2,** (range of occurrence) распределе́ние; размеще́ние: *geographic distribution,* географи́ческое распределе́ние/размеще́ние.

distributive *adj.* распредели́тельный.

distributor *n.* **1,** (one who distributes) распредели́тель. **2,** *comm.* опто́вая фи́рма; опто́вый торго́вец. **3,** *mech.* распредели́тель.

district *n.* райо́н; о́круг. *Business district,* делово́й райо́н; делова́я часть го́рода. *Election district,* избира́тельный о́круг; избира́тельный уча́сток. *District of Columbia,* о́круг Колу́мбия. —*adj.* райо́нный; окружно́й. —**district attorney,** окружно́й прокуро́р.

distrust *n.* недове́рие. —*v.t.* не доверя́ть. —**distrustful,** *adj.* недове́рчивый.

disturb *v.t.* **1,** (bother; interrupt) меша́ть; беспоко́ить. *I hope I'm not disturbing you,* наде́юсь, что я вам не меша́ю. *I don't want to disturb the boss,* не хочу́ беспоко́ить нача́льника. *He is not to be disturbed,* его́ нельзя́ (*or* не на́до) беспоко́ить. **2,** (disrupt) наруша́ть: *disturb the balance,* наруша́ть равнове́сие. **3,** (upset emotionally; distress) расстра́ивать; огорча́ть.

disturbance *n.* **1,** (interruption; intrusion) беспоко́йство. **2,** *often pl.* (public disorder) волне́ния; беспоря́дки.

disturbed *adj.* **1,** (troubled) обеспоко́енный; расстро́енный. **2,** (emotionally unstable) душевнобольно́й.

disturbing *adj.* беспоко́йный; трево́жный.

disunity *n.* отсу́тствие еди́нства; разобщённость.

disuse *n. Fall into disuse,* вы́йти из употребле́ния.

disyllabic *adj.* двусло́жный.

ditch *n.* кана́ва; ров. —*v.t. Ditch a plane over water,* де́лать вы́нужденную поса́дку на́ воду.

ditto *n.* то же. —**ditto marks,** зна́ки повторе́ния.

ditty *n.* частушка.

diuretic *adj.* мочего́нный. —*n.* мочего́нное сре́дство.

diurnal *adj.* дневно́й.

divan *n.* тахта́.

dive *v.i.* **1,** (plunge headfirst into water) ныря́ть. **2,**

(leap; dart) ныря́ть: *dive into the crowd/bushes,* нырну́ть в толпу́/ в кусты́/. **3,** *aero.* пики́ровать. —*n.* **1,** (plunge into water) прыжо́к в во́ду. **2,** *aero.* пики́рование; пике́. *Go into a dive,* войти́ в пике́. **3,** *colloq.* (cheap place) кабачо́к.

dive bomber пики́рующий бомбардиро́вщик.

diver *n.* **1,** *sports* ныря́льщик. **2,** (deep-sea diver) водола́з. *Pearl diver,* иска́тель же́мчуга.

diverge *v.i.* расходи́ться. —**divergence,** *n.* расхожде́ние.

divergent *adj.* **1,** (diverging) расходя́щийся. **2,** (differing) разли́чный.

diverse *adj.* разнообра́зный; ра́зный.

diversify *v.t.* разнообра́зить. —**diversification,** *n.* диверсифика́ция.

diversion *n.* **1,** (turning aside) отво́д; отвлече́ние. **2,** (amusement) развлече́ние. **3,** *mil.* демонстра́ция.

diversionary *adj., mil.* отвлека́ющий; демонстрати́вный; диверсио́нный.

diversity *n.* разнообра́зие.

divert *v.t.* **1,** (draw off in another direction) отвлека́ть: *divert attention from,* отвлека́ть внима́ние от. *Divert traffic,* направля́ть движе́ние в объе́зд. *Divert a river,* изменя́ть ру́сло реки́. **2,** (entertain) развлека́ть.

divest *v.t.* лиша́ть. *Divest oneself of,* отка́зываться от.

divide *v.t.* **1,** (separate into parts) разделя́ть; дели́ть; разбива́ть. *Divide something in half,* разделя́ть/ дели́ть что́-нибудь попола́м. *Divide a field into plots,* дели́ть *or* разделя́ть *or* разбива́ть по́ле на уча́стки. *Divide a book into chapters,* разби́ть кни́гу на гла́вы. *Divide the children into groups,* дели́ть *or* разделя́ть *or* разбива́ть дете́й на гру́ппы. *Divide one's time between...,* дели́ть своё вре́мя ме́жду... *The book is divided into two parts,* кни́га разделена́ (*or* де́лится) на две ча́сти; кни́га состои́т из двух часте́й. **2,** often fol. by *up* (give out in shares) дели́ть; разделя́ть: *divide up the loot,* дели́ть/разделя́ть добы́чу. **3,** (separate; be a boundary between) отделя́ть: *The Rio Grande divides the United States and Mexico,* Ри́о-Гра́нде отделя́ет США от Ме́ксики. **4,** *math.* дели́ть: *divide forty by eight,* дели́ть со́рок на во́семь. **5,** *fig.* (set apart) разъединя́ть: *the things that divide us,* то, что нас разъединя́ет. *Opinions were divided,* мне́ния раздели́лись. —*v.i.* разделя́ться; дели́ться: *The road divides,* доро́га разделя́ется/ де́лится. *Divide up into two groups,* разделя́ться *or* разбива́ться на две гру́ппы.

dividend *n.* **1,** *finance* дивиде́нд. **2,** *math.* дели́мое.

divider *n.* **1,** (partition) перегоро́дка. **2,** *pl.* (pair of compasses) ци́ркуль.

dividing *adj.* раздели́тельный: *dividing line,* раздели́тельная ли́ния.

divination *n.* гада́ние; ворожба́.

divine *adj.* **1,** (of or from God) боже́ственный; бо́жий. *Divine gift,* бо́жий дар. **2,** *colloq.* (wonderful; heavenly) боже́ственный: *a divine voice,* боже́ственный го́лос. *His playing was divine,* игра́л он боже́ственно. —*v.t.* предуга́дывать; разга́дывать. *Divine the future,* предуга́дывать бу́дущее. *Divine*

someone's intentions, разгада́ть чьи́-нибудь наме́рения.

diving *n.* **1,** *sports* прыжки́ в во́ду. **2,** (deep-sea diving) водола́зное де́ло. —**diving board,** трампли́н. —**diving helmet,** водола́зный шлем. —**diving suit,** водола́зный костю́м; скафа́ндр.

divinity *n.* **1,** (divine nature) боже́ственность. **2,** (deity) божество́. **3,** (study of religion) богосло́вие.

divisible *adj.* **1,** (capable of being divided) дели́мый. **2,** *math.* кра́тный: *divisible by two,* кра́тный двум. *Six is divisible by three,* шесть дели́тся на три; шесть — кра́тное трём. —**divisibility,** *n.* дели́мость.

division *n.* **1,** (act of dividing or being divided) деле́ние; разделе́ние; разде́л. *Division of labor,* разделе́ние труда́. **2,** (part; section) отде́л. **3,** (military unit) диви́зия. **4,** *math.* деле́ние.

divisional *adj., mil.* дивизио́нный.

divisive *adj.* раско́льнический.

divisor *n., math.* дели́тель.

divorce *n.* разво́д. —*adj.* бракоразво́дный: *divorce case,* бракоразво́дное де́ло. —*v.t.* **1,** (get a divorce from) разводи́ться с. **2,** *fig.* (detach; cut off) отрыва́ть: *divorced from the real world,* ото́рванный от жи́зни. —**divorced,** *adj.* разведённый. *They are divorced,* они́ в разво́де. —**divorcée,** *n.* разведённая.

divulge *v.t.* разглаша́ть. —**divulgence,** *n.* разглаше́ние.

dizziness *n.* головокруже́ние.

dizzy *adj.* **1,** (giddy): *I am dizzy,* у меня́ кру́жится голова́. **2,** [*also,* **dizzying**] (causing dizziness) головокружи́тельный: *dizzying height,* головокружи́тельная высота́.

do¹ (doo) *v.t.* **1,** (attend to) де́лать: *What are you doing?,* что вы де́лаете? *Do one's lessons,* де́лать уро́ки. *Do the dishes,* мыть посу́ду. *Do a lot of reading,* мно́го чита́ть. *There is nothing you can do about it,* ничего́ не поде́лаешь. **2,** (work at) рабо́тать; занима́ться: *What do you do for a living?; what sort of work do you do?,* кем вы рабо́таете?; чем вы занима́етесь? **3,** (cause) причиня́ть. *Do harm to,* причиня́ть *or* наноси́ть вред (+ *dat.*); причиня́ть *or* де́лать зло (+ *dat.*). *Do someone good,* приноси́ть по́льзу (+ *dat.*). **4,** (render; perform; carry out) де́лать; выполня́ть. *Do one's duty,* выполня́ть свой долг. *Do research,* проводи́ть иссле́дование. *Do someone a favor/service,* сде́лать кому́-нибудь одолже́ние. *What can I do for you?,* чем могу́ быть поле́зен (поле́зна)? **5,** fol. by *to* (hurt) де́лать: *What did you do to him?,* что вы ему́ сде́лали? *What did he ever do to you?,* что он тако́е вам сде́лал? *What did you do to your leg?,* что случи́лось с ва́шей ного́й? **6,** (travel at the rate of) де́лать: *do sixty miles an hour,* де́лать шестьдеся́т миль в час. —*v.i.* **1,** (act; behave) де́лать: *Do as you are told,* де́лайте, как вам ве́лено. **2,** (fare) *How are you doing?,* как (ва́ши) дела́? *How did he do?,* как у него́ получи́лось? **3,** (be suitable) годи́ться; подходи́ть. *That won't do,* э́то не подойдёт (*or* не пойдёт). **4,** (be sufficient) хвата́ть: *That will do,* хва́тит!; э́того хва́тит! *Fifty dollars will do,* пяти́десяти до́лларов бу́дет доста́точно.

—*v.aux.* **1,** *in forming questions: Do you speak Russian?*, вы говори́те по-ру́сски? **2,** *in forming neg. sentences: I do not speak Russian*, я не говорю́ по-ру́сски. **3,** *to add emphasis: Do pay us a visit!*, пожа́луйста, заходи́те *or* приходи́те к нам! *Do be quiet*, да замолчи́те же! **4,** *to replace a verb previously expressed or understood: Do you know how to cook? Yes, I do.*, уме́ете ли вы гото́вить? Да, уме́ю. *You don't know how to cook. Yes, I do.*, вы не уме́ете гото́вить. Непра́вда, уме́ю. —**do away with,** уничтожа́ть; поко́нчить с. —**do in,** *slang* **1,** (kill) прика́нчивать. **2,** (be the undoing of) (по)губи́ть. —**do not,** *see* **don't.** —**do over,** переде́лывать. —**do with, 1,** (lay; leave) дева́ть: *What did I do with my glasses?*, куда́ я дел (де́ла) мои́ очки́? **2,** (make use of) распоряжа́ться; располага́ть: *know what to do with one's time*, уме́ть распоряжа́ться/располага́ть свои́м вре́менем. **3,** (use; enjoy): *You could do with a haircut*, вам не меша́ло бы постри́чься. *I could do with a drink*, я бы вы́пил что́-нибудь. *Could I do with a glass of beer right now!*, мне сейча́с стака́н пи́ва! —**do without,** обходи́ться без. *See also* **doing, done, don't.**

do² (do) *n., music* до.

docile *adj.* послу́шный; поко́рный. —**docility,** *n.* поко́рность.

dock *n.* **1,** (place where a ship stands) док: *dry dock,* сухо́й док. **2,** (pier) при́стань. **3,** (prisoner's stand) скамья́ подсуди́мых: *in the dock,* на скамье́ подсуди́мых. —*v.i.* **1,** (of a ship) прича́ливать. **2,** (of space vehicles) стыкова́ться. —*v.t.* (deduct from) уре́зывать.

docket *n., law* спи́сок дел.

docking *n., aerospace* стыко́вка.

dockyard *n.* верфь.

doctor *n.* **1,** (physician) врач. **2,** (holder of a doctorate) до́ктор. —*v.t.* **1,** (treat) лечи́ть. **2,** (tamper with) подде́лывать; фальсифици́ровать. —**doctoral,** *adj.* до́кторский. —**doctorate,** *n.* до́кторская сте́пень.

doctrine *n.* доктри́на.

doctrinaire *n.* доктринёр. —*adj.* доктринёрский.

document *n.* докуме́нт. —*v.t.* документи́ровать.

documentary *adj.* документа́льный. —*n.* документа́льный фильм.

documentation *n.* документа́ция.

dodder *v.i.* **1,** (tremble) трясти́сь. **2,** (wobble along) ковыля́ть; шата́ться. *A doddering old man,* ковыля́ющий стари́к; стари́к, е́ле передвига́ющий но́ги.

dodge *v.t.* уклоня́ться от; увёртываться от; уви́ливать от. —*n.* увёртка.

doe *n.* **1,** (female deer) олену́ха. **2,** (female of other animals) са́мка.

doeskin *n.* за́мша.

doff *v.t.* снима́ть.

dog *n.* соба́ка. —*adj.* соба́чий: *dog collar,* соба́чий оше́йник. —*v.t.* **1,** (track; pursue) гна́ться по пята́м за; увя́зываться за. *Dog someone's footsteps,* сле́довать по пята́м за. **2,** *fig.* (haunt; hound) пресле́довать: *dogged by misfortune,* пресле́дуемый несча́стьями. —**a dog's age,** це́лая ве́чность. —**a**

dog's life, соба́чья жизнь. —**dog tired,** уста́лый как соба́ка. —**go do the dogs,** пойти́ пра́хом. —**it is raining cats and dogs,** дождь льёт как из ведра́. —**let sleeping dogs lie,** не буди́ ли́ха, пока́ спит ти́хо.

doge *n.* дож.

dog-eared *adj.* растрёпанный.

dogfight *n., aero.* возду́шный бой.

dogfish *n.* морска́я соба́ка.

dogged *adj.* упо́рный; насто́йчивый.

doggerel *n.* ви́рши.

doggone *adj., colloq.* прокля́тый. —**doggone it!,** чёрт побери́!

doggy *n.* соба́чка.

doghouse *n.* конура́.

dogma *n.* до́гма. —**dogmatic,** *adj.* догмати́ческий. —**dogmatism,** *n.* догмати́зм. —**dogmatist,** *n.* догма́тик.

dogmeat *n.* мя́со соба́к.

dog sled на́рты.

dogwood *n.* кизи́л.

doily *n.* салфе́точка.

doing *n. Big doings,* больши́е собы́тия. *It is mainly their doing,* э́то в основно́м де́ло их рук. *That will take some doing,* э́то потре́бует нема́ло уси́лий.

doldrums *n.pl.* **1,** *naut.* штилевы́е по́лосы. **2,** (low spirits) пода́вленное настрое́ние; уны́ние.

dole *n.* **1,** (handout) пода́чка. **2,** *Brit.* (unemployment insurance) посо́бие (по безрабо́тице): *be on the dole,* получа́ть посо́бие по безрабо́тице. —*v.t.* [*usu.* **dole out**] выдава́ть.

doleful *adj.* ско́рбный; жа́лобный.

doll *n.* ку́кла. *Play with dolls,* игра́ть в ку́клы. —*v.t.* [*usu. passive*] разоде́ть: *all dolled up,* весь разоде́тый; вся разоде́тая (как ку́кла).

dollar *n.* до́ллар. *Dollar bill,* до́лларовая бума́жка *or* купю́ра. —**in dollars and cents,** в де́нежном выраже́нии.

dollhouse *n.* ку́кольный до́мик.

dolly *n.* **1,** (doll) ку́колка. **2,** (cart) теле́жка.

dolomite *n.* доломи́т.

dolphin *n.* дельфи́н.

dolt *n.* глупе́ц; болва́н; тупи́ца.

domain *n.* **1,** (territory; realm) владе́ние; террито́рия. **2,** (sphere; field) о́бласть; сфе́ра; круг.

dome *n.* ку́пол.

domestic *adj.* **1,** (of the home) дома́шний. *Domestic animals,* дома́шние живо́тные. *Domestic quarrel,* семе́йная ссо́ра. **2,** (internal) вну́тренний: *domestic policy,* вну́тренняя поли́тика. **3,** (produced at home; not imported) оте́чественный. —*n.* (servant) слуга́; прислу́га. —**domestic science,** домово́дство.

domesticate *v.t.* прируча́ть; одома́шнивать. —**domesticated,** *adj.* ручно́й; приручённый. —**domestication,** *n.* прируче́ние; одома́шнивание.

domicile *n.* местожи́тельство.

dominance *n.* госпо́дство.

dominant *adj.* госпо́дствующий; домини́рующий.

dominate *v.t.* **1,** (control) госпо́дствовать: *dominate the sea/air,* госпо́дствовать на мо́ре/ в во́здухе/.

Dominate other nations, госпо́дствовать над други́ми стра́нами. **2,** (tower over) домини́ровать над; госпо́дствовать над.

domination *n.* госпо́дство.

domineer *v.t. & i.* вла́ствовать (над); кома́ндовать (над).

domineering *adj.* вла́стный.

dominion *n.* **1,** (sovereignty; rule) влады́чество. **2,** *pl.* (territory under one's control) владе́ния. **3,** (self-governing member of the British Commonwealth) доминио́н.

domino *n.* **1,** (masquerade costume) домино́. **2,** *pl.* (game) домино́. **3,** (tile used in this game) кость.

don *v.t.* надева́ть.

donate *v.t.* же́ртвовать; дари́ть. *Donate money to charity,* же́ртвовать де́ньги на благотвори́тельные це́ли. *Donate a painting to a museum,* дари́ть карти́ну музе́ю. *Donate blood,* дава́ть кровь.

donation *n.* поже́ртвование.

done *adj.* **1,** (carried out) сде́лан: *The deed is done,* де́ло сде́лано. **2,** (finished) (о)ко́нчен. *Are you done?,* вы зако́нчили? *Are you done with the screwdriver?,* отвёртка бо́льше вам не нужна́? **3,** (adequately cooked) гото́в: *Is the meat done yet?,* мя́со уже́ гото́во? **4,** (socially acceptable) при́нят: *That is not done,* э́то не при́нято. —**done for,** пропа́вший; поги́бший. *We're done for,* мы пропа́ли; мы поги́бли; с на́ми поко́нчено; с на́ми всё ко́нчено.

donkey *n.* осёл.

donor *n.* же́ртвователь. *Blood donor,* до́нор.

don't *contr. of* **do not.** *In neg. imperatives rendered with* не: *Don't cry!,* не плачь!; не пла́чьте! *Don't forget!,* не забу́дь!; не забу́дьте! *Don't (do that)!,* не на́до! *Don't let me detain you!,* не хочу́ вас заде́рживать. *Don't let this happen again!,* чтобы э́того бо́льше не́ было!

doom *n.* ги́бель. *Sense of doom,* чу́вство обречённости. —*v.t.* обрека́ть: *doomed to failure,* обречённый на прова́л.

doomsday *n.* день Стра́шного суда́. —**till doomsday,** до второ́го прише́ствия.

door *n.* дверь. *The door to the room,* дверь ко́мнаты. *Walk out the door,* выходи́ть за дверь. *Stand outside the door,* стоя́ть за две́рью. *Someone is at the door,* кто́-то пришёл. —*adj.* дверно́й: *door lock,* дверно́й замо́к. —**behind closed doors,** при закры́тых дверя́х. —**go from door to door,** ходи́ть из до́ма в дом. —**next door,** ря́дом. —**out of doors,** на дворе́. —**show someone the door,** показа́ть *or* указа́ть кому́-нибудь на дверь.

doorbell *n.* (дверно́й) звоно́к. *Ring the doorbell,* звони́ть в дверь. *The doorbell rang,* разда́лся звоно́к в дверь. *Hear the doorbell ring,* услы́шать звоно́к в дверь.

doorkeeper *n.* привра́тник.

doorknob *n.* дверна́я ру́чка.

doorman *n.* швейца́р.

doormat *n.* полови́к.

doorpost *n.* (дверно́й) кося́к.

doorstep *n.* поро́г. —**camp on someone's doorstep,** обива́ть поро́ги у кого́-нибудь. —**lay the blame on someone's doorstep,** возлага́ть вину́ на кого́-нибудь.

doorway *n.* дверно́й проём. *Stand in the doorway,* стоя́ть в дверя́х.

dope *n., slang* **1,** (drug) нарко́тик; дурма́н. **2,** (dumbbell) глупе́ц. **3,** (information) информа́ция: *the latest dope,* после́дняя информа́ция. —*v.t., colloq.* **1,** (drug) накача́ть нарко́тиками. **2,** *fol. by* **out** (figure out) разга́дывать. —**dope addict; dope fiend,** наркома́н.

dopey *adj., colloq.* глу́пый.

dormant *adj.* **1,** (sleeping) спя́щий. **2,** (inactive) усну́вший: *dormant volcano,* усну́вший вулка́н. —**lie dormant,** быть забы́тым; быть отло́женным (в сто́рону).

dormer window слухово́е окно́.

dormitory *n.* общежи́тие.

dormouse *n.* со́ня.

dorsal *adj.* спинно́й.

dosage *n.* дозиро́вка.

dose *n.* до́за: *in small doses,* небольши́ми до́зами.

dossier *n.* досье́.

dot *n.* то́чка. *Dots and dashes,* то́чки и тире́. *Polka dots,* горо́шек. —*v.t.* **1,** (mark with a dot) ста́вить то́чку на. **2,** (stud) усе́ивать: *The fields are dotted with flowers,* поля́ усе́яны цвета́ми. —**on the dot, 1,** with the time of day, ро́вно: *at six o'clock on the dot,* ро́вно в шесть часо́в. **2,** (exactly on time) мину́та в мину́ту.

dotage *n.* ста́рческое слабоу́мие. *Be in one's dotage,* впада́ть в де́тство.

dote *v.i.* [*usu.* **dote on** *or* **upon**] души́ не ча́ять в; носи́ть на рука́х.

dotted *adj.* в кра́пинку; в горо́шек. —**dotted line,** пункти́рная ли́ния; пункти́р.

dotterel *n.* си́вка глу́пая; хруста́н.

double *adj.* двойно́й; двоя́кий. *Double portion,* двойна́я по́рция. *Double bed,* двуспа́льная крова́ть. *Double room,* ко́мната *or* но́мер на двои́х. *Double chin,* двойно́й подборо́док. *Double exposure,* двойна́я *or* двукра́тная экспози́ция. *Double pneumonia,* двусторо́ннее воспале́ние лёгких. *Double standard,* двойно́й станда́рт; двойна́я ме́рка. *Double rose,* махро́вая ро́за. —*adv.* вдво́е бо́льше; вдвойне́. *Double the price,* вдво́е доро́же. *At double the price,* по двойно́й цене́. —*n.* **1,** (perfect likeness) двойни́к. **2,** *pl., tennis* па́рная игра́. *Mixed doubles,* сме́шанные па́ры. —*v.t.* удва́ивать; увели́чивать вдво́е. *Double the dose,* удва́ивать до́зу. —*v.i.* удва́иваться; увели́чиваться *or* возраста́ть вдво́е. —**double back,** возвраща́ться по свои́м следа́м. —**double up,** скрю́чивать(ся): *He was doubled up in pain,* он скрю́чился (*or* его́ скрю́чило) от бо́ли. —**on the double,** бего́м; на бегу́. —**see double,** двои́ться в глаза́х: *I am seeing double,* у меня́ двои́тся в глаза́х.

double-barreled *adj.* двуство́льный.

double bass контраба́с.

double bassoon контрафаго́т.

double-breasted *adj.* двубо́ртный.

double-cross *v.t.*, *colloq.* обма́нывать; надува́ть.

double-dealer *n.* двуру́шник. —**double-dealing,** *adj.* двуру́шнический. —*n.* двуру́шничество.

double-decker *n.* двухэта́жный авто́бус. *Double-decker bridge*, двухъя́русный мост.

double-edged *adj.* обоюдоо́стрый. —**double-edged sword,** па́лка о двух конца́х.

double entendre двусмы́сленность.

double-lock *v.t.* запира́ть на два оборо́та.

double-space *v.t.* печа́тать че́рез два интерва́ла.

doubly *adv.* вдвойне́: *I am doubly sorry for them*, мне их вдвойне́ жа́лко.

doubt *n.* сомне́ние: *without a doubt*, без вся́кого сомне́ния. *Have doubts about someone*, сомнева́ться в ком-нибудь. —*v.t.* сомнева́ться в: *I doubt that*, я в э́том сомнева́юсь. *Doubt someone's honesty*, сомнева́ться в чьей-нибудь че́стности. *I doubt if he'll agree*, я сомнева́юсь (в том), что он согласи́тся. —**be in doubt,** сомнева́ться: *When in doubt — ask*, е́сли сомнева́ешься, спроси́. *The outcome is still in doubt*, исхо́д де́ла ещё не я́сен. —**no doubt, 1,** (undoubtedly) без сомне́ния; несомне́нно. **2,** (probably) наве́рно.

doubtful *adj.* **1,** (tending to doubt): *be doubtful*, сомнева́ться. **2,** (questionable; unlikely) сомни́тельный: *That is doubtful*, э́то сомни́тельно.

doubtless *adv.* **1,** (undoubtedly) несомне́нно. **2,** (probably) наве́рно. *Also,* **doubtlessly.**

douche *n.* душ; облива́ние.

dough *n.* **1,** (flour paste) те́сто. **2,** *slang* (money) моне́та.

doughnut *n.* по́нчик.

doughty *adj.* сто́йкий; отва́жный.

dour *adj.* мра́чный; угрю́мый.

douse *v.t.* **1,** (immerse) погружа́ть; окуна́ть. **2,** (drench) обдава́ть; облива́ть; ока́чивать. **3,** (extinguish) туши́ть; гаси́ть. *Douse a fire*, залива́ть костёр.

dove *n.* го́лубь.

dovecote *n.* голубя́тня.

dovetail *n.* ла́сточкин хвост. —*v.t.* увя́зывать. —*v.i.* увя́зываться; впи́сываться.

dowager *n.* **1,** (widow) вдова́. *Dowager queen*, вдо́вствующая короле́ва. **2,** *colloq.* (elderly woman) матро́на.

dowdy *adj.* безвку́сный; неэлега́нтный.

dowel *n.* шпо́нка; штифт; штырь.

down *adv.* **1,** (to a lower position; toward the ground) вниз: *look down*, смотре́ть вниз. ♦*Usu. rendered by a single verb: sit down*, сесть; *lie down*, лечь; *go (or come) down*, сойти́; *climb down*, слезть; *fall down*, упа́сть; *knock down*, повали́ть; *sbit to be feet; tear down*, снести́; *burn down*, сгоре́ть; *write down*, записа́ть; *calm down*, успоко́ить(ся). **2,** (as a down payment) нали́чными: *forty dollars down and the rest in monthly installments*, со́рок до́лларов нали́чными, а остально́е ежеме́сячными взно́сами. —*adj. The sun is down*, со́лнце зашло́. *Her temperature is down*, её температу́ра пони́зилась. *He is*

down with the flu, он боле́ет гри́ппом. *Strike a man when he is down*, бить лежа́чего. —*prep.* с: *fall down the stairs*, упа́сть с ле́стницы; *slide down the banister*, съе́хать по пери́лам. *Sail down the river*, плыть вниз по реке́. —*n.* пух: *eider down*, гага́чий пух. —*v.t.* **1,** (shoot down) сбива́ть. **2,** (drink) вы́пить за́лпом. —**down and out,** разорённый; в нищете́. —**down to,** вплоть до. —**down with...!,** доло́й (+ *acc.*).

downcast *adj.* уны́лый; пону́рый.

downfall *n.* паде́ние; круше́ние; ги́бель.

downgrade *n.* склон; укло́н. —*v.t.* **1,** (demote) понижа́ть. **2,** (minimize) умаля́ть.

downhearted *adj.* па́вший ду́хом; уны́лый. *Don't be downhearted!*, не уныва́й!

downhill *adv.* под го́ру; под укло́н.

down payment зада́ток: *make a down payment*, дава́ть *or* вноси́ть зада́ток.

downpour *n.* ли́вень.

downright *adj.* я́вный; сплошно́й; су́щий. —*adv.* про́сто; пря́мо: *It's downright amazing!*, э́то про́сто/пря́мо удиви́тельно!

downstairs *adv.* **1,** (location) внизу́. **2,** (motion) вниз. —*n.* ни́жний эта́ж.

downstream *adv.* вниз по тече́нию.

downtime *n.* просто́й.

downtown *n.* центр го́рода; делова́я часть го́рода. —*adj.* центра́льный. —*adv.* в центр(е) го́рода.

downtrodden *adj.* заби́тый; за́гнанный.

downward *adv.* [*also,* **downwards**] вниз; кни́зу; под укло́н. —*adj.* под укло́н: *downward movement*, движе́ние под укло́н.

downy *adj.* пуши́стый; пухо́вый.

dowry *n.* прида́ное.

doze *v.i.* дрема́ть. *Doze off*, задрема́ть; забыва́ться.

dozen *n.* дю́жина.

drab *adj.* бесцве́тный; се́рый; однообра́зный. —**drabness,** *n.* бесцве́тность; се́рость; однообра́зие.

drachma *n.* дра́хма.

draconian *adj.* драко́новский.

draft *n.* **1,** (preliminary version) набро́сок; эски́з. *First/rough draft*, чернови́к. *Final draft*, оконча́тельная реда́кция. *Draft resolution*, прое́кт резолю́ции. **2,** (current of air) сквозня́к: *sit in a draft*, сиде́ть на сквозняке́. *There is a draft in here*, здесь сквози́т. *There is a draft from the window*, от окна́ ду́ет. **3,** (device to regulate air intake) тя́га. **4,** (conscription) во́инская пови́нность. **5,** *finance* чек. **6,** *naut.* (depth of a vessel below the water) оса́дка. —*adj.* **1,** (for hauling) тя́гловый. *Draft animals*, (живо́е) тя́гло; рабо́чий *or* тя́гловый скот. *Draft horse*, упряжна́я ло́шадь. **2,** (drawn from a cask) разливно́й: *draft beer*, разливно́е пи́во. —*v.t.* **1,** (compose in preliminary form) составля́ть: *draft a letter*, составля́ть письмо́. *Draft a constitution*, вы́работать прое́кт конститу́ции. **2,** (conscript) призыва́ть (на вое́нную слу́жбу). *Also, chiefly Brit.,* **draught.**

draft board призывно́й пункт.

draftee *n.* призывни́к.

draftsman *also,* **draughtsman** *n.* чертёжник.

drafty *also,* **draughty** *adj. It is drafty in here,* здесь сквози́т.

drag *v.t.* **1,** (pull along the ground) тащи́ть; волочи́ть. *Drag in,* вта́скивать. *Drag out,* выта́скивать. *I could hardly drag myself to work,* я е́ле дотащи́лся до рабо́ты. *Drag one's feet,* волочи́ть но́ги; *fig.* ме́длить. **2,** (dredge, as a river) очища́ть (дно реки́). **3,** (force to go against one's will) тащи́ть. **4,** *fol. by* **out** (prolong) тяну́ть; затя́гивать; растя́гивать. —*v.i.* **1,** (trail along) тащи́ться; волочи́ться. **2,** *fol. by* **on** *or* **out** (progress slowly; last a long time) тяну́ться; затя́гиваться. —*n.* **1,** (hindrance) то́рмоз; обу́за. **2,** *colloq.* (draw, as on a cigarette) затя́жка.

dragnet *n.* **1,** (net) бре́день. **2,** (network for catching a criminal) обла́ва.

dragon *n.* драко́н.

dragonfly *n.* стрекоза́.

dragoon *n.* драгу́н.

drain *v.t.* **1,** (draw off, as water) отводи́ть. **2,** (draw water from, as a lake) отводи́ть во́ду из; осуша́ть; дрени́ровать. **3,** (drink all the contents of) осуша́ть. **4,** *surgery* дрени́ровать. **5,** *fig.* (exhaust; consume totally) истоща́ть. —*v.i.* вытека́ть. *The river drains into the ocean,* река́ впада́ет в океа́н. —*n.* **1,** (channel; pipe) водосто́к; (водо)сто́чная труба́. **2,** (continuous outflow) уте́чка. —**go down the drain,** пройти́ да́ром.

drainage *n.* дрена́ж; осуше́ние. —*adj.* дрена́жный; осуши́тельный; отво́дный; водоотво́дный.

drainpipe *n.* водосто́чная труба́.

drake *n.* се́лезень.

drama *n.* дра́ма. *Drama critic,* театра́льный кри́тик.

dramatic *adj.* **1,** (of drama; stirring) драмати́ческий. **2,** (striking; drastic) ре́зкий: *dramatic change,* ре́зкая переме́на.

dramatically *adv.* ре́зко; кру́то: *change dramatically,* ре́зко/кру́то измени́ться.

dramatics *n.* драмати́ческое иску́сство. —**dramatize,** *v.t.* драматизи́ровать. —**dramaturgy,** *n.* драматурги́я.

drape *v.t.* драпирова́ть. *The coffin was draped in black,* гроб был обтя́нут чёрным. —*n.* = **drapery.**

drapery *n., usu. pl.* драпиро́вка.

drastic *adj.* круто́й; ре́зкий. *Drastic measures,* круты́е ме́ры. *Drastic changes,* ре́зкие переме́ны. *Drastic reduction,* ре́зкое сниже́ние. —**drastically,** *adv.* ре́зко.

draught *n.* = **draft.**

draughtboard *n., Brit.* ша́шечная доска́.

draughts *n.pl., Brit.* ша́шки.

draughtsman *n.* = **draftsman.**

draughty *adj.* = **drafty.**

draw *v.t.* **1,** (sketch) рисова́ть: *draw a picture,* рисова́ть карти́ну. *Draw a line,* проводи́ть ли́нию *or* черту́. *Draw a circle,* черти́ть круг. *Draw a map,* черти́ть ка́рту. **2,** (make, as a comparison or distinction) де́лать; проводи́ть. **3,** (derive, as a conclusion) де́лать (вы́вод); выводи́ть (заключе́ние). *Draw a lesson from,* извлека́ть уро́к из. *Draw strength from,* че́рпать си́лы из. **4,** (pull) тащи́ть: *The horse draws the carriage,* ло́шадь та́щит каре́ту. *A carriage drawn by six horses,* каре́та, влеко́мая шестью́ лошадьми́. **5,** (pull so as to close) задёргивать: *draw the curtain/blind,* задёргивать занаве́ску/што́ру. **6,** (pull tight) натя́гивать: *draw the bow,* натя́гивать лук. *Draw the rope tight,* ту́го (*or* потуже) затя́гивать верёвку. **7,** (move in a given direction) отводи́ть: *draw someone aside,* отводи́ть кого́-нибудь в сто́рону. **8,** (take out; withdraw) вынима́ть; выхва́тывать. *Draw one's sword,* вынима́ть шпа́гу из но́жен. *Draw a knife/gun,* выхва́тывать нож/пистоле́т. *Draw a card from the deck,* тяну́ть ка́рту из коло́ды. **9,** (bring out, as a liquid) че́рпать: *draw water from a well,* че́рпать во́ду из коло́дца. *Draw blood,* пуска́ть кровь. *Draw a bath for someone,* нали́ть кому́-нибудь ва́нну. **10,** (attract) привлека́ть: *draw visitors,* привлека́ть посети́телей. *Draw a large audience,* собира́ть большу́ю аудито́рию. *Draw criticism,* подверга́ться кри́тике. *Draw someone's attention to,* обраща́ть чьё-нибудь внима́ние на. *Draw someone into a conversation,* вовлека́ть кого́-нибудь в разгово́р. *He feels drawn to his homeland,* его́ тя́нет на ро́дину. **11,** (elicit) вызыва́ть: *draw loud applause,* вызыва́ть гро́мкие аплодисме́нты. *Draw enemy fire,* вызыва́ть ого́нь проти́вника. **12,** (get or receive by chance) *rendered by* выпада́ть (+ *dat.*): *He drew a tough assignment,* ему́ вы́пало тру́дное зада́ние. **13,** (get or pick at random) тяну́ть: *draw lots,* тяну́ть жре́бий. **14,** (earn): *draw a salary,* получа́ть зарпла́ту. *Draw interest,* приноси́ть проце́нты. **15,** (issue, as a check) выпи́сывать. **16,** (inhale) вдыха́ть. *Draw air into one's lungs,* набира́ть во́здуха в лёгкие. *Draw a breath,* передохну́ть. **17,** *naut.* име́ть оса́дку в: *The ship draws 15 feet,* парохо́д име́ет оса́дку в пятна́дцать фу́тов. —*v.i.* **1,** (sketch) рисова́ть. **2,** (move in a certain direction): *draw near,* приближа́ться; *draw even with,* поравня́ться с; *draw to a close,* подходи́ть *or* идти́ *or* бли́зиться *or* приближа́ться к концу́. **3,** (draw lots) тяну́ть жре́бий. *Draw for partners,* выбира́ть партнёров по жре́бию. **4,** (play to a tie) сыгра́ть вничью́; сде́лать ничью́. **5,** (take in air) тяну́ть: *The chimney isn't drawing,* труба́ не тя́нет. —*n.* (tied game) ничья́. —**draw back, 1,** (pull back) отдёргивать. **2,** (step back) отпря́нуть. —**draw in,** вбира́ть; втя́гивать. —**draw off, 1,** (siphon off) отводи́ть. **2,** *mil.* отводи́ть; оття́гивать (войска́). —**draw out,** выта́гивать. —**draw up, 1,** (compose; draft) составля́ть; разраба́тывать. **2,** (pull up, as a chair) подставля́ть; пододвига́ть. **3,** (pull up, as one's legs or knees) поджима́ть. **4,** *fol. by* **to** (pull up to) подъезжа́ть (к). *See also* **drawn.**

drawback *n.* недоста́ток.

drawbridge *n.* подъёмный мост; разводно́й мост.

draw curtain раздвижно́й за́навес.

drawer *n.* **1,** (sliding container) я́щик (стола́). *Chest of drawers,* комо́д. **2,** *comm.* трасса́нт. **3,** *pl.* (undergarment) кальсо́ны.

drawing *n.* **1,** (art) рисова́ние; черче́ние. *Mechanical drawing,* механи́ческое черче́ние. **2,** (picture) рису́нок. **3,** (sketch; design) чертёж. **4,** (selection of tickets in a lottery) ро́зыгрыш.

drawing board чертёжная доска́.

drawing pin *Brit.* (thumbtack) кно́пка.

drawing room 1, (living room) гости́ная. **2,** (private compartment on a train) купе́.

drawl *n.* протя́жное произноше́ние. —*v.i.* говори́ть врастя́жку; растя́гивать слова́.

drawn *adj.* **1,** (pulled out of the sheath) наголо́: *with swords drawn:* с ша́шками наголо́. **2,** (haggard) измождённый. *He looks drawn,* он осу́нулся. *Her cheeks are drawn,* её щёки втяну́лись. **3,** (tied, as of a game) ниче́йный.

drawn-out *adj.* затяжно́й.

dray *n.* ломова́я теле́га. —**dray horse,** ломова́я ло́шадь. —**drayman,** *n.* ломово́й изво́зчик.

dread *v.t.* боя́ться; страши́ться. —*n.* страх; боя́знь. —*adj.* стра́шный; гро́зный.

dreadful *adj.* стра́шный; ужа́сный.

dreadnought *n.* дредно́ут.

dream *n.* **1,** (thoughts while asleep) сон; сновиде́ние. *Bad dream,* дурно́й сон. *I had a dream,* я ви́дел(а) сон. *Walk around in a dream,* ходи́ть, как во сне. **2,** (cherished hope) мечта́; грёза. —*v.i.* **1,** (have a dream; have dreams) ви́деть *or* сни́ться сон/сны. *Am I dreaming?,* э́то мне сни́тся? *I dreamt about you,* вы мне сни́лись; я вас ви́дел(а) во сне. **2,** *fol. by of* (envision, as in a dream) мечта́ть: *dream of taking a trip abroad,* мечта́ть о пое́здке за грани́цу. *Dream of becoming an actress,* мечта́ть стать актри́сой. **3,** *fol. by of* (consider doing) сни́ться: *I never even dreamt of it,* э́то мне да́же и не сни́лось. *I wouldn't dream of it!,* и не поду́маю!; об э́том не мо́жет быть и ре́чи. —*v.t.* сни́ться: *I dreamt that...,* мне (при)сни́лось, что... *I never dreamt that...,* мне не приходи́ло в го́лову, что... *You must have dreamt it,* вам э́то присни́лось. —**dream up, 1,** (devise) приду́мывать. **2,** (concoct) выду́мывать.

dreamer *n.* мечта́тель.

dreamland *n.* **1,** (sleep) сон. **2,** = **dreamworld.**

dreamworld *n.* мир грёз; ца́рство грёз.

dreamy *adj.* мечта́тельный.

dreary *adj.* мра́чный; па́смурный; хму́рый. —**dreariness,** *n.* мра́чность.

dredge *n.* дра́га. —*v.t.* **1,** (clear out) очища́ть (дно реки́). **2,** *fol. by up* (bring up; remove) выла́вливать.

dregs *n.pl.* **1,** (residue) подо́нки; гу́ща. **2,** *fig.* (worst portion) подо́нки: *the dregs of society,* подо́нки о́бщества.

drench *v.t.* прома́чивать; выма́чивать. *Get drenched,* промока́ть; вымока́ть.

dress *n.* **1,** (woman's garment) пла́тье. **2,** (apparel) оде́жда; пла́тье. —*adj.* **1,** (for a dress): *dress fabric,* мате́рия на пла́тье. **2,** *mil.* пара́дный: *dress uniform,* пара́дная фо́рма. —*v.t.* **1,** (put clothes on) одева́ть. *Get dressed,* одева́ться. *Dressed in black,* оде́т(а) в чёрное. **2,** (adorn) украша́ть; убира́ть. **3,** (bandage) перевя́зывать. **4,** (prepare for cooking) чи́стить; разде́лывать; свежева́ть. **5,** (curry, as leather) выде́лывать. **6,** *mil.* выра́внивать. —*v.i.* **1,** (put on one's

clothes; wear clothes) одева́ться: *dress well/warmly,* хорошо́/тепло́ одева́ться. *Dress for dinner,* (пере)одева́ться к обе́ду. **2,** *mil.* (come into alignment) равня́ться: *Dress right!,* напра́во — равня́йся! —**dress down,** *colloq.* дать нагоня́й *or* взбу́чку (+ *dat.*). —**dress up,** наряжа́ться; приоде́ться; разряжа́ться. *Dress up as,* переодева́ться (+ *instr.*); наряжа́ться (+ *instr.*).

dress circle бельэта́ж.

dresser *n.* **1,** (one who dresses in a certain way): *She is a good dresser,* она́ хорошо́ одева́ется. **2,** (chest of drawers) комо́д.

dressing *n.* **1,** (act of putting clothes on) одева́ние. **2,** (bandage) перевя́зка. **3,** (sauce) припра́ва. **4,** (stuffing) начи́нка; фарш. —**dressing gown,** хала́т. —**dressing room, 1,** (of an actor or performer) убо́рная. **2,** (in a gymnasium, public bath, etc.) раздева́лка. **3,** (for trying on clothes) приме́рочная. —**dressing table,** туале́тный сто́лик; туале́т.

dressing-down *n.* нагоня́й; взбу́чка.

dressmaker *n.* портни́ха.

dress rehearsal генера́льная репети́ция.

drib *n., in* **in dribs and drabs,** че́рез час по ча́йной ло́жке.

dribble *v.i.* **1,** (drip) ка́пать. **2,** (drool) пуска́ть слю́ни. —*v.t. & i., basketball* вести́ (мяч).

dried *adj.* сушёный; сухо́й. —**dried milk,** сухо́е молоко́.

drier *n.* = **dryer.**

drift *v.i.* **1,** (move with the current) плыть; дрейфова́ть. *Drift downstream,* плыть вниз по тече́нию. **2,** (move aimlessly) идти́ самотёком. *Let things drift,* пусти́ть де́ло на самотёк. *Drift from place to place,* переходи́ть с ме́ста на ме́сто. **3,** (stray) отклоня́ться: *drift off course,* отклоня́ться от ку́рса. *Drift away from old friends,* отходи́ть от ста́рых друзе́й. *We drifted apart,* на́ши пути́ разошли́сь. **4,** (pile up, as of snow) намета́ть; нава́ливать (*both impers.*). —*v.t.* намета́ть (*impers.*): *The wind drifted the snow,* ве́тром намело́ сне́гу. —*n.* **1,** *naut; aero.* дрейф; снос. **2,** (snowdrift) зано́с; сугро́б. **3,** (meaning) смысл: *get the drift of the conversation,* улови́ть смысл разгово́ра.

drifter *n.* бродя́га.

driftwood *n.* плавни́к.

drill *n.* **1,** (tool for making holes) сверло́; дрель. **2,** (dentist's drill) бормаши́на. **3,** (training or classroom exercise) трениро́вка. **4,** *mil.* строева́я подгото́вка; трениро́вка. —*v.t.* **1,** (make, as a hole) сверли́ть; просве́рливать. **2,** *dent.* сверли́ть: *drill a tooth,* сверли́ть зуб. **3,** (teach; train) обуча́ть; трениров́а́ть. **4,** *mil.* муштрова́ть. —*v.i.* **1,** (bore holes) бури́ть; сверли́ть. *Drill for oil,* бури́ть нефть. **2,** *fol. by* **through** (bore through) бури́ть: *drill through rock,* бури́ть го́рную поро́ду. **3,** (practice) упражня́ться; трениров́а́ться. **4,** *mil.* проводи́ть строеву́ю подгото́вку.

drilling *n.* буре́ние. —*adj.* бурово́й; бури́льный. *Drilling rig,* бурова́я устано́вка.

drillmaster *n.* инстру́ктор строево́й подгото́вки.

drily *adv.* = **dryly**.

drink *v.t. & i.* пить: *What would you like to drink?*, что вы бу́дете пить? *Would you like something to drink?*, хоти́те чтó-нибудь вы́пить? *Drink to someone's health*, пить за чьё-нибудь здорóвье. —*n.* напи́ток: *food and drinks*, едá и напи́тки. *Would you like a drink of water?*, вам чегó-нибудь воды́? *Can I get you a drink?*, вам чегó-нибудь нали́ть? *Would you like another drink?*, хоти́те ещё вы́пить? *Have two drinks before dinner*, вы́пить две рю́мочки пéред обéдом. —**drink in**, впи́тывать. —**drive to drink**, доводи́ть до пья́нства. —**take to drink**, спивáться.

drinkable *adj.* гóдный для питья́.

drinker *n.* пью́щий. *He is a heavy drinker*, он си́льно пьёт.

drinking *n.* питьё: *the drinking of wine*, питьё винá. *Drinking ruined his life*, пья́нство погуби́ло егó жизнь. —*adj.* питьевóй: *drinking water*, питьевáя водá. *The quality of the drinking water*, кáчество водопровóдной воды́. —**drinking bout**, запóй; попóйка. —**drinking companion**, собуты́льник. —**drinking fountain**, фонтáнчик. —**drinking song**, застóльная пéсня.

drip *v.i.* **1,** (of a liquid) кáпать: *Water was dripping from the faucet*, водá кáпала из крáна. *The faucet is dripping*, из крáна кáпает. *His hands were dripping with blood*, кровь стекáла с егó рук. **2,** (of a candle) оплывáть; отекáть. —*v.t.* кáпать (+ *instr.*). —*n.* кáпанье.

dripping *adj.* кáпающий: *dripping faucet*, кáпающий кран. —*adv.*, in **dripping wet,** мóкрый, хоть вы́жми (*or* выжимáй). —*n.*, *usu. pl.* вы́текший сок.

drive *v.t.* **1,** (propel) дви́гать: *Steam drives the mechanism*, пар дви́жет механи́зм. **2,** (operate, as a car) води́ть (маши́ну). **3,** (transport in a vehicle) вози́ть; отвози́ть. *Drive someone to the airport*, отвози́ть когó-нибудь в аэропóрт. *Drive someone around town*, вози́ть *or* катáть когó-нибудь по гóроду. **4,** (lead; herd, as cattle) гнать. **5,** (force; chase; press) загоня́ть: *drive into a corner*, загоня́ть в у́гол. *Drive the invaders from the country*, прогоня́ть захвáтчиков из страны́. **6,** (hammer) вбивáть; забивáть: *drive a nail into a wall*, вбивáть/забивáть гвоздь в стéну. *Drive a wedge between*, вбивáть клин мéжду. **7,** (bring to a certain state or act) доводи́ть (до). *Drive to despair*, доводи́ть до отчáяния; приводи́ть в отчáяние. *Drive mad*, своди́ть с умá. *He was driven to suicide*, он был доведён до самоуби́йства. **8,** *sports* (hit; kick) забивáть; посылáть: *He drove the ball into the net*, он заби́л мяч в ворóта; он послáл мяч в сéтку. —*v.i.* **1,** (operate a vehicle) води́ть маши́ну. *Drive faster!*, езжáйте быстрéе! **2,** (go in a vehicle) éхать (на маши́не). *Drive to/around town*, éхать в гóрод; éздить по гóроду. *Drive into the garage*, въезжáть в гарáж. *Drive onto the ferry*, въезжáть на парóм. *Drive across the bridge*, переезжáть чéрез мост. **3,** *fol. by* **at** (mean; intend) гнуть; клони́ть: *What are you driving at?*, кудá ты гнёшь?; к чему́ ты клóнишь? —*n.* **1,** (ride in a car) ездá; прогу́лка. *A two-hour drive*, два часá езды́. *Go*

for a drive, éздить на прогу́лку; катáться на маши́не; прокати́ться; проéхаться. *Take for a drive*, катáть; прокати́ть; повози́ть. **2,** (campaign) похóд: *economy drive*, похóд за эконóмию. **3,** (energy; ambition) энéргия. *Sexual drive*, половóе влечéние. **4,** *mech.* передáча; привóд: *belt drive*, ремённая передáча; ремённый привóд. *Front-wheel drive*, передний привóд. **5,** *sports* удáр. —**drive away, 1,** (repel) прогоня́ть; отгоня́ть. **2,** (depart in a vehicle) укати́ть; (of a vehicle) укати́ться. —**drive back, 1,** (force back) оттесня́ть. **2,** (return by car) éхать обрáтно. —**drive home, 1,** (transport to one's home) отвози́ть домóй. **2,** (go home in a vehicle) éхать домóй. **3,** (make someone understand) внушáть: *drive home to someone the fact that...*, внушáть комý-нибудь, что... —**drive off,** = drive away. —**drive out, 1,** (chase out; expel) выгоня́ть. **2,** (exit in a vehicle) выезжáть. —**drive up,** взви́нчивать (цéны). —**drive up to,** подъезжáть к.

drivel *v.i.* **1,** (drool) пускáть слю́ни. **2,** (talk foolishly) порóть чушь; нести́ вздор. —*n.* **1,** (saliva) слю́ни. **2,** (foolish talk) чушь; вздор. —**driveling,** *adj.* слюня́вый.

driver *n.* **1,** (of a car or truck) води́тель; шофёр. **2,** (of a carriage) ку́чер; извóзчик. **3,** (of cattle) погóнщик; гуртовщи́к. —**driver's licence,** води́тельские правá.

drive shaft приводнóй вал.

driveway *n.* подъéзд (к дóму).

driving *n.* вождéние; ездá. *Careless driving*, неосторóжная ездá. *Drunk driving*, вождéние в нетрéзвом состоя́нии. —*adj.* **1,** *mech.* веду́щий: *driving wheel*, веду́щее колесó. **2,** (heavy, as of rain) проливнóй.

drizzle *n.* и́зморось. —*v.i.* мороси́ть: *It is drizzling*, мороси́т.

droll *adj.* забáвный. —**drollery,** *n.* шу́тки; юмóр.

dromedary *n.* дромадéр.

drone *n.* **1,** (hum) гул. **2,** (bee; *also fig.* idler) тру́тень. —*v.i.* **1,** (hum) жужжáть. **2,** *fol. by* **on** (speak in a monotonous tone) бубни́ть; дудéть.

drool *v.i.* пускáть слю́ни.

droop *v.i.* свисáть; отвисáть; обвисáть; поникáть; ни́кнуть. *The flowers are beginning to droop*, цветы́ начинáют вя́нуть.

drop *n.* **1,** (liquid globule) кáпля: *drop of blood*, кáпля крóви. *Not touch a drop*, кáпли в рот не брать. **2,** *pl.* (liquid medicine) кáпли: *eye drops*, глазны́е кáпли. *Cough drops*, таблéтки от кáшля. **3,** *pl.* (small pieces of candy) дражé. **4,** (fall; decrease) падéние; сниже́ние; понижéние. —*v.t.* **1,** (accidentally let fall) роня́ть: *You dropped your comb*, вы урони́ли гребéнь. **2,** (deposit) опускáть: *drop a letter in the mailbox*, опускáть письмó в почтóвый я́щик. *Drop one's ballot in the box*, опускáть бюллетéнь в избирáтельную у́рну. **3,** (let fall from an airplane) сбрáсывать: *drop bombs*, сбрáсывать бóмбы. *Drop by parachute*, сбрáсывать на парашю́те. **4,** (let off, as from a vehicle) высáживать. **5,** (remove, as from a committee or list) исключáть; выводи́ть. **6,** (omit; delete) исключáть; опускáть. **7,** (give up; abandon) бро́сить; отказа́ться от. *Drop the subject*, оста́вить те́му. *Drop a demand*, отказа́ться от тре́бования. *Drop charges against*, снима́ть обвине́ния с (+ *gen.*). **8,** (send, as a note) присыла́ть; черкну́ть: *Drop me a line*, пришли́те мне ве́сточку; черкни́те мне не́сколько строк. **9,** (lower, as a price) снижа́ть. **10,** *colloq.* (utter casually) оброни́ть. *Drop a hint*, сде́лать намёк. **11,** *Drop anchor*, бро́сить я́корь. **12,** *Drop a stitch*, спусти́ть пе́тлю. —*v.i.* **1,** (fall) па́дать. *Drop out of one's hands*, вы́пасть из рук. *Be ready to drop*, вали́ться с ног от уста́лости. *You could have heard a pin drop*, слы́шно бы́ло, как му́ха пролети́т. **2,** (decline) па́дать; снижа́ться; пойти́ вниз. — **at the drop of a hat,** по мале́йшему по́воду. —**drop back,** отступа́ть. —**drop by/in/over,** заходи́ть. —**drop in the bucket,** ка́пля в мо́ре. —**drop off, 1,** (let off, as from a vehicle) выса́живать. **2,** (leave off while en route elsewhere) завози́ть: *drop off a package on the way*, завезти́ паке́т по доро́ге. **3,** (fall asleep) засыпа́ть. **4,** (decrease) па́дать; снижа́ться. —**drop out, 1,** (slip out) выпада́ть: *The tray dropped out of my hands*, подно́с вы́пал из мои́х рук. **2,** (withdraw) выходи́ть; выбыва́ть; отсе́иваться. *Drop out of school*, бро́сить шко́лу. *Drop out of a race* (*of a runner*), сходи́ть с диста́нции; (*of a political candidate*) вы́быть из борьбы́. **3,** *Drop out of sight*, исче́знуть и́з виду.

droplet *n.* ка́пелька.

dropout *n.* тот, кто бро́сил шко́лу. *Dropout rate*, проце́нт отсе́ва.

dropper *n.* ка́пельница; пипе́тка.

droppings *n.pl.* помёт.

dropsy *n.* водя́нка.

droshky *n.* дро́жки.

dross *n.* ока́лина.

drought *n.* за́суха.

drove *n.* ста́до; гурт. —**in droves,** то́лпами.

drover *n.* гуртовщи́к; пого́нщик.

drown *v.i.* тону́ть. *Drowning man*, утопа́ющий. —*v.t.* **1,** (cause to drown) топи́ть. *Drown oneself*, (у)топи́ться. *Drown one's sorrows in drink*, топи́ть го́ре в вине́. **2,** *fol. by* **out** (muffle, as sound) заглуша́ть; глуши́ть; подавля́ть; покрыва́ть.

drowning *n.* утопле́ние.

drowse *v.i.* дрема́ть.

drowsiness *n.* сонли́вость; дремо́та; забытьё.

drowsy *adj.* со́нный; сонли́вый; дремо́тный. *I feel drowsy*, меня́ кло́нит ко сну. *Wine makes me drowsy*, от вина́ меня́ кло́нит ко сну.

drub *v.t.* **1,** (beat) дуба́сить. **2,** (defeat) разбива́ть.

drubbing *n.* **1,** (beating) побо́и. **2,** (defeat) разгро́м.

drudgery *n.* кропотли́вая рабо́та.

drug *n.* **1,** (medication) (лека́рственный *or* лече́бный) препара́т. **2,** (narcotic) нарко́тик. **3,** *sports* до́пинг. —*v.t.* накача́ть нарко́тиками. —**drug addict,** наркома́н.

druggist *n.* апте́карь.

drugstore *n.* апте́ка.

drum *n.* бараба́н. —*v.i.* **1,** (beat a drum) бить в бараба́н. **2,** (tap) бараба́нить *or* постуки́вать

па́льцами (*e.g.* по́ столу). —*v.t.* [*usu.* **drum in** *or* **into**] вда́лбливать (в го́лову кому́-нибудь).

drumbeat *n.* бараба́нный бой; бараба́нная дробь.

drummer *n.* бараба́нщик.

drumstick *n.* **1,** (stick for beating a drum) бараба́нная па́лочка. **2,** (leg of a fowl) но́жка.

drunk *adj. & n.* пья́ный. *Get drunk*, напи́ться; опьяне́ть.

drunkard *n.* пья́ница.

drunken *adj.* пья́ный: *in a drunken state*, в пья́ном ви́де. *Drunken revelry*, пья́ный кутёж. —**drunkenness,** *n.* пья́нство.

dry *adj.* сухо́й: *dry bread/pavement/climate*, сухо́й хлеб/тротуа́р/кли́мат. *Dry land*, су́ша. *Dry wine*, сухо́е вино́. *Wipe something dry*, вы́тереть что-нибудь на́сухо. *The laundry is not dry yet*, бельё ещё не вы́сохло. —*v.t.* **1,** (wipe) вытира́ть: *dry one's hands/ the dishes/*, вытира́ть ру́ки/посу́ду. *Dry oneself*, вытира́ться. *Dry one's eyes*, осуша́ть глаза́. **2,** (rid of moisture) суши́ть: *dry one's hair/shoes*, суши́ть во́лосы/боти́нки. —*v.i.* со́хнуть; суши́ться. *Hang something up/out to dry*, ве́шать/выве́шивать/разве́шивать что-нибудь посуши́ть/суши́ться/ для просу́шки/. —**dry up; run dry, 1,** (become completely dry) высыха́ть; иссыха́ть; пересыха́ть; иссяка́ть. **2,** (be used up; become unproductive) иссяка́ть.

dry cleaning хими́ческая чи́стка; химчи́стка.

dry dock сухо́й док.

dryer *also*, **drier** *n.* суши́лка. *Hair dryer*, фен.

dry goods галантере́я.

dry ice сухо́й лёд.

dryly *also*, **drily** *adv.* су́хо.

dry measure ме́ра сыпу́чих тел.

dryness *n.* су́хость.

dry run репети́ция.

dual *adj.* **1,** (double) двойно́й; двоя́кий; дво́йственный. *Dual purpose*, двоя́кая цель. *Dual citizenship*, двойно́е гражда́нство. **2,** (joint) совме́стный: *dual ownership*, совме́стное владе́ние.

dualism *n.* дуали́зм. —**dualistic,** *adj.* дуалисти́ческий.

duality *n.* дво́йственность.

dub *v.t.* **1,** (knight) посвяща́ть (в ры́цари). **2,** (nickname) прозыва́ть; окрести́ть. **3,** *motion pictures* дубли́ровать.

dubious *adj.* **1,** (doubtful): *be dubious*, сомнева́ться. **2,** (of doubtful worth) сомни́тельный: *a dubious honor*, сомни́тельная честь.

ducal *adj.* ге́рцогский.

ducat *n.* **1,** (old coin) дука́т. **2,** *slang* (ticket) биле́т.

duchess *n.* герцоги́ня.

duchy *n.* ге́рцогство. *Grand duchy*, вели́кое кня́жество.

duck *n.* у́тка. —*adj.* [*also*, **duck's**] ути́ный: *duck feathers*, ути́ные пе́рья. —*v.t.* **1,** (immerse) окуна́ть. **2,** (dodge) уверну́ться от. —*v.i.* **1,** (so as to avoid a blow) нырну́ть. **2,** (in order to pass under something) нагну́ть го́лову. **3,** *fol. by* **out** (leave suddenly) улизну́ть. —**like water off a duck's back,** как с гу́ся вода́.

duckbill *n.* утконо́с.
duckling *n.* утёнок. —**ugly duckling,** га́дкий утёнок.
duckweed *n.* ря́ска.
duct *n.* прото́к; кана́л. *Bile duct,* жёлчный прото́к.
ductile *adj.* ко́вкий; тягу́чий.
ductless gland железа́ вну́тренней секре́ции.
due *adj.* **1,** (owed; payable) причита́ющийся: *the amount due you,* причита́ющаяся вам су́мма. *Five rubles are due you,* вам причита́ется *or* полага́ется пять рубле́й. *The bill is/falls due on May 1,* счёт подлежи́т упла́те пе́рвого ма́я. **2,** (proper) до́лжный: *with due regard for,* с до́лжным внима́нием к. *With all due respect to,* при всём (моём) уваже́нии к. *Give credit where it is due,* отда́ть до́лжное кому́ сле́дует. **3,** (expected) до́лжен: *He is due here at noon,* он до́лжен прийти́ в по́лдень. *When is the train due in?,* когда́ прибыва́ет *or* прихо́дит по́езд? *He is due for a promotion,* он до́лжен получи́ть повыше́ние. *He is due to become the next prime minister,* он наме́чен в но́вые премье́р-мини́стры. —*adv.* пря́мо на: *due north,* пря́мо на се́вер. —*n.* **1,** (that which one deserves) до́лжное: *give someone his due,* отда́ть до́лжное (+ *dat.*). **2,** *pl.* (fee) взно́сы: *membership dues,* чле́нские взно́сы. —**due to,** из-за; по. *Due to the illness of the director,* из-за боле́зни дире́ктора. *Due to circumstances beyond our control,* по не зави́сящим от нас обстоя́тельствам. *Death was due to asphyxiation,* смерть была́ вы́звана удуше́нием. —**in due course; in due time,** в своё вре́мя.
duel *n.* дуэ́ль; поеди́нок. —*v.i.* дра́ться на дуэ́ли. —**duelist,** *n.* дуэли́ст.
duet *n.* дуэ́т.
dugout *n.* земля́нка; *mil.* убе́жище; блинда́ж.
duke *n.* ге́рцог. *Grand duke,* вели́кий князь. —**dukedom,** *n.* ге́рцогство.
dulcet *adj.* сла́дкий; благозву́чный; мелоди́чный.
dulcimer *n.* цимба́лы.
dull *adj.* **1,** (blunt) тупо́й. **2,** (not bright; not shiny) ту́склый. **3,** (gloomy; cloudy) мра́чный; па́смурный. **4,** (boring) ску́чный. **5,** (mentally slow; obtuse) тупо́й. **6,** (not acute, as of pain) тупо́й. **7,** (not distinct, as of a sound) глухо́й; тупо́й. —*v.t.* **1,** (make less sharp) тупи́ть; притупля́ть. **2,** (cloud, as the senses) мути́ть; притупля́ть. —*v.i.* тупи́ться.
dullard *n.* тупи́ца.
dullness *n.* ту́пость.
duly *adv.* **1,** (properly) до́лжным о́бразом; надлежа́щим о́бразом. **2,** (at the proper time) своевре́менно.
dumb *adj.* **1,** (mute) немо́й. **2,** (of animals) бессло́весный. **3,** *colloq.* (stupid) глу́пый.
dumbbell *n.* **1,** (weight for exercise) ги́ря; ганте́ль. **2,** *slang* (dolt) болва́н; глупе́ц.
dumbfound *also,* **dumfound** *v.t.* ошара́шивать.
dummy *n.* **1,** (mannequin) манеке́н. **2,** *printing* маке́т. **3,** (substitute; fake) подставно́е лицо́. **4,** *cards* болва́н. **5,** *slang* (dolt) болва́н; тупи́ца. —*adj.* подставно́й.
dump *v.t.* **1,** (drop heavily) вали́ть; сва́ливать: *dump*

something on the ground, вали́ть/сва́ливать что́-нибудь на зе́млю. *Dump wastes into the river,* сбра́сывать отхо́ды в ре́ку. **2,** (throw out) выбра́сывать; выва́ливать. **3,** *comm.* выбра́сывать: *dump goods on the market,* выбра́сывать това́р на ры́нок. *Dump shares of stock,* сбра́сывать а́кции. **4,** (transfer, as something burdensome) сва́ливать: *dump the work on someone,* сва́ливать рабо́ту на кого́-нибудь. —*n.* **1,** (field for rubbish) сва́лка. **2,** *mil.* (storage place) склад: *ammunition dump,* склад боеприпа́сов. —**in the dumps,** в уны́нии.
dumpling *n.* клёцка; галу́шка.
dump truck самосва́л.
dunce *n.* глупе́ц; тупи́ца. —**dunce cap,** дура́цкий колпа́к.
dunderhead *n.* о́лух; остоло́п; растя́па.
dune *n.* дю́на; песча́ный холм; барха́н.
dung *n.* помёт; наво́з.
dungarees *n.pl.* рабо́чие брю́ки.
dung beetle наво́зный жук; наво́зник.
dungeon *n.* темни́ца.
dunghill *n.* наво́зная ку́ча.
dunk *v.t.* **1,** (immerse) погружа́ть; окуна́ть. **2,** (dip, as a doughnut) мака́ть.
duo *n.* па́ра; дуэ́т.
duodenal *adj.* двенадцатипе́рстный. —**duodenum,** *n.* двенадцатипе́рстная кишка́.
dupe *n.* проста́к. —*v.t.* надува́ть; наставля́ть нос (+ *dat.*).
duplex *adj.* двойно́й. —*n.* **1,** (house) двухкварти́рный дом. **2,** (apartment) двухэта́жная кварти́ра.
duplicate *n.* дублика́т; дубле́т; ко́пия. *In duplicate,* в двух экземпля́рах. —*adj.* дублика́тный. —*v.t.* дубли́ровать. —**duplication,** *n.* дубли́рование.
duplicator *n.* мно́жительная маши́на.
duplicitous *adj.* двули́чный. —**duplicity** *n.* двули́чие; двули́чность.
durability *n.* про́чность.
durable *adj.* про́чный. —**durable goods,** това́ры дли́тельного по́льзования.
duralumin *n.* дюралюми́ний; дюра́ль. —*adj.* дюралюми́ниевый; дюра́левый.
duration *n.* продолжи́тельность; дли́тельность. *For the duration of,* на вре́мя (+ *gen.*). *Of short duration,* непродолжи́тельный; недолгове́чный.
duress *n.* принужде́ние. *Under duress,* по принужде́нию.
during *prep.* во вре́мя (+ *gen.*); за (+ *acc.*); в тече́ние (+ *gen.*). *During the war/lesson,* во вре́мя войны́/уро́ка. *During that time,* за э́то вре́мя. *During the last year,* за после́дний год. *During the winter,* в тече́ние зимы́. *I'm home during the day,* днём я до́ма. *It rained during the night,* но́чью шёл дождь. *During the last two weeks,* в тече́ние после́дних двух неде́ль.
durum *n.* твёрдая пшени́ца. *Also,* **durum wheat.**
dusk *n.* су́мерки. *From dawn till dusk,* от зари́ до зари́.
dust *n.* **1,** (tiny bits, as of earth) пыль. **2,** (mortal remains) прах. —*v.t.* **1,** (wipe the dust from) стира́ть

пыль с. **2,** (sprinkle with a powdery substance) опы́ливать: *dust the crops,* опы́ливать посе́вы. —*v.i.* стира́ть пыль. —**bite the dust,** упа́сть. —**shake the dust from one's feet,** отрясти́ прах от свои́х ног.

dustbin *n., Brit.* му́сорный я́щик; му́сорный бак *or* бачо́к.

duster *n.* **1,** (cloth for dusting) пы́льная тря́пка. **2,** (protective smock) пы́льник.

dust jacket суперобло́жка.

dustman *n., Brit.* му́сорщик.

dustpan *n.* сово́к (для му́сора).

dust storm пы́льная бу́ря.

dusty *adj.* пы́льный. *Get dusty,* пыли́ться.

Dutch *adj.* голла́ндский. —*n.* **1,** (language) голла́ндский язы́к. **2,** *preceded by* **the** (people) голла́ндцы.

Dutchman *n.* голла́ндец. —**Dutchwoman,** *n.* голла́ндка.

duteous *adj.* послу́шный. *Also,* **dutiful.**

duty *n.* **1,** (obligation) долг; обя́занность. *Do one's duty,* выполня́ть свой долг. *Sense of duty,* чу́вство до́лга. *I consider it my duty to warn you,* счита́ю свои́м до́лгом (*or* свое́й обя́занностью) предупреди́ть вас. **2,** *pl.* (responsibilities in one's job) обя́занности: *official duties,* служе́бные обя́занности. *He was relieved of his duties,* он был освобождён от обя́занностей. **3,** (being on the job) дежу́рство. *Night duty,* ночно́е дежу́рство. *Be on duty,* дежу́рить; нести́ дежу́рство. *Go off duty,* сменя́ться с дежу́рства. **4,** (military service) слу́жба. *On active duty,* на действи́тельной слу́жбе. *Guard duty,* карау́льная слу́жба. **5,** (tariff) по́шлина; тамо́женный сбор. *Pay duty,* (у)плати́ть по́шлину. —*adj.* дежу́рный: *duty officer,* дежу́рный офице́р. —**in line of duty,** при исполне́нии служе́бных обя́занностей.

duty-free *adj.* беспо́шлинный. —*adv.* беспо́шлинно.

dwarf *n.* ка́рлик. —*v.t.* затмева́ть. —**dwarfish,** *adj.* ка́рликовый.

dwell *v.i.* **1,** (reside) жить. **2,** *fol. by* **on** (linger) остана́вливаться: *dwell on a subject,* остана́вливаться на вопро́се. —**dweller,** *n.* жи́тель; обита́тель.

dwelling *n.* жили́ще.

dwindle *v.i.* уменьша́ться; истоща́ться.

dye *n.* кра́ска; краси́тель. —*v.t.* кра́сить; окра́шивать.

dyed *adj.* кра́шеный. —**dyed-in-the-wool,** *adj.* твердоло́бый.

dyeing *n.* кра́шение. —**dyer,** *n.* краси́льщик.

dyestuff *n.* кра́сящее вещество́.

dye works краси́льня.

dying *n.* умира́ние. —*adj.* **1,** (about to die) умира́ющий. **2,** (uttered just before death) предсме́ртный. —**till one's dying day,** до са́мой сме́рти; до гро́ба; по гроб жи́зни.

dyke *n.* = **dike.**

dynamic *adj.* динами́ческий. —**dynamics,** *n.* дина́мика. —**dynamism,** *n.* динами́зм.

dynamite *n.* динами́т. —*adj.* динами́тный. —*v.t.* взрыва́ть динами́том.

dynamo *n.* дина́мо.

dynamometer *n.* динамо́метр; силоме́р.

dynasty *n.* дина́стия. —**dynastic,** *adj.* династи́ческий.

dyne *n., physics* ди́на.

dysentery *n.* дизентери́я.

dyspepsia *n.* диспепси́я.

dysprosium *n.* диспро́зий.

dystrophy *n.* дистрофи́я.

E

E, e пя́тая бу́ква англи́йского алфави́та. —*n.* (musical note) ми.

each *adj. & pron.* ка́ждый: *each participant,* ка́ждый уча́стник. *Each of them,* ка́ждый из них. *To each his own,* ка́ждому своё. —*adv.* (apiece) шту́ка: *ten cents each,* де́сять це́нтов шту́ка. *They received five rubles each,* ка́ждый получи́л по пять рубле́й. —**each other,** друг дру́га: *love each other,* люби́ть друг дру́га. *Write to each other,* писа́ть друг дру́гу. *They resemble each other,* они́ похо́жи друг на дру́га. *Respect each other's opinion,* уважа́ть мне́ние друг

дру́га. *Shake each other's hand,* пожа́ть друг дру́гу ру́ку. ♦*Also with the refl. verb: see each other,* ви́деться; *scratch each other,* цара́паться.

eager *adj.* **1,** (ardent) усе́рдный: *eager pupil,* усе́рдный учени́к. *Eager fans,* стра́стные боле́льщики. **2,** *fol. by inf.* (anxious): *I am eager to see him,* мне о́чень хо́чется уви́деть его́. *I am eager to begin,* мне не те́рпится нача́ть.

eagerly *adv.* жа́дно; с жа́дностью; с нетерпе́нием.

eagerness *n.* пыл; рве́ние; задо́р.

eagle *n.* орёл. *Bald eagle,* орла́н. *Golden eagle,*

бе́ркут. —*adj.* орли́ный: *eagle eye,* орли́ный взгляд. —**eagle owl,** фи́лин.

eaglet *n.* орлёнок.

ear *n.* **1,** (organ of hearing) у́хо. *Whisper in someone's ear,* шепта́ть *or* говори́ть на́ ухо (+ *dat.*). **2,** (sense of hearing) слух: *ear for music,* музыка́льный слух. *Play by ear,* игра́ть по слу́ху. **3,** (of corn) поча́ток; (of wheat, oats, etc.) ко́лос. —*adj.* ушно́й: *ear drops,* ушны́е ка́пли. —**be all ears,** во все у́ши слу́шать; превраща́ться в слух; быть весь (вся) внима́ние. —**in one ear and out the other,** в одно́ у́хо вошло́, в друго́е вы́шло. —**up to one's ears,** по́ уши (в рабо́те, в долга́х, *etc.*).

earache *n.* боль в у́хе; ушна́я боль.

eardrum *n.* бараба́нная перепо́нка.

earflap *n.* нау́шник.

earl *n.* граф.

early *adj.* ра́нний: *in early autumn,* ра́нней о́сенью. *It is still early,* ещё ра́но. *Since early childhood,* с ра́ннего де́тства. *The plane/train was early,* самолёт приземли́лся/ по́езд при́был/ ра́ньше вре́мени *or* ра́ньше сро́ка. *He is an early riser,* он ра́но встаёт. *In early spring,* ра́нней весно́й. *In the early 1960s,* в нача́ле шестидеся́тых годо́в. *He is in his early forties,* ему́ лет со́рок с небольши́м. *Early elections,* досро́чные вы́боры. *Early release from prison,* досро́чное освобожде́ние из тюрьмы́. —*adv.* ра́но: *go to bed early,* ложи́ться ра́но. *A day earlier,* днём ра́ньше. *As early as March,* ещё *or* уже́ в ма́рте. *At the earliest,* са́мое ра́нее. *Arrive early for the meeting,* прийти́ до нача́ла собра́ния. —**early bird,** ра́нняя пта́шка. —**early warning system,** систе́ма да́льнего обнаруже́ния; систе́ма ра́ннего предупрежде́ния *or* оповеще́ния.

earmark *v.t.* предназнача́ть; выделя́ть.

earmuff *n.* нау́шник.

earn *v.t.* **1,** (receive in payment for labor) зараба́тывать. *Earn a living,* зараба́тывать на жизнь. *Earned income,* трудовы́е дохо́ды. **2,** (bring in; produce) приноси́ть: *earn interest,* приноси́ть проце́нты. **3,** (gain; deserve) заслужи́ть: *earn the right,* заслужи́ть пра́во.

earnest *adj.* **1,** (intent in purpose) серьёзный; добросо́вестный; испра́вный. **2,** (marked by deep feeling) и́скренний. —**in earnest, 1,** (not joking) всерьёз. *Are you in earnest?,* вы э́то всерьёз?; вы э́то серьёзно? **2,** (with determination) вплотну́ю.

earnings *n.pl.* **1,** (wages) за́работок. **2,** (profit) вы́ручка; поступле́ния. *Export earnings,* э́кспортные поступле́ния.

earphone *n.* нау́шник.

earring *n.* серьга́.

earshot *n.* преде́л слы́шимости: *within earshot,* в преде́лах слы́шимости.

earth *n.* **1,** *often cap.* (the planet) Земля́: *revolve around the earth,* враща́ться вокру́г Земли́. *The earth's axis/crust,* земна́я ось/кора́. **2,** (the ground; this world) земля́: *fall to earth,* упа́сть на зе́млю. *Peace on earth,* мир на земле́. —**on earth,** *rendered variously in Russian: Why on earth did he say that?,*

почему́ же он э́то сказа́л? *Why on earth should I do that?,* с како́й ста́ти мне де́лать э́то? *How on earth did you find out?,* как вы смогли́ узна́ть э́то?

earthen *adj.* **1,** (made of earth) земляно́й. **2,** (made of baked clay) гли́няный.

earthenware *n.* гли́няная посу́да; гонча́рные изде́лия. —*adj.* гли́няный.

earthly *adj.* **1,** (worldly) земно́й: *earthly cares,* земны́е забо́ты. **2,** (possible; conceivable): *of no earthly use,* соверше́нно бесполе́зный. *For no earthly reason,* без вся́кой причи́ны.

earthquake *n.* землетрясе́ние. *Earthquake-proof,* сейсмосто́йкий.

earthwork *n.* **1,** *usu. pl.* (embankment; fortification) земляно́е укрепле́ние. **2,** (excavation) земляны́е рабо́ты.

earthworm *n.* земляно́й червь.

earthy *adj.* **1,** (of or like earth) земли́стый. **2,** (coarse) risqué) солёный.

ear trumpet слухова́я тру́бка; слухово́й рожо́к.

earwax *n.* ушна́я се́ра.

ease *n.* **1,** (freedom from pain, worry, or trouble) поко́й. *A life of ease,* споко́йная жизнь; приво́льная жизнь. **2,** (facility) лёгкость: *with ease,* с лёгкостью. *The ease with which he scaled the wall,* лёгкость, с кото́рой он взобра́лся на сте́ну. —*v.t.* (facilitate; alleviate) облегча́ть. *Ease the pain,* облегча́ть *or* смягча́ть боль. *Ease tension,* разряжа́ть напряжённость. **2,** (move slowly and carefully) (осторо́жно) подвига́ть. **3,** *fol. by* **out** (oust gently) вытесня́ть. —*v.i.* смягча́ться; успока́иваться. —**at ease, 1,** (relaxed) споко́йный. *Set someone's mind at ease,* успока́ивать кого́-нибудь. *My mind is at ease,* у меня́ на душе́ споко́йно. *I felt ill at ease,* я чу́вствовал себя́ нело́вко; мне ста́ло не по себе́. **2,** *mil.* во́льно. *At ease!,* во́льно!

easel *n.* мольбе́рт.

easily *adv.* **1,** (with ease) легко́; без труда́. *Easily defeat one's opponent,* легко́ победи́ть проти́вника. **2,** (without much cause) бы́стро: *tire easily,* бы́стро устава́ть. **3,** (without question; by far) несомне́нно; беспо́рно. *Easily the best,* беспо́рно са́мый лу́чший. **4,** (very possibly) вполне́ вероя́тно: *You may easily be right,* вполне́ вероя́тно, что вы пра́вы.

east *n.* восто́к. *The East,* Восто́к. —*adj.* восто́чный: *east wind,* восто́чный ве́тер. —*adv.* на восто́к; к восто́ку. *East of,* к восто́ку от; восто́чнее (+ *gen.*).

Easter *n.* па́сха. —*adj.* пасха́льный.

easterly *adj.* восто́чный.

eastern *adj.* восто́чный. —**easternmost,** *adj.* са́мый восто́чный.

eastward *adv.* к восто́ку; в восто́чном направле́нии. —*adj.* восто́чный.

easy *adj.* лёгкий: *easy lesson/test/way,* лёгкий уро́к/ экза́мен/спо́соб. —**be on easy street,** жить в доста́тке *or* в дово́льстве. —**come easy to,** дава́ться легко́ (+ *dat.*). —**easier said than done,** ле́гче сказа́ть, чем сде́лать. —**easy come, easy go,** как на́жито, так и про́жито. —**take it easy, 1,** (remain calm) не волнова́ться. **2,** (not hurry) не торопи́ться. **3,** (relax; rest) отдыха́ть.

easy chair кре́сло.

easygoing *adj.* **1,** (good-natured) ужи́вчивый. **2,** (leisurely) неторопли́вый.

eat *v.t. & i.* есть; ку́шать. *Have you already eaten?,* вы уже́ пое́ли? *I do not eat meat,* я не ем мя́са. —**eat away,** разъеда́ть; изъеда́ть. —**eat into,** въеда́ться в; изъеда́ть. —**eat one's heart out,** изводи́ться. —**eat one's words,** брать наза́д свои́ слова́. —**eat out,** обе́дать в рестора́не. —**eat up,** съесть; пожира́ть. —**what's eating you?,** что вас гло́жет?

eatable *adj.* съедо́бный.

eater *n.* едо́к: *poor eater,* плохо́й едо́к.

eau de Cologne одеколо́н.

eaves *n.* стреха́.

eavesdrop *v.i.* подслу́шивать.

ebb *n.* отли́в. *Ebb and flow,* прили́в и отли́в. —*v.i.* убыва́ть; угаса́ть. —**ebb tide,** отли́в.

ebonite *n.* эбони́т.

ebony *n.* чёрное де́рево; эбе́новое де́рево. —*adj.* эбе́новый.

ebullient *adj.* кипу́чий. —**ebullience,** *n.* кипу́честь.

eccentric *adj.* **1,** (odd) эксцентри́чный. **2,** *math.* эксцентри́ческий. —*n.* чуда́к; оригина́л.

eccentricity *n.* **1,** (eccentric nature) эксцентри́чность. **2,** (peculiarity; quirk) стра́нность.

ecclesiastic *adj.* церко́вный; духо́вный. *Also,* **ecclesiastical.**

echelon *n.* **1,** (step-like formation) эшело́н; ступе́нчатое расположе́ние. **2,** (section of a military force) эшело́н: *rear echelon,* второ́й *or* тылово́й эшело́н. **3,** (level of authority) инста́нция; звено́.

echidna *n.* ехи́дна.

echo *n.* э́хо; о́тзвук; отголо́сок. —*v.i.* откли́ка́ться *or* отдава́ться э́хом. —*v.t.* вто́рить.

éclair *n.* экле́р.

eclectic *adj.* эклекти́ческий; эклекти́чный. —*n.* эклекти́к. —**eclecticism,** *n.* эклекти́зм.

eclipse *n.* затме́ние. —*v.t.* затмева́ть.

ecliptic *n.* экли́птика.

ecology *n.* эколо́гия. —**ecological,** *adj.* экологи́ческий.

economic *adj.* экономи́ческий; хозя́йственный.

economical *adj.* **1,** (thrifty) эконо́мный. **2,** (efficient; avoiding waste) экономи́чный.

economics *n.* эконо́мика.

economist *n.* экономи́ст.

economize *v.i.* эконо́мить; соблюда́ть эконо́мию.

economy *n.* **1,** (economic system or condition) эконо́мика; хозя́йство. **2,** (thrift) эконо́мия; эконо́мность; бережли́вость.

ecstasy *n.* восто́рг; экста́з.

ecstatic *adj.* восто́рженный; экстати́ческий. *She was ecstatic,* она́ была́ в восто́рге.

ectoplasm *n.* эктопла́зма.

ecumenical *adj.* вселе́нский. —**ecumenical council,** вселе́нский собо́р.

eczema *n.* экзе́ма.

eddy *n.* водоворо́т.

edelweiss *n.* эдельве́йс.

edema *also,* **oedema** *n., med.* отёк.

Eden *n.* Эде́м.

edge *n.* **1,** (border; brink) край: *edge of a table/cliff/city,* край стола́/обры́ва/го́рода. *Edge of a forest,* опу́шка. *At the water's edge,* на са́мом берегу́; у са́мой воды́. **2,** (cutting part of a blade) остриё. **3,** *colloq.* (advantage) преиму́щество; переве́с. —*v.t.* **1,** (trim) окаймля́ть. **2,** *Edge one's way,* пробира́ться; проти́скиваться. —*v.i.* подвига́ться: *edge forward,* подвига́ться вперёд. —**on edge,** в не́рвном состоя́нии. —**take the edge off,** притупля́ть.

edgewise *adv.* бо́ком; бочко́м. —**get a word in edgewise,** вверну́ть слове́чко.

edging *n.* кайма́; кант; бордю́р; обши́вка; оторо́чка; вы́пушка.

edgy *adj.* не́рвный; раздражи́тельный.

edible *adj.* съедо́бный. —**edibles,** *n.pl.* съестно́е.

edict *n.* ука́з.

edification *n.* назида́ние: *for the edification of,* в назида́ние (+ *dat.*).

edifice *n.* зда́ние; сооруже́ние.

edify *v.t.* поуча́ть; наставля́ть. —**edifying,** *adj.* поучи́тельный; назида́тельный.

edit *v.t.* редакти́ровать. *Edit a film,* монти́ровать фильм. —**edit out,** вычёркивать.

edition *n.* **1,** (of a book) изда́ние. **2,** (of a newspaper) вы́пуск : *the morning edition,* у́тренний вы́пуск.

editor *n.* реда́ктор. *Editor's note,* «от реда́кции». *Letter to the editor,* письмо́ в реда́кцию. —**editor in chief,** гла́вный реда́ктор.

editorial *adj.* редакцио́нный; реда́кторский. *Editorial board,* редакцио́нная колле́гия. —*n.* редакцио́нная статья́.

educate *v.t.* воспи́тывать. —**educated,** *adj.* образо́ванный.

education *n.* образова́ние; воспита́ние; просвеще́ние. *Higher education,* вы́сшее образова́ние. *Sex education,* полово́е воспита́ние. *Minister of education,* мини́стр просвеще́ния.

educational *adj.* **1,** (pert. to education) образова́тельный; воспита́тельный. **2,** (providing instruction) уче́бный: *educational film,* уче́бный фильм; *educational institution,* уче́бное заведе́ние. **3,** (instructive) поучи́тельный.

educator *n.* воспита́тель; педаго́г.

eel *n.* у́горь.

eerie *adj.* таи́нственный; при́зрачный; жу́ткий.

efface *v.t.* **1,** (erase) стира́ть. **2,** (blot out; obliterate) изгла́живать.

effect *n.* **1,** (result) сле́дствие: *the effect of an illness,* сле́дствие боле́зни. *Cause and effect,* причи́на и сле́дствие. **2,** (influence) влия́ние; де́йствие; возде́йствие; эффе́кт. *Have an effect (on),* ока́зывать влия́ние/(воз)де́йствие (на); (по)де́йствовать (на); отража́ться на; ска́зываться на; возыме́ть де́йствие; дать *or* произвести́ эффе́кт. *Have its effect,* сде́лать своё де́ло. *Have a harmful/depressing/sobering effect on,* вре́дно/угнета́юще/отрезвля́юще де́йствовать на. *Have little effect on,* ма́ло поде́йствовать на. *The medicine has taken effect,* лека́рство поде́йствовало. **3,** (force) си́ла; де́йствие: *go into ef-*

fect, вступи́ть в си́лу/де́йствие. *Put a law into effect,* вводи́ть зако́н в де́йствие. **4,** (impression purposely produced) эффе́кт: *done for effect,* рассчи́танный на эффе́кт. *Sound effects,* шумовы́е эффе́кты. **5,** (meaning) смысл. *To the effect that,* о том, что... *Something to that effect,* что́-то в э́том ду́хе. *Statements to this effect,* заявле́ния на э́тот счёт. **6,** (specific scientific phenomenon) эффе́кт: *Doppler effect,* эффе́кт До́плера. **7,** *pl.* (belongings) иму́щество; пожи́тки. *Personal effects,* ли́чные ве́щи. —*v.t.* производи́ть; соверша́ть; осуществля́ть. —**in effect, 1,** (in force) в си́ле. *A curfew is in effect,* де́йствует коменда́нтский час. **2,** (in essence) факти́чески; по существу́.

effective *adj.* **1,** (producing the desired result) де́йственный; эффекти́вный. **2,** (in force) де́йству-ющий; в си́ле. *Become effective,* вступа́ть в си́лу.

effectively *adv.* **1,** (in an effective manner) эффекти́вно. **2,** (in effect) факти́чески.

effectiveness *n.* де́йственность; эффекти́вность.

effectual *adj.* эффекти́вный; де́йственный.

effectuate *v.t.* соверша́ть; осуществля́ть.

effeminate *adj.* женоподо́бный.

effervesce *v.i.* **1,** (give off bubbles of gas) шипе́ть. **2,** *fig.* (show exhilaration) кипе́ть.

effervescence *n.* **1,** (bubbling state) шипу́честь. **2,** (vivacity) кипу́честь.

effervescent *adj.* **1,** (sparkling) игри́стый; шипу́чий. **2,** (exuberant) кипу́чий.

effete *adj.* **1,** (exhausted) истощённый. **2,** (barren) беспло́дный.

efficacious *adj.* де́йственный; эффекти́вный. —**efficacy,** *n.* де́йственность; эффекти́вность.

efficiency *n.* эффекти́вность.

efficient *adj.* **1,** (systematic; not wasteful) эффекти́в-ный. **2,** (competent; thorough) де́льный; аккура́т-ный; расторо́пный; исполни́тельный. —**efficiently,** *adv.* эффекти́вно; аккура́тно.

effigy *n.* чу́чело. —**burn/hang in effigy,** сжечь/ пове́сить чу́чело (кого́-нибудь).

effort *n.* уси́лие: *without effort,* без уси́лия; без уси́лий. *Make an effort to,* де́лать уси́лия для. *Make every effort,* прилага́ть все уси́лия. *Efforts to revive him were unsuccessful,* попы́тки оживи́ть его́ оказа́лись безуспе́шными.

effortless *adj.* сде́ланный без уси́лий; гла́дкий. —**effortlessly,** *adv.* без уси́лий; игра́ючи.

effrontery *n.* на́глость; наха́льство.

effulgent *adj.* лучеза́рный.

effusion *n.* излия́ние.

effusive *adj.* экспанси́вный. *Be effusive in one's praise (of),* рассыпа́ться в похвала́х (+ *dat.*).

egalitarian *adj.* эгалита́рный.

egg *n.* яйцо́. —*adj.* яи́чный: *egg yoke,* яи́чный желто́к. —*v.t.* [*usu.* **egg on**] подстрека́ть; подбива́ть; нау́ськивать. —**put all one's eggs in one basket,** поста́вить всё на одну́ ка́рту.

egghead *n., slang* интеллиге́нт.

eggplant *n.* баклажа́н.

eggshell *n.* яи́чная скорлупа́.

egg white бело́к.

ego *n.* **1,** (the self) ли́чность. **2,** (conceit) самомне́ние. **3,** (self-esteem) самолю́бие.

egocentric *adj.* эгоцентри́ческий.

egoism *n.* эгои́зм; себялю́бие. —**egoist,** *n.* эго́ист. —**egoistic,** *adj.* эгоисти́ческий.

egotism *n.* эготи́зм. —**egotist,** *n.* эготи́ст. —**egotisti-cal,** *adj.* эгоисти́ческий; эгоисти́чный.

egregious *adj.* вопию́щий.

egress *n.* вы́ход.

egret *n.* бе́лая ца́пля.

Egyptian *adj.* еги́петский. —*n.* египтя́нин. —**Egyptian vulture,** стервя́тник.

Egyptology *n.* египтоло́гия. —**Egyptologist,** *n.* египто́лог.

eider *n.* га́га. —*adj.* гага́чий. —**eiderdown,** *n.* гага́чий пух.

eight *adj.* во́семь. —*n.* **1,** (cardinal number) во́семь. **2,** *cards* восьмёрка. —**figure (of) eight,** восьмёрка.

eighteen *n. & adj.* восемна́дцать. —**eighteenth,** *adj.* восемна́дцатый.

eighth *adj.* восьмо́й. —*n.* восьма́я; восьма́я часть. *One-eighth,* одна́ восьма́я; восьма́я часть. *One-eighth of the earth's surface,* восьма́я часть пове́рхности Земли́. *Three-eighths,* три восьмы́х.

eight hundred восемьсо́т. —**eight-hundredth,** *adj.* восьмисо́тый.

eighty *n. & adj.* во́семьдесят. —**eightieth,** *adj.* восьмидеся́тый.

einsteinium *n.* эйнште́йний.

either *adj.* **1,** (one or the other of two) любо́й: *in either case,* в любо́м слу́чае. **2,** (each of two; one and the other) о́ба: *on either side of the street,* по обе́им сторона́м у́лицы. —*pron.* **1,** (either one) любо́й; и тот и друго́й. *Were either of you there?,* кто́-то из вас был там? **2,** *in neg. sentences* (neither one) ни тот ни друго́й: *I don't like either of them/ either one/,* мне не нра́вится ни тот ни друго́й. —*adv.* то́же: *I don't know either,* я то́же не зна́ю. —**either ... or,** и́ли ... и́ли. —**either way, 1,** (by either of two possible methods) и так и так. **2,** (in either case) в любо́м слу́чае.

ejaculate *v.t.* изверга́ть. —**ejaculation,** *n.* семяизлия́ние.

eject *v.t.* **1,** (emit; discharge) выбра́сывать; изверга́ть. **2,** (expel; evict) исключа́ть; выгоня́ть. —*v.i., aero.* катапульти́роваться.

ejection *n.* **1,** (discharging) выбра́сывание. **2,** (expulsion) исключе́ние. —**ejection seat,** катапу́льта; катапульти́руемое кре́сло.

eke *v.t.* [*usu.* **eke out**] *Eke out a living,* перебива́ться ко́е-ка́к. *Eke out a narrow victory,* с трудо́м вы́рвать побе́ду.

elaborate *adj.* **1,** (worked out carefully and thoroughly) тща́тельно разрабо́танный. **2,** (intricate; ornate) замыслова́тый; зате́йливый. **3,** (lavish; plush) пы́шный; роско́шный. —*v.t.* разраба́тывать. —*v.i.* вда-ва́ться в подро́бности. *Elaborate on a subject,* развива́ть те́му.

elaboration *n.* уточне́ние: *require no further elaboration,* не тре́бовать уточне́ния.

eland *n.* оленебы́к.

elapse *v.i.* **1,** (pass) проходи́ть; протека́ть. **2,** (expire) истека́ть.

elastic *adj.* **1,** (resilient) упру́гий; эласти́чный. **2,** (flexible; adaptable) ги́бкий. —*n.* рези́нка; ла́стик.

elasticity *n.* **1,** (resiliency) упру́гость; эласти́чность. **2,** (flexibility) ги́бкость.

elated *adj.* обра́дованный. —**elation,** *n.* восто́рг; ликова́ние.

elbow *n.* ло́коть. —*v.t.* толка́ть ло́ктем. *Elbow one's way,* прота́лкиваться. —**at one's elbow,** под руко́й. —**rub elbows with,** якша́ться с.

elbowroom *n.* просто́р.

elder *adj.* ста́рший. —*n.* **1,** (older person) ста́рший. **2,** (person of authority) старе́йшина. **3,** (shrub) бузина́.

elderberry *n.* я́года бузины́.

elderly *adj.* пожило́й.

eldest *adj.* ста́рший.

elect *v.t.* **1,** (vote into office) избира́ть; выбира́ть. *Elected representative,* вы́борный *or* и́збранный представи́тель. **2,** *fol. by inf.* (choose; decide) реши́ть.

election *n.* **1,** (act of choosing) избра́ние. **2,** *often pl.* (popular vote) вы́боры: *elections to/for Congress,* вы́боры в Конгре́сс. *Be defeated in the elections,* потерпе́ть пораже́ние на вы́борах. —*adj.* избира́тельный; предвы́борный: *election campaign,* избира́тельная/предвы́борная кампа́ния.

elective *adj.* **1,** (chosen by election) вы́борный: *elective office,* вы́борная до́лжность. **2,** (optional) факультати́вный.

elector *n.* вы́борщик. —**electoral,** *adj.* избира́тельный. —**electorate,** *n.* избира́тели.

electric *adj.* электри́ческий. *Electric power,* электроэне́ргия. *Electric shock,* уда́р электри́ческим то́ком. *Electric train,* электропо́езд. *Electric sign,* светова́я рекла́ма.

electrical *adj.* электри́ческий. —**electrical engineer,** инжене́р-эле́ктрик; электроте́хник. —**electrical engineering,** электроте́хника.

electric chair электри́ческий стул.

electric eye фотоэлеме́нт.

electrician *n.* (электро)монтёр; эле́ктрик.

electricity *n.* электри́чество.

electrification *n.* электрифика́ция.

electrify *v.t.* **1,** (charge with electricity) электризова́ть. **2,** (provide with electric power) электрифици́ровать. **3,** *fig.* (charge with excitement) электризова́ть.

electrocardiogram *n.* электрокардиогра́мма.

electrocardiograph *n.* электрокардио́граф.

electrocute *v.t.* **1,** (kill accidentally by electricity) убива́ть электри́ческим то́ком. **2,** (execute) казни́ть на электри́ческом сту́ле.

electrocution *n.* казнь на электри́ческом сту́ле.

electrode *n.* электро́д.

electrolysis *n.* электро́лиз.

electrolyte *n.* электроли́т.

electromagnet *n.* электромагни́т. —**electromagnetic,** *adj.* электромагни́тный. —**electromagnetism,** *n.* электромагнети́зм.

electron *n.* электро́н. —*adj.* электро́нный: *electron microscope,* электро́нный микроско́п.

electronic *adj.* электро́нный. —**electronically,** *adv.* с по́мощью электро́нной аппарату́ры.

electronics *n.* электро́ника.

electrostatics *n.* электроста́тика. —**electrostatic,** *adj.* электростати́ческий.

elegance *n.* элега́нтность; изя́щество.

elegant *adj.* элега́нтный; изя́щный. —**elegantly,** *adv.* элега́нтно; изя́щно.

elegiac *adj.* элеги́ческий. —**elegiacs,** *n.pl.* элеги́ческие стихи́.

elegy *n.* эле́гия.

element *n.* **1,** (in most meanings) элеме́нт: *chemical element,* хими́ческий элеме́нт. *Consist of a number of elements,* состоя́ть из ря́да элеме́нтов. *The criminal element,* престу́пный элеме́нт. *The element of surprise,* внеза́пность. **2,** (customary environment) стихи́я: *be in one's element,* быть в свое́й стихи́и. **3,** (trace) до́ля: *element of truth,* до́ля и́стины. *Element of doubt,* тень сомне́ния. **4,** (fundamentals) осно́вы; элеме́нты. **5,** *pl.* (weather conditions) стихи́я; стихи́и: *battle/withstand the elements,* боро́ться с стихи́ей; противостоя́ть стихи́ям.

elemental *adj.* стихи́йный: *elemental force,* стихи́йная си́ла.

elementary *adj.* **1,** (fundamental) элемента́рный. **2,** (pert. to the first years of schooling) нача́льный: *elementary school,* нача́льная шко́ла.

elephant *n.* слон.

elephantiasis *n.* слоно́вая боле́знь; слоно́вость.

elephant seal морско́й слон.

elevate *v.t.* **1,** (raise) поднима́ть; повыша́ть; возвыша́ть. **2,** (promote) возводи́ть: *elevate to the rank of...,* возводи́ть в ранг (+ *gen.*).

elevated *adj.* **1,** (raised, as of a railway) надзе́мный. **2,** *fig.* (lofty) возвы́шенный; припо́днятый.

elevation *n.* **1,** (act of elevating) подня́тие. **2,** (height; altitude) высота́. **3,** (raised area) возвы́шенность.

elevator *n.* лифт. *Grain elevator,* элева́тор. —**elevator operator,** лифтёр; лифтёрша.

eleven *n.* & *adj.* оди́ннадцать. —**eleventh,** *adj.* оди́ннадцатый.

elf *n.* эльф.

elicit *v.t.* **1,** (draw out; obtain) выявля́ть: *elicit the facts,* выявля́ть фа́кты. *Elicit information,* выве́дывать информа́цию. **2,** (evoke) вызыва́ть: *elicit applause,* вызыва́ть аплодисме́нты. *Elicit no reply,* не принести́ отве́та.

eligibility *n.* пра́во: *eligibility for a position,* пра́во на заня́тие до́лжности.

eligible *adj.* **1,** (qualified) име́ющий пра́во. *Be eligible to vote,* име́ть пра́во го́лоса; облада́ть пра́вом го́лоса. **2,** (desirable for marriage) вы́годный: *eligible bachelor,* вы́годный жени́х.

eliminate *v.t.* **1,** (get rid of) устраня́ть; ликви́дировать. **2,** (rule out, as a possibility) исключа́ть. **3,** *sports* выводи́ть. *Be eliminated,* выбыва́ть. **4,** *physiol.* (excrete) выделя́ть.

elimination *n.* **1,** (getting rid of) устране́ние;

ликвида́ция. **2,** *physiol.* (secretion) выделе́ние. **—process of elimination,** ме́тод исключе́ния.

elite *n.* эли́та. *Social elite,* сли́вки *or* цвет о́бщества.

elixir *n.* эликси́р.

elk *n.* лось.

ellipse *n.* э́ллипс.

ellipsis *n.* э́ллипсис; э́ллипс.

ellipsoid *n.* эллипсо́ид.

elliptical *adj.* эллипти́ческий.

elm *n.* вяз; ильм.

elocution *n.* ора́торское иску́сство.

elongate *v.t.* удлиня́ть. **—elongated,** *adj.* удлинён-ный; продолгова́тый.

elope *v.i.* бежа́ть (с возлю́бленным).

eloquence *n.* красноре́чие. **—eloquent,** *adj.* красноречи́вый.

else *adj.* **1,** (different) друго́й: *something else,* что́-то друго́е; *someone else,* кто́-то друго́й; *no one else,* никто́ друго́й. *Everything else,* всё остально́е. *Everyone else,* все други́е; все остальны́е. *I have something else in mind,* у меня́ друго́е на уме́. *Is there anyone else I can talk to?,* могу́ ли я поговори́ть с ке́м-то (*or* с ке́м-нибудь) други́м? *There was nothing else I could do,* ничего́ друго́го мне не остава́лось де́лать. **2,** (additional) ещё: *What else do you need?,* что ещё вам ну́жно? *Would you like to speak to someone else (i.e. in addition)?,* хоти́те поговори́ть с ке́м-то (*or* с ке́м-нибудь) ещё? ♦*With negatives,* бо́льше: *nothing else,* бо́льше ничего́. *Nothing else happened,* ничего́ бо́льше не случи́лось. *We have nothing else to offer them,* нам не́чего бо́льше им предложи́ть. *No one else knows about it,* никто́ бо́льше не зна́ет об э́том. *There was no one else there,* никого́ бо́льше не́ было там. *There was no place else to go,* идти́ бо́льше бы́ло не́куда. **—adv.** ещё: *Where else did you go?,* куда́ ещё вы е́здили? *Let's go somewhere else,* пойдём ещё куда́-нибудь. ♦*With negatives,* бо́льше: *nowhere else in the world,* бо́льше нигде́ в ми́ре. **—or else...,** а то; а не то; ина́че. **—someone else's,** чужо́й.

elsewhere *adv.* (где́-нибудь) в друго́м ме́сте; (куда́-нибудь) в друго́е ме́сто.

elucidate *v.t.* разъясня́ть; поясня́ть; освеща́ть. **—elucidation,** *n.* разъясне́ние; освеще́ние.

elude *v.t.* избега́ть; увёртываться от; ускольза́ть от.

elusive *adj.* неулови́мый. **—elusiveness,** *n.* неулови́мость.

emaciate *v.t.* истоща́ть. **—emaciated,** *adj.* истощён-ный; измождённый; исхуда́лый; то́щий.

emanate *v.i.* **1,** (of heat, light, etc.) излуча́ться. **2,** (originate) исходи́ть; истека́ть.

emanation *n.* эмана́ция.

emancipate *v.t.* освобожда́ть; эмансипи́ровать; раскрепоща́ть. **—emancipation,** *n.* освобожде́ние; эмансипа́ция; раскрепоще́ние. **—emancipator,** *n.* освободи́тель; эмансипа́тор.

emasculate *v.t.* выхола́щивать (*lit. & fig.*).

embalm *v.t.* бальзами́ровать. **—embalmer,** *n.* бальза-ми́ровщик.

embankment *n.* **1,** (along a river) на́бережная. **2,** (to

support a roadway) на́сыпь. *Plunge over an embank-ment,* свали́ться под отко́с.

embargo *n.* эмба́рго: *arms embargo,* эмба́рго на ору́жие.

embark *v.i.* **1,** (go aboard a vessel) сади́ться на парохо́д. **2,** *fol. by* **on** *or* **upon** (start out on) пуска́ться в: *embark on a voyage,* пуска́ться в пла́вание.

embarkation *n.* поса́дка (на парохо́д).

embarrass *v.t.* конфу́зить; ста́вить в нело́вкое положе́ние. **—embarrassed,** *adj.* смущённый. *Be embarrassed,* смуща́ться. **—embarrassing,** *adj.* нело́вкий; конфу́зный. **—embarrassment,** *n.* смуще́ние; конфу́з.

embassy *n.* посо́льство.

embed *v.t.* **1,** (implant firmly) вде́лывать. **2,** (fix, as in one's memory) вреза́ть (в па́мять); запечатлева́ть (в па́мяти).

embellish *v.t.* **1,** (beautify) украша́ть. **2,** (embroider; exaggerate) приукра́шивать.

embellishment *n.* украше́ние.

ember *n.* тле́ющий у́голь. *Live embers,* горя́чие у́гли.

embezzle *v.t.* растра́чивать. **—embezzlement,** *n.* рас-тра́та. **—embezzler,** *n.* растра́тчик.

embitter *v.t.* озлобля́ть; ожесточа́ть.

emblem *n.* эмбле́ма. **—emblematic,** *adj.* эмблема-ти́ческий. *Be emblematic of,* символизи́ровать.

embody *v.t.* воплоща́ть; олицетворя́ть. **—embodi-ment,** *n.* воплоще́ние; олицетворе́ние.

embolism *n.* эмболи́я; заку́порка.

emboss *v.t.* **1,** (cover with raised figures, as a surface) украша́ть *or* лепи́ть (что́-нибудь) релье́фом. **2,** (raise upon a surface, as a design) чека́нить; гофрирова́ть.

embossed *adj.* **1,** (having raised designs) релье́фный; тиснёный. **2,** (raised) релье́фный; вы́пуклый; тиснёный. **—embossing,** *n.* тисне́ние.

embrace *v.t.* **1,** (hug) обнима́ть. **2,** (include; encom-pass) охва́тывать. **3,** (take up; adopt) принима́ть. **—v.i.** обнима́ться. *They embraced,* они́ обняли́сь; он обня́лся с ней. **—n.** объя́тие.

embrasure *n.* **1,** (opening for a door or window) проём. **2,** (opening through which a gun may be fired) амбразу́ра; бойни́ца.

embroider *v.t.* **1,** (decorate with needlework) вышива́ть. **2,** *fig.* (embellish, as a story) приукра́ши-вать. **—v.i.** вышива́ть. **—embroidered,** *adj.* вы́ши-тый; расши́тый.

embroidery *n.* **1,** (needlework) вышива́ние; вы́шивка. **2,** (embroidered design) вы́шивка.

embroil *v.t.* впу́тывать; втя́гивать.

embryo *n.* заро́дыш; зача́ток; эмбрио́н.

embryology *n.* эмбриоло́гия. **—embryologist,** *n.* эмбрио́лог.

embryonic *adj.* заро́дышевый; эмбриона́льный. *In an embryonic state,* в зача́точном состоя́нии.

emerald *n.* изумру́д. **—adj.** изумру́дный.

emerge *v.i.* **1,** (come out) выходи́ть: *emerge from the shadows,* выходи́ть из те́ни. **2,** (come into being) возника́ть. **3,** (come to light) всплыва́ть; выплыва́ть.

emergence *n.* **1,** (coming out) вы́ход. **2,** (coming into being) возникнове́ние.

emergency *n.* э́кстренный слу́чай; кра́йняя необходи́мость. *In case of emergency,* в э́кстренном слу́чае; в э́кстренных слу́чаях. *State of emergency,* чрезвыча́йное положе́ние. —*adj.* **1,** (used in an emergency) авари́йный: *emergency brake/signal,* авари́йный то́рмоз/сигна́л. *Emergency exit,* запа́сный вы́ход **2,** (occurring or invoked in an emergency) чрезвыча́йный: *emergency meeting,* чрезвыча́йное собра́ние. *Emergency powers,* чрезвыча́йные полномо́чия. *Emergency landing,* вы́нужденная *or* авари́йная поса́дка.

emeritus *adj.* в отста́вке. *Professor emeritus,* заслу́женный профе́ссор в отста́вке.

emery *n.* нажда́к. —*adj.* нажда́чный.

emetic *adj.* рво́тный. —*n.* рво́тное; рво́тное сре́дство.

emigrant *n.* эмигра́нт.

emigrate *v.i.* эмигри́ровать. *Apply to emigrate,* подава́ть заявле́ние о вы́езде (*or* на вы́езд).

emigration *n.* эмигра́ция.

émigré *n.* эмигра́нт.

eminence *n.* **1,** (exalted position) знамени́тость. **2,** (elevation; hill) возвы́шенность.

eminent *adj.* выдаю́щийся; знамени́тый.

eminently *adv.* весьма́; вполне́: *eminently satisfactory/ successful,* весьма́ удовлетвори́тельно; вполне́ уда́чно.

emir *n.* эми́р. —**emirate,** *n.* эмира́т.

emissary *n.* эмисса́р.

emission *n.* **1,** (act of emitting) испуска́ние. **2,** *physics* эми́ссия. **3,** *pl.* (something emitted) вы́бросы: *emissions into the atmosphere,* вы́бросы в атмосфе́ру.

emit *v.t.* испуска́ть; издава́ть: *emit a sound/odor,* испуска́ть/издава́ть звук/за́пах. *Emit light,* испуска́ть свет.

emotion *n.* **1,** (any feeling) чу́вство; эмо́ция. *Mixed emotions,* сме́шанные чу́вства. **2,** (mental agitation) волне́ние: *overcome with emotion,* охва́чен волне́нием. *Speak with emotion,* говори́ть эмоциона́льно.

emotional *adj.* **1,** (pert. to the emotions) душе́вный: *emotional state,* душе́вное состоя́ние. **2,** (easily aroused to emotion; appealing to emotions) эмоциона́льный. *Emotional speech,* эмоциона́льная *or* патети́ческая речь.

empathize *v.i.* [*usu.* **empathize with**] входи́ть в (чьё-нибудь положе́ние).

empathy *n.* сочу́вствие; отзы́вчивость.

emperor *n.* импера́тор.

emphasis *n.* ударе́ние; акце́нт; упо́р. *Lay/place* (*the*) *emphasis on,* де́лать упо́р/ударе́ние/акце́нт на. *Pronounce with emphasis,* произноси́ть подчёркнуто. *From now on the emphasis will be on...,* отны́не упо́р бу́дет де́латься на...

emphasize *v.t.* подчёркивать.

emphatic *adj.* реши́тельный; категори́ческий: *emphatic gesture,* реши́тельный жест; *emphatic de-*

nial, категори́ческое опроверже́ние. —**emphatically,** *adv.* реши́тельно; категори́чески.

emphysema *n.* эмфизе́ма.

empire *n.* импе́рия: *the Roman Empire,* Ри́мская импе́рия.

empirical *adj.* эмпири́ческий. —**empiricism,** *n.* эмпири́зм. —**empiricist,** *n.* эмпи́рик.

emplacement *n., mil.* огнева́я пози́ция: *gun emplacement,* оруди́йная огнева́я пози́ция.

employ *v.t.* **1,** (use) испо́льзовать; применя́ть. **2,** (hire) нанима́ть. *Are you employed?,* вы рабо́таете?; вы устро́ены? *The factory employs 300 workers,* на фа́брике рабо́тают (*or* за́нято) три́ста рабо́чих. —*n.* слу́жба: *be in the employ of...,* быть на слу́жбе у.

employee *n.* слу́жащий.

employer *n.* нанима́тель; работода́тель.

employment *n.* **1,** (use) испо́льзование; примене́ние. **2,** (work) рабо́та: *seek employment,* иска́ть рабо́ту. **3,** (being employed; percentage of population employed) за́нятость: *full/seasonal employment,* по́лная/сезо́нная за́нятость. —**employment agency,** бюро́ по на́йму *or* по трудоустро́йству.

empower *v.t.* уполномо́чивать.

empress *n.* императри́ца.

emptiness *n.* пустота́.

empty *adj.* пусто́й: *empty glass/bus/hall,* пусто́й стака́н/авто́бус/зал. *Empty seat,* свобо́дное ме́сто. *Empty words/promises,* пусты́е слова́/обеща́ния. *The stores were empty,* в магази́нах бы́ло пу́сто. *The house stands empty,* дом стои́т пусто́й; дом пусту́ет. —*v.t.* **1,** (remove the contents of) опора́жнивать. *Empty one's pockets,* выкла́дывать всё из карма́нов. *Empty the ashtrays,* чи́стить пе́пельницы. **2,** (toss out) выбра́сывать: *empty the trash from the wastebasket,* выбра́сывать сор из корзи́ны. **3,** *fol. by* **into** (pour into) вылива́ть (в); высыпа́ть (в). —*v.i.* **1,** (become empty) (о)пусте́ть; опора́жниваться. **2,** *fol. by* **into** (flow into, as of a river) впада́ть (в); нести́ свои́ во́ды (в).

empty-handed *adj.* с пусты́ми рука́ми; ни с чем.

empty-headed *adj.* пустоголо́вый.

emu *n.* э́му.

emulate *v.t.* равня́ться по: *emulate one's predecessors,* равня́ться по свои́м предше́ственникам. *Emulate one's father's success,* доби́ться того́ же успе́ха, что и оте́ц.

emulsion *n.* эму́льсия.

enable *v.t.* позволя́ть; дава́ть возмо́жность (+ *dat.*).

enact *v.t.* **1,** (make into law) принима́ть; утвержда́ть. **2,** (act out) разы́грывать. —**enactment,** *n.* приня́тие; утвержде́ние.

enamel *n.* эма́ль. —*adj.* эма́левый; эмалиро́ванный. —*v.t.* покрыва́ть эма́лью; эмалирова́ть. —**enamelware,** *n.* эмалиро́ванная посу́да.

enamored *also,* **enamoured** *adj.* влюблён. *Be enamored of,* увлека́ться (+ *instr.*).

encamp *v.i.* располага́ться ла́герем.

encampment *n.* **1,** (setting up a camp) расположе́ние ла́герем. **2,** (camp; campsite) (вре́менный) ла́герь.

encase *v.t.* вде́лывать.

encephalitis *n.* энцефали́т.

enchant *v.t.* очаро́вывать; восхища́ть; пленя́ть; обвора́живать.

enchanted *adj.* **1**, (captivated) зачаро́ванный; очаро́ванный. **2**, (having a seemingly magical quality) заколдо́ванный; зачаро́ванный.

enchanting *adj.* очарова́тельный; обая́тельный; обворожи́тельный; восхити́тельный.

enchantment *n.* очарова́ние; восхище́ние; обая́ние.

enchantress *n.* чаровни́ца; чароде́йка.

encipher *v.t.* шифрова́ть.

encircle *v.t.* окружа́ть. —**encirclement,** *n.* окруже́ние.

enclave *n.* анкла́в.

enclose *v.t.* **1**, (fence in) огора́живать; загора́живать; обноси́ть. **2**, (insert) вкла́дывать (в конве́рт); прилага́ть (к письму́). *Enclosed herewith,* при сём прилага́ется. **3**, (place between, as in parentheses) заключа́ть; брать (в ско́бки).

enclosure *n.* **1**, (act of enclosing) огора́живание. **2**, (enclosed area) огоро́женное ме́сто. **3**, (fence) огра́да. **4**, (something enclosed with a letter) вложе́ние; приложе́ние.

encode *v.t.* шифрова́ть; коди́ровать.

encomium *n.* панеги́рик.

encompass *v.t.* **1**, (encircle) окружа́ть. **2**, (take in; include) охва́тывать.

encore *interj.* бис. —*n. Give an encore,* испо́лнить что́-нибудь на бис; биси́ровать.

encounter *v.t.* встреча́ть; ста́лкиваться с: *encounter resistance,* встреча́ть сопротивле́ние; *encounter difficulties,* ста́лкиваться с тру́дностями. —*n.* **1**, (meeting) встре́ча: *chance encounter,* случа́йная встре́ча. **2**, (contact; clash) столкнове́ние.

encourage *v.t.* **1**, (hearten) ободря́ть; подба́дривать; обнадёживать. **2**, (spur on; stimulate) поощря́ть. **3**, (help bring about) спосо́бствовать.

encouragement *n.* ободре́ние; поощре́ние. *Words of encouragement,* поощри́тельные слова́.

encouraging *adj.* обнадёживающий; ободри́тельный. *Initial results are encouraging,* пе́рвые результа́ты обнадёживают.

encroach *v.i.* [*usu.* **encroach upon**] посяга́ть (на); вторга́ться (в); покуша́ться (на). —**encroachment,** *n.* посяга́тельство; покуше́ние.

encrust *v.t.* инкрусти́ровать.

encrypt *v.t.* шифрова́ть. —**encryption,** *n.* шифрова́ние.

encumber *v.t.* **1**, (hinder; hamper) стесня́ть. **2**, (clutter; obstruct) загроможда́ть.

encumbrance *n.* **1**, (hindrance) препя́тствие; поме́ха. **2**, (burden) бре́мя; обу́за.

encyclical *n.* энци́клика.

encyclopedia *also,* **encyclopaedia** *n.* энциклопе́дия. —**encyclopedic,** *adj.* энциклопеди́ческий.

end *n.* **1**, (extremity; conclusion) коне́ц: *the end of the street,* коне́ц у́лицы. *From end to end,* из конца́ в коне́ц; от одного́ конца́ до друго́го. *Come to an end,* конча́ться; приходи́ть к концу́. *Come to a bad end,* пло́хо ко́нчить. *Put an end to,* поко́нчить с;

положи́ть коне́ц (+ *dat.*). *To the bitter end,* до са́мого конца́; до после́дней ка́пли кро́ви. *The crisis is at an end,* кри́зис зако́нчился. **2**, (goal; purpose) цель: *toward this end,* с э́той це́лью. *The end justifies the means,* цель опра́вдывает сре́дства. **3**, (death) смерть; кончи́на. *Meet one's end,* встре́тить свой коне́ц; найти́ свою́ смерть. —*adj.* коне́чный: *end product,* коне́чный проду́кт; *end result,* коне́чный результа́т; *end user,* коне́чный по́льзователь. —*v.t.* **1**, (conclude) конча́ть; зака́нчивать; заключа́ть. **2**, (halt; put a stop to) прекраща́ть. —*v.i.* конча́ться; зака́нчиваться. *All's well that ends well,* всё хорошо́, что хорошо́ конча́ется. *End in disaster,* ко́нчиться катастро́фой. —**at loose ends,** без де́ла; не у дел. —**be the end of,** своди́ть в моги́лу. —**end up,** очути́ться. *End up in jail,* угоди́ть в тюрьму́. *End up with nothing,* оста́ться ни с чем. —**in the end,** в конце́ концо́в. —**make ends meet,** своди́ть концы́ с конца́ми. —**no end of,** отбо́ю нет от; хоть отбавля́й. —**on end,** по це́лым: *for weeks on end,* по це́лым неде́лям. —**stand on end, 1**, (set upright) ста́вить стойма́; ста́вить на ребро́; ста́вить на попа́. **2**, (bristle, as of one's hair) встава́ть *or* станови́ться ды́бом. —**to the ends of the earth,** на край све́та (*or* земли́).

endanger *v.t.* подверга́ть опа́сности; ста́вить под угро́зу.

endear *v.t.* сде́лать дороги́м се́рдцу. *Endear oneself to,* покоря́ть се́рдце (+ *gen.*). —**endearing,** *adj.* подкупа́ющий; обезору́живающий.

endearment *n.* ла́ска. —**term of endearment,** ласка́тельное и́мя.

endeavor *also,* **endeavour** *v.t.* пыта́ться; стара́ться. —*n.* **1**, (attempt) попы́тка. **2**, (undertaking) предприя́тие; зате́я.

endemic *adj.* энземи́ческий.

end game *chess* э́ндшпиль.

ending *n.* оконча́ние: *verb/chess/nerve endings,* глаго́льные/ша́хматные/не́рвные оконча́ния. *The story has a happy ending,* расска́з име́ет счастли́вый коне́ц.

endive *n.* энди́вий.

endless *adj.* бесконе́чный; несконча́емый. —**endlessly,** *adv.* без конца́; бесконе́чно.

endocrine *adj.* эндокри́нный. —**endocrine glands,** эндокри́нные же́лезы; же́лезы вну́тренней секре́ции.

endocrinology *n.* эндокриноло́гия.

endorse *v.t.* **1**, *finance* индосси́ровать. **2**, (support, as a candidate) подде́рживать кандидату́ру (+ *gen.*). **3**, (express one's agreement with) присоединя́ться к.

endorsement *n.* **1**, (support) подде́ржка. **2**, (signature on the back of a check) переда́точная на́дпись; индоссаме́нт; жи́ро.

endow *v.t.* **1**, (provide with funds) обеспе́чивать. **2**, provide with, as a certain quality) наделя́ть; одаря́ть; награжда́ть.

endowment *n.* **1**, (bequest) дар; поже́ртвование. **2**, (natural gift) дарова́ние; одарённость.

endurance *n.* выно́сливость. *Beyond endurance,*

невыноси́мый. *Endurance test,* испыта́ние на вы-
но́сливость.

endure *v.t.* терпе́ть; выноси́ть; переноси́ть; выде́р-
живать. *Endure pain,* терпе́ть *or* переноси́ть боль.
Endure hardship, терпе́ть лише́ния. —*v.i.* просу-
ществова́ть. *His name/memory will endure forever,*
его́ и́мя бу́дет жить ве́чно; па́мять о нём оста́нется
наве́чно.

enduring *adj.* про́чный: *enduring peace,* про́чный
мир.

endwise *adv.* **1,** (on end) стоймя́. **2,** (lengthwise) в
длину́. **3,** (with the end foremost) концо́м вперёд.
Also, **endways.**

enema *n.* кли́зма.

enemy *n.* враг; неприя́тель; проти́вник. —*adj.*
вра́жеский; неприя́тельский. *Come under enemy
fire,* попа́сть под ого́нь проти́вника.

energetic *adj.* энерги́чный. —**energetically,** *adv.*
энерги́чно.

energize *v.t.* **1,** (activate; invigorate) побужда́ть к
де́йствию. **2,** *electricity* сообща́ть эне́ргию (+ *dat.*).

energy *n.* **1,** (capacity for vigorous action) эне́ргия: *full
of energy,* по́лон эне́ргии. **2,** *pl.* (efforts) эне́ргия;
си́лы: *direct one's energies to,* направля́ть свою́
эне́ргию/ свои́ си́лы/ на (+ *acc.*). **3,** (source of usable
power) эне́ргия: *atomic energy,* а́томная эне́ргия.
(*U.S.*) *Department of Energy,* министе́рство энер-
ге́тики. *Energy crisis,* энергети́ческий кри́зис.

enervate *v.t.* обесси́ливать; расслабля́ть.

enfeeble *v.t.* ослабля́ть; обесси́ливать. —**enfeebled,**
adj. одряхле́вший.

enfold *v.t.* **1,** (surround with a covering) заку́тывать. **2,**
(embrace) обнима́ть.

enforce *v.t.* осуществля́ть. *Enforce a ban,* осу-
ществля́ть запре́т; обеспе́чивать соблюде́ние
запре́та.

enforcement *n.* осуществле́ние. *Law enforcement,*
правоохране́ние.

enfranchise *v.t.* предоставля́ть избира́тельные права́
(+ *dat.*).

engage *v.t.* **1,** (hire) нанима́ть. **2,** (occupy; absorb) за-
нима́ть; поглоща́ть. *Engage someone in conversa-
tion,* занима́ть кого́-нибудь разгово́ром. *Engage
someone's attention,* занима́ть *or* поглоща́ть чьё-
нибудь внима́ние. *The work engages much of my
time,* рабо́та занима́ет/поглоща́ет у меня́ мно́го
вре́мени. **3,** (meet in battle) вступа́ть в бой с. —*v.i.*
1, *fol. by* **in** (involve oneself; take part) занима́ться (+
instr.): *engage in sports,* занима́ться спо́ртом. **2,**
(mesh) сцепля́ться.

engaged *adj.* **1,** (occupied) за́нятый. *Be engaged in,*
быть за́нятым (+ *instr.*); занима́ться (+ *instr.*). **2,**
(betrothed) помо́лвленный; обручённый. *Become
engaged to,* обруча́ться с. *She is engaged to...,* она́
обручена́ с (+ *instr.*).

engagement *n.* **1,** (betrothal) помо́лвка; обруче́ние.
Break off one's engagement, расто́ргнуть помо́лвку;
расстро́ить сва́дьбу. **2,** (appointment) свида́ние;
встре́ча. *We have a prior engagement,* у нас други́е
пла́ны; мы уже́ приглашены́. **3,** (battle) бой. —*adj.*

обруча́льный: *engagement ring,* обруча́льное
кольцо́.

engaging *adj.* привлека́тельный; подкупа́ющий.

engender *v.t.* порожда́ть; зарожда́ть.

engine *n.* **1,** (motor) дви́гатель; мото́р; маши́на. **2,**
(locomotive) парово́з; локомоти́в. —**engine room,**
маши́нное отделе́ние.

engineer *n.* **1,** (one trained in a branch of engineering)
инжене́р. **2,** (locomotive operator) машини́ст. —*v.t.*
соверша́ть: *engineer an escape,* соверши́ть побе́г.
Engineer a victory, кова́ть побе́ду.

engineering *n.* инжене́рное де́ло; те́хника; техно-
ло́гия. —**chemical engineering,** хими́ческая техно-
ло́гия. —**civil engineering,** строи́тельная те́хника.
—**electrical engineering,** электроте́хника. —**mechanical engineering,** машинострое́ние.

English *adj.* англи́йский. —*n.* **1,** (language) англи́й-
ский язы́к. *Speak English,* говори́ть по-англи́йски.
2, *preceded by* **the** (people) англича́не.

English horn англи́йский рожо́к.

Englishman *n.* англича́нин. —**Englishwoman,** *n.* ан-
глича́нка.

engrain *v.* = **ingrain.**

engrave *v.t.* гравирова́ть.

engraver *n.* гравёр; ре́зчик.

engraving *n.* **1,** (art) гравирова́ние; гравиро́вка. **2,**
(engraved plate) гравю́ра.

engross *v.t.* поглоща́ть. *Be engrossed in,* быть
поглощённым в; углубля́ться в; погружа́ться в.
Become engrossed in a book, зачита́ться кни́гой.
—**engrossing,** *adj.* увлека́тельный; захва́тывающий.

engulf *v.t.* **1,** (of flames, darkness, etc.) охва́тывать. **2,**
(of waves, the sea, etc.) поглоща́ть.

enhance *v.t.* увели́чивать; повыша́ть. *Enhance the
prestige of,* подня́ть авторите́т (+ *gen.*).

enigma *n.* зага́дка. —**enigmatic,** *adj.* зага́дочный.

enjoin *v.t.* **1,** (order; direct) предпи́сывать. **2,** (forbid;
prohibit) запреща́ть.

enjoy *v.t.* **1,** (have a good time at): *Did you enjoy the
play?,* пье́са вам понра́вилась? *I enjoyed talking to
you,* мне бы́ло о́чень прия́тно разгова́ривать с
ва́ми. **2,** (relish; admire) наслажда́ться: *enjoy life/
music/ the scenery/,* наслажда́ться жи́знью/му́зы-
кой/пейза́жем. *Enjoy reading,* люби́ть чита́ть; по-
луча́ть удово́льствие от чте́ния. **3,** (have, as an advantage) облада́ть: *enjoy good health, etc.*) по́льзоваться; облада́ть.
—**enjoy oneself,** хорошо́ проводи́ть вре́мя; полу-
ча́ть (большо́е) удово́льствие.

enjoyable *adj.* прия́тный.

enjoyment *n.* **1,** (pleasure) удово́льствие; насла-
жде́ние. **2,** (possession) облада́ние.

enlarge *v.t.* **1,** (make larger) расширя́ть. **2,** *photog.*
увели́чивать. —*v.i.* **1,** (become larger) расширя́ться;
увели́чиваться. **2,** *fol. by* **upon** (treat in greater detail)
распространя́ться о.

enlargement *n.* **1,** (act of enlarging) увеличе́ние;
расшире́ние. **2,** (enlarged copy) увеличе́ние.

enlarger *n., photog.* увеличи́тель; увеличи́тельный
аппара́т.

enlighten *v.t.* **1,** (bring knowledge to) просвеща́ть. **2,**

(inform) осведомля́ть. —**enlightened**, *adj.* просвещённый. —**enlightening**, *adj.* поучи́тельный. —**enlightenment**, *n.* просвеще́ние.

enlist *v.i.* поступа́ть (доброво́льцем); (за)вербова́ться. —*v.t.* **1,** (gain the support of) привлека́ть; вербова́ть. **2,** (secure, as someone's services) заруча́ться. —**enlisted man,** военнослу́жащий рядово́го соста́ва.

enlistment *n.* **1,** (act of enlisting) поступле́ние (на вое́нную слу́жбу). **2,** (term) срок слу́жбы.

enliven *v.t.* оживля́ть.

en masse в ма́ссе; ско́пом. *The cabinet submitted its resignation en masse,* кабине́т по́дал в отста́вку в по́лном соста́ве.

enmity *n.* вражда́; неприя́знь.

ennoble *v.t.* облагора́живать.

ennui *n.* ску́ка; тоска́.

enormity *n.* **1,** (heinousness) чудо́вищность. **2,** (heinous crime) злодея́ние.

enormous *adj.* огро́мный; грома́дный. —**enormously**, *adv.* чрезвыча́йно; о́чень и о́чень.

enough *adj.* доста́точно (+ *gen.*): *enough money,* доста́точно де́нег. *Be enough,* хвата́ть: *That will be enough for today,* на сего́дня хва́тит. *There is enough room for everyone,* на всех хвата́ет ме́ста. —*adv.* **1,** (sufficiently) доста́точно: *old enough to understand,* доста́точно взро́слый, что́бы поня́ть. **2,** (adequately) дово́льно: *He plays well enough,* он игра́ет дово́льно хорошо́. **3,** *in* **oddly enough,** как ни стра́нно; **sure enough,** *see* sure. —*n.* доста́точно: *I've had enough,* мне уже́ доста́точно. —*interj.* доста́точно!; хва́тит! *Enough of this nonsense!,* бро́сьте э́ти глу́пости!

en passant 1, (in passing) мимохо́дом. **2,** *chess* на прохо́де.

enquire *v.* = **inquire.** —**enquiry**, *n.* = **inquiry.**

enrage *v.t.* беси́ть; разъяря́ть; приводи́ть в я́рость.

enraged *adj.* разъярённый. *Become enraged,* приходи́ть в я́рость.

enrapture *v.t.* восхища́ть; восторга́ть.

enrich *v.t.* обогаща́ть. *Enriched uranium,* обогащённый ура́н. —**enrichment**, *n.* обогаще́ние.

enroll *also,* **enrol** *v.t.* запи́сывать; зачисля́ть. —*v.i.* запи́сываться; зачисля́ться.

enrollment *also,* **enrolment** *n.* **1,** (act of enrolling) зачисле́ние. **2,** (number of students enrolled) число́ уча́щихся.

en route по (*or* в) пути́; по (*or* в) доро́ге.

ensconce *v.t.* устра́ивать. *Ensconce oneself,* устра́иваться; засе́сть.

ensemble *n.* **1,** (group) анса́мбль. **2,** (attire) наря́д.

enshrine *v.t.* храни́ть; сохраня́ть. *Enshrined in our hearts forever,* наве́чно сохранён в на́ших сердца́х.

enshroud *v.t.* оку́тывать.

ensign *n.* **1,** (flag) зна́мя; флаг. **2,** (emblem) значо́к; эмбле́ма. **3,** (naval rank) мла́дший лейтена́нт.

enslave *v.t.* порабоща́ть. —**enslavement**, *n.* порабоще́ние. —**enslaver**, *n.* поработи́тель.

ensnare *v.t.* пойма́ть в лову́шку.

ensue *v.i.* **1,** (follow) сле́довать. **2,** (result) вытека́ть. —**ensuing**, *adj.* после́дующий; вытека́ющий.

ensure *v.t.* обеспе́чивать: *ensure success/victory,* обеспе́чивать успе́х/побе́ду. *Ensure that this does not happen again,* доби́ться, что́бы э́то не повторя́лось.

entail *v.t.* влечь за собо́й; быть свя́занным с.

entangle *v.t.* запу́тывать. *Become entangled in,* пу́таться в; запу́тываться в.

enter *v.t.* **1,** (go into; come into) входи́ть в: *enter the hall,* входи́ть в зал. *Enter the hospital,* лечь в больни́цу. *Enter production,* поступа́ть в произво́дство. *Enter one's head,* приходи́ть в го́лову (+ *dat.*). **2,** (join; enroll in) поступа́ть в; вступа́ть в. *Enter a university,* поступа́ть в университе́т. *Enter a contest,* включи́ться в ко́нкурс. *Enter the war,* вступи́ть в войну́. *Enter the political arena,* выходи́ть на полити́ческую аре́ну. **3,** (pierce; penetrate) вонза́ться в; пробива́ть. **4,** (begin, as a new era) вступа́ть в. **5,** (place, as on a list) вноси́ть; заноси́ть; впи́сывать; зачисля́ть. **6,** (place; register, as in school) запи́сывать. **7,** (submit formally) заявля́ть: *enter a protest,* заяви́ть проте́ст. —*v.i.* входи́ть. —**enter into,** вступа́ть в; входи́ть в: *enter into an agreement,* вступи́ть/войти́ в соглаше́ние. *Enter into one's calculations,* входи́ть в чьи-нибудь расчёты.

enteritis *n.* энтери́т.

enterprise *n.* **1,** (undertaking; business operation) предприя́тие. **2,** (economic activity) предпринима́тельство: *private enterprise,* ча́стное предпринима́тельство. **3,** (initiative) предприи́мчивость.

enterprising *adj.* предприи́мчивый.

entertain *v.t.* **1,** (amuse) развлека́ть; забавля́ть; занима́ть. **2,** (extend hospitality to) принима́ть; угоща́ть. **3,** (consider) обду́мывать. *Entertain the notion of…,* поду́мывать о… *Entertain a motion,* принима́ть предложе́ние к рассмотре́нию. **4,** (harbor, as illusions) пита́ть. —*v.i.* принима́ть госте́й. —**entertainer**, *n.* арти́ст эстра́ды. —**entertaining**, *adj.* занима́тельный.

entertainment *n.* **1,** (entertaining of guests) приём (госте́й); угоще́ние. **2,** (diversion) развлече́ние. **3,** (show; performance) варьете́.

enthrall *also,* **enthral** *v.t.* **1,** (captivate) увлека́ть; захва́тывать; завлека́ть. **2,** *obs.* (enslave) порабоща́ть. —**enthralling**, *adj.* увлека́тельный; захва́тывающий.

enthrone *v.t.* возводи́ть на престо́л.

enthusiasm *n.* энтузиа́зм; увлече́ние; воодушевле́ние; подъём. —**enthusiast**, *n.* энтузиа́ст; охо́тник. —**enthusiastic**, *adj.* восто́рженный; по́лный энтузиа́зма.

entice *v.t.* зама́нивать; перема́нивать; завлека́ть; прельща́ть.

enticement *n.* **1,** (act of enticing) зама́нивание. **2,** (something that entices) прима́нка.

enticing *adj.* зама́нчивый; завлека́тельный.

entire *adj.* **1,** *preceded by the* (all; all of) весь: *the entire day/cost,* весь день; вся сто́имость. **2,** *preceded by an* (whole) це́лый: *an entire day/army,* це́лый день; це́лая а́рмия.

entirely *adv.* **1,** (completely) соверше́нно; совсе́м; вполне́; целико́м; всеце́ло. *Not entirely sure,* не совсе́м уве́рен. *An entirely different matter,* совсе́м друго́е де́ло. **2,** (solely) исключи́тельно: *entirely through one's own efforts,* исключи́тельно свои́ми со́бственными уси́лиями.

entirety *n.* полнота́. *In its entirety,* во всей полноте́; со всей полното́й.

entitle *v.t.* **1,** (qualify; authorize) дава́ть пра́во (+ *dat.*). *Be entitled to,* име́ть пра́во на. **2,** (name) озагла́вливать. *A book entitled...,* кни́га под назва́нием... *The book is entitled...,* кни́га называ́ется...

entity *n.* вещь: *separate entities,* ра́зные ве́щи.

entomb *v.t.* погреба́ть.

entomology *n.* энтомоло́гия. —**entomological,** *adj.* энтомологи́ческий. —**entomologist,** *n.* энтомо́лог.

entourage *n.* окруже́ние.

entrails *n.pl.* вну́тренности; требуха́.

entrance[1] (**en-trens**) *n.* **1,** (act of entering) вход. *No entrance!,* вхо́да нет!; вход воспрещён! *Make a grand entrance,* торже́ственно войти́. **2,** (place to enter) вход; ход. *Back entrance,* чёрный ход. *The entrance to the subway,* вход в метро́. **3,** *theat.* вы́ход (на сце́ну). —*adj.* входно́й; вступи́тельный. *Entrance examination,* вступи́тельный экза́мен.

entrance[2] (**en-trans**) *v.t.* очаро́вывать; завора́живать.

entrant *n.* уча́стник (состяза́ния).

entrap *v.t.* пойма́ть в лову́шку.

entreat *v.t.* умоля́ть; упра́шивать. —**entreaty,** *n.* мольба́.

entrée *n.* **1,** (right of entry) пра́во вхо́да. *Have entrée,* быть вхо́жим. **2,** (main course) второ́е (блю́до).

entrench *v.t.* **1,** (fortify with a trench) ока́пывать. **2,** (establish firmly) укореня́ть. *Become entrenched,* укореня́ться.

entrepreneur *n.* предпринима́тель.

entrust *v.t.* доверя́ть; вверя́ть; поруча́ть. *Entrust one's fate/ an important assignment/ to,* вве́рить свою́ судьбу́ (+ *dat.*); дове́рить отве́тственное зада́ние (+ *dat.*). *They were entrusted with the care of the children,* им бы́ло поручено́ воспита́ние дете́й.

entry *n.* **1,** (act of entering) вход; въезд. *Entry permit,* разреше́ние на въезд. **2,** (application to compete) зая́вка. *Entry blank,* анке́та. **3,** (opening; passage) вход; прохо́д. **4,** (notation) за́пись; отме́тка. **5,** (item in a reference book) статья́.

entwine *v.t.* **1,** (intertwine) вплета́ть; сплета́ть. *Become entwined,* переплета́ться. **2,** (twine around) обвива́ть; увива́ть; оплета́ть. —*v.i.* [*usu.* **entwine around**] обвива́ться вокру́г.

enumerate *v.t.* перечисля́ть.

enumeration *n.* **1,** (act of enumerating) перечисле́ние. **2,** (list; catalogue) пе́речень.

enunciate *v.t.* **1,** (articulate) выгова́ривать. **2,** (state systematically) излага́ть. —*v.i.* произноси́ть.

enunciation *n.* **1,** (pronunciation) вы́говор. **2,** (formal statement) изложе́ние.

envelop *v.t.* охва́тывать; оку́тывать; обвола́кивать. *Enveloped in fog,* оку́танный тума́ном.

envelope *n.* конве́рт.

envelopment *n.* охва́т.

envenom *v.t.* отравля́ть.

enviable *adj.* зави́дный.

envious *adj.* зави́стливый. *Be envious of,* зави́довать (+ *dat.*).

environment *n.* окруже́ние; среда́; обстано́вка. *The environment,* окружа́ющая среда́. *A wholesome environment,* здоро́вая обстано́вка. —**environmental,** *adj.* свя́занный с окружа́ющей средо́й. —**environmentalist,** *n.* сторо́нник охра́ны окружа́ющей среды́.

environs *n.pl.* окре́стности. *Live in the environs of Moscow,* жить под Москво́й.

envisage *v.t.* предусма́тривать.

envision *v.t.* **1,** (picture in the mind) представля́ть. **2,** (provide for in the future) предусма́тривать.

envoy *n.* **1,** (messenger) посла́нец; по́сланный. **2,** (diplomat) посла́нник.

envy *n.* за́висть. *To the envy of,* на за́висть (+ *dat.*). —*v.t.* зави́довать: *I don't envy him,* я ему́ не зави́дую.

enzyme *n.* ферме́нт.

eon *n.* ве́чность.

epaulet *also,* **epaulette** *n.* эполе́т; эполе́та.

ephemeral *adj.* недолгове́чный; преходя́щий; эфеме́рный.

epic *n.* эпи́ческая поэ́ма; эпопе́я. —*adj.* эпи́ческий.

epicenter *also,* **epicentre** *n.* эпице́нтр.

epicure *n.* эпикуре́ец. —**epicurean,** *adj.* эпикуре́йский.

epidemic *n.* эпиде́мия. —*adj.* эпидеми́ческий.

epidemiology *n.* эпидемиоло́гия. —**epidemiologist,** *n.* эпидемио́лог.

epidermis *n.* эпиде́рмис.

epiglottis *n.* надгорта́нник.

epigram *n.* эпигра́мма. —**epigrammatic,** *adj.* эпиграмма́ти́ческий.

epigraph *n.* **1,** (inscription) на́дпись; эпи́граф. **2,** (opening quotation) эпи́граф.

epilepsy *n.* эпиле́псия. —**epileptic,** *adj.* эпилепти́ческий. —*n.* эпиле́птик.

epilogue *n.* эпило́г; послесло́вие.

Epiphany *n.* креще́ние; богоявле́ние.

episcopal *adj.* епи́скопский.

Episcopalian *adj.* епископа́льный. —*n.* член епископа́льной це́ркви.

episode *n.* эпизо́д. —**episodic,** *adj.* эпизоди́ческий.

epistemology *n.* тео́рия позна́ния.

epistle *n.* эпи́стола. —**epistolary,** *adj.* эпистоля́рный.

epitaph *n.* надгро́бная на́дпись; эпита́фия.

epithelium *n.* эпите́лий. —**epithelial,** *adj.* эпителиа́льный.

epithet *n.* **1,** (descriptive word or phrase) эпи́тет. **2,** (disparaging word or phrase) руга́тельство. *Hurl epithets at,* осыпа́ть (кого́-нибудь) бра́нью.

epitome *n.* **1,** (perfect example; embodiment) воплоще́ние. **2,** (summary) конспе́кт.

epitomize *v.t.* **1,** (typify) воплоща́ть. **2,** (summarize) конспекти́ровать.

epoch *n.* эпо́ха. —**epochal,** *adj.* эпоха́льный.

Epsom salt *also,* **Epsom salts** англи́йская соль.

equable *adj.* **1,** (not fluctuating) ро́вный; равноме́рный. **2,** (tranquil; serene) ро́вный; уравнове́шенный.

equal *adj.* ра́вный: *equal parts,* ра́вные ча́сти. *Equal rights,* равнопра́вие. *Equal partner,* равнопра́вный партнёр. *In equal measure,* в ра́вной (*or* в одина́ковой) ме́ре. *Of equal height,* одина́кового ро́ста. *Other things being equal,* при про́чих ра́вных усло́виях. *Speak two languages with equal facility,* говори́ть на двух языка́х одина́ково свобо́дно. *All citizens are equal before the law,* все гра́ждане равны́ пе́ред зако́ном. —*v.t.* **1,** (be equal to) равня́ться (+ *dat.*): *Six plus three equals nine,* шесть плюс три равня́ется (*or* равно́) девяти́. *Let x equal y,* пусть икс ра́вен и́греку. *No one can equal him in ability,* никто́ не мо́жет сравни́ться с ним в спосо́бности. **2,** (duplicate; tie) повторя́ть: *equal a record,* повторя́ть реко́рд. —*n.* ра́вный; ро́вня. *He has no equal,* ему́ нет ра́вного; он не име́ет себе́ ра́вного. *Treat someone as an equal,* относи́ться к кому́-нибудь как к ра́вному. —**equal to,** на высоте́ (+ *gen.*): *equal to the occasion,* на высоте́ положе́ния. *He is not equal to the task,* э́та зада́ча ему́ не под си́лу.

equality *n.* ра́венство. *Achieve equality with,* сравня́ться с.

equalize *v.t.* ура́внивать. —**equalization,** *n.* уравне́ние.

equally *adv.* **1,** (in equal parts) по́ровну. **2,** (to an equal degree) одина́ково; в ра́вной ме́ре; в одина́ковой ме́ре. **3,** (by the same token) ра́вным о́бразом.

equal sign знак ра́венства.

equanimity *n.* споко́йствие; самооблада́ние; хладнокро́вие.

equate *v.t.* [*often* **equate with**] равня́ть (с); прира́внивать (к); отождествля́ть (с).

equation *n.* уравне́ние.

equator *n.* эква́тор. —**equatorial,** *adj.* экваториа́льный.

equestrian *adj.* ко́нный.

equiangular *adj.* равноуго́льный.

equidistant *adj.* на ра́вном (*or* на одина́ковом) расстоя́нии.

equilateral *adj.* равносторо́нний.

equilibrium *n.* равнове́сие.

equine *adj.* лошади́ный.

equinox *n.* равноде́нствие.

equip *v.t.* обору́довать; снаряжа́ть; оснаща́ть. *Fully equipped,* со всем обору́дованием.

equipment *n.* обору́дование; снаряже́ние; аппарату́ра; те́хника. *The laboratory contains the latest equipment,* лаборато́рия обору́дована нове́йшей те́хникой.

equitable *adj.* справедли́вый; беспристра́стный.

equity *n.* **1,** (fairness) справедли́вость. **2,** *finance* акти́вы.

equivalence *n.* эквивале́нтность.

equivalent *adj.* равноси́льный; равнозна́чный; эквивале́нтный. *Equivalent amount,* эквивале́нтная су́мма. *This is equivalent to a declaration of war,* э́то равноси́льно объявле́нию войны́. —*n.* эквивале́нт.

equivocal *adj.* двусмы́сленный.

equivocate *v.i.* говори́ть обиняка́ми; виля́ть.

equivocation *n.* двусмы́сленность; укло́нчивость. *Without equivocation,* недвусмы́сленно; без экиво́ков.

era *n.* э́ра; эпо́ха.

eradicate *v.t.* **1,** (destroy; wipe out) уничтожа́ть: *eradicate pests,* уничтожа́ть вреди́телей. **2,** *fig.* (eliminate; put an end to) искореня́ть; уничтожа́ть; ликвиди́ровать. —**eradication,** *n.* искорене́ние; уничтоже́ние; ликвида́ция.

erase *v.t.* **1,** (rub out) стира́ть. *Erase the blackboard,* стира́ть с доски́. **2,** (obliterate, as from one's mind) изгла́живать (из па́мяти). **3,** (nullify) перечёркивать.

eraser *n.* **1,** (for something written in pencil) рези́нка; ла́стик. **2,** (for blackboards) тря́пка.

erasure *n.* подчи́стка.

erbium *n.* э́рбий.

ere *prep., poetic* до; пе́ред. —*conj., poetic* пре́жде чем.

erect *adj.* прямо́й: *erect posture,* пряма́я оса́нка. *Erect position,* стоя́чее положе́ние. *Stand erect,* держа́ться пря́мо. *With one's head erect,* с по́днятой голово́й. —*v.t.* **1,** (build) сооружа́ть; возводи́ть; воздвига́ть. *Erect a monument,* ста́вить па́мятник.

erection *n.* **1,** (construction) сооруже́ние; возведе́ние. **2,** *physiol.* эре́кция.

erg *n.* эрг.

ergo *adv.* сле́довательно.

ergot *n.* спорынья́.

ermine *n.* горноста́й. —*adj.* горноста́евый.

erode *v.t.* **1,** (wear away, as of the wind) выве́тривать. **2,** (wash away, as of water) размыва́ть. **3,** (eat into, as of acid) разъеда́ть. **4,** *fig.* (undermine; weaken) подта́чивать. —*v.i.* подрыва́ться.

erosion *n.* эро́зия; выве́тривание; размы́в.

erotic *adj.* эроти́ческий. —**eroticism,** *n.* эроти́зм.

err *v.i.* ошиба́ться; заблужда́ться.

errand *n.* поруче́ние. *Go on an errand,* пойти́/пое́хать по поруче́нию. *Send on an errand,* посла́ть с поруче́нием. *Run errands for,* быть у кого́-нибудь на посы́лках *or* на побегу́шках. —**errand boy,** рассы́льный.

errant *adj.* **1,** (wandering) стра́нствующий; блужда́ющий. **2,** (having gone astray) заблу́дший; сби́вшийся с пути́.

erratic *adj.* неусто́йчивый; неро́вный.

erratum *n.* опеча́тка.

erroneous *adj.* ошибочный; неве́рный; ло́жный. —**erroneously,** *adv.* оши́бочно; по оши́бке.

error *n.* оши́бка. *Be in error,* ошиба́ться; заблужда́ться.

ersatz *adj.* суррога́тный.

erstwhile *adj.* пре́жний.

erudite *adj.* учёный; зна́ющий; эруди́рованный.

erudition *n.* эруди́ция; учёность; начи́танность.

erupt *v.i.* **1,** (of a volcano) изверга́ться. **2,** (of a rash) высыпа́ть; выступа́ть. **3,** *fig.* (of an argument, fight, etc.) вспы́хивать; разгора́ться.

eruption *n.* **1,** (of a volcano) изверже́ние. **2,** (rash) сыпь.

erysipelas *n.* рóжа.

escalate *v.i.* перераста́ть. —**escalation,** *n.* перераста́ние; эскала́ция.

escalator *n.* эскала́тор.

escapade *n.* вы́ходка; проде́лка.

escape *v.i.* **1,** (get free) бежа́ть; убега́ть. *Escape from prison,* бежа́ть из тюрьмы́. *The lion/bird escaped from its cage,* лев убежа́л/ пти́ца улете́ла/ из кле́тки. **2,** (avoid injury, danger, etc.) спаса́ться. *We barely escaped,* мы едва́ спасли́сь; мы едва́ но́ги унесли́. *Escape with minor injuries,* отде́латься лёгкими ране́ниями. **3,** (leak out; seep out) утека́ть; вытека́ть. *Gas escaped from the pipe,* газ вытека́л из трубы́. —*v.t.* **1,** (manage to avoid) спаса́ться от: *escape death,* спаса́ться от сме́рти. *There is no escaping the fact that...,* никуда́ не уйти́ от того́, что... **2,** (be unnoticed or forgotten by) ускольза́ть от: *escape someone's notice,* ускольза́ть от чьего́-нибудь внима́ния. *Nothing escapes him,* от него́ ничто́ не укро́ется. *His name escapes me,* не могу́ припо́мнить его́ и́мени. **3,** (slip out inadvertently, as from one's lips) срыва́ться (с языка́). —*n.* **1,** (breaking out) побе́г; бе́гство. **2,** (avoidance of near disaster) спасе́ние: *miraculous escape,* чуде́сное спасе́ние. *Have a narrow escape,* едва́ спасти́сь.

escapee *n.* бегле́ц.

escarpment *n.* отко́с; *mil.* эска́рп.

eschew *v.t.* сторони́ться; чужда́ться.

escort *n.* **1,** (one who accompanies) провожа́тый. **2,** (for a lady) кавале́р. **3,** (armed guard) конвои́р. *Under police escort,* под конво́ем полице́йских. **4,** *mil.* (single ship or plane) конво́йр; конво́йный; (a number of ships or planes) конво́й; эско́рт. *Fighter escort,* сопровожде́ние истреби́телями. —*v.t.* **1,** (accompany) провожа́ть; проводи́ть (*impfv.*): *escort someone to the door/ through the gate/,* провожа́ть кого́-нибудь до две́ри; провести́ кого́-нибудь че́рез воро́та. **2,** (lead away or out) уводи́ть; выводи́ть. **3,** *mil.* конвои́ровать; эскорти́ровать.

escutcheon *n.* щит герба́.

Eskimo *n.* эскимо́с. —*adj.* эскимо́сский.

esophagus also, **oesophagus** *n.* пищево́д.

esoteric *adj.* малодосту́пный; мудрёный; зау́мный.

espalier *n.* шпале́ра.

especial *adj.* осо́бенный; осо́бый.

especially *adv.* **1,** (to a particularly large degree) осо́бенно: *especially pleased,* осо́бенно рад. *What especially struck me,* что меня́ осо́бенно порази́ло. **2,** (specifically) специа́льно: *especially for you,* специа́льно для вас. *I came especially to...,* я пришёл (пришла́) специа́льно для того́, чтобы... **3,** (the more so) осо́бенно: *especially now/if/when,* осо́бенно тепе́рь/е́сли/когда́. *Especially since...,* тем бо́лее, что...

Esperanto *n.* эспера́нто.

espionage *n.* шпиона́ж. —*adj.* шпио́нский: *espionage activity,* шпио́нская де́ятельность.

esplanade *n.* эспла́на́да.

espouse *v.t.* **1,** (advocate; support) отста́ивать: *espouse*

a cause, отста́ивать де́ло. **2,** (profess, as an idea, principle, etc.) испове́довать.

espy *v.t.* рассмотре́ть; разгляде́ть.

esquire *n.* эсквайр.

essay *n.* о́черк. —*v.t.* **1,** (try out) про́бовать. **2,** (attempt) пыта́ться. —**essayist,** *n.* очерки́ст.

essence *n.* **1,** (fundamental nature; heart; crux) су́щность; существо́; суть. **2,** (extract) эссе́нция. —**in essence,** в су́щности; по существу́; по су́ти де́ла.

essential *adj.* **1,** (absolutely necessary) необходи́мый. *Essential condition,* необходи́мое *or* обяза́тельное *or* непреме́нное усло́вие. *Accuracy is essential,* здесь необходи́ма то́чность. *Water is essential to life,* вода́ необходи́ма для жи́зни. *It is essential that you be there,* необходи́мо, чтобы вы бы́ли там. **2,** (fundamental) суще́ственный: *an essential difference,* суще́ственная ра́зница. *Omit an essential detail,* пропуска́ть суще́ственную подро́бность. —*n., usu. pl.* **1,** (necessities) необходи́мое: *the basic essentials,* са́мое необходи́мое. **2,** (heart; crux) суть: *get down to the essentials,* добра́ться до су́ти де́ла. *Reduce to its essentials,* своди́ть (что-нибудь) к основно́му *or* к основны́м пу́нктам. **3,** (fundamentals) осно́вы; элеме́нты.

essentially *adv.* в су́щности; по существу́.

essential oil эфи́рное ма́сло.

establish *v.t.* **1,** (found) осно́вывать: *establish a museum/newspaper,* основа́ть музе́й/газе́ту. **2,** (bring about; set up) устана́вливать: *establish order/ relations/ a dictatorship/,* установи́ть поря́док/отноше́ния/диктату́ру. **3,** (ascertain; prove) устана́вливать: *establish a fact/ the cause of something/ one's innocence/,* установи́ть факт/ причи́ну чего́-нибудь/ свою́ невино́вность/. —**establish oneself,** устра́иваться.

establishment *n.* **1,** (act of establishing) установле́ние; основа́ние. **2,** (institution) учрежде́ние; заведе́ние. **3,** (influential or controlling group) исте́блишмент.

estate *n.* **1,** (piece of landed property) име́ние; поме́стье; уса́дьба. **2,** (possessions of a deceased person) иму́щество; состоя́ние. **3,** (social class in feudal times) сосло́вие.

esteem *v.t.* **1,** (respect) уважа́ть; цени́ть. **2,** (regard; deem) счита́ть. —*n.* уваже́ние; почёт. *Hold in high esteem,* высоко́ цени́ть. *Be held in high esteem,* по́льзоваться почётом.

esthete also **aesthete** *n.* эсте́т. —**esthetic,** *adj.* эстети́ческий. —**esthetics,** *n.* эсте́тика.

estimable *adj.* досто́йный уваже́ния; уважа́емый.

estimate *v.t.* оце́нивать; исчисля́ть. *Estimate the cost,* исчисля́ть сто́имость. *Damage is estimated at $10,000,* убы́тки оце́ниваются в де́сять ты́сяч до́лларов. *Estimated cost,* сме́тная сто́имость. *Estimated time of arrival,* расчётное вре́мя прибы́тия. —*n.* оце́нка; сме́та.

estimation *n.* мне́ние; сужде́ние. *Go up in someone's estimation,* повы́ситься *or* вы́играть в чьём-нибудь мне́нии; вы́расти в чьих-нибудь глаза́х. *Go down in someone's estimation,* теря́ть *or* проигра́ть в чьём-нибудь мне́нии; упа́сть в чьи́х-нибудь глаза́х.

Estonian *adj.* эсто́нский. —*n.* **1,** (person) эсто́нец; эсто́нка. **2,** (language) эсто́нский язы́к.

estrange *v.t.* отдаля́ть; отчужда́ть; разобща́ть. *He is estranged from his wife,* он разошёлся с жено́й.

estrangement *n.* отдале́ние; отчужде́ние; разобщённость.

estrogen *also,* **oestrogen** *n.* эстроге́н.

estuary *n.* лима́н.

et cetera и так да́лее; и тому́ подо́бное.

etch *v.t.* гравирова́ть; трави́ть. *Etched design,* тра́вленый узо́р. *Be etched in one's memory,* вре́заться в па́мять; запечатле́ться в па́мяти.

etcher *n.* гравёр.

etching *n.* **1,** (process) гравирова́ние; травле́ние. **2,** (figure so made) гравю́ра; офо́рт.

eternal *adj.* ве́чный: *eternal friendship,* ве́чная дру́жба.

eternally *adv.* ве́чно. *I am eternally grateful to you,* я бу́ду вам ве́чно благода́рен (благода́рна).

eternity *n.* ве́чность. *Seem like an eternity,* каза́ться ве́чностью. —**for all eternity,** на ве́чные времена́; наве́чно.

ether *n.* эфи́р. —**ethereal,** *adj.* эфи́рный.

ethical *adj.* эти́ческий; эти́чный.

ethics *n.pl.* э́тика.

Ethiopian *adj.* эфио́пский. —*n.* эфио́п; эфио́пка.

ethnic *adj.* этни́ческий.

ethnography *n.* этногра́фия. —**ethnographer,** *n.* этно́граф. —**ethnographic,** *adj.* этнографи́ческий.

ethnology *n.* этноло́гия. —**ethnological,** *adj.* этнологи́ческий. —**ethnologist,** *n.* этно́лог.

ethyl *n.* эти́л. —*adj.* эти́ловый. —**ethyl alcohol,** эти́ловый *or* ви́нный спирт.

ethylene *n.* этиле́н.

etiquette *n.* этике́т.

Etruscan *adj.* этру́сский.

étude *n.* этю́д.

etymology *n.* этимоло́гия. —**etymological,** *adj.* этимологи́ческий. —**etymologist,** *n.* этимо́лог.

eucalyptus *n.* эвкали́пт. —*adj.* эвкали́птовый.

Eucharist *n.* прича́стие; евхари́стия.

Euclidean *adj.* эвкли́дов: *Euclidean geometry,* эвкли́дова геоме́трия.

eugenics *n.* евге́ника. —**eugenic,** *adj.* евгени́ческий.

eulogize *v.t.* восхваля́ть. —**eulogy,** *n.* надгро́бная речь; надгро́бное сло́во; панеги́рик.

eunuch *n.* е́внух.

euphemism *n.* эвфеми́зм. —**euphemistic,** *adj.* эвфемисти́ческий. —**euphemistically,** *adv.* для прили́чия: *euphemistically called...,* для прили́чия называ́емый...

euphonic *adj.* благозву́чный.

euphonious *adj.* благозву́чный. —**euphoniousness,** *n.* благозву́чность.

euphony *n.* благозву́чие.

euphoria *n.* эйфори́я.

Eurasian *adj.* евразийский.

eureka *interj.* э́врика!

European *adj.* европе́йский. —*n.* европе́ец. *The Europeans,* европе́йцы.

europium *n.* евро́пий.

Eustachian tube евста́хиева труба́.

evacuate *v.t.* **1,** (remove during an emergency) эвакуи́ровать. **2,** (vacate) освобожда́ть. **3,** (excrete) выделя́ть. —**evacuation,** *n.* эвакуа́ция. —**evacuee,** *n.* эвакуи́рованный.

evade *v.t.* уклоня́ться от; избега́ть; ускольза́ть от. *Evade responsibility,* уклоня́ться *or* уходи́ть от отве́тственности. *Evade taxes,* уклоня́ться от упла́ты нало́гов. *Evade a question,* уклоня́ться от отве́та.

evaluate *v.t.* оце́нивать. —**evaluation,** *n.* оце́нка.

evanescent *adj.* мимолётный; мину́тный.

evangelical *adj.* евангели́ческий.

evangelist *n.* **1,** *cap., Bib.* евангели́ст. **2,** (preacher) пропове́дник.

evaporate *v.t.* испаря́ть. —*v.i.* испаря́ться; улету́чиваться. —**evaporated milk,** сгущённое молоко́.

evaporation *n.* испаре́ние.

evasion *n.* **1,** (avoidance) уклоне́ние: *tax evasion,* уклоне́ние от упла́ты нало́гов. *Evasion of military service,* уклоне́ние от вое́нной слу́жбы. **2,** (subterfuge) уло́вка; увёртка.

evasive *adj.* укло́нчивый. —**evasiveness,** *n.* укло́нчивость.

eve *n.* кану́н. *On the eve of,* в кану́н (+ *gen.*); накану́не (+ *gen.*). —**Christmas Eve,** соче́льник. —**New Year's Eve,** кану́н Но́вого го́да.

even *adj.* **1,** (level) ро́вный: *even ground,* ро́вная земля́. **2,** *fol. by* with (on a level with) вро́вень с. *Draw even with,* поравня́ться с. **3,** (regular; constant) ро́вный; равноме́рный: *an even tempo,* ро́вный/равноме́рный темп. **4,** (calm; tranquil) ро́вный; уравнове́шенный. *Even disposition,* ро́вный хара́ктер. **5,** (divisible by two) чётный: *even number,* чётное число́. **6,** (exact) *rendered by* ро́вно: *an even dozen,* ро́вно дю́жина. **7,** (having settled debts, scores, etc.) кви́ты; в расчёте: *Now we are even,* тепе́рь мы с ва́ми кви́ты/ в расчёте/. —*adv.* да́же: *even in winter,* да́же зимо́й. *What is even worse...,* что ещё ху́же... —*v.t.* **1,** (smooth; level) выра́внивать; ровня́ть. **2,** (equalize) равня́ть. *Even the score,* сравня́ть счёт. —*v.i.* [*usu.* **even out**] выра́вниваться. —**break even,** оста́ться при свои́х. —**even if,** да́же е́сли; хотя́ бы. —**even so,** всё равно́; хоть бы и так. —**even though,** хотя́ (и); несмотря́ на то, что. *Even though there are many others,* хотя́ и существу́ют мно́гие други́е. *Even though I didn't want to,* несмотря́ на то, я не хоте́л(а). —**get even with,** распла́чиваться с; рассчи́тываться с; расквита́ться с.

even-handed *adj.* беспристра́стный.

evening *n.* ве́чер. *In the evening,* ве́чером. *This evening,* сего́дня ве́чером. *Good evening!,* до́брый ве́чер! *He works evenings,* он рабо́тает по вечера́м. —*adj.* вече́рний: *evening dress,* вече́рнее пла́тье.

evenly *adv.* ро́вно; равноме́рно. *Divide evenly,* дели́ть по́ровну. *Evenly divided,* равноме́рно разделён. *Evenly matched teams,* равноси́льные кома́нды.

evenness *n.* ро́вность.

event *n.* **1,** (occurrence) собы́тие. **2,** (item on a sports program) но́мер. —**in any event,** во вся́ком слу́чае. —**in the event of,** в слу́чае (+ *gen.*). —**in the event that,** в том слу́чае, е́сли...

even-tempered *adj.* с ро́вным хара́ктером; уравнове́шенный.

eventful *adj.* по́лный собы́тий.

eventual *adj.* коне́чный: *eventual outcome,* коне́чный исхо́д.

eventuality *n.* (возмо́жный) слу́чай; случа́йность.

eventually *adv.* в конце́ концо́в.

eventuate *v.i.* **1,** *fol. by* **in** (result in) ко́нчиться (+ *instr.*). **2,** (develop; happen) получи́ться; случи́ться.

ever *adv.* **1,** (at any time) когда́-нибудь; когда́-либо. *Have you ever been there?,* вы когда́-нибудь быва́ли там? *The best film I ever saw,* са́мый лу́чший фильм, кото́рый я когда́-либо ви́дел. *More than ever before,* бо́льше, чем когда́-либо ра́ньше. ♦*In neg. constructions,* никогда́: *No one has ever been there,* никто́ никогда́ не́ был там. **2,** (at all times) всегда́: *ever ready,* всегда́ гото́в. *The ever increasing importance of...,* всё возраста́ющая ва́жность (+ *gen.*). —*particle: Thank you ever so much!,* большо́е вам спаси́бо! *What ever do you mean by that?,* что же, со́бственно, вы хоти́те э́тим сказа́ть? —**ever since,** с тех пор (как). —**hardly ever,** почти́ никогда́.

evergreen *adj.* вечнозелёный. —*n.* вечнозелёное расте́ние.

everlasting *adj.* ве́чный.

evermore *adv.,* **in for evermore,** навсегда́; наве́чно.

ever-present *adj.* безотлу́чный.

every *adj.* **1,** (each) ка́ждый: *every day,* ка́ждый день; *in every case,* в ка́ждом слу́чае. *Every country we visited,* в каку́ю бы страну́ мы ни прие́хали. **2,** (all possible) все: *try every remedy,* про́бовать все сре́дства. *Have every reason to suppose,* име́ть все основа́ния предполага́ть. *I wish you every success,* жела́ю вам вся́ческих успе́хов. **3,** (each sequentially) ка́ждый: *every three hours,* ка́ждые три часа́; *every few minutes,* ка́ждые не́сколько мину́т. —**every now and then; every once in a while; every so often,** вре́мя от вре́мени. —**every one,** все без исключе́ния. —**every other,** че́рез; ка́ждый второ́й; ка́ждые два. *Every other day,* че́рез день. —**every time,** вся́кий раз: *every time he speaks,* вся́кий раз, когда́ он говори́т. —**every which way,** *colloq.* врассыпну́ю; вразбро́с. —**in every way, 1,** (in every respect) во всех отноше́ниях. **2,** (using every method) вся́чески.

everybody *pron.* все: *Everybody is present,* все налицо́.

everyday *adj.* повседне́вный; жите́йский; бу́дничный. *Everyday occurrence,* обы́чное явле́ние. *Items of everyday use,* предме́ты повседне́вного спро́са.

everyone *pron.* **1,** (all people) все: *This applies to everyone,* э́то отно́сится ко всем. **2,** (each person) ка́ждый: *Everyone is free to...,* ка́ждый во́лен (+ *inf.*).

everything *pron.* всё: *Everything is all right,* всё в

поря́дке. *There is a time for everything,* всему́ своё вре́мя.

everywhere *adv.* везде́; всю́ду; повсю́ду. *Everywhere we went,* всю́ду, куда́ мы приезжа́ли. *From everywhere,* отовсю́ду.

evict *v.t.* выселя́ть. —**eviction,** *n.* выселе́ние.

evidence *n.* **1,** (something that tends to prove) доказа́тельство; свиде́тельство. *To cite as evidence,* приводи́ть (что́-нибудь) в доказа́тельство. *There is little evidence to support this theory,* в по́льзу э́той тео́рии име́ется ма́ло доказа́тельств. **2,** (testimony) показа́ния; свиде́тельство. *Give evidence,* дава́ть показа́ния; свиде́тельствовать. **3,** (incriminating information)ули́ки: *circumstantial evidence,* ко́свенные ули́ки. *There is no evidence against him,* про́тив него́ нет никаки́х ули́к. —*v.t.* **1,** (indicate) свиде́тельствовать о. **2,** (evince) проявля́ть. —**in evidence,** заме́тный; на виду́.

evident *adj.* очеви́дный. *It is evident that...,* очеви́дно, что... —**evidently,** *adv.* очеви́дно; по-ви́димому.

evil *n.* зло: *good and evil,* добро́ и зло. *A necessary evil,* необходи́мое зло. *Choose the lesser of two evils,* из двух зол выбира́ть ме́ньшее. —*adj.* злой; дурно́й: *evil spirit,* злой дух; *evil thoughts,* дурны́е мы́сли.

evildoer *n.* злоде́й.

evil eye дурно́й глаз.

evince *v.t.* проявля́ть; выка́зывать.

eviscerate *v.t.* потроши́ть.

evoke *v.t.* вызыва́ть: *evoke sympathy,* вызыва́ть сочу́вствие.

evolution *n.* эволю́ция. —**evolutionary,** *adj.* эволюцио́нный.

evolve *v.t.* развива́ть; разраба́тывать. —*v.i.* развива́ться; эволюциони́ровать.

ewe *n.* овца́.

ex- *prefix* бы́вший: *ex-president,* бы́вший президе́нт.

exacerbate *v.t.* обостря́ть. —**exacerbation,** *n.* обостре́ние.

exact *adj.* то́чный: *exact copy,* то́чная ко́пия; *exact meaning,* то́чный смысл. —*v.t.* взы́скивать. *Exact payment,* взима́ть пла́ту. *Exact tribute,* налага́ть дань. —**exact sciences,** то́чные нау́ки.

exacting *adj.* тре́бовательный; взыска́тельный.

exactitude *n.* то́чность.

exactly *adv.* **1,** (in an exact manner) то́чно. **2,** (precisely) ро́вно: *five dollars exactly,* ро́вно пять до́лларов. **3,** (just) как раз: *exactly what I need,* как раз то, что мне ну́жно. **4,** (specifically) и́менно: *Where exactly does he live?,* где и́менно он живёт? **5,** (quite so) вот и́менно; соверше́нно ве́рно. —**not exactly,** не совсе́м; (э́то) не совсе́м так.

exactness *n.* то́чность.

exaggerate *v.t. & i.* преувели́чивать. —**exaggeration,** *n.* преувеличе́ние.

exalt *v.t.* **1,** (raise in status) возвыша́ть. **2,** (glorify) возвели́чивать. **3,** (extol) восхваля́ть.

exaltation *n.* восто́рг; упое́ние; экзальта́ция.

exalted *adj.* высо́кий; возвы́шенный.

exam *n.* экза́мен.

examination *n.* **1,** (scrutiny) осмо́тр; рассмотре́ние. *Physical examination,* медици́нский осмо́тр; медици́нское освиде́тельствование. **2,** (test of knowledge) экза́мен. —**examination paper,** экзаменацио́нная рабо́та.

examine *v.t.* **1,** *med.* осма́тривать; обсле́довать (больно́го). *You should have your eyes examined,* вы должны́ прове́рить ва́ши глаза́. **2,** (scrutinize) рассма́тривать; осма́тривать. *Examine a painting,* рассма́тривать карти́ну. *Examine baggage,* осма́тривать бага́ж. **3,** (study, as a proposal or issue) рассма́тривать. **4,** (question, as a witness) допра́шивать. **5,** (give a test to) экзаменова́ть.

examiner *n.* **1,** (inspector) контролёр. **2,** (one who gives an examination) экзамена́тор.

example *n.* приме́р. —**for example,** наприме́р.

exasperate *v.t.* выводи́ть из себя́; изводи́ть. —**exasperating,** *adj.* доса́дный. —**exasperation,** *n.* доса́да; раздраже́ние.

excavate *v.t.* раска́пывать. —**excavation,** *n.* раско́пка; *pl.* раско́пки.

exceed *v.t.* **1,** (be more than; go beyond) превыша́ть: *exceed ten dollars,* превыша́ть де́сять до́лларов; *exceed the speed limit,* превыша́ть дозво́ленную ско́рость. **2,** (surpass) превосходи́ть: *exceed all expectations,* превосходи́ть все ожида́ния.

exceedingly *adv.* чрезвыча́йно.

excel *v.t.* превосходи́ть; опережа́ть. —*v.i.* отлича́ться. *He excels at sports/mathematics,* он отли́чный спортсме́н; он силён в матема́тике.

excellence *n.* отли́чное ка́чество. *For excellence in studies,* за отли́чную учёбу.

Excellency *n.* превосходи́тельство: *Your Excellency,* ва́ше превосходи́тельство.

excellent *adj.* отли́чный; прекра́сный; превосхо́дный. —**excellently,** *adv.* отли́чно.

excelsior *n.* стру́жка.

except *prep.* кро́ме; за исключе́нием (+ *gen.*). *Every day except Sunday,* ка́ждый день, кро́ме воскресе́нья. —*conj.* кро́ме как; ра́зве то́лько: *except in the summertime,* кро́ме как (*or* ра́зве то́лько) в ле́тнее вре́мя. —*v.t.* исключа́ть. *Present company excepted,* исключа́я прису́тствующих. —**except for,** за исключе́нием (+ *gen.*); е́сли не счита́ть.

excepting *prep.* исключа́я; за исключе́нием (+ *gen.*).

exception *n.* исключе́ние. *Exception to the rule,* исключе́ние из пра́вила. *With the exception of,* за исключе́нием (+ *gen.*). *Make an exception in your case,* де́лать исключе́ние для вас. —**take exception (to),** возража́ть (про́тив).

exceptional *adj.* исключи́тельный. —**exceptionally,** *adv.* исключи́тельно.

excerpt *n.* вы́держка; отры́вок; вы́писка; извлече́ние. —*v.t.* выпи́сывать; выбира́ть (отры́вки).

excess *n.* **1,** (surplus) изли́шек; избы́ток. **2,** *usu. pl.* (instances of immoderation) изли́шества; переги́бы; эксце́ссы. —*adj.* ли́шний: *excess weight,* ли́шний вес. *Excess profits,* сверхпри́быль. *Pay for excess baggage,* доплати́ть за ли́шний вес. —**in excess of,** сверх (+ *gen.*); свы́ше (+ *gen.*).

—**to excess,** до изли́шества. *Drink to excess,* перепива́ть.

excessive *adj.* чрезме́рный; непоме́рный; изли́шний. —**excessively,** *adv.* чрезме́рно.

exchange *v.t.* **1,** (trade for another) меня́ть; обме́нивать: *exchange one book for another,* меня́ть/обме́нивать одну́ кни́гу на другу́ю. **2,** (interchange) меня́ться; обме́ниваться (+ *instr.*): *exchange gifts,* меня́ться/обме́ниваться пода́рками. *Exchange pawns* (*in chess*), разме́ниваться пе́шками. *Exchange glances,* перегля́дываться. **3,** (change, as money) разме́нивать. *Exchange francs for marks,* меня́ть фра́нки на ма́рки. —*n.* **1,** (swap) обме́н: *exchange of currency,* обме́н валю́ты; *exchange of views,* обме́н мне́ниями *or* взгля́дами. *In exchange for,* в обме́н на. *Receive in exchange,* получи́ть взаме́н. **2,** *chess* разме́н. **3,** (central place for brokers, merchants, etc.) би́ржа: *stock/grain/commodity exchange,* фо́ндовая/хле́бная/това́рная би́ржа. **4,** *finance* валю́та: *foreign exchange,* иностра́нная валю́та. *Bill of exchange,* ве́ксель. *Rate of exchange,* курс валю́ты; валю́тный курс; обме́нный курс.

exchequer *n.* казначе́йство; казна́.

excise *n.* [*also,* **excise tax**] акци́з. —*v.t.* **1,** *med.* выреза́ть; иссека́ть. **2,** (delete) исключа́ть; вычёркивать. —**excision,** *n., med.* иссече́ние.

excitable *adj.* возбуди́мый. —**excitability,** *n.* возбуди́мость.

excitation *n.* возбужде́ние.

excite *v.t.* **1,** (rouse; stir up) возбужда́ть; волнова́ть. **2,** (evoke) возбужда́ть; вызыва́ть.

excited *adj.* возбуждённый; взволно́ванный. *Get excited,* волнова́ться.

excitement *n.* возбужде́ние; волне́ние.

exciting *adj.* волну́ющий; захва́тывающий.

exclaim *v.t. & i.* восклица́ть.

exclamation *n.* восклица́ние. —**exclamation point,** восклица́тельный знак.

exclamatory *adj.* восклица́тельный.

exclude *v.t.* исключа́ть. —**excluding,** *prep.* исключа́я. —**exclusion,** *n.* исключе́ние.

exclusive *adj.* **1,** (sole) исключи́тельный: *exclusive right,* исключи́тельное пра́во. **2,** (admitting only a select group) для и́збранных. *Exclusive circle,* за́мкнутый круг. **3,** (unrelated; separate): *be mutually exclusive,* взаи́мно исключа́ть друг дру́га. —**exclusive of,** не счита́я; исключа́я.

exclusively *adv.* исключи́тельно.

exclusivity *n.* исключи́тельность.

excommunicate *v.t.* отлуча́ть от це́ркви. —**excommunication,** *n.* отлуче́ние (от це́ркви).

excoriate *v.t.* бичева́ть; разноси́ть.

excrement *n.* испражне́ния; кал.

excrescence *n.* наро́ст; (*on trees*) наплы́в.

excrete *v.t.* выделя́ть. —**excretion,** *n.* выделе́ние. —**excretory,** *adj.* выдели́тельный; выводно́й.

excruciating *adj.* мучи́тельный.

exculpate *v.t.* опра́вдывать.

excursion *n.* экску́рсия. *Go on an excursion,* е́хать на экску́рсию. *Take on an excursion,* везти́ (кого́-нибудь) на экску́рсию. —*adj.* экскурси́онный.

excusable *adj.* прости́тельный; извини́тельный.

excuse *v.t.* **1,** (forgive; pardon) извиня́ть; проща́ть. *Excuse me!*, извини́те!; прости́те! *Excuse the interruption!*, извини́те/прости́те за беспоко́йство! **2,** (justify; make all right) опра́вдывать. **3,** (release; let off) отпуска́ть; освобожда́ть: *excuse from classes*, отпуска́ть с заня́тий; освобожда́ть от заня́тий. *He asked to be excused from the meeting*, он проси́л отпусти́ть его́ с собра́ния. —*n.* **1,** (pretext) отгово́рка; предло́г. *Stop making excuses!*, прекрати́ иска́ть отгово́рки! **2,** (valid reason) извине́ние; оправда́ние. *That's no excuse!*, э́то не оправда́ние/извине́ние. —**excuse oneself**, извиня́ться; проси́ть проще́ния.

execrable *adj.* отврати́тельный; гну́сный.

execrate *v.t.* **1,** (denounce) проклина́ть. **2,** (detest) ненави́деть.

execute *v.t.* **1,** (carry out; perform) выполня́ть; исполня́ть: *execute an order*, вы́полнить/испо́лнить прика́з. **2,** (put to death) казни́ть. *Execute by a firing squad*, расстре́ливать.

execution *n.* **1,** (carrying out; performance) выполне́ние; исполне́ние. **2,** (putting to death) казнь. *Execution by a firing squad*, расстре́л.

executioner *n.* пала́ч.

executive *adj.* **1,** (exercising authority) исполни́тельный: *executive committee*, исполни́тельный комите́т. **2,** (of an executive!), администрати́вный: *executive duties*, администрати́вные обя́занности. —*n.* руководя́щий рабо́тник.

executor *n.* душеприка́зчик.

exemplary *adj.* приме́рный; образцо́вый.

exemplify *v.t.* служи́ть приме́ром (+ *gen.*).

exempt *v.t.* освобожда́ть. —*adj.* [*usu.* **exempt from**] освобождённый (от); не подлежа́щий (+ *dat.*).

exemption *n.* **1,** (act of exempting) освобожде́ние. **2,** (tax deduction) льго́та (по нало́гу).

exercise *n.* **1,** (physical activity) физи́ческие упражне́ния; заря́дка. *Do one's exercises*, де́лать заря́дку. *You should get more exercise*, вам ну́жно бо́льше физи́ческих упражне́ний. **2,** (that which develops proficiency) упражне́ние: *exercises for the piano*, упражне́ния для фортепья́но. **3,** (performance, as of duties) исполне́ние; отправле́ние. **4,** (act of using or exerting) осуществле́ние; примене́ние; проявле́ние. **5,** *pl.* (ceremonies) торжества́. *Graduation exercises*, выпускно́й акт. **6,** *mil.* уче́ние. —*v.t.* **1,** (train) упражня́ть: *exercise one's muscles*, упражня́ть мы́шцы. **2,** (use; put into play) осуществля́ть: *exercise leadership/control/authority*, осуществля́ть руково́дство/контро́ль/полномо́чия. *Exercise a right*, осуществля́ть пра́во; (вос)по́льзоваться пра́вом. **3,** (execute; discharge, as duties) исполня́ть; выполня́ть. **4,** (display; observe, as caution) проявля́ть; соблюда́ть. **5,** (exert, as influence) ока́зывать. **6,** (worry; upset) расстра́ивать. —*v.i.* де́лать заря́дку. —**exercise book**, тетра́дь.

exert *v.t.* **1,** (strain) напряга́ть. *Exert oneself*, напряга́ться. *Exert every effort*, прилага́ть все уси́лия;

напряга́ть все си́лы. **2,** (exercise; bring to bear) ока́зывать: *exert pressure*, ока́зывать давле́ние.

exertion *n.* напряже́ние; напряже́ние сил.

exhale *v.t. & i.* выдыха́ть. —**exhalation,** *n.* вы́дох; выдыха́ние.

exhaust *v.t.* **1,** (tire out) изнуря́ть; истоща́ть. **2,** (use up; deplete) исче́рпывать; истоща́ть: *exhaust supplies*, исче́рпывать/истоща́ть запа́сы. *Exhaust a mine*, истоща́ть *or* вы́работать рудни́к. *My patience is exhausted*, моё терпе́ние ко́нчилось *or* ло́пнуло. **3,** (deal with completely) исче́рпывать: *exhaust a subject*, исче́рпывать те́му. *Exhaust every possibility*, исче́рпывать все возмо́жности. —*n., mech.* вы́хлоп. —*adj.* выхлопно́й; вытяжно́й: *exhaust pipe*, выхлопна́я труба́; *exhaust fan*, вытяжно́й вентиля́тор.

exhausted *adj.* **1,** (tired out) изнурённый; изму́ченный. *Be exhausted*, заму́читься; вы́биться из сил; быть без ног. **2,** (depleted) исче́рпанный; истощённый.

exhausting *adj.* утоми́тельный; изнури́тельный.

exhaustion *n.* **1,** (extreme fatigue) изнуре́ние; истоще́ние; изнеможе́ние. *In a state of exhaustion*, в по́лном изнеможе́нии. **2,** (depletion) истоще́ние.

exhaustive *adj.* исче́рпывающий.

exhibit *v.t.* **1,** (put on show) выставля́ть; экспони́ровать. **2,** (manifest; give evidence of) проявля́ть. —*n.* экспона́т.

exhibition *n.* **1,** (public display) вы́ставка: *exhibition of paintings*, вы́ставка карти́н. **2,** (display; manifestation) проявле́ние. —**exhibition hall,** вы́ставочный зал.

exhibitor *n.* экспоне́нт.

exhilarate *v.t.* развесели́ть; оживля́ть. —**exhilaration,** *n.* весёлость; припо́днятое настрое́ние.

exhort *v.t.* призыва́ть; увещева́ть. —**exhortation,** *n.* увеща́ние.

exhume *v.t.* выка́пывать; вырыва́ть; эксгуми́ровать. —**exhumation,** *n.* эксгума́ция.

exigency *n.* **1,** (urgency) неотло́жность. **2,** (urgent situation) (кра́йний) слу́чай. **3,** *pl.* (requirements) потре́бности.

exile *n.* **1,** (banishment) изгна́ние; ссы́лка. *Live in exile*, жить в изгна́нии *or* в ссы́лке. **2,** (one who is exiled) изгна́нник; ссы́льный. —*v.t.* изгоня́ть; ссыла́ть. *He was exiled to Siberia*, он был со́слан в Сиби́рь.

exist *v.i.* существова́ть. *Cease to exist*, переста́ть существова́ть; прекрати́ть своё существова́ние. *Exist without water*, существова́ть без воды́. *Various theories exist*, существу́ют ра́зные тео́рии. *As if they never existed*, как бу́дто их никогда́ не́ было.

existence *n.* существова́ние. *Be in existence*, существова́ть. *Come into existence*, возника́ть; появля́ться. *Go out of existence*, переста́ть существова́ть. *The best plane in existence*, са́мый лу́чший самолёт из всех существу́ющих. *Lead a miserable existence*, влачи́ть жа́лкое существова́ние.

existent *adj.* существу́ющий.

existential *adj.* экзистенциа́льный. —**existentialism,**

n. экзистенциали́зм. —**existentialist,** *adj.* экзистен-циа́льный. —*n.* экзистенциали́ст.

exit *n.* вы́ход: *rush for the exits,* бро́ситься к вы́ходам. —*v.i.* **1,** (go out) выходи́ть. **2,** (stage direction) «он/она́ ухо́дит». —**exit visa,** выездна́я ви́за.

exodus *n.* **1,** (outpouring of people) (ма́ссовый) ухо́д *or* отъе́зд. **2,** *cap., Bib.* исхо́д; (*book*) Исхо́д.

exonerate *v.t.* опра́вдывать. —**exoneration,** *n.* оправда́ние.

exophthalmic goiter базе́дова боле́знь.

exorbitant *adj.* непоме́рный.

exorcise *also,* **exorcize** *v.t.* изгоня́ть (злых ду́хов). —**exorcism,** *n.* изгна́ние злых ду́хов.

exotic *adj.* экзоти́ческий.

expand *v.t.* **1,** (increase the scope of) расширя́ть: *expand trade,* расширя́ть торго́влю. **2,** (enlarge, as a book) дополня́ть: *expanded edition,* допо́лненное изда́ние. **3,** *math.* разлага́ть. —*v.i.* **1,** (become larger) расширя́ться. **2,** *fol. by* **on** (discuss more fully) распространя́ться на (те́му).

expandable *adj.* раздвижно́й.

expanse *n.* простра́нство; просто́р; ширь. *Huge expanse of territory,* огро́мное простра́нство терри-то́рии.

expansion *n.* **1,** (enlargement) расшире́ние. **2,** (extension of one's territory) экспа́нсия.

expansionism *n.* экспансиони́зм. —**expansionist,** *adj.* экспансиони́стский; захва́тнический.

expansive *adj.* экспанси́вный.

expatiate *v.i.* распространя́ться (о).

expatriate *n.* экспатриа́нт. —*v.t.* экспатрии́ровать. —**expatriation,** *n.* экспатриа́ция.

expect *v.t.* **1,** (anticipate) ожида́ть; ждать: *be expecting company,* ожида́ть *or* ждать госте́й. *It was to be expected,* э́того сле́довало ожида́ть. *I did not expect to meet you here,* я вас не ожида́л(а) *or* предполага́л(а) встре́тить здесь. *The patient is expected to live,* ожида́ют, что больно́й вы́живет. *I expect you to be there,* я наде́юсь, что вы бу́дете там. **2,** *fol. by inf.* (plan; intend) ду́мать; предполага́ть; рассчи́тывать: *When do you expect to arrive?,* когда́ вы ду́маете/предполага́ете/рассчи́тываете прие́хать? **3,** (consider due or obligated) тре́бовать: *expect too much of,* тре́бовать сли́шком мно́го от. —**be expecting,** ждать *or* ожида́ть ребёнка; быть в положе́нии.

expectancy *n.* выжида́ние; предвкуше́ние. —**life expectancy,** продолжи́тельность жи́зни.

expectant *adj.* ожида́ющий. *Expectant mother,* бере́менная же́нщина. —**expectantly,** *adv.* с выжида́-нием.

expectation *n.* ожида́ние: *contrary to all expectations,* вопреки́ всем ожида́ниям.

expectorate *v.i.* **1,** (cough up phlegm) отха́ркивать. **2,** (spit) ха́ркать. —*v.t.* отха́ркивать.

expedient *adj.* целесообра́зный; вы́годный. —**expediency,** *n.* целесообра́зность.

expedite *v.t.* **1,** (speed up) ускоря́ть. *Expedite a matter,* продви́нуть де́ло. **2,** (do quickly) (бы́стро) выпол-ня́ть. —**expediter,** *n.* толка́ч.

expedition *n.* экспеди́ция. —**expeditionary,** *adj.* экспедицио́нный.

expeditious *adj.* бы́стрый; операти́вный.

expel *v.t.* **1,** (discharge; eject) выбра́сывать; извер-га́ть. *Expel air from the lungs,* выпуска́ть во́здух из лёгких. **2,** (dismiss) исключа́ть; выгоня́ть: *expel from school,* исключа́ть/выгоня́ть из шко́лы.

expend *v.t.* тра́тить; затра́чивать; расхо́довать.

expendable *adj.* ли́шний.

expenditure *n.* **1,** (act of expending) затра́та; расхо́дование. **2,** (that which is expended) тра́та; за-тра́та; расхо́д. *Military expenditures,* вое́нные расхо́ды.

expense *n.* **1,** (financial outlay) расхо́д. *Go to expense,* тра́тить де́ньги; тра́титься. *Go to great expense,* идти́ на больши́е расхо́ды. *Put to expense,* вводи́ть в расхо́д. *At one's own expense,* на свои́ сре́дства; на *or* за свой счёт. **2,** *pl.* (costs) расхо́ды; изде́ржки; затра́ты. —**at the expense of,** за *or* на счёт (+ *gen.*). *At government expense,* на казённый счёт. *Jokes at my expense,* шу́тки на мой счёт *or* по моему́ а́дресу.

expensive *adj.* дорого́й: *expensive coat/ring/wine,* дорого́е пальто́/кольцо́/вино́.

experience *n.* **1,** (accumulated knowledge) о́пыт: *practical experience,* практи́ческий о́пыт. *From personal experience,* на своём ли́чном о́пыте. *From one's own experience,* на со́бственном о́пыте; по со́бствен-ному о́пыту. *From bitter experience,* на го́рьком о́пыте; по го́рькому о́пыту. *Learn from the experience of others,* учи́ться на о́пыте други́х. **2,** (something experienced) слу́чай: *a funny experience,* заба́вный слу́чай. *It was a new experience for me,* мне э́то бы́ло в нови́нку. —*v.t.* испы́тывать; пережива́ть. *Experience difficulties,* испы́тывать тру́дности.

experienced *adj.* о́пытный.

experiment *n.* о́пыт; экспериме́нт. —*v.i.* произ-води́ть о́пыты; эксперименти́ровать.

experimental *adj.* эксперимента́льный; о́пытный. *On an experimental basis,* на осно́ве экспериме́нта; на эксперимента́льной ба́зе.

experimentation *n.* эксперименти́рование.

expert *n.* экспе́рт; специали́ст; знато́к. —*adj.* иску́с-ный; о́пытный: *an expert mechanic,* иску́сный/о́пыт-ный меха́ник. *Expert advice,* экспер́тный сове́т.

expertise *n.* специа́льные зна́ния.

expiate *v.t.* искупа́ть. —**expiation,** *n.* искупле́ние. —**expiatory,** *adj.* искупи́тельный.

expiration *n.* **1,** (ending) истече́ние. *Expiration date,* да́та истече́ния сро́ка де́йствия. **2,** (exhalation) вы-дыха́ние.

expire *v.i.* **1,** (elapse, as of a time period) истека́ть. **2,** (become invalid) теря́ть си́лу. *Your passport has expired,* срок де́йствия ва́шего па́спорта истёк; у вас просро́чен(ный) па́спорт. **3,** (exhale) выдыха́ть. **4,** (breathe one's last) испусти́ть дух.

explain *v.t.* объясня́ть: *explain the rules to someone,* объясня́ть пра́вила кому́-нибудь. —**explain away,** опра́вдывать. —**explain oneself,** объясня́ть своё поведе́ние.

explainable *adj.* объясни́мый.

explanation *n.* объясне́ние: *an explanation for such behavior*, объясне́ние тако́го поведе́ния. *An act like that defies explanation*, тако́й посту́пок не объясни́шь (*or* нельзя́ объясни́ть).

explanatory *adj.* объясни́тельный; разъясни́тельный; поясни́тельный. —**explanatory note**, примеча́ние.

expletive *n.* бра́нное сло́во; руга́тельство.

explicable *adj.* объясни́мый.

explicit *adj.* я́сный; то́чный; определённый. —**explicitly**, *adv.* я́сно; определённо.

explode *v.i.* взрыва́ться. —*v.t.* **1,** (set off) взрыва́ть. **2,** *fig.* (refute, as a theory) разбива́ть; уничтожа́ть; опроверга́ть. *Explode a myth*, разве́ять миф.

exploit *v.t.* эксплуати́ровать: *exploit resources/workers*, эксплуати́ровать ресу́рсы/рабо́чих. *Exploit an advantage/opportunity*, воспо́льзоваться преиму́ществом/возмо́жностью. —*n.* по́двиг. —**exploitation**, *n.* эксплуата́ция. —**exploiter**, *n.* эксплуата́тор.

exploration *n.* **1,** (traveling and studying) иссле́дование. **2,** (prospecting) разве́дка: *exploration for oil*, разве́дка не́фти; нефтеразве́дка.

exploratory *adj.* **1,** (involving research or exploration) иссле́довательский. **2,** *geol.* разве́дочный. **3,** *med.* про́бный: *exploratory operation*, про́бная опера́ция. **4,** *fig.* (sounding out the possibilities) зонди́рующий.

explore *v.t.* **1,** (travel into and study) иссле́довать: *explore the Amazon basin*, иссле́довать бассе́йн Амазо́нки. **2,** (look into; investigate) изуча́ть; иссле́довать; рассма́тривать. *Explore a question*, изуча́ть вопро́с. *Explore the possibilities*, иссле́довать возмо́жности. —*v.i.* [*usu.* **explore for**] разве́дывать.

explorer *n.* иссле́дователь.

explosion *n.* взрыв. —**population explosion**, демографи́ческий взрыв.

explosive *adj.* **1,** (liable to explode) взры́вчатый; взрывно́й. *Explosive device*, взрывно́е устро́йство. *Explosive bullet*, разрывна́я пу́ля. **2,** *fig.* (highly volatile) взрывоопа́сный: *explosive situation*, взрывоопа́сное положе́ние. —*n.* взры́вчатое вещество́; *pl.* взрывча́тка.

exponent *n.* **1,** (advocate) сторо́нник; пропове́дник. **2,** *math.* показа́тель; экспоне́нт. —**exponential**, *adj.* экспоненциа́льный.

export *v.t.* вывози́ть; экспорти́ровать. —*n., often pl.* вы́воз; э́кспорт. —*adj.* вывозно́й; э́кспортный. *Export license*, лице́нзия на э́кспорт.

exportation *n.* вы́воз.

exporter *n.* экспортёр.

expose *v.t.* **1,** (bare) раскрыва́ть. **2,** (leave unprotected) подставля́ть: *expose one's face to the sun*, подставля́ть лицо́ со́лнцу. *Expose one's flank to the enemy*, подставля́ть свой фланг проти́внику. **3,** (bring to light; unmask) разоблача́ть: *expose corruption*, разоблача́ть корру́пцию. **4,** *fol. by* **to** (subject to) подверга́ть (+ *dat.*): *expose to danger*, подверга́ть опа́сности. *Expose plants to light*, выставля́ть расте́ния на свет. **5,** *photog.* экспони́ровать. *Accidentally expose the film*, засвети́ть плёнку.

exposé *n.* разоблаче́ние.

exposed *adj.* **1,** (not protected) неприкры́тый: *with one's head exposed*, с неприкры́той голово́й. *Exposed flank*, неприкры́тый *or* откры́тый фланг. **2,** *photog.* (of film) экспони́рованный.

exposer *n.* обличи́тель; изоблачи́тель.

exposition *n.* **1,** (presentation of subject matter) изложе́ние; переска́з. **2,** (large exhibition) вы́ставка.

expository *adj.* объясни́тельный; разъясни́тельный.

expostulate *v.i.* [*usu.* **expostulate with**] увещева́ть. —**expostulation**, *n.* увеща́ние.

exposure *n.* **1,** (act of exposing) раскры́тие; разоблаче́ние. **2,** (condition of being exposed): *die from exposure*, поги́бнуть от хо́лода. *Avoid excessive exposure to the sun*, возде́рживаться от чрезме́рного пребыва́ния на со́лнце. **3,** (direction faced): *The room has a southern exposure*, ко́мната выхо́дит на юг. **4,** *photog.* вы́держка; экспози́ция. —**exposure meter**, экспози́метр; экспоно́метр.

expound *v.t.* **1,** (set forth) излага́ть. **2,** (interpret) разъясня́ть. —*v.i.* [*usu.* **expound on**] рассужда́ть (о); распространя́ться (о). *Expound on a subject*, рассужда́ть *or* распространя́ться на те́му.

express *v.t.* выража́ть; выска́зывать. *Express one's opinion*, вы́разить/вы́сказать своё мне́ние. —*adj.* **1,** (explicit) я́сный; то́чный; чёткий. **2,** (specific) специа́льный: *for the express purpose of*, специа́льно для того́, что́бы. **3,** (rapid) сро́чный: *express telegram*, сро́чная телегра́мма. *Express train*, курье́рский по́езд; экспре́сс. *Express mail*, экспре́сс по́чта. —*adv.* экспре́ссом. —*n.* (train) экспре́сс. —**express oneself**, **1,** (make oneself understood) объясня́ться. **2,** (state one's opinion) выража́ться; выска́зываться.

expression *n.* выраже́ние. *Idiomatic expression*, идиомати́ческое выраже́ние. *Expression on one's face*, выраже́ние лица́. *Read with expression*, чита́ть с выраже́нием. —**expressionless**, *adj.* невырази́тельный.

expressive *adj.* вырази́тельный. —**expressiveness**, *n.* вырази́тельность.

expressly *adv.* **1,** (explicitly) я́сно. **2,** (specifically) специа́льно; наро́чно.

expressway *n.* автостра́да; автомагистра́ль.

expropriate *v.t.* экспроприи́ровать. —**expropriation**, *n.* экспроприа́ция.

expulsion *n.* исключе́ние; изгна́ние.

expunge *v.t.* вычёркивать.

expurgate *v.t.* вычёркивать нежела́тельные места́ в (кни́ге).

exquisite *adj.* **1,** (extremely beautiful) прекра́сный. **2,** (keen; discriminating) изы́сканный; утончённый: *exquisite taste*, изы́сканный/утончённый вкус.

extant *adj.* сохрани́вшийся; существу́ющий.

extemporaneous *adj.* импровизи́рованный. —**extemporaneously**, *adv.* без подгото́вки; экспро́мтом.

extemporize *v.t. & i.* импровизи́ровать.

extend *v.t.* **1,** (hold out; stretch across) протя́гивать. *Extend one's hand*, протя́гивать *or* подава́ть ру́ку. *Extend a rope across the yard*, протя́гивать верёвку через двор. **2,** (make longer) удлиня́ть: *extend a road,* удлиня́ть доро́гу. *Extend a road to the shore,* подводи́ть доро́гу к бе́регу. **3,** (make larger; expand, as property) расширя́ть. **4,** (prolong in time) продлева́ть: *extend one's vacation,* продли́ть о́тпуск; *extend a visa,* продли́ть ви́зу (*or* срок ви́зы). **5,** (give; grant; accord) ока́зывать: *extend aid/hospitality to,* ока́зывать по́мощь/гостеприи́мство (+ *dat.*). *Extend credit to,* открыва́ть *or* предоставля́ть креди́т (+ *dat.*). **6,** (give; convey) передава́ть; приноси́ть. *Extend regards/ an invitation/,* передава́ть приве́т/приглаше́ние. *Extend one's apologies,* приноси́ть извине́ния. *Extend one's thanks,* приноси́ть *or* вырази́ть благода́рность. *Extend sympathy,* выража́ть сочу́вствие. —*v.i.* **1,** (stretch) тяну́ться; растя́гиваться; простира́ться. *The line extended for two blocks,* о́чередь протяну́лась *or* растяну́лась на два кварта́ла. **2,** *fol. by* **to** (reach or affect additionally) распространя́ться (на). —**extend oneself,** утружда́ть себя́.

extended *adj.* **1,** (stretched out) протя́нутый; распростёртый. **2,** (lengthy; prolonged) дли́тельный; продолжи́тельный. **3,** (enlarged in scope) расши́ренный.

extension *n.* **1,** (making longer) удлине́ние. **2,** (expansion) расшире́ние. **3,** (addition, as to a house) пристро́йка. **4,** (extra time allowed a debtor) отсро́чка; продле́ние. **5,** (internal telephone number) доба́вочный: *extension five,* доба́вочный пять. —**extension cord,** удлини́тельный шнур; удлини́тель. —**extension ladder,** раздвижна́я ле́стница.

extensive *adj.* **1,** (vast) обши́рный. **2,** (broad in scope) широ́кий; обши́рный. *Extensive menu,* обши́рное меню́. *Extensive knowledge,* обши́рные зна́ния. *Extensive damage,* больши́е поврежде́ния. *Extensive repairs,* кру́пный ремо́нт. *Extensive coverage in the press,* широ́кое освеще́ние в печа́ти.

extensively *adv.* мно́го: *read/travel extensively,* мно́го чита́ть/путеше́ствовать.

extent *n.* **1,** (length) протяже́ние; протяжённость. **2,** (degree) сте́пень; ме́ра: *to a certain extent,* в/до не́которой *or* изве́стной сте́пени; в изве́стной ме́ре. *To the extent that I am able,* в ме́ру мои́х сил. **3,** (scope) сте́пень; разме́р: *extent of the damage,* сте́пень поврежде́ния; разме́р уще́рба. *To the full extent of the law,* по всей стро́гости зако́на.

extenuate *v.t.* смягча́ть. —**extenuating circumstances,** смягча́ющие вину́ обстоя́тельства.

exterior *adj.* нару́жный; вне́шний. —*n.* нару́жность; вне́шность.

exterminate *v.t.* уничтожа́ть; истребля́ть; выводи́ть; мори́ть; трави́ть. —**extermination,** *n.* уничтоже́ние; истребле́ние.

external *adj.* вне́шний; нару́жный. *For external use only,* то́лько для нару́жного употребле́ния.

extinct *adj.* **1,** (of an animal, bird, etc.) вы́мерший. *Become extinct,* вымира́ть; выводи́ться. **2,** (of a volcano) поту́хший. **3,** (of a language) мёртвый.

extinction *n.* **1,** (extinguishing) гаше́ние; туше́ние. **2,** (dying out) вымира́ние: *doomed to extinction,* обречён на вымира́ние.

extinguish *v.t.* **1,** (put out) гаси́ть; туши́ть : *extinguish the lights/candles/fire,* гаси́ть *or* туши́ть свет/све́чи/ пожа́р. *Extinguish all cigarettes!,* погаси́те *or* поту́шите все сигаре́ты! **2,** (end, as hopes) убива́ть.

extirpate *v.t.* искореня́ть; выкорчёвывать; вырыва́ть с ко́рнем. —**extirpation,** *n.* искорене́ние.

extol *v.t.* превозноси́ть; расхва́ливать; восхваля́ть.

extort *v.t.* **1,** (obtain using threats) вымога́ть (де́ньги). **2,** (wring, as a confession or promise) вырыва́ть (призна́ние); исто́ргнуть (обеща́ние). —**extortion,** *n.* вымога́тельство. —**extortionist,** *n.* вымога́тель.

extra *adj.* **1,** (additional) дополни́тельный: *extra expenses,* дополни́тельные расхо́ды. *Postage is extra,* за пересы́лку берётся осо́бая пла́та. *Pay two dollars extra,* припла́чивать два до́ллара. **2,** (spare) ли́шний: *Have you an extra pencil?,* есть у вас ли́шний каранда́ш? —*adv.* осо́бенно; осо́бо. *Of extra fine quality,* осо́бенно высо́кого ка́чества. —*n.* **1,** *theat.* (supernumerary) стати́ст. **2,** (special edition) э́кстренный вы́пуск.

extract *v.t.* **1,** (draw out; remove) извлека́ть; удаля́ть; выта́скивать; вырыва́ть. *Extract a tooth,* удали́ть *or* вы́рвать *or* вы́тащить зуб. **2,** (remove from the ground; mine) добыва́ть. **3,** (obtain by pressing or squeezing) извлека́ть; выжима́ть. **4,** (copy out; choose for quotation) выпи́сывать; выбира́ть. **5,** (obtain, as a promise, confession, etc.) вырыва́ть; вынужда́ть; исторга́ть. **6,** *math.* извлека́ть. —*n.* **1,** (excerpt) извлече́ние; вы́держка; вы́писка. **2,** (concentrate) вы́тяжка; экстра́кт; насто́й.

extraction *n.* **1,** (act of extracting) извлече́ние; удале́ние; добы́ча. **2,** (origin; descent) происхожде́ние: *of Russian extraction,* ру́сского происхожде́ния.

extracurricular *adj.* внекла́ссный: *extracurricular activities,* внекла́ссная рабо́та; внекла́ссные мероприя́тия.

extradite *v.t.* выдава́ть. —**extradition,** *n.* вы́дача.

extramarital *adj.* внебра́чный.

extraneous *adj.* **1,** (coming from outside; foreign) посторо́нний. **2,** (irrelevant) не име́ющий отноше́ния (к чему́-нибудь).

extraordinarily *adv.* чрезвыча́йно; в вы́сшей сте́пени.

extraordinary *adj.* **1,** (remarkable; exceptional) чрезвыча́йный; исключи́тельный; необыча́йный; экстраордина́рный. **2,** (special, as of a meeting) чрезвыча́йный; внеочередно́й. **3,** (of an envoy) чрезвыча́йный.

extrapolate *v.t. & i.* экстраполи́ровать. —**extrapolation,** *n.* экстраполя́ция.

extraterrestrial *adj.* внеземно́й.

extraterritorial *adj.* экстерриториа́льный.

extravagance *n.* расточи́тельность.

extravagant *adj.* **1,** (wasteful) расточи́тельный. **2,** (excessive) непоме́рный: *extravagant demands,* непоме́рные тре́бования.

extreme *adj.* кра́йний: *extreme caution/poverty,* кра́йняя осторо́жность/нищета́. *Extreme measures/ views,* кра́йние ме́ры/взгля́ды. *Extreme old age,* глубо́кая ста́рость. —*n.* кра́йность: *to an extreme,* до кра́йности. *Go to extremes,* вдава́ться в кра́йности. *Go from one extreme to the other,* ударя́ться из одно́й кра́йности в другу́ю.

extremely *adv.* кра́йне; чрезвыча́йно.

extremism *n.* экстреми́зм.

extremist *n.* экстреми́ст. —*adj.* экстреми́стский.

extremity *n.* **1,** (end; edge) коне́ц; край; оконе́чность. **2,** *pl.* (appendages of the body) коне́чности.

extricate *v.t.* выпу́тывать; выта́скивать. *Extricate oneself,* выпу́тываться; выкара́бкиваться. *Extricate someone from the wreckage,* извлека́ть кого́-нибудь из-под обло́мков.

exuberance *n.* жизнера́достность.

exuberant *adj.* кипу́чий; жизнера́достный.

exude *v.t.* **1,** (discharge) выделя́ть. **2,** *fig.* (radiate) излуча́ть: *exude confidence,* излуча́ть уве́ренность. —*v.i.* выделя́ться; проступа́ть.

exult *v.i.* ликова́ть; торжествова́ть. —**exultant,** *adj.* лику́ющий; торжеству́ющий. —**exultation,** *n.* ликова́ние; торжество́.

eye *n.* **1,** (organ of sight) глаз. *With tears in his eyes,* со слеза́ми на глаза́х. **2,** (of a needle) ушко́. —*adj.* глазно́й. *Eye doctor,* глазно́й врач; окули́ст. —*v.t.* разгля́дывать; загля́дываться на; засма́триваться на. —**an eye for an eye,** о́ко за о́ко. —**be all eyes,** смотре́ть во все глаза́. —**before one's very eyes,** на чьи́х-нибудь глаза́х; на глаза́х у кого́-нибудь. —**by eye,** на глаз; на глазо́к. —**close one's eyes to,** за-

крыва́ть глаза́ на. —**give someone the eye; make eyes at,** де́лать *or* стро́ить гла́зки (+ *dat.*). —**have an** (*or* **one's**) **eye on,** име́ть на приме́те. —**in the eyes of,** в глаза́х (+ *gen.*). —**keep an eye on,** присма́тривать за. —**look someone in the eye,** смотре́ть кому́-нибудь в глаза́. —**more than meets the eye,** бо́льше, чем ка́жется на пе́рвый взгляд. —**open someone's eyes to,** открыва́ть кому́-нибудь глаза́ на. —**see eye to eye,** сходи́ться во взгля́дах; быть одного́ мне́ния. —**with one's eyes open,** зна́я, на что идёт.

eyeball *n.* глазно́е я́блоко. *I am up to my eyeballs with work,* я за́нят (*or* у меня́ рабо́ты) по го́рло.

eyebrow *n.* бровь.

eyecup *n.* глазна́я ва́нночка.

eyeglasses *n.pl.* очки́.

eyelash *n.* ресни́ца.

eyelet *n.* пе́телька.

eyelid *n.* ве́ко.

eye patch повя́зка на глазу́.

eyepiece *n.* окуля́р.

eyeshade *n.* нагла́зник.

eyesight *n.* зре́ние.

eye socket глазна́я впа́дина; глазни́ца.

eyesore *n.* безобра́зие.

eyestrain *n.* утомле́ние гла́за.

eyetooth *n.* глазно́й зуб.

eyewash *n.* примо́чка для глаз.

eyewitness *n.* очеви́дец.

F

F, f шеста́я бу́ква английского алфави́та. —*n.* **1,** (musical note) фа. **2,** (failing grade) едини́ца.

fa *n., music* фа.

fable *n.* ба́сня. —**fabled,** *adj.* басносло́вный; ска́зочный.

fabric *n.* **1,** (cloth) ткань; мате́рия; материа́л. **2,** *fig.* (basic structure) строй; строе́ние. *The social fabric,* обще́ственный строй.

fabricate *v.t.* **1,** (manufacture) производи́ть. **2,** (make up; invent) фабрикова́ть; выду́мывать; измышля́ть.

fabrication *n.* **1,** (manufacture) произво́дство. **2,** (falsehood) вы́думка; вы́мысел; измышле́ние; фи́кция.

fabulist *n.* баснопи́сец.

fabulous *adj.* басносло́вный; ска́зочный.

façade *n.* фаса́д.

face *n.* **1,** (of a human being) лицо́. *Look someone in*

the face, смотре́ть кому́-нибудь в лицо́. *Laugh/ blow smoke/ in someone's face,* рассмея́ться/пуска́ть дым/ кому́-нибудь в лицо́. *Slap someone in the face,* дать пощёчину (+ *dat.*). *It's written all over your face,* э́то у вас на лице́ напи́сано. **2,** (of a clock) цифербла́т. **3,** (surface) лицо́; лик. *Face of the moon,* лик луны́. *Vanish from the face of the earth,* исче́знуть с лица́ земли́. **4,** (expression; countenance) лицо́; ми́на; физионо́мия. *Long face,* вы́тянутое лицо́. *Make a sour face,* сде́лать ки́слое лицо́. **5,** (exaggerated expression) грима́са. *Make faces,* грима́сничать; де́лать *or* стро́ить грима́сы *or* ро́жи. **6,** (front; main side) лицева́я сторона́; лицо́. **7,** (dignity) лицо́: *loss of face,* поте́ря лица́. *Save face,* сохраня́ть лицо́. —*v.t.* **1,** (front; look out on) смотре́ть; выходи́ть (*with* в *or* на). **2,** (turn or be turned toward) стоя́ть лицо́м к: *face the audience,* стоя́ть лицо́м к аудито́рии. *He sat facing me,* он сиде́л напро́тив меня́ (*or* лицо́м ко мне). *We sat facing each other,* мы сиде́ли друг про́тив (*or* напро́тив) дру́га. **3,** (confront; be confronted with) стоя́ть пе́ред: *face a choice,* стоя́ть пе́ред вы́бором. *The problems facing us,* пробле́мы, стоя́щие пе́ред на́ми. *We are faced with a difficult task,* нам предстои́т тру́дная зада́ча. *He faces life imprisonment,* ему́ грози́т пожи́зненное тюре́мное заключе́ние. **4,** (confront squarely) смотре́ть в лицо́ *or* в глаза́ (+ *dat.*): *face death/ the truth/,* смотре́ть сме́рти/пра́вде в лицо́/глаза́. *Let's face it!,* посмо́трим пра́вде в глаза́; ска́жем че́стно. **5,** (cover with a layer of something) облицо́вывать; обкла́дывать. —*v.i.* выходи́ть: *The room faces west,* ко́мната выхо́дит на за́пад. —**face down,** лицо́м вниз; ничко́м. —**face to face,** лицо́м к лицу́; оди́н на оди́н. —**face up,** лицо́м кве́рху. —**in the face of,** пе́ред лицо́м (+ *gen.*). —**on the face of it,** на пе́рвый взгляд. —**to one's face,** в лицо́ (+ *dat.*).

face card фигу́ра.

face cream крем для лица́.

faceless *adj.* безли́кий; безли́чный.

face powder пу́дра для лица́.

facet *n.* **1,** (of a gem) грань; фасе́т(ка). **2,** *fig.* (aspect) сторона́.

facetious *adj.* шутли́вый; шу́точный.

face towel полоте́нце для лица́.

face value номина́льная сто́имость. —**take at face value,** принима́ть за чи́стую моне́ту.

facial *adj.* лицево́й. *Facial features,* черты́ лица́. *Facial expression,* выраже́ние лица́. —*n.* масса́ж лица́.

facile *adj.* бе́глый; бо́йкий.

facilitate *v.t.* **1,** (make easier) облегча́ть. **2,** (promote; stimulate) спосо́бствовать.

facility *n.* **1,** (ease) лёгкость. *With facility,* легко́; бе́гло; с лёгкостью. **2,** (aptitude) спосо́бности. **3,** *pl.* (conveniences; services) сре́дства; удо́бства; услу́ги. *Communications facilities,* сре́дства свя́зи. **4,** *pl.* (buildings used for a certain function) помеще́ние: *storage facilities,* складски́е помеще́ния.

facing *n.* **1,** (outer covering) облицо́вка. **2,** (trim) кант; отде́лка.

facsimile *n.* факси́миле.

fact *n.* факт. *It is a fact that...,* факт, что... *The fact that...,* то, что... *The fact is...,* де́ло в том, что... —**after the fact,** за́дним число́м. —**as a matter of fact,** *see* **matter.** —**in fact,** факти́чески; на са́мом де́ле. —**know for a fact,** знать то́чно; знать наверняка́.

faction *n.* фра́кция. —**factional,** *adj.* фракцио́нный.

factious *adj.* фракцио́нный.

factor *n.* **1,** (contributing element) фа́ктор; обстоя́тельство. *You forgot one important factor,* вы забы́ли об одно́м ва́жном обстоя́тельстве. **2,** (agent) комиссионе́р. **3,** *math.* мно́житель; сомно́житель; коэффицие́нт. —*v.t.* разлага́ть на мно́жители.

factory *n.* заво́д; фа́брика. *Watch/cement factory,* часово́й/цеме́нтный заво́д. *Furniture/shoe factory,* ме́бельная/обувна́я фа́брика. *Work in a factory,* рабо́тать на заво́де/ на фа́брике/. —*adj.* заводско́й;

фабри́чный: *factory worker,* заводско́й/фабри́чный рабо́чий.

factual *adj.* факти́ческий.

faculty *n.* **1,** *usu. pl.* (power of the mind) спосо́бности: *mental faculties,* у́мственные спосо́бности. *The faculty of speech,* дар ре́чи. *In full possession of one's faculties,* в по́лном рассу́дке. *Lose possession of one's faculties,* вы́жить из ума́. **2,** (knack) спосо́бности: *a faculty for languages,* спосо́бности к языка́м. **3,** (department of a university) факульте́т. **4,** (teaching staff) преподава́тельский соста́в.

fad *n.* пове́трие.

fade *v.i.* **1,** (lose color) линя́ть; выцвета́ть; (*from the sun*) выгора́ть. **2,** (wither) вя́нуть; блёкнуть. **3,** (grow dim) блёкнуть. **4,** (grow inaudible) замира́ть. **5,** (lessen; wane) га́снуть; угаса́ть: *Hopes are fading,* наде́жды га́снут/угаса́ют. **6,** (disappear gradually) исчеза́ть: *fade into the distance,* исчеза́ть вдали́. *Fade from view,* скрыва́ться и́з виду. *Fade from memory,* стере́ться в па́мяти. —*v.t.* обесцве́чивать: *Sunlight fades the fabric,* со́лнце обесцве́чивает ткань.

faded *adj.* вы́цветший.

faeces *n.* = **feces.**

fag *v.t.* утомля́ть. *Be fagged out,* заму́читься.

fagot *also,* **faggot** *n.* вяза́нка хво́роста.

Fahrenheit *adj.* Фаренге́йт: *forty degrees Fahrenheit,* со́рок гра́дусов по Фаренге́йту.

fail *v.i.* **1,** (be unsuccessful) не удава́ться; терпе́ть неуда́чу; прова́ливаться. **2,** (stop working; cease to function) отказа́ть; отказа́ться рабо́тать. **3,** (decline; deteriorate) слабе́ть; сдава́ть. *His eyesight is failing,* его́ зре́ние слабе́ет; зре́ние ему́ изменя́ет. **4,** (become insolvent) прогора́ть. **5,** (receive a failing grade) прова́ливаться. —*v.t.* **1,** (be of no help to) изменя́ть: *His strength failed him,* си́лы ему́ измени́ли. *Words fail me,* не нахожу́ слов. **2,** (disappoint; let down) подводи́ть: *Don't fail me!,* не подведи́те меня́! **3,** *fol. by inf.* (not do): *He failed to answer,* он не отве́тил. *I fail to see the difference,* не ви́жу ра́зницы. *The parachute failed to open,* парашю́т не откры́лся. **4,** (not pass) прова́ливаться на (*e.g.* экза́мене) *or* по (*e.g.* хи́мии). **5,** (not give a passing grade to) прова́ливать. —**without fail,** обяза́тельно; в обяза́тельном поря́дке.

failing *n.* недоста́ток; сла́бость. —*adj.* **1,** (not passing, as of a mark) неудовлетвори́тельный. **2,** (deteriorating, as of eyesight) слабе́ющий. *She is in failing health,* у неё сла́бое здоро́вье. —*prep.* за неиме́нием (+ *gen.*). *Failing which,* ина́че; в проти́вном слу́чае.

failure *n.* **1,** (lack of success) неуда́ча; прова́л. *End in failure,* ко́нчиться неуда́чей *or* прова́лом. *Doomed to failure,* обречён на прова́л. *Crop failure,* неурожа́й. **2,** (one who is unsuccessful) неуда́чник. **3,** (non-performance) неисполне́ние: *failure to carry out an order,* неисполне́ние распоряже́ния. *Failure to appear,* нея́вка. **4,** (malfunctioning) ава́рия; отка́з; неиспра́вность. *Mechanical failure,* механи́ческая неиспра́вность. *Engine/power failure,* отка́з двигателя/электропита́ния. **5,** (a becoming bankrupt) крах; банкро́тство.

faint *adj.* **1,** (weak; dim; slight) сла́бый: *faint mark,* сла́бый след; *faint hope,* сла́бая наде́жда. *Faint resemblance,* отдалённое схо́дство. *I haven't the faintest idea,* я не име́ю ни мале́йшего поня́тия. **2,** (ready to faint): *feel faint,* чу́вствовать дурноту́. *I feel faint,* мне ду́рно. —*n.* о́бморок: *in a dead faint,* в глубо́ком о́бмороке. *Fall into a dead faint,* упа́сть за́мертво. —*v.i.* упа́сть в о́бморок.

fainthearted *adj.* малоду́шный. —**faintheartedness,** *n.* малоду́шие.

faintly *adv.* **1,** (dimly) сла́бо; нея́сно. **2,** (slightly) слегка́.

faintness *n.* **1,** (dimness) сла́бость. **2,** (weak feeling) дурнота́.

fair *adj.* **1,** (beautiful; lovely) прекра́сный. **2,** (light, as of skin) све́тлый. **3,** (blond) белоку́рый. **4,** (clear; sunny) я́сный. *Fair weather,* хоро́шая пого́да. **5,** (just and honest) справедли́вый. *Fair judge/trial/verdict,* справедли́вый судья́/суд/пригово́р. *Fair share/deal,* справедли́вая до́ля/сде́лка. *Fair play,* че́стная игра́. **6,** (reasonable) подходя́щий. *Fair price,* подходя́щая *or* схо́дная цена́. *Fair offer,* прие́млемое предложе́ние. *It is fair to assume that...,* резо́нно предположи́ть, что... **7,** (fairly large) изря́дный: *a fair amount,* изря́дное коли́чество. **8,** (average; so-so) так себе́; посре́дственный; сно́сный. —*adv.* че́стно; поря́дочно; по пра́вилам. —*n.* **1,** (market) я́рмарка. **2,** (exposition) вы́ставка: *world's fair,* всеми́рная вы́ставка. —**bid fair,** обеща́ть. —**fair copy,** чистово́й экземпля́р; чистови́к. —**fair enough!,** согла́сен!; согла́сна! —**fair sex,** прекра́сный пол. —**fair to middling,** так себе́; сно́сно; ни ша́тко ни ва́лко.

fair-haired *adj.* **1,** (light-haired) белоку́рый; ру́сый; световоло́сый. **2,** (favorite) излю́бленный.

fairly *adv.* **1,** (justly) справедли́во; че́стно. **2,** (rather) дово́льно: *fairly well,* дово́льно хорошо́.

fairness *n.* справедли́вость. —**in all fairness,** справедли́вости ра́ди.

fairy *n.* фе́я. —**fairyland,** *n.* ска́зочная страна́; волше́бное ца́рство. —**fairy tale,** (волше́бная) ска́зка.

fait accompli соверши́вшийся факт. *Present someone with a fait accompli,* поста́вить кого́-нибудь пе́ред фа́ктом.

faith *n.* **1,** (trust; confidence) ве́ра; дове́рие. *Put one's faith in,* полага́ться на. *Lose faith in,* разуве́риться в; изуве́риться в. **2,** (belief in God) ве́ра: *faith in God,* ве́ра в бо́га. *Man of faith,* ве́рующий. **3,** (religious denomination) ве́ра; вероиспове́дание. —**bad faith,** недобросо́вестность. *In bad faith,* недобросо́вестно. —**good faith,** и́скренность. *In good faith,* и́скренне; по чи́стой со́вести. —**keep faith with,** остава́ться ве́рен/верна́ (+ *dat.*). —**take on faith,** принима́ть на ве́ру.

faithful *adj.* ве́рный. *Remain faithful to,* остава́ться ве́рен/верна́ (+ *dat.*). —*n., preceded by* the, правове́рные.

faithfully *adv.* ве́рно: *faithfully serve,* ве́рно служи́ть. *Promise faithfully,* твёрдо обеща́ть. *Faithfully obey,* беспрекосло́вно слу́шаться.

faithfulness *n.* ве́рность.

fake *v.t.* **1,** (feign) притворя́ться (+ *instr.*). **2,** (forge) подде́лывать. —*v.i.* притворя́ться. —*adj.* подде́льный; подло́жный; фальши́вый. —*n.* подде́лка; фальши́вка.

faker *n.* обма́нщик; притво́рщик. —**fakery,** *n.* обма́н.

falcon *n.* со́кол. —**falconry,** *n.* соколи́ная охо́та.

fall *v.i.* **1,** (lose one's footing; drop; come down) па́дать (*pfv.* упа́сть): *fall to the ground/ on the ice/ down the stairs/,* упа́сть на зе́млю/ на льду/ с ле́стницы. *Fall to one's knees,* бро́ситься на коле́ни. *Fall in battle,* пасть в бою́. *Prices fell,* це́ны упа́ли. *Rain fell during the night,* но́чью шёл дождь. *Dusk is falling,* спуска́ются су́мерки. *Shadows are falling,* те́ни ложа́тся. *His face fell,* его́ лицо́ вы́тянулось. **2,** (be caught or captured) попада́ть: *fall into a trap,* попа́сть в лову́шку. *Fall into the hands of,* попа́сть в ру́ки (+ *gen.*). *Fall victim to,* пасть же́ртвой (+ *gen.*). **3,** (be conquered or overthrown) пасть: *The fortress fell,* кре́пость па́ла. *Fall from power,* лиши́ться вла́сти. **4,** (occur) наступа́ть: *Night fell,* наступи́ла ночь. *New Year's Day falls on a Wednesday,* Но́вый год выпада́ет *or* прихо́дится на сре́ду. *The stress falls on the first syllable,* ударе́ние па́дает на пе́рвый слог. **5,** (come by lot or chance) па́дать; выпада́ть: *The lot fell upon him,* ему́ вы́пал жре́бий; жре́бий пал на него́. **6,** (pass into a particular state): *fall asleep,* засыпа́ть; *fall ill,* заболева́ть; *fall silent,* замолка́ть; умолка́ть; *fall in love,* влюбля́ться. *Fall into disrepair,* приходи́ть в ве́тхость *or* в него́дность. **7,** (come within; come under) относи́ться: *fall into a certain category,* относи́ться к тако́й-то катего́рии. *Fall into the category of,* подпада́ть под катего́рию (+ *gen.*). *Fall into three categories,* дели́ться на три катего́рии. *Fall within one's jurisdiction,* входи́ть в чью-нибудь компете́нцию. **8,** *fol. by inf.* (begin): *They fell to quarreling among themselves,* они́ поссо́рились ме́жду собо́й. —*n.* **1,** (loss of footing; drop; decline) паде́ние. *Take a bad fall,* си́льно разби́ться. *Fall in prices,* паде́ние цен. *The fall of the Roman Empire,* паде́ние Ри́мской импе́рии. **2,** *pl.* (waterfall) водопа́д: *Niagara Falls,* Ниага́рский водопа́д. **3,** (autumn) о́сень. *In the fall,* о́сенью. —*adj.* осе́нний: *fall weather,* осе́нняя пого́да. —**fall apart,** распада́ться; разва́ливаться. —**fall back,** отступа́ть; отка́тываться. —**fall back on,** прибега́ть к. —**fall behind, 1,** *literally* зава́ливаться за (+ *acc.*). **2,** (lag behind) отстава́ть. —**fall down,** па́дать. —**fall flat,** прова́ливаться. —**fall for, 1,** (be tricked, as by a ruse) попада́ться на (у́дочку). **2,** (be captivated by) влюбля́ться в; увлека́ться (+ *instr.*). —**fall in, 1,** (cave in) обва́ливаться; прова́ливаться. **2,** *mil.* стро́иться. *Fall in!,* станови́сь! —**fall in with,** попа́сть в: *fall in with a bad crowd,* попа́сть в плоху́ю компа́нию. —**fall off, 1,** (tumble from) упа́сть с; свали́ться с; сорва́ться с. **2,** (decline) уменьша́ться; упа́сть. —**fall out, 1,** *literally* выпада́ть; выва́ливаться. **2,** *mil.* выходи́ть из стро́я. —**fall over,** опроки́дываться. —**fall short of,** не достига́ть. *Fall short of expectations,* обма́нывать ожида́ния. —**fall through, 1,** *literally* упа́сть в: *fall through a crack,* упа́сть в тре́щину. *Fall through the ice,* провали́ться под лёд. **2,** (fail to come about) прова́ливаться; расстра́иваться; срыва́ться.

fallacious *adj.* оши́бочный; ло́жный. —**fallaciousness,** *n.* оши́бочность.

fallacy *n.* **1,** (false notion; error) оши́бка. **2,** (fallaciousness) оши́бочность.

fallen *adj.* па́вший; па́дший. —**fallen arches,** плоскосто́пие. —**fallen woman,** па́дшая же́нщина.

fallible *adj.* подве́рженный оши́бкам.

falling *adj.* па́дающий. —**falling star,** па́дающая звезда́.

falling-out *n.* ссо́ра. *They have had a falling-out,* они́ в ссо́ре; они́ рассо́рились; ме́жду ни́ми пробежа́ла чёрная ко́шка.

Fallopian tubes фалло́пиевы тру́бы.

fallout *n.* **1,** (particles) радиоакти́вные оса́дки. **2,** (descent of same) выпаде́ние радиоакти́вных оса́дков.

fallow *adj.* парово́й. *Fallow land,* земля́ под па́ром. *Lie fallow,* лежа́ть под па́ром. —**fallow deer,** лань.

false *adj.* **1,** (incorrect; insincere) ло́жный: *false rumor,* ло́жный слух; *false modesty,* ло́жная скро́мность. *False advertising,* лжи́вая рекла́ма. **2,** (forged) фальши́вый: *false passport,* фальши́вый па́спорт. **3,** (of hair, a mustache, etc.) накладно́й. —**false alarm,** ло́жная трево́га. —**false note,** фальши́вая *or* неве́рная но́та. —**false start,** фальста́рт; неве́рный старт. —**false step,** ло́жный шаг. —**false teeth,** вставны́е зу́бы. —**under a false name,** под чужи́м и́менем.

falsehood *n.* ложь; непра́вда; вы́мысел.

falsely *adv.* ло́жно.

falseness *n.* ло́жность; фальшь.

falsetto *n.* фальце́т; фи́стула. —*adj.* фальце́тный.

falsification *n.* фальсифика́ция.

falsifier *n.* фальсифика́тор.

falsify *v.t.* фальсифици́ровать.

falsity *n.* **1,** (falseness) ло́жность. **2,** (falsehood) ложь.

falter *v.i.* **1,** (waver) дро́гнуть: *His voice faltered,* его́ го́лос дро́гнул. *In a faltering voice,* слабе́ющим *or* замира́ющим го́лосом. *Faltering gait,* нетвёрдая *or* неве́рная похо́дка. **2,** (lose strength or momentum) теря́ть си́лу.

fame *n.* сла́ва; изве́стность. —**famed,** *adj.* просла́вленный.

familiar *adj.* **1,** (well-known) знако́мый: *a familiar voice,* знако́мый го́лос. *His face is familiar to me,* его́ лицо́ мне знако́мо. **2,** *fol. by* **with** (having knowledge of) знако́мый с; в ку́рсе (+ *gen.*). *Become familiar with,* знако́миться с; ознакомля́ться с. **3,** (unduly intimate) фамилья́рный; развя́зный; бесцеремо́нный.

familiarity *n.* **1,** (knowledge) знако́мство. **2,** (undue intimacy) фамилья́рность; бесцеремо́нность.

familiarization *n.* ознакомле́ние.

familiarize *v.t.* знако́мить; ознакомля́ть. *Familiarize oneself with,* знако́миться с; ознакомля́ться с.

family *n.* **1,** (parents and children) семья́. *It runs in the*

family, э́то (у него́/неё) семе́йная черта́; э́то у него́/неё в роду́. **2,** *biol.* семе́йство. **3,** (of languages) семья́. —*adj.* семе́йный; фами́льный. *Family ties,* ро́дственные свя́зи. *Family friend,* друг семьи́. —**family man,** семе́йный челове́к. —**family name,** фами́лия. —**family planning,** плани́рование семьи́. —**family tree,** родосло́вное де́рево; родосло́вная. —**in the family way,** в интере́сном положе́нии.

famine *n.* го́лод. —**feast or famine,** то гу́сто, то пу́сто.

famished *adj.* голо́дный как соба́ка; умира́ющий от го́лода.

famous *adj.* знамени́тый. *Be famous for,* сла́виться (+ *instr.*).

fan *n.* **1,** (manual device) ве́ер. **2,** (machine) вентиля́тор. **3,** *colloq.* (devotee) боле́льщик: *baseball fan,* боле́льщик бейсбо́ла. **4,** *colloq.* (admirer) покло́нник: *I'm a big fan of yours,* я ваш большо́й покло́нник. —*v.t.* **1,** (cool with a fan) обма́хивать. *Fan oneself,* обма́хиваться. **2,** (direct air on, as a fire) раздува́ть. **3,** *fig.* (stir up; foment) раздува́ть. —*v.i.* [*usu.* **fan out**] развёртываться ве́ером.

fanatic *n.* фана́тик. —*adj.* [*also,* **fanatical**] фанати́ческий; фанати́чный. —**fanaticism,** *n.* фанати́зм.

fan belt реме́нь вентиля́тора.

fanciful *adj.* **1,** (imaginary; unreal) фантасти́ческий. **2,** (whimsical) капри́зный.

fancy *n.* **1,** (imagination) фанта́зия: *flight of fancy,* полёт фанта́зии. **2,** (whim) при́хоть; причу́да; фанта́зия. *Passing fancy,* мимолётная при́хоть. **3,** (liking) увлече́ние. *Catch the fancy of,* полюби́ться (+ *dat.*); пригляну́ться (+ *dat.*). *He took a fancy to...,* ему́ полюби́лся (полюби́лась) *or* пригляну́лся (пригляну́лась) (+ *nom.*). —*adj.* **1,** (elaborate) замыслова́тый; зате́йливый: *fancy design,* замыслова́тый/зате́йливый узо́р. **2,** *colloq.* (high, as of prices) ду́тый. —*v.t.* **1,** (imagine) вообража́ть; представля́ть себе́. *Fancy oneself as a writer,* вообража́ть *or* мнить себя́ писа́телем. **2,** (suppose; surmise) предполага́ть; вообража́ть. **3,** (like): *What do you fancy?,* что вам нра́вится? **4,** (feel like): *I don't fancy...,* у меня́ нет охо́ты (+ *inf. or* на + *acc.*).

fanfare *n.* **1,** (flourish of trumpets) фанфа́ра. **2,** (ballyhoo) шуми́ха. *Without fanfare,* без зате́й.

fang *n.* клык.

fantastic *adj.* фантасти́ческий.

fantasy *n.* **1,** (creative imagination) фанта́зия. *Live in a fantasy world,* жить в фантасти́ческом ми́ре. **2,** (something existing only in the imagination) фанта́стика; фанта́зия.

far *adj.* **1,** (distant) A, *used predicatively,* далеко́: *Moscow is far away,* Москва́ далеко́. *Not far from here,* недалеко́ отсю́да. B, *used as a modifier,* далёкий: *the far north,* далёкий се́вер. **2,** (more distant) да́льний: *in the far corner,* в да́льнем углу́. —*adv.* **1,** (a long way) далеко́: *leave far behind,* оставля́ть далеко́ позади́. **2,** *in comparisons* (by a great deal) гора́здо; намно́го: *far better,* гора́здо/намно́го лу́чше. —**as far as, 1,** (up to) до: *We drove as far as*

Boston, мы дое́хали до Бо́стона. **2,** (to the extent that) наско́лько: *as far as I know,* наско́лько я зна́ю. *As far as possible,* наско́лько возмо́жно; по (ме́ре) возмо́жности. *As far as I am concerned,* что каса́ется меня́. **—by far; far and away,** несомне́нно; бесспо́рно. **—far and wide,** повсю́ду; вдоль и поперёк. **—far be it from me to...,** я далёк от того́, что́бы... **—far from, 1,** *literally* далеко́ от. **2,** (by no means) далеко́ не: *far from dumb,* далеко́ не глуп. **—far from it,** далеко́ не так; ничего́ подо́бного. **—far into,** вглубь (+ *gen.*): *far into the woods,* вглубь ле́са. *Far into the night,* до глубо́кой но́чи. *Look far into the future,* загля́дывать в далёкое бу́дущее. **—go far,** далеко́ пойти́: *He will go far,* он далеко́ пойдёт. **—go too far,** зайти́ сли́шком далеко́; хвати́ть че́рез край. **—how far?,** ско́лько на́до е́хать?; ско́лько киломе́тров? **—so far,** пока́ что; пока́ ещё; до сих пор. **—so far, so good,** пока́ всё хорошо́.

faraway *adj.* **1,** (distant) далёкий; отдалённый. **2,** (dreamy, as of a look) отсу́тствующий.

farce *n.* фарс. **—farcical,** *adj.* смешно́й.

fare *v.i.* пожива́ть: *How are you faring?,* как вы пожива́ете? **—n. 1,** (price of a trip) пла́та за прое́зд; сто́имость прое́зда. *What is the fare to Washington?,* ско́лько сто́ит прое́зд до Вашингто́на?; ско́лько сто́ит биле́т в Вашингто́н (*or* до Вашингто́на)? **2,** (paying passenger) пассажи́р. **3,** (food) пи́ща; пита́ние; стол.

Far East да́льний восто́к. **—Far Eastern,** дальневосто́чный.

farewell *n.* проща́ние. *Bid farewell to,* проща́ться с. **—adj.** проща́льный; напу́тственный. **—interj.** проща́й(те)!

farfetched *adj.* наду́манный; притя́нутый за́ уши.

far-flung *adj.* обши́рный; раздо́льный; разветвлённый.

farina *n.* ма́нная крупа́. **—farinaceous,** *adj.* мучни́стый.

farm *n.* фе́рма. *Collective farm,* колхо́з. **—adj.** сельскохозя́йственный: *farm products/machinery,* сельскохозя́йственные проду́кты/маши́ны. **—v.t. 1,** (cultivate) обраба́тывать. **2,** *fol. by* **out** (let out) отдава́ть на о́ткуп. **—v.i.** занима́ться се́льским хозя́йством.

farmer *n.* фе́рмер.

farm hand сельскохозя́йственный рабо́чий.

farmhouse *n.* дом на фе́рме.

farming *n.* земледе́лие.

farmland *n.* па́хотная земля́.

farmstead *n.* уса́дьба.

farmyard *n.* ско́тный двор.

faro *n.* фарао́н; банк.

far-off *adj.* далёкий; да́льний.

far-reaching *adj.* далеко́ иду́щий.

farrow *n.* опоро́с.

farsighted *adj.* **1,** *med.* дальнозо́ркий. **2,** (having or showing foresight) дальнови́дный. **—farsightedness,** *n.* дальнозо́ркость.

farther *adv. & adj.* да́льше. *Not a step farther!,* ни

шагу да́льше! *Nothing could be farther from the truth,* ничто́ не мо́жет быть да́льше от пра́вды.

farthing *n.* фа́ртинг.

fascinate *v.t.* увлека́ть. **—fascinating,** *adj.* увлека́тельный.

fascination *n.* **1,** (state of being fascinated) увлече́ние. **2,** (charm; attraction) очарова́ние.

fascism *n.* фаши́зм.

fascist *n.* фаши́ст. **—adj.** фаши́стский.

fashion *n.* **1,** (current style; vogue) мо́да: *be in fashion,* быть в мо́де. *The latest fashion,* после́дняя мо́да. *Fashion magazine,* журна́л мод. *Fashion show,* пока́з моде́лей оде́жды. **2,** (way; manner) о́браз; спо́соб; мане́ра. *In this fashion,* таки́м о́бразом. *Behave in a strange fashion,* вести́ себя́ стра́нно. **—v.t.** выде́лывать. *Fashion out of clay,* вы́лепить (что́-нибудь) из гли́ны. **—after a fashion,** не́которым о́бразом; в своём ро́де.

fashionable *adj.* **1,** (in style) мо́дный. *Become fashionable,* А, (of clothes) входи́ть в мо́ду. В, (of a practice) стать мо́дно. **2,** (high-class) фешене́бельный.

fashionably *adv.* мо́дно.

fashion plate мо́дник; мо́дная карти́нка.

fast *adj.* **1,** (swift) бы́стрый; ско́рый. *Fast horse,* бы́страя ло́шадь. *Fast train,* ско́рый по́езд. **2,** (of a timepiece): *My watch is* (*ten minutes*) *fast,* мои́ часы́ спеша́т (на де́сять мину́т). **3,** (loyal; close, as of friends) ве́рный. **4,** (not fading) про́чный: *fast colors,* про́чные кра́ски. **—adv. 1,** (rapidly) бы́стро: *run fast,* бежа́ть бы́стро. **2,** (firmly) кре́пко. *Stand fast,* сто́йко держа́ться. **3,** *He is fast asleep,* он кре́пко спит. **—v.i.** пости́ться. **—n.** пост: *observe a fast:* соблюда́ть пост.

fast-acting *adj.* быстроде́йствующий.

fasten *v.t.* **1,** (fix firmly in place) скрепля́ть: *fasten something with a pin,* скрепля́ть что́-нибудь була́вкой. **2,** (attach) прикрепля́ть: *fasten a mirror to the wall,* прикрепля́ть зе́ркало к стене́. **3,** (hook; buckle) застёгивать; пристёгивать. *Fasten one's seat belt,* пристегну́ть привязно́й ре́мень. **—v.i. 1,** *fol. by* **to** *or* **onto** (attach to) прикрепля́ться (к). **2,** (button; hook; clasp) застёгиваться.

fastener *n.* застёжка.

fastidious *adj.* **1,** (neat) чистопло́тный. **2,** (discriminating) разбо́рчивый.

fast-moving *adj.* быстрохо́дный.

fastness *n.* **1,** (remote and secure place) тверды́ня. **2,** (firmness) про́чность.

fast-selling *adj.* хо́дкий; ходово́й.

fat *adj.* **1,** (obese) по́лный; то́лстый; ту́чный. *Get fat,* полне́ть; толсте́ть. **2,** (of fat): *the fat content of milk,* содержа́ние жи́ра в молоке́; жи́рность молока́. **—n.** жир; са́ло.

fatal *adj.* **1,** (mortal; lethal) смерте́льный. **2,** (causing ruin; disastrous) роково́й: *fatal mistake,* рокова́я оши́бка. *Fatal consequences,* ги́бельные после́дствия.

fatalism *n.* фатали́зм. **—fatalist,** *n.* фатали́ст. **—fatalistic,** *adj.* фаталисти́ческий.

fatality *n.* смерте́льный слу́чай: *no fatalities,* ни одного́ смерте́льного слу́чая.

fatally *adv.* смерте́льно.

fate *n.* **1,** (invisible force) судьба́. *Fate brought them together,* судьба́ их свела́. **2,** (what happens to someone) судьба́; у́часть. *The fate of mankind,* судьба́ челове́чества. *He met a horrible fate,* его́ пости́гла стра́шная судьба́/у́часть.

fated *adj.* суждено́: *We were not fated to...,* нам не суждено́ бы́ло (+ *inf.*).

fateful *adj.* **1,** (momentous) роково́й; судьбоно́сный. **2,** (telltale) проро́ческий.

father *n.* **1,** (male parent) оте́ц. **2,** *pl.* (ancestors) пре́дки. **3,** (God) Оте́ц: *Heavenly Father,* Оте́ц Небе́сный. *Our Father (prayer),* О́тче наш. **4,** (priest) оте́ц: *Father Michael,* оте́ц Михаи́л. —*v.t.* роди́ть; производи́ть.

fatherhood *n.* отцо́вство.

father-in-law *n.* **1,** (husband's father) свёкор. **2,** (wife's father) тесть.

fatherland *n.* оте́чество.

fatherly *adj.* оте́ческий.

fathom *n.* морска́я саже́нь. —*v.t.* проника́ть в; разга́дывать; разбира́ть.

fatigue *n.* утомле́ние; уста́лость. —*v.t.* утомля́ть. —*v.i.* устава́ть. —**fatiguing,** *adj.* утоми́тельный.

fatten *v.t.* корми́ть на убо́й; отка́рмливать; раска́рмливать.

fattening *adj.* жи́рный. *Avoid fattening foods,* избега́ть жиро́в.

fatty *adj.* жи́рный; жирово́й. —**fatty acid,** жи́рная кислота́.

fatuous *adj.* глу́пый; дура́цкий.

faucet *n.* (водопрово́дный) кран.

fault *n.* **1,** (responsibility; blame) вина́. *It's my fault,* (э́то) моя́ вина́; я винова́т(а). *It's all the director's fault,* всему́ вино́й дире́ктор. *It's all your fault,* э́то всё вы винова́ты. **2,** (flaw; defect) недоста́ток. **3,** *geol.* сдвиг. —*v.t.* придира́ться к; критикова́ть. —**at fault,** винова́т. —**find fault with,** придира́ться к. —**to a fault,** чрезме́рно.

faultfinder *n.* приди́ра; критика́н.

faultless *adj.* безупре́чный; безукори́зненный.

faulty *adj.* неиспра́вный; дефе́ктный; брако́ванный; поро́чный.

faun *n.* фавн.

fauna *n.* фа́уна.

faux pas ло́жный шаг.

favor *also,* **favour** *n.* **1,** (good turn) одолже́ние; услу́га; любе́зность; ми́лость. *Do someone a favor,* сде́лать одолже́ние (+ *dat.*); оказа́ть услу́гу (+ *dat.*). *Ask someone a favor,* попроси́ть кого́-нибудь об услу́ге. *I have a favor to ask of you,* у меня́ к вам про́сьба. *You would be doing me a big favor,* вы меня́ э́тим о́чень обя́жете. **2,** (friendly regard; approval) ми́лость; благоскло́нность; расположе́ние. *Out of favor,* в неми́лости. *Find favor in someone's eyes,* сниска́ть чьё-нибудь расположе́ние. *Look upon with favor,* относи́ться благоскло́нно к. *Gain favor among,* находи́ть подде́ржку у. —*v.t.* **1,** (oblige) удоста́ивать; благоволи́ть. *He favored us with his presence,* он удосто́ил нас свои́м прису́тствием.

Kindly favor us with a reply, благоволи́те нам отве́тить. **2,** (show partiality toward; prefer) ока́зывать предпочте́ние (+ *dat.*). **3,** (be in favor of; advocate) быть за; стоя́ть за; выступа́ть за. **4,** (facilitate; aid) благоприя́тствовать. **5,** (resemble) уроди́ться в. —**in favor of, 1,** (for; supporting) за: *be in favor of,* быть/стоя́ть/выступа́ть за. **2,** (to the advantage of) в по́льзу (+ *gen.*): *3-2 in favor of...,* три-два в по́льзу (+ *gen.*). *The matter was settled in our favor,* де́ло реши́лось в на́шу по́льзу.

favorable *also,* **favourable** *adj.* благоприя́тный; вы́годный. *Favorable impression,* благоприя́тное впечатле́ние. *In a favorable light,* в вы́годном све́те. *Favorable wind,* попу́тный ве́тер. *On favorable terms,* на льго́тных усло́виях. *Favorable balance of trade,* акти́вный торго́вый бала́нс.

favorably *also,* **favourably** *adv.* благоскло́нно: *be favorably disposed toward,* относи́ться благоскло́нно к. *Compare favorably with, see* **compare.**

favorite *also,* **favourite** *adj.* люби́мый; излюбленный. —*n.* **1,** (that best liked) люби́мец; фавори́т. **2,** *sports* фавори́т.

favoritism *also,* **favouritism** *n.* фаворити́зм; протекциони́зм.

favour *n.* & *v.* = **favor.** —**favourable,** *adj.* = **favorable.** —**favourite,** *adj.* & *n.* = **favorite.** —**favouritism,** *n.* = **favoritism.**

fawn *n.* молодо́й оле́нь. —*v.i.* [*usu.* **fawn on** *or* **upon**] раболе́пствовать (пе́ред); пресмыка́ться (пе́ред); лебези́ть (пе́ред).

fax machine факси́мильный аппара́т.

faze *v.t., colloq.* смуща́ть; расстра́ивать.

fealty *n.* ве́рность.

fear *n.* **1,** (fright) страх: *fear of the unknown,* страх пе́ред неизве́стностью. **2,** (concern) опасе́ние: *arouse fears,* вызыва́ть опасе́ния. —*v.t.* & *i.* боя́ться: *fear trouble,* боя́ться неприя́тностей; *fear for one's life,* боя́ться за свою́ жизнь. —**for fear of/that,** из стра́ха, что; боя́сь, что; из боя́зни, что.

fearful *adj.* **1,** (dreadful) стра́шный. **2,** (apprehensive): *be fearful that...,* боя́ться, что...

fearless *adj.* бесстра́шный; неустраши́мый. —**fearlessness,** *n.* бесстра́шие; неустраши́мость.

fearsome *adj.* стра́шный; гро́зный.

feasibility *n.* осуществи́мость.

feasible *adj.* выполни́мый; исполни́мый; осуществи́мый. *Feasible task,* поси́льная зада́ча.

feast *n.* **1,** (sumptuous meal) пир. **2,** (religious festival) пра́здник. —*v.i.* **1,** (have a feast) пирова́ть. **2,** *fol. by* **on** (eat) ла́комиться (+ *instr.*). —*v.t.* че́ствовать. —**feast one's eyes on,** любова́ться (+ *instr.*); упива́ться (+ *instr.*).

feat *n.* по́двиг.

feather *n.* перо́. *Light as a feather,* лёгкий, как пёрышко. —**birds of a feather,** одного́ по́ля я́года; два сапога́ па́ра. *Birds of a feather flock together,* моря́к моряка́ (*or* рыба́к рыбака́) ви́дит издалека́. —**feather in one's cap,** большо́е достиже́ние; предме́т го́рдости. —**feather one's nest,** нагре́ть ру́ки; наби́ть себе́ карма́н; свить себе́ тёплое гнёздышко.

feather bed пери́на; пухови́к.

feathered *adj.* оперённый; перна́тый.

feather grass ковы́ль.

feathery *adj.* **1,** (covered with feathers) перна́тый. **2,** (light; soft) пуши́стый.

feature *n.* **1,** (characteristic) черта́; осо́бенность. *Distinguishing feature,* отличи́тельная черта́. **2,** *pl.* (facial appearance) черты́ лица́. **3,** (highlight) гвоздь. —*adj.* передово́й: центра́льный: *feature article,* передова́я/центра́льная статья́. —*v.t.* отводи́ть важне́йшее ме́сто (+ *dat.*); помеща́ть на ви́дном ме́сте; выводи́ть в гла́вной ро́ли. *The film features...,* в фи́льме ... игра́ет гла́вную роль.

febrile *adj.* лихора́дочный.

February *n.* февра́ль. —*adj.* февра́льский.

feces *also,* **faeces** *n.pl.* кал; испражне́ния.

feckless *adj.* **1,** (careless; irresponsible) неради́вый. **2,** (ineffectual) сла́бый: *feckless attempt,* сла́бая попы́тка.

fecund *adj.* плодови́тый. —**fecundity,** *n.* плодови́тость.

federal *adj.* федера́льный; федерати́вный; сою́зный. —**Federal Assembly,** Федера́льное собра́ние.

federalism *n.* федерали́зм. —**federalist,** *n.* федерали́ст.

federate *v.t. & i.* объединя́ть(ся) в сою́з. —**federated,** *adj.* федерати́вный.

federation *n.* федера́ция; сою́з. *The Russian Federation,* Росси́йская Федера́ция.

fee *n.* **1,** (for professional services) гонора́р; пла́та. *Charge a fee,* взима́ть пла́ту. **2,** (for admission, membership, etc.) пла́та; взнос.

feeble *adj.* **1,** (infirm) нéмощный; хи́лый. **2,** *fig.* (ineffective) сла́бый: *feeble attempt,* сла́бая попы́тка.

feeble-minded *adj.* слабоу́мный. —**feeble-mindedness,** *n.* слабоу́мие.

feed *v.t.* **1,** (give food to; help to eat) корми́ть: *feed the baby/monkeys,* корми́ть ребёнка/обезья́н. **2,** (provide as food) ска́рмливать. *Feed oats to the horses,* ска́рмливать овёс лошадя́м; корми́ть лошаде́й овсо́м. **3,** (keep nourished; sustain) корми́ть; прокорми́ть; пита́ть. *Feed one's family,* корми́ть семьёй. *Feed the population,* прокорми́ть населе́ние. **4,** *in* **feed oneself,** есть самостоя́тельно. *Be able to feed oneself,* мочь сам (сама́) есть. *That's how I feed (i.e. support) myself,* э́тим я кормлю́сь. **5,** (insert) вкла́дывать; вноси́ть: *feed paper into a copying machine,* вкла́дывать бума́гу в копирова́льную маши́ну; *feed data into a computer,* вноси́ть да́нные в компью́тер. —*v.i.* корми́ться; пита́ться: *feed on hay,* корми́ться/пита́ться се́ном. —*n.* корм. —**fed up,** сыт по го́рло (+ *instr.*). *I am fed up with it,* э́то мне надое́ло *or* осточерте́ло.

feedback *n.* обра́тная связь.

feedbag *n.* то́рба.

feeder *n.* **1,** (branch line) ве́тка. **2,** *electricity* фи́дер.

feed grain фура́жное зерно́.

feeding *n.* кормле́ние; пита́ние. —**feeding bottle,** де́тский рожо́к. —**feeding trough,** корму́шка.

feel *v.t.* **1,** (sense; experience) чу́вствовать; ощуща́ть:

feel pain, чу́вствовать/ощуща́ть боль. **2,** (touch) щу́пать; ощу́пывать; прощу́пывать; потро́гать. *Feel someone's pulse,* (по)щу́пать пульс у кого́-нибудь. *Feel how cold my hands are!,* потро́гайте, каки́е у меня́ холо́дные ру́ки! **3,** *in* **feel one's way,** идти́ на о́щупь; пробира́ться о́щупью. **4,** (think; believe) счита́ть. —*v.i.* **1,** (be in a certain physical condition) чу́вствовать себя́: *How do you feel?,* как вы себя́ чу́вствуете? *Feel ill,* пло́хо себя́ чу́вствовать. **2,** (have a certain feeling) име́ть чу́вство: *I feel as if I haven't eaten for three days,* у меня́ тако́е чу́вство, бу́дто не ел (е́ла) три дня. **3,** (experience some emotion): *feel sorry for,* жале́ть. *Feel bad about,* сожале́ть о. **4,** (seem, as to the touch) каза́ться: *The water feels warm,* вода́ ка́жется тёплой. *It feels like silk,* на о́щупь э́то похо́же на шёлк. **5,** (grope) ша́рить: *feel in one's pocket,* ша́рить в карма́не. **6,** (have an opinion about): *How do you feel about this?,* как вы отно́ситесь к э́тому? *I feel very strongly about it,* я твёрдо убеждён в э́том. —*n.* ощуще́ние; осяза́ние; чутьё. *Get the feel of,* осво́иться с. *Have a feel for music,* хорошо́ чу́вствовать му́зыку. —**feel for, 1,** (grope for) иска́ть о́щупью. **2,** (sympathize with) сочу́вствовать (+ *dat.*); страда́ть за; боле́ть душо́й за. —**feel like,** хоте́ться (+ *dat.*); име́ть охо́ту; быть не прочь. —**make itself felt,** дава́ть себя́ знать; дава́ть себя́ чу́вствовать.

feeler *n.* **1,** *zool.* у́сик. **2,** *fig.* (hint) про́бный шар. *Put out a feeler,* заки́нуть у́дочку.

feeling *n.* **1,** (emotion; sense) чу́вство: *feeling of pride,* чу́вство го́рдости. *Play with feeling,* игра́ть с чу́вством; игра́ть с душо́й. **2,** (sensation) ощуще́ние. *I have no feeling in my arm,* у меня́ рука́ онеме́ла. **3,** *pl.* (sensibilities) самолю́бие: *hurt someone's feelings,* задева́ть чьё-нибудь самолю́бие. **4,** (impression; opinion) впечатле́ние; мне́ние. *I have the feeling that...,* у меня́ тако́е впечатле́ние, что... **5,** (presentiment) предчу́вствие.

feign *v.t.* притворя́ться. *Feign illness,* притворя́ться *or* сказа́ться больны́м (больно́й). *Feign surprise,* разыгра́ть удивле́ние. —**feigned,** *adj.* притво́рный.

feint *n.* финт. —*v.i.* сде́лать финт.

feldspar *n.* полево́й шпат.

felicitate *v.t.* поздравля́ть. —**felicitation,** *n.* поздравле́ние.

felicitous *adj.* уда́чный; ме́ткий.

felicity *n.* **1,** (great happiness) сча́стье; блаже́нство. **2,** (aptness) ме́ткость.

feline *adj.* коша́чий.

fell *v.t.* **1,** (cut down) руби́ть; сруба́ть; выруба́ть. **2,** (knock down) вали́ть; сбива́ть с ног.

fellow *n.* челове́к; па́рень; ма́лый. —*adj.* това́рищ по; со-: *fellow worker,* това́рищ по рабо́те; *fellow citizen,* согражда́нин. *Fellow countryman,* соотéчественник.

fellowship *n.* **1,** (comradeship) това́рищество. **2,** (grant) стипе́ндия.

fellow traveler *also,* **fellow traveller** попу́тчик.

felon *n.* престу́пник. —**felonious,** *adj.* престу́пный. —**felony,** *n.* уголо́вное преступле́ние.

felt *n.* во́йлок; фетр. —*adj.* во́йлочный; фе́тровый.
female *adj.* же́нский. *Female doctor,* же́нщина-врач. *Female deer,* са́мка оле́ня. *Female cat,* ко́шка. *Female horse,* кобы́ла. —*n.* **1,** (woman) же́нщина. **2,** (female animal) са́мка; ма́тка.
feminine *adj.* **1,** (female) же́нский. **2,** (womanly) же́нственный. **3,** *gram.* же́нского ро́да. *Feminine gender,* же́нский род.
femininity *n.* же́нственность.
feminism *n.* feminíзм. —**feminist,** *n.* feminíст; feminíстка. —*adj.* feminíстский; feministíческий.
femur *n.* бе́дренная кость.
fence *n.* забо́р; огра́да. —*v.t.* **1,** *fol. by* **in** (enclose) загора́живать; огора́живать. **2,** *fol. by* **off** (separate) отгора́живать; выгора́живать. —*v.i.* (engage in fencing) фехтова́ть.
fencer *n.* фехтова́льщик.
fencing *n.* фехтова́ние.
fend *v.t.* [*usu.* **fend off**] отража́ть; отбива́ть. —**fend for oneself,** забо́титься о себе́. *He was left to fend for himself,* он был предоста́влен самому́ себе́.
fender *n.* крыло́.
fennel *n.* фе́нхель.
ferment *n.* **1,** (substance producing fermentation) ферме́нт; заква́ска. **2,** *fig.* (unrest) броже́ние. —*v.i.* броди́ть; переброди́ть. —*v.t.* вызыва́ть броже́ние в; заква́шивать.
fermentation *n.* броже́ние.
fermented *adj.* переброди́вший.
fermium *n.* фе́рмий.
fern *n.* па́поротник.
ferocious *adj.* свире́пый; лю́тый. —**ferocity,** *n.* свире́пость; лю́тость.
ferret *n.* хорёк. —*v.t.* [*usu.* **ferret out**] выве́дывать; выпы́тывать.
ferric oxide о́кись желе́за.
Ferris wheel чёртово колесо́.
ferrotype *n.* ферроти́пия.
ferrous *adj.* желе́зистый. —**ferrous metals,** чёрные мета́ллы. —**ferrous oxide,** за́кись желе́за. —**ferrous sulfate,** желе́зный купоро́с.
ferrule *n.* наконе́чник.
ferry *n.* [*also,* **ferryboat**] паро́м. —*v.t.* перевози́ть; переправля́ть. —**ferryman,** *n.* паро́мщик; перево́зчик.
fertile *adj.* плодоро́дный: *fertile soil,* плодоро́дная по́чва. *Fertile imagination,* бога́тое/живо́е/пы́лкое воображе́ние.
fertility *n.* **1,** (of the soil) плодоро́дие. **2,** *biol.* плодови́тость.
fertilization *n.* **1,** (of the soil) удобре́ние. **2,** *biol.* оплодотворе́ние.
fertilize *v.t.* **1,** (spread fertilizer on) удобря́ть. **2,** *biol.* оплодотворя́ть. *Fertilized egg,* оплодотворённое яйцо́.
fertilizer *n.* удобре́ние.
ferule *n.* феру́ла.
fervent *adj.* горя́чий; стра́стный; пы́лкий. —**fervently,** *adv.* горячо́.

fervid *adj.* горя́чий; пы́лкий; пла́менный.
fervor *also,* **fervour** *n.* жар; пыл; задо́р.
fester *v.i.* гнои́ться.
festering *n.* гное́ние; нагное́ние. —*adj.* гно́йный.
festival *n.* **1,** (holiday) пра́зднество. **2,** (music, film, youth, etc.) фестива́ль. *Film festival,* кинофестива́ль.
festive *adj.* пра́здничный; торже́ственный.
festivity *n.* **1,** (gaiety; mirth) весе́лье. **2,** *pl.* (festive proceedings) пра́зднества; торжества́.
festoon *n.* **1,** (hanging decoration) гирля́нда. **2,** (ornamental carving) фесто́н. —*v.t.* украша́ть.
fetal *also,* **foetal** *adj.* пло́дный.
fetch *v.t.* идти́ за; сходи́ть за; приноси́ть; приводи́ть.
fetching *adj.* привлека́тельный; хоро́шенький; коке́тливый.
fete *also,* **fête** *n.* пра́зднество. —*v.t.* че́ствовать.
fetid *adj.* злово́нный; воню́чий.
fetish *n.* фети́ш.
fetlock *n.* щётка.
fetter *n., usu. pl.* **1,** (chains) пу́ты; кандалы́. **2,** *fig.* (shackles) око́вы; пу́ты. —*v.t.* пу́тать (ло́шадь).
fettle *n.* состоя́ние; настрое́ние.
fetus *also,* **foetus** *n.* плод; заро́дыш.
feud *n.* вражда́. —*v.i.* враждова́ть.
feudal *adj.* феода́льный. —**feudalism,** *n.* феодали́зм.
fever *n.* **1,** (high temperature) жар. **2,** (disease) лихора́дка: *yellow fever,* жёлтая лихора́дка. **3,** *fig.* (enthusiasm; craze) лихора́дка; горя́чка: *speculative fever,* биржева́я лихора́дка/горя́чка. —**fever pitch,** нака́л. *Reach a fever pitch,* дости́гнуть нака́ла; дойти́ *or* накали́ться до преде́ла.
feverish *adj.* лихора́дочный. *I feel feverish,* меня́ знобит; меня́ лихора́дит.
few *adj.* **1,** (not many) ма́ло; немно́гие. *There were very few people there,* там бы́ло ма́ло наро́ду. *Few people know about it,* ма́ло кто зна́ет об э́том. *With few exceptions,* за немно́гими исключе́ниями. *Few events of recent years have so...,* то́лько немно́гие собы́тия (*or* ма́ло како́е собы́тие) после́дних лет так... **2,** *usu. preceded by* **a** (a certain small number of) не́сколько: *in a few minutes,* че́рез не́сколько мину́т; *in a few words,* в не́скольких слова́х. *Every few days,* ка́ждые не́сколько дней. *Quite a few,* дово́льно мно́го. —*pron.* немно́гие: *one of the few who...,* оди́н (одна́) из тех немно́гих, кото́рые... —**few and far between,** о́чень ре́дкие; наперечёт.
fez *n.* фе́ска.
fiancé *n.* жени́х. —**fiancée,** *n.* неве́ста.
fiasco *n.* фиа́ско.
fiat *n.* декре́т; ука́з.
fib *n.* вы́думка; непра́вда. —*v.i.* врать; привира́ть. —**fibber,** *n.* вы́думщик.
fiber *also,* **fibre** *n.* **1,** (filament) волокно́. **2,** *fig.* (inner strength) хара́ктер. —**fiberglass,** *n.* стекловолокно́. —**fiber optics,** волоко́нная о́птика.
fibrin *n.* фибри́н.
fibrinogen *n.* фибриноге́н.
fibrous *adj.* волокни́стый.
fibula *n.* ма́лая берцо́вая кость.

fickle *adj.* непостоя́нный; изме́нчивый.

fiction *n.* **1,** (literature) беллетри́стика; худо́жественная литерату́ра. **2,** (fabrication) фи́кция; вы́мысел. —**fictional,** *adj.* беллетристи́ческий.

fictitious *adj.* **1,** = **fictional. 2,** (false) вы́думанный; вы́мышленный; фикти́вный.

fiddle *n.* скри́пка. —*v.i.* **1,** *colloq.* (play the violin) игра́ть на скри́пке. **2,** *fol.* by **with** (fidget with) вози́ться с; игра́ть (+ *instr.*). —*v.t.* [*usu.* **fiddle away**] растра́чивать. —**fit as a fiddle,** совсе́м здоро́в; как нельзя́ лу́чше. —**play second fiddle,** игра́ть втору́ю скри́пку.

fiddler *n.* скрипа́ч.

fiddlesticks *interj.* вздор!; чепуха́!

fidelity *n.* **1,** (faithfulness) ве́рность. **2,** (accuracy) то́чность.

fidget *v.i.* **1,** (move restlessly) ёрзать; егози́ть; суети́ться. **2,** *fol.* by **with** (fuss with) игра́ть (+ *instr.*). —*n.* непосе́да; егоза́; юла́. —**fidgety,** *adj.* суетли́вый; егозли́вый; непосе́дливый.

fie *interj.* фи!

fief *n.* феод.

field *n.* **1,** (piece of open land) по́ле: *cornfield,* кукуру́зное по́ле. **2,** (piece of land used for a particular purpose) площа́дка: *landing field,* поса́дочная площа́дка. **3,** *sports* по́ле; площа́дка: *athletic/playing field,* спорти́вное по́ле; спорти́вная площа́дка; *soccer/football field,* футбо́льное по́ле. **4,** (place containing a natural resource) месторожде́ние; про́мысел: *oil fields,* месторожде́ния не́фти; нефтяны́е про́мыслы. *Coal field,* месторожде́ние угля́; у́гольный бассе́йн. **5,** *fig.* (sphere, as of knowledge) о́бласть; о́трасль. *Work in one's field,* рабо́тать по специа́льности. —*adj.* полево́й: *field gun,* полево́е ору́дие; *field hospital,* полево́й го́спиталь. —**field of vision,** по́ле зре́ния.

field glasses полево́й бино́кль.

field goal гол с игры́.

field hockey хокке́й на траве́.

field marshal фельдма́ршал.

field mouse полева́я мышь.

fiend *n.* и́зверг; изуве́р.

fiendish *adj.* зве́рский; изуве́рский.

fierce *adj.* **1,** (ferocious) свире́пый; лю́тый. **2,** (violent, as of a storm) нето́вый. **3,** (bitter; intense, as of a struggle) жесто́кий; ожесточённый.

fiery *adj.* **1,** (ablaze) о́гненный. **2,** (impassioned) пла́менный; о́гненный; огнево́й; горя́чий. *Fiery speech,* пла́менная речь.

fife *n.* ду́дка.

fifteen *n. & adj.* пятна́дцать.

fifteenth *adj.* пятна́дцатый. —*n.* пятна́дцатая; пятна́дцатая часть. *One-fifteenth,* одна́ пятна́дцатая; пятна́дцатая часть.

fifth *adj.* пя́тый. —*n.* пя́тая; пя́тая часть. *One-fifth,* одна́ пя́тая; пя́тая часть. *One-fifth of the population,* пя́тая часть населе́ния. *Three-fifths,* три пя́тых. —**fifth column,** пя́тая коло́нна. —**fifth wheel,** пя́тое колесо́ в теле́ге; пя́тая спи́ца в колесни́це.

fiftieth *adj.* пятидеся́тый. —*n.* пятидеся́тая; пяти-

деся́тая часть. *One-fiftieth,* одна́ пятидеся́тая; пятидеся́тая часть.

fifty *n. & adj.* пятьдеся́т.

fig *n.* **1,** (tree) инжи́р; фи́га; фи́говое де́рево; смоко́вница. **2,** (fruit) инжи́р; фи́га; ви́нная я́года; смо́ква. **3,** (insulting gesture) шиш; ку́киш; фи́га. —**fig leaf,** фи́говый листо́к.

fight *v.i.* **1,** (engage in fisticuffs) дра́ться. **2,** (take part in combat) сража́ться: *fight bravely,* сража́ться хра́бро. **3,** (wage war) воева́ть: *England fought against Germany,* А́нглия воева́ла с Герма́нией. **4,** (wage a campaign) боро́ться: *fight for an idea,* боро́ться за иде́ю; *fight against injustice,* боро́ться про́тив несправедли́вости. —*v.t.* **1,** (combat physically) дра́ться с. **2,** (combat in war) сража́ться с; боро́ться с: *fight the enemy,* сража́ться/боро́ться с враго́м. **3,** (wage; carry on, as a war or battle) вести́. *Fight a duel,* дра́ться на дуэ́ли. **4,** (try to do away with) боро́ться с: *fight crime/poverty,* боро́ться с престу́пностью/нището́й. **5,** *Fight one's way,* пробива́ться (*e.g.* сквозь толпу́). —*n.* **1,** (fistfight) дра́ка: *start a fight,* затея́ть дра́ку. *Get into a fight with,* подра́ться с. **2,** (fighting; boxing match) бой: *lose the fight,* проигра́ть бой. *Surrender without a fight,* сда́ться без бо́я. **3,** *fig.* (battle; campaign) борьба́: *the fight against crime,* борьба́ с престу́пностью. —**fight back, 1,** (not yield) отбива́ться. **2,** (try to suppress, as tears) боро́ться с. —**fight off,** отбива́ть; отбива́ться от: *fight off an attack/ one's attackers/,* отбива́ть нападе́ние; отбива́ться от напада́ющих. *Fight off sleep,* боро́ться со сном.

fighter *n.* **1,** (combatant) бое́ц. **2,** (pugilist) боксёр. **3,** (strong advocate, as of a cause) боре́ц. **4,** (fighter plane) истреби́тель. —**fighter-pilot,** лётчик-истреби́тель.

fighting *n.* бой. *Heavy fighting,* тяжёлые *or* упо́рные бои́. —*adj.* **1,** (pert. to combat) боево́й. *Fighting spirit,* боево́й дух. **2,** (militant, as of a speech) вои́нственный.

figment *n.* вы́мысел; вы́думка. *Figment of the imagination,* плод *or* игра́ воображе́ния.

figurative *adj.* перено́сный. —**figuratively,** *adv.* о́бразно: *figuratively speaking,* о́бразно говоря́.

figure *n.* **1,** (number) ци́фра: *exact figures,* то́чные ци́фры. *Bad at figures,* слаб в арифме́тике. **2,** (form; shape; anything visible by its outline) фигу́ра. *She has a nice figure,* у неё хоро́шая фигу́ра. **3,** (sculptured representation) фигу́ра: *wax figure,* восково́я фигу́ра. **4,** (diagram in a textbook) рису́нок. **5,** (personage) фигу́ра; ли́чность; де́ятель. **6,** *geom.* фигу́ра. —*v.t.* **1,** (calculate) рассчи́тывать; подсчи́тывать. **2,** *colloq.* (think; reckon) полага́ть; счита́ть. **3,** *fol. by* **out** (reason out) сообража́ть: *figure out what is going on,* сообража́ть, что происхо́дит. **4,** *fol. by* **out** (understand) понима́ть: *I can't figure him out,* не могу́ его́ поня́ть. —*v.i.* **1,** (appear prominently) фигури́ровать. **2,** *fol. by* **on** (count on) рассчи́тывать на. —**figure of speech,** оборо́т ре́чи.

figured *adj.* фигу́рный; узо́рчатый.

figurehead *n.* номина́льный глава́.

figure skating фигу́рное ката́ние. —**figure skater,** фигури́ст; фигури́стка.

figurine *n.* фигу́рка; статуэ́тка.

filament *n.* **1,** (fine thread or fiber) волокно́. **2,** (of a bulb) нить; волосо́к.

filbert *n.* фунду́к.

filch *v.t.* стащи́ть; стяну́ть.

file *n.* **1,** (cabinet) шкаф; (folder) па́пка; скоросшива́тель. **2,** (record) де́ло; досье́. *Card file,* картоте́ка. *Newspaper file,* газе́тная подши́вка. **3,** (line) ряд; шере́нга; коло́нна; верени́ца. *Single file,* гуська́м. **4,** *chess* вертика́ль. **5,** (tool) напи́льник. *Nail file,* пи́лка для ногте́й. —*v.t.* **1,** (smooth with a file) подпи́ливать. **2,** (store in a file) подшива́ть (к де́лу). **3,** (submit; lodge; register) подава́ть: *file an application/complaint/appeal,* подава́ть заявле́ние/жа́лобу/апелля́цию. *File suit against,* подава́ть в суд на (+ *acc.*); предъявля́ть иск к. *File a claim/protest,* заяви́ть прете́нзию/проте́ст. —*v.i.* **1,** (march in file) идти́ коло́нной; идти́ гуська́м. *File in,* входи́ть гуська́м. *File out,* выходи́ть гуська́м. **2,** (make application) подава́ть заявле́ние. *File for divorce,* возбужда́ть де́ло о разво́де; подава́ть на разво́д.

filet *n.* филе́.

filial *adj.* сыно́вний; доче́рний.

filigree *n.* филигра́нь. —*adj.* филигра́нный.

filing cabinet шкаф (для хране́ния докуме́нтов).

filings *n.pl.* опи́лки.

fill *v.t.* **1,** (make full) наполня́ть: *fill the pail with water,* напо́лнить ведро́ водо́й. *The room was filled with smoke,* ко́мната напо́лнилась ды́мом. *Fill a hole with dirt,* заполня́ть *or* засыпа́ть *or* забра́сывать я́му землёй. *Fill one's pipe,* набива́ть тру́бку. **2,** (occupy the whole of) заполня́ть: *People filled the hall,* зал запо́лнили лю́ди. *Music filled the air,* во́здух напо́лнила му́зыка. **3,** (plug up; close) затыка́ть: *fill the cracks,* затыка́ть ще́ли. *Fill a gap (fig.),* восполня́ть пробе́л. **4,** (complete, as an order for merchandise) выполня́ть (зака́з). *Fill a prescription,* изготовля́ть лека́рство (по реце́пту). **5,** (satisfy, as a need) удовлетворя́ть. **6,** (occupy, as an office) заполня́ть: *fill a vacancy,* запо́лнить вака́нсию. **7,** (put a filling in, as a tooth) пломбирова́ть. —**eat one's fill,** нае́сться до́сыта *or* вво́лю. —**fill in, 1,** (fill, as cracks) затыка́ть. **2,** (fill up, as a hole) засыпа́ть; зака́пывать. **3,** (write in) впи́сывать; проставля́ть. *Fill in the blanks,* заполня́ть про́пуски. **4,** (occupy, as time) заполня́ть. **5,** *fol. by* **for** (be a substitute for) заменя́ть. **6,** *fol. by* **on** (provide with information about) вводи́ть в курс (+ *gen.*). —**fill out, 1,** (complete, as a questionnaire) заполня́ть. **2,** (become fuller or more rounded) полне́ть; округля́ться. —**fill up, 1,** (make full) наполня́ть. *Fill up the water in the radiator,* долива́ть воды́ в радиа́тор. **2,** (become full) наполня́ться.

filler *n.* **1,** (substance to increase bulk) наполни́тель. **2,** (substance to fill cracks) шпаклёвка. **3,** (filling, as for pies) начи́нка.

fillet *n.* **1,** (band) ле́нта. **2,** (of meat or fish) филе́; вы́резка.

filling *n.* **1,** (act of filling) наполне́ние. **2,** (for pastry, cake, etc.) фарш; начи́нка. **3,** (for a tooth) пло́мба. **4,** *textiles* (weft; woof) уто́к. —*adj.* (of food) сы́тный. —**filling station,** бензозапра́вочная ста́нция; автозапра́вочная ста́нция; бензоколо́нка.

fillip *n.* **1,** (snap of the fingers) щелчо́к. **2,** *fig.* (stimulus) толчо́к.

filly *n.* кобы́лка.

film *n.* **1,** (thin layer) плёнка. **2,** *photog.* плёнка; фотоплёнка. **3,** (movie) фильм; карти́на. *Film crew,* съёмочная гру́ппа. —*v.t.* **1,** (photograph) снима́ть; засня́ть. **2,** (make a movie of) экранизи́ровать.

filmmaker *n.* продю́сер.

filmy *adj.* похо́жий на плёнку; вя́зкий.

filter *n.* фильтр. —*v.t.* **1,** (strain) фильтрова́ть; процежива́ть. **2,** *fol. by* **out** (remove) отсе́ивать. —*v.i.* [*often* **filter into**] проса́чиваться (в); проника́ть (в).

filth *n.* грязь.

filthy *adj.* гря́зный.

filtration *n.* фильтра́ция.

fin *n.* плавни́к.

final *adj.* **1,** (last) после́дний; коне́чный; заключи́тельный; заверша́ющий. *The final outcome,* коне́чный результа́т. *The final score,* оконча́тельный счёт. *Final examination,* ито́говый экза́мен. **2,** (definitive) оконча́тельный: *The decision of the court is final,* реше́ние суда́ — оконча́тельное. —*n.* **1,** = **final exam. 2,** *pl., sports* фина́л.

finale *n.* фина́л.

finalist *n.* финали́ст.

finality *n.* оконча́тельность. *With an air of finality,* повели́тельным то́ном.

finally *adv.* наконе́ц.

finance *n., often pl.* фина́нсы. —*v.t.* финанси́ровать.

financial *adj.* фина́нсовый. *Financial difficulties,* фина́нсовые *or* материа́льные затрудне́ния. *Financial support/gain,* материа́льная подде́ржка/вы́года.

financier *n.* финанси́ст.

finch *n.* вьюро́к. *Bullfinch,* снеги́рь. *Chaffinch,* зя́блик. *Goldfinch,* щего́л.

find *v.t.* **1,** (locate; discover) находи́ть (*pfv.* найти́): *find the money,* найти́ де́ньги; *find a mistake,* найти́ оши́бку. *Find a country on the map,* найти́ страну́ на ка́рте. **2,** (discover on arrival) находи́ть; застава́ть. *Find a note on the table,* найти́ запи́ску на столе́. *Find the door open,* найти́ дверь откры́той. *Find someone at home,* заста́ть кого́-нибудь до́ма. *I found him talking to Sasha,* я заста́л его́ бесе́дующим с Са́шей. **3,** (consider; think) находи́ть: *find the book interesting,* находи́ть кни́гу интере́сной. *Find it amusing that...,* находи́ть заба́вным, что... *I find that hard to believe,* мне тру́дно э́тому (*or* в э́то) пове́рить. **4,** (reach; attain) попада́ть: *find its mark,* попада́ть в цель. **5,** (adjudge) признава́ть: *find the defendant guilty,* призна́ть подсуди́мого вино́вным. *The doctor found the child to be healthy,* врач нашёл ребёнка здоро́вым. **6,** *in* **find fault with,** придира́ться к. **7,** *in* **find (the) time,** находи́ть *or* выбира́ть вре́мя. —*n.* нахо́дка: *a real find,* настоя́щая нахо́дка. —**be found,** находи́ться. *Kangaroos are* *found only in Australia,* кенгуру́ во́дятся то́лько в Австра́лии. *He is nowhere to be found,* его́ нигде́ нет. —**find oneself, 1,** (perceive oneself to be somewhere) оказа́ться; очути́ться. **2,** (become aware) лови́ть себя́: *find oneself doing something,* лови́ть себя́ на том, что (+ *verb*). **3,** (discover where one's talents lie) найти́ себя́. —**find out,** узнава́ть.

finding *n.* **1,** (verdict) реше́ние. **2,** *usu. pl.* (results of an inquiry) вы́воды. **3,** *pl.* (accessories used in dressmaking) прикла́д.

fine *adj.* **1,** (very good; excellent) прекра́сный; отли́чный. *Fine person,* прекра́сный челове́к. *Fine young man,* сла́вный па́рень. *In fine shape,* в отли́чном состоя́нии. *How are you? Fine!,* как вы пожива́ете? Хорошо́! *I'm feeling fine,* я чу́вствую себя́ отли́чно. **2,** (clear; cloudless) хоро́ший; я́сный; пого́жий. *Fine weather,* хоро́шая пого́да. *Fine day,* я́сный *or* пого́жий день. *One fine day (fig.),* в оди́н прекра́сный день. **3,** (of high quality) то́нкий: *fine wines,* то́нкие ви́на. *Fine workmanship,* то́нкая рабо́та. **4,** (of thread, lace, etc.) то́нкий. **5,** (of sand, dust, rain, print, etc.) ме́лкий. **6,** (of a comb, net, sieve, etc.) ча́стый. **7,** (subtle) то́нкий. *Fine point,* то́нкость. —*adv.* **1,** (into small particles) то́нко; ме́лко. **2,** (O.K.; swell) хорошо́. *That suits me fine,* э́то меня́ вполне́ устра́ивает. —*n.* штраф: *a ten-dollar fine,* штраф в де́сять до́лларов; *a fine of $1000,* штраф в разме́ре ты́сячи до́лларов. —*v.t.* штрафова́ть: *He was fined $100,* его́ штрафова́ли (*or* он был оштрафо́ван) на сто до́лларов.

fine arts изя́щные *or* изобрази́тельные иску́сства.

fine-grained *adj.* мелкозерни́стый.

finely *adv.* то́нко; ме́лко. *Finely sliced onions,* то́нко/ме́лко наре́занный лук.

fineness *n.* то́нкость.

finery *n.* наря́ды.

finesse *n.* то́нкость.

finger *n.* па́лец. *Eat with one's fingers,* есть рука́ми. *Count on one's fingers,* счита́ть на па́льцах. *You can count them on the fingers of one hand,* их мо́жно счита́ть по па́льцам. —*v.t.* перебира́ть. —**not lay a finger on,** па́льцем не тро́гать. —**not lift a finger,** па́лец о па́лец не уда́рить; па́льцем не шевельну́ть. —**put one's finger on it,** попа́сть в са́мую то́чку. —**put the finger on,** *slang* доноси́ть на.

finger board гриф.

fingering *n., music* аппликату́ра.

finger mark пятно́ от па́льца.

fingernail *n.* но́готь.

fingerprint *n.* отпеча́ток па́льца. —*v.t.* снима́ть отпеча́тки па́льцев с (+ *gen.*).

fingertip *n.* ко́нчик па́льца. —**have at one's fingertips,** име́ть под руко́й.

finical *adj.* привере́дливый. *Also,* **finicky.**

finish *v.t.* **1,** (complete) конча́ть; зака́нчивать: *finish a story,* ко́нчить/зако́нчить расска́з. *Finish dinner,* ко́нчить/зако́нчить обе́д. *Finish speaking,* ко́нчить говори́ть; договори́ть. *Finish a cigarette,* ко́нчить *or* докури́ть сигаре́ту. **2,** (ruin) дока́нчивать; доко́нать. **3,** (give a desired surface to) отде́лывать. —*v.i.*

1, (complete something being done) зака́нчивать: *Have you finished?,* вы зако́нчили? *Let someone finish (i.e. speaking),* дать кому́-нибудь договори́ть. **2,** (come to an end) конча́ться. **3,** *fol. by with* (finish using): *Have you finished with the scissors?,* но́жницы бо́льше вам не нужны́? **4,** *sports* финиши́ровать. *Finish first,* финиши́ровать *or* прийти́ пе́рвым; занима́ть пе́рвое ме́сто. —*n.* **1,** (end) коне́ц. *Fight to the finish,* борьба́ не на жизнь, а на́ смерть. **2,** *sports* фи́ниш. *Finish line,* фи́нишная черта́; фи́нишная пряма́я. **3,** (surface texture) отде́лка; полиро́вка: *bronze finish,* бро́нзовая отде́лка; *dull finish,* ту́склая полиро́вка. *The table has an oak finish,* стол отде́лан под дуб. —**finish off, 1,** (complete) зака́нчивать. **2,** (eat or drink) прика́нчивать. **3,** (kill; destroy) добива́ть; прика́нчивать; дока́нчивать.

finished *adj.* **1,** (having completed something): *Are you finished?,* вы зако́нчили? **2,** (completed) зако́нченный. **3,** (completely processed) гото́вый. *Finished product,* гото́вое изде́лие; фабрика́т. **4,** (highly skilled; polished) зако́нченный. **5,** (done for) пропа́вший; поги́бший: *We're finished,* мы пропа́ли; мы поги́бли.

finishing *adj.* заверша́ющий: *finishing blow,* заверша́ющий уда́р. *Finishing touches,* после́дние штрихи́.

finite *adj.* коне́чный.

Finn *n.* финн; фи́нка. —**Finnish,** *adj.* фи́нский. —*n.* фи́нский язы́к.

Finno-Ugric *adj.* фи́нно-уго́рский.

fiord *n.* фио́рд.

fir *n.* пи́хта. —*adj.* пи́хтовый.

fire *n.* **1,** (flames) ого́нь. *Be on fire,* быть в огне́; горе́ть. **2,** (campfire) костёр: *sit around the fire,* сиде́ть вокру́г костра́. **3,** (conflagration) пожа́р: *forest fire,* лесно́й пожа́р. **4,** (shooting) ого́нь; обстре́л. *Open fire on,* откры́ть ого́нь *or* стрельбу́ по. *Be under fire,* быть под обстре́лом. *Come under enemy fire,* попа́сть под ого́нь проти́вника. —*adj.* пожа́рный: *fire hydrant,* пожа́рный кран. —*v.t.* **1,** (shoot, as a gun) стреля́ть из. **2,** (propel) пуска́ть; стреля́ть: *fire a bullet,* пуска́ть пу́лю; *fire bullets,* стреля́ть пу́лями. *Fire a shot,* сде́лать *or* произвести́ вы́стрел. *Fire two shots,* вы́стрелить два ра́за. **3,** (discharge from a position) увольня́ть; прогоня́ть; выгоня́ть с рабо́ты. **4,** (stoke, as a furnace) топи́ть. **5,** (bake in a kiln) обжига́ть. **6,** *fol. by* **up** (rouse; excite) зажига́ть; воспламеня́ть. —*v.i.* **1,** (shoot) стреля́ть. *Fire on,* стреля́ть в; бить по; вести́ ого́нь по. *Fire at a target,* стреля́ть в мише́нь *or* по мише́ни. *Fire into a crowd,* стреля́ть в толпу́. *Fire back,* отстре́ливаться. **2,** (go off) вы́стрелить. —**catch fire,** загоре́ться. —**come under fire, 1,** (come under gunfire) попа́сть под обстре́л. **2,** (come under criticism) попа́сть под обстре́л кри́тики. —**hang fire,** дать осе́чку. —**play with fire,** игра́ть *or* шути́ть с огнём. —**set fire to; set on fire,** поджига́ть.

fire alarm пожа́рная трево́га.

firearm *n.* огнестре́льное ору́жие.

fireball *n.* **1,** (large meteor) боли́д. **2,** (cloud formed by a nuclear blast) о́гненный шар.

firebird *n.* жар-пти́ца.

fire bomb зажига́тельная бо́мба.

firebrand *n.* **1,** (piece of smoldering wood) головёшка. **2,** (one who inflames passions) пла́менный ора́тор.

firecracker *n.* пета́рда.

fire engine пожа́рная маши́на.

fire escape пожа́рная ле́стница.

fire extinguisher огнетуши́тель.

firefighter *n.* пожа́рный.

firefly *n.* светля́к; светлячо́к.

firehouse *n.* пожа́рное депо́.

fire irons ками́нные щипцы́.

fireman *n.* **1,** (firefighter) пожа́рный. **2,** (stoker) кочега́р.

fireplace *n.* ками́н.

fireplug *n.* пожа́рный кран; гидра́нт.

firepower *n.* огнева́я мощь.

fireproof *adj.* огнесто́йкий; несгора́емый.

firescreen *n.* ками́нная решётка.

fireside *n.* оча́г.

fire station пожа́рное депо́.

firewood *n.* дрова́. *Chop down trees for firewood,* руби́ть дере́вья на дрова́.

fireworks *n.* фейерве́рк.

firing *n.* **1,** (shooting) стрельба́. *Firing practice,* уче́бная стрельба́. **2,** (laying off) увольне́ние. —**firing line,** огнево́й рубе́ж; ли́ния огня́. —**firing pin,** уда́рник. —**firing range,** стре́льбище; полиго́н.

firm *adj.* твёрдый; про́чный. *Firm ground,* твёрдая по́чва. *Firm foundation,* про́чный фунда́мент. *Firm handshake,* кре́пкое рукопожа́тие. *Firm tone,* твёрдый тон. *Firm belief,* твёрдое убежде́ние. —*adv.* твёрдо: *stand firm,* держа́ться твёрдо; твёрдо стоя́ть на своём. —*n.* фи́рма: *law firm,* юриди́ческая фи́рма.

firmament *n.* небе́сный свод; небосво́д.

firmly *adv.* твёрдо; про́чно; кре́пко.

firmness *n.* твёрдость.

first *adj.* пе́рвый: *the first time,* пе́рвый раз. *Nicholas I,* Никола́й Пе́рвый. *The first thing that comes to mind,* пе́рвое, что прихо́дит в го́лову. *The first person I saw,* пе́рвым, кого́ я ви́дел(а). —*adv.* **1,** (before the other or others) пе́рвым: *come in first,* прийти́ пе́рвым. *He hit me first,* он уда́рил меня́ пе́рвым. *This method was first suggested by...,* э́тот ме́тод пе́рвым предложи́л (+ *nom.*). **2,** (before doing something else) снача́ла: *Think first!,* снача́ла поду́майте! **3,** (for the first time) впервы́е: *when I first saw her,* когда́ я впервы́е уви́дел(а) её. **4,** (sooner; preferably) скоре́е: *I'd die first,* я скоре́е умру́. —*n.* пе́рвый. *May 1st,* пе́рвое ма́я. *On May 1,* пе́рвого ма́я. *(On) the first of the month,* пе́рвого числа́. *He/she was the first to leave,* он ушёл пе́рвым; она́ ушла́ пе́рвой. *It's the first I've heard of it,* пе́рвый раз слы́шу; впервы́е об э́том слы́шу. *Let me be the first to congratulate you,* разреши́те мне пе́рвым (пе́рвой) вас поздра́вить. —**at first,** снача́ла. —**first of all,** пре́жде всего́. —**in the first place,** во-пе́рвых. —**not**

know the first thing about..., ничего́ не понима́ть в; ничего́ не знать о.

first aid ско́рая по́мощь; пе́рвая по́мощь. —**first-aid kit,** апте́чка; *mil.* санита́рная су́мка. —**first-aid station,** медпу́нкт.

first-born *n.* пе́рвенец.

first-class *adj.* **1,** (first-rate) первокла́ссный. **2,** (most expensive, as of accommodations) пе́рвого кла́сса. —*adv.* пе́рвым кла́ссом: *travel first-class,* е́хать пе́рвым кла́ссом.

first cousin двою́родный брат; двою́родная сестра́.

firsthand *adj. & adv.* из пе́рвых рук.

firstly *adv.* во-пе́рвых.

first name и́мя.

first-rate *adj.* первокла́ссный.

fiscal *adj.* фина́нсовый. —**fiscal year,** фина́нсовый год.

fish *n.* ры́ба. —*adj.* ры́бный. *Fish soup,* ры́бный суп; уха́. —*v.i.* **1,** (go fishing) лови́ть *or* уди́ть ры́бу; рыба́чить. **2,** *fol. by* **for** (attempt to catch) уди́ть. **3,** *fol. by* **for** (seek indirectly) напра́шиваться на: *fish for compliments,* напра́шиваться на комплиме́нты. —*v.t.* [*usu.* **fish out**] выла́вливать. —**drink like a fish,** пить как бо́чка; пить запо́ем. —**fish in troubled waters,** лови́ть ры́бу в му́тной воде́. —**neither fish nor fowl,** ни ры́ба ни мя́со.

fishbone *n.* ры́бья кость.

fishbowl *n.* аква́риум.

fish cake ры́бная котле́та.

fisher *n.* (animal) и́лька.

fisherman *n.* рыба́к; рыболо́в.

fishery *n.* **1,** (business of fishing) ры́бный про́мысел. **2,** (fishing ground) ры́бные места́.

fishhook *n.* (рыболо́вный) крючо́к.

fishing *n.* ры́бная ловля́. *Go fishing,* идти́/уйти́ на ры́бную ло́влю (*or* на рыба́лку). —*adj.* рыболо́вный. —**fishing boat,** ры́ба́чья ло́дка. —**fishing line,** леса́; ле́ска. —**fishing rod,** у́дочка; уди́лище. —**fishing tackle,** рыболо́вная снасть. —**fishing village,** рыба́цкий *or* рыба́чий посёлок.

fishpond *n.* пруд для разведе́ния ры́бы; садо́к.

fish story охо́тничий расска́з.

fish tank аква́риум.

fishy *adj.* **1,** (suggestive of fish) ры́бный. **2,** (expressionless) ры́бий: *fishy eyes,* ры́бьи глаза́. **3,** *colloq.* (questionable; suspicious) сомни́тельный. *Something is fishy here,* тут что́-то нела́дно.

fission *n.* **1,** *physics* расщепле́ние; деле́ние: *nuclear fission,* я́дерное расщепле́ние *or* деле́ние; расщепле́ние *or* деле́ние ядра́. **2,** *biol.* деле́ние (кле́ток). —**fissionable,** *adj.* расщепля́ющийся.

fissure *n.* тре́щина; рассе́лина; расще́лина.

fist *n.* кула́к. —**fistfight,** *n.* кула́чный бой.

fisticuffs *n.pl.* **1,** (fistfight) кула́чный бой. **2,** (pugilism) бокс.

fistula *n.* фи́стула; свищ.

fit *v.t.* **1,** (be the right size for) быть впо́ру (+ *dat.*); быть в са́мый раз (+ *dat.*); подходи́ть (+ *dat.*); сиде́ть на (+ *prepl.*). *The dress fits you well,* пла́тье вам впо́ру; пла́тье вам подхо́дит; пла́тье хорошо́ на вас сиди́т. *The key fits the lock,* ключ подхо́дит к замку́. **2,** (be appropriate to) быть подходя́щим для; подходи́ть к; соотве́тствовать (+ *dat.*). *Something to fit the occasion,* что́-то, подходя́щее для э́того слу́чая. *The description/nickname fits him,* описа́ние ему́ соотве́тствует; про́звище ему́ (*or* к нему́) подхо́дит. **3,** (find room for; squeeze into) умеща́ть: *fit everything into the suitcase,* умеща́ть всё в чемода́н. *Fit something into one's schedule,* вти́снуть что́-нибудь в расписа́ние. **4,** (tailor; adjust) пригоня́ть. **5,** *fol. by* **out** (equip) снаряжа́ть; оснаща́ть. —*v.i.* **1,** (be the right size) быть впо́ру; сиде́ть хорошо́. **2,** (be able to go into something) входи́ть; вмеща́ться; помеща́ться; умеща́ться; укла́дываться. *Fit in one's pocket,* помеща́ться в карма́не. *Fit on one page,* умеща́ться на одно́й страни́це. *Fit through the door,* проходи́ть в дверь. *Fit around the table,* умеща́ться за столо́м. **3,** *fol. by* **in** (be suitable; blend in) впи́сываться: *She didn't fit in,* она́ не вписа́лась. *Fit in with the overall picture,* впи́сываться в о́бщую карти́ну. *That fits in with my plans,* э́то совпада́ет с мои́ми пла́нами. —*adj.* **1,** (in proper condition) го́дный; приго́дный; спосо́бный. *Fit to drink,* го́дный для питья́. *Fit for military service,* го́дный к вое́нной слу́жбе. *Fit to stand trial,* спосо́бен предста́ть пе́ред судо́м. *Not fit for anything,* ни на что не спосо́бен. *I am not fit to be seen,* я не могу́ показа́ться. **2,** (in good physical condition) здоро́вый; в хоро́шем состоя́нии. *Keep fit,* сохраня́ть своё здоро́вье. —*n.* **1,** (seizure; spell) припа́док; при́ступ. *Epileptic fit,* эпилепти́ческий припа́док. *Fit of coughing,* при́ступ ка́шля. **2,** (outburst) поры́в: *fit of rage,* поры́в гне́ва. **3,** (manner of fitting): *be a good fit,* хорошо́ сиде́ть. —**by** (*or* in) **fits and starts,** уры́вками; скачка́ми. —**fit to be tied,** вне себя́ от гне́ва. —**see fit,** счита́ть ну́жным (+ *inf.*). *Do as you see fit,* де́лайте, как вы счита́ете ну́жным. *He will do as he sees fit,* он посту́пит так, как ему́ заблагорассу́дится.

fitch *n.* хорёк. *Also,* **fitchew.**

fitful *adj.* поры́вистый; преры́вистый. *Fitful sleep,* беспоко́йный сон. —**fitfully,** *adv.* беспоко́йно: *sleep fitfully,* спать беспоко́йно.

fitness *n.* го́дность; приго́дность. —**physical fitness,** физи́ческая подгото́вка.

fitter *n.* **1,** (of machinery) монтёр; сбо́рщик; сле́сарь. **2,** (of clothes) портно́й.

fitting *adj.* досто́йный: *fitting reward/rebuke,* досто́йная награ́да/о́тповедь. —*n.* **1,** (trying on) приме́рка: *have a fitting,* сде́лать приме́рку. **2,** *pl.* (fixtures) армату́ра. —**fittingly,** *adv.* досто́йно.

five *adj.* пять. —*n.* **1,** (cardinal number) пять. **2,** (written numeral; school grade) пятёрка. **3,** *cards* пятёрка.

fivefold *adj.* пятикра́тный. —*adv.* впя́теро.

five hundred пятьсо́т. —**five-hundredth,** *adj.* пятисо́тый.

Five-Year Plan пятиле́тка; пятиле́тний план.

fix *v.t.* **1,** (repair) чини́ть; нала́живать; ремонти́ровать: *fix a watch/radio/car,* чини́ть часы́; нала́живать радиоприёмник; ремонти́ровать маши́ну.

Have something fixed, отда́ть что́-нибудь в ремо́нт *or* в почи́нку. **2,** *fol. by* **up** (decorate, as a room) обставля́ть; отде́лывать. **3,** (fasten securely) укрепля́ть; закрепля́ть. *Fix a mirror to the wall,* прикрепля́ть зе́ркало к стене́. *Fix a stake in the ground,* забива́ть кол в зе́млю. **4,** (direct steadily, as one's gaze) устремля́ть; прико́вывать; фикси́ровать. **5,** (set, as a date) назнача́ть; определя́ть. **6,** (prepare, as a meal) гото́вить. **7,** (determine, as blame) устана́вливать (вино́вность). **8,** *photog.* закрепля́ть; фикси́ровать. **9,** *colloq.* (get even with) разде́лываться с. *I'll fix him!,* я ему́ зада́м! —*n.,* *colloq.* переде́лка. *Get into a fix,* попа́сть в переде́лку; сесть в лу́жу.

fixation *n.* навя́зчивая иде́я.

fixed *adj.* **1,** (repaired) отремонти́рованный. *My car is fixed,* моя́ маши́на отремонти́рована; моя́ маши́на в поря́дке. **2,** (stationary; immobile) неподви́жный: *fixed point,* неподви́жная то́чка. **3,** (not fluctuating) фикси́рованный: *fixed price,* фикси́рованная цена́. **4,** (provided for) обеспе́ченный: *well fixed,* хорошо́ обеспе́ченный. *She is well fixed,* она́ живёт в доста́тке. *How are you fixed for money?,* как у вас с деньга́ми? —**fixed bayonets,** примкну́тые штыки́. —**fixed idea,** навя́зчивая иде́я.

fixture *n.* прибо́р; дета́ль; *pl.* армату́ра.

fizz *v.i.* шипе́ть. —*n.* шипе́ние.

fizzle *v.i.* **1,** (hiss) шипе́ть. **2,** *colloq.* (peter out) выдыха́ться.

flabbergast *v.t.,* *colloq.* ошара́шивать.

flabby *adj.* дря́блый; вя́лый; обрю́згший; обрю́зглый. *Become flabby,* обрю́згнуть. —**flabbiness,** *n.* дря́блость.

flaccid *adj.* дря́блый; отви́слый.

flag *n.* флаг. —*v.t.* [*usu.* **flag down**] (hail; signal to stop) оклика́ть. —*v.i.* (slacken; wane) слабе́ть; ослабева́ть. *The conversation flagged,* разгово́р (ча́сто) замолка́л.

flagellate *v.t.* бичева́ть. —**flagellation,** *n.* бичева́ние.

flagman *n.* сигна́льщик.

flag officer фла́гман.

flagpole *n.* флагшто́к.

flagrant *adj.* гру́бый; вопию́щий: *flagrant violation,* гру́бое/вопию́щее наруше́ние.

flagship *n.* фла́гманский кора́бль; фла́гман.

flagstaff *n.* флагшто́к.

flagstone *n.* плита́; плитня́к. —*adj.* плитняко́вый.

flail *n.* цеп. —*v.t.* **1,** (thresh) молоти́ть. **2,** (beat) колоти́ть.

flair *n.* спосо́бности: *a flair for music/languages,* спосо́бности к му́зыке/языка́м.

flak *n.* зени́тная артилле́рия; зени́тный ого́нь.

flake *n.,* *usu. pl.* хло́пья. *Corn flakes,* кукуру́зные хло́пья. *Soap flakes,* мы́льная стру́жка. —*v.i.* [*usu.* **flake off**] шелуши́ться; лупи́ться; сы́паться. —**flaky,** *adj.* слоёный.

flamboyant *adj.* цвети́стый; пы́шный; показно́й.

flame *n.* **1,** (fire) пла́мя: *burst into flames,* вспы́хнуть пла́менем. *Be in flames,* быть в огне́. **2,** *colloq.* (sweetheart) зазно́ба. —*v.i.* пыла́ть. —**flame thrower,** огнемёт.

flaming *adj.* **1,** (ablaze) пыла́ющий. **2,** (intense; ardent) пла́менный.

flamingo *n.* флами́нго.

flammable *adj.* огнеопа́сный.

flange *n.* **1,** (for a pipe) фла́нец. **2,** (for a wheel) ребо́рда.

flank *n.* фланг. —*v.t.* фланки́ровать. *He was flanked by two bodyguards,* у него́ по бока́м стоя́ли два телохрани́теля. —**flanking,** *adj.* фланго́вый.

flannel *n.* флане́ль. —*adj.* флане́льный.

flap *v.t.* взма́хивать; маха́ть; хло́пать (кры́льями). —*v.i.* развева́ться: *flap in the wind,* развева́ться на ветру́ *or* по ве́тру. —*n.* **1,** (flapping, as of wings) взмах. **2,** (of a garment or tent) пола́; (of a pocket) кла́пан. **3,** *aero.* закры́лок.

flare *n.* **1,** (burst of flame) вспы́шка. **2,** (bright light for illumination or signaling) освети́тельная раке́та; сигна́льная раке́та. **3,** (expanding part) растру́б; клёш. *Flared skirt,* ю́бка клёш. —*v.i.* [*usu.* **flare up**] **1,** (flame up brightly) возгора́ться. **2,** (suddenly become angry) вспыли́ть. **3,** *fig.* (break out; erupt) разгора́ться; вспы́хивать. *Tempers flared,* стра́сти разгоре́лись.

flash *n.* **1,** (of light) вспы́шка; про́блеск. *Flash of lightning,* вспы́шка мо́лнии. **2,** (instant) миг: *in a flash,* ми́гом; в оди́н миг. **3,** *pl.* (sudden manifestations, as of wit) блёстки (остроу́мия). —*v.i.* **1,** (shine brightly or suddenly) сверка́ть: *Lightning flashed,* сверкну́ла мо́лния. *A flashing light,* мига́ющий свет. *His eyes flashed with anger,* его́ глаза́ сверка́ли гне́вом. **2,** *fol. by* **by, past, across** (pass suddenly and swiftly) мелькну́ть; промелькну́ть. *An idea flashed across my mind,* у меня́ (про)мелькну́ла *or* блесну́ла мысль; меня́ осени́ла мысль. —*v.t.* **1,** (shine) свети́ть: *flash a light in someone's eyes,* свети́ть кому́-нибудь в глаза́. **2,** (send at great speed) сообщи́ть (с быстрото́й мо́лнии). *Flash a signal,* подава́ть сигна́л. **3,** *colloq.* (display ostentatiously) выставля́ть; демонстри́ровать.

flash bulb ла́мпа-вспы́шка; блиц.

flasher *n.* мига́лка.

flash gun вспы́шка.

flashlight *n.* карма́нный фона́рь.

flashy *adj.* крича́щий; крикли́вый.

flask *n.* **1,** (for carrying liquids) фля́га; фля́жка. **2,** (for use in a laboratory) ко́лба.

flat *adj.* **1,** (level) пло́ский: *flat surface,* пло́ская пове́рхность. **2,** (not hilly or mountainous) равни́нный. **3,** (lacking zest, as of a drink) вы́дохшийся. **4,** (dull; insipid) пло́ский; пре́сный. **5,** (uniform, as of a rate or tax) единообра́зный; еди́ный. **6,** (absolute; point-blank) категори́ческий. **7,** *music* бемо́ль: *E-flat,* ми-бемо́ль. —*adv.* **1,** (prostrate) плашмя́; врастя́жку. *Lie flat,* ложи́ться плашмя́; распласта́ться. *Flat on one's back,* на́взничь; пласто́м. **2,** (in full contact) вплотну́ю: *flat against the wall,* вплотну́ю к стене́. **3,** (completely) соверше́нно: *flat broke,* соверше́нно разорённый. **4,** (exactly) ро́вно: *in two minutes flat,* ро́вно за две мину́ты. **5,** *music* не в лад. *Sing flat,* фальши́вить. —*n.* **1,** (apartment) кварти́ра. **2,** (low-lying area) бассе́йн: *salt flats,* соляны́е бассе́йны. **3,** *pl.* (flat-heeled shoes) ту́фли без каблука́. **4,** = **flat tire.** —**fall flat,** не уда́ться; провали́ться. —**flat tire,** спу́щенная ши́на *or* покры́шка: *We had a flat tire,* у нас спусти́ла ши́на/покры́шка.

flat-bottomed *adj.* плоскодо́нный.

flatcar *n.* платфо́рма; ваго́н-платфо́рма.

flat-chested *adj.* плоскогру́дый.

flatfoot *n.* пло́ская стопа́; плоскосто́пие.

flatfooted *adj.* страда́ющий плоскосто́пием. —**catch flatfooted,** *colloq.* заста́ть враспло́х.

flatiron *n.* утю́г.

flatly *adv.* (categorically) наотре́з.

flatness *n.* пло́скость.

flatten *v.t.* сплю́щивать; расплю́щивать. *The earth is flattened at the poles,* земля́ сплю́щена у по́люсов. *The storm flattened the crops,* бу́рей поби́ло *or* приби́ло посе́вы. —*v.i.* [*usu.* **flatten out**] **1,** (become flat) сплю́щиваться. **2,** *aero.* (resume a horizontal line of flight) выра́вниваться.

flatter *v.t.* льстить. *I am flattered,* мне ле́стно; я польщён (польщена́). *Flatter oneself that...,* обольща́ться тем, что...

flatterer *n.* льстец.

flattering *adj.* **1,** (intended to flatter) льсти́вый. **2,** (complimentary) ле́стный.

flattery *n.* лесть.

flatulence *n.* скопле́ние га́зов; метеори́зм.

flatware *n.* столо́вые прибо́ры.

flatworm *n.* пло́ский червь.

flaunt *v.t.* выставля́ть напока́з; афиши́ровать; козыря́ть; брави́ровать; коке́тничать; щеголя́ть (*last four with instr.*).

flavor *also,* **flavour** *n.* **1,** (distinctive taste) вкус. **2,** (kind of ice cream) сорт (моро́женого). **3,** (distinctive quality) при́вкус. —*v.t.* приправля́ть.

flavoring *also,* **flavouring** *n.* припра́ва.

flavour *n. & v.* = **flavor.** —**flavouring,** *n.* = **flavoring.**

flaw *n.* поро́к; брак; изъя́н. —*v.t.* по́ртить.

flawed *adj.* **1,** (containing an imperfection) с изъя́ном. **2,** *fig.* (defective) ущерб́ный. **3,** *fig.* (unsound; illogical) поро́чный.

flawless *adj.* безупре́чный; безукори́зненный. —**flawlessly,** *adv.* безупре́чно; безукори́зненно.

flax *n.* лён. —**flaxen,** *adj.* льняно́й. *Flaxen hair,* льняны́е во́лосы.

flay *v.t.* **1,** (strip off the skin of) сдира́ть ко́жу с; обдира́ть. **2,** *fig.* (criticize severely) хлеста́ть.

flea *n.* блоха́. —**fleabite,** *n.* блоши́ный уку́с. —**flea market,** толку́чка.

fleck *n.* пятно́; кра́пинка. —*v.t.* испещря́ть. *Hair flecked with gray,* во́лосы с про́седью.

fledged *adj.* опери́вшийся. *Become fully fledged,* опери́ться.

fledgling *n.* птене́ц.

flee *v.i.* бежа́ть; убега́ть; спаса́ться бе́гством. *Flee in panic,* бежа́ть в па́нике. *Flee abroad,* бежа́ть за грани́цу. —*v.t.* бежа́ть из; убега́ть из. *Flee the country,* бежа́ть из страны́.

fleece *n.* руно́. —*v.t.* (swindle) обира́ть; обдира́ть.

fleecy *adj.* **1,** (soft and light) пуши́стый. **2,** (of clouds) пе́ристый.

fleet *n.* **1,** (of warships) флот. **2,** (of boats) флоти́лия: *whaling fleet,* китобо́йная флоти́лия. **3,** (of vehicles) парк. —*adj.* бы́стрый; быстроно́гий. —*v.i.* бежа́ть; лете́ть.

fleet-footed *adj.* быстроно́гий.

fleeting *adj.* **1,** (momentary) мимолётный. **2,** *phonet.* (of a vowel) бе́глый.

Fleming *n.* флама́ндец. —**Flemish,** *adj.* флама́нд-ский. —*n.* флама́ндский язы́к.

flesh *n.* **1,** (soft substance of the body) мя́коть; мя́со. *Flesh wound,* пове́рхностная ра́на. **2,** (the body as distinguished from the soul) плоть. —**in the flesh,** во плоти́. —**it makes my flesh creep,** у меня́ моро́з подира́ет по ко́же; у меня́ мура́шки бе́гают по спине́. —**of one's own flesh and blood,** чья́-нибудь плоть и кровь.

flesh-colored *adj.* теле́сный; теле́сного цве́та.

fleshy *adj.* мяси́стый.

flex *v.t.* гнуть; сгиба́ть. *Flex one's muscles,* напряга́ть му́скулы.

flexible *adj.* ги́бкий. —**flexibility,** *n.* ги́бкость.

flick *n.* щелчо́к. —*v.t.* **1,** (strike deftly) щёлкать. **2,** (remove with a quick snap) сма́хивать.

flicker *v.i.* **1,** (glimmer) мерца́ть; мига́ть; трепета́ть. **2,** *fol. by* **out** (go out) га́снуть; угаса́ть. —*n.* **1,** (wavering light) мерца́ние. **2,** (glimmer, as of hope) про́блеск (наде́жды).

flier *also,* **flyer** *n.* лётчик.

flight *n.* **1,** (act of flying) полёт. *Be in flight,* быть в полёте. **2,** (trip made by air) полёт; перелёт. **3,** (scheduled trip of an airplane) рейс: *flight 242,* рейс две́сти со́рок два. *What flight are you taking?,* каки́м ре́йсом вы лети́те? **4,** (abrupt departure) бе́гство: *put to flight,* обраща́ть в бе́гство; *take flight,* обраща́ться в бе́гство. **5,** (set of stairs) марш. **6,** (flock of birds) ста́я. **7,** (group of airplanes) звено́. **8,** (soaring beyond normal limits) полёт: *flight of fantasy,* полёт фанта́зии. —**flight deck,** полётная па́луба (авиано́сца). —**flight engineer,** бортмеха́ник. —**flight path,** траекто́рия полёта. —**flight recorder,** бортово́й самопи́сец. —**flight testing,** лётные испыта́ния.

flightless *adj.* бескры́лый.

flighty *adj.* легкомы́сленный; ве́треный.

flimsy *adj.* **1,** (lacking solidity) непро́чный. **2,** (poor, as of an excuse) сла́бый. —**flimsiness,** *n.* непро́чность.

flinch *v.i.* **1,** (wince, as from pain) вздра́гивать. **2,** (draw back; shrink, as from fear) дро́гнуть.

fling *v.t.* кида́ть; мета́ть; швыря́ть. *Fling open,* распа́хивать. —*n.* **1,** (toss) бросо́к. **2,** *colloq.* (try) попы́тка. *Have a fling at,* попро́бовать.

flint *n.* креме́нь.

flip *v.t.* **1,** (toss) броса́ть. **2,** (toss into the air, as a coin) подбра́сывать. **3,** (flick) сма́хивать. **4,** (turn rapidly, as a dial) верте́ть; крути́ть. **5,** (activate, as a switch) повора́чивать (выключа́тель). **6,** *fol. by* **over** (invert) перевёртывать. —*v.i.* **1,** *fol. by* **over** (turn over) переве́ртываться. **2,** *fol. by* **through** (leaf through) перели́стывать; полиста́ть.

flippant *adj.* де́рзкий. —**flippancy,** *n.* де́рзость.

flipper *n.* ласт.

flirt *v.i.* коке́тничать; флиртова́ть. —*n.* коке́тка. —**flirtation,** *n.* коке́тство; флирт. —**flirtatious,** *adj.* коке́тливый.

flit *v.i.* порха́ть.

float *v.i.* **1,** (not sink) пла́вать; не тону́ть; держа́ться на воде́. **2,** (drift) плыть; нести́сь. *Float downstream,* плыть вниз по тече́нию. *Float to the surface,* всплыва́ть *or* выплыва́ть на пове́рхность. —*v.t.* **1,** (ship by water, as logs) сплавля́ть. **2,** (arrange for, as a loan) размеща́ть (заём). —*n.* поплаво́к.

floating *adj.* **1,** (on water) пла́вающий; плаву́чий. *Floating bridge,* плаву́чий *or* наплавно́й мост. **2,** *finance* оборо́тный: *floating capital,* оборо́тный капита́л. **3,** *med.* блужда́ющий: *floating kidney,* блужда́ющая по́чка.

flock *n.* **1,** (of sheep, goats, etc.) ста́до. **2,** (of birds) ста́я. **3,** (congregation) па́ства. **4,** (crowd) толпа́. —*v.i.* толпи́ться; стека́ться; (ва́лом) вали́ть.

floe *n.* плаву́чая льди́на.

flog *v.t.* сечь; поро́ть; хлеста́ть; стега́ть.

flood *n.* **1,** (deluge) наводне́ние. *The Flood,* всеми́рный пото́п. **2,** *fig.* (huge flow or influx) пото́к. —*v.t.* **1,** (overwhelm with water) затопля́ть; залива́ть. *Many homes were flooded,* мно́гие дома́ бы́ли зато́плены. *The roads are flooded,* доро́ги зали́ты водо́й. **2,** *fig.* (overwhelm) наводня́ть; зава́ливать: *flood the market with cheap goods,* наводня́ть/зава́ливать ры́нок дешёвыми това́рами.

floodgate *n.* шлюз; шлю́зные воро́та.

flooding *n.* затопле́ние; наводне́ние.

floodlight *n.* проже́ктор.

flood plain (залива́я) по́йма.

flood tide прили́в.

floodwaters *n.pl.* по́лая вода́. *The floodwaters are rising/receding,* вода́ прибыва́ет/убыва́ет.

floor *n.* **1,** (in a room) пол: *He fell to the floor,* он упа́л на́ пол. *She was lying on the floor,* она́ лежа́ла на полу́. **2,** (storey of a building) эта́ж: *on the sixth floor,* на шесто́м этаже́. **3,** (bottom) дно: *ocean floor,* океа́нское *or* морско́е дно. **4,** (right to speak) сло́во: *take the floor,* брать сло́во; *ask for the floor,* проси́ть сло́ва. *Questions from the floor,* вопро́сы с ме́ста. —*v.t.* **1,** (knock to the ground) вали́ть на́ пол. **2,** *colloq.* (stun) оглуши́ть.

floorboard *n.* полови́ца.

flooring *n.* насти́л.

floor lamp торше́р.

floor polish масти́ка.

floor show варьете́.

floorspace *n.* жила́я пло́щадь; жилпло́щадь.

flop *v.i.* **1,** (fall) бро́ситься; плю́хаться; бу́хаться; хло́паться. *Flop into an armchair,* бро́ситься в кре́сло. **2,** *slang* (fail) прова́ливаться. —*n., colloq.* неуда́ча; фиа́ско.

flophouse *n., colloq.* ночле́жка.

floppy disk ги́бкий диск.

flora *n.* фло́ра.

floral *adj.* цвето́чный. *Floral design,* узо́р из цвето́в.

floriculture *n.* цветово́дство.

florid *adj.* цвети́стый; витиева́тый.

florin *n.* флори́н.

florist *n.* торго́вец цвета́ми. *Florist's shop,* цвето́чный магази́н.

flotilla *n.* флоти́лия.

flounce *n.* обо́рка.

flounder *n.* (fish) ка́мбала. —*v.i.* **1,** (move with great difficulty) бара́хтаться. **2,** *fig.* (fare badly) хрома́ть на о́бе ноги́.

flour *n.* мука́. —*adj.* мучно́й: *flour sack,* мучно́й мешо́к.

flourish *v.i.* процвета́ть. —*n.* **1,** (dramatic gesture) ро́счерк. **2,** (embellishment in handwriting) завито́к; завиту́шка. **3,** (florid bit of writing) завито́к; завиту́шка. *Rhetorical flourishes,* ритори́ческие завиту́шки. **4,** (sound of trumpets) фанфа́ра; туш.

flout *v.t.* бро́сить вы́зов (+ *dat.*); попира́ть.

flow *v.i.* течь; ли́ться. *Flow out to sea,* вытека́ть в мо́ре. *The Volga flows into the Caspian Sea,* Во́лга впада́ет в Каспи́йское мо́ре. *The Danube flows through eight countries.* Дуна́й течёт *or* протека́ет че́рез во́семь стран. —*n.* **1,** (of a fluid) тече́ние. *Flow of blood,* кровотече́ние. **2,** *fig.* (steady movement) пото́к; тече́ние; ход. —**a lot of water has flown under the bridge since then,** мно́го воды́ утекло́ с тех пор.

flower *n.* цвето́к (*pl.* цветы́). —*adj.* цвето́чный: *flower show,* цвето́чная вы́ставка. —*v.i.* цвести́; расцвета́ть. —**flower bed,** клу́мба; цветни́к. —**flower girl,** цвето́чница.

flowering *adj.* цвету́щий; цветко́вый.

flowerpot *n.* цвето́чный горшо́к; вазо́н.

flowery *adj.* цвети́стый; кра́сочный; витиева́тый.

flowing *adj.* **1,** (smooth and continuous) пла́вный. **2,** (hanging loosely at full length) свиса́ющий.

flu *n.* грипп.

fluctuate *v.i.* колеба́ться. —**fluctuation,** *n.* колеба́ние.

flue *n.* дымохо́д.

fluency *n.* пла́вность; бе́глость.

fluent *adj.* пла́вный; бе́глый; свобо́дный. —**fluently,** *adv.* свобо́дно; бе́гло. *Speak Russian fluently,* свобо́дно владе́ть ру́сским языко́м.

fluff *n.* пух; пушо́к. —*v.t.* [*usu.* **fluff up**] взбива́ть; (рас)пуши́ть. —**fluffy,** *adj.* пуши́стый; пы́шный.

fluid *n.* жи́дкость. —*adj.* жи́дкий; теку́чий. —**fluidity,** *n.* теку́честь.

fluke *n.* **1,** (fish) ка́мбала. **2,** (part of an anchor) ла́па. **3,** *slang* (lucky chance) игра́ слу́чая.

flunk *v.t., colloq.* **1,** (fail, as an exam) сре́заться на (экза́мене). **2,** (give a failing grade to) сре́зать. —*v.i., colloq.* сре́заться.

flunky *also,* **flunkey** *n.* лаке́й.

fluoresce *v.i.* флуоресци́ровать.

fluorescence *n.* свече́ние; флуоресце́нция.

fluorescent *adj.* флуоресци́рующий. —**fluorescent lamp,** люминесце́нтная ла́мпа.

fluoride *n.* фтори́д. ♦*In combinations,* фто́ристый: *sodium fluoride,* фто́ристый на́трий.

fluorine *n.* фтор.

fluorite *n.* плавико́вый шпат.

fluorocarbon *n.* фторуглеро́д.

fluorspar *n.* плавико́вый шпат.

flurry *n.* **1,** *pl.* (of snow) снежи́нки. **2,** (sudden burst) поры́в.

flush *v.t.* **1,** (purge) промыва́ть; очища́ть. *Flush the toilet,* спусти́ть во́ду в убо́рной. *Flush something down the toilet,* спусти́ть что́-нибудь в убо́рную. **2,** (drive from cover) выку́ривать. **3,** (redden) румя́нить. —*v.i.* красне́ть; багрове́ть; румя́ниться; але́ть. —*n.* кра́ска: *flush of anger,* кра́ска гне́ва. —*adj.* [*usu.* **flush with** *or* **against**] вро́вень (с); впритьı́к (к).

fluster *v.t.* конфу́зить. *Become flustered,* теря́ться; растеря́ться; конфу́зиться.

flute *n.* фле́йта.

fluted *adj.* рифлёный.

flutist *n.* флейти́ст.

flutter *v.i.* развева́ться; ре́ять; полоска́ться.

flux *n.* **1,** (continual change): *in a state of flux,* в состоя́нии измене́ния; в состоя́нии неопределённости. **2,** *metall.* флюс; пла́вень.

fly *v.i.* **1,** (general term) лете́ть; лета́ть. *The little bird cannot fly,* пти́чка не мо́жет лета́ть. *First we fly to London,* снача́ла мы лети́м в Ло́ндон. *Sparks flew in all directions,* и́скры лете́ли во все сто́роны. *Time flies,* вре́мя лети́т. **2,** (wave, as of a flag) развева́ться. **3,** *fol. by* **into** (burst into) приходи́ть в: *fly into a rage,* приходи́ть в я́рость. —*v.t.* **1,** (operate, as an aircraft) вести́; управля́ть. **2,** (float, as a kite) пуска́ть; запуска́ть (змея́). **3,** (transport by aircraft) перевози́ть (по во́здуху); перебра́сывать. **4,** (fly across) перелета́ть: *fly the Atlantic,* перелета́ть (че́рез) Атланти́ческий океа́н. **5,** (complete, as a sortie or mission) соверша́ть (вы́лет). —*n.* **1,** (insect) му́ха. *He wouldn't hurt a fly,* он и му́хи не оби́дит; он па́льцем никого́ не тро́нет. *Dying like flies,* мрут как му́хи. **2,** (on trousers) ши́ринка. —**fly across,** перелета́ть (че́рез); лете́ть че́рез. —**fly away,** улета́ть. —**fly by,** пролета́ть. —**fly in, 1,** (arrive by plane) прилета́ть. **2,** (deliver by air) доставля́ть (самолётом). —**fly in the face of,** идти́ вразре́з с; противоре́чить. —**fly in the ointment,** ло́жка дёгтя в бо́чке мёда. —**fly off,** улета́ть: *fly off to California,* улете́ть в Калифо́рнию. *The papers flew off the table,* бума́ги слете́ли со стола́. —**fly open,** распахну́ться. —**fly past,** пролета́ть ми́мо. —**let fly,** пуска́ть. —**on the fly,** на лету́.

flycatcher *n.* мухоло́вка.

flyer *n.* = flier.

flying *n.* полёты; лётное де́ло. *Fear of flying,* страх пе́ред полётами *or* самолётами. —*adj.* **1,** (that flies) лета́ющий; летучий. *Flying fish,* летучая ры́ба. *Flying saucer,* лета́ющая таре́лка. **2,** (used for flying) лета́тельный: *flying machine,* лета́тельный аппара́т. **3,** (suitable for flying) лётный: *flying weather,* лётная пого́да. —**with flying colors,** с бле́ском.

flying squirrel летя́га.

flyleaf *n.* фо́рзац.

flypaper *n.* липу́чая бума́га от мух; липу́чка от мух.

fly swatter хлопу́шка.

flytrap *n.* мухоло́вка.

flywheel *n.* махово́е колесо́; махови́к.

foal *n.* жеребёнок. —*v.t.* рожа́ть. —*v.i.* жереби́ться.

foam *n.* пе́на. —*v.i.* пе́ниться. —**foam rubber,** гу́б-чатая рези́на.

foamy *adj.* пе́нистый.

focal *adj.* фо́кусный: *focal length,* фо́кусное рассто-я́ние. —**focal point,** фо́кус; центр; средото́чие.

focus *n.* фо́кус: *be in focus,* быть в фо́кусе. *Be the focus of attention,* быть в це́нтре внима́ния. —*v.t.* **1,** (adjust the focus of) фокуси́ровать. *Automatic focusing,* автомати́ческая фокусиро́вка; автомати́ческая наво́дка на ре́зкость. **2,** (concentrate) сосре-дото́чивать. *Focus attention on,* заостря́ть *or* сосредото́чивать *or* концентри́ровать внима́ние на (+ *prepl.*).

fodder *n.* корм; фура́ж.

foe *n.* враг.

foetal *adj.* = **fetal.** —**foetus,** *n.* = **fetus.**

fog *n.* тума́н. *Be in a fog,* быть как в тума́не. —*v.t.* тума́нить; затума́нивать. —*v.i.* [*usu.* **fog up**] вспо-те́ть; запотева́ть.

fogginess *n.* тума́нность.

foggy *adj.* тума́нный. *It is foggy today,* сего́дня тума́н; сего́дня тума́нно. *I haven't the foggiest notion,* я не име́ю ни мале́йшего поня́тия.

foghorn *n.* наутофо́н.

foible *n.* сла́бое ме́сто; сла́бая сторона́; сла́бость.

foil *v.t.* расстра́ивать; срыва́ть. —*n.* **1,** (thin sheet of metal) фо́льга. *Tin foil,* станио́ль. **2,** (sword) рапи́р.

foist *v.t.* навя́зывать; всуча́ть.

fold *v.t.* [*often* **fold up**] скла́дывать. *Fold one's hands,* скла́дывать ру́ки. *Fold up a map,* скла́дывать ка́рту. —*v.i.* **1,** [*often* **fold up**] (be able to be folded) скла́ды-ваться. *A bed that folds up,* складна́я крова́ть. **2,** *colloq.* (fail and close down) прогоре́ть. —*n.* **1,** (in paper or cloth; of skin) скла́дка. *Lie in folds,* ложи́ться скла́дками. **2,** (of a tent) пола́; (of a screen) ство́рка. **3,** (pen) заго́н. —**fold back,** отки́дывать. —**fold under,** подвёртывать.

folder *n.* па́пка; скоросшива́тель.

folding *adj.* **1,** (of a chair, table, etc.) складно́й; раскладно́й; откидно́й. **2,** (of doors) (дву)ство́р-чатый.

foliage *n.* листва́.

folio *n.* **1,** (sheet) лист. **2,** (book) фолиа́нт; фо́лио.

folk *n.* лю́ди: *simple folk,* просты́е лю́ди. —*adj.* наро́дный: *folk song,* наро́дная пе́сня.

folklore *n.* фолькло́р.

follicle *n.* фолли́кул.

follow *v.t.* **1,** (go after; come after) сле́довать за; идти́ за: *Follow me!,* сле́дуйте *or* иди́те за мной! *Summer follows spring,* за весно́й идёт ле́то. **2,** (watch; trail; keep track of) следи́ть за: *We're being followed,* за на́ми следя́т. *Follow current events,* следи́ть за теку́щими собы́тиями. **3,** (proceed along, as a road) идти́ по; е́хать по. *Follow the coast,* идти́/е́хать вдоль бе́рега. **4,** (heed; obey) сле́довать (+ *dat.*): *fol-low someone's advice,* сле́довать чьему́-нибудь сове́ту. *Follow someone's example,* сле́довать чьему́-нибудь приме́ру; брать приме́р с (+ *gen.*). *Follow orders,* выполня́ть прика́зы. **5,** (understand the logic of) понима́ть. —*v.i.* (come next or as a result) сле́довать. *From this it follows that...,* из э́того сле́дует, что... —**as follows,** сле́дующее: *The telegram reads as follows,* телегра́мма гласи́т сле́дую-щее. *Your duties are as follows,* ва́ши обя́занности заключа́ются в сле́дующем. *The story is briefly as follows,* исто́рия вкра́тце такова́.

follower *n.* после́дователь.

following *adj.* сле́дующий. *The following day,* на друго́й день. *The following morning,* нау́тро. —*prep.* по́сле: *following the meeting,* по́сле собра́ния. —*n.* **1,** (group of followers or fans) после́дователи; покло́нники. **2,** *preceded by* **the** (what follows) сле́дующее.

folly *n.* глу́пость; безу́мие. *Act of folly,* безу́мный посту́пок.

foment *v.t.* раздува́ть; разжига́ть. *Foment hatred,* разжига́ть не́нависть.

fond *adj.* **1,** *fol. by* **of** (liking): *be fond of,* люби́ть. **2,** (cherished, as of a wish) заве́тный. *Exceed one's fondest expectations,* превзойти́ чьи́-нибудь лу́чшие ожида́ния.

fondle *v.t.* ласка́ть.

fondness *n.* расположе́ние: *have a special fondness for,* испы́тывать осо́бое расположе́ние к.

font *n.* **1,** (receptacle for holy water) купе́ль. **2,** *printing* (typeface) шрифт.

food *n.* пи́ща; еда́; продово́льствие; проду́кты. *Nourishing food,* пита́тельная пи́ща *or* еда́. *Baby food,* де́тское пита́ние. *Frozen foods,* заморо́женные проду́кты. —*adj.* продово́льственный. *Food store,* продово́льственный магази́н. *Food prices,* це́ны на продово́льствие. *Food shortage,* нехва́тка продово́льствия. *Food parcel,* продукто́вая посы́лка. *Food poisoning,* пищево́е отравле́ние. *Food riots,* голо́дные бу́нты. —**food for thought,** пи́ща для ума́; пи́ща для размышле́ния.

foodstuff *n., usu. pl.* пищевы́е проду́кты; продо-во́льственные това́ры.

fool *n.* **1,** (stupid person) дура́к. *I was a fool to believe him,* я дура́к, что пове́рил ему́. **2,** (jester) шут. —*adj.* дура́цкий; шутовско́й: *fool's cap,* дура́цкий/ шутовско́й колпа́к. —*v.t.* обма́нывать; дура́чить; провести́. —*v.i.* **1,** (jest) шути́ть: *I'm not fooling,* я не шучу́. *Don't fool with him!,* с ним не шути́! **2,** *fol. by* **with** (play with carelessly) игра́ть (+ *instr.*); вози́ться с; балова́ться с. —**fool around,** дура́читься. —**make a fool of,** оста́вить в дурака́х; дура́чить. —**make a fool of oneself,** оста́ться в ду-рака́х; опростоволо́ситься. —**nobody's fool,** ма́лый не про́мах. —**play the fool,** валя́ть дурака́.

foolhardy *adj.* безрассу́дный. —**foolhardiness,** *n.* безрассу́дство.

foolish *adj.* глу́пый: *foolish person/question,* глу́пый челове́к/вопро́с.

foolishly *adv.* глу́по: *act foolishly,* поступа́ть глу́по. *I*

foolishly went outside without a coat, не поду́мав, я вы́шел (вы́шла) и́з дому без пальто́.
foolishness *n.* глу́пость. *Enough of this foolishness!,* бро́сьте э́ти глу́пости!
foot *n.* **1,** (of humans) нога́. *Be on one's feet,* быть на нога́х. *Get/jump to one's feet,* встать/вскочи́ть на́ ноги. **2,** (of animals) ла́па. **3,** (base) подно́жие. **4,** (lower end; bottom) коне́ц. *At the foot of the stairs,* внизу́ ле́стницы. *At the foot of the bed,* в нога́х крова́ти. **5,** (of a mountain, hill, etc.) подно́жие; подо́шва. **6,** (measure of length) фут. **7,** *pros.* стопа́. —*adj.* ножно́й: *foot brake,* ножно́й то́рмоз. —**get cold feet,** стру́сить. —**get to one's feet,** вставáть на́ ноги. —**get on one's feet** (*fig.*), стать на́ ноги. —**on foot,** пешко́м. —**put one's best foot forward,** показа́ть това́р лицо́м. —**put one's foot in it,** попа́сть впроса́к; сесть в лу́жу. —**set foot on,** ступи́ть на: *set foot on the moon,* ступи́ть на Луну́. *I will not set foot in there,* мое́й ноги́ там не бу́дет; нога́ моя́ туда́ не сту́пит.
footage *n.* **1,** (length expressed in feet) длина́ (в фу́тах). **2,** *motion pictures* метра́ж.
foot-and-mouth disease я́щур.
football *n.* **1,** (game) футбо́л. **2,** (ball) футбо́льный мяч.
footbridge *n.* мо́стик; пешехо́дный мост.
foothill *n.* предго́рье. *The foothills of the Caucasus,* кавка́зские предго́рья.
foothold *n.* то́чка опо́ры: *gain a foothold,* найти́ то́чку опо́ры.
footing *n.* **1,** (firm placing of the feet): *keep one's footing,* удержа́ться на нога́х; *lose one's footing,* оступи́ться. **2,** (position; standing): *on an equal footing,* наравне́; на ра́вных усло́виях; на ра́вной ноге́. *Place on a war footing,* перестро́ить на вое́нный лад.
footlights *n.pl.* ра́мпа.
footman *n.* лаке́й; скорохо́д.
footnote *n.* примеча́ние; сно́ска.
footprint *n.* след; отпеча́ток ноги́.
foot soldier пехоти́нец.
footstep *n., usu. pl.* **1,** (footprints) следы́. **2,** (sound of someone walking) шаги́. —**follow in the footsteps of,** идти́ по стопа́м (+ *gen.*).
footstool *n.* скаме́йка для ног.
footwear *n.* о́бувь.
fop *n.* фат; франт; щёголь; хлыщ. —**foppery,** *n.* фа́товство́; щего́льство. —**foppish,** *adj.* фатова́тый; франтова́тый.
for *prep.* **1,** (used for; intended for; as regards) для: *Do it for me!,* сде́лайте э́то для меня́! *A book for children,* кни́га для дете́й. *Bad for one's health,* вре́дно для здоро́вья. *Pose for a portrait,* пози́ровать для портре́та. *What is this for?,* к чему́ э́то? ♦*Also with* на: *material for a dress,* материа́л на пла́тье; *the lesson for tomorrow,* уро́к на за́втра; *plans for the summer,* пла́ны на ле́то; *a room for two,* ко́мната на двои́х; *the demand for oil,* спрос на нефть; *closed for repairs,* закры́то на ремо́нт; *play for money,* игра́ть на де́ньги. *What's for sup-*

per?, что на у́жин? *A good memory for names,* хоро́шая па́мять на имена́. *Stretch for many miles,* простира́ться на мно́го миль. *The meeting is set for Wednesday,* собра́ние назна́чено на сре́ду. *Put aside for a rainy day,* бере́чь на чёрный день. **2,** (in favor of; in exchange for; in recognition of; as punishment for) за (+ *acc.*): *vote for,* голосова́ть за; *pay for,* плати́ть за; *fight for,* боро́ться за. *An eye for an eye,* о́ко за о́ко. *An award for bravery,* награ́да за му́жество. *The penalty for lateness,* наказа́ние за опозда́ние. *Thanks for your help!,* спаси́бо за по́мощь! ♦*But notice: in exchange for dollars,* в обме́н на до́ллары. **3,** (towards; with respect to) к: *pity for someone,* жа́лость к кому́-нибудь. *An aptitude for languages,* спосо́бности к языка́м. ♦*But notice: sympathy for someone,* сочу́вствие кому́-нибудь. *Concern for others,* забо́та о други́х. **4,** (seeking) о; за. *A cry/request for help,* крик/про́сьба о по́мощи. *Turn to someone for advice,* обрати́ться к кому́-нибудь за сове́том. *Suit for damages,* иск о возмеще́нии убы́тков. **5,** (to fetch; to buy) за (+ *instr.*): *go for some cigarettes,* сходи́ть за сигаре́тами; *send for the doctor,* посла́ть за врачо́м. *The line for tickets,* о́чередь за биле́тами. **6,** (indicating destination) в (+ *acc.*): *leave for Washington,* уезжа́ть в Вашингто́н. ♦*But notice: the train for Washington,* по́езд на Вашингто́н. **7,** (indicating duration of time) *usu. omitted in Russian: wait for two hours,* ждать два часа́. *Live in France for two years,* прожи́ть два го́да во Фра́нции. ♦*Also,* в тече́ние: *for the last two weeks,* в тече́ние после́дних двух неде́ль. ♦*With pl. nouns, usu. rendered by the instr. case: stand in line for hours,* выста́ивать часа́ми в о́череди. *Remain in power for decades,* десятиле́тиями остаа́ться у вла́сти. *For days on end,* по це́лым дням. *I haven't seen you for ages,* не ви́дел(а) вас це́лую ве́чность. **8,** (for a period of time begun as action is completed) на (+ *acc.*): *lie down for an hour,* приле́чь на час. *Come in for a minute!,* зайди́те на мину́ту! *Stay for three days,* оста́ться на три дня (*but* остава́ться три дня). **9,** (in view of the normal character of) для: *very warm for May,* о́чень тепло́ для ма́я. *Not bad for a beginner,* непло́хо для начина́ющего. **10,** (in place of) за (+ *acc.*): *Give her a kiss for me!,* поцелу́йте её за меня́! *Sign for the chairman,* распиши́ться за председа́теля. *A substitute for sugar,* замени́тель *or* суррога́т са́хара. **11,** (from; because of) от: *jump for joy,* пры́гать от ра́дости. **12,** (owing to) за (+ *instr.*): *for lack of evidence,* за отсу́тствием ули́к. *For many reasons,* по мно́гим причи́нам. **13,** (to help cure) от: *Have you anything for a headache?,* у вас есть что́-нибудь от головно́й бо́ли? **14,** (despite; notwithstanding) при: *for all his knowledge,* при всех его́ зна́ниях. *For all that,* при всём том. —*conj.* (because; inasmuch as) и́бо; поско́льку.
forage *n.* фура́ж; корм. —*adj.* кормово́й: *forage crops,* кормовы́е культу́ры. —*v.i.* [*usu.* **forage for**] разы́скивать.
foray *n.* набе́г; налёт.

forbear *v.t.* (refrain from) уде́рживаться от; воздёрживаться от. —*v.i.* (have patience) терпе́ть. —*n.* = **forebear.**

forbearance *n.* **1,** (abstinence) воздержа́ние. **2,** (patient endurance) терпели́вость.

forbid *v.t.* запреща́ть; воспреща́ть. *I forbid to you go,* я запреща́ю тебе́ идти́. —**God forbid!,** не дай бог!; бо́же упаси́!

forbidden *adj.* **1,** *used predicatively,* запрещено́: *It is forbidden,* э́то запрещено́. *Strictly forbidden,* стро́го воспреща́ется. *They are forbidden to...,* им запреща́ется (+ *inf.*). **2,** *modifier,* запре́тный: *forbidden fruit,* запре́тный плод.

forbidding *adj.* непристу́пный; неприве́тливый.

force *n.* **1,** (strength; power) си́ла: *the force of a blow,* си́ла уда́ра. **2,** (physical pressure or coercion) си́ла: *by force,* си́лой; наси́льно. *The use of force,* примене́ние си́лы. **3,** (validity) си́ла: *remain in force,* остава́ться в си́ле. **4,** *pl., mil.* си́лы: *armed forces,* вооружённые си́лы. —*v.t.* **1,** (compel) заставля́ть; вынужда́ть; принужда́ть. *Force oneself,* де́лать над собо́й уси́лие. *Force oneself to eat,* заставля́ть себя́ есть; есть че́рез си́лу. *He was forced to...,* он был вы́нужден (+ *inf.*). **2,** (cause to move against resistance) вта́лкивать; вгоня́ть. *He was forced into a car,* его́ втолкну́ли в маши́ну. *Force the crowd back,* оса́живать толпу́. *Force the enemy back,* оттесня́ть проти́вника. *Force one's way into/through,* вла́мываться в; пробива́ться сквозь. *Force out of power,* вытесня́ть из правле́ния. **3,** (break open, as a door or lock) взла́мывать. **4,** (impose) навя́зывать: *force one's opinion on someone,* навя́зывать своё мне́ние кому́-нибудь. **5,** (produce by effort) вы́давить: *force a smile,* вы́давить улы́бку. **6,** (make grow faster, as plants) выгоня́ть. —**by force of arms,** си́лой ору́жия. —**by force of habit,** в си́лу привы́чки. —**join forces,** соединя́ть *or* объединя́ть си́лы.

forced *adj.* **1,** (compulsory) принуди́тельный: *forced labor,* принуди́тельный труд. **2,** (emergency, as of a landing) вы́нужденный. **3,** (unnatural, as of a smile) натя́нутый. —**forced entry,** взлом. —**forced feeding,** наси́льственное кормле́ние. —**forced march,** *mil.* форси́рованный марш.

force-feed *v.t.* наси́льственно корми́ть.

forceful *adj.* реши́тельный: *forceful measures,* реши́тельные ме́ры.

forceps *n.* хирурги́ческие щипцы́.

forcible *adj.* наси́льственный. —**forcibly,** *adv.* наси́льно; наси́льственно; принуди́тельно.

ford *n.* брод. —*v.t.* переходи́ть вброд.

fore *n.* пере́дний план: *come to the fore,* выдвига́ться на пере́дний план.

fore-and-aft *adj.* продо́льный. *Fore-and-aft sail,* косо́й па́рус.

forearm *n.* предпле́чье.

forebear *also,* **forbear** *n.* пре́док.

forebode *v.t.* предвеща́ть. —**foreboding,** *n.* дурно́е предчу́вствие.

forecast *n.* прогно́з; предсказа́ние. *Weather forecast,* прогно́з *or* сво́дка пого́ды. —*v.t.* предска́зывать.

forecaster *n.* предсказа́тель. *Weather forecaster,* сино́птик.

forecastle *n.* бак.

forefather *n.* пре́док.

forefinger *n.* указа́тельный па́лец.

forefront *n.* аванга́рд. *In the forefront,* в аванга́рде; в пе́рвых ряда́х.

forego *v.* = **forgo.**

foregoing *adj.* предше́ствующий; вышеука́занный. —**the foregoing,** предыду́щее.

foregone *adj.* проше́дший. —**foregone conclusion,** зара́нее изве́стный результа́т. *The result was a foregone conclusion,* в исхо́де не́ было сомне́ний.

foreground *n.* пере́дний план.

forehand *n., tennis* уда́р спра́ва. —*adj.* спра́ва.

forehead *n.* лоб.

foreign *adj.* **1,** (of another country) иностра́нный; чужо́й: *foreign language,* иностра́нный язы́к; *foreign country,* чужа́я страна́. *Foreign car,* иностра́нная маши́на. *Foreign goods,* заграни́чные това́ры. **2,** (conducted with other nations) вне́шний: *foreign policy,* вне́шняя поли́тика; *foreign trade,* вне́шняя торго́вля. *Foreign aid,* иностра́нная по́мощь. **3,** (extraneous) иноро́дный; посторо́нний: *foreign body,* иноро́дное/посторо́ннее те́ло. **4,** (alien; strange) чу́ждый: *Jealousy is foreign to his nature,* ре́вность ему́ чужда́.

foreigner *n.* иностра́нец.

foreign minister мини́стр иностра́нных дел.

foreleg *n.* пере́дняя нога́; пере́дняя ла́па.

forelock *n.* чуб; чёлка; вихо́р.

foreman *n.* ма́стер; бригади́р; прора́б; деся́тник.

foremast *n.* фок-ма́чта.

foremost *adj.* **1,** (in front) пере́дний; передово́й. **2,** (leading; outstanding) выдаю́щийся. —*adv.* вперёд. —**first and foremost,** пре́жде всего́.

forenoon *n.* вре́мя до полу́дня; у́тро.

forensic *adj.* суде́бный.

foreordain *v.t.* предопределя́ть; предначерта́ть.

forerunner *n.* предше́ственник; предве́стник.

foresail *n.* фок.

foresee *v.t.* предви́деть.

foreseeable *adj.* *It was not foreseeable,* э́того нельзя́ бы́ло предви́деть. —**in the foreseeable future,** в обозри́мом бу́дущем.

foreshadow *v.t.* предвеща́ть.

foreshorten *v.t., art* взять в раку́рсе. —**foreshortened,** *adj.* в раку́рсе.

foresight *n.* предусмотри́тельность.

foreskin *n.* кра́йняя плоть.

forest *n.* лес. —*adj.* лесно́й: *forest fire,* лесно́й пожа́р. —**not see the forest for the trees,** за дере́вьями ле́са не ви́дно.

forestall *v.t.* предупрежда́ть; предвосхища́ть.

forester *n.* лесни́чий.

forestry *n.* лесно́е хозя́йство; лесово́дство.

foretaste *n.* предвкуше́ние.

foretell *v.t.* предска́зывать.

forethought *n.* предусмотри́тельность.

forever *adv.* **1,** (for all time) ве́чно; навсегда́;

наве́к(и). *Live forever,* жить ве́чно. **2,** (constantly) ве́чно: *They are forever arguing,* они́ ве́чно спо́рят.

forewarn *v.t.* предостерега́ть.

foreword *n.* предисло́вие.

forfeit *v.t.* лиша́ться; теря́ть. *Forfeit a right,* теря́ть пра́во. —*n.* **1,** (penalty) неусто́йка. **2,** *pl.* (game) фа́нты. **—forfeiture,** *n.* поте́ря; лише́ние.

forge *n.* **1,** (smithy) ку́зница. **2,** (furnace) горн. —*v.t.* **1,** (shape, as metal) кова́ть. **2,** *fig.* (fashion; hammer out) кова́ть: *forge a victory,* кова́ть побе́ду. *Forge an alliance,* образова́ть сою́з. **3,** (make a fraudulent copy of) подде́лывать: *forge someone's signature,* подде́лать чью-нибудь по́дпись. —*v.i.* [*usu.* **forge ahead**] продвига́ться вперёд; вы́скочить вперёд. **—forged,** *adj.* подде́льный; подло́жный. **—forger,** *n.* подде́лыватель; фальшивомоне́тчик.

forgery *n.* **1,** (act of forging) подло́г; подде́лка. **2,** (something forged) подде́лка.

forget *v.t. & i.* забыва́ть: *Don't forget!,* не забу́дьте! *Forgot how to do something,* разучи́ться (+ *inf.*). *I completely forgot about it,* я соверше́нно забы́л(а) об э́том. *I forgot to lock the door,* я забы́л(а) запере́ть дверь.

forgetful *adj.* забы́вчивый. **—forgetfulness,** *n.* забы́вчивость.

forget-me-not *n.* незабу́дка.

forgivable *adj.* прости́тельный.

forgive *v.t.* проща́ть: *Forgive me for being late,* прости́те меня́ за опозда́ние. *I shall never forgive you for this,* я вам э́того никогда́ не прощу́.

forgiveness *n.* проще́ние: *forgiveness for one's sins,* проще́ние грехо́в. *Ask for someone's forgiveness,* проси́ть проще́ния у кого́-нибудь.

forgo *also,* **forego** *v.t.* отка́зываться от; возде́рживаться от; поступа́ться (+ *instr.*).

forgotten *adj.* забы́тый.

fork *n.* **1,** (eating utensil) ви́лка. **2,** (in a road) разветвле́ние; развви́лка. —*v.i.* разветвля́ться; раздва́иваться.

forked *adj.* раздвое́нный; разветвлённый. *Forked lightning,* зигзагообра́зная мо́лния.

forlorn *adj.* жа́лкий: *forlorn appearance,* жа́лкий вид. **—forlorn hope,** (о́чень) сла́бая наде́жда.

form *n.* **1,** (outward appearance) фо́рма: *form and content,* фо́рма и содержа́ние. **2,** (type; variety) фо́рма: *form of energy,* фо́рма эне́ргии. *Form of government,* фо́рма *or* о́браз правле́ния. *Low forms of life,* ни́зшие фо́рмы жи́зни. *Familiar form of address,* обраще́ние на «ты.» **3,** (character) фо́рма; вид. *Take the form of,* принима́ть фо́рму (+ *gen.*). *In the form of,* в ви́де (+ *gen.*). *In its present form,* в его́ ны́нешнем ви́де. *In abridged form,* в сокращённом ви́де. **4,** (document to be filled out) анке́та; бланк. **5,** (fitness) фо́рма. *Be in good form,* быть в фо́рме; быть в уда́ре. **6,** (correct social behavior) фо́рма; тон: *for form's sake; as a matter of form,* для фо́рмы; для проформы. *A sign of poor form,* при́знак дурно́го то́на. **7,** *gram.* фо́рма: *short form of adjectives,* кра́ткая фо́рма прилага́тельных. **8,** (mold; dummy) фо́рма: *form for hats,* фо́рма для шляп. —*v.t.* **1,**

(make; put together; organize) образова́ть; составля́ть; формирова́ть. *Form a circle,* образова́ть круг; стать в круг. *Form a group,* образова́ть *or* соста́вить гру́ппу. *Form a plan,* соста́вить *or* вы́работать план. *Form a government,* образова́ть *or* формирова́ть прави́тельство. **2,** (give form or shape to) формирова́ть: *form character,* формирова́ть хара́ктер. **3,** (develop in one's mind) составля́ть: *form an opinion,* соста́вить себе́ мне́ние. **4,** (develop, as a habit) выраба́тывать в себе́ (привы́чку). **5,** (make up; constitute) составля́ть; образова́ть: *form a single whole,* составля́ть/образова́ть еди́ное це́лое. *Form the boundary between,* образова́ть грани́цу ме́жду. *Form the basis of,* лежа́ть в осно́ве (+ *gen.*). —*v.i.* образова́ться; формирова́ться. *Puddles formed from the rain,* от дождя́ образова́лись лу́жи. *Long lines formed,* вы́строились дли́нные о́череди.

formal *adj.* **1,** (in various meanings) форма́льный: *formal logic,* форма́льная ло́гика. **2,** (official) официа́льный: *formal protest,* официа́льный проте́ст. **3,** (of clothes) пара́дный: *formal attire,* пара́дное пла́тье. **4,** (stiff; constrained) церемо́нный.

formaldehyde *n.* формальдеги́д.

formalism *n.* формали́зм. **—formalist,** *n.* формали́ст. **—formalistic,** *adj.* формалисти́ческий.

formality *n.* форма́льность. *It's merely a formality,* э́то пуста́я форма́льность.

formalize *v.t.* оформля́ть.

formally *adv.* форма́льно.

format *n.* форма́т.

formation *n.* **1,** (act or process of forming) образова́ние; формирова́ние: *formation of a committee,* образова́ние/формирова́ние комите́та. *Formation of character,* формирова́ние *or* становле́ние хара́ктера. **2,** (something formed) образова́ние: *rock formations,* го́рные *or* ска́льные образова́ния. **3,** *mil.* строй; построе́ние. *In formation,* в строю́; стро́ем. **4,** *geol.* форма́ция.

former *adj.* **1,** (earlier) пре́жний: *in former times,* в пре́жнее вре́мя. **2,** (ex-) бы́вший: *the former mayor,* бы́вший мэр. *The former Soviet Union,* бы́вший Сове́тский Сою́з. **3,** (opp. of latter) пе́рвый.

formerly *adv.* ра́ньше; пре́жде.

formic *adj.* муравьи́ный: *formic acid,* муравьи́ная кислота́.

formidable *adj.* **1,** (awesome) гро́зный. **2,** (hard to accomplish, as of a task) тяжёлый. **3,** (strikingly impressive) внуши́тельный.

formless *adj.* бесфо́рменный.

form letter станда́ртное письмо́.

formula *n.* фо́рмула.

formulate *v.t.* **1,** (express in precise form) формули́ровать. **2,** (devise; shape) определя́ть (поли́тику); разраба́тывать (план).

formulation *n.* **1,** (expressing) формулиро́вка. **2,** (devising; shaping) определе́ние; разрабо́тка.

fornication *n.* внебра́чная связь.

forsake *v.t.* **1,** (leave; abandon) броса́ть; покида́ть. **2,** (give up; renounce) отка́зываться от; отрека́ться от.

forswear *v.t.* зарека́ться от.

fort *n.* форт.

forte *adj. & adv., music* фо́рте. —*n.* (strong point) си́льная сторона́.

forth *adv.* **1,** (forward) вперёд. *Step forth,* выступа́ть. **2,** (outward) нару́жу. *Spew forth,* изверга́ть. —**and so forth,** и так да́лее; и тому́ подо́бное; и про́чее. —**back and forth,** взад и вперёд.

forthcoming *adj.* **1,** (impending) предстоя́щий. **2,** (produced when wanted): *No reply was forthcoming,* отве́та не после́довало.

forthright *adj.* прямоду́шный; прямолине́йный. —**forthrightness,** *n.* прямоду́шие; прямота́.

forthwith *adv.* неме́дленно.

fortieth *adj.* сороково́й. —*n.* сорокова́я; сорокова́я часть. *One-fortieth,* одна́ сорокова́я; сорокова́я часть.

fortification *n.* укрепле́ние; фортифика́ция.

fortify *v.t.* **1,** (strengthen; provide with defenses) укрепля́ть. **2,** (reinforce; invigorate) подкрепля́ть.

fortissimo *adj. & adv.* форти́ссимо.

fortitude *n.* сто́йкость; вы́держка.

fortnight *n.* две неде́ли.

fortnightly *adj.* происходя́щий раз в две неде́ли; (*of a publication*) двухнеде́льный. —*adv.* раз в две неде́ли.

fortress *n.* кре́пость.

fortuitous *adj.* случа́йный; неча́янный. —**fortuitousness; fortuity,** *n.* случа́йность.

fortunate *adj.* счастли́вый: *fortunate occurrence,* счастли́вый слу́чай. *It was fortunate that...,* хорошо́, что... *Those fortunate enough to...,* те, кому́ посчастли́вилось (+ *inf.*).

fortunately *adv.* к сча́стью.

fortune *n.* **1,** (fate) судьба́: *Fortune smiled on us,* судьба́ нам улыба́лась. **2,** (luck) сча́стье; уда́ча. *I had the good fortune to...,* я име́л(а) сча́стье (+ *inf.*); мне посчастли́вилось (+ *inf.*). **3,** (great amount of wealth or money) состоя́ние: *make a fortune,* нажи́ть состоя́ние; *spend a fortune,* потра́тить це́лое состоя́ние. *Cost a fortune,* обойти́сь *or* влете́ть в копе́ечку. —**tell fortunes,** гада́ть; ворожи́ть. *Tell someone's fortune,* предсказа́ть чье-нибудь бу́дущее.

fortuneteller *n.* гада́лка; ворожея́. —**fortunetelling,** *n.* гада́ние; ворожба́.

forty *n. & adj.* со́рок.

forum *n.* фо́рум.

forward *adv.* вперёд. *Step/come forward,* выступа́ть. *A step forward (fig.),* шаг вперёд. —*adj.* **1,** (toward the front) поступа́тельный: *forward motion,* поступа́тельный ход; движе́ние вперёд. **2,** (in the front) пере́дний; передово́й. *Forward position (mil.),* передова́я пози́ция. **3,** (presumptuous) развя́зный. —*v.t.* **1,** (send) отправля́ть. **2,** (send to a further destination) пересыла́ть; переправля́ть; переадресо́вывать. **3,** (promote; advance) продвига́ть. —*n., sports* напада́ющий; фо́рвард. —**forward march!,** ша́гом марш!

fossil *n.* окамене́лость; ископа́емое. —*adj.* ископа́емый: *fossil remains,* ископа́емые оста́тки; *fossil*

fuel, ископа́емое то́пливо. —**fossilized,** *adj.* ископа́емый.

foster *v.t.* **1,** (promote; stimulate) спосо́бствовать: *foster mutual understanding,* спосо́бствовать взаимопонима́нию. **2,** (create; cultivate) се́ять: *foster discontent,* се́ять недово́льство. *Foster an illusion,* создава́ть иллю́зию. —*adj.* приёмный: *foster father,* приёмный оте́ц.

foul *adj.* га́дкий; скве́рный; ме́рзкий. *Foul weather,* га́дкая *or* скве́рная пого́да. *Foul odor,* проти́вный за́пах. *Foul air,* нечи́стый во́здух. *Foul language,* скверносло́вие. *In a foul mood,* в скве́рном настрое́нии. —*v.t.* **1,** (soil; defile) загрязня́ть; зага́живать. **2,** *fol. by* **up** (bungle) напу́тать. —*n., sports* фол: *personal foul,* персона́льный фол. —**foul play,** преступле́ние: *signs of foul play,* при́знаки совершённого преступле́ния.

found *v.t.* осно́вывать; учрежда́ть. *The city was founded by...,* го́род был осно́ван (+ *instr.*).

foundation *n.* **1,** (supporting part of a building) фунда́мент. *Shake something to its foundations,* потрясти́ что-нибудь до основа́ния. **2,** (basis) основа́ние. (*Be*) *without foundation,* не име́ть (под собо́й) основа́ния; ни на чём не осно́ван(о); не име́ть под собо́й по́чвы. **3,** (endowed institution) фонд.

founder *n.* **1,** (one who has founded or established something) основа́тель; учреди́тель. **2,** (caster of metals) лите́йщик. —*v.i.* **1,** (sink) тону́ть. **2,** (fail) срыва́ться.

foundling *n.* подки́дыш; найдёныш. *Foundling home,* прию́т; детдо́м.

foundry *n.* лите́йный заво́д. *Iron foundry,* чугуноли́тейный заво́д *or* цех.

fount *n.* кла́дезь.

fountain *n.* **1,** (large) фонта́н. **2,** (drinking fountain) фонта́нчик; авторучка. —**fountain pen,** авторучка.

four *adj.* четы́ре. —*n.* **1,** (cardinal number) четы́ре. **2,** (written numeral; school grade) четвёрка. **3,** *cards* четвёрка. —**on all fours,** ползко́м; на четвере́ньках.

fourfold *adj.* четырёхкра́тный. —*adv.* вче́тверо.

four hundred четы́реста. —**four-hundredth,** *adj.* четырёхсо́тый.

four-legged *adj.* четвероно́гий.

fourteen *n. & adj.* четы́рнадцать. —**fourteenth,** *adj.* четы́рнадцатый.

fourth *adj.* четвёртый. —*n.* **1,** (quarter) че́тверть: *three-fourths,* три че́тверти. **2,** *music* ква́рта. —**in the fourth place,** в-четвёртых.

four-wheel *also,* **four-wheeled** *adj.* четырёхколёсный. —**four-wheel drive,** приво́д на четы́ре колеса́.

fowl *n.* дома́шняя пти́ца. —**neither fish nor fowl,** ни ры́ба ни мя́со.

fowler *n.* птицело́в. —**fowling,** *n.* птицело́вство.

fox *n.* лиса́; лиси́ца. —*adj.* ли́сий: *fox fur,* ли́сий мех.

foxglove *n.* наперстя́нка.

foxhole *n., mil.* яче́йка.

fox terrier фокстерье́р.

foxtrot *n.* фокстро́т.

foxy *adj.* ли́сий; хи́трый.

foyer *n.* фойе́; вестибю́ль.

fracas *n.* шу́мная ссо́ра; дебо́ш.

fraction *n.* **1,** *math.* дробь. **2,** *fol. by* **of** (small portion) деся́тая до́ля (+ *gen.*). —**fractional,** *adj.* дро́бный.

fractious *adj.* **1,** (cross) злой. **2,** (unruly) непоко́рный.

fracture *n.* перело́м. —*v.t.* лома́ть; перела́мывать; прола́мывать. *Fracture one's skull,* проломи́ть себе́ го́лову *or* че́реп.

fragile *adj.* хру́пкий; ло́мкий. —**fragility,** *n.* хру́пкость; ло́мкость.

fragment *n.* обло́мок; оско́лок. —*v.t.* дроби́ть; раздробля́ть.

fragmentary *adj.* отры́вочный: *fragmentary information,* отры́вочные све́дения.

fragmentation *n.* **1,** (splitting up) дробле́ние. **2,** (state of being divided) раздро́бленность. —**fragmentation bomb,** оско́лочная бо́мба.

fragrance *n.* арома́т; благоуха́ние.

fragrant *adj.* души́стый; арома́тный; благоуха́нный.

frail *adj.* хру́пкий; тщеду́шный. —**frailty,** *n.* хру́пкость; тщеду́шие.

frame *n.* **1,** (for a picture) ра́ма; ра́мка. **2,** (of a window or door) ра́ма. **3,** (for eyeglasses) опра́ва. **4,** (of a building) карка́с; о́стов; сруб; коро́бка. **5,** (build, as of the human body) (те́ло)сложе́ние. **6,** *motion pictures* кадр. —*v.t.* **1,** (put into a frame) вставля́ть в ра́му; обрамля́ть. **2,** (devise; formulate) составля́ть; формули́ровать. **3,** *colloq.* (falsely incriminate) ло́жно обвиня́ть; состря́пать де́ло (*or* обвине́ние) про́тив. —**frame of mind,** настрое́ние; расположе́ние ду́ха. —**frame of reference,** систе́ма взгля́дов; то́чка зре́ния.

frame house карка́сный дом.

framework *n.* **1,** (skeleton; structure) карка́с; о́стов; сруб. **2,** (basic structure) ра́мки: *within the framework of,* в ра́мках (+ *gen.*).

franc *n.* франк.

franchise *n.* **1,** (suffrage) пра́во го́лоса. **2,** (concession granted by a government) привиле́гия.

francium *n.* фра́нций.

frank *adj.* открове́нный.

frankfurter *n.* соси́ска.

frankincense *n.* ла́дан.

frankly *adv.* **1,** (in a frank manner) открове́нно. **2,** (to be frank; in truth) открове́нно говоря́.

frankness *n.* открове́нность.

frantic *adj.* отча́янный. *Frantic attempt,* отча́янная *or* я́ростная попы́тка. *Frantic efforts,* отча́янные *or* бе́шеные уси́лия. *I am frantic,* я в отча́янии.

fraternal *adj.* бра́тский. —**fraternal twins,** двуяйцо́вые близнецы́.

fraternity *n.* **1,** (brotherhood) бра́тство. **2,** (fraternal organization) бра́тия.

fraternize *v.i.* брата́ться. —**fraternization,** *n.* брата́ние.

fratricide *n.* братоуби́йство. —**fratricidal,** *adj.* братоуби́йственный.

fraud *n.* **1,** (criminal deception) обма́н; моше́нничество. **2,** (a cheat) обма́нщик; самозва́нец.

fraudulent *adj.* обма́нный; жу́льнический; моше́ннический. —**fraudulently,** *adv.* обма́ном; обма́нным путём.

fraught *adj.* [*usu.* **fraught with**] чрева́тый (+ *instr.*).

fray *n.* **1,** (brawl) дра́ка. **2,** (battle) бой. —*v.t.* обтрепа́ть. —*v.i.* обтрепа́ться. —**frayed,** *adj.* обтрёпанный.

freak *n.* уро́д. *Freak of nature,* капри́з *or* шу́тка приро́ды. —**freakish,** *adj.* капри́зный; чудакова́тый.

freckle *n.* весну́шка. —**freckled; freckle-faced,** *adj.* весну́шчатый.

free *adj.* **1,** (independent; unrestricted; unburdened; not occupied) свобо́дный: *free country/press,* свобо́дная страна́/печа́ть. *Free from worry,* свобо́дный от забо́т. *Are you free this evening?,* вы свобо́дны сего́дня ве́чером? **2,** *fol. by inf.* (at liberty) во́лен (во́льна): *You are free to leave,* ты во́лен (во́льна) уйти́. **3,** (not costing anything) беспла́тный: *Admission is free,* вход беспла́тный. —*adv.* [*also,* **free of charge**] беспла́тно; да́ром; безвозме́здно. —*v.t.* освобожда́ть. *Free oneself,* освобожда́ться. *Free someone from the wreckage,* извлека́ть кого́-нибудь из-под обло́мков. *Free up funds,* высвобожда́ть сре́дства. —**free city,** во́льный го́род. —**free enterprise,** свобо́дное предпринима́тельство. —**free fall,** свобо́дное паде́ние. —**free hand,** свобо́да де́йствий: *give someone a free hand,* дать кому́-нибудь по́лную свобо́ду де́йствий. —**free love,** свобо́дная любо́вь. —**free port,** откры́тый порт. —**free speech,** свобо́да сло́ва. —**free thought,** свободомы́слие; вольноду́мство. —**free throw,** *basketball* штрафно́й бросо́к. —**free trade,** свобо́дная торго́вля. —**free translation,** во́льный перево́д. —**free verse,** во́льный стих. —**set free,** выпуска́ть *or* отпуска́ть на свобо́ду *or* на во́лю.

freedom *n.* свобо́да. —**freedom-loving,** *adj.* свободолюби́вый.

free-for-all *n.* о́бщая сва́лка.

freelance *adj.* внешта́тный.

freely *adv.* свобо́дно. *Perspire freely,* си́льно поте́ть.

Freemason *n.* франкмасо́н. —**Freemasonry,** *n.* франкмасо́нство.

freestyle *n., swimming* во́льный стиль.

freethinker *n.* вольноду́мец; свободомы́слящий. —**freethinking,** *adj.* вольноду́мный; свободомы́слящий.

freeze *v.i.* **1,** (from the cold) мёрзнуть; замерза́ть. *I am freezing,* я мёрзну. *The crops are freezing,* посе́вы мёрзнут. *The river froze over,* река́ замёрзла. *The pipes froze,* тру́бы замёрзли. *Freeze to death,* поги́бнуть от хо́лода; замёрзнуть. **2,** (from fear, shock, etc.) цепене́ть; ледене́ть; замира́ть: *freeze in horror,* цепене́ть/ледене́ть/замира́ть от у́жаса. *Freeze in one's tracks,* останови́ться как вко́панный. **3,** *fol. by* **to** (become attached by freezing) примерза́ть (к). —*v.t.* замора́живать; моро́зить. —*n.* **1,** (freezing weather) моро́з. **2,** (of prices, wages, etc.) замора́живание: *price freeze,* замора́живание цен.

freezer *n.* морози́льник.

freezing *adj.* моро́зный: *freezing weather,* моро́зная пого́да. *Freezing cold,* жесто́кий хо́лод. *Freezing temperature,* температу́ра ни́же нуля́ (по Це́льсию). *Shut the window! It is freezing in here!,* закро́й окно́! Здесь стра́шно хо́лодно! —**freezing point,** то́чка замерза́ния.

freight *n.* **1,** (goods being transported) това́р; груз. **2,** (transportation of goods) перево́зка. **3,** (charge for such transportation) пла́та за прово́з. *What will be the freight charges?,* ско́лько бу́дет сто́ить перево́зка? —*adj.* това́рный; грузово́й: *freight train,* това́рный по́езд; *freight traffic,* грузово́е движе́ние.

freighter *n.* грузово́е су́дно.

French *adj.* францу́зский. —*n.* **1,** (language) францу́зский язы́к. *Speak French,* говори́ть по-францу́зски. **2,** *preceded by* the (people) францу́зы.

French curve лека́ло.

French horn валто́рна.

Frenchman *n.* францу́з. —**Frenchwoman,** *n.* францу́женка.

frenetic *adj.* лихора́дочный; кипу́чий.

frenzy *n.* исступле́ние. —**frenzied,** *adj.* исступлённый.

freon *n.* фрео́н.

frequency *n.* **1,** (rate of occurrence) частота́: *frequency of cases,* частота́ слу́чаев. **2,** *radio* частота́: *low frequencies,* ни́зкие часто́ты. —**frequency modulation,** часто́тная модуля́ция.

frequent *adj.* ча́стый. *Become more frequent,* уча́щаться. —*v.t.* ча́сто посеща́ть.

frequentative *adj., gram.* многокра́тный.

frequently *adv.* ча́сто.

fresco *n.* фре́ска.

fresh *adj.* **1,** (not used, treated, or spoiled) све́жий: *fresh air,* све́жий во́здух; *fresh linen,* све́жее бельё; *fresh eggs/vegetables,* све́жие я́йца/о́вощи. *Fresh in one's memory,* свеж (свежо́) в па́мяти. **2,** (not salt, as of water) пре́сный. **3,** *colloq.* (impudent) наха́льный.

freshen *v.t.* освежа́ть. —*v.i.* [*usu.* **freshen up**] **1,** (become fresh) свеже́ть. **2,** (make oneself clean and fresh) освежа́ться.

freshly *adv.* свеже-: *freshly baked,* свежевы́печенный; *freshly painted,* свежеокра́шенный; свежевы́крашенный.

freshman *n.* первоку́рсник; но́венький.

freshness *n.* **1,** (newness) све́жесть. **2,** (insolence) наха́льство.

fresh-water *adj.* пресново́дный.

fret *v.i.* му́читься. —*n., music* лад. —**fretful,** *adj.* раздражи́тельный; капри́зный.

fret saw ло́бзик.

fretwork *n.* резна́я рабо́та.

Freudian *adj.* фрейди́стский.

friable *adj.* ры́хлый; сыпу́чий; рассы́пчатый.

friar *n.* мона́х; и́нок.

fricassee *n.* фрикасе́.

fricative *adj.* фрикати́вный.

friction *n.* **1,** (rubbing together; resistance) тре́ние. **2,** (conflict; disagreement) тре́ния. —**friction tape,** изоляцио́нная ле́нта.

Friday *n.* пя́тница. —**Good Friday,** страстна́я пя́тница.

fried *adj.* жа́реный. *Fried eggs,* яи́чница-глазу́нья.

friend *n.* друг. *Be friends,* дружи́ть. *Become friends,* дружи́ться. *Make a lot of friends,* заводи́ть мно́го друзе́й; подружи́ться со мно́гими людьми́. *She has difficulty making friends,* ей тру́дно заводи́ть друзе́й *or* знако́мства.

friendliness *n.* приве́тливость; дружелю́бие.

friendly *adj.* **1,** (outgoing) приве́тливый: *friendly neighbors,* приве́тливые сосе́ди. **2,** (amicable) дру́жеский; дружелю́бный. *Friendly tone,* дру́жеский тон. *Be on friendly terms with,* быть в дру́жеских отноше́ниях с; быть на дру́жеской ноге́ с. **3,** (not hostile or antagonistic) дру́жественный: *friendly countries,* дру́жественные стра́ны. *Friendly relations (between countries),* дру́жественные отноше́ния. **4,** (given as a friend) дру́жеский: *friendly advice,* дру́жеский сове́т.

friendship *n.* дру́жба.

frieze *n.* фриз.

frigate *n.* фрега́т. —**frigate bird,** фрега́т.

fright *n.* **1,** (sudden fear) испу́г. *Give someone (quite) a fright,* напуга́ть кого́-нибудь. **2,** *colloq.* (grotesque person or thing) страши́лище.

frighten *v.t.* пуга́ть. *Be frightened,* пуга́ться. —**frighten away** *or* **off,** спуга́ть.

frightening *adj.* пуга́ющий; стра́шный. *With frightening speed,* с пуга́ющей быстрото́й. *Frightening rumors,* трево́жные слу́хи. *It is frightening,* жу́тко.

frightful *adj.* ужа́сный; стра́шный. —**frightfully,** *adv.* ужа́сно: *frightfully expensive,* ужа́сно дорого́й.

frigid *adj.* холо́дный; ледяно́й.

frigidity *n., physiol.* полова́я хо́лодность; фриги́дность.

frill *n.* обо́рка.

fringe *n.* **1,** (trimming) бахрома́. **2,** (outer edge) край. —**fringe benefits,** дополни́тельные льго́ты.

fringed *adj.* бахро́мчатый.

frisk *v.i.* (frolic) резви́ться. —*v.t., colloq.* (search) обы́скивать.

frisky *adj.* ре́звый; игри́вый.

fritter *n.* ола́дья. —*v.t.* [*usu.* **fritter away**] растра́чивать.

frivolity *n.* легкомы́слие.

frivolous *adj.* легкомы́сленный.

fro *adv., in* **to and fro,** взад и вперёд.

frock *n.* **1,** (dress) пла́тье. **2,** (monk's habit) ря́са. —**frock coat,** сюрту́к.

frog *n.* лягу́шка. —**frog in one's throat,** хрипота́. —**frogs' legs,** лягу́шечьи ла́пки.

frogman *n.* водола́з-подрывни́к.

frolic *v.i.* резви́ться; вози́ться. —**frolicsome,** *adj.* ре́звый; шаловли́вый.

from *prep.* **1,** (away from; a certain distance from) от: *move away from the window,* отходи́ть от окна́. *Far from home,* далеко́ от до́ма. *Three miles from the airport,* в трёх ми́лях от аэропо́рта. **2,** (from a place) из: *arrive from Paris,* прие́хать из Пари́жа; *news from America,* но́вости из Аме́рики. ♦*With certain* *nouns*, с: *from work*, с рабо́ты; *from the post office*, с по́чты; *from the south*, с ю́га. *From head to toe*, с головы́ до ног. *From all over the world*, со всего́ ми́ра. **3**, (from a person) A, (where the subject initiates the action) у: *buy from*, покупа́ть у; *take from*, брать у; *find out from*, узна́ть у; *get from*, получи́ть у. B, (where the subject is the recipient of the action) от: *learn/hear from*, узна́ть от; *receive a letter from a friend*, получи́ть письмо́ от дру́га. **4**, (from out of) из: *drink from a glass*, пить из стака́на; *remove from one's pocket*, вынима́ть из карма́на. *Rescue a child from a burning building*, спасти́ ребёнка из горя́щего зда́ния. **5**, (off of; down from; up from) с: *dismount from a horse*, сойти́ с ло́шади; *take a book from the shelf*, доста́ть кни́гу с по́лки; *fall from the sky*, па́дать с не́ба; *rise from one's chair*, встава́ть со сту́ла; *take off from the deck of a carrier*, взлета́ть с па́лубы авиано́сца. *Get up from the table*, встава́ть из-за стола́. *Hang from the ceiling*, висе́ть на потолке́. *Rise from the ashes*, возрожда́ться из пе́пла. **6**, *with numbers, time, etc.* от; с: *from four to six*, от четырёх до шести́; *from morning till evening*, с утра́ до ве́чера; *from Monday to Friday*, с понеде́льника до пя́тницы. *From this moment onward*, с э́того моме́нта. **7**, (from a source or origin) из: *from the newspapers*, из газе́т; *from a good family*, из хоро́шей семьи́. *From Russian to English*, с ру́сского на англи́йский. *Wine is made from grapes*, вино́ де́лают из виногра́да. *From this it follows that..*, из э́того сле́дует, что... **8**, (because of) от: *suffer from insomnia*, страда́ть от бессо́нницы; *shiver from the cold*, дрожа́ть от хо́лода. **9**, *with various verbs*, от: *differ from*, отлича́ться от; *keep from laughing*, удержа́ться от сме́ха; *hide from the police*, пря́таться от поли́ции; *save from disaster*, избавля́ть от катастро́фы; *protect one's eyes from the sun*, защища́ть глаза́ от со́лнца. **10**, *with various verbs*, из: *disappear from view*, скры́ться и́з виду; *return from a vacation*, верну́ться из о́тпуска; *strike from the list*, вы́черкнуть из спи́ска; *expel from the party*, исключи́ть из па́ртии; *subtract three from eight*, вычита́ть три из восьми́.

front *n*. **1**, (foremost part or side) пере́дняя часть; пере́дняя сторона́; фаса́д; перёд; (*of a vehicle*) передо́к. *Sit in the front* (*of a car*), сиде́ть впереди́. *In the front of the book*, в нача́ле кни́ги. **2**, *mil.* фронт: *at the front*, на фро́нте. **3**, *meteorol.* фронт: *cold front*, холо́дный фронт. **4**, (coalition) фронт: *united front*, еди́ный фронт. **5**, *colloq.* (person used as a cover) подставно́е лицо́. —*adj*. **1**, (at the front) пере́дний: *front wheel*, пере́днее колесо́. *Front door*, пара́дная дверь. *Front row*, пе́рвый ряд. *Front page*, пе́рвая страни́ца *or* полоса́. *Front sight*, му́шка. *On the front lines*, на фро́нте; на ли́нии фро́нта. **2**, (from the front) спе́реди: *front view*, вид спе́реди. **3**, (used as a cover) подставно́й: *front organization*, подставна́я организа́ция. —*v.t.* выходи́ть в *or* на. —**in front**, впереди́. —**in front of**, перед.

frontal *adj*. **1**, (from the front) спе́реди: *frontal view*, вид спе́реди. **2**, *mil.* лобово́й; фронта́льный: *frontal*

assault, лобова́я *or* фронта́льная ата́ка; ата́ка в лоб. **3**, (of the forehead) ло́бный. —**frontally**, *adv*. в лоб.

frontier *n*. грани́ца.

frontispiece *n*. фронтиспи́с.

frontline *adj*. фронтово́й; строево́й. *Frontline soldier*, фронтови́к.

front-wheel drive пере́дний приво́д; приво́д на пере́дние колёса.

frost *n*. **1**, (freezing temperature) моро́з: *ten degrees of frost*, де́сять гра́дусов моро́за. **2**, (hoarfrost) и́ней; и́зморозь.

frostbite *n*. отморо́жение; обморо́жение. *Suffer frostbite*, обмора́живаться.

frostbitten *adj*. отморо́женный; обморо́женный. *My ears are frostbitten*, я отморо́зил/обморо́зил себе́ у́ши.

frosted *adj*. покры́тый и́неем. —**frosted glass**, ма́товое стекло́.

frosting *n*. глазу́рь.

frosty *adj*. **1**, (freezing) моро́зный. **2**, (cold and unfriendly) ледяно́й: *frosty reception*, ледяно́й приём.

froth *n*. пе́на. —*v.t.* пе́нить. —*v.i.* пе́ниться.

frothy *adj*. пе́нистый.

frown *v.i.* **1**, (contract the brows) хму́риться; хму́рить *or* насу́пить бро́ви; хму́рить лицо́. **2**, *fol. by* **on** (disapprove of) смотре́ть ко́со (на). —*n*. хму́рое лицо́; нахму́ренные *or* насу́пленные бро́ви.

frozen *adj*. **1**, (cold; numb; icebound) замёрзший: *frozen lake*, замёрзшее о́зеро. *My hands are frozen*, у меня́ замёрзли ру́ки. **2**, (preserved through freezing) моро́женый; заморо́женный.

fructose *n*. фрукто́за.

frugal *adj*. **1**, (thrifty) бережли́вый. **2**, (meager) ску́дный. —**frugality**, *n*. бережли́вость. —**frugally**, *adv*. ску́по: *live frugally*, жить ску́по.

fruit *n*. **1**, (juicy edible thing to eat) фрукт; (*in the collective sense*) фру́кты: *I like fruit*, я люблю́ фру́кты. **2**, (yield of a plant or tree) плод: *The acorn is the fruit of the oak tree*, жёлудь — плод ду́ба. *Forbidden fruit*, запре́тный плод. **3**, *fig.* (results) плоды́: *bear fruit*, приноси́ть плоды́. *The fruits of one's labor*, плоды́ свои́х трудо́в. —*adj.* фрукто́вый: *fruit juice*, фрукто́вый сок. *Fruit tree*, фрукто́вое *or* плодо́вое де́рево.

fruitcake *n*. фрукто́вый торт.

fruitful *adj*. плодотво́рный.

fruition *n*. осуществле́ние. *Reach fruition*, осуществля́ться.

fruitless *adj*. беспло́дный.

frustrate *v.t.* расстра́ивать; срыва́ть: *frustrate someone's plans*, расстра́ивать/срыва́ть чьи-нибудь пла́ны.

frustration *n*. **1**, (act of frustrating) расстро́йство; срыв. **2**, (feeling of being frustrated) фрустра́ция.

fry *v.t.* жа́рить. —*v.i.* жа́риться.

frying pan сковорода́; сковоро́дка. —**out of the frying pan into the fire**, из огня́ да в по́лымя.

fuchsia *n*. фу́ксия.

fuchsin *also*, **fuchsine** *n*. фукси́н.

fudge *n*. мя́гкая шокола́дная конфе́та.

fuel *n.* то́пливо; горю́чее. —**add fuel to the fire,** подлива́ть ма́сла в ого́нь.

fuel-efficient *adj.* малолитра́жный.

fuel gauge бензиноме́р.

fuel pump то́пливный насо́с.

fuel tank то́пливный бак; бак горю́чего.

fugitive *n.* бегле́ц. —*adj.* бе́глый.

fugue *n., music* фу́га.

fulcrum *n.* то́чка опо́ры.

fulfill *also,* **fulfil** *v.t.* выполня́ть; исполня́ть. —**fulfillment,** *n.* выполне́ние; исполне́ние.

full *adj.* **1,** (filled; complete; rounded out) по́лный: *full plate,* по́лная таре́лка; *full account,* по́лный отчёт. *Full of water,* по́лон воды́. *Full of mistakes,* по́лон оши́бок. *Full of holes,* весь в ды́рах. *Assume full power,* принима́ть полноту́ вла́сти. **2,** (sated) сы́тый. **3,** (whole) це́лый: *a full hour,* це́лый час. **4,** *Full brother,* родно́й брат; *full sister,* родна́я сестра́. **5,** *Full member,* действи́тельный *or* полнопра́вный член. —*v.t.* валя́ть: *to full cloth,* валя́ть сукно́. —**full force,** на всю мощь. *Turn the water on full force,* откры́ть во́ду на всю мощь *or* на по́лную кату́шку. —**full of oneself,** поглощён собо́й. —**full speed ahead!,** по́лный ход! —**full well,** прекра́сно: *I know full well,* я прекра́сно зна́ю. —**in full,** по́лностью; сполна́: *paid in full,* по́лностью опла́чено. *Write your name in full,* напиши́те ва́ше и́мя по́лностью. —**to the full** *or* **fullest,** в по́лной ме́ре. *Develop to the full,* разверну́ться во всю ширь.

full-blooded *adj.* полнокро́вный.

fuller *n.* валя́льщик.

full-face *adv.* анфа́с.

full-fledged *adj.* полноце́нный.

full house по́лный зал; по́лный сбор; аншла́г.

full-length *adj.* **1,** (of a dress) до по́ла. **2,** (of a portrait) во весь рост. **3,** (unabridged) по́лный. *Full-length film,* полнометра́жный фильм.

full moon по́лная луна́; полнолу́ние.

fullness *n.* полнота́.

full professor профе́ссор.

full-scale *adj.* **1,** (the same size as the original) в нату́ра́льную величину́. **2,** (all-out) развёрнутый.

full stop 1, (halt; standstill) по́лная остано́вка. **2,** (period) то́чка.

full-time *adj. & adv.* на по́лную ста́вку: *full-time work,* рабо́та на по́лную ста́вку. *Work full-time,* рабо́тать на по́лную ста́вку; рабо́тать по́лный день.

fully *adv.* вполне́; по́лностью; в по́лной ме́ре. *Fully equipped,* по́лностью обору́дованный. *I fully agree,* я вполне́ согла́сен (согла́сна). *Be fully aware,* отдава́ть себе́ по́лный отчёт.

fulmar *n.* глупы́ш.

fulminate *v.i.* мета́ть гро́мы и мо́лнии. *Fulminate against,* громи́ть. —**fulminate of mercury,** грему́чая ртуть.

fulsome *adj.* гру́бый; слаща́вый. *Fulsome flattery,* гру́бая лесть.

fumble *v.i.* **1,** (grope about) ша́рить: *fumble in one's*

pockets, ша́рить в карма́нах. **2,** *fol. by* **for** (grope for) нащу́пывать. **3,** *fol. by* **with** (handle clumsily) вози́ться с. —*v.t.* (fail to hold) роня́ть; теря́ть.

fume *n., usu. pl.* чад; испаре́ния. *Exhaust fumes,* вы́хлопны́е га́зы. —*v.i.* **1,** (emit fumes) чади́ть. **2,** (fret; rage) рвать и мета́ть.

fumigate *v.t.* оку́ривать. —**fumigation,** *n.* оку́ривание.

fun *n.* заба́ва; поте́ха. —**for the fun of it,** из спорти́вного интере́са. —**have fun, 1,** (live it up) весели́ться. **2,** (have a good time) хорошо́ проводи́ть вре́мя. —**in** (*or* **for) fun,** в шу́тку. —**make fun of**; **poke fun at,** шути́ть над; смея́ться над; подшу́чивать над; посме́иваться над; подсме́иваться над.

function *n.* **1,** (role) фу́нкция. **2,** (social affair) ве́чер; приём. **3,** *math.* фу́нкция. —*v.i.* рабо́тать; де́йствовать; функциони́ровать. —**functional,** *adj.* функциона́льный.

functionary *n.* чино́вник.

fund *n.* **1,** (money reserved for a specific purpose) фонд. **2,** *pl.* (money available) сре́дства. *Fund-raising campaign,* кампа́ния по сбо́ру средств. **3,** (store; supply) запа́с: *fund of knowledge,* запа́с зна́ний. —*v.t.* финанси́ровать.

fundamental *adj.* основно́й; коренно́й; принципиа́льный. *The fundamental purpose of...,* основна́я цель (+ *gen.*). *Fundamental changes,* коренны́е измене́ния. *Fundamental difference,* принципиа́льная ра́зница.

fundamentalism *n.* фундаментали́зм. —**fundamentalist,** *n.* фундаментали́ст.

fundamentally *adv.* коренны́м о́бразом; принципиа́льно. *Be fundamentally different,* принципиа́льно отлича́ться (друг от дру́га).

fundamentals *n.pl.* осно́вы; азы́. *Fundamentals of algebra,* осно́вы а́лгебры.

funding *n.* финанси́рование. *Receive funding,* получа́ть материа́льную подде́ржку.

funeral *n.* по́хороны. *At the funeral,* на похорона́х. —*adj.* похоро́нный; погреба́льный; тра́урный. *Funeral home/parlor,* похоро́нное бюро́. *Funeral procession,* похоро́нная *or* погреба́льная проце́ссия. *Funeral cortege,* тра́урное ше́ствие. *Funeral service,* заупоко́йная слу́жба; отпева́ние. *Funeral pyre,* погреба́льный костёр.

funereal *adj.* гробово́й; тра́урный.

fungous *adj.* грибко́вый.

fungus *n.* грибо́к.

funicular *adj.* кана́тный. *Funicular railway,* фуникулёр.

funnel *n.* воро́нка.

funny *adj.* **1,** (amusing) смешно́й; заба́вный: *funny story,* смешна́я/заба́вная исто́рия. *That's funny,* смешно́. **2,** *colloq.* (strange; odd) стра́нный: *That's funny!,* стра́нное де́ло! —**funny bone,** локтева́я кость.

fur *n.* мех; *pl.* пушни́на; меха́. —*adj.* **1,** (made of fur) мехово́й: *fur collar,* мехово́й воротни́к. **2,** (pert. to fur) пушно́й: *fur auction,* пушно́й аукцио́н. —**fur-**

bearing, *adj.* пушнóй. —**fur-lined,** *adj.* на мехý; подбúтый мéхом.

furious *adj.* **1,** (extremely angry): *be furious,* быть в я́рости; óчень разозлúться. **2,** (violent; intense; fierce) я́ростный: *furious battle,* я́ростный бой.

furlough *n.* óтпуск.

furnace *n.* печь; горн.

furnish *v.t.* **1,** (fit out with furniture) обставля́ть; меблировáть. **2,** (provide; give) окáзывать (пóмощь); давáть (информáцию); представля́ть (доказáтельства). **3,** (supply) снабжáть: *furnish the guests with linen,* снабжáть гостéй бельём. —**furnished,** *adj.* меблирóванный.

furnishings *n.pl.* меблирóвка; убрáнство.

furniture *n.* мéбель; обстанóвка. —*adj.* мéбельный: *furniture store,* мéбельный магазúн.

furor *also,* **furore** *n.* шумúха; фурóр.

furrier *n.* меховщúк; скорня́к.

furrow *n.* бороздá. —*v.t.* бороздúть. *Furrowed brow,* морщúнистый *or* изборождённый лоб.

furry *adj.* пушúстый.

fur seal (морскóй) кóтик.

further *adj.* дальнéйший. *For further information,* за дальнéйшими свéдениями. *Until further notice,* впредь до распоряжéния; до осóбого распоряжéния. *Without further ado,* без дальнéйших церемóний. *I have nothing further to say,* бóльше мне нéчего сказáть. —*adv.* **1,** (onward; forward) дáльше: *Not a step further!,* ни шáгу дáльше! **2,** (more; additionally) бóльше: *I didn't question him further,* я бóльше егó не расспрáшивал. *This further complicates the situation,* э́то ещё бóльше осложня́ет ситуáцию. —*v.t.* продвигáть; способствовать. *Further one's career,* продвúнуть карьéру. *Further one's goal,* способствовать достижéнию цéли.

furtherance *n.* продвижéние.

furthermore *adv.* крóме тогó; сверх тогó; к тому́ же.

furthermost *adj.* сáмый дáльний.

furtive *adj.* сдéланный украдкой; воровáтый; крáдущийся. *Cast a furtive glance at,* посмотрéть украдкой на. —**furtively,** *adv.* украдкой; крáдучись.

furuncle *n.* фурýнкул.

fury *n.* **1,** (rage) я́рость; бéшенство. **2,** (violence, as of a storm) неúстовство. **3,** *cap., myth.* фýрия.

fuse *n.* **1,** *electricity* прóбка; плáвкий предохранúтель. *A fuse blew,* прóбка перегорéла. **2,** (powder wick) запáл; шнур. **3,** [*also,* **fuze**] (detonating device) взрывáтель; трýбка. —*v.t.* **1,** (melt) плáвить; сплавля́ть. **2,** (blend) сливáть. —*v.i.* **1,** (melt) плáвиться. **2,** (merge; blend) сливáться.

fuselage *n.* фюзеля́ж.

fusible *adj.* плáвкий.

fusillade *n.* стрельбá; обстрéл.

fusion *n.* **1,** (act of fusing; state of being fused) плáвка. **2,** (union; merger) слия́ние. **3,** *physics* сúнтез. —**fusion bomb,** термоя́дерная бóмба.

fuss *n.* **1,** (bustle) суетá; возня́. **2,** (stir) шум; скандáл. *Make/raise a fuss,* поднимáть шум; скандáлить. —*v.i.* **1,** (bustle) суетúться. **2,** *fol. by* **with** (fiddle with) возúться (с). **3,** *fol. by* **over** (show excessive care or concern) носúться (с). **4,** *colloq.* (complain) хны́кать.

fussy *adj.* **1,** (exacting) въéдливый. **2,** (finicky) привередливый.

futile *adj.* тщéтный; напрáсный; бесполéзный. —**futility,** *n.* тщéтность.

future *adj.* бýдущий: *future generations,* бýдущие поколéния. —*n.* [*usu.* **the future**] бýдущее. *In the future,* в бýдущем; в дальнéйшем.

futurism *n.* футурúзм. —**futuristic,** *adj.* футуристúческий.

fuze *n.* = **fuse** (*in sense #3*).

fuzz *n.* пух.

fuzzy *adj.* **1,** (having fuzz) пушúстый. **2,** (blurred; vague) смýтный.

G

G, g седьмáя бýква англúйского алфавúта. —*n.* (musical note) соль.

gab *n., colloq.* болтовня́. —*v.i., colloq.* болтáть; трепáть языкóм. —**gift of gab,** дар слóва.

gabardine *n.* габардúн. —*adj.* габардúновый.

gabby *adj., colloq.* болтлúвый; разговóрчивый.

gable *n.* щипéц. —**gable roof,** двускáтная крýша.

gad *v.i.* [*usu.* **gad about**] шля́ться; слоня́ться.

gadfly *n.* **1,** (insect) óвод. **2,** (annoying person) надоéда.

gadget *n.* приспособлéние.

gadolinium *n.* гадолúний.

Gaelic *adj.* гэ́льский. —*n.* гэ́льский язы́к.

gaff *n.* рыболóвный багóр.

gaffe *n.* оплóшность. *Commit a gaffe,* допустúть оплóшность; попáсть впросáк.

gag n. **1,** (silencer) кляп. **2,** slang (joke) шу́тка. —v.t. засу́нуть кляп в рот (+ dat.). —v.i. (choke) дави́ться.

gaiety n. весе́лье; весёлость.

gaily adv. ве́село.

gain v.t. **1,** (get; win; acquire) получа́ть; завоёвывать; доби́ться. Gain recognition, получи́ть or завоева́ть призна́ние. Gain one's freedom, завоева́ть свобо́ду. Gain an advantage, получи́ть преиму́щество; доби́ться преиму́щества. Gain experience, приобрета́ть о́пыт. Gain someone's confidence, завоева́ть or заслужи́ть чьё-нибудь дове́рие; войти́ в дове́рие к. **2,** (achieve) доби́ться: gain one's end, доби́ться свое́й це́ли. What did you gain by that?, чего́ вы э́тим доби́лись?; что вы вы́гадали на э́том? **3,** (increase in) набира́ть: gain strength/altitute, набира́ть си́лу/высоту́. Gain weight, прибавля́ть в ве́се; поправля́ться. Gain ten pounds, приба́вить де́сять фу́нтов. **4,** (receive, as an impression) выноси́ть (впечатле́ние). I gained the impression that..., у меня́ созда́лось or сложи́лось впечатле́ние, что... —v.i. **1,** (benefit) выи́грывать, выга́дывать. Stand to gain, быть в вы́игрыше. Gain in someone's estimation, выи́грывать в чьём-нибудь мне́нии. **2,** fol. by **on** (draw nearer to) догоня́ть; нагоня́ть. —n. **1,** (benefit) вы́года; вы́игрыш. **2,** pl. (that which is gained) вы́игрыш; завоева́ния. Gains and losses, приобрете́ния и поте́ри. **3,** (increase) увеличе́ние; приро́ст. —**gain ground, 1,** (make progress) продвига́ться вперёд; де́лать успе́хи. **2,** fol. by **on** (draw nearer to) догоня́ть; нагоня́ть. —**gain time, 1,** (of a timepiece) идти́ вперёд. **2,** (obtain a delay to one's advantage) вы́играть вре́мя.

gainer n. тот, кто выи́грывает. Be the gainer, быть в вы́игрыше.

gainful adj. **1,** (profitable) дохо́дный; при́быльный. **2,** (paid) опла́чиваемый. —**gainfully,** adv. с опла́той. Be gainfully employed, име́ть опла́чиваемую рабо́ту; рабо́тать за де́ньги.

gainsay v.t. отрица́ть; опроверга́ть.

gait n. **1,** (walk; step) похо́дка; по́ступь. **2,** (of a horse) аллю́р.

gaiters n.pl. ге́тры.

gal n., colloq. де́вушка.

gala adj. пра́здничный; торже́ственный; пара́дный.

galactic adj. галакти́ческий.

galaxy n. **1,** astron. гала́ктика. **2,** (brilliant assemblage) плея́да.

gale n. **1,** (strong wind) шторм. Winds of gale force, ве́тры штормово́й си́лы. **2,** (outburst) раска́т: gales of laughter, раска́ты сме́ха.

galena n. галени́т; свинцо́вый блеск.

gall n. **1,** (bile) жёлчь. **2,** colloq. (effrontery) на́глость. **3,** bot. галл. —v.t. раздража́ть; обижа́ть. It galls me, мне оби́дно.

gallant adj. **1,** (brave; daring) хра́брый; до́блестный. **2,** (chivalrous) гала́нтный.

gallantry n. **1,** (valor) до́блесть. **2,** (courtly manner) гала́нтность.

gall bladder жёлчный пузы́рь.

gallery n. галере́я. —**art gallery, 1,** (private establishment) худо́жественный сало́н. **2,** (museum) карти́нная галере́я. —**shooting gallery,** тир.

galley n. **1,** (ship) гале́ра. **2,** (ship's kitchen) ка́мбуз. **3,** printing (proof) гра́нка.

Gallic adj. га́лльский. —**Gallicism,** n. галлици́зм.

galling adj. оби́дный. It is galling, оби́дно.

gallinule n. водяна́я ку́рочка.

gallium n. га́ллий.

gallivant v.i. шля́ться.

gallnut n. черни́льный оре́шек.

gallon n. галло́н.

galloon n. галу́н; позуме́нт.

gallop n. гало́п. At a gallop, гало́пом; вскачь. Full gallop, карье́р. —v.i. галопи́ровать. Gallop off, ускака́ть. —v.t. пуска́ть (ло́шадь) гало́пом.

gallows n. ви́селица.

gallstone n. жёлчный ка́мень.

galore adv. хоть отбавля́й.

galosh n. гало́ша.

galvanic adj. гальвани́ческий.

galvanize v.t. **1,** electricity; metall. гальванизи́ровать. **2,** fig. (rouse to action) возбужда́ть; побужда́ть.

gambit n. гамби́т.

gamble v.i. **1,** (play for stakes) игра́ть в аза́ртные и́гры. **2,** (take a chance) рискова́ть. —v.t. **1,** (risk) рискова́ть. **2,** fol. by **away** (squander by gambling) прои́грывать. —n. риско́ванная игра́.

gambler n. игро́к; картёжник.

gambling n. аза́ртная игра́. —adj. иго́рный: gambling house/parlor/casino, иго́рный дом.

gambol v.i. резви́ться.

game n. **1,** (form of play or sport) игра́: children's games, де́тские и́гры. Board game, насто́льная игра́. Olympic games, Олимпи́йские и́гры. Join in the game, включи́ться в игру́. **2,** (single contest) па́ртия; матч. Win three games, вы́играть три па́ртии. Football game, футбо́льный матч. **3,** (scheme) игра́: play a double game, вести́ двойну́ю игру́. See through someone's game, ви́деть кого́-нибудь наскво́зь. **4,** (animals or birds hunted for food) дичь. Big game, кру́пный зверь; кру́пная дичь. —adj. **1,** (of animals or birds) промысло́вый. Game laws, зако́ны об охо́те. **2,** (plucky; courageous) сме́лый; сто́йкий. **3,** colloq. (ready; willing) гото́вый. **4,** (lame) хромо́й. —**game bag,** ягдта́ш.

gamely adv. сто́йко; отва́жно.

gamete n. гаме́та.

gaming adj. иго́рный: gaming table, иго́рный стол.

gamma globulin га́мма-глобули́н.

gamma rays га́мма-лучи́.

gamut n. га́мма: the whole gamut of emotions, це́лая га́мма ощуще́ний. —**run the gamut,** быть/быва́ть са́мые ра́зные.

gander n. гуса́к. —**take a gander,** slang взгляну́ть.

gang n. **1,** (band, as of thieves) ба́нда; ша́йка. **2,** (crew of workers) брига́да. —v.i. [usu. **gang up on**] обру́шиваться на.

gangling adj. долговя́зый.

ganglion n. не́рвный у́зел; га́нглий.

gangplank *n.* схо́дни.

gangrene *n.* гангре́на. —**gangrenous,** *adj.* гангрено́зный.

gangster *n.* га́нгстер.

gangway *n.* **1,** (passageway) прохо́д. **2,** (gangplank) схо́дни. —*interj.* посторони́тесь!

gannet *n.* о́луша.

gantlet *n.* = **gauntlet** (*in sense #3*).

gaol *n.* = **jail.**

gap *n.* **1,** (opening; breach) брешь; проло́м. **2,** (break; lacuna) пробе́л: *fill a gap,* восполня́ть пробе́л. **3,** (disparity) разры́в: *the generation gap,* разры́в поколе́ний. **4,** (mountain pass) го́рный прохо́д.

gape *v.i.* **1,** (stare open-mouthed) глазе́ть; зева́ть. **2,** (be wide open) зия́ть: *gaping wound,* зия́ющая ра́на.

garage *n.* гара́ж. *Public garage; parking garage,* автостоя́нка.

garb *n.* наря́д; одея́ние.

garbage *n.* му́сор; отбро́сы. —**garbage can,** му́сорный я́щик; му́сорный бак *or* бачо́к. —**garbage collector,** му́сорщик.

garble *v.t.* **1,** (make unintelligible) искажа́ть. **2,** (misrepresent) перевира́ть. **3,** (pronounce indistinctly) глота́ть.

garden *n.* сад. *Vegetable garden,* огоро́д. —*adj.* садо́вый; огоро́дный.

gardener *n.* садо́вник; садово́д.

gardenia *n.* гарде́ния.

gardening *n.* садово́дство.

gargantuan *adj.* гига́нтский.

gargle *v.i.* полоска́ть го́рло.

garish *adj.* крича́щий; крикли́вый; бро́ский.

garland *n.* гирля́нда; вено́к. —*v.t.* украша́ть гирля́ндами.

garlic *n.* чесно́к.

garment *n.* **1,** (article of clothing) предме́т оде́жды. **2,** *pl.* (clothing) оде́жда. —**garment factory,** шве́йная фа́брика.

garner *v.t.* **1,** (store) скла́дывать в амба́р. **2,** (win; obtain) получа́ть: *garner first prize,* получи́ть пе́рвую пре́мию.

garnet *n.* грана́т.

garnish *v.t.* **1,** (embellish) приукра́шивать. **2,** *cooking* гарни́ровать. —*n.* гарни́р.

garret *n.* черда́к; мансáрда.

garrison *n.* гарнизо́н.

garrulous *adj.* болтли́вый; говорли́вый; разгово́рчивый.

garter *n.* подвя́зка.

gas *n.* **1,** (vapor) газ: *natural gas,* приро́дный газ. *Tear gas,* слезоточи́вый газ. *Poison gas,* ядови́тый газ; отравля́ющее вещество́. *Turn on the gas,* включи́ть газ. **2,** (gasoline) бензи́н. **3,** *med.* га́зы. —*adj.* **1,** (pert. to gas) га́зовый: *gas range,* га́зовая плита́. **2,** (pert. to gasoline) бензи́новый. —*v.t.* отравля́ть *or* умерщвля́ть га́зом; *mil.* поража́ть га́зом. —*v.i.* [*usu.* **gas up**] *colloq.* заправля́ться. —**step on the gas,** дать газ.

gas burner га́зовая горе́лка; га́зовая конфо́рка.

gas chamber га́зовая ка́мера.

gaseous *adj.* газообра́зный.

gash *n.* глубо́кий поре́з. —*v.t.* си́льно поре́зать.

gasket *n.* прокла́дка. —**blow a gasket,** *slang* вы́йти из себя́.

gaslight *n.* **1,** (light) га́зовое освеще́ние. **2,** (lamp) га́зовая ла́мпа.

gas main га́зовая магистра́ль.

gas mask противога́з.

gas meter га́зовый счётчик; газоме́р.

gasoline *n.* бензи́н. —*adj.* бензи́новый.

gasp *v.i.* задыха́ться. —*v.t.* [*usu.* **gasp out**] говори́ть задыха́ющимся го́лосом. —*n.* вздох. —**to the last gasp,** до после́днего издыха́ния.

gas station бензозапра́вочная ста́нция *or* коло́нка; автозапра́вочная ста́нция; бензоколо́нка.

gas tank бензоба́к.

gastric *adj.* желу́дочный. —**gastric juice,** желу́дочный сок. —**gastric ulcer,** я́зва желу́дка.

gastritis *n.* гастри́т.

gastrointestinal *adj.* желу́дочно-кише́чный.

gastronome *n.* гастроно́м. —**gastronomic,** *adj.* гастрономи́ческий. —**gastronomy,** *n.* гастроно́мия.

gate *n.* **1,** (entrance) воро́та: *open the gate,* откры́ть воро́та. *The gates to the palace,* воро́та дворца́. *Be at the city gates,* быть у воро́т го́рода. **2,** (swinging door in a picket fence) кали́тка. **3,** (movable barrier) шлагба́ум. **4,** (box-office receipts) сбо́ры. —**give (someone) the gate,** *colloq.* вы́бросить за воро́та.

gatehouse *n.* сторо́жка (у воро́т).

gatekeeper *n.* привра́тник.

gateway *n.* воро́та; вход.

gather *v.t.* **1,** (pick; collect) собира́ть: *gather firewood,* собира́ть дрова́; *gather data,* собира́ть да́нные. *Gather in the harvest,* собира́ть урожа́й. *Gather dust,* пыли́ться. **2,** (infer) заключа́ть: *From this I gather that...,* из э́того я заключа́ю, что... *I gather from what he said that...,* из его́ слов я по́нял (*or* я сде́лал вы́вод), что... *As far as I can gather,* наско́лько я могу́ суди́ть. **3,** (gain, as speed) набира́ть; развива́ть (ско́рость). *Gather momentum,* разгоня́ться. **4,** (draw into folds) собира́ть. —*v.i.* собира́ться; сходи́ться; съезжа́ться. *A crowd gathered,* собрала́сь толпа́. *Gather around the fire,* собира́ться вокру́г костра́. *Gather together in a circle,* собира́ться в круг. *Gather from all over the world,* съе́хаться со всех концо́в ми́ра. —*n.,* *usu. pl.* сбо́рки.

gathering *n.* **1,** (collecting) сбор; собира́ние. *Hunting and gathering,* охо́та и собира́тельство. **2,** (an assemblage) собра́ние; сбор; сбо́рище; слёт.

gaudy *adj.* крича́щий; пёстрый.

gauge *n.* **1,** (instrument for measuring) измери́тель. *Pressure gauge,* мано́метр. *Fuel gauge,* бензиноме́р. **2,** *R.R.* колея́: *broad gauge,* широ́кая колея́. **3,** (standard of measurement) кали́бр. **4,** *fig.* (standard; yardstick) мери́ло. —*v.t.* **1,** (measure) измеря́ть. **2,** (estimate; assess) оце́нивать; суди́ть о.

gaunt *adj.* исхуда́лый; измождённый.

gauntlet *n.* **1,** (glove) (ла́тная) перча́тка. **2,** *fig.* (challenge): *throw down/ take up/ the gauntlet,* броса́ть/ поднима́ть перча́тку. **3,** [*also,* **gantlet**] (form of punishment): *run the gauntlet,* проходи́ть сквозь строй; *make someone run the gauntlet,* прогоня́ть кого́-нибудь сквозь строй.

gauze *n.* **1,** (fabric) газ. **2,** (material used for bandages) ма́рля. —*adj.* ма́рлевый. —**gauzy,** *adj.* прозра́чный.

gavel *n.* молото́к.

gawk *v.i.* глазе́ть; зева́ть.

gay *adj.* **1,** (merry) весёлый. **2,** *colloq.* (homosexual) голубо́й. —*n., colloq.* (homosexual) голубо́й.

gaze *n.* при́стальный взгляд. —*v.i.* смотре́ть; вгля́дываться.

gazelle *n.* газе́ль.

gazette *n.* (официа́льная) газе́та.

gazetteer *n.* географи́ческий спра́вочник.

gear *n.* **1,** (toothed wheel) шестерня́. **2,** (adjustment relative to speed) переда́ча; ско́рость: *first/second gear,* пе́рвая/втора́я переда́ча/ско́рость. *In first/second gear,* на пе́рвой/второ́й переда́че. *Be in gear,* стоя́ть на переда́че. *High/low gear,* вы́сшая/ни́зшая переда́ча. *Reverse gear,* за́дний ход. *Shift gears,* переключи́ть переда́чу. **3,** (devise; mechanism) устро́йство. *Landing gear,* поса́дочное устро́йство; шасси́. **4,** (equipment) принадле́жности; снасть. —*v.t.* (adjust; adapt) приводи́ть в соотве́тствие (с).

gearbox *n.* коро́бка переда́ч; коро́бка скоросте́й.

gearshift *n.* переключе́ние переда́ч.

Geiger counter счётчик Ге́йгера.

geisha *n.* ге́йша.

gelatin *n.* желати́н. —**gelatinous,** *adj.* желати́новый.

geld *v.t.* холости́ть; кастри́ровать.

gelding *n.* ме́рин.

gem *n.* драгоце́нный ка́мень.

Gemini *n.* Близнецы́.

gemstone *n.* драгоце́нный ка́мень.

gendarme *n.* жанда́рм. —**gendarmerie,** *n.* жандарме́рия.

gender *n.* род: *feminine gender,* же́нский род.

gene *n.* ген.

genealogy *n.* генеало́гия; родосло́вие; родосло́вная. —**genealogical,** *adj.* генеалоги́ческий; родосло́вный.

general *n.* (military officer) генера́л. —*adj.* **1,** (not specific or restricted) о́бщий: *general rule/opinion,* о́бщее пра́вило/мне́ние. *General reader,* широ́кий *or* ма́ссовый чита́тель. *General anesthetic,* о́бщий нарко́з. *General practitioner,* врач о́бщей пра́ктики. **2,** (widespread; nationwide) всео́бщий: *general strike,* всео́бщая забасто́вка. *The general public,* широ́кая пу́блика. **3,** (chief; highest ranking) генера́льный: *general staff,* генера́льный штаб. *Secretary-general,* генера́льный секрета́рь. —**in general,** вообще́.

General Assembly Генера́льная Ассамбле́я.

general delivery до востре́бования.

generalissimo *n.* генерали́ссимус.

generality *n.* обобще́ние. *Talk in generalities,* говори́ть о́бщими слова́ми.

generalization *n.* обобще́ние.

generalize *v.i.* обобща́ть; говори́ть о́бщими слова́ми; де́лать о́бщий вы́вод.

generally *adv.* **1,** (usually) обы́чно; как пра́вило. **2,**

(in general) вообще́: *generally speaking,* вообще́ говоря́. **3,** (popularly; commonly) обще-: *generally known,* общеизве́стный; *generally accepted,* общепри́нятый. *As is generally thought,* как при́нято счита́ть.

generate *v.t.* **1,** *electricity* выраба́тывать (электро-эне́ргию). **2,** *fig.* (give rise to) порожда́ть.

generation *n.* **1,** (stage in natural descent) поколе́ние. *From generation to generation,* из поколе́ния в поколе́ние; из ро́да в род. **2,** (production of electricity) генера́ция.

generator *n.* генера́тор.

generic *adj.* **1,** (general) о́бщий: *generic term,* о́бщий те́рмин. **2,** *biol.* родово́й.

generosity *n.* ще́дрость.

generous *adj.* ще́дрый: *generous person/gift,* ще́дрый челове́к/пода́рок. —**generously,** *adv.* ще́дро.

genesis *n.* **1,** (origin) происхожде́ние; возникнове́ние; ге́незис. **2,** *cap.* (book of the Bible) Бытие́; Кни́га Бытия́.

genetic *adj.* генети́ческий. —**genetic code,** генети́ческий код. —**genetic engineering,** ге́нная инжене́рия.

genetics *n.* гене́тика. —**geneticist,** *n.* гене́тик.

genial *adj.* серде́чный; доброду́шный. —**geniality,** *n.* серде́чность; доброду́шие.

genie *n.* джин. —**let the genie out of the bottle,** вы́пустить джи́на из буты́лки.

genital *adj.* полово́й; деторо́дный. —**genitalia; genitals,** *n.pl.* половы́е *or* деторо́дные о́рганы.

genitive *adj.* роди́тельный: *genitive case,* роди́тельный паде́ж.

genius *n.* **1,** (person) ге́ний. **2,** (extraordinary talent) гениа́льность. *Man of genius,* гениа́льный челове́к.

genocide *n.* геноци́д.

genre *n.* жанр. —**genre painting,** жа́нровая жи́вопись; жанр.

genteel *adj.* **1,** (well-bred) благовоспи́танный. **2,** (elegant; polished) изя́щный.

gentian *n.* горечка́вка.

gentile *also,* **Gentile** *n.* неевре́й. —*adj.* неевре́йский.

gentility *n.* **1,** (noble birth) родови́тость. **2,** (delicacy; refinement) изя́щество.

gentle *adj.* **1,** (not violent) лёгкий: *gentle nudge,* лёгкий толчо́к; *gentle breeze,* лёгкий ветеро́к. **2,** (mild; not harsh) мя́гкий; не́жный: *gentle voice,* мя́гкий/не́жный го́лос. **3,** (delicate; subtle) то́нкий; делика́тный: *gentle hint/reminder,* то́нкий намёк; делика́тное напомина́ние. **4,** (docile) сми́рный: *gentle dog,* сми́рная соба́ка. **5,** (not steep) отло́гий.

gentlefolk *n.* дворя́нство.

gentleman *n.* джентльме́н; господи́н. *Ladies and gentlemen!,* да́мы и господа́! —**gentlemen's agreement,** джентльме́нское соглаше́ние.

gentlemanly *adj.* джентльме́нский.

gentleness *n.* мя́гкость; не́жность.

gently *adv.* мя́гко; не́жно.

gentry *n.* дворя́нство.

genuflect *v.i.* преклоня́ть коле́но (*or* коле́на).

genuine *adj.* **1,** (authentic) по́длинный; настоя́щий;

неподде́льный. **2**, (sincere) неподде́льный: *genuine joy*, неподде́льная ра́дость. —**genuinely**, *adv.* и́скренне.

genus *n.* род.

geocentric *adj.* геоцентри́ческий.

geodesy *n.* геоде́зия. —**geodetic**, *adj.* геодези́ческий.

geography *n.* геогра́фия. —**geographer**, *n.* гео́граф. —**geographic; geographical**, *adj.* географи́ческий.

geology *n.* геоло́гия. —**geological**, *adj.* геологи́ческий. —**geologist**, *n.* гео́лог.

geometry *n.* геоме́трия. —**geometric; geometrical**, *adj.* геометри́ческий.

geophysics *n.* геофи́зика. —**geophysical**, *adj.* геофизи́ческий.

geopolitics *n.* геополи́тика. —**geopolitical**, *adj.* геополити́ческий.

Georgian *adj.* грузи́нский. —*n.* **1**, (person) грузи́н; грузи́нка. **2**, (language) грузи́нский язы́к.

geothermal *adj.* геотерма́льный; геотерми́ческий.

geranium *n.* гера́нь.

gerbil *n.* песча́нка.

geriatrics *n.* гериатри́я. —**geriatric**, *adj.* гериатри́ческий.

germ *n.* микро́б. —**germ warfare**, бактериологи́ческая война́.

German *adj.* герма́нский; неме́цкий. —*n.* **1**, (person) не́мец; не́мка. **2**, (language) неме́цкий язы́к. *Speak German*, говори́ть по-неме́цки.

germane *adj.* относя́щийся к де́лу.

Germanic *adj.* герма́нский.

germanium *n.* герма́ний.

German measles красну́ха.

German shepherd неме́цкая овча́рка.

germinal *adj.* заро́дышевый; зача́точный.

germinate *v.i.* пуска́ть ростки́; прораста́ть. —**germination**, *n.* прораста́ние.

gerontology *n.* геронтоло́гия.

gerund *n.* геру́ндий.

gestation *n.* бере́менность.

gesticulate *v.i.* жестикули́ровать. —**gesticulation**, *n.* жестикуля́ция.

gesture *n.* жест. —*v.i.* де́лать жест.

get *v.t.* **1**, (receive) получа́ть: *get a letter*, получи́ть письмо́. **2**, (obtain) достава́ть; получа́ть: *get tickets*, доста́ть биле́ты; *get permission*, получи́ть разреше́ние. *Where can I get...?*, где я могу́ доста́ть/получи́ть...? **3**, (fetch; bring) взять; принести́; сходи́ть (*pfv.*) за. *Get one's coat*, взять пальто́. *Get my shoes*, принеси́ мне боти́нки. *Get some cigarettes*, сходи́ть за сигаре́тами. *Can I get you a drink?*, вам чего́-нибудь нали́ть? **4**, (bring; deliver) доставля́ть: *get the manuscript to the printer*, доста́вить ру́копись в типогра́фию. *Get (something heavy) home*, везти́ *or* тащи́ть (что́-нибудь) домо́й. **5**, (catch, as an illness) получа́ть: *get pneumonia*, получи́ть воспале́ние лёгких. **6**, (make; prepare, as a meal) гото́вить. **7**, (cause to happen): *get the work done*, зако́нчить рабо́ту. *Get something fixed*, отдава́ть что́-нибудь в почи́нку. *Get one's feet wet*, промочи́ть но́ги. *I can't get the door (to) open*, не могу́ откры́ть дверь. **8**,

(spill) *rendered by* па́чкать: *get ink on one's fingers*, испа́чкать ру́ки черни́лами (*or* в черни́лах). *Get a stain on one's tie*, посади́ть пятно́ на га́лстук. **9**, (induce; prevail upon) заста́вить; убеди́ть; уговори́ть. **10**, (apprehend; nab) пойма́ть; схвати́ть. **11**, (succeed in shooting or swatting) попа́сть в. *I got him!*, попа́л! **12**, (be sentenced to): *He got ten years*, ему́ да́ли де́сять лет. **13**, *colloq.* (hear) расслы́шать. **14**, *colloq.* (understand) понима́ть. —*v.i.* **1**, (arrive) приходи́ть; приезжа́ть: *when I got home*, когда́ я пришёл/прие́хал домо́й. **2**, (reach) попа́сть; добра́ться до. *How do I get there?*, как мне туда́ попа́сть? *Get to one's feet*, встава́ть на́ ноги. *Get to the end/truth*, добра́ться до конца́/и́стины. *Where have we gotten to?*, куда́ мы зашли́? *Where have my glasses gotten to?*, куда́ де́лись мои́ очки́? *At last we're getting somewhere*, наконе́ц у нас что́-то получа́ется. **3**, (become) станови́ться: *get better*, стать лу́чше. ♦ *Usu. rendered by individual verbs: get dressed*, одева́ться; *get tired*, устава́ть; *get sick*, заболева́ть; *get well*, оправля́ться; поправля́ться; *get lost*, заблуди́ться; *get wet*, промока́ть; *get angry*, серди́ться; *get dark*, темне́ть; *get married*, жени́ться; вы́йти за́муж; *get ready*, гото́виться; *get stuck*, застрева́ть; *get used to*, привыка́ть к; *get caught in the rain*, попа́сть под дождь. **4**, *fol. by* **to** (begin) принима́ться за: *get to work*, принима́ться за рабо́ту. *We got to talking*, мы разговори́лись; у нас завяза́лся разгово́р. **5**, *fol. by* **to** (have the opportunity) приходи́ться (+ *dat.*): *I don't get to see her often*, мне ре́дко прихо́дится ви́деться *or* встреча́ться с ней. —**get about**, передвига́ться. —**get across, 1**, (reach the opposite side of) перебира́ться (че́рез). **2**, (transmit; convey) передава́ть. —**get along, 1**, (fare; progress) пожива́ть. **2**, (manage) обходи́ться; устра́иваться. *Get along without*, обходи́ться без. *Get along on 5,000 rubles a month*, обходи́ться пятью́ ты́сячами рубле́й в ме́сяц. **3**, (be compatible) ла́дить; ужива́ться. *They could not get along*, они́ не ла́дили; они́ не могли́ ужи́ться; они́ не сошли́сь хара́ктерами. —**get around, 1**, (walk) передвига́ться. **2**, (travel from place to place) е́здить: *How did you get around?*, на чём вы е́здили? **3**, (travel, as of news) распространя́ться; разноси́ться. **4**, (circumvent) обходи́ть. **5**, *fol. by* **to** (find time to) успе́ть; удосу́житься. —**get at, 1**, (reach and touch) добира́ться до. **2**, (imply) клони́ть: *What are you getting at?*, к чему́ ты кло́нишь? —**get away, 1**, (go away) уходи́ть; уезжа́ть. *Get away from me!*, прочь от меня́! *Get away for a few days*, уезжа́ть на не́сколько дней. **2**, (escape) убега́ть; уходи́ть. *The fish got away*, ры́ба ускользну́ла. —**get away with, 1**, (make off with) утащи́ть. **2**, (escape unpunished) сходи́ть с рук: *He got away with it*, э́то сошло́ ему́ с рук. *You'll never get away with it*, э́то вам да́ром не пройдёт. —**get back, 1**, (recover) верну́ть; получи́ть обра́тно. **2**, (return) возвраща́ться. **3**, (step back) отступа́ть наза́д. —**get behind, 1**, (fall behind) отстава́ть. **2**, (give support to) подде́рживать. —**get by, 1**, (sneak past) проскользну́ть ми́мо. **2**, *colloq.*

(manage) обходи́ться; устра́иваться. —**get down, 1,** (come down; lower oneself) сходи́ть; спуска́ться; опуска́ться. *Get down on one knee,* опуска́ться на одно́ коле́но. *Get down on one's hands and knees,* стать на четвере́ньки. **2,** (write down; record) запи́сывать. **3,** (depress) угнета́ть. *Don't let it get you down!,* не расстра́ивайтесь из-за э́того! —**get down to,** бра́ться за; засе́сть за. *Get down to business,* приступи́ть к де́лу. —**get in, 1,** (enter) входи́ть; влеза́ть. **2,** (arrive) приходи́ть; приезжа́ть; прибыва́ть. **3,** (manage to say) вверну́ть. **4,** (receive, as a supply of merchandise) получи́ть. —**get into, 1,** (step into) сади́ться в; влеза́ть в: *get into the car,* сади́ться/влеза́ть в маши́ну. *Get into the elevator,* входи́ть в лифт. *Get into the bathtub,* сади́ться в ва́нну. **2,** (lie down in) ложи́ться в: *get into bed,* ложи́ться в посте́ль *or* в крова́ть. **3,** (manage to enter) попа́сть в; влеза́ть в. *Get into the house,* попа́сть в дом; (*of burglars*) влезть в дом. **4,** (arrive in) приезжа́ть в; прибыва́ть в. **5,** (put into with difficulty) попа́сть (+ *instr.*): *get the key into the lock,* попа́сть ключо́м в замо́к. **6,** (squeeze into) умеща́ть: *get everything into the suitcase,* умеща́ть всё в чемода́не. **7,** (fit into) умеща́ться в; влеза́ть в. **8,** (seep into) затека́ть в: *Water got into the basement,* вода́ затекла́ в подва́л. *Sand got into my shoes,* песо́к попа́л мне в ту́фли. **9,** (become involved in) попа́сть в: *get into trouble,* попа́сть в беду́. *Get into a fight,* подра́ться. *Get into an argument,* поспо́рить. **10,** (put on) напя́ливать. **11,** *Get into debt,* влезть в долги́. **12,** *Get into the habit of,* привыка́ть (+ *inf.*). **13,** *What's gotten into you?,* кака́я му́ха (*or* блоха́) вас укуси́ла? —**get it,** *colloq.* **1,** (understand) понима́ть. **2,** (be punished) доста́ться (+ *dat.*); попа́сть (+ *dat.*): *He'll get it for doing that,* ему́ доста́нется/попадёт за э́то. —**get off, 1,** (debark) выходи́ть; сходи́ть: *get off a bus,* вы́йти из авто́буса; *get off a train,* сойти́ с по́езда. **2,** (dismount) сходи́ть; слеза́ть. **3,** (remove; take off) снима́ть. **4,** (send off) отправля́ть. **5,** (escape) отде́лываться: *get off cheap,* дёшево отде́латься. —**get on, 1,** (mount; board) сади́ться на *or* в. **2,** (put on) надева́ть. **3,** = **get along** (*sense #1*). **4,** *Get on one's nerves,* де́йствовать на не́рвы (+ *dat.*). **5,** *He is getting on in years,* он (уже́) пожило́й; он (уже́) в года́х. —**get out, 1,** (leave) уйти́. *Get out!,* вон отсю́да! **2,** (become known) вы́йти нару́жу. **3,** (take out) вынима́ть. **4,** (help to escape) вызволя́ть. —**get out of, 1,** (step or climb out of) выходи́ть из; вылеза́ть из. *Get out of bed,* встава́ть с посте́ли. *Let's get out of the rain,* дава́йте уйдём с дождя́. **2,** (depart from) выходи́ть: *Let's get out of here!,* дава́йте вы́йдем отсю́да! *Get out of here!,* убира́йтесь!; прочь отсю́да! *Get out of the way!,* прочь с доро́ги! *Get out of my sight!,* прочь с глаз мои́х! **3,** (escape from) выбира́ться из. **4,** (evade doing something) избега́ть (+ *inf.*); увильну́ть от. **5,** (remove) вынима́ть: *get the key out of the lock,* вынима́ть ключ из замка́. **6,** (elicit from) вырыва́ть; выве́дывать. **7,** (learn) выноси́ть: *get something out of a lecture,* выноси́ть что-нибудь из ле́кции. **8,** *Get

out of debt,* выходи́ть из долго́в. **9,** *Get out of the habit of,* отвыка́ть (+ *inf.*). —**get over, 1,** (recover from) оправля́ться от (боле́зни). *Get over the shock,* опра́виться *or* опо́мниться от потрясе́ния. **2,** (overcome) преодолева́ть: *get over one's shyness/ sense of guilt/,* преодоле́ть ро́бость/ чу́вство вины́/. **3,** *fol. by* **with** (finish) поко́нчить с. **4,** *with* **can't** *or* **couldn't** (not but wonder) (не мочь) надиви́ться. —**get through, 1,** (make or force one's way through) проби́ва́ться сквозь. **2,** (finish, as a book or course) одолева́ть; оси́ливать. **3,** (manage to survive) пережива́ть; выде́рживать. **4,** (reach its destination) доходи́ть. **5,** *fol. by* (reach on the phone) дозвони́ться (к). **6,** *fol. by* **to** (make oneself understood) доходи́ть (до). —**get together,** встреча́ться. —**get up, 1,** (stand up; rise) встава́ть: *get up early in the morning,* встава́ть ра́но у́тром. *Get up from the table,* встава́ть из-за стола́. *Get up from a chair,* встава́ть со сту́ла. *Get up on a chair,* стать *or* встать на стул. **2,** *fol. by* **to** (read as far as) доходи́ть (до). **3,** (summon) собира́ться с: *get up the courage/nerve,* собра́ться с ду́хом. *See also* **got.**

getaway *n.* побе́г. *Make a clean getaway,* убежа́ть, не оста́вив и следа́.

get-together *n.* сбо́рище.

getup *n., colloq.* наря́д.

geyser *n.* ге́йзер.

ghastly *adj.* стра́шный; ужа́сный; жу́ткий.

gherkin *n.* корнишо́н.

ghetto *n.* ге́тто.

ghost *n.* привиде́ние; при́зрак. —**give up the ghost,** испусти́ть дух. —**not a ghost of a chance,** ни мале́йшего ша́нса.

ghostly *adj.* при́зрачный.

ghoul *n.* вампи́р. —**ghoulish,** *adj.* жу́ткий; чудо́вищный.

giant *n.* гига́нт; велика́н; исполи́н. —*adj.* гига́нтский; исполи́нский.

gibberish *n.* набо́р слов; тараба́рщина.

gibbet *n.* ви́селица.

gibbon *n.* гиббо́н.

gibe *v.t. & i.* издева́ться (над); насмеха́ться (над). —*n.* издёвка; насме́шка.

giblets *n.pl.* потроха́; ли́вер.

giddap *interj.* гей!

giddiness *n.* головокруже́ние.

giddy *adj.* **1,** (dizzy) чу́вствующий головокруже́ние. **2,** (causing giddiness, as of a height) головокружи́тельный. **3,** (frivolous) легкомы́сленный.

giddyap *interj.* гей!

gift *n.* **1,** (present) пода́рок. **2,** (talent) дар; дарова́ние.

gifted *adj.* дарови́тый; одарённый.

gift horse дарёный конь: *Don't look a gift horse in the mouth,* дарёному коню́ в зу́бы не смо́трят.

gift shop магази́н пода́рков.

gift-wrap *v.t.* заверну́ть в пода́рочную бума́гу.

gig *n.* **1,** (carriage) кабриоле́т; одноко́лка. **2,** (boat) ги́чка.

gigantic *adj.* гига́нтский; исполи́нский.

giggle *v.i.* хихи́кать.

gigolo *n.* сутенёр.

gild *v.t.* золоти́ть.

gilded *adj.* золочёный; позоло́ченный; вы́золоченный. —**gilded cage,** золочёная кле́тка.

gilding *n.* **1,** (process) золоче́ние. **2,** (substance) позоло́та.

gills *n.pl.* жа́бры. —**stuffed to the gills,** сыт по го́рло.

gillyflower *n.* левко́й.

gilt *adj.* золочёный; позоло́ченный; вы́золоченный. —*n.* позоло́та.

gimlet *n.* бура́в; бура́вчик.

gimmick *n., colloq.* уло́вка; трюк; приём.

gin *n.* (liquor) джин. —**cotton gin,** хлопко-очисти́тельная маши́на.

ginger *n.* имби́рь. —*adj.* имби́рный.

gingerbread *n.* имби́рный пря́ник; коври́жка.

gingerly *adj.* осмотри́тельный; осторо́жный. —*adv.* осмотри́тельно; осторо́жно.

gingivitis *n.* воспале́ние дёсен.

ginseng *n.* женьше́нь.

Gipsy *n. & adj.* = **Gypsy.**

giraffe *n.* жира́ф.

gird *v.t.* опоя́сывать; подпоя́сывать.

girder *n.* ба́лка; прого́н.

girdle *n.* по́яс; корсе́т.

girl *n.* **1,** (female child) де́вочка. **2,** (young woman) де́вушка. **3,** (female servant) служа́нка.

girlfriend *n.* подру́га; прия́тельница.

girlhood *n.* деви́чество.

girlish *adj.* де́вичий; деви́ческий.

girth *n.* **1,** (circumference) обхва́т. **2,** (band) подпру́га; чересседе́льник.

gist *n.* суть; су́щность.

give *v.t.* **1,** (hand over; provide) дава́ть: *Give me a cigarette,* да́йте мне сигаре́ту. *Give advice/lessons/evidence,* дава́ть сове́т/уро́ки/показа́ния. *Give one's word,* дава́ть че́стное сло́во. *I'll give you an example,* я вам приведу́ приме́р. *Give help to the needy,* ока́зывать по́мощь нужда́ющимся. **2,** (make a present of) дари́ть; преподноси́ть. *Give someone a gift,* де́лать кому́-нибудь пода́рок. **3,** (convey) передава́ть: *Give him my regards,* переда́йте ему́ приве́т. **4,** (impart, as strength or confidence) придава́ть. **5,** (organize; hold) дава́ть; устра́ивать: *give a dinner/concert,* дава́ть обе́д/конце́рт; *give a party,* устра́ивать вечери́нку. **6,** *with certain nouns,* отдава́ть: *give an order,* отда́ть прика́з; *give one's life,* отда́ть свою́ жизнь. *I'd give anything to...,* всё отда́м, чтобы... **7,** *with certain nouns,* подава́ть: *give alms,* подава́ть ми́лостыню; *give someone hope,* подава́ть кому́-нибудь наде́жду. **8,** *with certain nouns, rendered equally by* дава́ть *and* подава́ть: *give someone a signal/idea,* дава́ть *or* подава́ть кому́-нибудь сигна́л/иде́ю. **9,** *with certain nouns,* де́лать: *give a report,* де́лать докла́д; *give someone a hint/warning/discount,* де́лать кому́-нибудь намёк/предупрежде́ние/ски́дку. **10,** *with certain nouns,* доставля́ть: *give someone pleasure/trouble,* доставля́ть кому́-нибудь удово́льствие/неприя́тности. **11,** *with various miscellaneous nouns: give a lecture,* чита́ть ле́кцию; *give a course,* вести́ *or* чита́ть курс; *give an examination,* принима́ть экза́мен; *give thanks,* приноси́ть благода́рность. **12,** *in various set expressions: give birth,* рожа́ть; *give rise to,* порожда́ть. **13,** (care to the extent of): *I don't give a damn,* мне плева́ть на э́то. —*v.i.* **1,** (make charitable donations) дава́ть; же́ртвовать. **2,** (yield to physical pressure) поддава́ться. —**give away, 1,** (give freely) раздава́ть. **2,** (reveal; betray) выдава́ть. *Give oneself away,* вы́дать себя́. —**give back,** возвраща́ть; отдава́ть. *Leningrad was given back its old name of St. Petersburg,* Ленингра́ду верну́ли его́ ста́рое назва́ние Санкт-Петербу́рг. —**give in (to),** уступа́ть (+ *dat.*); поддава́ться (+ *dat.*); склоня́ться (пе́ред). *Give in to the demands of...,* уступи́ть тре́бованиям (+ *gen.*). *She gave in to him,* она́ ему́ отдала́сь. —**give off,** испуска́ть; выделя́ть. *Give off an odor,* издава́ть за́пах. —**give out, 1,** (distribute) раздава́ть; выдава́ть. **2,** (be exhausted, as of supplies) иссяка́ть; истоща́ться. —**give over (to),** посвяща́ть (+ *dat.*); отдава́ть (+ *dat.*). —**give to understand,** дать поня́ть. —**give up, 1,** (yield; relinquish) уступа́ть; сдава́ть; отка́зываться от; сложи́ть с себя́. *Give up one's seat to,* уступа́ть ме́сто (+ *dat.*). *Give up power,* отказа́ться от вла́сти. *Give up the post of...,* отказа́ться от *or* уйти́ с поста́ (+ *gen.*). **2,** (surrender) сдава́ться: *I give up!,* сдаю́сь! *Give oneself up,* сдава́ться; прийти́ с пови́нной. **3,** (abandon, as hope) оставля́ть (наде́жду). *Give up for lost,* счита́ть поги́бшим. **4,** (abandon, as an idea, attempt, etc.) отка́зываться от. **5,** (cease; drop; quit) бро́сить. —**give way,** *see* **way.**

given *adj.* **1,** [*usu.* **the given**] (present) да́нный: *under the given circumstances,* при да́нных обстоя́тельствах. **2,** [*usu.* **a given**] (stated; specified) устано́вленный: *in a given amount of time,* в устано́вленный срок. *At any given moment,* в ка́ждый конкре́тный моме́нт. *At a given signal,* по сигна́лу. **3,** *fol. by* **to** (prone to) скло́нный (к): *given to exaggeration,* скло́нен к преувеличе́ниям. —*n.* да́нность: *take as a given,* принима́ть *or* воспринима́ть как да́нность; относи́ться (к чему́-нибудь) как к да́нности. —*prep.* при: *given the situation,* при тако́м положе́нии дел. *They were surprisingly cheerful given their situation,* они́ бы́ли удиви́тельно ве́селы для свое́й ситуа́ции. —**given name,** и́мя.

gizzard *n.* му́скульный желу́док.

glacial *adj.* леднико́вый. —**glacial epoch,** леднико́вый пери́од.

glacier *n.* ледни́к; гле́тчер.

glad *adj.* **1,** (happy; pleased) рад: *I am glad to see you,* я рад (ра́да) вас ви́деть. *I'll be glad to answer any questions,* я охо́тно отве́чу на ва́ши вопро́сы. **2,** (bringing joy) ра́достный: *glad tidings,* ра́достное изве́стие.

gladden *v.t.* ра́довать.

glade *n.* поля́на; лужа́йка.

gladiator *n.* гладиа́тор.

gladiolus *n.* гладио́лус.

gladly *adv.* охо́тно; с удово́льствием.

gladness *n.* ра́дость.

glamorous *also,* **glamourous** *adj.* чару́ющий; очарова́тельный.

glamour *also,* **glamor** *n.* ча́ры; очарова́ние.

glance *n.* (бы́стрый) взгляд. *Passing glance,* мимолётный взгляд. *Exchange glances,* перегля́дываться. —*v.i.* **1,** (give a quick look at) взгля́дывать: *glance at one's watch,* взгляну́ть на часы́. *Glance over one's shoulder,* посмотре́ть че́рез плечо́. **2,** *fol.* **by over** *or* **through** (look or read over quickly) просма́тривать; загля́дывать в (+ *acc.*). **3,** *fol.* **by off** (strike and be deflected) скользну́ть по; отскочи́ть от. *Glancing blow,* скользя́щий уда́р. —**at a glance,** с пе́рвого взгля́да. —**at first glance,** на пе́рвый взгляд; с пе́рвого взгля́да.

gland *n.* железа́: *thyroid gland,* щитови́дная железа́. *Pituitary gland,* гипо́физ. —**swollen glands,** гла́нды.

glanders *n.* сап.

glandular *adj.* желе́зистый.

glandule *n.* желёзка.

glare *n.* **1,** (dazzling light) сверка́ние. **2,** (angry stare) свире́пый взгляд. —*v.i.* **1,** (shine very brightly) сверка́ть. **2,** (stare fiercely) свире́по смотре́ть.

glaring *adj.* **1,** (dazzlingly bright) я́ркий; ре́зкий; ослепи́тельный. **2,** (flagrant) гру́бый; вопию́щий. *Glaring error,* гру́бая оши́бка.

glass *n.* **1,** (substance) стекло́: *broken glass,* би́тое стекло́. *Cut oneself on a piece of glass,* поре́заться о стекло́. **2,** (container) стака́н: *a glass of water,* стака́н воды́. *Wineglass,* бока́л. *Raise one's glass to,* поднима́ть бока́л за (+ *acc.*). **3,** *pl.* (eyeglasses) очки́: *He was wearing glasses,* он был в очка́х. *Opera glasses,* театра́льный бино́кль. —*adj.* стекля́нный: *glass vase/door,* стекля́нная ва́за/дверь.

glass blower стеклоду́в.

glassful *n.* стака́н.

glassware *n.* стекля́нные изде́лия.

glass wool стеклова́та.

glassworks *n.* стеко́льный заво́д.

glassy *adj.* **1,** (smooth, as of the surface of a lake) зерка́льный. **2,** (blank, as of a stare) стекля́нный.

glaucoma *n.* глауко́ма.

glaze *n.* глазу́рь. —*v.t.* **1,** (fit with glass) застекля́ть. **2,** (apply a glaze to) глазурова́ть (посу́ду); глазирова́ть (фру́кты).

glazed *adj.* глазуро́ванный; глазиро́ванный.

glazier *n.* стеко́льщик.

gleam *n.* про́блеск. *Gleam in one's eye,* огонёк в глаза́х. —*v.i.* блесте́ть.

glean *v.t.* **1,** (collect, as grain) подбира́ть (коло́сья). **2,** (gather, as information) че́рпать; почерпну́ть.

glee *n.* ра́дость; ликова́ние. —**glee club,** хорово́й кружо́к.

gleeful *adj.* ра́достный; лику́ющий.

glen *n.* доли́на; лощи́на.

glib *adj.* бо́йкий.

glide *v.i.* **1,** (move smoothly) скользи́ть. **2,** *aero.* плани́ровать. —*n.* **1,** (smooth easy movement) скольже́ние. **2,** (powerless flight) плани́рование.

glider *n.* планёр. *Glider pilot,* планери́ст.

glimmer *v.i.* мерца́ть. —*n.* **1,** (faint light) мерца́ние. **2,** (flicker, as of hope) про́блеск (наде́жды).

glimpse *n.* мимолётный взгляд. —*v.t.* [*also,* **catch a glimpse of**] уви́деть ме́льком.

glint *n.* вспы́шка; блеск.

glisten *v.i.* блесте́ть.

glitter *v.i.* блесте́ть; сверка́ть. —**all that glitters is not gold,** не всё то зо́лото, что блести́т.

glittering *adj.* блестя́щий; блиста́тельный.

gloaming *n.* су́мерки.

gloat *v.i.* злора́дствовать.

global *adj.* мирово́й; всеми́рный; глоба́льный. *Global war,* глоба́льная война́. *Global economy,* мирова́я эконо́мика. *On a global scale,* во всеми́рном масшта́бе; в масшта́бе ми́ра.

globe *n.* **1,** (sphere) шар. **2,** (the earth) земно́й шар. **3,** (spherical model of the earth) гло́бус.

globular *adj.* шарово́й; шарови́дный.

globule *n.* **1,** (tiny sphere) ша́рик. **2,** (drop) ка́пля.

gloom *n.* **1,** (darkness) мрак. **2,** (melancholy feeling) мра́чность; уны́ние.

gloominess *n.* мра́чность; угрю́мость.

gloomy *adj.* **1,** (dark; dismal) мра́чный; хму́рый. **2,** (melancholy; morose) мра́чный; угрю́мый; хму́рый; па́смурный.

glorify *v.t.* прославля́ть. —**glorification** *n.* прославле́ние.

glorious *adj.* **1,** (possessing or deserving glory) сла́вный. **2,** *colloq.* (delightful) чуде́сный.

glory *n.* сла́ва. —*v.i.* [*usu.* **glory in**] наслажда́ться (+ *instr.*); упива́ться (+ *instr.*).

gloss *n.* **1,** (luster) лоск; гля́нец. **2,** (commentary) гло́сса. —*v.t.* [*usu.* **gloss over**] сма́зывать; зама́зывать; затушёвывать.

glossary *n.* глосса́рий.

glossy *adj.* лощёный; глянцеви́тый; гля́нцевый.

glottis *n.* голосова́я щель.

glove *n.* перча́тка. *Boxing glove,* боксёрская перча́тка. —**fit like a glove,** сиде́ть как влито́й. —**treat with kid gloves,** делика́тничать с.

glow *v.i.* **1,** (shine; beam) свети́ться. **2,** (smolder) тлеть. **3,** *fig.* (radiate, as with emotion) сия́ть. —*n.* **1,** (luminosity) за́рево. **2,** (flush; redness) румя́нец.

glower *v.i.* смотре́ть исподло́бья; смотре́ть во́лком; смотре́ть зве́рем.

glowing *adj.* **1,** (burning) тле́ющий. **2,** (rich and warm, as of colors) я́ркий. **3,** (ruddy; healthy) румя́ный. **4,** (highly enthusiastic) восто́рженный.

glowworm *n.* светля́к.

gloxinia *n.* глокси́ния.

glucose *n.* глюко́за.

glue *n.* клей. —*v.t.* кле́ить; прикле́ивать. *Glue together,* скле́ивать; слепля́ть. *We sat glued to the TV set,* мы не могли́ оторва́ться от телеви́зора.

glum *adj.* мра́чный; угрю́мый; хму́рый.

glut *n.* избы́ток. —*v.t.* пресыща́ть. *Glut the market,* наводня́ть ры́нок това́рами.

gluten *n.* клейкови́на.

glutton *n.* обжо́ра. —**gluttonous,** *adj.* прожо́рливый. —**gluttony,** *n.* обжо́рство.

glycerin *also,* **glycerine** *n.* глицери́н.

glycogen *n.* гликоге́н.

gnarl *n.* сучо́к.

gnarled *adj.* **1,** (knotty) сучкова́тый. **2,** (twisted, as of fingers) сучкова́тый; коря́вый.

gnash *v.t.* скрежета́ть (зуба́ми).

gnat *n.* мо́шка.

gnaw *v.t. & i.* грызть; глода́ть. *Gnaw a hole,* выгрыза́ть дыру́. —**gnawing,** *adj.* (of a pain) сверля́щий.

gneiss *n.* гнейс.

gnome *n.* гном.

gnu *n.* гну.

go *v.i.* **1,** (proceed on foot) идти́: *go to the theater,* идти́ в теа́тр; *go for a walk,* идти́ гуля́ть. *Who goes there?,* кто идёт? **2,** (travel by vehicle) е́хать: *go to California,* е́хать в Калифо́рнию. *Go for a ride,* е́здить на прогу́лку; ката́ться на маши́не. *Go by plane,* лете́ть на самолёте. **3,** (leave; depart) уходи́ть. *It's time to go,* пора́ идти́ *or* уходи́ть. **4,** (engage in an activity): *go swimming,* купа́ться; *go skiing,* ходи́ть на лы́жах; *go shopping,* идти́ за поку́пками. **5,** (proceed; progress) идти́; проходи́ть. *Things are going badly,* дела́ иду́т пло́хо. *Everything went well,* всё прошло́ хорошо́. *The operation went well,* опера́ция прошла́ хорошо́. **6,** (belong) до́лжен быть. *Where do these things go?,* где должны́ быть э́ти ве́щи?; куда́ положи́ть э́ти ве́щи? *They go on the top shelf,* они́ должны́ быть на ве́рхней по́лке. **7,** *used with various adjectives: go mad,* сходи́ть с ума́; *go broke,* прогоре́ть; *go bad,* испо́ртиться; *go free,* остава́ться на свобо́де; *go hungry,* голода́ть; *go barefoot,* ходи́ть босико́м; *go unnoticed,* пройти́ незаме́ченным. **8,** (be phrased) гласи́ть: *as the saying goes,* как гласи́т погово́рка; как говори́тся. **9,** (be in harmony) подходи́ть (к); идти́ (к); гармони́ровать (с); сочета́ться (с). *These colors go well together,* э́ти цвета́ хорошо́ сочета́ются. *The tie doesn't go with the suit,* га́лстук не подхо́дит *or* не идёт к костю́му. **10,** (fail) слабе́ть. *His eyesight is going,* зре́ние у него́ слабе́ет; он теря́ет зре́ние. —*v.t. Used mainly in set expressions: go shares with,* войти́ в до́лю с. *We are going the same way,* нам с ва́ми по пути́. —*n. Used mainly in idiomatic expressions: on the go,* на нога́х; в движе́нии. *Have a go at,* попыта́ться. *From the word "go",* с са́мого нача́ла. —**be going to,** собира́ться: *What are you going to do?,* что вы собира́етесь де́лать? *I'm not going to worry about it,* я об э́том не бу́ду беспоко́иться. —**go about,** принима́ться за: *I don't know how to go about it,* я не зна́ю, как приня́ться за э́то. *Go about one's business,* занима́ться свои́ми дела́ми. —**go against, 1,** (oppose) идти́ про́тив. **2,** (act contrary to) поступа́ть вопреки́. **3,** (be contrary to) противоре́чить; идти́ вразре́з с. **4,** (be decided against): *The decision went against him,* де́ло реши́лось не в его́ по́льзу. —**go ahead!,** дава́йте! —**go along, 1,** (proceed) идти́. **2,** *fol. by* **with** (accompany) сопровожда́ть. **3,** (consent) соглаша́ться. **4,** *fol. by* **with** (agree with) быть согла́сным с. —**go around,**

1, (walk around) обходи́ть. **2,** (revolve around) враща́ться вокру́г. **3,** (extend all the way around) окружа́ть. **4,** (fit around) сходи́ться на: *The belt won't go around his waist,* по́яс не схо́дится на его́ та́лии. **5,** (circulate, as of rumors) ходи́ть; распространя́ться; проноси́ться; распуска́ться. **6,** (suffice for all) хвата́ть: *There is not enough to go around,* на всех не хва́тит. —**go away,** уходи́ть; уезжа́ть. —**go back, 1,** (return) возвраща́ться: *go back to the store,* возвраща́ться в магази́н. *Go back to the beginning,* нача́ть снача́ла. **2,** (resume after a long break) сно́ва пойти́ (+ *inf.*): *go back to school/work,* сно́ва пойти́ учи́ться/рабо́тать. **3,** *fol. by* **to** (date back) относи́ться (к); восходи́ть (к). *The history of Egypt goes back 5,000 years,* исто́рия Еги́пта насчи́тывает пять ты́сяч лет. **4,** *Go back on one's word,* наруша́ть своё сло́во; идти́ на попя́тную. —**go by, 1,** (pass by) проходи́ть ми́мо. **2,** (pass, as of time) проходи́ть: *The years go by,* го́ды прохо́дят. **3,** (act in accordance with) поступа́ть по: *go by the rules,* поступа́ть по пра́вилам. *You can't go by what he says,* нельзя́ доверя́ть тому́, что он говори́т. **4,** (be known as): *He goes by the name of...,* он изве́стен под и́менем (+ *nom.*). —**go down, 1,** (descend) сходи́ть; спуска́ться: *go down the stairs,* сходи́ть/спуска́ться по ле́стнице (*or* с ле́стницы). **2,** (set, as of the sun) сади́ться; заходи́ть. **3,** (sink, as of a ship) идти́ ко дну. **4,** (subside, as of swelling) опада́ть; спада́ть. **5,** (fall, as of prices) снижа́ться. **6,** (drop, as of temperature) понижа́ться. **7,** *Go down the wrong way (of food),* попа́сть не в то го́рло. **8,** *Go down in history,* войти́ в исто́рию. —**go for, 1,** (fetch) идти́ за (+ *instr.*). **2,** (be used for a certain purpose) идти́ на (+ *acc.*): *go for export,* идти́ на э́кспорт. **3,** (be applicable to) относи́ться к. **4,** (be sold for) продава́ться за (+ *acc.*). **5,** *slang* (take a fancy to) увлека́ться (+ *instr.*). —**go in, 1,** (enter) входи́ть. **2,** (fit) входи́ть; вмеща́ться; умеща́ться. —**go in for,** занима́ться (+ *instr.*). —**go into, 1,** (enter) входи́ть в. *The nail won't go into the wall,* гвоздь не идёт *or* не ле́зет в сте́ну. *Go into effect,* входи́ть в си́лу. *Go into detail,* вдава́ться в подро́бности. **2,** (fit into) входи́ть в; вмеща́ться в; умеща́ться в. **3,** (be invested in) уходи́ть на: *A lot of work went into that,* мно́го рабо́ты ушло́ на э́то. **4,** *She went into labor,* у неё начали́сь ро́ды. —**go off, 1,** (slip or slide off) сходи́ть: *The train went off the tracks,* по́езд сошёл с ре́льсов. **2,** (depart) уходи́ть: *go off to war,* уходи́ть на войну́. **3,** (detonate, as of a bomb) взрыва́ться; (discharge, as of a firearm) вы́стрелить. **4,** (of an alarm clock) зазвони́ть. **5,** (happen; proceed) проходи́ть: *go off well,* проходи́ть успе́шно. —**go on, 1,** (continue) продолжа́ть; продолжа́йте! *Oh, go on!,* да брось ты! *Life goes on,* жизнь продолжа́ется. *We can't go on like this,* так да́льше не мо́жет продолжа́ться. *If things go on like this,* е́сли так пойдёт да́льше. **2,** (happen) происходи́ть; де́латься: *What's going on?,* что происхо́дит?; что де́лается? *While all this was going on,* пока́ всё э́то шло. **3,** (appear, as on stage) выходи́ть (на сце́ну). **4,** (be turned on, as of light) зажига́ться. **—go out, 1,** (go outside) выходи́ть на у́лицу. *Go out on deck,* выходи́ть на па́лубу. **2,** (stop burning) га́снуть; ту́хнуть. *The lights went out,* свет пога́с. **—go out of,** выходи́ть из: *go out of the house,* выходи́ть и́з дому. *Go out of style,* выходи́ть из мо́ды. *Go out of control,* потеря́ть управле́ние. *Go out of one's mind,* сходи́ть с ума́. **—go out with,** встреча́ться с. **—go over, 1,** (cross over; shift) переходи́ть. **2,** (tumble over) сва́ливаться: *The car went over the cliff,* маши́на свали́лась со скалы́. **3,** (look over) просма́тривать; разбира́ть. **4,** (examine) осма́тривать. **5,** (repeat) повторя́ть. **6,** (fare) проходи́ть. *Go over big,* име́ть большо́й успе́х. **—go round,** враща́ться. **—go through, 1,** (fit through) проходи́ть в; пролеза́ть в. **2,** (pass, as a red light) прое́хать на; проскочи́ть на (кра́сный свет). **3,** (pass through) пережива́ть; проходи́ть: *go through a period of transition,* пережива́ть пери́од перехо́да; *go through several stages of development,* проходи́ть не́сколько ста́дий разви́тия. **4,** (experience; endure) проходи́ть; пережива́ть. *She has gone through a lot,* она́ мно́го пережила́. **5,** (look over; sort out) разбира́ть. **6,** (search) обша́ривать. **7,** (repeat) повторя́ть. **8,** (be completed, as of a deal) состоя́ться. **9,** (spend; squander) промота́ть. **10,** *The book has gone through several editions,* кни́га вы́держала не́сколько изда́ний. **—go under, 1,** (sink) тону́ть. **2,** (go bankrupt) прогоре́ть. **—go up, 1,** (ascend) поднима́ться: *go up the stairs,* поднима́ться по ле́стнице. *The curtain went up,* за́навес подня́лся. **2,** (increase) расти́; повыша́ться. *Prices are going up,* це́ны расту́т. *Go up in price,* повыша́ться в цене́; дорожа́ть. **3,** (be built) стро́иться. **—go without,** обходи́ться без. *Go without dinner,* оста́ться без обе́да. *See also* **going** *and* **gone.**

goad *v.t.* **1,** (prod, as cattle) погоня́ть; подгоня́ть. **2,** (incite) подстрека́ть; подбива́ть.

go-ahead *n., colloq.* разреше́ние (сде́лать что́-нибудь). *Give (someone) the go-ahead to...,* дать (кому́-нибудь) добро́ на (+ *acc.*).

goal *n.* **1,** (aim; objective) цель. **2,** *sports* (scoring area) воро́та. **3,** *sports* (point scored) гол.

goalie *n.* врата́рь. *Also,* **goalkeeper.**

goal line ли́ния воро́т.

goal post сто́йка воро́т.

goat *n.* (female) коза́; (male) козёл. **—***adj.* [*also,* **goat's**] ко́зий: *goat's milk,* ко́зье молоко́. **—get someone's goat,** *colloq.* разозли́ть; вы́вести из себя́.

goatee *n.* козли́ная боро́дка.

goat meat козля́тина.

goatskin *n.* ко́зья шку́ра. **—***adj.* козло́вый; козли́ный.

goatsucker *n.* козодо́й.

gobble *v.t.* пожира́ть.

go-between *n.* посре́дник.

goblet *n.* бока́л; ку́бок.

goblin *n.* домово́й; ле́ший.

goby *n.* бычо́к.

god *also,* **God** *n.* бог. *God's will,* бо́жья во́ля. *God's punishment,* ка́ра госпо́дня. **—by God,** кляну́сь бо́гом. **—for God's sake,** ра́ди бо́га. **—God bless you!** *(after a sneeze),* бу́дьте здоро́вы! **—God forbid!,** не дай бог!; бо́же упаси́! **—God knows!,** бог его́ зна́ет! **—God willing,** е́сли бог даст. **—good God!; my God!,** бо́же мой! **—thank God!,** сла́ва бо́гу!

godchild *n.* кре́стник; кре́стница.

goddaughter *n.* кре́стница; крёстная дочь.

goddess *n.* боги́ня.

godfather *n.* кре́стный оте́ц; крёстный.

god-fearing *adj.* богобоя́зненный.

godforsaken *adj.* захолу́стный. *Godforsaken place,* захолу́стье; трущо́ба; медве́жий у́гол.

godless *adj.* безбо́жный. **—godlessness,** *n.* безбо́жие.

godly *adj.* на́божный; благочести́вый.

godmother *n.* крёстная мать; крёстная.

godson *n.* кре́стник; крёстный сын.

goggle *v.i.* тара́щить глаза́; де́лать кру́глые глаза́. **—goggle-eyed,** *adj.* пучегла́зый. **—goggles,** *n.pl.* защи́тные очки́.

going *n.* **1,** (act of going) хожде́ние. **2,** (departure) отъе́зд. **—***adj.* **1,** (present) теку́щий: *at the going rate,* по теку́щим тари́фам. **2,** (operating and doing well) соли́дный; рента́бельный: *a going concern,* соли́дная компа́ния; рента́бельное предприя́тие.

goiter *also,* **goitre** *n.* зоб. *Exophthalmic goiter,* ба́зедова боле́знь.

gold *n.* зо́лото. **—***adj.* золото́й: *a gold chain,* золота́я цепо́чка. **—be worth its weight in gold,** быть на вес зо́лота. **—have a heart of gold,** име́ть золото́е се́рдце.

gold dust золото́й песо́к.

golden *adj.* золото́й; золоти́стый. **—golden age,** золото́й век. **—golden calf,** золото́й теле́ц. **—golden eagle,** бе́ркут. **—Golden Fleece,** золото́е руно́. **—Golden Horde,** Золота́я орда́. **—golden mean,** золота́я середи́на.

goldeneye *n.* го́голь.

goldenrod *n.* золота́рник.

goldfinch *n.* щего́л.

goldfish *n.* золота́я ры́бка. *Goldfish bowl,* аква́риум с золоты́ми ры́бками.

gold leaf суса́льное зо́лото.

gold mine 1, *often pl.* (mine producing gold ore) золоты́е при́иски. **2,** *fig.* (source of great wealth) золото́е дно.

gold plate накладно́е зо́лото. **—gold-plate,** *v.t.* золоти́ть. **—gold-plated,** *adj.* накладно́го зо́лота; позоло́ченный.

goldsmith *n.* золоты́х дел ма́стер.

gold standard золото́й станда́рт.

golf *n.* гольф. **—golf club,** клю́шка. **—golf course,** площа́дка для го́льфа.

gonad *n.* **1,** (testicle) яи́чко. **2,** (ovary) яи́чник.

gondola *n.* гондо́ла. **—gondolier,** *n.* гондолье́р.

gone *adj.* **1,** (departed; away) уше́дший; в отъе́зде. **2,** (missing) пропа́вший. **3,** (dead) уме́рший; бо́льше нет в живы́х. **4,** (over): *The pain is gone,* боль прошла́. —**gone by,** было́й: *in days gone by,* в былы́е времена́.

gong *n.* гонг.

gonococcus *n.* гоноко́кк.

gonorrhea *also,* **gonorrhoea** *n.* гоноре́я; три́ппер.

good *adj.* **1,** (general term) хоро́ший: *good manners,* хоро́шие мане́ры. *Good news,* хоро́шая но́вость; хоро́шее изве́стие. *That's good,* э́то хорошо́. *Smell good,* хорошо́ па́хнуть. ♦*In certain set expressions,* до́брый: *Good morning!,* до́брое у́тро! *Good evening!,* до́брый ве́чер! *Good sign,* до́брый знак. *The good old days,* до́брое ста́рое вре́мя. **2,** (pleasant) прия́тный: *It was good to see you,* бы́ло прия́тно вас ви́деть; рад был (ра́да была́) вас ви́деть. *Have a good time,* хорошо́ провести́ вре́мя. **3,** *fol. by* at (having a knack for) спосо́бный (к); силён (в): *good at languages/ mathematics,* спосо́бный к языка́м; силён (сильна́) в матема́тике. **4,** *fol. by* for (of use; helpful) поле́зный: *good for one's health,* поле́зен для здоро́вья. *Exercise is good for you,* физи́ческие упражне́ния вам на по́льзу. *This medicine is good for a cough,* э́то лека́рство поле́зно (*or* помога́ет) от ка́шля. *Not be good for anything,* ни на что не годи́ться. **5,** (kind) до́брый; любе́зный: *Be so good as to...,* бу́дьте добры́/любе́зны (+ *imperative*). *Very good of you,* о́чень любе́зно с ва́шей стороны́. **6,** (honorable) до́брый. *Good intentions,* до́брые *or* благи́е наме́рения. *One's good name,* своё до́брое и́мя. **7,** (sound) уважи́тельный: *a good reason,* уважи́тельная причи́на. *With good reason,* с по́лным основа́нием. **8,** (valid) действи́тельный: *good for six months,* действи́телен на шесть ме́сяцев. **9,** (considerable) изря́дный: *a good distance,* изря́дное расстоя́ние. *A good while,* дово́льно до́лго. **10,** (not less than) до́брый: *a good hour,* до́брый час. *A good half-hour/ two hours/,* до́брых полчаса́/ два часа́/. —*n.* **1,** (something good; what is right) добро́: *good and evil,* добро́ и зло. *Do good,* де́лать добро́. **2,** (benefit; advantage) по́льза; бла́го. *For the good of the cause,* для по́льзы де́ла; в интере́сах де́ла. *For the good of mankind,* на бла́го челове́чества. *Do someone good,* быть *or* идти́ на по́льзу (+ *dat.*); принести́ по́льзу (+ *dat.*). *What's the good of it?,* кака́я от э́того по́льза? *What good will it do you?,* кака́я вам от э́того по́льза? *What's the good of arguing?,* что по́льзы (*or* како́й смысл) спо́рить? *It will lead to no good,* э́то ни к чему́ хоро́шему не приведёт. *What good is money if there's nothing to buy?,* к чему́ де́ньги, е́сли не́чего купи́ть? —**as good as...,** всё равно́, что... —**be up to no good,** замышля́ть недо́брое. —**come to no good,** пло́хо ко́нчить. —**for good,** навсегда́; оконча́тельно. —**good and...,** *colloq.* здо́рово; поря́дком: *good and tired,* здо́рово/поря́дком уста́л. —**make good,** *see* make. —**to the good,** в вы́игрыше.

goodbye *interj.* до свида́ния! —*n.* проща́ние. *Say goodbye (to),* проща́ться (с).

good-for-nothing *adj.* никчёмный. —*n.* шалопа́й.

Good Friday страстна́я пя́тница.

good-hearted *adj.* добросерде́чный.

good-looking *adj.* **1,** (pretty; handsome) краси́вый;

хоро́ш собо́й; хоро́шенький; милови́дный. **2,** (smart; stylish) наря́дный.

goodly *adj.* (rather large) поря́дочный; изря́дный.

good-natured *adj.* доброду́шный.

good-neighbor *adj.* доброcосе́дский.

goodness *n.* доброта́. —*interj.* го́споди! —**for goodness' sake,** ра́ди бо́га! —**thank goodness!,** сла́ва бо́гу!

goods *n.* **1,** (merchandise) изде́лия; това́р(ы). *Leather goods,* ко́жаные изде́лия. *Canned goods,* консе́рвы. *Consumer goods,* потреби́тельские това́ры; това́ры широ́кого потребле́ния. *Goods and services,* това́ры и услу́ги. **2,** (personal possessions) ве́щи; иму́щество. **3,** (fabric) мате́рия.

good will до́брая во́ля: *people of good will,* лю́ди до́брой во́ли. —**goodwill,** *adj.* до́брой во́ли: *goodwill mission,* ми́ссия до́брой во́ли.

goose *n.* гусь. —*adj.* гуси́ный: *goose feathers,* гуси́ные пе́рья.

gooseberry *n.* крыжо́вник.

goose flesh гуси́ная ко́жа. *Also,* **goose pimples.**

goose step гуси́ный шаг.

gopher *n.* **1,** (burrowing rodent) го́фер. **2,** (ground squirrel) су́слик.

Gordian knot го́рдиев у́зел.

gore *n.* **1,** (blood) кровь. **2,** (gusset) клин. —*v.t.* забода́ть.

gorge *n.* уще́лье. —*v.t.* обка́рмливать. *Gorge oneself,* нае́сться до́сыта *or* до отва́ла.

gorgeous *adj.* великоле́пный; прекра́сный.

gorilla *n.* гори́лла.

gory *adj.* **1,** (covered with blood) окрова́вленный. **2,** (involving much bloodshed) крова́вый.

goshawk *n.* тетереви́ятник.

gosling *n.* гусёнок.

gospel *n.* ева́нгелие. —**gospel truth,** свята́я и́стина *or* пра́вда.

gossamer *n.* **1,** (cobweb) паути́на. **2,** (fabric) газ.

gossip *n.* **1,** (talk) спле́тня; пересу́ды. **2,** (person) спле́тник; спле́тница. —*v.i.* спле́тничать.

got *v.,* past tense of **get.** —**have got, 1,** (having): *Have you got a match?,* у вас есть спи́чка? *What have you got to say?,* что вы мо́жете сказа́ть? *What have you got against him?,* что вы име́ете про́тив него́? **2,** *fol. by inf.* (must) на́до: *I've got to go,* мне на́до идти́.

Goth *n.* гот.

Gothic *adj.* **1,** (of architecture, script, etc.) готи́ческий. **2,** (of the language) го́тский. —*n.* **1,** (architecture) го́тика. **2,** (language) го́тский язы́к.

gouache *n.* гуа́шь.

gouge *v.t.* **1,** (make grooves or holes in) долби́ть. **2,** *fol. by* out (cut out) выда́лбливать. **3,** *fol. by* out (put out, as an eye) выка́лывать. **4,** *colloq.* (cheat; overcharge) обжу́ливать. —*n.* **1,** (tool) долото́. **2,** (groove) вы́емка.

goulash *n.* гуля́ш.

gourd *n.* **1,** (calabash) горля́нка. **2,** (pumpkin) ты́ква.

gourmand *n.* **1,** (glutton) обжо́ра. **2,** = **gourmet.**

gourmet *n.* гурма́н; гастроно́м.

gout *n.* пода́гра.

govern *v.t.* **1,** (rule over) пра́вить; управля́ть: *govern a country,* пра́вить/управля́ть страно́й. **2,** (determine) определя́ть. **3,** *gram.* управля́ть. —*v.i.* пра́вить.

governess *n.* гуверна́нтка; воспита́тельница.

government *n.* **1,** (governing body of a nation) прави́тельство: *the Canadian government,* кана́дское прави́тельство. *The three branches of government,* три ве́тви вла́сти. *Work for the government,* быть на госуда́рственной слу́жбе. **2,** (administration; rule) правле́ние; управле́ние. *Form of government,* фо́рма *or* о́браз правле́ния. *Organs of local government,* о́рганы ме́стного управле́ния. —*adj.* госуда́рственный; прави́тельственный. *Government workers/employees,* госуда́рственные слу́жащие. *Government building,* прави́тельственное зда́ние.

governmental *adj.* прави́тельственный.

governor *n.* **1,** *polit.* губерна́тор. **2,** *mech.* регуля́тор. —**governorship,** *n.* губерна́торство.

gown *n.* **1,** (long dress) пла́тье: *evening gown,* вече́рнее пла́тье. **2,** (long robe) ма́нтия.

grab *v.t.* **1,** (grasp; snatch) хвата́ть; хвата́ться за; схва́тывать; выхва́тывать. **2,** (seize; take possession of) захва́тывать.

grace *n.* **1,** (beauty; elegance) гра́ция; изя́щество: *grace of movement,* гра́ция/изя́щество движе́ний. **2,** (proper behavior; sense of what is right): *social graces,* пра́вила хоро́шего то́на. *He conceded defeat with good grace,* он призна́л своё пораже́ние с досто́инством. *At least he had the grace to apologize,* по кра́йней ме́ре, он набра́лся сме́лости извини́ться. **3,** (favor) ми́лость: *by God's grace,* бо́жьей ми́лостью. *Be in someone's good graces,* быть в ми́лости у кого́-нибудь; быть у кого́-нибудь на хоро́шем счету́. *Fall from grace,* впасть в неми́лость. **4,** (extension): отсро́чка: *receive a month's grace,* получи́ть ме́сячную отсро́чку. **5,** (prayer at meals) моли́тва: *say grace,* чита́ть моли́тву. **6,** *cap.* (title of respect) све́тлость: *Your Grace,* ва́ша све́тлость. —*v.t.* украша́ть: *Flowers graced the table,* стол украша́ли цветы́.

graceful *adj.* **1,** (moving with grace) грацио́зный: *graceful dancer,* грацио́зный танцо́р. *Graceful movements,* грацио́зные *or* изя́щные движе́ния. **2,** (well-proportioned) изя́щный; стро́йный.

gracefully *adv.* **1,** (with grace of movement) грацио́зно. **2,** (with good grace) с досто́инством.

gracefulness *n.* грацио́зность.

grace note форшла́г.

grace period льго́тный срок.

gracious *adj.* любе́зный: *gracious hostess,* любе́зная хозя́йка; *gracious words,* любе́зные слова́. —*interj.* бо́же мой! —**graciously,** *adv.* любе́зно. —**graciousness,** *n.* любе́зность.

gradation *n.* града́ция.

grade *n.* **1,** (school class or year) класс: *in the fourth grade,* в четвёртом кла́ссе. **2,** (mark in school) отме́тка; оце́нка; балл. *A good grade on one's composition,* хоро́шая отме́тка за сочине́ние. *A grade of "four" in physics,* отме́тка «четы́ре» по фи́зике. **3,** (rank) зва́ние; чин. **4,** (quality) сорт; ка́чество. **5,**

(slope) склон; укло́н. *Steep grade,* круто́й склон. —*v.t.* **1,** (classify) сортирова́ть. **2,** (give a grade to) ста́вить отме́тку *or* оце́нку (+ *dat.*). **3,** (level) ука́зывать; нивели́ровать. —**make the grade,** быть на до́лжной высоте́.

grader *n.* **1,** (machine for grading) гре́йдер. **2,** (pupil): *third grader,* учени́к тре́тьего кла́сса.

grade school нача́льная шко́ла.

gradient *n.* **1,** (slope) склон; укло́н. **2,** *physics* (rate of change) градие́нт.

gradual *adj.* постепе́нный: *gradual change/improvement,* постепе́нное измене́ние/улучше́ние. —**gradually,** *adv.* постепе́нно.

graduate *v.t. & i.* ко́нчить; око́нчить (шко́лу *or* университе́т). *Graduating class,* выпускно́й класс; вы́пуск. —*n.* выпускни́к. —**graduate school,** аспиранту́ра: *go to graduate school,* пойти́ в аспиранту́ру. —**graduate student,** аспира́нт.

graduated *adj.* **1,** (containing gradations) градуи́рованный. **2,** (of a tax) прогресси́вный.

graduation *n.* **1,** (completion of studies) оконча́ние. **2,** (commencement exercises) выпускно́й акт.

graffiti *n.* на́дписи и рису́нки на стена́х и забо́рах; граффи́ти.

graft *v.t.* **1,** *horticulture* привива́ть. **2,** *surgery* переса́живать. —*n.* **1,** *horticulture* черено́к. **2,** *surgery* переса́дка: *skin graft,* переса́дка ко́жи. **3,** (corruption) по́дкуп.

grain *n.* **1,** (seed; crops) зерно́; хлеб. **2,** (particle) зерно́; крупи́нка; крупи́ца. *Grain of sand,* песчи́нка. *Grain of truth,* зерно́ *or* крупи́ца *or* до́ля и́стины. **3,** (arrangement of fibers or layers) волокно́: *parallel to the grain,* паралле́льно волокну́. **4,** (unit of weight) гран. —**against the grain,** про́тив ше́рсти.

grain elevator элева́тор.

grain exchange хле́бная би́ржа.

grainy *adj.* зерни́стый; крупча́тый.

gram *also,* **gramme** *n.* грамм.

grammar *n.* **1,** (structure of a language) грамма́тика. **2,** (book on grammar) уче́бник грамма́тики. —**grammarian,** *n.* граммати́ст. —**grammatical,** *adj.* граммати́ческий.

gramme *n.* = **gram.**

gramophone *n.* граммофо́н.

granary *n.* **1,** (storehouse for grain) амба́р; зернохрани́лище. **2,** (grain-producing region) жи́тница.

grand *adj.* **1,** (magnificent; luxurious) великоле́пный. *Live in grand style,* жить широко́; жить на широ́кую но́гу. **2,** (marked by pomp) торже́ственный: *grand opening,* торже́ственное откры́тие; *grand finale,* торже́ственный фина́л. **3,** *colloq.* (fine; splendid) чуде́сный. **4,** (overall) о́бщий: *grand total,* о́бщий ито́г.

grandchild *n.* внук; вну́чка. —**grandchildren,** *n.pl.* вну́ки.

granddaughter *n.* вну́чка.

grand duke вели́кий князь. —**grand duchy,** вели́кое кня́жество.

grandeur *n.* **1,** (splendor) великоле́пие. **2,** (greatness) грандио́зность. —**delusions of grandeur,** ма́ния вели́чия.

grandfather *n.* де́душка; дед.

grandiloquent *adj.* высокопа́рный; напы́щенный. —**grandiloquence,** *n.* высокопа́рность; напы́щенность.

grandiose *adj.* грандио́зный. —**grandiosity,** *n.* грандио́зность.

grand jury большо́е жюри́.

grandmaster *n.* **1,** (of a monastic order) маги́стр. **2,** *chess* гроссме́йстер.

grandmother *n.* ба́бушка.

grandnephew *n.* внуча́тый племя́нник.

grandniece *n.* внуча́тая племя́нница.

grandparent *n.* де́душка; ба́бушка.

grand piano роя́ль.

grand slam большо́й шлем.

grandson *n.* внук.

grandstand *n.* трибу́на.

grange *n.* уса́дьба.

granite *n.* грани́т. —*adj.* грани́тный.

grant *v.t.* **1,** (give; bestow) предоставля́ть; дава́ть. *Grant freedom/ rights/ a loan/ to someone,* предоставля́ть кому́-нибудь свобо́ду/права́/заём. *Grant permission/ a delay/,* дава́ть разреше́ние/отсро́чку. *Grant a pension to,* назнача́ть пе́нсию (+ *dat.*). **2,** (consent to carry out) удовлетворя́ть: *grant a request/wish,* удовлетворя́ть про́сьбу/жела́ние. **3,** (concede; allow) допуска́ть: *I'll grant that...,* допуска́ю, что... *Granted she is no beauty,* пусть она́ не краса́вица. —*n.* дота́ция; безвозвра́тная ссу́да. —**take for granted, 1,** (assume as obvious) счита́ть само́ собо́й разуме́ющимся. **2,** (fail to appreciate) принима́ть как до́лжное.

granular *adj.* зерни́стый.

granulate *v.t.* гранули́ровать. —**granulated sugar,** са́харный песо́к.

granulation *n.* грануля́ция.

granule *n.* зёрнышко.

grape *n.* виногра́дина; *pl.* виногра́д. —*adj.* виногра́дный: *grape wine,* виногра́дное вино́.

grapefruit *n.* гре́йпфрут.

grape sugar виногра́дный са́хар.

grapevine *n.* **1,** (plant) виногра́дная лоза́. **2,** (rumors) слу́хи; то́лки: *The grapevine has it that...,* иду́т то́лки о том, что...

graph *n.* гра́фик; диагра́мма.

graphic *adj.* **1,** (illustrated by graphs) графи́ческий. **2,** (vivid) о́бразный; нагля́дный: *graphic description,* о́бразное описа́ние; *graphic example,* нагля́дный приме́р. —**graphic artist,** гра́фик; рисова́льщик. —**graphic arts,** гра́фика; графи́ческое иску́сство.

graphically *adv.* нагля́дно; о́бразно; воо́чию.

graphite *n.* графи́т. —*adj.* графи́товый.

graph paper бума́га в кле́тку.

grapnel *n.* ко́шка.

grapple *v.i.* **1,** (fight; wrestle) схва́тываться; сцепля́ться. **2,** *fol. by* **with** (contend with, as a problem) би́ться (над); схва́тываться (с).

grappling iron ко́шка.

grasp *v.t.* **1,** (seize; grab) хвата́ть; хвата́ться за; схва́тывать. **2,** (comprehend) схва́тывать; воспринима́ть; постига́ть. —*v.i.* [*usu.* **grasp at**] хвата́ться за; ухвати́ться за: *grasp at a straw,* хвата́ться за соло́минку; *grasp at an opportunity,* ухвати́ться за слу́чай. —*n.* **1,** (firm hold; grip) хва́тка. **2,** (comprehension) понима́ние: *beyond one's grasp,* вы́ше чьего́-нибудь понима́ния.

grasping *adj.* **1,** (prehensile) це́пкий. **2,** (avaricious) жа́дный; а́лчный.

grass *n.* трава́. *Keep off the grass!,* по траве́ не ходи́ть!

grasshopper *n.* кузне́чик.

grassland *n.* травяно́е уго́дье.

grass snake уж.

grass widow соло́менная вдова́.

grassy *adj.* травяно́й; травяни́стый.

grate *n.* решётка. —*v.t.* тере́ть: *grate carrots,* тере́ть морко́вь. —*v.i.* **1,** (make a harsh grinding sound) скрежета́ть. **2,** *fol. by* **on** (irritate) коро́бить. *Grate on one's ear,* ре́зать у́хо *or* слух (+ *dat.*).

grateful *adj.* благода́рный; призна́тельный. *I am very grateful to you,* я вам о́чень благода́рен (-рна). —**gratefully,** *adv.* с благода́рностью.

grater *n.* тёрка.

gratification *n.* **1,** (act of gratifying) удовлетворе́ние. **2,** (sense of satisfaction) удовлетворе́ние; удово́льствие.

gratify *v.t.* **1,** (give satisfaction to) доставля́ть удово́льствие (+ *dat.*); ра́довать. **2,** (satisfy; indulge, as a desire) удовлетворя́ть. —**gratifying,** *adj.* отра́дный.

grating *n.* решётка. —*adj.* ре́зкий; скрипу́чий.

gratis *adv.* беспла́тно; да́ром; безвозме́здно.

gratitude *n.* благода́рность; призна́тельность.

gratuitous *adj.* **1,** (freely given) безвозме́здный. **2,** (uncalled-for) неуме́стный: *gratuitous remarks,* неуме́стные замеча́ния. *Gratuitous insult,* ниче́м не вы́званное оскорбле́ние.

gratuity *n.* чаевы́е.

grave *n.* моги́ла. —*adj.* **1,** (serious) серьёзный: *a grave matter,* серьёзное де́ло; *grave appearance,* серьёзный вид; *in grave danger,* в серьёзной опа́сности. **2,** (critical) тяжёлый; тя́жкий: *a grave illness,* тяжёлая/тя́жкая боле́знь. *In grave condition,* в тяжёлом состоя́нии. **3,** *phonet.* тупо́й: *grave accent,* тупо́е ударе́ние. —**dig one's own grave,** само́му себе́ рыть моги́лу. —**have one foot in the grave,** стоя́ть одно́й ного́й в моги́ле. —**turn over in one's grave,** переверну́ться в гробу́.

gravedigger *n.* моги́льщик.

gravel *n.* **1,** (mixture of pebbles and sand) гра́вий. **2,** *med.* мочево́й песо́к.

gravely *adv.* тяжело́: *gravely ill,* тяжело́ бо́лен.

graven *adj.* вы́сеченный. —**graven image,** и́дол; куми́р.

graveside *n.* край моги́лы. —*adj.* надгро́бный: *graveside speech,* надгро́бная речь.

gravestone *n.* моги́льная плита́; моги́льный ка́мень; надгро́бная плита́; надгро́бие.

graveyard *n.* кла́дбище; пого́ст.

gravitate *v.i.* тяготе́ть: *gravitate toward politics,* тяготе́ть к поли́тике.

gravitation *n.* тяготе́ние; притяже́ние; гравита́ция.

gravitational *adj.* гравитацио́нный. —**gravitational field,** гравитацио́нное по́ле.

gravity *n.* **1,** (seriousness) тя́жесть; серьёзность. *The gravity of the problem,* тя́жесть пробле́мы. *A matter of the utmost gravity,* де́ло велича́йшей серьёзности. **2,** *physics* тя́жесть; тяготе́ние; притяже́ние. *Center of gravity,* центр тя́жести. *The force of gravity,* си́ла тяготе́ния. *The earth's gravity,* земно́е притяже́ние. *The law of gravity,* зако́н (всеми́рного) тяготе́ния.

gravy *n.* со́ус; подли́вка. —**gravy boat,** со́усник; судо́к.

gray *also,* **grey** *adj.* се́рый; (*of hair*) седо́й; (*of a horse*) си́вый. —*n.* се́рый цвет. *Hair flecked with gray,* во́лосы с про́седью. —**gray matter,** се́рое вещество́ (мо́зга). —**turn gray,** сере́ть; (*of hair*) седе́ть.

gray-haired *adj.* седо́й; седоволо́сый.

graze *v.t.* **1,** (brush lightly, as of a bullet) задева́ть; скользну́ть по. **2,** (put to pasture) пасти́. —*v.i.* пасти́сь. —**grazing land,** па́стбищные уго́дья.

grease *n.* **1,** (melted fat) топлёное са́ло; жир. *Grease spot,* жи́рное пятно́. **2,** (lubricant) сма́зка; мазь. **3,** (ointment) мазь. —*v.t.* сма́зывать. —**grease the palm of,** подма́зывать.

grease monkey *slang* сма́зчик.

grease paint грим.

greasy *adj.* **1,** (smeared with grease) са́льный; жи́рный. **2,** (containing grease, as of food) жи́рный.

great *adj.* **1,** (eminent; outstanding) вели́кий: *a great writer,* вели́кий писа́тель. *Peter the Great,* Пётр Вели́кий. **2,** (large) большо́й: *a great distance,* большо́е расстоя́ние. *To a great extent,* в значи́тельной сте́пени. *Pose the greatest danger,* представля́ть наибо́льшую опа́сность. **3,** (far beyond the ordinary) большо́й; кру́пный: *a great victory,* больша́я/кру́пная побе́да. *A great honor,* больша́я честь. *A great loss,* больша́я поте́ря. *Great friends,* больши́е друзья́. *With great pleasure,* с больши́м удово́льствием. **4,** *colloq.* (splendid) чуде́сный: *have a great time,* чуде́сно провести́ вре́мя. —*adv., colloq.* прекра́сно; чу́дно. *Feel great,* прекра́сно чу́вствовать себя́.

great-aunt *n.* двою́родная ба́бушка.

great circle большо́й круг.

Great Dane да́тский дог.

Greater *adj.* Большо́й: *Greater London,* Большо́й Ло́ндон.

great-granddaughter *n.* пра́внучка.

great-grandfather *n.* пра́дед.

great-grandmother *n.* праба́бка; праба́бушка.

great-grandson *n.* пра́внук.

great-great-granddaughter *n.* прапра́внучка.

great-great-grandfather *n.* прапра́дед.

great-great-grandmother *n.* прапраба́бка; прапраба́бушка.

great-great-grandson *n.* прапра́внук.

greatly *adv.* о́чень; си́льно: *differ greatly from,* о́чень/си́льно отлича́ться от. *Greatly exceed,* намно́го превыша́ть. *He will be greatly missed,* его́ о́чень бу́дет не хвата́ть.

greatness *n.* вели́чие.

great-uncle *n.* двою́родный де́душка.

grebe *n.* пога́нка.

greed *n.* жа́дность; а́лчность.

greedy *adj.* жа́дный; а́лчный. —**greedily,** *adv.* жа́дно. —**greediness,** *n.* = **greed.**

Greek *adj.* гре́ческий. —*n.* **1,** (person) грек; греча́нка. **2,** (language) гре́ческий язы́к.

green *adj.* зелёный. *Be green with envy,* ло́паться от за́висти. —*n.* **1,** (color) зелёный цвет. **2,** *pl.* (leafy vegetables) зе́лень. **3,** (grassy lawn) лужа́йка.

greenery *n.* зе́лень.

green-eyed *adj.* зеленогла́зый.

greengrocer *n.* зеленщи́к.

greenhorn *n.* новичо́к; молокосо́с.

greenhouse *n.* тепли́ца; оранжере́я.

greenish *adj.* зеленова́тый.

green light зелёный свет. —**give someone the green light,** дать кому́-нибудь зелёную у́лицу.

greet *v.t.* **1,** (say hello to) здоро́ваться с. **2,** (welcome) приве́тствовать. **3,** (meet in a specified manner) встреча́ть: *He was greeted with applause,* его́ встре́тили аплодисме́нтами.

greeting *n.* **1,** (salutation) приве́тствие. **2,** *pl.* (regards) приве́т.

gregarious *adj.* **1,** (living in herds) ста́дный. **2,** (fond of company) общи́тельный; компане́йский.

Gregorian *adj.* григориа́нский. —**Gregorian calendar,** григориа́нский календа́рь.

gremlin *n.* чертёнок.

grenade *n.* грана́та: *hand grenade,* ручна́я грана́та. —**grenade launcher,** гранатомёт.

grenadier *n.* гренаде́р.

grey *adj. & n.* = **gray.**

greyhound *n.* борза́я.

grid *n.* **1,** (grating) решётка. **2,** (lines dividing a map) се́тка. **3,** *electricity* се́тка.

griddle *n.* сковоро́дка.

gridiron *n.* **1,** (cooking utensil) ра́шпер. **2,** (football field) футбо́льное по́ле.

grief *adj.* го́ре. —**come to grief,** потерпе́ть неуда́чу. —**good grief!,** бо́же мой!

grief-stricken *adj.* уби́тый го́рем.

grievance *n.* **1,** (wrong; injustice) оби́да. **2,** (complaint) прете́нзия.

grieve *v.t.* огорча́ть; печа́лить. —*v.i.* горева́ть; скорбе́ть; печа́литься; сокруша́ться.

grievous *adj.* **1,** (distressing) мучи́тельный. **2,** (severe; serious) тяжёлый; тя́жкий. *Grievous insult,* кро́вная *or* смерте́льная оби́да.

griffin *n.* гриф; грифо́н.

griffon *n.* (dog) грифо́н. —**griffon vulture,** сип.

grill *n.* **1,** (gridiron) ра́шпер. **2,** (grilled meat) жа́реное (на ра́шпере) мя́со. —*v.t.* **1,** (broil) жа́рить. **2,** *colloq.* (interrogate) допра́шивать.

grille *n.* решётка.

grilled *adj.* жа́реный.

grim *adj.* **1,** (horrible) жу́ткий; стра́шный: *a grim sight/reminder,* жу́ткое зре́лище; стра́шное напомина́ние. **2,** (forbidding; stern) суро́вый: *a grim look on one's face,* суро́вое выраже́ние лица́. **3,** (resolute; relentless) непоколеби́мый: *grim determination,* непоколеби́мая реши́мость.

grimace *n.* грима́са; ужи́мка. —*v.i.* де́лать грима́су; грима́сничать.

grime *n.* грязь; са́жа. —**grimy,** *adj.* гря́зный; запа́чканный.

grin *v.i.* усмеха́ться; ухмыля́ться; ска́лить зу́бы; расплыва́ться в улы́бке. —*n.* усме́шка. —**grin and bear it,** де́лать хоро́шую ми́ну при плохо́й игре́.

grind *v.t.* **1,** (reduce to small particles) моло́ть; разма́лывать; измельча́ть; размельча́ть; растира́ть. *Grind coffee,* моло́ть ко́фе. *Grind meat,* пропуска́ть мя́со че́рез мясору́бку. *Grind into powder,* измельча́ть *or* растира́ть в порошо́к. **2,** (shape by friction) шлифова́ть: *grind a lens,* шлифова́ть ли́нзу. **3,** (sharpen) точи́ть. **4,** (grate, as one's teeth) скрежета́ть (зуба́ми) **5,** (press; force) вда́вливать (в зе́млю); вта́птывать; зата́птывать. —*v.i.* (grate) скрежета́ть. *Grind to a halt,* останови́ться с ля́згом; *fig.* (за)сто́пориться. —*n.* **1,** (degree of fineness) помо́л. **2,** *colloq.* (monotonous routine) коле́я́. **3,** *colloq.* (laborious study) зубрёжка. **4,** *colloq.* (one who so studies) зубрёжка. —**grind away,** *colloq.* **1,** (work steadily) рабо́тать без у́стали. **2,** (study hard) зубри́ть. —**grind down, 1,** (make smooth) шлифова́ть. **2,** (oppress) заму́чить; забива́ть. —**grind out,** *colloq.* штампова́ть. —**grind up,** дроби́ть; измельча́ть.

grinder *n.* **1,** (person) точи́льщик. *Organ grinder,* шарма́нщик. **2,** (machine for crushing) дроби́лка. *Meat grinder,* мясору́бка. *Coffee grinder,* кофемо́лка; кофе́йная ме́льница. **3,** (grindstone) точи́льный стано́к.

grinding *n.* **1,** (pulverizing) растира́ние. **2,** (sharpening) точе́ние. **3,** (grating, as of wheels) скре́жет. —*adj.* мучи́тельный. *Grinding poverty,* кра́йняя нищета́.

grindstone *n.* точи́льный ка́мень. —**keep one's nose to the grindstone,** рабо́тать не поклада́я рук.

grip *v.t.* **1,** (hold tenaciously) кре́пко держа́ться за. **2,** (seize, as of fear) овладева́ть; охва́тывать; обуя́ть. **3,** (engross) захва́тывать. *Grip someone's attention,* завладе́ть чьи́м-нибудь внима́нием. —*n.* **1,** (strong hold) хва́тка: *firm grip,* кре́пкая хва́тка. *Be in the grips of a crisis,* быть в тиска́х кри́зиса. **2,** (small suitcase) чемода́нчик; саквоя́ж. —**come to grips with,** схва́тываться с.

gripe *v.t., colloq.* (annoy) раздража́ть. —*v.i., colloq.* (grouse) ворча́ть. —*n., colloq.* жа́лоба. —**griper,** *n.* ворчу́н.

grippe *n.* грипп.

gripping *adj.* захва́тывающий.

grisly *adj.* жу́ткий; жу́ткий.

grist *n.* зерно́ для помо́ла. —**be grist for** (*or* **bring grist to**) **someone's mill,** лить во́ду на чью́-нибудь ме́льницу.

gristle *n.* хрящ. —**gristly,** *adj.* хрящева́тый.

grit *v.t.* сти́скивать: *grit one's teeth,* сти́скивать зу́бы. —*n.* (pluck) вы́держка.

grizzly bear гри́зли.

groan *v.i.* стона́ть. —*n.* стон.

groats *n.pl.* крупа́.

grocer *n.* бакале́йщик.

groceries *n.pl.* проду́кты; бакале́я; гастроно́мия.

grocery store продукто́вый *or* продово́льственный *or* бакале́йный магази́н; гастроно́м.

grog *n.* грог.

groggy *adj.* обалде́лый; одуре́лый.

groin *n.* пах.

groom *n.* **1,** (stableboy) ко́нюх. **2,** (bridegroom) жени́х. —*v.t.* хо́лить: *well-groomed,* хо́леный.

groove *n.* желобо́к.

grope *v.i.* **1,** (feel one's way) идти́ о́щупью. **2,** *fol. by* **for** (search for clumsily) нащу́пывать; иска́ть о́щупью.

grosbeak *n.* дубоно́с.

gross *adj.* **1,** (fat; heavy) то́лстый; ту́чный. **2,** (crude; flagrant) гру́бый. **3,** (total; without deductions) валово́й: *gross national product,* валово́й национа́льный проду́кт. *Gross weight,* вес бру́тто. —*n.* (144) гросс.

grotesque *adj.* **1,** *art* гроте́скный. **2,** (outlandish) абсу́рдный; карикату́рный.

grotto *n.* грот.

grouch *n., colloq.* брюзга́. —*v.i.* брюзжа́ть. —**grouchy,** *adj.* брюзгли́вый.

ground *n.* **1,** (surface of the earth) земля́: *lie on the ground,* лежа́ть на земле́. **2,** (earth; soil) по́чва: *hard ground,* твёрдая по́чва. **3,** (area used for a specific purpose) площа́дка. *Parade ground,* плац. *Training ground,* уче́бное по́ле. **4,** *pl.* (area surrounding a building) террито́рия: *on the grounds of the embassy,* на террито́рии посо́льства. **5,** *pl.* (basis; valid reason) основа́ние; по́вод. *On what grounds?,* на како́м основа́нии? *Grounds for divorce,* по́вод для разво́да. **6,** *pl.* (dregs; sediment) гу́ща: *coffee grounds,* кофе́йная гу́ща. **7,** *painting* грунт. —*adj.* **1,** (made fine by grinding) мо́лотый; толчёный. **2,** *mil.* (operating on the ground) сухопу́тный; назе́мный: *ground troops,* сухопу́тные/назе́мные войска́. —*v.t.* **1,** (cancel, as a flight) отменя́ть; запреща́ть. **2,** *usu. passive* (teach; instruct) подко́вывать: *well-grounded in mathematics,* хорошо́ подко́ван по матема́тике. **3,** *electricity* заземля́ть. —**be on firm ground,** стоя́ть на твёрдой по́чве. —**burn to the ground,** сжечь *or* сгоре́ть дотла́. —**cover a lot of ground, 1,** (by traveling) покрыва́ть большо́е расстоя́ние. **2,** (in a book, lecture, etc.) косну́ться мно́го вопро́сов. —**cut the ground from under one's feet,** выбива́ть по́чву из-под ног у кого́-нибудь. —**find common ground,** найти́ о́бщий язы́к. —**from the ground up,** с нуля́. —**gain ground,** *see* gain. —**get off the ground, 1,** (of an airplane) оторва́ться от земли́. **2,** (make initial progress) сдви́нуться с ме́ста. —**give ground, 1,** (retreat) отступа́ть. **2,** (yield) сдава́ть пози́ции. —**shift one's ground,** перемени́ть пози́цию. —**stand one's ground,** устоя́ть; стоя́ть на своём.

ground beetle жужелица.

ground floor пе́рвый эта́ж; ни́жний эта́ж.

ground glass притёртое стекло́.

ground hog суро́к.

grounding *n.* подгото́вка: *a good grounding in chemistry,* хоро́шая подгото́вка по хи́мии.

groundless *adj.* необосно́ванный; беспричи́нный; беспо́чвенный; неоснова́тельный; безоснова́тельный; не име́ющий под собо́й по́чвы. *Groundless accusations/fears,* необосно́ванные обвине́ния; беспричи́нные опасе́ния.

ground speed путева́я ско́рость.

ground squirrel су́слик.

groundswell *n.* мёртвая зыбь.

ground water грунтовы́е во́ды.

groundwork *n.* фунда́мент. *Lay the groundwork,* закла́дывать фунда́мент; подгота́вливать по́чву.

group *n.* гру́ппа. *Literary group,* литерату́рный кружо́к. —*adj.* группово́й: *group portrait,* группово́й портре́т. —*v.t.* группирова́ть. —*v.i.* группирова́ться.

grouping *n.* группиро́вка.

grouse *n.* *Black grouse,* те́терев. *Hazel grouse,* ря́бчик. *Wood grouse,* глуха́рь. —*v.i., colloq.* (grumble) ворча́ть.

grove *n.* ро́ща: *orange grove,* апельси́новая ро́ща.

grovel *v.i.* пресмыка́ться; низкопокло́нничать.

grow *v.i.* **1,** (increase in size) расти́: *grow in height,* расти́ в высоту́. *Grow three inches,* вы́расти на три дю́йма. *Let one's hair grow,* отра́щивать *or* отпуска́ть во́лосы. **2,** (increase) расти́; увели́чиваться; уси́ливаться: *Interest is growing,* интере́с (к чему́-нибудь) растёт/увели́чивается/уси́ливается. **3,** (become) станови́ться. *Grow old,* старе́ть. *Grow tired,* устава́ть. —*v.t.* **1,** (cultivate) выра́щивать; разводи́ть: *grow vegetables,* выра́щивать/разводи́ть о́вощи. **2,** (develop, as a beard or mustache) отра́щивать; отпуска́ть. —**grow into, 1,** *literally* враста́ть в: *grow into the soil,* враста́ть в по́чву. **2,** (develop into) выраста́ть в. —**grow out of,** выраста́ть из. —**grow together,** сраста́ться. —**grow up,** расти́; выраста́ть; подраста́ть. *He/she is quite grown up,* он совсе́м вы́рос; она́ совсе́м вы́росла.

grower *n. Rendered by the suffix* -вод: *tobacco grower,* табаково́д; *cotton grower,* хлопково́д.

growing *adj.* расту́щий. —**growing pains,** боле́зни ро́ста.

growl *v.i.* рыча́ть; ворча́ть. —*n.* рыча́ние; ворча́ние.

grown *adj.* взро́слый: *They have two grown sons,* у них два взро́слых сы́на.

grownup *n.* взро́слый; большо́й.

growth *n.* **1,** (development; increase; expansion) рост: *slow growth,* ме́дленный рост. *Economic growth,* экономи́ческий рост. *Population growth,* рост *or* прирост населе́ния. **2,** (tumor) новообразова́ние; наро́ст; о́пухоль.

grub *n.* **1,** (larva) личи́нка. **2,** *slang* (food) харчи́. —*v.t.* (clear of roots; root out) выкорчёвывать. —*v.i.* **1,** (rummage) ры́ться. **2,** (toil) труди́ться.

grubby *adj.* неря́шливый; гря́зный.

grudge *n.* зло́ба. *Have/bear a grudge against,* пита́ть *or* (за)таи́ть зло́бу к *or* про́тив; (за)таи́ть оби́ду на; *colloq.* име́ть зуб про́тив. —*v.t.* = **begrudge.**

grudging *adj.* неохо́тный. —**grudgingly,** *adv.* неохо́тно; нехотя́; с неохо́той; скрепя́ се́рдце.

gruel *n.* каши́ца; размазня́.

grueling *also,* **gruelling** *adj.* изнури́тельный.

gruesome *adj.* ужа́сный; жу́ткий.

gruff *adj.* гру́бый: *gruff voice,* грубый го́лос.

grumble *v.i.* брюзжа́ть; ропта́ть; ворча́ть. —**grumbler,** *n.* брюзга́; ворчу́н.

grumpy *adj.* брюзгли́вый; ворчли́вый.

grunt *v.i.* хрю́кать. —*n.* хрю́канье.

guano *n.* гуа́но.

guarantee *n.* гара́нтия; руча́тельство; поручи́тельство. *A two-year guarantee,* гара́нтия *or* руча́тельство на два го́да. —*v.t.* гаранти́ровать; руча́ться за.

guarantor *n.* поручи́тель; гара́нт.

guard *v.t.* охраня́ть; стере́чь; сторожи́ть; карау́лить. *The border is well guarded,* грани́ца хорошо́ охраня́ется. —*v.i.* [*usu.* **guard against**] бере́чься (+ *gen.*); остерега́ться (+ *gen.*). —*n.* **1,** (one who guards) сто́рож; часово́й; охра́нник; вахтёр. *Prison guard,* надзира́тель. **2,** (unit that guards) карау́л; стра́жа; охра́на. *Guard of honor,* почётный карау́л. *Palace guard,* дворцо́вая охра́на. *Changing of the guard,* сме́на карау́ла. **3,** *often pl.* (unit of troops) гва́рдия: *National Guard,* Национа́льная гва́рдия. *Red Guards,* Кра́сная гва́рдия. **4,** (state of watchfulness) бди́тельность: *relax/lower one's guard,* ослабля́ть бди́тельность. *Be on one's guard,* быть насторо́же; быть начеку́; гляде́ть в о́ба. *Catch off guard,* заста́ть враспло́х. *Put on one's guard,* наста́раживать. **5,** (device that protects) щит: *mudguard,* щит от гря́зи. **6,** *sports* защи́тник. —*adj.* карау́льный: *guard duty,* карау́льная слу́жба. —**stand guard,** стоя́ть на часа́х/ в карау́ле/ на стра́же/. —**under guard,** под охра́ной; под конво́ем.

guarded *adj.* **1,** (watched; protected) охраня́емый: *a well guarded building,* хорошо́ охраня́емое зда́ние. **2,** (cautious; circumspect) осторо́жный; насторо́женный: *guarded comments,* осторо́жные/насторо́женные замеча́ния. *Guarded prognosis,* сде́ржанный прогно́з.

guardhouse *n.* **1,** (house used by a guard) карау́льная. **2,** (military prison) гауптва́хта.

guardian *n.* **1,** (protector) блюсти́тель; страж. *Guardian of the law,* блюсти́тель поря́дка. **2,** (one assigned to care for a minor) опеку́н; попечи́тель. —**guardian angel,** а́нгел-храни́тель.

guardianship *n.* опе́ка; опеку́нство; попечи́тельство.

guardsman *n.* гварде́ец.

gubernatorial *adj.* губерна́торский.

gudgeon *n.* песка́рь.

guerrilla *n.* партиза́н. —*adj.* партиза́нский: *guerrilla warfare,* партиза́нская война́.

guess *v.t. & i.* **1,** (make a guess) дога́дываться; уга́дывать; отга́дывать. *Guess someone's intentions,* догада́ться о чьи́х-нибудь наме́рениях; угада́ть *or* отгада́ть чьи́-нибудь наме́рения. *Guess who came to see us!*, угада́йте *or* отгада́йте, кто к нам пришёл! *You'll never guess!*, ни за что не угада́ете *or* догада́етесь. **2,** (think; suppose) полага́ть. —*n.* дога́дка.

guesser *n.* отга́дчик.

guesswork *n.* дога́дки; гада́ние. *By guesswork,* науга́д.

guest *n.* гость. *Guest of honor,* почётный гость. —**guest conductor,** приглашённый дирижёр.

guest room ко́мната для госте́й.

guffaw *v.i.* хохота́ть. —*n.* хо́хот.

guidance *n.* **1,** (direction) руково́дство. **2,** (advice) консульта́ция. **3,** *aerospace* наведе́ние.

guide *v.t.* **1,** (lead; conduct) вести́: *guide someone along a path,* вести́ кого́-нибудь по тропи́нке. **2,** (supervise; give guidance to) руководи́ть. *Be guided by,* руково́дствоваться (+ *instr.*). —*n.* **1,** (person who guides) гид; проводни́к. *Tour guide,* экскурсово́д. **2,** (guidebook) путеводи́тель. **3,** (manual; handbook) руково́дство: *a guide to automotive repairs,* руково́дство по авторемо́нту. **4,** (something that shows the way) руково́дство: *a guide to action,* руково́дство к де́йствию.

guidebook *n.* путеводи́тель.

guided missile управля́емая раке́та; управля́емый реакти́вный снаря́д.

guided tour экску́рсия с ги́дом.

guideline *n.* руково́дство.

guidepost *n.* указа́тельный столб.

guiding *adj.* руководя́щий: *guiding principle,* руководя́щий при́нцип.

guild *n.* ги́льдия; цех.

guilder *n.* гу́льден.

guile *n.* хи́трость.

guillemot *n.* чи́стик.

guillotine *n.* гильоти́на. —*v.t.* гильотини́ровать.

guilt *n.* вина́; вино́вность. *Admit one's guilt,* признава́ть свою́ вину́. *Sense of guilt,* чу́вство вины́.

guiltless *adj.* неви́нный; невино́вный.

guilty *adj.* **1,** (having done wrong) винова́тый. **2,** (having committed a crime) вино́вный. *Guilty party,* вино́вник. *Guilty of murder,* вино́вный в уби́йстве. *He was found guilty,* его́ призна́ли вино́вным. **3,** (showing or feeling guilt) винова́тый: *guilty look,* винова́тый вид. *Guilty conscience,* нечи́стая со́весть. —**plead guilty,** признава́ть себя́ вино́вным. —**plead not guilty,** не признава́ть себя́ вино́вным. —**verdict of "guilty",** обвини́тельный пригово́р. —**verdict of "not guilty",** оправда́тельный пригово́р.

guinea *n.* гине́я.

guinea fowl цеза́рка. *Also,* **guinea hen.**

guinea pig 1, (rodent) морска́я сви́нка. **2,** (person used in experiments) подо́пытный кро́лик.

guise *n.* вид: *in the guise of,* под ви́дом (+ *gen.*).

guitar *n.* гита́ра. —**guitarist,** *n.* гитари́ст.

gulf *n.* **1,** (body of water) зали́в. **2,** (chasm) про́пасть.

gull *n.* ча́йка.

gullet *n.* **1,** (esophagus) пищево́д. **2,** (throat) гло́тка.

gullible *adj.* легкове́рный. —**gullibility,** *n.* легкове́рие.

gully *n.* овра́г.

gulp *v.t. & i.* (бы́стро) глота́ть; хлеба́ть. *Don't gulp down your food!,* не глота́й еду́!; не глота́й, не жуя́ *or* не (раз)жева́в! —*n.* глото́к: *in one gulp,* одни́м глотко́м; за́лпом.

gum *n.* **1,** (substance) каме́дь; гу́мми. **2,** (chewing gum) жева́тельная рези́нка; жва́чка. **3,** (flesh in which the teeth are set) десна́. —*v.t.* **1,** (glue in place) накле́ивать. **2,** *fol. by* **up,** *slang* (botch up) напу́тать. —**gum arabic,** гуммиара́бик.

gumbo *n.* ба́мия; о́кра.

gumboil *n.* флюс.

gummy *adj.* кле́йкий; ли́пкий.

gun *n.* **1,** (portable firearm) ружьё. **2,** (pistol) пистоле́т. **3,** (heavy weapon) ору́дие; пу́шка. *Coastal/shore guns,* береговы́е ору́дия. *Machine gun,* пулемёт. —*adj.* оруди́йный: *gun sight,* оруди́йный прице́л. —*v.t.* **1,** (race, as an engine) дава́ть по́лный газ (+ *dat.*). **2,** *fol. by* **down** (shoot; kill) застрели́ть. **3,** *fol. by* **for** (seek to catch) охо́титься за; (seek to obtain) стреми́ться к. —**stick to one's guns,** стоя́ть на своём. —**under the gun,** под уда́ром.

gunboat *n.* канони́рская ло́дка; канони́рка. —**gunboat diplomacy,** «диплома́тия канони́рок».

gun carriage лафе́т.

gunfire *n.* оруди́йный ого́нь. *Exchange of gunfire,* перестре́лка.

gunman *n.* банди́т.

gunner *n.* артиллери́ст; пулемётчик; стрело́к.

gunnery *n.* артиллери́йское де́ло. *Gunnery school,* артиллери́йская шко́ла.

gunpoint *n.,* *in* **at gunpoint,** под ду́лом пистоле́та.

gunpowder *n.* по́рох.

gunshot *n.* вы́стрел. *Gunshot wound,* огнестре́льная ра́на.

gunsmith *n.* оруже́йный ма́стер; оруже́йник; руже́йник.

gunwale *n.* планши́р.

gurgle *v.i.* бу́лькать. —*n.* бу́льканье.

gush *v.i.* хлы́нуть; бры́згать; бить; бить *or* бры́згать фонта́ном. *Blood gushed from the wound,* кровь хлы́нула *or* бры́знула из ра́ны.

gusset *n.* клин.

gust *n.* поры́в: *gust of wind,* поры́в ве́тра.

gustatory *adj.* вкусово́й.

gusto *n.* смак. *With gusto,* со сма́ком; взахлёб.

gusty *adj.* **1,** (of wind) поры́вистый. **2,** (of weather conditions) ве́треный.

gut *n.* **1,** (intestine) кишка́. **2,** *pl., slang* (courage) дух: *He hasn't the guts to...,* у него́ не хвата́ет ду́ха (+ *inf.*). —*adj., colloq.* **1,** (instinctive, as of a reaction) инстинкти́вный. **2,** (basic, as of an issue) жи́зненно ва́жный. —*v.t.* **1,** (remove the intestines from) потроши́ть. **2,** (destroy) опустоша́ть. —**hate someone's guts,** *colloq.* смерте́льно ненави́деть кого́-нибудь.

gutta-percha *n.* гуттапе́рча.

gutter *n.***1,** (alongside a street or road) сто́чная кана́ва. **2,** (of a roof) водосто́чный жёлоб; водосто́чная кана́ва.

guttersnipe *n.* беспризо́рник; у́личный мальчи́шка.

guttural *adj.* горта́нный; горлово́й.

guy *n., colloq.* па́рень; ма́лый. *Nice guy,* сла́вный ма́лый.

guzzle *v.t.* лака́ть.

gym *n., colloq.* = **gymnasium.**

gymnasium *n.* гимнасти́ческий зал; спорти́вный зал; спортза́л.

gymnast *n.* гимна́ст; гимна́стка. —**gymnastic,** *adj.* гимнасти́ческий. —**gymnastics,** *n.pl.* гимна́стика.

gym suit спорти́вный костю́м.

gynecology *also,* **gynaecology** *n.* гинеколо́гия. —**gy-**

necological, *adj.* гинекологи́ческий. —**gynecologist,** *n.* гинеко́лог.

gyp *n., slang* **1,** (swindler) жу́лик; плут. **2,** (swindle) афе́ра. —*v.t., colloq.* обжу́ливать.

gypsum *n.* гипс.

Gypsy *also,* **Gipsy** *n.* цыга́н; цыга́нка. —*adj.* цыга́нский. —**gypsy moth,** непа́рный шелкопря́д.

gyrate *v.i.* враща́ться (по кру́гу); крути́ться. —**gyration,** *n.* враще́ние.

gyrfalcon *n.* кре́чет.

gyrocompass *n.* гироко́мпас.

gyroscope *n.* гироско́п.

H

H, h восьма́я бу́ква англи́йского алфави́та.

haberdasher *n.* галантере́йщик.

haberdashery *n.* **1,** (goods) галантере́я. **2,** (shop) галантере́йный магази́н; галантере́я.

habit *n.* **1,** (customary practice) привы́чка: *bad habit,* дурна́я привы́чка. *Drug habit,* наркома́ния. *Be in the habit of,* име́ть привы́чку *or* обыкнове́ние (+ *inf.*). *It has become a habit with him,* Э́то вошло́ у него́ в привы́чку. **2,** *pl.* (mannerisms) пова́дки: *study the habits of a wolf,* изуча́ть пова́дки во́лка. **3,** (garb): *riding habit,* амазо́нка; *monk's habit,* мона́шеская ря́са.

habitable *adj.* го́дный для жилья́.

habitat *n.* среда́; стихи́я.

habitation *n.* жильё: *unfit for human habitation,* неприго́дный для жилья́.

habitual *adj.* **1,** (customary) привы́чный; обы́чный. **2,** (of the nature of a habit) застаре́лый; закорене́лый. *Habitual drunkenness,* застаре́лое пья́нство. **3,** (inveterate) закорене́лый; отъя́вленный. *Habitual liar,* отъя́вленный лгун.

habitually *adv.* постоя́нно; ве́чно.

habituate *v.t.* приуча́ть.

habitué *n.* завсегда́тай.

hack *n.* **1,** (tool) кайло́. **2,** (banal writer) халту́рщик. —*adj.* халту́рный. —*v.t.* руби́ть; разруба́ть. *Hack to death,* заруби́ть.

hacking *adj.* надса́дный: *hacking cough,* надса́дный ка́шель.

hackneyed *adj.* изби́тый; зата́сканный.

hacksaw *n.* ножо́вка.

hackwork *n.* халту́ра.

haddock *n.* пи́кша.

Hades *n.* ад; преиспо́дняя.

haematite *n.* = **hematite.**

haematology *n.* = **hematology.**

haemoglobin *n.* = **hemoglobin.** —**haemophilia,** *n.* = **hemophilia.** —**haemorrhage,** *n.* = **hemorrhage.** —**haemorrhoid,** *n.* = **hemorrhoid.**

hafnium *n.* га́фний.

haft *n.* черено́к.

hag *n.* ве́дьма; карга́.

haggard *adj.* изможде́нный; исхуда́лый.

haggle *v.i.* торгова́ться. *Haggle over every penny,* торгова́ться из-за ка́ждой копе́йки.

hagiography *n.* агиогра́фия.

hail *n.* град. *Hail of bullets,* град пуль. —*v.t.* **1,** (call) оклика́ть. *Hail a taxi,* подозва́ть такси́. **2,** (greet; welcome) приве́тствовать. **3,** (acclaim) расхва́ливать. —*v.i.* **1,** (be hailing): *It is hailing,* идёт град. **2,** *fol. by* **from** (be from) быть ро́дом из: *He hails from Michigan,* он ро́дом из Мичига́на.

hailstone *n.* гра́дина.

hailstorm *n.* гроза́ с гра́дом.

hair *n.* **1,** (of a human being) во́лосы: *red hair,* ры́жие во́лосы. *Comb one's hair,* причёсываться. *A single hair,* во́лос. *Tuft of hair,* клок воло́с. **2,** (of an animal) шерсть: *camel's hair,* верблю́жья шерсть. —*adj.* волосяно́й. *Hair net,* се́тка для воло́с. —**split hairs,** спо́рить о мелоча́х; вдава́ться в то́нкости. —**tear one's hair,** рвать на себе́ во́лосы.

hairbreadth *also,* **hairsbreadth** *n., in* **within a hairbreadth of,** на волосо́к (*or* на волоске́) от.

hairbrush *n.* щётка для воло́с.

haircut *n.* стри́жка. *Get a haircut,* стри́чься; пострига́ться.

hairdo *n.* причёска.

hairdresser *n.* парикма́хер.

hair dryer фен.

hairpiece *n.* пари́к; накла́дка.

hairpin *n.* шпи́лька.

hair-raising *adj.* душераздира́ющий.

hair shirt власяни́ца.

hair spray лак для воло́с.

hairspring *n.* волосо́к (в часа́х).

hairstyle *n.* причёска.

hairy *adj.* волоса́тый.

Haitian *adj.* гаитя́нский. —*n.* гаитя́нин; гаитя́нка.

hake *n.* хек.

halberd *n.* алеба́рда.

halcyon *n.* зиморо́док. —*adj.* споко́йный; бла́гостный.

hale *adj.* кре́пкий; здоро́вый. —*v.t.* тащи́ть: *hale into court*, тащи́ть в суд. —**hale and hearty**, бо́дрый; ядрёный.

half *n.* полови́на: *half of the money*, полови́на де́нег. *One and a half*, полтора́. *Two and a half*, два с полови́ной. *Half past four*, полови́на пя́того. *At half past twelve*, в полови́не пе́рвого. *In half the time*, в два ра́за быстре́е. ♦*Often rendered by the prefixes* пол- *and* полу-: *half an hour*, полчаса́; *a half-turn*, полуоборо́т. —*adj.* полови́нный: *a half share*, полови́нная до́ля. *A half portion*, полпо́рции. *At half strength*, в полови́нном соста́ве. —*adv.* наполови́ну: *half done*, наполови́ну сде́лано. ♦*Also with* вдво́е *and comp. adj. of opp. meaning*: *half as much*, вдво́е ме́ньше. *He is half my age*, он вдво́е моло́же меня́. *Be half the price of*, быть вдво́е дешевле (+ *gen.*). —**go halves with**, войти́ в до́лю с. —**half again as many** *or* **much**, в полтора́ ра́за бо́льше. —**in half, 1,** (into two parts) попола́м: *divide in half*, дели́ть попола́м. **2,** (by half) наполови́ну; вдво́е: *reduce the deficit in half*, уменьша́ть дефици́т наполови́ну/вдво́е. *His popularity dropped in half*, его́ популя́рность упа́ла вдво́е. —**listen with half an ear**, слу́шать кра́ем у́ха *or* вполу́ха. —**that's not the half of it**, э́то далеко́ не всё.

half-asleep *adj. Be half-asleep*, быть в полусне́. *While half-asleep*, сквозь сон.

halfback *n.* полузащи́тник.

half-baked *adj.* **1,** (incompletely baked) недопечённый. **2,** *fig.* (crude; not well planned) доморо́щенный.

half-blooded *adj.* полукро́вный; нечистокро́вный.

half-breed *n.* полукро́вка.

half brother сво́дный брат; брат по отцу́; брат по ма́тери.

half-dead *adj.* полумёртвый.

half-dozen *n.* полдю́жины.

half-empty *adj.* полупусто́й; наполови́ну пусто́й.

halfhearted *adj.* нереши́тельный; неохо́тный.

half-hour *n.* полчаса́. *Every half-hour*, ка́ждые полчаса́.

half-life *n.* пери́од полураспа́да.

half-mast *n.* приспу́щенный флаг. *Lower a flag to half-mast*, приспуска́ть флаг.

half-measure *n.* полуме́ра.

half-moon *n.* полуме́сяц.

half note полови́нная но́та.

half-price *n.* полцены́: *at half-price*, за полцены́. *Pay half-price*, заплати́ть полцены́.

half sister сво́дная сестра́; сестра́ по отцу́; сестра́ по ма́тери.

half slip ни́жняя ю́бка.

half-staff *n.* = **half-mast**.

half tone *music* полуто́н.

halftone *n., art* полуто́н.

half-truth *n.* полупра́вда.

half-turn *n.* полуоборо́т.

halfway *adv.* на полупути́: *stop halfway*, остана́вливаться на полупути́. *Turn back halfway*, возвраща́ться с полупути́. *Meet someone halfway*, идти́ навстре́чу (+ *dat.*). *Fly halfway around the world*, лете́ть че́рез полови́ну земно́го ша́ра. —*adj.* **1,** (midway): *the halfway point*, полпути́. **2,** (inadequate; indecisive) полови́нчатый.

half-wit *n.* дура́к; болва́н. —**half-witted,** *adj.* слабоу́мный.

halibut *n.* па́лтус.

hall *n.* **1,** (large public room or building) зал. *Town/city hall*, ра́туша. **2,** (vestibule) пере́дняя; прихо́жая. **3,** (corridor) коридо́р.

hallelujah *interj.* аллилу́йя.

hallmark *n.* **1,** (of precious metals) про́ба. **2,** (indication of excellence) при́знак; крите́рий.

halloo *interj.* ату́!; улюлю́! —*v.i.* улюлю́кать.

hallow *v.t.* освяща́ть. *Hallowed ground*, свята́я земля́.

Halloween *n.* кану́н дня всех святы́х (= *Allhallows eve*).

hallucination *n.* галлюцина́ция.

hallway *n.* **1,** (vestibule) пере́дняя; прихо́жая. **2,** (corridor) коридо́р.

halo *n.* орео́л.

halogen *n.* галоге́н.

halt *v.t.* **1,** (bring to a stop) остана́вливать. **2,** (cease; terminate) прекраща́ть. —*v.i.* остана́вливаться. —*n.* **1,** (stop) остано́вка. **2,** (cessation) прекраще́ние. —**call a halt to**, прекрати́ть; положи́ть коне́ц (+ *dat.*). —**come to a halt, 1,** (stop moving) остана́вливаться. **2,** (end) прекраща́ться.

halter *n.* **1,** (strap for confining an animal) недоу́здок. **2,** (woman's garment) лиф.

halting *adj.* **1,** (unsteady) неве́рный: *halting gait*, неве́рная похо́дка. **2,** (hesitant) свя́занный: *halting speech*, свя́занная речь.

halvah *also,* **halva** *n.* халва́.

halve *v.t.* **1,** (divide in two) дели́ть попола́м. **2,** (reduce by half) уменьша́ть вдво́е *or* наполови́ну.

halyard *n.* фал.

ham *n.* **1,** (meat) ветчина́. *Ham sandwich*, бутербро́д с ветчино́й. **2,** *slang* (one who overacts) позёр. **3,** [*usu.* **ham operator**] *colloq.* (amateur radio operator) радиолюби́тель.

hamburger *n.* ру́бленая котле́та.

Hamitic *adj.* хами́тский.

hamlet *n.* дереву́шка.

hammer *n.* **1,** (tool) молото́к. *Large hammer*, мо́лот. **2,** (of a gun) куро́к. **3,** *sports* мо́лот: *hammer throw*, мета́ние мо́лота. —*v.t.* **1,** (drive in with a hammer) вбива́ть; забива́ть: *hammer a nail into a wall,* вбива́ть/забива́ть гвоздь в сте́ну. **2**, *fol. by* **out** (shape with a hammer) выбива́ть. *Hammer out a dent,* выбива́ть вмя́тину молотко́м. **3**, *fig.* (drum in by continual repetition) вбива́ть в го́лову. **4**, *fol. by* **out,** *fig.* (forge, as an agreement) выраба́тывать. —*v.i.* **1**, (use a hammer) рабо́тать *or* стуча́ть молотко́м. **2**, (knock; pound) колоти́ть.

hammerhead *n.* мо́лот-ры́ба.

hammock *n.* гама́к; подвесна́я ко́йка.

hamper *v.t.* меша́ть; затрудня́ть; препя́тствовать. *Hamper progress,* препя́тствовать прогре́ссу. *Hamper the work of the committee,* меша́ть рабо́те комите́та. —*n.* корзи́на.

hamster *n.* хомя́к.

hand *n.* **1**, (part of the body) рука́: *right hand,* пра́вая рука́. **2**, (of a clock) стре́лка: *minute hand,* мину́тная стре́лка. **3**, *often pl.* (worker; personnel) рабо́чий; (рабо́чие) ру́ки. *Hired hand,* наёмный рабо́чий. *There are not enough hands available,* не хвата́ет рабо́чих рук. *All hands on deck!,* все наве́рх! **4**, (help; assistance) по́мощь: *give/lend someone a helping hand,* подава́ть кому́-нибудь ру́ку по́мощи. **5**, (handwriting) по́черк; рука́. **6**, (permission to marry) рука́: *ask for someone's hand,* проси́ть руки́ кого́-нибудь. **7**, *colloq.* (round of applause) аплодисме́нты. **8**, *cards* ка́рты: *a bad hand,* плохи́е ка́рты. —*adj.* ручно́й: *hand luggage,* ручно́й бага́ж; *hand brake,* ручно́й то́рмоз. *Hand towel,* полоте́нце для рук. —*v.t.* **1**, (give) передава́ть: *Hand me my hat,* переда́йте мне шля́пу. **2**, (present) вруча́ть: *hand the ambassador a statement,* вручи́ть заявле́ние послу́. —**at hand, 1**, (nearby) под руко́й. **2**, (about to occur) на носу́. *Victory is at hand,* побе́да близка́. —**at the hands of,** от рук (+ *gen.*). —**by hand, 1**, (manually) ручны́м спо́собом. *This carpet is made by hand,* э́тот ковёр — ручно́й рабо́ты; э́тот ковёр сде́лан ручны́м спо́собом. *Copy by hand,* писа́ть от руки́. **2**, (in person) вручну́ю: *deliver by hand,* доставля́ть вручну́ю. —**first hand,** из пе́рвых рук. —**from hand to hand,** из рук в ру́ки. —**get off one's hands,** сбыва́ть с рук. —**get one's hands on,** добира́ться до: *Wait till I get my hands on him!,* я ещё до него́ доберу́сь! *Everything they could get their hands on,* всё, что им попа́лось под ру́ку. —**get out of hand, 1**, (of a person) отбива́ться от рук. **2**, (of a situation) выходи́ть из-под контро́ля. —**hand down, 1**, (pass on) передава́ть: *The legend was handed down from generation to generation,* леге́нда передава́лась из поколе́ния в поколе́ние. **2**, (deliver; render, as a verdict) выноси́ть (пригово́р). —**hand in,** подава́ть; сдава́ть. —**hand in hand,** рука́ о́б руку. *Go hand in hand with (fig.),* идти́ рука́ о́б руку с. —**hand it to,** *colloq.* отдава́ть до́лжное (+ *dat.*). —**hand out,** выдава́ть; раздава́ть. —**hand over,** передава́ть; отдава́ть; сдава́ть. —**hands down,** легко́; без труда́. —**hands off!,** ру́ки прочь! —**hands up!,** ру́ки вверх! —**have a hand in,** приложи́ть ру́ку к; игра́ть роль в. —**have one's hands full,** име́ть рабо́ты по го́рло. *I have my hands full,* у меня́

хлопо́т по́лон рот. —**have on one's hands,** име́ть на рука́х: *I have two small children on my hands,* у меня́ на рука́х дво́е ма́леньких дете́й. —**know like the back of one's hand,** знать как свои́ пять па́льцев. —**live from hand to mouth,** перебива́ться с хле́ба на квас. —**on hand, 1**, (available) на рука́х; под руко́й. **2**, (present) налицо́. —**on the one hand,** с одно́й стороны́. —**on the other hand, 1**, (from another standpoint) с друго́й стороны́. **2**, (by contrast) напро́тив. —**play into the hands of,** игра́ть на́ руку (+ *dat.*). —**reveal** *or* **tip one's hand,** раскры́ть свои́ ка́рты. —**strengthen someone's hand,** уси́ливать чьи́-нибудь пози́ции. —**take in hand,** брать в ру́ки; прибира́ть к рука́м; брать в оборо́т. —**take into one's own hands,** брать в свои́ ру́ки. —**tie someone's hands,** свя́зывать ру́ки (+ *dat.*); свя́зывать (+ *acc.*) по рука́м и нога́м. *My hands are tied,* у меня́ свя́заны ру́ки; я свя́зан по рука́м и нога́м. —**try one's hand at,** про́бовать свои́ си́лы (*or* себя́) в (+ *prepl.*).

handbag *n.* су́мка; су́мочка.

handball *n.* гандбо́л; ручно́й мяч.

handbill *n.* рекла́мный листо́к.

handbook *n.* руково́дство.

handcar *n.* дрези́на.

handcart *n.* ручна́я теле́жка.

hand cream крем для рук.

handcuff *v.t.* надева́ть нару́чники на. —**handcuffs,** *n.pl.* нару́чники.

handful *n.* **1**, (as much as the hand will hold) горсть; при́горшня. **2**, (small number) го́рстка; ку́чка: *a handful of volunteers,* го́рстка/ку́чка доброво́льцев. *Only a handful survived,* вы́жили едини́цы.

hand grenade ручна́я грана́та.

handgun *n.* ручно́е огнестре́льное ору́жие.

handicap *n.* **1**, *sports* гандика́п. **2**, (disadvantage) недоста́ток. **3**, (disability) физи́ческий недоста́ток. —*v.t.* **1**, (put a handicap on) дава́ть гандика́п (+ *dat.*). **2**, (put at a disadvantage) препя́тствовать; затрудня́ть.

handicapped *adj.* с физи́ческими недоста́тками.

handicraft *n.* **1**, (craft) ремесло́. **2**, *pl.* (products so made) куста́рные изде́лия. —**handicraftsman,** *n.* реме́сленник; куста́рь.

handily *adv.* **1**, (deftly) ло́вко. **2**, (easily) без труда́.

handiwork *n.* **1**, (manual work) ручна́я рабо́та. **2**, (work; creation) де́ло рук. *It's his handiwork,* э́то его́ рук де́ло.

handkerchief *n.* носово́й плато́к.

handle *n.* ру́чка; рукоя́тка. *Ax handle,* топори́ще. —*v.t.* **1**, (touch) тро́гать. **2**, (manipulate; treat) обраща́ться с: *handle with care,* обраща́ться с осторо́жностью. **3**, (operate) управля́ть; обраща́ться с. **4**, (deal with) справля́ться с. **5**, (deal in) торгова́ть (+ *instr.*). —*v.i. This car handles easily,* э́той маши́ной легко́ управля́ть. —**fly off the handle,** *colloq.* лезть на́ стену.

handlebar *n.* руль (велосипе́да).

handling *n.* обраще́ние.

handmade *adj.* ручно́й рабо́ты: *This tie is handmade,* э́тот га́лстук — ручно́й рабо́ты.

hand organ шарма́нка.

handout *n.* пода́чка.

handrail *n.* пери́ла; по́ручни.

handsaw *n.* ручна́я пила́; ножо́вка.

handshake *n.* пожа́тие (руки́); рукопожа́тие.

handsome *adj.* **1,** (good-looking) краси́вый. **2,** (considerable) изря́дный: *a handsome sum,* изря́дная су́мма.

handstand *n.* сто́йка. *Do a handstand,* стать на́ руки; де́лать сто́йку на рука́х.

hand-to-hand *adj.* рукопа́шный: *hand-to-hand combat,* рукопа́шный бой.

handwriting *n.* по́черк.

handwritten *adj.* от руки́; руко́й напи́санный; рукопи́сный; собственноручный.

handy *adj.* **1,** (dexterous) ло́вкий; иску́сный. **2,** (within easy reach) под руко́й. **3,** (convenient; useful) удо́бный; поле́зный. —**come in handy,** приходи́ться кста́ти; пригоди́ться.

hang *v.t.* **1,** (fasten from above) ве́шать: *hang a picture,* ве́шать карти́ну. *Hang a door,* наве́шивать дверь. *Hang wallpaper,* кле́ить обо́и. **2,** (execute) ве́шать. *Hang oneself,* ве́шаться. *He was hanged,* он был пове́шен. **3,** (let droop, as one's head) ве́шать; поника́ть; пону́рить. **4,** (decorate with hanging things) уве́шивать; обве́шивать; заве́шивать. **5,** *in* **hang fire,** дать осе́чку. —*v.i.* висе́ть: *hang from the ceiling,* висе́ть на потолке́. *Hang by its tail,* висе́ть на хвосте́. *Hang by a thread, see* **thread.** —*n.* сноро́вка. *Get the hang of,* напрактикова́ться в (+ *prepl.*); наловчи́ться (+ *inf.*); наби́ть ру́ку на (+ *prepl.*). —**hang around, 1,** (spend time idly) слоня́ться; окола́чиваться, **2,** *fol. by* **with** (keep company with) води́ться с; якша́ться с. —**hang down,** свиса́ть; повиса́ть; обвиса́ть; отвиса́ть. —**hang on, 1,** (hold on) держа́ться. **2,** (hold the line) не ве́шать (*or* не класть) тру́бку. **3,** (persist, as of a cold) упо́рствовать. **4,** *Hang on every word,* лови́ть ка́ждое сло́во. —**hang on to,** держа́ться за; приде́рживать; повиса́ть на. —**hang onto,** (retain) оставля́ть (себе́); не выбра́сывать. —**hang out, 1,** (hang up, as wash) выве́шивать. **2,** (lean out) высо́вываться. **3,** *colloq.* (spend one's time) крути́ться. —**hang over,** висе́ть над; нависа́ть над. —**hang up, 1,** (place on a hanger or hook) ве́шать. **2,** (a telephone receiver) ве́шать; класть; броса́ть (тру́бку).

hangar *n.* анга́р.

hanger *n.* ве́шалка.

hanger-on *n.* нахле́бник; прижива́льщик.

hanging *n.* **1,** (execution) пове́шение: *death by hanging,* казнь че́рез пове́шение. **2,** *usu. pl.* (something hung on a wall) драпиро́вки. —*adj.* вися́чий: *hanging lamp,* вися́чая ла́мпа.

hangman *n.* пала́ч.

hangnail *n.* заусе́ница.

hangover *n.* **1,** (remnant) пережи́ток. **2,** (aftereffect of intoxication) похме́лье.

hank *n.* мото́к.

hanker *v.i.* жа́ждать. —**hankering,** *n.* жела́ние; жа́жда.

haphazard *adj.* беспоря́дочный; бессисте́мный. —**haphazardly,** *adv.* беспоря́дочно; как попа́ло.

hapless *adj.* несча́стный; злополу́чный.

happen *v.i.* **1,** (take place) случа́ться; происходи́ть. *What happened?,* что случи́лось? *Nothing happened,* ничего́ не случи́лось. *It happens to everybody,* э́то быва́ет со все́ми. *As often happens,* как э́то ча́сто быва́ет. *It happened in Riga,* де́ло бы́ло в Ри́ге. *It so happens that...,* случи́лось так, что... *As if nothing happened,* как ни в чём не быва́ло. *Don't let it happen again!,* чтобы э́того бо́льше не́ было! **2,** *fol. by* **to** (become of; befall) случа́ться с: *What happened to him?,* что случи́лось с ним? **3,** *fol. by inf.* (chance) *Did you happen to see where I left my glasses?,* вы случа́йно не ви́дели куда́ я дел (де́ла) свои́ очки́? **4,** *fol. by* **on** *or* **upon** (run into; come upon) натыка́ться на; ната́лкиваться на.

happening *n.* слу́чай; собы́тие.

happenstance *n.* случа́йность: *by pure happenstance,* по чи́стой случа́йности.

happily *adv.* **1,** (in happiness) счастли́во: *live happily,* жить счастли́во. **2,** (gladly) с ра́достью. **3,** (luckily) к сча́стью.

happiness *n.* сча́стье.

happy *adj.* **1,** (joyous; contented) счастли́вый: *happy child/day/marriage,* счастли́вый ребёнок/день/брак. *Happy life,* счастли́вая жизнь. *You've made me very happy,* вы меня́ о́чень обра́довали. **2,** (pleased) счастли́вый; рад. *I'm very happy to see you,* я о́чень рад (ра́да) вас ви́деть. *I'm happy that you're here at last,* я сча́стлив(а), что вы наконе́ц пришли́. *We're very happy for you,* мы о́чень ра́ды за вас. *I'll be happy to do it,* я бу́ду рад (ра́да) сде́лать э́то; мне бу́дет прия́тно сде́лать э́то; я с удово́льствием сде́лаю э́то. **3,** (satisfactory, as of an outcome) счастли́вый; благополу́чный. *Happy ending,* счастли́вый коне́ц. **4,** (fortunate) уда́чный: *happy choice,* уда́чный вы́бор. —**Happy Birthday!,** (Поздравля́ю вас) с днём рожде́ния! —**happy medium,** золота́я середи́на. —**Happy New Year!,** с Но́вым го́дом!

happy-go-lucky *adj.* беззабо́тный; беспе́чный.

hara-kiri *n.* хараки́ри.

harass *v.t.* **1,** (harry; torment) издева́ться над; изводи́ть; трави́ть. **2,** (pester; molest) пристава́ть к. **3,** *mil.* изма́тывать. —**harassment,** *n.* издева́тельство; тра́вля.

harbinger *n.* предве́стник.

harbor *also,* **harbour** *n.* га́вань; порт. —*v.t.* **1,** (shelter) укрыва́ть; приюти́ть. *Harbor a criminal,* укрыва́ть престу́пника. **2,** (entertain in the mind) пита́ть; (за)таи́ть. *Harbor illusions,* пита́ть иллю́зии; *harbor a grudge,* пита́ть *or* (за)таи́ть зло́бу. —**harbor pilot,** ло́цман.

hard *adj.* **1,** (not soft) твёрдый; жёсткий. *Hard surface,* твёрдая пове́рхность. *Hard as a rock,* твёрдый как ка́мень. *Hard seat/bed/mattress,* жёсткое сиде́нье; жёсткая крова́ть; жёсткий матра́с. **2,** (difficult) тру́дный: *hard problem,* тру́дная зада́ча. *It's hard to say,* тру́дно сказа́ть. **3,** (rigorous; trying) тяжёлый: *hard work/life,* тяжёлая рабо́та/жизнь.

Hard times, тяжёлые времена́. **4,** (industrious) трудолюби́вый: *hard worker,* трудолюби́вый рабо́тник. **5,** (of or with great force) си́льный: *hard blow,* си́льный уда́р. **6,** (strict; stern) жёсткий; стро́гий. —*adv.* **1,** (with great effort) тяжело́; уси́ленно. *Work/breathe hard,* тяжело́ рабо́тать/дыша́ть. *Study hard,* приле́жно учи́ться; уси́ленно занима́ться. *Try hard,* о́чень стара́ться. *Try hard to persuade someone,* уси́ленно угова́ривать кого́-нибудь. **2,** (with great force) си́льно: *hit hard,* си́льно уда́рить. *It is raining hard,* идёт си́льный дождь. **3,** (with sorrow or distress) тяжело́: *take something hard,* тяжело́ переноси́ть *or* пережива́ть что́-нибудь. —**hard and fast,** жёсткий: *hard and fast rules,* жёсткие пра́вила. —**hard cash,** нали́чные де́ньги. —**hard currency,** твёрдая валю́та. —**hard disk,** жёсткий диск. —**hard labor,** ка́торга; ка́торжные рабо́ты. —**hard line,** жёсткая ли́ния. —**hard liquor,** спиртны́е напи́тки. —**hard luck,** невезе́ние. —**hard of hearing,** туго́й на́ ухо. —**hard palate,** твёрдое нёбо. —**hard up,** не при деньга́х; стеснённый в деньга́х. —**hard water,** жёсткая вода́.

hard-boiled *adj.* **1,** (of eggs) круто́й: *hard-boiled egg,* круто́е яйцо́; яйцо́ вкруту́ю. **2,** *colloq.* (unsentimental) чёрствый; твердока́менный.

hardbound *adj.* в твёрдой обло́жке; в переплёте. *Also,* **hard-cover.**

hard-earned *adj.* кро́вный: *hard-earned money,* кро́вные де́ньги.

harden *v.t.* **1,** (make hard) де́лать (бо́лее) твёрдым; закаля́ть. **2,** (toughen) закаля́ть; ожесточа́ть. **3,** (make more rigorous, as demands) ужесточа́ть. —*v.i.* тверде́ть; затвердева́ть; (of metals) закаля́ться.

hardened *adj.* **1,** (having become hard) затверде́лый; закалённый. *Hardened steel,* закалённая сталь. **2,** (inveterate) закорене́лый: *hardened criminal,* закорене́лый престу́пник.

hardening *n.* затверде́ние. —**hardening of the arteries,** артериосклеро́з.

hardheaded *adj.* **1,** (practical; realistic) практи́чный; тре́звый. **2,** (stubborn) упря́мый.

hardhearted *adj.* жесткосе́рдный. —**hardheartedness,** *n.* жестокосе́рдие.

hardiness *n.* вынос́ливость.

hardly *adv.* **1,** (scarcely) едва́; е́ле; с трудо́м. *We could hardly keep up with him,* мы едва́ *or* е́ле поспева́ли за ним. *I can hardly understand him,* я с трудо́м его́ понима́ю. **2,** (almost not at all) почти́; ма́ло. *There was hardly anyone there,* там почти́ никого́ не́ было. *Hardly anyone knows,* ма́ло кто зна́ет об э́том. *Hardly ever,* почти́ никогда́; ма́ло когда́. **3,** (almost surely not) едва́ ли; вряд ли. *That is hardly possible,* едва́ ли э́то возмо́жно. *He will hardly come now,* вряд ли он уже́ придёт.

hardness *n.* твёрдость; жёсткость.

hardship *n.* лише́ние: *suffer hardships,* терпе́ть лише́ния.

hardware *n.* **1,** (tools and household items) скобяно́й това́р; скобяны́е изде́лия. *Hardware store,* скобя-

но́й магази́н. **2,** (computers and other devices) техни́ческое обеспе́чение.

hard-working *adj.* трудолюби́вый.

hardy *adj.* **1,** (robust) кре́пкий; выно́сливый; живу́чий. **2,** (adventuresome) сме́лый. **3,** (frost-resistant) морозосто́йкий.

hare *n.* за́яц.

harebrained *adj.* легкомы́сленный; безрассу́дный.

harelip *n.* за́ячья губа́.

harem *n.* гаре́м.

hark *v.i.* слу́шать. —*interj.* слу́шай! —**hark back, 1,** (return) возвраща́ться. **2,** (date back) восходи́ть.

harken *v.* = **hearken.**

harlequin *n.* арлеки́н; шут.

harlot *n.* проститу́тка.

harm *n.* вред; зло; уще́рб. *He wishes you no harm,* он не жела́ет вам зла. *It won't do any harm,* вреда́ от э́того не бу́дет. *I see no harm in it,* я не ви́жу в э́том ничего́ плохо́го. *It won't do any harm to...,* не повреди́т, е́сли... *What harm is there in asking?,* что стра́шного в том, е́сли мы спро́сим? *Do more harm than good,* принести́ бо́льше вреда́, чем по́льзы. —*v.t.* вреди́ть; наноси́ть *or* причиня́ть вред (+ *dat.*). *No one was harmed,* никто́ не пострада́л. *Don't harm her!,* не тро́гайте её! —**out of harm's way,** от греха́ пода́льше.

harmful *adj.* вре́дный.

harmless *adj.* безвре́дный; безоби́дный.

harmonic *adj.* гармони́ческий. —*n.,* music оберто́н.

harmonica *n.* губна́я гармо́ника.

harmonious *adj.* гармони́чный; согла́сный; сла́женный. —**harmoniously,** *adv.* согла́сно; сла́женно.

harmonium *n.* фисгармо́ния.

harmonize *v.t.* **1,** (bring into accord) согласо́вывать. **2,** *music* гармонизи́ровать. —*v.i.* гармони́ровать.

harmony *n.* **1,** *music* гармо́ния. **2,** (accord) гармо́ния; согла́сие. *Harmony of interests,* гармо́ния интере́сов. *Live in harmony,* жить в согла́сии.

harness *n.* у́пряжь; сбру́я. —*v.t.* **1,** (put a harness on) запряга́ть. **2,** *fig.* (utilize the potential of) испо́льзовать. —**harness races,** бега́.

harp *n.* а́рфа. —*v.i.* [usu. **harp on**] тверди́ть (о). —**harp on the same string,** тверди́ть *or* зала́дить одно́ и то же; тяну́ть всё ту же пе́сню; дуде́ть в одну́ ду́дку.

harpist *n.* арфи́ст; арфи́стка.

harpoon *n.* острога́; гарпу́н. —*v.t.* бить острого́й/гарпуно́м; гарпу́нить.

harpsichord *n.* клавеси́н.

harquebus *n.* пища́ль.

harridan *n.* ста́рая карга́.

harrier *n.* (bird) лунь.

harrow *n.* борона́. —*v.t.* борони́ть. —**harrowing,** *adj.* душераздира́ющий.

harry *v.t.* му́чить; трави́ть; изводи́ть. *A harried look,* изму́ченный вид.

harsh *adj.* **1,** (grating to the ear) ре́зкий: *harsh voice,* ре́зкий го́лос. **2,** (severe; grim; cruel) ре́зкий; жёсткий; суро́вый; жесто́кий. *Harsh words,* ре́зкие *or* жёсткие слова́. *Harsh criticism,* ре́зкая *or* о́страя кри́тика. *Harsh climate,* суро́вый кли́мат. *Harsh sentence,* суро́вый *or* жесто́кий пригово́р. —**harshly,** *adv.* ре́зко; жесто́ко. —**harshness,** *n.* ре́зкость; суро́вость.

hart *n.* рога́ч.

harum-scarum *adv.* как попа́ло; очертя́ го́лову.

harvest *n.* **1,** (crop) урожа́й. *Poor harvest,* неурожа́й; недоро́д. *Gather in the harvest,* собира́ть урожа́й. **2,** (gathering in of a crop) жа́тва; сбор *or* убо́рка урожа́я. *Harvest time,* вре́мя жа́твы. —*v.t.* собира́ть: *harvest the crops,* собира́ть урожа́й. *Harvest grain,* убира́ть хлеб.

harvester *n.* убо́рочная маши́на; жа́твенная маши́на; жне́йка; жа́тка; комба́йн.

hash *n.* **1,** (food) ру́бленое мя́со. **2,** (mishmash) мешани́на.

hashish *n.* гаши́ш.

hasp *n.* пробо́й.

hassle *n., colloq.* перебра́нка; препира́тельство.

hassock *n.* пуф.

haste *n.* поспе́шность; торопли́вость; спе́шка. *In haste,* поспе́шно; на́спех; второпя́х. *In my haste,* в спе́шке; второпя́х; впопыха́х. —**haste makes waste,** поспеши́шь — люде́й насмеши́шь. —**make haste,** спеши́ть; торопи́ться.

hasten *v.i.* спеши́ть; торопи́ться. *He hastened to add that...,* он поспеши́л доба́вить, что... —*v.t.* торопи́ть; ускоря́ть; приближа́ть.

hastily *adv.* поспе́шно; на́скоро; на́спех; второпя́х.

hasty *adj.* поспе́шный; торопли́вый. *Be hasty in one's conclusions,* торопи́ться с вы́водами.

hat *n.* шля́па. —*adj.* шля́пный: *hat shop,* шля́пный магази́н. —**at the drop of a hat,** чуть что; по мале́йшему по́воду. —**keep under one's hat,** пома́лкивать о. —**take off one's hat to,** снима́ть шля́пу пе́ред; преклоня́ться пе́ред. —**talk through one's hat,** нести́ чушь.

hatband *n.* око́лыш.

hatbox *n.* карто́нка для шля́пы.

hatch *v.t.* **1,** (bring forth, as young) выси́живать; выводи́ть. **2,** (incubate, as an egg) наси́живать. **3,** *fig.* (devise, as plans) вына́шивать. *Hatch a plot,* устра́ивать *or* организова́ть за́говор. **4,** (mark with lines) штрихова́ть. —*v.i.* выводи́ться; вылупля́ться. —*n.* люк: *escape hatch,* авари́йный люк.

hatchet *n.* топо́рик.

hate *v.t.* **1,** (detest) ненави́деть: *hate onions/liars/war,* ненави́деть лук/лгуно́в/войну́. **2,** (dislike doing) о́чень не люби́ть *or* не хоте́ть; ненави́деть: *hate writing letters,* о́чень не люби́ть (*or* ненави́деть) писа́ть пи́сьма. *I hate to interrupt, but...,* извини́те, что перебива́ю, но... *I hate to spend money for that,* мне жаль тра́тить де́ньги на э́то. —*n.* не́нависть.

hated *adj.* ненави́стный.

hateful *adj.* ненави́стный.

hatpin *n.* була́вка для шля́пы; шля́пная була́вка.

hatrack *n.* ве́шалка для шляп.

hatred *n.* не́нависть: *hatred of war,* не́нависть к войне́. *Feel hatred toward,* чу́вствовать не́нависть к.

hatter *n.* шля́пный ма́стер; шля́пник; ша́почник.

haughty *adj.* надме́нный; высокоме́рный. —**haughtiness,** *n.* надме́нность; высокоме́рие.

haul *v.t.* **1,** (drag) тяну́ть; тащи́ть. **2,** (transport) перевози́ть. **3,** *fol. by in* (pull in, as a fish) выта́скивать. **4,** *fol. by down* (pull down) спуска́ть. —*n.* **1,** (distance covered) рейс. **2,** (of fish) уло́в. **3,** (of loot) добы́ча. —**haul off,** *colloq.* размахну́ться: *haul off and strike someone,* размахну́ться и уда́рить кого́-нибудь. —**over the long haul,** в долгосро́чном пла́не.

haulage *n.* перево́зка.

haunch *n.* бедро́; ля́жка.

haunt *v.t.* **1,** (dwell in, as of a ghost) обита́ть. *Haunted house,* дом с привиде́ниями. **2,** (obsess, as of a thought) пресле́довать; му́чить. *Haunting melody,* навя́зчивый моти́в. —*n.* люби́мое ме́сто.

have *v.t.* **1,** (possess) име́ть: *have the right/opportunity/misfortune,* име́ть пра́во/возмо́жность/несча́стье. ♦*Most commonly rendered, however, by* у: *Do you have a match?,* у вас есть спи́чка? *I have no time,* у меня́ нет вре́мени. **2,** (receive) получа́ть: *I've had no news from him,* я не получа́л(а) от него́ изве́стий. **3,** (do; perform; carry on) *rendered by various verbs: have a look,* посмотре́ть; *have a talk with,* поговори́ть с; *have an argument,* поспо́рить. **4,** (cause to do or be done): *Have him come in,* попроси́те его́ войти́. *Have a new suit made,* де́лать себе́ но́вый костю́м. *Have one's picture taken,* снима́ться. **5,** (cause to be treated) отдава́ть: *have (something) fixed,* отдава́ть (что́-нибудь) в ремо́нт; *have cleaned,* отдава́ть в чи́стку; *have washed,* отдава́ть в сти́рку. **6,** (experience) *rendered by* у: *She has a cold,* у неё на́сморк. *He had a heart attack,* у него́ был серде́чный припа́док. *Have a dream,* ви́деть сон. *Have a good time,* хорошо́ проводи́ть вре́мя. **7,** (harbor) пита́ть; испы́тывать. *Have warm feelings toward,* испы́тывать тёплые чу́вства к. *Have an aversion to,* име́ть отвраще́ние к. **8,** (feel and show): *have mercy on,* щади́ть; *have pity on,* сжа́литься над. **9,** (eat; drink): *have tea,* пить чай. *Have supper,* у́жинать. *What will you have to drink?,* что вы бу́дете пить? *Will you have some tea?,* чай бу́дете пить? **10,** (bear; beget) роди́ть: *She had a son,* у неё роди́лся сын. *Have puppies/kittens,* приноси́ть щеня́т/котя́т. **11,** (permit; tolerate) потерпе́ть: *I won't have such conduct,* я не потерплю́ тако́го поведе́ния. **12,** *fol. by it* (declare; state) гласи́ть: *Legend has it that...,* леге́нда гласи́т, что... *Rumor has it,* хо́дят слу́хи, что... —*v.aux.* **1,** *used to form the perfect tenses: I have already eaten,* я уже́ пое́л(а). *I haven't/hadn't seen her for three years,* я не ви́дел её три го́да. **2,** *in contrary-to-fact sentences,* е́сли бы: *Had I only known!,* е́сли бы я то́лько знал (зна́ла)! ♦*Also rendered by the imperative: Had he lived a little longer,* проживи́ он чуть до́льше. *Had the blast occurred ten minutes earlier,* произойди́ взрыв на де́сять мину́т ра́ньше. **3,** *fol. by inf., expressing obligation,* на́до; ну́жно; до́лжен: *I have to go,* мне на́до/ну́жно идти́; я до́лжен (должна́) идти́. *You don't have to thank me,* не на́до благодари́ть меня́.

—**have against,** име́ть про́тив: *I have nothing against him,* я ничего́ про́тив него́ не име́ю. —**have it in for,** име́ть зуб на; быть на (+ *acc.*) в прете́нзии. —**have it out with,** объясня́ться с. —**have on,** быть в (+ *prepl.*); быть оде́тым в (+ *acc.*): *have a raincoat on,* быть в плаще́. *What else did she have on?,* что ещё на ней бы́ло наде́то? —**have to do with, 1,** (have a connection with) име́ть отноше́ние к. *What has this to do with me?,* како́е э́то име́ет отноше́ние ко мне?; при чём тут я? **2,** (associate with) име́ть де́ло с: *He refused to have anything to do with me,* он отказа́лся име́ть де́ло со мной.

haven *n.* **1,** (harbor) га́вань. **2,** (shelter) убе́жище; прию́т.

haversack *n.* вещево́й мешо́к; ра́нец.

havoc *n.* опустоше́ние. —**play havoc with,** приводи́ть в расстро́йство.

Hawaiian *adj.* гава́йский.

hawk *n.* я́стреб. —*v.t. & i.* (peddle) торгова́ть вразно́с. —**hawker,** *n.* разно́счик.

hawk-eyed *adj.* зо́ркий.

hawser *n.* пе́рлинь.

hawthorn *n.* боя́рышник.

hay *n.* се́но. —*adj.* сенно́й. —**hit the hay,** *colloq.* отпра́виться на боко́вую. —**make hay while the sun shines,** куй желе́зо, пока́ горячо́.

haycock *n.* копна́.

hay fever сенна́я лихора́дка.

hayfield *n.* сеноко́с.

hayloft *n.* сенова́л.

haystack *n.* стог се́на; скирд (*or* скирда́) се́на.

hazard *n.* опа́сность; риск. —*v.t.* **1,** (risk) рискова́ть. **2,** (venture) осме́ливаться: *hazard a guess,* осме́литься догада́ться. —**hazardous,** *adj.* опа́сный; риско́ванный.

haze *n.* ды́мка; мгла; ма́рево.

hazel *n.* **1,** (tree) оре́шник; лещи́на. **2,** (nut) лесно́й оре́х. —*adj.* светло-кори́чневый.

hazel grouse ря́бчик. *Also,* **hazel hen.**

hazelnut *n.* лесно́й оре́х.

hazy *adj.* **1,** (misty) тума́нный; мгли́стый. **2,** (vague) сму́тный; тума́нный.

he *pers. pron.* он: *He is ill,* он бо́лен; *he left,* он ушёл. *He is not here,* его́ нет. —**he who,** тот, кто...; кто..., тот... *He who laughs last laughs best,* хорошо́ смеётся тот, кто смеётся после́дним. *See also* **him.**

head *n.* **1,** (part of the body) голова́. *A head taller than...,* вы́ше (+ *gen.*) на го́лову. **2,** (top part; head end) глава́: *at the head of the table,* во главе́ стола́. *Go to the head of the line,* пройти́ без о́череди. **3,** (of a pin, match, etc.) голо́вка; (of a nail) шля́пка. **4,** (of cabbage) коча́н. **5,** (of a bed) изголо́вье. **6,** (unit, as of cattle) голова́. **7,** (chief) глава́: *head of the family,* глава́ семьи́. *Head of state,* глава́ госуда́рства. *Department head,* нача́льник отде́ла; заве́дующий отде́лом. *He was made head of the institute,* он был поста́влен во главе́ институ́та. **8,** (mind; brain) голова́; ум: *clear head,* я́сная голова́; я́сный ум. *Do figures in one's head,* счита́ть в уме́. **9,** (person): *ten dollars a/per head,* по де́сять до́лларов с головы́ *or*

с но́са. —*adj.* **1,** (of or for the head) головно́й. **2,** (chief) гла́вный; ста́рший: *head physician,* гла́вный/ста́рший врач. —*v.t.* **1,** (set the course of) направля́ть: *head a ship northward,* направля́ть парохо́д на се́вер. *Which way are we headed?,* в каку́ю сто́рону мы е́дем? **2,** (be the head of) возглавля́ть. *Headed by,* во главе́ с. **3,** *fol. by* **off** (intercept; avert) пресека́ть. —*v.i.* (move in a specified direction) направля́ться; брать курс. *Head north,* направля́ться *or* направля́ть свой путь *or* брать курс на се́вер. —**come into one's head,** взбрести́ в го́лову. —**come to a head,** назре́ть. —**from head to toe,** с головы́ до ног. —**get it into one's head,** вбива́ть себе́ в го́лову. —**get it through someone's head,** вбива́ть в го́лову (+ *dat.*). —**go to one's head, 1,** (intoxicate) ударя́ть в го́лову (+ *dat.*). **2,** (make conceited) вскружи́ть го́лову (+ *dat.*). —**head and shoulders above,** на́ голову вы́ше (+ *gen.*). —**head over heels, 1,** (tumbling) ку́барем; кувырко́м; вверх торма́шками. **2,** (completely) по́ уши (влюблён, в долга́х, *etc.*). —**heads or tails?,** орёл и́ли ре́шка? —**keep one's head,** не теря́ть головы́. —**keep one's head above water,** держа́ться на пове́рхности. —**lose one's head,** потеря́ть го́лову. —**make head or tail of,** разбира́ться в. —**over one's head, 1,** (too difficult for) вы́ше (чьего́-нибудь) понима́ния. **2,** (bypassing) че́рез (чью-нибудь) го́лову. —**put out of one's head,** вы́бросить (*e.g.* мысль) из головы́. —**stand** (*e.g.* **the truth**) **on its head,** поста́вить (пра́вду) с ног на́ голову. —**take it into one's head,** взду́мать (+ *inf.*). —**talk someone's head off,** загова́ривать. —**two heads are better than one,** ум хорошо́ (*or* одна́ голова́ хорошо́), а два лу́чше. —**use one's head,** шевели́ть мозга́ми.

headache *n.* головна́я боль. *I have a headache,* у меня́ боли́т голова́.

headband *n.* головна́я повя́зка.

head cold на́сморк.

headdress *n.* головно́й убо́р.

headfirst *adv.* голово́й вперёд; вниз голово́й.

heading *n.* ру́брика.

headland *n.* мыс.

headless *adj.* безголо́вый.

headlight *n.* фа́ра.

headline *n.* заголо́вок; ша́пка.

headlong *adv.* **1,** (headfirst) голово́й вперёд; вниз голово́й. **2,** (at breakneck speed) стреми́тельно; стремгла́в; о́прометью. **3,** (rashly) очертя́ го́лову; напропалу́ю. —*adj.* стреми́тельный; безогля́дный.

headmaster *n.* дире́ктор (шко́лы).

head-on *adv.* в лоб; но́сом. —*adj.* прямо́й: *head-on collision,* прямо́е столкнове́ние.

headphone *n.* нау́шник.

headquarters *n.pl.* **1,** (place of command) штаб. **2,** (main building) штаб-кварти́ра.

headrest *n.* подголо́вник.

headset *n.* головно́й телефо́н.

head start фо́ра.

headstone *n.* **1,** (tombstone) надгро́бный ка́мень. **2,** *obs.* (cornerstone) краеуго́льный ка́мень.

headstrong *adj.* упря́мый; своево́льный.

headwaiter *n.* метрдоте́ль.

headwaters *n.pl.* исто́ки; верхо́вье.

headway *n.* продвиже́ние вперёд; прогре́сс. *Make headway,* продвига́ться вперёд; прогресси́ровать.

head wind встре́чный ве́тер.

heady *adj.* опьяня́ющий.

heal *v.t.* зале́чивать. *Physician, heal thyself,* врачу́, исцели́ся сам. —*v.i.* зажива́ть: *The wound/scar has healed,* ра́на зажила́; рубе́ц за́жил.

healer *n.* исцели́тель; цели́тель.

health *n.* здоро́вье. *Public health,* здравоохране́ние. *World Health Organization,* Всеми́рная организа́ция здравоохране́ния. *He is in good health,* он здоро́в; у него́ хоро́шее здоро́вье; он облада́ет хоро́шим здоро́вьем. *She is in poor health,* у неё сла́бое здоро́вье. —**to your health!,** за ва́ше здоро́вье!

healthful *adj.* здоро́вый; целе́бный.

healthy *adj.* здоро́вый: *healthy child/climate,* здоро́вый ребёнок/кли́мат. *Healthy food,* здоро́вая пи́ща.

heap *n.* ку́ча; гру́да. *Heap of rubble,* гру́да разва́лин. —*v.t.* **1,** *often fol. by* **up** (pile up) нагроможда́ть. **2,** (shower) осыпа́ть: *heap ridicule on,* осыпа́ть (кого́-нибудь) насме́шками.

hear *v.t.* **1,** (catch the sound of) слы́шать: *hear the music,* слы́шать му́зыку. *I can't hear you,* не слы́шу вас. *I can't hear a thing,* мне ничего́ не слы́шно. *You can hear the sound of the waves,* слы́шен шум волн. *I heard someone approaching from behind,* я слы́шал(а), как кто́-то подходи́л сза́ди. **2,** (learn) слы́шать: *Have you heard the news?,* вы слы́шали но́вость? *I hear he's thinking of resigning,* я слы́шал, что он ду́мает уйти́ в отста́вку. *What is this I hear about...?,* что тако́е, я слы́шал(а), что... **3,** *law* слу́шать: *hear a case,* слу́шать де́ло. —*v.i.* **1,** (be able to perceive sound) слы́шать: *He can't hear,* он не слы́шит. **2,** *fol. by* **of** *or* **about** (learn of) слы́шать (о): *hear about the earthquake,* слы́шать о землетрясе́нии. *It's the first I've heard of it,* пе́рвый раз слы́шу. **3,** *fol. by* **from** (get mail or a call from) получи́ть изве́стие от. *Let us hear from you,* да́йте нам знать о вас. *What do you hear from home?,* что вам пи́шут из до́ма? *I haven't heard a word from him,* он мне ни стро́чки не написа́л; он мне ничего́ не сообщи́л. **4,** *fol. by* **of** (consider; consent to) слы́шать (о): *I won't hear of it!,* я об э́том и слы́шать не хочу́. —**hear out,** выслу́шивать.

hearing *n.* **1,** (sense) слух. *Hard of hearing,* туго́й на́ ухо. *Lose one's hearing,* (о)гло́хнуть. **2,** *law* слу́шание. **3,** (earshot) слы́шимость: *within hearing,* в преде́лах слы́шимости. —**hearing aid,** слухово́й аппара́т.

hearken *also,* **harken** *v.i.* слу́шать. *Hearken to,* внима́ть (+ *dat.*).

hearsay *n.* слу́хи; молва́. *Through hearsay,* по слу́хам; понаслы́шке.

hearse *n.* катафа́лк; похоро́нные дро́ги; погреба́льная колесни́ца.

heart *n.* **1,** (organ of the body) се́рдце. **2,** (center)

центр; се́рдце: *in the heart of Europe,* в са́мом це́нтре (*or* в се́рдце) Евро́пы. **3,** (essence; crux) суть; су́щность: *get to the heart of the matter,* добра́ться до су́ти де́ла. **4,** *pl., cards* че́рви: *ace of hearts,* туз черве́й. —*adj.* серде́чный: *heart muscle,* серде́чная мы́шца. —**at heart,** в глубине́ души́. —**by heart,** наизу́сть. —**lose heart,** па́дать ду́хом; уныва́ть. —**not have the heart to,** не хвата́ть ду́ху (with y): *I haven't the heart to...,* у меня́ не хвата́ет ду́ху (+ *inf.*). —**take heart,** ободря́ться; воспря́нуть ду́хом. —**take to heart,** принима́ть бли́зко к се́рдцу. —**with a heavy heart,** с тяжёлым се́рдцем; с бо́лью в се́рдце. —**with all one's heart,** всем се́рдцем; всей душо́й. —**with one's heart in one's mouth,** с замира́нием се́рдца.

heartache *n.* душе́вная боль.

heart attack серде́чный припа́док; инфа́ркт.

heartbeat *n.* сердцебие́ние.

heartbreaking *adj.* (душе)раздира́ющий. *It is heartbreaking,* се́рдце *or* душа́ разрыва́ется.

heartbroken *adj.* уби́тый го́рем.

heartburn *n.* изжо́га.

heart disease боле́знь се́рдца. *Suffer from heart disease,* страда́ть боле́знью се́рдца. *Treatment of heart disease,* лече́ние боле́зней се́рдца.

hearten *v.t.* ободря́ть; подба́дривать.

heart failure разры́в се́рдца; парали́ч се́рдца.

heartfelt *adj.* серде́чный; душе́вный; задуше́вный.

hearth *n.* оча́г.

heartily *adv.* **1,** (warmly; cordially) серде́чно. **2,** (with a hearty appetite) с аппети́том; пло́тно. **3,** (completely) вполне́: *I heartily agree/approve,* я вполне́ согла́сен/одобря́ю. **4,** (emphatically) о́чень: *heartily recommend,* о́чень рекомендова́ть. **5,** (lustily): *laugh heartily,* смея́ться от души́; хохота́ть.

heartless *adj.* бессерде́чный; безду́шный. —**heartlessness,** *n.* бессерде́чие; бессерде́чность; безду́шие.

heart-rending *adj.* (душе)раздира́ющий; надры́вный; исто́шный.

heart-shaped *adj.* сердцеви́дный.

heartsick *adj.* (о́чень) огорчён; (о́чень) расстро́ен.

heart-to-heart *adj.* инти́мный; серде́чный. *Heart-to-heart talk,* разгово́р по душа́м.

heartwarming *adj.* ра́достный.

hearty *adj.* **1,** (cordial, as of a welcome) серде́чный; раду́шный. **2,** (solid, as of a meal) пло́тный; сы́тный. **3,** (big, as of one's appetite) хоро́ший; отли́чный.

heat *n.* **1,** (hot temperature or weather) жара́: *unbearable heat,* невыноси́мая жара́. **2,** *physics* теплота́; тепло́: *give off heat,* выделя́ть тепло́. **3,** (heating system) отопле́ние: *steam heat,* парово́е отопле́ние. **4,** (excitement; strong feelings) жар; пыл. *In the heat of battle,* в пылу́ сраже́ния. *In the heat of the moment,* сгоряча́. **5,** (sexual excitement) те́чка: *The dog is in heat,* у соба́ки те́чка. **6,** *sports* забе́г; *swimming* заплы́в. —*v.t.* **1,** (provide with heat) топи́ть; ота́пливать. *The apartment is not heated,* кварти́ра не ота́пливается. **2,** *often fol. by* **up** (warm up) нагрева́ть; согрева́ть; разогрева́ть. —*v.i.* [*usu.* **heat up**] нагрева́ться; согрева́ться.

heated *adj.* **1,** (having central heating) с отопле́нием. **2,** (warmed) нагре́тый. **3,** (vehement, as of an argument) жа́ркий; горя́чий. —**heatedly,** *adv.* горячо́: *argue heatedly,* спо́рить горячо́.

heater *n.* нагрева́тельный прибо́р; нагрева́тель; обогрева́тель. *Electric heater,* электри́ческий нагрева́тель *or* обогрева́тель.

heath *n.* **1,** (uncultivated land) пу́стошь. **2,** (shrub) э́рика.

heathen *n.* язы́чник. —*adj.* язы́ческий.

heather *n.* ве́реск.

heating *n.* **1,** (providing of heat) отопле́ние: *central heating,* центра́льное отопле́ние. **2,** (warming up) нагрева́ние. —*adj.* отопи́тельный; нагрева́тельный. —**heating oil,** отопи́тельная нефть. —**heating pad,** электри́ческая гре́лка.

heat lightning зарни́ца.

heat rash потни́ца.

heat-resistant *adj.* теплосто́йкий.

heat shield теплово́й экра́н.

heatstroke *n.* теплово́й уда́р.

heat wave полоса́ си́льной жары́.

heave *v.t.* **1,** (hurl) броса́ть; швыря́ть. **2,** *Heave a sigh,* испусти́ть вздох. —*v.i.* **1,** (rise and fall rhythmically) вздыма́ться. **2,** *colloq.* (retch) рвать. —*n.* бросо́к. —**heave ho!,** раз, два, дру́жно! —**heave to,** *naut.* лечь в дрейф.

heaven *n.* не́бо. —**be in seventh heaven,** быть на седьмо́м не́бе. —**for heaven's sake!,** ра́ди бо́га! —**heaven forbid!,** не дай бог!; бо́же упаси́! —**heavens!,** бо́же мой! —**thank heaven!,** сла́ва бо́гу! —**move heaven and earth,** пусти́ть в ход все сре́дства.

heavenly *adj.* **1,** (of the heavens) небе́сный: *heavenly body,* небе́сное те́ло. **2,** (divine; sublime) боже́ственный.

heaves *n.pl.* запа́л.

heavily *adv.* тяжело́: *breathe heavily,* тяжело́ дыша́ть. *Heavily armed/guarded,* уси́ленно вооружённый/охраня́емый. *Heavily in debt,* круго́м в долга́х. *Perspire heavily,* си́льно поте́ть.

heaviness *n.* тя́жесть.

heavy *adj.* **1,** (weighty) тяжёлый: *heavy object/suitcase/blow,* тяжёлый предме́т/чемода́н/уда́р. *Heavy feeling in one's head,* тяжёлая голова́; тя́жесть в голове́. **2,** (difficult; arduous) тяжёлый: *heavy work,* тяжёлая рабо́та; *heavy breathing,* тяжёлое дыха́ние. **3,** (intense) си́льный: *heavy rain/snow,* си́льный дождь/снегопа́д; *a heavy cold,* си́льный на́сморк. *Under heavy guard,* под си́льной охра́ной. *Heavy traffic,* интенси́вное движе́ние. *Heavy fighting,* тяжёлые *or* упо́рные бои́. *He is a heavy drinker,* он си́льно пьёт. **4,** (severe, as of losses) тяжёлый; большо́й; кру́пный; серьёзный. *Heavy damage,* больши́е *or* си́льные повреждё́ния. *Pay a heavy price for,* заплати́ть дорого́й цено́й за. **5,** (grave) тяжёлый: *heavy responsibility,* тяжёлая отве́тственность. **6,** (large, as of industry, artillery, etc.) тя-

жёлый. **7,** (ponderous, as of writing) тяжёлый; тяжелове́сный. **8,** (hard to digest) тяжёлый. **9,** (choppy, as of the sea) бу́рный. **10,** (gloomy, as of the sky) мра́чный; хму́рый. —**hang heavy,** ме́дленно тяну́ться. —**with a heavy heart,** с тяжёлым се́рдцем; с бо́лью в се́рдце.

heavy-handed *adj.* неуклю́жий; нело́вкий.

heavyset *adj.* призе́мистый; корена́стый.

heavy water тяжёлая вода́.

heavyweight *n.* тяжелове́с. —*adj.* тяжелове́сный.

Hebrew *adj.* (древне)евре́йский. —*n.* **1,** (person) евре́й. **2,** (ancient language) древнеевре́йский язы́к. **3,** (modern language) иври́т.

heckle *v.t.* прерыва́ть кри́ками.

hectare *n.* гекта́р.

hectic *adj.* сумато́шный; бу́рный; горя́чий.

hedge *n.* жива́я и́згородь. —*v.t.* [*usu.* **hedge in**] обноси́ть и́згородью. —*v.i.* (equivocate) виля́ть.

hedgehog *n.* ёж.

hedonism *n.* гедони́зм. —**hedonist,** *n.* гедони́ст. —**hedonistic,** *adj.* гедонисти́ческий.

heed *v.t.* слу́шать; слу́шаться; прислу́шиваться к. *Heed a warning,* слу́шать предостереже́ние. *Heed someone's advice,* (по)слу́шаться чьего́-нибудь сове́та; прислу́шиваться к чьему́-нибудь сове́ту. —*n.* внима́ние: *pay no heed to,* не обраща́ть (никако́го) внима́ния на. —**heedless,** *adj.* не обраща́ющий внима́ния.

heel *n.* **1,** (part of the foot) пя́тка; пята́. **2,** (part of a shoe) каблу́к. **3,** (part of a stocking) пя́тка. —**head over heels,** *see* **head.** —**on the heels of,** вслед за. —**take to one's heels,** бро́ситься *or* пусти́ться наутёк; улепётывать; дать тя́гу; смота́ть у́дочки; показа́ть пя́тки. —**under the heel of,** под пято́й (+ *gen.*).

hefty *adj.* **1,** (burly) ро́слый; дю́жий. **2,** (substantial) поря́дочный; изря́дный: *a hefty sum,* поря́дочная/ изря́дная су́мма.

hegemony *n.* гегемо́ния.

heifer *n.* тёлка.

height *n.* **1,** (size; altitude) высота́: *a building of enormous height,* зда́ние огро́мной высоты́. *Fall from a height of 200 feet,* упа́сть с высоты́ двухсо́т фу́тов. **2,** (of a person) рост: *They are the same height,* они́ одного́ ро́ста. *Tall weeds the height of a man,* бурья́н в рост челове́ка. **3,** (high point of land) возвы́шенность; *pl.* высо́ты. *The Golan Heights,* Гола́нские высо́ты. **4,** *fol. by* **of** (greatest degree) верх: *the height of folly,* верх глу́пости. *At the height of its glory,* на верши́не его́ сла́вы. **5,** (time of greatest activity) разга́р: *at the height of the season,* в разга́р (*or* в разга́ре) сезо́на. *Be at its height,* быть в разга́ре.

heighten *v.t.* **1,** (raise) повыша́ть. **2,** (intensify) повыша́ть; уси́ливать. *Heighten tension,* уси́ливать напряжённость. —*v.i.* повыша́ться; уси́ливаться.

heinous *adj.* гну́сный. —**heinousness,** *n.* гну́сность.

heir *n.* насле́дник. *Heir to the throne,* насле́дник престо́ла. —**heiress,** *n.* насле́дница.

heirloom *n.* фами́льное сокро́вище.

helicopter *n.* вертолёт.

heliograph *n.* гелио́граф.

heliotrope *n.* гелиотро́п.

heliport *n.* вертодро́м.

helium *n.* ге́лий.

hell *n.* ад. —*interj.* чёрт возьми́! —**a hell of a...,** а́дский; черто́вский. *A hell of a long way,* чертовски́ далеко́. —**as hell,** черто́вски: *mad as hell,* черто́вски серди́т. —**catch hell,** *slang* получи́ть по ша́пке. —**come hell or high water,** во что бы то ни ста́ло. —**for the hell of it,** про́сто так. —**give someone hell,** *colloq.* распека́ть. —**go through hell,** переноси́ть му́ки а́да. —**go to hell!,** иди́те к чёрту! —**like hell, 1,** (with all one's might) как чёрт: *work like hell,* рабо́тать как чёрт. **2,** (terribly) черто́вски: *It hurts like hell,* черто́вски бо́льно. **3,** *as an exclamation,* чёрта с два!; как бы не так! —**raise hell,** *colloq.* поднима́ть шум. —**to hell with,** чёрт с; а ну (+ *gen.*): *To hell with him!,* чёрт с ним!; а ну его́! *To hell with it!,* к чёрту! —**what the hell...?,** како́го чёрта: *What the hell is he doing there?,* како́го чёрта он там де́лает?

hellebore *n.* чемери́ца.

Hellenic *adj.* э́ллинский.

hellish *adj.* а́дский.

hello *interj.* здра́вствуйте! ♦*When answering the telephone,* алло́!; слу́шаю!

helm *n.* руль; штурва́л. *Be at the helm,* стоя́ть у руля́.

helmet *n.* шлем; ка́ска.

helmsman *n.* рулево́й; штурва́льный; ко́рмчий.

help *v.t.* **1,** (aid; assist) помога́ть. *Help someone up,* помо́чь кому́-нибудь встать. *Help someone on/off with his coat,* пода́ть кому́-нибудь пальто́; помо́чь кому́-нибудь снять пальто́. **2,** (assist in accomplishing) спосо́бствовать: *help to achieve our goal,* спосо́бствовать достиже́нию на́шей це́ли. **3,** (wait on) обслу́живать. **4,** (serve) класть: *help oneself to,* класть себе́ на таре́лку (+ *gen.*). *May I help you to some meat?,* мо́жно вам положи́ть мя́са? *Help yourself!,* угоща́йтесь, пожа́луйста! **5,** (prevent; change): *I can't help it,* ничего́ не могу́ поде́лать. *It can't be helped,* ничего́ не поде́лаешь. —*v.i.* помога́ть: *He did nothing to help,* он ниче́м не помо́г. —*n.* **1,** (aid; assistance) по́мощь. *You were a big help,* вы нам о́чень помогли́. **2,** (workers) рабо́чие. **3,** (household help) прислу́га; слу́ги. —*interj.* на по́мощь! —**not help** (**doing something**), не мочь не (+ *inf.*): *I couldn't help noticing that...,* я не мог (могла́) не заме́тить, что... *I couldn't help laughing,* я не мог удержа́ться от сме́ха. *I can't help thinking that...,* я не могу́ освободи́ться от мы́сли, что... *You can't help feeling sorry for him,* нельзя́ не сочу́вствовать ему́. —**so help me God!,** да помо́жет мне бог.

helper *n.* помо́щник.

helpful *adj.* **1,** (useful) поле́зный. **2,** (accommodating) услу́жливый. *He was very helpful to us,* он нам о́чень помо́г.

helping *n.* по́рция. *Second helping,* доба́вка. —*adj., in* **lend a helping hand,** подава́ть ру́ку по́мощи.

helpless *adj.* беспо́мощный; бесси́льный. —**helplessness,** *n.* беспо́мощность; бесси́лие.

help-wanted ad объявле́ние о на́йме.

helter-skelter *adv.* как попа́ло; врассыпну́ю; вкривь и вкось.

hem *n.* рубе́ц. —*v.t.* **1,** (sew a hem in) подруба́ть. **2,** *fol. by* **in** (encircle and immobilize) сти́скивать; сжима́ть. —*v.i., in* **hem and haw,** тяну́ть и мя́млить; ни шьёт, не по́рет.

he-man *n., colloq.* настоя́щий мужчи́на.

hematite *also,* **haematite** *n.* кра́сный железня́к; желе́зный блеск.

hematology *also,* **haematology** *n.* гематоло́гия.

hemisphere *n.* полуша́рие.

hemlock *n.* **1,** (poisonous plant) болиголо́в. *Water hemlock,* цику́та. **2,** (evergreen tree) тсу́га.

hemoglobin *also,* **haemoglobin** *n.* гемоглоби́н.

hemophilia *also,* **haemophilia** *n.* гемофили́я; кровоточи́вость.

hemorrhage *also,* **haemorrhage** *n.* кровоизлия́ние. —*v.i.* кровоточи́ть.

hemorrhoid *also,* **haemorrhoid** *n., usu. pl.* геморро́й.

hemp *n.* **1,** (plant) конопля́. **2,** (fiber) пенька́. —*adj.* конопля́ный; пенько́вый.

hemstitch *n.* ажу́рная стро́чка.

hen *n.* ку́рица.

henbane *n.* белена́.

hence *adv.* **1,** (therefore) сле́довательно; отсю́да. **2,** (from now) че́рез: *a week hence,* че́рез неде́лю.

henceforth *adv.* впредь; отны́не; с э́того вре́мени. *Also,* **henceforward.**

henchman *n.* приспе́шник.

henhouse *n.* куря́тник.

henna *n.* хна.

henpecked *adj.* под башмако́м (у жены́).

hepatic *adj.* печёночный.

hepatica *n.* печёночница; переле́ска.

hepatitis *n.* воспале́ние пе́чени; гепати́т.

heptagon *n.* семиуго́льник. —**heptagonal,** *adj.* семиуго́льный.

her *pers. pron.* **1,** *used as dir. obj. of a verb,* её: *Ask her,* спроси́ её. **2,** *used as indir. obj. of a verb,* ей: *Give her the keys,* дай ей ключи́. **3,** *used as obj. of a prep.,* неё; ней: *from her,* от неё; *with her,* с ней. —*poss. adj.* её: *her brother,* её брат. ♦*When the possessor is the subject of the sentence,* свой: *She helped her father,* она́ помога́ла своему́ отцу́. *She cut her finger,* она́ поре́зала себе́ па́лец.

herald *n.* **1,** *hist.* геро́льд. **2,** (messenger) ве́стник. —*v.t.* возвеща́ть. —**heraldic,** *adj.* геральди́ческий. —**heraldry,** *n.* гера́льдика.

herb *n.* трава́. —**herbaceous,** *adj.* травяно́й; травяни́стый. —**herbarium,** *n.* герба́рий. —**herbicide,** *n.* гербици́д.

herbivorous *adj.* травоя́дный.

Hercules *n.* Геркуле́с.

herd *n.* ста́до: *herd of elephants,* ста́до слоно́в. —*v.t.* **1,** (tend) пасти́. **2,** (drive, as if in a herd) гнать. *Herd into a pen,* загоня́ть в заго́н. *Herd together,* сгоня́ть. —**herd instinct,** ста́дный инсти́нкт.

herdsman *n.* гуртовщи́к.

here *adv.* **1,** (in this place) здесь; тут. *Wait here!,* подожди́те здесь. *He is not here,* его́ нет. *From here,* отсю́да. *Look who's here!,* посмотри́, кто пришёл! **2,** (to this place) сюда́: *Come here!,* иди́ сюда́! **3,** *used to indicate something,* вот: *Here I am!,* вот и я!; *here he comes!,* вот он идёт! *Here are your glasses,* вот ва́ши очки́. —**here and now,** сейча́с же. —**here and there,** ко́е-где́; места́ми; там и тут; то тут, то там. —**here's to...,** за (+ *acc.*): *Here's to our hosts!,* за на́ших хозя́ев!

hereabout *also,* **hereabouts** *adv.* поблизости.

hereafter *adv.* впредь; отны́не; в дальне́йшем.

hereby *adv.* сим; настоя́щим.

hereditary *adj.* насле́дственный.

heredity *n.* насле́дственность.

herein *adv.* в э́том; здесь.

hereinafter *adv.* в дальне́йшем: *hereinafter referred to as...,* в дальне́йшем имену́емый...

heresy *n.* е́ресь.

heretic *n.* ерети́к. —**heretical,** *adj.* ерети́ческий.

hereto *adv.* при сём: *attached hereto,* при сём прилага́ется.

heretofore *adv.* до э́того; до сих пор; до сего́ вре́мени.

herewith *adv.* при сём: *enclosed herewith,* при сём прилага́ется.

heritage *n.* насле́дие.

hermaphrodite *n.* гермафроди́т.

hermetic *adj.* гермети́ческий. —**hermetically,** *adv.* гермети́чески.

hermit *n.* отше́льник; затво́рник; пусты́нник.

hernia *n.* гры́жа. —**hernial,** *adj.* грыжево́й.

hero *n.* геро́й. *He received a hero's welcome,* его́ приве́тствовали как геро́я.

heroic *adj.* герои́ческий; геро́йский. —**heroically,** *adv.* герои́чески; геро́йски.

heroin *n.* герои́н.

heroine *n.* герои́ня.

heroism *n.* герои́зм; геро́йство.

heron *n.* ца́пля.

herpes *n.* лиша́й.

herring *n.* сельдь; селёдка.

herringbone *n.* ёлочка: *in herringbone style,* ёлочкой; в ёлочку.

hers *poss. pron.* её: *This umbrella is hers,* э́тот зо́нтик её. *An uncle of hers,* оди́н её дя́дя. *My dress is red — hers is blue,* моё пла́тье кра́сное — её си́нее.

herself *pers. pron.* **1,** *used for emphasis,* (она́) сама́: *She did it herself,* она́ сама́ э́то сде́лала. **2,** *used reflexively,* себя́: *She bought it for herself,* она́ купи́ла э́то для себя́. *She hurt herself,* она́ уши́блась. —**by herself, 1,** (alone) одна́. **2,** (without help) сама́. —**she is not herself,** она́ сама́ не своя́.

hesitancy *n.* колеба́ние. *Without hesitancy,* без колеба́ний; не колебля́сь.

hesitant *adj.* колеблющийся; нереши́тельный. *In a hesitant tone of voice,* нереши́тельным то́ном. *She is hesitant to ask,* она́ стесня́ется попроси́ть; она́ не реша́ется попроси́ть. —**hesitantly,** *adv.* нереши́тельно.

hesitate *v.i.* **1,** (waver) колеба́ться: *He hesitated before agreeing,* он колеба́лся, пре́жде чем согласи́ться. **2,** (be reluctant) стесня́ться: *I hesitate to say,* я стесня́юсь сказа́ть.

hesitation *n.* колеба́ние. *Without (a moment's) hesitation,* без колеба́ний; не коле́блясь; не разду́мывая; не заду́мываясь; недо́лго ду́мая.

heterodox *adj.* не ортодокса́льный; ерети́ческий.

heterogeneous *adj.* разноро́дный. —**heterogeneity,** *n.* разноро́дность.

hew *v.t.* **1,** (chop) руби́ть; теса́ть. **2,** (carve) высека́ть; вытёсывать. —*v.i.* [*usu.* **hew to**] приде́рживаться: *hew to the party line,* приде́рживаться парти́йной ли́нии.

hex *n.* дурно́й глаз. —*v.t.* сгла́зить.

hexagon *n.* шестиуго́льник. —**hexagonal,** *adj.* шестиуго́льный.

hey *interj.* эй!; гей!

heyday *n.* зени́т; расцве́т.

hi *interj.* приве́т!

hiatus *n.* **1,** (gap) пробе́л. **2,** (break) переры́в. **3,** *ling.* зия́ние.

hibernate *v.i.* залега́ть в зи́мнюю спя́чку. —**hibernation,** *n.* зи́мняя спя́чка.

hibiscus *n.* гиби́скус.

hiccup *also,* **hiccough** *v.i.* ика́ть. —**hiccups,** *n.pl.* ико́та.

hick *n.* провинциа́л; дереве́нщина. —*adj., colloq.* провинциа́льный.

hickory *n.* гико́ри.

hidden *adj.* скры́тый; та́йный.

hide *v.t.* пря́тать; скрыва́ть. *Hide something in the drawer,* пря́тать что́-нибудь в я́щик(е) стола́. —*v.i.* пря́таться; скрыва́ться: *hide in the basement/ under the bed/ behind a tree/,* пря́таться/скрыва́ться в подва́л(е)/ под крова́ть(ю)/ за де́рево(м)/. —*n.* шку́ра: *cowhide,* коро́вья шку́ра.

hide-and-seek *n.* пря́тки.

hideaway *n.* тайни́к.

hidebound *adj.* ограни́ченный; узколо́бый.

hideous *adj.* отврати́тельный; уро́дливый. —**hideousness,** *n.* уро́дство; безобра́зие.

hideout *n.* тайни́к.

hiding *n.* пря́танье; скры́тие. *In hiding,* в бега́х. *Go into hiding,* скрыва́ться. —**hiding place,** тайни́к.

hierarchy *n.* иера́рхия. —**hierarchical,** *adj.* иерархи́ческий.

hieroglyph *also,* **hieroglyphic** *n.* иеро́глиф. —**hieroglyphic,** *adj.* иероглифи́ческий.

high *adj.* **1,** (lofty) высо́кий: *high mountain,* высо́кая гора́. *High ceiling/fence,* высо́кий потоло́к/забо́р. *On a high level,* на высо́ком у́ровне. *Hold one's head high,* держа́ть *or* нести́ го́лову высоко́. **2,** (having a specified height): *That building is 100 meters high,* э́то зда́ние в сто ме́тров высото́й. **3,** (above average) высо́кий: *high temperature,* высо́кая температу́ра; *high quality,* высо́кое ка́чество. *High prices,* высо́кие *or* дороги́е це́ны. *High speed,* больша́я ско́рость. *High hopes,* ра́дужные наде́жды. *A high honor,* высо́кая честь. *Have a high opinion of,* быть высо́кого мне́ния о. *Play for high stakes,* игра́ть по большо́й; вести́ кру́пную игру́. **4,** (high-pitched) высо́кий: *high notes,* высо́кие но́ты. **5,** (of high rank) высокопоста́вленный: *high official,* высокопоста́вленный чино́вник. *Hold a high position in the government,* занима́ть высо́кое ме́сто в прави́тельстве. **6,** (gay) весёлый: *high spirits,* весёлое настрое́ние. **7,** *colloq.* (tipsy) под хмелько́м; навеселе́. **8,** *High winds,* си́льный ве́тер. **9,** *The high seas,* откры́тое мо́ре. **10,** *High crimes,* госуда́рственные преступле́ния. —*adv.* высоко́: *aim high,* ме́тить высоко́. —*n.* вы́сшая то́чка. *Reach a record high,* достига́ть реко́рдного у́ровня. *Reach record highs,* расти́ до реко́рдных высо́т. —**high and dry,** на мели́. *Leave high and dry,* оста́вить с но́сом. —**high and mighty,** высокоме́рный. —**it is high time,** давно́ уже́ пора́. —**look high and low,** иска́ть всю́ду и везде́. —**on high,** в высоте́; в вышине́. *From on high,* с высоты́. *See also* **higher.**

highbrow *n.* интеллиге́нт.

highchair *n.* высо́кий де́тский сту́льчик.

high-class *adj.* фешене́бельный.

high command вы́сшее *or* гла́вное кома́ндование.

higher *adj., comp. of* **high.** —**higher education,** вы́сшее образова́ние. —**higher mathematics,** вы́сшая матема́тика.

high-flown *adj.* высокопа́рный; напы́щенный; треску́чий.

high-handed *adj.* самово́льный; вла́стный. —**high-handedness,** *n.* своево́лие; самово́лие; самоду́рство.

high-heeled *adj.* на высо́ких каблука́х.

high jump прыжо́к в высоту́.

highland *n.* наго́рье. —**highlander,** *n.* го́рец.

high-level *adj.* на высо́ком у́ровне.

highlight *n.* **1,** *art; photog.* световой эффе́кт. **2,** *fig.* (high point; feature) гвоздь. —*v.t.* оттеня́ть; высве́чивать; обознача́ть.

highly *adv.* **1,** (to a high degree) высоко́. *Highly developed,* высокора́звитый. *Highly seasoned,* о́стро припра́вленный. **2,** (extremely) весьма́: *highly probable/successful,* весьма́ вероя́тно/успе́шный. **3,** (with high approval or praise) высоко́: *value highly,* высоко́ цени́ть. *Think highly of,* быть высо́кого мне́ния о. *Speak highly of,* ле́стно отозва́ться о.

high-minded *adj.* иде́йный. —**high-mindedness,** *n.* иде́йность.

Highness *n.* высо́чество: *Your Highness,* ва́ше высо́чество.

high-paid *adj.* высокоопла́чиваемый.

high-pitched *adj.* высо́кий.

high-powered *adj.* (of a weapon) кру́пного кали́бра; (of a telescope or microscope) си́льный.

high-priced *adj.* дорогосто́ящий.

high priest первосвяще́нник.

high-ranking *adj.* высокопоста́вленный.

high-rise *adj.* многоэта́жный; высо́тный.

high school сре́дняя шко́ла.

high sign усло́вленный знак.

high society вы́сшее о́бщество; вы́сший свет.

high-sounding *adj.* гро́мкий; широковеща́тельный; треску́чий.

high-speed *adj.* скоростно́й; быстрохо́дный. *High-speed train,* скоростно́й по́езд. *High-speed computer,* быстроде́йствующая электро́нно-вычисли́тельная маши́на.

high-strung *adj.* не́рвный; нерво́зный.

high-tension *adj.* высо́кого напряже́ния.

high tide вы́сшая то́чка отли́ва.

high treason госуда́рственная изме́на.

highway *n.* шоссе́; магистра́ль.

highwayman *n.* разбо́йник.

hijack *v.t.* угоня́ть; похища́ть (самолёт). —**hijacker,** *n.* похити́тель (самолёта). —**hijacking,** *n.* уго́н (самолёта); похище́ние (самолёта); нападе́ние (на самолёт).

hike *v.i.* ходи́ть пешко́м. —*v.t., colloq.* (raise) повыша́ть. —*n.* **1,** (long walk) похо́д. **2,** (increase) повыше́ние: *price/wage hike,* повыше́ние цен/зарпла́ты.

hilarious *adj.* **1,** (gay) весёлый. **2,** (screamingly funny) умори́тельный. —**hilarity,** *n.* весе́лье.

hill *n.* холм. *Climb a hill,* взбира́ться на́ гору. *Roll down the hill,* кати́ться с горы́.

hillock *n.* хо́лмик; го́рка; приго́рок.

hillside *n.* склон горы́; склон холма́; косого́р.

hilltop *n.* верши́на холма́.

hilly *adj.* холми́стый.

hilt *n.* рукоя́тка; эфе́с. —**to the hilt,** по́лностью; до конца́.

him *pers. pron.* **1,** *used as dir. obj. of a verb,* его́: *Ask him,* спроси́ его́. **2,** *used as indir. obj. of a verb,* ему́: *Give him a dollar,* дай ему́ до́ллар. **3,** *used as obj. of a prep.,* него́; нему́; нём; ним: *from him,* от него́; *about him,* о нём.

himself *pers. pron.* **1,** *used for emphasis,* (он) сам: *He did it himself,* он сам э́то сде́лал. **2,** *used reflexively,* себя́: *He bought himself a coat,* он купи́л себе́ пальто́. *He hurt himself,* он уши́бся. —**by himself, 1,** (alone) оди́н. **2,** (without help) сам. —**he is not himself,** он сам не свой.

hind *adj.* за́дний: *hind legs,* за́дние ла́пы.

hinder *v.t.* меша́ть; препя́тствовать. *Hinder progress,* препя́тствовать прогре́ссу.

Hindi *n.* хи́нди.

hindrance *n.* препя́тствие; поме́ха.

hindsight *n.* ретроспе́кция. *In hindsight,* за́дним число́м (говоря́).

Hindu *n.* инду́с. —*adj.* инду́сский. —**Hinduism,** *n.* индуи́зм.

hinge *n.* **1,** (joint) пе́тля; шарни́р. **2,** (for a postage stamp) накле́йка. —*v.i.* [*usu.* **hinge on**] (depend on) зави́сеть (от).

hinny *n.* лоша́к.

hint *n.* намёк. —*v.t.* намека́ть. —*v.i.* [*usu.* **hint at**] намека́ть (на).

hinterland *n.* глушь; захолу́стье.

hip *n.* бедро́. *With one's hands on one's hips,* упере́в ру́ки в бока́. —**shoot from the hip,** *colloq.* руби́ть сплеча́.

hipbone *n.* тáзовая кость.

hippopotamus *n.* бегемóт; гиппопотáм.

hire *v.t.* **1,** (employ) нанимáть. **2,** (rent) брать напрокáт. —*n.* наём. *Be for hire,* сдавáться напрокáт.

hired *adj.* наёмный. *Hired hand,* наёмный рабóчий.

hireling *n.* наёмник; наймúт.

his *poss. adj. & pron.* егó: *his aunt,* егó тётя. *An aunt of his,* однá егó тётя. ♦*When the possessor is the subject of the sentence,* свой: *He sold his house,* он прóдал свой дом. *He broke his leg,* он сломáл нóгу.

hiss *v.i.* **1,** (give off a hissing sound) шипéть. **2,** (whistle disapproval) свистéть; шúкать. —*v.t.* освúстывать (+ *acc.*); шúкать (+ *dat.*). —*n.* = **hissing.**

hissing *n.* **1,** (sound of escaping air) шипéние. **2,** (sound of disapproval) свист. —*adj.* шипя́щий.

histology *n.* гистолóгия.

historian *n.* истóрик.

historic *adj.* истори́ческий.

historical *adj.* истори́ческий. —**historically,** *adv.* истори́чески.

historiography *n.* историогрáфия. —**historiographer,** *n.* историóграф.

history *n.* истóрия. *History lesson,* урóк истóрии. *History teacher,* учи́тель истóрии. *History department,* истори́ческий факультéт.

histrionic *adj.* театрáльный. —**histrionics,** *n.pl.* театрáльность.

hit *v.t.* **1,** (deal a blow to) ударя́ть: *hit someone in the face,* удáрить когó-нибудь по лицý *or* в лицó. *Hit a ball,* удáрить по мячý. **2,** (strike against) ударя́ться о *or* в. *Hit one's head on the door,* удáриться головóй о дверь. *The car hit a tree,* маши́на наскочи́ла *or* налетéла на дéрево. **3,** (strike, as a target) попадáть в. **4,** (reach; attain) достигáть: *The temperature hit 100°,* температýра дости́гла ста грáдусов. *Hit a high note,* взять высóкую нóту. **5,** *usu. passive* (affect severely): *be hard hit by the flood,* си́льно пострадáть от наводнéния. *Those hardest hit by inflation,* те, по комý больнéе всегó удáрила инфля́ция. —*v.i.* **1,** (strike, as of a storm) обрýшиваться. **2,** *fol. by* **on** *or* **upon** (come up with, as an idea) нападáть (на); набрести́ (на); додýматься (до). —*n.* **1,** (blow) удáр. **2,** (striking of a target) попадáние: *direct hit,* прямóе попадáние. **3,** (success) успéх: *be a big hit,* имéть большóй успéх. **4,** (film) боеви́к. —**hit back,** давáть сдáчи (+ *dat.*). —**hit it off,** сойти́сь харáктерами. *Hit it off with,* лáдить с. —**hit or miss,** как попáло; наудáчу; наобýм. —**hit the road,** *slang* отпрáвиться в путь.

hitch *v.t.* **1,** (tie; fasten) привя́зывать; прикрепля́ть. *Hitch a horse to a wagon,* запрягáть *or* впрягáть лóшадь в телéжку. *Hitch a car onto a train,* прицепля́ть вагóн к пóезду. **2,** (pull up with a jerk) подтя́гивать: *hitch up one's trousers,* подтя́гивать брю́ки. —*n.* **1,** (tug; jerk) рывóк. **2,** (delay; complication) зами́нка: *without a hitch,* без зами́нки. **3,** *colloq.* (period of service) срок (слýжбы).

hitchhike *v.i.* éхать на попýтной маши́не; «голосовáть» на дорóге.

hitching post кóновязь.

hither *adv.* сюдá.

hitherto *adv.* до сих пор.

Hittite *adj.* хéттский. —**Hittites,** *n.pl.* хéтты.

hive *n.* **1,** (beehive) ýлей. **2,** *pl.* (skin condition) крапи́вница.

hoard *n.* запáс. —*v.t.* закупáть впрок; запря́тывать про запáс.

hoarfrost *n.* и́ней; и́зморозь.

hoarse *adj.* хри́плый; си́плый. *Be hoarse,* хрипéть. *Become hoarse,* (о)хри́пнуть. *Talk oneself hoarse,* договори́ться до хрипоты́. —**hoarsely,** *adv.* хри́пло.

hoarseness *n.* хрипотá.

hoary *adj.* **1,** (gray or white with age) седóй. **2,** (ancient; venerable) почтéнный.

hoax *n.* шýтка; мистификáция.

hobble *v.i.* ковыля́ть. *Hobble along,* идти́ прихрáмывая. —*v.t.* (fetter) тренóжить; пýтать.

hobby *n.* хóбби.

hobbyhorse *n.* конь-качáлка.

hobgoblin *n.* **1,** (elf) домовóй. **2,** (bugaboo) жýпел.

hobnob *v.i.* води́ть компáнию; якшáться.

hobo *n.* бродя́га; бося́к.

hock *v.t., colloq.* заклáдывать. —*n., colloq., usu. in* **in hock,** в заклáде.

hockey *n.* хоккéй. —*adj.* хоккéйный: *hockey game,* хоккéйный матч. —**hockey player,** хоккеи́ст. —**hockey stick,** клю́шка.

hockshop *n.* ломбáрд.

hocus-pocus *n.* фóкус-пóкус.

hodgepodge *n.* мешани́на; ералáш.

hoe *n.* моты́га. —*v.t.* моты́жить.

hogwash *n.* **1,** (swill) пóйло (для свинéй). **2,** (nonsense) чепухá.

hoi polloi плебс; простонарóдье.

hoist *v.t.* поднимáть. *Hoist a flag,* подня́ть *or* вы́бросить *or* вы́кинуть флаг. —*n.* **1,** (act of hoisting) подъём. **2,** (hoisting device) подъёмник.

hold *v.t.* **1,** (grip) держáть: *hold in one's hand,* держáть в рукé. *Hold hands,* держáться зá руки. *Hold one's nose,* зажимáть нос. **2,** (keep in a certain position) держáть. *Hold one's head high,* держáть *or* нести́ гóлову высокó. **3,** (bear the weight of) удéрживать: *The hook will not hold the mirror,* крючóк не удéржит зéркала. **4,** (detain) держáть; задéрживать. *Hold (someone) prisoner,* держáть (когó-нибудь) в пленý. *He was held for questioning,* егó задержáли для допрóса. **5,** (delay the departure of) задéрживать: *hold a train,* задéрживать пóезд. **6,** (set aside until needed or requested) оставля́ть. *Hold in reserve,* держáть про запáс. **7,** (prevent from being captured) удéрживать: *hold the bridge,* удéрживать мост. **8,** (conduct) проводи́ть; вести́; устрáивать. *Hold a meeting,* проводи́ть собрáние. *Hold a meeting with someone,* провести́ встрéчу с кéм-нибудь. *The meeting will be held on Tuesday,* собрáние состои́тся во втóрник. *Hold talks,* вести́ переговóры. *Hold elections,* проводи́ть вы́боры. *Hold a wedding,* сыгрáть свáдьбу. **9,** (occupy, as a job or office) занимáть. **10,** (have room for; accommodate) вмещáть. **11,** (have; own) имéть; владéть.

Hold shares, владе́ть а́кциями. *Hold the rank of captain,* име́ть *or* носи́ть зва́ние капита́на. *He holds the world record for...,* ему́ принадлежи́т мирово́й реко́рд по... **12,** (maintain, as an opinion) приде́рживаться. **13,** (command, as attention) владе́ть. **14,** (consider; regard) счита́ть: *We hold these truths to be self-evident,* мы счита́ем самоочеви́дными сле́дующие и́стины. *Hold in high esteem,* высоко́ цени́ть; *hold sacred,* свя́то чтить; *hold in contempt,* относи́ться с презре́нием к. *You will be held responsible,* с вас бу́дут спра́шивать за э́то. **15,** (believe; maintain) утвержда́ть. **16,** (rule) постановля́ть: *The court held that...,* суд постанови́л, что... **17,** *Hold one's breath,* затаи́ть дыха́ние; *hold one's tongue, see* **tongue. 18,** *Not hold water,* не выде́рживать кри́тики. —*v.i.* **1,** (retain a hold) держа́ться: *hold tight,* держа́ться кре́пко. **2,** (not break or give way) держа́ть; выде́рживать. *The brakes aren't holding,* тормоза́ не де́ржат. *The glue isn't holding,* клей не де́ржит. *The rope held,* верёвка вы́держала. **3,** (stand firm) вы́стоять; устоя́ть: *The fortress held,* кре́пость вы́стояла *or* устоя́ла. **4,** (be true or valid) остава́ться в си́ле. —*n.* **1,** (grip) сжа́тие; хва́тка. *Take/catch/grab hold of,* ухвати́ться за. *Lose hold of,* упуска́ть. **2,** (of a ship) трюм. **3,** *wrestling* захва́т. **4,** (sway; control) власть; влия́ние. —**get (a) hold of, 1,** (get a grip on) ухвати́ться за. **2,** *colloq.* (obtain) раздобы́ть. **3,** *colloq.* (reach, as by telephone) связа́ться с; дозвони́ться до *or* к. **4,** *Get hold of oneself,* взять себя́ в ру́ки. —**hold against,** ста́вить в вину́ *or* в упрёк (+ *dat.*). —**hold aside,** сберега́ть. —**hold back, 1,** (restrain) уде́рживать; сде́рживать. *What's holding him back?,* что его́ сде́рживает? *Hold back the tears,* сде́рживать *or* уде́рживать слёзы; уде́рживаться от слёз. **2,** (withhold) заде́рживать; приде́рживать. **3,** (not reveal) недогова́ривать; ута́ивать. **4,** (retard) заде́рживать. —**hold down, 1,** (pin down) прижима́ть к земле́. **2,** (keep down, as prices) уде́рживать. **3,** *colloq.* (have; keep, as a job) уде́рживаться на (рабо́те). *Hold down two jobs,* рабо́тать на двух рабо́тах; рабо́тать по совмести́тельству. —**hold forth,** разглаго́льствовать. —**hold good,** остава́ться в си́ле. —**hold it!,** стой!; стоп! —**hold off, 1,** (check the advance of) уде́рживать. **2,** (delay in doing something) повремени́ть. —**hold on, 1,** (grasp something) держа́ться. **2,** (not hang up) не ве́шать (*or* не класть) тру́бку; подожда́ть у телефо́на. —**hold one's own,** *see* **own.** —**hold on to, 1,** (hold so as not to fall) держа́ться за (+ *acc.*): *hold on to the banister,* держа́ться за пери́ла. **2,** (hold in place) приде́рживать: *hold on to one's hat,* приде́рживать шля́пу. —**hold onto,** (retain) уде́рживать (за собо́й); оставля́ть (себе́). —**hold out, 1,** (proffer) протя́гивать. **2,** (offer, as hope) подава́ть (наде́жду). **3,** (stand firm) держа́ться; продержа́ться; устоя́ть; вы́стоять. **4,** (last; suffice) хвата́ть. —**hold still,** не шевели́ться. —**hold up, 1,** (raise) подноси́ть: *hold up to the light,* подноси́ть к све́ту. **2,** (support; keep from falling) подде́рживать; уде́рживать. **3,** (delay) заде́рживать. **4,** (expose; exhibit): *hold up as an example/ a model/,* ста́вить в приме́р/образе́ц. *Hold up to ridicule,* поднима́ть на́ смех. **5,** (last; continue to function) выде́рживать. **6,** (rob) гра́бить.

holder *n.* **1,** (possessor) держа́тель; облада́тель. *Holder of an order,* кавале́р о́рдена. **2,** (device) держа́тель. *Cigarette holder,* мундшту́к.

holding *n.* **1,** (conducting, as elections) проведе́ние. **2,** *usu. pl.* (property) владе́ния; (money) вкла́ды. —**holding pattern,** маршру́т ожида́ния.

holdover *n.* пережи́ток.

holdup *n., colloq.* **1,** (delay) заде́ржка. **2,** (robbery) налёт.

hole *n.* **1,** (opening; tear) дыра́; ды́рка. *Hole in the roof,* дыра́ в кры́ше. *Hole in one's stocking,* ды́рка на чулке́. *Bullet hole,* пулева́я пробо́ина. **2,** (in the ground) я́ма: *dig a hole,* рыть я́му. **3,** (animal's burrow) нора́; но́рка. **4,** *golf* лу́нка. **5,** *colloq.* (small dingy quarters) конура́. —*v.i.* [*usu.* **hole up**] скрыва́ться.

holiday *n.* **1,** (commemorative day) пра́здник. **2,** *Brit.* (vacation) о́тпуск. —*adj.* пра́здничный.

holiness *n.* **1,** (sanctity) свя́тость. **2,** *cap.* (papal title) святе́йшество: *His Holiness,* его́ святе́йшество.

holler *v.i., colloq.* ора́ть; вопи́ть. —*n., colloq.* вопль.

hollow *adj.* **1,** (having a cavity within) по́лый: *hollow sphere,* по́лый шар. **2,** (sunken, as of cheeks) впа́лый. **3,** (muffled, as of a sound) глухо́й. **4,** (meaningless; shallow) пусто́й. —*n.* углубле́ние; впа́дина; вы́емка; ложби́на; лощи́на; котлови́на. *Hollow of the hand,* горсть; при́горшня. *Hollow in a tree,* дупло́. —*v.t.* [*usu.* **hollow out**] долби́ть; выда́лбливать.

holly *n.* па́дуб; остроли́ст.

hollyhock *n.* штокро́за.

holmium *n.* го́льмий.

holocaust *n.* катастро́фа. *The (Nazi) Holocaust,* Катастро́фа.

holography *n.* гологра́фия.

holster *n.* кобура́.

holy *adj.* свято́й; свяще́нный. —**Holy Alliance,** Свяще́нный сою́з. —**Holy Ghost,** свято́й дух. —**holy of holies,** свята́я святы́х. —**Holy Roman Empire,** Свяще́нная Ри́мская импе́рия. —**Holy Scripture,** свяще́нное писа́ние. —**Holy See,** па́пский престо́л. —**Holy Thursday,** страстно́й четве́рг. —**holy water,** свята́я вода́. —**Holy Week,** свята́я *or* страстна́я неде́ля.

homage *n.* по́чести: *pay homage to,* ока́зывать *or* воздава́ть по́чести (+ *dat.*).

home *n.* дом. *Leave home,* уходи́ть *or* уезжа́ть из до́ма. *There's no place like home,* в гостя́х хорошо́, а до́ма лу́чше. —*adj.* дома́шний: *home address,* дома́шний а́дрес. *Home delivery,* доста́вка на́ дом. *The home team,* хозя́ева по́ля. —*adv.* **1,** (to one's home) домо́й: *go home,* идти́ домо́й. *Come/get home,* прийти́ домо́й. *On the way home,* по пути́ домо́й. *Write a letter home,* написа́ть письмо́ домо́й. *Take work home,* брать рабо́ту на́ дом. **2,** (at home) до́ма: *He is not home,* его́ нет до́ма. —**at home, 1,** (in one's house) до́ма. *Work at home,* рабо́тать до́ма *or* на дому́. **2,** *sports* на своём по́ле. **3,** (comfortable; at ease) как до́ма: *feel at home,* чу́вствовать себя́ как до́ма. *Make yourself at home!,* бу́дьте как до́ма! —**bring home to,** внуша́ть; втолкова́ть. —**from home,** из до́ма: *mail from home,* пи́сьма из до́ма. *Far from home,* далеко́ от до́ма. *Run away from home,* убежа́ть из до́ма. *I'm calling from home,* я звоню́ из до́ма. —**to one's home,** к себе́: *invite to one's home,* пригласи́ть к себе́. *I have never been to their home,* я никогда́ не́ был у них. —**strike home,** попа́сть не в бровь, а в глаз.

homebody *n.* домосе́д.

homebred *adj.* доморо́щенный.

home-brew *n.* самого́н.

homecoming *n.* возвраще́ние домо́й.

home economics домово́дство.

home front вну́тренний фронт.

homeland *n.* ро́дина; оте́чество.

homeless *adj.* бездо́мный; бесприю́тный; беспризо́рный. *Hundreds of people have been left homeless,* со́тни люде́й оста́лись без кро́ва. —*n., preceded by* **the,** бездо́мные.

homely *adj.* **1,** (unattractive) некраси́вый; невзра́чный. **2,** (unpretentious; plain) просто́й.

homemade *adj.* **1,** (of something made or built) дома́шнего изготовле́ния; самоде́льный. **2,** (of something cooked or brewed) дома́шний; дома́шнего приготовле́ния.

homemaker *n.* дома́шняя хозя́йка.

homeopathy *also,* **homoeopathy** *n.* гомеопа́тия. —**homeopath,** *n.* гомеопа́т. —**homeopathic,** *adj.* гомеопати́ческий.

homeowner *n.* домовладе́лец.

home rule самоуправле́ние.

homesick *adj.* тоску́ющий по до́му *or* по ро́дине. *Be homesick,* тоскова́ть по до́му *or* по ро́дине. —**homesickness,** *n.* тоска́ по до́му *or* по ро́дине.

homespun *adj.* **1,** (woven at home) домотка́ный. **2,** (simple; unpretentious) доморо́щенный.

homestead *n.* уса́дьба.

home town родно́й го́род.

homeward *adv.* домо́й; к до́му. *Homeward bound,* возвраща́ющийся домо́й.

homework *n.* дома́шнее зада́ние; дома́шняя рабо́та. *Do one's homework,* (при)гото́вить уро́ки *or* дома́шние зада́ния.

homicide *n.* уби́йство.

homily *n.* поуче́ние.

homing pigeon почто́вый го́лубь.

hominy *n.* мамалы́га.

homoeopathy *n.* = homeopathy.

homogeneous *adj.* одноро́дный. —**homogeneity,** *n.* одноро́дность.

homogenize *v.t.* гомогенизи́ровать.

homonym *n.* омо́ним.

homosexual *n.* гомосексуали́ст. —*adj.* гомосексуа́льный. —**homosexuality,** *n.* гомосексуали́зм.

hone *v.t.* точи́ть: *hone a razor,* точи́ть бри́тву.

honest *adj.* че́стный. *To be honest...,* че́стно говоря́. —**honest to goodness!,** че́стное сло́во!

honestly *adv.* **1,** (in an honest manner) че́стно. **2,** (really; truly) че́стное сло́во: *I honestly don't know,* че́стное сло́во, не зна́ю!

honesty *n.* че́стность. —**in all honesty,** че́стно говоря́; по со́вести (говоря́); положа́ ру́ку на́ сердце.

honey *n.* **1,** (sweet substance) мёд. **2,** *colloq.* (term of endearment) дорого́й; ми́лый. —*adj.* медо́вый.

honeybee *n.* медоно́сная пчела́.

honey cake коври́жка.

honeycomb *n.* со́ты.

honeydew *n.* медвя́ная роса́. —**honeydew melon,** зи́мняя дыня.

honeyed *adj.* медо́вый; слаща́вый; прито́рный.

honeymoon *n.* медо́вый ме́сяц.

honeysuckle *n.* жи́молость.

honk *n.* (sound of a car horn) гудо́к. —*v.i.* гуде́ть. —*v.t.* дать: *honk the horn,* дать гудо́к.

honor *also,* **honour** *n.* **1,** (integrity; reputation; privilege) честь. *Consider it an honor,* счита́ть за честь. *A party in your honor,* вечери́нка в ва́шу честь. *Do someone the honor of...,* оказа́ть кому́-нибудь честь (+ *inf.*). *It is my honor to introduce...,* име́ю честь предста́вить... **2,** (esteem) почёт. *Place of honor,* почётное ме́сто. **3,** *pl.* (ceremonies of respect) по́чести: *with military honors,* с во́инскими по́честями. **4,** *cap.* (title of respect) честь: *Your Honor,* ва́ша честь. **5,** *pl.* (credit awarded to outstanding students) отли́чие: *graduate with honors,* око́нчить с отли́чием. **6,** *pl., cards* онёры. —*v.t.* **1,** (show special respect for) почита́ть; чтить; почти́ть. *Honor thy father and thy mother,* почита́й *or* чти отца́ твоего́ и мать твою́. *Honor the memory of our fallen heroes,* чтить *or* почти́ть (па́мять) на́ших па́вших геро́ев. **2,** (pay tribute to; salute) че́ствовать: *honor the victors,* че́ствовать победи́телей. **3,** (bring honor or distinction to) ока́зывать честь (+ *dat.*). **4,** (observe; abide by) выполня́ть; соблюда́ть; приде́рживаться. —**do honor to,** де́лать честь (+ *dat.*). —**in honor of,** в честь (+ *gen.*). —**on my honor; word of honor,** че́стное сло́во.

honorable *also,* **honourable** *adj.* **1,** (honest; upright) че́стный: *honorable people/intentions,* че́стные лю́ди/наме́рения. **2,** (preserving one's dignity) почётный: *honorable peace,* почётный мир. **3,** *preceded by* **the** (title of respect) уважа́емый; почётный. —**honorable discharge,** *mil.* увольне́ние с положи́тельной характери́стикой.

honorarium *n.* гонора́р.

honorary *adj.* почётный: *honorary member,* почётный член.

honored *also,* **honoured** *adj.* почётный: *honored guest,* почётный гость. *I am honored to...,* счита́ю за честь (+ *inf.*).

honor guard почётный карау́л.

honor roll доска́ почёта.

honour *n. & v.* = honor. —**honourable,** *adj.* = honorable. —**honoured,** *adj.* = honored.

hood *n.* **1,** (head covering) капюшо́н. **2,** (cover of an engine) капо́т.

hooded *adj.* **1,** (wearing a hood) в капюшо́не. **2,** (containing a hood) с капюшо́ном. —**hooded seal,** хохла́ч.

hoodlum *n.* хулига́н.

hoodwink *v.t.* обма́нывать; провести́; обжу́ливать.

hoof *n.* копы́то. —**hoofed,** *adj.* копы́тный.

hook *n.* **1,** (metal device) крюк; крючо́к. *Leave the receiver off the hook,* не ве́шать тру́бку; забы́ть пове́сить тру́бку. **2,** *boxing* хук: *left hook,* хук сле́ва. —*v.t.* **1,** (fasten) застёгивать (на крючо́к). **2,** (attach; hitch) прицепля́ть. **3,** *fol. by* **up** (connect) подключа́ть. **4,** (catch, as a fish) выу́живать. —*v.i.* **1,** (fasten) застёгиваться: *The dress hooks in back,* пла́тье застёгивается сза́ди. **2,** *fol. by* **onto** (be attached to) пристёгиваться (к); прицепля́ться (к). —**by hook or by crook,** каки́м бы то ни́ было спо́собом; все́ми пра́вдами и непра́вдами; не мытьём, так ка́таньем. —**hook, line, and sinker,** по́лностью; целико́м.

hooked *adj.* **1,** (curved like a hook) крючкова́тый. *Hooked nose,* горба́тый нос; нос с горби́нкой. **2,** *fol. by* **on,** *slang* (addicted to) поме́шанный (на).

hookup *n.* **1,** (network) сеть. **2,** *colloq.* (connection) связь.

hookworm *n.* глист.

hooky *n., in* **play hooky,** прогу́ливать уро́ки.

hooligan *n.* хулига́н. —**hooliganism,** *n.* хулига́нство.

hoop *n.* о́бруч.

hoopla *n.* шум; шуми́ха.

hoopoe *n.* удо́д.

hoop skirt кринoли́н.

hooray *interj.* ура́!

hoosegow *n., colloq.* куту́зка.

hoot *n.* **1,** (cry of an owl) крик (совы́). **2,** (toot) гудо́к. —*v.i.* (of an owl) у́хать. —*v.t.* (jeer) освисты́вать.

hop *v.i.* **1,** (leap, as of a frog) пры́гать. **2,** (jump on one foot) пры́гать *or* скака́ть на одно́й ноге́. —*v.t.* вска́кивать на: *hop a train,* вскочи́ть на по́езд. —*n.* **1,** (jump) прыжо́к; скачо́к. **2,** *colloq.* (short flight) рейс. **3,** (plant) хмель. **4,** *pl.* (flavoring for beer) хмель. —**hop, step, and jump,** тройно́й прыжо́к.

hope *n.* наде́жда: *Don't lose hope!,* не теря́йте наде́жды! —*v.t. & i.* наде́яться. *I hope so,* наде́юсь, что да; *I hope not,* наде́юсь, что нет. *Hope for the best,* наде́яться на лу́чшее. *I hope to see you again soon,* наде́юсь ско́ро вас сно́ва уви́деть. —**hope against hope,** наде́яться вопреки́ всему́.

hopeful *adj.* **1,** (having hope): *be hopeful,* наде́яться; пита́ть наде́жды. **2,** (giving hope) обнадёживающий; подаю́щий наде́жды.

hopefully *adv.* **1,** (with hope) с наде́ждой. **2,** (if all goes well) на́до наде́яться, что...

hopeless *adj.* **1,** (offering no hope) безнадёжный; безвы́ходный; безысхо́дный. **2,** *colloq.* (worthless; without merit) беспо́мощный. —**hopelessly,** *adv.* безнадёжно. *She is hopelessly in love,* она́ безнадёжно влюблена́. —**hopelessness,** *n.* безнадёжность; безвы́ходность; безысхо́дность.

hopper *n.* бу́нкер.

hopscotch *n.* кла́ссы.

horde *n.* по́лчище; орда́.

horizon *n.* **1,** (line between the earth and the sky) горизо́нт: *sink below the horizon,* сади́ться за горизо́нт. **2,** *often pl.* (range of interests) кругозо́р: *expand one's horizons,* расширя́ть кругозо́р.

horizontal *adj.* горизонта́льный. —*n.* горизонта́ль. —**horizontal bar,** *sports* перекла́дина; турни́к.

horizontally *adv.* горизонта́льно.

hormone *n.* гормо́н.

horn *n.* **1,** (bonelike growth) рог. **2,** (instrument sounded by blowing) рог: *blow a horn,* труби́ть в рог. **3,** (brass-wind instrument) рожо́к. *English horn,* англи́йский рожо́к. **4,** (of an automobile) гудо́к; кла́ксон. **5,** *The Horn of Africa,* рог Áфрики. —**blow one's own horn,** труби́ть о себе́. —**draw/pull in one's horns,** бить отбо́й. —**horn of plenty,** рог изоби́лия. —**take the bull by the horns,** брать быка́ за рога́.

hornbeam *n.* граб.

hornblende *n.* роговáя обмáнка.

horned *adj.* рога́тый.

hornet *n.* ше́ршень. —**hornets' nest,** оси́ное гнездо́.

hornless *adj.* безро́гий; комо́лый.

horn-rimmed *adj.* роговой: *horn-rimmed glasses,* рого́вые очки́.

horny *adj.* **1,** (made of a hornlike substance) роговой. **2,** (calloused; tough) мозо́листый.

horoscope *n.* гороско́п.

horrendous *adj.* = **horrible**.

horrible *adj.* стра́шный; ужа́сный.

horrid *adj.* ужа́сать; проти́вный.

horrify *v.t.* ужаса́ть; приводи́ть в у́жас. *Be horrified,* ужаса́ться; приходи́ть в у́жас. —**horrifying,** *adj.* ужаса́ющий.

horror *n.* **1,** (terror) у́жас. **2,** *pl.* (that which horrifies) у́жасы: *the horrors of war,* у́жасы войны́. —**horror movie,** фильм у́жасов.

hors d'oeuvre заку́ска.

horse *n.* **1,** (animal) ло́шадь; конь. **2,** (frame) ра́ма. *Sawhorse,* ко́злы. **3,** *gymnastics* конь; кобы́ла. —*adj.* лошади́ный; ко́нный. —*v.i.* [*usu.* **horse around**] *colloq.* озорнича́ть; прока́зничать; дури́ть. —**back the wrong horse,** поста́вить не на ту ло́шадь. —**change horses in midstream,** меня́ть лошаде́й во вре́мя перепра́вы. —**from the horse's mouth,** из первоисто́чника. —**horse of a different color,** совсе́м друго́й коленко́р. —**play the horses,** игра́ть на ска́чках. —**work like a horse,** рабо́тать как вол.

horseback *adv.* верхо́м: *ride horseback,* е́здить верхо́м. *Be on horseback,* быть верхо́м. —**horseback riding,** верхова́я езда́. *Go horseback riding,* ката́ться верхо́м.

horse breeder конево́д. —**horse breeding,** коне́во́дство; коннозаво́дство.

horsecar *n.* ко́нка.

horse chestnut ко́нский кашта́н.

horsecloth *n.* попо́на.

horse doctor конова́л.

horse-drawn *adj.* ко́нный.

horseflesh *n.* кони́на.

horsefly *n.* слепе́нь.

horsehair *n.* ко́нский во́лос. —*adj.* волосяно́й: *horsehair mattress,* волосяно́й матра́с.

horsehide *n.* ко́нская шку́ра.

horselaugh *n.* хо́хот.

horseman *n.* вса́дник; нае́здник. —**horsemanship,** *n.* иску́сство верхово́й езды́; нае́здничество.

horsemeat *n.* кони́на.

horseplay *n.* баловство́; озорство́.

horsepower *n.* лошади́ная си́ла.

horse race ска́чка; заё́зд. —**horse racing,** ска́чки.

horseradish *n.* хрен.

horseshoe *n.* подко́ва.

horsetail *n.* (plant) хвощ.

horse thief конокра́д.

horsetrader *n.* бары́шник.

horsewhip *n.* хлыст. —*v.t.* отхлеста́ть.

horsewoman *n.* вса́дница; нае́здница; амазо́нка.

horticulture *n.* садово́дство. —**horticultural,** *adj.* садово́дческий. —**horticulturist,** *n.* садово́д.

hosanna *n.* оса́нна.

hose *n.* **1,** (device for squirting water) шланг; кишка́; рука́в. **2,** (stockings) чулки́. —*v.t.* полива́ть: *hose the deck,* полива́ть па́лубу.

hosiery *n.* чуло́чные изде́лия.

hospitable *adj.* гостеприи́мный.

hospital *n.* больни́ца; *mil.* го́спиталь. *Children's hospital,* де́тская больни́ца. *Maternity hospital,* роди́льный дом. *Be in the hospital,* быть *or* лежа́ть в больни́це. —*adj.* больни́чный; госпита́льный. —**hospital ship,** госпита́льное *or* санита́рное су́дно.

hospitality *n.* гостеприи́мство.

hospitalization *n.* **1,** (being hospitalized) госпитализа́ция. **2,** (insurance) страхова́ние на слу́чай госпитализа́ции.

hospitalize *v.t.* помеща́ть в больни́цу; госпитализи́ровать.

host *n.* **1,** (one who entertains) хозя́ин. **2,** (multitude) мно́жество; тьма. —**play host to,** *sports* принима́ть на своём по́ле.

hostage *n.* зало́жник. *Hold someone hostage,* держа́ть кого́-нибудь зало́жником.

hostel *n.* турба́за. *Youth hostel,* молодёжная турба́за.

hostelry *n.* постоя́лый двор.

hostess *n.* хозя́йка.

hostile *adj.* **1,** (antagonistic) вражде́бный; неприя́зненный. **2,** (being or belonging to an enemy) вра́жеский: *hostile countries/forces,* вра́жеские стра́ны/си́лы.

hostility *n.* **1,** (antagonism) вражда́; вражде́бность; неприя́знь. *With hostility,* вражде́бно. **2,** *pl.* (warfare) вое́нные де́йствия.

hot *adj.* **1,** (of the weather, temperature, etc.) жа́ркий: *a hot day,* жа́ркий день. *I am hot,* мне жа́рко. **2,** (of an object, liquid, etc.) горя́чий: *hot water,* горя́чая вода́; *hot soup/iron/shower,* горя́чий суп/утю́г/душ. **3,** (highly spiced) о́стрый. **4,** (impassioned; fiery) горя́чий. —**get into hot water,** попа́сть в беду́; попа́сть как кур во́ щи. —**hot on the trail of,** по горя́чим следа́м (+ *gen.*). —**not so hot,** так себе́.

hot air 1, *literally* нагре́тый во́здух. **2,** *colloq.* (empty talk) пустосло́вие.

hotbed *n.* **1,** (glass-covered bed of soil) парни́к. **2,** *fig.* (breeding ground) оча́г.

hot-blooded *adj.* горя́чий; пы́лкий; стра́стный.

hot cake блин. —**sell** (*or* **go**) **like hot cakes,** раскупа́ться нарасхва́т.

hot chocolate шокола́д.

hot dog *colloq.* соси́ска.

hotel *n.* гости́ница.

hothead *n.* горя́чая голова́; кипято́к. —**hotheaded,** *adj.* горя́чий; вспы́льчивый.

hothouse *n.* тепли́ца; оранжере́я. —*adj.* тепли́чный; оранжере́йный; парнико́вый.

hot line ли́ния «горя́чей свя́зи».

hotly *adv.* горячо́.

hot spot горя́чая то́чка.

hot spring горя́чий (минера́льный) исто́чник.

hot-tempered *adj.* горя́чий; вспы́льчивый; запа́льчивый.

hot-water bottle гре́лка.

hound *n.* охо́тничья соба́ка; го́нчая. —*v.t.* **1,** (pursue relentlessly) пресле́довать; трави́ть. **2,** *colloq.* (nag; pester) пристава́ть к.

hour *n.* час: *two hours,* два часа́. *Hour after hour,* час за ча́сом. *Hour by hour,* час о́т часу. *An eight-hour day,* восьмичасово́й рабо́чий день. *He is paid by the hour,* он на почасово́й опла́те; он почасови́к.

hourglass *n.* песо́чные часы́.

hour hand часова́я стре́лка.

hourly *adj.* **1,** (occurring every hour) ежеча́сный. **2,** (per hour) часово́й; почасово́й: *hourly wages,* часова́я/почасова́я опла́та. —*adv.* ежеча́сно.

house *n.* **1,** (dwelling place) дом. *At my house,* у меня́. *To my house,* ко мне. **2,** (building) зда́ние; дом. *Schoolhouse,* шко́льное зда́ние. *Rooming house,* пансио́н. *Movie house,* кино́. *Opera house,* о́перный теа́тр. *House of worship,* моли́твенный дом. **3,** (household) дом: *She runs the house,* она́ ведёт весь дом. *Wake up the whole house,* разбуди́ть весь дом. **4,** (institution) дом: *house of correction,* исправи́тельный дом. **5,** (business establishment) фи́рма. *Publishing house,* изда́тельство. **6,** (theater; audience) зал: *full house,* по́лный зал. **7,** (legislative body) пала́та: *House of Representatives,* пала́та представи́телей. *House of Commons,* пала́та общин. *House of Lords,* пала́та ло́рдов. **8,** (dynasty) дом: *House of Tudor,* дом Тюдо́ров. —*adj.* дома́шний: *house arrest,* дома́шний аре́ст. *House plant,* ко́мнатное расте́ние. —*v.t.* **1,** (provide quarters for) помеща́ть. *Be housed,* помеща́ться; размеща́ться. **2,** (serve as the headquarters of) вмеща́ть. —**bring down the house,** вызыва́ть взрыв сме́ха *or* аплодисме́нтов. —**house of cards,** ка́рточный до́мик. —**keep house,** вести́ (дома́шнее) хозя́йство. —**on the house,** за счёт предприя́тия.

houseboat *n.* плаву́чий дом.

housebreaker *n.* взло́мщик.

house call вы́зов на́ дом. *Make house calls,* явля́ться на вы́зовы на́ дом.

housecoat *n.* капо́т.

housefly *n.* ко́мнатная му́ха.

household *n.* семья́; домоча́дцы. *Run the household,* вести́ дома́шнее хозя́йство. —*adj.* дома́шний; хозя́йственный. *Household goods,* хозя́йственные това́ры. *Household items,* предме́ты дома́шнего обихо́да. *Household appliances,* бытовы́е прибо́ры. *Household chores,* хло́поты по хозя́йству.

housekeeper *n.* 1, (housewife) хозя́йка. 2, (woman hired to run a house) эконо́мка.

housekeeping *n.* веде́ние хозя́йства; дома́шнее хозя́йство; домово́дство.

housemaid *n.* го́рничная; домрабо́тница.

housetop *n., in* **from the housetops,** во всеуслы́шание; на всех перекрёстках.

housewarming *n.* новосе́лье.

housewife *n.* дома́шняя хозя́йка; домохозя́йка.

housework *n.* рабо́та по хозя́йству. *Help with the housework,* помога́ть по хозя́йству.

housing *n.* 1, (living quarters) жили́ще; жильё. *Poor housing,* неудовлетвори́тельные жили́щные усло́вия. *Provide with housing,* обеспе́чивать жильём. *Shortage of housing,* нехва́тка жилья́. 2, (casing) кожу́х. —*adj.* жили́щный: *housing conditions,* жили́щные усло́вия. *Housing allowance,* кварти́рное дово́льствие.

hovel *n.* лачу́га; хиба́ра.

hover *v.i.* 1, (remain suspended in the air) ре́ять. 2, *fol. by* **over** (stick close to) стоя́ть над (чьей-нибудь) душо́й. 3, (waver) колеба́ться. *Hover between life and death,* быть ме́жду жи́знью и сме́ртью.

hovercraft *n.* су́дно на возду́шной поду́шке.

how *adv.* 1, (in what manner; in what state) как: *How is this done?,* как э́то де́лается? *How are you?,* как вы пожива́ете? *How does the story end?,* чем конча́ется расска́з? 2, (to what extent) наско́лько: *How true is this?,* наско́лько э́то ве́рно? *How tall are you?,* како́го вы ро́ста? *How high is this building?,* како́й высоты́ э́то зда́ние? 3, *in exclamations,* как: *How strange!,* как стра́нно! *How awful!,* како́й у́жас! *How kind of you!,* как э́то ми́ло с ва́шей стороны́! *How you have changed!,* как вы измени́лись! —**and how!,** ещё бы! —**how about...?,** как насчёт...? *How about me/ the others!?,* а как же я?; а как же други́е? *Well, how about it?,* ну как? *How about starting right now?,* а что, е́сли начнём сейча́с? *How about a cup of tea?,* как насчёт ча́шки ча́ю? —**how come?,** почему́ же? *How come you're not asleep?,* что же ты не спишь? —**how do you do?,** 1, (hello) здра́вствуйте! 2, *on being introduced,* о́чень прия́тно! —**how far?,** *see* **far.** —**how long?,** *see* **long.** —**how many?; how much?,** ско́лько?: *how many books/times?,* ско́лько книг/раз?; *how much money?,* ско́лько де́нег? *How much will it cost?,* ско́лько э́то бу́дет сто́ить? —**how so?,** как же так?

however *conj.* одна́ко: *Now, however, it turns out that...,* тепе́рь выясня́ется, одна́ко, что... —*adv.* как (бы) ни: *However hard he tried,* как он ни стара́лся. *However much you want to,* ско́лько бы вы ни хоте́ли.

howitzer *n.* га́убица.

howl *v.i.* 1, (of an animal or the wind) выть; завыва́ть. 2, (cry out) реве́ть; вопи́ть. 3, (laugh loudly) хохота́ть. —*n.* вой; рёв; вопль.

howler *n.* гру́бая оши́бка.

howling monkey реву́н.

hub *n.* 1, (of a wheel) сту́пица. 2, (center; focal point) у́зел; средото́чие. *Rail hub,* железнодоро́жный у́зел.

hubbub *n.* гам; гвалт; галдёж.

hubcap *n.* колпа́к (сту́пицы).

huckleberry *n.* черни́ка.

huckster *n.* торга́ш; бары́шник.

huddle *v.i.* 1, (crowd together) жа́ться; тесни́ться; юти́ться; сбива́ться. 2, *fol. by* **up** (hunch up, as from the cold) ёжиться; жа́ться; сжима́ться.

hue *n.* 1, (color) цвет; кра́ска. 2, (shade) отте́нок. —**hue and cry,** шум: *raise a hue and cry,* поднима́ть шум.

huff *n.* вспы́шка гне́ва. *Get into a huff,* уда́риться в амби́цию. —*v.i.* (blow) дуть; фу́кать. *Huff and puff,* задыха́ться.

huffy *adj.* оби́дчивый.

hug *v.t.* 1, (embrace) обнима́ть. 2, (stick close to) пристава́ть к; держа́ться (+ *gen.*): *hug the shore,* пристава́ть к бе́регу; держа́ться бе́рега. —*v.i.* обнима́ться. —*n.* объя́тие.

huge *adj.* огро́мный; грома́дный.

Huguenot *n.* гугено́т.

hulk *n.* 1, (remains of an old ship) ко́рпус корабля́. 2, (huge bulky thing) грома́да; махи́на. —**hulking,** *adj.* неуклю́жий; медве́жий.

hull *n.* 1, (shell; husk) шелуха́. 2, (body of a ship) ко́рпус (корабля́). —*v.t.* шелуши́ть; лущи́ть. *Hulled grain,* лущёное зерно́.

hullabaloo *n.* шуми́ха; ажиота́ж; тарара́м.

hum *v.i.* 1, (sing without words) напева́ть. 2, (buzz) жужжа́ть. 3, *colloq.* (be full of activity) кипе́ть. —*v.t.* напева́ть. —*n.* 1, (of insects) жужжа́ние. 2, (of voices) гул; го́мон.

human *adj.* челове́ческий; людско́й. —**human being,** челове́к. —**human nature,** челове́ческая приро́да. —**human race,** челове́ческий род. —**human rights,** права́ челове́ка.

humane *adj.* гума́нный; челове́чный. —**humanely,** *adv.* гума́нно. —**humaneness,** *n.* гума́нность; челове́чность.

humanism *n.* гумани́зм.

humanist *n.* гумани́ст. —**humanistic,** *adj.* гумани́сти́ческий.

humanitarian *adj.* гума́нный; гуманита́рный. —*n.* благотвори́тель; филантро́п.

humanity *n.* 1, (mankind) челове́чество. 2, (humaneness) гума́нность; челове́чность. 3, *pl.* (literature, fine arts, etc.) гуманита́рные нау́ки.

humanize *v.t.* очелове́чивать.

humankind *n.* челове́чество.

humanly *adv. Everything that is/was humanly possible,* всё, что в челове́ческих си́лах. *Not humanly possible,* вы́ше челове́ческих сил.

humble *adj.* **1,** (not proud or self-assertive) смире́нный; поко́рный. *Your humble servant,* ваш поко́рный слуга́. *Humble request,* поко́рная про́сьба. **2,** (of low social rank) ни́зкий: *of humble origin,* ни́зкого происхожде́ния. **3,** (unpretentious) скро́мный: *humble abode,* скро́мное жили́ще. —*v.t.* унижа́ть; принижа́ть. *Humble oneself,* унижа́ться. —**humbly,** *adv.* смире́нно; поко́рно.

humdrum *adj.* однообра́зный; бу́дничный.

humid *adj.* вла́жный.

humidifier *n.* увлажни́тель.

humidify *v.t.* увлажня́ть.

humidity *n.* вла́жность.

humiliate *v.t.* унижа́ть. —**humiliating,** *adj.* унизи́тельный. —**humiliation,** *n.* униже́ние.

humility *n.* смире́ние; смире́нность.

hummingbird *n.* коли́бри.

hummock *n.* **1,** (low mound) ко́чка. **2,** (ridge in an ice field) торо́с.

humor *also,* **humour** *n.* **1,** (drollery; sense or use of same) ю́мор: *sense of humor,* чу́вство ю́мора. **2,** (mood) настрое́ние: *in good humor,* в хоро́шем настрое́нии. *Out of humor,* не в ду́хе. —*v.t.* ублажа́ть; ува́жить.

humoresque *n.* юморе́ска.

humorist *n.* юмори́ст.

humorous *adj.* **1,** (amusing) заба́вный; смешно́й. **2,** (containing humor) юмористи́ческий.

humour *n. & v.* = **humor.**

hump *n.* горб.

humpback *n.* **1,** (hump) горб. **2,** (person so afflicted) горбу́н; горба́тый. —**humpbacked,** *adj.* горба́тый.

humus *n.* перегно́й; гу́мус.

Hun *n.* гунн.

hunch *n.* **1,** (hump) горб. **2,** (feeling; premonition) предчу́вствие; интуи́ция. —*v.t.* го́рбить; суту́лить: *hunch one's back,* го́рбить/суту́лить спи́ну. —*v.i.* го́рбиться.

hunchback *n.* = **humpback.** —**hunchbacked,** *adj.* = **humpbacked.**

hunched *adj.* [*usu.* **hunched over**] сго́рбленный. *Sit hunched over the typewriter,* сиде́ть согну́вшись над пи́шущей маши́нкой.

hundred *adj.* сто. *One/two/three hundred dollars,* сто/ две́сти/три́ста до́лларов. —*n.* **1,** (cardinal number) сто. **2,** *pl.* (groups of 100) со́тни (+ *gen.*): *hundreds of people,* со́тни люде́й. *Number in the hundreds,* насчи́тываться *or* исчисля́ться со́тнями. *The number of victims could run into the hundreds,* число́ жертв мо́жет дойти́ до со́тен; счёт же́ртвам мо́жет пойти́ на со́тни.

hundredfold *adj.* стокра́тный. —*adv.* во́ сто крат.

hundredth *adj.* со́тый. *See also* **one-hundredth.**

Hungarian *adj.* венге́рский. —*n.* **1,** (person) венгр; венге́рка. **2,** (language) венге́рский язы́к.

hunger *n.* **1,** (craving for food) го́лод. **2,** *fig.* (great desire) жа́жда: *hunger for knowledge,* жа́жда зна́ний. —*adj.* голо́дный: *hunger pangs,* голо́дные му́ки. —*v.i.* [*usu.* **hunger for**] жа́ждать (+ *gen.*). —**die of hunger,** умира́ть с го́лоду; умира́ть голо́дной

сме́ртью. *I am dying of hunger (i.e. very hungry),* я умира́ю от го́лода; я стра́шно проголода́лся.

hunger strike голодо́вка: *go on a hunger strike,* объявля́ть голодо́вку. *He is in the fifth day of a hunger strike,* он голода́ет уже́ пять дней.

hungrily *adv.* жа́дно; с жа́дностью.

hungry *adj.* **1,** (wanting or needing food) голо́дный: *hungry wolf,* голо́дный волк. *I am hungry,* мне хо́чется есть; я го́лоден (голодна́). *Go hungry,* голода́ть. **2,** *fol. by* **for** (craving) жа́ждущий; жа́дный (к *or* до). *Be hungry for,* жа́ждать (+ *gen.*). *Hungry for knowledge,* жа́ждущий зна́ний; жа́дный до зна́ний.

hunk *n.* ломо́ть: *hunk of bread,* ломо́ть хле́ба.

hunky-dory *adj., slang, in* **everything is hunky-dory,** всё идёт как по ма́слу.

hunt *v.t.* **1,** (try to kill, as game) охо́титься на: *hunt bear,* охо́титься на медве́дей. **2,** (chase; pursue) пресле́довать. **3,** *fol. by* **down** (track down) затрави́ть; вы́следить. —*v.i.* **1,** (go hunting) охо́титься. **2,** *fol. by* **for** (search for) разы́скивать. —*n.* **1,** (hunting) охо́та. **2,** (search) по́иски.

hunter *n.* охо́тник.

hunting *n.* охо́та: *duck hunting,* охо́та на у́ток. *Go hunting,* идти́ на охо́ту. —*adj.* охо́тничий: *hunting season,* охо́тничий сезо́н.

huntsman *n.* = **hunter.**

hurdle *n.* **1,** (barrier) барье́р; препя́тствие. **2,** *pl.* (hurdle race) барье́рный бег; бег с препя́тствиями. —*v.t.* **1,** (clear, as a barrier) брать (барье́р). **2,** (overcome) преодолева́ть.

hurl *v.t.* **1,** (throw; fling) мета́ть; швыря́ть. **2,** (utter vehemently) осыпа́ть: *hurl insults at,* осыпа́ть (кого́-нибудь) оскорбле́ниями. —**hurl back,** отбива́ть: *hurl back the enemy,* отбива́ть проти́вника.

hurly-burly *n.* суматоха; переполо́х.

hurrah *interj.* ура́! *Also,* **hurray.**

hurricane *n.* урага́н.

hurried *adj.* торопли́вый; поспе́шный. —**hurriedly,** *adv.* торопли́во; поспе́шно; на́скоро; на́спех; второпя́х.

hurry *v.i.* [*also,* **hurry up**] спеши́ть; торопи́ться. *Hurry up!,* скоре́й!; быстре́е!; потора́пливайтесь! *Hurry about one's business,* спеши́ть по свои́м дела́м. —*v.t.* торопи́ть. —*n.* спе́шка; торопли́вость; поспе́шность. *Be in a hurry,* спеши́ть; торопи́ться. *There is no hurry,* не на́до спеши́ть; э́то не к спе́ху.

hurt *v.t.* **1,** (cause pain or discomfort to) причиня́ть боль (+ *dat.*). *It hurts me to walk,* мне бо́льно ходи́ть. *The sun hurts my eyes,* от со́лнца глаза́м бо́льно. **2,** (injure) повреждать; ушиба́ть: *hurt one's leg,* повреди́ть/ушиби́ть себе́ но́гу. *Hurt oneself,* ушиби́ться. *No one was hurt,* никто́ не пострада́л. **3,** (be detrimental to; damage) вреди́ть; по́ртить. *Hurt our cause,* вреди́ть на́шему де́лу. **4,** (wound the feelings of) задева́ть; обижа́ть. *Be hurt by a remark,* оби́деться на замеча́ние. —*v.i.* **1,** (be painful) боле́ть: *My stomach hurts,* у меня́ боли́т живо́т. *Does it hurt?,* вам бо́льно? *Where does it hurt?,* где боли́т? *It hurts to lie on my back,* бо́льно лежа́ть на спине́. **2,** (cause harm) меша́ть: *It wouldn't hurt to ask,* не меша́ло бы спроси́ть. *Excessive caution never hurts,* чрезме́рная осторо́жность никогда́ не меша́ет.

hurtle *v.i.* **1,** (rush violently) нести́сь; мча́ться. **2,** *fol. by* **against** (collide with) вреза́ться (в).

husband *n.* муж. —*v.t.* (conserve) эконо́мить.

husbandry *n.* земледе́лие. —**animal husbandry,** животново́дство.

hush *v.i.* молча́ть. —*v.t.* **1,** (call upon to be silent) ши́кать на. **2,** *fol. by* **up** (keep from public notice) зама́лчивать; замя́ть. —*n.* тишина́; молча́ние. *A hush fell over the hall,* в за́ле наступи́ла тишина́. —*interj.* ти́ше!; тсс!; шш!

husk *n.* шелуха́. —*v.t.* шелуши́ть; лущи́ть.

husky *adj.* **1,** (hoarse) си́плый; хри́плый. **2,** (burly) ро́слый; дю́жий. —*n.* (dog) ла́йка.

hussar *n.* гуса́р.

hussy *n.* же́нщина лёгкого поведе́ния.

hustle *v.t.* затолка́ть. —*v.i.* торопи́ться; суети́ться. —*n.* [*often* **hustle and bustle**] суета́; суматоха.

hustler *n.* **1,** (petty racketeer) живодёр. **2,** (go-getter) хлопоту́н.

hut *n.* хи́жина.

hyacinth *n.* гиаци́нт.

hybrid *n.* по́месь; гибри́д. —*adj.* гибри́дный; разноро́дный; сме́шанный.

hydra *n.* ги́дра.

hydrangea *n.* горте́нзия.

hydrant *n.* водоразбо́рный кран; водоразбо́рная коло́нка; гидра́нт. *Fire hydrant,* пожа́рный кран; пожа́рная коло́нка; пожа́рный гидра́нт.

hydrate *n.* гидра́т.

hydraulic *adj.* гидравли́ческий. —**hydraulics,** *n.* гидра́влика.

hydrocarbon *n.* углеводоро́д.

hydrochloric acid соля́ная кислота́.

hydrodynamics *n.* гидродина́мика.

hydroelectric *adj.* гидроэлектри́ческий. *Hydroelectric station,* гидроэлектроста́нция.

hydrofluoric acid плавико́вая кислота́.

hydrofoil *n.* **1,** (winglike structure) подво́дное крыло́. **2,** (craft) су́дно на подво́дных кры́льях.

hydrogen *n.* водоро́д. —*adj.* водоро́дный. —**hydrogen bomb,** водоро́дная бо́мба. —**hydrogen peroxide,** пе́рекись водоро́да. —**hydrogen sulfide,** сероводоро́д.

hydrology *n.* гидроло́гия.

hydrolysis *n.* гидро́лиз.

hydrometer *n.* гидро́метр.

hydrophobia *n.* водобоя́знь; бе́шенство.

hydroplane *n.* **1,** (boat) гли́ссер. **2,** (seaplane) гидросамолёт.

hydrostatics *n.* гидроста́тика.

hydroxide *n.* гидроо́кись.

hyena *n.* гие́на.

hygiene *n.* гигие́на.

hygienic *adj.* **1,** (pert. to hygiene) гигиени́ческий. **2,** (clean; sanitary) гигиени́чный.

hymen *n.* де́вственная плева́.

hymn *n.* гимн. —**hymnal,** *n.* сбо́рник ги́мнов.

hyperbola *n.* гипе́рбола.

hyperbole *n.* гипе́рбола.

hyperbolic *adj.* гиперболи́ческий.

hypercritical *adj.* приди́рчивый.

hyperinflation *n.* гиперинфля́ция.

hypertension *n.* гипертони́я.

hyphen *n.* дефи́с; чёрточка.

hyphenate *v.t.* писа́ть че́рез дефи́с *or* че́рез чёрточку.

hypnosis *n.* гипно́з. —**hypnotic,** *adj.* гипноти́ческий. —**hypnotism,** *n.* гипноти́зм. —**hypnotist,** *n.* гипнотизёр. —**hypnotize,** *v.t.* гипнотизи́ровать.

hypo *n., photog.* фикса́ж.

hypochondria *n.* ипохо́ндрия. —**hypochondriac,** *n.* ипохо́ндрик.

hypocrisy *n.* лицеме́рие.

hypocrite *n.* лицеме́р.

hypocritical *adj.* лицеме́рный. *Be hypocritical,* лицеме́рить; фальши́вить; криви́ть душо́й.

hypodermic *adj.* подко́жный. *Hypodermic needle,* игла́ для подко́жных впры́скиваний.

hypotenuse *n.* гипотену́за.

hypothesis *n.* гипо́теза.

hypothesize *v.i.* стро́ить гипо́тезу. —*v.t.* предполага́ть.

hypothetical *adj.* предположи́тельный; гада́тельный; гипотети́ческий.

hyrax *n.* дама́н.

hyssop *n.* иссо́п.

hysterectomy *n.* удале́ние ма́тки.

hysteria *n.* истери́я. —**hysterical,** *adj.* истери́ческий. *Become hysterical,* впада́ть в исте́рику. —**hysterics,** *n.pl.* исте́рика.

I

I, i девя́тая бу́ква англи́йского алфави́та. —**dot the "i's" and cross the "t's",** ста́вить то́чки над «и».

I *pers. pron.* я: *I don't know,* я не зна́ю. *You and I,* мы с ва́ми. *See also* **me.**

iamb *n.* ямб. —**iambic,** *adj.* ямби́ческий. *Iambic pentameter,* пятисто́пный ямб. *Iambic tetrameter,* четырёхсто́пный ямб.

Iberian *adj.* ибери́йский.

ibex *n.* **1,** (alpine goat) козеро́г. **2,** (Asiatic variety) сиби́рский козёл.

ibidem *adv.* [*usu. abbreviated to* **ibid.**] там же.

ibis *n.* и́бис.

ice *n.* лёд: *slip on the ice,* поскользну́ться на льду. —*adj.* ледяно́й. —*v.t.* замора́живать. —*v.i.* [*usu.* **ice up**] обледене́ть. —**break the ice,** разби́ть *or* слома́ть лёд.

ice age леднико́вый пери́од.

ice bag пузы́рь со льдом.

iceberg *n.* а́йсберг.

iceboat *n.* бу́ер.

icebound *adj.* **1,** (held fast by ice) затёртый льда́ми: *The ship is icebound,* су́дно затёрло льда́ми. **2,** (blocked by ice, as of a river) ско́ванный льда́ми.

icebox *n.* холоди́льник.

icebreaker *n.* (ship) ледоко́л.

icecap *n.* леднико́вый покро́в.

ice-cold *adj.* ледяно́й; холо́дный как лёд.

ice cream моро́женое.

ice cube ку́бик льда.

iced tea чай со льдом.

ice field плаву́чая льди́на. *Also,* **ice floe.**

ice hockey хоккей с ша́йбой.

Icelander *n.* исла́ндец. —**Icelandic,** *adj.* исла́ндский. —*n.* исла́ндский язы́к.

ice pack пузы́рь со льдом.

ice skate конёк. —**ice-skate,** *v.i.* [*also,* **go ice-skating**] ката́ться на конька́х.

ice water вода́ со льдом.

ichneumon *n.* ихневмо́н.

ichthyology *n.* ихтиоло́гия.

icicle *n.* сосу́лька.

icing *n.* **1,** (frosting, as for a cake) глазу́рь. **2,** *aero.* обледене́ние.

icon *n.* ико́на. *Icon painter,* иконопи́сец. —*adj.* ико́нный. —**icon case,** кио́т. —**icon lamp,** лампа́да.

iconoclasm *n.* иконобо́р(че)ство. —**iconoclast,** *n.* иконобо́рец. —**iconoclastic,** *adj.* иконобо́рческий.

iconostasis *n.* иконоста́с.

icy *adj.* **1,** (ice-covered, as of roads) обледене́лый. **2,** (freezing cold) ледяно́й: *icy wind,* ледяно́й ве́тер. **3,** *fig.* (frosty; hostile) ледяно́й: *icy stare/reception,* ледяно́й взгляд/приём.

idea *n.* **1,** (original thought) иде́я; мысль: *brilliant idea,* блестя́щая иде́я/мысль. *Where did you get that idea?,* с чего́ вы э́то взя́ли? **2,** (notion; mental picture) представле́ние: *have a general idea of...,* име́ть о́бщее представле́ние о. *Not have the slightest idea,* не име́ть ни мале́йшего поня́тия *or* представле́ния.

ideal *n.* идеа́л. —*adj.* идеа́льный.

idealism *n.* идеали́зм. —**idealist,** *n.* идеали́ст. —**idealistic,** *adj.* идеалисти́ческий.

idealize *v.t.* идеализи́ровать.

identical *adj.* одина́ковый; тожде́ственный; иденти́чный. —**identical twins,** по́лные близнецы́.

identically *adv.* одина́ково.

identification *n.* **1,** (act of identifying) опозна́ние. **2,** (that which serves to identify) удостовере́ние ли́чности.

identify *v.t.* **1,** (establish the identity of) опознава́ть: *identify the victims of the earthquake,* опозна́ть же́ртвы землетрясе́ния. **2,** (name; give the name of) называ́ть: *identify one's source of information,* назва́ть исто́чник информа́ции. *Identify oneself,* назва́ть себя́; назва́ться. **3,** *fol. by* **with** (associate) отождествля́ть (с). —*v.i.* [*usu.* **identify with**] отождествля́ть себя́ с. —**identifying,** *adj.* опознава́тельный.

identity *n.* **1,** (sameness) то́ждество; тожде́ственность. **2,** (fact of being someone) ли́чность. —**identity card,** удостовере́ние ли́чности.

ideogram *n.* идеогра́мма. *Also,* **ideograph.**

ideology *n.* идеоло́гия. —**ideological,** *adj.* идеологи́ческий; иде́йный. —**ideologist; ideologue,** *n.* идео́лог.

ides *n.pl.* и́ды: *the ides of March,* и́ды ма́рта.

idiocy *n.* **1,** (mental deficiency) идиоти́зм. **2,** (extreme foolishness) идио́тство.

idiom *n.* **1,** (idiomatic expression) идиомати́ческое выраже́ние. **2,** (language; dialect) язы́к; го́вор; наре́чие. —**idiomatic,** *adj.* идиомати́ческий.

idiosyncrasy *n.* стра́нность; причу́да; вы́верт; заско́к.

idiot *n.* идио́т. —**idiotic,** *adj.* идио́тский; дура́цкий.

idle *adj.* **1,** (doing nothing; not occupied) без де́ла; пра́здный. **2,** (not in operation) безде́йствующий. *Stand idle,* проста́ивать. *The plant has been idle for three days,* заво́д стои́т уже́ тре́тий день. **3,** (casual) пра́здный: *idle curiosity,* пра́здное любопы́тство. *Idle fantasy,* досу́жая фанта́зия. **4,** (meaningless) пусто́й: *idle chatter,* пуста́я болтовня́. —*v.i.* **1,** (loaf) безде́льничать. **2,** (of a motor) рабо́тать вхолосту́ю; рабо́тать на холосто́м ходу́. —*v.t.* **1,** (put out of work) оставля́ть без рабо́ты. **2,** *fol. by* **away** (while away) корота́ть.

idleness *n.* безде́лье; пра́здность.

idler *n.* безде́льник.

idly *adv.* пра́здно; сложа́ ру́ки. *Sit idly by,* сиде́ть сложа́ ру́ки.

idol *n.* **1,** (image of a god) и́дол; истука́н. **2,** (object of great admiration) и́дол; куми́р.

idolater *n.* идолопокло́нник. —**idolatrous,** *adj.* идол-опокло́ннический. —**idolatry,** *n.* идолопокло́нство.

idolize *v.t.* обожа́ть; боготвори́ть.

idyll *also,* **idyl** *n.* иди́ллия. —**idyllic,** *adj.* идилли́ческий.

if *conj.* **1,** (in the event that; on condition that) е́сли: *if he wishes to,* е́сли он хо́чет; *if he comes,* е́сли он придёт. ♦*In contrary-to-fact sentences,* е́сли бы: *if I had known,* е́сли бы я знал. *If I were you,* на ва́шем ме́сте. **2,** (whether) ли : *I don't know if she's coming,* я не зна́ю, придёт ли она́ (и́ли нет). *Open the door and see if it's raining,* откро́й дверь и посмотри́, идёт ли дождь. —**as if,** *see* **as.** —**if it were not for...,** е́сли бы не (+ *nom.*). —**if not, 1,** (if that is not the case) е́сли нет. **2,** (not to say) что́бы (*or* е́сли) не сказа́ть: *difficult, if not impossible,* тру́дно, что́бы/е́сли не сказа́ть невозмо́жно. **3,** (other than) как не: *Who, if not us?,* кто, как не мы? —**if only, 1,** (be it only) хотя́ бы: *if only for a few minutes,* хотя́ бы на не́сколько мину́т. **2,** *to express a profound wish,* е́сли (бы) то́лько; о, е́сли бы; лишь бы. *If only I had known!,* е́сли бы я то́лько знал!

igloo *n.* и́глу.

igneous *adj.* **1,** (of fire) о́гненный. **2,** *geol.* изве́рженный.

ignite *v.t.* зажига́ть; воспламеня́ть. —*v.i.* загора́ться; воспламеня́ться.

ignition *n.* зажига́ние; воспламене́ние. *Turn on the ignition,* включи́ть зажига́ние. —**ignition key,** ключ зажига́ния. —**ignition switch,** выключа́тель зажига́ния.

ignoble *adj.* неблагоро́дный.

ignominious *adj.* позо́рный; бессла́вный. —**ignominy,** *n.* позо́р; бессла́вие.

ignoramus *n.* неве́жда; неуч; профа́н.

ignorance *n.* **1,** (lack of education or enlightenment) неве́жество. **2,** (lack of knowledge or information about something) незна́ние; неве́дение; неосведом-лённость.

ignorant *adj.* **1,** (knowing very little; uninformed) неве́жественный. **2,** (lacking knowledge of a certain field) несве́дущий: *ignorant of physics,* несве́дущий в фи́зике. **3,** (unaware) неосведомлённый.

ignore *v.t.* не обраща́ть внима́ния на; игнори́ровать.

iguana *n.* игуа́на.

ilk *n.* род: *of that ilk,* тако́го ро́да.

ill *adj.* **1,** (sick) больно́й. *Feel ill,* пло́хо себя́ чу́вствовать. *I began to feel ill,* мне ста́ло пло́хо. *Become ill,* заболева́ть. *He suddenly became ill,* ему́ внеза́пно ста́ло пло́хо. **2,** (bad) дурно́й: *ill omen,* дурно́е предзнаменова́ние. *Ill health,* сла́бое здоро́вье. *Ill effects,* отрица́тельные после́дствия. —*adv.* **1,** (badly) ду́рно: *speak ill of,* ду́рно говори́ть о. **2,** (hardly) едва́ ли: *We can ill afford to lose him,* едва́ ли мы обойдёмся без него́. —*n.* **1,** (evil; harm) зло; вред. **2,** *pl.* (troubles; problems) бе́ды: *social ills,* социа́льные бе́ды. —**ill at ease,** нело́вко: *feel ill at ease,* чу́вствовать себя́ нело́вко.

ill-advised *adj.* неблагоразу́мный.

ill-bred *adj.* невоспи́танный.

ill-considered *adj.* неблагоразу́мный; неразу́мный.

ill-defined *adj.* неопределённый.

ill-disposed *adj.* не располо́жен (к).

illegal *adj.* незако́нный; нелега́льный; противо-зако́нный. —**illegality,** *n.* незако́нность; нелега́льность; противозако́нность. —**illegally,** *adv.* незако́нно; нелега́льно.

illegible *adj.* неразбо́рчивый. —**illegibility,** *n.* неразбо́рчивость.

illegitimate *adj.* **1,** (unlawful) незако́нный. **2,** (born out of wedlock) внебра́чный; незаконнорождён-ный. —**illegitimacy,** *n.* незако́нность.

ill-fated *adj.* злополу́чный; злосча́стный.

illicit *adj.* незако́нный; недозво́ленный.

illiteracy *n.* негра́мотность. —**illiterate,** *adj.* не-гра́мотный; безгра́мотный. —*n.* негра́мотный.

ill-mannered *adj.* невоспи́танный.

illness *n.* боле́знь.

illogical *adj.* нелоги́чный. —**illogically,** *adv.* не-логи́чно.

ill-starred *adj.* злополу́чный; злосча́стный.

ill-tempered *adj.* злой; раздражи́тельный.

ill-timed *adj.* несвоевре́менный.

illuminate *v.t.* освеща́ть. —**illuminated manuscript,** лицева́я ру́копись.

illuminating *adj.* **1,** (providing light) освети́тельный. **2,** *fig.* (enlightening) поучи́тельный.

illumination *n.* освеще́ние.

illusion *n.* иллю́зия. —**optical illusion,** опти́ческий обма́н; обма́н зре́ния.

illusory *adj.* иллюзо́рный; обма́нчивый; при́зрач-ный. *Also,* **illusive.**

illustrate *v.t.* иллюстри́ровать. —**illustration,** *n.* иллюстра́ция. —**illustrative,** *adj.* иллюстрати́вный. —**illustrator,** *n.* иллюстра́тор.

illustrious *adj.* знамени́тый; выдаю́щийся; просла́вленный.

ill will зло́ба; недоброжела́тельность; недобро-жела́тельство. *Bear someone no ill will,* не держа́ть зла на (+ *acc.*).

ill-wisher *n.* недоброжела́тель.

image *n.* **1,** (representation; conception) о́браз; изображе́ние. *Visual image,* зри́тельный о́браз. *Mirror* *image,* зерка́льное изображе́ние. *He is the image of his father,* он вы́литый оте́ц; он весь в отца́. **2,** (public perception) и́мидж.

imagery *n.* о́бразность.

imaginable *adj.* кото́рый мо́жно себе́ предста́вить.

imaginary *adj.* вообража́емый; мни́мый. *Imaginary line,* вообража́емая *or* усло́вная ли́ния.

imagination *n.* воображе́ние. *It's just your imagination,* э́то вам то́лько ка́жется (*or* мере́щится).

imaginative *adj.* име́ющий большу́ю си́лу воображе́ния.

imagine *v.t. & i.* **1,** (visualize in the mind) вообража́ть; представля́ть себе́. *I can imagine!,* вообража́ю! *You can't imagine!,* вы себе́ не мо́жете предста́вить! *You're just imagining it,* э́то вам то́лько ка́жется. **2,** (suppose) ду́мать; полага́ть. *I imagine around six,* ду́маю, о́коло шести́.

imbalance *n.* дисбала́нс: *trade imbalance,* торго́вый дисбала́нс.

imbecile *n.* слабоу́мный; идио́т; глупе́ц. —**imbecilic,** *adj.* идио́тский; дура́цкий. —**imbecility,** *n.* слабоу́мие; идиоти́зм.

imbed *v.* = **embed.**

imbibe *v.t.* **1,** (drink) пить. **2,** (absorb) впи́тывать.

imbue *v.t.* внуша́ть; вселя́ть; привива́ть.

imitate *v.t.* подража́ть (+ *dat.*); имити́ровать (+ *acc.*).

imitation *n.* **1,** (act of imitating) подража́ние; имита́ция. **2,** (fake) имита́ция. —*adj.* иску́сственный. *Imitation pearl,* имита́ция же́мчуга. *In imitation walnut,* под оре́х. —**imitative,** *adj.* подража́тельный. —**imitator,** *n.* подража́тель; имита́тор.

immaculate *adj.* безукори́зненно чи́стый. —**Immaculate Conception,** непоро́чное зача́тие.

immaterial *adj.* **1,** (not consisting of matter) невеще́ственный. **2,** (all the same): *It's immaterial to me,* мне э́то безразли́чно.

immature *adj.* незре́лый. —**immaturity,** *n.* незре́лость.

immeasurable *adj.* неизмери́мый. —**immeasurably,** *adv.* неизмери́мо.

immediacy *n.* неотло́жность.

immediate *adj.* **1,** (instant; prompt) неме́дленный: *an immediate reply,* неме́дленный отве́т. **2,** (nearest; next in order) ближа́йший; непосре́дственный. *In the immediate future,* в ближа́йшем бу́дущем. *In the immediate vicinity (of),* в непосре́дственной бли́зости (от). *Immediate superior,* непосре́дственный нача́льник.

immediately *adv.* **1,** (right then) неме́дленно; сра́зу; сейча́с же; то́тчас же. **2,** (right now) сейча́с; неме́дленно.

immemorial *adj.* незапа́мятный. —**since time immemorial,** с незапа́мятных времён.

immense *adj.* огро́мный. —**immensely,** *adv.* о́чень; весьма́. —**immensity,** *n.* огро́мные разме́ры (чего́-нибудь).

immerse *v.t.* погружа́ть. —**immersion,** *n.* погруже́ние.

immigrant *n.* иммигра́нт.

immigrate *v.i.* иммигри́ровать.

immigration *n.* иммигра́ция. —*adj.* иммиграцио́нный.

imminent *adj.* бли́зкий; надвига́ющийся. *His imminent departure,* его́ бли́зкий отъе́зд. *In imminent danger,* в непосре́дственной опа́сности.

immobile *adj.* неподви́жный. —**immobility,** *n.* неподви́жность.

immobilize *v.t.* **1,** (prevent from getting around) де́лать неподви́жным; лиша́ть подви́жности. **2,** *med.* иммобилизова́ть.

immoderate *adj.* неуме́ренный. —**immoderation,** *n.* неуме́ренность; невозде́ржанность.

immodest *adj.* нескро́мный. —**immodesty,** *n.* нескро́мность.

immolate *v.t.* приноси́ть в же́ртву. —**immolation,** *n.* жертвоприноше́ние.

immoral *adj.* безнра́вственный. —**immorality,** *n.* безнра́вственность.

immortal *adj.* бессме́ртный. —**immortality,** *n.* бессме́ртие.

immortalize *v.t.* обессме́ртить; увекове́чивать. —**immortalization,** *n.* увекове́чение.

immovable *adj.* неподви́жный; недви́жимый.

immune *adj.* **1,** (protected from a certain disease) невоспри́имчивый. *She is immune to the mumps,* у неё иммуните́т про́тив сви́нки. **2,** (exempt) свобо́дный. —**immune system,** имму́нная систе́ма.

immunity *n.* **1,** *med.* иммуните́т; невоспри́имчивость. **2,** *law* неприкоснове́нность. —**diplomatic immunity,** дипломати́ческая неприкоснове́нность; дипломати́ческий иммуните́т.

immunize *v.t.* иммунизи́ровать. —**immunization,** *n.* иммуниза́ция.

immutable *adj.* непрело́жный.

imp *n.* чертёнок; бесёнок; постре́л.

impact *n.* **1,** (force of a collision) уда́р: *The plane broke up on impact,* самолёт развали́лся при уда́ре о зе́млю. **2,** *fig.* (effect) возде́йствие. *Have an impact on,* оказа́ть возде́йствие на.

impair *v.t.* по́ртить; вреди́ть.

impairment *n.* по́рча; вред; ухудше́ние. *Visual impairment,* по́рча зре́ния. *Hearing impairment,* ухудше́ние слу́ха.

impale *v.t.* **1,** (pierce) пронза́ть. **2,** (kill or torture by fixing on a stake) сажа́ть на́ кол.

impart *v.t.* **1,** (transmit, as a quality) придава́ть; сообща́ть. **2,** (reveal; pass along, as knowledge) сообща́ть; передава́ть.

impartial *adj.* беспристра́стный. —**impartiality,** *n.* беспристра́стие.

impassable *adj.* непроходи́мый; непрое́зжий. —**impassability,** *n.* непроходи́мость.

impasse *n.* тупи́к.

impassioned *adj.* стра́стный; пы́лкий; горя́чий.

impassive *adj.* бесстра́стный. —**impassivity,** *n.* бесстра́стие.

impatience *n.* нетерпе́ние.

impatient *adj.* нетерпели́вый. *Grow/become impatient,* теря́ть терпе́ние. *He is impatient to leave,* ему́ не те́рпится уйти́.

impatiently *adv.* нетерпели́во. *Wait impatiently,* ждать с нетерпе́нием.

impeachment *n.* импи́чмент.

impeccable *adj.* безупре́чный; безукори́зненный.

impecunious *adj.* безде́нежный.

impede *v.t.* препя́тствовать; меша́ть. *Impede the movement of...,* препя́тствовать/меша́ть движе́нию *or* продвиже́нию (+ *gen.*).

impediment *n.* **1,** (obstruction) препя́тствие. **2,** (defect) дефе́кт: *speech impediment,* дефе́кт ре́чи.

impel *v.t.* побужда́ть; заставля́ть: *What impelled him to...?,* что побуди́ло/заста́вило его́ (+ *inf.*).

impending *adj.* предстоя́щий; надвига́ющийся.

impenetrability *n.* непроница́емость; непроходи́мость.

impenetrable *adj.* **1,** (impossible to pierce or break through) непроница́емый; непробива́емый. **2,** (impossible to walk or travel across) непроходи́мый. **3,** (impossible to see through) непрогля́дный.

impenitent *adj.* нераска́явшийся.

imperative *adj.* **1,** (essential) необходи́мый: *It is imperative that we be on time,* нам необходи́мо прийти́ во́время. **2,** *gram.* повели́тельный. —*n.* **1,** (compelling requirement) императи́в. **2,** *gram.* повели́тельное наклоне́ние; императи́в.

imperceptible *adj.* незаме́тный; неощути́мый. —**imperceptibly,** *adv.* незаме́тно.

imperfect *adj.* несоверше́нный.

imperfection *n.* **1,** (state of being imperfect) несоверше́нство. **2,** (defect; flaw) недоста́ток; дефе́кт; несоверше́нство.

imperfective *adj., gram.* несоверше́нный: *imperfective aspect,* несоверше́нный вид.

imperforate *adj.* беззубцо́вый.

imperial *adj.* импе́рский; импера́торский.

imperialism *n.* империали́зм. —**imperialist,** *n.* империали́ст. —**imperialistic,** *adj.* империалисти́ческий.

imperil *v.t.* подверга́ть опа́сности; ста́вить под угро́зу.

imperious *adj.* повели́тельный; вла́стный; императи́вный.

imperishable *adj.* **1,** (not subject to decay) непо́ртящийся. **2,** (enduring; everlasting) неруши́мый; нетле́нный.

impermanent *adj.* непостоя́нный. —**impermanence,** *n.* непостоя́нство.

impermeable *adj.* непроница́емый. —**impermeability,** *n.* непроница́емость.

impermissible *adj.* недопусти́мый; непозволи́тельный.

impersonal *adj.* безли́чный.

impersonate *v.t.* подража́ть; выдава́ть себя́ за.

impertinent *adj.* де́рзкий; на́глый; наха́льный. —**impertinence,** *n.* де́рзость; на́глость; наха́льство.

imperturbable *adj.* невозмути́мый. —**imperturbability,** *n.* невозмути́мость.

impervious *adj.* **1,** (impenetrable) непроница́емый. **2,** *fol. by* **to** (not open to; not influenced by) глух (к).

impetuosity *n.* опроме́тчивость.

impetuous *adj.* опроме́тчивый; поры́вистый. —**impetuously,** *adv.* опроме́тчиво.

impetus *n.* и́мпульс; толчо́к; побужде́ние.

impiety *n.* непочти́тельность.

impinge *v.i.* [*usu.* **impinge upon**] посяга́ть на; покуша́ться на.

impish *adj.* прока́зливый; шаловли́вый.

implacable *adj.* неумоли́мый. *Implacable enemies,* непримири́мые враги́.

implant *v.t.* **1,** (set firmly in the ground) вка́лывать. **2,** *med.* вживля́ть. **3,** *fig.* (instill; inculcate) привива́ть; укореня́ть; насажда́ть.

implantation *n.* вживле́ние; имплрнта́ция.

implausible *adj.* невероя́тный; неправдоподо́бный.

implement *n.* ору́дие; инструме́нт. —*v.t.* осуществля́ть: *implement an idea,* осуществля́ть иде́ю. —**implementation,** *n.* осуществле́ние.

implicate *v.t.* вовлека́ть; заме́шивать; впу́тывать.

implication *n.* **1,** (act of involving) вовлече́ние. **2,** (inference) намёк. **3,** (application; significance) значе́ние.

implicit *adj.* **1,** (understood; implied) подразумева́емый. *Be implicit,* подразумева́ться. *Implicit agreement,* молчали́вое соглаше́ние. **2,** (unreserved; absolute) беспрекосло́вный. *Implicit faith,* слепа́я ве́ра.

implore *v.t.* умоля́ть.

imply *v.t.* намека́ть; хоте́ть сказа́ть. *I did not mean to imply that...,* я не хоте́л(а) э́тим сказа́ть, что...

impolite *adj.* неве́жливый. —**impoliteness,** *n.* неве́жливость.

impolitic *adj.* нетакти́чный; беста́ктный; неполити́чный.

imponderable *adj.* нея́сный; неопределённый; неизве́стный.

import *v.t.* ввози́ть; импорти́ровать. —*n.* **1,** *pl.* (goods imported) ввоз; и́мпорт. **2,** (significance; importance) значе́ние; ва́жность. —*adj.* и́мпортный; ввозны́й: *import duty,* и́мпортная/ввозна́я по́шлина.

importance *n.* ва́жность: *of particular importance,* осо́бой ва́жности. *Be of great importance to,* име́ть большо́е значе́ние для. *Attach great importance to,* придава́ть большо́е значе́ние (+ *dat.*). *Assume an air of importance,* принима́ть ва́жный вид; напуска́ть на себя́ ва́жность.

important *adj.* ва́жный: *important person/event/discovery,* ва́жное лицо́/собы́тие/откры́тие. *It's not important,* э́то не ва́жно. *The project was important to me,* прое́кт был ва́жен для меня́.

importation *n.* ввоз; и́мпорт.

imported *adj.* ввозно́й; и́мпортный.

importer *n.* импортёр.

importunate *adj.* навя́зчивый; назо́йливый; неотвя́зный.

importune *v.t.* докуча́ть; надоеда́ть.

impose *v.t.* **1,** (levy; introduce) налага́ть; вводи́ть. *Impose a fine/ban,* налага́ть штраф/запре́т. *Impose a tax,* вводи́ть нало́г. *Impose a tax/duty on,* облага́ть (+ *acc.*) нало́гом/по́шлиной. *Impose restrictions,* вводи́ть ограниче́ния. *Impose sanctions,* применя́ть *or* налагáть *or* вводить сáнкции. *Impose sentence,* выносить пригово́р. **2,** (force) навя́зывать: *impose one's will on someone,* навя́зывать кому́-нибудь свою́ во́лю. —*v.i.* [*usu.* **impose upon**] эксплуати́ровать.

imposing *adj.* внуши́тельный; представи́тельный; импозáнтный.

imposition *n.* **1,** (levying) наложе́ние; обложе́ние. **2,** (taking advantage) эксплуатáция. *I think it's an imposition on your part,* по-мо́ему вы сли́шком мно́го от (+ *gen.*) тре́буете.

impossibility *n.* невозмо́жность.

impossible *adj.* невозмо́жный: *It/that is impossible,* э́то невозмо́жно. *It is impossible to...,* нельзя́ (+ *inf.*). *Impossible task,* невыполни́мая задáча. *Impossible dream,* неисполни́мая мечтá. —*n., preceded by* **the** невозмо́жное: *wish for the impossible,* желáть невозмо́жного.

impost *n.* налóг; пóдать.

impostor *n.* самозвáнец.

impotence *n.* **1,** (helplessness) бесси́лие. **2,** *med.* импоте́нция; половóе бесси́лие.

impotent *adj.* **1,** (helpless) бесси́льный. **2,** *med.* импоте́нтный.

impound *v.t.* **1,** (shut up in a pound) загоня́ть. **2,** (seize and hold in legal custody) аресто́вывать; конфисковáть.

impoverish *v.t.* **1,** (reduce to poverty) доводи́ть до нищеты́. **2,** (exhaust, as soil) истощáть. —**impoverished,** *adj.* обедне́вший; обнищáлый. *Become impoverished,* (об)нищáть. —**impoverishment,** *n.* обедне́ние; обнищáние.

impracticable *adj.* невыполни́мый; неисполни́мый; неосуществи́мый. —**impracticability,** *n.* невыполни́мость; неисполни́мость; неосуществи́мость.

impractical *adj.* непракти́чный. —**impracticality,** *n.* непракти́чность.

imprecate *v.t.* призывáть (прокля́тие) на чью́-нибудь го́лову. —**imprecation,** *n.* прокля́тие.

imprecise *adj.* нето́чный. —**imprecision,** *n.* нето́чность.

impregnable *adj.* непристу́пный.

impregnate *v.t.* **1,** (make pregnant) оплодотворя́ть. **2,** (saturate) пропи́тывать. —**impregnation,** *n.* оплодотворе́ние.

impresario *n.* антрепренёр; импресáрио.

impress *v.t.* **1,** (imprint) дéлать о́ттиск с. **2,** (produce a marked effect upon) производи́ть впечатле́ние на; импони́ровать. **3,** (establish firmly in one's mind) внушáть: *impress upon someone the fact that...,* внушáть кому́-нибудь, что... **4,** (force into military service) наси́льно вербовáть.

impression *n.* **1,** (imprint) о́ттиск; отпечáток. **2,** (effect produced on the mind) впечатле́ние: *What are your impressions?,* каки́е у вас впечатле́ния? *Make a good/deep impression on,* производи́ть хоро́шее/глубо́кое впечатле́ние на (+ *acc.*). *I got the impression that...,* у меня́ создало́сь *or* сложи́лось впечатле́ние, что...; я вы́нес впечатле́ние, что... *I was under the impression that...,* я ду́мал(а), что...

impressionable *adj.* впечатли́тельный.

impressionism *n.* импрессиони́зм. —**impressionist,** *n.* импрессиони́ст. —*adj.* [*also,* **impressionistic**] импрессиони́стический; импрессиони́стский.

impressive *adj.* впечатля́ющий; внуши́тельный; представи́тельный.

impressment *n.* наси́льственная вербо́вка.

imprint *n.* о́ттиск. —*v.t.* отти́скивать.

imprison *v.t.* заключáть (в тюрьму́); сажáть (в тюрьму́).

imprisonment *n.* (тюре́мное) заключе́ние. *Life imprisonment,* пожи́зненное заключе́ние.

improbability *n.* маловероя́тность; неправдоподо́бие.

improbable *adj.* маловероя́тный; неправдоподо́бный. *It is improbable that...,* маловероя́тно, что...

impromptu *adj.* импровизи́рованный. —*adv.* экспро́мтом.

improper *adj.* **1,** (incorrect) непрáвильный: *improper use of a word,* непрáвильное употребле́ние сло́ва. **2,** (unseemly) неприли́чный: *improper behavior,* неприли́чное поведе́ние. **3,** (inappropriate) неподходя́щий: *improper dress,* неподходя́щая оде́жда. —**improper fraction,** непрáвильная дробь.

improperly *adv.* **1,** (incorrectly) непрáвильно. **2,** (in an unseemly manner) неприли́чно.

impropriety *n.* **1,** (being improper or inappropriate) неприли́чие; неуме́стность. **2,** (improper act) просту́пок.

improve *v.t.* улучшáть. —*v.i.* улучшáться.

improvement *n.* улучше́ние: *a marked improvement in his condition,* заме́тное улучше́ние его́ состоя́ния.

improvident *adj.* непредусмотри́тельный; нерасчётливый. —**improvidence,** *n.* непредусмотри́тельность; нерасчётливость.

improvise *v.t. & i.* импровизи́ровать. —**improvisation,** *n.* импровизáция. —**improviser,** *n.* импровизáтор.

imprudent *adj.* неблагоразу́мный; неосмотри́тельный. —**imprudence,** *n.* неблагоразу́мие; неосмотри́тельность.

impudent *adj.* де́рзкий; нáглый. —**impudence,** *n.* де́рзость; нáглость.

impugn *v.t.* оспáривать; подвергáть сомне́нию.

impulse *n.* **1,** (impelling force) толчо́к; и́мпульс. **2,** (sudden inclination) поры́в; и́мпульс: *yield to a sudden impulse,* поддавáться мину́тному поры́ву; подчиня́ться внезáпному и́мпульсу.

impulsive *adj.* импульси́вный.

impunity *n.* безнакáзанность. *With impunity,* безнакáзанно.

impure *adj.* нечи́стый.

impurity *n.* **1,** (state of being impure) нечистотá. **2,** *pl.* (foreign matter) нечисто́ты.

impute *v.t.* **1,** (charge) инкримини́ровать: *impute a crime to someone,* инкримини́ровать кому́-нибудь преступле́ние. **2,** (attribute) припи́сывать.

in *prep.* **1,** (in a certain place or condition) в (+ *prepl.*): *in Moscow,* в Москве́; *in the room,* в ко́мнате; *in the car,* в маши́не; *in one's hand,* в руке́; *in order,* в поря́дке; *in good condition,* в хоро́шем состоя́нии. *Stand in line,* стоя́ть в о́череди. ♦*With certain nouns,* на: *in one's arms,* на рука́х; *in the sun,* на со́лнце; *in the sky,* на не́бе; *in the south,* на ю́ге; *in orbit,* на орби́те. **2,** (into; arriving in) в (+ *acc.*): *arrive in Moscow,* прие́хать в Москву́. *Dip a pen in ink,* обмакну́ть перо́ в черни́ла. *Put something in a box,* положи́ть что́-нибудь в я́щик. *Put someone in prison,* посади́ть кого́-нибудь в тюрьму́. **3,** (with months, years, centuries) в (+ *prepl.*): *in August,* в а́вгусте; *in 1900,* в ты́сяча девятисо́том году́. ♦*Sometimes with the acc.: in that month,* в э́тот (*or* в тот) ме́сяц; *in past years,* в про́шлые го́ды; *in the space age,* в косми́ческий век. **4,** (with seasons, parts of the day) *rendered by the instr. case: in the morning,* у́тром; *in the evening,* ве́чером; *in the fall,* о́сенью. **5,** (with expressions of time, indicating how long it takes or took to complete a task) за: *read a book in two days,* чита́ть кни́гу за два дня. *Cover the distance in less than two hours,* покры́ть расстоя́ние ме́ньше чем за два часа́. ♦*To emphasize rapidity,* в: *I got dressed in three minutes,* я оде́лся (оде́лась) в три мину́ты. **6,** (over the course of) за (+ *acc.*): *for the first time in many years,* впервы́е за мно́го лет. *Receive three packages in one week,* получи́ть три посы́лки за одну́ неде́лю. **7,** (indicating a certain amount of time from now) че́рез: *He will be here in ten minutes,* он придёт че́рез де́сять мину́т. **8,** (with languages) по-; на (+ *prepl.*): *in Russian,* по-ру́сски; на ру́сском языке́. **9,** (with weather conditions) в (+ *acc.*): *in such weather/heat,* в таку́ю пого́ду/жару́. **10,** (in the person of) в лице́ (+ *gen.*): *a true friend in him,* ве́рный друг в его́ лице́. **11,** *with gerunds, rendered by the verbal adverb: in taking this step,* пойдя́ на тако́й шаг. **12,** *expressing various relationships,* в (+ *prepl.*): *in any case,* во вся́ком слу́чае; *in the light of,* в све́те (+ *gen.*); *poor in arithmetic,* слаб в арифме́тике; *tight in the waist,* у́зок в та́лии; *live in peace,* жить в ми́ре; *fall in battle,* пасть в бою́. **13,** *expressing various relationships, rendered by the instr. case: in a loud voice,* гро́мким го́лосом; *rich in vitamins,* бога́т витами́нами; *paint in oils,* писа́ть ма́слом; *end in disaster,* ко́нчиться катастро́фой. ♦*Sometimes with the acc.: in reply to,* в отве́т на; *dressed in black,* оде́т(а) в чёрное. **14,** *in various miscellaneous expressions: in fact,* факти́чески; на са́мом де́ле; *in reality,* в действи́тельности; *in jest,* в шу́тку; *in short,* коро́че говоря́; *in passing,* мимохо́дом; вскользь. —*adj.* **1,** (at home) до́ма. **2,** (in one's office) у себя́. **3,** (having arrived) прибы́вший. *The train is in,* по́езд при́был *or* пришёл. *The tide is in,* сейча́с прили́в. —*adv. Usu. rendered by a prefixed verb: come in,* входи́ть; *drop in,* заходи́ть; *cave in,* обвали́ться. —**in for,** *rendered by* ждать, ожида́ть, *or* предстоя́ть: *I know what I'm in for,* я зна́ю, что меня́ ждёт. *He is in for a big surprise,* его́ ждёт *or* ожида́ет большо́й сюрпри́з. *You are in for a disappointment,* вас ожида́ет разочарова́ние. *We are in for a cold winter,* нам предстои́т холо́дная зима́. —**in on, 1,** (having a part in) прича́стный к. **2,** (having

knowledge of) посвящён в: *in on the secret,* посвящён в та́йну. —**in that,** тем, что...: *The situation is unique in that...,* ситуа́ция уника́льна тем, что... —**know all the ins and outs,** знать все ходы́ и вы́ходы.

inability *n.* неспосо́бность; неуме́ние.

in absentia зао́чно: *be tried in absentia,* суди́ться зао́чно.

inaccessible *adj.* недосту́пный. —**inaccessibility,** *n.* недосту́пность.

inaccurate *adj.* нето́чный. —**inaccuracy,** *n.* нето́чность.

inaction *n.* безде́йствие.

inactive *adj.* безде́йственный; бездея́тельный. —**inactivity,** *n.* безде́йствие; бездея́тельность.

inadequacy *n.* **1,** (state of being inadequate) недоста́точность. **2,** (failing; lack) недоста́ток.

inadequate *adj.* недоста́точный; не отвеча́ющий тре́бованиям.

inadmissible *adj.* недопусти́мый.

inadvertence *n.* **1,** (carelessness) невнима́тельность; небре́жность. **2,** (oversight) недосмо́тр; опло́шность.

inadvertent *adj.* **1,** (not duly attentive) невнима́тельный; небре́жный. **2,** (unintentional) неча́янный. —**inadvertently,** *adv.* неча́янно; невзнача́й; не́хотя.

inadvisable *adj.* нецелесообра́зный.

inalienable *adj.* неотъе́млемый.

inane *adj.* глу́пый; ну́дный.

inanimate *adj.* неодушевлённый.

inanity *n.* глу́пость.

inapplicable *adj.* неприми́мый.

inappropriate *adj.* неуме́стный; неподходя́щий.

inarticulate *adj.* нечленоразде́льный; невня́тный.

inasmuch as так как; поско́льку; ввиду́ того́, что.

inattention *n.* невнима́ние. —**inattentive,** *adj.* невнима́тельный.

inaudible *adj.* неслы́шный.

inaugural *n.* вступи́тельный. *Inaugural address,* речь при вступле́нии в до́лжность.

inaugurate *v.t.* **1,** (induct into office) вводи́ть в до́лжность. **2,** (introduce; launch) вводи́ть. —**inauguration,** *n.* инаугура́ция.

inauspicious *adj.* неблагоприя́тный; неутеши́тельный.

inborn *adj.* врождённый; прирождённый. *Also,* **inbred.**

incalculable *adj.* несме́тный; неисчисли́мый.

incandescence *n.* нака́л; кале́ние.

incandescent *adj.* накалённый. —**incandescent lamp,** ла́мпа нака́ливания.

incantation *n.* заклина́ние; за́говор.

incapable *adj.* неспосо́бный: *incapable of telling a lie,* неспосо́бный на ложь.

incapacitate *v.t.* де́лать нетрудоспосо́бным. —**incapacitated,** *adj.* нетрудоспосо́бный. —**incapacitation,** *n.* поте́ря трудоспосо́бности. —**incapacity,** *n.* нетрудоспосо́бность.

incarcerate *v.t.* заключа́ть (в тюрьму́); заточа́ть (в тюрьму́). —**incarceration,** *n.* (тюре́мное) заключе́ние; заточе́ние.

incarnate *adj.* воплощённый. *The devil incarnate,* исча́дие а́да. —*v.t.* воплоща́ть. —**incarnation,** *n.* воплоще́ние.

incautious *adj.* неосторо́жный.

incendiary *adj.* зажига́тельный: *incendiary bomb,* зажига́тельная бо́мба. *Incendiary speeches,* зажига́тельные ре́чи.

incense *n.* фимиа́м; ла́дан. *Burn incense,* кури́ть ла́даном. —*v.t.* приводи́ть в я́рость. —**incensed,** *adj.* разгне́ванный. *Become incensed,* приходи́ть в я́рость.

incentive *n.* побужде́ние; толчо́к; сти́мул.

inception *n.* нача́ло.

inceptive *adj.* нача́льный. —**inceptive verb,** начина́тельный глаго́л.

incertitude *n.* неуве́ренность.

incessant *adj.* беспреста́нный; бесконе́чный; непреста́нный. —**incessantly,** *adv.* беспреста́нно; бесконе́чно.

incest *n.* кровосмеше́ние. —**incestuous,** *adj.* кровосмеси́тельный.

inch *n.* дюйм. —*v.i.* ползти́: *inch forward,* ползти́ вперёд. —**every inch a...,** с головы́ до ног; до мо́зга косте́й. —**inch by inch,** пядь за пя́дью. —**not yield** (*or* **budge) an inch,** не уступи́ть ни пя́ди (земли́); не уступи́ть ни на йо́ту. —**within an inch of,** на волосо́к (*or* на волоске́) от. *Beat within an inch of one's life,* избива́ть до полусме́рти; бить сме́ртным бо́ем.

inchoate *adj.* **1,** (in a rudimentary stage) зача́точный. **2,** (lacking order; shapeless) бесфо́рменный.

incidence *n.* **1,** (prevalence) распростране́ние. *Incidence of a disease,* заболева́емость. **2,** *physics* паде́ние: *angle of incidence,* у́гол паде́ния.

incident *n.* происше́ствие; слу́чай; инциде́нт. *Without incident,* без происше́ствий. *Amusing incident,* заба́вный слу́чай. *Border incident,* пограни́чный инциде́нт. —*adj.* [*usu.* **incident to**] свя́занный с.

incidental *adj.* **1,** *fol. by* **to** (associated with) свя́занный (с). **2,** (minor; secondary) побо́чный. *Incidental expenses,* случа́йные расхо́ды.

incidentally *adv.* ме́жду про́чим; кста́ти.

incinerate *v.t.* испепеля́ть; сжига́ть дотла́. —**incinerator,** *n.* мусоросжига́тельная печь.

incipient *adj.* нача́льный.

incise *v.t.* **1,** (cut into) надреза́ть. **2,** (carve; engrave) выреза́ть; насека́ть.

incision *n.* разре́з; надре́з.

incisive *adj.* **1,** (trenchant) то́нкий. **2,** (keen; penetrating) проница́тельный.

incisor *n.* резе́ц.

incite *v.t.* возбужда́ть; подстрека́ть. *Incite the people to rebellion,* подстрека́ть наро́д к мятежу́. —**incitement,** *n.* подстрека́тельство.

inclement *adj.* нена́стный. *Inclement weather,* нена́стье; непого́да.

inclination *n.* **1,** (slant; slope) накло́н; наклоне́ние. *Angle of inclination,* у́гол накло́на. **2,** (tendency; disposition) скло́нность; накло́нность.

incline *v.t.* наклоня́ть; склоня́ть: *incline one's head,* наклоня́ть/склоня́ть го́лову. —*v.i.* наклоня́ться; склоня́ться. —*n.* склон; накло́н; укло́н; скат; пока́тость. *Steep incline,* круто́й склон.

inclined *adj.* **1,** (sloping) накло́нный. *Inclined plane,* накло́нная пло́скость. **2,** *fol. by* **to** (tending toward) скло́нный (к). *I am inclined to think that...,* я скло́нен (склонна́) ду́мать, что...; я склоня́юсь к мне́нию, что...

include *v.t.* включа́ть: *include a question on the agenda,* включи́ть вопро́с в пове́стку дня. *The delegation includes...,* в делега́цию (*or* в соста́в делега́ции) вхо́дят...; в делега́цию включа́ется... *The price of the ticket includes...,* в сто́имость биле́та вхо́дит... *This category includes...,* к э́той катего́рии отно́сятся... —**including,** *prep.* включа́я.

inclusion *n.* включе́ние.

inclusive *adj.* **1,** *fol. by* **of** (including) включа́я. **2,** (within the limits mentioned) включи́тельно.

incognito *adv.* инко́гнито.

incoherent *adj.* бессвя́зный; несвя́зный. —**incoherence,** *n.* бессвя́зность; несвя́зность.

incombustible *adj.* невоспламеня́емый.

income *n.* дохо́д. —**income tax,** подохо́дный нало́г.

incoming *adj.* входя́щий; вступа́ющий.

incommensurable *adj.* несоизмери́мый. —**incommensurability,** *n.* несоизмери́мость.

incommensurate *adj.* несоразме́рный.

incommode *v.t.* затрудня́ть; меша́ть; беспоко́ить. —**incommodious,** *adj.* неудо́бный.

incommunicado *adj. & adv.* без пра́ва сообще́ния.

incomparable *adj.* **1,** (not comparable) несравни́мый. **2,** (matchless; unsurpassed) несравне́нный. —**incomparably,** *adv.* несравне́нно.

incompatible *adj.* несовмести́мый. —**incompatibility,** *n.* несовмести́мость.

incompetence *n.* **1,** (lack of ability) некомпете́нтность. **2,** *law* недееспосо́бность.

incompetent *adj.* **1,** (lacking the necessary ability) некомпете́нтный. **2,** *law* недееспосо́бный.

incomplete *adj.* непо́лный; незако́нченный. —**completeness,** *n.* неполнота́.

incomprehensible *adj.* непоня́тный; непостижи́мый. —**incomprehensibility,** *n.* непоня́тность; непостижи́мость. —**incomprehensibly,** *adv.* непоня́тно.

incomprehension *n.* непонима́ние.

inconceivable *adj.* невообрази́мый.

inconclusive *adj.* неоконча́тельный.

incongruous *adj.* несообра́зный. —**incongruity,** *n.* несообра́зность.

inconsequential *adj.* несуще́ственный; не име́ющий значе́ния.

inconsiderate *adj.* невнима́тельный.

inconsistent *adj.* непосле́довательный. —**inconsistency,** *n.* непосле́довательность.

inconsolable *adj.* безуте́шный; неуте́шный.

inconspicuous *adj.* незаме́тный; примеме́тный.

inconstant *adj.* непостоя́нный. —**inconstancy,** *n.* непостоя́нство.

incontestable *adj.* неоспори́мый; бесспо́рный.

incontinence *n.* **1,** (immoderate behavior) невозде́ржанность. **2**, *med.* недержа́ние. —**incontinent,** *adj.* невозде́ржанный.

incontrovertible *adj.* неопровержи́мый.

inconvenience *n.* неудо́бство. —*v.t.* затрудня́ть. —**inconvenient,** *adj.* неудо́бный.

incorporate *v.t.* **1**, (combine) объединя́ть. **2**, *fol. by* **into** (make a part of) включа́ть в соста́в (+ *gen.*); присоединя́ть (к). **3**, (form into a corporation) инкорпори́ровать. —*v.i.* объединя́ться.

incorporation *n.* включе́ние в соста́в; присоедине́ние; инкорпора́ция.

incorporeal *adj.* бестеле́сный.

incorrect *adj.* непра́вильный; неве́рный. —**incorrectly,** *adv.* непра́вильно; неве́рно.

incorrigible *adj.* неисправи́мый.

incorruptible *adj.* неподку́пный. —**incorruptibility,** *n.* неподку́пность.

increase *v.t.* увели́чивать: *increase the dose,* увели́чивать до́зу; *increase production,* увели́чивать произво́дство. *Increase prices,* повыша́ть це́ны. *Increase (the) pressure,* увели́чивать *or* повыша́ть давле́ние. —*v.i.* увели́чиваться; возраста́ть; расти́. —*n.* увеличе́ние; рост; приро́ст. *Population increase,* увеличе́ние *or* приро́ст населе́ния. *Price increase,* повыше́ние цен. *Tax increase,* увеличе́ние *or* повыше́ние нало́гов. *Wage increase,* приба́вка *or* надба́вка к зарпла́те. *Increase in the cost of living,* рост сто́имости жи́зни.

increasing *adj.* возраста́ющий. *An ever increasing number of people,* всё бо́льшее коли́чество люде́й.

increasingly *adv.* всё бо́лее: *The work is becoming increasingly difficult,* рабо́та стано́вится всё бо́лее тру́дной.

incredible *adj.* невероя́тный. —**incredibly,** *adv.* невероя́тно; до невероя́тности.

incredulity *n.* недове́рие. —**incredulous,** *adj.* недове́рчивый.

increment *n.* прираще́ние.

incriminate *v.t.* изоблича́ть. —**incriminating,** *adj.* изобличи́тельный.

incubate *v.t.* сиде́ть на (я́йцах). —**incubation,** *n.* инкуба́ция. —**incubator,** *n.* инкуба́тор.

inculcate *v.t.* внуша́ть; вселя́ть; внедря́ть.

incumbent *adj.* **1**, *fol. by* **on** *or* **upon** (obligatory) надлежа́щий: *It is incumbent on us to help,* нам надлежи́т помо́чь. **2**, (in office) стоя́щий у вла́сти. —*n.* тот, кто стои́т у вла́сти.

incur *v.t.* **1**, (bring on oneself) навлека́ть на себя́: *incur suspicion,* навлека́ть на себя́ подозре́ние. **2**, (suffer, as losses) нести́ (убы́тки). **3**, (contract, as debts) де́лать (долги́).

incurable *adj.* неизлечи́мый.

incursion *n.* вторже́ние; наше́ствие; набе́г.

indebted *adj.* [*usu.* **indebted to**] в долгу́ (у *or* пе́ред); обя́зан (+ *dat.*). *I am much indebted to you,* я мно́гим вам обя́зан(а). —**indebtedness,** *n.* задо́лженность.

indecency *n.* неприли́чие.

indecent *adj.* неприли́чный. —**indecently,** *adv.* неприли́чно.

indecipherable *adj.* **1**, (of a coded message)

неподдаю́щийся расшифро́вке. **2**, (of handwriting) неразбо́рчивый.

indecision *n.* нереши́тельность; нереши́мость.

indecisive *adj.* нереши́тельный. —**indecisiveness,** *n.* нереши́тельность.

indeclinable *adj.* несклоня́емый.

indecorous *adj.* некорре́ктный; неприли́чный.

indeed *adv.* в са́мом де́ле; действи́тельно. *I am very glad indeed,* я действи́тельно о́чень рад (ра́да). *Yes, indeed!,* о да!; да, да! —*interj.* да ну!; вот ещё.

indefatigable *adj.* неутоми́мый. —**indefatigability,** *n.* неутоми́мость.

indefensible *adj.* **1**, *mil.* непригодный для оборо́ны. **2**, (inexcusable) непрости́тельный.

indefinable *adj.* неопредели́мый.

indefinite *adj.* неопределённый: *for an indefinite period,* на неопределённый срок. *Indefinite leave of absence,* бессро́чный о́тпуск. —**indefinite article,** неопределённый арти́кль *or* член.

indefinitely *adv.* на неопределённое вре́мя.

indelible *adj.* **1**, (that cannot be erased) несмыва́емый: *indelible ink,* несмыва́емые черни́ла. *Indelible pencil,* хими́ческий каранда́ш. **2**, (permanent; lasting) неизглади́мый: *indelible impression,* неизглади́мое впечатле́ние.

indelicate *adj.* неделика́тный; некорре́ктный; нескро́мный. —**indelicacy,** *n.* неделика́тность.

indemnify *v.t.* возмеща́ть; компенси́ровать. —**indemnification,** *n.* возмеще́ние.

indemnity *n.* **1**, (compensation) возмеще́ние; компенса́ция. **2**, (protection) гара́нтия.

indent *v.t.* **1**, (space in from the margin) писа́ть с абза́ца; писа́ть с о́тступом. **2**, (notch) зазу́бривать. —*v.i.* отступа́ть: *indent slightly,* отступа́ть немно́го.

indentation *n.* **1**, (notch) зазу́брина. **2**, [*also,* **indention**] (spacing in from the margin) абза́ц; о́тступ.

independence *n.* **1**, (freedom from foreign rule) незави́симость. **2**, (self-sufficiency) самостоя́тельность.

independent *adj.* **1**, (autonomous) незави́симый. **2**, (self-sufficient; done on one's own) самостоя́тельный. —**independently,** *adv.* незави́симо; самостоя́тельно.

in-depth *adj.* глубо́кий; углублённый.

indescribable *adj.* неописуемый.

indestructible *adj.* неразруши́мый.

indeterminate *adj.* неопределённый.

index *n.* **1**, (alphabetical list) указа́тель. **2**, *math.; econ.* показа́тель; и́ндекс. *Price index,* и́ндекс цен. —*v.t.* **1**, (provide with an index) снабжа́ть указа́телем. **2**, (make an index of) заноси́ть в указа́тель. —**index card,** катало́жная ка́рточка. —**index finger,** указа́тельный па́лец.

India ink тушь.

Indian *n.* **1**, (American) индеец. **2**, (of India) инди́ец. —*adj.* **1**, (of America) инде́йский. **2**, (of India) инди́йский. —**Indian Ocean,** Инди́йский океа́н. —**Indian summer,** ба́бье ле́то.

indicate *v.t.* **1**, (point out) ука́зывать (на): *indicate the road/date,* ука́зывать доро́гу/да́ту. *Indicate mistakes/*

shortcomings, ука́зывать на оши́бки/недоста́тки. **2,** (designate; show on a map) обознача́ть. **3,** (be a sign of) ука́зывать на; говори́ть о.

indication *n.* указа́ние; обозначе́ние; при́знак. *Indications of trouble,* при́знаки неприя́тностей. *There is every indication that...,* всё говори́т о том, что...

indicative *adj.* **1,** (revealing) показа́тельный. *Be indicative of,* ука́зывать на; говори́ть о. **2,** *gram.* изъяви́тельный: *indicative mood,* изъяви́тельное наклоне́ние.

indicator *n.* **1,** (needle, dial, etc.) указа́тель; индика́тор. **2,** *fig.* (general indication) показа́тель.

indict *v.t.* обвиня́ть; предъявля́ть обвине́ние (+ *dat.*); привлека́ть к уголо́вной отве́тственности.

indictment *n.* **1,** (act of indicting) обвине́ние. **2,** (formal written accusation) обвини́тельный акт; обвини́тельное заключе́ние.

indifference *n.* равноду́шие; безразли́чие. *With indifference,* равноду́шно; безразли́чно.

indifferent *adj.* **1,** (unconcerned; apathetic) безразли́чный; равноду́шный; безуча́стный. **2,** (mediocre) посре́дственный.

indigence *n.* нужда́; нищета́.

indigenous *adj.* коренно́й; тузе́мный.

indigent *adj.* неиму́щий; обездо́ленный.

indigestible *adj.* неудобовари́мый.

indigestion *n.* несваре́ние желу́дка; расстро́йство пищеваре́ния.

indignant *adj.* негоду́ющий; возмущённый. *Be indignant,* негодова́ть; возмуща́ться.

indignation *n.* негодова́ние; возмуще́ние.

indignity *n.* оскорбле́ние; униже́ние: *suffer indignities,* подверга́ться оскорбле́ниям/униже́ниям.

indigo *n.* инди́го. —*adj.* цве́та инди́го.

indirect *adj.* **1,** (roundabout) непрямо́й; обхо́дный; око́льный. **2,** (not pertaining or following directly) ко́свенный; непрямо́й: *indirect answer,* ко́свенный/непрямо́й отве́т. *Indirect evidence,* ко́свенные ули́ки. —**indirect object,** ко́свенное дополне́ние.

indirectly *adv.* ко́свенно; ко́свенным о́бразом; ко́свенным путём.

indiscernible *adj.* неразличи́мый.

indiscreet *adj.* неделика́тный; нескро́мный; беста́ктный.

indiscretion *n.* нело́вкость; беста́ктность: *commit an indiscretion,* допусти́ть нело́вкость; соверши́ть беста́ктность.

indiscriminate *adj.* **1,** (not discriminating) неразбо́рчивый. **2,** (random; haphazard) огу́льный. —**indiscriminately,** *adv.* без разбо́ра; без вы́бора.

indispensable *adj.* незамени́мый.

indisposed *adj.* **1,** (unwell) нездоро́вый. **2,** (disinclined) не расположён.

indisposition *n.* **1,** (ailment) недомога́ние. **2,** (disinclination) нерасположе́ние.

indisputable *adj.* неоспори́мый; бесспо́рный.

indissoluble *adj.* **1,** (incapable of being dissolved) нераствори́мый. **2,** (lasting; permanent) неразры́вный; нерасторжи́мый; неруши́мый. —**indissolubly,** *adv.* неразры́вно.

indistinct *adj.* **1,** (hard to see or read) неотчётливый; нея́сный. **2,** (hard to hear) невня́тный; нея́сный.

indistinguishable *adj.* неразличи́мый.

indium *n.* и́ндий.

individual *adj.* отде́льный; индивидуа́льный. —*n.* ли́чность; лицо́; индивиду́ум; осо́ба; о́собь. *Suspicious-looking individual,* подозри́тельная ли́чность. *The role of the individual in history,* роль ли́чности в исто́рии.

individualism *n.* индивидуали́зм. —**individualist,** *n.* индивидуали́ст. —**individuality,** *n.* индивидуа́льность.

individually *adv.* отде́льно; в отде́льности.

indivisible *adj.* недели́мый; неразделИ́мый; неразде́льный. —**indivisibility,** *n.* недели́мость.

indoctrinate *v.t.* обраба́тывать. —**indoctrination,** *n.* обрабо́тка.

Indo-European *adj.* индоевропе́йский.

indolent *adj.* лени́вый; вя́лый. —**indolence,** *n.* лень; вя́лость.

indomitable *adj.* неукроти́мый.

Indonesian *adj.* индонези́йский. —*n.* индонези́ец.

indoor *adj.* **1,** (situated inside) вну́тренний. *Indoor plumbing,* водопрово́д. **2,** (enclosed) закры́тый: *indoor pool/stadium,* закры́тый бассе́йн/стадио́н. **3,** (taking place inside) ко́мнатный: *indoor games,* ко́мнатные и́гры.

indoors *adv.* в до́ме; внутри́ до́ма; в закры́том помеще́нии. *Stay indoors,* сиде́ть до́ма; не выходи́ть на у́лицу.

indorse *v.* = endorse.

indubitable *adj.* несомне́нный. —**indubitably,** *adv.* несомне́нно.

induce *v.t.* **1,** (cause; prompt) побужда́ть; заставля́ть: *What induced him to...?,* что побуди́ло/заста́вило его́ (+ *inf.*)? **2,** (persuade; prevail upon) уговори́ть. **3,** (cause; bring on) вызыва́ть; навева́ть. *Induce labor,* провоци́ровать схва́тки; вызыва́ть родову́ю де́ятельность.

inducement *n.* побужде́ние; сти́мул.

induct *v.t.* **1,** (install in office) вводи́ть в до́лжность. **2,** *mil.* зачисля́ть на вое́нную слу́жбу.

inductee *n.* призывни́к.

induction *n.* **1,** (installation in office) введе́ние в до́лжность. **2,** *mil.* зачисле́ние на вое́нную слу́жбу. **3,** *electricity; logic* инду́кция. —**induction center,** призывно́й пункт. —**induction coil,** индукцио́нная кату́шка.

inductive *adj.* индукти́вный.

indulge *v.t.* потво́рствовать; потака́ть. —*v.i.* [*usu.* **indulge in**] предава́ться (+ *dat.*); балова́ться (+ *instr.*). *Indulge in a cigar,* балова́ться сига́рой. *Indulge in fantasy,* предава́ться фанта́зиям.

indulgence *n.* потво́рство; потака́ние; побла́жка; снисходи́тельность.

indulgent *adj.* снисходи́тельный.

industrial *adj.* промы́шленный; индустриа́льный.

industrialist *n.* промы́шленник.

industrialization *n.* индустриализа́ция.

industrialize *v.t.* индустриализи́ровать. *Industrialized countries,* индустриа́льные стра́ны.

industrious *adj.* трудолюби́вый; приле́жный. —**industriousness,** *n.* трудолю́бие; прилежа́ние.

industry *n.* **1,** (branch of the economy) промы́шленность; инду́стрия. *Heavy industry,* тяжёлая промы́шленность. *Key industries,* веду́щие *or* ключевы́е о́трасли промы́шленности. **2,** (diligence) трудолю́бие.

inebriate *v.t.* опьяня́ть. —**inebriated,** *adj.* пья́ный; опьяне́вший.

inedible *adj.* несъедо́бный.

ineffable *adj.* невырази́мый; несказа́нный; неопису́емый.

ineffective *adj.* неэффекти́вный; безрезульта́тный. *Also,* **ineffectual.**

inefficacy *n.* неэффекти́вность.

inefficient *adj.* неэффекти́вный. —**inefficiency,** *n.* неэффекти́вность.

ineligible *adj.* не име́ющий пра́ва; не могу́щий быть и́збранным.

inept *adj.* неуме́лый; безда́рный. —**ineptitude,** *n.* неуме́ние; безда́рность.

inequality *n.* нера́венство.

inequitable *adj.* несправедли́вый; неравнопра́вный. —**inequity,** *n.* несправедли́вость.

ineradicable *adj.* **1,** (indelible, as of ink) несмыва́емый. **2,** (ingrained) неискорени́мый.

inert *adj.* **1,** *chem.* ине́ртный: *inert gases,* ине́ртные га́зы. **2,** (sluggish) ине́ртный.

inertia *n.* **1,** *physics* ине́рция. **2,** *fig.* (disinclination to move or act) ине́рция; ине́ртность.

inescapable *adj.* неизбе́жный; немину́емый.

inestimable *adj.* неоцени́мый.

inevitable *adj.* неизбе́жный. —**inevitability,** *n.* неизбе́жность. —**inevitably,** *adv.* неизбе́жно.

inexact *adj.* нето́чный. —**inexactness; inexactitude,** *n.* нето́чность.

inexcusable *adj.* непрости́тельный.

inexhaustible *adj.* неистощи́мый; неисчерпа́емый; неиссяка́емый.

inexorable *adj.* неумоли́мый; непрекло́нный.

inexpensive *adj.* дешёвый; недорого́й. —**inexpensively,** *adv.* дёшево; недо́рого.

inexperience *n.* нео́пытность. —**inexperienced,** *adj.* нео́пытный.

inexplicable *adj.* необъясни́мый.

inexpressible *adj.* невырази́мый.

inexpressive *adj.* невырази́тельный.

inextricably *adv.* неразры́вно: *inextricably linked,* неразры́вно свя́занный.

infallible *adj.* непогреши́мый. —**infallibility,** *n.* непогреши́мость.

infamous *adj.* позо́рный; гну́сный.

infamy *n.* **1,** (shame) позо́р. **2,** (infamous nature) гну́сность.

infancy *n.* младе́нчество. *Since infancy,* с ра́ннего де́тства.

infant *n.* младе́нец. —*adj.* де́тский: *infant mortality,* де́тская сме́ртность.

infanticide *n.* детоуби́йство.

infantile *adj.* де́тский; младе́нческий. —**infantile paralysis,** де́тский парали́ч.

infantry *n.* пехо́та. —*adj.* пехо́тный: *infantry regiment,* пехо́тный полк. —**infantryman,** *n.* пехоти́нец.

infatuated *adj.* Be infatuated with, безу́мно увле́чься (+ *instr.*). —**infatuation,** *n.* увлече́ние.

infeasible *adj.* невыполни́мый; неисполни́мый; неосуществи́мый.

infect *v.t.* заража́ть. *The wound became infected,* ра́на воспали́лась.

infection *n.* инфе́кция; зараже́ние; зара́за.

infectious *adj.* **1,** *med.* зара́зный; инфекцио́нный. **2,** *fig.* (of a smile, laughter, etc.) зарази́тельный.

infer *v.t.* **1,** (deduce) заключа́ть; выводи́ть. **2,** (imply) намека́ть; хоте́ть сказа́ть.

inference *n.* вы́вод; заключе́ние.

inferior *adj.* **1,** (lower in rank) бо́лее ни́зкий. *Inferior in rank,* ни́же по чи́ну. **2,** (of poor or poorer quality) неполноце́нный; недоброка́чественный. *Of inferior quality,* ни́зкого ка́чества. *Be greatly inferior to,* си́льно (*or* во мно́гом *or* намно́го) уступа́ть (+ *dat.*).

inferiority *n.* неполноце́нность; недоброка́чественность. —**inferiority complex,** ко́мплекс неполноце́нности.

infernal *adj.* **1,** (hellish) а́дский. **2,** *colloq.* (damnable) прокля́тый.

inferno *n.* ад.

infertile *adj.* **1,** (unable to produce offspring) беспло́дный. **2,** (barren, as of soil) неплодоро́дный; беспло́дный. —**infertility,** *n.* беспло́дие; неплодоро́дность.

infest *v.t.* наводня́ть. *Be infested with,* кише́ть (+ *instr.*). *Lice-infested,* вши́вый.

infidel *n.* неве́рный.

infidelity *n.* неве́рность; изме́на.

infighting *n.* бли́жний бой.

infiltrate *v.t.* проса́чиваться в; проника́ть в. —**infiltration,** *n.* проса́чивание; проникнове́ние.

infinite *adj.* бесконе́чный; безграни́чный; беспреде́льный. —**infinitely,** *adv.* бесконе́чно; (*with comp. adjectives*) неизмери́мо.

infinitesimal *adj.* бесконе́чно ма́лый.

infinitive *n.* неопределённая фо́рма глаго́ла; инфинити́в.

infinity *n.* бесконе́чность.

infirm *adj.* не́мощный.

infirmary *n.* небольша́я больни́ца; лазаре́т.

infirmity *n.* не́мощь.

inflame *v.t.* **1,** (set on fire) зажига́ть. **2,** (arouse, as passions) разжига́ть. —**inflamed,** *adj.* воспалённый. *Become inflamed,* воспаля́ться.

inflammable *adj.* горю́чий; огнеопа́сный. —**inflammability,** *n.* воспламеня́емость.

inflammation *n.* воспале́ние.

inflammatory *adj.* **1,** *med.* воспали́тельный. **2,** (tending to incite) зажига́тельный.

inflatable *adj.* надувно́й.

inflate *v.t.* **1,** (fill with air) надува́ть; нака́чивать. **2,** (raise or increase unduly) раздува́ть; вздува́ть. *Inflated figures,* разду́тые ци́фры. *Inflated prices,* вздутые *or* дутые *or* взвинченные цены. *Inflated military budgets,* раздутые военные бюджеты. —*v.i.* надуваться.

inflation *n.* **1,** (act of inflating) надувание. **2,** *econ.* инфляция. —**inflationary,** *adj.* инфляционный.

inflect *v.t.* **1,** (change the pitch of, as one's voice) модулировать. **2,** *gram.* склонять; спрягать. *Inflected language,* флективный язык.

inflection *also,* **inflexion** *n.* **1,** (of the voice) модуляция. **2,** *gram.* флексия.

inflexible *adj.* **1,** (stiff; rigid) негибкий; несгибаемый. **2,** (intransigent; uncompromising) негибкий; несгибаемый; непреклонный. —**inflexibility,** *n.* непреклонность.

inflexion *n.* = **inflection.**

inflict *v.t.* наносить: *inflict losses/ heavy damage/ on,* наносить потери/ большие повреждения/ (+ *dat.*). *Inflict punishment on,* подвергать (кого-нибудь) наказанию.

inflow *n.* приток; наплыв.

influence *n.* **1,** (impact; effect) влияние; воздействие. *Be a good influence on,* хорошо влиять на. *Under the influence of alcohol,* под воздействием алкоголя. **2,** (connections; pull) блат. —*v.t.* влиять на; воздействовать на. *Influence the outcome of something,* влиять на исход чего-нибудь.

influential *adj.* влиятельный.

influenza *n.* грипп.

influx *n.* наплыв; прилив; приток.

inform *v.t.* сообщать; извещать; осведомлять; уведомлять; ставить в известность; информировать. *Keep me informed about what happens,* держите меня в курсе дел. —*v.i.* [*usu.* **inform on** *or* **against**] доносить (на).

informal *adj.* **1,** (casual) без формальностей. *Informal dress,* будничная одежда. **2,** (unofficial) неофициальный. —**informality,** *n.* отсутствие формальностей.

informant *n.* осведомитель; информатор; информант.

information *n.* сведения; информация; справка. *For your information,* к вашему сведению. —*adj.* справочный: *information bureau,* справочное бюро.

informative *adj.* поучительный; содержательный.

informed *adj.* осведомлённый; информированный: *well-informed sources,* хорошо осведомлённые/информированные источники.

informer *n.* осведомитель; доносчик.

infraction *n.* нарушение.

infrared *adj.* инфракрасный.

infrastructure *n.* инфраструктура.

infrequent *adj.* редкий. —**infrequently,** *adv.* редко.

infringe *v.t.* нарушать. —*v.i.* [*usu.* **infringe on** *or* **upon**] посягать (на); ущемлять: *infringe upon someone's rights,* посягать на *or* ущемлять чьи-нибудь права.

infringement *n.* **1,** (violation) нарушение. **2,** (encroachment) посягательство; ущемление.

infuriate *v.t.* приводить в ярость; разъярять; бесить.

infuse *v.t.* вливать; вселять; внушать. —**infusion,** *n.* вливание.

ingenious *adj.* гениальный; хитроумный: *ingenious solution/device,* гениальное/хитроумное решение/ устройство.

ingenuity *n.* изобретательность.

ingenuous *adj.* бесхитростный; простодушный.

ingest *v.t.* глотать; проглатывать.

inglorious *adj.* бесславный.

ingot *n.* слиток.

ingrain *v.t.* укоренять. —**ingrained,** *adj.* укоренившийся; закоренелый; закоснелый. *Become ingrained,* закоренеть; укореняться.

ingratiate *v.t. Ingratiate oneself with,* заискивать перед; снискать (чью-нибудь) милость.

ingratiating *adj.* **1,** (pleasing) подкупающий. **2,** (meant to gain favor) заискивающий; вкрадчивый; льстивый.

ingratitude *n.* неблагодарность.

ingredient *n.* составная часть; ингредиент.

ingrown *adj.* **1,** (grown into the flesh) вросший. **2,** (inborn) врождённый.

inhabit *v.t.* обитать в *or* на. —**inhabitant,** *n.* житель; обитатель. —**inhabited,** *adj.* обитаемый.

inhalation *n.* вдыхание.

inhalator *n.* ингалятор.

inhale *v.t. & i.* вдыхать. —*v.i.* (draw in tobacco smoke) затягиваться.

inhaler *n.* ингалятор.

inherent *adj.* **1,** (intrinsic) присущий. **2,** (inborn) врождённый. —**inherently,** *adv.* по своему существу.

inherit *v.t.* наследовать; получить по наследству.

inheritance *n.* **1,** (act of inheriting) наследование. **2,** (something inherited) наследство. —**inheritance tax,** налог на наследство.

inherited *adj.* унаследованный.

inhibit *v.t.* стеснять; тормозить. —**inhibited,** *adj.* стеснённый; стеснительный. —**inhibition,** *n.* стеснение.

inhospitable *adj.* негостеприимный; неприветливый.

inhuman *adj.* **1,** (cruel; barbarous) бесчеловечный. **2,** (not human) нечеловеческий.

inhumane *adj.* бесчеловечный; негуманный.

inhumanity *n.* бесчеловечность.

inimical *adj.* **1,** *fol. by* **to** (detrimental) вредный (для). **2,** (hostile) враждебный.

inimitable *adj.* неподражаемый; неповторимый.

iniquitous *adj.* гнусный; порочный.

iniquity *n.* **1,** (wickedness) гнусность; порочность. **2,** *usu. pl.* (transgression) грех; проступок; прегрешение. —**den of iniquity,** притон разврата.

initial *adj.* начальный; первоначальный; исходный. —*n.* инициал. —*v.t.* **1,** (place one's initials on) ставить инициалы на; подписывать инициалами. **2,** (tentatively approve, as a treaty or document) парафировать.

initially *adv.* сначала; вначале.

initiate *v.t.* **1,** (begin; launch) вводить; быть инициатором (+ *gen.*). **2,** (introduce to a subject) знакомить. **3,** (admit; induct) вводить; посвящать.

initiation *n.* посвяще́ние. *Initiation fee,* вступи́тельный взнос.

initiative *n.* инициати́ва; почи́н. *Take the initiative,* взять инициати́ву в свои́ ру́ки.

initiator *n.* инициа́тор; зачина́тель; застре́льщик.

inject *v.t.* **1,** *med.* впры́скивать; вводи́ть. **2,** (introduce, as a new element) вводи́ть. **3,** (interject) вставля́ть.

injection *n.* инъе́кция; впры́скивание; влива́ние; уко́л. *Give an injection to,* сде́лать инъе́кцию *or* уко́л (+ *dat.*).

injector *n.* форсу́нка: *fuel injector,* форсу́нка горю́чего.

injudicious *adj.* неблагоразу́мный; неразу́мный.

injunction *n.* **1,** (order) предписа́ние. **2,** *law* суде́бный запре́т.

injure *v.t.* **1,** (cause physical harm to) поврежда́ть; ушиба́ть. *Be injured,* пострада́ть; получи́ть повреждéние *or* ранéние (ранéния). *No one was injured,* никто́ не пострада́л. **2,** (be injurious to) вреди́ть.

injured *adj.* **1,** (damaged; hurt) уши́бленный; ра́неный; повреждённый. **2,** (offended) оби́женный. **3,** *law* потерпе́вший: *the injured party,* потерпе́вшая сторона́.

injurious *adj.* вре́дный. *Smoking is injurious to health,* куре́ние вреди́т здоро́вью.

injury *n.* **1,** (physical harm) поврежде́ние; ране́ние; тра́вма. *Suffer serious injuries,* получи́ть тяжёлые поврежде́ния *or* тра́вмы. **2,** (damage) вред.

injustice *n.* несправедли́вость. *Do someone an injustice,* быть несправедли́вым к кому́-нибудь.

ink *n.* черни́ла: *write in ink,* писа́ть черни́лами. *Printer's ink,* типогра́фская кра́ска. —*adj.* черни́льный: *ink spot,* черни́льное пятно́.

inkblot *n.* кля́кса.

inkling *n.* **1,** (hint; suggestion) намёк. **2,** (vague idea) представле́ние.

ink pad поду́шка для штемпеле́й; штéмпельная поду́шка.

inkstand *n.* черни́льный прибо́р.

inkwell *n.* черни́льница.

inky *adj.* покры́тый черни́лами; в черни́лах.

inlaid *adj.* инкрусти́рованный; моза́ичный. *Inlaid table,* сто́лик с инкруста́цией.

inland *adj.* вну́тренний: *inland waterways,* вну́тренние во́дные пути́. *Inland sea,* вну́треннее *or* закры́тое мо́ре. —*adv.* внутрь страны́; в глубь страны́.

inlaw *n.* ро́дственник со стороны́ му́жа *or* жены́; сво́йственник.

inlay *v.t.* **1,** (set flush into a surface) влепля́ть. **2,** (decorate by inserting such designs) инкрусти́ровать. —*n.* **1,** (inlaid work) моза́ика; инкруста́ция. **2,** *dent.* пло́мба.

inlet *n.* **1,** (bay) бу́хта. **2,** (creek) за́водь; зато́н.

inmate *n.* **1,** (in a prison) заключённый. **2,** (in an asylum) больно́й.

inn *n.* постоя́лый двор; тракти́р.

innards *n.pl.* вну́тренности.

innate *adj.* врождённый; прирождённый; приро́дный.

inner *adj.* вну́тренний. —**inner ear,** вну́треннее у́хо. —**inner sole,** стéлька. —**inner tube,** ка́мера.

innermost *adj.* **1,** (farthest in) са́мый глубо́кий. **2,** (most intimate, as of feelings) сокрове́нный.

innkeeper *n.* тракти́рщик.

innocence *n.* **1,** (absence of guilt) невино́вность: *prove one's innocence,* доказа́ть свою́ невино́вность. **2,** (lack of sophistication) неви́нность.

innocent *adj.* **1,** (not guilty) невино́вный: *He is innocent,* он невино́вен. *Innocent of a crime,* невино́вный в преступле́нии. *Plead innocent,* не признава́ть себя́ вино́вным. *He was found innocent,* его́ призна́ли невино́вным. **2,** (naïve; harmless) неви́нный: *innocent girl/victim/prank,* неви́нная де́вушка/же́ртва/ша́лость. —**right of innocent passage,** пра́во ми́рного прохо́да.

innocuous *adj.* безвре́дный; безоби́дный.

innovate *v.i.* вводи́ть но́вшества. —**innovation,** *n.* но́вшество; нововведе́ние. —**innovative,** *adj.* нова́торский. —**innovator,** *n.* нова́тор.

innuendo *n.* инсинуа́ция.

innumerable *adj.* бесчи́сленный; несчётный; бессчётный; неисчисли́мый.

inoculate *v.t.* де́лать приви́вку (+ *dat.*); прививáть. *Inoculate someone for smallpox,* приви́ть кому́-нибудь о́спу. —**inoculation,** *n.* приви́вка.

inoffensive *adj.* безоби́дный.

inoperable *adj.* неопера́бельный.

inoperative *adj.* безде́йствующий. *Become inoperative,* выходи́ть из стро́я.

inopportune *adj.* несвоевре́менный.

inordinate *adj.* чрезме́рный; непоме́рный.

inorganic *adj.* неоргани́ческий.

input *n.* ввод.

inquest *n.* сле́дствие; дозна́ние.

inquire *v.i.* **1,** (ask; seek information) спра́шивать; справля́ться; поинтересова́ться; осведомля́ться. **2,** *fol. by* **into** (investigate; study) рассле́довать; иссле́довать.

inquiry *n.* **1,** (request for information) запро́с. *Make inquiries about,* наводи́ть спра́вки о. **2,** (investigation) рассле́дование; сле́дствие. *Committee of inquiry,* сле́дственная коми́ссия.

inquisition *n.* инквизи́ция.

inquisitive *adj.* пытли́вый; любозна́тельный. —**inquisitiveness,** *n.* пытли́вость; любозна́тельность.

inquisitor *n.* инквизи́тор.

inroad *n.* **1,** (incursion) набе́г. **2,** *usu. pl.* (encroachment) посяга́тельство.

insane *adj.* **1,** (mad) сумасше́дший; душевнобольно́й; умалишённый. **2,** *law* невменя́емый. —**insane asylum,** сумасше́дший дом; дом (для) умалишённых; психиатри́ческая больни́ца.

insanity *n.* **1,** (mental condition) сумасше́ствие; умопомеша́тельство. **2,** *law* невменя́емость. **3,** (folly) безу́мие.

insatiable *adj.* ненасы́тный.

inscribe *v.t.* **1,** (autograph; dedicate, as a book or photograph) надпи́сывать. **2,** (write): *inscribe one's name in a book,* расписа́ться в кни́ге. **3,** (engrave; carve) выреза́ть. **4,** *geom.* впи́сывать.

inscription *n.* на́дпись. *Inscription in a book,* на́дпись на кни́ге.

inscrutable *adj.* непостижи́мый; неисповеди́мый.

insect *n.* насеко́мое.

insecticide *n.* инсектици́д.

insecure *adj.* **1,** (not safe) небезопа́сный. **2,** (lacking confidence or assurance) неуве́ренный в себе́. —**insecurity,** *n.* неуве́ренность в себе́.

insemination *n.* оплодотворе́ние; осемене́ние. *Artificial insemination,* иску́сственное оплодотворе́ние/ осемене́ние.

insensate *adj.* бесчу́вственный.

insensible *adj.* бесчу́вственный; нечувстви́тельный. —**insensibility,** *n.* бесчу́вствие; нечувстви́тельность.

insensitive *adj.* нечувстви́тельный; бесчу́вственный; нечу́ткий. —**insensitivity,** *n.* нечувстви́тельность; бесчу́вствие.

inseparable *adj.* **1,** (of two people) неразлу́чный. **2,** (of objects, concepts, etc.) неотдели́мый; неразде́льный. —**inseparability,** *n.* неразлу́чность; неотдели́мость.

insert *v.t.* **1,** (place inside) вкла́дывать; вставля́ть; опуска́ть. *Insert the key into the lock,* вкла́дывать ключ в замо́к. *Insert a coin into the machine,* опуска́ть моне́ту в автома́т. **2,** (add; enter) вноси́ть; вставля́ть. *Insert a name on a list,* вноси́ть фами́лию в спи́сок. *Insert a clause in a treaty,* вставля́ть статью́ в догово́р. —*n.* вкла́дка.

insertion *n.* **1,** (act of inserting) вкла́дывание; внесе́ние. **2,** (something inserted) вста́вка.

inset *n.* **1,** (in a book) вкле́йка. **2,** (in a dress) вста́вка.

inside *prep.* внутри́: *inside the house,* внутри́ до́ма. —*adv.* **1,** (motion) внутрь: *go/look inside,* войти́/загляну́ть внутрь. *Come inside!,* зайди́те! **2,** (location) внутри́. —*adj.* **1,** (interior) вну́тренний: *inside wall,* вну́тренняя стена́. **2,** *colloq.* (known to only a few) секре́тный: *inside information,* секре́тная информа́ция. —*n.* **1,** (interior) вну́тренняя часть; вну́тренность. *From/on the inside,* изнутри́. **2,** *pl.,* *colloq.* (innards) вну́тренности. —**inside out, 1,** (reversed) наизна́нку. *Turn inside out,* вы́вернуть (наизна́нку). **2,** *colloq.* (thoroughly) вдоль и поперёк; на зубо́к.

insidious *adj.* кова́рный. —**insidiousness,** *n.* кова́рство.

insight *n.* **1,** (discernment) зо́ркость; проница́тельность. **2,** (illuminating glimpse) прозре́ние.

insignia *n.pl.* зна́ки разли́чия.

insignificant *adj.* незначи́тельный. —**insignificance,** *n.* незначи́тельность.

insincere *adj.* неи́скренний. —**insincerity,** *n.* неи́скренность.

insinuate *v.i.* **1,** (introduce gradually) незаме́тно внуша́ть. *Insinuate oneself into someone's confidence,* втира́ться в чьё-нибудь дове́рие. **2,** (hint; suggest) намека́ть.

insinuation *n.* намёк; инсинуа́ция.

insipid *adj.* **1,** (tasteless) невку́сный; пре́сный. **2,** (dull) бесцве́тный; пре́сный.

insist *v.t. & i.* наста́ивать. *She insisted on going,* она́ наста́ивала на том, что́бы пойти́. *He insists on the following conditions,* он наста́ивает на сле́дующих усло́виях. *Well, all right, if you insist,* ну ла́дно, е́сли/раз (уж) вы наста́иваете.

insistence *n.* настоя́ние: *at my insistence,* по моему́ настоя́нию.

insistent *adj.* насто́йчивый; настоя́тельный. *He was insistent,* он наста́ивал на э́том. —**insistently,** *adv.* настоя́тельно.

insofar as 1, (as far as) наско́лько. **2,** (to the full extent that) посто́льку, поско́льку.

insole *n.* сте́лька.

insolent *adj.* на́глый; де́рзкий. —**insolence,** *n.* на́глость; наха́льство; де́рзость.

insoluble *adj.* **1,** (not soluble) нераствори́мый. **2,** (not solvable) неразреши́мый.

insolvent *adj.* несостоя́тельный; неплатёжеспосо́бный. —**insolvency,** *n.* несостоя́тельность; неплатёжеспосо́бность.

insomnia *n.* бессо́нница.

inspect *v.t.* **1,** (examine; conduct an inspection of) осма́тривать: *inspect a school/ the motor/ someone's luggage/,* осма́тривать шко́лу/мото́р/бага́ж. **2,** (review, as troops) производи́ть смотр (+ *dat.*).

inspection *n.* **1,** (examination) осмо́тр; досмо́тр; инспе́кция; реви́зия. *Customs inspection,* тамо́женный осмо́тр *or* досмо́тр. *On-site inspection,* инспе́кция на места́х. **2,** *mil.* (review) смотр.

inspector *n.* инспе́ктор; контролёр; реви́зор. *Customs inspector,* тамо́женник.

inspiration *n.* **1,** (feeling of being inspired) вдохнове́ние. **2,** (one who inspires) вдохнови́тель. **3,** (inspired idea) блестя́щая мысль.

inspire *v.t.* **1,** (animate; stir) вдохновля́ть; воодушевля́ть. **2,** (arouse; produce, as an emotion) внуша́ть; вселя́ть. *Inspire confidence,* внуша́ть дове́рие. —**inspired,** *adj.* вдохнове́нный.

instability *n.* неусто́йчивость; нестаби́льность.

install *v.t.* **1,** (fix in position for use) устана́вливать; ста́вить; проводи́ть. **2,** (induct) вводи́ть в до́лжность.

installation *n.* **1,** (act of installing) устано́вка; проведе́ние. **2,** (something installed) устано́вка. **3,** (induction) введе́ние в до́лжность. **4,** *mil.* ба́за; объе́кт.

installment also, **instalment** *n.* **1,** (payment) взнос. *On the installment plan,* в рассро́чку. **2,** (part of a published article) вы́пуск. *In installments,* отде́льными вы́пусками; по частя́м.

instance *n.* **1,** (example) приме́р: *for instance,* наприме́р. **2,** (case) слу́чай: *in this instance,* в да́нном слу́чае. **3,** *law* инста́нция: *court of first instance,* суд пе́рвой инста́нции.

instant *n.* мгнове́ние; миг; мину́та; моме́нт. *This instant,* сию́ мину́ту. —*adj.* момента́льный; мгнове́нный. —**instant coffee,** быстрораствори́мый ко́фе.

instantaneous *adj.* момента́льный; мгнове́нный.

instantly *adv.* момента́льно; мгнове́нно.

instead *adv.* вме́сто (*must be followed by a word in the gen. case*): *Instead we went to the movies,* вме́сто э́того мы пошли́ в кино́. *He is ill, so I came instead,* он бо́лен, а я пришёл вме́сто него́. —**instead of,** вме́сто (+ *gen.*): *drink beer instead of wine,* пить пи́во вме́сто вина́. ♦*When followed by the -ing form of a verb,* вме́сто того́, что́бы (+ *inf.*): *instead of going to the theater,* вме́сто того́, что́бы пойти́ в теа́тр.

instep *n.* подъём.

instigate *v.t.* **1,** (foment; provoke) провоци́ровать. **2,** (spur; goad) подстрека́ть. —**instigation,** *n.* подстрека́тельство. —**instigator,** *n.* подстрека́тель; зачи́нщик.

instill *also,* **instil** *v.t.* внуша́ть; вселя́ть; влива́ть; привива́ть. *Instill confidence in,* внуша́ть дове́рие (+ *dat.*). *Instill hope in,* вселя́ть наде́жду в (+ *acc.*). *Instill in the children a love of music,* привива́ть де́тям любо́вь к му́зыке.

instinct *n.* инсти́нкт.

instinctive *adj.* инстинкти́вный. —**instinctively,** *adv.* нево́льно; безотчётно; инстинкти́вно.

institute *n.* институ́т. —*v.t.* **1,** (establish) устана́вливать; учрежда́ть. **2,** (initiate; introduce) вводи́ть; заводи́ть. *Institute reforms,* проводи́ть рефо́рмы.

institution *n.* **1,** (organization) учрежде́ние; заведе́ние. *Institution of higher learning,* вы́сшее уче́бное заведе́ние. **2,** (established custom) институ́т: *the institution, of marriage,* институ́т бра́ка. **3,** (place of confinement) дом (для) умалишённых; психиатри́ческая больни́ца.

instruct *v.t.* **1,** (teach) обуча́ть. **2,** (order; direct) прика́зывать; веле́ть.

instruction *n.* **1,** (teaching) обуче́ние. **2,** *pl.* (directions) указа́ния; наставле́ние; инстру́кция. —**instructional,** *adj.* уче́бный; инструкти́вный.

instructive *adj.* поучи́тельный.

instructor *n.* инстру́ктор.

instrument *n.* **1,** (implement) инструме́нт; прибо́р; ору́дие. *Surgical instruments,* хирурги́ческие инструме́нты. *Precision instruments,* то́чные прибо́ры. *Instrument of torture,* ору́дие пы́тки. **2,** (means; agency) ору́дие. **3,** (musical instrument) инструме́нт. **4,** (gauge) прибо́р: *instrument landing,* поса́дка по прибо́рам. *Instrument panel,* прибо́рная доска́. **5,** (legal document) гра́мота: *instruments of ratification,* ратификацио́нные гра́моты.

instrumental *adj.* **1,** (serving to achieve an end): *be instrumental in,* сыгра́ть реша́ющую роль в. **2,** *music* инструмента́льный. **3,** *gram.* твори́тельный: *instrumental case,* твори́тельный паде́ж.

instrumentalist *n.* инструментали́ст.

instrumentality *n. Through the instrumentality of,* при посре́дстве (+ *gen.*); че́рез посре́дство (+ *gen.*).

insubordinate *adj.* самово́льный. —**insubordination,** *n.* неподчине́ние; неповинове́ние.

insufferable *adj.* невыноси́мый; нестерпи́мый; несно́сный.

insufficiency *n.* недоста́точность.

insufficient *adj.* недоста́точный: *insufficient quantity,* недоста́точное коли́чество. *Insufficient information,* недоста́точные све́дения. *Insufficient funds,* недоста́ток средств. —**insufficiently,** *adv.* недоста́точно.

insular *adj.* островно́й.

insulate *v.t.* изоли́ровать. —**insulation,** *n.* изоля́ция. —**insulator,** *n.* изоля́тор.

insulin *n.* инсули́н.

insult *v.t.* оскорбля́ть. —*n.* оскорбле́ние; оби́да. —**insulting,** *adj.* оскорби́тельный; оби́дный.

insuperable *adj.* непреодоли́мый.

insurance *n.* страхова́ние. —*adj.* страхово́й: *insurance company,* страхова́я компа́ния. *Insurance policy/agent,* страхово́й по́лис/аге́нт.

insure *v.t.* **1,** (guarantee) обеспе́чивать. **2,** (take out insurance for) страхова́ть. —**insurer,** *n.* страхо́вщик.

insurgency *n.* восста́ние; мяте́ж.

insurgent *n.* повста́нец; мяте́жник. —*adj.* повста́нческий; мяте́жный.

insurmountable *adj.* непреодоли́мый.

insurrection *n.* восста́ние; мяте́ж.

intact *adj.* це́лый; в це́лости; в сохра́нности. *Be preserved intact,* сохраня́ться в неприкоснове́нности.

intake *n.* впуск.

intangible *adj.* неосяза́емый.

integer *n.* це́лое число́; це́лое.

integral *adj.* **1,** (essential) неотъе́млемый: *integral part,* неотъе́млемая часть. **2,** *math.* интрега́льный: *integral calculus,* интегра́льное исчисле́ние. —*n., math.* интегра́л.

integrate *v.t.* **1,** (combine into a whole) интегри́ровать. **2,** (desegregate) десегреги́ровать.

integrated *adj.* ко́мплексный. *Integrated circuit,* интегра́льная схе́ма.

integration *n.* **1,** (combining into a whole) интегра́ция. **2,** (desegregation) десегрега́ция.

integrity *n.* **1,** (uprightness; honesty) че́стность. **2,** (entirety) це́лостность: *territorial integrity,* территориа́льная це́лостность.

integument *n.* покро́в.

intellect *n.* ум; ра́зум; интелле́кт.

intellectual *adj.* у́мственный; интеллектуа́льный. —*n.* интеллиге́нт; интеллектуа́л. —**intellectual property,** интеллектуа́льная со́бственность.

intelligence *n.* **1,** (mental ability) ум; у́мственные спосо́бности. **2,** (collection of secret information; organization engaged in same) разве́дка; (information so collected) разве́дывательные да́нные. —*adj.* разве́дывательный; разве́дочный. —**intelligence quotient,** показа́тель у́мственных спосо́бностей. —**intelligence test,** испыта́ние у́мственных спосо́бностей.

intelligent *adj.* **1,** (endowed with intellect) разу́мный. **2,** (smart; clever) у́мный.

intelligentsia *n.* интеллиге́нция.

intelligible *adj.* поня́тный; толко́вый; вразуми́тельный. —**intelligibility,** *n.* поня́тность.

intemperance *n.* невозде́ржность; невоздержа́ние.

intemperate *adj.* **1,** (given to excesses; excessive) неуме́ренный; невозде́ржанный. **2,** (improper; rude) невоздержанный: *intemperate language,* невоздержанный язык.

intend *v.t.* **1,** (have in mind; plan) собираться; намереваться. *What do you intend to do?,* что вы намерены делать? **2,** (design for a specific purpose) предназначать: *intended for children,* предназначен для детей.

intense *adj.* **1,** (keenly felt) сильный: *intense heat/hatred,* сильная жара/ненависть. *Intense pain,* сильная or острая боль. *Intense pressure,* сильное давление. **2,** (strenuous; heated) напряжённый: *intense struggle,* напряжённая борьба.

intensify *v.t.* **1,** (increase; step up) усиливать; усугублять. *Intensify one's efforts,* усугублять усилия. **2,** (make more acute) обострять. —*v.i.* обостряться. —**intensification,** *n.* усиление; обострение.

intensity *n.* интенсивность.

intensive *adj.* интенсивный. —**intensive care,** интенсивная терапия.

intent *n.* **1,** (intention) намерение. **2,** *law* умысел: *malicious intent,* злой умысел. —*adj.* **1,** (firmly fixed or directed) пристальный; сосредоточенный. **2,** *fol. by* **on** (determined) полный решимости. —**to all intents and purposes,** фактически.

intention *n.* намерение. *Have no intention of,* (отнюдь) не собираться (+ *inf.*).

intentional *adj.* намеренный; преднамеренный; умышленный. —**intentionally,** *adv.* намеренно; нарочно; умышленно.

intently *adv.* пристально; напряжённо; сосредоточенно. *Listen intently,* слушать напряжённо *or* сосредоточенно. *Stare intently into the distance,* смотреть пристально *or* напряжённо вдаль.

inter *v.t.* хоронить; погребать.

interact *v.i.* взаимодействовать. —**interaction,** *n.* взаимодействие.

intercede *v.i.* **1,** (plead in behalf of another) хлопотать; ходатайствовать; вступаться; заступаться. **2,** (mediate) посредничать.

intercept *v.t.* перехватывать. —**interception,** *n.* перехват. —**interceptor,** *n., aero.* истребитель-перехватчик.

intercession *n.* заступничество; ходатайство. —**intercessor,** *n.* заступник; ходатай.

interchange *v.t.* меняться (+ *instr.*); обмениваться (+ *instr.*). —*v.i.* меняться местами. —*n.* **1,** (instance of interchanging) (взаимный) обмен. **2,** (multilevel highway intersection) развязка.

interchangeable *adj.* взаимозаменяемый. —**interchangeably,** *adv. These words are used interchangeably,* эти слова взаимозаменяемы.

intercity *adj.* междугородный.

interconnect *v.i.* соединяться. *The bedrooms interconnect,* спальни соединены между собой. —**interconnected,** *adj.* взаимосвязанный. —**interconnection,** *n.* взаимосвязь.

intercontinental *adj.* межконтинентальный.

intercourse *n.* **1,** (dealings) общение; сношения. **2,** (copulation) половая связь.

interdependence *n.* взаимозависимость. —**interdependent,** *adj.* взаимозависимый.

interdict *v.t.* **1,** (forbid) запрещать. **2,** *mil.* воспрещать.

interdiction *n.* **1,** (act of forbidding) запрет; запрещение. **2,** *mil.* воспрещение.

interest *n.* **1,** (curiosity) интерес: *interest in music,* интерес к музыке. *Be of interest,* представлять интерес. *Broad range of interests,* широкий круг интересов. **2,** (advantage; benefit) интересы: *It is in your interest,* это в ваших интересах. *In the public interest,* в общественных интересах. *Protect one's interests,* защищать свои интересы. **3,** (payment for the use of money) процент; проценты: *interest on a loan,* процент(ы) по займу. *Charge interest,* брать проценты. *At low interest,* под низкий процент. *At 10% interest,* под десять процентов. **4,** (legal share) доля: *a half interest,* половинная доля. —*v.t.* интересовать. *This will interest you,* это вам будет интересно. —**in the interest of,** в интересах (+ *gen.*); ради. —**with interest,** с лихвой: *repay with interest,* отплатить с лихвой.

interested *adj.* заинтересованный: *interested party,* заинтересованная сторона. *Be interested in,* интересоваться (+ *instr.*); быть заинтересованным в (+ *prepl.*). *He is not interested,* ему не интересно.

interest-free *adj.* беспроцентный.

interesting *adj.* интересный.

interethnic *adj.* межнациональный.

interfere *v.i.* **1,** (meddle; intervene) вмешиваться. **2,** *fol. by* **with** (hinder; obstruct) мешать.

interference *n.* **1,** (act of interfering) вмешательство. **2,** (static) помехи.

interim *n.* промежуток. *In the interim,* тем временем. —*adj.* временный; промежуточный. *Interim agreement,* временное соглашение.

interior *adj.* внутренний. —*n.* **1,** (inner part; inside) внутренность; внутренняя часть. *Deep into the interior of the country,* вглубь страны. **2,** (of a house) интерьер. —**interior decorator,** декоратор.

interject *v.t.* вставлять; ввёртывать.

interjection *n.* междометие.

interlace *v.t.* **1,** (intertwine) сплетать; переплетать. **2,** (intersperse) пересыпать.

interlard *v.t.* пересыпать.

interlay *v.t.* перекладывать; прокладывать.

interlock *v.t.* сцеплять. —*v.i.* сцепляться.

interloper *n.* незваный гость; пришлый человек.

interlude *n.* **1,** (interval) промежуток. **2,** *music* интерлюдия.

intermarriage *n.* смешанный брак; брак между людьми различной расы. —**intermarry,** *v.i.* вступать в смешанный брак.

intermediary *n.* посредник. —*adj.* **1,** (intermediate) промежуточный. **2,** (acting as a mediator) посреднический.

intermediate *adj.* **1,** (situated in between) промежуточный. **2,** (between elementary and secondary) средний. —**intermediate-range,** *adj.* средней дальности.

interment *n.* погребение.

intermezzo *n.* интермеццо.

interminable *adj.* бесконе́чный; несконча́емый.
intermingle *v.t.* сме́шивать; перемеша́ивать. —*v.i.* сме́шиваться.
intermission *n.* **1**, (recess) переры́в. **2**, *theat.* антра́кт.
intermittent *adj.* перемежа́ющийся; преры́вистый. *Intermittent showers,* перемежа́ющиеся *or* переходя́щие дожди́. —**intermittently,** *adv.* с переры́вами.
intern *n.* интёрн. —*v.i.* служи́ть интёрном. —*v.t.* (confine) интерни́ровать.
internal *adj.* вну́тренний. —**internal bleeding,** вну́треннее кровотече́ние. —**internal-combustion engine,** дви́гатель вну́треннего сгора́ния. —**internal injuries,** вну́тренние поврежде́ния. —**internal medicine,** терапи́я.
internally *adv.* вну́тренне. *Take medicine internally,* принима́ть лека́рство внутрь.
international *adj.* междунаро́дный. —**International Date Line,** Ли́ния переме́ны да́ты.
Internationale *n.* Интернациона́л.
internationalism *n.* интернационали́зм.
internecine *adj.* **1**, (marked by great slaughter) истреби́тельный. **2**, (internal) междоусо́бный.
internist *n.* терапе́вт.
internment *n.* интерни́рование. —**internment camp,** ла́герь для интерни́рованных.
interplanetary *adj.* межплане́тный.
interplay *n.* взаимоде́йствие.
interpolate *v.t.* **1**, (interject; interpose) вставля́ть. **2**, *math.* интерполи́ровать. —**interpolation,** *n.* интерполя́ция.
interpose *v.t.* **1**, (place between others) ста́вить (ме́жду). **2**, (interject, as a comment) вставля́ть.
interpret *v.t.* **1**, (translate orally) переводи́ть. **2**, (explain; construe) толкова́ть; истолко́вывать; трактова́ть; интерпрети́ровать. *This should not be interpreted as...,* э́то не должно́ толкова́ться как...
interpretation *n.* **1**, (translation) перево́д. **2**, (explanation) толкова́ние; истолкова́ние; тракто́вка; интерпрета́ция. *Open to various interpretations,* откры́т для ра́зных толкова́ний.
interpreter *n.* **1**, (translator) перево́дчик. **2**, (commentator) толкова́тель; истолкова́тель; интерпрета́тор.
interregnum *n.* междуца́рствие.
interrelated *adj.* взаимоде́йствующий; взаимосвя́занный.
interrelation *n.* взаимоотноше́ние. —**interrelationship,** *n.* взаи́мная связь.
interrogate *v.t.* допра́шивать. —**interrogation,** *n.* допро́с.
interrogative *adj.* вопроси́тельный.
interrupt *v.t.* прерыва́ть; перебива́ть; обрыва́ть. *Interrupt a speaker,* перебива́ть *or* прерыва́ть ора́тора. *Interrupt a conversation/meeting/vacation,* прерыва́ть разгово́р/собра́ние/о́тпуск. —*v.i.* перебива́ть: *Don't interrupt!,* не перебива́й(те)!
interruption *n.* **1**, (act of interrupting) прерыва́ние. *Interruption of telephone service,* наруше́ние телефо́нной свя́зи. *Interruption of pregnancy,* прерыва́ние бере́менности. **2**, (instance of interrupting) поме́ха: *without any interruptions,* без вся́ких

поме́х. *Excuse the interruption!,* извини́те за беспоко́йство! **3**, (break) переры́в: *without interruption,* без переры́ва.
intersect *v.t.* пересека́ть. —*v.i.* пересека́ться.
intersection *n.* **1**, (of lines) пересече́ние. **2**, (of streets, roads, etc.) перекрёсток; пересече́ние.
intersperse *v.t.* **1**, (place at various intervals) размеща́ть. **2**, (interlace, as with comments) пересыпа́ть; пестри́ть.
interstellar *adj.* межзвёздный.
intertwine *v.t.* сплета́ть; переплета́ть. *Our lives became intertwined,* на́ши су́дьбы сплели́сь. —*v.i.* сплета́ться; переплета́ться.
interval *n.* **1**, (space; gap; break) промежу́ток; интерва́л. *At two-mile/ two-minute/ intervals,* с интерва́лом в две ми́ли/мину́ты. **2**, *Brit.* (intermission) антра́кт.
intervene *v.i.* **1**, (intercede) вме́шиваться: *intervene in a conflict,* вмеша́ться в конфли́кт. **2**, (occur in the meantime) происходи́ть (тем вре́менем). *In the intervening period,* тем вре́менем.
intervention *n.* вмеша́тельство; интерве́нция. *Surgical intervention,* хирурги́ческое *or* операти́вное вмеша́тельство.
interview *n.* **1**, (meeting to evaluate) встре́ча. **2**, (for a publication, on TV, etc.) интервью́. *Interview with a newspaper,* интервью́ газе́те. —*v.t.* брать интервью́ у; интервьюи́ровать. —**interviewer,** *n.* интервьюе́р.
interweave *v.t.* сплета́ть; переплета́ть.
intestate *adj.* без завеща́ния; не оста́вив завеща́ния.
intestine *n.* кишка́; *pl.* кишки́; кише́чник. —**intestinal,** *adj.* кише́чный.
intimacy *n.* инти́мность; бли́зость.
intimate[1] (in-ti-mit) *adj.* инти́мный: *intimate circle,* инти́мный круг. *Intimate friend,* бли́зкий друг. *Intimate knowledge of a subject,* основа́тельное знако́мство с предме́том. *On intimate terms with,* в бли́зких/инти́мных отноше́ниях с. *Become intimate with,* сойти́сь с.
intimate[2] (in-ti-mate) *v.t.* намека́ть.
intimately *adv.* инти́мно. *Intimately connected with,* те́сно свя́занный с.
intimation *n.* намёк.
intimidate *v.t.* запу́гивать. —**intimidation,** *n.* запу́гивание.
into *prep.* в (+ *acc.*): *walk into a room,* входи́ть в ко́мнату; *fall into a trap,* попа́сть в лову́шку. *Fire into the air/crowd,* стреля́ть в во́здух/толпу́. *Put into operation,* вводи́ть в де́йствие. *Get into trouble,* попа́сть в беду́. ♦*With certain verbs,* на: *divide into parts,* дели́ть на ча́сти. *Run into an old acquaintance,* ната́лкиваться на ста́рого знако́мого. *Translate into Russian,* переводи́ть на ру́сский язы́к.
intolerable *adj.* нетерпи́мый.
intolerant *adj.* нетерпи́мый. —**intolerance,** *n.* нетерпи́мость.
intonation *n.* интона́ция.
intone *v.i.* говори́ть нараспе́в *or* речитати́вом. —*v.t.* чита́ть *or* произноси́ть нараспе́в/речитати́вом.
intoxicate *v.t.* пьяни́ть; опьяня́ть. —**intoxicated,** *adj.*

пья́ный; хмельно́й; опьяне́вший. *While intoxicated,* в состоя́нии опьяне́ния. —**intoxicating,** *adj.* опьяня́ющий; хмельно́й. —**intoxication,** *n.* опьяне́ние.

intractable *adj.* несгово́рчивый; неподатливый.

intransigent *adj.* непрекло́нный. —**intransigence,** *n.* непрекло́нность.

intransitive *adj.* непереходный.

intravenous *adj.* внутриве́нный.

intrepid *adj.* неустраши́мый; бесстра́шный.

intricacy *n.* **1,** (complexity) запу́танность; сло́жность. **2,** *pl.* (intricate details) хитросплете́ния.

intricate *adj.* запу́танный; замыслова́тый; сло́жный.

intrigue *n.* интри́га; *pl.* интри́ги; про́иски. —*v.t.* (fascinate) интригова́ть. —*v.i.* (engage in intrigue) интригова́ть. —**intriguing,** *adj.* интригу́ющий.

intrinsic *adj.* вну́тренний. *Intrinsic value,* вну́тренняя *or* действи́тельная це́нность. —**intrinsically,** *adv.* в су́щности свое́й; по своему́ существу́.

introduce *v.t.* **1,** (present so as to make acquainted) знако́мить; представля́ть. *Introduce someone to someone,* (по)знако́мить кого́-нибудь с ке́м-нибудь. *Allow me to introduce...,* разреши́те мне предста́вить (+ *acc.*). **2,** (present to an audience) представля́ть. **3,** (institute) вводи́ть; заводи́ть. *Introduce a new method,* вводи́ть но́вый ме́тод. **4,** (offer, as a bill) вноси́ть. —**introduce oneself,** представля́ться; (от)рекомендова́ться.

introduction *n.* **1,** (presentation) представле́ние: *introduction of a speaker,* представле́ние ора́тора. *A flowery introduction,* кра́сочное представле́ние. **2,** (opening portion, as of a book) введе́ние; вступле́ние. **3,** (instituting) введе́ние. **4,** (elementary phase of study) введе́ние: *introduction to philosophy,* введе́ние в филосо́фию. **5,** *music* интроду́кция.

introductory *adj.* вступи́тельный; вво́дный. *Introductory course,* вво́дный курс.

introspection *n.* самонаблюде́ние; самоана́лиз; интроспе́кция. —**introspective,** *adj.* интроспекти́вный.

intrude *v.i.* вторга́ться. *Intrude into someone's affairs,* вторга́ться *or* вме́шиваться в чьи́-нибудь дела́. *I hope I'm not intruding,* наде́юсь, что я вам не меша́ю *or* помеша́ю. —*v.t.* навя́зывать: *intrude one's opinion on someone,* навя́зывать своё мне́ние кому́-нибудь.

intruder *n.* **1,** (interloper) незва́ный гость. **2,** (housebreaker) взло́мщик.

intrusion *n.* **1,** (encroachment) вторже́ние: *intrusion of (a country's) airspace,* вторже́ние в возду́шное простра́нство. **2,** (interruption) беспоко́йство: *Pardon the intrusion!,* извини́те за беспоко́йство!

intrusive *adj.* навя́зчивый.

intuition *n.* интуи́ция.

intuitive *adj.* интуити́вный. —**intuitively,** *adv.* интуити́вно; по наи́тию.

inundate *v.t.* **1,** (flood) затопля́ть. **2,** *fig.* (overwhelm) наводня́ть. —**inundation,** *n.* наводне́ние.

inure *v.t.* приуча́ть; закаля́ть. *Inured to hardships,* приу́чен к лише́ниям.

invade *v.t. & i.* вторга́ться (в): *invade a neighboring*

state, вто́ргнуться в сосе́днее госуда́рство. —**invader,** *n.* захва́тчик.

invalid[1] (in-va-lid) *n.* инвали́д.

invalid[2] (in-val-id) *adj.* **1,** (null; void) недействи́тельный: *declare the election invalid,* призна́ть вы́боры недействи́тельными. **2,** (unsound, as of an argument) необосно́ванный. **3,** (illegitimate, as of an excuse) неуважи́тельный.

invalidate *v.t.* де́лать недействи́тельным; аннули́ровать.

invaluable *adj.* неоцени́мый; бесце́нный.

invariable *adj.* неизме́нный. —**invariably,** *adv.* неизме́нно.

invasion *n.* вторже́ние; наше́ствие. *Invasion of,* вторже́ние в (+ *acc.*); наше́ствие на (+ *acc.*). *Invasion of privacy,* вторже́ние в ча́стную жизнь.

invective *n.* брань; ру́гань.

inveigh *v.i.* [*usu.* **inveigh against**] ра́товать (про́тив).

inveigle *v.t.* **1,** (talk into) ула́мывать. **2,** (wangle) выпра́шивать.

invent *v.t.* **1,** (devise; create) изобрета́ть: *The telephone was invented by Alexander Graham Bell,* телефо́н изобрёл Алекса́ндер Гре́йам Белл. **2,** (fabricate; concoct) выду́мывать; сочиня́ть; измышля́ть.

invention *n.* **1,** (act of inventing; something invented) изобрете́ние. **2,** (fabrication) вы́думка; измышле́ние.

inventive *adj.* изобрета́тельный. —**inventiveness,** *n.* изобрета́тельность.

inventor *n.* изобрета́тель.

inventory *n.* **1,** (stock-taking) о́пись; инвента́рь; инвентариза́ция; учёт; переучёт. *Take inventory,* де́лать о́пись; составля́ть инвента́рь. *Closed for inventory,* закры́т на учёт. **2,** (stock on hand) инвента́рь; запа́с. —*v.t.* опи́сывать; инвентаризи́ровать.

inverse *adj.* обра́тный; противополо́жный. —*n.* противополо́жность. —**inversely,** *adv.* обра́тно: *inversely proportional to,* обра́тно пропорциона́льный (+ *dat.*).

inversion *n.* **1,** (act of inverting) переворачивание. **2,** (reversal of order) перестано́вка. **3,** *gram.; chem.; meteorol.* инве́рсия.

invert *v.t.* **1,** (turn upside down) переворачивать. **2,** (reverse the order of) переставля́ть.

invertebrate *adj.* беспозвоно́чный. —*n.* беспозвоно́чное. *The invertebrates,* беспозвоно́чные.

inverted *adj.* **1,** (turned upside down) переверну́тый. **2,** (reverse) обра́тный: *inverted order,* обра́тный поря́док. —**inverted commas,** *Brit.* кавы́чки.

invest *v.t.* **1,** (put, as money, effort, etc.) вкла́дывать. **2,** (give power to) облека́ть. —*v.i.* [*usu.* **invest in**] вкла́дывать де́ньги в (+ *acc.*).

investigate *v.t.* **1,** (subject to an official probe) рассле́довать. **2,** (explore scientifically) иссле́довать.

investigation *n.* **1,** (official probe) рассле́дование; сле́дствие. *Federal Bureau of Investigation,* Федера́льное бюро́ рассле́дований. **2,** (scientific study) иссле́дование.

investigator *n.* сле́дователь. —**investigatory,** *adj.* сле́дственный.

investiture *n.* инвеститу́ра.

investment *n.* вложе́ние; капиталовложе́ние; инве́сти́ция; вклад.

investor *n.* вкла́дчик; инвести́тор; инве́стор.

inveterate *adj.* закоренéлый; застарéлый; зая́длый.

invidious *adj.* оскорби́тельный; оби́дный.

invigorate *v.t.* бодри́ть; оживля́ть. —**invigorating,** *adj.* бодря́щий; живи́тельный.

invincible *adj.* непобеди́мый. —**invincibility,** *n.* непобеди́мость.

inviolable *adj.* неруши́мый; неприкоснове́нный. —**inviolability,** *n.* неруши́мость; неприкоснове́нность.

inviolate *adj.* **1,** (not violated) не нару́шенный. *Keep inviolate,* свя́то храни́ть. **2,** (not profaned) нетро́нутый.

invisible *adj.* неви́димый. —**invisible ink,** симпати́ческие черни́ла.

invitation *n.* приглаше́ние.

invite *v.t.* **1,** (request the presence of) приглаша́ть: *invite someone to dinner,* пригласи́ть кого́-нибудь на у́жин *or* у́жинать. *Invite oneself to the meeting,* напроси́ться на встре́чу. **2,** (request politely): *invite questions from the audience,* предложи́ть задава́ть вопро́сы. **3,** (tend to bring on; lay oneself open to) напра́шиваться на: *invite trouble,* напра́шиваться на неприя́тности.

inviting *adj.* привлека́тельный; зама́нчивый; соблазни́тельный.

invocation *n.* **1,** (appeal to a higher power) обраще́ние. **2,** (opening prayer) моли́тва.

invoice *n.* факту́ра; накладна́я; счёт.

invoke *v.t.* **1,** (call on for help) обраща́ться к. **2,** (appeal for) моли́ть о: *invoke God's help,* моли́ть бо́га о по́мощи. **3,** (resort to; put into force) вводи́ть в де́йствие. **4,** (summon by incantation) заклина́ть.

involuntary *adj.* нево́льный; непроизво́льный.

involve *v.t.* **1,** (entail) влечь за собо́й; быть свя́занным с. *What does the job involve?,* в чём состои́т э́та рабо́та? *The job involves a lot of traveling,* рабо́та свя́зана с разъе́здами. **2,** (implicate; embroil) вовлека́ть. *Get involved in,* ввя́зываться в; впу́тываться в. *Become involved with a woman,* связа́ться *or* спу́таться с же́нщиной. **3,** (absorb; engross) поглоща́ть.

involved *adj.* **1,** (concerned) заинтересо́ванный. **2,** *fol. by* **in** (a party to) прича́стный (к). **3,** (complex) запу́танный.

involvement *n.* **1,** (act of involving) вовлече́ние. **2,** (state of being involved) вовлечённость; прича́стность. *Degree of involvement,* сте́пень вовлечённости.

invulnerable *adj.* неуязви́мый. —**invulnerability,** *n.* неуязви́мость.

inward *adj.* вну́тренний. —*adv.* [*also,* **inwards**] внутрь. —**inwardly,** *adv.* вну́тренне; в душе́.

iodine *n.* йод.

ion *n.* ио́н. —**ionic,** *adj.* ио́нный.

ionize *v.t.* иониз́ировать. —**ionization,** *n.* иониза́ция.

ionosphere *n.* ионосфе́ра.

iota *n.* йо́та. *Not one iota,* ни на йо́ту.

IQ *abbr.* показа́тель у́мственных спосо́бностей.

Iranian *adj.* ира́нский. —*n.* ира́нец; ира́нка.

Iraqi *adj.* ира́кский.

irascible *adj.* вспы́льчивый. —**irascibility,** *n.* вспы́льчивость.

irate *adj.* гне́вный; разгне́ванный. *Be irate,* зли́ться.

ire *n.* гнев.

iridescent *adj.* ра́дужный; перели́вчатый. —**iridescence,** *n.* ра́дужность.

iridium *n.* ири́дий.

iris *n.* **1,** (of the eye) ра́дужная оболо́чка. **2,** (flower) и́рис; каса́тик.

Irish *adj.* ирла́ндский. —*n., preceded by* **the** ирла́ндцы. —**Irishman,** *n.* ирла́ндец.

irk *v.t.* раздража́ть; досажда́ть; надоеда́ть. —**irksome,** *adj.* доса́дный; надое́дливый.

iron *n.* **1,** (metal) желе́зо. *Spinach contains iron,* шпина́т соде́ржит желе́зо. **2,** (flatiron) утю́г. **3,** (instrument of iron): *soldering iron,* пая́льник. *Fire irons,* ками́нные щипцы́. **4,** (shackles) кандалы́: *in irons,* в кандала́х. —*adj.* желе́зный: *iron ore,* желе́зная руда́. *Iron will, iron resolve,* желе́зная во́ля. —*v.t.* **1,** (press) утю́жить; гла́дить. **2,** *fol. by* **out** (remove by ironing) разгла́живать (утюго́м). **3,** *fol. by* **out** (smooth over, as differences) сгла́живать; ула́живать. —*v.i.* утю́жить. —**Iron Age,** желе́зный век. —**iron curtain,** желе́зный за́навес.

ironclad *adj.* желе́зный: *ironclad guarantee,* желе́зная гара́нтия.

ironic *adj.* ирони́ческий. *Also,* **ironical.**

ironically *adv.* **1,** (in an ironic manner) ирони́чески. **2,** (it is ironic that) по иро́нии судьбы́.

ironing *n.* утю́жка; гла́женье. —**ironing board,** гла́ди́льная доска́.

ironworks *n.* чугунолите́йный заво́д.

irony *n.* иро́ния.

irradiate *v.t.* **1,** (illuminate) освеща́ть; озаря́ть. **2,** (expose to rays or radiation) облуча́ть. —**irradiation,** *n.* иррадиа́ция; облуче́ние.

irrational *adj.* **1,** (not reasoning; senseless) неразу́мный; нерассуди́тельный. **2,** *math.* иррациона́льный. —**irrationality,** *n.* неразу́мность; нерассуди́тельность.

irreconcilable *adj.* непримири́мый. —**irreconcilability,** *n.* непримири́мость.

irrecoverable *adj.* непоправи́мый; невозвра́тный.

irrefutable *adj.* неопровержи́мый.

irregular *adj.* **1,** (not symmetrical) непра́вильный: *irregular features,* непра́вильные черты́. **2,** (uneven in occurrence) нерегуля́рный. **3,** (spasmodic) нерóвный: *irregular heartbeat,* нерóвное бие́ние се́рдца. **4,** *gram.* непра́вильный: *irregular verb,* непра́вильный глаго́л. **5,** *mil.* нерегуля́рный.

irregularity *n.* непра́вильность; нерегуля́рность.

irrelevance *also,* **irrelevancy** *n.* неуме́стность. *That is an irrelevance,* э́то не отно́сится к де́лу.

irrelevant *adj.* неуме́стный; не относя́щийся к де́лу.

irreligious *adj.* не ве́рующий.

irremovable *adj.* неустрани́мый.

irreparable *adj.* непоправи́мый; невозвра́тный; невосполни́мый; невознагради́мый. *Irreparable damage,* непоправи́мый вред *or* уще́рб. *Irreparable loss,* невозвра́тная *or* невосполни́мая поте́ря *or* утра́та.

irreplaceable *adj.* незамени́мый.

irrepressible *adj.* **1,** (impossible to hold back) неудержи́мый. **2,** (impossible to discourage) неугомо́нный.

irreproachable *adj.* безукори́зненный; безупре́чный.

irresistibility *n.* неотрази́мость.

irresistible *adj.* **1,** (that cannot be stopped) неотрази́мый: *irresistible force,* неотрази́мая си́ла. **2,** (impossible to resist, as of a desire, temptation, etc.) непреодоли́мый; неодоли́мый. *He made me an irresistible offer,* он сде́лал предложе́ние, от кото́рого я не мог отказа́ться. **3,** (having an overpowering appeal) неотрази́мый: *her irresistible beauty,* её неотрази́мая красота́.

irresolute *adj.* нереши́тельный.

irrespective *adj., in* **irrespective of,** незави́симо от; безотноси́тельно к.

irresponsibility *n.* безотве́тственность.

irresponsible *adj.* безотве́тственный. —**irresponsibly,** *adv.* безотве́тственно.

irretrievable *adj.* непоправи́мый; невозвра́тный.

irreverence *n.* непочте́ние. —**irreverent** *adj.* непочти́тельный.

irreversible *adj.* необрати́мый.

irrevocable *adj.* беспорово́тный.

irrigate *v.t.* ороша́ть. —**irrigation,** *n.* ороше́ние; ирриrа́ция.

irritable *adj.* раздражи́тельный. —**irritability,** *n.* раздражи́тельность.

irritant *n.* раздражи́тель.

irritate *v.t.* раздража́ть: *He irritates me,* он меня́ раздража́ет. *This brand of soap irritates my skin,* э́тот сорт мы́ла раздража́ет мою́ ко́жу.

irritation *n.* раздраже́ние. *Skin irritation,* раздраже́ние ко́жи.

is *v. see* be.

ischemia *also,* **ischaemia** *n.* ишеми́я.

isinglass *n.* **1,** (gelatin) ры́бий клей. **2,** (mica) слюда́.

Islam *n.* исла́м. —**Islamic,** *adj.* мусульма́нский.

island *n.* о́стров. —**islander,** *n.* островитя́нин.

isle *n.* острово́к.

isobar *n.* изоба́ра.

isolate *v.t.* изоли́ровать; обособля́ть.

isolated *adj.* **1,** (cut off) изоли́рованный; обосо́бленный. **2,** (rare; exceptional) едини́чный: *isolated cases,* едини́чные слу́чаи.

isolation *n.* изоля́ция; обособле́ние; о́торванность. *In isolation,* изоли́рованно. —**isolation ward,** изоля́тор.

isolationism *n.* изоляциони́зм.

isolationist *n.* изоляциони́ст. —*adj.* изоляциони́стский.

isomer *n.* изоме́р.

isosceles *adj.* равнобе́дренный.

isotope *n.* изото́п.

Israeli *adj.* изра́ильский. —*n.* израильтя́нин; израильтя́нка.

issuance *n.* **1,** (handing out) вы́дача. **2,** (putting out) вы́пуск. **3,** (promulgation) изда́ние.

issue *n.* **1,** = issuance. **2,** (something issued, as of bonds, stamps, etc.) вы́пуск. **3,** (single number of a periodical) но́мер; вы́пуск. **4,** (point in question) вопро́с. *At issue,* под вопро́сом. *That's not at issue,* об э́том спо́ру нет. **5,** (progeny) пото́мки; пото́мство. —*v.t.* **1,** (give; grant; hand out) выдава́ть: *issue a visa,* выдава́ть ви́зу. **2,** (put out, as stamps, money, etc.) выпуска́ть. **3,** (put forth officially) издава́ть: *issue an edict,* изда́ть ука́з. *Issue an order,* отда́ть *or* изда́ть прика́з. *Issue a warning to,* сде́лать предупрежде́ние (+ *dat.*). *Issue a reprimand to,* вы́нести вы́говор (+ *dat.*). *Issue an ultimatum to,* предъяви́ть ультима́тум (+ *dat.*). —*v.i.* (flow out) исходи́ть; вытека́ть. —**make an issue of,** де́лать исто́рию из; де́лать из (+ *gen.*) предме́т спо́ра. —**take issue with,** **1,** (a person) возража́ть (+ *dat.*). **2,** (a statement) оспа́ривать.

isthmus *n.* перешее́к.

it *pron.* **1,** *pers.* он; она́; оно́: *I don't know how good it is,* я не зна́ю наско́лько он хоро́ш. *Where did you put it?,* куда́ вы его́ положи́ли? ♦*Frequently omitted in Russian: Give it to me,* да́йте мне. *Did you find it?,* нашли́? *Would you like to see it?,* хоти́те посмотре́ть? *I don't like it when...,* я не люблю́, когда́... **2,** *indef.* э́то: *It is I,* э́то я. *It's Anna calling,* А́нна звони́т. *I already knew about it,* я уже́ знал (зна́ла) об э́том. **3,** *impers.: It seems,* ка́жется. *It is raining,* идёт дождь. *It is cold,* хо́лодно. *It's hard to say,* тру́дно сказа́ть. *It's time to go,* пора́ идти́.

Italian *adj.* италья́нский. —*n.* **1,** (person) италья́нец; италья́нка. **2,** (language) италья́нский язы́к. *Speak Italian,* говори́ть по-италья́нски.

italic *n., usu. pl.* курси́в; курси́вный шрифт. *In italics,* курси́вом. —*adj.* курси́вный. —**italicize,** *v.t.* выделя́ть курси́вом.

itch *n.* зуд. —*v.i.* **1,** (have or produce an itch) чеса́ться; зуде́ть. *My nose itches,* у меня́ че́шется/зуди́т нос. **2,** (cause itching, as of rough material) шерсти́ть. **3,** (have an urge): *I am itching to* (+ *verb*), у меня́ ру́ки че́шутся *or* зудя́т; мне не те́рпится; меня́ так и подмыва́ет (*all followed by inf.*).

itchy *adj.* **1,** (of material) колю́чий. **2,** (of a part of one's body) зудя́щий.

item *n.* **1,** (article) предме́т. **2,** (unit) статья́: *item of export/expense,* статья́ э́кспорта/расхо́да. **3,** (on an agenda) пункт; вопро́с. **4,** (in a newspaper) заме́тка; сообще́ние. **5,** (on a program) но́мер.

itemize *v.t.* перечисля́ть по пу́нктам; ука́зывать в отде́льности.

itinerant *adj.* стра́нствующий; бродя́чий.

itinerary *n.* маршру́т.

its *poss. adj.* его́; её: *its* (*e.g. a dog's*) *owner,* его́/её хозя́ин. ♦*When the possessor is the subject of the sentence,* свой: *care for its young,* бере́чь свои́х детёнышей. *Everything was in its place,* всё бы́ло на своём ме́сте. ♦*Often omitted: chew its cud,* жева́ть жва́чку; *lose its luster,* теря́ть блеск *or* лоск.

itself *pron.* **1,** *used for emphasis,* сам: *The room itself is not large,* сама́ ко́мната небольша́я. **2,** *used reflexively,* себя́; сам себя́. *It speaks for itself,* э́то говори́т само́ за себя́. —**by itself, 1,** (alone) оди́н. *The house stands by itself,* дом стои́т особняко́м. **2,** (without help) сам: *The door closes by itself,* дверь сама́ закрыва́ется.

ivory *n.* слоно́вая кость.

ivy *n.* плющ. *Ivy-covered walls,* сте́ны, покры́тые плющо́м.

J

J, j деся́тая бу́ква англи́йского алфави́та.

jab *v.t. & i.* ты́кать. —*n.* тычо́к.

jabber *v.i.* болта́ть; тарато́рить.

jack *n.* **1,** (lever) домкра́т. **2,** (socket) гнездо́. **3,** *cards* вале́т. —*v.t.* [*usu.* **jack up**] **1,** (hoist with a jack) поднима́ть домкра́том. **2,** (raise, as prices) набива́ть; взви́нчивать.

jackal *n.* шака́л.

jackass *n.* осёл.

jackdaw *n.* га́лка.

jacket *n.* **1,** (man's sport coat) пиджа́к. **2,** (man's outer garment, as a lumberjacket) ку́ртка. **3,** (woman's garment) жаке́т; ко́фта. **4,** (casing; covering) кожу́х. **5,** (dust jacket) суперобло́жка. **6,** (skin of a potato) кожура́. *Potatoes boiled in their jackets,* карто́фель в мунди́ре.

jackhammer *n.* пневмати́ческий отбо́йный молото́к.

jack-of-all-trades *n.* ма́стер на все ру́ки.

jackpot *n.* банк. —**hit the jackpot,** сорва́ть банк.

jack rabbit за́яц.

jacksnipe *n.* га́ршнеп.

jackstraws *n.pl.* бирю́льки.

jade *n.* **1,** (mineral) нефри́т. **2,** (old horse) кля́ча; одёр.

jaded *adj.* **1,** (worn out) изму́ченный. **2,** (satiated) пресы́щенный.

jaeger *n.* (bird) помо́рник.

jag *n.* зубе́ц.

jagged *adj.* зубча́тый; зазу́бренный. *Jagged coastline,* изре́занный бе́рег.

jaguar *n.* ягуа́р.

jail *n.* тюрьма́. —*adj.* тюре́мный: *jail term,* срок тюре́много заключе́ния. —*v.t.* посади́ть в тюрьму́.

jailbreak *n.* побе́г *or* бе́гство из тюрьмы́.

jailer *also,* **jailor** *n.* тюре́мщик.

jalopy *n.* драндуле́т; колыма́га.

jalousie *n.* жалюзи́.

jam *v.t.* **1,** (force; wedge) впи́хивать; вкли́нивать. **2,** (catch, as one's fingers in a door) защемля́ть; ущемля́ть; прищемля́ть. **3,** (cause to become unworkable) закли́нивать. **4,** (crowd; pack) запру́-

живать: *People jammed the streets,* лю́ди запруди́ли у́лицы. *The aisles were jammed,* прохо́ды бы́ли заби́ты. *The place was jammed,* наро́ду бы́ло битко́м наби́то. **5,** (interfere with, as a broadcast) глуши́ть; заглуша́ть. **6,** *Jam on the brakes,* ре́зко затормози́ть. —*v.i.* **1,** (fail to operate; stick) заеда́ть; закли́нивать (*both impers.*): *The door/wheels jammed,* дверь заклини́ло; колёса зае́ло. **2,** (crowd) набива́ться: *jam into the elevator,* набива́ться в лифт. —*n.* **1,** (congestion) зато́р: *traffic jam,* зато́р у́личного движе́ния; про́бка. **2,** (fruit preserve) варе́нье; джем; пови́дло. **3,** *colloq.* (predicament) переде́лка; переплёт.

Jamaican *adj.* яма́йский. —*n.* яма́ец; яма́йка.

jamb *n.* коса́к.

jamming *n., radio* заглуше́ние.

jam-packed *adj., colloq.* битко́м наби́тый.

jangle *v.i.* звя́кать. —*v.t.* **1,** (cause to jangle) звя́кать (+ *instr.*). **2,** (irritate, as nerves) трепа́ть (не́рвы). —*n.* звя́канье.

janitor *n.* убо́рщик.

January *n.* янва́рь. —*adj.* янва́рский.

Japanese *adj.* япо́нский. *He* (*she*) *is Japanese,* он япо́нец; она́ япо́нка. —*n.* **1,** (language) япо́нский язы́к. *Speak Japanese,* говори́ть по-япо́нски. **2,** *preceded by* **the** (people) япо́нцы.

jar *n.* **1,** (container) ба́нка. **2,** (jolt) толчо́к. —*v.t.* потряса́ть. —*v.i.* **1,** *fol. by* on (grate on) коро́бить. **2,** *fol. by* **with** (clash) дисгармони́ровать (с).

jargon *n.* жарго́н.

jasmine *n.* жасми́н. —*adj.* жасми́нный; жасми́новый.

jasper *n.* я́шма. —*adj.* я́шмовый.

jaundice *n.* желту́ха.

jaundiced *adj.* **1,** (having jaundice) поражённый желту́хой. **2,** (prejudiced) предвзя́тый; предубеждённый.

jaunt *n.* прогу́лка.

jaunty *adj.* **1,** (sprightly) бо́йкий; задо́рный. **2,** (stylish) мо́дный; шика́рный.

javelin *n.* копьё; дро́тик. —**javelin throw,** *sports* мета́ние копья́.

jaw *n.* чéлюсть. *In the jaws of death*, в когтя́х
сме́рти.

jawbone *n.* чéлюсть; челюстна́я кость.

jay *n.* со́йка.

jazz *n.* джаз. —*adj.* джа́зовый.

jealous *adj.* ревни́вый. *Be jealous of*, ревнова́ть;
зави́довать. —**jealously**, *adv.* ревни́во.

jealousy *n.* рéвность.

jeans *n.pl.* джи́нсы.

jeep *n.* джип; ви́ллис.

jeer *v.t.* издева́ться над; насмеха́ться над. —*v.i.*
издева́тельски крича́ть. —*n.* издёвка.

Jehovah *n.* Иего́ва. —**Jehovah's Witnesses,** свидé-
тели Иего́вы.

jejune *adj.* сухо́й; бесцвéтный.

jell *v.i.* **1,** (congeal) застыва́ть. **2,** *fig.* (take definite
form) определя́ться.

jellied *adj.* заливно́й: *jellied sturgeon*, заливна́я
осетри́на.

jelly *n.* желé.

jellyfish *n.* медýза.

jeopardize *v.t.* ста́вить под угро́зу.

jeopardy *n.* опа́сность. *Be in jeopardy*, находи́ться
под угро́зой. *Place in jeopardy*, ста́вить под угро́зу.
—**double jeopardy,** втори́чное привлечéние к суду́
за то же преступлéние.

jerboa *n.* тушка́нчик.

jerk *v.t.* дёргать. —*v.i.* дёрнуться. —*n.* **1,** (tug)
рыво́к. **2,** *slang* (dope) болва́н.

jerky *adj.* поры́вистый; рéзкий.

jersey *n.* фуфа́йка.

jest *n.* шýтка: *in jest*, в шýтку. —*v.i.* шути́ть.

jester *n.* шут: *court jester*, придво́рный шут.

Jesuit *n.* иезуи́т. —*adj.* иезуи́тский.

Jesus *n.* Иисýс.

jet *n.* **1,** (spurt; gush) струя́. **2,** (spout; nozzle) жиклёр.
3, (mineral) гага́т. **4,** (plane) реакти́вный самолёт.
—*adj.* реакти́вный: *jet propulsion*, реакти́вное движéние. *Jet pump*, стру́йный насо́с. —*v.i.* бить
струёй.

jet-black *adj.* чёрный как смоль.

jet-propelled *adj.* реакти́вный.

jet stream стру́йное течéние.

jettison *v.t.* выбра́сывать за́ борт.

jetty *n.* **1,** (breakwater) мол. **2,** (wharf) при́стань.

Jew *n.* еврéй.

jewel *n.* драгоцéнный ка́мень; драгоцéнность.

jeweler *also,* **jeweller** *n.* ювели́р.

jewelry *also,* **jewellery** *n.* драгоцéнности. *Jewelry
store*, ювели́рный магази́н.

Jewish *adj.* еврéйский. —**Jewry,** *n.* еврéйство.

jib *n.* (sail) кли́вер. —**jib boom,** утлéгарь.

jibe *v.i.* **1,** = gibe. **2,** *colloq.* (agree; square) сходи́ться.

jiffy *n., colloq.* миг; мгновéние. *In a jiffy*, ми́гом; в
два счёта.

jig *n.* джи́га: *dance a jig*, танцева́ть джи́гу. —**in jig
time,** *colloq.* в два счёта. —**the jig is up,** *colloq.* игра́
зако́нчена *or* око́нчена.

jigger *n.* рю́мочка.

jiggle *v.t.* шевели́ть.

jigsaw puzzle составна́я карти́нка.

jilt *v.t.* броса́ть; оставля́ть.

jimmy *n.* отмы́чка; воровско́й лом. —*v.t.* [*usu.*
jimmy open] взла́мывать.

jimsonweed *n.* дурма́н.

jingle *v.t. & i.* звенéть. —*n.* **1,** (sound) звон. **2,** (humorous verse) часту́шка.

jinks *n.pl.* [*usu.* **high jinks**] шýмное весéлье.

jinx *n., colloq.* дурно́й глаз. —*v.t.* сгла́зить.

jitters *n.pl., colloq.* нéрвность. *Have the jitters*,
нéрвничать. *It gives me the jitters*, от э́того меня́
броса́ет в дрожь.

jittery *adj., colloq.* нéрвный.

job *n.* **1,** (piece of work) рабо́та; труд. *By the job*,
сдéльно; поуро́чно. *Odd jobs*, случа́йная рабо́та. **2,**
(task; chore) рабо́та; зада́ние. **3,** (position of employment) рабо́та; слýжба; мéсто. *Look for a job*, иска́ть
рабо́ту. *Change jobs*, меня́ть рабо́ту. *Get a job*,
устро́иться (на рабо́ту). *He has a good job*, он хо-
рошо́ устро́ен. *Take a second job*, брать втору́ю
рабо́ту. *Soft job*, тёплое мéсте́чко. **4,** *pl., econ.* ра-
бо́чие места́: *create jobs*, создава́ть (но́вые)
рабо́чие места́. *The loss of 100 jobs*, потéря ста
рабо́чих мест. —**give up as a bad job,** *colloq.*
махну́ть руко́й на (+ *acc.*); поста́вить крест на (+
acc. or prepl.). —**lie down on the job,** *colloq.*
рабо́тать спустя́ рукава́. —**on the job, 1,** (at work)
на слýжбе. **2,** (while at work) в рабо́чем поря́дке.

jobber *n.* оптови́к; торго́вый посрéдник.

jobless *adj.* безрабо́тный.

jockey *n.* жокéй.

jockstrap *n.* суспензо́рий.

jocose *adj.* шутли́вый; игри́вый.

jocular *adj.* шутли́вый; шýточный.

jocund *adj.* весёлый.

jog *v.i.* бéгать (трусцо́й). —*v.t.* (nudge) подта́л-
кивать. —**jogger,** *n.* бегу́н.

join *v.t.* **1,** (bring together; link; unite) соединя́ть;
свя́зывать. *Join hands*, бра́ться за́ руки. *Join forces*,
соединя́ть *or* объединя́ть си́лы. *Join the two halves
of the city*, соединя́ть о́бе ча́сти го́рода. **2,** (attach to
each other) соединя́ть; присоединя́ть. *Join two
pipes*, соединя́ть трýбы. **3,** (meet and accompany)
присоединя́ться к. *Would you care to join us?*,
хоти́те присоедини́ться к нам? **4,** (become a part of;
participate in) присоединя́ться к; примыка́ть к: *join
the crowd/rebellion*, присоединя́ться *or* примыка́ть
к толпé/ к восста́нию/. **5,** (become a member of; enroll in) вступа́ть в; запи́сываться в: *join the party*,
вступи́ть в па́ртию; *join a library*, записа́ться в библиотéку. *Join the ranks of*, вступи́ть *or* записа́ться в
ряды́ (+ *gen.*). *Join a club*, вступи́ть в члéны (*or*
стать члéном) клýба. **6,** (enlist in, as a branch of military service) поступа́ть в *or* на. **7,** (connect with) со-
единя́ться с. —*v.i.* **1,** (come together) соединя́ться;
сходи́ться. **2,** (become members) присоединя́ться.
3, *fol. by* **in** (take part with others) присоединя́ться
(к); включа́ться (в). *Join in the demonstration*, при-
соединя́ться к демонстра́ции. *Join in the conversa-
tion/discussion*, включи́ться в разгово́р/диску́ссию.

Join in singing, подхва́тывать пе́сню; подпева́ть. **4,** *fol. by* **up** (enlist) поступа́ть на вое́нную слу́жбу.

joiner *n.* (carpenter) столя́р.

joint *n.* **1,** *anat.* суста́в. **2,** (juncture, as of two pipes) стык. **3,** (coupling) шарни́р: *universal joint,* универса́льный шарни́р. —*adj.* **1,** (done or executed together) совме́стный: *joint venture,* совме́стное предприя́тие. **2,** (shared with another) совме́стный; о́бщий; со-: *joint ownership,* совме́стное владе́ние; *joint account,* о́бщий счёт; *joint owner,* совладе́лец. **3,** (consisting of more than one element) объединённый: *joint commission,* объединённая коми́ссия. *Joint Chiefs of Staff,* объединённый комите́т нача́льников штабо́в. —**out of joint,** вы́вихнутый.

jointly *adv.* совме́стно; сообща́; в па́ре.

joint-stock company акционе́рное о́бщество.

joke *n.* шу́тка; остро́та. *Practical joke,* ро́зыгрыш; мистифика́ция. —*v.i.* шути́ть: *You're joking!,* вы шу́тите! *Joking aside,* шу́тки в сто́рону.

joker *n.* **1,** (one who jokes) шутни́к. **2,** *cards* джо́кер.

jokester *n.* шутни́к.

jokingly *adv.* шутя́; в шу́тку.

jolly *adj.* весёлый. —*adv., Brit., colloq.* о́чень.

jolt *n.* толчо́к. *The news came as quite a jolt,* но́вость нас си́льно потрясла́. —*v.t.* трясти́; встря́хивать.

jonquil *n.* жонки́ль.

Jordanian *adj.* иорда́нский.

josh *v.i.* шути́ть. —*v.t.* подшу́чивать над; подтру́нивать над.

jostle *v.t.* толка́ть; пиха́ть. —*v.i.* толка́ться.

jot *v.t.* [*usu.* **jot down**] запи́сывать; набра́сывать.

joule *n.* джо́уль.

journal *n.* **1,** (daily record) дневни́к. **2,** (publication) газе́та; журна́л.

journalism *n.* журнали́стика. —**journalist,** *n.* журнали́ст. —**journalistic,** *adj.* журнали́стский.

journey *n.* пое́здка; путеше́ствие. *Set out on a journey,* отпра́виться в путеше́ствие. —*v.i.* путеше́ствовать.

joust *n.* ры́царский поеди́нок. —*v.i.* би́ться на поеди́нке.

jovial *adj.* весёлый. —**joviality,** *n.* весёлость.

jowl *n.* **1,** (jaw) че́люсть. **2,** (cheek) щека́. **3,** (dewlap of cattle) подгру́док.

joy *n.* ра́дость; отра́да. —**joyful,** *adj.* ра́достный. —**joyless,** *adj.* безра́достный. —**joyous,** *adj.* ра́достный.

jubilant *adj.* лику́ющий. *Be jubilant,* ликова́ть. —**jubilation,** *n.* ликова́ние.

jubilee *n.* юбиле́й.

Judaic *adj.* иуде́йский.

Judaism *n.* иудаи́зм; уде́йство.

Judas *n.* Иу́да.

judge *n.* **1,** (one who judges; magistrate) судья́. **2,** *pl.* (in a sport or contest) жюри́. **3,** (connoisseur) цени́тель; знато́к. *Be a good judge of,* быть знатоко́м (+ gen.); знать толк в. *I am no judge of such matters,* я не судья́ в э́том де́ле. —*v.i.* суди́ть. *Judging by,* судя́ по. *Judge for yourself,* посуди́те са́ми. *It is not for me to judge,* не мне суди́ть. —*v.t.* **1,** (form an

opinion about) суди́ть о: *judge someone by his appearance,* суди́ть о ко́м-нибудь по вне́шности. *Don't judge him too severely,* не суди́те его́ сли́шком стро́го. **2,** (deem) счита́ть: *judge it advisable to...,* счита́ть целесообра́зным (+ *inf.*). *The costs were judged to be too high,* изде́ржки бы́ли сочтены́ сли́шком больши́ми.

judgeship *n.* суде́йская до́лжность.

judgment *n.* **1,** (faculty of judging wisely) рассуди́тельность; благоразу́мие. *Show good judgment,* суди́ть здра́во. **2,** (opinion) мне́ние; взгляд; сужде́ние. *In my judgment,* на мой взгляд. **3,** (legal decision) реше́ние: *pronounce judgment,* выноси́ть реше́ние; *defer judgment,* откла́дывать реше́ние. **4,** (conclusion) сужде́ние: *make a final judgment,* выноси́ть оконча́тельное сужде́ние. **5,** (verdict; assessment) суд: *the judgment of history,* суд исто́рии. —**Judgment Day,** Су́дный день; Стра́шный суд.

judicial *adj.* суде́бный; юриди́ческий.

judiciary *adj.* суде́бный; юриди́ческий. —*n.* судоустро́йство.

judicious *adj.* благоразу́мный; рассуди́тельный. —**judiciously,** *adv.* благоразу́мно.

judo *n.* дзюдо́.

jug *n.* кувши́н; жбан.

juggle *v.t.* **1,** (toss and catch) жонгли́ровать. **2,** *fig.* (manipulate, as facts) подтасо́вывать; жонгли́ровать; передёргивать. —**juggler,** *n.* жонглёр. —**juggling,** *n.* жонглёрство.

jugular vein яре́мная ве́на.

juice *n.* сок: *tomato juice,* тома́тный сок. —**juicer,** *n.* соковыжима́лка.

juicy *adj.* со́чный. —**juiciness,** *n.* со́чность.

jujitsu *n.* джи́у-джи́тсу; япо́нская борьба́.

Julian calendar юлиа́нский календа́рь.

July *n.* ию́ль. —*adj.* ию́льский.

jumble *v.t.* пу́тать; перепу́тывать. —*n.* пу́таница.

jumbo *adj.* большо́й; гига́нтский.

jump *v.i.* **1,** (leap) пры́гать; скака́ть. *Jump to one's feet,* вскочи́ть на́ ноги. *Jump overboard,* бро́ситься за́ борт. **2,** (start in astonishment or fright) вздра́гивать. **3,** (rise abruptly in amount) подска́кивать. **4,** *Jump to a conclusion,* поспеши́ть с вы́водом. —*v.t.* **1,** (jump over) перепры́гивать. *Jump rope,* пры́гать че́рез скака́лку. **2,** (go off, as a track) сходи́ть с (ре́льсов). **3,** *Jump ship,* спры́гнуть с корабля́ *or* с бо́рта су́дна. **4,** *colloq.* (attack suddenly) набра́сываться на. —*n.* прыжо́к; скачо́к. —**jump at,** ухвати́ться за: *jump at the offer,* ухвати́ться за предложе́ние. —**jump back,** отпры́гивать; отска́кивать; отпря́нуть. —**jump into,** впры́гивать в. *Jump into the water,* бро́ситься в во́ду. —**jump off,** спры́гивать; соска́кивать: *jump off a horse,* спры́гнуть *or* соскочи́ть с ло́шади. *Jump off a (moving) streetcar,* вы́прыгнуть *or* вы́скочить из (иду́щего) трамва́я; соскочи́ть с (иду́щего) трамва́я. *Jump off a bridge/cliff,* бро́ситься с моста́/ с обры́ва/. —**jump on, 1,** (board or mount quickly) вскочи́ть в *or* на. **2,** *colloq.* (rebuke; assail) набра́сываться на. —**jump out (of),** выпры́гивать из; выбра́сываться из;

выска́кивать из. *Jump out of bed,* вскочи́ть *or* соскочи́ть с посте́ли. *Jump out the window,* вы́броситься из окна́. *Jump out of the way of an oncoming vehicle,* отскочи́ть от приближа́ющейся маши́ны. —**jump over,** перепры́гивать; переска́кивать. —**jump up,** вска́кивать.

jumper *n.* **1,** (one who jumps) прыгу́н. **2,** (dress) пла́тье (без рукаво́в). **3,** (loose smock) блу́за.

jumping-off place плацда́рм.

jump rope скака́лка.

jumpy *adj.* не́рвный.

junction *n.* **1,** (of roads) у́зел; стык. *Railway junction,* железнодоро́жный у́зел. **2,** (of rivers) слия́ние.

juncture *n.* **1,** (joint) ме́сто соедине́ния. **2,** (point in time) моме́нт: *at this juncture,* в э́тот моме́нт.

June *n.* ию́нь. —*adj.* ию́ньский.

jungle *n.* джу́нгли. —**jungle fever,** тропи́ческая лихора́дка; тропи́ческая маляри́я.

junior *adj.* мла́дший: *junior partner,* мла́дший партнёр. *John Smith, Jr.,* Джон Смит мла́дший. —*n.* **1,** (younger person): *He is ten years my junior,* он моло́же меня́ на де́сять лет. **2,** (third-year student) студе́нт тре́тьего ку́рса. *She is a junior,* она́ на тре́тьем ку́рсе.

juniper *n.* можжеве́льник.

junk *n.* **1,** (old or worthless things) старьё; ру́хлядь; хлам; барахло́; дребеде́нь; дрянь. *Junk dealer,* старьёвщик. **2,** (boat) джо́нка.

Junker *n.* ю́нкер.

junket *n.* моло́чный кисе́ль.

junkman *n.* старьёвщик.

junta *n.* ху́нта.

Jupiter *n.* Юпи́тер.

Jurassic *adj.* ю́рский.

juridical *adj.* юриди́ческий.

jurisdiction *n.* **1,** (right to exercise official authority) юрисди́кция. **2,** (domain over which such authority extends) компете́нция; ве́дение; подчине́ние. *Beyond/outside my jurisdiction,* вне мое́й компете́нции.

jurisprudence *n.* юриспруде́нция; законове́дение.

jurist *n.* юри́ст.

juror *n.* прися́жный; прися́жный заседа́тель.

jury *n.* **1,** (in a court of law) прися́жные; жюри́. *Jury trial,* суд прися́жных. **2,** (in a contest) жюри́.

just *adj.* **1,** (fair; right; proper) справедли́вый: *just decision,* справедли́вое реше́ние; *just war,* справедли́вая война́. *Just cause,* пра́вое де́ло. **2,** (deserved) заслу́женный: *just reward,* заслу́женная награ́да. *Get one's just reward/deserts,* получи́ть по заслу́гам. —*adv.* **1,** (precisely) как раз; и́менно. *Just in time,* как раз во́время. *Just what I need,* как раз то, что мне ну́жно. *You're just the person I wanted to see,* вы и́менно тот, кого́ я хоте́л(а) ви́деть. *Just like in Moscow,* совсе́м как в Москве́. *He is just like you,* он тако́й же, как вы. *That's just the point!,* в том-то и де́ло! **2,** (barely) едва́: *I just made it,* едва́ успе́л!

There's just enough room, ме́ста едва́ хвата́ет. **3,** (only; merely) то́лько; про́сто. *He lives just a few miles from here,* он живёт всего́ в не́скольких ми́лях отсю́да. *I just wanted to ask...,* я то́лько хоте́л(а) спроси́ть... *He is just a child,* да он ещё ребёнок. **4,** (almost at the point of) то́лько сейча́с: *We are just leaving,* мы то́лько сейча́с ухо́дим. *We were just leaving,* мы как раз собира́лись уходи́ть. *The trouble is just beginning,* неприя́тности ещё то́лько начина́ются. **5,** (only a moment ago) то́лько что: *He just left,* он то́лько что ушёл. —*particle* то́лько: *Just think!,* поду́мать то́лько! *Just you try!,* то́лько попро́буйте! *Just look at him!,* вы то́лько посмотри́те на него́! *Just what do you mean by that?,* что вы, со́бственно, хоти́те э́тим сказа́ть? —**just about, 1,** (almost; very nearly) почти́: *just about everything,* почти́ всё. **2,** (on the point of) вот-во́т: *He is just about to leave,* он вот-во́т уйдёт. *I was just about to call you,* я как раз собира́лся вам звони́ть. —**just a minute!,** одну́ мину́тку! —**just as, 1,** *with adjectives,* сто́лько же. **2,** (at the moment when) в тот моме́нт, когда́... **3,** (in the same way that) подо́бно тому́, как...; то́чно так же, как... —**just as soon,** *see* soon. —**just as well,** с тем же успе́хом. *It's just as well,* ну что же. —**just in case,** на вся́кий слу́чай. —**just now, 1,** (at this instant) сейча́с. **2,** (a moment ago) то́лько сейча́с. —**just then,** в тот моме́нт. —**just the same,** всё равно́.

justice *n.* **1,** (administration of law) правосу́дие; юсти́ция. *Minister of justice,* мини́стр юсти́ции. *The scales of justice,* весы́ правосу́дия. **2,** (fairness) справедли́вость: *sense of justice,* чу́вство справедли́вости. *Justice triumphed,* справедли́вость восторжествова́ла. **3,** (judge) судья́: *justice of the peace,* мирово́й судья́. *Supreme Court justice,* член верхо́вного суда́. —**bring to justice,** привлека́ть к отве́тственности. —**do justice (to),** отдава́ть до́лжное (+ *dat.*). *The picture doesn't do her justice,* фотогра́фия не де́лает ей комплиме́нта.

justifiable *adj.* зако́нный; позволи́тельный. —**justifiably,** *adv.* по пра́ву.

justification *n.* оправда́ние. *There is no justification for that,* э́тому нет оправда́ния.

justify *v.t.* опра́вдывать.

justly *adv.* **1,** (fairly) справедли́во. **2,** (rightly; deservedly) по пра́ву: *There is much of which we can be justly proud,* есть мно́гое тако́е, чем мы по пра́ву мо́жем горди́ться.

jut *v.i.* [*usu.* **jut out**] выдава́ться; выступа́ть; торча́ть.

jute *n.* джут.

juvenile *adj.* ю́ный; ю́ношеский; малоле́тний. —*n.* ю́ноша; подро́сток; малоле́тний. —**juvenile delinquency,** де́тская престу́пность.

juxtapose *v.t.* **1,** (place side by side) помеща́ть бок о́ бок. **2,** (contrast) сопоставля́ть.

K

K, k оди́ннадцатая бу́ква англи́йского алфави́та.

Kaiser *n.* ка́йзер.

kaleidoscope *n.* калейдоско́п. —**kaleidoscopic,** *adj.* калейдоскопи́ческий.

kangaroo *n.* кенгуру́.

kaolin *n.* каоли́н.

kapok *n.* капо́к.

karakul *n.* = **caracul**.

karat *n.* **1,** (24th part of pure gold) про́ба. ♦*The Russian system, however, is based on 1,000: 18-karat gold,* зо́лото 750-ой про́бы. **2,** = **carat**.

karate *n.* карата́.

kasha *n.* ка́ша.

kayak *n.* байда́рка; ка́як.

keel *n.* киль. —*v.i.* [*usu.* **keel over**] **1,** (capsize) опроки́дываться. **2,** (faint away) упа́сть без чувств. —**be on an even keel,** идти́ ро́вным ку́рсом; приде́рживаться ро́вного ку́рса.

keen *adj.* **1,** (sharp; acute; sensitive) о́стрый; то́нкий. *Keen eyesight,* о́строе зре́ние. *Keen eye,* зо́ркий *or* ме́ткий глаз. *Keen sense of hearing,* о́стрый *or* то́нкий *or* чу́ткий слух. *Keen sense of smell,* то́нкое обоня́ние. *Keen mind,* о́стрый ум. *A keen judge of people,* то́нкий знато́к люде́й. *Keen interest,* живо́й *or* о́стрый интере́с. **2,** (avid; enthusiastic) стра́стный. *Be keen on,* увлека́ться (+ *instr.*). *I'm not keen on going,* мне не хо́чется идти́.

keenly *adv.* жи́во: *be keenly interested in,* жи́во интересова́ться (+ *instr.*). *Keenly disappointed,* глубоко́ разочаро́ван. *Be keenly aware that...,* отдава́ть себе́ по́лный отчёт в том, что...

keenness *n.* острота́; то́нкость.

keep *v.t.* **1,** (hold in a specified place) держа́ть; храни́ть. *Keep one's hands in one's pockets,* держа́ть ру́ки в карма́нах. *Keep money in the bank,* держа́ть *or* храни́ть де́ньги в ба́нке. *Keep things in a safe place,* храни́ть ве́щи в надёжном ме́сте. **2,** (maintain in a certain state) держа́ть; содержа́ть: *keep the cards/house in order,* держа́ть ка́рты/ содержа́ть дом/ в поря́дке. *Keep one's room clean,* держа́ть/ содержа́ть ко́мнату в чистоте́. *Keep one's feet warm,* держа́ть но́ги в тепле́. *Keep the windows closed,* держа́ть о́кна закры́тыми. *Keep something secret,* храни́ть *or* держа́ть что́-нибудь в секре́те *or* в та́йне. *Keep me informed,* держи́те меня́ в ку́рсе дел. **3,** (not throw away; retain) храни́ть; сохраня́ть;

оставля́ть (себе́); уде́рживать. *Keep old letters,* храни́ть ста́рые пи́сьма. *Keep a copy for oneself,* оста́вить себе́ экземпля́р. *Keep the change!,* оста́вьте себе́ сда́чу! **4,** (maintain; preserve) сохраня́ть: *keep order,* сохраня́ть поря́док. *Keep watch,* сторожи́ть. *Keep a secret,* храни́ть/сохраня́ть секре́т *or* та́йну. *Keep in mind,* име́ть в виду́. *Keep one's seat,* остава́ться сиде́ть. *Keep one's feet,* уде́рживаться на нога́х. **5,** (maintain at home) держа́ть: *keep a dog,* держа́ть соба́ку; *keep servants,* держа́ть прислу́гу. **6,** (carry out; fulfill) сдержа́ть: *keep one's word,* сдержа́ть своё сло́во; *keep a promise,* сдержа́ть обеща́ние. **7,** (observe) соблюда́ть: *keep the laws,* соблюда́ть зако́н. *Keep an appointment,* прийти́ на свида́ние. **8,** (maintain; perform) вести́: *keep score,* вести́ счёт; *keep a diary,* вести́ дневни́к; *keep the books,* вести́ кни́ги; *keep count of,* вести́ счёт (+ *dat.*); *keep house,* вести́ (дома́шнее) хозя́йство. *Keep company with,* води́ть компа́нию с. *My watch keeps good time,* мои́ часы́ хорошо́ иду́т. **9,** (withhold; not reveal) скрыва́ть: *keep information from the public,* скрыва́ть/ута́ивать информа́цию от пу́блики. **10,** (delay) заде́рживать: *Don't let me keep you!,* не хочу́ вас заде́рживать. *Keep someone waiting,* заставля́ть кого́-нибудь ждать. **11,** *fol. by* **from** (prevent) не дава́ть (+ *dat.*): *keep someone from interfering,* не дать кому́-нибудь вмеша́ться. *Keep from laughing,* удержа́ться от сме́ха. —*v.i.* **1,** (persist; continue) продолжа́ть. *Prices keep going up,* це́ны всё расту́т. *I kept imagining that...,* мне всё каза́лось, что... **2,** (remain) держа́ться: *keep to the right,* держа́ться пра́вой стороны́. *Keep off the grass!,* по траве́ не ходи́ть! *Keep quiet,* молча́ть. *Keep warm,* гре́ться. **3,** (not spoil) держа́ться; сохраня́ться. —*n.* **1,** (livelihood; support) содержа́ние. **2,** (stronghold of a castle) гла́вная ба́шня (за́мка). —**for keeps,** навсегда́. —**keep away, 1,** (not let come near) не подпуска́ть (к): *keep the children away from the fire,* не подпуска́ть дете́й к огню́. **2,** (remain at a distance) держа́ться на расстоя́нии *or* в стороне́; не подходи́ть. *Keep away from me!,* держи́тесь от меня́ пода́льше! —**keep back, 1,** (hold back) уде́рживать; сде́рживать. **2,** (not move forward) держа́ться сза́ди. *Keep back!,* наза́д! —**keep down, 1,** (keep low, as one's head) пригиба́ть. **2,** *Keep your voices down!,* говори́те ти́ше! **3,** *Keep down expenses,* эконо́мить. —**keep in,** держа́ть: *keep the children in,* держа́ть дете́й до́ма; не выпуска́ть дете́й на у́лицу. *Keep a pupil in after school,* оставля́ть ученика́ по́сле уро́ков. —**keep on, 1,** (continue) продолжа́ть; не перестава́ть. **2,** (not remove) не снима́ть. **3,** (continue to employ) оставля́ть. —**keep out, 1,** (not let in) не пуска́ть; не пропуска́ть. **2,** (stay outside) не входи́ть. *Keep out!,* вход воспрещён! **3,** *fol. by* **of** (keep away from; steer clear of) избега́ть; держа́ться в стороне́ от. *Keep out of the sun,* избега́ть находи́ться на со́лнце. *Keep out of trouble,* избега́ть неприя́тностей. *Keep out of my sight!,* с глаз доло́й!; уйди́ с глаз мои́х! *You keep out of this!,* а ты не вме́шивайся! —**keep to oneself, 1,** (not reveal) держа́ть при себе́. **2,** (remain aloof) держа́ться особняко́м. —**keep up, 1,** (maintain) подде́рживать: *keep up a correspondence,* подде́рживать перепи́ску. *Keep up the good work!,* продолжа́йте та́кже хорошо́ рабо́тать и да́льше! *Keep up one's spirits,* не уныва́ть; не па́дать ду́хом. **2,** (maintain the pace) идти́ в но́гу; не отстава́ть. **3,** (continue; not cease) продолжа́ться. *If this keeps up,* е́сли так пойдёт да́льше. **4,** (prevent from sleeping) не дава́ть спать. —**keep up with, 1,** (keep pace with) идти́ в но́гу с; не отстава́ть от; поспева́ть за; угна́ться за. **2,** (keep track of) следи́ть за: *keep up with world events,* следи́ть за мировы́ми собы́тиями.

keeper *n.* храни́тель. *Lighthouse keeper,* смотри́тель маяка́.

keeping *n.* хране́ние. —**in keeping with,** соотве́тствующий (+ *dat.*); сообра́зный с.

keepsake *n.* пода́рок на па́мять.

keg *n.* бочо́нок. —**powder keg,** порохова́я бо́чка; порохово́й по́греб.

ken *n.* круг позна́ний. *Beyond one's ken,* вы́ше чьего́-нибудь понима́ния.

kennel *n.* конура́.

kept woman содержа́нка; коко́тка.

kerb *n., Brit.* = **curb** (*in sense #1*).

kerchief *n.* плато́к; косы́нка.

kernel *n.* **1,** (grain or seed) зерно́. **2,** (edible part of a nut) ядро́. **3,** *in* **kernel of truth,** зерно́ и́стины.

kerosene *also,* **kerosine** *n.* кероси́н. —*adj.* кероси́новый.

kestrel *n.* пустельга́.

ketchup *n.* ке́тчуп; тома́тный со́ус.

kettle *n.* **1,** (teakettle) ча́йник. **2,** (pot) котело́к. —**kettle of fish,** исто́рия: *That's a pretty kettle of fish!,* вот так исто́рия.

kettledrum *n.* лита́вра.

key *n.* **1,** (for a lock) ключ: *the key to the apartment,* ключ от кварти́ры. **2,** (of a piano, typewriter, etc.) кла́виша. **3,** (code; solution) ключ: *the key to the mystery,* ключ к та́йне. **4,** (explanatory table) ключ. **5,** *fig.* (vital element) зало́г: *the key to his success,* зало́г его́ успе́ха. **6,** *music* тона́льность; лад. *Key of B-flat,* тона́льность си бемо́ль. *Sing off key,* петь не в тон *or* фальши́во; фальши́вить. **7,** (tone; style; mood) тон. —*adj.* ключево́й: *key figure,* ключева́я фигу́ра; *key role,* ключева́я роль. *Key question,* узлово́й *or* стержнево́й вопро́с. —*v.t.* **1,** (adapt)

приспособля́ть. **2,** *fol. by* **up** (arouse) взви́нчивать: *keyed up,* взви́нченный.

keyboard *n.* клавиату́ра. *Keyboard instrument,* кла́вишный инструме́нт.

keyhole *n.* замо́чная сква́жина.

key punch кла́вишный перфора́тор.

key ring кольцо́ для ключе́й.

khaki *n.* защи́тный цвет; ха́ки. —**khaki-colored,** *adj.* защи́тного цве́та; цве́та ха́ки.

khan *n.* хан. —**khanate,** *n.* ха́нство.

kibitzer *n.* непро́шеный зри́тель.

kick *v.t.* **1,** (strike with the foot) ударя́ть ного́й; дава́ть пинка́ (+ *dat.*); пина́ть ного́й. **2,** (propel with the foot, as a ball) поддава́ть (ного́й). **3,** *sports* (score, as a goal) забива́ть (гол). **4,** *slang* (overcome, as a habit) избавля́ться от (привы́чки). —*v.i.* **1,** (of a person, esp. a child) дры́гать нога́ми. **2,** (of a horse) брыка́ть(ся); ляга́ть(ся); бить за́дом. **3,** *colloq.* (complain; grumble) ворча́ть. —*n.* **1,** (blow with the foot) пино́к. **2,** *sports* уда́р: *free kick,* свобо́дный уда́р. **3,** (recoil of a firearm) отда́ча. **4,** *colloq.* (pleasure) удово́льствие: *get a kick out of,* получи́ть удово́льствие от. *For kicks,* про́сто так; ра́ди удово́льствия. **5,** *colloq.* (complaint) жа́лоба. —**kick off, 1,** (toss off, as one's shoes) сбра́сывать. **2,** (start, as a campaign) начина́ть. —**kick out,** выгоня́ть; выши-ба́ть. —**kick up,** поднима́ть: *kick up dust,* подни-ма́ть пыль; *kick up a fuss,* поднима́ть шум.

kid *n.* **1,** (young goat) козлёнок. **2,** (leather) ла́йка; шевро́. **3,** *colloq.* (child) ребёнок; малы́ш. —*adj.* **1,** made of kidskin) ла́йковый; шевро́вый. **2,** *colloq.* (younger) мла́дший. —*v.t., colloq.* **1,** (try to fool) обма́нывать: *Whom are you kidding?,* кого́ вы об-ма́нываете? *Let's stop kidding ourselves,* дава́йте не бу́дем себя́ обма́нывать. *You're just kidding yourself,* вы сам себя́ обма́нываете. **2,** (tease) дразни́ть; подтру́нивать над. —*v.i., colloq.* шути́ть: *You're kid-ding!,* вы шу́тите! —**treat with kid gloves,** дели-ка́тничать с.

kidder *n.* зубоска́л.

kidnap *v.t.* похища́ть. —**kidnaper,** *n.* похити́тель. —**kidnaping,** *n.* похище́ние.

kidney *n.* по́чка. —**kidney bean,** фасо́ль. —**kidney stones,** по́чечные ка́мни.

kidskin *n.* ла́йка; шевро́. —*adj.* ла́йковый; шев-ро́вый.

kill *v.t.* убива́ть. *Be killed,* поги́бнуть. *Kill oneself,* поко́нчить с собо́й; уби́ть себя́. *Thou shalt not kill,* не уби́й. *Kill chickens,* ре́зать кур. *Kill cockroaches,* трави́ть тарака́нов. *Kill the pain,* успока́ивать боль. *Kill time,* убива́ть вре́мя. *Kill a bill,* провали́ть за-конопрое́кт. *Frost killed the flowers,* моро́з погуби́л цветы́. *My feet are killing me,* у меня́ стра́шно боля́т но́ги. *Dressed to kill,* разоде́т в пух и прах. —**kill two birds with one stone,** уби́ть двух за́йцев одни́м уда́ром.

killer *n.* уби́йца. —**killer whale,** коса́тка.

killing *n.* **1,** (murder) уби́йство. **2,** *colloq.* (sudden large profit) куш. —*adj.* уби́йственный.

kiln *n.* обжига́тельная печь.

kilocycle *n.* килогéрц.

kilogram *also,* **kilogramme** *n.* килогрáмм.

kilometer *also,* **kilometre** *n.* километр.

kiloton *n.* килотóнна.

kilowatt *n.* киловáтт. —**kilowatt-hour,** *n.* киловáтт-чác.

kilt *n.* шотлáндская юбка.

kilter *n., in* **out of kilter,** не в порядке.

kimono *n.* кимонó.

kin *n.* родня; родные; рóдственники. —**next of kin,** ближáйшие рóдственники.

kind *n.* род; вид; сорт. *All kinds of,* всякого рóда (+ *nom.*). *A mandarin is a kind of orange,* мандарин — вид апельсина. *The first such book of its kind,* пéрвая такóго рóда книга. *What kind of books do you like best?,* какие книги вы любите бóльше всегó? *What kind of person is he?,* что он за человéк? *Something of the kind,* чтó-то в этом рóде. *Nothing of the kind,* ничегó подóбного. —*adj.* **1,** (kindly) дóбрый: *kind man,* дóбрый человéк. *Kind heart/face,* дóброе сéрдце/лицó. **2,** (considerate) любéзный; милый: *very kind of you,* óчень любéзно/мило с вáшей сторонs. **3,** (cordial) сердéчный: (*with*) *kind regards,* с сердéчным привéтом. —**be so kind as to...,** будьте добры *or* любéзны (+ *imperative*); не сочтите за труд (+ *imperative*). —**in kind, 1,** (in goods) натýрой. **2,** (in like manner) той же монéтой. —**kind of,** *colloq.* кáк-то: *He is acting kind of strange,* он ведёт себя кáк-то стрáнно. —**one of a kind,** не имéющий себé подóбных.

kindergarten *n.* дéтский сад.

kindhearted *adj.* добросердéчный; отзывчивый. —**kindheartedness,** *n.* добросердéчие; отзывчивость.

kindle *v.t.* разжигáть; зажигáть.

kindling *n.* **1,** (act of kindling) разжигáние. **2,** (kindling wood) растóпка.

kindly *adj.* дóбрый; добродýшный. —*adv.* **1,** (graciously) любéзно: *She kindly offered to help,* онá любéзно предложила помóчь. **2,** (favorably) хорошó: *kindly disposed toward,* хорошó располóжен к. *Take kindly to,* хорошó относиться к. *Not take kindly to,* плóхо относиться к. **3,** *when making a request,* будьте добры (+ *imperative*). —**thank you kindly!,** сердéчно благодарю вас!

kindness *n.* **1,** (quality of being kind) добротá. **2,** (kind act; favor) любéзность. **3,** (solicitude) внимáние.

kindred *adj.* рóдственный.

kinescope *n.* кинескóп.

kinetic *adj.* кинетический. —**kinetic energy,** кинетическая энéргия; живáя сила.

kinetics *n.* кинéтика.

kinfolk *n.* родные; родня.

king *n.* **1,** (sovereign) корóль. **2,** (most powerful creature) царь: *the king of beasts/birds,* царь зверéй/птиц. **3,** (tycoon) корóль: *oil king,* нефтянóй корóль. **4,** *cards; chess* корóль. *King of spades,* корóль пик. *King's bishop,* королéвский слон. **5,** *checkers* дáмка. —**live like a king,** жить бáрином.

kingbolt *n.* шквóрень.

kingdom *n.* **1,** (monarchy) королéвство: *United Kingdom,* Соединённое Королéвство. **2,** *fig.* (realm) цáрство: *animal kingdom,* живóтное цáрство.

kingfisher *n.* зиморóдок.

kinglet *n.* (bird) королёк.

kingly *adj.* королéвский; цáрственный.

kingpin *n.* **1,** = **kingbolt. 2,** *colloq.* (key figure) главáрь.

kink *n.* **1,** (bend; loop; knot) загиб; пéтля; ýзел. **2,** (cramp; crick) сýдорога. —**kinky,** *adj.* (of hair) курчáвый.

kinsfolk *n.pl.* родные; родня.

kinship *n.* родствó.

kinsman *n.* рóдственник.

kiosk *n.* киóск.

kipper *n.* копчёная селёдка.

kiss *v.t.* целовáть. *Kiss someone's hand,* целовáть рýку (+ *dat.*). *Kiss someone on the cheek,* целовáть когó-нибудь в щёку. —*v.i.* (of two people) целовáться. —*n.* поцелýй.

kisser *n., slang* мóрда; рыло; хáря.

kit *n.* **1,** (set of equipment) набóр; комплéкт. *First-aid kit,* аптéчка; *mil.* санитáрная сýмка. **2,** (container for same; case) сýмка; ящик.

kitchen *n.* кýхня. —*adj.* кýхонный: *kitchen table,* кýхонный стол.

kite *n.* **1,** (device that flies) змей. **2,** (bird) кóршун.

kitten *n.* котёнок.

kittiwake *n.* моёвка.

kitty *n.* **1,** (kitten) котёнок; киска. **2,** (pool or reserve of money) фонд. **3,** (money bet in a game) кон: *put money in the kitty,* стáвить дéньги на кон.

kiwi *n.* киви-киви.

kleptomania *n.* клептомáния. —**kleptomaniac,** *n.* клептомáн.

knack *n.* снорóвка. *Get the knack of,* принорáвливаться к; наловчиться (+ *inf.*).

knapsack *n.* рюкзáк; рáнец; котóмка; вещевóй мешóк.

knave *n.* **1,** (rascal) плут; мошéнник. **2,** *Brit., cards* валéт.

knead *v.t.* месить; замéшивать; мять.

knee *n.* колéно. *On one's hands and knees,* на четверéньках. —*adj.* колéнный: *knee joint,* колéнный сустáв. —**bring to one's knees,** стáвить (когó-нибудь) на колéни.

kneecap *n.* колéнная чáшка; колéнная чáшечка.

knee-deep *adj.* по колéно; по колéни.

kneel *v.i.* **1,** (assume a kneeling position) становиться на колéни. **2,** (be in a kneeling position) стоять на колéнях.

kneepad *n.* наколéнник.

knell *n.* похорóнный звон. —**sound the death knell for,** предвещáть конéц (+ *gen.*).

knickers *n.* бриджи.

knickknack *n.* безделýшка; вещица; финтифлюшка.

knife *n.* нож. *Bread/butter knife,* нож для хлéба/мáсла. —*adj.* ножевóй: *knife wound,* ножевáя рáна. —*v.t.* рéзать *or* колóть ножóм.

knight *n.* **1,** (medieval warrior) ры́царь. **2,** *chess* конь. —*v.t.* посвяща́ть в ры́цари. —**knight-errant,** *n.* стра́нствующий ры́царь. —**knighthood,** *n.* ры́царство. —**knightly,** *adj.* ры́царский.

knit *v.t.* **1,** (weave) вяза́ть: *knit a sweater,* вяза́ть сви́тер. **2,** (contract, as one's eyebrows) хму́рить; сдви́нуть. *Knit one's brow (i.e. forehead),* мо́рщить лоб. —*v.i.* **1,** (do knitting) вяза́ть. **2,** (grow together, as of bones) сраста́ться.

knitted *adj.* вя́заный; трикота́жный. *Knitted fabric,* трикота́ж.

knitting *n.* вяза́ние. —*adj.* вяза́льный. —**knitting needle,** (вяза́льная) спи́ца; вяза́льная игла́.

knob *n.* **1,** (handle of a door) (дверна́я) ру́чка. **2,** (lump; protuberance) ши́шка; буго́р. —**knobby,** *adj.* шишкова́тый.

knock *v.i.* стуча́ть (в дверь). —*v.t.* **1,** (hit; strike) ударя́ть; бить; колоти́ть. *Knock someone to the ground,* повали́ть кого́-нибудь на зе́млю. *Be knocked unconscious,* лиши́ться созна́ния. **2,** (bang) ударя́ться; сту́каться. *Knock heads,* сту́кнуться голова́ми. *Knock one's head on the door,* уда́риться голово́й о дверь. **3,** (make by striking) пробива́ть: *knock a hole in the wall,* пробива́ть отве́рстие в стене́. **4,** *colloq.* (criticize) придира́ться к. —*n.* **1,** (rap, as on a door) стук. **2,** (blow) уда́р. **3,** (engine noise) стук. —**knock about,** *colloq.* слоня́ться; шата́ться; околачиваться. —**knock down,** сбива́ть с ног; вали́ть; сва́ливать. *He was knocked down by a bicycle,* его́ сбил велосипе́д. —**knock loose,** расша́тывать. —**knock off, 1,** (dislodge; topple) сбива́ть: *knock off one's feet,* сбива́ть с ног. *Knock someone's hat off,* сбить ша́пку с чье́й-нибудь головы́. *Knock the snow off one's boots,* сбить снег с сапо́г. *Knock off the bandage while asleep,* сбить повя́зку во сне. *Knock a glass off the table,* урони́ть стака́н со стола́. **2,** *colloq.* (deduct) сбавля́ть; ски́дывать; ска́щивать. **3,** *colloq.* (compose quickly; dash off) (на)строчи́ть. **4,** *slang* (quit work) шаба́шить. —**knock out, 1,** (dislodge) выбива́ть. *Three of his teeth were knocked out,* у него́ вы́биты три зу́ба. **2,** (exhaust completely) истомля́ть. **3,** *boxing* нокаути́ровать. **4,** *mil.* (destroy) выводи́ть из стро́я; подбива́ть. —**knock over,** опроки́дывать. —**knock together,** скола́чивать; сбива́ть.

knockdown *n., boxing* нокда́ун.

knocker *n.* дверно́й молото́к.

knock-kneed *adj.* кривоно́гий.

knockout *n., boxing* нока́ут.

knoll *n.* хо́лмик; буго́р; приго́рок.

knot *n.* **1,** (in rope) у́зел: *a knot in the rope,* у́зел на верёвке. **2,** (in wood) сук; сучо́к. **3,** (nautical mile per hour) у́зел. —*v.t.* завя́зывать узло́м. *My shoelaces are knotted,* у меня́ на шнурка́х узлы́.

knothole *n.* свищ.

knotted *adj.* **1,** (tied with a knot) завя́занный узло́м. **2,** (full of knots) узлова́тый.

knotty *adj.* **1,** (full of knots, as of wood) сучкова́тый. **2,** *fig.* (difficult; intricate) запу́танный.

knout *n.* кнут.

know *v.t. & i.* знать: *I don't know,* я не зна́ю. *Who knows?,* кто его́ зна́ет? *Know what's what,* знать что к чему́. *As far as I know,* наско́лько я зна́ю. *For all one knows,* чего́ до́брого. *How should I know?,* отку́да же я зна́ю? *How was I to know?,* как же я мог (могла́) знать? *One never knows,* никогда́ не зна́ешь. *Get to know someone,* позна́ть кого́-нибудь. —*n., in* **in the know,** в ку́рсе де́ла. —**know better,** знать: *I should have known better than to do that,* я до́лжен был (должна́ была́) знать, что не сле́дует де́лать э́того. —**know how,** уме́ть: *know how to swim,* уме́ть пла́вать. *I don't know how to answer that question,* я не зна́ю, как отве́тить на э́тот вопро́с.

knowing *adj.* **1,** (knowledgeable; astute) зна́ющий; то́нкий. **2,** (of a smile, glance, etc.) многозначи́тельный.

knowingly *adv.* **1,** (deliberately) созна́тельно; наме́ренно; заве́домо. **2,** (as if having secret information) многозначи́тельно.

know-it-all *n.* всезна́йка.

knowledge *n.* зна́ние. *With/without the knowledge of,* с/без ве́дома (+ *gen.*). *Deny any knowledge of...,* отрица́ть осведомлённость о... *It has come to my knowledge that...,* мне ста́ло изве́стно, что... *It is common knowledge that...,* общеизве́стно, что... —**to (the best of) my knowledge,** наско́лько мне изве́стно. *Not to my knowledge,* наско́лько мне изве́стно — нет.

knowledgeable *adj.* зна́ющий; све́дущий; гра́мотный; осведомлённый. —**knowledgeability,** *n.* зна́ния; гра́мотность; осведомлённость.

known *adj.* изве́стный: *a known fact,* изве́стный факт. *As is known...,* как изве́стно. *It is known that...,* изве́стно, что... *Known for one's generosity,* изве́стен свое́й ще́дростью. *He is known as an expert on art,* он изве́стен как знато́к иску́сства; он слывёт знатоко́м иску́сства. —**make known,** раскрыва́ть; разглаша́ть.

knuckle *n.* **1,** (joint of the finger) костя́шка. **2,** (animal joint used as food) но́жка. —*v.i.* **1,** *fol. by* **down** (apply oneself vigorously) запряга́ться. **2,** *fol. by* **under** (give in; yield) подчиня́ться.

koala *n.* коа́ла.

kohlrabi *n.* кольра́би.

kolinsky *n.* колоно́к.

kopeck *n.* копе́йка.

Koran *n.* кора́н.

Korean *adj.* коре́йский. —*n.* **1,** (person) коре́ец; корея́нка. **2,** (language) коре́йский язы́к.

kosher *adj.* коше́рный.

kowtow *v.i.* [*usu.* **kowtow to**] низкопокло́нничать; раболе́пствовать; расша́ркиваться (*all with* пе́ред).

Kremlin *n.* Кремль. —*adj.* кремлёвский.

krypton *n.* крипто́н.

kulak *n.* кула́к.

Kurd *n.* курд. *The Kurds,* ку́рды. —**Kurdish,** *adj.* ку́рдский. —*n.* ку́рдский язы́к.

Kuwaiti *adj.* куве́йтский.

Kyrgyz *n.* кирги́з. —*adj.* кирги́зский.

L

L, l двена́дцатая бу́ква англи́йского алфави́та.

la *n., music* ля.

label *n.* ярлы́к; этике́тка; би́рка. —*v.t.* накле́ивать ярлы́к на (*also fig.*).

labial *adj.* губно́й.

labor *also,* **labour** *n.* **1,** (work; toil) труд: *manual/child labor,* ручно́й/де́тский труд. *Capital and labor,* капита́л и труд. *Department of Labor,* министе́рство труда́. **2,** (manpower) рабо́чая си́ла: *labor costs/shortage,* сто́имость/недоста́ток рабо́чей си́лы. **3,** (trade unions) профсою́зы. **4,** (childbirth) ро́ды; родовы́е поту́ги. *Be in labor,* быть в ро́дах. *Induce labor,* провоци́ровать схва́тки; вызыва́ть родову́ю де́ятельность. —*v.i.* **1,** (toil) труди́ться. **2,** *fol. by* **under** (be afflicted with): *labor under a delusion,* быть в заблужде́нии. —*adj.* **1,** (pert. to work or workers) трудово́й: *labor laws,* трудово́е законода́тельство. **2,** (pert. to trade unions) профсою́зный: *the labor movement,* профсою́зное движе́ние. **3,** (pert. to childbirth) родово́й: *labor pains,* родовы́е поту́ги/схва́тки/му́ки.

laboratory *n.* лаборато́рия. *Language laboratory,* кабине́т иностра́нных языко́в. —*adj.* лаборато́рный: *laboratory experiments,* лаборато́рные о́пыты.

labored *also,* **laboured** *adj.* **1,** (done with difficulty) затруднённый. **2,** (ponderous) вы́мученный.

laborer *also,* **labourer** *n.* рабо́чий.

labor-intensive *adj.* трудоёмкий.

laborious *adj.* кропотли́вый.

labor union профсою́з.

labour *n. & v.* = **labor.** —**Labour,** *adj.* лейбори́стский: *Labour Party,* лейбори́стская па́ртия. —**Labourite,** *n.* лейбори́ст.

labyrinth *n.* лабири́нт.

lace *n.* **1,** (fabric) кру́жево. **2,** (cord, as for shoes) шнуро́к. —*adj.* кружевно́й. —*v.t.* шнурова́ть. —*v.i.* [*usu.* **lace into**] *colloq.* обру́шиваться на.

lacerate *v.t.* разрыва́ть; раздира́ть. —**laceration,** *n.* разры́в; рва́ная ра́на.

lachrymal *adj.* слёзный. —**lachrymose,** *adj.* слезли́вый.

lack *n.* **1,** (shortage) недоста́ток: *for lack of money,* за недоста́тком де́нег. **2,** (absence) отсу́тствие: *lack of ability,* отсу́тствие спосо́бностей. *For lack of evidence,* за отсу́тствием (*or* за неиме́нием) ули́к.

—*v.t.* **1,** (not have) не име́ть: *lack experience,* не име́ть о́пыта. *The building lacks an elevator,* в до́ме нет ли́фта. *He lacks self-confidence,* он неуве́рен в себе́. *Lacking the most basic conveniences,* лишённый элемента́рных удо́бств. **2,** (not have enough of) не хвата́ть (*impers.*); недостава́ть (*impers.*). *He lacks the strength to...,* ему́ не хвата́ет сил, что́бы... —*v.i.* не хвата́ть: *There is only one thing lacking,* одного́ то́лько не хвата́ет.

lackadaisical *adj.* хала́тный; неради́вый.

lackey *n.* лаке́й; прислу́жник.

lackluster *also,* **lacklustre** *adj.* **1,** (lacking brightness) ту́склый. **2,** *fig.* (uninspired) пре́сный.

laconic *adj.* лакони́чный; немногосло́вный.

lacquer *n.* лак. —*v.t.* лакирова́ть. —**lacquerware,** *n.* лакиро́ванные изде́лия.

lacrosse *n.* лякро́сс.

lactation *n.* лакта́ция.

lacteal *adj.* моло́чный.

lactic *adj.* моло́чный. —**lactic acid,** моло́чная кислота́.

lactose *n.* моло́чный са́хар; лакто́за.

lacuna *n.* пробе́л; про́пуск.

lad *n.* па́рень; ю́ноша.

ladder *n.* ле́стница.

laden *adj.* нагру́женный; перегру́женный.

ladies' man волоки́та; женолю́б; ловела́с; ба́бник; да́мский уго́дник. *Also,* **lady's man.**

ladies' room да́мская убо́рная; да́мский туале́т.

ladle *n.* поло́вник. —*v.t.* разлива́ть.

lady *n.* **1,** (woman) да́ма. *Ladies and gentlemen,* да́мы и господа́. *Ladies' wear,* да́мская оде́жда. **2,** (woman of rank or nobility) ле́ди. *The First Lady,* пе́рвая ле́ди. —**lady of the house,** хозя́йка до́ма.

ladybug *n.* бо́жья коро́вка. *Also,* **ladybird.**

lady in waiting фре́йлина.

lady-killer *n., colloq.* покори́тель серде́ц; сердцее́д.

ladylike *adj.* же́нственный; воспи́танный; прили́чный.

ladylove *n.* да́ма се́рдца; зазно́ба.

lag *v.i.* отстава́ть: *lag behind the others,* отстава́ть от остальны́х. —*n.* отстава́ние; запа́здывание.

lager *n.* лёгкое пи́во.

laggard *n. & adj.* отстаю́щий.

lagoon *n.* лагу́на.

lair *n.* ло́говище; берло́га.

laity *n.* миря́не.

lake *n.* о́зеро.

lama *n.* ла́ма. —**Lamaism,** *n.* ламаи́зм. —**lamasery,** *n.* ламаи́стский монасты́рь.

lamb *n.* **1,** (animal) ягнёнок; бара́шек. **2,** (meat) (молода́я) бара́нина. —**lamb chop,** бара́нья отбивна́я.

lambaste *v.t., colloq.* **1,** (beat) колоти́ть. **2,** (berate) хлеста́ть.

lambskin *n.* бара́шек; мерлу́шка. —*adj.* бара́шковый; мерлу́шковый.

lame *adj.* **1,** (crippled) хромо́й. **2,** (poor, as of an excuse) сла́бый. —**lameness,** *n.* хромота́.

lament *v.t. & i.* сокруша́ться (о); се́товать (на). —**lamentable,** *adj.* плаче́вный; приско́рбный. —**lamentation,** *n.* причита́ние; се́тование.

laminated *adj.* сло́истый.

lamp *n.* ла́мпа. *Floor lamp,* торше́р.

lamplighter *n.* фона́рщик.

lampoon *n.* шарж; па́сквиль. —*v.t.* шаржи́ровать.

lamppost *n.* фона́рный столб.

lamprey *n.* мино́га.

lampshade *n.* абажу́р.

lance *n.* **1,** (weapon) пи́ка. **2,** (surgical knife) ланце́т. —*v.t.* вскрыва́ть; разреза́ть.

lancet *n.* (knife) ланце́т. —**lancet arch,** стре́льчатая а́рка. —**lancet window,** стре́льчатое окно́.

land *n.* **1,** (ground) земля́. *Sight land,* уви́деть *or* узре́ть зе́млю. *Own land,* владе́ть землёй. *Dry land,* су́ша. **2,** (country) страна́; край. *Native land,* ро́дина. —*adj.* земе́льный: *land reform,* земе́льная рефо́рма. —*v.t.* **1,** (set down, as an aircraft) посади́ть. *Land a man on the moon,* вы́садить челове́ка на Луну́. **2,** (catch, as a fish) вы́тащить (ры́бу). **3,** (deliver, as a blow) наноси́ть (уда́р). **4,** *colloq.* (obtain) получи́ть. *Land a job,* попа́сть на рабо́ту. *Land a husband,* подцепи́ть себе́ му́жа. —*v.i.* **1,** (put into port) выса́живаться. **2,** (touch down, as of an aircraft) приземля́ться; опуска́ться; спуска́ться; де́лать поса́дку. *Land on water,* сесть на́ воду. *Land on the moon,* сесть *or* опусти́ться на Луну́; прилуни́ться. **3,** (fall; strike) попа́сть; прийти́сь. **4,** *colloq.* (end up; wind up) попа́сть; угоди́ть: *land in jail,* попа́сть/угоди́ть в тюрьму́.

landed *adj.* **1,** (owning land) поме́стный: *the landed gentry,* поме́стное дворя́нство. **2,** (consisting of land) земе́льный.

landing *n.* **1,** (of an aircraft) поса́дка. **2,** (debarkation) вы́садка. **3,** *mil.* вы́садка; деса́нт; вы́садка деса́нта. **4,** (platform, as on stairs) площа́дка. —**landing craft,** деса́нтное су́дно. —**landing field,** поса́дочная площа́дка. —**landing gear,** шасси́. —**landing strip,** взлётно-поса́дочная полоса́.

landlady *n.* хозя́йка.

landless *adj.* безземе́льный.

landlocked *adj.* не име́ющий вы́хода к мо́рю.

landlord *n.* хозя́ин.

landmark *n.* **1,** (prominent object to go by) ориенти́р. **2,** (major event) ве́ха. *Landmark event,* эта́пное собы́тие.

land mine фуга́с.

landowner *n.* поме́щик; землевладе́лец.

land rover вездехо́д.

landscape *n.* пейза́ж; ландша́фт. —**landscape architecture,** садо́во-па́рковое иску́сство.

landslide *n.* обва́л; о́ползень.

lane *n.* **1,** (narrow path) доро́жка. **2,** (narrow street) у́личка. **3,** (marked division on a highway) ряд; полоса́. **4,** (on a running track or swimming pool) доро́жка. **5,** *naut.* (морско́й) путь.

language *n.* **1,** (idiom; tongue; human speech) язы́к: *foreign language,* иностра́нный язы́к. *The origin of language,* происхожде́ние языка́. **2,** (form or manner of expression): *strong language,* си́льные выраже́ния. *Bad language,* брань; ру́гань; скверносло́вие. *Watch your language!,* следи́ за свое́й ре́чью!; следи́ за языко́м!; следи́, как ты говори́шь!; не выража́йся! —*adj.* языково́й: *language barrier,* языково́й барье́р.

languid *adj.* вя́лый; то́мный.

languish *v.i.* **1,** (lose vigor; droop) вя́нуть; ча́хнуть. **2,** (live under dispiriting conditions) томи́ться; изныва́ть.

languor *n.* вя́лость; то́мность; исто́ма. —**languorous,** *adj.* вя́лый; то́мный.

lanky *adj.* долговя́зый.

lanolin *n.* ланоли́н.

lantern *n.* фона́рь.

lanthanum *n.* ланта́н.

Laotian *adj.* лао́сский.

lap *n.* **1,** (area between the waist and knees) коле́ни: *sit on one's mother's lap,* сиде́ть у ма́тери на коле́нях. **2,** (secure place) ло́но: *in the lap of nature,* на ло́не приро́ды. *Live in the lap of luxury,* утопа́ть в ро́скоши. **3,** (front part of a skirt for carrying things) подо́л. **4,** (one circuit of a racecourse) круг. **5,** *swimming* заплы́в. —*v.t.* [*usu.* **lap up**] (lick up) лака́ть. —*v.i.* (of waves) плеска́ть.

lap dog ко́мнатная соба́чка.

lapel *n.* отворо́т; ла́цкан.

lapidary *n.* грани́льщик. —*adj.* грани́льный.

lapis lazuli ля́пис-лазу́рь.

Lapp *n.* [*also,* **Laplander**] саа́м. —*adj.* [*also,* **Lappish**] саа́мский.

lap robe по́лость; плед.

lapse *n.* **1,** (slip; failure) ля́псус. *Lapse of memory,* прова́л па́мяти. **2,** (interval, as of time) промежу́ток. —*v.i.* **1,** *fol. by* **into** (slip into; sink into) впада́ть (в). **2,** (expire) теря́ть си́лу.

lapwing *n.* чи́бис; пи́галица.

larceny *n.* кра́жа; воровство́. —**larcenous,** *adj.* воровско́й.

larch *n.* ли́ственница.

lard *n.* (топлёное свино́е) са́ло; шпик. —*v.t.* **1,** (apply lard to) шпигова́ть. **2,** *fig.* (sprinkle; intersperse) шпигова́ть; пересыпа́ть.

larder *n.* кладова́я.

large *adj.* большо́й; кру́пный. *Large room/crowd,* больша́я ко́мната/толпа́. *Large type,* кру́пный шрифт. *Large sum of money,* больша́я *or* кру́пная су́мма де́нег. *Have you anything in a larger size?*, у вас есть что́-нибудь бо́льшего разме́ра? —**at large, 1,** (at liberty) на свобо́де. **2,** (general) широ́кий: *the public at large*, широ́кая пу́блика. —**by and large,** в це́лом; в основно́м. —**in large part,** во мно́гом.

large intestine то́лстая кишка́.

largely *adv.* **1,** (to a great extent) во мно́гом. **2,** (for the most part) в основно́м.

large-scale *adj.* крупномасшта́бный; большо́го *or* кру́пного масшта́ба. *Large-scale map*, крупно-масшта́бная ка́рта.

largesse *also,* **largess** *n.* ще́дрость.

largo *adj. & adv.* ла́рго.

lariat *n.* арка́н; лассо́.

lark *n.* жа́воронок.

larkspur *n.* живоко́сть; шпо́рник.

larva *n.* личи́нка. —**larval,** *adj.* личи́ночный.

laryngeal *adj.* горта́нный. —**laryngitis,** *n.* ларинги́т.

larynx *n.* горта́нь.

lascivious *adj.* похотли́вый. —**lasciviousness,** *n.* похотли́вость.

laser *n.* ла́зер. —*adj.* ла́зерный: *laser beam*, ла́зерный луч. *Laser-guided bomb*, бо́мба с ла́зерным наведе́нием.

lash *n.* **1,** (whip) плеть; бич. **2,** (stroke of a whip) уда́р пле́тью. **3,** (eyelash) ресни́ца. —*v.t.* **1,** (flog) хлеста́ть; стега́ть; сечь. **2,** (dash against) хлеста́ть в *or* о (+ *acc.*). *The waves lashed the shore*, во́лны хлеста́ли о бе́рег. *The wind lashed our faces*, Ве́тер хлеста́л (*or* сёк) в лицо́. **3,** (shake violently, as one's tail) хлеста́ть (хвосто́м). **4,** (tie) привя́зывать. —**lash out against,** обру́шиваться на.

lashing *n.* по́рка.

lass *n.* де́вушка; деви́ца.

lassitude *n.* вя́лость; исто́ма.

lasso *n.* лассо́; арка́н. —*v.t.* арка́нить.

last *adj.* **1,** (final) после́дний. *At the last moment*, в са́мый после́дний моме́нт. *The last time I was in England*, в после́дний раз, когда́ я был (была́) в А́нглии. **2,** (just past; most recent) про́шлый: *last week*, на про́шлой неде́ле; *last month*, в про́шлом ме́сяце; *last March*, в ма́рте э́того (*or* про́шлого) го́да; *last year*, в про́шлом году́; *last Sunday*, в про́шлое воскресе́нье; *last summer*, про́шлым ле́том; ле́том про́шлого го́да. *Last night*, вчера́ ве́чером. *At our last meeting*, на про́шлом собра́нии. *Last time we discussed...*, в про́шлый раз мы обсуди́ли... **3,** (least likely) ме́ньше всего́: *That's the last thing I expected*, э́того я ожида́л(а) ме́ньше всего́. —*adv.* **1,** (after all others) после́дним: *come in last*, прийти́ после́дним. *He spoke last*, он вы́ступил по́сле всех. **2,** (for the last time) в после́дний раз. **3,** (finally; lastly) наконе́ц. —*n.* **1,** (final one) после́дний: *the last of the Mohicans*, после́дний из моги́ка́н. *He was the last to leave*, он ушёл после́дним; он ушёл по́сле всех. *The last I heard, he was...*, после́днее, что я о нём слы́шал — он... *See the last of someone*, ви́деть кого́-нибудь в после́дний раз. **2,** (shoe mold) коло́дка. —*v.i.* **1,** (continue; remain in existence) продолжа́ться; дли́ться: *last (for) two*

hours, продолжа́ться/дли́ться два часа́. *The warm weather will last until Sunday*, тёплая пого́да продержи́тся до воскресе́нья. **2,** (remain in good condition) сохраня́ться; проноси́ться (*pfv.*). *These shoes will last a long time*, э́ти боти́нки проно́сятся до́лго. *This house was built to last a hundred years*, э́тот дом был постро́ен на сто лет. *When we build something, we build it to last*, когда́ мы стро́им, мы стро́им наве́чно. **3,** (live; survive) вы́держать; продержа́ться. **4,** (be enough; suffice) хвата́ть. *Supplies should last until spring*, запа́сов должно́ хвати́ть до весны́. —*v.t.* **1,** (complete) проходи́ть: *last the distance*, проходи́ть всю диста́нцию. **2,** *fol. by* out (survive) вы́держать. **3,** (be enough for) хвата́ть: *last someone a lifetime*, хвати́ть (+ *dat.*) на всю жизнь. —**at last,** наконе́ц. —**at long last,** наконе́ц-то. —**before last,** позапро́шлый: *the year before last*, в позапро́шлом году́. *The night before last*, позавчера́ ве́чером. —**for last,** на коне́ц; напосле́док: *save the best for last*, оста́вить *or* прибере́чь са́мое лу́чшее на коне́ц *or* напосле́док. —**last but not least,** после́днее по поря́дку, но не по ва́жности. —**last name,** фами́лия. —**last straw,** после́дняя ка́пля. —**last word,** после́днее сло́во: *have the last word*, сказа́ть после́днее сло́во. *The last word in technical equipment*, после́днее сло́во те́хники. —**next to last,** предпосле́дний. —**to the last,** до после́днего: *fight to the last*, би́ться до после́днего.

lasting *adj.* про́чный: *lasting peace*, про́чный мир. —*n.* (cloth) ла́стик.

lastly *adv.* наконе́ц.

latch *n.* щеко́лда; защёлка; шпингале́т. —*v.t.* запира́ть за щеко́лду. —*v.i.* [*usu.* **latch onto**] хвата́ться за.

late *adj.* **1,** (tardy; at an advanced time) по́здний: *late hour/arrival*, по́здний час/прихо́д. *In late autumn*, по́здней о́сенью. *In late October*, в конце́ октября́. *It is getting late*, уже́ по́здно. *Be late*, опа́здывать. *You're late*, вы опозда́ли. **2,** *preceded by* the (deceased) поко́йный. —*adv.* по́здно; с опозда́нием. *Till late at night*, по́здно; до по́здней но́чи. *Be/come an hour late*, опозда́ть на час; прийти́ с опозда́нием на час. —**of late,** в *or* за после́днее вре́мя; с неда́вних пор. *See also* **later** *and* **latest**.

latecomer *n.* опозда́вший.

lately *adv.* в *or* за после́днее вре́мя.

lateness *n.* опозда́ние; запозда́ние; запа́здывание.

latent *adj.* скры́тый; латент́ный; подспу́дный.

later *adv.* **1,** (comp. degree of late) по́зже; поздне́е. *No later than...*, не по́зже/поздне́е (+ *gen.*) *or* чем. *A little later*, попо́зже. **2,** (later on) пото́м. *An hour later*, че́рез час. *A little while later*, немно́го погодя́. *See you later!*, пока́!; уви́димся! —*adj.* бо́лее по́здний: *They arrived on a later train*, они́ прие́хали бо́лее по́здним по́ездом. —**sooner or later,** ра́но и́ли по́здно.

lateral *adj.* боково́й. —**lateral vision,** боково́е зре́ние.

latest *adj.* нове́йший; после́дний. *The latest news*, после́дние изве́стия. —**at the latest,** са́мое поздне́е.

latex *n.* ла́текс.

lath *n.* дра́нка; пла́нка; ре́йка.

lathe *n.* тока́рный стано́к.

lather *n.* (мы́льная) пе́на. —*v.t.* мы́лить; намы́ливать.

Latin *adj.* лати́нский. —*n.* лати́нский язы́к; латы́нь.

Latin American латиноамерика́нский.

latitude *n.* **1,** *geog.* широта́. **2,** (freedom to maneuver) свобо́да де́йствий.

latrine *n.* отхо́жее ме́сто.

latter *adj.* **1,** (second of two) после́дний (из двух). **2,** (nearer the end) после́дний: *in the latter part of the year,* в после́дней ча́сти го́да.

lattice *n.* решётка. —**latticed,** *adj.* решётчатый. —**latticework,** *n.* решётчатая констру́кция.

Latvian *adj.* латви́йский; латы́шский. —*n.* **1,** (person) латви́ец; латы́ш. **2,** (language) латы́шский язы́к.

laud *v.t.* восхваля́ть; превозноси́ть. —**laudable,** *adj.* похва́льный. —**laudatory,** *adj.* хвале́бный.

laugh *v.i.* смея́ться. *What are you laughing at?,* чему́ вы смеётесь? *Laugh at a joke,* смея́ться шу́тке. *Don't laugh!,* не сме́йтесь! *Don't make me laugh!,* не смеши́те меня́! *It was impossible to look at him without laughing,* невозмо́жно бы́ло смотре́ть на него́ без сме́ха. *He who laughs last laughs best,* хорошо́ смеётся тот, кто смеётся после́дним. —*n.* смех. *We had a good laugh,* мы хорошо́ посмея́лись. *He had the last laugh,* в конце́ концо́в посмея́лся он. —**laugh off,** смея́ться над.

laughable *adj.* смехотво́рный.

laughing *n.* смех. —*adj.* шу́точный: *no laughing matter,* не шу́точное де́ло. —**laughing gas,** веселя́щий газ.

laughingstock *n.* посме́шище. *Make a laughingstock of,* выставля́ть на посме́шище; выставля́ть в сме́шном ви́де; де́лать из (+ *gen.*) посме́шище.

laughter *n.* смех. *The sound of laughter,* звук сме́ха.

launch *v.t.* **1,** (set afloat) спуска́ть (на́ воду). **2,** (set in flight) запуска́ть. **3,** (initiate) открыва́ть; предпринима́ть; пуска́ть в ход. *Launch a campaign,* разверну́ть кампа́нию. *Launch an offensive,* предприня́ть *or* повести́ наступле́ние. —*v.i.* [*usu.* **launch into**] пуска́ться: *launch into an explanation,* пуска́ться в объясне́ния. —*n.* **1,** (act of launching) за́пуск; пуск. **2,** (boat) ка́тер. —**launch pad,** пускова́я *or* ста́ртовая площа́дка. —**launch vehicle,** раке́таноси́тель; ракетоноси́тель.

launcher *n.* (пускова́я) устано́вка. *Rocket launcher,* раке́тная *or* реакти́вная устано́вка. *Grenade launcher,* гранатомёт.

launching *n.* **1,** (of a ship) спуск на́ воду. **2,** (of a satellite) за́пуск. —**launching pad,** пускова́я *or* ста́ртовая площа́дка.

launder *v.t.* стира́ть. —**laundress,** *n.* пра́чка.

laundry *n.* **1,** (items to be laundered) бельё: *do the laundry,* стира́ть бельё. *Take in laundry,* брать бельё в сти́рку. **2,** (business establishment) пра́чечная.

laureate *n.* лауреа́т.

laurel *n.* **1,** (tree) лавр. **2,** *pl.* (fame; honor) ла́вры.

—*adj.* ла́вровый; лавро́вый. *Laurel wreath,* лавро́вый вено́к. —**rest on one's laurels,** почива́ть на ла́врах.

lava *n.* ла́ва.

lavaliere *n.* подве́ска.

lavatory *n.* убо́рная.

lavender *n.* лава́нда. —*adj.* **1,** (pert. to the shrub) лава́ндовый. **2,** (pale purple) бле́дно-лило́вый.

lavish *adj.* **1,** (very generous) ще́дрый: *lavish in one's praise,* ще́дрый на похвалы́. **2,** (sumptuous; grand) пы́шный; роско́шный. —*v.t.* расточа́ть. *Lavish praise upon,* расточа́ть похвалы́ (+ *dat.*); рассыпа́ться в похвала́х (+ *dat.*). *Lavish gifts upon,* засыпа́ть (кого́-нибудь) пода́рками. *Lavish care upon,* окружа́ть (кого́-нибудь) забо́той.

law *n.* **1,** (rule of law; scientific principle) зако́н: *break the law,* наруша́ть зако́н. *It's against the law,* э́то противозако́нно. *The law of gravity,* зако́н (всеми́рного) тяготе́ния. **2,** (jurisprudence) пра́во: *criminal law,* уголо́вное пра́во. *Study law,* изуча́ть пра́во. *Practice law,* занима́ться адвокату́рой. —**take the law into one's own hands,** распра́виться без суда́.

law-abiding *adj.* законопослу́шный.

lawbreaker *n.* правонаруши́тель.

lawful *adj.* зако́нный.

lawless *adj.* беззако́нный. —**lawlessness,** *n.* беззако́ние.

lawmaker *n.* законода́тель.

lawn *n.* газо́н; лужа́йка. —**lawn mower,** газонокоси́лка.

law school юриди́ческий факульте́т.

lawsuit *n.* суде́бный проце́сс; иск.

lawyer *n.* юри́ст; адвока́т.

lax *adj.* небре́жный; хала́тный. *Lax discipline,* сла́бая дисципли́на. *Lax morals,* лёгкие нра́вы.

laxative *n.* слаби́тельное.

laxity *n.* небре́жность; хала́тность. *Also,* **laxness.**

lay *v.t.* **1,** (put or place horizontally) класть: *lay the wounded man on a stretcher,* класть ра́неного на носи́лки. *Lay a wreath on a grave,* возложи́ть вено́к на моги́лу. **2,** (install; place in position) прокла́дывать: *lay a pipeline,* прокла́дывать трубопрово́д. *Lay bricks,* класть кирпичи́. *Lay a floor,* настила́ть пол. *Lay a floor with tiles,* укла́дывать пол пли́тками. *Lay a foundation,* подводи́ть фунда́мент. *Lay (railroad) tracks,* укла́дывать ре́льсы. *Lay mines,* ста́вить *or* закла́дывать ми́ны. **3,** (spread, as a tablecloth, carpet, etc.) класть (ковёр); стлать (ска́терть). **4,** (produce, as eggs) класть; нести́. **5,** (locate): *The scene is laid in France,* де́йствие происхо́дит во Фра́нции. **6,** *with various abstract nouns:* lay plans, стро́ить пла́ны; lay the blame on, возлага́ть *or* вали́ть вину́ на; lay emphasis on, де́лать упо́р на; lay claim to, see **claim.** **7,** *in fig. expressions involving parts of the body:* lay (one's) hands on, распра́виться с; lay eyes on, (у)ви́деть; lay a finger on, тро́нуть па́льцем. **8,** (bet) держа́ть пари́ на. —*v.i.* (of a hen) нести́сь. —*adj.* (secular) мирско́й; све́тский. —*n.* (ballad) песнь. *The Lay of*

Igor's Host, Сло́во о полку́ И́гореве. —**lay aside/away/by,** откла́дывать (в сто́рону). —**lay bare,** обнажа́ть; выкла́дывать. —**lay down, 1,** (place in a horizontal position) класть; укла́дывать. **2,** (give up; surrender) сложи́ть: *lay down one's arms/life,* сложи́ть ору́жие/го́лову. **3,** (state authoritatively, as rules) устана́вливать. *Lay down conditions,* ста́вить усло́вия. *Lay down the law,* установи́ть твёрдое пра́вило. —**lay low,** свали́ть; повали́ть; срази́ть. —**lay off, 1,** (discharge) увольня́ть; рассчи́тывать. **2,** *colloq.* (stop; give up) бро́сить. —**lay of the land,** положе́ние веще́й. —**lay oneself open to,** дава́ть основа́ние для. —**lay out, 1,** (spread out) раскла́дывать; выкла́дывать. **2,** (design) плани́ровать; разбива́ть. **3,** (spend, as money) тра́тить. —**lay to rest,** хорони́ть. —**lay up, 1,** (store) заготовля́ть впрок. **2,** (confine to bed) укла́дывать. *He has been laid up for two weeks,* он лежи́т уже́ две неде́ли. —**lay waste,** опустоша́ть.

layer *n.* **1,** (stratum) слой; пласт. *Layer of dust/fat,* слой пы́ли/жи́ра. *Layer of snow,* пласт сне́га. **2,** (workman who lays something) укла́дчик: *track layer,* укла́дчик путе́й. **3,** (hen as an egg producer) несу́шка. *Good layer,* но́ская ку́рица.

layette *n.* прида́ное.

layman *n.* миря́нин.

layoff *n.* **1,** (dismissal) увольне́ние. **2,** (period of inactivity) переры́в.

layout *n.* **1,** (arrangement) расположе́ние; устро́йство; плани́ровка. **2,** (design; format, as of a newspaper) оформле́ние.

layover *n.* остано́вка (в пути́).

laze *v.i.* не́житься; лентя́йничать.

laziness *n.* лень; ле́ность.

lazy *adj.* лени́вый. *He is too lazy to write to you,* он сли́шком лени́вый, что́бы писа́ть вам; он ле́нится написа́ть вам.

lazybones *n., colloq.* лентя́й; лежебо́ка.

lead[1] (led) *n.* **1,** (heavy metal) свине́ц. **2,** (graphite, as used in pencils) графи́т. —*adj.* свинцо́вый. —**lead pencil,** просто́й *or* графи́товый каранда́ш. —**lead poisoning,** отравле́ние свинцо́м.

lead[2] (leed) *v.t.* **1,** (guide) вести́: *lead someone by the hand,* вести́ кого́-нибудь за́ руку. *Lead troops into battle,* вести́ войска́ в бой. **2,** (direct) руководи́ть: *lead an expedition,* руководи́ть экспеди́цией. **3,** (initiate and head) возглавля́ть: *lead a rebellion,* возглавля́ть восста́ние. **4,** (march at the head of) идти́ во главе́ (+ *gen.*). **5,** (be ahead of) опережа́ть: *lead one's opponent by six points,* опережа́ть проти́вника на шесть очко́в. **6,** *Lead the way,* идти́ впереди́. **7,** (induce; prompt) побужда́ть. *This leads me to believe that...,* из э́того я заключа́ю, что... **8,** (live, as a certain kind of life) вести́. *Lead a miserable existence,* влачи́ть жа́лкое существова́ние. **9,** *cards* идти́ с: *lead an ace,* идти́ с туза́. —*v.i.* **1,** (serve as a route) вести́: *This road leads to town,* э́та доро́га ведёт к го́роду. **2,** *fol. by* **to** (tend toward a certain result) вести́ (к); привести́ (к): *lead to nothing,* ни к чему́ не вести́ *or* привести́. **3,** (be in the lead)

лиди́ровать. *Be leading by two points,* быть впереди́ на два очка́. **4,** *cards: Who leads?,* чей ход? —*n.* **1,** (first place in a contest) ли́дерство. *Be in the lead,* лиди́ровать. *Take the lead,* выходи́ть вперёд. **2,** (distance in front): *have a long lead,* быть далеко́ впереди́. **3,** (role of leader) инициати́ва: *take the lead,* взять инициати́ву в свои́ ру́ки. **4,** (example) приме́р: *follow someone's lead,* сле́довать чьему́-нибудь приме́ру. **5,** *theat.* гла́вная роль. **6,** *cards* ход. **7,** *electricity* про́вод. —*adj.* веду́щий: *lead aircraft,* веду́щий самолёт. *Lead role,* гла́вная роль. *Lead article,* передова́я статья́. —**lead away,** уводи́ть. —**lead in,** вводи́ть. —**lead off, 1,** (lead away) уводи́ть. **2,** (begin) начина́ть; открыва́ть: *lead off the discussion,* начина́ть/открыва́ть диску́ссию. —**lead on,** води́ть за́ нос. —**lead out,** выводи́ть. —**lead up to, 1,** (precede; result in) вести́ к; приводи́ть к. **2,** (approach gradually) подходи́ть к.

leaded *adj.* (of gasoline) этили́рованный.

leaden *adj.* свинцо́вый: *leaden skies,* свинцо́вое не́бо.

leader *n.* руководи́тель; вождь; ли́дер. —**leadership,** *n.* руково́дство.

lead-in *n.* ввод.

leading *adj.* веду́щий: *play a leading role,* игра́ть веду́щую роль. —**leading lady,** премье́рша. —**leading light,** свети́ло; све́точ; корифе́й. —**leading man,** премье́р. —**leading question,** наводя́щий вопро́с.

leaf *n.* **1,** (of a tree or plant) лист: *The leaves are falling,* ли́стья па́дают. *Tea/tobacco leaf,* ча́йный/таба́чный лист. **2,** (of a book) лист. **3,** (for a table) доска́. **4,** (of a door or gate) ство́рка; полотни́ще. **5,** *in gold/silver leaf,* суса́льное зо́лото/серебро́. —*v.t.* [*usu* **leaf through**] перели́стывать. —**take a leaf from someone's book,** брать приме́р с. —**turn over a new leaf,** исправля́ться.

leaflet *n.* листо́вка.

leafy *adj.* ли́ственный.

league *n.* ли́га; сою́з. *League of Nations,* Ли́га на́ций. *Hanseatic League,* Ганзе́йский сою́з. —**in league with,** в сою́зе с; в сго́воре с.

leak *n.* течь: *spring a leak,* дать течь. *Gas leak,* уте́чка га́за. *News leak,* уте́чка информа́ции. —*v.i.* **1,** (admit water) течь; протека́ть. **2,** *fol. by* **into** (seep onto) затека́ть (в); протека́ть (в). —*v.t.* **1,** (allow to escape) пропуска́ть: *leak oil,* пропуска́ть ма́сло. **2,** (reveal clandestinely) разглаша́ть. —**leak out, 1,** (seep out) вытека́ть. **2,** *fig.* (become known) вы́йти нару́жу; проса́чиваться.

leakage *n.* уте́чка.

leaky *adj.* име́ющий течь; протека́ющий.

lean *v.i.* **1,** (incline one's body) наклоня́ться: *lean over the cradle,* наклоня́ться над колыбе́лью. *Lean over the railing,* перегиба́ться че́рез пери́ла. *Lean out of the window,* высо́вываться из окна́. *Lean back in the chair,* отки́дываться в кре́сле. **2,** (not be erect; slant) наклоня́ться. **3,** *fol. by* **against** (rest against) прислоня́ться (к). **4,** *fol. by* **on** (support oneself on; depend on) опира́ться (на). **5,** *fol. by* **toward** (favor slightly) склоня́ться (к): *lean toward the view that...,* склоня́ться к мне́нию, что... —*v.t.* **1**, (tilt) наклоня́ть. **2**, (prop) прислоня́ть; упира́ть: *lean something against the wall*, прислоня́ть что́-нибудь к стене́; упира́ть что́-нибудь в сте́ну. —*adj.* **1**, (thin) худо́й. **2**, (not fatty, as of meat) нежи́рный; по́стный. **3**, *Lean years*, неурожа́йные го́ды.

leaning *n.* скло́нность; накло́нность. —*adj.* накло́нный.

leanness *n.* худоба́.

leap *v.i.* пры́гать; скака́ть. *Leap to one's feet*, вскочи́ть на́ ноги. *Leap out of bed*, вскочи́ть *or* соскочи́ть с посте́ли. *Leap over the fence*, перескочи́ть че́рез забо́р. —*n.* прыжо́к; скачо́к. —**by leaps and bounds**, о́чень бы́стро; стреми́тельно. *The town is growing by leaps and bounds*, городо́к растёт не по дням, а по часа́м.

leapfrog *n.* чехарда́.

leap year високо́сный год.

learn *v.t.* **1**, (gain knowledge or mastery of) научи́ться; вы́учить; вы́учиться. *Learn a great deal*, научи́ться мно́гому. *Learn how to swim*, научи́ться пла́вать. *Where did you learn your Russian?*, где вы (так) вы́учили ру́сский? *I studied Russian for three years but never really learned it*, я учи́л ру́сский язы́к три го́да, но (так и) не вы́учил его́. *You have a lot to learn, see* **lot**. **2**, (memorize) зау́чивать. *Learn by heart*, зау́чивать *or* выу́чивать (что́-нибудь) наизу́сть. **3**, (find out) узнава́ть: *learn the truth*, узна́ть пра́вду. —*v.i.* **1**, (gain knowledge) учи́ться: *learn from experience/ one's mistakes/*, учи́ться на о́пыте/оши́бках. **2**, *fol. by* **of** *or* **about** (find out about) узнава́ть (о).

learned *adj.* зна́ющий; учёный.

learner *n.* учени́к: *slow learner*, сла́бый учени́к.

learning *n.* **1**, (acquiring knowledge) уче́ние. **2**, (erudition) учёность. *Book learning*, кни́жная учёность.

lease *n.* догово́р об аре́нде; аре́ндный догово́р. *Two-year lease*, аре́нда на два го́да. *The lease expires in December*, срок аре́нды истека́ет в декабре́. —*v.t.* **1**, (rent) брать в аре́нду. **2**, (let) сдава́ть в аре́нду. —**new lease on life**, втора́я мо́лодость.

leaseholder *n.* аренда́тор.

leash *n.* при́вязь; поводо́к.

least *adj.* мале́йший; наиме́ньший: *not the least doubt*, ни мале́йшего сомне́ния; *the line of least resistance*, ли́ния наиме́ньшего сопротивле́ния. —*adv.* **1**, *before adjectives*, наиме́нее: *the least important question*, наиме́нее ва́жный вопро́с. *The least interesting part of the book*, наиме́нее интере́сная (*or* са́мая неинтере́сная) часть кни́ги. **2**, *with verbs*, ме́ньше всего́: *what I like least*, что мне нра́вится ме́ньше всего́. —*n.* [*usu.* **the least**] са́мое ме́ньшее; са́мое ма́лое. *It was the least I could do*, э́то таки́е пустяки́; э́то мне ничего́ не сто́ило. *That's the least of my worries*, э́то меня́ ме́ньше всего́ беспоко́ит. —**at least**, по кра́йней ме́ре; по ме́ньшей ме́ре; не ме́нее (+ *gen.*); хоть; хотя́ бы. *Cost at least ten dollars*, сто́ить по кра́йней ме́ре де́сять до́лларов. *At least it's not raining*, по кра́йней ме́ре дождь не идёт. *Say a word at least!*,

скажи́те хотя́ бы сло́во! *You might at least say you're sorry!*, вы могли́ бы, по кра́йней ме́ре, извини́ться! —**at the least**, са́мое ме́ньшее; са́мое ма́лое. —**not in the least**, ниско́лько; ни в мале́йшей сте́пени. —**not the least bit** (+ *adj.*), ниско́лько не; совсе́м не. —**to say the least**, по ме́ньшей ме́ре; е́сли (*or* что́бы) не сказа́ть бо́льше.

leather *n.* ко́жа. —*adj.* ко́жаный.

leatherette *n.* дермати́н; ледери́н.

leave *v.i.* уходи́ть; уезжа́ть: *He left*, он ушёл. *She left for Florida*, она́ уе́хала во Флори́ду. *Are you leaving already?*, вы уже́ ухо́дите? *The train/plane leaves at eight*, по́езд отхо́дит/ самолёт вылета́ет/ в во́семь часо́в. *The train has already left*, по́езд уже́ ушёл. —*v.t.* **1**, (go out of) выходи́ть из: *leave the room/house*, выходи́ть из ко́мнаты/ и́з дому/. *The train is leaving the station*, по́езд отхо́дит от ста́нции. **2**, (depart from) уходи́ть из; уезжа́ть из: *leave home*, уходи́ть/уезжа́ть из до́ма. *Leave the meeting*, уходи́ть с собра́ния. *Leave the table*, встава́ть из-за стола́. *What time do you leave work?*, во ско́лько вы ухо́дите с рабо́ты? *The train leaves New York at six*, по́езд ухо́дит из Нью-Йо́рка в шесть часо́в. **3**, (quit; withdraw from) уходи́ть из *or* с; выходи́ть из. *Leave school*, уходи́ть из шко́лы; бро́сить шко́лу. *Leave the party*, выходи́ть из па́ртии. **4**, (go without taking; deposit; let remain) оставля́ть: *leave the children at home*, оставля́ть дете́й до́ма. *Leave a note for someone*, оставля́ть кому́-нибудь запи́ску. *Leave far behind*, оставля́ть далеко́ позади́. *Leave the door open*, оставля́ть дверь откры́той. *Leave in peace*, оставля́ть в поко́е. **5**, (forget) забы́ть; оста́вить: *leave the tickets home*, забы́ть/оста́вить биле́ты до́ма. **6**, (forsake) уходи́ть от; покида́ть; оставля́ть; бро́сить. *He left his wife*, он ушёл от жены́; он бро́сил жену́. *Don't leave me!*, не покида́йте меня́! **7**, (entrust) предоставля́ть: *Leave it to me to decide*, предоста́вьте реша́ть э́то мне. *I leave this task to others*, э́ту зада́чу я предоставля́ю други́м. **8**, (be survived by) оста́вить по́сле себя́: *He left no survivors*, он не оста́вил по́сле себя́ насле́дников. *He leaves a wife and two children*, по́сле него́ оста́лись жена́ и дво́е дете́й. **9**, (bequeath) оставля́ть: *leave someone a fortune*, оставля́ть кому́-нибудь состоя́ние. **10**, *in subtraction: Seven minus three leaves four*, семь ми́нус три равня́ется четырём. —*n.* **1**, (permission) разреше́ние: *by your leave*, с ва́шего разреше́ния. **2**, *mil.* (furlough) о́тпуск; побы́вка. *Absence without leave*, самово́льная отлу́чка. **3**, *in* **take leave of**, проща́ться с; **take one's leave**, уходи́ть. —**be left**, оста́ться: *be left homeless*, оста́ться без кро́ва. *There is nothing left*, ничего́ не оста́лось. *How much time is left?*, ско́лько вре́мени оста́лось? *I have only one stamp left*, у меня́ оста́лась то́лько одна́ ма́рка. *He has two years left to serve of his sentence*, ему́ оста́лось два го́да до оконча́ния сро́ка наказа́ния. —**leave alone**, *see* **alone**. —**leave aside**, оставля́ть в стороне́: *leaving aside the question of...*, оставля́я в стороне́ вопро́с о... —**leave back**, оста́вить на второ́й год (в шко́ле). —**leave behind,** *see* **behind.** —**leave off, 1,** (drop off, as from a car) выса́живать. **2,** (omit) пропуска́ть. *Leave (someone) off the list,* не включи́ть в спи́сок. **3,** (stop) остана́вливаться: *Where did we leave off?,* где мы останови́лись? —**leave out,** пропуска́ть.

leaven *n.* заква́ска; опа́ра. —*v.t.* заква́шивать.

leavings *n.pl.* оста́тки.

Lebanese *adj.* лива́нский.

lecher *n.* развра́тник; распу́тник. —**lecherous,** *adj.* развра́тный; распу́тный. —**lechery,** *n.* развра́т; распу́тство.

lectern *n.* **1,** (speaker's stand) пюпи́тр. **2,** (reading desk in a church) анало́й.

lecture *n.* **1,** (discourse) ле́кция. *Attend a lecture,* прису́тствовать на ле́кции. *Attend lectures,* посеща́ть ле́кции. **2,** (reprimand) нота́ция. —*v.i.* чита́ть ле́кции. —*v.t.* поуча́ть. —**lecture hall,** лекцио́нный зал; аудито́рия.

lecturer *n.* ле́ктор.

ledge *n.* **1,** (small shelf) по́лочка. **2,** (on the side of a cliff) вы́ступ; усту́п.

ledger *n.* гла́вная кни́га; гроссбу́х.

leech *n.* пия́вка.

leek *n.* поре́й; лук-поре́й.

leer *v.i.* смотре́ть и́скоса. —*n.* косо́й взгляд.

leery *adj., colloq.* подозри́тельный; скепти́ческий. *Be leery of,* относи́ться подозри́тельно/скепти́чески к.

lees *n.pl.* гу́ща; муть.

leeward *adj.* подве́тренный.

leeway *n.* свобо́да де́йствий.

left[1] *adj.* ле́вый: *left hand,* ле́вая рука́. —*adv.* нале́во: *turn left,* повора́чивать нале́во. —*n.* **1,** (side opp. to right) ле́вая сторона́. *On/to my left,* сле́ва от меня́; по ле́вую ру́ку от меня́. *Hebrew is written from right to left,* на иври́те пи́шут спра́ва нале́во. **2,** *polit.* [*usu.* **the Left**] ле́вые.

left[2] *past tense and past part. of* **leave.** *See* **leave.**

left-hand *adj.* ле́вый.

left-handed *adj.* **1,** (favoring the left hand): *I am left-handed,* я левша́. **2,** *fig.* (backhanded) сомни́тельный: *left-handed compliment,* сомни́тельный комплиме́нт.

leftist *n.* лева́к. —*adj.* лева́цкий.

leftovers *n.pl.* оста́тки: *leftovers from last night's dinner,* оста́тки вчера́шнего обе́да.

left-wing *adj.* ле́вый.

leg *n.* **1,** (part of the body) нога́: *long legs,* дли́нные но́ги. *Break one's leg,* слома́ть но́гу. **2,** (of a piece of furniture) но́жка. **3,** (of a pair of trousers) штани́на. **4,** (piece of meat) нога́: *leg of mutton,* бара́нья нога́. **5,** (stage of a journey) эта́п. —**be on one's last legs,** дожива́ть после́дние дни. —**pull someone's leg,** шути́ть над ке́м-нибудь.

legacy *n.* насле́дие.

legal *adj.* **1,** (pert. to law) правово́й; юриди́ческий. *Legal question,* юриди́ческий вопро́с. *Legal norms,* правовы́е но́рмы. *From a legal standpoint,* с юриди́ческой *or* правово́й то́чки зре́ния. *Have no legal*

force, не име́ть юриди́ческой си́лы. **2,** (pert. to lawyers or lawsuits) суде́бный: *legal costs,* суде́бный изде́ржки. *Take legal action,* начина́ть суде́бный проце́сс. **3,** (lawful; legitimate) зако́нный; лега́льный. —**legal tender,** зако́нное платёжное сре́дство.

legality *n.* зако́нность; лега́льность.

legalize *v.t.* узако́нивать; легализи́ровать. —**legalization,** *n.* узаконе́ние; легализа́ция.

legally *adv.* **1,** (in a legal manner) зако́нно; зако́нным путём; лега́льно. **2,** (from a legal point of view) юриди́чески. *Legally obligated,* юриди́чески *or* по зако́ну обя́занный. *Be legally entitled to,* име́ть зако́нное пра́во на; по зако́ну име́ть пра́во на.

legation *n.* ми́ссия.

legato *adj. & adv.* лега́то.

legend *n.* леге́нда; преда́ние. *Biblical legend,* библе́йское преда́ние; библе́йское сказа́ние. —**legendary,** *adj.* легенда́рный.

legerdemain *n.* ло́вкость рук.

leggings *n.pl.* гама́ши; кра́ги.

legibility *n.* разбо́рчивость.

legible *adj.* разбо́рчивый. —**legibly,** *adv.* разбо́рчиво.

legion *n.* легио́н. —**legionnaire,** *n.* легионе́р.

legislation *n.* законода́тельство. —**legislative,** *adj.* законода́тельный. —**legislator,** *n.* законода́тель. —**legislature,** *n.* легислату́ра.

legitimate *adj.* **1,** (lawful) зако́нный. **2,** (valid, as of an excuse) уважи́тельный. **3,** (born in wedlock) законорождённый. —**legitimacy,** *n.* зако́нность.

legitimize *v.t.* узако́нивать.

legless *adj.* безно́гий.

legroom *n.* ме́сто для ног.

leguminous *adj.* бобо́вый; стручко́вый.

leisure *n.* досу́г: *at one's leisure,* на досу́ге. —*adj.* свобо́дный: *leisure time,* свобо́дное вре́мя. *The leisure class,* пра́здный класс.

leisurely *adj.* неторопли́вый. —*adv.* неторопли́во.

leitmotif *n.* лейтмоти́в.

lemming *n.* ле́мминг.

lemon *n.* лимо́н. —*adj.* лимо́нный: *lemon tree,* лимо́нное де́рево. —**lemonade,** *n.* лимона́д.

lemur *n.* лему́р.

lend *v.t.* **1,** (let have temporarily) одолжа́ть; дава́ть: *Could you lend me a pencil?,* вы не мо́жете одолжи́ть/дать мне каранда́ш? **2,** (give as a loan) одолжа́ть; ссужа́ть; дава́ть взаймы́. **3,** (give; contribute) подава́ть: *lend a helping hand,* подава́ть ру́ку по́мощи. **4,** (give; impart) придава́ть: *lend dignity to,* придава́ть досто́инство (+ *dat.*). **5,** *fol. by* **itself** (be suitable) поддава́ться (+ *dat.*): *not lend itself to translation,* не поддава́ться перево́ду.

lender *n.* кредито́р.

length *n.* **1,** (distance from end to end) длина́: *twelve feet in length,* в двена́дцать фу́тов длино́й. **2,** (extent) протяже́ние: *along the entire length of the river,* на всём протяже́нии реки́. *Walk the length of the street,* проходи́ть (всю) у́лицу. **3,** (duration) продолжи́тельность. *Length of service,* стаж. *For a certain length of time,* на определённый срок. **4,** (piece, as of cloth) отре́з; отре́зок. **5,** *horse racing* ко́рпус: *win by two lengths,* опереди́ть други́х на два ко́рпуса. —**at length,** подро́бно. —**go to any length,** идти́ на всё. —**go to great lengths,** прилага́ть больши́е уси́лия; лезть из ко́жи вон. —**keep at arm's length,** держа́ть на почти́тельном расстоя́нии.

lengthen *v.t.* удлиня́ть: *lengthen a skirt,* удлиня́ть ю́бку. —*v.i.* удлиня́ться.

lengthwise *adv.* в длину́; вдоль.

lengthy *adj.* дли́тельный; продолжи́тельный. *Lengthy discussion,* дли́тельное обсужде́ние; продолжи́тельная диску́ссия.

lenient *adj.* снисходи́тельный; нестро́гий. *Lenient teacher,* нестро́гий учи́тель. —**leniency,** *n.* снисхожде́ние; снисходи́тельность.

Leninism *n.* ленини́зм. —**Leninist,** *n.* ле́нинец. —*adj.* ле́нинский.

lens *n.* **1,** (glass) ли́нза; объекти́в. **2,** (of the eye) хруста́лик. —**lens cap,** кры́шка объекти́ва.

Lent *n.* вели́кий пост. —**Lenten,** *adj.* великопо́стный.

lentil *n.* чечеви́ца. —*adj.* чечеви́чный.

lento *adj. & adv.* ле́нто.

Leo *n.* Лев.

leopard *n.* леопа́рд.

leotard *n.* трико́.

leper *n.* прокажённый. —**leper colony,** коло́ния прокажённых.

leprosy *n.* прока́за. —**leprous,** *adj.* прокажённый.

lesbian *n.* лесбия́нка. —*adj.* лесби́йский.

lesion *n.* пораже́ние; повражде́ние.

less *adj.* ме́ньше: *less time,* ме́ньше вре́мени. *A little less sugar,* немно́жко ме́ньше са́хара. —*adv.* **1,** *before adjectives,* ме́нее: *less likely,* ме́нее вероя́тно. **2,** *after verbs,* ме́ньше: *smoke less,* ме́ньше кури́ть. —*n.* ме́ньше: *eat less,* ме́ньше есть. *Less than I expected,* ме́ньше, чем я ожида́л(а). *He finished the job in less than an hour,* он зако́нчил рабо́ту ме́ньше чем за час. *I'll be back in less than an hour,* я верну́сь ра́ньше чем че́рез час. *He lived here less than a year,* он про́жил здесь ме́нее го́да. *The less I hear about it, the better,* чем ме́ньше я слы́шу об э́том, тем лу́чше. —*prep.* за вы́четом (+ *gen.*). —**less and less,** всё ме́ньше и ме́ньше; (*before adjectives*) всё ме́нее (+ *adj.*). —**more or less,** бо́лее и́ли ме́нее. —**much less, 1,** *literally* гора́здо ме́ньше. **2,** *before adjectives,* гора́здо ме́нее. **3,** (especially) тем бо́лее.

lessee *n.* аренда́тор.

lessen *v.t.* уменьша́ть. *Lessen international tension,* уменьша́ть *or* ослабля́ть *or* разряжа́ть междунаро́дную напряжённость. —*v.i.* уменьша́ться.

lesser *adj.* ме́ньший: *a lesser offense,* ме́ньший просту́пок. *To a lesser degree,* в ме́ньшей сте́пени. *An official of lesser rank,* сотру́дник ме́ньшего ра́нга. —**the lesser of two evils,** ме́ньшее из двух зол.

lesson *n.* уро́к: *music lessons,* уро́ки му́зыки. *Give/ take lessons,* дава́ть/брать уро́ки. *Study one's les-*

sons, учи́ть уро́ки. *Serve as a lesson to,* послужи́ть уро́ком (+ *dat.*). *Learn one's lesson* (*fig.*), получи́ть хоро́ший уро́к. *Learn a lesson from,* извле́чь уро́к из. *Let this be a lesson to you,* э́то бу́дет тебе́ уро́ком. —**teach someone a lesson,** проучи́ть кого́-нибудь; дать *or* преподда́ть кому́-нибудь уро́к.

lest *conj.* **1,** (so that...not) чтобы не: *lest the reader think that...,* чтобы чита́тель не поду́мал, что... *Lest any doubts remain,* чтобы не остава́лось сомне́ний. **2,** (for fear that) как бы не: *lest something worse should happen,* как бы ху́же не́ было.

let *v.t.* **1,** (allow) разреша́ть; позволя́ть; дава́ть. *Let the children play outside,* разреша́ть/позволя́ть де́тям игра́ть на дворе́; отпуска́ть дете́й игра́ть на дворе́. *Let him speak,* дай ему́ говори́ть. *Let me think,* да́йте мне поду́мать. *Let me help you,* дава́йте я вам помогу́. *Let an opportunity slip by,* упусти́ть возмо́жность. *Don't let this happen again!,* чтобы э́того бо́льше не́ было! ♦*Also with* пусть: *Let him go,* пусть он идёт. *Let him wait!,* пусть подождёт! *Just let him try!,* пусть он то́лько попро́бует! **2,** (rent; give out) сдава́ть внаём *or* в аре́нду. *Let a contract,* сдава́ть подря́д. *House to let,* сдаётся дом. —*v.aux.* **1,** [*usu.* **let's**] *in suggestions, rendered by the 1st person pl.:* *Let's go!,* пойдём(те)! ♦*Also by* дава́й, дава́йте *and* бу́дем: *Let's take the bus,* дава́й(те) возьмём (*or* ся́дем на) автóбус. *Let's not argue about it,* дава́йте не спо́рить об э́том. *Let's hope so,* бу́дем наде́яться. *Let's not waste time,* дава́йте не бу́дем теря́ть вре́мени. **2,** *acquiescence,* пусть: *Let it rain!,* пусть бу́дет дождь. **3,** *assumption,* пусть: *Let x equal y,* пусть икс ра́вен и́греку. —**let alone,** *see* **alone.** —**let down, 1,** (lower) опуска́ть; спуска́ть. **2,** (undo, as one's hair) распуска́ть. **3,** (fail to keep one's word to) подводи́ть; обма́нывать. —**let go (of),** отпуска́ть; пуска́ть. *Let go!,* отпусти́(те). —**let have,** уступа́ть: *I'll let you have it for ten dollars,* я уступлю́ вам э́то за де́сять до́лларов. —**let in,** пуска́ть; допуска́ть; впуска́ть; пропуска́ть. —**let in on,** посвяща́ть в: *let someone in on a secret,* посвяща́ть кого́-нибудь в та́йну. —**let know,** дать знать. —**let off, 1,** (emit, as steam) выпуска́ть (пары́). **2,** (drop off, as a passenger) выса́живать. **3,** (release with light punishment): *He was let off with a fine,* он отде́лался штра́фом. *The judge let him off with a fine,* судья́ ограни́чился штра́фом. —**let on,** *colloq.* (*usu. neg.*) (никому́ не) говори́ть, что...; (не) подава́ть ви́ду, что... —**let out, 1,** (release) выпуска́ть: *let the bird out of the cage,* выпуска́ть пти́цу из кле́тки. *Let the water out of the bathtub,* спуска́ть во́ду из ва́нны. *Let the air out of a tire,* спуска́ть ши́ну. *Let out one's feelings,* отводи́ть ду́шу. *Don't let him out of your sight!,* не спуска́йте с него́ глаз! **2,** (loosen) распуска́ть. **3,** (make longer) выпуска́ть. **4,** (emit) испуска́ть: *let out a scream,* испусти́ть крик. —**let through,** пропуска́ть. —**let up, 1,** (slacken) ослабева́ть. **2,** (abate, as of a storm) зати́хать.

letdown *n.* разочарова́ние.

lethal *adj.* смертоно́сный; смерте́льный. *Lethal*

weapon, смертоно́сное ору́жие. *Lethal dose,* смерте́льная до́за.

lethargic *adj.* летарги́ческий; вя́лый. —**lethargy,** *n.* летарги́я; вя́лость.

Lett *n.* латы́ш.

letter *n.* **1,** (of the alphabet) бу́ква. **2,** (message sent by mail) письмо́: *There's a letter for you,* вам письмо́. —*v.t.* помеча́ть бу́квами. —**letter of the law,** бу́ква зако́на. —**man of letters,** литера́тор. —**to the letter,** то́чка в то́чку; в то́чности.

letter carrier почтальо́н.

letterhead *n.* на́дпись (на почто́вой бума́ге).

lettering *n.* на́дпись: *hand lettering,* на́дпись от руки́.

letter of credit аккредити́в.

letter-perfect *adj.* соверше́нно то́чный.

Lettish *adj.* латы́шский. —*n.* латы́шский язы́к.

lettuce *n.* сала́т.

letup *n.* переры́в; остано́вка. *Without letup,* безостано́вочно.

leucocyte *n.* = **leukocyte.**

leukemia *also,* **leukaemia** *n.* лейко́з; лейкеми́я; белокро́вие.

leukocyte *also,* **leucocyte** *n.* лейкоци́т.

levee *n.* да́мба.

level *n.* **1,** (elevation; standard) у́ровень: *water level,* у́ровень воды́. *On/at a high level,* на высо́ком у́ровне. *On a level with,* наравне́ с; наряду́ с; вро́вень с. **2,** (instrument) ватерпа́с; нивели́р; у́ровень. —*adj.* ро́вный: *level ground,* ро́вная ме́стность. —*v.t.* **1,** (make level) выра́внивать; сра́внивать (*pfv.* сровня́ть). **2,** (knock down; raze) сра́внивать/ сровня́ть с землёй. **3,** (aim) наводи́ть. **4,** (direct, as an accusation) выдвига́ть (про́тив); возводи́ть (на); броса́ть (+ *dat.*). **5,** *surveying* нивели́ровать. —**do one's level best,** сде́лать всё, что в чьи́х-нибудь си́лах. —**on the level,** *colloq.* че́стный.

levelheaded *adj.* уравнове́шенный; здравомы́слящий.

lever *n.* рыча́г.

leverage *n.* **1,** (action of a lever) де́йствие рычага́. **2,** *fig.* (power to influence) рычаги́: *use leverage,* испо́льзовать рычаги́.

leviathan *n.* левиафа́н.

Leviticus *n.* Леви́т.

levity *n.* легкомы́слие.

levy *v.t.* **1,** (impose) облага́ть (нало́гом); налага́ть (штраф). **2,** (collect) взима́ть; взы́скивать. —*n.* сбор; нало́г.

lewd *adj.* **1,** (lascivious) похотли́вый. **2,** (obscene) са́льный. —**lewdness,** *n.* похотли́вость.

lexical *adj.* лекси́ческий; слова́рный.

lexicography *n.* лексикогра́фия. —**lexicographer,** *n.* лексико́граф. —**lexicographic,** *adj.* лексикографи́ческий.

lexicon *n.* **1,** (wordbook; dictionary) лексико́н; слова́рь. **2,** (vocabulary) ле́ксика; лексико́н; слова́рь.

liability *n.* **1,** (state of being liable) отве́тственность. **2,** *pl.* (debts; obligations) пасси́в.

liable *adj.* **1,** (legally obligated): *be liable for damages,*

нести́ материа́льную отве́тственность за убы́тки. **2,** *fol. by* **to** (subject to) подлежа́щий (+ *dat.*); подве́рженный (+ *dat.*). *Be liable to prosecution,* подлежа́ть суде́бному пресле́дованию. **3,** (likely) *rendered by* мочь: *You're liable to catch cold,* ты мо́жешь простуди́ться. *He is liable to come at any moment,* он мо́жет прийти́ в любо́й моме́нт. *He is liable to do anything,* он спосо́бен на всё.

liaison *n.* **1,** (means of contact) связь. **2,** (adulterous relationship) (любо́вная) связь. **3,** *phonet.* слия́ние зву́ков.

liar *n.* лгун; лжец.

libation *n.* возлия́ние.

libel *n.* клевета́. *Libel suit,* иск за клевету́. —*v.t.* клевета́ть на. —**libelous,** *adj.* клеветни́ческий.

liberal *adj.* **1,** *polit.* либера́льный. **2,** (generous; ample) ще́дрый. **3,** (of an education) гуманита́рный. *Liberal arts,* гуманита́рные нау́ки. —*n.* либера́л. —**liberalism,** *n.* либерали́зм. —**liberality,** *n.* ще́дрость.

liberalize *v.t.* де́лать бо́лее либера́льным.

liberate *v.t.* освобожда́ть. —**liberation,** *n.* освобожде́ние. —**liberator,** *n.* освободи́тель.

libertine *n.* распу́тник; развра́тник.

liberty *n.* **1,** (freedom) свобо́да. *The Statue of Liberty,* ста́туя свобо́ды. **2,** *pl.* (action going beyond normal limits) во́льности: *permit someone certain liberties,* позво́лить кому́-нибудь не́которые во́льности. *Take liberties,* позво́лить себе́ во́льности. *Take liberties with,* фамилья́рничать с. —**at liberty,** на свобо́де. *At liberty to,* во́лен (+ *inf.*). —**take the liberty of,** позво́лить себе́ (+ *inf.*); брать на себя́ сме́лость (+ *inf.*).

Libra *n.* Весы́.

librarian *n.* библиоте́карь. —**librarianship,** *n.* библиоте́чное де́ло.

library *n.* библиоте́ка. *Record library,* фоноте́ка. *Film library,* фильмоте́ка. —*adj.* библиоте́чный: *library book,* библиоте́чная кни́га. —**library science,** библиотекове́дение.

libretto *n.* либре́тто. —**librettist,** *n.* либретти́ст.

Libyan *adj.* ливи́йский.

license *n.* **1,** (official permit) разреше́ние; свиде́тельство; лице́нзия. *Marriage license,* бра́чное свиде́тельство. *Driver's license,* води́тельские права́. *Pilot's license,* права́ на управле́ние самолётом. **2,** (freedom) во́льность: *poetic license,* поэти́ческая во́льность. —*v.t.* разреша́ть; санкциони́ровать. —**license plate,** номерно́й знак.

licentious *adj.* распу́тный; распу́щенный. —**licentiousness,** *n.* распу́тство; распу́щенность.

lichen *n.* лиша́йник; лиша́й.

lick *v.t.* **1,** (pass the tongue over) лиза́ть; обли́зывать. *Lick off,* сли́зывать. **2,** (touch lightly, as of flames) лиза́ть. **3,** *colloq.* (defeat soundly) поби́ть. —**lick one's chops,** обли́зываться. —**lick one's wounds,** зали́зывать ра́ны. —**lick someone's boots,** лиза́ть пя́тки (+ *dat.*).

licking *n.* **1,** (act of licking) лиза́ние. **2,** *colloq.* (thrashing) по́рка; взбу́чка.

lickspittle *n.* лизоблю́д; подхали́м.

licorice *also,* **liquorice** *n.* лакри́ца. —*adj.* лакри́чный.

lid *n.* кры́шка.

lie *v.i.* **1,** (be in a recumbent position; rest on a horizontal surface) лежа́ть: *She was lying on the floor,* она́ лежа́ла на полу́. *Snow lay on the ground,* снег лежа́л на земле́. **2,** *fol. by* **down** (assume a recumbent position) ложи́ться (*pfv.* лечь): *lie down on the ground,* лечь на зе́млю. **3,** (be situated) лежа́ть. *The city lies midway between...,* го́род лежи́т *or* стои́т на полпути́ ме́жду... *The truth lies somewhere in between,* пра́вда — где́-то посереди́не. **4,** (be in a certain condition) лежа́ть: *lie idle,* лежа́ть без употребле́ния; *lie fallow,* лежа́ть под па́ром; *lie in ruins,* лежа́ть в разва́линах. *Lie at anchor,* стоя́ть на я́коре. **5,** (be buried) поко́иться: *Here lies...,* здесь поко́ится прах (+ *gen.*). **6,** *fol. by* **in** (be) состоя́ть в; заключа́ться в: *The difficulty lies in the fact that...,* тру́дность состои́т/заключа́ется в том, что... **7,** (make false statements) лгать; врать: *You're lying!,* лжёшь! —*n.* ложь: *It's all a lie,* э́то всё ложь. —**lie ahead,** предстоя́ть. —**lie around/about,** валя́ться. —**lie in wait for,** подстерега́ть. —**lie low,** залега́ть; отлёживаться; притаи́ться. —**see which way the land lies,** зонди́ровать по́чву. —**take lying down,** прогла́тывать (оскорбле́ние).

lie detector дете́ктор лжи. *Lie detector test,* прове́рка на дете́кторе лжи.

lien *n.* пра́во аре́ста: *obtain a lien on someone's property,* получи́ть пра́во аре́ста чьего́-нибудь иму́щества.

lieu *n., in* **in lieu of,** вме́сто (+ *gen.*).

lieutenant *n.* лейтена́нт. *First lieutenant,* ста́рший лейтена́нт. *Second lieutenant,* мла́дший лейтена́нт. —**lieutenant colonel,** подполко́вник. —**lieutenant commander,** капита́н тре́тьего ра́нга. —**lieutenant general,** генера́л-полко́вник. —**lieutenant governor,** ви́це-губерна́тор.

life *n.* жизнь: *all one's life,* всю жизнь. *City/family life,* городска́я/семе́йная жизнь. *Happy/bitter life,* счастли́вая/го́рькая жизнь. *Is there life on Mars?,* есть ли жизнь на Ма́рсе? *Result in great loss of life,* унести́ мно́го челове́ческих жи́зней. *Life of a battery,* срок слу́жбы аккумуля́тора. —*adj.* пожи́зненный: *life imprisonment,* пожи́зненное заключе́ние. *He was given a life sentence,* его́ приговори́ли к пожи́зненному заключе́нию. —**bring back to life,** воскреша́ть. —**come to life,** ожива́ть; оживля́ться. —**for dear life,** изо всех сил. —**for life,** на всю жизнь. *Be appointed for life,* назнача́ться пожи́зненно. —**for the life of me,** хоть убе́й. —**life-and-death struggle,** борьба́ не на жизнь, а на́ смерть. —**life of the party,** душа́ о́бщества. —**lose one's life,** лиши́ться жи́зни; поги́бнуть. —**matter of life and death,** вопро́с жи́зни и сме́рти. —**not on your life,** ни за что на све́те. —**take one's life in one's hands,** рискова́ть жи́знью. —**take one's own life,** лиши́ть себя́ жи́зни. —**true to life,** как в жи́зни: *In the movie everything was true to life,* в фи́льме всё бы́ло как в жи́зни.

life belt спаса́тельный по́яс; про́бковый по́яс.

lifeboat *n.* спаса́тельная ло́дка *or* шлю́пка.

life buoy спаса́тельный круг.

life expectancy продолжи́тельность жи́зни.

lifeguard *n.* спаса́тель.

life insurance страхова́ние жи́зни.

life jacket спаса́тельный жиле́т.

lifeless *adj.* мёртвый; ме́ртвенный; безжи́зненный; бездыха́нный.

lifelike *adj.* жи́зненный.

lifelong *adj.* на всю жизнь: *lifelong friend,* друг на всю жизнь. *Lifelong desire,* заве́тное жела́ние.

life preserver спаса́тельный по́яс.

life raft спаса́тельный плот.

lifesaver *n.* спаси́тель.

life-size *also,* **life-sized** *adj.* в натура́льную величину́.

lifetime *n.* жизнь: *in one's lifetime,* при чье́й-нибудь жи́зни. *Not in my lifetime,* не при мое́й жи́зни. *I have seen a lot in my lifetime,* я мно́го повида́л(а) на своём веку́. *Lifetime employment,* пожи́зненная за́нятость. *It's the chance of a lifetime,* тако́й слу́чай представля́ется раз в жи́зни.

lifework *n.* де́ло *or* труд (чье́й-нибудь) жи́зни.

lift *v.t.* **1,** (raise) поднима́ть: *The trunk is too heavy to lift,* сунду́к тако́й тяжёлый, что его́ не подня́ть. *Lift someone's spirits,* поднима́ть дух *or* настрое́ние кого́-нибудь. **2,** (eliminate; end) отменя́ть; снима́ть. *Lift sanctions/ a curfew/,* отменя́ть са́нкции/ коменда́нтский час/. *Lift restrictions/ a ban/ a blockade/,* снима́ть ограниче́ния/запре́т/блока́ду. **3,** *Lift out of context,* вы́рвать из конте́кста. —*v.i.* **1,** (of fog) поднима́ться. —*n.* **1,** (instance of lifting): *give something a lift,* поднима́ть что́-нибудь. **2,** (free ride): *give a lift to,* подвози́ть. **3,** (machine for lifting) подъёмная маши́на; подъёмник. **4,** *Brit.* (elevator) лифт. **5,** (part of the heel of a shoe) набо́йка. **6,** *fig.* (elevation of one's spirits): *give someone a lift,* подба́дривать кого́-нибудь. —**lift off,** *aerospace* отрыва́ться от земли́.

liftoff *n.* отры́в от земли́.

ligament *n.* свя́зка.

ligature *n.* лигату́ра.

light *n.* **1,** (illumination) свет: *dim light,* ту́склый свет. *Read in good light,* чита́ть при хоро́шем све́те. *Turn out the light(s):* (по)туши́ть свет. *The lights went out,* свет пога́с. **2,** (source of illumination) фона́рь: *street light,* у́личный фона́рь. *The lights of a city,* огни́ го́рода. **3,** (traffic light) светофо́р. *Red light,* кра́сный свет. **4,** (for a cigarette): *Can you give me a light?,* разреши́те прикури́ть! **5,** (aspect) свет: *see something in its true light,* ви́деть что́-нибудь в и́стинном све́те. —*adj.* **1,** (not dark; bright) све́тлый: *light hair/colors,* све́тлые во́лосы/кра́ски. *It is getting light,* света́ет; рассвета́ет. *It is already light,* уже́ светло́. ♦ *With colors,* светло-: *light gray,* светло-се́рый. **2,** (of or pert. to light) светово́й: *light wave,* светова́я волна́. **3,** (not heavy; not serious) лёгкий: *light suitcase/breakfast/breeze,* лёгкий чемода́н/за́втрак/ветеро́к. *Light reading,* лёгкое чте́ние. *Light sentence,* мя́гкий пригово́р. *Be a light* *sleeper,* чу́тко спать. —*adv.* легко́. *Travel light,* путеше́ствовать налегке́. —*v.t.* **1,** (ignite; turn on, as a lamp, match, etc.) зажига́ть. *Light a fire,* разжига́ть ого́нь *or* костёр. *Light a stove,* зата́пливать плиту́. *Light (up) a cigarette,* заку́ривать сигаре́ту. **2,** *often fol. by* **up** (illuminate) освеща́ть; озаря́ть. —*v.i.* **1,** (ignite) зажига́ться. **2,** *fol. by* **up** (brighten, as of one's face) освеща́ться; озаря́ться; (of one's eyes) загоре́ться; засвети́ться. **3,** *fol. by* **on** *or* **upon** (come upon) ната́лкиваться на. **4,** *fol. by* **into** (attack violently) обру́шиваться на. —**bring to light,** выявля́ть. —**come to light,** обнару́живаться; вскрыва́ться; всплыва́ть; выплыва́ть. —**in (the) light of,** в све́те (+ *gen.*). —**make light of,** относи́ться легко́ к. —**see the light,** прозре́ть.

light bulb ла́мпочка.

lighted *adj.* зажжённый. *Lighted candle,* горя́щая свеча́.

lighten *v.t.* **1,** (make less heavy) облегча́ть. **2,** (make lighter, as colors) де́лать светле́е. —*v.i.* облегча́ться.

lighter *n.* **1,** (igniting device) зажига́лка. **2,** (boat) ли́хтер.

light-fingered *adj.* на́ руку нечи́ст.

light-haired *adj.* световоло́сый.

lightheaded *adj.* **1,** (giddy; dizzy) *I feel lightheaded,* у меня́ кру́жится голова́. **2,** (frivolous; silly) легкомы́сленный.

lighthearted *adj.* беззабо́тный; весёлый.

lighthouse *n.* мая́к.

lighting *n.* **1,** (act of lighting) зажига́ние: *lighting of candles,* зажига́ние свеч. **2,** (illumination) освеще́ние. —*adj.* освети́тельный: *lighting system,* освети́тельная сеть.

lightly *adv.* **1,** (gently; not heavily) легко́; слегка́. *Tread lightly,* легко́ ступа́ть. *Dressed lightly,* легко́ оде́т. **2,** (slightly) слегка́: *lightly salted,* слегка́ солёный. **3,** (not as a serious matter) несерьёзно. *Take lightly,* не принима́ть всерьёз. **4,** (with little or no penalty) легко́; дёшево: *get off lightly,* легко́/ дёшево отде́латься.

light meter экспози́метр; экспоно́метр.

lightness *n.* **1,** (brightness) све́тлость. **2,** (not being heavy) лёгкость.

lightning *n.* мо́лния. *He was/ two people were/ killed by lightning,* его́/двои́х уби́ло мо́лнией. —*adj.* молниено́сный: *with lightning speed,* с молниено́сной быстрото́й. —*v.i. It is lightning,* мо́лния сверка́ет. —**lightning bug,** светля́к. —**lightning rod,** громоотво́д; молниеотво́д.

lightproof *adj.* светонепроница́емый.

lightweight *adj.* лёгкий; легкове́сный. —*n., sports* легкове́с.

light year светово́й год.

lignite *n.* лигни́т.

likable *also,* **likeable** *adj.* симпати́чный.

like *v.t.* **1,** (be fond of) люби́ть: *He likes music,* он лю́бит му́зыку; *she likes to dance,* она́ лю́бит танцева́ть. **2,** (enjoy) *rendered by* нра́виться: *How did you like the movie?,* как вам понра́вился фильм? **3,** (wish) хоте́ть: ·*I would like a cup of tea,* я бы

хоте́л(а) ча́шку ча́ю. —*v.i.* хоте́ть: *Do as you like,* де́лайте, как хоти́те. *Ask any questions you like,* задава́йте каки́е уго́дно вопро́сы. —*prep.* **1,** (similar to) похо́ж на: *She is like her mother,* она́ похо́жа на свою́ мать. *It was like a bad dream,* э́то бы́ло похо́же на дурно́й сон. *A man like that,* тако́й челове́к. *He is just like you,* он тако́й же, как вы. *All Russians are like that,* все ру́сские таковы́. *Like most Russians, he...,* подо́бно большинству́ ру́сских, он... *What is he like?,* что он собо́й представля́ет?; что он за челове́к? *She is like a sister to me,* она́ мне как сестра́. *I've never seen anything like it,* я ничего́ подо́бного не ви́дел(а). **2,** (in a manner similar to) как: *act like a madman,* поступа́ть как безу́мец. *Don't talk like that!,* не говори́те так! *It's like trying to...,* э́то сло́вно пыта́ться (+ *inf.*). **3,** (characteristic of) похо́же; типи́чно: *That's just (or not) like him,* э́то на него́ (не) похо́же; э́то (не) типи́чно для него́. *It's not like him to be late,* опа́здывать на него́ не похо́же. —*conj.* как: *This car runs like new,* э́та маши́на как но́вая. *Love me like I am!,* люби́ меня́ таки́м, како́й я есть; люби́ меня́ тако́й, кака́я я есть. —*adj.* **1,** (similar) подо́бный: *in like manner,* подо́бным (же) о́бразом; (equal) ра́вный: *a like amount,* ра́вная су́мма. —*n.* **1,** (anything similar): *and the like,* и тому́ подо́бное. *I have never seen the like of it,* я никогда́ не ви́дел ничего́ подо́бного. *We'll not see the likes of him again,* таки́х, как он мы бо́льше не уви́дим. *A disaster the likes of which we have never seen,* катастро́фа, ра́вная кото́рой мы ещё не ви́дели. **2,** *pl.* (preferences): *likes and dislikes,* симпа́тии и антипа́тии. —**like it or not,** хо́чешь не хо́чешь; нра́вится тебе́ и́ли нет.

likeable *adj.* = likable.

likelihood *n.* вероя́тность. *In all likelihood,* по всей вероя́тности.

likely *adj.* **1,** (probable; credible) вероя́тный; правдоподо́бный. *A likely story,* правдоподо́бный расска́з. *He is likely to be late,* он, вероя́тно, опозда́ет. *That is not likely to happen,* вряд ли э́то случи́тся. **2,** (suitable) подходя́щий. —*adv.* вероя́тно. *Quite likely,* вполне́ вероя́тно. *More likely,* скоре́е. *Most likely,* скоре́е всего́.

like-minded *adj. Like-minded person,* единомы́шленник.

liken *v.t.* уподобля́ть: *liken oneself to...,* уподобля́ть себя́ (+ *dat.*). *Liken chess to war,* уподобля́ть ша́хматы войне́.

likeness *n.* **1,** (similarity) схо́дство; подо́бие. **2,** (image) ко́пия: *a perfect likeness,* то́чная ко́пия. **3,** (guise) личи́на: *in the likeness of,* под личи́ной (+ *gen.*).

likewise *adv.* **1,** (in the same manner) подо́бным о́бразом. **2,** (by the same token) ра́вным о́бразом. **3,** (also; too) та́кже.

liking *n.* симпа́тия; расположе́ние. *Take a liking to,* полюби́ть. *Be to someone's liking,* быть по душе́ (+ *dat.*).

lilac *n.* сире́нь. —*adj.* сире́невый.

lilt *n.* ритм. —**lilting,** *adj.* перели́вчатый.

lily *n.* ли́лия. —**lily of the valley,** ла́ндыш.

lima bean ли́мская фасо́ль.

limb *n.* **1,** (branch) сук; ветвь. **2,** (arm; leg) член. —**out on a limb,** *colloq.* в ша́тком (*or* в ско́льзком) положе́нии. —**tear from limb to limb,** разорва́ть *or* растерза́ть на ча́сти.

limber *adj.* **1,** (flexible; pliant) ги́бкий. **2,** (agile; nimble) прово́рный. —*v.t. & i.* [*usu.* **limber up**] размина́ть(ся).

limbo *n.* неопределённость. *In a state of limbo,* в подве́шенном состоя́нии; в состоя́нии неопределённости.

lime *n.* **1,** (citrus fruit; tree that bears it) лайм. **2,** (linden tree) ли́па. **3,** (calcium oxide, used in cement) и́звесть.

limelight *n.* огни́ ра́мпы. *Be in the limelight,* быть в це́нтре внима́ния. *Come into the limelight,* попа́сть в центр внима́ния.

limerick *n.* стихотворе́ние из пяти́ строк.

limestone *n.* известня́к. —*adj.* известняко́вый.

limewater *n.* известко́вая вода́.

limit *n.* преде́л; грани́ца. *Speed limit,* преде́льная ско́рость. *Time limit,* преде́льный срок. *City limits,* преде́лы *or* черта́ го́рода. *There is a limit to my patience,* моему́ терпе́нию есть преде́л. *That's the limit!,* э́то уж сли́шком!; э́то уже́ после́днее де́ло! —*v.t.* ограни́чивать: *limit the size of the classes/number of students/,* ограни́чивать чи́сленность кла́ссов/число́ студе́нтов/. —**off limits,** закры́т: *off limits to foreigners,* закры́т для иностра́нцев.

limitation *n.* **1,** (restriction) ограниче́ние. **2,** (drawback; weakness) недоста́ток.

limited *adj.* ограни́ченный. —**limited edition,** малотира́жное изда́ние. —**limited monarchy,** ограни́ченная мона́рхия.

limitless *adj.* безграни́чный; беспреде́льный.

limonite *n.* бу́рый железня́к.

limousine *n.* лимузи́н.

limp *v.i.* хрома́ть. —*n.* хромота́. *Have a limp; walk with a limp,* хрома́ть. —*adj.* дря́блый; вя́лый. *Go limp,* мя́кнуть; размяка́ть.

limpid *adj.* прозра́чный.

linage *n.* число́ строк.

linchpin *n.* **1,** *mech.* чека́. **2,** *fig.* (mainstay) станово́й хребе́т.

linden *n.* ли́па.

line *n.* **1,** (thin continuous mark) ли́ния; черта́. *Draw a line,* провести́ черту́. **2,** (line of writing) строка́; стро́чка. *The third line from the bottom,* тре́тья строка́ сни́зу. *Read between the lines,* чита́ть ме́жду строк. **3,** (row; file) ли́ния; ряд. **4,** (queue) о́чередь: *stand in line,* стоя́ть в о́череди. **5,** (border) грани́ца: *the state line,* грани́ца шта́та. **6,** *sports* ли́ния: *starting line,* ста́ртовая ли́ния. **7,** *pl.* (contour) ли́нии; очерта́ния. **8,** *pl.* (wrinkles) скла́дки; морщи́ны. **9,** (rope; string) верёвка: *hang the clothes on the line,* ве́шать бельё на верёвку. **10,** (fishing line) ле́ска; леса́. **11,** (course of movement or action) ли́ния: *line of flight,* ли́ния полёта; *line of fire* ли́ния огня́. **12,** *mil.* ли́ния: *front line,* ли́ния фро́нта. *Behind enemy lines,* в тылу́ проти́вника. **13,** (system of transportation) ли́ния: *bus line,* авто́бусная ли́ния. **14,** *R.R.* ли́ния. *Main line,* магистра́ль. *Branch line,* ве́тка. **15,** (wires to connect electricity; telephone connection) ли́ния; про́вод: *power lines,* ли́нии электропереда́чи; *telephone line,* телефо́нный про́вод. *The line is busy,* ли́ния занята́. *Direct line,* прямо́й про́вод. *The chief is on the line,* нача́льник на про́воде. *The voice on the other end of the line,* го́лос на друго́м конце́ про́вода. **16,** *pl.* (actor's part) роль: *memorize one's lines,* зау́чивать роль. **17,** (attitude; policy) ли́ния: *take a hard line,* занима́ть жёсткую ли́нию. **18,** (succession of descendants) ли́ния: *the male line,* мужска́я ли́ния. *He is next in line for the throne,* он прямо́й насле́дник престо́ла. —*v.t.* **1,** (mark with lines) линова́ть. **2,** *fol. by* **up** (arrange in a line) выстра́ивать. **3,** (put a lining in) де́лать *or* подшива́ть подкла́дку к; подбива́. **4,** (fill; cram) заставля́ть: *The shelves are lined with books,* по́лки заста́влены кни́гами. **5,** (form a line along) вы́строиться вдоль. —*v.i.* [*usu.* **line up**] выстра́иваться. —**all along the line,** по всех отноше́ниях; во всём. —**bring into line,** приводи́ть в соотве́тствие. —**draw the line,** проводи́ть чёткую черту́ (*or* грань). —**drop me a line,** пришли́те мне ве́сточку; черкни́те мне не́сколько слов. —**get a line on,** разузна́ть о. —**hold the line, 1,** *mil.* держа́ть оборо́ну. **2,** (stand firm) держа́ться. **3,** (not hang up the telephone) не ве́шать тру́бку. —**in line with,** в соотве́тствии с. —**in the line of duty,** при исполне́нии служе́бных обя́занностей. —**lay it on the line,** *colloq.* говори́ть напрями́к. —**line of work,** род заня́тий. —**not in/out of my line,** не по мое́й ча́сти. —**out of line, 1,** (not aligned) не в ряд. **2,** (improper; uncalled-for) неуме́стный.

lineage *n.* родосло́вная; происхожде́ние.

lineal *adj.* прямо́й: *lineal descendant,* прямо́й пото́мок.

linear *adj.* лине́йный. —**linear equation,** лине́йное уравне́ние. —**linear measure,** лине́йная ме́ра; ме́ра длины́.

lined *adj.* **1,** (ruled) лино́ванный; в лине́йку. **2,** (wrinkled) морщи́нистый. **3,** (having a lining) на подкла́дке.

lineman *n.* лине́йный монтёр.

linen *n.* **1,** (fabric) полотно́; холст. **2,** (articles made of linen or other cloth) бельё: *bed linen,* посте́льное бельё. —*adj.* **1,** (made of linen) льняно́й; полотня́ный; холщёвый. **2,** (for linen) бельево́й: *linen closet,* бельево́й шкаф.

liner *n.* **1,** (ship) ла́йнер. **2,** (plane) возду́шный ла́йнер. **3,** (lining) подкла́дка.

linesman *n.* **1,** *sports* судья́ на ли́нии. **2,** = **lineman.**

lineup *n.* соста́в (кома́нды). *Starting lineup,* ста́ртовый соста́в.

linger *v.i.* **1,** (tarry) заде́рживаться. **2,** (continue to exist; remain alive) протяну́ть.

lingerie *n.* да́мское бельё. *Lingerie department,* бельево́й отде́л.

lingo *n.* жарго́н.

linguist *n.* языкове́д; лингви́ст. —**linguistic,** *adj.* языково́й; лингвисти́ческий. —**linguistics,** *n.* языкозна́ние; лингви́стика.

liniment *n.* втира́ние.

lining *n.* подкла́дка: *silk lining,* шёлковая подкла́дка. *Brake lining,* тормозна́я накла́дка. —**every cloud has a silver lining,** нет ху́да без добра́.

link *n.* **1,** (part of a chain) звено́. **2,** (tie; connection) связь. —*v.t.* соединя́ть; свя́зывать. *The bridge links the two halves of the city,* мост соединя́ет о́бе ча́сти го́рода. —*v.i.* [*usu.* **link up**] соединя́ться; смыка́ться. —**linking verb,** глаго́л-свя́зка.

linkage *n.* **1,** (act of linking; coupling) сцепле́ние. *Genetic linkage,* сцепле́ние ге́нов. **2,** (connection) связь. **3,** (linking of two issues) увя́зка.

linnet *n.* конопля́нка; реполо́в.

linoleum *n.* лино́леум.

linotype *n.* линоти́п.

linseed *n.* льняно́е се́мя. —**linseed oil,** льняно́е ма́сло.

lint *n.* **1,** (fluff) пушо́к. **2,** (substance formerly used for dressing wounds) ко́рпия.

lintel *n.* перемы́чка; прито́лока.

lion *n.* лев. —*adj.* [*also,* **lion's**] льви́ный: *lion skin,* льви́ная шку́ра. —**lion's share,** льви́ная до́ля.

lioness *n.* льви́ца.

lionize *v.t.* поднима́ть на щит.

lip *n.* губа́. —**be on everyone's lips,** быть у всех на уста́х. —**keep a stiff upper lip,** храбри́ться. —**my lips are sealed,** у меня́ рот на замке́. —**none of your lip!,** без де́рзостей! —**pay lip service to,** признава́ть то́лько на слова́х.

lip reading чте́ние с губ.

lipstick *n.* губна́я пома́да.

liquefy *v.t.* сжижа́ть. *Liquefied gas,* сжи́женный газ. —**liquefaction,** *n.* сжиже́ние.

liqueur *n.* ликёр.

liquid *n.* жи́дкость. —*adj.* **1,** (fluid) жи́дкий. **2,** *finance* ликви́дный: *liquid assets,* ликви́дные сре́дства. —**liquid measure,** ме́ра жи́дкости.

liquidate *v.t.* ликвиди́ровать. —**liquidation,** *n.* ликвида́ция.

liquidity *n.* ликви́дность.

liquor *n.* спиртны́е напи́тки.

liquorice *n.* = licorice.

lira *n.* ли́ра.

lisp *n.* шепеля́вость; сюсю́канье. —*v.i.* шепеля́вить; сюсю́кать.

lissome *also,* **lissom** *adj.* **1,** (supple) ги́бкий. **2,** (agile) прово́рный.

list *n.* **1,** (enumeration) спи́сок. *He was last on the list,* в спи́ске он стоя́л после́дним. **2,** (tilt, as of a ship) крен. —*v.t.* **1,** (make a list of) составля́ть спи́сок (+ *gen.*). **2,** (include in a list) вноси́ть в спи́сок. *Be listed,* чи́слиться; зна́читься. —*v.i.* (of a boat or ship) крени́ться. *The boat is listing,* ло́дку кло́нит на́ бок.

listen *v.i.* слу́шать: *listen to the music/ one's parents/,* слу́шать му́зыку/роди́телей/. *Listen to* (*someone's*) *advice,* слу́шать сове́ты; прислу́шиваться к сове́там.

listener *n.* слу́шатель.

listening *n.* слу́шание. —**listening device,** подслу́шивающее устро́йство. —**listening post,** пункт *or* пост подслу́шивания.

listless *adj.* вя́лый; апати́чный. —**listlessly,** *adv.* вя́ло. —**listlessness,** *n.* вя́лость.

list price прейскура́нтная цена́.

litany *n.* лита́ния.

liter *also,* **litre** *n.* литр.

literacy *n.* гра́мотность.

literal *adj.* **1,** (reflecting the exact meaning) буква́льный. **2,** (word for word) досло́вный. —**literally,** *adv.* буква́льно; досло́вно.

literary *adj.* литерату́рный.

literate *adj.* гра́мотный.

literature *n.* литерату́ра.

lithe *adj.* **1,** (supple) ги́бкий. **2,** (graceful) стро́йный.

lithium *n.* ли́тий.

lithograph *n.* литогра́фия; литогра́фский о́ттиск. —*v.t.* литографи́ровать. —**lithographer,** *n.* лито́граф. —**lithographic,** *adj.* литогра́фский. —**lithography,** *n.* литогра́фия.

lithosphere *n.* литосфе́ра.

Lithuanian *adj.* лито́вский. —*n.* **1,** (person) лито́вец; лито́вка. **2,** (language) лито́вский язы́к.

litigate *v.i.* суди́ться. —**litigation,** *n.* иск; суде́бное де́ло.

litmus *n.* ла́кмус. —**litmus paper,** ла́кмусовая бума́га.

litre *n.* = liter.

litter *n.* **1,** (trash) сор; му́сор. **2,** (stretcher) носи́лки. **3,** (animals born at one time) помёт; вы́водок. —*v.t.* сори́ть; засоря́ть; замусо́рить. *Litter the floor,* сори́ть на́ пол; засоря́ть *or* заму́сорить пол. *Litter the room,* сори́ть в ко́мнате; засоря́ть *or* заму́сорить ко́мнату. *The floor is littered with paper,* на полу́ разбро́сана бума́га. —*v.i.* сори́ть: *"Do not litter!",* не сори́ть!

little *adj.* **1,** (small in size) ма́ленький; небольшо́й. **2,** (small in amount) ма́ло: *little time/hope,* ма́ло вре́мени/наде́жды. *Little cause for alarm,* ма́ло основа́ний для трево́ги. *Have little effect on,* ма́ло поде́йствовать на. —*adv.* ма́ло: *too little,* сли́шком ма́ло. *Things have changed very little,* де́ло о́чень ма́ло измени́лось. *Little did he suspect that...,* совсе́м не подозрева́л, что... —*n.* ма́ло; ма́лое; ма́ло что. *I ate very little,* я ел (е́ла) о́чень ма́ло. *Be satisfied with little,* дово́льствоваться ма́лым. *Little has changed,* ма́ло что измени́лось. *Little remains of..,* ма́ло что оста́лось от... *We see very little of them,* мы ре́дко ви́димся с ни́ми. *I have little to add,* мне почти́ не́чего доба́вить. —**a little,** немно́го: *a little water,* немно́го воды́; *a little tired,* немно́го уста́л; *a little better,* немно́го лу́чше. ♦ *With comp. adjectives, also rendered by the prefix* по-: *a little later,* попо́зже; *a little louder,* погро́мче. —**as little as,** всего́ лишь: *for as little as $100,* всего́ лишь за сто до́лларов. *As little as a year ago,* ещё год наза́д. —**little by little,** понемно́гу; ма́ло-пома́лу. —**what little,** то немно́гое, что: *I did what little I could,* я сделал то немно́гое, что мог. *From what little is known about him*, из того́ немно́гого, что изве́стно о нём.

little finger мизи́нец.

little-known *adj.* малоизве́стный.

liturgy *n.* литурги́я. —**liturgical**, *adj.* литурги́ческий.

livable *also,* **liveable** *adj.* **1,** (nice to live in) удо́бный для жилья́. **2,** (endurable, as of life) сно́сный.

live¹ (liv) *v.i. & t.* жить: *live next door*, жить ря́дом. *Live forever*, жить ве́чно. *Live to a ripe old age*, дожи́ть до ста́рости. *Live a normal life*, жить норма́льной жи́знью. *Live a long life*, прожи́ть до́лгую жизнь. *Had he lived one year longer*, прожи́ви он ещё оди́н год. —**live down**, искупа́ть; загла́живать. —**live for**, жить (+ *instr.*): *live for one's son*, жить свои́м сы́ном. *I have nothing to live for*, мне не́зачем жить. —**live it up**, *colloq.* разгу́ливаться. —**live off, 1,** (use to live on) жить на (+ *acc.*): *live off one's savings*, жить на свои́ сбереже́ния. **2,** (sponge off) жить за счёт (+ *gen.*). —**live on, 1,** (support oneself on) жить на (+ *acc.*): *live on a pension*, жить на пе́нсию. *What are they living on?*, на что они́ живу́т?; на каки́е сре́дства они́ живу́т? *You can't live on that*, на э́то жить нельзя́; на э́то прожи́ть невозмо́жно. *I have enough to live on*, мне хвата́ет на жизнь. *It's hardly enough to live on*, э́того едва́ хвата́ет на жизнь. *I have nothing to live on*, мне не́ на что жить. **2,** (subsist on) пита́ться (+ *instr.*): *live on fruit*, пита́ться фру́ктами. **3,** (not fade from memory) жить. *His name will live on*, его́ и́мя не умрёт. —**live out**, дожива́ть: *live out one's last days*, дожива́ть после́дние дни. —**live through**, пережива́ть. —**live up to, 1,** (abide by) соблюда́ть; выполня́ть. *Live up to a promise*, сдержа́ть *or* вы́полнить обеща́ние. *Live up to an agreement*, приде́рживаться догово́ра. *Live up to (one's end of) a bargain*, вы́полнить усло́вия сде́лки. **2,** (satisfy) опра́вдывать: *live up to expectations/ one's reputation/*, опра́вдывать ожида́ния/ свою́ репута́цию/. —**live with, 1,** (cohabit with) жить с. **2,** (learn to accept) мири́ться с. *Learn to live with*, притерпе́ться к.

live² (laiv) *adj.* **1,** (alive) живо́й: *live animals*, живы́е живо́тные. **2,** (burning) горя́чий: *live coals*, горя́чие у́гли. **3,** (active, as of a volcano) де́йствующий. **4,** (charged with electricity) под напряже́нием. **5,** (not exploded) боево́й: *live ammunition*, боевы́е патро́ны. **6,** (broadcast while being performed) прямо́й: *live broadcasting*, прямо́е веща́ние; прямо́й эфи́р.

liveable *adj.* = **livable**.

livelihood *n.* сре́дства к жи́зни. *Earn one's livelihood*, зараба́тывать на жизнь.

liveliness *n.* жи́вость; оживлённость.

lively *adj.* **1,** (active) живо́й: *lively baby*, живо́й ребёнок. **2,** (brisk; bouncy) задо́рный: *lively dance/tune*, задо́рный та́нец/моти́в. **3,** (animated) оживлённый: *lively discussion*, оживлённая диску́ссия. —*adv.* in **step lively!**, скоре́й!; побыстре́е!

liven *v.t.* [*usu.* **liven up**] оживля́ть. —*v.i.* [*usu.* **liven up**] оживля́ться.

liver *n.* **1,** (organ) пе́чень. **2,** (meat) печёнка. —*adj.* печёночный: *liver extract*, печёночный экстра́кт.

liveried *adj.* в ливре́е; ливре́йный.

liverwort *n.* печёночник.

liverwurst *n.* ли́верная колбаса́.

livery *n.* ливре́я. —**livery stable**, пла́тная коню́шня.

livestock *n.* (дома́шний) скот; живо́й инвента́рь.

livid *adj.* **1,** (pale) (ме́ртвенно) бле́дный. **2,** (incensed) разъярённый; вне себя́ от я́рости.

living *n.* **1,** (manner or means of living) жизнь: *cost of living*, сто́имость жи́зни; *standard of living*, у́ровень жи́зни. *Earn a living*, зараба́тывать на жизнь. **2,** preceded by **the** (those who are alive) живы́е. —*adj.* **1,** (alive; in use) живо́й. *People no longer living*, лю́ди, кото́рых уже́ нет в живы́х. **2,** (pert. to living) жили́щный: *living conditions*, жили́щные усло́вия. *Living quarters*, жило́е помеще́ние.

living room гости́ная. *Living room furniture*, ме́бель для гости́ной.

lizard *n.* я́щерица.

llama *n.* ла́ма.

lo *interj.* вот! —**lo and behold!**, и вот!; и вдруг!

load *n.* **1,** (something carried) груз; тя́жесть. *Heavy load*, тяжёлый груз. *Carry a load on one's back*, нести́ груз/тя́жесть на спине́. **2,** (work performed) нагру́зка: *teaching load*, преподава́тельская нагру́зка; *peak load*, максима́льная нагру́зка. **3,** *fig.* (burden) бре́мя; тя́жесть; но́ша. *Load off one's shoulders*, тя́жесть *or* гора́ с плеч. *Load off one's mind*, ка́мень с души́ свали́лся. **4,** *pl., fol. by of, colloq.* (a great deal of) ма́сса (+ *gen.*): *We have loads of time*, у нас ма́сса вре́мени. —*v.t.* **1,** (place on a conveyance; place cargo on) грузи́ть; нагружа́ть: *load grain onto trucks*, грузи́ть/нагружа́ть зерно́ на грузовики́; *load trucks with grain*, грузи́ть/нагружа́ть грузовики́ зерно́м. **2,** (place; insert) вставля́ть. *Load film into a camera*, вставля́ть *or* заправля́ть плёнку в фотоаппара́т. **3,** (put ammunition or film into) заряжа́ть. **4,** often fol. by **down** (fill; cover; weigh down) зава́ливать. —*v.i.* **1,** (take on cargo) грузи́ться. **2,** fol. by **into** (board in large numbers) грузи́ться (в); погружа́ться (в): *load into a bus*, грузи́ться/ погружа́ться в авто́бус.

loaded *adj.* **1,** (carrying a load) загру́женный; нагру́женный; гружёный. **2,** (filled to capacity) перепо́лненный. **3,** (ready to fire) заря́женный: *loaded gun*, заря́женный пистоле́т. **4,** (overburdened) зава́ленный: *loaded with work*, зава́лен рабо́той. **5,** *slang* (rich) при деньга́х. *He is loaded*, он купа́ется в зо́лоте. **6,** *slang* (drunk) пья́ный. *Get loaded*, напива́ться.

loading *n.* погру́зка. —*adj.* погру́зочный: *loading machine*, погру́зочная маши́на.

loaf *n.* буха́нка. *Long loaf*, бато́н. *Round loaf*, карава́й. —*v.i.* безде́льничать; ло́дырничать.

loafer *n.* **1,** (idler) безде́льник; ло́дырь. **2,** (casual shoe) спорти́вная ту́фля.

loam *n.* сугли́нок; су́песь. —**loamy**, *adj.* сугли́нистый.

loan *n.* заём; ссу́да. *A loan of two million dollars*, заём в два миллио́на до́лларов. —*v.t.* одолжа́ть; ссу-жа́ть; дава́ть взаймы́.

loan translation ка́лька.

loanword *n.* заи́мствованное сло́во.

loath *adj.* неохо́тный. *Be loath to,* не хоте́ть (+ *inf.*).

loathe *v.t.* ненави́деть. —**loathing,** *n.* отвраще́ние; омерзе́ние. —**loathsome,** *adj.* отврати́тельный; омерзи́тельный.

lob *v.t.* высоко́ подбра́сывать (мяч).

lobby *n.* **1,** (hall; anteroom) вестибю́ль; фойе́; (*of a hotel*) холл. **2,** *polit.* ло́бби. —**lobbyist,** *n.* лобби́ст.

lobe *n.* до́ля. *Ear lobe,* мо́чка.

lobster *n.* ома́р.

lobule *n.* до́лька.

local *adj.* ме́стный: *local newspaper,* ме́стная газе́та. *6:00 local time,* шесть часо́в по ме́стному вре́мени. —*n.* **1,** (local resident) ме́стный жи́тель. **2,** (local train) при́городный по́езд. —**local anesthetic,** ме́стный нарко́з. —**local color,** ме́стный колори́т.

locale *n.* ме́сто де́йствия.

locality *n.* ме́стность; райо́н.

localize *v.t.* локализова́ть. —**localization,** *n.* локали-за́ция.

locally *adv.* в э́тих места́х; в э́тих края́х; в э́том райо́не.

locate *v.t.* **1,** (place; situate) располага́ть: *locate a factory near a river,* располага́ть фа́брику у реки́. *Be located somewhere,* находи́ться где́-нибудь; быть располо́женным где́-нибудь. **2,** (find) найти́; разы́ска́ть. *Locate a town on a map,* найти́ городо́к на ка́рте.

location *n.* **1,** (place where something is) местона-хожде́ние. **2,** (site) местоположе́ние. *Move to a new location,* переходи́ть на но́вое ме́сто. **3,** *motion pictures* нату́ра: *on location,* на нату́ре.

locative *adj.,* in **locative case,** предло́жный паде́ж; ме́стный паде́ж.

locator *n.* лока́тор: *sound locator,* звуково́й лока́тор.

lock *n.* **1,** (on a door or box) замо́к. **2,** (of a canal) шлюз. **3,** (curl of hair) ло́кон. —*v.t.* **1,** [*also,* **lock up**] (secure with a lock; confine) запира́ть; закрыва́ть: *lock the door,* запира́ть/закрыва́ть дверь. *Lock something in the desk,* запира́ть что́-нибудь в стол. *Lock oneself in one's room,* запира́ться в свое́й ко́мнате. **2,** (interlock) сцепля́ться: *lock horns/bumpers,* сце-пля́ться рога́ми/буфера́ми. *Be locked in mortal combat,* сцепля́ться в смерте́льной схва́тке. —*v.i.* запира́ться: *The door won't lock,* дверь не запира́ется. —**lock, stock and barrel,** целико́м; по́лностью; «со все́ми потроха́ми». —**under lock and key,** под замко́м.

locker *n.* (запира́ющийся) шка́фчик. —**locker room,** раздева́лка.

locket *n.* медальо́н.

lockjaw *n.* тризм; столбня́к.

lockout *n.* лока́ут.

locksmith *n.* сле́сарь.

locomotion *n.* передвиже́ние.

locomotive *n.* локомоти́в; парово́з. —*adj.* дви́жу-щий.

locus *n.* геометри́ческое ме́сто то́чек.

locust *n.* саранча́.

locution *n.* оборо́т ре́чи; рече́ние.

lode *n.* (ру́дная) жи́ла.

lodestar *n.* путево́дная звезда́.

lodge *n.* **1,** (hut; cabin) до́мик; сторо́жка. *Hunting lodge,* охо́тничий до́мик. **2,** (base for outdoor activity) ба́за: *skiing lodge,* лы́жная ба́за. **3,** (fraternal society) ло́жа. —*v.t.* **1,** (house) помеща́ть; вселя́ть. **2,** (file; register): *lodge a complaint,* подава́ть жа́лобу; *lodge a protest,* заяви́ть *or* вы́разить проте́ст. —*v.i.* **1,** (be housed) помеща́ться. **2,** (become embedded) засе́сть: *The bullet lodged in his shoulder,* пу́ля засе́ла у него́ в плече́.

lodger *n.* жиле́ц.

lodging *n.* помеще́ние; жильё. *Lodging for the night,* ночле́г.

loft *n.* **1,** (attic) черда́к. **2,** (hayloft) сенова́л. **3,** (balcony, as for a choir) хо́ры.

lofty *adj.* высо́кий; возвы́шенный. —**loftiness,** *n.* возвы́шенность.

log *n.* **1,** (piece of timber) бревно́. **2,** (same used for burning) поле́но. **3,** *pl.* (timber floated down a river) лес. **4,** (daily record) формуля́р. *Ship's log,* ва́хтен-ный *or* бортово́й *or* судово́й журна́л. —*adj.* бреве́нчатый. *Log cabin,* бреве́нчатый до́мик; изба́. —*v.t.* **1,** (enter in a log) вноси́ть в журна́л. **2,** (cover, as a certain distance) пройти́; прое́хать. *Log 2,000 flying hours,* налета́ть две ты́сячи часо́в. —**sleep like a log,** спать как суро́к.

logarithm *n.* логари́фм. —**logarithmic,** *adj.* лога-рифми́ческий.

loge *n.* ло́жа.

logger *n.* лесору́б.

loggerheads *n.pl.,* in **at loggerheads,** не в лада́х; на ножа́х. *Set at loggerheads,* ста́лкивать лба́ми (+ *acc.*).

logic *n.* ло́гика. —**logical,** *adj.* логи́ческий; логи́чный. —**logically,** *adv.* логи́чески; логи́чно. —**logician,** *n* ло́гик.

logistics *n.* тыл и снабже́ние; тылово́е обеспе́чение; материа́льно-техни́ческое обеспе́чение. —**logistical,** *adj.* тылово́й.

loin *n.* **1,** (part of the back) поясни́ца. **2,** *pl.* (region of the thigh and groin) пах. —**loincloth,** *n.* набе́дренная повя́зка.

loiter *v.i.* **1,** (drift about) слоня́ться. **2,** (dawdle) ме́шкать. —**loiterer,** *n.* лоды́рь.

loll *v.i.* валя́ться; не́житься.

lollipop *n.* ледене́ц (на па́лочке).

lone *adj.* одино́кий: *a lone gunman,* одино́кий банди́т.

loneliness *n.* одино́чество.

lonely *adj.* **1,** (lonesome) одино́кий. *Lead a lonely existence,* жить одино́ко. **2,** (solitary) уедине́нный. **3,** (little frequented) глухо́й: *a lonely street,* глуха́я у́лица.

loner *n., colloq.* дика́рь; бирю́к.

lonesome *adj.* одино́кий.

lone wolf одино́чка; бирю́к.

long *adj.* **1,** (of considerable length) дли́нный: *long dress*, дли́нное пла́тье; *long line*, дли́нная о́чередь; *long hair*, дли́нные во́лосы. *A long distance*, большо́е расстоя́ние. *A long book*, больша́я кни́га. *A long trip* (*in distance*), да́льняя пое́здка; далёкое путеше́ствие. *The dress is two inches too long*, пла́тье длинне́е на два дю́йма. *We* (*still*) *have a long way to go*, нам ещё далеко́ éхать. **2,** (having a specified length): длино́й; в длину́: *This table is six feet long*, э́тот стол в шесть фу́тов длино́й; э́тот стол имéет шесть фу́тов в длину́. **3,** (of considerable duration) до́лгий; дли́нный. *Long life*, до́лгая жизнь. *A long silence*, до́лгое молча́ние. *Long trip* (*in time*), до́лгий путь; до́лгое путеше́ствие. *Long speech/pause*, дли́нная речь/па́уза. *After a long illness*, по́сле дли́тельной боле́зни. *We had a long talk*, у нас была́ до́лгая бесе́да. *That won't happen for a long time*, э́то случи́тся о́чень не ско́ро. **4,** (taking a long time): *I won't be long*, я не до́лго; я не надо́лго. *He was not long in answering*, он не заме́длил с отве́том. **5,** *Long face*, вы́тянутое лицо́. —*adv.* **1,** (for a long time in the past or future) до́лго: *Did you have to wait long?*, вам пришло́сь до́лго ждать? *It was long believed that...*, до́лгое вре́мя счита́лось, что... *He hasn't long to live*, ему́ оста́лось недо́лго жить. *Independence did not last for long*, незави́симость дли́лась недо́лго. **2,** (for a long time up to and including the present) давно́: *Have you been waiting long?*, вы давно́ ждёте? **3,** (for the duration of) напролёт: *all night long*, всю ночь напролёт. —*n.* мно́го вре́мени: *It won't take long*, э́то не займёт мно́го вре́мени. —*v.i.* **1,** *fol. by* **for** (await eagerly) о́чень ждать; ждать с нетерпе́нием; ждать не дожда́ться. *Long for spring to arrive*, ждать не дожда́ться наступле́ния весны́. **2,** *fol. by inf.* (earnestly desire) жа́ждать: *long to see someone*, жа́ждать уви́деть кого́-нибудь. —**any longer**; **no longer,** бо́льше не; ужé не: *It's no longer a joke*, э́то ужé не шу́тка. —**as long as, 1,** (for all the time that) пока́: *as long as I live*, пока́ я жив (жива́). *As long as you like*, ско́лько хоти́те. **2,** (seeing that; inasmuch as) так как; ввиду́ того́, что. **3,** (provided that) éсли то́лько; лишь бы. *As long as he is not there*, éсли то́лько его́ там не бу́дет; лишь бы его́ нé было там. —**at long last,** наконéц-то. —**before long,** в ско́ром врéмени. —**for a long time, 1,** (in the past or future) до́лго. **2,** (up to and including the present) давно́. **3,** (following the action described) надо́лго: *He went away for a long time*, он уéхал надо́лго. —**how long?, 1,** (for how much time) ско́лько врéмени?; как до́лго? *How long have you been waiting?*, ско́лько вы ужé ждёте? **2,** (until when) до каки́х пор? **3,** (in length): *How long is this carpet?*, какова́ длина́ э́того ковра́?; како́й длины́ э́тот ковёр? —**in the long run,** *see* **run.** —**long after,** до́лгое врéмя по́сле. —**long ago,** давно́. —**long before,** задо́лго до. —**long live...!,** да здра́вствует (+ *nom.*). —**so long, 1,** (for such a long time) так до́лго. **2,** (goodbye) до свида́ния!; пока́!

long-awaited *adj.* долгожда́нный.

long-distance *adj.* на да́льнее расстоя́ние; на дли́нную диста́нцию: *long-distance flight*, полёт на да́льнее расстоя́ние; *long-distance race*, бег на дли́нную диста́нцию. *Long-distance train*, по́езд да́льнего слéдования. *Long-distance telephone call*, междугоро́дный телефо́нный разгово́р.

longevity *n.* долгове́чность; долголе́тие.

long-haired *adj.* длинноволо́сый.

longhand *n.* по́черк. *Written in longhand*, напи́санный от руки́.

longing *n.* стремле́ние; жа́жда. —*adj.* тоску́ющий: *a longing look*, тоску́ющий взгляд. —**longingly,** *adv.* с тоско́й; тоскли́во.

longitude *n.* долгота́. —**longitudinal,** *adj.* продо́льный.

long-lasting *adj.* про́чный; сто́йкий.

long-legged *adj.* длинноно́гий.

long-lived *adj.* долговéчный; многолéтний.

long-playing *adj.* долгоигра́ющий.

long-range *adj.* **1,** (of a weapon or aircraft) да́льнего дéйствия; дальнобо́йный. **2,** (long-term, as of plans or planning) долгосро́чный; перспекти́вный.

longshoreman *n.* (порто́вый) гру́зчик; до́кер.

long shot 1, *horse racing* аутса́йдер. **2,** (unpromising venture): *It's a long shot*, ша́нсов ма́ло. —**not by a long shot,** нико́им о́бразом; далеко́ не. *Not everyone by a long shot*, далеко́ не все.

long-sleeved *adj.* с дли́нными рукава́ми.

long-standing *adj.* да́вний; давни́шний.

long-suffering *adj.* многострада́льный.

long-term *adj.* долгосро́чный.

long wave дли́нная волна́. —**long-wave,** *adj.* длинново́лновый.

longways *adv.* в длину́; вдоль.

long-winded *adj.* многосло́вный.

look *v.i.* **1,** (use one's sense of sight) смотрéть: *Look this way!*, смотри́те сюда́! *Look at one's watch*, (по)смотрéть на часы́. *Look at oneself in the mirror*, смотрéться в зéркало. *Look who's here!*, посмотри́, кто пришёл! **2,** (appear; seem) вы́глядеть; имéть (како́й-нибудь) вид: *She looks well*, она́ вы́глядит хорошо́; у неё хоро́ший вид. *You look as if you want to leave*, у вас тако́й вид, бу́дто вы хоти́те уйти́. *The dress looks well on you*, пла́тье вам идёт. *You can't go there looking like that*, нельзя́ пойти́ туда́ в тако́м ви́де. —*v.t.* **1,** (face squarely) смотрéть (+ *dat.*): *look someone in the face*, смотрéть кому́-нибудь в лицо́. **2,** (appear to be a certain age) вы́глядеть: *look one's age*, вы́глядеть на свой во́зраст. *She doesn't look her age*, она́ вы́глядит моло́же свои́х лет. *He looks about 40*, ему́ на вид о́коло сорока́. *He is 35, but looks 25*, ему́ три́дцать пять, но вы́глядит он на два́дцать пять. —*n.* **1,** (glance) взгляд: *angry look*, серди́тый взгляд. *Have a look at*, посмотрéть (+ *acc.*). **2,** (expression) выраже́ние лица́. *A look of sadness*, выраже́ние гру́сти. **3,** (appearance) вид; о́блик; нару́жность; внéшность. *Judge something by its looks*, суди́ть о чём-нибудь по внéшнему ви́ду. —**look after,** присма́тривать за; уха́живать за; следи́ть за; смотрéть за. —**look ahead,** смотрéть or заглянýть вперёд. —**look around, 1,** (turn around and look back) оборáчиваться. **2,** (look all around) смотрéть кругóм; осмáтриваться; оглядываться. —**look away,** смотрéть в стóрону. —**look back,** оглядываться (назáд). —**look down on,** смотрéть свысокá на; пренебрегáть. —**look for,** искáть. —**look forward to,** óчень ждать; ждать с нетерпéнием; предвкушáть. *I'll look forward to it,* я с удовóльствием бýду ждать. —**look here!,** послýшайте! —**look in on,** заглянýть к. —**look into,** рассмáтривать; расслéдовать. *Look into the future,* заглянýть в бýдущее. —**look like, 1,** (resemble) быть похóжим на; вýглядеть (+ *instr.*). *She looks like you,* онá похóжа на вас. *He looks like an old man,* он вýглядит старикóм. *That outfit makes you look like an old woman,* э́тот наряд дéлает тебя старýхой. **2,** (be of a certain appearance): *What does he look like?,* какóв он собóй? **3,** *colloq.* (seem as if): *It looks like rain,* похóже, что бýдет дождь. —**look out, 1,** *literally* выгля́дывать. *Look out the window,* смотрéть *or* выгля́дывать в окнó *or* из окнá. **2,** (be careful) быть осторóжным; глядéть в óба. *Look out!,* осторóжно! **3,** *fol. by* **for** (beware of) берéчься (+ *gen.*). **4,** *fol. by* **for** (protect) берéчь. **5,** *fol. by* **on** (face) выходи́ть; смотрéть (*with* в *or* на). —**look over, 1,** *literally* смотрéть чéрез; загля́дывать чéрез: *look over one's shoulder,* смотрéть/загля́дывать чéрез плечó. *Look over a cliff,* смотрéть со скалы́. **2,** (examine; inspect) (по)смотрéть: *look over the new apartment,* посмотрéть нóвую кварти́ру. **3,** (read quickly; scan) просмáтривать. —**look through, 1,** (peep through) смотрéть в; загля́дывать в. *Look through a telescope,* смотрéть в телескóп. *Look through a hole in the fence,* смотрéть в (*or* чéрез) ды́рку в забóре. **2,** (read through) просмáтривать. —**look to,** рассчи́тывать на. —**look up, 1,** *literally* поднимáть *or* вски́нуть глазá. **2,** (seek in a reference book) искáть; смотрéть: *look up a word in the dictionary,* искáть/смотрéть слóво в словарé. **3,** *fol. by* **to** (admire; respect) преклоня́ться пéред; смотрéть на (+ *acc.*) сни́зу вверх. **4,** *colloq.* (call on; visit) заходи́ть к; заглянýть к. **5,** *colloq.* (get better) поправля́ться: *Things are looking up,* делá поправля́ются. —**look upon,** считáть; рассмáтривать.

looking glass зéркало.

lookout *n.* **1,** (act of watching) наблюдéние: *keep a lookout,* вести́ наблюдéние. *Be on the lookout,* быть насторожé. *Be on the lookout for,* подстерегáть. **2,** (place for keeping watch) наблюдáтельный пункт.

loom *n.* ткáцкий станóк. —*v.i.* **1,** (appear) виднéться; вырисóвываться; мáячить. **2,** (impend) надвигáться. *Loom on the horizon* (*fig.*), мáячить на горизóнте.

loon *n.* гагáра.

loony *adj., slang* сумасбрóдный.

loop *n.* **1,** (doubled cord) пéтля. **2,** *aero.* мёртвая пéтля: *loop the loop,* дéлать мёртвую пéтлю. —*v.t.* обмáтывать.

loophole *n.* лазéйка: *leave oneself a loophole,* остáвить себé лазéйку.

loose *adj.* **1,** (not tight or taut) слáбый: *loose knot,* слáбый ýзел. **2,** (loose-fitting) свобóдный: *loose collar,* свобóдный воротни́к. *Loose clothing,* свобóдная *or* простóрная одéжда. **3,** (not firmly fastened; not firmly in place) шатáющийся: *I have a loose tooth,* у меня́ зуб шатáется. *You have a button loose,* у вас пýговица болтáется. **4,** (not dense, as of soil) ры́хлый. **5,** (dissolute) распýтный. *Loose morals,* лёгкие нрáвы. —*adv.* свобóдно. —*v.t.* **1,** (loosen) ослабля́ть. **2,** (shoot; let fly) стреля́ть; пускáть. —**at loose ends,** без дéла; не у дел. —**break loose,** вырывáться; срывáться. —**come loose, 1,** (come untied) развя́зываться; отвя́зываться. **2,** (be dislodged from a fixed position) расшáтываться; ослабевáть. —**loose bowels,** понóс. —**loose talk,** кривотóлки. —**loose tongue,** язы́к без костéй. —**loose translation,** нетóчный перевóд. —**on the loose,** на свобóде. —**set/let/turn loose,** отпускáть. —**work loose,** выпýтываться; вывёртываться.

loose-fitting *adj.* свобóдный; ширóкий.

loose-leaf *adj.* с вкладны́ми листáми.

loosely *adv.* **1,** (not tightly) свобóдно: *fit loosely,* сидéть свобóдно. **2,** (not strictly) ширóко: *interpret loosely,* ширóко толковáть.

loosen *v.t.* **1,** (make less tight) ослабля́ть; отпускáть; распускáть. *Loosen someone's tongue,* развязáть комý-нибудь язы́к. **2,** (make less dense, as soil) рыхли́ть; разрыхля́ть. —*v.i.* ослабевáть.

loot *n.* добы́ча. —*v.t.* грáбить; разгрáбить. —**looter,** *n.* граби́тель. —**looting,** *n.* грабёж; разграблéние.

lop *v.t.* [*usu.* **lop off**] отрубáть; обрубáть.

lope *v.i.* бежáть вприпры́жку.

lop-eared *adj.* лопоýхий; вислоýхий.

lopsided *adj.* кривобóкий; однобóкий.

loquacious *adj.* болтли́вый; говорли́вый; разговóрчивый. —**loquaciousness,** *n.* болтли́вость; говорли́вость; разговóрчивость.

lord *n.* **1,** (ruler; master) влады́ка; повели́тель; властели́н. **2,** (British title) лорд: *House of Lords,* палáта лóрдов. **3,** *cap.* (God) бог; госпóдь: *Oh, Lord!; Good Lord!,* гóсподи!; бóже мой! —*v.i., usu. in* **lord it over,** комáндовать над; влáствовать над.

lordly *adj.* бáрственный.

lordship *n.* свéтлость: *Your Lordship,* вáша свéтлость.

lore *n.* знáния.

lorgnette *n.* лорнéт.

lorry *n., Brit.* грузови́к.

lose *v.t.* **1,** (misplace) теря́ть: *lose one's glasses,* (по)теря́ть очки́. *The letter was lost,* письмó потеря́лось *or* пропáло. **2,** (suffer the loss of) теря́ть; лишáться; утрáчивать. *Lose one's voice/appetite/job/balance,* теря́ть гóлос/аппети́т/рабóту/равновéсие. *Lose a leg,* потеря́ть нóгу. *Lose a son,* потеря́ть *or* лиши́ться сы́на. *Lose confidence/consciousness,* теря́ть увéренность/сознáние; лиши́ться увéренности/сознáния. *Lose faith/interest/hope,* теря́ть *or* утрáчивать вéру/интерéс/надéжду. *What have we got to lose?,* что нам теря́ть?; что мы мóжем проигрáть при э́том? **3,** (fail to win; gamble away) проигрывать: *lose a game/case/war/ an election/ ten dollars/*, проигра́ть па́ртию/де́ло/войну́/ на вы́борах/ де́сять до́лларов/. **4,** (miss, as an opportunity) упуска́ть; пропуска́ть. **5,** *colloq.* (elude; shake off) ускольза́ть от. —*v.i.* проигрывать: *We (we've) lost*, проигра́ли. —**lose heart,** па́дать ду́хом; уныва́ть. —**lose one's head,** потеря́ть го́лову. —**lose one's life,** лиши́ться жи́зни; поги́бнуть. —**lose one's mind,** сходи́ть с ума́. —**lose one's temper,** выходи́ть из себя́. —**lose one's way,** заблуди́ться; сбива́ться с пути́ *or* с доро́ги. —**lose patience,** теря́ть терпе́ние; выходи́ть из терпе́ния. —**lose sight of,** *see* **sight.** —**lose time, 1,** (waste valuable time) теря́ть вре́мя. *There is no time to be lost*, нельзя́ теря́ть ни мину́ты. **2,** (of a timepiece) отстава́ть. —**lose weight,** теря́ть в ве́се; убавля́ть в ве́се. *Lose twenty pounds*, теря́ть два́дцать фу́нтов; похуде́ть на два́дцать фу́нтов. *See also* **lost.**

loser *n.* проигра́вший. *Come out the loser*, быть в про́игрыше. *He is a poor loser*, он не уме́ет досто́йно прои́грывать.

losing *adj.* **1,** (that lost) проигра́вший: *the losing team*, проигра́вшая кома́нда. **2,** (likely to fail) про́игрышный: *losing proposition*, про́игрышное де́ло. *Fight a losing battle*, вести́ безнаде́жную борьбу́.

loss *n.* **1,** (act of losing; that which is lost) поте́ря; утра́та. *Loss of consciousness*, поте́ря созна́ния. *Loss of strength*, упа́док сил. *Weight loss*, поте́ря в ве́се. *Suffer a grave loss*, понести́ тяжёлую утра́ту. **2,** (money lost; opp. of profit) убы́ток. *Sell at a loss*, продава́ть в убы́ток/ с убы́тком/ невы́годно/. *Suffer huge losses*, потерпе́ть *or* понести́ огро́мные убы́тки. *Enterprises operating at a loss*, убы́точные предприя́тия. **3,** (defeat in a game) про́игрыш; пораже́ние. **4,** *pl.* (casualties) поте́ри: *suffer heavy losses*, понести́ больши́е поте́ри. **5,** *pl.* (what is lost in gambling) убы́тки; про́игрыш. —**be at a loss,** теря́ться в дога́дках. *I am at a loss for words*, не нахожу́ слов. *He is never at a loss for words*, он за сло́вом в карма́н не ле́зет. *I was at a loss as to how to answer*, я не нашёлся (нашла́сь), что отве́тить. —**throw for a loss,** озада́чивать.

lost *adj.* **1,** (missing; misplaced; gone) поте́рянный. *Make up for lost time*, наверста́ть поте́рянное вре́мя. *All is not lost*, не всё поте́ряно. **2,** (having lost one's way) заблу́дший. *Be/get lost*, заблуди́ться. *Get lost in a crowd*, потеря́ться *or* замеша́ться в толпе́. **3,** (killed, drowned, sunk, etc.) поги́бший. *Give up for lost*, счита́ть поги́бшим. **4,** (engrossed) погружённый: *lost in thought*, погружённый в размышле́ния. **5,** (missed, as of an opportunity) пропу́щенный; упу́щенный. **6,** (helpless) как без рук: *I am lost without him*, без него́ я как без рук. **7,** *fol. by* **on** *or* **upon** (unheeded): *The lesson was not lost upon him*, уро́к не прошёл для него́ да́ром; уро́к пошёл ему́ на по́льзу. —**lost and found department,** бюро́ нахо́док. —**lost cause,** ги́блое де́ло. —**lost sheep,** заблу́дшая овца́.

lot *n.* **1,** (object used to determine something by chance) жре́бий: *draw lots*, тяну́ть жре́бий. *Decide*

something by lot, реши́ть что́-нибудь по жре́бию. *The lot fell upon him*, жре́бий пал на него́. **2,** (fate; portion) судьба́; у́часть. *Cast one's lot with*, связа́ть свою́ судьбу́ с. *Fall to someone's lot*, вы́пасть на чью́-нибудь до́лю. **3,** (plot of land) уча́сток. *Parking lot*, стоя́нка (автомоби́лей); автостоя́нка. **4,** (batch; quantity) па́ртия. **5,** *colloq.* [*also pl.* **lots**] мно́го: *a lot of money*, мно́го де́нег. *Read a lot*, мно́го чита́ть. *Have lots to do*, име́ть мно́го дел. *I've heard a lot about you*, я мно́го о вас слы́шал(а). *You have a lot to learn*, у вас мо́жно (*or* вы мо́жете *or* вам на́до) мно́гому научи́ться; вам есть чему́ поучи́ться. *You have a lot to be proud of*, вам есть чем горди́ться. —*adv.* гора́здо; намно́го: *a lot easier*, гора́здо/намно́го ле́гче.

lotion *n.* (космети́ческая) жи́дкость. *Hand lotion*, жи́дкость для рук. *Skin lotion*, лосьо́н.

lottery *n.* лотере́я. *Win something in a lottery*, вы́играть что́-нибудь по лотере́е *or* по лотере́йному биле́ту. —*adj.* лотере́йный.

lotto *n.* лото́.

lotus *n.* ло́тос.

loud *adj.* **1,** (strongly audible) гро́мкий: *in a loud voice*, гро́мким го́лосом. *Loud noise*, си́льный шум. **2,** *colloq.* (garish) крича́щий; крикли́вый; бро́ский. —*adv.* гро́мко. *Out loud*, вслух. —**loud and clear,** во весь го́лос; в по́лный го́лос.

loudly *adv.* гро́мко.

loudmouth *n.* крику́н. —**loudmouthed,** *adj.* крикли́вый.

loudness *n.* гро́мкость.

loudspeaker *n.* громкоговори́тель; репроду́ктор; дина́мик.

lounge *n.* **1,** (public room) сало́н. **2,** (sofa) куше́тка. —*v.i.* [*usu.* **lounge around**] не́житься; валя́ться.

lour *v.* = **lower**[2].

louse *n.* **1,** (insect) вошь. **2,** *slang* (contemptible person) подле́ц. —**louse up,** *slang* напу́тать.

lousy *adj.* **1,** (infested with lice) вши́вый. **2,** *slang* (rotten; miserable) парши́вый; дрянно́й.

lout *n.* хам; неве́жа; у́валень.

lovable *adj.* ми́лый; сла́вный.

love *n.* любо́вь. *Love of/for music*, любо́вь к му́зыке. *In love*, влюблён. *Fall in love (with)*, влюби́ться в. *Marry for love*, жени́ться *or* вы́йти за́муж по любви́. —*adj.* любо́вный: *love letter*, любо́вное письмо́; *love song*, любо́вная песнь. *Love story*, расска́з *or* по́весть о любви́. *Love affair*, рома́н. —*v.t. & i.* люби́ть: *I love you*, я тебя́ люблю́. *I'd love to go*, мне о́чень хоте́лось бы пойти́. *I'd love to!*, с (больши́м) удово́льствием!

lovely *adj.* прекра́сный; преле́стный; чуде́сный. —**loveliness,** *n.* красота́; пре́лесть.

lover *n.* **1,** (person in love) влюблённый. **2,** (enthusiast) люби́тель. **3,** (paramour) любо́вник.

love seat дива́н на двои́х.

loving *adj.* **1,** (feeling love) лю́бящий. **2,** (tender) любо́вный. —**loving cup,** кругова́я ча́ша.

lovingly *adv.* любо́вно; с любо́вью.

low *adj.* **1,** (not high) ни́зкий: *low ceiling*, ни́зкий потоло́к. *Low prices,* ни́зкие це́ны. *Low pressure,* ни́зкое давле́ние. *Low gear,* пе́рвая переда́ча. *At low altitude,* на небольшо́й высоте́. **2,** (poor; inferior) ни́зкий; плохо́й: *low quality,* ни́зкое ка́чество; *low mark,* плоха́я отме́тка. *Have a low opinion of,* быть невысо́кого *or* плохо́го мне́ния о. **3,** (not loud) негро́мкий; ти́хий: *in a low voice,* негро́мким/ти́хим го́лосом. **4,** (low-pitched; deep) ни́зкий. **5,** (humble in origin) ни́зкий: *of low station,* ни́зкого происхожде́ния. **6,** (base; mean) по́длый; ни́зкий. **7,** (dejected) уны́лый. *Low spirits,* уны́ние. **8,** *fol. by* **on** (not well supplied with): *We're low on gas,* бензи́н конча́ется. —*adv.* **1,** (at or to a low level) ни́зко: *bow low,* ни́зко кла́няться. **2,** (softly) ти́хо. —*n.* ни́зшая то́чка. *Prices reached a new low,* це́ны пони́зились до но́вого преде́ла. —*v.i.* (bellow) мыча́ть. —**lay low,** свали́ть; повали́ть; срази́ть. —**lie low,** залега́ть; отлёживаться; притаи́ться. —**run low,** конча́ться; истоща́ться; быть на исхо́де.

low-cut *adj.* с ни́зким вы́резом.

lower[1] (**lo**-er) *v.t.* **1,** (let down) спуска́ть; опуска́ть: *lower the flag/curtain,* спуска́ть *or* опуска́ть флаг/за́навес. *Lower the coffin into the grave,* опусти́ть гроб в моги́лу. *Lower one's eyes,* опусти́ть глаза́. **2,** (reduce) снижа́ть; понижа́ть: *lower prices/ the temperature/,* снижа́ть *or* понижа́ть це́ны/температу́ру. **3,** (weaken, as someone's resistance) ослабля́ть. **4,** (reduce the volume of) понижа́ть: *lower one's voice,* понижа́ть го́лос. **5,** in **lower oneself,** унижа́ться. —*adj.* ни́жний: *lower berth,* ни́жняя по́лка; *lower deck,* ни́жняя па́луба. *Lower House,* ни́жняя пала́та. *Lower class,* ни́зший класс. *Lower back,* поясни́ца.

lower[2] (**lau**-er) *also,* **lour** *v.i.* смотре́ть во́лком; смотре́ть зве́рем.

lower case строчны́е бу́квы.

low-fat *adj.* нежи́рный: *low-fat milk,* нежи́рное молоко́.

low-grade *adj.* недоброка́чественный; низкосо́ртный; низкопро́бный.

low-interest *adj.* под ни́зкий проце́нт: *low-interest loans,* за́ймы под ни́зкий проце́нт.

lowland *n.* ни́зменность; *pl.* низи́ны.

lowly *adj.* **1,** (of low rank) ни́зкий. **2,** (humble; meek) скро́мный; смире́нный.

low-lying *adj.* ни́зменный; низи́нный.

low-necked *adj.* с ни́зким вы́резом; декольте́.

low-paid *adj.* низкоопла́чиваемый: *low-paid worker,* низкоопла́чиваемый рабо́тник.

low-paying *adj.* низкоопла́чиваемый: *low-paying job,* низкоопла́чиваемая рабо́та.

low-powered *adj.* маломо́щный; малоси́льный; слабоси́льный.

low-priced *adj.* дешёвый.

low tide ни́зшая то́чка отли́ва.

lox *n.* сёмга.

loyal *adj.* ве́рный; лоя́льный. *Remain loyal to,* остава́ться ве́рен/лоя́льным (+ *dat.*). —**loyalty,** *n.* ве́рность; лоя́льность.

lozenge *n.* лепёшка; табле́тка.

lubricant *n.* сма́зочный материа́л; сма́зочное вещество́; сма́зка.

lubricate *v.t.* сма́зывать. —**lubrication,** *n.* сма́зка; сма́зывание. —**lubricator,** *n.* маслёнка.

lucid *adj.* я́сный: *lucid exposition,* я́сное изложе́ние. *Lucid mind,* све́тлый ум. *Lucid intervals,* про́блески созна́ния.

luck *n.* уда́ча; сча́стье; везе́ние. *Good luck!,* жела́ю вам уда́чи. *The element of luck,* фа́ктор везе́ния. *Try one's luck,* попыта́ть сча́стья. *I had the good luck to...,* мне посчастли́вилось (+ *inf.*). —**as luck would have it,** как наро́чно; как назло́; как на беду́; как на грех. —**bad luck,** несча́стье: *I had the bad luck to...,* я име́л(а) несча́стье (+ *inf.*). —**be in luck,** повезти́ (+ *dat.*): *You are in/ out of/ luck,* вам (не) повезло́. —**for (good) luck,** на сча́стье.

luckily *adv.* к сча́стью. *Luckily for me,* на моё сча́стье.

luckless *adj.* несчастли́вый; незада́чливый.

lucky *adj.* счастли́вый; уда́чливый. —**be lucky,** повезти́ (+ *dat.*): *He is lucky at cards,* ему́ везёт в ка́ртах. *It is lucky for you that...,* ва́ше сча́стье, что...; вам повезло́, что...

lucrative *adj.* прибы́льный; дохо́дный.

lucre *n.* нажи́ва. —**filthy lucre,** презре́нный мета́лл.

ludicrous *adj.* смешно́й; неле́пый; смехотво́рный.

lug *v.t.* тащи́ть; волочи́ть.

luggage *n.* бага́ж. *Hand luggage,* ручно́й бага́ж; ручна́я кладь.

lugubrious *adj.* печа́льный; гру́стный; мра́чный.

lukewarm *adj.* теплова́тый; чуть тёплый.

lull *v.t.* усыпля́ть; убаю́кивать. —*n.* зати́шье: *lull in the fighting,* зати́шье в боя́х. *Lull in the conversation,* па́уза в разгово́ре.

lullaby *n.* колыбе́льная пе́сня.

lumbago *n.* простре́л; люмба́го.

lumbar *adj.* поясни́чный.

lumber *n.* лес; лесоматериа́л. —*adj.* лесно́й. —*v.i.* (move heavily) громыха́ть. —**lumberjack,** *n.* лесору́б. —**lumber jacket,** ку́ртка. —**lumberyard,** *n.* лесно́й склад.

luminary *n.* свети́ло.

luminescence *n.* свече́ние; люминесце́нция. —**luminescent,** *adj.* светя́щийся; люминесце́нтный.

luminosity *n.* освещённость.

luminous *adj.* светя́щийся: *luminous dial,* светя́щийся цифербла́т.

lummox *n., colloq.* у́валень; простофи́ля.

lump *n.* **1,** (shapeless mass) ком; комо́к: *lump of dirt,* ком/комо́к гря́зи *or* земли́. **2,** (piece, as of sugar) кусо́к. **3,** (swelling; bump) ши́шка. —*v.t.* [*usu.* **lump together**] вали́ть в одну́ ку́чу; стричь под одну́ гребёнку. —**lump in one's throat,** ком/комо́к/ клубо́к в го́рле. *I felt a lump in my throat,* ком подступи́л *or* подкати́л к го́рлу.

lump sugar кусково́й *or* ко́лотый *or* пилёный са́хар; рафина́д.

lump sum единовре́менно выпла́чиваемая су́мма. *Pay (out) in a lump sum,* заплати́ть всё сра́зу; выпла́чивать единовре́менно.

lumpy *adj.* с комка́ми.

lunacy *n.* безу́мие. *It's lunacy!*, э́то бред!

lunar *adj.* лу́нный.

lunatic *n.* душевнобольно́й; сумасше́дший. *Lunatic asylum,* сумасше́дший дом.

lunch *n.* обе́д; ленч. *Have lunch,* обе́дать. —*adj.* обе́денный: *lunch break,* обе́денный переры́в.

luncheon *n.* обе́д. —**luncheonette,** *n.* заку́сочная.

lung *n.* лёгкое. —*adj.* лёгочный. *Lung cancer,* рак лёгких. —**at the top of one's lungs,** во весь го́лос; во всё го́рло; во всю гло́тку.

lunge *v.i.* дёрнуться. —*n.* наско́к; вы́пад.

lupus *n.* волча́нка.

lurch *v.i.* покачну́ться. —*n.* толчо́к. —**leave in the lurch,** поки́нуть в беде́.

lure *n.* **1,** (decoy) прима́нка. **2,** (power of attracting) притяга́тельная си́ла: *the lure of the Orient,* притяга́тельная си́ла Восто́ка. —*v.t.* завлека́ть; зама́нивать; прима́нивать. *Lure into a trap,* зама́нивать в лову́шку. *Lure out of one's hiding place,* выма́нивать из тайника́.

lurid *adj.* **1,** (glowing) о́гненный. **2,** (shocking) жу́ткий.

lurk *v.i.* таи́ться: *lurk in the bushes,* таи́ться в куста́х. *Danger lurked at every turn,* опа́сности подстерега́ли на ка́ждом шагу́.

luscious *adj.* ла́комый; со́чный.

lush *adj.* **1,** (luxuriant, as of foliage) бу́йный; пы́шный; ту́чный; роско́шный. **2,** (succulent) со́чный. —*n., slang* (drunkard) пья́ница.

lust *n.* **1,** (sexual desire) по́хоть; вожделе́ние. **2,** (any overwhelming desire) жа́жда; страсть. —*v.i.* [*usu.* **lust for or after**] жа́ждать (+ *gen.*).

luster *also,* **lustre** *n.* блеск; лоск; гля́нец. *Lose its luster,* теря́ть блеск *or* лоск; тускне́ть.

lustful *adj.* похотли́вый.

lustre *n.* = luster.

lustrous *adj.* глянцеви́тый; гля́нцевый.

lusty *adj.* кре́пкий; дю́жий.

lute *n.* лю́тня.

lutetium *n.* люте́ций.

Lutheran *adj.* лютера́нский. —*n.* лютера́нин. —**Lutheranism,** *n.* лютера́нство.

luxuriant *adj.* пы́шный; бу́йный; роско́шный.

luxuriate *v.i.* [*usu.* **luxuriate in**] не́житься (в *or* на); наслажда́ться (+ *instr.*).

luxurious *adj.* роско́шный.

luxury *n.* ро́скошь. —*adj.* люкс: *luxury hotel,* гости́ница-люкс. *Luxury item,* предме́т ро́скоши.

lycée *n.* лице́й.

lye *n.* щёлок.

lying *adj.* **1,** (recumbent) лежа́щий; лежа́чий. **2,** (false) лжи́вый; ло́жный. —*n.* лганьё; враньё.

lymph *n.* ли́мфа. *Lymph nodes,* лимфати́ческие узлы́. —**lymphatic,** *adj.* лимфати́ческий.

lynch *v.t.* линчева́ть. —**lynching,** *n.* линчева́ние; самосу́д.

lynx *n.* рысь.

lyre *n.* ли́ра.

lyric *n.* **1,** (lyric poem) ли́рика. **2,** *pl.* (words of a song) текст. —*adj.* [*also,* **lyrical**] лири́ческий.

lyricism *n.* лири́зм.

M

M, m трина́дцатая бу́ква англи́йского алфави́та.

macabre *adj.* жу́ткий.

macadam *n.* ще́бень. —*adj.* щебёночный. —*v.t.* мости́ть ще́бнем.

macaque *n.* мака́ка.

macaroni *n.* макаро́ны.

macaroon *n.* минда́льное пече́нье.

macaw *n.* а́ра; ара́ра.

mace *n.* **1,** (club) булава́. **2,** (staff of office) жезл. **3,** (spice) муска́тный цвет.

Macedonian *adj.* македо́нский.

Machiavellian *adj.* макиаве́ллевский.

machination *n., usu. pl.* махина́ции; ко́зни.

machine *n.* маши́на; стано́к: *washing machine,* стира́льная маши́на; *milling machine,* фре́зерный стано́к. —*adj.* маши́нный: *machine parts,* маши́нные ча́сти. *Machine translation,* маши́нный перево́д.

machine gun пулемёт. —**machine-gun,** *v.t.* обстре́ливать пулемётным огнём. —**machine gunner,** пулемётчик.

machinery *n.* **1,** (machines collectively) маши́ны. **2,** (system; organization) аппара́т.

machine shop механи́ческий цех; механи́ческая мастерска́я.

machine tool стано́к.

machinist *n.* машини́ст.

mackerel *n.* ску́мбрия; макре́ль.

mackintosh *n.* макинто́ш; плащ.

macrocosm *n.* макроко́см.

mad *adj.* **1,** (insane) сумасше́дший. *Drive mad,* своди́ть с ума́. *Go mad,* сходи́ть с ума́. **2,** (reckless; foolish) безу́мный. **3,** (rabid) бе́шеный. **4,** *fol. by* **about** (infatuated) без ума́ (от). **5,** *colloq.* (angry) серди́тый. *Get mad,* серди́ться. *He is mad at me,* он серди́т на меня́. —**like mad,** сломя́ го́лову; как угоре́лый. *Run like mad,* бежа́ть как угоре́лый *or* как бе́шеный.

madam *n.* мада́м; суда́рыня; госпожа́.

madcap *n.* сумасбро́д; сорване́ц; сорвиголова́.

madden *v.t.* **1,** (drive mad) своди́ть с ума́. **2,** (make furious) беси́ть. —**maddening,** *adj.* доса́дный.

madder *n.* (plant) маре́на.

Madeira *n.* (wine) маде́ра.

mademoiselle *n.* мадемуазе́ль.

made-to-order *adj.* сде́ланный на зака́з.

madhouse *n.* сумасше́дший дом.

madly *adv.* безу́мно. *Madly in love with,* безу́мно влюблён (влюблена́) в (+ *acc.*); без ума́ от; пыла́ющий любо́вью к.

madman *n.* сумасше́дший; безу́мец.

madness *n.* **1,** (insanity) сумасше́ствие. **2,** (folly) безу́мие. *It's madness!,* э́то бред!

Madonna *n.* мадо́нна.

madrigal *n.* мадрига́л.

maelstrom *n.* водоворо́т; вихрь.

maestro *n.* ма́эстро.

Mafia *n.* ма́фия.

magazine *n.* **1,** (publication) журна́л. **2,** (of a firearm) магази́н. **3,** (storage place) по́греб: *powder magazine,* порохово́й по́греб. —*adj.* журна́льный: *magazine article,* журна́льная статья́.

magenta *n.* фукси́н. —*adj.* кра́сно-лило́вый.

maggot *n.* личи́нка.

Magi *n.pl.* волхвы́.

magic *n.* ма́гия; волшебство́. *As if by magic,* как бу́дто по волшебству́. —*adj.* [*also,* **magical**] маги́ческий; волше́бный. *Magic lantern,* волше́бный фона́рь. *Magic wand,* волше́бная па́лочка.

magician *n.* **1,** (sorcerer; wizard) волше́бник; чароде́й. **2,** (entertainer who performs magic tricks) фо́кусник; иллюзиони́ст.

magisterial *adj.* **1,** (of or pert. to a magistrate) суде́бный. **2,** (imperious) повели́тельный.

magistracy *n.* магистрату́ра.

magistrate *n.* судья́.

Magna Carta Вели́кая ха́ртия во́льностей.

magnanimity *n.* великоду́шие. —**magnanimous,** *adj.* великоду́шный.

magnate *n.* магна́т.

magnesia *n.* магне́зия.

magnesium *n.* ма́гний.

magnet *n.* магни́т.

magnetic *adj.* **1,** *physics* магни́тный: *magnetic field,* магни́тное по́ле. *Magnetic tape,* магни́тная ле́нта. *Magnetic pole,* магни́тный по́люс. *Magnetic storm,* магни́тная бу́ря. **2,** *fig.* (powerfully attractive) магнети́ческий. —**magnetics,** *n.* магнети́зм. —**magnetism,** *n.* магнети́зм.

magnetite *n.* магнети́т.

magnetize *v.t.* намагни́чивать.

magneto *n.* магне́то.

magnetron *n.* магнетро́н.

magnification *n.* увеличе́ние.

magnificence *n.* великоле́пие.

magnificent *adj.* великоле́пный. —**magnificently,** *adv.* великоле́пно.

magnify *v.t.* **1,** (enlarge) увели́чивать. **2,** (exaggerate) преувели́чивать. —**magnifying glass,** увеличи́тельное стекло́; лу́па.

magnitude *n.* **1,** (size; brightness) величина́. *Star of the first magnitude,* звезда́ пе́рвой величины́. **2,** (significance) ва́жность. —**order of magnitude,** поря́док величины́.

magnolia *n.* магно́лия.

magpie *n.* соро́ка.

Magyar *n.* мадья́р. —*adj.* мадья́рский.

maharajah *also,* **maharaja** *n.* магара́джа.

mahogany *n.* кра́сное де́рево. —*adj.* кра́сного де́рева.

maid *n.* **1,** (young woman) де́ва; деви́ца; де́вушка. **2,** (housemaid) го́рничная; домрабо́тница; (chambermaid) го́рничная; убо́рщица. —**old maid,** ста́рая де́ва.

maiden *n.* де́ва; деви́ца; де́вушка. —*adj.* **1,** (unmarried) незаму́жняя. **2,** (initial) пе́рвый: *maiden voyage,* пе́рвый рейс.

maidenhead *n.* де́вственная плева́.

maidenhood *n.* деви́чество.

maidenly *adj.* деви́чий.

maiden name де́вичья фами́лия.

mail *n.* **1,** (letters) по́чта; пи́сьма. *By mail,* по по́чте. *Mail delivery/pickup,* доста́вка/вы́емка пи́сем. **2,** (armor) кольчу́га. —*adj.* почто́вый: *mail train,* почто́вый по́езд. —*v.t.* **1,** (deposit in a mailbox) опуска́ть (в почто́вый я́щик). **2,** (send by mail) посыла́ть по по́чте.

mailbag *n.* почто́вый мешо́к. *Also,* **mail pouch.**

mailbox *n.* почто́вый я́щик.

mailed fist брони́рованный кула́к.

mailman *n.* почтальо́н.

mail-order *adj.* посы́лочный: *mail-order house,* посы́лочная фи́рма.

maim *v.t.* кале́чить; уве́чить.

main *adj.* гла́вный; основно́й: *the main reason,* гла́вная/основна́я причи́на. *The main thing,* (са́мое) гла́вное. *The main street,* гла́вная *or* центра́льная у́лица. *The main course,* второ́е (блю́до). —*n.* магистра́ль: *water main,* водопрово́дная магистра́ль. —**in the main,** в основно́м. —**with might and main,** изо всех сил; во всю мочь.

mainland *n.* матери́к.

mainly *adv.* в основно́м; гла́вным о́бразом; бо́льшей ча́стью.

mainmast *n.* грот-ма́чта.

mainsail *n.* грот.

mainspring *n.* **1,** (of a watch) ходова́я пружи́на. **2,** *fig.* (chief source or motive) гла́вная пружи́на.

mainstay *n.* станово́й хребе́т.

mainstream *n.* гла́вное тече́ние; гла́вное ру́сло:

outside the mainstream, в стороне́ от гла́вного тече́ния/ ру́сла.

maintain *v.t.* **1,** (assert; claim) утвержда́ть: *He maintains that...,* он утвержда́ет, что... *Maintain one's innocence,* наста́ивать на свое́й невино́вности. **2,** (keep; keep up) подде́рживать; сохраня́ть; выде́рживать. *Maintain order,* подде́рживать *or* сохраня́ть поря́док. *Maintain one's balance,* сохраня́ть *or* выде́рживать равнове́сие. *Maintain diplomatic relations,* подде́рживать дипломати́ческие отноше́ния. *Maintain the pace,* выде́рживать темп. **3,** (preserve; retain) сохраня́ть: *maintain peace/neutrality/ one's composure/,* сохраня́ть мир/нейтралите́т/самооблада́ние. **4,** (own; keep up) держа́ть: *maintain two residences,* держа́ть две резиде́нции. **5,** (support; provide for) содержа́ть. **6,** (keep in good condition or repair) содержа́ть в хоро́шем состоя́нии; содержа́ть в испра́вности.

maintenance *n.* **1,** (keeping up) поддержа́ние. **2,** (upkeep) содержа́ние. **3,** (servicing) техни́ческое обслу́живание; ухо́д. *Maintenance manual,* руково́дство по обслу́живанию и эксплуата́ции.

maître d'hôtel метрдоте́ль.

maize *n.* ма́ис.

majestic *adj.* вели́чественный.

majesty *n.* **1,** (grandeur) вели́чие. **2,** *cap.* (title) вели́чество: *Your Majesty,* ва́ше вели́чество.

major *n.* **1,** (military officer) майо́р. **2,** *music* мажо́р: *key of F-major,* тона́льность фа-мажо́р. **3,** (main field of study) основно́й предме́т. —*adj.* **1,** (greater) бо́льший: *the major part,* бо́льшая часть. **2,** (important; significant) ва́жный; значи́тельный. *A major role,* ва́жная *or* ви́дная роль. **3,** (prominent) кру́пный: *a major writer,* кру́пный писа́тель. **4,** (broad in scope) капита́льный: *major repairs,* капита́льный ремо́нт. **5,** *music* мажо́рный. —*v.i.* специализи́роваться: *major in chemistry,* специализи́роваться в хи́мии.

majordomo *n.* мажордо́м.

major general генера́л-лейтена́нт.

majority *n.* **1,** (more than half of the total) большинство́: *in the majority of cases,* в большинстве́ слу́чаев. *By a large majority,* значи́тельным большинство́м. *Be in the majority,* быть в большинстве́. *By a three vote majority,* большинство́м в три го́лоса. **2,** (full legal age) совершенноле́тие.

make *v.t.* **1,** (accomplish; carry out; commit) де́лать; соверша́ть: *make a mistake,* де́лать/соверша́ть оши́бку; *make an attempt,* де́лать попы́тку; *make an offer,* де́лать предложе́ние; *make a choice,* де́лать вы́бор; *make progress,* де́лать успе́хи; *make a deal,* соверша́ть сде́лку. **2,** (produce; manufacture) де́лать; производи́ть; выраба́тывать; изготовля́ть. *Make a movie,* ста́вить *or* снима́ть фильм. *What is this made of?,* из чего́ э́то сде́лано? *Japanese-made cars,* маши́ны япо́нского произво́дства. **3,** (sew) шить: *He is making me a suit,* он шьёт мне костю́м. *She makes all her own clothes,* она́ шьёт себе́ всё сама́. **4,** (produce; cause) производи́ть: *make an impression,* производи́ть впечатле́ние. *Make a scene,* устра́и-

вать сце́ну. **5,** (produce as a result) де́лать: *make no secret of,* не де́лать секре́та из. *Make enemies,* нажи́ть враго́в. *Make a joke of,* превраща́ть *or* обраща́ть в шу́тку. *Make a mess of,* напу́тать. **6,** (cause to be or become) де́лать: *make someone unhappy,* де́лать кого́-нибудь несча́стным. *Make public,* предава́ть гла́сности. *Make something impossible,* де́лать что́-нибудь невозмо́жным. *I made him my assistant,* я сде́лал его́ свои́м помо́щником. ♦*Often rendered by a single verb: make happy,* ра́довать; *make angry,* серди́ть; *make shorter,* укора́чивать. **7,** (cause to; force to) заставля́ть: *make someone wait,* заставля́ть кого́-нибудь ждать. *Make someone promise,* брать сло́во с. **8,** (prompt to; impel to) побужда́ть: *What made you do it?,* что вас побуди́ло э́то сде́лать? *What makes you think that...?,* почему́ вы ду́маете, что...? **9,** (amount to; constitute) составля́ть. *Two and two make four,* два и два равно́ четырём. *One swallow does not make a summer,* одна́ ла́сточка весны́ не де́лает. **10,** (turn out to be; become) ока́зываться. *He will make a good teacher,* из него́ вы́йдет хоро́ший учи́тель. **11,** (utter; issue) де́лать: *make a remark/ an announcement/,* де́лать замеча́ние/заявле́ние. **12,** (establish; enact, as laws or rules) устана́вливать. **13,** (arrange, as an appointment or date) назнача́ть. **14,** (draw up, as a list or will) составля́ть. **15,** (pay) вноси́ть: *make a payment,* вноси́ть пла́ту. *Make a down payment,* дава́ть *or* вноси́ть зада́ток. **16,** (earn) зараба́тывать: *make a living,* зараба́тывать на жизнь. *Make a profit,* получи́ть при́быль. *Make a fortune,* нажи́ть состоя́ние. **17,** (arrive in time for; catch) успева́ть на *or* к. **18,** (cook) гото́вить: *make dinner,* гото́вить обе́д. *Make coffee,* вари́ть ко́фе. *Make tea,* зава́ривать чай. **19,** *with certain nouns,* дава́ть: *make a promise,* дава́ть обеща́ние; *make a recommendation,* дава́ть рекоменда́цию. *Make room for,* дава́ть ме́сто (+ *dat.*). **20,** *with certain nouns,* идти́ на: *make concessions,* идти́ на усту́пки; *make sacrifices,* идти́ на же́ртвы. **21,** *used with various other nouns: make a bed,* убира́ть *or* постели́ть *or* пригото́вить посте́ль; *make a speech,* говори́ть *or* произноси́ть речь; *make a request,* обраща́ться с про́сьбой; *make a bet,* держа́ть *or* заключа́ть пари́; *make a decision,* принима́ть реше́ние; *make changes,* вноси́ть измене́ния; *make sense,* име́ть смысл; *make many acquaintances,* завяза́ть мно́го знако́мств. **22,** *Make oneself understood,* объясня́ться; *make oneself at home,* быть как до́ма; *make oneself comfortable,* устро́иться поудо́бнее. —*n.* **1,** (brand) ма́рка. *Cars of all makes,* маши́ны всех ма́рок. **2,** (manufacture) изде́лие; произво́дство. *Of foreign make,* иностра́нного произво́дства. —**make as if; make as though,** де́лать вид; притворя́ться. —**make do,** обходи́ться: *make do with what we have on hand,* обходи́ться име́ющимися запа́сами. —**make for, 1,** (head for) направля́ться к. **2,** (make a dash for) бро́ситься к. **3,** (tend to create) спосо́бствовать; соде́йствовать. **4,** *Made for each other,* со́зданы друг для дру́га. —**make good, 1,** (be successful)

преуспева́ть. **2,** *fol. by* **on** (carry out; live up to) вы-
полня́ть. **—make it, 1,** (achieve a certain thing)
попа́сть. **2,** *fol. by* **to** (reach) добра́ться (до). **3,** (be
on time) успе́ть. **4,** (*judge; estimate*): *I make it twenty
miles,* по-мо́ему, здесь два́дцать миль. *What time do
you make it?,* ско́лько вре́мени на ва́ших часа́х? **5,**
Make it a rule to, взять себе́ за пра́вило (+ *inf.*).
—make of, понима́ть: *What do you make of his remarks?,* как вы понима́ете его́ замеча́ния? *I don't
know what to make of it,* я не зна́ю, что об э́том
и ду́мать. **—make off with,** уноси́ть; утащи́ть.
—make out, 1, (discern) различа́ть; разбира́ть;
распознава́ть. **2,** (be able to read) разбира́ть. **3,**
(comprehend) понима́ть. *There is no making him out,*
его́ не поня́ть. **4,** (draw up) составля́ть. **5,** (fill out)
заполня́ть. **6,** (write out, as a bill, check, etc.)
выпи́сывать. **7,** (represent as being) изобража́ть.
Make oneself out to be a..., изобража́ть *or* стро́ить
из себя́ (+ *acc.*). **8,** *colloq.* (manage; get along) об-
ходи́ться. *How are you making out?,* как у вас дела́?
—make over, 1, (remake) переде́лывать. **2,** (transfer;
sign over) передава́ть. **—make up, 1,** (put together;
compose; constitute) составля́ть. **2,** (invent; concoct)
выду́мывать. **3,** (straighten up, as a bed or hotel
room) убира́ть. **4,** (be reconciled) мири́ться. **5,** *theat.*
гримирова́ть. **6,** *printing* верста́ть. **—make up for,**
восполня́ть; возмеща́ть; навёрстывать. *Make up
for lost time,* возмести́ть/наверста́ть поте́рянное
вре́мя. **—make way,** *see* **way.**

maker *n.* **1,** (manufacturer) производи́тель; фаб-
рика́нт. *Car maker,* производи́тель автомоби́лей.
♦*Often in combinations: dressmaker,* портни́ха;
peacemaker, миротво́рец. **2,** *cap.* (God) творе́ц;
созда́тель.

makeshift *adj.* вре́менный; подру́чный.

make-up *n.* **1,** (composition) соста́в. **2,** (nature; disposition) нату́ра; хара́ктер. **3,** (cosmetics) косме́тика.
Put on/ use/ wear make-up, кра́ситься. **4,** *theat.* грим.
Make-up artist, гримёр. **5,** *printing* вёрстка. *Make-up
man,* метранпа́ж.

makeweight *n.* дове́сок.

making *n.* **1,** (creation) созда́ние. **2,** (manufacture)
произво́дство. **3,** *pl.* (potential ability) зада́тки;
да́нные: *He has the makings of a fine writer,* у него́
зада́тки хоро́шего писа́теля; у него́ все да́нные,
чтобы стать хоро́шим писа́телем.

malachite *n.* малахи́т. **—***adj.* малахи́товый.

maladjusted *adj.* неприспосо́бленный. **—maladjustment,** *n.* неприспосо́бленность.

maladroit *adj.* неуклю́жий; нело́вкий.

malady *n.* боле́знь.

Malaga *n.* (wine) мала́га.

malaise *n.* недомога́ние.

malapropos *adj.* неуме́стный. **—***adv.* некста́ти.

malaria *n.* маляри́я. **—malarial,** *adj.* маляри́йный.

Malay *adj.* мала́йский. **—***n.* **1,** (person) мала́ец;
мала́йка. **2,** (language) мала́йский язы́к.

malcontent *n. & adj.* недово́льный.

male *adj.* мужско́й; мужско́го по́ла. **—***n.* **1,** (man)
мужчи́на. **2,** (male animal) саме́ц.

malediction *n.* прокля́тие.

malefactor *n.* престу́пник; правонаруши́тель; зло-
де́й.

maleficent *adj.* вре́дный; зловре́дный.

malevolent *adj.* зло́бный; недоброжела́тельный.
—malevolence, *n.* зло́ба; недоброжела́тельство.

malfeasance *n.* должностно́е преступле́ние.

malformation *n.* уро́дство. **—malformed,** *adj.*
уро́дливый.

malfunction *n.* неиспра́вность; отка́з. **—***v.i.* отка́зы-
вать.

malice *n.* зло́ба; злость.

malicious *adj.* **1,** (spiteful) зло́бный; зло́стный. **2,** *law*
злой; злонаме́ренный. *Malicious act,* злонаме́рен-
ный посту́пок. *Malicious intent,* злой у́мысел.
—maliciously, *adv.* зло́бно; зло; со зло́бой.

malign *v.t.* клевета́ть на; поро́чить. **—***adj.* па́губный.

malignancy *n.* злока́чественная о́пухоль.

malignant *adj.* **1,** (malicious) зло́бный. **2,** (pernicious)
па́губный. **3,** *med.* злока́чественный.

malinger *v.i.* притворя́ться больны́м; симули́ровать
боле́знь. **—malingerer,** *n.* симуля́нт.

mall *n.* **1,** (public promenade) алле́я; бульва́р. **2,** (enclosed shopping center) закры́тый торго́вый центр.

mallard *n.* кря́ква.

malleable *adj.* ко́вкий. **—malleability,** *n.* ко́вкость.

mallet *n.* колоту́шка.

mallow *n.* ма́льва; просви́рник.

malnutrition *n.* недоеда́ние.

malodorous *adj.* злово́нный; воню́чий.

malpractice *n.* небре́жное лече́ние.

malt *n.* со́лод.

maltose *n.* мальто́за; солодо́вый са́хар.

maltreat *v.t.* ду́рно *or* пло́хо обраща́ться с. **—mal-
treatment,** *n.* дурно́е *or* плохо́е обраще́ние.

mama *also,* **mamma** *n.* ма́ма. **—mama's boy,** ма́-
менькин сыно́к.

mammal *n.* млекопита́ющее.

mammary *adj.* грудно́й; моло́чный.

mammoth *n.* ма́монт. **—***adj.* огро́мный; гига́нтский;
колосса́льный.

man *n.* **1,** (person) челове́к: *a nice man,* симпати́ч-
ный челове́к. *Man in the street,* «челове́к с у́лицы».
Man of action, челове́к де́йствия *or* де́ла. *Man of letters,* литера́тор. *All men are mortal,* все лю́ди
сме́ртны. **2,** (male human being) мужчи́на: *for men
only,* то́лько для мужчи́н. *Men's clothing,* мужска́я
оде́жда. **3,** (mankind) челове́к: *Man is a rational being,* челове́к — разу́мное существо́. **4,** (type of early
human) челове́к: *primitive man,* первобы́тный
челове́к. **—***v.t.* **1,** (furnish with men) (у)комплек-
това́ть: *man a regiment,* (у)комплектова́ть полк. **2,**
(take stations at) станови́ться в *or* на. *Man one's
post,* стать на пост. **—to a man,** все поголо́вно; все
как оди́н; до еди́ного челове́ка.

manacle *n.* нару́чник. **—***v.t.* надева́ть нару́чники на;
ско́вывать.

manage *v.t.* **1,** (direct; administer) управля́ть;
заве́довать; руководи́ть (all with instr.). **2,** (handle)
справля́ться с: *manage one's affairs,* справля́ться с

делами. **3,** *fol. by inf.* (contrive; succeed) суметь; ухитряться; умудряться; изловчиться. —*v.i.* (make out; get along) обходиться; устраиваться: *We'll manage somehow,* мы как-нибудь обойдёмся *or* устроимся. *Manage on 5,000 rubles a month,* существовать на пять тысяч рублей в месяц.

management *n.* **1,** (act of managing) управление; руководство. *Management techniques,* методы управления. **2,** (those who manage) правление; дирекция; администрация.

manager *n.* заведующий; управляющий; руководитель; директор. *Store manager,* заведующий магазином; директор магазина. *Bank manager,* управляющий банком. *Factory manager,* директор завода. *Project manager,* руководитель проекта.

managerial *adj.* руководящий: *managerial position,* руководящая должность. *Managerial abilities,* организаторские способности.

manatee *n.* ламантин.

Manchu *adj.* маньчжурский. —*n.* **1,** (person) маньчжур. **2,** (language) маньчжурский язык.

mandarin *n.* **1,** (Chinese official) мандарин. **2,** *cap.* (language) мандаринский язык. **3,** (tangerine) мандарин.

mandate *n.* **1,** (instruction from constituents) наказ (избирателей). **2,** (charge to administer a territory) мандат.

mandatory *adj.* обязательный.

mandible *n.* нижняя челюсть.

mandolin *n.* мандолина.

mandrake *n.* мандрагора.

mandrel *also,* **mandril** *n.* оправка.

mandrill *n.* мандрил.

mane *n.* грива.

maneuver *also,* **manoeuvre** *n.* манёвр. *Be on maneuvers,* быть на манёврах. —*v.t.* маневрировать (+ *instr.*). —*v.i.* маневрировать; лавировать. —**maneuverable,** *adj.* манёвренный. —**maneuverability,** *n.* манёвренность.

manganese *n.* марганец.

manganite *n.* манганит.

mange *n.* чесотка; парша.

manger *n.* ясли. —**dog in the manger,** собака на сене.

mangle *v.t.* **1,** (mutilate; disfigure) калечить. **2,** (spoil; ruin) коверкать. **3,** (press in a mangle) катать. —*n.* каток (для белья).

mango *n.* манго.

mangy *adj.* паршивый; шелудивый; облезлый.

manhandle *v.t.* грубо обращаться с.

manhole *n.* люк; лаз.

manhood *n.* возмужалость; зрелость.

man-hour *n.* человеко-час.

manhunt *n.* полицейская облава.

mania *n.* мания. —**maniac,** *n.* маньяк. —**maniacal,** *adj.* маниакальный.

manic *adj.* маниакальный. —**manic-depressive,** *adj.* маниакально-депрессивный.

manicure *n.* маникюр. —*v.t. Manicure someone's nails,* делать маникюр (+ *dat.*). —**manicurist,** *n.* маникюрша.

manifest *v.t.* проявлять. *Manifest itself,* проявляться; выражаться. —*adj.* очевидный; явный. —**manifestation,** *n.* проявление.

manifesto *n.* манифест.

manifold *adj.* разнообразный; разносторонний. —*n.* (pipe) трубопровод.

manikin *n.* манекен.

manioc *n.* маниока.

manipulate *v.t.* манипулировать. —**manipulation,** *n.* манипуляция. —**manipulator,** *n.* манипулятор.

mankind *n.* человечество.

manlike *adj.* человекоподобный.

manly *adj.* мужественный. —**manliness,** *n.* мужественность.

man-made *adj.* искусственный.

manna *n.* манна. *Manna from heaven,* манна небесная.

manned *adj.* пилотируемый; с человеком на борту.

mannequin *n.* манекен.

manner *n.* **1,** (way) способ; образ. *In this manner,* таким образом; *in like manner,* подобным образом. **2,** (mode of behavior) манера. **3,** *pl.* (social ways) манеры: *good manners,* хорошие манеры. *Table manners,* поведение за столом. *Comedy of manners,* комедия нравов. —**all manner of,** всевозможные. —**by no manner of means,** никоим образом. —**in a manner of speaking,** так сказать; если можно так выразиться. —**in the manner of,** на манер (+ *gen.*).

mannered *adj.* манерный.

mannerism *n.* **1,** (excessive use of an affected style) манерность. **2,** (peculiarity of manner) манера.

mannerly *adj.* вежливый; воспитанный.

mannish *adj.* мужеподобный.

manoeuvre *n. & v.* = **maneuver.**

man-of-war *n.* военный корабль.

manometer *n.* манометр. —**manometric,** *adj.* манометрический.

manor *n.* поместье. —**manor house,** помещичий дом.

manorial *adj.* помещичий.

manpower *n.* рабочая сила; рабочие руки.

mansard *n.* мансардная крыша. *Also,* **mansard roof.**

manservant *n.* слуга.

mansion *n.* особняк.

manslaughter *n.* непредумышленное убийство; убийство по неосторожности.

mantel *n.* каминная полка. *Also,* **mantelpiece.**

mantilla *n.* мантилья.

mantis *n.* богомол.

mantle *n.* **1,** (cloak) мантия. **2,** (incandescent hood) калильная сетка. **3,** *fig.* (covering) покров.

manual *adj.* ручной: *manual labor,* ручной труд. *Manual training,* уроки по труду. —*n.* **1,** (book of instructions) руководство. **2,** *mil.* наставление. *Field manual,* боевой устав. —**manually,** *adv.* вручную.

manufacture *v.t.* производить; изготовлять; вырабатывать; выделывать; фабриковать. *Manufactured goods,* промышленные товары. —*n.* производство; изготовление; выработка; выделка; фабрикация.

—**manufacturer,** *n.* фабрика́нт; промы́шленник.

manure *n.* наво́з; удобре́ние.

manuscript *n.* ру́копись.

many *adj.* мно́го: *many times,* мно́го раз; *in many cases,* во мно́гих слу́чаях. *He resembles ... in many ways,* он мно́гим (*or* во мно́гом) похо́ж на (+ *acc.*). —*pron.* мно́гие: *many of them,* мно́гие из них. *Many believe that...,* мно́гие счита́ют, что... *It seemed to many that...,* мно́гим каза́лось, что... —**a great many,** о́чень мно́го. —**as many,** сто́лько же. *Twice as many,* в два ра́за (*or* вдво́е) бо́льше. —**as many as,** 1, (the same quantity) сто́лько же..., ско́лько и...: *as many adults as children,* сто́лько же взро́слых, ско́лько и дете́й. *Take as many as you like,* бери́те (сто́лько), ско́лько вам уго́дно. **2,** (before numbers, emphasizing a large amount) це́лые; це́лых; до. —**how many?,** ско́лько? —**so many,** так мно́го; сто́лько. *I told him in so many words that...,* я так и сказа́л ему́, что... —**the many,** большинство́. —**too many,** сли́шком мно́го.

many-sided *adj.* многосторо́нний.

Maori *n. & adj.* ма́ори.

map *n.* ка́рта. *City map,* план го́рода. —*v.t.* **1,** (make a map of) наноси́ть на ка́рту; картографи́ровать. **2,** *fol. by* **out** (plan) намеча́ть: *map out one's route,* намеча́ть маршру́т. —**map maker,** карто́граф. —**map making,** картогра́фия.

maple *n.* клён. —*adj.* клено́вый. —**maple sugar,** клено́вый са́хар. —**maple syrup,** клено́вый сиро́п.

mar *v.t.* **1,** (spoil) по́ртить; омрача́ть; отравля́ть. *The parade was marred by an accident,* пара́д омрачи́лся несча́стным слу́чаем. **2,** (disfigure) уро́довать; обезобра́живать; безобра́зить. *Mar the (appearance of the) landscape,* обезобра́живать пейза́ж.

marabou *n.* марабу́.

maraschino *n.* мараски́н.

marasmus *n.* мара́зм.

marathon *n.* марафо́нский бег.

maraud *v.i.* мароде́рствовать. —**marauder,** *n.* мароде́р. —**marauding,** *n.* мароде́рство. —*adj.* мароде́рский.

marble *n.* **1,** (mineral) мра́мор. **2,** (little ball) ша́рик: *play marbles,* игра́ть в ша́рики. —*adj.* мра́морный.

march *v.i.* марширова́ть. —*n.* **1,** *mil.* марш; похо́д; перехо́д. *A two-day march,* двухдне́вный перехо́д. **2,** (demonstration) марш: *protest march,* марш проте́ста. **3,** *music* марш. **4,** (progress) ход: *march of events,* ход собы́тий. —**on the march,** на ма́рше; на похо́де.

March *n.* март. —*adj.* ма́ртовский.

marching *n.* марширо́вка. —*adj.* похо́дный; марширо́вочный.

marchioness *n.* марки́за.

marchpane *n.* марципа́н.

Mardi gras ма́сленица.

mare *n.* кобы́ла.

margarine *n.* маргари́н.

margin *n.* **1,** (edge of a page) поля́ (страни́цы): *write in the margin,* писа́ть на поля́х. **2,** (border; edge) край. **3,** (reserve) запа́с: *margin of safety,* запа́с без-

опа́сности; запа́с про́чности. **4,** (difference, as in votes) переве́с: *by a narrow margin,* с незначи́тельным переве́сом.

marginal *adj.* **1,** (written in the margin) напи́санный на поля́х: *marginal note,* заме́тка на поля́х. **2,** (slight; minimal) незначи́тельный. **3,** (barely profitable) малоприбыльный.

marginalia *n.pl.* маргина́лии.

marginally *adv.* немно́го; слегка́; чуть-чу́ть.

marigold *n.* **1,** (African or French marigold) ба́рхатцы. **2,** (pot marigold) ноготки́.

marijuana *n.* марихуа́на.

marinade *n.* марина́д.

marinate *v.t.* маринова́ть. —**marinated,** *adj.* марино́ванный.

marine *adj.* морско́й: *marine animals,* морски́е живо́тные. —*n.* **1,** (seagoing soldier) морско́й пехоти́нец. **2,** *pl.* (Marine Corps) морска́я пехо́та. —**merchant marine,** торго́вый флот.

mariner *n.* моря́к; матро́с.

marionette *n.* марионе́тка.

marital *adj.* супру́жеский; бра́чный. *Marital status,* семе́йное положе́ние.

maritime *adj.* морско́й; примо́рский.

marjoram *n.* майора́н.

mark *n.* **1,** (written line or symbol) ме́тка; поме́тка. *Make a mark on the page,* де́лать поме́тку на страни́це. **2,** (scratch, scar, etc.) след: *tire marks,* следы́ шин. **3,** (grade) отме́тка; оце́нка; балл. **4,** (effect; impression) отпеча́ток: *leave its mark,* накла́дывать свой отпеча́ток. **5,** (target) цель: *hit the mark,* попа́сть *or* бить в цель. *Be wide of the mark,* бить ми́мо це́ли; *fig.* попа́сть па́льцем в не́бо. **6,** (sign; true indication) ве́рный при́знак: *the mark of a true connoisseur,* ве́рный при́знак знатока́. **7,** (standard): *up to the mark,* на до́лжной высоте́. **8,** (starting line in a race) старт: *On your mark, get set, go!,* на старт, внима́ние, марш! **9,** (monetary unit) ма́рка. —*v.t.* **1,** (place a mark on) ме́тить; отмеча́ть; помеча́ть; обознача́ть. *Mark the place in a book,* отмеча́ть *or* помеча́ть *or* закла́дывать ме́сто в кни́ге. **2,** (indicate; show) ука́зывать. *The prices are clearly marked,* це́ны чётко ука́заны *or* проста́влены. *The roads are poorly marked,* доро́ги пло́хо обозна́чены. *The lanes (in the roads) are poorly marked,* доро́ги пло́хо разме́чены. **3,** (grade) ста́вить отме́тку (отме́тки) за. **4,** (celebrate; commemorate) отмеча́ть; ознаменова́ть. *To mark the anniversary,* в ознаменова́ние юбиле́я. **5,** (signify; represent) знаменова́ть (собо́й). *Mark the beginning of a new era,* знаменова́ть нача́ло но́вой эпо́хи. **6,** (be a feature of) ознаменова́ть: *a century marked by great discoveries,* век, ознамено́ванный больши́ми откры́тиями. —**mark down,** уце́нивать. —**mark my words,** попо́мните моё сло́во. —**mark off,** отсчи́тывать: *mark off ten paces,* отсчи́тывать де́сять шаго́в. —**mark time,** топта́ться на ме́сте. —**mark up, 1,** (cover with markings) испещря́ть. **2,** (raise the price of) наце́нивать.

marked *adj.* **1,** (having a mark or marks) ме́ченый.

Marked cards, краплёные ка́рты. **2,** (strikingly evident) заме́тный: *a marked improvement,* заме́тное улучше́ние.

marker *n.* **1,** (one who marks) ме́тчик. **2,** (device for marking) флома́стер. **3,** (indicator) знак. *Boundary marker,* пограни́чный *or* межево́й знак; пограни́чная ве́ха. **4,** (chip; counter) фи́шка.

market *n.* **1,** (marketplace) ры́нок; база́р. *Fish market,* ры́бный ры́нок *or* база́р. *Go to market,* идти́ на ры́нок. **2,** (outlet for sale) ры́нок: *foreign market(s),* вне́шний ры́нок. *Be on the market,* продава́ться. *Put on the market,* выпуска́ть на ры́нок. *Come onto the market,* поступа́ть на ры́нок. **3,** (desire to buy; demand) спрос. *Find a ready market,* находи́ть лёгкий *or* бы́стрый сбыт. **4,** (stock market) би́ржа: *play the market,* игра́ть на би́рже. —*adj.* ры́ночный: *market economy,* ры́ночная эконо́мика; *market price,* ры́ночная цена́. *Market basket,* корзи́на для прови́зии. —*v.t.* продава́ть; сбыва́ть. —**black market,** чёрный ры́нок.

marketplace *n.* **1,** (public place for a market) база́р; база́рная пло́щадь. **2,** (buying and selling of goods) ры́нок.

marking *n.* **1,** (mark) ме́тка. **2,** (coloration) окра́ска; расцве́тка.

marksman *n.* (ме́ткий) стрело́к. —**marksmanship,** *n.* ме́ткость.

markup *n.* наце́нка.

marl *n.* ме́ргель.

marmalade *n.* джем; пови́дло.

marmoset *n.* марты́шка.

marmot *n.* суро́к.

maroon *adj.* бордо́; цве́та бордо́; бордо́вый. —*v.t.* выса́живать (на необита́емом о́строве). *Marooned by the flood,* отре́занный наводне́нием. *Be marooned in the sticks,* застря́ть в глуши́.

marquee *n.* театра́льный наве́с.

marquis *n.* марки́з. —**marquise,** *n.* марки́за.

marriage *n.* брак; жени́тьба; заму́жество. —**relative by marriage,** сво́йственник.

married *adj.* **1,** (of a man) жена́т; *modifier* жена́тый. **2,** (of a woman) за́мужем; *modifier* заму́жняя. **3,** (of two or many people) жена́ты: *They are not married,* они́ не жена́ты. *Married people,* жена́тые. *Married couple,* супру́жеская чета́ *or* па́ра. *Married life,* супру́жеская жизнь. —**get married, 1,** (of a man) жени́ться. **2,** (of a woman) выходи́ть за́муж. **3,** (of two people) пожени́ться.

marrow *n.* ко́стный мозг. —**to the marrow,** до мо́зга косте́й.

marry *v.t.* **1,** (get married to) A, (of a man) жени́ться на (+ *prepl.*). B, (of a woman) выходи́ть за́муж за (+ *acc.*). *I have asked her to marry me,* я сде́лал ей предложе́ние. **2,** *usu. fol. by* **off** (give in marriage) A, (a son) жени́ть. B, (a daughter) выдава́ть за́муж. **3,** (perform the marriage ceremony for) A, (in a religious ceremony) венча́ть; (in a civil ceremony) расписы́вать. —*v.i.* вступа́ть в брак; жени́ться; выходи́ть за́муж; (*of two people*) пожени́ться.

Mars *n.* Марс.

Marsala *n.* (wine) марсала́.

Marseillaise *n.* Марселье́за.

marsh *n.* боло́то; топь.

marshal *n.* **1,** (military rank) ма́ршал. **2,** (law-enforcement official) суде́бный исполни́тель. —*v.t.* **1,** (array, as for battle) выстра́ивать. **2,** (assemble, as thoughts, facts, etc.) собира́ть.

marsh gas боло́тный газ.

marshland *n.* боло́тистая ме́стность.

marshmallow *n.* (candy) зефи́р. —**marsh mallow,** (plant) алте́й.

marsh marigold калу́жница.

marshy *adj.* боло́тистый; то́пкий.

marsupial *n. & adj.* су́мчатый.

marten *n.* куни́ца.

martial *adj.* вое́нный; во́инский. —**martial law,** вое́нное положе́ние.

Martian *n.* марсиа́нин. —*adj.* марсиа́нский.

martyr *n.* му́ченик. —*v.t.* подверга́ть му́ченической сме́рти. —**martyrdom,** *n.* му́ченичество.

marvel *n.* чу́до; ди́во. —*v.i.* диви́ться; изумля́ться.

marvelous *also,* **marvellous** *adj.* удиви́тельный; изуми́тельный; чу́дный; чуде́сный. —**marvelously,** *adv.* удиви́тельно; изуми́тельно; чу́дно; чуде́сно.

Marxism *n.* маркси́зм. —**Marxian,** *adj.* маркси́стский. —**Marxist,** *n.* маркси́ст. —*adj.* маркси́стский.

marzipan *n.* марципа́н.

mascara *n.* тушь.

mascot *n.* талисма́н.

masculine *adj.* **1,** (male) мужско́й. **2,** (manly) му́жественный. **3,** *gram.* мужско́го ро́да. *Masculine gender,* мужско́й род. —**masculinity,** *n.* му́жественность.

mash *n.* **1,** (brewing mixture) су́сло. **2,** (feed for livestock) по́йло; ме́сиво. —*v.t.* размина́ть. *Mashed potatoes,* карто́фельное пюре́.

mask *n.* ма́ска; личи́на. —*v.t.* маскирова́ть. —**masked,** *adj.* замаскиро́ванный.

masochism *n.* мазохи́зм. —**masochist,** *n.* мазохи́ст. —**masochistic,** *adj.* мазохи́стский.

mason *n.* **1,** (worker in stone) ка́менщик. **2,** *cap.* (Freemason) масо́н.

Masonic *adj.* масо́нский.

masonry *n.* **1,** (work in stone) ка́менная кла́дка. **2,** *cap.* (Freemasonry) масо́нство.

masquerade *n.* маскара́д. —*v.i.* выдава́ть себя́ (за).

mass *n.* **1,** (body of matter) ма́сса: *a mass of clay,* гли́няная ма́сса. **2,** (great amount) ма́сса: *a mass of information,* ма́сса информа́ции. **3,** *physics* ма́сса: *critical mass,* крити́ческая ма́сса. **4,** *pl., preceded by* **the** (the common people) ма́ссы. **5,** *cap.* (church service) ме́сса; обе́дня. —*adj.* ма́ссовый: *mass production,* ма́ссовое произво́дство; *mass media,* сре́дства ма́ссовой информа́ции. —*v.t.* масси́ровать: *troops massed at the border,* войска́, масси́рованные на грани́це. —*v.i.* масси́роваться.

massacre *n.* резня́; бо́йня; избие́ние. —*v.t.* выреза́ть; изруби́ть.

massage *n.* масса́ж. —*v.t.* масси́ровать; растира́ть.

masseur *n.* массажи́ст. —**masseuse,** *n.* массажи́стка.

massive *adj.* **1,** (huge; heavy and solid) масси́вный. **2,** (enormous in scope) огро́мный.

mast *n.* ма́чта.

master *n.* **1,** (one having control over another) хозя́ин; господи́н. *Master of the house/ situation/ one's fate/,* хозя́ин до́ма/ положе́ния/ свое́й судьбы́/. *The dog's master,* хозя́ин соба́ки. *Serve two masters,* служи́ть двум господа́м. **2,** (expert; skilled craftsman) ма́стер: *chess master,* ша́хматный ма́стер. *The great masters,* вели́кие мастера́. *Past master,* иску́сник. **3,** (holder of a master's degree) маги́стр: *Master of Arts,* маги́стр гуманита́рных нау́к. *Master's degree,* маги́стр; сте́пень маги́стра. **4,** (captain of a merchant ship) капита́н. —*adj.* **1,** (highly skilled): *master craftsman,* ма́стер. *Master storyteller,* ма́стер расска́за. **2,** (being master) госпо́дствующий. *Master race,* ра́са госпо́д. **3,** (comprehensive): *master plan,* генера́льный план. **4,** (brilliantly executed) мастерско́й: *master stroke,* мастерско́й уда́р. **5,** (original, as of a copy) по́длинный. **6,** *mech.* (of a switch, cylinder, etc.) гла́вный. —*v.t.* **1,** (bring under control) одолева́ть; оси́лить. **2,** (learn thoroughly) усва́ивать; овладева́ть.

masterful *adj.* **1,** (expert) мастерско́й. **2,** (domineering) вла́стный.

master key отмы́чка.

masterly *adj.* мастерско́й.

mastermind *v.t.* заду́мывать; замышля́ть.

master of ceremonies конферансье́.

masterpiece *n.* шеде́вр.

master sergeant старшина́.

mastery *n.* **1,** (control; dominion) госпо́дство. **2,** (command, as of a subject) владе́ние; овладе́ние. *Mastery of a language,* владе́ние языко́м.

masthead *n.* (of a newspaper) ша́пка.

mastic *n.* масти́ка. —*adj.* масти́ковый.

masticate *v.t. & i.* жева́ть. —**mastication,** *n.* жева́ние.

mastiff *n.* дог.

mastitis *n.* грудни́ца; масти́т.

mastodon *n.* мастодо́нт.

masturbate *v.i.* мастурби́ровать; онани́ровать. —**masturbation,** *n.* мастурба́ция; онани́зм.

mat *n.* **1,** (small rug) ко́врик; цино́вка. *Doormat,* полови́к. **2,** (something placed under a dish or vase) подсти́лка. **3,** *sports* ковёр. **4,** (dull surface) ма́товая пове́рхность. —*adj.* ма́товый. —*v.t.* (tangle) запу́тывать. —*v.i.* запу́тываться.

match *n.* **1,** (device for igniting) спи́чка. **2,** (equal; peer) ро́вня. *No match for,* не чета́ (+ *dat.*). *Meet one's match,* найти́ ра́вного проти́вника. **3,** (suitable or possible mate) па́ра; па́ртия: *She is not a good match for him,* она́ ему́ не па́ра/па́ртия. **4,** (combination; marriage) па́ртия: *a good match,* хоро́шая па́ртия. **5,** (contest) состяза́ние; матч: *wrestling match,* состяза́ние по борьбе́; *chess match,* ша́хматный матч. —*v.t.* **1,** (be equal to; rival) сравни́ться с; равня́ться с. *The climate here is hard to match,* тру́дно найти́ ме́сто с таки́м кли́матом. **2,** (correspond to) соотве́тствовать (+ *dat.*). *The copy matches*

the original, ко́пия повторя́ет оригина́л. **3,** (go well with) гармони́ровать с; сочета́ться с; подходи́ть к. *A dress with matching shoes,* пла́тье с подо́бранными к ней ту́флями. *Choose a tie to match one's suit,* подбира́ть га́лстук под цвет костю́ма (*or* в тон костю́му). **4,** *fol. by* **up** (pair; mate) сва́тать. **5,** (pit; place in opposition) противопоставля́ть. *Match wits,* состяза́ться в остроу́мии. *Evenly matched teams,* равноси́льные кома́нды. —*v.i.* гармони́ровать: *The shirt and tie don't match,* руба́шка и га́лстук не гармони́руют (друг с дру́гом).

matchbox *n.* спи́чечная коро́бка.

matchless *adj.* несравне́нный; бесподо́бный.

matchmaker *n.* сват; сва́ха. —**matchmaking,** *n.* сватовство́.

mate *n.* **1,** (one of a pair) па́ра. **2,** (spouse) супру́г; супру́га. **3,** (associate; buddy) това́рищ; напа́рник. **4,** (of an animal) па́ра. **5,** *naut.* помо́щник капита́на. **6,** *chess* мат. —*v.t.* **1,** (pair for breeding) спа́ривать; случа́ть. **2,** *chess* де́лать мат (+ *dat.*). *Mating attack,* ма́товая ата́ка. —*v.i.* спа́риваться.

material *n.* **1,** (that of which something is made) материа́л: *building materials,* строи́тельные материа́лы. *Raw materials,* сырьё. **2,** (textile fabric) материа́л; мате́рия: *material for a dress,* материа́л/мате́рия на пла́тье. **3,** *pl.* (implements) принадле́жности: *writing materials,* пи́сьменные принадле́жности. **4,** (data to be worked on) материа́л: *material for a book,* материа́л для кни́ги. —*adj.* **1,** (physical) материа́льный; веще́ственный. *Material well-being,* материа́льное благополу́чие. *Material evidence,* веще́ственные доказа́тельства. **2,** (significant; substantial) суще́ственный. **3,** *Material witness,* ва́жный свиде́тель.

materialism *n.* материали́зм. —**materialist,** *n.* материали́ст. —**materialistic,** *adj.* материалисти́ческий.

materialize *v.i.* осуществля́ться; реализова́ться.

materially *adv.* **1,** (in a material sense) материа́льно: *materially well-off,* материа́льно обеспе́ченный. **2,** (significantly) суще́ственно; суще́ственным о́бразом.

matériel *n.* материа́льная часть.

maternal *adj.* **1,** (motherly) матери́нский. **2,** (on one's mother's side of the family) по ма́тери; со стороны́ ма́тери; с матери́нской стороны́. *My maternal grandfather,* мой дед по ма́тери.

maternity *n.* матери́нство. —**maternity clothes,** оде́жда для бере́менной же́нщины. —**maternity hospital,** роди́льный дом; роддо́м. —**maternity leave,** о́тпуск по бере́менности и ро́дам; декре́тный о́тпуск. —**maternity ward,** роди́льное отделе́ние.

mathematics *n.* матема́тика. —**mathematical,** *adj.* математи́ческий. —**mathematician,** *n.* матема́тик.

matin *n., usu. pl.* у́треня; зау́треня.

matinee *n.* дневно́й спекта́кль.

mating *n.* спа́ривание. —**mating call,** токова́ние. —**mating season,** бра́чный пери́од.

matins *n., pl. of* **matin.**

matriarch *n.* мать. —**matriarchal,** *adj.* матриарха́льный. —**matriarchy,** *n.* матриарха́т.

matricide *n.* матереубийство.

matriculate *v.i.* зачисляться (в высшее учебное заведение). —**matriculation,** *n.* зачисление (в высшее учебное заведение).

matrimony *n.* супружество; брак. —**matrimonial,** *adj.* супружеский; брачный; матримониальный.

matrix *n.* матрица.

matron *n.* матрона.

matted *adj.* спутанный.

matter *n.* **1,** (substance) вещество; материя. *Organic matter,* органическое вещество. **2,** (something printed) материал: *reading matter,* материал для чтения. **3,** (affair; question) вопрос; дело. *A matter of taste,* дело вкуса. *It is only a matter of time,* это лишь дело времени. *A matter of life and death,* вопрос жизни и смерти. *As matters stand,* при данном положении дел. *That is another matter,* это другое дело; это другой разговор. *It is no laughing matter,* это не шуточное дело. *In a matter of minutes,* в считанные минуты. —*v.i.* иметь значение. *It doesn't matter,* ничего; неважно; не имеет значения. —**as a matter of fact, 1,** (in point of fact) на самом деле; фактически. **2,** (now that you mention it) представьте себе: *As a matter of fact, yes,* представьте себе, да. **3,** (in this connection) между прочим. —**for that matter,** если (уж) на то пошло. —**no matter how/what/when** *etc.,* как бы ни/ что бы ни/ когда бы ни, *etc. No matter how he tried,* как он ни старался. —**something is the matter,** что-то не так. —**what is the matter?,** в чём дело?; что такое? —**what is the matter with you?,** что с вами?

matter-of-fact *adj.* сухой; прозаичный.

matting *n.* рогожа.

mattock *n.* мотыга.

mattress *n.* матрас; матрац.

maturation *n.* созревание.

mature *adj.* зрелый. —*v.i.* созревать. —*v.t.* доводить до зрелости. —**maturity,** *n.* зрелость.

matutinal *adj.* утренний.

matzo *n.* маца.

maudlin *adj.* слезливый.

maul *n.* колотушка; кувалда. —*v.t.* терзать; растерзать.

Maundy Thursday страстной четверг.

Mauser *n.* маузер.

mausoleum *n.* мавзолей.

mauve *adj.* лиловый.

maverick *n.* **1,** (unbranded calf) телёнок без клейма. **2,** (independent person) индивидуалист.

mawkish *adj.* приторный; слащавый.

maxim *n.* изречение; сентенция.

maximal *adj.* максимальный.

maximize *v.t.* доводить до максимума.

maximum *n.* максимум. —*adj.* максимальный; предельный: *maximum speed,* максимальная/предельная скорость.

may *v.aux.* **1,** *expressing possibility or contingency,* мочь: *It may rain,* может пойти дождь. *They may have gone home already,* они могли уже уйти домой. ♦*Also rendered by* возможно: *I may be late,* я,

возможно, опоздаю. *It may be true,* возможно, это правда. **2,** *requesting or granting permission,* мочь; можно: *May I come in?,* можно войти? *You may go now,* вы можете теперь идти. **3,** *expressing a wish, hope, or prayer,* пусть; да: *May all your dreams come true!,* пусть/да сбудутся все ваши мечты! *May he rest in peace,* мир праху его. —**be that as it may,** как бы то ни было. —**come what may,** будь, что будет.

May *n.* май. —*adj.* майский.

maybe *adv.* может быть.

May Day Первое мая; праздник Первого мая. —**May-Day,** *adj.* первомайский.

mayfly *n.* подёнка.

mayhem *n.* **1,** *law* нанесение увечья. **2,** (havoc) хаос.

mayonnaise *n.* майонез.

mayor *n.* мэр.

maze *n.* лабиринт.

mazurka *n.* мазурка.

me *pers. pron.* **1,** *used as dir. obj. of a verb,* меня: *He loves me,* он меня любит. **2,** *used as indir. obj. of a verb,* мне: *Show me!,* покажите мне. **3,** *used as obj. of a prep.,* меня; мне; мной: *about me,* обо мне; *with me,* со мной.

mead *n.* мёд.

meadow *n.* луг.

meadowsweet *n.* таволга.

meager *also,* **meagre** *adj.* **1,** (scanty) скудный; скупой; бедный. *Meager supplies,* скудные *or* скупые запасы. *Meager supper,* скудный *or* бедный ужин. **2,** (lean) худой; тощий.

meal *n.* **1,** (repast) еда. *Two tablets before/after meals,* две таблетки перед едой/ после еды/. *Eat three meals a day,* есть три раза в день. *Cook one's own meals,* готовить самому (самой) себе. **2,** (ground grain) мука: *corn meal,* кукурузная мука.

mealy *adj.* мучнистый.

mean *v.t.* **1,** (signify; denote) значить: *What does this mean?,* что это значит? *The name means nothing to me,* это имя мне ничего не говорит. **2,** *fol. by inf.* (intend) собираться; хотеть. *I've been meaning to write you for a long time,* я долго собирался (*or* давно хотел) написать вам. *By the way, I meant to ask you...,* кстати, я хотел(а) вас спросить... *I mean to succeed in this job,* я собираюсь преуспеть на этой должности. **3,** (intentionally plan or wish) хотеть: *I didn't mean to offend you,* я не хотел(а) вас обидеть. *He means you no harm,* он не желает вам зла. **4,** (intend to express) хотеть сказать; подразумевать. *What do you mean by that?,* что вы хотите этим сказать?; что вы подразумеваете под этим? *By ... I mean...,* под ... я подразумеваю... *What do you mean, you don't know?,* как не знаешь? **5,** (have in mind) иметь в виду: *Whom do you mean?,* кого вы имеете в виду? **6,** (matter) значить: *mean a great deal to,* много значить для. **7,** *fol. by* **it** (be serious): *Do you really mean it?,* вы это серьёзно? *I mean it,* я говорю серьёзно. *I mean that sincerely,* я говорю искренне; я действительно так думаю. *You don't mean it!,* вы шутите! **8,** (intend; design) предназнача́ть: *The book is meant for the general reader,* кни́га предназна́чена для широ́кого чита́теля. **9,** *usu.* passive (destine): *He was not meant to be a soldier,* ему́ не суждено́ бы́ло быть солда́том. *They were meant for each other,* они́ со́зданы друг для дру́га. *It wasn't meant to be,* ви́дно, не судьба́. —*v.i. Mean well,* име́ть до́брые наме́рения. —*adj.* **1,** (nasty) злой: *a mean old man,* злой стари́к. *Be mean to someone,* пло́хо *or* гру́бо обраща́ться с ке́м-нибудь. **2,** (malicious) ни́зкий; по́длый; злой: *mean trick,* ни́зкий/по́длый посту́пок; зла́я шу́тка. **3,** (average) сре́дний: *mean distance,* сре́днее расстоя́ние. —*n.* **1,** (something between extremes) середи́на: *golden mean,* золота́я середи́на. **2,** *math.* сре́днее число́. **3,** *pl.* (method; instrument) сре́дства: *means of production,* сре́дства произво́дства. *The end justifies the means,* цель опра́вдывает сре́дства. **4,** *pl.* (money; wealth) сре́дства: *man of means,* челове́к со сре́дствами. *People of modest means,* лю́ди скро́много доста́тка. *Live beyond one's means,* жить не по сре́дствам. —**by all means, 1,** (without fail) обяза́тельно. **2,** (of course) коне́чно; пожа́луйста. —**by means of,** посре́дством (+ *gen.*); путём (+ *gen.*); при по́мощи (+ *gen.*). —**by no means, 1,** *fol. by an adj.* (not the least bit) совсе́м не; отню́дь не. **2,** *as an exclamation* (not at all) нет, что вы! —**not ... by any means,** совсе́м не: *not cheap by any means,* совсе́м не дёшево.

meander *v.i.* **1,** (follow a winding course) извива́ться. **2,** (ramble; wander) броди́ть. —**meandering,** *adj.* изви́листый.

meaning *n.* значе́ние; смысл. *The word has several meanings,* сло́во име́ет не́сколько значе́ний. *The meaning of life,* смысл жи́зни. *What is the meaning of this?,* что всё э́то зна́чит?

meaningful *adj.* **1,** (having meaning) зна́чащий. **2,** (significant) многозначи́тельный.

meaningless *adj.* бессмы́сленный; не име́ющий смы́сла; ничего́ не зна́чащий.

meanness *n.* зло́ба; ни́зость; по́длость.

meantime *n., usu. in* **in the meantime,** тем вре́менем; ме́жду тем. —*adv.* = **in the meantime.** *Also,* **meanwhile.**

measles *n.* корь. *German measles,* красну́ха.

measly *adj., colloq.* ничто́жный; мизе́рный.

measurable *adj.* **1,** (that can be measured) измери́мый. **2,** (appreciable) заме́тный; ощути́мый.

measure *n.* **1,** (unit or system of measurement) ме́ра: *measure of length,* ме́ра длины́; *dry measure,* ме́ра сыпу́чих тел. **2,** (action; step) ме́ра: *drastic measures,* круты́е ме́ры. **3,** (degree; extent) ме́ра; сте́пень. *In large measure,* в большо́й *or* в значи́тельной ме́ре. *In some measure,* до не́которой сте́пени; в изве́стной ме́ре. **4,** *music* разме́р; такт. —*v.t.* **1,** (determine the size of) измеря́ть. **2,** (appraise; gauge) оце́нивать. **3,** (bring into comparison) ме́риться: *measure one's strength against,* ме́риться си́лами с. **4,** *fol. by* **off** (mark off) отмеря́ть. —*v.i.* име́ть (разме́ры): *The room measures ten feet in length,* ко́мната име́ет де́сять фу́тов в длину́. —be-

yond **measure,** неизмери́мо; чрезвыча́йно. —**for good measure,** в прида́чу. —**measure one's length,** растяну́ться во всю длину́. —**measure up,** быть на высоте́. *Measure up to expectations,* опра́вдывать ожида́ния. —**take one's measure, 1,** (take someone's measurements) снима́ть ме́рку с (+ *gen.*). **2,** (size up) присма́триваться к. —**to measure,** по ме́рке: *made to measure,* сши́тый по ме́рке.

measured *adj.* **1,** (ascertained by measurement) изме́ренный. **2,** (regular; steady; deliberate) ме́рный; разме́ренный.

measurement *n.* **1,** (measuring) измере́ние. **2,** *usu. pl.* (size found by measuring) ме́рка: *take someone's measurements,* снима́ть ме́рку с (+ *gen.*).

meat *n.* мя́со. —*adj.* мясно́й. —**meatballs,** *n.pl.* тёфтели; битки́. —**meat grinder,** мясору́бка. —**meat loaf,** мясно́й руле́т. —**meat pie,** пиро́г с мя́сом.

meaty *adj.* **1,** (fleshy) мяси́стый. **2,** *fig.* (full of substance) содержа́тельный.

mechanic *n.* меха́ник.

mechanical *adj.* **1,** (pert. to machinery) механи́ческий: *mechanical failure,* механи́ческая неиспра́вность. *Mechanical toy,* заводна́я игру́шка. *Mechanical aptitude,* техни́ческие спосо́бности. **2,** *fig.* (automatic; done without thinking) машина́льный; механи́ческий. —**mechanical drawing,** техни́ческое черче́ние. —**mechanical engineer,** меха́ник; инжене́р-меха́ник. —**mechanical engineering,** машинострое́ние.

mechanics *n.* меха́ника.

mechanism *n.* механи́зм.

mechanize *v.t.* механизи́ровать; машинизи́ровать. —**mechanization,** *n.* механиза́ция; машиниза́ция.

medal *n.* меда́ль: *a medal for bravery,* меда́ль за хра́брость. —**medalist,** *n.* медали́ст.

medallion *n.* медальо́н.

medallist *n.* = **medalist.**

meddle *v.i.* вме́шиваться: *meddle in someone's personal life,* вме́шиваться в чью́-нибудь ли́чную жизнь. —**meddlesome,** *adj.* вме́шивающийся не в свои́ дела́. —**meddling,** *n.* вмеша́тельство.

media *n.pl.* сре́дства ма́ссовой информа́ции.

mediaeval *adj.* = **medieval.**

median *adj.* сре́дний. —*n.* медиа́на.

mediate *v.i.* посре́дничать. —*v.t.* ула́живать: *mediate a dispute,* ула́живать спор. —**mediation,** *n.* посре́дничество. —**mediator,** *n.* посре́дник.

medical *adj.* медици́нский.

medication *n.* медикаме́нты; лека́рство.

medicinal *adj.* лека́рственный; целе́бный.

medicine *n.* **1,** (the science) медици́на: *study medicine,* изуча́ть медици́ну. **2,** (something taken when ill) лека́рство: *strong medicine,* си́льное лека́рство. *A shortage of medicines,* недоста́ток медикаме́нтов. —**give someone a taste of his own medicine,** отплати́ть кому́-нибудь той же моне́той.

medicine cabinet (дома́шняя) апте́ка; апте́чный шкаф. *Also,* **medicine chest.**

medicine man зна́харь; шама́н.

medieval *also,* **mediaeval** *adj.* средневеко́вый.

mediocre *adj.* посре́дственный; заУря́дный.

mediocrity *n.* посре́дственность. *A mediocrity,* посре́дственность; середня́к.

meditate *v.i.* размышля́ть; разду́мывать; заду́мываться. —**meditation,** *n.* размышле́ние; разду́мье. —**meditative,** *adj.* заду́мчивый.

medium *n.* **1,** (mean) середи́на: *happy medium,* золота́я середи́на. **2,** (means) сре́дство: *medium of exchange,* сре́дство обме́на. *Through the medium of,* посре́дством (+ *gen.*); че́рез посре́дство (+ *gen.*). **3,** (substance through which something is transmitted) среда́. **4,** (culture medium) пита́тельная среда́. **5,** (spiritualist) ме́диум. —*adj.* сре́дний: *of medium height,* сре́днего ро́ста. *Medium bomber,* сре́дний бомбардиро́вщик. —**medium-range,** *adj.* сре́днего ра́диуса де́йствия; (*of missiles*) сре́дней да́льности. —**medium-sized,** *adj.* сре́дней величины́; сре́днего разме́ра. *See also* **media.**

medlar *n.* мушмула́.

medley *n.* **1,** (hodgepodge) мешани́на; ме́сиво. **2,** *music* попурри́.

medulla *n.* **1,** (marrow) ко́стный мозг. **2,** (inner part of an organ) мозгово́й слой. —**medulla oblongata,** продолгова́тый мозг.

medusa *n.* меду́за.

meek *adj.* кро́ткий; смире́нный. —**meekness,** *n.* кро́тость; смире́ние.

meerschaum *n.* (морска́я) пе́нка. —*adj.* пе́нковый.

meet *v.t.* **1,** (come upon; join) встреча́ть: *meet a friend/ a train/ resistance/,* встреча́ть дру́га/по́езд/сопротивле́ние. **2,** (make the acquaintance of) знако́миться с. *Meet some interesting people,* познако́миться с интере́сными людьми́. *I would like you to meet my wife,* позво́льте познако́мить вас с мое́й жено́й. **3,** (conform to; satisfy) отвеча́ть (+ *dat.*); удовлетворя́ть: *meet the requirements,* отвеча́ть/ удовлетворя́ть тре́бованиям. *Meet world standards,* отвеча́ть мировы́м станда́ртам. *Meet the needs of...,* удовлетворя́ть ну́жды (+ *gen.*). *Meet someone's demands,* удовлетвори́ть чьи́-нибудь тре́бования. **4,** *Meet one's death/end,* найти́ свою́ смерть; встре́тить свой коне́ц. —*v.i.* **1,** (come upon or join each other) встреча́ться: *meet in the park,* встреча́ться в па́рке. **2,** (become acquainted) знако́миться. *Have you met?,* вы знако́мы? **3,** *fol. by* **with** (confer with) встреча́ться с; совеща́ться с. **4,** *fol. by* **with** (encounter) встреча́ть; встреча́ться с; ста́лкиваться с. *Meet with approval,* встре́тить одобре́ние. *Meet with difficulties,* встреча́ться *or* ста́лкиваться с тру́дностями. **5,** (gather; assemble) собира́ться; сходи́ться. **6,** (come together in battle or competition) встреча́ться; сходи́ться: *meet in the* (*boxing*) *ring/ on the battlefield/,* встре́титься/ сойти́сь на ри́нге/ на по́ле би́твы/. **7,** (intersect) сходи́ться. —*n.* соревнова́ние: *track meet,* легкоатлети́ческое соревнова́ние.

meeting *n.* **1,** (encounter) встре́ча: *chance meeting,* случа́йная встре́ча. **2,** (scheduled appointment) встре́ча; свида́ние. **3,** (gathering to discuss something) собра́ние: *attend a meeting,* прису́тствовать на собра́нии.

megacycle *n.* мегаге́рц.

megalith *n.* мегали́т.

megalomania *n.* ма́ния вели́чия.

megaphone *n.* ру́пор; мегафо́н.

megaton *n.* мегато́нна.

megawatt *n.* мегава́тт.

melancholia *n.* меланхо́лия. —**melancholic,** *adj.* меланхоли́ческий.

melancholy *n.* уны́ние; тоска́; грусть; меланхо́лия. —*adj.* уны́лый; тоскли́вый; меланхоли́ческий.

mélange *n.* смеше́ние; смесь.

melee *n.* сва́лка.

meliorate *v.t.* улучша́ть. —*v.i.* улучша́ться. —**melioration,** *n.* улучше́ние.

mellifluous *adj.* медоточи́вый; сладкозву́чный.

mellow *adj.* **1,** (fully flavored; full-bodied) со́чный: *mellow voice,* со́чный го́лос. **2,** *colloq.* (genial) добро́душный. *Become mellow with age,* подобре́ть с года́ми. —*v.t.* смягча́ть. —*v.i.* добре́ть.

melodic *adj.* мелоди́ческий. —**melodics,** *n.* мело́дика.

melodious *adj.* мелоди́чный; певу́чий. —**melodiousness,** *n.* мелоди́чность; певу́честь.

melodrama *n.* мелодра́ма. —**melodramatic,** *adj.* мелодрамати́ческий; театра́льный.

melody *n.* мело́дия.

melon *n.* ды́ня. *Melon field,* бахча́.

melt *v.t.* **1,** (reduce to a liquid state) A, (butter, snow, ice, etc.) топи́ть; раста́пливать. *The sun melted the snow,* со́лнце растопи́ло снег. B, (metals) пла́вить; расплавля́ть. **2,** (dissolve) растворя́ть. —*v.i.* **1,** (turn to liquid) A, (of snow, ice cream, butter, etc.) та́ять. B, (of metals) пла́виться. **2,** (dissolve) растворя́ться. **3,** (fade away; dwindle) улету́чиваться. *Melt into the background,* слива́ться с фо́ном. *Melt into the crowd,* смеша́ться с толпо́й. —**melt in one's mouth,** та́ять во рту.

melted *adj.* (of snow) та́лый; (of butter) топлёный; (of metals) распла́вленный.

melting *n.* плавле́ние; пла́вка. *Melting point,* то́чка плавле́ния. —**melting pot,** плави́льный котёл.

member *n.* член. *Member of parliament,* член парла́мента; парламента́рий.

membership *n.* **1,** (status of a member) чле́нство. *Admit to membership* (*in*), принима́ть в чле́ны (+ *gen.*). **2,** (members collectively) чле́ны. **3,** (number of members) коли́чество чле́нов. —*adj.* чле́нский: *membership dues,* чле́нские взно́сы.

membrane *n.* плева́; перепо́нка; оболо́чка. —**membranous,** *adj.* перепо́нчатый.

memento *n.* па́мятный пода́рок; сувени́р.

memo *n., colloq.* = **memorandum.**

memoirs *n.pl.* мемуа́ры.

memorable *adj.* па́мятный; знамена́тельный.

memorandum *n.* **1,** (reminder) па́мятная запи́ска; мемора́ндум. **2,** (informal communication) делова́я *or* докладна́я запи́ска; мемора́ндум. **3,** *dipl.* мемора́ндум.

memorial *n.* па́мятник; мемориа́л. —*adj.* мемори-а́льный. *Memorial plaque,* мемориа́льная *or* па́мят-ная доска́. *Memorial service,* заупоко́йная слу́жба.

memorialize *v.t.* увекове́чивать па́мять (+ *gen. or with* о).

memorize *v.t.* запомина́ть; зау́чивать *or* выу́чивать наизу́сть.

memory *n.* **1,** (capacity to remember) па́мять. *From memory,* на па́мять; по па́мяти. *Within my memory,* на мое́й па́мяти. *Good memory for names,* хоро́шая па́мять на имена́. *The first case in memory,* пе́рвый слу́чай на па́мяти. **2,** (recollection) воспомина́ние: *memories of childhood,* воспомина́ния де́тства. *Bring back memories of the past,* напомина́ть про́-шлое *or* о про́шлом. **3,** (commemoration) па́мять: *in memory of,* в па́мять (+ *gen.*); па́мяти (+ *gen.*). **4,** (of a computer) па́мять.

menace *n.* угро́за. —*v.t.* угрожа́ть; грози́ть. —**men-acing,** *adj.* гро́зный; угрожа́ющий.

menagerie *n.* звери́нец.

mend *v.t.* **1,** (repair) чини́ть. **2,** (darn) што́пать. **3,** *in* **mend one's ways,** исправля́ться. —*v.i.* (of bones) сраста́ться. —**be on the mend,** выздора́вливать. *He is on the mend,* у него́ де́ло идёт на попра́вку.

mendacious *adj.* лжи́вый; ло́жный. —**mendacity,** *n.* лжи́вость.

mendelevium *n.* менделе́вий.

mendicant *n.* ни́щий. —*adj.* ни́щенствующий. —**mendicancy,** *n.* ни́щенство.

menial *adj.* чёрный: *menial tasks,* чёрная рабо́та.

meningitis *n.* менинги́т.

menopause *n.* кли́макс.

Menshevik *n.* меньшеви́к. —*adj.* меньшеви́стский.

men's room мужска́я убо́рная; мужско́й туале́т.

menstrual *adj.* менструа́льный.

menstruate *v.i.* менструи́ровать. —**menstruation,** *n.* менструа́ция.

mensuration *n.* измере́ние.

mental *adj.* **1,** (pert. to the mind) у́мственный: *mental faculties,* у́мственные спосо́бности. **2,** (taking place in the mind) мы́сленный: *mental image,* мы́сленный о́браз. **3,** (pert. to the mentally ill) душе́вный; психи́ческий: *mental illness,* душе́вная/психи́че-ская боле́знь. *Mental case; mental patient,* ду-шевнобольно́й; психи́чески больно́й. *Mental hospi-tal,* психиатри́ческая больни́ца.

mentality *n.* склад ума́; психоло́гия; менталите́т; мента́льность.

mentally *adv.* **1,** (in one's mind) мы́сленно. **2,** (as re-gards one's mental faculties) у́мственно; психи́-чески. *Mentally ill,* душевнобольно́й; психи́чески больно́й. *Mentally retarded,* у́мственно отста́лый.

menthol *n.* менто́л. —**mentholated,** *adj.* менто́-ловый.

mention *v.t.* упомина́ть: *mention someone's name,* упомина́ть чьё-нибудь и́мя. *I'll mention it to him,* я ему́ скажу́ об э́том. *As has already been mentioned,* как уже́ упомина́лось... —*n.* упомина́ние: *at the mention of,* при упомина́нии (+ *gen.*). *He made no mention of it,* он не упомина́л об э́том. —**don't**

mention it!, не́ за что!; пожа́луйста; не сто́ит благода́рности. —**not to mention,** не говоря́ уже́ о.

mentor *n.* наста́вник; воспита́тель.

menu *n.* меню́.

meow *also,* **miaow** *v.i.* мяу́кать. —*n.* мяу́канье.

mercantile *adj.* **1,** (commercial) торго́вый; ком-ме́рческий. **2,** (pert. to mercantilism) меркант́иль-ный. —**mercantilism,** *n.* меркантили́зм.

mercenary *adj.* **1,** (selfish) коры́стный. **2,** (serving for ray) наёмный. —*n.* наёмник.

merchandise *n.* това́р.

merchant *n.* купе́ц; торго́вец. *Arms merchants,* торго́вцы ору́жием. —**merchant marine,** торго́вый флот. —**merchant ship,** торго́вое су́дно.

merciful *adj.* милосе́рдный; сострада́тельный.

merciless *adj.* безжа́лостный; беспоща́дный; не-ща́дный; немилосе́рдный. —**mercilessly,** *adv.* без-жа́лостно; беспоща́дно; неща́дно; немилосе́рдно.

mercurial *adj.* **1,** [*also,* **mercuric**] (of mercury) рту́тный. **2,** (volatile) изме́нчивый; переме́нчивый. —**mercuric chloride,** сулема́. —**mercuric oxide,** о́кись рту́ти. —**mercuric sulfide,** серни́стая ртуть.

mercury *n.* **1,** (element) ртуть. **2,** *cap.* (god; planet) Мерку́рий. —*adj.* рту́тный: *mercury barometer,* рту́тный баро́метр.

mercy *n.* милосе́рдие; ми́лость; поща́да. *Show mercy toward,* проявля́ть милосе́рдие к. *Have/take mercy on,* щади́ть. —*interj.* го́споди! —**at the mercy of,** во вла́сти (+ *gen.*). *Throw oneself at the mercy of,* отда́ться на ми́лость (+ *gen.*).

mercy killing уби́йство из милосе́рдия.

mere *adj.* просто́й: *mere mortals,* просты́е сме́ртные. *He is a mere child,* да он ещё ребёнок. *At the mere thought of,* при одно́й мы́сли о.

merely *adv.* то́лько; про́сто.

meretricious *adj.* показно́й; мишу́рный.

merganser *n.* кроха́ль.

merge *v.t.* объединя́ть. —*v.i.* слива́ться; объ-единя́ться.

merger *n.* слия́ние; объедине́ние.

meridian *n.* меридиа́н.

meringue *n.* мере́нга.

merino *n.* мерино́с. —*adj.* мерино́совый.

merit *n.* **1,** (positive quality; virtue) заслу́га; досто́ин-ство. *Be without merit,* не выде́рживать кри́тики. **2,** *pl.* (intrinsic rights and wrongs) существо́: *the merits of a case,* существо́ де́ла. —*v.t.* заслу́живать.

meritorious *adj.* похва́льный. *Award for meritorious service,* награ́да за заслу́ги.

merlin *n.* (bird) де́рбник.

mermaid *n.* руса́лка.

merrily *adv.* ве́село.

merriment *n.* весе́лье.

merry *adj.* весёлый. *Merry Christmas!,* с Рождество́м (христо́вым)! —**make merry,** весели́ться. —**the more the merrier,** чем бо́льше, тем лу́чше.

merry-go-round *n.* карусе́ль.

merrymaker *n.* весельча́к. —**merrymaking,** *n.* весе́лье.

mesa *n.* столо́вая гора́; плоского́рье.

mesh *n.* очко́; яче́йка. —*v.i.* (engage) сцепля́ться.

mesmerism *n.* гипно́з; гипноти́зм. —**mesmerist,** *n.* гипнотизёр. —**mesmerize,** *v.t.* гипнотизи́ровать.

meson *n.* мезо́н.

Mesozoic *adj.* мезозо́йский.

mess *n.* **1,** (dirty or untidy condition) грязь: *What a mess!,* кака́я грязь! *The room was a mess,* в ко́мнате был разгро́м. **2,** (confused state) пу́таница; неразбери́ха. *Make a mess of,* напу́тать; прова́ливать. **3,** (trouble) беда́. *Get into a mess,* попа́сть в беду́ *or* в переплёт *or* в переде́лку. **4,** (group taking meals together; a meal so taken) о́бщий стол; (place where it is eaten) столо́вая. *Officers' mess,* офице́рский клу́б-столо́вая. —*v.t.* [*usu.* **mess up**] **1,** (soil) (за)па́чкать. **2,** (disarrange) (пере)пу́тать. **3,** (spoil) по́ртить; расстра́ивать. **4,** (bungle; botch) напу́тать. —*v.i.* **1,** *fol. by* **around** *or* **about** (putter) вози́ться. **2,** *fol. by* **in** (meddle) сова́ться (в). **3,** *fol. by* **with** (tussle with) тро́гать: *Don't mess with him!,* не тро́гайте его́!

message *n.* **1,** (communication) сообще́ние; донесе́ние. **2,** (written note) запи́ска. **3,** (verbal communication to be passed on): *Is there any message?,* что ему́ (ей) переда́ть? *Did he leave a message?,* он проси́л что́-нибудь переда́ть? **4,** (formal address) посла́ние.

messenger *n.* **1,** (one bringing a message or news) ве́стник. **2,** (errand boy) посы́льный; курье́р. *Send something by messenger,* посыла́ть что́-нибудь с посы́льным.

mess hall столо́вая.

Messiah *n.* месси́я. —**Messianic,** *adj.* мессиа́нский.

messy *adj.* **1,** (untidy; disorderly) неопря́тный. **2,** (complicated; unpleasant) неприя́тный.

mestizo *n.* мети́с.

metabolism *n.* обме́н веще́ств. —**metabolic,** *adj.* относя́щийся к обме́ну веще́ств: *metabolic disease,* боле́знь обме́на веще́ств.

metacarpus *n.* пясть.

metal *n.* мета́лл. —*adj.* металли́ческий. —**metallic,** *adj.* металли́ческий.

metalliferous *adj.* металлоно́сный.

metalloid *n.* металло́ид.

metallurgy *n.* металлу́ргия. —**metallurgic,** *adj.* металлурги́ческий. —**metallurgist,** *n.* металлу́рг.

metalworker *n.* сле́сарь; металли́ст.

metamorphosis *n.* **1,** *biol.* метаморфо́з. **2,** *fig.* (complete transformation) метаморфо́за.

metaphor *n.* мета́фора. —**metaphorical,** *adj.* метафори́ческий.

metaphysics *n.* метафи́зика. —**metaphysical,** *adj.* метафизи́ческий. —**metaphysician; metaphysicist,** *n.* метафи́зик.

metastasis *n.* метаста́з.

metatarsus *n.* плюсна́. —**metatarsal,** *adj.* плюсневой.

mete *v.t.* [*usu.* **mete out**] выделя́ть; распределя́ть. *Mete out punishment,* определя́ть наказа́ние.

meteor *n.* метео́р.

meteoric *adj.* **1,** (of a meteor) метео́рный. **2,** *fig.* (daz-

zlingly fast) головокружи́тельный.

meteorite *n.* метеори́т.

meteorology *n.* метеороло́гия. —**meteorological,** *adj.* метеорологи́ческий. —**meteorologist,** *n.* метеоро́лог.

meter *also,* **metre** *n.* **1,** (unit of length) метр. **2,** (measuring instrument) счётчик: *gas meter,* га́зовый счётчик. *Water meter,* водоме́р. **3,** *pros.* разме́р; метр. **4,** *music* ритм.

methane *n.* мета́н.

methanol *n.* метано́л.

method *n.* ме́тод; спо́соб. —**methodical,** *adj.* методи́ческий; методи́чный.

Methodist *n.* методи́ст. —*adj.* методи́стский. —**Methodism,** *n.* методи́зм.

methodology *n.* методоло́гия. —**methodological,** *adj.* методологи́ческий.

methyl *n.* мети́л. —**methyl alcohol,** мети́ловый спирт.

methylene *n.* метиле́н.

meticulous *adj.* аккура́тный; дото́шный. —**meticulousness,** *n.* аккура́тность.

metre *n.* = **meter.**

metric *adj.* метри́ческий. —**metric system,** метри́ческая систе́ма мер.

metrics *n.* ме́трика.

metronome *n.* метроно́м.

metropolis *n.* кру́пный го́род.

metropolitan *adj.* городско́й: *metropolitan police,* городска́я мили́ция. *Metropolitan New York,* Большо́й Нью-Йо́рк. —*n.* (archbishop) митрополи́т.

mettle *n.* зака́лка; вы́держка. *Prove one's mettle,* прояви́ть себя́.

Mexican *adj.* мексика́нский. —*n.* мексика́нец; мексика́нка.

mezzanine *n.* бельэта́ж.

mezzo-soprano *n.* ме́ццо-сопра́но.

mi *n., music* ми.

miaow *v. & n.* = **meow.**

miasma *n.* миа́змы.

mica *n.* слюда́. —*adj.* слюдяно́й.

microbe *n.* микро́б.

microbiology *n.* микробиоло́гия. —**microbiologist,** *n.* микробио́лог.

microcircuit *n.* микросхе́ма.

microcosm *n.* микроко́см.

microelectronics *n.* микроэлектро́ника.

microfilm *n.* микрофи́льм.

micrometer *n.* микро́метр.

micron *n.* микро́н.

microorganism *n.* микрооргани́зм.

microphone *n.* микрофо́н.

microscope *n.* микроско́п. *Examine something under a microscope,* рассма́тривать что́-нибудь в микроско́п *or* под микроско́пом.

microscopic *adj.* микроскопи́ческий.

mid- *prefix* в середи́не (+ *gen.*): *in mid-June,* в середи́не ию́ня.

midair *n., in* **in midair,** на лету́; на весу́. *Midair collision,* столкнове́ние в во́здухе.

midday *n.* по́лдень. —*adj.* полу́денный; полдне́вный.

middle *n.* середи́на. —*adj.* сре́дний: *the middle window*, сре́днее окно́. *Steer a middle course*, держа́ться сре́днего ку́рса. —**in the middle of**, в середи́не (+ *gen.*); посреди́ (+ *gen.*); посереди́не (+ *gen.*); посреди́ (+ *gen.*). *In the middle of May*, в середи́не ма́я. *In the middle of the night*, среди́ но́чи.

middle age сре́дний во́зраст. —**middle-aged,** *adj.* сре́дних лет.

Middle Ages сре́дние века́; средневеко́вье. *In the Middle Ages*, в сре́дние века́; в средневеко́вье.

middle class сре́дний класс. —**middle-class,** *adj.* сре́днего кла́сса.

middle distance *sports* сре́дняя диста́нция: *middle distance runner*, бегу́н на сре́днюю диста́нцию.

middle ear сре́днее у́хо.

Middle East Бли́жний Восто́к. *Middle East countries*, ближневосто́чные стра́ны.

Middle English среднеангли́йский язы́к.

middle finger сре́дний па́лец.

middle game *chess* ми́ттельшпиль.

middleman *n.* посре́дник.

middle name второ́е и́мя.

middleweight *n.* средневе́с. —*adj.* сре́днего ве́са.

middling *adj.* сре́дний; посре́дственный. —**fair to middling,** так себе́; сно́сно; ни ша́тко ни ва́лко.

midge *n.* мо́шка.

midget *n.* ка́рлик. —*adj.* ка́рликовый.

midnight *n.* по́лночь. *Stay up till midnight*, сиде́ть до по́лночи. —*adj.* полно́чный; полу́ночный; полуно́чный. —**burn the midnight oil,** по́здно заси́живаться за рабо́той.

midshipman *n.* курса́нт вое́нно-морско́го учи́лища.

midst *n.* середи́на. *In the midst of*, в середи́не (+ *gen.*); среди́ (+ *gen.*). *In our midst*, среди́ нас.

midway *adj., in* **the midway point,** полпути́; полдоро́ги. —*adv.* на полпути́; на полдоро́ге. *Lie midway between...*, лежа́ть на полпути́ ме́жду...

midwife *n.* акуше́рка; повива́льная ба́бка. —**midwifery,** *n.* акуше́рство.

mien *n.* вид; ми́на.

miff *v.t., colloq.* обижа́ть: *somewhat miffed*, не́сколько оби́жен.

might[1] *v.aux* мочь (+ бы): *Who might that be?*, кто бы э́то мог быть? *I might have guessed it*, я мог (могла́) бы об э́том догада́ться. *You might have offered to help*, вы могли́ бы предложи́ть свою́ по́мощь. *You might at least have said something about it*, вы хоть сказа́ли бы об э́том. *I might (just) as well have stayed home*, с тем же успе́хом я мог бы сиде́ть до́ма.

might[2] *n.* мощь; могу́щество. *Military might*, вое́нная мощь. —**might makes right,** кто силён, тот и прав. —**with all one's might,** изо всех сил; во всю мочь; со всего́ разма́ху.

mightily *adv.* усе́рдно; изо всех сил.

mighty *adj.* **1,** (powerful) могу́чий; могу́щественный: *mighty nation*, могу́чая/могу́щественная страна́. **2,** (great; huge) могу́чий: *a mighty river*, могу́чая река́.

—*adv., colloq.* о́чень: *mighty kind of you*, о́чень любе́зно с ва́шей стороны́.

mignonette *n.* резеда́.

migraine *n.* мигре́нь.

migrant *n.* переселе́нец. —*adj.* кочу́ющий.

migrate *v.i.* **1,** (of people) мигри́ровать; переселя́ться. **2,** (of birds) соверша́ть перелёт; перелета́ть; кочева́ть.

migration *n.* **1,** (of people) мигра́ция; переселе́ние. **2,** (of birds) перелёт.

migratory *adj.* **1,** (of people) кочу́ющий. **2,** (of birds) перелётный.

milch *adj.* моло́чный; до́йный.

mild *adj.* **1,** (gentle in disposition) мя́гкий: *a mild man*, мя́гкий челове́к. **2,** (moderate; temperate) мя́гкий: *mild weather*, мя́гкая пого́да. **3,** (not severe) мя́гкий; лёгкий: *a mild reproach*, мя́гкий упрёк; *a mild case*, лёгкий слу́чай (заболева́ния). **4,** (not strong, as tobacco) лёгкий; некре́пкий.

mildew *n.* **1,** (plant disease) мучни́стая роса́. **2,** (mold) пле́сень. —**mildewed,** *adj.* запле́сневелый.

mildly *adv.* **1,** (in a mild manner) мя́гко. **2,** (slightly; somewhat) не́сколько: *mildly surprised*, не́сколько удивлён. —**to put it mildly,** мя́гко выража́ясь.

mild-mannered *adj.* с мя́гким хара́ктером.

mildness *n.* мя́гкость.

mile *n.* ми́ля. *How many miles do you have on your car?*, ско́лько миль прошла́ ва́ша маши́на? —**miss by a mile,** промахну́ться на киломе́тр.

mileage *n.* расстоя́ние в ми́лях. *This car gets good gas mileage*, э́та маши́на расхо́дует ма́ло бензи́на.

milepost *n.* верстово́й столб.

milestone *n.* **1,** = **milepost. 2,** (momentous event) ве́ха.

milieu *n.* среда́; окруже́ние.

militancy *n.* вои́нственность.

militant *adj.* вои́нственный; вои́нствующий. —*n.* боеви́к.

militarily *adv.* с вое́нной то́чки зре́ния; в вое́нном отноше́нии.

militarism *n.* милитари́зм. —**militarist,** *n.* милитари́ст. —**militaristic,** *adj.* милитаристи́ческий.

militarize *v.t.* милитаризи́ровать. —**militarization,** *n.* милитариза́ция.

military *adj.* вое́нный. —*n., preceded by* **the** вое́нные. —**military science,** вое́нная нау́ка; вое́нное де́ло.

militate *v.i.* **1,** [*usu.* **militate in favor of**] (work in one's favor) спосо́бствовать (+ *dat.*); (be an argument for) говори́ть в по́льзу (+ *gen.*). **2,** [*usu.* **militate against**] (work against) быть поме́хой (+ *dat.*); (be an argument against) говори́ть не в по́льзу (+ *gen.*).

militia *n.* мили́ция; ополче́ние. —**militiaman,** *n.* милиционе́р; ополче́нец.

milk *n.* молоко́. —*adj.* моло́чный: *milk diet*, моло́чная дие́та. —*v.t.* дои́ть: *milk a cow*, дои́ть коро́ву. —**there's no use crying over spilt milk,** что с во́зу упа́ло, то пропа́ло.

milking *n.* дое́ние; до́йка. —**milking machine,** дои́льная маши́на.

milkmaid *n.* доя́рка.

milkman *n.* моло́чник.

milk shake молочный коктейль.

milksop *n.* баба; тряпка; мокрая курица.

milky *adj.* молочный. —**Milky Way,** Млечный Путь.

mill *n.* **1,** (apparatus or building for grinding) мельница. *Coffee mill,* кофейная мельница. **2,** (factory) фабрика; завод: *paper mill,* бумажная фабрика; *steel mill,* сталелитейный завод. **3,** (machine for rolling metal) прокатный стан. —*v.t.* **1,** (grind) молоть. **2,** (roll, as metal) прокатывать; вальцевать. **3,** (shape, as metal) фрезеровать. —*v.i.* [*usu.* **mill around** *or* **about**] толочься. —**go through the mill,** пройти огонь и воду.

millennium *n.* тысячелетие.

millepede *n.* = **millipede.**

miller *n.* мельник.

millet *n.* **1,** (cereal grass) просо. **2,** (food grain) пшено.

milligram *n.* миллиграмм.

millimeter *also,* **millimetre** *n.* миллиметр.

milliner *n.* модистка.

millinery *n.* дамские шляпы. —**millinery shop,** шляпный магазин.

milling *n.* **1,** (grinding) размол. **2,** (rolling, as of metal) прокатка; вальцовка. **3,** (shaping, as of metal) фрезерование. —**milling cutter,** фреза. —**milling machine,** фрезерный станок.

million *n.* миллион.

millionaire *n.* миллионер.

millionth *adj.* миллионный. —*n.* миллионная часть.

millipede *also,* **millepede** *n.* многоножка.

millrace *n.* мельничный лоток.

millstone *n.* жёрнов. *Millstone around one's neck,* камень на шее.

milquetoast *n., slang* тихоня.

milt *n.* молоки.

mime *n.* **1,** (pantomime) пантомима. **2,** (farce performed in ancient times) мим. **3,** (mimic) мимист.

mimeograph *n.* ротатор. —*v.t.* размножать на ротаторе.

mimic *v.t.* передразнивать. —*n.* **1,** (one adept at mimicking) имитатор. **2,** (stage performer) мимист.

mimicry *n.* **1,** (imitating) мимика. **2,** *biol.* мимикрия.

mimosa *n.* мимоза.

minaret *n.* минарет.

mince *v.t.* **1,** (chop) крошить; рубить. **2,** (lessen the force of): *not mince words,* не стесняться в выражениях. —*v.i.* **1,** (speak or behave daintily) жеманиться. **2,** (walk daintily or affectedly) семенить ногами.

mincemeat *n.* **1,** *obs.* (chopped meat) рубленое мясо. **2,** (pie filling) фарш. —**make mincemeat of,** стереть в порошок.

mind *n.* ум. *On one's mind,* на уме. *To my mind,* по-моему; на мой взгляд. —*v.t.* **1,** (pay attention to) обращать внимание на. *Mind one's own business,* не вмешиваться в чужие дела. **2,** (obey) слушаться. **3,** (look after) присматривать за (+ *instr.*). **4,** (object to) быть прочь; возражать против. *I don't mind staying home,* я не прочь сидеть дома. *I wouldn't mind a cup of tea,* не откажусь от чашки чая. **5,** (take care not to): *Mind you don't slip!,* осторожно, не оступитесь! *Mind you're not late!,* смотрите, не опоздайте! —*v.i.* **1,** (be obedient) слушаться. **2,** (object) возражать; иметь что́-нибудь против: *If you don't mind,* если вы не возражаете; если вы не имеете ничего против. *Do you mind if I smoke?,* вы не возражаете, если я закурю? —**bear/have/keep in mind,** иметь в виду. *I'll bear/keep that in mind,* я это учту. —**be in one's right mind,** быть в своём (*or* в здравом) уме. —**be of one mind,** быть одного мнения. —**bring/call/recall to mind,** напоминать; воскрешать в памяти. —**change one's mind,** передумать; раздумать; изменить своё решение. *Get someone to change his/her mind,* переубедить кого́-нибудь. —**come to mind,** приходить на ум *or* на память. —**cross one's mind,** приходить в голову (+ *dat.*). —**give someone a piece of one's mind,** сказать кому́-нибудь пару тёплых слов. —**go out of** (*or* **lose**) **one's mind,** сходить с ума. —**keep one's mind on,** сосредоточиваться на. —**make up one's mind,** решить; решиться; собраться. *I can't make up my mind,* я не могу решить. —**never mind!,** ничего; неважно; всё равно. —**out of one's mind,** сумасшедший. *Are you out of your mind?,* вы с ума сошли? —**put out of one's mind,** выбросить из головы. —**read someone's mind,** читать чьи́-нибудь мысли. —**slip someone's mind,** выскочить из головы. —**speak one's mind,** высказываться.

mindful *adj.* [*usu.* **mindful of**] имея в виду; отдавая себе отчёт (в).

mindless *adj.* **1,** (senseless) бессмысленный. **2,** *fol. by* **of** (heedless; unmindful) не обращая внимания (на).

mind's eye духовное око.

mine[1] *poss. pron.* мой: *This hat is mine,* это моя шляпа. *A friend of mine,* один мой друг; один из моих друзей. *He is no friend of mine,* он мне не друг.

mine[2] *n.* **1,** (pit) шахта; рудник; прииск. *Coal mine,* угольная шахта; *copper mine,* медный рудник. *Salt mine,* соляная шахта; соляной рудник; *pl.* соляные промыслы. *Gold/diamond mines,* золотые/алмазные прииски. **2,** (charge of explosives) мина. *Land mine,* фугас. —*v.t.* **1,** (extract, as ore, coal, etc.) добывать. **2,** (lay explosives under) минировать; закладывать мины под. —*v.i.* производить горные работы.

mine detector миноискатель.

minefield *n.* минное поле.

minelayer *n.* (минный) заградитель.

miner *n.* шахтёр; горняк.

mineral *n.* минерал; *pl.* минералы; полезные ископаемые. *Rich in minerals,* богат полезными ископаемыми. —*adj.* минеральный: *mineral resources,* минеральные ресурсы; ресурсы полезных ископаемых; богатства недр.

mineralogy *n.* минералогия. —**mineralogical,** *adj.* минералогический. —**mineralogist,** *n.* минералог.

mineral oil минеральное масло.

mineral wool минеральная вата.

minesweeper *n.* тральщик.

mingle *v.i.* **1,** (become mixed) смешиваться. **2,** (associate) общаться; вращаться.

miniature *n.* миниатю́ра. —*adj.* миниатю́рный.

miniaturization *n.* миниатюриза́ция.

minimal *adj.* минима́льный.

minimize *v.t.* **1,** (reduce to a minimum) доводи́ть до ми́нимума. **2,** (belittle) преуменьша́ть; умаля́ть.

minimum *n.* ми́нимум. —*adj.* минима́льный. —**minimum wage,** ми́нимум за́работной пла́ты.

mining *n.* го́рное де́ло. —*adj.* го́рный: *mining engineer,* го́рный инжене́р.

minion *n.* **1,** (servile follower) приспе́шник; клевре́т. **2,** (favorite) ба́ловень: *minion of fortune,* ба́ловень судьбы́.

minister *n.* **1,** (officer of state) мини́стр. **2,** (envoy) посла́нник. **3,** (clergyman) па́стор. —*v.i.* [*usu.* **minister to**] служи́ть; помога́ть.

ministerial *adj.* министе́рский. *On the ministerial level,* на у́ровне мини́стров.

ministration *n.* оказа́ние по́мощи.

ministry *n.* **1,** (governmental department) министе́рство. **2,** (clergy) духове́нство.

mink *n.* но́рка. —*adj.* но́рковый.

minnow *n.* голья́н.

minor *adj.* **1,** (unimportant) незначи́тельный: *minor defects,* незначи́тельные недоста́тки. **2,** (of lesser importance) ме́лкий; второстепе́нный. *Minor role,* второстепе́нная роль. *Minor repairs,* ме́лкий ремо́нт. *Minor injuries,* лёгкие ране́ния. **3,** *music* мино́рный: *minor key,* мино́рная тона́льность. —*n.* **1,** (one under legal age) несовершенноле́тний. **2,** *music* мино́р: *Prelude in C-sharp minor,* прелю́дия до-диез мино́р. —**minor piece,** *chess* лёгкая фигу́ра.

minority *n.* **1,** (less than half of a total) меньшинство́: *be in the minority,* оказа́ться *or* оста́ться в меньшинстве́. **2,** (distinct group) меньшинство́: *ethnic minorities,* этни́ческие меньшинства́. **3,** (period of being under legal age) несовершенноле́тие.

minstrel *n.* менестре́ль.

mint *n.* **1,** (plant) мя́та. **2,** (confection) мя́тная конфе́та. **3,** (place where money is coined) моне́тный двор. —*adj.* **1,** (containing mint) мя́тный. **2,** (of a postage stamp) негашёный. —*v.t.* чека́нить: *mint coins,* чека́нить моне́ты.

mintage *n.* чека́нка.

minuend *n.* уменьша́емое.

minuet *n.* менуэ́т.

minus *prep.* **1,** (less) ми́нус: *six minus three,* шесть ми́нус три. **2,** (lacking) без. —*n.* (drawback) ми́нус. —*adj.* отрица́тельный. —**minus sign,** (знак) ми́нус.

minuscule *adj.* кро́хотный; малю́сенький.

minute[1] (**min**-it) *n.* **1,** (60th part of an hour or degree) мину́та. *This minute!,* сию́ мину́ту! *Just a minute!,* одну́ мину́т(к)у! *Any minute,* с мину́ты на мину́ту. *The minute he arrives,* как то́лько он придёт. **2,** *pl.* (record) протоко́л. —**minute hand,** мину́тная стре́лка.

minute[2] (mai-**noot**) *adj.* **1,** (tiny) ме́лкий. **2,** (painstaking; detailed) подро́бный. —**minutely,** *adv.* подро́бно; до то́нкостей.

minutiae *n.pl.* ме́лочи.

miracle *n.* чу́до. *He escaped by a miracle,* он спа́сся каки́м-то чу́дом.

miraculous *adj.* **1,** (as if by a miracle) чуде́сный: *miraculous escape,* чуде́сное спасе́ние. **2,** (seeming to work miracles) чудотво́рный; чудоде́йственный. —**miraculously,** *adv.* чу́дом.

mirage *n.* мира́ж; ма́рево.

mire *n.* **1,** (bog) тряси́на. **2,** (mud) грязь. —*v.t. Become mired in,* завяза́ть в; увяза́ть в; погряза́ть в.

mirror *n.* зе́ркало. —*v.t.* отража́ть. —**mirror image,** зерка́льное изображе́ние.

mirth *n.* весе́лье. —**mirthful,** *adj.* весёлый.

misadventure *n.* злоключе́ние.

misanthrope *n.* человеконенави́стник; мизантро́п. —**misanthropic,** *adj.* человеконенави́стнический; мизантропи́ческий. —**misanthropy,** *n.* человеконенави́стничество; мизантро́пия.

misapply *v.t.* непра́вильно применя́ть.

misapprehension *n.* заблужде́ние. *Be under a misapprehension,* заблужда́ться ; быть в заблужде́нии.

misappropriate *v.t.* растра́чивать; расхища́ть. —**misappropriation,** *n.* растра́та; хище́ние; расхище́ние.

misbegotten *adj.* внебра́чный; незаконнорождённый.

misbehave *v.i.* ду́рно вести́ себя́. —**misbehavior,** *n.* дурно́е поведе́ние.

miscalculate *v.t.* непра́вильно подсчи́тывать. —*v.i.* просчи́тываться. —**miscalculation,** *n.* просчёт.

miscarriage *n.* вы́кидыш. *Have a miscarriage,* име́ть вы́кидыш. *She had a miscarriage,* у неё был вы́кидыш. —**miscarriage of justice,** суде́бная оши́бка.

miscarry *v.i.* **1,** (go wrong; fail) дава́ть осе́чку. **2,** (have a miscarriage) вы́кинуть.

miscast *v.t., usu. passive. She is miscast in the part,* она́ не годи́тся для э́той ро́ли; роль ей не подхо́дит.

miscegenation *n.* ра́совое смеше́ние.

miscellaneous *adj.* **1,** (not falling into a single category) ра́зные; (*as a heading*) ра́зное. **2,** (made up of different elements) разноро́дный.

miscellany *n.* **1,** (miscellaneous collection) смесь. **2,** (collection of writings) сбо́рник.

mischance *n.* несча́стье; несча́стный слу́чай. *If by some mischance...,* е́сли по несча́стной случа́йности...; е́сли на беду́.

mischief *n.* озорство́; баловство́; ша́лости. *Make mischief,* озорнича́ть; бедоку́рить. —**mischief-maker,** *n.* озорни́к; шалу́н; прока́зник; бедоку́р.

mischievous *adj.* озорно́й; шаловли́вый.

misconception *n.* заблужде́ние.

misconduct *n.* **1,** (in public office) должностно́е преступле́ние. **2,** *mil.* наруше́ние дисципли́ны.

misconstrue *v.t.* превра́тно истолко́вывать; перетолко́вывать.

miscount *v.t.* просчи́тывать. —*v.i.* просчи́тываться; обсчи́тываться. —*n.* просчёт.

miscreant *n.* злоде́й; негодя́й.

misdeal *v.t. & i.* ошиба́ться при сда́че (карт). —*n.* непра́вильная сда́ча.

misdeed *n.* просту́пок.

misdemeanor *also,* **misdemeanour** *n.* просту́пок.

misdirect *v.t.* **1,** (give wrong directions to) сбива́ть с доро́ги. **2,** (address to the wrong person) отправля́ть не по а́дресу. *Your remarks are misdirected,* ва́ши замеча́ния напра́влены не по а́дресу.

miser *n.* скупе́ц; скря́га.

miserable *adj.* **1,** (unhappy; wretched) жа́лкий; несча́стный. *Make one's life miserable,* отравля́ть чью́-нибудь жизнь. **2,** (awful; rotten) скве́рный; отврати́тельный. **3,** (despicable) жа́лкий; презре́нный. **4,** (squalid) жа́лкий; убо́гий.

miserly *adj.* скупо́й. —**miserliness,** *n.* ску́пость.

misery *n.* **1,** (suffering; distress) страда́ние. *Her life is a misery,* её жизнь — су́щий ад. *Make someone's life a misery,* загуби́ть чью́-нибудь жизнь. **2,** (poverty) нищета́. —**put out of one's misery,** положи́ть коне́ц чьи́м-нибудь страда́ниям.

misfire *v.i.* дава́ть осе́чку. —*n.* осе́чка.

misfortune *n.* несча́стье.

misgiving *n.* **1,** (doubt) сомне́ние. **2,** (apprehension) опасе́ние.

misguided *adj.* **1,** (mistaken) оши́бочный. **2,** (deluded) заблужда́ющийся.

mishandle *v.t.* **1,** (treat roughly) пло́хо обраща́ться с. **2,** (mismanage) напу́тать.

mishap *n.* злоключе́ние; ава́рия. *Without mishap,* благополу́чно; без происше́ствий.

mishear *v.t.* непра́вильно *or* нето́чно рассл́ышать. —*v.i.* ослы́шаться.

mishmash *n.* мешани́на.

misinform *v.t.* непра́вильно информи́ровать. —**misinformation,** *n.* непра́вильная информа́ция.

misinterpret *v.t.* неве́рно *or* превра́тно истолко́вывать; перетолко́вывать. —**misinterpretation,** *n.* неве́рное истолкова́ние.

misjudge *v.t.* непра́вильно оце́нивать. —**misjudgment,** *n.* оши́бка; просчёт.

mislay *v.t.* затеря́ть; заложи́ть.

mislead *v.t.* вводи́ть в заблужде́ние. —**misleading,** *adj.* вводя́щий в заблужде́ние; обма́нчивый.

mismanage *v.t.* пло́хо вести́ *or* управля́ть. —**mismanagement,** *n.* бесхозя́йственное веде́ние дел; бесхозя́йственность.

mismatch *n.* плоха́я па́ртия.

misnomer *n.* непра́вильное назва́ние.

misogynist *n.* женоненави́стник. —**misogyny,** *n.* женоненави́стничество.

misplace *v.t.* **1,** (put in the wrong place) класть не на ме́сто. **2,** (mislay; lose) затеря́ть; заложи́ть.

misprint *n.* опеча́тка.

mispronounce *v.t.* непра́вильно произноси́ть. —**mispronunciation,** *n.* непра́вильное произноше́ние.

misquote *v.t.* непра́вильно *or* нето́чно (про)цити́ровать. —**misquotation,** *n.* непра́вильная цита́та.

misread *v.t.* **1,** (read incorrectly) непра́вильно проче́сть. **2,** (interpret incorrectly) неве́рно истолко́вывать.

misrepresent *v.t.* искажа́ть; извраща́ть. —**misrepresentation,** *n.* искаже́ние; извраще́ние.

misrule *n.* плохо́е правле́ние.

miss *v.t.* **1,** (fail to hit) не попа́сть в (цель). *The plane missed the runway,* самолёт не попа́л в лётную полосу́. **2,** (fail to catch) пропуска́ть. **3,** (fail to attend) пропуска́ть. **4,** (fail to meet) не заста́ть. **5,** (fail to understand or appreciate) не понима́ть. **6,** (fail to hear) прослу́шать. **7,** (let slip by) упуска́ть; пропуска́ть. *Miss an opportunity,* упусти́ть возмо́жность. **8,** (be late for, as a train) опа́здывать на. **9,** (escape; avoid, as a mishap): *He narrowly missed being killed,* он чуть не поги́б. **10,** (overlook) прогляде́ть; не заме́тить. *Miss a turn (i.e. in the road),* прое́хать поворо́т. **11,** (feel the absence of) не хвата́ть (*impers.*); скуча́ть по. *I miss you,* мне вас не хвата́ет. *We missed you,* нам вас не хвата́ло. *We shall miss you,* нам бу́дет не хвата́ть вас; мы бу́дем скуча́ть по вас. *I miss my sister,* мне не хвата́ет мое́й сестры́; я скуча́ю по свое́й сестре́. *You were sorely missed,* вас о́чень не хвата́ло. **12,** (lack) не хвата́ть (*impers.*): недостава́ть (*impers.*). *The book is missing a few pages,* в кни́ге не хвата́ет не́скольких страни́ц. —*v.i.* промахну́ться; не попа́сть в цель. —*n.* **1,** (failure to hit) про́мах; непопада́ние. **2,** (young lady) мисс.

misshapen *adj.* уро́дливый.

missile *n.* **1,** (any projectile) снаря́д. **2,** *mil.* раке́та; реакти́вный снаря́д. *Ballistic missile,* баллисти́ческая раке́та. —*adj.* раке́тный: *missile strike,* раке́тный уда́р.

missing *adj.* отсу́тствующий; недостаю́щий. *Be missing,* отсу́тствовать; не хвата́ть; недостава́ть; не оказа́ться. *Missing in action,* пропа́вший без вести. *Be missing from the list,* отсу́тствовать в спи́ске. —**missing link,** недостаю́щее звено́.

mission *n.* **1,** (assignment; trip) ми́ссия: *rescue mission,* спаса́тельная ми́ссия. *Goodwill mission,* ми́ссия до́брой во́ли. **2,** (combat operation) боева́я зада́ча. **3,** (military flight) (боево́й) вы́лет. **4,** (legation) ми́ссия; представи́тельство. *U.S. Mission to the UN,* представи́тельство США при ООН. **5,** (delegation) ми́ссия: *trade mission,* торго́вая ми́ссия. **6,** *relig.* ми́ссия.

missionary *n.* миссионе́р. —*adj.* миссионе́рский.

missive *n.* посла́ние.

misspell *v.t.* непра́вильно писа́ть. —**misspelling,** *n.* орфографи́ческая оши́бка. —**misspelt,** *adj.* непра́вильно напи́санный.

misspend *v.t.* растра́чивать; расточа́ть. *Misspent youth,* растра́ченная мо́лодость.

misstate *v.t.* ло́жно излага́ть; искажа́ть. —**misstatement,** *n.* ло́жное заявле́ние; искаже́ние.

misstep *n.* ло́жный шаг.

mist *n.* лёгкий тума́н; ды́мка.

mistake *n.* оши́бка. *By mistake,* по оши́бке. *Make a mistake,* ошиба́ться; де́лать оши́бку. —*v.t.* **1,** (misinterpret) непра́вильно понима́ть. **2,** *fol. by* **for** (take for someone else) принима́ть за (+ *acc.*).

mistaken *adj.* **1,** (in error): *You are mistaken,* вы ошиба́етесь. **2,** (erroneous) оши́бочный: *mistaken identity,* оши́бочное опозна́ние. —**mistakenly,** *adv.* оши́бочно; по оши́бке.

mister *n.* ми́стер; господи́н.

mistletoe *n.* оме́ла.

mistranslate *v.t.* непра́вильно переводи́ть. —**mistranslation,** *n.* непра́вильный перево́д.

mistreat *v.t.* ду́рно обраща́ться с. —**mistreatment,** *n.* дурно́е обраще́ние.

mistress *n.* **1,** (lady of the house; owner) хозя́йка. **2,** (paramour) любо́вница.

mistrial *n.* непра́вильное суде́бное разбира́тельство.

mistrust *n.* недове́рие. *Mistrust of,* недове́рие к. —*v.t.* не доверя́ть (+ *dat.*). —**mistrustful,** *adj.* недове́рчивый.

misty *adj.* **1,** (characterized by mist) тума́нный. **2,** (obscured by mist) затума́ненный.

misunderstand *v.t.* непра́вильно поня́ть. —**misunderstanding,** *n.* недоразуме́ние.

misuse *v.t.* **1,** (use incorrectly) непра́вильно употребля́ть. **2,** (abuse) злоупотребля́ть. —*n.* **1,** (incorrect use) непра́вильное употребле́ние. **2,** (abuse) злоупотребле́ние.

mite *n.* **1,** (parasite) клещ. **2,** (tiny person) кро́шка. **3,** (small contribution) ле́пта. —**a mite,** чу́точку: *a mite better,* чу́точку лу́чше.

miter *also,* **mitre** *n.* **1,** (headdress) ми́тра. **2,** (beveled joint) скос. —*v.t.* ска́шивать.

mitigate *v.t.* смягча́ть. *Mitigating circumstances,* смягча́ющие вину́ обстоя́тельства.

mitosis *n.* мито́з.

mitre *n. & v.* = **miter.**

mitten *n.* рукави́ца; ва́режка.

mix *v.t.* **1,** (blend into a single mass) меша́ть; сме́шивать: *mix paints,* меша́ть/сме́шивать кра́ски. *Rain mixed with snow,* дождь со сне́гом. **2,** (make by mixing something) гото́вить: *mix a salad,* (при)гото́вить сала́т. **3,** (combine) сочета́ть; совмеща́ть. *Mix business with pleasure,* сочета́ть прия́тное с поле́зным. —*v.i.* **1,** (become mixed) сме́шиваться. **2,** (associate; mingle) обща́ться; враща́ться. —*n.* смесь. —**mix up, 1,** (mix thoroughly) сме́шивать. **2,** (confuse; jumble) пу́тать; сме́шивать. *Get mixed up,* пу́таться. *You're mixing him up with someone else,* вы пу́таете его́ с ке́м-то други́м. **3,** (involve) заме́шивать; впу́тывать. *Get mixed up in,* заме́шиваться в; впу́тываться в.

mixed *adj.* сме́шанный. *Mixed feelings,* сме́шанные чу́вства. —**mixed marriage,** сме́шанный брак. —**mixed number,** сме́шанное число́.

mixer *n.* меша́лка; смеси́тель; ми́ксер.

mixture *n.* смесь.

mix-up *n.* недоразуме́ние; неувя́зка.

mizzen *n.* биза́нь. —**mizzenmast,** *n.* биза́нь-ма́чта.

mnemonic *adj.* мнемони́ческий. —**mnemonics,** *n.* мнемо́ника.

moan *n.* стон. —*v.i.* стона́ть.

moat *n.* крепостно́й ров.

mob *n.* толпа́. *Mobs of people,* то́лпы наро́да. —*v.t.* **1,** (crowd around) напада́ть толпо́й на. **2,** (jam) набива́ться в. *The place was mobbed,* наро́ду бы́ло битко́м наби́то.

mobile *adj.* подвижно́й; моби́льный; передвижно́й.

Mobile warfare, манёвренная война́. —**mobility,** *n.* подви́жность; моби́льность.

mobilize *v.t.* мобилизова́ть. —*v.i.* мобилизова́ться. —**mobilization,** *n.* мобилиза́ция.

mobster *n., colloq.* га́нгстер.

moccasin *n.* **1,** (shoe) мокаси́н. **2,** (snake) мокаси́новая змея́.

mocha *n.* мо́кко.

mock *v.t.* издева́ться над; насмеха́ться над; высме́ивать. —*adj.* инсцени́рованный: *mock trial,* инсцени́рованный суде́бный проце́сс.

mockery *n.* **1,** (ridicule; derision) издева́тельство; осмея́ние. **2,** (travesty) паро́дия: *mockery of justice,* паро́дия на правосу́дие.

mocking *adj.* издева́тельский; насме́шливый.

mockingbird *n.* пересме́шник.

mock-up *n.* маке́т.

modal *adj.* мода́льный.

mode *n.* **1,** (way; manner) спо́соб. *Mode of living,* о́браз жи́зни. **2,** (style; fashion) мо́да: *dress in the latest mode,* одева́ться по после́дней мо́де.

model *n.* **1,** (small-scale reproduction) моде́ль; маке́т. **2,** (make; design) моде́ль: *the latest model cars,* после́дние моде́ли автомоби́лей. **3,** (standard; ideal) образе́ц: *take as a model,* принима́ть за образе́ц. **4,** (one who poses) нату́рщик; нату́рщица. **5,** (one who displays clothes by wearing them) манеке́нщик; манеке́нщица. —*adj.* **1,** (used for purposes of demonstration) показа́тельный: *model school,* показа́тельная шко́ла. **2,** (exemplary) образцо́вый; приме́рный. *Model pupil,* приме́рный учени́к. **3,** (being a miniature version): *model airplane,* моде́ль самолёта. —*v.t.* **1,** (make figures of) лепи́ть. **2,** (display by wearing) демонстри́ровать (на себе́); пока́зывать. **3,** (pattern after) создава́ть по образцу́ (+ *gen.*): *Its constitution is modeled after that of the U.S.,* её конститу́ция со́здана по образцу́ америка́нской. —*v.i.* рабо́тать манеке́нщиком (-щицей).

modeler *also,* **modeller** *n.* моде́льщик.

modeling *also,* **modelling** *n.* **1,** (making of figures) ле́пка. **2,** (working as a model): *do modeling,* рабо́тать манеке́нщиком (-щицей). —**modeling clay,** гли́на для ле́пки.

modeller *n.* = **modeler.**

modem *n.* моде́м.

moderate *adj.* уме́ренный: *moderate speed,* уме́ренная ско́рость; *moderate demands,* уме́ренные тре́бования. *Moderate prices,* уме́ренные *or* досту́пные це́ны. *The moderate wing of the party,* уме́ренное крыло́ па́ртии. —*n.* уме́ренный. —*v.t.* смягча́ть; умеря́ть. —*v.i.* **1,** (become less extreme or severe) смягча́ться: *The weather moderated,* пого́да смягчи́лась. **2,** (act as moderator) служи́ть веду́щим.

moderately *adv.* **1,** (in moderation) уме́ренно; в ме́ру. **2,** (fairly; more or less) дово́льно; в ме́ру: *moderately well,* дово́льно/ в ме́ру/ хорошо́.

moderation *n.* **1,** (act of moderating) смягче́ние. **2,** (restraint; temperance) уме́ренность; воздержа́ние; возде́ржанность. *Moderation in eating,* воздержа́ние в пи́ще; возде́ржанность в еде́. **—in moderation,** уме́ренно.

moderator *n.* веду́щий.

modern *adj.* совреме́нный: *modern art*, совреме́нное иску́сство; *modern methods of treatment*, совреме́нные ме́тоды лече́ния. *Modern history*, но́вая исто́рия. *Modern languages*, но́вые языки́. *Modern dance*, та́нец модэ́рн.

modernism *n.* модерни́зм. **—modernist**, *n.* модерни́ст. **—modernistic**, *adj.* модерни́стский. **—modernity**, *n.* совреме́нность.

modernize *v.t.* модернизи́ровать. **—modernization**, *n.* модерниза́ция.

modest *adj.* скро́мный: *modest person/house/income*, скро́мный челове́к/дом/дохо́д. **—modestly**, *adv.* скро́мно. **—modesty**, *n.* скро́мность.

modicum *n.* чу́точка; ка́пелька.

modification *n.* видоизмене́ние; модифика́ция. *Make modifications in the design*, вноси́ть измене́ния в констру́кцию.

modifier *n.*, *gram.* определе́ние; атрибу́т.

modify *v.t.* **1**, (alter) видоизменя́ть; модифици́ровать. **2**, (moderate) смягча́ть. **3**, *gram.* определя́ть.

modish *adj.* мо́дный.

modulate *v.t.* модули́ровать. **—v.i.** перелива́ться. **—modulation**, *n.* модуля́ция. **—modulator**, *n.* модуля́тор.

module *n.* **1**, (unit of measurement) мо́дуль. **2**, (space vehicle) отсе́к.

modulus *n.* мо́дуль.

Mogul *n.* **1**, *hist.* мого́л. **2**, *l.c.* (powerful person) магна́т.

mohair *n.* мохе́р. **—adj.** мохе́ровый.

Mohammedan *n.* магомета́нин. **—adj.** магомета́нский. **—Mohammedanism**, *n.* магомета́нство; мусульма́нство.

moire *n.* муа́р. **—moiré**, *adj.* муа́ровый.

moist *adj.* вла́жный.

moisten *v.t.* сма́чивать.

moisture *n.* вла́жность; вла́га.

molar *n.* коренно́й зуб.

molasses *n.* па́тока.

mold *also*, **mould** *n.* **1**, (fungus) пле́сень; гниль. **2**, (matrix) фо́рма. **3**, (cast; model) сле́пок. **4**, *fig.* (distinctive character) заква́ска. **5**, *fig.* (fixed pattern) шабло́н. **—v.t. 1**, (make) формова́ть. **2**, *fig.* (shape) формирова́ть: *mold someone's character*, формирова́ть чей-нибудь хара́ктер.

molder *also*, **moulder** *v.i.* рассыпа́ться (в пыль).

molding *also*, **moulding** *n.* лепно́е украше́ние.

moldy *also*, **mouldy** *adj.* запле́сневелый.

mole *n.* **1**, (blemish) ро́динка. **2**, (rodent) крот.

molecule *n.* моле́кула. **—molecular**, *adj.* молекуля́рный.

molehill *n.* крото́вая нора́. **—make a mountain out of a molehill**, де́лать из му́хи слона́.

mole rat слепы́ш.

moleskin *n.* **1**, (fur) крото́вый мех; крот. **2**, (cloth) молески́н. **—adj.** крото́вый; молески́новый.

molest *v.t.* пристава́ть к; беспоко́ить.

mollify *v.t.* **1**, (placate) уми́лостивить. **2**, (make less intense) смягча́ть.

mollusk *also*, **mollusc** *n.* моллю́ск.

mollycoddle *v.t.*, *colloq.* изне́живать. **—n.**, *colloq.* не́женка.

Molotov cocktail буты́лка с зажига́тельной сме́сью.

molt *also*, **moult** *v.i.* линя́ть.

molten *adj.* распла́вленный; жи́дкий. *Molten lava*, жи́дкая ла́ва.

molybdenum *n.* молибде́н. **—molybdic**, *adj.* молибде́новый.

mom *n.*, *colloq.* ма́ма.

moment *n.* **1**, (instant; point in time) моме́нт: *at that moment*, в тот моме́нт. *At the moment*, в да́нный моме́нт. *At any moment*, в любо́й моме́нт; в любу́ю мину́ту. *For the moment*, пока́. **2**, (importance) ва́жность; значе́ние.

momentarily *adv.* **1**, (for a moment) на мину́ту. **2**, (very soon) че́рез не́сколько мину́т. **3**, (any moment) с мину́ты на мину́ту.

momentary *adj.* мгнове́нный. *Catch a momentary glimpse of*, уви́деть ме́льком.

momentous *adj.* знамена́тельный; торже́ственный: *momentous event*, знамена́тельное собы́тие; *momentous occasion*, торже́ственный слу́чай.

momentum *n.* ине́рция; разго́н. *Gain/gather momentum*, набира́ть темп; разгоня́ться. *Lose momentum*, теря́ть темп.

mommy *n.* ма́ма; мама́ша.

monarch *n.* мона́рх. **—monarchical**, *adj.* монархи́ческий. **—monarchism**, *n.* монархи́зм.

monarchist *n.* монархи́ст. **—adj.** монархи́ческий.

monarchy *n.* мона́рхия.

monastery *n.* монасты́рь. **—monasterial**, *adj.* монасты́рский.

monastic *adj.* мона́шеский. *Monastic vows*, мона́шеские обе́ты. **—monasticism**, *n.* мона́шество.

Monday *n.* понеде́льник.

monetary *adj.* де́нежный; моне́тный. *International Monetary Fund*, Междунаро́дный валю́тный фонд.

money *n.* де́ньги: *a lot of money*, мно́го де́нег. *Cost a lot of money*, сто́ить больши́х де́нег. *Play for money*, игра́ть на де́ньги. *There is no money to pay the workers*, не́чем плати́ть рабо́чим. **—adj.** де́нежный: *money market*, де́нежный ры́нок.

moneybag *n.* **1**, (sack for money) мешо́к для де́нег. **2**, *pl.*, *colloq.* (rich man) золото́й *or* де́нежный мешо́к; толстосу́м.

money box копи́лка; кубы́шка.

moneychanger *n.* меня́ла.

moneylender *n.* ростовщи́к.

moneymaking *adj.* дохо́дный; при́быльный.

money order де́нежный перево́д.

Mongol *n.* монго́л. **—adj.** монго́льский. *Also*, **Mongolian**.

mongoose *n.* мангу́ста.

mongrel *n.* **1**, (plant or animal of mixed breed) по́месь; мети́с. **2**, (dog of mixed breed) дворня́га; дворня́жка. **—adj.** нечистокро́вный.

moniker *also*, **monicker** *n.*, *slang* про́звище; кли́чка.

monism *n.* мони́зм. —**monistic,** *adj.* монисти́ческий.

monitor *n.* **1,** (pupil with special duties) ста́роста. **2,** (TV monitor) монито́р; контро́льный кинеско́п. —*v.t.* наблюда́ть за; контроли́ровать. —**monitor lizard,** вара́н.

monk *n.* мона́х.

monkey *n.* обезья́на. —*v.i.* [*usu.* monkey with] *slang* вози́ться с. —**make a monkey out of,** *slang* оста́вить в дурака́х.

monkey business *slang* чуда́чества.

monkey wrench францу́зский ключ. —**throw a monkey wrench into the works,** вставля́ть па́лки в колёса.

monkhood *n.* мона́шество.

monkshood *n.* (plant) акони́т.

monochromatic *adj.* одноцве́тный; монохромати́ческий.

monocle *n.* моно́кль.

monogamy *n.* единобра́чие; монога́мия. —**monogamous,** *adj.* единобра́чный; монога́мный.

monogram *n.* ве́нзель; моногра́мма.

monograph *n.* моногра́фия. —**monographic,** *adj.* монографи́ческий.

monolith *n.* моноли́т. —**monolithic,** *adj.* моноли́тный.

monologue *n.* моноло́г.

mononucleosis *n.* мононуклео́з.

monoplane *n.* монопла́н.

monopolist *n.* монополи́ст. —**monopolistic,** *adj.* монополисти́ческий.

monopolize *v.t.* монополизи́ровать. —**monopolization,** *n.* монополиза́ция.

monopoly *n.* монопо́лия.

monorail *n.* однopéльсовая желе́зная доро́га.

monosyllabic *adj.* односло́жный. —**monosyllable,** *n.* односло́жное сло́во.

monotheism *n.* монотеи́зм; единобо́жие. —**monotheistic,** *adj.* монотеисти́ческий.

monotone *n.* моното́нная речь; моното́нное пе́ние. *In a monotone,* моното́нно. —*adj.* моното́нный; однотонный.

monotonous *adj.* **1,** (unchanging in tone) моното́нный. **2,** (tedious; repetitious) однообра́зный. —**monotony,** *n.* однообра́зие.

monotype *n.* моноти́п.

monsieur *n.* мосье́.

Monsignor *n.* монсеньёр.

monsoon *n.* муссо́н.

monster *n.* **1,** (fantastic creature) чудо́вище. **2,** (ugly or grotesque creature) чудо́вище; уро́д. **3,** (vicious or depraved person) чудо́вище; и́зверг.

monstrosity *n.* **1,** (state of being monstrous) чудо́вищность. **2,** (very ugly thing) уро́д.

monstrous *adj.* чудо́вищный; зве́рский.

montage *n.* монта́ж.

month *n.* ме́сяц. *A month's vacation,* ме́сячный о́тпуск.

monthly *adj.* ежеме́сячный. *Average monthly wage,* сре́дняя ме́сячная зарпла́та. —*adv.* ежеме́сячно. —*n.* ежеме́сячник.

monument *n.* па́мятник. —**monumental,** *adj.* монумента́льный.

moo *v.i.* мыча́ть. —*n.* мыча́ние.

mooch *v.t., slang* **1,** (obtain by begging) выкля́нчивать; стреля́ть. **2,** (steal) стащи́ть; стяну́ть.

mood *n.* **1,** (frame of mind) настрое́ние: *in a bad mood,* в плохо́м настрое́нии. **2,** *gram.* наклоне́ние: *subjunctive mood,* сослага́тельное наклоне́ние. —**in the mood,** располо́жен. *I am not in the mood for work today,* я не располо́жен(a) (*or* у меня́ нет расположе́ния) сего́дня рабо́тать. *He is not in the mood for jokes,* ему́ не до шу́ток.

moody *adj.* **1,** (gloomy; sullen) угрю́мый. **2,** (subject to changes of mood) капри́зный.

moon *n.* луна́. *To the moon,* на Луну́. —**once in a blue moon,** в ко́и-то ве́ки.

moonbeam *n.* луч луны́.

moon landing прилуне́ние.

moonlight *n.* лу́нный свет. —**moonlit,** *adj.* лу́нный: *moonlit night,* лу́нная ночь.

moonshine *n., colloq.* самого́н. —**moonshiner,** *n., colloq.* самого́нщик.

moonstone *n.* лу́нный ка́мень.

moor *n.* (tract of land) пу́стошь. —*v.t., naut.* прича́ливать; швартова́ть. —*v.i., naut.* прича́ливать; швартова́ться.

Moor *n.* мавр.

moorage *n.* прича́л.

mooring *n.* **1,** (tying up) прича́л. **2,** *often pl.* (lines, cables, etc.) швартóвы. —**mooring line,** швартóв; чал; ча́лка; прича́л; прича́льный кана́т.

Moorish *adj.* маврита́нский.

moose *n.* лось.

moot *adj.* спо́рный.

mop *n.* **1,** (cleaning tool) шва́бра. **2,** (mass of hair) копна́ (воло́с). —*v.t.* **1,** (clean) мыть шва́брой. **2,** (wipe) вытира́ть. **3,** *fol. by* **up,** *mil.* очища́ть от проти́вника.

mope *v.i.* хандри́ть.

moped *n.* мопе́д.

moraine *n.* море́на.

moral *adj.* мора́льный; нра́вственный. *Moral code/ duty,* мора́льный ко́декс/долг. *Moral support/victory,* мора́льная подде́ржка/побе́да. —*n.* **1,** *pl.* (standards of behavior) мора́ль; нра́вственность. *Loose morals,* лёгкие нра́вы. **2,** (lesson) мора́ль: *the moral of the fable,* мора́ль ба́сни.

morale *n.* мора́льный дух; мора́льное состоя́ние.

moralist *n.* морали́ст. —**moralistic,** *adj.* нравоучи́тельный.

morality *n.* мора́ль; нра́вственность.

moralize *v.i.* морализова́ть.

morally *adv.* **1,** (from a moral point of view) мора́льно. **2,** (virtuously) мора́льно; нра́вственно. **3,** (virtually) практи́чески: *morally certain,* практи́чески уве́рен.

morass *n.* боло́то; тряси́на.

moratorium *n.* морато́рий.

moray *n.* муре́на. *Also,* **moray eel.**

morbid *adj.* **1,** (unhealthy) боле́зненный: *morbid*

curiosity, боле́зненное любопы́тство. **2,** (gruesome) жу́ткий. —**morbidity,** *n.* боле́зненность.

mordant *adj.* ко́лкий; язви́тельный. —*n.* протра́ва.

more *adj.* **1,** (greater in quantity) бо́льше: *It will take more time,* на э́то пона́добится бо́льше вре́мени. *More people than I expected,* бо́льше люде́й, чем я ожида́л(а). *I have more helpers than I need,* у меня́ есть бо́льше помо́щников, чем мне ну́жно. **2,** (additional) ещё: *Would you like some more tea?,* хоти́те ещё ча́ю? *I need more (i.e. additional) time,* мне ну́жно ещё вре́мя. *I need three more days,* мне ну́жно ещё три дня. —*n.* **1,** (a greater quantity) бо́льше: *more than 100 people,* бо́льше ста люде́й. *More than enough,* бо́льше *or* бо́лее чем доста́точно. *More than ever before,* бо́льше, чем когда́-либо ра́ньше. *It's more than we need,* э́то бо́льше, чем нам ну́жно. *More than meets the eye,* бо́льше, чем ка́жется на пе́рвый взгляд. *You should read more,* тебе́ сле́дует бо́льше чита́ть. *Cost more,* сто́ить доро́же. **2,** (an additional quantity) ещё: *Would you like some more?,* хоти́те ещё? *What more can I say?,* что я могу́ ещё сказа́ть? *What more could one ask for?,* о чём ещё мо́жно мечта́ть? ♦*In neg. sentences,* бо́льше: *I have nothing more to say,* мне бо́льше не́чего сказа́ть. —*adv.* **1,** used to form the comp. degree of adjectives and adverbs, бо́лее: *more interesting,* бо́лее интере́сный. *More quickly,* быстре́е. **2,** (to a greater extent) бо́льше; скоре́е. *I like this one more,* э́тот/э́та/э́то мне бо́льше нра́вится. *He is more like his father,* он бо́льше (*or* скоре́е) похо́ж на отца́. *It is more a matter of taste,* э́то скоре́е де́ло вку́са. *It sounds more like...,* э́то звучи́т скоре́е как... —**all the more,** всё бо́лее (+ *adj.*). —**(all) the more so since/because...,** тем бо́лее, что... —**any more,** *see* **any.** —**more and more,** всё бо́льше и бо́льше; (*with adjectives*) всё бо́лее (+ *adj.*). —**more or less,** бо́лее и́ли ме́нее. —**no more,** бо́льше нет; бо́льше не. *We have no more money,* у нас бо́льше нет де́нег. *I'll have no more of it!,* с меня́ дово́льно!; я бо́льше не бу́ду э́того терпе́ть! *He is no more,* его́ бо́льше нет; его́ не ста́ло. *Say no more!,* всё я́сно! —**once more,** ещё раз. —**the more..., the more...,** чем бо́льше..., тем бо́льше... —**what's more,** бо́лее того́; бо́льше того́.

morel *n.* сморчо́к.

moreover *adv.* кро́ме того́; сверх того́; к тому́ же.

mores *n.pl.* нра́вы.

morganatic *adj.* морганати́ческий.

morgue *n.* поко́йницкая; морг.

moribund *adj.* умира́ющий.

Mormon *n.* мормо́н. —*adj.* мормо́нский.

morning *n.* у́тро. *This morning,* сего́дня у́тром. *Tomorrow morning,* за́втра у́тром. *The next morning,* нау́тро. *Monday morning,* в понеде́льник у́тром. —*adj.* у́тренний: *morning newspaper,* у́тренняя газе́та. —**good morning!,** до́брое у́тро! —**in the morning,** у́тром. *Two o'clock in the morning,* два часа́ но́чи. *Eight o'clock in the morning,* во́семь часо́в утра́.

morning coat визи́тка.

morning-glory *n.* ипоме́я.

morning sickness тошнота́ бере́менных (по утра́м).

morning star у́тренняя звезда́.

Moroccan *adj.* марокка́нский.

morocco *n.* сафья́н. —*adj.* сафья́нный; сафья́новый.

moron *n.* слабоу́мный; идио́т. —**moronic,** *adj.* слабоу́мный; идио́тский.

morose *adj.* мра́чный; угрю́мый; па́смурный. —**moroseness,** *n.* мра́чность; угрю́мость.

morpheme *n.* морфе́ма.

morphine *n.* мо́рфий. *Morphine addict,* морфини́ст.

morphology *n.* морфоло́гия. —**morphological,** *adj.* морфологи́ческий.

Morse code а́збука Мо́рзе.

morsel *n.* кусо́чек: *tasty morsel,* ла́комый кусо́чек.

mortal *adj.* **1,** (subject to death) сме́ртный: *Man is mortal,* челове́к — сме́ртен. **2,** (fatal) смерте́льный: *mortal blow,* смерте́льный уда́р. **3,** (fought to the death) сме́ртный: *mortal combat,* сме́ртный бой. **4,** (bitter; implacable) смерте́льный: *mortal enemy,* смерте́льный враг. **5,** (extreme; dire) смерте́льный: *mortal fear,* смерте́льный страх. —*n.* сме́ртный: *a mere mortal,* просто́й сме́ртный. —**mortal remains,** бре́нные оста́нки. —**mortal sin,** сме́ртный грех.

mortality *n.* сме́ртность: *infant mortality,* де́тская сме́ртность. *Mortality rate,* сме́ртность.

mortally *adv.* смерте́льно; на́смерть. *Mortally wounded,* смерте́льно ра́нен.

mortar *n.* **1,** (mixing bowl) сту́пка; сту́па. **2,** (cement) строи́тельный раство́р. **3,** (military weapon) миномёт; морти́ра. —*adj., mil.* миномётный: *mortar fire,* миномётный ого́нь.

mortgage *n.* закладна́я; ипоте́ка. —*v.t.* закла́дывать.

mortician *n.* дире́ктор похоро́нного бюро́.

mortification *n.* **1,** (humiliation) униже́ние. **2,** (self-denial) умерщвле́ние (пло́ти).

mortify *v.t.* **1,** (humiliate) унижа́ть. **2,** (discipline, as the body) умерщвля́ть (плоть). —**mortifying,** *adj.* унизи́тельный.

mortise *n.* паз; гнездо́.

mortuary *n.* похоро́нное бюро́. —*adj.* похоро́нный; погреба́льный.

mosaic *n.* моза́ика. —*adj.* моза́ичный.

Moslem *n.* мусульма́нин. —*adj.* мусульма́нский.

mosque *n.* мече́ть.

mosquito *n.* кома́р. —**mosquito bite,** уку́с комара́.

moss *n.* мох. —**moss-grown,** *adj.* замше́лый; обомше́лый. —**mossy,** *adj.* мши́стый.

most *adj.* **1,** (in the greatest amount) наибо́льшее коли́чество: *receive the most votes,* получи́ть наибо́льшее коли́чество голосо́в. **2,** (the majority of) большинство́ (+ *gen.*): *most people,* большинство́ люде́й; *in most cases,* в большинстве́ слу́чаев. —*n.* **1,** (the majority) большинство́; бо́льшая часть: *most of them,* большинство́ из них; *most of whom,* большинство́ кото́рых; *most of the time,* бо́льшую часть вре́мени. *He spent most of his life abroad,* основну́ю часть жи́зни он провёл за грани́цей. *She did most of the talking,* в основно́м говори́ла она́. **2,** *preceded by* **the** (the greatest amount) са́мое большее: *the most I can do,* са́мое бо́льшее, что я могу́ сде́лать. *He has the most to lose,* он потеря́ет (*or* потеря́л бы) бо́льше всех. —*adv.* **1,** (in or to the greatest extent) бо́льше всего́: *what I need most,* что мне ну́жно бо́льше всего́. **2,** *used to form the superl. degree of adjectives,* са́мый: *the most difficult part,* са́мая тру́дная часть. *Most likely,* скоре́е всего́. **3,** (very; highly) о́чень; о́чень и о́чень: *most appreciative,* о́чень (и о́чень) призна́телен. *You've been most kind,* о́чень любе́зно с ва́шей стороны́. —**at (the) most,** са́мое бо́льшее; от си́лы; ма́ксимум. —**for the most part,** гла́вным о́бразом; бо́льшей ча́стью; в большинстве́ (своём). —**make the most of,** максима́льно испо́льзовать.

mostly *adv.* гла́вным о́бразом; бо́льшей ча́стью; в основно́м.

mote *n.* пыли́нка; сори́нка.

motel *n.* моте́ль.

moth *n.* **1,** (night-flying insect) ба́бочка; мотылёк. **2,** (clothes moth) моль.

mothball *n.* **1,** *pl.* (substance) нафтали́н. **2,** (single ball of same) ша́рик нафтали́на. —*v.t.* (put away for future use) (за)консерви́ровать.

moth-eaten *adj.* изъе́денный мо́лью.

mother *n.* мать. —*adj.* **1,** (maternal) матери́нский. **2,** (native) родно́й. —**mother country,** ро́дина; оте́чество. —**mother tongue,** родно́й язы́к.

motherhood *n.* матери́нство.

mother-in-law *n.* **1,** (husband's mother) свекро́вь. **2,** (wife's mother) тёща.

motherland *n.* ро́дина; оте́чество.

motherless *adj.* лишённый ма́тери.

motherly *adj.* матери́нский.

mother-of-pearl *n.* перламу́тр. —*adj.* перламу́тровый.

mother superior игу́менья; настоя́тельница.

motif *n.* моти́в.

motion *n.* **1,** (movement) движе́ние; ход. *Set in motion,* приводи́ть в движе́ние; пусти́ть в ход; дать ход (+ *dat.*). **2,** (gesture) жест. **3,** (proposal to be put to a vote) предложе́ние. **4,** *law* хода́тайство. —*v.t.* пока́зывать же́стом. *He motioned me to a chair,* он указа́л мне на стул. —*v.i.* жестикули́ровать. *He motioned to me to sit down,* он же́стом пригласи́л меня́ сесть.

motionless *adj.* неподви́жный; без движе́ния. *Stand motionless,* стоя́ть неподви́жно.

motion picture 1, (movie) кинофи́льм; кинокарти́на. **2,** *pl.* (the art or field of movie-making) кино́; кинематогра́фия.

motivate *v.t.* побужда́ть. —**motivation,** *n.* побужде́ние.

motive *n.* моти́в; побужде́ние. —*adj.* дви́жущий; дви́гательный.

motley *adj.* пёстрый.

motor *n.* мото́р; дви́гатель. —*adj.* мото́рный. —*v.i.* е́хать *or* ката́ться на маши́не.

motorbike *n.* мопе́д.

motorboat *n.* мото́рная ло́дка.

motorbus *n.* авто́бус.

motorcade *n.* корте́ж (автомоби́лей); автоколо́нна.

motorcar *n.* автомоби́ль.

motorcycle *n.* мотоци́кл. *Motorcycle races,* мотого́нки. —**motorcyclist,** *n.* мотоцикли́ст.

motorist *n.* автомобили́ст.

motorized *adj.* моторизо́ванный.

motorman *n.* **1,** (engineer on a train) машини́ст. **2,** (tram driver) вагоновожа́тый.

motor nerve дви́гательный нерв.

motor scooter мотороллер.

motor ship теплохо́д.

motor vehicle автомаши́на.

mottle *v.t.* испещря́ть. —**mottled,** *adj.* кра́пчатый.

motto *n.* деви́з.

mould *n. & v.* = **mold.** —**moulder,** *v.* = **molder.** —**moulding,** *n.* = **molding.** —**mouldy,** *adj.* = **moldy.**

moult *v.* = **molt.**

mound *n.* буго́р. *Burial mound,* курга́н; моги́льный холм.

mount *v.t.* **1,** (climb, as stairs) поднима́ться по; взбира́ться по. **2,** (go up and stand on) всходи́ть на: *mount the rostrum/scaffold,* всходи́ть на трибу́ну/эшафо́т. **3,** (get up on, as a horse) сади́ться на. **4,** (set, as a jewel) вставля́ть *or* вде́лывать в опра́ву; оправля́ть. **5,** (display, as a picture) накле́ивать на карто́н; кантова́ть. **6,** (set in position, as a gun) устана́вливать. **7,** (launch, as an attack) предпринима́ть. —*v.i.* **1,** (get up on a horse) сади́ться на ло́шадь. **2,** (rise; increase) расти́; возраста́ть. **3,** *fol. by up* (pile up; accumulate) накопля́ться. —*n.* **1,** *used in names of mountain peaks,* гора́: *Mount Everest,* гора́ Эвере́ст. **2,** (horse) верхова́я ло́шадь; ло́шадь под седло́м. **3,** (setting, as for a jewel) опра́ва. **4,** (for a picture) паспарту́. **5,** (stand, as for a weapon) устано́вка. **6,** (supporting structure) крепле́ние. *Engine mount,* у́зел крепле́ния дви́гателя.

mountain *n.* гора́. —*adj.* го́рный: *mountain air,* го́рный во́здух.

mountain ash ряби́на.

mountain climbing альпини́зм. —**mountain climber,** альпини́ст.

mountaineer *n.* **1,** (highlander) го́рец. **2,** (mountain climber) альпини́ст.

mountain goat сне́жная коза́.

mountain lion пу́ма; кугуа́р.

mountainous *adj.* гори́стый; го́рный.

mountaintop *n.* верши́на (горы́).

mountebank *n.* зна́харь; шарлата́н.

mounted *adj.* ко́нный: *mounted police,* ко́нная поли́ция.

mounting *n.* устано́вка; крепле́ние.

mourn *v.i.* **1,** (grieve) горева́ть; скорбе́ть. **2,** (be in mourning) быть в тра́уре; носи́ть тра́ур. —*v.t.* опла́кивать. *Mourn the loss of someone,* опла́кивать кого́-нибудь; скорбе́ть о ко́м-нибудь.

mourner *n.* скорбя́щий.

mournful *adj.* ско́рбный; тра́урный; жа́лобный; плаче́вный.

mourning *n.* тра́ур: *in mourning,* в тра́уре. *Be in mourning for,* быть в тра́уре по; носи́ть тра́ур по. *Go into mourning,* наде́ть тра́ур. —*adj.* тра́урный: *mourning band,* тра́урная повя́зка.

mourning cloak (butterfly) тра́урница.

mouse *n.* мышь.

mousetrap *n.* мышело́вка.

mousse *n.* мусс.

moustache *n.* = mustache.

mousy *adj.* мыши́ный.

mouth *n.* **1,** *anat.* рот: *in one's mouth,* во рту. *Breathe through one's mouth,* дыша́ть ртом. *Have five mouths to feed,* име́ть пять ртов в семье́. **2,** (opening) жерло́; у́стье. *Mouth of a cave,* вход в пеще́ру. **3,** (of a river) у́стье. —*v.t.* произноси́ть. —**by word of mouth,** из уст в уста́. —**down at the mouth,** па́вший ду́хом; в уны́нии. —**keep one's mouth shut,** заткну́ться. —**live from hand to mouth,** *see* **hand.** —**put words in someone's mouth,** вложи́ть слова́ в чьи-нибудь уста́. —**you took the words right out of my mouth,** и́менно э́то я хоте́л(а) сказа́ть.

mouthful *n.* глото́к. *You said a mouthful,* э́тим вы мно́гое сказа́ли.

mouthpiece *n.* **1,** (part that goes in the mouth) мундшту́к. **2,** *colloq.* (spokesman) ру́пор.

mouthwash *n.* полоска́ние.

movable *adj.* **1,** (that can be moved) подвижно́й; передвижно́й. **2,** *law* (of property) дви́жимый. —**movables,** *n.pl., law* дви́жимость.

move *v.t.* **1,** (change the location or position of) дви́гать: *move furniture,* дви́гать ме́бель; *move one's legs,* дви́гать нога́ми. **2,** (move from one place to another; transfer) передвига́ть; перемеща́ть; переноси́ть; переводи́ть; переставля́ть. *Move one's office to another building,* перемеща́ть кабине́т в друго́е зда́ние. *Move the capital to another city,* переноси́ть столи́цу в друго́й го́род. *Move troops up to the border,* передвига́ть *or* подтя́гивать войска́ к грани́це. **3,** (prompt; cause) побужда́ть. **4,** (touch the feelings of) тро́гать; растро́гать. *We were very moved,* мы бы́ли о́чень тро́нуты. *Move to tears,* тро́гать (кого́-нибудь) до слёз. **5,** (propose) предлага́ть. **6,** *chess* игра́ть (+ *instr.*); идти́ (+ *instr.*). **7,** (evacuate, as the bowels) очища́ть. —*v.i.* **1,** (change location or position) дви́гаться; сдвига́ться; передвига́ться. *Don't move!,* не дви́гайтесь!; не шевели́тесь! *Move to another room,* переходи́ть в другу́ю ко́мнату. **2,** (change residence) переезжа́ть: *move to Chicago,* переезжа́ть в Чика́го. **3,** (shift) переходи́ть: *move to a different subject,* переходи́ть к друго́й те́ме. **4,** (be active; circulate) враща́ться: *move in scholarly circles,* враща́ться в учёных круга́х. —*n.* **1,** (movement) движе́ние: *the slightest move,* мале́йшее движе́ние. *One (false) move and I'll shoot!,* одно́ (неве́рное) движе́ние, и я бу́ду стреля́ть! **2,** (change of residence) перее́зд. **3,** (step; maneuver) ход; шаг. **4,** (play, as in games) ход: *He resigned on the 47th move,* он сда́лся на со́рок седьмо́м ходу́. —**get a move on!,** *colloq.* потора́пливайтесь! —**move about,** передвига́ться. —**move aside,** отодвига́ть(ся). —**move away,** уезжа́ть. —**move back, 1,** (step back) отодвига́ться. **2,** (move to where one used to live) возвраща́ться. —**move in/into,** въезжа́ть (в); вселя́ться (в). —**move in with,** переезжа́ть (жить)

к. —**move out,** съезжа́ть; выезжа́ть. —**move over,** подвига́ться. —**move up, 1,** (advance in rank or status) продвига́ться. **2,** (schedule earlier) переноси́ть *or* передвига́ть на бо́лее ра́нний срок. —**on the move,** в разъе́здах.

movement *n.* **1,** (motion) движе́ние; передвиже́ние. *Troop movement,* движе́ние *or* передвиже́ние войск. *Freedom of movement,* свобо́да передвиже́ния. **2,** (organized campaign) движе́ние: *the trade union movement,* профсою́зное движе́ние. **3,** *music* (portion of a work) часть.

mover *n.* перево́зчик.

movie *n.* **1,** (motion picture) фильм; кинофи́льм. *Make a movie,* ста́вить *or* создава́ть фильм. *Make a movie out of,* экранизи́ровать. **2,** *pl.* (showing) кино́: *go to the movies,* ходи́ть в кино́. *See three movies a week,* ходи́ть в кино́ три ра́за в неде́лю. —**movie camera,** киноаппара́т; кинока́мера. —**movie film,** киноплёнка. —**movie projector,** кинопрое́ктор. —**movie star,** кинозвезда́. —**movie theater,** кинотеа́тр.

moving *adj.* **1,** (that moves; in motion) дви́жущийся: *moving parts,* дви́жущиеся ча́сти; *moving target,* дви́жущаяся цель. **2,** (stirring the emotions) тро́гательный. —**moving allowance,** подъёмные (де́ньги). —**moving van,** ме́бельный фурго́н.

mow *v.t.* **1,** (cut down, as grass) коси́ть. **2,** (cut the grass from, as a lawn) подстрига́ть. —**mow down,** коси́ть.

mower *n.* **1,** (person) коса́рь; косе́ц. **2,** (machine) коси́лка.

Mr. *abbr.* ми́стер; господи́н.

Mrs. *abbr.* ми́ссис; госпожа́.

much *adj.* мно́го: *much time,* мно́го вре́мени. *There is much truth in what he says,* в его́ слова́х мно́го пра́вды. —*adv.* **1,** (to a great extent or degree) о́чень: *I want very much to go,* я о́чень хочу́ пойти́. *I am much indebted to you,* я вам мно́гим обя́зан. **2,** (by far) гора́здо; намно́го: *much better,* гора́здо/намно́го лу́чше. **3,** (often; a lot) ча́сто; мно́го: *Do you travel much?,* вы ча́сто/мно́го разъезжа́ете? **4,** (nearly; about) почти́: *much the same,* почти́ тако́й же. —*n.* мно́го; мно́гое: *leave much to be desired,* оставля́ть жела́ть мно́го лу́чше. *We don't see much of him,* мы ре́дко ви́дим его́. *There is much we still don't know,* мы мно́гого ещё не зна́ем. *I agree with much of what you say,* в основно́м я согла́сен с тем, что вы говори́те. *Much of my time is taken up with the children,* де́ти отнима́ют у меня́ мно́го вре́мени. —**as much... as,** сто́лько же...; ско́лько и: *He has as much energy as you do,* у него́ сто́лько же эне́ргии, ско́лько и у вас. *I don't have as much money as he has,* у меня́ нет сто́лько де́нег, ско́лько у него́. *Take as much as you like,* возьми́те, ско́лько хоти́те. *A fur coat can cost as much as $10,000,* шу́ба мо́жет сто́ить де́сять ты́сяч до́лларов. —**how much?,** *see* **how.** —**make much of,** придава́ть большо́е значе́ние (+ *dat.*). —**much as,** как ни: *much as I hate to,* как э́то ни оби́дно. *Much as I would like to,* при всём моём жела́нии. —**much less,** *see* **less.** —**much to my...,** к моему́ вели́кому...: *much to my surprise,* к моему́ вели́кому удивле́нию. —**nothing much,** ничего́ осо́бенного. —**not much of a...,** нева́жный: *He is not much of a swimmer,* он нева́жно пла́вает. —**so much,** *see* **so.** —**so much the better/worse,** тем лу́чше/ху́же. —**too much,** сли́шком мно́го; сли́шком. —**too much for,** не под си́лу (+ *dat.*).

mucilage *n.* **1,** (gummy secretion) (расти́тельная) слизь. **2,** (glue) (расти́тельный) клей.

muck *n.* **1,** (filth) грязь. **2,** (manure) наво́з.

mucous *adj.* сли́зистый. —**mucous membrane,** сли́зистая оболо́чка.

mucus *n.* слизь.

mud *n.* грязь. —*adj.* грязево́й: *mud bath,* грязева́я ва́нна. *Mud hut,* глиноби́тная земля́нка. —**drag through the mud,** втопта́ть в грязь. —**hurl/sling mud at,** забра́сывать (кого́-нибудь) гря́зью.

muddle *v.t.* **1,** (mix up; confuse) пу́тать. **2,** (bungle) напу́тать. —*v.i.* [*usu.* **muddle through**] выкру́чиваться. —*n.* пу́таница; неразбери́ха.

muddy *adj.* гря́зный. —*v.t.* **1,** (soil with mud) испа́чкать гря́зью. **2,** (make turbid) мути́ть. —**muddy the waters,** мути́ть во́ду.

mudguard *n.* брызгови́к; щит от гря́зи.

mudslide *n.* о́ползень.

mudslinger *n.* клеветни́к; злопыха́тель.

muezzin *n.* муэдзи́н.

muff *n.* му́фта. —*v.t.* **1,** (fail to catch) пропусти́ть. **2,** (bungle) упусти́ть: *muff a chance,* упусти́ть слу́чай. *Muff one's lines,* сма́зать свою́ ре́плику.

muffin *n.* сдо́бная бу́лка.

muffle *v.t.* **1,** (cover up; wrap) заку́тывать. **2,** (deaden, as sound) глуши́ть; заглуша́ть.

muffler *n.* **1,** (scarf) кашне́. **2,** (silencing device) глуши́тель.

mufti *n.* **1,** (civilian garb) шта́тская оде́жда; шта́тское. **2,** (Moslim jurist) му́фтий.

mug *n.* **1,** (vessel) кру́жка: *beer mug,* пивна́я кру́жка. **2,** *slang* (face) мо́рда; ро́жа; ры́ло; ха́ря. —*v.t., colloq.* гра́бить. —**mugger,** *n., colloq.* налётчик.

muggy *adj.* сыро́й; гнило́й.

mulatto *n.* мула́т.

mulberry *n.* **1,** (tree) ту́товое де́рево; шелкови́ца. **2,** (fruit) ту́товая я́года.

mulch *n.* му́льча.

mule *n.* мул. *Mule team,* упря́жка му́лов. *Stubborn as a mule,* упря́мый как осёл. —**muleteer,** *n.* пого́нщик му́лов.

mull *v.i.* [*usu.* **mull over**] обду́мывать.

mullah *n.* мулла́.

mullet *n.* **1,** (gray mullet) кефа́ль. **2,** (red mullet) барабу́лька; султа́нка.

multicolored *also,* **multicoloured** *adj.* многоцве́тный; многокра́сочный.

multifaceted *adj.* многогра́нный; разносторо́нний.

multifarious *adj.* разнообра́зный.

multiform *adj.* многообра́зный.

multilateral *adj.* многосторо́нний.

multilingual *adj.* многоязы́чный; разноязы́чный.

multimillionaire *n.* мультимиллионе́р; миллиарде́р.

multinational *adj.* многонациона́льный.

multiparty *adj.* многопарти́йный.

multiple *adj.* **1,** (numerous) многочи́сленный. *Receive multiple injuries,* получи́ть мно́го поврежде́ний. **2,** (involving more than one element): *multiple births,* многопло́дные ро́ды; *multiple warhead,* разделя́ющаяся боеголо́вка. —*n.* кра́тное: *least common multiple,* о́бщее наиме́ньшее кра́тное. —**multiple sclerosis,** рассе́янный склеро́з.

multiplicand *n.* мно́жимое.

multiplication *n.* умноже́ние. —**multiplication table,** табли́ца умноже́ния.

multiplicity *n.* мно́жество. *A multiplicity of cases,* мно́жество случа́ев; многочи́сленные слу́чаи.

multiplier *n., math.* мно́житель.

multiply *v.t.* мно́жить; умножа́ть: *multiply six by eight,* мно́жить/умножа́ть шесть на во́семь. —*v.i.* **1,** (perform multiplication) мно́жить; умножа́ть. **2,** (increase) мно́житься; умножа́ться. **3,** (propagate) размножа́ться; разводи́ться.

multipurpose *adj.* универса́льный.

multistage *adj.* многоступе́нчатый.

multistoried *adj.* многоэта́жный. *Also,* **multistory.**

multitude *n.* мно́жество. —**multitudinous,** *adj.* многочи́сленный.

mum *adj., colloq.* ни гугу́. *Keep mum,* пома́лкивать. —**mum's the word,** (об э́том) ни гугу́.

mumble *v.t. & i.* бормота́ть. —*n.* бормота́нье.

mummy *n.* **1,** (embalmed body) му́мия. **2,** *colloq.* (mother) ма́мочка.

mumps *n.* сви́нка.

munch *v.t. & i.* ча́вкать.

mundane *adj.* земно́й; мирско́й; жите́йский.

municipal *adj.* городско́й; муниципа́льный.

municipality *n.* муниципалите́т.

munificent *adj.* ще́дрый. —**munificence,** *n.* ще́дрость.

munition *n., usu. pl.* боеприпа́сы; вое́нное иму́щество. *Munitions factory,* вое́нный заво́д.

mural *n.* (стенна́я) ро́спись. —*adj.* стенно́й.

murder *n.* уби́йство. *The murder weapon,* ору́дие уби́йства. —*v.t.* **1,** (kill) убива́ть. **2,** (butcher) кове́ркать: *murder the English language,* кове́ркать англи́йский язы́к. —**murderer,** *n.* уби́йца. —**murderous** *adj.* уби́йственный.

murky *adj.* **1,** (dark; gloomy) мра́чный. **2,** (turbid) му́тный.

murmur *n.* **1,** (sound) ро́пот: *murmur of voices,* ро́пот голосо́в. *Without a murmur,* безро́потно. **2,** *med.* шум (в се́рдце). —*v.i.* ропта́ть.

murrain *n.* падёж.

murre *n.* ка́йра.

muscat *n.* муска́т. —*adj.* муска́тный.

muscatel *n.* муска́т.

muscle *n.* мы́шца; му́скул. —*adj.* мы́шечный: *muscle tone,* мы́шечный то́нус. —*v.i.* [*usu.* **muscle in**] *colloq.* пробива́ться.

Muscovite *n.* москви́ч.

muscular *adj.* **1,** (of or done by the muscles) мы́шечный; му́скульный. **2,** (brawny) му́скулистый. —**muscular dystrophy,** мы́шечная дистрофи́я.

musculature *n.* мускулату́ра.

muse *v.i.* размышля́ть; заду́мываться. —*n.* му́за.

museum *n.* музе́й. —**museum piece,** музе́йная ре́дкость.

mush *n.* ка́ша.

mushroom *n.* гриб. —*v.i.* разраста́ться. —**mushroom cloud,** грибови́дное облако.

mushy *adj.* **1,** (soft; pulpy) мя́гкий. **2,** *colloq.* (excessively sentimental) слаща́вый.

music *n.* **1,** (general term) му́зыка. *Set words to music,* положи́ть слова́ на му́зыку. **2,** (written score) но́ты: *play from/without music,* игра́ть по но́там/ без нот/. —*adj.* музыка́льный; но́тный. *Music stand,* но́тный пюпи́тр; пульт.

musical *adj.* музыка́льный: *musical instrument,* музыка́льный инструме́нт. —*n.* мю́зикл. —**musical comedy,** музыка́льная коме́дия.

musicale *n.* музыка́льный ве́чер.

music box музыка́льная шкату́лка; музыка́льный я́щик.

music hall мю́зик-хо́лл.

musician *n.* музыка́нт.

musicology *n.* музыкове́дение. —**musicologist,** *n.* музыкове́д.

musk *n.* му́скус.

musk deer кабарга́.

musket *n.* мушке́т. —**musketeer,** *n.* мушкетёр.

musk ox овцебы́к.

muskrat *n.* онда́тра.

Muslim *n. & adj.* = **Moslem.**

muslin *n.* мусли́н; кисея́. —*adj.* мусли́новый; кисе́йный.

muss *v.t.* растрепа́ть; еро́шить; взлохма́чивать.

mussel *n.* ми́дия.

must *v.aux.* **1,** *expressing necessity,* до́лжен; на́до: *I must go,* мне на́до идти́; я до́лжен (должна́) идти́. **2,** *expressing strong probability,* должно́ быть: *He must be here,* он, должно́ быть, здесь. *You must have heard about it,* вы, должно́ быть, слы́шали об э́том. **3,** *used negatively, expressing prohibition,* нельзя́; не на́до; не до́лжен: *You mustn't say such things,* не на́до так говори́ть; нельзя́ (*or* не на́до) говори́ть таки́х веще́й. *We must not be seen together,* нас не должны́ ви́деть вме́сте. *This must not happen again!,* чтобы э́того бо́льше не́ было!

mustache *also,* **moustache** *n.* усы́.

mustang *n.* муста́нг.

mustard *n.* горчи́ца. —**mustard gas,** горчи́чный газ; иприт. —**mustard oil,** горчи́чное ма́сло. —**mustard plaster,** горчи́чник.

muster *v.t.* **1,** (assemble) собира́ть. **2,** (summon, as strength, courage, etc.) набира́ться (+ *gen.*); собира́ться с. **3,** *fol. by* **out** (discharge) увольня́ть (с вое́нной слу́жбы); демобилизова́ть. —*v.i.* собира́ться. —*n.* **1,** (assemblage, as of troops) сбор; смотр. **2,** (list; roll) именно́й спи́сок. —**pass muster,** оказа́ться на высоте́.

musty *adj.* за́тхлый.

mutate *v.t.* видоизменя́ть. —*v.i.* видоизменя́ться.

mutation *n.* **1,** *biol.* мута́ция. **2,** *phonet.* перегласо́вка.

mute *adj.* немо́й. —*n.* **1,** (one incapable of speech) немо́й. **2,** *music* сурди́нка. —*v.t.* **1,** *music* надева́ть сурди́нку на. **2,** (muffle) приглуша́ть.

muted *adj.* приглушённый.

muteness *n.* немота́; онеме́ние.

mutilate *v.t.* уве́чить; уро́довать; кале́чить. *Mutilated bodies,* изуро́дованные тру́пы. —**mutilation,** *n.* уве́чье.

mutineer *n.* мяте́жник; бунтовщи́к.

mutinous *adj.* мяте́жный; бунта́рский.

mutiny *n.* мяте́ж; бунт. —*v.i.* подня́ть мяте́ж; бунтова́ть.

mutter *v.t. & i.* бормота́ть.

mutton *n.* бара́нина. —*adj.* бара́ний: *mutton chop,* бара́нья котле́та.

mutual *adj.* **1,** (given and received in kind) взаи́мный; обою́дный. *Mutual assistance,* взаимопо́мощь. **2,** (possessed in common) о́бщий: *mutual acquaintances,* о́бщие знако́мые.

mutuality *n.* взаи́мность; обою́дность.

mutually *adv.* взаи́мно; обою́дно. *Mutually advantageous/beneficial,* взаимовы́годный. *Be mutually exclusive,* взаи́мно исключа́ть друг дру́га.

muzhik *n.* мужи́к.

muzzle *n.* **1,** (of a firearm) ду́ло; жерло́. **2,** (snout) мо́рда; ры́ло. **3,** (covering for an animal's mouth) намо́рдник. —*v.t.* **1,** (put a muzzle on) надева́ть намо́рдник на. **2,** *fig.* (silence; gag) заста́вить замолча́ть.

my *poss. adj.* мой (моя́, моё, мои́): *my mother,* моя́ мать. *My two helpers,* два мои́х помо́щника. *It's in my office,* он (она́, оно́) у меня́ в кабине́те. ♦*When the possessor is the subject of the sentence,* свой: *I finished my work,* я зако́нчил свою́ рабо́ту. —*interj.* бо́же мой!; ну и ну!

myopia *n.* близору́кость; миопи́я. —**myopic,** *adj.* близору́кий.

myriad *n.* мириа́ды. —*adj.* бесчи́сленный; несме́тный.

myriapod *n.* многоно́жка.

myrrh *n.* ми́рра.

myrtle *n.* мирт. —*adj.* ми́ртовый.

myself *pers. pron.* **1,** *used for emphasis,* (я) сам: *I don't know myself,* я сам (сама́) не зна́ю. **2,** *used reflexively,* себя́: *I bought myself a dress,* я купи́ла себе́ пла́тье. *I hurt myself,* я уши́бся (уши́блась). —**by myself, 1,** (alone) оди́н (одна́). **2,** (without help) сам (сама́). —**to myself,** себе́; про себя́.

mysterious *adj.* таи́нственный; зага́дочный. —**mysteriously,** *adv.* таи́нственно.

mystery *n.* **1,** (enigma) та́йна; зага́дка. **2,** (mysteriousness) та́йна; таи́нственность. **3,** (mystery story) детекти́вный рома́н.

mystic *adj.* мисти́ческий. —*n.* ми́стик. —**mystical,** *adj.* мисти́ческий.

mysticism *n.* ми́стика; мистици́зм.

mystify *v.t.* озада́чивать. —**mystification,** *n.* озада́ченность.

mystique *n.* таи́нственность.

myth *n.* миф. —**mythical,** *adj.* мифи́ческий

mythology *n.* мифоло́гия. —**mythological,** *adj.* мифологи́ческий.

N

N, n четы́рнадцатая бу́ква англи́йского алфави́та.

nab *v.t., colloq.* схвати́ть.

nadir *n.* **1,** *astron.* нади́р. **2,** *fig.* (low point) ни́зшая то́чка.

nag *v.t.* придира́ться к; пристава́ть к; пили́ть. —*n.* **1,** (person who nags) придира́. **2,** (old horse) кля́ча.

nagging *n.* пристава́ние. —*adj.* **1,** (of a person) надое́дливый. **2,** (of a pain) но́ющий. **3,** (of a thought, question, etc.) назо́йливый; неотвя́зный. *Nagging fear,* тупо́й страх.

nail *n.* **1,** (of a finger or toe) но́готь. **2,** (metal fastener) гвоздь. —*v.t.* **1,** (fasten with a nail or nails) приби-ва́ть; набива́ть: *nail a notice to the wall,* приби́ть объявле́ние к стене́; *nail a plaque on the door,* наби́ть доще́чку на дверь. **2,** *fol. by* **up** (seal up with nails) забива́ть; зака́лачивать. **3,** *fol. by* **down** (fasten down with nails) забива́ть; прибива́ть. **4,** *fig.* (rivet) пригвожда́ть: *nailed to one's seat,* пригво-ждённый к ме́сту. **5,** *fol. by* **down** (clinch) заключ-и́ть: *nail down an agreement,* заключи́ть согла-ше́ние. **6,** *colloq.* (seize; nab) схвати́ть. —**hit the nail on the head,** попа́сть в (са́мую) то́чку; попа́сть не в бровь, а в глаз.

nail file пи́лка (для ногте́й).

nail polish лак для ногте́й.

naïve *adj.* наи́вный. —**naïveté,** *n.* наи́вность.

naked *adj.* го́лый; наго́й; обнажённый. *Run around naked,* пробега́ть в го́лом ви́де; пробега́ть на-гишо́м. *The naked truth,* го́лая и́стина. *Naked ag-gression,* неприкры́тая агре́ссия. —**with the naked eye,** просты́м гла́зом; невооружённым гла́зом.

nakedness *n.* нагота́.

name *n.* **1,** (first name; Christian name) и́мя: *a com-mon/pretty name,* распространённое/краси́вое и́мя. *What is your name?,* как вас зову́т? *My name is...,* меня́ зову́т (+ *nom.*). **2,** (last name; surname) фами́лия: *a man by the name of Smith,* челове́к по фами́лии Смит. *He goes by the name of Sokolov,* он изве́стен под и́менем Со́колова. **3,** (appellation) назва́ние: *the name of the city,* назва́ние го́рода. *The movie is based on a novel of the same name by...,* фильм со́здан по одноимённому рома́ну (+ *gen.*). **4,** (reputation) и́мя: *make a name for oneself,* сде́лать себе́ и́мя. **5,** *colloq.* (celebrity) и́мя: *big names,* кру́пные имена́. —*v.t.* **1,** (give a name, to; call) дава́ть и́мя (+ *dat.*); называ́ть: *They named her Olga,*

ей да́ли и́мя О́льга; её назва́ли О́льгой. *The city was named after...,* го́род был на́зван и́менем *or* в честь (+ *gen.*). **2,** (state; recount by name) называ́ть: *Name your price,* назови́те ва́шу це́ну. *Name the signs of the zodiac,* назови́те зна́ки зодиа́ка. **3,** (ap-point; designate) назнача́ть. —**by name,** поимённо: *mention by name,* называ́ть поимённо. —**call (some-one) names,** руга́ть; обруга́ть. —**give one's name,** называ́ть своё и́мя; называ́ть себя́. —**in name only,** то́лько номина́льно. —**in the name of, 1,** *literally* на и́мя (+ *gen.*): *reserve a room in the name of Clark,* за-каза́ть но́мер на и́мя Кла́рка. **2,** (for the sake of) во и́мя (+ *gen.*): *in the name of justice,* во и́мя справедли́вости. **3,** (by the authority of) и́менем (+ *gen.*): *in the name of the law,* и́менем зако́на. —**name names,** называ́ть имена́: *I don't want to name names,* я не хочу́ называ́ть имён. —**to one's name,** за душо́й: *He hasn't a penny to his name,* у него́ за душо́й ни гроша́.

name day имени́ны.

nameless *adj.* безымя́нный. *Someone who shall re-main nameless,* лицо́, кото́рого мы не бу́дем назы-ва́ть.

namely *adv.* а и́менно.

nameplate *n.* доще́чка; табли́чка.

namesake *n.* тёзка.

nanny *n.* ня́ня. —**nanny goat,** коза́.

nap *n.* **1,** (brief sleep) сон. *Take a nap,* поспа́ть; сосну́ть; вздремну́ть. **2,** (fuzzy surface) ворс; начёс. —*v.i.* **1,** (be asleep) спать. **2,** (be off one's guard) дрема́ть. *Catch someone napping,* заста́ть кого́-нибудь враспло́х.

napalm *n.* напа́лм. —*adj.* напа́лмовый.

nape *n.* загри́вок.

naphtha *n.* лигрои́н.

naphthalene *n.* нафтали́н.

naphthol *n.* нафто́л.

napkin *n.* салфе́тка.

nappy *n., Brit.* пелёнка.

narcissus *n.* нарци́сс.

narcotic *n.* нарко́тик. —*adj.* наркоти́ческий.

nard *n.* нард.

narrate *v.t.* **1,** (relate; recount) расска́зывать о. **2,** (provide the running commentary for): *The film was narrated by...,* текст в фи́льме чита́л (+ *nom.*).

narration *n.* **1,** (act of narrating) расска́зывание. **2,** (a narrative) повествова́ние. **3,** (running commentary for a film) коммента́рий; текст.

narrative *n.* повествова́ние. —*adj.* повествова́тельный.

narrator *n.* **1,** (storyteller) расска́зчик. **2,** (of a film) ди́ктор; коммента́тор.

narrow *adj.* **1,** (not wide) у́зкий: *narrow street/bridge/ passageway,* у́зкий переу́лок/мост/прохо́д. **2,** (tight) у́зкий; те́сный: *narrow in the waist,* у́зок/те́сен в та́лии. **3,** (limited in scope) у́зкий: *narrow subject/ perspective,* у́зкая те́ма/перспекти́ва. *Narrow circle of friends,* у́зкий *or* те́сный круг друзе́й. **4,** (uncomfortably close) незначи́тельный: *win a narrow victory,* победи́ть с незначи́тельным переве́сом. *Have a narrow escape,* едва́ спасти́сь; едва́ но́ги унести́. —*v.t.* су́живать: *narrow the debate,* су́живать пре́ния. —*v.i.* су́живаться: *The road narrows,* доро́га су́живается. —**narrow down to,** своди́ть(ся) к.

narrow-gauge *adj.* узкоколе́йный.

narrowly *adv.* чуть; е́ле-е́ле. *He narrowly missed being killed,* он чуть не поги́б.

narrow-minded *adj.* у́зкий; ограни́ченный; узколо́бый.

narrowness *n.* у́зость.

narwhal *n.* нарва́л.

nary *adj., colloq.* ни оди́н: *nary a person,* ни одного́ челове́ка.

nasal *adj.* **1,** (pert. to the nose; pronounced through the nose) носово́й. **2,** (having a nasal quality) гнуса́вый.

nascent *adj.* зарожда́ющийся. *Nascent republic,* молода́я респу́блика.

nasturtium *n.* насту́рция.

nasty *adj.* **1,** (nauseating; disgusting) проти́вный; отврати́тельный: *nasty odor,* проти́вный/отврати́тельный за́пах. **2,** (very bad) скве́рный: *nasty habit/weather,* скве́рная привы́чка/пого́да. *He is in for a nasty surprise,* его́ ждёт больша́я неприя́тность. **3,** (causing harm or discomfort) серьёзный; доса́дный: *nasty accident,* серьёзная ава́рия; *nasty cough,* доса́дный ка́шель. **4,** (ill-tempered; unpleasant) скве́рный: *nasty disposition,* скве́рный хара́ктер. *He has a nasty temper,* у него́ вспы́льчивый хара́ктер. *Be nasty to,* пло́хо относи́ться к. **5,** (malicious; mean) злой: *nasty trick,* зла́я шу́тка.

natal *adj.* относя́щийся к рожде́нию.

nation *n.* страна́. *The United Nations,* Объединённые На́ции.

national *adj.* национа́льный; госуда́рственный. —*n.* граждани́н; по́дданный. *Foreign nationals,* иностра́нные гра́ждане.

National Guard национа́льная гва́рдия.

nationalism *n.* национали́зм.

nationalist *n.* национали́ст. —*adj.* националисти́ческий. —**nationalistic,** *adj.* националисти́ческий.

nationality *n.* **1,** (national origin) национа́льность. **2,** (body of people) национа́льность; наро́дность. *The nationality question,* национа́льный вопро́с.

nationalize *v.t.* национализи́ровать. —**nationalization,** *n.* национализа́ция.

nationhood *n.* госуда́рственность.

nationwide *adj.* всенаро́дный.

native *adj.* **1,** (of the land of one's birth) родно́й: *one's native land,* родна́я страна́; родно́й край; ро́дина. **2,** (indigenous) тузе́мный. *Native New Yorker,* уроже́нец Нью-Йо́рка. —*n.* **1,** (one born in a particular place) уроже́нец. *He is a native of Kiev,* он ро́дом из Ки́ева. **2,** (original inhabitant; aborigine) тузе́мец.

nativity *n.* **1,** (birth) рожде́ние. **2,** *cap.* (birth of Christ) рождество́ Христо́во.

natty *adj.* наря́дный; щеголева́тый.

natural *adj.* **1,** (arising from nature) есте́ственный; приро́дный. *Natural boundary,* есте́ственная грани́ца. *A natural desire,* есте́ственное жела́ние. *Natural phenomenon,* явле́ние приро́ды. *Natural ability,* приро́дные спосо́бности. *Natural disaster,* стихи́йное бе́дствие. *Die a natural death,* умере́ть есте́ственной сме́ртью. **2,** (not artificial or affected) есте́ственный: *natural expression,* есте́ственное выраже́ние лица́. **3,** (having certain abilities innately) прирождённый: *a natural comedian,* прирождённый ко́мик. **4,** *music* бека́р: *D-natural,* ре-бека́р. —**natural gas,** приро́дный газ. —**natural resources,** есте́ственные *or* приро́дные ресу́рсы. —**natural science,** есте́ственные нау́ки. —**natural selection,** есте́ственный отбо́р.

naturalism *n.* натурали́зм.

naturalist *n.* естествоиспыта́тель; натурали́ст.

naturalize *v.t.* натурализова́ть. —**naturalization,** *n.* натурализа́ция.

naturally *adv.* **1,** (in accordance with the laws of nature) есте́ственно. **2,** (by nature) по приро́де; по нату́ре; натура́льно. **3,** (without affectation) есте́ственно: *behave naturally,* вести́ себя́ есте́ственно. **4,** (as one might expect; of course) коне́чно; разуме́ется; есте́ственно.

nature *n.* **1,** (universe) приро́да: *the laws of nature,* зако́ны приро́ды. **2,** (temperament; disposition) нату́ра. *By nature,* по нату́ре; по приро́де. *It is not her nature to show off,* рисова́ться не в её хара́ктере. **3,** (essential characteristics) хара́ктер: *the nature of the work,* хара́ктер рабо́ты. *By its very nature,* по са́мой свое́й су́щности. **4,** (sort; kind) род: *things of that nature,* тако́го ро́да ве́щи. —**in the nature of things,** в поря́дке веще́й; в приро́де веще́й.

naught *n.* нуль. *All for naught,* всё напра́сно. *Go for naught,* пропа́сть да́ром. *Come to naught,* своди́ться к нулю́ *or* на нет.

naughty *adj.* **1,** (mischievous) шаловли́вый. *Naughty child,* шалу́н. *Be naughty,* шали́ть. **2,** (indecent) риско́ванный; двусмы́сленный.

nausea *n.* тошнота́. —**nauseate,** *v.t.* вызыва́ть тошноту́ у. —**nauseating,** *adj.* тошнотво́рный.

nauseous *adj.* **1,** (nauseating) тошнотво́рный. **2,** (nauseated): *I feel nauseous,* меня́ тошни́т. *I felt nauseous,* меня́ тошни́ло; тошнота́ подкати́ла к го́рлу.

nautical *adj.* морско́й. —**nautical mile,** морска́я ми́ля.

nautilus *n.* кора́блик.

naval *adj.* морско́й; вое́нно-морско́й. *Naval academy,* вое́нно-морско́е учи́лище. *Naval battle,* морско́й бой. *Naval warfare,* война́ на мо́ре.

nave *n.* кора́бль.

navel *n.* пупо́к.

navigable *adj.* судохо́дный. —**navigability,** *n.* судохо́дность.

navigate *v.t.* **1,** (sail through) переплыва́ть. **2,** (steer; operate) управля́ть. —*v.i.* **1,** (sail) пла́вать (на су́дне). **2,** *colloq.* (walk) передвига́ться.

navigation *n.* **1,** (sailing; shipping) судохо́дство; навига́ция; морепла́вание. *Freedom of navigation,* свобо́да судохо́дства. **2,** (the science) навига́ция; кораблевожде́ние. —**navigational,** *adj.* навигаци́онный.

navigator *n.* **1,** (on a ship or aircraft) шту́рман. **2,** (explorer) морепла́ватель.

navy *n.* (вое́нно-морско́й) флот.

navy blue тёмноси́ний цвет. —**navy-blue,** *adj.* тёмноси́ний.

navy yard вое́нно-морска́я верфь.

nay *adv.* нет. —*n.* про́тив: *three ayes, two nays,* три за, два про́тив. *The nays have it,* большинство́ про́тив.

Nazi *n.* наци́ст. —*adj.* наци́стский. —**Nazism,** *n.* наци́зм.

Neanderthal *adj.* неандерта́льский. —**Neanderthal man,** неандерта́лец.

near *adj.* бли́зкий: *The end is near,* коне́ц бли́зок. *It's quite near,* э́то совсе́м бли́зко. *In the near future,* в ско́ром *or* в ближа́йшем бу́дущем; в ближа́йшее вре́мя. *The nearest way to town,* кратча́йший путь в го́род. —*adv.* бли́зко. *Draw near,* бли́зиться; приближа́ться. —*prep.* о́коло; у; во́зле; бли́зко от *or* к; недалеко́ от. *Near here,* недалеко́ отсю́да; побли́зости. *Sit near me,* сядь о́коло меня́. *Sit near each other,* сиде́ть бли́зко друг к дру́гу. *The post office is near the station,* по́чта недалеко́ от вокза́ла. *Be near death,* быть при́ сме́рти. —*v.t. & i.* бли́зиться (к): приближа́ться (к): *be nearing an end,* бли́зиться/приближа́ться к концу́. —**near at hand,** бли́зко; под руко́й; на носу́. —**near miss,** попада́ние близ це́ли.

nearby *adj.* бли́зкий; сосе́дний; близлежа́щий. *Their house is right nearby,* их дом совсе́м бли́зко *or* совсе́м ря́дом. —*adv.* бли́зко; вблизи́; побли́зости.

nearly *adv.* почти́; едва́ ли не; чуть ли не. ♦*With verbs,* едва́ не; чуть не: *He nearly drowned,* он едва́ не *or* чуть не утону́л. —**not nearly,** совсе́м не; соверше́нно не: *not nearly ready,* совсе́м не гото́в; *not nearly enough,* соверше́нно недоста́точно.

nearness *n.* бли́зость.

nearsighted *adj.* близору́кий. —**nearsightedness,** *n.* близору́кость.

neat *adj.* **1,** (tidy) опря́тный; аккура́тный; чистопло́тный. **2,** *colloq.* (adroit) ло́вкий. —**neatly,** *adv.* опря́тно; аккура́тно. —**neatness,** *n.* опря́тность; аккура́тность.

nebula *n.* тума́нность.

nebulous *adj.* сму́тный; нея́сный; тума́нный.

necessarily *adv.* обяза́тельно.

necessary *adj.* необходи́мый; ну́жный: *necessary information,* необходи́мые/ну́жные све́дения. *A necessary evil,* необходи́мое зло. *Necessary to life,* необходи́м для жи́зни. *When/if necessary,* при необходи́мости; в слу́чае необходи́мости. *No, thank you. It's not necessary,* нет спаси́бо. В э́том нет необходи́мости. *It will be necessary to...,* придётся (+ *inf.*). *Consider it necessary to...,* счита́ть ну́жным/необходи́мым (+ *inf.*).

necessitate *v.t.* де́лать необходи́мым; тре́бовать.

necessity *n.* **1,** (the fact of being necessary) необходи́мость; на́добность. *Out of necessity,* по необходи́мости. **2,** (something that is necessary) необходи́мая вещь. *The basic necessities,* са́мое необходи́мое; предме́ты пе́рвой необходи́мости.

neck *n.* **1,** (part of the body) ше́я. **2,** (of a garment) во́рот: *shirt with an open neck,* руба́шка с откры́тым во́ротом. *V-neck,* треуго́льный вы́рез. **3,** (of a bottle) го́рлышко; го́рло. **4,** (of a violin; of the uterus) ше́йка. **5,** (of land) переше́ек. —*adj.* ше́йный. —**get it in the neck,** *colloq.* получи́ть по ше́е. —**neck and neck,** голова́ в го́лову. —**risk one's neck,** лезть в пе́тлю. —**stick one's neck out,** ста́вить себя́ под уда́р.

neckerchief *n.* ше́йный плато́к.

necklace *n.* ожере́лье.

neckline *n.* вы́рез: *low neckline,* глубо́кий вы́рез.

necktie *n.* га́лстук.

necrosis *n.* некро́з.

nectar *n.* некта́р.

nee *also,* **née** *adj.* урождённая.

need *n.* **1,** (poverty) нужда́: *live in dire need,* жить в нужде́. **2,** (necessity) на́добность; нужда́; необходи́мость; потре́бность. *No need to...,* нет на́добности/нужды́ (+ *inf.*). *There is no need for that,* в э́том нет необходи́мости. *In case of dire need,* в слу́чае кра́йней нужды́ *or* необходи́мости. *The need for discipline,* необходи́мость дисципли́ны. *An urgent need for reform,* назре́вшая потре́бность в рефо́рме. **3,** *pl.* (wants; requirements) ну́жды; потре́бности. —*v.t.* **1,** (have need of) нужда́ться в: *need help,* нужда́ться в по́мощи. *Need no introduction,* не нужда́ться в представле́нии. ♦*More commonly rendered by* ну́жен: *I need a new suit,* мне ну́жен но́вый костю́м; *I need money,* мне нужны́ де́ньги. *What do you need that for?,* для чего́ э́то вам ну́жно? **2,** (require) тре́бовать: *The house needs repair,* дом тре́бует ремо́нта. *These flowers need a lot of water,* э́ти цветы́ тре́буют мно́го воды́. —*v.aux.* (have to) *rendered by* на́до *or* ну́жно: *You need to rest more,* вам на́до бо́льше отдыха́ть. *You need not be afraid,* вам не ну́жно боя́ться. *You need not worry,* вы мо́жете не беспоко́иться. —**be in need of,** нужда́ться в; тре́бовать. —**if need be,** е́сли ну́жно.

needle *n.* **1,** (sewing implement) игла́; иго́лка. **2,** (knitting needle) (вяза́льная) спи́ца. **3,** (of a compass) стре́лка. **4,** (hypodermic needle) игла́ (для подко́жных впры́скиваний). **5,** (for a phonograph) (граммофо́нная) игла́. **6,** (used in engraving) (гравирова́льная) игла́. **7,** (needle-shaped leaf) игла́.

Pine needles, хвоя. —*v.t., colloq.* поддева́ть; подка́лывать; подпуска́ть шпи́льки (+ *dat.*). —**be on pins and needles,** быть *or* сиде́ть как на иго́лках. —**needle in a haystack,** иго́лка в сто́ге се́на.

needless *adj.* нену́жный; бесполе́зный. —**needless to say,** разуме́ется; не́чего и говори́ть.

needlessly *adv.* бесполе́зно.

needlework *n.* шитьё; вышива́ние; рукоде́лие. —**needleworker,** *n.* рукоде́льница.

needy *adj.* нужда́ющийся. —*n., preceded by* **the** нужда́ющиеся.

ne'er-do-well *n.* никчёмный челове́к; него́дник; шалопа́й.

nefarious *adj.* гну́сный.

negate *v.t.* **1,** (nullify) своди́ть на нет *or* к нулю́. **2,** (contradict; refute) опроверга́ть. —**negation,** *n.* отрица́ние.

negative *adj.* отрица́тельный: *negative answer/influence,* отрица́тельный отве́т; отрица́тельное влия́ние. *Negative electric charge,* отрица́тельный электри́ческий заря́д. —*n.* **1,** *gram.* отрица́ние. **2,** *photog.* негати́в. —**in the negative,** отрица́тельно: *answer in the negative,* отве́тить отрица́тельно.

neglect *v.t.* **1,** (fail to give proper attention to) пренебрега́ть; запуска́ть; забра́сывать. *Neglect one's studies,* пренебрега́ть заня́тиями; запуска́ть *or* забра́сывать заня́тия. *Neglect one's children,* забра́сывать дете́й. **2,** *fol. by inf.* (fail to) забыва́ть: *neglect to mention,* забы́ть упомяну́ть; не упомяну́ть. —*n.* **1,** (act of neglecting) пренебреже́ние. **2,** (state of neglect) запу́щенность; забро́шенность; запусте́ние. *Suffer from neglect,* страда́ть от забро́шенности. *In a state of neglect,* в запу́щенном состоя́нии; в заго́не.

neglectful *adj.* небре́жный; невнима́тельный.

negligee *n.* неглиже́.

negligence *n.* небре́жность. *Criminal negligence,* престу́пная небре́жность *or* хала́тность.

negligent *adj.* небре́жный; хала́тный; невнима́тельный.

negligible *adj.* незначи́тельный; ничто́жный.

negotiable *adj.* **1,** (capable of being negotiated) подлежа́щий обсужде́нию: *This question is not negotiable,* э́тот вопро́с не подлежи́т обсужде́нию. **2,** *finance* оборо́тный: *negotiable instrument,* оборо́тный докуме́нт.

negotiate *v.i.* вести́ перегово́ры. —*v.t.* **1,** (conduct negotiations over) вести́ перегово́ры по *or* о. **2,** (conclude through negotiations) заключа́ть. **3,** *colloq.* (traverse; surmount) преодолева́ть.

negotiation *n., usu. pl.* перегово́ры. —**negotiator,** *n.* лицо́, веду́щее перегово́ры.

Negro *n.* негр. —*adj.* негритя́нский.

Negroid *adj.* негро́идный.

neigh *v.i.* ржать.

neighbor *also,* **neighbour** *n.* **1,** (person living nearby) сосе́д. **2,** (fellow being) бли́жний.

neighborhood *also,* **neighbourhood** *n.* райо́н; окру́га. —**in the neighborhood of, 1,** (near) по сосе́дству с. **2,** (approximately) о́коло; приблизи́тельно. *Some-*

where in the neighborhood of sixty dollars, что́-то о́коло шести́десяти до́лларов.

neighboring *also,* **neighbouring** *adj.* сосе́дний.

neighborly *also,* **neighbourly** *adj.* доброросе́дский.

neighbour *n.* = **neighbor.** —**neighbourhood,** *n.* = **neighborhood.**

neither *adj.* ни тот, ни друго́й; ни оди́н из. *In neither case,* ни в том, ни в друго́м слу́чае. *Neither side objected,* ни одна́ из сторо́н не возража́ла; о́бе стороны́ не возража́ли. —*pron.* **1,** *when standing alone,* ни тот, ни друго́й. **2,** (not one or the other) ни тот, ни друго́й; ни оди́н из. *Neither of them is here,* ни того́, ни друго́го нет. *Neither of them wants to go,* ни оди́н из них не хо́чет пойти́. *Neither of the accusations is true,* ни одно́ из обвине́ний не справедли́во. *Neither is suspected of anything,* ни тот, ни друго́й ни в чём не подозрева́ется. —*conj.* **1,** *used with* **nor,** ни..., ни...: *neither for nor against,* ни за, ни про́тив. **2,** (nor) то́же не: *neither do I,* я то́же не (хочу́, зна́ю, *etc.*). —**neither here nor there,** ни к селу́, ни к го́роду.

nemesis *n.* Немези́да.

neoclassical *adj.* неокласси́ческий. —**neoclassicism,** *n.* неоклассици́зм.

neodymium *n.* ниоди́мий.

neolithic *adj.* неолити́ческий.

neologism *n.* неологи́зм.

neon *n.* нео́н. —*adj.* нео́новый.

neophyte *n.* **1,** *eccles.* неофи́т; новообращённый. **2,** (novice) новичо́к; неофи́т.

neoplasm *n.* новообразова́ние.

nephew *n.* племя́нник.

nephrite *n.* нефри́т.

nephritis *n.* нефри́т.

nepotism *n.* кумовство́; семе́йственность; непоти́зм.

Neptune *n.* Непту́н.

neptunium *n.* непту́ний.

nerve *n.* **1,** *physiol.* нерв: *sciatic nerve,* седа́лищный нерв. *Get on one's nerves,* де́йствовать на не́рвы (+ *dat.*). *Calm one's nerves,* успока́ивать не́рвы. **2,** (courage; daring) му́жество. *Lose one's nerve,* оробе́ть; стру́сить. **3,** *Strain every nerve,* напряга́ть все си́лы. **4,** *colloq.* (audacity) на́глость; наха́льство. —*adj.* не́рвный: *nerve centers,* не́рвные це́нтры.

nerve gas не́рвно-паралити́ческое отравля́ющее вещество́.

nerve-racking *adj.* мучи́тельный.

nervous *adj.* не́рвный. *Be nervous,* волнова́ться; не́рвничать. —**nervous breakdown,** не́рвный срыв; невростени́я. —**nervous system,** не́рвная систе́ма.

nervousness *n.* не́рвность; нерво́зность.

nest *n.* гнездо́. —*v.i.* гнезди́ться. —**nest egg,** сбереже́ния на чёрный день.

nestle *v.i.* **1,** (cuddle) прижима́ться; льнуть. **2,** (lie sheltered) юти́ться.

nestling *n.* птене́ц.

net *n.* **1,** (for fishing, hunting, etc.) сеть. **2,** (for catching butterflies) сачо́к. **3,** (for the hair) се́тка. **4,** (for tennis, badminton, etc.) се́тка. **5,** (for hockey, soccer, etc.) воро́та. —*adj.* чи́стый: *net profit,* чи́стая при́быль. *The net result,* коне́чный результа́т. —*v.t.* **1,** (ensnare) пойма́ть (се́тью). **2,** (earn) выруча́ть.

nether *adj.* ни́жний. —**nethermost,** *adj.* са́мый ни́жний. —**nether world,** преиспо́дняя.

netting *n.* се́тка. *Mosquito netting,* накома́рник.

nettle *n.* крапи́ва. —*v.t.* уязвля́ть; уколо́ть.

network *n.* сеть: *television network,* телевизио́нная сеть.

neural *adj.* не́рвный.

neuralgia *n.* невралги́я. —**neuralgic,** *adj.* невралги́ческий.

neuritis *n.* воспале́ние не́рва; неври́т.

neurology *n.* невроло́гия. —**neurological,** *adj.* неврологи́ческий. —**neurologist,** *n.* невро́лог; невропато́лог.

neuron *n.* нейро́н.

neurosis *n.* невро́з.

neurosurgery *n.* нейрохирурги́я. —**neurosurgeon,** *n.* нейрохиру́рг.

neurotic *adj.* невроти́ческий.

neuter *adj.* сре́дний; сре́днего ро́да. —*n.* сре́дний род.

neutral *adj.* нейтра́льный. —*n.* **1,** (country) нейтра́льное госуда́рство. **2,** (gear) нейтра́льная ско́рость. —**neutrality,** *n.* нейтралите́т.

neutralize *v.t.* нейтрализова́ть. —**neutralization,** *n.* нейтрализа́ция.

neutron *n.* нейтро́н. —*adj.* нейтро́нный. —**neutron bomb,** нейтро́нная бо́мба.

never *adv.* никогда́. *He is never home,* он никогда́ не быва́ет до́ма. *I have never seen anything like it,* я никогда́ не ви́дел(а) ничего́ подо́бного. ♦*Also rendered by* так и не: *I never found out,* я так и не узна́л(а). *He never regained consciousness,* он так и пришёл в созна́ние. *The problem may never arise,* пробле́ма мо́жет (так) и не возни́кнуть. *The killer was never found,* уби́йцу так и не нашли́. —**better late than never,** лу́чше по́здно, чем никогда́. —**never again,** никогда́ бо́льше: *I never saw him again,* я его́ никогда́ бо́льше не ви́дел(а). *He was never seen again,* бо́льше его́ никогда́ не ви́дели. —**never before,** никогда́ ещё. *Now as never before,* тепе́рь, как никогда́ пре́жде. —**never mind,** *see* **mind.** —**now or never,** тепе́рь и́ли никогда́.

never-ending *adj.* несконча́емый; непрекраща́ющийся.

nevermore *adv.* никогда́ бо́льше.

nevertheless *adv.* тем не ме́нее.

new *adj.* но́вый. *What's new?,* что но́вого?; что слы́шно? —**new potatoes,** молодо́й карто́фель. —**new wine,** молодо́е вино́.

newborn *adj.* новорождённый.

newcomer *n.* прише́лец; прие́зжий; новоприбы́вший.

New Deal Но́вый курс.

Newfoundland *n.* (dog) водола́з; ньюфа́ундленд.

newly *adv.* вновь: *the newly elected president,* вновь и́збранный президе́нт.

newlyweds *n.pl.* новобра́чные; молодожёны.

new moon новолу́ние; молодо́й ме́сяц.

newness *n.* новизна́.

news *n.* но́вости; изве́стия; ве́сти. *Piece of news,* но́вость; изве́стие; весть. *It's news to me,* э́то для меня́ но́вость. —**news agency,** телегра́фное аге́нтство.

newsboy *n.* газе́тчик.

newscast *n.* переда́ча после́дних изве́стий.

newsletter *n.* информацио́нный бюллете́нь.

newsman *n.* **1,** (reporter) репортёр; корреспонде́нт. **2,** (dealer) газе́тчик.

newspaper *n.* газе́та. —*adj.* газе́тный: *newspaper clipping,* газе́тная вы́резка. —**newspaperman,** *n.* журнали́ст.

newsprint *n.* газе́тная бума́га.

newsreel *n.* кинохро́ника.

newsstand *n.* газе́тный кио́ск.

newt *n.* трито́н.

New Testament Но́вый заве́т.

New World Но́вый свет.

New Year Но́вый год. *Happy New Year!,* с Но́вым го́дом!

next *adj.* **1,** (coming after the present one) сле́дующий: *the next stop,* сле́дующая остано́вка. *Next time,* в сле́дующий раз. *Who is next?,* кто сле́дующий? **2,** *with intervals or periods of time,* сле́дующий; бу́дущий: *next week,* на сле́дующей/бу́дущей неде́ле; *next year,* в сле́дующем/бу́дущем году́. *Next summer,* сле́дующим ле́том. *The next day,* на сле́дующий (*or* на друго́й) день. *The next morning,* нау́тро. **3,** (adjacent) сосе́дний: *in the next room,* в сосе́дней ко́мнате. —*adv.* **1,** (after that) пото́м; да́льше. *What happened next?,* что случи́лось пото́м? *What next?,* (а) что же да́льше? *Not know what to do next,* не знать, что де́лать да́льше. **2,** (again) в сле́дующий раз; сно́ва: *when next we meet,* когда́ мы сно́ва встре́тимся. —**next to, 1,** (beside; alongside) у; ря́дом; во́зле; по́дле. *We sat next to each other,* мы сиде́ли ря́дом. **2,** (almost; nearly) почти́: *next to impossible,* почти́ невозмо́жно. **3,** (after; indicating that something is second best) по́сле: *Next to tennis, my favorite sport is swimming,* по́сле те́нниса, мой люби́мый вид спо́рта — пла́вание. —**next to last,** предпосле́дний. —**next to nothing,** почти́ ничего́. *I bought it for next to nothing,* я купи́л э́то за гроши́. —**than the next,** оди́н друго́го (+ *comp. adj.*): *one taller than the next,* оди́н друго́го вы́ше.

next door ря́дом; в сосе́днем до́ме. *Next door to,* ря́дом с. *Next-door neighbor,* сосе́д по до́му. *The girl next door,* сосе́дская де́вушка.

nib *n.* ко́нчик; остриё.

nibble *v.t. & i.* **1,** (eat in small bites) грызть; обгрыза́ть. **2,** (bite, as of a fish) клева́ть. —*n.* **1,** (small bite; morsel) кусо́чек. **2,** (bite, in fishing): *not a nibble,* ни одна́ ры́ба не клю́нула.

nice *adj.* **1,** (fine; pleasant) хоро́ший; прия́тный: *nice weather,* хоро́шая/прия́тная пого́да. *Have a nice time,* хорошо́ провести́ вре́мя. **2,** (likable; gracious) ми́лый; симпати́чный; любе́зный. *A nice man,* ми́лый/симпати́чный челове́к. *Be nice to someone,* хорошо́ относи́ться к кому́-нибудь. *Very nice of you,* о́чень ми́ло *or* любе́зно с ва́шей стороны́. **3,** (proper) прили́чный; поря́дочный. *A nice girl,* прили́чная де́вушка. *That's not nice,* э́то некраси́во. **4,** (well-executed) ло́вкий; уда́чный. **5,** (subtle) то́нкий: *a nice distinction,* то́нкое разли́чие. **—nice and...,** и краси́во: *It's nice and warm in here!,* здесь так тепло́ и краси́во!

nice-looking *adj.* милови́дный; хоро́шенький.

nicely *adv.* хорошо́; прили́чно.

nicety *n.* **1,** (fine point) то́нкость. **2,** *pl.* (proprieties) прили́чия.

niche *n.* ни́ша.

nick *n.* ще́рбина; цара́пина. **—***v.t.* цара́пать. **—in the nick of time,** как раз во́время; в са́мый после́дний моме́нт.

nickel *n.* **1,** (element) ни́кель. **2,** (five-cent coin) пята́к. **—***adj.* ни́келевый.

nickel plate никелиро́вка. **—nickel-plate,** *v.t.* никелирова́ть.

nickname *n.* про́звище; кли́чка. *A man with the nickname...,* челове́к по кли́чке (+ *nom.*). **—***v.t.* прозыва́ть; окрести́ть.

nicotine *n.* никоти́н.

niece *n.* племя́нница.

nifty *adj.*, *colloq.* **1,** (splendid; first-rate) чу́дный. **2,** (stylish) шика́рный.

Nigerian *adj.* нигери́йский.

niggardly *adj.* **1,** (stingy) скупо́й; ска́редный. **2,** (meager) ску́дный.

niggling *adj.* ме́лочный.

nigh *adv.* **1,** (near) бли́зко. *Draw nigh,* приближа́ться. **2,** *fol. by* **onto** (nearly) чуть ли не.

night *n.* ночь. *At night,* но́чью; по ноча́м. *Last night,* вчера́ ве́чером; вчера́ но́чью. *Tomorrow night,* за́втра ве́чером. *Saturday night,* в суббо́ту ве́чером. *Spend the night,* ночева́ть; переночева́ть. *Stop for the night,* останови́ться на́ ночь. *Lock the doors at night,* закрыва́ть две́ри на́ ночь. *He went to school at night,* он учи́лся вечера́ми *or* по вечера́м. **—***adj.* ночно́й: *the night train,* ночно́й по́езд; *the night shift,* ночна́я сме́на. **—good night!,** споко́йной но́чи!

night blindness кури́ная слепота́.

nightcap *n.* **1,** (cap worn in bed) ночно́й колпа́к. **2,** *colloq.* (drink before retiring) стака́нчик спиртно́го на́ ночь.

nightclothes *n.pl.* ночно́е бельё.

night club ночно́й клуб.

nightfall *n.* наступле́ние но́чи; наступле́ние темноты́. *Before nightfall,* за́светло.

nightgown *n.* ночна́я руба́шка; ночна́я соро́чка.

nightingale *n.* солове́й.

night light ночни́к.

nightly *adj.* ежено́щный. **—***adv.* ежено́щно; ка́ждую ночь.

nightmare *n.* кошма́р. *I had a nightmare,* мне присни́лся кошма́р; я ви́дел во сне кошма́р. **—nightmarish,** *adj.* кошма́рный.

night owl полуно́чник.

night school вече́рняя шко́ла.

nightshade *n.* паслён.

nightshirt *n.* ночна́я руба́шка; ночна́я соро́чка.

nightstick *n.* дуби́нка.

night table ночно́й сто́лик; ту́мбочка.

nighttime *n.* ночно́е вре́мя; ночь.

night watch ночно́й дозо́р; *naval* ночна́я ва́хта. **—night watchman,** ночно́й сто́рож.

nihilism *n.* нигили́зм. **—nihilist,** *n.* нигили́ст. **—nihilistic,** *adj.* нигилисти́ческий.

nil *n.* нуль; ничего́. *The chances of that are practically nil,* ша́нсов на э́то практи́чески нет; ша́нсы на э́то почти́ нулевы́е.

nimble *adj.* прово́рный.

nimbus *n.* нимб.

nincompoop *n.* простофи́ля; дурале́й; растя́па.

nine *adj.* де́вять. **—***n.* **1,** (cardinal number) де́вять. **2,** *cards* девя́тка.

nine hundred девятьсо́т. **—nine-hundredth,** *adj.* девятисо́тый.

nineteen *n. & adj.* девятна́дцать. **—nineteenth,** *adj.* девятна́дцатый.

ninety *n. & adj.* девяно́сто. **—ninetieth,** *adj.* девяно́стый.

ninny *n.* простофи́ля; дурале́й.

ninth *adj.* девя́тый. **—***n.* девя́тая; девя́тая часть. *One-ninth,* одна́ девя́тая; девя́тая часть.

niobium *n.* нио́бий.

nip *v.t.* **1,** (pinch) щипа́ть; ущипну́ть. **2,** *fol. by* **off** (snip; cut off) отщи́пывать. **3,** (damage, as of frost) поби́ть; тро́нуть. **4,** (check; head off) пресека́ть. *Nip in the bud,* подавля́ть в заро́дыше; пресека́ть в ко́рне. **—***n.* **1,** (pinch) щипо́к. **2,** (cold) моро́зец: *There is a nip in the air,* во́здух па́хнет моро́зцем. **3,** *colloq.* (small drink) рю́мочка. **—nip and tuck,** голова́ в го́лову.

nipper *n.* **1,** (claw) клешня́. **2,** *pl.* (pincers) кле́щи.

nipple *n.* **1,** (on the breast) соско́к. **2,** (for a nursing bottle) со́ска. **3,** (threaded pipe) ни́ппель.

nippy *adj. It is nippy outside,* на дворе́ моро́зит.

nirvana *n.* нирва́на.

nit *n.* гни́да.

niter *also,* **nitre** *n.* сели́тра.

nit-pick *v.i., colloq.* придира́ться.

nitrate *n.* соль азо́тной кислоты́; нитра́т. ♦*In compounds,* сели́тра: *sodium nitrate,* на́триевая сели́тра. *Silver nitrate,* ля́пис.

nitre *n.* = **niter.**

nitric *adj.* азо́тный. **—nitric acid,** азо́тная кислота́. **—nitric oxide,** о́кись азо́та.

nitrite *n.* соль азо́тистой кислоты́; нитри́т.

nitrogen *n.* азо́т.

nitroglycerin *also,* **nitroglycerine** *n.* нитроглицери́н.

nitrous *adj.* азо́тистый. **—nitrous acid,** азо́тистая кислота́. **—nitrous oxide,** за́кись азо́та.

nitwit *n., slang* простофи́ля; балда́; балбе́с.

no *adv.* **1,** (opp. of yes) нет: *yes or no,* да и́ли нет. *No, thank you,* спаси́бо, нет. *Not take no for an answer,* не принима́ть отка́за. *He doesn't know how to say no,* он не уме́ет отка́зывать. **2,** *with comp. adjectives* (not at all) не: *no bigger than a postage stamp*, не бо́льше почто́вой ма́рки. *She is no better today*, ей сего́дня (ниско́лько) не лу́чше. —*adj.* никако́й: *no comment*, никаки́х коммента́риев. *There can be no doubt*, не мо́жет быть никако́го сомне́ния. *She is no beauty*, никака́я она́ не краса́вица. ♦*Often rendered by* не *or* нет: *spare no effort*, не щади́ть уси́лий. *No smoking!*, не кури́ть! *I have no time*, у меня́ нет вре́мени. *There is no time for anything*, ни на что нет вре́мени. —*n.* отка́з: *an emphatic "no"*, реши́тельный отка́з. *The noes have it*, большинство́ про́тив.

nobelium *n.* нобе́лий.

Nobel Prize Но́белевская пре́мия.

nobility *n.* **1,** (aristocracy) дворя́нство. **2,** (quality of being noble) благоро́дство.

noble *adj.* благоро́дный: *a noble act*, благоро́дный посту́пок. *Of noble birth*, родови́тый; благоро́дного происхожде́ния. —*n.* дворяни́н.

nobleman *n.* дворяни́н.

nobody *pron.* никто́: *Nobody knows*, никто́ не зна́ет. *There was nobody home*, никого́ не́ было до́ма. ♦*With infinitives*, не́кого: *There was nobody to send to the store*, посла́ть в магази́н бы́ло не́кого. *There is nobody to replace him*, не́кому его́ замени́ть. *He has nobody to play with*, ему́ не́ с кем игра́ть. —*n.*, *preceded by* **a**, ничто́жество; ничто́; пусто́е ме́сто.

nocturnal *adj.* ночно́й.

nocturne *n.* ноктю́рн.

nod *n.* киво́к. —*v.t.* кива́ть (голово́й). —*v.i.* **1,** (nod one's head) кива́ть (голово́й). *Nod in assent*, кивну́ть голово́й в знак согла́сия. **2,** (drowse) клева́ть но́сом. —**nodding acquaintance,** ша́почное знако́мство.

node *n.* у́зел. *Lymph nodes*, лимфати́ческие узлы́.

nodule *n.* узело́к.

Noel *n.* рождество́.

noggin *n.*, *colloq.* башка́.

noise *n.* шум. *Make noise*, шуме́ть.

noiseless *adj.* бесшу́мный. —**noiselessly,** *adv.* бесшу́мно.

noisily *adv.* шу́мно.

noisome *adj.* **1,** (foul) проти́вный. **2,** (harmful) вре́дный.

noisy *adj.* шу́мный; шумли́вый. *It is very noisy in here*, здесь о́чень шу́мно.

nomad *n.* коче́вник. —**nomadic,** *adj.* кочево́й; кочу́ющий.

no man's land ничья́ земля́.

nomenclature *n.* номенклату́ра.

nominal *adj.* номина́льный.

nominate *v.t.* **1,** (propose for an elected position) выдвига́ть (на до́лжность); выставля́ть (чью́-нибудь) кандидату́ру. **2,** (recommend for an honor or award) выдвига́ть; представля́ть: *nominate for a prize/ an award/*, выдвига́ть (кого́-нибудь) на пре́мию; представля́ть (кого́-нибудь) к награ́де.

nomination *n.* кандидату́ра; выдвиже́ние кандида́том. *Second the nomination*, подде́рживать кандидату́ру (кого́-нибудь). *Decline the nomination*, отка́-

зывать в выдвиже́нии кандида́том. *Seek the Presidential nomination*, добива́ться выдвиже́ния кандида́том на пост президе́нта.

nominative *adj.* имени́тельный: *nominative case*, имени́тельный паде́ж.

nominee *n.* кандида́т.

nonaggression *n.* ненападе́ние. *Nonaggression pact*, пакт о ненападе́нии.

nonalcoholic *adj.* безалкого́льный.

nonaligned *adj.* неприсоедини́вшийся. —**nonalignment,** *n.* неприсоедине́ние.

nonbeliever *n.* неве́рующий.

nonbelligerent *adj.* невою́ющий.

nonbinding *adj.* ни к чему́ не обя́зывающий.

nonbreakable *adj.* небью́щийся.

nonchalance *n.* беззабо́тность; непринуждённость. —**nonchalant,** *adj.* беззабо́тный; непринуждённый.

noncombatant *n.* & *adj.* нестроево́й.

noncommissioned officer сержа́нт; у́нтер-офице́р.

noncommittal *adj.* укло́нчивый.

noncompliance *n.* невыполне́ние; несоблюде́ние.

nonconductor *n.* непроводни́к.

noncontagious *adj.* незара́зный.

nondescript *adj.* неприме́тный; ни то ни сё.

nondrinker *n.* непью́щий.

none *pron.* **1,** (no one) никто́: *None of them came*, никто́ из них не пришёл. *None of us wanted to go*, никто́ из нас не хоте́л пойти́. **2,** (not any) ни оди́н: *None of them was any good*, ни оди́н из них не́ был хоро́ш. *He saw none of this*, он не ви́дел ничего́ э́того. *None of this concerns me*, всё э́то меня́ не каса́ется. *He would have none of it*, он об э́том и слы́шать не хоте́л. —*adv.* ниско́лько; ничу́ть: *He is none the worse for it*, ему́ от э́того ниско́лько не ху́же. —**none other than,** как бы ино́й, как.

nonentity *n.* ничто́жество; ничто́; пусто́е ме́сто.

nonessential *adj. Nonessential items*, ве́щи, в кото́рых нет абсолю́тной необходи́мости.

nonetheless *adv.* тем не ме́нее.

nonexistence *n.* небытие́. —**nonexistent,** *adj.* несуществу́ющий.

nonferrous *adj.* цветно́й.

nonflammable *adj.* несгора́емый; невоспламеня́емый.

nonfulfillment *also*, **nonfulfilment** *n.* невыполне́ние.

noninterference *n.* невмеша́тельство.

nonintervention *n.* невмеша́тельство.

non-Jew *n.* нееврей. —**non-Jewish,** *adj.* нееврейский.

nonpayment *n.* неупла́та; неплатёж.

nonperishable *adj.* непо́ртящийся.

nonpermanent *adj.* непостоя́нный: *nonpermanent members of the Security Council*, непостоя́нные чле́ны Сове́та Безопа́сности.

nonplus *v.t.* ста́вить в тупи́к; озада́чивать.

nonproductive *adj.* непроизводи́тельный.

nonproliferation *n.* нераспростране́ние.

nonrecognition *n.* непризна́ние.

non-Russian *adj.* неру́сский.

nonsense *n.* ерунда́; чепуха́; глу́пости; вздор. —**nonsensical,** *adj.* глу́пый; вздо́рный.

nonsmoker *n.* некуря́щий.

nonstop *adj.* безостано́вочный; беспоса́дочный. —*adv.* безостано́вочно.

nonuse *n.* неприменéние: *nonuse of force,* непримене́ние си́лы.

nonvoting *adj. Nonvoting member,* член с совеща́тельным го́лосом.

nonworking *adj.* нера́бочий.

noodle *n.* **1,** (food) лапша́. *Noodle pudding,* лапше́вник. *Noodle soup,* лапша́. **2,** *slang* (head) башка́.

nook *n.* уголо́к; закоу́лок.

noon *n.* по́лдень. —*adj.* [*also,* **noonday**] полу́денный; полдне́вный.

no one никто́. *See* **nobody.**

noose *n.* пе́тля.

nor *conj.* **1,** (neither) то́же: *nor do I; nor am I,* я то́же. ♦*In longer sentences, rendered with the conjunction* и: *Nor do I agree with...,* не согла́сен я и с... *Nor is there any doubt that...,* нет сомне́ния и в том, что... *Nor was the weather any better the next day,* но и на сле́дующий день пого́да была́ не лу́чше. **2,** (and besides) да и (вообще́): *I have not seen him, nor do I wish to,* я его́ не ви́дел(а), да и вообще́ не хочу́. —**neither... nor,** ни..., ни...: *neither for nor against,* ни за, ни про́тив.

norm *n.* но́рма; нормати́в. *Norms of behavior,* но́рмы поведе́ния. *Become the norm,* стать но́рмой.

normal *adj.* норма́льный. —*n.* **1,** (natural condition) норма́льное состоя́ние. *Return to normal,* войти́ в норма́льную колею́ (*or* в норма́льное ру́сло); сно́ва нала́живаться. **2,** *math.* норма́ль.

normalcy *n.* норма́льность.

normalize *v.t.* нормализова́ть. —**normalization,** *n.* нормализа́ция.

normally *adv.* **1,** (in a normal manner) норма́льно. **2,** (ordinarily) обы́чно.

Norman *adj.* норма́ндский: *the Norman Conquest,* Норма́ндское завоева́ние А́нглии.

normative *adj.* нормати́вный.

Norse *adj.* норма́ннский. —**Norseman,** *n.* норма́нн.

north *n.* се́вер. —*adj.* се́верный: *north wind,* се́верный ве́тер. *North Korea,* Се́верная Коре́я. *North Cape,* Нордка́п. —*adv.* на се́вер; к се́веру. *North of,* к се́веру от; се́вернее (+ *gen.*).

North America Се́верная Аме́рика. —**North American,** североамерика́нский.

northeast *n.* се́веро-восто́к. —*adj.* се́веро-восто́чный. —*adv.* к се́веро-восто́ку; на се́веро-восто́к.

northeaster *n.* норд-о́ст.

northeasterly *adj.* се́веро-восто́чный. —*adv.* к се́веро-восто́ку.

northeastern *adj.* се́веро-восто́чный.

northerly *adj.* се́верный.

northern *adj.* се́верный. *Northern Hemisphere,* Се́верное полуша́рие. *Northern Ireland,* Се́верная Ирла́ндия.

northerner *n.* северя́нин.

northern lights се́верное сия́ние.

northernmost *adj.* са́мый се́верный.

North Pole Се́верный по́люс.

North Star Поля́рная звезда́.

northward *adv.* к се́веру; в се́верном направле́нии. —*adj.* се́верный.

northwest *n.* се́веро-за́пад. —*adj.* се́веро-за́падный. —*adv.* к се́веро-за́паду; на се́веро-за́пад.

northwester *n.* норд-ве́ст.

northwesterly *adj.* се́веро-за́падный. —*adv.* к се́веро-за́паду.

northwestern *adj.* се́веро-за́падный.

Norwegian *adj.* норве́жский. —*n.* **1,** (person) норве́жец; норве́жка. **2,** (language) норве́жский язы́к.

nose *n.* **1,** (of a person) нос. *Breathe/speak through one's nose,* дыша́ть но́сом; говори́ть в нос. **2,** (of a ship or aircraft) нос. —*v.i.* [*usu.* **nose about** *or* **around**] разню́хивать. —**as plain as the nose on your face,** я́сный как бо́жий день. —**follow one's nose,** идти́ куда́ глаза́ глядя́т. —**have a nose for,** име́ть нюх на. —**lead by the nose,** вести́ на поводу́. —**look down one's nose at,** смотре́ть свысока́ на. —**not see farther than the end of one's nose,** не ви́деть да́льше своего́ но́са. —**on the nose,** то́чно; в (са́мую) то́чку. —**pay through the nose,** плати́ть бе́шеные де́ньги; плати́ть втри́дорога. —**poke one's nose into someone else's affairs,** сова́ть нос в чужи́е дела́. —**turn up one's nose,** задира́ть нос. —**under one's (very) nose,** под (са́мым) но́сом; под но́сом. *From under one's very nose,* из-под са́мого но́са.

nosebleed *n.* кровотече́ние и́з носу.

nose cone носово́й ко́нус.

nose dive 1, *aero.* пики́рование; пике́. **2,** (sharp drop) ре́зкое паде́ние.

nose drops ка́пли от на́сморка.

nosegay *n.* буке́тик цвето́в.

nosey *adj.* = **nosy.**

nostalgia *n.* ностальги́я: *nostalgia for the past,* ностальги́я по про́шлому.

nostalgic *adj.* ностальги́ческий. *Feel nostalgic,* испы́тывать ностальги́ю.

nostril *n.* ноздря́.

nosy *also,* **nosey** *adj.* (не в ме́ру) любопы́тный.

not *adv.* **1,** *expressing negation,* не: *not today,* не сего́дня. *He did not come,* он не пришёл. *I am not angry,* я не сержу́сь. **2,** *expressing the absence of something,* нет: *He is not here,* его́ нет. **3,** *in replies,* нет: *Why not?,* почему́ нет? *Not yet,* нет ещё. *I hope not,* наде́юсь, что нет. —**not a ...,** ни; ни оди́н: *not a word,* ни (одного́) сло́ва. *Not a bit of difference,* ни мале́йшей ра́зницы. —**not at all, 1,** (not in the least) совсе́м не; ниско́лько не: *not at all tired,* совсе́м/ниско́лько не уста́л. *Am I disturbing you? No, not at all,* я вам не меша́ю? Нет, что вы! **2,** *in reply to an expression of thanks,* пожа́луйста!; не́ за что! —**not that...,** не то, что; не то, чтобы: *It's not that I'm ill, I'm just tired,* я не то, что бо́лен а про́сто уста́л. *Not that I know of,* наско́лько мне изве́стно, нет. —**or not,** и́ли нет: *Are you going or not?,* вы идёте и́ли нет? *Like it or not,* хо́чешь не хо́чешь.

notable *adj.* **1,** (noteworthy) примеча́тельный. *Be no-*

table for, отлича́ться (+ *instr.*). **2,** (distinguished) зна́тный. —*n., usu. pl.* зна́тные лю́ди.

notably *adv.* **1,** (strikingly) удиви́тельно. **2,** (particularly) осо́бенно.

notarize *v.t.* засвиде́тельствовать.

notary *n.* нота́риус. *Also,* **notary public.**

notation *n.* **1,** (note) заме́тка; за́пись. **2,** (system of signs or symbols) нота́ция: *chess notation,* ша́хматная нота́ция.

notch *n.* **1,** (on a flat surface) зару́бка. **2,** (on a cutting edge) зазу́брина. **3,** (deep gorge) тесни́на. —*v.t.* заруба́ть; зазу́бривать.

note *n.* **1,** (short informal letter) запи́ска. **2,** (official communication between governments) но́та. **3,** *usu. pl.* (something written down for future reference) запи́ска; заме́тка; за́пись: *take/make notes,* де́лать заме́тки/за́писи. *Lecture from notes,* чита́ть ле́кцию по за́писям. *Take notes of a lecture,* запи́сывать ле́кцию. **4,** *pl.* (record of impressions) заме́тки: *travel notes,* путевы́е заме́тки. **5,** (explanatory comment) заме́тка: *note in the margin,* заме́тка на поля́х. *Explanatory note,* примеча́ние. **6,** *music* но́та: *high note,* высо́кая но́та. **7,** (negotiable instrument) биле́т: *treasury note,* казначе́йский биле́т. *Promissory note,* ве́ксель; долгово́е обяза́тельство. **8,** (trace; touch) но́тка: *note of anxiety,* но́тка беспоко́йства. **9,** (notice; attention) внима́ние: *worthy of note,* досто́йный внима́ния. **10,** (distinction) изве́стность. *A writer of note,* небезызве́стный писа́тель. —*v.t.* **1,** (notice) замеча́ть. **2,** (make mention of; point out) отмеча́ть. **3,** *fol. by* **down** (record) запи́сывать. —**compare notes,** обме́ниваться впечатле́ниями. —**make a note of,** запи́сывать; отмеча́ть. —**take note of, 1,** (make a mental note of) брать на заме́тку; примеча́ть. **2,** (notice; pay attention to) обраща́ть внима́ние на.

notebook *n.* тетра́дь; записна́я кни́жка.

noted *adj.* изве́стный; знамени́тый.

note pad блокно́т.

notepaper *n.* почто́вая бума́га.

noteworthy *adj.* примеча́тельный; достопримеча́тельный.

nothing *n.* **1,** (not anything) ничего́: *What did you do? Nothing,* что ты сде́лал? Ничего́. *Nothing of the kind,* ничего́ подо́бного. *He said nothing,* он ничего́ не сказа́л. *Quarrel over nothing,* ссо́риться из-за ничего́ *or* из-за пустяко́в. *Be left with nothing,* оста́ться ни с чем. ♦*Less commonly,* ничто́: *Nothing bothers him,* ничто́ не беспоко́ит его́. *That's nothing compared to...,* э́то ничто́ по сравне́нию с... ♦*Before infinitives,* не́чего: *I have nothing to say,* мне не́чего сказа́ть. *You have nothing to fear,* вам не́чего боя́ться. *There was nothing more to talk about,* бо́льше говори́ть бы́ло не о чем. **2,** *preceded by a* (nonentity) ничто́жество; пусто́е ме́сто. —*adv.* совсе́м не: *nothing like it used to be,* совсе́м не то, что бы́ло. —**for nothing, 1,** (free; at no cost) беспла́тно; да́ром. **2,** (to no avail) напра́сно; да́ром. **3,** (for no reason) зря. —**have nothing to do with, 1,** (bear no relation to) не име́ть никако́го отноше́ния

к; совсе́м не каса́ться. *Sergey has nothing to do with this,* Серге́й тут ни при чём. **2,** (refuse to associate with) не жела́ть име́ть ничего́ о́бщего с. —**nothing but,** то́лько; оди́н. *Nothing but the best,* то́лько са́мое лу́чшее. *He gives me nothing but trouble,* он мне доставля́ет одни́ неприя́тности. —**nothing to it,** про́ще просто́го. —**to say nothing of,** не говоря́ уже́ о.

notice *v.t.* замеча́ть: *notice mistakes in the report,* заме́тить оши́бки в докла́де. *I noticed he was limping a bit,* я заме́тил, что (*or* как) он прихра́мывал. —*n.* **1,** (attention) внима́ние: *take notice of,* обраща́ть внима́ние на. *Take no notice of,* не обраща́ть внима́ния на; оставля́ть без внима́ния. *Bring to someone's notice,* доводи́ть до чьего́-нибудь све́дения. **2,** (notification) извеще́ние; уведомле́ние; предупрежде́ние. *Dismissal notice,* уведомле́ние об увольне́нии. *Give notice to,* ста́вить (кого́-нибудь) в изве́стность. *Give notice of,* сде́лать предупрежде́ние о. *Until further notice,* впредь до дальне́йшего уведомле́ния; до осо́бого распоряже́ния. *I realize this is very short notice,* я понима́ю, что даю́ вам ма́ло вре́мени. **3,** (announcement) объявле́ние: *post a notice,* вы́весить объявле́ние. **4,** (review) о́тзыв: *receive favorable notices,* получи́ть благоприя́тные о́тзывы. —**at a moment's notice,** по пе́рвому тре́бованию; в любо́й моме́нт.

noticeable *adj.* заме́тный. —**noticeably,** *adv.* заме́тно.

notification *n.* **1,** (act of notifying) извеще́ние; уведомле́ние; осведомле́ние; оповеще́ние. **2,** (notice given or received) извеще́ние; уведомле́ние.

notify *v.t.* извеща́ть; уведомля́ть; осведомля́ть; оповеща́ть.

notion *n.* **1,** (concept; idea) поня́тие; представле́ние. *I haven't the foggiest notion,* я не име́ю ни мале́йшего поня́тия. **2,** *pl.* (small miscellaneous articles) галантере́я.

notoriety *n.* изве́стность.

notorious *adj.* заве́домый; пресловутый.

notwithstanding *adv.* тем не ме́нее. —*prep.* несмотря́ на.

nougat *n.* нуга́.

nought *n.* = **naught.**

noun *n.* существи́тельное; и́мя существи́тельное. *Common noun,* и́мя нарица́тельное. *Proper noun,* и́мя со́бственное.

nourish *v.t.* пита́ть. —**nourishing,** *adj.* пита́тельный.

nourishment *n.* пита́ние. *Take nourishment,* принима́ть пи́щу.

nova *n.* но́вая звезда́.

novel *n.* рома́н. —*adj.* но́вый; необыкнове́нный. —**novelist,** *n.* романи́ст.

novella *n.* новелла.

novelty *n.* **1,** (quality of being new) новизна́; но́вость. **2,** (something new) но́вость; нови́нка; но́вшество.

November *n.* ноя́брь. —*adj.* ноя́брьский.

novice *n.* **1,** (beginner) новичо́к. **2,** *eccles.* послу́шник.

novocaine *n.* новокаи́н.

now *adv.* **1,** (at the present time) тепе́рь; сейча́с. **2,** (at once) сейча́с; сейча́с же. —*particle* так: *Now, what was I saying?*, так, о чём я говори́л(а)? *Come now!*, ну вот ещё! —**by now,** уже́: *He should have been here by now,* он уже́ до́лжен быть здесь. —**for now,** пока́. —**from now,** че́рез: *a year from now,* че́рез год. —**from now on,** впредь; отны́не. —**now and then,** вре́мя от вре́мени; кое́-когда́. —**now that...,** тепе́рь, когда́... —**until now,** до сих пор.

nowadays *adv.* в на́ше вре́мя; в тепе́решнее вре́мя; ны́нче.

nowhere *adv.* **1,** (in no place) нигде́. *He is nowhere to be found,* его́ нигде́ нет. **2,** (to no place) никуда́. ♦*With infinitives,* не́где; не́куда: *nowhere to sit,* не́где сесть; *nowhere to go,* не́куда идти́. —**from out of nowhere,** отку́да ни возьми́сь. —**get nowhere,** ничего́ не доби́ться. —**in the middle of nowhere,** у чёрта на кули́чках. —**lead nowhere,** ни к чему́ не привести́. —**nowhere near,** далеко́ не; совсе́м не; соверше́нно не: *nowhere near full,* далеко́ не по́лон; *nowhere near ready,* совсе́м не гото́в; *nowhere near enough,* соверше́нно недоста́точно.

noxious *adj.* вре́дный; па́губный. *Noxious fumes,* вре́дные испаре́ния.

nozzle *n.* сопло́; брандспо́йт.

nth *adj.* э́нный: *to the nth degree,* в э́нной сте́пени.

nuance *n.* отте́нок; нюа́нс.

nub *n.* **1,** (knob; lump) ши́шка. **2,** *colloq.* (gist; point) суть.

nuclear *adj.* я́дерный: *nuclear weapons,* я́дерное ору́жие. *Nuclear energy,* я́дерная *or* а́томная эне́ргия. *Nuclear power plant,* а́томная электроста́нция. *Nuclear-free zone,* безъя́дерная зо́на.

nucleus *n.* ядро́.

nude *adj.* наго́й; го́лый; обнажённый. —*n.* обнажённая фигу́ра. —**in the nude,** в го́лом ви́де.

nudge *v.t.* толка́ть ло́ктем; подта́лкивать ло́ктем. —*n.* толчо́к ло́ктем.

nudity *n.* нагота́.

nugget *n.* саморо́док.

nuisance *n.* **1,** (annoying thing) доса́да: *What a nuisance!,* кака́я доса́да! **2,** (pest) надое́да. *Make a nuisance of oneself,* прока́зничать; озорнича́ть.

null *adj.* [*often* **null and void**] недействи́тельный; не име́ющий зако́нной си́лы.

nullification *n.* аннули́рование.

nullify *v.t.* **1,** (make null and void) аннули́ровать. **2,** (negate) своди́ть на нет *or* к нулю́.

numb *adj.* **1,** (from the cold) окочене́лый; окочене́вший. **2,** (from paralysis) онеме́лый. **3,** (from emotion) оцепене́лый. *Become numb,* (о)кочене́ть; (о)неме́ть; (о)цепене́ть. —*v.t.* ско́вывать: *The cold numbed our hands,* хо́лод скова́л нам ру́ки.

number *n.* **1,** (numeral) число́: *even number,* чётное число́. *Theory of numbers,* тео́рия чи́сел. **2,** (numeral used to identify something) но́мер: *telephone number,* но́мер телефо́на. **3,** (quantity) число́; коли́чество: *a large number of workers,* большо́е число́/коли́чество рабо́чих. **4,** (indefinite quantity)

ряд: *in a number of cases,* в ря́де слу́чаев; *for a number of reasons,* по ря́ду причи́н. *A number of people,* не́которые лю́ди; не́сколько челове́к. *On a number of occasions,* не́сколько раз. **5,** (item on a musical program) но́мер. **6,** *gram.* (singular or plural) число́. —*v.t.* **1,** (assign numbers to) нумерова́ть. **2,** (amount to; contain) насчи́тывать: *The garrison numbered 300 men,* гарнизо́н насчи́тывал три́ста челове́к. **3,** *fol. by* **among** (count among) причисля́ть (к); относи́ть к числу́ (+ *gen.*). **4,** *His days are numbered,* его́ дни сочтены́. —*v.i.* **1,** (be or reach a certain amount) насчи́тываться; исчисля́ться: *number in the thousands,* насчи́тываться/исчисля́ться ты́сячами. *Hotels in the city number about twenty,* в го́роде насчи́тывается о́коло двадцати́ гости́ниц. **2,** *fol. by* **among** (be one of) принадлежа́ть к числу́ (+ *gen.*). —**any number of,** мно́го; нема́ло. —**without number,** без числа́; без счёта.

numbered *adj.* нумеро́ванный; номерно́й.

numbering *n.* нумера́ция. *Numbering machine,* нумера́тор.

numberless *adj.* бесчи́сленный.

Numbers *n., Bib.* Чи́сла. *Book of Numbers,* Кни́га Чи́сел.

numbness *n.* онеме́ние.

numeral *n.* **1,** (number) ци́фра. *Roman numerals,* ри́мские ци́фры. **2,** *gram.* (Russian part of speech) (и́мя) числи́тельное.

numeration *n.* нумера́ция.

numerator *n.* числи́тель.

numerical *adj.* числово́й; чи́сленный; цифрово́й. *Numerical superiority,* чи́сленное превосхо́дство. *Numerical data,* цифровы́е да́нные. —**numerically,** *adv.* чи́сленно.

numerous *adj.* многочи́сленный.

numismatics *n.* нумизма́тика. —**numismatic,** *adj.* нумизмати́ческий. —**numismatist,** *n.* нумизма́т.

numskull *n.* блух; тупи́ца; болва́н.

nun *n.* мона́хиня.

nuncio *n.* ну́нций.

nunnery *n.* же́нский монасты́рь.

nuptial *adj.* бра́чный; сва́дебный. —**nuptials,** *n.pl.* сва́дьба.

nurse *n.* **1,** (one who tends the sick) медсестра́; сиде́лка. *Male nurse,* медбра́т. **2,** (nursemaid) ня́ня. —*v.t.* **1,** (suckle) корми́ть. *Nursing mother,* кормя́щая мать. **2,** (take care of) уха́живать за; ня́нчить. *Nurse back to health,* выха́живать. **3,** (treat gently) бере́чь. **4,** (take steps to cure, as a cold) лечи́ть. **5,** (harbor, as a grudge) пита́ть; таи́ть.

nursemaid *n.* ня́ня; ня́нька.

nursery *n.* **1,** (children's room) де́тская. **2,** (day nursery) я́сли. **3,** (place where plants are raised) пито́мник; расса́дник. —**nursery rhymes,** де́тские пе́сенки; де́тские стишки́. —**nursery school,** де́тский сад.

nursing *n.* **1,** (suckling) кормле́ние (гру́дью). **2,** (profession) ухо́д за больны́ми. *Study nursing,* учи́ться на медсестру́. *School of nursing,* шко́ла медсестёр. —**nursing bottle,** рожо́к. —**nursing home,** дом для престаре́лых.

nurture *v.t.* леле́ять: *nurture a child/hope,* леле́ять ребёнка/наде́жду.

nut *n.* **1,** (fruit) оре́х. **2,** (what goes with a bolt) га́йка. **3,** *slang* (crazy person) чуда́к; сумасбро́д; псих.

nutcracker *n.* щипцы́ для оре́хов.

nuthatch *n.* по́ползень.

nutmeg *n.* **1,** (seed) муска́тный оре́х; муска́т. **2,** (tree) муска́тник; муска́тное де́рево. —*adj.* муска́тный.

nutria *n.* ну́трия.

nutrient *n.* пита́тельное вещество́.

nutrition *n.* **1,** (nourishment) пита́ние. **2,** (study of proper diet) диетоло́гия; диете́тика. —**nutritional,** *adj.* пищево́й; пита́тельный. —**nutritious,** *adj.* пита́тельный.

nuts *adj., slang* **1,** (crazy) сумасше́дший. *Go nuts,* свихну́ться; спя́тить. **2,** *fol. by* **about** (mad about) без ума́ (от). —*interj., slang* тьфу!

nutshell *n., in* **in a nutshell,** вкра́тце; в двух слова́х.

nutty *adj.* **1,** (having or made with nuts) оре́ховый. **2,** *slang* (crazy; ridiculous) глу́пый.

nuzzle *v.t.* тере́ться но́сом о.

nylon *n.* **1,** (fabric) нейло́н. **2,** *pl.* (stockings) нейло́новые чулки́. —*adj.* нейло́новый.

nymph *n.* ни́мфа.

nymphomania *n.* нимфома́ния. —**nymphomaniac,** *n.* нимфома́нка.

O

O, o пятна́дцатая бу́ква англи́йского алфави́та. —*interj.* о!; ах!

oaf *n.* ду́рень; тупи́ца; о́лух. —**oafish,** *adj.* придуркова́тый.

oak *n.* дуб. —*adj.* дубо́вый.

oakum *n.* па́кля.

oar *n.* весло́. —**oarlock,** *n.* уклю́чина.

oarsman *n.* гребе́ц.

oasis *n.* оа́зис.

oat *n., usu. pl.* овёс. —*adj.* овся́ный.

oath *n.* **1,** (solemn promise) прися́га; кля́тва. *Under oath,* под прися́гой. *Take the oath,* приноси́ть *or* принима́ть прися́гу. *Take/swear an oath,* дава́ть кля́тву *or* прися́гу. *Oath of allegiance,* кля́тва (в) ве́рности. **2,** (swearword) прокля́тие.

oatmeal *n.* овся́ная ка́ша; овся́ная крупа́; овся́нка; толокно́; геркуле́с.

obdurate *adj.* **1,** (obstinate) упря́мый. **2,** (hardhearted) чёрствый. —**obduracy,** *n.* упря́мство.

obedient *adj.* послу́шный. —**obedience,** *n.* послуша́ние; повинове́ние.

obeisance *n.* **1,** (bow) покло́н. **2,** (deference) почте́ние.

obelisk *n.* обели́ск.

obese *adj.* по́лный; ту́чный; гру́зный. —**obesity,** *n.* ту́чность; ожире́ние; полнота́.

obey *v.t.* **1,** (mind; heed) слу́шаться (+ *acc. or gen.*); повинова́ться (+ *dat.*). **2,** (observe; carry out) подчиня́ться (+ *dat.*): *obey an order/ the law/,* подчиня́ться прика́зу/зако́ну. —*v.i.* слу́шаться.

obfuscate *v.t.* затемня́ть. —**obfuscation,** *n.* затемне́ние.

obituary *n.* некроло́г.

object[1] (**ob**-jekt) *n.* **1,** (material thing) предме́т: *inanimate object,* неодушевлённый предме́т. **2,** (that to which something is directed) объе́кт; предме́т: *object of attention,* объе́кт/предме́т внима́ния. **3,** (goal; purpose) цель. **4,** *gram.* дополне́ние.

object[2] (ub-**jekt**) *v.i.* возража́ть: *No one objected,* никто́ не возража́л. *Object to a remark,* возража́ть про́тив замеча́ния. *Object to the use of...,* возража́ть про́тив по́льзования (+ *gen.*).

objection *n.* возраже́ние. *Have no objection,* не возража́ть; не име́ть возраже́ний; ничего́ не име́ть про́тив.

objectionable *adj.* нежела́тельный; неприя́тный; неуго́дный.

objective *n.* **1,** (goal; purpose) цель. **2,** *mil.* объе́кт. —*adj.* объекти́вный. —**objective case,** объе́ктный паде́ж.

objectivity *n.* объекти́вность.

object lesson нагля́дный уро́к.

obligate *v.t.* обя́зывать. —**obligated,** *adj.* обя́занный.

obligation *n.* обяза́тельство. *Under an obligation,* обя́зан. *Under no obligation,* ниско́лько не обя́зан.

obligatory *adj.* обяза́тельный.

oblige *v.t.* **1,** (compel) обя́зывать. **2,** (place under a debt of gratitude) обя́зывать: *You will oblige me greatly,* вы меня́ о́чень обя́жете. **3,** (do a favor for): *Could you oblige me with an answer?,* вы не могли́ бы дать мне отве́т?

obliged *adj.* обя́занный: *You are not obliged to answer,* вы не обя́заны отвеча́ть. *I am much obliged to you,* я вам мно́гим обя́зан.

obliging *adj.* услу́жливый; предупреди́тельный.

oblique *adj.* **1,** (slanting) косо́й. **2,** (indirect) ко́свенный.

obliquely *adv.* **1,** (at an angle) ко́со; на́искось; вкось. **2,** (indirectly) ко́свенно.

obliterate *v.t.* **1,** (efface) изгла́живать. **2,** (wipe out) уничтожа́ть. —**obliteration,** *n.* уничтоже́ние.

oblivion *n.* забве́ние. *Sink into oblivion,* ка́нуть в ве́чность *or* в Ле́ту.

oblivious *adj.* [*usu.* oblivious of *or* to] не име́ющий поня́тия о; в по́лном неве́дении (относи́тельно).

oblong *adj.* продолгова́тый. —*n.* продолгова́тая фигу́ра.

obloquy *n.* **1,** (abusive language) злосло́вие. **2,** (disgrace) позо́р.

obnoxious *adj.* неприя́тный; проти́вный.

oboe *n.* гобо́й. —**oboist,** *n.* гобои́ст.

obscene *adj.* непристо́йный.

obscenity *n.* непристо́йность: *utter obscenities,* говори́ть непристо́йности.

obscurant *n.* мракобе́с; обскура́нт. —**obscurantism,** *n.* мракобе́сие; обскуранти́зм.

obscure *adj.* **1,** (dark) тёмный. **2,** (unclear; vague) нея́сный; сму́тный. **3,** (hardly known) безве́стный. —*v.t.* затемня́ть; затмева́ть; завола́кивать; затушёвывать; застила́ть. *Clouds obscured the stars,* ту́чи закры́ли звёзды.

obscurity *n.* **1,** (lack of clarity) нея́сность. **2,** (state of being unknown) неизве́стность; безве́стность. *Live in obscurity,* жить в неизве́стности *or* в безве́стности.

obsequious *adj.* уго́дливый; раболе́пный; подобостра́стный. —**obsequiousness,** *n.* уго́дливость; раболе́пие; подобостра́стие.

observable *adj.* заме́тный.

observance *n.* **1,** (compliance with) соблюде́ние: *observance of the rules,* соблюде́ние пра́вил. **2,** (celebration) пра́зднование: *observance of Easter,* пра́зднование Па́схи.

observant *adj.* **1,** (perceptive) наблюда́тельный. **2,** (religious) благочести́вый.

observation *n.* **1,** (act of observing) наблюде́ние: *keep under observation,* держа́ть под наблюде́нием. **2,** (something observed) наблюде́ние: *personal observations,* ли́чные наблюде́ния. **3,** (remark) замеча́ние. —**observation post,** наблюда́тельный пост. —**observation tower,** наблюда́тельная *or* смотрова́я вы́шка.

observatory *n.* обсервато́рия.

observe *v.t.* **1,** (watch) наблюда́ть: *observe the sunrise,* наблюда́ть восхо́д со́лнца. **2,** (notice) замеча́ть: *observe someone leaving the building,* заме́тить, как кто́-то выходи́л из до́ма. **3,** (comply with; obey) соблюда́ть: *observe the law,* соблюда́ть зако́н. *Observe neutrality,* соблюда́ть нейтралите́т. **4,** (remark) замеча́ть. **5,** (celebrate) отмеча́ть; пра́здновать.

observer *n.* наблюда́тель.

obsess *v.t.* пресле́довать. *Obsessed by,* одержи́мый (+ *instr.*).

obsession *n.* одержи́мость. —**obsessive,** *adj.* навя́зчивый.

obsolescent *adj.* устарева́ющий; отжива́ющий. —**obsolescence,** *n.* мора́льный изно́с.

obsolete *adj.* устаре́лый; устаре́вший. *Become obsolete,* устарева́ть; изжи́ть себя́.

obstacle *n.* препя́тствие. —**obstacle course,** полоса́ препя́тствий.

obstetrics *n.* акуше́рство. —**obstetric,** *adj.* акуше́рский. —**obstetrician,** *n.* акуше́р.

obstinate *adj.* упря́мый. —**obstinacy,** *n.* упря́мство.

obstreperous *adj.* шу́мный; бу́йный; непоко́рный.

obstruct *v.t.* **1,** (bar; block) прегражда́ть; загражда́ть; загора́живать. **2,** (hinder; impede) препя́тствовать. **3,** (cut off from sight) заслоня́ть.

obstruction *n.* **1,** (blocking) прегражде́ние. **2,** (impediment) прегра́да; загражде́ние. **3,** (delaying tactics) обстру́кция. **4,** *med.* непроходи́мость; заку́порка.

obstructionism *n.* обструкциони́зм.

obstructionist *n.* обструкциони́ст. —*adj.* обструкцио́нный.

obtain *v.t.* получа́ть; достава́ть; добыва́ть. *Obtain permission/ a loan/,* получа́ть разреше́ние/заём. *Obtain tickets/medicine,* достава́ть биле́ты/лека́рство. *Obtain food,* добыва́ть пи́щу. *Obtain information,* получа́ть *or* добыва́ть све́дения. —*v.i.* (be in effect) существова́ть.

obtrude *v.t.* **1,** (thrust forward) высо́вывать. **2,** (thrust forward unasked) навя́зывать. —*v.i.* навя́зываться; вторга́ться.

obtrusive *adj.* навя́зчивый.

obtuse *adj.* тупо́й. *Obtuse angle,* тупо́й у́гол. —**obtuseness,** *n.* ту́пость.

obverse *adj.* лицево́й. —*n.* лицева́я сторона́.

obviate *v.t.* устраня́ть; предупрежда́ть.

obvious *adj.* очеви́дный; я́вный. *Obvious to all,* очеви́дно для всех. —**obviously,** *adv.* очеви́дно; я́вно.

ocarina *n.* окари́на.

occasion *n.* **1,** (event) собы́тие; слу́чай. *This happy occasion,* э́то ра́достное собы́тие. *Specially prepared for the occasion,* специа́льно пригото́влен для э́того слу́чая. *This hall is for special occasions,* э́тот зал для осо́бых собы́тий *or* слу́чаев. **2,** (particular time) раз: *on several occasions,* не́сколько раз. **3,** (opportunity) слу́чай: *take the occasion,* по́льзоваться слу́чаем. **4,** (cause; grounds) по́вод: *occasion for a quarrel,* по́вод для ссо́ры. —*v.t.* вызыва́ть; обусло́вливать. —**have occasion to,** приходи́ться (+ *dat.*): *I frequently had occasion to...,* мне ча́сто приходи́лось (+ *inf.*). —**on occasion,** от слу́чая к слу́чаю. —**on the occasion of,** по слу́чаю (+ *gen.*). —**rise to the occasion,** быть на высоте́ положе́ния.

occasional *adj.* быва́ющий вре́мя от вре́мени. *Take an occasional drink,* вре́мя от вре́мени выпива́ть.

occasionally *adv.* иногда́; вре́мя от вре́мени.

occident *n., often cap.* За́пад. —**occidental,** *adj.* за́падный.

occipital *adj.* заты́лочный.

occlude *v.t.* заку́поривать. —**occlusion,** *n.* заку́порка.

occult *adj.* таи́нственный; окку́льтный. —**occultism,** *n.* оккульти́зм.

occupancy *n.* заня́тие; заселе́ние.

occupant *n.* жиле́ц. *The occupants of the car,* е́дущие *or* е́хавшие в маши́не.

occupation *n.* **1,** (act of occupying) заня́тие. **2,** *mil.* оккупа́ция. *Army of occupation,* оккупацио́нная а́рмия. **3,** (what one does with one's time) заня́тие. **4,** (type of work; profession) заня́тие; профе́ссия. *What is your occupation?,* чем вы занима́етесь?; кем вы рабо́таете?

occupational *adj.* профессиона́льный. —**occupational therapy,** трудотерапи́я.

occupy *v.t.* **1,** (fill; take up; inhabit) занима́ть: *occupy a seat/house/post,* занима́ть ме́сто/дом/пост. *Be occupied with,* занима́ться (+ *instr.*); быть за́нятым (+ *instr.*). **2,** *mil.* оккупи́ровать; занима́ть.

occur *v.i.* **1,** (happen) случа́ться; происходи́ть; быва́ть. *Occur infrequently,* ре́дко быва́ть. **2,** (exist; be found) встреча́ться; води́ться. **3,** *fol. by* **to** (come to mind) приходи́ть в го́лову (+ *dat.*): *It never occurred to me,* э́то мне никогда́ не приходи́ло в го́лову.

occurrence *n.* слу́чай; происше́ствие; явле́ние.

ocean *n.* океа́н. —*adj.* океа́нский: *ocean liner,* океа́нский парохо́д; *ocean currents,* океа́нские тече́ния. —**oceanic,** *adj.* океа́нский.

oceanography *n.* океаногра́фия. —**oceanographer,** *n.* океано́граф. —**oceanographic,** *adj.* океанографи́ческий.

ocelot *n.* оцело́т.

ocher *also,* **ochre** *n.* о́хра.

o'clock *adv., in* **one o'clock,** час; **two o'clock,** два часа́; **five o'clock,** пять часо́в.

octagon *n.* восьмиуго́льник. —**octagonal,** *adj.* восьмиуго́льный.

octahedron *n.* восьмигра́нник. —**octahedral,** *adj.* восьмигра́нный.

octane *n.* окта́н.

octave *n.* окта́ва.

octavo *n.* восьму́шка.

octet *n.* окте́т.

October *n.* октя́брь. —*adj.* октя́брьский.

octopus *n.* осьмино́г; спрут.

ocular *adj.* глазно́й.

oculist *n.* окули́ст.

odd *adj.* **1,** (strange; queer) стра́нный: *odd name/behavior,* стра́нное и́мя/поведе́ние. **2,** (not even) нечётный: *odd number,* нечётное число́. **3,** (not paired) непа́рный. **4,** (one of an incomplete set) разро́зненный. **5,** (about; some) с ли́шним: *forty odd years ago,* со́рок с ли́шним лет тому́ наза́д. **6,** (occasional) случа́йный: *odd jobs,* случа́йная рабо́та. *At odd moments,* ме́жду де́лом.

oddity *n.* **1,** (strangeness) стра́нность. **2,** (strange person or thing) стра́нный челове́к; стра́нное де́ло; чуда́к.

oddly *adv.* стра́нно. *Oddly enough,* как ни стра́нно.

odds *n.pl.* **1,** (in betting): *I'll give you 2-1 odds,* ста́влю два про́тив одного́. **2,** (chances) ша́нсы: *The odds are in your favor,* ша́нсы на ва́шей стороне́. *The odds are that...,* скоре́е всего́... **3,** (advantage): *against*

overwhelming odds, про́тив значи́тельно превосходя́щих сил. *Give someone a knight odds* (*in chess*), дать кому́-нибудь фо́ру коня́. —**at odds,** в ссо́ре; не в лада́х. —**by all odds,** несомне́нно; бесспо́рно. —**odds and ends,** ме́лкие ве́щи; ме́лочь.

ode *n.* о́да.

odious *adj.* гну́сный; ненави́стный; одио́зный.

odium *n.* **1,** (hatred) не́нависть. **2,** (opprobrium) позо́р.

odometer *n.* одо́метр.

odontology *n.* одонтоло́гия.

odor *also,* **odour** *n.* за́пах.

odoriferous *adj.* души́стый; паху́чий.

odorless *also,* **odourless** *adj.* не име́ющий за́паха.

odorous *adj.* души́стый; паху́чий.

odour *n.* = **odor.** —**odourless,** *adj.* = **odorless.**

odyssey *n.* одиссе́я.

oedema *n.* = **edema.**

oesophagus *n.* = **esophagus.**

oestrogen *n.* = **estrogen.**

of *prep.* **1,** (denoting possession, relation, a quantity or part of something, the contents of something) *rendered by the gen. case: the name of the city,* назва́ние го́рода; *the works of Chekhov,* произведе́ния Че́хова; *a glass of water,* стака́н воды́; *a piece of meat,* кусо́к мя́са; *a pound of sugar,* фунт са́хару. **2,** (with the names of cities or countries) *not rendered in Russian* (*nom. case follows*): *the city of Moscow,* го́род Москва́; *the State of Israel,* Госуда́рство Изра́иль; *the Kingdom of Denmark,* Короле́вство Да́ния; *in the Republic of India,* в Респу́блике И́ндия. **3,** (from; designating origin or material) из: *articles of gold,* изде́лия из зо́лота; *made of silk,* сде́лан из шёлка. **4,** (consisting of — when followed by a number) из: *a group of twenty demonstrators,* гру́ппа из двадцати́ демонстра́нтов; *a column of 100 tanks,* коло́нна из ста та́нков. **5,** (from among) из: *some of us,* не́которые из нас; *an acquaintance of mine,* оди́н из мои́х знако́мых. **6,** (on one's part) с (чье́й-нибудь) стороны́: *very kind of you,* о́чень любе́зно с ва́шей стороны́. **7,** (indicating direction from) от: *south of the city,* к ю́гу от го́рода. **8,** (indicating cause) от: *die of cancer,* умира́ть от ра́ка. **9,** (about; concerning) о: *news of the accident,* весть о́б аи́и. *Rumors of a possible coup,* слу́хи о возмо́жном переворо́те. *Think a great deal of oneself,* мно́го вообража́ть (*or* ду́мать) о себе́. **10,** (with dates) *with the gen. case: the Fourth of July,* четвёртое ию́ля. *My letter of May 5th,* моё письмо́ от пя́того ма́я. **11,** (in telling time) без: *twenty of two,* без двадцати́ два. **12,** *with various miscellaneous verbs: smell of onions,* па́хнуть лу́ком; *accuse someone of stealing,* обвиня́ть кого́-нибудь в кра́же. *He was cured of tuberculosis,* он вы́лечился от туберкулёза. *She was robbed of her purse and glasses,* у неё укра́ли су́мку и очки́.

off *adv.* прочь: *Hands off!,* ру́ки прочь! ♦*Usu. rendered by a prefixed verb: take off,* снима́ть; *cut off,* отреза́ть; *jump off,* спры́гивать; *see off,* провожа́ть. —*adj.* **1,** (not turned on) вы́ключенный: *The light is* *off*, свет вы́ключен. **2,** (canceled) отменён. *The picnic is off*, пикни́к отменя́ется *or* отменён. *The deal is off*, сде́лка не состоя́лась; сде́лка расстро́илась. *The wedding is off*, сва́дьба не состои́тся. **3,** (free from one's job): *I'm off on Friday; I have* (*this*) *Friday off*, я не рабо́таю в пя́тницу; в пя́тницу у меня́ выходно́й. *I have Fridays off*, я не рабо́таю по пя́тницам; пя́тница у меня́ выходно́й. *Ask for a day off*, проси́ть выходно́й. *Can I have tomorrow off?*, могу́ ли я за́втра взять выходно́й *or* отгу́л? *Take two days off*, взять два дня выходны́х; отгу́ливать два дня. **4,** (in error): *be off in one's calculations*, ошиба́ться в расчётах. **5,** (away; into the future): *Christmas is two months off*, до рождества́ оста́лось два ме́сяца. **6,** (in a certain state): *well off*, обеспе́ченный. *You'd be better off if you stayed home*, вам бы лу́чше оста́ться до́ма. **7,** (about to go somewhere): *We must be off*, нам пора́ уходи́ть. *Well, I'm off to town*, ну, я пошёл (пошла́) в го́род. **8,** (declining): *Production is off*, произво́дство упа́ло. —*prep.* **1,** (from off; down from) с: *fall off the chair*, упа́сть со сту́ла. *The train went off the tracks*, по́езд сошёл с ре́льсов. *Eat off paper plates*, есть из бума́жных таре́лок. **2,** (away from): *Keep off the grass!*, по траве́ не ходи́ть! **3,** (distant from) от: *100 miles off the coast*, в ста ми́лях от бе́рега. *Just off the main square*, в двух шага́х от гла́вной пло́щади. **4,** (deviating from) от: *stray/drift off course*, отклоня́ться от ку́рса. **5,** (deducted from) ни́же: *ten dollars off the usual price*, де́сять до́лларов ни́же обы́чной цены́. **6,** *with various nouns: off duty*, не дежу́рит; *off balance*, потеря́вший равнове́сие; *off limits*, закры́т; *off one's game*, не в фо́рме. —*interj.* вон!; прочь! *Off with you!*, убира́йтесь вон! *Off with his head!*, го́лову с плеч! —**off and on,** с переры́вами.

offal *n.* требуха́.

off-color *also,* **off-colour** *adj.* **1,** (imperfect, as of a gem) нечи́стой воды́. **2,** (risqué) риско́ванный; сомни́тельный.

offence *n.* = **offense.**

offend *v.t.* обижа́ть; оскорбля́ть. *Don't be offended!,* не обижа́йтесь! *Be offended by a remark*, оби́деться на замеча́ние. *Offend the eye*, ре́зать (кому́-нибудь) глаз. *Easily offended*, оби́дчивый.

offender *n.* **1,** (one who offends) оби́дчик. **2,** (wrongdoer) правонаруши́тель. *Juvenile offender*, малоле́тний престу́пник.

offense *also,* **offence** *n.* **1,** (affront) оби́да. *No offense meant*, не в оби́ду будь ска́зано. **2,** (attack) нападе́ние: *The best defense is* (*a good*) *offense*, лу́чшее сре́дство защи́ты — нападе́ние. **3,** (misdeed; transgression) просту́пок. **4,** *law* преступле́ние; правонаруше́ние. *Criminal offense*, уголо́вное преступле́ние. *Capital offense*, преступле́ние, наказу́емое сме́ртью. —**give offense** (**to**), обижа́ть кого́-нибудь. —**take offense,** обижа́ться; оскорбля́ться.

offensive *adj.* **1,** (disagreeable; nasty) неприя́тный; проти́вный: *offensive odor*, неприя́тный/проти́вный за́пах. **2,** (insulting) оби́дный; оскорби́тельный: *offensive remark*, оби́дное/оскорби́тельное замеча-ние. **3,** *mil.* наступа́тельный: *offensive weapons*, наступа́тельное ору́жие. —*n.* наступле́ние: *go on the offensive*, идти́ в наступле́ние.

offer *v.t.* **1,** (present for approval or acceptance) предлага́ть: *offer one's services*, предлага́ть свои́ услу́ги. *Offer one's hand*, подава́ть ру́ку. *Offer one's apologies*, приноси́ть свои́ извине́ния. *Offer one's condolences*, выража́ть своё соболе́знование. *Offer* (*up*) *a prayer*, возноси́ть моли́тву. **2,** (provide) предоставля́ть: *offer opportunities*, предоставля́ть возмо́жности. *Offer hope*, подава́ть наде́жду. *Offer a wide choice*, предоставля́ть бога́тый вы́бор. **3,** *fol. by inf.* (volunteer) предлага́ть; вызыва́ться: *She offered to help*, она́ предложи́ла/вы́звалась помо́чь. **4,** (put up, as resistance) ока́зывать. —*n.* предложе́ние: *make an offer*, де́лать предложе́ние.

offering *n.* **1,** (gift; contribution) приноше́ние. **2,** (sacrifice) жертвоприноше́ние.

offhand *adv.* без подгото́вки; экспро́мтом. —*adj.* **1,** (impromptu) импровизи́рованный. **2,** (casual; brusque) бесцеремо́нный.

office *n.* **1,** (place of business) конто́ра; канцеля́рия. *He is at the office*, он на рабо́те. **2,** (private room for work) кабине́т. **3,** (high position) до́лжность. *Take/enter office*, вступи́ть в до́лжность (*e.g.* президе́нта). *Term of office*, срок полномо́чий. *Out of office*, не у госуда́рственных дел. **4,** (administrative body) бюро́. **5,** (government department) министе́рство; ве́домство; управле́ние. **6,** *pl.* (services) услу́ги: *good offices*, до́брые услу́ги. —*adj.* конто́рский; канцеля́рский; служе́бный. *Office worker*, конто́рский слу́жащий. *Office supplies*, канцеля́рские принадле́жности. *Office hours*, служе́бные *or* приёмные часы́.

office boy рассы́льный; посы́льный.

officeholder *n.* должностно́е лицо́.

officer *n.* **1,** *mil.* офице́р. **2,** (person in authority) должностно́е лицо́. **3,** (elected official, as of a club) член правле́ния. **4,** (policeman) полице́йский. —*adj.* [*usu.* **officer's** *or* **officers'**] офице́рский.

official *adj.* **1,** (authorized; formal) официа́льный: *official spokesman*, официа́льный представи́тель. *Official language*, госуда́рственный язы́к. **2,** (connected with one's work) служе́бный: *official duties*, служе́бные обя́занности. —*n.* чино́вник; сотру́дник; официа́льное *or* должностно́е лицо́. *Embassy official*, сотру́дник посо́льства. *Customs official*, тамо́женник.

officialdom *n.* чино́вничество.

officially *adv.* официа́льно.

officiate *v.i.* **1,** (preside) председа́тельствовать (на собра́нии). **2,** (conduct a service) соверша́ть богослуже́ние. *Officiate at a wedding*, соверша́ть обря́д бракосочета́ния.

officious *adj.* назо́йливый; навя́зчивый.

offing *n., in* **be in the offing,** предстоя́ть; гото́виться.

off-season *n.* мёртвый сезо́н. —*adj. & adv.* не в сезо́нное вре́мя.

offset *v.t.* возмеща́ть; компенси́ровать. —*n., printing* офсе́т. —**offset printing,** офсе́тная печа́ть.

offshoot *n.* отро́сток; ответвле́ние.

offshore *adj.* прибре́жный. *Offshore drilling,* буре́ние в мо́ре. —*adv.* недалеко́ от бе́рега.

offside *adj., sports* вне игры́.

offspring *n.* **1,** (child as related to its parent) пото́мок; о́тпрыск. **2,** (descendants; progeny) пото́мство: *produce offspring,* производи́ть пото́мство.

offstage *adj.* закули́сный. —*adv.* за кули́сами; за кули́сы.

off-white *adj.* белёсый; белова́тый.

off-year *adj. Off-year elections,* промежу́точные вы́боры.

often *adv.* ча́сто. *How often?,* как ча́сто? —**every so often,** вре́мя от вре́мени. —**more often than not,** ча́ще всего́.

ogle *v.i.* де́лать *or* стро́ить гла́зки; игра́ть глаза́ми.

ogre *n.* велика́н-людое́д.

oh *interj.* о!; ах!; ох!

ohm *n.* ом.

oho *interj.* ого́!

oil *n.* **1,** (viscous substance) ма́сло: *olive/castor/linseed oil,* оли́вковое/касто́ровое/льняно́е ма́сло. *Check/change the oil,* прове́рить/смени́ть ма́сло. **2,** (petroleum) нефть: *import oil,* ввози́ть *or* импорти́ровать нефть. *The demand for oil,* спрос на нефть. **3,** *art* ма́сло; ма́сляные кра́ски: *paint in oils,* писа́ть ма́слом *or* ма́сляными кра́сками. —*adj.* ма́сляный; нефтяно́й. *Oil filter,* ма́сляный фильтр. *The oil industry,* нефтяна́я промы́шленность. *Oil production,* добы́ча не́фти. —*v.t.* сма́зывать: *oil the hinges on the door,* сма́зывать дверны́е пе́тли. *A well-oiled machine* (*fig.*), хорошо́ отла́женная маши́на.

oilcan *n.* маслёнка.

oilcloth *n.* клеёнка.

oiler *n.* **1,** (device for oiling) маслёнка. **2,** (ship) нефтеналивно́е су́дно.

oil field месторожде́ние не́фти.

oil lamp ма́сляная ла́мпа.

oil painting карти́на, напи́санная ма́сляными кра́сками.

oil shale нефтено́сный сла́нец.

oil well нефтяна́я сква́жина.

oily *adj.* ма́сленый; масляни́стый. *Oily skin,* жи́рная ко́жа.

ointment *n.* мазь.

O.K. *interj.* хорошо́!; ла́дно! —*adj.* ничего́; норма́льно. *Everything is O.K.,* всё норма́льно.

okapi *n.* ока́пи.

okra *n.* ба́мия; о́кра.

old *adj.* ста́рый. *Old man,* стари́к. *Old woman,* стару́шка. *Old friend,* ста́рый *or* да́вний друг. *Old furniture,* ста́рая ме́бель. *Old custom,* ста́рый обы́чай. *Get/grow old,* старе́ть; ста́риться. *Live to be very old,* дожи́ть до глубо́кой ста́рости; дожи́ть до прекло́нных лет. *How old are you?,* ско́лько вам лет? *I am ten years old,* мне де́сять лет. *You are not old enough,* ты недоста́точно взро́слый. *This newspaper is two weeks old,* э́та газе́та двухнеде́льной да́вности. —**in days of old,** в старину́. *See also* **older.**

old age ста́рость. *In one's old age,* на ста́рости лет. *Old age pension,* пе́нсия по ста́рости. —**old age home,** дом для престаре́лых.

Old Believer старове́р; старообря́дец.

olden *adj.* было́й; да́вний. *In olden times,* в старину́.

Old English древнеангли́йский язы́к.

older *comp. adj.* ста́рший: *my older sister,* моя́ ста́ршая сестра́. *She is older than me,* она́ ста́рше меня́. *Older people,* пожилы́е лю́ди.

old-fashioned *adj.* старомо́дный.

old guard ста́рая гва́рдия.

old hand тёртый кала́ч; стре́ляный воробе́й.

old maid ста́рая де́ва.

Old Testament Ве́тхий заве́т. *Old Testament prophet,* ветхозаве́тный проро́к.

old-time *adj.* стари́нный; ста́рых времён. *Old-time resident,* старожи́л.

old-timer *n.* старожи́л.

old wives' tale ба́бья ска́зка.

Old World Ста́рый свет.

oleaginous *adj.* масляни́стый.

oleander *n.* олеа́ндр.

oleomargarine *n.* маргари́н.

oleoresin *n.* живи́ца.

olfactory *adj.* обоня́тельный.

oligarchy *n.* олига́рхия. —**oligarch,** *n.* олига́рх. —**oligarchic,** *adj.* олигархи́ческий.

olive *n.* оли́ва; оли́вка; масли́на. —*adj.* оли́вковый; масли́чный. —**olive branch,** оли́вковая *or* масли́чная ветвь. —**olive-green,** *adj.* оли́вковый. —**olive oil,** оли́вковое *or* прова́нское ма́сло. —**olive tree,** оли́ва; масли́на; оли́вковое де́рево.

Olympiad *n.* олимпиа́да.

Olympian *adj.* олимпи́йский.

Olympic *adj.* олимпи́йский. —**Olympic games,** Олимпи́йские и́гры.

Olympics *n.pl.* олимпиа́да.

omega *n.* оме́га.

omelet *also,* **omelette** *n.* омле́т.

omen *n.* предзнаменова́ние.

ominous *adj.* злове́щий: *an ominous sign,* злове́щий при́знак; *an ominous silence,* злове́щая тишина́.

omission *n.* упуще́ние; про́пуск.

omit *v.t.* пропуска́ть: *omit a word,* пропуска́ть сло́во. *Omit an essential detail,* пропуска́ть суще́ственную подро́бность.

omnibus *n.* **1,** *obs.* (bus) авто́бус. **2,** (anthology) антоло́гия; сбо́рник. —*adj.* о́бщий; всеобъе́млющий.

omnipotent *adj.* всемогу́щий. —**omnipotence,** *n.* всемогу́щество.

omnipresent *adj.* вездесу́щий.

omniscient *adj.* всеве́дущий. —**omniscience,** *n.* всеве́дение.

omnivorous *adj.* всея́дный.

on *prep.* **1,** (indicating position upon) на (+ *prepl.*): *Your keys are on the dresser,* ва́ши ключи́ (лежа́т) на комо́де. *The picture is hanging on the wall,* карти́на виси́т на стене́. *Drive on the left,* е́хать по ле́вой стороне́ у́лицы (*or* доро́ги). **2,** (onto) на (+ *acc.*): *put the books on the shelf,* положи́ть кни́ги на по́лку.

Lie down on the floor, лечь на́ пол. *Set foot on the moon,* ступи́ть на Луну́. **3,** (inside, as a vehicle) в (+ *prepl.*): *fall asleep on the train/plane/bus,* засну́ть в по́езде/ в самолёте/ в авто́бусе. *Seat on a train,* ме́сто в по́езде. **4,** *with various nouns,* на: *on a diet,* на дие́те; *on that subject,* на э́ту те́му; *based on facts,* осно́ванный на фа́ктах; *a tax on cigarettes,* нало́г на сигаре́ты; *on the following conditions,* на сле́дующих усло́виях. *Run on gasoline,* рабо́тать на бензи́не. *Pin one's hopes on,* возлага́ть наде́жды на (+ *acc.*). *Live on one's earnings,* жить на свой за́работок. *Spend money on books,* тра́тить де́ньги на кни́ги. **5,** (indicating point of contact) по (+ *dat.*); о (+ *acc.*); в (+ *acc.*). *Knock on the door,* стуча́ть в дверь. *Choke on a bone,* дави́ться ко́стью. *Stumble on a stone,* споткну́ться о ка́мень. *Tap someone on the shoulder,* сту́кнуть кого́-нибудь по плечу́. *Bang one's fist on the table,* уда́рить кулако́м по́ столу. *Kiss someone on the cheek,* целова́ть кого́-нибудь в щёку. *Wipe one's hands on one's apron,* вытира́ть ру́ки о пере́дник. *Cut one's finger on a piece of glass,* поре́зать себе́ па́лец о стекло́. **6,** (in one's possession) при: *I have no money on me,* у меня́ при себе́ нет де́нег. **7,** (being a member of) в: *be on a certain team,* быть в како́й-нибудь кома́нде. *He is on the board/committee,* он член правле́ния/комите́та. **8,** (through the medium of) по: *appear on television,* выступа́ть по телеви́дению. **9,** (about; concerning) о: *an essay on war,* о́черк о войне́. *A book on art,* кни́га по иску́сству. *My opinion on this subject,* моё мне́ние по э́тому вопро́су. **10,** (on the basis of) по: *on my advice/recommendation,* по моему́ сове́ту; по мое́й рекоменда́ции. **11,** (during) в; во вре́мя. *On that day,* в тот день. *Be killed on a polar expedition,* поги́бнуть во вре́мя поля́рной экспеди́ции. **12,** (at the moment of) по (+ *prepl.*); при: *on his arrival,* по прие́зде; *on entering the room,* при вхо́де в ко́мнату. *On reaching the age of 21,* по достиже́нии двадцати́ одного́ го́да. *On hearing the news,* услы́шав но́вости. **13,** (with dates) *rendered by the gen. case:* *on July 4th,* четвёртого ию́ля. **14,** (with days of the week) в (+ *acc.*): *on Wednesday,* в сре́ду. ♦*In the meaning "each" or "every,"* по (+ *dat. pl.*): *on Wednesday(s),* по среда́м. **15,** *colloq.* (at the expense of): *This is on me,* я угоща́ю. *Drinks are on the house,* все напи́тки за счёт заведе́ния. **16,** *in various miscellaneous expressions: on foot,* пешко́м; *on board,* на борту́; *on fire,* в огне́; *on time,* во́время; *on purpose,* наро́чно; *on trial,* под судо́м. —*adv.* да́льше: *go on,* идти́ да́льше. *Read on!,* чита́йте да́льше! ♦ *Usu. rendered by a prefixed verb: put on,* надева́ть; *turn on,* включа́ть. —*adj.* **1,** (being worn) наде́тый: *What did she have on?,* что бы́ло на ней наде́то? *Your hat is on backwards,* у вас шля́па наде́та за́дом наперёд. *He had nothing on,* он был в го́лом ви́де. **2,** (turned on) включён: *The light is on,* свет включён. **3,** (in progress) *rendered by the verb* идти́: *What's on today?,* что идёт сего́дня? *The exam is on,* идёт экза́мен. **4,** (not canceled) в си́ле. —**on and off,** попереме́нно; то..., то... —**on and on,** без конца́.

onager *n.* она́гр.
on-board *adj.* бортово́й.
once *adv.* **1,** (one time) раз; оди́н раз. *Once a month,* раз в ме́сяц. *Once is enough,* оди́н раз — доста́точно. *More than once,* не раз. *Not once,* ни ра́зу. **2,** (on a certain occasion in the past) одна́жды; ка́к-то раз. **3,** (formerly) не́когда; когда́-то: *The ruins of a once great city,* руи́ны не́когда большо́го го́рода. —*conj.* как то́лько; раз. *Once he finds out about it,* как то́лько он узна́ет об э́том. —**all at once, 1,** (all simultaneously) все *or* всё вме́сте; сра́зу. **2,** (suddenly) вдруг. —**at once, 1,** (right now) сейча́с; неме́дленно. **2,** (just then; immediately) сра́зу; неме́дленно. —**for once,** на э́тот раз. —**just this once,** хотя́ бы на э́тот раз. —**once again; once more,** ещё раз. —**once and for all,** раз (и) навсегда́. —**once in a while,** вре́мя от вре́мени. —**once or twice,** раз-друго́й; ра́за два. —**once upon a time,** одна́жды; жил-был.
oncology *n.* онколо́гия.
oncoming *adj.* встре́чный: *oncoming train,* встре́чный по́езд.
one *n.* оди́н. ♦*In counting,* раз: *one, two, three,* раз, два, три. —*adj.* **1,** (a single) оди́н (одна́, одно́): *one time,* оди́н раз; *one portion,* одна́ по́рция; *one summer,* одно́ ле́то. *One watch,* одни́ часы́. *One o'clock,* час. *Act One,* де́йствие пе́рвое. **2,** (only) еди́нственный: *the one man who can do it,* еди́нственный, кто мо́жет э́то сде́лать. *With the one difference that...,* с той то́лько ра́зницей, что... **3,** (united) еди́ный. —*indef. pron.* **1,** (single element in a group) оди́н (одна́): *one of them,* оди́н/одна́ из них. *Which one is yours?,* како́й из э́тих ваш? **2,** (a person) *rendered variously in Russian: One never knows,* никогда́ не зна́ешь. *The one in the red dress,* та в кра́сном пла́тье. *One must observe the rules,* на́до соблюда́ть пра́вила. *If one is to believe the author,* е́сли ве́рить а́втору. *One is never too old to learn,* век живи́ — век учи́сь. ♦*Possessive,* свой; себе́: *love one's country,* люби́ть свою́ ро́дину; *cut one's finger,* поре́зать себе́ па́лец; *tear one's hair,* рвать на себе́ во́лосы. **3,** (item) *omitted in Russian: the red one,* кра́сный (кра́сная, кра́сное). *Buy a new one,* купи́ть но́вый (но́вую, но́вое). **4,** *preceded by* **the** (specific person or thing) тот: *not the one I wanted,* не тот, кото́рый я хоте́л(а). **5,** (the kind of person) тако́й: *He is not one to back down,* он не тако́й, чтобы отступа́ть. —**at one with,** заодно́ с; солида́рный с. —**one and all,** все до одного́; все до еди́ного. —**one another,** *see* **another.** —**one at a time,** по одному́; поодино́чке. —**one by one, 1,** (one at a time) по одному́. **2,** (one after the other) оди́н за други́м. —**one on one,** оди́н на оди́н; с гла́зу на глаз.
one-armed *adj.* однору́кий.
one-celled *adj.* однокле́точный.
one-day *adj.* однодне́вный.
one-eyed *adj.* одногла́зый.
one hundred сто. —**one-hundredth,** *adj.* со́тый. —*n.* со́тая; со́тая часть. *One one-hundredth,* одна́ со́тая; со́тая часть.
one-legged *adj.* одноно́гий.

one-man *adj.* единоли́чный: *one-man rule,* единоли́чная власть; *one-man business,* единоли́чное предприя́тие. *One-man show,* моноспекта́кль.

oneness *n.* **1,** (unity) еди́нство. **2,** (sameness) то́ждество.

one-room *adj.* однокомнатный.

onerous *adj.* тя́гостный; обремени́тельный.

oneself *pres. pron.* **1,** *used reflexively,* себя́: *underestimate oneself,* недооце́нивать себя́; *speak for oneself,* говори́ть за себя́; *kill oneself,* поко́нчить с собо́й. ♦*Often rendered by the reflexive verb: hurt oneself,* ушиби́ться; *shoot oneself,* застрели́ться. **2,** *used for emphasis,* сам: *One has to experience it oneself,* на́до самому́ э́то испыта́ть. —**be oneself,** быть сами́м собо́й. —**by oneself, 1,** (alone) оди́н (одна́). **2,** (without help) сам (сама́). —**not oneself,** не по себе́ (+ *dat.*); сам не свой (сама́ не своя́). —**to oneself,** себе́; про себя́. *Say to oneself,* говори́ть себе́. *Talk to oneself,* говори́ть с сами́м собо́й. *Read to oneself,* чита́ть про себя́. *Keep to oneself,* держа́ться особняко́м. *Keep one's thoughts to oneself,* держа́ть свои́ мы́сли при себе́.

one-sided *adj.* односторо́нний; однобо́кий. *One-sided interpretation,* однобо́кое толкова́ние.

one-story *adj.* одноэта́жный.

one-time *adj.* **1,** (former) бы́вший. **2,** (done only once) ра́зовый; однокра́тный; единовре́менный.

one-volume *adj.* однотомный.

one-way *adj.* **1,** (moving in one direction) односторо́нний. *One-way street,* у́лица с односторо́нним движе́нием. **2,** (not including a return, as of a trip) в оди́н коне́ц.

one-year *adj.* одногоди́чный.

ongoing *adj.* поступа́тельный.

onion *n.* лу́ковица; голо́вка лу́ка; *pl.* лук.

onlooker *n.* зри́тель.

only *adv.* **1,** (merely; exclusively) то́лько; лишь: *only one thing,* то́лько/лишь одно́. *I only wanted to ask...,* я то́лько хоте́л(а) спроси́ть... *Only then did it become clear that...,* то́лько тогда́ ста́ло я́сно, что... *He was wearing only a shirt,* он был в одно́й руба́шке. *For reasons known only to him,* по одному́ ему́ изве́стным причи́нам. **2,** (as recently as) ещё; не да́лее как: *only yesterday,* ещё вчера́; не да́лее как вчера́. —*adj.* еди́нственный: *the only way out,* еди́нственный вы́ход. *Only child,* еди́нственный ребёнок. *The only one of its kind,* еди́нственный в своём ро́де. *The only possible way,* еди́нственно возмо́жный спо́соб. *The only thing I can say,* еди́нственно, что я могу́ сказа́ть. *He is the only one who can do it,* он еди́нственный, кто мо́жет э́то сде́лать. *I was the only one there,* я оди́н был там; я одна́ была́ там. *And he is not the only one!,* да и не то́лько он! *I was not the only one who disagreed,* не я оди́н не согласи́лся; но. *Only be careful!,* то́лько бу́дьте осторо́жны! —**have only to,** сто́ит то́лько: *One has only to ask,* сто́ит то́лько попроси́ть. —**if only,** *see* **if.** —**not only,** не то́лько. —**only too,** то́лько: *I would be only too happy to do it,* мне бу́дет то́лько прия́тно э́то сде́лать.

onomatopoeia *n.* звукоподража́ние.

onrush *n.* наплы́в; прито́к.

onset *n.* нача́ло; наступле́ние.

on-site *adj.* на места́х.

onslaught *n.* на́тиск.

onstage *adv.* на сце́ну: *walk onstage,* выходи́ть на сце́ну.

onto *prep.* на (+ *acc.*): *climb onto the roof,* влезть на кры́шу.

ontology *n.* онтоло́гия. —**ontological,** *adj.* онтологи́ческий

onus *n.* бре́мя; отве́тственность.

onward *adv.* вперёд. *From this moment onward,* с э́того моме́нта. —*adj.* поступа́тельный.

onyx *n.* о́никс. —*adj.* о́никсовый.

oodles *n.pl.,* *colloq.* у́йма.

ooze *v.i.* сочи́ться; проступа́ть.

opacity *n.* непрозра́чность.

opal *n.* опа́л. —*adj.* опа́ловый.

opalescent *adj.* ра́дужный.

opaline *adj.* опа́ловый.

opaque *adj.* непрозра́чный; светонепроница́емый. —**opaqueness,** *n.* непрозра́чность.

open *v.t.* открыва́ть: *open the window/ one's eyes/ a meeting/,* открыва́ть окно́/глаза́/собра́ние. *Open a drawer,* выдвига́ть я́щик стола́. *Open a package,* вскрыва́ть посы́лку. *Open fire,* откры́ть ого́нь *or* стрельбу́. —*v.i.* **1,** (become open; begin) открыва́ться: *The window won't open,* окно́ не открыва́ется. **2,** *fol. by* **to** (turn to) открыва́ть: *Open to page 106,* откро́йте сто шесту́ю страни́цу. **3,** *fol. by* **up** (expand, as of a table) раздвига́ться. **4,** (spread apart, as of buds) распуска́ться. **5,** *fol. by* **on** *or* **onto** (give access to) выходи́ть в *or* на. —*adj.* откры́тый: *The door is open,* дверь откры́та. *Open wound,* откры́тая ра́на. *The open sea,* откры́тое мо́ре. *Open question,* откры́тый вопро́с. *Be open to question,* быть под вопро́сом. *Open to the public,* откры́т для пу́блики. *The job is still open,* ме́сто ещё не за́нято. —*n.* [*usu.* **the open**]. *Out in the open,* на откры́том во́здухе. *Operate in the open,* де́йствовать откры́то. *Come out/ bring out/ into the open,* вы́йти/вы́вести нару́жу. —**open up to,** открыва́ться (+ *dat.*).

open-air *adj.* откры́тый; на откры́том во́здухе; под откры́тым не́бом.

open-ended *adj.* бессро́чный.

opener *n.* открыва́лка: *bottle opener,* открыва́лка для буты́лок. *Can opener,* консе́рвный нож. —**for openers,** *colloq.* для нача́ла.

open-hearted *adj.* чистосерде́чный. —**open-heartedness,** *n.* чистосерде́чие.

open-hearth *adj.* марте́новский: *open-hearth furnace,* марте́новская печь; марте́н.

opening *n.* **1,** (act of opening) откры́тие. **2,** (hole; gap) отве́рстие. **3,** (vacancy) вака́нсия. **4,** *theat.* премье́ра. **5,** *chess* дебю́т. —*adj.* **1,** (first; initial) пе́рвый; нача́льный. **2,** (introductory) вступи́тельный: *opening remarks,* вступи́тельное сло́во.

openly *adv.* откры́то; в откры́тую.

open-minded *adj.* непредубеждённый.

open-mouthed *adj.* с откры́тым ртом; рази́нув рот.

openness *n.* откры́тость; гла́сность.

openwork *n.* ажу́рная рабо́та; ажу́р; мере́жка.

opera *n.* о́пера. —*adj.* о́перный. —**opera glasses,** театра́льный бино́кль. —**opera house,** о́перный теа́тр.

operate *v.i.* **1,** (function) рабо́тать; де́йствовать. *The buses are not operating today,* автобу́сы сего́дня не хо́дят. **2,** (carry on certain activities) де́йствовать; ору́довать. **3,** (perform surgery) опери́ровать. *Operate on someone,* опери́ровать кого́-нибудь. —*v.t.* **1,** (manage, as an enterprise) управля́ть; заве́довать. **2,** (handle, as a machine) управля́ть; обраща́ться с; обслу́живать.

operatic *adj.* о́перный.

operating *adj.* **1,** *med.* операцио́нный: *operating table,* операцио́нный стол. *Operating room,* операцио́нная. **2,** *econ.* эксплуатацио́нный: *operating costs/expenses,* эксплуатацио́нные расхо́ды.

operation *n.* **1,** (functioning) де́йствие. *Put into operation,* вводи́ть в де́йствие; вводи́ть в строй. *Be in operation,* рабо́тать; де́йствовать; быть в эксплуата́ции. **2,** *pl.* (actions; procedures) рабо́ты: *rescue operations,* спаса́тельные рабо́ты. **3,** *med.* опера́ция: *heart operation,* опера́ция на се́рдце. **4,** (handling) управле́ние: *operation of a motor vehicle,* управле́ние автомаши́ной. **5,** *mil.* опера́ция; *pl.* де́йствия. *Amphibious operation,* морска́я деса́нтная опера́ция. *Combat operations,* боевы́е де́йствия. **6,** *finance* опера́ция.

operational *adj.* **1,** (in use; operating) де́йствующий. **2,** *mil.* операти́вный.

operative *adj.* **1,** (in operation) де́йствующий. **2,** (in force; valid) де́йствующий; действи́тельный. **3,** *med.* операти́вный. —*n.* аге́нт; сы́щик.

operator *n.* **1,** (one who works a machine) опера́тор; машини́ст. *Lathe operator,* то́карь. *Crane operator,* машини́ст подъёмного кра́на; кранови́к. *Radio operator,* ради́ст. **2,** (telephone operator) телефони́стка. **3,** (owner; director) владе́лец; управля́ющий.

operetta *n.* опере́тта.

ophthalmology *n.* офтальмоло́гия. —**ophthalmologist,** *n.* офтальмо́лог.

opiate *n.* **1,** (drug) нарко́тик. **2,** (that which dulls the senses) о́пиум: *the opiate of the masses,* о́пиум наро́дных масс.

opinion *n.* мне́ние. *In my opinion,* по моему́ мне́нию; по-мо́ему. *Have a high opinion of,* быть высо́кого мне́ния о.

opinionated *adj.* упря́мый; своево́льный.

opium *n.* о́пиум; о́пий. *Opium den,* кури́льня о́пиума.

opossum *n.* опо́ссум.

opponent *n.* проти́вник; (*specifically in a game*) партнёр; (*in a debate*) оппоне́нт.

opportune *adj.* **1,** (appropriate; suitable) подходя́щий: *opportune moment,* подходя́щий моме́нт. **2,** (timely) своевре́менный.

opportunism *n.* оппортуни́зм. —**opportunist,** *n.* оппортуни́ст. —**opportunistic,** *adj.* оппортунисти́ческий.

opportunity *n.* возмо́жность; (удо́бный) слу́чай. *Take the/this opportunity to...,* по́льзоваться слу́чаем (+ *inf.*). *At the first convenient opportunity,* при пе́рвом удо́бном слу́чае. *At every opportunity,* при ка́ждой возмо́жности.

oppose *v.t.* **1,** (work to defeat) проти́виться; противостоя́ть. *Oppose someone at every turn,* проти́виться кому́-нибудь на ка́ждом шагу́. **2,** (be against) выступа́ть *or* возража́ть про́тив. **3,** (compete against) состяза́ться с. **4,** (set in opposition) противопоставля́ть: *oppose force with force,* противопоставля́ть си́лу си́ле.

opposed *adj.* про́тив: *be strongly opposed to something,* быть реши́тельно про́тив чего́-нибудь. *Nine in favor, five opposed,* де́вять за, пять про́тив. —**as opposed to,** в отли́чие от.

opposing *adj.* проти́вный: *opposing sides,* проти́вные сто́роны. *Opposing views,* противополо́жные взгля́ды.

opposite *adj.* **1,** (facing) противополо́жный: *the opposite shore,* противополо́жный бе́рег. *On opposite sides of the street,* по ра́зные сто́роны у́лицы. **2,** (reverse) обра́тный: *in the opposite direction,* в обра́тном направле́нии. **3,** (contrary) противополо́жный: *opposite views,* противополо́жные взгля́ды. *The opposite sex,* противополо́жный пол. —*n.* противополо́жность; противополо́жное; обра́тное. *He is the complete opposite of his brother,* он по́лная противополо́жность своему́ бра́ту. *Yesterday you were saying the opposite,* вчера́ вы утвержда́ли противополо́жное/обра́тное. —*adv.* напро́тив: *sit opposite,* сиде́ть напро́тив. —*prep.* про́тив; напро́тив. *Sit opposite each other,* сиде́ть друг про́тив дру́га.

opposition *n.* **1,** (resistance) противоде́йствие; оппози́ция: *meet with opposition,* встре́тить противоде́йствие/оппози́цию. **2,** (state of being opposed) возраже́ние: *my opposition to this bill,* моё возраже́ние про́тив э́того законопрое́кта. **3,** *polit.* оппози́ция. **4,** *astron.* противостоя́ние. —*adj.* оппозицио́нный: *the opposition party,* оппозицио́нная па́ртия.

oppress *v.t.* угнета́ть; притесня́ть. —**oppression,** *n.* угнете́ние; притесне́ние; гнёт.

oppressive *adj.* **1,** (causing distress) гнету́щий; угнета́ющий; томи́тельный. *Oppressive heat,* томи́тельная жара́. *Oppressive thoughts,* гнету́щие мы́сли. **2,** (tyrannical) деспоти́ческий.

oppressor *n.* угнета́тель; притесни́тель; наси́льник.

opprobrious *adj.* **1,** (scurrilous) оскорби́тельный. **2,** (shameful) позо́рный. —**opprobrium,** *n.* позо́р.

opt *v.i.* [*usu.* **opt for**] выбира́ть; остана́вливать свой вы́бор на.

optic *adj.* глазно́й; зри́тельный. —**optic nerve,** глазно́й/зри́тельный нерв.

optical *adj.* зри́тельный; опти́ческий. —**optical illusion,** опти́ческий обма́н; обма́н зре́ния.

optician *n.* о́птик.

optics *n.* о́птика.

optimism *n.* оптими́зм. —**optimist,** *n.* оптими́ст. —**optimistic,** *adj.* оптимисти́ческий. *I am optimistic,* я настро́ен оптимисти́чески.

optimum *adj.* наилу́чший; оптима́льный. —*n.* о́птимум.

option *n.* вы́бор.

optional *adj.* необяза́тельный; факультати́вный.

optometrist *n.* о́птик.

opulent *adj.* пы́шный; роско́шный; бога́тый. —**opulence,** *n.* пы́шность.

opus *n.* о́пус.

or *conj.* **1,** (introducing an alternative) и́ли: *yes or no,* да и́ли нет. *Tea or coffee?,* чай и́ли ко́фе? **2,** (otherwise; lest) а то; ина́че. *Careful, or you'll fall,* осторо́жно, а то упадёте. —**or so,** о́коло: *an hour or so,* о́коло ча́са. *In a month or so,* приблизи́тельно че́рез ме́сяц. —**or what?,** что: *Is he joking, or what?,* он, что, шу́тит?; *is he crazy, or what?,* он, что, с ума́ сошёл?

oracle *n.* ора́кул.

oral *adj.* **1,** (spoken) у́стный. **2,** (of the mouth) ротово́й.

orally *adv.* **1,** (verbally) у́стно. **2,** (by mouth) в рот.

orange *n.* апельси́н. —*adj.* **1,** (of or pert. to oranges) апельси́новый; апельси́нный. **2,** (color) ора́нжевый. —**orange blossom,** помера́нцевый цвет. —**orange grove,** апельси́новая ро́ща. —**orange juice,** апельси́новый сок. —**orange tree,** апельси́новое де́рево.

orangutan *also,* **orangoutang** *n.* орангута́нг.

orate *v.i.* ора́торствовать; разглаго́льствовать.

oration *n.* речь.

orator *n.* ора́тор. —**oratorical,** *adj.* ора́торский.

oratorio *n.* орато́рия.

oratory *n.* **1,** (art of public speaking) ора́торское иску́сство. **2,** (eloquence) красноре́чие.

orb *n.* шар; сфе́ра.

orbit *n.* орби́та. *Be in orbit,* быть на орби́те. *Go into orbit,* вы́йти на орби́ту. *Put in orbit,* вы́вести на орби́ту. —*v.t. & i.* дви́гаться по орби́те (вокру́г). *Orbiting station,* орбита́льная ста́нция. —**orbital,** *adj.* орбита́льный.

orchard *n.* фрукто́вый сад. *Apple orchard,* я́блоневый сад.

orchestra *n.* **1,** (large group of musicians) орке́стр. **2,** (main floor of a theater) парте́р. —**orchestral,** *adj.* оркестро́вый.

orchestrate *v.t.* оркестрова́ть; инструментова́ть. —**orchestration,** *n.* оркестро́вка; инструменто́вка.

orchid *n.* орхиде́я.

ordain *v.t.* **1,** (decree) предпи́сывать. **2,** (predestine) предопределя́ть. **3,** (confer holy orders upon) посвяща́ть (в духо́вный сан).

ordeal *n.* тяжёлое испыта́ние; мыта́рство; иску́с.

order *n.* **1,** (sequence; methodical arrangement; proper condition) поря́док: *in alphabetical order,* в алфави́тном поря́дке. *Everything is in order,* всё в поря́дке. *Put one's affairs in order,* приводи́ть свои́ дела́ в поря́док. **2,** (command) прика́з; распоряже́ние. *The order to attack,* прика́з наступа́ть *or* о на-

ступле́нии. *By order of...,* по прика́зу (+ *gen.*). *Doctor's orders,* предписа́ния врача́. *Follow orders,* выполня́ть приказа́ния. *I am under orders to...,* мне прика́зано (+ *inf.*). **3,** (direction to buy or sell) зака́з: *rush order,* сро́чный зака́з. *Fill an order,* выполня́ть зака́з. *Take someone's order* (*in a restaurant*), принима́ть зака́з. **4,** *law* распоряже́ние; о́рдер. *Court order,* суде́бное реше́ние. *Issue an order for someone's arrest,* вы́дать о́рдер на че́й-нибудь аре́ст. **5,** (restaurant portion) по́рция: *two orders of peas,* две по́рции горо́ха. **6,** (scientific classification) отря́д: *The order Piciformes includes the woodpecker,* к отря́ду *Piciformes* отно́сятся дя́тлы. **7,** (medal) о́рден: *the Order of Lenin,* о́рден Ле́нина. **8,** (regime) поря́док; строй. *The old order,* ста́рый поря́док. **9,** *mil.* поря́док; строй. *Order of battle,* боево́й поря́док. **10,** (society; brotherhood) о́рден: *monastic order,* мона́шеский о́рден. —*v.t.* **1,** (command; direct) прика́зывать: *order the driver to stop,* приказа́ть води́телю останови́ться. *The doctor ordered me to rest,* врач веле́л мне отдыха́ть. **2,** (issue an order for) отдава́ть распоряже́ние о; прика́зывать (+ *inf.*); распоряжа́ться (+ *inf.*): *order the arrest of,* отда́ть распоряже́ние об аре́сте (+ *gen.*); приказа́ть *or* распоряди́ться арестова́ть (+ *acc.*). **3,** (place an order for) зака́зывать: *order dinner,* зака́зывать обе́д. *Order something by mail,* вы́писать что́-нибудь по по́чте. *Order something from the jeweler/ drugstore,* заказа́ть что́-нибудь ювели́ру/ в апте́ке/. **4,** (arrange; manage) устра́ивать: *order one's life,* устра́ивать жизнь. —*v.i.* зака́зывать: *Are you ready to order?,* бу́дете зака́зывать? —**call to order,** призыва́ть к поря́дку. —**in order that/to,** для того́, что́бы. —**in short order,** в спе́шном поря́дке. —**on order,** зака́зан(ный). —**on the order of, 1,** (resembling) вро́де (+ *gen.*); наподо́бие (+ *gen.*). **2,** (approximately) поря́дка (+ *gen.*). —**order about,** кома́ндовать над; помыка́ть (+ *instr.*). —**order arms!,** *mil.* к ноге́! —**order out,** показа́ть на дверь; вы́ставить за дверь. *Order a pupil out of the room,* выгоня́ть ученика́ из кла́сса. —**out of order,** не в поря́дке. *The elevator is out of order,* лифт не рабо́тает. —**to order,** на зака́з: *made to order,* сде́ланный на зака́з. *She has all her clothes made to order,* она́ всегда́ шьёт себе́ пла́тья на зака́з.

orderly *adj.* **1,** (tidy) аккура́тный. **2,** (without disruption) организо́ванный; упоря́доченный. *Orderly demonstration,* ми́рная демонстра́ция. —*n.* **1,** *mil.* ордина́рец. **2,** (hospital aide) санита́р.

ordinal number поря́дковое числи́тельное.

ordinance *n.* ука́з; постановле́ние.

ordinarily *adv.* обы́чно.

ordinary *adj.* **1,** (not exceptional) обы́чный; обыкнове́нный: *an ordinary house,* обыкнове́нный дом; *an ordinary occurrence,* обы́чное явле́ние. **2,** (average) рядово́й; обыкнове́нный: *ordinary citizen,* рядово́й граждани́н; *ordinary people,* обыкнове́нные лю́ди. **3,** (relatively poor or inferior) заура́дный; посре́дственный. —**out of the ordinary,** из ря́да вон выходя́щий.

ordinate *n., math.* ордина́та.

ordination *n.* посвяще́ние (в духо́вный сан); рукоположе́ние.

ordnance *n.* артилле́рия. *Piece of ordnance,* артиллери́йское ору́дие.

ore *n.* руда́: *iron ore,* желе́зная руда́.

organ *n.* **1,** (musical instrument) орга́н. *Barrel organ,* шарма́нка. **2,** (part of the body) о́рган: *organs of speech,* о́рганы ре́чи. **3,** (organization; body) о́рган. **4,** (publication) о́рган: *press organ,* о́рган печа́ти. *House organ,* многотира́жка. —*adj.* орга́нный: *organ music,* орга́нная му́зыка.

organdy *n.* то́нкая кисея́.

organ grinder шарма́нщик.

organic *adj.* органи́ческий.

organism *n.* органи́зм.

organist *n.* органи́ст.

organization *n.* организа́ция.

organizational *adj.* организацио́нный; организа́торский. *Organizational ability,* организа́торские спо́собности.

organize *v.t.* устра́ивать; организова́ть. —*v.i.* организова́ться. —**organizer,** *n.* организа́тор.

orgasm *n.* орга́зм.

orgy *n.* о́ргия; разгу́л. —**orgiastic,** *adj.* разгу́льный.

orient *v.t.* ориенти́ровать. *Orient oneself; become oriented,* ориенти́роваться.

Orient *n.* Восто́к.

Oriental *adj.* восто́чный. —*n.* азиа́т. —**Orientalist,** *n.* востокове́д.

orientation *n.* **1,** (bearings) ориента́ция; ориенти́ровка. **2,** (leaning) ориента́ция.

orifice *n.* отве́рстие.

origin *n.* **1,** (beginning; original source) происхожде́ние; возникнове́ние. *A word of Latin origin,* сло́во лати́нского происхожде́ния. *Have its origin in,* вести́ своё нача́ло от. **2,** (ancestry) происхожде́ние: *of Russian origin,* ру́сского происхожде́ния; ру́сский по происхожде́нию.

original *adj.* **1,** (first; earliest) первонача́льный: *lose its original shape,* теря́ть первонача́льную фо́рму. *The original inhabitants of Australia,* коренны́е жи́тели Австра́лии. **2,** (not imitated; creative) оригина́льный; самобы́тный. **3,** (being that from which a copy or translation is made) по́длинный. —*n.* по́длинник; оригина́л: *read in the original,* чита́ть в по́длиннике *or* в оригина́ле. —**original sin,** перворо́дный грех.

originality *n.* оригина́льность; самобы́тность.

originally *adv.* **1,** (at first) снача́ла; первонача́льно. **2,** (by origin) ро́дом.

originate *v.t.* создава́ть; порожда́ть. —*v.i.* зарожда́ться; исходи́ть; брать нача́ло. *The idea originated with him,* э́та мысль зароди́лась у него́. *The fire originated in the basement,* пожа́р начался́ *or* возни́к в подва́ле. —**originator,** *n.* а́втор; созда́тель.

oriole *n.* **1,** (European bird) и́волга. **2,** (American bird) трупиа́л.

Orion *n.* Орио́н.

ornament *n.* украше́ние. —*v.t.* украша́ть. —**ornamental,** *adj.* декорати́вный. —**ornamentation,** *n.* украше́ние.

ornate *adj.* вы́чурный.

ornery *adj., colloq.* злой; упря́мый; сварли́вый.

ornithology *n.* орнитоло́гия. —**ornithological,** *adj.* орнитологи́ческий. —**ornithologist,** *n.* орнито́лог.

orotund *adj.* **1,** (sonorous) зву́чный. **2,** (pompous) напы́щенный.

orphan *n.* сирота́. —*adj.* **1,** (for orphans) сиро́тский. **2,** (orphaned) осироте́лый. —*v.t.* де́лать сирото́й. *Be orphaned,* (о)сироте́ть.

orphanage *n.* сиро́тский дом; сиро́тский прию́т.

orphanhood *n.* сиро́тство.

orthodontia *n.* ортодонти́я.

orthodox *adj.* **1,** (pert. to the Orthodox Church) правосла́вный. **2,** (adhering to traditional practice) правове́рный; ортодокса́льный. *Orthodox Jew,* ортодокса́льный евре́й. —**Orthodox Church,** правосла́вная це́рковь.

orthodoxy *n.* **1,** (religion of the Orthodox Church) правосла́вие. **2,** (conformity) ортодо́ксия.

orthography *n.* орфогра́фия; правописа́ние. —**orthographic,** *adj.* орфографи́ческий.

orthopedic *also,* **orthopaedic** *adj.* ортопеди́ческий. —**orthopedics,** *n.* ортопе́дия. —**orthopedist,** *n.* ортопе́д.

ortolan *n.* садо́вая овся́нка.

oryx *n.* сернобы́к.

oscillate *v.i.* кача́ться; колеба́ться. —**oscillation,** *n.* кача́ние; колеба́ние. —**oscillator,** *n.* генера́тор; осцилля́тор; вибра́тор.

oscillograph *n.* осцилло́граф.

oscilloscope *n.* осциллоско́п.

osier *n.* и́ва.

osmium *n.* о́смий.

osmosis *n.* о́смос.

osprey *n.* скопа́.

osseous *adj.* ко́стный; кости́стый.

ossify *v.i.* костене́ть. —**ossification,** *n.* окостене́ние. —**ossified,** *adj.* окостене́лый; окостене́вший.

ostensible *adj.* **1,** (apparent) ви́димый. **2,** (professed) официа́льный. —**ostensibly,** *adv.* я́кобы.

ostentation *n.* показна́я ро́скошь; пара́дность; мишура́. —**ostentatious,** *adj.* показно́й; мишу́рный.

osteology *n.* остеоло́гия. —**osteologist,** *n.* остео́лог.

osteoporosis *n.* остеопоро́з.

ostracize *v.t.* изгоня́ть. —**ostracism,** *n.* изгна́ние; остраки́зм.

ostrich *n.* стра́ус. —*adj.* стра́усовый: *ostrich egg/feather,* стра́усовое яйцо́/перо́.

other *adj.* **1,** *preceded by the,* A, (being the remaining one of two) друго́й: *the other hand/room/car,* друга́я рука́/ко́мната/маши́на. B, (being the remaining ones of many) остальны́е: *the other children,* остальны́е де́ти. **2,** (different) друго́й; ино́й: *in other countries,* в други́х стра́нах. *In other words,* други́ми слова́ми; ина́че говоря́. *Somehow or other,* так и́ли ина́че. *For some reason or other,* по той и́ли ино́й причи́не. **3,** (additional) *rendered by* ещё: *Have you any other* *brothers?*, у вас есть ещё бра́тья? *How many other people were there?*, ско́лько ещё люде́й бы́ло там? **4,** (opposite; reverse) обра́тный; друго́й. *In the other direction*, в обра́тную сто́рону. *On the other side of the river*, по ту сто́рону (*or* на друго́й стороне́) реки́. —*n. & pron.* друго́й; остальны́е. *One left, the other stayed*, оди́н ушёл, друго́й оста́лся. *Some prefer beer, others wine*, одни́ предпочита́ют пиво́, други́е вино́. *One is connected to the other*, одно́ с други́м свя́зано. *What happened to the others?*, что случи́лось с остальны́ми? *Each accused the other of...*, ка́ждый обвиня́л друго́го в (+ *prepl.*). *Have you any others?*, у вас есть ещё каки́е-нибудь? —**each other,** *see* **each.** —**none other than,** не кто ино́й, как. —**other people's** (+ *noun*), чужо́й. —**other than,** кро́ме. —**other things being equal,** при про́чих ра́вных усло́виях. —**some other time,** ка́к-нибудь в друго́й раз. —**the other day,** на днях. —**the other way round,** как раз наоборо́т.

otherwise *adv.* **1,** (differently) ина́че; по-друго́му. *Sergey thought otherwise*, Серге́й ду́мал ина́че. *The facts speak otherwise*, фа́кты говоря́т о друго́м. *Otherwise known as...*, ина́че называ́емый... *Unless otherwise indicated*, е́сли нет други́х указа́ний. **2,** (if not) ина́че; а то; в проти́вном слу́чае. *Otherwise, I won't know*, ина́че, я не бу́ду знать. **3,** (in all other respects) в остально́м.

otter *n.* вы́дра. *Sea otter*, морска́я вы́дра; кала́н.

Ottoman *adj.* оттома́нский. *The Ottoman Empire*, Оттома́нская импе́рия.

ottoman *n.* **1,** (divan) оттома́нка; тахта́. **2,** (footstool) скаме́йка для ног.

ouch *interj.* ай!; ой!

ought *v.aux.* *Generally rendered by* до́лжен, сле́довать, *or the subjunctive mood: He ought to be grateful to you*, он до́лжен быть вам благода́рен. *She ought to be here at any moment*, она́ должна́ прийти́ в любо́й моме́нт. *You ought to see a doctor*, вам сле́дует (*or* вам бы) пойти́ к врачу́.

ounce *n.* **1,** (unit of weight) у́нция. **2,** (small amount; bit) ка́пля; чу́точка.

our *poss. adj.* наш: *our house*, наш дом; *our street*, на́ша у́лица; *our friends*, на́ши друзья́.

ours *poss. pron.* наш. *A friend of ours*, оди́н наш друг; оди́н из на́ших друзе́й. *Their room is on the first floor and ours is on the second*, их ко́мната на пе́рвом этаже́, а на́ша — на второ́м.

ourselves *pers. pron.* **1,** *used for emphasis*, (мы) са́ми: *We don't know ourselves*, мы са́ми не зна́ем. **2,** *used reflexively*, себя́: *We underestimated ourselves*, мы недооцени́ли себя́. —**by ourselves, 1,** (alone) одни́. **2,** (without help) са́ми.

oust *v.t.* вытесня́ть; выгоня́ть. —**ouster,** *n.* вытесне́ние.

out *adj.* **1,** (not in; away): *He is out*, он вы́шел; его́ нет. *Out to lunch*, ушёл обе́дать. **2,** (not turned on) вы́ключен: *The light is out*, свет вы́ключен. **3,** (visible in the sky): *The sun is out*, вы́шло со́лнце; *the stars are out*, появи́лись звёзды. **4,** (extended; outstretched) протя́нутый: *a beggar with his hand out*, ни́щий с протя́нутой руко́й. **5,** (known) раскры́т. *The secret is out*, секре́т раскры́т; секре́т стал всем изве́стен. **6,** (checked out, as of a library book) на рука́х. **7,** (over; ended): *before the week is out*, до конца́ неде́ли. **8,** (unconscious) без созна́ния. **9,** (not to be considered) исключён: *London is out*, Ло́ндон исключён. **10,** (no longer in style): *Narrow ties are out*, у́зкие га́лстуки вы́шли из мо́ды. **11,** *colloq.* (having lost) в про́игрыше. *I am out 100 dollars*, у меня́ про́игрыш в сто до́лларов. —*adv.* **1,** (outside) на дворе́: *It's hot out*, на дворе́ жа́рко. **2,** (to the outside) нару́жу: *The news leaked out*, но́вость вы́шла нару́жу. ♦*Usu. rendered by a prefixed verb: go out*, выходи́ть; *take out*, вынима́ть; *throw out*, выбра́сывать; *leave out*, пропуска́ть; *start out*, отправля́ться; *break out*, вспы́хивать; *fill out*, заполня́ть. —*prep.* за: *throw/drop/hang something out the window*, вы́бросить/урони́ть/выве́шивать что́-нибудь за окно́. *Look out the window*, смотре́ть *or* выгля́дывать в окно́ *or* из окна́. *Walk out the door*, выходи́ть за дверь. *The smell of ... out the window*, за́пах (+ *gen.*) за окно́м. —*interj.* вон! —**on the outs,** в ссо́ре; не в ладу́; в ко́нтрах. —**out for,** жа́ждущий (+ *gen.*): *He is out for blood/revenge*, он жа́ждет кро́ви/ме́сти. —**out of, 1,** (from within) из: *walk out of the room*, выходи́ть из ко́мнаты; *drink out of a glass*, пить из стака́на. **2,** (from) с (+ *gen.*): *get up out of one's chair*, встать со сту́ла. *Leap out of bed*, вскочи́ть *or* соскочи́ть с посте́ли. *Come in out of the rain/cold*, зайти́ в дом от дождя́/ от хо́лода/. **3,** (through) из: *lean out of the window*, высо́вываться из окна́. **4,** (beyond the limits of) за; вне: *out of town*, за́ городом; в отъе́зде. *Out of danger*, вне опа́сности. *Out of turn*, не в о́череди. *Pass out of sight*, скрыва́ться и́з виду. **5,** (from; made of) из: *made out of wood*, сде́ланный из де́рева. **6,** (from; as a result of) из: *out of curiosity*, из любопы́тства. *Out of necessity*, по необходи́мости. *Out of spite*, назло́; со зла. *The argument arose out of a misunderstanding*, спор возни́к из-за недоразуме́ния. **7,** (from among) из: *in 99 cases out of 100*, в девяно́сто девяти́ слу́чаях из ста. *One out of every 25*, ка́ждый два́дцать пя́тый. **8,** (not having) без: *out of work*, без рабо́ты. *We are out of gas*, у нас вы́шел *or* ко́нчился бензи́н. **9,** (not in a condition of) не в поря́дке; не в поря́дке; *out of step*, не в но́гу; *out of sorts*, не в ду́хе.

outage *n.* переры́в: *power outage*, переры́в в пода́че эне́ргии.

out-and-out *adj.* отъя́вленный: *an out-and-out liar*, отъя́вленный лгун. *Out-and-out lie*, я́вная ложь.

outargue *v.t.* переспо́рить.

outboard motor подвесно́й мото́р.

outbound *adj.* уходя́щий; отбыва́ющий.

outbreak *n.* вспы́шка. *Outbreak of violence*, вспы́шка *or* всплеск наси́лия. *Outbreak of war*, нача́ло *or* возникнове́ние войны́.

outbuilding *n.* надво́рная постро́йка.

outburst *n.* взрыв; вспы́шка.

outcast *n.* изгна́нник; па́рия; отве́рженный. —*adj.* отве́рженный.

outclass *v.t.* превосходи́ть; оставля́ть далеко́ позади́.

outcome *n.* исхо́д; результа́т. *Final outcome*, коне́чный результа́т.

outcry *n.* **1,** (shout) крик; вы́крик. **2,** (public protest) шум.

outdated *adj.* устаре́лый; устаре́вший.

outdistance *v.t.* обгоня́ть; перегоня́ть; опережа́ть.

outdo *v.t.* превосходи́ть. *He was not to be outdone*, он не оста́лся в долгу́. —**outdo oneself**, превосходи́ть (самого́) себя́.

outdoor *adj.* откры́тый: *outdoor swimming pool*, откры́тый бассе́йн. *Outdoor games*, подвижны́е и́гры.

outdoors *adv.* **1,** (location) на дворе́; на (откры́том) во́здухе. **2,** (motion) на у́лицу; нару́жу; на во́здух.

outdrink *v.t.* перепива́ть.

outer *adj.* **1,** (external) вне́шний; нару́жный: *outer covering*, вне́шняя/нару́жная оболо́чка. *Outer layer of the skin*, нару́жный слой ко́жи. *Outer garments*, ве́рхняя оде́жда. *Outer Mongolia*, Вне́шняя Монго́лия. **2,** (farther from the center) да́льний; кра́йний. *Outer limits*, кра́йние преде́лы. —**outer space**, ко́смос.

outermost *adj.* са́мый да́льний от середи́ны; кра́йний.

outfit *n.* **1,** (set of equipment) снаряже́ние. **2,** (set of clothing) наря́д. **3,** *colloq.* (group) гру́ппа; па́ртия; компа́ния. —*v.t.* снаряжа́ть; экипирова́ть.

outflank *v.t.* обходи́ть.

outflow *n.* истече́ние; уте́чка.

outfox *v.t.* перехитри́ть.

outgoing *adj.* **1,** (going out; leaving) уходя́щий; исходя́щий. **2,** (extroverted) общи́тельный; компане́йский.

outgrow *v.t.* **1,** (surpass in growth) перераста́ть. **2,** (grow too big to wear) выраста́ть из. **3,** (grow too old for) стать сли́шком больши́м для. **4,** (get rid of in the course of growing up) избавля́ться от; отде́лываться от.

outgrowth *n.* **1,** (excrescence) отро́сток; о́тпрыск. **2,** (consequence) проду́кт; результа́т.

outguess *v.t.* перехитри́ть.

outhouse *n.* отхо́жее ме́сто.

outing *n.* прогу́лка; похо́д; экску́рсия.

outlandish *adj.* дико́винный.

outlast *v.t.* **1,** (remain in existence longer than) пережива́ть. **2,** (overcome after a long struggle) переси́ливать.

outlaw *n.* банди́т; разбо́йник. —*v.t.* запреща́ть; объявля́ть вне зако́на.

outlay *n.* расхо́д; тра́та.

outlet *n.* **1,** (passage for letting something out) выходно́е *or* выпускно́е отве́рстие. *Outlet to the sea*, вы́ход к мо́рю. **2,** (means of release or expression) вы́ход; отду́шина. *Seek an outlet for*, иска́ть вы́ход (+ *dat.*). **3,** (electrical outlet) (штепсельная розетка. **4,** (commercial market) ры́нок.

outline *n.* **1,** (line forming the outer edge) очерта́ния; ко́нтур. **2,** (sketch) набро́сок; эски́з. **3,** (short summary) схе́ма. —*v.t.* **1,** (sketch) оче́рчивать. **2,** (de-

scribe in general terms) намеча́ть. —**in broad outline**, в о́бщих черта́х.

outlive *v.t.* пережива́ть.

outlook *n.* **1,** (prospect) ви́ды; перспекти́вы. **2,** (mental attitude) кругозо́р; воззре́ние.

outlying *adj.* окра́инный; перифери́йный. *Outlying areas*, окра́ина; перифери́я; места́.

outmoded *adj.* устаре́лый; устаре́вший.

outnumber *v.t.* превосходи́ть чи́сленностью *or* чи́сленно *or* по чи́сленности; чи́сленно преоблада́ть над. *We were outnumbered 5:1*, нас бы́ло ме́ньше в пять раз. *Blacks outnumber whites 3:1*, не́гров в три ра́за бо́льше, чем бе́лых.

out-of-date *adj.* устаре́лый.

out-of-the-way *adj.* отдалённый; захолу́стный.

out-of-town *adj.* иногоро́дный: *out-of-town guests*, иногоро́дные го́сти.

outpace *v.t.* опережа́ть; обгоня́ть.

outpatient *n.* амбулато́рный (*or* приходя́щий) больно́й.

outplay *v.t.* переи́грывать.

outpost *n.* **1,** *mil.* аванпо́ст; форпо́ст. **2,** (outlying settlement) форпо́ст; окра́ина.

outpouring *n.* излия́ние.

output *n.* проду́кция; вы́пуск; вы́работка.

outrage *n.* **1,** (vicious act) безобра́зие; бесчи́нство; надруга́тельство. *It's an outrage!*, (э́то) безобра́зие!; (э́то) возмути́тельно! **2,** (resentful anger) возмуще́ние; негодова́ние. —*v.t.* **1,** (offend) оскорбля́ть. **2,** (infuriate) возмуща́ть. *Be outraged*, возмуща́ться.

outrageous *adj.* **1,** (grossly offensive) возмути́тельный; вопию́щий. **2,** (exorbitant) непоме́рный: *outrageous demands*, непоме́рные тре́бования. *Outrageous prices*, бе́шеные це́ны.

outrageously *adv.* **1,** (in an outrageous manner) возмути́тельно. **2,** (terribly) ужа́сно: *outrageously expensive*, ужа́сно дорого́й.

outrank *v.t.* быть ста́рше по зва́нию, чем.

outrigger *n.* утле́гарь.

outright *adj.* по́лный: *an outright loss*, по́лная ги́бель. *Outright refusal*, прямо́й отка́з. *Outright grant*, безвозвра́тная ссу́да. —*adv.* **1,** (straight to one's face) (пря́мо) в лицо́. **2,** (on the spot) на ме́сте; напова́л.

outrun *v.t.* **1,** (run faster than) обгоня́ть; перегоня́ть; опережа́ть. **2,** (elude by running) убежа́ть от. **3,** (exceed) превыша́ть.

outsell *v.t.* продава́ться лу́чше чем.

outset *n.* нача́ло. *At the outset*, снача́ла. *From the outset*, с са́мого нача́ла.

outshine *v.t.* затмева́ть.

outside *adv.* **1,** (location) снару́жи; на у́лице; на дворе́. *Wait outside*, ждать снару́жи. *It's cold outside*, на у́лице *or* на дворе́ хо́лодно. **2,** (motion) нару́жу; на у́лицу. *Let's go outside*, пойдём на у́лицу; дава́йте вы́йдем на у́лицу. *Come in from outside*, войти́ с у́лицы. —*adj.* **1,** (external) нару́жный; вне́шний. *Outside wall*, нару́жная стена́. *Cut off from the outside world*, отре́зан от вне́шнего ми́ра. **2,** (coming from without) посторо́нний: *outside help*, посторо́нняя по́мощь. **3,** (remote; slight) небольшо́й: *an outside chance,* небольшо́й шанс; небольша́я вероя́тность. —*prep.* вне; за (+ *instr.*); за преде́лами (+ *gen.*). *Outside the city,* вне го́рода; за́ городом; в при́городе. *Outside the country,* за преде́лами страны́. *Outside the window,* за окно́м. *Wait outside the room/door,* ждать за две́рью. —*n.* нару́жная сторона́. *On the outside,* снару́жи. —*at the outside,* са́мое бо́льшее. —*outside of,* кро́ме.

outsider *n.* **1,** (one not part of a group) посторо́нний. **2,** *sports* (long shot) аутса́йдер.

outskirts *n.pl.* окра́ина: *on the city outskirts,* на окра́ине го́рода.

outsmart *v.t.* перехитри́ть. *Outsmart oneself,* перехитри́ть самого́ себя́.

outspoken *adj.* прямо́й; открове́нный.

outspread *adj.* распростёртый.

outstanding *adj.* **1,** (distinguished; extraordinary) выдаю́щийся: *outstanding writer,* выдаю́щийся писа́тель. *Outstanding achievement,* выдаю́щееся достиже́ние. **2,** (unsettled, as of an issue) спо́рный. **3,** (unpaid) неупла́ченный.

outstretched *adj.* распростёртый.

outstrip *v.t.* обгоня́ть; опережа́ть.

outtalk *v.t.* переговори́ть.

outvote *v.t. We were outvoted,* мы оказа́лись в меньшинстве́.

outward *adj.* вне́шний; нару́жный. —*adv.* [also, **outwards**] нару́жу. —**outwardly,** *adv.* вне́шне; снару́жи; на вид.

outwear *v.t.* изна́шивать.

outweigh *v.t.* переве́шивать: *outweigh all other considerations,* переве́шивать все остальны́е соображе́ния.

outwit *v.t.* перехитри́ть.

ouzel *n.* **1,** (water ouzel) оля́пка. **2,** (ring ouzel) белозо́бый дрозд.

oval *adj.* ова́льный. —*n.* ова́л.

ovarian *adj. Ovarian cancer,* рак яи́чников.

ovary *n.* **1,** *anat.* яи́чник. **2,** *bot.* за́вязь.

ovate *adj.* яйцеви́дный.

ovation *n.* ова́ция. *Give an ovation to,* устро́ить ова́цию (+ *dat.*).

oven *n.* духо́вка; печь.

over *prep.* **1,** (above) над: *a roof over one's head,* кры́ша над голово́й; *fly over the city,* пролете́ть над го́родом; *lean over the cradle,* наклоня́ться над колыбе́лью. *Appear over the horizon,* показа́ться из-за горизо́нта. *It was hard to hear over the noise,* тру́дно бы́ло слы́шать из-за шу́ма. **2,** (higher than) вы́ше: *The water was over our heads,* вода́ была́ вы́ше головы́. **3,** (above and across) че́рез: *jump over the fence,* перепры́гнуть че́рез забо́р; *lean over the railing,* перегиба́ться че́рез пери́ла; *glance over one's shoulder,* посмотре́ть *or* загляну́ть че́рез плечо́; *look over the edge,* загляну́ть че́рез край. **4,** (down from the edge of) с (+ *gen.*): *fall over a cliff,* упа́сть со скалы́; сорва́ться с обры́ва *or* со скалы́. *Push a rock over a cliff,* столкну́ть ка́мень с обры́ва. *Tumble over an embankment,* свали́ться под отко́с.

5, (throughout) на; по: *over a wide area,* на большо́й террито́рии. *Over an area of...,* на пло́щади (+ *gen.*). *Over the entire length of the road,* на всём протяже́нии (*or* по всей протяжённости) доро́ги. *Scattered over a number of countries,* разбро́саны по ря́ду стран. **6,** (along the surface of) по: *run one's fingers over the keyboard,* пробежа́ть па́льцами по клавиату́ре. **7,** (so as to cover) пове́рх; на. *A patch over one's eye,* повя́зка на глазу́. *Wear a sweater over one's shirt,* наде́ть сви́тер пове́рх руба́шки. *Pull the blanket over oneself,* натяну́ть на себя́ одея́ло. *Pull one's hat down over one's eyes,* надви́нуть шля́пу на глаза́. **8,** (indicating violent contact from above) по; о: *beat someone over the head,* бить кого́-нибудь по голове́; *trip over the rug,* споткну́ться о ковёр. **9,** (more than) бо́льше; свы́ше: *over an hour,* бо́льше ча́са; *over 2,000 dollars,* свы́ше двух ты́сяч до́лларов. *People over forty,* те, кому́ за со́рок. **10,** (on; through the medium of) по: *over the radio,* по ра́дио. **11,** (about) о: *argue over something,* спо́рить о чём-нибудь. *Quarrel over nothing,* ссо́риться из-за ничего́. *Fight over a girl,* дра́ться из-за де́вушки. *The argument over whether to raise taxes,* спор вокру́г вопро́са о повыше́нии нало́гов. **12,** (during; in the course of) за; с; в тече́ние: *over the past six months,* за после́дние шесть ме́сяцев; *over time,* со вре́менем; *over the years,* с года́ми; *over the next ten years,* в тече́ние ближа́йших десяти́ лет. **13,** (while engaged in or partaking of) за (+ *instr.*): *discuss the question over dinner,* обсужда́ть вопро́с за обе́дом. **14,** (compared to) по сравне́нию с: *a threefold increase over last year,* трёхкра́тное увеличе́ние по сравне́нию с про́шлым го́дом. **15,** *with certain abstract nouns,* над; пе́ред. *Victory over the enemy,* побе́да над враго́м. *Advantage over one's rival,* преиму́щество пе́ред сопе́рником. *Give someone preference over...,* отдава́ть кому́-нибудь предпочте́ние пе́ред. —*adv. Usu. rendered by a prefixed verb.* **1,** (once more; again) пере-: *do over,* переде́лывать. *Start life over,* начина́ть жизнь за́ново. **2,** (across; transferring) пере-: *cross over,* переходи́ть; *hand over,* передава́ть. *Walk over to the window,* переходи́ть к окну́. *Come over and see us,* зайди́те к нам. **3,** (inverting; overturning) пере-: *turn over,* перевёртывать(ся); *roll over,* перева́ливаться. *Knock over,* опроки́дывать. **4,** (thoroughly; through) об-; про-: *talk over,* обсужда́ть; *think over,* обду́мывать; проду́мывать; *read over,* прочита́ть. **5,** (cursorily) про-: *look/glance over,* просма́тривать. **6,** *after numbers,* бо́льше; вы́ше. *Children five and over,* де́ти от пяти́ лет и ста́рше. —*adj.* око́нченный: *The meeting is over,* собра́ние око́нчено. *The war is over,* война́ ко́нчилась *or* око́нчилась. —**all over, 1,** (everywhere) всю́ду. *All over the world,* по всему́ ми́ру. *From all over the world,* со всех концо́в ми́ра. *I ache all over,* у меня́ всё те́ло боли́т. **2,** (finished) ко́нчен: *It's all over,* всё ко́нчено. *It's all over between them,* ме́жду ни́ми всё ко́нчено. **3,** *often fol. by* **again** (again completely) за́ново. *Start all over (again),* начина́ть всё снача́ла.

—**over again,** снача́ла; сно́ва. —**over against,** про́тив. —**over and above,** сверх того́, что. —**over and over,** сно́ва и сно́ва. —**over here,** здесь; тут. —**over there,** вон там.

overabundance n. избы́ток. —**overabundant,** adj. избы́точный.

overact v.i. переи́грывать; шаржи́ровать.

overage[1] (o-ve-rij) n. избы́ток; изли́шек.

overage[2] (o-ver-ayj) adj. вы́шедший из во́зраста: He is overage, он вы́шел из во́зраста.

overall adj. о́бщий: overall length, о́бщая длина́. Overall impression, о́бщее впечатле́ние.

overalls n.pl. рабо́чий хала́т; комбинезо́н; спецоде́жда; ро́ба.

overbearing adj. вла́стный.

overblown adj. разду́тый.

overboard adv. за́ борт; за бо́ртом. Toss overboard, вы́бросить за́ борт. Jump overboard, бро́ситься за́ борт. —**go overboard,** colloq. перегну́ть па́лку. —**man overboard!,** челове́к за бо́ртом! —**wash overboard,** смыва́ть (impers.): He was washed overboard, его́ смы́ло за́ борт; его́ смы́ло волно́й (с су́дна).

overburden v.t. перегружа́ть; переобременя́ть.

overcast adj. о́блачный; хму́рый; па́смурный. The sky is/became overcast, не́бо покры́лось or затяну́лось or обложи́ло ту́чами.

overcharge v.t. **1,** (charge too high a price) брать ли́шнее с. **2,** (overload, as a battery) перезаряжа́ть. —v.i. брать ли́шнее.

overcoat n. пальто́.

overcome v.t. **1,** (surmount; get over) преодолева́ть. Overcome difficulties, преодоле́ть тру́дности. Overcome one's shyness, преодоле́ть ро́бость. **2,** (defeat) одолева́ть; поборо́ть. **3,** (fell): They were overcome by smoke, они́ потеря́ли созна́ние от ды́ма. **4,** (seize, as of an emotion) охва́тывать; одолева́ть. Overcome with emotion, охва́чен волне́нием.

overconfident adj. чрезме́рно уве́ренный. —**overconfidence,** n. чрезме́рная уве́ренность.

overcook v.t. перева́ривать; пережа́ривать.

overcritical adj. приди́рчивый.

overcrowd v.t. переполня́ть. —**overcrowded,** adj. те́сный; перепо́лненный; ску́ченный. —**overcrowding,** n. теснота́; переполне́ние; ску́ченность.

overdo v.t. **1,** (carry too far) утри́ровать. **2,** = **overcook.** —**overdo it, 1,** (overexert oneself) переутомля́ться. **2,** (go too far) переба́рщивать; зарыва́ться; перестара́ться; переса́ливать.

overdone adj. **1,** (done to excess) утри́рованный. **2,** (overcooked) пережа́ренный.

overdose n. сли́шком больша́я до́за; чрезме́рная до́за.

overdraft n. превыше́ние креди́та (в ба́нке).

overdraw v.t. превыша́ть оста́ток (счёта в ба́нке).

overdress v.t. одева́ть сли́шком наря́дно.

overdue adj. **1,** comm. просро́ченный. **2,** (late): The train is overdue, по́езд опа́здывает or запа́здывает. These changes are long overdue, э́ти переме́ны сле́довало провести́ давно́.

overeat v.i. перееда́ть; объеда́ться.

overemphasize v.t. преувели́чивать.

overestimate v.t. переоце́нивать. —**overestimation,** n. переоце́нка.

overexert v.t. перенапряга́ть. —**overexertion,** n. перенапряже́ние.

overexpenditure n. перерасхо́д.

overexpose v.t., photog. переде́рживать. —**overexposure,** n., photog. переде́ржка.

overfeed v.t. перека́рмливать; зака́рмливать.

overfill v.t. переполня́ть.

overflow v.i. ли́ться че́рез край; перелива́ться (че́рез край). The bathtub overflowed, ва́нна перепо́лнилась. —v.t. перелива́ться че́рез. The river overflowed its banks, река́ вы́шла из берего́в. —n. **1,** (overflowing) разли́в. **2,** (that which overflows) изли́шек воды́. —adj. An overflow crowd, по́лный зал. —**filled to overflowing,** перепо́лненный.

overfulfill also, **overfulfil** v.t. перевыполня́ть. —**overfulfillment,** n. перевыполне́ние.

overgrown adj. **1,** (covered, as with vegetation) заро́сший: The field is overgrown with weeds, по́ле заросло́ со́рной траво́й. **2,** (grown excessively) переро́сший.

overhand adj. & adv., sports све́рху.

overhang v.t. нависа́ть над; висе́ть над.

overhaul v.t. **1,** (examine for possible revision) пересма́тривать. **2,** (renovate) ремонти́ровать. **3,** (overtake) догоня́ть. —n. восстанови́тельный ремо́нт.

overhead adv. наверху́; над голово́й. Directly overhead, над са́мой голово́й. —adj. **1,** (elevated) возду́шный; надзе́мный. **2,** (suspended) подвесно́й. **3,** comm. (of costs) накладны́е. —n. накладны́е расхо́ды.

overhear v.t. подслу́шать; услы́шать.

overheat v.t. перегрева́ть. —v.i. перегрева́ться.

overindulge v.t. балова́ть; потво́рствовать. —v.i. перееда́ть; объеда́ться.

overindulgence n. **1,** (excessive leniency) баловство́. **2,** (immoderation) неуме́ренность.

overindulgent adj. **1,** (too lenient) сли́шком снисходи́тельный. **2,** (immoderate) неуме́ренный.

overjoyed adj. вне себя́ от ра́дости.

overkill n. многокра́тное уничтоже́ние.

overland adj. сухопу́тный; назе́мный. —adv. по су́ше; на су́ше.

overlap v.i. части́чно совпада́ть.

overlay v.t. **1,** (place over) накла́дывать. **2,** (coat; cover) устила́ть. —n. покры́шка.

overload v.t. перегружа́ть. —n. перегру́зка.

overlong adj. растя́нутый.

overlook v.t. **1,** (fail to notice) просмотре́ть. **2,** (lose sight of) упуска́ть и́з виду. **3,** (ignore) смотре́ть сквозь па́льцы на. **4,** (afford a view of) выходи́ть в or на. **5,** (rise above) возвыша́ться над.

overly adv. чрезме́рно; сли́шком.

overnight adv. **1,** (for the night) на́ ночь: stay overnight, оста́ться на́ ночь. **2,** (very quickly; suddenly) момента́льно. —adj. **1,** (lasting or staying through the night): overnight stop, ночле́г. Overnight guests, го́сти, остаю́щиеся на́ ночь. **2,** (very rapid; instant) momentа́льный.

overpass *n.* эстакáда.

overpay *v.t.* переплáчивать. *He is overpaid,* ему́ переплáчивают. —**overpayment,** *n.* переплáта.

overplay *v.t.* **1,** (overact) переи́грывать. **2,** (exaggerate) преувели́чивать. —**overplay one's hand,** перестарáться; зайти́ сли́шком далеко́.

overpopulate *v.t.* перенаселя́ть. —**overpopulated,** *adj.* перенаселённый. —**overpopulation,** *n.* перенаселе́ние; перенаселённость.

overpower *v.t.* одолевáть; переси́ливать. —**overpowering,** *adj.* подавля́ющий; неотрази́мый.

overproduction *n.* перепроизво́дство.

overrate *v.t.* переоце́нивать.

override *v.t.* **1,** (disregard; wave aside) отмáхиваться от. **2,** (nullify, as a Presidential veto) аннули́ровать; опроки́дывать.

overriding *adj.* важне́йший; реша́ющий; первостепе́нный.

overripe *adj.* перезре́лый.

overrule *v.t.* **1,** (set aside) отменя́ть; аннули́ровать. **2,** (disallow) отклоня́ть; отвергáть.

overrun *v.t.* **1,** (invade and conquer) завоёвывать: *overrun a country,* завоевáть страну́. *Overrun the enemy's defenses,* прорвáть оборо́ну проти́вника. **2,** (swarm over) наводня́ть. *Be overrun with mice,* кише́ть мышáми. —*n.* превыше́ние: *cost overrun,* превыше́ние сто́имости.

overseas *adj.* замо́рский; заграни́чный. —*adv.* **1,** (location) за мо́рем; за грани́цей. **2,** (motion) за мо́ре; за грани́цу. —**overseas cap,** *mil.* пило́тка.

oversee *v.t.* надзирáть за; наблюдáть за. —**overseer,** *n.* надзирáтель; надсмо́трщик.

overshadow *v.t.* затмевáть; заслоня́ть.

overshoe *n.* галóша.

overshoot *v.t. Overshoot one's target; overshoot a landing field,* давáть перелёт.

oversight *n.* **1,** (failure to notice something) недосмо́тр; просмо́тр; упуще́ние. **2,** (supervision) надзо́р.

oversimplify *v.t.* упрощáть. —**oversimplification,** *n.* упрощён(че)ство.

oversize *adj.* бо́льше обы́чного разме́ра. *Also,* **oversized.**

oversleep *v.i.* просыпáть.

overstaff *v.t. The agency is overstaffed,* в учрежде́нии разду́тые штáты.

overstate *v.t.* **1,** (exaggerate) преувели́чивать. **2,** (inflate, as figures) завышáть. —**overstatement,** *n.* преувеличе́ние.

overstay *v.t., in* **overstay one's welcome,** загости́ться.

overstep *v.t.* переступáть: *overstep the bounds of propriety,* переступи́ть грани́цы прили́чия. *Overstep the time limit, chess* просро́чить вре́мя.

oversupply *n.* избы́ток.

overt *adj.* откры́тый; неприкры́тый; я́вный.

overtake *v.t.* **1,** (catch up with) догоня́ть. **2,** (pass after catching up with) обгоня́ть. **3,** (befall) постигáть.

overtax *v.t.* **1,** (tax too heavily) обременя́ть сли́шком

высо́кими налóгами. **2,** (overexert) перенапрягáть; надрывáть.

overthrow *v.t.* свергáть. —*n.* сверже́ние.

overtime *n.* **1,** (extra time worked) сверхуро́чное вре́мя. **2,** (extra work) сверхуро́чная рабо́та; перерабо́тка. **3,** (payment for same) сверхуро́чные. **4,** *sports* дополни́тельное вре́мя. —*adj.* сверхуро́чный. —*adv.* сверхуро́чно: *work overtime,* рабо́тать сверхуро́чно.

overtone *n.* **1,** *music* оберто́н. **2,** *usu. pl.* (implications) скры́тые намёки.

overture *n.* **1,** *music* увертю́ра. **2,** *usu. pl.* (offer to negotiate) предложе́ние: *peace overtures,* ми́рные предложе́ния. **3,** *usu. pl.* (flirtatious advances) заи́грывания; ухáживания.

overturn *v.t.* опроки́дывать. —*v.i.* опроки́дываться; перевёртываться.

overused *adj.* затáсканный.

overview *n.* обзо́р.

overweening *adj.* **1,** (arrogant) высокоме́рный. **2,** (excessive) чрезме́рный.

overweight *adj.* ве́сящий бо́льше (*or* вы́ше) поло́женного ве́са. *I am ten pounds overweight,* я ве́шу на де́сять фу́нтов бо́льше/вы́ше поло́женного.

overwhelm *v.t.* **1,** (overpower; crush) разбивáть; (раз)громи́ть; сокрушáть. **2,** (swamp) завáливать: *overwhelmed with work,* завáлен рабо́той. **3,** (overcome, as with emotion) охвáтывать. *Overwhelmed with grief,* уби́тый го́рем.

overwhelming *adj.* подавля́ющий. *Overwhelming majority,* подавля́ющее большинство́. *Overwhelming victory,* реши́тельная побе́да. *Against overwhelming odds,* про́тив значи́тельно превосходя́щих сил.

overwind *v.t.* перевёртывать (*pfv.* переверте́ть).

overwork *v.t.* переутомля́ть. —*v.i.* переутомля́ться; перерабáтывать. —*n.* переутомле́ние.

oviduct *n.* яйцево́д.

oviparous *adj.* яйцеклáду́щий; яйцеро́дный.

ovulation *n.* овуля́ция.

ovule *n.* **1,** *biol.* яйцекле́тка. **2,** *bot.* семяпо́чка.

ovum *n.* яйцо́.

owe *v.t.* **1,** (have as an obligation to pay) задолжáть: *He owes me money,* он задолжáл мне де́ньги. *He owes me five dollars,* он мне до́лжен пять до́лларов. *How much do I owe?,* ско́лько с меня́? *You owe ten rubles,* с вас (прихо́дится) де́сять рубле́й. *I owe you an apology,* я до́лжен (должнá) извини́ться пе́ред вáми. **2,** (be obligated for) *rendered by* обя́зан: *I owe my life to you,* я вам обя́зан(а) жи́знью. *I owe everything to my teacher,* я всем обя́зан(а) моему́ учи́телю. *He owes his success to the fact that...,* он обя́зан свои́м успе́хом тому́, что...

owing to из-за; благодаря́ (+ *dat.*); всле́дствие (+ *gen.*); по причи́не (+ *gen.*).

owl *n.* совá. —**owlish** *adj.* сови́ный.

own *v.t.* владе́ть: *own a house/car,* владе́ть до́мом/ маши́ной. —*v.i.* [*usu.* **own up**] признáться (во всём). *Own up to the fact that...,* признáться, что... —*adj.* со́бственный: *see with one's own eyes,* ви́деть (что́-нибудь) со́бственными глазáми. *A house of* *one's own*, свой со́бственный дом. *For reasons of his own*, по каки́м-то свои́м соображе́ниям. *Go one's own way*, идти́ свое́й доро́гой. *She makes all her own clothes*, она́ шьёт себе́ всё сама́. *I have enough problems of my own*, у меня́ доста́точно со́бственных пробле́м. —**come into one's own**, вступи́ть в свои́ права́. —**hold one's own**, держа́ться. *He can hold his own against the best players*, он мо́жет поспо́рить с лу́чшими игрока́ми. —**on one's own, 1**, (alone; independently) в одино́чку; самостоя́тельно. *Leave on one's own*, предоставля́ть самому́ себе́. *He acted on his own*, он де́йствовал на со́бственный страх и риск. **2**, (on one's own initiative) самочи́нно. —**to each his own**, ка́ждому своё.

owner *n.* владе́лец; со́бственник; хозя́ин. *The owner of the house*, владе́лец до́ма. —**ownerless**, *adj.* бесхозя́йный.

ownership *n.* владе́ние; со́бственность. *Ownership of property*, владе́ние иму́ществом. *Ownership of land*, владе́ние землёй; со́бственность на зе́млю. *Ownership of the means of production*, со́бственность на сре́дства произво́дства.

ox *n.* вол.

oxalic acid щаве́левая кислота́.

oxeye daisy нивя́ник.

oxford *n.* полуботи́нок. *Also*, **oxford shoe**.

oxidation *n.* окисле́ние.

oxide *n.* о́кись; о́кисел. *Ferric oxide*, о́кись желе́за. *Ferrous oxide*, за́кись желе́за.

oxidize *v.t.* окисля́ть. —*v.i.* окисля́ться.

oxygen *n.* кислоро́д. —*adj.* кислоро́дный. —**oxygen mask**, кислоро́дная ма́ска. —**oxygen tent**, кислоро́дная пала́тка.

oyster *n.* у́стрица. —*adj.* у́стричный: *oyster shell*, у́стричная ра́ковина.

ozocerite *n.* озокери́т.

ozone *n.* озо́н.

P

P, p шестна́дцатая бу́ква англи́йского алфави́та.

pace *n.* **1**, (step) шаг: *step off twenty paces*, отсчи́тывать два́дцать шаго́в. **2**, (rate of speed when walking) шаг: *at a brisk pace*, бы́стрым ша́гом. *Quicken one's pace*, уско́рить шаг; приба́вить ша́гу. **3**, (rate of speed of an activity) темп; те́мпы: *the pace of construction*, те́мпы строи́тельства. *Quicken the pace*, ускоря́ть темп (те́мпы). *At a snail's pace*, черепа́шьим ша́гом. **4**, (gait of a horse) и́ноходь. —*v.t.* **1**, (walk back and forth across) расха́живать по; проха́живаться по. **2**, *fol. by* **off** (measure by paces) отмеря́ть. **3**, *fol. by* **oneself** (set a pace for oneself) задава́ть себе́ темп. —*v.i.* **1**, (walk deliberately) шага́ть; расха́живать. **2**, (of a horse) идти́ и́ноходью. —**keep pace with**, идти́ в но́гу с; идти́ наравне́ с; поспева́ть за. —**off the pace**, позади́: *keep off the pace*, держа́ться позади́. —**put through one's paces**, подверга́ть испыта́ниям. —**set the pace**, задава́ть темп.

pacemaker *n., med.* стимуля́тор се́рдца.

pacer *n.* иноходе́ц.

pachyderm *n.* толстоко́жее живо́тное.

pacific *adj.* **1**, (peaceful; calm) споко́йный; ти́хий. **2**, (not warlike) ми́рный; миролюби́вый. —**Pacific Ocean**, Ти́хий океа́н.

pacification *n.* умиротворе́ние.

pacifier *n.* **1**, (one who pacifies) миротво́рец. **2**, (for a baby to suck on) со́ска; пусты́шка.

pacifism *n.* пацифи́зм. —**pacifist**, *n.* пацифи́ст. —*adj.* пацифи́стский.

pacify *v.t.* **1**, (quiet; calm) усмиря́ть. **2**, (establish peace in) умиротворя́ть.

pack *n.* **1**, (carried by a person) кото́мка; ра́нец. **2**, (carried by an animal) вьюк. **3**, (of cigarettes) па́чка. **4**, (of cards) коло́да. **5**, (of dogs, wolves, etc.) ста́я; сво́ра. **6**, (gang; band) ша́йка; сво́ра. **7**, *med.* обёртывание. **8**, *in* **pack of lies**, сплошна́я ложь. —*v.t.* **1**, (put in a suitcase; fill, as a suitcase) укла́дывать; упако́вывать. **2**, (put in a box, bag, etc.) упако́вывать; запако́вывать. **3**, (cram) заполня́ть; набива́ть. *The hall was packed*, зал был битко́м наби́т. *Play to packed houses*, де́лать по́лные сбо́ры; идти́ с аншла́гом. **4**, *fol. by* **down** (press down firmly) уплотня́ть. **5**, *fol. by* **off** (send off) отсыла́ть. —*v.i.* **1**, *often fol. by* **up** (pack one's things) укла́дываться; упако́вываться. *He is busy packing*, он за́нят упако́вкой веще́й. **2**, (form into a solid mass) уплотня́ться. —**send packing**, спрова́живать; выпрова́живать.

package *n.* **1**, (bundle) паке́т. **2**, (parcel) посы́лка. —*v.t.* фасова́ть. —**package deal**, ко́мплексное соглаше́ние.

packaging *n.* фасо́вка; расфасо́вка.

pack animal вью́чное живо́тное.

packer *n.* упако́вщик.

packet *n.* **1,** (small package) паке́т; па́чка. **2,** (ship) пакетбо́т.

packing *n.* **1,** (act) упако́вка. **2,** (material) упако́вка; наби́вка. —*adj.* упако́вочный. —**packing case,** упако́вочный я́щик. —**packing house,** консе́рвная фа́брика.

packsaddle *n.* вью́чное седло́.

pact *n.* пакт; догово́р.

pad *n.* **1,** (cushionlike object) поду́шечка. **2,** (writing tablet) блокно́т. **3,** (floating leaf, as of a lily) лист. **4,** (stamp pad) поду́шечка для штемпеле́й. —*v.t.* **1,** (line with padding) подбива́ть ва́той *or* волоса́ми. **2,** (expand unduly) раздува́ть; размазывать.

padding *n.* наби́вка; прокла́дка.

paddle *n.* **1,** (oar) весло́; гребо́к. **2,** (stick for administering punishment) па́лка. **3,** *sports* (racket) раке́тка. —*v.t.* **1,** (row) грести́. **2,** (spank) бить па́лкой. —**paddle wheel,** гребно́е колесо́.

paddock *n.* заго́н.

paddy *n.* [*usu.* rice paddy] ри́совое по́ле.

padlock *n.* вися́чий замо́к. —*v.t.* запира́ть на вися́чий замо́к.

paean *n.* хвале́бная песнь.

paediatrics *n.* = pediatrics. —**paediatric,** *adj.* = pediatric. —**paediatrician,** *n.* = pediatrician.

pagan *n.* язы́чник. —*adj.* язы́ческий. —**paganism,** *n.* язы́чество.

page *n.* **1,** (of a book, newspaper, etc.) страни́ца. **2,** (attendant) паж. —*v.t.* (call; summon) вызыва́ть.

pageant *n.* **1,** (dramatic presentation) спекта́кль. **2,** (costumed procession) ше́ствие; пара́д. —**pageantry,** *n.* по́мпа; блеск; великоле́пие.

page proofs вёрстка; корректу́ра в листа́х.

pagination *n.* пагина́ция.

pagoda *n.* па́года.

paid *adj.* опла́чиваемый; пла́тный. *Paid vacation,* опла́чиваемый о́тпуск. *Paid worker,* пла́тный рабо́тник. *Paid advertisement,* пла́тное объявле́ние. *Well paid,* хорошо́ опла́чиваемый.

pail *n.* ведро́: *garbage pail,* му́сорное ведро́. *Milk pail,* подо́йник.

pain *n.* **1,** (feeling of discomfort) боль: *pain in one's chest,* боль в груди́. *Cry out in pain,* вскри́кнуть от бо́ли. *Are you in much pain?,* вам о́чень бо́льно? **2,** *pl.* (efforts) стара́ния. *Take pains,* прилага́ть стара́ния; о́чень стара́ться. —*v.t.* огорча́ть. *It pains me to think about it,* мне бо́льно ду́мать об э́том. —**on pain of,** под стра́хом (+ *gen.*): *on pain of death,* под стра́хом сме́рти.

pained *adj.* огорчённый: *pained look,* огорчённый вид.

painful *adj.* **1,** (hurting) больно́й. *Is it painful?,* вам бо́льно? **2,** (causing pain) боле́зненный: *painful bite,* боле́зненный уку́с. **3,** (unpleasant; agonizing) мучи́тельный. *It is painful to watch,* бо́льно смотре́ть на э́то. *He died a painful death,* он у́мер *or* умира́л мучи́тельной сме́ртью; он умира́л тяжело́.

painfully *adv.* боле́зненно; мучи́тельно. *Painfully familiar,* до бо́ли знако́мый.

painkiller *n.* болеутоля́ющее сре́дство.

painless *adj.* безболе́зненный. —**painlessly,** *adv.* безболе́зненно.

painstaking *adj.* тща́тельный; стара́тельный. —**painstakingly,** *adv.* тща́тельно; стара́тельно.

paint *n.* кра́ска: *coat of paint,* слой кра́ски. *"Wet paint!",* осторо́жно! окра́шено! —*v.t.* **1,** (coat with paint) кра́сить. *Paint something green,* кра́сить что́-нибудь в зелёный цвет. **2,** (make, as a picture; make a picture of) писа́ть. *This picture was painted by...,* э́та карти́на была́ напи́сана (+ *instr.*). **3,** (apply cosmetics to) кра́сить. **4,** (swab) сма́зывать. **5,** *fig.* (describe; depict) рисова́ть; изобража́ть. *Paint a gloomy picture,* рисова́ть мра́чную карти́ну. —*v.i.* рисова́ть *or* писа́ть кра́сками. *Paint in oils,* рисова́ть *or* писа́ть ма́сляными кра́сками; писа́ть ма́слом.

paintbrush *n.* кисть; маля́рная кисть.

painted *adj.* кра́шеный.

painter *n.* **1,** (house painter) маля́р. **2,** (artist) худо́жник; живопи́сец. *Sign painter,* худо́жник по вы́вескам.

painting *n.* **1,** (the art) жи́вопись. **2,** (a painted picture) карти́на; ро́спись.

pair *n.* па́ра: *pair of shoes/pants,* па́ра сапо́г/брюк. *Pair of scissors,* но́жницы. *In pairs,* па́рами; попа́рно. —*v.t.* спа́ривать; случа́ть. —*v.i.* [*usu.* **pair off**] разделя́ться попа́рно.

pajamas *also,* **pyjamas** *n.* пижа́ма.

Pakistani *adj.* пакиста́нский. —*n.* пакиста́нец; пакиста́нка.

pal *n., colloq.* прия́тель; това́рищ; дружо́к. —*v.i.* [*usu.* **pal around**] дружи́ть (с).

palace *n.* дворе́ц. *Buckingham Palace,* Букинге́мский дворе́ц. —*adj.* дворцо́вый: *palace guard,* дворцо́вая стра́жа; *palace coup,* дворцо́вый переворо́т.

palatable *adj.* **1,** (fit to be eaten) вку́сный. **2,** (agreeable; acceptable) прие́млемый.

palatal *adj.* **1,** (pert. to the palate) нёбный. **2,** *phonet.* палата́льный.

palatalize *v.t.* палатализова́ть. —**palatalization,** *n.* палатализа́ция.

palate *n.* **1,** (roof of the mouth) нёбо. **2,** (sense of taste) вкус.

palatial *adj.* роско́шный; великоле́пный.

palaver *n.* пуста́я болтовня́.

pale *adj.* **1,** (pallid; not bright) бле́дный: *pale cheeks/colors,* бле́дные щёки/кра́ски. *Pale moon,* бле́дная луна́. **2,** (denoting a light shade) бледно-: *pale green,* бледно-зелёный. —*n.* **1,** (stake) кол. **2,** (boundary) грани́ца; преде́лы. *The Pale of Settlement,* черта́ осе́длости. —*v.i.* **1,** (turn pale) бледне́ть. **2,** *fol. by* **before** (suffer in comparison with) бледне́ть (пе́ред); ме́ркнуть (пе́ред); тускне́ть (пе́ред).

Paleo-Asiatic *adj.* палеоазиа́тский.

paleography *n.* палеогра́фия. —**paleographer,** *n.* палео́граф. —**paleographic,** *adj.* палеографи́ческий.

paleolithic *adj.* палеолити́ческий.

paleontology *n.* палеонтоло́гия. —**paleontologist,** *n.* палеонто́лог. —**paleontological,** *adj.* палеонтологи́ческий.

Paleozoic *adj.* палеозо́йский.

Palestinian *adj.* палести́нский. —*n.* палести́нец; палести́нка.

palette *n.* пали́тра. —**palette knife,** шпа́тель.

paling *n.* частоко́л; тын.

palisade *n.* палиса́д.

pall *n.* **1,** (covering for a coffin) покро́в. **2,** (gloom) мра́чность. *Cast a pall over,* омрача́ть. —*v.i.* [*usu.* **pall on**] приеда́ться (+ *dat.*); пригля́дываться (+ *dat.*).

palladium *n.* палла́дий.

pallbearer *n.* челове́к, несу́щий гроб.

pallet *n.* **1,** (straw mattress) тюфя́к. **2,** (pawl) соба́чка.

palliate *v.t.* облегча́ть; смягча́ть.

palliative *n.* паллиати́в. —*adj.* паллиати́вный.

pallid *adj.* бле́дный. —**pallor,** *n.* бле́дность.

palm *n.* **1,** (of the hand) ладо́нь. **2,** (tree) па́льма. —*adj.* па́льмовый. —*v.t.* [*usu.* **palm off**] всуча́ть; подсо́вывать. —**know like the palm of one's hand,** знать как свои́ пять па́льцев.

palmist *n.* хирома́нт. —**palmistry,** *n.* хирома́нтия.

palm oil па́льмовое ма́сло.

Palm Sunday ве́рбное воскресе́нье.

palpable *adj.* **1,** (tangible) осяза́емый; ощути́мый. **2,** (obvious) очеви́дный; я́вный.

palpitate *v.i.* трепета́ть. —**palpitation,** *n.* тре́пет; трепета́ние. *Heart palpitations,* учащённое сердцебие́ние.

palsy *n.* парали́ч.

paltry *adj.* ничто́жный; пустяко́вый. *Paltry wage,* ни́щенская зарпла́та.

pampas *n.pl.* пампа́сы.

pamper *v.t.* балова́ть; не́жить; изне́живать.

pamphlet *n.* **1,** (small unbound book) брошю́ра. **2,** (political article published in same) памфле́т. —**pamphleteer,** *n.* памфлети́ст.

pan *n.* **1,** (frying pan) сковорода́; (roasting pan) жаро́вня; (baking pan) про́тивень. **2,** (dishpan) таз для мытья́ посу́ды; (dustpan) сово́к. —*v.t.* **1,** (separate, as gold) промыва́ть. **2,** *colloq.* (criticize severely) раскритикова́ть; разруга́ть. —**pan out,** *colloq.* вы́гореть.

panacea *n.* панаце́я; универса́льное сре́дство.

Panama hat пана́ма.

Panamanian *adj.* пана́мский.

pancake *n.* блин; ола́дья.

panchromatic *adj.* панхромати́ческий.

pancreas *n.* поджелу́дочная железа́. —**pancreatic,** *adj.* поджелу́дочный.

panda *n.* па́нда.

pandemic *n.* пандеми́я.

pandemonium *n.* гвалт; хао́с; бедла́м.

pander *v.i.* **1,** (act as a pander) сво́дничать. **2,** *fol. by* **to** (cater to) потво́рствовать. —*n.* [*also,* **panderer**] сво́дник.

pane *n.* (око́нное) стекло́.

panegyric *n.* панеги́рик. —**panegyrist,** *n.* панеги́рист.

panel *n.* **1,** (section of a wall, door, etc.) пане́ль; филёнка. **2,** (board with instruments or controls) щит; щито́к. *Instrument panel,* прибо́рная доска́. *Control panel,* щит управле́ния; пульт. **3,** *art* панно́. **4,** (committee) коми́ссия. *Panel of judges,* суде́йская колле́гия. —*v.t.* обшива́ть пане́лями *or* филёнками.

paneled *also,* **panelled** *adj.* филёночный; филёнчатый. *Wood-paneled,* обши́тый де́ревом.

paneling *also,* **panelling** *n.* пане́ль.

pang *n., usu. pl.* му́ки; бо́ли: *hunger pangs,* му́ки го́лода; голо́дные бо́ли. *Pangs of childbirth,* родовы́е му́ки *or* поту́ги. —**pangs of conscience,** угрызе́ния со́вести.

pangolin *n.* я́щер.

panhandler *n.* попроша́йка.

panic *n.* па́ника. —*v.t.* наводи́ть па́нику на. —*v.i.* впада́ть в па́нику; поддава́ться па́нике; паникова́ть.

panicky *adj.* пани́ческий. *Get panicky,* впада́ть в па́нику.

panicle *n.* метёлка.

panic-stricken *adj.* пани́ческий; охва́ченный па́никой.

panoply *n.* **1,** (suit of armor) доспе́хи. **2,** (magnificent array) блеск.

panorama *n.* панора́ма. —**panoramic,** *adj.* панора́мный.

pansy *n.* аню́тины гла́зки.

pant *v.i.* пыхте́ть; задыха́ться; запыха́ться; отдува́ться. —*n.* вздох.

pantheism *n.* пантеи́зм. —**pantheist,** *n.* пантеи́ст. —**pantheistic,** *adj.* пантеисти́ческий.

pantheon *n.* пантео́н.

panther *n.* панте́ра.

panties *n.pl.* тру́сики.

pantomime *n.* пантоми́ма. —*adj.* пантомими́ческий; пантоми́мный.

pantry *n.* кладова́я.

pants *n.pl.* брю́ки; штаны́. *Pants pocket,* карма́н брюк. *Pants leg,* штани́на.

pantyhose *n.* колго́тки.

pap *n.* ка́шка.

papa *n.* па́па.

papacy *n.* па́пство. —**papal,** *adj.* па́пский.

papaya *n.* ды́нное де́рево.

paper *n.* **1,** (material) бума́га. **2,** (newspaper) газе́та. **3,** (treatise) докла́д: *deliver a paper,* чита́ть докла́д. **4,** (written work for school) сочине́ние. *Term paper,* курсова́я рабо́та. **5,** (document) бума́га; докуме́нт. —*adj.* бума́жный: *paper money,* бума́жные де́ньги. —*v.t.* **1,** (cover with wallpaper) окле́ивать (обо́ями). **2,** *fol. by* **over** (cover up) зама́зывать. —**on paper, 1,** (in writing) в пи́сьменной фо́рме. **2,** (in theory) на бума́ге.

paperback *n.* кни́га в бума́жной обло́жке.

paper clip скре́пка.

paperhanger *n.* обо́йщик.

paperweight *n.* пресс-папье́.

paper work делопроизво́дство.

papier-mâché *n.* папье́-маше́.

papoose *n.* инде́йский ребёнок.

paprika *n.* кра́сный пе́рец; па́прика.

papule *n.* па́пула.

papyrus *n.* папи́рус.

par *n.* **1,** (equal status): *be/rank on a par with,* быть наравне́ с; стоя́ть в одно́м ряду́ с. *Place on a par with,* ста́вить в оди́н ряд с. **2,** (normal state or level): *up to par,* на до́лжной высоте́; *below par,* не на высоте́. **3,** *finance* номина́л. —*adj.* **1,** *finance* номина́льный: *par value,* номина́льная цена́. **2,** (normal; up to par) норма́льный.

parable *n.* при́тча.

parabola *n.* пара́бола. —**parabolic,** *adj.* параболи́ческий.

parachute *n.* парашю́т. —*v.i.* пры́гать *or* вы́броситься с парашю́том. —**parachutist,** *n.* парашюти́ст.

parade *n.* пара́д. —*v.i.* ше́ствовать. —*v.t.* (flaunt) щеголя́ть. —**parade ground,** плац.

paradigm *n.* паради́гма.

paradise *n.* рай.

paradox *n.* парадо́кс. —**paradoxical,** *adj.* парадокса́льный.

paraffin *n.* парафи́н.

paragon *n.* образе́ц.

paragraph *n.* абза́ц; пара́граф. *Begin a new paragraph,* начина́ть с но́вой (*or* с кра́сной) строки́.

parakeet *n.* ма́ленький попуга́й.

parallax *n.* паралла́кс.

parallel *adj.* паралле́льный: *parallel lines,* паралле́льные ли́нии. —*adv.* паралле́льно. *Parallel to,* паралле́льно (+ *dat.*). —*n.* паралле́ль: *the 40th parallel,* сорокова́я паралле́ль. *Draw a parallel,* проводи́ть паралле́ль. —*v.t.* **1,** (run parallel to) идти́ паралле́льно (+ *dat.*). **2,** (be analogous to) соотве́тствовать (+ *dat.*). —**parallel bars,** паралле́льные бру́сья.

parallelepiped *n.* параллелепи́пед.

parallelism *n.* параллели́зм.

parallelogram *n.* параллелогра́мм.

paralyse *v.t.* = **paralyze.**

paralysis *n.* парали́ч. —**paralytic,** *adj.* паралити́ческий; парали́чный. —*n.* парали́тик.

paralyze *also,* **paralyse** *v.t.* парализова́ть. —**paralyzed,** *adj.* парализо́ван(ный).

paramecium *n.* ту́фелька; парамéция.

parameter *n.* пара́метр.

paramilitary *adj.* полувое́нный.

paramount *adj.* **1,** (first in rank or title) верхо́вный. **2,** (overriding) первостепе́нный. *Of paramount importance,* велича́йшей *or* первостепе́нной ва́жности.

paramour *n.* любо́вник; любо́вница.

paranoia *n.* парано́йя. —**paranoiac,** *n.* парано́ик. —**paranoid,** *adj.* парано́ический.

parapet *n.* **1,** (low wall or railing) парапе́т. **2,** (breastwork) бру́ствер.

paraphernalia *n.* принадле́жности.

paraphrase *n.* перефрази́ровка. —*v.t.* перефрази́ровать.

paraplegia *n.* параплеги́я. —**paraplegic,** *adj.* больно́й параплеги́ей.

parapsychology *n.* парапсихоло́гия. —**parapsychologist,** *n.* парапсихо́лог.

parasite *n.* **1,** *biol.* парази́т. **2,** (sponger) туне́ядец; дармое́д; прихлеба́тель; парази́т. —**parasitic,** *adj.* паразити́ческий; парази́тный. —**parasitism,** *n.* паразити́зм.

parasol *n.* со́лнечный зо́нтик.

parathyroid gland околощитови́дная железа́; паращитови́дная железа́.

paratrooper *n.* парашюти́ст.

paratyphoid *n.* парати́ф. *Also,* **paratyphoid fever.**

parcel *n.* **1,** (package sent through the mail) посы́лка. **2,** (package; bundle) паке́т. **3,** (plot of land) уча́сток (земли́). —*v.t.* [*usu.* **parcel out**] выделя́ть; распределя́ть. —**part and parcel,** неотъе́млемая часть.

parch *v.t.* иссуша́ть. *My throat is parched,* у меня́ в го́рле пересо́хло. *My lips are parched,* мои́ гу́бы запекли́сь. *The ground is parched,* земля́ пересо́хла.

parchment *n.* перга́мент. —*adj.* перга́ментный.

pardon *v.t.* **1,** (forgive) проща́ть; извиня́ть. *Pardon me!,* прости́те!; извини́те! *Pardon the expression,* извини́те за выраже́ние. **2,** (release from punishment) поми́ловать. —*n.* **1,** (forgiveness) проще́ние. *I beg your pardon, see* **beg. 2,** (release from punishment) поми́лование. —**pardonable,** *adj.* прости́тельный.

pare *v.t.* **1,** (peel) чи́стить. **2,** *often fol. by* **down** (reduce) сокраща́ть; уре́зывать.

parent *n., usu. pl.* роди́тели. —**parentage,** *n.* происхожде́ние. —**parental,** *adj.* роди́тельский.

parentheses *n.pl.* ско́бки. —**parenthesize,** *v.t.* заключа́ть в ско́бки. —**parenthetic(al),** *adj.* вво́дный. —**parenthetically,** *adv.* в ско́бках.

parenthood *n.* отцо́вство; матери́нство.

paresis *n.* паре́з.

par excellence превосхо́дный; замеча́тельный.

pariah *n.* па́рия.

pari-mutuel *n., usu. pl.* тотализа́тор.

paring knife нож для чи́стки фру́ктов и овоще́й; фрукто́вый нож.

parish *n.* (церко́вный) прихо́д. —*adj.* прихо́дский: *parish priest,* прихо́дский свяще́нник. —**parishioner,** *n.* прихожа́нин.

Parisian *adj.* пари́жский. —*n.* парижа́нин.

parity *n.* парите́т.

park *n.* парк. —*v.t.* **1,** (a car) ста́вить; припарко́вывать (маши́ну). **2,** *colloq.* (place) оставля́ть; положи́ть. *Park oneself somewhere,* расположи́ться; усе́сться.

parka *n.* па́рка.

parking *n.* стоя́нка. *No parking!,* стоя́нка запрещена́! —**parking lights,** подфона́рники. —**parking lot,** стоя́нка (автомоби́лей); автостоя́нка. —**parking place,** ме́сто стоя́нки (автомоби́ля).

parkway *n.* шоссе́.

parlance *n.* язы́к: *legal parlance,* юриди́ческий язы́к. *In common parlance,* в просторе́чии.

parley *n.* перегово́ры. —*v.i.* вести́ перегово́ры.

parliament *n.* парла́мент. *Member of parliament,* член парла́мента; парламента́рий. —**parliamentar-**

ianism, *n.* парламентари́зм. —**parliamentary,** *adj.* парла́ментский; парламента́рный.

parlor *also,* **parlour** *n.* **1,** (sitting room) гости́ная. **2,** (establishment): *beauty parlor,* космети́ческий кабине́т; *ice cream parlor,* кафе́-моро́женое. *Funeral parlor,* похоро́нное бюро́. —**parlor car,** сало́н-ваго́н. —**parlor games,** ко́мнатные и́гры.

parochial *adj.* **1,** (of a parish) прихо́дский. **2,** (narrow; provincial) у́зкий; ограни́ченный. —**parochial school,** прихо́дская шко́ла.

parody *n.* паро́дия. —*v.t.* пароди́ровать. —**parodist,** *n.* пароди́ст.

parole *n.* усло́вно-досро́чное освобожде́ние. —*v.t.* освобожда́ть под че́стное сло́во.

paroxysm *n.* парокси́зм.

parquet *n.* парке́т. —*adj.* парке́тный. —**parquetry,** *n.* парке́т.

parrot *n.* попуга́й. —*v.t.* **1,** (repeat) повторя́ть как попуга́й. **2,** (say the same things as) подпева́ть; перепева́ть.

parry *v.t.* **1,** (ward off) отража́ть; отбива́ть; пари́ровать. **2,** (evade) уклоня́ться от: *parry a question,* уклоня́ться от отве́та.

parse *v.t.* разбира́ть.

parsimonious *adj.* скупо́й. —**parsimony,** *n.* ску́пость.

parsley *n.* петру́шка.

parsnip *n.* пастерна́к.

parson *n.* прихо́дский свяще́нник.

part *n.* **1,** (portion; element) часть: *part of the whole,* часть це́лого. *Parts of the body,* ча́сти те́ла. *Spare parts,* запасны́е ча́сти. *Part One,* Часть пе́рвая. *Part of speech,* часть ре́чи. *Principal parts of a sentence,* гла́вные чле́ны предложе́ния. **2,** (role) роль: *bit part,* выходна́я роль. **3,** *pl.* (locality) края́: *in these parts,* в э́тих края́х. **4,** (in one's hair) пробо́р. **5,** *music* па́ртия. —*adj.* части́чный: *a part interest in,* части́чная до́ля (+ *gen.*). *Part owner,* совладе́лец. —*adv.* части́чно: *She is part Russian and part French,* она́ части́чно ру́сская и части́чно францу́женка. —*v.t.* **1,** (separate) разлуча́ть. *Till death do us part,* пока́ смерть не разлучи́т нас. **2,** (comb with a part): *part one's hair,* де́лать себе́ пробо́р. *Part one's hair in the middle/ on the side/,* носи́ть во́лосы на прямо́й/косо́й пробо́р. —*v.i.* **1,** (divide) разделя́ться; расступа́ться; раздвига́ться. **2,** (part company) расстава́ться; расходи́ться; разлуча́ться. *We parted friends,* мы расста́лись *or* разошли́сь друзья́ми. **3,** *fol. by* with (give up; let go; relinquish) расстава́ться с. —**do one's part,** де́лать своё де́ло. —**for my part,** я, со свое́й стороны́; что каса́ется меня́. —**for the most part,** *see* most. —**in large part,** во мно́гом. —**in part,** ча́стью; части́чно; отча́сти. —**in parts,** по частя́м. —**on the part of,** со стороны́ (+ *gen.*). —**take part in,** принима́ть уча́стие в; уча́ствовать в. —**want no part of,** *colloq.* ника́к не хоте́ть впу́тываться в.

partake *v.i.* **1,** *fol. by* in (take part in) принима́ть уча́стие (в). **2,** *fol. by* of (take, as food) пое́сть. —**partake oneself,** угоща́ться.

parthenogenesis *n.* партеногене́з.

Parthenon *n.* Парфено́н.

partial *adj.* **1,** (involving only a part) части́чный. **2,** (biased) пристра́стный. **3,** *fol. by* to (particularly fond of) пристра́стный (к).

partiality *n.* пристра́стие; пристра́стность.

partially *adv.* части́чно; отча́сти.

participant *n.* уча́стник.

participate *v.i.* уча́ствовать: *participate in a demonstration,* уча́ствовать в демонстра́ции. —**participation,** *n.* уча́стие.

participle *n.* прича́стие. —**participial,** *adj.* прича́стный.

particle *n.* **1,** (speck) части́ца: *particle of dust,* части́ца пы́ли. **2,** (tiny amount) части́ца; крупи́ца. *Not a particle of difference,* ни мале́йшей ра́зницы. **3,** *physics* части́ца: *elementary particle,* элемента́рная части́ца. **4,** *gram.* части́ца. —**particle beam,** пучо́к части́ц.

particular *adj.* **1,** (special; unusual) осо́бенный; осо́бый. *Nothing in particular,* ничего́ осо́бенного. *For no particular reason,* без осо́бой причи́ны. **2,** (specific; individual) ча́стный: *a particular case,* ча́стный слу́чай. *At this particular time,* в да́нный моме́нт. *Why did you choose this particular color?,* почему́ вы вы́брали и́менно э́тот цвет? **3,** (fussy) разбо́рчивый; привере́дливый. —*n.* подро́бность: *go into the particulars,* вдава́ться в подро́бности. —**in particular,** в ча́стности; в осо́бенности.

particularity *n.* осо́бенность.

particularly *adv.* осо́бенно: *Victor was particularly helpful,* Ви́ктор нам осо́бенно помога́л. *Did you enjoy the play? Not particularly,* пье́са вам понра́вилась? Не осо́бенно; не о́чень.

parting *n.* расстава́ние; разлу́ка; проща́ние. *At parting,* на проща́ние. —*adj.* проща́льный; напу́тственный. *Parting words,* проща́льные слова́; напу́тственное сло́во; напу́тствие. —**parting of the ways,** распу́тье. *We reached a parting of the ways,* мы разошли́сь; на́ши пути́ разошли́сь.

partisan *n.* **1,** (adherent) сторо́нник. **2,** (guerrilla) партиза́н. —*adj.* **1,** (biased) пристра́стный. **2,** (of guerrillas) партиза́нский. —**partisanship,** *n.* пристра́стие.

partition *n.* **1,** (dividing up) разде́л: *the partition of Poland,* разде́л По́льши. **2,** (something that divides) перегоро́дка. —*v.t.* **1,** (divide into sections by means of a partition) перегора́живать; разгора́живать. **2,** *fol. by* off (separate by a partition) отгора́живать.

partitive *adj., gram.* раздели́тельный.

partly *adv.* ча́стью; части́чно; отча́сти.

partner *n.* **1,** (in business) компаньо́н; това́рищ; партнёр. **2,** (in a game) партнёр. **3,** (in dancing) кавале́р; да́ма. —**partnership,** *n.* това́рищество; партнёрство.

partridge *n.* куропа́тка.

part-time *adj. & adv.* на полста́вки. *Part-time work,* рабо́та на полста́вки. *Work part-time,* рабо́тать на полста́вки; рабо́тать непо́лный день.

partway *adv.* полпути́: *I'll walk you partway,* я пройду́ с ва́ми полпути́.

party *n.* **1,** (social gathering) вечери́нка; ве́чер. **2,** (political party) па́ртия. **3,** (group of people organized for a purpose) гру́ппа: *search party,* по́исковая гру́ппа. **4,** *mil.* (detachment; detail) кома́нда; па́ртия. *Rescue party,* спаса́тельная кома́нда. **5,** *law* сторона́: *interested party,* заинтересо́ванная сторона́. *Party to an agreement,* уча́стник соглаше́ния. *Be a party to,* быть прича́стным к. *Through a third party,* че́рез тре́тье лицо́. —*adj.* парти́йный: *party congress,* парти́йный съезд. —**party line, 1,** (of telephones) телефо́н сме́шанного по́льзования. **2,** *polit.* парти́йная ли́ния.

paschal *adj.* пасха́льный. —**paschal lamb,** пасха́льный а́гнец.

pasha *n.* паша́.

pass *v.t.* **1,** (go by; go past) проходи́ть ми́мо; проезжа́ть ми́мо; минова́ть. **2,** (go beyond) проходи́ть; проезжа́ть. **3,** (overtake) обгоня́ть. *No passing!,* не обгоня́ть!; обго́н воспрещён! **4,** (hand over) передава́ть: *Please pass the salt!,* переда́йте мне соль, пожа́луйста! *Pass a note to the speaker,* переда́ть запи́ску ора́тору. **5,** (complete successfully, as a test) сдать; вы́держать. *Pass a physical examination,* пройти́ медици́нский осмо́тр. **6,** (enact, as a bill) принима́ть. **7,** (while away, as time) корота́ть. **8,** (pronounce, as a sentence or verdict) выноси́ть. **9,** (excrete; void) испуска́ть. **10,** *sports* пасова́ть; передава́ть. —*v.i.* **1,** (move ahead; move past; extend) проходи́ть. *Let pass,* пропуска́ть. *Let me pass!,* да́йте мне пройти́! **2,** (elapse; go by) проходи́ть: *A whole year passed,* прошёл це́лый год. *Time passes quickly,* вре́мя идёт бы́стро. **3,** (go by; be over) проходи́ть; минова́ть: *The storm/danger has passed,* гроза́ прошла́; опа́сность минова́ла. **4,** (be transferred) переходи́ть; передава́ться; достава́ться. **5,** (be approved or adopted) проходи́ть. **6,** *cards* пасова́ть. —*n.* **1,** (passage between mountains) перева́л: *the Khyber Pass,* Ха́йберский перева́л. **2,** (permit) про́пуск. **3,** (free ticket) контрама́рка. **4,** *mil.* (leave) о́тпуск; побы́вка. **5,** *sports* пас; переда́ча. **6,** *cards* пас. —**come to pass,** произойти́; случи́ться. —**make a pass at,** приста́ть к. —**pass around,** пусти́ть по кру́гу. —**pass away,** сконча́ться. —**pass by,** проходи́ть ми́мо; проходи́ть стороно́й. —**pass for,** сходи́ть за. —**pass off,** выдава́ть: *pass oneself off as a physician,* выдава́ть себя́ за врача́. —**pass on, 1,** (give to the next person) передава́ть. **2,** (die) умира́ть. —**pass out, 1,** (hand out) раздава́ть. **2,** *colloq.* (faint) потеря́ть созна́ние; упа́сть в о́бморок. —**pass over, 1,** (skip; disregard) пропуска́ть; обходи́ть. *Pass over in silence,* обходи́ть молча́нием. **2,** (fail to promote) обходи́ть. —**pass through,** проходи́ть че́рез; проезжа́ть че́рез. *I am just passing through,* я здесь прое́здом. —**pass up,** *colloq.* пропуска́ть.

passable *adj.* **1,** (traversable) проходи́мый. **2,** (barely satisfactory) сно́сный.

passage *n.* **1,** (passing) перехо́д; прохожде́ние; прохо́д; прое́зд. **2,** (passageway) прохо́д; перехо́д; прое́зд. **3,** (voyage) перее́зд. *Book passage,* брать

билет на парохо́д. **4,** (lapse, as of time) тече́ние (вре́мени). **5,** (enactment, as of a law) приня́тие. **6,** (portion of something written) отры́вок. **7,** *music* пасса́ж.

passageway *n.* прохо́д; перехо́д; коридо́р.

passbook *n.* сберега́тельная кни́жка.

passed pawn *chess* проходна́я пе́шка.

passenger *n.* пассажи́р. —*adj.* пассажи́рский. *Passenger car,* легково́й автомоби́ль. —**passenger pigeon,** стра́нствующий го́лубь.

passer-by *n.* прохо́жий; встре́чный.

passing *adj.* **1,** (going by) проходя́щий. *Passing car,* попу́тная маши́на. *With each passing year,* с ка́ждым го́дом; год о́т году. **2,** (quick; cursory) бе́глый: *passing glance,* бе́глый взгляд. **3,** (transitory) мимолётный: *passing fancy,* мимолётная при́хоть. **4,** (casual, as of a remark) попу́тный. **5,** (satisfactory, as of a grade) перехо́дный. —*n.* **1,** (act of passing) прохожде́ние. **2,** (death) кончи́на. —**in passing,** мимохо́дом; вскользь.

passion *n.* страсть: *Passions flared,* стра́сти разгоре́лись. *A passion for music,* страсть к му́зыке; увлече́ние му́зыкой. *Fit of passion,* поры́в *or* вспы́шка гне́ва.

passionate *adj.* стра́стный. —**passionately,** *adv.* стра́стно.

passive *adj.* **1,** (not active) пасси́вный: *passive role,* пасси́вная роль. *Passive vocabulary,* пасси́вный слова́рь; пасси́вный запа́с слов. **2,** *gram.* страда́тельный: *passive voice,* страда́тельный зало́г.

passivity *n.* пасси́вность.

passkey *n.* отмы́чка.

Passover *n.* па́сха.

passport *n.* па́спорт. —*adj.* па́спортный: *passport department,* па́спортный отде́л.

password *n.* паро́ль; про́пуск.

past *adj.* **1,** (of a former time) про́шлый: *past wars,* про́шлые во́йны. *The times are past when...,* прошли́ те времена́, когда́... **2,** *preceded by* **the** (just gone by) после́дний; мину́вший; исте́кший. *During the past year,* за после́дний/исте́кший год. **3,** (former) бы́вший: *past president,* бы́вший президе́нт. **4,** *gram.* проше́дший: *past tense,* проше́дшее вре́мя. —*n.* **1,** (past time) про́шлое. *In the past,* в про́шлом. *A thing of the past,* де́ло про́шлое. *Become a thing of the past,* отойти́ *or* уйти́ в про́шлое. **2,** *gram.* проше́дшее вре́мя. —*prep.* **1,** (by) ми́мо: *slip past the guard,* проскользну́ть ми́мо сто́рожа. **2,** (beyond) за: *past the city limits,* за преде́лами го́рода. *Just past the station,* сра́зу за вокза́лом *or* по́сле вокза́ла. *Well past midnight,* далеко́ за́ полночь. **3,** *in telling time:* *half-past six,* полови́на седьмо́го; *twenty past one,* два́дцать мину́т второ́го. —*adv.* ми́мо. ♦*Often with the prefix* про-: *fly past,* пролета́ть; *dart past,* промча́ться.

paste *n.* **1,** (soft, creamy substance) па́ста: *toothpaste,* зубна́я па́ста; *tomato paste,* тома́т-па́ста. **2,** (adhesive) (мучно́й) клей; клейстер. **3,** (dough) те́сто: *puff paste,* слоёное те́сто. —*v.t.* **1,** (affix) накле́ивать. *Paste together,* скле́ивать. *Paste stamps in* *an album,* вкле́ивать ма́рки в альбо́м. **2,** (cover with pasted material) окле́ивать. **3,** *slang* (smack) тре́снуть.

pasteboard *n.* карто́н.

pastel *n.* пасте́ль. —*adj.* пасте́льный.

pastern *n.* ба́бка.

pasteurize *v.t.* пастеризова́ть. —**pasteurization,** *n.* пастериза́ция.

pastime *n.* времяпрепровожде́ние.

past master иску́сник.

pastor *n.* па́стор; па́стырь.

pastoral *adj.* **1,** (bucolic) пастора́льный. **2,** (of a pastor) па́стырский; па́сторский. *Pastoral duties,* па́стырские обя́занности. —*n.* пастора́ль.

pastorale *n.* пастора́ль.

pastry *n.* конди́терские изде́лия; пиро́жное. —**pastry cook; pastry chef,** конди́тер. —**pastry shop,** конди́терская.

pasturage *n.* **1,** (grass) подно́жный корм. **2,** (land) па́стбище. **3,** (grazing) пастьба́.

pasture *n.* па́стбище. —*v.i.* пасти́сь. —**put out to pasture, 1,** *literally* (вы)пуска́ть на подно́жный корм. **2,** (allow or compel to retire) увольня́ть в отста́вку.

pat *v.t.* похло́пывать; гла́дить; погла́живать; трепа́ть. *Pat someone on the back,* похло́пывать *or* погла́живать кого́-нибудь по спине́. *Pat someone on the head,* гла́дить кого́-нибудь по голове́. —*n.* **1,** (tap) хлопо́к. **2,** (small piece, as of butter) кусо́чек; комо́к. —*adj.* гото́вый: *a pat answer for everything,* гото́вый отве́т на всё. —**give (someone) a pat on the back,** гла́дить по голо́вке. —**have down** (*or* **know**) **pat,** знать назубо́к. —**stand pat,** стоя́ть на своём.

patch *n.* **1,** (covering, as for mending) запла́та. **2,** (bandage) повя́зка: *eye patch,* повя́зка на глазу́. **3,** (small plot) уча́сток; клочо́к. **4,** (small piece or area) клочо́к: *patch of fog,* клочо́к тума́на; *patch of blue,* клочо́к лазу́ри. *Patch of sunlight,* со́лнечный блик. —*v.t.* **1,** (mend) лата́ть; накла́дывать запла́ту на. **2,** *fol. by* **up** (settle; resolve) ула́живать.

patch pocket накладно́й карма́н.

patchwork *n.* **1,** (fabric made of patches) лоскутная рабо́та: *patchwork quilt,* лоску́тное одея́ло. **2,** (jumble) мешанина; ералаш.

pate *n.* башка́.

pâté *n.* паште́т.

patent *n.* пате́нт. —*adj.* **1,** (of or pert. to patents) пате́нтный. **2,** (patented) патенто́ванный. **3,** (obvious) я́вный: *a patent lie,* я́вная ложь. —*v.t.* патентова́ть. —**patent leather,** лакиро́ванная ко́жа. —**patent medicine,** патенто́ванное лека́рство.

paternal *adj.* **1,** (of one's father) отцо́вский. **2,** (fatherly) оте́ческий.

paternalistic *adj.* оте́ческий.

paternity *n.* отцо́вство.

path *n.* **1,** (footway) тропи́нка; тропа́; доро́жка. *Winding path,* изви́листая тропи́нка. **2,** (course) путь: *destroy everything in its path,* уничтожа́ть всё на своём пути́.

pathetic *adj.* жа́лкий; плаче́вный.

pathology *n.* патоло́гия. —**pathological,** *adj.* патологи́ческий. —**pathologist,** *n.* пато́лог.

pathos *n.* тро́гательность.

pathway *n.* тропи́нка; тропа́; доро́жка.

patience *n.* терпе́ние.

patient *adj.* терпели́вый. *Be patient!,* име́йте терпе́ние! —*n.* больно́й; пацие́нт. —**patiently,** *adv.* терпели́во.

patio *n.* па́тио.

patois *n.* ме́стный го́вор.

patriarch *n.* патриа́рх. —**patriarchal,** *adj.* патриарха́льный. —**patriarchate,** *n.* патриа́рхия. —**patriarchy,** *n.* патриарха́т.

patrician *n.* патри́ций.

patricide *n.* отцеуби́йство.

patrimony *n.* отцо́вское насле́дие.

patriot *n.* патрио́т. —**patriotic,** *adj.* патриоти́ческий. —**patriotism,** *n.* патриоти́зм.

patrol *v.t.* патрули́ровать. —*n.* дозо́р; патру́ль. *Be on patrol,* быть в дозо́ре. —*adj.* дозо́рный; патру́льный. *Patrol boat,* дозо́рное су́дно; сторожево́й ка́тер. —**patrolman,** *n.* полице́йский.

patron *n.* **1,** (benefactor) покрови́тель. *Patron of the arts,* мецена́т. **2,** (customer) покупа́тель; клие́нт. *Patron of a restaurant,* посети́тель рестора́на.

patronage *n.* покрови́тельство; проте́кция.

patronize *v.t.* **1,** (sponsor) покрови́тельствовать. **2,** (be a regular customer of) покупа́ть в. —**patronizing,** *adj.* покрови́тельственный: *patronizing attitude,* покрови́тельственное отноше́ние.

patronymic *n.* о́тчество. *Also,* **patronymic name.**

patter *n.* **1,** (drumming sound) стук; шум. *The patter of rain,* шум дождя́. *The patter of feet,* то́пот ног. **2,** (rapid-fire speech) скорогово́рка. **3,** (cant; jargon) жарго́н. —*v.i.* постуки́вать; бараба́нить.

pattern *n.* **1,** (decorative design) узо́р. **2,** (diagram used in making garments) вы́кройка. **3,** (model; example) образе́ц: *on the pattern of,* по образцу́ (+ *gen.*). *Set the pattern for,* стать образцо́м для. **4,** *aero.* маршру́т: *holding pattern,* маршру́т ожида́ния; *landing pattern,* маршру́т захо́да на поса́дку. —*v.t.* [*usu.* **pattern after**] де́лать (что́-нибудь) по образцу́ (+ *gen.*). *Pattern oneself after,* брать приме́р с.

patty *n.* **1,** (flat piece of chopped meat) котле́та. **2,** (small pie) пирожо́к.

paucity *n.* ску́дность.

paunch *n.* **1,** (potbelly) брюшко́; пу́зо. **2,** (rumen) рубе́ц. —**paunchy,** *adj.* пуза́тый.

pauper *n.* бедня́к; ни́щий. *He died a pauper,* он у́мер в нищете́.

pause *n.* па́уза; переры́в; переды́шка. *After a slight pause,* по́сле небольшо́й па́узы. —*v.i.* де́лать па́узу; остана́вливаться. —**give one pause,** наводи́ть на размышле́ния; заставля́ть кого́-нибудь призаду́маться.

pave *v.t.* мости́ть. —**pave the way,** прокла́дывать путь; подгота́вливать по́чву.

paved *adj.* мощёный.

pavement *n.* тротуа́р; пане́ль.

pavilion *n.* павильо́н.

paving *n.* мощéние. —**paving block/stone,** торéц; *pl.* брусчáтка.

paw *n.* лáпа. —*v.t.* облáпить.

pawl *n.* собáчка.

pawn *n., chess* пéшка. —*v.t.* заклáдывать; отдавáть в залóг. —**pawnbroker,** *n.* залогодержáтель. —**pawnshop,** *n.* ломбáрд. —**pawn ticket,** ломбáрдная квитáнция.

pay *v.t.* **1,** (give in payment; settle) платúть: *pay ten dollars,* платúть дéсять дóлларов. *Pay a bill,* платúть по счёту; оплáчивать счёт. *Pay a fine,* платúть штраф. *Pay a debt,* выплáчивать *or* уплáчивать *or* отдавáть долг. *Pay cash,* платúть налúчными. *Pay a high price,* платúть высóкую цéну. **2,** (give money to; remunerate) платúть (+ *dat.*): *pay the doctor,* платúть врачу́. *Pay the cashier,* платúть кассúру; платúть в кáссу. **3,** *fol. by inf.* (be worthwhile) стóить: *It doesn't pay to argue with him,* не стóит с ним спóрить. **4,** (offer in wages): *The job pays 20,000 a year,* зарплáта — двáдцать ты́сяч в год. **5,** *used with certain nouns: pay a visit on,* нанестú визúт (+ *dat.*); *pay attention to,* обращáть внимáние на; *pay someone a compliment,* сдéлать кому́-нибудь комплимéнт. —*v.i.* **1,** (make payment) платúть: *pay in rubles,* платúть рубля́ми *or* в рубля́х. **2,** (offer wages): *The job pays well,* рабóта хорошó оплáчивается. **3,** (be worthwhile) стóить. **4,** (be profitable) окупáться. **5,** (suffer or be punished for something) поплатúться: *pay with one's life,* поплатúться жúзнью. —*n.* плáта; зарплáта; жáлованье; оклáд. *Receive no pay,* не получáть зарплáты. *Base pay,* основнóй оклáд. *In the pay of,* на зарплáте у. *Vacation without pay,* неоплáчиваемый óтпуск; óтпуск без сохранéния содержáния. —**pay back, 1,** (a person) отплáчивать (+ *dat.*). **2,** (money) возвращáть. *Pay back a loan,* выплáчивать *or* возвращáть заём. —**pay for, 1,** *literally* платúть за. **2,** (suffer the consequences of) платúться за; отвéтить за; расплáчиваться за. *Pay for one's mistakes,* платúться *or* расплáчиваться за свои́ оши́бки. *You'll pay for this!,* вы за э́то поплáтитесь! **3,** *Pay for itself,* окупáться. —**pay off, 1,** (pay in full) выплáчивать; расплáчиваться с; рассчúтываться с; погашáть. *Pay off a loan,* платúть по займу́; погашáть ссу́ду. **2,** (settle up with) расплáчиваться с; рассчúтываться с. **3,** (bribe) подкупáть. **4,** (give money to under duress) откупáться от. **5,** (yield a profit; be successful) окупáться. —**pay out, 1,** (disburse) выплáчивать. **2,** *naut.* (let out, as a rope) травúть. —**pay up,** выплáчивать. *You're all paid up,* вы пóлностью рассчитáлись *or* расплатúлись. *See also* **paid.**

payable *adj. Be payable,* подлежáть уплáте. *A check payable to...,* чек на и́мя (+ *gen.*).

paycheck *n.* полу́чка.

payday *n.* платёжный день.

payee *n.* получáтель (дéнег).

payer *n.* платéльщик.

paying *adj.* **1,** (who pays) плáтный. **2,** (profitable) рентáбельный.

payload *n.* **1,** *comm.* полéзный груз. **2,** *aero.* полéзная нагру́зка.

paymaster *n.* кассúр; казначéй.

payment *n.* **1,** (act of paying) плáта; оплáта; уплáта; платёж. **2,** (something paid) платёж. *Down payment,* задáток. *Balance of payments,* платёжный балáнс.

payoff *n.,* *colloq.* **1,** (money paid to a winner) вы́игрыш. **2,** (bribe) взя́тка. **3,** (climax) развя́зка.

pay phone телефóн-автомáт. *Call from a pay phone,* звонúть из автомáта.

payroll *n.* платёжная вéдомость: *on the payroll,* в платёжной вéдомости. *Be on the payroll of,* быть на зарплáте у.

pea *n.* горóшина; *pl.* горóх; горóшек. —*adj.* горóховый: *pea soup,* горóховый суп.

peace *n.* **1,** (absence of war) мир: *at peace,* в мúре. *Live in peace,* жить в мúре. *Make peace with,* заключúть мир с. **2,** (peace of mind) покóй: *leave in peace,* оставля́ть в покóе. *Know no peace,* не знать покóя. *May he rest in peace,* мир прáху егó. **3,** (public order) (обществéнный) поря́док: *keep the peace,* блюстú поря́док; *disturb the peace,* нарушáть обществéнный поря́док. —*adj.* мúрный. *Peace treaty,* договóр о мúре; мúрный договóр. —**hold** (*or* **keep**) **one's peace,** придержáть язы́к.

peaceable *adj.* мúрный.

peaceful *adj.* **1,** (not involving war) мúрный: *for peaceful purposes,* в мúрных цéлях. **2,** (tranquil) спокóйный: *peaceful scene,* спокóйный вид *or* пейзáж. —**peacefully,** *adv.* мúрно; спокóйно.

peacekeeping *n.* поддержáние *or* сохранéние мúра. *Peacekeeping force,* войскá по поддержáнию мúра.

peace-loving *adj.* миролюбúвый.

peacemaker *n.* миротвóрец.

peacetime *n.* мúрное врéмя.

peach *n.* пéрсик. —*adj.* пéрсиковый. —**peach tree,** пéрсик; пéрсиковое дéрево.

peacock *n.* павлúн. *Peacock feathers,* павлúньи пéрья.

peahen *n.* пáва.

pea jacket бушлáт.

peak *n.* **1,** (of a mountain) пик; вершúна. **2,** (of a cap) козырёк. **3,** *fig.* (high point; acme) вершúна; вы́сшая тóчка. *Reach its peak,* достигáть вы́сшей тóчки *or* наивы́сшего у́ровня. *At the peak of his career,* на вершúне своéй карьéры. —*adj.* максимáльный: *peak load,* максимáльная нагру́зка. *In peak form,* в наилу́чшей фóрме.

peaked *adj.* **1,** (having a peak) с козырькóм. *Peaked cap,* картỳз. **2,** (pale and drawn) измождённый.

peal *n.* **1,** (of a bell) звон; трезвóн. **2,** (of thunder, laughter, etc.) раскáт. —*v.i.* гремéть; трезвóнить.

peanut *n.* арáхис; землянóй орéх. —**peanut butter,** пáста из тёртого арáхиса.

pear *n.* гру́ша. —*adj.* гру́шевый.

pearl *n.* жéмчуг. *A single pearl,* жемчу́жина; жемчу́жное зернó. —*adj.* жемчу́жный. —**pearl barley,** перлóвая крупá. —**pearl oyster,** жемчу́жница.

pearly *adj.* жемчу́жный.

peasant *n.* крестья́нин. —*adj.* крестья́нский. —**peasantry**, *n.* крестья́нство.

peat *n.* торф. —*adj.* торфяно́й: *peat bog,* торфяно́е боло́то. —**peat moss,** торфяно́й мох.

pebble *n.* ка́мешек; голы́ш; га́лька. —*adj.* га́лечный: *pebble beach,* га́лечный пляж.

pecan *n.* пека́н.

peccadillo *n.* грешо́к.

peccary *n.* пе́кари.

peck *v.t. & i.* клева́ть. *Peck out,* выклёвывать. —*n.* клево́к.

pectoral *adj.* грудно́й: *pectoral muscles,* грудны́е мы́шцы. *Pectoral cross,* напе́рсный крест.

peculiar *adj.* **1,** (unique; particular) осо́бенный; своеобра́зный; специфи́ческий. *Problems peculiar to women,* пробле́мы, специфи́ческие для же́нщин. **2,** (odd) стра́нный. —**peculiarity,** *n.* стра́нность.

pecuniary *adj.* де́нежный.

pedagogue *n.* педаго́г. —**pedagogic(al),** *adj.* педагоги́ческий. —**pedagogy,** *n.* педаго́гика.

pedal *n.* педа́ль. —*v.t.* вести́ (велосипе́д). —*v.i.* **1,** (work a pedal) нажима́ть педа́ль. **2,** (ride a bicycle) е́хать на велосипе́де.

pedant *n.* педа́нт; буквое́д. —**pedantic,** *adj.* педанти́чный. —**pedantry,** *n.* педанти́зм; буквое́дство.

peddle *v.t. & i.* торгова́ть вразно́с; торгова́ть с лотка́. *Peddle a theory,* носи́ться с тео́рией.

peddler *n.* коробе́йник; разно́счик.

pederast *n.* педера́ст. —**pederasty,** *n.* педера́стия.

pedestal *n.* пьедеста́л; постаме́нт; подно́жие.

pedestrian *n.* пешехо́д. —*adj.* **1,** (of or for pedestrians) пешехо́дный. **2,** (unimaginative; dull) прозаи́чный.

pediatrics *also,* **paediatrics** *n.* педиатри́я. —**pediatric,** *adj.* педиатри́ческий. —**pediatrician,** *n.* педиа́тр.

pedicel *n.* цветоно́жка.

pedicure *n.* педикю́р.

pedigree *n.* **1,** (lineage) происхожде́ние. **2,** (list of ancestors) родосло́вная. —**pedigreed,** *adj.* поро́дистый; племенно́й; чистокро́вный.

pediment *n.* фронто́н.

pedlar *n.* = **peddler.**

pedometer *n.* шагоме́р; педо́метр.

peek *n.* бы́стрый взгляд; взгляд укра́дкой. —*v.i.* подгля́дывать: *No peeking!,* не подгля́дывать!

peel *n.* ко́рка; кожура́; шелуха́. *Orange peel,* апельси́нная ко́рка. *Banana peel,* бана́новая кожура́. —*v.t.* **1,** (pare, as potatoes, fruit, etc.) чи́стить. **2,** *fol. by* **off** (remove) снима́ть (ко́рку); откле́ивать (ма́рку). —*v.i.* **1,** (shed skin) лупи́ться: *My face is peeling,* у меня́ лу́пится лицо́. **2,** *often fol. by* **off** (come off) сходи́ть; шелуши́ться; осыпа́ться; лупи́ться; облу́пливаться; облеза́ть. —**keep an eye peeled,** смотре́ть в о́ба.

peelings *n.pl.* очи́стки; шелуха́: *potato peelings,* карто́фельные очи́стки; карто́фельная шелуха́.

peep *v.i.* **1,** (look furtively) загля́дывать; подгля́дывать: *peep through a keyhole,* загля́дывать/подгля́дывать в замо́чную сква́жину. **2,** (come partly into view) выгля́дывать; прогля́дывать: *peep*

through/ out from behind/ the clouds, прогля́дывать сквозь ту́чи; выгля́дывать из-за туч. **3,** (chirp) пища́ть. —*n.* **1,** (glimpse) бы́стрый взгляд. *Have a peep at,* взгляну́ть на. **2,** (chirp) писк. **3,** (sound) звук.

peephole *n.* глазо́к.

peer *n.* **1,** (equal) ра́вный. **2,** (person one's own age) све́рстник. **3,** (nobleman) пэр. —*v.i.* всма́триваться; вгля́дываться. *Peer into the distance/darkness,* всма́триваться/вгля́дываться в даль/ в темноту́/. *Peer into a telescope,* смотре́ть в телеско́п. *Peer out the window,* выгля́дывать из окна́.

peerage *n.* **1,** (rank) пэ́рство. **2,** (peers collectively) сосло́вие пэ́ров.

peerless *adj.* несравне́нный; бесподо́бный.

peeve *v.t.* раздража́ть. —*n., in* **pet peeve,** люби́мая мозо́ль. —**peeved,** *adj.* раздражённый. —**peevish,** *adj.* сварли́вый.

peg *n.* **1,** (conical pin) ко́лышек. **2,** (such a pin on a stringed instrument) коло́к. —*v.t.* **1,** (fasten with a peg) прикрепля́ть ко́лышком. **2,** *fig.* (tie) привя́зывать: *pegged to the American dollar,* привя́зан к америка́нскому до́ллару. —**take (someone) down a peg,** сбива́ть спесь с (+ *gen.*).

Pegasus *n.* Пега́с.

peg leg деревя́нная нога́; деревя́шка.

peg top кубарь.

peignoir *n.* пенью́ар.

pejorative *adj.* уничижи́тельный.

pelican *n.* пелика́н.

pellagra *n.* пелла́гра.

pellet *n.* **1,** (small round ball) ша́рик. **2,** (small lead shot) дроби́н(к)а.

pellicle *n.* ко́жица; плёнка.

pell-mell *adv.* **1,** (in total disorder) впереме́шку. **2,** (in wild haste) сломя́ го́лову.

pellucid *adj.* прозра́чный.

pelt *n.* шку́ра. —*v.t.* (bombard) забра́сывать; засыпа́ть. —*v.i.* (beat down) бараба́нить.

pelvis *n.* таз. —**pelvic,** *adj.* та́зовый.

pen *n.* **1,** (quill pen) перо́; (fountain pen, ball-point, etc.) ру́чка. *Fountain pen,* авторучка. **2,** (enclosure for animals) заго́н. *Pigpen,* свина́рник. —*v.t.* **1,** (write; compose) писа́ть; сочиня́ть. **2,** (confine in a pen) загоня́ть в заго́н.

penal *adj.* **1,** (prescribing punishment) уголо́вный: *penal code,* уголо́вный ко́декс. **2,** (of or for prisoners) штрафно́й: *penal colony,* штрафна́я коло́ния. *Penal battalion,* штрафно́й батальо́н. —**penal servitude,** ка́торга; ка́торжные рабо́ты.

penalize *v.t.* штрафова́ть.

penalty *n.* **1,** (punishment) наказа́ние; взыска́ние; штраф; пе́ня. *Death penalty,* сме́ртная казнь. *Pay the penalty,* поплати́ться. **2,** *sports* штраф. —*adj.* штрафно́й: *penalty kick,* штрафно́й уда́р.

penance *n.* покая́ние.

pence *n.pl.* пенс: *six pence,* шесть пе́нсов.

penchant *n.* скло́нность; накло́нность. *Have a penchant for neatness,* отлича́ться аккура́тностью.

pencil *n.* каранда́ш. —*adj.* каранда́шный: *pencil*

drawing, каранда́шный рису́нок. —*v.t.* писа́ть (карандашо́м). *Pencil one's eyebrows,* подводи́ть бро́ви. —**pencil case,** пена́л. —**pencil sharpener,** точи́лка.

pendant *n.* куло́н; подве́ска.

pending *adj.* ожида́ющий реше́ния. —*prep.* в ожида́нии (+ *gen.*); впредь до.

pendulum *n.* ма́ятник.

penetrate *v.t.* пробива́ть; проника́ть в. *The bullet penetrated the wall,* пу́ля проби́ла сте́ну. *The car's headlights penetrated the darkness,* фа́ры маши́ны проби́ли темноту́. *Penetrate the building's security system,* прони́кнуть в дом че́рез охра́ну. *Penetrate the enemy's defenses,* прорва́ть оборо́ну проти́вника. *Penetrate someone's mind,* прони́кнуть в чьи́-нибудь мы́сли.

penetrating *adj.* **1,** (of cold, wind, etc.) прони́зывающий. **2,** (keen; discerning) проница́тельный.

penetration *n.* проникнове́ние.

penguin *n.* пингви́н.

penholder *n.* ру́чка (для пера́).

penicillin *n.* пеницилли́н.

peninsula *n.* полуо́стров. —**peninsular,** *adj.* полуостровно́й.

penis *n.* мужско́й половой член.

penitence *n.* раска́яние; покая́ние.

penitent *adj.* ка́ющийся. *Penitent look,* покая́нный вид.

penitentiary *n.* ка́торжная тюрьма́.

penknife *n.* перочи́нный нож(ик).

penmanship *n.* каллигра́фия; чистописа́ние.

pen name псевдони́м.

pennant *n.* вы́мпел.

penniless *adj.* безде́нежный; без копе́йки; без гроша́.

penny *n.* (American coin) моне́та в оди́н цент; (British coin) пе́нни; пенс. —**a penny for your thoughts,** о чём ты заду́мался? —**cost a pretty penny,** обойти́сь в копе́ечку; бить *or* уда́рить по карма́ну. —**not have a penny to one's name,** не име́ть ни копе́йки (*or* ни гроша́) за душо́й.

penny pincher скопидо́м; скуперда́й.

pension *n.* пе́нсия: *old-age pension,* пе́нсия по ста́рости. —*v.t.* [*usu.* **pension off**] увольня́ть на пе́нсию. —**pensioner,** *n.* пенсионе́р.

pensive *adj.* заду́мчивый; вду́мчивый. —**pensiveness,** *n.* заду́мчивость.

pentagon *n.* **1,** (geometric figure) пятиуго́льник. **2,** *cap.* (headquarters of U.S. Defense Dept.) Пентаго́н. —**pentagonal,** *adj.* пятиуго́льный.

pentahedron *n.* пятигра́нник.

pentameter *n.* пятисто́пный стих; пента́метр. *Iambic pentameter,* пятисто́пный ямб. —*adj.* пятисто́пный.

Pentateuch *n.* пятикни́жие.

pentathlon *n.* пятибо́рье.

Pentecost *n.* пятидеся́тница.

penthouse *n.* кварти́ра на ве́рхнем этаже́.

pent-up *adj.* затаённый.

penultimate *adj.* предпосле́дний.

penumbra *n.* полуте́нь.

penurious *adj.* **1,** (stingy) скупо́й. **2,** (poor) бе́дный.

penury *n.* нужда́; нищета́.

peon *n.* пео́н. —**peonage,** *n.* пеона́ж.

peony *n.* пио́н.

people *n.* **1,** (persons) лю́ди. *One hundred people,* сто челове́к. *What will people say?,* что ска́жут лю́ди? *Many people believe that...,* мно́гие счита́ют, что... **2,** (nation) наро́д: *the Chinese people,* кита́йский наро́д. —*v.t.* населя́ть. —**people's,** *adj.* наро́дный: *people's republic,* наро́дная респу́блика.

pep *n., colloq.* эне́ргия; прыть. —*v.t.* [*usu.* **pep up**] оживля́ть.

pepper *n.* пе́рец. —*v.t.* **1,** (season) пе́рчить. **2,** (pelt) забра́сывать; осыпа́ть. —**pepper shaker,** пе́речница.

peppermint *n.* **1,** (herb) пе́речная мя́та. **2,** (candy) мя́тный ледене́ц.

pepsin *n.* пепси́н.

peptic ulcer я́звенная боле́знь.

peptone *n.* пепто́н.

per *prep.* **1,** (for each) в; за: *ten miles per hour,* де́сять миль в час; *ten cents per item,* де́сять це́нтов за шту́ку. *Two dollars per person,* два до́ллара с челове́ка. *One box per customer,* одну́ коро́бку в одни́ ру́ки. **2,** [*often,* **as per**] (according to) в соотве́тствии с.

peradventure *adv., archaic* мо́жет быть; возмо́жно.

perambulator *n.* де́тская коля́ска.

per annum в год.

percale *n.* перка́ль.

per capita на ду́шу населе́ния.

perceive *v.t.* **1,** (become aware of through the senses) воспринима́ть; ощуща́ть. **2,** (come to understand) понима́ть; осознава́ть.

percent *n.* проце́нт: *one percent,* оди́н проце́нт; *fifty percent,* пятьдеся́т проце́нтов. *I am 100% certain,* я уве́рен(а) на сто проце́нтов.

percentage *n.* **1,** (percent) проце́нт. **2,** (part; proportion) часть; до́ля; проце́нт; уде́льный вес. *Constitute a small percentage of...,* составля́ть ма́лый проце́нт от (+ *gen.*). **3,** (fee; commission) проце́нты: *work on percentage,* рабо́тать на проце́нтах. —**percentagewise,** *adv.* в проце́нтном отноше́нии.

perceptible *adj.* заме́тный; ощути́мый.

perception *n.* **1,** (act of perceiving) восприя́тие. **2,** (mental image) представле́ние. **3,** (keenness of mind) проница́тельность.

perceptive *adj.* проница́тельный; то́нкий; зо́ркий. *Perceptive comment,* то́нкое замеча́ние.

perch *n.* **1,** (fish) о́кунь. **2,** (roost) насе́ст. —*v.i.* уса́живаться.

perchance *adv.* случа́йно.

perchloric acid хло́рная кислота́.

percolate *v.t.* проце́живать. —*v.i.* **1,** (seep; ooze) проса́чиваться. **2,** (start bubbling up) кипе́ть. —**percolator,** *n.* кофе́йник с си́течком.

percussion *n.* **1,** (striking together of two bodies) столкнове́ние; уда́р. **2,** *med.* перку́ссия. —**percussion cap,** ка́псюль; писто́н. —**percussion instrument,** уда́рный инструме́нт.

per diem 1, (per day) за день. **2,** (daily allowance) суточные деньги.

perdition *n.* проклятие: *condemn to perdition,* предавать проклятию.

peregrination *n.* странствие.

peregrine falcon сапсан.

peremptory *adj.* **1,** (barring further action) безапелляционный. **2,** (allowing no room for disagreement) повелительный.

perennial *adj.* **1,** (perpetual) вечный. **2,** *bot.* многолетний. —*n., bot.* многолетнее растение.

perfect *adj.* **1,** (complete; exact) совершенный: *a perfect circle,* совершенный круг; *a perfect resemblance,* совершенное сходство. **2,** (flawless) безупречный: *in perfect condition,* в безупречном состоянии; *in perfect English,* на безупречном английском языке. *Far from perfect,* далёк от совершенства. **3,** (ideal) идеальный; образцовый; превосходный. *Perfect weather,* идеальная погода. *The perfect man for the position,* идеальный человек для этой должности. —*v.t.* совершенствовать; отрабатывать; доводить до совершенства. —*n., gram.* перфект.

perfection *n.* **1,** (state of being perfect) совершенство. *To perfection,* в совершенстве. **2,** (act of perfecting) совершенствование.

perfective *adj., gram.* совершенный. —*n., gram.* совершенный вид.

perfectly *adv.* **1,** (to perfection) в совершенстве: *speak Russian perfectly,* говорить по-русски в совершенстве. *These shoes fit (me) perfectly,* эти ботинки (мне) как раз впору. **2,** (completely; fully) совершенно: *perfectly obvious,* совершенно очевидно. *I know perfectly well that...,* я прекрасно знаю, что... **3,** (without a hitch) безотказно: *work perfectly,* работать безотказно.

perfidious *adj.* вероломный. —**perfidy,** *n.* вероломство.

perforate *v.t.* перфорировать. —*adj.* = **perforated.**

perforated *adj.* **1,** (pierced with holes) перфорированный. **2,** (of stamps) зубцовый. —**perforated ulcer,** прободная язва.

perforation *n.* **1,** *med.* прободение; перфорация. **2,** (on stamps) перфорация; зубцовка.

perforator *n.* перфоратор.

perforce *adv.* волей-неволей.

perform *v.t.* **1,** (execute; carry out) выполнять; исполнять. *Perform one's duties,* выполнять *or* исполнять *or* нести свои обязанности. *Perform military service,* нести военную службу. *Perform an operation,* сделать операцию. *Perform an experiment,* проводить опыт. *Perform a feat,* совершить подвиг. *Perform a ritual,* совершить обряд. *Perform a trick,* показать фокус. **2,** (give a performance of) исполнять: *perform a symphony,* исполнить симфонию. —*v.i.* **1,** (give a performance) играть; выступать. **2,** (function; operate) работать. *The car performs well,* машина идёт хорошо.

performance *n.* **1,** (carrying out) выполнение; исполнение. *In performance of one's duties,* при исполнении служебных обязанностей. **2,** (rendition) исполнение; игра. *Give a brilliant performance,* блестяще исполнить роль. **3,** (show) представление; спектакль; сеанс. **4,** (efficiency of operation) ходовые качества. *Performance tests,* ходовые испытания.

performer *n.* исполнитель.

perfume *n.* духи. *Perfume bottle,* флакон для духов. —*v.t.* душить. —**perfumer,** *n.* парфюмер. —**perfumery,** *n.* парфюмерия.

perfunctory *adj.* поверхностный; механический. —**perfunctorily,** *adv.* поверхностно; мельком.

perhaps *adv.* может быть.

pericardium *n.* околосердечная сумка ; перикард.

pericarp *n.* околоплодник.

perigee *n.* перигей.

perihelion *n.* перигелий.

peril *n.* опасность; риск. *At one's own peril,* на свой страх и риск. —*v.t.* ставить под угрозу. —**perilous,** *adj.* опасный; рискованный.

perimeter *n.* периметр.

period *n.* **1,** (in history) период. *The postwar period,* послевоенный период. *The Jurassic Period,* юрский период. **2,** (interval of time) срок; период: *brief period,* короткий срок/период. *Waiting period,* срок ожидания. *Period of incubation,* инкубационный период. **3,** (dot placed at the end of a sentence) точка. **4,** (division of a school day) урок. **5,** (division of a game) период; тайм. —*adj.* стильный: *period furniture,* стильная мебель.

periodic *adj.* периодический.

periodical *adj.* периодический. —*n.* периодическое издание; *pl.* периодика.

periodically *adv.* **1,** (at regular intervals) периодически. **2,** (from time to time) время от времени.

peripatetic *adj.* странствующий.

peripheral *adj.* **1,** (away from the center) периферический. **2,** *fig.* (incidental; tangential) несущественный; второстепенный. —**peripheral vision,** периферическое зрение.

periphery *n.* периферия.

periphrasis *n.* перифраза.

periscope *n.* перископ.

perish *v.i.* гибнуть; погибать. *Perish in a fire,* погибнуть во время пожара. —**perish the thought!,** упаси Бог!; Боже упаси!

perishable *adj.* скоропортящийся. —*n., usu. pl.* скоропортящиеся продукты.

peristalsis *n.* перистальтика. —**peristaltic,** *adj.* перистальтический.

peristyle *n.* перистиль.

peritoneum *n.* брюшина. —**peritonitis,** *n.* воспаление брюшины; перитонит.

periwinkle *n.* **1,** (plant) барвинок. **2,** (mollusk) литорина.

perjure *v.t.* [*usu.* **perjure oneself**] лжесвидетельствовать. —**perjurer,** *n.* лжесвидетель; клятвопреступник. —**perjury,** *n.* лжесвидетельство; клятвопреступление.

perk *v.t.* [*usu.* **perk up**] оживлять; ободрять. —*v.i.*

[*usu.* **perk up**] оживать; оживляться; воспрянуть духом. —**perky,** *adj.* бойкий; задорный.

permafrost *n.* вечная мерзлота.

permanence *n.* постоянство.

permanent *adj.* постоянный: *permanent job/residence/address,* постоянная работа; постоянное местожительство; постоянный адрес. —*n.* = **permanent wave.**

permanently *adv.* на долгое время; навсегда. *Permanently damaged,* непоправимо повреждён. *Settle permanently in New York,* окончательно поселиться в Нью-Йорке; осесть в Нью-Йорке.

permanent wave перманент; шестимесячная завивка.

permeable *adj.* проницаемый. —**permeability,** *n.* проницаемость.

permeate *v.t.* пропитывать; пронизывать.

Permian *adj.* пермский.

permissible *adj.* позволительный; допустимый; дозволенный.

permission *n.* разрешение; позволение. *Permission to enter the house,* разрешение на вход в дом. *With your permission,* с вашего разрешения.

permissive *adj.* не строгий; снисходительный. —**permissiveness,** *n.* вседозволенность.

permit *v.t.* **1,** (give permission to) разрешать; позволять: *Permit me to...,* разрешите/позвольте мне (+ *inf.*). *No one is permitted to...,* никому не разрешается *or* позволено (+ *inf.*). **2,** (allow to happen) допускать. **3,** (enable) позволять: *This will permit me to...,* это позволит мне (+ *inf.*). —*v.i.* позволять: *if time permits,* если время позволяет; *weather permitting,* если погода позволит. —*n.* пропуск; разрешение. *Gun permit,* разрешение на владение огнестрельным оружием. *Residence permit,* прописка; вид на жительство.

permutation *n.* перестановка.

pernicious *adj.* пагубный; вредный. —**pernicious anemia,** злокачественное малокровие.

perorate *v.i.* ораторствовать; разглагольствовать.

peroxide *n.* **1,** (chemical) перекись. **2,** (antiseptic) перекись водорода.

perpendicular *adj.* перпендикулярный. —*n.* перпендикуляр.

perpetrate *v.t.* совершать: *perpetrate a crime,* совершить преступление. —**perpetration,** *n.* совершение (преступления). —**perpetrator,** *n.* виновник (преступления).

perpetual *adj.* вечный. —**perpetual check,** *chess* вечный шах. —**perpetual motion,** вечное движение.

perpetually *adv.* вечно.

perpetuate *v.t.* увековечивать. —**perpetuation,** *n.* увековечение.

perpetuity *n.* вечность. —**in perpetuity,** навечно.

perplex *v.t.* приводить в недоумение; озадачивать. —**perplexed,** *adj.* недоуменный; недоумевающий; озадаченный. —**perplexing,** *adj.* недоуменный. —**perplexity,** *n.* недоумение; озадаченность.

perquisite *n.* льгота.

per se сам по себе.

persecute *v.t.* преследовать. —**persecution,** *n.* преследование; гонение. —**persecutor,** *n.* преследователь; гонитель.

persevere *v.i.* упорствовать. —**perseverance,** *n.* упорство; настойчивость.

Persian *adj.* персидский. —*n.* **1,** (person) перс; персиянка. **2,** (language) персидский язык. —**Persian carpet,** персидский ковёр. —**Persian cat,** сибирская кошка. —**Persian lamb,** каракуль.

persiflage *n.* беззлобная насмешка.

persimmon *n.* хурма.

persist *v.i.* **1,** (refuse to give up) упорствовать. **2,** (continue to exist) сохраняться.

persistence *n.* упорство; настойчивость; настоятельность.

persistent *adj.* **1,** (refusing to relent) упорный; настойчивый; настоятельный. *Persistent cough,* упорный кашель. **2,** (repeated; continuous) бесконечный.

person *n.* **1,** (human being) человек: *a nice person,* симпатичный человек. *An important person,* важное лицо. **2,** *gram.* лицо: *first person,* первое лицо. —**in person,** лично; собственной персоной. —**in the person of,** в лице (+ *gen.*). —**on one's person,** при себе. *Carry on one's person,* носить с собой.

personable *adj.* симпатичный; располагающий.

personage *n.* **1,** (person) лицо: *historic personage,* историческое лицо. **2,** (character in a play, history, etc.) персонаж.

personal *adj.* личный: *my personal opinion,* моё личное мнение. *Personal computer,* персональный компьютер. *Close personal friend,* близкий друг. *Get personal,* переходить на личности. —**personal pronoun,** личное местоимение.

personality *n.* личность.

personally *adv.* лично: *Personally I'm against it,* лично я против этого. *Experience something personally,* испытать что-нибудь на себе. *Take something personally,* принимать что-нибудь на свой счёт.

persona non grata персона нон грата.

personify *v.t.* олицетворять. —**personification,** *n.* олицетворение.

personnel *n.* кадры; персонал; личный состав. *Personnel department,* отдел кадров. *Reduction in personnel,* сокращение штатов.

perspective *n.* **1,** *art* перспектива. **2,** (viewpoint) свет. *In a different perspective,* в другом свете; в другом ракурсе. *Keep things in perspective,* широко смотреть на вещи. —*adj.* перспективный.

perspicacious *adj.* проницательный. —**perspicacity,** *n.* проницательность.

perspiration *n.* пот; испарина.

perspire *v.i.* потеть.

persuade *v.t.* **1,** (induce; prevail on) уговаривать; убеждать; склонять: *persuade someone to come,* уговорить/убедить/склонить кого-нибудь прийти. **2,** (cause to believe; convince) убеждать: *persuade someone to the contrary,* убедить кого-нибудь в обратном.

persuasion *n*. **1,** (act of persuading) убежде́ние. *After considerable persuasion,* по́сле до́лгих угово́ров. **2,** (religious belief) вероиспове́дание.

persuasive *adj*. убеди́тельный. **—persuasively,** *adv*. убеди́тельно. **—persuasiveness,** *n*. убеди́тельность.

pert *adj*. **1,** (impudent) развя́зный. **2,** (lively) задо́рный.

pertain *v.i.* [*usu.* **pertain to**] относи́ться (к).

pertinacious *adj*. **1,** (stubborn) упря́мый. **2,** (persistent) упо́рный. **—pertinacity,** *n*. упря́мство; упо́рство.

pertinent *adj*. уме́стный; относя́щийся к де́лу. **—pertinence,** *n*. уме́стность.

perturb *v.t.* смуща́ть; волнова́ть.

perturbation *n., astron.* пертурба́ция.

peruse *v.t.* **1,** (read carefully) внима́тельно прочита́ть. **2,** (read casually; scan) просма́тривать. **—perusal,** *n*. прочте́ние.

Peruvian *adj*. перуа́нский.

pervade *v.t.* наполня́ть; насыща́ть; пропи́тывать; прони́зывать; распространя́ться по. **—pervasive,** *adj*. распространя́ющийся повсю́ду.

perverse *adj*. **1,** (contrary) упря́мый. **2,** (perverted) поро́чный.

perversion *n*. извраще́ние.

perversity *n*. **1,** (contrariness) упря́мство. **2,** (depravity) извращённость; поро́чность.

pervert *v.t.* **1,** (distort; twist) извраща́ть. **2,** (lead astray; corrupt) совраща́ть. **—***n*. извращённый челове́к.

perverted *adj*. поро́чный; извращённый; противоесте́ственный.

peseta *n*. песе́та; пезе́та.

pesky *adj., colloq.* надое́дливый; доку́чливый.

peso *n*. пе́со; пе́зо.

pessimism *n*. пессими́зм. **—pessimist,** *n*. пессими́ст. **—pessimistic,** *adj*. пессимисти́ческий. *I am pessimistic,* я настро́ен пессимисти́чески.

pest *n*. **1,** (annoying person) надое́да. **2,** (destructive insect) вреди́тель.

pester *v.t.* надоеда́ть; докуча́ть; донима́ть; пристава́ть к.

pesticide *n*. пестици́д; ядохимика́т.

pestilence *n*. чума́.

pestle *n*. пест; пе́стик.

pet *n*. **1,** (animal) дома́шнее живо́тное. **2,** (favorite) люби́мец; ба́ловень. **—***adj*. **1,** (of an animal) ручно́й: *pet monkey,* ручна́я обезья́на. **2,** (favorite) люби́мый. **—***v.t.* гла́дить: *pet the dog,* гла́дить соба́ку. **—pet name,** уменьши́тельное *or* ласка́тельное и́мя. **—pet store,** зоомагази́н.

petal *n*. лепесто́к.

petard *n*. пета́рда.

petcock *n*. спускно́й кран.

peter *v.i.* [*usu.* **peter out**] выдыха́ться; захлёбываться.

petiole *n*. черешо́к.

petit bourgeois мещани́н. **—petit-bourgeois,** *adj*. мелкобуржуа́зный; меща́нский. **—petite bourgeoisie,** ме́лкая буржуази́я; меща́нство.

petition *n*. **1,** (document signed by many) пети́ция. **2,** (formal request) хода́тайство. **—***v.t.* обраща́ться с пети́цией к. **—***v.i.* хода́тайствовать. *Petition for early release,* хода́тайствовать (*or* подава́ть хода́тайство) о досро́чном освобожде́нии (из тюрьмы́). **—petitioner,** *n*. проси́тель.

petrel *n*. буреве́стник; качу́рка.

petrified *adj*. **1,** (having turned to stone) окамене́лый. **2,** (terrified) оцепене́вший. *We were petrified,* мы дрожа́ли от стра́ха.

petrify *v.t.* превраща́ть в ка́мень. **—***v.i.* (о)камене́ть.

petrochemical *n*. нефтехими́ческий проду́кт. **—***adj*. нефтехими́ческий.

petrol *n., Brit.* бензи́н.

petroleum *n*. нефть. **—***adj*. нефтяно́й.

petticoat *n*. ни́жняя ю́бка.

pettifoggery *n*. крючкотво́рство.

pettiness *n*. ме́лочность.

petty *adj*. **1,** (minor; trivial) ме́лкий; ме́лочный. **2,** (small-minded) ме́лочный. **—petty cash,** де́ньги на ме́лкие расхо́ды. **—petty larceny,** ме́лкая кра́жа. **—petty officer,** старшина́.

petulant *adj*. раздражи́тельный; сварли́вый. **—petulance,** *n*. раздражи́тельность.

petunia *n*. пету́ния.

pew *n*. (церко́вная) скамья́.

pewit *n*. чи́бис; пи́галица.

pewter *n*. сплав на оловя́нной осно́ве. **—***adj*. оловя́нный.

phaeton *n*. фаэто́н.

phagocyte *n*. фагоци́т.

phalanx *n*. фала́нга.

phalarope *n*. плаву́нчик.

phallic *adj*. фалли́ческий. **—phallus,** *n*. фа́ллос.

phantasmagoria *n*. фантасмаго́рия. **—phantasmagoric,** *adj*. фантасмагори́ческий.

phantom *n*. при́зрак; виде́ние; фанто́м.

Pharaoh *n*. фарао́н.

pharisee *n*. фарисе́й. **—pharisaic,** *adj*. фарисе́йский.

pharmaceutical *adj*. апте́карский; фармацевти́ческий. **—pharmaceutics,** *n*. фармаце́втика.

pharmacist *n*. фармаце́вт; апте́карь; прови́зор.

pharmacology *n*. фармаколо́гия. **—pharmacological,** *adj*. фармакологи́ческий. **—pharmacologist,** *n*. фармако́лог.

pharmacopoeia *n*. фармакопе́я.

pharmacy *n*. **1,** (the science) фармаце́втика; фарма́ция. **2,** (drugstore) апте́ка.

pharynx *n*. зев.

phase *n*. фа́за; фа́зис. **—***v.t.* [*usu.* **phase in** *or* **phase out**] постепе́нно вводи́ть *or* упраздня́ть. **—phased,** *adj*. поэта́пный.

pheasant *n*. фаза́н.

phenobarbital *n*. люмина́л; фенобарбита́л.

phenol *n*. фено́л.

phenomenal *adj*. феномена́льный.

phenomenon *n*. **1,** (observable fact) явле́ние. **2,** (marvel; wonder) фено́мен.

phial *n*. пузырёк; флако́н; скля́нка.

philander *v.i.* флиртова́ть. **—philanderer,** *n*. воло-ки́та; ухажёр.

philanthropy *n.* филантро́пия. —**philanthropic,** *adj.* филантропи́ческий. —**philanthropist,** *n.* филантро́п.

philately *n.* филатели́я. —**philatelic,** *adj.* филателисти́ческий. —**philatelist,** *n.* филатели́ст.

philharmonic *adj.* филармони́ческий. —*n.* **1,** (orchestra) симфони́ческий орке́стр. **2,** (group supporting same) филармо́ния.

philippic *n.* фили́ппика.

Philippine *adj.* филиппи́нский.

philodendron *n.* филоде́ндрон.

philology *n.* филоло́гия. —**philological,** *adj.* филологи́ческий. —**philologist,** *n.* фило́лог.

philosopher *n.* фило́соф. —**philosophic(al),** *adj.* филосо́фский. —**philosophically,** *adv.* филосо́фски. —**philosophize,** *v.i.* филосо́фствовать.

philosophy *n.* филосо́фия.

phlebitis *n.* флеби́т.

phlebotomy *n.* кровопуска́ние.

phlegm *n.* **1,** (mucus) мокро́та. **2,** (apathy) фле́гма. —**phlegmatic,** *adj.* флегмати́чный.

phloem *n.* флоэ́ма.

phlox *n.* флокс.

phobia *n.* фо́бия.

Phoenician *adj.* финики́йский. —*n.* финики́ец. *The Phoenicians,* финики́йцы.

phoenix *n.* фе́никс.

phone *n., colloq.* телефо́н. *Phone call,* вы́зов (по телефо́ну); телефо́нный звоно́к. *Phone number,* но́мер телефо́на. *Pick up the phone!,* возьми́те тру́бку! —*v.t. & i., colloq.* звони́ть.

phoneme *n.* фоне́ма. —**phonemic,** *adj.* фонемати́ческий.

phonetic *adj.* фонети́ческий. —**phonetics,** *n.* фоне́тика.

phoney *adj.* = phony.

phonograph *n.* граммофо́н; патефо́н; прои́грыватель. *Phonograph record,* грампласти́нка.

phonology *n.* фоноло́гия.

phony *also,* **phoney** *adj., slang* подде́льный; ли́повый.

phooey *interj.* тьфу!

phosgene *n.* фосге́н.

phosphate *n.* фосфа́т.

phosphorescence *n.* свече́ние; фосфоресце́нция. —**phosphorescent,** *adj.* фосфоресци́рующий.

phosphorus *n.* фо́сфор. —**phosphoric; phosphorous,** *adj.* фо́сфорный.

photo *n., colloq.* фотогра́фия; фо́то.

photo album альбо́м для фо́то.

photocopier *n.* копирова́льная маши́на; фостоста́т. —**photocopy,** *n.* фотоко́пия.

photoelectric *adj.* фотоэлектри́ческий. —**photoelectric cell,** фотоэлеме́нт.

photoengraving *n.* фотогравю́ра.

photogenic *adj.* фотогени́чный.

photograph *n.* фотогра́фия; фотосни́мок. —*v.t.* фотографи́ровать. —*v.i. I do not photograph well,* я пло́хо выхожу́ на фотогра́фии.

photographer *n.* фото́граф.

photographic *adj.* фотографи́ческий.

photography *n.* фотогра́фия.

photogravure *n.* фотогравю́ра.

photo lab фотолаборато́рия.

photometer *n.* фото́метр.

photon *n.* фото́н.

photosphere *n.* фотосфе́ра.

photostat *n.* фотоко́пия.

photosynthesis *n.* фотоси́нтез.

phrase *n.* фра́за; оборо́т. —*v.t.* формули́ровать. —**phrase book,** разгово́рник.

phraseology *n.* фразеоло́гия. —**phraseological,** *adj.* фразеологи́ческий.

phrenology *n.* френоло́гия.

phylactery *n.* филакте́рия.

phylum *n.* тип.

physical *adj.* физи́ческий. —*n., colloq.* медици́нский осмо́тр. —**physical education,** физи́ческое воспита́ние; физи́ческая культу́ра; физкульту́ра. —**physical examination,** медици́нский осмо́тр. —**physical exercise,** физи́ческие упражне́ния. —**physical science,** физи́ческие нау́ки. —**physical training = physical education.**

physically *adv.* физи́чески.

physician *n.* врач.

physicist *n.* фи́зик.

physics *n.* фи́зика. *Physics department,* физи́ческий факульте́т.

physiognomy *n.* физионо́мия.

physiology *n.* физиоло́гия. —**physiological,** *adj.* физиологи́ческий. —**physiologist,** *n.* физио́лог.

physiotherapy *n.* физиотерапи́я. —**physiotherapist,** *n.* физиотерапе́вт.

physique *n.* телосложе́ние.

pianissimo *adj. & adv.* пиани́ссимо.

pianist *n.* пиани́ст.

piano *n.* роя́ль; фортепья́но. *Upright piano,* пиани́но. —*adj.* фортепья́нный: *piano concerto,* фортепья́нный конце́рт. *Piano bench,* скаме́йка для роя́ля. *Piano lessons,* уро́ки игры́ на роя́ле. —*adv.* пиа́но.

pianoforte *n.* фортепья́но.

piaster *also,* **piastre** *n.* пиа́стр.

pica *n.* ци́церо.

picaresque *adj.* плутовско́й.

picayune *adj.* пустяко́вый; ерундо́вый; ме́лочный.

piccolo *n.* пи́кколо.

pick *n.* **1,** (tool) кирка́. **2,** (choice) вы́бор. *Take your pick,* выбира́йте. **3,** (choicest part) лу́чшая часть; цвет. —*v.t.* **1,** (select) выбира́ть; подбира́ть. **2,** (gather, as berries) собира́ть. **3,** (pluck, as flowers) рвать; срыва́ть. **4,** (pry open, as a lock) взла́мывать. **5,** (provoke, as a fight or quarrel) лезть в (дра́ку); иска́ть (ссо́ры). **6,** *Pick one's nose/teeth,* ковыря́ть в носу́/ в зуба́х/. **7,** *Pick someone's pocket,* залеза́ть в карма́н (+ *dat.*). —*v.i.* (select) выбира́ть. —**pick on,** придира́ться к. —**pick out, 1,** (select) выбира́ть. **2,** (distinguish; discern) различа́ть. **3,** (play by ear) подбира́ть: *pick out a tune on the piano,* подбира́ть моти́в на роя́ле. —**pick up, 1,** (take up from the ground or floor) поднима́ть; подбира́ть. **2,** (lift, as a telephone receiver) снима́ть; поднима́ть; брать (тру́бку). *Pick up the phone!*, возьми́те тру́бку! **3,** (call for) заходи́ть за; заезжа́ть за. **4,** (go and collect) идти́ за; забира́ть. **5,** (give a lift to on the road) подвози́ть. **6,** (take on, as a passenger or freight) забира́ть. *Pick up survivors,* подобра́ть уцеле́вших. **7,** (acquire casually) приобрета́ть; подхва́тывать; подцепля́ть. **8,** (learn superficially) нахвата́ться. **9,** (gain, as speed) набира́ть; развива́ть (ско́рость). **10,** (find, as a trail or scent) напада́ть на (след). **11,** (receive, as a radio signal) лови́ть; ула́вливать. **12,** (give added energy to) подба́дривать. **13,** (take into custody) заде́рживать: *pick up for questioning,* заде́рживать для допро́са. **14,** *colloq.* (improve) поправля́ться.

pickax *also,* **pickaxe** *n.* кирка́.

picker *n.* сбо́рщик.

pickerel *n.* щу́ка.

picket *n.* **1,** (stake) кол. **2,** (protester) пике́тчик. **3,** *mil.* пике́т. —*v.t. & i.* пикети́ровать. —**picket fence,** часто-ко́л. —**picket line,** пике́т.

pickings *n.pl.* объе́дки.

pickle *n.* (солёный) огуре́ц. —*v.t.* соли́ть; заса́ливать; маринова́ть. —**pickled,** *adj.* солёный. *Pickled herring,* сельдь в рассо́ле.

pickpocket *n.* карма́нный вор; карма́нник.

pickup *n.* **1,** (acceleration): *The car has good pickup,* маши́на хорошо́ (*or* бы́стро) набира́ет ско́рость. **2,** (collection of mail) вы́емка. **3,** *colloq.* (improvement) оживле́ние. —**pickup truck,** пика́п.

picky *adj., colloq.* привере́дливый.

picnic *n.* пикни́к. *Go on a picnic,* устро́ить пикни́к.

pictograph *n.* пиктогра́мма. —**pictographic,** *adj.* пиктографи́ческий. —**pictography,** *n.* пиктогра́фия.

pictorial *adj.* **1,** (graphic) живопи́сный; изобрази́тельный; о́бразный. **2,** (containing pictures) иллюстри́рованный.

picture *n.* **1,** (drawing or painting) карти́на. **2,** (photograph) фотогра́фия; сни́мок; ка́рточка. *Take a picture of,* фотографи́ровать; снима́ть. *Take pictures,* фотографи́ровать. *Have one's picture taken,* снима́ться. **3,** (movie) фильм. **4,** (image on a TV screen) изображе́ние. **5,** (vivid description) карти́на: *a picture of life in ancient Rome,* карти́на жи́зни в дре́внем Ри́ме. **6,** (mental image) представле́ние: *have a clear picture of,* име́ть я́сное представле́ние о. **7,** (general situation) карти́на: *a gloomy picture,* мра́чная карти́на. *Be out of the picture,* не фигури́ровать. *I get the picture,* я понима́ю в чём де́ло. **8,** (embodiment) воплоще́ние: *the picture of health,* воплоще́ние здоро́вья. —*adj.* карти́нный: *picture gallery,* карти́нная галере́я. —*v.t.* **1,** (visualize) представля́ть себе́. *Picture in one's mind,* представля́ть в уме́. **2,** (depict) изобража́ть.

picture postcard откры́тка с ви́дом.

picturesque *adj.* живопи́сный.

picture tube кинеско́п.

piddling *adj.* ничто́жный; пустяко́вый.

pie *n.* пиро́г; пирожо́к.

piebald *adj.* пе́гий.

piece *n.* **1,** (portion) кусо́к: *piece of bread/meat,* кусо́к хле́ба/мя́са. *Piece of paper,* бума́жка. *Piece of candy,* конфе́та. *Piece of advice,* сове́т. *Cut the pie into five pieces,* разре́зать пиро́г на пять часте́й. **2,** *pl.* (fragments) куски́; клочки́: *tear to pieces,* рвать на куски́ *or* в клочки́. *Smash to pieces,* разбива́ть вдре́безги. **3,** (item) шту́ка. *Piece of furniture,* ме́бель. *Five pieces of luggage,* пять мест. *Three-piece suit,* костю́м-тро́йка. *Sell by the piece,* продава́ть пошту́чно. **4,** (artistic creation) произведе́ние: *piece of art,* произведе́ние иску́сства. *Museum piece,* музе́йная ре́дкость. **5,** (coin) моне́та: *fifty-cent piece,* моне́та в пятьдеся́т це́нтов. **6,** (firearm) ору́дие: *artillery piece,* артиллери́йское ору́дие. **7,** *chess* фигу́ра. —*v.t.* [*usu.* **piece together**] составля́ть по кусо́чкам. —**give someone a piece of one's mind,** сказа́ть кому́-нибудь па́ру тёплых слов. —**go to pieces,** потеря́ть го́лову. —**speak one's piece,** вы́сказать своё мне́ние.

piecemeal *adv.* по частя́м.

piecework *n.* сде́льная рабо́та; акко́рдная рабо́та. —**pieceworker,** *n.* сде́льщик.

pier *n.* **1,** (wharf) при́стань. **2,** (of a bridge) бык. **3,** (between windows) просте́нок.

pierce *v.t.* пронза́ть; прока́лывать; протыка́ть; пробива́ть; прони́зывать. *The bullet pierced his helmet,* пу́ля проби́ла его́ ка́ску. *The searchlight pierced the darkness,* луч проже́ктора прониза́л темноту́. *Have one's ears pierced,* проколо́ть у́ши.

piercing *adj.* **1,** (shrill) пронзи́тельный. **2,** (biting, as of a wind) прони́зывающий.

pier glass трюмо́.

pier table подзерка́льник.

piety *n.* на́божность; благоче́стие.

pig *n.* свинья́. *Baby pig,* поросёнок.

pigeon *n.* го́лубь.

pigeonhole *v.t.* класть под сукно́.

pigeon-toed *adj.* косола́пый.

piggyback *adv.* на спине́; на зако́рках.

piggy bank копи́лка (в ви́де поросёнка).

pigheaded *adj.* крепколо́бый.

pig iron чугу́н в чу́шках.

piglet *n.* поросёнок.

pigment *n.* пигме́нт. —**pigmentation,** *n.* пигмента́ция. —**pigmented,** *adj.* пигме́нтный.

pigpen *n.* свина́рник.

pigskin *n.* **1,** (leather) свина́я ко́жа. **2,** *colloq.* (football) футбо́льный мяч.

pigsty *n.* **1,** (pigpen) свина́рник. **2,** (filthy place) хлев.

pigtail *n.* коси́чка; мыши́ный *or* кры́си́ный хво́стик.

pika *n.* пищу́ха.

pike *n.* **1,** (fish) щу́ка. **2,** (spear) пи́ка.

pilaf *also,* **pilaff** *n.* пила́в; плов.

pilaster *n.* пиля́стра.

pile *n.* **1,** (heap) ку́ча; гру́да; ки́па. *A pile of money,* ку́ча де́нег. **2,** (foundation for a pier) сва́я. **3,** (soft nap) ворс. —*v.t.* **1,** [*usu.* **pile up**] (make a pile of) скла́дывать; нагроможда́ть. **2,** (load) нава́ливать. **3,** (cover) зава́ливать: *The table is piled with books,* стол зава́лен кни́гами. **4,** *fol. by* **up** (run up, as debts) наде́лать (долго́в). —*v.i.* **1,** *fol. by* **up** (form a pile) нагроможда́ться. **2,** *fol. by* **up** (accumulate) накопля́ться; (*of debts*) нараста́ть. **3,** *fol. by* **into** *or* **onto** (board in large numbers) грузи́ться (в); погружа́ться (в).

pile driver копёр.

piles *n.pl.* геморро́й.

pilfer *v.t.* красть; тащи́ть; стяну́ть. —**pilferage,** *n.* ме́лкая кра́жа.

pilgrim *n.* пало́мник; пилигри́м. —**pilgrimage,** *n.* пало́мничество.

pill *n.* пилю́ля.

pillage *v.t.* гра́бить. —*v.i.* мародёрствовать. —*n.* грабёж; мародёрство.

pillar *n.* **1,** (column) столб. *Pillar of smoke,* столб ды́ма. **2,** *fig.* (mainstay) столп: *the pillars of society,* столпы́ о́бщества.

pillbox *n.* **1,** (box for pills) коро́бочка для пилю́ль. **2,** *mil.* дот.

pillory *n.* позо́рный столб. —*v.t.* пригвожда́ть *or* ста́вить *or* выставля́ть к позо́рному столбу́.

pillow *n.* поду́шка. —**pillowcase,** *n.* на́волочка.

pilot *n.* **1,** (of an aircraft) пило́т; лётчик. **2,** (harbor pilot) ло́цман. —*v.t.* вести́; управля́ть; пилоти́ровать. —*adj.* о́пытный; про́бный; эксперимента́льный. *Pilot program,* эксперимента́льная програ́мма.

pilot fish ло́цман.

pilothouse *n.* рулева́я ру́бка.

pimento *n.* **1,** [*also,* **pimiento**] (variety of pepper) стручко́вый пе́рец. **2,** = **allspice.**

pimp *n.* сво́дник.

pimpernel *n.* о́чный цвет.

pimple *n.* прыщ. —**pimply,** *adj.* прыща́вый; угрева́тый.

pin *n.* **1,** (small metal fastener) була́вка: *safety pin,* англи́йская була́вка. **2,** (bar or rod that fastens) штифт; штырь; шпи́лька. **3,** (brooch) брошь; бро́шка: *a gold pin,* золота́я брошь/бро́шка. **4,** (badge) значо́к: *college pin,* университе́тский значо́к. **5,** *bowling* ке́гля. —*v.t.* **1,** (fasten with a pin) прика́лывать: *pin a medal on someone,* приколо́ть меда́ль к чье́й-нибудь груди́. *Pin up,* подка́лывать. *Pin together,* ска́лывать. **2,** (immobilize) прижима́ть: *pin a boxer to the ropes,* прижима́ть боксёра к кана́там. *Pin (someone) down,* прижима́ть к земле́; подмина́ть под себя́. *Pin down the enemy,* ско́вывать проти́вника. *Pinned under the wreckage,* зажа́т под обло́мками. **3,** *fig.* (place; lay) возлага́ть: *pin one's hopes/ the blame/ on someone,* возлага́ть наде́жды/вину́ на кого́-нибудь. **4,** *fol. by* **down** (get to commit oneself) доби́ться (от кого́-нибудь) определённого отве́та. —**be on pins and needles,** быть *or* сиде́ть как на иго́лках. —**you could have heard a pin drop,** слы́шно бы́ло, как му́ха пролети́т.

pinafore *n.* передни́к; фа́ртук.

pince-nez *n.* пенсне́.

pincers *n.pl.* **1,** (tool) кле́щи; пинце́т. **2,** (claw) клешня́. —**pincers movement,** клещи́.

pinch *v.t.* **1,** (nip) щипа́ть; ущипну́ть. *Pinch oneself*

(*to make sure one is not dreaming*), ущипну́ть себя́. **2,** *colloq.* (steal) красть; тащи́ть. —*v.i.* (of a shoe) жать. —*n.* **1,** (nip) щипо́к. **2,** (bit, as of salt) щепо́ть; щепо́тка; (of tobacco) поню́шка. **3,** (emergency) кра́йний слу́чай: *in a pinch,* в кра́йнем слу́чае. —**pinch pennies,** жа́ться; стесня́ть себя́ в сре́дствах.

pincushion *n.* поду́шечка для була́вок.

pine *n.* сосна́. —*adj.* сосно́вый; хво́йный: *pine cone,* сосно́вая ши́шка; *pine tar,* хво́йный дёготь. —*v.i.* **1,** *fol. by* **away** (waste away) ча́хнуть; томи́ться. **2,** *fol. by* **for** (long for) тоскова́ть по; томи́ться по; вздыха́ть по *or* о.

pineal *adj.* шишкови́дный. —**pineal gland,** шишкови́дная железа́.

pineapple *n.* анана́с. —*adj.* анана́сный; анана́совый: *pineapple juice,* анана́сный/анана́совый сок.

ping *n.* звон.

ping-pong *n.* пинг-по́нг.

pinhole *n.* була́вочная ды́рка.

pinion *n.* шестерня́.

pink *adj.* ро́зовый. —*n.* **1,** (flower) гвозди́ка. **2,** (color) ро́зовый цвет. —**in the pink,** в расцве́те сил.

pinkeye *n.* о́стрый зара́зный конъюнктиви́т.

pinkie *also,* **pinky** *n.* мизи́нец.

pin money де́ньги на була́вки.

pinnacle *n.* верши́на. *The pinnacle of power,* верши́на вла́сти.

pinnate *adj.* пе́ристый.

pinpoint *n.* остриё була́вки. —*v.t.* то́чно определя́ть.

pinprick *n.* була́вочный уко́л.

pint *n.* пи́нта.

pintail *n.* шилохво́сть.

pinto *n.* пе́гая ло́шадь.

pioneer *n.* пионе́р. —*adj.* пионе́рский.

pious *adj.* **1,** (devout) на́божный; благочести́вый. **2,** (sanctimonious) ха́нжеский.

pip *n.* **1,** (bird disease) типу́н. **2,** (spot on a playing card) очко́.

pipe *n.* **1,** (tube) труба́. *Drainpipe,* водосто́чная труба́. **2,** (for smoking) тру́бка. **3,** (musical instrument) свире́ль. —*adj.* тру́бочный: *pipe tobacco,* тру́бочный таба́к. —*v.t.* передава́ть че́рез трубу́ *or* че́рез трубопрово́д. —**pipe down,** *colloq.* сба́вить тон. *Pipe down!,* молчи́! —**pipe up,** заговори́ть.

pipe dream несбы́точная мечта́.

pipeline *n.* трубопрово́д. *Oil pipeline,* нефтепрово́д. *Gas pipeline,* газопрово́д.

pipe organ орга́н.

piper *n.* волы́нщик.

piping *n.* **1,** (tubing) тру́бы; систе́ма труб. **2,** (edging for dresses) кант; вы́пушка. —**piping hot,** с пы́лу, с жа́ру.

pipistrelle *n.* нетопы́рь.

pipsqueak *n., colloq.* ме́лкая со́шка.

piquant *adj.* пика́нтный. —**piquancy,** *n.* пика́нтность.

pique *n.* оби́да; доса́да. —*v.t.* **1,** (cause resentment in) уязвля́ть; уколо́ть. **2,** (arouse) возбужда́ть.

piqué *n.* пике́. —*adj.* пике́йный.

piquet *n.* (card game) пике́т.

piracy *n.* пира́тство.

pirate *n.* пира́т. —*adj.* пира́тский: *pirate ship*, пира́тский кора́бль. —*v.t. Pirate a book*, пира́тски изда́ть кни́гу. *Pirate an invention*, укра́сть изобрете́ние. —**piratical,** *adj.* пира́тский.

pirouette *n.* пируэ́т.

piscatorial *adj.* рыболо́вный; рыба́цкий.

Pisces *n.* Ры́бы.

pistachio *n.* фиста́шка. —*adj.* фиста́шковый.

pistil *n.* пе́стик.

pistol *n.* пистоле́т. *Toy pistol*, пуга́ч.

piston *n.* **1,** (of an engine) по́ршень. **2,** (of a wind instrument) писто́н. —*adj.* поршнево́й: *piston engine*, поршнево́й дви́гатель; *piston ring*, поршнево́е кольцо́; *piston rod*, поршнево́й шток.

pit *n.* **1,** (stone of a fruit) ко́сточка. **2,** (hole) я́ма. **3,** (mine) ша́хта. **4,** *anat.* впа́дина. *Armpit*, подмы́шка. *In the pit of the stomach*, под ло́жечкой. **5,** (place where an orchestra sits) орке́стр; оркестро́вая я́ма. —*v.t.* **1,** (remove the pit from) вынима́ть ко́сточку из. **2,** (set in competition) противопоставля́ть.

pitch *v.t.* **1,** (throw) броса́ть; кида́ть. *Pitch hay*, мета́ть *or* вороши́ть се́но. **2,** (erect, as a tent) разбива́ть; раски́дывать. —*v.i.* **1,** (fall headlong) сва́ливаться. **2,** (toss, as of a ship) кача́ть; кача́ться. —*n.* **1,** (resin) смола́. **2,** (slope) скат; укло́н; накло́н. **3,** (tossing of a ship) ка́чка. **4,** *music* высота́. *Absolute pitch*, абсолю́тный слух. **5,** (degree of intensity) нака́л: *reach fever pitch*, дойти́ до нака́ла. —**pitch in,** внести́ свою́ ле́пту.

pitchblende *n.* смоляна́я обма́нка.

pitch-dark *adj.* непрогля́дный. *It is pitch-dark in here*, темны́м-темно́; темно́, хоть глаз вы́коли; здесь ни зги не ви́дно.

pitched battle генера́льное сраже́ние.

pitcher *n.* **1,** (vessel) кувши́н. **2,** *sports* подаю́щий.

pitchfork *n.* ви́лы.

piteous *adj.* жа́лкий.

pitfall *n.* подво́дный ка́мень.

pith *n.* сердцеви́на. —**pithy,** *adj.* вырази́тельный; содержа́тельный.

pitiable *adj.* = **pitiful.**

pitiful *adj.* жа́лкий.

pitiless *adj.* безжа́лостный.

pittance *n.* (жа́лкие) гроши́.

pituitary gland гипо́физ.

pity *n.* **1,** (compassion) жа́лость. *Have/take pity on*, сжа́литься над. *Move to pity*, разжа́лобить. **2,** (cause for sorrow) *rendered by* жаль: *It's a pity that...*, жаль, что... *What a pity!*, как жаль!; кака́я жа́лость! —*v.t.* жале́ть. *I pity him*, я жале́ю его́; мне жаль его́.

pivot *n.* сте́ржень; шкво́рень. —*v.i.* враща́ться. —**pivotal,** *adj.* центра́льный; стержнево́й.

pizza *n.* пи́цца.

pizzicato *adj.* щипко́вый. —*adv.* щипко́м; пиццика́то; пиччика́то.

placard *n.* плака́т; афи́ша.

placate *v.t.* умиротворя́ть; уми́лостивить.

place *n.* ме́сто: *from place to place*, с ме́ста на ме́сто. *Place of birth*, ме́сто рожде́ния. *What would you do in my place?*, что вы сде́лаете на моём ме́сте? *Set a place (at the table) for...*, поста́вить прибо́р для. *Come over to my place*, заходи́те ко мне. *Have you a place to stay?*, вам (*or* у вас) где останови́ться? *Even in those places where...*, да́же там, где... *George is ill, so I came in his place*, Джордж бо́лен, а я пришёл вме́сто него́. —*v.t.* **1,** (put; set) класть; ста́вить. *Place the pie in the oven*, класть пиро́г в духо́вку. *Place chairs around the table*, расставля́ть сту́лья вокру́г стола́. *Place a ring on someone's finger*, наде́ть кольцо́ на чей-нибудь па́лец. **2,** (put in an institution or establishment) помеща́ть: *He was placed in a mental institution*, его́ помести́ли в психиатри́ческую больни́цу. *Place under arrest*, посади́ть под аре́ст. *Place a child in school*, отдава́ть ребёнка в шко́лу. **3,** (put in a certain situation) ста́вить: *place in a difficult position*, ста́вить в затрудни́тельное положе́ние. **4,** (order; list) помеща́ть: *place an ad*, помеща́ть рекла́му. *Place an order*, де́лать зака́з. *Place orders*, размеща́ть зака́зы. *Place a telephone call*, зака́зывать разгово́р по телефо́ну. **5,** (name; identify) *I can't place him*, не могу́ вспо́мнить, кто он тако́й. **6,** (repose; pin) возлага́ть (наде́жду); ока́зывать (дове́рие). —*v.i.* занима́ть (како́е-нибудь ме́сто): *place third*, заня́ть тре́тье ме́сто. —**fall into place,** стать *or* встать на свои́ места́. —**in place of,** вме́сто (+ *gen.*). —**in places,** места́ми. —**in the first place,** во-пе́рвых. —**in the second place,** во-вторы́х. —**know one's place,** знать своё ме́сто. —**no place,** не́где; не́куда: *There is no place to park*, не́где поста́вить маши́ну; *I have no place to sit*, мне не́куда сесть. —**out of place, 1,** (not in the proper place) не на (своём) ме́сте; не на тех места́х. **2,** (inappropriate) не к ме́сту; неуме́стный. —**put someone in his place,** поста́вить кого́-нибудь на ме́сто. —**take place,** име́ть ме́сто; происходи́ть; состоя́ться. —**take the place of,** заменя́ть.

placebo *n.* безоби́дное сре́дство.

placement *n.* **1,** (act of placing) помеще́ние; размеще́ние. **2,** (placing persons in jobs) расстано́вка.

place name географи́ческое назва́ние.

placenta *n.* плаце́нта; де́тское ме́сто.

place setting прибо́р.

placid *adj.* споко́йный; безмяте́жный; невозмути́мый.

plagiarism *n.* литерату́рное воровство́; плагиа́т. —**plagiarist,** *n.* плагиа́тор.

plagiarize *v.t.* заи́мствовать (чужо́е произведе́ние).

plague *n.* **1,** (disease) чума́. **2,** (calamity; scourge) бич. —*v.t.* му́чить: *be plagued by doubts*, му́читься сомне́ниями.

plaice *n.* ка́мбала.

plaid *n.* шотла́ндка. —*adj.* клетчатый; в кле́тку.

plain *n.* равни́на. —*adj.* **1,** (clear; unambiguous) я́сный; поня́тный. *In plain English*, поня́тным англи́йским языко́м. *In plain view of everyone*, у всех на виду́. *As plain as the nose on your face*, ясне́е я́сного. **2,** (simple; unpretentious) просто́й: *plain folk,* просты́е лю́ди; *plain food,* проста́я пи́ща. **3,** (downright) чи́стый; су́щий: *plain nonsense,* чи́стый/ су́щий вздор. **4,** (having no design) одноцве́тный; гла́дкий. **5,** (unattractive) некраси́вый; невзра́чный. **6,** (not encoded) откры́тый: *plain text,* откры́тый текст.

plainclothesman *n.* сы́щик в шта́тской оде́жде.

plainly *adv.* **1,** (clearly) я́сно. **2,** (simply) про́сто: *dress plainly,* одева́ться про́сто.

plain-spoken *adj.* открове́нный; прямоду́шный.

plaintiff *n.* исте́ц; предъяви́тель и́ска.

plaintive *adj.* жа́лобный.

plait *n.* коса́. —*v.t.* плести́; заплета́ть.

plan *n.* план. —*v.t.* **1,** (draw up plans for) плани́ровать; заду́мывать; намеча́ть. *Plan a trip,* плани́ровать *or* заду́мать пое́здку. *Everything worked out as planned,* всё вы́шло, как бы́ло заду́мано. **2,** *fol. by inf.* (intend; expect) собира́ться; намерева́ться; предполага́ть. *We stayed longer than planned,* мы пробы́ли до́льше, чем предполага́ли. —*v.i.* стро́ить пла́ны.

plane *n.* **1,** (flat surface) пло́скость. **2,** (tool) руба́нок. **3,** (airplane) самолёт. *Plane ticket,* авиабиле́т; биле́т на самолёт. *Plane fare,* сто́имость биле́та на самолёт. *Plane crash,* авиацио́нная катастро́фа. **4,** *fig.* (level) у́ровень: *on a high moral plane,* на высо́ком нра́вственном у́ровне. —*v.t.* строга́ть.

plane geometry планиме́трия.

planer *n.* строга́льщик.

planet *n.* плане́та. —**planetarium,** *n.* планета́рий. —**planetary,** *adj.* плане́тный.

plane tree плата́н; чина́р(а).

plank *n.* доска́; пла́нка. —*v.t.* настила́ть; обшива́ть.

planking *n.* до́ски; обши́вка.

plankton *n.* планкто́н.

planned *adj.* заплани́рованный. *Planned economy,* пла́новое хозя́йство.

planner *n.* **1,** (economic planner) планови́к. **2,** (designer) планиро́вщик: *city planner,* планиро́вщик городо́в.

planning *n.* плани́рование; планиро́вка. *Family planning,* плани́рование семьи́. *City/urban planning,* градострои́тельство. *Planning department,* пла́новый отде́л.

plant *n.* **1,** (living organism) расте́ние. **2,** (factory) заво́д. **3,** (complete apparatus) устано́вка: *power plant,* силова́я устано́вка. —*v.t.* **1,** (place in the ground) сажа́ть: *plant a tree,* сажа́ть де́рево. **2,** (furnish with plants, as a field) заса́живать; уса́живать. **3,** (place firmly) упира́ться (+ *instr.*). **4,** (place surreptitiously) подкла́дывать; подбра́сывать. *Plant a bomb,* подложи́ть бо́мбу.

plantain *n.* подоро́жник.

plantation *n.* планта́ция.

planter *n.* **1,** (plantation owner) планта́тор. **2,** (machine for planting) сажа́лка.

planting *n.* **1,** (act of planting) поса́дка. **2,** *usu. pl.* (group of plants under cultivation) поса́дки; насажде́ния.

plant louse тля.

plaque *n.* **1,** (engraved plate) доска́; дощёчка; табли́чка. **2,** (on the teeth) зубно́й налёт.

plasma *n.* пла́зма.

plaster *n.* **1,** (substance for coating walls) штукату́рка. **2,** (substance applied to the body) пла́стырь. **3,** (plaster of Paris) гипс. —*adj.* штукату́рный; ги́псовый. —*v.t.* **1,** (cover with plaster) штукату́рить. **2,** (cover all over) облепля́ть. —**plaster cast, 1,** (copy of a statue) ги́псовый сле́пок. **2,** *med.* гипс.

plasterer *n.* штукату́р.

plastic *n.* пластма́сса; пла́стик. —*adj.* **1,** (made of plastic) пластма́ссовый; пла́стиковый. **2,** (pert. to modeling) пласти́ческий. **3,** (capable of being molded) пласти́чный. —**plastic arts,** пла́стика. —**plastic bomb,** пла́стиковая бо́мба. —**plastic surgery,** пласти́ческая хирурги́я. *Have plastic surgery,* сде́лать пласти́ческую опера́цию.

plasticine *n.* пластили́н.

plat du jour дежу́рное блю́до.

plate *n.* **1,** (dish) таре́лка. **2,** (sheet of metal) пласти́нка. —**clean one's plate,** съесть всё до́чиста.

plateau *n.* плоского́рье; плато́.

plate glass зерка́льное стекло́.

platelet *n., usu. pl.* кровяна́я пласти́нка.

platen *n.* ва́лик.

platform *n.* **1,** (landing alongside railway tracks) платфо́рма; перро́н. **2,** (stage; rostrum) трибу́на; помо́ст. **3,** (of a railway car or streetcar) площа́дка; та́мбур. **4,** (of a political party) платфо́рма.

plating *n.* покры́тие; обши́вка. *Armor plating,* броневая́ плита́.

platinum *n.* пла́тина. —*adj.* пла́тиновый.

platitude *n.* о́бщее ме́сто; бана́льность.

platonic *adj.* платони́ческий.

platoon *n.* взвод. *Platoon leader,* взво́дный.

platter *n.* блю́до.

platypus *n.* утконо́с.

plaudit *n., usu. pl.* **1,** (applause) аплодисме́нты. **2,** (praise) восто́рженные о́тзывы.

plausible *adj.* правдоподо́бный. *Plausible excuse,* благови́дный предло́г. —**plausibility,** *n.* правдоподо́бие.

play *v.i.* **1,** (engage in recreation or a game) игра́ть: *play in the sand,* игра́ть на песке́. *Play with a doll/ with dolls/,* игра́ть с ку́клой/ в ку́клы/. *Play with blocks,* игра́ть ку́биками *or* в ку́бики. *Play with matches/fire,* игра́ть со спи́чками/ с огнём/. **2,** (perform on a musical instrument; give out sounds) игра́ть: *continue playing,* продолжа́ть игра́ть. *An orchestra was playing,* игра́л орке́стр. **3,** *fol. by* **with** (fiddle with) игра́ть (+ *instr.*): *play with one's keys,* игра́ть ключа́ми. *Play with a knife,* балова́ться ножо́м. **4,** (of a film, show, etc.) идти́. **5,** (pretend to be) притворя́ться (+ *instr.*): *play dead,* притворя́ться мёртвым. **6,** (operate, as of a fountain) бить. **7,** in **play for time,** оття́гивать вре́мя; стара́ться вы́играть вре́мя. **8,** *in* **play into the hands of,** игра́ть на́ руку (+ *dat.*). —*v.t.* **1,** (engage in, as a game) игра́ть в (+ *acc.*): *play ball/chess/cards,* игра́ть в мяч/ша́хматы/ка́рты. *Know how to play that game,* уме́ть игра́ть в э́ту игру́. **2**, (perform on, as a musical instrument) игра́ть на (+ *prepl.*): *play the violin,* игра́ть на скри́пке. **3**, (compete against) игра́ть с. **4**, (perform) игра́ть: *play a role,* игра́ть роль; *play Hamlet,* игра́ть Гамле́та. *Play the fool,* валя́ть дурака́. **5**, (gamble at) игра́ть на (+ *prepl.*): *play the horses,* игра́ть на ска́чках; *play the stock market,* игра́ть на би́рже. **6**, (lead, as a card) идти́ с (+ *gen.*); (move, as a chess piece) игра́ть (+ *instr.*); идти́ (+ *instr.*). **7**, *Play a record,* (по)ста́вить пласти́нку. **8**, *Play tricks,* шали́ть. **9**, *Play a joke/trick on,* сыгра́ть шу́тку с. —*n.* **1**, (recreation) игра́: *at play,* за игро́й. **2**, (act or manner of playing) игра́: *Play began,* начала́сь игра́. *Rough play,* гру́бая игра́. *It's your play,* вам игра́ть. *In play,* в игре́. *Out of play,* вне игры́. **3**, (drama) пье́са. **4**, (slack, as in rope) игра́; слабина́. **5**, (brisk movement) игра́: *the play of light/colors,* игра́ све́та/цвето́в. **6**, *in play on words,* игра́ слов. —**bring into play,** пуска́ть в ход. —**come into play,** пойти́ в ход. —**play around,** шали́ть. —**play down,** преуменьша́ть; принижа́ть. —**play on** *or* **upon,** игра́ть на: *play on someone's emotions/weaknesses,* игра́ть на чьи́х-нибудь чу́вствах/сла́бостях. —**play up,** подчёркивать; выпя́чивать. —**play up to,** заи́грывать с; уго́дничать пе́ред; подма́зываться к.

play-acting *n.* актёрство; позёрство. —**play-actor,** *n.* позёр.

playbill *n.* **1**, (poster) афи́ша. **2**, (printed program) програ́мма.

playboy *n.* пове́са; гуля́ка; жуи́р; шалопа́й.

player *n.* **1**, (contestant) игро́к. *Basketball player,* баскетболи́ст. *Chess player,* шахмати́ст. **2**, (actor) актёр. **3**, (of a musical instrument) *used in combinations: trumpet player,* труба́ч.

player piano пиано́ла.

playful *adj.* игри́вый; ре́звый; шаловли́вый. —**playfulness,** *n.* игри́вость; ре́звость; шаловли́вость.

playgoer *n.* театра́л.

playground *n.* площа́дка для игр.

playhouse *n.* теа́тр.

playing *adj.* игра́ющий. —**playing card,** игра́льная ка́рта. —**playing field,** спорти́вное по́ле; спорти́вная площа́дка. —**playing time,** *sports* игрово́е вре́мя.

playmate *n.* друг де́тства.

playoff *n., sports* ро́зыгрыш.

playpen *n.* мане́ж.

plaything *n.* игру́шка.

playwright *n.* драмату́рг.

plaza *n.* пло́щадь.

plea *n.* **1**, (entreaty) про́сьба; мольба́: *a plea for help,* про́сьба/мольба́ о по́мощи. *A plea for mercy,* про́сьба о поми́ловании. **2**, *law* заявле́ние: *plea of not guilty,* заявле́ние о свое́й неви́новности.

plead *v.i.* **1**, (beg) умоля́ть; упра́шивать: *plead with someone for help,* умоля́ть/упра́шивать кого́-нибудь о по́мощи. *Plead for mercy,* проси́ть поща́ды. **2**, *law* (put forward a plea): *plead guilty,* признава́ть себя́ вино́вным. *Plead not guilty,* не признава́ть себя́

вино́вным. —*v.t.* **1**, (argue; present, as a case) вести́ (де́ло). **2**, (offer as justification) ссыла́ться на; отгова́риваться (+ *instr.*).

pleading *adj.* умоля́ющий; проси́тельный.

pleasant *adj.* прия́тный: *pleasant person/voice/conversation,* прия́тный челове́к/го́лос/разгово́р.

pleasantly *adv.* прия́тно: *I was pleasantly surprised,* я был (была́) прия́тно удивлён (удивлена́).

pleasantry *n.* любе́зность. *Exchange pleasantries with,* любе́зничать с.

please *v.t.* нра́виться; угожда́ть. *You can't please everyone,* на всех не уго́дишь. *He is a hard man to please,* ему́ тру́дно угоди́ть. —*v.i.* **1**, (give satisfaction) дава́ть удовлетворе́ние. **2**, (wish; like) хоте́ть: *Do as you please,* де́лайте, как хоти́те. —*imperative* **1**, *in polite requests,* пожа́луйста; бу́дьте добры́; бу́дьте любе́зны. **2**, *in earnest entreaties,* я вас о́чень прошу́! —**if you please, 1**, (if you would be so kind) пожа́луйста; с ва́шего разреше́ния. **2**, *used ironically,* предста́вьте себе́!; поду́майте то́лько! —**please God,** дай Бог.

pleased *adj.* рад; дово́лен. *Pleased to meet you!,* о́чень рад (ра́да) познако́миться с ва́ми! *You will be pleased to learn that...,* вам бу́дет прия́тно узна́ть, что...

pleasing *adj.* прия́тный; привлека́тельный.

pleasurable *adj.* прия́тный.

pleasure *n.* **1**, (satisfaction) удово́льствие: *with pleasure,* с удово́льствием. **2**, (wish; choice; preference) жела́ние. *What is your pleasure?,* что вам уго́дно? —*adj.* увесели́тельный: *pleasure trip,* увесели́тельная пое́здка.

pleat *n.* скла́дка. —*v.t.* плиссирова́ть. —**pleated,** *adj.* скла́дчатый; в скла́дку; плиссиро́ванный.

plebeian *adj.* плебе́йский. —*n.* плебе́й.

plebiscite *n.* плебисци́т.

plectrum *n.* плектр.

pledge *n.* **1**, (vow) заро́к. *Pledge of allegiance,* кля́тва ве́рности. **2**, (security) зало́г. —*v.t.* **1**, (solemnly promise) обя́зываться (+ *inf.*); кля́сться в (+ *prepl.*). *Pledge allegiance,* кля́сться в ве́рности. **2**, (leave as security) закла́дывать; отдава́ть в зало́г.

Pleiades *n.pl.* плея́ды.

plenary *adj.* **1**, (complete; absolute) по́лный. **2**, (fully attended) плена́рный: *plenary session,* плена́рное заседа́ние.

plenipotentiary *adj.* полномо́чный.

plentiful *adj.* оби́льный; изоби́льный. *Fruit right now is plentiful,* фру́кты сейча́с в изоби́лии.

plenty *n.* изоби́лие: *the horn of plenty,* рог изоби́лия. *I have plenty to eat,* у меня́ есть что пое́сть. *There was plenty to tell,* расска́зывать бы́ло что. —*adj., colloq.* о́чень; изря́дно. —**plenty of,** мно́го; мно́жество (+ *gen.*).

plenum *n.* пле́нум.

plethora *n.* **1**, *med.* полнокро́вие. **2**, (superabundance) изоби́лие.

pleura *n.* пле́вра. —**pleural,** *adj.* плевра́льный.

pleurisy *n.* плеври́т.

Plexiglas *n.* плексигла́с.

plexus *n., anat.* сплете́ние: *solar plexus,* со́лнечное сплете́ние.

pliable *adj.* ги́бкий. —**pliability,** *n.* ги́бкость.

pliant *adj.* = **pliable.**

pliers *n.pl.* кле́щи; плоскогу́бцы.

plight *n.* плаче́вное состоя́ние.

plimsolls *n.pl., Brit.* = **sneakers.**

plinth *n.* пли́нтус.

plod *v.i.* брести́; тащи́ться; плести́сь.

plop *v.i.* бултыха́ться. —*adv.* булты́х.

plot *n.* **1,** (piece of ground) уча́сток. **2,** (conspiracy) за́говор: *a plot to overthrow the government,* за́говор с це́лью сверже́ния прави́тельства. **3,** (story line) фа́була; сюже́т; интри́га. —*v.t.* **1,** (trace) наноси́ть (на ка́рту). **2,** (make secret plans for) замышля́ть. —*v.i.* устра́ивать за́говор.

plotter *n.* загово́рщик.

plough *n. & v.* = **plow.** —**ploughing,** *n.* = **plowing.** —**ploughman,** *n.* = **plowman.** —**ploughshare,** *n.* = **plowshare.**

plover *n.* ржа́нка; зуёк. *Golden plover,* си́вка.

plow *also,* **plough** *n.* плуг. —*v.t.* **1,** (use a plow on) паха́ть. **2,** *fol. by* **up** (turn up) распа́хивать. —*v.i.* **1,** (use a plow) паха́ть. **2,** *fol. by* **into** (run into) вре́заться в. **3,** *fol. by* **through** (work one's way through) оси́ливать: *plow through a book,* оси́лить кни́гу.

plowing *also,* **ploughing** *n.* па́хота; вспа́шка.

plowman *also,* **ploughman** *n.* па́харь.

plowshare *also,* **ploughshare** *n.* ле́мех; сошни́к. —**beat swords into plowshares,** перекова́ть мечи́ на ора́ла.

ploy *n.* приём.

pluck *v.t.* **1,** (pick) рвать; срыва́ть. **2,** (snatch) выдёргивать. **3,** (pull out the feathers of) щипа́ть; ощи́пывать; общи́пывать. **4,** (pull at, as the strings of a musical instrument) щипа́ть. —*n.* (courage; fortitude) сме́лость; сто́йкость. —**plucky,** *n.* сме́лый.

plug *n.* **1,** (stopper) про́бка; заты́чка; вту́лка. **2,** (two-pronged electrical device) штэ́псель; ви́лка. **3,** = **fireplug.** —*v.t.* **1,** [*often* **plug up**] (stop up) затыка́ть; заку́поривать. *Plug a gap,* заткну́ть дыру́. **2,** *fol. by* **in** (connect) вставля́ть (в розе́тку); включа́ть (в сеть).

plum *n.* сли́ва. —*adj.* сли́вочный: *plum brandy,* сли́вочная насто́йка.

plumage *n.* опере́ние.

plumb *n.* [*also,* **plumb line**] **1,** (device for finding the exact perpendicular) отве́с. **2,** (device for determining the depth of water) лот. —*adj.* отве́сный; вертика́льный. —*v.t.* **1,** (test the depth of) измеря́ть глубину́ (+ *gen.*). **2,** *fig.* (go deep into) проника́ть в.

plumber *n.* водопрово́дчик. —**plumbing,** *n.* водопрово́д.

plume *n.* **1,** (feather) перо́. **2,** (ornament for a hat or helmet) плюма́ж; султа́н.

plummet *v.i.* па́дать (как ка́мень); лете́ть вниз.

plump *adj.* по́лный; пу́хлый. —*v.i.* бу́хаться.

plunder *v.t.* гра́бить; разгра́бить. —*n.* **1,** (robbery) грабёж. **2,** (booty) добы́ча.

plunge *v.t.* **1,** (thrust, as a dagger) вонза́ть; вса́живать. **2,** (throw into, as darkness, despair, etc.) погружа́ть; вверга́ть; поверга́ть. *The city was plunged into darkness,* го́род погрузи́лся (*or* был погружён) в темноту́. *Plunge a country into war,* вверга́ть страну́ в войну́. —*v.i.* **1,** (dive; dash headlong) бро́ситься: *plunge into the water,* бро́ситься в во́ду. *Plunge down an embankment,* свали́ться под отко́с. *The plane plunged into a lake,* самолёт упа́л в о́зеро. *The car plunged into the crowd,* маши́на вре́залась в толпу́. **2,** *fig.* (plummet) лете́ть вниз. —*n.* **1,** (dive) ныро́к. **2,** (sudden decline) ре́зкое паде́ние.

plunger *n.* плу́нжер.

plunk *v.t.* **1,** (strum) бренча́ть. **2,** *fol. by* **down** (toss down) бро́сить: *plunk down a dollar on the counter,* бро́сить до́ллар на прила́вок.

pluperfect *adj.* давнопрошё́дший. —*n.* давнопрошё́дшее вре́мя.

plural *adj.* мно́жественный. *Plural noun,* существи́тельное мно́жественного числа́. —*n.* мно́жественное число́.

pluralism *n.* плюрали́зм.

plurality *n.* **1,** (largest number of votes but less than 50%) относи́тельное большинство́. **2,** (excess of votes over nearest competitor) переве́с.

plus *prep.* плюс: *two plus two,* два плюс два. *Plus or minus three,* плюс-ми́нус три. —*n.* (advantage) плюс: *a big plus,* большо́й плюс. —**plus sign,** (знак) плюс.

plush *n.* (fabric) плюш. —*adj.* **1,** (of this fabric) плю́шевый. **2,** [*also,* **plushy**] *colloq.* (luxurious) роско́шный.

Pluto *n.* Плуто́н.

plutocracy *n.* плутокра́тия. —**plutocrat,** *n.* плутокра́т. —**plutocratic,** *adj.* плутократи́ческий.

plutonium *n.* плуто́ний.

ply *v.t.* **1,** (do work with; wield) рабо́тать (+ *instr.*). *Ply the oars,* налега́ть на вёсла. **2,** (practice, as a trade) подвиза́ться на (како́м-нибудь по́прище). **3,** (address constantly with, as questions) засыпа́ть (вопро́сами). **4,** (keep supplying with) по́тчевать: *ply with wine,* по́тчевать вино́м. **5,** (traverse regularly) борозди́ть: *ply the seas,* борозди́ть моря́. —*v.i.* (travel back and forth) курси́ровать; снова́ть. —*n.* слой: *three-ply wood,* трёхсло́йная фане́ра.

plywood *n.* фане́ра. —*adj.* фане́рный.

p.m. *abbr.* дня; ве́чера: *at 2 p.m.,* в два часа́ дня; *at 9 p.m.,* в де́вять часо́в ве́чера.

pneumatic *adj.* пневмати́ческий. —**pneumatic drill,** пневмати́ческое сверло́.

pneumonia *n.* воспале́ние лёгких.

poach *v.t.* вари́ть (без скорлупы́). *Poached egg,* яйцо́-пашо́т. —*v.i.* занима́ться браконье́рством. *Poach on,* вторга́ться в.

poacher *n.* браконье́р. —**poaching,** *n.* браконье́рство.

pochard *n.* ныро́к.

pocket *n.* **1,** (of a garment) карма́н. **2,** *billiards* лу́за. **3,** (small area) у́зел; оча́г. *Pocket of resistance,* оча́г сопротивле́ния. **4,** *in* **air pocket,** возду́шная я́ма. —*adj.* карма́нный: *pocket comb,* карма́нная расчёска. —*v.t.* **1,** (put in one's pocket) класть в карма́н. **2,** (take dishonestly) класть (себе́) в карма́н; прикарма́нивать. —**out of pocket,** в убы́тке; в про́игрыше.

pocket billiards лу́зный билья́рд.

pocketbook *n.* су́мка; су́мочка. —**put a hole in one's pocketbook,** бить *or* ударя́ть по карма́ну.

pocketknife *n.* карма́нный нож.

pocket money карма́нные де́ньги.

pockmark *n.* о́спина; ряби́на.

pockmarked *adj.* **1,** (scarred from smallpox) в о́спинах; изры́тый о́спой; рябо́й. **2,** (damaged by shells, bombs, etc.) вы́щербленный.

pod *n.* стручо́к. *Peas in the pod,* стручко́вый горо́х. —**like two peas in a pod,** как две ка́пли воды́.

podiatrist *n.* специали́ст по лече́нию ног. —**podiatry,** *n.* лече́ние заболева́ний ног.

podium *n.* помо́ст.

pozdol *n.* подзо́л.

poem *n.* стихотворе́ние; поэ́ма.

poet *n.* поэ́т. —**poetess,** *n.* поэте́сса.

poetic *adj.* поэти́ческий. —**poetic license,** поэти́ческая во́льность.

poetical *adj.* поэти́ческий.

poetry *n.* поэ́зия; стихи́.

pogrom *n.* погро́м.

poignancy *n.* тро́гательность.

poignant *adj.* **1,** (cutting; harsh) о́стрый. **2,** (touching) тро́гательный.

point *n.* **1,** (sharp end) ко́нчик; острие́. *Come to a point,* заостря́ться. **2,** (point in space) пункт; то́чка. *The furthermost point,* са́мый да́льний пункт. *The shortest distance between two points,* наиме́ньшее расстоя́ние ме́жду двумя́ то́чками. *Point of the compass,* страна́ све́та. **3,** (stage; juncture) то́чка; пункт: *starting point,* нача́льный пункт; *boiling point,* то́чка кипе́ния; *turning point,* поворо́тный пункт. *Reach the point where...,* дойти́ до того́, что... **4,** (specific moment in time) моме́нт. *At this point I should like to...,* здесь я хоте́л бы (+ *inf.*). **5,** (item; element) пункт: *the main points of the plan,* основны́е пу́нкты пла́на. *Fine point,* то́нкость. *Point of interest,* достопримеча́тельность. **6,** (essence; gist) суть; существо́. *Come to the point,* говори́ть по существу́ *or* напрями́к. *The point is...,* де́ло в том, что... *That's just the point,* в то́м-то и де́ло. *That's not the point,* не в э́том де́ло. *You've missed my point,* вы меня́ непра́вильно по́няли. **7,** (idea advanced, esp. a valid one): *I don't get your point,* я не понима́ю, что вы хоти́те сказа́ть (*or* куда́ вы гнёте). *He has a point there!,* в э́том он прав. **8,** (purpose; use; advantage) смысл: *What's the point of it?,* како́й смысл в э́том? *There is no point arguing with him,* нет смы́сла (*or* не сто́ит) с ним спо́рить. *There is no point in even trying,* не́чего и пыта́ться. **9,** (unit of scoring) очко́: *win on points,* победи́ть по очка́м. **10,** (characteristic) сторона́; ме́сто: *weak points,* сла́бые сто́роны/места́. *Have one's good points,* име́ть свои́ хоро́шие сто́роны. **11,** (promontory; cape) мыс; нос. **12,** *print-*

ing пункт: *12-point type,* шрифт в двена́дцать пу́нктов. —*v.t.* **1,** (direct, as a weapon) направля́ть; наводи́ть; наставля́ть. **2,** *Point one's finger at,* пока́зывать *or* ука́зывать па́льцем на (+ *acc.*). **3,** (show by pointing) ука́зывать: *point the way to someone,* ука́зывать путь кому́-нибудь. **4,** *fol. by* **out** (indicate; explain) ука́зывать (на): *point out someone's mistakes,* ука́зывать кому́-нибудь на оши́бки. *He pointed out that...,* он указа́л, что... (*or* на то, что...). *Point him out to me,* укажи́те мне на него́. **5,** *fol. by* **up** (emphasize; make clear) заостря́ть. —*v.i.* **1,** (motion with one's finger) пока́зывать па́льцем: *Don't point!,* не пока́зывай па́льцем! **2,** *fol. by* **to** (motion toward) пока́зывать на; ука́зывать на. **3,** (be turned in a given direction) ука́зывать на: *The needle points south,* стре́лка ука́зывает на юг. **4,** *fol. by* **to** (indicate; suggest) говори́ть о: *Everything points to the fact that...,* всё говори́т о том, что... —**be on the point of,** как раз собира́ться (+ *inf.*). —**beside the point,** *see* **beside.** —**case in point,** хоро́ший приме́р э́того. —**in point of fact,** факти́чески; на са́мом де́ле. —**make a point of; make it a point to,** взять себе́ за пра́вило (+ *inf.*). —**point of view,** то́чка зре́ния. —**point by point,** по пу́нктам; пункт за пу́нктом. —**up to a point,** до не́которой *or* изве́стной сте́пени.

pointblank *adj.* **1,** (fired straight at the mark) прямо́й. **2,** (explicit) категори́ческий. —*adv.* **1,** (straight at the mark) в упо́р. **2,** (without hesitation or equivocation) наотре́з; напрями́к.

pointed *adj.* **1,** (coming to a point) заострённый; остроконе́чный. **2,** (sharp; incisive) о́стрый; ме́ткий. **3,** (deliberately emphasized) подчёркнутый; демонстрати́вный.

pointedly *adv.* подчёркнуто: *He was pointedly rude,* он был подчёркнуто груб.

pointer *n.* **1,** (indicator) стре́лка; указа́тель. **2,** (rod used in classrooms) па́лочка; ука́зка. **3,** (dog) лега́вая соба́ка; по́йнтер. **4,** *colloq.* (tip; advice) сове́т.

pointless *adj.* бессмы́сленный; бесце́льный; беспредме́тный. *It is pointless to...,* нет смы́сла (+ *inf.*).

poise *n.* **1,** (equilibrium) равнове́сие. **2,** (composure) уравнове́шенность. —*v.t.* уравнове́шивать.

poised *adj.* **1,** (composed) уравнове́шенный. **2,** *fol. by* **to** (suspended in readiness) гото́вый (к).

poison *n.* яд; отра́ва. —*adj.* ядови́тый. —*v.t.* отравля́ть. *Poisoned arrows,* отра́вленные стре́лы. —**poison gas,** ядови́тый газ; отравля́ющее вещество́.

poisoning *n.* отравле́ние: *food poisoning,* пищево́е отравле́ние.

poisonous *adj.* ядови́тый: *poisonous snake,* ядови́тая змея́.

poke *v.t.* **1,** (jab) ты́кать; толка́ть. *Poke someone in the ribs,* толкну́ть кого́-нибудь в бок. *Poke one's finger at someone,* ты́кать па́льцем в кого́-нибудь. **2,** (thrust) сова́ть: *poke one's nose into,* сова́ть нос в. **3,** (stir, as a fire) меша́ть; переме́шивать (у́гли). **4,**

(make, as a hole) протыка́ть. —*v.i.* **1,** *fol. by* **around** *or* **about** (search leisurely) ры́ться. **2,** *fol. by* **along** (plod along) таска́ться. **3,** *fol. by* **out** (protrude) торча́ть. —*n.* тычо́к. —**buy a pig in a poke,** купи́ть кота́ в мешке́. —**poke fun at,** *see* **fun.**

poker *n.* **1,** (rod for stirring a fire) кочерга́. **2,** (card game) по́кер.

poky *also,* **pokey** *adj.* те́сный. —*n., slang* (jail) куту́зка.

polar *adj.* поля́рный. —**polar bear,** бе́лый *or* поля́рный медве́дь. —**polar fox,** песе́ц.

polarity *n.* поля́рность.

polarize *v.t.* поляризова́ть. —**polarization,** *n.* поляриза́ция.

pole *n.* **1,** (long stick) шест; жердь. **2,** (upright post) столб. **3,** (of the earth) по́люс: *North Pole,* Се́верный по́люс.

Pole *n.* поля́к; по́лька. *The Poles,* поля́ки.

poleax *also,* **poleaxe** *n.* секи́ра.

polecat *n.* хорёк.

polemic *adj.* поле́мика. —*adj.* [*also,* **polemical**] полеми́ческий. —**polemicist,** *n.* полеми́ст. —**polemics,** *n.* поле́мика.

pole vault прыжо́к с шесто́м. —**pole-vault,** *v.i.* пры́гать с шесто́м.

police *n.* поли́ция; мили́ция. —*adj.* полице́йский: *police station,* полице́йский уча́сток. —*v.t.* **1,** (keep order in) охраня́ть; патрули́ровать. **2,** (clean up) чи́стить; убира́ть.

policeman *n.* **1,** (in Russia) милиционе́р. **2,** (elsewhere) полице́йский; полисме́н.

police state полице́йское госуда́рство.

policy *n.* **1,** (course of government action) поли́тика; курс: *foreign policy,* вне́шняя поли́тика; внешнеполити́ческий курс. *Policy of nonalignment,* поли́тика неприсоедине́ния. *Pursue a policy of...,* проводи́ть курс на (+ *acc.*). **2,** (contract of insurance) по́лис.

poliomyelitis *n.* полиомиели́т.

polish *v.t.* **1,** (shine) полирова́ть; шлифова́ть. *Polish furniture,* полирова́ть ме́бель. *Polish diamonds,* полирова́ть *or* шлифова́ть алма́зы. *Polish one's shoes,* чи́стить боти́нки. *Polish the floor,* натира́ть пол. **2,** (refine; perfect) шлифова́ть. —*n.* **1,** (glossy finish) полиро́вка. **2,** (polishing substance) лак; политу́ра. *Nail polish,* лак для ногте́й. *Shoe polish,* гутали́н; ва́кса. *Floor polish,* масти́ка. **3,** *fig.* (elegance; refinement) лоск. —**polish off,** поко́нчить с.

Polish *adj.* по́льский. —*n.* по́льский язы́к. *Speak Polish,* говори́ть по-по́льски.

polished *adj.* **1,** (shiny) полиро́ванный; шлифо́ванный. *Polished diamond,* шлифо́ванный бриллиа́нт. **2,** (elegant) изы́сканный; лощёный. **3,** (finished; flawless) зако́нченный.

polisher *n.* полиро́вщик; шлифова́льщик.

Politburo *n.* политбюро́.

polite *adj.* **1,** (courteous) ве́жливый: *polite letter/reminder,* ве́жливое письмо́/напомина́ние. *Polite toward one's elders,* ве́жлив со ста́ршими; ве́жлив по отноше́нию к ста́ршим. *She is polite to everyone,*

она́ ве́жлива со все́ми. **2,** (refined) прили́чный: *polite society,* прили́чное о́бщество. —**politely,** *adv.* ве́жливо. —**politeness,** *n.* ве́жливость.

politic *adj.* полити́чный.

political *adj.* полити́ческий. —**political prisoner,** политзаключённый.

politician *n.* **1,** (one engaged in politics) полити́ческий де́ятель; поли́тик. **2,** (political opportunist) полити́кан.

politicize *v.t.* политизи́ровать. —**politicization,** *n.* политиза́ция.

politics *n.* поли́тика.

polity *n.* о́браз правле́ния.

polka *n.* по́лька.

polka dots горо́шек. —**polka-dot,** *adj.* в горо́шек: *polka-dot necktie,* га́лстук в горо́шек.

poll *n.* **1,** (vote) голосова́ние. **2,** *pl.* (voting place) избира́тельный уча́сток. *Go to the polls,* идти́ на вы́боры; идти́ голосова́ть. **3,** (survey of opinion) опро́с. —*v.t.* **1,** (receive, as votes) получа́ть; собира́ть. **2,** (survey; canvass) опра́шивать.

pollen *n.* пыльца́.

pollinate *v.t.* опыля́ть. —**pollination,** *n.* опыле́ние.

polling booth каби́на для голосова́ния.

polling place избира́тельный уча́сток; избира́тельный пункт; помеще́ние для голосова́ния.

polliwog *n.* голова́стик.

poll tax поду́шный нало́г; избира́тельный нало́г.

pollute *v.t.* загрязня́ть. —**pollutant,** *n.* загрязня́ющее вещество́. —**pollution,** *n.* загрязне́ние.

polo *n.* по́ло.

polonaise *n.* полоне́з.

polonium *n.* поло́ний.

polo shirt те́нниска.

poltroon *n.* трус.

polyandry *n.* полиа́ндрия; многому́жие.

polychromatic *adj.* многоцве́тный; многокра́сочный.

polyclinic *n.* поликли́ника.

polyester *n.* полиэфи́р. —*adj.* полиэфи́рный.

polyethylene *n.* полиэтиле́н. —*adj.* полиэтиле́новый.

polygamy *n.* многобра́чие; многожёнство; полига́мия. —**polygamist,** *n.* многожёнец. —**polygamous,** *adj.* многобра́чный; полига́мный; полигами́ческий.

polyglot *adj.* многоязы́чный; разноязы́чный. —*n.* полигло́т.

polygon *n.* многоуго́льник. —**polygonal,** *adj.* многоуго́льный.

polyhedron *n.* многогра́нник. —**polyhedral,** *adj.* многогра́нный.

polymer *n.* полиме́р. —**polymeric,** *adj.* полиме́рный.

Polynesian *adj.* полинези́йский. —*n.* полинези́ец.

polynomial *n.* многочле́н. —*adj.* многочле́нный.

polyp *n.* поли́п.

polystyrene *n.* полистиро́л.

polysyllabic *adj.* многосло́жный.

polytechnic *adj.* политехни́ческий.

polytheism *n.* политеи́зм; многобо́жие. —**polytheist,**

n. политеи́ст. —**polytheistic,** *adj.* политеисти́ческий.

pomade *n.* пома́да. —*v.t.* пома́дить.

pomegranate *n.* грана́т.

pommel *n.* (of a saddle) лука́. —*v.t.* (beat) колоти́ть.

pomp *n.* пы́шность; по́мпа.

pompon *n.* помпо́н.

pompous *adj.* напы́щенный; наду́тый. —**pomposity,** *n.* напы́щенность.

poncho *n.* по́нчо.

pond *n.* пруд.

ponder *v.t.* обду́мывать; размышля́ть о. *Ponder a decision,* обду́мывать реше́ние. *Ponder one's next move,* обду́мывать сле́дующий ход. *Ponder the fate of...,* размышля́ть о судьбе́ (+ *gen.*).

ponderous *adj.* тяжёлый; тяжелове́сный.

pond scum ти́на.

pondweed *n.* рдест.

pontiff *n.* **1,** (Pope) па́па. **2,** (bishop) епи́скоп. —**pontifical,** *adj.* па́пский; епи́скопский.

pontificate *n.* понтифика́т. —*v.i.* ора́торствовать.

pontoon *n.* (boat) понто́н. —**pontoon bridge,** понто́нный мост.

pony *n.* по́ни. —**pony tail,** (hairstyle) хво́стик.

pooch *n., colloq.* соба́чка.

poodle *n.* пу́дель.

pool *n.* **1,** (puddle) лу́жа. **2,** (swimming pool) бассе́йн для пла́вания. **3,** (billiards) (лу́зный) билья́рд. **4,** (combination of resources) фонд. —*v.t.* объединя́ть. *Pool one's resources,* объединя́ть ресу́рсы; устро́ить скла́дчину.

pool table билья́рд.

poop *n., naut.* ют; полуют. —**poop deck,** па́луба юта.

poor *adj.* **1,** (needy) бе́дный: *poor family/country,* бе́дная семья́/страна́. **2,** (unfortunate) бе́дный: *Poor Sasha!,* бе́дный Са́ша! *Poor man/fellow/woman/creature!,* несча́стный (несча́стная); бедня́га. **3,** (bad) плохо́й; сла́бый: *poor memory,* плоха́я/сла́бая па́мять. *Poor grades,* плохи́е отме́тки. *Poor student,* сла́бый учени́к. *Poor quality,* ни́зкое ка́чество. *Poor harvest,* плохо́й урожа́й; неурожа́й. *Read in poor light,* чита́ть при плохо́м све́те. *She is in poor health,* у неё сла́бое здоро́вье. *My French is poor,* мой францу́зский плохо́й *or* сла́бый. —*n., preceded by* **the** бе́дный; беднота́.

poorbox *n.* кру́жка.

poorhouse *n.* богаде́льня.

poorly *adv.* пло́хо; сла́бо; нева́жно.

pop *n.* **1,** (sound) хлопо́к. **2,** (drink) газиро́ванная вода́. **3,** *colloq.* (dad) па́па; папа́ша. —*v.i.* **1,** (make a short explosive sound) хло́пать; тре́снуть. **2,** *fol. by* **up** *or* **out** (appear suddenly) пока́зываться. **3,** *fol. by* **in** (drop in for a moment) загляну́ть. **4,** (of one's eyes) широко́ раскрыва́ться. *His eyes nearly popped out of his head,* у него́ глаза́ на лоб поле́зли. —*v.t.* **1,** (put quickly or suddenly) сова́ть; всо́вывать. *Pop one's head out the window,* высо́вывать го́лову из окна́. **2,** *in* **pop the question,** (propose) сде́лать предложе́ние.

popcorn *n.* возду́шная кукуру́за.

Pope *n.* па́па.

popgun *n.* пуга́ч.

poplar *n.* то́поль. —*adj.* то́полевый; тополи́ный.

poplin *n.* попли́н. —*adj.* попли́новый.

poppy *n.* мак. *Poppy seeds,* мак.

poppycock *n., colloq.* чушь; галиматья́; белиберда́.

populace *n.* населе́ние.

popular *adj.* **1,** (well-liked; enjoyed by many) популя́рный. **2,** (of the people) наро́дный. *Popular front,* наро́дный фронт. *Popular vote,* всенаро́дное голосова́ние. *By popular demand,* по тре́бованию пу́блики. **3,** (within the means of most people) досту́пный.

popularity *n.* популя́рность.

popularize *v.t.* популяризи́ровать. —**popularization,** *n.* популяриза́ция.

populate *v.t.* населя́ть; заселя́ть. *Densely/sparsely populated,* густонаселённый; малонаселённый.

population *n.* населе́ние. —**population explosion,** демографи́ческий взрыв.

Populist *n.* попули́ст; *Russian hist.* наро́дник. —*adj.* попули́стский; *Russian hist.* наро́днический. —**Populism,** *n.* наро́дничество.

populous *adj.* лю́дный; многолю́дный; густонаселённый.

porcelain *n.* фарфо́р. —*adj.* фарфо́ровый.

porch *n.* крыльцо́.

porcupine *n.* дикобра́з.

pore *n.* по́ра. —*v.i.* [*usu.* **pore over**] корпе́ть (над); копте́ть (над).

pork *n.* свини́на. —*adj.* свино́й: *pork chop,* свина́я котле́та; свина́я отбивна́я.

pornography *n.* порногра́фия. —**pornographic,** *adj.* порнографи́ческий.

porous *adj.* по́ристый; ноздрева́тый. —**porosity,** *n.* по́ристость.

porphyry *n.* порфи́р.

porpoise *n.* морска́я свинья́.

porridge *n.* ка́ша.

port *n.* **1,** (harbor; seaport) порт. **2,** (left side of a vessel) ле́вый борт. **3,** (wine) портве́йн. —**port of call,** порт захо́да.

portable *adj.* перено́сный; портати́вный.

portage *n.* **1,** (act of carrying) перено́ска. **2,** (route over which boats are carried) во́лок.

portal *n.* **1,** (imposing entrance) порта́л. **2,** (factory gate) проходно́й пункт.

portend *v.t.* предвеща́ть.

portent *n.* **1,** (omen) предзнаменова́ние; предве́стие. **2,** (significance) значе́ние.

portentous *adj.* **1,** (ominous) злове́щий. **2,** (momentous) знамена́тельный.

porter *n.* **1,** (baggage carrier) носи́льщик. **2,** (handyman) убо́рщик.

portfolio *n.* портфе́ль. *Minister without portfolio,* мини́стр без портфе́ля.

porthole *n.* иллюмина́тор.

portico *n.* по́ртик.

portion *n.* **1,** (part of a whole) часть; до́ля. **2,** (single serving of food) по́рция. —*v.t.* [*usu.* **portion out**] распределя́ть; выделя́ть.

portly *adj.* по́лный; доро́дный.

portrait *n.* портре́т. *Portrait gallery,* портре́тная галере́я. *Portrait painter,* портрети́ст.

portray *v.t.* изобража́ть. —**portrayal,** *n.* изображе́ние.

Portuguese *adj.* португа́льский. *He (she) is Portuguese,* он португа́лец; она́ португа́лка. —*n.* **1,** (language) португа́льский язы́к. *Speak Portuguese,* говори́ть по-португа́льски. **2,** *preceded by* **the** (people) португа́льцы.

portulaca *n.* портула́к.

pose *n.* по́за. —*v.i.* **1,** (assume a certain position) пози́ровать: *pose for a portrait,* пози́ровать для портре́та. *Pose for photographers,* пози́ровать фото́графам. **2,** *fol. by* **as** (represent oneself as) выдава́ть себя́ (за). —*v.t.* **1,** (put, as a question) ста́вить; задава́ть; предлага́ть. *Pose a riddle,* задава́ть зага́дку. **2,** (present) представля́ть: *pose difficulties,* представля́ть тру́дности. *Pose a threat to,* представля́ть *or* создава́ть угро́зу (+ *dat. or* **для**).

posh *adj., colloq.* роско́шный.

position *n.* **1,** (posture) положе́ние; по́за: *in a sitting/ uncomfortable position,* в сидя́чем/неудо́бном положе́нии; в сидя́чей/неудо́бной по́зе. **2,** (location) положе́ние; местоположе́ние. *The country's geographic position,* географи́ческое положе́ние страны́. *Report one's position,* сообща́ть своё местоположе́ние. **3,** (proper place) ме́сто: *Take up your positions!,* займи́те ва́ши места́! *Out of position,* не на своём ме́сте. **4,** (situation) положе́ние: *put someone in an awkward position,* ста́вить кого́-нибудь в нело́вкое положе́ние. *Be in a position to...,* быть в состоя́нии (+ *inf.*). *What would you do in my position?,* что бы вы сде́лали на моём ме́сте? **5,** (job) ме́сто: *seek a position as a reporter,* иска́ть ме́ста репортёра. **6,** (point of view; stand) пози́ция: *state one's position,* изложи́ть свою́ пози́цию. **7,** *mil.* пози́ция: *forward position,* передова́я пози́ция. **8,** *chess* пози́ция: *winning position,* вы́игрышная пози́ция. —*v.t.* ста́вить; помеща́ть. *Position oneself at the entrance,* стать у вхо́да.

positional *adj.* позицио́нный.

positive *adj.* **1,** (affirmative; favorable) положи́тельный: *a positive reaction,* положи́тельная реа́кция. **2,** (certain) уве́ренный: *I am positive that...,* я (абсолю́тно) уве́рен(а), что... **3,** *math.; electricity* положи́тельный. **4,** *photog.* позити́вный. —*n., photog.* позити́в. —**positively,** *adv.* положи́тельно.

positivism *n.* позитиви́зм.

positron *n.* позитро́н.

possess *v.t.* **1,** (have; own) облада́ть: *possess talent,* облада́ть тала́нтом. **2,** (come over) овладева́ть: *Fear possessed him,* им овладе́л страх. *What possessed you do that?,* что вас заста́вило сде́лать э́то?

possessed *adj.* **1,** *fol. by* **of** (having) облада́ющий. **2,** (obsessed) одержи́мый.

possession *n.* **1,** (fact of possessing) облада́ние; владе́ние. *Possession of a weapon,* владе́ние ору́жием. *Be in someone's possession,* быть в чьём-нибудь распоряже́нии. *Take/ come into/ possession*

of, вступи́ть во владе́ние (+ *instr.*). *How did this letter come into your possession?,* как к вам попа́ло э́то письмо́? **2,** (territory belonging to an outside country) владе́ние. **3,** *pl.* (belongings) иму́щество.

possessive *adj.* **1,** (desiring to possess) со́бственнический. **2,** *gram.* притяжа́тельный.

possessor *n.* облада́тель.

possibility *n.* возмо́жность: *the possibility of error,* возмо́жность оши́бки. *There is little possibility of that,* ша́нсов на э́то ма́ло. *There are two possibilities,* существу́ют два вариа́нта.

possible *adj.* возмо́жный. *If possible,* е́сли возмо́жно. *That is not possible,* э́то невозмо́жно. *That's entirely possible,* э́то вполне́ возмо́жно. *It is very possible that...,* о́чень мо́жет быть, что... *Do everything possible,* де́лать всё возмо́жное. *Make it possible to,* позволя́ть (+ *inf.*). —**as...as possible,** как мо́жно (+ *comparative*): *as soon as possible,* как мо́жно скоре́е. *Be as objective as possible,* быть по возмо́жности объекти́вным.

possibly *adv.* возмо́жно: *I may possibly be late,* я, возмо́жно, опозда́ю. *As soon as I possibly can,* как то́лько я смогу́. *He could not possibly have done it,* не мо́жет быть, чтобы он сде́лал э́то.

possum *n., colloq.* = **opossum.** —**play possum,** притворя́ться мёртвым.

post *n.* **1,** (upright pole) столб. **2,** (station) пункт; пост: *observation post,* наблюда́тельный пункт; *control post,* контро́льный пост. *Border post,* пограни́чная заста́ва. **3,** (assigned position) пост: *remain at one's post,* остава́ться на своём посту́. **4,** (camp; base) городо́к: *military post,* вое́нный городо́к. **5,** (appointed public office) пост; до́лжность: *appointed to the post of...,* назна́чен на пост/ до́лжность (+ *gen.*). **6,** (mail) по́чта. —*v.t.* **1,** (put up; hang up) выве́шивать; раскле́ивать. *Post a notice,* выве́шивать объявле́ние. **2,** (station, as a sentry) ста́вить; выставля́ть (часово́го); расставля́ть; разводи́ть (часовы́х). **3,** (assign) прикомандирова́ть. **4,** (keep informed) держа́ть в ку́рсе. *Well posted on politics,* в ку́рсе поли́тики. **5,** *comm.* (transfer to a ledger) переноси́ть в гроссбу́х. **6,** *chiefly Brit.* (mail) отправля́ть; опуска́ть (в почто́вый я́щик). **7,** *in* **post bond for,** брать на пору́ку.

postage *n.* почто́вые расхо́ды; сто́имость пересы́лки. *Pay the postage,* (у)плати́ть за пересы́лку. —**postage stamp,** почто́вая ма́рка.

postal *adj.* почто́вый: *postal rates,* почто́вый тари́ф.

postcard *n.* почто́вая ка́рточка; откры́тка.

postdate *v.t.* дати́ровать (что́-нибудь) бо́лее по́здним число́м.

poster *n.* плака́т; афи́ша.

posterior *adj.* **1,** (rear) за́дний. **2,** (subsequent) после́дующий. —*n.* зад.

posterity *n.* пото́мство: *the verdict of posterity,* суд пото́мства.

postgraduate *n.* аспира́нт. *Postgraduate studies,* аспиранту́ра.

posthaste *adv.* сломя́ го́лову; момента́льно.

posthumous *adj.* посме́ртный. —**posthumously,** *adv.* посме́ртно.

postilion *also,* **postillion** *n.* форе́йтор.

postman *n.* почтальо́н.

postmark *n.* почто́вый шт́емпель. —*v.t.* штемпелева́ть.

postmaster *n.* почтме́йстер. —**postmaster general,** мини́стр почт.

post-mortem *n.* **1,** (autopsy) вскры́тие. **2,** *colloq.* (post-game analysis) ана́лиз игры́.

postnatal *adj.* послеродово́й.

post office по́чта. *Go to the post office,* идти́ на по́чту.

postoperative *adj.* послеоперацио́нный.

postpaid *adj. & adv.* с опла́ченными почто́выми расхо́дами.

postpone *v.t.* откла́дывать. *The meeting has been postponed until tomorrow,* собра́ние отло́жено на *or* до за́втра; собра́ние перенесли́ на за́втра. —**postponement,** *n.* отсро́чка.

post road почто́вый тракт.

postscript *n.* **1,** (to a letter) припи́ска; постскри́птум. **2,** (to a book or article) послесло́вие.

postulate *n.* постула́т. —*v.t.* постули́ровать.

posture *n.* **1,** (position) положе́ние. **2,** (way of standing) оса́нка: *poor posture,* плоха́я оса́нка. **3,** *fig.* (stance) пози́ция.

postwar *adj.* послевое́нный.

posy *n.* **1,** (flower) цвето́к. **2,** (bouquet) буке́т.

pot *n.* **1,** (for cooking) кастрю́ля; котело́к. *Coffeepot,* кофе́йник. **2,** (for plants) горшо́к: *flowerpot,* цвето́чный горшо́к. —**go to pot,** *slang* вы́лететь в трубу́.

potable *adj.* го́дный для питья́.

potash *n.* пота́ш.

potassium *n.* ка́лий. —**potassium bromide,** бро́мистый ка́лий. —**potassium carbonate,** углеки́слый ка́лий. —**potassium chloride,** хло́ристый ка́лий. —**potassium cyanide,** циа́нистый ка́лий. —**potassium iodide,** йо́дистый ка́лий. —**potassium nitrate,** ка́лиевая *or* кали́йная сели́тра.

potato *n.* карто́фелина; *pl.* карто́фель. —*adj.* карто́фельный. —**potato beetle** (*or* **bug**), (колора́дский) карто́фельный жук. —**potato chips,** чи́псы.

potbelly *n., colloq.* пу́зо; брю́хо. —**potbellied,** *adj., colloq.* пуза́тый.

pot cheese творо́г.

Potemkin village потёмкинская дере́вня.

potency *n.* си́ла.

potent *adj.* **1,** (powerful, as of a weapon) мо́щный. **2,** (effective, as of a drug or medicine) сильноде́йствующий. **3,** (strong, as of a drink) кре́пкий. **4,** (convincing; cogent) си́льный; убеди́тельный.

potentate *n.* власте́ли́н.

potential *adj.* потенциа́льный. —*n.* потенциа́л. —**potentiality,** *n.* возмо́жности.

pothole *n.* уха́б; ры́твина; вы́боина; колдо́бина.

potion *n.* зе́лье. *Love potion,* любо́вный напи́ток.

potpourri *n.* мешани́на; винегре́т.

pot shot вы́стрел в упо́р. *Take a pot shot at,* вы́стрелить в (кого́-нибудь) в упо́р.

pottage *n.* похлёбка.

potted *adj.* **1,** (kept in a pot, as of plants) горше́чный. **2,** *slang* (drunk) пья́ный.

potter *n.* гонча́р. —*v.i.* = **putter.** —**potter's wheel,** гонча́рный круг.

pottery *n.* гонча́рные *or* гли́няные изде́лия; гли́няная посу́да.

pouch *n.* **1,** (small bag) су́мка; мешо́чек. *Tobacco pouch,* кисе́т. **2,** (of a kangaroo) су́мка. —**diplomatic pouch,** дипломати́ческая по́чта.

poultice *n.* припа́рка.

poultry *n.* дома́шняя пти́ца.

pounce *v.i.* [*usu.* **pounce on** *or* **upon**] набра́сываться (на); обру́шиваться (на); налета́ть (на).

pound *n.* **1,** (measure of weight; monetary unit) фунт. **2,** (enclosure for stray animals) заго́н. —*v.t.* **1,** (bang) ударя́ть; колоти́ть: *pound one's fist on the table,* ударя́ть/колоти́ть кулако́м по́ столу. **2,** [*also intrans.* **pound on**] (strike heavily) ударя́ть (в *or* по); колоти́ть (в *or* по). **3,** (crush; pulverize) толо́чь; дроби́ть; размельча́ть. —*v.i.* колоти́ться: *My heart was pounding,* у меня́ се́рдце колоти́лось.

poundage *n.* вес (в фу́нтах).

pour *v.t.* **1,** (a liquid) налива́ть; лить. *Pour oneself a glass of juice,* налива́ть себе́ стака́н со́ка. *Pour tea for the guests,* разлива́ть гостя́м чай. **2,** (a dry substance) сы́пать: *pour something into a sack,* сы́пать что́-нибудь в мешо́к. *Pour sand on a fire,* сы́пать песо́к (*or* песко́м) на костёр. —*v.i.* ли́ться; лить. *It is pouring,* идёт си́льный дождь; дождь так и льёт. *Tears were pouring down her cheeks,* слёзы кати́лись у неё по щека́м. *Sunlight poured through the window,* со́лнечный свет ли́лся че́рез окно́. —**pour in, 1,** (stream into a place) вали́ть. **2,** (arrive in great numbers) сы́паться. —**pour out, 1,** *literally* вылива́ть. **2,** (give vent to, as one's feelings) излива́ть. *Pour out one's heart to,* излива́ть ду́шу (+ *dat.*). **3,** (come streaming out) высыпа́ть: *pour out into the streets,* высыпа́ть на у́лицы.

pout *v.i.* ду́ться; надува́ть гу́бы.

poverty *n.* бе́дность; нищета́. *Live in poverty,* жить в нищете́ *or* в нужде́. *Poverty of ideas,* убо́жество иде́й. —**poverty line,** черта́ бе́дности: *live below the poverty line,* жить за черто́й бе́дности. —**poverty-stricken,** *adj.* ни́щий; обедне́вший; обнища́лый.

powder *n.* **1,** (substance of fine particles) порошо́к: *tooth powder,* зубно́й порошо́к. **2,** (talcum) пу́дра: *face powder,* пу́дра для лица́. *Baby powder,* де́тская присы́пка. **3,** (gunpowder) по́рох. —*adj.* порохово́й: *powder magazine,* порохово́й по́греб. —*v.t.* пу́дрить. *Powder one's nose,* пу́дриться. —**keep one's powder dry,** держа́ть по́рох сухи́м.

powdered *adj.* напу́дренный: *powdered wig,* напу́дренный пари́к. —**powdered eggs,** яи́чный порошо́к. —**powdered milk,** моло́чный порошо́к. —**powdered sugar,** са́харная пу́дра.

powder keg порохова́я бо́чка; порохово́й по́греб.

powder puff пухо́вка.

powder room да́мская убо́рная; да́мский туале́т.

powdery *adj.* порошкообра́зный.

power *n.* **1,** (strength; might) мощь; могу́щество. *Military/air power,* вое́нная/возду́шная мощь. *The power of the printed word,* власть печа́тного сло́ва. **2,** (political control) власть: *be/remain in power,* быть/оста́ться у вла́сти. *Seize power,* захвати́ть власть. **3,** (form of energy) эне́ргия: *electric power,* электроэне́ргия. *Nuclear power,* я́дерная *or* а́томная эне́ргия. **4,** (electricity) электри́чество: *The power is out,* нет электри́чества. **5,** (capacity to exert force or energy) си́ла; мо́щность: *horsepower,* лошади́ная си́ла; *engine power,* мо́щность дви́гателя. *Lose power,* теря́ть мо́щность. **6,** (large nation) держа́ва: *a world power,* мирова́я держа́ва. **7,** *pl.* (faculties) си́лы: *mental powers,* у́мственные си́лы. **8,** *pl.* (authority) полномо́чия: *broad powers,* широ́кие полномо́чия. **9,** *math.* сте́пень: *ten to the sixth power,* де́сять в шесто́й сте́пени. —*adj.* **1,** (generating or transmitting power) силово́й. *Power station,* силова́я ста́нция; электроста́нция. *Power lines,* ли́нии электропереда́чи. **2,** (driven by a motor) механи́ческий: *power tool,* механи́ческий инструме́нт. *Power saw,* мотопила́. —*v.t.* дви́гать: *The plane is powered by two large engines,* самолёт дви́жут два больши́х мото́ра. —**do everything in one's power,** де́лать всё, что в чьи́х-нибудь си́лах. —**the powers that be,** власть иму́щие. —**under one's own power,** со́бственными си́лами; свои́м хо́дом.

powerful *adj.* си́льный; мо́щный; могу́чий. *Powerful engine/weapon,* мо́щный дви́гатель; мо́щное ору́жие. *Powerful army,* си́льная *or* могу́чая а́рмия. *Powerful nation,* могу́чая *or* могу́щественная страна́. *Powerful argument,* си́льный до́вод. —**powerfully,** *adv.* си́льно.

powerless *adj.* бесси́льный.

power of attorney дове́ренность.

power pack блок пита́ния.

power plant 1, (source of power) силова́я устано́вка. **2,** (power station) электроста́нция.

pox *n.* о́спа.

practicable *adj.* осуществи́мый; реа́льный. —**practicability,** *n.* осуществи́мость.

practical *adj.* практи́ческий; практи́чный: *practical person,* практи́чный челове́к; *practical advice,* практи́ческий сове́т. *Practical application,* практи́ческое примене́ние. *Put one's knowledge to practical use,* применя́ть свои́ зна́ния на пра́ктике. —**for all practical purposes,** факти́чески.

practicality *n.* практи́чность.

practical joke ро́зыгрыш; мистифика́ция.

practically *adv.* **1,** (in a practical way) практи́чески. **2,** (virtually; in effect) практи́чески: *practically impossible,* практи́чески невозмо́жно. **3,** (almost) почти́: *practically all week,* почти́ всю неде́лю. —**practically speaking,** факти́чески.

practice *also,* **practise** *n.* **1,** (repeated exercise) пра́ктика: *conversational practice,* пра́ктика разгово́рной ре́чи. *Swimming practice,* трениро́вка по пла́ванию. *Choir practice,* репети́ция хо́ра. *Be out of practice,* не име́ть пра́ктики. **2,** (usage; performance) пра́ктика. *In practice,* на пра́ктике; на де́ле. *Put into practice,* применя́ть *or* осуществля́ть *or* проводи́ть на пра́ктике; вводи́ть в пра́ктику; проводи́ть *or* претворя́ть в жизнь. **3,** (habitual way of doing things) привы́чка; обы́чай. *Make it a practice to; make a practice of,* взять себе́ за пра́вило (+ *inf.*). *It is not our practice to...,* у нас не при́нято (+ *inf.*). *As has been the practice heretofore,* как э́то практикова́лось до сих пор. **4,** (professional activity or clientele) пра́ктика: *legal practice,* адвока́тская пра́ктика. *He has a large practice,* у него́ больша́я пра́ктика. **5,** *pl.* (questionable activities) дела́: *shady practices,* тёмные дела́. —*adj.* про́бный: *practice shot/jump,* про́бный вы́стрел/прыжо́к. —*v.t.* **1,** (observe; exercise) практикова́ть. *Practice thrift,* соблюда́ть эконо́мию. *Practice one's religion,* испове́довать свою́ рели́гию. **2,** (drill oneself in) упражня́ться в *or* на; практикова́ться в. *Practice the piano,* упражня́ться на роя́ле. **3,** (pursue, as a profession): *practice law/medicine,* быть адвока́том/врачо́м. —*v.i.* **1,** (drill) упражня́ться; практикова́ться. **2,** (pursue one's profession) практикова́ть.

practiced *also,* **practised** *adj.* о́пытный; уме́лый.

practitioner *n. General practitioner,* врач о́бщей пра́ктики; врач о́бщего про́филя; врач по всем боле́зням.

praetor *n.* пре́тор.

Praetorian Guard преториа́нская гва́рдия.

pragmatic *adj.* прагмати́ческий. —**pragmatism,** *n.* прагмати́зм. —**pragmatist,** *n.* прагмати́ст.

prairie *n.* пре́рия; степь.

praise *v.t.* хвали́ть: *praise a book/movie,* хвали́ть кни́гу/фильм. *Praise someone for his courage,* хвали́ть кого́-нибудь за хра́брость. —*n.* похвала́. *In praise of,* в похвалу́ (+ *dat.*). *Unanimous in their praise of...,* единоду́шны в похвала́х (+ *dat.*). —**praise to the skies,** превозноси́ть до небе́с. —**sing the praises of,** петь дифира́мбы (+ *dat.*).

praiseworthy *adj.* похва́льный.

pram *n., colloq.* = **perambulator.**

prance *v.i.* **1,** (on a horse) гарцева́ть. **2,** (swagger; strut) ва́жничать; ходи́ть го́голем.

prank *n.* вы́ходка; прока́за; проде́лка; ша́лость. *Play pranks,* прока́зничать. —**prankish,** *adj.* прока́зливый. —**prankster,** *n.* прока́зник.

praseodymium *n.* празеоди́м.

prate *v.i.* болта́ть; треща́ть.

prattle *v.i.* лепета́ть. —*n.* ле́пет.

prawn *n.* креве́тка.

pray *v.i.* моли́ться: *pray to God,* моли́ться бо́гу; *pray for rain,* моли́ться о дожде́. —*v.t. & i.* (beg; beseech) умоля́ть.

prayer *n.* моли́тва: *say a prayer,* чита́ть моли́тву. *Call to prayer,* звать к моли́тве. *Kneel in prayer,* моли́ться на коле́нях. —**prayer book,** моли́твенник. —**prayer service,** моле́ние.

praying mantis богомо́л.

preach *v.t.* **1,** (advocate) пропове́довать. **2,** (deliver, as a sermon) чита́ть; произноси́ть. —*v.i.* (deliver a sermon) пропове́довать. —**preacher,** *n.* пропове́дник.

preamble *n.* преа́мбула: *preamble to the constitution,* преа́мбула конститу́ции.

prearranged *adj.* зара́нее усло́вленный; усло́вный.

precancerous *adj.* предра́ковый.

precarious *adj.* ненадёжный; ша́ткий. *Precarious position,* ша́ткое положе́ние. *Precarious situation,* ненадёжная ситуа́ция.

precaution *n.* предосторо́жность. *Take precautions,* принима́ть (ме́ры) предосторо́жности. —**precautionary,** *adj., in* **precautionary measures,** ме́ры предосторо́жности.

precede *v.t.* предше́ствовать: *events preceding the trial,* собы́тия, предше́ствовавшие проце́ссу. *In the years preceding World War I,* в го́ды, предше́ствовавшие пе́рвой мирово́й войне́.

precedence *n.* приорите́т. *Take precedence over,* име́ть приорите́т над; преоблада́ть над; превали́ровать над.

precedent *n.* прецеде́нт: *set a precedent,* создава́ть прецеде́нт.

preceding *adj.* предше́ствующий; предыду́щий.

precept *n.* заве́т; наставле́ние.

precinct *n.* уча́сток; о́круг.

precious *adj.* **1,** (highly valuable) драгоце́нный: *precious stones,* драгоце́нные ка́мни. **2,** (held dear) дорого́й: *precious memories,* дороги́е воспомина́ния. **3,** (vitally important) драгоце́нный; дорого́й. *Waste precious time,* теря́ть драгоце́нное вре́мя. *Time was precious,* вре́мя бы́ло до́рого. **4,** (delightful) преле́стный: *a precious child,* преле́стный ребёнок. **5,** (affected, as of a style) мане́рный. —**precious metals,** благоро́дные мета́ллы.

precipice *n.* обры́в.

precipitate *v.t.* приводи́ть к; вызыва́ть. —*adj.* = **precipitous.**

precipitation *n.* оса́дки.

precipitous *adj.* **1,** (steep) круто́й; обры́вистый. **2,** (hasty; rash) опроме́тчивый.

precise *adj.* **1,** (accurate; exact) то́чный: *precise measurement,* то́чное измере́ние. *To be precise...,* что́бы быть то́чным... *Or to be more precise...,* и́ли точне́е... **2,** (punctilious) аккура́тный. **3,** (particular) как раз: *at that precise moment,* как раз в тот моме́нт.

precisely *adv.* **1,** (in a precise manner) то́чно. **2,** (just; exactly) и́менно: *precisely for this reason,* и́менно по э́той причи́не.

precision *n.* то́чность. —*adj.* то́чный: *precision instruments,* то́чные прибо́ры. *Precision bombing,* прице́льное бомбомета́ние.

preclude *v.t.* исключа́ть возмо́жность (+ *gen.*): *preclude escape,* исключа́ть возмо́жность побе́га. *Preclude someone's attending the meeting,* меша́ть кому́-нибудь прису́тствовать на собра́нии.

precocious *adj.* развито́й; ра́звит не по года́м.

preconceived *adj.* предвзя́тый.

preconception *n.* предвзя́тое мне́ние.

precondition *n.* **1,** (prerequisite) предпосы́лка. **2,** (prior stipulation) предвари́тельное усло́вие.

precursor *n.* **1,** (predecessor) предше́ственник. **2,** (harbinger) предве́стник.

predate *v.t.* **1,** (come before) предше́ствовать. **2,** (put an earlier date on) поме́тить за́дним число́м.

predator *n.* хи́щник.

predatory *adj.* **1,** (characterized by plundering) граби́тельский. **2,** (rapacious, as of a bird) хи́щный.

predecessor *n.* предше́ственник.

predestine *v.t.* предопределя́ть; предначерта́ть. —**predestination,** *n.* предопределе́ние.

predetermine *v.t.* предопределя́ть; предреша́ть. —**predetermination,** *n.* предопределе́ние.

predicament *n.* затрудни́тельное положе́ние.

predicate *n.* сказу́емое; предика́т. —*v.t.* осно́вывать: *On what is this predicated?,* на чём э́то осно́вано? —**predicative,** *adj.* предикати́вный.

predict *v.t. & i.* предска́зывать: *predict the future,* предска́зывать бу́дущее. *Predict a brilliant future for someone,* предсказа́ть кому́-нибудь блестя́щее бу́дущее. —**predictable,** *adj.* предсказу́емый. —**prediction,** *n.* предсказа́ние.

predilection *n.* пристра́стие; скло́нность.

predispose *v.t.* предрасполага́ть. —**predisposed,** *adj.* предрасполо́женный. —**predisposition,** *n.* предрасположе́ние.

predominance *n.* преоблада́ние. —**predominant,** *adj.* преоблада́ющий. —**predominantly,** *adv.* преиму́щественно. *The population is predominantly Catholic,* основна́я часть населе́ния — като́лики.

predominate *v.i.* преоблада́ть; госпо́дствовать; домини́ровать.

preeminent *adj.* выдаю́щийся. —**preeminence,** *n.* превосхо́дство.

preempt *v.t.* присва́ивать. —**preemptive,** *adj.* упрежда́ющий: *preemptive strike,* упрежда́ющий уда́р.

preen *v.t.* **1,** (smooth with the beak) чи́стить клю́вом. **2,** (primp) прихора́шивать.

prefabricated *adj.* сбо́рный.

preface *n.* предисло́вие. —*v.t.* предпосыла́ть: *preface one's report with a story,* предпосла́ть докла́ду расска́з. —**prefatory,** *adj.* вступи́тельный; вво́дный.

prefect *n.* префе́кт. —**prefecture,** *n.* префекту́ра.

prefer *v.t.* **1,** (like better) предпочита́ть: *prefer beer to wine,* предпочита́ть пи́во вину́. **2,** (file) предъявля́ть: *prefer charges against,* предъяви́ть обвине́ние (+ *dat.*). *See also* **preferred.**

preferable *adj.* предпочти́тельный. *Plastic is preferable to wood,* пластма́сса предпочти́тельнее де́рева. —**preferably,** *adv.* лу́чше; скоре́е.

preference *n.* предпочте́ние: *give preference to,* отдава́ть *or* ока́зывать предпочте́ние (+ *dat.*). *What is your preference?,* что вы предпочита́ете?

preferential *adj.* льго́тный. *Preferential tariff,* предпочти́тельный тари́ф.

preferred *adj.* предпочти́тельный. —**preferred stock,** привилегиро́ванные а́кции.

prefix *n.* приста́вка; пре́фикс. —*v.t.* присоединя́ть приста́вку к (сло́ву). —**prefixed,** *adj.* приста́вочный. —**prefixion,** *n.* префикса́ция.

preflight *adj.* предполётный.

pregnancy *n.* бере́менность.

pregnant *adj.* бере́менная. *She is pregnant,* она́ бере́менна; она́ в положе́нии. *Become pregnant,* стать бере́менной; (за)бере́менеть.

prehensile *adj.* цепкий.
prehistoric *adj.* доисторический.
prehistory *n.* предыстория.
prejudge *v.t.* предрешать.
prejudice *n.* **1,** (bias) предрассудок; предубеждение; предвзятость. *Racial prejudice,* расовые предрассудки. **2,** (detriment) ущерб. —*v.t.* **1,** (cause prejudice in) предубеждать. **2,** (harm) наносить ущерб (+ *dat.*).
prejudiced *adj.* предубеждённый. *He is prejudiced against me,* он относится ко мне предубеждённо; против меня он настроен предубеждённо.
prejudicial *adj.* вредный. *Be prejudicial to the interests of the workers,* ущемлять интересы рабочих.
prelate *n.* прелат.
preliminary *adj.* предварительный.
prelude *n.* прелюдия.
premarital *adj.* добрачный.
premature *adj.* **1,** (occurring earlier than normal) преждевременный: *premature birth/death,* преждевременные роды; преждевременная смерть. *Premature child,* недоношенный ребёнок; недоносок. **2,** (too hasty) поспешный: *premature conclusion,* поспешный вывод. —**prematurely,** *adv.* преждевременно.
premeditated *adj.* преднамеренный; умышленный. —**premeditation,** *n.* преднамеренность.
premier *adj.* первый. —*n.* премьер-министр; премьер.
première *n.* премьера.
premise *n.* **1,** (assumption) посылка; предпосылка. *False premise,* ложная посылка. **2,** *pl.* (building and grounds) помещение.
premium *n.* премия. *At a premium,* нарасхват.
premonition *n.* предчувствие: *a premonition of trouble,* предчувствие беды.
prenatal *adj.* предродовой. *Prenatal care,* гигиена беременной.
preoccupation *n.* **1,** (absorption) одержимость. **2,** (something that preoccupies) забота.
preoccupied *adj.* **1,** (lost in thought) погружённый в мысли. **2,** (totally involved) поглощённый.
preoccupy *v.t.* поглощать.
preordain *v.t.* предопределять.
prepaid *adj.* уплаченный *or* оплаченный заранее.
preparation *n.* **1,** (act of preparing something or getting something ready) приготовление; подготовка. *The preparation of food,* приготовление пищи. *Preparation for an examination,* подготовка к экзамену. **2,** *usu. pl.* (steps taken to prepare) приготовления. *Make preparations for,* готовиться к. **3,** (something prepared; a substance) препарат.
preparatory *adj.* приготовительный; подготовительный. —**preparatory to,** прежде чем.
prepare *v.t.* готовить; приготовлять; подготавливать. —*v.i.* готовиться; приготовляться; подготавливаться. *Prepare for an exam,* готовиться к экзамену. *Prepare to depart,* готовиться к отъезду.
prepared *adj.* готовый: *prepared for anything,* готов на всё; *prepared to negotiate,* готов вести пере-

говоры. *I was not prepared for that,* я не был готов к этому.
preparedness *n.* готовность; подготовленность.
prepay *v.t.* уплачивать *or* оплачивать заранее.
preponderance *n.* перевес; преобладание. —**preponderant,** *adj.* преобладающий.
preposition *n.* предлог.
prepositional *adj.* предложный. *Prepositional case,* предложный падеж.
prepossessing *adj.* располагающий; приятный; привлекательный.
preposterous *adj.* нелепый; абсурдный; дикий.
prerequisite *n.* предпосылка.
prerevolutionary *adj.* дореволюционный.
prerogative *n.* прерогатива; привилегия.
presage *v.t.* предвещать.
presbyter *n.* пресвитер.
Presbyterian *n.* пресвитерианин; пресвитерианец. —*adj.* пресвитерианский.
preschool *adj.* дошкольный.
prescience *n.* предвидение. —**prescient,** *adj.* проницательный.
prescribe *v.t.* **1,** (set down to be followed) предписывать: *prescribe the rules,* предписывать правила. *Within the prescribed period,* в положенный срок. **2,** (order the use of, as medicine) прописывать.
prescription *n.* **1,** (instruction; directive) предписание. **2,** *med.* рецепт. **3,** *law* давность.
presence *n.* присутствие; наличие. *In the presence of,* при; в присутствии (+ *gen.*). *In my presence,* в моём присутствии; при мне. *Make one's presence felt,* заявить о себе; сказать своё слово. —**presence of mind,** присутствие духа.
present *adj.* **1,** (now going on; current) настоящий; теперешний; нынешний; данный. *At the present time,* в настоящее время. *At the present moment,* в данный момент. *The present regime,* теперешний режим. **2,** (here; on hand) присутствующий. *Be present,* присутствовать; быть налицо. **3,** (this; now being discussed) данный; настоящий. *In the present case,* в данном случае. **4,** *gram.* настоящий: *the present tense,* настоящее время. —*n.* **1,** *preceded by* **the** (present time) настоящее. *At present,* сейчас; в настоящее время. *For the present,* пока. **2,** (gift) подарок: *birthday present,* подарок ко дню рождения. —*v.t.* **1,** (give; offer) представлять: *present facts/ evidence/ a plan/ a paper/,* представлять факты/ доказательства/план/доклад. **2,** (produce; show) предъявлять; представлять: *present one's documents,* предъявлять/представлять документы. **3,** (hand over; submit) вручать: *present one's credentials,* вручить свои верительные грамоты. **4,** (give or award formally) вручать; преподносить. *Present an award,* вручить награду. *She was presented with a bouquet of roses,* ей преподнесли букет роз. **5,** (introduce) представлять: *May I present...,* разрешите мне представить... **6,** (offer, as problems or difficulties) представлять. **7,** (give, as a play) показывать; ставить. —**present arms,** взять на караул. —**present itself,** являться; представляться.

presentable *adj.* прили́чный; презента́бельный.

presentation *n.* **1,** (submitting; introducing) представле́ние. **2,** (producing; showing) предъявле́ние. **3,** (awarding; bestowing) вруче́ние. **4,** (a performance) представле́ние.

present-day *adj.* совреме́нный: *meet present-day needs,* отвеча́ть совреме́нным тре́бованиям. *By present-day standards,* по ме́ркам на́шего вре́мени.

presentiment *n.* предчу́вствие.

presently *adv.* **1,** (soon) ско́ро; вско́ре. **2,** (at present) сейча́с; в настоя́щее вре́мя.

preservation *n.* **1,** (act of preserving) сохране́ние. **2,** (state of being preserved) сохра́нность. *In an excellent state of preservation,* в прекра́сной сохра́нности.

preservative *n.* консерва́нт.

preserve *v.t.* **1,** (keep; maintain) сохраня́ть: *preserve historical monuments,* сохраня́ть истори́ческие па́мятники. *Well preserved,* хорошо́ сохрани́вшийся. **2,** (prepare, as food, for future use) консерви́ровать. —*n.* **1,** (restricted area) запове́дник. **2,** *pl.* (confection) варе́нье.

preside *v.i.* председа́тельствовать (на собра́нии).

president *n.* **1,** (chief executive) президе́нт. **2,** (presiding officer) председа́тель: *Mr. President,* господи́н председа́тель. **3,** (of a university) ре́ктор. —**presidency,** *n.* президе́нтство. —**presidential,** *adj.* президе́нтский.

presidium *n.* прези́диум.

press *v.t.* **1,** (push, as a button) нажима́ть на (кно́пку). **2,** (clasp; squeeze) жать: *press someone's hand,* жать кому́-нибудь ру́ку. *Press to one's bosom,* прижима́ть к груди́. **3,** (squeeze out the juice from) дави́ть; жать. **4,** (work in a press) прессова́ть: *press cotton,* прессова́ть хло́пок. **5,** (iron) гла́дить. **6,** (urge) угова́ривать: *press someone to go,* угова́ривать кого́-нибудь пойти́. **7,** (put pressure on) торопи́ть: *press someone for an answer,* торопи́ть кого́-нибудь с отве́том. **8,** (be insistent about) наста́ивать на: *press a matter,* наста́ивать на чём-нибудь. *I will not press the point,* я не бу́ду наста́ивать на э́том. **9,** *usu. passive* (put under pressure) стесня́ть: *pressed for money,* стеснённый в деньга́х. *I am pressed for time,* у меня́ вре́мени в обре́з. **10,** (bring, as charges) предъявля́ть (обвине́ние). **11,** *in* **press one's luck,** искуша́ть *or* испы́тывать судьбу́. —*v.i.* **1,** (push hard) нажима́ть; нада́вливать; прида́вливать. *Press hard!,* нажми́ кре́пко! **2,** *fol. by* **on** *or* **against** (push against; exert pressure on) дави́ть: *press on a nerve,* дави́ть на нерв. **3,** *fol. by* **against** (lean hard against) прижима́ться (к); приника́ть (к). **4,** (advance forcibly) пробира́ться; прота́лкиваться. *Press forward,* протолкну́ться вперёд. —*n.* **1,** (instance of pressing) нажа́тие: *by a press of the button,* нажа́тием на кно́пку. **2,** (device for pressing or crushing) пресс: *hydraulic press,* гидравли́ческий пресс; *wine press,* дави́льный пресс. *Printing press,* печа́тный стано́к. **3,** (newspapers collectively) печа́ть; пре́сса. *A free press,* свобо́дная печа́ть/пре́сса. *Freedom of the press,* свобо́да печа́ти. **4,** (printing) печа́ть: *go to press,* поступи́ть в печа́ть. **5,** (crush) да́вка. **6,** *weightlifting* жим. —*adj.* корреспонде́нтский: *press card/corps,* корреспонде́нтский биле́т/ко́рпус.

press box ло́жа пре́ссы.

press conference пресс-конфере́нция.

presser *n.* прессовщи́к.

pressing *n.* гла́женье. —*adj.* неотло́жный; сро́чный. *Pressing engagement,* неотло́жная встре́ча.

pressman *n.* **1,** (one who works a press) прессовщи́к. **2,** (operator of a printing press) печа́тник.

pressmark *n., Brit.* шифр.

pressrun *n.* тира́ж.

pressure *n.* давле́ние: *blood pressure,* кровяно́е давле́ние. *Air pressure,* давле́ние во́здуха. *He declined, citing the pressure of work,* он отказа́лся, сосла́вшись на за́нятость. —*v.t.* ока́зывать давле́ние на. —**pressure gauge,** мано́метр.

pressurized *adj.* гермети́ческий: *pressurized cabin,* гермети́ческая каби́на.

prestidigitation *n.* ло́вкость рук. —**prestidigitator,** *n.* фо́кусник.

prestige *n.* прести́ж; авторите́т. —**prestigious,** *adj.* прести́жный.

presto *adv., music* пре́сто.

presumably *adv.* предположи́тельно. *He presumably will decline the offer,* предполага́ется, что он отка́жется от предложе́ния.

presume *v.t.* **1,** (assume) полага́ть; предполага́ть. *I presume you've heard the news,* я полага́ю, что вы слы́шали но́вость. *The rest are presumed dead,* предполага́ется, что остальны́е поги́бли. **2,** *fol. by inf.* (dare; venture) осме́ливаться; бра́ться; реша́ться. *I do not presume to judge,* не беру́сь суди́ть. *Whether this is true or not I would not presume to say,* так ли э́то и́ли нет — сказа́ть не реша́юсь. —*v.i.* [*usu.* **presume on** *or* **upon**] злоупотребля́ть.

presumption *n.* **1,** (supposition) предположе́ние. **2,** *law* презу́мпция: *presumption of innocence,* презу́мпция невино́вности. **3,** (effrontery) на́глость; самонаде́янность. *Have the presumption to...,* име́ть на́глость (+ *inf.*).

presumptive *adj.* предположи́тельный. —**heir presumptive,** вероя́тный насле́дник.

presumptuous *adj.* самонаде́янный.

presuppose *v.t.* предполага́ть.

pretence *n.* = **pretense.**

pretend *v.t. & i.* притворя́ться; де́лать вид. *Pretend to be asleep,* притворя́ться спя́щим. *I pretended I didn't know,* я де́лал вид, что не знал. *Stop pretending!,* переста́ньте притворя́ться! —**pretended,** *adj.* притво́рный.

pretender *n.* претенде́нт.

pretense *also,* **pretence** *n.* **1,** (pretending; falseness) притво́рство; по́за. **2,** (claim) прете́нзия. *Make no pretense of,* не претендова́ть на. **3,** (pretext) предло́г. *Under false pretenses,* обма́нным путём.

pretension *n.* прете́нзия; притяза́ние. *Have pretensions of,* претендова́ть на.

pretentious *adj.* претенцио́зный; с прете́нзиями. —**pretentiousness,** *n.* претенцио́зность.

pretext *n.* предло́г: *On/under what pretext?*, под каки́м предло́гом?

prettily *adv.* краси́во; ми́ло.

pretty *adj.* **1,** (pleasing to the eye) хоро́шенький; милови́дный; краси́вый. *Pretty girl,* хоро́шенькая/ милови́дная де́вушка. *Pretty face,* милови́дное лицо́. *Pretty dress,* краси́вое пла́тье. **2,** (pleasing to the ear, as of a song or voice) прия́тный; краси́вый. **3,** *colloq.* (quite a large) изря́дный: *a pretty sum,* изря́дная су́мма. **4,** *ironic* (fine; nice) хоро́шенький: *a pretty mess,* хоро́шенькая исто́рия. —*adv.* дово́льно; доста́точно. *Pretty good,* неду́рно; так себе́; ничего́. *Pretty much,* почти́; бо́лее и́ли ме́нее. *Things are pretty much the same,* в основно́м всё по- ста́рому. —*v.t.* [*usu.* **pretty up**] приукра́шивать.

pretzel *n.* кре́ндель.

prevail *v.i.* **1,** *often fol.* by **over** (triumph; win out) (вос)торжествова́ть (над); брать верх (над); пре- облада́ть (над). **2,** (be in use; be current) су- ществова́ть. **3,** *fol.* by **upon** (persuade) убеди́ть; уго- вори́ть; упроси́ть; умоли́ть.

prevailing *adj.* преоблада́ющий; госпо́дствующий. *Prevailing winds,* преоблада́ющие ве́тры.

prevalent *adj.* распространённый. —**prevalence,** *n.* распростране́ние.

prevaricate *v.i.* **1,** (speak evasively) уви́ливать. **2,** (lie) привира́ть.

prevent *v.t.* **1,** (keep from happening) предупрежда́ть; предотвраща́ть; не допуска́ть. *Prevent illness,* предупрежда́ть боле́знь. *Prevent a disaster,* преду- прежда́ть *or* предотвраща́ть катастро́фу. *Prevent war,* предотвраща́ть войну́. *Will he be able to prevent this?,* суме́ет ли он э́того не допусти́ть? **2,** (stop from doing something) меша́ть; не позволя́ть: *Ill- ness prevented me from coming,* боле́знь помеша́ла/ не позво́лила/ мне прийти́.

prevention *n.* предупрежде́ние; предотвраще́ние. *Prevention of disease,* профила́ктика боле́зней.

preventive *adj.* предупреди́тельный; предохра- ни́тельный. —**preventive medicine,** предупре- ди́тельная *or* профилакти́ческая медици́на. —**pre- ventive war,** превенти́вная война́.

preview *n.* **1,** (of a movie) предвари́тельный пока́з *or* просмо́тр. **2,** (advance view) предвари́тельный взгляд (на бу́дущее).

previous *adj.* предыду́щий: *the previous day/issue,* предыду́щий день/но́мер. —**previous to,** до; пре́жде.

previously *adv.* ра́ньше. *A previously unknown writer,* ра́нее неизве́стный писа́тель.

prewar *adj.* дово́енный; предвое́нный.

prey *n.* **1,** (animal killed by another) добы́ча: *stalk one's prey,* высле́живать добы́чу. **2,** (victim) же́ртва: *fall prey to,* пасть же́ртвой (+ *gen.*). —*v.i.* [*usu.* **prey on** *or* **upon**] **1,** (seek and take for food) охо́титься на; лови́ть; пита́ться (+ *instr.*). **2,** (plun- der) гра́бить. **3,** (victimize) эксплуати́ровать. **4,** *Prey on one's mind,* пресле́довать. —**bird of prey,** хи́щная пти́ца.

price *n.* цена́. *The price of bread,* цена́ хле́ба; цена́ на хлеб. *At any price,* любо́й цено́й. *The price of the ticket includes...,* в сто́имость биле́та вхо́дит... —*v.t.* **1,** (set a price on) расце́нивать. **2,** *colloq.* (ask the price of) прице́ниваться к.

priceless *adj.* бесце́нный. *Priceless opportunity,* бес- це́нная возмо́жность. *This ring is priceless,* э́тому кольцу́ нет цены́.

price list прейскура́нт.

price tag ярлы́к с указа́нием цены́.

prick *v.t.* **1,** (pierce accidentally) уколо́ть: *prick one's finger,* уколо́ть себе́ па́лец. **2,** (puncture, as a bubble or balloon) прока́лывать. —*n.* уко́л: *pinprick,* була́- вочный уко́л. —**prick up one's ears,** насторожи́ть *or* навостри́ть у́ши; насторожи́ться.

prickle *n.* шип; колю́чка.

prickly *adj.* колю́чий; ко́лкий. —**prickly heat,** потни́ца. —**prickly pear,** опу́нция.

pride *n.* **1,** (pleasure; satisfaction) го́рдость. *Pride in one's country,* го́рдость за свою́ страну́. *Take pride in,* горди́ться (+ *instr.*). **2,** (conceit; self-esteem) самолю́бие; го́рдость. *Hurt someone's pride,* заде́ть чьё-нибудь самолю́бие. **3,** (that of which one is proud) го́рдость. —*v.t.* [*usu.* **pride oneself on**] горди́ться (+ *instr.*).

priest *n.* свяще́нник. *Pagan priest,* жрец. —**priest- hood,** *n.* свяще́нство; духове́нство. —**priestly,** *adj.* свяще́ннический.

prim *adj.* чо́порный.

primacy *n.* пе́рвенство; прима́т.

prima donna примадо́нна.

primarily *adv.* преиму́щественно; в основно́м; пре́жде всего́.

primary *adj.* **1,** (first) перви́чный. **2,** (first in impor- tance) основно́й: *the primary purpose,* основна́я цель. *The primary task,* первоочередна́я зада́ча. —*n.* перви́чные вы́боры. —**primary color,** основно́й цвет. —**primary school,** нача́льная шко́ла. —**pri- mary source,** первоисто́чник.

primate *n.* **1,** *eccles.* прима́с. **2,** *zool.* прима́т.

prime *adj.* **1,** (chief; paramount) основно́й: *prime req- uisite,* основно́е тре́бование. *A prime example,* я́ркий приме́р. *Of prime concern,* велича́йшей ва́жности. **2,** (of the finest quality) первосо́ртный. —*n.* расцве́т. *In one's prime; in the prime of life,* во цве́те лет; в расцве́те сил. —*v.t.* **1,** (make ready) подготавля́ть. **2,** (set, as a gun) вставля́ть запа́л в. **3,** (fill, as a pump) наполня́ть (водо́й). —**prime cost,** себесто́имость. —**prime minister,** премье́р- мини́стр. —**prime number,** просто́е число́; недели́мое число́.

primer[1] (prim-er) *n.* (beginning reading book) бук- ва́рь.

primer[2] (prai-mer) *n.* (detonating device) запа́л; ка́п- сюль.

primeval *adj.* первобы́тный.

priming *n.,* *painting* грунт.

primitive *adj.* **1,** (earliest) первобы́тный: *primitive man,* первобы́тный челове́к. **2,** (plain; crude) при- мити́вный.

primogeniture *n.* перворо́дство.

primordial *adj.* иско́нный; изнача́льный.

primp *v.i.* прихора́шиваться.

primrose *n.* первоцве́т; при́мула.

prince *n.* **1,** (in tsarist Russia) князь. **2,** (in other countries) принц.

princely *adj.* кня́жеский. *A princely sum,* огро́мная су́мма.

princess *n.* **1,** *pre-rev.* (prince's wife) княги́ня; (prince's daughter) княжна́. **2,** (outside Russia) принце́сса.

principal *adj.* гла́вный; основно́й: *the principal reason,* гла́вная/основна́я причи́на. —*n.* **1,** (head of a school) дире́ктор. **2,** *finance* капита́л: *principal and interest,* капита́л и проце́нты.

principality *n.* кня́жество.

principally *adv.* гла́вным о́бразом; преиму́щественно.

principle *n.* при́нцип. *A man of principle,* принципиа́льный челове́к. *A matter of principle,* де́ло при́нципа; принципиа́льный вопро́с. —**in principle,** в при́нципе. —**on principle,** из при́нципа.

print *n.* **1,** (impression) отпеча́ток: *footprint,* отпеча́ток ноги́. **2,** (type) шрифт; печа́ть. *Large print,* кру́пный шрифт. **3,** *photog.* отпеча́ток. **4,** (engraving, woodcut, etc.) гравю́ра; лубо́к; эста́мп. **5,** (fabric with a printed design) набивно́й си́тец. —*adj.* си́тцевый: *a print dress,* си́тцевое пла́тье. —*v.t.* **1,** (produce from type; publish in print) печа́тать. **2,** (produce from a negative) отпеча́тывать. **3,** (write in block letters) писа́ть печа́тными бу́квами. **4,** *textiles* набива́ть. —**in print, 1,** (still being published) печа́тается. **2,** (in the press) в печа́ти; печа́тно. *See one's name in print,* ви́деть своё и́мя в печа́ти. —**out of print,** бо́льше не печа́тается.

printed *adj.* печа́тный; напеча́танный; отпеча́танный; *(of fabric)* набивно́й. —**printed matter,** бандеро́ль. —**the printed word,** печа́тное сло́во.

printer *n.* **1,** (person) печа́тник; типо́граф. *Send a manuscript to the printer,* посла́ть ру́копись в типогра́фию; сдать ру́копись в набо́р. **2,** (device that prints) печа́тающее устро́йство; при́нтер. —**printer's ink,** типогра́фская кра́ска.

printing *n.* **1,** (act) печа́тание. **2,** (art) печа́тное де́ло; полиграфи́я. **3,** (quantity printed at one time) тира́ж. **4,** *textiles* наби́вка. —**printing press,** печа́тный стано́к.

prior *adj.* предвари́тельный: *prior condition,* предвари́тельное усло́вие. *By prior agreement,* по предвари́тельному соглаше́нию. *We have a prior engagement,* у нас други́е пла́ны; нас уже́ пригласи́ли. —*n.* (of a monastery) прио́р; настоя́тель. —**prior to,** до: *prior to Christmas,* до рождества́. *Prior to leaving for Europe,* пре́жде чем (*or* пе́ред тем, как) уе́хать в Евро́пу.

priority *n.* приорите́т: *Priority is given to...,* приорите́т отдаётся (+ *dat.*). *Give top priority to,* ста́вить во главу́ угла́. *Our Number one priority,* на́ша зада́ча но́мер оди́н.

priory *n.* монасты́рь.

prism *n.* при́зма. —**prismatic,** *adj.* призмати́ческий.

prison *n.* тюрьма́: *put in prison,* сажа́ть в тюрьму́. *Two years in prison,* два го́да тюре́много заключе́ния. —*adj.* тюре́мный: *prison cell,* тюре́мная ка́мера. *Long prison term,* дли́тельный срок заключе́ния.

prisoner *n.* **1,** (one held for a crime) заключённый. *Political prisoner,* полити́ческий заключённый. **2,** (in war) пле́нный: *take prisoners,* брать пле́нных. *Prisoner of war,* военнопле́нный. *Take prisoner,* взять в плен. *Be taken prisoner,* попа́сть в плен. *Hold prisoner,* держа́ть в плену́.

pristine *adj.* первобы́тный.

privacy *n.* уедине́ние; та́йна. *The right to privacy,* пра́во на (ли́чную) та́йну. *Invasion of privacy,* вторже́ние в ча́стную жизнь.

private *adj.* ча́стный: *private house/matter/lessons,* ча́стный дом; ча́стное де́ло; ча́стные уро́ки. *Private property,* ча́стная со́бственность. *Private enterprise,* ча́стное предпринима́тельство. *The private sector,* ча́стный се́ктор. *Private meeting,* закры́тое собра́ние. —*n., mil.* рядово́й. —**in private,** наедине́; с гла́зу на глаз.

privately *adv.* наедине́; ча́стным о́бразом; в ча́стном поря́дке.

privation *n.* лише́ние: *suffer privations,* терпе́ть лише́ния.

privatize *v.t.* приватизи́ровать. —**privatization,** *n.* приватиза́ция.

privilege *n.* привиле́гия; льго́та. —**privileged,** *adj.* привилегиро́ванный. *I am privileged to...,* име́ю честь (+ *inf.*).

privy *adj.* [*usu.* **privy to**] посвящённый (в). —*n.* отхо́жее ме́сто. —**Privy Council,** та́йный сове́т.

prize *n.* пре́мия; приз. —*adj.* **1,** (given as a prize) призово́й. **2,** (having won a prize) премиро́ванный. —*v.t.* цени́ть; дорожи́ть.

prize fight боксёрское состяза́ние. —**prize fighter,** боксёр.

prizewinner *n.* призёр.

pro *n.* **1,** (argument in favor): *the pros and cons,* до́воды за и про́тив. **2,** *colloq.* (professional) профессиона́л.

pro- *prefix* про-: *pro-American,* проамерика́нский.

probability *n.* вероя́тность. *In all probability,* по всей вероя́тности.

probable *adj.* вероя́тный. *Highly probable,* весьма́ вероя́тно.

probably *adv.* вероя́тно; наве́рно; пожа́луй. *Most probably,* скоре́е всего́.

probate *n.* утвержде́ние (завеща́ния).

probation *n.* усло́вное освобожде́ние. *He was given a year on probation,* он получи́л год усло́вно.

probe *n.* **1,** (instrument) зонд; щуп. **2,** (investigation) рассле́дование. —*v.t.* **1,** *med.* зонди́ровать. **2,** (investigate) вника́ть в; рассле́довать. —**space probe,** косми́ческий зонд.

probity *n.* че́стность; поря́дочность.

problem *n.* **1,** (difficult question or matter) пробле́ма. **2,** (arithmetical problem) зада́ча. —**problem child,** тру́дный ребёнок.

problematic *adj.* проблемати́ческий; проблемати́чный. *Also,* **problematical.**

proboscis *n.* хо́бот.

procedure *n.* процеду́ра; поря́док. —**procedural,** *adj.* процеду́рный.

proceed *v.i.* **1,** (go forward) идти́; е́хать; сле́довать. *Proceed with caution,* идти́ *or* е́хать осторо́жно. *Proceed down the main street,* сле́довать по центра́льной у́лице. *Proceed across the square,* проходи́ть че́рез пло́щадь. *Proceed into the living room,* переходи́ть в гости́ную. **2,** (begin) приступа́ть: *proceed with the vote,* приступи́ть к голосова́нию. *I don't know how to proceed,* я не зна́ю, как приступи́ть к э́тому де́лу. *She proceeded to criticize him,* она́ ста́ла критикова́ть его́. **3,** (move toward completion) идти́; проходи́ть. *Matters are proceeding normally,* дела́ иду́т норма́льно. **4,** (continue) продолжа́ть: *Please proceed!,* продолжа́йте, пожа́луйста! **5,** *fol. by* **on** *or* **from** (begin in one's reasoning) исходи́ть из: *proceed on the assumption that...,* исходи́ть из того́, что...

proceedings *n.pl.* **1,** (action taking place) происходя́щее. **2,** (legal action) судопроизво́дство. *Institute criminal proceedings against,* возбуди́ть уголо́вное де́ло про́тив. **3,** (records; minutes) протоко́л.

proceeds *n.pl.* вы́ручка.

process *n.* проце́сс. *In the process of,* в проце́ссе (+ *gen.*). *Right now I'm in the process of...,* сейча́с я за́нят (+ *instr.*). —*v.t.* **1,** (treat) обраба́тывать; перераба́тывать. **2,** (handle, as a document) оформля́ть; обраба́тывать.

procession *n.* ше́ствие; проце́ссия.

proclaim *v.t.* провозглаша́ть: *proclaim independence,* провозглаша́ть незави́симость.

proclamation *n.* **1,** (act of proclaiming) провозглаше́ние. **2,** (formal public announcement) объявле́ние; проклама́ция.

proclivity *n.* скло́нность; накло́нность; тенде́нция.

proconsul *n.* проко́нсул.

procrastinate *v.i.* ме́длить; ме́шкать; тяну́ть вре́мя. —**procrastination,** *n.* промедле́ние; проволо́чка. —**procrastinator,** *n.* копу́н; копу́ша.

procreate *v.t.* производи́ть пото́мство. —**procreation,** *n.* деторожде́ние.

proctor *n.* **1,** (person supervising an examination) надзира́тель. **2,** *law* (agent; representative) пове́ренный.

procure *v.t.* достава́ть; добыва́ть.

procurement *n.* **1,** (acquisition) приобрете́ние. **2,** (purchase by the government) заку́пки; загото́вки.

procurer *n.* сво́дник.

prod *v.t.* **1,** (poke) ты́кать. **2,** (urge; goad) подгоня́ть. —*n.* тычо́к.

prodigal *adj.* расточи́тельный. —**prodigal son,** блу́дный сын.

prodigality *n.* расточи́тельность; мотовство́.

prodigious *adj.* огро́мный; колосса́льный.

prodigy *n.* чу́до. *Child prodigy,* вундерки́нд.

produce *v.t.* **1,** (manufacture; bring into being) производи́ть: *produce wheat/cars,* производи́ть

пшени́цу/маши́ны. *Produce offspring,* производи́ть пото́мство. **2,** (show; offer for inspection) предъявля́ть; представля́ть; пока́зывать. *Produce evidence,* представля́ть доказа́тельства. **3,** (bring about) приноси́ть; дава́ть. *Produce income,* приноси́ть дохо́д. *Produce results,* дава́ть *or* приноси́ть результа́ты. **4,** (bring to the stage or screen) ста́вить. —*n.* сельскохозя́йственные проду́кты.

producer *n.* **1,** (one who produces) производи́тель. **2,** *theat., motion pictures* режиссёр; постано́вщик. **3,** (filmmaker in Western countries) продю́сер.

product *n.* **1,** (something produced or manufactured) проду́кт; изде́лие; *pl.* това́ры; проду́кция. *By-product,* побо́чный проду́кт. *Industrial product,* промы́шленное изде́лие. *Gross national product,* валово́й национа́льный проду́кт. *Agricultural products,* сельскохозя́йственные това́ры; сельскохозя́йственная проду́кция. **2,** *fig.* (result; outgrowth) плод; порожде́ние. *Product of the imagination,* плод воображе́ния. *The product of many years of work,* плод многоле́тнего труда́. **3,** *math.* произведе́ние.

production *n.* **1,** (act of producing) произво́дство: *steel production,* произво́дство ста́ли. *Oil production,* добы́ча не́фти. *Go into production,* поступи́ть в произво́дство. **2,** *theat.* постано́вка: *a new production of Swan Lake,* Лебеди́ное о́зеро в но́вой постано́вке. —*adj.* произво́дственный: *production plan,* произво́дственный план. —**production line,** пото́чная ли́ния.

productive *adj.* **1,** (producing) производи́тельный; продукти́вный. **2,** (fruitful) плодотво́рный.

productivity *n.* производи́тельность; продукти́вность.

profanation *n.* оскверне́ние; профана́ция.

profane *adj.* **1,** (irreverent; blasphemous) нечести́вый; богоху́льный. **2,** (vulgar; coarse) вульга́рный; гру́бый. **3,** (secular) све́тский. —*v.t.* оскверня́ть.

profanity *n.* брань; ру́гань; *pl.* са́льности.

profess *v.t.* **1,** (openly declare or admit) заявля́ть о; (откры́то) признава́ть. *Profess one's love,* призна́ться в любви́. **2,** (avow, as a religion) испове́довать.

profession *n.* **1,** (occupation) профе́ссия: *a lawyer by profession,* юри́ст по профе́ссии. *The medical profession,* врачи́. **2,** (open declaration) заявле́ние. **3,** (avowal of a religion) испове́дание.

professional *adj.* профессиона́льный. *Professional man,* челове́к, владе́ющий профе́ссией. —*n.* профессиона́л.

professor *n.* профе́ссор. *Assistant professor,* ассисте́нт. *Associate professor,* доце́нт. —**professorial,** *adj.* профе́ссорский. —**professorship,** *n.* профе́ссорство; профессу́ра.

proffer *v.t.* предлага́ть. *Proffer one's hand,* протяну́ть ру́ку.

proficiency *n.* уме́ние; на́вык; сноро́вка. *Proficiency in a language,* зна́ние языка́.

proficient *adj.* иску́сный; уме́лый.

profile *n.* про́филь.

profit *n.* **1,** (monetary gain) при́быль. *Sell at a profit,* продава́ть с при́былью; продава́ть вы́годно. *Make a $1,000 profit,* получи́ть ты́сячу до́лларов при́были. **2,** (benefit) по́льза; вы́года. —*v.t.* приноси́ть по́льзу (+ *dat.*). —*v.i.* [*usu.* **profit from**] извлека́ть по́льзу (из).

profitability *n.* при́быльность; дохо́дность; рента́бельность.

profitable *adj.* **1,** (yielding a profit) при́быльный; вы́годный; дохо́дный; рента́бельный. **2,** (beneficial) поле́зный.

profitably *adv.* с по́льзой: *spend one's time profitably,* проводи́ть вре́мя с по́льзой.

profiteer *n.* спекуля́нт. —*v.i.* спекули́ровать. —**profiteering,** *n.* спекуля́ция.

profligacy *n.* **1,** (dissoluteness) распу́тство. **2,** (reckless extravagance) расточи́тельность.

profligate *adj.* **1,** (dissolute) распу́тный; развра́тный. **2,** (recklessly extravagant) расточи́тельный. —*n.* распу́тник; развра́тник.

profound *adj.* глубо́кий: *profound knowledge/changes,* глубо́кие зна́ния/изменения. *Profound grief,* глубо́кое го́ре. *Profound difference,* огро́мная ра́зница. *Profound consequences,* далеко́ иду́щие после́дствия. —**profoundly,** *adv.* глубоко́.

profundity *n.* глубина́.

profuse *adj.* **1,** (abundant) оби́льный. **2,** (lavish): *be profuse in one's praise,* рассыпа́ться в похвала́х.

profusely *adv. Multiply profusely,* бы́стро размножа́ться. *Bleed profusely,* истека́ть кро́вью. *Perspire profusely,* облива́ться по́том. *Apologize profusely,* рассыпа́ться в извине́ниях.

profusion *n.* изоби́лие.

progenitor *n.* родонача́льник.

progeny *n.* пото́мство.

prognosis *n.* прогно́з.

prognosticate *v.t. & i.* прогнози́ровать; предска́зывать. —**prognostication,** *n.* прогнози́рование; предсказа́ние. —**prognosticator,** *n.* предсказа́тель.

program *also,* **programme** *n.* програ́мма. —*v.t.* программи́ровать. —**programmed,** *adj.* програ́ммный; программи́рованный. —**programmer,** *n.* программи́ст.

programming *n.* программи́рование. —**programming language,** язы́к программи́рования.

progress *n.* прогре́сс; успе́хи. *Make progress,* де́лать успе́хи. —*v.i.* **1,** (make progress) прогресси́ровать; продвига́ться. **2,** (get along) идти́: *How is your work progressing?,* как идёт ва́ша рабо́та? —**be in progress,** идти́: *Examinations are in progress,* иду́т экза́мены. *An investigation is in progress,* ведётся сле́дствие.

progression *n.* **1,** (advancement) продвиже́ние. **2,** *math.* прогре́ссия: *geometric progression,* геометри́ческая прогре́ссия.

progressive *adj.* прогресси́вный. *Progressive income tax,* прогресси́вный подохо́дный нало́г. *Progressive disease,* прогресси́рующее заболева́ние.

progressively *adv.* неукло́нно: *get progressively worse,* неукло́нно ухудша́ться; станови́ться всё ху́же.

prohibit *v.t.* запреща́ть: *prohibit the carrying of weapons,* запреща́ть ноше́ние ору́жия. S*trictly prohibited,* стро́го запреща́ется *or* воспреща́ется; стро́го запрещено́. —**prohibition,** *n.* запреще́ние.

prohibitive *adj.* запрети́тельный. *Prohibitive prices,* недосту́пные це́ны.

project *n.* прое́кт. —*v.t.* **1,** (plan) проекти́ровать: *a projected highway,* проекти́рованное шоссе́. **2,** (estimate) вычисля́ть: *projected earnings,* вы́численная вы́ручка. **3,** (convey; get across) передава́ть; внуша́ть. **4,** (show on a screen) проекти́ровать. —*v.i.* (protrude) выдава́ться; выступа́ть.

projectile *n.* снаря́д.

projection *n.* **1,** (something jutting out) вы́ступ. **2,** (system used in mapmaking) прое́кция. **3,** (showing on a screen) прое́кция. **4,** (advance estimate) оце́нка; прогно́з. —**projection booth,** проекцио́нная бу́дка.

projectionist *n.* киномеха́ник.

projector *n.* проекцио́нный аппара́т *or* фона́рь; прое́ктор. *Movie projector,* кинопрое́ктор.

prolapse *n.* выпаде́ние; опуще́ние.

proletarian *n.* пролета́рий. —*adj.* пролета́рский. —**proletariat,** *n.* пролетариа́т.

proliferate *v.i.* размножа́ться; распространя́ться. —**proliferation,** *n.* распростране́ние.

prolific *adj.* плодови́тый.

prolix *adj.* многосло́вный; простра́нный.

prologue *n.* проло́г.

prolong *v.t.* продлева́ть. —**prolongation,** *n.* продле́ние. —**prolonged,** *adj.* дли́тельный; продолжи́тельный.

promenade *n.* **1,** (stroll) прогу́лка. **2,** (mall) бульва́р. —*v.i.* прогу́ливаться. —**promenade deck,** прогу́лочная па́луба.

Prometheus *n.* Промете́й.

promethium *n.* проме́тий.

prominence *n.* **1,** (fame) изве́стность: *come into prominence,* приобрета́ть изве́стность. **2,** (bulge) вы́ступ.

prominent *adj.* **1,** (leading; well-known) ви́дный; изве́стный. **2,** (major; important) ви́дный: *play a prominent role,* игра́ть ви́дную роль. **3,** (protruding) выдаю́щийся вперёд; оттопы́ренный.

promiscuous *adj.* лёгкого поведе́ния; распу́тный. —**promiscuity,** *n.* лёгкое поведе́ние.

promise *v.t. & i.* обеща́ть: *I promise you I won't be late,* обеща́ю вам, что не опозда́ю. *The movie promises to be interesting,* фильм обеща́ет быть интере́сным. *Make someone promise,* брать сло́во с. —*n.* **1,** (pledge) обеща́ние. **2,** (basis for expectation): *show great promise,* подава́ть больши́е наде́жды. *A violinist of great promise,* многообеща́ющий скрипа́ч. —**Promised Land,** земля́ обетова́нная.

promising *adj.* многообеща́ющий; перспекти́вный.

promissory note *n.* ве́ксель; долгово́е обяза́тельство.

promontory *n.* мыс.

promote *v.t.* **1,** (raise in rank) продвига́ть; повыша́ть в чи́не. *He was promoted at work,* он получи́л повыше́ние по слу́жбе. *He was promoted to captain,* ему́ присво́или зва́ние капита́на; его́ произвели́ в капита́ны. **2,** (move up to the next grade in school) переводи́ть. **3,** (foster; further) спосо́бствовать; содействовать: *promote mutual understanding,* спосо́бствовать/соде́йствовать взаимопонима́нию. **4,** (publicize) реклами́ровать. **5,** *chess* превраща́ть (пе́шку).

promotion *n.* **1,** (advancement in rank) повыше́ние *or* продвиже́ние по слу́жбе; *mil.* присвое́ние зва́ния; произво́дство. **2,** (furtherance) продвиже́ние; поощре́ние. **3,** (publicity) рекла́ма. **4,** *chess* превраще́ние (пе́шки).

promotional *adj.* рекла́мный.

prompt *adj.* **1,** (done without delay) бы́стрый; сро́чный. *Prompt reply,* бы́стрый отве́т. *Take prompt measures,* принима́ть сро́чные ме́ры. **2,** (punctual) аккура́тный. —*v.t.* **1,** (induce) побужда́ть: *What prompted you to do that?,* что вас побуди́ло сде́лать э́то? **2,** (serve as the cause of) диктова́ть: *The decision was prompted by...,* реше́ние бы́ло продикто́вано (*or* диктова́лось) (+ *instr.*). **3,** (give rise to; occasion) вызыва́ть. **4,** (assist with a reminder) подска́зывать. **5,** *theat.* суфли́ровать. —*v.i.* подска́зывать: *No prompting!,* не подска́зывать! —**prompter,** *n.* суфлёр. —**promptly,** *adv.* бы́стро; сра́зу.

promptness *n.* **1,** (speed) быстрота́. **2,** (punctuality) аккура́тность.

promulgate *v.t.* издава́ть; опубликова́ть; обнаро́довать. —**promulgation,** *n.* изда́ние; опубликова́ние; обнаро́дование.

prone *adj.* **1,** (prostrate) лежа́щий ничко́м. *Prone position,* положе́ние лёжа. **2,** *fol. by* **to** (inclined) скло́нный (к); подве́рженный (+ *dat.*). *Prone to error,* подве́рженный оши́бкам. *Prone to violence,* скло́нный к наси́лию.

prong *n.* зубе́ц.

pronoun *n.* местоиме́ние. —**pronominal,** *adj.* местоиме́нный.

pronounce *v.t.* **1,** (articulate) произноси́ть: *pronounce a word incorrectly,* непра́вильно произноси́ть сло́во. **2,** (declare to be) объявля́ть; признава́ть: *I pronounce you man and wife,* объявля́ю вас му́жем и жено́й. *Pronounce someone guilty/insane,* призна́ть кого́-нибудь вино́вным/душевнобольны́м. **3,** (announce, as a sentence) произноси́ть; объявля́ть; оглаша́ть; зачи́тывать (пригово́р). *Pronounce judgment,* выноси́ть реше́ние.

pronounced *adj.* заме́тный; я́рко вы́раженный. *He walks with a pronounced limp,* он заме́тно хрома́ет.

pronouncement *n.* **1,** (act of announcing) объявле́ние. *Pronouncement of sentence,* произнесе́ние *or* оглаше́ние пригово́ра. **2,** (formal declaration) (официа́льное) заявле́ние; постановле́ние.

pronunciation *n.* произноше́ние.

proof *n.* **1,** (conclusive evidence) доказа́тельство. *To cite as proof,* приводи́ть (что́-нибудь) в доказа́тельство. **2,** *printing* корректу́ра; гра́нка; о́ттиск. *Page proofs,* вёрстка; корректу́ра в листа́х.

proofread *v.t.* корректи́ровать. —*v.i.* держа́ть *or* пра́вить корректу́ру. —**proofreader,** *n.* корре́ктор.

—**proofreading,** *n.* корректу́ра; пра́вка корректу́ры.

prop *v.t.* **1,** *fol. by* **up** (hold up; support) подпира́ть. **2,** *fol. by* **against** (lean against) прислоня́ть (к). —*n.* **1,** (support) подпо́ра; подпо́рка. **2,** *pl., theat.* реквизи́т; бутафо́рия.

propaganda *n.* пропага́нда. —**propagandist,** *n.* пропаганди́ст. —**propagandistic,** *adj.* пропаганди́стский. —**propagandize,** *v.t.* пропаганди́ровать.

propagate *v.t.* **1,** (breed) размножа́ть. **2,** (disseminate) распространя́ть; пропове́довать. —*v.i.* размножа́ться.

propagation *n.* **1,** (reproduction) размноже́ние. **2,** (dissemination) распростране́ние; про́поведь.

propane *n.* пропа́н.

propel *v.t.* дви́гать; приводи́ть в движе́ние.

propellant *n.* **1,** (explosive charge) мета́тельное взры́вчатое вещество́. **2,** (fuel for a rocket) раке́тное то́пливо.

propeller *n.* **1,** (of an aircraft) (возду́шный) винт; пропе́ллер. **2,** (of a boat) гребно́й винт. —**propellerdriven,** *adj.* винтово́й.

propensity *n.* скло́нность; накло́нность; предрасположе́ние.

proper *adj.* **1,** (appropriate) подходя́щий; надлежа́щий; до́лжный; подоба́ющий. *Find the proper tools,* находи́ть подходя́щие инструме́нты. *At the proper time,* в надлежа́щее вре́мя. **2,** (correct) пра́вильный: *the proper approach,* пра́вильный подхо́д. **3,** (socially correct) прили́чный; присто́йный: *proper behavior,* прили́чное/присто́йное поведе́ние. **4,** (in the narrow sense) со́бственно: *the city proper,* со́бственно го́род. **5,** *gram.* со́бственное: *proper noun,* и́мя со́бственное. **6,** *math.* пра́вильный: *proper fraction,* пра́вильная дробь.

properly *adv.* как сле́дует; до́лжным о́бразом; надлежа́щим о́бразом. —**properly speaking,** со́бственно говоря́.

propertied *adj.* иму́щий.

property *n.* **1,** (that which is owned) со́бственность; иму́щество: *personal property,* ли́чная со́бственность; ли́чное иму́щество. **2,** (attribute) сво́йство: *the chemical properties of alcohol,* хими́ческие сво́йства алкого́ля. **3,** *pl., theat.* реквизи́т; бутафо́рия. —**property man,** бутафо́р. —**property tax,** нало́г на недви́жимость.

prophecy *n.* проро́чество; прорица́ние. —**prophesy,** *v.t. & i.* проро́чить; прорица́ть.

prophet *n.* проро́к. —**prophetic,** *adj.* проро́ческий.

prophylactic *adj.* профилакти́ческий. —*n.* профилакти́ческое сре́дство. —**prophylaxis,** *n.* профила́ктика.

propinquity *n.* **1,** (nearness) бли́зость. **2,** (kinship) родство́.

propitiate *v.t.* уми́лостивить.

propitious *adj.* благоприя́тный; подходя́щий.

proponent *n.* сторо́нник; пропове́дник.

proportion *n.* **1,** *math.* пропо́рция; пропорциона́льность. *Geometric proportion,* геометри́ческая пропо́рция. *Direct/inverse proportion,* пряма́я/обра́тная пропорциона́льность. **2,** (balance; symmetry) соразмéрность. *Sense of proportion,* чу́вство мéры. **3,** *pl.* (size; scope) размéры: *reach catastrophic proportions,* достигáть катастрофи́ческих размéров. —*v.t.* соразмеря́ть. —**in proportion to,** соразмéрно (+ *dat.*); пропорционáльно (+ *dat.*). —**out of proportion,** чрезмéрно; сверх мéры. *Out of proportion to,* несоразмéрно с. *The matter was blown up out of proportion,* дéло бы́ло разду́то сверх мéры.

proportional *adj.* пропорционáльный: *directly proportional to...,* пря́мо пропорционáльный (+ *dat.*). *Proportional representation,* пропорционáльное представи́тельство. *Also,* **proportionate.**

proportionally *adv.* пропорционáльно. *Also,* **proportionately.**

proposal *n.* предложéние. *Proposal of marriage* предложéние (о брáке).

propose *v.t.* **1,** (suggest) предлагáть. *Propose a new approach,* предложи́ть нóвый подхóд. *Propose a toast,* предложи́ть тост. *He proposed selling the factory,* он предложи́л продáть завóд. **2,** *fol. by inf.* (intend) предполагáть: *What do you propose to do?,* что вы предполагáете сдéлать? —*v.i.* [*usu.* **propose to**] сдéлать (+ *dat.*) предложéние (о брáке); (по)свáтать; (по)свáтаться к *or* за.

proposition *n.* **1,** (proposal) предложéние. **2,** (thesis) положéние. **3,** *logic* выскáзывание. **4,** *colloq.* (undertaking) дéло: *a tough proposition,* слóжное дéло.

propound *v.t.* выдвигáть: *propound a theory,* выдвигáть теóрию.

proprietary *adj.* сóбственнический; хозя́йский.

proprietor *n.* сóбственник; владéлец; хозя́ин.

propriety *n.* прили́чие. *Observe the proprieties,* соблюдáть прили́чия.

propulsion *n.* движéние вперёд; приведéние в движéние. *Jet propulsion,* реакти́вное движéние.

pro rata пропорционáльно.

prorate *v.t.* распределя́ть пропорционáльно.

prorogue *v.t.* распускáть (парлáмент).

prosaic *adj.* прозаи́ческий; прозаи́чный.

proscenium *n.* просцéниум; авансцéна.

proscribe *v.t* **1,** (prohibit) запрещáть. **2,** (outlaw) объявля́ть вне закóна.

proscription *n.* запрéт; запрещéние.

prose *n.* прóза. *Work of prose,* прозаи́ческое произведéние. —*adj.* прозаи́ческий. *Prose writer,* прозáик.

prosecute *v.t.* **1,** *law* отдавáть под суд; предавáть суду́; преслéдовать (когó-нибудь) судéбным поря́дком. **2,** (conduct, as a war) вести́.

prosecution *n.* **1,** (conducting) ведéние. **2,** *law* (prosecuting) судéбное преслéдование. **3,** (party initiating criminal proceedings) обвинéние. *Witness for the prosecution,* свидéтель обвинéния.

prosecutor *n.* обвини́тель. *Public prosecutor,* прокуро́р.

proselyte *n.* новообращённый; прозели́т. —**proselytize,** *v.t.* обращáть (в свою́ вéру). —*v.i.* искáть прозели́тов.

prosody *n.* просóдия. —**prosodic,** *adj.* просоди́ческий.

prospect *n.* **1,** (outlook; chance) перспекти́ва; *pl.* ви́ды; перспекти́вы. *The prospects for success,* ви́ды на успéх. **2,** (likely candidate) кандидáт. —*v.t.* развéдывать. —*v.i.* [*usu.* **prospect for**] искáть: *prospect for gold,* искáть зóлото. —**be in prospect,** быть в перспекти́ве.

prospective *adj.* **1,** (future) бу́дущий. **2,** (potential) возмóжный.

prospector *n.* развéдчик; изыскáтель. *Prospector for gold,* золотоискáтель; старáтель.

prospectus *n.* проспéкт.

prosper *v.i.* процветáть. —**prosperity,** *n.* процветáние.

prosperous *adj.* зажи́точный; состоя́тельный; обеспéченный.

prostate *n.* предстáтельная железá; простáта.

prosthesis *n.* протéз. —**prosthetic,** *adj.* протéзный.

prostitute *n.* проститу́тка. —**prostitution,** *n.* проститу́ция.

prostrate *adj.* **1,** (flat; prone) распростёртый. *Lie prostrate,* лежáть ничкóм. **2,** (exhausted) истощённый. —*v.t.* **1,** *fol. by* **oneself** (lie face down in humility) пáдать ниц. **2,** (exhaust) истощáть.

prostration *n.* **1,** (act of prostrating oneself) земнóй поклóн. **2,** (complete exhaustion) изнеможéние; прострáция. *Heat prostration,* тепловóй удáр.

protactinium *n.* протакти́ний.

protagonist *n.* протагони́ст.

protect *v.t.* защищáть; охраня́ть; предохраня́ть; огражда́ть; оберегáть; уберéчь. *Protect one's face from the cold,* защищáть *or* предохраня́ть *or* оберегáть лицó от хóлода. *Protect one's young from predators,* защищáть *or* охраня́ть детёнышей от хи́щников.

protection *n.* защи́та; охрáна; предохранéние; огражде́ние.

protectionism *n.* протекциони́зм.

protective *adj.* **1,** (serving to protect) защи́тный: *protective helmet,* защи́тный шлем. **2,** (carefully protecting) забóтливый: *an overly protective mother,* сли́шком забóтливая мать. *Be protective of,* бéрежно забóтиться о. —**protective coloration,** защи́тная *or* покрови́тельственная окрáска. —**protective tariff,** покрови́тельственный тари́ф.

protector *n.* защи́тник.

protectorate *n.* протекторáт.

protégé *n.* протеже́; стáвленник.

protein *n.* белóк; протеи́н. —*adj.* белкóвый.

protest *n.* протéст. *In protest against,* в знак протéста прóтив. —*v.i.* протестовáть. —*v.t.* **1,** (raise a protest against) протестовáть прóтив: *protest a decision,* протестовáть прóтив решéния. **2,** (assert) заявля́ть: *protest one's innocence,* заявля́ть о своéй невинóвности.

Protestant *n.* протестáнт. —*adj.* протестáнтский. —**Protestantism,** *n.* протестанти́зм; протестáнтство.

protestation *n.* (торжéственное) заявлéние. *Protestations of one's innocence,* заявлéния о своéй невинóвности.

protester *n.* протестáнт.

protocol *n.* протоко́л: *adhere to protocol*, приде́рживаться протоко́ла. *Chief of protocol*, заве́дующий протоко́льным отде́лом. *Sign a protocol*, подписа́ть протоко́л.

proton *n.* прото́н.

protoplasm *n.* протопла́зма.

prototype *n.* прототи́п; проо́браз; первоо́браз.

protoxide *n.* за́кись.

protozoa *n.pl.* просте́йшие.

protract *v.t.* тяну́ть; затя́гивать. —**protracted,** *adj.* дли́тельный; затяжно́й.

protractor *n.* транспорти́р.

protrude *v.i.* выдава́ться; торча́ть; выпира́ть. —*v.t.* высо́вывать. —**protruding,** *adj.* оттопы́ренный.

protrusion *n.* вы́ступ.

protuberance *n.* бугоро́к; вы́пуклость. —**protuberant,** *adj.* вы́пуклый.

proud *adj.* го́рдый: *proud man*, го́рдый челове́к. *Proud father*, счастли́вый оте́ц. *Be proud of*, горди́ться (+ *instr.*). *He is too proud to...*, он сли́шком горд, что́бы... —**do someone proud,** де́лать честь (+ *dat.*).

proud flesh ди́кое мя́со.

proudly *adv.* го́рдо; с го́рдостью.

prove *v.t.* дока́зывать: *prove one's innocence*, доказа́ть свою́ невино́вность. *Prove a hypothesis*, доказа́ть гипо́тезу. —*v.i.* (turn out to be) оказа́ться; показа́ть себя́; прояви́ть себя́; зарекомендова́ть себя́ (*all with instr.*). *The rumor proved to be false*, слух оказа́лся ло́жным. *He proved to be an able leader*, он показа́л себя́ (*or* прояви́л себя́) спосо́бным руководи́телем. —**prove itself,** оправда́ть себя́ (на пра́ктике). —**prove oneself,** показа́ть себя́; прояви́ть себя́.

proven *adj.* **1,** (demonstrated) дока́занный. **2,** (tested and found valid) испы́танный: *proven method*, испы́танный ме́тод.

provenance *n.* происхожде́ние.

provender *n.* корм; фура́ж.

proverb *n.* посло́вица. —**Book of Proverbs,** Кни́га при́тчей Соломо́новых.

proverbial *adj.* воше́дший в посло́вицу.

provide *v.t.* **1,** (supply with something useful) снабжа́ть; обеспе́чивать: *provide the children with warm clothes*, снабжа́ть/обеспе́чивать дете́й тёплой оде́ждой. *Provide the workers with housing*, обеспе́чивать рабо́чих жильём. **2,** (give; furnish) ока́зывать; предоставля́ть: *provide assistance to*, ока́зывать/предоставля́ть по́мощь (+ *dat.*). *Provide information*, предоставля́ть информа́цию. **3,** (give; afford, as pleasure) доставля́ть. **4,** (stipulate) предусма́тривать. —*v.i.* [*usu.* **provide for**] **1,** (furnish with means of subsistence) содержа́ть; обеспе́чивать. **2,** (allow for) предусма́тривать.

provided *conj.* при усло́вии, что; е́сли то́лько.

providence *n.* **1,** (foresight) предусмотри́тельность. **2,** *cap.* (divine care) провиде́ние.

provident *adj.* предусмотри́тельный; запа́сливый.

providential *adj.* провиденциа́льный.

providing *conj.* = **provided.**

province *n.* **1,** (division of a country) прови́нция. **2,** *pl.* (rural areas) прови́нция; периферия́. **3,** *fig.* (sphere of knowledge or activity) о́бласть зна́ний; сфе́ра; компете́нция.

provincial *adj.* провинциа́льный. —*n.* провинциа́л. —**provincialism,** *n.* провинциали́зм.

proving ground испыта́тельный полиго́н.

provision *n.* **1,** (supplying) снабже́ние. **2,** (clause in a legal document) положе́ние. **3,** (stipulation; proviso) усло́вие. **4,** *pl.* (victuals) прови́зия. —**make provision for,** предусма́тривать.

provisional *adj.* вре́менный: *provisional government*, вре́менное прави́тельство.

proviso *n.* усло́вие; огово́рка.

provocation *n.* провока́ция. *Without provocation*, без вся́кого по́вода. *At the slightest provocation*, по мале́йшему по́воду.

provocative *adj.* вызыва́ющий; провокацио́нный.

provoke *v.t.* **1,** (excite to a certain action; bring about) провоци́ровать: *provoke unrest*, провоци́ровать волне́ния; *provoke the workers to strike*, провоци́ровать рабо́чих на забасто́вку. **2,** (evoke, as an emotion) вызыва́ть: *provoke someone's anger*, вызыва́ть гнев у кого́-нибудь. **3,** (vex) раздража́ть.

provost *n.* ре́ктор; дека́н. —**provost marshal,** нача́льник вое́нной поли́ции.

prow *n.* нос (су́дна).

prowess *n.* **1,** (bravery) до́блесть; у́даль. **2,** (skill) мастерство́.

prowl *v.i.* ры́скать; кра́сться. —**prowl car,** маши́на полице́йского патруля́.

prowler *n.* взло́мщик.

proximity *n.* бли́зость: *in close proximity to*, в непосре́дственной бли́зости от.

proxy *n.* **1,** (person authorized to act for another) дове́ренный. **2,** (authority) полномо́чие. —**by proxy,** по дове́ренности.

prude *n.* челове́к стро́гих нра́вов.

prudence *n.* благоразу́мие; рассуди́тельность.

prudent *adj.* благоразу́мный; рассуди́тельный; расчётливый. —**prudently,** *adv.* благоразу́мно.

prudish *adj.* чо́порный; пурита́нский.

prune *n.* черносли́в. —*v.t.* (trim) обреза́ть; подреза́ть.

prurient *adj.* похотли́вый.

Prussian *adj.* пру́сский. —*n.* прусса́к. —**Prussian blue,** берли́нская лазу́рь.

prussic acid сини́льная кислота́.

pry *v.t.* **1,** (open; loosen) открыва́ть; взла́мывать (при по́мощи рычага́). **2,** (worm out, as a secret) выве́дывать; выпы́тывать. —*v.i.* **1,** (snoop) подгля́дывать. **2,** *fol. by* **into** (meddle) сова́ть нос (в). —**prying,** *adj.* пытли́вый.

psalm *n.* псало́м.

Psalter *n.* псалты́рь.

pseudonym *n.* псевдони́м.

pseudoscience *n.* лженау́ка. —**pseudoscientific,** *adj.* лженау́чный.

pshaw *interj.* фи!

psoriasis *n.* псориа́з.

psyche *n.* пси́хика.

psychiatry *n.* психиатри́я. —**psychiatric,** *adj.* психиатри́ческий. —**psychiatrist,** *n.* психиа́тр.

psychic *adj.* психи́ческий; душе́вный.

psychoanalysis *n.* психоана́лиз. —**psychoanalyst,** *n.* специали́ст по психоана́лизу. —**psychoanalytic(al),** *adj.* психоаналити́ческий. —**psychoanalyze,** *v.t.* подверга́ть психоана́лизу.

psychology *n.* психоло́гия. —**psychological,** *adj.* психологи́ческий. —**psychologist,** *n.* психо́лог.

psychopath *n.* психопа́т. —**psychopathic,** *adj.* психопати́ческий. —**psychopathy,** *n.* психопа́тия.

psychosis *n.* психо́з.

psychosomatic *adj.* психосомати́ческий.

psychotherapy *n.* психотерапи́я. —**psychotherapist,** *n.* психотерапе́вт.

psychotic *adj.* психоти́ческий.

ptarmigan *n.* бе́лая куропа́тка.

PT boat торпе́дный ка́тер.

pterodactyl *n.* птероца́ктиль.

ptomaine *n.* тру́пный яд. —**ptomaine poisoning,** отравле́ние тру́пным я́дом.

pub *n., Brit.* пивна́я; каба́к.

puberty *n.* полова́я зре́лость.

public *adj.* **1,** (of or for the community at large) обще́ственный; публи́чный. *Public transportation,* обще́ственный тра́нспорт. *Public place,* обще́ственное ме́сто. *Public opinion,* обще́ственное мне́ние. *Public library,* публи́чная библиоте́ка. *Public health,* здравоохране́ние. **2,** (done or made in public; open) публи́чный. *Public trial,* публи́чный *or* откры́тый суд. *Public protest,* публи́чный *or* обще́ственный проте́ст. *Public execution,* публи́чная казнь. *Public speaking,* ора́торское иску́сство. **3,** (of the government) госуда́рственный; казённый. *Public funds,* госуда́рственные сре́дства; казённые де́ньги; обще́ственные фо́нды. *Public service,* госуда́рственная слу́жба. *Public law,* госуда́рственное пра́во. —*n.* пу́блика: *the general public,* широ́кая пу́блика. *Open to the public,* откры́т для пу́блики. *The British public,* англи́йская обще́ственность. —**in public,** публи́чно; на лю́дях. *Appear in public,* появи́ться *or* показа́ться на лю́дях. —**make public,** предава́ть гла́сности.

public-address system систе́ма звукоусиле́ния.

publication *n.* **1,** (act of publishing) изда́ние; опублико́ва́ние; публика́ция. *Year of publication,* год изда́ния. *This is not for publication,* э́то не подлежи́т оглаше́нию. **2,** (something published) изда́ние; публика́ция.

publicist *n.* публици́ст.

publicity *n.* **1,** (notice by the public) гла́сность; огла́ска. *Receive publicity,* получи́ть огла́ску. **2,** (advertising) рекла́ма. *Publicity campaign,* рекла́мная кампа́ния.

publicize *v.t.* предава́ть гла́сности; реклами́ровать.

publicly *adv.* публи́чно.

publish *v.t.* **1,** (print and issue) издава́ть. *Published works,* печа́тные труды́. **2,** (print in a certain publication) публикова́ть. —**publisher,** *n.* изда́тель.

publishing *n.* изда́тельское де́ло. —**publishing house,** изда́тельство.

puck *n., hockey* ша́йба.

pucker *v.t.* мо́рщить. —*v.i.* мо́рщиться. —*n.* **1,** (pleat) скла́дка. **2,** (wrinkle) морщи́на.

pudding *n.* пу́динг.

puddle *n.* лу́жа.

pudgy *adj.* пу́хлый.

puerile *adj.* ребя́ческий. —**puerility,** *n.* ребя́чество.

puerperal *adj.* роди́льный. —**puerperal fever,** роди́льная горя́чка.

Puerto Rican 1, *used adjectivally,* пуэрторика́нский. **2,** *used as a noun,* пуэрторика́нец; пуэрторика́нка.

puff *n.* **1,** (of air, wind, etc.) дунове́ние. **2,** (of smoke) клуб. **3,** (draw at a cigarette) затя́жка. **4,** (powder puff) пухо́вка. **5,** (pastry) сло́йка. —*v.t.* **1,** (emit forcibly) пуска́ть. **2,** *fol. by* **up** (swell; inflate) надува́ть; раздува́ть. —*v.i.* **1,** (pant) пыхте́ть; отдува́ться. **2,** *fol. by* **on** (smoke) попы́хивать (+ *instr.*). **3,** *fol. by* **up** (swell up) вздува́ться.

puffin *n.* ту́пик.

puff paste сло́еное те́сто. —**puff pastry,** сло́еный пиро́г.

puffy *adj.* одутлова́тый. *Become puffy,* отека́ть.

pug *n.* (dog) мопс; мо́ська.

pugilism *n.* бокс. —**pugilist,** *n.* боксёр.

pugnacious *adj.* драчли́вый. —**pugnacity,** *n.* драчли́вость.

pug nose курно́сый нос. —**pug-nosed,** *adj.* курно́сый.

pulchritude *n.* красота́.

pull *v.t.* **1,** (draw; drag) тащи́ть: *The horse is pulling the cart,* ло́шадь та́щит теле́гу. **2,** (tug; yank) тяну́ть: *pull the rope,* тяну́ть верёвку. *Pull someone's hair,* дёргать кого́-нибудь за́ волосы. **3,** (draw into a certain position) натя́гивать: *pull a blanket over oneself,* натяну́ть на себя́ одея́ло. *Pull one's cap down over one's ears,* надви́нуть шля́пу на́ уши. **4,** (remove) вырыва́ть: *pull a tooth,* вы́рвать зуб. *Six bodies were pulled from the water,* из воды́ извлечены́ шесть тру́пов. **5,** (strain, as a muscle) растя́гивать. —*v.i.* тяну́ть. *Pull at someone's sleeve,* дёргать кого́-нибудь за рука́в. *Pull at one's beard,* тереби́ть бо́роду. —*n.* **1,** (tug; jerk) рыво́к. **2,** (pulling power) тя́га; натяже́ние. **3,** *slang* (influence) блат; зару́чка. —**pull ahead of,** обгоня́ть; опережа́ть. —**pull apart, 1,** (separate) разнима́ть; разводи́ть; раста́скивать. **2,** (criticize; pan) раскритикова́ть; разруга́ть. —**pull away, 1,** (jerk away; yank away) отта́скивать: *pull someone away from the window,* оттащи́ть кого́-нибудь от окна́. **2,** (seize) вырыва́ть: *pull away the matches from the child,* вы́рвать спи́чки у ребёнка. **3,** (drive away) отъезжа́ть. —**pull back, 1,** (draw back suddenly) отдёргивать. **2,** *mil.* (order to withdraw) отводи́ть. **3,** (step back) отступа́ть. —**pull down, 1,** (lower, as a shade) опуска́ть. **2,** (take down; remove) снима́ть. **3,** (tear down, as a building) сноси́ть. —**pull in, 1,** (draw in) втя́гивать. **2,** (arrive) прибыва́ть. —**pull into, 1,** *literally* вта́скивать в. **2,** (roll into; enter) подходи́ть к:

The train pulled into the station, поезд подошёл к станции. —**pull off, 1,** (remove) стя́гивать; ста́скивать; сдёргивать. **2,** (move over to the side of) съезжа́ть: *pull off the road,* съезжа́ть с доро́ги. **3,** *colloq.* (accomplish; engineer) соверша́ть. —**pull on,** натя́гивать: *pull on one's shoes,* натяну́ть сапоги́. —**pull oneself together,** взять себя́ в ру́ки. —**pull out, 1,** (remove) выта́скивать; выдёргивать. **2,** (withdraw, as troops) выводи́ть. **3,** (pull open, as a drawer) выдвига́ть. **4,** (depart) отходи́ть: *The train is pulling out of the station,* по́езд отхо́дит от ста́нции. **5,** *The plane pulled out of a dive,* самолёт вы́шел из пике́. —**pull over,** подъезжа́ть: *pull over to the curb,* подъезжа́ть к тротуа́ру. —**pull together,** де́йствовать сообща́. —**pull through, 1,** *literally* прота́скивать. **2,** (recover from an illness) выжива́ть; выкара́бкиваться. *Pull through an illness,* опра́виться от боле́зни. —**pull up, 1,** (pull into position) подтя́гивать: *pull up one's socks/trousers,* подтя́гивать носки́/брю́ки. **2,** (raise, as a shade) поднима́ть. **3,** (move closer) подвига́ть: *Pull up a chair!,* подви́ньте стул бли́же! *Pull up a chair for someone,* подвига́ть *or* подставля́ть стул кому́-нибудь. **4,** (uproot) вырыва́ть. *Pull up weeds,* вырыва́ть *or* поло́ть сорняки́. **5,** (drive forward slightly) е́хать вперёд. **6,** *fol. by* **to** (drive up to) подъезжа́ть (к). **7,** *Pull up stakes,* сня́ться с ме́ста.

pullet *n.* ку́рочка; молода́я ку́рица.

pulley *n.* шкив; блок.

pullover *n.* пуло́вер; дже́мпер.

pulmonary *adj.* лёгочный. *Pulmonary artery,* лёгочная арте́рия.

pulp *n.* **1,** (juicy part of a fruit) мя́коть. **2,** (material used in making paper) древе́сная ма́сса. **3,** (part of a tooth) пу́льпа. —**beat to a pulp,** не оста́вить живо́го ме́ста на (+ *prepl.*).

pulpit *n.* ка́федра.

pulpy *adj.* мяси́стый.

pulsar *n.* пульса́р.

pulsate *v.i.* пульси́ровать. —**pulsation,** *n.* пульса́ция.

pulse *n.* пульс. *Pulse rate,* частота́ пу́льса.

pulverize *v.t.* измельча́ть; размельча́ть; превраща́ть в порошо́к.

puma *n.* пу́ма.

pumice *n.* пе́мза.

pummel *v.t.* колоти́ть; дуба́сить.

pump *n.* **1,** (device) насо́с; по́мпа. *Gasoline pump,* бензоколо́нка. *Stomach pump,* желу́дочный зонд. **2,** (shoe) ло́дочка. —*v.t.* **1,** (propel by means of a pump) кача́ть: *pump water/oil,* кача́ть во́ду/нефть. *Pump air,* нагнета́ть во́здух. **2,** *fol. by* **out** (remove by means of a pump) выка́чивать; отка́чивать. **3,** *fol. by* **up** (inflate) нака́чивать. **4,** (shake vigorously) трясти́. **5,** (fire, as bullets) пуска́ть (пу́ли в кого́-нибудь). **6,** *colloq.* (question closely) выспра́шивать.

pumpernickel *n.* чёрный хлеб.

pumping *n.* кача́ние. —**pumping station,** насо́сная ста́нция; водока́чка.

pumpkin *n.* ты́ква.

pun *n.* каламбу́р; игра́ слов. —*v.i.* каламбу́рить.

punch *n.* **1,** (blow) уда́р (кулако́м). **2,** (hole puncher) дыроко́л; (for punching a ticket) компо́стер. **3,** (perforating device) перфора́тор: *key punch,* кла́вишный перфора́тор. **4,** (beverage) пунш. —*v.t.* **1,** (strike) ударя́ть кулако́м. *Punch someone in the nose,* дать (+ *dat.*) в нос. **2,** (make, as a hole) пробива́ть. **3,** (validate, as a ticket) компости́ровать. **4,** (form with a machine that punches) штампова́ть. —**punch card,** перфока́рта. —**punch press,** штампова́льный *or* штампо́вочный пресс.

punching bag боксёрский мешо́к.

punctilious *adj.* щепети́льный.

punctual *adj.* аккура́тный; пунктуа́льный. —**punctuality,** *n.* аккура́тность; пунктуа́льность. —**punctually,** *adv.* аккура́тно.

punctuate *v.t.* **1,** (insert punctuation marks in) ста́вить зна́ки препина́ния в. **2,** (intersperse) пересыпа́ть.

punctuation *n.* пунктуа́ция. —**punctuation marks,** зна́ки препина́ния.

puncture *v.t.* прока́лывать. —*n.* проко́л.

pundit *n.* учёный; мудре́ц.

pungent *adj.* о́стрый; пика́нтный: *pungent sauce,* о́стрый/пика́нтный со́ус. *Pungent odor,* о́стрый *or* ре́зкий за́пах. —**pungency,** *n.* острота́.

punish *v.t.* нака́зывать: *punish a child for disobedience,* наказа́ть ребёнка за непослуша́ние.

punishable *adj.* наказу́емый. *Be punishable by death,* кара́ться сме́ртной ка́знью.

punishment *n.* наказа́ние: *in/as punishment for,* в наказа́ние за (+ *acc.*).

punitive *adj.* кара́тельный.

punk *n., slang* хулига́н; молодчик. —*adj., slang* дрянно́й; парши́вый.

punster *n.* каламбури́ст.

puny *adj.* **1,** (frail; sickly) щу́плый. **2,** (insignificant) ничто́жный.

pup *n.* **1,** (puppy) щено́к. **2,** (young of certain animals) детёныш.

pupa *n.* ку́колка.

pupil *n.* **1,** (student) учени́к; уча́щийся. **2,** (of the eye) зрачо́к.

puppet *n.* **1,** (animated figure) ку́кла; марионе́тка. **2,** *fig.* (person controlled by another) марионе́тка. —*adj.* **1,** (pert. to puppets) ку́кольный: *puppet show,* ку́кольный теа́тр. **2,** *fig.* (controlled by someone else) марионе́точный.

puppy *n.* щено́к.

purblind *adj.* подслепова́тый.

purchase *v.t.* покупа́ть. —*n.* **1,** (act of purchasing) ку́пля; поку́пка. **2,** (something purchased) поку́пка. —**purchase price,** покупна́я цена́.

purchaser *n.* покупа́тель.

purchasing power покупа́тельная спосо́бность.

pure *adj.* чи́стый: *pure gold,* чи́стое зо́лото; *pure chance,* чи́стая случа́йность; *pure nonsense,* чи́стый вздор.

purée *n.* пюре́.

purely *adv.* чи́сто: *purely by chance,* чи́сто случа́йно.

purgative *adj.* слаби́тельный. —*n.* слаби́тельное.

purgatory *n.* чисти́лище.

purge *v.t.* **1,** (rid of impurities) очища́ть. **2,** *fig.* (rid of undesirable elements) чи́стить. **3,** (remove and do away with) ликвиди́ровать. —*n.* чи́стка.

purify *v.t.* очища́ть. —**purification,** *n.* очи́стка; очище́ние.

purism *n.* пури́зм. —**purist,** *n.* пури́ст.

Puritan *n.* пурита́нин. —*adj.* пурита́нский. —**puritanical,** *adj.* пурита́нский.

purity *n.* чистота́.

purl *v.i.* журча́ть.

purloin *v.t.* красть; ута́скивать.

purple *adj.* лило́вый.

purport *v.t.* претендова́ть (на). —*n.* смысл.

purpose *n.* цель: *the purpose of my trip,* цель мое́й пое́здки. *Answer/serve the purpose,* отвеча́ть це́ли. —**on purpose,** наро́чно. —**to all intents and purposes,** факти́чески. —**to no purpose,** напра́сно.

purposeful *adj.* целеустремлённый.

purposely *adv.* наро́чно; наме́ренно; умы́шленно.

purr *v.i.* мурлы́кать. —*n.* мурлы́канье.

purse *n.* **1,** (change purse) кошелёк. **2,** (handbag) су́мка; су́мочка. **3,** (prize money) приз; пре́мия. —*v.t., in* **purse one's lips,** поджима́ть *or* подбира́ть *or* мо́рщить гу́бы.

purser *n.* казначе́й.

purslane *n.* портула́к.

pursuance *n.* выполне́ние; исполне́ние. —**in pursuance of,** во исполне́ние (+ *gen.*).

pursuant *adj. & adv.* [*usu.* **pursuant to**] согла́сно; соотве́тственно (+ *dat.*).

pursue *v.t.* **1,** (chase; seek) пресле́довать: *pursue a fugitive/goal,* пресле́довать беглеца́/цель. **2,** (conduct; carry out) проводи́ть: *pursue a policy,* проводи́ть поли́тику. **3,** (take up; engage in) занима́ться (+ *instr.*). *Pursue a career,* де́лать *or* составля́ть карье́ру. **4,** (continue) продолжа́ть: *pursue one's studies,* продолжа́ть учёбу.

pursuer *n.* пресле́дователь: *elude one's pursuers,* ускользну́ть от пресле́дователей.

pursuit *n.* **1,** (act of pursuing) пресле́дование; пого́ня. *Set out in pursuit of,* пусти́ться в пого́ню за. **2,** (act of seeking) пого́ня; стремле́ние: *the pursuit of happiness,* пого́ня за сча́стьем; стремле́ние к сча́стью. **3,** (activity; avocation) заня́тие.

purvey *v.t.* поставля́ть. —**purveyor,** *n.* поставщи́к.

purview *n.* сфе́ра; компете́нция.

pus *n.* гной.

push *v.t.* **1,** (propel; shove) толка́ть: *push a baby carriage,* толка́ть де́тскую коля́ску. *Push something over a cliff,* столкну́ть что́-нибудь с обры́ва. *Push one's way through a crowd,* прота́лкиваться сквозь толпу́. **2,** (press, as a button) нажима́ть на. **3,** (urge on) подта́лкивать. **4,** (prosecute vigorously) прота́лкивать: *push a matter,* прота́лкивать де́ло. **5,** *colloq.* (be approaching) rendered by сту́кнуть: *He is pushing fifty,* ему́ ско́ро сту́кнет пятьдеся́т. **6,** *slang* (sell, as drugs) торгова́ть (нарко́тиками). —*v.i.* **1,** (exert force on something) толка́ть: *Push harder!,* толкни́те посильне́е! **2,** (shove) толка́ться: *Don't push!,* не толка́йтесь! —*n.* толчо́к. *Give someone a*

push, толкну́ть кого́-нибудь. —**push away,** отта́лкивать. —**push back,** отбра́сывать; оттесня́ть. —**push off, 1,** (force off) ста́лкивать. **2,** (depart in a boat) отта́лкиваться от бе́рега. **3,** *colloq.* (leave; depart) уходи́ть; убира́ться. —**push on,** продолжа́ть путь. —**push out,** выта́лкивать. —**push through, 1,** (shove through) прота́лкивать. **2,** *fig.* (force through, as a resolution) прота́скивать.

push button кно́пка.

pushcart *n.* ручна́я теле́жка.

pushy *adj., colloq.* пробивно́й; напо́ристый.

pusillanimous *adj.* малоду́шный. —**pusillanimity,** *n.* малоду́шие.

puss *n.,* **1,** (cat) ко́шечка; кис(к)а. **2,** *slang* (face) ха́ря.

pussy *n.* ко́шечка; кис(к)а. *Also,* **pussy cat.**

pussy willow ве́рба.

pustule *n.* гнойничо́к.

put *v.t.* **1,** (lay) класть: *put the book on the table,* класть кни́гу на стол. *Where did I put my glasses?,* куда́ я дел (де́ла) мои́ очки́? **2,** (stand) ста́вить: *put the flowers in water,* ста́вить цветы́ в во́ду. **3,** (place) помеща́ть; класть; ста́вить. *Put an ad in the newspaper,* помеща́ть объявле́ние в газе́те. *Put sugar in the tea,* класть са́хар в чай. *Put one's hands in one's pockets,* класть ру́ки в карма́ны. *Put one's ear to the door,* прикла́дывать у́хо к две́ри. *Put the letter in the envelope,* вложи́ть письмо́ в конве́рт. *Put a stamp on an envelope,* накле́ить ма́рку на конве́рт. *Put a child in kindergarten,* отдава́ть ребёнка в де́тский сад. *Put a patient in the hospital,* помеща́ть *or* класть больно́го в больни́цу. *Put someone in prison,* посади́ть кого́-нибудь в тюрьму́. *Put a period at the end of a sentence,* ста́вить то́чку в конце́ предложе́ния. *Put a word in brackets,* ста́вить сло́во в ско́бки. *Put one's signature on,* ста́вить свою́ по́дпись под (+ *instr.*). *Put obstacles in someone's way,* ста́вить препя́тствия кому́-нибудь. *Put in an awkward position,* ста́вить в нело́вкое положе́ние. *Put yourself in my place,* поста́вьте себя́ на моё ме́сто. **4,** (bring to a certain state): *put at ease,* успока́ивать. *Put in order,* приводи́ть в поря́док. *Put to work,* уса́живать за рабо́ту. *Put to bed,* укла́дывать. *Put to death,* казни́ть; предава́ть сме́рти. *Put to flight,* обрати́ть в бе́гство. *Put to shame,* пристыди́ть. **5,** (cause to take effect): *put an end to,* поко́нчить с; положи́ть коне́ц (+ *dat.*). *Put into effect/operation,* вводи́ть в де́йствие. *Put into circulation,* пуска́ть в обраще́ние. **6,** (apply; expend) вкла́дывать; класть: *put a lot of work into,* вкла́дывать/класть мно́го труда́ в. *Put one's heart and soul into,* вкла́дывать всю ду́шу в. **7,** (cause to undergo) подверга́ть: *put to the test,* подверга́ть испыта́нию. *Put on trial,* предава́ть суду́. *Put to expense,* вводи́ть в расхо́д. *Put to a vote,* поста́вить на голосова́ние. **8,** (exert) ока́зывать: *put pressure on,* ока́зывать давле́ние на. **9,** (express) выража́ть: *put into words,* выража́ть словами. *To put it mildly,* мя́гко выража́ясь. *I don't know how to put it,* я не зна́ю, как э́то сказа́ть. *Let me put the question another way,* позво́льте мне сформули́ровать вопро́с ина́че. **10,**

(pose, as a question) ста́вить; задава́ть. **11,** (render; set): *put words to music,* положи́ть слова́ на му́зыку. **12,** (attach; attribute): *put the blame on,* вали́ть вину́ на. *Put a wrong interpretation on,* дава́ть непра́вильное толкова́ние (+ *dat.*). **13,** (invest; deposit) класть; вкла́дывать; помеща́ть. *Put money in a savings account,* класть де́ньги в сберка́ссу. **14,** (estimate at a certain figure) оце́нивать: *put the number at two million,* оце́нивать о́бщее число́ в два миллио́на. **15,** (bet) ста́вить: *put two dollars on a horse,* ста́вить два до́ллара на ло́шадь. **16,** *sports: put the shot,* толка́ть ядро́. —*v.i.* *Used in certain set expressions: put into port,* заходи́ть в порт; *put out to sea,* выходи́ть в мо́ре. —**put aside,** откла́дывать (в сто́рону); сберега́ть. —**put away, 1,** (remove from sight) убира́ть. **2,** (save; reserve) откла́дывать. **3,** *colloq.* (commit, as to jail) сажа́ть. **4,** *colloq.* (consume) съесть; вы́пить. —**put back, 1,** (restore to its place) ста́вить на ме́сто. **2,** (turn back, as a clock) ста́вить *or* переводи́ть наза́д. —**put down, 1,** (set down) класть; ста́вить (на́ пол *or* на зе́млю). *Put down the receiver,* класть (положи́ть) тру́бку. **2,** (write down) запи́сывать. **3,** (suppress, as a revolt) подавля́ть. **4,** *fol. by* to (attribute) относи́ть на счёт (+ *gen.*). **5,** (pay in a lump sum) дать в зада́ток. **6,** (land) приземля́ться. **7,** *Put down roots,* пуска́ть ко́рни. —**put forth, 1,** (sprout) пуска́ть. **2,** (exert, as effort) прилага́ть. **3,** (advance, as a proposal) выдвига́ть. —**put forward,** выдвига́ть: *put forward a plan,* выдвига́ть план. —**put in, 1,** (insert) вкла́дывать; вставля́ть. *Put in a light bulb,* ввинти́ть ла́мпочку. *Put in stitches,* наложи́ть швы. *Put in a good word for,* замо́лвить словечко за. **2,** (install) ста́вить. **3,** (plant) сажа́ть. **4,** (enter, as a claim) предъявля́ть. **5,** *fol. by* for (apply for) подава́ть заявле́ние о. **6,** *colloq.* (expend, as time) тра́тить. **7,** *Put in an appearance,* появля́ться. —**put off, 1,** (make get off) выса́живать; сса́живать. **2,** (postpone) откла́дывать. **3,** *colloq.* (repel) отта́лкивать. —**put on, 1,** (don) надева́ть. **2,** (apply) накла́дывать: *put on a bandage,* накла́дывать повя́зку. *Put on make-up,* кра́ситься. *Put on the brakes,* тормози́ть. **3,** (turn on, as a light) включа́ть. **4,** (stage, as a play) ста́вить. **5,** (assume; affect) напуска́ть на себя́. **6,** (gain, as weight) прибавля́ть в (ве́се). *Put on ten pounds,* поправля́ться на де́сять фу́нтов; прибавля́ть де́сять фу́нтов. **7,** *Put on a record,* (по)ста́вить пласти́нку. **8,** *Put on some tea,* (по)ста́вить ча́йник. **9,** *Put on extra trains,* пуска́ть дополни́тельные поезда́. —**put out, 1,** (extend) протя́гивать. **2,** (lay out) выкла́дывать. **3,** (take out, as garbage) выноси́ть. **4,** (stick out) высо́вывать. **5,** (extinguish) туши́ть. **6,** (gouge out, as an eye) выка́лывать. **7,** (manufacture; publish) выпуска́ть. **8,** (inconvenience) затрудня́ть. *Put oneself out,* утружда́ть себя́; дать себе́ нема́ло труда́. **9,** (vex) обижа́ть. *Be put out,* быть оби́женным. **10,** *Put out of action,* выводи́ть из стро́я. *Put out of one's head,* выбра́сывать из головы́. —**put over,** (postpone)

переноси́ть. —**put right,** нала́живать; поправля́ть. —**put through, 1,** (implement) проводи́ть. **2,** (cause to undergo) подверга́ть (+ *dat.*). **3,** (connect by phone) соединя́ть. —**put together, 1,** (place together) составля́ть. **2,** (assemble) собира́ть. **3,** (put back in one piece) скла́дывать. **4,** (amass) накопля́ть. **5,** (combined) взя́тые вме́сте: *more than all the rest put together,* бо́льше, чем все остальны́е взя́тые вме́сте. —**put up, 1,** (erect) стро́ить; воздвига́ть. **2,** (hang; post) ве́шать; взве́шивать. **3,** (preserve; can) консерви́ровать. **4,** (advance; invest, as money) вкла́дывать. *Put up the money for a venture,* фина́нси́ровать предприя́тие. *Put up bail,* вноси́ть зало́г. **5,** (give lodging to) устра́ивать; помеща́ть; приюти́ть (на́ ночь); пуска́ть ночева́ть *or* на ночле́г. **6,** (offer): *put up for sale,* пуска́ть в прода́жу. *Put up resistance,* ока́зывать сопротивле́ние. **7,** *fol. by* **with** (endure; tolerate) терпе́ть; выноси́ть; мири́ться с. **8,** *fol. by* **to** (incite; goad) подбива́ть; подучивать; подгова́ривать.

putative *adj.* предполага́емый.

putrefaction *n.* гние́ние; разложе́ние.

putrefy *v.i.* гнить. —*v.t.* гнои́ть.

putrid *adj.* **1,** (decomposed) гнило́й. **2,** (foul, as of an odor) тру́пный. **3,** (foul-smelling) воню́чий.

putsch *n.* путч.

puttee *n., usu. pl.* кра́ги; обмо́тки.

putter *v.i.* вози́ться: *putter in the garden,* вози́ться в саду́.

putty *n.* зама́зка; шпаклёвка. —*v.t.* зама́зывать; шпаклева́ть. —**putty knife,** шпа́тель.

puzzle *n.* зага́дка; головоло́мка. *Jigsaw puzzle,* соста́вная карти́нка. *Crossword puzzle,* кроссво́рд. —*v.t.* **1,** (perplex) приводи́ть в недоуме́ние; озада́чивать. **2,** *fol. by* **out** (solve) разга́дывать; распу́тывать. —*v.i.* [*usu.* **puzzle over**] би́ться над; лома́ть себе́ го́лову над.

puzzled *adj.* недоуме́нный; недоумева́ющий. *Be puzzled,* недоумева́ть.

puzzlement *n.* недоуме́ние.

puzzling *adj.* недоуме́нный: *puzzling question,* недоуме́нный вопро́с. *I find his behavior puzzling,* его́ поведе́ние приводи́т меня́ в недоуме́ние.

pygmy *n.* пигме́й.

pyjamas *n.* = **pajamas.**

pylon *n.* пило́н.

pyorrhea *also,* **pyorrhoea** *n.* пиоре́я.

pyramid *n.* пирами́да. —**pyramidal,** *adj.* пирами́дальный.

pyre *n.* погреба́льный костёр.

pyrite *n.* пири́т.

pyrites *n.* колчеда́н.

pyrography *n.* выжига́ние.

pyromania *n.* пирома́ния.

pyrotechnics *n.* пироте́хника.

Pyrrhic victory пи́ррова побе́да.

Pythagorean theorum пифаго́рова теоре́ма.

python *n.* пито́н.

Q

Q, q семна́дцатая бу́ква англи́йского алфави́та.

quack *n.* **1,** (duck's cry) кря́канье. **2,** (false doctor) зна́харь; шарлата́н. —*adj.* шарлата́нский. —*v.i.* кря́кать.

quackery *n.* зна́харство; шарлата́нство.

quadrangle *n.* четырёхуго́льник. —**quadrangular,** *adj.* четырёхуго́льный.

quadrant *n.* квадра́нт.

quadratic *adj.* квадра́тный.

quadrennial *adj.* происходя́щий раз в четы́ре го́да.

quadrilateral *n.* четырёхуго́льник. —*adj.* четырёхсторо́нний.

quadrille *n.* кадри́ль.

quadrillion *n.* квадрильо́н.

quadruped *n.* четвероно́гое.

quadruple *adj.* четверно́й; четырёхкра́тный. —*v.t.* учетверя́ть. —*v.i.* увели́чиваться в четы́ре ра́за; учетверя́ться.

quadruplets *n.pl.* четверня́.

quadruplicate *n. In quadruplicate,* в четырёх экземпля́рах.

quaff *v.t.* пить за́лпом.

quagmire *n.* тряси́на.

quail *n.* пе́репел. —*v.i.* (flinch) дро́гнуть.

quaint *adj.* причу́дливый.

quake *v.i.* дрожа́ть; трясти́сь. —*n.* = **earthquake.**

Quaker *n.* ква́кер. —*adj.* ква́керский.

qualification *n.* **1,** (ability; competence) квалифика́ция. *He has all the necessary qualifications for the job,* у него́ все да́нные для э́той рабо́ты. **2,** (limitation; reservation) огово́рка.

qualified *adj.* **1,** (able; fit) компете́нтный. *Qualified for a position,* приго́дный для до́лжности. **2,** (limited; with reservations) ограни́ченный; с огово́рками.

qualifier *n., gram.* определе́ние; атрибу́т.

qualify *v.t.* **1,** (make eligible) дава́ть пра́во (+ *dat.*). **2,** (make less categorical): *qualify one's statement,* огова́риваться. **3,** *gram.* (modify) определя́ть. —*v.i.* выслу́живать: *qualify for a pension,* выслу́живать пе́нсию. *Qualify for the finals,* вы́йти в фина́л. *He qualifies on all counts,* он подхо́дит по всем статья́м.

qualifying *adj., sports* квалификацио́нный; отбо́рочный: *qualifying rounds,* квалификацио́нные/отбо́рочные соревнова́ния.

qualitative *adj.* ка́чественный. —**qualitative analysis,** ка́чественный ана́лиз.

quality *n.* ка́чество: *items of good quality,* изде́лия хоро́шего ка́чества. —*adj., colloq.* высо́кого ка́чества; добро́тный; доброка́чественный; высокока́чественный.

qualm *n., usu. pl.* **1,** (misgivings) сомне́ние. **2,** (compunctions) угрызе́ния со́вести.

quandary *n.* затрудни́тельное положе́ние; затрудне́ние.

quantitative *adj.* коли́чественный. —**quantitative analysis,** коли́чественный ана́лиз.

quantity *n.* **1,** (amount) коли́чество: *enormous quantity,* огро́мное коли́чество. *Buy in quantity,* покупа́ть в большо́м коли́честве. **2,** *math.* величина́: *unknown quantity,* неизве́стная величина́.

quantum *n., physics* квант. —*adj.* ква́нтовый: *quantum mechanics/theory,* ква́нтовая меха́ника/тео́рия.

quarantine *n.* каранти́н; изоля́ция. *Quarantine period,* каранти́нный срок. —*v.t.* подверга́ть каранти́ну; изоли́ровать.

quarrel *n.* ссо́ра. *They have had a quarrel,* они́ в ссо́ре. —*v.i.* ссо́риться: *They quareled among themselves,* они́ поссо́рились ме́жду собо́й. *I do not quarrel with that point,* я не оспа́риваю э́того утвержде́ния.

quarrelsome *adj.* вздо́рный; сварли́вый.

quarry *n.* **1,** (place of excavation) каменоло́мня; карье́р. **2,** (prey) добы́ча. —*v.t.* добыва́ть. *Quarry stone,* лома́ть ка́мень.

quart *n.* ква́рта.

quarter *n.* **1,** (one-fourth) че́тверть: *three quarters,* три че́тверти. *He is one-quarter Jewish,* он евре́й на че́тверть. **2,** (25-cent piece) четверта́к. **3,** (period of three months) кварта́л. **4,** (part of an academic year) че́тверть. **5,** (fifteen minutes) че́тверть: *a quarter of two,* без че́тверти два; *a quarter past seven,* че́тверть восьмо́го. **6,** (district of a city) кварта́л. **7,** (direction) сторона́: *from every quarter,* со всех сторо́н. **8,** *pl.* (place of lodging) помеще́ние; *mil.* кварти́ры. *Servants' quarters,* помеще́ние для прислу́ги. **9,** (part of an animal) часть: *hind quarters,* за́дняя часть. **10,** (mercy) поща́да. *Give someone no quarter,* не дава́ть поща́ды (+ *dat.*); не дава́ть спу́ска (+ *dat.*). —*v.t.* **1,** (divide in four) дели́ть на четы́ре ча́сти. **2,** (billet) расквартиро́вать. **3,** *hist.* (execute) четвертова́ть.

quarterdeck *n.* шка́нцы; ют.

quarterfinal *n.* четвертьфина́л. —*adj.* четверть-фина́льный.

quarterly *adj.* кварта́льный. —*adv.* покварта́льно. —*n.* журна́л, выходя́щий покварта́льно.

quartermaster *n.* интенда́нт; квартирме́йстер. —**quartermaster corps,** интенда́нтство.

quarter note *music* четвертна́я но́та.

quartet *n.* кварте́т.

quartz *n.* кварц. —*adj.* ква́рцевый.

quartzite *n.* кварци́т.

quasar *n.* кваза́р.

quash *v.t.* **1,** (suppress) подавля́ть. **2,** *law* (set aside) аннули́ровать.

quasi- *prefix* полу-: *quasi-official,* полуофициа́льный.

quatrain *n.* четверости́шие.

quaver *v.i.* **1,** (tremble; quake) дрожа́ть. **2,** (be tremulous, as of one's voice) дро́гнуть. —*n.* трель.

quay *n.* при́стань.

queasiness *n.* **1,** (nausea) тошнота́. **2,** (squeamishness) брезгли́вость.

queasy *adj.* **1,** (sick to one's stomach): *I felt queasy,* меня́ тошни́ло. **2,** (squeamish) брезгли́вый.

queen *n.* **1,** (sovereign) короле́ва. **2,** *cards* да́ма. **3,** *chess* ферзь. —*adj.* [*usu.* **queen's**] **1,** (of a queen) короле́вский. **2,** *chess* фе́рзевый: *queen's bishop,* фе́рзевый слон. *Queen's gambit,* фе́рзевый гамби́т. —**queen bee,** (пчели́ная) ма́тка. —**queen dowager,** вдо́вствующая короле́ва.

queer *adj.* стра́нный; чудакова́тый; эксцентри́чный. —**queerly,** *adv.* стра́нно.

quell *v.t.* **1,** (suppress) подавля́ть. **2,** (allay) успока́ивать.

quench *v.t.* **1,** (extinguish; put out) гаси́ть; туши́ть. **2,** (slake, as thirst) утоля́ть.

querulous *adj.* ворчли́вый; сварли́вый.

query *n.* вопро́с. —*v.t.* **1,** (ask questions of) расспра́шивать. **2,** (express doubts about) сомнева́ться в; ста́вить под вопро́с.

quest *n.* по́иски. *In quest of,* в по́исках (+ *gen.*).

question *n.* **1,** (query) вопро́с: *ask a question,* задава́ть вопро́с. **2,** (subject; issue) вопро́с: *the German question,* герма́нский вопро́с. *The question is...,* вопро́с (состои́т) в том, ... **3,** (doubt) сомне́ние. *Without question,* бесспо́рно. *Beyond question,* вне сомне́ния. *Open to question,* под вопро́сом. *Call into question,* ста́вить под вопро́с; ста́вить под сомне́ние. —*v.t.* **1,** (ask questions of) расспра́шивать. **2,** (interrogate) допра́шивать. **3,** (express uncertainty about) сомнева́ться в; ста́вить под сомне́ние; подверга́ть сомне́нию. —**in question, 1,** (under consideration) о кото́ром идёт речь: *the case in question,* слу́чай, о кото́ром идёт речь. **2,** (in dispute) под вопро́сом. —**it is a question of...,** речь идёт о... *It is not a question of money,* не в деньга́х де́ло; де́ньги тут ни при чём. —**that is out of the question,** об э́том не мо́жет быть и ре́чи; об э́том не́чего и ду́мать; э́то исключено́.

questionable *adj.* сомни́тельный.

questioning *n.* допро́с: *detain for questioning,* заде́рживать для допро́са.

question mark вопроси́тельный знак.

questionnaire *n.* анке́та; вопро́сник; опро́сный лист.

queue *n.* о́чередь. —*v.i.* [*usu.* **queue up**] стоя́ть в о́череди; станови́ться в о́чередь.

quibble *n.* **1,** (evasion of a point) уве́ртка. **2,** (minor criticism) приди́рка. —*v.i.* **1,** (cavil) придира́ться. **2,** (bicker) спо́рить. —**quibbler,** *n.* приди́ра.

quick *adj.* **1,** (rapid; swift) бы́стрый; ско́рый. *Be quick!,* скоре́е! **2,** (bright; alert) поня́тливый. *Quick to grasp things,* сообрази́тельный. **3,** (easily aroused) вспы́льчивый: *quick temper,* вспы́льчивый хара́ктер. —*adv.* бы́стро. *Come quick!,* иди́ скоре́й! —*n., in* cut to the quick, заде́ть за живо́е.

quick-acting *adj.* быстроде́йствующий.

quick-change artist трансформа́тор.

quicken *v.t.* **1,** (accelerate) ускоря́ть: *quicken the pace,* ускоря́ть шаг. *Quickened pulse,* учащённый пульс. **2,** (arouse; stir) волнова́ть. *Quicken the imagination,* волнова́ть *or* будора́жить воображе́ние. —*v.i.* ускоря́ться.

quicklime *n.* негашёная и́звесть.

quickly *adv.* бы́стро. *Come quickly!,* иди́ скоре́й!

quickness *n.* **1,** (rapidity) быстрота́. **2,** (keenness of mind) сообрази́тельность.

quicksand *n.* сыпу́чий песо́к.

quicksilver *n.* ртуть.

quick-tempered *adj.* вспы́льчивый.

quick-witted *adj.* сообрази́тельный; сме́тливый; дога́дливый.

quiescent *adj.* неподви́жный; споко́йный. —**quiescence,** *n.* поко́й; неподви́жность.

quiet *adj.* **1,** (making no noise; free from noise) ти́хий: *quiet neighbors,* ти́хие сосе́ди; *quiet street,* ти́хая у́лица. *Be/keep quiet,* молча́ть. *Keep something quiet,* зама́лчивать что́-нибудь. **2,** (calm; tranquil) споко́йный. *Lead a quiet life,* жить споко́йно. —*n.* тишина́! *Peace and quiet,* поко́й. —*interj.* ти́ше!; не шуме́ть! —*v.t.* успока́ивать: *quiet the crowd,* успока́ивать толпу́. —*v.i.* [*usu.* **quiet down**] успока́иваться.

quietude *n.* поко́й; споко́йствие.

quill *n.* **1,** (feather) перо́. **2,** (spine, as of a porcupine) игла́. **3,** (quill pen) перо́.

quilt *n.* стёганое одея́ло; стёганое покрыва́ло. —*v.t.* стега́ть. —**quilted,** *adj.* стёганый.

quince *n.* айва́.

quinine *n.* хини́н.

quintessence *n.* квинтэссе́нция.

quintet *n.* квинте́т.

quintuplets *n.pl.* пя́теро близнецо́в.

quip *n.* остро́та. —*v.i.* состри́ть.

quire *n.* (ру́сская) десть.

quirk *n.* причу́да; вы́верт; заско́к. *Quirk of fate,* игра́ судьбы́; игра́ слу́чая.

quit *v.t.* **1,** (cease) перестава́ть; бро́сить. *Quit crying,* перестава́ть пла́кать. *Quit yelling!,* бро́сьте крича́ть! **2,** (give up) бро́сить: *quit smoking,* бро́сить кури́ть. **3,** (resign from; leave) уходи́ть из *or* с; выходи́ть из; бро́сить. *Quit one's job,* уйти́ с рабо́ты; бро́сить рабо́ту. *Quit school,* бро́сить шко́лу. *Quit* *the party,* выходи́ть из па́ртии. *Quit the post of treasurer,* уходи́ть с поста́ казначе́я. **4,** (vacate) покида́ть; освобожда́ть. —*v.i.* **1,** (resign) уходи́ть. **2,** (leave one's job) уходи́ть с рабо́ты. **3,** (give up; stop trying) сдава́ться.

quite *adv.* **1,** (entirely) совсе́м; вполне́. *Not quite,* не совсе́м. *I quite agree,* я вполне́ согла́сен (согла́сна). **2,** (rather; very) дово́льно: *quite far from here,* дово́льно далеко́ отсю́да. *Quite a few,* дово́льно мно́го. *Quite a while,* дово́льно до́лго. **3,** *fol. by* **a** (considerable) изря́дный: *quite a distance,* изря́дное расстоя́ние. *It's quite a distance from here,* э́то дово́льно далеко́ (*or* поря́дочно) отсю́да. *It was quite a surprise,* э́то бы́ло большо́й неожи́данностью.

quits *adj.* кви́ты. —**call it quits, 1,** (stop work) ко́нчить рабо́ту; шаба́шить. **2,** (retire) вы́йти на пе́нсию; сойти́ со сце́ны.

quiver *v.i.* трепета́ть; дро́гнуть. —*n.* **1,** (tremor) тре́пет. **2,** (case for arrows) колча́н.

quixotic *adj.* донкихо́тский.

quiz *n.* **1,** (short test) опро́с; контро́льная рабо́та. **2,** (game) виктори́на. —*v.t.* **1,** (interrogate) допра́шивать. **2,** (give a short test to) проверя́ть зна́ния (+ *gen.*); опра́шивать.

quizzical *adj.* недоуме́нный; недоумева́ющий.

quorum *n.* кво́рум.

quota *n.* кво́та; но́рма.

quotation *n.* **1,** (words or passage quoted) цита́та. **2,** *finance* котиро́вка. —**quotation marks,** кавы́чки.

quote *v.t.* **1,** (cite) ссыла́ться на; цити́ровать. **2,** (name, as a price) называ́ть. —*n.* **1,** *colloq.* = quotation. **2,** *pl.* = quotation marks.

quotient *n.* ча́стное. —**intelligence quotient,** показа́тель у́мственных спосо́бностей.

R

R, r восемна́дцатая бу́ква англи́йского алфави́та. —**the three R's,** чте́ние, письмо́, арифме́тика.

rabbi *n.* равви́н. —**rabbinical,** *adj.* равви́нский.

rabbit *n.* кро́лик. —*adj.* кро́личий: *rabbit hole,* кро́личья нора́.

rabble *n.* толпа́. —**the rabble,** сброд; чернь; отре́бье.

rabid *adj.* **1,** (having rabies) бе́шеный. **2,** (fanatical) оголте́лый; махро́вый.

rabies *n.* бе́шенство; водобоя́знь.

raccoon *also,* **racoon** *n.* ено́т. —*adj.* ено́товый.

race *n.* **1,** (contest of speed) бег; забе́г; пробе́г; го́нки. *Boat race,* ло́дочные го́нки. *Horse race,* ска́чка; зае́зд. *The races,* ска́чки; бега́. **2,** (any contest) го́нка: *the arms race,* го́нка вооруже́ний. **3,** (ethnic group) ра́са. **4,** *in the human race,* челове́ческий род. —*adj.* *race relations,* ра́совые отноше́ния. —*v.i.* **1,** (compete in a race) бежа́ть; (*of a horse*) скака́ть. **2,** (dash) мча́ться. *Race by,* промча́ться. —*v.t.* **1,** (run against) бежа́ть наперегонки́ с. *I'll race you to the lake!,* дава́й побежи́м неперегонки́ до о́зера. **2,** (run at high speed, as an engine) дава́ть по́лный газ (+ *dat.*).

racecourse *n.* скакова́я доро́жка.

racehorse *n.* скакова́я ло́шадь.

raceme *n.* кисть; соцве́тие.

racer *n.* **1,** (racing driver) го́нщик. **2,** (horse) скакова́я ло́шадь; скаку́н. **3,** (automobile) го́ночный автомоби́ль.

racetrack *n.* ипподро́м.

racial *adj.* ра́совый.

racing *n.* бега́; ска́чки. —*adj.* **1,** (of racing) беговой; скаково́й. **2,** (used in racing) го́ночный: *racing car,* го́ночный автомоби́ль.

racism *n.* раси́зм. —**racist,** *n.* раси́ст. —*adj.* раси́стский.

rack *n.* **1,** (for coats, hats, etc.) ве́шалка. **2,** (for books or other standing objects) стелла́ж. **3,** (for luggage) по́лка; се́тка. **4,** (for bombs) бомбодержа́тель. **5,** (instrument of torture) ды́ба. **6,** (toothed bar) зубча́тая ре́йка. —*v.t.* **1,** [*also,* **wrack**] (afflict) изму́чить; (ис)терза́ть. *Racked with disease,* изму́ченный боле́знью. **2,** *fol. by* **up** (score) набира́ть (...очко́в); оде́ржать (побе́ду). **3,** *in* **rack one's brains,** лома́ть себе́ го́лову. —**go to rack and ruin,** пойти́ пра́хом.

racket *n.* **1,** (din) гам; гвалт. **2,** *sports* [*also,* **racquet**] (webbed bat) раке́тка. **3,** (fraud) рэ́кет. —**racketeer,** *n.* га́нгстер; рэкети́р.

raconteur *n.* расска́зчик.

racoon *n.* = raccoon.

racquet *n.* = racket (*in sense #2*).

racy *adj.* **1,** (lively) колори́тный. **2,** (risqué) солёный.

radar *n.* **1,** (system) радиолока́ция. **2,** (device) радиолока́тор. —*adj.* радиолокацио́нный.

radial *adj.* лучево́й; радиа́льный.

radiance *n.* сия́ние; блеск.

radiant *adj.* **1,** (sending out or transmitted by rays) лучи́стый: *radiant heat/energy,* лучи́стая теплота́/ эне́ргия. **2,** (beaming, as with joy) сия́ющий; лучеза́рный.

radiate *v.t.* **1,** (emit) излуча́ть. **2,** (manifest in a glowing manner) сия́ть; лучи́ться: *radiate happiness,* сия́ть/лучи́ться сча́стьем. —*v.i.* **1,** (spread out in rays) излуча́ться. **2,** (branch out) расходи́ться.

radiation *n.* излуче́ние; радиа́ция; лучеиспуска́ние. *Radiation treatment,* облуче́ние. —**radiation sickness,** лучева́я боле́знь. —**radiation therapy,** лучева́я терапи́я; радиотерапи́я.

radiator *n.* батаре́я отопле́ния; радиа́тор.

radical *adj.* **1,** *polit.* радика́льный. **2,** (drastic) коренно́й; радика́льный. —*n.* **1,** *polit.* радика́л. **2,** *math.* ко́рень. *Radical sign,* знак ко́рня; радика́л. **3,** *chem.* радика́л. —**radicalism,** *n.* радикали́зм. —**radically,** *adv.* коренны́м о́бразом; радика́льно.

radio *n.* **1,** (receiving set) радиоприёмник: *car radio,* автомоби́льный радиоприёмник. **2,** (broadcasting medium) ра́дио: *hear something over the radio,* услы́шать что́-нибудь по ра́дио. **3,** (small portable receiver and transmitter) ра́ция. —*v.t. & i.* ради́ровать. —**radio operator,** ради́ст. —**radio station,** радиоста́нция.

radioactive *adj.* радиоакти́вный. —**radioactivity,** *n.* радиоакти́вность.

radiogram *n.* радиогра́мма.

radiology *n.* **1,** (use of X-rays) рентгеноло́гия. **2,** (use of radiation) радиоло́гия. —**radiologist,** *n.* рентгено́лог; радио́лог.

radio-phonograph *n.* радио́ла.

radiotelegraphy *n.* радиотелеграфи́я.

radiotelephone *n.* радиотелефо́н. —**radiotelephony,** *n.* радиотелефони́я.

radiotherapy *n.* радиотерапи́я.

radish *n.* реди́ска; ре́дька; *pl.* реди́с; реди́ски.

radium *n.* ра́дий. —*adj.* ра́диевый.

radius *n.* ра́диус. *Within a radius of,* в ра́диусе (+ *gen.*).

radon *n.* радо́н.

raffle *n.* лотере́я. *Raffle ticket,* лотере́йный биле́т. —*v.t.* разы́грывать.

raft *n.* **1,** (float) плот. **2,** *colloq.* (large amount) у́йма; ку́ча.

rafter *n.* стропи́ло.

rag *n.* **1,** (piece of cloth) тря́пка: *dust rag,* пы́льная тря́пка. **2,** *pl.* (scraps of cloth) тряпьё; ве́тошь. **3,** *pl.* (shabby clothes; tatters) лохмо́тья; тряпьё; ру́бище; отре́пья. —*adj.* тряпи́чный: *rag paper,* тряпи́чная бума́га.

ragamuffin *n.* обо́рвыш.

rag doll тряпи́чная ку́кла.

rage *n.* **1,** (fury) я́рость; бе́шенство. *Fly into a rage,* приходи́ть в я́рость. **2,** *colloq.* (fad; craze) после́дний крик мо́ды. —*v.i.* **1,** (show violent anger) беси́ться; неи́стовствовать. **2,** (of a storm, fire, etc.) бушева́ть; свире́пствовать; неи́стовствовать. *The raging sea,* бушу́ющее мо́ре.

ragged *adj.* **1,** (tattered) поно́шенный; изо́рванный;

обо́рванный. **2,** (rough; jagged) шерохова́тый; зазу́бренный. —**run oneself ragged,** избе́гаться; забе́гаться.

raglan *n.* регла́н.

ragman *n.* тряпи́чник.

ragout *n.* рагу́.

ragweed *n.* амбро́зия.

raid *n.* **1,** *mil.* налёт; набе́г; рейд. *Air raid,* возду́шный налёт. **2,** (by the police) обла́ва; рейд. —*v.t.* **1,** *mil.* соверша́ть налёт/набе́г на. **2,** (of the police) нагря́нуть в *or* на.

rail *n.* **1,** (horizontal bar) попере́чина; перекла́дина. **2,** (handrail; railing) пери́ла; по́ручни. **3,** (railroad track) рельс. **4,** (railroad) желе́зная доро́га: *by rail,* по желе́зной доро́ге. **5,** (bird) пастушо́к. —*adj.* железнодоро́жный: *rail junction,* железнодоро́жный у́зел. —*v.i.* [*usu.* **rail at** *or* **against**] брани́ть. —**thin as a rail,** худо́й как ще́пка.

railing *n.* **1,** (fence) огра́да. **2,** (banister) пери́ла.

raillery *n.* беззло́бная насме́шка.

railroad *n.* желе́зная доро́га. —*adj.* железнодоро́жный.

railway *n.* = **railroad.**

raiment *n.* одея́ние.

rain *n.* дождь. *Stand in the rain,* стоя́ть под дождём. *Come in out of the rain,* зайти́ в дом от дождя́. *Let's get out of the rain,* дава́йте уйдём с дождя́. —*adj.* дождево́й: *rain water,* дождева́я вода́. —*v.i.* **1,** (be raining) идти́: *It is raining,* идёт дождь; *it's not raining,* дождь не идёт. *It rained all day,* весь день шёл дождь. *If it doesn't rain,* е́сли не бу́дет дождя́. **2,** *fig.* (fall like rain) сы́паться: *Bombs rained down on the city,* бо́мбы сы́пались на го́род. —*v.t.* **1,** (shower) обру́шивать. *Rain blows on someone,* обру́шивать уда́ры на кого́-нибудь; осыпа́ть кого́-нибудь уда́рами. **2,** *fol. by* **out** (force to cancel) отменя́ть из-за дождя́: *The game was rained out,* матч был отменён из-за дождя́. —**it is raining cats and dogs,** дождь льёт как из ведра́. —**rain or shine,** в любу́ю пого́ду; кака́я бы ни была́ пого́да.

rainbow *n.* ра́дуга. —**rainbow trout,** ра́дужная форе́ль.

raincoat *n.* плащ; дождеви́к.

raindrop *n.* дождева́я ка́пля.

rainfall *n.* коли́чество оса́дков.

rain hat шля́па от дождя́.

rainstorm *n.* ли́вень.

rainy *adj.* дождли́вый: *rainy weather,* дождли́вая пого́да. *The rainy season,* сезо́н дожде́й. —**put aside for a rainy day,** бере́чь на чёрный день.

raise *v.t.* **1,** (lift) поднима́ть: *raise one's hand,* поднима́ть ру́ку. *Raise the curtain/flag,* поднима́ть за́навес/флаг. *Raise our glasses to...,* подня́ть на́ши бока́лы за (+ *acc.*). *Raise the standard of living,* поднима́ть у́ровень жи́зни. *Raise a hand against,* поднима́ть ру́ку на (+ *acc.*). **2,** (increase) повыша́ть: *raise prices/taxes,* повыша́ть це́ны/нало́ги. *Raise the stakes/ante,* повыша́ть ста́вку. **3,** (rear) воспи́тывать; расти́ть. **4,** (cultivate) выра́щивать: *raise corn,* выра́щивать кукуру́зу. **5,** (breed) разводи́ть: *raise* *sheep,* разводи́ть ове́ц. **6,** (make louder, as one's voice) повыша́ть. *Raise one's voice at,* повыша́ть го́лос на (+ *acc.*). **7,** (collect, as money) собира́ть. **8,** (bring up, as a question) поднима́ть; ста́вить; возбужда́ть; выдвига́ть. *Raise an objection,* выдвинуть возраже́ние; предъяви́ть прете́нзию. **9,** (evoke, as doubts) вызыва́ть; возбужда́ть. **10,** (lift; increase, as hopes) возбужда́ть. **11,** (cause; stir up) поднима́ть: *raise a fuss,* поднима́ть шум; *raise a rebellion,* поднима́ть восста́ние. **12,** (cause to form, as a blister) натира́ть. **13,** *math.* возводи́ть (в сте́пень). **14,** *Raise from the dead,* оживля́ть; воскреша́ть. —*n.* повыше́ние зарпла́ты; приба́вка (к зарпла́те); надба́вка (к зарпла́те).

raised *adj.* **1,** (lifted) по́днятый. *Raised eyebrows,* припо́днятые бро́ви. **2,** (embossed) рельє́фный; вы́пуклый: *raised design,* рельє́фный узо́р; *raised letters,* вы́пуклые бу́квы.

raisin *n.* изю́мина; изю́минка; *pl.* изю́м.

rajah *also,* **raja** *n.* ра́джа.

rake *n.* **1,** (garden tool) гра́бли. **2,** (roué) пове́са; распу́тник. —*v.t.* **1,** (gather or smooth with a rake) грести́; сгреба́ть. *Rake leaves,* сгреба́ть ли́стья. **2,** (spray with gunfire) простре́ливать. **3,** *fol. by* **in** (amass in large quantities) загреба́ть: *rake in money,* загреба́ть де́ньги лопа́той. **4,** *fol. by* **up** (dig up from the past) вороши́ть. —**rake over the coals,** зада́ть жа́ру (+ *dat.*); взять под обстре́л.

rakish *adj.* **1,** (jaunty) лихо́й. **2,** (dissolute) распу́тный.

rally *v.t.* **1,** (bring together for a common purpose) спла́чивать. **2,** (summon; muster) набира́ться: *rally one's forces,* набра́ться сил. —*v.i.* **1,** (unite) спла́чиваться: *rally around their leaders,* спла́чиваться вокру́г свои́х ли́деров. **2,** (show a sudden improvement) оправля́ться. —*n.* **1,** (mass meeting) ми́тинг; слёт. **2,** (sudden improvement) улучше́ние; попра́вка.

ram *n.* **1,** (male sheep) бара́н. **2,** (battering ram; hydraulic ram) тара́н. —*v.t.* **1,** (force into a narrow space; jam) забива́ть; вти́скивать. **2,** [*also intrans.* **ram into**] (crash or smash into) наскочи́ть на; налете́ть на; тара́нить.

ramble *v.i.* **1,** (wander) броди́ть. **2,** (speak aimlessly) загова́риваться. *He tends to ramble,* он ча́сто уклоня́ется от те́мы.

rambling *adj.* **1,** (wandering) бродя́чий. **2,** (disconnected) бессвя́зный.

rambunctious *adj.*, *colloq.* бу́йный; непоко́рный.

ramification *n.* **1,** (branch) разветвле́ние. **2,** *pl.* (consequences) после́дствия.

ramp *n.* **1,** (inclined passageway) скат. **2,** (movable staircase for an airplane) трап: *descend the ramp,* спуска́ться по тра́пу.

rampage *n.* бу́йство. —*v.i.* [*also,* **go on a rampage**] бу́йствовать; буя́нить; бесчи́нствовать.

rampant *adj.* **1,** (growing unchecked, as of plants) бу́йный. **2,** *fig.* (spreading unchecked) безу́держный: *rampant inflation,* безу́держная инфля́ция.

rampart *n.* крепостно́й вал.

ramrod *n.* шо́мпол. —**ramrod straight,** как арши́н проглоти́л.

ramshackle *adj.* ве́тхий; обветша́лый.

ranch *n.* ра́нчо.

rancid *adj.* прого́рклый. *Turn rancid,* (про)го́ркнуть.

rancor *also,* **rancour** *n.* зло́ба; озлобле́ние. —**rancorous,** *adj.* зло́бный; злопа́мятный.

random *adj.* случа́йный: *random shot,* случа́йный вы́стрел. —**at random,** науда́чу; науга́д; наобу́м.

random access произво́льная вы́борка.

range *n.* **1,** (scope; extent) разма́х: *range of activities,* разма́х де́ятельности. *Range of vision,* кругозо́р. **2,** (of a weapon, transmitter, etc.) да́льность; досяга́емость. *Within range,* в преде́лах досяга́емости. *Out of range,* вне досяга́емости. *The gun has a range of 500 meters,* ору́дие бьёт на пятьсо́т ме́тров. **3,** (of an aircraft, missile, etc.) ра́диус де́йствия; ра́диус полёта. **4,** (distance) расстоя́ние: *at close range,* на бли́зком расстоя́нии. *Fire at close range,* стреля́ть в упо́р. **5,** (variety) круг: *range of interests,* круг интере́сов; *a broad range of questions,* широ́кий круг вопро́сов. *Range of colors,* га́мма цвето́в. **6,** (limits of variation) преде́лы: *fluctuate within a narrow range,* колеба́ться в у́зких преде́лах. **7,** *music* диапазо́н. **8,** (of mountains) хребе́т; го́рная цепь. **9,** (place for shooting practice) стре́льбище; полиго́н. **10,** (large stove) плита́. **11,** (grazing land) па́стбище. —*v.t.* выстра́ивать в ряд. *They ranged themselves along the sidewalk,* они́ вы́строились вдоль тротуа́ра. *Various groups were ranged against us,* разли́чные гру́ппы выступа́ли про́тив нас. —*v.i.* **1,** (wander) ры́скать. **2,** (vary within stated limits) колеба́ться. *The children's ages range from two to six,* во́зраст дете́й — от двух до шести́. **3,** *fol. by* **over** (cover; take in) охва́тывать: *range over many topics,* охва́тывать мно́го предме́тов.

range finder дально́мер.

ranger *n.* **1,** (forest guard) лесни́к; объе́здчик. **2,** *mil.* диверса́нт.

rangy *adj.* долговя́зый.

rank *n.* **1,** (grade; position) зва́ние; чин; ранг. *The rank of admiral,* адмира́льское зва́ние; адмира́льский чин. *An official of lesser rank,* сотру́дник ме́ньшего ра́нга. *Persons of rank,* зна́тные лю́ди. **2,** (category) ряд: *a writer of the first rank,* писа́тель пе́рвого ря́да. **3,** (column) шере́нга; ряд. *Close ranks,* смыка́ть *or* спла́чивать ряды́. *Break ranks,* расходи́ться. **4,** *pl.* (armed forces) строй; ряды́. *Join the ranks,* стать в строй. *Serve in the ranks of the army,* служи́ть в ряда́х а́рмии. **5,** *pl.* (enlisted men) рядовы́е: *rise from the ranks,* выдвига́ться (из рядовы́х в офице́ры). **6,** *pl.* (body of people) ряды́: *the ranks of the unemployed,* ряды́ безрабо́тных. *Take into their ranks,* принима́ть в свои́ ряды́. —*v.t.* **1,** (evaluate relative to each other) дава́ть оце́нку (+ *dat.*). **2,** *fol. by* **among** (consider; number) относи́ть к числу́ (+ *gen.*); причисля́ть к; ста́вить в ряду́ (+ *gen.*). —*v.i.* стоя́ть: *rank first,* стоя́ть на пе́рвом ме́сте. *Rank on a par with,* стоя́ть в одно́м ряду́ с; быть наравне́ с. *Rank among the finest,* принадлежа́ть к числу́ са́мых лу́чших. *A major ranks above a captain,* майо́р по чи́ну (*or* по зва́нию) вы́ше капита́на. —*adj.* **1,** (luxuriant) роско́шный; бу́йный. **2,** (rancid) прого́рклый. **3,** (utter; gross) я́вный; су́щий. *Rank ingratitude,* чёрная неблагода́рность. *Rank injustice,* вопию́щая несправедли́вость. —**rank and file,** *mil.* рядово́й соста́в.

ranking *adj.* ста́рший.

rankle *v.i.* му́чить; глода́ть: *The memory still rankles,* воспомина́ние об э́том ещё му́чит/гло́жет меня́.

ransack *v.t.* **1,** (search thoroughly) ры́ться в; обша́ривать. **2,** (rob and leave in disarray) разгра́бить.

ransom *n.* вы́куп: *hold for ransom,* тре́бовать вы́купа за (+ *acc.*). —*v.t.* выкупа́ть.

rant *v.i.* неи́стовствовать; бесснова́ться; безу́мствовать. —**rant and rave,** рвать и мета́ть; мета́ть гро́мы и мо́лнии.

rap *n.* **1,** (quick, sharp blow) уда́р. **2,** (tapping sound) стук. **3,** *slang* (blame; punishment) наказа́ние: *beat the rap,* избежа́ть наказа́ния. *Take the rap for,* отдува́ться за (кого́-нибудь). —*v.t. & i.* ударя́ть (по); стуча́ть (в). —**not give/care a rap,** *colloq.* наплева́ть: *I don't give a rap,* мне наплева́ть на э́то.

rapacious *adj.* хи́щный.

rape *n.* **1,** (sexual violation) изнаси́лование. **2,** (plant) рапс; суре́пица. —*v.t.* наси́ловать. —**rape oil,** ра́псовое ма́сло; суре́пное ма́сло.

rapid *adj.* бы́стрый; стреми́тельный. *Rapid growth,* бу́рный рост. *Rapid pulse,* ча́стый пульс. —**rapidity,** *n.* быстрота́. —**rapidly,** *adv.* бы́стро.

rapids *n.pl.* поро́ги; стремни́на; быстрина́.

rapier *n.* рапи́ра.

rapist *n.* наси́льник.

rapport *n.* взаимопонима́ние; согла́сие.

rapprochement *n.* сближе́ние.

rapt *adj.* **1,** (enraptured) восхищённый. **2,** (engrossed) поглощённый. *Rapt attention,* напряжённое *or* при́стальное *or* сосредото́ченное внима́ние.

rapture *n.* восто́рг; упое́ние. —**rapturous,** *adj.* восто́рженный.

rara avis бе́лая воро́на.

rare *adj.* **1,** (uncommon) ре́дкий: *rare book/stamp/bird,* ре́дкая кни́га/ма́рка/пти́ца. **2,** (lightly cooked) с кро́вью; крова́вый. *I like my meat rare,* я предпочита́ю мя́со с кро́вью.

rarefy *v.t.* разрежа́ть. —**rarefied,** *adj.* разрежённый.

rarely *adv.* ре́дко.

rarity *n.* ре́дкость: *a great rarity,* больша́я ре́дкость.

rascal *n.* **1,** (scoundrel) подле́ц. **2,** (imp) постре́л; плути́шка.

rash *adj.* опроме́тчивый; необду́манный; безрассу́дный. —*n.* сыпь. *Heat rash,* потни́ца.

rasher *n.* ло́мтик беко́на.

rashly *adv.* опроме́тчиво; безрассу́дно.

rashness *n.* опроме́тчивость; безрассу́дство.

rasp *v.t.* скрести́. —*v.i.* скрипе́ть. —*n.* **1,** (sound) скре́жет. **2,** (tool) ра́шпиль.

raspberry *n.* мали́на. —*adj.* мали́новый: *raspberry jam,* мали́новое варе́нье.

rasping *adj.* скрипу́чий.

rat *n.* **1,** (rodent) кры́са. **2,** (contemptible person) гад. —*adj.* кры́синый: *rat poison,* кры́синый яд. —**smell a rat,** чу́ять недо́брое.

ratchet *n.* храпови́к; трещо́тка. —**ratchet wheel,** храпово́е колесо́.

rate *n.* **1,** (measurement relative to a standard) ста́вка; курс: *rate of interest,* ста́вка проце́нта; *wage rate,* ста́вка зарпла́ты. *Rate of exchange,* валю́тный курс. *The rate of the ruble to the dollar,* курс рубля́ по отноше́нию к до́ллару. *Rate of return,* но́рма при́были. *Birth rate,* рожда́емость. *Death rate,* сме́ртность. **2,** *often pl.* (price; cost) тари́ф; расце́нка. *Postal rates,* почто́вый тари́ф. *Advertising rates,* расце́нка объявле́ний. *Subscription rate,* цена́ подпи́ски; подписна́я цена́. **3,** (pace) темп: *rate of growth,* темп ро́ста. *Pulse rate,* частота́ пу́льса. *At this rate we'll never get there,* при тако́м те́мпе мы никогда́ не доберёмся. —*v.t.* **1,** (evaluate) оце́нивать. **2,** (consider; regard) счита́ть. **3,** *colloq.* (deserve) заслу́живать. —*v.i.* счита́ться: *He rates among the best,* он счита́ется одни́м из са́мых лу́чших. —**at any rate,** во вся́ком слу́чае.

rather *adv.* **1,** (fairly) дово́льно: *rather interesting,* дово́льно интере́сный. **2,** (preferably) скоре́е. *I would rather...,* я бы предпочёл (+ *inf.*). *I'd rather not say,* я бы предпочёл об э́том не говори́ть. *Which would you rather have?,* что вы предпочита́ете?; чего́ вам бо́льше хо́чется? **3,** (more correctly) верне́е; точне́е: *her sister, or rather her stepsister,* её сестра́, и́ли верне́е/точне́е, сво́дная сестра́. —**rather than,** вме́сто того́, чтобы...

rathole *n.* кры́синая нора́.

ratify *v.t.* ратифици́ровать. —**ratification,** *n.* ратифика́ция.

rating *n.* **1,** (evaluation) оце́нка. **2,** (numerical indicator of something) рейтинг. **3,** (scolding) нагоня́й.

ratio *n.* отноше́ние; соотноше́ние; коэффицие́нт. *The ratio of women to men,* соотноше́ние же́нщин и мужчи́н.

ration *n.* паёк; рацио́н. *Monthly ration,* ме́сячный паёк. *Meager rations,* ску́дный паёк. —*v.t.* нормирова́ть. *Bread is rationed,* хлеб выдаётся по ка́рточкам *or* по тало́нам. —**ration card,** продово́льственная ка́рточка; тало́н. *See also* **rationing.**

rational *adj.* **1,** (able to reason; reasonable) разу́мный; рассу́дочный; рациона́льный. *Man is a rational being,* челове́к — разу́мное существо́. **2,** *math.* рациона́льный.

rationale *n.* моти́в: *the rationale behind a decision,* моти́в для реше́ния.

rationalism *n.* рационали́зм. —**rationalist,** *n.* рационали́ст. —**rationalistic,** *adj.* рационалисти́ческий.

rationality *n.* рациона́льность.

rationalize *v.t.* **1,** (give plausible excuses for) опра́вдывать. **2,** (apply modern methods of efficiency to) рационализи́ровать.

rationally *adv.* разу́мно.

rationing *n.* ка́рточная систе́ма; нормирова́ние. *Introduce rationing,* вводи́ть ка́рточную систе́му.

rattan *n.* рота́нг. —*adj.* рота́нговый.

rattle *v.i.* **1,** (shake with quick sharp sounds) дребезжа́ть. **2,** (move with such sounds) громыха́ть: *rattle along the road,* громыха́ть по доро́ге. —*v.t.* **1,** (shake noisily) греме́ть: *rattle the dishes,* греме́ть посу́дой. *The wind rattled the windows,* стёкла дребезжа́ли от ве́тра. **2,** *colloq.* (fluster) сбива́ть с то́лку. *Get rattled,* (рас)теря́ться. **3,** *fol. by* **off** (recite rapidly) отбараба́нить. —*n.* **1,** (sound) дребезжа́ние. **2,** (sound in one's throat) хрип: *death rattle,* предсме́ртный хрип. **3,** (baby's toy) погрему́шка. **4,** (noisemaker) трещо́тка.

rattlesnake *n.* грему́чая змея́.

rattletrap *n.* колыма́га.

rattrap *n.* крысоло́вка.

raucous *adj.* **1,** (loud and harsh) хри́плый; ре́зкий. **2,** (rowdy; disorderly) шумли́вый; бу́йный.

ravage *v.t.* разоря́ть; опустоша́ть. *War-ravaged country,* страна́, разорённая *or* опустошённая войно́й. —*n., usu. pl.* опустоши́тельное де́йствие: *the ravages of time,* опустоши́тельное де́йствие вре́мени.

rave *v.i.* **1,** (speak incoherently) бре́дить. **2,** *fol. by* **about** (praise enthusiastically) быть в восто́рге от; расхва́ливать. —*adj., colloq.* восто́рженный: *rave notices,* восто́рженные о́тзывы.

ravel *v.t.* **1,** (fray) обтрепа́ть. **2,** (disentangle) распу́тывать. —*v.i.* обтрепа́ться.

raven *n.* во́рон. —*adj.* чёрный как смоль.

ravenous *adj.* **1,** (voracious; gluttonous) прожо́рливый. *Ravenous appetite,* во́лчий аппети́т. **2,** (rapacious) хи́щный.

ravine *n.* ущé́лье; овра́г.

raving *adj.* **1,** (wild) бу́йный: *raving maniac,* бу́йный сумасше́дший. **2,** (ravishing) восхити́тельный. —*n., often pl.* бред; бре́дни.

ravish *v.t.* **1,** (enrapture) восхища́ть. **2,** (rape) растлева́ть. —**ravishing,** *adj.* восхити́тельный.

raw *adj.* **1,** (uncooked) сыро́й: *raw vegetables,* сырье́ о́вощи. **2,** (untreated; unprocessed) необрабо́танный: *raw data,* необрабо́танные да́нные. ♦ *Often rendered by* -сыре́ц: *raw silk,* шёлк-сыре́ц; *raw whisky,* спирт-сыре́ц. **3,** (cold and damp) сыро́й. **4,** (exposed; irritated) обо́дранный. *Raw wound,* жива́я ра́на. **5,** (untrained) зелёный. **6,** (bawdy) са́льный. —**in the raw,** нагишо́м.

rawboned *adj.* костля́вый.

rawhide *n.* сыромя́ть. —*adj.* сыромя́тный.

raw material сырьё.

ray *n.* **1,** (beam, as of light) луч. **2,** *pl.* (radiation) лучи́: *gamma rays,* га́мма-лучи́. **3,** (glimmer, as of hope) луч; и́скра; про́блеск (наде́жды). **4,** (fish) скат.

rayon *n.* иску́сственный шёлк; виско́за.

raze *v.t.* сноси́ть; срыва́ть (*pfv.* срыть); сровня́ть с землёй; разруша́ть до основа́ния.

razor *n.* бри́тва. —**razor blade,** ле́звие бри́твы.

re *n., music* ре.

reach *v.t.* **1,** (get to) достига́ть; доходи́ть до; доезжа́ть до; (*with difficulty*) добира́ться до. *Reach the opposite shore,* дости́гнуть противополо́жного бе́рега. *Reach one's destination,* добра́ться до ме́ста назначе́ния. *The letter/news did not reach me,*

письмо́/изве́стие до меня́ не дошло́. **2,** (extend as far as) доходи́ть до: *Her dress reaches the floor,* её пла́тье дохо́дит до по́ла. **3,** *fol. by* **out** (extend, as one's hand) протя́гивать. **4,** (be able to touch) достава́ть до; дотя́гиваться до. **5,** (obtain and hand over) передава́ть: *Reach me the salt,* переда́йте, пожа́луйста, соль. **6,** (attain) достига́ть: *reach one's goal,* достига́ть свое́й це́ли. *Reach supersonic speed,* достига́ть сверхзвуково́й ско́рости. **7,** (come to, as a conclusion or agreement) приходи́ть к. **8,** (get in touch with, as by phone) связа́ться с; дозвони́ться к. —*v.i.* **1,** *often fol. by* **out** (extend one's hand) протя́гивать ру́ку. *Reach across the table,* тяну́ться че́рез стол. *Reach into one's pocket,* тяну́ться *or* лезть в карма́н. *I can't reach that high,* я не могу́ дотя́гиваться так высоко́. *A hand reached out from the crowd,* из толпы́ протяну́лась рука́. **2,** *fol. by* **for** (attempt to grasp) тяну́ться за *or* к. —*n.* **1,** (range) досяга́емость: *within reach,* в преде́лах досяга́емости; *out of reach,* вне досяга́емости. **2,** *pl.* (of a river) тече́ние: *the upper reaches of the Volga,* ве́рхнее тече́ние Во́лги; верхо́вье Во́лги.

react *v.i.* реаги́ровать.

reaction *n.* реа́кция. —**chain reaction,** цепна́я реа́кция.

reactionary *adj.* реакцио́нный. —*n.* реакционе́р.

reactivate *v.t.* **1,** (restore to service) вводи́ть вновь в де́йствие *or* в эксплуата́цию; расконсерви́ровать. **2,** *mil.* сно́ва сформирова́ть.

reactive *adj.* реакти́вный.

reactor *n.* реа́ктор.

read *v.t. & i.* чита́ть: *read a book/letter,* чита́ть кни́гу/письмо́. *Read music,* чита́ть но́ты. *Read aloud,* чита́ть вслух. *Know how to read,* уме́ть чита́ть. *Read to the children,* чита́ть де́тям. *Read someone's lips,* чита́ть с чьи́х-нибудь губ. *Read someone's mind,* чита́ть чьи-нибудь мы́сли. ♦ *Other meanings:* —*v.t.* **1,** (make out) разбира́ть: *read someone's handwriting,* разбира́ть чей-нибудь по́черк. **2,** (interpret) оце́нивать; истолко́вывать. *I read the situation differently,* я оце́ниваю ситуа́цию ина́че; я истолко́вываю э́то ина́че. **3,** (take a reading of, as a meter) снима́ть показа́ния (счётчика). **4,** (indicate; register) пока́зывать: *The thermometer reads 40°,* термо́метр пока́зывает со́рок гра́дусов. **5,** *Brit.* (study) изуча́ть: *read law,* изуча́ть пра́во. —*v.i.* **1,** (have a particular wording) гласи́ть; говори́ться: *The telegram reads as follows,* телегра́мма гласи́т сле́дующее; в телегра́мме говори́тся сле́дующее. **2,** (admit of being read) чита́ться: *The book reads like a detective story,* кни́га чита́ется как детекти́в. —**read between the lines,** чита́ть ме́жду строк. —**read out,** зачи́тывать; оглаша́ть. —**read out of,** исключа́ть из. —**read over; read through,** прочита́ть. —**read up on,** почита́ть о.

readable *adj.* удобочита́емый. *The book is very readable,* кни́га легко́ чита́ется.

readdress *v.t.* переадресо́вывать.

reader *n.* **1,** (person who reads) чита́тель. *He is a slow/avid reader,* он ме́дленно чита́ет; он чита́ет запоём. **2,** (professional reciter) чтец. **3,** *Brit.* (lecturer) ле́ктор. **4,** (textbook) хрестома́тия.

readership *n.* круг чита́телей.

readily *adv.* **1,** (willingly; promptly) охо́тно. **2,** (easily) легко́; без труда́.

readiness *n.* гото́вность. *Hold in readiness,* держа́ть нагото́ве. *All is in readiness,* всё гото́во.

reading *n.* **1,** (act of reading; recital) чте́ние: *on the first reading,* в пе́рвом чте́нии. **2,** (interpretation) толкова́ние. **3,** (indication on a meter) показа́ния; отсчёт. —**reading desk,** пюпи́тр. —**reading glasses,** очки́ для чте́ния. —**reading room,** чита́льный зал; чита́льня.

readjust *v.t.* (сно́ва) регули́ровать. —*v.i.* приспособля́ться (к). —**readjustment,** *n.* приспособле́ние.

readout *n.* счи́тывание информа́ции.

ready *adj.* гото́вый: *Are you ready?,* вы гото́вы? *Ready for use,* гото́вый для употребле́ния. *Ready for takeoff,* гото́вый к вы́лету. *Ready for anything,* гото́в ко всему́. *Ready (i.e. willing) to do anything,* гото́в на всё. *Get ready to leave,* гото́виться к отъе́зду. *Get ready to go to work,* собира́ться на рабо́ту. *Ready cash,* нали́чные де́ньги. —*v.t.* гото́вить. —**at the ready,** на изгото́вку.

ready-made *adj.* гото́вый: *ready-made clothes,* гото́вая оде́жда.

reaffirm *v.t.* вновь подтвержда́ть.

reagent *n.* реакти́в; реаге́нт.

real *adj.* **1,** (actual; existing) действи́тельный; реа́льный: *the real world,* действи́тельный *or* реа́льный мир. *Real life,* действи́тельная *or* реа́льная *or* настоя́щая *or* жива́я жизнь. **2,** (genuine) настоя́щий; натура́льный. *Real flowers,* живы́е цветы́. **3,** (true, as of a friend, reason, etc.) настоя́щий; и́стинный. —*adv., colloq.* о́чень: *get up real early,* встава́ть о́чень ра́но. —**real estate,** недви́жимое иму́щество; недви́жимость. —**real number,** действи́тельное число́. —**real wages,** реа́льная за́работная пла́та.

realign *v.t.* перестра́ивать. —**realignment,** *n.* перестро́йка; перестано́вка.

realism *n.* реали́зм. —**realist,** *n.* реали́ст. —**realistic,** *adj.* реалисти́ческий; реа́льный.

reality *n.* действи́тельность; реа́льность. *Become a reality,* стать действи́тельностью. —**in reality,** в действи́тельности; на са́мом де́ле.

realization *n.* **1,** (recognition; awareness) понима́ние; созна́ние; осозна́ние. **2,** (becoming a reality) осуществле́ние; реализа́ция.

realize *v.t.* **1,** (be or become aware of) понима́ть; созна́вать; осознава́ть; представля́ть; отдава́ть себе́ отчёт в. *Realize one's mistake,* созна́ть *or* осозна́ть свою́ оши́бку. *I realize you're in a hurry,* я понима́ю, что вы спеши́те. *Many people do not yet realize that...,* мно́гие лю́ди ещё не представля́ют, что... **2,** (achieve; bring about) осуществля́ть; реализова́ть. *Realize one's dream,* осуществи́ть свою́ мечту́. *Be realized,* осуществля́ться; сбыва́ться. **3,** (gain; obtain) получа́ть; выруча́ть. *Realize a profit,* получи́ть при́быль. *The money realized from the sale,* де́ньги, вы́рученные от прода́жи.

really *adv.* **1,** (actually; in actual fact) действи́тельно; на са́мом де́ле. *Better than it really is,* лу́чше чем оно́ есть на са́мом де́ле. *No one really knows,* никто́ то́лком не зна́ет. **2,** (truly; indeed) действи́тельно; в са́мом де́ле. *The meal really turned out well,* еда́ в са́мом де́ле оказа́лась хоро́шей. —**really?,** неуже́ли?: *Do you really think that....?,* неуже́ли вы ду́маете, что...? *Did I really say that?,* неужели я это говори́л(а).

realm *n.* **1,** (kingdom) короле́вство; ца́рство. **2,** (sphere) о́бласть; сфе́ра.

realtor *n.* аге́нт по прода́же недви́жимости. —**realty,** *n.* недви́жимое иму́щество.

ream *n.* **1,** (quantity of paper) стопа́. **2,** *usu. pl., colloq.* (large amount) ма́сса; ку́ча; у́йма.

reamer *n.* развёртка.

reap *v.t.* **1,** (cut; gather) жать. **2,** *fig.* (gain as a reward) пожина́ть: *reap the benefits of,* пожина́ть плоды́ (+ gen.).

reaper *n.* **1,** (one who reaps) жнец. **2,** (reaping machine) жа́твенная маши́на; жа́тка; жне́йка.

reappear *v.i.* сно́ва появля́ться.

reapportion *v.t.* перераспределя́ть. —**reapportionment,** *n.* перераспределе́ние.

reappraise *v.t.* переоце́нивать; пересма́тривать. —**reappraisal,** *n.* переоце́нка; пересмо́тр.

rear *n.* **1,** (back part) за́дняя часть; зад. *In the rear of the hall,* в за́дней ча́сти за́ла. *From the rear,* сза́ди. **2,** (tail end) хвост: *at the rear of the column,* в хвосте́ коло́нны. **3,** *mil.* тыл. —*adj.* **1,** (back) за́дний: *rear wheel,* за́днее колесо́. **2,** (from the back): *rear view,* вид сза́ди. **3,** (located in the back part of a house) чёрный: *rear door,* чёрный ход. **4,** *mil.* тылово́й. —*v.t.* **1,** (elevate) поднима́ть: *rear one's head,* поднима́ть го́лову. **2,** (raise; bring up) воспи́тывать; расти́ть. —*v.i.* (of a horse) станови́ться на дыбы́. —**bring up the rear,** замыка́ть ше́ствие; *mil.* быть в обо́зе.

rear admiral контр-адмира́л.

rear end 1, (tail end) хвост. **2,** (buttocks) зад.

rear guard арьерга́рд. —**rearguard,** *adj.* арьерга́рдный.

rearm *v.t.* перевооружа́ть. —*v.i.* перевооружа́ться. —**rearmament,** *n.* перевооруже́ние.

rearrange *v.t.* **1,** (move around) переставля́ть: *rearrange the furniture,* переставля́ть ме́бель. **2,** *music* перекла́дывать. —**rearrangement,** *n.* перестано́вка.

rear-view mirror зе́ркало за́днего ви́да.

rearward *adv.* наза́д. —*adj.* за́дний; обра́тный.

reason *n.* **1,** (cause; motive) причи́на. *By reason of...,* по причи́не (+ gen.). *For the reason that...,* по той причи́не, что... *For some reason or other,* по той и́ли ино́й причи́не. *For no reason,* без вся́кой причи́ны. *The reason he left,* причи́на, по кото́рой он ушёл. *What is the reason for this?,* в чём причи́на? *There are several reasons for this,* причи́н (к) тому́ не́сколько. *That is not the only reason,* не то́лько поэ́тому. *He gave no reason for his decision,* он не объясни́л своего́ реше́ния. *Give me a reason!,* объясни́те почему́! **2,** (basis; justification) основа́ние:

with good reason, с по́лным основа́нием. *There is reason to believe that...,* есть основа́ние полага́ть, что... **3,** (ability to think) ра́зум; рассу́док. **4,** (common sense; sanity) рассу́док: *devoid of reason,* лишён рассу́дка. —*v.i.* **1,** (think logically) рассужда́ть. **2,** *fol. by* with (try to persuade) урезо́нивать. —*v.t.* рассуди́ть: *He reasoned that...,* он рассуди́л, что... —**bring to reason,** образу́мить; урезо́нить; наводи́ть на ум. —**listen to reason,** прислу́шиваться к го́лосу рассу́дка. —**stand to reason,** само́ собо́й разуме́ться. —**within reason,** разу́мный: *any offer within reason,* вся́кое разу́мное предложе́ние.

reasonable *adj.* **1,** (amenable to reason; logical) разу́мный; рассуди́тельный; благоразу́мный. *Be reasonable!,* бу́дьте благоразу́мным! *It is reasonable to assume that...,* резо́нно предположи́ть, что... **2,** (fair; within reason) разу́мный: *a reasonable offer,* разу́мное предложе́ние. **3,** (fair; pretty good) неплохо́й: *reasonable prospects,* неплохи́е перспекти́вы. **4,** (not excessive) досту́пный: *reasonable prices,* досту́пные це́ны. **5,** (not expensive) недорого́й.

reasonably *adv.* **1,** (sensibly) разу́мно. **2,** (fairly) дово́льно: *reasonably well,* дово́льно хорошо́. *Reasonably certain,* бо́лее и́ли ме́нее уве́рен(а).

reasoning *n.* рассужде́ние: *sound reasoning,* здра́вое рассужде́ние. *Line of reasoning,* аргумента́ция.

reassess *v.t.* переоце́нивать; пересма́тривать. —**reassessment,** *n.* переоце́нка; пересмо́тр.

reassign *v.t.* назнача́ть (*or* переводи́ть) на но́вую до́лжность. *He was reassigned to headquarters,* его́ перевели́ в штаб. —**reassignment,** *n.* назначе́ние на но́вую до́лжность.

reassure *v.t.* ободря́ть; обнадёживать. —**reassurance,** *n.* ободре́ние. —**reassuring,** *adj.* ободри́тельный; обадря́ющий; успокои́тельный.

rebandage *v.t.* перебинтова́ть.

rebate *n.* **1,** (discount) ски́дка. **2,** (refund) возвра́т.

rebel *v.i.* восстава́ть; бунтова́ть. *Rebel against one's oppressors,* восста́ть про́тив свои́х угнета́телей. —*n.* повста́нец; бунта́рь; бунто́вщи́к; мяте́жник. —*adj.* повста́нческий; мяте́жный: *rebel troops,* повста́нческие/мяте́жные войска́.

rebellion *n.* восста́ние; бунт; мяте́ж.

rebellious *adj.* **1,** (inclined to rebel) мяте́жный. **2,** (opposing any control) непоко́рный. —**rebelliousness,** *n.* непоко́рность.

rebirth *n.* возрожде́ние.

reborn *adj. Be reborn,* возрожда́ться.

rebound *v.i.* отска́кивать. —*n.* рикоше́т. *On the rebound,* рикоше́том.

rebuff *n.* отпо́р. —*v.t.* дать отпо́р (+ *dat.*).

rebuild *v.t.* перестра́ивать; (за́ново) отстра́ивать.

rebuke *n.* упрёк; вы́говор; замеча́ние; о́тповедь. —*v.t.* упрека́ть: *rebuke someone for his remark,* упрекну́ть кого́-нибудь за своё замеча́ние.

reburial *n.* перезахороне́ние.

rebury *v.t.* перехорони́ть; перезахорони́ть.

rebus *n.* ре́бус.

rebut *v.t.* опроверга́ть. —**rebuttal,** *n.* опроверже́ние.

recalcitrant *adj.* непоко́рный. —**recalcitrance,** *n.* непоко́рность.

recall *v.t.* **1,** (summon back) отзыва́ть: *recall an ambassador,* отозва́ть посла́. **2,** (remember) по́мнить; вспо́мнить. **3,** (reminisce about) вспомина́ть. **4,** (bring back to mind) напомина́ть. —*n.* **1,** (summons to return) отзы́в. **2,** (ability to remember) па́мять.

recant *v.t.* отрека́ться от. —*v.i.* (публи́чно) ка́яться.

recapitulate *v.t. & i.* сумми́ровать; резюми́ровать. —**recapitulation,** *n.* сумми́рование; резюме́.

recapture *v.t.* брать обра́тно; сно́ва захва́тывать; отбива́ть.

recarve *v.t. Recarve the map of the world,* перекра́ивать ка́рту ми́ра.

recast *v.t.* **1,** (remold) перелива́ть. **2,** (rework) переде́лывать.

recede *v.i.* **1,** (move back) отступа́ть: *recede into the background,* отступа́ть на за́дний план. **2,** (subside, as of floodwaters) убыва́ть; сбыва́ть; идти́ на у́быль. —**receding forehead,** пока́тый лоб.

receipt *n.* **1,** (act of receiving) получе́ние: *upon receipt of,* по получе́нии (+ *gen.*). *Acknowledge receipt of,* подтверди́ть получе́ние (+ *gen.*). **2,** (note acknowledging payment) распи́ска; квита́нция. **3,** *pl.* (proceeds; income) вы́ручка; поступле́ния. *Box-office receipts,* сбо́ры.

receivable *adj.* подлежа́щий упла́те.

receive *v.t.* **1,** (get; have inflicted on one) получа́ть: *receive permission,* получи́ть разреше́ние; *receive a blow,* получи́ть уда́р. **2,** (admit; greet) принима́ть: *receive guests,* принима́ть госте́й. **3,** (pick up, as a signal) принима́ть. **4,** (deal in, as stolen goods) укрыва́ть.

receiver *n.* **1,** (part of a telephone) тру́бка. **2,** (instrument for receiving signals) приёмник.

recent *adj.* **1,** (having just occurred) неда́вний: *recent trip/attempt,* неда́вняя пое́здка/попы́тка. **2,** (just past) после́дний: *in recent years,* в *or* за после́дние го́ды. *The events of recent weeks,* собы́тия после́дних неде́ль.

recently *adv.* неда́вно; в *or* за после́днее вре́мя. *Until recently,* до неда́внего вре́мени. —**as recently as,** ещё; не да́лее как: *as recently as last year,* ещё/ не да́лее как/ в про́шлом году́.

receptacle *n.* **1,** (container) вмести́лище. **2,** *bot.* цветоло́же.

reception *n.* **1,** (social gathering; manner of being received) приём: *at a reception honoring...,* на приёме в честь (+ *gen.*). *He was given a warm reception,* ему́ оказа́ли тёплый приём. **2,** *radio; television* приём. *Poor reception,* плохо́й приём; плоха́я слы́шимость. —**reception room,** приёмная.

receptionist *n.* секрета́рша (в приёмной).

receptive *adj.* восприи́мчивый. —**receptivity; receptiveness,** *n.* восприи́мчивость.

recess *n.* **1,** (short break between sessions) переры́в. **2,** (break between school terms or legislative sessions) кани́кулы. *Summer recess,* ле́тние кани́кулы. *Parliament is in recess,* парла́мент распу́щен на кани́-

кулы. **3,** (hollow place) углубле́ние. **4,** *usu. pl.* (inner place, as of the heart) тайни́к. —*v.t.* **1,** (set back into a recess) отодвига́ть наза́д. **2,** (adjourn) закрыва́ть. —*v.i.* де́лать переры́в; закрыва́ться на кани́кулы.

recession *n.* спад.

recessive *adj.* рецесси́вный.

recharge *v.t.* перезаряжа́ть.

rechristen *v.t.* перекре́щивать.

recidivism *n.* рецидиви́зм. —**recidivist,** *n.* рецидиви́ст.

recipe *n.* реце́пт.

recipient *n.* получа́тель.

reciprocal *adj.* взаи́мный; обою́дный. —*n., math.* обра́тная величина́.

reciprocate *v.t.* отвеча́ть. *Reciprocate someone's feelings,* отвеча́ть на чьи-нибудь чу́вства; отвеча́ть кому́-нибудь взаи́мностью. —*v.i.* отпла́чивать: *We would like to reciprocate somehow,* нам бы хоте́лось вам че́м-то отплати́ть. —**reciprocating engine,** поршнево́й дви́гатель.

reciprocity *n.* взаи́мность; обою́дность.

recital *n.* **1,** (narration) изложе́ние. **2,** *music* конце́рт: *piano recital,* фортепья́нный конце́рт.

recitation *n.* **1,** (public reading) деклама́ция. *Recitation of poetry,* чте́ние стихо́в. **2,** (school exercise) отве́т (уро́ка).

recitative *n., music* речитати́в.

recite *v.t.* чита́ть; деклами́ровать. *Recite poetry,* чита́ть стихи́. *Recite one's prayers,* чита́ть моли́твы. *Recite one's lesson,* отвеча́ть уро́к. —**reciter,** *n.* деклама́тор.

reckless *adj.* безрассу́дный. —**recklessly,** *adv.* безрассу́дно. —**recklessness,** *n.* безрассу́дство.

reckon *v.t.* **1,** (figure; compute) счита́ть; подсчи́тывать. **2,** (regard) счита́ть; рассма́тривать. **3,** *colloq.* (think; suppose) ду́мать; полага́ть. —**reckon on,** рассчи́тывать на. —**reckon with, 1,** (settle accounts with) распла́чиваться с. **2,** (take into account) счита́ться с.

reckoning *n.* расчёт; счёт. —**day of reckoning,** день (*or* час) распла́ты. —**dead reckoning,** счисле́ние пути́.

reclaim *v.t.* **1,** (claim back) тре́бовать обра́тно. **2,** (cultivate, as land) поднима́ть; осва́ивать.

reclamation *n.* мелиора́ция.

recline *v.i.* полулежа́ть.

recluse *n.* затво́рник; отше́льник.

recognition *n.* **1,** (identification) узнава́ние. *Beyond recognition,* неузнава́емо; до неузнава́емости. **2,** (acknowledgment; acclaim) призна́ние: *gain recognition,* получи́ть призна́ние. *In recognition of his services,* в знак призна́ния его́ заслу́г.

recognize *v.t.* **1,** (identify from previous contact) узнава́ть: *I hardly recognize you,* я с трудо́м узна́л(а) вас. **2,** (formally acknowledge) признава́ть: *recognize a new nation,* признава́ть но́вую страну́. *A recognized authority,* при́знанный авторите́т. **3,** (realize; be aware of) сознава́ть: *recognize the danger,* сознава́ть опа́сность. **4,** (give the floor to) дава́ть *or* предоставля́ть сло́во (+ *dat.*).

recoil *v.i.* **1,** (shrink back) отска́кивать; отпря́нуть; отшатну́ться. **2,** (of a firearm) отдава́ть; отка́тываться. —*n.* отда́ча; отка́т. —**recoilless,** *adj.* безотка́тный.

recollect *v.t.* вспомина́ть; припомина́ть.

recollection *n.* **1,** (capacity to remember) па́мять: *within my recollection,* на мое́й па́мяти. *To the best of my recollection,* наско́лько я по́мню. **2,** (something remembered) воспомина́ние.

recommend *v.t.* рекомендова́ть: *recommend someone for a position / for admission to a club/,* рекомендова́ть кого́-нибудь на до́лжность/ в клуб/. *Recommend someone for promotion,* выдвига́ть кого́-нибудь (на повыше́ние). *Recommend someone for an award,* представля́ть кого́-нибудь к награ́де. *Can you recommend a good doctor?,* мо́жете ли вы порекомендова́ть мне хоро́шего врача́? *You were recommended to me by...,* вас мне рекомендова́л(а)... *That is not recommended,* э́то не рекоменду́ется.

recommendation *n.* рекоменда́ция. *On/at your recommendation,* по ва́шей рекоменда́ции. —**letter of recommendation,** рекоменда́тельное письмо́.

recompense *v.t.* вознагражда́ть; компенси́ровать. —*n.* вознагражде́ние; компенса́ция.

reconcile *v.t.* **1,** (restore to good terms; make content) мири́ть; примиря́ть. *They became reconciled,* они́ примири́лись. *Become reconciled to; reconcile oneself to,* мири́ться с; примиря́ться с. **2,** (adjust; resolve) ула́живать: *reconcile differences,* ула́живать разногла́сия. *Reconcile contradictions,* примиря́ть противоре́чия.

reconciliation *n.* **1,** (bringing or coming together) примире́ние. **2,** (adjustment, as of differences) ула́живание.

recondite *adj.* замыслова́тый; мудрёный.

recondition *v.t.* ремонти́ровать.

reconnaissance *n.* разве́дка; рекогносциро́вка. —*adj.* разве́дывательный.

reconnoiter *also,* **reconnoitre** *v.t.* разве́дывать; рекогносци́ровать. —*v.i.* вести́ разве́дку.

reconsider *v.t.* пересма́тривать. —*v.i.* переду́мывать: *Won't you reconsider?,* вы не переду́маете?; а, мо́жет быть, переду́маете? —**reconsideration,** *n.* пересмо́тр.

reconstruct *v.t.* **1,** (rebuild) перестра́ивать; реконструи́ровать. **2,** (put together from clues) восстана́вливать; воссоздава́ть.

reconstruction *n.* перестро́йка; реконстру́кция. *Period of reconstruction,* восстанови́тельный пери́од.

reconvene *v.i.* сно́ва собира́ться.

recook *v.t.* перева́ривать.

record *n.* **1,** (written account) за́пись; учёт: *keep record of,* вести́ за́пись/учёт (+ *gen.*). **2,** (official account of proceedings) протоко́л. **3,** (recorded facts about someone) спи́сок: *work record,* трудово́й *or* послужно́й спи́сок. *Attendance record,* посеща́емость. *Criminal record,* уголо́вное про́шлое; суди́мости. **4,** (best achievement) реко́рд: *the record for the 100-meter dash,* реко́рд в бе́ге на сто ме́тров. **5,** (for a phonograph) пласти́нка; грампласти́нка. —*adj.* реко́рдный: *a* *record number of...,* рекóрдное числó (+ *gen.*). *In record time,* с рекóрдным врéменем; в рекóрдный срок. *Record harvest,* небывáло высóкий урожáй. —*v.t.* **1,** (set down in writing; keep a record of) запи́сывать; регистри́ровать. *Record one's impressions in a notebook,* запи́сывать свои́ впечатлéния в тетрáдь (*or* в тетрáди). *A seismograph records earthquakes,* сейсмóграф регистри́рует землетрясéния. *Last year more than 100 such incidents were recorded,* в прóшлом годý бы́ло зарегистри́ровано бóлее ста таки́х слýчаев. **2,** (transcribe, as sound) запи́сывать на плёнку *or* на пласти́нку. *Record one's voice,* запи́сывать свой гóлос на плёнку; наговáривать пласти́нку. —**a matter of record,** неоспори́мый факт. —**off the record,** неофициáльно; не для печáти. —**on the record,** официáльно: *go on the record,* заяви́ть официáльно. —**on record,** зарегистри́рованный: *the worst earthquake on record,* сáмое си́льное из когдá-либо зарегистри́рованных землетрясéний.

recorder *n.* **1,** (recording device) самопи́сец: *flight recorder,* бортовóй самопи́сец. *Tape recorder,* магнитофóн. **2,** (person who takes notes or minutes) протоколи́ст.

record holder рекордсмéн; рекорди́ст.

recording *n.* **1,** (taking down) зáпись; запи́сывание. **2,** (entering) занесéние. **3,** (something on a record or tape) зáпись. *Sound recording,* звукозáпись. *Make a recording,* записáть пласти́нку.

record player граммофóн; прои́грыватель.

recount *v.t.* **1,** (relate) расскáзывать. **2,** (count again) пересчи́тывать. —*n.* пересчёт.

recoup *v.t.* оты́грывать. *Recoup one's losses,* оты́грываться.

recourse *n.* ресýрс. *Have recourse to,* прибегáть к. *Have no other recourse but to...,* не имéть никакóго другóго вы́хода, крóме...

recover *v.t.* получáть обрáтно; возвращáть. *Recover one's wallet,* получи́ть свой бумáжник обрáтно. *Recover lost territory,* возвращáть (себé) утрáченную террито́рию. *Recover a debt,* взыскáть долг. —*v.i.* **1,** (regain one's health) выздорáвливать; оправля́ться; поправля́ться. *Recover from an illness,* оправля́ться от болéзни. *He is recovering slowly,* он мéдленно выздорáвливает. **2,** (regain one's composure) приходи́ть в себя́; оправля́ться: *recover from the shock,* прийти́ в себя́ от шóка; опрáвиться от шóка.

re-cover *v.t.* перекрывáть.

recovery *n.* **1,** (getting back) возвращéние. **2,** (getting well) выздоровлéние. *I wish you a speedy recovery,* желáю вам скóрого выздоровлéния. *He is on the road to recovery,* у негó дéло идёт на попрáвку. **3,** (improvement after a decline) оживлéние: *economic recovery,* оживлéние эконóмики. —**recovery room,** послеоперациóнная палáта.

re-create *v.t.* воссоздавáть; пересоздавáть.

recreation *n.* развлечéние.

recrimination *n.*, *usu. pl.* взаи́мные обвинéния.

recruit *v.t.* вербовáть; набирáть. —*n.* новобрáнец. —**recruiter,** *n.* вербóвщик. —**recruiting; recruitment,** *n.* вербóвка.

rectal *adj.* относя́щийся к прямóй кишкé.

rectangle *n.* прямоугóльник. —**rectangular,** *adj.* прямоугóльный.

rectify *v.t.* исправля́ть. —**rectifiable,** *adj.* исправи́мый. —**rectification,** *n.* исправлéние.

rectilinear *adj.* прямолинéйный.

rectitude *n.* прáведность.

rector *n.* **1,** (clergyman) прихóдский свящéнник. **2,** (university head) рéктор.

rectum *n.* прямáя кишкá.

recumbent *adj.* лежáчий; лежáщий.

recuperate *v.i.* выздорáвливать; оправля́ться; восстанáвливать си́лы. —**recuperation,** *n.* выздоровлéние.

recur *v.i.* повторя́ться; возвращáться; происходи́ть вновь. *Should the symptoms recur...,* éсли симптóмы повторя́тся... —**recurrence,** *n.* повторéние; возврáт; рециди́в.

recurrent *adj.* повтóрный; повторя́ющийся; периоди́ческий.

recycle *v.t.* втори́чно испóльзовать; возвращáть в оборóт.

red *adj.* крáсный: *red dress,* крáсное плáтье. *Red hair,* ры́жие вóлосы. *Turn red,* краснéть. *Paint something red,* крáсить чтó-нибудь в крáсный цвет. —*n.* **1,** (color) крáсный цвет. *The woman in red,* жéнщина в крáсном. *Red is my favorite color,* крáсный — мой люби́мый цвет. **2,** *pl.* (communists) крáсные. —**in the red, 1,** (showing a loss) с убы́тком. **2,** (in debt) в долгáх. —**see red,** *colloq.* приходи́ть в я́рость.

red-blooded *adj.* полнокрóвный.

Red Cross Крáсный Крест.

red deer благорóдный олéнь.

redden *v.t.* румя́нить. —*v.i.* краснéть.

reddish *adj.* краснова́тый.

redeem *v.t.* **1,** (buy back; pay off) выкупáть. **2,** (cash in) реализовáть. **3,** (rescue; liberate) избавля́ть. **4,** (make amends for) искупáть. —**redeemer,** *n.* избави́тель.

redemption *n.* **1,** (paying off) вы́куп. **2,** (deliverance) спасéние; избавлéние.

redeploy *v.t.* передислоци́ровать.

redesign *v.t.* переконструи́ровать; реконструи́ровать.

red-handed *adj.* с поли́чным: *catch red-handed,* поймáть с поли́чным.

redhead *n.* ры́жий. —**redheaded,** *adj.* ры́жий; рыжеволóсый.

red-hot *adj.* накалённый *or* раскалённый докраснá; калёный.

redistribute *v.t.* перераспределя́ть; переделя́ть. —**redistribution,** *n.* перераспределéние; передéл.

red lead (свинцóвый) сýрик.

red light крáсный свет. *Stop at a red light,* останови́ться на крáсный свет. *Go through a red light,* проéхать на крáсный свет; проскочи́ть (на) крáсный свет.

redness *n.* краснотá. *Redness in one's cheeks,* румя́нец.

redo *v.t.* передéлывать.

redolent *adj.* **1,** (fragrant) души́стый; благоуха́нный. **2,** *fol. by* **of** (smelling of) па́хнущий (+ *instr.*). —**redolence,** *n.* благоуха́ние.

redouble *v.t.* **1,** (double again) втори́чно удва́ивать. **2,** (increase greatly) удва́ивать; усугубля́ть.

redoubt *n.* **1,** (small defensive fortification) реду́т. **2,** (earthenwork within a fortification) редю́йт.

redoubtable *adj.* **1,** (fearsome) гро́зный. **2,** (estimable) почте́нный.

redound *v.i. Redound to the credit of,* де́лать честь (+ *gen.*). *Redound to the advantage of,* благоприя́тствовать (+ *dat.*).

red pepper кра́сный пе́рец; стручко́вый пе́рец.

redpoll *n.* чечётка.

redress *v.t.* **1,** (set right, as a wrong) загла́живать (вину́). **2,** (restore, as a balance) восстана́вливать (равнове́сие). —*n.* возмеще́ние убы́тков: *demand redress,* тре́бовать возмеще́ния убы́тков.

redskin *n.* красноко́жий.

redstart *n.* горихво́стка.

red tape волоки́та.

reduce *v.t.* **1,** (lessen) уменьша́ть; сокраща́ть: *reduce expenses,* уменьша́ть/сокраща́ть расхо́ды. *Reduce to a minimum,* доводи́ть до ми́нимума. **2,** (lower, as a price) понижа́ть; снижа́ть. **3,** (put in a simpler form) своди́ть: *reduce to a simple formula,* своди́ть к просто́й фо́рмуле. *Reduce to a common denominator,* приводи́ть к о́бщему знамена́телю. **4,** (bring to an extreme state) *rendered by various verbs: reduce to dust,* обрати́ть в прах; *reduce to rubble,* превраща́ть в разва́лины; *reduce to poverty,* доводи́ть до нищеты́; *reduce to naught,* своди́ть на нет *or* к нулю́. —*v.i.* худе́ть; убавля́ть в ве́се.

reduction *n.* **1,** (lessening) уменьше́ние; сокраще́ние. **2,** (lowering) пониже́ние; сниже́ние. **3,** (discount) ски́дка. **4,** *math.* приведе́ние (к о́бщему знамена́телю). **5,** *in various technical senses,* реду́кция.

redundancy *n.* **1,** (state of being redundant) нену́жность. **2,** (redundant word or phrase) избы́точность.

redundant *adj.* **1,** (superfluous) изли́шний; ли́шний. **2,** (wordy; verbose) многосло́вный. **3,** (needlessly repeating something) избы́точный: *That word is redundant,* э́то сло́во избы́точно.

reduplicate *v.t.* удва́ивать. —**reduplication,** *n.* удвое́ние.

redwood *n.* секво́йя.

reed *n.* **1,** (plant) тростни́к; камы́ш. **2,** (primitive musical instrument) свире́ль. **3,** *music* (vibrating piece) язычо́к. —*adj.* тростнико́вый; камышо́вый. —**reed instrument,** язычко́вый инструме́нт.

re-educate *v.t.* перевоспи́тывать. —**re-education,** *n.* перевоспита́ние.

reedy *adj.* **1,** (full of reeds) тростнико́вый. **2,** (of thin, sharp tone) то́нкий.

reef *n.* риф; подво́дный ка́мень; подво́дная скала́.

reek *v.i.* воня́ть. —**reek of/with,** воня́ть (+ *instr.*); рази́ть; нести́ (*both impers. with instr.*). *He reeks of vodka,* от него́ рази́т/несёт во́дкой.

reel *n.* **1,** (for thread, rope, etc.) кату́шка. **2,** (for movie film) ро́лик. **3,** (for fishing) кату́шка. *Rod and reel,*

у́дочка со спи́ннингом. —*v.t.* **1,** (wind) нама́тывать. **2,** *fol. by* **in** (pull in, as a fish) выта́гивать. **3,** *fol. by* **off** (recite fluently) отбараба́нить. —*v.i.* **1,** (stagger) шата́ться. **2,** (whirl) кружи́ться.

re-elect *v.t.* переизбира́ть. —**re-election,** *n.* переизбра́ние.

re-enlist *v.i.* продлева́ть контра́кт на вое́нную слу́жбу.

re-enter *v.t.* сно́ва входи́ть в.

re-equip *v.t.* переобору́довать.

re-establish *v.t.* восстана́вливать. —**re-establishment,** *n.* восстановле́ние.

re-evaluate *v.t.* переоце́нивать.

re-examine *v.t.* **1,** (scrutinize again) сно́ва осма́тривать *or* рассма́тривать. **2,** (review; reconsider) пересма́тривать.

refashion *v.t.* преобразо́вывать; перекра́ивать.

refectory *n.* **1,** (in a school) столо́вая. **2,** (in a monastery) тра́пезная.

refer *v.t.* **1,** (send; direct) отсыла́ть; направля́ть. *Refer the reader to the previous chapter,* отсыла́ть чита́теля к предыду́щей главе́. *Refer a patient to a specialist,* направля́ть больно́го к специали́сту. **2,** (submit for consideration) передава́ть: *refer the matter to a committee,* передава́ть де́ло в коми́ссию. —*v.i.* [*usu.* **refer to**] **1,** (pertain to) относи́ться к. **2,** (allude to) ссыла́ться на. *To whom are you referring?,* кого́ вы име́ете в виду́? **3,** (consult, as a dictionary) обраща́ться к.

referee *n.* судья́. —*v.t. & i.* суди́ть: *referee a match,* суди́ть матч.

reference *n.* **1,** (act of referring to or consulting) спра́вка: *for reference only,* то́лько для спра́вок. **2,** (allusion) ссы́лка; упомина́ние. *Make reference to,* ссыла́ться на; упомина́ть. **3,** (note) ссы́лка: *cross-reference,* перекрёстная ссы́лка. **4,** (recommendation) о́тзыв; рекоменда́ция; спра́вка с ме́ста рабо́ты. *Character reference,* характери́стика; аттеста́ция. —*adj.* спра́вочный: *reference material,* спра́вочный материа́л. —**with reference to,** в связи́ с; в отноше́нии (+ *gen.*).

reference book спра́вочник.

reference point ориенти́р; ориентиро́вочный пункт; то́чка отсчёта.

referendum *n.* всенаро́дное голосова́ние; рефере́ндум.

refill *v.t.* сно́ва наполня́ть. *May I refill your glass?,* мо́жно вам нали́ть ещё?

refine *v.t.* **1,** (purify) очища́ть. *Refine oil,* перераба́тывать нефть. **2,** (polish, as one's manners) облагора́живать. **3,** (perfect) соверше́нствовать.

refined *adj.* **1,** (purified) очи́щенный. **2,** (cultivated; polished) утончённый; изя́щный; изы́сканный.

refinement *n.* **1,** (elegance of manner) утончённость; изя́щество; изы́сканность. *Lack of refinement,* некульту́рность. **2,** (subtle improvement) усоверше́нствование.

refinery *n.* очисти́тельный заво́д. *Oil refinery,* нефтеперего́нный заво́д. *Sugar refinery,* са́харный *or* рафина́дный заво́д.

reflect *v.t.* отража́ть: *reflect light,* отража́ть свет. *Reflect someone's views,* отража́ть чьи-нибудь взгля́ды. —*v.i.* **1,** (meditate) размышля́ть: *reflect on a problem,* размышля́ть над пробле́мой. **2,** *fol. by* **on** *or* **upon** (tend to discredit) броса́ть тень (на). —**reflecting telescope,** зерка́льный телеско́п; рефле́ктор.

reflection *n.* **1,** (act of reflecting; image reflected) отраже́ние. **2,** (serious thought) размышле́ние. *On reflection,* пораски́нув умо́м. **3,** (something that discredits) тень.

reflective *adj.* **1,** (reflecting) отража́ющий. **2,** (thoughtful) вду́мчивый.

reflector *n.* рефле́ктор; отража́тель.

reflex *n.* рефле́кс. —*adj.* рефлекто́рный: *reflex reaction,* рефлекто́рная реа́кция. —**reflex camera,** зерка́льный фотоаппара́т.

reflexive *adj.* возвра́тный: *reflexive verb,* возвра́тный глаго́л.

reforge *v.t.* переко́вывать.

reform *v.t.* **1,** (introduce changes in) реформи́ровать; преобразо́вывать. **2,** (cause to mend one's ways) исправля́ть. —*v.i.* исправля́ться. —*n.* рефо́рма; преобразова́ние. *Land reform,* земе́льная рефо́рма. *Calendar/spelling reform,* рефо́рма календаря́/правописа́ния. —*adj.* реформи́стский: *reform movement,* реформи́стское движе́ние.

re-form *v.t.* **1,** (form again) вновь формирова́ть. **2,** *mil.* (line up differently) перестра́ивать; (reorganize) переформирова́ть. —*v.i., mil.* перестра́иваться.

reformation *n.* **1,** (change; reshaping) преобразова́ние. **2,** *cap., hist.* реформа́ция.

reformatory *n.* исправи́тельный дом; исправи́тельная коло́ния.

reformed *adj.* испра́вленный. —**Reformed Church,** реформа́тская це́рковь.

reformer *n.* реформа́тор; преобразова́тель.

reformist *n.* реформи́ст. —*adj.* реформи́стский.

reform school = **reformatory.**

refract *v.t.* преломля́ть. —**refracting,** *adj.* преломля́ющий. *Refracting telescope,* рефра́ктор. —**refraction,** *n.* преломле́ние; рефра́кция. —**refractor,** *n.* рефра́ктор.

refractory *adj.* **1,** (obstinate) упря́мый; непоко́рный. **2,** (heat-resistant) огнеупо́рный.

refrain *v.i.* [*usu.* **refrain from**] возде́рживаться (от); уде́рживаться (от). —*n.* припе́в; рефре́н.

refresh *v.t.* освежа́ть. —**refresher course,** повтори́тельный курс; переподгото́вка. —**refreshing,** *adj.* освежа́ющий; освежи́тельный.

refreshment *n.* **1,** (act of refreshing) освеже́ние. **2,** *pl.* (food, drink, etc.) угоще́ние.

refrigerate *v.t.* охлажда́ть; замора́живать. —**refrigeration,** *n.* охлажде́ние; замора́живание.

refrigerator *n.* холоди́льник.

refuel *v.t.* дозаправля́ть. —*v.i.* дозаправля́ться; заправля́ться горю́чим. *Refueling stop,* остано́вка для заправки горю́чим. *Without refueling,* без дозапра́вки.

refuge *n.* убе́жище; прию́т; приста́нище. *Take refuge,* укрыва́ться.

refugee *n.* бе́женец. *Refugee camp,* ла́герь для бе́женцев.

refund *v.t.* возвраща́ть (де́ньги). —*n.* возвра́т (де́нег).

refurbish *v.t.* обновля́ть; ремонти́ровать.

refusal *n.* отка́з.

refuse[1] (ri-fyooz) *v.t.* **1,** *fol. by inf.* (decline to) отка́зываться (+ *inf.*): *He refused to answer,* он отказа́лся отве́тить. **2,** (decline to accept) отка́зываться от: *refuse help/ an offer/,* отказа́ться от по́мощи/предложе́ния. **3,** (decline to give) отка́зывать: *refuse help to someone,* отка́зывать кому́-нибудь в по́мощи. **4,** (turn down the request of) отка́зывать (+ *dat.*): *She refused him,* она́ ему́ отказа́ла. —*v.i.* отка́зываться: *He flatly refused,* он отказа́лся наотре́з.

refuse[2] (ref-yoos) *n.* му́сор; сор; отбро́сы.

refute *v.t.* опроверга́ть. —**refutation,** *n.* опроверже́ние.

regain *v.t.* возвраща́ть (себе́); верну́ть (себе́): *regain territory,* возвраща́ть/верну́ть себе́ террито́рию. *Regain the world championship title,* возврати́ть/верну́ть себе́ зва́ние чемпио́на ми́ра. *Regain consciousness,* приходи́ть в созна́ние *or* в себя́; очну́ться. *Regain one's strength,* восстана́вливать свои́ си́лы. *Regain one's balance,* сбаланси́ровать. *Regain one's eyesight,* прозре́ть. *Regain one's composure,* овладе́ть собо́й.

regal *adj.* **1,** (of a king) короле́вский. **2,** *fig.* (magnificent; stately) ца́рственный; ца́рский.

regale *v.t.* угоща́ть; по́тчевать.

regalia *n.pl.* рега́лии. *In full regalia,* при всех рега́лиях.

regard *v.t.* **1,** (look at; watch) смотре́ть на; разгля́дывать. *Regard someone suspiciously,* смотре́ть на *or* разгля́дывать кого́-нибудь подозри́тельно. **2,** (look upon; consider) счита́ть; рассма́тривать. *We regard this action as unjustified,* мы счита́ем э́тот посту́пок неопра́вданным. *He is regarded as an impostor,* его́ рассма́тривают как самозва́нца. *Regard someone highly,* быть высо́кого мне́ния о. *He is highly regarded,* он по́льзуется больши́м уваже́нием; его́ о́чень уважа́ют. *Regard something with favor,* относи́ться к чему́-нибудь благоскло́нно. **3,** (concern) каса́ться. *As regards...,* что каса́ется (+ *gen.*). —*n.* **1,** (consideration; esteem) уваже́ние: *out of regard for,* из уваже́ния к. *Without regard to,* безотноси́тельно к. *Have a high regard for someone,* высоко́ цени́ть кого́-нибудь. *Have no regard for others,* не счита́ться с други́ми. **2,** (attention) внима́ние: *pay no regard to,* не обраща́ть (никако́го) внима́ния на. **3,** *pl.* (greetings) приве́т: *best regards,* серде́чный приве́т. *Give one's regards to,* кла́няться (+ *dat.*); передава́ть приве́т (+ *dat.*). **4,** (relation; connection) отноше́ние: *in this regard,* в э́том отноше́нии. *You need not worry in that regard,* на э́тот счёт мо́жете быть споко́йны. —**in/with regard to,** в отноше́нии (+ *gen.*); относи́тельно; в связи́ с; что каса́ется.

regarding *prep.* относи́тельно; каса́ющийся; по по́воду.

regardless *adv., colloq.* невзира́я ни на что. —**regardless of,** незави́симо от; вне зави́симости от; безотноси́тельно к; невзира́я на.

regatta *n.* рега́та.

regency *n.* ре́гентство.

regenerate *v.t.* перерожда́ть. —*v.i.* перерожда́ться.

regeneration *n.* **1,** (renewal) перерожде́ние. **2,** *mech.; biol.* регенера́ция. —**regenerative,** *adj.* регенерати́вный.

regent *n.* ре́гент.

regicide *n.* цареуби́йство.

regime *n.* режи́м.

regimen *n.* режи́м.

regiment *n.* полк. —*v.t.* дисциплини́ровать. —**regimental,** *adj.* полково́й. —**regimentation,** *n.* стро́гая дисципли́на.

region *n.* ме́стность; о́бласть; райо́н; регио́н. —**regional,** *adj.* областно́й; региона́льный.

register *n.* **1,** (record) ве́домость; реги́стр; рее́стр. **2,** (book containing such a record) журна́л; реги́стр; рее́стр. *Guest register,* кни́га для посети́телей. **3,** *music* (range) реги́стр. —*v.t.* **1,** (record) регистри́ровать; брать на учёт. **2,** (indicate, as of a mechanical device) пока́зывать: *A thermometer registers temperature,* термо́метр пока́зывает температу́ру. **3,** (show, as emotion) проявля́ть; обнару́живать: *register surprise,* проявля́ть/обнару́живать удивле́ние. **4,** (express; voice) выража́ть: *The students registered their displeasure,* студе́нты выража́ли своё недово́льство. **5,** (insure delivery of, as a letter) посыла́ть (письмо́) заказны́м. *Registered letter,* заказно́е письмо́. —*v.i.* **1,** (sign up) регистри́роваться; отмеча́ться; стать *or* встать на учёт. *Register at a hotel,* пропи́сываться в гости́нице. **2,** (make an impression): *The name doesn't register with me,* э́то и́мя мне ничего́ не говори́т. —**cash register,** ка́сса.

registrar *n.* регистра́тор.

registration *n.* регистра́ция; за́пись. —*adj.* регистрацио́нный. *Registration office,* регистрату́ра.

registry *n.* **1,** = **registration. 2,** (place of registration) регистрату́ра.

regress *v.i.* регресси́ровать. —**regression,** *n.* регре́сс. —**regressive,** *adj.* регресси́вный.

regret *v.t.* сожале́ть о; жале́ть о: *regret one's decision,* сожале́ть/жале́ть о своём реше́нии. *I regret that I will be unable to come,* я сожале́ю, что не смогу́ прийти́. *We regret to inform you,* мы с сожале́нием сообща́ем вам. —*n.* **1,** (troubled feeling) сожале́ние. *I have no regrets,* я не сожале́ю об э́том. **2,** *pl.* (polite refusal) извине́ния: *Tanya sends her regrets,* Та́ня прино́сит *or* передаёт свои́ извине́ния.

regretful *adj.* по́лный сожале́ния. *Be regretful,* сожале́ть.

regrettable *adj.* досто́йный сожале́ния; приско́рбный. —**regrettably,** *adv.* к сожале́нию.

regroup *v.t.* перегруппиро́вывать. —*v.i.* перегруппиро́вываться. —**regrouping,** *n.* перегруппиро́вка.

regular *adj.* **1,** (recurring at set times) регуля́рный: *at regular intervals,* с регуля́рными интерва́лами. **2,** (even, as of one's pulse) регуля́рный. *Regular heartbeat,* пра́вильное сердцебие́ние. **3,** (steady) постоя́нный: *regular customer,* постоя́нный клие́нт. **4,** (customary) обы́чный: *one's regular place,* чьё-нибудь обы́чное ме́сто. **5,** (regularly scheduled) очередно́й: *regular session,* очередно́е заседа́ние. **6,** (symmetrical, as of features) пра́вильный. **7,** *gram.* пра́вильный: *regular verb,* пра́вильный глаго́л. **8,** *mil.* регуля́рный; ка́дровый. **9,** *colloq.* (out-and-out) настоя́щий. **10,** *slang* (likable) сла́вный: *a regular guy,* сла́вный ма́лый.

regularity *n.* регуля́рность; пра́вильность.

regularly *adv.* регуля́рно.

regulate *v.t.* регули́ровать.

regulation *n.* **1,** (act of regulating) регули́рование. **2,** (rule) пра́вило. **3,** *pl.* (set of rules) пра́вила; уста́в. —*adj.* уста́вный; устано́вленный.

regulator *n.* регуля́тор.

regurgitate *v.t.* изрыга́ть; отры́гивать.

rehabilitate *v.t.* реабилити́ровать. —**rehabilitation,** *n.* реабилита́ция.

rehash *n.* повторе́ние; перепе́в.

rehearsal *n.* репети́ция. *Dress rehearsal,* генера́льная репети́ция.

rehearse *v.t. & i.* репети́ровать.

reheat *v.t.* разогрева́ть; подогрева́ть.

reign *n.* **1,** (period of rule) ца́рствование. *During the reign of Peter I,* в ца́рствование Петра́ Пе́рвого; при Петре́ Пе́рвом. **2,** (rule) власть: *reign of law,* власть зако́на. *Reign of terror,* разгу́л терро́ра. —*v.i.* **1,** (of a monarch) ца́рствовать. **2,** *fig.* (of silence, peace, etc.) цари́ть; воцаря́ться. —**reigning,** *adj.* ца́рствующий.

reimburse *v.t.* возмеща́ть; опла́чивать. *You will be fully reimbursed for your expenses,* вам бу́дут по́лностью опла́чены ва́ши расхо́ды. —**reimbursement,** *n.* возмеще́ние.

rein *n.* **1,** (for a horse) по́вод (*pl.* пово́дья); вожжа́ (*pl.* во́жжи). **2,** *The reins of government,* бразды́ правле́ния. —*v.t.* [*usu.* **rein in**] **1,** (stop or slow down, as a horse) оса́живать. **2,** *fig.* (restrain; curb) одёргивать. —**give free rein to,** дава́ть во́лю (+ *dat.*). —**keep a tight rein on,** держа́ть в узде́.

reincarnate *v.t.* перевоплоща́ть. —**reincarnation,** *n.* перевоплоще́ние.

reindeer *n.* се́верный оле́нь. *Young reindeer,* пы́жик. —**reindeer moss,** оле́ний мох; я́гель.

reinforce *v.t.* уси́ливать; укрепля́ть; подкрепля́ть. —**reinforced concrete,** железобето́н.

reinforcement *n.* **1,** (strengthening) усиле́ние; укрепле́ние; подкрепле́ние. **2,** *pl., mil.* подкрепле́ния.

reinstate *v.t.* восстана́вливать в (пре́жней) до́лжности. —**reinstatement,** *n.* восстановле́ние в до́лжности.

reinsure *v.t.* перестрахо́вывать. —**reinsurance,** *n.* перестрахо́вка.

reinterpret *v.t.* переосмы́сливать.

reinvest *v.t.* сно́ва вкла́дывать (де́ньги).

reissue *v.t.* переиздава́ть. —*n.* переизда́ние.

reiterate *v.t.* повторя́ть; тверди́ть. —**reiteration,** *n.* повторе́ние.

reject *v.t.* **1,** (turn down) отклоня́ть; отверга́ть: *reject an offer,* отклони́ть/отве́ргнуть предложе́ние. **2,** (rebuff) отка́зывать: *reject a suitor,* отказа́ть жениху́. **3,** (discard because of defects) бракова́ть. **4,** (fail to accept, as a transplanted organ) оттрга́ть. —*n.* брак; брако́ванное изде́лие.

rejection *n.* **1,** (turning down; being turned down) отка́з; отклоне́ние. **2,** *med.* отторже́ние.

rejoice *v.i.* ра́доваться;икова́ть. —**rejoicing,** *n.* икова́ние.

rejoin *v.t.* **1,** (meet again after an interval) присоединя́ться к. **2,** (come back to) возвраща́ться к. **3,** (resume membership in) сно́ва присоединя́ться к.

rejoinder *n.* возраже́ние; ре́плика.

rejuvenate *v.t.* омола́живать. —**rejuvenation,** *n.* омоложе́ние.

relapse *v.i.* [*usu.* **relapse into**] (сно́ва) впада́ть в; (сно́ва) предава́ться (+ *dat.*). —*n.* рециди́в: *suffer a relapse,* переноси́ть рециди́в. —**relapsing fever,** возвра́тный тиф.

relate *v.t.* **1,** (tell) расска́зывать: *relate a story,* рассказа́ть исто́рию. **2,** (establish a connection between) свя́зывать. —*v.i.* [*usu.* **relate to**] относи́ться к.

related *adj.* **1,** (connected) свя́занный. *The two murders are not related,* оба уби́йства не свя́заны друг с дру́гом. *Job-related injury,* произво́дственная тра́вма. **2,** (kindred) ро́дственный: *related languages,* ро́дственные языки́. *Be related to,* быть в родстве́ с; быть сродни́ (+ *dat.*). *We are not related,* мы не ро́дственники. *How is he related to you?,* кем он вам прихо́дится? *Armenian is distantly related to English,* армя́нский язы́к име́ет отдалённое родство́ с англи́йским.

relation *n.* **1,** (connection) отноше́ние; связь. *Bear no relation to,* не име́ть никако́го отноше́ния к. **2,** (relative; kin) ро́дственник. **3,** *pl.* (dealings; intercourse) отноше́ния: *friendly/international/diplomatic relations,* дру́жеские/междунаро́дные/дипломати́ческие отноше́ния. *Sexual relations,* полова́я связь. —**in relation to,** в отноше́нии (+ *gen.*).

relationship *n.* **1,** (connection) отноше́ние; связь. **2,** (kinship) родство́. *What is her relationship to you?,* кем она́ вам прихо́дится? **3,** (connection between people) отноше́ния: *close relationship,* бли́зкие отноше́ния. **4,** (liaison; affair) связь: *intimate relationship,* инти́мная связь.

relative *n.* ро́дственник; *fem.* ро́дственница; *pl.* ро́дственники; родны́е; родня́. *Distant relative,* да́льний ро́дственник. *Relative by marriage,* сво́йственник. —*adj.* **1,** (comparative; not absolute) относи́тельный: *relative quiet,* относи́тельная тишина́. *Everything is relative,* всё относи́тельно. **2,** *fol. by* **to** (pertaining; relevant) относя́щийся (к): *the documents relative to the case,* докуме́нты, относя́щиеся к де́лу. *The value of the dollar relative to the yen,* курс до́ллара по отноше́нию к ие́не. **3,** *gram.* относи́тельный: *relative pronoun,* относи́тельное местоиме́ние.

relatively *adv.* относи́тельно: *relatively happy,* относи́тельно сча́стлив. *Relatively speaking,* вообще́ говоря́.

relativity *n.* относи́тельность. *Theory of relativity,* тео́рия относи́тельности.

relax *v.t.* **1,** (make less tight or strict) ослабля́ть. *Relax the muscles,* рассла́бить мы́шцы. **2,** (make less tense) разряжа́ть. —*v.i.* **1,** (become less tight) ослабева́ть. **2,** (take it easy) расслабля́ться; отдыха́ть.

relaxation *n.* **1,** (making less tight or strict) ослабле́ние. **2,** (making less tense) разря́дка: *relaxation of tension,* разря́дка напряжённости. **3,** (rest) о́тдых.

relaxed *adj.* непринуждённый.

relay *n.* **1,** (shift) сме́на. *Work in relays,* рабо́тать посме́нно. **2,** (race) эстафе́та. **3,** *electricity* реле́. —*v.t.* передава́ть: *relay information,* передава́ть информа́цию. —**relay race,** эстафе́та; эстафе́тный бег.

re-lay *v.t.* перекла́дывать. *Re-lay a floor,* перестила́ть пол.

relearn *v.t.* переу́чиваться (+ *dat.*).

release *v.t.* **1,** (let out; set free) выпуска́ть; освобожда́ть: *release from prison,* выпуска́ть/освобожда́ть из тюрьмы́. *Release a bird from a cage,* выпуска́ть *or* отпуска́ть пти́цу из кле́тки. **2,** (let go of) отпуска́ть; пуска́ть. **3,** (let loose against a target) выпуска́ть; пуска́ть: *release bombs,* выпуска́ть бо́мбы; *release an arrow,* пусти́ть стрелу́ из лу́ка. **4,** (disengage, as a brake) отпуска́ть (то́рмоз); (cause to snap, as a shutter) спуска́ть (затво́р). **5,** (relieve, as from an obligation) освобожда́ть. **6,** (allow to be published) обнаро́довать: *release documents,* обнаро́довать докуме́нты. —*n.* **1,** (act of releasing) освобожде́ние. **2,** (something issued or produced) вы́пуск. **3,** (discharge; dismissal) увольне́ние. —**press release,** сообще́ние для пре́ссы. —**shutter release,** *photog.* спускова́я кно́пка.

relegate *v.t.* **1,** (consign) отодвига́ть: *relegate to the background,* отодвига́ть на за́дний план. **2,** (refer; delegate) передава́ть.

relent *v.i.* смягча́ться.

relentless *adj.* неотсту́пный: *relentless pursuit,* неотсту́пное пресле́дование. —**relentlessly,** *adv.* неотсту́пно.

relevance *n.* **1,** (relation) отноше́ние (к де́лу). **2,** (timeliness) актуа́льность.

relevant *adj.* **1,** (pertinent) относя́щийся к де́лу. *The question is no longer relevant,* вопро́с отпада́ет. **2,** (timely) актуа́льный.

reliable *adj.* **1,** (of a person) надёжный. **2,** (of information, a source, etc.) достове́рный. —**reliability,** *n.* надёжность; достове́рность.

reliance *n.* **1,** (dependence) зави́симость: *his reliance on his parents,* его́ зави́симость от роди́телей. **2,** (trust) дове́рие. *Place one's reliance on,* наде́яться на. **3,** (something relied on) наде́жда; опо́ра.

reliant *adj.* *Be reliant on,* полага́ться на; рассчи́тывать на.

relic *n.* **1,** (ancient object) рели́кт. **2,** (memento of the past) рели́квия: *relics of the past,* рели́квии про́шлого. **3,** (object of religious worship) рели́квия.

relief *n.* **1,** (easing of pain or anxiety) облегче́ние. *Sigh* *with relief*, вздохну́ть с облегче́нием (*or* облег-чённо). **2,** (replacement) сме́на. **3,** (emergency aid) по́мощь. **4,** (financial assistance) посо́бие. **5,** (raised decoration) рельéф. *In relief*, рельéфно. —**relief map,** рельéфная ка́рта.

relieve *v.t.* **1,** (alleviate) облегча́ть: *relieve the pain*, облегча́ть боль. *Relieve boredom*, разве́ять ску́ку. *Relieve the monotony*, вноси́ть разнообра́зие. **2,** (reduce, as tension or pressure) ослабля́ть. **3,** (free from anxiety) успока́ивать. *Feel relieved*, чу́вствовать облегче́ние. **4,** (free, as from a burden) освобожда́ть. **5,** (furnish aid to) ока́зывать по́мощь (+ *dat.*). **6,** (remove; release) освобожда́ть: *relieved of his post/duties*, освобождён от до́лжности/ от обя́занностей/. **7,** (replace) сменя́ть. —**relieve oneself,** «облегча́ться».

religion *n.* рели́гия. *Freedom of religion*, свобо́да вероисповéдания.

religiosity *n.* религио́зность.

religious *adj.* религио́зный: *religious man/custom*, религио́зный челове́к/обы́чай. *Religious persecution*, религио́зное пресле́дование.

religiously *adv.* свя́то: *observe one's diet religiously*, свя́то соблюда́ть дие́ту.

relinquish *v.t.* **1,** (give up) отка́зываться от: *relinquish one's rights*, отка́зываться от свои́х прав. *Relinquish one's seat/place to someone*, уступи́ть ме́сто кому́-нибудь. **2,** (let go): *relinquish one's hold on*, выпуска́ть из рук.

relish *n.* **1,** (enjoyment; zest) смак. **2,** (condiment) припра́ва. —*v.t.* наслажда́ться; смакова́ть. *I don't relish the prospect*, перспекти́ва мне не улыба́ется.

relive *v.t.* сно́ва пережива́ть.

reload *v.t.* **1,** (transfer to another vehicle) перегружа́ть. **2,** (load again, as a vehicle) сно́ва грузи́ть. **3,** (refill, as a camera or gun) перезаряжа́ть.

relocate *v.t.* перемеща́ть; переселя́ть. —*v.i.* пере-езжа́ть; переселя́ться. —**relocation,** *n.* пере́езд (к но́вому ме́сту рабо́ты).

reluctance *n.* неохо́та; нежела́ние.

reluctant *adj.* неохо́тный. *I am reluctant to...*, мне не хо́чется (+ *inf.*). —**reluctantly,** *adv.* неохо́тно; с неохо́той; не́хотя.

rely *v.i.* [*usu.* **rely on**] полага́ться на: *You can rely on him completely*, на него́ мо́жно вполне́ положи́ться. *I am relying on you for/to help*, я рассчи́тываю на ва́шу по́мощь.

remain *v.i.* остава́ться: *remain at home*, остава́ться до́ма. *Remain standing/seated*, остава́ться стоя́ть/ сиде́ть. *Remain friends*, оста́ться друзья́ми. *Remain silent*, храни́ть молча́ние. *Remain calm*, сохраня́ть споко́йствие. *Little remains of...*, ма́ло что оста́лось от... *Nothing remains of the city*, от го́рода ничего́ не оста́лось. *Much remains to be done*, мно́го остаётся сде́лать. *He remained faithful to his principles*, он оста́лся ве́рен свои́м при́нципам.

remainder *n.* оста́ток.

remaining *adj.* остально́й: *the remaining passengers*, остальны́е пассажи́ры. *In the time remaining*, в оста́вшееся вре́мя.

remains *n.pl.* **1,** (remnants) оста́тки. **2,** (dead body) оста́нки; прах. *Mortal remains*, бре́нные оста́нки.

remake *v.t.* переде́лывать.

remand *v.t.* возвраща́ть: *remand to custody*, возвраща́ть под стра́жу.

remark *n.* замеча́ние: *a crude remark*, грубое замеча́ние. —*v.t.* замеча́ть: *He remarked to me that...*, он заме́тил мне, что... —*v.i.* [*usu.* **remark on**] (comment on) де́лать замеча́ние (о).

remarkable *adj.* замеча́тельный; удиви́тельный. —**remarkably,** *adv.* удиви́тельно.

remarry *v.i.* вступа́ть в но́вый брак.

rematch *n.* матч-рева́нш.

remeasure *v.t.* перемеря́ть.

remediable *adj.* исправи́мый.

remedial *adj.* корректи́вный: *remedial reading*, корректи́вное чте́ние.

remedy *n.* сре́дство: *remedy for a cough*, сре́дство от ка́шля. —*v.t.* **1,** (cure) выле́чивать. **2,** (correct) поправля́ть: *remedy the situation*, поправля́ть положе́ние.

remember *v.t.* **1,** (recall) по́мнить: *What do you remember about him?*, что вы по́мните о нём? *Remember what I told you*, запо́мните то, что я вам сказа́л(а). *I can't remember his name*, я не могу́ вспо́мнить его́ и́мени. **2,** (mention in sending regards) передава́ть приве́т; кла́няться: *Remember me to your sister*, переда́йте приве́т/ кла́няйтесь/ ва́шей сестре́. *He asked to be remembered to you*, он проси́л переда́ть вам приве́т. —*v.i.* по́мнить: *I don't remember*, я не по́мню. *I'll remember*, я бу́ду по́мнить. *Try to remember*, постара́йтесь вспо́мнить *or* запо́мнить.

remembrance *n.* **1,** (memory) па́мять: *in remembrance of*, в па́мять (+ *gen.*). **2,** (memento) сувени́р: *a remembrance of our trip*, сувени́р о на́шей пое́здке.

remind *v.t.* напомина́ть: *Remind me to ask him*, напо́мните мне спроси́ть его́. *He reminds me of my brother*, он напомина́ет мне моего́ бра́та. —**which reminds me,** а кста́ти...

reminder *n.* напомина́ние: *after repeated reminders*, по́сле неоднокра́тных напомина́ний.

reminisce *v.i.* вспомина́ть: *reminisce about the past*, вспомина́ть о про́шлом.

reminiscence *n.* воспомина́ние.

reminiscent *adj.* Be reminiscent of, напомина́ть.

remiss *adj.* небре́жный; невнима́тельный. *Be remiss in one's duties*, пренебрега́ть свои́ми обя́занностями.

remission *n.* **1,** (pardon) отпуще́ние: *remission of sins*, отпуще́ние грехо́в. **2,** *med.* реми́ссия.

remit *v.t.* **1,** (send, as payment) переводи́ть; пересыла́ть. **2,** (pardon; forgive) проща́ть; отпуска́ть. **3,** (slacken) ослабля́ть. **4,** (refrain from exacting) проща́ть; снима́ть.

remittance *n.* перево́д (де́нег); пересы́лка.

remnant *n.* **1,** (remainder) оста́ток. **2,** (vestige) пережи́ток. **3,** (leftover piece of cloth) оста́ток.

remodel *v.t.* переде́лывать.

remold *v.t.* переко́вывать.

remonstrance *n.* увеща́ние.

remonstrate *v.i.* **1,** *fol. by* **with** (exhort) увещева́ть. **2,** *fol. by* **against** (protest; object) возража́ть; протестова́ть (про́тив).

remorse *n.* раска́яние. —**remorseful,** *adj.* по́лный раска́яния. —**remorseless,** *adj.* безжа́лостный.

remote *adj.* отдалённый: *remote place/resemblance/ recollection,* отдалённое ме́сто/схо́дство/воспомина́ние. *The chances of that are remote,* ша́нсы на э́то незначи́тельные. —**not the remotest,** ни мале́йшего (поня́тия, представле́ния, *etc.*). —**remote control,** дистанцио́нное управле́ние.

remoteness *n.* отдалённость.

remount *v.t. & i.* сно́ва сесть (на ло́шадь).

removable *adj.* съёмный; сменя́емый.

removal *n.* **1,** (taking out; taking away) удале́ние. **2,** (taking down) съёмка. **3,** (moving to another place) перемеще́ние. **4,** (dismissal, as from office) смеще́ние (с до́лжности) отстране́ние (от до́лжности).

remove *v.t.* **1,** (take away) убира́ть; удаля́ть. **2,** (take out; draw out) вынима́ть. **3,** (take off; take down) снима́ть. **4,** (take out; extract; remove, as a splinter or nail) удаля́ть; выта́скивать. **5,** (move to another place) перемеща́ть. **6,** (eradicate, as a stain) выводи́ть. **7,** (take off, as paint or rust) удаля́ть. **8,** (straighten out, as a dent) исправля́ть. **9,** (eliminate; get rid of) устраня́ть. **10,** (dismiss, as from office) смеща́ть (с до́лжности); отстраня́ть (от до́лжности).

remunerate *v.t.* вознагражда́ть.

remuneration *n.* вознагражде́ние. *Without remuneration,* безвозме́здно.

remunerative *adj.* вы́годный; дохо́дный.

renaissance *n.* **1,** (rebirth) возрожде́ние. **2,** *cap., hist.* Возрожде́ние.

renal *adj.* по́чечный.

rename *v.t.* переименова́ть. *The city was renamed in honor of Lincoln,* го́роду бы́ло присво́ено и́мя Ли́нкольна.

renascence *n.* возрожде́ние. —**renascent,** *adj.* возрожда́ющийся.

rend *v.t.* рвать; разрыва́ть; раздира́ть. *Rend the air,* раздира́ть *or* сотряса́ть во́здух.

render *v.t.* **1,** (give; provide) ока́зывать: *render assistance,* ока́зывать соде́йствие. *Render homage,* ока́зывать *or* воздава́ть по́чести. *For services rendered,* за услу́ги. **2,** (submit, as a bill) предъявля́ть. **3,** (hand down, as a verdict) выноси́ть (пригово́р). **4,** (cause to be or become) *rendered by various verbs: render harmless,* обезвре́живать; *render lifeless,* обескро́вливать. **5,** (translate) переводи́ть. **6,** (depict) изобража́ть. **7,** (perform) исполня́ть. **8,** (melt, as fat) топи́ть.

rendezvous *n.* **1,** (meeting) свида́ние. **2,** (meeting place) ме́сто свида́ния. —*v.i.* встреча́ться.

rendition *n.* **1,** (performance) исполне́ние. **2,** (translation) перево́д.

renegade *n.* отщепе́нец; ренега́т.

renege *v.i.* **1,** *fol. by* **on** (go back on) наруша́ть; не сдержа́ть. **2,** *cards* (revoke) де́лать рено́нс. —*n., cards* рено́нс.

renew *v.t.* **1,** (resume; extend) возобновля́ть: *renew one's subscription,* возобнови́ть подпи́ску. **2,** (make new again) обновля́ть. *With renewed vigor,* со све́жими си́лами. —**renewal,** *n.* возобновле́ние; обновле́ние.

rennet *n.* сычу́г.

rennin *n.* сычу́жный ферме́нт; сычу́жина.

renounce *v.t.* отрека́ться от; отка́зываться от. *Renounce one's citizenship,* отказа́ться от гражда́нства.

renovate *v.t.* обновля́ть; ремонти́ровать. —**renovation,** *n.* обновле́ние; восстанови́тельный ремо́нт.

renown *n.* сла́ва; изве́стность. *A writer of world renown,* писа́тель с мировы́м и́менем.

renowned *adj.* знамени́тый; просла́вленный. *Be renowned for,* сла́виться (+ *instr.*).

rent *n.* **1,** (payment for lodgings) кварти́рная пла́та. *Pay the rent,* плати́ть за кварти́ру. *How much rent do you pay?,* ско́лько вы пла́тите за кварти́ру?; кака́я у вас кварти́рная пла́та? **2,** *econ.* ре́нта. —*v.t.* **1,** (obtain the use of, as an apartment) снима́ть; брать внаём; (a car, equipment, etc.) брать напрока́т. **2,** (give the use of, as an apartment) сдава́ть; дава́ть внаём; (a car, equipment, etc.) дава́ть напрока́т. —**for rent,** сдаётся внаём.

rental *n.* **1,** (of an apartment) аре́нда; (of a car, equipment, etc.) прока́т. **2,** (money paid for use) аре́ндная пла́та; пла́та за прока́т.

renter *n.* аренда́тор.

renumber *v.t.* перенумерова́ть.

renunciation *n.* отрече́ние; отка́з.

reoccur *v.i.* повторя́ться.

reopen *v.t.* вновь открыва́ть: *reopen the discussion,* вновь открыва́ть диску́ссию. *Reopen a case,* возобнови́ть де́ло. *Reopen old wounds,* береди́ть ста́рые ра́ны. —*v.i.* вновь открыва́ться.

reorder *v.t.* **1,** (order again) сно́ва зака́зывать. **2,** (restructure) перестра́ивать. —*v.i.* сде́лать повто́рный зака́з. —*n.* повто́рный зака́з.

reorganization *n.* реорганиза́ция; перестро́йка; переустро́йство; преобразова́ние.

reorganize *v.t.* реорганизова́ть; перестра́ивать; переустра́ивать; преобразо́вывать.

repaint *v.t.* перекра́шивать.

repair *v.t.* чини́ть; исправля́ть; ремонти́ровать. *Repair the damage,* исправля́ть повреждё́ние. —*v.i.* (go) направля́ться. —*n.* **1,** (act of repairing; being repaired) ремо́нт; почи́нка. *Be under repair,* быть в ремо́нте. *Closed for repairs,* закры́то на ремо́нт. **2,** (working condition) испра́вность: *in good repair,* в испра́вности. —*adj.* ремо́нтный: *repair shop,* ремо́нтная мастерска́я. *Shoe repair shop,* ателье́ по ремо́нту о́буви.

repairable *adj.* исправи́мый. *Is it repairable?,* мо́жно э́то испра́вить?

repairman *n.* ма́стер по ремо́нту; ремо́нтник. *TV repairman,* ма́стер по ремо́нту телеви́зоров.

reparable *adj.* исправи́мый.

reparations *n.pl.* репара́ции.

repast *n.* еда́.

repatriate *v.t.* репатрии́ровать. —*n.* репатриа́нт. —**repatriation**, *n.* репатриа́ция.

repay *v.t.* **1,** (pay off, as a debt, loan, etc.) возвраща́ть; отдава́ть; выпла́чивать. **2,** (return a favor on the part of) отпла́чивать (+ *dat.*): *How can I ever repay you?*, как я могу́ отплати́ть вам? *I owe you a debt that can never be repaid*, я у вас в неопла́тном долгу́.

repayment *n.* **1,** (of money) возвра́т; вы́плата: *repayment of a debt/loan*, возвра́т до́лга; вы́плата за́йма. **2,** (returning a favor or ill turn) отпла́та.

repeal *v.t.* отменя́ть; аннули́ровать. —*n.* отме́на; аннули́рование.

repeat *v.t.* повторя́ть: *repeat a question/mistake*, повторя́ть вопро́с/оши́бку. *Repeat gossip*, передава́ть *or* распространя́ть спле́тни. *Don't repeat this to anyone!*, никому́ э́того не говори́те! *Repeat oneself/itself*, повторя́ться. —*n.* повторе́ние. —*adj.* повто́рный: *repeat order*, повто́рный зака́з.

repeated *adj.* неоднокра́тный; многокра́тный. *After repeated attempts*, по́сле неоднокра́тных попы́ток. —**repeatedly**, *adv.* неоднокра́тно; многокра́тно.

repeater *n.* **1,** (pupil not promoted) второго́дник. **2,** (person more than once in jail) рецидиви́ст.

repeating *adj.* (of a firearm) магази́нный. —**repeating decimal**, периоди́ческая дробь.

repel *v.t.* **1,** (ward off) отража́ть; отбива́ть. **2,** (arouse repulsion in) отта́лкивать.

repellent *adj.* отта́лкивающий: *repellent sight*, отта́лкивающий вид. *Water-repellent*, водоотта́лкивающий. —*n.* *Insect repellent*, сре́дство от насеко́мых.

repent *v.t. & i.* раска́иваться (в); ка́яться (в). *Repent (for) one's sins*, раска́иваться *or* ка́яться в свои́х греха́х.

repentance *n.* раска́яние; покая́ние. *Letter of repentance*, покая́нное письмо́.

repentant *adj.* **1,** (feeling repentance) ка́ющийся: *repentant sinner*, ка́ющийся гре́шник. **2,** (showing repentance) покая́нный: *repentant look*, покая́нный вид.

repercussion *n.*, *usu. pl.* после́дствия.

repertoire *n.* репертуа́р.

repertory *n.* **1,** (repertoire) репертуа́р. **2,** (repository) храни́лище. —*adj.* репертуа́рный.

repetition *n.* повторе́ние. *Avoid unnecessary repetition*, избега́ть нену́жных повторе́ний. *Draw by repetition of moves (in chess)*, ничья́ повторе́нием хо́дов.

repetitious *adj.* повторя́ющийся. *Become repetitious*, нача́ть повторя́ться. *Also*, **repetitive**.

rephrase *v.t.* перефрази́ровать.

replace *v.t.* **1,** (put back) класть *or* ста́вить обра́тно. **2,** (find a substitute for) заменя́ть: *replace old furniture*, заменя́ть ста́рую ме́бель. *Replace a window pane*, поста́вить но́вое стекло́. *Replace an employee with someone who is more experienced*, замени́ть слу́жащего ке́м-то бо́лее о́пытным. *He will be hard to replace*, тру́дно бу́дет его́ замени́ть. **3,** (take the place of) заменя́ть; сменя́ть; вытесня́ть. *There is no one to replace him*, его́ не́кому замени́ть. *A replaced*

B as prime minister, А смени́л Б на посту́ премье́р-мини́стра. *Electricity replaced gas as a means of illumination*, электри́чество замени́ло/вы́теснило газ как сре́дство освеще́ния.

replaceable *adj.* замени́мый.

replacement *n.* **1,** (act of replacing; one who replaces) заме́на: *find a replacement for someone*, найти́ заме́ну кому́-нибудь *or* для кого́-нибудь. **2,** *mil.* пополне́ние; *pl.* пополне́ния.

replay *v.t.* переи́грывать.

replenish *v.t.* пополня́ть; обновля́ть. —**replenishment**, *n.* пополне́ние; обновле́ние.

replete *adj.* изоби́лующий: *be replete with*, изоби́ловать (+ *instr.*).

replica *n.* ко́пия.

reply *v.t. & i.* отвеча́ть: *reply to an invitation*, отвеча́ть на приглаше́ние. *She replied that...*, она́ отве́тила, что... —*n.* отве́т: *in reply to*, в отве́т на.

report *n.* **1,** (formal account) докла́д; отчёт. *A report on the progress of the negotiations*, докла́д о хо́де перегово́ров. *A report on one's trip*, отчёт о свое́й пое́здке. **2,** (item of news; communiqué) сообще́ние: *reports in the press*, сообще́ния в печа́ти. *Weather report*, сво́дка пого́ды. **3,** (message; communication) сообще́ние; донесе́ние: *reports from the battlefield*, сообще́ния/донесе́ния с по́ля би́твы. **4,** (assessment) о́тзыв: *a favorable report*, благоприя́тный о́тзыв. **5,** (rumor) слух; молва́. —*v.t.* **1,** (convey; relate) сообща́ть (о): *report the latest news*, сообща́ть после́дние изве́стия. *Report an incident to the police*, сообщи́ть о (*or* заяви́ть о) происше́ствии в мили́цию. **2,** (make a charge against to someone in authority) жа́ловаться на: *I'll report him to the police*, я бу́ду жа́ловаться на него́ в мили́цию. —*v.i.* **1,** (give a report) докла́дывать: *report to the congress*, докла́дывать съе́зду; *report on the situation*, докла́дывать обстано́вку. **2,** (present oneself; appear) явля́ться. *Report for work*, явля́ться *or* выходи́ть на рабо́ту. **3,** *fol. by* **to** (be subordinate to) отчи́тываться (пе́ред).

report card та́бель (успева́емости).

reportedly *adv.* по слу́хам. *He is reportedly looking for a new job*, говоря́т, что он и́щет но́вую рабо́ту.

reporter *n.* репортёр.

repose *n.* **1,** (rest) о́тдых; отдохнове́ние. **2,** (tranquillity) поко́й; споко́йствие. —*v.t.* (place, as trust) возлага́ть. —*v.i.* **1,** (lie at rest) лежа́ть. **2,** (rest; relax) отдыха́ть. **3,** (rest in death) поко́иться; почива́ть.

repository *n.* храни́лище.

reprehensible *adj.* предосуди́тельный.

represent *v.t.* **1,** (symbolize; stand for) представля́ть; изобража́ть. *This figure represents good and this one evil*, э́та фигу́ра представля́ет добро́, а э́та — зло. *Phonetic symbols represent sounds*, фонети́ческие зна́ки изобража́ют зву́ки. **2,** (serve as the agent or representative of) представля́ть. **3,** (be; constitute) представля́ть (собо́й). *Represent nothing new*, не представля́ть собо́й ничего́ но́вого. —**represent oneself as**, изобража́ть из себя́ (+ *acc.*); выдава́ть себя́ за.

representation *n.* **1,** (being represented) представи́тельство: *proportional representation,* пропорциона́льное представи́тельство. **2,** (picture; image) изображе́ние. **3,** (formal statement or protest) представле́ние: *make representations to,* де́лать представле́ния (+ *dat.*).

representative *n.* представи́тель. —*adj.* **1,** (based on the principle of representation) представи́тельный. **2,** (typical) характе́рный. —**House of Representatives,** пала́та представи́телей.

repress *v.t.* подавля́ть; сде́рживать.

repression *n.* **1,** (suppression) подавле́ние. **2,** (practice of repressing) репре́ссия. *Political repression,* полити́ческие репре́ссии.

repressive *adj.* репресси́вный.

reprieve *n.* отсро́чка приведе́ния в исполне́ние (сме́ртного) пригово́ра.

reprimand *n.* вы́говор. —*v.t.* де́лать вы́говор (+ *dat.*).

reprint *v.t.* перепеча́тывать. —*n.* перепеча́тка; о́ттиск.

reprisal *n., often pl.* отве́тная ме́ра: *economic reprisals,* отве́тные экономи́ческие ме́ры.

reprise *n.* репри́за.

reproach *v.t.* упрека́ть; укоря́ть. —*n.* упрёк; уко́р. *Beyond reproach,* безупре́чный. —**reproachful,** *adj.* укори́зненный.

reprobate *n.* распу́тник. —*adj.* распу́тный.

reprobation *n.* порица́ние; осужде́ние.

reproduce *v.t.* воспроизводи́ть: *reproduce a picture,* воспроизводи́ть карти́ну. —*v.i.* размножа́ться: *reproduce by cellular division,* размножа́ться кле́точным деле́нием.

reproduction *n.* **1,** (act of reproducing) воспроизведе́ние. **2,** (copy; facsimile) репроду́кция. **3,** (propagation) размноже́ние.

reproductive *adj.* воспроизводи́тельный. *Reproductive organs,* о́рганы размноже́ния.

reproof *n.* вы́говор; замеча́ние; упрёк; о́тповедь.

reprove *v.t.* упрека́ть; сде́лать вы́говор *or* замеча́ние (+ *dat.*).

reptile *n.* пресмыка́ющееся.

republic *n.* респу́блика.

republican *n.* республика́нец. —*adj.* республика́нский.

republish *v.t.* переиздава́ть. —**republication,** *n.* переизда́ние.

repudiate *v.t.* **1,** (renounce; disavow) отрека́ться от; отка́зываться от. **2,** (reject as untrue) отрица́ть. **3,** (reject with disapproval) отверга́ть.

repudiation *n.* **1,** (disavowal) отрече́ние; отка́з. **2,** (rejection; rebuff) отпо́р.

repugnance *n.* отвраще́ние.

repugnant *adj.* отта́лкивающий; отврати́тельный. *Be repugnant to,* отта́лкивать.

repulse *v.t.* **1,** (repel) отража́ть; отбива́ть. **2,** (rebuff) дать отпо́р (+ *dat.*). —*n.* отпо́р.

repulsion *n.* **1,** (repulsing) отраже́ние. **2,** (repugnance) отвраще́ние.

repulsive *adj.* отта́лкивающий; отврати́тельный.

repurchase *v.t.* перекупа́ть.

reputable *adj.* соли́дный; по́льзующийся хоро́шей репута́цией.

reputation *n.* репута́ция.

repute *n.* репута́ция.

reputed *adj.* предполага́емый. —**be reputed to be,** слыть (+ *instr.*): *He is reputed to be an expert,* он слывёт знатоко́м.

request *n.* про́сьба: *a request for help,* про́сьба о по́мощи. *At the request of,* по про́сьбе (+ *gen.*). —*v.t.* проси́ть: *request permission,* проси́ть разреше́ния; *request an appointment,* проси́ть о свида́нии. *It is requested that each person bring a gift,* про́сят, чтобы ка́ждый принёс пода́рок. —**on/by request,** по про́сьбе; по тре́бованию.

requiem *n.* панихи́да; ре́квием.

require *v.t.* тре́бовать: *require constant care,* тре́бовать постоя́нного ухо́да. *The law requires all citizens to register,* зако́н тре́бует, чтобы все гра́ждане зарегистри́ровались.

required *adj.* **1,** (needed; necessary) необходи́мый; тре́буемый. *The required amount,* необходи́мое коли́чество. **2,** (compulsory) обяза́тельный: *required subject,* обяза́тельный предме́т. **3,** *fol. by* **to** (obligated) обя́зан: *You are not required to attend,* вы не обя́заны прису́тствовать.

requirement *n.* **1,** (condition; prerequisite) тре́бование: *meet the requirements,* отвеча́ть тре́бованиям. **2,** (need) потре́бность.

requisite *adj.* необходи́мый; тре́буемый.

requisition *v.t.* реквизи́ровать. —*n.* тре́бование; зая́вка.

requital *n.* взаи́мность: *without requital,* без взаи́мности.

requite *v.t.* **1,** (return) отпла́чивать. *Requite someone's love,* отвеча́ть кого́-нибудь взаи́мностью. **2,** (avenge) вымеща́ть (оби́ду).

reread *v.t.* перечи́тывать.

resale *n.* перепрода́жа.

reschedule *v.t.* переноси́ть: *reschedule the meeting for Wednesday,* переноси́ть собра́ние на сре́ду. *Reschedule a debt,* отсро́чить упла́ту до́лга.

rescind *v.t.* отменя́ть; аннули́ровать. —**rescission,** *n.* отме́на; аннули́рование.

rescue *v.t.* спаса́ть; избавля́ть. *Rescue a drowning man,* спасти́ утопа́ющего. *Rescue a child from a burning building,* спасти́ ребёнка из горя́щего зда́ния. —*n.* спасе́ние. *Come to the rescue of,* приходи́ть на по́мощь (+ *dat.*). —*adj.* спаса́тельный: *rescue operations,* спаса́тельные опера́ции *or* рабо́ты; *rescue team/party,* спаса́тельная кома́нда. *Rescue worker,* спаса́тель.

rescuer *n.* спаси́тель.

research *n.* иссле́дование; изыска́ния. *Do research,* проводи́ть иссле́дование. —*adj.* иссле́довательский: *research work,* иссле́довательская рабо́та. *Research institute,* нау́чно-иссле́довательский институ́т. *Research associate,* нау́чный сотру́дник. —*v.t.* иссле́довать. —**researcher,** *n.* иссле́дователь.

resection *n., med.* резе́кция.

resell *v.t.* перепродава́ть.

resemblance *n.* сходство: *bear a certain resemblance to,* иметь некоторое сходство с.

resemble *v.t.* быть похожим на: *He resembles his father,* он похож на отца. *The building resembled an old castle,* здание напоминало старый замок.

resent *v.t.* обижаться на; негодовать на. *He resented your remarks very much,* он очень обиделся на ваши замечания. —**resentful,** *adj.* обиженный. —**resentment,** *n.* обида.

reservation *n.* **1,** (limiting condition) оговорка: *without reservation,* без оговорок; безоговорочно. **2,** (advance order) броня. *I have a (room) reservation,* у меня забронирован *or* зарезервирован *or* заказан номер; у меня броня. *Make a reservation,* бронировать место; сделать предварительный заказ. **3,** (reserve for Indians) резервация.

reserve *v.t.* **1,** (set aside) откладывать: *Reserve one copy for me,* отложите один экземпляр для меня. *Reserve a book in the library,* откладывать книгу в библиотеке. *These seats are reserved for tourists,* эти места предназначены для туристов. **2,** (secure in advance) бронировать; заказывать. *Reserve a room in a hotel,* бронировать номер в гостинице. *Reserve a table for two,* заказать стол на двоих. **3,** (retain for oneself, as a right) сохранять *or* оставлять за собой. **4,** (defer) откладывать. *Reserve judgment,* воздержаться от суждения. —*n.* **1,** (something kept for future use) запас; резерв. *Oil reserves,* запасы нефти. *Reserves of ammunition,* запас боеприпасов. *Hold in reserve,* держать про запас. **2,** (reservation of public land) заповедник: *forest reserve,* лесной заповедник. **3,** (qualification; reservation) оговорка: *without reserve,* без оговорок. **4,** (reticence) сдержанность. **5,** *often pl., mil.* запас; резерв: *be in the reserves,* быть в запасе; быть в резерве. **6,** *finance* резервный фонд. **7,** *sports* запасной игрок. —*adj.* запасной. *Reserve officer,* офицер запаса.

reserved *adj.* **1,** (secured in advance) забронированный. *Reserved seat,* нумерованное место. **2,** (reticent) сдержанный.

reservist *n.* резервист; запасной.

reservoir *n.* водохранилище.

reset *v.t.* **1,** *med.* вправлять. **2,** *printing* перебирать.

resettle *v.t.* переселять. —*v.i.* переселяться. —**resettlement,** *n.* переселение.

reshoot *v.t.* переснимать.

reshuffle *v.t.* перетасовывать. —*n.* перетасовка. *Cabinet reshuffle,* перестановки в кабинете (*or* в составе кабинета).

reside *v.i.* проживать; жить.

residence *n.* **1,** (act of residing) проживание; жительство. *Take up residence,* поселяться. *Residence permit,* прописка; вид на жительство. *Permanent residence abroad,* постоянное жительство за границей. **2,** (dwelling place) местожительство; местопребывание; резиденция.

resident *n.* житель. —**residential,** *adj.* жилой: *residential area,* жилой район.

residue *n.* остаток. —**residual,** *adj.* остаточный.

resign *v.i.* **1,** (give up one's office or position) уходить в отставку. *Resign!,* в отставку! **2,** (withdraw) выходить: *resign from the commission,* выходить из комиссии. **3,** *chess* сдаваться. —*v.t.* отказываться от (должности). —**resign oneself to; become resigned to,** мириться с; покоряться (+ *dat.*).

resignation *n.* **1,** (act of resigning) отставка: *submit one's resignation,* подавать в отставку. *Announce one's resignation,* заявить об уходе в отставку. **2,** (being resigned to something) смирение.

resilient *adj.* упругий. —**resilience,** *n.* упругость.

resin *n.* смола. —**resinous,** *adj.* смолистый.

resist *v.t.* **1,** (try to stop) сопротивляться: *resist the invaders,* сопротивляться захватчикам. *Resist someone's advances,* отвергать чьи-нибудь ухаживания. **2,** (withstand, as temptation) устоять против *or* перед; удержаться от. *The offer is hard to resist,* трудно отказаться от этого предложения. **3,** (restrain oneself) удержаться: *I couldn't resist teasing him,* я не мог удержаться, чтобы не подразнить его. **4,** (withstand the effect of) не поддаваться (+ *dat.*): *resist rust,* не поддаваться ржавчине. —*v.i.* сопротивляться; оказывать сопротивление.

resistance *n.* **1,** (act of resisting) сопротивление. *Resistance movement,* движение сопротивления. **2,** *med.* устойчивость; сопротивляемость. —**follow the path** (*or* **line**) **of least resistance,** идти по линии наименьшего сопротивления.

resistant *adj.* стойкий; устойчивый. *Become resistant to antibiotics,* стать устойчивым к антибиотикам. *Heat-resistant,* теплостойкий. *Rust-resistant,* нержавеющий. *Crease-resistant,* немнущийся.

resolute *adj.* решительный; твёрдый. —**resoluteness,** *n.* решительность; решимость; твёрдость.

resolution *n.* **1,** (act of solving or resolving) разрешение; решение. **2,** (formal expression of a group's opinion) резолюция. **3,** (vow; pledge) зарок.

resolve *v.t.* **1,** (solve; settle) разрешать: *resolve a conflict,* разрешать конфликт. **2,** (express by resolution) постановлять. **3,** (decide) решать; решаться. —*n.* решимость. —**resolving power,** разрешающая способность.

resonance *n.* резонанс. —**resonant,** *adj.* звучный; гулкий.

resonator *n.* резонатор.

resort *v.i.* [*usu.* **resort to**] прибегать к; идти на: пойти на. *Resort to force,* прибегать к силе. *Resort to guile,* идти на хитрость. *Resort to drastic measures,* пойти на крутые меры. —*n.* **1,** (vacation spot) курорт. **2,** (recourse) ресурс: *last resort,* последний ресурс. *As a last resort,* в крайнем случае; как последнее средство. *Have resort to,* прибегать к. *Without resort to,* не прибегая к. —*adj.* курортный: *resort area,* курортный район.

resound *v.i.* **1,** (sound; be heard) раздаваться; резонировать. **2,** (be filled with the sound of) оглашаться (+ *instr.*).

resounding *adj.* **1,** (reverberating) звонкий; звучный; зычный; гулкий; раскатистый. **2,** (decisive) решительный.

resource *n.* **1,** (source of help) ресурс. **2,** (assets;

wealth) ресу́рсы; бога́тства: *natural resources,* приро́дные ресу́рсы; есте́ственные бога́тства.

resourceful *adj.* нахо́дчивый. —**resourcefulness,** *n.* нахо́дчивость.

respect *v.t.* уважа́ть: *respect one's elders/ someone's feelings/ human rights/,* уважа́ть ста́рших/ чьи́-нибудь чу́вства/ права́ челове́ка/. *Respect someone's wishes,* учи́тывать чьи́-нибудь жела́ния. —*n.* **1,** (deference; due regard) уваже́ние: *respect for one's elders,* уваже́ние к ста́ршим; *respect for the law,* уваже́ние к зако́ну. *With all due respect to,* при всём моём уваже́нии к. **2,** *pl.* (expressions of esteem) почте́ние: *pay one's respects to,* (за)свиде́тельствовать почте́ние (+ *dat.*). *Pay one's last respects to,* отдава́ть после́дний долг *or* после́дние по́чести (+ *dat.*). **3,** (aspect) отноше́ние: *in many respects,* во мно́гих отноше́ниях. *In all other respects,* в остально́м; во всём остально́м. —**in/with respect to,** в отноше́нии (+ *gen.*).

respectability *n.* респекта́бельность.

respectable *adj.* **1,** (proper; presentable) прили́чный; респекта́бельный. **2,** (fairly good or large) прили́чный; поря́дочный: *a respectable amount,* прили́чная/поря́дочная су́мма.

respected *adj.* уважа́емый.

respectful *adj.* почти́тельный; уважи́тельный.

respectfully *adv.* почти́тельно; уважи́тельно. —**respectfully yours,** с почте́нием.

respecting *prep.* относи́тельно; по отноше́нию к.

respective *adj.* свой: *in their respective places,* ка́ждый на своём ме́сте.

respectively *adv.* соотве́тственно.

respiration *n.* дыха́ние. —**respirator,** *n.* респира́тор. —**respiratory,** *adj.* дыха́тельный.

respite *n.* передышка. *Without respite,* без передышки.

resplendent *adj.* блиста́тельный. —**resplendence,** *n.* блеск.

respond *v.i.* отвеча́ть; отзыва́ться; отклика́ться. *Respond to an appeal,* отвеча́ть *or* отзыва́ться *or* отклика́ться на призы́в. *Respond to treatment,* поддава́ться лече́нию.

response *n.* **1,** (answer) отве́т. **2,** (reaction) о́тклик.

responsibility *n.* **1,** (accountability) отве́тственность. *Position of responsibility,* отве́тственный пост. *The responsibility for a crime,* отве́тственность на преступле́ние. *Acknowledge one's responsibility,* признава́ть свою́ отве́тственность. **2,** (duty) обя́занность: *broad range of responsibilities,* широ́кий круг обя́занностей.

responsible *adj.* **1,** (accountable) отве́тственный. *Be responsible for,* отвеча́ть за; быть отве́тственным за; нести́ отве́тственность за. *Be responsible to,* нести́ отве́тственность пе́ред. **2,** (being the cause of): *the person responsible for the crime,* вино́вник преступле́ния. *He is responsible for my being here,* я здесь благодаря́ ему́. **3,** (reliable) отве́тственный: *responsible person,* отве́тственный челове́к. **4,** (entailing great responsibility) отве́тственный: *responsible position,* отве́тственный пост.

responsive *adj.* отзы́вчивый.

rest *n.* **1,** (relaxation) о́тдых. *Day of rest,* день о́тдыха. *Take a short rest,* немно́го отдохну́ть. **2,** (peace and quiet) поко́й. **3,** (absence of motion) поко́й: *at rest,* в поко́е. *Come to rest,* сади́ться. **4,** *music* па́уза. **5,** (the remainder) оста́ток; остально́е. *The rest of the way/money,* оста́ток пути́/де́нег. *The rest of the time,* остально́е вре́мя. *How about the rest?,* как насчёт остально́го? **6,** (the remaining ones) остальны́е. —*v.i.* **1,** (relax) отдыха́ть: *rest from one's labors,* отдыха́ть от рабо́ты. **2,** (lean; be supported) опира́ться; поко́иться. **3,** *fol. by* **on** *or* **with** (fall; lie, as of blame, responsibility, etc.) лежа́ть (на). **4,** (remain for action): *The decision rests with you,* реше́ние за ва́ми. *Let the matter rest there,* оста́вить де́ло как есть. **5,** *fol. by* **on** (be based on) поко́иться (на): *rest on three principles,* поко́иться на трёх при́нципах. —*v.t.* **1,** (place) класть; ста́вить: *rest one's elbows on the table,* класть ло́кти на стол. **2,** (lean) прислоня́ть. **3,** (allow to rest) дать отдохну́ть: *rest one's eyes/ the horses/,* дать глаза́м/лошадя́м отдохну́ть. —**eternal rest,** ве́чный поко́й. *Go to one's eternal rest,* засну́ть ве́чным сном. —**lay to rest,** хорони́ть. —**may he rest in peace,** мир пра́ху его́. —**put to rest,** рассе́ивать (сомне́ния). —**rest!** (*military command*), во́льно!

restate *v.t.* вновь заявля́ть.

restaurant *n.* рестора́н.

restful *adj.* споко́йный. *Restful color,* споко́йный цвет.

rest home дом о́тдыха.

restitution *n.* **1,** (restoration) восстановле́ние. **2,** (reimbursement) возмеще́ние убы́тков. *Make restitution,* возмеща́ть убы́тки.

restive *adj.* **1,** (restless) беспоко́йный; непосе́дливый. **2,** (balky, as of a horse) норови́стый.

restless *adj.* беспоко́йный; непосе́дливый. —**restlessness,** *n.* беспоко́йство; непосе́дливость.

restoration *n.* **1,** (bringing back) восстановле́ние. **2,** (repair; rebuilding) восстанови́тельные рабо́ты. **3,** (bringing back to its original state) реставра́ция. **4,** (restoring of a monarchy) реставра́ция.

restore *v.t.* **1,** (bring back; re-establish) восстана́вливать: *restore order,* восстанови́ть поря́док. *Restore someone to health,* возврати́ть кому́-нибудь здоро́вье. *Be restored to health,* восстанови́ть своё здоро́вье. *The king was restored to the throne,* коро́ль был возвращён на престо́л. **2,** (bring back to its original state) реставри́ровать: *restore an old church,* реставри́ровать стари́нную це́рковь. **3,** (return; give back) возвраща́ть: *restore citizenship to,* возвраща́ть гражда́нство (+ *dat.*).

restorer *n.* реставра́тор.

restrain *v.t.* сде́рживать; уде́рживать; обу́здывать. —**restrain oneself,** сде́рживаться; уде́рживаться; обу́здывать себя́.

restrained *adj.* сде́ржанный.

restraint *n.* **1,** (act of restraining) обузда́ние. *Under no restraint,* ниче́м не обу́зданный. **2,** (reserve; constraint) сде́ржанность: *show/exercise restraint,* проявлять сде́ржанность. **3,** (limitation) ограниче́ние: *wage restraints,* ограниче́ния зарабо́тной пла́ты.

restrict *v.t.* ограни́чивать: *restrict imports of cars,* ограни́чивать ввоз автомоби́лей. *Restricted area,* запре́тная зо́на.

restriction *n.* ограниче́ние: *restrictions on exports/ travel,* ограниче́ния на э́кспорт/пое́здки.

restrictive *adj.* ограничи́тельный.

rest room туале́т; убо́рная.

restructure *v.t.* перестра́ивать.

result *n.* результа́т; ито́г; сле́дствие. *As a result (of),* в результа́те (+ *gen.*). *Without results,* безрезульта́тно. *Election results,* ито́ги вы́боров. —*v.i.* **1,** (happen) вытека́ть; происходи́ть; проистека́ть. **2,** *fol. by* **in** (lead to) приводи́ть (к); конча́ться (+ *instr.*).

resume *v.t.* **1,** (start again after a break) возобновля́ть: *resume debate/negotiations,* возобновля́ть пре́ния/ перегово́ры. **2,** (assume again) сно́ва принима́ть. *Resume one's seat,* сно́ва сесть. —*v.i.* возобновля́ться: *Work resumed after a brief interruption,* рабо́та возобнови́лась по́сле небольшо́го переры́ва.

résumé *n.* резюме́. *Job résumé,* послужно́й спи́сок.

resumption *n.* возобновле́ние.

resurgence *n.* возрожде́ние. —**resurgent,** *adj.* возрожда́ющий.

resurrect *v.t.* воскреша́ть.

resurrection *n.* **1,** (returning to life) воскресе́ние; возрожде́ние. **2,** *fig.* (revival) возрожде́ние; воскреше́ние.

resuscitate *v.t.* оживля́ть; приводи́ть в созна́ние. —**resuscitation,** *n.* оживле́ние; реанима́ция.

retail *n.* ро́зничная прода́жа. —*adj.* ро́зничный: *retail store,* ро́зничный магази́н. —*adv.* в ро́зницу. —*v.t. & i.* продава́ть(ся) в ро́зницу. —**retailer,** *n.* ро́зничный торго́вец.

retain *v.t.* **1,** (keep possession of) уде́рживать: *retain power,* уде́рживать власть. *Retain the championship,* отстоя́ть зва́ние чемпио́на. *Retain the post of...,* сохраня́ть *or* оставля́ть за собо́й пост (+ *gen.*). **2,** (maintain; keep) сохраня́ть: *retain control over,* сохраня́ть контро́ль над. **3,** (hold within) заде́рживать: *retain moisture,* заде́рживать вла́гу. **4,** (remember) уде́рживать в па́мяти; запомина́ть. **5,** (hire) нанима́ть.

retainer *n.* **1,** (servant) приближённый. **2,** (fee) (предвари́тельный) гонора́р.

retaining wall подпо́рная сте́нка.

retake *v.t.* **1,** (recapture) отбива́ть; отвоёвывать. **2,** (photograph again) пересни́мать. **3,** (take again, as an examination) пересдава́ть; переде́рживать.

retaliate *v.i.* **1,** (repay in kind) отпла́чивать тем же. **2,** *mil.* наноси́ть отве́тный уда́р. —**retaliation,** *n.* отпла́та; отве́тный уда́р. —**retaliatory,** *adj.* отве́тный.

retard *v.t.* заде́рживать; замедля́ть; тормози́ть.

retardation *n.* **1,** (act of retarding) торможе́ние. **2,** (mental deficiency) у́мственная отста́лость *or* неразви́тость.

retarded *adj.* отста́лый. *Mentally retarded,* у́мственно отста́лый.

retch *v.i.* рвать. —**retching,** *n.* рво́та.

retell *v.t.* переска́зывать.

retention *n.* **1,** (keeping for oneself) удержа́ние. **2,** (maintaining; keeping) сохране́ние. **3,** (holding within) задержа́ние. **4,** (ability to remember) па́мять.

retentive *adj.* це́пкий: *retentive memory,* це́пкая па́мять.

rethink *v.t.* взгляну́ть на (что-нибудь) по-друго́му.

reticent *adj.* сде́ржанный; молчали́вый. —**reticence,** *n.* сде́ржанность; молчали́вость.

retie *v.t.* перевя́зывать.

retighten *v.t.* перетя́гивать.

retina *n.* сетча́тка; се́тчатая оболо́чка; рети́на. —**detached retina,** отсло́йка сетча́тки; отсло́йка се́тчатой оболо́чки.

retinue *n.* сви́та.

retire *v.i.* **1,** (give up one's work or career) уходи́ть на пе́нсию *or* в отста́вку. *Retire from the stage,* сойти́ *or* уйти́ со сце́ны. *Retire from the army,* уйти́ в отста́вку из а́рмии. **2,** (withdraw) удаля́ться. **3,** (go to bed) ложи́ться спать. —*v.t.* **1,** (force to retire) отправля́ть на пе́нсию *or* на поко́й; увольня́ть в отста́вку. **2,** (withdraw from circulation) изыма́ть из обраще́ния. **3,** *mil.* (take out of service) снима́ть с вооруже́ния.

retired *adj.* на пе́нсии; в отста́вке; отставно́й. *Lt. Col. (ret.),* подполко́вник в отста́вке. *Retired persons,* пенсионе́ры.

retiree *n.* пенсионе́р.

retirement *n.* **1,** (act of retiring) ухо́д на пе́нсию; отста́вка. *Retirement age,* пенсио́нный во́зраст. *Send into retirement,* отправля́ть в отста́вку *or* на поко́й. **2,** (seclusion) уедине́ние.

retiring *adj.* скро́мный; засте́нчивый.

retort *v.i.* (ре́зко) отве́тить. —*n.* **1,** (quick, sharp reply) возраже́ние; ре́плика. **2,** (vessel) ко́лба; рето́рта.

retouch *v.t.* **1,** (touch up) подправля́ть. **2,** *photog.* ретуши́ровать. —**retoucher,** *n.* ретушёр. —**retouching,** *n.* ре́тушь.

retrace *v.t.* **1,** (go back over, as one's steps) возвраща́ться по (свои́м следа́м). **2,** (trace the history of) просле́живать.

retract *v.t.* **1,** (pull in) втя́гивать. *Retract the landing gear,* убира́ть шасси́. **2,** (take back; disavow) отка́зываться от; брать наза́д.

retraction *n.* опроверже́ние: *print a retraction,* печа́тать опроверже́ние.

retrain *v.t.* переу́чивать; переквалифици́ровать. —**retraining,** *n.* переквалифика́ция.

retreat *v.i.* отступа́ть: *retreat from danger,* отступа́ть пе́ред опа́сностью. *Retreat a few steps,* отступи́ть на не́сколько шаго́в. *The order to retreat,* прика́з об отступле́нии. —*n.* **1,** (withdrawal) отступле́ние. *Beat a retreat,* бить отбо́й. **2,** (signal to retreat; bugle call at sunset) отбо́й. *Sound retreat,* дава́ть *or* бить отбо́й. **3,** (secluded place) прию́т; приста́нище.

retrench *v.i.* сокраща́ть расхо́ды; эконо́мить.

retrial *n.* повто́рное слу́шание де́ла; пересу́д.

retribution *n.* возме́здие; распла́та. *Retribution will* *be swift,* возме́здие не заста́вит себя́ ждать; расчёт бу́дет ко́роток; с ним бу́дет коро́ткий расчёт (*or* коро́ткий разгово́р).

retrieval *n.* возвраще́ние. *Retrieval of information,* по́иск информа́ции.

retrieve *v.t.* брать обра́тно; возвраща́. —**retriever,** *n.* охо́тничья соба́ка.

retroactive *adj.* име́ющий обра́тную си́лу (*or* обра́тное де́йствие). *Make retroactive to January 1,* счита́ть вступи́вшим в си́лу с пе́рвого января́.

retrograde *adj.* обра́тный: *retrograde motion,* обра́тное движе́ние.

retrogress *v.i.* регресси́ровать. —**retrogression,** *n.* регре́сс. —**retrogressive,** *adj.* регресси́вный.

retro-rocket *n.* тормозна́я раке́та.

retrospect *n., in* **in retrospect,** ретроспекти́вно (смотря́); за́дним число́м (говоря́).

retrospection *n.* ретроспе́кция. —**retrospective,** *adj.* ретроспекти́вный.

retry *v.t.* сно́ва слу́шать (де́ло); сно́ва суди́ть (обвиня́емого).

return *v.i.* возвраща́ться: *return home,* возвраща́ться домо́й; *return from vacation,* возвраща́ться из о́тпуска. —*v.t.* **1,** (give back) возвраща́ть; отдава́ть. *Return a book to the library,* возвраща́ть *or* сдава́ть кни́гу в библиоте́ку. *Return a wallet to its owner,* возвраща́ть бума́жник владе́льцу. **2,** (put back) класть *or* ста́вить обра́тно. **3,** (reciprocate) отвеча́ть на. *Return the fire,* откры́ть отве́тный ого́нь. *Return the enemy's fire,* отве́тить на ого́нь проти́вника. *Return a salute,* отда́ть честь в свою́ о́чередь. *Return a favor,* отвеча́ть услу́гой на услу́гу. *Return a visit,* нанести́ отве́тный визи́т; прийти́ с отве́тным визи́том. *Have him return my call,* пусть он мне позвони́т; попроси́те его́ мне позвони́ть. **4,** (yield, as a profit) приноси́ть. **5,** (render, as a verdict) выноси́ть. **6,** (elect) избира́ть; (re-elect) переизбира́ть. **7,** *sports* отбива́ть (мяч). —*n.* **1,** (act of returning) возвраще́ние; возвра́т. *On his return from Europe,* по возвраще́нии из Евро́пы. **2,** (profit; yield) дохо́д; отда́ча. **3,** (report, as on taxes) деклара́ция. **4,** *pl.* (election returns) результа́ты вы́боров. —*adj.* **1,** (in the opposite direction) обра́тный: *return ticket/address,* обра́тный биле́т/а́дрес. *By return mail,* с обра́тной по́чтой. **2,** (done or held in return) отве́тный: *return visit,* отве́тный визи́т. *Return match,* матч-рева́нш. —**in return,** взаме́н: *receive nothing in return,* ничего́ не получи́ть взаме́н. —**in return for,** в отве́т на; в обме́н на; в отпла́ту за. —**many happy returns of the day,** поздравля́ю вас с днём рожде́ния; жела́ю вам до́лгих лет жи́зни.

retype *v.t.* перепеча́тывать.

reunification *n.* воссоедине́ние.

reunion *n.* встре́ча; сбор.

reunite *v.t.* воссоединя́ть. *Be reunited,* воссоединя́ться.

reupholster *v.t.* перебива́ть.

reuse *v.t.* повто́рно испо́льзовать.

revamp *v.t.* **1,** (renovate) обновля́ть. **2,** (revise) перекра́ивать.

revanchism *n.* реванши́зм. —**revanchist,** *n.* реванши́ст. —*adj.* реванши́стский.

reveal *v.t.* **1,** (show; uncover; display) пока́зывать; обнару́живать: *reveal one's face/feelings,* пока́зывать/ обнару́живать своё лицо́/ свои́ чу́вства/. **2,** (disclose; divulge) раскрыва́ть. *Reveal a secret,* раскры́ть *or* откры́ть секре́т. —**revealing,** *adj.* показа́тельный; знамена́тельный.

reveille *n.* побу́дка; подъём; (у́тренняя) заря́.

revel *v.i.* **1,** (carouse) пирова́ть; кути́ть. **2,** *fol. by in* (delight in) наслажда́ться (+ *instr.*); упива́ться (+ *instr.*).

revelation *n.* **1,** (act of revealing) раскры́тие. **2,** (something revealed) разоблаче́ние: *revelations of corruption,* разоблаче́ния корру́пции. **3,** (striking discovery) открове́ние: *It was quite a revelation to me,* для меня́ э́то бы́ло настоя́щим открове́нием. **4,** *cap., Bib.* апока́липсис.

reveler *also,* **reveller** *n.* кути́ла; гуля́ка.

revelry *n.* весе́лье.

revenge *n.* **1,** (vengeance) месть; мще́ние. *In revenge for,* в отме́стку за. *Take revenge,* мстить. **2,** (reversal of a defeat) рева́нш: *gain revenge,* взять рева́нш. —*v.t.* мстить за; вымеща́ть.

revengeful *adj.* мсти́тельный.

revenue *n.* дохо́д.

reverberate *v.i.* отража́ться; отдава́ться. —**reverberation,** *n.* ревербера́ция.

revere *v.t.* почита́ть; благогове́ть пе́ред.

reverence *n.* **1,** (veneration) почте́ние; благогове́ние. **2,** *cap.* (title) преподо́бие.

reverend *adj., usu. cap.* его́ преподо́бие (+ *name*).

reverent *adj.* почти́тельный; благогове́йный.

reverie *n.* мечта́ние; мечта́тельность. *Indulge in reverie,* предава́ться мечта́м.

reversal *n.* **1,** (complete change) измене́ние; переме́на: *reversal of direction,* измене́ние/переме́на направле́ния. **2,** *law* отме́на; аннули́рование: *reversal of a decision,* отме́на/аннули́рование реше́ния.

reverse *adj.* обра́тный: *in reverse order,* в обра́тном поря́дке. *The reverse side,* обра́тная *or* оборо́тная сторона́. *Reverse gear,* за́дний ход. —*n.* **1,** *preceded by* **the** (opposite) обра́тное; противополо́жное. *Quite the reverse,* совсе́м наоборо́т. **2,** (setback) неуда́ча. **3,** (backward motion) за́дний ход: *put the car in reverse,* дать за́дний ход. —*v.t.* **1,** (turn about) повора́чивать круго́м. **2,** (turn inside out) вывёртывать. **3,** (turn upside down) перевёртывать. **4,** (change completely) по́лностью изменя́ть: *reverse one's opinion,* по́лностью измени́ть своё мне́ние. **5,** (transpose) переставля́ть: *reverse two chapters in a book,* переставля́ть две главы́ в кни́ге. *Reverse the order of something,* измени́ть поря́док чего́-нибудь. *Now the situation is reversed,* тепе́рь де́ло обстои́т как раз наоборо́т. **6,** *law* (set aside; overturn) отменя́ть; аннули́ровать. —**reverse oneself,** дава́ть за́дний ход.

reversible *adj.* **1,** (that can be reversed) обрати́мый. **2,** (worn on either side) двусторо́нний. —**reversibility,** *n.* обрати́мость.

reversion *n.* возвраще́ние.
revert *v.i.* **1,** (return) возвраща́ться: *revert to one's old habits,* возвраща́ться к ста́рым привы́чкам. **2,** *law* переходи́ть.
revet *v.t.* облицо́вывать. —**revetment,** *n.* облицо́вка.
review *n.* **1,** (reconsideration) пересмо́тр. *The decision is subject to review,* реше́ние подлежи́т пересмо́тру. *The matter is under review,* де́ло сейча́с рассма́тривается. **2,** (critique) реце́нзия; о́тзыв. *Book review,* реце́нзия на кни́гу. *Get rave reviews,* получи́ть восто́рженные о́тзывы. **3,** (survey) обзо́р. **4,** (restudying of lessons) повторе́ние. **5,** *mil.* смотр: *review of the troops,* смотр войска́м. **6,** (journal) обозре́ние. —*v.t.* **1,** (reconsider) пересма́тривать: *review a case,* пересма́тривать де́ло. **2,** (go over) просма́тривать: *review one's notes,* просмотре́ть запи́ски. *Review a lesson,* повторя́ть уро́к. **3,** (think back on) перебира́ть: *review in one's mind,* перебира́ть в уме́. **4,** (write a review of) рецензи́ровать. **5,** *mil.* принима́ть (пара́д); производи́ть смотр (войска́м).
reviewer *n.* рецензе́нт.
reviewing stand трибу́на.
revile *v.t.* поноси́ть; руга́ть.
revise *v.t.* **1,** (alter; change) пересма́тривать. **2,** (re-edit; rework) перераба́тывать. *Revised edition,* испра́вленное изда́ние.
revision *n.* **1,** (act of revising) пересмо́тр (програ́ммы); перерабо́тка (кни́ги). **2,** (change; correction) измене́ние; попра́вка. **3,** (revised edition) перерабо́тка.
revisionism *n.* ревизиони́зм. —**revisionist,** *n.* ревизиони́ст. —*adj.* ревизиони́стский.
revisit *v.t.* вновь посеща́ть.
revitalize *v.t.* оживля́ть; обновля́ть.
revival *n.* **1,** (resuscitation) оживле́ние. **2,** (restoration; renascence) оживле́ние; возрожде́ние. **3,** (restaging) возобновле́ние (постано́вки).
revive *v.t.* **1,** (resuscitate) оживля́ть; приводи́ть в себя́ *or* в созна́ние *or* в чу́вство. **2,** (bring back; restore) возрожда́ть; воскреша́ть: *revive a custom,* возрожда́ть/воскреша́ть обы́чай. **3,** (show or stage again) возобновля́ть постано́вку (+ *gen.*). —*v.i.* **1,** (regain consciousness) очну́ться. **2,** (regain vigor) ожива́ть: *The flowers revived in water,* цветы́ в воде́ о́жили. **3,** (come back into existence) воскреса́ть; возрожда́ться. *Hope revived,* наде́жда воскре́сла.
revocation *n.* отме́на; аннули́рование.
revoke *v.t.* отменя́ть; аннули́ровать. *His driver's license was revoked,* он был лишён води́тельских прав; у него́ бы́ли ото́браны води́тельские права́. —*v.i.,* *cards* рено́нс.
revolt *v.i.* (rebel) восстава́ть. —*v.t.* (disgust) вызыва́ть отвраще́ние у; отта́лкивать. —*n.* восста́ние; мяте́ж. —**revolting,** *adj.* отврати́тельный; омерзи́тельный.
revolution *n.* **1,** (political upheaval; momentous change) револю́ция. **2,** (rotation) оборо́т: *70 revolutions per minute,* се́мьдесят оборо́тов в мину́ту.
revolutionary *adj.* революцио́нный. —*n.* [*also,* **revolutionist**] революционе́р.

revolutionize *v.t.* революционизи́ровать.
revolve *v.i.* враща́ться; верте́ться: *revolve around the sun,* враща́ться/верте́ться вокру́г Со́лнца. *The investigation revolves around one question,* сле́дствие враща́ется (*or* сосредото́чено) вокру́г одного́ вопро́са. *Her whole life revolves around her daughter,* она́ живёт свое́й до́черью; вся её жизнь в до́чери.
revolver *n.* револьве́р.
revolving *adj.* враща́ющийся. —**revolving door,** враща́ющаяся дверь; верту́шка.
revue *n.* обозре́ние; ревю́.
revulsion *n.* отвраще́ние.
reward *n.* награ́да; вознагражде́ние. *Get one's just reward,* получи́ть по заслу́гам. —*v.t.* награжда́ть; вознагражда́ть. *Our patience has been rewarded,* на́ше терпе́ние вознаграждено́. —**rewarding,** *adj.* вы́годный; поле́зный.
rewind *v.t.* перема́тывать.
reword *v.t.* переде́лывать; перепи́сывать; перефрази́ровать.
rework *v.t.* перераба́тывать.
rewrite *v.t.* **1,** (write again) перепи́сывать. **2,** (revise) перераба́тывать.
rhapsody *n.* рапсо́дия.
rhenium *n.* ре́ний.
rheostat *n.* реоста́т.
rhetoric *n.* рито́рика. —**rhetorical,** *adj.* ритори́ческий.
rheumatic *adj.* ревмати́ческий. —*n.* ревма́тик. —**rheumatic fever,** суставно́й ревмати́зм.
rheumatism *n.* ревмати́зм.
rhinestone *n.* иску́сственный бриллиа́нт.
rhinoceros *n.* носоро́г.
rhizome *n.* корневи́ще.
rhodium *n.* ро́дий.
rhododendron *n.* рододе́ндрон.
rhombic *adj.* ромби́ческий.
rhomboid *n.* ромбо́ид.
rhombus *n.* ромб.
rhubarb *n.* реве́нь. —*adj.* реве́нный.
rhyme *n.* ри́фма. —*v.t.* рифмова́ть. —*v.i.* рифмова́ться. —**without rhyme or reason,** ни с того́ ни с сего́.
rhymer *n.* рифма́ч; рифмоплёт. *Also,* **rhymester.**
rhythm *n.* ритм. —**rhythmic; rhythmical,** *adj.* ритми́ческий; ритми́чный. —**rhythmics,** *n.* ри́тмика.
rib *n.* **1,** *anat.* ребро́. *Poke someone in the ribs,* толкну́ть кого́-нибудь в бок. **2,** (raised stripe in cloth) ру́бчик. —*v.t., colloq.* (tease) поддра́знивать.
ribald *adj.* скабрёзный; неприли́чный. —**ribaldry,** *n.* скабрёзность.
ribbed *adj.* **1,** (lined with ridges) ребри́стый; ру́бчатый. **2,** (fluted; corrugated) рифлёный.
ribbon *n.* **1,** (ornamental band; military decoration) ле́нта. *Typewriter ribbon,* ле́нта для пи́шущей маши́нки. **2,** *pl.* (shreds) кло́чья.
rice *n.* рис. —*adj.* ри́совый: *rice pudding,* ри́совый пу́динг.
rich *adj.* **1,** (wealthy) бога́тый: *rich widow/country,* бога́тая вдова́/страна́. *Rich in iron/vitamins,* бога́т

желе́зом/витами́нами. *Get rich,* (раз)богате́ть. **2,** (fertile) ту́чный; плодоро́дный. **3,** (fattening) жи́рный. **4,** (deep; vivid; mellow) со́чный; густо́й. *—n., preceded by* **the** бога́тые; богачи́.

riches *n.pl.* бога́тство.

richly *adv.* **1,** (lavishly) бога́то. **2,** (fully) вполне́: *richly deserved,* вполне́ заслу́женный.

richness *n.* **1,** (wealth) бога́тство. **2,** (fertility) ту́чность; плодоро́дие. **3,** (vividness, as of sound or color) густота́.

rick *n.* стог; скирд; скирда́.

rickets *n.* рахи́т.

rickety *adj.* ша́ткий; расша́танный.

rickshaw *n.* ри́кша.

ricochet *n.* рикоше́т. *—v.i.* рикошети́ровать.

rid *v.t.* избавля́ть; освобожда́ть; очища́ть. *Rid the house of mice,* очища́ть дом от мыше́й. **—get rid of,** отде́лываться от; избавля́ться от.

riddance *n.* избавле́ние. **—good riddance!,** ска́тертью доро́га!

riddle *n.* зага́дка. *—v.t.* **1,** (pierce with holes or bullets) изреше́чивать. **2,** *fig.* (affect every part of) проника́ть: *riddled with graft,* прони́кнут корру́пцией.

ride *v.i.* **1,** (be conveyed in a vehicle) е́хать; е́здить. *Ride in a carriage,* е́хать в коля́ске. **2,** (sit on and be carried by a horse) е́здить верхо́м: *teach someone how to ride,* научи́ть кого́-нибудь е́здить верхо́м. **3,** (handle, as of a car) идти́; ходи́ть: *The car rides well,* маши́на хорошо́ идёт/хо́дит. **4,** *fol. by* **on** (depend on) зави́сеть от: *A lot is riding on the outcome,* мно́го зави́сит от исхо́да де́ла. *—v.t.* **1,** (be transported by or on) е́хать на; е́здить на; ката́ться на. *Ride a bicycle,* е́хать/е́здить на велосипе́де; *ride a horse,* е́здить верхо́м; *ride a camel,* е́здить верхо́м на верблю́де; *ride a merry-go-round,* ката́ться на карусе́ли; *ride the waves,* ката́ться на волна́х. **2,** *usu. passive* (beset) му́чить: *be ridden by doubts,* му́читься сомне́ниями. **3,** *colloq.* (tease) высме́ивать. **4,** *fol. by* **out** (weather, as a storm) выде́рживать. *—n.* **1,** (act of riding) езда́: *a ten-minute ride,* де́сять мину́т езды́. **2,** (leisurely drive) прогу́лка: *go for a ride,* е́здить на прогу́лку; ката́ться на маши́не; прокати́ться; прое́хаться. *Take for a ride,* ката́ть; прокати́ть; повози́ть. **—ride at anchor,** стоя́ть на я́коре. **—ride away; ride off,** отъезжа́ть; уезжа́ть.

rider *n.* **1,** (one who rides horseback) вса́дник; нае́здник; верхово́й; седо́к; ездо́к. **2,** (passenger) седо́к. **3,** (clause added to a document) дополне́ние; добавле́ние.

ridge *n.* **1,** (range of hills) гряда́; кряж. **2,** (strip of earth raised by a plow) гре́бень. **3,** (rib on material) ру́бчик. **4,** (apex of a roof) конёк; гре́бень.

ridicule *n.* осмея́ние; насме́шка. *Object/target of ridicule,* предме́т насме́шек; мише́нь для насме́шек. *Hold up to ridicule,* поднима́ть на́ смех. *—v.t.* насмеха́ться над; осме́ивать; высме́ивать.

ridiculous *adj.* смешно́й; неле́пый; смехотво́рный. *Don't be ridiculous!,* не глупи́те! **—ridiculously,**

adv. до смешно́го. *Be ridiculously expensive,* сто́ить безу́мно до́рого.

riding *n.* езда́: *horseback riding,* верхова́я езда́. **—riding breeches,** рейту́зы; галифе́. **—riding habit,** амазо́нка. **—riding master,** бере́йтор. **—riding school,** шко́ла верхово́й езды́; мане́ж.

rife *adj.* **1,** (widespread) распространённый. **2,** *fol. by* **with** (full; abounding) по́лный; изоби́лующий. *The country is rife with rumors,* страна́ полна́ слу́хов (*or* слу́хами).

riffraff *n.* сброд; чернь; подо́нки.

rifle *n.* винто́вка. *—adj.* винто́вочный; руже́йный; стрелко́вый. *Rifle butt,* прикла́д. *Rifle fire,* ого́нь из стрелко́вого ору́жия. *Rifle battalion,* стрелко́вый баталь́он. *—v.t.* **1,** (force open) взла́мывать. **2,** (cut spiral grooves in) нареза́ть. **—rifleman,** *n.* стрело́к. **—riflery,** *n.* стрелко́вое де́ло.

rift *n.* **1,** (crack) тре́щина; рассе́лина. **2,** *fig.* (disagreement) тре́щина; раско́л.

rig *v.t.* **1,** (fit out, as a ship) оснаща́ть. **2,** *fol. by* **up** (construct hastily) скола́чивать. **3,** (control fraudulently) манипули́ровать; фальсифици́ровать. *—n.* **1,** (arrangement of sails) осна́стка. **2,** (device) устано́вка. *Oil rig,* нефтяна́я вы́шка. *Drilling rig,* бурова́я устано́вка; бурова́я вы́шка.

rigging *n.* сна́сти; осна́стка; такела́ж.

right *adj.* **1,** (correct) пра́вильный; пра́вый; ве́рный. *The right answer,* пра́вильный отве́т. *You are right,* вы пра́вы. *That's right,* пра́вильно. *Quite right,* соверше́нно пра́вильно. *Is my watch right?,* мои́ часы́ иду́т ве́рно? *Something is not right here,* здесь что́-то не так. *You did the right thing,* вы пра́вильно сде́лали. *You made the right decision,* вы реши́ли пра́вильно; вы при́няли пра́вильное реше́ние. *You were right to insist,* вы пра́вильно сде́лали, что наста́ивали на э́том. **2,** (the one wanted or needed) тот: *Is this the right train?,* э́то тот по́езд? *You've come to the right place,* вы попа́ли туда́, куда́ сле́дует. **3,** (appropriate) подходя́щий: *choose the right moment,* выбира́ть подходя́щий моме́нт. **4,** (opp. of left) пра́вый: *one's right eye,* пра́вый глаз; *the right side of the road,* пра́вая сторона́ доро́ги. **5,** (designating the side as of cloth) пра́вый; лицево́й. *Right side up,* лицо́м кве́рху. **6,** *polit.* пра́вый: *the right wing of the party,* пра́вое крыло́ па́ртии. **7,** *math.* (of an angle) прямо́й; (of a triangle) прямоуго́льный. *—adv.* **1,** (correctly) пра́вильно: *He can't do anything right,* он ничего́ не мо́жет сде́лать пра́вильно. *You guessed right,* угада́ли. **2,** *usu. neg.* (as it should) (не) так: *Something doesn't sound right,* что́-то звучи́т не так. *Nothing ever goes right for him,* у него́ всё идёт не так. **3,** (to the right) напра́во: *turn right,* повора́чивать напра́во. **4,** (immediately) сейча́с: *I'll be right back,* я сейча́с верну́сь. **5,** (directly) пря́мо: *right from the store,* пря́мо из магази́на. *Come right in!,* войди́те, пожа́луйста! **6,** (exactly; just) как раз: *right in the middle,* как раз в середи́не. *He is standing right over there,* вот он там стои́т. **7,** (all the way): *right to the end,* до са́мого конца́. *The bullet went right through him,* пу́ля прошла́ навы́лет.

8, *colloq.* (very) о́чень; здо́рово: *right happy,* о́чень рад. *He was right angry,* он здо́рово рассерди́лся. —*n.* **1,** (that which is right) справедли́вость. *Tell right from wrong,* отлича́ть добро́ от зла. **2,** (just claim) пра́во: *civil rights,* гражда́нские права́. *The right to vote/ bear arms/,* пра́во го́лоса/ носи́ть ору́жие/. *The right of asylum/self-defense/,* пра́во убе́жища; пра́во на самозащи́ту. *Have the right to,* име́ть пра́во (+ *inf.*). **3,** (side opp. the left) пра́вая сторона́: *keep to the right,* держа́ться пра́вой стороны́. *To the right; on the right,* напра́во; спра́ва. *On/to his right,* спра́ва от него́; по пра́вую ру́ку от него́. **4,** *polit.* [*usu.* **the right**] пра́вые. —*v.t.* **1,** (return to an even keel) выра́внивать. **2,** (return to an upright position) выпрямля́ть. **3,** (redress, as a wrong) исправля́ть (зло). —**all right,** *see* **all right.** —**be in one's right mind,** быть в своём (*or* в здра́вом) уме́. —**be in the right,** быть пра́вым. —**by rights,** по справедли́вости. —**in one's own right,** сам; сам по себе́. —**put right,** нала́живать; поправля́ть. —**right after,** сра́зу по́сле (+ *gen.*). —**right away, 1,** (right now) сейча́с; сейча́с же. **2,** (right then) сра́зу. —**right itself, 1,** (regain a vertical position) выра́вниваться. **2,** (correct itself; return to normal) нала́живаться. —**right now, 1,** (at present) сейча́с. **2,** (immediately) сейча́с; сейча́с же. —**right you are!,** соверше́нно ве́рно!

righteous *adj.* пра́ведный. —**righteousness,** *n.* пра́ведность.

rightful *adj.* зако́нный. —**rightfully,** *adv.* справедли́во.

right-hand *adj.* пра́вый. —**right-hand man,** пра́вая рука́.

right-handed *adj.* по́льзующийся пра́вой руко́й.

rightist *n. & adj.* пра́вый.

rightly *adv.* **1,** (correctly) пра́вильно. **2,** (fairly) справедли́во. **3,** (justly; deservedly) по пра́ву. —**and rightly so,** да и соверше́нно справедли́во.

rightness *n.* пра́вильность; правота́.

right of way пра́во прохо́да; пра́во прое́зда.

right-wing *adj.* пра́вый.

rigid *adj.* **1,** (stiff; not bending) жёсткий; негну́щийся. **2,** *fig.* (inflexible) жёсткий; неги́бкий. *Rigid rules,* жёсткие пра́вила.

rigidity *n.* жёсткость.

rigor *also,* **rigour** *n.* **1,** (strictness) стро́гость. **2,** (severity) суро́вость. **3,** *pl.* (hardships) тя́готы.

rigor mortis тру́пное окочене́ние.

rigorous *adj.* **1,** (rigidly precise) стро́гий. **2,** (full of rigors; harsh) суро́вый.

rigour *n.* = **rigor.**

rile *v.t., colloq.* раздража́ть; досажда́ть.

rill *n.* ручеёк.

rim *n.* **1,** (edge) край: *the rim of a canyon,* край уще́лья. **2,** (of glasses) опра́ва. **3,** (outer part of a wheel) о́бод. **4,** *basketball* кольцо́ (корзи́ны).

rime *n.* **1,** = **rhyme. 2,** (hoarfrost) и́ней.

rind *n.* кожура́; ко́жица; ко́рка.

ring *n.* **1,** (circular band) кольцо́: *engagement ring,* обруча́льное кольцо́. *Diamond ring,* бриллиа́нт-

овый пе́рстень. *The rings of Saturn,* ко́льца Сату́рна. **2,** (circle) круг; кольцо́: *form a ring,* стать в круг. *Rings under one's eyes,* круги́ под глаза́ми. *Blow smoke rings,* пуска́ть ко́льца ды́ма. **3,** (arena, as for a circus) аре́на; мане́ж. **4,** (boxing ring) ринг: *meet in the ring,* сходи́ться на ри́нге. **5,** (illegal band) ша́йка; ба́нда. *Smuggling ring,* ша́йка контрабанди́стов. **6,** (sound of a bell) звон; звоно́к. *Give someone a ring,* позвони́ть кому́-нибудь. —*v.t.* **1,** (cause to sound, as a bell) звони́ть в (ко́локол); дава́ть (звоно́к). **2,** [*also, Brit.* **ring up**] (call on the telephone) звони́ть (+ *dat.*). **3,** (encircle) окружа́ть. —*v.i.* **1,** (of a bell, telephone, alarm clock, etc.) звони́ть. *The telephone rang/ is ringing/,* телефо́н зазвони́л/звони́т. **2,** (ring a bell) звони́ть; дава́ть звоно́к. **3,** *Ring in one's ears,* звуча́ть в уша́х. *My ears are ringing,* у меня́ звени́т в уша́х. —**ring a bell,** *see* **bell.** —**ring for,** вызыва́ть. —**ring in,** встреча́ть (Но́вый год). —**ring off,** дать отбо́й. —**ring out,** раздава́ться; гря́нуть: *A shot rang out,* разда́лся/гря́нул вы́стрел. —**ring true,** звуча́ть и́скренне. *Much of the article rings true,* во мно́гом э́та статья́ права́ *or* правди́льная.

ringer *n.* **1,** (person who rings a bell) звона́рь. **2,** *slang* (person who greatly resembles another) двойни́к.

ring finger безымя́нный па́лец.

ringing *n.* звон. —*adj.* зво́нкий.

ringleader *n.* зачи́нщик; глава́рь.

ringlet *n.* **1,** (small ring) коле́чко. **2,** (of hair) завито́к; кудря́шка.

ringworm *n.* стригу́щий лиша́й.

rink *n.* като́к.

rinse *v.t.* полоска́ть; опола́скивать. *Rinse out,* выпола́скивать. —*n.* полоска́ние.

riot *n.* **1,** (wild disturbance) дебо́ш. **2,** (public demonstration) бунт; *pl.* беспоря́дки. **3,** *colloq.* (something extremely funny) умо́ра. **4,** *A riot of color,* всевозмо́жные цвета́. —*v.i.* бунтова́ть. —**read the riot act to,** чита́ть нота́цию (+ *dat.*). —**run riot,** бу́йствовать; буя́нить.

rioter *n.* бунтовщи́к.

riotous *adj.* **1,** (rioting) бунту́ющий. **2,** (boisterous) бу́йный.

rip *v.t.* рвать; разрыва́ть. *Rip open,* распа́рывать. —*v.i.* рва́ться; разрыва́ться. —*n.* проре́ха. —**rip into,** обру́шиваться на. —**rip off, 1,** (tear off) срыва́ть. **2,** *slang* (swindle) содра́ть. —**rip up,** разрыва́ть.

ripcord *n.* вытяжно́й трос (парашю́та).

ripe *adj.* спе́лый; зре́лый. *Is this melon ripe?,* э́та ды́ня спе́лая? *Cut open the melon to see if it is ripe,* разре́зать ды́ню чтобы посмотре́ть, спе́лая ли она́. *The time is ripe,* вре́мя назре́ло. *Live to a ripe old age,* дожи́ть до ста́рости.

ripen *v.i.* спеть; зреть; поспева́ть; созрева́ть.

ripeness *n.* спе́лость; зре́лость.

riposte *n.* **1,** *fencing* отве́тный вы́пад. **2,** (quick rejoinder) ре́плика.

ripple *n.* **1,** (small wave) рябь; зыбь. *Ripples on the water,* круги́ на воде́. **2,** (slight sound): *ripple* *of laughter/applause*, небольша́я (*or* кра́ткая) вспы́шка сме́ха/аплодисме́нтов. —*v.t. & i.* ряби́ть.

ripsaw *n.* продо́льная пила́.

rise *v.i.* **1**, (ascend) поднима́ться: *rise into the air*, поднима́ться в во́здух. *Rise to the surface*, поднима́ться *or* всплыва́ть на пове́рхность. *The water/river/barometer is rising*, вода́ прибыва́ет; река́/баро́метр поднима́ется. *Her spirits rose*, у неё подняло́сь настрое́ние. *Rise to the defense of one's country*, встать на защи́ту ро́дины. **2**, (stand; get up) встава́ть. **3**, (extend upward) возвыша́ться. **4**, (of the sun, moon, etc.) всходи́ть; восходи́ть; встава́ть; поднима́ться. **5**, (originate, as of a river) брать нача́ло. **6**, (increase, as of prices, temperature, etc.) поднима́ться; повыша́ться; расти́; возраста́ть. **7**, (move up professionally) выдвига́ться; продвига́ться. *He rose to the rank of colonel*, он дослужи́лся до полко́вника. **8**, (rebel) поднима́ться; восстава́ть: *rise against the regime*, поднима́ться/восстава́ть про́тив режи́ма. **9**, (return to life) воскреса́ть. —*n.* **1**, (ascent) восхо́д; подъём. **2**, (raised ground) возвы́шенность. **3**, (increase) повыше́ние; рост. *Be on the rise*, быть на подъёме. **4**, (emergence, of an empire) возвыше́ние. —**give rise to**, вызыва́ть; порожда́ть; дать нача́ло (+ *dat.*); дать по́вод к *or* для; вызыва́ть к жи́зни. *Give rise to doubts*, вызыва́ть/порожда́ть сомне́ния. *Give rise to numerous jokes*, дать по́вод для мно́гих остро́т. —**rise above**, стать вы́ше (+ *gen.*).

riser *n. He is an early riser*, он ра́но встаёт.

rising *adj.* **1**, (ascending) восходя́щий. *A rising star* (*fig.*), восходя́щая звезда́. **2**, (growing, as of a generation) подраста́ющий.

risk *n.* риск. *Take a risk*, идти́ на риск. *At the risk of…*, рискуя́ (+ *inf.*). *At one's own risk*, на свой страх и риск. —*v.t.* рискова́ть (+ *instr. or inf.*): *risk one's life*, рискова́ть жи́знью; *risk being killed*, рискова́ть быть уби́тым.

risky *adj.* риско́ванный.

risqué *adj.* риско́ванный.

rite *n.* обря́д.

ritual *n.* ритуа́л. —*adj.* ритуа́льный; обря́довый.

ritzy *adj., colloq.* роско́шный; шика́рный.

rival *n.* сопе́рник. —*adj.* сопе́рничающий. —*v.t.* сопе́рничать с. —**rivalry,** *n.* сопе́рничество.

river *n.* река́. —*adj.* речно́й. —**riverbank,** *n.* речно́й бе́рег; бе́рег реки́. —**river bed,** ру́сло. —**riverboat,** *n.* речно́е су́дно; речно́й парохо́д.

rivet *n.* заклёпка. —*v.t.* **1**, (fasten with rivets) клепа́ть. **2**, *fig.* (fix rigidly in place) прико́вывать; пригвожда́ть: *riveted to the spot*, прико́ванный/пригвождённый к ме́сту. —**riveter,** *n.* клепа́льщик.

rivulet *n.* ручéй.

roach *n.* **1**, (cockroach) тарака́н. **2**, (fish) плотва́; тара́нь.

road *n.* **1**, (path; highway) доро́га: *narrow road*, у́зкая доро́га. *The main road*, гла́вная магистра́ль. **2**, *fig.* (avenue) путь: *the road to success*, путь к успе́ху. —*adj.* доро́жный: *road surface*, доро́жное покры́тие. —**be on the road, 1**, (be traveling) разъезжа́ть. **2**, (be on tour) гастроли́ровать. **3**, *sports* быть *or* игра́ть на вы́езде; быть *or* игра́ть на чужо́м по́ле.

roadbed *n.* полотно́.

roadblock *n.* **1**, (barrier) загражде́ние *or* заса́да на доро́ге. *Set up roadblocks*, перекры́ть доро́ги. **2**, *fig.* (obstacle) зава́л на пути́.

road map путева́я ка́рта.

roadside *adj.* придоро́жный.

road sign доро́жный знак.

roadstead *n., naut.* рейд.

road test доро́жное испыта́ние.

roadway *n.* мостова́я.

roam *v.i. & t.* **1**, (walk around aimlessly) броди́ть; блужда́ть: *roam (about) the streets*, броди́ть/блужда́ть по у́лицам. **2**, (wander far and wide) стра́нствовать; скита́ться: *roam the world*, стра́нствовать/скита́ться по све́ту *or* по́ миру.

roan *adj.* ча́лый.

roar *v.i.* реве́ть. *Roar with laughter*, покати́ться *or* пока́тываться со́ смеху. —*v.t.* выкри́кивать: *The crowd roared its approval*, толпа́ выкри́кивала одобре́ние. —*n.* рёв.

roaring *adj.* реву́щий. *We sat by a roaring fire*, мы сиде́ли у пыла́ющего ками́на.

roast *v.t.* жа́рить. —*v.i.* жа́риться. —*adj.* жа́реный: *roast lamb*, жа́реная бара́нина. *Roast beef*, ро́стбиф. —*n.* жарко́е.

roasted *adj.* жа́реный: *roasted coffee*, жа́реный ко́фе. *Roasted nuts*, калёные оре́хи.

roasting pan жаро́вня.

rob *v.t.* **1**, (steal from) гра́бить; обкра́дывать: *rob a house*, гра́бить/обкра́дывать дом. *He was robbed of $200*, у него́ укра́ли две́сти до́лларов. **2**, (deprive of something) лиша́ть; отнима́ть. *Rob someone of sleep*, отнима́ть сон у кого́-нибудь.

robber *n.* граби́тель. —**robbery,** *n.* грабёж; ограбле́ние.

robe *n.* **1**, (long, loose garment) ма́нтия. **2**, (bathrobe) хала́т. —*v.t.* облача́ть.

robin *n.* мали́новка; заря́нка.

robot *n.* ро́бот; автома́т. —**robotics,** *n.* робото́техника.

robust *adj.* кре́пкий; дю́жий.

rock *n.* **1**, (large stone) ка́мень. **2**, (substance) поро́да: *drill through rock*, бури́ть по поро́де. **3**, (cliff) скала́: *The Rock of Gibraltar*, Гибралта́рская скала́. **4**, (reef) (подво́дная) скала́. —*v.t.* **1**, (move gently; cause to sway) кача́ть; раска́чивать. *Rock to sleep*, ука́чивать; баю́кать. *Don't rock the boat!*, не раска́чивайте ло́дку! **2**, (shake violently) потряса́ть; сотряса́ть. —*v.i.* кача́ться. —**on the rocks, 1**, (in difficulty) на мели́. **2**, (of drinks) со льдом. —**rock crusher,** камнедроби́лка. —**rock crystal,** го́рный хруста́ль. —**rock salt,** ка́менная соль.

rocker *n.* **1**, (rocking chair) кача́лка. **2**, (runner of a rocking chair) по́лоз. —**off one's rocker,** *slang* сумасше́дший: *Are you off your rocker?*, ты с ума́ сошёл?

rocket *n.* **1**, (projectile; space vehicle) раке́та. **2**, (firework) шути́ха. —*adj.* раке́тный: *rocket launcher*, раке́тная устано́вка. —*v.i.* взмыва́ть: *rocket into* *space,* взмывáть в кóсмос. —**rocketry,** *n.* ракéтная тéхника.

rocking chair качáлка.

rocking horse конь-качáлка.

rocky *adj.* **1,** (stony) скалúстый. **2,** (shaky) шáткий.

rococo *n.* рококó. —*adj.* в стúле рококó.

rod *n.* **1,** (slender, straight stick) прут. **2,** (bar) стéржень. **3,** (whip; switch) рóзга. —**curtain rod,** пáлка для штор. —**fishing rod,** ýдочка; удúлище. —**lightning rod,** громоотвóд; молниеотвóд. —**piston rod,** поршневóй шток.

rodent *n.* грызýн.

roe *n.* **1,** (fish eggs; hard roe) икрá. **2,** (milt; soft roe) молóки. **3,** (roe deer) косýля.

roebuck *n.* самéц косýли.

roe deer косýля.

rogue *n.* плут; мошéнник. —**roguish,** *adj.* жуликовáтый.

roil *v.t.* **1,** (make turbid) мутúть. **2,** (annoy) раздражáть.

role *n.* роль: *play a role,* игрáть роль.

roll *v.t.* **1,** (cause to roll; move by rolling) катúть: *roll the ball,* катúть мяч. **2,** (flatten; shape, as dough) катáть; раскáтывать. **3,** (smooth the surface of, as a road) укáтывать. **4,** (turn, as in bread crumbs) валять (в сухаря́х). **5,** (make, as a cigarette) крутúть; скрýчивать. **6,** (flatten into a sheet, as metal) прокáтывать; вальцевáть. **7,** (throw, as dice) бросáть. **8,** (move in circles, as one's eyes) вращáть (глазáми). —*v.i.* **1,** (move by turning over and over) катúться. *The ball rolled under the bed,* мяч покатúлся (*or* закатúлся) под кровáть. *Tanks rolled into the city,* тáнки вошлú в гóрод. *He is rolling in money,* он купáется в зóлоте. *Heads will roll,* полетят гóловы. **2,** (toss, as of a ship) качáть (*impers.*). **3,** (sound, as of a drum) грохотáть. —*n.* **1,** (anything rolled up) свúток; свёрток; рулóн. **2,** (of film) кассéта. *Two rolls of film,* две кассéты плёнки; две плёнки. **3,** (small bread or biscuit) бýлка; бýлочка. **4,** (list of names) вéдомость; реéстр. *Roll of honor,* доскá почёта. *Call the roll,* дéлать переклúчку. **5,** (swaying of a ship) кáчка. **6,** (sound of drums) барабáнный бой. **7,** (sound of thunder) раскáты (грóма). —**roll down, 1,** (move downward by rolling) скáтывать. *Roll down one's sleeves,* рассýчивать рукавá. **2,** (slide down) катúться; скáтываться: *The ball rolled down the hill,* мяч покатúлся *or* скатúлся с горы́. *Tears rolled down her cheeks,* слёзы катúлись *or* скатúлись по её щекáм. —**roll out, 1,** (come rolling out) выкáтываться. **2,** (spread out) расстилáть: *roll out the red carpet for,* расстилáть крáсный ковёр пéред. —**roll over,** перевáливаться. —**roll up, 1,** (form into a roll) свёртывать; скáтывать. **2,** (turn up, as one's sleeves) засýчивать. **3,** (arrive by vehicle) подъезжáть.

roll call переклúчка; повéрка. —**roll-call vote,** поимéнное голосовáние.

roller *n.* **1,** (caster) колéсико; рóлик. **2,** (heavy cylinder for smoothing roads) катóк. —**roller bearing,** рóликовый подшúпник. —**roller coaster,** америкáнские гóры.

roller skate рóлик; конёк на рóликах; рóликовый конёк. —**roller-skate,** *v.i.* катáться на рóликах.

rollick *v.i.* резвúться; возúться.

rolling *n.* **1,** (moving by turning over and over) катáние. **2,** (swaying of a ship or vehicle) кáчка. **3,** (flattening of metal) прокáтка. —*adj.* **1,** (moving on wheels or rollers) на колёсах. **2,** (pert. to the rolling of metal) прокáтный. **3,** (undulating) волнúстый: *rolling country,* волнúстая мéстность. —**rolling mill,** прокáтный стан; вальцóвая мéльница. —**rolling pin,** скáлка. —**rolling stock,** подвижнóй состáв.

roly-poly *adj.* пýхлый.

Roman *adj.* рúмский. *Roman numerals,* рúмские цúфры. —*n.* рúмлянин.

Roman Catholic 1, *used as a noun,* катóлик. **2,** *used adjectivally,* рúмско-католúческий.

romance *n.* **1,** (love affair) ромáн. **2,** (fascination; appeal) ромáнтика. **3,** (romantic tale) ромáн. **4,** *music* ромáнс. —*adj., cap.* ромáнский: *Romance languages,* ромáнские языкú.

Romanesque *adj.* ромáнский. —*n.* ромáнский стиль.

Romanian *also,* **Rumanian** *adj.* румы́нский. —*n.* **1,** (person) румы́н; румы́нка. **2,** (language) румы́нский язы́к.

romantic *adj.* романтúческий; романтúчный. —**romanticism,** *n.* романтúзм; ромáнтика. —**romanticist,** *n.* ромáнтик. —**romanticize,** *v.t.* романтизúровать.

romp *v.i.* возúться; резвúться.

rondo *n.* рóндо.

roof *n.* кры́ша. *Roof of the mouth,* нёбо. —**roofer,** *n.* крóвельщик. —**roofing,** *n.* крóвля.

rook *n.* **1,** (bird) грач. **2,** *chess* ладья́. —*v.t., colloq.* (cheat; swindle) обсчúтывать.

rookery *n.* лéжбище.

rookie *n.* новичóк.

room *n.* **1,** (part of a house or building) кóмната. *Three-room apartment,* трёхкóмнатная квартúра. **2,** (in a hotel) нóмер: *room for two,* нóмер на двоúх. *What is your room number?,* какóй у вас нóмер? *Order breakfast in one's room,* заказáть зáвтрак в нóмер. **3,** (space) мéсто: *make room for,* давáть мéсто (+ *dat.*). *Take up too much room,* занимáть слúшком мнóго мéста. —*adj.* кóмнатный: *room temperature,* кóмнатная температýра. —*v.i.* жить. —**room and board,** стол и квартúра; пансиóн.

roomer *n.* пансионéр.

roominess *n.* вместúтельность.

rooming house пансиóн.

roommate *n.* сосéд по кóмнате. *They are roommates,* онú живýт в однóй кóмнате.

roomy *adj.* простóрный; вместúтельный.

roost *n.* насéст. —*v.i.* садúться на насéст; сидéть на насéсте. —**rule the roost,** вертéть всем дóмом.

rooster *n.* петýх.

root *n.* кóрень: *root of a tree/tooth/word,* кóрень дéрева/зýба/слóва. *Square root,* квадрáтный кóрень. *Pull up by the roots,* вы́рвать (чтó-нибудь) с кóрнем. *Have its roots in,* уходúть своúми корня́ми в (+ *acc.*). *The roots go much deeper,* кóрни ухóдят мно́го глу́бже. —*v.t.* **1,** *usu. passive* (implant deeply) укореня́ть. *Be rooted in,* корени́ться в; (быть) укоренён в (+ *prepl.*). *Rooted to the spot,* прико́ванный к ме́сту. **2,** *fol. by* **out** (eliminate completely) вырыва́ть с ко́рнем; искореня́ть. —*v.i.* [*usu.* **root for**] боле́ть (за). —**root and branch,** в ко́рне; коренны́м о́бразом. —**root of all evil,** ко́рень зла. —**take root,** укореня́ться.

rooter *n.* боле́льщик.

rootlet *n.* корешо́к.

rope *n.* верёвка; кана́т. *Jump rope,* скака́лка. —*adj.* верёвочный: *rope ladder,* верёвочная ле́стница. —*v.t.* **1,** (fasten by a rope) привя́зывать *or* свя́зывать верёвкой. **2,** (lasso) лови́ть арка́ном. **3,** *fol. by* **off** (fence off) отгора́живать; оцепля́ть. **4,** *fol. by* **in** (entice) втя́гивать. —**know the ropes,** знать все ходы́ и вы́ходы. —**learn the ropes,** ориенти́роваться. —**reach the end of one's rope,** дойти́ до то́чки.

rorqual *n.* полоса́тик.

rosary *n.* чётки.

rose *n.* **1,** (flower) ро́за. **2,** (color) ро́зовый цвет. —*adj.* ро́зовый.

roseate *adj.* ро́зовый.

rosebud *n.* буто́н ро́зы.

rosebush *n.* ро́за; ро́зовый куст.

rose-colored *also,* **rose-coloured** *adj.* ро́зовый. —**see through rose-colored glasses,** смотре́ть сквозь ро́зовые очки́.

rosemary *n.* розмари́н.

Rosetta Stone Розе́ттский ка́мень.

rosette *n.* розе́тка.

rose water ро́зовая вода́.

rosewood *n.* ро́зовое де́рево; палиса́ндр. —*adj.* палиса́ндровый.

rosin *n.* канифо́ль.

roster *n.* спи́сок; рее́стр. *Duty roster,* наря́д дежу́рств; гра́фик дежу́рств; лист наря́дов.

rostrum *n.* трибу́на; ка́федра.

rosy *adj.* **1,** (rose-colored) ро́зовый; румя́ный. **2,** *fig.* (bright; cheerful; optimistic) ро́зовый; ра́дужный. *Paint a rosy picture of,* представля́ть в ро́зовом/ра́дужном све́те. —**rosy-cheeked,** *adj.* розовощёкий.

rot *v.i.* гнить; загнива́ть; ту́хнуть. —*v.t.* гнои́ть. —*n.* **1,** (decay) гние́ние. **2,** (anything rotten) гниль; прель. **3,** (plant disease) гниль. **4,** *slang* (nonsense) вздор.

rotary *adj.* враща́тельный; поворо́тный; ротацио́нный. —**rotary engine,** ротацио́нный дви́гатель. —**rotary press,** ротацио́нная (печа́тная) маши́на.

rotate *v.i.* **1,** (turn) враща́ться. *The earth rotates on its axis,* Земля́ враща́ется вокру́г свое́й оси́. **2,** (alternate) чередова́ться. —*v.t.* **1,** (cause to turn) враща́ть: *rotate a wheel,* враща́ть колесо́. *Rotate the handle,* повора́чивать ру́чку. **2,** (alternate) чередова́ть. *Rotate crops,* чередова́ть *or* сменя́ть культу́ры. **3,** (interchange, as tires) переставля́ть (ши́ны).

rotation *n.* **1,** (rotary motion) враще́ние. **2,** (alternation) чередова́ние. *In rotation,* по о́череди. —**rotation of crops,** севооборо́т. —**rotation of the seasons,** круговоро́т времён го́да.

rote *adj.* зау́ченный; зазу́бренный. *Rote learning,* зубрёжка. —**by rote,** машина́льно. *Learn by rote,* зубри́ть.

rotor *n.* ро́тор.

rotten *adj.* **1,** (decayed) гнило́й; ту́хлый. *Rotten apple,* гнило́е я́блоко. *Rotten egg,* ту́хлое яйцо́. *Rotten teeth,* гнилы́е *or* испо́рченные зу́бы. **2,** (mean; despicable) ни́зкий; по́длый. **3,** *colloq.* (very bad; miserable) парши́вый; дрянно́й; отврати́тельный.

rottenness *n.* **1,** (decayed state) гни́лость; ту́хлость. **2,** (meanness) ни́зость; по́длость.

rotund *adj.* **1,** (round; plump) пу́хлый. **2,** (sonorous) зву́чный.

rotunda *n.* рото́нда.

roué *n.* распу́тник.

rouge *n.* румя́на. —*v.t.* румя́нить.

rough *adj.* **1,** (not smooth; coarse) гру́бый; шерша́вый; шерохова́тый. *Rough skin/material,* гру́бая *or* шерша́вая ко́жа/ткань. *Rough surface,* шерохова́тая пове́рхность. *Rough road,* неро́вная доро́га. *Rough terrain,* пересечённая ме́стность. *We had a rough crossing,* нас си́льно кача́ло во вре́мя перее́зда. **2,** (not gentle) гру́бый: *rough handling/treatment,* гру́бое обраще́ние. **3,** (preliminary, as of something written) черново́й. *Rough draft/copy,* чернови́к. **4,** (choppy, as of the sea) бу́рный. **5,** (approximate) гру́бый: *a rough estimate,* гру́бый подсчёт. *A rough idea of,* о́бщее представле́ние о. **6,** *colloq.* (difficult; unpleasant) тру́дный; тяжёлый; неприя́тный. —*adv.* гру́бо: *play rough,* игра́ть гру́бо. —*v.t.* **1,** *fol. by* **up** (beat up) поби́ть. **2,** *fol. by* **out** (sketch) набра́сывать. —**in the rough,** вчерне́; на́черно. —**rough it,** жить *or* обходи́ться без удо́бств.

roughage *n.* гру́бая пи́ща.

roughen *v.t.* де́лать гру́бым. —*v.i.* грубе́ть.

rough-hew *v.t.* обтёсывать. —**rough-hewn,** *adj.* гру́бо обтёсанный.

roughly *adv.* **1,** (not gently) гру́бо. **2,** (approximately) приблизи́тельно: *roughly forty miles,* приблизи́тельно со́рок миль. —**roughly speakng,** гру́бо говоря́.

roughneck *n.* буя́н.

roughness *n.* гру́бость; шерохова́тость.

roughshod *adj.* подко́ванный на шипы́. —**ride roughshod over,** попира́ть.

roulade *n.* **1,** *music* рула́да. **2,** (meat pie) пирожо́к.

roulette *n.* руле́тка. —**roulette wheel,** руле́тка.

round *adj.* кру́глый: *round table,* кру́глый стол. *The earth is round,* Земля́ име́ет кру́глую фо́рму; Земля́ име́ет фо́рму ша́ра. *In round figures,* кру́глым счётом; в кру́глых ци́фрах. —*n.* **1,** (unit of ammunition) вы́стрел; патро́н. **2,** *often pl.* (tour) обхо́д: *make one's rounds,* де́лать обхо́д. *Make the round of all the stores,* обходи́ть все магази́ны. **3,** (of a tournament, negotiations, etc.) тур. **4,** *boxing* ра́унд. **5,** (burst, as of applause) взрыв. —*v.t.* **1,** (make round) округля́ть; закругля́ть. **2,** (go round, as a bend, turn, etc.) огиба́ть (поворо́т). —*adv.* **1,** (around) вокру́г; круго́м. *Go round,* враща́ться. **2,** (throughout): *the*

year round, кру́глый год. —*prep.* = **around**.
—**round off, 1,** (finish into rounded form) округля́ть; закругля́ть. **2,** (state as a round number) округля́ть. —**round out, 1,** (fill out; become round) округля́ться. **2,** (complete) заверша́ть. *Round out a collection,* (у)комплектова́ть колле́кцию. —**round the clock,** кру́глые су́тки. —**round up, 1,** (assemble) собира́ть. **2,** (herd together) сгоня́ть. **3,** (seize and arrest) производи́ть обла́ву на.

roundabout *adj.* око́льный; обхо́дный; кру́жный. —*n., Brit.* = **traffic circle**.

rounded *adj.* закруглённый; округлённый.

roundhouse *n.* парово́зное депо́.

roundish *adj.* круглова́тый.

roundly *adv.* **1,** (sharply; severely) ре́зко. **2,** (thoroughly; soundly) здо́рово.

round robin кругова́я систе́ма.

round-shouldered *adj.* суту́лый.

round-the-clock *adj.* круглосу́точный.

round trip пое́здка туда́ и обра́тно. *Round-trip ticket,* биле́т туда́ и обра́тно.

roundup *n.* **1,** (of cattle) заго́н. **2,** (raid and arrest) обла́ва: *roundup of suspected persons,* обла́ва на подозрева́емые ли́ца. **3,** (summary) обзо́р; обозре́ние.

rouse *v.t.* **1,** (waken) буди́ть; поднима́ть. *Rouse the neighbors,* подня́ть сосе́дей. **2,** (stir; arouse) поднима́ть: *rouse the nation to fight,* поднима́ть наро́д на борьбу́. **3,** (excite) возбужда́ть: *rouse someone's curiosity,* возбужда́ть чьё-нибудь любопы́тство.

rousing *adj.* **1,** (stirring) волну́ющий. **2,** (enthusiastic) восто́рженный: *rousing welcome,* восто́рженный приём.

rout *v.t.* **1,** (put to flight) обраща́ть в бе́гство. **2,** (defeat overwhelmingly) громи́ть; разби́ть на́голову. **3,** (drive out) выгоня́ть. *Rout out of bed,* поднима́ть с посте́ли. —*n.* разгро́м.

route *n.* **1,** (road; way) путь: *the shortest route to town,* кратча́йший путь в го́род. **2,** (itinerary) маршру́т: *the route of a trip,* маршру́т путеше́ствия. *Bus route,* маршру́т авто́буса. —*v.t.* направля́ть: *route the traffic through the park,* направля́ть движе́ние че́рез парк. —**en route,** по (*or* в) пути́; по (*or* в) доро́ге.

routine *n.* режи́м; распоря́док; колея́. *Daily routine,* распоря́док дня. *Settle into a routine,* войти́ в колею́. —*adj.* обы́чный; очередно́й; бу́дничный. —**routinely,** *adv.* автомати́чески.

rove *v.i.* броди́ть; скита́ться; стра́нствовать.

rover *n.* скита́лец. —**land rover,** вездехо́д.

roving *adj.* бродя́чий. —**roving ambassador,** посо́л по осо́бым поруче́ниям.

row[1] (ro) *n.* ряд: *row of houses,* ряд домо́в. *In the third row,* в тре́тьем ряду́. —*v.t. & i.* грести́. *Row a boat,* грести́ на ло́дке. —**in a row, 1,** (in a line) в ряд; в ряду́. **2,** (consecutively) подря́д.

row[2] (rau) *n.* сканда́л; дебо́ш; скло́ка; сва́ра.

rowan *n.* ряби́на. —**rowanberry,** *n.* ряби́на.

rowboat *n.* гребна́я ло́дка; гребна́я шлю́пка; весёльная ло́дка.

rowdy *n.* буя́н; хулига́н; скандали́ст; безобра́зник. —*adj.* бу́йный. —**rowdiness,** *n.* хулига́нство.

rower *n.* гребе́ц.

rowing *n.* гре́бля; гребно́й спорт. —*adj.* гребно́й.

rowlock *n.* уклю́чина.

royal *adj.* короле́вский. *Of royal blood,* короле́вской *or* ца́рской кро́ви. *Royal Philharmonic Society,* короле́вское филармони́ческое о́бщество. *A royal reception,* короле́вский приём.

royalism *n.* роялизм. —**royalist,** *n.* роялист. —*adj.* роялисти́ческий.

royalty *n.* **1,** (royal persons) чле́ны короле́вской семьи́. **2,** *pl.* (fees) а́вторский гонора́р.

rub *v.t.* **1,** (stroke hard) тере́ть; потира́ть; растира́ть: *rub one's eyes,* тере́ть глаза́; *rub one's hands,* потира́ть ру́ки; *rub someone's back,* растира́ть кому́-нибудь спи́ну. *Rub one's injured knee,* потира́ть уши́бленное коле́но. *Rub two sticks together,* тере́ть две па́лки друг о дру́га. *Rub one's back with alcohol,* натира́ть спи́ну спи́ртом. **2,** (stroke in order to clean) протира́ть: *rub the table with a cloth,* протира́ть стол тря́пкой. **3,** (apply with pressure) растира́ть. *Rub cream into one's face,* растира́ть *or* натира́ть лицо́ кре́мом. **4,** (chafe) тере́ть; натира́ть; стира́ть. *The collar is rubbing my neck,* воротни́к натира́ет мне ше́ю. —*v.i.* (apply repeated pressure) тере́ть: *Keep rubbing!,* продолжа́йте тере́ть! **2,** (chafe) тере́ть: *The shoe rubs,* боти́нок (*or* ту́фля) трёт. **3,** *fol. by* **against** (scrape) тере́ться о (+ *acc.*). —*n.* **1,** (vigorous stroking): *give something a good rub,* хороше́нько потере́ть что́-нибудь. **2,** (difficulty; catch) загво́здка: *That's the rub,* вот в чём загво́здка. —**rub down,** обтира́ть. —**rub in, rub it in,** растравля́ть ра́ну; пили́ть кого́-нибудь. —**rub off,** стира́ться. —**rub off on,** передава́ться (+ *dat.*). —**rub out,** стира́ть. —**rub the wrong way,** гла́дить (кого́-нибудь) про́тив ше́рсти.

rubber *n.* **1,** (raw rubber) каучу́к. **2,** (processed rubber) рези́на. **3,** (overshoe) гало́ша. **4,** *cards* ро́ббер. —*adj.* рези́новый. —**rubber band,** рези́нка.

rubberize *v.t.* прорези́нивать.

rubber plant 1, (plant yielding crude rubber) каучу́к. **2,** (ornamental house plant) фи́кус.

rubber stamp штамп; штемпель; гриф.

rubbish *n.* **1,** (refuse) хлам; му́сор; сор. **2,** (nonsense) вздор; чепуха́; глу́пости.

rubble *n.* **1,** (rough broken stones) рва́ный ка́мень. **2,** (ruins) разва́лины; обло́мки. *Reduce to rubble,* превраща́ть в разва́лины.

rubdown *n.* обтира́ние; масса́ж.

rube *n., slang* дереве́нщина.

rubella *n.* красну́ха.

Rubicon *n.,* in **cross the Rubicon,** перейти́ Рубико́н.

rubicund *adj.* румя́ный.

rubidium *n.* руби́дий.

ruble *n.* рубль.

rubric *n.* ру́брика.

ruby *n.* руби́н. —*adj.* руби́новый.

rucksack *n.* рюкза́к.

ruckus *n., colloq.* шум; гвалт; бата́лия.

rudder *n.* руль.

ruddy *adj.* румя́ный.

rude *adj.* грубый; неве́жливый. *Be rude to someone,* груби́ть кому́-нибудь. —**rudeness,** *n.* грубость; неве́жливость.

rudiment *n.* **1,** *pl.* (fundamentals) осно́вы; элеме́нты; нача́тки. **2,** (incompletely developed organ) рудимента́рный о́рган; рудиме́нт.

rudimentary *adj.* **1,** (elementary) элемента́рный. **2,** (incompletely developed) рудимента́рный; зача́точный.

rue *v.t.* **1,** (feel remorse for) раска́иваться в. **2,** (come to regret) сожале́ть о. —**rue the day,** проклина́ть тот день, когда́...

rueful *adj.* печа́льный; уны́лый; ско́рбный.

ruff *n.* **1,** (frilled collar) брыжи. **2,** (bird) турухта́н. **3,** (fish) ёрш. —*v.t. & i., cards* = **trump.**

ruffian *n.* хулига́н; буя́н.

ruffle *n.* обо́рка. —*v.t.* **1,** (disturb) ряби́ть: *ruffle the surface of the lake,* ряби́ть пове́рхность о́зера. **2,** (fluster) смуща́ть; конфу́зить. **3,** (erect, as feathers) еро́шить. *The hen ruffled its feathers,* ку́рица нахо́хлилась.

rug *n.* ковёр: *spot on the rug,* пятно́ на ковре́.

rugby *n.* ре́гби.

rugged *adj.* **1,** (rough, as of terrain) пересечённый; изре́занный. **2,** (wrinkled; furrowed) грубый: *rugged features,* грубые черты́ лица́. **3,** (trying; harsh) тяжёлый; суро́вый. **4,** (robust; sturdy) кре́пкий; дю́жий.

ruin *n.* **1,** (destruction; downfall) ги́бель; круше́ние. **2,** (financial collapse) разоре́ние. **3,** *pl.* (remains of something destroyed) разва́лины; руи́ны. *Lie in ruins,* лежа́ть в разва́линах. —*v.t.* **1,** (destroy; damage irreparably) губи́ть: *ruin the crops,* губи́ть посе́вы. *Ruin someone's health,* губи́ть *or* разруша́ть *or* расстра́ивать чьё-нибудь здоро́вье. *My dress is ruined,* моё пла́тье соверше́нно испо́рчено; моё пла́тье пропа́ло. *The snowstorm ruined our plans,* мете́ль сорвала́ на́ши пла́ны. *Drinking ruined his life,* пья́нство погуби́ло *or* испо́ртило его́ жизнь. **2,** (bankrupt) разоря́ть.

ruination *n.* ги́бель.

ruinous *adj.* ги́бельный; губи́тельный; па́губный; разори́тельный.

rule *n.* **1,** (regulation) пра́вило: *the rules of the game,* пра́вила игры́. **2,** (act of governing) правле́ние; управле́ние. *Self-rule,* самоуправле́ние. **3,** (domination; sway) власть: *under colonial rule,* под колониа́льной вла́стью. **4,** (measuring stick) лине́йка. —*v.t.* **1,** (govern) пра́вить; управля́ть: *rule the country,* пра́вить/управля́ть страно́й. **2,** (decide authoritatively) постанови́ть: *The court ruled that...,* суд постанови́л, что... *The referee ruled that...,* судья́ реши́л *or* объяви́л, что... **3,** (mark with lines) линова́ть; графи́ть. **4,** *fol. by* **out** (eliminate from consideration) исключа́ть; сбра́сывать со счето́в. —*v.i.* **1,** (reign; govern) пра́вить. **2,** (issue a decision) выноси́ть реше́ние: *rule in favor of,* выноси́ть реше́ние в по́льзу (+ *gen.*). —**as a rule,** как пра́вило. —**make it a rule,** взять себе́ за пра́вило.

ruled *adj.* лино́ванный; в лине́йку; графлёный; разграфлённый.

ruler *n.* **1,** (one who governs) прави́тель. **2,** (measuring stick) лине́йка.

ruling *n.* постановле́ние; реше́ние. —*adj.* пра́вящий. —**ruling circles,** пра́вящие круги́. —**ruling classes,** пра́вящие *or* госпо́дствующие кла́ссы.

rum *n.* ром.

Rumanian *adj. & n.* = **Romanian.**

rumba *n.* ру́мба.

rumble *v.i.* **1,** (roar) громыха́ть; грохота́ть; греме́ть; рокота́ть. **2,** (gurgle, as of the stomach) урча́ть; бурча́ть. **3,** (move with such a sound) громыха́ть; грохота́ть. —*n.* гро́хот; ро́кот. —**rumble seat,** откидно́е сиде́нье.

rumen *n.* рубе́ц.

ruminant *n.* жва́чное живо́тное. —*adj.* жва́чный.

ruminate *v.i.* **1,** (chew the cud) жева́ть жва́чку. **2,** (ponder) разду́мывать; размышля́ть.

rumination *n.* размышле́ние.

rummage *v.t. & i.* ры́ться в; обша́ривать.

rumor *also,* **rumour** *n.* слух. —*v.t. It is rumored that...,* хо́дят слу́хи, что...

rump *n.* **1,** (hind part of an animal) крестец. **2,** (buttocks) зад; я́годицы.

rumple *v.t.* мять. —*v.i.* мя́ться. —**rumpled,** *adj.* измя́тый: *rumpled suit,* измя́тый костю́м.

rump steak ромште́кс.

rumpus *n.* шум; гам; гвалт.

run *v.i.* **1,** (dash; jog) бежа́ть: *run fast,* бежа́ть быстро. *Run home/upstairs,* побежа́ть домо́й/наве́рх. *Run to the store for some cigarettes,* побежа́ть *or* сбе́гать в магази́н за сигаре́тами. **2,** (operate; function) ходи́ть; рабо́тать. *The trains aren't running,* поезда́ не хо́дят. *The elevator isn't running,* лифт не рабо́тает. *The car runs smoothly,* маши́на идёт безотка́зно. *Run on electricity,* рабо́тать на электри́честве. *Leave the motor running,* не выключа́ть мото́ра. **3,** (extend) идти́; пролега́ть; проходи́ть. *The road runs along the coast,* доро́га идёт *or* пролега́ет вдоль бе́рега. *The tunnel runs under the river,* тунне́ль прохо́дит под реко́й. **4,** (stream; flow) ли́ться. *The water ran out of the bathtub,* вода́ вы́текла из ва́нны. *Leave the water running,* оставля́ть кран откры́тым. *My nose is running,* у меня́ из носу течёт. **5,** (spread, as of colors or dyes) линя́ть; (of ink) растека́ться; расплыва́ться. **6,** (be in force) быть действи́тельным; остава́ться в си́ле. *The lease runs for two years,* срок де́йствия аре́нды — два го́да. **7,** (be on, as of a play) идти́. **8,** (be a candidate) баллоти́роваться; выставля́ть свою́ кандидату́ру. *Run for president,* баллоти́роваться в президе́нты *or* на пост президе́нта. **9,** (come in; finish) приходи́ть: *run last,* приходи́ть после́дним. **10,** *used with various adjectives: run dry,* высыха́ть; *run low,* истоща́ться; *run late,* опа́здывать; *run short, see* **short.** *Feelings ran high,* стра́сти разгоре́лись *or* разыгра́лись. —*v.t.* **1,** (cover by running) пробега́ть: *run five miles,* пробега́ть пять миль. *He ran a good race,* он пробежа́л хорошо́. *The race will be run to-*

morrow, забег состоится завтра. **2,** (take; drive) отвозить: *I'll run you to the station,* я вас отвезу на вокзал. **3,** (chase) прогонять: *run someone out of town,* прогнать кого-нибудь из города. **4,** (cause to move quickly) пробегать: *run one's fingers over the keyboard,* пробегать пальцами по клавиатуре. **5,** (manage; govern; conduct) руководить; управлять; вести. *Run a department,* руководить отделом. *Run the country,* руководить *or* управлять страной. *Run a meeting,* вести собрание. **6,** (print; carry, as a story) печатать; помещать. **7,** (break through; go past): прорывать: *run a blockade,* прорвать блокаду. *Run a red light,* проехать на красный свет. **8,** (extend; install, as a wire or cable) прокладывать; проводить. **9,** *used with various nouns: run a risk,* рисковать; *run errands,* быть на посылках. *He is running a temperature,* у него температура. **—n. 1,** (act of running) бег; пробег; пробёжка. *Early-morning run,* утренняя пробёжка. *Set off at a run,* пуститься *or* броситься бегом. **2,** (single trip) рейс: *maiden run,* первый рейс. **3,** (streak, as of luck; spell, as of weather) полоса. **4,** (series of performances): *The play had a long run,* пьеса шла долго. **5,** (unrestricted use): *Give the children the run of the house,* распустить детей по дому. *We had the run of the house,* дом был в нашем полном распоряжении. **6,** (tear in one's stocking) спустившаяся петля: *I have a run in my stocking,* у меня на чулке спустилась петля. **7,** *Run on a bank,* натиск вкладчиков на банк. **8,** *music* рулада. **—in the long run,** в долгосрочном плане; в длительной перспективе. **—in the short run,** в краткосрочном плане; в краткосрочной перспективе; в ближней *or* ближайшей перспективе. **—on the run, 1,** (while in motion) на ходу. **2,** (hurriedly) второпях. **3,** (fleeing from justice) в бегах. **—run across, 1,** *literally* перебегать. **2,** (encounter by chance) наталкиваться на; случайно встречаться с. **—run after,** бежать за. **—run along,** побежать: *Well, I'll be running along,* ну, я побегу. **—run around with,** водиться с; путаться с. **—run away,** убегать: *run away from home,* убегать из дома. *The dog ran away from its master,* собака сбежала от хозяина. **—run down, 1,** *literally* сбегать с: *run down the stairs,* сбегать с лестницы. **2,** (run along; run through) пробегать по: *run down the street,* пробегать по улице. *A chill ran down my spine,* по моей спине пробежала дрожь. **3,** *fol. by* **to** (make a short trip to) побежать (в); сходить (в); сбегать (в); съездить (в). **4,** (flow down) сбегать: *The streams run down from the mountains,* ручьи сбегают с гор. *Tears ran down her cheeks,* слёзы сбегали по её щекам. **5,** (pursue and catch) настигать. **6,** (knock over with a vehicle) наехать на. **7,** (read over rapidly) пробегать. **8,** (disparage) порочить. **9,** (of a clock) стать; (of a battery) разряжаться. **—run into, 1,** *literally* вбегать в. **2,** (collide with) сталкиваться с; наехать на; налететь на. **3,** (encounter by chance) наталкиваться на; случайно встречаться с. **4,** (experience, as difficulties) сталкиваться с; встречаться с. **5,** (cost) стоить: *run into a lot of*

money, стоить больших денег. **6,** (add up to) исчисляться: *Losses ran into the millions,* убытки исчислялись миллионами. **—run off, 1,** (go off) сходить: *The car ran off the road,* машина сошла с дороги. **2,** (run away) убегать. **3,** (flow off; drain) стекать. **4,** (print) печатать; отпечатывать. **—run out, 1,** *literally* выбегать. **2,** (expire) истекать: *Time is running out,* время истекает. **3,** (be used up) выходить; кончаться; истощаться; иссякать; быть на исходе. *We ran out of gas,* у нас кончился бензин. *His luck ran out,* счастье ему изменило. **—run over, 1,** (overflow) переливаться через. *My cup runneth over,* моя чаша переполнена. **2,** (knock down and crush with a vehicle) (за)давить; переехать. *He was run over by a car,* он попал под машину. **3,** (review again quickly) повторять. **4,** (exceed) превышать. **—run through, 1,** *literally* пробегать через. **2,** (review again quickly) повторять. **3,** (plunge) пронзать: *run a bayonet through someone,* пронзать кого-нибудь штыком. **4,** (squander) проживать; проматывать. **—run up, 1,** *literally* взбегать на *or* по. **2,** (hoist, as a flag) выкинуть. **3,** (pile up, as debts) наделать (долгов).

runaway *adj.* бежавший; беглый. *Runaway slave,* беглый раб. *Runaway victory,* лёгкая победа. *Runaway inflation,* безудержная инфляция.

rundown *n.* краткое изложение; сводка.

run-down *adj.* **1,** (tired; worn out) переутомлённый. **2,** (in poor condition) обветшалый; обшарпанный.

rune *n.* руна.

rung *n.* ступенька.

runic *adj.* рунический.

run-in *n.* склока; перебранка.

runner *n.* **1,** (one who runs) бегун. **2,** (messenger) посыльный. **3,** (smuggler) контрабандист. **4,** (blade, as of a sled) полоз. **5,** (strip of carpet) дорожка. **6,** (trailing plant stem) усик.

running *n.* **1,** (act of running; jogging) бег. *Take up running,* бегать; начать бегать. **2,** (chances of winning) шансы: *be in the running,* иметь шансы; *be out of the running,* потерять все шансы. **—adj. 1,** (moving fast) бегущий. **2,** (used for running) беговой: *running track,* беговая дорожка. **3,** (continuous) непрерывный. **—adv.** подряд: *three years running,* три года подряд. **—running board,** подножка. **—running broad jump,** прыжок с разбега. **—running head,** колонтитул. **—running water,** водопровод.

runoff *n.* **1,** (of water) сток. **2,** (new election) повторные выборы; повторное голосование.

run-of-the-mill *adj.* заурядный; дюжинный.

runt *n.* недоросток; коротыш(ка).

runway *n.* лётная полоса; взлётно-посадочная полоса.

rupee *n.* рупия.

rupture *n.* **1,** (break) разрыв. **2,** (hernia) грыжа. **—v.t.** прорывать. *Ruptured spleen,* разрыв селезёнки. **—v.i.** прорываться.

rural *adj.* сельский; деревенский.

ruse *n.* уловка.

rush *v.i.* **1,** (hurry) спеши́ть; торпи́ться: *I'm rushing to the airport,* я спешу́/тороплю́сь в аэропо́рт. **2,** (dash) бро́ситься; ри́нуться: *rush to the aid of,* бро́ситься/ри́нуться на по́мощь (+ *dat.*). **3,** (flow rapidly) хлы́нуть. *A rushing river,* стреми́тельная река́. *Blood rushed to her cheeks,* кровь бро́силась ей в щёки; кровь прилила́ к её щека́м. —*v.t.* **1,** (force to move hastily) торопи́ть: *Don't rush me!,* не торопи́те меня́! **2,** (whisk) мчать. *He was rushed to the hospital,* его́ сро́чно доста́вили в больни́цу. —*n.* **1,** (hurry) спе́шка: *What's the rush?,* к чему́ така́я спе́шка? *There is no rush,* не на́до спеши́ть. *I'm in a big rush,* я о́чень тороплю́сь. **2,** (dash) бросо́к. *Gold rush,* золота́я лихора́дка. **3,** (heavy flow, as of air) поры́в; (of blood) прили́в. **4,** (grasslike plant) тростни́к; камы́ш; си́тник. —*adj.* **1,** (urgent) сро́чный: *rush order,* сро́чный зака́з. **2,** (made of rush) тростнико́вый; камышо́вый. —**rush hours,** часы́пик.

rusk *n.* сла́дкий суха́рь.

russet *adj.* кра́снобу́рый.

Russia leather юфть.

Russian *adj.* ру́сский; росси́йский. *The Russian language,* ру́сский язы́к. *Russian literature,* ру́сская литерату́ра. *The Russian Federation,* Росси́йская Федера́ция. *The Russian Empire,* Росси́йская импе́рия. *A Russian citizen,* росси́йский граждани́н.

The Russian parliament, росси́йский парла́мент. —*n.* **1,** (ethnic Russian) ру́сский; ру́сская. *The Russians,* ру́сские. **2,** (citizen of Russia) россия́нин; россия́нка. **3,** (language) ру́сский язы́к. *Do you speak Russian?,* вы говори́те (*or* разгова́риваете) порусски?

Russify *v.t.* русифици́ровать. *Become Russified,* обрусе́ть. —**Russification,** *n.* русифика́ция.

Russophile *n.* русофи́л.

Russophobe *n.* русофо́б. —**Russophobia,** *n.* русофо́бство.

rust *n.* ржа́вчина. —*adj.* (rust-colored) ржа́вый. —*v.i.* ржа́веть.

rustic *adj.* дереве́нский.

rustle *v.i.* шелесте́ть; шурша́ть. —*v.t.* шелесте́ть (+ *instr.*). —*n.* ше́лест; шо́рох.

rusty *adj.* ржа́вый; заржа́вленный. *Get rusty,* ржа́веть. *My French is a bit rusty,* я подзабы́л(а) свой францу́зский.

rut *n.* коле́я; колдо́бина.

rutabaga *n.* брю́ква.

ruthenium *n.* руте́ний.

ruthless *adj.* безжа́лостный. —**ruthlessly,** *adv.* безжа́лостно. —**ruthlessness,** *n.* беажа́лостность.

rye *n.* рожь. —*adj.* ржано́й: *rye bread,* ржано́й хлеб.

ryegrass *n.* плёвел.

S

S, s девятна́дцатая бу́ква англи́йского алфави́та.

Sabbath *n.* суббо́та: *observe the Sabbath,* соблюда́ть суббо́ту.

sabbatical *n.* годи́чный о́тпуск.

saber *also,* **sabre** *n.* са́бля; ша́шка. —**saber rattling,** бряца́ние ору́жием.

sable *n.* со́боль. —*adj.* собо́лий; соболи́ный.

sabotage *n.* сабота́ж; диве́рсия. —*v.t.* саботи́ровать. —**saboteur,** *n.* сабота́жник; диверса́нт.

sabre *n.* = **saber.**

sac *n.* мешо́чек.

saccharin *n.* сахари́н.

saccharine *adj.* **1,** (of or like sugar) са́харистый. **2,** (cloyingly sweet) са́харный; слаща́вый; при́торный.

sacerdotal *adj.* свяще́ннический.

sack *n.* мешо́к: *sack of potatoes,* мешо́к с карто́фелем. *Flour sack,* мешо́к из-под муки́. —*v.t.* **1,** (plunder) гра́бить; разгра́бить; громи́ть. **2,** *slang* (fire) выгоня́ть с рабо́ты. —**get the sack,** *slang* вы́лететь с рабо́ты.

sackcloth *n.* **1,** (sacking) мешкови́на; дерю́га; холст. **2,** (symbol of penitence) власяни́ца.

sacking *n.* мешкови́на; дерю́га.

sacrament *n.* та́инство. —**sacramental,** *adj.* относя́щийся к та́инству; свяще́нный.

sacred *adj.* свяще́нный; свято́й. *Sacred duty,* свяще́нный долг. *Hold something sacred,* свя́то чтить что́-нибудь.

sacrifice *n.* **1,** (giving up of something) же́ртва: *make sacrifices,* идти́ на же́ртвы. **2,** (religious offering) жертвоприноше́ние. *Make sacrifices to the gods,* приноси́ть же́ртвы бога́м. —*v.t.* же́ртвовать; приноси́ть в же́ртву. *Sacrifice one's life,* же́ртвовать (свое́й) жи́знью. *Sacrifice a pawn* (*in chess*), же́ртвовать пе́шкой. —**sacrificial,** *adj.* же́ртвенный.

sacrilege *n.* святота́тство; кощу́нство. —**sacrilegious,** *adj.* святота́тственный; кощу́нственный.

sacristy *n.* ри́зница.

sacrosanct *adj.* свяще́нный; неприкоснове́нный.

sacrum *n.* кресте́ц.

sad *adj.* печа́льный; гру́стный: *sad face,* печа́льное/гру́стное лицо́; *sad story,* печа́льная/гру́стная исто́рия. *Sad news,* печа́льная но́вость. *In a sad state,* в плаче́вном состоя́нии. *I was sad,* мне бы́ло гру́стно. *Why are you so sad?,* почему́ вы тако́й гру́стный (така́я гру́стная)? *I was very sad to hear the news,* я был о́чень огорчён услы́шать но́вость.

sadden *v.t.* печа́лить. *Saddened by the news,* опеча́лен но́востью.

saddle *n.* седло́: *jump into the saddle,* вскочи́ть в седло́. *Saddle of lamb,* седло́ бара́на. —*v.t.* **1,** (put a saddle on) седла́ть. **2,** (burden) обременя́ть: *saddled with debts,* обременён долга́ми. *Saddle someone with a job,* взва́ливать рабо́ту на кого́-нибудь. —**saddlebag,** *n.* седе́льная *or* перемётная сума́. —**saddlecloth,** *n.* потни́к. —**saddle horse,** верхова́я ло́шадь. —**saddler,** *n.* седе́льный ма́стер; седе́льник; шо́рник.

sadism *n.* сади́зм. —**sadist,** *n.* сади́ст. —**sadistic,** *adj.* сади́стский.

sadly *adv.* печа́льно; гру́стно. *Be sadly mistaken,* серьёзно ошиба́ться. *Be sadly lacking in,* о́чень *or* о́стро нужда́ться в (+ *prepl.*). ♦*As an introductory word,* к несча́стью.

sadness *n.* печа́ль; грусть.

safari *n.* охо́тничья экспеди́ция.

safe *adj.* **1,** (free from danger) безопа́сный; в безопа́сности. *From a safe distance,* с безопа́сного расстоя́ния. *It is safe here,* здесь безопа́сно. *Keep in a safe place,* храни́ть в надёжном ме́сте. *I feel safe here,* здесь я чу́вствую себя́ в безопа́сности. **2,** (unharmed) невреди́мый: *The boy is safe,* ма́льчик невреди́м. **3,** (without mishap) благополу́чный: *safe return,* благополу́чное возвраще́ние. **4,** (careful) осторо́жный: *a safe driver,* осторо́жный води́тель. **5,** (dependable) надёжный: *in safe hands,* в надёжных рука́х. —*n.* сейф. —**play safe,** де́йствовать наверняка́. —**safe and sound,** цел и невреди́м; в це́лости и сохра́нности. —**to be on the safe side,** для бо́льшей ве́рности; для перестрахо́вки; на вся́кий слу́чай.

safe-conduct *n.* осо́бая охра́на. *Safe-conduct pass,* охра́нная гра́мота; охра́нный лист.

safeguard *n.* гара́нтия; ме́ра предосторо́жности. —*v.t.* охраня́ть; защища́ть.

safe house я́вка.

safekeeping *n.* хране́ние; сохране́ние: *turn over for safekeeping,* отдава́ть на хране́ние/сохране́ние.

safely *adv.* **1,** (without mishap) благополу́чно. **2,** (without fear of being wrong) с уве́ренностью; сме́ло.

safety *n.* безопа́сность. —**safety catch,** предохрани́тель. —**safety pin,** англи́йская була́вка. —**safety razor,** безопа́сная бри́тва. —**safety valve,** предохрани́тельный кла́пан.

safflower *n.* сафло́р.

saffron *n.* шафра́н.

sag *v.i.* прогиба́ться; провиса́ть. —*n.* проги́б.

saga *n.* са́га.

sagacious *adj.* проница́тельный; прозорли́вый. —**sagacity,** *n.* проница́тельность; прозорли́вость.

sage *n.* **1,** (wise man) мудре́ц. **2,** (shrub) шалфе́й. —*adj.* му́дрый: *sage advice,* му́дрый сове́т.

sagebrush *n.* полы́нь.

Sagittarius *n.* Стреле́ц.

sail *n.* **1,** (piece of canvas to propel a ship) па́рус. **2,** (ride on a sailing vessel) прогу́лка под паруса́ми. *Go for a sail,* идти́ ката́ться на па́русной ло́дке. —*v.i.* **1,** (travel by ship or boat) плыть; пла́вать. *Sail down the river,* плыть вниз по реке́. *Sail across the ocean,* переплы́ть океа́н. *Sail around the world,* соверши́ть кругосве́тное пла́вание. **2,** (set sail) отплыва́ть; отходи́ть: *The ship sails at noon,* кора́бль отплыва́ет *or* отхо́дит в по́лдень. **3,** (soar; glide) плыть; пари́ть. —*v.t.* **1,** (handle; steer) вести́; управля́ть. **2,** (travel on or over) плыть; пла́вать (по *or* в). *Sail the seas,* плыть по мо́рю *or* по́ морю. —**sail into, 1,** *literally* входи́ть в; вплыва́ть в. **2,** (assail) обру́шиваться на; ополча́ться на. —**set sail,** отплыва́ть; отходи́ть.

sailboat *n.* па́русная ло́дка.

sailfish *n.* па́русник.

sailing *n.* **1,** (the sport) па́русный спорт. **2,** (riding in a sailboat) пла́вание; ката́ние на (па́русной) ло́дке. **3,** (departure from port) отплы́тие. —**sailing vessel,** па́русное су́дно; па́русник.

sailor *n.* моря́к; матро́с. —*adj.* [*also,* **sailor's**] матро́сский: *sailor suit,* матро́сский костю́м.

saint *n.* свято́й: *St. Peter,* св. Пётр. *St. Patrick's Day,* день св. Па́трика. *St. Petersburg,* Санкт-Петербу́рг. *St. Louis,* Сент-Лу́ис. *St. Lawrence River,* река́ Свято́го Лавре́нтия. *St. Basil's Cathedral,* храм Васи́лия Блаже́нного.

Saint Bernard сенберна́р.

sainthood *n.* лик святы́х: *confer sainthood upon,* причисля́ть к ли́ку святы́х.

saintly *adj.* свято́й; подоба́ющий свято́му.

Saint Vitus' dance пля́ска свято́го Ви́тта; ви́ттова пля́ска.

sake *n., in* **for the sake of,** ра́ди (+ *gen.*). *Do it for my/ your own/ sake,* сде́лайте э́то ра́ди меня́; сде́лайте э́то для себя́. —**for goodness' sake!,** ра́ди бо́га!

salacious *adj.* са́льный; скабрёзный.

salad *n.* сала́т. —**salad bowl,** сала́тник. —**salad dressing,** припра́ва к сала́ту.

salamander *n.* салама́ндра.

salami *n.* колбаса́ твёрдого копче́ния; саля́ми.

salary *n.* жа́лованье; зарпла́та; окла́д.

sale *n.* **1,** (selling) прода́жа; сбыт. *Put on/ up for/ sale,* пуска́ть в прода́жу. **2,** (clearance sale) распрода́жа. **3,** *pl.* (business of selling) сбыт: *sales department,* отде́л сбы́та. **4,** *pl.* (volume of business) объём прода́ж: *Sales are off/down,* объём прода́ж упа́л. —**for sale,** продаётся. *It is not for sale,* не продаётся.

saleslady *n.* продавщи́ца. *Also,* **salesgirl; saleswoman.**

salesman *n.* **1,** [*also,* **salesclerk**] (seller in a store) продаве́ц. **2,** (traveling agent) коммивояжёр.

sales slip квита́нция.

sales tax нало́г на поку́пки.

salient *adj.* **1,** (protruding) выдаю́щийся. **2,** (noteworthy) примеча́тельный. *The salient points of the plan,* основны́е пу́нкты пла́на. —*n., mil.* вы́ступ; клин.

saline *adj.* соляно́й; солево́й. —**salinity,** *n.* солёность.

saliva *n.* слюна́. —**salivary,** *adj.* слю́нный. —**salivate,** *v.i.* выделя́ть слюну́.

sallow *adj.* желтова́тый; земли́стый.

sally *n.* **1,** *mil.* вы́лазка. **2,** (witticism) остро́та; ре́плика. —*v.i.* [*usu.* **sally forth**] отправля́ться.

salmon *n.* **1,** (fish) лосо́сь. **2,** (food) лососи́на. *Smoked salmon,* сёмга. —*adj.* **1,** (of salmon) лососёвый. **2,** (pinkish orange) ора́нжево-ро́зового цве́та.

salon *n.* сало́н.

saloon *n.* бар; пивна́я.

salt *n.* соль. *Smelling salts,* нюхательная соль. —*adj.* соляно́й: *salt mines,* соляны́е ко́пи. *Salt water,* солёная вода́. *Salt marsh,* солонча́к. —*v.t.* соли́ть; заса́ливать. —**rub salt on a wound,** растравля́ть ра́ну; сы́пать соль на ра́ну. —**salt away,** откла́дывать; накопля́ть. —**salt of the earth,** соль земли́. —**take with a grain of salt,** относи́ться скепти́чески к.

saltcellar *n.* соло́нка.

salted *adj.* солёный.

saltiness *n.* солёность.

saltpeter *also,* **saltpetre** *n.* сели́тра.

salt shaker соло́нка.

saltworks *n.* солева́рня; солева́ренный заво́д.

saltwort *n.* соля́нка.

salty *adj.* солёный.

salubrious *adj.* здоро́вый; целе́бный.

salutary *adj.* благотво́рный.

salutation *n.* приве́тствие. —**salutatory,** *adj.* приве́тственный.

salute *n.* **1,** (with the hand) отда́ние че́сти; во́инское приве́тствие. **2,** (with guns) салю́т: *21-gun salute,* салю́т из двадцати́ одного́ ору́дия *or* двадцатью́ одни́м оруди́йным за́лпом. —*v.t.* **1,** *mil.* отдава́ть честь (+ *dat.*). **2,** (hail) приве́тствовать. —*v.i.* отдава́ть честь.

salvage *n.* **1,** (act of saving) спасе́ние. **2,** (property saved from destruction) спасённое иму́щество. —*adj.* спаса́тельный: *salvage ship,* спаса́тельное су́дно. —*v.t.* спаса́ть: *salvage something from the fire,* спасти́ что́-нибудь от пожа́ра.

salvation *n.* спасе́ние.

salve *n.* (целе́бная) мазь.

salvo *n.* залп.

samarium *n.* сама́рий.

same *adj.* **1,** (the one just mentioned; one and the same) тот же; тот са́мый; тот же са́мый: *the same day,* в тот же день; *in the same place,* в *or* на том же са́мом ме́сте. *The same thing,* то же са́мое. *I got the same grade as you,* я получи́л(а) ту же отме́тку, что и вы. *England and Great Britain are not the same,* А́нглия и Великобрита́ния — не одно́ и то же. **2,** (one; applying to both or all) оди́н: *live under*

the same roof, жить под одно́й кры́шей. *They are the same age,* они́ одного́ во́зраста; они́ одни́х лет. **3,** (alike; identical) одина́ковый: *to the same degree,* в одина́ковой ме́ре. *All politicians are the same,* все поли́тики одина́ковы. **4,** (unchanged) тако́й же; пре́жний. *Remain the same,* остава́ться пре́жним (пре́жней). —*pron.* [*usu.* **the same**] то же са́мое; одно́ и то же. *The same to you!,* и вам того́ же!; и вас та́кже! *That's the same as saying...,* э́то всё равно́, что сказа́ть... —*adv.* [*usu.* **the same**] одина́ково. *They are pronounced the same,* они́ произно́сятся одина́ково. —**all the same, 1,** [*also,* **just the same**] (anyway) всё же; всё ещё; всё равно́. *Thank you just the same,* всё же благодарю́ вас. **2,** *fol. by* **to** (making no difference) всё равно́; безразли́чно: *It's all the same to me,* мне всё равно́; мне безразли́чно. —**at the same time,** *see* time.

sameness *n.* **1,** (identity) то́ждество. **2,** (monotony) однообра́зие.

samovar *n.* самова́р.

sample *n.* **1,** (typical example) образе́ц; обра́зчик; про́ба. **2,** *statistics* вы́борка: *random sample,* случа́йная вы́борка. —*adj.* про́бный: *sample copy,* про́бный экземпля́р. —*v.t.* про́бовать: *sample the cake,* про́бовать торт.

sampling *n.* вы́борка.

samurai *n.* самура́й.

sanatorium *n.* санато́рий.

sanctify *v.t.* освяща́ть. —**sanctification,** *n.* освяще́ние.

sanctimony *n.* ха́нжество. —**sanctimonious,** *adj.* ха́нжеский.

sanction *n.* **1,** (official permission) са́нкция. **2,** *usu. pl.* (punitive measures) са́нкции: *impose sanctions,* применя́ть са́нкции. —*v.t.* санкциони́ровать.

sanctity *n.* **1,** (saintliness) свя́тость. **2,** (inviolability) неприкоснове́нность: *the sanctity of the home/individual,* неприкоснове́нность жили́ща/ли́чности.

sanctuary *n.* **1,** (sacred place) святи́лище. **2,** (place of refuge) убе́жище. **3,** (animal preserve) запове́дник.

sanctum *n.* убе́жище.

sand *n.* песо́к. *Play in the sand,* игра́ть на песке́. *Dig in the sand,* копа́ться *or* ры́ться в песке́. —*adj.* песо́чный; песча́ный. —*v.t.* **1,** (sprinkle with sand) посыпа́ть песко́м. **2,** (sandpaper) натира́ть нажда́чной бума́гой.

sandal *n.* санда́лия; босоно́жка.

sandalwood *n.* санда́л.

sandbag *n.* мешо́к с песко́м.

sandbank *n.* песча́ная мель *or* о́тмель; перека́т; ба́нка. *Also,* **sand bar.**

sandbox *n.* песо́чница.

sanderling *n.* песча́нка.

sand fly моски́т.

sandpaper *n.* нажда́чная бума́га; шку́рка. —*v.t.* натира́ть нажда́чной бума́гой.

sandpiper *n.* песо́чник; перево́зчик.

sandstone *n.* песча́ник.

sandstorm *n.* песча́ная бу́ря.

sandwich *n.* бутербро́д.

sandy *adj.* **1,** (consisting of sand) песча́ный. **2,** (of the color of sand) песо́чный.

sane *adj.* **1,** (of sound mind) в здра́вом уме́; норма́льный. **2,** (sensible; rational) разу́мный.

sanguinary *adj.* **1,** (bloody) крова́вый. **2,** (bloodthirsty) кровожа́дный.

sanguine *adj.* **1,** (ruddy) румя́ный. **2,** (optimistic) оптимисти́ческий.

sanitarium *n.* санато́рий.

sanitary *adj.* санита́рный; гигиени́ческий; оздорови́тельный. —**sanitary napkin,** гигиени́ческая салфе́тка.

sanitation *n.* **1,** (protection of public health) санитари́я. **2,** (disposal of sewage) убо́рка му́сора; канализа́ция.

sanity *n.* рассу́док: *lose one's sanity,* теря́ть рассу́док. *Fear for someone's sanity,* боя́ться за чей-нибудь рассу́док.

Sanskrit *n.* санскри́т. —*adj.* санскри́тский.

Santa Claus дед-моро́з.

sap *n.* **1,** (juice of a plant) сок. **2,** *slang* (fool) простофи́ля. **3,** *mil.* (trench) са́па. —*v.t.* подта́чивать: *sap someone's strength,* подта́чивать чьи́-нибудь си́лы.

sapling *n.* де́ревце; деревцо́.

sapper *n., mil.* сапёр.

sapphire *n.* сапфи́р. —*adj.* сапфи́рный; сапфи́ровый.

sapwood *n.* за́болонь.

sarcasm *n.* сарка́зм. —**sarcastic,** *adj.* саркасти́ческий; язви́тельный. —**sarcastically,** *adv.* саркасти́чески.

sarcophagus *n.* саркофа́г.

sardine *n.* сарди́на; сарди́нка. —**like sardines,** как се́льди в бо́чке.

sardonic *adj.* сардони́ческий.

sari *n.* са́ри.

sartorial *adj.* портня́жный.

sash *n.* **1,** (band worn around the waist) куша́к. **2,** (window frame) око́нная ра́ма; око́нный переплёт.

sassy *adj., colloq.* наха́льный.

Satan *n.* сатана́. —**satanic,** *adj.* сатани́нский.

satchel *n.* ра́нец; су́мка.

sate *v.t.* пресыща́ть.

sateen *n.* сати́н. —*adj.* сати́новый.

satellite *n.* **1,** (moon) спу́тник. *Artificial satellite,* иску́сственный спу́тник. *Satellite pictures/photography,* сни́мки/фотогра́фия со спу́тника. **2,** *fig.* (nation dominated by another) сателли́т.

satiate *v.t.* **1,** (satisfy) насыща́ть. **2,** (surfeit) пресыща́ть. —**satiation; satiety,** *n.* насыще́ние; пресыще́ние; сы́тость.

satin *n.* атла́с. —*adj.* атла́сный.

satire *n.* сати́ра. —**satirical,** *adj.* сатири́ческий. —**satirist,** *n.* сати́рик. —**satirize,** *v.t.* высме́ивать; осме́ивать.

satisfaction *n.* удовлетворе́ние; удовлетворённость. *With satisfaction,* с удовлетворе́нием; удовлетворённо.

satisfactory *adj.* удовлетвори́тельный. —**satisfactorily,** *adv.* удовлетвори́тельно.

satisfied *adj.* дово́льный: *I am satisfied,* я дово́лен; я дово́льна.

satisfy *v.t.* удовлетворя́ть: *satisfy the teacher/ the requirements/, someone's needs/,* удовлетворя́ть учи́теля/ тре́бованиям/ чьи́-нибудь потре́бности.

satrap *n.* сатра́п. —**satrapy,** *n.* сатра́пия.

saturate *v.t.* насыща́ть; пропи́тывать.

saturation *n.* насыще́ние. —**saturation point,** то́чка насыще́ния.

Saturday *n.* суббо́та.

Saturn *n.* Сату́рн.

saturnine *adj.* мра́чный; молчали́вый.

satyr *n.* сати́р.

sauce *n.* со́ус; подли́вка.

saucepan *n.* кастрю́ля.

saucer *n.* блю́дце; блю́дечко. —**flying saucer,** лета́ющая таре́лка.

saucy *adj.* де́рзкий; наха́льный.

Saudi *adj.* сау́довский.

sauerkraut *n.* ки́слая *or* ква́шеная капу́ста.

sauna *n.* са́уна.

saunter *v.i.* прогу́ливаться; проха́живаться.

sausage *n.* колбаса́.

sauterne *n.* соте́рн.

savage *adj.* **1,** (uncivilized) ди́кий: *savage tribes,* ди́кие племена́. **2,** (ferocious) свире́пый: *savage beast,* свире́пый зверь. **3,** (brutal; vicious) зве́рский: *savage attack,* зве́рское нападе́ние. —*n.* дика́рь.

savagery *n.* ди́кость.

savanna *also,* **savannah** *n.* сава́нна.

savant *n.* учёный.

save *v.t.* **1,** (rescue) спаса́ть: *save someone's life,* спасти́ чью́-нибудь жизнь. *Save someone from death,* спасти́ кого́-нибудь от сме́рти. **2,** (retain; not throw away) храни́ть; бере́чь; сохраня́ть. **3,** (hold aside) бере́чь; сберега́ть: *save something for a special occasion,* бере́чь/сберега́ть что́-нибудь для осо́бого слу́чая. *Save me a seat!,* займи́те мне ме́сто. **4,** (conserve) бере́чь: *save one's strength,* бере́чь свои́ си́лы. **5,** (reduce the expenditure of, as time or money) бере́чь; эконо́мить. *Save ten dollars,* сэконо́мить де́сять до́лларов. **6,** (spare) избавля́ть: *That will save me a lot of trouble,* э́то изба́вит меня́ от мно́гих хлопо́т. **7,** (collect as a hobby) собира́ть: *save stamps,* собира́ть почто́вые ма́рки. **8,** *fol. by* **up** (keep and gradually amass) копи́ть. —*v.i.* **1,** (economize) эконо́мить: *save on fuel,* эконо́мить на то́пливе. **2,** *often fol. by* **up** (put money aside) копи́ть де́ньги. —*prep.* кро́ме; за исключе́нием (+ *gen.*). —**save the day,** спасти́ положе́ние.

saving *n.* **1,** (rescuing) спасе́ние. **2,** (reduction in cost) эконо́мия. **3,** *pl.* (money saved up) сбереже́ния. —**savings bank,** сберега́тельный банк; сберега́тельная ка́сса.

savior *also,* **saviour** *n.* спаси́тель.

savor *also,* **savour** *n.* вкус; смак. —*v.t.* вкуша́ть; смакова́ть.

savory *also,* **savoury** *adj.* **1,** (appetizing) вку́сный. **2,** (piquant) пика́нтный. —*n.* (plant) чабёр.

savvy *n., slang* смётка. —*adj., slang* смётливый.

saw *n.* **1,** (cutting tool) пила́. **2,** (maxim; saying) изрече́ние. —*v.t. & i.* пили́ть. *Saw in half,* распи́ливать попола́м. —**saw off,** отпи́ливать. *Sawed-off rifle,* обре́з.

sawdust *n.* опи́лки.

sawfish *n.* ры́ба-пила́.

sawhorse *n.* ко́злы.

sawmill *n.* лесопи́льный заво́д; лесопи́лка.

sawyer *n.* пи́льщик.

saxifrage *n.* камнело́мка.

Saxon *n.* сакс. —*adj.* саксо́нский.

saxophone *n.* саксофо́н.

say *v.t.* **1,** (utter; state) говори́ть (*pfv.* сказа́ть). *What did you say?,* что вы сказа́ли? *They say he is dissatisfied,* говоря́т, что он недово́лен. *I have nothing to say,* мне не́чего сказа́ть. *That says it all,* э́тим всё ска́зано. **2,** (recite) чита́ть: *say one's prayers,* чита́ть моли́твы. **3,** (assert) утвержда́ть: *He says he's innocent,* он утвержда́ет, что он невино́вен. **4,** (assume) допуска́ть: *Let's say it's true,* допу́стим, что э́то так. **5,** (read; go, as of a law or proverb) гласи́ть: *The law says...,* зако́н гласи́т, что.. —*n.* сло́во: *Have one's say,* сказа́ть своё сло́во; выска́зывать своё мне́ние; выска́зываться. —**as they say,** как говоря́т; что называ́ется. —**if I (one) may so,** с позволе́ния сказа́ть; е́сли мо́жно так вы́разиться. —**I should say so!,** ещё бы! —**it goes without saying,** само́ собо́й разуме́ется; не́чего и говори́ть. —**not to say,** чтобы (*or* е́сли) не сказа́ть: *a difficult assignment, not to say dangerous,* тру́дное зада́ние, чтобы (*or* е́сли) не сказа́ть опа́сное. —**that is to say,** то есть. —**when all is said and done,** в конце́ концо́в; в коне́чном счёте. —**you can say that again!,** и не говори́те!; ещё бы! —**you don't say!,** да что вы говори́те! —**you might say,** мо́жно сказа́ть.

saying *n.* погово́рка; изрече́ние. *As the saying goes,* как говори́тся.

scab *n.* струп.

scabbard *n.* но́жны.

scabies *n.* чесо́тка.

scads *n.pl., colloq.* ма́сса; у́йма.

scaffold *n.* **1,** (platform for a gallows) эшафо́т. **2,** (raised wooden framework) подмо́стки. —**scaffolding,** *n.* (строи́тельные) леса́.

scald *v.t.* обва́ривать; ошпа́ривать. *Scald oneself,* обва́риваться; ошпа́риваться.

scale *n.* **1,** (instrument for weighing) весы́. **2,** (scope) масшта́б: *on a large scale,* в большо́м масшта́бе. **3,** (series of marks for measuring, as on a thermometer) шкала́. **4,** (projection on a map) масшта́б: *large-scale map,* ка́рта кру́пного масшта́ба. **5,** (graded system of classification) шкала́; ле́стница: *wage scale,* шкала́ зарабо́тной пла́ты; *social scale,* обще́ственная ле́стница. **6,** *music* га́мма. **7,** *pl.* (of fish and reptiles) чешуя́. —*v.t.* **1,** (have a weight of) ве́сить. **2,** (climb to the top of) взбира́ться на. **3,** *fol. by* **down** (reduce) понижа́ть; снижа́ть. **4,** (remove the scales from) снима́ть чешую́ с; чи́стить. —**tip the scales,** склони́ть *or* перетяну́ть ча́шу весо́в (*e.g.* в чью́-нибудь по́льзу). —**tip the scales at,** ве́сить.

scalene *adj., math.* разносторо́нний.

scallion *n.* зелёный лук.

scallop *n.* **1,** (mollusk) гребешо́к. **2,** *pl.* (decorative curves forming an edge) фесто́ны. —**scalloped,** *adj.* фесто́нный; фесто́нчатый.

scalp *n.* **1,** (skin on the top of the head) ко́жа головы́. **2,** (portion of this taken in battle) скальп. —*v.t.* скальпи́ровать.

scalpel *n.* ска́льпель.

scaly *adj.* чешу́йчатый.

scamp *n.* негодя́й; мерза́вец.

scamper *v.i.* **1,** (race; dash) мча́ться. **2,** (frolic) резви́ться; снова́ть.

scan *v.t.* **1,** (scrutinize) рассма́тривать. *Scan the horizon,* оки́нуть *or* обвести́ горизо́нт взгля́дом. **2,** (glance over) просма́тривать; пробега́ть.

scandal *n.* сканда́л. —**scandalize,** *v.t.* скандализи́ровать. —**scandalous,** *adj.* сканда́льный.

Scandinavian *adj.* скандина́вский. —*n.* скандина́в.

scandium *n.* ска́ндий.

scant *adj.* **1,** (meager) ску́дный: *scant resources,* ску́дные ресу́рсы. **2,** (hardly any) почти́ никако́й. *Pay scant attention,* е́ле обраща́ть внима́ние. **3,** (not quite the amount needed) всего́ на: *miss by a few scant inches,* промахну́ться всего́ на не́сколько дю́ймов.

scanty *adj.* ску́дный: *scanty supplies/information,* ску́дные запа́сы/све́дения. —**scantily,** *adv. Scantily attired,* едва́ оде́тый.

scapegoat *n.* козёл отпуще́ния.

scar *n.* **1,** (mark) рубе́ц; шрам. **2,** *fig.* (lasting effect) след. —*v.t.* оставля́ть рубцы́ *or* шра́мы на; обезобра́живать. —*v.i.* рубцева́ться.

scarab *n.* скарабе́й.

scarce *adj.* **1,** (in short supply) дефици́тный: *scarce commodity,* дефици́тный това́р. **2,** (rarely seen) ре́дкий. —**make oneself scarce,** не пока́зываться; не попада́ться на глаза́.

scarcely *adv.* едва́; е́ле; с трудо́м. *Scarcely enough,* едва́ доста́точно. *He is scarcely breathing,* он е́ле ды́шит. *I could scarcely make out the road,* я с трудо́м различа́л(а) доро́гу.

scarcity *n.* **1,** (dearth) нехва́тка; дефици́т. **2,** (rarity) ре́дкость.

scare *v.t.* **1,** (frighten) пуга́ть. *I'm scared,* мне стра́шно. *Be scared to death,* испуга́ться до́ смерти. **2,** *fol. by* **away** *or* **off** (drive away) спу́гивать. —*v.i.* пуга́ться. *He doesn't scare easily,* его́ не так легко́ испуга́ть. —*n. Give someone a scare,* напуга́ть кого́-нибудь. *Have quite a scare,* о́чень перепуга́ться.

scarecrow *n.* пу́гало; чу́чело.

scaremonger *n.* паникёр.

scarf *n.* шарф.

scarlet *adj.* а́лый. —*n.* а́лый цвет. —**scarlet fever,** скарлати́на.

scar tissue рубцо́вая ткань.

scary *adj., colloq.* пуга́ющий; стра́шный.

scat *interj.* прочь!; поди́ прочь!; прочь отсю́да!

scathing *adj.* хлёсткий; разно́сный; разгро́мный; уничтожа́ющий.

scatter *v.t.* **1,** (strew) разбра́сывать; рассыпа́ть. *Scatter seeds,* рассе́ять семена́. *The wreckage was scattered over a wide area,* обло́мки бы́ли разбро́саны на большо́м расстоя́нии. **2,** (disperse; rout) рассе́ивать; разгоня́ть. —*v.i.* рассе́иваться; рассыпа́ться; разбега́ться. *Scatter in all directions,* бро́ситься врассыпну́ю.

scatterbrain *n.* ве́треник; рази́ня. —**scatterbrained,** *adj.* ве́треный; безголо́вый.

scavenge *v.i.* иска́ть отбро́сы; ры́ться в му́соре. —**scavenger,** *n.* живо́тное, пита́ющееся па́далью.

scenario *n.* сцена́рий.

scene *n.* **1,** (place where something occurs) ме́сто: *the scene of the crime,* ме́сто преступле́ния; *the scene of bitter fighting,* ме́сто ожесточённых боёв. *Appear on the scene,* яви́ться на сце́ну. *Pass from the scene,* сойти́ со сце́ны. **2,** (division of an act of a play) сце́на; явле́ние; карти́на. *Act One, Scene Two,* де́йствие пе́рвое, сце́на втора́я. **3,** (part or setting of a play, movie or story) сце́на: *love scenes,* любо́вные сце́ны. *Scenes from a movie,* ка́дры из фи́льма. *The scene is laid in ancient Rome,* де́йствие происхо́дит в дре́внем Ри́ме. **4,** (sight) вид; зре́лище. *The scene from the window,* вид из окна́. *Peaceful scene,* споко́йный вид. **5,** (subject of a painting) пейза́ж: *winter scene,* зи́мний пейза́ж. **6,** (image; picture) карти́на: *scenes from childhood,* карти́ны де́тства; *a scene of utter desolation,* карти́на по́лного запусте́ния. **7,** (display of temper) сце́на: *make a scene,* устро́ить сце́ну. —**behind the scenes,** за кули́сами. *Direct a campaign from behind the scenes,* руководи́ть кампа́нией из-за кули́с.

scenery *n.* **1,** (features of a landscape) пейза́ж. **2,** *theat.* декора́ции. —**change of scenery, 1,** *theat.* переме́на декора́ций. **2,** *fig.* (change of surroundings) переме́на обстано́вки.

scenic *adj.* **1,** (pert. to stage effects) сцени́ческий: *scenic effects,* сцени́ческие эффе́кты. **2,** (having beautiful scenery) живопи́сный.

scent *n.* **1,** (odor) за́пах; арома́т. **2,** (trail of an animal) след: *pick up the scent,* напа́сть на след. **3,** (sense of smell) чутьё. **4,** (perfume) духи́. —*v.t.* **1,** (smell) обоня́ть. **2,** (sense; suspect) чу́ять. **3,** (perfume) души́ть.

scepter *also,* **sceptre** *n.* ски́петр.

sceptic *n.* = **skeptic.** —**sceptical,** *adj.* = **skeptical.** —**scepticism,** *n.* = **skepticism.**

sceptre *n.* = **scepter.**

schedule *n.* расписа́ние; гра́фик. *Tight schedule,* жёсткий *or* напряжённый гра́фик. *On schedule,* по расписа́нию; в срок. *Ahead of schedule,* до сро́ка; ра́ньше сро́ка; ра́ньше расписа́ния. *Be behind schedule,* отстава́ть от гра́фика; вы́биться из гра́фика *or* расписа́ния; опа́здывать. —*v.t.* назнача́ть; намеча́ть: *The conference is scheduled for May 5th,* конфере́нция назна́чена *or* назнача́ется *or* наме́чена *or* намеча́ется на пя́тое ма́я. *He is scheduled to become the new prime minister,* он наме́чен в но́вые премье́р-мини́стры.

schematic *adj.* схемати́ческий.

scheme *n.* **1,** (plan of action) план. **2,** (underhanded plot) махина́ция; интри́га. **3,** (diagram) схе́ма. **4,** (orderly combination) сочета́ние. *Color scheme,* сочета́ние цвето́в; расцве́тка. —*v.i.* интригова́ть; вести́ интри́гу. —**schemer,** *n.* интрига́н.

scherzo *n.* ске́рцо.

schism *n.* раско́л; схи́зма. —**schismatic,** *adj.* раско́льнический.

schist *n.* сла́нец.

schizophrenia *n.* шизофрени́я. —**schizophrenic,** *adj.* шизофрени́ческий. —*n.* шизофре́ник.

schnitzel *n.* шни́цель.

scholar *n.* учёный.

scholarly *adj.* учёный. *Scholarly appearance,* профе́ссорский вид. *Scholarly term,* нау́чный те́рмин.

scholarship *n.* **1,** (learning) учёность. **2,** (grant) стипе́ндия.

scholastic *adj.* шко́льный; уче́бный.

school *n.* **1,** (place of learning) шко́ла: *go to school,* ходи́ть в шко́лу. *Law school,* юриди́ческий факульте́т. **2,** (classes) заня́тия; уро́ки. *Miss school,* пропусти́ть заня́тия. *Keep in after school,* оставля́ть (кого́-нибудь) по́сле уро́ков. *School starts on Monday,* заня́тия начина́ются в понеде́льник. **3,** (trend in the arts) шко́ла: *the impressionist school,* импрессиони́стская шко́ла. **4,** (large group of fish) кося́к. —*adj.* шко́льный; уче́бный. *School age,* шко́льный во́зраст. *School year,* уче́бный год. —*v.t.* **1,** (educate) воспи́тывать. *He was schooled in England,* он получи́л образова́ние в А́нглии. **2,** (train; discipline) приуча́ть. —**a man of the old school,** челове́к ста́рого зака́ла. —**school of thought,** то́чка зре́ния: *There are two schools of thought on this question,* на э́тот счёт существу́ют две разли́чных то́чки зре́ния. —**tell tales out of school,** выноси́ть сор из избы́.

schoolbook *n.* уче́бник.

schoolboy *n.* шко́льник. —**schoolchildren,** *n.pl.* шко́льники. —**schoolgirl,** *n.* шко́льница.

schoolhouse *n.* шко́льное зда́ние.

schooling *n.* образова́ние.

schoolteacher *n.* учи́тель; учи́тельница.

schooner *n.* шху́на.

sciatic *adj.* седа́лищный: *sciatic nerve,* седа́лищный нерв.

sciatica *n.* и́шиас.

science *n.* нау́ка. —**science fiction,** нау́чная фанта́стика.

scientific *adj.* нау́чный. —**scientifically,** *adv.* нау́чно.

scientist *n.* **1,** (eminent figure in a field of science) учёный. **2,** (person engaged in scientific research) нау́чный рабо́тник.

scimitar *n.* ятага́н.

scintilla *n.* ка́пелька; крупи́ца; тень. *Not a scintilla of evidence,* ни мале́йших доказа́тельств.

scintillate *v.i.* и́скриться. —**scintillating,** *adj.* блестя́щий.

scion *n.* о́тпрыск.

scissors *n.* но́жницы.

sclerosis *n.* склеро́з. —**sclerotic,** *adj.* склероти́ческий.

scoff *v.i.* [*usu.* **scoff at**] смея́ться над.

scold *v.t.* брани́ть. —**scolding,** *n.* вы́говор; нагоня́й.

scoop *n.* сово́к; ковш; черпа́к. —*v.t.* **1,** *fol. by* **up** (gather up) че́рпать; заче́рпывать. **2,** *fol. by* **out** (remove) выче́рпывать.

scoot *v.i., colloq.* бежа́ть; удира́ть.

scooter *n.* самока́т. —**motor scooter,** мотоpо́ллер.

scope *n.* **1,** (range; extent) разма́х; масшта́б. *Be beyond the scope of,* выходи́ть за ра́мки (+ *gen.*). **2,** (opportunity to function) просто́р: *provide scope for,* дава́ть просто́р (+ *dat.*). **3,** (outlook; intellect) круго́зор: *broaden one's scope,* расширя́ть круго́зор.

scorch *v.t.* опа́ливать; подпа́ливать; пали́ть. —**scorched-earth policy,** страте́гия вы́жженной земли́.

scorching *adj.* паля́щий.

score *n.* **1,** (in sports and games) счёт: *What's the score?,* како́й счёт? *Keep score,* вести́ счёт. *By a score of 2-0,* со счётом два-ноль. **2,** (achievement in a test or competition) результа́т: *achieve the best score,* показа́ть лу́чший результа́т. **3,** (account) счёт: *Have no fear on that score,* на э́тот счёт мо́жете быть споко́йны. **4,** *pl.* (grievance demanding satisfaction) счёты: *settle scores with,* своди́ть счёты с. **5,** (twenty) два́дцать; два деся́тка; *pl.* деся́тки; не́сколько деся́тков; мно́жество. **6,** *music* партиту́ра. **7,** (mark; incision) след; зару́бка. —*v.t.* **1,** *sports: score a goal,* заби́ть гол. *Score a point,* получи́ть *or* вы́играть очко́. *Score ten points,* набра́ть де́сять очко́в. **2,** (achieve) получи́ть; доби́ться. *Score a victory,* одержа́ть побе́ду. **3,** (denounce) осужда́ть. **4,** *music* оркестрова́ть. —*v.i.* получи́ть очко́; заби́ть гол. *Score first; be the first to score,* откры́ть счёт. —**know the score,** знать что к чему́.

scoreboard *n.* табло́.

scorekeeper *n.* судья́.

scoreless *adj.* нулево́й: *scoreless tie,* нулева́я ничья́.

scorn *n.* презре́ние. —*v.t.* презира́ть. —**scornful,** *adj.* презри́тельный.

Scorpio *n.* Скорпио́н.

scorpion *n.* скорпио́н.

Scotch *adj.* шотла́ндский. —*n.* **1,** *preceded by* **the** (people) шотла́ндцы. **2,** (whiskey) (шотла́ндское) ви́ски.

scotch *v.t.* опроверга́ть: *scotch a rumor,* опрове́ргнуть слух.

Scotchman *n.* шотла́ндец.

scot-free *adj.* безнака́занный.

Scotsman *n.* шотла́ндец.

Scottish *adj.* шотла́ндский. —**Scottish terrier,** шотла́ндский терье́р.

scoundrel *n.* подле́ц; негодя́й; мерза́вец; прохво́ст.

scour *v.t.* **1,** (clean thoroughly) чи́стить; отчища́ть. **2,** (range over in search of something) ры́скать по: *scour the woods,* ры́скать по ле́су.

scourge *n.* бич. *The scourge of war,* бич войны́.

scout *n.* **1,** (agent) разве́дчик; лазу́тчик. **2,** (boy scout) ска́ут. —*v.t.* разве́дывать. —*v.i.* [*usu.* **scout around**] ры́скать (в по́исках чего́-нибудь).

scow *n.* шала́нда.

scowl *v.i.* хму́риться. —*n.* серди́тый взгляд.

scraggly *adj.* нечёсаный; взъеро́шенный.

scram *v.i., slang* убира́ться.

scramble *v.i.* **1,** (climb hurriedly) кара́бкаться: *scramble up a tree,* кара́бкаться на де́рево. **2,** (dash) бро́ситься: *scramble for cover/safety,* бро́ситься в укры́тие/ в безопа́сное ме́сто/. *The boys scrambled for the coins,* ма́льчики бро́сились за моне́тами. —*v.t.* (mix up; jumble) переме́шивать. —*n.* сва́лка. —**scrambled eggs,** яи́чница-болту́нья.

scrap *n.* **1,** (fragment) обры́вок; обре́зок; (*of paper*) клочо́к; (*of material*) лоску́т; (*of bread*) кусо́чек. **2,** *pl.* (bits of food) объе́дки. **3,** (waste metal) лом; ути́ль. **4,** *slang* (fight; quarrel) дра́ка; потасо́вка. —*adj.* ути́льный. *Scrap iron,* желе́зный лом; ути́льное желе́зо. *Scrap metal,* металлоло́м. *Scrap heap,* сва́лка. —*v.t.* **1,** (junk) сдава́ть на слом. *Be scrapped,* идти́ на слом. **2,** (drop, as a project) бро́сить. —*v.i., slang* (quarrel) вздо́рить.

scrapbook *n.* альбо́м для вы́резок.

scrape *v.t.* **1,** (rub the surface of) скрести́; скобли́ть. **2,** (injure; abrade) сса́живать. —*n.* **1,** (abrasion) сса́дина. **2,** (fight; scrap) потасо́вка. **3,** (predicament) переде́лка; передря́га. —**scrape along,** ко́е-как перебива́ться. —**scrape off,** соска́бливать; отска́бливать. —**scrape up; scrape together,** наскрести́; скола́чивать; выкра́ивать.

scraper *n.* скребо́к.

scrapper *n., colloq.* драчу́н; задира; забия́ка.

scrappy *adj., slang* драчли́вый.

scratch *n.* цара́пина. —*v.t.* **1,** (tear the skin of; damage the surface of) цара́пать: *scratch one's face/ the table/,* цара́пать лицо́/стол. **2,** (rub to relieve itching) чеса́ть: *Scratch my back!,* почеши́ мне спи́ну! *Scratch one's head (in puzzlement),* чеса́ть заты́лок *or* в заты́лке. **3,** *fol. by* **out** (cross out) вычёркивать. **4,** (withdraw from a contest) снима́ть с состяза́ний. —*v.i.* **1,** (have a tendency to scratch) цара́паться. **2,** (rub to relieve itching) чеса́ться: *Stop scratching!,* переста́нь чеса́ться! **3,** (produce a grating sound) скрипе́ть: *The pen scratches,* перо́ скрипи́т. *A cat was scratching at the door,* ко́шка цара́палась в дверь. —**scratch the surface,** скользи́ть по пове́рхности. —**start from scratch,** начина́ть с нуля́. —**up to scratch,** на до́лжной высоте́.

scratch pad блокно́т.

scratch paper бума́га для заме́ток.

scratchy *adj.* скрипу́чий.

scrawl *n.* кара́кули; мара́нье. —*v.t.* (на)цара́пать. *Slogans were scrawled all over the wall,* стена́ была́ испи́сана ло́зунгами.

scrawny *adj.* костля́вый; сухопа́рый.

scream *v.i.* **1,** (yell) крича́ть: *scream from the pain,* крича́ть от бо́ли; *scream with delight,* крича́ть от восто́рга. *Scream for help,* звать на по́мощь. **2,** (whistle; roar) реве́ть: *Sirens screamed,* реве́ли сире́ны. —*v.t.* **1,** (utter with a scream) выкри́кивать. **2,** *Scream one's head off,* ора́ть во всё го́рло. —*n.* **1,** (shriek) (пронзи́тельный) крик. **2,** *colloq.* (very funny person) умо́ра.

screech *n.* визг; клёкот. —*v.i.* визжа́ть; клекота́ть.

screen *n.* **1,** (partition; anything that covers or protects) ши́рма. *Smoke screen,* дымова́я заве́са. **2,** (mesh for a window to keep out insects) се́тка. **3,** (surface for projecting pictures) экра́н. **4,** (motion pictures collectively) кино́; экра́н. *Adapt for the screen,* экранизи́ровать. —*v.t.* **1,** (shield) прикрыва́ть. **2,** *fol. by* **off** (separate by a screen) отгора́живать ши́рмой. **3,** (separate and select) фильтрова́ть.

screw *n.* винт. —*v.t.* **1,** (fasten by turning) завёртывать: *screw the lid tight,* заверну́ть кры́шку. *Screw in a bulb,* вви́нчивать *or* вве́ртывать ла́мпочку. *Screw a nut onto a bolt,* нави́нчивать га́йку на болт. **2,** (attach with a screw) привви́нчивать: *screw a lock onto a door,* привви́нчивать замо́к к две́ри. *Screw something into a wall,* вви́нчивать что́-нибудь в сте́ну. **3,** *fol. by* **up** (contort) мо́рщить. *Screw up one's eyes,* щу́рить глаза́; щу́риться. **4,** *fol. by* **up,** *slang* (botch) напу́тать. —*v.i.* [*usu.* **screw in/into** *or* **on/onto**] завинчиваться; вви́нчиваться (в); нави́нчиваться (на). —**he has a screw loose,** *slang* у него́ ви́нтика не хвата́ет. —**put the screws on,** нажима́ть на. —**tighten the screws,** зави́нчивать га́йки.

screwball *n., slang* сумасбро́д; чуда́к.

screwdriver *n.* отвёртка.

screw propeller гребно́й винт.

screwy *adj., slang* **1,** (crazy) сумасбро́дный. **2,** (odd) чудакова́тый.

scribble *v.t. & i.* цара́пать; мара́ть. *Scribble off a letter,* черкну́ть *or* строчи́ть письмо́. *Scribble all over something,* исчёркивать что́-нибудь. —*n.* кара́кули; мара́нье. —**scribbler,** *n.* писа́ка.

scribe *n.* **1,** (copier of manuscripts) писе́ц. **2,** *Bib.* кни́жник.

scrimmage *n.* **1,** (tussle) сва́лка. **2,** *football* сва́лка вокру́г мяча́.

scrimp *v.i.* скупи́ться.

scrip *n.* бума́жные де́ньги.

script *n.* **1,** (copy of something to be read) текст. **2,** (system of writing) письмо́: *the Arabic script,* ара́бское письмо́.

scriptural *adj.* библе́йский.

Scripture *n., usu. pl.* свяще́нное писа́ние.

scrofula *n.* золоту́ха.

scroll *n.* сви́ток.

scrotum *n.* мошо́нка.

scrounge *v.t., colloq.* выкля́нчивать. —*v.i., colloq.* [*usu.* **scrounge around**] ры́скать.

scrub *v.t.* **1,** (rub hard so as to clean) тере́ть (щёткой с мы́лом). **2,** *colloq.* (cancel) отменя́ть.

scruff *n.* загри́вок. —**seize by the scruff of one's neck,** схвати́ть за́ ворот; взять за ши́ворот.

scruffy *adj.* неря́шливый.

scrumptious *adj., colloq.* великоле́пный; о́чень вку́сный.

scruple *n., usu. pl.* угрызе́ния со́вести. *Have no scruples,* не стесня́ться в сре́дствах. —*v.i.* стесня́ться; со́веститься.

scrupulous *adj.* **1,** (honest) со́вестливый. **2,** (meticulous) добросо́вестный; скрупулёзный. —**scrupu-**

lously, *adv.* свя́то: *scrupulously observe,* свя́то соблюда́ть (что́-нибудь).

scrutinize *v.t.* (при́стально) рассма́тривать.

scrutiny *n.* рассмотре́ние. *Come under the scrutiny of,* стать объе́ктом внима́ния (+ *gen.*).

scuffle *n.* дра́ка; сва́лка; потасо́вка. —*v.i.* дра́ться.

scull *n.* **1,** (single long oar) кормово́е весло́. **2,** (one of a pair of short oars) па́рное весло́. **3,** (boat) гребна́я ло́дка. —*v.t. & i.* грести́.

scullery *n.* судомо́йня.

sculpt *v.t.* лепи́ть.

sculptor *n.* ску́льптор.

sculptural *adj.* скульпту́рный.

sculpture *n.* **1,** (art) скульпту́ра; вая́ние. **2,** (piece of sculptured work) скульпту́ра; извая́ние. —*v.t.* лепи́ть. *Sculptured figure,* лепна́я фигу́ра.

scum *n.* **1,** (extraneous matter on liquid) на́кипь. **2,** (riffraff) подо́нки.

scurrilous *adj.* гру́бый; оскорби́тельный; непристо́йный.

scurry *v.i.* снова́ть.

scurvy *n.* цинга́; скорбу́т.

scutch *v.t.* трепа́ть. —*n.* трепа́ло.

scuttle *v.t.* затопля́ть (кора́бль).

scythe *n.* коса́.

Scythian *adj.* ски́фский. —*n.* скиф.

sea *n.* мо́ре. *The Black Sea,* Чёрное мо́ре. *Put (out) to sea,* выходи́ть в мо́ре. *Go off to sea,* уходи́ть в мо́ре. *Perish at sea,* поги́бнуть в мо́ре. *Sail the seas,* плыть по мо́рю *or* по́ морю. *Spend one's whole life at sea,* провести́ всю жизнь на мо́ре. —*adj.* морско́й: *sea water,* морска́я вода́. —**be all at sea,** быть как в лесу́.

sea anemone акти́ния.

seabed *n.* морско́е дно.

seaboard *n.* побере́жье.

sea breeze морско́й бриз; примо́рский ве́тер.

seacoast *n.* побере́жье.

sea cow морска́я коро́ва.

sea dog морско́й волк.

sea elephant морско́й слон.

seafarer *n.* морепла́ватель; морехо́д.

seafood *n.* морски́е проду́кты.

seagoing *adj.* океа́нский; да́льнего пла́вания.

sea gull ча́йка.

sea horse морско́й конёк.

sea kale морска́я капу́ста.

seal *n.* **1,** (imprint; stamp for making same) печа́ть: *affix a seal to,* ста́вить печа́ть на (+ *acc.*). *The Great Seal of the United States,* госуда́рственная печа́ть США. **2,** (wax to secure an envelope) печа́ть: *break the seal,* взлома́ть печа́ть. **3,** (something that closes tightly) пло́мба. **4,** (sign; token) знак: *seal of approval,* знак одобре́ния. **5,** (marine animal) тюле́нь. *Fur seal,* ко́тик. —*v.t.* **1,** (close, as an envelope) закле́ивать; запеча́тывать. **2,** *often fol. by* **up** (close tightly) заде́лывать; забива́ть; зама́зывать; залепля́ть; опеча́тывать; пломбирова́ть. *Sealed room,* опеча́танная ко́мната. *Sealed railroad car,* запломбиро́ванный ваго́н. *My lips are sealed,* у меня́ рот на замке́. **3,** *fol.* **by off** (cordon off) оцепля́ть. **4,** (affix a seal to) скрепля́ть печа́тью: *signed, sealed and delivered,* подпи́сано, скреплено́ печа́тью и вручено́. **5,** (settle finally) реши́ть: *His fate is sealed,* его́ судьба́ решена́.

sealed move *chess* запи́санный ход.

sea level у́ровень мо́ря.

sealing wax сургу́ч.

sea lion морско́й лев.

sealskin *n.* ко́тик. —*adj.* ко́тиковый; тюле́невый.

seam *n.* шов. —*v.t.* сшива́ть. —**come apart at the seams,** треща́ть по всем швам; расползáться.

seaman *n.* матро́с; моря́к.

seamless *adj.* **1,** (of stockings) без шва. **2,** (of pipes) бесшо́вный.

seamstress *n.* швея́; белошве́йка.

seamy *adj., in* **the seamy side,** теневáя сторонá; изнáнка: *the seamy side of life,* теневáя сторонá жи́зни; изнáнка жи́зни.

séance *n.* спирити́ческий сеáнс.

seaplane *n.* гидроплáн; гидросамолёт.

seaport *n.* **1,** (harbor) морско́й порт. **2,** (city) портóвый гóрод.

sear *v.t.* опáливать. *Searing heat,* паля́щая жарá.

search *v.i.* [*often* **search for**] искáть. *Search for one's keys,* искáть ключи́. *I've searched everywhere,* я всю́ду искáл(а). —*v.t.* обы́скивать: *search a house/ suspect,* обы́скивать дом/подозревáемого. *Search the woods,* обы́скивать лес. —*n.* **1,** (for something missing or desired) пóиски: *in search of,* в пóисках (+ *gen.*). *Set out in search of,* отпрáвиться на пóиски (+ *gen.*). **2,** (of a suspected person or place) óбыск. *Search of an apartment,* óбыск в квартúре. —**search party,** поискóвая грýппа. —**search warrant,** óрдер на óбыск.

searching *adj.* **1,** (extremely thorough) тщáтельный. **2,** (penetrating, as of a look) испытýющий.

searchlight *n.* прожéктор.

seascape *n.* морскóй пейзáж; марúна.

seashell *n.* ракýшка.

seashore *n.* бéрег мóря; морскóй бéрег. *A house at the seashore,* дом на берегý мóря. *Relax at the seashore,* отдыхáть на мóре *or* у мóря.

seasick *adj.* **Be seasick,** укáчивать (*impers.*): *I got seasick,* меня́ укачáло. —**seasickness,** *n.* морскáя болéзнь.

seaside *n.* бéрег мóря; примóрье. —*adj.* примóрский: *seaside resort,* примóрский курóрт. *Seaside cottage,* дáча на мóре.

season *n.* **1,** (quarter of the year) врéмя гóда: *the four seasons,* четы́ре врéмени гóда. **2,** (period of the year marked by some characteristic or activity) сезóн: *the hunting season,* охóтничий сезóн; *the rainy season,* сезóн дождéй. *Strawberries are out of season,* клубнúке сейчáс не сезóн. —*adj.* сезóнный: *season ticket,* сезóнный билéт. —*v.t.* **1,** (flavor) приправля́ть; заправля́ть; сдáбривать. **2,** (inure; harden) закаля́ть. —*v.i.* (become seasoned) созревáть.

seasonal *adj.* сезóнный.

seasoning *n.* припрáва.

seat *n.* **1,** (place to sit) мéсто: *reserved seat,* нумерóванное мéсто. *Take a seat,* садúться. *Take your seats,* занимáйте свои́ местá. *Have a seat!,* присáживайтесь! *Change one's seat,* пересáживаться. *Seat in parliament,* мéсто в парлáменте. *We sat in the cheap seats,* мы сидéли на дешёвых местáх. **2,** (that on which one sits) сидéнье: *seat of a chair,* сидéнье стýла. *Back seat,* зáднее сидéнье. **3,** (back part of trousers) зад; сидéнье. *Tight in the seat,* у́зки в шагý. **4,** (center; site) местопребывáние: *seat of government,* местопребывáние прави́тельства. *Seat of learning,* центр просвещéния. —*v.t.* **1,** (place on a seat) сажáть; усáживать. *Seat the guests,* рассадúть гостéй. **2,** (hold; accommodate) вмещáть. —**be seated, 1,** (sit down) садúться. *Please be seated,* прошý садúться. **2,** (be sitting down) сидéть.

seat belt привязнóй ремéнь; ремéнь безопáсности.

seating *n.* сидя́чие местá. —**seating capacity,** числó мест. *The stadium has a seating capacity of 100,000,* стадиóн вмещáет сто ты́сяч человéк.

sea urchin морскóй ёж.

sea wall стéнка нáбережной.

seaway *n.* фарвáтер.

seaweed *n.* (морскáя) вóдоросль.

seaworthy *adj.* гóдный для плáвания; морехóдный.

sebaceous glands сáльные жéлезы.

secant *n.* **1,** *geom.* секýщая. **2,** *trig.* сéканс.

secede *v.i.* выходúть. *Secede from,* выходúть из состáва (+ *gen.*). —**secession,** *n.* вы́ход.

seclude *v.t.* уединя́ть. —**secluded,** *adj.* уединённый; укрóмный.

seclusion *n.* уединéние. *In seclusion,* в уединéнии; уединённо; взаперти́.

second *adj.* вторóй. *Alexander II,* Алексáндр Вторóй. *Come in second,* прийти́ вторы́м. *For the second time,* втори́чно; повтóрно. *The second largest city in the country,* вторóй по величинé гóрод в странé. *He is second to none,* он никомý не уступáет. —*n.* **1,** (unit of time or angular measure) секýнда. *Just a second!,* однý секýнд(очк)у! однý минýт(к)у! **2,** (attendant in boxing, a duel, etc.) секундáнт. **3,** *music* секýнда. **4,** *pl.* (imperfect merchandise) второсóртный товáр; слегкá брако́ванный товáр. —*v.t.* поддéрживать: *second the motion,* поддéрживать предложéние. —**in the second place,** во-вторы́х.

secondary *adj.* **1,** (of less importance) второстепéнный. **2,** (of education, school, etc.) срéдний. —**secondary sex characteristics,** втори́чные половы́е при́знаки.

second-class *adj.* второклáссный; второразря́дный. *Second-class passengers,* пассажи́ры вторóго клáсса. *Second-class coach,* жёсткий вагóн. —*adv.* вторы́м клáссом: *travel second-class,* éхать вторы́м клáссом.

second cousin *see* **cousin.**

second hand секýндная стрéлка.

secondhand *adj.* подéржанный: *secondhand furniture,* подéржанная мéбель. *Secondhand bookstore,* букинисти́ческий магази́н. —*adv.* (not from the original source) из вторы́х рук; с чужи́х слов.

second-in-command замести́тель команди́ра.

second lieutenant мла́дший лейтена́нт.

secondly *adv.* во-вторы́х.

second nature втора́я нату́ра.

second-rate *adj.* второсо́ртный; второразря́дный.

second thought разду́мье: *He had second thoughts,* его́ взя́ло разду́мье. —**on second thought,** по зре́лом размышле́нии; пораски́нув умо́м.

second wind второ́е дыха́ние. *Get one's second wind,* обрести́ второ́е дыха́ние.

secrecy *n.* секре́тность. *In great secrecy,* под больши́м секре́том. *I have been sworn to secrecy,* с меня́ взя́ли кля́тву молча́ть.

secret *n.* секре́т; та́йна. *In secret,* та́йно; втайне; тайко́м. —*adj.* секре́тный; та́йный: *secret weapon,* секре́тное/та́йное ору́жие. *Secret agent,* секре́тный аге́нт. *Secret police,* та́йная поли́ция. *Secret ambition,* та́йная мечта́. *Keep (something) secret,* держа́ть *or* храни́ть в секре́те *or* в та́йне. *Secret passage,* потайно́й ход.

secretarial *adj.* секрета́рский.

secretariat *n.* секретариа́т.

secretary *n.* **1,** (clerical assistant) секрета́рь; секрета́рша. **2,** (official; officer) секрета́рь. **3,** (cabinet officer) мини́стр; секрета́рь. *Secretary of state,* госуда́рственный секрета́рь. *Secretary of the treasury,* мини́стр фина́нсов. *Foreign secretary,* мини́стр иностра́нных дел. —**secretary-general,** генера́льный секрета́рь.

secrete *v.t.* **1,** (conceal) укрыва́ть; пря́тать. **2,** *physiol.* выделя́ть. —**secretion,** *n.* секре́ция; выделе́ние.

secretive *adj.* скры́тный. —**secretiveness,** *n.* скры́тность.

secretly *adv.* та́йно; втайне; тайко́м.

secretory *adj.* выдели́тельный.

sect *n.* се́кта.

sectarian *adj.* секта́нтский. —*n.* секта́нт. —**sectarianism,** *n.* секта́нтство.

section *n.* **1,** (portion, as of a road) отре́зок. **2,** (part, as of a fence or bookcase) се́кция. **3,** (of an aircraft) часть: *tail section,* хвостова́я часть. *First-class section,* сало́н пе́рвого кла́сса. **4,** (view in a given plane) сече́ние; разре́з: *cross section,* попере́чное сече́ние; попере́чный разре́з. *Conic section,* кони́ческое сече́ние. **5,** (district; neighborhood) райо́н. **6,** (division of an organization) отде́л; се́кция. **7,** (division of a book or newspaper) отде́л; разде́л; (of a law) пара́граф. **8,** (slice, as of an orange) до́лька. **9,** (slice of something used for microscopic study) срез. **10,** (incision) сече́ние: *Caesarean section,* ке́сарево сече́ние.

sectional *adj.* **1,** (made up of sections) секцио́нный; разбо́рный; составно́й. **2,** (regional) ме́стный.

sector *n.* **1,** (part of a circle) се́ктор. **2,** *mil.* уча́сток. **3,** (division) се́ктор: *the private sector,* ча́стный се́ктор. *The service sector,* сфе́ра обслу́живания.

secular *adj.* све́тский; мирско́й.

secularize *v.t.* секуляризи́ровать. —**secularization,** *n.* секуляриза́ция.

secure *adj.* **1,** (safe) безопа́сный: *secure place,*

безопа́сное ме́сто. *Feel secure,* чу́вствовать себя́ в безопа́сности. **2,** (firm) про́чный; кре́пкий: *secure footing,* про́чная опо́ра; *secure grip,* кре́пкая хва́тка. —*v.t.* **1,** (firmly fasten) закрепля́ть. **2,** (make safe) обезопа́сить. **3,** (make certain; ensure) обеспе́чивать: *secure the peace,* обеспе́чивать мир. **4,** (gain; obtain) заруча́ться: *secure the support of,* заручи́ться подде́ржкой (+ *gen.*). *Secure a loan,* заручи́ться за́ймом. —**securely,** *adv.* про́чно: *tie securely,* про́чно привя́зывать.

security *n.* **1,** (safety; protection) безопа́сность: *national security,* национа́льная *or* госуда́рственная безопа́сность. *Provide security,* обеспе́чивать безопа́сность. **2,** (material well-being) обеспе́чение; обеспе́ченность: *financial security,* материа́льное обеспе́чение; материа́льная обеспе́ченность. **3,** (pledge; deposit) зало́г: *leave something as security,* оста́вить что́-нибудь в зало́г. **4,** *pl.* (stocks, bonds, etc.) це́нные бума́ги. —*adj.* *Security guard,* сто́рож; охра́нник. *Security measures,* ме́ры безопа́сности. —**security clearance, 1,** (investigation) прове́рка благонадёжности. **2,** (access) до́пуск.

Security Council Сове́т Безопа́сности.

sedan *n.* легково́й автомоби́ль. —**sedan chair,** портше́з.

sedate *adj.* степе́нный; чи́нный. —*v.t.* дава́ть успокои́тельное сре́дство (+ *dat.*).

sedation *n.* успокое́ние. *Place under sedation,* дава́ть успокои́тельное сре́дство (+ *dat.*).

sedative *n.* успокои́тельное *or* успока́ивающее сре́дство; успокои́тельное.

sedentary *adj.* сидя́чий: *sedentary position/work,* сидя́чее положе́ние; сидя́чая рабо́та.

sedge *n.* осо́ка.

sediment *n.* **1,** (matter that settles at the bottom) оса́док. **2,** *geol.* отложе́ние.

sedimentary *adj.* оса́дочный: *sedimentary rock,* оса́дочная го́рная поро́да.

sedition *n.* подстрека́тельство к мятежу́. —**seditious,** *adj.* мяте́жный; бунта́рский.

seduce *v.t.* соблазня́ть; обольща́ть; совраща́ть. —**seducer,** *n.* соблазни́тель; обольсти́тель; совраща́тель. —**seduction,** *n.* обольще́ние. —**seductive,** *adj.* соблазни́тельный; обольсти́тельный.

sedulous *adj.* приле́жный; стара́тельный.

see *v.t.* & *i.* **1,** (perceive visually; have the power of sight) ви́деть: *see a man/car/difference,* ви́деть челове́ка/маши́ну/ра́зницу. *Can you see?,* вам ви́дно? *See in the dark,* ви́деть в темноте́. *I saw him come in,* я ви́дел, как он вошёл. *I didn't see anyone enter,* я не ви́дел, чтобы кто́-нибудь входи́л. *I never saw him smile,* я никогда́ не ви́дел, чтобы он улыба́лся. **2,** (view) смотре́ть: *see a play,* смотре́ть пье́су. *See the sights,* осма́тривать достопримеча́тельности. *There is nothing to see there,* там не́чего смотре́ть; там нет ничего́ интере́сного. *Would you like to see it?,* хоти́те посмотре́ть? *I'll go see,* я пойду́ посмотре́ть. **3,** (understand) понима́ть: *I see,* я понима́ю. *I see what you mean,* я понима́ю, что вы име́ете в виду. —*v.t.* **1,** (consult) обраща́ться к. *See a* *doctor,* обрати́ться к врачу́; показа́ться врачу́; сове́товаться с врачо́м. *Can I see you for a moment?,* мо́жно вас на мину́ту? **2,** (receive) принима́ть: *He refused to see me,* он отказа́лся приня́ть меня́. *The doctor will see you now,* врач вас тепе́рь при́мет. **3,** (visit; meet) ви́деть; встреча́ть: *We rarely see each other,* мы ре́дко ви́димся/встреча́емся. *He came to see me last night,* он пришёл ко мне вчера́ ве́чером. *No one is allowed to see her,* к ней никого́ не пуска́ют. *She is seeing other men,* она́ встреча́ется с други́ми. **4,** (escort) провожа́ть: *see someone to the door,* провожа́ть кого́-нибудь до двере́й. **5,** (find out; ascertain) смотре́ть; узнава́ть. *See what he wants,* посмотри́те *or* узна́йте *or* спроси́те, что он хо́чет. *See who is at the door,* посмотри́те, кто стучи́т *or* звони́т (в дверь). *Let's see what happens,* посмо́трим, что бу́дет. *I'll see what I can do,* я посмотрю́, что я смогу́ сде́лать. *He waited to see if anyone else was coming,* он ждал, не придёт ли ещё кто́-нибудь. **6,** (sense) ви́деть: *I don't see any need for that,* я не ви́жу в э́том никако́й необходи́мости. *I don't see anything funny about that,* я не ви́жу в э́том ничего́ смешно́го. **7,** (experience) ви́деть. *I have seen a lot in my time,* я мно́го повида́л(а) на своём веку́. *This car has seen better days,* э́та маши́на знава́ла лу́чшие времена́. **8,** (visualize) представля́ть (себе́). *I can't see myself doing that,* я не могу́ предста́вить себя́ в э́той ро́ли. **9,** (regard) ви́деть: *They see him as a savior,* они́ ви́дят в нём спаси́теля; он ви́дится им спаси́телем. **10,** (interpret) рассма́тривать: *His hesitancy is seen as a sign of weakness,* его́ колеба́ние рассма́тривается как при́знак сла́бости. **11,** (admire) находи́ть: *What does she see in him?,* что она́ в нём нашла́? —*n.* престо́л: *Holy See,* па́пский престо́л. —**let me see!,** да́йте мне поду́мать. —**see fit, see for oneself,** воо́чию убеди́ться. *I want to see for myself,* Я хочу́ убеди́ться сам (сама́). —**see here!,** послу́шайте! —**see off,** провожа́ть: *see someone off on the train,* провожа́ть кого́-нибудь на по́езд. —**see things,** каза́ться (+ *dat.*); чу́диться (+ *dat.*): *You're seeing things!,* вам то́лько ка́жется/чу́дится. —**see through, 1,** *literally* ви́деть че́рез. **2,** (not be fooled by) ви́деть наскво́зь; раскуси́ть. **3,** (carry through to the end) доводи́ть до конца́. **4,** (carry through a difficult time) хвата́ть: *This money should see you through the week,* э́тих де́нег должно́ вам хвати́ть до конца́ неде́ли. —**see to,** забо́титься о; занима́ться (+ *instr.*): *I'll see to that myself,* я сам (сама́) позабо́чусь об э́том; я сам (сама́) э́тим займу́сь. —**see (to it) that...,** смотре́ть, что́бы; позабо́титься о том, что́бы; следи́ть *or* проследи́ть за тем, что́бы; доби́ться того́, что́бы; распоряди́ться, что́бы. *See that he stays where he is,* (по)смотри́те, что́бы он оста́лся на ме́сте.

seed *n.* **1,** (that which can grow into a new plant) се́мя. **2,** (of fruits, sunflowers, etc.) семечко. **3,** *fig.* (source) се́мя: *seeds of rebellion,* семена́ бу́нта. —*adj.* семенно́й: *seed coat,* семенна́я оболо́чка. —*v.t.* засева́ть (*e.g.* сад) семена́ми. —**go to seed, 1,** (shed seeds) пойти́ в семена́. **2,** (deteriorate) опуска́ться.

seeder *n.* се́ялка.

seedless *adj.* бессемя́нный.

seedling *n.* се́янец; *pl.* расса́да.

seedy *adj.* потрёпанный; потёртый.

seeing *conj.* [*usu.* **seeing that**] поско́льку; ввиду́ того́, что...

Seeing Eye dog соба́ка-поводы́рь.

seek *v.t.* **1,** (try to find) иска́ть: *seek one's long-lost sister,* иска́ть свою́ давно́ пропа́вшую сестру́. **2,** (try to obtain) иска́ть; добива́ться. *Seek work/help/advice/ the cause,* иска́ть рабо́ту/по́мощи/сове́та/причи́ну. *Seek recognition/ an advantage,* добива́ться призна́ния/преиму́щества. **3,** *fol. by inf.* (endeavor) пыта́ться; стреми́ться.

seeker *n.* иска́тель.

seem *v.i.* каза́ться: *He seems ill,* он ка́жется больны́м. *It seems to me that...,* мне ка́жется, что... *It may seem strange to you,* вам э́то мо́жет показа́ться стра́нным. *I seem to have misplaced my glasses,* я, ка́жется, затеря́л (*or* куда́-то дел) свои́ очки́. *It is not as easy as it seems,* э́то не так про́сто, как ка́жется. *I can't seem to get used to it,* я ника́к не могу́ привы́кнуть к э́тому.

seeming *adj.* ка́жущийся; ви́димый.

seemingly *adv.* каза́лось бы. *A seemingly small amount,* каза́лось бы (*or* как бу́дто бы) небольша́я су́мма.

seemly *adj.* прили́чный; присто́йный.

seep *v.i.* проса́чиваться. —**seepage,** *n.* проса́чивание.

seer *n.* проро́к; прови́дец.

seesaw *n.* каче́ли.

seethe *v.i.* кипе́ть; бурли́ть. *Seethe with anger,* кипе́ть гне́вом.

segment *n.* **1,** (section) отре́зок. **2,** *geom.* сегме́нт.

segregate *v.t.* отделя́ть. —**segregation,** *n.* сегрега́ция.

seismic *adj.* сейсми́ческий.

seismograph *n.* сейсмо́граф.

seismology *n.* сейсмоло́гия. —**seismological,** *adj.* сейсмологи́ческий. —**seismologist,** *n.* сейсмо́лог.

seize *v.t.* **1,** (grasp) хвата́ть; схва́тывать. *Seize by the arm,* схвати́ть за́ руку. **2,** (take by force) захва́тывать; завладева́ть. *Seize power,* захвати́ть власть. **3,** (confiscate) изыма́ть; конфискова́ть. **4,** (take prompt advantage of) ухвати́ться за: *seize the opportunity,* ухвати́ться за возмо́жность. **5,** (overwhelm, as of fear) овладева́ть; охва́тывать; обуя́ть. *Panic seized the crowd,* толпу́ охвати́ла па́ника.

seizure *n.* **1,** (act of seizing) захва́т. **2,** (confiscation) конфиска́ция. **3,** *med.* при́ступ; припа́док. *Epileptic seizure,* эпилепти́ческий припа́док.

seldom *adv.* ре́дко.

select *v.t.* выбира́ть; отбира́ть; подбира́ть; избира́ть. *Select a book/quotation,* выбира́ть кни́гу/цита́ту. *Select a tie to go with one's shirt,* подбира́ть га́лстук к руба́шке. *Select someone to be one's successor,* избира́ть кого́-нибудь свои́м прее́мником. —*adj.* [*also,* **selected**] и́збранный: *selected works,* и́збранные сочине́ния. *A select circle of people,* и́збранный круг люде́й.

selection *n.* **1,** (act of selecting) отбо́р; подбо́р. **2,** (assortment) вы́бор; ассортиме́нт: *a large selection of* *merchandise,* хоро́ший вы́бор/ассортиме́нт това́ров. **3,** *biol.* отбо́р: *natural selection,* есте́ственный отбо́р. —**selection committee,** отбо́рочная коми́ссия.

selective *adj.* вы́борочный; избира́тельный. —**selective service,** во́инская пови́нность.

selectively *adv.* вы́борочно; с вы́бором; с (больши́м) разбо́ром.

selectivity *n.* разбо́рчивость.

selenite *n.* селени́т.

selenium *n.* селе́н.

self *n. One's own self,* со́бственная персо́на. *My other self,* моё второ́е я. *He is only a shadow of his former self,* от него́ оста́лась одна́ тень.

self-addressed *adj.* адресо́ванный самому́ себе́.

self-assurance *n.* самоуве́ренность; самонаде́янность. —**self-assured,** *adj.* самоуве́ренный; самонадеянный.

self-centered *also,* **self-centred** *adj.* эгоцентри́ческий.

self-complacent *adj.* самодово́льный. —**self-complacency,** *n.* самодово́льство.

self-confidence *n.* уве́ренность в себе́. *Lack of self-confidence,* неуве́ренность в себе́. —**self-confident,** *adj.* уве́ренный в себе́.

self-conscious *adj.* засте́нчивый; стесни́тельный; стыдли́вый.

self-contained *adj.* **1,** (existing on its own) самодовле́ющий. **2,** *mech.* автоно́мный: *self-contained equipment,* автоно́мное обору́дование.

self-control *n.* самооблада́ние; вы́держка. —**self-controlled,** *adj.* вы́держанный.

self-criticism *n.* самокри́тика. —**self-critical,** *adj.* самокрити́чный.

self-deception *n.* самообма́н.

self-defense *also,* **self-defence** *n.* самозащи́та; самооборо́на. *In self-defense,* в поря́дке самозащи́ты; защища́ясь.

self-denial *n.* самоотрече́ние.

self-designation *n.* самоназва́ние.

self-destruction *n.* самоуничтоже́ние.

self-determination *n.* самоопределе́ние.

self-discipline *n.* самодисципли́на.

self-educated *adj. Self-educated person,* самоу́чка.

self-effacing *adj.* держа́щийся в тени́.

self-employed *adj.* рабо́тающий на себя́.

self-esteem *n.* самоуваже́ние.

self-evident *adj.* самоочеви́дный.

self-explanatory *adj.* не тре́бующий разъясне́ния.

self-governing *adj.* самоуправля́ющийся. —**self-government,** *n.* самоуправле́ние.

self-immolation *n.* самосожже́ние.

self-importance *n.* ва́жность: *assume an air of self-importance,* напуска́ть на себя́ ва́жность. —**self-important,** *adj.* ва́жный.

self-inflicted *adj.* нанесённый самому́ себе́.

self-interest *n.* коры́сть; корыстолю́бие; своекоры́стие.

selfish *adj.* **1,** (of a person) эгоисти́ческий; эгоисти́чный. **2,** (of interests, motives, etc.) коры́стный. —**selfishness,** *n.* эгои́зм.

selfless *adj.* самоотве́рженный; беззаве́тный. —**selflessness,** *n.* самоотве́рженность.

self-management *n.* самоуправле́ние.

self-portrait *n.* автопортре́т.

self-possessed *adj.* вы́держанный.

self-preservation *n.* самосохране́ние.

self-propelled *adj.* самохо́дный; самодви́жущийся.

self-reliant *adj.* самостоя́тельный. —**self-reliance,** *n.* самостоя́тельность.

self-respect *n.* чу́вство со́бственного досто́инства; самолю́бие; самоуваже́ние. —**self-respecting,** *adj.* уважа́ющий себя́.

self-restraint *n.* сде́ржанность.

self-righteous *adj.* ха́нжеский. —**self-righteousness,** *n.* ха́нжество.

self-sacrifice *n.* самопоже́ртвование.

selfsame *adj.* тот же са́мый.

self-satisfaction *n.* самодово́льство. —**self-satisfied,** *adj.* самодово́льный.

self-seeking *adj.* своекоры́стный.

self-service *n.* самообслу́живание. *Self-service store,* магази́н самообслу́живания.

self-starter *n.* самопу́ск.

self-study *n.* самообразова́ние; самовоспита́ние.

self-styled *adj.* самозва́н(н)ый.

self-sufficient *adj.* **1,** (able to get along on one's own) самостоя́тельный. **2,** *econ.* самообеспе́ченный. *The country is self-sufficient in food,* страна́ сама́ обеспе́чивает себя́ продово́льствием. —**self-sufficiency,** *n.* самообеспе́ченность.

self-supporting *adj.* самостоя́тельный.

self-taught *adj. Rendered by* самоу́чка: *self-taught engineer,* инжене́р-самоу́чка.

self-willed *adj.* самово́льный.

sell *v.t.* **1,** (transfer for money) продава́ть: *She was selling flowers,* она́ продава́ла цветы́. *I sold my house,* я про́дал свой дом. **2,** (deal in; carry) торгова́ть (+ *instr.*). *The store sells bicycles,* в магази́не продаю́тся велосипе́ды; магази́н торгу́ет велосипе́дами. —*v.i.* **1,** (engage in selling) продава́ть. **2,** (be sold) продава́ться; расходи́ться. *Be selling well,* хорошо́ продава́ться/расходи́ться/идти́. *Sell for 25 rubles (each),* продава́ться по два́дцать пять рубле́й. *What are eggs selling for?,* почём я́йца? —**sell off,** распродава́ть. —**sell oneself, 1,** (sell one's services) продава́ться; продава́ть себя́. **2,** *colloq.* (convince others of one's worth) набива́ть себе́ це́ну. —**sell out, 1,** (sell completely) распрода́ть: *The book is sold out,* кни́га распро́дана. *The book sold out immediately,* кни́га разошла́сь момента́льно; кни́гу неме́дленно раскупи́ли. **2,** *colloq.* (betray one's cause) продава́ться: *sell out to the enemy,* продава́ться врагу́.

seller *n.* продаве́ц.

selling *n.* прода́жа. —**selling price,** прода́жная цена́.

sellout *n. The show is a complete sellout,* пьеса де́лает по́лные сбо́ры.

seltzer *n.* [*usu.* **seltzer water**] се́льтерская вода́.

selvage *n.* кро́мка.

semantic *adj.* семанти́ческий; смыслово́й. —**semantics,** *n.* сема́нтика.

semaphore *n.* семафо́р.

semblance *n.* **1,** (likeness; copy) подо́бие. **2,** (outward appearance) ви́димость: *a semblance of order,* ви́димость поря́дка.

semelfactive *adj., gram.* однокра́тный.

semen *n.* се́мя; спе́рма.

semester *n.* семе́стр.

semiannual *adj.* полугодово́й.

semiautomatic *adj.* полуавтомати́ческий.

semicircle *n.* полукру́г. —**semicircular,** *adj.* полукру́глый.

semicolon *n.* то́чка с запято́й.

semiconductor *n.* полупроводни́к.

semiconscious *adj.* полусозна́тельный; полубессозна́тельный; в полу(бес)созна́тельном состоя́нии. —**semiconsciousness,** *n.* полу(бес)созна́тельное состоя́ние; забытьё.

semidarkness *n.* полумра́к; полутьма́; су́мрак.

semifinal *n.* полуфина́л. *Advance to the semifinals,* вы́йти в полуфина́л. —*adj.* полуфина́льный. —**semifinalist,** *n.* полуфинали́ст.

semiliterate *adj.* полугра́мотный; малогра́мотный.

seminal *adj.* **1,** *biol.* семенно́й: *seminal fluid,* семенна́я жи́дкость. **2,** *fig.* (breaking new ground) основополага́ющий.

seminar *n.* семина́р. *Attend a seminar,* прису́тствовать на семина́ре.

seminary *n.* семина́рия.

semiprecious *adj.* самоцве́тный. *Semiprecious stone,* самоцве́т.

Semitic *adj.* семи́тский; семити́ческий.

semitrailer *n.* полуприце́п.

senate *n.* сена́т. —**senator,** *n.* сена́тор. —**senatorial,** *adj.* сена́торский.

send *v.t.* посыла́ть; присыла́ть; отправля́ть: *send a package/messenger,* посыла́ть/присыла́ть/отправля́ть посы́лку/курье́ра. *Send a telegram,* дать *or* посла́ть *or* отпра́вить телегра́мму. *Send regards,* посыла́ть *or* передава́ть приве́т. *Send a pupil from the room,* удаля́ть *or* выгоня́ть ученика́ из кла́сса. *He was sent to prison,* его́ отпра́вили в тюрьму́. *Send flames high into the air,* вы́бросить языки́ пла́мени в во́здух. —**send away,** усыла́ть; отсыла́ть. —**send away for,** выпи́сывать. —**send for,** посыла́ть за (+ *instr.*). —**send in, 1,** (submit) подава́ть; посыла́ть: *send in an application,* подава́ть заявле́ние; *send in an article to a newspaper,* посыла́ть статью́ в газе́ту. **2,** (direct to enter) впуска́ть: *Shall I send him in?,* его́ впусти́ть? *Send him in!,* пусть он войдёт! —**send off,** отсыла́ть. —**send out, 1,** (mail out) высыла́ть; рассыла́ть: *send out a package,* высыла́ть посы́лку; *send out invitations,* рассыла́ть приглаше́ния. *Send something out to be repaired,* отпра́вить что́-нибудь в ремо́нт. **2,** *fol. by* **for** (order; have delivered) посыла́ть за. **3,** (assign; dispatch) засыла́ть: *send out spies,* засыла́ть шпио́нов. **4,** (transmit, as a signal) передава́ть.

sender *n.* отправи́тель.

send-off *n.* про́воды.

senile *adj.* ста́рческий. *He is senile,* он страда́ет ста́рческим слабоу́мием. —**senility,** *n.* ста́рческое слабоу́мие; ста́рческий мара́зм.

senior *adj.* **1,** (older) ста́рший: *senior member,* ста́рший член. *John Smith, Sr.,* Джон Смит ста́рший. *He is in his senior year,* он на ста́ршем (*or* на после́днем) ку́рсе. **2,** (high-ranking) отве́тственный; высокопоста́вленный: *senior official,* отве́тственный рабо́тник; высокопоста́вленный чино́вник. *Senior position,* отве́тственный пост. —*n.* **1,** (elder) ста́рший. *Three years my senior,* ста́рше меня́ на три го́да. **2,** (student in one's final year) старшеку́рсник.

seniority *n.* старшинство́.

sensation *n.* **1,** (feeling) чу́вство; ощуще́ние. *I have no sensation in my right arm,* у меня́ пра́вая рука́ онеме́ла. **2,** (great excitement; that which causes it) сенса́ция.

sensational *adj.* **1,** (causing great excitement) сенсацио́нный. **2,** (extraordinary; phenomenal) потряса́ющий.

sense *n.* **1,** (faculty) чу́вство: *the five senses,* пять чувств. *Sense of smell,* обоня́ние. *Sense of touch,* осяза́ние. *Sense organs,* о́рганы чувств. *Alcohol dulls the senses,* алкого́ль притупля́ет чу́вства. **2,** (awareness; appreciation) чу́вство: *sense of duty,* чу́вство до́лга; *sense of humor,* чу́вство ю́мора. *Lose all sense of time,* потеря́ть вся́кое представле́ние о вре́мени. **3,** (good judgment) ум: *He had the (good) sense to...,* у него́ хвати́ло ума́ (+ *inf.*). **4,** *pl.* (rationality) ум: *take leave of one's senses,* сойти́ с ума́. *Bring to one's senses,* наводи́ть на ум; вразумля́ть. *Come to one's senses,* опо́мниться; образу́миться; оду́маться; бра́ться за ум. **5,** (logic; point) смысл: *common sense,* здра́вый смысл. *Make no sense at all,* не име́ть никако́го смы́сла. *There is no sense in...,* нет смы́сла (+ *inf.*). *Talk sense,* говори́ть де́ло. **6,** (meaning) смысл: *in the literal sense of the word,* в буква́льном смы́сле э́того сло́ва. —*v.t.* чу́вствовать; ощуща́ть; чу́ять. *Sense danger,* чу́вствовать *or* чу́ять опа́сность. *I sensed that something was wrong,* я почу́вствовал(а) что́-то нела́дное. —**in a sense,** в изве́стном смы́сле. —**make sense of,** понима́ть; разбира́ться в.

senseless *adj.* **1,** (making no sense) бессмы́сленный: *senseless acts of violence,* бессмы́сленные а́кты наси́лия. **2,** (unconscious) без созна́ния. *Beat senseless,* бить до бесчу́вствия. —**senselessly,** *adv.* бессмы́сленно.

senselessness *n.* **1,** (irrationality) бессмы́сленность. **2,** (unconsciousness) бесчу́вствие.

sensibility *n.* **1,** (ability to perceive) чувстви́тельность. **2,** *pl.* (feelings; pride) чу́вства (прили́чия); самолю́бие.

sensible *adj.* разу́мный; благоразу́мный; рассуди́тельный. —**sensibly,** *adv.* разу́мно.

sensitive *adj.* **1,** (perceptive; responsive; tender) чувстви́тельный: *sensitive skin/film,* чувстви́тельная ко́жа/плёнка. *Sensitive to light,* чувстви́тельный к све́ту. **2,** (easily offended) оби́дчивый. **3,** (involving secret matters) секре́тный; засекре́ченный. —**sensitivity,** *n.* чувстви́тельность.

sensor *n.* да́тчик.

sensory *adj.* сенсо́рный. *Sensory nerve,* чувстви́тельный нерв.

sensual *adj.* чу́вственный; сладостра́стный. —**sensuality,** *n.* чу́вственность; сладостра́стие.

sensuous *adj.* чу́вственный.

sentence *n.* **1,** (group of words) предложе́ние; фра́за. *Incomplete sentence,* непо́лное предложе́ние. *Put a period at the end of a sentence,* ста́вить то́чку в конце́ предложе́ния. **2,** (penalty pronounced) пригово́р. *Death sentence,* сме́ртный пригово́р. *Serve out a sentence,* отбыва́ть срок наказа́ния. —*v.t.* пригова́ривать; осужда́ть. *He was sentenced to five years in prison,* он был приговорён к пяти́ года́м (*or* осуждён на пять лет) тюре́много заключе́ния. *He was sentenced to death,* он был приговорён к сме́рти *or* к сме́ртной ка́зни; он был осуждён на смерть *or* на сме́ртную казнь.

sententious *adj.* сентенцио́зный.

sentiment *n.* **1,** *usu. pl.* (feelings) чу́вства: *lofty sentiments,* высо́кие чу́вства. *Pacifist sentiments,* пацифи́стские настрое́ния. **2,** (opinion) мне́ние: *public sentiment,* обще́ственное мне́ние.

sentimental *adj.* сентимента́льный. *These things are of sentimental value to me,* э́ти ве́щи мне до́роги как па́мять. —**sentimentality,** *n.* сентимента́льность.

sentinel *n.* часово́й.

sentry *n.* часово́й; карау́льный. —**sentry box,** карау́льная *or* постова́я бу́дка. —**sentry post,** сторожево́й пост.

sepal *n.* чашели́стик.

separate *v.t.* **1,** (set apart) отделя́ть: *separate the boys from the girls,* отделя́ть ма́льчиков от де́вочек. **2,** (form a barrier or boundary between) разделя́ть: *The two plots are separated by a fence,* о́ба уча́стка разделены́ забо́ром. **3,** (pull apart, as two combatants) разнима́ть; разводи́ть. **4,** (force to part company) разъединя́ть; разлуча́ть. **5,** *used passively* (drift away from) отделя́ться: *be separated from the group,* отделя́ться от гру́ппы. *Become separated in a crowd,* потеря́ть друг дру́га в толпе́. —*v.i.* **1,** (become divided) отделя́ться. **2,** (part company) разлуча́ться. **3,** (break up without a divorce) расходи́ться; разъезжа́ться. —*adj.* отде́льный: *separate entrance,* отде́льный вход. *Conclude a separate peace,* заключи́ть сепара́тный мир. —**separately,** *adv.* отде́льно; в отде́льности.

separation *n.* **1,** (dividing) отделе́ние. **2,** (parting company) разлу́ка. —**separation of powers,** разделе́ние власте́й.

separatism *n.* сепарати́зм. —**separatist,** *n.* сепарати́ст. —*adj.* сепарати́стский.

separator *n.* сепара́тор.

sepia *n.* се́пия. —*adj.* кори́чневый.

sepsis *n.* се́псис.

September *n.* сентя́брь. —*adj.* сентя́брьский.

septic *adj.* септи́ческий.

sepulcher *also,* **sepulchre** *n.* моги́ла; склеп. —**sepulchral,** *adj.* моги́льный; замоги́льный.

sequel *n.* продолже́ние.

sequence *n.* поря́док; после́довательность. *In sequence,* по поря́дку. *In strict sequence,* в стро́гой после́довательности. *Sequence of events,* ход собы́тий. *Sequence of tenses, gram.* согласова́ние времён.

sequester *v.t.* **1,** (seclude) уединя́ть: *a sequestered life,* уединённая жизнь. **2,** *law* аресто́вывать; налага́ть аре́ст *or* секве́стр на; секвестрова́ть. —**sequestration,** *n.* аре́ст; секве́стр.

sequin *n.* блёстка.

sequoia *n.* секво́йя.

seraglio *n.* сера́ль.

seraph *n.* серафи́м.

Serb *n.* серб. —**Serbian,** *adj.* се́рбский. —*n.* се́рбский язы́к.

Serbo-Croatian *adj.* сербохорва́тский; сербохорва́тский.

serenade *n.* серена́да. —*v.t.* петь серена́ду (+ *dat.*).

serene *adj.* **1,** (unclouded) безо́блачный. **2,** (tranquil; untroubled) споко́йный; безмяте́жный; безо́блачный. —**serenity,** *n.* споко́йствие; безмяте́жность.

serf *n.* крепостно́й. —**serfdom,** *n.* крепостно́е пра́во; крепостни́чество.

serge *n.* са́ржа. —*adj.* са́ржевый.

sergeant *n.* сержа́нт.

serial *adj.* многосери́йный. —*n.* по́весть в не́скольких частя́х; фильм в не́скольких се́риях.

serialize *v.t.* издава́ть се́риями.

serial number **1,** (of a serviceman) ли́чный но́мер. **2,** (of a manufactured product) поря́дковый но́мер.

sericulture *n.* шелково́дство.

series *n.* **1,** (set) се́рия: *series of experiments,* се́рия о́пытов. *Series of lectures,* курс *or* цикл ле́кций. *Series of concerts,* цикл конце́ртов. **2,** (number of; succession of) ряд: *a whole series of disasters,* це́лый ряд катастро́ф. **3,** *math.* ряд.

serious *adj.* серьёзный: *serious tone/step/student,* серьёзный тон/шаг/студе́нт; *serious error/illness,* серьёзная оши́бка/боле́знь. *A serious case of malaria,* тяжёлый слу́чай маляри́и. *Are you serious?,* вы э́то серьёзно? *I'm serious,* я говорю́ серьёзно.

seriously *adv.* **1,** (in earnest) серьёзно: *talk seriously,* говори́ть серьёзно. *Take seriously,* принима́ть *or* воспринима́ть всерьёз. **2,** (gravely) тяжело́: *seriously ill/injured,* тяжело́ бо́лен/ра́нен.

seriousness *n.* серьёзность. *In all seriousness,* серьёзно; со всей серьёзностью.

sermon *n.* про́поведь. *Sermon on the Mount,* Наго́рная про́поведь.

sermonize *v.i.* пропове́довать. —**sermonizer,** *n.* пропове́дник; резонёр.

serology *n.* сероло́гия.

serpent *n.* змея́. —**serpentine,** *adj.* змееви́дный.

serrate *adj.* зубча́тый; зазу́бренный. *Also,* **serrated.**

serum *n.* сы́воротка.

servant *n.* (man) слуга́; (woman) служа́нка; прислу́га. *Servants,* слу́ги; прислу́га. —**civil servant,** госуда́рственный слу́жащий.

serve *v.t.* **1,** (work for; be in the service of) служи́ть (+ *dat.*): *serve one's country,* служи́ть свое́й ро́дине; *serve two masters,* служи́ть двум господа́м. *If* *memory serves me correctly,* éсли пáмять мне не изменя́ет. **2,** (provide with goods or services) обслу́живать: *serve a customer/district,* обслу́живать покупа́теля/райо́н. *Are you being served?,* вас обслу́живают? **3,** (prepare and offer, as food or a meal) подава́ть; сервирова́ть: *serve tea,* подава́ть/сервирова́ть чай. *We were served tea,* нам по́дали чай; нас пои́ли ча́ем. *Dinner is served!,* обе́д по́дан! **4,** (present; deliver, as a legal document) вруча́ть. **5,** (complete, as a prison term) отбыва́ть: *serve one's sentence,* отбыва́ть срок наказа́ния. *Serve five years in prison,* (от)сиде́ть пять лет в тюрьме́. **6,** *Serve the purpose,* отвеча́ть це́ли. **7,** *sports* подава́ть (мяч). —*v.i.* **1,** (perform service) служи́ть: *serve in the navy,* служи́ть во фло́те. **2,** *fol. by* **as** (function as) служи́ть (+ *instr.*): *serve as a judge/bedroom/pretext,* служи́ть судьёй/спа́льней/предло́гом. **3,** (be suitable or usable) годи́ться. **4,** *sports* подава́ть. —*n.,* *sports* пода́ча. —**it serves him right,** так ему́ и на́до; туда́ ему́ и доро́га.

server *n.* **1,** (waiter) подава́льщик. **2,** (tray) подно́с; (utensil) лопа́тка. **3,** *sports* игро́к, подаю́щий мяч.

service *n.* **1,** (performance of duty) слу́жба: *military service,* вое́нная слу́жба. **2,** (work professionally performed) обслу́живание: *medical service,* медици́нское обслу́живание. *Poor service,* пло́хое обслу́живание. **3,** (public facility) слу́жба: *weather service,* слу́жба пого́ды. **4,** (transportation or communications) сообще́ние; связь. *Air service,* возду́шное сообще́ние. *Rail/bus service,* железнодоро́жное/авто́бусное сообще́ние *or* движе́ние. *Mail/telephone service,* почто́вая/телефо́нная связь. **5,** (help given another) услу́га: *offer one's services,* предлага́ть свои́ услу́ги. **6,** *pl.* (deeds performed) заслу́ги: *in recognition of one's services,* в знак призна́ния чьих-нибудь заслу́г. **7,** (armed forces) вое́нная слу́жба: *drafted into the service,* при́зван на вое́нную слу́жбу. **8,** (set of dishes) серви́з: *tea service,* ча́йный серви́з. **9,** (religious ceremony) богослуже́ние; слу́жба. *Church service,* церко́вная слу́жба; *funeral/memorial service(s);* заупоко́йная слу́жба. *Conduct a service,* соверши́ть богослуже́ние; отслужи́ть слу́жбу. **10,** *sports* пода́ча. —*adj.* обслу́живающий: *service personnel,* обслу́живающий персона́л. *Service entrance,* служе́бный вход. *Service elevator,* грузово́й лифт. *Service record,* послужно́й спи́сок. —*v.t.* обслу́живать: *service a car,* обслу́живать автомоби́ль. —**at your service,** к ва́шим услу́гам. —**be in service,** рабо́тать; де́йствовать. —**be of service,** быть поле́зным. —**"out of service",** «не рабо́тает».

serviceable *adj.* поле́зный; приго́дный.

service cap фура́жка.

service charge допла́та за обслу́живание.

service life срок слу́жбы.

serviceman *n.* **1,** (member of the armed forces) военнослу́жащий. **2,** (repairman) ма́стер по ремо́нту; ремо́нтник.

service station бензозапра́вочная ста́нция; автозапра́вочная ста́нция.

servile *adj.* рабол́епный; подобостра́стный. —**servility,** *n.* рабол́епие; подобостра́стие; уго́дничество.

serving *n.* по́рция.

servitude *n.* ра́бство. —**penal servitude,** ка́торга; ка́торжные рабо́ты.

sesame *n.* кунжу́т; сеза́м. —*adj.* кунжу́тный. —**open sesame!,** сеза́м, откро́йся!

session *n.* **1,** (meeting) заседа́ние; се́ссия. *Joint session,* совме́стное заседа́ние. *Be in session,* заседа́ть. **2,** (school term): *summer session,* ле́тние ку́рсы.

set *v.t.* **1,** (put; place) ста́вить; класть: *set the package on the table,* ста́вить/класть посы́лку на стол. **2,** (arrange, as a table) накрыва́ть (на). *Set the table for six,* накры́ть стол на шесть прибо́ров. **3,** (adjust to a certain setting) ста́вить: *set the alarm for 6:00,* ста́вить буди́льник на шесть часо́в. *Set one's watch by the radio,* ста́вить *or* установи́ть часы́ по ра́дио. **4,** (mount, as a gem) оправля́ть; обде́лывать. **5,** (arrange, as one's hair) укла́дывать. **6,** (lay, as a trap) ста́вить. **7,** *med.* вправля́ть; сра́щивать: *set a bone,* вправля́ть/сра́щивать кость. **8,** (fix, as a date) назнача́ть; намеча́ть (срок); (a price) назнача́ть; устана́вливать (це́ну). **9,** (establish) устана́вливать: *set a limit,* устана́вливать преде́л. *Set a record,* устана́вливать *or* ста́вить реко́рд. *Set a precedent,* создава́ть прецеде́нт. *Set an example,* подава́ть приме́р. *Set the pace/tone,* задава́ть темп/тон. **10,** (assign; lay down) ста́вить: *set a goal/task for oneself,* ста́вить себе́ цель/зада́чу. *Set conditions,* ста́вить *or* выдвига́ть усло́вия. **11,** (cause): *set someone thinking,* наводи́ть кого́-нибудь на размышле́ния. *Set tongues wagging,* вызыва́ть мно́го то́лков (*or* кривото́лков.) **12,** *printing* набира́ть: *set something in boldface,* набра́ть что́-нибудь жи́рным шри́фтом. **13,** (bring to a certain state) *rendered by various verbs: set free,* освобожда́ть; *set in motion,* приводи́ть в движе́ние; *set at ease,* успока́ивать; *set on fire,* поджига́ть; *set to music,* положи́ть на му́зыку. —*v.i.* **1,** (sink below the horizon) заходи́ть; сади́ться; зака́тываться. **2,** *fol. by* **to** (begin) бра́ться; принима́ться. *Set to work in earnest,* бра́ться вплотну́ю за рабо́ту. **3,** (solidify; congeal) затвердева́ть; засты́ва́ть. —*n.* **1,** (group of matching things) набо́р; компле́кт; гарниту́р; прибо́р. *Set of tools,* набо́р/компле́кт инструме́нтов. *Desk set,* пи́сьменный прибо́р. *Set of china,* фарфо́ровый серви́з. *Set of underwear,* гарниту́р белья́. *Chess set,* ша́хматы. *Set of stamps,* се́рия ма́рок. **2,** *Television set,* телеви́зор. **3,** (group of people) о́бщество; свет. *The smart set,* мо́дный свет. **4,** *theat.* декора́ция; обстано́вка. *Gorgeous sets,* великоле́пные декора́ции. **5,** *motion pictures* съёмочная площа́дка. **6,** *tennis* сет. **7,** *math.* мно́жество: *theory of sets,* тео́рия мно́жеств. —*adj.* **1,** (fixed) устано́вленный; определённый: *at a set time,* в устано́вленное/определённое вре́мя. **2,** (rigid; unchanging) неизме́нный. *Set pattern,* шабло́н. *Set expression* (*i.e.* turn of speech), усто́йчивое словосочета́ние. **3,** (determined) *He is set on going,* он твёрдо реши́л пое́хать. *Dead set against,* категори́чески про́тив. **4,** *colloq.* (ready) гото́вый. *Get* *set*, гото́виться. —**set about,** приступа́ть к. —**set against, 1,** (balance; compare) противопоставля́ть. **2,** (prejudice against) восстана́вливать про́тив; настра́ивать про́тив; вооружа́ть про́тив. —**set apart,** выделя́ть; отлича́ть. —**set aside, 1,** (lay aside) откла́дывать (в сто́рону). **2,** (allocate) отводи́ть: *set aside time for reading,* отводи́ть вре́мя для чте́ния. **3,** (annul) отменя́ть. —**set back, 1,** (move back, as a clock) ста́вить *or* переводи́ть наза́д. **2,** (hinder the progress of) заде́рживать: *The fire set us back six months,* пожа́р задержа́л на́шу рабо́ту на шесть ме́сяцев. **3,** *The house is set back from the road,* дом стои́т в стороне́ от доро́ги. **4,** *colloq.* (cost) сто́ить; обходи́ться. *How much did it set you back?,* во ско́лько э́то вам обошло́сь? —**set down, 1,** (put down) ста́вить; класть. **2,** (land, as an aircraft) посади́ть. **3,** (put in writing) запи́сывать; пи́сьменно излага́ть. —**set forth, 1,** (state; express) излага́ть. **2,** (start out) отправля́ться (в путь). —**set in,** устана́вливаться; водворя́ться; воцаря́ться. *Winter has set in,* установи́лась зима́. —**set off, 1,** (start; touch off) вызыва́ть; порожда́ть. *Set off a chain reaction,* вызыва́ть цепну́ю реа́кцию. **2,** (cause to go off or explode) взрыва́ть: *set off a bomb,* взорва́ть бо́мбу. *Set off fireworks,* пуска́ть *or* устра́ивать фейерве́рк. **3,** (set in relief; make prominent) оттеня́ть. **4,** (start out) отправля́ться (в путь). —**set out, 1,** (display) выставля́ть. **2,** (start out) отправля́ться (в путь); дви́гаться в путь. **3,** *fol. by inf.* (undertake) взя́ться: *set out to prove that...,* взя́ться доказа́ть, что... —**set up,** устра́ивать; создава́ть; организова́ть. *Set up house,* обзавести́сь хозя́йством. *Set up camp,* разбива́ть ла́герь; располага́ться ла́герем. —**set upon, 1,** (attack) напада́ть на. **2,** (cause to attack) натра́вливать (соба́ку) на.

setback *n.* неуда́ча.

settee *n.* небольшо́й дива́н.

setter *n.* лега́вая соба́ка; се́ттер.

setting *n.* **1,** (surroundings; background) окруже́ние; обстано́вка. **2,** (mount, as for a jewel) опра́ва. **3,** (position, as on a dial) устано́вка. **4,** (place setting) прибо́р. **5,** *Setting of the sun,* захо́д со́лнца.

settle *v.t.* **1,** (resolve, as a dispute, issue, etc.) реша́ть; разреша́ть; ула́живать; урегули́ровать. *The matter is settled,* вопро́с исче́рпан. **2,** (populate; colonize) заселя́ть; осва́ивать. **3,** (cause to come to rest) прибива́ть: *The rain settled the dust,* дождь приби́л пыль. **4,** (calm, as one's nerves or stomach) успока́ивать. **5,** (dispose of; pay) опла́чивать; упла́чивать: *settle an account,* оплати́ть счёт; уплати́ть по счёту. *Settle one's debts,* распла́чиваться с долга́ми. *Settle scores with,* своди́ть счёты с. —*v.i.* **1,** (establish residence) поселя́ться; обосно́вываться; оседа́ть. **2,** (come to rest) сади́ться; оседа́ть. *The dust settled,* пыль се́ла *or* осе́ла *or* улегла́сь. **3,** (become clear, as of liquids) отста́иваться; устоя́ться. —**settle down, 1,** (calm down; quiet down) успока́иваться. **2,** (lead a more settled life) остепени́ться. **3,** *fol. by* **to** (sit down and begin) уса́живаться за (+ *acc.*); располага́ться (+ *inf.*). —**settle for,** дово́льствоваться

(+ *instr.*): *settle for a draw,* дово́льствоваться ничье́й. —**settle on/upon, 1,** (decide upon) остана́вливаться на; облюбова́ть. **2,** (agree upon) догова́риваться о. —**settle up,** рассчи́тываться; распла́чиваться.

settlement *n.* **1,** (resolution, as of a dispute) урегули́рование; разреше́ние. **2,** (agreement) соглаше́ние. **3,** (settling of a new region) заселе́ние. **4,** (small settled area) поселе́ние; селе́ние; посёлок. **5,** (payment) расчёт.

settler *n.* поселе́нец; переселе́нец.

setup *n.* организа́ция; структу́ра; устро́йство.

seven *adj.* семь. —*n.* **1,** (cardinal number) семь. **2,** *cards* семёрка.

sevenfold *adj.* семикра́тный. —*adv.* в семь раз.

seven hundred семьсо́т. —**seven-hundredth,** *adj.* семисо́тый.

seventeen *n. & adj.* семна́дцать. —**seventeenth,** *adj.* семна́дцатый.

seventh *adj.* седьмо́й. —*n.* **1,** (fraction) седьма́я; седьма́я часть. *One-seventh,* одна́ седьма́я; седьма́я часть. **2,** *music* се́птима. —**be in seventh heaven,** быть на седьмо́м не́бе.

seventy *n. & adj.* се́мьдесят. *In the 1970s,* в семидеся́тых года́х. —**seventieth,** *adj.* семидеся́тый.

sever *v.t.* **1,** (cut off) отреза́ть; отруба́ть; отка́лывать. **2,** (break off, as ties) порыва́ть; разрыва́ть.

several *adj.* не́сколько: *several times,* не́сколько раз. —*n.* не́которые: *several of them,* не́которые из них.

severance *n.* разры́в. —**severance pay,** выходно́е посо́бие.

severe *adj.* **1,** (harsh) суро́вый; стро́гий. *Severe winter,* суро́вая зима́. *Severe sentence,* суро́вый/стро́гий пригово́р. *Severe blow,* жесто́кий *or* чувстви́тельный уда́р. *Severe criticism,* о́страя *or* ре́зкая кри́тика. **2,** (acute; intense) си́льный; жесто́кий: *severe pain/frost,* си́льная/жесто́кая боль; си́льный/жесто́кий моро́з. *A severe shortage of...,* о́стрый недоста́ток (+ *gen.*). *Suffer severe damage,* си́льно пострада́ть.

severely *adv.* **1,** (harshly) суро́во; стро́го; жесто́ко. *Don't punish him too severely,* не нака́зывайте его́ сли́шком стро́го. **2,** (seriously) си́льно; жесто́ко. *Severely damaged,* си́льно повреждён. *He was severely beaten,* он был жесто́ко изби́т.

severity *n.* суро́вость; стро́гость.

sew *v.t. & i.* шить: *Do you know how to sew?,* вы уме́ете шить? *Sew* (*i.e. fix*) *a dress,* зашива́ть пла́тье. —**sew on,** пришива́ть: *sew a button onto a shirt,* пришива́ть пу́говицу к руба́шке. —**sew together,** сшива́ть. —**sew up,** зашива́ть.

sewage *n.* нечисто́ты; сто́чные во́ды. —**sewage pipe,** канализацио́нная труба́. —**sewage system,** канализа́ция.

sewer *n.* сто́чная труба́. —**sewerage,** *n.* канализа́ция.

sewing *n.* шитьё. —**sewing machine,** швейная маши́на.

sex *n.* **1,** (male or female) пол: *the opposite sex,* противополо́жный пол. *Equality of the sexes,* ра́венство поло́в. **2,** (sexual activity, feelings, etc.) секс: *a book* *about sex*, кни́га о се́ксе. *Have sex with*, вступи́ть в полову́ю связь с. —*adj.* полово́й: *the sex act*, полово́й акт; *sex education*, полово́е воспита́ние.

sexless *adj.* беспо́лый.

sextant *n.* секста́нт.

sextet *also,* **sextette** *n.* N. секстет.

sexton *n.* церко́вный сто́рож; понома́рь.

sexual *adj.* полово́й; сексуа́льный. —**sexuality,** *n.* сексуа́льность.

shabbily *adv.* **1,** (poorly) бе́дно: *shabbily dressed*, бе́дно оде́тый. **2,** (meanly) по́дло.

shabbiness *n.* убо́гость.

shabby *adj.* **1,** (threadbare) поно́шенный; потёртый; потрёпанный. **2,** (run-down; dilapidated) ве́тхий; убо́гий. **3,** (mean; unfair) по́длый; ни́зкий.

shack *n.* лачу́га; хи́жина.

shackle *n., usu. pl.* канда́лы; око́вы. —*v.t.* зако́вывать в канда́лы; ско́вывать.

shade *n.* **1,** (darkness; dark area) тень: *in the shade*, в тени́. **2,** (gradation of color) оттёнок. **3,** (nuance) оттёнок; нюа́нс: *shade of meaning*, оттёнок/нюа́нс значе́ния. **4,** (window shade) што́ра. **5,** (small degree): *She is a shade better today*, ей немно́го лу́чше сего́дня. —*v.t.* **1,** (screen from light) затеня́ть; заслоня́ть. *Shade one's eyes from the sun*, защища́ть *or* прикрыва́ть глаза́ от со́лнца. **2,** (add shading to) отеня́ть; тушева́ть; штрихова́ть.

shading *n.* **1,** (small variation) разли́чие. **2,** *drawing* тушёвка; штрихо́вка.

shadow *n.* тень: *cast a shadow*, отбра́сывать тень. *Shadows are falling*, те́ни ложа́тся. *Emerge from the shadows*, выходи́ть из те́ни. *Not a shadow of doubt*, ни те́ни сомне́ния. *He is only a shadow of his former self*, от него́ оста́лась одна́ тень. —*v.t.* (trail) следи́ть за; высле́живать; просле́живать. —**shadow boxing,** бой с те́нью.

shadowy *adj.* тёмный; сму́тный.

shady *adj.* **1,** (in the shade at a given time) теневой; (generally in the shade) тени́стый. **2,** *colloq.* (dubious; underhanded) тёмный; сомни́тельный; нечи́стый.

shaft *n.* **1,** (long body, as of a spear) дре́вко. **2,** (beam, as of light) сноп (све́та); просве́т. **3,** (bar transmitting motion) вал: *drive shaft*, приводно́й вал. **4,** (pole to which an animal is hitched) огло́бля; ды́шло. **5,** (passage, as in a mine or for an elevator) ша́хта.

shaggy *adj.* косма́тый; лохма́тый; мохна́тый.

shah *n.* шах.

shake *v.t.* **1,** (agitate) трясти́: *shake a tree*, трясти́ де́рево. *Shake one's watch*, встря́хивать часы́. *Shake well before using*, взба́лтывать пе́ред употребле́нием. **2,** (rock; jolt) потряса́ть; сотряса́ть: *The blast shook nearby buildings*, взрыв потря́с/сотря́с близлежа́щие дома́. **3,** (brandish) потряса́ть: *shake one's fists*, потряса́ть кулака́ми. *Shake one's fist at*, грози́ть кулако́м (+ *dat.*). **4,** (shock; unnerve) потряса́ть: *I was shaken by the news*, я был потрясён (я была́ потрясена́) но́востью. **5,** (weaken; undermine) колеба́ть; пошатну́ть: *shake one's faith in*, колеба́ть/пошатну́ть чью-нибудь ве́ру в (+ *acc.*). **6,** *in* **shake hands,** пожима́ть ру́ки. *Shake hands with*,

пожима́ть ру́ку (+ *dat.*). *They shook hands*, они́ пожа́ли друг дру́гу ру́ки. **7,** *in* **shake one's head,** (по)кача́ть *or* мота́ть голово́й. —*v.i.* дрожа́ть; трясти́сь; сотряса́ться. *They were shaking from the cold*, они́ дрожа́ли от хо́лода. *The ground shook from the explosions*, земля́ трясла́сь *or* сотряса́лась *or* содрога́лась от взры́вов. *His voice was shaking with emotion*, его́ го́лос дро́гнул от волне́ния. —*n.* **1,** (an act of shaking) встря́ска. **2,** *pl.* [*usu.* **the shakes**] (trembling) дрожь. *It gives me the shakes*, от э́того меня́ броса́ет в дрожь. **3,** (drink) кокте́йль: *milk shake*, моло́чный кокте́йль. **4,** *colloq.* (jiffy) миг. *In two shakes*, в два счёта. —**no great shakes,** *colloq.* не ахти́ како́й. —**shake down,** стря́хивать: *shake down a thermometer*, стря́хивать термо́метр. —**shake off, 1,** (brush off) отря́хивать; стря́хивать. **2,** (get rid of, as a feeling) избавля́ться от; отде́лываться от; сбра́сывать; стря́хивать. *Shake off a cold*, изба́виться от просту́ды. **3,** (elude) отрыва́ться от; отвя́зываться от. —**shake out,** вытря́хивать; вытряса́ть. —**shake up, 1,** (shake hard) встря́хивать; взба́лтывать. **2,** (unnerve) потряса́ть. **3,** (shuffle) перетасо́вывать.

shake-up *n.* перетасо́вка.

shaky *adj.* ша́ткий; нетвёрдый; зы́бкий.

shale *n.* (гли́нистый) сла́нец. *Oil shale*, нефтено́сный сла́нец. —**shale oil,** сла́нцевое ма́сло.

shall *v.aux.* **1,** *used to form the future tense: What shall we do?*, что мы бу́дем де́лать? **2,** *used to make a polite suggestion: Shall we dance?*, потанцу́ем?

shallot *n.* шало́т.

shallow *adj.* **1,** (not deep) ме́лкий: *shallow river*, ме́лкая река́. **2,** *fig.* (lacking depth) пове́рхностный; пусто́й.

sham *n.* **1,** (fraudulent imitation) подде́лка. **2,** (pretense) притво́рство.

shaman *n.* шама́н. —**shamanism,** *n.* шама́нство.

shambles *n.* разгро́м: *The room was a shambles*, в ко́мнате был по́лный разгро́м.

shame *n.* **1,** (feeling of guilt) стыд. *Shame on you!*, сты́дно!; как вам не сты́дно! **2,** (disgrace; dishonor) позо́р. *Bring shame upon*, (о)позо́рить (кого́-нибудь). **3,** (a pity) жаль: *What a shame!*, как жаль! *It's a shame that...*, жаль, что... —*v.t.* **1,** (make ashamed) стыди́ть. **2,** (disgrace) позо́рить. —**put to shame, 1,** (make ashamed) пристыди́ть; устыди́ть. **2,** (excel; outshine) затмева́ть; заткну́ть за́ пояс.

shameful *adj.* позо́рный; посты́дный.

shameless *adj.* бессты́дный. —**shamelessly,** *adv.* бессты́дно. —**shamelessness,** *n.* бессты́дство.

shampoo *n.* **1,** (act of washing) мытьё. *Give oneself a shampoo*, помы́ть го́лову. **2,** (soaplike preparation) шампу́нь. —*v.t.* мыть (го́лову).

shamrock *n.* трили́стник.

shank *n., anat.* го́лень.

shanty *n.* хиба́ра; лачу́га.

shape *n.* **1,** (physical form) фо́рма: *oval shape*, ова́льная фо́рма. *Give shape to*, придава́ть фо́рму (+ *dat.*). *Get all out of shape*, потеря́ть фо́рму. *Bend out of shape*, криви́ть; искривля́ть. **2,** *colloq.* (condition) состоя́ние: *in bad shape*, в плохо́м состоя́нии. **3**, *colloq.* (good physical condition) фо́рма: *out of shape*, не в фо́рме. *Get in/into shape*, обрести́ фо́рму. *Get out of shape*, потеря́ть фо́рму. —*v.t.* **1**, (give shape to) формова́ть. *Shaped like a cigar*, име́ющий фо́рму сига́ры. **2**, (cause to develop in a certain way) определя́ть: *shape policy*, определя́ть поли́тику. **3**, (adjust; adapt) приспособля́ть. —**shape up**, *colloq.* **1**, (turn out; develop) скла́дываться. **2**, (start behaving or performing properly) исправля́ться. —**take shape**, скла́дываться; оформля́ться; определя́ться.

shapeless *adj.* бесфо́рменный.

shapely *adj.* стро́йный; ста́тный.

share *n.* **1**, (portion) до́ля: *divide into equal shares*, разделя́ть на ра́вные до́ли. *One's rightful share*, чья́-нибудь зако́нная до́ля. *Do one's share*, вноси́ть свою́ до́лю. **2**, (unit of corporate stock) а́кция; пай. —*v.t.* **1**, (use jointly) дели́ть; дели́ться; разделя́ть. *Share a room with*, дели́ть ко́мнату с; жить в одно́й ко́мнате с. *Share power*, дели́ть *or* разделя́ть власть. *Share one's last piece of bread with*, дели́ть после́дний кусо́к хле́ба с; дели́ться после́дним куско́м хле́ба с. *Share thoughts*, дели́ться мы́слями. *Share a common boundary*, име́ть о́бщую грани́цу. *Share first place in a tournament*, подели́ть пе́рвое ме́сто в турни́ре. **2**, (hold or experience jointly) разделя́ть: *share someone's opinion/fate*, разделя́ть чьё-нибудь мне́ние/ чью́-нибудь судьбу́/. —*v.i.* [*usu.* **share in**] уча́ствовать в: *share in the expenses*, уча́ствовать в расхо́дах. —**go shares with**, войти́ в до́лю с.

sharecropper *n.* испо́льщик; издо́льщик.

shareholder *n.* акционе́р; па́йщик.

shark *n.* аку́ла.

sharp *adj.* **1**, (having a fine cutting edge) о́стрый: *sharp knife*, о́стрый нож. **2**, (acute; pungent) о́стрый: *sharp pain*, о́страя боль; *sharp cheese*, о́стрый сыр. *He has a sharp tongue*, у него́ о́стрый язы́к. **3**, (keen; acute) зо́ркий: *sharp eyes*, зо́ркие глаза́. **4**, (abrupt) круто́й: *sharp turn*, круто́й поворо́т. **5**, (sudden; precipitous) ре́зкий: *a sharp drop in prices*, ре́зкое паде́ние цен. **6**, (clever; astute) бо́йкий; шу́стрый. **7**, (clearly defined; distinct) чёткий; ре́зкий. *Sharp image*, чёткое изображе́ние. *Sharp contrast*, ре́зкий контра́ст. *Sharp features*, ре́зкие черты́ лица́. **8**, *music* дие́з. *F-sharp*, фа-дие́з. —*adv.* ро́вно: *at six o'clock sharp*, ро́вно в шесть часо́в.

sharpen *v.t.* точи́ть; заостря́ть. *Sharpen a pencil*, точи́ть *or* чини́ть каранда́ш.

sharpener *n.* точи́лка.

sharp-eyed *adj.* зо́ркий; остроглазый; глаза́стый.

sharply *adv.* о́стро; ре́зко. *Sharply criticize*, о́стро критикова́ть; подверга́ть о́строй кри́тике. *Curtail production sharply*, ре́зко сокраща́ть произво́дство.

sharpness *n.* **1**, (cutting quality) острота́. **2**, (clarity; definition) ре́зкость; чёткость.

sharpshooter *n.* иску́сный стрело́к; сна́йпер.

sharp-tongued *adj.* о́стрый на язы́к; языка́стый.

shashlik *n.* шашлы́к.

shatter *v.t.* **1**, (smash to pieces) разбива́ть (вдре́безги). **2**, (dash, as hopes) разбива́ть; разруша́ть. **3**, (demolish, as a theory or myth) разбива́ть. —*v.i.* разби́ться (вдре́безги).

shattering *adj.* сокруши́тельный: *shattering blow*, сокруши́тельный уда́р.

shatterproof *adj.* небью́щийся.

shave *v.t.* **1**, (cut, as a beard; cut the beard of) брить. *Shave off*, сбрива́ть. *With shaved heads*, с бри́тыми голова́ми. **2**, (plane) строга́ть. —*v.i.* бри́ться: *I haven't shaved for three days*, я три дня не бри́лся. —*n.* бритьё. *I need a shave*, мне на́до побри́ться. —**have a close shave**, едва́ спасти́сь; быть на волосо́к от ги́бели.

shaver *n.* **1**, (razor) (электри́ческая) бри́тва. **2**, *colloq.* (youngster) юне́ц.

shaving *n.* **1**, (act of one who shaves) бритьё. **2**, *pl.* (pieces of thinly sliced wood) стру́жка. —**shaving brush**, помазо́к; ки́сточка для бритья́. —**shaving cream**, крем для бритья́.

shawl *n.* шаль.

she *pers. pron.* она́: *She left*, она́ ушла́. *She is not here*, её нет. *See also* **her**.

she- *combining form, denoting the female of animals*, -и́ца; -и́ха: *she-lion*, льви́ца; *she-elephant*, слони́ха.

sheaf *n.* **1**, (of hay, grain, etc.) сноп. **2**, (of papers) свя́зка.

shear *v.t.* **1**, (cut off; cut the fleece from) стричь. **2**, *fol. by* **off** (slice off) отсека́ть. —**shears**, *n.pl.* но́жницы.

sheatfish *n.* сом.

sheath *n.* но́жны.

sheathe *v.t.* вкла́дывать в но́жны.

shed *v.t.* **1**, (pour forth, as blood, tears, light, etc.) пролива́ть. **2**, (cast off, as leaves, skin, etc.) сбра́сывать; роня́ть. —*v.i.* линя́ть. —*n.* сара́й: *woodshed*, дровяно́й сара́й.

sheen *n.* блеск; лоск.

sheep *n.* (domesticated) овца́; (wild) бара́н. —*adj.* ове́чий; бара́ний. —**black sheep**, парши́вая овца́ (в семье́). —**lost sheep**, заблу́дшая овца́.

sheep dog овча́рка.

sheepfold *n.* овча́рня.

sheepish *adj.* засте́нчивый; стыдли́вый.

sheepskin *n.* овчи́на. —*adj.* овчи́нный; бара́ний.

sheer *adj.* **1**, (extremely thin) прозра́чный; сквозно́й. **2**, (precipitous) отве́сный. **3**, (utter; absolute) сплошно́й; чи́стый; су́щий. *It's sheer madness*, э́то про́сто безу́мие.

sheet *n.* **1**, (for a bed) простыня́. **2**, (of paper, metal, etc.) лист. *Sheet of paper*, лист бума́ги. **3**, (list) ве́домость: *expense sheet*, ве́домость расхо́дов. **4**, (continuous expanse) пелена́: *sheet of fog*, пелена́ тума́на. *Sheet of ice*, сплошно́й лёд. —**white/pale as a sheet**, бе́лый/бле́дный как полотно́.

sheeting *n.* **1**, (material for bedsheets) просты́нное полотно́. **2**, (thin plates, as of metal) обши́вка.

sheet metal листово́й мета́лл.

sheik *also*, **sheikh** *n.* шейх.

sheldrake *n.* пега́нка.

shelf *n.* по́лка. *Empty shelves (in a store)*, пусты́е по́лки. —**continental shelf**, шельф.

shell *n.* **1,** (hard covering of a mollusk) ра́ковина. **2,** (of a turtle) па́нцирь; щит. **3,** (of a fruit or seed) оболо́чка. **4,** (of a nut or egg) скорлупа́. **5,** (sea shell) ра́ковина; раку́шка. **6,** (framework) о́стов; сруб. **7,** (projectile) снаря́д: *artillery shell,* артиллери́йский снаря́д. **8,** (cartridge) ги́льза: *spent shell,* стре́ляная *or* пуста́я ги́льза. —*v.t.* **1,** (remove from a shell) лущи́ть; шелуши́ть. *Shell peas,* лущи́ть горо́х. **2,** (bombard) обстре́ливать: *shell enemy positions,* обстре́ливать пози́ции проти́вника. **3,** *fol. by* out, *colloq.* (spend) тра́тить. —**come out of one's shell,** вы́йти из свое́й скорлупы́. —**withdraw into one's shell,** уйти́ в свою́ скорлупу́.

shellac *n.* шелла́к. —*v.t.* покрыва́ть шелла́ком.

shellfish *n.* моллю́ск.

shelter *n.* **1,** (something affording protection) убе́жище; укры́тие. *Bomb shelter,* бомбоубе́жище. **2,** (refuge) убе́жище; прию́т; приста́нище; кров. *Take shelter,* укрыва́ться. —*v.t.* **1,** (protect) укрыва́ть. **2,** (give refuge to) приюти́ть.

shelve *v.t.* **1,** (put on a shelf) ста́вить *or* класть на по́лку. **2,** (put off) откла́дывать; класть под сукно́; откла́дывать в до́лгий я́щик.

shelving *n.* стелла́ж.

shenanigans *n.pl., colloq.* чуда́чества.

shepherd *n.* пасту́х. *Shepherd's crook,* пасту́ший по́сох. —*v.t.* води́ть: *shepherd tourists around town,* води́ть тури́стов по го́роду.

sherbet *n.* шербе́т.

sheriff *n.* шери́ф.

sherry *n.* хе́рес.

shh *interj.* шш!

shield *n.* щит. —*v.t.* защища́ть; заслоня́ть; прикрыва́ть. *Shield someone from a blow,* защища́ть *or* заслоня́ть кого́-нибудь от уда́ра. *Shield one's eyes from the sun,* защища́ть *or* прикрыва́ть глаза́ от со́лнца. —**heat shield,** теплово́й экра́н.

shift *v.t.* **1,** (move; transfer) передвига́ть; перемеща́ть; перекла́дывать. *Shift the furniture,* передвига́ть ме́бель. *Shift the responsibility,* перекла́дывать отве́тственность. *Shift the blame on,* перекла́дывать *or* свали́ть вину́ на (+ *acc.*). **2,** (change; switch) перемени́ть; переводи́ть; переключа́ть. *Shift gears,* переключи́ть ско́рость. *Shift one's ground,* переме́нить пози́цию. *Shift the conversation to another subject,* перевести́ разгово́р на другу́ю те́му. —*v.i.* **1,** (move) передвига́ться; перемеща́ться. *Shift from foot to foot,* перемина́ться *or* переступа́ть с ноги́ на́ ногу. *The ground shifted under our feet,* земля́ сдви́нулась под нога́ми. **2,** (switch) переходи́ть; переключа́ться. *Shift to the offensive,* переходи́ть в наступле́ние. *The wind shifted,* ве́тер перемени́лся. *The scene shifts to London,* де́йствие перено́сится в Ло́ндон. **3,** (get along) обходи́ться: *shift for oneself,* обходи́ться без посторо́нней по́мощи. —*n.* **1,** (movement) перемеще́ние. **2,** (change; switch) сдвиг. **3,** (work period) сме́на. *Work in shifts,* рабо́тать посме́нно. *Work the morning shift,* рабо́тать в у́треннюю сме́ну. **4,** (gearshift) переда́ча: *automatic shift,* ав-

тома́тическая переда́ча. —**shift work,** сме́нная *or* посме́нная рабо́та.

shifting *adj.* переме́нный: *shifting winds,* переме́нный ве́тер. *Shifting sands,* зыбу́чие пески́. *Shifting stress,* подви́жное ударе́ние.

shiftless *adj.* неради́вый; непутёвый.

shifty *adj.* увёртливый; изворо́тливый.

Shiite *n.* шии́т. —*adj.* шии́тский.

shillelagh *n.* дуби́нка.

shilling *n.* ши́ллинг.

shimmer *v.i.* мерца́ть.

shin *n.* го́лень. —**shinbone,** *n.* больша́я берцо́вая кость.

shine *v.i.* **1,** (emit light) свети́ть; свети́ться. *The sun is shining,* со́лнце све́тит. **2,** (gleam) блесте́ть; сия́ть. **3,** (excel) блиста́ть. —*v.t.* **1,** (polish) полирова́ть. *Shine shoes,* чи́стить боти́нки. **2,** (point; direct, as light) свети́ть (+ *instr.*): *shine the light in the corner,* свети́ть фонарём в у́гол. *Shine the light over here!,* посвети́те сюда́! *Don't shine the light in my eyes!,* не свети́те мне в глаза́! —*n.* **1,** (luster) лоск; блеск; гля́нец. **2,** (shoeshine): *get a shine,* почи́стить боти́нки. —**take a shine to,** *colloq.* полюби́ть.

shiner *n.* **1,** (fish) голья́н. **2,** *slang* (black eye) фона́рь.

shingle *n.* **1,** (wood tile) дра́нка; *pl.* гонт. **2,** (small sign) вы́веска.

shingles *n., med.* опоя́сывающий лиша́й.

shinguard *n.* щито́к.

shining *adj.* сия́ющий; блестя́щий.

Shinto *n.* синтои́зм. *Also,* **Shintoism.**

shiny *adj.* **1,** (glossy) блестя́щий. **2,** (rubbed or worn smooth) лосня́щийся.

ship *n.* **1,** (large vessel) парохо́д; су́дно. *Go by ship,* е́хать на парохо́де. *Cargo ship,* грузово́е су́дно. **2,** (naval vessel) кора́бль. *Warship,* вое́нный кора́бль. —*adj.* [*often* **ship's**] судово́й: *ship doctor,* судово́й врач. —*v.t.* **1,** (send to a destination) отправля́ть; перевози́ть; отгружа́ть. **2,** *fol. by* off (send away) отсыла́ть. —*v.i.* [*usu.* **ship out**] отправля́ться; отплыва́ть.

shipbuilder *n.* кораблестрои́тель; судострои́тель.

shipbuilding *n.* кораблестрое́ние; судострое́ние.

ship canal судохо́дный кана́л.

shipment *n.* **1,** (shipping of goods) отпра́вка; отгру́зка. **2,** (a consignment of goods) па́ртия.

shipowner *n.* судовладе́лец.

shipper *n.* грузоотправи́тель.

shipping *n.* **1,** (shipment) отгру́зка; отпра́вка. **2,** (movement of ships carrying cargo) судохо́дство: *closed to shipping,* закры́т для судохо́дства. **3,** (ships collectively) суда́. —*adj.* судохо́дный: *shipping company,* судохо́дная компа́ния.

shipshape *adj.* в по́лном поря́дке.

shipwreck *n.* кораблекруше́ние. *Be shipwrecked,* потерпе́ть кораблекруше́ние.

shipyard *n.* верфь; судове́рфь.

shire *n.* гра́фство.

shirk *v.t.* уклоня́ться от; уви́ливать от. —**shirker,** *n.* прогу́льщик.

shirt *n.* руба́шка; соро́чка. *Shirt pocket,* карма́н

руба́шки. —**keep one's shirt on,** *slang* не горячи́ться; не кипяти́ться. —**lose one's shirt,** *slang* проигра́ться.

shirt front мани́шка.

shirtsleeve *n.* рука́в руба́шки. *In one's shirtsleeves,* без пиджака́.

shirttail *n.* низ руба́шки. *Your shirttail is hanging out,* у вас вы́лезла руба́шка.

shish kebab шашлы́к.

shiver *v.i.* дрожа́ть; трясти́сь. —*n.* дрожь. *It gives me the shivers,* меня́ от э́того броса́ет в дрожь; у меня́ моро́з по ко́же подира́ет.

shoal *n.* мель; о́тмель.

shock *n.* **1,** (sudden jolt) уда́р; толчо́к; сотрясе́ние. **2,** (sudden emotional disturbance) потрясе́ние: *It was a great shock to us,* э́то бы́ло для нас больши́м потрясе́нием. **3,** *med.* шок. *Everyone was in a state of shock,* все бы́ли в состоя́нии шо́ка. **4,** (jolt of electricity) (электри́ческий) уда́р. *I got a shock,* меня́ уда́рило то́ком. **5,** (mass, as of hair) копна́; ша́пка (воло́с). —*v.t.* **1,** (startle; horrify) потряса́ть. **2,** (offend; scandalize) шоки́ровать.

shock absorber амортиза́тор.

shocking *adj.* **1,** (extremely upsetting) стра́шный; ужаса́ющий. **2,** (outrageous) возмути́тельный; сканда́льный.

shock troops уда́рные войска́.

shock wave уда́рная волна́.

shoddy *adj.* недоброка́чественный.

shoe *n.* **1,** (general term) боти́нок. *What size shoe do you wear?,* како́й но́мер о́буви вы но́сите? **2,** (lady's) ту́фля. **3,** (for a horse) подко́ва. **4,** *mech.* башма́к; коло́дка: *brake shoe,* тормозно́й башма́к; тормозна́я коло́дка. —*adj.* обувно́й: *shoe store,* обувно́й магази́н. —*v.t.* обува́ть: *well shod,* хорошо́ обу́тый. *Shoe a horse,* подкова́ть ло́шадь. —**be in someone's shoes,** быть на чьём-нибудь ме́сте; быть в чьей-нибудь шку́ре. —**fill someone's shoes,** занима́ть чьё-нибудь ме́сто.

shoehorn *n.* рожо́к.

shoelace *n.* шнуро́к (для боти́нок).

shoemaker *n.* сапо́жник.

shoe polish гутали́н; ва́кса; сапо́жный крем; сапо́жная мазь.

shoeshine *n.* чи́стка сапо́г. —**shoeshine boy,** чи́стильщик сапо́г.

shoetree *n.* коло́дка.

shoo *interj.* кш!; вон! —*v.t.* [*usu.* **shoo away**] ши́кать на.

shoot *v.t.* **1,** (discharge; fire) пуска́ть: *shoot an arrow,* пуска́ть стрелу́. **2,** (fire at and hit) стреля́ть в (и ра́нить): *shoot a burglar,* стреля́ть во взло́мщика (и ра́нить его́). *Shoot someone in the leg,* вы́стрелить кому́-нибудь в но́гу. **3,** (fire and kill) застрели́ть. *Shoot oneself,* застрели́ться. **4,** (hunt and kill) стреля́ть; застрели́ть: *shoot deer,* стреля́ть оле́ней; *shoot a deer,* застрели́ть оле́ня. **5,** (execute) расстре́ливать. **6,** *fol. by* **down** (bring down by shooting) сбива́ть. **7,** (fire, as a gun) стреля́ть (из ружья́). **8,** (propel with great force) запуска́ть. *Shoot forth lava,*

изверга́ть ла́ву. **9,** (photograph) снима́ть; засня́ть. **10,** *sports* посыла́ть (мяч). **11,** *games* игра́ть: *shoot dice/pool/marbles,* игра́ть в ко́сти/билья́рд/ша́рики. **12,** *Shoot rapids,* переправля́ться че́рез поро́ги. —*v.i.* **1,** (fire a weapon) стреля́ть: *Don't shoot!,* не стреля́йте! **2,** (flash; dart) мча́ться; нести́сь. *Shoot past,* промча́ться; проноси́ться; промелькну́ть. *Shoot ahead,* вы́рваться *or* рвану́ться вперёд. *The horse shot out of the gate,* ло́шадь вы́летела из-за барье́ра. *Flames shot up into the air,* пла́мя взвило́сь в во́здух. **3,** *hockey* бить; *basketball* броса́ть. **4,** *fol. by* **up** (soar, as of prices, temperature, etc.) подска́кивать. **5,** *fol. by* **up** (grow rapidly) вы́расти; вы́тянуться; вы́махать. **6,** *fol. by* **for** (aim for; strive for) ме́тить (в). —*n.* отро́сток; росто́к; побе́г. —**shoot back, 1,** (return fire) отвеча́ть огнём. **2,** *colloq.* (retort) найти́сь. —**shoot off one's mouth,** *slang* проболта́ться. —**shoot the breeze,** *colloq.* болта́ть. —**shoot the works,** *slang* идти́ ва-ба́нк.

shooting *n.* **1,** (firing of weapons) стрельба́. **2,** (filming) съёмка. —*adj.* **1,** (pert. to shooting) стрелко́вый: *shooting match,* стрелко́вое состяза́ние. **2,** (stabbing, as of pain) стреля́ющий; ко́лющий. —**shooting gallery,** тир. —**shooting star,** па́дающая звезда́.

shop *n.* **1,** (small store) магази́н; ла́вка. **2,** (place where work is done) мастерска́я: *repair shop,* ремо́нтная мастерска́я. **3,** (division in a factory) цех; мастерска́я: *machine shop,* механи́ческий цех; механи́ческая мастерска́я. —*adj.* цехово́й: *shop foreman,* цехово́й ма́стер. —*v.i.* [*also,* **go shopping**] ходи́ть по магази́нам; де́лать поку́пки. —**talk shop,** говори́ть о служе́бных дела́х.

shopkeeper *n.* ла́вочник.

shoplifter *n.* магази́нный вор.

shopper *n.* покупа́тель.

shopping bag су́мка для поку́пок; хозя́йственная су́мка.

shopping center *also,* **shopping centre** торго́вый центр.

shopping list спи́сок поку́пок; спи́сок того́, что купи́ть.

shopworn *adj.* залежа́лый.

shore *n.* бе́рег: *on the opposite shore,* на противополо́жном берегу́. —*v.t.* [*usu.* **shore up**] подпира́ть.

shoreline *n.* берегова́я ли́ния.

short *adj.* **1,** (not long) коро́ткий: *short skirt,* коро́ткая ю́бка. *Short hair/sleeves,* коро́ткие во́лосы/рукава́. *Short walk,* небольша́я *or* коро́ткая прогу́лка. *I'm going for a short walk,* я иду́ прогуля́ться. *It's a short walk,* туда́ идти́ недалеко́. *The dress is two inches short,* пла́тье вам коро́тко *or* коро́тко. *The dress is two inches short,* пла́тье коро́че на два дю́йма. *The shortest distance between two points,* наиме́ньшее расстоя́ние ме́жду двумя́ то́чками. **2,** (not of long duration) коро́ткий: *short winter/memory/life,* коро́ткая зима́/па́мять/жизнь. *A short time ago,* неда́вно. *The days are getting shorter,* дни стано́вятся коро́че. **3,** (brief; concise) коро́ткий; кра́ткий: *short speech/article*, коро́ткая *or* кра́ткая речь/статья́; *short letter*, коро́ткое *or* кра́ткое письмо́. *Short book*, небольша́я *or* ма́ленькая кни́га. **4**, (not tall) ни́зкого ро́ста; ма́ленького ро́ста: *a short man*, челове́к ни́зкого/ма́ленького ро́ста. **5**, (insufficient) недоста́точный. *Be in short supply*, быть дефици́тным. **6**, *fol.* by *of* (not having enough of): *We are short of milk*, у нас не хвата́ет молока́. *I am short of cash/money*, я не при деньга́х; у меня́ с деньга́ми ту́го. **7**, (brusque; curt) ре́зкий: *He was short with me*, он был ре́зок со мной. —*adv.* коро́тко: *cut one's hair short*, коро́тко постри́чь во́лосы. —*n.* **1**, (short film) короткометра́жный фильм. **2**, *pl.* (short pants) *see* shorts. **3**, = **short circuit.** —**cut short**, обрыва́ть. —**fall short of**, не достига́ть: *fall short of the mark*, не достига́ть це́ли. —**for short**, сокращённо; для кра́ткости. —**in short**, коро́че говоря́. —**in short order**, в спе́шном поря́дке. —**nothing short of**, про́сто: *It was nothing short of miraculous*, э́то бы́ло про́сто чу́до. —**run short**, истоща́ться: *Their supplies were running short*, их запа́сы истоща́лись. *Time is running short*, вре́мя истека́ет. —**short of**, кро́ме; поми́мо. —**stop short**, внеза́пно останови́ться; (when speaking) останови́ться на полусло́ве; осе́чься. —**to make a long story short**, коро́че говоря́.

shortage *n.* недоста́ток; нехва́тка; дефици́т.

shortbread *n.* песо́чное пече́нье; рассы́пчатое пече́нье.

shortcake *n.* песо́чный торт.

shortchange *v.t., colloq.* обсчи́тывать.

short circuit коро́ткое замыка́ние.

shortcoming *n.* недоста́ток.

shortcut *n.* коро́ткий путь. *Take a shortcut*, сре́зать у́гол.

shorten *v.t.* укора́чивать; сокраща́ть: *shorten a dress*, укора́чивать пла́тье; *shorten an article*, сокраща́ть статью́.

shortening *n.* **1**, (making shorter) сокраще́ние. **2**, (pastry ingredient) сдо́ба.

shortfall *n.* дефици́т; недобо́р.

shorthand *n.* стеногра́фия. *Take down in shorthand*, стенографи́ровать. *Can you take shorthand?*, вы уме́ете стенографи́ровать?

short-lived *adj.* недолгове́чный.

shortly *adv.* ско́ро; вско́ре. *Shortly before*, незадо́лго до. *Shortly after*, вско́ре по́сле. *Shortly thereafter*, вско́ре. *I'll be there shortly*, я ско́ро приду́.

shortness *n.* коро́ткость. —**shortness of breath**, оды́шка.

short-range *adj.* бли́жнего де́йствия; с ма́лым ра́диусом де́йствия.

shorts *n.pl.* трусы́; тру́сики; шо́рты.

shortsighted *adj.* близору́кий; недальнови́дный. —**shortsightedness**, *n.* близору́кость; недальнови́дность.

short story расска́з; нове́лла. *Short story writer*, нове́ллист.

short-tempered *adj.* вспы́льчивый.

short-term *adj.* краткосро́чный.

short wave коро́ткая волна́. —**short-wave**, *adj.* коротково́лновый.

shot *n.* **1**, (discharge of a firearm) вы́стрел: *without firing a shot*, без еди́ного вы́стрела. *I heard a shot*, я услы́шал вы́стрел. **2**, (one who shoots) стрело́к. *He is a good shot*, он хоро́ший стрело́к; он хорошо́ стреля́ет. **3**, (small pellets) дробь. *Buckshot*, кру́пная дробь. **4**, (picture) сни́мок. **5**, *sports* бросо́к; уда́р. *Penalty shot*, штрафно́й уда́р. *Take a shot*, де́лать бросо́к. *Put the shot*, толка́ть ядро́. **6**, (inoculation) приви́вка: *flu shot*, приви́вка от (or про́тив) гри́ппа. **7**, *colloq.* (drink of liquor) глото́к (спиртно́го). **8**, *colloq.* (attempt) попы́тка. —*adj.* **1**, (streaked): *shot with gold*, с золоты́м отли́вом. **2**, *colloq.* (worn out) изно́шенный: *These pants are shot*, э́ти брю́ки износи́лись. *My nerves are shot*, у меня́ не́рвы расшата́лись. —**call the shots**, распоряжа́ться. —**like a shot**, пу́лей: *take off like a shot*, бро́ситься *or* понести́сь пу́лей.

shotgun *n.* дробови́к. *Sawed-off shotgun*, обре́з.

shot-put *n.* толка́ние ядра́.

should *v.aux.* **1**, *expressing mild obligation or advisability*: *Should I leave?*, мне уйти́? *What should I wear?*, что мне наде́ть? *What should we order for dessert?*, что нам заказа́ть на десе́рт? *You should write a book about it*, вы бы об э́том кни́гу написа́ли. *You shouldn't have done it*, вы не должны́ бы́ли де́лать э́того. *It should be borne in mind that...*, сле́дует име́ть в виду́, что... **2**, *expressing expectation*, до́лжен: *He should be here soon*, он до́лжен ско́ро прийти́. **3**, *expressing condition or assumption*, е́сли: *should the need arise*, е́сли возни́кнет необходи́мость. *Should I be late*, (в слу́чае) е́сли я опозда́ю. *Should you be in Philadelphia,...* бу́дете в Филаде́льфии,... **4**, *used in polite requests*, бы: *I should like to ask...*, я бы хоте́л(а) спроси́ть...

shoulder *n.* **1**, (part of the body) плечо́: *broad shoulders*, широ́кие пле́чи. *Wear a coat over one's shoulders*, носи́ть пальто́ внаки́дку. **2**, (side of a road) обо́чина. —*v.t.* **1**, (place on one's shoulders) взва́ливать на пле́чи. **2**, (assume; bear) брать на себя́; брать на пле́чи. —**give someone the cold shoulder**, хо́лодно встре́тить. —**have a good head on one's shoulders**, име́ть го́лову на плеча́х. —**shoulder to shoulder**, плечо́м к плечу́. —**straight from the shoulder**, начистоту́.

shoulder blade лопа́тка.

shoulder strap ля́мка; *mil.* пого́н.

shout *v.i.* крича́ть: *shout for help*, крича́ть о по́мощи; *shout to a passer-by*, крича́ть прохо́жему. *Don't shout at me!*, не кричи́(те) на меня́! —*v.t.* крича́ть; выкри́кивать. *Shout hurrah*, крича́ть ура́. *Shout slogans*, выкри́кивать ло́зунги. *Shout someone's name*, вы́крикнуть чьё-нибудь и́мя. —*n.* крик; вы́крик; во́зглас. *A shout for help*, крик о по́мощи. —**shout down**, перекрича́ть.

shove *v.t.* толка́ть; пиха́ть. —*v.i.* толка́ться: *Don't shove!*, не толка́йтесь! —*n.* толчо́к. —**shove aside**, отта́лкивать; отпи́хивать. —**shove off**, **1**, (push off from shore) отта́лкиваться от бе́рега. **2**, *colloq.* (depart) уходи́ть; отправля́ться.

shovel *n.* лопа́та. —*v.t.* разгреба́ть: *shovel snow,* разгреба́ть снег. *Shovel snow from the sidewalk,* сгреба́ть снег с тротуа́ра.

show *v.t.* **1,** (make visible; point out; demonstrate) пока́зывать: *show one's ticket,* пока́зывать биле́т; *show someone the way,* пока́зывать кому́-нибудь доро́гу. *I'll show you how to do it,* я вам покажу́, как э́то де́лается. **2,** (display publicly) выставля́ть: *show merchandise in the window,* выставля́ть това́ры в *or* на витри́не. **3,** (reveal; evince) проявля́ть; обнару́живать: *show courage,* проявля́ть/обнару́живать му́жество. *Show no signs of life,* не подава́ть при́знаков жи́зни. **4,** (extend) ока́зывать: *show kindness to,* ока́зывать любе́зность (+ *dat.*). *Show respect for,* ока́зывать уваже́ние (+ *dat.*). **5,** (guide; escort) проводи́ть; провожа́ть. *Show someone to his room/ to the door/ around town/,* проводи́ть кого́-нибудь в свою́ ко́мнату; провожа́ть кого́-нибудь до двере́й; пока́зывать кому́-нибудь го́род. *I'll show you the way out,* я вас вы́веду. **6,** (prove; demonstrate) пока́зывать; дока́зывать; устана́вливать. **7,** (indicate; suggest; reflect) говори́ть о: *It shows a lack of self-confidence,* э́то говори́т о неуве́ренности в себе́. **8,** (indicate; register) пока́зывать: *The clock shows 3:00,* часы́ пока́зывают три часа́. **9,** *colloq.* (teach a lesson to) показа́ть: *I'll show him!,* я ему́ покажу́! **10,** *Show one's face,* показа́ться. *Not show one's face,* не каза́ть глаз *or* но́са. **11,** *Show oneself to be...,* показа́ть себя́ (+ *instr.*). —*v.i.* быть ви́дным; быть заме́тным; видне́ться. *Your slip is showing,* у вас видна́ ни́жняя ю́бка. *The stain hardly shows,* пятно́ почти́ не заме́тно. —*n.* **1,** (a presentation of entertainment) спекта́кль. **2,** (single performance) сеа́нс. **3,** (exhibition) вы́ставка: *air show,* авиацио́нная вы́ставка; *dog show,* вы́ставка соба́к. **4,** (pointed display) демонстра́ция: *show of strength/force,* демонстра́ция си́лы. **5,** (that which is intended to impress) эффе́кт. *Done for show,* сде́ланный напока́з; рассчи́танный на эффе́кт. **6,** *Show of hands,* подня́тие рук. —**show in,** вводи́ть. —**show off, 1,** (flaunt) щеголя́ть (+ *instr.*); выставля́ть напока́з. **2,** (make a great display of oneself) рисова́ться; красова́ться. —**show out,** провожа́ть до двере́й. —**show up, 1,** (arrive) явля́ться. **2,** *colloq.* (prove superior to) затмева́ть; утира́ть нос (+ *dat.*).

showcase *n.* витри́на.

showdown *n.* развя́зка.

shower *n.* **1,** (shower bath) душ: *take a shower,* принима́ть душ. **2,** (light rain) дождь; до́ждик; *pl.* дожди́. **3,** (torrent; profusion) град. —*v.t.* **1,** (cover; pelt) засыпа́ть; забра́сывать: *shower the town with volcanic ash,* засы́пать дере́вню вулкани́ческим пе́плом; *shower the visitors with leaflets,* заброса́ть прие́зжих листо́вками. **2,** *fig.* (deluge) засыпа́ть; осыпа́ть; забра́сывать (*e.g.* пода́рками). *Shower with praise,* осыпа́ть (кого́-нибудь) похвала́ми. —*v.i.* принима́ть душ. —**shower room,** душева́я.

showing *n.* **1,** (act of showing) пока́з. **2,** (overall performance) результа́т: *make a good showing,* показа́ть хоро́ший результа́т.

showman *n.* антрепренёр.

showroom *n.* вы́ставочный зал; демонстрацио́нный зал; сало́н.

show trial показа́тельный суд.

showy *adj.* показно́й; мишу́рный.

shrapnel *n.* шрапне́ль. *Shrapnel wound,* оско́лочная ра́на.

shred *n.* клок; клочо́к; лоску́т. *Tear to shreds,* разрыва́ть в кло́чья *or* в клочки́. *Not a shred of evidence,* ни мале́йших доказа́тельств. —*v.t.* измельча́ть; кромса́ть. *Shred cabbage,* шинкова́ть капу́сту. *Shred documents,* уничтожа́ть докуме́нты.

shrew *n.* **1,** (animal) землеро́йка. **2,** (scolding woman) меге́ра; фу́рия. *"The Taming of the Shrew",* «Укроще́ние стропти́вой».

shrewd *adj.* **1,** (of a person) проница́тельный; расчётливый. **2,** (of an action) ло́вкий. —**shrewdness,** *n.* проница́тельность.

shriek *n.* пронзи́тельный крик. —*v.i.* пронзи́тельно крича́ть.

shrift *n., in* **make short shrift of,** (бы́стро) распра́виться с.

shrike *n.* сорокопу́т.

shrill *adj.* ре́зкий; пронзи́тельный.

shrimp *n.* **1,** (crustacean) креве́тка. **2,** *colloq.* (small person) коро́ты́ш(ка); недоро́сток.

shrine *n.* **1,** (tomb of a saint) ра́ка. **2,** (revered site) святы́ня.

shrink *v.i.* **1,** (of fabric) сади́ться. **2,** (become smaller) сжима́ться. **3,** (draw back; recoil) отпря́нуть. **4,** *fol. by* **from** (avoid) уклоня́ться от; отступа́ть (пе́ред); пасова́ть (пе́ред). —*v.t.* **1,** (cause shrinkage in) вызыва́ть уса́дку (+ *gen.*). **2,** (reduce in size) сжима́ть.

shrinkage *n.* уса́дка.

shrivel *v.i.* смо́рщиваться; съёживаться.

shroud *n.* **1,** (burial cloth) са́ван. **2,** (that which covers or envelops) пелена́. —*v.t.* оку́тывать. *Shrouded in secrecy,* оку́танный та́йной; покры́т мра́ком неизве́стности.

Shrovetide *n.* ма́сленица.

shrub *n.* куст. —**shrubbery,** *n.* куста́рник.

shrug *v.t. & i.* пожима́ть (плеча́ми). —*n.* пожима́ние (плеч). —**shrug off,** отма́хиваться от.

shuck *n.* **1,** (husk) шелуха́. **2,** (shell) скорлупа́. —*v.t.* лущи́ть; шелуши́ть.

shucks *interj.* чёрт побери́!

shudder *v.i.* содрога́ться: *shudder at the thought of...,* содрога́ться при мы́сли о... —*n.* содрога́ние.

shuffle *v.t.* **1,** (drag, as one's feet) ша́ркать (нога́ми); волочи́ть (но́ги). **2,** (mix, as cards) тасова́ть. —*v.i.* **1,** *fol. by* **along** (walk by dragging one's feet) волочи́ться. **2,** (mix the cards) тасова́ть. —*n.* **1,** (of feet) ша́рканье. **2,** (mixing of cards) тасо́вка.

shun *v.t.* избега́ть; сторони́ться.

shunt *v.t.* **1,** (turn aside) отводи́ть. **2,** *R.R.* переводи́ть на запа́сный путь.

shut *v.t.* закрыва́ть: *Shut the door!,* закро́й(те) дверь! —*v.i.* закрыва́ться. —*adj.* закры́тый: *The windows were shut,* о́кна бы́ли закры́ты. —**shut down,** закрыва́ть(ся). —**shut off, 1,** (turn off) отключа́ть. **2,** (halt, as debate) прекраща́ть. **3,** (isolate) отгора́живать. —**shut out, 1,** (keep out) не допуска́ть. *Shut out the light,* не пропуска́ть све́та. **2,** *sports* сде́лать суху́ю (+ *dat.*). —**shut up, 1,** (incarcerate) заточа́ть. **2,** *colloq.* (stop talking) замолча́ть. *Shut up!,* заткни́сь!

shutout *n., sports* суха́я.

shutter *n.* **1,** (for a window) ста́вень; ста́вня. **2,** (of a camera) затво́р. *Shutter release,* спускова́я кно́пка. —*v.t.* закрыва́ть ста́внями.

shuttle *n.* челно́к. *Space shuttle,* косми́ческий челно́к. —*v.i.* курси́ровать; снова́ть. —**shuttle diplomacy,** «челно́чная» диплома́тия.

shuttlecock *n.* вола́н.

shy *adj.* **1,** (timid) ро́бкий; засте́нчивый. **2,** *colloq.* (lacking; short): *We are shy a few dollars,* нам не хвата́ет не́скольких до́лларов. —*v.i.* **1,** (rear, as of a horse) отпря́нуть. **2,** [*usu.* **shy away from**] (avoid) уклоня́ться от. —*v.t.* (throw) броса́ть.

shyness *n.* ро́бость; засте́нчивость.

si *n., music* си.

Siamese *adj.* сиа́мский. —**Siamese twins,** сиа́мские близнецы́.

Siberian *adj.* сиби́рский. —*n.* сибиря́к.

sibilant *n. & adj.* **1,** (ж,ч,ш,щ) шипя́щий. **2,** (с,з) свистя́щий.

sibling *n.* родно́й брат; родна́я сестра́.

sic *v.t.* натра́вливать. —**sic 'im!,** ату́ его́!

sick *adj.* **1,** (ill) больно́й: *sick child,* больно́й ребёнок. *I was sick,* я был бо́лен; я была́ больна́. **2,** (nauseous): *I feel sick to my stomach,* меня́ тошни́т. **3,** (mentally ill) душевнобольно́й. **4,** (perverted) извращённый: *sick mind,* извращённый ум. **5,** (extremely upset) о́чень огорчён. *I am sick at heart,* у меня́ боли́т душа́. **6,** (disgusted): *Talk like that makes me sick,* таки́е разгово́ры мне претя́т; меня́ тошни́т от таки́х разгово́ров. **7,** *fol. by of* (fed up with): *I am sick of staying home,* мне надое́ло сиде́ть до́ма. —*n.,* *preceded by* **the** больны́е: *tend the sick,* уха́живать за больны́ми. —**take sick,** заболева́ть.

sick bay лазаре́т.

sicken *v.t.* прети́ть. *It sickens me,* мне прети́т (*or* меня́ тошни́т) от э́того.

sickening *adj.* тошнотво́рный; отврати́тельный.

sickle *n.* серп.

sick leave о́тпуск по боле́зни. *He is on sick leave,* он на больни́чном (листе́).

sickly *adj.* боле́зненный; хи́лый. —**sickliness,** *n.* боле́зненность.

sickness *n.* боле́знь.

side *n.* **1,** (in most meanings) сторона́: *the right side of the road,* пра́вая сторона́ доро́ги. *The two sides of a coin,* о́бе стороны́ моне́ты. *On the other side of the river,* по ту сто́рону реки́. *Stand to one side,* держа́ться в стороне́. *Whose side are you on?,* вы на чьей стороне́? *Time is on our side,* вре́мя рабо́тает на нас. *A relative on his mother's side,* ро́дственник со стороны́ ма́тери. **2,** (part of the body) бок: *lie on one's/its side,* лежа́ть на боку́. *I have a pain in my*

side, у меня́ ко́лет в боку́. **3,** (of an object) *rendered by various nouns: side of a box/ship/canyon/mountain,* сте́нка я́щика; бок корабля́; стена́ каньо́на; склон горы́. **4,** (of a geometric figure) грань: *A cube has six sides,* куб име́ет шесть гра́ней. **5,** (area immediately adjacent) край: *along the side of the road,* по кра́ю доро́ги. *Stand on the side of the road,* стоя́ть на обо́чине доро́ги. *Stand at someone's side,* стоя́ть ря́дом с ке́м-нибудь. **6,** *naut.* борт: *starboard side,* пра́вый борт. **7,** (of beef) бок: *side of mutton,* бара́ний бок. —*adj.* **1,** (located on one side) боково́й: *side door,* боковая́ дверь; *side entrance,* боково́й вход. **2,** (from one side) сбо́ку: *side view,* вид сбо́ку. **3,** (incidental) побо́чный: *side effects,* побо́чное де́йствие. —*v.i.* [*usu.* **side with**] станови́ться *or* встава́ть на сто́рону (+ *gen.*). —**from side to side,** из стороны́ в сто́рону; с бо́ку на́ бок. —**on all sides,** со всех сторо́н. —**on the side,** на стороне́: *do work on the side,* подраба́тывать на стороне́. —**on the** (+ *adj.*) **side,** дово́льно (+ *adj.*). *It's on the chilly side today,* холоднова́то сего́дня. —**side by side,** ря́дом; бок о́ бок. —**take someone's side,** брать *or* принима́ть *or* держа́ть чью́-нибудь сто́рону; стать на чью́-нибудь сто́рону.

sideboard *n.* буфе́т; серва́нт.

sideburns *n.pl.* бакенба́рды.

sidecar *n.* коля́ска (мотоци́кла).

sidekick *n., colloq.* партнёр; това́рищ.

sideline *n.* **1,** (additional work) побо́чная рабо́та. *He does this as a sideline,* он занима́ется э́тим ме́жду де́лом. **2,** *sports* боковая́ ли́ния. —**on the sidelines,** в стороне́; на обо́чине.

sidelong *adj.* косо́й: *sidelong glance,* косо́й взгляд.

sidestep *v.t.* исходи́ть (стороно́й); уклоня́ться от.

side street переу́лок; боковая́ у́лица.

sidetrack *n.* запа́сный путь. —*v.t.* **1,** *R.R.* переводи́ть на запа́сный путь. **2,** (divert; shunt aside): *I got sidetracked along the way,* я задержа́лся в доро́ге. *The bill got sidetracked in Congress,* обсужде́ние законопрое́кта в конгре́ссе бы́ло отло́жено.

sidewalk *n.* тротуа́р.

sideways *adv.* бо́ком; бочко́м.

siding *n.* запа́сный путь.

sidle *v.i.* ходи́ть бо́ком; пробира́ться бочко́м. *Sidle up to,* пробра́ться бочко́м к.

siege *n.* оса́да; блока́да. *Under siege,* в оса́де. —**lay siege to,** осажда́ть. —**state of siege,** оса́дное положе́ние.

sienna *n.* сие́на.

sieve *n.* решето́; си́то. —**memory like a sieve,** дыря́вая па́мять.

sift *v.t.* **1,** (pass through a sieve) просе́ивать. **2,** (consider carefully) взве́шивать. —*v.i.* [*usu.* **sift through**] ры́ться в.

sigh *v.i.* вздыха́ть. —*n.* вздох.

sight *n.* **1,** (vision; eyesight) зре́ние: *lose one's sight,* лиши́ться зре́ния. *Lose the sight of one eye,* ослепну́ть на оди́н глаз. **2,** (field of vision) по́ле зре́ния: *come within sight,* попа́сть в по́ле зре́ния. *The end is in sight,* коне́ц уже́ ви́ден. *There was not a* *house in sight*, не́ было ви́дно ни одного́ до́ма. *There is no relief in sight*, никако́го облегче́ния не предви́дится. *Not let out of one's sight*, не спуска́ть глаз с (+ *gen.*); не упуска́ть и́з виду. *Pass out of sight*, скрыва́ться и́з виду. *Out of my sight!*, с глаз мои́х доло́й. **3,** (something seen; spectacle) вид; зре́лище. *At the sight of*, при ви́де (+ *gen.*). *A horrible sight*, ужа́сное зре́лище. *The sight of hungry children*, вид голо́дных дете́й. *I can't stand the sight of blood*, я не выношу́ ви́да кро́ви. **4,** *pl.* (places worth seeing) достопримеча́тельности: *see the sights*, осма́тривать достопримеча́тельности. **5,** (mechanism on a gun) прице́л. —*v.t.* уви́деть: *sight land*, уви́деть зе́млю. —**a darned sight,** *colloq.* гора́здо; несравне́нно (+ *comp.*). —**catch sight of,** уви́деть; зави́деть. —**from sight,** с листа́: *play from sight*, игра́ть с листа́. —**know by sight,** знать в лицо́. —**lose sight of, 1,** (see no longer) (по)теря́ть и́з виду. **2,** (fail to realize) упуска́ть и́з виду; (по)теря́ть и́з виду. —**love at first sight,** любо́вь с пе́рвого взгля́да. —**out of sight, out of mind,** с глаз доло́й, из се́рдца вон. —**shoot on sight,** стреля́ть без предупрежде́ния. —**sight unseen,** загла́зно; за глаза́.

sighted *adj.* ви́дящий; зря́чий.

sightless *adj.* неви́дящий; незря́чий.

sight-read *v.t. & i.* чита́ть с листа́.

sightseeing *n.* осмо́тр достопримеча́тельностей. *Go sightseeing*, осма́тривать достопримеча́тельности. *Sightseeing tour of the city*, экску́рсия по го́роду. —**sightseer,** *n.* тури́ст; экскурса́нт.

sight translation перево́д с листа́.

sign *n.* **1,** (mark; symbol; signal; token; omen) знак: *minus sign*, знак ми́нус. *Secret sign*, та́йный знак. *A sign of respect*, знак уваже́ния. *A good sign*, до́брый знак. *Sign of the times*, зна́мение вре́мени. *The signs of the zodiac*, зна́ки зодиа́ка. **2,** (display board) вы́веска. *Road sign*, доро́жный знак. *Street sign*, табли́чка с назва́нием у́лицы. *Neon sign*, нео́новая рекла́ма. **3,** (evidence; trace; indication) при́знак: *signs of life*, при́знаки жи́зни. *Signs of an economic upturn*, при́знаки оживле́ния эконо́мики. —*v.t.* подпи́сывать: *sign a letter*, подписа́ть письмо́. *Sign a statement*, подписа́ть заявле́ние; подписа́ться под заявле́нием. *Sign one's name*, подпи́сываться; распи́сываться. —*v.i.* подпи́сываться; распи́сываться. *Sign on the dotted line*, расписа́ться на пункти́рной ли́нии. *Sign in his name*, подписа́ться его́ и́менем. *Sign for a parcel*, расписа́ться в получе́нии посы́лки. —**sign off,** зака́нчивать переда́чу. —**sign out,** отмеча́ться. —**sign up (for),** запи́сываться (в *or* на).

signal *n.* сигна́л: *distress signal*, сигна́л бе́дствия. *Hand signal*, знак руко́й. *Turn signal*, указа́тель поворо́та. *At a given signal*, по сигна́лу; по зна́ку. —*adj.* знамена́тельный: *a signal achievement*, знамена́тельное достиже́ние. —*v.t.* **1,** (give a signal to) подава́ть сигна́л *or* знак (+ *dat.*). **2,** (indicate) говори́ть о. —*v.i.* подава́ть сигна́л; сигнализи́ровать.

signalman *n.* сигна́льщик; *mil.* связи́ст.

signatory *n.* подписа́вший.

signature *n.* **1,** (name written by oneself) по́дпись. *Over the signature of*, за по́дписью (+ *gen.*). *For the signature of*, на по́дпись (+ *gen.*). *Collect signatures on a petition*, собира́ть по́дписи под пети́цией. **2,** *printing* печа́тный лист.

signboard *n.* вы́веска.

signer *n.* подписа́вший.

signet *n.* печа́тка.

significance *n.* значе́ние: *be of great significance*, име́ть большо́е значе́ние.

significant *adj.* значи́тельный: *significant discovery/ increase*, значи́тельное откры́тие/увеличе́ние. *Be significant*, име́ть значе́ние. *It is significant that...*, характе́рно, что...; знамена́тельно, что... —**significantly,** *adv.* значи́тельно.

signify *v.t.* **1,** (mean; denote) зна́чить; означа́ть. **2,** (make known; indicate) ука́зывать: *signify by raising their hands*, ука́зывать подня́тием рук.

sign language нема́я а́збука; язы́к же́стов.

sign painter худо́жник по вы́вескам; оформи́тель *or* изготови́тель вы́весок.

signpost *n.* указа́тельный столб; ве́ха.

Sikh *n.* сикх.

silage *n.* си́лос.

silence *n.* **1,** (absence of sound) тишина́. **2,** (failure to speak) молча́ние. *In silence*, мо́лча. —*interj.* помолчи́те! —*v.t.* **1,** (make silent) заста́вить замолча́ть. **2,** (suppress; still) заглуша́ть.

silencer *n.* глуши́тель.

silent *adj.* **1,** (making no sound; tacit; taciturn) молчали́вый; безмо́лвный. *Keep silent*, молча́ть. *Fall silent*, замолка́ть; умолка́ть. *Remain silent*, храни́ть молча́ние. *Silent prayer*, безмо́лвная моли́тва. **2,** (not pronounced): *The "k" is silent*, бу́ква "k" не произно́сится. **3,** (of a film) немо́й.

silently *adv.* мо́лча.

silhouette *n.* силуэ́т.

silica *n.* кремнезём.

silica gel силикаге́ль.

silicate *n.* силика́т.

siliceous *adj.* кремни́стый.

silicic *adj.* кре́мниевый: *silicic acid*, кре́мниевая кислота́.

silicon *n.* кре́мний.

silicone *n.* силико́н.

silk *n.* шёлк. *Raw silk*, шёлк-сыре́ц. —*adj.* шёлковый: *silk thread/shirt*, шёлковая нить/руба́шка.

silken *adj.* шелкови́стый.

silkworm *n.* (ту́товый) шелкопря́д; шелкови́чный червь.

silky *adj.* шелкови́стый.

silliness *n.* глу́пость.

silly *adj.* глу́пый. *Don't be silly!*, не говори́те глу́пости! *Laugh oneself silly*, смея́ться до упа́ду.

silo *n.* **1,** (for grain) си́лосная ба́шня. **2,** (for a missile) ша́хта.

silt *n.* ил. —*v.i.* [*usu.* **silt up**] заноси́ть и́лом (*impers.*): *The canal silted up*, кана́л занесло́ и́лом. —**silty,** *adj.* и́листый.

silver *n.* серебро́. —*adv.* сере́бряный: *silver coin,* серебряная монета. *Silver mines,* серебряные прииски *or* рудники. —*v.t.* серебрить.

silver fox черно-бурая лисица.

silver nitrate ляпис.

silver plate 1, (coating of silver) накладное серебро. **2,** (silverware) столовое серебро; серебряная посуда. —**silver-plate,** *v.t.* серебрить. —**silver-plated,** *adj.* посеребрённый.

silversmith *n.* серебряных дел мастер.

silverware *n.* столовое серебро; столовые приборы.

silvery *adj.* серебристый.

similar *adj.* **1,** (alike) сходный; похожий; подобный. *Similar goals,* сходные цели. *Similar tastes,* похожие *or* сходные вкусы. *A rabbit is similar to a hare,* кролик подобен зайцу; кролик похож на зайца. **2,** *geom.* подобный.

similarity *n.* сходство: *a great similarity between them,* большое сходство между ними. *The similarity between Victor and his father,* сходство Виктора с отцом.

similarly *adv.* подобным образом.

simile *n.* сравнение.

simmer *v.i.* закипать. —**simmer down,** успокаиваться.

simper *v.i.* ухмыляться.

simple *adj.* простой: *simple woman/task/food/life,* простая женщина/задача/пища/жизнь. *It's not so simple,* это не так просто. —**simple fracture,** простой перелом. —**simple interest,** простые проценты. —**simple sentence,** простое предложение.

simple-hearted *adj.* простодушный; простосердечный. —**simple-heartedness,** *n.* простодушие; простосердечие.

simple-minded *adj.* слабоумный.

simpleton *n.* простак.

simplicity *n.* простота.

simplify *v.t.* упрощать. —**simplification,** *n.* упрощение. —**simplified,** *adj.* упрощённый.

simplistic *adj.* упрощенческий.

simply *adv.* просто: *live/dress simply,* жить/одеваться просто. *It's simply outrageous,* это просто безобразие.

simulate *v.t.* симулировать; притворяться. —**simulation,** *n.* симуляция. —**simulator,** *n.* тренажёр.

simultaneity *n.* одновременность.

simultaneous *adj.* одновременный. *Simultaneous translation,* синхронный перевод. —**simultaneously,** *adv.* одновременно.

sin *n.* грех. *It is a sin to...,* грех *or* грешно (+ *inf.*). *Ugly as sin,* страшен (страшна) как смертный грех. —*v.i.* грешить.

since *adv.* **1,** (between then and now) с тех пор: *I have lived here ever since,* я живу здесь с тех пор. *He has since changed his mind,* он потом передумал. **2,** (ago) уже: *long since forgotten,* давно уже забыт. —*prep.* с (+ *gen.*); со времени (+ *gen.*): *since childhood,* с детства; *since yesterday,* со вчерашнего дня; *since the war,* со времени войны. ♦ *Also* после: *for the first time since his illness,* впервые после его болезни. *His first visit to Moscow since his departure*

in 1978, его первый визит в Москву после отъезда в 1978г. —*conj.* **1,** (during the time after) с тех пор, как: *since he arrived,* с тех пор, как он приехал. **2,** (because; inasmuch as) поскольку; так как. *Since there are no objections, we can proceed with the vote,* поскольку нет возражений, мы можем приступить к голосованию. —**since then,** с тех пор. —**since when?,** с каких пор?

sincere *adj.* искренний.

sincerely *adv.* искренний; искренно. *I mean that sincerely,* я говорю искренне; я действительно так думаю. —**sincerely yours,** искренне ваш.

sincerity *n.* искренность. —**in all sincerity,** от чистого сердца.

sine *n.,* *math.* синус.

sinecure *n.* синекура.

sinew *n.* сухожилие. —**sinewy,** *adj.* жилистый.

sinful *adj.* грешный.

sing *v.t. & i.* петь: *Can you sing?,* вы поёте? *Sing us a song,* спойте нам песню.

singe *v.t.* **1,** (burn slightly) подпаливать. **2,** (burn off the feathers of) опаливать: *singe a goose,* опаливать гуся.

singer *n.* певец; певица.

singing *n.* пение.

single *adj.* **1,** (only one) единый; один. *A single purpose,* единая цель. *Made from a single piece of material,* сделанный из одного куска материи. *Every single one,* все до одного; все до единого. *Not a single word,* ни одного (*or* ни единого) слова. *He was killed by a single shot,* он был убит единым *or* одиночным выстрелом. *Not a single shot was fired,* не было сделано ни одного выстрела. **2,** (unmarried) A, (of a man) неженатый; холостой. B, (of a woman) незамужняя. *Single mother,* мать-одиночка. **3,** (for use by one person) одиночный. *Single room,* комната *or* номер на одного. *Single bed,* односпальная кровать. —*v.t.* [*usu.* **single out**] выделять; отличать. —*n.* **1,** = **single room. 2,** *pl.,* *tennis* игры в одиночном разряде.

single-breasted *adj.* однобортный.

single combat *adj.* одиночный бой; единоборство.

single-engine *adj.* одномоторный.

single file колонна по одному. *Proceed single file,* идти гуськом.

single-handed *adj. & adv.* без посторонней помощи. *Also,* **single-handedly,** *adv.*

single-minded *adj.* целеустремлённый.

single-track *adj.* одноколейный.

singly *adv.* **1,** (separately; alone) один; в одиночку. **2,** (one at a time) поодиночке.

singsong *adj.* монотонный. *In a singsong voice,* нараспев.

singular *adj.* **1,** (unique) исключительный. **2,** (peculiar; distinctive) своеобразный. **3,** *gram.* единственный. —*n.,* *gram.* единственное число. —**singularity,** *n.* своеобразие. —**singularly,** *adv.* необычайно.

sinister *adj.* зловещий.

sink *v.i.* **1,** (go beneath the surface) погружаться: *sink into quicksand,* погружаться в сыпучий песок. **2,**

(go down in water) тону́ть: *sinking ship*, то́нущий кора́бль. *The ship sank*, кора́бль затону́л. *Sink to the bottom*, идти́ ко дну. **3,** (descend slowly) опуска́ться; сади́ться; оседа́ть. *Sink into a chair*, опуска́ться в кре́сло. *Sink below the horizon*, сади́ться за горизо́нт. *The foundation is sinking*, фунда́мент оседа́ет. **4,** (pass gradually into a given condition) впада́ть; погружа́ться: *sink into poverty/ despair*, впада́ть/погружа́ться в нищету́/ в отча́яние/. *Sink into a deep sleep*, погружа́ться в глубо́кий сон. **5,** (be near death) га́снуть. **6,** *My heart sank*, у меня́ се́рдце упа́ло *or* за́мерло; у меня́ душа́ ушла́ в пя́тки. **7,** *fol. by in* (penetrate the mind) запечатлева́ться. —*v.t.* **1,** (cause to sink) топи́ть: *The ship was sunk*, кора́бль был пото́плен. **2,** (drive into something) вонза́ть; втыка́ть; вса́живать. *Sink one's teeth into*, впива́ться зуба́ми в (+ *acc.*). **3,** (dig, as a well) рыть. *Sink an oil well*, бури́ть нефтяну́ю сква́жину. **4,** *basketball* забра́сывать: *sink a shot*, забро́сить мяч в корзи́ну. **5,** *colloq.* (invest) вса́живать. —*n.* ра́ковина: *kitchen sink*, ку́хонная ра́ковина.

sinker *n., fishing* грузи́ло.

sinking fund амортизацио́нный фонд.

sinner *n.* гре́шник.

sinuous *adj.* изви́листый.

sinus *n.* па́зуха; си́нус. —**sinusitis,** *n.* синуси́т.

sip *v.t.* потя́гивать; отпива́ть; прихлёбывать. *Sip lemonade through a straw*, соса́ть лимона́д че́рез соло́минку. —*n.* ма́ленький глото́к. *Take a sip of*, отпи́ть; прихлебну́ть; пригу́бить.

siphon *n.* сифо́н. —*v.t.* слива́ть *or* спуска́ть сифо́ном.

sir *n.* сэр; су́дарь.

sire *n.* **1,** (progenitor) производи́тель. **2,** (form of address for a sovereign) госуда́рь. —*v.t.* роди́ть; производи́ть.

siren *n.* сире́на: *air-raid siren*, сире́на возду́шной трево́ги.

sirloin *n.* филе́.

sirocco *n.* сиро́кко.

sisal *n.* сиза́ль.

siskin *n.* чиж.

sissy *n., colloq.* не́женка.

sister *n.* сестра́.

sister-in-law *n.* **1,** (husband's sister) золо́вка. **2,** (wife's sister) своя́ченица. **3,** (brother's wife or spouse's brother's wife) неве́стка.

sit *v.i.* **1,** [*usu.* **sit down**] (take a seat) сади́ться: *Sit down!*, сади́тесь! *Sit down to dinner*, сади́ться за обе́д. **2,** (be in a sitting position) сиде́ть: *He was sitting on the floor*, он сиде́л на полу́. *Where do you want to sit?*, где вы хоти́те сиде́ть? **3,** (be located) стоя́ть: *The house sits on a hill*, дом стои́т на холму́. **4,** (remain inactive or unused) сиде́ть: *sit home all day*, весь день сиде́ть до́ма. *Sit idle*, проста́ивать. **5,** (pose) пози́ровать. **6,** (be in session) заседа́ть. —*v.t.* сажа́ть; уса́живать: *sit someone down to work*, сажа́ть/уса́живать кого-нибудь за рабо́ту. —**sit back,** отки́дываться. —**sit out,** вы́сидеть до конца́;

пересиде́ть. —**sit through,** просиде́ть. —**sit up, 1,** (rise to a sitting position) приподнима́ться. *Sit up in bed*, сесть в посте́ли. **2,** (stay up late) не ложи́ться спать; заси́живаться до по́здней но́чи. *Sit up all night*, просиде́ть всю ночь. —**sit well with,** устра́ивать.

sit-down strike сидя́чая забасто́вка; италья́нская забасто́вка.

site *n.* **1,** (place where something is) местоположе́ние. **2,** (place where something takes place) ме́сто: *crash site*, ме́сто ава́рии. *Building site*, строи́тельная пло́щадка; стро́йка.

sitting *n.* **1,** (act of sitting) сиде́ние. **2,** (session) сеа́нс. *At one sitting*, в оди́н присе́ст. —*adj.* сидя́чий: *sitting position*, сидя́чее положе́ние. —**sitting room,** гости́ная.

situate *v.t.* располага́ть. —**situated,** *adj.* располо́женный.

situation *n.* **1,** (state of affairs) положе́ние; обстано́вка; ситуа́ция. *The international situation*, междунаро́дное положе́ние; междунаро́дная обстано́вка. *Awkward situation*, нело́вкое положе́ние. *My situation is this*, моя́ ситуа́ция такова́. **2,** (position of employment) ме́сто; рабо́та.

six *adj.* шесть. —*n.* **1,** (cardinal number) шесть. **2,** *cards* шестёрка.

sixfold *adj.* шестикра́тный. —*adv.* в шесть раз.

six hundred шестьсо́т. —**six-hundredth,** *adj.* шестисо́тый.

six-shooter *n., colloq.* шестизаря́дный револьве́р.

sixteen *n. & adj.* шестна́дцать. —**sixteenth,** *adj.* шестна́дцатый.

sixth *adj.* шесто́й. —*n.* **1,** (fraction) шеста́я; шеста́я часть. *One-sixth*, одна́ шеста́я; шеста́я часть. *One-sixth of the earth's surface*, шеста́я часть пове́рхности Земли́. **2,** *music* се́кста. —**sixth sense,** шесто́е чу́вство.

sixty *n. & adj.* шестьдеся́т. *In the 1960s*, в шестидеся́тых года́х. —**sixtieth,** *adj.* шестидеся́тый.

sizable *also,* **sizeable** *adj.* значи́тельный; поря́дочный.

size *n.* **1,** (largeness) величина́; разме́р: *the size of an object*, величина́/разме́р предме́та. *The size of an army*, чи́сленность а́рмии. *Small-size photograph*, фотогра́фия ма́лого форма́та. *Hailstones the size of one's fist*, град величино́й/разме́ром с (*or* в) кула́к. *Equal in size to…*, ра́вен по разме́рам (+ *dat.*). *Be twice the size of*, быть в два ра́за (*or* вдво́е) бо́льше (+ *gen.*). *Line up in size order*, стро́иться по ро́сту. **2,** (standard measure for shoes, clothes, etc.) разме́р; но́мер: *What size shoe do you wear?*, како́й разме́р/ но́мер о́буви вы но́сите? *I wear size eight*, я ношу́ восьмо́й разме́р/но́мер. *Two sizes too big*, вели́к на два разме́ра/но́мера. *Have you anything in a larger size?*, у вас есть что-нибудь бо́льшего разме́ра? **3,** *colloq.* (state of affairs): *That's about the size of it*, вот как обстои́т де́ло. —*v.t.* [*usu.* **size up**] оце́нивать. *Size up the situation*, оце́нивать обстано́вку; уясни́ть себе́ положе́ние. *Size someone up*, присма́триваться к кому-нибудь. *He's got you sized up*, он вас раскуси́л.

sizeable *adj.* = **sizable**.

sizzle *v.i.* шипе́ть.

skate *n.* **1,** (ice skate) конёк; (roller skate) ро́лик; конёк на ро́ликах. **2,** (fish) скат. —*v.i.* [*also,* **go skating**] ката́ться на конька́х *or* на ро́ликах. —**skater**, *n.* конькобе́жец.

skating *n.* ката́ние на конька́х; конькобе́жный спорт. *Speed skating*, скоростно́й бег на конька́х. —**skating rink,** като́к.

skedaddle *v.i., slang* улепётывать.

skein *n.* мото́к.

skeletal *adj.* скеле́тный.

skeleton *n.* **1,** *anat.* скеле́т; костя́к. **2,** (inner framework) о́стов; карка́с. —**skeleton key,** отмы́чка.

skeptic *also,* **sceptic** *n.* ске́птик.

skeptical *also,* **sceptical** *adj.* скепти́ческий. *I am skeptical*, я настро́ен(а) скепти́чески. *Be skeptical about,* относи́ться скепти́чески к. —**skeptically,** *adv.* скепти́чески.

skepticism *also,* **scepticism** *n.* скептици́зм.

sketch *n.* **1,** (rough drawing) набро́сок; эски́з; зарисо́вка. **2,** (short essay or outline) о́черк. **3,** (short play; skit) скетч. —*v.t.* **1,** (draw in rough outline) набра́сывать; зарисо́вывать. **2,** *fig.* (outline; describe) обрисо́вывать; оче́рчивать.

sketchy *adj.* схемати́ческий; пове́рхностный.

skewer *n.* ве́ртел.

ski *n.* лы́жа. —*adj.* лы́жный: *ski suit,* лы́жный костю́м. —*v.i.* ходи́ть на лы́жах. *Go skiing,* идти́/ пойти́ на лы́жах.

skid *v.i.* **1,** (slip because of lack of traction) заноси́ть (*impers.*): *The car skidded,* маши́ну занесло́. **2,** (slide instead of revolving) идти́ ю́зом.

skier *n.* лы́жник.

skiff *n.* скиф; я́лик.

skiing *n.* лы́жный спорт.

ski jump лы́жный трампли́н.

skilful *adj.* = **skillful**.

skill *n.* **1,** (expertness) мастерство́; уме́ние; иску́сство. *Chess is a game of skill,* ша́хматы тре́буют мастерства́. **2,** (a specific ability) на́вык; квалифика́ция. *Reading skills,* на́выки чте́ния.

skilled *adj.* **1,** (skillful) иску́сный: *skilled craftsmen,* иску́сные реме́сленники. **2,** (highly trained) квалифици́рованный: *both skilled and unskilled workers,* и квалифици́рованные и неквалифици́рованные рабо́чие.

skillet *n.* сковорода́; сковоро́дка.

skillful *also,* **skilful** *adj.* иску́сный; уме́лый. —**skillfully,** *adv.* иску́сно; уме́ло.

skim *v.t.* **1,** (remove from the top of a liquid) снима́ть: *skim the cream from the milk,* снима́ть сли́вки с молока́. **2,** (read superficially) (бе́гло) просма́тривать. **3,** (glide lightly over) скользи́ть по: *skim the surface,* скользи́ть по верха́м *or* по пове́рхности. —*v.i.* **1,** (glide) скользи́ть. **2,** *fol. by* **through** *or* **over** (read superficially) (бе́гло) просма́тривать.

skimmer *n.* шумо́вка.

skim milk сня́тое *or* обезжи́ренное молоко́.

skimp *v.i.* скупи́ться; эконо́мничать.

skimpy *adj.* **1,** (meager) ску́дный. **2,** (not quite large enough) ку́цый.

skin *n.* **1,** (tissue covering the body) ко́жа. *Wear something next to the skin,* наде́ть что́-нибудь на го́лое те́ло. **2,** (hide; pelt) ко́жа; шку́ра. **3,** (thin skin, as of a sausage) ко́жица. **4,** (rind; peel) кожура́; ко́рка. *Potato skins,* карто́фельная шелуха́; карто́фельные очи́стки. **5,** (film on the surface of milk) пе́нка. **6,** (vessel for holding liquids) мех. —*adj.* ко́жный: *skin disease,* ко́жная боле́знь. *Skin rash,* накожная сыпь. *Skin cancer,* рак ко́жи. —*v.t.* **1,** (remove the skin from) сдира́ть ко́жу с; обдира́ть; свежева́ть. **2,** (scrape; abrade) сса́живать: *skin one's knee,* сса́живать себе́ коле́но. —**by the skin of one's teeth,** с грехо́м попола́м. —**save one's skin,** спасти́ свою́ шку́ру. —**skin and bones,** ко́жа да ко́сти. —**soaked to the skin,** промо́кший до косте́й.

skin-deep *adj.* пове́рхностный.

skin diver аквалангист. —**skin diving,** подво́дное пла́вание (с аквала́нгом).

skinflint *n., colloq.* скря́га; скопидо́м; сквалы́га.

skinny *adj.* то́щий; худо́й; сухоща́вый; сухопа́рый.

skip *v.i.* **1,** (move with light springing steps) бежа́ть вприпры́жку. **2,** (move quickly from point to point) переска́кивать: *skip from place to place,* переска́кивать с одного́ ме́ста на друго́е. **3,** *fol. by* **over** (jump over; omit) переска́кивать: *skip over a puddle/page,* переска́кивать лу́жу/страни́цу. —*v.t.* **1,** (jump over) переска́кивать. *Skip rope,* пры́гать че́рез скака́лку. **2,** (omit; bypass) пропуска́ть: *skip a line,* пропуска́ть стро́чку. *Skip a grade,* переска́кивать че́рез класс. *My heart skipped a beat,* у меня́ се́рдце ёкнуло. **3,** *colloq.* (depart hurriedly from) удра́ть от: *skip town,* удра́ть от го́рода. —*n.* прыжо́к; скачо́к.

skipper *n.* шки́пер.

skirmish *n.* сты́чка; схва́тка; перестре́лка. —*v.i.* перестре́ливаться.

skirt *n.* ю́бка. —*v.t.* (go around; avoid) огиба́ть; обходи́ть (что́-нибудь) стороно́й.

skit *n.* скетч; сце́нка.

skittish *adj.* норови́стый.

skittles *n.* ке́гли.

skua *n.* большо́й помо́рник.

skulduggery *also,* **skullduggery** *n.* надува́тельство.

skulk *v.i.* кра́сться.

skull *n.* че́реп. *Fracture one's skull,* проломи́ть себе́ го́лову *or* че́реп. *Skull and crossbones,* че́реп да ко́сти.

skullcap *n.* ермо́лка; тюбете́йка; скуфья́.

skullduggery *n.* = **skulduggery**.

skunk *n.* **1,** (animal) скунс; воню́чка. **2,** *colloq.* (vile person) гад.

sky *n.* не́бо: *high in the sky,* высоко́ в не́бе. *Appear in the sky,* появи́ться на не́бе. *Fall from the sky,* па́дать с не́ба. —**out of a clear blue sky,** ни с того́ ни с сего́; как снег на́ голову. —**praise to the skies,** превозноси́ть до небе́с.

sky-high *adv.* до небе́с; высоко́-высоко́.

skylark *n.* полево́й жа́воронок.

skylight *n.* застеклённая кры́ша; светово́й люк; фона́рь.

skyline *n.* очерта́ние небоскрёбов на фо́не не́ба.

skyrocket *v.i.* подска́кивать.

skyscraper *n.* небоскрёб.

skyward *adv.* к не́бу; в не́бо.

slab *n.* плита́.

slack *adj.* **1,** (not taut) сла́бый; свобо́дный. **2,** (slow; sluggish) ме́дленный: *slack pace,* ме́дленный темп. **3,** (weak; lax) сла́бый: *slack discipline,* сла́бая дисципли́на. **4,** (marked by a slowdown in activity) вя́лый. *Slack period,* глуха́я пора́. —*n.* слабина́: *take up the slack,* выбира́ть слабину́. —*v.i.* [*usu.* **slack off**] ослабева́ть; спада́ть.

slacken *v.t.* **1,** (loosen; relax) ослабля́ть. **2,** (slow down) замедля́ть. —*v.i.* ослабева́ть.

slacker *n.* лентя́й; прогу́льщик.

slacks *n.pl.* брю́ки.

slag *n.* шлак.

slake *v.t.* **1,** (quench, as thirst) утоля́ть. **2,** (treat with water, as lime) гаси́ть.

slalom *n.* сла́лом.

slam *v.t.* **1,** (shut with force) хло́пать; захло́пывать: *slam the door in someone's face,* хло́пнуть две́рью *or* захло́пнуть дверь пе́ред чьи́м-нибудь но́сом. **2,** (throw or apply with force) хло́пать: *slam the book on the table,* хло́пнуть кни́гой по́ столу. *Slam down the telephone,* бро́сить тру́бку. *Slam on the brakes,* ре́зко тормози́ть. —*v.i.* **1,** (shut noisily) захло́пываться. **2,** *fol. by* **into** (run into) вре́заться в; налете́ть на. —*n.* **1,** (act of slamming) хло́панье. **2,** *cards* шлем.

slander *n.* клевета́. —*v.t.* клевета́ть на. —**slanderer,** *n.* клеветни́к. —**slanderous,** *adj.* клеветни́ческий.

slang *n.* жарго́н. —*adj.* жарго́нный.

slant *v.t.* **1,** (set at an angle) наклоня́ть. **2,** *colloq.* (write so as to express a bias) искажа́ть. —*v.i.* коси́ться. —*n.* накло́н; укло́н; склон. *On a slant,* ко́со.

slanted *adj.* (biased) пристра́стный; тенденцио́зный.

slanting *adj.* **1,** (oblique) накло́нный; пока́тый; косо́й. *Slanting position,* накло́нное положе́ние. *Slanting roof,* пока́тая кры́ша. **2,** (of eyes) раско́сый.

slap *v.t.* шлёпать; хло́пать. *Slap someone's face,* дать пощёчину (+ *dat.*). —*n.* шлепо́к. *Slap in the face,* пощёчину.

slapdash *adj.* безала́берный; неря́шливый. —*adv.* кое-ка́к; на ско́рую ру́ку; спустя́ рукава́.

slapstick *n.* фарс.

slash *v.t.* **1,** (cut severely) поре́зать; руби́ть. *Slash tires,* вспа́рывать ши́ны. *Slash one's wrists,* вскрыть себе́ на рука́х ве́ны. **2,** (reduce drastically) уре́зывать. —*n.* **1,** (sweeping stroke) взмах. **2,** (sign [/]) дробь: 8/10, во́семь дробь де́сять.

slashing *adj.* ре́зкий; хлёсткий: *slashing (verbal) attack,* ре́зкий/хлёсткий вы́пад.

slat *n.* пла́нка; пласти́нка.

slate *n.* **1,** (mineral) сла́нец; ши́фер. **2,** (writing plate) гри́фельная доска́. **3,** (list of candidates) спи́сок кандида́тов. —*adj.* **1,** (of slate) сла́нцевый; ши́ферный. **2,** (slate-colored) цве́та сла́нца. —*v.t.* [*usu. passive*] намеча́ть: *He is slated to become the new prime*

minister, он наме́чен в но́вые премье́р-мини́стры. —**wipe the slate clean,** всё прости́ть.

slattern *n.* **1,** (slob) неря́ха; грязну́ля. **2,** (slut) шлю́ха.

slaughter *n.* **1,** (of animals) забо́й; убо́й. *Lead to the slaughter,* вести́ на убо́й. **2,** (massacre) резня́; бо́йня; избие́ние. *The slaughter of thousands of people,* уби́йство ты́сяч люде́й. —*v.t.* **1,** (kill, as animals) забива́ть; ре́зать; коло́ть; зака́лывать. **2,** (massacre) выреза́ть.

slaughterhouse *n.* бо́йня; скотобо́йня.

Slav *n.* славяни́н. *The Slavs,* славя́не.

slave *n.* раб. —*adj.* ра́бский; нево́льничий. *Slave labor,* ра́бский труд. *Slave market,* нево́льничий ры́нок. *Slave trade,* работорго́вля. —*v.i.* труди́ться. *Slave away,* тяну́ть ля́мку. *Slave over,* корпе́ть над. —**slaveowner,** *n.* рабовладе́лец.

slaver *n.* слюни́. —*v.i.* пуска́ть слю́ни.

slavery *n.* ра́бство. *They were sold into slavery,* они́ бы́ли про́даны в ра́бство.

Slavic *adj.* славя́нский. —**Slavicist,** *n.* слави́ст.

slavish *adj.* ра́бский: *slavish obedience,* ра́бское повинове́ние.

Slavonic *adj.* славя́нский.

Slavophile *n.* славянофи́л.

slaw *n.* = coleslaw.

slay *v.t.* убива́ть. —**slayer,** *n.* уби́йца.

sleazy *adj.* **1,** (flimsy) непро́чный. **2,** (run-down) убо́гий.

sled *n.* **1,** (for traveling over distances) са́ни. *Dog sled,* на́рты. **2,** (for children) са́нки. —*v.i.* [*usu.* **go sledding**] ката́ться на са́нках.

sledge *n.* са́ни; са́нки.

sledgehammer *n.* мо́лот; кува́лда.

sleek *adj.* прили́занный.

sleep *v.i.* спать. *Go to sleep,* ложи́ться спать. *I slept badly,* мне пло́хо спало́сь. —*n.* сон: *deep sleep,* глубо́кий сон. *Have a good night's sleep,* вы́спаться. —**put to sleep, 1,** (put to bed) укла́дывать (в посте́ль). **2,** (make drowsy) усыпля́ть; нагоня́ть сон на. **3,** (put to death, as a sick animal) усыпля́ть. —**sleep it off,** проспа́ться. —**sleep through,** просыпа́ть. *Sleep through a lecture,* проспа́ть всю ле́кцию. —**sleep with,** спать с.

sleeper *n.* **1,** (one who sleeps): *He is a light/heavy sleeper,* он чу́тко/кре́пко спит. **2,** (sleeping car) спа́льный ваго́н. **3,** *Brit.* (railroad tie) шпа́ла.

sleepiness *n.* сонли́вость.

sleeping *adj.* **1,** (asleep) спя́щий. **2,** (of or for sleep) спа́льный. —**sleeping bag,** спа́льный мешо́к. —**sleeping car,** спа́льный ваго́н. —**sleeping pill,** снотво́рная табле́тка. —**sleeping sickness,** со́нная боле́знь.

sleepless *adj.* бессо́нный. *Spend a sleepless night,* провести́ бессо́нную ночь; провести́ ночь без сна.

sleepwalker *n.* луна́тик. —**sleepwalking,** *n.* луна́тизм.

sleepy *adj.* со́нный; сонли́вый. —**be sleepy,** хоте́ть спать: *I am sleepy,* я хочу́ спать.

sleepy-eyed *adj.* за́спанный.

sleepyhead *n.* со́ня; со́нная тете́ря.

sleet *n.* дождь со сне́гом.

sleeve *n.* рука́в: *short sleeves,* коро́ткие рукава́. —**have something up one's sleeve,** име́ть что́-то на уме́; замышля́ть что́-то.

sleeveless *adj.* без рукаво́в; безрука́вный. *Sleeveless jacket,* безрука́вка.

sleigh *n.* са́ни; са́нки. —*v.i.* [*usu.* **go sleighing** *or* **sleigh riding**] ката́ться на са́нках. —**sleigh bells,** бубе́нчики.

sleight of hand ло́вкость рук.

slender *adj.* **1,** (thin) то́нкий. **2,** (gracefully slim) стро́йный. **3,** (meager) ску́дный. **4,** (slight; feeble, as of hope) сла́бый.

sleuth *n.* **1,** (detective) сы́щик; шпик; ище́йка. **2,** (bloodhound) ище́йка.

slew *n., colloq.* ма́сса; у́йма.

slice *n.* ло́мтик. *Slice of bread,* кусо́к хле́ба. —*v.t.* **1,** (divide into slices) ре́зать; нареза́ть. **2,** *fol. by* **off** (cut off) отреза́ть. **3,** *sports* ре́зать; среза́ть (мяч).

slick *adj.* **1,** (slippery) ско́льзкий. **2,** (sleek, as of hair) прили́занный. **3,** *colloq.* (clever; tricky) хи́трый. —*v.t.* [*usu.* **slick down**] прилажи́ивать. —*n.* покрыва́ло: *oil slick,* нефтяно́е покрыва́ло.

slide *v.i.* **1,** (slip; glide) скользи́ть: *slide on the ice,* скользи́ть по льду. *Slide down a pole,* соска́льзывать по шесту́. *Slide down the banister,* съе́хать по пери́лам. **2,** (move easily, as of a drawer) задвига́ться; выдвига́ться. **3,** *fol. by* **off** (slip off) соска́льзывать. —*v.t.* задвига́ть: *slide the suitcase under the bed,* задвига́ть чемода́н под крова́ть. —*n.* **1,** (act of sliding) скольже́ние. **2,** (inclined track) скат. **3,** (avalanche) обва́л; о́ползень. **4,** (transparency) диапозити́в. **5,** (specimen holder) предме́тное стекло́.

slide rule логарифми́ческая лине́йка.

sliding *adj.* скользя́щий; задвижно́й; выдвижно́й; раздвижно́й. *Sliding door,* раздвижна́я дверь. *Sliding scale,* скользя́щая шкала́. —**sliding board,** го́рка.

slight *adj.* **1,** (not great) небольшо́й: *a slight increase,* небольшо́е увеличе́ние. *Cause slight damage,* причиня́ть незначи́тельный уро́н. *The risk is slight,* риск невели́к. **2,** (not severe or heavy) лёгкий: *a slight cold,* лёгкий на́сморк. *A slight accent,* лёгкий акце́нт. *A slight temperature,* повы́шенная температу́ра. **3,** (short; brief) небольшо́й: *a slight pause,* небольшо́й переры́в. **4,** (slender; slim) то́нкий. —*v.t.* **1,** (neglect) пренебрега́ть. **2,** (treat discourteously) обижа́ть; трети́ровать. —*n.* оби́да; щелчо́к.

slightest *adj.* мале́йший: *I haven't the slightest idea,* я не име́ю ни мале́йшего поня́тия. *Not in the slightest,* ничу́ть; ни на йо́ту.

slighting *adj.* оби́дный: *slighting remark,* оби́дное замеча́ние.

slightly *adv.* слегка́; немно́го. *Slightly wounded,* легко́ ра́неный. *Be slightly damaged,* получи́ть небольши́е поврежде́ния. *Bend over slightly,* слегка́ нагну́ться.

slim *adj.* **1,** (thin; slender) то́нкий; стро́йный. **2,** (mea-

ger) ску́дный. **3,** (poor, as of a chance) сла́бый. —*v.i.* [*usu.* **slim down**] худе́ть.

slime *n.* **1,** (mud) грязь. **2,** (animal secretion) слизь.

slimy *adj.* **1,** (covered with slime) сли́зистый. **2,** (repulsive) га́дкий.

sling *n.* **1,** (support for an injured arm) пе́ревязь: *He has his arm in a sling,* у него́ рука́ на пе́ревязи. **2,** (rifle strap) руже́йный реме́нь. **3,** (device for shooting stones) праща́. **4,** = **slingshot.** —*v.t.* броса́ть; швыря́ть. *Sling a gun over one's shoulder,* заки́нуть ружьё за плечо́. *Sling mud at,* забра́сывать (кого́-нибудь) гря́зью.

slingshot *n.* рога́тка.

slink *v.i.* кра́сться; идти́ кра́дучись. *Slink away,* ускольза́ть.

slip *v.i.* **1,** (lose one's footing) поскользну́ться: *slip on the ice,* поскользну́ться на льду. **2,** (slide out of place) скользи́ть. *The knife slipped,* нож скользну́л. *Slip off the table,* соскользну́ть со стола́. *Slip from one's fingers,* вы́скользнуть из па́льцев. **3,** (move quickly or furtively) скользну́ть. *Slip in/into,* проска́льзывать (в); вкра́дываться (в); прокра́дываться (в). *Slip out (of),* выска́льзывать (из). *Slip away (from),* ускольза́ть (от); улизну́ть (из). *Slip by/past,* скользну́ть (ми́мо); проска́льзывать (ми́мо). **4,** *fol. by* **over, down to,** *etc.* (run a quick errand) сбе́гать (в). **5,** *fol. by* **into** (put on quickly) наки́нуть. **6,** *fol. by* **by** (pass imperceptibly, as of time) проноси́ться; промелькну́ть. **7,** (decline in vigor) сдава́ть. —*v.t.* **1,** (place in one quick motion) надева́ть: *slip a ring on someone's finger,* наде́ть кому́-нибудь кольцо́ на па́лец; *slip a pair of handcuffs on someone,* наде́ть на кого́-нибудь нару́чники. **2,** (pass stealthily) сова́ть; подсо́вывать; подбра́сывать; подкла́дывать. *Slip someone a ruble/ a note/,* су́нуть кому́-нибудь рубль; подбро́сить кому́-нибудь запи́ску. *Slip a message under the door,* подсу́нуть сообще́ние под дверь. **3,** *fol. by* **on** (put on quickly) наки́нуть. **4,** *fol. by* **off** (take off quickly) сбро́сить. **5,** (escape, as one's mind) вы́скочить; вы́лететь (из головы́). —*n.* **1,** (mistake; lapse) оши́бка. *Slip of the tongue,* обмо́лвка; огово́рка. **2,** (woman's undergarment) комбина́ция. *Your slip is showing,* у вас видна́ ни́жняя ю́бка. **3,** (pillowcase) на́волочка. **4,** (piece of paper) листо́к (бума́ги). *Order slip,* бланк зака́за. *Sales slip,* квита́нция. **5,** (plant cutting) черено́к. **6,** (docking place) прича́л. —**give someone the slip,** ускольза́ть от; отрыва́ться от. —**let slip, 1,** (miss, as an opportunity) упуска́ть. **2,** (utter unintentionally) отпуска́ть. —**slip through someone's fingers,** проскочи́ть *or* проскользну́ть у кого́-нибудь ме́жду па́льцами (*or* па́льцев). —**slip up,** *colloq.* оплоша́ть.

slipcover *n.* чехо́л.

slipknot *n.* скользя́щий у́зел.

slippage *n.* скольже́ние; проска́льзывание.

slipper *n.* (дома́шняя) ту́фля; шлёпанец.

slippery *adj.* **1,** (smooth; slick) ско́льзкий. **2,** (shifty; elusive) увёртливый; изворо́тливый.

slipshod *adj.* небре́жный; неря́шливый. *In a slipshod manner,* спустя́ рукава́.

slip-up *n.*, *colloq.* неувязка.

slit *n.* щель; разрез; прорез; прорезь. —*v.t.* разрезать. *Slit someone's throat,* перерезать горло (+ *dat.*). *Slit open an envelope,* вскрыть конверт. —**slit trench,** щель.

slither *v.i.* **1,** (slide) скользить. **2,** (move like a snake) ползти.

sliver *n.* щепка; лучина.

slob *n.*, *slang* неряха; грязнуля; растрёпа.

slobber *v.i.* пускать слюни. —*n.* слюни.

sloe *n.* тёрн.

slogan *n.* лозунг.

sloop *n.* шлюп.

slop *n.* помои. —*v.t.* расплёскивать. —**slop basin,** полоскательница.

slope *n.* склон; наклон; уклон; откос; скат; спуск. *Steep slope,* крутой спуск; круча; крутизна. —*v.i.* иметь наклон. *Slope downward,* идти *or* спускаться под уклон. *Slope forty degrees,* иметь наклон в сорок градусов. —**sloping,** *adj.* наклонный; покатый; пологий; отлогий.

sloppy *adj.* **1,** (muddy) грязный. **2,** (untidy; slipshod) неряшливый. —**sloppiness,** *n.* неряшливость.

slosh *v.i.* шлёпать (по грязи).

slot *n.* **1,** (long opening) щель. **2,** (round opening for a coin) отверстие.

sloth *n.* **1,** (animal) ленивец. **2,** (indolence) леность. —**slothful,** *adj.* ленивый; инертный.

slot machine игровой автомат.

slouch *v.i.* сутулиться; горбиться. —*n.* **1,** (bent posture) сутулость. **2,** (incompetent person): *He is no slouch,* он не лыком шит.

slough *v.t.* **1,** (shed) сбрасывать. **2,** *cards* сбрасывать. —*v.i.* [*usu.* **slough off**] сходить; шелушиться.

Slovak *n.* **1,** (person) словак. **2,** (language) словацкий язык. —*adj.* словацкий.

Slovene *n.* словенец. —**Slovenian,** *adj.* словенский. —*n.* словенский язык.

slovenly *adj.* неряшливый. —**slovenliness,** *n.* неряшливость; неряшество.

slow *adj.* **1,** (not fast) медленный: *slow pace,* медленный ход. *On a slow fire,* на медленном огне. *Be slow in replying,* замедлить с ответом. **2,** (behind time, as of a clock): *My watch is slow,* мои часы отстают. **3,** (dull-witted) тупой. —*adv.* медленно. —*v.t.* [*usu.* **slow down**] замедлять. —*v.i.* [*usu.* **slow down**] замедлять ход; замедляться.

slowdown *n.* замедление.

slowly *adv.* медленно.

slow motion замедленная съёмка. —**slow-motion,** *adj.* замедленный.

slowness *n.* медленность.

slowpoke *n.*, *colloq.* медлительный человек.

slow-witted *adj.* тупой; непонятливый; несообразительный.

sludge *n.* грязь; ил.

slug *n.* **1,** (bullet) пуля. **2,** (object used in place of a coin) жетон. **3,** *printing* шпон. **4,** (mollusk) слизняк; слизень. —*v.t.* (punch) тузить.

sluggard *n.* лентяй; лежебока.

sluggish *adj.* вялый; медлительный; инертный. —**sluggishly,** *adv.* вяло. —**sluggishness,** *n.* вялость.

sluice *n.* шлюз. —**sluice gate,** шлюзные ворота.

slum *n.* трущоба.

slumber *n.* сон. —*v.i.* спать; дремать.

slump *n.* спад. —*v.i.* **1,** (fall heavily) валиться. *Slump into a chair,* опуститься в кресло. **2,** (decline suddenly) резко падать.

slung shot кистень.

slur *v.t.* **1,** (pronounce indistinctly) глотать (слова). *His speech is slurred,* у него язык заплетается. **2,** [*usu.* **slur over**] (pass over lightly) смазывать. **3,** (disparage) порочить. —*n.* **1,** (stain) пятно (на репутации). *Cast slurs on someone's reputation,* чернить чью-нибудь репутацию. **2,** (disparaging remark) инсинуация. **3,** *music* лига.

slush *n.* слякоть; талый снег. —**slushy,** *adj.* слякотный.

slut *n.* **1,** (slovenly woman) неряха. **2,** (loose woman) шлюха.

sly *adj.* хитрый. —**on the sly,** тайком; потихоньку.

slyly *adv.* хитро.

smack *v.t.* **1,** (slap) хлопать; шлёпать. **2,** *Smack one's lips,* чмокать губами. —*v.i.* [*usu.* **smack of**] попахивать (+ *instr.*); отдавать (+ *instr.*). *It smacks of favoritism,* это попахивает протекционизмом. *Smack of dishonesty,* отдавать нечестностью. —*n.* **1,** (slap) шлепок. **2,** (trace; suggestion) привкус. —*adv.*, *colloq.* прямо: *run smack into a tree,* врезаться прямо в дерево.

small *adj.* **1,** (little; not large) маленький; небольшой. *Small child/house/town,* маленький ребёнок/дом/город. *Small print,* мелкий шрифт. *Small income,* небольшой доход. *On a small scale,* в небольшом масштабе. *She is a small eater,* она мало ест. *These shoes are too small,* эти ботинки (мне) малы. **2,** (operating on a limited scale) мелкий: *a small business,* мелкое предприятие; *small depositor,* мелкий вкладчик. **3,** *in small letter,* маленькая *or* строчная буква. —*n.*, *in small of the back,* поясница.

small arms стрелковое оружие. *Small arms fire,* огонь из стрелкового оружия.

small-bore *adj.* малокалиберный.

small change мелкие деньги; разменная монета.

small fry *colloq.* мелкая сошка; *collective* мелюзга; мелкота.

small intestine тонкая кишка.

small-minded *adj.* мелкий; мелочный.

smallpox *n.* (чёрная) оспа.

small talk салонный разговор.

smart *adj.* **1,** (bright; clever) умный. **2,** (brisk; vigorous) быстрый: *at a smart pace,* быстрым ходом. **3,** (stylish) шикарный; нарядный. —*v.i.* **1,** (sting; burn) саднить; щипать (*impers.*). *My eyes are smarting,* у меня щипит глаза. **2,** (suffer keenly) мучиться. —**smart aleck,** *colloq.* умник.

smarten *v.t.* [*usu.* **smarten up**] **1,** (improve in appearance) прихорашивать. **2,** (make more aware) вразумлять. —*v.i.* [*usu.* **smarten up**] образумиться.

smartly *adv.* **1,** (stylishly) шикарно. **2,** (with brisk and precise movements) чётко.

smash *v.t.* **1,** (break to pieces) разбива́ть: *smash a vase*, разби́ть ва́зу. *Smash up a car*, разби́ть маши́ну. *Smash down a door*, вы́ломать дверь. *Smash something to the ground*, разби́ть что́-нибудь о зе́млю. **2,** (defeat utterly) разбива́ть; громи́ть. —*v.i.* **1,** (break to pieces) разбива́ться. **2,** *fol. by* **into** (crash into) вре́заться в; налете́ть на. —*n.* (hard blow) тума́к.

smash hit *The play was a smash hit*, пье́са име́ла огро́мный успе́х.

smashing *adj., colloq.* потряса́ющий.

smattering *n.* пове́рхностное зна́ние.

smear *v.t.* **1,** (cover with grease, paint, etc.) ма́зать. **2,** (spread on; apply) нама́зывать; разма́зывать. **3,** (soil) ма́зать; па́чкать. **4,** (smudge, as ink) разма́зывать. **5,** (defame) черни́ть. —*v.i.* разма́зываться. —*n.* **1,** (spot; smudge) пятно́. **2,** *med.* мазо́к. **3,** (slander) клевета́.

smell *v.i.* **1,** (have a certain odor) па́хнуть: *smell good*, хорошо́ па́хнуть. *He smells bad*, от него́ пло́хо па́хнет. *Smell of fish*, па́хнуть ры́бой. **2,** (be malodorous) попа́хивать. —*v.t.* **1,** (catch the smell of) чу́вствовать за́пах (+ *gen.*). *I don't smell anything*, я не чу́вствую никако́го за́паха. **2,** (test by smelling; sniff) ню́хать: *Smell this perfume!*, поню́хайте э́ти духи́! **3,** (sense the presence of) чу́ять: *smell a rat*, чу́ять недо́брое. —*n.* за́пах: *a strange smell*, стра́нный за́пах. *There is a smell of smoke*, па́хнет ды́мом. —**sense of smell, 1,** (of a person) обоня́ние. **2,** (of an animal) чутьё; нюх.

smelling salts ню́хательная соль.

smelly *adj.* ду́рно па́хнущий; злово́нный.

smelt *n.* (fish) ко́рюшка. —*v.t.* (fuse; melt) пла́вить; выплавля́ть. —**smelter,** *n.* плави́льщик. —**smelting,** *n.* пла́вка.

smidgen *also,* **smidgeon** *n., colloq.* чу́точка.

smile *v.i.* улыба́ться. *Fortune smiled on them*, им улыбну́лось сча́стье. —*n.* улы́бка.

smirk *n.* усме́шка. —*v.i.* ухмыля́ться.

smite *v.t.* **1,** (strike; kill; afflict) поража́ть. **2,** (affect strongly) охва́тывать: *smitten with love*, охва́ченный любо́вью. **3,** (captivate) увлека́ть; восхища́ть.

smith *n.* кузне́ц.

smithereens *n.pl.,* **in smash to smithereens,** разбива́ть вдре́безги.

smithy *n.* ку́зница.

smock *n.* блу́за; хала́т.

smog *n.* ды́мная мгла; «смог».

smoke *n.* **1,** (vapor) дым: *tobacco smoke*, таба́чный дым. **2,** (an instance of smoking): *have a smoke*, покури́ть. —*adj.* дымово́й: *smoke signal*, дымово́й сигна́л. —*v.i.* **1,** (indulge in smoking) кури́ть. *No smoking!*, не кури́ть! *I don't smoke*, я не курю́; я не куря́щий. *Do you mind if I smoke?*, вы не возража́ете, е́сли я закурю́? **2,** (give off smoke) дыми́ть; дыми́ться; кури́ться. —*v.t.* **1,** (a cigarette, pipe, opium, etc.) кури́ть. *Smoke two packs of cigarettes a day*, кури́ть *or* выку́ривать две па́чки сигаре́т в день. **2,** (treat or preserve with smoke) копти́ть. **3,** *fol. by* **out** (drive out) выку́ривать. —**go up in smoke,** взлете́ть на во́здух.

smoked *adj.* копчёный: *smoked fish*, копчёная ры́ба. *Smoked salmon*, сёмга.

smoke detector пожа́рная сигнализа́ция.

smokehouse *n.* копти́льня.

smoke pot дымова́я ша́шка.

smoker *n.* куря́щий; кури́льщик.

smoke screen дымова́я заве́са.

smokestack *n.* дымова́я труба́.

smoking *n.* **1,** (of a cigarette, cigar, etc.) куре́ние. **2,** (treatment with smoke) копче́ние. —**smoking car,** ваго́н для куря́щих.

smoky *adj.* ды́мный. —**smoky quartz,** ды́мчатый кварц.

smolder *also,* **smoulder** *v.i.* **1,** (burn) тлеть. **2,** (exist in a suppressed state) таи́ться. *Smoldering resentment*, затаённая зло́ба.

smooth *adj.* **1,** (not rough) гла́дкий: *smooth surface/skin*, гла́дкая пове́рхность/ко́жа. **2,** (not jerky) пла́вный; споко́йный. *Smooth gait*, пла́вная похо́дка. *Smooth trip/flight*, споко́йный рейс. —*v.t.* **1,** (make smooth) сгла́живать; прига́живать. **2,** *fol. by* **out** (remove the wrinkles from) разгла́живать; расправля́ть. *Smooth out the wrinkles*, расправля́ть скла́дки. **3,** *fol. by* **out** (make even; level) выра́внивать. **4,** *fol. by* **out** *or* **over** (make less acute) сгла́живать. *Smooth out our differences*, ула́живать на́ши разногла́сия.

smoothbore *adj.* гладкоство́льный.

smoothly *adv.* гла́дко: *go smoothly*, проходи́ть гла́дко.

smoothness *n.* гла́дкость.

smooth-spoken *adj.* сладкоречи́вый.

smorgasbord *n.* шве́дский стол.

smother *v.t.* души́ть; удуша́ть. —*v.i.* задыха́ться.

smoulder *v.* = **smolder.**

smudge *n.* пятно́. —*v.t.* разма́зывать. —*v.i.* разма́зываться. —**smudge pot,** дымова́я ша́шка.

smug *adj.* самодово́льный.

smuggle *v.t.* **1,** (bring into a country illegally) провози́ть (контраба́ндой). **2,** (convey surreptitiously) проноси́ть: *smuggle a gun into prison*, проноси́ть пистоле́т в тюрьму́. —**smuggler,** *n.* контрабанди́ст. —**smuggling,** *n.* контраба́нда.

smugness *n.* самодово́льство.

smut *n.* **1,** (sooty matter) са́жа. **2,** (plant disease) головня́. **3,** (obscene writing) непристо́йность.

snack *n.* заку́ска. *Have a snack*, закуси́ть. —**snack bar,** заку́сочная; буфе́т.

snaffle *n.* тре́нзель.

snafu *n., slang* пу́таница.

snag *n.* **1,** (tree stump sticking out of the water) коря́га. **2,** *fig.* (hitch) заце́пка; зами́нка; загво́здка. *Hit a snag*, наскочи́ть на мель. —*v.t.* зацепля́ть. —*v.i.* зацепля́ться; задева́ть: *snag on a nail*, зацепля́ться/задева́ть за гвоздь.

snail *n.*ули́тка. —**at a snail's pace,** черепа́шьим ша́гом.

snake *n.* змея́. —*v.i.* змеи́ться. —**snake in the grass,** подколо́дная змея́.

snakebite *n.* уку́с змеи́.

snake charmer заклина́тель змей.

snap *v.i.* **1,** (break suddenly) ло́пнуть; порва́ться; оборва́ться. **2,** *fol. by* **at** (bite suddenly) ца́пать (за); (lunge at menacingly) огрыза́ться (на). **3,** (speak or retort sharply) отре́зать; отруби́ть; огрыза́ться. *Snap at someone*, огрыза́ться на кого́-нибудь. **4,** *Snap to attention*, вы́тянуться в сто́йке «сми́рно». —*v.t.* **1,** (cause to make a sharp sound) щёлкать: *snap one's fingers*, щёлкать па́льцами. **2,** (release, as a shutter) щёлкать (затво́ром *or* затво́р). **3,** (take, as a picture) сде́лать (сни́мок). **4,** (break) порва́ть; оборва́ть. **5,** *fol. by* **up** (buy quickly) раскупа́ть; расхва́тывать. —*n.* **1,** (sharp sound) щелчо́к. **2,** (fastening device) застёжка; кно́пка. **3,** (motion with the fingers) щелчо́к. **4,** (brief spell) полоса́. *Cold snap*, похолода́ние. **5,** (cookie) пря́ник: *ginger snap*, имби́рный пря́ник. **6,** *slang* (easy task) пустяки́; ерунда́. —*adj.* скоропали́тельный: *snap judgment*, скоропали́тельное сужде́ние. —**snap back,** оправля́ться. —**snap out of,** избавля́ться от. —**snap shut, 1,** *transitively,* защёлкивать. **2,** *intransitively,* защёлкиваться.

snapdragon *n.* льви́ный зев; льви́ная пасть.

snappy *adj.* **1,** (brisk) бы́стрый; живо́й. **2,** (cold and invigorating) холоднова́тый. **3,** *colloq.* (stylish) бро́ский. —**make it snappy!,** жи́во!; поскоре́е!

snapshot *n.* сни́мок; фотосни́мок.

snare *n.* сило́к; тенёта. —*v.t.* **1,** (catch; trap) пойма́ть в лову́шку. **2,** (entice; inveigle) зама́нивать; завлека́ть.

snarl *v.i.* **1,** (growl) рыча́ть; огрыза́ться. **2,** (become entangled) запу́тываться. —*v.t.* запу́тывать. —*n.* **1,** (growl) рыча́ние. **2,** (tangle) пу́таница.

snatch *v.t.* **1,** (grab) хвата́ть; выхва́тывать; вырыва́ть; урыва́ть. **2,** *fol. by* **up** (buy quickly) раскупа́ть; расхва́тывать. —*v.i.* [*usu.* **snatch at**] хвата́ться за; ухвати́ться за. —*n.* **1,** (act of snatching) хва́тка. **2,** *weightlifting* рыво́к. **3,** (bit) обры́вок; отры́вок: *Snatches of a conversation*, обры́вки/отры́вки разгово́ра. **4,** (brief period of time): *work in snatches*, рабо́тать уры́вками.

snazzy *adj., slang* бро́ский; шика́рный.

sneak *v.i.* кра́сться. *Sneak into*, вкра́дываться в; прокра́дываться в; лезть в. *Sneak out of*, вы́скользнуть из. *Sneak up to*, подкра́дываться к. —*v.t.* проноси́ть; прота́скивать. *Sneak a gun into school*, проноси́ть пистоле́т в шко́лу. —*adj.* внеза́пный: *sneak attack*, внеза́пное нападе́ние. —*n.* пройдо́ха.

sneakers *n.pl.* та́почки; ке́ды; кроссо́вки.

sneaky *adj.* лука́вый; проны́рливый.

sneer *n.* (презри́тельная) усме́шка. —*v.i.* **1,** (make a sneer) усмеха́ться. **2,** *fol. by* **at** (express contempt for) насмеха́ться (над).

sneeze *v.i.* чиха́ть. —*n.* чих.

snicker *v.i.* хихи́кать. —*n.* хихи́канье.

snide *adj.* язви́тельный; ехи́дный.

sniff *v.i.* шмы́гать но́сом. —*v.t.* **1,** (breathe in forcibly) вдыха́ть. **2,** (try to smell by sniffing) ню́хать. **3,** *fol. by* **out** (detect by sniffing; uncover) разню́хивать; выню́хивать. —*n.* вдох но́сом.

sniffle *v.i.* **1,** (breathe with difficulty) сопе́ть; шмы́гать но́сом. **2,** (cry intermittently) всхли́пывать. —**sniffles,** *n.pl.* на́сморк.

snip *v.t.* **1,** (cut; slip) ре́зать. **2,** *fol. by* **off** (cut off) отреза́ть; отхва́тывать; отпа́рывать. —*n.* **1,** (piece snipped off) кусо́чек; обре́зок. **2,** (stroke) взмах; движе́ние: *with one snip of the scissors*, одни́м взма́хом/движе́нием но́жниц.

snipe *n.* кули́к; бека́с. —**great snipe,** ду́пель.

sniper *n.* сна́йпер.

snitch *v.t., slang* (swipe) стащи́ть. —*v.i.* [*usu.* **snitch on**] *slang* (tell on) я́бедничать (на).

snivel *v.i.* **1,** (run at the nose) распуска́ть со́пли. **2,** (complain; whine) хны́кать; распуска́ть ню́ни.

snob *n.* сноб. —**snobbery,** *n.* сноби́зм. —**snobbish,** *adj.* чва́нный; спеси́вый. —**snobbishness,** *n.* сноби́зм.

snoop *v.i., colloq.* подгля́дывать; подслу́шивать. —**snoop around,** ры́скать; шныря́ть.

snooty *adj., colloq.* чва́нный; спеси́вый.

snooze *v.i., colloq.* вздремну́ть. —*n., colloq.* коро́ткий сон.

snore *v.i.* храпе́ть. —*n.* храп. —**snorer,** *n.* храпу́н.

snorkel *n.* шно́ркель.

snort *v.i.* фы́ркать. —*n.* **1,** (snorting sound) фы́рканье. **2,** *slang* (short drink) глото́к (спиртно́го); рю́мочка.

snot *n.* со́пли.

snotty *adj.* **1,** (covered with snot) сопли́вый. **2,** *slang* (saucy) наха́льный.

snout *n.* ры́ло; мо́рда.

snow *n.* снег. *Tracks in the snow*, следы́ на снегу́. *Heavy snow*, си́льный снегопа́д. —*adj.* сне́жный. —*v.i.* снежи́ть. *It is snowing*, идёт снег. —*v.t.* **1,** *fol. by* **in** *or* **under** (cover or obstruct with snow) зава́ливать *or* заноси́ть сне́гом. *The city is snowed in*, го́род занесло́ сне́гом. **2,** *fol. by* **under** (overwhelm, as with work) зава́ливать (рабо́той).

snowball *n.* снежо́к; сне́жный ком. *Throw snowballs*, игра́ть в снежки́; броса́ться снежка́ми. *Throw a snowball at someone/ through the window/*, бро́сить снежко́м в кого́-нибудь/ в окно́/. —*v.i.* расти́ как сне́жный ком.

snowbank *n.* сне́жный зано́с.

snowbound *adj.* занесённый *or* зава́ленный сне́гом.

snow bunting пу́ночка.

snow-clad *adj.* засне́женный. *Also,* **snow-covered.**

snowdrift *n.* сугро́б; сне́жный зано́с; сне́жный зава́л.

snowdrop *n.* подсне́жник.

snowfall *n.* снегопа́д.

snowflake *n.* снежи́нка; *pl.* хло́пья сне́га.

snow leopard барс.

snow line снегова́я ли́ния.

snow maiden снегу́рка; снегу́рочка.

snowman *n.* сне́жная ба́ба.

snowmobile *n.* снегохо́д.

snowplow *also,* **snowplough** *n.* снегоочисти́тель; снегово́й плуг.

snowshoe *n.* снегосту́п.

snowstorm *n.* мете́ль; вью́га; сне́жная бу́ря.

snow-white *adj.* белосне́жный.

snowy *adj.* сне́жный. —**snowy owl,** бе́лая сова́.

snub *v.t.* трети́ровать. —*n.* щелчо́к. —*adj.* (of the nose) вздёрнутый.

snub-nosed *adj.* курно́сый.

snuff *n.* **1,** (powdered tobacco) ню́хательный таба́к. **2,** (charred end of a candle) нага́р. —*v.t.* ню́хать. —**snuff out, 1,** (extinguish) туши́ть. **2,** (suppress; destroy) разруша́ть. *Snuff out human lives,* погуби́ть челове́ческие жи́зни. —**up to snuff,** на до́лжной высоте́.

snuffbox *n.* табаке́рка.

snug *adj.* **1,** (cozy) ую́тный. **2,** (compact; tight-fitting) те́сный.

snuggle *v.i.* [*usu.* **snuggle up to**] прижима́ться (к); прилаека́ться (к).

so *adv.* **1,** (to the extent indicated; to a high degree) так: *so soon,* так ско́ро; *so long,* так до́лго. *I am so sorry!,* мне так жаль! ♦*Before long-form adjectives,* тако́й: *She is so beautiful!,* она́ така́я краси́вая? **2,** (thus; in that manner; to that effect) так: *He said so,* он так сказа́л. *I told him so,* я ему́ так и сказа́л(а). *I think/hope so,* ду́маю/наде́юсь, что да. *I don't think so,* ду́маю, что нет. *Let us hope so,* бу́дем наде́яться. *By so doing,* э́тим; при э́том. *It so happened that...,* случи́лось так, что... *It was so named because...,* он бы на́зван так, потому́ что... **3,** (then; it turns out) так; так что; зна́чит. *So you know her!,* так вы её зна́ете? *So if you want to go...,* так что, е́сли вам хо́чется пойти́... *So you've come after all!,* зна́чит, вы всё-таки пришли́? **4,** (also; likewise) то́же: *so do I,* я то́же. **5,** *expressing disagreement with a neg. statement: You don't know how to cook. I do so!,* вы не уме́ете гото́вить. Непра́вда, уме́ю! —*adj.* так: *Isn't that so?,* не так ли? *That is not so,* э́то не так; э́то не ве́рно. *Is that so!,* да что вы говори́те! —*conj.* поэ́тому: *It was raining, so we stayed home,* шёл дождь, и поэ́тому мы оста́лись до́ма. —**and so,** ита́к. —**and so on; and so forth,** и так да́лее. —**or so,** *see* **or.** —**so as to,** с тем, что́бы. —**so be it,** так и быть; пусть бу́дет так. —**so far,** *see* **far.** —**so long!,** пока́!; до свида́нья! —**so long as,** е́сли то́лько; лишь бы. —**so many; so much, 1,** (such a large amount or number) так мно́го; сто́лько. *In so many places,* в сто́льких места́х. *After so many years,* по́сле сто́льких лет. **2,** (a specific amount or number) сто́лько-то. —**so much for...,** вот тебе́ и...: *So much for our trip to Europe!,* вот тебе́ и пое́здка в Евро́пу! —**so much the better/worse,** тем лу́чше/ху́же. —**so that,** с тем, что́бы. —**so what?,** ну и что?; что с того́?

soak *v.t.* **1,** (keep in water) мочи́ть; зама́чивать; выма́чивать. **2,** (drench) прома́чивать. *Get soaked,* промока́ть. **3,** *fol. by* **up** (absorb) впи́тывать; вса́сывать. **4,** *fol. by* **off** (remove, as a stamp) отма́чивать. —*v.i.* **1,** (stay immersed in water) пролежа́ть в воде́; мо́кнуть. **2,** *fol. by* **through** (seep through) проса́чиваться (сквозь). —**soaking wet,** мо́крый, хоть вы́жми (*or* выжима́й).

so-and-so *n.* тако́й-то: *Mr. So-and-so,* господи́н тако́й-то.

soap *n.* мы́ло. *I got soap in my eyes,* мне в глаза́ попа́ло мы́ло. —*adj.* мы́льный: *soap bubble,* мы́льный пузы́рь. —*v.t.* мы́лить; намы́ливать.

soap dish мы́льница.

soap flakes мы́льная стру́жка.

soap powder мы́льный порошо́к.

soapstone *n.* мы́льный ка́мень.

soapsuds *n.pl.* мы́льная пе́на.

soapwort *n.* мыльня́нка.

soapy *adj.* мы́льный.

soar *v.i.* **1,** (fly high into the air) взлета́ть; взвива́ться; взмыва́ть. **2,** (glide) пари́ть; ре́ять. **3,** (shoot up, as of prices) подска́кивать.

sob *v.i.* рыда́ть. —*n.* рыда́ние.

sober *adj.* тре́звый; в тре́звом состоя́нии. *A sober assessment of the situation,* тре́звая оце́нка обстано́вки. —*v.t.* отрезвля́ть; вытрезвля́ть. *Have a sobering effect upon,* де́йствовать (на кого́-нибудь) отрезвля́юще. —*v.i.* [*usu.* **sober up**] трезве́ть; отрезвля́ться; вытрезвля́ться. —**sobering-up station,** вытрезви́тель.

soberly *adv.* тре́зво.

sobriety *n.* тре́звость.

sobriquet *n.* про́звище; кли́чка.

so-called *adj.* так называ́емый.

soccer *n.* футбо́л.

sociable *adj.* общи́тельный; компане́йский. —**sociability,** *n.* общи́тельность.

social *adj.* **1,** (pert. to society) обще́ственный; социа́льный: *social status,* обще́ственное/социа́льное положе́ние. *Social strata,* слои́ о́бщества. **2,** (involving relations between people) дру́жеский: *social visit,* дру́жеский визи́т. *Social gathering,* встре́ча друзе́й. —**social sciences,** обще́ственные нау́ки. —**social security,** социа́льное обеспе́чение.

socialism *n.* социали́зм. —**socialist,** *n.* социали́ст. —*adj.* [*also,* **socialistic**] социалисти́ческий.

socialize *v.t.* социализи́ровать; обобществля́ть. *Socialized medicine,* госуда́рственное медици́нское обслу́живание. —*v.i.* (associate; consort) обща́ться. —**socialization,** *n.* социализа́ция; обобществле́ние.

society *n.* о́бщество: *feudal society,* феода́льное о́бщество. *High society,* вы́сшее о́бщество; вы́сший свет. *A scientific society,* нау́чное о́бщество.

sociology *n.* социоло́гия. —**sociological,** *adj.* социологи́ческий. —**sociologist,** *n.* социо́лог.

sock *n.* **1,** (short stocking) носо́к. **2,** *slang* (a punch) тума́к. —*v.t.,* *slang* тра́хнуть.

socket *n.* **1,** (electric outlet) розе́тка; гнездо́. **2,** (for an electric bulb) патро́н. **3,** *anat.* впа́дина. *Eye socket,* глазна́я впа́дина; глазни́ца. *Socket of a tooth,* ячейка.

socle *n.* цо́коль.

sod *n.* дёрн. —*v.t.* обкла́дывать дёрном.

soda *n.* **1,** (sodium or sodium compound) со́да. **2,** (carbonated drink) газиро́ванная вода́. —**soda fountain,** сто́йка. —**soda water,** со́довая вода́.

sodden *adj.* промо́кший; пропи́танный вла́гой.

sodium *n.* на́трий. —**sodium bicarbonate,** двууглеки́слый на́трий. —**sodium carbonate,** углеки́слый на́трий. —**sodium chloride,** хло́ристый на́трий. —**sodium fluoride,** фто́ристый на́трий. —**sodium hydroxide,** е́дкий натр. —**sodium nitrate,** на́триевая сели́тра. —**sodium phosphate,** фосфа́т на́трия. —**sodium sulfate,** сернокисл́ый на́трий. —**sodium-vapor lamp,** на́триевая ла́мпа.

sodomy *n.* педера́стия; скотоло́жство.

sofa *n.* дива́н; софа́.

soft *adj.* **1,** (not hard) мя́гкий: *soft pillow,* мя́гкая поду́шка. **2,** (not loud) ти́хий: *in a soft voice,* ти́хим го́лосом. **3,** (not bright; subdued) мя́гкий: *soft light,* мя́гкий свет; *soft colors,* мя́гкие тона́. **4,** (out of condition; flabby) дря́блый; не в фо́рме. **5,** (easy to digest) лёгкий: *soft foods,* лёгкая пи́ща. **6,** (nonalcoholic) безалкого́льный. *Soft drinks,* безалкого́льные *or* прохлади́тельные напи́тки. **7,** *colloq.* (easy): *soft job,* тёплое месте́чко. —**have a soft spot in one's heart for,** пита́ть сла́бость к.

soft-boiled egg яйцо́ всмя́тку.

soft coal битумино́зный у́голь.

softcover *adj.* в мя́гком переплёте.

soften *v.t.* смягча́ть: *soften the blow,* смягча́ть уда́р. —*v.i.* смягча́ться.

softhearted *adj.* мягкосерде́чный. —**softheartedness,** *n.* мягкосерде́чие; мягкосерде́чность.

soft landing мя́гкая поса́дка.

softly *adv.* **1,** (gently) мя́гко. **2,** (quietly) ти́хо.

softness *n.* мя́гкость.

soft palate мя́гкое нёбо.

soft-spoken *adj.* ти́хий; кро́ткий.

software *n.* програ́ммное обеспе́чение.

soggy *adj.* сыро́й; отсыре́лый.

soil *n.* **1,** (top layer of the earth's surface) по́чва: *rich soil,* плодоро́дная по́чва. **2,** *fig.* (country; land) земля́: *on foreign soil,* на чужо́й земле́. —*v.t.* па́чкать: *soil one's clothes,* па́чкать оде́жду. —*v.i.* па́чкаться. *This fabric soils easily,* материа́л легко́ па́чкается; э́то о́чень ма́ркий материа́л. —**soil science,** почвове́дение. —**soil scientist,** почвове́д.

soirée *n.* ве́чер; вечери́нка.

sojourn *v.i.* жить; прожива́ть. —*n.* пребыва́ние.

sol *n., music* соль.

solace *n.* утеше́ние.

solar *adj.* со́лнечный. *Solar system,* со́лнечная систе́ма. *Solar energy,* со́лнечная эне́ргия.

solarium *n.* соля́рий.

solar plexus со́лнечное сплете́ние.

solder *n.* припо́й. —*v.t.* пая́ть. *Solder together,* спа́ивать. —**solderer,** *n.* пая́льщик. —**soldering iron,** пая́льник.

soldier *n.* солда́т. *Play soldier,* игра́ть в солда́тики. —**soldier of fortune,** кондотье́р.

soldierly *adj.* вое́нный; во́инский.

sole *n.* **1,** (of the foot) ступня́; подо́шва. **2,** (of a shoe) подмётка; подо́шва. *Inner sole,* сте́лька. **3,** (fish) ка́мбала. —*v.t.* ста́вить подмётку на; подши́вать. —*adj.* еди́нственный: *the sole reason,* еди́нственная причи́на; *sole owner,* еди́нственный владе́лец.

solecism *n.* солеци́зм.

solely *adv.* еди́нственно; то́лько; исключи́тельно.

solemn *adj.* торже́ственный: *solemn occasion/oath,* торже́ственный слу́чай; торже́ственная кля́тва.

solemnity *n.* торже́ственность. *With great solemnity,* торже́ственно.

solemnly *adv.* торже́ственно: *I solemnly swear,* я торже́ственно кляну́сь.

solenoid *n.* солено́ид.

solfeggio *n.* сольфе́джио.

solicit *v.t.* проси́ть; выпра́шивать; хода́тайствовать о. *Solicit alms,* проси́ть ми́лостыню; попроша́йничать. *Solicit contributions,* собира́ть поже́ртвования. *Solicit votes,* собира́ть голоса́. —**solicitation,** *n.* хода́тайство.

solicitor *n.* **1,** (one who solicits) проси́тель. **2,** (lawyer) адвока́т.

solicitous *adj.* забо́тливый. —**solicitude,** *n.* забо́тливость.

solid *adj.* **1,** (of firm structure) твёрдый: *solid body/state,* твёрдое те́ло/состоя́ние. *Solid food,* твёрдая пи́ща. *Solid fuel,* твёрдое то́пливо. *Solid waste,* твёрдые отхо́ды. **2,** (sturdily built) соли́дный; про́чный: *solid building,* соли́дное/про́чное зда́ние. *Solid foundation,* про́чный фунда́мент. **3,** (upstanding; reliable) соли́дный: *solid person,* соли́дный челове́к; *solid company,* соли́дная компа́ния. **4,** (unbroken) сплошно́й: *solid line/wall,* сплошна́я ли́ния/стена́. **5,** (pure; unalloyed) чи́стый: *of solid gold,* из чи́стого зо́лота. **6,** (plain; without a design) однотонный: *solid color,* однотонная кра́ска. **7,** (three-dimensional) куби́ческий; трёхме́рный. **8,** (uninterrupted) це́лый. *A solid hour,* би́тый час. —*n.* твёрдое те́ло.

solidarity *n.* солида́рность; сплочённость.

solid geometry стереоме́трия.

solidify *v.i.* затвердева́ть; отвердева́ть. —*v.t.* **1,** (harden) де́лать твёрдым. **2,** (consolidate) упро́чивать: *solidify one's position,* упро́чить своё положе́ние.

solidity *n.* твёрдость.

solidly *adv.* про́чно; соли́дно. *Solidly built,* кре́пкого сложе́ния; *(of a building)* про́чно постро́ен. *Be solidly behind,* стоя́ть горо́й за.

solid-state *adj.* твердоте́льный: *solid-state amplifier,* твердоте́льный усили́тель. —**solid-state physics,** фи́зика твёрдого те́ла.

soliloquize *v.i.* произноси́ть моноло́г.

soliloquy *n.* моноло́г.

solitaire *n.* **1,** (gem) солите́р. **2,** (card game) пасья́нс.

solitary *adj.* **1,** (lone) одино́кий; одино́чный. *A solitary house on the hill,* одино́кий до́мик на приго́рке. **2,** (single; sole) едини́чный: *a solitary instance,* едини́чный слу́чай. *Not a single solitary person,* ни еди́ной души́. **3,** (avoiding the company of others) одино́кий: *a solitary existence,* одино́кая жизнь. *Lead a solitary existence,* жить одино́ко. **4,** (secluded; remote) уединённый; обосо́бленный. —**solitary confinement,** одино́чное заключе́ние.

solitude *n.* одино́чество; уедине́ние. *A life of solitude,* уединённая жизнь. *Live in solitude,* жить уединённо.

solo *n.* **1,** (composition) со́ло: *solo for violin*, со́ло для скри́пки. **2,** (performance) со́льная па́ртия; со́льный но́мер. —*adj.* со́льный: *give a solo performance*, исполня́ть со́льную па́ртию. *Solo flight*, одино́чный полёт. —**soloist**, *n.* соли́ст; соли́стка.

solstice *n.* солнцестоя́ние.

soluble *adj.* раствори́мый. —**solubility**, *n.* раствори́мость.

solution *n.* **1,** (answer to a problem) реше́ние: *find a solution to the problem*, найти́ реше́ние пробле́мы. **2,** (answer to a puzzle or mystery) разга́дка. **3,** (resolution of a question or issue) разреше́ние. **4,** (mixture of various substances) раство́р: *saline solution*, соляно́й *or* солево́й раство́р.

solvable *adj.* разреши́мый.

solve *v.t.* реша́ть; разреша́ть; разга́дывать. *Solve a (mathematical) problem*, реши́ть зада́чу. *Solve economic problems*, разреши́ть экономи́ческие пробле́мы. *Solve a riddle*, реши́ть *or* разгада́ть зага́дку. *Solve a mystery*, разгада́ть та́йну *or* зага́дку. *Solve a crime*, раскры́ть преступле́ние.

solvency *n.* платёжеспосо́бность.

solvent *adj.* **1,** (able to pay one's debts) платёжеспосо́бный. **2,** (dissolving another substance) растворя́ющий. —*n.* растворя́ющее вещество́; раствори́тель.

Somali *adj.* сома́ли́йский.

somatic *adj.* сомати́ческий.

somber *also*, **sombre** *adj.* **1,** (gloomy) мра́чный; хму́рый; па́смурный. **2,** (morose) мра́чный; угрю́мый.

some *adj.* **1,** (of an unspecified quantity) *rendered by the gen. case: Would you like some tea?*, хоти́те ча́ю? *Have/take some meat!*, возьми́те себе́ мя́са! ◆*With abstract nouns*, не́который: *some time/doubt*, не́которое вре́мя/сомне́ние. *For some time now*, с не́которых пор. *To some extent*, в *or* до не́которой сте́пени. **2,** (a few) не́сколько: *some apples/stamps*, не́сколько я́блок/ма́рок. **3,** (rather a lot of) нема́ло: *It took some effort*, понадо́билось нема́ло уси́лий. *It's some distance from here*, э́то дово́льно далеко́ (*or* поря́дочно) отсю́да. **4,** (certain ones) не́который: *some people*, не́которые лю́ди. **5,** (unspecified) како́й-то; како́й-нибудь. *Some man was asking for you*, вас спра́шивал како́й-то челове́к. **6,** *slang* (quite a) вот э́то; ну и. *Some singer!*, вот э́то певе́ц! *Some weather!*, ну и пого́да! —*pron.* **1,** (a certain amount) *not rendered in Russian: Would you like some?*, хоти́те?; хоти́те попро́бовать? *I already have some*, у меня́ уже́ есть. **2,** (certain ones) не́которые: *some of my friends*, не́которые из мои́х друзе́й; не́которые мои́ друзья́. *Some believe that...*, не́которые счита́ют, что... **3,** (certain ones as opposed to others) одни́: *Some want to go, others do not*, одни́ хотя́т пойти́, други́е нет. —*adv.* (approximately) о́коло; до; како́й-нибудь. *Some forty miles*, каки́е-нибудь со́рок миль. —**and then some**, *colloq.* и ещё сверх того́. —**some other time**, ка́к-нибудь в друго́й раз.

somebody *pron.* кто́-то; кто́-нибудь. *Somebody else*, кто́-то друго́й; кто́-нибудь друго́й. *Somebody's*

чей-то; чей-нибудь. —*n.*, *colloq.* ва́жная персо́на; ва́жная осо́ба.

someday *adv.* когда́-то; когда́-нибудь; ка́к-нибудь.

somehow *adv.* ка́к-то; ка́к-нибудь; каки́м-то о́бразом. *We'll manage somehow*, мы ка́к-нибудь устро́имся. *It sounds strange somehow*, э́то звучи́т ка́к-то стра́нно. —**somehow or other**, так и́ли ина́че.

someone *pron.* кто́-то; кто́-нибудь. *Someone else*, кто́-то друго́й; кто́-нибудь друго́й. *Someone else's*, чужо́й. *Someone's*, чей-то; чей-нибудь.

someplace *adv.* = **somewhere**.

somersault *n.* са́льто; са́льто-морта́ле. —*v.i.* кувырка́ться.

something *pron.* что́-то; что́-нибудь; ко́е-что. *Something is happening*, что́-то происхо́дит. *Would you like something to drink?*, хоти́те что́-нибудь вы́пить? *I want to ask you something*, я хочу́ вас ко́е-что спроси́ть. *Something else*, что́-то друго́е; что́-нибудь друго́е. *Something like that*, что́-то в э́том ро́де. *Or something*, и́ли что́-то в э́том ро́де.

sometime *adv.* когда́-то; когда́-нибудь.

sometimes *adv.* иногда́: *Sometimes the temperature reaches 100˚*, иногда́ температу́ра достига́ет ста гра́дусов. *Sometimes it seems that...*, иногда́ (*or* ино́й раз) ка́жется, что...

somewhat *adv.* немно́го; не́сколько; слегка́.

somewhere *adv.* где́-то; где́-нибудь; куда́-то; куда́-нибудь. *Somewhere else*, где́-то в друго́м ме́сте.

somnambulate *v.i.* ходи́ть во сне. —**somnambulism**, *n.* лунати́зм. —**somnambulist**, *n.* луна́тик.

somnolent *adj.* **1,** (sleepy) со́нный; сонли́вый. **2,** (causing drowsiness) снотво́рный. —**somnolence**, *n.* сонли́вость; дремо́та.

son *n.* сын.

sonar *n.* **1,** (method) гидролока́ция. **2,** (device) гидролока́тор.

sonata *n.* сона́та.

song *n.* пе́сня. *Break/burst into song*, запе́ть. —**for a song**, за бесце́нок; за гроши́.

songbird *n.* пе́вчая пти́ца.

songbook *n.* пе́сенник.

songster *n.* певе́ц. —**songstress**, *n.* певи́ца.

songwriter *n.* пе́сенник.

sonic *adj.* звуково́й. —**sonic boom**, звуково́й уда́р; сверхзвуково́й хлопо́к.

son-in-law *n.* зять.

sonnet *n.* соне́т.

sonny *n.* сыно́к.

sonorous *adj.* зву́чный; зво́нкий.

soon *adv.* ско́ро. *Soon after*, вско́ре по́сле. *Write soon!*, напиши́те поскоре́е! *See you soon!*, до (ско́рой) встре́чи! *Too soon*, сли́шком ра́но. *How soon can you get here?*, как ско́ро вы смо́жете прийти́? —**as soon as**, как то́лько: *as soon as he arrives*, как то́лько он придёт. *I came as soon as I could*, я пришёл, как то́лько смог; я пришла́, как то́лько смогла́. —**just as soon**, скоре́е; лу́чше. *I'd just as soon stay home*, я предпочёл (предпочла́) бы оста́ться до́ма.

sooner *adv.* **1,** (earlier) скоре́е; ра́ньше. **2,** (preferably) скорее: *I would sooner die,* я скоре́е умру́. —**no sooner,** едва́: *No sooner did we start out than the car broke down,* едва́ мы отпра́вились в путь, как маши́на слома́лась. —**no sooner said than done,** ска́зано — сде́лано. —**sooner or later,** ра́но и́ли по́здно. —**the sooner the better,** чем ра́ньше, тем лу́чше.

soot *n.* са́жа; ко́поть.

soothe *v.t.* успока́ивать: *soothe the pain,* успока́ивать боль. *Soothing effect,* успока́ивающее де́йствие.

soothsayer *n.* предсказа́тель; прорица́тель.

sooty *adj.* в са́же; закопте́лый; закопчённый.

sop *v.t.* **1,** (soak) нама́чивать. **2,** *fol. by* **up** (absorb) впи́тывать. —*n.* пода́чка.

sophism *n.* софи́зм. —**sophist,** *n.* софи́ст. —**sophistic,** *adj.* софисти́ческий.

sophisticated *adj.* **1,** (urbane) искушённый; уто́нченный; изы́сканный. **2,** (technologically advanced) совреме́нный; соверше́нный; сло́жный. —**sophistication,** *n.* утончённость; изы́сканность.

sophistry *n.* софи́стика.

sophomore *n.* студе́нт-второку́рсник. *She is a sophomore,* она́ на второ́м ку́рсе.

soporific *adj.* **1,** *med.* снотво́рный; усыпля́ющий. **2,** (boring) усыпи́тельный.

sopping *adj.* промо́кший. —**sopping wet,** мо́крый, хоть вы́жми. —*n.v.* выжима́й).

soprano *n.* сопра́но. —*adj.* сопра́новый; сопра́нный.

sorcerer *n.* колду́н; чароде́й. —**sorceress,** *n.* колду́нья; чароде́йка.

sordid *adj.* гря́зный. *A sordid affair,* гря́зное де́ло; гря́зная исто́рия.

sore *adj.* **1,** (hurting) больно́й: *sore finger,* больно́й па́лец. *I have a sore throat,* у меня́ боли́т го́рло. **2,** *fig.* (painful; irritating) больно́й: *sore point; sore subject,* больно́й вопро́с. **3,** *colloq.* (offended; angry) оби́женный; серди́тый. —*n.* боля́чка; я́зва.

sorely *adv.* **1,** (grievously) до бо́ли: *sorely distressed,* до бо́ли огорчён. **2,** (greatly) о́чень: *You were sorely missed,* вас о́чень не хвата́ло. *I am sorely tempted,* э́то о́чень соблазни́тельно. *Sorely disappointed,* глубоко́ разочаро́ван.

soreness *n.* боле́зненное ощуще́ние; боль.

sorghum *n.* со́рго.

sorrel *n.* **1,** (plant) щаве́ль. *Wood sorrel,* кисли́ца. **2,** (color) кра́сно-кори́чневый цвет.

sorrow *n.* печа́ль; го́ре; скорбь. *To my sorrow,* на своё го́ре.

sorrowful *adj.* печа́льный; ско́рбный. —**sorrowfully,** *adv.* ско́рбно; сокрушённо.

sorry *adj.* **1,** (feeling sympathy) жаль: *I am sorry,* мне жаль. *Feel sorry for,* сочу́вствовать (+ *dat.*); жале́ть (+ *acc.*). *I feel sorry for her,* я сочу́вствую ей; я жале́ю её; мне её жаль. *Feel sorry for oneself,* жале́ть себя́. **2,** (feeling regret): *be sorry,* сожале́ть; жале́ть. *I am sorry now that I did it,* тепе́рь я сожале́ю, что сде́лал(а) э́то. **3,** (expressing one's apologies): *I'm sorry!,* прости́те!; прошу́ извине́ния. **4,** (pitiful) жа́лкий; плаче́вный: *a sorry sight,* жа́лкое зре́лище; *in a sorry state,* в плаче́вном состоя́нии.

sort *n.* род; сорт; вид. *A sort of,* вро́де (+ *gen.*); не́что вро́де (+ *gen.*). *All sorts of,* всевозмо́жные; вся́кого ро́да (+ *nom.*). *Something of the sort,* что́-то в э́том ро́де. *Nothing of the sort,* ничего́ подо́бного. *What sort of person is he?,* что он за челове́к? —*v.t.* [*also,* **sort out**] разбира́ть; сортирова́ть; перебира́ть. —**after a sort**; **of sorts,** не́которым о́бразом. —**out of sorts,** не в ду́хе. —**sort of,** бо́лее и́ли ме́нее: *I'm sort of glad,* я бо́лее и́ли ме́нее рад (ра́да). *Are you acquainted? Sort of,* вы знако́мы? Вро́де как бы.

sorter *n.* **1,** (person) сортиро́вщик. **2,** (machine) сортиро́вочная маши́на.

sortie *n.* **1,** (sudden attack by besieged forces) вы́лазка. **2,** (mission by a single plane) (боево́й) вы́лет.

so-so *adj.* нева́жный; сно́сный. —*adv.* так себе́; сно́сно.

sot *n.* го́рький пья́ница.

soufflé *n.* суфле́.

soul *n.* душа́. *A simple soul,* проста́я душа́. *There was not a soul present,* там не́ было ни души́. *Put one's heart and soul into,* вкла́дывать всю ду́шу в (+ *acc.*). *Don't tell a soul!,* никому́ не говори́те!; об э́том ни гугу́!

sound *n.* **1,** (what can be heard) звук: *not a sound,* ни зву́ка. *The sound of footsteps,* звук *or* шум шаго́в. *Without making a sound,* бесшу́мно. *Don't make a sound!,* ни зву́ка! **2,** (strait) проли́в: *Long Island Sound,* проли́в Лонг-А́йленд. **3,** (inlet) зали́в. *Puget Sound,* Пю́джет-Са́унд. —*v.i.* **1,** (make a sound) звуча́ть; раздава́ться. *The trumpets sounded,* тру́бы труби́ли. *The whistle sounded,* разда́лся гудо́к. *The all-clear sounded,* разда́лся отбо́й. *The engine sounds fine,* мото́р звучи́т хорошо́. **2,** (seem) звуча́ть: *sound logical,* звучи́т логи́чно. *Sound incredible,* каза́ться невероя́тным. *It sounds strange somehow,* э́то звучи́т ка́к-то стра́нно. —*v.t.* **1,** (cause to sound) труби́ть в: *sound the trumpets,* труби́ть в тру́бы. *Sound the horn,* дать гудо́к. *Sound the bells,* звони́ть в колокола́. *Sound the alarm,* бить *or* заби́ть *or* ударя́ть трево́гу *or* (в) наба́т. *Sound retreat,* дава́ть *or* бить отбо́й. **2,** (pronounce; articulate) произноси́ть. **3,** (fathom; probe) зонди́ровать. **4,** *fol. by* **out** (solicit the opinion of) зонди́ровать; расспра́шивать. —*adj.* **1,** (healthy) здоро́вый. *Of sound mind,* в здра́вом уме́; *law* вменя́емый. **2,** (free from defect or harm) испра́вный. *In sound condition,* в хоро́шем состоя́нии; в испра́вности. *Safe and sound,* цел и невреди́м. **3,** (sensible; logical) здра́вый; основа́тельный; обосно́ванный. *Sound idea,* здра́вая мысль. *Sound advice,* у́мный *or* де́льный сове́т. *Sound arguments,* основа́тельные до́воды. *Sound decision,* обосно́ванное реше́ние. **4,** (solid; firm) про́чный: *a sound basis for further development,* про́чная осно́ва для дальне́йшего разви́тия. **5,** (financially strong or secure) соли́дный: *a sound company,* соли́дная компа́ния. *A sound investment,* надёжный вклад. **6,** (of sleep) кре́пкий. **7,** (thorough) здоро́вый: *a sound thrashing,* здоро́вая по́рка. **8,** (pert. to sound) звуково́й: *sound barrier,* звуково́й барье́р. —*adv. She is sound asleep,* она́ кре́пко спит.

—**sound off, 1,** *mil.* откликáться. **2,** *colloq.* (express one's views) выскáзываться.

sound effects шумовы́е эффéкты.

sounding board дéка.

soundless *adj.* беззвýчный.

soundly *adv.* **1,** (so as not to be awakened) крéпко: *sleep soundly,* крéпко спать. **2,** (thoroughly; decisively) здóрово: *Our team was soundly beaten,* нáша комáнда былá здóрово разби́та.

soundman *n.* звукооперáтор; акýстик.

soundness *n.* **1,** (solidity) прóчность. **2,** (logic; validity) основáтельность.

soundproof *adj.* звуконепроницáемый. *These walls are soundproof,* э́ти стéны не пропускáют звук.

sound track звуковáя дорóжка.

soup *n.* суп. —*adj.* суповóй: *soup tureen,* суповáя ми́ска.

soup kitchen бесплáтная столóвая; бесплáтный питáтельный пункт.

soupspoon *n.* столóвая лóжка.

sour *adj.* **1,** (having a sharp acid taste) ки́слый: *sour milk,* ки́слое молокó. **2,** (cross; peevish) злой; ки́слый. *Sour disposition,* злой харáктер. *In a sour mood,* в дурнóм *or* в ки́слом настроéнии. *Make a sour face,* сдéлать ки́слое лицó. **3,** (bad; unsuccessful): *The marriage went sour,* брак не удáлся. —*v.i.* **1,** (turn sour) ки́снуть; скисáть; прокисáть. **2,** *fol. by* **on** (become disenchanted with) разочарóвываться в. —*v.t.* **1,** (spoil, as relations) пóртить. **2,** (disenchant) разочарóвывать. *Sour someone on traveling,* отбивáть у когó-нибудь охóту к поéздкам. —**sour grapes!,** зéлен виногрáд!

source *n.* **1,** (beginning of a stream or river) истóк. **2,** (that from which something comes) истóчник: *source of energy,* истóчник энéргии. **3,** (something that provides information) истóчник: *reliable source,* достовéрный истóчник.

sour cream сметáна.

souse *v.t.* **1,** (pickle) маринóвать. **2,** (plunge into a liquid) погружáть; окунáть. **3,** (drench; soak) промáчивать. **4,** *slang* (intoxicate) опьянять. —*n., slang* (drunkard) пья́ница.

south *n.* юг. —*adj.* ю́жный: *the south bank,* ю́жный бéрег. *South Korea,* Ю́жная Корéя. —*adv.* на юг; к ю́гу. *South of,* к ю́гу от; южнéе (+ *gen.*).

South America Ю́жная Амéрика. —**South American,** южноамерикáнский.

southeast *n.* ю́го-востóк. —*adj.* ю́го-востóчный. —*adv.* к ю́го-востóку; на ю́го-востóк.

southeaster *n.* зюйд-óст.

southeasterly *adj.* ю́го-востóчный. —*adv.* к ю́го-востóку.

southeastern *adj.* ю́го-востóчный.

southerly *adj.* ю́жный: *southerly winds,* ю́жный вéтер.

southern *adj.* ю́жный. *Southern California,* ю́жная Калифóрния. *Southern Cross,* Ю́жный Крест. *Southern Hemisphere,* Ю́жное полушáрие.

southerner *n.* южáнин.

southernmost *adj.* сáмый ю́жный.

southpaw *n., slang* левшá.

South Pole Ю́жный пóлюс.

southward *adv.* к ю́гу; в ю́жном направлéнии. —*adj.* ю́жный.

southwest *n.* ю́го-зáпад. —*adj.* ю́го-зáпадный. —*adv.* к ю́го-зáпаду; на ю́го-зáпад.

southwester *n.* зюйд-вéст.

southwesterly *adj.* ю́го-зáпадный. —*adv.* к ю́го-зáпаду.

southwestern *adj.* ю́го-зáпадный.

souvenir *n.* сувени́р. *Souvenir shop,* магази́н сувени́ров. *Keep it as a souvenir!,* возьми́те на пáмять! —**souvenir sheet,** *philately* блок.

sovereign *n.* **1,** (ruler) госудáрь; суверéн. **2,** (British coin) соверéн. —*adj.* суверéнный. —**sovereignty,** *n.* суверенитéт.

soviet *n.* совéт. *The Supreme Soviet,* Верхóвный совéт. —**Soviet,** *adj.* совéтский: *the Soviet Union,* Совéтский Сою́з.

sow[1] (so) *v.t.* **1,** (scatter) сéять: *sow wheat,* сéять пшени́цу. **2,** (plant seed in) засевáть: *sow a field with rye,* засевáть пóле рóжью. **3,** *fig.* (implant) сéять: *sow suspicion,* сéять подозрéние. —*v.i.* сéять: *As you sow so you shall reap,* что посéешь, то и пожнёшь.

sow[2] (sau) *n.* свиномáтка.

sower *n.* сéятель.

sowing *n.* сев; посéв; засéв.

soy *n.* соя. *Also,* **soya.**

soybean *n.* сóя; сóевый боб. —*adj.* сóевый: *soybean oil,* сóевое мáсло.

soy sauce сóя.

spa *n.* курóрт с минерáльными вóдами.

space *n.* **1,** (infinite expanse) прострáнство: *time and space,* врéмя и прострáнство. **2,** (room) мéсто; плóщадь. *Take up a lot of space,* занимáть мнóго мéста. *Living space,* жилáя плóщадь. *Advertising space,* реклáмная плóщадь. **3,** (place available for a particular purpose) мéсто: *parking space,* мéсто стоя́нки маши́ны. **4,** (interval) промежýток; интервáл. *Leave a space between lines,* оставля́ть промежýток мéжду стрóчками. *Within a space of three days,* в течéние трёх дней. **5,** *pl.* (great expanse) простóры: *wide open spaces,* широ́кие простóры. **6,** (outer space) кóсмос. *A flight into space,* полёт в кóсмос. —*adj.* косми́ческий: *space flight,* косми́ческий полёт. —*v.t.* расставля́ть с промежýтками. *Space the letters farther apart,* увели́чивать промежýток мéжду бýквами. *Evenly spaced tables,* столы́, распо́ложенные на рáвном расстоя́нии друг от дрýга.

spacecraft *n.* косми́ческий аппарáт.

spaceman *n.* космонáвт.

space probe косми́ческий зонд.

spaceship *n.* косми́ческий корáбль.

space suit скафáндр.

spacious *adj.* простóрный; вмести́тельный. —**spaciousness,** *n.* вмести́тельность.

spade *n.* **1,** (tool) лопáта; зáступ. **2,** *pl., cards* пи́ки. —**call a spade a spade,** называ́ть вéщи свои́ми имена́ми. —**spade work,** подготови́тельная рабóта.

spaghetti *n.* тóнкие макарóны; спагéтти.

span *n.* **1,** (distance from thumb to little finger) пядь. **2,** (distance between vertical supports) пролёт. **3,** (spread) разма́х: *wingspan*, разма́х кры́льев. **4,** (period of time) отре́зок: *a short span of time*, небольшо́й отре́зок вре́мени. —*v.t.* **1,** (extend across) протя́гиваться че́рез. *The bridge spans the river*, мост соединя́ет берега́ реки́. **2,** *fig.* (encompass, as a period of time) охва́тывать.

spangle *n.* блёстка.

Spaniard *n.* испа́нец; испа́нка.

spaniel *n.* спание́ль.

Spanish *adj.* испа́нский. —*n.* испа́нский язы́к. *Speak Spanish*, говори́ть по-испа́нски. —**Spanish fly,** шпа́нская му́шка; шпа́нка. —**Spanish moss,** испа́нский *or* луизиа́нский мох.

spank *v.t.* шлёпать.

spanking *n.* шлёпка. —*adv., colloq.* соверше́нно: *spanking new,* соверше́нно но́вый.

spanner *n., Brit.* га́ечный ключ.

spar *n.* **1,** *naut.* ранго́утное де́рево. **2,** *aero.* лонжеро́н. **3,** (mineral) шпат. —*v.i.* **1,** (box) дра́ться на кула́чках. **2,** (argue) препира́ться; пререка́ться.

spare *v.t.* **1,** (show mercy toward) щади́ть: *spare the women and children,* щади́ть же́нщин и дете́й. *Spare someone's life/feelings,* щади́ть чью-нибудь жизнь/чьи-нибудь чу́вства/. **2,** (use sparingly) щади́ть; жале́ть. *Spare no expense/effort,* не жале́ть расхо́дов/уси́лий. **3,** (give up conveniently) обходи́ться без: *I can't spare him,* без него́ не могу́ обходи́ться. *Spare time for something,* уделя́ть вре́мя чему́-нибудь. *Can you spare a dollar?,* вы мо́жете дать мне до́ллар?; нет ли у вас ли́шнего до́ллара? *We haven't a moment to spare,* у нас нет ни одно́й свобо́дной мину́ты. **4,** (save) избавля́ть: *spare someone trouble,* избавля́ть кого́-нибудь от хлопо́т. —*adj.* **1,** (extra) ли́шний: *a spare bedroom,* ли́шняя спа́льня. **2,** (in reserve) запасно́й: *spare parts,* запасны́е ча́сти. *Spare tire,* запасна́я ши́на *or* покры́шка. **3,** (not taken up by regular duties) свобо́дный: *spare time,* свобо́дное вре́мя. *When I have a spare moment,* когда́ у меня́ бу́дет свобо́дная мину́та.

spareribs *n.pl.* свины́е рёбра.

sparing *adj.* скупо́й: *sparing with words,* скупо́й на слова́. —**sparingly,** *adv.* ску́по.

spark *n.* и́скра. —*v.i.* искри́ть; —*v.t.* вызыва́ть; порожда́ть. *Spark a riot,* вызыва́ть бунт.

sparkle *v.i.* **1,** (glitter) сверка́ть; блесте́ть; и́скриться. **2,** (effervesce) игра́ть. —*n.* сверка́ние.

sparkler *n.* **1,** (firecracker) шути́ха. **2,** *colloq.* (diamond) солите́р.

sparkling *adj.* **1,** (glittering) и́скрящийся; искри́стый. **2,** (effervescent) игри́стый; шипу́чий: *sparkling wines,* игри́стые/шипу́чие ви́на. **3,** (outstanding; brilliant) блестя́щий.

spark plug запа́льная свеча́.

sparrow *n.* воробе́й. —*adj.* [*also,* **sparrow's**] воробьи́ный: *sparrow's nest,* воробьи́ное гнездо́. —**sparrow hawk,** перепеля́тник.

sparse *adj.* ре́дкий: *sparse hair,* ре́дкие во́лосы. *Sparse vegetation,* ску́дная расти́тельность.

sparsely *adv. Sparsely populated,* малонаселённый.

sparseness *n.* ре́дкость. *Also,* **sparsity.**

Spartan *adj.* спарта́нский. —*n.* спарта́нец.

spasm *n.* спазм; спа́зма.

spasmodic *adj.* **1,** (convulsive) спазмати́ческий. **2,** (uneven; irregular) скачкообра́зный.

spastic *adj.* спасти́ческий.

spat *n.* **1,** (petty quarrel) перебра́нка; размо́лвка. **2,** *usu. pl.* (short cloth gaiters) ге́тры. —*v.i.* (squabble) препира́ться.

spate *n.* пото́к.

spatial *adj.* простра́нственный.

spatter *v.t.* **1,** (scatter in drops) бры́згать; разбры́згивать. **2,** (splash; spot; soil) бры́згать; забры́згивать; обры́згивать. —*v.i.* разбры́згиваться.

spatula *n.* шпа́тель.

spawn *v.i.* мета́ть икру́. —*v.t.* (give rise to) порожда́ть.

spawning *n.* мета́ние икры́; не́рест. —**spawning ground,** нерести́лище.

spay *v.t.* удаля́ть яи́чники у.

speak *v.t. & i.* говори́ть: *speak to someone,* говори́ть с ке́м-нибудь. *Speak the truth,* говори́ть пра́вду. *Speak Russian,* говори́ть *or* разгова́ривать по-ру́сски. *Speak five languages,* говори́ть на пяти́ языка́х; знать пять языко́в. *Speak at a meeting,* выступа́ть на собра́нии. *Speaking of...,* кста́ти о... *Frankly speaking,* открове́нно говоря́. —**so to speak,** так сказа́ть. —**speak for oneself,** говори́ть за себя́. *It speaks for itself,* э́то говори́т само́ за себя́. —**speak one's mind,** вы́сказать своё мне́ние. —**speak out,** выска́зываться. —**speak up,** говори́ть гро́мче. —**speak up for,** заступа́ться за. —**speak well for,** говори́ть в по́льзу (+ *gen.*). —**speak well of,** хорошо́ отзыва́ться о. —**to speak of,** осо́бенный: *nothing to speak of,* ничего́ осо́бенного. *We've had no rain to speak of,* у нас почти́ не́ было дожде́й.

speaker *n.* **1,** (person speaking) тот, кто говори́т; говоря́щий. **2,** (person giving a speech) выступа́ющий; ора́тор; докла́дчик. **3,** (one who speaks a certain language) говоря́щий; носи́тель. *The number of speakers of German,* число́ говоря́щих на неме́цком языке́. **4,** (presiding officer) спи́кер. **5,** (loudspeaker) громкоговори́тель.

speaking *n.* разгово́р. *Public speaking,* ора́торское иску́сство. —**in a manner of speaking,** *see* **manner.** —**not be on speaking terms,** не говори́ть (*or* не разгова́ривать) друг с дру́гом.

spear *n.* **1,** (weapon) копьё. **2,** (for spearing fish) острога́. —*v.t.* пронза́ть копьём; бить (ры́бу) острого́й.

spearhead *n.* **1,** (head of a spear) острие́. **2,** *mil.* острие́: *the spearhead of the attack,* острие́ ата́ки. —*v.t.* возглавля́ть; стоя́ть во главе́ (+ *gen.*).

special *adj.* **1,** (distinctive; particular) осо́бенный; осо́бый: *special case,* осо́бенный/осо́бый слу́чай. *Special assignment,* осо́бое зада́ние. *Require special effort,* тре́бовать осо́бых уси́лий. *Nothing special,* ничего́ осо́бенного. **2,** (separate) осо́бый: *special section,* осо́бый разде́л. **3,** (having a particular purpose) специа́льный: *special course/flight/correspondent*, специа́льный курс/полёт/корреспонде́нт. **4,** (extra) специа́льный; э́кстренный: *special edition*, специа́льный/ э́кстренный вы́пуск.

specialist *n.* специали́ст.

speciality *n.* = specialty.

specialization *n.* специализа́ция.

specialize *v.i.* специализи́роваться. —**specialized,** *adj.* специа́льный: *specialized terms*, специа́льные те́рмины.

specially *adv.* специа́льно: *specially selected*, специа́льно отобранный.

specialty *also*, **speciality** *n.* специа́льность. —**specialty of the house,** фи́рменное блю́до.

specie *n.* зво́нкая моне́та.

species *n.* вид: *a rare species of monkey*, ре́дкий вид обезья́н.

specific *adj.* **1,** (explicit) конкре́тный: *specific purpose*, конкре́тная цель; *specific proposal*, конкре́тное предложе́ние. **2,** (individual; particular) отде́льный: *in each specific case*, в ка́ждом отде́льном слу́чае. **3,** *physics* уде́льный: *specific gravity*, уде́льный вес. —*n.*, *usu. pl.* подро́бности.

specifically *adv.* **1,** (specially) осо́бо; специа́льно: *I specifically asked for...*, я осо́бо/специа́льно попроси́л(а)... **2,** (in particular) в ча́стности.

specification *n.* **1,** (act of specifying) специфика́ция. **2,** *pl.* (detailed description) техни́ческие усло́вия.

specify *v.t.* **1,** (indicate clearly) ука́зывать: *specify the time*, ука́зывать вре́мя. **2,** (stipulate) предусма́тривать: *The law specifies that...*, зако́н предусма́тривает, что...

specimen *n.* **1,** (example; sample) экземпля́р: *a rare specimen of fish*, ре́дкий экземпля́р ры́бы. **2,** *med.* про́ба: *urine specimen*, про́ба мочи́.

specious *adj.* благови́дный.

speck *n.* **1,** (spot) пя́тнышко; кра́пинка. **2,** (small particle) части́ца. *Speck of dust*, пыли́нка; сори́нка.

speckle *n.* кра́пинка. —*v.t.* испещря́ть. —**speckled,** *adj.* (of material) в кра́пинку; кра́пчатый; (of an animal) рябо́й.

spectacle *n.* **1,** (sight) зре́лище. **2,** *pl.* (glasses) очки́. —**make a spectacle of oneself,** обраща́ть на себя́ внима́ние.

spectacular *adj.* грандио́зный; потряса́ющий.

spectator *n.* зри́тель.

specter *also*, **spectre** *n.* при́зрак.

spectral *adj.* **1,** (ghostly) при́зрачный. **2,** (produced by a spectrum) спектра́льный.

spectre *n.* = specter.

spectroscope *n.* спектроско́п. —**spectroscopic,** *adj.* спектроскопи́ческий.

spectrum *n.* спектр.

speculate *v.i.* **1,** (ponder) размышля́ть. **2,** (conjecture) стро́ить дога́дки. **3,** (engage in risky ventures) спекули́ровать.

speculation *n.* **1,** (conjecture) дога́дка: *a matter of sheer speculation*, чи́стая дога́дка. **2,** (engaging in risky ventures) спекуля́ция.

speculative *adj.* **1,** (based on an assumption) умозри́тельный; спекуляти́вный. **2,** (involving risk) спекуляти́вный.

speculator *n.* спекуля́нт.

speech *n.* речь: *organs of speech*, о́рганы ре́чи. *Make a speech*, говори́ть *or* произноси́ть речь. *Freedom of speech*, свобо́да сло́ва. —*adj.* речево́й. *Speech defect*, дефе́кт ре́чи.

speechless *adj.* **1,** (incapable of speech) немо́й. **2,** (at a loss for words) онеме́вший. *Be speechless*, онеме́ть; потеря́ть дар ре́чи; лиши́ться да́ра сло́ва. *We were speechless with astonishment*, мы онеме́ли от изумле́ния.

speechwriter *n.* соста́витель рече́й.

speed *n.* ско́рость. *At high speed*, с большо́й ско́ростью; на большо́й ско́рости. *At top speed*, по́лным хо́дом; во весь опо́р. *Full speed ahead!*, по́лный ход! —*v.t.* [*usu.* **speed up**] ускоря́ть: *speed up the pace*, ускоря́ть темп. —*v.i.* **1,** (move rapidly; race) мча́ться. *Speed by*, промча́ться. *Speed away/off*, умча́ться; унести́сь. **2,** (go too fast) превыша́ть дозво́ленную ско́рость. **3,** *fol. by* **up** (go faster) ускоря́ть ход.

speedboat *n.* быстрохо́дный ка́тер.

speed limit дозво́ленная ско́рость. *Exceed the speed limit*, превыша́ть ско́рость.

speedometer *n.* спидо́метр.

speed skating скоростно́й бег на конька́х.

speedway *n.* **1,** (racing strip) автодро́м. **2,** (superhighway) автостра́да.

speedy *adj.* бы́стрый; ско́рый. *I wish you a speedy recovery*, жела́ю вам ско́рого выздоровле́ния.

spell *v.t.* **1,** *usu. passive* (write using certain letters) писа́ть: *How is this word spelled?*, как пи́шется э́то сло́во? *How do you spell your name?*, как пи́шется ва́ша фами́лия? *The word "harass" is spelled with one "r"*, сло́во «harass» пи́шется с одни́м «r». **2,** (name the letters of) сказа́ть по бу́квам: *Spell it for me, please*, скажи́те э́то по бу́квам, пожа́луйста. *Spell the word «воскресе́нье»*, назови́те по бу́квам сло́во «воскресе́нье». **3,** (be the letters of) образо́вывать. **4,** (signify; mean) означа́ть. **5,** (replace temporarily) сменя́ть. —*v.i.* *He spells poorly*, он негра́мотно пи́шет; у него́ хрома́ет орфогра́фия. —*n.* **1,** (compelling attraction) ча́ры. *Cast a spell over*, заколдо́вывать; око́лдовывать. **2,** (short period) полоса́: *spell of good weather*, полоса́ хоро́шей пого́ды. *Cold spell*, похолода́ние. **3,** (attack; fit) при́ступ: *coughing spell*, при́ступ ка́шля. *Fainting spell*, о́бморок. —**spell out,** уточня́ть; подро́бно излага́ть.

spellbound *adj.* очаро́ванный; зачаро́ванный; заворожённый.

spelling *n.* орфогра́фия; правописа́ние. *Correct spelling*, пра́вильная орфогра́фия. *Correct spelling of a word*, пра́вильное написа́ние сло́ва. —*adj.* орфографи́ческий: *spelling error*, орфографи́ческая оши́бка. *Spelling rules*, пра́вила правописа́ния. *Spelling reform*, орфографи́ческая рефо́рма; рефо́рма правописа́ния.

spend *v.t.* **1,** (expend) трáтить: *spend money*, трáтить дéньги. *Spend a fortune*, потрáтить цéлое состоя́ние. *Spend two hours fixing something*, трáтить два часá на почи́нку чего-нибудь. **2,** (pass) проводи́ть: *spend the summer at the seashore*, проводи́ть лéто на мóре. *Spend the night*, ночевáть. *Spend two years in China*, прожи́ть *or* пробы́ть два гóда в Китáе. *Spend six months in prison*, просидéть шесть мéсяцев в тюрьмé. **3,** (use up; exhaust) истощáть; исчéрпывать.

spending *n.* расхóды: *government spending*, прави́тельственные расхóды.

spendthrift *n.* расточи́тель; транжи́р; мот.

spent *adj.* **1,** (physically exhausted) изнурённый; измýченный. **2,** (used up) истощённый; исчéрпанный. *Spent fuel*, отрабóтанное *or* отрабóтавшее тóпливо. **3,** (fired) стрéляный: *spent shell*, стрéляная *or* пустáя ги́льза. *Spent bullet*, пýля на излёте.

sperm *n.* спéрма. **—sperm cell,** сперматозóид; жи́вчик. **—sperm whale,** кашалóт.

spew *v.t.* изверга́ть. **—***v.i.* изверга́ться: *Lava spewed forth from the volcano*, лáва изверга́лась из вулкáна.

sphere *n.* **1,** (round body) шар; сфéра. **2,** *fig.* (area) сфéра: *sphere of influence*, сфéра влия́ния. *Out of my sphere*, не в моéй сфéре; вне моéй сфéры.

spherical *adj.* сфери́ческий; шарообрáзный; шаровóй.

spheroid *n.* сферóид. **—spheroidal,** *adj.* сфероидáльный.

sphinx *n.* сфинкс.

spice *n.* **1,** (seasoning) пря́ность; спéция. **2,** (zest; piquancy) острота́; пикáнтность. **—***v.t.* приправля́ть. *Spice a story with jokes*, приправля́ть расскáз анекдóтами.

spick-and-span *adj.* чи́сто-нáчисто; безукори́зненно чи́стый.

spicy *adj.* **1,** (highly seasoned) пря́ный. **2,** *fig.* (titillating) солёный; пикáнтный.

spider *n.* паýк. **—spider web,** паути́на.

spigot *n.* **1,** (faucet) кран. **2,** (plug) прóбка; заты́чка.

spike *n.* **1,** (sharp-pointed projection) острие́. **2,** (large nail) косты́ль. **3,** (for athletic shoes) шип; шипóвка. **4,** (ear of grain) кóлос. **—***v.t.* **1,** (pierce with a spike) пронзáть; прокáлывать. **2,** (scotch, as a rumor) опроверга́ть.

spikenard *n.* нард.

spill *v.t.* **1,** (a liquid) пролива́ть; разлива́ть. *Spill coffee on one's dress*, пролива́ть кóфе (себé) на плáтье. *Spill wine on the tablecloth*, пролива́ть *or* разлива́ть винó на скáтерть *or* по скáтерти. *Spill soup over oneself*, облива́ться сýпом. *Blood was spilled*, кровь пролилáсь. **2,** (a dry substance) просыпáть; рассыпáть. *Spill salt on the tablecloth*, просыпáть соль на скáтерть. *Spill crumbs on the table*, рассыпáть крóшки на столé *or* пó столу. **—***v.i.* **1,** (of a liquid) пролива́ться; разлива́ться. *Spill over the top*, перелива́ться чéрез край. **2,** (of a dry substance) сы́паться; просыпáться; рассыпáться. **3,** (tumble out) выва́ливаться. *The bag burst and everything spilled onto the floor*, сýмка прорвалáсь, и всё вы-

вáлилось нá пол. **4,** (come rushing out) высыпáть: *People spilled out into the streets*, лю́ди вы́сыпали на ýлицу. **5,** (spread) переки́дываться: *spill into adjacent districts*, переки́дываться на сосéдние райóны. **—spill the beans,** *see* **bean.**

spillway *n.* водосли́в.

spin *v.t.* **1,** (make into thread) прясть: *spin flax*, прясть лён. *Spin a web*, плести́ *or* ткать паути́ну. **2,** (twirl) кружи́ть; вертéть. *Spin a top*, вертéть *or* пускáть волчóк. **3,** (relate; tell) плести́: *spin tales*, плести́ небыли́цы. **—***v.i.* **1,** (spin thread) прясть. **2,** (whirl) кружи́ться; крути́ться; вертéться. *Spin around*, крýто повернýться. *My head is spinning*, у меня́ крýжится головá; у меня́ головá идёт крýгом. **3,** (move along smoothly) кати́ться. **—***n.* **1,** (spinning motion) круже́ние. **2,** (short ride) прогýлка. *Go for a spin*, проéхаться; прокати́ться. **3,** *aero.* штóпор: *go into a spin*, входи́ть в штóпор.

spinach *n.* шпинáт.

spinal *adj.* спиннóй; спинномозговóй. **—spinal column,** спиннóй хребéт; позвонóчный столб; позвонóчник. **—spinal cord,** спиннóй мозг. **—spinal fluid,** спинномозговáя жи́дкость. **—spinal tap,** спинномозговáя пýнкция.

spindle *n.* **1,** (rod used in spinning) веретенó. **2,** (axle; shaft) шпи́ндель.

spindlelegs *n.pl.* журавли́ные нóги.

spine *n.* **1,** (backbone) позвонóчник; спиннóй хребéт. **2,** (quill) иглá. **3,** (thorn) шип. **4,** (stiff backing of a book) корешóк. **—spineless,** *adj.* бесхребéтный; бесхарáктерный.

spinet *n.* пиани́но.

spinner *n.* пряди́льщик; пряди́льщица; пря́ха.

spinning *n.* пряде́ние. **—***adj.* пряди́льный. **—spinning machine,** пряди́льная маши́на. **—spinning wheel,** пря́лка.

spinoff *n.* побóчный продýкт.

spinster *n.* стáрая дéва.

spiny *adj.* игли́стый. **—spiny anteater,** ехи́дна. **—spiny lobster,** лангýст.

spiral *n.* спирáль. **—***adj.* спирáльный. *Spiral staircase*, вита́я *or* винтовáя лéстница.

spire *n.* шпиль.

spirit *n.* **1,** (vital principle in man) дух: *the human spirit*, человéческий дух. **2,** *often pl.* (frame of mind) настроéние: *in low spirits*, в дурнóм настроéнии. *Lift someone's spirits*, поднимáть дух *or* настроéние когó-нибудь. *Keep one's spirits up*, не пáдать дýхом. **3,** (pervading attitude) дух: *fighting spirit*, боевóй дух. *In a spirit of cooperation*, в дýхе сотрýдничества. **4,** (energy; vivacity) жи́вость. *Play with spirit*, игрáть жи́во. **5,** (supernatural being) дух: *evil spirit*, злой дух. **6,** (real meaning or intent) дух: *the spirit of the law*, дух закóна. **7,** *pl.* (alcohol) спиртны́е напи́тки; спиртнóе. **8,** *pl.* (distillate) спирт: *spirits of camphor*, камфáрный спирт. **—***v.t.* [*usu.* **spirit away** *or* **off**] умчáть.

spirited *adj.* живóй; оживлённый; темперáментный.

spirit lamp спиртовáя лáмпа; спиртóвка.

spirit level ватерпáс.

spiritual *adj.* духо́вный. —*n.* негритя́нская религио́зная песнь.

spiritualism *n.* **1,** (belief in communication with the dead) спирити́зм. **2,** *philos.* спиритуали́зм.

spiritualist *n.* **1,** (medium) спири́т. **2,** *philos.* спиритуали́ст.

spirituality *n.* духо́вность.

spit *v.i.* плева́ть: *No spitting!,* не плева́ть! *Spit on the floor,* плю́нуть на́ пол. *Spit in someone's face,* плю́нуть кому́-нибудь в лицо́. —*v.t.* плева́ть (+ *instr.*). *Spit blood,* плева́ть *or* ха́ркать кро́вью. *Spit out the pits,* выплёвывать ко́сточки. —*n.* **1,** (saliva) плево́к. **2,** (rack for roasting meat) ве́ртел. **3,** (narrow point of land) коса́; стре́лка. —**the spit and** (*or* **spitting**) **image of,** живо́й портре́т (+ *gen.*).

spite *n.* зло́ба. *For/out of/spite,* назло́; со зла. —*v.t.* де́лать назло́ (+ *dat.*). *Do something in order to spite someone,* де́лать что́-нибудь назло́ (*or* в пи́ку) кому́-нибудь. —**in spite of,** несмотря́ на.

spiteful *adj.* зло́бный.

spittle *n.* плево́к.

spittoon *n.* плева́тельница.

spitz *n.* шпиц.

splash *v.t.* **1,** (scatter; dash) бры́згать; плеска́ть: *splash water in someone's face,* бры́згать/плеска́ть водо́й (*or* во́ду) в лицо́ кому́-нибудь. **2,** (spatter) забры́згивать. *A passing car splashed the pedestrians with mud,* прое́хавшая ми́мо маши́на обры́згала пешехо́дов гря́зью. —*v.i.* **1,** (fall or strike with a splash) плеска́ть; плеска́ться: *The waves splashed against the shore,* во́лны плеска́ли(сь) о бе́рег. **2,** (move about with splashes) плеска́ться; полоска́ться: *splash about in the water,* плеска́ться/полоска́ться в воде́. —*n.* **1,** (act or sound of splashing) плеск; всплеск. **2,** (that which is splashed) бры́зги.

splashdown *n.* приводне́ние.

splatter *v.t. & i.* = **spatter**.

spleen *n.* **1,** *anat.* селезёнка. **2,** (ill will) зло́ба. —**vent one's spleen,** сорва́ть зло́бу.

splendid *adj.* **1,** (magnificent) великоле́пный; пы́шный; роско́шный. **2,** *colloq.* (fine; excellent) великоле́пный; чу́дный; чуде́сный.

splendor *also,* **splendour** *n.* великоле́пие; пы́шность; блеск. *In all its splendor,* во всём (своём) бле́ске.

splenetic *adj.* **1,** *anat.* селезёночный. **2,** (peevish) жёлчный.

splice *v.t.* сра́щивать: *splice wires,* сра́щивать провода́.

splint *n.* лубо́к; ши́на.

splinter *n.* **1,** (fragment) оско́лок. **2,** (that which gets under the skin) зано́за. *Get a splinter in one's finger,* заноз́ить себе́ па́лец. —*v.t.* раздробля́ть: *splinter the party,* раздробля́ть па́ртию. —*v.i.* раздробля́ться.

split *v.t.* **1,** (cleave) раска́лывать; расщепля́ть: *split logs,* раска́лывать/расщепля́ть поле́нья. *Split the atom,* расщепля́ть а́том. **2,** (divide up and share) дели́ть: *split a bottle of wine,* дели́ть буты́лку вина́. **3,** (divide into opposing factions) раска́лывать: *split the party,* раска́лывать па́ртию. **4,** *fol. by* **up** (divide into smaller units) разбива́ть. —*v.i.* **1,** (break in two)

раска́лываться; расщепля́ться. *The ship split in two,* кора́бль расколо́лся на́двое. **2,** (burst; rip apart) ло́паться; распа́рываться. **3,** (divide into two or more groups or factions) разделя́ться; разбива́ться; раска́лываться; размежёвываться. **4,** *fol. by* **up** (separate; part company) расходи́ться. **5,** *fol. by* **off** (break off or away) отка́лываться. **6,** *My head is splitting,* у меня́ трещи́т голова́. —*n.* **1,** (break; tear) тре́щина. **2,** (division; schism) раско́л. **3,** *gymnastics* шпага́т. —*adj.* раско́лотый; расщеплённый. —**split decision,** *boxing* неединогла́сное реше́ние. —**split hairs,** спо́рить о мелоча́х; вдава́ться в то́нкости. —**split personality,** раздвое́ние ли́чности. —**split picture** (**on TV**), раздво́енное изображе́ние. —**split second,** *Split-second timing,* синхрониза́ция с то́чностью до секу́нды. —**split the difference,** подели́ть ра́зницу попола́м.

splitting *n.* расщепле́ние: *splitting of the atom,* расщепле́ние а́тома. —*adj. Splitting headache,* мучи́тельная головна́я боль. *I have a splitting headache,* у меня́ раска́лывается голова́.

splotch *n.* пятно́; кля́кса.

splurge *v.i.* раскоше́ливаться.

splutter *v.i.* **1,** (make hissing sounds) шипе́ть. **2,** (speak hurriedly or confusedly) лопота́ть.

spoil *v.t.* **1,** (damage; mar) по́ртить: *spoil someone's appetite,* по́ртить кому́-нибудь аппети́т. *The bad weather spoiled our vacation,* плоха́я пого́да испо́ртила нам о́тпуск. **2,** (pamper) балова́ть. —*v.i.* по́ртиться: *The meat spoiled,* мя́со испо́ртилось. —*n., usu. pl.* добы́ча. *The spoils of war,* вое́нная добы́ча; трофе́и. *To the victor belong the spoils,* трофе́и принадлежа́т победи́телю. —**be spoiling for a fight,** лезть в дра́ку.

spoilage *n.* по́рча.

spoiled *adj.* **1,** (damaged) испо́рченный. **2,** (pampered) избало́ванный; бало́ванный.

spoke *n.* спи́ца. —**put a spoke in someone's wheel,** вставля́ть па́лки в колёса (+ *dat.*).

spoken *adj.* у́стный. *The spoken language,* разгово́рный язы́к.

spokesman *n.* представи́тель.

sponge *n.* гу́бка. —*v.t.* вытира́ть *or* обтира́ть гу́бкой. *Sponge oneself down,* обтира́ться. —*v.i., colloq.* жить на чужо́й счёт. *Sponge off someone,* жить за счёт кого́-нибудь. —**throw/toss in the sponge,** *colloq.* призна́ть себя́ побеждённым.

sponge cake бискви́т.

sponger *n., colloq.* тунея́дец; дармое́д; прихлеба́тель; прижива́льщик.

spongy *adj.* гу́бчатый.

sponsor *n.* **1,** (guarantor; benefactor) спо́нсор. **2,** (initiator of a bill or resolution) а́втор. —*v.t.* **1,** (act as a sponsor for) руча́ться за. **2,** (pay for) финанси́ровать. **3,** (introduce, as a bill or resolution) вноси́ть.

sponsorship *n.* покрови́тельство; поручи́тельство.

spontaneity *n.* стихи́йность; непосре́дственность; самопроизво́льность.

spontaneous *adj.* **1,** (resulting from a natural impulse) стихи́йный; непосре́дственный. *Spontaneous upris-*

ing, стихи́йное восста́ние. *Spontaneous laughter*, непосре́дственный смех. **2,** (self-generated) самопрои́звольный; спонта́нный. —**spontaneous combustion,** самовоспламене́ние; самовозгора́ние. —**spontaneous generation,** самозарожде́ние.

spoof *n.* паро́дия; сати́ра. —*v.i.* шути́ть. —*v.t.* высме́ивать.

spook *n., colloq.* **1,** (ghost) привиде́ние; при́зрак. **2,** (secret agent) шпик.

spooky *adj.* при́зрачный; пуга́ющий.

spool *n.* шпу́лька; кату́шка.

spoon *n.* ло́жка. —*v.t.* че́рпать ло́жкой.

spoon bait блесна́.

spoonbill *n.* ко́лпица.

spoonful *n.* ло́жка.

sporadic *adj.* споради́ческий. —**sporadically,** *adv.* споради́чески; вре́мя от вре́мени.

spore *n.* спо́ра.

sport *n.* **1,** *usu. pl.* (athletic activity) спорт: *engage in sports*, занима́ться спо́ртом. **2,** (particular type of such activity) вид спо́рта: *my favorite sport*, мой люби́мый вид спо́рта. *Winter sports*, зи́мние ви́ды спо́рта. **3,** (jest) шу́тка: *say something in sport*, сказа́ть что́-нибудь в шу́тку. **4,** *colloq.* (good fellow) молоде́ц. *Be a sport!*, будь челове́ком! —*adj.* [*also*, **sports**] спорти́вный: *sport shirt*, спорти́вная руба́шка; *sports car*, спорти́вный автомоби́ль. —*v.t.* щеголя́ть в: *sport a new suit*, щеголя́ть в но́вом костю́ме. —**make sport of,** подшу́чивать над.

sporting *adj.* **1,** (used in sports) спорти́вный: *sporting goods*, спорти́вные това́ры. **2,** (fair) неплохо́й: *a sporting chance*, неплохи́е ша́нсы.

sportscaster *n.* спорти́вный коммента́тор.

sportsman *n.* спортсме́н. —**sportsmanlike,** *adj.* спортсме́нский. —**sportsmanship,** *n.* поведе́ние, подоба́ющее спортсме́ну.

sportswear *n.* спорти́вная оде́жда.

spot *n.* **1,** (stain; blemish) пятно́: *grease spot*, жи́рное пятно́. *Spots on one's face*, пя́тна на лице́. **2,** *usu. pl.* (marking on an animal or bird) пятно́; кра́пинка. **3,** (place; location) ме́сто: *a convenient spot*, удо́бное ме́сто. *Sore spot*, больно́е ме́сто. *Weak spot*, сла́бое ме́сто. *Riveted to the spot*, пригвождённый к ме́сту. *Have a soft spot in one's heart for*, пита́ть сла́бость к. **4,** (set of circumstances) положе́ние: *in a tight spot*, в затрудни́тельном положе́нии. —*v.t.* **1,** (stain) пятна́ть; зака́пать. **2,** (catch sight of; detect) заме́тить; уви́деть; рассмотре́ть; разгляде́ть; вы́смотреть. **3,** (give, as a certain number of points) дава́ть (не́сколько очко́в) вперёд. —*v.i.* па́чкаться: *spot easily*, легко́ па́чкаться. —**in spots,** места́ми. —**on the spot, 1,** (at once) тут же. **2,** (at the scene of action) на ме́сте. **3,** (in a difficult position) в тупике́. *Put on the spot*, ста́вить в тупи́к.

spot check вы́борочная прове́рка.

spotless *adj.* безукори́зненно чи́стый. —**spotlessly,** *adv. Spotlessly clean*, чи́сто-на́чисто; безукори́зненно чи́стый.

spotlight *n.* прожёктор. —**be in the spotlight,** быть в це́нтре внима́ния.

spotted *adj.* пятни́стый; кра́пчатый; рябо́й.

spotter *n., mil.* корректиро́вщик. —**spotter plane,** самолёт-корректиро́вщик.

spouse *n.* супру́г; супру́га.

spout *v.t.* **1,** (discharge with force) изверга́ть. **2,** (utter profusely) сы́пать. —*v.i.* **1,** (shoot out with force) хлы́нуть; бить струёй. **2,** (speak pompously) разглаго́льствовать. —*n.* **1,** (projection for pouring a liquid) но́сик. **2,** (stream of liquid) струя́.

sprain *n.* растяже́ние. —*v.t.* растя́гивать; подвёртывать. *Sprain one's ankle*, подверну́ть себе́ но́гу.

sprat *n.* ки́лька; шпро́та.

sprawl *v.i.* растя́гиваться; разва́ливаться. *Send someone sprawling*, повали́ть кого́-нибудь с ног. *He lay sprawled across the bed*, он лежа́л, распласта́вшись поперёк крова́ти.

spray *n.* **1,** (fine liquid particles) бры́зги. **2,** (atomizer) распыли́тель; пульвериза́тор; опры́скиватель. **3,** (liquid discharged from an atomizer) жи́дкость: *hair spray*, жи́дкость для воло́с. **4,** (branch) ве́точка. —*v.t.* **1,** (direct a spray of) обры́згивать; разбры́згивать. **2,** (treat with a spray) опры́скивать; распыля́ть. **3,** (rake, as with bullets) полива́ть (пу́лями).

sprayer *n.* распыли́тель; пульвериза́тор.

spray gun краскопу́льт.

spread *v.t.* **1,** *often fol. by* **out** (stretch out to its full extent) расстила́ть; раскла́дывать; растя́гивать: *spread a tablecloth*, расстила́ть ска́терть; *spread out a map/blanket*, раскла́дывать ка́рту/одея́ло. **2,** *usu. fol. by* **out** (lay out in display) раскла́дывать; выкла́дывать. **3,** (move apart; extend out) раздвига́ть; расставля́ть: *spread one's legs*, раздвига́ть/расставля́ть но́ги. *Spread one's wings*, расправля́ть кры́лья. **4,** (diffuse; disseminate) распространя́ть: *spread rumors*, распространя́ть слу́хи. *Flies spread disease*, му́хи распространя́ют боле́зни. **5,** (scatter; strew) рассыпа́ть; разбра́сывать. *Spread manure*, разбра́сывать наво́з. **6,** (smear) нама́зывать: *spread butter on bread*, нама́зывать ма́сло на хлеб. **7,** (extend over a period of time, as payments) рассро́чивать. —*v.i.* распространя́ться: *The fire spread quickly*, пожа́р бы́стро распространя́лся. *The news spread all over town*, но́вость обошла́ / облете́ла весь го́род; но́вость разнесла́сь по го́роду. —*n.* **1,** (diffusion; dissemination) распростране́ние: *prevent the spread of disease*, предотвраща́ть распростране́ние боле́зней. **2,** (expanse) разма́х: *wingspread*, разма́х кры́льев. **3,** (bedspread) покрыва́ло. **4,** (soft food) па́ста: *cheese spread*, сы́рная па́ста. **5,** (food set out on a table) угоще́ние. **6,** (differential, as between prices) разры́в. —**spread oneself thin,** разбра́сываться.

spreading *n.* распростране́ние: *the spreading of rumors*, распростране́ние слу́хов. —*adj.* **1,** (expanding in range) бы́стро распространя́ющийся. **2,** (of a tree) разве́систый; раски́дистый.

spree *n.* кутёж. *Go on a spree*, кути́ть; устра́ивать кутёж.

sprig *n.* ве́точка; побе́г.

sprightly *adj.* бо́дрый; задо́рный.

spring *v.i.* **1,** (leap) прыѓгать; вскаѓкивать. *Spring to one's feet,* вскочиѓть наѓ ноги. **2,** *fol. by* **up** (come into being; develop) возникаѓть; появляѓться; завяѓзываться. *New town are springing up everywhere,* повсюѓду возникаѓют ноѓвые городаѓ. *A conversation sprang up,* завязаѓлся разговоѓр. **3,** *fol. by* **from** (stem from; be due to) происходиѓть (от). **4,** *Spring open,* распахнуѓться; *spring shut,* захлоѓпнуться. —*v.t.* **1,** (release; actuate) пускаѓть в ход. **2,** (present or make known suddenly) преподносиѓть: *spring a surprise on,* преподносиѓть сюрприѓз (+ *dat.*). **3,** *Spring a leak,* дать течь. —*n.* **1,** (season) веснаѓ. *In spring,* весноѓй. **2,** (device for applying tension) пружиѓна; (*on vehicles*) рессоѓра. **3,** (elasticity) упруѓгость. **4,** (water rising from the ground) истоѓчник; ключ; родниѓк. *Hot springs,* горяѓчие истоѓчники. —*adj.* **1,** (of springtime) весеѓнний: *spring vacation,* весеѓнние каниѓкулы. **2,** (motivated by tension) пружиѓнный: *spring mattress,* пружиѓнный матраѓс. **3,** (flowing up from the ground) ключевоѓй; родникоѓвый.

springboard *n.* **1,** (used by athletes and acrobats) трамплиѓн. **2,** *fig.* (starting point; impetus) трамплиѓн; плацдаѓрм.

springtime *n.* веснаѓ; весеѓнняя пораѓ; весеѓннее вреѓмя.

springy *adj.* упруѓгий; пружиѓнистый.

sprinkle *v.t.* **1,** (scatter in drops) брыѓзгать: *sprinkle water on,* брыѓзгать водоѓй на (+ *acc.*). **2,** (scatter drops of something on) обрыѓзгивать; кропиѓть; окропляѓть; опрыѓскивать (*e.g.* что́-нибудь водоѓй). **3,** (scatter in particles) посыпаѓть: *sprinkle salt in the soup,* посыпаѓть соль в суп. **4,** (scatter particles of something on) посыпаѓть: *sprinkle the road with sand,* посыпаѓть дороѓгу пескоѓм. —*v.i.* (rain lightly) моросиѓть; накраѓпывать. —*n.* доѓждик; иѓзморось.

sprinkler *n.* разбрыѓзгиватель. —**sprinkler system,** дождеваѓльная устаноѓвка.

sprinkling *n.* **1,** (spraying of water) дождеваѓние. **2,** (small admixture) приѓмесь. —**sprinkling can,** леѓйка.

sprint *n.* **1,** (short race) спринт. **2,** (extra burst of speed) рывоѓк; бросоѓк. —*v.i.* броѓситься; помчаѓться; бежаѓть во весь опоѓр. —**sprinter,** *n.* сприѓнтер.

sprite *n.* эльф. *Water sprite,* водяноѓй.

sprocket *n.* зубеѓц. —**sprocket wheel,** цепноѓе колесоѓ.

sprout *v.i.* пускаѓть ростки́; прорастаѓть. —*v.t.* отраѓщивать. —*n.* отроѓсток;ростоѓк; побеѓг.

spruce *n.* (tree) ель. —*v.t. & i.* [*usu.* **spruce up**] наряжаѓть(ся); прихораѓшивать(ся).

spry *adj.* живоѓй; боѓйкий; боѓдрый; юѓркий. —**spryness,** *n.* жиѓвость; боѓдрость.

spud *n., colloq.* картоѓфелина.

spume *n.* пеѓна; наѓкипь.

spun *adj.* пряѓденый.

spunk *n., colloq.* боѓдрость дуѓха. —**spunky,** *adj., colloq.* боѓйкий; темпераѓментный.

spur *n.* **1,** (of a horseman) шпоѓра. **2,** (of a mountain) отроѓг. **3,** (branch line) веѓтка. **4,** *fig.* (stimulus) толчоѓк. —*v.t.* **1,** (urge on with spurs) пришпоѓривать. **2,** (stimulate; rouse) побуждаѓть: *spur to action,* побуждаѓть к деѓйствию. —**on the spur of the moment,** под влияѓнием минуѓты.

spurious *adj.* **1,** (counterfeit) подлоѓжный; поддеѓльный. **2,** (false; not true) лоѓжный: *spurious charges,* лоѓжные обвинеѓния.

spurn *v.t.* отвергаѓть; оттаѓлкивать.

spurt *n.* **1,** (gush of liquid) струяѓ. **2,** (sudden burst of speed) рывоѓк; бросоѓк. —*v.i.* **1,** (gush) бить струѓей; брыѓзгать; хлыѓнуть. *Blood spurted from the wound,* кровь брыѓзнула *or* хлыѓнула из раѓны. **2,** (put on a burst of speed) сдеѓлать рывоѓк *or* бросоѓк.

sputter *v.i.* **1,** (make hissing sounds) шипеѓть. **2,** (speak hurriedly or confusedly) лопотаѓть.

sputum *n.* плевоѓк.

spy *n.* шпиоѓн. —*adj.* шпиоѓнский: *spy ring,* шпиоѓнская организаѓция *or* сеть. —*v.i.* **1,** (engage in espionage) шпиоѓнить. *He was convicted of spying on behalf of...,* он был осуждёѓн за шпионаѓж в поѓльзу (+ *gen.*). **2,** *fol. by* **on** (watch furtively) подсмаѓтривать за. —*v.t.* (see; catch sight of) рассмотреѓть; разглядеѓть.

spyglass *n.* подзоѓрная трубаѓ.

squab *n.* (неопериѓвшийся) гоѓлубь.

squabble *n.* перебраѓнка; пререкаѓния. —*v.i.* вздоѓрить; пререкаѓться; препираѓться.

squad *n.* **1,** (smallest army unit) отделеѓние. **2,** (small organized group) отряѓд; наряѓд; комаѓнда; бригаѓда. *Rescue squad,* спасаѓтельная комаѓнда.

squadron *n.* **1,** *naval* эскаѓдра. **2,** (of cavalry) эскадроѓн. **3,** *aero.* эскадриѓлья.

squalid *adj.* убоѓгий: *squalid dwelling,* убоѓгое жилиѓще.

squall *n.* **1,** (yell) вопль. **2,** (storm) шквал. —*v.i.* ораѓть; вопиѓть.

squalor *n.* убоѓжество; убоѓгость. *Live in squalor,* жить в убоѓжестве.

squander *v.t.* растраѓчивать; расточаѓть; промаѓтывать. —**squanderer,** *n.* расточиѓтель.

square *n.* **1,** (equilateral rectangle) квадраѓт. **2,** (open area in a city) плоѓщадь: *Red Square,* Краѓсная плоѓщадь. *A demonstration in Pushkin Square,* демонстраѓция на плоѓщади Пуѓшкина. **3,** *math.* квадраѓт: *The square of three is nine,* три в квадраѓте равноѓ девятиѓ. **4,** (T-shaped or L-shaped instrument) угоѓльник; наугоѓльник; рейсшиѓна. **5,** *chess* клеѓтка; поѓле. *Advance a pawn one square,* передвиѓнуть пеѓшку впереёѓд на одну́ клеѓтку. —*adj.* **1,** (equal on all four sides) квадраѓтный: *a square table,* квадраѓтный стол. **2,** (expressing surface measures) квадраѓтный: *square meter,* квадраѓтный метр. *The room is five meters square,* коѓмната имеѓет размеѓры пять на пять меѓтров. **3,** (honest; fair; equitable) честный: *a square deal,* честная сдеѓлка. **4,** (paid-up; even) в расчёѓте; квиѓты: *We're all square,* мы с ваѓми в расчёѓте; мы с ваѓми квиѓты. **5,** *Square meal,* плоѓтный обеѓд. —*v.t.* **1,** (straighten, as one's shoulders) расправляѓть; распрямляѓть. **2,** (multiply by itself) возводиѓть в квадраѓт. *Ten squared equals 100,* деѓсять в квадраѓте равноѓ ста. *The area of a circle is* πr^2, плоѓщадь круѓга — πг квадраѓт. **3,** (settle, as accounts) своди́ть (счёѓты). **4,** (reconcile, as one statement with another) увяѓзывать. —*v.i.* [*usu.* **square with**] (be consistent) согласова́ться (с); вяза́ться (с). —*adv.* **1,** (at right angles) под прямы́м угло́м. **2,** [*usu.* **fair and square**] (fairly) че́стно. **3,** (directly) пря́мо: *look someone square in the eye,* смотре́ть кому́-нибудь пря́мо в глаза́.

squarely *adv.* пря́мо. *Face the facts squarely,* смотре́ть фа́ктам пря́мо в лицо́. *Confront a question squarely,* вплотну́ю подходи́ть к вопро́су.

square root квадра́тный ко́рень.

squash *n.* **1,** (vegetable) кабачо́к. **2,** (beverage) лимона́д. —*v.t.* **1,** (crush) расплю́щивать; (раз)дави́ть. **2,** (suppress) подавля́ть.

squat *v.i.* приседа́ть; сиде́ть на ко́рточках; сесть на ко́рточки. —*n.* приседа́ние. —*adj.* призе́мистый. —**squatter,** *n.* сква́ттер.

squaw *n.* индиа́нка.

squawk *v.i.* **1,** (cry hoarsely) клекота́ть. **2,** *slang* (complain) ворча́ть. —*n.* **1,** (hoarse cry) клёкот. **2,** *slang* (complaint) жа́лоба.

squeak *v.i.* скрипе́ть. —*n.* скрип. —**squeaky,** *adj.* скрипу́чий.

squeal *v.i.* **1,** (utter a loud, sharp sound) визжа́ть. **2,** *slang* (inform) доноси́ть. —*n.* визг. —**squealer,** *n.,* *slang* (informer) доно́счик; стука́ч.

squeamish *adj.* брезгли́вый. —**squeamishness,** *n.* брезгли́вость.

squeeze *v.t.* **1,** (press) сжима́ть; сти́скивать. *Squeeze a lemon,* дави́ть *or* жать лимо́н. *Squeeze someone's hand,* сжать чью́-нибудь ру́ку. **2,** (extract by squeezing) выжима́ть: *squeeze juice from an orange,* выжима́ть сок из апельси́на. **3,** (cram) вти́скивать: *squeeze everything into a suitcase,* вти́снуть всё в чемода́н. *Squeeze a lot into five days,* вти́снуть мно́го в пять дней. —*v.i.* **1,** (apply pressure) жать; сжима́ть. **2,** *fol. by* **in, into** *or* **through** (force one's way) вти́скиваться (в); проти́скиваться (в). —*n.* **1,** (act of squeezing) сжа́тие. **2,** (embrace) объя́тие. **3,** (cramming; crowding) да́вка. *It was something of a squeeze,* бы́ло тесноватo.

squeezer *n.* соковыжима́лка.

squelch *v.t.* пресека́ть; подавля́ть. *Squelch a rumor,* опрове́ргнуть слух.

squid *n.* кальма́р.

squiggle *n.* закорю́чка.

squint *v.i.* **1,** (screw up one's eyes) жму́риться; щу́риться. *Squint from the bright sun,* жму́риться от я́ркого со́лнца. **2,** (be cross-eyed) коси́ть. **3,** (look sideways) коси́ть глаза́ми. —*n.* косогла́зие.

squire *n.* **1,** (title) сквайр. **2,** (lady's escort) кавале́р. —*v.t.* сопровожда́ть.

squirm *v.i.* **1,** (wriggle) извива́ться; ко́рчиться. *Squirm out of,* вывёртываться из. **2,** (fret; worry) му́читься.

squirrel *n.* бе́лка. —*adj.* бе́личий: *squirrel coat,* бе́личья шу́ба.

squirt *v.t.* пуска́ть струёй. *Squirt water in someone's face,* пуска́ть стру́йку воды́ в лицо́ (+ *dat.*). —*v.i.* бить струёй. —*n.* струя́; стру́йка.

stab *v.t.* уда́рить (кого́-нибудь) ножо́м; коло́ть. *Stab to death,* заколо́ть. *Stab someone in the back,*

уда́рить кого́-нибудь (*or* нанести́ кому́-нибудь уда́р) ножо́м в спи́ну; *fig.* нанести́ кому́-нибудь преда́тельский уда́р. —*n.* уда́р (ножо́м). *Stab in the back,* уда́р *or* нож в спи́ну. —**stabbing pain,** ко́лющая боль. —**stab wound,** ко́лотая ра́на.

stability *n.* усто́йчивость; стаби́льность.

stabilize *v.t.* стабилизи́ровать. —*v.i.* стабилизи́роваться. —**stabilization,** *n.* стабилиза́ция. —**stabilizer,** *n.* стабилиза́тор.

stable *adj.* **1,** (steady; firm) усто́йчивый; стаби́льный. *Stable currency,* усто́йчивая валю́та. *Stable prices,* усто́йчивые *or* стаби́льные це́ны. **2,** *chem.* сто́йкий. —*n.* коню́шня. —*v.t.* ста́вить в коню́шню; держа́ть в коню́шне.

stableboy *n.* ко́нюх. *Also,* **stable hand.**

staccato *adj.* отры́вистый. —*adv.* стакка́то.

stack *n.* **1,** (orderly pile) ки́па: *stack of papers,* ки́па бума́г. *Stack of wood,* шта́бель дров. *Stack of logs,* поле́нница. **2,** (pile of hay or straw) стог; скирд; скирда́. **3,** *pl.* (library shelves) стелла́ж. —*v.t.* [*often* **stack up**] скла́дывать. *Stack hay,* смётывать се́но. —**stack the cards** *or* **deck,** подтасо́вывать ка́рты.

stadium *n.* стадио́н. *In the stadium,* на стадио́не.

staff *n.* **1,** (long stick) по́сох. **2,** (flagpole) дре́вко. **3,** (rod as a symbol of authority) жезл. **4,** (personnel) штат; соста́в. *Be on the staff,* быть *or* состоя́ть в шта́те. *Teaching staff,* преподава́тельский соста́в. *Staff reduction,* сокраще́ние шта́тов. **5,** *mil.* штаб: *the general staff,* генера́льный штаб. *Chief of staff,* нача́льник шта́ба. **6,** *music* но́тный стан; нотоно́сец. —*adj.* **1,** (permanent) шта́тный: *staff position,* шта́тная до́лжность. **2,** *mil.* штабно́й: *staff officer,* штабно́й офице́р. —*v.t.* обеспе́чивать персона́лом; *mil.* укомплекто́вывать ли́чным соста́вом.

stag *n.* **1,** (male deer) рога́ч. **2,** *adj., colloq.* (for men only) холостя́цкий. —**stag beetle,** рога́ч.

stage *n.* **1,** (theater platform) сце́на: *appear on stage,* выступа́ть на сце́не. **2,** (dais) помо́ст. **3,** (theatrical profession) сце́на: *retire from the stage,* уходи́ть со сце́ны. **4,** (step; phase) ста́дия; эта́п. *In stages,* по ста́диям. *At an early stage,* на ра́нней ста́дии. *Reach a critical stage,* вступи́ть в крити́ческую ста́дию. **5,** (leg of a journey) перего́н. **6,** *rocketry* ступе́нь. —*v.t.* **1,** (put on) ста́вить: *stage a play,* ста́вить пье́су. **2,** (adapt for the stage) инсцени́ровать. **3,** (carry out; hold) устра́ивать; проводи́ть; организова́ть: *Stage a strike,* проводи́ть забасто́вку. **4,** (make appear spontaneous) инсцени́ровать. —**set the stage for,** подгота́вливать по́чву для.

stagecoach *n.* дилижа́нс.

stage effects сцени́ческие эффе́кты.

stage fright страх пе́ред пу́бликой. *Suffer from stage fright,* стесня́ться пу́блики.

stagehand *n.* рабо́чий сце́ны.

stage manager режиссёр.

stage props реквизи́т; бутафо́рия.

stagger *v.i.* шата́ться; пошатну́ться. *He staggered out of the bar and collapsed,* шата́ясь, он вы́шел из ба́ра и свали́лся. —*v.t.* **1,** (shock; stun) потряса́ть; ошеломля́ть. **2,** (alternate) чередова́ть. *Staggered work* *schedule,* скользя́щий гра́фик рабо́ты. —**stagger-ing,** *adj.* потряса́ющий; ошеломля́ющий.

staging *n.* постано́вка (пье́сы). —**staging area,** *mil.* плацда́рм.

stagnant *adj.* **1,** (foul; polluted) стоя́чий; засто́йный. *Become stagnant,* заста́иваться. **2,** *fig.* (sluggish) вя́лый; ко́сный.

stagnate *v.i.* **1,** (become foul) заста́иваться. **2,** (become sluggish) косне́ть. —**stagnation,** *n.* засто́й.

staid *adj.* степе́нный; положи́тельный.

stain *n.* **1,** (spot; blemish) пятно́. **2,** (coloring substance) мори́лка. —*v.t.* **1,** (spot; soil) пятна́ть; па́чкать. **2,** (color; tint) мори́ть: *stain wood,* мори́ть де́рево. —*v.i.* па́чкаться.

stained *adj.* морёный: *stained oak,* морёный дуб. —**stained glass,** цветно́е стекло́. *Stained-glass window,* витра́ж.

stainless steel нержаве́ющая сталь.

stair *n.* **1,** (step) ступе́нька. **2,** *usu. pl.* (staircase) ле́стница.

staircase *n.* ле́стница. *Also,* **stairway.**

stairwell *n.* ле́стничная кле́тка; пролёт; прого́н.

stake *n.* **1,** (pointed stick) кол. **2,** (post for execution): *be burned at the stake,* поги́бнуть на костре́. **3,** (money wagered) ста́вка. *The stakes are high,* ста́вки велики́. *Play for high stakes,* игра́ть по большо́й; вести́ кру́пную игру́. **4,** (share; interest) до́ля. *Have a stake in the outcome,* быть заинтересо́ванным в исхо́де де́ла. —*v.t.* **1,** *fol. by* **out** *or* **off** (delineate) отмеча́ть ве́хами. *Stake out a claim,* заявля́ть прете́нзию. **2,** *fol. by* **out** (put under surveillance) установи́ть слёжку за. **3,** (bet; risk) ста́вить; ста́вить на ка́рту. *Stake one's all,* поста́вить всё на ка́рту. *Stake one's life on it,* руча́ться за что́-нибудь голово́й; дава́ть ру́ку (*or* го́лову) на отсече́ние. **4,** (provide with money or resources) финанси́ровать. —**at stake,** поста́влен на ка́рту. *The fate of the country was at stake,* реша́лась судьба́ страны́. —**pull up stakes,** сня́ться с ме́ста.

stalactite *n.* сталакти́т.

stalagmite *n.* сталагми́т.

stale *adj.* **1,** (no longer fresh) чёрствый: *stale bread,* чёрствый хлеб. *Stale air,* спёртый во́здух. *Become stale,* черстве́ть. **2,** (trite; hackneyed) изби́тый. *Stale news,* устаре́вшие но́вости.

stalemate *n.* **1,** *chess* пат. **2,** (deadlock) мёртвая то́чка; тупи́к. —*v.t.* заводи́ть в тупи́к. *The talks are stalemated,* перегово́ры зашли́ в тупи́к.

stalk *n.* сте́бель. —*v.i.* шага́ть. *Stalk out of the room,* демонстрати́вно уйти́ из ко́мнаты. —*v.t.* **1,** (pursue stealthily) выслёживать: *stalk its prey,* выслёживать добы́чу. **2,** (advance grimly across) броди́ть по: *Hunger stalked the land,* го́лод броди́л по стране́.

stall *n.* **1,** (compartment for an animal) сто́йло. **2,** (market booth) ларёк; пала́тка. **3,** *Brit.* (orchestra seat) кре́сло в парте́ре. —*v.t.* **1,** (put or lodge in a stall) ста́вить в сто́йло. **2,** (delay; check) заде́рживать; тормози́ть. *Negotiations are stalled,* перегово́ры зашли́ в тупи́к. **3,** *fol. by* **off** (delay; divert) заде́рживать. —*v.i.* **1,** (stop running, as of an engine)

гло́хнуть; захлёбываться. **2,** (get stuck) застрева́ть. **3,** (use delaying tactics) оття́гивать вре́мя.

stallion *n.* жеребе́ц.

stalwart *adj.* **1,** (robust) дю́жий; ро́слый. **2,** (loyal; staunch) ве́рный; сто́йкий. **3,** (brave; valiant) отва́жный; до́блестный. —*n.* сто́йкий сторо́нник.

stamen *n.* тычи́нка.

stamina *n.* выно́сливость.

stammer *v.i.* заика́ться. —*n.* заика́ние. —**stammer-er,** *n.* заи́ка. —**stammering,** *n.* заика́ние.

stamp *n.* **1,** (postage stamp) ма́рка: *30-cent stamp,* ма́рка за три́дцать це́нтов. **2,** (marking device; impression so made) печа́ть; штамп; ште́мпель. —*v.t.* **1,** (bring down forcibly) то́пать: *stamp one's feet,* то́пать нога́ми. *The stamping of feet,* то́пот ног. **2,** (impress with a mark) штампова́ть; штемпелева́ть. *Stamp a passport,* штампова́ть па́спорт; ста́вить штамп на па́спорт. **3,** *fol. by* **out** (extinguish by stamping on) зата́птывать. **4,** *fol. by* **out** (eradicate) искореня́ть. —*v.i.* то́пать нога́ми. —**stamp album,** альбо́м для ма́рок. —**stamp collecting,** собира́ние ма́рок. —**stamp collection,** колле́кция ма́рок. —**stamp collector,** филатели́ст. —**stamp pad,** поду́шка для штемпеле́й; ште́мпельная поду́шка.

stampede *n.* пани́ческое бе́гство. —*v.i.* броса́ться врассыпну́ю; обраща́ться в пани́ческое бе́гство.

stance *n.* по́за; положе́ние; *sports* сто́йка.

stanch *v.t.* остана́вливать (кровотече́ние). —*adj.* = **staunch.**

stanchion *n.* сто́йка; *naut.* пи́ллерс.

stand *v.i.* **1,** (be in an upright position) стоя́ть: *She was standing in the doorway,* она́ стоя́ла в дверя́х. *Stand (i.e. wait) in line,* стоя́ть *or* выста́ивать в о́череди. **2,** (station oneself somewhere standing) станови́ться (*pfv.* стать); встава́ть: *stand on a chair,* стать *or* встать на стул. *Stand (i.e. get) in line,* стать в о́чередь. *Stand on your tiptoes!,* стань на цы́почки! *Stand still!,* не дви́гайтесь! **3,** *often fol. by* **up** (get up; rise) встава́ть. **4,** (be placed or situated) стоя́ть: *The house stands on a hill,* дом стои́т на холме́. **5,** (be a certain height) быть ро́стом: *He stands six feet tall,* он ро́стом шесть фу́тов. **6,** (be; remain) стоя́ть: *The house stands empty,* дом стои́т пусто́й; дом пусту́ет. *Not a building was left standing,* ни одного́ зда́ния не оста́лось. *The door stood open,* дверь была́ на́стежь. *That is how matters stand,* вот как обстои́т де́ло. *Stand accused of,* обвиня́ться в. *The thermometer stands at zero,* термо́метр пока́зывает нуль. **7,** (remain in effect) остава́ться в си́ле: *The decision stands,* реше́ние остаётся в си́ле. *The record not did stand for long,* реко́рд продержа́лся недо́лго. **8,** *Brit.* (be a candidate) баллоти́роваться. —*v.t.* **1,** (set upright) ста́вить: *Stand the vase on the table,* ста́вить ва́зу на стол. *Stand the table against the wall,* ста́вить стол вплотну́ю к стене́. **2,** (endure) терпе́ть; выноси́ть. *I can't stand it,* я э́того терпе́ть не могу́. **3,** *Stand guard,* стоя́ть на часа́х/ в карау́ле/ на стра́же/. **4,** *Stand trial,* предста́ть пе́ред судо́м. **5,** *Stand a chance,* име́ть ша́нсы. —*n.* **1,** (instance of standing) стоя́ние: *a long stand in line,* до́лгое стоя́ние в о́череди. **2,** (small display table) стенд. **3,**

(support; base, as for a vase) подста́вка. *Music stand,* но́тный пюпи́тр. **4,** (raised platform for performers) эстра́да. **5,** (selling place) ларёк; кио́ск: *fruit stand,* фрукто́вый ларёк; *flower stand,* цвето́чный кио́ск. **6,** (parking place for taxis) стоя́нка. **7,** *pl.* (grandstand) трибу́на. **8,** (final defensive effort) сопротивле́ние: *make a stand,* ока́зывать сопротивле́ние. **9,** (view; opinion; position) пози́ция. *Take a stand,* занима́ть определённую пози́цию. **10,** (stop on a tour) гастро́ли: *one-night stand,* однодне́вные гастро́ли. —**stand aside, 1,** (of a person) сторони́ться. **2,** (of a crowd) расступа́ться. —**stand back,** отступа́ть; держа́ться на расстоя́нии. —**stand by, 1,** (remain aloof) держа́ться в стороне́. **2,** (stand ready) быть нагото́ве. **3,** (stand firmly behind) остава́ться ве́рен (+ *dat.*). **4,** (not depart from) приде́рживаться (+ *gen.*): *stand by one's principles,* приде́рживаться при́нципов. —**stand for, 1,** (represent; signify) означа́ть. **2,** (tolerate) терпе́ть. **3,** (advocate; favor) стоя́ть за. —**stand in for,** замеща́ть. —**stand out,** выделя́ться: *stand out in a crowd,* выделя́ться в толпе́. —**stand over,** стоя́ть над (чьей-нибудь) душо́й. —**stand up, 1,** (rise) встава́ть. *Stand up straight,* держа́ться пря́мо. *Everyone stood up when the teacher entered the classroom,* все вста́ли, когда́ учи́тель вошёл в класс. **2,** (set upright) ста́вить стоймя́. **3,** (prove durable) служи́ть: *These shoes have stood up well,* э́ти боти́нки хорошо́ послужи́ли. **4,** *slang* (disappoint) подводи́ть. —**stand up for,** заступа́ться за. *Stand up for one's rights,* отста́ивать свои́ права́. —**stand up to,** вы́стоять про́тив. —**stand up under,** выде́рживать.

standard *n.* **1,** (norm) станда́рт; но́рма; мери́ло; ме́рка. *Moral standards,* мора́льные но́рмы. *Double standard,* двойно́й станда́рт; двойна́я ме́рка. *Up to standard,* на до́лжной высоте́. **2,** (degree; level) у́ровень: *standard of living,* у́ровень жи́зни. **3,** (basis of a monetary system) станда́рт: *gold standard,* золото́й станда́рт. **4,** (banner) зна́мя; штанда́рт. —*adj.* станда́ртный; типово́й. *Standard textbook,* стаби́льный уче́бник. —**standard-bearer,** *n.* знамено́сец.

standardize *v.t.* стандартизи́ровать; норми́ровать; унифици́ровать. —**standardization,** *n.* стандартиза́ция; норми́рование; унифика́ция.

standee *n., colloq.* стоя́щий зри́тель; стоя́щий пасса́жи́р.

stand-in *n.* дублёр.

standing *n.* **1,** (act of standing) стоя́ние. **2,** (status) положе́ние. *Be in good standing,* быть на хоро́шем счету́. **3,** *pl., sports* положе́ние: *team standings,* положе́ние кома́нд. —*adj.* **1,** (upright; on one's feet) стоя́чий; стоя́щий. *Standing position,* стоя́чее положе́ние. **2,** *sports* (from a standing position) с ме́ста: *standing broad jump,* прыжо́к с ме́ста. **3,** (permanent) постоя́нный: *standing army,* постоя́нная а́рмия; *standing invitation,* постоя́нное приглаше́ние. —**of long standing,** да́вний: *a friendship of long standing,* да́вняя дру́жба.

standing room стоя́чие места́: *standing room only,* биле́ты то́лько на стоя́чие места́.

stand-off *n.* ничья́.

standoffish *adj.* необщи́тельный; холо́дный.

standpoint *n.* то́чка зре́ния.

standstill *n.* мёртвая то́чка. *Be at a standstill,* проста́ивать; быть на мёртвой то́чке. *Come to a standstill,* замира́ть; (за)сто́пориться. *Negotiations are at a standstill,* перегово́ры зашли́ в тупи́к.

stanza *n.* строфа́; купле́т.

staple *n.* **1,** (wire clamp) скоба́; ско́бка. **2,** (clip) скре́пка. **3,** (principal commodity) основно́й проду́кт. **4,** (raw material) сырьё. —*adj.* основно́й; гла́вный. —*v.t.* скрепля́ть.

star *n.* звезда́. *Movie star,* кинозвезда́. —*adj.* **1,** (of stars) звёздный: *star map,* звёздная ка́рта. **2,** (outstanding) выдаю́щийся. —*v.t.* **1,** (mark with an asterisk) помеча́ть звёздочкой. **2,** (feature): *The film stars...,* в фи́льме...игра́ет гла́вную роль. —*v.i.* игра́ть гла́вную роль; выступа́ть в гла́вной ро́ли. —**see stars,** *colloq.* све́та невзви́деть. *He saw stars,* у него́ и́скры из глаз посы́пались. —**thank one's lucky stars,** благодари́ть *or* благословля́ть судьбу́.

starboard *adj.* пра́вый. —*n.* пра́вый борт.

starch *n.* крахма́л. —*v.t.* крахма́лить. —**starched,** *adj.* накрахма́ленный; крахма́льный.

starchy *adj.* **1,** (containing starch) крахма́листый. *Starchy foods,* мучно́е. **2,** (stiffened with starch) накрахма́ленный.

stare *v.i.* смотре́ть при́стально; глазе́ть. *Stare at,* уста́виться на. *Stop staring!,* переста́нь глазе́ть! *What are you staring at?,* куда́ ты уста́вился? *Stare into the distance,* всма́триваться вдаль.

starfish *n.* морска́я звезда́.

stark *adj.* **1,** (bleak; desolate) пусты́нный: *stark landscape,* пусты́нный пейза́ж. **2,** (blunt; grim) жесто́кий: *stark reminder,* жесто́кое напомина́ние. **3,** (pure; sheer; utter) сплошно́й. *Stark contrast,* ре́зкий контра́ст. —*adv.* соверше́нно: *stark naked,* соверше́нно го́лый; *stark raving mad,* соверше́нно сумасше́дший.

starless *adj.* беззвёздный.

starlight *n.* свет звёзд.

starling *n.* скворе́ц.

starry *adj.* звёздный.

start *v.t.* **1,** (begin) начина́ть: *start work,* начина́ть рабо́ту. *She started to cry,* она́ начала́ пла́кать; она́ запла́кала. *It started/ is starting/ to rain/,* пошёл/ начина́ется дождь. **2,** (initiate) завя́зывать; заводи́ть; зате́ять. *Start a fight,* завяза́ть *or* зате́ять дра́ку. *Start an argument,* зате́ять спор. *Start a conversation,* завяза́ть *or* завести́ разгово́р. *Start a business,* завести́ де́ло. *Start a rumor,* пусти́ть слух. *Start a fire,* устро́ить пожа́р. *Start a war,* развяза́ть войну́. **3,** (set going, as an engine) запуска́ть (мото́р). *Start the car,* заводи́ть маши́ну. —*v.i.* **1,** (begin) начина́ть: *start from the beginning,* начина́ть снача́ла. *Starting April 1,* начина́я с пе́рвого апре́ля. **2,** (commence; originate) начина́ться: *The meeting starts at 10:00,* собра́ние начина́ется в де́сять часо́в. *The fire started in the basement,* пожа́р нача́лся *or* возни́к в подва́ле. **3,** (begin to move) тро́нуться: *The train started,* по́езд тро́нулся. **4,** (begin to function, as of an engine) заводи́ться. **5,** *fol. by* **out** (set out) отправля́ться в путь. **6,** (be a starter in a race) стартова́ть. **7,** (jump from fright) вздра́гивать. —*n.* **1,** (beginning) *From start to finish,* снача́ла до конца́. *I knew it from the start,* с са́мого нача́ла я э́то знал (зна́ла). **2,** (beginning of a race) старт: *false start,* неве́рный старт; фальста́рт. **3,** (sudden movement): *give a start,* вздра́гивать. *Give someone a start,* испуга́ть *or* напуга́ть кого́-нибудь. —**by fits and starts,** уры́вками.

starter *n.* **1,** *mech.* ста́ртер. **2,** (one who starts in a race) уча́стник (состяза́ния). **3,** (one who gives the signal to start in a race) ста́ртер. —**for starters,** *colloq.* для нача́ла.

starting line старт; ста́ртовая ли́ния.

starting point нача́льный пункт; отправно́й пункт; исхо́дная то́чка. *Take as a starting point,* класть в осно́ву; брать *or* принима́ть за осно́ву.

startle *v.t.* **1,** (frighten) испуга́ть: *You startled me!,* вы меня́ испуга́ли. **2,** (shock) потряса́ть: *We were startled by the news,* мы бы́ли потрясены́ но́востью. —**startling,** *adj.* поразительный; потряса́ющий.

starvation *n.* го́лод; голода́ние. *Die of starvation,* умира́ть с го́лоду; умира́ть голо́дной сме́ртью. —**starvation diet,** голо́дная дие́та. —**starvation wages,** ни́щенская зарпла́та.

starve *v.i.* **1,** (go continually hungry) голода́ть. *Starve to death,* умира́ть с го́лоду; умира́ть голо́дной сме́ртью. **2,** *colloq.* (be very hungry) быть о́чень голо́дным. *I'm starving,* я умира́ю от го́лода; я стра́шно проголода́лся. —*v.t.* мори́ть го́лодом: *starve oneself,* мори́ть себя́ го́лодом. *Starve into submission,* взять измо́ром.

starveling *n.* замо́рыш.

starving *adj.* голода́ющий.

stash *v.t., colloq.* [*usu.* **stash away**] припря́тывать.

state *n.* **1,** (condition) состоя́ние; положе́ние. *State of affairs,* положе́ние дел *or* веще́й. *State of health,* состоя́ние здоро́вья. *State of mind,* душе́вное состоя́ние. *State of emergency,* чрезвыча́йное положе́ние. *In a drunken state,* в пья́ном ви́де. **2,** (nation; government) госуда́рство: *sovereign state,* суваре́нное госуда́рство. *The State of Israel,* Госуда́рство Изра́иль. *Affairs of state,* госуда́рственные дела́. *Separation of church and state,* отделе́ние це́ркви от госуда́рства. **3,** (unit of a republic) штат: *United States,* Соединённые Шта́ты. —*adj.* **1,** (of a nation) госуда́рственный: *state secret,* госуда́рственная та́йна. (*The U.S.*) *State Department,* госуда́рственный департа́мент. **2,** (of a U.S. state): *state law,* зако́н шта́та; *state legislature,* легислату́ра шта́та. **3,** (marked by ceremony) торже́ственный: *state dinner,* торже́ственный обе́д. —*v.t.* **1,** (set forth) излага́ть: *state one's case,* излага́ть своё де́ло. *State one's opinion,* вы́сказать своё мне́ние. **2,** (announce; assert) заявля́ть: *He stated that...,* он заяви́л, что... *The resolution states...,* в резолю́ции говори́тся... —**lie in state,** поко́иться в откры́том гробу́.

stated *adj.* **1,** (announced) изло́женный; вы́сказанный. **2,** (fixed) устано́вленный; определённый.

statehood *n.* госуда́рственность.

stateless *adj.* не име́ющий гражда́нства; без гражда́нства.

stately *adj.* вели́чественный; велича́вый.

statement *n.* **1,** (act of stating) изложе́ние. *A statement of fact,* конста́ция фа́кта. **2,** (something stated; a declaration) заявле́ние: *make a statement,* сде́лать заявле́ние. **3,** *comm.* отчёт.

stateroom *n.* каю́та.

statesman *n.* госуда́рственный де́ятель.

static *adj.* **1,** *physics* стати́ческий: *static pressure,* стати́ческое давле́ние. **2,** (not moving or progressing) стати́чный. —*n.* поме́хи: *It was impossible to hear anything because of the static,* из-за поме́х ничего́ не́ было слы́шно. —**static electricity,** стати́ческое электри́чество.

statics *n.* ста́тика.

station *n.* **1,** (terminal) вокза́л; ста́нция: *railroad station,* железнодоро́жный вокза́л; железнодоро́жная ста́нция. *Bus station,* авто́бусная ста́нция. *The train was standing in the station,* по́езд стоя́л на вокза́ле. **2,** (establishment) ста́нция: *tracking station,* ста́нция слеже́ния. *Gas station,* бензозапра́вочная ста́нция; бензоколо́нка. *Police station,* полице́йский уча́сток; отделе́ние мили́ции. *Fire station,* пожа́рное депо́. *First-aid station,* медици́нский пункт. **3,** (duty post) пост: *battle station,* боево́й пост. **4,** (status in society) обще́ственное положе́ние. **6,** *radio* радиоста́нция. **6,** *mil.; naval* ба́за. —*v.t.* размеща́ть; располага́ть; дислоци́ровать (войска́). *Station a guard at the door,* ста́вить часово́го у две́ри. *Station oneself at the window,* стать у окна́. *He is stationed in Texas,* он слу́жит в Теха́се.

stationary *adj.* неподви́жный: *stationary target,* неподви́жная цель.

stationer *n.* торго́вец канцеля́рскими принадле́жностями.

stationery *n.* **1,** (paper) почто́вая бума́га. **2,** (supplies) канцеля́рские *or* писчебума́жные принадле́жности. —**stationery store,** писчебума́жный магази́н.

station house полице́йский уча́сток.

stationmaster *n.* нача́льник ста́нции.

statistical *adj.* статисти́ческий.

statistician *n.* стати́стик.

statistics *n.* **1,** (science) стати́стика. **2,** (figures) статисти́ческие да́нные.

statue *n.* ста́туя.

statuesque *adj.* скульпту́рный; ста́тный.

statuette *n.* статуэ́тка.

stature *n.* **1,** (height) рост. **2,** *fig.* (reputation) авторите́т.

status *n.* положе́ние; ста́тус. *Marital status,* семе́йное положе́ние. —**status quo,** ста́тус-кво.

statute *n.* стату́т; зако́н; положе́ние; законоположе́ние. —**statute law,** пи́саный зако́н. —**statute mile,** англи́йская ми́ля. —**statute of limitations,** срок да́вности.

statutory *adj.* устано́вленный зако́ном.

staunch *adj.* ве́рный; сто́йкий; убеждённый. *Staunch*

supporter, ве́рный *or* убеждённый сторо́нник. *A staunch advocate of reform,* сто́йкий сторо́нник рефо́рмы.

stave *n.* клёпка. —*v.t.* [*usu.* **stave off**] предотвраща́ть.

stay *v.i.* **1,** (remain) остава́ться: *stay home,* остава́ться до́ма. *Stay for dinner,* оста́ться обе́дать. **2,** (reside temporarily) жить; остана́вливаться: *stay at a hotel,* жить/остана́вливаться в гости́нице. *Stay with friends,* жить *or* остана́вливаться *or* гости́ть у друзе́й. *Where are you staying?,* где вы останови́лись? —*v.t.* **1,** (stop; halt) остана́вливать; приостана́вливать. *Stay the hand of,* останови́ть ру́ку (+ *gen.*). **2,** (assuage, as hunger) утоля́ть. **3,** *Stay the night,* оста́ться на́ ночь. **4,** *Stay the course,* вы́держать *or* (про)держа́ться до конца́. —*n.* **1,** (sojourn) пребыва́ние. **2,** (delay) отсро́чка: *stay of execution,* отсро́чка ка́зни. **3,** (collar support) ко́сточка. —**stay away,** отсу́тствовать; не приходи́ть. —**stay in,** остава́ться до́ма. —**stay out,** прогу́ливать: *stay out all night,* прогуля́ть всю ночь. —**stay put,** *colloq.* остава́ться на ме́сте. —**stay up,** не ложи́ться спать. *Stay up all night,* просиде́ть всю ночь.

stay-at-home *n.* домосе́д.

staying power выно́сливость.

staysail *n.* ста́ксель.

stead *n.* ме́сто. *In someone's stead,* вме́сто (+ *gen.*). —**stand (someone) in good stead,** пригоди́ться (+ *dat.*); сослужи́ть (+ *dat.*) хоро́шую слу́жбу.

steadfast *adj.* сто́йкий; непоколеби́мый; вы́держанный. —**steadfastness,** *n.* сто́йкость; непоколеби́мость; вы́держанность.

steadily *adv.* неукло́нно: *Their numbers are steadily decreasing,* коли́чество их неукло́нно уменьша́ется.

steady *adj.* **1,** (stable; firm) усто́йчивый: *steady ladder,* усто́йчивая ле́стница. *Steady on one's feet,* твёрдый на нога́х. *Sew with a steady hand,* шить твёрдой руко́й. **2,** (regular) постоя́нный: *steady job,* постоя́нная рабо́та; *steady customer,* постоя́нный клие́нт. **3,** (uninterrupted) непреры́вный; неукло́нный. *Steady downpour,* беспреры́вные дожди́. *Steady growth,* неукло́нный рост. **4,** (even) равноме́рный: *steady speed,* равноме́рная ско́рость. **5,** (reliable; not frivolous) степе́нный. —*v.t.* **1,** (prevent from tottering) де́лать усто́йчивым; приводи́ть в равнове́сие. **2,** (calm) успока́ивать: *steady one's nerves,* успока́ивать не́рвы.

steak *n.* бифште́кс; антреко́т.

steal *v.t.* **1,** (rob) красть. *His bicycle was stolen,* у него́ укра́ли велосипе́д. **2,** *fig.* (take furtively): *steal a glance at,* укра́дкой посмотре́ть на; *steal a kiss,* сорва́ть поцелу́й. —*v.i.* **1,** (commit theft) ворова́ть. **2,** (move furtively) кра́сться; подкра́дываться. *Steal into,* вкра́дываться в; прокра́дываться в. *Steal away,* ускольза́ть.

stealth *n., usu. in* **by stealth,** укра́дкой. —**stealthily,** *adv.* укра́дкой; кра́дучись. —**stealthy,** *adj.* сде́ланный укра́дкой: *stealthy glance,* взгляд укра́дкой.

steam *n.* пар; пары́. —*adj.* парово́й: *steam heat,* парово́е отопле́ние. —*v.t.* па́рить. *Steamed oysters,*

паровы́е у́стрицы. —*v.i.* **1,** (emit vapor) выпуска́ть пар. **2,** *fol. by* **up** (become covered with vapor) запотева́ть. **3,** (move by steam) плыть. *The ship steamed into port,* парохо́д вошёл в га́вань. —**let/blow off steam,** дава́ть вы́ход свои́м чу́вствам. —**under a full head of steam,** на всех пара́х. —**under one's own steam,** со́бственными си́лами; свои́м хо́дом.

steamboat *n.* парохо́д.

steam engine парова́я маши́на.

steamer *n.* (steamship) парохо́д. —**steamer rug,** плед. —**steamer trunk,** ба́ул.

steamroller *n.* парово́й като́к.

steam room пари́льня.

steamship *n.* парохо́д.

steam shovel землеро́йная маши́на; экскава́тор.

steamy *adj.* **1,** (filled with steam) напо́лненный па́ром. **2,** (hot and humid) зно́йный; вла́жный. *Steamy jungle,* вла́жные джу́нгли.

stearin *n.* стеари́н.

steatite *n.* стеати́т.

steed *n.* конь.

steel *n.* сталь. —*adj.* стально́й. *Steel mill,* сталелите́йный заво́д. —*v.t.* **1,** (plate with steel) покрыва́ть ста́лью. **2,** *fig.* (harden; make tough) закаля́ть.

steelworker *n.* сталелите́йщик; сталева́р. —**steelworks,** *n.* сталелите́йный заво́д.

steely *adj.* стально́й: *steely glance,* стально́й взгляд.

steelyard *n.* безме́н.

steep *adj.* **1,** (precipitous) круто́й: *steep hill/incline,* круто́й холм/склон. **2,** *colloq.* (high, as of a price) высо́кий; (expensive) дорого́й. —*v.t.* **1,** (soak) выма́чивать; зама́чивать. **2,** *fig.* (immerse; saturate) *steep oneself in a subject,* глубоко́ изуча́ть како́й-нибудь предме́т. *Be steeped in ignorance,* погряза́ть в неве́жестве.

steepen *v.t.* де́лать бо́лее круты́м.

steeple *n.* шпиль.

steeplechase *n.* ска́чки с препя́тствиями.

steeplejack *n.* верхола́з.

steeply *adv.* кру́то.

steepness *n.* круто́сть; крутизна́.

steer *v.t.* **1,** (make go in the right direction); управля́ть; пра́вить. *Steer a ship,* управля́ть су́дном. *Steer the conversation to a certain subject,* направля́ть разгово́р на каку́ю-нибудь те́му. **2,** (set and follow) держа́ться: *steer a middle course,* держа́ться сре́днего ку́рса. —*v.i. Steer clear of,* избега́ть; сторони́ться. —*n.* (ox) вол.

steerage *n.* **1,** (part of a ship) ни́зший класс. **2,** (steering) управле́ние.

steering *n.* рулево́е управле́ние. —**steering column,** рулева́я коло́нка. —**steering committee,** руководя́щий комите́т. —**steering wheel,** руль; рулево́е колесо́; штурва́л.

stein *n.* пивна́я кру́жка.

stellar *adj.* **1,** (consisting of stars) звёздный. **2,** (outstanding) превосхо́дный.

stem *n.* **1,** (of a plant) сте́бель. **2,** (of a glass) но́жка. **3,**

(of a pipe) черенóк. **4,** (of a ship) форштéвень. **5,** *ling.* оснóва. —*v.t.* останáвливать: *stem the flow of refugees,* останови́ть потóк бéженцев. —*v.i.* [*usu.* **stem from**] вытекáть из; проистекáть из.

stench *n.* вонь; смрад; зловóние.

stencil *n.* шаблóн; трафарéт. —*v.t.* наноси́ть по трафарéту.

stenography *n.* стеногрáфия. —**stenographer,** *n.* стенóграф; стенографи́ст; стенографи́стка. —**stenographic,** *adj.* стенографи́ческий.

stentorian *adj.* громовóй; зы́чный.

step *n.* **1,** (movement of the foot) шаг: *take a step,* сдéлать шаг. **2,** (in dancing) па. **3,** (on a staircase) ступéнь; ступéнька. *Flight of steps,* марш. *Climb the staircase two steps at a time,* поднимáться по лéстнице чéрез ступéньку. **4,** (action) шаг: *take steps,* предпринимáть шаги́. *In taking this step,* пойдя́ на такóй шаг. **5,** (degree of progress or retrogression) шаг: *a big step forward,* большóй шаг вперёд; *a step backward,* шаг назáд. —*v.i.* шагáть; ступáть. *Step this way, please!,* сюдá, пожáлуйста! —**in step,** в нóгу. *Keep in step,* идти́ в нóгу. —**out of step,** не в нóгу. *Be out of step with the times,* идти́ не в нóгу со врéменем (*or* с вéком). —**step aside, 1,** (to avoid a blow) уклоня́ться; отстраня́ться. **2,** (to allow someone to pass) сторони́ться. *Step aside for,* уступáть дорóгу (+ *dat.*). —**step back,** отступáть: *step back from the window,* отступи́ть от окнá. —**step by step,** шаг за шáгом. —**step down,** уйти́ с постá. —**step in, 1,** (enter) входи́ть. *Won't you step in?,* зайди́те, пожáлуйста! **2,** (step into) ступáть в; попáсть ногóй в: *step in a puddle,* ступи́ть в лу́жу; попáсть ногóй в лу́жу. —**step into,** входи́ть в: *step into the elevator,* входи́ть в лифт. *Will you please step into my office?,* зайди́те, пожáлуйста, ко мне (в кабинéт). —**step off, 1,** *literally* сходи́ть с. **2,** (mark off) отсчи́тывать: *step off ten paces,* отсчи́тывать дéсять шагóв. —**step on,** наступáть на. *Step on the gas,* дать газ. —**step on it,** поторáпливаться. *Step on it!,* живéй!; скорéй! —**step onto,** сходи́ть на: *step onto the platform,* сходи́ть на платфóрму. —**step out,** выходи́ть. —**step over,** переступáть; перешáгивать. —**step up, 1,** (step forward) проходи́ть. **2,** (increase) уси́ливать; нарáщивать.

stepbrother *n.* свóдный брат.

stepchild *n.* пáсынок.

stepdaughter *n.* пáдчерица.

stepfather *n.* óтчим.

stepladder *n.* стремя́нка.

stepmother *n.* мáчеха.

steppe *n.* степь.

stepping stone ступéнька на пути́: *stepping stone to success,* ступéнька на пути́ к успéху.

stepsister *n.* свóдная сестрá.

stepson *n.* пáсынок.

stereophonic *adj.* стереофони́ческий.

stereoscope *n.* стереоскóп. —**stereoscopic,** *adj.* стереоскопи́ческий. —**stereoscopy,** *n.* стереоскопи́я.

stereotype *n.* **1,** *printing* стереоти́п. **2,** (conventional type) шаблóн; трафарéт; штамп; стандáрт; стерео-

ти́п. —*v.t.* стереотипи́ровать. —**stereotyped,** *adj.* шаблóнный; трафарéтный; стереоти́пный.

sterile *adj.* **1,** (germ-free) стери́льный. **2,** (incapable of producing offspring) беспло́дный. **3,** *fig.* (devoid of substance) пустóй.

sterility *n.* **1,** (absence of germs) стери́льность. **2,** (inability to produce offspring) беспло́дие.

sterilize *v.t.* стерилизовáть. —**sterilization,** *n.* стерилизáция. —**sterilizer,** *n.* стерилизáтор.

sterlet *n.* стéрлядь.

sterling *n.* **1,** (standard for British coins) стéрлинг. *Pound sterling,* фунт стéрлингов. **2,** (silver) серебрó. —*adj.* **1,** (pert. to the pound sterling) стéрлинговый. **2,** (silver) серéбряный. **3,** (excellent; outstanding) превосхóдный.

stern *adj.* стрóгий; суро́вый. *Stern judge,* стрóгий судья́. *Stern look,* стрóгий *or* суро́вый взгляд. *Stern warning,* суро́вое предупреждéние. *Stern rebuke,* стрóгий вы́говор. *Stern measures,* стрóгие *or* суро́вые мéры. —*n.* (of a ship) кормá. —**sternness,** *n.* стрóгость; суро́вость.

sternpost *n.* ахтерштéвень.

sternum *n.* груди́на.

steroid *n.* стерóид.

stethoscope *n.* стетоскóп.

stevedore *n.* грýзчик.

stew *n.* тушёное мя́со; рагý. —*v.t.* туши́ть; пáрить. —*v.i.* **1,** (cook) туши́ться; пáриться. **2,** (fret; worry) волновáться; мýчиться.

steward *n.* **1,** (manager of a household) завхóз; экóном. **2,** (on a ship or plane) бортпроводни́к; стю́ард. —**stewardess,** *n.* бортпроводни́ца; стюардéсса.

stewed *adj.* **1,** (cooked by stewing) тушёный; пáреный. **2,** *slang* (drunk) под хмелькóм. —**stewed fruit,** компóт.

stewpan *n.* кастрю́ля.

stick *n.* **1,** (long slender piece of wood) пáлка; пáлочка. *Walking stick,* трость; пáлка. *Hockey stick,* клю́шка. **2,** (sticklike piece, as of chewing gum) пли́тка. *Stick of dynamite,* шáшка динами́та. **3,** *aero.* рýчка управлéния. **4,** *pl., colloq.* (rural districts) глушь. —*v.t.* **1,** (prick) колóть: *Something is sticking me,* чтó-то меня́ кóлет. **2,** (insert; pin) втыкáть; вкáлывать. *Stick a pin into something,* воткнýть булáвку во чтó-нибудь. *Stick a flower in one's lapel,* воткнýть цветóк в петли́цу. **3,** (thrust) совáть: *stick a pie in the oven,* сýнуть пирóг в духóвку. *Stick it in the drawer!,* брóсьте в я́щик! *Stick one's head in the door,* просýнуть гóлову в дверь. *Stick one's head out the window,* вы́сунуться из окнá. **4,** (glue) прикле́ивать; накле́ивать: *stick a stamp on an envelope,* прикле́ивать мáрку к конвéрту; накле́ивать мáрку на конвéрт. **5,** *colloq.* (impose upon) свáливать: *I got stuck with the job of doing the dishes,* на меня́ свали́ли мытьё посýды. —*v.i.* **1,** (adhere) кле́иться; закле́иваться; пристáвать. *The envelope doesn't stick,* конвéрт не закле́ивается. **2,** *fol. by* **to** (adhere to) ли́пнуть (к); прилипáть (к); пристáвать (к). **3,** (become embedded) застревáть. *The words stuck in* *his throat,* слова́ застря́ли у него́ в го́рле. **4,** (fail to operate; jam) заеда́ть (*impers.*): *The door stuck,* дверь зае́ло. **5,** (become permanent, as of a nickname) приставать; прилипа́ть; прикле́иваться. **6,** *fol.* **by to** (not deviate from) не отклоня́ться от; держа́ться; приде́рживаться. *Stick to the subject,* держа́ться те́мы. *Stick to the rules,* держа́ться *or* приде́рживаться пра́вил. —**stick around,** *colloq.* остава́ться побли́зости. —**stick by, 1,** (remain close to; continue to support) остава́ться ве́рен (+ *dat.*); не покида́ть. **2,** (not go back on) упо́рствовать в: *stick by a decision,* упо́рствовать в (при́нятом) реше́нии. —**stick out, 1,** (put out) высо́вывать; выставля́ть. *Stick out one's tongue,* вы́сунуть *or* показа́ть язы́к. **2,** (protrude) торча́ть: *The hull of the sunken ship was sticking out of the water,* ко́рпус затону́вшего корабля́ торча́л из воды́. **3,** (be conspicuous) отлича́ться; выдава́ться. —**stick together, 1,** (adhere) скле́иваться; слипа́ться; слепля́ться. **2,** (remain united) держа́ться вме́сте. —**stick up, 1,** (protrude upward) торча́ть; выдава́ться. **2,** *slang* (rob) гра́бить. **3,** *Stick 'em up!,* ру́ки вверх! —**stick up for,** заступа́ться за. *See also* **stuck.**

sticker *n.* накле́йка.

stickiness *n.* кле́йкость.

sticking plaster ли́пкий пла́стырь.

sticking point загво́здка; заце́пка.

stickleback *n.* колю́шка.

stickup *n., slang* налёт; грабёж; ограбле́ние.

sticky *adj.* **1,** (adhesive; gummy) ли́пкий; кле́йкий. **2,** (humid) вла́жный. **3,** *colloq.* (ticklish) щекотли́вый.

stiff *adj.* **1,** (rigid; unbending) жёсткий; негну́щийся. *Stiff brush,* жёсткая щётка. *Stiff cardboard,* твёрдый *or* негну́щийся карто́н. *Stiff collar,* крахма́льный воротничо́к. **2,** (sore and not moving easily) онеме́вший: *stiff joints,* онеме́вшие суста́вы. *I have a stiff neck,* мне наду́ло (в) ше́ю; у меня́ ше́я не повора́чивается. *My hands are stiff from the cold,* ру́ки мои́ окочене́ли от хо́лода. **3,** (hard to remove or operate) туго́й: *stiff door,* туга́я дверь. **4,** (awkward; constrained) натя́нутый; принуждённый. **5,** (moving with great force) си́льный. *Stiff wind,* си́льный *or* жесто́кий ве́тер. *Stiff current,* бы́строе тече́ние. **6,** (stout; resolute) упо́рный. *Stiff resistance,* упо́рное *or* жесто́кое сопротивле́ние. **7,** (harsh; severe) суро́вый: *stiff sentence,* суро́вый пригово́р. **8,** (difficult; demanding) тру́дный: *stiff exam,* тру́дный экза́мен. *Stiff requirements,* высо́кие тре́бования. *Stiff competition,* о́страя *or* жесто́кая конкуре́нция. **9,** (potent) кре́пкий: *stiff drink,* кре́пкий напи́ток. **10,** *colloq.* (high, as of a price) ду́тый. —*adv.* **1,** (so as to be stiff): *be frozen stiff,* окочене́ть от хо́лода. **2,** *colloq.* (to an extreme degree) до́ смерти: *be scared stiff,* перепуга́ться до́ смерти.

stiffen *v.t.* **1,** (make stiff) де́лать жёстким. **2,** (make tougher) ужесточа́ть: *stiffen one's demands,* ужесточа́ть свои́ тре́бования. **3,** (make more resolute) укрепля́ть: *stiffen someone's will,* укрепля́ть чью-нибудь во́лю. —*v.i.* станови́ться неподви́жным; кочене́ть.

stiffness *n.* **1,** (firmness) жёсткость. **2,** *med.* непо-

дви́жность: *stiffness in the joints,* неподви́жность суста́вов. **3,** (awkwardness) натя́нутость; принуждённость.

stifle *v.t.* **1,** (suffocate; smother) души́ть; удуша́ть. **2,** (suppress, as criticism or initiative) подавля́ть; дави́ть; глуши́ть; души́ть; зажима́ть.

stifling *adj.* уду́шливый: *stifling heat,* уду́шливая жара́. *It is stifling in here,* здесь ду́шно.

stigma *n.* **1,** (mark of shame) клеймо́ позо́ра. **2,** *bot.* ры́льце. —**stigmatize,** *v.t.* клейми́ть.

stiletto *n.* стиле́т.

still *adj.* **1,** (motionless) неподви́жный: *The air was still,* во́здух был неподви́жен. **2,** (tranquil) ти́хий: *still waters,* ти́хая вода́. **3,** (silent) безмо́лвный. *Be still!,* молчи́! —*adv.* **1,** (motionless) неподви́жно. *Sit still!,* сиди́те ти́хо!; сиди́те споко́йно!; сиди́те сми́рно! *He can't sit still,* ему́ не сиди́тся на ме́сте. *Time does not stand still,* вре́мя не стои́т на ме́сте. **2,** (yet) ещё; всё ещё: *She is still young,* она́ (всё) ещё молода́я. **3,** (all the same) всё же; всё-таки; всё равно́: *I still love him,* я всё же/ всё-таки/ всё равно́ люблю́ его́. **4,** *with comp. adjectives,* ещё: *still further,* ещё да́льше. —*n.* **1,** (silence; quiet) тишина́. *In the still of the night,* в ночно́й тиши́. **2,** (distilling apparatus) перего́нный куб. **3,** (distillery) винокуре́нный заво́д. —*v.t.* усмиря́ть: *still the crowd,* усмиря́ть толпу́. —*v.i.* успока́иваться. —*conj.* всё же; всё-таки; тем не ме́нее. *Still, you ought to go,* всё же/ тем не ме́нее/ вам сле́дует пойти́. —**still and all,** несмотря́ на всё э́то; тем не ме́нее.

stillborn *adj.* мертворождённый.

still life натюрмо́рт.

stillness *n.* **1,** (motionlessness) неподви́жность. **2,** (calm; quiet) тишина́.

stilt *n.* **1,** (tall pole) ходу́ля: *walk on stilts,* ходи́ть на ходу́лях. **2,** (post; support) сва́я. **3,** (wading bird) ходу́лочник.

stilted *adj.* ходу́льный: *stilted phrases,* ходу́льные фра́зы.

stimulant *n.* возбужда́ющее сре́дство.

stimulate *v.t.* возбужда́ть; поощря́ть; дава́ть толчо́к (+ *dat.*); стимули́ровать. *Stimulate the appetite,* возбужда́ть аппети́т. *Stimulate interest in,* возбужда́ть *or* поощря́ть интере́с к. *Stimulate discussion,* поощря́ть диску́ссию.

stimulation *n.* возбужде́ние; поощре́ние; стимули́рование.

stimulus *n.* сти́мул; возбуди́тель; толчо́к.

sting *v.t.* **1,** (wound, as of a bee) жа́лить. **2,** (cause severe pain to; burn) щипа́ть; жечь. **3,** *fig.* (hurt; distress) уязвля́ть. —*v.i.* **1,** (of a bee) жа́лить. **2,** (cause pain) жечь. —*n.* уку́с: *bee sting,* пчели́ный уку́с.

stinger *n.* (stinging organ) жа́ло.

stingily *adv.* ску́по.

stinginess *n.* ску́пость.

stinging *adj.* язви́тельный: *stinging rebuke,* язви́тельный упрёк.

stingray *n.* морско́й кот.

stingy *adj.* скупо́й. *Don't be (so) stingy!,* не скупи́тесь!

stink *v.i.* воня́ть; смерде́ть. —*v.t.* [*usu.* **stink up**] провоня́ть. —*n.* злово́ние; вонь; смрад.

stinking *adj.* воню́чий; злово́нный; смра́дный.

stint *v.t. & i.* скупи́ться (на): *not stint one's praise*, не скупи́ться на похвалы́. —*n.* **1,** (limitation; restriction) ограниче́ние. **2,** (short period of service) срок. —**stint oneself**, ограни́чивать себя́: *She stints herself in everything*, она́ ограни́чивает себя́ во всём. *He does not stint himself*, он ни в чём себя́ не ограни́чивает.

stipend *n.* **1,** (salary) жа́лованье. **2,** (scholarship) стипе́ндия.

stipple *v.t.* рисова́ть *or* гравирова́ть пункти́ром.

stipulate *v.t.* обусло́вливать; огова́ривать; предусма́тривать. —**stipulation,** *n.* усло́вие; огово́рка.

stir *v.t.* **1,** (agitate) меша́ть: *stir the coffee/fire*, меша́ть ко́фе/у́гли. **2,** (move slightly) шевели́ть: *The wind stirred the leaves*, ве́тер шевели́л ли́стья. **3,** (arouse, as an emotion) возбужда́ть; вызыва́ть. *Stir someone's wrath*, возбужда́ть гнев в ком-нибудь; вызыва́ть гнев у кого́-нибудь. **4,** (affect strongly; rouse) волнова́ть. *Stir the imagination*, волнова́ть *or* возбужда́ть воображе́ние. *Stir someone to action*, побужда́ть кого́-нибудь к де́йствию. **5,** *fol. by* **up** (incite; foment) возбужда́ть; разжига́ть: *stir up the crowd*, возбужда́ть толпу́; *stir up hatred*, разжига́ть не́нависть. *Stir up trouble*, мути́ть во́ду. —*v.i.* дви́гаться; шевели́ться. *I saw something stir in the bushes*, я уви́дел, как что́-то шевели́лось в куста́х. —*n.* **1,** (act of stirring): *give the soup a stir*, помеша́ть суп. **2,** (movement) движе́ние. **3,** (excited reaction) резона́нс: *create quite a stir*, вы́звать широ́кий резона́нс.

stirring *adj.* волну́ющий.

stirrup *n.* стре́мя. —**stirrup cup,** проща́льный ку́бок.

stitch *n.* **1,** *sewing* стежо́к. **2,** *knitting* пе́тля. **3,** *surgery* шов: *put in stitches*, накла́дывать швы. **4,** (sudden sharp pain) резь. *I have a stitch in my side*, у меня́ ко́лет в боку́. **5,** (article of clothing): *without a stitch on*, в чём мать родила́. —*v.t.* **1,** *sewing* строчи́ть; простра́чивать. **2,** *surgery* накла́дывать швы на (ра́ну). —**be in stitches,** *colloq.* надрыва́ть животы́ (со сме́ху).

St.-John's-wort *n.* зверобо́й.

stock *n.* **1,** (supply of merchandise) инвента́рь; ассорти́мент. *In stock*, в нали́чии. *Out of stock*, нет в прода́же; распро́дан. **2,** (reserve supply) запа́с. **3,** (corporate shares) а́кции; фо́нды. **4,** (lineage) род: *of good stock*, хоро́шего ро́да. *He is of peasant stock*, он происхо́дит из крестья́н (*or* из крестья́нской семьи́). **5,** (part of a firearm) ло́жа. **6,** (raw material) сырьё: *paper stock*, бума́жное сырьё. **7,** (broth from boiled meat) мясно́й отва́р. **8,** (livestock) скот. **9,** *Summer stock*, ле́тний теа́тр. **10,** *pl.* (instrument of punishment) коло́дки. —*adj.* **1,** (of the stock market) биржево́й. *Stock prices*, курс а́кций. **2,** (regularly on sale) основно́й. *Stock sizes*, станда́ртные разме́ры. **3,** (regularly used) шабло́нный: *stock phrases*, шабло́нные фра́зы. —*v.t.* **1,** (supply with merchan-

dise) снабжа́ть (това́рами). *Well-stocked stores*, хорошо́ снабжа́емые магази́ны. **2,** (have on hand) держа́ть. **3,** *Stock a pond with fish*, запусти́ть ры́бу в пруд. —*v.i.* [*usu.* **stock up**] запаса́ться. *Stock up on food*, запаса́ться продово́льствием; запаса́ть продово́льствие. —**take stock, 1,** (take inventory) составля́ть инвента́рь. **2,** *fol. by* **of** (inventory) инвентаризова́ть; переучи́тывать. **3,** *fig.* (evaluate a situation) подводи́ть ито́ги.

stockade *n.* **1,** (fence) частоко́л. **2,** (fort) форт. **3,** (prison) гауптва́хта.

stockbroker *n.* (биржево́й) ма́клер.

stock car го́ночный автомоби́ль.

stock company 1, *comm.* акционе́рная компа́ния. **2,** *theat.* театра́льная тру́ппа.

stock exchange фо́ндовая би́ржа.

stockfish *n.* вя́леная ры́ба.

stockholder *n.* акционе́р.

stocking *n.* чуло́к. *In one's stocking feet*, в одни́х чулка́х.

stock-in-trade *n.* непреме́нное ору́дие.

stock market фо́ндовая би́ржа.

stockpile *n.* запа́с: *stockpiles of nuclear weapons*, запа́сы я́дерного ору́жия. —*v.t.* накопля́ть; запаса́ть; де́лать запа́сы (+ *gen.*).

stocktaking *n.* инвентариза́ция; переучёт.

stocky *adj.* призе́мистый; корена́стый.

stockyard *n.* ско́тный двор; скотоприго́нный двор.

stodgy *adj.* ску́чный; ну́дный.

stoic *n.* сто́ик. —**stoical,** *adj.* стои́ческий. —**stoically,** *adv.* стои́чески; сто́йко. —**stoicism,** *n.* стоици́зм.

stoke *v.t.* **1,** (stir, as a fire) расшевели́ть (у́гли). **2,** (tend, as a furnace) топи́ть.

stoker *n.* **1,** (person) кочега́р; истопни́к. **2,** (device) сто́кер.

stole *n.* паланти́н.

stolen *adj.* кра́деный.

stolid *adj.* бесстра́стный.

stomach *n.* **1,** (digestive organ) желу́док. *On an empty stomach*, на голо́дный желу́док; натоща́к. **2,** (abdomen; belly) живо́т. —*v.t.* (tolerate) перева́ривать. —**stomach ache,** боль в животе́. *I have a stomach ache*, у меня́ боли́т живо́т. —**stomach pump,** желу́дочный зонд.

stomatology *n.* стоматоло́гия. —**stomatologist,** *n.* стомато́лог.

stomp *v.t. & i.* то́пать (нога́ми). *Stomp on*, топта́ть.

stone *n.* **1,** (substance) ка́мень: *pave with stone*, мости́ть ка́мнем. *Heart of stone*, ка́менное се́рдце. **2,** (small rock) ка́мень. *Precious stone*, драгоце́нный ка́мень. *Throw stones at*, броса́ть *or* заброса́ть (кого́-нибудь) камня́ми. **3,** (pit of fruits) ко́сточка. **4,** *med.* ка́мень: *kidney stone*, по́чечный ка́мень. —*adj.* ка́менный: *stone wall*, ка́менная стена́. —*v.t.* забива́ть камня́ми. —**leave no stone unturned,** сде́лать всё возмо́жное; пусти́ть в ход все сре́дства. —**not leave a stone standing,** ка́мня на ка́мне не оста́вить. —**within a stone's throw,** в двух шага́х; руко́й пода́ть.

Stone Age ка́менный век.

stonecutter *n.* камнере́з.
stone-deaf *adj.* соверше́нно глухо́й.
stonemason *n.* ка́менщик; каменотёс.
stonework *n.* ка́менная кла́дка.
stony *adj.* **1**, (of or like stone) ка́менный. **2**, (full of stones) камени́стый. **3**, *fig.* (unfeeling) ка́менный; окамене́лый. *Stony gaze*, ка́менный взгляд. **4**, *Stony silence*, гробово́е молча́ние.
stooge *n.*, *colloq.* **1**, *theat.* посме́шище. **2**, (underling) приспе́шник.
stool *n.* **1**, (seat) табуре́тка; табуре́т. **2**, (excrement) стул. —**fall between two stools**, сиде́ть ме́жду двух сту́льев.
stool pigeon стука́ч.
stoop *v.i.* **1**, (bend the body) наклоня́ться; нагиба́ться. **2**, (slouch) суту́литься. **3**, *fol. by* **to** (lower or degrade oneself) унижа́ться до; снисходи́ть до. —*n.* **1**, (slouch) суту́лость. **2**, (front steps) крыльцо́.
stooped *adj.* суту́лый.
stop *v.t.* **1**, (bring to a halt) остана́вливать: *stop a car/traffic/pain*, останови́ть маши́ну/движе́ние/боль. **2**, (terminate) прекраща́ть: *stop a war/payments/assistance*, прекрати́ть войну́/платежи́/по́мощь. *Stop that noise!*, прекрати́ э́тот шум! **3**, (cease) перестава́ть: *stop crying*, переста́ть пла́кать. **4**, (prevent) меша́ть; уде́рживать. *Stop someone from speaking*, меша́ть кому́-нибудь говори́ть. *Stop someone from committing suicide*, удержа́ть кого́-нибудь от самоуби́йства. **5**, *fol. by* **up** (block; plug) затыка́ть; заде́лывать; заку́поривать. —*v.i.* **1**, (come to a halt) остана́вливаться: *stop at a red light*, остана́вливаться на кра́сный свет. *My watch has stopped*, мои́ часы́ ста́ли *or* стоя́т *or* останови́лись. **2**, (pay a brief visit) заходи́ть; заезжа́ть: *stop in to see a friend*, заходи́ть/заезжа́ть к дру́гу. *Stop at the drugstore for some medicine*, заходи́ть/заезжа́ть в апте́ку за лека́рством. **3**, (cease) прекраща́ться; перестава́ть. *The rain has stopped*, дождь ко́нчился/переста́л/прошёл/прекрати́лся. *The noise stopped*, шум прекрати́лся. —*n.* **1**, (halt) остано́вка: *sudden stop*, внеза́пная остано́вка. *Come to an abrupt stop*, ре́зко останови́ться. *Make an unplanned stop*, сде́лать незаплани́рованную остано́вку. **2**, (place to stop) остано́вка: *bus stop*, авто́бусная остано́вка. *Get off at the next stop*, выходи́ть на сле́дующей остано́вке. **3**, *music* (of a fretted instrument) лад; (of an organ) реги́стр. —**pull out all the stops**, нажа́ть на все пружи́ны. —**put a stop to**, поко́нчить с; положи́ть коне́ц (+ *dat.*); пресека́ть. —**stop at nothing**, ни пе́ред чем не остана́вливаться. —**stop by**; **stop in**, зайти́; загляну́ть. —**stop off**, останови́ться в пути́. —**stop short**, *see* **short**.
stopgap *n.* паллиати́в. —*adj.* паллиати́вный.
stoplight *n.* **1**, (traffic light) светофо́р. **2**, (brake light) стоп-сигна́л.
stopover *n.* остано́вка в пути́.
stoppage *n.* прекраще́ние: *work stoppage*, прекраще́ние рабо́ты.
stopper *n.* про́бка.
stopwatch *n.* секундоме́р.

storage *n.* хране́ние: *put in storage*, отдава́ть *or* сдава́ть на хране́ние. `Storage facilities`, складски́е помеще́ния. —**storage battery**, аккумуля́торная батаре́я.
store *n.* **1**, (retail outlet) магази́н: *shoe/furniture store*, обувно́й/ме́бельный магази́н. **2**, (supply) запа́с; склад: *stores of food*, запа́сы продово́льствия; *store of weapons*, склад ору́жия. *Store of knowledge*, запа́с зна́ний. —*v.t.* **1**, (put away for safekeeping) храни́ть: *store something in the attic/ in a warehouse/*, храни́ть что́-нибудь на чердаке́/ на скла́де/. **2**, *often fol. by* **up** (put aside for future use) запаса́ть; заготовля́ть (впрок). —**be** *or* **lie in store**, предстоя́ть; ждать впереди́. *What lies in store for them?*, что их ждёт? —**hold in store**, держа́ть про запа́с. *Who knows what the future holds in store?*, кто зна́ет, что ждёт нас впереди́? —**set store by**, придава́ть значе́ние (+ *dat.*).
storehouse *n.* **1**, (warehouse) склад. **2**, *fig.* (abundant source) сокро́вищница: *storehouse of knowledge*, сокро́вищница зна́ний.
storekeeper *n.* **1**, (shopkeeper) ла́вочник. **2**, (keeper of supplies) кладовщи́к.
storeroom *n.* кладова́я; чула́н.
storey *n.* = **story** (*in sense #5*).
storied *adj.* легенда́рный; баснословный.
stork *n.* а́ист.
storm *n.* **1**, (windstorm) бу́ря; (thunderstorm) гроза́. *Dust storm*, пы́льная бу́ря. **2**, *naut.* шторм. **3**, *fig.* (outburst) бу́ря; взрыв. *A storm of protests*, бу́ря проте́ста. **4**, *mil.* штурм; при́ступ: *take by storm*, взять шту́рмом; взять при́ступом. —*v.i.* **1**, (rage) бушева́ть: *It is storming*, бушу́ет гроза́. **2**, (move with great force) проноси́ться: *Storm into the room*, ворва́ться в ко́мнату. *Storm out of the room*, бро́ситься вон из ко́мнаты в гне́ве. —*v.t.* штурмова́ть: *storm the town*, штурмова́ть го́род. —**take by storm**, *fig.* захвати́ть; увле́чь; покори́ть.
storm cloud (грозова́я) ту́ча.
storm trooper штурмови́к.
storm windows двойны́е ра́мы; вставны́е ра́мы.
stormy *adj.* бу́рный: *stormy sea*, бу́рное мо́ре. *Stormy weather*, нена́стье. *A stormy session of Congress*, бу́рное заседа́ние конгре́сса.
story *n.* **1**, (short literary work) расска́з; по́весть; ска́зка. *Short story*, новелла. *Love story*, расска́з *or* по́весть о любви́. *Detective story*, детекти́в. *The story of Cinderella*, ска́зка о Зо́лушке. **2**, (something related; account) исто́рия; расска́з. *Tell someone a story*, рассказа́ть кому́-нибудь исто́рию. *The story of one's life*, исто́рия свое́й жи́зни. *Get ahead of one's story*, забега́ть вперёд в расска́зе. **3**, (news event) собы́тие; (report on same) сообще́ние. **4**, *colloq.* (lie) расска́зывай: *Don't tell me stories!*, ска́зки мне не расска́зывай! **5**, [*also*, **storey**] (floor of a building) эта́ж. *Two-story house*, двухэта́жный дом. —**a long story**, до́лгая пе́сня. —**to make a long story short**, коро́че говоря́. —**that's a different story**, э́то друго́е де́ло.
storyteller *n.* **1**, (narrator) расска́зчик. **2**, *colloq.* (fibber) вы́думщик.

stout *adj.* **1,** (corpulent) по́лный; ту́чный; доро́дный. **2,** (sturdy) кре́пкий; про́чный. *On his stout back,* на его́ кре́пкой спине́. **3,** (resolute) сто́йкий: *stout defense,* сто́йкая оборо́на. *Stout resistance,* сто́йкое *or* упо́рное сопротивле́ние.

stouthearted *adj.* сто́йкий; отва́жный.

stove *n.* **1,** (coal or wood stove) печь. **2,** (electric or gas range) плита́.

stovepipe *n.* дымохо́д.

stow *v.t.* укла́дывать. —**stow away, 1,** (store) убира́ть; пря́тать. **2,** (hide aboard a ship) е́хать за́йцем.

stowaway *n.* безбиле́тный пассажи́р; «за́яц».

strabismus *n.* косогла́зие.

straddle *v.t.* сиде́ть верхо́м на.

strafe *v.t.* обстре́ливать.

straggle *v.i.* **1,** (move along separately) идти́ вразбро́д. **2,** (fall behind) отстава́ть. **3,** (stray) отбива́ться. —**straggler,** *n.* отста́вший.

straight *adj.* **1,** (not crooked; not curly) прямо́й: *straight line,* пряма́я ли́ния; *straight hair,* прямы́е во́лосы. **2,** (properly arranged) в поря́дке. *Put things straight,* приводи́ть дела́ в поря́док. **3,** (direct and candid) прямо́й; открове́нный. *Straight answer,* прямо́й отве́т. **4,** (consecutive) подря́д; *five straight days,* пять дней подря́д. **5,** *colloq.* (undiluted) чи́стый: *straight alcohol,* чи́стый спирт. **6,** *Straight razor,* опа́сная бри́тва. —*adv.* пря́мо: *drive straight to the airport,* пое́хать пря́мо в аэропо́рт. *Stand up straight,* держа́ться пря́мо. *Is my hat on straight?,* у меня́ шля́па пря́мо наде́та? —**get (something) straight,** вспомина́ть: *I can't get their names straight,* не могу́ вспо́мнить их имена́. *Get this straight!,* заруби́те себе́ э́то на носу́. —**set (someone) straight,** наставля́ть на путь и́стинный. —**straight ahead,** пря́мо. —**straight face,** бесстра́стное лицо́. *With a straight face,* не рассмея́вшись. —**straight away**; **straight off,** сра́зу.

straightedge *n.* лине́йка.

straighten *v.t.* **1,** (make straight) выпрямля́ть; распрямля́ть; выправля́ть. *Straighten one's back,* выпрямля́ть спи́ну. *Straighten a bent nail,* выпрямля́ть *or* распрямля́ть *or* выправля́ть согну́вшийся гвоздь. **2,** *fol by* **out** (remove and thus make a surface smooth) выправля́ть; расправля́ть: *straighten out a dent,* выправля́ть вмя́тину; *straighten out wrinkles,* расправля́ть морщи́ны. **3,** (adjust, as one's tie) поправля́ть. **4,** *fol. by* **up** (tidy up) убира́ть. **5,** *fol. by* **out** (set right) выправля́ть; нала́живать. —*v.i.* **1,** *fol. by* **up** (stand up straight) выпрямля́ться; распрямля́ться; разгиба́ться. **2,** *fol. by* **out** (become straight) распрямля́ться. **3,** *fol. by* **out** (return to normal) нала́живаться; образо́вываться.

straightforward *adj.* прямо́й; прямоду́шный. —**straightforwardness,** *n.* прямота́; прямоду́шие.

straightness *n.* прямизна́.

strain *v.t.* **1,** (exert to the utmost) напряга́ть: *strain every nerve,* напряга́ть все си́лы. **2,** (overtax) надрыва́ть. *Strain one's voice,* сорва́ть го́лос. *Strain one's eyes,* по́ртить себе́ глаза́; по́ртить зре́ние. **3,**

(injure; sprain) растя́гивать: *strain a muscle,* растя́гивать мы́шцу. **4,** (filter) протира́ть; цеди́ть; проце́живать. —*v.i.* напряга́ться. *Strain at the leash,* рва́ться с при́вязи. —*n.* **1,** (tension; pressure) напряже́ние: *nervous strain,* не́рвное напряже́ние. *Withstand the strain,* выде́рживать напряже́ние. **2,** (sprain) растяже́ние. **3,** (species) поро́да: *a new strain of cattle,* но́вая поро́да скота́. **4,** *pl.* (sounds of music) зву́ки: *the strains of a waltz,* зву́ки ва́льса.

strained *adj.* **1,** (aggravated; tense) натя́нутый; напряжённый: *strained relations,* натя́нутые/напряжённые отноше́ния. **2,** *med.* *Strained ligaments,* растяже́ние свя́зок. **3,** (passed through a strainer) протёртый.

strainer *n.* си́то; решето́.

strait *n.* **1,** (channel) проли́в. **2,** *pl.* (difficulty) затрудни́тельное положе́ние; стеснённые обстоя́тельства. *In dire straits,* в бе́дственном *or* в отча́янном положе́нии.

straiten *v.t.* стесня́ть. *In straitened circumstances,* в стеснённых обстоя́тельствах.

strait jacket смири́тельная руба́шка.

strait-laced *adj.* чо́порный; пурита́нский.

strand *v.t.* **1,** (drive or run aground) посади́ть на мель. **2,** [*also,* **leave stranded**] (leave in a helpless position) поки́нуть в беде́. —*n.* **1,** (of hair, rope, etc.) прядь. *Strand of wool,* шерсти́нка. **2,** (string, as of pearls, beads, etc.) ни́тка.

strange *adj.* **1,** (queer; odd) стра́нный: *strange man,* стра́нный челове́к; *strange occurrence,* стра́нное явле́ние. *It is strange,* стра́нно. *Strange as it seems,* как ни стра́нно. **2,** (unfamiliar) незнако́мый: *find oneself in a strange place,* очути́ться в незнако́мом ме́сте. **3,** (foreign) чужо́й: *in a strange country,* в чужо́й стране́. —**strangely,** *adv.* стра́нно. —**strangeness,** *n.* стра́нность.

stranger *n.* **1,** (person not known) незнако́мец. **2,** (outsider) посторо́нний. **3,** (newcomer) прие́зжий.

strangle *v.t.* души́ть; удави́ть. —*v.i.* задыха́ться.

stranglehold *n.* *Have a stranglehold on,* держа́ть в тиска́х.

strangulation *n.* **1,** (strangling) удавле́ние. **2,** *med.* ущемле́ние.

strap *n.* **1,** (general term) реме́нь. **2,** (of an undergarment) брете́ль(ка). —*v.t.* свя́зывать *or* скрепля́ть ремнём. *The prisoner was strapped in a chair,* заключённый был пристёгнут ремня́ми к сту́лу.

strapped *adj., colloq.* стеснённый в деньга́х.

strapping *adj.* ро́слый; дю́жий.

stratagem *n.* вое́нная хи́трость; уло́вка.

strategy *n.* страте́гия. —**strategic,** *adj.* стратеги́ческий. —**strategist,** *n.* страте́г.

stratification *n.* **1,** *geol.* наслое́ние; напластова́ние; стратифика́ция. **2,** *fig.* (division into strata) расслое́ние: *stratification of society,* расслое́ние о́бщества.

stratified *adj.* сло́истый. *Stratified society,* расслоённое о́бщество.

stratify *v.t.* рассла́ивать.

stratosphere *n.* стратосфе́ра.

stratum *n.* **1,** (layer) слой; пласт; просло́йка. **2,** *fig.* (class; division) слой; просло́йка.

stratus *n.* слои́стое о́блако.

straw *n.* **1,** (stalk of grain) соло́ма. **2,** (for sipping drinks) соло́минка. **—adj.** соло́менный: *straw hat,* соло́менная шля́па. **—grasp at a straw,** хвата́ться за соло́минку. **—the last straw,** после́дняя ка́пля; преде́л терпе́ния; ка́пля, перепо́лнившая ча́шу (терпе́ния).

strawberry *n.* (wild) земляни́ка; (cultivated) клубни́ка. **—adj.** земляни́чный; клубни́чный.

stray *v.i.* **1,** (wander off) отбива́ться: *stray from the flock,* отбива́ться от ста́да. **2,** (deviate) отклоня́ться; уклоня́ться: *stray off course,* отклоня́ться/ уклоня́ться от ку́рса. **—adj. 1,** (lost) заблуди́вшийся; бездо́мный. *Stray dog,* бродя́чая *or* бездо́мная соба́ка. **2,** (random; chance) случа́йный. *Stray bullet,* шальна́я пу́ля.

streak *n.* **1,** (thin line, as in marble) прожи́лка. **2,** (mark; smear) потёк; подтёк; *pl.* разво́ды. **3,** (flash, as of lightning) вспы́шка. **4,** (trace of a certain characteristic) жи́лка: *romantic streak,* романти́ческая жи́лка. *Person with a lazy streak,* челове́к с ленцо́й. **5,** (spell; run) полоса́. **6,** *sports* ше́ствие: *winning streak,* побе́дное ше́ствие. **—v.t.,** *usu. passive: hair streaked with gray,* во́лосы с про́седью. *The wallpaper is all streaked,* обо́и все в потёках. **—v.i. 1,** (form streaks) растека́ться. **2,** (dash; flash) проноси́ться; промелькну́ть. *Jet planes streaked by overhead,* реакти́вные самолёты проноси́лись над голова́ми. **—talk a blue streak,** *colloq.* говори́ть без у́молку.

stream *n.* **1,** (small river) руче́й. **2,** (current) тече́ние: *against the stream,* про́тив тече́ния. **3,** (steady flow) пото́к: *a stream of people,* пото́к люде́й; *a stream of invective,* пото́к руга́тельств. **—v.i. 1,** (flow rapidly) течь; ли́ться; хлы́нуть; струи́ться. *Tears were streaming down her cheeks,* слёзы текли́ *or* ли́лись *or* кати́лись у неё по щека́м. **2,** (move in large numbers) вали́ть. *Refugees were streaming out of the city,* пото́к бе́женцев повали́л из го́рода.

streamer *n.* серпанти́н.

streamline *v.t.* **1,** (shape so as to offer little wind resistance) придава́ть (+ *dat.*) обтека́емую фо́рму. **2,** (modernize) рационализи́ровать. **—streamlined,** *adj.* обтека́емый.

street *n.* у́лица. *Gorky Street is now Tverskaya,* у́лица Го́рького тепе́рь Тверска́я. *Wall Street,* Уо́лл-стри́т. *Take to the streets,* вы́сыпать на у́лицу. **—adj.** у́личный: *street scene,* у́личная сце́на; *street fighting,* у́личные бои́. **—man in the street,** рядово́й челове́к; «челове́к с у́лицы».

streetcar *n.* трамва́й.

street lamp у́личный фона́рь. *Also,* **street light.**

streetwalker *n.* у́личная де́вка/деви́ца/же́нщина.

strength *n.* **1,** (force; power) си́ла: *physical strength,* физи́ческая си́ла. *A man of enormous strength,* челове́к огро́мной си́лы. *I haven't the strength to go on,* я не в си́лах идти́ да́льше. **2,** (durability) про́чность: *tensile strength,* про́чность на разры́в. **3,** (potency) кре́пость. **4,** (complement of personnel) чи́сленность. *At full strength,* в по́лном соста́ве. *Bring up to full strength,* (у)комплектова́ть. **—on the strength of,** в си́лу (+ *gen.*); на основа́нии (+ *gen.*).

strengthen *v.t.* уси́ливать; укрепля́ть.

strenuous *adj.* **1,** (requiring great exertion) напряжённый: *strenuous work,* напряжённая рабо́та. *Strenuous exercise,* интенси́вное физи́ческое упражне́ние. **2,** (emphatic) реши́тельный: *strenuous objections,* реши́тельные возраже́ния.

streptococcus *n.* стрептоко́кк.

streptomycin *n.* стрептомици́н.

stress *n.* **1,** (physical pressure exerted) напряже́ние. **2,** (mental strain) стресс: *be under great stress,* быть под больши́м стре́ссом. **3,** (accent) ударе́ние: *The stress is on the first syllable,* ударе́ние па́дает на пе́рвый слог. **4,** (emphasis) ударе́ние. *Lay stress on,* де́лать ударе́ние/акце́нт/упо́р на. **—v.t. 1,** (emphasize) подчёркивать: *stress the importance of something,* подчёркивать ва́жность чего́-нибудь. **2,** (pronounce with emphasis) де́лать ударе́ние на. *Stressed syllable,* уда́рный слог.

stretch *v.t.* **1,** (expand; extend) растя́гивать; вытя́гивать. *Stretch one's legs,* размина́ть но́ги. *Stretch a canvas over a frame,* натя́гивать холст на ра́му. *Stretch a rope across the yard,* протя́гивать верёвку че́рез двор. *Have one's shoes stretched,* отда́ть ту́фли на растя́жку. **2,** *fol. by* **out** (put forth; hold out) протя́гивать. **3,** *Stretch one's luck,* искуша́ть судьбу́. **4,** *Stretch a point,* допусти́ть натя́жку. **—v.i. 1,** (be capable of being stretched) тяну́ться; растя́гиваться. **2,** (take a stretch) потя́гиваться. **3,** *fol. by* **out** (lie prone) растя́гиваться; вытя́гиваться. **4,** (extend) тяну́ться; растя́гиваться; простира́ться. *Stretch for many miles,* тяну́ться на мно́го миль. **—n. 1,** (act of stretching): *take a stretch,* потя́гиваться. **2,** (expanse) отре́зок: *stretch of land,* отре́зок земли́. **3,** (interval of time) срок: *three-month stretch,* трёхме́сячный срок. **—adj.** эласти́чный; безразме́рный: *stretch socks,* эласти́чные/безразме́рные носки́. **—at a stretch,** подря́д; за оди́н присе́ст.

stretchable *adj.* растяжи́мый; тягу́чий. **—stretchability,** *n.* растяжи́мость; тягу́честь.

stretcher *n.* носи́лки: *carry on a stretcher,* нести́ (кого́-нибудь) на носи́лках. **—stretcher-bearer,** *n.* санита́р; санита́р-носи́льщик.

strew *v.t.* **1,** (scatter) разбра́сывать; рассыпа́ть. *Papers were strewn all over the floor,* бума́ги бы́ли разбро́саны по всему́ по́лу. **2,** (cover with scattered things) засыпа́ть; усыпа́ть.

stricken *adj.* пострада́вший: *stricken areas,* пострада́вшие райо́ны. ♦ *Often as a combining form: grief-stricken,* уби́тый го́рем; *poverty-stricken,* ни́щий; обедне́вший; обнища́лый.

strict *adj.* стро́гий: *strict teacher/diet,* стро́гая учи́тельница/дие́та; *strict rules,* стро́гие пра́вила. *In the strict sense of the word,* в стро́гом смы́сле э́того сло́ва. *In strict confidence,* под больши́м секре́том.

strictly *adv.* стро́го: *strictly forbidden,* стро́го запреща́ется. *Strictly between us,* стро́го ме́жду на́ми.

—**strictly speaking,** стро́го говоря́; со́бственно говоря́.

strictness *n.* стро́гость.

stricture *n.* стро́гая кри́тика; осужде́ние.

stride *v.i.* шага́ть: *stride across the stage,* шага́ть че́рез сце́ну. —*n.* **1,** (long step) большо́й шаг. **2,** *pl.* (progress) успе́хи. *Make great strides,* де́лать больши́е шаги́; де́лать больши́е успе́хи; шагну́ть далеко́ вперёд. —**take in stride,** воспринима́ть споко́йно. —**throw off stride,** вы́бить из коле́й.

strident *adj.* ре́зкий. *Strident criticism,* ре́зкая кри́тика.

strife *n.* ра́спря; раздо́р; рознь. *Civil strife,* гражда́нский раздо́р.

strike *v.t.* **1,** (deliver a blow to; hit) ударя́ть: *strike someone in the face,* уда́рить кого́-нибудь по лицу́ *or* в лицо́. *Strike a horse with a whip,* ударя́ть *or* бить ло́шадь кнуто́м. **2,** (deliver, as a blow) наноси́ть (уда́р). **3,** (bang; knock) ударя́ться: *strike one's head on the door,* уда́риться голово́й о дверь. **4,** *mil.* (attack; hit) поража́ть: *strike enemy targets,* поража́ть це́ли проти́вника. **5,** (make impact against) уда́риться о; попа́сть в (+ *acc.*). *The boat struck a rock,* ло́дка уда́рилась о ска́лу. *The ship struck a mine,* кора́бль наскочи́л *or* налете́л на ми́ну. *The bullet struck him in the shoulder,* пу́ля попа́ла ему́ в плечо́. *Two bullets struck the general,* две пу́ли попа́ли в генера́ла. *He was struck by a car,* его́ сбил автомоби́ль. *The tree was struck by lightning,* в де́рево уда́рила мо́лния. *A hurricane struck the island,* урага́н обру́шился на о́стров. **6,** (cause to ignite, as a match) чи́ркнуть (спи́чкой). **7,** (mint, as a coin or medal) выбива́ть; чека́нить. **8,** (announce by striking) бить; проби́ть; ударя́ть. *The clock struck ten,* часы́ проби́ли де́сять часо́в. **9,** (discover) находи́ть: *strike oil,* найти́ нефть. **10,** (attack; afflict) поража́ть. *Strike dead,* сража́ть на́смерть. *Be struck dumb,* онеме́ть. *The disease strikes mainly young people,* боле́знь поража́ет в основно́м молодёжь. **11,** (impress; appear to; seem to) каза́ться: *He strikes me as an honest man,* он мне ка́жется че́стным челове́ком. *How does this strike you?,* как вам э́то нра́вится? **12,** (impress strongly) поража́ть; броса́ться в глаза́ (+ *dat.*). *One is immediately struck by the cleanliness of the city,* сра́зу броса́ется в глаза́ чистота́ го́рода. **13,** (implant, as an emotion) нагоня́ть; наводи́ть; вселя́ть. *Strike fear into the heart of,* нагоня́ть *or* наводи́ть страх на; вселя́ть страх в. **14,** (occur to; come to mind) приходи́ть (+ *dat.*) в го́лову; осени́ть; озаря́ть. **15,** *often fol. by* **off** *or* **from** (delete; drop) исключа́ть; вычёркивать. **16,** (assume, as a pose or attitude) стать в по́зу. **17,** (sound, as a note) брать (но́ту). **18,** (conclude, as an agreement) заключа́ть. *Strike a bargain,* пойти́ на сде́лку; уда́рить *or* бить по рука́м. **19,** (achieve, as a balance) подводи́ть (бала́нс). **20,** *Strike it rich,* напа́сть на золоту́ю жи́лу. —*v.i.* **1,** (deliver a blow) наноси́ть уда́р. *Strike while the iron is hot,* куй желе́зо, пока́ горячо́. **2,** (attack) ударя́ть. *The enemy struck at dawn,* враг уда́рил на рассве́те. **3,** (refuse to

work) бастова́ть. —*n.* **1,** (attack) уда́р: *air strike,* уда́р с во́здуха. **2,** (work stoppage) забасто́вка: *go (out) on strike,* выходи́ть на забасто́вку. —*adj.* забасто́вочный; ста́чечный: *strike fund,* забасто́вочный фонд; *strike committee,* ста́чечный комите́т. —**strike back,** нанести́ отве́тный уда́р. —**strike down, 1,** (knock down; afflict) сража́ть. **2,** (override; annul) отменя́ть. —**strike home,** *see* **home.** —**strike out, 1,** (cross out) зачёркивать. **2,** (fail) потерпе́ть неуда́чу. —**strike up, 1,** (initiate, as a conversation) завя́зывать; заводи́ть. **2,** (begin to play) заигра́ть.

strikebreaker *n.* штрейкбре́хер.

striker *n.* забасто́вщик; басту́ющий.

striking *adj.* **1,** (remarkable) порази́тельный; рази́тельный: *striking similarity,* порази́тельное/рази́тельное схо́дство. **2,** (on strike) басту́ющий. —**within striking distance,** в преде́лах досяга́емости.

strikingly *adv.* порази́тельно; рази́тельно. *Be strikingly beautiful,* поража́ть свое́й красото́й.

string *n.* **1,** (cord) верёвка; бечёвка. **2,** (on clothes) завя́зка: *apron string,* завя́зка передника́. **3,** (of pearls, beads, etc.) ни́тка. **4,** (of a musical instrument) струна́. **5,** *pl.* (musical instruments) стру́нные инструме́нты. **6,** (of a tennis racket) струна́. **7,** (bowstring) тетива́. **8,** (succession; series) ряд. **9,** *sports* соста́в: *first string,* пе́рвый соста́в. **10,** *pl.* (limiting conditions) усло́вия: *with no strings attached,* без каки́х-либо усло́вий. —*adj.* стру́нный: *string quartet,* стру́нный кварте́т. —*v.t.* **1,** (provide with strings) снабжа́ть стру́нами. **2,** (arrange on a string) нани́зывать. **3,** (extend; stretch) протя́гивать: *string a rope across the yard,* протя́гивать верёвку че́рез двор. **4,** *fol. by* **up,** *colloq.* (hang) ве́шать; вздёргивать. —**pull strings,** нажима́ть на та́йные пружи́ны. —**string (someone) along,** води́ть за́ нос.

string bean стручко́вая фасо́ль; фасо́ль в стручка́х.

stringed instrument стру́нный инструме́нт.

stringent *adj.* стро́гий. —**stringency,** *n.* стро́гость.

stringy *adj.* волокни́стый; жи́листый.

strip *v.t.* **1,** (undress) раздева́ть. **2,** *fol. by* **off** (take off; remove) снима́ть; срыва́ть (с себя́). **3,** (tear off) сдира́ть: *strip the bark from a tree,* сдира́ть кору́ с де́рева. **4,** (deprive; divest) лиша́ть: *He was stripped of his citizenship,* он был лишён гражда́нства. —*v.i.* раздева́ться; обнажа́ться. —*n.* **1,** (long narrow piece or area) полоса́; поло́ска. **2,** (airstrip) (взлётно-поса́дочная) полоса́.

stripe *n.* **1,** (band of different color) полоса́; поло́ска. *With blue and white stripes,* в бе́лую и си́нюю поло́ску. **2,** (insignia) наши́вка. **3,** (kind; ilk) род; тип. *Of every stripe,* всех масте́й. —**striped,** *adj.* полоса́тый; в поло́ску.

stripling *n.* ю́ноша; подро́сток.

strip mining откры́тая добы́ча угля́.

strive *v.i.* стреми́ться: *strive for success,* стреми́ться к успе́ху. *Strive to become independent,* стреми́ться стать самостоя́тельным.

stroboscope *n.* стробоско́п.

stroke *n.* **1,** (single movement) уда́р; взмах; мах: *with one stroke, одни́м уда́ром/взма́хом/ма́хом. *Deft stroke*, ло́вкий уда́р. **2**, (of a brush in painting) штрих; мазо́к. *With a stroke of the pen*, одни́м ро́счерком пера́. **3**, (of an oar) гребо́к; взмах весла́. **4**, swimming стиль. *Breast stroke*, брасс. *He can't swim a stroke*, он совсе́м не уме́ет пла́вать. **5**, (gentle caress) ла́ска. **6**, mech. ход: *stroke of a piston*, ход по́ршня. **7**, (sounding of a bell or chime) уда́р. *At the stroke of ten*, ро́вно в де́сять часо́в. **8**, med. уда́р; инсу́льт. **9**, *Stroke of luck*, уда́ча; *stroke of bad luck*, уда́р судьбы́. **10**, (effective or inspired action) ход; прие́м. *Master stroke*, мастерско́й уда́р. *Stroke of genius*, гениа́льная иде́я. —v.t. гла́дить: *stroke one's beard*, гла́дить бо́роду.

stroll v.i. гуля́ть; прогу́ливаться. —n. прогу́лка. *Go for a stroll*, идти́ гуля́ть; погуля́ть.

strong adj. **1**, (powerful; intense; forceful) си́льный: *strong swimmer*, си́льный пловец́; *strong medicine*, си́льное лека́рство. *Strong language*, си́льные выраже́ния. *Strong measures*, жёсткие or круты́е ме́ры. **2**, (robust) кре́пкий: *strong constitution*, кре́пкий органи́зм. *Grow stronger*, кре́пнуть. **3**, (capable of enduring stress) кре́пкий; про́чный. *Strong rope*, кре́пкая верёвка. **4**, (concentrated, as of coffee) кре́пкий. **5**, (keenly felt; clearly noticeable) си́льный; кре́пкий: *strong odor*, си́льный/кре́пкий за́пах. *Strong cigarettes*, кре́пкие сигаре́ты. *Strong accent*, си́льный акце́нт. *Strong resemblance*, большо́е схо́дство. **6**, (deeply held) твёрдый; глубо́кий: *strong beliefs*, твёрдые/глубо́кие убежде́ния. **7**, (numbering): *one hundred strong*, чи́сленностью в сто челове́к; в коли́честве ста челове́к.

strongarm adj., colloq. силово́й: *strongarm methods*, силовы́е ме́тоды.

strongbox n. несгора́емый я́щик.

stronghold n. кре́пость; тверды́ня.

strongly adv. си́льно: *which I strongly doubt*, в чём я си́льно сомнева́юсь. *Strongly recommend*, о́чень рекомендова́ть. *Strongly condemn*, реши́тельно or ре́зко осужда́ть. *Object strongly to*, реши́тельно or ре́зко возража́ть про́тив. *Be strongly opposed to*, быть реши́тельно про́тив. *He feels very strongly about it*, он твёрдо убеждён в э́том.

strong point 1, mil. опо́рный пункт. **2**, fig. (asset) си́льная сторона́.

strong-smelling adj. паху́чий.

strong-willed adj. волево́й; своево́льный; с хара́ктером.

strontium n. стро́нций.

strop n. точи́льный реме́нь.

structural adj. структу́рный: *structural changes*, структу́рные измене́ния. —**structural engineer**, инжене́р-строи́тель. —**structural linguistics**, структу́рная лингви́стика. —**structural steel**, строи́тельная сталь.

structure n. **1**, (arrangement of parts) структу́ра; строе́ние. *Structure of the atom*, строе́ние а́тома. **2**, (something built) строе́ние; сооруже́ние. —v.t. стро́ить; организова́ть.

struggle n. борьба́: *a bitter struggle*, ожесточённая

борьба́. *Power struggle*, борьба́ за власть. *The struggle for survival*, борьба́ за существова́ние. —v.i. боро́ться: *struggle with an assailant*, боро́ться с налётчиком. *Struggle to one's feet*, с трудо́м подня́ться на́ ноги. *Struggle to break loose*, вырыва́ться. *Struggle with a problem*, би́ться над зада́чей.

strum v.t. & i. тре́нькать; бренча́ть.

strumpet n. потаску́ха.

strut v.i. выступа́ть; ва́жно расха́живать; ходи́ть го́голем. —n. **1**, (swagger) ва́жная похо́дка. **2**, (brace) сто́йка; подко́с.

strychnine n. стрихни́н.

stub n. **1**, (fragment) огры́зок; (of a cigar) оку́рок. **2**, (counterfoil) корешо́к. —v.t. расшиба́ть: *stub one's toe*, расшиби́ть па́лец ноги́.

stubble n. **1**, (stubs of grain) жнивьё; стерня́. **2**, (rough growth, as of a beard) щети́на.

stubborn adj. **1**, (obstinate) упря́мый: *stubborn as a mule*, упря́мый как осёл. **2**, (persistent) упо́рный: *stubborn cough*, упо́рный ка́шель; *stubborn resistance*, упо́рное сопротивле́ние.

stubbornness n. **1**, (obstinacy) упря́мство. **2**, (persistence) упо́рство.

stubby adj. **1**, (short and thickset) то́лстый. **2**, (bristly, as of a beard) щети́нистый.

stucco n. штукату́рка. —adj. штукату́рный. —v.t. штукату́рить.

stuck adj. **1**, (mired): *get stuck in the mud*, застря́ть or завя́знуть в грязи́. **2**, (jammed): *The door is stuck*, дверь зае́ло. **3**, colloq. (stumped) в тупике́.

stud n. **1**, (shirt front ornament) за́понка. **2**, (projecting pin or spike) шип; штифт. **3**, (breeding) разво́д; заво́д. *Purchase for stud*, купи́ть на разво́д. —v.t. усыпа́ть; усе́ивать; уни́зывать. *Studded with diamonds*, усы́пан алма́зами.

student n. **1**, (pupil) учени́к; уча́щийся. **2**, (university student) студе́нт. —adj. студе́нческий: *student unrest*, студе́нческие волне́ния.

stud farm ко́нный заво́д; конево́дческая фе́рма.

studied adj. **1**, (not natural; affected) зау́ченный. **2**, (carefully considered) обду́манный.

studio n. **1**, (workroom) сту́дия; мастерска́я; ателье́. **2**, motion pictures киносту́дия; павильо́н. **3**, (for broadcasting) сту́дия; радиосту́дия; телесту́дия.

studious adj. приле́жный; стара́тельный. —**studiously**, adv. стара́тельно: *studiously avoid*, стара́тельно избега́ть.

study n. **1**, (studying) изуче́ние: *the study of history*, изуче́ние исто́рии. *Make a study of*, тща́тельно изуча́ть. **2**, pl. (academic pursuits) заня́тия; уче́ние; учёба. *Continue one's studies*, продолжа́ть учёбу. **3**, (scientific investigation) иссле́дование: *a study of the effects of weightlessness on the body*, иссле́дование по возде́йствию невесо́мости на органи́зм. **4**, (room reserved for study) кабине́т. —v.t. **1**, (take a course in) изуча́ть; учи́ть; учи́ться: *study Russian*, изуча́ть or учи́ть ру́сский язы́к; учи́ться ру́сскому языку́. *Study history/mathematics*, изуча́ть исто́рию/матема́тику. *Study music/drawing*, учи́ться му́зыке/

рисова́нию. **2,** (make a study of) изуча́ть; иссле́довать: *study a problem,* изуча́ть/иссле́довать пробле́му. *Study the origin/behavior of...,* изуча́ть происхожде́ние/поведе́ние (+ *gen.*). **3,** (examine) изуча́ть: *study a map/proposal,* изуча́ть ка́рту/предложе́ние. —*v.i.* **1,** (take courses) учи́ться: *study abroad,* учи́ться за грани́цей. *He is studying to be a doctor,* он у́чится на врача́; он у́чится чтобы быть врачо́м. **2,** (do one's lessons) занима́ться: *study hard,* уси́ленно занима́ться. **3,** *fol. by* **for** (prepare for) гото́виться (к): *study for an examination,* гото́виться к экза́мену.

stuff *n.* **1,** (any substance): *This medicine is powerful stuff,* э́то лека́рство си́льно де́йствует. **2,** (things; effects) ве́щи: *Leave this stuff here,* оста́вьте э́ти ве́щи здесь. *Put all this stuff in the closet,* положи́те всё э́то в шкаф. **3,** (anything eaten or drunk): *sweet stuff,* сла́сти. *I don't touch the stuff,* ка́пли в рот не беру́. **4,** (basic elements; character) заква́ска. *He is made of different stuff,* он из друго́го те́ста. **5,** *Kid stuff,* пустяко́вое де́ло; *rough stuff,* чуда́чества. **6,** *Know/do one's stuff, colloq.* знать/де́лать своё де́ло. —*v.t.* **1,** (fill; pack) набива́ть: *stuff a pillow with down,* набива́ть поду́шку пу́хом. *Stuff one's briefcase with papers,* набива́ть портфе́ль бума́гами. *Stuff one's head with facts,* забива́ть себе́ го́лову фа́ктами. **2,** (cram in) вти́скивать; запи́хивать: *stuff one's things in a suitcase,* вти́скивать/запи́хивать ве́щи в чемода́н. **3,** (put or thrust hastily) засо́вывать: *stuff money into one's pockets,* засо́вывать де́ньги в карма́ны. **4,** *cookery* начиня́ть; фарширова́ть. *Stuff the pies with meat,* начиня́ть пирожки́ мя́сом. **5,** (glut with food) наеда́ть; корми́ть как на убо́й. *Stuff oneself,* объеда́ться. *I'm stuffed,* я сыт (сыта́) по го́рло. **6,** *fol. by* **up** (plug; block) затыка́ть; забива́ть. *The sink is stuffed up,* ра́ковина засори́лась. *My nose is stuffed up,* мне заложи́ло нос; у меня́ нос зало́жен.

stuffed *adj.* фарширо́ванный: *stuffed peppers,* фарширо́ванный пе́рец. *Stuffed cabbage,* голубцы́. *Stuffed animal,* чу́чело.

stuffiness *n.* духота́.

stuffing *n.* **1,** (act of stuffing) наби́вка. **2,** (material for stuffing) наби́вка; фарш. **3,** *cookery* начи́нка; фарш.

stuffy *adj.* ду́шный; спёртый.

stultify *v.t.* ско́вывать; стесня́ть.

stumble *v.i.* **1,** (trip) спотыка́ться; оступа́ться. *He stumbled and fell,* он споткну́лся и упа́л. *She stumbled on the staircase,* она́ оступи́лась на ле́стнице. **2,** (stagger) шата́ться; пошатну́ться. **3,** (falter in speech) запина́ться. *Read a speech without stumbling,* чита́ть речь не запина́ясь *or* без запи́нки. **4,** *fol. by* **on, upon** *or* **across** (chance to meet or find) ната́лкиваться на; натыка́ться на; набрести́ на.

stumbling block ка́мень преткнове́ния.

stump *n.* **1,** (tree trunk) пень. **2,** (remaining part; stub) обру́бок; (*of an amputated limb*) культя́. —*v.t.* (baffle) ста́вить в тупи́к.

stun *v.t.* ошеломля́ть; оглуша́ть; потряса́ть.

stunning *adj.* **1,** (staggering, as of a blow) сокру-

ши́тельный. **2,** (shocking, as of news) ошеломля́ющий; сногсшиба́тельный. **3,** (outstanding; splendid) потряса́ющий. **4,** (gorgeous) великоле́пный.

stunt *n.* трюк: *acrobatic stunt,* акробати́ческий трюк. —*v.t.* остана́вливать: *stunt the growth of,* остана́вливать рост (+ *gen.*). —**stunt man,** каскадёр.

stupefaction *n.* отупе́ние; оцепене́ние; остолбене́ние.

stupefy *v.t.* **1,** (dull the senses of) дурма́нить. **2,** (astound) ошеломля́ть.

stupendous *adj.* колосса́льный; потряса́ющий.

stupid *adj.* глу́пый: *stupid person,* глу́пый челове́к; *stupid idea,* глу́пая иде́я. *What a stupid thing to do!,* как э́то глу́по!; кака́я глу́пость! —**stupidity,** *n.* глу́пость. —**stupidly,** *adv.* глу́по.

stupor *n.* отупе́ние; оцепене́ние; остолбене́ние; сту́пор. *In a stupor,* в состоя́нии отупе́ния/оцепене́ния. *In a drunken stupor,* отупе́в от пья́нства.

sturdy *adj.* **1,** (strong; stout) кре́пкий: *of sturdy build,* кре́пкого сложе́ния. **2,** (firm; steady) про́чный: *sturdy table/foundation,* про́чный стол/фунда́мент.

sturgeon *n.* **1,** (fish) осётр. *White sturgeon,* белу́га. **2,** (food) осетри́на.

stutter *v.i.* заика́ться. —*n.* заика́ние. —**stutterer,** *n.* заи́ка.

sty *n.* **1,** (pigpen) свина́рник. **2,** (inflammation of the eyelid) ячме́нь.

style *n.* **1,** (fashion) мо́да. *Be in style,* быть в мо́де. *The latest style,* после́дняя мо́да. **2,** (way a garment is made) фасо́н. **3,** (manner of expression or design) стиль: *writing style,* стиль письма́. *Lofty style,* возвы́шенный стиль. *Byzantine style,* византи́йский стиль. **4,** (way of doing things) стиль: *That's not my style,* э́то не в моём сти́ле. **5,** (way of reckoning dates) стиль: *Old/New Style,* по ста́рому/но́вому сти́лю. **6,** (elegance; grace) шик: *do something with style,* де́лать что́-нибудь с ши́ком. *Live in style,* жить на широ́кую но́гу. **7,** *bot.* сто́лбик. —*v.t.* модели́ровать: *style dresses,* модели́ровать пла́тья.

stylish *adj.* мо́дный. —**stylishly,** *adv.* мо́дно.

stylist *n.* **1,** (master of literary style) стили́ст. **2,** (designer) модельёр. **3,** *Hair stylist,* парикма́хер.

stylistic *adj.* стилисти́ческий. —**stylistics,** *n.* стили́стика.

stylize *v.t.* стилизова́ть. —**stylization,** *n.* стилиза́ция.

stylus *n.* гравирова́льная игла́.

stymie *v.t.* срыва́ть. *Be stymied,* зайти́ в тупи́к.

styptic *adj.* кровоостана́вливающий.

styrene *n.* стиро́л.

suave *adj.* обходи́тельный. —**suavity,** *n.* обходи́тельность.

subclass *n.* подкла́сс.

subcommittee *n.* подкоми́ссия; подкомите́т.

subconscious *adj.* подсозна́тельный. —*n., preceded by the* подсозна́ние.

subcontinent *n.* субконтине́нт.

subcontract *n.* субподря́д. —**subcontractor,** *n.* субподря́дчик.

subdivide *v.t.* подразделя́ть. —*v.i.* подразделя́ться. —**subdivision,** *n.* подразделе́ние.

subdue *v.t.* **1,** (conquer) покоря́ть; подчиня́ть. **2,** (overpower) укроща́ть; переси́ливать.

subdued *adj.* **1,** (less noisy or aggressive) пода́вленный; приглушённый. **2,** (less bright) нея́ркий; приглушённый.

subgroup *n.* подгру́ппа.

subheading *n.* подзаголо́вок. *Also,* **subhead.**

subject *n.* **1,** (topic) те́ма; предме́т. *Change the subject,* перемени́ть разгово́р. **2,** (academic course) предме́т: *I am taking three subjects,* я изуча́ю три предме́та. **3,** (recipient of treatment, examination, etc.) субъе́кт. **4,** (one who owes allegiance) по́дданный: *British subject,* брита́нский по́дданный. **5,** *gram.* подлежа́щее. —*adj.* **1,** (under the dominion of another) подчинённый: *subject peoples,* подчинённые наро́ды. **2,** *fol. by* **to** (under the authority of) подвла́стный (+ *dat.*): *subject to the laws of the kingdom,* подвла́стен зако́нам короле́вства. **3,** *fol. by* **to** (open to) подлежа́щий (+ *dat.*): *be subject to arrest,* подлежа́ть аре́сту. *The treaty is subject to revision,* догово́р подлежи́т пересмо́тру. *The decision is not subject to appeal,* реше́ние не подлежи́т обжа́лованию. **4,** *fol. by* **to** (prone to) подве́рженный (+ *dat.*): *subject to earthquakes/flooding,* подве́рженный землетрясе́ниям/наводне́нию. *He is subject to nervous fits,* он подве́ржен не́рвным припа́дкам. **5,** *fol. by* **to** (contingent on) зави́сящий (от). *All this is subject to the chief's approval,* всё э́то зави́сит от одобре́ния нача́льника. —*v.t.* **1,** (expose) подверга́ть: *He was subjected to harsh criticism,* он подве́ргся ре́зкой кри́тике. **2,** (subjugate) подчиня́ть; покоря́ть. —**subject matter,** содержа́ние; сюже́т.

subjection *n.* подчине́ние.

subjective *adj.* субъекти́вный. —**subjectivism,** *n.* субъективи́зм. —**subjectivity,** *n.* субъекти́вность.

subjugate *v.t.* покоря́ть; подчиня́ть. —**subjugation,** *n.* покоре́ние; подчине́ние.

subjunctive *adj.* сослага́тельный. —*n.* сослага́тельное наклоне́ние.

sublease *n.* субаре́нда. —*v.t.* [*also,* **sublet**] пересдава́ть.

sublimate *v.t., chem.* возгоня́ть; сублими́ровать. —*n.* сублима́т. —**corrosive sublimate,** сулема́.

sublimation *n.* возго́нка; сублима́ция.

sublime *adj.* вели́чественный; возвы́шенный. —**from the sublime to the ridiculous,** от вели́кого до смешно́го.

submachine gun пистоле́т-пулемёт; автома́т.

submarine *n.* подво́дная ло́дка. —*adj.* подво́дный: *submarine warfare,* подво́дная война́.

submerge *v.t.* погружа́ть (в во́ду). —*v.i.* погружа́ться (в во́ду).

submersion *n.* погруже́ние (в во́ду).

submission *n.* **1,** (presentation) представле́ние; пода́ча: *submission of evidence,* представле́ние доказа́тельств; *submission of an application,* пода́ча заявле́ния. **2,** (yielding) подчине́ние. *Starve into submission,* взять изма́ром.

submissive *adj.* поко́рный. —**submissiveness,** *n.* поко́рность.

submit *v.t.* **1,** (present for consideration) представля́ть; выдвига́ть; вноси́ть; подава́ть. *Submit a list of names,* представля́ть спи́сок имён. *Submit a proposal,* вноси́ть *or* выдвига́ть предложе́ние. *Submit an application,* подава́ть заявле́ние. **2,** (contend) утвержда́ть: *I submit that...,* сме́ю утвержда́ть, что... —*v.i.* уступа́ть; подчиня́ться; покоря́ться. *Submit to someone's demands,* уступа́ть чьи́м-нибудь тре́бованиям.

subnormal *adj.* **1,** (below normal) ни́же норма́льного. **2,** (of low intelligence) слабоу́мный.

subordinate *adj.* **1,** (lower-ranking) подчинённый. *Be subordinate to,* быть в подчине́нии у. **2,** *gram.* прида́точный: *subordinate clause,* прида́точное предложе́ние. —*n.* подчинённый. —*v.t.* подчиня́ть: *subordinate one's wishes to those of the majority,* подчиня́ть свои́ жела́ния жела́ниям большинства́.

subordination *n.* подчинённость; подчине́ние.

suborn *v.t.* подкупа́ть.

subpoena *n.* пове́стка в суд. —*v.t.* вызыва́ть в суд.

subscribe *v.i.* [*usu.* **subscribe to**] **1,** (take out a subscription to) подпи́сываться на. **2,** (receive regularly by subscription) выпи́сывать. **3,** (endorse; support) присоединя́ться к; подпи́сываться под (+ *instr.*).

subscriber *n.* подпи́счик.

subscription *n.* (to a magazine or newspaper) подпи́ска; (to a series of cultural events) абонеме́нт. *Subscription rate,* цена́ подпи́ски; подписна́я цена́.

subsequent *adj.* после́дующий; дальне́йший. —**subsequently,** *adv.* впосле́дствии; в дальне́йшем.

subservience *n.* подчине́ние. *Position of subservience,* подчинённое положе́ние.

subservient *adj.* **1,** (subordinate) подчинённый. **2,** (servile) раболе́пный.

subside *v.i.* **1,** (abate; wane) утиха́ть; затиха́ть; стиха́ть; уле́чься. **2,** (ease, as of pain) стиха́ть; смягча́ться; успока́иваться. **3,** (go down, as of fever or swelling) спада́ть. **4,** (recede, as of floodwaters) спада́ть; убыва́ть; идти́ на у́быль.

subsidiary *adj.* вспомога́тельный; подсо́бный. —*n.* доче́рнее предприя́тие; филиа́л.

subsidize *v.t.* субсиди́ровать.

subsidy *n.* субси́дия; дота́ция.

subsist *v.i.* **1,** (continue to exist) просуществова́ть. **2,** *fol. by* **on** (sustain oneself) пита́ться (+ *instr.*); корми́ться (+ *instr.*).

subsistence *n.* существова́ние; пропита́ние. *Means of subsistence,* сре́дства к существова́нию; сре́дства пропита́ния.

subsoil *n.* подпо́чва.

subsonic *adj.* дозвуково́й.

subspecies *n.* подви́д.

substance *n.* **1,** (material) вещество́: *a hard substance,* твёрдое вещество́. **2,** (essence; gist) су́щность; существо́; суть. *In substance,* в су́щности. **3,** (wealth): *a man of substance,* состоя́тельный челове́к. **4,** (density; body) твёрдость; пло́тность. **5,** *fig.* (solid quality) содержа́ние: *lacking substance,* бе́ден содержа́нием. *A report lacking in substance,* бессодержа́тельный докла́д. **6,** *philos.* субста́нция.

substandard *adj.* ни́зкого ка́чества; ни́же устано́вленного станда́рта.

substantial *adj.* **1,** (firm; solid) соли́дный: *a substantial building*, соли́дное зда́ние. *A substantial breakfast*, пло́тный за́втрак. **2,** (considerable; significant) суще́ственный; значи́тельный: *substantial improvement*, суще́ственное/значи́тельное улучше́ние. *Substantial amount*, значи́тельная су́мма. *Substantial pay increase*, значи́тельное повыше́ние зарпла́ты. *Substantial difference*, суще́ственная ра́зница. *Substantial income*, соли́дный дохо́д. **3,** (in essentials) основно́й. *We are in substantial agreement*, в основно́м мы схо́димся во взгля́дах; в основно́м мы договори́лись. —**substantially,** *adv.* суще́ственно; значи́тельно.

substantiate *v.t.* обосно́вывать. —**substantiation,** *n.* обоснова́ние.

substantive *adj.* суще́ственный: *substantive changes*, суще́ственные измене́ния. —*n., gram.* и́мя существи́тельное.

substation *n.* подста́нция.

substitute *n.* **1,** (replacement) заме́на; замести́тель. *Find a substitute for someone*, найти́ заме́ну для кого́-нибудь. **2,** *sports* запасно́й (игро́к). **3,** (synthetic product) замени́тель; суррога́т. —*adj.* **1,** (of a product) суррога́тный. **2,** (of a person): *substitute teacher*, замести́тель. —*v.t.* подставля́ть: *substitute one word for another*, подставля́ть одно́ сло́во вме́сто друго́го. —*v.i.* [*usu.* **substitute for**] заменя́ть; замеща́ть.

substitution *n.* **1,** (act of substituting) заме́на; замеще́ние. **2,** *math.* подстано́вка.

substratum *n.* субстра́т.

subsume *v.t.* подводи́ть: *subsume under a certain category*, подводи́ть под каку́ю-нибудь катего́рию.

subterfuge *n.* увёртка; уло́вка.

subterranean *adj.* подзе́мный.

subtitle *n.* **1,** (secondary title) подзаголо́вок. **2,** *motion pictures* субти́тр.

subtle *adj.* то́нкий: *subtle humor*, то́нкий ю́мор; *subtle hint*, то́нкий намёк; *subtle distinction*, то́нкое разли́чие. —**subtlety,** *n.* то́нкость. —**subtly,** *adv.* то́нко.

subtotal *n.* ча́стный ито́г.

subtract *v.t. & i.* вычита́ть. —**subtraction,** *n.* вычита́ние.

subtrahend *n.* вычита́емое.

subtropics *n.pl.* субтро́пика. —**subtropical,** *adj.* субтропи́ческий.

subunit *n., mil.* подразделе́ние.

suburb *n.* при́город; предме́стье; *pl.* при́городы; предме́стья; окре́стности. —**suburban,** *adj.* при́городный; да́чный. —**suburbanite,** *n.* жи́тель при́города.

subversion *n.* **1,** (subversive activities) подрывна́я де́ятельность. **2,** (overthrow) сверже́ние; ниспроверже́ние.

subversive *adj.* подрывно́й.

subvert *v.t.* **1,** (destroy; overthrow) сверга́ть; ниспроверга́ть. **2,** (corrupt) развраща́ть.

subway *n.* метро́; метрополите́н.

subzero *adj.* ни́же нуля́; ми́нусовый.

succeed *v.i.* **1,** (achieve one's goal) доби́ться успе́ха: *If you try hard enough, you'll succeed*, е́сли вы о́чень постара́етесь, то добьётесь успе́ха. **2,** (achieve a specified goal) удава́ться (*impers., with dat.*): *He succeeded in obtaining a loan*, ему́ удало́сь получи́ть заём. **3,** (achieve success) преуспева́ть: *succeed in life*, преуспева́ть в жи́зни. **4,** (turn out successfully) удава́ться; увенча́ться успе́хом. *The plan succeeded*, план уда́лся. *Our efforts succeeded*, на́ши уси́лия увенча́лись успе́хом. **5,** *fol. by* **to** (assume after someone else departs): *succeed to the presidency*, стать прее́мником президе́нта. *Succeed to the throne*, насле́довать престо́л. —*v.t.* **1,** (come after) сле́довать за; сменя́ть. *Succeed one's father* (*to the throne*), насле́довать отцу́. **2,** (take the place of) приходи́ть на сме́ну (+ *dat.*).

succeeding *adj.* после́дующий: *succeeding generations*, после́дующие поколе́ния.

success *n.* успе́х: *achieve success*, доби́ться успе́ха. *Without success*, безуспе́шно. *I wish you* (*every*) *success*, жела́ю вам успе́ха. —**be a success, 1,** (succeed in life) преуспева́ть. **2,** (turn out well) удава́ться: *The experiment was a success*, о́пыт уда́лся. *The play was a huge success*, пье́са име́ла огро́мный успе́х.

successful *adj.* **1,** (resulting in success) успе́шный; уда́чный: *successful attempt/outcome*, уда́чная попы́тка; успе́шный исхо́д. *The operation was successful*, опера́ция удала́сь. **2,** (achieving one's goal): *Were you successful in convincing him?*, вам удало́сь убеди́ть его́? **3,** (achieving professional success) преуспева́ющий: *successful lawyer*, преуспева́ющий адвока́т. *He was very successful in business*, он о́чень преуспе́л в би́знесе.

successfully *adv.* успе́шно; уда́чно.

succession *n.* **1,** (the coming of one after another) прее́мственность: *the succession of generations*, прее́мственность поколе́ний. **2,** (series) ряд; цепь: *a succession of disasters*, ряд/цепь катастро́ф. **3,** (succeeding to power): *succession to the throne*, престолонасле́дие. *War of the Austrian Succession*, война́ за Австри́йское насле́дство. —**in succession, 1,** (one after another) по поря́дку. **2,** (in a row; consecutively) подря́д.

successive *adj.* после́довательный. *Three successive years*, три го́да подря́д.

successor *n.* прее́мник.

succinct *adj.* сжа́тый; кра́ткий.

succor *also,* **succour** *n.* по́мощь; соде́йствие.

succotash *n.* блю́до из кукуру́зы и бобо́в.

succour *n.* = **succor.**

succulent *adj.* со́чный. —**succulence,** *n.* со́чность.

succumb *v.i.* **1,** (yield) уступа́ть; поддава́ться. *Succumb to pressure*, уступа́ть давле́нию. *Succumb to temptation*, поддава́ться собла́зну *or* искуше́нию. *He succumbed to her charms*, он подда́лся её ча́рам. **2,** (die) умере́ть: *succumb to an illness*, умере́ть от (како́й-нибудь) боле́зни.

such *adj. & adv.* тако́й: *in such cases*, в таки́х

случаях; *such a large house,* такóй большóй дом; *such tall buildings,* такúе высóкие здáния. *Such a long time ago,* так давнó. *In such a way that...,* так, что... *The situation is such that...,* ситуáция таковá, что... —*pron.* такóв: *Such is life,* таковá жизнь. —**and such,** и томý подóбное. —**as such,** как таковóй; сам по себé. —**no such thing,** ничегó такóго; ничегó подóбного. *I said no such thing,* я не говорúл(а) ничегó такóго/подóбного. —**such a thing,** такóе: *How could you say such a thing?,* как вы моглú сказáть такóе? *How could such a thing happen?,* как такóе моглó случúться? —**such and such,** такóй-то. *As of such and such a date,* с такóго-то числá. —**such as,** как напримéр: *large countries such as India,* большúе стрáны, как, напримéр, Úндия.

suck *v.t.* сосáть: *suck one's finger,* сосáть пáлец. —**give suck,** кормúть грýдью. —**suck in,** всáсывать; засáсывать.

sucker *n.* **1,** (person or thing that sucks) сосýн; сосунóк. **2,** *bot.; zool.* присóсок. **3,** *slang* (dupe) простáк.

suckle *v.t.* кормúть (грýдью). —*v.i.* сосáть.

suckling *n.* сосýн; сосунóк. —*adj.* груднóй; молóчный. *Suckling pig,* поросёнок.

sucrose *n.* сахарóза.

suction *n.* всáсывание. —**suction pump,** всáсывающий насóс.

sudden *adj.* внезáпный; неожúданный. *Sudden departure/downpour,* внезáпный отъéзд/лúвень. *Sudden death,* внезáпная *or* скоропостúжная смерть. *This is so sudden,* э́то так неожúданно. —**all of a sudden,** вдруг; внезáпно; ни с тогó ни с сегó.

suddenly *adv.* вдруг; внезáпно. —**suddenness,** *n.* внезáпность.

suds *n.pl.* **1,** (soapy water) мы́льная водá. **2,** (lather) мы́льная пéна.

sue *v.t. & i.* подавáть в суд (на); предъявля́ть иск (к); возбуждáть дéло *or* иск (о *or* прóтив); судúться (с). *Sue for damages,* предъявля́ть иск о возмещéнии убы́тков. *Sue for libel,* возбуждáть дéло о клеветé. *Sue for peace,* добивáться мúра. *He sued to get his job back,* он пóдал в суд, чтóбы егó восстановúли на рабóту.

suede *n.* зáмша. —*adj.* зáмшевый.

suffer *v.i.* страдáть: *suffer from the cold,* страдáть от хóлода; *suffer from a rare disease,* страдáть рéдкой болéзнью. *Suffer in translation,* теря́ть в перевóде. *His reputation will suffer,* егó репутáция пострадáет. —*v.t.* **1,** (undergo; experience) испы́тывать: *suffer pain,* испы́тывать боль; *suffer pangs of conscience,* испы́тывать угрызéния сóвести. *He suffered the same fate,* егó постúгла та же ýчасть. **2,** (sustain) потерпéть; понестú; получúть. *Suffer a defeat,* потерпéть поражéние. *Suffer losses,* понестú потéри. *Suffer an injury,* получúть повреждéние. **3,** (put up with) терпéть; выносúть. *Suffer fools,* терпéть дуракóв.

sufferance *n.* **1,** (passive permission) мúлость: *at the sufferance of,* по мúлости (+ *gen.*). **2,** (endurance) терпéние; терпелúвость.

sufferer *n.* страдáлец.

suffering *n.* страдáние. —*adj.* страдáющий.

suffice *v.i.* быть достáточным; хватáть. *That will suffice for today,* э́того хвáтит на сегóдня. *A few words will suffice,* нéсколько слов бýдет достáточно. —**suffice (it) to say,** достáточно сказáть.

sufficiency *n.* достáточность.

sufficient *adj.* достáточно: *sufficient fuel,* достáточно тóплива. *Five gallons are sufficient for such a short trip,* пять галлóнов достáточно для такóй корóткой поéздки. —**sufficiently,** *adv.* достáточно.

suffix *n.* сýффикс.

suffocate *v.t.* душúть; удушáть. —*v.i.* задыхáться. *I am suffocating,* мне дýшно.

suffocation *n.* удýшье: *die of suffocation,* умерéть от удýшья.

suffrage *n.* прáво гóлоса; избирáтельное прáво.

suffragette *n.* суфражúстка.

suffuse *v.t.* заливáть: *The room is suffused with light,* кóмната залитá свéтом.

sugar *n.* сáхар. —*adj.* сáхарный. —**sugar beet,** сáхарная свёкла. —**sugar bowl,** сáхарница. —**sugar cane,** сáхарный тростнúк. —**sugar loaf,** головá (*or* голóвка) сáхару. —**sugar refinery,** сáхарный *or* рафинáдный завóд.

sugar-coat *v.t.* покрывáть сáхаром; *fig.* подслáщивать.

sugary *adj.* **1,** (of or containing sugar) сáхарный; сáхаристый. **2,** *fig.* (cloyingly sweet) слащáвый; сáхарный; прúторный.

suggest *v.t.* **1,** (advise; recommend) предлагáть: *suggest a new approach,* предлагáть нóвый подхóд. *He suggested that I see a doctor,* он предложúл мне обратúться к врачý. **2,** (offer, as an idea or thought) подавáть; наводúть на. *Suggest a simple idea,* подáть простýю идéю. *Suggest a thought to someone,* навестú когó-нибудь на мысль. *That suggests a different thought,* э́то навóдит на другýю мысль. **3,** (indicate; lead to believe) говорúть о: *The evidence suggests that...,* улúки говоря́т о том, что... *Experience suggests that...,* óпыт подскáзывает, что... **4,** (imply) намекáть. *Are you suggesting that...?,* вы намекáете (*or* вы хотúте сказáть), что...? —**suggest itself,** напрáшиваться: *The following conclusion suggests itself,* напрáшивается слéдующий вы́вод.

suggestion *n.* **1,** (something suggested) предложéние. **2,** (faint trace; hint) намёк; нóтка. **3,** *physiol.* внушéние.

suggestive *adj.* **1,** *fol. by* **of** (recalling; resembling) напоминáющий. **2,** (suggesting something indecent) двусмы́сленный.

suicidal *adj.* самоубúйственный.

suicide *n.* самоубúйство. *Suicide note,* предсмéртная запúска. —**commit suicide,** покóнчить жизнь самоубúйством; покóнчить с собóй.

suit *n.* **1,** (outfit) костю́м: *three-piece suit,* костю́м-трóйка. *Bathing suit,* купáльный костю́м. *Space suit,* космúческий костю́м. *Suit of armor,* лáтные доспéхи. **2,** *law* иск; дéло; процéсс. *Divorce suit,* бракоразвóдный процéсс. *Libel suit,* иск за клевету́. *Suit for damages,* иск о возмеще́нии убы́тков. *Bring/file suit against,* подава́ть в суд на (+ *acc.*); предъявля́ть иск к. **3,** *cards* масть. *Follow suit,* ходи́ть в масть; *fig.* сле́довать чьему́-нибудь приме́ру. —*v.t.* **1,** (be right for) подходи́ть: *The job doesn't suit him,* рабо́та ему́ не подхо́дит. **2,** (please; be to someone's liking) устра́ивать: *It suits me fine,* э́то меня́ вполне́ устра́ивает. *Nothing suits him,* на него́ (*or* ему́) не уго́дишь. —**suit yourself,** де́лайте, как хоти́те. *See also* **suited.**

suitability *n.* го́дность; приго́дность.

suitable *adj.* **1,** (appropriate) подходя́щий: *suitable partner,* подходя́щий партнёр. **2,** (usable) го́дный; приго́дный. *Suitable for drinking,* го́дный для питья́. —**suitably,** *adv.* как сле́дует; до́лжным о́бразом.

suitcase *n.* чемода́н.

suite *n.* **1,** (of rooms) анфила́да. **2,** (of furniture) гарниту́р. **3,** (retinue) сви́та. **4,** *music* сюи́та.

suited *adj. Be suited for/to,* годи́ться: *He is not suited to be a teacher,* он не годи́тся в учителя́. *He is not suited for this type of work,* така́я рабо́та ему́ не подхо́дит.

suiting *n.* костю́мный материа́л.

suitor *n.* покло́нник.

sulfa drugs *also,* **sulpha drugs** сульфанилами́дные препара́ты.

sulfate *also,* **sulphate** *n.* сульфа́т; сернокисла́я соль. *See also* **ammonium/barium/copper/sodium sulfate.**

sulfide *also,* **sulphide** *n.* сульфи́д. ♦*In compounds,* серни́стый: *hydrogen sulfide,* серни́стый водоро́д.

sulfur *also,* **sulphur** *n.* се́ра. —*adj.* се́рный: *sulfur springs,* се́рные исто́чники. —**sulfur dioxide,** двуо́кись се́ры.

sulfuric *also,* **sulphuric** *adj.* се́рный. —**sulfuric acid,** се́рная кислота́.

sulfurous *also,* **sulphurous** *adj.* серни́стый.

sulk *v.i.* ду́ться.

sulky *adj.* наду́тый. —*n.* (carriage) одноме́стная двуко́лка.

sullen *adj.* угрю́мый; хму́рый; па́смурный. —**sullenness,** *n.* угрю́мость.

sully *v.t.* **1,** (soil) па́чкать; пятна́ть. **2,** (tarnish, as someone's reputation) пятна́ть.

sulphate *n.* = **sulfate.** —**sulphide,** *n.* = **sulfide.** —**sulphur,** *n.* = **sulfur.** —**sulphuric,** *adj.* = **sulfuric.** —**sulphurous,** *adj.* = **sulfurous.**

sultan *n.* султа́н. —**sultanate,** *n.* султана́т.

sultry *adj.* зно́йный. *It is sultry,* па́рит.

sum *n.* **1,** (total) су́мма; ито́г. **2,** (amount) су́мма: *a healthy sum of money,* изря́дная су́мма де́нег. —*v.t.* [*usu.* **sum up**] сумми́ровать; резюми́ровать; подыто́живать; подводи́ть ито́г (+ *gen.*). —*v.i.* [*usu.* **sum up**] подводи́ть ито́ги. *To sum up,* в ито́ге; коро́че говоря́. —**in sum,** одни́м сло́вом; коро́че говоря́. —**sum total,** о́бщий ито́г. —**the sum and substance,** са́мая суть (+ *gen.*).

sumac *n.* сума́х.

summarily *adv.* бесцеремо́нно.

summarize *v.t.* сумми́ровать; резюми́ровать.

summary *n.* сво́дка; резюме́; конспе́кт. —*adj.* **1,** (brief; general) сумма́рный. **2,** (without observing the formalities) бесцеремо́нный.

summation *n.* резюме́. —**in summation,** в ито́ге; подводя́ ито́ги.

summer *n.* ле́то. *In summer,* ле́том. —*adj.* ле́тний: *summer day,* ле́тний день. —*v.i.* проводи́ть ле́то.

summerhouse *n.* бесе́дка.

summer lightning зарни́ца.

summertime *n.* ле́то; ле́тнее вре́мя.

summery *adj.* ле́тний.

summit *n.* верши́на: *reach the summit,* добра́ться до верши́ны. —**summit conference,** встре́ча на вы́сшем у́ровне; встре́ча в верха́х.

summon *v.t.* **1,** (order to appear) вызыва́ть: *summon to a meeting,* вы́звать на собра́ние. **2,** (call together; convene) созыва́ть: *summon one's advisers,* созва́ть свои́х сове́тников. **3,** *fol. by* **up** (muster) собра́ться с; набра́ться (+ *gen.*): *summon up courage,* собра́ться с ду́хом; набра́ться хра́брости.

summons *n.* вы́зов; повестка (в суд).

sumptuous *adj.* роско́шный; пы́шный. —**sumptuousness,** *n.* пы́шность.

sun *n.* со́лнце: *lie in the sun,* лежа́ть на со́лнце. —*adj.* со́лнечный. —*v.t.* [*usu.* **sun oneself**] гре́ться на со́лнце.

sun bath со́лнечная ва́нна. —**sun-bathe,** *v.i.* принима́ть со́лнечную ва́нну; загора́ть.

sunbeam *n.* со́лнечный луч.

sunburn *n.* зага́р. —**sunburned; sunburnt,** *adj.* загоре́лый. *Get/become sunburned,* загора́ть.

sundae *n.* пломби́р.

Sunday *n.* воскресе́нье. —*adj.* воскре́сный: *Sunday issue,* воскре́сный но́мер.

sunder *v.t.* раска́лывать; разбива́ть.

sundew *n.* рося́нка.

sundial *n.* со́лнечные часы́.

sundown *n.* зака́т. *At sundown,* на зака́те.

sundries *n.pl.* ра́зное; вся́кая вся́чина.

sundry *adj.* разли́чный; ра́зный.

sunfish *n.* луна́-ры́ба.

sunflower *n.* подсо́лнечник. *Sunflower oil,* подсо́лнечное ма́сло. *Sunflower seeds,* се́мечки.

sunglasses *n.pl.* со́лнечные очки́; солнцезащи́тные очки́; очки́ от со́лнца.

sunken *adj.* **1,** (under water) зато́пленный; зато́нувший. **2,** (hollow, as of cheeks, eyes, etc.) впа́лый; запа́вший; углублённый.

sun lamp ла́мпа со́лнечного све́та.

sunlight *n.* со́лнечный свет.

sunlit *adj.* освещённый со́лнцем.

sunny *adj.* **1,** (bright with sunshine) со́лнечный. *It is sunny,* со́лнечно. **2,** *fig.* (cheerful) весёлый; ра́достный. —**sunny side up,** желтка́ми вверх.

sunrise *n.* восхо́д со́лнца. *At sunrise,* на заре́.

sunset *n.* захо́д со́лнца; зака́т. *At sunset,* на зака́те.

sunshade *n.* **1,** (parasol) зо́нтик. **2,** (awning) наве́с. **3,** (visor) козырёк.

sunshine *n.* **1,** (sunlight) со́лнечный свет. *In the sunshine,* на со́лнце. **2,** *fig.* (good cheer) весе́лье.

sunspot *n.* со́лнечное пятно́.

sunstroke *n.* со́лнечный уда́р.

suntan *n.* зага́р. —**suntanned,** *adj.* загоре́лый.

super *n., colloq.* = **superintendent** (*in sense #1*). —*adj., colloq.* чу́дный; превосхо́дный.

superabundance *n.* чрезме́рный избы́ток.

superannuated *adj.* **1,** (retired) в отста́вке. **2,** (past one's point of usefulness) отжи́вший свой век.

superb *adj.* превосхо́дный; великоле́пный.

supercharger *n.* нагнета́тель.

supercilious *adj.* высокоме́рный; надме́нный.

superconductor *n.* сверхпроводни́к. —**superconductivity,** *n.* сверхпроводи́мость.

superficial *adj.* пове́рхностный. —**superficiality,** *n.* пове́рхностность. —**superficially,** *adv.* пове́рхностно.

superfluous *adj.* изли́шний; ли́шний.

superhighway *n.* автостра́да; автомагистра́ль; скоростна́я доро́га.

superhuman *adj.* сверхчелове́ческий. *Superhuman efforts,* нечелове́ческие уси́лия.

superimpose *v.t.* накла́дывать.

superintend *v.t.* надзира́ть за; заве́довать; управля́ть.

superintendent *n.* **1,** (of a building) коменда́нт. **2,** (of a police department or military academy) нача́льник.

superior *adj.* **1,** (better) лу́чший: *far superior to,* намно́го лу́чше (+ *gen.*). *Our team proved superior,* на́ша кома́нда оказа́лась сильне́е. **2,** (higher in rank) ста́рший: *a superior officer,* ста́рший офице́р. **3,** (greater; preponderant) превосходя́щий: *superior forces,* превосходя́щие си́лы. **4,** (excellent) отли́чный; отме́нный. *A superior technician,* отли́чный те́хник. **5,** (haughty) высокоме́рный; надме́нный. —*n.* **1,** (one superior in rank) нача́льник; ста́рший. *One's immediate superior,* прямо́й нача́льник. *Bow to the will of one's superiors,* подчиня́ться во́ле ста́рших. **2,** (head of a monastery) настоя́тель. *Mother superior,* игу́менья; настоя́тельница. —**Lake Superior,** о́зеро Ве́рхнее. —**superior court,** вы́сший суд.

superiority *n.* превосхо́дство.

superlative *adj.* превосхо́дный: *superlative weather,* превосхо́дная пого́да. —**superlative degree,** *gram.* превосхо́дная сте́пень.

superman *n.* сверхчелове́к.

supermarket *n.* суперма́ркет; универса́м.

supernatural *adj.* сверхъесте́ственный.

supernumerary *adj.* сверхшта́тный. —*n., theat.* стати́ст.

superpower *n.* сверхдержа́ва.

superscript *n.* надстро́чный знак.

supersede *v.t.* заменя́ть; идти́ на сме́ну (+ *dat.*).

supersensitive *adj.* сверхчувстви́тельный.

supersonic *adj.* сверхзвуково́й.

superstition *n.* суеве́рие. —**superstitious,** *adj.* суеве́рный.

superstructure *n.* надстро́йка.

supertanker *n.* суперта́нкер.

supervise *v.t.* наблюда́ть за; надзира́ть за: *super-vise the children/work,* наблюда́ть *or* надзира́ть за детьми́/ за рабо́той/.

supervision *n.* наблюде́ние; надзо́р; присмо́тр; надсмо́тр. *Elections under U.N. supervision,* вы́боры под наблюде́нием ООН. *Require close supervision,* тре́бовать стро́гого надзо́ра.

supervisor *n.* **1,** (overseer) надзира́тель; надсмо́трщик. **2,** (immediate superior) нача́льник.

supervisory *adj.* руководя́щий: *supervisory personnel,* руководя́щие рабо́тники.

supine *adj.* **1,** (on one's back) лежа́щий на́взничь. **2,** (inactive; passive) безуча́стный.

supper *n.* у́жин. *Have supper,* у́жинать. *What's for supper?,* что на у́жин? —**the Last Supper,** та́йная ве́черя.

suppertime *n.* вре́мя у́жина.

supplant *v.t.* вытесня́ть; идти́ на сме́ну (+ *dat.*).

supple *adj.* ги́бкий.

supplement *n.* **1,** (anything added) дополне́ние. **2,** (addition to a publication) приложе́ние. —*v.t.* дополня́ть.

supplemental *adj.* дополни́тельный; доба́вочный. *Also,* **supplementary.**

suppliant *n.* проси́тель. —*adj.* умоля́ющий; проси́тельный. *Also,* **supplicant.**

supplicate· *v.t.* моли́ть; умоля́ть. —**supplication,** *n.* мольба́.

supplier *n.* поставщи́к.

supply *v.t.* **1,** (provide with what is needed) снабжа́ть; обеспе́чивать: *supply a factory with raw materials,* снабжа́ть фа́брику сырьём; *supply the children with clothing,* обеспе́чивать дете́й оде́ждой. **2,** (make available) поставля́ть. *Supply merchandise to a store,* поставля́ть това́р магази́ну; снабжа́ть магази́н това́ром. —*n.* **1,** (act of supplying) снабже́ние. *Supply lines,* ли́нии снабже́ния. *Supply depot,* склад снабже́ния. **2,** (stock) запа́с: *adequate supplies of fuel,* доста́точный запа́с то́плива. *Goods in short supply,* дефици́тные това́ры. *Supplies are running low,* запа́сы истоща́ются. *While the supply lasts,* пока́ запа́с не истощи́тся. **3,** *pl.* (materials; equipment) това́ры: *hardware supplies,* скобяны́е това́ры. *Office supplies,* канцеля́рские принадле́жности. **4,** *econ.* предложе́ние: *supply and demand,* спрос и предложе́ние.

support *v.t.* **1,** (hold up) подде́рживать; держа́ть: *Beams support the ceiling,* ба́лки подде́рживают/ де́ржат потоло́к. *The bridge could not support the weight of the trucks,* мост не вы́держал ве́са грузовико́в. **2,** (back) подде́рживать: *support a candidate/proposal,* подде́рживать кандида́та/предложе́ние. **3,** (provide for) содержа́ть; име́ть на иждиве́нии. *Support a family,* содержа́ть семью́. *He has a wife and three children to support,* у него́ на иждиве́нии жена́ и тро́е дете́й. *How does he support himself?,* чем он зараба́тывает на жизнь? **4,** (corroborate) подтвержда́ть. —*n.* **1,** (backing) подде́ржка: *moral support,* мора́льная подде́ржка. *Appeals in support of the prisoner,* обраще́ния в подде́ржку заключённого. *Speak in support of a* *proposal,* выступа́ть за предложе́ние. **2,** (base; prop) опо́ра; подпо́рка; подста́вка. **3,** (maintenance; assistance) содержа́ние; подде́ржка; иждиве́ние. *Child support,* де́ньги на содержа́ние ребёнка. *Provide with financial support,* ока́зывать (+ *dat.*) материа́льную подде́ржку. *Be left without visible means of support,* оста́ться без подде́ржки. **4,** *mil.* подде́ржка; обеспе́чение. *Artillery support,* подде́ржка артилле́рии.

supporter *n.* сторо́нник.

supporting *adj.* опо́рный: *supporting beam,* опо́рная ба́лка. **—supporting role,** вспомога́тельная роль.

supportive *adj.* отзы́вчивый; уча́стливый.

suppose *v.t.* **1,** (think; imagine) полага́ть: *I suppose so,* полага́ю, что да. *What do you suppose this means?,* что э́то, по-ва́шему, зна́чит? **2,** (assume) предполага́ть: *Let's just suppose for a moment that...,* предполо́жим на мину́ту, что... **3,** used to make a suggestion: *Suppose we do it this way,* дава́йте сде́лаем э́то так.

supposed *adj.* **1,** (assumed) предполага́емый: *the supposed cause of the crash,* предполага́емая причи́на ава́рии. **2,** (expected) до́лжен; поло́жено. *He is supposed to be here at noon,* он до́лжен прийти́ в по́лдень. *You are supposed to obey,* тебе́ поло́жено слу́шаться. *I am not supposed to drink,* мне пить не полага́ется. *It's supposed to rain today,* на сего́дня обеща́ли (*or* предска́зывали) дождь.

supposedly *adv.* предположи́тельно; я́кобы. *The money which he supposedly took,* де́ньги, кото́рые он я́кобы забра́л. *Supposedly, he will be there already,* предполага́ется, что он уже́ бу́дет там.

supposition *n.* предположе́ние.

suppository *n.* свеча́; све́чка.

suppress *v.t.* **1,** (quell; crush) подавля́ть; усмиря́ть. *Suppress a revolt,* подави́ть восста́ние. **2,** (repress, as a yawn, one's feelings, etc.) подавля́ть; сде́рживать. **3,** (hush up) зама́лчивать; замя́ть. **4,** (keep from being published) запреща́ть.

suppression *n.* подавле́ние.

suppurate *v.i.* гнои́ться. **—suppuration,** *n.* нагное́ние.

supremacy *n.* **1,** (supreme power) госпо́дство; главе́нство. **2,** (superiority) превосхо́дство: *military supremacy,* вое́нное превосхо́дство.

supreme *adj.* верхо́вный. *The Supreme Court,* Верхо́вный суд. *The supreme penalty,* вы́сшая ме́ра наказа́ния. *Make the supreme sacrifice,* же́ртвовать жи́знью.

supremely *adv.* в вы́сшей сте́пени. *Supremely confident of victory,* соверше́нно уве́ренный в побе́де.

surcease *n.* прекраще́ние; остано́вка.

surcharge *n.* припла́та; допла́та.

surcingle *n.* подпру́га.

sure *adj.* **1,** (certain; confident) уве́ренный: *I am sure of it,* я в э́том уве́рен(а). *I am sure he'll agree,* я уве́рен(а), что он согласи́тся. *You may be sure of that,* вы мо́жете быть уве́рены в э́том; вы мо́жете не сомнева́ться в э́том. **2,** (not disputed) несомне́нный: *One thing is sure,* одно́ несомне́нно. **3,** *fol.*

by **to** (bound to) несомне́нно; обяза́тельно: *He is sure to be there,* он несомне́нно/обяза́тельно бу́дет там. **4,** (reliable; unfailing; inevitable) ве́рный: *a sure sign,* ве́рный при́знак; *sure death,* ве́рная смерть. **5,** (confident; steady) уве́ренный: *sure hand,* уве́ренная рука́; *sure step,* уве́ренный шаг. —*adv., colloq.* коне́чно! **—be sure to,** не забы́ть (+ *inf.*). *Be sure not to...,* смотри́(те), не (+ *imperative*). **—for sure, 1,** (without fail) обяза́тельно. **2,** (for a certainty) наверняка́: *No one knows for sure,* никто́ не зна́ет наверняка́. **—make sure, 1,** (see to it that) позабо́титься (о том, что́бы); доби́ться (что́бы). **2,** (ascertain for certain) убеди́ться; удостове́риться. **—sure enough,** действи́тельно; на са́мом де́ле. **—to be sure, 1,** (certainly) что и говори́ть; не́чего сказа́ть; ничего́ не ска́жешь. **2,** (admittedly) пра́вда.

sure-footed *adj.* твёрдо стоя́щий на нога́х.

surely *adv.* несомне́нно; наверняка́; коне́чно. *Surely you don't believe that!,* вы, коне́чно, э́тому не ве́рите! **—slowly but surely,** ме́дленно, но ве́рно.

surety *n.* **1,** (certainty) уве́ренность. **2,** (guarantee) пору́ка. **3,** (guarantor) поручи́тель.

surf *n.* прибо́й; буруны́.

surface *n.* пове́рхность: *smooth surface,* гла́дкая пове́рхность. *Road surface,* доро́жное покры́тие. *Float to the surface,* всплыва́ть на пове́рхность. —*adj.* **1,** (moving over land) назе́мный: *surface forces,* назе́мные си́лы; (moving over water) надво́дный: *surface ship,* надво́дный кора́бль. **2,** (superficial) пове́рхностный: *surface judgments,* пове́рхностные сужде́ния. —*v.t.* (pave) мости́ть; зама́щивать. —*v.i.* (come to the surface) всплыва́ть. **—on the surface,** внешне.

surfeit *n.* **1,** (overindulgence) пресыще́ние. **2,** (excess) изли́шек. —*v.t.* пресыща́ть.

surge *n.* волна́; прито́к; прили́в. *Surge of energy,* прили́в эне́ргии. *Surge in the President's popularity,* всплеск популя́рности президе́нта. —*v.i.* **1,** (billow) вздыма́ться. **2,** (move in large numbers) хлы́нуть; нахлы́нуть. *The crowd surged forward,* толпа́ подала́сь вперёд.

surgeon *n.* хиру́рг.

surgery *n.* хирурги́я. *Undergo surgery,* подве́ргнуться опера́ции. **—surgical,** *adj.* хирурги́ческий.

surly *adj.* злой; ворчли́вый.

surmise *v.t. & i.* предполага́ть. —*n.* предположе́ние; дога́дка.

surmount *v.t.* **1,** (overcome) преодолева́ть: *surmount difficulties,* преодолева́ть тру́дности. **2,** *usu. passive* (place on top of) уве́нчивать: *surmounted by a dome,* уве́нчан ку́полом. **—surmountable,** *adj.* преодоли́мый.

surname *n.* фами́лия.

surpass *v.t.* **1,** (exceed) превосходи́ть: *surpass all expectations,* превосходи́ть все ожида́ния. **2,** (go beyond in achievement) перегоня́ть: *catch up to and surpass the United States,* догна́ть и перегна́ть США. **—surpassing,** *adj.* исключи́тельный; несравне́нный. *A woman of surpassing beauty,* же́нщина исключи́тельной красоты́.

surplice *n.* стиха́рь.

surplus *n.* избы́ток; изли́шек. —*adj.* избы́точный: *surplus merchandise,* избы́точные това́ры. —**surplus value,** приба́вочная сто́имость.

surprise *v.t.* **1,** (astonish) удивля́ть. *Be surprised,* удивля́ться. *I'm surprised at you,* я тебе́ удивля́юсь; ты меня́ удивля́ешь. *We were pleasantly surprised,* мы бы́ли прия́тно удивлены́. *I wouldn't be surprised if it rained,* меня́ не удиви́ло бы, е́сли бы пошёл дождь. **2,** (catch unawares) заста́ть враспло́х. —*n.* **1,** (astonishment) удивле́ние: *To my great surprise,* к моему́ большо́му удивле́нию. *He discovered to his surprise that...,* он с удивле́нием обнару́жил, что... *In surprise,* удивлённо. *The element of surprise,* внеза́пность. **2,** (unexpected development) неожи́данность; сюрпри́з. *It came as a complete surprise to me,* для меня́ э́то бы́ло (*or* яви́лось) по́лной неожи́данностью. —*adj.* неожи́данный; внеза́пный. *Surprise attack,* внеза́пное нападе́ние. —**take by surprise,** заста́ть враспло́х.

surprising *adj.* удиви́тельный: *a surprising turn of events,* удиви́тельный поворо́т собы́тий.

surprisingly *adv.* удиви́тельно; на удивле́ние: *surprisingly well,* удиви́тельно/ на удивле́ние/ хорошо́. *Surprisingly, he turned down the offer,* к на́шему удивле́нию (*or* как ни удиви́тельно), он отклони́л предложе́ние.

surrealism *n.* сюрреали́зм. —**surrealist,** *n.* сюрреали́ст. —**surrealistic,** *adj.* сюрреалисти́ческий.

surrender *v.t.* **1,** (yield; give up) сдава́ть: *surrender a fortress,* сдава́ть кре́пость. **2,** (relinquish) отка́зываться от: *surrender a right,* отказа́ться от пра́ва. —*v.i.* сдава́ться: *I surrender!,* я сдаю́сь! *Surrender to the enemy/police,* сдава́ться врагу́/мили́ции. —*n.* сда́ча; капитуля́ция.

surreptitious *adj.* та́йный. —**surreptitiously,** *adv.* тайко́м; исподтишка́.

surrey *n.* пролётка.

surrogate *n.* **1,** (substitute; deputy) замести́тель. **2,** *law* судья́ по насле́дственным дела́м. —**surrogate court,** суд по насле́дственным дела́м.

surround *v.t.* окружа́ть. *Surrounded on all sides,* окружён со всех сторо́н. *Surround oneself with,* окружа́ть себя́ (+ *instr.*). *The house is surrounded by a fence,* дом окружён *or* обнесён забо́ром. *The circumstances surrounding the incident,* обстоя́тельства, свя́занные с происше́ствием.

surrounding *adj.* окружа́ющий: *the surrounding countryside,* окружа́ющая ме́стность. —**surroundings,** *n.pl.* окруже́ние; среда́; окружа́ющая обстано́вка; окружа́ющее.

surtax *n.* доба́вочный нало́г.

surveillance *n.* надзо́р; наблюде́ние; сле́жка. *Place under surveillance,* взять под наблюде́ние; установи́ть надзо́р *or* сле́жку за (+ *instr.*).

survey *v.t.* **1,** (view; review) обозрева́ть. *Survey the situation,* уясни́ть себе́ положе́ние. **2,** (poll) опра́шивать. **3,** (measure, as land) межева́ть. —*n.* **1,** (review) обзо́р; обозре́ние. **2,** (poll) опро́с. **3,** (detailed study) обсле́дование. **4,** (measurement) съёмка: *aerial survey,* возду́шная съёмка; аэросъёмка. —*adj.* обзо́рный: *survey course,* обзо́рный курс. —**surveying,** *n.* межева́ние. —**surveyor,** *n.* землеме́р.

survival *n.* **1,** (fact of surviving) выжива́ние. *Survival of the fittest,* выжива́ние наибо́лее приспосо́бленных. **2,** (vestige) пережи́ток.

survive *v.i.* **1,** (remain alive) выжива́ть; уцеле́ть; остава́ться в живы́х. **2,** (continue in existence) сохраня́ться: *The custom has survived to this day,* обы́чай сохрани́лся по сей день. —*v.t.* **1,** (come through alive) уцеле́ть от; выжива́ть по́сле; пережива́ть; выде́рживать; остава́ться в живы́х по́сле. *Survive the harsh winter,* вы́держать суро́вую зи́му. **2,** (outlive) пережива́ть. *He is survived by his wife,* по́сле него́ оста́лась его́ жена́.

survivor *n.* **1,** (one who has survived an accident) оста́вшийся в живы́х; уцеле́вший. *There were no survivors,* никто́ не уцеле́л. **2,** (descendant; heir) насле́дник: *He left no survivors,* он не оста́вил по́сле себя́ насле́дников.

susceptibility *n.* подве́рженность; восприи́мчивость.

susceptible *adj.* [*usu.* **susceptible to**] подве́рженный (+ *dat.*); восприи́мчивый (к). *Susceptible to colds,* подве́рженный простуде. *Susceptible to flattery,* па́дкий на лесть.

suspect *v.t.* **1,** (believe possibly guilty; sense the existence of) подозрева́ть: *He is suspected of murder,* его́ подозрева́ют в уби́йстве. *Suspect arson/cancer,* подозрева́ть поджо́г/рак. **2,** (believe to be the case; surmise) полага́ть: *I suspect he'll be more careful from now on,* полага́ю, что отны́не он бу́дет бо́лее осторо́жным. —*n.* подозрева́емый. —*adj.* вызыва́ющий подозре́ние: *His actions are suspect,* его́ де́йствия вызыва́ют подозре́ние.

suspend *v.t.* **1,** (hang from above) подве́шивать: *Suspend a chandelier from the ceiling,* подве́сить лю́стру под потолко́м (*or* к потолку́). **2,** (halt temporarily) прерыва́ть; приостана́вливать; прекраща́ть. **3,** (debar temporarily) вре́менно отстраня́ть (от до́лжности, заня́тий, игры́, *etc.*). **4,** (revoke temporarily, as a rule) вре́менно отменя́ть. *His driver's license was suspended,* он был вре́менно лишён води́тельских прав. **5,** (defer) откла́дывать. *Suspend judgment,* возде́рживаться от сужде́ний.

suspended *adj.* подвесно́й. *Be suspended from the ceiling/ in midair/,* висе́ть на потолке́/ в во́здухе/. —**suspended animation,** бесчу́вствие. —**suspended sentence,** усло́вный пригово́р.

suspenders *n.pl.* подтя́жки; по́мочи.

suspense *n.* неизве́стность; неопределённость. *Keep in suspense,* держа́ть в неизве́стности. *The suspense is killing me,* неизве́стность *or* неопределённость му́чит меня́.

suspension *n.* **1,** (temporary halt) приостано́вка; приостановле́ние; прекраще́ние. **2,** (temporary debarment) вре́менное отстране́ние. **3,** (temporary revocation) вре́менная отме́на. *Suspension of one's driver's license,* лише́ние води́тельских прав. **4,** *mech.* подве́ска. —**suspension bridge,** вися́чий *or* подвесно́й мост. —**suspension points,** многото́чие.

suspicion *n.* подозре́ние: *be under suspicion,* быть под подозре́нием. *I have my suspicions,* у меня́ есть свои́ подозре́ния. *He was detained on suspicion of theft,* его́ задержа́ли по подозре́нию в кра́же.

suspicious *adj.* **1,** (causing or arousing suspicion) подозри́тельный: *a suspicious character* (*i.e.* person), подозри́тельная ли́чность. *Look suspicious,* вы́глядеть подозри́тельно. *A suspicious noise,* подозри́тельный шум. **2,** (feeling suspicion): *be suspicious of someone,* подозрева́ть кого́-нибудь. *I became suspicious,* я заподо́зрил что́-то; я стал подозрева́ть. *Something in his manner made me suspicious,* что́-то в его́ мане́ре вы́звало у меня́ подозре́ния. **3,** (tending to suspect evil) подозри́тельный. *I am suspicious by nature,* я по нату́ре подозри́телен. —**suspiciously,** *adv.* подозри́тельно. —**suspiciousness,** *n.* подозри́тельность.

sustain *v.t.* **1,** (hold up; support) подде́рживать; держа́ть. **2,** (support; maintain) подде́рживать: *sustain life,* подде́рживать жизнь. **3,** (experience; suffer) потерпе́ть; понести́. *Sustain losses,* понести́ поте́ри. *Sustain injuries,* получи́ть поврежде́ния. **4,** (strengthen the spirits of) подкрепля́ть. **5,** (uphold, as an objection) принима́ть: *Objection sustained,* возраже́ние принима́ется. **6,** (prolong, as a note) тяну́ть; протя́гивать.

sustenance *n.* пропита́ние.

suture *n.* шов; нить. —*v.t.* сшива́ть.

suzerain *n.* сюзере́н. —*adj.* сюзере́нный. —**suzerainty,** *n.* сюзеренитѐт.

svelte *adj.* стро́йный; ги́бкий.

swab *v.t.* **1,** (mob; scrub) дра́ить. **2,** *med.* (paint) сма́зывать: *swab with iodine,* сма́зывать йо́дом.

swaddle *v.t.* свива́ть; пелена́ть. —**swaddling clothes,** свива́льник.

swag *n., slang* добы́ча.

swagger *v.i.* ходи́ть с ва́жным ви́дом; выступа́ть. —*n.* ва́жная похо́дка.

Swahili *n.* суахи́ли.

swallow *v.i.* глота́ть. *It hurts me to swallow,* мне бо́льно глота́ть. —*v.t.* **1,** (pass into the stomach) глота́ть; прогла́тывать. **2,** (pronounce indistinctly) глота́ть; прогла́тывать (слова́). **3,** (endure, as an insult) прогла́тывать; стерпе́ть (оби́ду). **4,** (suppress) подавля́ть: *swallow one's pride,* подави́ть самолю́бие. **5,** *fol. by* up (engulf) поглоща́ть; заса́сывать. *The ship was swallowed up by the sea,* мо́ре поглоти́ло кора́бль. **6,** *colloq.* (believe credulously) ве́рить; принима́ть на ве́ру. *Swallow the bait,* попа́сться на у́дочку. —*n.* **1,** (gulp) глото́к. **2,** (bird) ла́сточка.

swallowtail *n.* (butterfly) па́русник; махао́н. —**swallow-tailed coat,** фрак.

swamp *n.* боло́то. —*v.t.* завали́ть: *swamped with work,* зава́лен рабо́той.

swampland *n.* боло́то.

swampy *adj.* боло́тистый; то́пкий.

swan *n.* ле́бедь. —*adj.* [*also,* **swan's**] лебя́жий; лебеди́ный. *Swan's-down,* лебя́жий пух. *Swan's*

neck, лебеди́ная ше́я. —**swan dive,** прыжо́к в во́ду ла́сточкой. —**swan song,** лебеди́ная пе́сня.

swank *n., slang* шик; форс. —*adj.* [*also,* **swanky**] *colloq.* шика́рный; роско́шный.

swap *v.t.* обме́нивать(ся); меня́ть(ся): *swap my bicycle for his,* обме́нивать/меня́ть мой велосипе́д на его́. *Swap bicycles,* обме́ниваться/меня́ться велосипе́дами. —*v.i.* меня́ться: *Let's swap!,* дава́йте поменя́емся! —*n.* обме́н.

swarm *n.* рой: *swarm of bees,* рой пчёл. —*v.i.* **1,** (of bees) рои́ться; (of insects) кише́ть; копоши́ться; (of people) кише́ть. **2,** *fol. by* **with** (teem with) кише́ть (+ *instr.*): *The city is swarming with tourists,* го́род киши́т тури́стами.

swarthy *adj.* сму́глый.

swashbuckler *n.* сорвиголова́.

swastika *n.* сва́стика.

swat *v.t., colloq.* **1,** (slap) шлёпать. **2,** (crush, as a fly) раздави́ть. —*n., colloq.* шлепо́к.

swatch *n.* обра́зчик.

swath *n.* проко́с. —**cut a wide swath, 1,** *mil.* де́йствовать на широ́ком фро́нте. **2,** *fig.* (attract notice) наде́лать мно́го шу́ма; привлека́ть всео́бщее внима́ние.

swathe *v.t.* заку́тывать; обма́тывать. *Swathed in bandages,* обмо́танный бинта́ми.

sway *v.i.* кача́ться; раска́чиваться; колеба́ться; колыха́ться. *Sway in the breeze,* колыха́ться на ветру́ *or* от ве́тра. *During the earthquake the building began to sway,* во вре́мя землетрясе́ния зда́ние на́чало кача́ться. —*v.t.* **1,** (cause to sway) кача́ть; колеба́ть; колыха́ть. **2,** (influence; persuade) склоня́ть. *Sway public opinion,* ока́зывать влия́ние на обще́ственное мне́ние. —*n.* **1,** (swaying movement) кача́ние; колеба́ние; колыха́ние. **2,** (power; dominion) власть. *Hold sway over,* вла́ствовать над; госпо́дствовать над.

swear *v.i.* **1,** (take an oath) кля́сться; присяга́ть; дава́ть кля́тву *or* прися́гу. *I swear to God!,* кляну́сь бо́гом! *I wouldn't swear to it,* я не могу́ покля́сться в э́том. **2,** (use profanity) руга́ться. *Swear at someone,* обруга́ть кого́-нибудь. —*v.t.* кля́сться. *Do you solemnly swear that...?,* вы торже́ственно кляне́тесь, что...? *Swear an oath,* дава́ть кля́тву *or* прися́гу. *Swear allegiance to,* кля́сться *or* присяга́ть в ве́рности (+ *dat.*). *Swear someone to secrecy,* взять с кого́-нибудь кля́тву молча́ть. *Make someone swear that...,* взять с кого́-нибудь кля́тву, что... —**swear by, 1,** (name in taking an oath) кля́сться (+ *instr.*). **2,** (have complete faith in) безграни́чно ве́рить в *or* доверя́ть. —**swear in,** приводи́ть к прися́ге. —**swear off,** зарека́ться (+ *instr.*); дать заро́к не (+ *inf.*). *See also* **sworn.**

swearword *n.* бра́нное сло́во; руга́тельство.

sweat *v.i.* **1,** (perspire) поте́ть. **2,** *fol. by* **over** (slave over) му́читься (над). —*v.t.* [*usu.* **sweat up**] *My shirt is all sweated up,* моя́ руба́шка намо́кла (*or* промо́кла) от по́та; моя́ руба́шка пропита́лась по́том. —*n.* пот: *in a sweat,* в поту́. *He broke out in a sweat,* его́ бро́сило в пот. —**by the sweat of one's brow,** в по́те лица́.

sweater *n.* свитер.

sweat gland потовая железа.

sweat shirt фуфайка.

sweatshop *n.* потогонная фабрика.

sweaty *adj.* потный. *I'm all sweaty,* я весь (вся) в поту.

Swede *n.* швед; шведка.

Swedish *adj.* шведский. —*n.* шведский язык.

sweep *v.t.* **1,** (clean or remove with a broom) мести; подметать: *sweep the floor,* мести/подметать пол. *Sweep something into the corner,* заметать что-нибудь в угол. **2,** (carry with great force) проносить. *He was swept out to sea,* его унесло в море. *A wave swept him overboard,* его смыло волной за борт. **3,** (engulf) охватывать: *Flames swept the building,* пламя охватило здание. *A wave of strikes swept the country,* волна забастовок захлестнула страну (*or* прокатилась по стране). —*v.i.* **1,** (use a broom) мести. **2,** (move swiftly) мчаться; проноситься. *Planes swept by overhead,* самолёты промчались над головами. *A wave swept over the deck,* волна набежала на палубу; волна захлестнула палубу. *A murmur swept through the crowd,* по толпе пронёсся ропот. —*n.* **1,** (motion; stroke) взмах; размах. *With a sweep of the hand,* взмахом руки. **2,** (scope; extent) размах; охват. **3,** (raid) облава: *conduct a sweep,* проводить облаву. —**sweep away, 1,** (remove with a broom) сметать: *sweep away the cobwebs,* смести паутину. **2,** (carry away with great force) сметать; уносить; сносить. *The leaves were swept away by the wind,* листья были сметены ветром. *The boat was swept away by the current,* лодку унесло *or* снесло течением. —**sweep off,** сметать. *Sweep off the porch,* подметать крыльцо. —**sweep out,** выметать. *Sweep out the basement,* выметать *or* подметать подвал. —**sweep up,** подметать: *sweep up the porch,* подметать крыльцо; *sweep up the refuse,* подметать сор.

sweeper *n.* подметальщик.

sweeping *adj.* **1,** (extending in a wide curve) широкий; размашистый: *with a sweeping motion of the hand,* широким/размашистым движением руки. **2,** (wide-ranging) огульный. *Sweeping generalization,* широкое обобщение. *Sweeping changes,* радикальные изменения. —*n.* **1,** (act of sweeping) подметание. **2,** *pl.* (litter) мусор; сор.

sweepstakes *n.* лотерея.

sweet *adj.* **1,** (having a sugary taste) сладкий: *sweet wine,* сладкое вино. **2,** (pleasant) сладкий; приятный. *Smell sweet,* приятно пахнуть. **3,** (likable; kind) милый: *sweet girl,* милая девушка. *Very sweet of you,* очень мило с вашей стороны. —*n.* **1,** *pl.* (confections) сласти; сладости; сладкое. **2,** *Brit.* (piece of candy) конфета. **3,** *Brit.* (dessert) сладкое.

sweet-and-sour *adj.* кисло-сладкий.

sweetbread *n.* сладкое мясо.

sweeten *v.t.* подслащивать. —**sweeten the pill,** золотить *or* подслащивать пилюлю.

sweetener *n.* сладкое вещество. *Also,* **sweetening.**

sweetheart *n.* возлюбленный; возлюбленная.

sweetly *adv.* сладко.

sweetmeat *n.* конфета; сласть.

sweetness *n.* сладость.

sweet pea душистый горошек.

sweet potato сладкий картофель; батат.

sweet-smelling *adj.* душистый; ароматный.

sweet tooth *colloq.* пристрастие к сластям. *Have a sweet tooth,* быть падким до сладкого. *Person with a sweet tooth,* сластёна; сладоежка; лакомка.

sweet william турецкая *or* бородатая гвоздика.

swell *v.i.* пухнуть; распухать; опухать. *Her cheek began to swell up,* у неё начала пухнуть щека. —*v.t.* надувать; раздувать. *Swell the ranks,* увеличивать ряды. —*adj., colloq.* отличный; чудный. *I'm feeling swell,* я отлично чувствую себя. *Have a swell time,* чудно провести время. —**get a swelled head,** зазнаваться; возгордиться; надуваться; заноситься; возомнить о себе. *See also* **swollen.**

swelling *n.* **1,** (condition) опухание; вздутие: *swelling of the joints,* опухание суставов; *swelling of the abdomen,* вздутие живота. **2,** (swollen area) опухоль; припухлость; вздутие.

swelter *v.i.* изнемогать от жары. —**sweltering,** *adj.* знойный; душный.

sweptback *adj.* стреловидный.

swerve *v.t. & i.* сворачивать (в сторону).

swift *adj.* быстрый: *swift current,* быстрое течение. —*n.* (bird) стриж. —**swiftly,** *adv.* быстро. —**swiftness,** *n.* быстрота.

swig *n., colloq.* большой глоток.

swill *n.* **1,** (garbage; slop) помои. **2,** (food for animals) пойло. —*v.t.* жадно пить; лакать.

swim *v.i.* плавать; плыть. *Swim away,* уплывать. *Go swimming,* купаться. *Do you know how to swim?,* вы умеете плавать? —*v.t.* проплывать; переплывать. *Swim two miles,* проплыть две мили. *Swim the English Channel,* переплыть Ла-Манш. —*n. Go for a swim,* поплавать; искупаться.

swimmer *n.* пловец; пловчиха.

swimming *n.* плавание. —*adj.* **1,** (that swims) плавающий. **2,** (of or for swimming) плавательный. —**swimming pool,** бассейн для плавания.

swimsuit *n.* купальный костюм.

swindle *v.t.* обжуливать. —*n.* афера. —**swindler,** *n.* мошенник; плут; жулик; аферист.

swine *n.* свинья.

swineherd *n.* свинопас.

swing *v.i.* **1,** (sway back and forth) качаться; раскачиваться. *The monkey was swinging from a branch,* обезьяна раскачивалась на ветке. *The pendulum swung to the left,* маятник качнулся влево. **2,** (turn on a pivot) вертеться. *Swing open,* распахиваться. **3,** *fol. by* **around** (turn around quickly) поворачиваться. **4,** (move laterally) сворачивать: *swing over to the right,* сворачивать направо. **5,** (shift) переходить: *swing over to our side,* переходить на нашу сторону. **6,** (aim or deliver a blow) размахиваться. **7,** *colloq.* (be executed by hanging) быть повешенным: *He'll swing for it,* его повесят за это. —*v.t.* **1,** (cause to swing back and forth; brandish) размахивать: *swing* *one's arms/ an ax/*, разма́хивать рука́ми/топоро́м. **2,** (turn) развора́чивать: *swing the car around,* развора́чивать маши́ну. **3,** *Swing an election,* реши́ть исхо́д вы́боров. —*n.* **1,** (swaying back and forth) кача́ние: *swing of a pendulum,* кача́ние ма́ятника. **2,** (stroke; sweep) разма́х; взмах. **3,** (shift) сдвиг. **4,** (playground device) каче́ли. **5,** (short trip) пое́здка; объе́зд. —**in full swing,** в (по́лном) разга́ре; в по́лном ходу́.

swingle *n.* трепа́ло; трепа́лка.

swingletree *n.* валёк.

swinish *adj.* свин́ский.

swipe *v.t., slang* (steal) стяну́ть; стащи́ть. —*n., colloq.* (blow) тума́к.

swirl *v.t.* крути́ть; кружи́ть; клуби́ть; взвива́ть. —*v.i.* кружи́ться; клуби́ться. *The dust swirled overhead,* пыль кружи́лась/клуби́лась над голова́ми. —*n.* вихрь; завихре́ние: *swirl of dust,* вихрь/завихре́ние пы́ли.

swish *v.t.* разма́хивать. *Swish one's tail,* пома́хивать *or* бить хвосто́м. —*v.i.* рассека́ть во́здух (со сви́стом). —*n.* **1,** (whistling sound) свист. **2,** (movement producing such a sound) взмах.

Swiss *adj.* швейца́рский. —*n., preceded by the,* швейца́рцы. —**Swiss cheese,** швейца́рский сыр.

switch *n.* **1,** (flexible rod) прут. **2,** *electricity* выключа́тель; переключа́тель. *Flip the switch,* поверну́ть выключа́тель. **3,** *R.R.* стре́лка. **4,** (change; shift) переме́на; перехо́д: *a switch in jobs,* переме́на рабо́ты; *a switch to part-time work,* перехо́д на рабо́ту на полста́вки. —*v.t.* **1,** (shift) переключа́ть: *switch the plant over to producing bicycles,* переключа́ть заво́д на произво́дство велосипе́дов. *Switch the meeting to the afternoon,* переноси́ть собра́ние на втору́ю полови́ну дня. **2,** (change to another) переключа́ться на. *Switch jobs,* переключа́ться на другу́ю рабо́ту; меня́ть рабо́ту. *Switch trains,* переса́живаться на друго́й по́езд. **3,** (exchange) меня́ться: *switch places,* меня́ться места́ми. —*v.i.* переходи́ть; переключа́ться: *switch to a different job,* переходи́ть/переключа́ться на другу́ю рабо́ту. *Switch to a different channel,* переключи́ться на друго́й кана́л. *Switch into French,* переходи́ть на францу́зский язы́к. *Switch to writing novels,* переключи́ться на созда́ние рома́нов. —**switch off,** выключа́ть. —**switch on,** включа́ть.

switchboard *n.* коммута́тор; распредели́тельный щит.

switchman *n.* стре́лочник.

switchyard *n.* сортиро́вочная ста́нция.

swivel *n.* вертлю́г. —*v.i.* враща́ться. —**swivel seat,** враща́ющееся *or* поворо́тное сиде́нье.

swollen *adj.* **1,** (of a part of one's body) опу́хший; распу́хший; вспу́хший; взду́тый; разду́тый. *Swollen glands/joints/ankles,* опу́хшие *or* распу́хшие же́лезы/суста́вы/лоды́жки. **2,** (of a river or stream) взду́тый; разду́тый; набу́хший; взбу́хший.

swoon *n.* о́бморок. —*v.i.* па́дать в о́бморок.

swoop *v.i.* [*usu.* swoop down on] устремля́ться (на); налета́ть (на); броса́ться (на). —**in one fell swoop,**

одни́м уда́ром; одни́м ма́хом.

sword *n.* меч; шпа́га. —**at swords' points,** на ножа́х. —**cross swords,** скрести́ть мечи́ *or* шпа́ги. —**put to the sword,** предава́ть мечу́. —**sword of Damocles,** дамо́клов меч.

swordfish *n.* меч-ры́ба.

swordplay *n.* фехтова́ние.

swordsman *n.* фехтова́льщик.

sworn *adj.* кля́твенный: *sworn oath,* кля́твенная прися́га. *Sworn testimony,* показа́ния под прися́гой. *Sworn enemy,* закля́тый враг.

sybarite *n.* сибари́т. —**sybaritic,** *adj.* сибари́тский.

sycamore *n.* **1,** (fig tree of the Middle East) сикомо́р. **2,** (maple tree of Eurasia) я́вор. **3,** (plane tree of America) за́падный плата́н; сикомо́р.

sycophant *n.* льстец; подхали́м.

syllable *n.* слог. —**syllabic,** *adj.* слогово́й.

syllabus *n.* програ́мма (ку́рса).

syllogism *n.* силлоги́зм. —**syllogistic,** *adj.* силлогисти́ческий.

sylph *n.* сильф. —**sylphid,** *n.* сильфи́д.

sylvan *adj.* лесно́й; леси́стый.

symbiosis *n.* симбио́з.

symbol *n.* си́мвол. —**symbolic,** *adj.* символи́ческий; символи́чный.

symbolism *n.* символи́зм; симво́лика.

symbolize *v.t.* символизи́ровать.

symmetry *n.* симметри́я. —**symmetrical,** *adj.* симметри́чный; симметри́ческий.

sympathetic *adj.* сочу́вственный; отзы́вчивый; чу́ткий. *Be sympathetic to,* сочу́вствовать (+ *dat.*). —**sympathetic nervous system,** симпати́ческая не́рвная систе́ма.

sympathetically *adv.* сочу́вственно; чу́тко.

sympathize *v.i.* [*usu.* sympathize with] сочу́вствовать (+ *dat.*).

sympathy *n.* **1,** (pity; compassion) сочу́вствие; сострада́ние. *Sympathy for someone,* сочу́вствие кому́-нибудь. *My sincere sympathy,* моё и́скреннее соболе́знование. **2,** (harmony of feeling) симпа́тия: *the sympathies of the crowd,* симпа́тии толпы́. *My sympathies are with the British,* мои́ симпа́тии на стороне́ англича́н. *Be in sympathy with,* симпатизи́ровать (+ *dat.*). —**sympathy strike,** ста́чка солида́рности.

symphonic *adj.* симфони́ческий.

symphony *n.* симфо́ния. *Symphony orchestra,* симфони́ческий орке́стр.

symposium *n.* симпо́зиум.

symptom *n.* симпто́м; при́знак.

symptomatic *adj.* **1,** *med.* симптомати́ческий. **2,** (indicative of something) симптомати́чный.

synagogue *n.* синаго́га.

synchronic *adj.* синхрони́ческий.

synchronize *v.t.* синхронизи́ровать. —**synchronization,** *n.* синхрониза́ция.

synchronous *adj.* синхро́нный.

syncopate *v.t.* синкопи́ровать. —**syncopation,** *n.* синко́па.

syncope *n.* **1,** *med.* о́бморок. **2,** *gram.* синко́па.

syndicate *n.* синдика́т. —*v.t.* объединя́ть в синдика́т.
syndrome *n.* синдро́м.
synod *n.* сино́д. —**synodal,** *adj.* синода́льный.
synonym *n.* сино́ним.
synonymous *adj.* синоними́ческий; синоними́чный; однозна́чный. *Be synonymous with,* быть синоними́чен (+ *dat.*).
synopsis *n.* конспе́кт; аннота́ция; рефера́т.
syntax *n.* си́нтаксис. —**syntactical,** *adj.* синтакси́ческий.
synthesis *n.* си́нтез.
synthesize *v.t.* обобща́ть; синтези́ровать.
synthesizer *n., music* синтеза́тор.
synthetic *adj.* синтети́ческий. —*n.* синте́тика.
syphilis *n.* си́филис. —**syphilitic,** *adj.* сифилити́ческий. —*n.* сифили́тик.
Syrian *adj.* сири́йский. —*n.* сири́ец; сири́йка.
syringe *n.* **1,** (bulb-shaped device) спринцо́вка. **2,** (hypodermic syringe) шприц. —*v.t.* спринцева́ть.
syrup *n.* сиро́п.
system *n.* **1,** (set arrangement or method) систе́ма: *the solar system,* со́лнечная систе́ма. *Public-address system,* систе́ма звукоусиле́ния. **2,** (political, social, economic) систе́ма; строй; устро́йство. **3,** *physiol.* аппара́т; систе́ма. *Respiratory system,* дыха́тельный аппара́т. *Digestive system,* пищевари́тельный аппара́т. *Nervous system,* не́рвная систе́ма. **4,** (the human body) органи́зм: *bad for one's system,* вре́дно для органи́зма. **5,** *mech.* систе́ма: *ignition system,* систе́ма зажига́ния. *Exhaust system,* вытяжно́е устро́йство. *Sprinkler system,* дождева́льная устано́вка. **6,** *mil.* систе́ма; ко́мплекс. *Weapon system,* систе́ма ору́жия. *Missile system,* раке́тный ко́мплекс. *Delivery system,* сре́дство доста́вки. **7,** (network) систе́ма; сеть. *Highway system,* доро́жная сеть. *Early-warning system,* систе́ма да́льнего обнаруже́ния; систе́ма ра́ннего предупрежде́ния *or* оповеще́ния.
systematic *adj.* системати́ческий. —**systematically,** *adv.* системати́чески.
systematize *v.t.* систематизи́ровать.
systole *n.* си́стола. —**systolic,** *adj.* систоли́ческий.

T

T, t двадца́тая бу́ква англи́йского алфави́та. —**to a T,** вполне́; точь-в-точь.
tab *n.* **1,** (flap to aid in handling) ушко́. **2,** *colloq.* (bill) счёт. —**keep tab** (*or* **tabs**) **on,** следи́ть за.
tabernacle *n.* **1,** (portable sanctuary) ски́ния. **2,** (house of worship) моле́льня. —**Feast of Tabernacles,** пра́здник ку́щей.
table *n.* **1,** (article of furniture) стол. *Night table,* ночно́й сто́лик; ту́мбочка. *Operating table,* операцио́нный стол. **2,** (chart with rows and columns) табли́ца. *Multiplication table,* табли́ца умноже́ния. **3,** (list; roster) та́бель. *Table of contents,* оглавле́ние; (*as a heading*) —*adj.* столо́вый: *table linen,* столо́вое бельё. —*v.t.* **1,** (postpone) откла́дывать. **2,** *Brit.* (submit for discussion) ста́вить на обсужде́ние. —**turn the tables on,** бить (кого́-нибудь) его́ же ору́жием. —**under the table,** из-под полы́.
tableau *n.* **1,** (dramatic scene) карти́на. **2,** (tableau vivant) жива́я карти́на.
tablecloth *n.* ска́терть.
table d'hôte табльдо́т.
tableland *n.* плоского́рье; столо́вая гора́.
tablespoon *n.* столо́вая ло́жка.
tablet *n.* **1,** (writing pad) блокно́т. **2,** (pill) табле́тка. **3,** (slab with writing) табли́чка; (same with sacred text) скрижа́ль.
table tennis насто́льный те́ннис.
tableware *n.* столо́вые прибо́ры.
taboo *also,* **tabu** *n.* табу́. —*adj.* запрещённый.
tabular *adj.* табли́чный. *In tabular form,* в ви́де табли́цы.
tabulate *v.t.* своди́ть в табли́цу. —**tabulator,** *n.* табуля́тор.
tachometer *n.* тахо́метр.
tacit *adj.* молчали́вый: *tacit consent,* молчали́вое согла́сие.
taciturn *adj.* молчали́вый; неразгово́рчивый. —**taciturnity,** *n.* молчали́вость; неразгово́рчивость.
tack *n.* **1,** (nail) гво́здик; кно́пка. **2,** *naut.* галс. **3,** (course of action) путь; курс. —*v.t.* **1,** (fasten) прибива́ть (гво́здиками). **2,** *fol. by* **on** (add on) прибавля́ть. —*v.i., naut.* лави́ровать. —**get down to brass tacks,** добра́ться до су́ти де́ла.
tackle *n.* снасть. *Fishing tackle,* рыболо́вная снасть; рыболо́вные принадле́жности. —*v.t.* **1,** (jump on and pin down) схва́тывать. **2,** (undertake) бра́ться за.
tacky *adj.* **1,** (sticky) кле́йкий; ли́пкий. **2,** *colloq.* (gaudy; showy) мишу́рный.

tact *n.* такт; такти́чность. —**tactful,** *adj.* такти́чный.
—**tactfully,** *adv.* такти́чно; с та́ктом.

tactic *n.* та́ктика. —**tactical,** *adj.* такти́ческий.
—**tactician** *n.* та́ктик.

tactics *n.* та́ктика.

tactile *adj.* осяза́тельный.

tactless *adj.* беста́ктный; нетакти́чный. —**tactlessness,** *n.* беста́ктность; нетакти́чность.

tadpole *n.* голова́стик.

taffeta *n.* тафта́. —*adj.* тафтяно́й.

taffy *n.* тяну́чка; ири́с.

tag *n.* **1,** (label) ярлы́к; ярлычо́к; этике́тка; би́рка.
Price tag, це́нник; ярлы́к с указа́нием цены́. **2,**
(game) пятна́шки; са́лки. —*v.t.* накле́ивать ярлы́к
на. —*v.i.* [*usu.* **tag along**] идти́ вслед. —**tag end,**
са́мый коне́ц.

taiga *n.* тайга́.

tail *n.* **1,** (of an animal or bird) хвост. **2,** (of an aircraft,
kite, comet, etc.) хвост. **3,** (of a coat) фа́лда. **4,** *pl.*
(tailcoat) фрак. **5,** *pl.* (reverse side of a coin) ре́шка:
Heads or tails?, орёл и́ли ре́шка? —*adj.* хвостово́й:
tail section, хвостова́я часть. —*v.t., colloq.* (shadow)
высле́живать. —*v.i.* [*usu.* **tail along**] идти́ вслед.
—**tail end,** са́мый коне́ц. *At the tail end,* в обо́зе.
—**turn tail,** пусти́ться наутёк.

tailcoat *n.* фрак.

taillight *n.* за́дняя фа́ра; за́дний фона́рь; за́дний
свет.

tailor *n.* портно́й. —*v.t.* **1,** (fit) подгоня́ть. **2,** *fig.*
(adapt): *tailor a speech to an audience,* сфор-
мули́ровать речь с учётом аудито́рии. —**tailor-
made,** *adj.* сши́тый на зака́з.

tailpipe *n.* выхлопна́я труба́.

tailspin *n., aero.* што́пор на хвост.

tail wind попу́тный ве́тер.

taint *v.t.* **1,** (infect; contaminate) по́ртить. **2,** (tarnish,
as one's reputation) пятна́ть. —*n.* **1,** (blemish) пятно́.
2, (trace of decay) душо́к. —**tainted,** *adj.* ту́хлый;
испо́рченный; с душко́м.

Taiwanese *adj.* тайва́ньский.

Tajik *n.* таджи́к. —*adj.* таджи́кский.

Taj Mahal Тадж-Маха́л.

take *v.t.* **1,** (grasp; get possession of) брать (*pfv.* взять).
Take someone by the hand, брать кого́-нибудь за́
руку. *Who took my briefcase?,* кто взял *or* забра́л
мой портфе́ль? *Take a book from the shelf,* взять *or*
доста́ть кни́гу с по́лки. **2,** (bring along) брать с
собо́й: *Should I take an umbrella?,* мне взять с собо́й
зо́нтик? **3,** (carry; deliver) относи́ть: *Take this letter
to the post office,* отнеси́те э́то письмо́ на по́чту. **4,**
(escort) вести́: *take someone to a museum,* повести́
кого́-нибудь в музе́й. *Take a child to school,* вести́
or отводи́ть ребёнка в шко́лу. **5,** (drive) отвози́ть:
take someone to the airport, отвози́ть кого́-нибудь в
аэропо́рт. **6,** (seize; capture) брать; захва́тывать:
take prisoners, брать/захва́тывать пле́нных. **7,** (accept) принима́ть: *take the offer,* принима́ть пред-
ложе́ние; *take gifts from strangers,* принима́ть
пода́рки от незнако́мцев. **8,** (require) тре́бовать: *It
took him two years to...,* ему́ потре́бовалось два

го́да, что́бы... *That will take decades,* на э́то уйду́т
десятиле́тия. **9,** (occupy) занима́ть: *take one's seat
at the table,* заня́ть ме́сто за столо́м. *All the seats are
taken,* все места́ за́няты; везде́ за́нято. *Is this seat
taken?,* здесь свобо́дно? **10,** (use up, as time)
занима́ть; отнима́ть. *I won't take much of your time,*
я у вас мно́го вре́мени не отниму́. *I don't want to
take too much of your time,* я не хочу́ злоу-
потребля́ть ва́шим вре́менем. **11,** (travel by means
of) брать; пое́хать на; сесть в *or* на. *Let's take a
taxi,* дава́йте возьмём (*or* ся́дем на) такси́. **12,** (follow, as a street or road) идти́ по; е́хать по. *Take
Broadway to 42nd Street,* иди́те *or* поезжа́йте по
Бродве́ю до Со́рок второ́й у́лицы. **13,** (win)
занима́ть; получа́ть: *take first place,* заня́ть пе́рвое
ме́сто; *take first prize,* получи́ть пе́рвую пре́мию.
14, (rent temporarily) снима́ть: *I took an apartment in
Brooklyn,* я снял (сняла́) кварти́ру в Бру́клине. **15,**
(measure, as one's temperature) измеря́ть. *Take someone's pulse,* счита́ть чей-нибудь пульс. *Take someone's measurements,* снима́ть ме́рку с кого́-нибудь.
16, (study) изуча́ть: *take French,* изуча́ть францу́з-
ский язы́к. **17,** (assume) принима́ть; брать на себя́.
Take command, принима́ть кома́ндование. *Take office,* вступи́ть в до́лжность. *Take the offensive,*
переходи́ть в наступле́ние. *Take the blame,* брать на
себя́ вину́. *Take the name Smith,* принима́ть
фами́лию Смит. **18,** (heed, as advice) сле́довать;
слу́шаться. *Take my advice!,* послу́шайтесь моего́
сове́та! *Take the hint,* поня́ть намёк. **19,** (interpret)
понима́ть: *take something literally,* понима́ть что́-
нибудь буква́льно (*or* в буква́льном смы́сле). **20,**
(receive or regard in a certain way) принима́ть;
воспринима́ть. *Take seriously,* принима́ть всерьёз.
Take something hard, тяжело́ переноси́ть *or* пере-
жива́ть что́-нибудь. *Take life as it is,* воспринима́ть
жизнь тако́й, кака́я она́ есть. **21,** (endure, as a joke,
criticism, etc.) терпе́ть. *He can't take a joke,* он не
понима́ет шу́ток. **22,** (charm) увлека́ть: *I was very
much taken with her,* я увлёкся е́ю. **23,** *gram.* тре́бо-
вать: *take the genitive case,* тре́бовать роди́тельного
падежа́. **24,** *chess* (capture) брать. **25,** *colloq.* (cheat;
dupe) надува́ть: *I was taken for 1,000 rubles,* меня́
наду́ли на ты́сячу рубле́й. **26,** with certain nouns,
брать: *take lessons,* брать уро́ки; *take a vacation,*
брать о́тпуск; *take a bribe,* брать взя́тку; *take prisoner,* взять в плен. **27,** with certain nouns,
принима́ть: *take food,* принима́ть пи́щу; *take medicine,* принима́ть лека́рство; *take poison,* принима́ть
яд; *take a bath,* принима́ть ва́нну; *take measures,*
принима́ть ме́ры; *take part,* принима́ть уча́стие;
take someone's side, принима́ть чью-нибудь
сто́рону. **28,** with certain nouns, де́лать: *take a step,*
де́лать шаг; *take a picture,* де́лать фотогра́фию;
take notes, де́лать заме́тки. **29,** used with various
other nouns: *take aim,* прице́ливаться; *take a bow,*
раскла́ниваться; *take a course,* (про)слу́шать курс;
take an examination, сдава́ть *or* держа́ть экза́мен;
take a look, посмотре́ть; *take a nap,* поспа́ть;
вздремну́ть; *take a poll,* производи́ть опро́с; *take a*

seat, присáживаться; *take a certain size,* носи́ть (какóй-нибудь) размéр; *take a trip,* соверша́ть поéздку; *take a walk,* погуля́ть; *take comfort,* утеша́ться; *take cover/shelter,* укры́ться; *take offense,* обижа́ться; *take office,* вступи́ть в дóлжность; *take pity on,* сжáлиться над; *take pride in,* горди́ться (+ *instr.*); *take revenge,* мстить; *take turns,* чередовáться. **30,** *used in various set expressions: take place,* происходи́ть; состоя́ться; имéть мéсто; *take the trouble to,* дать себé труд (+ *inf.*); *take by surprise,* застáть враспло́х; *take one's own life,* лиши́ть себя́ жи́зни. —*v.i.* **1,** (have the intended effect) дéйствовать. *The vaccination didn't take,* óспа не привилáсь *or* не принялáсь. **2,** (become): *take sick/ill,* заболéть. **3,** *fol. by* (go to; leave for) отправля́ться в: *take to the road,* отправля́ться в путь. *Take to the lifeboats,* брóситься к спасáтельным лóдкам. *Take to one's bed,* слечь в постéль. *People took to the streets,* лю́ди вы́сыпали на у́лицу. **4,** *fol. by inf.* (begin) стать: *She has taken to wearing large earrings,* онá стáла носи́ть больши́е сéрьги. *He has taken to writing poetry,* он стал писáть стихи́. **5,** *fol. by* **to** (develop a liking for) полюби́ть. **6,** *Take to drink,* спивáться. —*n.* (receipts) вы́ручка; сбор. —**take aback,** озадáчить; огоро́шить. —**take after, 1,** (pursue) брóситься за; погнáться за. **2,** (resemble) быть похóжим на; уроди́ться в. —**take along,** брать с собóй. —**take apart,** разбирáть. —**take aside,** отводи́ть в стóрону; отзывáть. —**take away, 1,** (carry away; lead away) забирáть; уноси́ть; уводи́ть; увози́ть. **2,** (remove) убирáть. **3,** (seize) отбирáть; отнимáть: *take away the candy from the child,* отбирáть/отнимáть конфéту у ребёнка. **4,** (eliminate, as pain) устраня́ть. —**take back, 1,** (return) возвращáть: *take a book back to a library,* возвращáть кни́гу в библиотéку. **2,** (accept return of) принимáть обрáтно. **3,** (retract) брать назáд. —**take down, 1,** (carry down) сноси́ть. **2,** (pull down) снимáть. **3,** (write down) запи́сывать. *Take down someone's testimony,* снимáть с когó-нибудь показáния. —**take for,** принимáть за: *I took him for a German,* я при́нял егó за нéмца. —**take in, 1,** (accept) брать. *Take in laundry,* брать бельё в сти́рку. **2,** (give shelter to) приюти́ть. *Take in lodgers,* брать *or* пускáть жильцóв. **3,** (shorten; narrow) собирáть; забирáть; ушивáть; су́живать. **4,** (include) охвáтывать. **5,** (trick) надувáть; провести́. **6,** (visit; tour) осмáтривать: *take in the sights,* осмáтривать достопримечáтельности. *Take in a movie,* пойти́ в кинó. —**take it, 1,** (assume; surmise) полагáть. **2,** (withstand difficulty) терпéть. —**take it out on,** сорвáть зло *or* злóбу на. —**take off, 1,** (remove) снимáть. **2,** (lose, as weight or so many pounds) сгоня́ть. *Take off excess fat,* сбрóсить ли́шний жир. **3,** (deduct) сбавля́ть; ски́дывать: *take a dollar off the price,* сбáвить/ски́нуть дóллар с цены́. **4,** (of an airplane) взлетáть; вылетáть. **5,** (rush off; dash off) понести́сь. *Take off after,* брóситься *or* пусти́ться вдогóнку за (+ *instr.*). **6,** *colloq.* (depart) уходи́ть; уезжáть. **7,** *I couldn't take my eyes off her,* я не мог

отвести́ *or* оторвáть от неё глаз. —**take on, 1,** (take on board) нагружáться (+ *instr.*); заправля́ться (+ *instr.*). **2,** (undertake; assume) брать *or* принимáть на себя́. **3,** (hire) брать *or* принимáть на рабóту; зачисля́ть. **4,** (acquire; assume) принимáть; приобретáть. **5,** (compete with) состязáться с. —**take out, 1,** (remove) вынимáть: *take out a handkerchief,* вынимáть платóк. *Take out a tooth,* удаля́ть зуб. *Take out stains,* выводи́ть пя́тна. *Take out of production,* снимáть с произвóдства. **2,** (escort) повести́: *take out to dinner,* повести́ (в ресторáн) обéдать. **3,** (obtain by application) брать: *take out a loan/patent,* брать заём/патéнт. *Take out insurance,* застрахóвываться. *Take out a subscription to,* подпи́сываться на. **4,** (vent) сорвáть; вымещáть: *take out one's anger on,* сорвáть/вымещáть злóбу на (+ *prepl.*). —**take over, 1,** (assume) принимáть: *take over someone's duties,* принимáть делá от когó-нибудь. *Take over as President,* приня́ть на себя́ обя́занности президéнта. **2,** (assume direction of) принимáть: *take over the class,* принимáть класс. **3,** (assume forcibly; seize) прибирáть к рукáм; брать в свои́ ру́ки. —**take up, 1,** (carry up) поднимáть. **2,** (lift up; roll up, as a carpet) снимáть; свёртывать. **3,** (occupy, as space) занимáть. **4,** (consume, as time) занимáть; отнимáть. **5,** (go in for) занимáться (+ *instr.*). **6,** (assume; begin, as an assignment) принимáть. *Take up one's duties,* приступáть к исполнéнию свои́х обя́занностей. **7,** (consider) рассмáтривать: *take up the question of...,* рассмáтривать вопрóс о... **8,** (discuss) обсуждáть. *I'll take the matter up with him,* я обсужу́ э́то дéло с ним; я пойду́ к нему́ с э́тим дéлом. **9,** (quickly accept or adopt) подхвáтывать. **10,** (remove the slack from) натя́гивать. **11,** *Take up arms,* брáться за ору́жие. **12,** *Take up residence,* селя́ться. —**take upon oneself,** брать на себя́. —**take up with,** гуля́ть с; пу́таться с.

take-home pay чи́стый зáработок; чи́стая полу́чка.

takeoff *n.* **1,** *aero.* взлёт; отры́в от земли́. **2,** *colloq.* (imitation) подражáние; карикату́ра.

taker *n. There were no takers,* никтó не при́нял предложéния (*or* пари́).

taking *n.* **1,** (act of taking) взя́тие. **2,** *pl.* (receipts) вы́ручка; сбор.

talc *n.* тальк.

talcum *n.* тальк. —*adj.* тáльковый. —**talcum powder,** тáльковый порошóк; тальк.

tale *n.* **1,** (story) рассказ; пóвесть. **2,** (folk tale; fairy tale) скáзка. **3,** (falsehood) скáзка.

talebearer *n.* сплéтник; я́бедник.

talent *n.* талáнт. —**talented,** *adj.* талáнтливый.

talisman *n.* талисмáн.

talk *v.i.* **1,** (speak) говори́ть: *The child is already able to talk,* ребёнок ужé говори́т. *My throat is so sore I can hardly talk,* гóрло у меня́ так боли́т, что я едвá могу́ говори́ть. **2,** (converse) говори́ть; разговáривать: *talk about politics,* говори́ть/разговáривать о поли́тике. *What is there to talk about?,* какóй мóжет быть разговóр? **3,** (gossip) поговáривать. *People are starting to talk,* ужé пошли́ тóлки. **4,** (yield information under duress) заговори́ть. —*v.t.* говори́ть; болта́ть. *Talk sense,* говори́ть де́ло. *Talk nonsense,* говори́ть чепуху́; болта́ть глу́пости; нести́ вздор. *Talk oneself hoarse,* договори́ться до хрипоты́. —*n.* **1,** (conversation) разгово́р. *Have a talk with,* погово-ри́ть с. *Small talk,* сало́нный разгово́р. **2,** (chat) бесе́да. **3,** *pl.* (high-level discussions) перегово́ры. **4,** (informal speech or lecture) докла́д: *He gave a talk on his trip to China,* он сде́лал докла́д о свое́й пое́здке в Кита́й. **5,** (type of speech) речь. *Baby talk,* де́тский ле́пет. **6,** (meaningless conversation) пусто́й раз-гово́р. *It's just talk,* э́то одни́ слова́. **7,** (rumors) разго-во́ры; то́лки; молва́. *There is talk that...,* погова́ривают, что... **8,** *in* **talk of the town,** при́тча во язы́цех. *It's the talk of the town,* об э́том все гово-ря́т. —**talk back,** груби́ть; дерзи́ть. —**talk down to,** говори́ть с (+ *instr.*) свысока́. —**talk into,** угово-ри́ть. —**talk out of,** отговори́ть от; отсове́товать (+ *inf.*). —**talk over,** обсужда́ть.

talkative *adj.* болтли́вый; разгово́рчивый; говор-ли́вый. —**talkativeness,** *n.* разгово́рчивость; го-ворли́вость.

talking-to *n., colloq.* взбу́чка; нагоня́й.

tall *adj.* **1,** (of considerable height) высо́кий: *a tall man,* высо́кий челове́к. *Tall tree,* высо́кое де́рево. *Tall building,* высо́кое *or* высо́тное зда́ние; высо́кий *or* высо́тный дом. *He is tall,* он высо́кого ро́ста. **2,** (having a specified height) ро́стом в: *six feet tall,* ро́стом в шесть фу́тов. *I am six feet tall,* мой рост шесть фу́тов. *How tall are you?,* како́й ваш рост?; како́го вы ро́ста? —**tall story,** небыли́ца.

tallow *n.* са́ло. —*adj.* са́льный: *tallow candle,* са́льная свеча́.

tally *n.* **1,** *obs.* (notched stick) би́рка. **2,** (score) счёт. —*v.t.* подсчи́тывать: *tally the votes,* подсчи́тывать голоса́. *Tally the results,* подводи́ть ито́ги. —*v.i.* (agree) совпада́ть; сходи́ться; вяза́ться.

tallyho *interj.* ату́!

Talmud *n.* талму́д. —**Talmudic,** *adj.* талмуди́ческий.

talon *n.* ко́готь.

tamarind *n.* тамари́нд.

tamarisk *n.* тамари́ск.

tambour *n.* пя́льцы.

tambourine *n.* бу́бен; тамбури́н.

tame *adj.* **1,** (domesticated) ручно́й; приручённый. **2,** (docile) поко́рный. **3,** (lacking excitement) пре́сный. —*v.t.* **1,** (domesticate) прируча́ть; укроща́ть. **2,** (bring under control, as passions) укроща́ть; смиря́ть.

tamer *n.* укроти́тель.

tamper *v.i.* [*usu.* **tamper with**] **1,** (meddle with) тро́гать. **2,** (fraudulently alter) фальсифици́ровать. **3,** (bribe) подкупа́ть.

tampon *n.* тампо́н.

tan *adj.* **1,** (light brown) светло-кори́чневый. **2,** (bronzed by the sun) загоре́лый. —*n.* **1,** (color) светло-кори́чневый цвет. **2,** (suntan) зага́р. —*v.t.* **1,** (cure, as leather) дуби́ть. **2,** *in* **tan one's hide,** спусти́ть шку́ру с (+ *gen.*).

tanager *n.* тана́гра.

tandem *n.* та́ндем. —**in tandem,** цу́гом. *Work in tan-dem,* рабо́тать в та́ндеме.

tang *n.* ре́зкий при́вкус.

tangent *n.* **1,** *geom.* каса́тельная. **2,** *trig.* та́нгенс. —**go off on a tangent,** отклоня́ться от те́мы.

tangential *adj.* **1,** *math.* тангенциа́льный. **2,** (not di-rectly related) не име́ющий прямо́го отноше́ния.

tangerine *n.* мандари́н.

tangible *adj.* осяза́емый; осяза́тельный; ощути́мый.

tangle *v.t.* запу́тывать; пу́тать. —*v.i.* **1,** (become en-tangled) запу́тываться; пу́таться. **2,** *fol. by* **with** (come into conflict with) ста́лкиваться (с). —*n.* **1,** (snarled or intricate mass) сплете́ние. **2,** (confused state) пу́таница. —**tangled,** *adj.* запу́танный.

tango *n.* та́нго.

tangy *adj.* о́стрый; с ре́зким при́вкусом.

tank *n.* **1,** (container) бак. *Gas tank,* бензоба́к. *Fish tank,* аква́риум. *Oil storage tank,* нефтехрани́лище. **2,** (military vehicle) танк. —*adj.* та́нковый: *tank army,* та́нковая а́рмия.

tankard *n.* кру́жка.

tank car цисте́рна.

tanker *n.* наливно́е су́дно; та́нкер. *Oil tanker,* нефте-наливно́е су́дно.

tanned *adj.* **1,** (treated by tanning) дублёный. **2,** (sun-burned) загоре́лый.

tanner *n.* дуби́льщик. —**tannery,** *n.* коже́венный заво́д; дуби́льня.

tannic *adj.* тани́нный. —**tannic acid,** дуби́льная кислота́.

tannin *n.* тани́н.

tanning *n.* **1,** (process of tanning hides) дубле́ние. **2,** *colloq.* (thrashing) взбу́чка.

tantalize *v.t.* му́чить; дразни́ть.

tantalum *n.* танта́л.

tantamount *adj.* [*usu.* **tantamount to**] равноси́льный (+ *dat.*).

tantrum *n.* при́ступ гне́ва.

tap *v.t.* **1,** (strike gently) сту́кнуть; похло́пать: *tap someone on the shoulder,* сту́кнуть/похло́пать кого́-нибудь по плечу́. **2,** (strike repeatedly against some-thing) посту́кивать: *tap a pencil on the table,* посту́кивать карандашо́м по́ столу. **3,** *fol. by* **out** (produce by tapping, as a message) высту́кивать. **4,** (wiretap) перехва́тывать. **5,** (draw upon, as re-sources) испо́льзовать. —*v.i.* **1,** (make repeated sounds by striking something) посту́кивать. **2,** *fol. by* **on** (rap gently) ти́хо сту́кать (в). —*n.* **1,** (light blow) стук. **2,** (faucet) кран. *Tap water,* вода́ из-под кра́на; водопрово́дная вода́. **3,** (leather affixed to a shoe) набо́йка. **4,** *med.* пу́нкция: *spinal tap,* спинномоз-гова́я пу́нкция. —**on tap, 1,** (served from a tap) раз-ливно́й. **2,** *colloq.* (ready for action or use) гото́вый; под руко́й.

tap dance чечётка. —**tap-dance,** *v.i.* отбива́ть чечётку.

tape *n.* **1,** (strip of material) ле́нта. *Adhesive tape,* ли́пкая ле́нта. **2,** (material used for recording) плёнка. *Magnetic tape,* магнитофо́нная ле́нта. **3,** (strip across the finish line) фи́нишная ле́нта. —*v.t.*

1, (fasten with tape) прикрепля́ть: *tape something to the wall,* прикрепля́ть что́-нибудь к стене́. **2,** *fol. by up* (bind with tape) перевя́зывать. **3,** (record on tape) запи́сывать на плёнку.

tape deck магнитофо́нная приста́вка.

tape measure руле́тка; сантиме́тр.

taper *n.* то́нкая свеча́. —*v.t.* заостря́ть. —*v.i.* [*usu.* **taper off**] **1,** (narrow toward one end) заостря́ться. **2,** *fig.* (diminish; subside) убыва́ть.

tape-record *v.t.* запи́сывать на плёнку. —**tape recorder,** магнитофо́н. —**tape recording,** магнитофо́нная за́пись.

tapestry *n.* гобеле́н.

tapeworm *n.* ле́нточный червь; солитёр.

tapioca *n.* тапио́ка.

tapir *n.* тапи́р.

taps *n.* (вече́рняя) заря́.

tar *n.* дёготь; смола́. —*v.t.* смоли́ть.

tarantula *n.* тара́нтул.

tardy *adj.* **1,** (late) запозда́лый. **2,** (slow) медли́тельный. —**tardiness,** *n.* опозда́ние; запозда́ние; запа́здывание.

tare *n.* **1,** (vetch) ви́ка. **2,** *comm.* та́ра.

target *n.* **1,** (object fired at in practice) мише́нь. **2,** (something aimed or fired at) цель: *moving target,* дви́жущаяся цель. **3,** *mil.* цель; объе́кт. *Hit the target,* поража́ть цель. **4,** *fig.* (object, as of criticism or ridicule) мише́нь; предме́т. **5,** (goal) цель; план. —**target date,** наме́ченная да́та. —**target practice,** уче́бная стрельба́.

tariff *n.* тари́ф. —*adj.* тари́фный: *tariff barriers,* тари́фные барье́ры.

tarnish *v.t.* **1,** (dim the luster of) лиша́ть бле́ска. **2,** (detract from, as one's reputation) пятна́ть; подма́чивать. —*v.i.* тускне́ть. —*n.* ту́склость.

tarpaulin *n.* брезе́нт.

tarragon *n.* эстраго́н.

tarred *adj.* смолёный.

tarry *v.i.* **1,** (delay) ме́длить. **2,** (stray) отстава́ть.

tarsus *n.* предплюсна́. —**tarsal,** *adj.* предплюсневой.

tart *adj.* **1,** (sour) ки́слый; те́рпкий. **2,** *fig.* (caustic) е́дкий; ко́лкий. —*n.* **1,** (pie) пиро́г. **2,** (loose woman) потаску́ха.

tartan *n.* шотла́ндка.

Tartar *n.* тата́рин. —*adj.* тата́рский.

tartar *n.* ви́нный ка́мень.

tartaric *adj.* винока́менный. —**tartaric acid,** ви́нная кислота́.

task *n.* зада́ча; зада́ние. —**take to task,** взять в рабо́ту; взять в оборо́т.

task force операти́вная гру́ппа.

taskmaster *n.* надсмо́трщик. *Hard taskmaster,* стро́гий нача́льник.

tassel *n.* кисть; ки́сточка.

taste *n.* вкус. *A matter of taste,* де́ло вку́са. *Take a taste of,* попро́бовать (что́-нибудь) на вкус. —*v.t.* **1,** (test the flavor of) про́бовать: *taste the soup,* попро́бовать суп. **2,** (detect the flavor of) чу́вствовать вкус (+ *gen.*): *Do you taste the garlic?,* вы чу́вствуете вкус чеснока́? **3,** (experience) вкуша́ть;

изве́дывать; отве́дывать. —*v.i.* име́ть (како́й-нибудь) вкус: *taste sour,* име́ть ки́слый вкус. *What does it taste like?,* как э́то на вкус?; каков он на вкус? *Taste like cider,* име́ть вкус си́дра. *Taste of garlic,* отдава́ть чесноко́м. —**in bad taste,** безвку́сно; беста́ктно. —**in good taste,** со вку́сом. —**to one's taste,** по вку́су (+ *dat.*); в чьём-нибудь вку́се.

taste bud вкусова́я по́чка.

tasteful *adj.* сде́ланный со вку́сом. —**tastefully,** *adv.* со вку́сом.

tasteless *adj.* безвку́сный. —**tastelessness,** *n.* безвку́сие.

taster *n.* дегуста́тор.

tasty *adj.* вку́сный.

Tatar *n.* тата́рин. —*adj.* тата́рский.

tatter *n., usu. pl.* лохмо́тья; тряпьё; ру́бище; отре́пья. —*v.t.* растрепа́ть.

tatterdemalion *n.* оборва́нец; обо́рвыш.

tattered *adj.* разо́рванный; обо́рванный; потрёпанный; растрёпанный.

tattle *v.i.* [*often* **tattle on**] я́бедничать (на).

tattler *n.* я́бедник; фиска́л. *Also,* **tattletale.**

tattoo *n.* татуиро́вка. —*v.t.* татуи́ровать.

taunt *v.t.* насмеха́ться над; издева́ться над. —*n.* насме́шка.

Taurus *n.* Теле́ц.

taut *adj.* туго́й; ту́го натя́нутый.

tautology *n.* тавтоло́гия. —**tautological,** *adj.* тавтологи́ческий.

tavern *n.* пивна́я; тракти́р; таве́рна; каба́к; бар. —**tavern keeper,** тракти́рщик.

tawdry *adj.* мишу́рный.

tawny *adj.* светло-кори́чневый. —**tawny owl,** неясы́ть.

tax *n.* нало́г. —*adj.* нало́говый: *tax revenues,* нало́говые дохо́ды. —*v.t.* **1,** (impose a tax on) облага́ть (+ *acc.*) нало́гом. **2,** (put a strain on) надрыва́ть. **3,** (try, as someone's patience) испы́тывать. —**tax collector,** сбо́рщик нало́гов.

taxable *adj.* облага́емый нало́гом; подлежа́щий обложе́нию нало́гом.

taxation *n.* обложе́ние (нало́гом); налогообложе́ние.

tax-exempt *adj.* освобождённый от нало́гов.

taxi *n.* такси́. —*v.i.* **1,** (travel by taxi) е́хать на такси́. **2,** *aero.* рули́ть; выру́ливать. *Taxi up to,* подру́ливать к.

taxicab *n.* такси́.

taxidermy *n.* наби́вка чу́чел. —**taxidermist,** *n.* наби́вщик чу́чел.

taxi driver шофёр такси́.

taximeter *n.* таксо́метр.

taxonomy *n.* таксоно́мия. —**taxonomic,** *adj.* таксономи́ческий.

taxpayer *n.* налогоплате́льщик.

tea *n.* чай: *cup of tea,* ча́шка ча́ю. *I'll put on some tea,* я поста́влю ча́йник. —*adj.* ча́йный: *tea service,* ча́йный серви́з.

tea bag мешо́чек *or* паке́тик с ча́ем.

tea caddy ча́йница.

teach *v.t.* **1,** (be a teacher of or in) преподава́ть: *teach Russian,* преподава́ть ру́сский язы́к. *Teach a course,* вести́ *or* чита́ть курс. *Teach school,* преподава́ть в шко́ле. *Teach a class,* вести́ класс. *Teach first grade,* преподава́ть в пе́рвом кла́ссе. **2,** (give instruction to) учи́ть; обуча́ть: *teach someone Russian,* учи́ть/ обуча́ть кого́-нибудь ру́сскому языку́. *Teach someone how to swim,* научи́ть кого́-нибудь пла́вать. *Teach oneself to play the piano,* научи́ться сам игра́ть на роя́ле. **3,** (make it clear to) учи́ть: *History teaches that...,* исто́рия у́чит, что... *We were always taught that...,* нас всегда́ учи́ли, что... *Teach someone a lesson,* проучи́ть кого́-нибудь; дать *or* препода́ть кому́-нибудь уро́к. *That'll teach him!,* э́то его́ нау́чит!; э́то послу́жит ему́ уро́ком! —*v.i.* преподава́ть.

teacher *n.* учи́тель; учи́тельница.

teaching *n.* **1,** (act or profession of teaching) преподава́ние. **2,** *usu. pl.* (precepts) уче́ние: *the teachings of Christ,* уче́ние Христа́. —*adj.* преподава́тельский; педагоги́ческий: *teaching experience,* преподава́тельский о́пыт; *teaching load,* педагоги́ческая нагру́зка.

teacup *n.* ча́йная ча́шка.

teahouse *n.* ча́йный до́мик.

teak *n.* тик. —*adj.* ти́ковый.

teakettle *n.* ча́йник.

teal *n.* чиро́к.

tea leaf ча́йный лист.

team *n.* **1,** *sports* кома́нда. **2,** (working group) брига́да; гру́ппа. **3,** (of horses, mules, etc. harnessed to a vehicle) упря́жка. —*adj.* кома́ндный: *team championship,* кома́ндное пе́рвенство. *Team sports,* кома́ндные ви́ды спо́рта. —*v.i.* [*usu.* **team up**] объединя́ться.

teammate *n.* това́рищ по кома́нде.

teamster *n.* **1,** *obs.* (driver of a team) пого́нщик. **2,** (truck driver) води́тель грузовика́.

teamwork *n.* сы́гранность.

teapot *n.* ча́йник.

tear[1] (teer) *n.* слеза́. *Be in tears,* быть в слеза́х. *Tears of joy,* слёзы ра́дости. *Moved to tears,* тро́нутый до слёз. *With tears in his/her eyes,* со слеза́ми на глаза́х. *Tears came to my eyes,* у меня́ на глаза́х показа́лись *or* вы́ступили слёзы; у меня́ на глаза́ наверну́лись слёзы. —*v.i.* слези́ться: *My eyes are tearing,* мои́ глаза́ слезя́тся.

tear[2] (tayr) *v.t.* **1,** (rip accidentally) рвать; разрыва́ть: *tear one's stocking,* рвать/разрыва́ть чуло́к. *Tear one's dress on a nail,* порва́ть/разорва́ть пла́тье о гвоздь. *Tear a muscle/ligament,* порва́ть мы́шцу/ свя́зку. **2,** *fol. by* **up** (rip up) разрыва́ть; рвать: *tear up a letter,* разрыва́ть/порва́ть письмо́. **3,** (make; open, as a hole) сде́лать (ды́рку); пробива́ть (отве́рстие). *Tear a hole in the wall,* проби́ть сте́ну. *Tear a hole in one's stocking,* протира́ть ды́рку в чулке́. **4,** (snatch) вырыва́ть; выхва́тывать: *tear something out of someone's hands,* вы́рвать/вы́хватить что́-нибудь из чьи́х-нибудь рук. **5,** *in* **tear one's hair,** рвать на себе́ во́лосы. —*v.i.* **1,** (rip) рва́ться: *This material tears* *easily,* э́та мате́рия легко́ рвётся. **2,** (race) нести́сь; мча́ться: *tear along the highway,* нести́сь/мча́ться по шоссе́. —*n.* проре́ха; дыра́; ды́рка. —*tear apart,* **1,** (tear to pieces; kill) растерза́ть. **2,** *colloq.* (criticize severely) разруга́ть. —**tear away,** отрыва́ть: *I couldn't tear myself away from the book,* я не мог (могла́) оторва́ться от кни́ги. —**tear down,** сноси́ть. —**tear off,** отрыва́ть; срыва́ть. —**tear open,** разрыва́ть. —**tear out,** вырыва́ть. —**tear to pieces, 1,** (rip up) рвать *or* разрыва́ть на куски́ *or* в клочки́; раздира́ть. **2,** (kill) терза́ть; растерза́ть; драть; задра́ть. *See also* **torn.**

teardrop *n.* слеза́; слези́нка.

tear duct слёзный прото́к.

tearful *adj.* слезли́вый: *tearful voice,* слезли́вый го́лос; *tearful farewell,* слезли́вое проща́ние.

tear gas слезоточи́вый газ.

tearoom *n.* ча́йная.

tear-stained *adj.* запла́канный.

teary *adj.* слезоточи́вый: *teary eyes,* слезоточи́вые глаза́.

tease *v.t.* дразни́ть; поддра́знивать. *Tease someone about his being so short,* дразни́ть кого́-нибудь из-за его́ ма́ленького ро́ста.

teaspoon *n.* ча́йная ло́жка.

teat *n.* сосо́к.

technetium *n.* техне́ций.

technical *adj.* техни́ческий.

technicality *n.* **1,** (technical term) техни́ческая дета́ль. **2,** (minute point) форма́льность.

technically *adv.* **1,** (from a technical point of view) техни́чески. **2,** (strictly speaking) форма́льно: *Technically you're correct,* форма́льно вы пра́вы.

technician *n.* те́хник.

technique *n.* **1,** (sophisticated method) приём. **2,** (technical skill) те́хника.

technology *n.* техноло́гия; те́хника. —**technological,** *adj.* технологи́ческий. —**technologist,** *n.* техно́лог.

teddy bear ми́шка.

tedious *adj.* ску́чный; утоми́тельный; кропотли́вый.

tedium *n.* ску́ка.

teem *v.i.* **1,** *fol. by* **with** (swarm; abound) кише́ть (+ *instr.*). **2,** (of rain) ливмя́ лить.

teenage *adj.* о́трочеcкий. *Teenage son,* сын-подро́сток. —**teenager,** *n.* подро́сток.

teeny *adj., colloq.* кро́хотный; кро́шечный.

teeter *v.i.* кача́ться; колеба́ться.

teethe *v.i. The child is teething,* у ребёнка проре́зываются зу́бы.

teetotaler *also,* **teetotaller** *n.* тре́звенник; непью́щий.

telecast *n.* телепереда́ча. —*v.t.* передава́ть по телеви́дению.

telecommunications *n.pl.* телесвя́зь; телекоммуника́ции.

telegram *n.* телегра́мма.

telegraph *n.* телегра́ф. —*adj.* телегра́фный. *Telegraph office,* телегра́ф. *Telegraph operator,* телеграфи́ст. —*v.t.* телеграфи́ровать.

telegrapher *n.* телеграфи́ст.

telegraphic *adj.* телегра́фный.

telegraphy *n.* телеграфи́я.

telemeter *n.* телеме́тр. —**telemetry,** *n.* телеметри́я.

teleology *n.* телеоло́гия. —**teleological,** *adj.* телеологи́ческий.

telepathy *n.* телепа́тия. —**telepathic,** *adj.* телепати́ческий.

telephone *n.* телефо́н. *Just a minute, I'm on the telephone!,* одну́ мину́ту, я разгова́риваю по телефо́ну. —*adj.* телефо́нный: *telephone book,* телефо́нная кни́га; *telephone call,* телефо́нный звоно́к; *telephone service,* телефо́нная связь; *telephone lines,* телефо́нные провода́. *Telephone number,* но́мер телефо́на. *Telephone bill,* счёт за телефо́н. *Telephone operator,* телефони́ст(ка). —*v.t.* звони́ть по телефо́ну; телефони́ровать.

telephonic *adj.* телефо́нный.

telephony *n.* телефони́я.

telephoto lens телеобъекти́в.

teleprompter *n.* телеподска́зчик.

telescope *n.* телеско́п. —**telescopic,** *adj.* телескопи́ческий.

teletype *n.* телета́йп.

televise *v.t.* пока́зывать по телеви́дению.

television *n.* телеви́дение. *Watch television,* смотре́ть телеви́зор. *Watch something on television,* смотре́ть что́-нибудь по телеви́дению *or* по телеви́зору. *What's on television?,* что идёт по телеви́зору? —*adj.* телевизио́нный: *television screen,* телевизио́нный экра́н. —**television set,** телеви́зор.

tell *v.t.* **1,** (utter) говори́ть (*pfv.* сказа́ть): *tell the truth,* говори́ть пра́вду; *tell a lie,* говори́ть непра́вду. **2,** (relate) расска́зывать: *tell a story,* расска́зывать исто́рию. **3,** (inform) говори́ть; сказа́ть (+ *dat.*): *Did you tell him this?,* вы ему́ сказа́ли об э́том? *Tell him your name!,* скажи́ ему́ твоё и́мя! *Can you tell me how to...?,* вы не ска́жете, как...? *I told you so!,* я тебе́ говори́л(а)! *Don't tell a soul!,* никому́ не говори́те! *I can't tell you how sorry I am,* слова́ми переда́ть не могу́, насколько мне жаль; не могу́ да́же сказа́ть, насколько мне жаль. *How many times must I tell you?,* сколько раз тебе́ повторя́ть? **4,** (order) сказа́ть; веле́ть. *Tell him to go away,* скажи́те ему́, чтобы он ушёл. *Do as you are told,* де́лайте, как вам ве́лено. *I told them not to wait for us,* я сказа́л, чтобы они́ не жда́ли нас. **5,** (determine; decide; know): *know how to tell time,* уме́ть называ́ть вре́мя. *Tell the difference,* различа́ть. **6,** (distinguish) отлича́ть: *tell one from the other,* отлича́ть оди́н от друго́го. **7,** (indicate) ука́зывать: *Clocks tell time,* часы́ ука́зывают вре́мя. —*v.i.* **1,** *usu. neg.* (divulge information): *Promise me you won't tell!,* обеща́йте никому́ не расска́зывать. **2,** (decide definitely; say) сказа́ть; знать. *It's hard to tell,* тру́дно сказа́ть; *Who can tell?,* кто зна́ет? *Time will tell,* вре́мя пока́жет. *There is no telling when...,* невозмо́жно сказа́ть, когда́... *How could I tell that...?,* отку́да мне бы́ло знать, что...? **3,** *fol. by* **of** (give an account of) расска́зывать (о). **4,** (have force or effect) ска́зываться. *The years are beginning to tell,* го́ды

начина́ют ска́зываться; го́ды беру́т своё. —**tell apart,** различа́ть. —**tell off,** *colloq.* брани́ть; отчи́тывать. —**tell on, 1,** [*also,* **tell upon**] (have an effect upon) ска́зываться на. **2,** *colloq.* (tattle on) я́бедничать на.

teller *n.* **1,** (narrator) расска́зчик. **2,** (bank clerk) касси́р.

telling *adj.* **1,** (having great force) си́льный. *Telling blow,* тяжёлый *or* чувстви́тельный уда́р. **2,** (revealing) многозначи́тельный.

telltale *adj.* показа́тельный: *telltale sign,* показа́тельный при́знак.

tellurium *n.* теллу́р.

temerity *n.* сме́лость.

temper *n.* **1,** (composure; equanimity): *keep one's temper,* владе́ть собо́й; *lose one's temper,* выходи́ть из себя́. **2,** (disposition) нрав; хара́ктер: *bad temper,* дурно́й нрав/хара́ктер. *Hot temper,* вспы́льчивость. **3,** (mood) настрое́ние. **4,** (anger; rage) гнев: *fit of temper,* при́ступ гне́ва. *Tempers flared,* стра́сти разгоре́лись. —*v.t.* **1,** *metall.* закаля́ть: *temper steel,* закаля́ть сталь. **2,** *fig.* (moderate) умеря́ть; смягча́ть.

tempera *n.* те́мпера. *In tempera,* те́мперой.

temperament *n.* темпера́мент; нрав.

temperamental *adj.* капри́зный; темпера́ментный.

temperance *n.* **1,** (moderation) уме́ренность. **2,** (abstinence) возде́ржанность.

temperate *adj.* уме́ренный: *a temperate climate,* уме́ренный кли́мат. —**Temperate Zone,** уме́ренный по́яс.

temperature *n.* **1,** (degree of heat or cold) температу́ра. **2,** (fever) повы́шенная температу́ра; жар. *He has a temperature,* у него́ температу́ра.

tempest *n.* бу́ря. —**tempest in a teapot,** бу́ря в стака́не воды́.

tempestuous *adj.* бу́рный.

template *n.* шабло́н.

temple *n.* **1,** (church) храм. **2,** (side of the head) висо́к.

templet *n.* = **template.**

tempo *n.* темп.

temporal *adj.* **1,** (pert. to time) временно́й. **2,** (temporary; transient) вре́менный; преходя́щий. **3,** (worldly; secular) мирско́й; све́тский.

temporarily *adv.* вре́менно: *He is temporarily out of work,* он вре́менно без рабо́ты. *The telephone is temporarily disconnected,* телефо́н вре́менно (*or* на вре́мя) отключён.

temporary *adj.* вре́менный: *temporary address,* вре́менный а́дрес; *temporary job,* вре́менная рабо́та. *Be temporary,* носи́ть вре́менный хара́ктер.

temporize *v.i.* оття́гивать вре́мя.

tempt *v.t.* соблазня́ть; искуша́ть. *I am tempted,* меня́ э́то соблазня́ет. *I was tempted to...,* у меня́ был собла́зн (+ *inf.*). *Tempt fate,* искуша́ть *or* испы́тывать судьбу́.

temptation *n.* собла́зн; искуше́ние: *yield to temptation,* поддава́ться собла́зну/искуше́нию.

tempter *n.* соблазни́тель; искуси́тель.

tempting *adj.* соблазни́тельный; зама́нчивый.

ten *adj.* де́сять. —*n.* **1,** (cardinal number) де́сять. **2,**

(written numeral) деся́тка. **3,** *cards* деся́тка. **4,** *pl.* (quantities of 10) деся́тки (+ *gen.*): *tens of thousands of...,* деся́тки ты́сяч (+ *gen.*).

tenable *adj.* разу́мный: *tenable argument,* разу́мный до́вод.

tenacious *adj.* це́пкий.

tenacity *n.* **1,** (firmness of hold) це́пкость. **2,** (persistence) упо́рство.

tenant *n.* жиле́ц; нанима́тель; аренда́тор; квартира́нт. —**tenant farmer,** фе́рмер-аренда́тор.

tend *v.t.* **1,** (care for) уха́живать за: *tend the sick,* уха́живать за больны́ми. **2,** (look after) присма́тривать за. *Tend sheep,* пасти́ ове́ц. *Tend the fire,* подде́рживать ого́нь. —*v.i.* [*usu.* **tend to**] **1,** (be inclined; have a tendency) склоня́ться; име́ть тенде́нцию. *He tends to exaggerate,* он скло́нен преувели́чивать. *I tend to agree,* в о́бщем я согла́сен. **2,** (mind) обраща́ть внима́ние (на).

tendency *n.* тенде́нция; скло́нность; накло́нность. *Aggressive tendencies,* агресси́вные тенде́нции. *A tendency toward obesity,* скло́нность к полноте́.

tendentious *adj.* тенденцио́зный. —**tendentiousness,** *n.* тенденцио́зность.

tender *adj.* **1,** (gentle; delicate) не́жный: *tender skin,* не́жная ко́жа; *tender caress,* не́жная ла́ска. *Tender age,* не́жный во́зраст. **2,** (sensitive; painful) чувстви́тельный: *tender spot,* чувстви́тельное ме́сто. **3,** (soft, as of meat) мя́гкий. —*n.* **1,** (offer) предложе́ние. **2,** (money) платёжное сре́дство: *legal tender,* зако́нное платёжное сре́дство. **3,** R.R. те́ндер. **4,** *naut.* плаву́чая ба́за. —*v.t.* предлага́ть. *Tender one's resignation,* подава́ть в отста́вку.

tenderhearted *adj.* мягкосерде́чный. —**tenderheartedness,** *n.* мягкосерде́чие; мягкосерде́чность.

tenderloin *n.* вы́резка.

tenderly *adv.* не́жно.

tenderness *n.* не́жность.

tendon *n.* сухожи́лие.

tendril *n.* у́сик.

tenement *n.* (убо́гий) жило́й дом.

tenet *n.* положе́ние; устано́вка.

tenfold *adj.* десятикра́тный. —*adv.* в де́сять раз; вде́сятеро.

tennis *n.* те́ннис. —*adj.* те́ннисный: *tennis court,* те́ннисный корт; *tennis racket,* те́ннисная раке́тка. *Tennis player,* тенниси́ст; тенниси́стка. *Tennis shoes,* кроссо́вки.

tenon *n.* шип.

tenor *n.* **1,** *music* те́нор. **2,** (purport; thrust) смысл. —*adj.* теноро́вый. —**tenor clef,** теноро́вый ключ.

tenpins *n.* ке́гли.

tense *adj.* напряжённый: *tense atmosphere,* напряжённая атмосфе́ра. —*v.t.* напряга́ть: *tense one's muscles,* напряга́ть мы́шцы. —*v.i.* напряга́ться. —*n.,* *gram.* вре́мя: *present tense,* настоя́щее вре́мя.

tensile *adj.* растяжи́мый. —**tensile strength,** растяжи́мость; про́чность на разры́в.

tension *n.* **1,** (strain; strained relations) напряже́ние; напряжённость. *International tension,* междунаро́дная напряжённость. **2,** *electricity* напряже́ние.

tent *n.* пала́тка; шатёр. —*adj.* пала́точный: *tent city,* пала́точный городо́к.

tentacle *n.* щу́пальце.

tentative *adj.* предвари́тельный; усло́вный. —**tentatively,** *adv.* усло́вно.

tenterhook *n., in* be on tenterhooks, быть *or* сиде́ть как на иго́лках *or* как на у́гольях.

tenth *adj.* деся́тый. —*n.* деся́тая; деся́тая часть. *One-tenth,* одна́ деся́тая; деся́тая часть. *One-tenth of the population,* деся́тая часть населе́ния. *Three-tenths,* три деся́тых.

tenuous *adj.* **1,** (thin) то́нкий. **2,** (not firm or strong) непро́чный.

tenure *n.* **1,** (holding of a position) пребыва́ние: *one's tenure in office,* пребыва́ние у вла́сти *or* в до́лжности. **2,** (permanence of a position) несменя́емость.

tepid *adj.* теплова́тый.

terbium *n.* те́рбий.

tercentenary *adj.* трёхсотле́тний. —*n.* трёхсотле́тие.

term *n.* **1,** (period of time) срок: *term of office,* срок полномо́чий. *Prison term,* срок тюре́много заключе́ния. *Be elected for a four-year term,* избира́ться сро́ком на четы́ре го́да. **2,** (semester) семе́стр. **3,** (word or phrase) те́рмин: *technical term,* техни́ческий те́рмин. **4,** *pl.* (manner of expression) выраже́ния: *in flattering terms,* в ле́стных выраже́ниях. **5,** *pl.* (provisions, as of a contract) усло́вия: *on favorable terms,* на льго́тных усло́виях. **6,** *pl.* (relations) отноше́ния: *be on good terms with,* быть в хоро́ших отноше́ниях с; быть в ладу́ (*or* в лада́х) с; быть на дру́жеской (*or* на коро́ткой) ноге́ с. **7,** *math.* член. —*v.t.* называ́ть; характеризова́ть. —**come to terms,** приходи́ть к соглаше́нию; догова́риваться. —**come to terms with,** мири́ться с (чём-нибудь). —**in terms of,** с то́чки зре́ния (+ *gen.*); в пла́не (+ *gen.*). —**in the near term,** в краткосро́чном пла́не; в краткосро́чной перспекти́ве; в бли́жней *or* ближа́йшей перспекти́ве.

termagant *n.* меге́ра; фу́рия.

terminal *n.* **1,** (terminus; station) вокза́л. *Bus terminal,* автовокза́л. *Air terminal,* аэровокза́л. **2,** *electricity* зажи́м. **3,** (for a computer) термина́л. —*adj.* **1,** (last; final) коне́чный. **2,** *med.* смерте́льный: *terminal illness,* смерте́льная боле́знь.

terminate *v.t.* **1,** (end; halt) прекраща́ть. **2,** (cancel; annul) расторга́ть. —*v.i.* конча́ться; ока́нчиваться.

termination *n.* **1,** (ending; halting) прекраще́ние. **2,** (annulment) расторже́ние.

terminology *n.* терминоло́гия.

terminus *n.* коне́чная ста́нция.

termite *n.* терми́т.

term paper курсова́я рабо́та.

tern *n.* кра́чка.

terrace *n.* терра́са. —**terraced,** *adj.* терра́сный.

terra cotta терракота. —**terra-cotta,** *adj.* террако́товый.

terrain *n.* ме́стность.

terrapin *n.* черепа́ха.

terrestrial *adj.* земно́й.

terrible *adj.* ужа́сный; стра́шный: *a terrible tragedy,* ужа́сная/стра́шная траге́дия.

terribly *adv.* ужа́сно; стра́шно. *I'm terribly sorry!*, A, (saddened) мне о́чень и о́чень жаль. B, (apologetic) я о́чень извиня́юсь.

terrier *n.* терье́р.

terrific *adj.* **1,** (very great; tremendous) огро́мный: *terrific speed,* огро́мная ско́рость. *Terrific noise,* стра́шный шум. **2,** *colloq.* (marvelous) чу́дный; потряса́ющий. *We had a terrific time,* мы чу́дно провели́ вре́мя.

terrified *adj. Be terrified,* ужаса́ться. *Be terrified of,* ужаса́ться *or* безу́мно боя́ться (+ *gen.*). *Terrified passengers,* напу́ганные *or* приведённые в у́жас *or* обезу́мевшие от стра́ха пассажи́ры. *Terrified look,* выраже́ние у́жаса.

terrify *v.t.* ужаса́ть; приводи́ть в у́жас. —**terrifying,** *adj.* ужаса́ющий.

territorial *adj.* территориа́льный. —**territorial waters,** территориа́льные во́ды.

territory *n.* террито́рия.

terror *n.* **1,** (intense fear) у́жас. **2,** (use of violence as a political weapon) терро́р.

terrorism *n.* террори́зм. —**terrorist,** *n.* террори́ст. —*adj.* террористи́ческий.

terrorize *v.t.* терроризи́ровать.

terror-stricken *adj.* объя́тый *or* охва́ченный у́жасом.

terry cloth махро́вая ткань.

terse *adj.* кра́ткий; сжа́тый. —**tersely,** *adv.* ску́по. —**terseness,** *n.* кра́ткость; сжа́тость.

tertiary *adj.* трети́чный.

test *n.* **1,** (trial) испыта́ние; про́ба. *Test of strength,* про́ба сил. *Underground nuclear test,* подзе́мное испыта́ние я́дерного ору́жия. *Put to the test,* подверга́ть испыта́нию. *Stand/withstand the test of time,* вы́держать прове́рку вре́менем. **2,** (school examination) экза́мен; контро́льная рабо́та; (*at the university level only*) зачёт. *Mathematics test,* экза́мен *or* зачёт по матема́тике. *Spelling test,* орфографи́ческий дикта́нт; контро́льная рабо́та по орфогра́фии. *I.Q. test,* прове́рка у́мственных спосо́бностей. **3,** *med.* ана́лиз: *blood test,* ана́лиз кро́ви. *Drug test,* прове́рка на нарко́тики; про́ба на до́пинг. —*adj.* испыта́тельный; про́бный: *test flight,* испыта́тельный/про́бный полёт. —*v.t.* испы́тывать; проверя́ть; испро́бовать. *Test (out) a new aircraft,* испы́тывать но́вый самолёт. *Test a metal for durability,* испы́тывать мета́лл на про́чность. *Test someone's knowledge of history,* прове́рить чьи́-нибудь зна́ния по исто́рии. *Test a theory out in practice,* прове́рить тео́рию на пра́ктике. —**test the waters,** зонди́ровать по́чву.

testaceous *adj.* па́нцирный.

testament *n.* завеща́ние. *Last will and testament,* духо́вное завеща́ние; после́дняя во́ля. —**New Testament,** Но́вый заве́т. —**Old Testament,** Ве́тхий заве́т.

testator *n.* завеща́тель. —**testatrix,** *n.* завеща́тельница.

tester *n.* испыта́тель.

testes *n.pl.* яи́чки.

testicle *n.* яи́чко.

testify *v.t. & i.* дава́ть показа́ния; пока́зывать; свиде́тельствовать. *He testified that...,* он показа́л, что...

testimonial *n.* рекоменда́ция; характери́стика. —*adj.* рекоменда́тельный. *Testimonial dinner,* обе́д в честь кого́-нибудь.

testimony *n.* **1,** (statement made under oath) показа́ния; свиде́тельство. **2,** (proof) свиде́тельство.

test pilot лётчик-испыта́тель.

test tube проби́рка.

testy *adj.* раздражи́тельный; брюзгли́вый.

tetanus *n.* столбня́к.

tête-à-tête *n.* бесе́да с гла́зу на глаз.

tether *n.* при́вязь. —*v.t.* привя́зывать. —**reach the end of one's tether,** дойти́ до то́чки.

tetragon *n.* четырёхуго́льник. —**tetragonal,** *adj.* четырёхуго́льный.

tetrahedron *n.* четырёхгра́нник. —**tetrahedral,** *adj.* четырёхгра́нный.

tetrameter *n.* четырёхсто́пный стих. *Iambic tetrameter,* четырёхсто́пный ямб. —*adj.* четырёхсто́пный.

Teuton *n.* тевто́н. —**Teutonic,** *adj.* тевто́нский.

text *n.* текст.

textbook *n.* уче́бник.

textile *n., usu. pl.* тексти́ль. —*adj.* тексти́льный.

textual *adj.* **1,** (pert. to a text) тексто́вой; текстуа́льный. **2,** (literal) текстуа́льный.

texture *n.* строе́ние; переплете́ние (тка́ни).

Thai *adj.* та́йский. —*n.* та́йский язы́к.

thallium *n.* та́ллий.

than *conj.* чем: *less strict than you,* ме́нее стро́гий (стро́гая), чем вы. *More than ever before,* бо́льше, чем когда́-либо ра́ньше. *Sooner than expected,* ра́ньше, чем мы ожида́ли. *Better late than never,* лу́чше по́здно, чем никогда́. ♦ *Also rendered by the genitive case: He is taller than you,* он вы́ше вас. *She is younger than the other students,* она́ моло́же други́х студе́нтов. *No later than thirty days after...,* не поздне́е тридцати́ дней по́сле...

thank *v.t.* благодари́ть: *thank someone for a gift,* благодари́ть кого́-нибудь за пода́рок. *There are no words to thank you enough,* слова́ми не вы́разить мою́ благода́рность (*or* наско́лько я благода́рен); не хвата́ет слов, что́бы вас отблагодари́ть. —**thank God!,** сла́ва бо́гу! —**thank you!,** спаси́бо!; благодарю́ вас. *Thank you very much!,* большо́е (вам) спаси́бо. *Thank you for the invitation,* спаси́бо за приглаше́ние. *No, thank you!,* нет, спаси́бо. *See also* **thanks.**

thankful *adj.* благода́рный. —**thankfulness,** *n.* благода́рность.

thankless *adj.* неблагода́рный.

thanks *n.pl.* благода́рность: *Please accept my thanks,* прими́те мою́ благода́рность. —*interj.* спаси́бо: *Thanks for the good advice,* спаси́бо за хоро́ший сове́т. *Thanks for coming!,* спаси́бо, что пришли́! —**thanks to,** благодаря́ (+ *dat.*).

thanksgiving *n.* **1,** (giving of thanks) благодаре́ние. **2,** *cap.* (American holiday) День Благодаре́ния.

that *adj.* тот: *that house,* тот дом; *at that time,* в то вре́мя. *—dem. pron.* э́то: *That's all,* э́то всё; *that's not the point,* де́ло не в э́том. *Is that you, Nina?,* э́то ты, Ни́на? *That's what I came for,* для э́того я и пришёл. *Who was that you were talking to?,* с кем э́то вы разгова́ривали? *That is the question!,* вот в чём вопро́с. *—rel. pron.* кото́рый: *the book that was lying on the table,* кни́га, кото́рая лежа́ла на столе́. *The air that we breathe,* во́здух, кото́рым мы ды́шим. *The company that bears his name,* компа́ния, нося́щая его́ и́мя. ♦*After* тот *and* всё — что: *everything that happened,* всё, что случи́лось. *All's well that ends well,* всё хорошо́, что хорошо́ конча́ется. *He is not the man (that) he was,* он не тот (челове́к), что был. *—conj.* что; что́бы. *I admit that I was wrong,* я признаю́, что был непра́в (что была́ неправа́). *He demanded that we apologize,* он потре́бовал, что́бы мы извини́лись. *—adv.* так; тако́й. *I can't walk that far,* я не могу́ идти́ так далеко́. *—and all that,* и всё тако́е. *—at that, see* at. *—by that,* э́тим. *—for all that,* при всём том. *—in that,* тем, что. *—like that,* так. *—so that,* с тем, что́бы. *—that is,* то есть. *—that much,* так мно́го; сто́лько. *—that which,* то, что. *—this and that, see* this.

thatch *n.* кро́вельная соло́ма. *—v.t.* крыть соло́мой. *Thatched roof,* соло́менная кры́ша.

thaw *n.* о́ттепель. *—v.i.* та́ять; отта́ивать. *—v.t.* раста́пливать; отта́ивать.

the *def. art. Not rendered in Russian: the Kremlin,* Кремль. *The Bible says...,* Би́блия гласи́т... *The end of the road,* коне́ц доро́ги. *The 20th century,* двадца́тый век. *the..., the...,* чем..., тем...: *The sooner the better,* чем ра́ньше, тем лу́чше.

theater *also,* **theatre** *n.* **1,** (playhouse) теа́тр. *Theater tickets,* биле́ты в теа́тр. **2,** *mil.* теа́тр: *theater of operations,* теа́тр вое́нных де́йствий. *—***theatergoer,** *n.* театра́л. *—***theatrical,** *adj.* театра́льный.

theatrics *n.pl.* **1,** (art of the theater) театра́льное иску́сство. **2,** (histrionics) театра́льность.

thee *pers. pron., archaic* тебя́; тебе́; тобо́й.

theft *n.* воровство́; кра́жа. *Theft of government property,* хище́ние *or* расхище́ние госуда́рственной со́бственности.

their *poss. adj.* их: *their mother,* их мать. ♦*When the possessor is the subject of the sentence,* свой: *They sold their house,* они́ про́дали свой дом. *They brought their daughter with them,* они́ привели́ с собо́й свою́ дочь.

theirs *poss. pron.* их: *a friend of theirs,* оди́н из их друзе́й. *Is this our luggage or theirs?,* э́тот бага́ж наш и́ли их?

theism *n.* теи́зм. *—***theist,** *n.* теи́ст. *—***theistic,** *adj.* теисти́ческий.

them *pers. pron.* **1,** *used as dir. obj. of a verb,* их: *I saw them,* я ви́дел их. **2,** *used as indir. obj. of a verb,* им: *Give them the money,* да́йте им де́ньги. **3,** *used as obj. of a prep.* них; ним; ни́ми.

thematic *adj.* темати́ческий.

theme *n.* те́ма.

themselves *pers. pron.* **1,** *used for emphasis,* (они́) са́ми: *They don't know themselves,* они́ са́ми не зна́ют. **2,** *used reflexively,* себя́: *They behaved themselves badly,* они́ пло́хо вели́ себя́. *They cannot agree among themselves,* они́ не мо́гут договори́ться ме́жду собо́й. *—***by themselves, 1,** (alone) одни́. **2,** (without help) са́ми.

then *adv.* **1,** (at that time) тогда́; в то вре́мя. *We were young then,* тогда́ мы бы́ли молоды́ми. *Where were you living then?,* где вы жи́ли в то вре́мя? **2,** (afterward; next) пото́м; зате́м: *First we go to London, and then to Paris,* снача́ла мы пое́дем в Ло́ндон, а пото́м/зате́м в Пари́ж. **3,** (in that case) тогда́; так; то. *What will you do then?,* что вы бу́дете де́лать тогда́? *Then say so!,* так и скажи́те! *If he is ill, then we shouldn't go there,* е́сли он бо́лен, то не на́до идти́ туда́. **4,** (so) зна́чит: *Then you're not coming,* зна́чит, вы не идёте. *—adj., preceded by* **the** тогда́шний. *—***but then,** зато́; впро́чем. *—***by then,** к тому́ вре́мени. *By then I knew that...,* тогда́ я знал, что... *—***now and then,** вре́мя от вре́мени; ко́е-когда́. *—***since then,** с тех пор. *—***then and there,** тут же. *—***till then,** до тех пор.

thence *adv.* **1,** (from there) отту́да. **2,** (from that time) с тех пор. **3,** (therefore) отсю́да; поэ́тому.

thenceforth *adv.* с тех пор; с того́ вре́мени. *Also,* **thenceforward.**

theocracy *n.* теокра́тия. *—***theocratic,** *adj.* теократи́ческий.

theologian *n.* богосло́в.

theological *adj.* богосло́вский; теологи́ческий. *Theological seminary,* духо́вная семина́рия.

theology *n.* богосло́вие; теоло́гия.

theorem *n.* теоре́ма.

theoretical *adj.* теорети́ческий. *—***theoretically,** *adv.* теорети́чески; в тео́рии.

theoretician *n.* теоре́тик. *Also,* **theorist.**

theorize *v.i.* теоретизи́ровать.

theory *n.* тео́рия.

theosophy *n.* теосо́фия. *—***theosophical,** *adj.* теосо́фский; теософи́ческий. *—***theosophist,** *n.* теосо́ф.

therapeutic *adj.* терапевти́ческий.

therapist *n.* физиотерапе́вт. *Speech therapist,* логопе́д.

therapy *n.* терапи́я. *Physical therapy,* физиотерапи́я. *Speech therapy,* логопе́дия.

there *adv.* **1,** (in that place) там. *From there,* отту́да. **2,** (to that place) туда́: *there and back,* туда́ и обра́тно. **3,** (from that place) отту́да: *He left there,* он уе́хал отту́да. **4,** *used to call attention,* вот; вон: *There he is!,* вот он!; *there he goes!,* вон он идёт! **5,** (in that matter) здесь: *I disagree with you there,* здесь я с ва́ми не согла́сен. *You've got me there!,* здесь я попа́лся. **6,** (at that point) в (*or* на) э́том; э́тим. *He didn't stop there,* он на э́том не останови́лся. *The matter didn't end there,* э́тим де́ло не ко́нчилось. *There the similarity ends,* на э́том схо́дство зака́нчивается. *—interj.* **1,** *to express satisfaction,* ну вот! **2,** *to express sympathy,* ну ну! *—***not all there,** *colloq.* (у него́/неё) не все до́ма. *—***over there,** вон там.

—**there and then,** тут же. —**there is; there are,** есть; имеется (имеются). *There is reason to believe that...,* есть основание полагать, что... *There is nothing/ no one/ there,* там ничего/никого нет. *There is nothing I can do,* я ничего не могу сделать. *There is nothing to worry about,* беспокоиться не о чем. *There is no telling when...,* нельзя сказать, когда... *There is no stopping him,* его не остановишь. *There is nothing you can do about it,* ничего не поделаешь. —**there was; there were,** был; было. *There was no one there,* там никого не было. *There were three of them,* их было трое.

thereabout *adv.* **1,** (near that place) поблизости. **2,** (approximately) около этого: *ten miles or thereabout,* десять миль или что-нибудь около этого. *Also,* **thereabouts.**

thereafter *adv.* с этого (*or* с того) времени; в дальнейшем.

thereby *adv.* тем самым.

therefore *adv.* поэтому.

therein *adv.* в этом.

thereupon *adv.* **1,** (following that) вслед за тем. **2,** (because of that) вследствие того.

thermal *adj.* тепловой; термический. —**thermal energy,** тепловая энергия.

Thermit *also,* **Thermite** *n.* термит.

thermocouple *n.* термопара.

thermodynamics *n.* термодинамика. —**thermodynamic,** *adj.* термодинамический.

thermometer *n.* термометр; градусник.

thermonuclear *adj.* термоядерный.

thermos *n.* термос. *Also,* **thermos bottle.**

thermostat *n.* термостат.

thesaurus *n.* тезаурус.

these *dem.adj. & pron.* эти: *these houses,* эти дома. *I'll take these,* я возьму эти. *These are my children,* это мои дети. *One of these days,* на днях.

thesis *n.* **1,** (proposition) тезис; положение. **2,** (dissertation) диссертация.

Thespian *adj.* трагический; драматический. —*n.* трагический актёр.

they *pers. pron.* они: *They left,* они ушли. *They say that...,* говорят, что... *See also* **them.**

thick *adj.* **1,** (not thin) толстый: *thick carpet,* толстый ковёр; *thick book,* толстая книга. **2,** (having a specified thickness) в ... толщиной: *six inches thick,* в шесть дюймов толщиной. **3,** (dense; not watery) густой: *thick fog/soup/syrup,* густой туман/суп/сироп. **4,** (heavy, as of an accent) сильный. —*adv. Slice the bread thick,* нарезать хлеб толстыми ломтями. —*n.* гуща: *in the thick of the fight,* в гуще боя. *In the thick of the forest,* в чаще *or* в гуще леса. —**lay it on thick,** сгущать краски. —**thick and fast,** градом.

thicken *v.t.* **1,** (make thicker or broader) утолщать. **2,** (make more dense) сгущать: *thicken a solution,* сгущать раствор. —*v.i.* густеть; сгущаться. *The plot thickens,* интрига становится всё сложнее.

thicket *n.* чаща; чащоба.

thickheaded *adj.* тупоголовый; тупоумный; твердолобый.

thick-lipped *adj.* толстогубый; губастый.

thickness *n.* **1,** (size) толщина. **2,** (density) густота. **3,** (layer) слой.

thickset *adj.* коренастый; приземистый; кряжистый.

thick-skinned *adj.* толстокожий.

thief *n.* вор. *Stop, thief!,* держите вора! *Gang of thieves,* шайка *or* банда воров.

thieve *v.i.* воровать. —**thievery,** *n.* воровство. —**thievish,** *adj.* вороватый.

thigh *n.* бедро. —**thighbone,** *n.* бедренная кость.

thimble *n.* напёрсток.

thin *adj.* **1,** (not thick) тонкий: *thin ice,* тонкий лёд. *Thin line/waist/shirt,* тонкая линия/талия/рубашка. **2,** (not fat) худой. *She has gotten very thin,* она очень похудела. **3,** (not dense) редкий. *His hair is getting thin,* волосы у него редеют. **4,** (watery) жидкий: *thin soup,* жидкий суп. —*adv.* тонко: *slice the bread thin,* нарезать хлеб тонко. —*v.t.* [*usu.* **thin out**] (make less dense) разрежать. —*v.i.* **1,** *fol. by* **out** (become less dense) редеть: *The crowds have thinned out,* толпы поредели. **2,** *fol. by* **down** (slim down) худеть. —**wear thin, 1,** (become worn) изнашиваться; стираться. **2,** *fig.* (of patience) истощаться; иссякать.

thine *poss. pron. & adj., archaic* твой.

thing *n.* **1,** (object) вещь: *What do you call this thing?,* как называется эта вещь? *What is that thing lying there in the corner?,* что это лежит в углу?; что за штука в углу лежит? *I haven't a thing to wear,* мне нечего надеть. *I couldn't eat another thing,* я наелся досыта. **2,** *pl.* (clothes; belongings) вещи: *Put away your things,* уберите свои вещи. **3,** (matter; factor; circumstance) дело: *It's a strange thing,* странное дело! *Other things being equal,* при прочих равных условиях. *Then another thing happened,* потом произошло ещё кое-что. *It is one thing to..., it is another to...,* одно дело (+ *inf.*), другое дело (+ *inf.*). ♦*Often omitted in Russian: the same thing,* то же самое. *The first thing (that)...,* первое, что... *The main thing is to...,* самое главное, чтобы... *It's a good thing (that)...,* хорошо, что... *Only one thing bothers me,* меня беспокоит лишь одно. *Such a thing could not happen here,* такое не может случиться здесь. *It comes to the same thing,* это всё равно; это одно и то же. **4,** (act; task) дело: *I have a number of things to do,* у меня много дел; мне многое надо сделать. *You did the right thing,* вы правильно сделали. **5,** *pl.* (state of affairs) дела: *How are things?,* как дела? **6,** (creature) существо. *Poor thing!,* бедняжка! —**for one thing,** во-первых. —**a thing or two,** кое-что.

think *v.i.* **1,** (exercise one's mind) думать: *Let me think,* дайте мне подумать. *I'll think about it,* я подумаю об этом. *Just think!,* подумать только! *I don't think so,* не думаю; думаю, что нет. *I thought so; I thought as much,* я так и думал(а). *Without thinking, I turned on the light,* не подумав, я включил(а) свет. **2,** (reason) мыслить: *think logically,* логически мыслить. *The ability to think,* способность мыслить. —*v.t.* **1,** (have in mind; imagine): *Who would have* *thought it?*, кто бы мог подумать? *How could you think such a thing?*, как вы могли подумать такое?; как у вас могла появиться такая мысль? **2,** (believe; suppose) полагать; считать. *There is no reason to think that...*, нет оснований полагать, что... *I think he's wrong*, я считаю, что он неправ. *I think it unlikely*, я считаю это маловероятным. *Do as you think best*, делайте, как вы считаете лучше. *What do you think it means?*, как вы думаете, что это значит? *People will think you're crazy*, вас сочтут за сумасшедшего. **—come to think of it,** если подумать. **—think better of it,** одуматься. **—think nothing of,** *rendered by* ничего не стоит (+ *dat.*): *He thinks nothing of running five miles*, ему ничего не стоит пробежать пять миль. *He thinks nothing of hurting a person's feelings*, ему ничего не стоит обидеть человека. **—think of, 1,** (think about; have an opinion about; be concerned about) думать о: *We think of you constantly*, мы постоянно думаем о вас. *What do you think of him?*, что вы думаете о нём? *He is well thought of*, о нём хорошо отзываются. *He thinks a great deal of himself*, он много думает (*or* воображает) о себе. *She thinks only of herself*, она думает только о себе. **2,** (intend) думать; подумывать: *She is thinking of getting married*, она думает/подумывает выйти замуж. **3,** (recall) вспоминать; припоминать: *I can't think of his name*, не могу вспомнить/припомнить его имя. **4,** (figure out; come up with) придумывать: *What will he think of next?*, что он придумает завтра? *I couldn't think of anything to say*, я не мог (могла) придумать, что сказать. **5,** (choose) задумать: *think of a number*, задумать какое-нибудь число. **—think out** *or* **through,** продумывать. **—think over,** обдумывать. **—think twice** (before), подумать хорошенько (прежде чем...). **—think up, 1,** (devise) придумывать. **2,** (concoct) выдумывать.

thinkable *adj.* мыслимый.

thinker *n.* мыслитель.

thinking *adj.* мыслящий. **—***n.* мышление. *Way of thinking*, образ мышления. *To my way of thinking*, по моему мнению; на мой взгляд. *Revolution in thinking*, революция в умах.

think tank исследовательский центр.

thinly *adv.* тонко: *thinly sliced bread*, тонко нарезанные ломтики хлеба. *Thinly veiled threat*, едва скрываемая угроза.

thinner *n.* разбавитель: *paint thinner*, разбавитель красок.

thinness *n.* тонкость; худоба.

thin-skinned *adj.* **1,** (having a thin skin) тонкокожий. **2,** (sensitive) обидчивый; чувствительный.

third *adj.* третий. *The third world*, третий мир. **—***n.* **1,** (fraction) треть: *two-thirds*, две трети. *The job is only one-third done*, работа сделана только на треть. *By a two-thirds vote*, большинством в две трети голосов. **2,** *music* терция. **—in the third place,** в-третьих.

third-class *adv.* третьим классом: *travel third-class*, ехать третьим классом.

third degree допрос с пристрастием.

third-rate *adj.* третьесортный; третьестепенный.

thirst *n.* жажда. **—***v.i.* [*usu.* **thirst for**] жаждать (+ *gen.*). *Be thirsting for battle*, рваться в бой.

thirsty *adj.* жаждущий. *I am thirsty*, я хочу пить.

thirteen *n.* & *adj.* тринадцать. **—thirteenth,** *adj.* тринадцатый.

thirty *n.* & *adj.* тридцать. **—thirtieth,** *adj.* тридцатый.

this *adj.* этот: *this house*, этот дом; *this book*, эта книга; *this place*, это место; *this one*, этот; *this time*, на этот раз; *this week*, на этой неделе; *this month*, в этом месяце; *this year*, в этом году; *this minute*, сию минуту; *this morning*, сегодня утром; *this Wednesday*, в эту среду. **—***dem. pron.* это: *What does this mean?*, что это значит? *This is the last time*, это — последний раз. *What floor is this?*, какой это этаж? *Whose glove is this?*, чья это перчатка? **—***adv.* так: *this quiet*, так тихо; *this soon*, так скоро. **—like this,** так. **—this and that,** то и сё; то да сё. *Talk about this and that*, поговорить о том, о сём. **—this is,** это: *This is my sister*, это моя сестра. **—this is how, where,** *etc.*, вот как; вот где, *etc.*

thistle *n.* чертополох.

thither *adv.* туда.

thong *n.* **1,** (strap) ремень. **2,** (lash of a whip) плеть.

thoracic *adj.* грудной. **—thoracic duct,** грудной проток.

thorax *n.* грудная клетка.

thorium *n.* торий.

thorn *n.* шип; колючка. **—thorn in one's flesh** (*or* **side**), бельмо на глазу.

thorn apple дурман.

thorny *adj.* **1,** (full of thorns) колючий. **2,** *fig.* (full of pitfalls) тернистый: *thorny path*, тернистый путь. **3,** *fig.* (controversial) спорный: *thorny question*, спорный вопрос.

thorough *adj.* **1,** (painstaking; complete) тщательный; основательный; доскональный. *A thorough analysis/examination of...*, тщательный анализ/осмотр (+ *gen.*). *Thorough knowledge of a subject*, основательное знание предмета. **2,** (utter; out-and-out) совершенный; отъявленный.

thoroughbred *adj.* чистокровный; породистый. **—***n.* чистокровная/породистая лошадь.

thoroughfare *n.* **1,** (main road) магистраль. **2,** (passage) проезд. *No thoroughfare*, нет проезда.

thoroughgoing *adj.* = **thorough.**

thoroughly *adv.* **1,** (carefully) тщательно; основательно. *Examine a patient thoroughly* тщательно осматривать больного. **2,** (completely) совершенно. *We were thoroughly trounced*, мы были здорово разбиты.

thoroughness *n.* тщательность; основательность; доскональность.

those *dem. adj.* & *pron.* те: *those buildings*, те здания. *Those wishing to go*, те, кто желает идти. *Those are my children*, это мои дети. *Those were my children*, то были мои дети. *I'll take one of those*, я возьму один из этих (вон там).

thou *pers. pron., archaic* ты. *Thou shalt not kill,* не убий.

though *conj.* **1,** (in spite of the fact that) хотя́: *though it is late,* хотя́ уже́ по́здно. *I am against the resolution, though I admit that...,* я про́тив резолю́ции, но признаю́, что...; хотя́ я про́тив резолю́ции, признаю́, что... **2,** (while) хотя́ и; хоть и: *Our house, though small, is very cozy,* наш дом, хотя́/хоть и небольшо́й, но о́чень ую́тный. —*adv.* всё же; всё-таки; впро́чем. *Do as you like, though,* впро́чем, де́лайте как хоти́те. —**as though,** бу́дто; как бу́дто; сло́вно. —**even though,** *see* **even.**

thought *n.* **1,** (idea) мысль. *At the thought of,* при мы́сли о. *The thought of his leaving made her sad,* мысль о его́ отъе́зде опеча́лила её. **2,** (thinking) мышле́ние. *Train of thought,* ход мы́слей. **3,** (reflection; meditation) размышле́ние; разду́мье. *Deep in thought,* в глубо́ком разду́мье. *Lost in thought,* погружён в размышле́ния. *After some thought,* по́сле не́которого разду́мья. **4,** (intention) наме́рение. *Have no thought of,* отню́дь не собира́ться (+ *inf.*). *She has no thought of getting married,* она́ и не ду́мает выходи́ть за́муж; у неё в по́мыслах нет выходи́ть за́муж. —**give thought to,** обду́мывать. *Give a lot of thought to,* мно́го ду́мать над. *See also* **second thought.**

thoughtful *adj.* **1,** (pensive) заду́мчивый; вду́мчивый. **2,** (considerate) забо́тливый; внима́тельный.

thoughtfulness *n.* забо́тливость; внима́тельность.

thoughtless *adj.* **1,** (ill-considered) необду́манный; безду́мный. **2,** (inconsiderate) невнима́тельный.

thoughtlessness *n.* недомы́слие.

thousand *n. & adj.* ты́сяча.

thousandfold *adj.* тысячекра́тный. —*adv.* в ты́сячу раз.

thousandth *adj.* ты́сячный. —*n.* **1,** (thousandth part) ты́сячная часть. **2,** (fraction) ты́сячная: *one thousandth,* одна́ ты́сячная.

Thracian *adj.* фраки́йский.

thrall *n.* **1,** (slave) раб. **2,** *fig.* (complete absorption): *be in the thrall of,* быть во вла́сти (+ *gen.*).

thrash *v.t.* поро́ть; колоти́ть. —*v.i.* [*usu.* **thrash about**] мета́ться; би́ться; бара́хтаться; трепыха́ться. —**thrash out,** подро́бно обсужда́ть.

thrashing *n.* трёпка; взбу́чка; по́рка.

thread *n.* **1,** (thin cord; fiber) ни́тка. **2,** (spiral ridge of a screw) наре́зка; резьба́. **3,** *fig.* (sequence) нить: *lose the thread of the conversation,* потеря́ть нить разгово́ра. —*v.t.* **1,** (pass through the eye of): *thread a needle,* продева́ть *or* вдева́ть ни́тку в иго́лку. **2,** (string) нани́зывать. **3,** (cut grooves in, as a screw) нареза́ть. **4,** *in* **thread one's way,** пробира́ться (сквозь). —**hang by a thread, 1,** (of a button) висе́ть *or* держа́ться на ни́точке. **2,** *fig.* (hang precariously in the balance) висе́ть на волоске́.

threadbare *adj.* потёртый; потрёпанный; изно́шенный.

threat *n.* угро́за. *The threat of war,* угро́за войны́. *A threat to peace,* угро́за ми́ру. *A threat to life,* угро́за для жи́зни. *He is always making threats,* он всегда́ угрожа́ет.

threaten *v.t.* грози́ть; угрожа́ть. *Don't threaten me!,* вы мне не грози́те! *Threaten to resign,* грози́ть (*or* грози́ться) уйти́ в отста́вку. *Threaten someone with a knife,* угрожа́ть кому́-нибудь ножо́м. *Threaten the very existence of,* грози́ть са́мому существова́нию (+ *gen.*). *They are threatened with extinction,* им грози́т/угрожа́ет вымира́ние.

threatening *adj.* угрожа́ющий: *threatening gesture,* угрожа́ющий жест. *Threatening weather,* мра́чная пого́да.

three *adj.* три: *three times,* три ра́за. *Three children,* тро́е дете́й. *Sleep three to a room,* ночева́ть по́ трое в ко́мнате. —*n.* **1,** (cardinal number) три. **2,** (written number; school grade) тро́йка. **3,** *cards* тро́йка.

three-colored *adj.* трёхцве́тный.

three-dimensional *adj.* трёхме́рный; (*optics; photog.*) объёмный.

threefold *adj.* тройно́й; троя́кий; троекра́тный; трёхкра́тный. *A threefold increase,* трёхкра́тное увеличе́ние. —*adv.* втро́е; втройне́.

three hundred три́ста. —**three-hundredth,** *adj.* трёхсо́тый.

three-legged *adj.* трено́гий.

three-quarter time трёхдо́льный разме́р.

three-room *adj.* трёхко́мнатный.

three-sided *adj.* трёхсторо́нний.

three-story *adj.* трёхэта́жный.

three-time *adj.* троекра́тный: *three-time champion,* троекра́тный чемпио́н.

three-way *adj.* тройно́й; трёхсторо́нний: *three-way exchange,* тройно́й/трёхсторо́нний обме́н.

three-wheel *adj.* трёхколёсный. *Also,* **three-wheeled.**

thresh *v.t.* молоти́ть.

thresher *n.* **1,** (one who threshes) молоти́льщик. **2,** (threshing machine) молоти́лка. **3,** (variety of shark) морска́я лиси́ца.

threshing *n.* молотьба́. *Threshing floor,* гумно́; ток.

threshold *n.* поро́г. *At the threshold of a new era,* на поро́ге но́вой эпо́хи.

thrice *adv.* три́жды.

thrift *n.* бережли́вость; расчётливость; эконо́мность.

thrifty *adj.* бережли́вый; расчётливый; эконо́мный; хозя́йственный.

thrill *v.t.* захва́тывать: *thrill the audience,* захва́тывать аудито́рию. *We were thrilled to hear the news,* мы бы́ли в восто́рге от но́вости. —*n.* о́строе ощуще́ние.

thriller *n.* три́ллер.

thrilling *adj.* захва́тывающий.

thrive *v.i.* процвета́ть.

throat *n.* го́рло. *Clear one's throat,* отка́шливаться. *Cut someone's throat,* перере́зать го́рло (+ *dat.*). —**cut one's own throat,** рыть самому́ себе́ я́му. —**jump down someone's throat,** набра́сываться на кого́-нибудь.

throaty *adj.* горлово́й; горта́нный.

throb *v.i.* си́льно би́ться; стуча́ть; пульси́ровать. *Throbbing pain,* ко́лющая боль. *My temples are throbbing,* у меня́ стучи́т в виска́х. —*n.* бие́ние; стук; пульса́ция.

throe *n.*, *usu. pl.* му́ки. *Throes of death*, (предсме́ртная) аго́ния; предсме́ртные су́дороги.

thrombosis *n.* тромбо́з.

throne *n.* престо́л; трон. —*adj.* тро́нный: *throne room*, тро́нный зал.

throng *n.* толпа́. —*v.i.* толпи́ться; стека́ться. —*v.t.* заполня́ть; запру́живать: *People thronged the square*, лю́ди запо́лнили/запруди́ли пло́щадь.

throttle *n.* дро́ссель. —*v.t.* души́ть.

through *prep.* **1,** (in and out of) че́рез; сквозь: *go through a tunnel*, е́хать че́рез тунне́ль; *make one's way through a crowd*, пробира́ться сквозь толпу́. *Fall through the ice*, провали́ться под лёд. *Breathe through one's mouth*, дыша́ть ртом. *The bullet went right through him*, пу́ля прошла́ навы́лет. ◆*With certain nouns*, в: *fit through the door*, проходи́ть в дверь; *climb through a window*, лезть в окно́; *look through a telescope*, смотре́ть в телеско́п; *speak through one's nose*, говори́ть в нос. **2,** (in the midst of) по: *walk through the mud*, идти́ по гря́зи; *fly through the air*, лете́ть по во́здуху. **3,** (to various places in) по: *travel through France*, е́здить по Фра́нции. **4,** (up to and including) по (+ *acc.*): *from May through September*, с ма́я по сентя́брь. *I'm staying through Sunday*, я бу́ду здесь по воскресе́нье. **5,** [*usu.* **all through**] (throughout) в тече́ние всего́: *all through dinner*, в тече́ние всего́ обе́да. *All through the night*, всю ночь напролёт. **6,** (because of) по: *through no fault of mine*, не по мое́й вине́. **7,** (through the medium of) че́рез: *speak through an interpreter*, говори́ть че́рез перево́дчика. **8,** (by means of) путём; посре́дством. *Achieve one's goals through revolution*, дости́гнуть це́лей путём револю́ции. ◆*Often with the prefix* про-: *look through a report*, просмотре́ть докла́д; *go through a red light*, прое́хать на кра́сный свет. *Pass through three stages of development*, проходи́ть три ста́дии разви́тия. *Less commonly*, пере-: *leaf through a book*, перели́стывать кни́гу; *live through a crisis*, пережи́ть кри́зис. —*adj.* **1,** (direct) прямо́й: *through train*, прямо́й по́езд. *Through flight*, беспереса́дочный полёт. **2,** (finished): *Are you through?*, вы зако́нчили? *Are you through with the hammer?*, вам бо́льше не ну́жен молото́к? —*adv.* **1,** (in space) насквозь: *soaked through and through насквозь*. *Let him through*, пропусти́те его́. **2,** (in time) напролёт: *the whole night through*, всю ночь напролёт. —**through and through, 1,** (thoroughly; throughout) насквозь: *soaked through and through*, промо́кший насквозь. **2,** (completely; in every respect) соверше́нно; до конца́.

throughout *prep.* **1,** (in every part of) по всему́; по всей (+ *dat.*): *throughout the country*, по всей стране́. **2,** (from the beginning to the end of) в тече́ние всего́/всей (+ *gen.*); в продолже́ние всего́/всей (+ *gen.*); на протяже́нии всего́/всей (+ *gen.*). —*adv.* повсю́ду; во всех отноше́ниях.

throw *v.t.* **1,** (toss) броса́ть; кида́ть. *Throw the ball to someone*, бро́сить мяч (+ *dat.*). *Throw a snowball at someone*, бро́сить снежко́м в (+ *acc.*). *Throw stones at someone*, броса́ть *or* забра́сывать (+ *acc.*) кам-

ня́ми. *Throw snowballs at each other*, броса́ть снежки́ (*or* снежка́ми) друг в дру́га. *Throw a stone through the window*, бро́сить *or* пусти́ть ка́мень (*or* ка́мнем) в окно́. *Throw something out the window*, вы́бросить что́-нибудь за окно́. *Throw someone into prison*, бро́сить кого́-нибудь в тюрьму́. *Throw troops into battle*, броса́ть войска́ в бой. **2,** *fol. by* **oneself** (lunge) бро́ситься; набро́ситься. *Throw oneself at*, набро́ситься на (+ *acc.*). *Throw oneself into someone's arms*, бро́ситься в чьи-нибудь объя́тия. **3,** (put on; lay over) набро́сить; наки́нуть: *throw a shawl over one's shoulders*, набро́сить/наки́нуть шаль на пле́чи. **4,** (unseat, as a rider) сбра́сывать. **5,** (put into a certain condition) приводи́ть: *throw into confusion*, приводи́ть в замеша́тельство. **6,** *colloq.* (give, as a big party) устра́ивать; задава́ть. —*v.i.* броса́ть; кида́ть. —*n.* **1,** (single act) бросо́к. **2,** (general act) мета́ние: *discus throw*, мета́ние ди́ска. —**throw away, 1,** (discard) выбра́сывать. **2,** (squander) растра́чивать. **3,** (fail to exploit, as an opportunity) упуска́ть. —**throw back,** отбра́сывать; отки́дывать. *Throw back one's head*, отки́нуть *or* заки́нуть *or* запроки́нуть го́лову. *Throw back the enemy*, отбро́сить врага́. —**throw off, 1,** (cast off) сбра́сывать: *throw off the blankets*, сбра́сывать одея́ла. **2,** (confuse; disconcert) сбива́ть: *I was counting and you threw me off*, я счита́л(а), а вы меня́ сби́ли. *Throw someone off the trail*, сбива́ть кого́-нибудь со сле́да. *Throw someone off balance*, выводи́ть кого́-нибудь из равнове́сия. **3,** (shake off; elude) отрыва́ться от. **4,** (emit) испуска́ть. —**throw open,** распа́хивать. —**throw out, 1,** (discard) выбра́сывать. **2,** (evict; eject) выгоня́ть. **3,** *Throw out of work*, уво́лить с рабо́ты. —**throw up, 1,** (erect) стро́ить; возводи́ть: *throw up barricades*, стро́ить/ возводи́ть баррика́ды. *Throw up a bridge*, стро́ить мост. **2,** (vomit) рвать (*impers.*): *He threw up*, его́ вы́рвало. **3,** *Throw up one's hands*, развести́ *or* всплесну́ть рука́ми.

throwaway *adj.* бро́совый.

thrower *n.* мета́тель.

throw-weight *n.* забра́сываемый вес.

thru *prep.*, *adj. & adv.* = **through.**

thrush *n.* **1,** (bird) дрозд. **2,** (disease) моло́чница.

thrust *v.t.* **1,** (push forcibly) сова́ть; засо́вывать. **2,** (plunge, as a dagger) вонза́ть. —*n.* **1,** (shove) толчо́к. **2,** (lunge) вы́пад. **3,** (of an engine, propeller, etc.) тя́га. **4,** *mil.* уда́р.

thruway *n.* автостра́да.

thud *n.* глухо́й звук.

thug *n.* громи́ла; моло́дчик; банди́т.

thulium *n.* ту́лий.

thumb *n.* большо́й па́лец. —*v.t.* **1,** (soil by handling) захва́тывать (*pfv.* захвата́ть). **2,** *fol. by* **through** (leaf through) перели́стывать. **3,** *in* **thumb a ride,** *colloq.* «голосова́ть» на доро́ге. —**he is all thumbs,** у него́ всё из рук ва́лится. —**thumb one's nose at,** показа́ть нос (+ *dat.*). —**turn thumbs down on,** реши́тельно отклоня́ть. —**under the thumb of,** под башмако́м *or* под каблуко́м у.

thumbnail *n.* ноготь большого пальца. —**thumbnail sketch,** краткое описание.

thumbscrew *n.* **1,** (screw turned by hand) барашек. **2,** (instrument of torture) тиски для больших пальцев.

thumbtack *n.* кнопка.

thump *n.* тяжёлый удар; тумак. —*v.t.* колотить. —*v.i.* колотиться: *My heart was thumping,* у меня сердце колотилось.

thunder *n.* гром. —*v.i.* **1,** (produce thunder; make a sound like thunder) греметь. *It is thundering,* гром гремит. *The applause thundered in our ears,* аплодисменты гремели в наших ушах. **2,** (move with a loud noise) грохотать: *thunder down the highway,* грохотать по шоссе.

thunderbolt *n.* удар молнии.

thunderclap *n.* удар грома.

thundercloud *n.* грозовая туча.

thunderous *adj.* громовой. *Thunderous applause,* бурные аплодисменты.

thundershower *n.* ливень.

thunderstorm *n.* гроза.

thunderstruck *adj.* как громом поражённый.

Thursday *n.* четверг.

thus *adv.* **1,** (in this manner) так; таким образом. **2,** (hence) так; поэтому. **3,** (thereby) тем самым. —**thus far,** пока что; пока ещё.

thwart *v.t.* расстраивать; срывать.

thy *poss. adj., archaic* твой.

thyme *n.* тимьян; чабрец.

thymus *n.* зобная железа.

thyroid *n.* [*also,* **thyroid gland**] щитовидная железа. —*adj.* щитовидный.

ti *n., music* си.

tiara *n.* тиара.

Tibetan *adj.* тибетский. —*n.* тибетский язык.

tibia *n.* большая берцовая кость.

tic *n.* тик: *nervous tic,* нервный тик.

tick *n.* **1,** (sound) тиканье. **2,** (parasite) клещ. **3,** (mark) птичка; галочка. —*v.i.* тикать. —*v.t.* [*usu.* **tick off**] **1,** (check off) отмечать птичкой/галочкой. **2,** (enumerate) перечислять. **3,** *slang* (anger; annoy) разозлить.

ticker *n.* тиккер.

ticket *n.* **1,** (token of admission) билет: *plane ticket,* билет на самолёт; *theater tickets,* билеты в театр. *Tickets to a show/match,* билеты на спектакль/матч. **2,** (check; receipt) номерок; квитанция. *Pawn ticket,* залоговая квитанция. *Lottery ticket,* лотерейный билет. **3,** (label; tag) этикетка; ярлык. **4,** (notification of a violation) штраф. *Issue a ticket to someone,* выписать кому-нибудь квитанцию о штрафе. **5,** (electoral slate) список кандидатов (какой-нибудь партии). —*v.t.* приклеивать этикетку *or* ярлык к. —**ticket collector,** билетёр; контролёр. —**ticket office; ticket window,** билетная касса.

ticking *n.* **1,** (sound) тиканье. **2,** (material) тик.

tickle *v.t. & i.* щекотать: *Don't tickle!,* не щекочи! *My throat tickles,* у меня в горле щекочет *or* першит. —*n.* щекотка; щекотание. —**be tickled to death,** захлёбываться от удовольствия.

ticklish *adj.* **1,** (sensitive to tickling): *be ticklish,* бояться щекотки. **2,** (delicate; tricky) щекотливый. —**ticklishness,** *n.* щекотливость.

tick-tack-toe *n.* (игра в) крестики и нолики.

tidal *adj.* приливный. —**tidal wave,** приливная волна; волна прилива.

tidbit *also,* **titbit** *n.* лакомый кусочек.

tiddlywinks *also,* **tiddledywinks** *n.* блошки.

tide *n.* **1,** (rise and fall of waters) приливы и отливы. *Flood tide,* прилив. *Ebb tide,* отлив. *High tide,* высшая точка прилива. *Low tide,* низшая точка отлива. *The tide is in/out,* сейчас прилив/отлив. **2,** (drift of events) дела; ход событий. *The tide has turned,* дела приняли иной оборот. *Turn the tide,* изменить ход событий. *Go against the tide,* идти против течения. —*v.t.* [*usu.* **tide over**] хватать: *This will tide us over till spring,* этого нам хватит до весны.

tidewater *n.* приливная вода.

tidiness *n.* опрятность; аккуратность.

tidings *n.pl.* вести; новости; известия.

tidy *adj.* **1,** (neat) опрятный; аккуратный. **2,** *colloq.* (considerable) порядочный; изрядный; кругленький. —*v.t.* [*usu.* **tidy up**] убирать; прибирать; приводить в порядок.

tie *v.t.* **1,** (fasten) завязывать: *tie one's shoelaces,* завязывать шнурки. *Tie one's shoes,* шнуровать ботинки. *Tie one's tie,* повязывать галстук. *Tie a knot,* завязывать узел. *Tie a horse to a post,* привязать лошадь к столбу. *Tie a rope around something,* обвязать что-нибудь верёвкой. *Tie someone's hands behind his back,* связать кому-нибудь руки за спиной. *Tie someone's hands* (*fig.*), связать кому-нибудь руки. **2,** *fol. by* **to** (confine; restrict) привязывать (к): *She is tied to the kitchen,* она привязана к кухне. **3,** (link) связывать: *closely tied to,* тесно связанный с. **4,** *sports* сыграть вничью с; сделать ничью с. *Tie the score,* сравнять счёт. *The score is tied,* счёт равный; счёт ничейный. *Tie a record,* повторять рекорд. —*v.i.* **1,** (be tied) завязываться: *The apron ties in front,* передник завязывается спереди. **2,** *sports: tie for first place,* поделить первое и второе место. —*n.* **1,** (necktie) галстук. **2,** (link; connection) связь. *Trade ties,* торговые связи. *Ties to the motherland,* связь с родиной. *Ties of friendship,* узы дружбы. **3,** (draw; stalemate) ничья: *end in a tie,* кончиться ничьей. **4,** *R.R.* шпала. —**tie down, 1,** *literally* привязывать. **2,** (restrict; confine) связывать: *tied down to a schedule,* связан расписанием. —**tie up, 1,** (bind) связывать: *tie up a watchman,* связывать сторожа. *Tie up hand and foot,* связать по рукам и ногам. **2,** (tie securely) привязывать: *The dog is tied up,* собака привязана. **3,** (tie with a string) перевязывать. **4,** (moor to a dock) причаливать; швартовать. **5,** (obstruct; halt) тормозить; приостанавливать: *tie up traffic,* тормозить/приостанавливать уличное движение. **6,** (keep busy) занимать: *I'm tied up right now,* я сейчас занят (занята).

tiepin *n.* заколка. *Also,* **tie clasp.**

tier *n.* я́рус. —**tiered,** *adj.* я́русный.

tie-up *n.* **1,** (stoppage) остано́вка. **2,** (jam, as of traffic) зато́р (у́личного движе́ния); про́бка.

tiff *n.* размо́лвка; перебра́нка.

tiger *n.* тигр. —*adj.* тигро́вый: *tiger skin,* тигро́вая шку́ра.

tiger lily тигро́вая ли́лия.

tight *adj.* **1,** (taut; fast) туго́й: *tight spring,* туга́я пружи́на. *Tight grip,* кре́пкая хва́тка. **2,** (fitting closely) те́сный; у́зкий. *These shoes are tight,* э́ти ту́фли мне узки́; э́ти ту́фли жмут. **3,** (crowded; cramped) те́сный: *tight quarters,* те́сное помеще́ние. **4,** (strict; rigid) стро́гий: *tight control,* стро́гий контро́ль. **5,** (affording little leeway) жёсткий. *Tight schedule,* жёсткий *or* напряжённый гра́фик. **6,** (difficult) пи́ковый: *a tight spot,* пи́ковое положе́ние. **7,** *colloq.* (stingy) скупо́й. **8,** *slang* (drunk) подвы́пивший. —*adv.* **1,** (taut) ту́го: *tie the knot tight,* ту́го завяза́ть у́зел. **2,** (firmly) кре́пко: *Hold tight!,* держи́тесь кре́пко! **3,** (with no openings) на́глухо; пло́тно. *Sealed up tight,* на́глухо закры́т. *The windows were shut tight,* о́кна бы́ли на́глухо *or* пло́тно закры́ты. —**sit tight,** выжида́ть. —**sleep tight!,** спи́те кре́пко! спи́те споко́йно!

tighten *v.t.* **1,** (pull tight; make taut) натя́гивать; затя́гивать; стя́гивать. *Tighten a rope/spring,* натя́гивать верёвку/пружи́ну. *Tighten a knot,* затя́гивать *or* стя́гивать у́зел. *Tighten the brakes,* подтя́гивать тормоза́. *Tighten the strings on a violin,* натя́гивать стру́ны на скри́пке. *Tighten the noose around someone's neck,* затя́гивать пе́тлю на ше́е у кого́-нибудь. **2,** (turn to a tight position) зави́нчивать; завёртывать: *tighten a screw,* зави́нчивать/завёртывать га́йку. *Tighten a faucet,* завёртывать кран. **3,** (compress; close) сжима́ть; смыка́ть: *tighten the ring around,* сжима́ть/смыка́ть кольцо́ вокру́г. *Tighten one's grip,* сжима́ть кре́пче. **4,** *fig.* (make more rigorous) уси́ливать; укрепля́ть; ужесточа́ть: *tighten control,* уси́ливать *or* ужесточа́ть контро́ль; *tighten the rules,* ужесточа́ть пра́вила; *tighten discipline,* уси́ливать *or* укрепля́ть дисципли́ну. *Tighten security,* принима́ть повы́шенные ме́ры безопа́сности. —*v.i.* **1,** (become taut) натя́гиваться. **2,** (tense up) напряга́ться. **3,** (become smaller; close in) сжима́ться; смыка́ться. —**tighten one's belt, 1,** *literally* затяну́ться по́ясом. **2,** (be more frugal) класть зу́бы на по́лку. —**tighten the screws,** зави́нчивать га́йки.

tight-fisted *adj.* скупо́й; скаре́дный; прижи́мистый.

tight-fitting *adj.* те́сный; в обтя́жку.

tight-lipped *adj.* за́мкнутый.

tightly *adv.* **1,** (tight) ту́го. **2,** (firmly) кре́пко. **3,** (so as to leave no openings) на́глухо; пло́тно. *Seal up tightly,* на́глухо заде́лать. *Close the door tightly,* пло́тно закры́ть дверь.

tightness *n.* теснота́. *I feel a tightness in my chest,* мне тесни́т грудь.

tightrope *n.* кана́т. *Walk a tightrope,* ходи́ть по кана́ту. —**tightrope walker,** канатохо́дец; эквилибри́ст; балансёр.

tights *n.pl.* трико́; рейту́зы.

tightwad *n.. slang* скопидо́м; скупердя́й.

tigress *n.* тигри́ца.

tilde *n.* ти́льда.

tile *n.* **1,** (glazed slab) ка́фель; изразе́ц. **2,** (roof tile) черепи́ца; (floor tile) пли́тка. —*v.t.* крыть черепи́цей.

tiled *adj.* (of a stove) ка́фельный; изразцо́вый; (of a roof) черепи́чный; (of a floor) пли́точный.

till *prep.* до: *till now,* до сих пор; *till then,* до э́того вре́мени; до тех пор; *till tomorrow,* до за́втра. *From morning till night,* с утра́ до ве́чера. *Till then!,* пока́! *Till we meet again!,* до сле́дующей встре́чи. —*conj.* пока́ не: *till he arrives,* пока́ он не придёт. *She is not coming till Sunday,* она́ придёт то́лько в воскресе́нье. —*n.* (cash box) ка́сса. —*v.t.* обраба́тывать; возде́лывать: *till the soil,* обраба́тывать/возде́лывать зе́млю.

tillage *n.* обрабо́тка.

tiller *n.* земледе́лец.

tilt *v.t.* наклоня́ть: *tilt one's head to one side,* наклоня́ть го́лову на́бок. *Tilt a chair backward,* наклоня́ть стул наза́д. —*v.i.* **1,** (slant) наклоня́ться. **2,** *fol. by* **over** (tip over) опроки́дываться. —*n.* **1,** (slant) накло́н. **2,** (joust) поеди́нок. —**full tilt,** по́лным хо́дом; во весь опо́р.

timber *n.* лес; лесоматериа́л; древеси́на. —**timber line,** грани́ца распростране́ния ле́са.

timbre *n.* тембр.

time *n.* **1,** (general term) вре́мя: *all the time,* всё вре́мя; *at the time,* в то вре́мя; *any time,* в любо́е вре́мя. *Dinner time,* обе́денное вре́мя. *7:00 Moscow time,* семь часо́в по моско́вскому вре́мени. *I have no time,* у меня́ нет вре́мени; мне не́когда. **2,** (occasion) раз: *three times,* три ра́за; *this time,* на э́тот раз. **3,** (period; interval) срок: *in a short time,* в коро́ткий срок. **4,** *often pl.* (historical period or conditions) времена́: *hard times,* тяжёлые времена́. *In Dante's time,* во времена́ Да́нте. *Since ancient times,* с дре́вних времён. *Times have changed,* времена́ измени́лись. **5,** *music* такт: *in time to the music,* в такт му́зыке. *Three-quarter time,* трёхдо́льный разме́р. **6,** *pl.,* in multiplication, rendered by два́жды, три́жды, пя́тью, ше́стью, *etc.: Three times seven is twenty-one,* три́жды семь — два́дцать оди́н. *Three times as large as,* в три ра́за бо́льше (+ *gen.*). —*v.t.* **1,** (set for a certain time) приуро́чивать: *time one's visit so as to fall on her birthday,* приуро́чить визи́т к её дню рожде́ния. **2,** (measure the time of) хронометри́ровать: *time a race,* хронометри́ровать забе́г. —**ahead of time,** заблаговре́менно. —**at no time,** никогда́; ни ра́зу. —**at one time, 1,** (simultaneously) одновре́менно; ра́зом. **2,** (at a certain time in the past) одно́ вре́мя. —**at the same time, 1,** (simultaneously) в то же (са́мое) вре́мя; одновре́менно. **2,** (besides; however) вме́сте с тем. *At the same time he is very modest,* вме́сте с тем он о́чень скро́мный. *At the same time I must warn you that...,* вме́сте с тем я до́лжен предупреди́ть вас, что... —**at times,** иногда́; времена́ми. —**(at) what time?,** в кото́ром часу́?; во ско́лько? *What time does the plane leave?*, во ско́лько вылета́ет самолёт? —**do time,** *colloq.* отбыва́ть срок. —**for the time being,** пока́; до поры́ до вре́мени. —**from time to time,** вре́мя от вре́мени; по времена́м. —**have a good time,** хорошо́ провести́ вре́мя. —**in due time,** в своё вре́мя. —**in good time,** своевре́менно. —**in no time,** в два счёта. —**in one's time,** в своё вре́мя. *I have seen a lot in my time,* я мно́го повида́л(а) на своём веку́. —**in the course of time,** с тече́нием вре́мени. —**in time, 1,** (on time) во́время. *Be in time for the meeting,* приходи́ть во́время на собра́ние; успева́ть на собра́ние. **2,** (eventually) со вре́менем. —**it is time,** пора́: *It is time to go,* пора́ идти́. —**many a time,** мно́го раз. —**once upon a time,** одна́жды; жил-был. —**one at a time,** по одному́; поодино́чке. —**on time, 1,** (punctually; on schedule) во́время: *get there on time,* попа́сть туда́ во́время. *The train is on time,* по́езд идёт по расписа́нию. **2,** (on installment) в рассро́чку. —**over time,** со вре́менем: *wear out over time,* изна́шиваться со вре́менем. —**take one's time,** не спеши́ть; не торопи́ться. —**time after time; time and time again,** раз за ра́зом. —**what time is it?,** кото́рый тепе́рь час?; ско́лько вре́мени сейча́с?

time bomb бо́мба заме́дленного де́йствия.

time clock та́бельные часы́.

time-consuming *adj.* отнима́ющий мно́го вре́мени.

time exposure больша́я вы́держка.

time-honored *adj.* освящённый века́ми.

timekeeper *n.* **1,** (one who records the hours worked by employees) та́бельщик. **2,** *sports* хронометри́ст.

timeless *adj.* вневре́менный.

time limit преде́льный срок. *Overstep the time limit* (*in chess*), превыша́ть лими́т вре́мени.

timely *adj.* своевре́менный; уме́стный. —**timeliness,** *n.* своевре́менность; уме́стность.

time-out *n.* переры́в.

timepiece *n.* часы́; хроно́метр.

timer *n.* **1,** (timepiece) хроно́метр. **2,** (timekeeper) хронометри́ст.

time study хронометра́ж.

timetable *n.* расписа́ние; гра́фик.

time trouble *chess* цейтно́т.

time zone часово́й по́яс.

timid *adj.* ро́бкий; засте́нчивый; боязли́вый. —**timidity,** *n.* ро́бость; засте́нчивость. —**timidly,** *adv.* ро́бко.

timing *n.* расчёт вре́мени; синхрониза́ция. *Timing device,* часово́й механи́зм.

timorous *adj.* боязли́вый; пугли́вый.

timothy *n.,* *bot.* тимофе́евка. *Also,* **timothy grass.**

tin *n.* **1,** (metal) о́лово. **2,** (tin plate) жесть. **3,** [*also,* **tin can**] (container) ба́нка; жестя́нка. —*adj.* оловя́нный; жестяно́й.

tincture *n.* тинкту́ра; насто́йка.

tinder *n.* трут. —**tinderbox,** *n.* порохова́я бо́чка (*fig.*).

tine *n.* зубе́ц.

tin foil станио́ль.

tinge *n.* отте́нок; при́месь; налёт. —*v.t.* **1,** (tint) подкра́шивать. *Tinged with blue,* с голубова́тым отте́нком. **2,** (give a slight trace to) придава́ть отте́нок (+ *dat.*). *Her voice was tinged with sadness,* в её го́лосе чу́вствовался отте́нок гру́сти. *Admiration tinged with envy,* восхище́ние с при́месью за́висти.

tingle *v.i.* пощи́пывать (*impers.*): *My cheeks are tingling,* щёки у меня́ пощи́пывает. *Tingle with excitement,* трепета́ть от возбужде́ния.

tinker *n.* ме́дник. —*v.i.* (putter) вози́ться.

tinkle *v.i.* звя́кать. —*v.t.* звя́кать (+ *instr.*). —*n.* звя́канье.

tinny *adj.* оловя́нный. *Tinny sound,* металли́ческий звук.

tin plate жесть. —**tin-plate,** *v.t.* луди́ть. —**tin-plated,** *adj.* лужёный.

tinsel *n.* **1,** (thin strips of something shiny) блёстки. **2,** (something superficially showy) мишура́.

tinsmith *n.* луди́льщик; жестя́нщик.

tint *n.* отте́нок. —*v.t.* подкра́шивать. *Tinted glasses,* ды́мчатые очки́.

tintype *n.* ферроти́пия.

tiny *adj.* кро́хотный; кро́шечный; малю́сенький.

tip *n.* **1,** (point; end) ко́нчик. **2,** (piece attached to the end of something) наконе́чник. **3,** (gratuity) чаевы́е. *Give someone a tip,* дава́ть кому́-нибудь на чай. **4,** (piece of advice) сове́т. —*v.t.* **1,** (tilt) наклоня́ть. **2,** *fol. by* **over** (overturn) опроки́дывать. **3,** (give a gratuity to) дава́ть (+ *dat.*) на чай. **4,** *fol. by* **off** (notify; warn) сообща́ть; предупрежда́ть. —*v.i.* **1,** (tilt) наклоня́ться. **2,** *fol. by* **over** (overturn) опроки́дываться. —**it is on the tip of my tongue,** э́то ве́ртится у меня́ на языке́. —**tip one's hand,** раскры́ть свои́ ка́рты. —**tip one's hat,** приподнима́ть шля́пу.

tipoff *n.,* *colloq.* намёк; предупрежде́ние.

tipple *v.i.* выпива́ть. —**tippler,** *n.* пья́ница.

tipsy *adj.* подвы́пивший; под хмелько́м; навеселе́.

tiptoe *n.* цы́почки: *on tiptoe; on one's tiptoes,* на цы́почках; на цы́почки. —*v.i.* ходи́ть на цы́почках.

tiptop *adj.* отли́чный: *in tiptop shape,* в отли́чном состоя́нии.

tirade *n.* тира́да.

tire[1] *v.i.* **1,** (become weary) устава́ть; утомля́ться: *tire easily,* бы́стро устава́ть/утомля́ться. **2,** *fol. by* **of** (lose interest in) устава́ть (+ *inf.*). *I never tire of looking at...,* не могу́ насмотре́ться *or* налюбова́ться на (+ *acc.*). —*v.t.* утомля́ть.

tire[2] *also,* **tyre** *n.* ши́на; покры́шка.

tired *adj.* уста́лый. *I am tired,* я уста́л(а). *Get tired,* устава́ть. *I am tired of waiting,* я уста́л(а) ждать. *I am tired of doing the same thing,* мне надое́ло де́лать одно́ и то же.

tireless *adj.* неутоми́мый. —**tirelessly,** *adv.* не устава́я; без у́стали.

tiresome *adj.* **1,** (tiring) утоми́тельный. **2,** (annoying) надое́дливый.

tiring *adj.* утоми́тельный.

tissue *n.* **1,** (structural material) ткань: *nerve tissue,* не́рвная ткань. **2,** (piece of soft absorbent paper) бумага: *toilet tissue,* туалетная бумага. **3,** *fig.* (web, as of lies) сплетение; паутина (лжи). —**tissue paper,** папиросная бумага.

tit *n.* (titmouse) синица. —**tit for tat,** той же монетой.

titan *n.* титан. —**titanic,** *adj.* титанический.

titanium *n.* титан.

titbit *n.* = **tidbit.**

tithe *n.* десятина.

titillate *v.t.* щекотать: *titillate the senses,* щекотать чувства. *Titillating stories,* двусмысленные анекдоты. —**titillation,** *n.* щекотание; щекотка.

title *n.* **1,** (name, as of a book) заглавие; название. **2,** (designation of rank or profession) звание: *the title of full professor,* звание профессора. **3,** (designation of nobility) титул: *confer a title on,* присваивать титул (+ *dat.*). **4,** *law* право собственности. **5,** *sports* чемпионское звание. *The heavyweight title,* звание чемпиона по тяжёлому весу. **6,** (subtitle) титр. —*v.t.* озаглавливать. —**title page,** заглавный лист; титульный лист. —**title role,** заглавная роль.

titled *adj.* титулованный.

titmouse *n.* синица.

titter *v.i.* хихикать. —*n.* хихиканье.

tittle-tattle *n.* тары-бары.

titular *adj.* номинальный: *titular head of state,* номинальный глава государства.

TNT тол; тротил; тринитротолуол.

to *prep.* **1,** (indicating destination) в (+ *acc.*): *go to the store/theater,* идти в магазин/ в театр/; *go to London/ England,* ехать в Лондон/ в Англию/. *His visit to Moscow,* его визит в Москву. *Return a book to the library,* возвращать книгу в библиотеку. ♦*Before certain nouns,* на: *go to the post office,* идти на почту; *go to work,* ехать на работу; *fall to the ground,* упасть на землю; *travel to Cuba,* ехать на Кубу; *fly to the moon,* лететь на Луну; *bring goods to market,* приносить товары на рынок. ♦*Also after certain nouns,* на: *the road to Moscow,* дорога на Москву; *the train to Vienna,* поезд на Вену. **2,** (toward) к: *Come to me,* иди ко мне. *Walk to the river,* идти к реке. **3,** (as far as; till) до: *to the end of the street,* до конца улицы; *soaked to the skin,* промокший до костей; *to a certain extent,* до некоторой степени; *from four to six o'clock,* от четырёх до шести часов. *To this day,* по сей день. **4,** (so as to be firmly fixed to) к: *tie to a post,* привязать к столбу; *nail to the wall,* прибить к стене; *pin to the ropes,* прижать к канатам. **5,** *introducing the indirect object,* rendered by the dative case: *It seems to me,* мне кажется. *I gave the letter to him,* я дал ему письмо. *Return a wallet to its owner,* возвращать бумажник владельцу. **6,** *used to form the infinitive: to read,* читать; *to dance,* танцевать. *She offered to help,* она предложила помочь. *The order to retreat,* приказ об отступлении. *An operation to remove a bullet,* операция по удалению пули. *A plot to overthrow the government,* заговор с целью свержения правительства. *Establish a commission to investigate the accident,* создавать комиссию для расследова-

ния катастрофы. *You are to leave at once,* вы должны немедленно уйти. *You are not to do that again!,* вы не должны больше этого делать. *He was not to remain in the post for long,* в этой должности ему долго быть не пришлось. *I wish to be correctly understood,* хочу, чтобы меня поняли правильно. **7,** (in one's behavior toward) к: *He is very kind to her,* он очень добр к ней. *Polite to one's relatives,* вежлив со своими родственниками. **8,** (producing or resulting in) к: *to my surprise,* к моему удивлению. **9,** (belonging to) от: *the key to the apartment,* ключ от квартиры. *The door to the room,* дверь комнаты. *The entrance to the building,* вход в здание. **10,** *in toasts,* за (+ *acc.*): *To our hosts!,* за наших хозяев! *Drink to someone's health,* пить за чьё-нибудь здоровье. **11,** (to the accompaniment of) под (+ *acc.*): *dance to the music,* танцевать под музыку. **12,** *used in telling time: a quarter to three,* без четверти три. **13,** *with various nouns and verbs,* в: *introduction to physics,* введение в физику; *shift to the offensive,* переходить в наступление. **14,** *with various nouns and verbs,* на: *spring to one's feet,* вскочить на ноги; *tear to pieces,* разорвать на куски; *come to someone's aid,* прийти на помощь (+ *dat.*); *made to order,* сделанный на заказ; *from Russian to English,* с русского на английский. **15,** *in various constructions,* к: *face to face,* лицом к лицу; *deaf to our pleas,* глух к нашим просьбам; *come to an end,* приходить к концу; *sentence to death,* приговаривать к смертной казни. **16,** *in certain combinations,* для: *open to the public,* открыт для публики; *mean a great deal to,* много значить для; *be of interest to all,* представлять интерес для всех. *It's news to me,* это для меня новость. —**as to,** что касается. —**to and fro,** взад и вперёд.

toad *n.* жаба.

toadstool *n.* поганка.

toady *n.* подхалим. —*v.i.* подхалимничать (перед). —**toadyism,** *n.* подхалимство.

toast *n.* **1,** (toasted bread) поджаренный хлеб. **2,** (short speech preceding a drink in someone's honor) тост. —*v.t.* **1,** (brown) поджаривать. **2,** (pay tribute to) провозглашать тост за (+ *acc.*).

toaster *n.* тостер.

toastmaster *n.* тамада.

tobacco *n.* табак. —*adj.* табачный: *tobacco leaves,* табачные листья. —**tobacco grower,** табаковод. —**tobacco pouch,** кисет.

toboggan *n.* салазки. —*v.i.* кататься на салазках.

tocsin *n.* набат.

today *n. & adv.* сегодня. *What is today's date?,* какое сегодня число? *As of today,* на сегодняшний день. *Today's lesson,* сегодняшний урок.

toddle *v.i.* ковылять. —**toddler,** *n.* ребёнок, начинающий ходить.

toe *n.* **1,** (digit of the foot) палец ноги; палец на ноге. **2,** (tip of a stocking or shoe) носок. —**on one's toes,** начеку; настороже. —**toe the line** (*or* **mark**), **1,** *sports* встать на стартовую линию. **2,** (conform to the rules) ходить по струнке.

toenail *n.* ноготь на пальце ноги.

toffee *also,* **toffy** *n.* тянучка; ирис.

toga *n.* тога.

together *adv.* вместе: *go together,* идти вместе. *Tie together,* связывать. *Paste together,* склеивать. *Rub two sticks together,* тереть две палки друг о друга. —**together with,** вместе с.

toil *n.* (тяжёлый) труд. —*v.i.* трудиться. —**toiler,** *n.* труженик.

toilet *n.* **1,** (receptacle) унитаз. **2,** (lavatory) уборная; туалет. **3,** [*also,* **toilette**] (dressing; grooming) туалет. —*adj.* туалетный. —**toilet paper,** туалетная бумага. —**toilet seat,** стульчак. —**toilet water,** туалетная вода.

toiletries *n.pl.* туалетные принадлежности.

token *n.* **1,** (sign; symbol) знак; залог: *as a token of,* в знак *or* в залог (+ *gen.*). **2,** (keepsake) сувенир. **3,** (coin; counter) жетон. —*adj.* символический: *token payment,* символический взнос. —**by the same token,** равным образом.

tolerable *adj.* **1,** (endurable) терпимый; сносный. **2,** (passable) сносный; приличный. —**tolerably,** *adv.* [*also,* **tolerably well**] сносно.

tolerance *n.* **1,** (toleration) терпимость. *Religious tolerance,* религиозная терпимость. *Tolerance for/of other people's views,* терпимость к чужим взглядам. **2,** *mech.* допуск.

tolerant *adj.* терпимый. *Be tolerant of,* относиться терпимо к.

tolerate *v.t.* **1,** (bear; endure) терпеть: *tolerate pain,* терпеть боль. **2,** (allow; permit) терпеть; допускать. *Tolerate injustice,* допускать несправедливость. *I will not tolerate such behavior,* я не потерплю такого поведения. —**toleration,** *n.* терпимость.

toll *n.* **1,** (fee) сбор: *pay a toll,* платить сбор. *Toll collector,* сборщик платы. **2,** (peal of a bell) звон. **3,** (extent of losses) потери. *Death toll,* число погибших; число жертв. *The hurricane took a heavy toll of lives,* ураган унёс много человеческих жизней. —*adj.* платный: *toll bridge,* платный мост. *Toll call,* междугородный телефонный разговор. —*v.t.* звонить в (церковный колокол). —*v.i.* звонить: *for whom the bell tolls,* по ком звонит колокол. —**take its toll,** брать своё: *Time had taken its toll,* время брало своё.

tollgate *n.* застава (где взимается сбор).

toluene *n.* толуол.

tomahawk *n.* томагавк.

tomato *n.* помидор; томат. —*adj.* томатный: *tomato juice,* томатный сок. *Tomato paste,* томат-паста.

tomb *n.* гробница. —**Tomb of the Unknown Soldier,** могила Неизвестного солдата.

tomboy *n.* сорванец.

tombstone *n.* надгробный камень; надгробная плита; надгробие.

tomcat *n.* кот.

tome *n.* том.

tomfoolery *n.* **1,** (foolish behavior) дурачества. **2,** (nonsense) чепуха.

Tommy gun автомат.

tommyrot *n., slang* вздор; галиматья.

tomorrow *n. & adv.* завтра: *The meeting is scheduled for tomorrow,* собрание намечено на завтра. *Beginning tomorrow,* начиная с завтрашнего дня. —*adj.* [*usu.* **tomorrow's**] завтрашний: *tomorrow's date,* завтрашнее число. —**the day after tomorrow,** послезавтра. —**tomorrow morning,** завтра утром. —**tomorrow evening; tomorrow night,** завтра вечером.

tomtit *n.* синица.

tom-tom *n.* тамтам.

ton *n.* тонна.

tonal *adj.* тональный. —**tonality,** *n.* тональность.

tone *n.* **1,** (quality of sound or color) тон: *light tones,* светлые тона. *By his tone of voice,* то его тону. **2,** *physiol.* тонус: *muscle tone,* мышечный тонус. **3,** *fig.* (general tenor) тон: *set the tone,* задать тон. —*v.t.* **1,** *fol. by* **down** (moderate; soften) смягчать; тушевать. **2,** *fol. by* **up,** *physiol.* тонизировать.

tone poem симфоническая поэма.

tongs *n.pl.* щипцы; клещи.

tongue *n.* язык. *Loose tongue,* язык без костей. *Mother tongue,* родной язык. *Smoked tongue,* копчёный язык. *Tongue of a shoe,* язычок ботинка. *Tongues of flame,* языки пламени. —**hold one's tongue,** придержать язык; проглотить язык; держать язык за зубами. —**with tongue in cheek,** в шутку.

tongue-lashing *n.* нагоняй; разнос.

tongue-tie *n.* косноязычие. —*v.t.* связать язык (+ *dat.*). —**tongue-tied,** *adj.* косноязычный.

tongue twister скороговорка.

tonic *n.* **1,** (agent to increase body tone) тонизирующее средство. **2,** (for a drink) тоник: *gin and tonic,* джин с тоником. —*adj.* тонический.

tonight *n. & adv.* сегодня вечером.

tonnage *n.* тоннаж.

tonsil *n.* миндалина; миндалевидная железа; гланда.

tonsillectomy *n.* удаление миндалин.

tonsillitis *n.* воспаление миндалин; тонзиллит.

tonsorial *adj.* парикмахерский.

tonsure *n.* тонзура.

too *adv.* **1,** (also; as well) тоже; также. *I'm sorry too,* мне тоже жаль. **2,** (excessively) слишком: *too far,* слишком далеко. —**not too,** не очень: *not too clever,* не очень умён. —**only too,** только: *I will be only too happy to...,* я буду только рад (+ *inf.*). —**too bad,** *see* **bad.** —**too many,** слишком много. —**too much,** слишком много; слишком. *Have too much to drink,* выпить лишнего. *I ate too much,* я объелся. —**too much for,** не под силу (+ *dat.*).

tool *n.* **1,** (hand-held implement) инструмент; орудие: *carpenter's tools,* плотничные инструменты; *farm tools,* сельскохозяйственные орудия. **2,** (person manipulated by another) орудие; марионетка. *A tool in the hands of...,* орудие в руках (+ *gen.*). —*v.t.* **1,** (shape with a tool) обрабатывать. **2,** *fol. by* **up** (provide with tools) оборудовать инструментами. —*v.i.* [*usu.* **tool along**] (ride; drive) ехать; катиться.

—**toolbox,** *n.* я́щик для инструме́нтов. —**toolmaker,** *n.* инструмента́льщик.

toot *n.* гудо́к. —*v.t. & i.* гуде́ть.

tooth *n.* **1,** (in the mouth) зуб (*pl.* зу́бы). **2,** (projecting point, as of a saw) зуб (*pl.* зу́бья, зу́бьев); зубе́ц. —**armed to the teeth,** вооружённый до зубо́в. —**in the teeth of,** вопреки́; напереко́р. *In the teeth of the wind,* пря́мо про́тив ве́тра. —**show one's teeth,** пока́зывать ко́гти. —**tooth and nail,** изо всех сил; все́ми си́лами.

toothache *n.* зубна́я боль. *I have a toothache,* у меня́ боля́т зу́бы.

toothbrush *n.* зубна́я щётка.

toothed *adj.* зубча́тый.

toothless *adj.* беззу́бый.

toothpaste *n.* зубна́я па́ста.

toothpick *n.* зубочи́стка.

toothpowder *n.* зубно́й порошо́к.

toothy *adj.* зуба́стый.

top *n.* **1,** (highest part) верх; верху́шка; верши́на; маку́шка. *At the top of the stairs/hill/page,* на верху́ ле́стницы; на верши́не холма́; вверху́ страни́цы. *Climb to the very top,* забра́ться на са́мый верх. *From the top,* све́рху. **2,** (lid; cover) кры́шка. **3,** (toy) волчо́к. **4,** *pl.* (above-ground part of a plant) ботва́. —*adj.* **1,** (highest) ве́рхний: *on the top shelf,* на ве́рхней по́лке. **2,** (best) лу́чший; пе́рвый: *top pupil,* лу́чший/пе́рвый учени́к. —*v.t.* **1,** (be at the top of): *top the list,* стоя́ть пе́рвым в спи́ске. **2,** (place something on top of) покрыва́ть. *Top fruit with whipped cream,* покрыва́ть фру́кты взби́тыми сли́вками. **3,** (exceed; surpass) превыша́ть; превосходи́ть. *Top the previous record,* превыша́ть пре́жний реко́рд. **4,** *fol. by off* (climax) доверша́ть. —**at top speed,** во весь опо́р. —**blow one's top,** *colloq.* взорва́ться. —**from top to bottom,** све́рху до́низу. —**on top,** наверху́. *Come out on top,* прийти́ пе́рвым; взять верх. —**on top of, 1,** (on) на: *on top of the refrigerator,* на холоди́льнике. **2,** (in addition to) кро́ме; сверх. *On top of everything* (else), сверх всего́. **3,** (following upon) вслед за. **4,** (in control of) на высоте́ (+ *gen.*): *on top of the situation,* на высоте́ положе́ния. —**on top of the world,** *colloq.* на седьмо́м не́бе; на верху́ блаже́нства. —**sleep like a top,** спать как суро́к. —**to top it off,** в доверше́ние всего́.

topaz *n.* топа́з. —*adj.* топа́зовый.

topcoat *n.* пальто́.

topflight *adj.* первокла́ссный; превосхо́дный.

topgallant *n.* [*also,* **topgallant sail**] бра́мсель. —**topgallant mast,** брам-сте́ньга.

top hat цили́ндр.

topic *n.* те́ма; предме́т.

topical *adj.* **1,** (pert. to a topic) темати́ческий. **2,** (of current interest) актуа́льный.

topknot *n.* хохо́л.

topmast *n.* сте́ньга.

topnotch *adj., colloq.* первокла́ссный.

topography *n.* топогра́фия. —**topographer,** *n.* топо́граф. —**topographical,** *adj.* топографи́ческий.

topology *n.* тополо́гия.

topple *v.t.* **1,** (overturn) вали́ть; опроки́дывать. **2,** (overthrow) сверга́ть. —*v.i.* (с)вали́ться: *topple over a cliff,* свали́ться со скалы́; *topple into the water,* свали́ться в во́ду. —**topple over,** опроки́дываться.

topsail *n.* то́псель; ма́рсель.

top-secret *adj.* соверше́нно секре́тный.

topside *adv.* на па́лубе. —**topsides,** *n.pl.* надво́дная часть.

topsoil *n.* ве́рхний слой по́чвы; по́чвенный покро́в.

topsy-turvy *adv.* вверх дном; ши́ворот-навы́ворот.

toque *n.* ток.

Torah *n.* то́ра.

torch *n.* **1,** (flaming light) фа́кел. **2,** (device used in welding and soldering) горе́лка: *acetylene torch,* ацетиле́новая горе́лка. **3,** *Brit.* (flashlight) карма́нный фона́рь. **4,** *fig.* (source of enlightenment) фа́кел; све́точ: *the torch of knowledge,* фа́кел/све́точ зна́ния. —**torchbearer,** *n.* фа́кельщик.

torchlight *n.* свет фа́кела. *Torchlight procession,* фа́кельное ше́ствие.

toreador *n.* тореадо́р.

torment *v.t.* му́чить; терза́ть. *Torment an animal,* му́чить живо́тное. *Be tormented by doubts,* му́читься *or* терза́ться сомне́ниями. —*n.* му́ка; муче́ние. —**tormentor,** *n.* мучи́тель.

torn *adj.* **1,** (ripped) рва́ный; по́рванный; разо́рванный. *Your trousers are torn in the back,* брю́ки у вас по́рваны/разо́рваны сза́ди. **2,** *med.* по́рванный: *torn muscle/ligament,* по́рванная мы́шца/свя́зка. **3,** (plagued; racked): *be torn by dissension,* раздира́ться разногла́сиями. *Be torn with conflicting emotions,* терза́ться противоречи́выми чу́вствами.

tornado *n.* смерч.

torpedo *n.* торпе́да. —*v.t.* торпеди́ровать. —**torpedo boat,** торпе́дный ка́тер.

torpid *adj.* **1,** (sluggish) вя́лый. **2,** (numb) онеме́лый.

torpor *n.* оцепене́ние; отупе́ние.

torrent *n.* пото́к. *Come down in torrents,* ливмя́ лить. —**torrential,** *adj.* проливно́й.

torrid *adj.* **1,** (scorching) паля́щий. **2,** *fig.* (heated; ardent) горя́чий. —**Torrid Zone,** тропи́ческий по́яс.

torsion *n.* круче́ние.

torso *n.* **1,** (of the human body) ту́ловище. **2,** (statue) торс.

tort *n.* правонаруше́ние.

tortoise *n.* черепа́ха.

tortoise shell черепа́ха. —**tortoise-shell,** *adj.* черепа́ховый.

tortuous *adj.* изви́листый.

torture *n.* **1,** (inflicting of pain) пы́тка; истяза́ние. *Be subjected to torture,* подверга́ться пы́тке. **2,** *fig.* (agony) му́ка; муче́ние: *sheer/pure torture,* настоя́щая му́ка; чи́стое муче́ние. —*v.t.* подверга́ть пы́тке; пыта́ть; истяза́ть. —**torture chamber,** засте́нок.

torturer *n.* истяза́тель.

Tory *n.* то́ри.

toss *v.t.* **1,** (throw) броса́ть; кида́ть; мета́ть. *Toss one's hat in the air,* бро́сить шля́пу в во́здух. *Toss a ball back and forth,* перебра́сываться мячо́м. *Toss into* *prison,* бро́сить в тюрьму́. *Toss money around* (*fig.*), сори́ть *or* сы́пать деньга́ми. **2,** (flip, as a coin) подбра́сывать (моне́ту). **3,** (jerk upward, as the head) вски́дывать. **4,** (fling about) кача́ть; подбра́сывать: *The waves tossed the ship,* во́лны кача́ли/подбра́сывали су́дно. **5,** *fol. by* **off** (drink down) вы́пить за́лпом. —*v.i.* **1,** (be thrown about) кача́ть; броса́ть; швыря́ть (*impers.*): *The boat is tossing,* ло́дку броса́ет/кача́ет/швыря́ет. **2,** (shift about restlessly) мета́ться: *toss in one's sleep,* мета́ться во сне. —*n.* бросо́к. *Toss of a coin,* жеребьёвка. —**toss aside,** отбра́сывать. —**toss out,** выбра́сывать; вышвы́ривать.

tot *n.* малы́ш.

total *n.* су́мма; ито́г; (*at the bottom of a column of figures*) итого́. *A total of...,* в о́бщей сло́жности. —*adj.* **1,** (overall) о́бщий: *the total amount/cost,* о́бщая су́мма/сто́имость. *The total number of...,* о́бщее число́; сумма́рное коли́чество (+ *gen.*). **2,** (complete; utter) по́лный: *total victory,* по́лная побе́да. *Total eclipse,* по́лное затме́ние. *In total darkness/isolation,* в по́лной темноте́/изоля́ции. *The house is a total loss,* от до́ма ничего́ не оста́лось. **3,** (all-out, as of war) тота́льный. —*v.t.* **1,** (add up) сумми́ровать; подыто́живать; подводи́ть ито́г (+ *dat.*). **2,** (amount to) составля́ть. *Military assistance totaling 100 million dollars,* вое́нная по́мощь на су́мму ста миллио́нов до́лларов. **3,** *slang* (demolish) разби́ть вдре́безги.

totalitarian *adj.* тоталита́рный. —**totalitarianism,** *n.* тоталитари́зм.

totality *n.* совоку́пность.

totalizator *n.* тотализа́тор.

totally *adv.* по́лностью; целико́м; соверше́нно. *Totally demolished,* по́лностью *or* соверше́нно разру́шен. *I totally agree,* я вполне́ согла́сен.

tote *v.t., colloq.* нести́; тащи́ть. *Tote a gun,* име́ть при себе́ ору́жие.

totem *n.* тоте́м. —**totemism,** *n.* тотеми́зм.

totter *v.i.* шата́ться; ковыля́ть.

toucan *n.* тука́н.

touch *v.t.* **1,** (place one's hand on) тро́гать; прикаса́ться к; дотра́гиваться до. *Don't touch me!,* не тро́гай меня́! **2,** (come into contact with) каса́ться; прикаса́ться к; достава́ть. *Touch bottom,* каса́ться дна; достава́ть до дна. *He can touch the ceiling with his hand,* он мо́жет достава́ть руко́й до потолка́. **3,** *usu. neg.* (eat some of) притра́гиваться к; прикаса́ться к. **4,** (border) соприкаса́ться с. **5,** (injure slightly) тро́нуть (*impers.*): *Frost touched the plants,* моро́зом тро́нуло расте́ния. **6,** (move emotionally) тро́гать; растро́гать. —*v.i.* тро́гать: "*Do not touch*", не тро́гать! —*n.* **1,** (act of touching; feeling of being touched) прикоснове́ние: *at the slightest touch,* при мале́йшем прикоснове́нии. **2,** (sense of touch) осяза́ние. *To the touch,* на о́щупь. **3,** (tinge; dash) отте́нок; при́месь; налёт. *Touch of salt,* чу́точка *or* щепо́тка со́ли. *A touch of sadness in his voice,* отте́нок печа́ли в его́ го́лосе. **4,** (slight attack, as of illness) лёгкий при́ступ. **5,** (manner of playing an instrument) туше́. **6,** *in* **finishing touches,** после́дние

штрихи́; оконча́тельная отде́лка. —**in touch with, 1,** (in communication with) в конта́кте с. *Get in touch with,* связа́ться с. *Keep in touch with,* подде́рживать связь с. **2,** (informed about) в ку́рсе (+ *gen.*). —**lose touch with,** потеря́ть связь с; оторва́ться от. —**touch down,** приземля́ться. —**touch off, 1,** (detonate) взрыва́ть. **2,** (initiate; trigger) вызыва́ть. —**touch on** *or* **upon,** затра́гивать; каса́ться. —**touch up,** подкра́шивать.

touched *adj.* **1,** (affected with emotion) тро́нут; растро́ганный. **2,** *colloq.* (unbalanced) тро́нутый.

touchiness *n.* оби́дчивость.

touching *adj.* тро́гательный.

touch-me-not *n.* недотро́га.

touchstone *n.* **1,** (testing stone) проби́рный ка́мень; осело́к. **2,** *fig.* (criterion; standard) про́бный ка́мень; осело́к.

touch-type *v.i.* печа́тать на маши́нке вслепу́ю. —**touch-typing,** *n.* слепо́й ме́тод печа́тания на маши́нке.

touchy *adj.* **1,** (easily offended) оби́дчивый. **2,** (delicate) щекотли́вый.

tough *adj.* **1,** (firm; durable) про́чный: *tough leather,* про́чная ко́жа. **2,** (hard to chew) жёсткий: *tough meat,* жёсткое мя́со. **3,** (difficult) тру́дный: *tough job,* тру́дная зада́ча. **4,** (robust; rugged) выно́сливый. **5,** *colloq.* (unfortunate): *tough luck; a tough break,* незада́ча; невезе́ние.

toughen *v.t.* **1,** (make more robust) закаля́ть. **2,** (make more stringent, as rules) ужесточа́ть.

toughness *n.* **1,** (durability) про́чность. **2,** (strength of character) зака́л; зака́лка.

toupee *n.* пари́к; накла́дка.

tour *n.* **1,** (organized trip) турне́; экску́рсия. *Walking tour,* пе́шая экску́рсия. *Sightseeing tour of the city,* экску́рсия по го́роду. **2,** (round of public appearances) гастро́ли; турне́. *Be on tour,* быть на гастро́лях; гастроли́ровать. **3,** *mil.* срок: *tour of duty,* срок слу́жбы. —*v.i.* **1,** (travel) путеше́ствовать. **2,** (give public appearances) гастроли́ровать. —*v.t.* соверша́ть турне́ по; объезжа́ть.

touring *adj.* гастро́льный. *Touring company,* гастро́льная *or* прие́зжая тру́ппа.

tourism *n.* тури́зм.

tourist *n.* тури́ст. —*adj.* тури́стский. —**tourist class,** тре́тий класс.

tourmaline *n.* турмали́н.

tournament *n.* турни́р.

tourniquet *n.* жгут.

tousle *v.t.* еро́шить; взлохма́чивать.

tow *v.t.* тяну́ть *or* тащи́ть на букси́ре; букси́ровать. —*n.* **1,** (act of towing) буксиро́вка. **2,** (fiber) па́кля; куде́ль. —**take in tow,** брать на букси́р.

toward *prep.* **1,** (in the direction of) к: *swim toward shore,* плыть к бе́регу. *He had his back turned toward me,* он стоя́л ко мне спино́й. **2,** (with respect to) к: *animosity toward someone,* вражда́ к кому́-нибудь. *His attitude toward me,* его́ отноше́ние ко мне. *Politeness toward one's subordinates,* ве́жливость по отноше́нию к подчинённым. *America's* *policy toward Japan,* поли́тика США в отноше́нии Япо́нии. **3,** (near in point of time) к; под: *toward evening,* к ве́черу; под ве́чер. *Toward the end of his life,* под коне́ц жи́зни. **4,** (in furtherance of) для: *money toward one's education,* де́ньги для получе́ния образова́ния. *Also,* **towards.**

towboat *n.* букси́р.

towel *n.* полоте́нце.

tower *n.* ба́шня; вы́шка. *The Eiffel Tower,* Э́йфелева ба́шня. —*v.i.* [*usu.* **tower over** *or* **above**] вы́ситься (над); возвыша́ться (над). —**tower of strength,** надёжная опо́ра.

towering *adj.* **1,** (very high) высо́кий; возвыша́ющийся. **2,** (outstanding) выдаю́щийся. **3,** (intense, as of rage) неи́стовый.

towheaded *adj.* белобры́сый.

towing *n.* буксиро́вка.

towline *n.* букси́р; бечева́.

town *n.* го́род. *Small town,* (ма́ленький) городо́к. *Out of town,* в отъе́зде. —**town crier,** глаша́тай. —**town hall,** ра́туша. —**town planning,** градостройтельство.

townsfolk *n.pl.* горожа́не; городски́е жи́тели.

townsman *n.* горожа́нин.

towpath *n.* бечевни́к.

towrope *n.* букси́р; бечева́.

tow truck авари́йная маши́на.

toxemia *n.* токсеми́я.

toxic *adj.* отравля́ющий; токси́ческий; ядови́тый. *Toxic substance/agent,* отравля́ющее *or* токси́ческое вещество́.

toxicology *n.* токсиколо́гия. —**toxicological,** *adj.* токсикологи́ческий. —**toxicologist,** *n.* токсико́лог.

toxin *n.* токси́н.

toy *n.* игру́шка. —*adj.* игру́шечный. *Toy pistol,* игру́шечный пистоле́т; пуга́ч. —*v.i.* [*usu.* **toy with**] игра́ть (+ *instr.*). *Toy with the idea of,* поду́мывать о.

trace *n.* **1,** (mark; track) след. *Disappear without a trace,* исче́знуть *or* пропа́сть бессле́дно. *There is no trace of him,* его́ и след просты́л. **2,** (barely perceptible sign) след: *not a trace of anxiety,* ни мале́йшего следа́ волне́ния. *Not a trace of evidence,* ни мале́йших доказа́тельств. *A trace of sadness in his voice,* отте́нок печа́ли в его́ го́лосе. **3,** (part of a harness) постро́мка. —*v.t.* **1,** (sketch) черти́ть. *Trace one's route on a map,* черти́ть маршру́т на ка́рте. **2,** (make a tracing of) кальки́ровать. **3,** (track down) высле́живать. **4,** (outline the development of) просле́живать. *Trace one's ancestry back to...,* see **ancestry.**

tracer *n.* запро́с (о пропа́вшей посы́лке). —**tracer bullet,** трасси́рующая пу́ля.

trachea *n.* трахе́я. —**tracheal,** *adj.* трахе́йный. —**tracheotomy,** *n.* трахеотоми́я.

trachoma *n.* трахо́ма.

tracing *n.* ка́лька. —**tracing paper,** бума́жная ка́лька.

track *n.* **1,** (mark; trace; trail) след: *tracks in the snow,* следы́ на снегу́. *Put someone on the track of,* наводи́ть кого́-нибудь на след (+ *gen.*). **2,** (rail)

рельс; путь; колея́. *Sidetrack,* запа́сный путь. *Trolley tracks,* трамва́йные пути́ *or* ре́льсы. *Lay tracks,* укла́дывать ре́льсы. *Go off the tracks,* сходи́ть с ре́льсов. *What track does the train leave on?,* с како́го пути́ (*or* с како́й платфо́рмы) отхо́дит по́езд? **3,** *sports* доро́жка; трек. *Running track,* бегова́я доро́жка. **4,** (track and field) лёгкая атле́тика. **5,** (method of proceeding) путь: *on the right/wrong track,* на ве́рном/ло́жном пути́. —*v.t.* **1,** (follow the tracks of) выслеживать. **2,** *fol. by* **down** (pursue and capture) вы́следить. **3,** (monitor the course of) следи́ть за. **4,** *fol. by* **up** (leave footprints in or on) следи́ть (*pfv.* наследи́ть) в *or* на (+ *prepl.*). —**in one's tracks,** на ме́сте. *Stop dead in one's tracks,* останови́ться, как вко́панный. —**keep track of, 1,** (monitor the movements of) уследи́ть за: *You can't keep track of everyone,* за все́ми не уследи́шь. **2,** (remain informed about) следи́ть за. **3,** (keep a record of) запи́сывать: *keep track of one's expenses,* запи́сывать расхо́ды. —**lose track of, 1,** (lose the trail of) потеря́ть след (+ *gen.*). **2,** (lose touch with) (по)теря́ть и́з виду. *We lost track of each other,* мы потеря́ли друг дру́га и́з виду. **3,** (lose count of) (по)теря́ть счёт (+ *dat.*). —**make tracks,** *colloq.* дать тя́гу. —**throw (someone) off the track,** сбива́ть (кого́-нибудь) со сле́да.

tracked *adj.* (of vehicles) гу́сеничный.

tracking station ста́нция слеже́ния.

trackman *n.* укла́дчик путе́й. *Also,* **track layer.**

track meet состяза́ние по лёгкой атле́тике.

tract *n.* **1,** (expanse) масси́в. **2,** *anat.* тракт; пути́: *digestive tract,* пищевари́тельный тракт; *respiratory tract,* дыха́тельные пути́; *urinary tract,* мочевы́е пути́. **3,** (brief treatise) тракта́т.

tractable *adj.* **1,** (docile) сгово́рчивый. **2,** (malleable) ко́вкий.

tractile *adj.* тягу́чий; ко́вкий.

traction *n.* **1,** (pulling power) тя́га. **2,** (friction that prevents skidding) сцепле́ние (с гру́нтом). **3,** *med.* вытяже́ние.

tractive *adj.* тя́говый.

tractor *n.* **1,** (farm vehicle) тра́ктор. **2,** (truck for pulling trailers) тяга́ч; тра́ктор. —**tractor-trailer,** *n.* тра́ктор *or* тяга́ч с прице́пом; тра́кторный прице́п.

trackwalker *n.* путево́й обхо́дчик.

trade *n.* **1,** (commerce) торго́вля: *foreign trade,* вне́шняя торго́вля. **2,** (craft) ремесло́: *learn a trade,* учи́ться ремеслу́. **3,** (exchange) обме́н. *Make a trade,* соверши́ть обме́н; обменя́ться. —*adj.* торго́вый; внешнеторго́вый. *Trade relations,* торго́вые отноше́ния. *Trade deficit,* дефици́т вне́шней торго́вли; внешнеторго́вый дефици́т. —*v.t.* **1,** (swap) меня́ться: *trade places,* меня́ться места́ми. **2,** (give in exchange for) обме́нивать: *trade cigarettes for vodka,* обме́нивать сигаре́ты на во́дку. —*v.i.* **1,** (swap) меня́ться: *Let's trade,* дава́й поменя́емся. **2,** (engage in trade) торгова́ть: *trade with other countries,* торгова́ть с други́ми стра́нами.

trademark *n.* фабри́чная ма́рка; фи́рменный знак.

trader *n.* торго́вец. *Fur trader,* торго́вец меха́ми.

trade school реме́сленное учи́лище.

tradesman *n.* торго́вец.

trade union профсою́з.

trade wind пасса́т.

trading *n.* торго́вля. —*adj.* торго́вый; торгу́ющий. *Trading company,* торго́вая компа́ния. —**trading post,** факто́рия.

tradition *n.* тради́ция. —**traditional,** *adj.* традицио́нный.

traduce *v.t.* клевета́ть на; черни́ть; поро́чить.

traffic *n.* **1,** (movement of vehicles) движе́ние: *heavy traffic,* интенси́вное движе́ние. **2,** (trade) торго́вля: *drug traffic,* торго́вля нарко́тиками. —*v.i.* [*usu.* **traffic in**] торгова́ть (+ *instr.*). —**traffic circle,** кольцева́я развя́зка. —**traffic jam,** зато́р у́личного движе́ния; про́бка. —**traffic light,** светофо́р. —**traffic manager,** диспе́тчер. —**traffic sign,** доро́жный знак. —**traffic signal,** доро́жный сигна́л.

trafficker *n.* торго́вец: *drug trafficker,* торго́вец нарко́тиками; деле́ц наркоби́знеса.

tragedian *n.* тра́гик. —**tragedienne,** *n.* траги́ческая актри́са.

tragedy *n.* **1,** (form of drama; calamity) траге́дия. *End in tragedy,* ко́нчиться траги́чно. **2,** (tragic nature) траги́чность; траги́зм.

tragic *adj.* траги́ческий; траги́чный. *It is tragic,* э́то траги́чно. —**tragically,** *adv.* траги́чески; траги́чно. *End tragically,* ко́нчиться траги́чно.

tragicomedy *n.* трагикоме́дия. —**tragicomic,** *adj.* трагикоми́ческий.

trail *n.* **1,** (tracks) след: *pick up the trail,* напа́сть на след. *Leave a trail behind,* оставля́ть за собо́й след. *Be hot on the trail of,* идти́ по горя́чим следа́м (+ *gen.*). **2,** (stream) след: *trail of blood,* крова́вый след. *Leave behind a trail of dust,* оставля́ть за собо́й столб пы́ли. **3,** (path) тропа́; тропи́нка. *Blaze a trail,* прокла́дывать путь. —*v.t.* **1,** (drag loosely) тащи́ть; волочи́ть. **2,** (follow; shadow) высле́живать; просле́живать. **3,** (lag behind, as in a contest) отстава́ть от. —*v.i.* **1,** (be dragged) тащи́ться; волочи́ться. **2,** (move slowly along) тащи́ться; плести́сь. **3,** *sports* (be behind) отстава́ть: *trail by three points,* отстава́ть на три очка́. **4,** *fol. by* **off** (fade away) замира́ть.

trailblazer *n.* пионе́р; нова́тор; следопы́т.

trailer *n.* прице́п.

train *n.* **1,** *R.R.* по́езд: *the train to/for Boston,* по́езд на Бо́стон. **2,** (long line of vehicles) цепь; верени́ца. *Wagon train,* обо́з. **3,** (sequence) ход: *train of thought,* ход мы́слей. **4,** (of a dress) шлейф. —*adj.* поездно́й: *train crew,* поездна́я брига́да. *Train service,* железнодоро́жное сообще́ние. *Train schedule,* расписа́ние поездо́в. *Train wreck,* круше́ние по́езда. —*v.t.* **1,** (instruct systematically) гото́вить; обуча́ть. *Train teachers,* гото́вить учителе́й. *Train soldiers for combat,* обуча́ть солда́т для боевы́х де́йствий. *Dogs specially trained to sniff out explosives,* соба́ки, специа́льно обу́ченные/натрениро́ванные выню́хивать взрывча́тку. **2,** (teach to act properly or in a certain way) воспи́тывать; приуча́ть. *Train children to be*

self-reliant, воспи́тывать дете́й быть самостоя́тельными. *Train oneself to get up early,* приуча́ть себя́ ра́но встава́ть. **3,** (make physically sound; prepare for an athletic contest) тренирова́ть. *Train one's ear,* тренирова́ть слух. **4,** (teach to perform tricks, as an animal) дрессирова́ть. **5,** (aim) наводи́ть. —*v.i.* тренирова́ться.

trained *adj.* **1,** (of a person) обу́ченный; подгото́вленный; (на)трениро́ванный. *Trained nurse,* медсестра́. *Poorly trained army,* пло́хо обу́ченная а́рмия. **2,** (of an animal) (на)трениро́ванный; (of circus animals) дрессиро́ванный.

trainee *n.* стажёр; практика́нт.

trainer *n.* **1,** (of athletes) тре́нер. **2,** (of animals) дресси́ровщик. **3,** (training device) тренажёр.

training *n.* **1,** (of people) обуче́ние; подгото́вка; трениро́вка. *Voice training,* постано́вка го́лоса. **2,** (of animals) дрессиро́вка. —*adj.* уче́бный; трениро́вочный. *Training program,* курс обуче́ния/подгото́вки. *Training flight,* трениро́вочный полёт.

trait *n.* черта́: *character trait,* черта́ хара́ктера.

traitor *n.* преда́тель; изме́нник. *Traitor to one's country,* изме́нник ро́дины. —**traitorous,** *adj.* преда́тельский; изме́ннический.

trajectory *n.* траекто́рия.

tram *n.* трамва́й.

trammel *n., usu. pl.* **1,** (shackles) пу́ты. **2,** (hindrance) око́вы. —*v.t.* ско́вывать.

tramp *v.i.* то́пать; топота́ть. *Tramp all over town,* исходи́ть весь го́род. —*n.* (vagabond) бродя́га; бося́к.

trample *v.t. & i.* **1,** [*also,* **trample on** *or* **down**] (press down; mash) топта́ть; раста́птывать; выта́птывать. **2,** (crush and injure severely) зата́птывать: *trample to death,* зата́птывать на́смерть. **3,** [*also,* **trample on**] *fig.* (flout, as someone's rights) попира́ть.

trampoline *n.* бату́т.

tramway *n.* подвесна́я кана́тная доро́га.

trance *n.* транс: *in a trance,* в тра́нсе.

tranquil *adj.* споко́йный; безмяте́жный. *Tranquil sea,* споко́йное мо́ре. *Tranquil life,* безмяте́жная жизнь.

tranquilize *also,* **tranquillize** *v.t.* успока́ивать.

tranquilizer *also,* **tranquillizer** *n.* успокои́тельное сре́дство; транквилиза́тор.

tranquillity *n.* споко́йствие.

transact *v.t.* **1,** (carry on) вести́: *transact business,* вести́ дела́. **2,** (complete) заключа́ть: *transact a deal,* заключи́ть сде́лку.

transaction *n.* **1,** (act of transacting) веде́ние (дел). **2,** (business deal) сде́лка.

transatlantic *adj.* трансатланти́ческий.

transcend *v.t.* **1,** (go beyond the range of) выходи́ть за преде́лы (+ *gen.*). **2,** (rise above; excel) превосходи́ть.

transcendent *adj.* **1,** (surpassing) исключи́тельный; непревзойдённый. **2,** *philos.* трансценде́нтный.

transcendental *adj.* **1,** *philos.* трансцендента́льный. **2,** *math.* трансценде́нтный.

transcontinental *adj.* трансконтинента́льный.

transcribe *v.t.* **1,** (make a written copy of) перепи́сывать. **2,** (tape-record) запи́сывать на плёнку. **3,** (represent by phonetic symbols) транскриби́ровать.

transcript *n.* ко́пия. *Stenographic transcript,* стеногра́мма. *Academic transcript,* академи́ческая спра́вка.

transcription *n.* **1,** *ling.* транскри́пция: *phonetic transcription,* фонети́ческая транскри́пция. **2,** (recording) звукоза́пись. **3,** *music* транскри́пция.

transept *n.* трансе́пт.

transfer *v.t.* **1,** (move to another place) переноси́ть; перемеща́ть. **2,** (move to a different job, school, etc.) переводи́ть; перемеща́ть; перечисля́ть. **3,** (shift; remit, as funds) переводи́ть; перечисля́ть. **4,** (make over possession of) передава́ть. —*v.i.* **1,** (change affiliation) переходи́ть; переводи́ться. **2,** (change trains, buses, etc.) переса́живаться. —*n.* **1,** (carrying; conveying) перено́с; перенесе́ние; перемеще́ние. **2,** (change of jobs or affiliation) перево́д; перемеще́ние; перечисле́ние. **3,** (shift or remittal of funds) перево́д; перечисле́ние. **4,** (shifting to another person) переда́ча: *transfer of property,* переда́ча иму́щества. *Transfer of power,* перехо́д вла́сти. **5,** (change of trains, buses, etc.) переса́дка. **6,** (ticket for same) переса́дочный *or* транзи́тный биле́т.

transferable *adj.* могу́щий быть пе́реданным. —**"not transferable"**, без пра́ва переда́чи.

transference *n.* перенесе́ние; перемеще́ние. *Thought transference,* переда́ча мы́слей.

Transfiguration *n., relig.* преображе́ние.

transfigure *v.t.* преобража́ть.

transfix *v.t.* **1,** (impale) пронза́ть. **2,** (rivet to the spot) прико́вывать к ме́сту.

transform *v.t.* **1,** (change the appearance of) преобража́ть. **2,** (change the basic nature of) преобразо́вывать: *The country has been transformed,* страна́ преобразова́лась. **3,** (turn into something else) превраща́ть. **4,** *electricity; physics* преобразо́вывать.

transformation *n.* превраще́ние; преобразова́ние; преображе́ние. *Undergo a transformation,* подве́ргнуться превраще́нию *or* преобразова́нию.

transformer *n.* преобразова́тель; трансформа́тор.

transfuse *v.t.* перелива́ть. —**transfusion,** *n.* перелива́ние: *blood transfusion,* перелива́ние кро́ви.

transgress *v.t.* наруша́ть; переступа́ть. —*v.i.* греши́ть. —**transgression,** *n.* грех; прегреше́ние; правонаруше́ние. —**transgressor,** *n.* гре́шник; правонаруши́тель.

transient *adj.* **1,** (fleeting) преходя́щий; мимолётный; скороте́чный. **2,** (staying for a short time) прое́зжий. —*n.* прое́зжий.

transistor *n.* транзи́стор.

transit *n.* **1,** (passage) перее́зд. *Be in transit,* быть в пути́. **2,** (process of conveying) транзи́т; перево́зка. *Damaged in transit,* испо́рчен при перево́зке. —*adj.* переса́дочный; транзи́тный.

transition *n.* перехо́д. *The transition to a market economy,* перехо́д к ры́ночной эконо́мике. —*adj.* [*also,* **transitional**] перехо́дный: *transition period,* перехо́дный пери́од.

transitive *adj.* перехо́дный: *transitive verb,* перехо́дный глаго́л.

transitory *adj.* преходя́щий; мимолётный; скороте́чный.

translate *v.t. & i.* переводи́ть: *translate from Russian to English,* переводи́ть с ру́сского на англи́йский.

translation *n.* перево́д. *Read something in translation,* чита́ть что́-нибудь в перево́де.

translator *n.* перево́дчик.

transliterate *v.t.* транслитери́ровать. —**transliteration,** *n.* транслитера́ция.

translucent *adj.* полупрозра́чный. *Be translucent,* просве́чивать.

transmigration *n.* **1,** (migration) переселе́ние. **2,** *relig.* переселе́ние душ.

transmission *n.* переда́ча. —**transmission belt,** переда́точный *or* приводно́й реме́нь. —**transmission line,** ли́ния переда́чи.

transmit *v.t.* передава́ть. *Transmit a disease,* передава́ть боле́знь. —**transmittal,** *n.* переда́ча.

transmitter *n.* (ра́дио)переда́тчик.

transoceanic *adj.* трансокеа́нский; заокеа́нский.

transom *n.* **1,** (small window above a door) фраму́га. **2,** (crossbeam) перекла́дина.

transparency *n.* **1,** (quality of being transparent) прозра́чность. **2,** (slide) диапозити́в.

transparent *adj.* **1,** (not opaque) прозра́чный. **2,** (easily detected; obvious) я́вный.

transpire *v.i.* **1,** (become known) обнару́живаться. **2,** (occur) происходи́ть.

transplant *v.t.* переса́живать. —*n.* переса́дка. *Heart transplant,* переса́дка се́рдца.

transplantation *n.* переса́дка.

transport *v.t.* **1,** (convey) перевози́ть; транспорти́ровать. **2,** (carry away with emotion) охва́тывать. *Transported with joy,* охва́чен ра́достью; вне себя́ (*or* не по́мня себя́) от ра́дости. —*n.* **1,** (act of transporting) тра́нспорт; перево́зка. *Public transport,* обще́ственный тра́нспорт. **2,** (ship) тра́нспорт: *troop transport,* войсково́й тра́нспорт.

transportable *adj.* транспорта́бельный.

transportation *n.* перево́зка; тра́нспорт.

transporter *n.* транспортёр: *tank transporter,* та́нковый транспортёр.

transpose *v.t.* **1,** (interchange) переставля́ть. **2,** *music* транспони́ровать.

transposition *n.* **1,** (act of transposing) перестано́вка. **2,** *music* транспониро́вка. **3,** *chess* перестано́вка ходо́в.

transship *v.t.* перегружа́ть; перева́ливать.

transshipment *n.* перегру́зка; перева́лка. *Transshipment point,* перегру́зочный *or* перева́лочный пункт; перева́лка.

trans-Siberian *adj.* транссиби́рский.

transverse *adj.* попере́чный.

trap *n.* западня́; лову́шка. —*v.t.* пойма́ть в западню́. *People were trapped in the building,* лю́ди, находя́щиеся в до́ме, оказа́лись в лову́шке.

trap door люк.

trapeze *n.* трапе́ция.

trapezoid *n.* трапе́ция.

trapper *n.* звероло́в.

trappings *n.pl.* **1,** (adornments) украше́ния; декора́ции. **2,** (items associated with something) си́мволы: *the trappings of monarchy,* си́мволы мона́рхии.

trapshooting *n.* стрельба́ по таре́лочкам; сте́ндовая стрельба́.

trash *n.* **1,** (refuse) отбро́сы; му́сор; сор. **2,** (worthless literature) макулату́ра. **—trash can,** му́сорный я́щик.

trashy *adj.* **1,** (like junk) дрянно́й. **2,** (of literature) бульва́рный.

trauma *n.* **1,** (bodily injury) тра́вма. **2,** (emotional shock) психи́ческая тра́вма. **—traumatic,** *adj.* травмати́ческий. **—traumatize,** *v.t.* травми́ровать. **—traumatology,** *n.* травматоло́гия.

travail *n.* **1,** (hard work) тяжёлый труд. **2,** (anguish) му́ка.

travel *v.i.* путеше́ствовать; разъезжа́ть. *Travel abroad,* е́хать за грани́цу; путеше́ствовать за грани́цей. *The job involves a lot of traveling,* рабо́та свя́зана с разъе́здами. *The news traveled fast,* но́вость бы́стро распространя́лась. *The train was traveling 100 miles an hour,* по́езд шёл со ско́ростью ста миль в час. *Light travels at 186,000 miles per second,* ско́рость све́та — сто во́семьдесят шесть ты́сяч миль в секу́нду. **—***v.t.* объезжа́ть. *Travel the world,* объе́хать весь свет. *Travel 2,000 miles,* прое́хать две ты́сячи миль. *A much-traveled road,* нае́зженная доро́га. **—***n.* **1,** (traveling) пое́здки. *A ban on travel,* запре́т на пое́здки. **2,** *pl.* (series of trips) разъе́зды. **—***adj.* доро́жный: *travel expenses,* доро́жные расхо́ды. *Travel notes,* путевы́е заме́тки. *Travel allowance,* командиро́вочные де́ньги.

travel agency бюро́ путеше́ствий; туристи́ческое бюро́; туристи́ческое аге́нтство.

traveler *also,* **traveller** *n.* путеше́ственник; пу́тник. **—traveler's check,** доро́жный чек.

traveling *also,* **travelling** *adj.* **1,** (moving from place to place) передвижно́й: *traveling exhibition,* передвижна́я вы́ставка. **2,** (of or for travel) доро́жный: *traveling clothes,* доро́жный костю́м. **—traveling bag,** саквоя́ж. **—traveling companion,** спу́тник; попу́тчик. **—traveling salesman,** коммивояжёр.

traverse *v.t.* пересека́ть. **—***n.* попере́чина. **—***adj.* попере́чный.

travesty *n.* паро́дия: *travesty of justice,* паро́дия на справедли́вость.

trawl *n.* трал. **—***v.t.* тра́лить. **—trawler,** *n.* тра́улер.

tray *n.* **1,** (for food or utensils) подно́с. **2,** (of a street peddler) лото́к.

treacherous *adj.* **1,** (perfidious) преда́тельский; вероло́мный; кова́рный. **2,** (dangerous) ско́льзкий: *treacherous path,* ско́льзкий путь.

treachery *n.* преда́тельство; вероло́мство; кова́рство.

treacle *n.* па́тока.

tread *v.i.* **1,** (step; walk) ступа́ть: *tread lightly,* ступа́ть легко́. **2,** *fol. by* **on** (step on) наступа́ть на. **—***v.t.* идти́

по: *tread a certain path,* идти́ по како́му-нибудь пути́. **—***n.* **1,** (stepping; footsteps) шаги́. **2,** (surface of a tire) проте́ктор. **—tread water,** плыть сто́я.

treadle *n.* педа́ль.

treadmill *n.* топча́к. *Be on a treadmill,* верте́ться как бе́лка в колесе́.

treason *n.* изме́на.

treasonable *adj.* изме́ннический; преда́тельский. *Also,* **treasonous.**

treasure *n.* сокро́вище. *Buried treasure,* клад. **—***v.t.* дорожи́ть: *treasure a friendship,* дорожи́ть дру́жбой.

treasure house сокро́вищница.

treasurer *n.* казначе́й.

treasury *n.* казначе́йство. *Secretary of the Treasury,* мини́стр фина́нсов. **—***adj.* казначе́йский: *treasury note,* казначе́йский биле́т.

treat *v.t.* **1,** (behave in a certain manner toward) обраща́ться с; обходи́ться с; поступа́ть с. *Treat someone as an equal,* обраща́ться с ке́м-нибудь как с ра́вным. *How is life treating you?,* как вам живётся? **2,** (regard in a certain way and act accordingly) относи́ться к: *treat something as a joke,* относи́ться к чему́-нибудь как к шу́тке. **3,** (subject to a process) обраба́тывать: *treat with acid,* обраба́тывать кислото́й. **4,** *med.* лечи́ть: *treat someone for hypertension,* лечи́ть кого́-нибудь от гипертони́и; *treat an infection with antibiotics,* лечи́ть инфе́кцию антибио́тиками. **5,** (entertain at one's own expense) угоща́ть. **6,** (deal with, as a subject) трактова́ть о. **—***v.i.* угоща́ть. **—***n.* **1,** (something paid for by someone else): *It's my treat; the treat's on me,* я угоща́ю. **2,** *colloq.* (something very enjoyable) удово́льствие: *Seeing him was a real treat,* ви́деть его́ бы́ло одно́ удово́льствие.

treatise *n.* тракта́т.

treatment *n.* **1,** (way in which one treats another) обраще́ние; обхожде́ние. **2,** (medical treatment) лече́ние. *Undergo treatment,* лечи́ться; проходи́ть курс лече́ния. *A new treatment for asthma,* но́вый ме́тод лече́ния а́стмы. **3,** (processing) обрабо́тка. **4,** (handling of a subject) тракто́вка.

treaty *n.* догово́р. *Treaty obligations,* догово́рные обяза́тельства.

treble *adj.* **1,** (threefold) тройно́й. **2,** *music* дискантовый. **—***n., music* ди́скант. **—***v.t.* утра́ивать. **—***v.i.* утра́иваться. **—treble clef,** скрипи́чный ключ.

tree *n.* де́рево. *Christmas tree,* рожде́ственская ёлка. *Family tree,* родосло́вное де́рево.

tree frog древе́сница; ква́кша.

treeless *adj.* безле́сный.

tree-lined *adj.* обса́женный дере́вьями.

treetops *n.pl.* верху́шки дере́вьев.

trefoil *n.* трили́стник.

trek *v.i.* тащи́ться; переселя́ться. **—***n.* путеше́ствие; переселе́ние.

trellis *n.* шпале́ры; трелья́ж.

tremble *v.i.* дрожа́ть: *tremble with fear,* дрожа́ть от стра́ха. *His voice trembled,* у него́ дрожа́л го́лос. *In a trembling voice,* дрожа́щим го́лосом.

tremendous *adj.* огро́мный; грома́дный. —**tremendously,** *adv.* чрезвыча́йно; о́чень и о́чень.

tremolo *n.* тре́моло; вибра́ция.

tremor *n.* дрожь; тре́пет. *Earth tremor,* подзе́мный толчо́к.

tremulous *adj.* дрожа́щий; тре́петный.

trench *n.* **1,** (ditch) ров; кана́ва. **2,** *mil.* око́п; транше́я. —**trench coat,** плащ. —**trench fever,** транше́йная лихора́дка. —**trench foot,** транше́йная стопа́. —**trench warfare,** око́пная война́.

trenchant *adj.* о́стрый; то́нкий.

trend *n.* направле́ние; тенде́нция; тече́ние. *Trend of thought,* ход мы́слей. *New trends in the arts,* но́вые тече́ния в иску́сстве.

trepak *n.* трепа́к.

trepidation *n.* тре́пет: *fear and trepidation,* страх и тре́пет.

trespass *v.i.* **1,** (enter another's property unlawfully) наруша́ть грани́цу. **2,** *fol. by* **on** (encroach upon) посяга́ть (на). —**trespasser,** *n.* наруши́тель.

tress *n.* **1,** (lock; ringlet) ло́кон. **2,** *pl.* (hair) во́лосы.

trestle *n.* **1,** (wooden frame) ко́злы. **2,** (bridge) эстака́да.

trey *n.* тро́йка.

triad *n.* **1,** (group of three) триа́да. **2,** *music* трезву́чие.

trial *n.* **1,** *law* суд; (суде́бный) проце́сс. *The trial of...,* суд над... *Be on trial,* быть под судо́м. *Stand trial,* предста́ть пе́ред судо́м. *Put on trial,* предава́ть суду́. **2,** (test) про́ба; испыта́ние. *Take on trial,* взять (что́-нибудь) на про́бу. *Method of trial and error,* ме́тод проб и оши́бок. **3,** *pl., sports* отбо́рочные соревнова́ния. **4,** (hardship; ordeal) испыта́ние. —*adj.* **1,** *law Trial judge,* судья́ на проце́ссе. *Trial lawyer,* юри́ст, ча́сто выступа́ющий на суде́. **2,** (experimental) про́бный; испыта́тельный. *Trial period/run,* испыта́тельный срок/пробе́г. —**trial balance,** про́бный бала́нс. —**trial balloon,** про́бный шар.

triangle *n.* **1,** (figure) треуго́льник. **2,** (drawing instrument) уго́льник. —**triangular,** *adj.* треуго́льный.

triangulation *n.* триангуля́ция.

Triassic *adj.* триа́совый.

tribal *adj.* племенно́й; родово́й.

tribe *n.* пле́мя: *warring tribes,* вою́ющие племена́. *The ten lost tribes of Israel,* де́сять исче́знувших коле́н Изра́илевых.

tribesman *n.* член пле́мени.

tribulation *n.* **1,** (suffering) страда́ние. **2,** (misfortune) несча́стье.

tribunal *n.* трибуна́л.

tribune *n.* трибу́н.

tributary *n.* прито́к.

tribute *n.* **1,** (enforced payment) дань. **2,** (testimonial) дань; до́лжное: *pay tribute to,* отда́ть дань/до́лжное (+ *dat.*).

tricentennial *adj. & n.* = **tercentenary.**

triceps *n.* трёхгла́вая мы́шца.

trichina *n.* трихи́на.

trichinosis *n.* трихинеллёз.

trick *n.* **1,** (ruse) обма́н; хи́трость; подво́х. *I suspect a*

trick, мне ка́жется, здесь како́й-то подво́х (*or* что́-то нечи́сто). **2,** (prank; practical joke) шу́тка; ша́лость: проде́лка; прока́за; вы́ходка. *Play a trick on,* сыгра́ть шу́тку с. *Dirty/mean trick,* зла́я шу́тка; по́длость. *Play a dirty trick on,* подложи́ть свинью́ (+ *dat.*). *None of your tricks!,* без фо́кусов! **3,** (stunt; feat) трюк; фо́кус. *Card trick,* ка́рточный фо́кус. **4,** (knack) сноро́вка: *There's a trick to it,* тут сноро́вка нужна́. **5,** *cards* взя́тка. —*adj.* трю́ковый: *trick photography,* трю́ковая съёмка. *Trick lock,* замо́к с секре́том. —*v.t.* обма́нывать; надува́ть: *We've been tricked,* нас обману́ли/наду́ли. —**he doesn't miss a trick,** от него́ ничто́ не укро́ется. —**that'll do the trick,** вот так э́то срабо́тает (*or* полу́чится).

trickery *n.* обма́н; надува́тельство.

trickle *v.i.* сочи́ться: *Blood trickled from the wound,* кровь сочи́лась из ра́ны. *Tears trickled down her cheeks,* слёзы ползли́ у неё по щека́м. —*n.* стру́йка: *a trickle of perspiration,* стру́йка по́та.

trickster *n.* обма́нщик; плут.

tricky *adj.* **1,** (deceptive; sly) хи́трый: *tricky methods,* хи́трые приёмы. **2,** (intricate) хи́трый; сло́жный; мудрёный. *A tricky game,* хи́трая игра́. **3,** (delicate) щекотли́вый: *a tricky situation,* щекотли́вое положе́ние.

tricolor *also,* **tricolour** *adj.* трёхцве́тный. —*n.* трёхцве́тный флаг.

tricot *n.* трико́.

tricycle *n.* трёхколёсный велосипе́д.

trident *n.* трезу́бец.

tried *adj.* испы́танный.

trifle *n.* пустя́к; ме́лочь. —*v.i.* [*usu.* **trifle with**] игра́ть; шути́ть (*both with instr.*). *Trifle with someone's feelings,* игра́ть чьи́ми-нибудь чу́вствами. *He is not to be trifled with,* с ним шу́тки пло́хи. —*v.t.* [*usu.* **trifle away**] растра́чивать. —**a trifle,** немно́жко: *a trifle annoyed,* немно́жко раздражён.

trifler *n.* безде́льник; лени́вец.

trifling *adj.* ничто́жный; пустяко́вый. *A trifling amount,* ничто́жная су́мма. *No trifling matter,* не шу́точное де́ло.

trigger *n.* соба́чка; гашётка; спусково́й крючо́к. *Pull the trigger,* спуска́ть куро́к. —*v.t.* вызыва́ть: *trigger an outburst of indignation,* вызыва́ть взрыв негодова́ния.

trigonometry *n.* тригономе́трия. —**trigonometric,** *adj.* тригонометри́ческий.

trihedron *n.* трёхгра́нник. —**trihedral,** *adj.* трёхгра́нный.

trilateral *adj.* трёхсторо́нний.

trill *n.* трель. —*v.i.* пуска́ть *or* выводи́ть трель.

trillion *n.* (U.S. — 10^{12}) триллио́н; (Brit. — 10^{18}) миллио́н триллио́нов.

trilogy *n.* трило́гия.

trim *v.t.* **1,** (clip; prune) подстрига́ть; подреза́ть; обреза́ть; подра́внивать. **2,** (adorn) отде́лывать: *trim with lace,* отде́лывать кружева́ми. **3,** (reduce; pare) уре́зывать. —*n.* **1,** (haircut) *give someone a trim,* подра́внивать во́лосы (+ *dat.*). **2,** (trimming) отде́лка: *lace trim,* кружевна́я отде́лка. **3,** (proper condition) гото́вность; фо́рма. *In fighting trim*, в боево́й гото́вности. —*adj.* **1**, (neat; tidy) опря́тный; аккура́тный. **2**, (well-proportioned) стро́йный.

trimester *n.* триме́стр.

trimming *n.* **1**, (decoration; ornament) отде́лка; обши́вка; бордю́р. **2**, *pl.* (side dishes) гарни́р.

trinitrotoluene *n.* тринитротолуо́л; троти́л.

Trinity *n.* тро́ица.

trinket *n.* безделу́шка.

trinomial *n.* трёхчле́н. —*adj.* трёхчле́нный.

trio *n.* три́о.

triode *n.* трио́д.

trip *n.* пое́здка; путеше́ствие. *Go on a trip*, соверши́ть пое́здку. *How was your trip?*, как прошла́ пое́здка? *Take something along on a trip*, брать что́-нибудь в доро́гу. *We made the trip in five hours*, мы дое́хали за пять часо́в. —*v.i.* **1**, (stumble) спотыка́ться; оступа́ться. *Trip over the rug*, споткну́ться о ковёр. **2**, (run lightly; skip) семени́ть нога́ми; бежа́ть вприпры́жку. —*v.t.* **1**, (release, as a mechanism) спуска́ть. **2**, (cause to stumble) подставля́ть но́жку (+ *dat.*); дава́ть подно́жку (+ *dat.*). **3**, *fol. by* up (cause to make a slip or error) сбива́ть.

tripartite *adj.* трёхсторо́нний; тро́йственный.

tripe *n.* **1**, (food) рубе́ц. **2**, *colloq.* (rubbish) чушь.

triphammer *n.* па́дающий мо́лот.

triple *adj.* тройно́й; троя́кий; тро́йственный. —*v.t.* увели́чивать втро́е; утра́ивать. —*v.i.* увели́чиваться *or* возраста́ть втро́е; утра́иваться.

triplet *n.* **1**, *pl.* (three offspring born together) тро́йня. **2**, *music* трио́ль.

triplicate *n. In triplicate*, в трёх экземпля́рах.

tripod *n.* трено́га; трено́жник; штати́в.

triptych *n.* три́птих.

trisect *v.t.* дели́ть на три ра́вные ча́сти.

trisyllabic *adj.* трёхсло́жный.

trite *adj.* бана́льный; изби́тый.

tritium *n.* три́тий.

triton *n.* трито́н.

triumph *n.* **1**, (victory) побе́да; торжество́; триу́мф. **2**, (exultation over victory) торжество́. —*v.i.* побежда́ть; торжествова́ть. *Triumph in battle*, победи́ть в бою́. *Justice triumphed*, справедли́вость восторжествова́ла.

triumphal *adj.* торже́ственный; триумфа́льный.

triumphant *adj.* **1**, (victorious) победоно́сный. **2**, (exultant in triumph) торжеству́ющий. —**triumphantly**, *adv.* с торжество́м.

triumvir *n.* триумви́р. —**triumvirate**, *n.* триумвира́т.

trivalent *adj.* трёхвале́нтный.

trivet *n.* **1**, (for holding pots over a fire) тага́н. **2**, (for holding hot dishes) подста́вка.

trivia *n.pl.* ме́лочи.

trivial *adj.* ме́лкий; ничто́жный; пустяко́вый. *Trivial details*, ме́лкие подро́бности. —**triviality**, *n.* ме́лочь.

trochaic *adj.* хореи́ческий; трохеи́ческий.

troche *n.* табле́тка.

trochee *n.* хоре́й; трохе́й.

troika *n.* тро́йка.

Trojan *adj.* троя́нский. —**Trojan horse**, троя́нский конь. —**Trojan War**, Троя́нская война́.

troll *n., folklore* тролль. —*v.t. & i.* (sing) распева́ть.

trolley *n.* **1**, (streetcar) трамва́й. **2**, (small truck) вагоне́тка. **3**, (device for conducting current) токоприёмник. —*adj.* трамва́йный: *trolley tracks*, трамва́йные пути́ *or* ре́льсы. —**trolley bus**, тролле́йбус. —**trolley car**, трамва́й.

trollop *n.* **1**, (slovenly woman) неря́ха; грязну́ля. **2**, (prostitute) потаску́ха.

trombone *n.* тромбо́н. —**trombonist**, *n.* тромбони́ст.

troop *n.* **1**, (group) гру́ппа; отря́д. **2**, *pl.* (soldiers collectively) войска́. —*adj.* войсково́й. *Troop train*, во́инский эшело́н. —*v.t., in* **troop the colors**, выноси́ть зна́мя.

trooper *n.* **1**, (cavalryman) кавалери́ст. **2**, (policeman) полице́йский. —**swear like a trooper**, руга́ться как изво́зчик.

troopship *n.* войсково́й тра́нспорт.

trope *n.* троп.

trophy *n.* **1**, (prize) приз; ку́бок. **2**, (memento of war) трофе́й.

tropic *n.* тро́пик. —**Tropic of Cancer**, тро́пик Ра́ка. —**Tropic of Capricorn**, тро́пик Козеро́га.

tropical *adj.* тропи́ческий.

tropics *n.pl.* тро́пики.

troposphere *n.* тропосфе́ра.

trot *n.* **1**, (gait of a horse) рысь. *At a trot*, ры́сью; на рыся́х. **2**, (jogging gait of a person) рысца́. —*v.i.* **1**, (of a horse) идти́ ры́сью. **2**, (of a person) труси́ть.

trotter *n.* рыси́стая ло́шадь; рыса́к.

trotting races рыси́стые бега́.

troubadour *n.* трубаду́р; менестре́ль.

trouble *n.* **1**, (difficult or distressing situation) беда́; неприя́тность. *Get into trouble*, попа́сть в беду́. *He is in trouble*, у него́ неприя́тности. *Get someone in trouble*, причиня́ть кому́-нибудь неприя́тности. *Ask for trouble*, напра́шиваться на неприя́тности. *Give someone a lot of trouble*, доставля́ть кому́-нибудь мно́го хлопо́т. **2**, (problem) беда́: *The trouble is...*, беда́ в том, что... *What's the trouble?*, в чём де́ло? *That's just the trouble*, в то́м-то и беда́. **3**, (difficulty) труд: *without any trouble*, без труда́. *I'm having trouble opening the safe*, я ника́к не могу́ откры́ть сейф. **4**, (extra effort) труд; хло́поты. *Take the trouble to*, дать себе́ труд *or* взять на себя́ труд *or* не счесть за труд (+ *inf.*); потруди́ться (+ *inf.*). *Will it be much trouble?*, э́то вас не затрудни́т? *It will be no trouble*, э́то не соста́вит труда́. *It's not worth the trouble*, не сто́ит труда́. *Thank you for all the trouble you've taken*, спаси́бо за все ва́ши хло́поты. **5**, (malfunction) неиспра́вность: *engine trouble*, неиспра́вность дви́гателя. *Stomach trouble*, расстро́йство желу́дка. *Heart trouble*, больно́е се́рдце. —*v.t.* **1**, (worry; bother; upset) беспоко́ить: *What's troubling you?*, что вас беспоко́ит? **2**, (bother; inconvenience) беспоко́ить; затрудня́ть: *Don't trouble yourself!*, не беспоко́йтесь! *May I trouble you for a match?*, мо́жно попроси́ть у вас спи́чку?

troubled *adj.* беспоко́йный; трево́жный.

troublemaker *n.* смутья́н.

troublesome *adj.* беспоко́йный.

trough *n.* **1,** (container) коры́то. *Feeding trough*, кормỳшка. *Kneading trough*, квашня́. **2,** (long narrow depression) впа́дина; котлови́на.

trounce *v.t.* **1,** (thrash) колоти́ть. **2,** *colloq.* (defeat decisively) разбива́ть.

troupe *n.* трỳппа.

trousers *n.pl.* брю́ки; штаны́.

trousseau *n.* прида́ное.

trout *n.* форе́ль.

trowel *n.* **1,** (for turning up earth) лопа́тка; садо́вый садо́к. **2,** (for smoothing plaster) мастеро́к.

truancy *n.* прогỳл.

truant *n.* прогỳльщик. **—play truant,** прогỳливать уро́ки; стать прогỳльщиком.

truce *n.* переми́рие. *Flag of truce*, парламентёрский флаг.

truck *n.* **1,** (motor vehicle) грузови́к. **2,** (cart) теле́жка; вагоне́тка. —*v.t.* перевози́ть на грузовике́.

trucker *n.* води́тель грузовика́.

truck farm огоро́дное хозя́йство. **—truck farmer,** огоро́дник. **—truck farming,** огоро́дничество.

truckle *v.i.* [*usu.* **truckle to**] раболе́пствовать (пе́ред); уго́дничать (пе́ред).

truculent *adj.* **1,** (fierce) свире́пый. **2,** (pugnacious) драчли́вый. **3,** (scathing) хлёсткий.

trudge *v.i.* брести́; тащи́ться; плести́сь.

true *adj.* **1,** (accurate; correct) ве́рный; и́стинный. *It/that is true*, э́то пра́вда; э́то ве́рно. *Is it true that...?*, пра́вда ли, что...? *Too good to be true*, сли́шком хорошо́, что́бы быть пра́вдой. *True, he is rarely at home*, пра́вда, он ре́дко быва́ет до́ма. *The theory still holds true today*, тео́рия остаётся пра́вильной (*or* ве́рной) и сего́дня. **2,** (factual) правди́вый: *a true story*, правди́вая исто́рия; правди́вый расска́з. **3,** (actual) действи́тельный: *the true state of affairs*, действи́тельное положе́ние веще́й. *The true value of something*, и́стинная *or* по́длинная це́нность чего́-нибудь. **4,** (rightful) зако́нный: *its true owner*, зако́нный владе́лец. **5,** (faithful) ве́рный: *a true friend*, ве́рный друг. *Remain true to*, остава́ться ве́рен (+ *dat.*). **6,** (on target) ме́ткий. *His aim was true*, он ме́тко прице́лился. **7,** *astron.* и́стинный: *true north*, и́стинный се́вер. **—come true,** осуществля́ться; сбыва́ться; опра́вдываться. **—true to life,** *see* life.

truffle *n.* трю́фель.

truism *n.* изби́тая *or* прописна́я *or* а́збучная и́стина; трюи́зм.

truly *adv.* **1,** (indeed) пои́стине; действи́тельно. **2,** (sincerely) и́скренне. **—yours truly,** пре́данный вам.

trump *n.* ко́зырь. *Play one's trump card*, пусти́ть в ход после́дний ко́зырь. —*v.i.* козыря́ть. —*v.t.* бить *or* крыть ко́зырем. **—trump up,** фабрикова́ть: *trumped-up charges*, сфабрико́ванные обвине́ния.

trumpet *n.* труба́. *The sound of trumpets*, звук труб; трỳбный звук. —*v.t.* (proclaim loudly) труби́ть о.

trumpeter *n.* **1,** (musician) труба́ч. **2,** (herald) глаша́тай.

truncate *v.t.* усека́ть. **—truncated,** *adj.* усечённый.

truncheon *n.* **1,** (cudgel) дуби́на. **2,** (staff) жезл.

trundle *n.* колёсико. —*v.t.* кати́ть. —*v.i.* кати́ться. **—trundle bed,** крова́ть на колёсиках.

trunk *n.* **1,** (of a tree) ствол. **2,** (of an elephant) хо́бот. **3,** (torso) тỳловище. **4,** (large box or case) сундỳк. **5,** (of an automobile) бага́жник. **6,** *pl.* (for swimming) пла́вки.

truss *n.* **1,** (support, as for a bridge) фе́рма. **2,** (device worn to support a hernia) грыжево́й банда́ж.

trust *n.* **1,** (confidence in another's honesty) дове́рие: *place one's trust in*, ока́зывать дове́рие (+ *dat.*). **2,** (monopoly) трест. —*v.t.* **1,** (have confidence in) доверя́ть: *He is not to be trusted*, емỳ нельзя́ доверя́ть. *Trust someone with one's money*, доверя́ть кому́-нибудь свои́ де́ньги. **2,** (rely on) полага́ться на. *Trust one's memory*, полага́ться на свою́ па́мять. *Trust someone's judgment*, полага́ться на чьё-нибудь мне́ние. **3,** (assume confidently) наде́яться; полага́ть. *I trust you're well*, я полага́ю, вы здоро́вы. *I trust you'll be able to come*, я наде́юсь, что вы смо́жете прийти́. —*v.i.* **1,** *fol. by* **in** (put one's trust in) доверя́ться (+ *dat.*). **2,** *in* **trust to luck,** полага́ться на слỳчай.

trustee *n.* опекỳн; попечи́тель. **—trusteeship,** *n.* опе́ка; попечи́тельство.

trustful *adj.* дове́рчивый. *Also,* **trusting.**

trust territory подопе́чная террито́рия.

trustworthy *adj.* заслỳживающий дове́рия; надёжный. **—trustworthiness,** *n.* надёжность.

trusty *adj.* ве́рный.

truth *n.* пра́вда. **—in truth,** на са́мом де́ле. **—to tell the truth...,** по пра́вде говоря́; по пра́вде сказа́ть.

truthful *adj.* правди́вый. **—truthfulness,** *n.* правди́вость.

try *v.t.* **1,** *fol. by inf.* (attempt) пыта́ться; стара́ться: *try to find out*, пыта́ться/стара́ться узна́ть. **2,** (taste) про́бовать: *Try the soup!*, попро́буйте суп! **3,** (test) про́бовать: *try a new remedy*, про́бовать но́вое сре́дство. *Try one's luck*, попыта́ть сча́стья. *Try one's hand at*, про́бовать си́лы в (+ *prepl.*). **4,** (strain) испы́тывать: *try one's patience*, испы́тывать чьё-нибудь терпе́ние. **5,** (put on trial) суди́ть: *He was tried for murder*, его́ суди́ли за уби́йство. *He was tried and executed*, он был суди́м и казнён. **6,** (hear, as a case) слỳшать (де́ло). —*v.i.* стара́ться: *I'll try*, я постара́юсь. *Try hard*, о́чень стара́ться. —*n.* попы́тка: *on the first try*, с пе́рвой попы́тки. *It's worth a try*, сто́ит попыта́ться. **—try on,** примеря́ть. **—try out, 1,** (experiment with) испы́тывать; про́бовать. **2,** (compete) про́боваться: *try out for a part*, про́боваться на роль. *Try out for the basketball team*, проходи́ть отбо́р в баскетбо́льную кома́нду.

trying *adj.* трỳдный; тяжёлый.

tryout *n.* про́ба (на роль).

try square уго́льник.

tryst *n.* любо́вное свида́ние.

tsar *n.* царь. **—tsarevitch,** *n.* царе́вич. **—tsarevna,** *n.* царе́вна. **—tsarina,** *n.* цари́ца. **—tsarism,** *n.* цари́зм. **—tsarist,** *adj.* ца́рский.

tsetse fly (му́ха) цеце́.

T-shirt *n.* ма́йка.

T square рейсши́на.

tub *n.* **1,** (large container) ка́дка; лоха́нь; уша́т. **2,** (bathtub) ва́нна. **3,** *colloq.* (old boat) посу́дина.

tuba *n.* ту́ба.

tubby *adj.* пу́хлый; ту́чный.

tube *n.* **1,** (hollow cylinder) тру́бка. **2,** (inner tube for a tire) ка́мера. **3,** (radio component) ла́мпа. **4,** (container for glue, toothpaste, etc.) тю́бик. **5,** *anat.* труба́.

tubeless *adj.* бе́ска́мерный.

tuber *n.* клу́бень.

tubercle *n.* бугоро́к. **—tubercle bacillus,** туберкулёзная па́лочка.

tubercular *adj.* туберкулёзный.

tuberculosis *n.* туберкулёз. **—tuberculous,** *adj.* туберкулёзный.

tuberose *n.* туберо́за.

tuberous *adj.* клубнево́й; буго́рчатый.

tubing *n.* тю́бинг.

tubular *adj.* тру́бчатый.

tuck *v.t.* **1,** (place so as to be held firmly) заправля́ть: *tuck one's shirt into one's trousers,* заправля́ть руба́шку в брю́ки. **2,** (fold under something) подбира́ть; подгиба́ть; подвёртывать; подтыка́ть. *Tuck in a blanket,* подвёртывать *or* подтыка́ть одея́ло. **3,** (place snugly) засо́вывать: *tuck something into one's pocket,* засо́вывать что́-нибудь в карма́н. *Tuck a child into bed,* уложи́ть ребёнка в посте́ль. **—***n.* вы́тачка.

tucker *v.t., colloq.* [*usu.* **tucker out**] изнуря́ть. *Be tuckered out,* изма́яться; быть без ног.

Tuesday *n.* вто́рник.

tuft *n.* **1,** (of hair) вихо́р; клок воло́с. **2,** (of grass) пук; пучо́к.

tug *v.t. & i.* тяну́ть; дёргать. **—***n.* **1,** (strong pull): *give a tug,* потяну́ть; дёрнуть. **2,** (tugboat) букси́р. **—tug of war,** перетя́гивание кана́та.

tugboat *n.* букси́р.

tuition *n.* **1,** (fee) пла́та за обуче́ние. **2,** (teaching) обуче́ние: *free tuition,* беспла́тное обуче́ние.

tulip *n.* тюльпа́н. **—***adj.* тюльпа́нный.

tulle *n.* тюль. **—***adj.* тю́левый.

tumble *v.i.* **1,** (fall; drop) па́дать; вали́ться. *Tumble down the stairs,* упа́сть с ле́стницы. *Tumble over a cliff,* свали́ться *or* сорва́ться со скалы́. *Come tumbling down,* ру́хнуть; обру́шиваться; сва́ливаться; обва́ливаться. *Prices tumbled,* це́ны упа́ли. **2,** (do somersaults) кувырка́ться. **—***n.* паде́ние.

tumble-down *adj.* ве́тхий; обветша́лый; полуразру́шенный.

tumbler *n.* **1,** (glass) стака́н. **2,** (of a lock) сува́льда. **3,** (gymnast) акроба́т. **4,** (pigeon) ту́рман.

tumbleweed *n.* перекати́-по́ле.

tumid *adj.* распу́хший.

tummy *n., colloq.* живо́тик.

tumor *also,* **tumour** *n.* о́пухоль.

tumult *n.* сумато́ха.

tumultuous *adj.* шу́мный; бу́рный. *Tumultuous applause,* бу́рные аплодисме́нты.

tuna *n.* туне́ц.

tundra *n.* ту́ндра.

tune *n.* **1,** (melody) моти́в; напе́в. **2,** (proper pitch or key) лад: *sing in tune,* петь в лад. *The piano is out of tune,* роя́ль расстро́ен. **—***v.t.* **1,** (a musical instrument) настра́ивать. **2,** (an engine) (от)регули́ровать. **3,** *fol. by* **in** (adjust a radio to receive) настра́ивать радиоприёмник на; настра́иваться на. **—be in tune with the times,** идти́ в но́гу со вре́менем. **—call the tune,** зака́зывать му́зыку. **—change one's tune,** запе́ть друго́е; запе́ть на друго́й лад. **—dance to someone's tune,** пляса́ть под чью́-нибудь ду́дку. **—to the tune of,** на су́мму (+ *gen.*).

tuneful *adj.* мелоди́чный.

tuner *n.* настро́йщик: *piano tuner,* настро́йщик роя́ля.

tune-up *n.* регулиро́вка: *engine tune-up,* регулиро́вка дви́гателя.

tung oil ту́нговое ма́сло.

tungsten *n.* вольфра́м. **—***adj.* вольфра́мовый.

tung tree тунг; ту́нговое де́рево.

tunic *n.* **1,** (garment worn in ancient times) туни́ка. **2,** (uniform coat) ки́тель.

tuning *n.* настро́йка. **—tuning fork,** камерто́н.

tunnel *n.* тунне́ль. **—***v.i.* **1,** (build a tunnel) прокла́дывать тунне́ль: *tunnel through a mountain,* прокла́дывать тунне́ль че́рез го́ру. **2,** *fol. by* **under** (dig one's way) подка́пывать; подка́пываться под.

tunny *n., Brit.* = **tuna.**

turban *n.* тюрба́н; чалма́.

turbid *adj.* му́тный. **—turbidity,** *n.* му́тность.

turbine *n.* турби́на.

turbojet *adj.* турбореакти́вный. **—***n.* турбореакти́вный самолёт.

turboprop *adj.* турбовинтово́й. **—***n.* турбовинтово́й самолёт.

turbot *n.* тюрбо́.

turbulence *n.* **1,** (commotion; agitation) волне́ние. **2,** *aero.* болта́нка.

turbulent *adj.* бу́рный; бу́йный; бурли́вый. *Turbulent sea/river,* бу́рное мо́ре; бу́рная река́.

tureen *n.* ми́ска. *Soup tureen,* су́пница; су́пник; супова́я ми́ска.

turf *n.* **1,** (matted grass) дёрн. **2,** (grass part of a racetrack) трава́. **3,** (horse racing) ска́чки.

turgid *adj.* **1,** (swollen) опу́хший. **2,** (bombastic) напы́щенный.

Turk *n.* ту́рок. *The Turks,* ту́рки.

turkey *n.* инде́йка. **—talk turkey,** *colloq.* говори́ть без обиняко́в.

Turkic *adj.* тю́ркский.

Turkish *adj.* туре́цкий. **—***n.* туре́цкий язы́к. **—Turkish bath,** туре́цкая ба́ня. **—Turkish delight,** раха́т-луку́м. **—Turkish towel,** махро́вое полоте́нце.

turmeric *n.* курку́ма.

turmoil *n.* беспоря́док; сумя́тица.

turn *v.t.* **1,** (change the position or direction of) повора́чивать: *turn one's head,* повора́чивать го́лову; *turn a key in a lock,* повора́чивать ключ в замке́. **2,** (cause to revolve) враща́ть: *turn a wheel,* вращáть колесó. **3**, (aim; direct) направля́ть; обраща́ть. *Turn one's attention to*, направля́ть внима́ние на. *Turn a gun on oneself*, обрати́ть ору́жие про́тив себя́ (и застрели́ться). **4**, (shape in a lathe) точи́ть. **5**, *in various combinations: turn the page*, перевёртывать страни́цу; *turn the corner*, заверну́ть *or* поверну́ть за́ угол; *turn one's back on*, поверну́ться спино́й к; отвора́чиваться от; *turn somersaults*, кувырка́ться; *turn one's ankle*, подверну́ть но́гу. **6**, *in various idiomatic expressions: turn a deaf ear to*, пропуска́ть ми́мо уше́й; *turn one's stomach*, прети́ть; *turn the other cheek*, подставля́ть другу́ю щёку; *turn someone's head*, кружи́ть го́лову (+ *dat.*); *turn to one's advantage*, обраща́ть в свою́ по́льзу. *He turned forty*, ему́ испо́лнилось со́рок лет. —*v.i.* **1**, (change direction) повора́чивать: *turn (to the) right*, повора́чивать напра́во. **2**, (face in a different direction) повора́чиваться: *turn toward someone*, повора́чиваться к кому́-нибудь. **3**, (be able to be turned) повора́чиваться: *The key won't turn*, ключ не повора́чивается. **4**, (rotate) враща́ться. **5**, (become) станови́ться: *turn cold*, станови́ться хо́лодно. *Turn traitor*, стать преда́телем. ♦*Also rendered by various verbs: turn sour*, ки́снуть; *turn gray*, седе́ть; *turn pale*, поблед́нéть. **6**, (shift) переходи́ть: *The conversation turned to politics*, разгово́р перешёл к поли́тике. **7**, (change color) желте́ть: *The leaves are turning*, ли́стья желте́ют. **8**, (become sour or rancid) проки́са́ть. —*n.* **1**, (change of direction; rotation) поворо́т: *turn to the right*, поворо́т напра́во. *Make a turn*, де́лать поворо́т. *With one turn of the key*, одни́м поворо́том ключа́. *The first turn on the left*, пе́рвый поворо́т нале́во. **2**, (occasion; chance) о́чередь: *wait one's turn*, ждать свое́й о́череди. *In turn*, по о́череди; поочерёдно; попереме́нно. *Out of turn*, вне о́череди. *Take turns*, чередова́ться. *When my turn came*, когда́ пришла́ *or* наступи́ла моя́ о́чередь; когда́ пришёл *or* наступи́л мой черёд. **3**, (action; deed) услу́га: *ill turn*, плоха́я услу́га. *One good turn deserves another*, долг платежо́м кра́сен. **4**, (change in trend) поворо́т; оборо́т: *turn of events*, поворо́т/оборо́т собы́тий. *Take a turn for the worse*, принима́ть дурно́й оборо́т. *Things have taken a turn for the better*, де́ло пошло́ на лад. **5**, *in various expressions: turn of mind*, склад ума́; *turn of speech*, оборо́т ре́чи; *turn of the century*, нача́ло ве́ка. —**at every turn**, на ка́ждом шагу́. —**turn against, 1**, (set against) восстана́вливать *or* настра́ивать про́тив. **2**, (renounce; betray) пойти́ про́тив. —**turn around, 1**, (face in the opposite direction) повора́чиваться (круго́м); обора́чиваться. **2**, (reverse the direction of) повора́чивать (*e.g.* стул); развора́чивать (маши́ну). —**turn aside, 1**, (turn and face a different way) сверну́ть в сто́рону. **2**, (brush aside, as a question) отма́хиваться от. —**turn away, 1**, (turn so as not to be visible) отвора́чивать. *Turn away one's eyes*, отвора́чивать *or* отводи́ть глаза́. **2**, (refuse admittance to) прогоня́ть; не пуска́ть. **3**, (turn one's back) отвора́чиваться. —**turn back, 1**, (fold back)

отгиба́ть. **2**, (set back, as a clock) поверну́ть *or* перевести́ наза́д. **3**, (turn around and return) поверну́ть наза́д *or* обра́тно; возвраща́ться наза́д. **4**, (force to turn around and return) завора́чивать. **5**, (repulse) отража́ть. —**turn down, 1**, (fold down) отвора́чивать; загиба́ть; отгиба́ть. *Turn down the page*, загиба́ть страни́цу. *Turn down one's collar*, опуска́ть воротни́к. **2**, (turn into, as a narrow street) свора́чивать в *or* на; повора́чивать в. *Turn down a path*, свора́чивать на тропи́нку. **3**, (reject) отклоня́ть; отверга́ть; отка́зываться от. *Turn down an offer*, отклони́ть *or* отве́ргнуть предложе́ние. *Turn down an invitation*, отклони́ть приглаше́ние; отказа́ться от приглаше́ния. *Turn down a part*, отказа́ться от ро́ли. *Turn down someone's request*, отказа́ть кому́-нибудь в про́сьбе. *They turned him down*, ему́ отказа́ли. **4**, (reduce) уменьша́ть; убавля́ть: *turn down the volume*, уменьша́ть/убавля́ть звук *or* гро́мкость. *Turn down the radio*, сде́лать ра́дио поти́ше. —**turn in, 1**, (hand in) сдава́ть. **2**, (inform on) доноси́ть на. **3**, *colloq.* (go to bed) ложи́ться спать. **4**, *Turn oneself in*, сдава́ться власт́ям; прийти́ *or* яви́ться с пови́нной. —**turn into, 1**, (make a turn into) свора́чивать в; повора́чивать в. **2**, (transform into) обраща́ть в; превраща́ть в. **3**, (be transformed into) превраща́ться в; обраща́ться в. —**turn loose**, отпуска́ть; выпуска́ть. —**turn off, 1**, (leave, as a road) свора́чивать с. **2**, (switch off, as a light) туши́ть; гаси́ть; выключа́ть; (a motor) выключа́ть. *Turn off the water*, закрыва́ть кран. —**turn on, 1**, (switch on) включа́ть; зажига́ть. *Turn on the water*, открыва́ть кран. **2**, (attack) набро́ситься на. —**turn out, 1**, (extinguish) туши́ть; гаси́ть; выключа́ть. **2**, (eject) выгоня́ть. **3**, (produce) выпуска́ть. **4**, (come; appear) выходи́ть: *turn out for the rally*, выходи́ть на ми́тинг; *turn out to greet the President*, выходи́ть приве́тствовать президе́нта. **5**, (prove to be) ока́зываться (+ *instr.*): *turn out to be an old acquaintance*, оказа́ться ста́рым знако́мым. *It turned out to be a nice day*, день вы́дался хоро́ший. **6**, (end up) вы́ясниться; оберну́ться. *As it turned out*, как вы́яснилось. *It turned out that...*, оказа́лось *or* вы́яснилось, что... *Turn out well*, ко́нчиться *or* обойти́сь благополу́чно. *Things turned out differently*, дела́ оберну́лись ина́че. —**turn over, 1**, (invert) перевёртывать. **2**, (roll over) перевёртываться: *The car turned over*, маши́на переверну́лась. *Turn over in one's grave*, переверну́ться в гробу́. **3**, (hand over) передава́ть; отдава́ть; сдава́ть. **4**, (start, as of an engine) заводи́ться. —**turn to, 1**, (appeal to; refer to) обраща́ться к: *turn to someone for help*, обраща́ться к кому́-нибудь за по́мощью. **2**, (open to a certain page) открыва́ть (каку́ю-нибудь страни́цу). **3**, (begin; take up) бра́ться за; принима́ться за. **4**, (change into) превраща́ться в: *turn to stone*, превраща́ться в ка́мень. *Our joy turned to sorrow*, на́ша ра́дость смени́лась го́рем. —**turn up, 1**, (fold up) подвёртывать. *Turn up one's collar*, поднима́ть воротни́к. **2**, (loosen, as soil) взрыхля́ть. **3**, (uncover; discover) раскрыва́ть; обнару́живать. **4**, (increase) увели́чивать: *turn up the volume,* увели́чивать звук *or* гро́мкость. *Turn up the radio,* сде́лать ра́дио погро́мче. **5,** (arrive; appear) явля́ться; появля́ться; приходи́ть; пока́зываться; ока́зываться; подверну́ться. **6,** (be found) найти́сь. **7,** *Turn up one's nose,* задира́ть нос. **—turn upon, 1,** (attack) набро́ситься на. **2,** (hinge on) зави́сеть от.

turnabout *n.* **1,** (turn) поворо́т круго́м. **2,** *fig.* (reversal) поворо́т на сто во́семьдесят гра́дусов.

turncoat *n.* перебе́жчик; ренега́т.

turndown *adj.* отложно́й: *turndown collar,* отложно́й воротни́к.

turner *n.* то́карь.

turning *n.* поворо́т. **—adj.** враща́ющийся. **—turning point,** поворо́тный пункт; перело́м.

turnip *n.* ре́па.

turnout *n.* **1,** (gathering) собра́ние. **2,** (number of people assembled): *a large turnout,* мно́го наро́ду. *Heavy turnout for an election,* высо́кий проце́нт уча́стия в вы́борах.

turnover *n.* оборо́т. *Turnover of personnel,* теку́честь ка́дров. **—turnover tax,** нало́г с оборо́та.

turnpike *n.* автомагистра́ль; автостра́да.

turnstile *n.* турнике́т.

turntable *n.* **1,** *R.R.* поворо́тный круг. **2,** (of a phonograph) диск.

turpentine *n.* скипида́р.

turpitude *n.* развра́т; развращённость: *moral turpitude,* нра́вственный развра́т; нра́вственная развращённость.

turquoise *n.* бирюза́. **—adj.** бирюзо́вый.

turret *n.* **1,** (small tower) ба́шенка. **2,** (revolving structure for a gun) оруди́йная ба́шня. **—turret lathe,** револьве́рный стано́к.

turtle *n.* черепа́ха. **—adj.** черепа́ховый: *turtle soup,* черепа́ховый суп.

turtledove *n.* го́рлица.

tusk *n.* клык; би́вень.

tussle *n.* дра́ка; сва́лка. **—v.i.** дра́ться.

tut *interj.* фи!; цыц!

tutelage *n.* **1,** (guardianship) опе́ка. **2,** (instruction) обуче́ние.

tutelary *adj.* опеку́нский.

tutor *n.* репети́тор; гуверне́р. **—v.t.** репети́ровать. **—v.i.** дава́ть ча́стные уро́ки. **—tutorial,** *adj.* репети́торский.

tutu *n.* па́чка.

tuxedo *n.* смо́кинг.

twaddle *v.i.* пустосло́вить. **—n.** пустосло́вие. **—twaddler,** *n.* пустосло́в; пустоме́ля.

twang *n.* гнуса́вость. *Nasal twang,* гнуса́вый го́лос.

tweak *v.t.* ущипну́ть. **—n.** щипо́к.

tweed *n.* твид.

tweet *n.* ще́бет. **—v.i.** щебета́ть; чири́кать.

tweezers *n.pl.* пинце́т; щи́пчики.

twelfth *adj.* двена́дцатый. **—n.** двена́дцатая; двена́дцатая часть. *One-twelfth,* одна́ двена́дцатая; двена́дцатая часть. **—Twelfth Night,** соче́льник.

twelve *n. & adj.* двена́дцать.

twentieth *adj.* двадца́тый. **—n.** двадца́тая; двадца́тая

часть. *One-twentieth,* одна́ двадца́тая; двадца́тая часть.

twenty *n. & adj.* два́дцать.

twice *adv.* **1,** (two times) два́жды; два ра́за. **2,** (doubly) вдво́е; в два ра́за: *twice as much,* вдво́е *or* в два ра́за бо́льше. *At twice the price,* по двойно́й цене́. *He is twice her age,* он вдво́е ста́рше её. **—once or twice,** раз-друго́й; ра́за два.

twiddle *v.t.* игра́ть (+ *instr.*); верте́ть. **—twiddle one's thumbs,** бить баклу́ши.

twig *n.* прут; ве́тка; ве́точка.

twilight *n.* су́мерки: *at twilight,* в су́мерки; в су́мерках.

twin *n.* близне́ц; *pl.* близнецы́; двойня́. **—adj. 1,** (being a twin or twins): *twin brothers,* бра́тья-близнецы́. **2,** (forming an identical pair) спа́ренный: *twin engines,* спа́ренные мото́ры. *Twin beds,* две односпа́льные крова́ти.

twine *n.* бечёвка; шпага́т. **—v.t.** обвива́ть. **—v.i.** ви́ться. *Twine around,* обвива́ться вокру́г.

twin-engine *adj.* двухмото́рный. *Also,* **twin-engined.**

twinge *n.* при́ступ бо́ли. *Twinge of conscience,* угрызе́ние со́вести.

twinkle *v.i.* мерца́ть; мига́ть. **—n.** мерца́ние; мига́ние.

twinkling *n.* **1,** (gleam) мерца́ние; мига́ние. **2,** (instant) мгнове́ние. **—in the twinkling of an eye,** в мгнове́ние о́ка.

twirl *v.t.* кружи́ть; верте́ть. *Twirl a baton,* верте́ть па́лочкой. *Twirl one's mustache,* крути́ть усы́.

twist *v.t.* **1,** (turn; wind) крути́ть; закру́чивать. *Twist the handle,* крути́ть рукоя́тку. *The rope became twisted,* верёвка закрути́лась. **2,** (make by twisting) вить; крути́ть; скру́чивать; сучи́ть. **3,** (wrench; sprain) подверну́ть; вы́вернуть. **4,** (warp; distort) искажа́ть. **—v.i. 1,** (squirm; writhe) ко́рчиться. **2,** (wind, as of a road) извива́ться; ви́ться. **3,** *fol. by* **around** (twine around) обвива́ться (вокру́г). **—n. 1,** (twisting motion) круче́ние. *Give something a twist,* закрути́ть что́-нибудь. **2,** (bend; curve) поворо́т; изги́б. **3,** *fig.* (unexpected turn or change) поворо́т; оборо́т. **4,** (loaf of bread) вито́й хлеб; вита́я бу́лка; плетёнка. **—twist around one's little finger,** вить верёвки из. **—twist someone's arm,** вы́вернуть *or* вы́крутить кому́-нибудь ру́ку. *Twist someone's arms behind his back,* скрути́ть кому́-нибудь ру́ки за́ спину *or* за спино́й.

twisted *adj.* **1,** (entangled, as of threads) запу́танный. **2,** (bent, as of wreckage) искорёженный. **3,** (perverted) извращённый.

twit *v.t.* поддева́ть; подка́лывать.

twitch *v.t.* дёргать; подёргивать. **—v.i.** дёргаться; подёргиваться. **—n.** подёргивание: *nervous twitch,* не́рвное подёргивание.

twitter *v.i.* щебета́ть; чири́кать. **—n.** щебет; чири́канье.

two *adj.* два; две: *two rubles,* два рубля́; *two kopecks,* две копе́йки. *Two children,* дво́е дете́й. *The two brothers are not at all alike,* о́ба бра́та нисколько непохо́жи друг на дру́га. **—n. 1,** (cardinal number) два. **2,** (written number; school grade) дво́йка. **3,** *cards* дво́йка. —**in two,** на́двое; попола́м. —**two by two,** по́ два; по́ двое; попа́рно.

two-faced *adj.* двули́чный; двули́кий.

twofold *adj.* двойно́й; двоя́кий; двукра́тный. —*adv.* вдво́е; вдвойне́.

two-headed *adj.* двугла́вый.

two hundred две́сти. —**two-hundredth,** *adj.* двух-со́тый.

two-legged *adj.* двуно́гий.

two-party *adj.* двухпарти́йный.

two-room *adj.* двухко́мнатный.

two-sided *adj.* двусторо́нний.

twosome *n.* па́ра.

two-story *adj.* двухэта́жный.

two-syllable *adj.* дву(х)сло́жный.

two-time *adj.* двукра́тный: *two-time champion,* двукра́тный чемпио́н.

two-volume *adj.* двухто́мный.

two-way *adj.* двусторо́нний. *Two-way street,* у́лица с двусторо́нним движе́нием.

two-wheel *adj.* двухколёсный. *Also,* **two-wheeled.**

tycoon *n., colloq.* магна́т.

tyke *n.* малы́ш.

type *n.* **1,** (kind; class) тип; род: *a new type of weapon,* но́вый тип/род ору́жия. *The men were of two types,* мужчи́ны бы́ли двух родо́в. **2,** (print) печа́ть; шрифт. *Set in type,* набира́ть. —*v.t.* (categorize) классифици́ровать. —*v.t. & i.* (write on a typewriter) писа́ть на пи́шущей маши́нке; печа́тать на маши́нке.

typeface *n.* шрифт.

typescript *n.* машинопи́сный текст.

typesetter *n.* набо́рщик.

typewriter *n.* пи́шущая маши́нка.

typewritten *adj.* машинопи́сный: *eight typewritten pages,* во́семь машинопи́сных страни́ц.

typhoid *n.* (брюшно́й) тиф. —*adj.* тифо́зный. —**typhoid fever,** тифо́зная лихора́дка; брюшно́й тиф.

typhoon *n.* тайфу́н.

typhus *n.* (сыпно́й) тиф.

typical *adj.* типи́чный; характе́рный. *Typical of,* типи́чно для; характе́рно для.

typically *adv.* типи́чно. *His reaction was typically American,* его́ реа́кция была́ типи́чно америка́нская. *A Scandinavian is typically reserved,* типи́чный скандина́в — сде́ржан; скандина́вы обы́чно сде́ржанные. *Deer are typically shy,* оле́ни обы́чно *or* в основно́м ро́бкие.

typify *v.t.* служи́ть типи́чным приме́ром (+ *gen.*).

typing *n.* машинопись. *Typing course,* курс маши́нописи.

typist *n.* машини́стка.

typographer *n.* типо́граф; печа́тник.

typographical *also,* **typographic** *adj.* типогра́фский. —**typographical error,** типогра́фская оши́бка.

typography *n.* типогра́фское де́ло; типогра́фское иску́сство.

tyrannical *adj.* тирани́ческий.

tyrannize *v.t.* тира́нить.

tyranny *n.* тирани́я; тира́нство.

tyrant *n.* тира́н; наси́льник.

tyre *n.* = **tire**[2].

tyro *n.* новичо́к.

U

U, u два́дцать пе́рвая бу́ква англи́йского алфави́та.

ubiquitous *adj.* вездесу́щий.

udder *n.* вы́мя.

ugh *interj.* фу!

ugliness *n.* уро́дство; уро́дливость; безобра́зие.

ugly *adj.* **1,** (unsightly) некраси́вый; безобра́зный. **2,** (nasty; disagreeable) неприя́тный; скве́рный. *Ugly odor,* неприя́тный *or* проти́вный за́пах. *In an ugly mood,* в скве́рном настрое́нии. *Ugly habit,* скве́рная привы́чка. —**ugly duckling,** га́дкий утёнок.

ukase *n.* ука́з.

Ukrainian *adj.* украи́нский. —*n.* **1,** (person) украи́нец; украи́нка. **2,** (language) украи́нский язы́к.

ukulele *n.* гава́йская гита́ра.

ulcer *n.* я́зва.

ulcerate *v.t.* изъязвля́ть. —*v.i.* изъязвля́ться. —**ulceration,** *n.* изъязвле́ние.

ulcerous *adj.* я́звенный.

ulterior *adj.* скры́тый. —**ulterior motive,** за́дняя мысль; скры́тый моти́в.

ultimate *adj.* коне́чный; оконча́тельный. *The ultimate purpose of something,* коне́чная цель чего́-нибудь. *The ultimate weapon,* абсолю́тное ору́жие. —*n.* [*usu.* **the ultimate in**] вы́сшая сте́пень (+ *gen.*).

ultimately *adv.* в конце́ концо́в; в коне́чном ито́ге; в коне́чном счёте.

ultimatum *n.* ультима́тум.

ultra- *prefix* ультра-.

ultramarine *n.* ультрамари́н. —*adj.* ультрамари́новый.

ultramodern *adj.* ультрасовреме́нный.

ultrasonic *adj.* ультразвуково́й.

ultraviolet *adj.* ультрафиоле́товый.

umber *n.* у́мбра.

umbilical *adj.* пупо́чный. —**umbilical cord,** пупови́на.

umbilicus *n.* пупо́к.

umbra *n.* тень.

umbrage *n.* оби́да. *Take umbrage,* обижа́ться; уда́риться в амби́цию.

umbrella *n.* зо́нтик; зонт.

umlaut *n.* умля́ут.

umpire *n.* **1,** *sports* судья́. **2,** (one empowered to settle a dispute) арби́тр. —*v.t.* суди́ть.

umpteen *adj., colloq.* мно́го; бесчи́сленные. *Umpteen reasons,* ты́сяча причи́н. —**umpteenth,** *adj., colloq. For the umpteenth time,* в кото́рый раз.

unable *adj.* не в состоя́нии. *I am unable to come today,* я не могу́ прийти́ сего́дня.

unabridged *adj.* по́лный; несокращённый.

unaccented *adj.* безуда́рный.

unacceptable *adj.* неприе́млемый. —**unacceptability,** *n.* неприе́млемость.

unaccompanied *adj.* без сопровожде́ния.

unaccountable *adj.* **1,** (inexplicable) необъясни́мый. **2,** (not responsible) безотчётный. —**unaccountably,** *adv.* по непоня́тной причи́не.

unaccounted-for *adj.* пропа́вший бе́з вести.

unaccustomed *adj.* **1,** *fol. by* **to** (unused to): *be/become unaccustomed to,* не привыка́ть к; отвыка́ть от. **2,** (unfamiliar) непривы́чный.

unacquainted *adj.* незнако́мый.

unadorned *adj.* неприкра́шенный: *the unadorned truth,* неприкра́шенная и́стина.

unadulterated *adj.* **1,** (undiluted) чи́стый; це́льный. **2,** *fig.* (sheer; utter) чи́стый; сплошно́й.

unaffected *adj.* **1,** (not affected): *I am unaffected by the decision,* реше́ние меня́ не каса́ется. **2,** (without affectation) непринуждённый; есте́ственный.

unafraid *adj. Be unafraid of,* не боя́ться; не страши́ться.

unaided *adj.* без (посторо́нней) по́мощи. *With the unaided eye,* невооружённым гла́зом.

unalike *adj.* непохо́жий.

unalterable *adj.* неизме́нный; неизменя́емый. —**unalterably,** *adv.* категори́чески: *unalterably opposed,* категори́чески про́тив.

unambiguous *adj.* недвусмы́сленный; однозна́чный. —**unambiguously,** *adv.* недвусмы́сленно; однозна́чно.

unanimity *n.* единоду́шие; единогла́сие.

unanimous *adj.* единоду́шный; единогла́сный. —**unanimously,** *adv.* единоду́шно; единогла́сно.

unannounced *adj.* без докла́да: *walk in unannounced,* входи́ть без докла́да.

unanswered *adj.* без отве́та: *go unanswered,* оста́ться без отве́та.

unappealing *adj.* непривлека́тельный; неаппети́тный.

unappetizing *adj.* неаппети́тный.

unapproachable *adj.* недосту́пный.

unarmed *adj.* невооружённый; безору́жный.

unassailable *adj.* **1,** (impregnable) непристу́пный. **2,** (incontrovertible) неоспори́мый; неопроверж́имый.

unassisted *adj.* без (посторо́нней) по́мощи.

unassuming *adj.* непритяза́тельный; скро́мный.

unattached *adj.* **1,** (not connected) неприкреплённый. **2,** (unmarried) нежена́тый; незаму́жняя.

unattainable *adj.* недостижи́мый.

unattended *adj.* без ухо́да; без присмо́тра.

unattractive *adj.* непривлека́тельный; некраси́вый.

unauthorized *adj.* самово́льный; недозво́ленный.

unavailable *adj.* не име́ющийся в нали́чии. *Further information is unavailable at this time,* никаки́х бо́льше све́дений сейча́с нет.

unavailing *adj.* тще́тный; напра́сный; бесполе́зный; безрезульта́тный; безуспе́шный. *All our efforts were unavailing,* все на́ши уси́лия бы́ли напра́сными (*or* пропа́ли да́ром).

unavoidable *adj.* неизбе́жный; немину́емый.

unavoidably *adv.* неизбе́жно; немину́емо. *I was unavoidably delayed,* я задержа́лся по незави́сящим от меня́ обстоя́тельствам; я не мог освободи́ться ра́ньше.

unaware *adj. Be unaware* (*of*), не знать (о); не отдава́ть себе́ отчёта (в).

unawares *adv.* врасплóх: *catch unawares,* заста́ть врасплóх.

unbalanced *adj.* неуравнове́шенный; несбаланси́рованный. *Become mentally unbalanced,* повреди́ться в уме́.

unbandage *v.t.* разбинто́вывать.

unbearable *adj.* невыноси́мый; непереноси́мый; нестерпи́мый; несно́сный. —**unbearably,** *adv.* невыноси́мо.

unbeaten *adj.* не име́вший *or* не потерпе́вший пораже́ния.

unbecoming *adj.* **1,** (not attractive or flattering) не к лицу́. **2,** (unseemly; indecorous) неприли́чный; неподоба́ющий; не к лицу́. *It is unbecoming of him to...,* ему́ не к лицу́ (+ *inf.*).

unbeknown *adj.* неве́домый. *Unbeknown to me,* без моего́ ве́дома. *Also,* **unbeknownst.**

unbelievability *n.* невероя́тность.

unbelievable *adj.* невероя́тный. —**unbelievably,** *adv.* невероя́тно; до невероя́тности.

unbeliever *n.* неве́рующий. —**unbelieving,** *adj.* неве́рующий.

unbend *v.t.* распрямля́ть; выпрямля́ть; разгиба́ть; отгиба́ть. —**unbending,** *adj.* несгиба́емый; непрекло́нный.

unbiased *adj.* беспристра́стный.

unbind *v.t.* развя́зывать; отвя́зывать.

unbleached *adj.* небелёный; суро́вый.

unblemished *adj.* незапя́тнанный: *unblemished reputation,* незапя́тнанная репута́ция.

unboiled *adj.* сыро́й: *drink unboiled water,* пить сыру́ю во́ду.

unborn *adj.* (ещё) не рождённый *or* роди́вшийся.

unbound *adj.* (of a book) без переплёта.

unbounded *adj.* неограни́ченный; безме́рный.

unbraid *v.t.* расплета́ть.

unbreakable *adj.* небью́щийся.

unbridle *v.t.* разну́здывать.

unbridled *adj.* 1, (having no bridle) разну́зданный. 2, *fig.* (unrestrained) необу́зданный.

unbroken *adj.* 1, (intact) це́лый. 2, (continuous) сплошно́й: *unbroken line,* сплошна́я ли́ния. *Unbroken string of successes,* сплошно́й ряд уда́ч.

unbuckle *v.t.* расстёгивать.

unburden *v.t.* снима́ть бре́мя с. —**unburden oneself,** отводи́ть ду́шу.

unbutton *v.t.* расстёгивать.

uncalled-for *adj.* 1, (unnecessary) нену́жный. 2, (out of place) неуме́стный.

uncanceled *also,* **uncancelled,** *adj.* (of stamps) нега́шёный.

uncanny *adj.* необъясни́мый.

uncared-for *adj.* безнадзо́рный; забро́шенный.

unceasing *adj.* непреста́нный; беспреста́нный.

uncensored *adj.* не подве́ргшийся цензу́ре.

unceremonious *adj.* бесцеремо́нный. —**unceremoniuosly,** *adv.* бесцеремо́нно.

uncertain *adj.* 1, (unsure) неуве́ренный: *in an uncertain tone of voice,* неуве́ренным то́ном. *I am uncertain about what to do,* я не зна́ю, что де́лать. 2, (indefinite; unclear) неопределённый; нея́сный: *The outcome is uncertain,* исхо́д де́ла нея́сен (*or* под вопро́сом). —**in no uncertain terms,** недвусмы́сленно.

uncertainty *n.* 1, (lack of confidence) неуве́ренность. 2, (lack of definite information) неопределённость; неизве́стность.

unchain *v.t.* 1, (release from a chain) спуска́ть с це́пи. 2, *fig.* (set free) раско́вывать.

unchallengeable *adj.* неоспори́мый.

unchallenged *adj.* 1, (having no rivals) не име́ющий сопе́рников. 2, (not answered or disputed) без возраже́ний: *allow to go unchallenged,* пропуска́ть без возраже́ний; ничего́ не говори́ть в отве́т.

unchanging *adj.* неизме́нный; неизменя́емый.

uncharacteristic *adj.* нехаракте́рный.

uncharted *adj.* неиссле́дованный.

unchecked *adj.* беспрепя́тственный.

uncivil *adj.* неве́жливый; неучти́вый.

uncivilized *adj.* 1, (primitive) нецивилизо́ванный. 2, (crude) некульту́рный.

unclaimed *adj.* невостре́бованный.

unclassified *adj.* несекре́тный.

uncle *n.* дя́дя.

unclean *adj.* нечи́стый. —**uncleanliness,** *n.* нечистота́. —**uncleanly,** *adj.* нечи́стый.

unclear *adj.* нея́сный.

unclench *v.t.* разжима́ть.

unclog *v.t.* прочища́ть.

uncoil *v.t.* разма́тывать; раскру́чивать.

uncomfortable *adj.* 1, (feeling or causing discomfort) неудо́бный: *uncomfortable chair,* неудо́бный стул;

uncomfortable position, неудо́бное положе́ние. *I am uncomfortable,* мне неудо́бно. 2, (awkward) нело́вкий: *uncomfortable situation,* нело́вкое положе́ние. *Feel uncomfortable,* чу́вствовать себя́ нело́вко. —**uncomfortably,** *adv.* неудо́бно.

uncommitted *adj.* неприсоедини́вшийся.

uncommon *adj.* ре́дкий; необыкнове́нный. —**uncommonly,** *adv.* необыкнове́нно.

uncommunicative *adj.* молчали́вый; неразгово́рчивый.

uncomplaining *adj.* безро́потный.

uncompleted *adj.* незако́нченный; незавершённый.

uncomplicated *adj.* несло́жный.

uncomplimentary *adj.* неле́стный.

uncompromising *adj.* бескомпроми́ссный.

unconcealed *adj.* нескрыва́емый: *with unconcealed pride,* с нескрыва́емой го́рдостью.

unconcern *n.* беззабо́тность; беспе́чность. —**unconcerned,** *adj.* беззабо́тный; беспе́чный.

unconditional *adj.* безогово́рочный; безусло́вный. —**unconditional surrender,** безогово́рочная капитуля́ция.

unconditionally *adv.* без вся́ких усло́вий.

unconfirmed *adj.* неподтверждённый.

unconnected *adj.* не свя́занный: *The two events are unconnected,* э́ти два собы́тия не свя́заны друг с дру́гом.

unconquerable *adj.* непобеди́мый.

unconscionable *adj.* бессо́вестный.

unconscious *adj.* 1, (having lost consciousness): *He is unconscious,* он без созна́ния; он в бессозна́тельном состоя́нии. *He was beaten unconscious,* его́ изби́ли до бесчу́вствия. *The blow knocked him unconscious,* уда́р лиши́л его́ созна́ния. 2, (involuntary) бессозна́тельный; безотчётный.

unconsciousness *n.* бессозна́тельное состоя́ние; беспа́мятство; бесчу́вствие.

unconstitutional *adj.* неконституцио́нный.

unconstrained *adj.* непринуждённый; раско́ванный.

uncontrollable *adj.* неукроти́мый; неудержи́мый; безу́держный. *Uncontrollable anger,* неукроти́мый гнев. *Uncontrollable desire,* неудержи́мое жела́ние. *Uncontrollable laughter,* безу́держный смех.

uncontrolled *adj.* неконтроли́руемый; бесконтро́льный.

unconventional *adj.* необы́чный; оригина́льный.

unconvinced *adj.* не убеждён. *I remain unconvinced,* я остаю́сь при своём мне́нии.

unconvincing *adj.* неубеди́тельный.

uncooked *adj.* сыро́й.

uncooperative *adj.* несгово́рчивый.

uncoordinated *adj.* несогласо́ванный.

uncork *v.t.* отку́поривать; раску́поривать.

uncountable *adj.* неисчисли́мый. —**uncounted,** *adj.* несчётный; бесчи́сленный.

uncouple *v.t.* расцепля́ть; отцепля́ть.

uncouth *adj.* гру́бый; неотёсанный.

uncover *v.t.* 1, (remove the cover from; make visible) открыва́ть. 2, (discover, as a plot or evidence) раскрыва́ть.

uncritical *adj.* некрити́ческий.

uncrowned *adj.* некороно́ванный.

unction *n.* **1,** (act of anointing) миропома́зание. *Extreme unction,* собо́рование. **2,** (oil; ointment) еле́й; мазь.

unctuous *adj.* еле́йный.

uncultivated *adj.* **1,** (untilled) необрабо́танный; невозде́ланный. **2,** (unrefined) некульту́рный.

uncultured *adj.* некульту́рный.

uncut *adj.* **1,** (not sliced) неразре́занный. **2,** (not abridged) по́лный; несокращённый. **3,** (not ground or polished) неотшлифо́ванный.

undamaged *adj.* невреди́мый; неповреждённый.

undaunted *adj.* неустраши́мый; бесстра́шный.

undecided *adj.* **1,** (not settled) нерешённый. **2,** (not having reached a decision) в нереши́тельности; в нереши́мости. *I am still undecided as to what to do,* я ещё не реши́л(а), что сде́лать.

undecipherable *adj.* неразбо́рчивый.

undeclared *adj.* необъя́вленный: *undeclared war,* необъя́вленная война́.

undefeated *adj.* не име́вший *or* не потерпе́вший пораже́ния.

undefended *adj.* незащищённый.

undemanding *adj.* нетре́бовательный; невзыска́тельный.

undemocratic *adj.* недемократи́ческий; антидемократи́ческий.

undeniable *adj.* неоспори́мый; бесспо́рный.

undependable *adj.* ненадёжный.

under *prep.* **1,** (below) под (+ *instr.*): *under the table/tree,* под столо́м; под де́ревом. *Under water,* под водо́й. *From under the table,* из-под стола́. *Live under the same roof,* жить под одно́й кры́шей. *Examine something under a microscope,* рассма́тривать что́-нибудь в микроско́п *or* под микроско́пом. ♦*With verbs of motion,* под (+ *acc.*): *The ball rolled under the bed,* мяч закати́лся под крова́ть. *Slip something under the door,* подсу́нуть что́-нибудь под дверь. **2,** (less than) ме́ньше чем: *sell for under two dollars,* продава́ться ме́ньше чем, за два до́ллара. *Children under sixteen not admitted,* де́ти до шестна́дцати (лет) не допуска́ются. **3,** (according to) по; согла́сно. *Under the terms of the treaty,* по усло́виям догово́ра. **4,** (in view of) при: *under the circumstances,* при таки́х обстоя́тельствах. **5,** (under the guidance of) у: *study under Stravinsky,* учи́ться у Страви́нского. **6,** (while subject to the rule of) при: *under Stalin,* при Ста́лине; *under the old regime,* при ста́ром режи́ме. *Live under communism,* жить при коммуни́зме. **7,** (subject to the authority of) под: *He has ten people under him,* он име́ет под свои́м нача́лом де́сять сотру́дников. **8,** *with various nouns,* под: *under oath,* под прися́гой; *under arrest,* под аре́стом; *under arms,* под ружьём; *under lock and key,* под замко́м; *under the leadership of,* под руково́дством (+ *gen.*); *under an assumed name,* под чужи́м и́менем. *Be under repair/siege,* быть в ремо́нте; быть в оса́де. ♦*Also with the refl. verb: be under construction,* стро́иться; *be under discussion,*

обсужда́ться; *be under consideration,* рассма́триваться. —*adv.* **1,** (to a place below) вниз. *The swimmer went under,* плове́ц утону́л. *The business went under,* де́ло прогоре́ло. **2,** (less) ме́ньше: *five dollars or under,* пять до́лларов и́ли (да́же) ме́ньше. *Children six and under,* де́ти до шести́ лет. —**under way,** see **way.**

underage *adj.* несовершенноле́тний; малоле́тний.

underbodice *n.* ли́фчик.

underbrush *n.* подле́сок.

undercarriage *n.* шасси́.

undercharge *v.t.* брать сли́шком дёшево с.

underclothes *n.pl.* ни́жнее бельё.

undercook *v.t.* недовари́ть; недожа́рить.

undercover *adj.* та́йный; секре́тный. *Undercover agent,* та́йный аге́нт.

undercurrent *n.* **1,** (lower current) подво́дное тече́ние. **2,** (latent manifestation): *undercurrent of discontent,* скры́тое недово́льство.

undercut *v.t.* **1,** = **undersell. 2,** (undermine) подрыва́ть; вести́ подко́п под.

underdeveloped *adj.* недора́звитый. *Underdeveloped countries,* слабора́звитые стра́ны.

underdone *adj.* недожа́ренный; с кро́вью.

underdrawers *n.pl.* кальсо́ны.

underestimate *v.t.* недооце́нивать; преуменьша́ть. —**underestimation,** *n.* недооце́нка; преуменьше́ние.

underexpose *v.t., photog.* недоде́рживать. —**underexposure,** *n.* недоде́ржка.

underfed *adj. Be underfed,* недоеда́ть.

underfoot *adv.* под нога́ми. *Trample underfoot,* зата́птывать.

undergarment *n.* предме́т ни́жнего белья́.

undergo *v.t.* проходи́ть; подверга́ться (+ *dat.*). *Undergo tests/training,* проходи́ть испыта́ния/подгото́вку. *Undergo an operation,* подве́ргнуться опера́ции. *Undergo interrogation,* подве́ргнуться допро́су. *Undergo changes,* претерпе́ть измене́ния. *Undergo treatment,* лечи́ться; проходи́ть курс лече́ния.

undergraduate *n.* студе́нт университе́та.

underground *n.* **1,** (clandestine movement) подпо́лье. *Go underground,* уйти́ в подпо́лье. **2,** *Brit.* = **subway.** —*adj.* **1,** (subterranean) подзе́мный. **2,** (clandestine) подпо́льный.

undergrowth *n.* подле́сок; за́росли.

underhand *adj.* = **underhanded.** —*adj. & adv., sports* сни́зу.

underhanded *adj.* обма́нный; надува́тельский.

underlie *v.t.* **1,** (lie under) лежа́ть под. **2,** (be the basis of) лежа́ть в осно́ве (+ *gen.*); лечь в осно́ву (+ *gen.*).

underline *v.t.* подчёркивать.

underling *n.* приспе́шник.

underlying *adj.* лежа́щий в осно́ве; основно́й.

undermine *v.t.* подрыва́ть: *undermine one's health,* подрыва́ть здоро́вье. *Undermine the foundations of society,* подрыва́ть осно́вы о́бщества.

underneath *adv.* внизу́; ни́же. —*prep.* под: *underneath the rug,* под ковро́м.

undernourished *adj. Be undernourished,* недоеда́ть.

underpaid *adj.* низкоопла́чиваемый.

underpants *n.pl.* **1,** (shorts; panties) трусы́; тру́сики. **2,** (long drawers) кальсо́ны.

underpass *n.* подзе́мный перехо́д.

underpay *v.t.* опла́чивать (кого́-нибудь) сли́шком ни́зко. —*v.i.* недопла́чивать: *underpay by ten dollars,* недопла́чивать де́сять до́лларов.

underpopulated *adj.* малонаселённый.

underprivileged *adj.* неиму́щий; малоиму́щий.

underproduction *n.* недопроизво́дство.

underrate *v.t.* недооце́нивать; преуменьша́ть.

underripe *adj.* недоспе́лый; недозре́лый.

underscore *v.t.* подчёркивать.

undersea *adj.* подво́дный.

undersecretary *n.* замести́тель мини́стра.

undersell *v.t.* продава́ть деше́вле, чем.

undershirt *n.* ни́жняя руба́шка.

undershorts *n.pl.* трусы́.

underside *n.* изна́нка.

undersigned *n., preceded by* **the,** нижеподписа́вшийся.

undersized *adj.* малоро́слый; низкоро́слый.

underskirt *n.* ни́жняя ю́бка.

understand *v.t. & i.* понима́ть: *understand Russian,* понима́ть по-ру́сски. *I don't understand,* я не понима́ю. —*v.t.* **1,** (hear) слы́шать: *I understand that...,* я слы́шал(а), что... **2,** (assume without stating) подразумева́ть: *The subject (of the sentence) is understood,* подлежа́щее подразумева́ется. —**give to understand,** дать поня́ть. —**make oneself understood,** объясня́ться.

understandable *adj.* поня́тный. —**understandably,** *adv.* поня́тно; поня́тное де́ло.

understanding *n.* **1,** (comprehension) понима́ние. **2,** (an agreement) договорённость; соглаше́ние. —*adj.* **1,** (comprehending) понима́ющий. **2,** (sympathetic) отзы́вчивый.

understate *v.t.* **1,** (describe with restraint) преуменьша́ть. **2,** (misrepresent) занижа́ть.

understatement *n.* преуменьше́ние. *That's an understatement!,* э́то сли́шком мя́гкое выраже́ние; э́то сли́шком сла́бо ска́зано; так сказа́ть — ничего́ не сказа́ть.

understudy *n.* дублёр. —*v.t.* дубли́ровать.

undertake *v.t.* **1,** (take upon oneself; agree to do) предпринима́ть; бра́ться за. *Undertake a trip,* предпринима́ть пое́здку. *Undertake a job/ an assignment/,* бра́ться за рабо́ту/поруче́ние. **2,** fol. by inf. (pledge) обя́зываться.

undertaker *n.* владе́лец похоро́нного бюро́.

undertaking *n.* предприя́тие; начина́ние.

undertone *n. In an undertone,* вполго́лоса.

undertow *n.* подво́дное тече́ние.

undervalue *v.t.* недооце́нивать.

underwater *adj.* подво́дный.

underwear *n.* ни́жнее бельё.

underweight *adj.* ве́сящий ме́ньше (*or* ни́же) поло́женного ве́са. *I am ten pounds underweight,* я ве́шу на де́сять фу́нтов ме́ньше/ни́же поло́женного ве́са.

underworld *n.* **1,** (criminal element) престу́пный мир; уголо́вщина. **2,** (hell) преиспо́дняя.

underwrite *v.t.* гаранти́ровать: *underwrite a loan,* гаранти́ровать размеще́ние за́йма.

underwriter *n.* страхо́вщик.

undeserved *adj.* незаслу́женный.

undesirable *adj.* нежела́тельный. —*n., usu. pl.* сомни́тельные элеме́нты.

undetected *adj.* необнару́женный.

undetermined *adj.* неопределённый.

undeveloped *adj.* неразвито́й.

undignified *adj.* недосто́йный.

undiplomatic *adj.* недипломати́чный.

undisciplined *adj.* недисциплини́рованный.

undiscriminating *adj.* неразбо́рчивый.

undisguised *adj.* неприкры́тый; нескрыва́емый.

undismayed *adj.* необескура́женный.

undisputed *adj.* неоспори́мый.

undistinguished *adj.* заря́дный; непримеча́тельный.

undisturbed *adj.* **1,** (not worried) необеспоко́енный. **2,** (uninterrupted, as of sleep) безмяте́жный.

undivided *adj.* безразде́льный. *One's undivided attention,* по́лное внима́ние.

undo *v.t.* **1,** (reverse the doing of) своди́ть на нет. *Undo an error,* исправля́ть оши́бку. *Undo everything that has been done,* перечеркну́ть всё, что бы́ло сде́лано. **2,** (unfasten) расстёгивать; отстёгивать; развя́зывать.

undoing *n. Be/prove the undoing of,* (по)губи́ть кого́-нибудь.

undone *adj.* **1,** (not done) незако́нченный. **2,** (unfastened): *come undone,* расстёгиваться; отстёгиваться; развя́зываться.

undoubted *adj.* несомне́нный; бесспо́рный. —**undoubtedly,** *adv.* несомне́нно; бесспо́рно.

undreamed-of *adj.* во сне не сни́вшийся; невообрази́мый.

undress *v.t.* раздева́ть. —*v.i.* раздева́ться. —**undressed,** *adj.* разде́тый.

undrinkable *adj.* непри́годный для питья́.

undue *adj.* изли́шний; чрезме́рный: *undue haste,* изли́шняя/чрезме́рная поспе́шность.

undulate *v.i.* **1,** (ripple) ряби́ть. **2,** (flutter) колыха́ться. —**undulating,** *adj.* волни́стый; волнообра́зный.

unduly *adv.* чрезме́рно; чересчу́р; сли́шком. *I hope you were not unduly alarmed,* наде́юсь, что вы не сли́шком (*or* не о́чень) встрево́жились.

undying *adj.* неугаси́мый; неувяда́емый; неме́ркнущий.

unearned *adj.* **1,** (not earned) нетрудово́й: *unearned income,* нетрудово́й дохо́д. **2,** (not deserved) незаслу́женный.

unearth *v.t.* **1,** (dig up from the earth) выка́пывать; вырыва́ть; отка́пывать; отрыва́ть. **2,** (find; discover) выка́пывать; отка́пывать; раска́пывать.

unearthly *adj.* неземно́й; нозде́шний. *At this unearthly hour,* в таку́ю рань.

uneasy *adj.* беспоко́йный; неспоко́йный. *Feel uneasy,* стесня́ться. —**uneasiness** *n.* беспоко́йство.

uneatable *adj.* несъедо́бный.

uneconomical *adj.* неэконо́мный; бесхозя́йственный.

uneducated *adj.* необразо́ванный.

unemployed *adj.* безрабо́тный. —*n., preceded by* **the** безрабо́тные.

unemployment *n.* безрабо́тица. *Unemployment insurance/benefits,* посо́бие по безрабо́тице.

unencouraging *adj.* неутеши́тельный.

unending *adj.* несконча́емый.

unendurable *adj.* невыноси́мый; непереноси́мый; несно́сный; нестерпи́мый.

unenforceable *adj.* неосуществи́мый.

unenlightened *adj.* непросвещённый.

unenterprising *adj.* непредприи́мчивый; безынициати́вный.

unenthusiastic *adj.* лишённый энтузиа́зма. *The critics were unenthusiastic,* кри́тики бы́ли не в восто́рге; кри́тики относи́лись хо́лодно (к чему́-нибудь).

unenviable *adj.* незави́дный.

unequal *adj.* **1,** (not equal in amount; not equitable) нера́вный. *Unequal battle,* нера́вный бой. *Unequal treaty,* неравнопра́вный догово́р. **2,** *fol. by* **to** (not up to): *He proved unequal to the task,* зада́ча оказа́лась ему́ не под си́лу.

unequaled *also,* **unequalled** *adj.* непревзойдённый. *An achievement unequaled since,* достиже́ние, ра́вных кото́рому не́ было с тех пор.

unequivocal *adj.* недвусмы́сленный; однозна́чный. —**unequivocally,** *adv.* недвусмы́сленно; однозна́чно.

unerring *adj.* безоши́бочный.

unethical *adj.* неэти́чный.

uneven *adj.* **1,** (not level or straight) неро́вный. **2,** (not uniform or consistent) неравноме́рный. **3,** (odd, as of a number) нечётный. —**unevenly,** *adv.* неро́вно; неравноме́рно. —**unevenness,** *n.* неро́вность; неравноме́рность.

uneventful *adj.* без происше́ствий: *The trip was uneventful,* пое́здка прошла́ без происше́ствий.

unexampled *adj.* беспримѐрный.

unexcelled *adj.* непревзойдённый.

unexceptionable *adj.* безупре́чный.

unexceptional *adj.* ниче́м не выделя́ющийся; заурядный.

unexpected *adj.* неожи́данный. —**unexpectedly,** *adv.* неожи́данно.

unexplainable *adj.* необъясни́мый.

unexplained *adj.* невы́ясненный. *He died under unexplained circumstances,* он у́мер при невы́ясненных обстоя́тельствах.

unexplored *adj.* неиссле́дованный; неизве́данный; неразве́данный.

unexposed *adj., photog.* неэкспони́рованный.

unexpressed *adj.* невы́сказанный.

unexpressive *adj.* невырази́тельный.

unfailing *adj.* **1,** (constant; unflagging) неосла́бный. **2,** (devoted; staunch) неизме́нный. —**unfailingly,** *adv.* неукосни́тельно.

unfair *adj.* **1,** (inequitable) несправедли́вый. **2,** (un-

ethical) нече́стный. —**unfairly,** *adv.* несправедли́во. —**unfairness,** *n.* несправедли́вость.

unfaithful *adj.* неве́рный. *Be unfaithful to,* изменя́ть; обма́нывать.

unfamiliar *adj.* незнако́мый. —**unfamiliarity,** *n.* незнако́мство.

unfasten *v.t.* **1,** (detach) открепля́ть. **2,** (unbutton; untie) расстёгивать; отстёгивать; отвя́зывать.

unfathomable *adj.* **1,** (impossible to measure) неизмери́мый. **2,** (impossible to understand) непостижи́мый.

unfavorable *also,* **unfavourable** *adj.* неблагоприя́тный. *Unfavorable balance of trade,* пасси́вный торго́вый бала́нс.

unfeasible *adj.* невыполни́мый; неосуществи́мый.

unfeeling *adj.* бесчу́вственный.

unfeigned *adj.* непритво́рный; неподде́льный.

unfetter *v.t.* раско́вывать.

unfilled *adj.* **1,** (vacant) вака́нтный. *Unfilled position,* вака́нсия. **2,** (not executed) невы́полненный: *unfilled orders,* невы́полненные зака́зы.

unfinished *adj.* незако́нченный.

unfit *adj.* него́дный; непригóдный.

unflagging *adj.* неосла́бный; неусы́пный.

unflappable *adj., colloq.* невозмути́мый.

unflattering *adj.* неле́стный.

unfledged *adj.* неопери́вшийся.

unflinching *adj.* непоколеби́мый; неукло́нный.

unfold *v.t.* развёртывать. —*v.i.* **1,** (open out) развёртываться. **2,** *fig.* (develop, as of events or a situation) развора́чиваться.

unforeseen *adj.* непредви́денный.

unforgettable *adj.* незабыва́емый; незабве́нный.

unforgivable *adj.* непрости́тельный.

unfortunate *adj.* **1,** (unlucky; hapless) несча́стный. **2,** (regrettable; inappropriate) неуда́чный. —**unfortunately,** *adv.* к сожале́нию; к несча́стью.

unfounded *adj.* необосно́ванный; неоснова́тельный; беспо́чвенный. *The charge is completely unfounded,* обвине́ние ни на чём не осно́вано.

unfreeze *v.t.* размора́живать.

unfriendliness *n.* недружелю́бие; неприве́тливость.

unfriendly *adj.* недружелю́бный; неприве́тливый.

unfrock *v.t.* расстрига́ть; лиша́ть духо́вного са́на.

unfulfilled *adj.* **1,** (not realized) невы́полненный. **2,** (broken; unkept) несде́ржанный.

unfurl *v.t.* развёртывать; распуска́ть.

unfurnished *adj.* немеблиро́ванный.

ungainly *adj.* неуклю́жий; нескла́дный.

ungird *v.t.* распоя́сывать.

unglue *v.t.* откле́ивать; раскле́ивать. *Come unglued,* откле́иваться; раскле́иваться.

ungodly *adj.* **1,** (not believing in God) безбо́жный. **2,** *colloq.* (horrible) ди́кий. *At this ungodly hour,* в таку́ю рань.

ungovernable *adj.* неуправля́емый.

ungraceful *adj.* нестро́йный; нескла́дный.

ungracious *adj.* нелюбе́зный; неприве́тливый. —**ungraciousness,** *n.* неприве́тливость.

ungrammatical *adj.* негра́мотный; безгра́мотный.

ungrateful *adj.* неблагода́рный.

unguarded *adj.* **1,** (unprotected) незащищённый. **2,** (indiscreet) неосторо́жный; неосмотри́тельный.

unguent *n.* мазь.

ungulate *adj.* копы́тный. —*n.* копы́тное живо́тное.

unhampered *adj.* беспрепя́тственный.

unhand *v.t.* отнима́ть ру́ки от.

unhandy *adj.* **1,** (inconvenient) неудо́бный. **2,** (clumsy) безру́кий.

unhappiness *n.* недово́льство; неудово́льствие.

unhappy *adj.* **1,** (sad) гру́стный: *Why are you so unhappy?*, почему́ вы тако́й гру́стный (така́я гру́стная)? *You look unhappy,* у вас несча́стный вид. **2,** (unfortunate; miserable) несчастли́вый; несча́стный: *unhappy life,* несчастли́вая/несча́стная жизнь. **3,** (not successful; unsatisfactory) несчастли́вый; неблагополу́чный. *Unhappy ending,* несчастли́вый коне́ц. *Unhappy outcome,* неблагополу́чный исхо́д. **4,** (dissatisfied) недово́лен: *unhappy with the results,* недово́лен результа́тами. **5,** (inappropriate) неуда́чный: *an unhappy choice,* неуда́чный вы́бор.

unharmed *adj.* невреди́мый.

unharness *v.t.* распряга́ть; отпряга́ть; выпряга́ть.

unhealthy *adj.* нездоро́вый.

unheard-of *adj.* неслы́ханный.

unheated *adj.* нето́пленый; неота́пливаемый.

unheeded *adj. His warnings went unheeded,* его́ предупрежде́ния оста́лись без внима́ния.

unhelpful *adj.* бесполе́зный: *unhelpful advice,* бесполе́зный сове́т. *He was completely unhelpful,* он совсе́м не помо́г.

unhesitatingly *adv.* без колеба́ний.

unhindered *adj.* беспрепя́тственный.

unhinge *v.t.* **1,** (remove from its hinges) снима́ть с пе́тель. **2,** (unbalance; upset) расша́тывать. *His mind became unhinged,* он тро́нулся умо́м.

unhitch *v.t.* отцепля́ть; расцепля́ть.

unholy *adj.* **1,** (wicked) нечести́вый. **2,** *colloq.* (dreadful) су́щий: *unholy hell,* су́щий ад.

unhook *v.t.* **1,** (detach) отцепля́ть; расцепля́ть. **2,** (unbutton) расстёгивать.

unhurried *adj.* неторопли́вый; неспе́шный.

unhurt *adj.* невреди́мый.

Uniate *also,* **Uniat** *n.* униа́т. —*adj.* униа́тский.

unicameral *adj.* однопала́тный.

unicorn *n.* единоро́г.

unidentified *adj.* неопо́знанный.

unification *n.* объедине́ние.

uniform *n.* фо́рма; обмундирова́ние. *In uniform,* в фо́рме. —*adj.* **1,** (of a uniform) фо́рменный: *uniform dress,* фо́рменная оде́жда. **2,** (regular; unchanging) ро́вный; равноме́рный. *Uniform temperature,* ро́вная температу́ра. **3,** (the same everywhere) единообра́зный: *a uniform system,* единообра́зная систе́ма.

uniformed *adj.* оде́тый в фо́рму.

uniformity *n.* единообра́зие.

uniformly *adv.* всегда́; во всех слу́чаях; без исключе́ния.

unify *v.t.* объединя́ть. *Under a unified command,* под еди́ным кома́ндованием.

unilateral *adj.* односторо́нний. —**unilaterally,** *adv.* в односторо́ннем поря́дке.

unimaginable *adj.* невообрази́мый.

unimpeachable *adj.* безукори́зненный; безупре́чный.

unimpeded *adj.* беспрепя́тственный.

unimportant *adj.* нева́жный: *unimportant question,* нева́жный вопро́с. *Unimportant detail,* несуще́ственная дета́ль.

unimpressed *adj. I was unimpressed,* э́то на меня́ не произвело́ никако́го впечатле́ния.

uninformed *adj.* неосведомлённый; несве́дущий.

uninhabitable *adj.* непригодный для жилья́.

uninhabited *adj.* **1,** (of a region, island, etc.) необита́емый; безлю́дный. **2,** (of a house, apartment, etc.) необжи́тый.

uninhibited *adj.* нестеснённый; раско́ванный.

uninitiated *adj.* непосвящённый.

uninjured *adj.* невреди́мый.

uninspired *adj.* безду́шный; бескры́лый.

uninsured *adj.* незастрахо́ванный.

unintelligent *adj.* неу́мный.

unintelligible *adj.* непоня́тный; невразуми́тельный. —**unintelligibility,** *n.* непоня́тность.

unintentional *adj.* ненаме́ренный; нево́льный; неумы́шленный. —**unintentionally,** *adv.* ненаме́ренно; нево́льно; неумы́шленно.

uninteresting *adj.* неинтере́сный.

uninterrupted *adj.* непреры́вный; беспреры́вный; беспере́бойный.

uninvited *adj.* незва́ный; непро́шеный. *He came to the wedding uninvited,* он пришёл на сва́дьбу без приглаше́ния.

uninviting *adj.* неприве́тливый.

union *n.* **1,** (joining together) соедине́ние; объедине́ние; слия́ние. *Marital union,* бра́чный сою́з. **2,** (a confederation) сою́з; объедине́ние. *Universal Postal Union,* Всеми́рный почто́вый сою́з. **3,** (labor union) профсою́з. —*adj.* профсою́зный: *union dues,* профсою́зные взно́сы.

unionize *v.t. & i.* объединя́ть(ся) в профсою́з.

unique *adj.* уника́льный; еди́нственный в своём ро́де. *Unique situation/opportunity,* уника́льная ситуа́ция/возмо́жность.

unisexual *adj.* однопо́лый.

unison *n.* унисо́н. —**in unison,** в унисо́н.

unit *n.* **1,** (basic element or amount) едини́ца: *unit of measurement,* едини́ца измере́ния. *Monetary unit,* де́нежная едини́ца. **2,** *mil.* часть: *artillery unit,* артиллери́йская часть. **3,** (apparatus) устано́вка; блок; у́зел; агрега́т.

unite *v.t.* соединя́ть; объединя́ть. —*v.i.* соединя́ться; объединя́ться. *"Workers of the world, unite!",* Пролета́рии всех стран, соединя́йтесь!

united *adj.* соединённый; объединённый. *United front,* еди́ный фронт. *A united people,* сплочённый наро́д. —**United Kingdom,** Соединённое Короле́вство. —**United Nations,** Объединённые На́ции. —**United States,** Соединённые Шта́ты.

unity *n.* **1,** (oneness; sameness) еди́нство. **2,** (quality of being united) еди́нство; едине́ние; сплочённость.

universal *adj.* **1,** (worldwide) всеобщий; всемирный. *Universal suffrage,* всеобщее избирательное право. *Universal language,* всемирный язык. **2,** (touching everything) универсальный: *a universal principle,* универсальный принцип. —**universal joint,** универсальный шарнир.

universality *n.* универсальность.

universally *adv.* во всём мире; всеми. *Universally recognized,* всеми признанный.

universe *n.* вселенная. *The origin of the universe,* происхождение мира.

university *n.* университет. —*adj.* университетский.

unjust *adj.* несправедливый.

unjustified *adj.* неоправданный.

unjustly *adv.* несправедливо.

unkempt *adj.* **1,** (uncombed) нечёсаный. **2,** (untidy) неопрятный; неряшливый; нечистоплотный.

unkept *adj.* несдержанный.

unkind *adj.* недобрый.

unknown *adj.* **1,** (not known) неизвестный; безвестный. **2,** *math.* неизвестный. —*n., math.* неизвестное; искомое. —**fear of the unknown,** страх перед неизвестностью.

unlace *v.t.* расшнуровывать.

unlawful *adj.* незаконный; противозаконный. —**unlawfully,** *adv.* незаконно.

unleaded *adj.* (of gasoline) неэтилированный.

unleash *v.t.* спускать с привязи *or* с поводка. *Unleash a war,* развязать *or* разжигать войну.

unleavened *adj.* пресный. *Unleavened bread,* пресный хлеб; маца́.

unless *conj.* если не: *unless I am mistaken,* если я не ошибаюсь. *Unless I hear to the contrary,* если я не услышу чего-нибудь иного.

unlighted *adj.* неосвещённый.

unlike *adj.* непохожий. —*prep.* **1,** (differing from) непохожий на. ♦*When introducing a contrasting situation,* в отличие от; не в пример (+ *dat.*). **2,** (not typical of) нетипично (для); нехарактерно (для). *That's unlike him,* это на него не похоже.

unlikelihood *n.* маловероятность.

unlikely *adj.* маловероятный: *It is extremely unlikely that...,* крайне маловероятно, чтобы...

unlimber *v.t.* разминать. —*v.i.* разминаться.

unlimited *adj.* неограниченный.

unlined *adj.* **1,** (of paper) нелинованный. **2,** (with no lining) без подкладки.

unlisted *adj.* не включённый в список. *We have an unlisted number,* наш номер не внесён в телефонную книгу.

unlit *adj.* неосвещённый.

unload *v.t.* **1,** (remove cargo from, as a ship) разгружать. **2,** (remove, as cargo) выгружать. **3,** (remove the ammunition from) разряжать. **4,** *colloq.* (sell; get rid of) спускать. —*v.i.* разгружаться.

unloaded *adj.* незаряженный: *unloaded rifle,* незаряженная винтовка.

unloading *n.* **1,** (of a ship) разгрузка. **2,** (of cargo) выгрузка.

unlock *v.t.* отпирать. —*v.i.* отпираться. —**unlocked,** *adj.* незапертый.

unloved *adj.* нелюбимый.

unlucky *adj.* **1,** (having no luck) неудачливый; незадачливый. *We were very unlucky,* нам очень не повезло. **2,** (bringing bad luck) несчастливый: *unlucky number,* несчастливая цифра.

unmanageable *adj.* неуправляемый.

unmanned *adj.* беспилотный.

unmannerly *adj.* невоспитанный; некультурный.

unmarried *adj.* (of a man) неженатый; (of a woman) незамужняя.

unmask *v.t.* разоблачать.

unmentionable *adj.* нецензурный. —**unmentionables,** *n.pl., colloq.* «невыразимые».

unmerciful *adj.* немилосердный; беспощадный.

unmindful *adj.* [*usu.* **unmindful of**] не обращая внимания (на).

unmistakable *adj.* **1,** (that cannot be confused) верный: *unmistakable sign,* верный признак. **2,** (allowing no misunderstanding) недвусмысленный.

unmitigated *adj.* **1,** (thoroughgoing; out-and-out) отъявленный. **2,** (total; utter) полный.

unmoved *adj.* безучастный.

unnamed *adj.* неназванный.

unnatural *adj.* неестественный.

unnavigable *adj.* несудоходный.

unnecessary *adj.* ненужный: *exercise unnecessary caution,* проявлять ненужную осторожность.

unnerve *v.t.* нервировать; расстраивать; лишать присутствия духа. —**unnerved,** *adj.* расстроенный; развинченный.

unnoticed *adj.* незамеченный: *go unnoticed,* пройти незамеченным.

unobservant *adj.* ненаблюдательный.

unobtainable *adj.* недоступный.

unoccupied *adj.* **1,** (with no one inside) незанятый: *unoccupied house,* незанятый дом. *The lavatory is unoccupied,* уборная свободна. **2,** (not held by anyone) вакантный: *The position is unoccupied at present,* место сейчас вакантно.

unofficial *adj.* неофициальный.

unopened *adj.* неоткрытый.

unopposed *adj.* без соперников. *Run unopposed,* баллотироваться в одиночку *or* в единственном числе.

unorganized *adj.* неорганизованный.

unorthodox *adj.* необычный; оригинальный.

unpack *v.t.* распаковывать. —*v.i.* распаковываться.

unpaid *adj.* **1,** (not yet paid) неоплаченный; неуплаченный. **2,** (receiving no pay) не получающий платы. **3,** (not compensated, as of labor) безвозмездный.

unpainted *adj.* некрашеный.

unpalatable *adj.* невкусный.

unparalleled *adj.* беспримерный; беспрецедентный.

unpardonable *adj.* непростительный.

unpatriotic *adj.* непатриотический; непатриотичный.

unpaved *adj.* немощёный.

unpersuasive *adj.* неубеди́тельный.

unpin *v.t.* отка́лывать.

unplanned *adj.* незаплани́рованный. *Unplanned economy,* беспла́новое хозя́йство.

unpleasant *adj.* неприя́тный. —**unpleasantness,** *n.* неприя́тность.

unplug *v.t.* отключа́ть.

unpolished *adj.* неотполиро́ванный; неотшлифо́ванный.

unpopular *adj.* непопуля́рный. —**unpopularity,** *n.* непопуля́рность.

unprecedented *adj.* беспрецеде́нтный; небыва́лый; неви́данный.

unpredictable *adj.* непредсказу́емый.

unprejudiced *adj.* непредубеждённый.

unpremeditated *adj.* непреднаме́ренный; непредумы́шленный.

unprepared *adj.* неподгото́вленный. *Catch unprepared,* заста́ть враспло́х.

unpretentious *adj.* непритяза́тельный; неприхотли́вый; незате́йливый.

unpreventable *adj.* неотврати́мый; неизбе́жный; немину́емый.

unprincipled *adj.* беспринци́пный.

unprintable *adj.* непеча́тный; нецензу́рный.

unproductive *adj.* непродукти́вный; непроизводи́тельный. —**unproductiveness,** *n.* непродукти́вность; непроизводи́тельность.

unprofitable *adj.* **1,** (not yielding a profit) невы́годный; беспри́быльный; нерента́бельный; убы́точный. **2,** (not accomplishing anything) безрезульта́тный.

unpromising *adj.* не подаю́щий наде́жды; неперспекти́вный.

unpronounceable *adj.* не(удобо)произноси́мый.

unpropitious *adj.* неблагоприя́тный.

unprotected *adj.* незащищённый; беззащи́тный.

unproved *adj.* недока́занный. *Also,* **unproven.**

unprovoked *adj.* неспровоци́рованный.

unpublished *adj.* неопублико́ванный; неи́зданный.

unpunished *adj.* безнака́занный. *Go unpunished,* оста́ться безнака́занным.

unqualified *adj.* **1,** (not fit) не име́ющий (соотве́тствующей) квалифика́ции. **2,** (unreserved) безоговоро́чный: *unqualified support,* безоговоро́чная подде́ржка.

unquenchable *adj.* **1,** (inextinguishable) неугаси́мый. **2,** (insatiable) неутоли́мый.

unquestionable *adj.* неоспори́мый; бесспо́рный. —**unquestionably,** *adv.* бесспо́рно.

unquestioned *adj.* несомне́нный; неоспори́мый.

unquestioning *adj.* беспрекосло́вный.

unravel *v.t.* **1,** (untangle) распу́тывать. **2,** (solve) распу́тывать; разга́дывать; раскрыва́ть. —*v.i.* располза́ться.

unreadable *adj.* неудобочита́емый.

unready *adj.* него́товый.

unreal *adj.* нереа́льный.

unrealistic *adj.* нереа́льный.

unrealizable *adj.* неосуществи́мый; несбы́точный.

unreasonable *adj.* **1,** (impossible to reason with) неразу́мный. **2,** (excessive; unfair) непоме́рный. —**unreasonableness,** *n.* неразу́мность.

unreasoning *adj.* неразу́мный; нерассуди́тельный.

unreceptive *adj.* невосприи́мчивый.

unrecognizable *adj.* неузнава́емый.

unrecognized *adj.* непри́знанный.

unreel *v.t.* разма́тывать.

unrefined *adj.* **1,** (raw) неочи́щенный. **2,** (lacking refinement) невоспи́танный.

unrehearsed *adj.* нерепети́рованный.

unrelated *adj.* [*usu.* **unrelated to**] не име́ющий отноше́ния (к).

unrelenting *adj.* **1,** (relentless) неотсту́пный. **2,** (not relaxing or slackening) неосла́бный.

unreliable *adj.* ненадёжный. —**unreliability,** *n.* ненадёжность.

unrelieved *adj.* беспросве́тный: *unrelieved boredom,* беспросве́тная тоска́.

unremitting *adj.* неосла́бный.

unremunerative *adj.* невы́годный; беспри́быльный.

unrepentant *adj.* нераска́явшийся. *He remains unrepentant,* он всё ещё не раска́ялся.

unrequited *adj.* без взаи́мности; безотве́тный.

unreserved *adj.* **1,** (not reserved, as of a seat) незаброни́рованный; (of a car on a train) бесплацка́ртный. **2,** (unqualified; unconditional) безоговоро́чный.

unresolved *adj.* неразрешённый; нерешённый.

unresponsive *adj.* неотзы́вчивый.

unrest *n.* **1,** (worry; concern) беспоко́йство; волне́ние. **2,** (disturbances; agitation) волне́ния; беспоря́дки.

unrestrained *adj.* несде́ржанный; необу́зданный; безуде́ржный.

unrestricted *adj.* неограни́ченный.

unripe *adj.* незре́лый; неспе́лый.

unrivaled *also,* **unrivalled** *adj.* не име́ющий себе́ ра́вных; непревзойдённый.

unroll *v.t.* развёртывать; раска́тывать.

unruffled *adj.* безмяте́жный.

unruled *adj.* нелино́ванный.

unruly *adj.* непоко́рный; бу́йный.

unsaddle *v.t.* рассёдлывать.

unsafe *adj.* опа́сный. *Unsafe bridge,* ненадёжный мост.

unsaid *adj.* *Leave* (something) *unsaid,* недогова́ривать чтó-нибудь.

unsalable *also,* **unsaleable** *adj.* неходово́й.

unsanitary *adj.* антисанита́рный.

unsatisfactory *adj.* неудовлетвори́тельный. —**unsatisfactorily,** *adv.* неудовлетвори́тельно.

unsatisfied *adj.* неудовлетворённый.

unsaturated *adj.* ненасы́щенный.

unsavory *also,* **unsavoury** *adj.* **1,** (having an unpleasant taste) невку́сный. **2,** (disreputable) сомни́тельный; тёмный.

unscathed *adj.* невреди́мый. *Emerge unscathed,* вы́йти сухи́м из воды́.

unscheduled *adj.* вне расписа́ния; незаплани́рованный.

unscientific *adj.* ненау́чный.

unscramble *v.t.* **1,** (unravel) распу́тывать. **2,** (decipher) расшифро́вывать.

unscrew *v.t.* отви́нчивать; разви́нчивать; выви́нчивать; вывёртывать; отвёртывать.

unscrupulous *adj.* бессо́вестный; недобросо́вестный; беспринци́пный; неразбо́рчивый в сре́дствах. —**unscrupulousness,** *n.* неразбо́рчивость в сре́дствах.

unseal *v.t.* распеча́тывать; вскрыва́ть.

unseasonable *adj.* не по сезо́ну.

unseat *v.t.* **1,** (throw from the saddle) сбра́сывать. **2,** (remove from office) смеща́ть с до́лжности.

unsecured *adj.* необеспе́ченный.

unseeing *adj.* неви́дящий; незря́чий.

unseemly *adj.* неподоба́ющий; неблагови́дный.

unseen *adj.* неви́димый. —**sight unseen,** за глаза́; заглазно.

unselfish *adj.* бескоры́стный. —**unselfishness,** *n.* бескоры́стие.

unsettle *v.t.* **1,** (make unstable) подрыва́ть; расша́тывать. **2,** (disconcert) расстра́ивать; выбива́ть из колеи́.

unsettled *adj.* **1,** (unstable; disturbed) неспоко́йный; неустро́енный. **2,** (unresolved) неразрешённый; неурегули́рованный. **3,** (unpaid) неопла́ченный. **4,** (not populated) незаселённый.

unshackle *v.t.* раско́вывать.

unshakable *also,* **unshakeable** *adj.* непоколеби́мый.

unshaven *adj.* небри́тый.

unsheathe *v.t.* обнажа́ть; вынима́ть из но́жен.

unshoe *v.t.* раско́вывать (ло́шадь).

unsightly *adj.* некраси́вый; непригля́дный.

unsigned *adj.* неподпи́санный. *Unsigned letter,* анони́мное письмо́.

unsinkable *adj.* непотопля́емый.

unskilful *adj.* = **unskillful.**

unskilled *adj.* неквалифици́рованный.

unskillful *also,* **unskilful** *adj.* неиску́сный; неуме́лый.

unsmiling *adj.* неулы́бчивый.

unsnarl *v.t.* распу́тывать.

unsociable *adj.* необщи́тельный; нелюди́мый. —**unsociability,** *n.* необщи́тельность; нелюди́мость.

unsold *adj.* непро́данный; залежа́лый: *unsold merchandise,* непро́данный/залежа́лый това́р. *Remain unsold,* не находи́ть сбы́та.

unsolder *v.t.* распа́ивать.

unsolicited *adj.* непро́шеный: *unsolicited advice,* непро́шеный сове́т.

unsolved *adj.* нерешённый; неразрешённый; неразга́данный; нераскры́тый. *Unsolved crime,* нераскры́тое преступле́ние.

unsophisticated *adj.* неискушённый; бесхи́тростный; безыску́сный.

unsought *adj.* непро́шеный.

unsound *adj.* **1,** (not healthy) нездоро́вый. **2,** (not solid or firm) непро́чный. **3,** (not valid; fallacious) необосно́ванный.

unsparing *adj.* беспоща́дный. *Be unsparing in one's criticism,* беспоща́дно критикова́ть.

unspeakable *adj.* невырази́мый; несказа́нный.

unspecified *adj.* неука́занный.

unspoiled *adj.* неиспо́рченный.

unspoken *adj.* невы́сказанный.

unsportsmanlike *adj.* недосто́йный спортсме́на; неспорти́вный.

unstable *adj.* **1,** (not stable) неусто́йчивый; нестаби́льный. *Emotionally unstable,* психи́чески неусто́йчивый; неуравнове́шенный. **2,** *chem.* несто́йкий.

unstained *adj.* незапя́тнанный.

unsteadily *adv.* нетвёрдо; ша́тко.

unsteady *adj.* неусто́йчивый; нетвёрдый; ша́ткий. *Unsteady gait,* нетвёрдая *or* неве́рная похо́дка. *Be unsteady on one's feet,* нетвёрдо держа́ться на нога́х.

unstinting *adj.* *Be unstinting in,* не скупи́ться на (+ *acc.*).

unstitch *v.t.* распа́рывать; поро́ть.

unstressed *adj.* безуда́рный.

unstuck *adj., in* **come unstuck, 1,** (come loose) откле́иваться; раскле́иваться. **2,** *colloq.* (go awry) раскле́иваться.

unsubstantiated *adj.* бездоказа́тельный; беспо́чвенный.

unsuccessful *adj.* неуда́чный; неуда́вшийся; безуспе́шный. *Be unsuccessful,* не уда́ться; не име́ть успе́ха. *Efforts to revive him were unsuccessful,* попы́тки оживи́ть его́ оказа́лись безуспе́шными. —**unsuccessfully,** *adv.* безуспе́шно.

unsuitability *n.* непригодность.

unsuitable *adj.* неподходя́щий.

unsuited *adj.* непригодный: *unsuited for this type of work,* непригодный к э́той рабо́те.

unsullied *adj.* незапя́тнанный.

unsung *adj.* невоспе́тый: *unsung hero,* невоспе́тый геро́й.

unsupervised *adj.* безнадзо́рный; бесконтро́льный.

unsupported *adj.* **1,** (not buttressed) не име́ющий опо́ры. **2,** (unsubstantiated) бездоказа́тельный.

unsure *adj.* неуве́ренный: *unsure of oneself,* неуве́ренный в себе́.

unsurpassed *adj.* непревзойдённый.

unsuspecting *adj.* ни о чём не подозрева́ющий.

unsympathetic *adj.* несочу́вствующий. *Be unsympathetic to,* не сочу́вствовать (+ *dat.*).

unsystematic *adj.* бессисте́мный; беспоря́дочный.

untalented *adj.* нетала́нтливый; бестала́нный; безда́рный.

untamable *also,* **untameable** *adj.* неукроти́мый.

untangle *v.t.* распу́тывать.

untapped *adj.* неиспо́льзованный: *untapped resouces,* неиспо́льзованные ресу́рсы.

untarnished *adj.* незапя́тнанный.

untenable *adj.* **1,** (unsound, as of an argument) несостоя́тельный. **2,** (that cannot be defended or saved) безвы́ходный: *in an untenable position,* в безвы́ходном положе́нии.

untested *adj.* неиспы́танный.

unthinkable *adj.* немы́слимый.

unthinking *adj.* безду́мный.

untidy *adj.* неопря́тный; неаккура́тный. —**untidiness,** *n.* неопря́тность.

untie *v.t.* развя́зывать; отвя́зывать.

until *prep.* до: *until spring,* до весны́. *Until tomorrow!,* до за́втра! *Postpone until next week,* отложи́ть до бу́дущей неде́ли (*or* на бу́дущую неде́лю). —*conj.* пока́ не: *Wait until he comes,* подожди́те, пока́ он не придёт. *Until their demands are met,* пока́ их тре́бования не удовлетворя́т. *Considered innocent until proven guilty,* счита́ется невино́вным, пока́ его́ вино́вность не бу́дет дока́зана. —**not until,** то́лько: *not until ten o'clock,* то́лько в де́сять часо́в. *He did not return until the next morning,* он верну́лся то́лько на сле́дующее у́тро.

untilled *adj.* невозде́ланный; необрабо́танный.

untimely *adj.* **1,** (ill-timed) несвоевре́менный; неуме́стный. **2,** (premature, as of a death) преждевре́менный; безвре́менный.

untiring *adj.* неуста́нный; неутоми́мый.

unto *prep., poetic & archaic* = **to.**

untold *adj.* **1,** (not told) нерасска́занный. **2,** (incalculable) несчётный; несме́тный. *An untold number of times,* несчётное число́ раз.

untouchable *n., usu. pl.* неприкаса́емые.

untouched *adj.* нетро́нутый.

untoward *adj.* **1,** (unfavorable) неблагоприя́тный. **2,** (unfortunate) несча́стный: *untoward incident,* несча́стный слу́чай. **3,** (improper; inappropriate) неподходя́щий; неуме́стный.

untrained *adj.* неподгото́вленный; необу́ченный.

untranslatable *adj.* непереводи́мый.

untried *adj.* неиспы́танный.

untrodden *adj.* нехо́женый.

untroubled *adj.* безмяте́жный.

untrue *adj.* неве́рный. *That is untrue,* э́то неве́рно. *Be untrue to,* быть неве́рен (+ *dat.*).

untrustworthy *adj.* ненадёжный.

untruth *n.* непра́вда. —**untruthful,** *adj.* ло́жный; лжи́вый.

unturned *adj., in* **leave no stone unturned,** *see* **stone.**

untwist *v.t.* раскру́чивать; откру́чивать.

unusable *adj.* неприго́дный. *Become unusable,* приходи́ть в него́дность.

unused *adj.* **1,** (not made use of) неиспо́льзованный. **2,** *fol. by* (unaccustomed) не привы́кший (к). **3,** *philately* негаше́ный.

unusual *adj.* необы́чный; необыкнове́нный.

unusually *adv.* необы́чно: *unusually large,* необы́чно большо́й. *The weather was unusually warm,* пого́да была́ необы́чно тёплой.

unutterable *adj.* невырази́мый; несказа́нный.

unvarnished *adj.* **1,** (not varnished) нелакиро́ванный. **2,** (undisguised) неприкра́шенный: *the unvarnished truth,* неприкра́шенная и́стина.

unvarying *adj.* неизме́нный.

unveil *v.t.* открыва́ть; раскрыва́ть.

unverifiable *adj.* не поддаю́щийся прове́рке.

unverified *adj.* непрове́ренный.

unversed *adj.* несве́дущий.

unvoiced *adj., phonet.* глухо́й.

unwanted *adj.* нежела́нный. *Unwanted merchandise,* неходово́й това́р.

unwarranted *adj.* неопра́вданный.

unwary *adj.* неосторо́жный.

unwavering *adj.* непоколеби́мый; незы́блемый.

unwed *adj.* незаму́жняя. —**unwed mother,** мать-одино́чка.

unwelcome *adj.* нежела́тельный: *unwelcome visitor,* нежела́тельный посети́тель.

unwell *adj.* нездоро́вый. *He is unwell,* ему́ нездоро́вится.

unwholesome *adj.* нездоро́вый: *unwholesome food,* нездоро́вая пи́ща; *unwholesome influence,* нездоро́вое влия́ние.

unwieldy *adj.* громо́здкий.

unwilling *adj.* неохо́тный. *Be unwilling to,* не хоте́ть (+ *inf.*). —**unwillingly,** *adv.* неохо́тно; не́хотя. —**unwillingness,** *n.* неохо́та; нежела́ние.

unwind *v.t.* разма́тывать; раскру́чивать. —*v.i.* **1,** (become unwound) разма́тываться; раскру́чиваться. **2,** (relax) рассе́иваться.

unwise *adj.* неу́мный; неразу́мный; неблагоразу́мный.

unwitting *adj.* нево́льный; ненаме́ренный. —**unwittingly,** *adv.* нево́льно; ненаме́ренно.

unworkable *adj.* непракти́чный; неосуществи́мый.

unworried *adj.* необеспоко́енный.

unworthy *adj.* недосто́йный. *Unworthy of respect,* недосто́ин уваже́ния. *He is unworthy of her,* он её недосто́ин.

unwrap *v.t.* развёртывать.

unwritten *adj.* непи́саный: *unwritten law,* непи́саный зако́н.

unyielding *adj.* неусту́пчивый; неподатливый.

up *adv.* **1,** (to a higher level) вверх; наве́рх: *Hands up!,* ру́ки вверх! ♦*Usu. rendered by a prefixed verb:* go up, поднима́ться; *stand up,* встава́ть; *climb up,* влеза́ть. **2,** (at a high or higher level) наверху́: *What are you doing up there?,* что ты де́лаешь там наверху́? *They live three floors up,* они́ живу́т тремя́ этажа́ми вы́ше. **3,** *used as an intensifier:* eat up, съесть; *tear up,* разорва́ть; *dry up,* вы́сохнуть. —*adj.* **1,** (having risen): *The sun is up,* со́лнце взошло́. *Prices are up,* це́ны подняли́сь. **2,** (awake; out of bed) на нога́х. *The children are already up,* де́ти уже́ вста́ли. *I was up all night,* я не спал всю ночь. **3,** (over; finished) ко́нчен: *Your time is up,* ва́ше вре́мя зако́нчилось *or* истекло́. *The game/jig is up,* и́гра зако́нчена *or* око́нчена. **4,** *colloq.* (going on): *What's up?,* в чём де́ло? *Something is up,* что́-то происхо́дит. —*prep.* **1,** (to a high or higher place on) вверх по: *up the stairs,* вверх по ле́стнице. *The dog chased the cat up a tree,* соба́ка загнала́ ко́шку на де́рево. **2,** (farther along) да́льше по: *just up the road,* чуть да́льше по э́той доро́ге. —*v.t.* повыша́ть: *up the price,* повыша́ть це́ну. —*v.i.* взять: *He up and left,* он взял и ушёл. —*n., in* **ups and downs,** перипети́и; взлёты и паде́ния. —**up against, 1,** (touching) вплотну́ю к: *place the table up against the* *wall,* поста́вить стол вплотну́ю к стене́. **2,** (confronted by): *He is up against a tough opponent,* ему́ противостои́т си́льный проти́вник. —**up against it,** *colloq.* ту́го: *He is up against it,* ему́ ту́го прихо́дится. —**up and about,** на нога́х. —**up and down, 1,** *literally* вверх и вниз. *Jump up and down,* подпры́гивать. **2,** (back and forth) взад и вперёд: *walk up and down the room,* ходи́ть взад и вперёд по ко́мнате. **3,** *Swear up and down,* кля́сться и божи́ться. —**up to, 1,** (to; as far as) по (+ *acc.*); до: *up to one's waist,* по по́яс; *up to the ceiling,* до потолка́. *Up to one's ears in debt,* по́ уши в долга́х. **2,** (until) до: *up to now,* до сих пор. **3,** (as many as; a maximum of) до: *up to 300 volunteers,* до трёхсо́т доброво́льцев. *He faces up to ten years in prison,* ему́ грози́т до десяти́ лет тюрьмы́. **4,** (approaching) к: *walk up to someone,* подходи́ть к кому́-нибудь. **5,** (incumbent upon) за: *It's up to you,* де́ло за ва́ми. *Whom is the final decision up to?,* за кем остаётся оконча́тельное реше́ние? **6,** (equal to): *up to the mark,* на до́лжной высоте́. *I am not up to the task,* э́та зада́ча мне не под си́лу. **7,** *colloq.* (plotting): *What is he up to?,* что он замышля́ет?; что он заду́мал? *He is up to something,* он что́-то затева́ет.

up-and-coming *adj., colloq.* многообеща́ющий.

upas *n.* анча́р.

upbraid *v.t.* упрека́ть; порица́ть.

upbringing *n.* воспита́ние.

upcoming *adj.* предстоя́щий.

update *v.t.* дополня́ть; включа́ть (са́мые) после́дние да́нные в.

upend *v.t.* опроки́дывать.

upgrade *n.* подъём. —*v.t.* **1,** (raise to a higher rank) возводи́ть. **2,** (raise the quality of) соверше́нствовать.

upheaval *n.* переворо́т; потрясе́ние.

uphill *adv.* в го́ру. —*adj.* **1,** (upward) иду́щий в го́ру. **2,** (difficult) тру́дный; тяжёлый.

uphold *v.t.* **1,** (defend) отста́ивать; защища́ть: *uphold the rights of...,* отста́ивать/защища́ть права́ (+ *gen.*). *Uphold a principle,* отста́ивать при́нцип. **2,** (approve) утвержда́ть: *uphold a sentence,* утвержда́ть пригово́р.

upholster *v.t.* обива́ть. *Upholstered chair,* оби́тый стул. —**upholsterer,** *n.* обо́йщик; драпиро́вщик. —**upholstery,** *n.* оби́вка.

upkeep *n.* содержа́ние.

upland *n.* наго́рье.

uplift *v.t.* поднима́ть. *Uplift one's spirits,* поднима́ть чьё-нибудь настрое́ние.

upon *prep.* **1,** (resting on) на: *high upon the hill,* высоко́ на холме́. **2,** (at the time of) по: *upon (his/her) arrival,* по прие́зде. **3,** (after) за: *row upon row,* ряд за ря́дом. **4,** *fol. by* **us** (having arrived): *Winter is upon us,* наступи́ла зима́. **5,** *in verbal combinations: come upon,* набрести́ на; *look upon,* рассма́тривать; *rely upon,* полага́ться на. —**once upon a time,** одна́жды; жил-был. —**upon my word!,** че́стное сло́во!

upper *adj.* ве́рхний: *upper berth,* ве́рхняя по́лка; *upper house,* ве́рхняя пала́та. *Upper class,* вы́сший

класс. *The Upper Nile,* ве́рхнее тече́ние Ни́ла. *Upper respiratory tract,* ве́рхние дыха́тельные пути́. —**gain the upper hand,** брать *or* одержа́ть верх.

upper case прописны́е бу́квы.

uppercut *n., boxing* апперко́т.

upper crust верху́шки о́бщества.

uppermost *adj.* са́мый ве́рхний. *Be uppermost in one's mind,* бо́льше всего́ занима́ть чьи-нибудь мы́сли.

upright *adj.* **1,** (erect) прямо́й; стоя́чий. **2,** (honorable) че́стный; пра́ведный. —*adv.* пря́мо; стоймя́. —*n.* сто́йка. —**upright piano,** пиани́но.

uprising *n.* восста́ние.

uproar *n.* шум; гам; гвалт.

uproarious *adj.* шу́мный; бу́рный; бу́йный.

uproot *v.t.* **1,** (remove from the ground) вырыва́ть с ко́рнем; корчева́ть; выкорчёвывать. **2,** (force to leave a familiar place) срыва́ть с ме́ста. *Uproot oneself,* снима́ться с ме́ста. *Uproot people from their homes,* выгоня́ть люде́й из свои́х домо́в.

upset *v.t.* **1,** (tip over) опроки́дывать. **2,** (distress) ун-нерве) расстра́ивать. **3,** (disrupt) наруша́ть; расстра́ивать: *upset the balance,* наруша́ть равнове́сие; *upset someone's plans,* расстра́ивать чьи-нибудь пла́ны. **4,** *Upset one's stomach,* расстра́ивать желу́док. —*adj.* расстро́енный: *She is very upset,* она́ о́чень расстро́ена. —*n., sports* неожи́данный результа́т. —**upset stomach,** расстро́йство желу́дка.

upsetting *adj.* трево́жный: *upsetting news,* трево́жные ве́сти.

upshot *n.* исхо́д; развя́зка.

upside down вверх дном; вверх нога́ми. *Turn upside down,* переверну́ть вверх дном/нога́ми.

upstage *v.t.* затмева́ть.

upstairs *adv.* **1,** (location) наверху́. **2,** (direction) наве́рх. —*n.* ве́рхняя часть (до́ма).

upstanding *adj.* **1,** (erect) прямо́й; стоя́чий. **2,** (honorable) че́стный; прямо́й.

upstart *n.* вы́скочка.

upstream *adv.* вверх по тече́нию; про́тив тече́ния. *A few miles upstream from...,* в не́скольких ми́лях вы́ше по тече́нию от...

upsurge *n.* подъём: *upsurge of patriotism,* подъём патриоти́ческих чувств.

up-to-date *adj.* совреме́нный.

upturn *n.* оживле́ние.

upward *also,* **upwards** *adv.* наве́рх; вверх. —**upwards of,** свы́ше (+ *gen.*).

uraemia *n.* = **uremia.** —**uraemic,** *adj.* = **uremic.**

uranium *n.* ура́н. —*adj.* ура́новый.

Uranus *n.* Ура́н.

urban *adj.* городско́й. *Urban planning/development,* градострои́тельство. *Urban renewal,* перестро́йка городо́в.

urbane *adj.* ве́жливый; обходи́тельный.

urchin *n.* мальчи́шка. —**sea urchin,** морско́й ёж.

Urdu *n.* урду́.

urea *n.* мочеви́на.

uremia *also,* **uraemia** *n.* уреми́я. —**uremic; uraemic,** *adj.* уреми́ческий

urethra *n.* мочеиспуска́тельный кана́л; уре́тра.

urge *v.t.* **1,** (try hard to persuade) убежда́ть: *They urged us to stay,* они́ нас убежда́ли оста́ться. **2,** *usu. fol. by* **on** (drive onward) подгоня́ть; погоня́ть; понука́ть. **3,** (advocate strongly) призыва́ть к: *urge calm,* призыва́ть к споко́йствию. —*n.* побужде́ние; стремле́ние; позы́в.

urgency *n.* сро́чность; неотло́жность. *A matter of great urgency,* сро́чное *or* неотло́жное де́ло.

urgent *adj.* сро́чный; неотло́жный; спе́шный; наста́ятельный; безотлага́тельный; назре́вший. *Urgent matter,* сро́чное *or* неотло́жное *or* спе́шное де́ло. *Urgent need,* наста́ятельная необходи́мость; сро́чная на́добность; назре́вшая потре́бность. *Urgent request,* наста́ятельная про́сьба. *Urgent measures,* сро́чные ме́ры. *Be in urgent need of repair,* наста́ятельно тре́бовать ремо́нта.

urgently *adv.* сро́чно; безотлага́тельно. *Urgently request,* наста́ятельно проси́ть.

uric *adj.* мочево́й. —**uric acid,** мочева́я кислота́.

urinal *n.* писсуа́р.

urinalysis *n.* ана́лиз мочи́.

urinary *adj.* мочево́й: *urinary tract,* мочевы́е пути́.

urinate *v.i.* мочи́ться. —**urination,** *n.* мочеиспуска́ние.

urine *n.* моча́.

urn *n.* **1,** (vase) ва́за. **2,** (vase for holding the ashes of a cremated body) у́рна. **3,** (container for brewing coffee or tea) самова́р.

urology *n.* уроло́гия. —**urological,** *adj.* урологи́ческий. —**urologist,** *n.* уро́лог.

Ursa Major Больша́я Медве́дица. —**Ursa Minor,** Ма́лая Медве́дица.

us *pers. pron.* **1,** *used as dir. obj. of a verb,* нас: *They drove us home,* они́ нас отвезли́ домо́й. **2,** *used as indir. obj. of a verb,* нам: *Tell us a story,* расскажи́те нам исто́рию. **3,** *used as obj. of a prep.* нас; нам; на́ми: *with us,* с на́ми; *without us,* без нас.

usable *also,* **useable** *adj.* го́дный к употребле́нию.

usage *n.* употребле́ние. *Proper usage,* пра́вильное употребле́ние слов.

use *v.t.* **1,** (employ; utilize) употребля́ть; по́льзоваться; испо́льзовать; применя́ть. *Use a hammer,* по́льзоваться молотко́м; испо́льзовать молото́к. *Use a pencil/dictionary,* по́льзоваться карандашо́м/словарём. *Use salt in one's food,* употребля́ть соль в пи́щу. *Use drugs,* употребля́ть нарко́тики. *Use a method,* испо́льзовать *or* применя́ть ме́тод. *Use an expression,* употребля́ть выраже́ние. *Use force,* применя́ть си́лу. *Use one's connections,* по́льзоваться свои́ми свя́зями. **2,** (consume) испо́льзовать; потребля́ть; расхо́довать. *Use raw materials,* испо́льзовать сырьё. **3,** *fol. by* **up** (consume completely; exhaust) тра́тить: *I've used up all my film,* я истра́тил(а) всю плёнку. **4,** (profit by; do well with): *That coat could use a cleaning,* не меша́ло бы вы́чистить э́то пальто́. *I could use $50 right now,* мне бы сейча́с (не помеша́ли) пятьдеся́т до́лларов. —*v.i., used only in the past tense, fol. by* **to, 1,** (do customarily) *rendered by the imperfective aspect: We used*

to visit them every week, мы их посеща́ли ка́ждую неде́лю. **2,** (formerly) ра́ньше; когда́-то. *They used to live in Kiev,* ра́ньше они́ жи́ли в Ки́еве. *There used to be a theater here,* когда́-то здесь был теа́тр. —*n.* **1,** (employment; utilization) употребле́ние; по́льзование; испо́льзование; примене́ние. *Be in use,* быть в употребле́нии; употребля́ться. *Go out of use,* вы́йти из употребле́ния. *The use of force,* примене́ние си́лы. *Have many uses,* применя́ться для разли́чных це́лей. **2,** (control, as of one's limbs): *have the use of one's legs,* владе́ть нога́ми. *He has lost the use of his right arm,* у него́ отняла́сь (*or* не де́йствует) пра́вая рука́. **3,** (benefit; advantage) по́льза: *be of use,* приноси́ть по́льзу. *Of no use,* бесполе́зный. *There is no use asking him,* нет смы́сла (*or* не сто́ит) его́ спра́шивать. *What's the use of arguing?,* како́й смысл спо́рить?; к чему́ спо́рить? —**have no use for, 1,** (have no need for) не нужда́ться в. *I have no use for it,* э́то мне соверше́нно не ну́жно. **2,** (dislike strongly) не выноси́ть: *I have no use for him,* я не выношу́ его́. —**make use of,** по́льзоваться; испо́льзовать. —**put to use,** применя́ть.

useable *adj.* = **usable.**

used *adj.* **1,** (having been used) испо́льзованный. **2,** (secondhand) поде́ржанный. **3,** (canceled, as of a stamp) гашёный. **4,** *fol. by* **to** (accustomed) привы́кший (к). *Get used to,* привыка́ть к.

useful *adj.* поле́зный. *Useful to someone,* поле́зен кому́-нибудь *or* для кого́-нибудь. *Be useful to,* пригоди́ться (+ *dat.*).

usefulness *n.* поле́зность. *Outlive one's/its usefulness,* отжи́ть свой век.

useless *adj.* бесполе́зный. —**uselessly,** *adv.* бесполе́зно; да́ром. —**uselessness,** *n.* бесполе́зность.

user *n.* по́льзователь.

usher *n.* билетёр. —*v.t.* **1,** (escort) провожа́ть. *Usher someone into a room,* вводи́ть кого́-нибудь в ко́мнату. **2,** *fol. by* **in** (herald) возвеща́ть: *usher in a new era,* возвеща́ть но́вую э́ру.

usherette *n.* билетёрша.

usual *adj.* обыкнове́нный; обы́чный. *At the usual time,* в обы́чное вре́мя. —**as usual,** как обы́чно. —**than usual,** чем обы́чно; обы́чного.

usually *adv.* обы́чно; обыкнове́нно.

usurer *n.* ростовщи́к. —**usurious,** *adj.* ростовщи́ческий.

usurp *v.t.* узурпи́ровать. —**usurpation,** *n.* узурпа́ция. —**usurper,** *n.* узурпа́тор.

usury *n.* ростовщи́чество.

utensil *n.* посу́да; *pl.* у́тварь; посу́да. *Kitchen utensils,* ку́хонная посу́да/у́тварь.

uterus *n.* ма́тка. —**uterine,** *adj.* ма́точный; утро́бный.

utilitarian *adj.* утилита́рный. —**utilitarianism,** *n.* утилитари́зм.

utility *n.* **1,** (usefulness) поле́зность. **2,** (public service company) предприя́тие обще́ственного по́льзования. **3,** *pl.* (gas, electricity, etc.) (дома́шние) удо́бства; коммуна́льные услу́ги. —**utility player,** *sports* запасно́й игро́к.

utilize *v.t.* испо́льзовать; утилизи́ровать. —**utilization,** *n.* испо́льзование; утилиза́ция.

utmost *adj.* велича́йший: *of the utmost importance,* велича́йшей ва́жности; *handle with the utmost care,* обраща́ться (с че́м-нибудь) с велича́йшей осторо́жностью. —*n.* **1,** (greatest possible degree) вы́сшая сте́пень. *To the utmost,* до после́днего; вовсю́. **2,** (best of one's abilities) всё возмо́жное: *do one's utmost,* де́лать всё возмо́жное.

utopia *n.* уто́пия. —**utopian,** *adj.* утопи́ческий. —**utopianism,** *n.* утопи́зм.

utter *v.t.* **1,** (give off; give out) издава́ть; испуска́ть. *Utter a sound,* издава́ть звук. *Utter a sigh,* испусти́ть вздох. **2,** (say, as a word) произноси́ть. *Not utter a word,* не пророни́ть ни сло́ва. —*adj.*

по́лный; полне́йший; чи́стый; сплошно́й. *Utter nonsense,* сплошна́я ерунда́; чи́стый вздор. *Utter incompetence,* полне́йшая некомпете́нтность.

utterance *n.* выска́зывание. *Give utterance to,* выска́зывать; дать вы́ход (+ *dat.*).

utterly *adv.* соверше́нно. *Utterly destroyed,* по́лностью *or* соверше́нно разру́шен.

uttermost *adj.* **1,** (outmost) са́мый отдалённый. **2,** (extreme; utmost) кра́йний; преде́льный.

U-turn *n.* разворо́т. *Make a U-turn,* развора́чиваться.

uvula *n.* язычо́к; нёбная занаве́ска. —**uvular,** *adj.* язычко́вый.

Uzbek *n.* **1,** (person) узбе́к. **2,** (language) узбе́кский язы́к. —*adj.* узбе́кский.

V, v два́дцать втора́я бу́ква англи́йского алфави́та.

vacancy *n.* **1,** (unfilled position) вака́нсия. **2,** (untenanted quarters) свобо́дная ко́мната *or* кварти́ра; (in a hotel) свобо́дный но́мер.

vacant *adj.* **1,** (empty) пусто́й. **2,** (unoccupied) свобо́дный. **3,** (not filled, as of a position) вака́нтный. **4,** (blank, as of a stare) отсу́тствующий.

vacate *v.t.* освобожда́ть.

vacation *n.* о́тпуск; (*from school*) кани́кулы. *Be on vacation,* быть в о́тпуске. —*adj.* отпускно́й: *vacation time,* отпускно́е вре́мя. —*v.i.* отдыха́ть.

vaccinate *v.t.* привива́ть о́спу (+ *dat.*); вакцини́ровать.

vaccination *n.* приви́вка о́спы; оспопривива́ние; вакцина́ция. *The vaccination didn't take,* о́спа не привила́сь *or* не приняла́сь.

vaccine *n.* вакци́на.

vacillate *v.i.* колеба́ться. —**vacillation,** *n.* колеба́ние.

vacuity *n.* пустота́.

vacuole *n.* вакуо́ль.

vacuous *adj.* пусто́й.

vacuum *n.* безвозду́шное простра́нство; ва́куум; пустота́. —*v.t.* пылесо́сить. —**vacuum cleaner,** пылесо́с. —**vacuum pump,** ва́куум-насо́с. —**vacuum tube,** электро́нная ла́мпа.

vagabond *n.* бродя́га; бося́к.

vagary *n.* капри́з; причу́да.

vagina *n.* влага́лище. —**vaginal,** *adj.* влага́лищный.

vagrancy *n.* бродя́жничество.

vagrant *n.* бродя́га. —*adj.* бродя́чий.

vague *adj.* сму́тный; нея́сный; тума́нный; рас-

плы́вчатый; неопределённый. *Vague recollection,* сму́тное воспомина́ние. *Vague answer,* расплы́вчатый отве́т. *Vague resemblance,* отдалённое схо́дство. *I haven't the vaguest notion,* не име́ю ни мале́йшего поня́тия.

vaguely *adv.* сму́тно: *I vaguely remember,* я сму́тно по́мню.

vagueness *n.* нея́сность; неопределённость.

vain *adj.* **1,** (futile) тще́тный; напра́сный. *Vain attempt,* тще́тная попы́тка. *Vain efforts,* тще́тные *or* напра́сные уси́лия. *In the vain hope of...,* в тще́тной наде́жде (+ *inf.*). **2,** (conceited) тщесла́вный. —**in vain,** напра́сно; тще́тно; да́ром. *It was all in vain,* всё бы́ло напра́сно. *All our efforts were in vain,* все на́ши уси́лия пропа́ли да́ром (*or* бы́ли бесполе́зны).

vainglorious *adj.* тщесла́вный; хвастли́вый. —**vainglory,** *n.* тщесла́вие; хвастли́вость.

vainly *adv.* тще́тно; напра́сно.

valance *n.* **1,** (for a bed) по́лог. **2,** (across the top of a window) карни́з.

vale *n.* доли́на; дол.

valedictory *adj.* проща́льный. —*n.* проща́льная речь.

valence *n.* вале́нтность.

valerian *n.* валерья́на.

valet *n.* камерди́нер.

valiant *adj.* хра́брый; до́блестный.

valid *adj.* **1,** (having legal force) действи́тельный: *a valid passport,* действи́тельный па́спорт. **2,** (sound; well-founded) обосно́ванный: *valid objections,* обосно́ванные возраже́ния. **3,** (legitimate, as of a reason or excuse) уважи́тельный.

validate *v.t.* оформля́ть: *validate a passport,* офо́рмить па́спорт.

validity *n.* **1,** (legal force) действи́тельность; зако́нность. **2,** (sound basis) обосно́ванность. *Have no validity,* не име́ть под собо́й по́чвы.

valise *n.* чемода́н.

valley *n.* доли́на. *Death Valley,* Доли́на Сме́рти.

valor also, **valour** *n.* до́блесть. **—valorous,** *adj.* до́блестный.

valuable *adj.* це́нный: *valuable postage stamp,* це́нная почто́вая ма́рка. *Valuable contribution,* це́нный вклад. *This ring is very valuable,* э́то кольцо́ представля́ет большу́ю це́нность. *Valuable time was lost,* пропа́ло (*or* бы́ло поте́ряно) драгоце́нное вре́мя. **—valuables,** *n.pl.* це́нные ве́щи; це́нности; драгоце́нности.

valuation *n.* оце́нка.

value *n.* **1,** (worth) це́нность. *The value of the dollar,* курс до́ллара. *Go up in value,* поднима́ться в цене́. *Be of great value,* представля́ть большу́ю це́нность. **2,** *econ.* сто́имость: *surplus value,* приба́вочная сто́имость. **3,** (numerical quantity) величина́; значе́ние. **4,** *pl.* (principles; standards) це́нности. **—v.t. 1,** (estimate the value of) оце́нивать. **2,** (prize; treasure) цени́ть; дорожи́ть. *Value a friendship,* цени́ть дру́жбу.

valued *adj.* це́нный.

valve *n.* **1,** *mech.; anat.* кла́пан. *Safety valve,* предохрани́тельный кла́пан. *Heart valve,* серде́чный кла́пан. **2,** (of a mollusk) ство́рка.

vamoose *v.i., slang* убира́ться; удира́ть.

vamp *n.* передо́к (боти́нка).

vampire *n.* **1,** *folklore* вампи́р; упы́рь; вурдала́к. **2,** = **vampire bat.**

vampire bat (true bloodsucker) кровосо́с; (non-bloodsucker) вампи́р.

van *n.* фурго́н: *moving van,* ме́бельный фурго́н.

vanadium *n.* вана́дий.

vandal *n.* ванда́л; хулига́н. **—vandalism,** *n.* вандали́зм; хулига́нство. **—vandalize,** *v.t.* наноси́ть уще́рб (+ *dat.*).

vane *n.* **1,** (weathercock) флю́гер. **2,** (revolving blade of a windmill) крыло́.

vanguard *n.* аванга́рд; передово́й отря́д.

vanilla *n.* вани́ль. **—adj.** вани́льный.

vanish *v.i.* исчеза́ть. *Vanish into thin air,* как в во́ду ка́нуть. *All hope vanished,* все наде́жды разлете́лись.

vanity *n.* **1,** (pride; conceit) тщесла́вие. **2,** (futility) тще́тность. *Vanity of vanities,* суета́ суе́т. **3,** (dressing table) туале́тный сто́лик; туале́т. **—vanity case,** несессе́р.

vanquish *v.t.* побежда́ть.

vantage point 1, (position with a commanding view) кома́ндная пози́ция; кома́ндная высота́. **2,** *fig.* (perspective; viewpoint) то́чка зре́ния.

vapid *adj.* пусто́й; пре́сный; бессодержа́тельный; бесцве́тный.

vapor also, **vapour** *n.* пар. **—vapor trail,** конденсацио́нный след.

vaporize *v.t.* испаря́ть. **—v.i.** испаря́ться. **—vaporization,** *n.* парообразова́ние. **—vaporizer,** *n.* испари́тель.

vaporous *adj.* парообра́зный.

vapour *n.* = **vapor.**

variable *adj.* переме́нный. **—n.** переме́нная величина́.

variance *n.* **1,** (difference) расхожде́ние. *Be at variance with,* расходи́ться с; противоре́чить. **2,** (variation; fluctuation) измене́ние.

variant *n.* вариа́нт. **—adj.** ра́зный; разли́чный.

variation *n.* **1,** (change; fluctuation) измене́ние; колеба́ние. **2,** (anything somewhat different) вариа́нт; вариа́ция. **3,** *music* вариа́ция.

varicolored also, **varicoloured** *adj.* разноцве́тный.

varicose *adj.* варико́зный. **—varicose veins,** расшире́ние вен.

varied *adj.* **1,** (assorted) разли́чный. **2,** (diverse) разнообра́зный.

variegate *v.t.* **1,** (mark with different colors) испестря́ть. **2,** (diversify) разнообра́зить.

variegated *adj.* **1,** (having diverse colors) пёстрый. **2,** (having different forms) разнообра́зный.

variety *n.* **1,** (diversity) разнообра́зие. **2,** (number) ряд: *for a variety of reasons,* по (це́лому) ря́ду причи́н. **3,** (type) род; сорт: *items of every variety,* вся́кого ро́да това́ры. **4,** (subspecies) разнови́дность: *varieties of wheat,* разнови́дности пшени́цы. **—variety show,** варьете́. **—variety store,** галантере́йный магази́н.

various *adj.* ра́зный; разли́чный: *various kinds of...,* ра́зного/разли́чного ро́да (+ *nom.*). *For various reasons,* по ра́зным причи́нам.

varnish *n.* лак. **—v.t.** лакирова́ть.

vary *v.t.* **1,** (modify) изменя́ть. **2,** (make diverse) разнообра́зить. **—v.i. 1,** (change) меня́ться; изменя́ться. **2,** (fluctuate) колеба́ться. *With varying (degrees of) success,* с ра́зной сте́пенью успе́ха. **3,** (differ) расходи́ться; быть ра́зным. *Opinions vary,* мне́ния расхо́дятся. *Methods vary,* ме́тоды быва́ют ра́зные. *The punishment will vary,* наказа́ние бу́дет ра́зным. *The results varied,* результа́ты бы́ли ра́зные. *Estimates of the cost vary,* сто́имость оце́нивают по-ра́зному. *Treatment varies depending on the case,* лече́ние различа́ется в зави́симости от слу́чая.

vascular *adj.* сосу́дистый.

vase *n.* ва́за.

vaseline *n.* вазели́н.

vassal *n.* васса́л. **—adj.** васса́льный.

vast *adj.* **1,** (of great extent or size) огро́мный; обши́рный; грома́дный; необозри́мый. *Vast expanse of water,* огро́мное простра́нство воды́. **2,** (great in number or degree) огро́мный: *a vast difference/improvement,* огро́мная ра́зница; огро́мное улучше́ние.

vastly *adv.* значи́тельно; в огро́мной сте́пени. *The patient is vastly improved,* больно́му значи́тельно лу́чше. *The two countries are vastly different,* э́ти две страны́ си́льно отлича́ются друг от дру́га.

vastness *n.* необозри́мость.

vat *n.* чан.

Vatican *n.* Ватика́н.

vaudeville *n.* эстра́да; варьете́; водеви́ль. —*adj.* эстра́дный.

vault *n.* **1,** (arched roof or chamber) свод. **2,** (safe storage place) храни́лище; сейф. **3,** (burial vault) склеп. **4,** (leap) прыжо́к. *Pole vault,* прыжо́к с шесто́м. —*v.i.* пры́гать. *Vault over a fence,* перепры́гнуть (че́рез) забо́р. —**vaulted,** *adj.* сво́дчатый.

vaunted *adj.* хвалёный.

veal *n.* теля́тина. —*adj.* теля́чий: *veal cutlet,* теля́чья отбивна́я.

vector *n.* ве́ктор. —*adj.* ве́кторный: *vector analysis,* ве́кторный ана́лиз.

veer *v.t. & i.* свора́чивать (в сто́рону). *Veer around,* ре́зко повора́чиваться круго́м.

vegetable *n.* о́вощ. —*adj.* овощно́й; расти́тельный. *Vegetable garden,* огоро́д. —**vegetable kingdom,** расти́тельный мир. —**vegetable oil,** расти́тельное ма́сло.

vegetarian *n.* вегетариа́нец. —*adj.* вегетариа́нский.

vegetate *v.i.* **1,** (grow) расти́. **2,** (live an uneventful life) прозяба́ть.

vegetation *n.* **1,** (plant life) расти́тельность. **2,** (process of vegetating) вегета́ция.

vehement *adj.* бу́рный; горя́чий: *vehement argument/ protest,* бу́рный *or* горя́чий спор/проте́ст. —**vehemence,** *n.* горя́чность.

vehicle *n.* **1,** (conveyance) маши́на. *Motor vehicle,* автомаши́на. *Space vehicle,* косми́ческий кора́бль. **2,** *fig.* (means) сре́дство: *vehicle to success,* сре́дство (для) достиже́ния успе́ха.

veil *n.* **1,** (light fabric worn over the face) вуа́ль. **2,** (bridal veil) фата́. **3,** (face-covering worn by Moslem women) чадра́. **4,** (anything that covers or conceals) заве́са. *Veil of clouds,* пелена́ туч. —*v.t.* **1,** (cover with a veil) закрыва́ть вуа́лью *or* чадро́й. **2,** *fig.* (conceal; hold back) скрыва́ть; завуали́ровать: *veiled threat,* скры́тая/завуали́рованная угро́за. —**take the veil,** постри́чься в мона́хини.

vein *n.* **1,** (blood vessel) ве́на; жи́ла; жи́лка. **2,** (when showing through the skin) прожи́лка. **3,** (of a leaf) жи́лка. **4,** (in marble) жи́лка; прожи́лка. **5,** (lode) жи́ла. **6,** *fig.* (mood; tone; style) дух; тон; стиль. *In the same vein,* в том же ду́хе. **7,** *fig.* (streak; tendency) жи́лка.

velar *adj.* веля́рный; занденёбный.

vellum *n.* **1,** (parchment) (то́нкий) перга́мент. **2,** (paper) веле́невая бума́га.

velocity *n.* ско́рость.

velodrome *n.* велодро́м.

velour *also,* **velours** *n.* велю́р. —*adj.* велю́ровый.

velvet *n.* ба́рхат. —*adj.* ба́рхатный.

velveteen *n.* вельве́т; плис. —*adj.* вельве́товый; пли́совый.

velvety *adj.* бархати́стый.

venal *adj.* прода́жный. —**venality,** *n.* прода́жность.

vender *n.* = **vendor.**

vendetta *n.* кро́вная месть.

vending machine автома́т.

vendor *also,* **vender** *n.* продаве́ц; торго́вец. *Street vendor,* у́личный торго́вец; лото́чник.

veneer *n.* **1,** (thin layer of wood) фане́ра. **2,** *fig.* (superficial display) (вне́шний) лоск.

venerable *adj.* почте́нный; масти́тый.

venerate *v.t.* благогове́ть пе́ред. —**veneration,** *n.* благогове́ние.

venereal *adj.* венери́ческий: *venereal disease,* венери́ческая боле́знь.

Venetian *adj.* венециа́нский. —**Venetian blinds,** подъёмные жалюзи́.

Venezuelan *adj.* венесуэ́льский.

vengeance *n.* месть; мще́ние. *Take vengeance,* мстить. —**with a vengeance,** с лихво́й.

vengeful *adj.* мсти́тельный.

venial *adj.* прости́тельный.

venison *n.* оле́нина.

venom *n.* яд. —**venomous,** *adj.* ядови́тый.

venous *adj.* вено́зный.

vent *n.* отду́шина. —*v.t.* [*also,* **give vent to**] излива́ть; срыва́ть; вымеща́ть; дать вы́ход *or* во́лю (+ *dat.*).

ventilate *v.t.* прове́тривать; вентили́ровать. —**ventilation,** *n.* прове́тривание; вентиля́ция. —**ventilator,** *n.* вентиля́тор.

ventral *adj.* брюшно́й.

ventricle *n.* желу́дочек.

ventriloquism *n.* чревовеща́ние. —**ventriloquist,** *n.* чревовеща́тель.

venture *n.* зате́я; предприя́тие. *Joint venture,* совме́стное предприя́тие. —*v.t.* **1,** (bet; stake) ста́вить. **2,** (dare to put forward; hazard) осме́ливаться: *venture a guess,* осме́литься догада́ться. —*v.i.* осме́ливаться: *venture out on the street at night,* осме́ливаться выходи́ть на у́лицу но́чью.

venturesome *adj.* сме́лый; отва́жный.

Venus *n.* Вене́ра.

veracity *n.* правди́вость.

veranda *n.* вера́нда.

verb *n.* глаго́л. —*adj.* глаго́льный: *verb endings,* глаго́льные оконча́ния.

verbal *adj.* **1,** (oral) у́стный: *verbal agreement,* у́стное соглаше́ние. **2,** (consisting of words) слове́сный: *verbal description,* слове́сное описа́ние. *Verbal battle,* слове́сная война́. **3,** *gram.* глаго́льный; отглаго́льный. —**verbal adverb,** дееприча́стие. —**verbal noun,** отглаго́льное существи́тельное.

verbalize *v.t.* выража́ть слова́ми.

verbally *adv.* у́стно.

verbatim *adj.* досло́вный. —*adv.* досло́вно; сло́во в сло́во.

verbena *n.* вербе́на.

verbiage *n.* пусты́е слова́; пустосло́вие.

verbose *adj.* многосло́вный. —**verbosity,** *n.* многосло́вие.

verdant *adj.* зелёный.

verdict *n.* пригово́р; верди́кт. *Verdict of "guilty",* обвини́тельный пригово́р. *Verdict of "not guilty",* оправда́тельный пригово́р. *The verdict of history,* пригово́р исто́рии.

verdigris *n.* медя́нка; ярь-медя́нка.

verdure *n.* зе́лень.

verge *n.* грань: *on the verge of,* на гра́ни (+ *gen.*). *She was on the verge of tears,* она́ была́ гото́ва распла́каться. —*v.i.* [*usu.* **verge on**] грани́чить с: *verge on lunacy,* грани́чить с безу́мием.

verify *v.t.* проверя́ть. —**verifiable,** *adj.* поддаю́щийся контро́лю. —**verification,** *n.* прове́рка; контро́ль.

verily *adv., archaic* пои́стине; вои́стину.

verisimilitude *n.* правдоподо́бие.

veritable *adj.* настоя́щий; и́стинный.

verity *n.* и́стина. *The eternal verities,* ве́чные и́стины.

vermicelli *n.* вермише́ль.

vermiform *adj.* червеобра́зный. —**vermiform appendix,** червеобра́зный отро́сток.

vermilion *n.* **1,** (pigment) ки́новарь. **2,** (color) я́рко-кра́сный цвет. —*adj.* я́рко-кра́сный.

vermin *n.* вреди́тели; парази́ты.

vermouth *n.* ве́рмут.

vernacular *n.* просторе́чие. —*adj.* просторе́чный.

vernal *adj.* весе́нний. —**vernal equinox,** весе́ннее равноде́нствие.

vernalize *v.t.* яровизи́ровать. —**vernalization,** *n.* яровиза́ция.

versatile *adj.* многосторо́нний; разносторо́нний. —**versatility,** *n.* многосторо́нность; разносторо́нность.

verse *n.* **1,** (line of poetry) стих. **2,** (stanza) строфа́; купле́т. **3,** (poetry) стихи́: *in verse,* в стиха́х.

versed *adj.* [*usu.* **versed in**] искушённый (в); све́дущий (в).

versification *n.* стихосложе́ние.

version *n.* ве́рсия; вариа́нт.

versus *prep.* про́тив.

vertebra *n.* позвоно́к. —**vertebral,** *adj.* позвоно́чный.

vertebrate *adj.* позвоно́чный. —*n.* позвоно́чное живо́тное.

vertex *n.* верши́на.

vertical *adj.* вертика́льный. —*n.* вертика́ль. —**vertically,** *adv.* вертика́льно.

vertigo *n.* головокруже́ние. —**vertiginous,** *adj.* головокружи́тельный.

verve *n.* жи́вость; подъём; огонёк.

very *adv.* **1,** (to a high degree) о́чень: *very glad,* о́чень рад. **2,** (precisely) же: *the very next day,* на сле́дующий же день; *the very same place,* то же са́мое ме́сто. **3,** *before superlatives,* са́мый: *the very best,* са́мый лу́чший. —*adj.* **1,** (absolute) са́мый: *from the very beginning,* с са́мого нача́ла; *in the very center of town,* в са́мом це́нтре го́рода. **2,** (precise) тот са́мый: *at that very moment,* в тот са́мый моме́нт. *This very minute,* сию́ же мину́ту. *The very man we read about,* тот са́мый челове́к, о кото́ром мы чита́ли. *You're the very person I wanted to see,* вы и́менно тот, кого́ я хоте́л(а) ви́деть. **3,** (mere) оди́н: *at the very thought of it,* при одно́й мы́сли об э́том. —**very much,** о́чень: *want very much to go,* о́чень хоте́ть идти́. *Thank you very much!,* большо́е (вам) спаси́бо! —**very well!,** хорошо́!; ла́дно!

vespers *n.pl.* вече́рня; всено́щная.

vessel *n.* **1,** (container) сосу́д. **2,** *anat.* сосу́д: *blood vessel,* кровено́сный сосу́д. **3,** (ship) су́дно; кора́бль. *Fishing vessel,* рыболо́вное су́дно.

vest *n.* жиле́т; жиле́тка. —*adj.* жиле́тный: *vest pocket,* жиле́тный карма́н. —*v.t.* **1,** (clothe, as in church vestments) облача́ть. **2,** (endow, as with power) облека́ть.

vestibule *n.* пере́дняя; прихо́жая.

vestige *n.* оста́ток; пережи́ток. —**vestigial,** *adj.* оста́точный; рудимента́рный.

vestment *n.* облаче́ние.

vestry *n.* ри́зница.

vet *n., colloq.* = **veterinarian.** —*v.t.* проверя́ть: *vet a manuscript,* проверя́ть ру́копись.

vetch *n.* ви́ка.

veteran *n.* ветера́н. —*adj.* ста́рый; быва́лый; матёрый.

veterinarian *n.* ветерина́р.

veterinary *adj.* ветерина́рный. —**veterinary medicine,** ветерина́рия.

veto *n.* ве́то. *Veto power,* пра́во ве́то. —*v.t.* налага́ть ве́то на.

vex *v.t.* досажда́ть; раздража́ть. —**vexation,** *n.* доса́да; раздраже́ние. —**vexatious,** *adj.* доса́дный.

via *prep.* че́рез.

viable *adj.* жизнеспосо́бный. —**viability,** *n.* жизнеспосо́бность.

viaduct *n.* виаду́к.

vial *n.* пузырёк; флако́н; скля́нка.

vibrant *adj.* **1,** (vibrating) вибри́рующий. **2,** (lively; pulsating) живо́й; оживлённый.

vibrate *v.i.* вибри́ровать. —**vibration,** *n.* вибра́ция. —**vibrator,** *n.* вибра́тор.

viburnum *n.* кали́на.

vicar *n.* вика́рий.

vicarious *adj.* чужо́й.

vice *n.* **1,** (immoral behavior; personal failing) поро́к. **2,** (vise) тиски́.

vice-admiral *n.* ви́це-адмира́л.

vice-consul *n.* ви́це-ко́нсул.

vice-president *n.* ви́це-президе́нт.

viceroy *n.* ви́це-коро́ль.

vice versa наоборо́т.

vicinity *n.* **1,** (proximity) сосе́дство; бли́зость. *In the vicinity of,* по сосе́дству с. *In the immediate vicinity (of),* в непосре́дственной бли́зости (от). *Somewhere in the vicinity of $200,000,* что́-то о́коло двухсо́т ты́сяч до́лларов. **2,** (neighborhood) окру́га; райо́н.

vicious *adj.* **1,** (savage; fierce) злой; свире́пый: *vicious dog,* зла́я/свире́пая соба́ка. **2,** (heinous; depraved) гну́сный: *vicious act/criminal,* гну́сный посту́пок/престу́пник. **3,** (malicious) зло́бный; зло́стный: *vicious remark,* зло́бное/зло́стное замеча́ние. —**vicious circle,** поро́чный *or* заколдо́ванный круг.

vicissitude *n.* превра́тность; перипети́я.

victim *n.* же́ртва; пострада́вший; потерпе́вший. *Flood victims,* пострада́вшие от наводне́ния. *Victims of crime,* потерпе́вшие от преступле́ний. *Fall victim to,* пасть *or* стать же́ртвой (+ *gen.*).

victimize *v.t.* надува́ть; обдира́ть.

victor *n.* победи́тель.
victorious *adj.* победоно́сный. *Be victorious,* побежда́ть.
victory *n.* побе́да.
victuals *n.pl.* пи́ща; я́ства; съестны́е припа́сы.
vicuna *also,* **vicuña** *n.* виго́нь. —*adj.* виго́невый.
video *n.* 1, (television) телеви́дение. 2, = **video cassete.** —*adj.* телевизио́нный. —**video cassette,** видеокассе́та. —**video cassette recorder,** видеомагнитофо́н. —**video tape,** видеоза́пись.
vie *v.i.* сопе́рничать; спо́рить; тяга́ться. *Vie with one another,* сопе́рничать друг с дру́гом. *Vie for first place,* соревнова́ться за *or* спо́рить за пе́рвое ме́сто. *Vie for the championship,* соревнова́ться за *or* оспа́ривать зва́ние чемпио́на. *Vie for the honor of,* спо́рить за че́сть (+ *inf.*).
Viennnese *adj.* ве́нский.
Vietnamese *adj.* вьетна́мский.
view *n.* 1, (sight) вид: *disappear from view,* исче́знуть *or* скры́ться и́з виду. *Come into view,* показа́ться. *In full view of everyone,* у всех на виду́; на глаза́х у всех. 2, (scene; vista) вид: *the view from the window,* вид из окна́. *Room with a view of the mountains,* ко́мната с ви́дом на го́ры. 3, (opinion) взгляд; мне́ние: *in my view,* на мой взгляд; по моему́ мне́нию. *In the justices' view,* на взгляд суде́й. *Exchange of views,* обме́н взгля́дами/мне́ниями. *We hold different views,* мы приде́рживаемся ра́зных взгля́дов; мы занима́ем ра́зные пози́ции. —*v.t.* 1, (look at; examine) осма́тривать. 2, (regard) рассма́тривать; смотре́ть на. *View something as a temporary phenomenon,* рассма́тривать что́-нибудь как вре́менное явле́ние. *View something with alarm,* смотре́ть на что́-нибудь с трево́гой. *How do you view the situation?,* как вы смо́трите на положе́ние дел? —**in view,** ви́дно. —**in view of,** ввиду́ (+ *gen.*). —**on view,** у всех на виду́. —**with a view to,** с це́лью (+ *inf. or gen.*); в це́лях (+ *gen.*).
viewer *n.* 1, (person who views) зри́тель. 2, (person watching television) телезри́тель.
view finder видоиска́тель; визи́р.
viewing *n.* просмо́тр: *a private viewing,* закры́тый просмо́тр.
viewpoint *n.* то́чка зре́ния.
vigil *n.* бде́ние. *Keep vigil,* дежу́рить; бо́дрствовать.
vigilant *adj.* бди́тельный. —**vigilance,** *n.* бди́тельность.
vignette *n.* 1, (ornamental design) винье́тка. 2, (literary piece) о́черк.
vigor *also,* **vigour** *n.* си́ла; бо́дрость. *With renewed vigor,* со све́жими си́лами.
vigorous *adj.* бо́дрый; энерги́чный. —**vigorously,** *adv.* энерги́чно.
vigour *n.* = **vigor.**
Viking *n.* ви́кинг.
vile *adj.* га́дкий; ме́рзкий; проти́вный; гну́сный. *Vile odor,* проти́вный за́пах. *Vile act,* га́дкий *or* ме́рзкий *or* гну́сный посту́пок. *Vile language,* скверносло́вие.
vilify *v.t.* поноси́ть; поро́чить; черни́ть. —**vilification,** *n.* поноше́ние.

villa *n.* ви́лла.
village *n.* дере́вня; село́. —*adj.* дереве́нский; се́льский. —**villager,** *n.* се́льский жи́тель.
villain *n.* 1, (scoundrel) злоде́й; негодя́й. 2, (of a story) отрица́тельный геро́й; злоде́й. —**villainous,** *adj.* злоде́йский. —**villainy,** *n.* злоде́йство.
vim *n.* прыть.
vindicate *v.t.* опра́вдывать; обеля́ть. —**vindication,** *n.* оправда́ние.
vindictive *adj.* мсти́тельный. —**vindictiveness,** *n.* мсти́тельность.
vine *n.* 1, (climbing or trailing plant) вью́щееся *or* ползу́чее расте́ние. 2, (grapevine) лоза́.
vinegar *n.* у́ксус. —*adj.* у́ксусный.
vineyard *n.* виногра́дник.
viniculture *n.* виногра́дарство.
vintage *n.* урожа́й: *This wine is vintage 1960,* э́то вино́ урожа́я 1960-го го́да. *An aircraft of World War II vintage,* самолёт времён второ́й мирово́й войны́. —*adj.* вы́сшего ка́чества. *Vintage wine,* ма́рочное вино́.
vinyl *n.* вини́л.
viol *n.* вио́ла. —**bass viol,** контраба́с.
viola *n.* альт; вио́ла.
violate *v.t.* 1, (break) наруша́ть: *violate a law/ an oath/,* наруша́ть зако́н/кля́тву. 2, (rape) растлева́ть.
violation *n.* 1, (act of violating) наруше́ние. *In violation of...,* в наруше́ние (+ *gen.*). *Border violation,* наруше́ние грани́цы. 2, (rape) растле́ние. —**violator,** *n.* наруши́тель.
violence *n.* 1, (physical force intended to harm) наси́лие: *resort to violence,* прибега́ть к наси́лию. 2, (great force; intensity) си́ла. —**do violence to,** искажа́ть; коверка́ть.
violent *adj.* 1, (fierce; powerful) неи́стовый; я́ростный; свире́пый; бу́рный. *Violent storm,* неи́стовая/я́ростная/свире́пая бу́ря. *Violent argument,* я́ростный/бу́рный спор. *Violent passions,* неи́стовые/бу́рные стра́сти. 2, (marked by death or violence) наси́льственный: *violent death,* наси́льственная смерть.
violet *n.* фиа́лка. —*adj.* фиоле́товый.
violin *n.* скри́пка. —*adj.* скрипи́чный: *violin concerto,* скрипи́чный конце́рт. —**violinist,** *n.* скрипа́ч.
violoncello *n.* виолонче́ль.
VIP *colloq.* ва́жное лицо́; ва́жная персо́на; высокопоста́вленное лицо́.
viper *n.* 1, (snake) гадю́ка. 2, (vicious person) гадю́ка; ехи́дна.
virago *n.* меге́ра.
viral *adj.* ви́русный.
virgin *n.* де́вственница. *She is still a virgin,* она́ ещё де́вушка *or* де́вственница. —*adj.* 1, (chaste) де́вственный. 2, *fig.* (unexploited) целинный. *Virgin forest,* де́вственный лес. *Virgin lands,* целинные зе́мли. *Virgin soil,* целина́. —**Virgin Mary,** Де́ва Мари́я; богоро́дица.
virginal *adj.* де́вственный; непоро́чный.
virginity *n.* де́вственность.
Virgo *n.* Де́ва.

virile *adj.* возмужа́лый. —**virility,** *n.* возмужа́лость.

virtual *adj.* факти́ческий. *He has become a virtual dictator,* факти́чески он стал дикта́тором. *That is a virtual impossibility,* э́то практи́чески невозмо́жно.

virtually *adv.* практи́чески; почти́: *virtually everyone,* практи́чески все; почти́ все.

virtue *n.* **1,** (moral excellence; admirable quality) доброде́тель. **2,** (merit; advantage) досто́инство. —**by virtue of,** в си́лу (+ *gen.*).

virtuoso *n.* виртуо́з. —**virtuosity,** *n.* виртуо́зность.

virtuous *adj.* доброде́тельный.

virulence *n.* **1,** *med.* вируле́нтность. **2,** (bitterness) я́рость.

virulent *adj.* **1,** (noxious; deadly) вируле́нтный. **2,** (bitterly hostile) я́ростный; зло́стный: *virulent attacks,* я́ростные/зло́стные нападки.

virus *n.* ви́рус.

visa *n.* ви́за.

visage *n.* **1,** (face) лицо́. **2,** (countenance) вид; выраже́ние лица́.

vis-à-vis *prep.* по отноше́нию к; в отноше́нии (+ *gen.*).

viscera *n.pl.* вну́тренности.

visceral *adj.* инстинкти́вный; интуити́вный.

viscose *n.* виско́за.

viscosity *n.* вя́зкость; тягу́честь.

viscount *n.* вико́нт.

viscous *adj.* вя́зкий; тягу́чий.

vise *n.* тиски́: *grip in a vise,* зажима́ть в тиски́.

visibility *n.* ви́димость.

visible *adj.* **1,** (in sight) ви́димый; ви́дный. *The lake is not visible from here,* отсю́да о́зера не ви́дно. *The moon is hardly visible behind the clouds,* луна́ чуть видна́ из-за туч. **2,** (noticeable; marked) заме́тный: *visible improvement,* ви́димое/заме́тное улучше́ние. *With no visible means of support,* без определённых средств к существова́нию.

visibly *adv.* заме́тно; я́вно: *He was visibly shaken,* он был заме́тно/я́вно потрясён.

vision *n.* **1,** (sense of sight) зре́ние. *Field of vision,* по́ле зре́ния. **2,** (foresight) проница́тельность. *A man of vision,* дальнови́дный челове́к. **3,** (mental image) представле́ние. *Visions of glory,* мечты́ о сла́ве. **4,** (revelation) виде́ние.

visionary *adj.* несбы́точный; непракти́чный. —*n.* мечта́тель; фантазёр.

visit *v.t.* **1,** (call on) навеща́ть; посеща́ть: *visit a friend,* навеща́ть/посеща́ть дру́га. **2,** (go to) посеща́ть; побыва́ть в. *Visit Paris,* посеща́ть Пари́ж; побыва́ть в Пари́же. *Visit a museum,* посеща́ть музе́й. —*v.i.* [*usu.* **visit with**] (по)вида́ться с; гости́ть у. —*n.* посеще́ние; визи́т. *During a visit to Bonn,* во вре́мя визи́та в Бонн; во вре́мя посеще́ния Бо́нна. *Pay a visit on,* наноси́ть визи́т (+ *dat.*). *A visit by a head of state,* визи́т главы́ госуда́рства. *Arrive on an official visit,* прибы́ть с официа́льным визи́том. *Pay an official visit to France,* пое́хать с официа́льным визи́том во Фра́нцию; посети́ть Фра́нцию с официа́льным визи́том. *My first visit to their apartment,* моё пе́рвое посеще́ние их кварти́ры.

visitation *n.* посеще́ние.

visiting *adj.* прие́зжий. —**visiting hours,** часы́ посеще́ния. —**visiting professor,** приглашённый профе́ссор.

visitor *n.* посети́тель.

visor *also,* **vizor** *n.* **1,** (of a cap) козырёк. **2,** (of a helmet) забра́ло.

vista *n.* вид; перспекти́ва.

visual *adj.* **1,** (produced by sight) зри́тельный: *visual impressions,* зри́тельные впечатле́ния. **2,** (serving to instruct) нагля́дный: *visual aids,* нагля́дные посо́бия.

visualize *v.t.* представля́ть себе́.

vital *adj.* **1,** (basic to survival) жи́зненный; насу́щный. *Vital interests,* жи́зненные *or* коренны́е *or* насу́щные интере́сы. *Vital necessity,* жи́зненная необходи́мость. *Vital organs,* жи́зненно ва́жные о́рганы. **2,** *fol. by* **to** (essential) необходи́мый (для): *vital to the success of,* абсолю́тно необходи́м для успе́ха (+ *gen.*). **3,** (utmost) первостепе́нный: *of vital importance,* первостепе́нной ва́жности.

vitality *n.* **1,** (ability to sustain life) жи́зненность. **2,** (vigor; energy) эне́ргия; энерги́чность.

vitally *adv.* жи́зненно: *vitally important,* жи́зненно ва́жный. *Vitally interested,* кро́вно заинтересо́ванный.

vitamin *n.* витами́н. —**vitamin B**^{1}, витами́н В^1 (*pronounced* бэ оди́н). —**vitamin C,** витами́н С (*pronounced* цэ).

vitiate *v.t.* **1,** (spoil) по́ртить. **2,** (invalidate) де́лать недействи́тельным. **3,** (make ineffectual) своди́ть на нет.

viticulture *n.* виногра́дарство.

vitreous *adj.* стекля́нный; стеко́льный.

vitriol *n.* купоро́с. *Blue/green/white vitriol,* ме́дный/желе́зный/ци́нковый купоро́с. —**oil of vitriol,** се́рная кислота́.

vitriolic *adj.* е́дкий; ехи́дный.

vituperation *n.* брань; ру́гань. —**vituperative,** *adj.* бра́нный; руга́тельный.

vivacious *adj.* живо́й; оживлённый. —**vivaciousness; vivacity,** *n.* жи́вость; оживлённость.

vivid *adj.* **1,** (intense, as of a color) я́ркий. **2,** (lively; striking) живо́й; я́ркий. *Vivid description,* я́ркое описа́ние. *Vivid memories,* живы́е/я́ркие воспомина́ния. *Vivid imagination,* живо́е *or* пы́лкое воображе́ние.

vividly *adv.* я́рко; жи́во. *Vividly remember,* жи́во по́мнить.

vividness *n.* я́ркость; жи́вость.

viviparous *adj.* живородя́щий.

vivisection *n.* вивисе́кция.

vixen *n.* **1,** (female fox) са́мка лиси́цы. **2,** (ill-tempered woman) меге́ра.

vizier *n.* визи́рь.

vizor *n.* = **visor.**

V-neck *n.* треуго́льный вы́рез.

vocabulary *n.* слова́рь; слова́рный запа́с; запа́с слов. *Vocabulary building,* накопле́ние словаря́.

vocal *adj.* **1,** (pert. to the voice) голосово́й. **2,** (meant to be sung) вока́льный. **3,** (vociferous) гро́мкий; шу́мный. *Vocal critic,* громогла́сный кри́тик. —**vocal cords,** голосовы́е свя́зки.

vocalist *n.* певе́ц; певи́ца.

vocation *n.* призва́ние.

vocational *adj.* профессиона́льно-техни́ческий: *vocational school/training,* профессиона́льно-техни́ческое учи́лище/обуче́ние.

vocative *adj.* зва́тельный: *vocative case,* зва́тельный паде́ж.

vociferous *adj.* гро́мкий; шу́мный.

vodka *n.* во́дка.

vogue *n.* мо́да. *Be in vogue,* быть в мо́де.

voice *n.* **1,** (sound made when speaking) го́лос: *in a loud voice,* гро́мким го́лосом. *Be in good voice,* быть в го́лосе. *Raise/lose one's voice,* повы́сить/потеря́ть го́лос. **2,** *gram.* зало́г: *passive voice,* страда́тельный зало́г. —*v.t.* выска́зывать: *voice one's opinion,* вы́сказать своё мне́ние. —**give voice to,** выража́ть. —**with one voice,** в оди́н го́лос.

voice box горта́нь.

voiced *adj., phonet.* зво́нкий.

voiceless *adj.* **1,** (having no voice) безголо́сый. **2,** *phonet.* глухо́й.

void *adj.* **1,** (invalid) недействи́тельный: *declare null and void,* объяви́ть недействи́тельным. **2,** *fol. by* **of** (utterly lacking) лишённый (+ *gen.*): *void of sense,* лишён смы́сла. **3,** (empty) пусто́й. —*n.* пустота́: *a void in one's life,* пустота́ в жи́зни. *Fill a void,* запо́лнить пустоту́. —*v.t.* (nullify) де́лать недействи́тельным; аннули́ровать. —*v.i., physiol.* опорожня́ть мочево́й пузы́рь; мочи́ться.

volatile *adj.* **1,** (evaporating rapidly) лету́чий. **2,** (changeable; fickle) изме́нчивый. **3,** (unstable; explosive) неусто́йчивый.

volatility *n.* **1,** *chem.* лету́честь. **2,** (changeability) изме́нчивость.

volcanic *adj.* вулкани́ческий.

volcano *n.* вулка́н.

vole *n.* полёвка.

volition *n.* во́ля. *Of one's own volition,* по свое́й во́ле; по до́брой во́ле; по со́бственному жела́нию.

volitional *adj.* волево́й.

volley *n.* **1,** (salvo) залп. **2,** *fig.* (torrent) град.

volleyball *n.* волейбо́л.

volt *n.* вольт. —**voltage,** *n.* напряже́ние; вольта́ж. —**voltmeter,** *n.* вольтме́тр.

voluble *adj.* говорли́вый; разгово́рчивый. —**volubility,** *n.* говорли́вость; разгово́рчивость.

volume *n.* **1,** (size; amount) объём: *volume of a sphere,* объём ша́ра; *volume of trade,* объём торго́вли. **2,** (book) том: *in two volumes,* в двух тома́х. **3,** (loudness) си́ла зву́ка; гро́мкость. *Turn down the volume,* уменьша́ть *or* убавля́ть звук *or* гро́мкость. —**speak volumes,** говори́ть о мно́гом.

volumetric *adj.* объёмный.

voluminous *adj.* обши́рный: *voluminous correspondence,* обши́рная перепи́ска.

voluntary *adj.* **1,** (done by free choice) доброво́льный. *On a voluntary basis,* на доброво́льной осно́ве; на

доброво́льных нача́лах. **2,** *physiol.* произво́льный. —**voluntarily,** *adv.* доброво́льно.

volunteer *n.* доброво́лец. *Are there any volunteers?,* есть жела́ющие?; есть охо́тники? —*adj.* доброво́льческий: *volunteer army,* доброво́льческая а́рмия. —*v.t.* предлага́ть: *volunteer one's services,* предлага́ть свои́ услу́ги. —*v.i.* вызыва́ться; пойти́ доброво́льцем. *Volunteer to help,* вы́зваться помо́чь. *Volunteer for the army,* пойти́ доброво́льцем в а́рмию.

voluptuous *adj.* чу́вственный.

vomit *v.i.* рвать (*impers.*): *He is vomiting,* его́ рвёт; *she vomited,* её вы́рвало. —*n.* рво́тная ма́сса. —**vomiting,** *n.* рво́та.

voodoo *n.* колдовство́.

voracious *adj.* прожо́рливый. *Voracious appetite,* во́лчий аппети́т. *He is a voracious reader,* он чита́ет запо́ем.

vortex *n.* вихрь; водоворо́т.

vote *n.* **1,** (choice expressed) го́лос: *win by ten votes,* вы́играть с переве́сом в де́сять голосо́в. **2,** (act of voting) голосова́ние: *put to a vote,* поста́вить на голосова́ние. *The vote on the resolution,* голосова́ние по по́воду резолю́ции. *Vote of confidence,* во́тум дове́рия. *By a majority vote,* большинство́м голосо́в. *By a 5-4 vote,* пятью́ голоса́ми про́тив четырёх. —*v.i.* голосова́ть: *vote for a candidate,* голосова́ть за кандида́та; *vote on a proposal,* голосова́ть предложе́ние. *The right to vote,* пра́во го́лоса. —*v.t.* **1,** (authorize by vote) одобря́ть; ассигнова́ть. **2,** *fol. by* **in** (elect) избира́ть. **3,** *fol. by* **down** (defeat; reject) прова́ливать.

voter *n.* избира́тель.

voting *n.* голосова́ние. —**voting booth,** каби́на для голосова́ния. —**voting member,** член с реша́ющим го́лосом.

vouch *v.i.* [*usu.* **vouch for**] руча́ться (за).

voucher *n.* о́рдер; квита́нция; ва́учер. *Expense voucher,* расхо́дный о́рдер.

vouchsafe *v.t.* удоста́ивать; соизволя́ть.

vow *n.* обе́т; кля́тва; заро́к. —*v.t. & i.* кля́сться (в).

vowel *n.* **1,** (letter) гла́сная бу́ква. **2,** (sound) гла́сный звук.

voyage *n.* путеше́ствие; пла́вание. —*v.i.* путеше́ствовать.

vulcanite *n.* эбони́т.

vulcanize *v.t.* вулканизи́ровать. —**vulcanization,** *n.* вулканиза́ция.

vulgar *adj.* гру́бый; по́шлый; вульга́рный. —**vulgarism,** *n.* вульгари́зм. —**vulgarity,** *n.* вульга́рность.

vulgarize *v.t.* опошля́ть; вульгаризи́ровать.

vulnerability *n.* уязви́мость.

vulnerable *adj.* уязви́мый: *vulnerable position,* уязви́мая пози́ция. *Vulnerable to attack,* уязви́мый для ата́ки.

vulture *n.* гриф.

W

W, w двадцать третья буква английского алфавита.

wacky *adj.*, *slang* чудаковатый; эксцентричный.

wad *n.* **1,** (small lump or mass) комок; кусочек. *Wad of cotton,* комок ваты. **2,** (bunch; roll) пачка: *wad of money,* пачка денег. **3,** (for a firearm) пыж.

wadded *adj.* ватный.

wadding *n.* вата; набивка.

waddle *v.i.* переваливаться (с боку на́ бок); ходить вперевалку; ходить вразвалку; ходить уточкой. —*n.* перевалка.

wade *v.i.* идти вброд. *Wade into the water,* входить в воду. *Wade across a river,* переходить реку вброд. —**wade through, 1,** (walk through) пробираться сквозь. **2,** (plow through; work one's way through) одолевать; осиливать (*e.g.* книгу).

wading bird болотная птица.

wafer *n.* **1,** (biscuit) сухое печенье. **2,** (bread used in the Eucharist) облатка.

waffle *n.* вафля. —**waffle iron,** вафельница.

waft *v.t.* навевать. —*v.i.* тянуть (*impers.*): *Cool air wafted in from the sea,* с моря тянуло свежим воздухом. —*n.* дуновение (воздуха).

wag *v.t.* вилять; махать (хвостом). *Wag one's tongue,* болтать языком; чесать язык. —*v.i.* вилять. *Set tongues wagging,* вызывать много толков (*or* кривотолков). —*n.* шутник; остряк; балагур.

wage *n.,* often *pl.* заработная плата; зарплата; жалованье. *A decent wage,* приличная зарплата. —*v.t.* вести (войну); проводить (кампанию). —**wage earner,** рабочий. —**wage scale,** шкала заработной платы.

wager *n.* пари. —*v.i.* держать пари; биться об заклад. —*v.t.* ставить.

wagon *also,* **waggon** *n.* повозка; телега; подвода. *Covered wagon,* фургон.

wagtail *n.* трясогузка.

waif *n.* уличный мальчишка; беспризорник.

wail *v.i.* выть; вопить. —*n.* вой; вопль. *The wail of air-raid sirens,* вой сирен воздушной тревоги.

wainscot *n.* панель.

waist *n.* талия. *Put one's arm around someone's waist,* обнять кого-нибудь за талию. *Take a dress in at the waist,* собрать платье в талии. ♦*In various expressions,* пояс: *bow from the waist,* кланяться в пояс; *strip to the waist,* раздеться до пояса; *in water up to one's waist,* по пояс в воде.

waistband *n.* пояс.

waistcoat *n.* жилет.

waistline *n.* талия.

wait *v.t. & i.* ждать. *Wait for the train,* ждать поезда. *Wait one's turn,* ждать своей очереди. *Wait for one's sister,* ждать свою сестру. *Wait for the rain to stop,* ждать, когда (*or* пока) перестанет дождь. *Don't wait for me,* не ждите меня. *I can't wait!,* жду не дождусь! я не могу дождаться! *Without waiting for an answer,* не дожидаясь ответа. —*n.* ожидание: *a long wait,* долгое ожидание. —**lie in wait for,** подстерегать. —**wait on,** обслуживать. *Wait on a table,* обслуживать стол. —**wait out,** выжидать; пережидать. —**wait up,** не ложиться спать.

waiter *n.* официант.

waiting *n.* ожидание. *Waiting period,* срок ожидания. —*adj.* выжидательный: *play a waiting game,* занимать выжидательную позицию.

waiting list очередь: *a long waiting list,* большая очередь. *Waiting list for housing,* очередь на жильё. *Be on the waiting list,* быть *or* стоять на очереди. *Put someone on the waiting list,* поставить кого-нибудь на очередь; записать кого-нибудь в очередь. *Put one's (own) name on the waiting list,* записаться в очередь.

waiting room 1, (in a railroad station) зал ожидания. **2,** (in a doctor's office) приёмная.

waitress *n.* официантка.

waive *v.t.* **1,** (give up; forgo) отказываться от; поступаться (+ *instr.*). *Waive a right,* отказаться от права. *Waive one's rights,* поступиться своими правами. **2,** (set aside; dispense with) делать исключение из: *waive a rule,* делать исключение из правила. *We'll waive the requirement in your case,* мы сделаем исключение для вас.

waiver *n.* исключение.

wake *v.t.* [*often* **wake up**] будить: *Wake me (up) at seven o'clock,* разбудите меня в семь часов. —*v.i.* [*usu.* **wake up**] просыпаться. —*n.* **1,** (for a dead person) поминки. **2,** (track of a ship) кильватер. **3,** (route passed over) *leave in its wake,* оставлять за собой; *bring in its wake,* влечь за собой. —**in the wake of,** по следам (+ *gen.*); по пятам (+ *gen.*).

waken *v.t.* будить. —*v.i.* просыпаться.

walk *v.i.* **1,** (take steps; proceed on foot) ходить; идти (пешком). *Walk slowly,* ходить/идти медленно.

Learn to walk, учи́ться ходи́ть. *Don't run, walk!,* не беги́те, иди́те ша́гом! *It's not far — I'll walk,* э́то недалеко́ — я пойду́ пешко́м. **2,** (stroll) ходи́ть; гуля́ть; прогу́ливаться; проха́живаться. *Walk in the park,* ходи́ть/гуля́ть в па́рке *or* по па́рку. —*v.t.* **1,** (walk along) ходи́ть по: *walk the streets at night,* ходи́ть по у́лицам но́чью. *Walk a tightrope,* ходи́ть по кана́ту. **2,** (traverse) проходи́ть: *walk five miles,* проходи́ть пять миль. *Walk the length of a street,* проходи́ть (всю) у́лицу. **3,** (accompany) провожа́ть: *walk someone home,* провожа́ть кого́-нибудь домо́й. **4,** (take for a walk) выгу́ливать: *walk the dog,* выгу́ливать соба́ку. —*n.* **1,** (act of walking; distance walked) ходьба́: *ten-minute walk,* де́сять мину́т ходьбы́. *20-km. walk, sports* ходьба́ на два́дцать киломе́тров. **2,** (stroll) прогу́лка. *Go for a walk,* идти́ гуля́ть. *Go for a short walk,* идти́ прогуля́ться. *I'm going for a walk,* я пойду́ погуля́ть; я пойду́ погуля́ю. *Take short walks,* соверша́ть коро́ткие прогу́лки. *Take for a walk,* води́ть гуля́ть; вести́ на прогу́лку. **3,** (manner of walking; gait) похо́дка. **4,** (slow pace) шаг: *slow a horse to a walk,* своди́ть ло́шадь на шаг. **5,** (path; promenade) алле́я; доро́жка. **6,** *in* **from all walks of life,** всех слоёв о́бщества. —**walk off,** уходи́ть. *Walk off the job,* объяви́ть забасто́вку. —**walk off with, 1,** (steal) утащи́ть. **2,** (win) взять; завоева́ть. —**walk out,** выходи́ть. *Walk out of a meeting,* поки́нуть собра́ние; поки́нуть зал; демонстрати́вно уйти́ с собра́ния. *Walk out of the talks,* уйти́ с перегово́ров. —**walk out on,** бро́сить; уйти́ от. —**walk up to,** подходи́ть к.

walker *n.* ходо́к.

walkie-talkie *n.* (портати́вная) ра́ция.

walking *adj.* ходя́чий. *It is within walking distance,* туда́ мо́жно дойти́ пешко́м. —*n.* ходьба́: *Walking is good for you,* ходьба́ тебе́ поле́зна. —**get one's walking papers,** быть уво́ленным; вы́лететь.

walking shoes о́бувь для ходьбы́.

walking stick па́лка; трость; клюка́.

walking tour пе́шая экску́рсия.

walkout *n.* **1,** (abrupt departure) демонстрати́вный ухо́д. **2,** (strike) забасто́вка.

wall *n.* **1,** (general term) стена́. **2,** *anat.* сте́нка: *abdominal wall,* брюшна́я сте́нка. —*adj.* стенно́й; насте́нный. *Wall newspaper,* стенна́я газе́та. —*v.t.* **1,** *fol. by* **in** (enclose) обноси́ть стено́й. **2,** *fol. by* **up** (board up) заде́лывать; замуро́вывать. **3,** *fol. by* **off** (partition off) отгора́живать. —**drive up a wall,** *colloq.* своди́ть с ума́; доводи́ть до сумасше́ствия. —**up against** (*or* **with one's back to) the wall,** припёртый к стене́.

wallet *n.* бума́жник.

walleye *n.* бельмо́.

wallflower *n.* **1,** (plant) лакфио́ль; желтофио́ль. **2,** *colloq.* (girl without a partner at a dance) де́вушка без кавале́ра.

wallop *n.* тума́к. —*v.t.* дать тумака́ (+ *dat.*).

wallow *v.i.* [*usu.* **wallow in**] **1,** (roll about in) валя́ться (в). **2,** *fig.* (indulge oneself to excess) погря́знуть (в); утопа́ть (в).

wallpaper *n.* обо́и. —*v.t.* окле́ивать (ко́мнату) обо́ями.

walnut *n.* **1,** (tree; wood) оре́х; оре́ховое де́рево. **2,** (nut) гре́цкий оре́х. —*adj.* оре́ховый.

walrus *n.* морж.

waltz *n.* вальс. —*v.i.* вальси́ровать.

wan *adj.* бле́дный.

wand *n.* па́лочка: *magic wand,* волше́бная па́лочка.

wander *v.i.* **1,** (walk or stroll aimlessly) броди́ть; блужда́ть: *wander around town,* броди́ть/блужда́ть по го́роду. **2,** (roam about the world) стра́нствовать; скита́ться. **3,** (fail to concentrate) блужда́ть: *His mind tends to wander,* его́ мы́сли ча́сто блужда́ют. —**wander into,** забрести́ в. —**wander off, 1,** [*also,* **wander away**] (stray) забрести́. *Wander off/away from the group,* отстава́ть от гру́ппы. **2,** [*also,* **wander from**] (digress) отклоня́ться от; отходи́ть от.

wanderer *n.* стра́нник; скита́лец.

wandering *n.* стра́нствие; скита́ние. —*adj.* бродя́чий; блужда́ющий.

wanderlust *n.* страсть к путеше́ствиям.

wane *v.i.* **1,** (of the moon) убыва́ть; идти́ на у́быль. **2,** *fig.* (fade; ebb) га́снуть; угаса́ть. *Hope is waning,* наде́жда га́снет *or* угаса́ет. *Interest is waning,* интере́с угаса́ет. *His popularity is waning,* его́ популя́рность тускне́ет. —*n., in* **on the wane,** на уще́рбе.

wangle *v.t.* выпра́шивать; раздобыва́ть; напроси́ться в *or* на. *Wangle a ticket/invitation,* вы́просить/раздобы́ть биле́т/приглаше́ние. *Wangle an invitation to a ball,* напроси́ться на бал. *Wangle an official trip abroad,* напроси́ться в зарубе́жную командиро́вку. *Wangle a secret from someone,* выве́дывать секре́т у кого́-нибудь.

want *v.t.* хоте́ть: *What do you want?,* что вы хоти́те? *What do you want me to do?,* что вы хоти́те, что́бы я сде́лал(а)? *I wanted to ask you...* я хоте́л(а) вас спроси́ть... *You are wanted on the phone,* вас про́сят к телефо́ну. *The boss wants to see you,* нача́льник вас про́сит к себе́. *He is wanted by the authorities,* он разы́скивается властя́ми. —*n.* **1,** (lack) недоста́ток. *For want of something better,* за неиме́нием лу́чшего. **2,** (poverty; need) нужда́: *freedom from want,* свобо́да от нужды́. *Be in want of,* нужда́ться в. **3,** *pl.* (needs) потре́бности.

want ad *colloq.* объявле́ние (в газе́те).

wanting *adj.* не име́ющий: *wanting in experience,* не име́ющий доста́точного о́пыта. *He was found wanting,* он оказа́лся не на высоте́.

wanton *adj.* **1,** (vicious; unprovoked) бессмы́сленный. **2,** (dissolute) распу́тный.

war *n.* война́. *Be at war,* быть в состоя́нии войны́. *Go to war,* пойти́ на войну́. *Go off to war,* уйти́ на войну́. *He was killed in the war,* он поги́б на войне́. —*adj.* вое́нный: *war game,* вое́нная игра́. —*v.i.* воева́ть: *warring parties,* вою́ющие сто́роны.

warble *v.i.* щёлкать. —*n.* трель.

warbler *n.* сла́вка.

war crime вое́нное преступле́ние. —**war criminal,** вое́нный престу́пник.

war cry боево́й клич.

ward *n.* **1,** (dependent) опека́емый; подопе́чный. **2,** (of a hospital) пала́та. *Maternity ward,* роди́льное отделе́ние. **3,** (district) райо́н. —*v.t.* [*usu.* **ward off**] отража́ть; отводи́ть.

warden *n.* сто́рож; объе́здчик: *forest warden,* лесно́й сто́рож/объе́здчик. *Prison warden,* тюре́мщик. *Game warden,* инспе́ктор по охра́не ди́чи.

warder *n.* **1,** (guard; watchman) сто́рож. **2,** *Brit.* = **prison warden.**

wardrobe *n.* **1,** (clothes closet) гардеро́б; платяно́й шкаф. **2,** (supply of clothes) гардеро́б.

ware *n.* **1,** *pl.* (merchandise) това́ры. **2,** *used in compounds,* изде́лия; посу́да: *hardware,* скобяны́е изде́лия; *earthenware,* гли́няная посу́да.

warehouse *n.* склад. *Store something in a warehouse,* храни́ть что́-нибудь на скла́де. —*adj.* складско́й: *warehouse facilities,* складски́е помеще́ния.

warfare *n.* война́: *submarine/guerrilla warfare,* подво́дная/партиза́нская война́.

warhead *n.* боева́я часть; боева́я голо́вка; боеголо́вка. *Nuclear warhead,* я́дерная боеголо́вка.

warhorse *n.* боево́й конь.

warily *adv.* осторо́жно; насторо́женно.

wariness *n.* осторо́жность; насторо́женность.

warlike *adj.* вои́нственный.

warm *adj.* тёплый: *warm milk/coat/summer,* тёплое молоко́/пальто́/ле́то. *Warm welcome,* тёплый приём. *It is warm,* тепло́. *Are you warm?,* вам тепло́? *The sun is warm,* со́лнце гре́ет. *Get warm,* согрева́ться. —*v.t.* [*also,* **warm up**] греть; нагрева́ть; согрева́ть: *warm up the food,* греть/нагрева́ть/согрева́ть пи́щу. *Warm one's feet by the fire,* греть но́ги у огня́. *Warm one's heart,* ра́довать се́рдце; согрева́ть ду́шу. —*v.i.* **1,** *fol. by* **up** (of the weather, temperature, etc.) тепле́ть. **2,** *fol. by* **up** (of a heating device, food on the stove, etc.) согрева́ться; нагрева́ться; (of an engine) прогрева́ться. **3,** *fol. by* **to** (get into the swing of) войти́ во вкус (+ *gen.*). *Warm to one's subject,* разговори́ться. —**warm oneself,** гре́ться. —**warm over,** разогрева́ть; подогрева́ть. *Warmed-over dinner,* разогре́тый обе́д. —**warm up,** (exercise; limber up) де́лать разми́нку; размина́ться. —**warm up to,** (бо́лее) тепло́ относи́ться к.

warm-blooded *adj.* теплокро́вный.

warmhearted *adj.* тёплый; серде́чный.

warmly *adv.* **1,** (so as to be warm) тепло́: *dress warmly,* тепло́ одева́ться. **2,** (cordially) тепло́; серде́чно.

warmonger *n.* поджига́тель войны́.

warmth *n.* тепло́; теплота́. *Give off warmth,* излуча́ть тепло́. *Warmth of feeling,* теплота́ чу́вства. *With great warmth,* с большо́й теплото́й.

warm-up *n.* разми́нка.

warn *v.t.* предупрежда́ть: *warn someone of the danger,* предупрежда́ть кого́-нибудь об опа́сности. *I'm warning you!,* предупрежда́ю (вас)! *I warned you not to do it,* я предупрежда́л(а) вас не де́лать э́того. *Don't say I didn't warn you!,* не говори́те, что я вас не предупрежда́л(а).

warning *n.* предупрежде́ние; предостереже́ние. *Fire without warning,* стреля́ть без предупрежде́ния. *Get off with a warning,* отде́латься предупрежде́нием. *Let this be a warning to you,* пусть э́то послу́жит вам предупрежде́нием. —*adj.* предупреди́тельный: *warning shot,* предупреди́тельный вы́стрел.

warp *v.t.* **1,** (twist; bend) коро́бить. *The door is badly warped,* дверь си́льно покоро́блена. **2,** (pervert) извраща́ть; коверка́ть. *Warped mind,* извращённый ум. —*v.i.* коро́биться; коро́бить (*impers.*). —*n.* **1,** (bend) коробле́ние; переко́с. **2,** *textiles* осно́ва.

warplane *n.* вое́нный самолёт.

warrant *n.* о́рдер; манда́т; наря́д. *Search warrant,* о́рдер на о́быск. —*v.t.* **1,** (justify) опра́вдывать. **2,** (merit) заслу́живать.

warrant officer (in the army) пра́порщик; (in the navy) ми́чман.

warranty *n.* гара́нтия; руча́тельство.

warren *n.* кро́личья нора́; кро́личий садо́к.

warrior *n.* во́ин.

warship *n.* вое́нный кора́бль.

wart *n.* борода́вка.

wart hog борода́вочник.

wartime *n.* вое́нное вре́мя.

wary *adj.* осторо́жный; насторо́женный. *Be wary of,* остерега́ться (+ *gen.*).

wash *v.t.* **1,** (clean; scrub) мыть; умыва́ть. *Wash one's hands,* мыть ру́ки. *Wash the dishes,* мыть посу́ду. **2,** (launder) стира́ть: *wash clothes,* стира́ть бельё. **3,** (flow over) омыва́ть: *Waves wash the shore,* во́лны омыва́ют бе́рег. —*v.i.* **1,** (get washed) мы́ться; умыва́ться. **2,** (do laundry) стира́ть. **3,** (be capable of being washed) стира́ться. *The sweater won't wash,* сви́тер нельзя́ стира́ть. **4,** (flow) набега́ть: *The waves washed over the deck,* во́лны набежа́ли на па́лубу. **5,** *colloq.* (stand up to scrutiny): *The story won't wash,* э́та исто́рия никого́ не убеди́т. —*n.* **1,** (act of washing) мытьё. **2,** (laundering) сти́рка: *fade in the wash,* линя́ть от сти́рки. *Do the wash,* стира́ть бельё. *The stains came out in the wash,* пя́тна отстира́лись. **3,** (things to be washed) бельё: *hang out the wash,* выве́шивать бельё. **4,** (liquid refuse) жи́жа. **5,** (liquid used for cleansing) примо́чка: *eyewash,* примо́чка для глаз. —**wash ashore,** *see* **ashore.** —**wash away,** размыва́ть (*impers.*); сноси́ть (*impers.*). *The road was washed away,* доро́гу размы́ло. *The bridge was washed away by the flood,* мост снесло́ водо́й. —**wash down,** запива́ть: *wash down medicine with water,* запива́ть лека́рство водо́й. —**wash off,** смыва́ть; отмыва́ть. —**wash one's hands of something,** умыва́ть ру́ки. —**wash out, 1,** (wash) стира́ть (*pfv.* вы́стирать). *Wash out one's socks,* вы́стирать носки́. **2,** (rinse out) спола́скивать. **3,** (remove) смыва́ть; отсти́рывать: *wash out a stain,* смыва́ть/отсти́рывать пятно́. **4,** (wash away) размыва́ть: *The flood washed out the road,* вода́ размы́ла доро́гу. —**wash overboard,** *see* **overboard.** —**wash up, 1,** (wash one's hands and face) умыва́ться. **2,** (deposit on the shore) наноси́ть *or* выноси́ть *or* выбра́сывать на бе́рег.

washable *adj. These shirts are washable,* э́ти руба́шки мо́жно стира́ть.

washbasin *n.* умыва́льник.

washboard *n.* стира́льная доска́.

washbowl *n.* умыва́льник.

washcloth *n.* ткань *or* полоте́нце для мытья́.

washed-out *adj.* **1,** (faded) полиня́вший. **2,** *colloq.* (tired; weak) лишён сил. **3,** *colloq.* (wan) бле́дный.

washed-up *adj.* ко́нченый. *He is washed-up as an actor,* он как актёр ко́нчился.

washer *n.* **1,** (person who washes) мо́йщик: *window washer,* мо́йщик о́кон. **2,** (washing machine) стира́льная маши́на. **3,** *mech.* ша́йба; прокла́дка.

washerwoman *n.* пра́чка.

washing *n.* мытьё; мо́йка; умыва́ние; (*of clothes*) сти́рка. —**washing machine,** стира́льная маши́на.

washrag *n.* = **washcloth.**

washroom *n.* убо́рная; туале́т.

washstand *n.* умыва́льник; рукомо́йник.

washtub *n.* лоха́нь; коры́то.

wasp *n.* оса́.

waste *v.t.* **1,** (spend needlessly) тра́тить (да́ром *or* по́пусту *or* зря). *Waste time,* теря́ть вре́мя. *Waste words; waste one's breath,* тра́тить слова́ да́ром *or* по́пусту *or* напра́сно; броса́ть слова́ на ве́тер. *His efforts were wasted,* его́ уси́лия пропа́ли да́ром. **2,** (fail to take advantage of) упуска́ть; прозева́ть (удо́бный слу́чай). —*v.i.* [*usu.* **waste away**] ча́хнуть. —*n.* **1,** (unnecessary expenditure) растра́та; пуста́я тра́та. *Waste of time,* поте́ря *or* растра́та вре́мени. *Waste of money,* пуста́я тра́та де́нег. *Waste of energy,* растра́та сил. **2,** (superfluous matter) отхо́ды; отбро́сы. *Industrial waste,* отхо́ды произво́дства. **3,** *physiol.* выделе́ния. —**go to waste, 1,** (never be used or consumed) пропада́ть. **2,** (go for nought) пропада́ть да́ром. —**lay waste,** опустоша́ть. —**waste products,** отхо́ды. *See also* **wasted.**

wastebasket *n.* корзи́на для бума́ги.

wasted *adj.* **1,** (squandered) растра́ченный. **2,** (fruitless; gone for naught) напра́сный; пропа́вший да́ром. **3,** (emaciated) истощённый: *wasted by disease,* истощённый боле́знью.

wasteful *adj.* расточи́тельный. —**wastefulness,** *n.* расточи́тельность.

wasteland *n.* пусты́ня.

wastrel *n.* **1,** (spendthrift) транжи́р. **2,** (good-for-nothing) шалопа́й.

watch *v.t.* **1,** (look at; observe) смотре́ть; наблюда́ть. *Watch television,* смотре́ть телеви́зор. *Watch the sun rise,* наблюда́ть восхо́д со́лнца. *Watch the boys playing ball,* смотре́ть, как ма́льчики игра́ют в мяч. **2,** (guard; keep an eye on; look after) смотре́ть за; следи́ть за; наблюда́ть за: *watch the children,* смотре́ть/следи́ть/наблюда́ть за детьми́. *Watch one's weight/language,* следи́ть за свои́м ве́сом/ за свое́й ре́чью/. —*v.i.* смотре́ть: *Watch how it's done,* посмотри́те, как э́то де́лается. *Watch where you're going!,* смотри́те, куда́ идёте! *Watch that he doesn't fall,* смотри́те, что́бы он не упа́л. —*n.* **1,** (timepiece) часы́. **2,** (observation) наблюде́ние. *Keep watch over,*

сторожи́ть; стере́чь; карау́лить. *Be on the watch for,* подстерега́ть. **3,** (guarding) стра́жа; *naval* ва́хта: *stand watch,* стоя́ть на стра́же *or* на ва́хте. *The night watch,* ночна́я стра́жа. —**watch for,** ждать; стере́чь; подстерега́ть. —**watch it!,** осторо́жно! —**watch oneself,** бере́чься. —**watch one's step, 1,** (be careful not to fall) стара́ться не оступи́ться. *Watch your step!,* осторо́жно, не оступи́тесь! **2,** (be prudent) бере́чься; быть осторо́жным; соблюда́ть осторо́жность. —**watch out,** бере́чься. *Watch out!,* осторо́жно! —**watch out for,** бере́чься (+ *gen.*); остерега́ться (+ *gen.*). —**watch over,** сторожи́ть; стере́чь; карау́лить.

watchband *n.* ремешо́к для часо́в.

watch chain цепо́чка для часо́в.

watchdog *n.* дворо́вая *or* сторожева́я соба́ка; сторожево́й пёс.

watchful *adj.* бди́тельный; насторо́женный. *Under the watchful eye of...,* под бди́тельным о́ком (+ *gen.*). *Keep a watchful eye on,* внима́тельно следи́ть за.

watchmaker *n.* часовщи́к.

watchman *n.* сто́рож.

watchtower *n.* сторожева́я ба́шня *or* вы́шка.

watchword *n.* **1,** (password) паро́ль. **2,** (motto) ло́зунг; деви́з.

water *n.* вода́: *a glass of water,* стака́н воды́. *Be under water,* быть под водо́й. *Mineral/territorial waters,* минера́льные/территориа́льные во́ды. *Ship something by water,* отправля́ть что́-нибудь во́дным путём. *Land a plane on the water,* посади́ть самолёт на́ воду. —*adj.* во́дный; водяно́й: *water sports,* во́дный спорт; *water vapor,* водяно́й пар. *Water glass,* стака́н для воды́. *Water bottle,* буты́лка из-под воды́. —*v.t.* **1,** (pour water on) полива́ть: *water the flowers,* полива́ть цветы́. **2,** (provide with water, as animals) пои́ть. **3,** *fol. by* **down** (dilute; weaken) разбавля́ть; разжижа́ть; *fig.* смягча́ть. —*v.i.* **1,** (of one's eyes) слези́ться. **2,** *My mouth is watering,* у меня́ слю́нки теку́т. *Mention of that makes my mouth water,* при упомина́нии об э́том у меня́ слю́нки теку́т. —**get into hot water,** *see* **hot.** —**of the first water,** чи́стой *or* чисте́йшей воды́. —**not hold water,** не выде́рживать кри́тики. —**spend money like water,** сори́ть деньга́ми. —**throw cold water on,** облива́ть (+ *acc.*) холо́дной водо́й.

water buffalo инди́йский (*or* водяно́й) бу́йвол.

water cannon водомёт.

water carrier водоно́с; водово́з.

water closet убо́рная.

watercolor *also,* **watercolour** *n., often pl.* акваре́ль. —*adj.* акваре́льный. —**watercolorist,** *n.* акваре́лист.

water-cooled *adj.* с водяны́м охлажде́нием.

watercress *n.* водяно́й кресс.

waterfall *n.* водопа́д.

waterfowl *n.* водопла́вающая пти́ца.

waterfront *n.* порт; райо́н по́рта.

watering *n.* **1,** (of plants) поли́вка. **2,** (of livestock) водопо́й. —**watering can,** ле́йка. —**watering place,** водопо́й.

waterless *adj.* безво́дный.

water lily водяна́я ли́лия; кувши́нка.

waterline *n.* ватерли́ния.

waterlogged *adj.* пропи́танный водо́й.

water main водопрово́дная магистра́ль.

watermark *n.* водяно́й знак.

watermelon *n.* арбу́з. —*adj.* арбу́зный: *watermelon pits*, арбу́зные ко́сточки.

water meter водоме́р.

water pipe водопрово́дная труба́.

water polo во́дное по́ло; ватерпо́ло.

water power во́дная эне́ргия.

waterproof *adj.* непромока́емый; водонепроница́емый. *Be waterproof*, не пропуска́ть воды́.

water-repellent *adj.* водоотта́лкивающий.

watershed *n.* водоразде́л.

water ski во́дная лы́жа. —**water-ski**, *v.i.* ката́ться на во́дных лы́жах. —**water-skiing**, *n.* воднолы́жный спорт.

waterspout *n.* **1,** (outlet for water) водосто́чная труба́. **2,** (tornado) смерч.

water sprite водяно́й.

water table у́ровень грунтовы́х вод.

watertight *adj.* **1,** (waterproof) водонепроница́емый; непромока́емый. **2,** *fig.* (impossible to refute) неопровержи́мый.

water tower водонапо́рная ба́шня.

water truck полива́льная маши́на.

waterway *n.* во́дный путь; во́дная арте́рия.

water wheel водяно́е колесо́.

watery *adj.* водяни́стый; жи́дкий.

watt *n.* ватт: *100-watt bulb*, ла́мпочка в сто ватт. —**wattage,** *n.* мо́щность (в ва́ттах).

wattle *n.* **1,** (interlaced twigs forming a fence) плете́нь. **2,** (fleshy skin hanging from the throat of certain fowl) борода́; серёжка. —**wattled,** *adj.* плетёный.

wave *n.* **1,** (of water) волна́: *float on the waves*, пла́вать на волна́х. **2,** (in one's hair) зави́вка. **3,** *physics* волна́: *sound wave*, звукова́я волна́. **4,** (motion with the hand) взмах. **5,** *fig.* (surge) волна́; прили́в; разгу́л. A *wave of strikes/discontent/enthusiasm*, волна́ забасто́вок; волна́ недово́льства; прили́в энтузиа́зма. *Crime wave*, разгу́л престу́пности. **6,** (period of intense cold or heat) полоса́: *heat wave*, полоса́ си́льной жары́. —*v.t.* **1,** (move back and forth; swing) маха́ть; пома́хать: *wave one's hand*, маха́ть/помаха́ть руко́й. *Wave a handkerchief*, маха́ть/помаха́ть платко́м. *Wave goodbye*, маха́ть/помаха́ть на проща́ние. *Wave a flag*, разма́хивать фла́гом. **2,** (curl, as hair) завива́ть. —*v.i.* **1,** (flutter) развева́ться: *The flag was waving in the wind*, флаг развева́лся на ветру́. **2,** (wave one's hand) маха́ть *or* помаха́ть руко́й. *Wave to someone*, маха́ть кому́-нибудь. *Wave to the crowd*, маха́ть руко́й толпе́. —**wave aside**, отма́хиваться от; отмета́ть. —**wave back**, маха́ть в отве́т.

wavelength *n.* длина́ волны́.

waver *v.i.* **1,** (sway; flutter) колыха́ться; развева́ться. **2,** (show hesitation) дро́гнуть; колеба́ться.

wavy *adj.* волни́стый: *wavy hair*, волни́стые во́лосы.

wax *n.* воск. —*adj.* восково́й: *wax figure*, восковáя фигу́ра. —*v.t.* вощи́ть. *Wax the floor*, натира́ть пол. —*v.i.* **1,** (of the moon) прибыва́ть; прибавля́ться. **2,** (become): *wax angry*, серди́ться; *wax calm*, успоко́иться.

waxen *adj.* восково́й.

wax museum музе́й восковы́х фигу́р; пано́птикум.

wax paper вощёная бума́га; воща́нка.

waxwing *n.* свиристе́ль.

waxy *adj.* восково́й.

way *n.* **1,** (route) путь; доро́га: *on the way home*, по пути́/ по доро́ге/ домо́й. *All the way*, всю доро́гу. *Part of the way*, часть пути́. *The shortest way to town*, кратча́йший путь в го́род. *Lose one's way*, заблуди́ться; сби́ться с пути́/ с доро́ги/. *I don't know the way to the station*, я не зна́ю доро́ги на ста́нцию. *Are you going my way?*, нам по пути́?; вам со мной по пути́? *I must be on my way*, ну, я пошёл (пошла́). *The children were on their way to school*, де́ти шли в шко́лу. *Block someone's way*, прегради́ть путь (+ *dat.*); загора́живать доро́гу (+ *dat.*). *Stand in someone's way*, стоя́ть на чьём-нибудь пути́; стоя́ть у кого́-нибудь поперёк доро́ги. **2,** (direction) сторона́: *He went that way*, он пошёл в ту сто́рону. *Which way are you going?*, вам в каку́ю сто́рону? *This way, please!*, сюда́, пожа́луйста! **3,** (position such as to be an obstacle): *be in the way*, меша́ть. *Get out of the way!*, не меша́йте!; прочь с доро́ги! *Keep out of the way*, держа́ться в стороне́. **4,** (manner; method) спо́соб; путь. *This way*, таки́м спо́собом; таки́м о́бразом. *Don't do it that way*, не де́лайте так. *Let's do it this way*, дава́йте сде́лаем так. *The same way*, так же. *In what way?*, каки́м о́бразом?; каки́м путём? *One way or another*, так и́ли ина́че. *One's own way*, на свой лад; по-сво́ему. *There is no other way to do it*, друго́го спо́соба/пути́ нет; ина́че (*or* по-друго́му) э́то сде́лать нельзя́. *Try in every way*, все́ми си́лами стара́ться. **5,** (respect) отноше́ние. *In a way*, в не́котором отноше́нии; в не́котором ро́де; в изве́стном смы́сле. *In many ways*, во мно́гих отноше́ниях. **6,** (distance): *a long way from here*, далеко́ отсю́да. *We have a long way to go*, нам ещё далеко́ е́хать. *We've come a long way*, мы прие́хали издалека́; мы проде́лали большо́й путь; *fig.* мы доби́лись мно́гого. **7,** (wish; will): *have one's way*, настоя́ть на своём. *Get one's way*, доби́ться своего́. *Have it your way*, пусть бу́дет по-ва́шему. **8,** *colloq.* (condition) состоя́ние. *He is in a bad way*, он в плохо́м состоя́нии; с ним де́ло пло́хо. **9,** *colloq.* (locality; region) райо́н: *out our way*, в на́шем райо́не. **10,** *pl.* (customs; manners) нра́вы. *Mend one's ways*, исправля́ться. —*adv.* далеко́: *way behind*, далеко́ позади́. *They are way ahead of us*, они́ намно́го опереди́ли нас. *Way back in 1906*, ещё в ты́сяча девятьсо́т шесто́м году́. —**by the way**, ме́жду про́чим; кста́ти. —**by way of, 1,** (via) че́рез. **2,** (as) в ка́честве (+ *gen.*): *by way of example*, в ка́честве приме́ра. *By way of proof*, в ви́де доказа́тельства. —**come one's way**, попада́ться (+ *dat.*). —**give way, 1,** (yield to physical pressure) подава́ться; поддава́ться: *The door gave way*, дверь подала́сь *or* поддала́сь. *The rope gave way*, верёвка порвала́сь. *The roof gave way*, кры́ша обвали́лась. *His legs gave way under him*, у него́ но́ги подкоси́лись *or* подломи́лись *or* подогну́лись. **2**, *fol. by* **to** (succumb to) поддава́ться (+ *dat.*); предава́ться (+ *dat.*): *give way to pressure*, поддава́ться давле́нию; *give way to despair*, предава́ться отча́янию. **3**, *fol. by* **to** (be replaced or succeeded by) сменя́ться (+ *instr.*); уступа́ть ме́сто (+ *dat.*). **—go out of one's way**, **1**, (make a detour) сде́лать крюк. **2**, (put oneself out) о́чень стара́ться: *I went out of my way to help him*, я о́чень стара́лся помо́чь ему́. *Don't go out of your way*, не стара́йтесь сли́шком си́льно. **—go the way of**, пойти́ путём (+ *gen.*). **—have a way with**, уме́ть обраща́ться с. **—in one's way**; **in its way**, в своём ро́де. **—in the way of**, **1**, (hindering): *stand in the way of progress*, тормози́ть прогре́сс. **2**, (in; by way of) в ка́честве (+ *gen.*). *What have you got in the way of fabrics?*, что у вас есть из материа́лов? **—lead the way**, идти́ впереди́. **—make one's way**, пробира́ться. **—make way**, сторони́ться; расступа́ться. *Make way for*, дать *or* уступи́ть доро́гу (+ *dat.*). **—open the way for**, открыва́ть путь к. **—out of the way**, **1**, (not on one's route) не по пути́. **2**, (not blocking anything; aside) в стороне́. **3**, (finished; disposed of) зако́нчен. **4**, *Put (someone) out of the way*, *colloq.* (kill) ликвиди́ровать; уложи́ть. **—under way**, *rendered by various verbs: Talks are under way*, перегово́ры начали́сь *or* иду́т *or* веду́тся. *Get under way*, начина́ть(ся); отправля́ться в путь. **—way of life**, о́браз *or* укла́д жи́зни. **—ways and means**, пути́ и сре́дства. **—way out**, вы́ход.

waybill *n.* накладна́я.

wayfarer *n.* пу́тник. **—wayfaring**, *adj.* стра́нствующий.

waylay *v.t.* напада́ть на; устра́ивать заса́ду на.

wayside *adj.* придоро́жный. *Wayside inn*, постоя́лый двор. **—***n.*, in **fall by the wayside**, выбыва́ть из стро́я.

way station попу́тная ста́нция; полустано́к.

wayward *adj.* заблу́дший; беспу́тный. *Wayward son*, заблу́дший сын. *Wayward existence*, беспу́тная жизнь.

we *pers. pron.* мы. *See also* **us**.

weak *adj.* сла́бый: *weak from hunger*, сла́бый от го́лода. *Weak link*, сла́бое звено́. *Weak tea*, сла́бый чай. *Weak point*, сла́бое ме́сто. *Weak argument*, сла́бый до́вод. *Grow weak*, слабе́ть; ослабева́ть. *Feel weak*, чу́вствовать сла́бость. *Have a weak spot in one's heart for*, име́ть *or* пита́ть сла́бость к.

weaken *v.t.* ослабля́ть. **—***v.i.* слабе́ть; ослабева́ть.

weakling *n.* тря́пка.

weakly *adj.* хи́лый. **—***adv.* сла́бо.

weakness *n.* сла́бость. *Have a weakness for*, име́ть *or* пита́ть сла́бость к. *Play on the weaknesses of*, игра́ть на сла́бостях (*or* на сла́бых стру́нках) (+ *gen.*).

weak-willed *adj.* безво́льный; слабово́льный; бесхара́ктерный.

weal *n.* **1**, (welt) рубе́ц; полоса́. **2**, *archaic* (welfare) бла́го; благосостоя́ние.

wealth *n.* **1**, (riches; prosperity) бога́тство: *acquire wealth*, приобрести́ бога́тство. *Man of wealth*, бога́ч; состоя́тельный челове́к. **2**, *fol. by* **of** (abundance) бога́тство; оби́лие (+ *gen.*). *A wealth of information*, ма́сса информа́ции. *A wealth of material*, бога́тый материа́л.

wealthy *adj.* бога́тый; зажи́точный; состоя́тельный.

wean *v.t.* **1**, (a child) отнима́ть от груди́. **2**, (break, as of a habit) отуча́ть (от).

weapon *n.* ору́жие (*always sing.*): *secret weapon*, секре́тное *or* та́йное ору́жие; *nuclear weapons*, я́дерное ору́жие. *Weapons of mass destruction*, ору́жие ма́ссового уничтоже́ния. *The murder weapon*, ору́дие уби́йства. *Weapons factory*, оборо́нный заво́д; оборо́нное предприя́тие; предприя́тие по произво́дству вооруже́ния.

weaponry *n.* вооруже́ние.

wear *v.t.* **1**, (have on) надева́ть: *What should I wear?*, что мне наде́ть? *I have nothing to wear*, мне не́чего наде́ть. *He is wearing a new suit*, на нём но́вый костю́м. *She was wearing a pink dress*, она́ была́ в ро́зовом пла́тье. *What are you going to wear to the party?*, что ты собира́ешься наде́ть на ве́чер? *I haven't worn this dress for a long time*, я давно́ не надева́ла э́то пла́тье. **2**, (wear habitually) носи́ть: *wear glasses*, носи́ть очки́. *He always wears a tie*, он всегда́ но́сит га́лстук; он всегда́ в га́лстуке. *He never wears a tie*, он никогда́ не но́сит (*or* надева́ет) га́лстука. *Wear one's hair short*, носи́ть коро́ткие во́лосы. *What size shoe do you wear?*, како́й но́мер о́буви вы но́сите? **3**, (bring to a certain state by wearing) изна́шивать: *wear a coat to shreds*, изна́шивать пальто́ до дыр. **4**, (cause by continued wear) протира́ть: *wear a hole in one's pocket*, протира́ть дыру́ в карма́не. **5**, (have; exhibit) име́ть: *wear a dejected look*, име́ть мра́чный вид. **—***v.i.* **1**, (hold up) носи́ться: *This skirt wears well*, э́та ю́бка хорошо́ но́сится. **2**, (show the effects of wear) изна́шиваться. **—***n.* **1**, (act of wearing or being worn) но́ска: *from long wear*, от до́лгой но́ски. *Clothes for winter wear*, зи́мняя оде́жда. **2**, (gradual deterioration from being worn) изно́с. *Show signs of wear*, обтрепа́ться. **3**, (clothes) оде́жда: *men's wear*, мужска́я оде́жда. **—wear and tear**, изно́с. **—wear away**, стира́ть. *The inscription is worn away*, на́дпись стёрлась. **—wear down**, **1**, (wear out, as footwear) ста́птывать. **2**, (become worn down) ста́птываться. **3**, (exhaust; weary) изнуря́ть. **4**, (overcome, as resistance) преодолева́ть; сломи́ть. **—wear off**, проходи́ть: *The pain wore off*, боль прошла́. **—wear out**, **1**, (wear until no longer usable) изна́шивать. **2**, (be no longer usable) изна́шиваться; (*of a machine*) сраба́тываться. **3**, (exhaust) изнуря́ть; измучи́ть. **—wear thin**, *see* **thin**.

weariness *n.* уста́лость; утомле́ние.

wearing *adj.* **1**, (intended for wearing): *wearing apparel*, оде́жда. **2**, (fatiguing; exhausting) утоми́тельный.

wearisome *adj.* томи́тельный.

weary *adj.* уста́лый; утомлённый. **—***v.t.* утомля́ть. **—***v.i.* устава́ть; утомля́ться.

weasel *n.* ласка.

weather *n.* погóда: *in good weather,* в хорóшую погóду. *Weather forecast,* прогнóз погóды. —*v.t.* **1,** (wear away by exposure to the elements) выве́тривать. **2,** (survive) выде́рживать: *weather a storm,* вы́держать бу́рю. —**keep one's weather eye open,** держáть у́хо востро́. —**under the weather, 1,** (ill) нездорóв. **2,** (drunk) под хмелькóм.

weather-beaten *adj.* обве́тренный.

weathercock *n.* флю́гер.

weatherman *n.* синóптик; метеорóлог.

weather map синопти́ческая кáрта.

weather satellite метеорологи́ческий спу́тник; метеоспу́тник.

weather vane флю́гер.

weave *v.t.* **1,** (form into fabric) ткать: *weave cloth,* ткать суднó. **2,** (make by weaving) плести́; ткать: *weave a basket,* плести́ корзи́ну; *weave a carpet,* ткать ковёр. **3,** (spin, as a tale) плести́. —*v.i.* **1,** (do weaving) ткать. **2,** (zigzag) петля́ть; виля́ть. —*n.* плете́ние; переплете́ние. *Close weave,* плóтное плете́ние.

weaver *n.* ткач.

weaving *n.* тканьё.

web *n.* **1,** (spider web) паути́на. **2,** *fig.* (tangle) сплете́ние; паути́на; клубóк. *Web of lies,* сплете́ние/паути́на лжи. *Web of intrigue,* клубóк интри́г. **3,** *zool.* (membrane) перепóнка.

webbed *adj.* перепóнчатый: *webbed feet,* перепóнчатые лáпы.

web-footed *adj.* с перепóнчатыми лáпами.

wed *v.t.* (of a man) жени́ться на (+ *prepl.*); (of a woman) выходи́ть зáмуж за. —*v.i.* жени́ться; выходи́ть зáмуж; вступáть в брак.

wedded *adj.* **1,** (married) *my lawfully wedded wife,* моя́ закóнная супру́га. **2,** *fol. by* **to** (tied) привя́занный: *I am not wedded to this job,* я не привя́зан(a) к э́той рабóте.

wedding *n.* свáдьба: *Were you at her wedding?,* вы бы́ли на её свáдьбе? —*adj.* свáдебный: *wedding cake/present,* свáдебный торт/подáрок. *Wedding day,* день свáдьбы. *Wedding dress,* свáдебное *or* подвене́чное плáтье. *Wedding palace,* дворе́ц бракосочетáния. *Wedding ring,* обручáльное кольцó.

wedge *n.* клин. *Drive a wedge between,* вбить клин ме́жду. —*v.t.* закли́нивать. *Become wedged,* закли́ниваться. —**wedge-shaped,** *adj.* клинови́дный; клинообрáзный.

wedlock *n.* брак. *Born out of wedlock,* рождённый вне брáка.

Wednesday *n.* средá.

wee *adj.* крóшечный; малю́сенький. —**a wee bit,** чуть-чу́ть.

weed *n.* сóрная травá; сорня́к. *Pull up weeds,* вырывáть *or* полóть сорняки́. *The garden is overrun with weeds,* сад зарóс сóрными трáвами; сад заглóх. —*v.t.* **1,** (clear of weeds) полóть; пропáлывать. **2,** *fol. by* **out** (eliminate) отсе́ивать. —**weedkiller,** *n.* гербици́д.

week *n.* неде́ля: *this week,* на э́той неде́ле. *A week's*

vacation, неде́льный óтпуск. *A week from Wednesday,* в сре́ду на сле́дующей неде́ле; че́рез неде́лю в сре́ду. *What day of the week is it today?,* какóй э́то день неде́ли?; какóй сегóдня день?

weekday *n.* бу́дний день.

weekend *n.* суббóта и воскресе́нье.

weekly *adj.* еженеде́льный: *weekly meeting,* еженеде́льное собрáние; *weekly magazine,* еженеде́льный журнáл. —*adv.* еженеде́льно. —*n.* еженеде́льник.

weep *v.i.* **1,** (cry) плáкать. **2,** *fol. by* **for** (mourn) оплáкивать. —*v.t.* (shed, as tears) проливáть.

weeping *n.* плач. —*adj.* плáчущий. —**weeping willow,** плаку́чая и́ва.

weevil *n.* долгонóсик.

weft *n., textiles* утóк.

weigh *v.t.* взве́шивать: *weigh merchandise,* взве́шивать товáры. *Weigh oneself,* взве́шиваться. *Weigh one's words,* взве́шивать свои́ словá. —*v.i.* **1,** (have a certain weight) ве́сить. *How much do you weigh?,* какóй у вас вес?; скóлько вы ве́сите? *I weigh 140 pounds,* мой вес (*or* я ве́шу) сто сóрок фу́нтов. **2,** (carry weight) име́ть вес. *Weigh in someone's favor,* говори́ть в чью-нибудь пóльзу. **3,** *fol. by* **on** (oppress): *weigh on one's mind,* гнести́ когó-нибудь; *weigh on one's conscience,* му́чить чью-нибудь сóвесть. —**weigh anchor,** снимáться с я́коря. —**weigh down,** отягощáть; оття́гивать; придáвливать. *Weighed down with packages/cares,* отягощён *or* обременён *or* придáвлен паке́тами/забóтами. *The snow weighs down on the roof,* снег дáвит на кры́шу. —**weigh out,** отве́шивать; разве́шивать.

weight *n.* **1,** (number of pounds or tons) вес: *the weight of a child at birth,* вес ребёнка при рожде́нии. *The weight of a space vehicle,* вес космÍческого корабля́. *Gain/lose weight,* прибавля́ть/теря́ть в ве́се. **2,** (heaviness) тя́жесть: *The branches were bent under the weight of the snow,* ве́тки гну́лись под тя́жестью сне́га. **3,** *fig.* (influence; importance) вес: *carry weight,* име́ть вес. *Attach great weight to,* придавáть большóе значе́ние (+ *dat.*). *His opinion carries great weight,* с егó мне́нием óчень считáются. **4,** *fig.* (burden) тя́жесть: *the weight of cares,* тя́жесть забóт. *The weight of evidence,* тя́жесть ули́к. **5,** (anything heavy, used for its weight) ги́ря. *Paperweight,* пресспапье́. **6,** *sports* ги́ря; штáнга; тя́жесть: *lift weights,* поднимáть ги́ри/тя́жести. —*v.t.* утяжеля́ть: *weight sacks with lead,* утяжеля́ть мешки́ свинцóм. —**throw one's weight around,** хозя́йничать. —**worth its weight in gold,** на вес зóлота.

weightless *adj.* невесóмый. —**weightlessness,** *n.* невесóмость.

weightlifter *n.* гиреви́к; штанги́ст; тяжелоатле́т. —**weightlifting,** *n.* подня́тие тя́жестей; тяжёлая атле́тика.

weighty *adj.* ве́ский; весóмый; уве́систый.

weir *n.* запру́да.

weird *adj.* **1,** (unearthly; eerie) тáинственный: *weird beings,* тáинственные существá. **2,** (odd) стрáнный; чудакóватый: *weird sounds,* стрáнные зву́ки; *weird character,* чудакóватый тип.

welcome *adj.* **1,** (gladly received) прия́тный: *welcome news,* прия́тное изве́стие. *A welcome guest,* жела́нный гость. **2,** *fol. by* **to** (gladly invited): *You are always welcome to come,* ми́лости про́сим. *You are welcome to use my car,* вы мо́жете взять мою́ маши́ну; моя́ маши́на к ва́шим услу́гам. —*n.* приём; встре́ча: *warm welcome,* тёплый приём; тёплая встре́ча. *Speech of welcome,* приве́тственная речь. —*v.t.* приве́тствовать: *welcome a delegation/proposal,* приве́тствовать делега́цию/предложе́ние. —*interj.* с прие́здом!; добро́ пожа́ловать! *Welcome to Moscow!,* добро́ пожа́ловать в Москву́! —**you are welcome!,** пожа́луйста!

weld *v.t.* **1,** (join by heating and fusing) сва́ривать. **2,** *fig.* (bring into close union) спла́чивать. —**welder,** *n.* сва́рщик.

welding *n.* сва́рка. —*adj.* сва́рочный: *welding torch,* сва́рочная горе́лка.

welfare *n.* **1,** (well-being) благосостоя́ние; благополу́чие. **2,** (support of the needy) социа́льное обеспе́чение. *Be on welfare,* получа́ть посо́бие.

well[1] *n.* коло́дец: *dig a well,* рыть *or* копа́ть коло́дец. *Oil well,* нефтяна́я сква́жина. —*adj.* коло́дезный: *well water,* коло́дезная вода́. —*v.i.* [*usu.* **well up**] (of emotions) вскипа́ть. *Tears welled up in her eyes,* слёзы наверну́лись на её глаза́.

well[2] *adv.* **1,** (satisfactorily; properly; excellently) хорошо́: *Everything went well,* всё прошло́ хорошо́. *Well said!,* хорошо́ ска́зано! *Turn out well,* ко́нчиться благополу́чно. *Shake well before using,* взба́лтывать пе́ред употребле́нием. *All's well that ends well,* всё хорошо́, что хорошо́ конча́ется. **2,** (fully; entirely) вполне́: *It may well be that...,* вполне́ возмо́жно, что... *Be well aware of...,* отдава́ть себе́ по́лный отчёт в (+ *prepl.*). **3,** (considerably; far) далеко́: *well past midnight,* далеко́ за́ по́лночь. —*adj.* **1,** (in good health) здоро́вый: *Are you well?,* вы здоро́вы? *Alive and well,* жив и здоро́в. *Get well,* выздора́вливать. *He looks well,* он хорошо́ вы́глядит. **2,** (satisfactory) хорошо́; в поря́дке. *All is well,* всё в поря́дке. —*interj.* **1,** used to introduce a statement, ну: *Well, I'm off!,* ну, я пошёл (пошла́). **2,** expressing surprise, вот как; вот тебе́ и на. —**as well,** а та́кже: *and in Paris as well,* а та́кже в Пари́же. —**as well as, 1,** (in addition) а та́кже: *as well as in a number of other countries,* а та́кже в ря́де други́х стран. **2,** (equally with) как..., так и...: *women as well as men,* как же́нщины, так и мужчи́ны. —**wish someone well,** жела́ть кому́-нибудь добра́.

well-behaved *adj.* благовоспи́танный. *The children were well-behaved,* де́ти вели́ себя́ хорошо́.

well-being *n.* благополу́чие; благосостоя́ние.

well-bred *adj.* (благо)воспи́танный.

well-developed *adj.* развито́й: *well-developed muscles,* разви́тые му́скулы.

well-done *adj.* **1,** (capably done) хорошо́ сде́ланный. **2,** (thoroughly cooked) (хорошо́) прожа́ренный.

well-dressed *adj.* хорошо́ оде́тый; наря́дный.

well-earned *adj.* заслу́женный.

well-fed *adj.* отко́рмленный; упи́танный.

well-founded *adj.* обосно́ванный; состоя́тельный.

well-groomed *adj.* хо́леный; вы́холенный; ухо́женный.

well-grounded *adj.* **1,** (well-founded) обосно́ванный. **2,** (knowledgeable) хорошо́ подко́ван (*e.g.* в хи́мии).

well-heeled *adj., colloq.* состоя́тельный.

well-informed *adj.* (хорошо́) осведомлённый; (хорошо́) информи́рованный.

well-intentioned *adj.* име́ющий до́брые наме́рения; благонаме́ренный.

well-known *adj.* изве́стный.

well-mannered *adj.* (благо)воспи́танный.

well-meaning *adj.* име́ющий до́брые наме́рения; благонаме́ренный.

well-nigh *adv.* почти́; чуть ли не.

well-off *adj.* зажи́точный; состоя́тельный; обеспе́ченный.

well-paid *adj.* хорошо́ опла́чиваемый.

well-preserved *adj.* хорошо́ сохрани́вшийся.

well-read *adj.* начи́танный.

well sweep жура́вль.

well-to-do *adj.* зажи́точный; состоя́тельный; обеспе́ченный.

well-trodden *adj.* проторённый; изби́тый.

well-versed *adj.* све́дущий.

well-wisher *n.* доброжела́тель. —**well-wishing,** *adj.* доброжела́тельный.

Welsh *adj.* уэ́льский; валли́йский. —*n.* уэ́льский/валли́йский язы́к. —**Welshman,** *n.* валли́ец.

welt *n.* **1,** (part of a shoe) рант. **2,** (cord trimming) обши́вка. **3,** (mark left by a whip or stick) рубе́ц; полоса́.

welter *n.* пу́таница: *welter of ideas,* пу́таница мы́слей.

welterweight *n.* полусредневе́с. —*adj.* полусре́днего ве́са.

welting *n.* обши́вка.

wench *n.* де́вка.

wend *v.t., in* **wend one's way,** направля́ть свои́ шаги́ *or* стопы́.

were *v., past tense of* **be.** —*subjunctive,* будь. *Were he alive today,* будь он сейча́с жив; живи́ он сего́дня. *If it weren't so late,* не будь так по́здно. *If I were you,* на ва́шем ме́сте. —**as it were,** так сказа́ть.

werewolf *n.* оборотень.

west *n.* за́пад. *The West,* За́пад. —*adj.* за́падный: *the West Coast,* за́падное побере́жье. —*adv.* на за́пад; к за́паду. *West of,* к за́паду от; за́паднее (+ *gen.*).

westerly *adj.* за́падный: *in a westerly direction,* в за́падном направле́нии. *Westerly winds,* за́падные ве́тры.

western *adj.* за́падный. —*n.* (movie) ве́стерн. —**westernmost,** *adj.* са́мый за́падный.

westward *adv.* к за́паду; в за́падном направле́нии. —*adj.* за́падный.

wet *adj.* мо́крый: *wet hands/shoes,* мо́крые ру́ки/боти́нки. *Wet pavement,* мо́крый тротуа́р. *"Wet paint!",* осторо́жно! окра́шено! *Get wet,* промока́ть. *Get one's feet wet,* промочи́ть но́ги. —*v.t.* мочи́ть; сма́чивать. *Wet one's bed,* де́лать под себя́.

—**he is still wet behind the ears,** у него молоко на губах не обсохло.

wet nurse корми́лица.

whack *n., colloq.* тума́к. —*v.t., colloq.* тра́хнуть; тре́снуть. —**out of whack,** *slang* не в поря́дке.

whale *n.* кит. —*adj.* кито́вый: *whale oil,* кито́вый жир.

whalebone *n.* кито́вый ус.

whaler *n.* **1,** (person) китобо́й. **2,** (ship) китобо́й; китобо́ец; китобо́йное су́дно.

whaling *n.* китобо́йный про́мысел. —*adj.* китобо́йный. —**whaling ship,** китобо́йное су́дно; китобо́й; китобо́ец.

whammy *n., slang* дурно́й глаз. *Put the whammy on,* сгла́зить (кого́-нибудь).

wharf *n.* при́стань.

what *pron.* **1,** *interr.* что?: *What happened?,* что случи́лось? *What is this?,* что э́то тако́е? *What do you want?,* что вы хоти́те? *What else do you need?,* что ещё вам ну́жно? *What is that building?,* что э́то за зда́ние? ♦*Often rendered by* как, како́й *and* како́в: *What is your name?,* как ва́ше и́мя?; как вас зову́т? *What is this called?,* как э́то называ́ется? *What do you think?,* как вы ду́маете? *What's the score?,* како́й счёт? *What is today's date?,* како́е сего́дня число́? *What is your phone number?,* како́й у вас но́мер телефо́на? *What's the latest news?,* каки́е после́дние но́вости? *What's the difference between...?,* кака́я ра́зница ме́жду...? *What is your opinion?,* каково́ ва́ше мне́ние? **2,** *rel.* что; то, что. *Did you find what you were looking for?,* вы нашли́, что иска́ли? *He got what he wanted,* он доби́лся, чего́ хоте́л. *Come what may,* будь, что бу́дет. *Say what you will,* что ни говори́те. *And what is worse,* а что ещё ху́же. *Just what I need,* как раз то, что мне ну́жно. *What he says is true,* то, что он говори́т — пра́вда. —*adj.* **1,** *interr.* како́й: *What clothes should I take?,* каку́ю оде́жду мне с собо́й взять? *What good will it do?,* кака́я от э́того по́льза? *What time is it?,* кото́рый тепе́рь час? **2,** *used in exclamations,* како́й: *What nonsense!,* кака́я чепуха́! *What a pleasant surprise!,* како́й прия́тный сюрпри́з! **3,** (as much; whatever) тот: *I forgot what little I knew,* я забы́л то немно́гое, что знал. *I gave him what money I had,* я дал ему́ все де́ньги, каки́е у меня́ бы́ли. —*adv.* **1,** *interr.*: *What does it matter?,* како́е э́то име́ет значе́ние? **2,** *used in exclamations,* како́й: *What lovely weather!,* кака́я чу́дная пого́да! —**what about...?,** а что с...?; а как же...?; как насчёт...? —**what for?,** заче́м? *What is that for?,* заче́м э́то?; к чему́ э́то? *What is that thing for?,* к чему́ (*or* для чего́) э́та шту́ка? —**what if...?,** а что е́сли...?; а вдруг...? —**what of it?,** ну и что?; ма́ло ли кто! —**what's more,** *see* more. —**what's what,** что к чему́. —**what then?,** что тогда́ (де́лать)? —**what with,** из-за; ввиду́.

whatever *pron.* **1,** (no matter what) что ни; что бы ни: *whatever happens,* что бы ни случи́лось. *Whatever the outcome,* незави́симо от исхо́да. **2,** (anything) что уго́дно; что хоти́те: *Do/take whatever you like,*

де́лайте, что хоти́те; возьми́те, что вам уго́дно. **3,** *expressing perplexity or wonderment,* что же: *Whatever can he want?,* что же он хо́чет? —*adj.* **1,** (no matter which) како́й бы ни: *whatever city you come to,* в како́й бы го́род вы ни прие́хали. *Whatever the reasons,* каковы́ бы ни́ были причи́ны. **2,** (absolutely) абсолю́тно; реши́тельно. *No doubt whatever,* абсолю́тно никако́го сомне́ния. *I know nothing whatever about it,* я реши́тельно ничего́ не зна́ю об э́том. *For no reason whatever,* без вся́кой причи́ны.

whatsoever *adv.* абсолю́тно; реши́тельно. *No doubt whatsoever,* абсолю́тно никако́го сомне́ния.

wheat *n.* пшени́ца. —*adj.* пшени́чный: *wheat field,* пшени́чное по́ле.

wheedle *v.t.* **1,** (cajole; coax) обха́живать. **2,** (get by cajolery) выпра́шивать; выма́нивать; выкля́нчивать.

wheel *n.* **1,** (circular device) колесо́: *rear wheel,* за́днее колесо́. *Potter's wheel,* гонча́рный круг. *Spinning wheel,* пря́лка. **2,** (steering wheel) руль: *be at the wheel,* быть за рулём. **3,** *slang* (big shot) ши́шка; туз. —*v.t.* кати́ть; вози́ть. *Wheel a baby carriage,* кати́ть де́тскую коля́ску. *Wheel a patient into/ out of/ the operating room,* ввози́ть больно́го в операцио́нную; вывози́ть больно́го из операцио́нной. —*v.i.* [*usu.* **wheel around** *or* **about**] кру́то поверну́ться. —**break on the wheel,** колесова́ть.

wheelbarrow *n.* та́чка.

wheelbase *n.* колёсная ба́за.

wheelchair *n.* инвали́дная коля́ска.

wheeled *adj.* колёсный.

wheel horse коренни́к; коренна́я ло́шадь.

wheelwright *n.* колёсный ма́стер.

wheeze *v.i.* дыша́ть с при́свистом; сопе́ть. —*n.* свистя́щее дыха́ние.

whelp *n.* щено́к. —*v.i.* щени́ться.

when *adv. & conj.* когда́: *When will you be ready?,* когда́ вы бу́дете гото́вы? *When she comes I'll ask her,* когда́ она́ придёт, я её спрошу́. *When in doubt — ask,* е́сли сомнева́ешься, спроси́. *We were about to leave when suddenly it began to rain,* мы ушли́ бы́ло, а (*or* как) вдруг пошёл дождь. *When startled the skunk emits a foul odor,* бу́дучи испу́ган, скунс издаёт проти́вный за́пах. ♦*With the -ing form of the verb,* при: *when crossing the border,* при перехо́де че́рез грани́цу. —*conj.* (considering that; since) е́сли: *Why ask him when he's bound to say no?,* заче́м его́ проси́ть, е́сли он обяза́тельно отка́жет? —**since when?,** с каки́х пор?

whence *adv.* отку́да. *From whence he came,* отку́да он пришёл.

whenever *adv. & conj.* когда́ (бы) ни; вся́кий раз, когда́. *Whenever you like,* когда́ хоти́те; когда́ вам уго́дно.

where *adv. & conj.* **1,** (in what or that place) где: *Where is he right now?,* где он сейча́с? *This is where I live,* вот где я живу́. *Stay where you are!,* остава́йтесь там, где вы сейча́с! *The right of everyone to live where he wishes,* пра́во ка́ждого жить там, где он хо́чет. *There have been cases where...,* быва́ли слу́чаи, когда́... **2,** (to what or that place) куда́: *Where are you going?,* куда́ вы идёте? *I don't know where this road leads,* я не зна́ю, куда́ ведёт э́та доро́га. *Let's go where there are not so many people,* пойдём туда́, где не так мно́го наро́ду. **3,** (from what place) отку́да: *Where are you from?,* отку́да вы? *I don't know where to begin,* я не зна́ю с чего́ нача́ть.

whereabouts *n.* местонахожде́ние. —*adv.* где?; о́коло како́го ме́ста?

whereas *conj.* **1,** (in view of the fact that) поско́льку; ввиду́ того́, что. **2,** (while on the one hand) в то вре́мя как; е́сли. **3,** (while on the other hand) тогда́ как; в то вре́мя как; ме́жду тем как.

whereby *adv.* при кото́ром; с по́мощью кото́рого; согла́сно кото́рому. *A new method whereby...,* но́вый ме́тод, при кото́ром (*or* с по́мощью кото́рого)... *A procedure whereby...,* поря́док, согла́сно кото́рому...

wherefore *adv., archaic* почему́? —*conj., archaic* почему́.

wherein *adv.* (in what way) в чём? —*conj.* (in which) в кото́ром.

whereof *adv. & conj.* о кото́ром; о чём. *In witness whereof,* в удостовере́нии чего́.

whereupon *conj.* по́сле чего́.

wherever *adv. & conj.* где бы ни; куда́ (бы) ни; везде́, где. *Wherever you are,* где бы вы ни́ были. *Wherever you look,* куда́ ни посмо́тришь. *Wherever he goes/went,* куда́ бы он ни пошёл. *Wherever I can,* где то́лько могу́. *Wherever possible,* везде́, где мо́жно; где то́лько возмо́жно. *Wherever you like,* где *or* куда́ хоти́те; где *or* куда́ вам уго́дно.

wherewithal *n.* необходи́мые сре́дства.

wherry *n.* я́лик.

whet *v.t.* **1,** (sharpen) точи́ть; отта́чивать. **2,** (stimulate, as the appetite) возбужда́ть; (раз)дразни́ть.

whether *conj.* ли: *Tell me whether you like it,* скажи́те мне, нра́вится ли э́то вам. *It is doubtful whether he knew about it,* сомни́тельно, чтобы он знал об э́том. *Whether you want to or not,* хо́чешь ты и́ли нет; хо́чешь не хо́чешь.

whetstone *n.* точи́льный ка́мень; осело́к; брусо́к.

whew *interj.* фу!

whey *n.* сы́воротка.

which *pron. & adj.* **1,** *interr.* како́й?: *Which newspapers do you read?,* каки́е газе́ты вы чита́ете? *Which way did he go?,* в каку́ю сто́рону он пошёл? *Which is your house?,* како́й дом ваш? *Which one do you want?,* како́й вы хоти́те? *Which (one) of you?,* кто из вас? *Which one of these umbrellas is yours?,* кото́рый из э́тих зо́нтиков ваш? *Which is worse — drugs or alcohol?,* что ху́же — нарко́тики и́ли алкого́ль? **2,** *rel.* кото́рый: *the book which you lent me,* кни́га, кото́рую вы мне одолжи́ли. *The play which you told me about,* пье́са, о кото́рой вы мне говори́ли. *This is the first case in which...,* э́то пе́рвый слу́чай, когда́... ♦ *When referring to a fact or circumstance,* что: *I did not answer, which made him even angrier,* я не отве́тил, что рассерди́ло его́ ещё бо́льше. **3,** (just mentioned) *rendered by* чего́: *in*

which case, в слу́чае чего́; *after which,* по́сле чего́. *Yet another obstacle, of which there are already too many,* ещё одно́ препя́тствие, кото́рых и так уже́ сли́шком мно́го.

whichever *pron. & adj.* како́й бы ни: *whichever country you go to,* в каку́ю бы страну́ вы ни пое́хали. *Take whichever one you want,* возьми́те како́й вам уго́дно.

whiff *n.* **1,** (puff; gust) дунове́ние. **2,** (slight odor) лёгкий за́пах; запашо́к. **3,** (inhalation): *take a whiff of,* понюха́ть (что́-нибудь).

while *conj.* **1,** (at the time that) пока́; когда́; в то вре́мя как. *While I was waiting for her,* пока́/когда́ я её ждал. *While in London,* бу́дучи в Ло́ндоне. *While on vacation,* во вре́мя о́тпуска. *While sitting by the fireplace,* си́дя у ками́на. **2,** (during all the time that; as long as) пока́: *while she is still here,* пока́ она́ здесь; *while there is still time,* пока́ ещё есть вре́мя. *Make hay while the sun shines,* куй желе́зо, пока́ горячо́. **3,** (whereas on the one hand) в то вре́мя как: *While most are in favor, some are opposed,* в то вре́мя как большинство́ за, не́которые выступа́ют про́тив. *While many disagree...,* хотя́ мно́гие несогла́сны... **4,** (whereas by contrast) а; тогда́ как. *Colorado is mountainous, while Kansas is flat,* Колора́до гори́стый, а Ка́нзас равни́нный. *The east is mainly industrial, while in the west agriculture predominates,* восто́к в основно́м промы́шленный, тогда́ как на за́паде преоблада́ет се́льское хозя́йство. —*n.* не́которое вре́мя: *a while ago,* не́которое вре́мя наза́д. *For a while,* не́которое вре́мя. *A short while,* недо́лго. *Quite a while,* дово́льно до́лго. *In a little while,* ско́ро. *After a while,* че́рез не́которое вре́мя. *All the while,* всё вре́мя. *He has been gone quite a while,* он ушёл уже́ давно́. —*v.t.* [*usu.* **while away**] корота́ть (вре́мя). —**be worth one's while,** сто́ить труда́. —**once in a while,** вре́мя от вре́мени.

whilst *conj.* = **while.**

whim *n.* при́хоть; причу́да; капри́з.

whimper *v.i.* **1,** (of a person, esp. a child) хны́кать. **2,** (of a dog) скули́ть. —*n.* хны́канье.

whimsical *adj.* прихотли́вый.

whimsy *n.* при́хоть; причу́да.

whine *v.i.* хны́кать; ныть. —*n.* нытьё; хны́канье. —**whiner,** *n.* ны́тик; ню́ня.

whinny *v.i.* ржать. —*n.* ржа́ние.

whip *n.* кнут; хлыст. —*v.t.* **1,** (thrash; flog) хлеста́ть; сечь; поро́ть; стега́ть. **2,** (beat, as eggs, cream, etc.) сбива́ть; взбива́ть. **3,** *fol. by* **out** (take out suddenly) выхва́тывать. —**whip up, 1,** (stir up; foment) разду́ва́ть. **2,** *colloq.* (cook in a hurry) состря́пать.

whipped cream взби́тые сли́вки.

whippet *n.* борза́я.

whipping *n.* по́рка; трёпка. —**whipping boy,** ма́льчик для битья́.

whippoorwill *n.* козодо́й.

whipsaw *n.* лучко́вая пила́.

whir *also,* **whirr** *v.i.* жужжа́ть. —*n.* жужжа́ние.

whirl *v.i.* **1,** (spin) кружи́ться. **2,** *fol. by* **around** (turn quickly around) кру́то поверну́ться. —*v.t.* **1,** (spin) верте́ть; кружи́ть. **2,** (swirl, as dust) крути́ть. —*n.* **1,** (rapid gyration) круже́ние. *My head is in a whirl,* у меня́ голова́ идёт кру́гом. **2,** *colloq.* (brief try): *give it a whirl,* попро́бовать.

whirligig *n.* юла́.

whirlpool *n.* водоворо́т.

whirlwind *n.* вихрь; смерч.

whirr *v. & n.* = **whir.**

whisk *v.t.* **1,** (carry swiftly) мчать; нести́; проноси́ть. *Whisk away,* умча́ть. **2,** *fol. by* **off** (brush away) сма́хивать.

whisk broom метёлка.

whisker *n., usu. pl.* **1,** (on a man's face) бакенба́рды. **2,** (of an animal) усы́.

whiskey *also,* **whisky** *n.* ви́ски.

whisper *v.t. & i.* шепта́ть. *Whisper in someone's ear,* шепта́ть кому́-нибудь на́ ухо. —*n.* шёпот. *In a whisper,* шёпотом. —**whisperer,** *n.* шепту́н.

whist *n.* вист.

whistle *v.i.* свисте́ть. *Whistle for a taxi,* сви́стом подозва́ть такси́. *The wind whistled through the trees,* ве́тер свисте́л в дере́вьях. *Bullets whistled by overhead,* пу́ли свисте́ли над на́шими голова́ми. —*v.t.* насви́стывать: *whistle a tune,* насви́стывать моти́в. —*n.* **1,** (device to be blown) свисто́к. **2,** (of a factory, train, etc.) гудо́к. **3,** (sound) свист. —**wet one's whistle,** промочи́ть го́рло.

whistler *n.* свисту́н.

whit *n.* йо́та: *not a whit,* ни на йо́ту. *Not care a whit about,* ни в грош не ста́вить.

white *adj.* бе́лый. *White meat/wine,* бе́лое мя́со/вино́. *White hair,* седы́е во́лосы. *The White House,* Бе́лый дом. —*n.* **1,** (color) бе́лый цвет. *All in white,* весь (вся) в бе́лом. **2,** (of an egg; of the eye) бело́к. **3,** (Caucasian) бе́лый. **4,** *chess* бе́лые: *White resigned,* бе́лые сдали́сь. —**turn white, 1,** (become white) беле́ть. **2,** (turn pale) побледне́ть; побеле́ть.

white bread бе́лый хлеб.

whitecap *n., usu. pl.* бара́шки; беляки́.

white-collar worker слу́жащий.

whitefish *n.* сиг.

white-haired *adj.* беловоло́сый; белоголо́вый.

white heat бе́лое кале́ние; бе́лый нака́л.

white-hot *adj.* раскалённый добела́.

white lead свинцо́вые бели́ла.

white lie неви́нная ложь.

whiten *v.t.* бели́ть.

whiteness *n.* белизна́.

whitewash *v.t.* **1,** (whiten with whitewash) бели́ть. **2,** *fig.* (gloss over) зама́зывать. —*n.* известко́вый раство́р. —**whitewashing,** *n.* побе́лка.

white whale белу́ха.

whither *adv.* куда́.

whiting *n.* бели́ла.

whitish *adj.* белёсый; белова́тый.

Whitmonday *n.* ду́хов день.

Whitsunday *n.* тро́ицын день; тро́ица.

whittle *v.t.* **1,** (cut out small chips from) строга́ть (ножо́м). **2,** (fashion by so doing) выреза́ть. **3,** *fol. by* **down** *or* **away** (reduce) уре́зывать.

whiz *also,* **whizz** *v.i.* **1,** (whir; hiss) свисте́ть. **2,** (rush past) промча́ться. —*n., slang* (marvel) фено́мен.

who *pron.* **1,** *interr.* кто?: *Who are you?,* кто вы? *Who is there?,* кто там? *Who knows?,* кто зна́ет? *Do you know who he is?,* вы зна́ете, кто он? *See who is at the door,* посмотри́те, кто стучи́т *or* звони́т (в дверь). **2,** *rel.* кото́рый: *the man who was just here,* челове́к, кото́рый то́лько сейча́с был здесь. *Was it you who broke the window?,* э́то вы разби́ли окно́? ♦*After* тот (та, те), все *and* вся́кий — кто: *those who came late,* те, кто опозда́л. *Everyone who was at the meeting,* все, кто был на собра́нии. *Anyone who is the least familiar with this question,* вся́кий, кто хоть ско́лько-нибудь знако́м с э́тим вопро́сом. *See also* **whom.**

whoa *interj.* тпру!

whoever *pron.* **1,** (no matter who) кто бы ни: *whoever you are,* кто бы вы ни́ были. *Whoever is right,* кто бы ни был прав. **2,** (whatever person) кто; тот, кто. *Whoever says that is mistaken,* кто говори́т э́то, ошиба́ется. **3,** *expressing perplexity or bewilderment,* кто?: *Whoever heard of such a thing?,* кто слыха́л подо́бное? *See also* **whomever.**

whole *adj.* **1,** (entire; complete) це́лый: *a whole piece,* це́лый кусо́к; *a whole year,* це́лый год. *Two whole days,* це́лых два дня. *A whole series of...,* це́лый ряд (+ *gen.*). *Swallow something whole,* проглоти́ть что-нибудь целико́м. **2,** *preceded by* **the** (all) весь: *the whole world,* весь мир. *The whole time we were in England it never rained once,* за всё вре́мя, что мы бы́ли в А́нглии, ни ра́зу не шёл дождь (*or* не́ было дождя́). **3,** (having none of the elements removed) це́льный: *whole milk,* це́льное молоко́; *whole blood,* це́льная кровь. —*n.* це́лое: *into a single whole,* в еди́ное це́лое. *The whole equals the sum of its parts,* це́лое есть су́мма всех его́ часте́й. —**as a whole,** в це́лом. —**a whole lot, 1,** (a great deal) мно́го. **2,** *fol. by a comp. adj.* гора́здо; намно́го. —**on the whole,** вздо́ общем; в о́бщем и це́лом.

wholehearted *adj.* беззаве́тный. *Wholehearted support,* горя́чая подде́ржка.

wholeness *n.* це́льность; це́лость.

whole note *music* це́лая но́та.

whole number це́лое число́; це́лое.

wholesale *adj.* **1,** *comm.* опто́вый. **2,** *fig.* (extensive; indiscriminate) огу́льный. *Wholesale looting,* пова́льный грабёж. —*adv.* опто́м.

wholesome *adj.* здоро́вый; поле́зный: *wholesome food,* здоро́вая/поле́зная пи́ща. *Wholesome influence,* благотво́рное влия́ние.

wholly *adv.* целико́м; по́лностью.

whom *pron., objective case of* **who,** кого́; кому́; кем; ком. *Whom do you have in mind?,* кого́ вы име́ете в виду́? *To whom did you give the money?,* кому́ вы да́ли де́ньги? *With whom were you speaking?,* с кем вы говори́ли?

whomever *pron., objective case of* **whoever.** *Invite whomever you like,* пригласи́те кого́ вам уго́дно.

whoop *v.i.* выкри́кивать; ги́кать. —*n.* вы́крик; во́зглас.

whooping cough коклю́ш.

whooping crane америка́нский жура́вль.

whopping *adj.*, *colloq.* огро́мный. *A whopping one million rubles*, це́лых миллио́н рубле́й.

whore *n.* проститу́тка. —**whorehouse,** *n.* публи́чный дом.

whorl *n.* **1,** (curve) вито́к; завито́к. **2,** *bot.* муто́вка.

whortleberry *n.* черни́ка.

whose *pron.* **1,** *interr.* чей?: *Whose hat is this?*, чья́ э́то шля́па? *Whose side are you on?*, вы на чьей стороне́? **2,** *rel.* кото́рого; кото́рой: *the girl whose book I borrowed*, де́вушка, кни́гу кото́рой я за́нял.

whosever *pron.* чей бы ни.

whosoever *pron.* кто бы ни.

why *adv.* почему́: *Why didn't you answer my letter?*, почему́ вы не отве́тили на моё письмо́? *I don't understand why he objects*, я не понима́ю, почему́ он возража́ет. *One of the reasons why...*, одна́ из причи́н того́, почему́... *I see no reason why you can't go*, я не зна́ю, почему́ бы тебе́ не пойти́. —*interj.* ведь: *Why everyone knows that!*, ведь э́то изве́стно всем! *Why it's Nina!*, да ведь э́то Ни́на! —**that's why,** вот почему́; потому́ и. *That's why I asked*, потому́ я и спроси́л(а). —**which is why,** потому́. —**why not?,** почему́ нет? *Why not ask him?*, почему́ бы не спроси́ть его́? —**why so?,** почему́ же?

wick *n.* фити́ль.

wicked *adj.* **1,** (evil) злой; дурно́й. *Wicked man*, дурно́й челове́к. *Wicked deed*, злой *or* дурно́й посту́пок. *Wicked thoughts*, дурны́е мы́сли. **2,** (harmful; grievous) жесто́кий: *a wicked blow*, жесто́кий уда́р. —**wickedness,** *n.* зло.

wicker *n.* плете́ние. —*adj.* плетёный: *wicker basket*, плетёная корзи́на.

wickerwork *n.* плете́ние; плетёные изде́лия.

wicket *n.* **1,** (small door or gate) кали́тка. **2,** *croquet* воро́та. **3,** *cricket* кали́тка.

wide *adj.* **1,** (broad; extensive) широ́кий: *wide street*, широ́кая у́лица. *Wide choice*, широ́кий *or* большо́й *or* бога́тый вы́бор. *By a wide margin*, с значи́тельным переве́сом. **2,** (having a specified width) широ́кий; в ширину́: *The river is two miles wide at this point*, в э́том ме́сте река́ в две ми́ли ширино́й; в э́том ме́сте река́ име́ет две ми́ли в ширину́. **3,** (astray; missing) ми́мо це́ли. *Be wide of the mark*, бить *or* попада́ть ми́мо це́ли; *fig.* попа́сть па́льцем в не́бо. —*adv.* **1,** (to the full extent of opening) широко́; на́стежь: *The windows were wide open*, о́кна бы́ли широко́ откры́ты; о́кна бы́ли на́стежь. **2,** (over a large area) широко́. *Far and wide*, вдоль и поперёк. **3,** (astray) в сто́рону; ми́мо це́ли.

wide-angle *adj.* широкоуго́льный.

wide-awake *adj.* совсе́м бо́дрый.

wide-eyed *adj.* с широко́ раскры́тыми глаза́ми. *Stare wide-eyed at*, смотре́ть на (+ *acc.*) больши́ми (*or* широко́ раскры́тыми) глаза́ми; вы́пучить глаза́ на (+ *acc.*).

widely *adv.* широко́. *Widely scattered*, широко́ разбро́санный. *Vary widely*, широко́ расходи́ться. *Travel widely*, мно́го путеше́ствовать.

widen *v.t.* расширя́ть: *widen a road*, расширя́ть доро́гу. —*v.i.* расширя́ться.

widespread *adj.* распространённый.

widgeon *n.* свия́зь.

widow *n.* вдова́. —**widowed,** *adj.* вдо́вый; овдове́вший. *Be/become widowed*, овдове́ть.

widower *n.* вдове́ц.

widowhood *n.* вдовство́.

width *n.* **1,** (breadth) ширина́. *Three feet in width*, в три фу́та ширино́й. **2,** (piece of material of a certain width) полоти́нще.

wield *v.t.* **1,** (brandish) разма́хивать: *a robber wielding a knife*, граби́тель, разма́хивая ножо́м. **2,** (handle) рабо́тать; ору́довать (*both with instr.*). **3,** (exercise, as power, influence, etc.) облада́ть; по́льзоваться.

wife *n.* жена́. *Take (someone) for a wife*, взять (кого́-нибудь) в жёны.

wig *n.* пари́к.

wiggle *v.t.* шевели́ть: *wiggle one's toes*, шевели́ть па́льцами ног. —*v.i.* ёрзать. *Wiggle out of*, выкру́чиваться из; выпу́тываться из.

wigwam *n.* вигва́м.

wild *adj.* **1,** (uncivilized; uncultivated; undomesticated) ди́кий: *wild animal*, ди́кое живо́тное. *Wild duck/rose/region*, ди́кая у́тка/ро́за/ме́стность. **2,** (boisterous; unruly) ди́кий; бу́йный. **3,** (fantastically impractical) ди́кий; сумасбро́дный; бредо́вый. **4,** (random; erratic) *rendered by the adv.* науга́д: *make a wild guess*, сказа́ть науга́д; *fire a wild shot*, стреля́ть науга́д. **5,** *fol. by about*, *colloq.* (mad about) без ума́ (от). —*adv.* ди́ко: *grow wild*, расти́ ди́ко. —*n.*, *often pl.* глушь; де́бри. *Live in the wild*, жить на во́ле. *Call of the wild*, зов приро́ды. —**run wild**, бу́йствовать; бу́йнить.

wild boar каба́н.

wildcat *n.* ди́кая ко́шка.

wilderness *n.* пусты́ня; глушь. —**voice in the wilderness,** глас вопию́щего в пусты́не.

wildfire *n.*, *in spread like wildfire*, распространя́ться с молниено́сной быстрото́й *or* со ско́ростью лесно́го пожа́ра.

wildflower *n.* дикорасту́щее расте́ние; *pl.* полевы́е цветы́.

wildlife *n.* ди́кие живо́тные.

wildly *adv.* ди́ко. *Wildly enthusiastic*, в ди́ком восто́рге.

wile *n.*, *usu. pl.* хи́трости; уло́вки.

wilful *adj.* = **willful.**

will[1] *v.aux.* **1,** *used to form the future tense: You will be sorry*, вы бу́дете сожале́ть об э́том. *The window won't open*, окно́ не открыва́ется. *Accidents will happen*, всегда́ быва́ют несча́стные слу́чаи. **2,** *in requests: Will you have a cup of tea?*, мо́жно вам предложи́ть ча́шку ча́ю? *Won't you sit down?*, сади́тесь, пожа́луйста! *Will you please be quiet!*, да замолчи́те же! **3,** *expressing probability: That will be Vera*, э́то, наве́рно, Ве́ра.

will[2] *n.* **1,** (in most meanings) во́ля: *the will of the people*, во́ля наро́да. *God's will*, бо́жья *or* бо́жия во́ля. *Good will*, до́брая во́ля. *Ill will*, недоброжела́тельство. *At will,* по жела́нию. *Of one's own free will,* по свое́й во́ле; по до́брой во́ле. *Against one's will,* не по свое́й во́ле; про́тив во́ли; понево́ле. *The will to win/live,* во́ля к побе́де/ к жи́зни/. *Where there's a will there's a way,* при жела́нии мо́жно всего́ доби́ться. **2,** (testament) завеща́ние. —*v.t.* **1,** (wish) хоте́ть: *Do what you will,* де́лай, что хо́чешь. *Say what you will,* что ни говори́те. **2,** (decree; ordain) распоряжа́ться. *Fate willed otherwise,* судьба́ распоряди́лась *or* реши́ла ина́че. *God has willed that...,* бо́жья во́ля (*or* бо́гу уго́дно), что... **3,** (bequeath) завеща́ть: *will property to one's children,* завеща́ть иму́щество де́тям. —**if you will,** е́сли хоти́те.

willful *also,* **wilful** *adj.* **1,** (deliberate) преднаме́ренный; умы́шленный. **2,** (headstrong) своево́льный. —**willfully,** *adv.* преднаме́ренно; умы́шленно.

willing *adj.* **1,** (ready; disposed) гото́вый: *I'm willing to help/wager,* я гото́в(а) помо́чь/ поби́ться об закла́д/. **2,** (acting or performing gladly) услу́жливый; стара́тельный. **3,** (readily given) доброво́льный. —**willingly,** *adv.* охо́тно; с гото́вностью. —**willingness,** *n.* гото́вность.

will-o'-the-wisp *n.* блужда́ющие огни́.

willow *n.* и́ва. —*adj.* и́вовый.

willow herb кипре́й.

willowy *adj.* стро́йный.

will power си́ла во́ли.

willy-nilly *adv.* во́лей-нево́лей.

wilt *v.i.* **1,** (wither) вя́нуть; ча́хнуть. **2,** (lose strength or vigor) изнемога́ть: *wilt from the heat,* изнемога́ть от жары́. —*v.t.* губи́ть: *The heat wilted the flowers,* жара́ погуби́ла цветы́.

wily *adj.* хи́трый; лука́вый.

win *v.i.* выи́грывать; побежда́ть: *Who won?,* кто вы́играл/победи́л? —*v.t.* **1,** (gain victory in) выи́грывать; побежда́ть в *or* на. *Win a game/bet/battle/war,* вы́играть игру́/пари́/сраже́ние/войну́. *Win a race/ argument,* победи́ть в бе́ге/ в спо́ре/. *Win an election,* победи́ть на вы́борах. **2,** (gain in competition) получа́ть; завоёвывать: *win first prize,* получи́ть пе́рвый приз; *win a gold medal,* завоева́ть золоту́ю меда́ль. **3,** (gain; earn) завоёвывать: *win one's freedom,* завоева́ть свобо́ду. *Win recognition,* завоева́ть *or* получи́ть *or* сниска́ть призна́ние. *Win concessions,* доби́ться усту́пок. *Win applause,* срыва́ть аплодисме́нты. *Win someone's heart,* покори́ть чье́-нибудь се́рдце. —*n.* побе́да; вы́игрыш. *Six wins and two losses,* шесть побе́д и два пораже́ния. —**win back,** оты́грывать. —**win over, 1,** (charm) располага́ть к себе́; привя́зывать к себе́. **2,** (prevail upon) склоня́ть *or* располага́ть в свою́ по́льзу. *Win over to one's side,* склоня́ть *or* привлека́ть на свою́ сто́рону.

wince *v.i.* вздра́гивать; мо́рщиться (от бо́ли).

winch *n.* лебёдка; во́рот.

wind[1] (wind) *n.* **1,** (air in motion) ве́тер: *against the wind,* про́тив ве́тра. *The flag was waving in the wind,* флаг развева́лся на ветру́. **2,** (breath) дыха́ние: *second wind,* второ́е дыха́ние. *Get one's wind,* отды́ша́ться. —**get wind of,** проню́хивать (о). —**see**

which way the wind blows, узна́ть, куда́ ве́тер ду́ет. —**something is in the wind,** что́-то затева́ется. *See also* **winded.**

wind[2] (waind) *v.t.* **1,** (turn) верте́ть: *wind a crank,* верте́ть рукоя́тку. **2,** (set going) заводи́ть: *wind a watch/toy,* заводи́ть часы́/игру́шку. **3,** (coil onto or around something) мота́ть. *Wind thread onto a spool,* намота́ть ни́тки на кату́шку. *Wind a scarf around one's head,* обмота́ть *or* оберну́ть *or* обви́ть шарф вокру́г головы́. *Wind the yarn into a ball,* смота́ть пря́жу в клубо́к. *Wind in a fishing line,* смота́ть у́дочку. —*v.i.* **1,** (extend in a curving or twisting path) ви́ться; извива́ться. *The road winds through the mountains,* доро́га вьётся по гора́м. **2,** *fol. by* **around** (twine around) обвива́ться (вокру́г); обма́тываться (вокру́г). —*n.* оборо́т; поворо́т: *one wind of the crank,* оди́н оборо́т/поворо́т рукоя́тки. —**wind up, 1,** (wind onto a spool) сма́тывать. **2,** (tighten the spring of) заводи́ть. **3,** (finish; conclude) зака́нчивать. **4,** (end up; find oneself) очути́ться. **5,** *usu. passive* (make tense) взви́нчивать: *all wound up,* взви́нченный.

windbag *n., slang* пустозво́н; пустосло́в; пустоме́ля; краснoба́й.

winded *adj.* запыха́вшийся.

windfall *n.* золото́й дождь; непредви́денный дохо́д. *Windfall profits,* непредви́денная при́быль; сверхпри́быль.

winding *adj.* **1,** (serving to wind) заводно́й; мота́льный: *winding mechanism,* заводно́й/мота́льный механи́зм. **2,** (twisting, as of a road) изви́листый. *Winding staircase,* вита́я ле́стница.

wind instrument духово́й инструме́нт.

windlass *n.* лебёдка; во́рот; *naut.* бра́шпиль.

windless *adj.* безве́тренный.

windmill *n.* ветряна́я ме́льница. —**tilt at windmills,** сража́ться с ветряны́ми ме́льницами.

window *n.* **1,** (opening to let in light) окно́. *Look out the window,* смотре́ть *or* выгля́дывать в окно́ *or* из окна́. *The windows rattled,* стёкла дребезжа́ли. **2,** (for a cashier, bank teller, etc.) око́шко. **3,** (display window in a store) витри́на: *merchandise in the window,* това́ры на витри́не. —*adj.* око́нный: *window curtain,* око́нная занаве́ска.

window dressing мишура́; декора́ции; показу́ха.

windowpane *n.* око́нное стекло́. *Windowpanes were blown out,* в о́кнах вы́летели стёкла.

window shade што́ра.

window-shop *v.i.* рассма́тривать витри́ны.

window sill подоко́нник. *On the window sill,* на подоко́нник(е); на окно́; на окне́.

windpipe *n.* дыха́тельное го́рло.

windscreen *n., Brit.* = **windshield.**

windshield *n.* передне́е стекло́; ветрово́е стекло́. —**windshield wiper,** стеклоочисти́тель; дво́рник.

windstorm *n.* бу́ря.

wind tunnel аэродинами́ческая труба́.

windward *adj.* наве́тренный.

windy *adj.* ве́треный. *It is windy,* ве́трено.

wine *n.* вино́. *Serve wine with dinner,* подава́ть вино́ к обе́ду. —*adj.* ви́нный: *wine cellar,* ви́нный по́греб. *Wine bottle,* буты́лка из-под вина́.

wineglass *n.* бока́л.

winegrower *n.* виноде́л. —**winegrowing,** *n.* виноде́лие. *Winegrowing region,* виноде́льческий райо́н.

wine list ка́рта (*or* ка́рточка) вин.

winemaker *n.* виноде́л. —**winemaking,** *n.* виноде́лие.

wine press дави́льный пресс; дави́льня.

wineskin *n.* бурдю́к; мех для вина́.

wing *n.* **1,** (of a bird; of a plane) крыло́. **2,** (of fowl, when eaten) кры́лышко. **3,** (extension of a building) фли́гель; крыло́. **4,** (side of a stage) кули́са: *in the wings,* за кули́сами. **5,** (political faction) крыло́. **6,** *Brit.* (fender) крыло́. —*v.t.* **1,** (shoot; wound) подстре́ливать. **2,** *in* **wing one's way,** пролета́ть. —**on the wing,** на лету́. —**take under one's wing,** брать под своё крыло́ *or* под своё покрови́тельство; брать под защи́ту. —**take wing,** вспорхну́ть.

winged *adj.* крыла́тый.

wingless *adj.* бескры́лый.

wingspan *n.* разма́х кры́льев. *Also,* **wingspread.**

wink *v.i.* мига́ть; морга́ть. —*n.* мига́ние. *Give someone a wink,* подми́гивать (+ *dat.*). *Not sleep a wink,* совсе́м не спать; не смыка́ть глаз. —**wink at, 1,** (signal with a wink) мига́ть (+ *dat.*); морга́ть (+ *dat.*); подми́гивать (+ *dat.*). **2,** (pretend not to notice) смотре́ть сквозь па́льцы на.

winner *n.* победи́тель. *Nobel Prize winner,* лауреа́т Нобелевской пре́мии.

winning *adj.* **1,** (victorious) победи́вший. *The winning team,* кома́нда-победи́тельница. *Winning streak,* побе́дное ше́ствие. **2,** (leading to victory) вы́игрышный: *winning ticket/move,* вы́игрышный биле́т/ ход. **3,** (captivating) подкупа́ющий; обезору́живающий. —*n.* **1,** (victory) побе́да. **2,** *pl.* (money won) вы́игрыш.

winnow *v.t.* **1,** (blow the chaff from) ве́ять. **2,** *fol. by* **out** (sift or separate out) отсе́ивать.

winnowing *n.* ве́яние. *Winnowing machine,* ве́ялка.

winsome *adj.* привлека́тельный; располага́ющий.

winter *n.* зима́. *In winter,* зимо́й. —*adj.* зи́мний: *winter sports,* зи́мний спорт; *winter clothes,* зи́мняя оде́жда. *Winter crops,* ози́мые культу́ры. —*v.i.* зимова́ть.

winterize *v.t.* утепля́ть; отепля́ть.

wintertime *n.* зима́; зи́мнее вре́мя.

wintry *adj.* зи́мний: *wintry weather,* зи́мняя пого́да.

wipe *v.t.* вытира́ть: *wipe the sweat from one's brow,* вытира́ть пот со лба; *wipe one's feet on the mat,* вытира́ть но́ги о полови́к. *Wipe one's nose,* утере́ть (себе́) нос. *Wipe one's glasses,* протира́ть очки́. *Wipe from the face of the earth,* стира́ть с лица́ земли́. —**wipe away,** вытира́ть; утира́ть: *wipe away the tears,* вытира́ть/утира́ть слёзы. —**wipe off,** стира́ть. —**wipe out,** уничтожа́ть. —**wipe up,** подтира́ть.

wire *n.* **1,** (metal strand) про́волока: *barbed wire,* колю́чая про́волока. **2,** (electric, telegraph, etc.) про́вод. **3,** (telegram) телегра́мма. —*adj.* про́волочный:

wire netting, про́волочная сеть. —*v.t.* **1,** (fasten with wire) скрепля́ть про́волокой. **2,** (install wiring in) прокла́дывать провода́ в. **3,** (send a telegram to) телеграфи́ровать.

wire cutter куса́чки.

wireless *n., Brit.* = **radio.** —*adj.* беспро́волочный.

wire service телегра́фное аге́нтство.

wiretap *v.t.* перехва́тывать. —**wiretapping,** *n.* перехва́т телефо́нных сообще́ний.

wiring *n.* прово́дка.

wiry *adj.* жи́листый.

wisdom *n.* му́дрость. —**wisdom tooth,** зуб му́дрости.

wise *adj.* **1,** (sagacious) му́дрый: *wise leader,* му́дрый вождь; *wise decision,* му́дрое реше́ние. **2,** (judicious) благоразу́мный: *You would be wise to follow his advice,* бы́ло бы благоразу́мно сле́довать его́ сове́ту. **3,** *fol. by* **to** (aware of) в ку́рсе: *wise to what is going on,* в ку́рсе де́ла. **4,** *slang* (impudent; fresh) наха́льный. **5,** *in* **wise guy,** у́мник. —**put wise,** *slang* вводи́ть в курс де́ла. —**wise up,** *slang* **1,** (become aware) образу́миться. **2,** (make aware) вразумля́ть.

wisecrack *n.* острота́.

wisely *adv.* благоразу́мно.

wish *v.t.* **1,** (want; desire) хоте́ть; жела́ть: *I do not wish to see him,* не хочу́/жела́ю его́ ви́деть. *I wish I could stay longer,* жаль, что не могу́ оста́ться подо́льше. *I wish I had known about it sooner,* (как) жаль *or* я жале́ю, что не знал об э́том ра́ньше. *I wish you would stop bothering me!,* нельзя́ ли не беспоко́ить меня́? **2,** (bid) жела́ть: *I wish you luck,* жела́ю вам сча́стья. *Wish someone happy birthday,* поздра́вить кого́-нибудь с днём рожде́ния. **3,** (inflict) жела́ть; навя́зывать. *I wouldn't wish this on anyone,* э́того я никому́ не жела́ю. *Who wished this job on us?,* кто навяза́л нам э́ту рабо́ту? —*v.i.* [*usu.* **wish for**] жела́ть: *wish for someone's recovery,* жела́ть чьего́-нибудь выздоровле́ния. *What more could one wish for?,* чего́ ещё мо́жно жела́ть? —*n.* **1,** (desire) жела́ние; охо́та. *Act against someone's wishes,* поступи́ть вопреки́ чьим-нибудь жела́ниям. *She got her wish,* она́ доби́лась, чего́ хоте́ла. **2,** *pl.* (expressed desire for someone's well-being) пожела́ние: *best wishes,* наилу́чшие пожела́ния.

wishful *adj. A wishful expression on one's face,* выраже́ние жела́ния на лице́. *Indulge in wishful thinking,* принима́ть жела́емое за действи́тельное.

wishy-washy *adj.* бесхара́ктерный; слабово́льный.

wisp *n.* **1,** (of hay, straw, etc.) пучо́к; клок. **2,** (of smoke, vapor, etc.) стру́йка.

wisteria *n.* глици́ния.

wistful *adj.* **1,** (melancholy) тоскли́вый. **2,** (pensive) заду́мчивый.

wit *n.* **1,** (wittiness) остроу́мие. *Man of great wit,* остроу́мный челове́к. **2,** (witty person) остря́к. **3,** *pl.* (innate intelligence) ум; мозги́. *Battle of wits,* поеди́нок умо́в. *Use one's wits,* шевели́ть мозга́ми. *Live by one's wits,* жить хи́тростью. **4,** *pl.* (sanity) рассу́док: *lose one's wits,* теря́ть рассу́док. —**be at one's wits' end,** дойти́ до то́чки. *I am at my wits' end,* у меня́ ум за ра́зум захо́дит. —**frighten out of**

one's wits, напуга́ть до́ сме́рти. —**keep one's wits about one,** не теря́ть головы́. —**to wit,** а и́менно.

witch *n.* ве́дьма.

witchcraft *n.* колдовство́.

witch doctor зна́харь.

witch hunt охо́та за ве́дьмами.

witch trial суд над ве́дьмами.

with *prep.* **1,** (in most meanings) с (+ *instr.*): *Come with me,* иди́те со мной. *Tea with lemon,* чай с лимо́ном. *A house with a fireplace,* дом с ками́ном. *Walk with a cane,* ходи́ть с па́лкой. *Read with difficulty,* чита́ть с трудо́м. *I agree with you,* я согла́сен с ва́ми. *Play/argue/cope/part with,* игра́ть/спо́рить/справля́ться/расстава́ться с. **2,** (by means of; using) *rendered by the instr. case: write with a pencil,* писа́ть карандашо́м; *work with one's hands,* рабо́тать рука́ми; *cut the meat with a knife,* ре́зать мя́со ножо́м. **3,** (at the home of) у: *stay with friends,* жить *or* гости́ть у друзе́й. **4,** (in the possession or care of) у: *leave the keys with the watchman,* оставля́ть ключи́ у сто́рожа. **5,** (in regard to): *satisfied with something,* дово́лен че́м-нибудь; *angry with me,* серди́т на меня́. **6,** (involving a material or substance) *rendered by the instr. case: covered with dust,* покры́ть пы́лью; *be filled with smoke,* напо́лниться ды́мом. *Line a coat with silk,* подбива́ть пальто́ шёлком. **7,** (from) от: *tremble with fear,* дрожа́ть от стра́ха; *beam with joy,* сия́ть от ра́дости; *be green with envy,* ло́паться от за́висти. **8,** (beginning with) с (+ *gen.*): *Let's start with you,* начнём с вас. *Begin the lecture with an anecdote,* нача́ть ле́кцию с анекдо́та. **9,** (having received) с (+ *gen.*): *with your permission,* с ва́шего разреше́ния. **10,** (to indicate proper spelling) на (+ *acc.*): *The word* анке́та *begins and ends with an* а, сло́во «анке́та» начина́ется и конча́ется на «а». *The names of the planets are written with a capital letter,* назва́ния плане́т пи́шутся с большо́й бу́квы. *The word "run-down" is spelled with a hyphen,* сло́во "run-down" пи́шется че́рез чёрточку.

withdraw *v.t.* **1,** (draw back; remove) отдёргивать: *withdraw one's hand,* отдёрнуть ру́ку. **2,** (remove; evacuate, as troops) выводи́ть. **3,** (retract) снима́ть: *withdraw one's offer/motion,* снима́ть своё предложе́ние. **4,** (retire) изыма́ть: *withdraw from circulation,* изыма́ть из обраще́ния. **5,** (take out, as money from a bank) снима́ть со счёта. —*v.i.* **1,** (leave; retire) удаля́ться. **2,** (drop out) выбыва́ть; выбыва́ть. **3,** *mil.* (retreat) отходи́ть; отступа́ть. **4,** *in* **withdraw into oneself,** уходи́ть в себя́; замыка́ться в себе́.

withdrawal *n.* **1,** (retreat) отхо́д. **2,** (pullout, as from occupied territory) ухо́д. **3,** (removal, as of troops) вы́вод. **4,** (dropping out) вы́ход. **5,** (removal, as from circulation) изъя́тие. **6,** (retraction of a motion) сня́тие. **7,** (removal, as of funds) сня́тие со счёта. *Make a withdrawal,* снима́ть де́ньги со счёта.

withdrawn *adj.* (retiring; reticent) сде́ржанный; за́мкнутый.

wither *v.i.* **1,** (shrivel) вя́нуть; увяда́ть; со́хнуть; отсыха́ть; блёкнуть. **2,** *fol. by* **away** (gradually cease to exist) отмира́ть: *"The state will wither away",* госуда́рство отмира́ет. —*v.t.* иссуша́ть.

withered *adj.* вя́лый; увя́дший; вы́сохший; блёклый.

withering *adj.* уничтожа́ющий: *withering look/crossfire,* уничтожа́ющий взгляд/ перекрёстный ого́нь/.

withers *n.pl.* хо́лка; загри́вок.

withhold *v.t.* **1,** (hold back, as money) уде́рживать; заде́рживать. *Withhold payment,* заде́рживать вы́плату. **2,** (refrain from giving) возде́рживаться от: *withhold comment,* возде́рживаться от коммента́риев. **3,** (refuse to grant) не дава́ть: *withhold permission,* не дава́ть разреше́ния. **4,** (not divulge) ута́ивать: *withhold information,* ута́ивать све́дения.

within *prep.* **1,** (inside) внутри́: *within the city walls,* внутри́ городски́х стен. *Within the city,* в преде́лах (*or* в черте́) го́рода. **2,** (not beyond) в; в преде́лах (+ *gen.*): *within reach/earshot,* в преде́лах досяга́емости/слы́шимости. *Within a radius of,* в ра́диусе (+ *gen.*). *Within the framework of,* в ра́мках (+ *gen.*). *Within ten paces of,* в десяти́ шага́х от. ♦*Also rendered by various other prepositions and constructions: within my recollection,* на мое́й па́мяти. *Live within one's means,* жить по свои́м сре́дствам. *Fall within one's jurisdiction,* входи́ть в чью-нибудь компете́нцию. *Come within six miles of the coast,* подойти́ на шесть миль к побере́жью. *Is it within walking distance?,* туда́ мо́жно дойти́ пешко́м? *Guess someone's age within a year,* угада́ть чей-нибудь во́зраст с то́чностью до го́да. *The planes passed within 100 feet of each other,* самолёты прошли́ на расстоя́нии ста фу́тов друг от дру́га. *The plane crashed within three miles of the airport,* самолёт разби́лся, не дотяну́в трёх миль до аэропо́рта. **3,** (not later than) в; в тече́ние (+ *gen.*): *within 24 hours,* в два́дцать четы́ре часа́; *within a year,* в тече́ние го́да. —*adv.* внутри́. *From within,* изнутри́.

without *prep.* **1,** (lacking; free from) без: *without exception,* без исключе́ния. *Get along without modern conveniences,* обходи́ться без совреме́нных удо́бств. **2,** (failing to do) без того́, что́бы (+ *inf.*); (+ *verbal adverb*). *Without saying a word,* не говоря́ (*or* не сказа́в) ни сло́ва. *Without saying goodbye to anyone,* ни с кем не простя́сь. **3,** (outside of) вне. —*adv.* снару́жи. *From without,* извне́. —**do** (*or* **go) without,** обходи́ться без.

withstand *v.t.* выде́рживать; устоя́ть пе́ред *or* про́тив; противостоя́ть. *Withstand an onslaught,* вы́держать на́тиск; устоя́ть про́тив на́тиска. *Withstand bombardment,* вы́держать бомбардиро́вку. *Withstand the elements,* противостоя́ть стихи́ям. *Withstand the test of time,* вы́держать прове́рку вре́менем.

witless *adj.* безмо́зглый.

witness *n.* свиде́тель. *Eyewitness,* очеви́дец. *Call someone as a witness,* призва́ть кого́-нибудь в свиде́тели. —*v.t.* **1,** (be present at; see) быть свиде́телем/очеви́дцем (+ *gen.*). **2,** (certify, as a signature) заверя́ть; удостоверя́ть. —**bear witness to,** свиде́тельствовать о. —**in witness whereof,** в удостовере́нии чего́.

witticism *n.* остро́та.

wittiness *n.* остроу́мие.

wittingly *adv.* созна́тельно; заве́домо.

witty *adj.* остроу́мный.

wizard *n.* **1,** (sorcerer) колду́н; чароде́й. **2,** *colloq.* (whiz) ге́ний.

wizardry *n.* колдовство́.

wizened *adj.* вы́сохший: *a wizened old man,* вы́сохший стари́к.

wobble *v.i.* шата́ться; пошатываться. —**wobbly,** *adj.* ша́ткий.

woe *n.* **1,** (distress) го́ре. *Tale of woe,* печа́льный расска́з. *Woe (be it) to him who...,* го́ре тому́, кто... **2,** *pl.* (misfortunes) бе́ды: *economic woes,* экономи́ческие бе́ды.

woebegone *adj.* удручённый; го́рестный.

woeful *adj.* **1,** (sad) го́рестный. **2,** (wretched) жа́лкий. —**knight of the woeful countenance,** ры́царь печа́льного о́браза.

wolf *n.* волк. —*adj.* [*also,* **wolf's**] во́лчий. —**wolf in sheep's clothing,** волк в ове́чьей шку́ре.

wolfhound *n.* (Irish) волкода́в; (Russian) борза́я.

wolverine *n.* росома́ха.

woman *n.* же́нщина. *Old woman,* стару́шка; стару́ха. —*adj.* **1,** (being a woman) же́нщина-: *woman doctor,* же́нщина-врач. **2,** [*usu.* **woman's** *or* **women's**] (of women) же́нский: *women's wear,* же́нская оде́жда. *Women's rights,* права́ же́нщин.

woman-hater *n.* женоненави́стник.

womanhood *n.* **1,** (maturity) зре́лость. **2,** (women collectively) же́нщины.

womanizer *n.,* *colloq.* ба́бник; женолю́б; ухажёр.

womankind *n.* же́нщины; же́нский пол.

womanly *adj.* же́нственный.

womb *n.* ма́тка; утро́ба.

wonder *v.t.* хоте́ть знать. *I wonder what he wants/ where she went/,* интере́сно, что он хо́чет/ куда́ она́ пошла́/. *I wonder what's wrong with my watch,* не понима́ю, что с мои́ми часа́ми. —*v.i.* **1,** *fol. by* **at** (marvel) удивля́ться (+ *dat.*). **2,** (have doubts) сомнева́ться: *I wonder,* я в э́том сомнева́юсь; я не уве́рен(а). *I wonder about his sincerity,* я сомнева́юсь в его́ и́скренности. *I wonder if she'll ever get married,* задаю́ себе́ вопро́с, вы́йдет ли она́ за́муж? —*n.* **1,** (awe) удивле́ние; изумле́ние: *watch in/with wonder,* смотре́ть с удивле́нием/изумле́нием. **2,** (a marvel; miracle) чу́до: *work wonders,* твори́ть чудеса́. *It's a wonder that...,* удиви́тельно, что... *The Seven Wonders of the World,* семь чуде́с све́та. —**no wonder,** не удиви́тельно; не ди́во; не мудрено́: *No wonder he's angry!,* не удиви́тельно/ не ди́во/ не мудрено́/, что он рассерди́лся. *And no wonder!,* и не удиви́тельно!; и немудрено́!

wonderful *adj.* чуде́сный; чу́дный; замеча́тельный. *Have a wonderful time,* чуде́сно провести́ вре́мя.

wonderfully *adv.* **1,** (marvelously) чуде́сно; чу́дно; замеча́тельно. **2,** (exceedingly; very) чрезвыча́йно; о́чень и о́чень.

wonderland *n.* страна́ чуде́с.

wonderment *n.* удивле́ние; изумле́ние.

wonder-working *adj.* чудоде́йственный; чудотво́рный.

wondrous *adj.* чу́дный; ди́вный.

wont *adj., used predicatively:* *be wont to,* име́ть привы́чку (+ *inf.*). —*n.* привы́чка; обыкнове́ние: *as was his wont,* по свое́й привы́чке; по своему́ обыкнове́нию.

woo *v.t.* уха́живать за.

wood *n.* **1,** (material) де́рево; древеси́на. **2,** (firewood) дрова́: *chop wood,* руби́ть/коло́ть дрова́. **3,** *usu. pl.* (forest) лес: *in the woods,* в лесу́. —*adj.* деревя́нный. —**out of the woods,** вне опа́сности.

wood alcohol древе́сный спирт.

wood block лубо́к.

woodchuck *n.* суро́к.

woodcock *n.* ва́льдшнеп.

woodcut *n.* гравю́ра на де́реве; лубо́к.

woodcutter *n.* лесору́б; дровосе́к.

wooded *adj.* леси́стый.

wooden *adj.* деревя́нный. *Wooden leg,* деревя́шка. *Wooden style of writing,* деревя́нный стиль письма́.

woodland *n.* леси́стая ме́стность.

wood louse мокри́ца.

woodman *n.* = **woodsman.**

woodpecker *n.* дя́тел.

wood pulp древе́сная ма́сса.

woods *see* **wood.**

woodshed *n.* дровяно́й сара́й.

woodsman *n.* лесору́б; лесни́к.

wood sorrel кисли́ца.

wood tar древе́сный дёготь.

woodwinds *n.pl.* деревя́нные духовы́е инструме́нты.

woodwork *n.* деревя́нные ча́сти (до́ма). —**woodworker,** *n.* деревообде́лочник. —**woodworking,** *adj.* деревообде́лочный.

woody *adj.* древе́сный; деревяни́стый.

woof *n., textiles* уто́к.

wool *n.* **1,** (yarn) шерсть. **2,** (fibrous matter) ва́та: *mineral wool,* минера́льная ва́та; *glass wool,* стеклова́та. —*adj.* шерстяно́й. —**pull the wool over someone's eyes,** втира́ть очки́ (+ *dat.*); пуска́ть пыль в глаза́ (+ *dat.*).

woolen *also,* **woollen** *adj.* шерстяно́й. —**woolens,** *n.pl.* шерстяны́е ве́щи.

woolly *adj.* шерсти́стый.

woozy *adj., slang* одуре́лый.

word *n.* **1,** (unit of speech) сло́во: *a rare word,* ре́дкое сло́во. *Harsh words,* ре́зкие слова́. *In one's own words,* свои́ми слова́ми. *Just say the word!,* скажи́те то́лько сло́во! *You can't get a word out of him,* из него́ ни сло́ва не вы́тянешь. *"Disappointed" isn't the word for it!,* «разочаро́ванный» — не то сло́во! **2,** *pl.* (lyrics) слова́; текст. *Set words to music,* класть слова́ на му́зыку. **3,** (promise) сло́во: *give one's word,* дава́ть (че́стное) сло́во; *keep one's word,* сдержа́ть (своё) сло́во. **4,** (news; information) изве́стие: *bring/receive word of his death,* приноси́ть/ получи́ть изве́стие о его́ сме́рти. *There hasn't been a word from him,* от него́ нет никако́го изве́стия; о нём (*or* от него́) ни слу́ху ни ду́ху. —*v.t.* выража́ть слова́ми; формули́ровать. *Carefully worded reply,* тща́тельно сформули́рованный отве́т. —**by word**

of mouth, у́стно; из уст в уста́. —**have a word with,** поговори́ть с. *May I have a word with you?*, мо́жно вас на полсло́ва? —**have words with,** кру́пно поговори́ть с; име́ть кру́пный разгово́р. —**in a word,** одни́м сло́вом. —**in other words,** други́ми слова́ми; ина́че говоря́. —**in so many words,** недвусмы́сленно. *I told her in so many words that…*, я так и сказа́л(а) ей, что… —**leave word,** проси́ть переда́ть. —**man of his word,** челове́к сло́ва; хозя́ин своего́ сло́ва. —**of few words,** немногосло́вный. —**send word,** сообща́ть; проси́ть переда́ть. —**take at one's word,** лови́ть на сло́ве. —**take one's word for it,** ве́рить (+ *dat.*) на́ слово. —**word for word,** сло́во в сло́во; досло́вно. —**word of honor,** че́стное сло́во.

wordbook *n.* слова́рь.

wording *n.* формулиро́вка; реда́кция.

wordy *adj.* многосло́вный.

work *n.* **1,** (labor) рабо́та: *hard work,* тяжёлая рабо́та. *Put a lot of work into,* вкла́дывать *or* класть мно́го труда́ в (+ *acc.*). **2,** (employment) рабо́та; слу́жба. *Look for work,* иска́ть рабо́ту. *Out of work,* без рабо́ты; безрабо́тный. *What sort of work do you do?,* кем вы рабо́таете? **3,** (place of employment) рабо́та: *He is at work today,* он сего́дня на рабо́те. *I'll phone you at work,* я позвоню́ вам на рабо́ту. **4,** (something done or produced) рабо́та: *stucco work,* лепна́я рабо́та. *That's his work,* э́то его́ рабо́та; э́то его́ рук де́ло. *The blast was the work of terrorists,* взрыв — де́ло рук террори́стов. **5,** (literary or artistic creation) произведе́ние; сочине́ние; труд; вещь. *Work of art,* произведе́ние иску́сства. *Literary work,* литерату́рное произведе́ние; литерату́рный труд. *The complete works of Chekhov,* по́лное собра́ние сочине́ний Че́хова. *Two works by Glinka,* два произведе́ния/сочине́ния (*or* две ве́щи) Гли́нки. **6,** (scholarly study) труд: *scientific work,* нау́чный труд. **7,** *pl.* (factory) заво́д: *glassworks,* стеко́льный заво́д. **8,** *pl., mil.* сооруже́ния: *defensive works,* оборони́тельные сооруже́ния. **9,** [*usu.* **the works**] *slang* (everything) всё: *shoot the works,* идти́ на всё; идти́ ва-ба́нк. —*v.i.* **1,** (do work) рабо́тать: *work as a draftsman,* рабо́тать чертёжником. *Work for someone,* рабо́тать на кого́-нибудь. *Work for a firm,* рабо́тать на фи́рме. **2,** (function) рабо́тать: *The radio doesn't work,* радиоприёмник не рабо́тает. **3,** (prove effective, as of medicine) де́йствовать; возыме́ть де́йствие. **4,** (accomplish its purpose) удава́ться: *The new method didn't work,* но́вый ме́тод не уда́лся. —*v.t.* **1,** (perform; accomplish) твори́ть: *work miracles/wonders,* твори́ть чудеса́. **2,** (operate) обраща́ться с: *know how to work a lathe,* уме́ть обраща́ться с то́карным станко́м. **3,** (till, as the soil; treat, as metal) обраба́тывать: *Work a mine,* разраба́тывать рудни́к. **4,** (manipulate, as dough; shape, as leather) меси́ть; заме́шивать (те́сто); обраба́тывать; мять (ко́жу). **5,** (make work, as subordinates) заставля́ть рабо́тать. **6,** *in* **work one's way,** прокла́дывать себе́ доро́гу. *Work one's way*

out of debt, вы́биться из долго́в. *Work one's way out of a tight spot,* выкру́чиваться из беды́. —**do its work,** сде́лать своё де́ло. —**go to work, 1,** (leave or report for work) идти́ на рабо́ту. **2,** (start to work) бра́ться за рабо́ту. —**work loose,** выпу́тываться; вывёртываться. —**work off, 1,** (pay off by working) отраба́тывать. **2,** (shed, as excess weight) сгоня́ть. —**work on, 1,** (do work on) рабо́тать над. **2,** (try to persuade) угова́ривать; склоня́ть. —**work out, 1,** (develop, as a plan) разраба́тывать; выраба́тывать. *Work out a compromise,* вы́работать компроми́сс. **2,** (solve) разга́дывать: *work out a puzzle,* разга́дывать зага́дку. **3,** (turn out) оберну́ться: *depending on how things work out,* смотря́ как де́ло обернётся. **4,** (end successfully) устро́иться: *Everything worked out,* всё устро́илось. *Everything will work out,* всё образу́ется. *Things didn't work out,* де́ло не вы́шло; де́ло не получи́лось. *The marriage didn't work out,* брак не уда́лся. **5,** *sports* тренирова́ться; размина́ться. —**work up, 1,** (develop) разраба́тывать. **2,** (arouse) возбужда́ть. *Work up an appetite,* нагуля́ть себе́ аппети́т. **3,** (agitate; upset) взви́нчивать. *All worked up,* взви́нченный.

workable *adj.* выполни́мый; осуществи́мый.

workaday *adj.* бу́дничный; повседне́вный.

workbench *n.* верста́к.

workbook *n.* тетра́дь.

workday *n.* **1,** (day on which one works) рабо́чий день; бу́дний день. **2,** (number of hours normally worked in one day) рабо́чий день: *seven-hour workday,* семичасово́й рабо́чий день.

worker *n.* **1,** (one who works) рабо́тник: *conscientious worker,* добросо́вестный рабо́тник. *Hard worker,* рабо́тяга. *Rescue worker,* спаса́тель. **2,** (hired employee) рабо́чий; трудя́щийся. *Factory worker,* заводско́й *or* фабри́чный рабо́чий. *Transport worker,* тра́нспортник. *Government workers,* госуда́рственные слу́жащие. *Meet the workers' demands,* удовлетворя́ть тре́бования рабо́чих.

work force рабо́чая си́ла: *less than 2% of the work force,* ме́ньше двух проце́нтов рабо́чей си́лы.

workhorse *n.* рабо́чая ло́шадь.

workhouse *n.* **1,** (prison) исправи́тельный дом. **2,** *Brit.* (poorhouse) рабо́тный дом.

working *adj.* рабо́тающий; рабо́чий. *Working mothers,* рабо́тающие ма́тери. *The working class,* рабо́чий класс. *Working clothes,* рабо́чая оде́жда. *Working conditions,* усло́вия труда́. *In working order,* испра́вный; в испра́вности. *Working knowledge of Russian,* практи́ческое владе́ние ру́сским языко́м. —**working capital,** оборо́тный капита́л. —**working group,** рабо́чая гру́ппа.

workingman *n.* рабо́чий.

workload *n.* нагру́зка.

workman *n.* рабо́тник.

workmanlike *adj.* иску́сный.

workmanship *n.* рабо́та; мастерство́; вы́делка; вы́работка. *Of marvelous workmanship,* великоле́пной рабо́ты.

workout *n.* трениро́вка.

workplace *n.* рабо́чее ме́сто: *accidents in the workplace*, несча́стные слу́чаи на рабо́чем ме́сте.

workroom *n.* рабо́чая ко́мната.

workshop *n.* мастерска́я.

workstation *n.* рабо́чая ста́нция.

workweek *n.* рабо́чая неде́ля.

world *n.* мир; свет. *The ancient world*, дре́вний мир. *The Old/New World*, Ста́рый/Но́вый свет. *The world of art*, мир иску́сства. *The next world*, тот свет. —*adj.* мирово́й: *a world record*, мирово́й реко́рд; *world events*, мировы́е собы́тия. *World champion*, чемпио́н ми́ра. —**be dead to the world,** спать мёртвым сном. —**bring/come into the world,** произвести́/появи́ться на свет. —**do someone a world of good,** о́чень идти́ на по́льзу (+ *dat.*); приноси́ть мно́го по́льзы (+ *dat.*). —**in the world, 1,** *literally* в ми́ре; на све́те. **2,** *used for emphasis: Where in the world have you been?*, куда́ же э́то вы пропа́ли? *Where in the world did you find it?*, где то́лько вы его́ нашли́? —**not for all the world,** ни за что на све́те. —**not long for this world,** не жиле́ц на э́том све́те. —**on top of the world,** на седьмо́м не́бе; на верху́ блаже́нства. —**out of this world,** из ря́да вон выходя́щий. —**think the world of,** быть о́чень высо́кого мне́ния о.

worldly *adj.* **1,** (earthly; mundane) мирско́й; жите́йский. **2,** (worldly-wise) быва́лый.

worldly-wise *adj.* вида́вший ви́ды; быва́лый.

world's fair всеми́рная вы́ставка.

world war мирова́я война́. *World War II*, втора́я мирова́я война́.

worldwide *adj.* мирово́й; всеми́рный.

worm *n.* червь; червя́к. *Intestinal worm*, глист. —*v.t.* **1,** *often fol. by* **out** (elicit, as a secret) выве́дывать. **2,** *in* **worm one's way into,** вкра́дываться в; втира́ться в. —*v.i.* [*usu.* **worm out of**] вывёртываться (из); выпу́тываться (из).

worm-eaten *adj.* черви́вый.

worm gear червя́чная шестерня́.

wormhole *n.* червото́чина.

worm wheel червя́чное колесо́.

wormwood *n.* полы́нь.

wormy *adj.* черви́вый.

worn *adj.* **1,** (showing the effects of wear) поно́шенный. *The soles/tires are worn*, подо́швы/ши́ны стёрлись. **2,** (haggard) изму́ченный; заму́ченный.

worn-out *adj.* **1,** (no longer fit for wear) изно́шенный. **2,** (exhausted) изнурённый. *I am worn-out*, я сме́ртельно уста́л(а); я соверше́нно изму́чился (изму́чилась). *Also*, **worn out.**

worried *adj.* **1,** (experiencing worry) обеспоко́енный: *I am very worried*, я о́чень обеспоко́ен(а). *I am worried about him*, я беспоко́юсь за него́. **2,** (showing worry) беспоко́йный: *a worried look*, беспоко́йный вид.

worrisome *adj.* беспоко́йный.

worry *v.t.* беспоко́ить: *It worries me a great deal*, э́то меня́ о́чень беспоко́ит. *Don't let it worry you*, пусть э́то вас не беспоко́ит. —*v.i.* беспоко́иться: *Don't*

worry!, не беспоко́йтесь! *There is nothing to worry about*, беспоко́иться не о чем. —*n.* **1,** (anxiety) беспоко́йство. **2,** (cause of anxiety) забо́та. *That's the least of my worries*, э́то меня́ ме́ньше всего́ беспоко́ит. *See also* **worried.**

worse *adj.* **1,** *modifier*, ху́дший: *in worse shape*, в ху́дшем состоя́нии. **2,** *predicate*, ху́же: *worse than I expected*, ху́же, чем я ожида́л(а). *He is worse today*, ему́ сего́дня ху́же. *It could have been worse*, могло́ бы быть и ху́же. *Make worse*, ухудша́ть. *Get/grow worse*, стать ху́же; ухудша́ться. —*adv.* ху́же: *Our team played even worse than yesterday*, на́ша кома́нда игра́ла да́же ху́же, чем вчера́. —*n.* [*usu.* **the worse**] ху́дшее: *change for the worse*, переме́на к ху́дшему. *Take a turn for the worse*, принима́ть дурно́й оборо́т. —**be none the worse for,** ничу́ть не страда́ть от. *He is none the worse for it*, ему́ от э́того ниско́лько не ху́же. —**go from bad to worse,** станови́ться всё ху́же и ху́же. —**so much the worse,** тем ху́же. —**what is worse; to make matters worse,** (и) что ещё ху́же. —**worse off,** в ху́дшем состоя́нии.

worsen *v.t.* ухудша́ть. —*v.i.* ухудша́ться: *The patient's condition has worsened*, состоя́ние больно́го ухудшилось.

worship *v.t.* **1,** (venerate, as a deity) поклоня́ться: *worship God*, поклоня́ться бо́гу. **2,** (idolize) обожа́ть; боготвори́ть. —*v.i.* моли́ться. —*n.* поклоне́ние: *the worship of idols*, поклоне́ние и́долам. *Freedom of worship*, свобо́да вероиспове́дания. *House of worship*, храм.

worshiper *also,* **worshipper** *n.* **1,** (person at prayer) моля́щийся. **2,** (fervent admirer) покло́нник.

worst *adj.* са́мый плохо́й; са́мый ху́дший; наиху́дший. *My worst mistake*, са́мая больша́я моя́ оши́бка. *One's worst enemy*, злейший враг. *At the worst possible time*, в са́мое неподходя́щее вре́мя. —*adv.* ху́же всего́; ху́же всех. *He was the worst dressed person there*, он был оде́т ху́же всех. —*n.* [*usu.* **the worst**] (са́мое) ху́дшее: *prepare for the worst*, гото́виться к ху́дшему. *Fear the worst*, боя́ться са́мого ху́дшего. *The worst is yet to come*, ху́дшее впереди́. *The worst of it is that...*, ху́же всего́ то, что... —**at worst,** в ху́дшем слу́чае. —**get the worst of it, 1,** (lose) быть в про́игрыше. **2,** (suffer most) страда́ть бо́льше всех. —**if worst comes to worst,** в кра́йнем слу́чае; на худо́й коне́ц. —**in the worst way,** *colloq.* о́чень; си́льно; стра́стно.

worsted *n.* камво́льная пря́жа; га́рус. —*adj.* камво́льный; га́русный.

worth *n.* **1,** (value) цена́; це́нность. *Know one's worth*, знать себе́ це́ну. *Show one's worth*, показа́ть себя́; прояви́ть себя́. **2,** *fol. by* **of** (amount to be had for a given sum) *rendered by* на: *a dollar's worth of stamps*, на до́ллар ма́рок. —*adj., used predicatively, rendered by the verb* сто́ить: *This painting is worth at least 10,000 dollars*, э́та карти́на сто́ит по кра́йней ме́ре де́сять ты́сяч до́лларов. *Be worth the expense*, сто́ить затра́т *or* расхо́дов. *Pay people what they are worth*, плати́ть лю́дям сто́лько, ско́лько они́ сто́ят.

Jewelry worth thousands of dollars, драгоце́нности на ты́сячи до́лларов. *The play is worth seeing,* пье́су сто́ит посмотре́ть. *He is worth 100,000 dollars,* он име́ет капита́л в сто ты́сяч до́лларов. **—for all one is worth,** изо всех сил; что есть сил.

worthiness *n.* досто́инство.

worthless *adj.* **1,** (of no value) ничего́ не сто́ящий. *Be worthless,* ничего́ не сто́ить. **2,** (useless; good-for-nothing) него́дный; никчёмный. **—worthlessness,** *n.* него́дность.

worthwhile *adj.* сто́ящий. *Be worthwhile,* сто́ить; име́ть смысл.

worthy *adj.* досто́йный: *a worthy adversary,* досто́йный проти́вник. *Worthy of attention,* досто́йный внима́ния. *He is not worthy of her,* он не сто́ит её; он недосто́ин её. *A job worthy of his talent,* ме́сто, подоба́ющее его́ тала́нту.

would *v.aux.* **1,** *used to express futurity: He said he would be here by six,* он сказа́л, что придёт к шести́ часа́м. **2,** *used to form the conditional mood,* бы: *I would go if I could,* я пошёл бы, е́сли б мог. **3,** *used to express a polite request or desire,* бы: *I would like a glass of milk,* я бы хоте́л(а) стака́н молока́. *I would rather stay home,* я бы предпочёл оста́ться до́ма. *Would you like to see it?,* хоти́те посмотре́ть? *Would you be so kind as to...?,* бу́дьте добры́, (+ *imperative*); вы не бу́дете так любе́зны (+ *inf.*). **4,** *used to express customary action: He would often drop in to say hello,* он ча́сто заходи́л, чтобы поздоро́ваться с на́ми. *She would sit for hours in front of the fireplace,* она́, быва́ло, сиде́ла це́лыми часа́ми пе́ред ками́ном. **5,** *used to express a strong wish: Would that he were here!,* о, е́сли бы он был здесь!

would-be *adj.* претенду́ющий на; с прете́нзией на.

wound *n.* ра́на; ране́ние. *Bullet wound to the head,* пулево́е ране́ние головы́. *—v.t.* ра́нить: *wounded in action,* ра́нен в бою́. *Three soldiers were wounded,* три солда́та бы́ли ра́нены *or* получи́ли ране́ния. *He was wounded in the chest,* он был ра́нен в грудь.

wounded *adj.* ра́неный. *Tend the wounded,* уха́живать за ра́неными.

woven *adj.* тка́ный.

wrack *v.t.* = **rack. —go to wrack and ruin,** пойти́ пра́хом.

wraith *n.* привиде́ние; при́зрак.

wrangle *v.i.* пререка́ться. *—n.* пререка́ния; перебра́нка.

wrap *v.t.* **1,** [*often* **wrap up**] (make a package of) завёртывать: *wrap a gift,* заверну́ть пода́рок. *Wrap something in paper,* заверну́ть *or* оберну́ть что́-нибудь в бума́гу. *Would you like it wrapped?,* вам э́то заверну́ть? **2,** (enclose snugly) заку́тывать; укýтывать; завёртывать: *wrap a child in a blanket,* заку́тывать/укýтывать/завёртывать ребёнка в одея́ло. **3,** *fol. by* **around** (wind around) обма́тывать; обвёртывать: *wrap a towel around one's head,* обма́тывать/обвёртывать полоте́нце вокру́г головы́. *Wrap one's arms around someone,* заключи́ть кого́-нибудь в объя́тия. **4,** *fol. by* **up,** *colloq.* (finish; conclude) зака́нчивать; заключа́ть. *—v.i.* [*usu.* **wrap**

around] обвива́ться (вокру́г). *—n.* шаль; наки́дка. **—under wraps,** под спу́дом. **—wrapped up in,** поглощён (+ *instr.*); погружён в; углублён в.

wrapper *n.* обёртка: *candy wrapper,* обёртка от конфе́ты.

wrapping *n.* обёртка. **—wrapping paper,** обёрточная бума́га.

wrath *n.* гнев. **—wrathful,** *adj.* гне́вный.

wreak *v.t.* наноси́ть. *Wreak havoc on,* разоря́ть; опусто́шать.

wreath *n.* **1,** (garland) вено́к. **2,** (puff, as of smoke) кольцо́.

wreathe *v.t.* свива́ть. *His face was wreathed in smiles,* его́ лицо́ расплыло́сь в улы́бке.

wreck *v.t.* разруша́ть; разбива́ть. *Wreck a car,* разби́ть маши́ну. *The blast wrecked the building,* зда́ние разру́шилось от взры́ва. *Wreck someone's hopes,* разру́шить *or* разби́ть чьи-нибудь наде́жды. *—n.* **1,** (crash) круше́ние: *train wreck,* круше́ние по́езда. **2,** (anything badly damaged; person in bad shape) разва́лина.

wreckage *n.* обло́мки.

wrecker *n.* **1,** (one who wrecks or destroys) разру́шитель. **2,** (company that tears down buildings) фи́рма, занима́ющаяся сно́сом домо́в. **3,** (truck) авари́йная маши́на.

wren *n.* крапи́вник.

wrench *n.* **1,** (tool) (га́ечный) ключ. *Monkey wrench,* францу́зский ключ. **2,** (sudden pull; yank) рыво́к. **3,** (sprain) вы́вих. **4,** (emotional shock) потрясе́ние. *—v.t.* **1,** (twist; sprain) вы́вихнуть; вы́вернуть. **2,** (wrest) вырыва́ть.

wrest *v.t.* вырыва́ть: *wrest a gun from one's assailant,* вы́рвать пистоле́т у налётчика; *wrest concessions from the company,* вы́рвать усту́пки у компа́нии.

wrestle *v.i.* **1,** *sports* боро́ться. **2,** *fol. by* **with** (struggle with, as a problem) би́ться (над). **—wrestler,** *n.* боре́ц.

wrestling *n.* борьба́. *Wrestling match,* встре́ча по борьбе́.

wretch *n.* **1,** (unfortunate person) несча́стный. **2,** (despicable person) негодя́й.

wretched *adj.* **1,** (miserable) жа́лкий: *wretched existence,* жа́лкое существова́ние. **2,** (squalid) убо́гий; жа́лкий: *wretched hovel,* убо́гая/жа́лкая лачу́га. **3,** (awful) отврати́тельный: *wretched performance,* отврати́тельное исполне́ние.

wriggle *v.i.* **1,** (squirm) извива́ться. **2,** *fol. by* **out** (extricate oneself) выпу́тываться; вывёртываться: *wriggle out of a predicament,* выпу́тываться/вывёртываться из затрудни́тельного положе́ния. *Wriggle out of a commitment,* уви́ливать от обяза́тельства.

wring *v.t.* **1,** (twist) скру́чивать. *Wring one's hands,* лома́ть себе́ ру́ки. *Wring someone's neck,* сверну́ть ше́ю (+ *dat.*). **2,** *fol. by* **out** (squeeze the water from) выжима́ть; отжима́ть. **3,** (obtain by pressure or coercion) вырыва́ть; исторга́ть. **—wringing wet,** мо́крый, хоть вы́жми (*or* выжима́й).

wringer *n.* пресс.

wrinkle *n.* морщи́на; скла́дка. *—v.t.* **1,** (crease) мять. **2,** (draw up; pucker) мо́рщить. *—v.i.* мя́ться.

wrinkled *adj.* **1,** (of one's face) морщи́нистый; смо́рщенный. *Become wrinkled,* мо́рщиться. **2,** (of fabric) мя́тый; измя́тый. *Become wrinkled,* мя́ться.

wrist *n.* запя́стье.

wristband *n.* напу́льсник.

wrist watch ручны́е *or* нару́чные часы́.

writ *n.* прика́з *or* распоряже́ние суда́; исполни́тельный лист. **—Holy Writ,** свяще́нное писа́ние.

write *v.t. & i.* писа́ть: *write a letter,* писа́ть письмо́. *Write a check,* вы́писать чек. *Write for advice/information,* писа́ть с про́сьбой дать сове́т/информа́цию. *Know how to write,* уме́ть писа́ть. *This pen writes well,* э́та ру́чка хорошо́ пи́шет. *Hebrew is written from right to left,* на иври́те пи́шут спра́ва нале́во. **—write away for,** вы́писать по по́чте. **—write down,** запи́сывать. **—write in,** впи́сывать. **—write off, 1,** *bookkeeping* спи́сывать. **2,** (dismiss as no longer a factor) сбра́сывать со счето́в. **3,** (acknowledge as a failure) махну́ть руко́й на. **—write out,** выпи́сывать. **—write up,** опи́сывать; писа́ть отчёт о. *See also* **written.**

writer *n.* писа́тель: *writer of children's stories,* де́тский писа́тель. *Prose writer,* проза́ик. *Fiction writer,* беллетри́ст. *Writer of novels,* а́втор рома́нов. *The writer of the letter,* а́втор письма́.

writhe *v.i.* ко́рчиться. *He was writhing in pain,* он ко́рчился (*or* его́ ко́рчило) от бо́ли.

writing *n.* **1,** (act of writing; ability to write) писа́ние; письмо́. *Reading, writing, arithmetic,* чте́ние, письмо́, арифме́тика. *He is good at writing,* он хорошо́ пи́шет. *Take up writing,* стать писа́телем. **2,** (something written on a surface): *read the writing on the blackboard,* чита́ть то, что напи́сано на доске́. *I can't read your writing,* не могу́ разобра́ть ваш по́черк. **3,** *pl.* (written works) произведе́ния; сочине́ния: *the writings of Plato,* произведе́ния/сочине́ния Плато́на. **4,** (characters of a language) письмо́: *hieroglyphic writing,* иероглифи́ческое письмо́. *The language was only recently reduced to writing,* язы́к то́лько неда́вно стал пи́сьменным. **—adj.** пи́счий; пи́сьменный: *writing paper,* пи́счая бума́га; *writing table,* пи́сьменный стол. **—in writing,** пи́сьменно; в пи́сьменной фо́рме; в пи́сьменном ви́де.

written *adj.* **1,** (having been written) напи́санный: *well written,* хорошо́ напи́санный. **2,** (in writing) пи́сьменный: *written exam,* пи́сьменный экза́мен. *In written form,* в пи́сьменной фо́рме; в пи́сьменном ви́де.

wrong *adj.* **1,** (incorrect) непра́вильный; неве́рный: *wrong answer,* непра́вильный/неве́рный отве́т. *You*

are wrong, вы непра́вы; вы ошиба́етесь. *My watch is wrong,* мои́ часы́ иду́т неве́рно. *Be on the wrong track,* быть на ло́жном пути́. **2,** *preceded by* **the** (not the one intended) не тот: *I took the wrong train,* я сел не на тот по́езд. *Begin at the wrong end,* начина́ть не с того́ конца́. *You have the wrong number,* вы не туда́ попа́ли. *You've come to the wrong place,* вы попа́ли не по а́дресу. **3,** (inappropriate) неподходя́щий; неполо́женный. *At the wrong time,* в неподходя́щее/неполо́женное вре́мя; не во́время. *That was the wrong thing to say,* э́то не на́до бы́ло говори́ть. *Did I say something wrong?,* я что́-то не так сказа́л(а)? **4,** (amiss) нела́дный: *Something is wrong,* что́-то нела́дно. *Something is wrong with the phone,* что́-то случи́лось (*or* не ла́дится) с телефо́ном. *What's wrong with you?,* что с ва́ми? *What's wrong with it/that?,* чем э́то пло́хо?; что в э́том плохо́го? **5,** (immoral) дурно́й; гре́шный. *It is wrong to kill,* убива́ть грешно́. **6,** (not intended to be seen) ле́вый. *The wrong side,* ле́вая сторона́; изна́нка. *Wrong side out,* наизна́нку. **—adv. 1,** (incorrectly) непра́вильно; неве́рно. *A number of words are spelled wrong,* не́сколько слов непра́вильно напи́сано. *I guessed wrong,* я не угада́л. *Don't get me wrong,* пойми́те меня́ пра́вильно. *You've got everything wrong,* вы всё перепу́тали. **2,** (inside out) наизна́нку: *You've got your shirt on wrong,* у вас руба́шка наде́та наизна́нку. **—n.** зло: *right a wrong,* испра́вить зло. *Tell right from wrong,* отлича́ть добро́ от зла. *Two wrongs don't make a right,* злом зла не попра́вишь. **—v.t.** обижа́ть: *wrong a friend,* обижа́ть дру́га. **—do wrong,** греши́ть. **—get (something) wrong,** пу́тать; перепу́тывать. **—go wrong, 1,** (go astray) заблуди́ться. **2,** (go awry) не вы́йти; не получи́ться. *Everything went wrong,* всё пошло́ насма́рку. **3,** (degenerate) опуска́ться. **—in the wrong,** винова́тый.

wrongdoer *n.* правонаруши́тель. **—wrongdoing,** *n.* правонаруше́ние.

wrongful *adj.* **1,** (improper; illegal) незако́нный. **2,** (unjust) несправедли́вый; ло́жный. **—wrongfully,** *adv.* несправедли́во; ло́жно.

wrongly *adv.* **1,** (incorrectly; improperly) непра́вильно. **2,** (unjustly) несправедли́во; ло́жно.

wrought *adj.* отде́ланный: *finely wrought,* то́нко отде́ланный. **—wrought iron,** сва́рочное желе́зо.

wrought-up *adj.* взви́нченный.

wry *adj.* **1,** (twisted) криво́й. *Wry smile,* крива́я улы́бка. *Make a wry face,* криви́ться; мо́рщиться. **2,** (ironic; perverse) то́нкий: *wry humor,* то́нкий ю́мор.

X

X, x два́дцать четвёртая бу́ква англи́йского алфави́та; икс. —*n.* **1,** *math.* икс: *Let x equal y,* пусть икс ра́вен и́греку. **2,** (mark in lieu of a signature) крест.

xenon *n.* ксено́н.

X-ray *n.* **1,** (picture) рентге́н; рентгеногра́мма; рентге́новский сни́мок. *Have X-rays taken,* идти́ на рентге́н. **2,** *pl.* (rays) рентге́новы лучи́; рентге́н. —*adj.* рентге́новский. —*v.t.* просве́чивать.

xylophone *n.* ксилофо́н.

Y

Y, y два́дцать пя́тая бу́ква англи́йского алфави́та; и́грек.

yacht *n.* я́хта. —**yachtsman,** *n.* яхтсме́н.

yak *n.* як.

yam *n.* **1,** (tropical plant) ямс. **2,** (sweet potato) бата́т.

yammer *v.i., colloq.* **1,** (whine; complain) ныть. **2,** (talk loudly) ора́ть.

yank *v.t., colloq.* дёргать. *Yank the covers off someone,* стащи́ть одея́ла с кого́-нибудь. —*n.* рыво́к.

Yankee *n.* я́нки.

yap *v.i.* **1,** (bark) тя́вкать. **2,** *slang* (jabber) тарато́рить.

yard *n.* **1,** (unit of length) ярд. **2,** (area surrounded by buildings) двор. *Barnyard,* пти́чий двор. *Lumber yard,* лесно́й склад. **3,** *R.R.* парк. *Freight yard,* това́рная ста́нция.

yardstick *n.* **1,** (measuring stick) ме́рка. **2,** *fig.* (standard) ме́рка; мери́ло.

yarn *n.* **1,** (spun fiber) пря́жа. **2,** *colloq.* (story) ро́ссказни.

yawl *n.* ял.

yawn *v.i.* **1,** (open the mouth, when sleepy) зева́ть. **2,** (gape, as of an opening) зия́ть: *yawning abyss,* зия́ющая про́пасть. —*n.* зево́к.

yaws *n.* фрамбе́зия.

ye *pers. pron., archaic* вы. —*def. art., archaic* = **the.**

yea *adv., archaic* да. —*n.* за: *ten yeas, two nays,* де́сять за, два про́тив.

year *n.* год. *Three years,* три го́да. *Five years,* пять лет. *Year after year,* из го́да в год. *He is in his second year at college,* он на второ́м ку́рсе университе́та.

yearbook *n.* ежего́дник.

yearling *n.* годова́лое живо́тное.

yearly *adj.* ежего́дный; годово́й. —*adv.* ежего́дно; раз в год.

yearn *v.i.* [*usu.* **yearn for**] **1,** (crave) жа́ждать. **2,** (long to see) тоскова́ть по.

yearning *n.* тоска́: *yearning for one's homeland,* тоска́ по ро́дине.

year-old *adj.* годова́лый.

yeast *n.* дро́жжи.

yell *v.i.* крича́ть. —*n.* крик.

yellow *adj.* жёлтый. —*n.* жёлтый цвет. —*v.i.* желте́ть. —**yellowed,** *adj.* пожелте́лый.

yellow fever жёлтая лихора́дка.

yellowhammer *n.* (обыкнове́нная) овся́нка.

yellowish *adj.* желтова́тый.

yellowjacket *n.* оса́.

yelp *v.i.* тя́вкать; визжа́ть; взви́згивать. —*n.* визг; взвизг.

Yemenite *also,* **Yemeni** *adj.* йе́менский.

yen *n.* **1,** (monetary unit) ие́на. **2,** *colloq.* (longing) жа́жда; страсть.

yes *adv.* да: *yes or no,* да и́ли нет. *Yes, sir!, mil.* так то́чно!; есть! —**yes man,** *colloq.* подпева́ла; подголо́сок.

yesterday *n. & adj.* вчера: *Yesterday was Tuesday,* вчера был вторник. *Since yesterday,* со вчерашнего дня. —*adj.* [*usu.* **yesterday's**] вчерашний: *yesterday's weather,* вчерашняя погода. —**the day before yesterday,** позавчера. —**yesterday morning,** вчера утром.

yet *adv.* ещё: *not yet,* нет ещё. *He hasn't come yet,* он ещё не пришёл. *Yet another example,* ещё один пример. *I'll beat him yet!,* я его ещё (когда-нибудь) побью! *Don't take your coat off yet!,* не снимайте пока пальто. ◆ *In interr. sentences,* уже: *Have you eaten yet?,* вы уже поели? *Has the mail come yet?,* почта уже пришла? —*conj.* но; однако. *Yet he keeps trying,* но он всё старается. —**as yet,** пока что; пока ещё; до сих пор.

yew *n.* тис.

Yiddish *n.* идиш: *speak Yiddish,* говорить на идише. —*adj.* на идише: *a Yiddish newspaper,* газета на идише.

yield *v.t.* **1,** (bear) приносить: *yield fruit,* приносить плоды. **2,** (produce; bring about) давать; приносить: *yield results/ a profit/,* давать *or* приносить результаты/прибыль. **3,** (give up; surrender) сдавать; уступать. *Yield the right of way,* уступать дорогу. *Yield the floor to,* давать *or* предоставлять слово (+ *dat.*). —*v.i.* **1,** (give in) уступать; поддаваться: *yield to pressure,* уступать/поддаваться давлению. *Yield to force,* уступать *or* подчиняться силе. *Yield to someone's demands,* уступать чьим-нибудь требованиям. *They refused to yield on this point,* в этом вопросе они стояли на своём. **2,** (give way) поддаться; подаваться: *The door yielded,* дверь поддалась *or* подалась. —*n.* **1,** (amount yielded) урожай; урожайность. *Yield of milk,* удой; надой. **2,** (return, as on an investment) доход; отдача.

yoga *n.* йога. —**yogi,** *n.* йог.

yogurt *also,* **yoghurt** *n.* йогурт.

yoke *n.* **1,** (device for coupling draft animals) ярмо. **2,** (for carrying buckets) коромысло. **3,** (of a dress) кокетка. **4,** *fig.* (oppressive domination) иго; гнёт; ярмо. —*v.t.* впрягать в ярмо. *Yoke to a plow,* впрягать (*e.g.* волов) в плуг.

yokel *n., colloq.* деревенщина.

yolk *n.* желток.

yonder *adj.* вон тот. —*adv.* вон там.

yore *n., in* **in days of yore,** во время оно; *since days of yore,* издавна.

you *pers. pron.* **1,** *sing.* (*familiar*) ты; (*polite*) вы. *You and I,* мы с вами. *You are right,* ты прав/права; вы правы. *You are very funny,* вы очень смешной (смешная). **2,** *pl.* вы: *the three of you,* вы втроём. *When are (the two of) you planning to get married?,*

когда вы собираетесь пожениться? **3,** (a person; anyone) *rendered by the 2nd person sing. of the verb:* *You get used to it after a while,* со временем привыкаешь. *There is nothing you can do,* ничего не поделаешь.

young *adj.* молодой: *young woman/bride/couple,* молодая женщина/невеста/чета. *Young children,* маленькие дети. *A lamb is a young sheep,* ягнёнок — молодая овца. *He died young,* он умер молодым. —*n.* **1,** *preceded by the* (young people) молодёжь. **2,** (offspring) детёныши. —**young and old alike,** от мала до велика; стар и млад.

younger *comp. adj.* младший: *my younger brother,* мой младший брат. *He is younger than me,* он моложе меня. *The younger generation,* молодое поколение. *That hairdo makes you look younger,* причёска вас молодит.

young-looking *adj.* моложавый.

youngster *n.* мальчик; юноша.

your *poss. adj.* **1,** *sing.* (*familiar*) твой; (*polite*) ваш: *your sisters,* твои/ваши сёстры. *Wash your hands!,* вымой руки! *It's in your coat pocket,* это у вас в кармане пиджака. *I have no objection to your going,* у меня нет возражений против того, чтобы вы пошли. ◆ *When the possessor is the subject of the sentence,* свой: *You forgot your glasses,* ты забыл свои очки. **2,** *pl.* ваш: *Where are your toys?,* где ваши игрушки?

yours *poss. pron.* твой; ваш: *Is this coat yours?,* это твоё/ваше пальто? *A friend of yours,* один ваш друг; один из ваших друзей. *I'm a big admirer of yours,* я ваш большой поклонник. —**yours truly,** преданный вам.

yourself *pers. pron.* **1,** *used for emphasis,* (ты) сам (сама); (вы) сами. **2,** *used reflexively,* себя. *Did you hurt yourself,* вы ушиблись? *You ought to be ashamed of yourself!,* как вам не стыдно! —**by yourself, 1,** (alone) один (одна). **2,** (without help) сам (сама, сами).

youth *n.* **1,** (quality of being young; one's early years) молодость; юность. *In my youth,* в молодости. **2,** (young man) юноша. **3,** (young people collectively) молодёжь. *Youth festival,* фестиваль молодёжи.

youthful *adj.* юный; молодой; юношеский. *Youthful appearance,* моложавый вид. *Youthful ardor,* юношеский/молодой задор.

ytterbium *n.* иттербий.

yttrium *n.* иттрий.

yuan *n.* юань.

yucca *n.* юкка.

Yugoslav *adj.* [*also,* **Yugoslavian**] югославский.

Yule *n.* святки. *Also,* **Yuletide.**

Z

Z, z двáдцать шестáя бýква англи́йского алфави́та. —**from A to Z,** от A до Я.

zeal *n.* усéрдие; рвéние. —**zealot,** *n.* фанáтик.

zealous *adj.* усéрдный; рети́вый; рéвностный; рья́ный. —**zealously,** *adv.* усéрдно; рети́во.

zebra *n.* зéбра.

zebu *n.* зéбу.

zenith *n.* зени́т.

zephyr *n.* зефи́р.

zeppelin *n.* цеппели́н.

zero *n.* нуль. —*adj.* нулевóй. —*v.t.* [*usu.* **zero in**] пристрéливать. —*v.i.* [*usu.* **zero in on**] пристрéливать; пристрéливаться по.

zest *n.* **1,** (keen enjoyment) смак. *Zest for life,* жизнерáдостность. **2,** (flavor) пикáнтность; изю́минка.

Zeus *n.* Зевс.

zigzag *n.* зигзáг. —*adj.* зигзагообрáзный. —*v.i.* дéлать зигзáги; петля́ть.

zinc *n.* цинк. —*adj.* ци́нковый. —**zinc oxide,** óкись ци́нка. —**zinc white,** ци́нковые бели́ла.

zinnia *n.* ци́нния.

Zionism *n.* сиони́зм. —**Zionist,** *n.* сиони́ст. —*adj.* сиони́стский.

zip *n.* **1,** (whizzing sound) свист. **2,** *colloq.* (vim; pep) прыть. —*v.t.* [*usu.* **zip up**] застёгивать (на мóлнию). —*v.i.* **1,** *colloq.* (move rapidly) мчáться. **2,** *slang* (make a quick errand) сбéгать.

zipper *n.* мóлния.

zircon *n.* цирки́н.

zirconium *n.* цирки́ний.

zither *n.* ци́тра.

zloty *n.* злóтый.

zodiac *n.* зодиáк.

zonal *adj.* зонáльный.

zone *n.* зóна; пóяс; полосá. *Time zone,* часовóй пóяс. —*v.t.* разделя́ть на зóны.

zoo *n.* зоопáрк.

zoology *n.* зоолóгия. —**zoological,** *adj.* зоологи́ческий. —**zoologist,** *n.* зоóлог.

zoom *v.i.* **1,** (fly suddenly upwards) взмывáть. **2,** *fig.* (rise rapidly) подскáкивать. **3,** (move rapidly) мчáться.

Zulu *n.* зулýс. —*adj.* зулýсский.

zwieback *n.* сухáрь.

zygote *n.* зигóта.

Russian-English
Section

A

А, а *n.neut.* first letter of the Russian alphabet. **—от А до Я,** from A to Z.

а *conj.* **1,** and: Хорошо́!, а вы?, fine!, and you? Сего́дня гу́сто, а за́втра пу́сто, feast today and fast tomorrow. **2,** but: Я приду́, а он нет, I'll come but he won't. Я ду́мал, что ты мужчи́на, а ты ещё ребёнок, I thought you were a man, but you are still a child. *—particle* and; so: А что случи́лось с Бори́сом?, and what ever happened to Boris? А что он сказа́л?, and/so what did he say? *—interj., expressing various emotions,* oh!; ah!: А!, что я наде́лал(а)!, oh!, what have I done! А, вот молоде́ц!, ah, that's a fine fellow!

абажу́р *n.* lampshade.

абба́т *n.* abbot. **—аббати́са,** *n.* abbess. **—абба́тство,** *n.* abbey.

аббревиату́ра *n.* **1,** abbreviation. **2,** acronym.

аберра́ция *n.* aberration.

абза́ц *n.* **1,** indentation; indention. **2,** paragraph.

абитурие́нт *n.* **1,** *obs.* person graduating secondary school. **2,** applicant/candidate for admission to a university.

абонеме́нт *n.* subscription (*to a series of concerts, lectures, etc.*).

абоне́нт *n.* **1,** user (*of a telephone*). **2,** member (*of a library*). **3,** subscriber (*to a series of cultural events*).

аборда́ж *n., naval* boarding (*of an enemy vessel*). **—брать на аборда́ж,** to board (an enemy vessel).

абориге́н *n.* aborigine.

або́рт *n.* abortion.

абрази́в *n.* abrasive. **—абрази́вный,** *adj.* abrasive.

абракада́бра *n.* abracadabra.

абрико́с *n.* **1,** apricot. **2,** apricot tree. **—абрико́совый,** *adj.* apricot.

а́брис *n.* outline; contour.

абсе́нт (сэ) *n.* absinthe.

абсолю́т *n.* absolute.

абсолюти́зм *n.* absolutism. **—абсолюти́ст,** *n.* absolutist. **—абсолюти́стский,** *adj.* absolutist.

абсолю́тно *adv.* absolutely.

абсолю́тный *adj.* absolute. **—абсолю́тный нуль, 1,** absolute zero. **2,** an absolute nothing (*said of a person*). **—абсолю́тный слух,** absolute (*or* perfect) pitch.

абсорби́ровать *v.impfv. & pfv.* [*pres.* **-рую, -руешь**] to absorb.

абсо́рбция *n.* absorption.

абстраги́ровать *v.impfv. & pfv.* [*pres.* **-рую, -руешь**] to abstract.

абстра́ктный *adj.* abstract. **—абстра́ктно,** *adv.* in an abstract manner; in the abstract.

абстракциони́зм *n.* abstract art. **—абстракциони́ст,** *n.* abstract artist.

абстра́кция *n.* abstraction.

абсу́рд *n.* absurdity. **—доводи́ть до абсу́рда,** to carry to the point of absurdity.

абсу́рдный *adj.* absurd; preposterous. **—абсу́рдность,** *n.f.* absurdity.

абсце́сс *n.* abscess.

абсци́сса *n.* abscissa.

абха́з *n.m.* [*fem.* **абха́зка**] Abkhaz (*one of a people inhabiting the Caucasus*). **—абха́зский,** *adj.* Abkhazian.

аванга́рд *n.* **1,** *mil.* advance guard. **2,** *fig.* vanguard: в аванга́рде, in the vanguard; in the forefront.

авангарди́зм *n.* avant-gardism. **—авангарди́ст,** *n.* member of the avant-garde; *pl.* avant-garde. **—авангарди́стский,** *adj.* avant-garde.

аванга́рдный *adj.* **1,** *mil.* vanguard (*attrib.*). **2,** *fig.* vanguard; leading: аванга́рдная роль, vanguard/leading role.

аванза́л *n.* anteroom; antechamber.

аванпо́ст *n., mil.* outpost.

ава́нс *n.* **1,** advance (*of money*). **2,** *pl., obs.* advances; overtures.

ависи́ровать *v.impfv. & pfv.* [*pres.* **-рую, -руешь**] to advance money to (an enterprise, organization, etc.).

ава́нсом *adv.* in advance.

авансце́на *n.* proscenium.

авантю́ра *n.* adventure; (risky) venture.

авантюри́зм *n.* adventurism.

авантюри́ст *n.* **1,** *obs.* adventurer. **2,** adventurist. **—авантюристи́ческий,** *adj.* adventuristic.

авантю́рный *adj.* **1,** speculative; risky. **2,** shady. **3,** (*of a story, novel, etc.*) adventure (*attrib.*).

ава́рец [*gen.* **-рца**] *n.m.* [*fem.* **-рка**] Avar (*one of a people inhabiting the Caucasus*). **—ава́рский,** *adj.* Avar.

авари́йность *n.f.* accident rate.

авари́йный *adj.* **1,** salvage (*attrib.*); wrecking (*attrib.*): авари́йная маши́на, wrecker; tow truck. **2,** emergency (*attrib.*): авари́йная поса́дка, emergency landing; crash landing. Авари́йный люк, escape hatch. **3,** unsafe.

ава́рия *n.* **1,** accident; crash; wreck. **2,** breakdown. **3,** mishap.

ава́ры *n.pl.* [*sing.* **ава́р**] Avars (*powerful Turkic people of the 6th–9th centuries*).

а́вгиев *adj., in* **а́вгиевы коню́шни**, Augean stables.

авгу́р *n.* augur.

а́вгуст *n.* August. —**а́вгустовский**, *adj.* August (*attrib.*).

авеню́ *n.f. indecl.* avenue.

авиа- *prefix* air-: авиаба́за, air base.

авиабиле́т *n.* plane ticket.

авиабо́мба *n.* aerial bomb.

авиакомпа́ния *n.* **1**, aircraft company. **2**, airline.

авиаконстру́ктор *n.* aircraft designer.

авиакосми́ческий *adj.* aerospace (*attrib.*).

авиали́ния *n.* air route.

авиамоде́ль (дэ) *n.f.* model airplane.

авиано́сец [*gen.* **-сца**] *n.* aircraft carrier.

авиапо́чта *n.* air mail.

авиа́тор *n.* aviator.

авиатра́сса *n.* air route.

авиацио́нный *adj.* **1**, aviation (*attrib.*). **2**, aeronautical. **3**, aircraft (*attrib.*); airplane (*attrib.*).

авиа́ция *n.* **1**, aviation. **2**, airplanes; aircraft.

авио́ника *n.* avionics.

авока́до *n. indecl.* avocado.

аво́сь *particle, colloq.* maybe; perhaps. —**на аво́сь**, hit or miss; by guesswork. Наде́яться *or* полага́ться на аво́сь, to trust to luck.

аво́ська [*gen. pl.* **-сек**] *n., colloq.* string bag.

авра́л *n.* **1**, *naval* job involving all hands. **2**, *colloq.* rush job. —**авра́льный**, *adj.* rush (*attrib.*); emergency.

авро́ра *n.* aurora.

австрали́ец [*gen.* **-и́йца**] *n.m.* [*fem.* **-и́йка**] Australian. —**австрали́йский**, *adj.* Australian.

австри́ец [*gen.* **-и́йца**] *n.m.* [*fem.* **-и́йка**] Austrian. —**австри́йский**, *adj.* Austrian.

авто- *prefix* **1**, self-; auto-: автопортре́т, self-portrait; автобиогра́фия, autobiography. **2**, automatic: автопило́т, automatic pilot. **3**, automobile: автозаво́д, automobile factory.

автоба́за *n.* motor transport depot.

автобиогра́фия *n.* autobiography. —**автобиографи́ческий**; **автобиографи́чный**, *adj.* autobiographical.

авто́бус *n.* bus. —**авто́бусный**, *adj.* bus (*attrib.*).

автовокза́л *n.* bus terminal.

авто́граф *n.* **1**, autograph. **2**, original handwritten manuscript.

автодро́м *n.* speedway.

автожи́р *n.* autogiro.

автозаво́д *n.* automobile factory.

автозапра́вочный *adj., in* **автозапра́вочная ста́нция**, gas station; service station.

автока́р *n.* self-propelled cart.

автоколо́нна *n.* column of automobiles; motorcade.

автокра́т *n.* autocrat. —**автокра́тия**, *n.* autocracy. —**автократи́ческий**, *adj.* autocratic.

автол *n.* motor oil.

автомагистра́ль *n.f.* superhighway; expressway; thruway.

автома́т *n.* **1**, any automatic device: телефо́н-автома́т, pay phone. **2**, vending machine. **3**, automaton; robot. **4**, submachine gun; Tommy gun.

автоматиза́ция *n.* automation: автоматиза́ция произво́дства, automation of production.

автоматизи́ровать *v.impfv. & pfv.* [*pres.* **-рую, -руешь**] to automate.

автома́тика *n.* automation: век автома́тики, the age of automation.

автомати́чески *adv.* automatically.

автомати́ческий *adj.* **1**, automatic; automatically operated. **2**, automatic; mechanical; involuntary.

автома́тчик *n.* soldier armed with a submachine gun.

автомаши́на *n.* motor vehicle.

автомеха́ник *n.* auto mechanic.

автомобили́ст *n.* motorist.

автомоби́ль *n.m.* automobile. —**автомоби́льный**, *adj.* automobile (*attrib.*); vehicle (*attrib.*); automotive.

автоно́мия *n.* **1**, autonomy. **2**, autonomous republic.

автоно́мный *adj.* **1**, autonomous. **2**, *mech.* self-contained.

автопило́т *n.* automatic pilot.

автопортре́т *n.* self-portrait.

а́втор *n.* **1**, author. **2**, (*with gen.*) writer (*of a letter, novels, etc.*); composer (*of a work of music*); creator (*of a work of art*).

авторемо́нт *n.* car repairs. —**авторемо́нтный**, *adj.* car-repair.

авторефера́т *n.* abstract (*by the author*).

авторизова́ть *v.impfv. & pfv.* [*pres.* **-зу́ю, -зу́ешь**] to authorize (the translation, reproduction, etc. of a literary work).

авторитари́зм *n.* authoritarianism.

авторита́рный *adj.* authoritarian.

авторите́т *n.* **1**, authority; prestige. **2**, an authority. —**авторите́тный**, *adj.* authoritative.

а́вторский *adj.* author's. —**а́вторское пра́во**, copyright.

а́вторство *n.* authorship.

авторучка [*gen. pl.* **-чек**] *n.* fountain pen.

автостоя́нка [*gen. pl.* **-нок**] *n.* **1**, parking lot. **2**, parking garage.

автостра́да *n.* superhighway; expressway; thruway.

автотра́нспорт *n.* motor transport.

автофурго́н *n.* van.

ага́ *interj.* aha!

ага́ва *n.* agave.

ага́т *n.* agate. —**ага́товый**, *adj.* agate.

агглютинати́вный *adj.* agglutinative. —**агглютина́ция**, *n.* agglutination.

аге́нт *n.* agent. —**аге́нтство**, *n.* agency.

агенту́ра *n.* **1**, intelligence agency; secret service. **2**, secret agents. —**аге́нтурный**, *adj.* intelligence (*attrib.*).

агиогра́фия *n.* hagiography.

агита́тор *n.* political agitator.

агита́ция *n.* political agitation; propaganda work. —**агитацио́нный**, *adj.* agitation (*attrib.*); propaganda (*attrib.*).

агити́ровать *v.impfv.* [*pres.* **-рую, -руешь**] **1**, to agitate (*politically*); carry on propaganda work. **2**, [*pfv.* **сагити́ровать**] *colloq.* to urge; try to persuade.

аги́тка [*gen. pl.* **-ток**] *n., colloq.* piece of art propaganda; propaganda play, novel, etc.

агитпу́нкт *n.* local agitation and propaganda headquarters.

а́гнец [*gen.* а́гнца] *n., obs.* lamb.

агностици́зм *n.* agnosticism. —**агно́стик,** *n.* agnostic. —**агности́ческий,** *adj.* agnostic.

аго́ния *n.* agony; throes of death.

агра́рный *adj.* agrarian.

агрега́т *n.* unit: силово́й агрега́т, power unit.

агресси́вный *adj.* aggressive. —**агресси́вность,** *n.f.* aggressiveness.

агре́ссия *n.* aggression. —**агре́ссор,** *n.* aggressor.

агроно́мия *n.* agronomy. —**агроно́м,** *n.* agronomist. —**агрономи́ческий,** *adj.* agronomic.

ад [*2nd loc.* аду́] *n.* hell.

ада́жио *adv. & n. indecl.* adagio.

ада́мов *adj.* Adam's. —**ада́мово я́блоко,** Adam's apple.

адапта́ция *n., biol.* adaptation.

ада́птер (тэ) *n., mech.* adapter.

адапти́роваться *v.impfv. & pfv.* [*pres.* -**ру́юсь,** -**ру́ешься**] (*with* к) to adjust (to); adapt (to).

адвока́т *n.* **1,** lawyer; attorney. **2,** advocate (*in court*). —**адвока́тский,** *adj.* lawyer's; lawyers'; legal.

адвокату́ра *n.* **1,** the practice of law. **2,** lawyers collectively; the bar.

адеква́тный (дэ) *adj.* **1,** appropriate. **2,** (*with dat.*) equal (to).

адено́ид (дэ) *n.* adenoid.

аде́пт (дэ) *n.* adherent; follower; supporter.

администрати́вный *adj.* administrative.

администра́тор *n.* administrator.

администра́ция *n.* administration; management; managing officials.

администри́ровать *v.impfv.* [*pres.* -**ру́ю, -ру́ешь**] to administer; manage.

адмира́л *n.* admiral.

адмиралте́йство *n.* **1,** admiralty. **2,** the Admiralty (*building*).

адмира́льский *adj.* admiral's.

адренали́н *n.* adrenalin.

а́дрес [*pl.* адреса́] *n.* address. —**по а́дресу** (+ *gen.*); **в а́дрес** (+ *gen.*); **по (чьему́-нибудь) а́дресу,** about; regarding; concerning; directed at/toward/against: по моему́ а́дресу, about me; directed against me. —**не по а́дресу,** to the wrong quarter, place or party.

адреса́т *n.* addressee.

а́дресный *adj.* address (*attrib.*). —**а́дресная кни́га,** directory. —**а́дресный стол; а́дресное бюро́,** address bureau.

адресова́ть *v.impfv. & pfv.* [*pres.* -**су́ю, -су́ешь**] to address (a letter, question, etc.). —**адресова́ться,** *refl.* **1,** to be addressed. **2,** (*with* к) to address (someone); apply (to).

а́дский *adj.* **1,** of hell. **2,** hellish. **3,** fiendish; diabolical. **4,** *colloq.* colossal; stupendous.

адсорби́ровать *v.impfv. & pfv.* [*pres.* -**ру́ю, -ру́ешь**] to adsorb.

адсо́рбция *n.* adsorption.

адъюта́нт *n.* aide-de-camp; adjutant.

адыге́ец [*gen.* -е́йца] *n.m.* [*fem.* -е́йка] Adygei (one of a people inhabiting the Caucasus). —**адыге́йский,** *adj.* Adygei.

аж *particle & conj., colloq.* **1,** even. **2,** (*before numbers*) as many as. **3,** (*before prepositions*) as far as; right up to.

ажиота́ж *n.* **1,** price fixing. **2,** *fig.* excitement.

ажу́р *n.* **1,** *obs.* openwork. **2,** *bookkeeping* current basis. —**в ажу́ре,** *colloq.* in perfect order; shipshape.

ажу́рный *adj.* **1,** openwork (*attrib.*). **2,** finely wrought; delicate. —**ажу́рная стро́чка,** hemstitch.

аз [*gen.* аза́] *n.* **1,** old name of the letter A. **2,** *pl.* letters. **3,** *pl., fig.* rudiments; elements; fundamentals. —**начина́ть с азо́в,** to start from the beginning. —**ни аза́ не знать,** not to know a thing.

аза́лия *n.* azalea.

аза́рт *n.* zeal; ardor; fervor. —**войти́ в аза́рт,** to get carried away.

аза́ртный *adj.* **1,** ardent; zealous; fervent. **2,** heated; impassioned. —**аза́ртная игра́, 1,** game of chance. **2,** gambling.

а́збука *n.* **1,** alphabet. **2,** alphabet book; primer. **3,** rudiments; ABC's.

а́збучный *adj.* **1,** *obs.* alphabetical. **2,** rudimentary. —**а́збучная и́стина,** obvious truth; truism.

азербайджа́нец [*gen.* -нца] *n.m.* [*fem.* -нка] Azerbaijani. —**азербайджа́нский,** *adj.* Azerbaijani.

азиа́т *n.m.* [*fem.* -а́тка] Asian; Asiatic. —**азиа́тский,** *adj.* Asian; Asiatic.

а́зимут *n.* azimuth.

азо́т *n.* nitrogen. —**азо́тистый,** *adj.* nitrous. —**азо́тный,** *adj.* nitric; nitrogen (*attrib.*).

а́ист *n.* stork.

ай *interj.* **1,** oh! **2,** ouch!

айва́ *n.* **1,** quince. **2,** quince tree. —**айво́вый,** *adj.* quince.

айда́ *interj., colloq.* go!; let's go!

а́йсберг (бэ) *n.* iceberg.

акаде́мия *n.* academy. —**акаде́мик,** *n.* academician. —**академи́ческий,** *adj.* academic.

ака́нт *also,* **ака́нф** *n.* acanthus.

а́канье *n.* pronunciation of unstressed Russian o as a.

а́кать *v.impfv.* to pronounce unstressed Russian o as a.

ака́ция *n.* acacia.

аквала́нг *n.* aqualung. —**акваланги́ст,** *n.* skin diver.

аквамари́н *n.* aquamarine. —**аквамари́новый,** *adj.* aquamarine.

акварели́ст *n.* watercolorist.

акваре́ль *n.f.* watercolors; watercolor painting. —**акваре́льный,** *adj.* watercolor (*attrib.*).

аква́риум *n.* **1,** aquarium. **2,** fishbowl; fish tank.

аквати́нта *n.* aquatint.

аквато́рия *n.* area of water (*on the globe*).

акведу́к *n.* aqueduct.

акклиматиза́ция *n.* acclimatization; acclimation.

акклиматизи́ровать *v.impfv. & pfv.* [*pres.* -**ру́ю, -ру́ешь**] to acclimatize; acclimate. —**акклиматизи́роваться,** *refl.* to become acclimatized; become acclimated.

аккомпанеме́нт *n., music* accompaniment.

аккомпаниа́тор *n.* accompanist.

аккомпани́ровать *v.impfv.* [*pres.* **-ру́ю, -ру́ешь**] (*with dat.*) *music* to accompany.

акко́рд *n.* **1,** *music* chord. **2,** *obs.* agreement; accord.

аккордео́н *n.* accordion. **—аккордеони́ст,** *n.* accordionist.

акко́рдный *adj.* by the piece: акко́рдная рабо́та, piecework.

аккредити́в *n.* letter of credit.

аккредитова́ть *v.impfv. & pfv.* [*pres.* **-ту́ю, -ту́ешь**] *dipl.* to accredit.

аккумуля́тор *n.* battery. **—аккумуля́торный,** *adj., in* аккумуля́торная батаре́я, storage battery.

аккура́тно *adv.* **1,** neatly. **2,** punctually. **3,** efficiently. **4,** *colloq.* regularly. **5,** *colloq.* cautiously.

аккура́тность *n.f.* **1,** meticulousness; care. **2,** tidiness; neatness. **3,** punctuality; promptness.

аккура́тный *adj.* **1,** neat; tidy. **2,** punctual; prompt. **3,** efficient; thorough.

акони́т *n.* aconite; monkshood.

акр *n.* acre.

акроба́т *n.* acrobat. **—акроба́тика,** *n.* acrobatics. **—акробати́ческий,** *adj.* acrobatic.

акро́поль *n.m.* acropolis.

акрости́х *n.* acrostic.

акселера́тор *n.* accelerator.

аксельба́нт *n.* aiguillette; aglet.

аксессуа́р *n.* **1,** accessory. **2,** *pl.* secondary features; background details (*of a painting, literary work, etc.*). **3,** *pl.* stage props.

аксио́ма *n.* axiom. **—аксиомати́ческий,** *adj.* axiomatic.

акт *n.* **1,** act: престу́пный акт: criminal act. **2,** document; deed. **3,** *law* act. **4,** *theat.* act. **5,** [*usu.* выпускно́й акт] graduation exercise; commencement.

актёр *n.* actor. **—актёрский,** *adj.* actor's; actors'.

актёрство *n.* **1,** acting (*as a profession*). **2,** affected behavior; play-acting.

акти́в *n.* **1,** most active members of an organization. **2,** *finance* assets. **3,** *bookkeeping & fig.* credit side of the ledger.

активиза́ция *n.* intensification.

активизи́ровать *v.impfv. & pfv.* [*pres.* **-ру́ю, -ру́ешь**] to step up; intensify.

активи́ст *n.* (political or social) activist.

акти́вно *adv.* actively.

акти́вность *n.f.* activity; participation; involvement.

акти́вный *adj.* **1,** active. **2,** *econ.* favorable.

акти́ний *n.* actinium.

акти́ния *n.* sea anemone.

а́ктовый *adj., in* а́ктовый зал, (school) auditorium; assembly hall.

актри́са *n.* actress.

актуа́льность *n.f.* **1,** timeliness; relevance. **2,** urgency.

актуа́льный *adj.* [*short form* **-лен, -льна**] **1,** timely; current; relevant. **2,** urgent.

аку́ла *n.* shark.

акупункту́ра *n.* acupuncture.

аку́стик *n.* soundman.

аку́стика *n.* acoustics. **—акусти́ческий,** *adj.* acoustic; acoustical.

акуше́р *n.* obstetrician. **—акуше́рка,** *n.* midwife. **—акуше́рский,** *adj.* obstetric.

акуше́рство *n.* **1,** obstetrics. **2,** midwifery.

акце́нт *n.* accent: говори́ть с акце́нтом, to speak with an accent. **—де́лать акце́нт на** (+ *prepl.*), to accentuate; emphasize; place the emphasis on.

акценти́ровать *v.impfv. & pfv.* [*pres.* **-ру́ю, -ру́ешь**] **1,** *phonet.* to accent; stress. **2,** *fig.* to accentuate.

акци́з *n.* excise; excise tax. **—акци́зный,** *adj.* excise (*attrib.*).

акционе́р *n.* stockholder; shareholder.

акционе́рный *adj.* stockholders'; joint-stock (*attrib.*): акционе́рное о́бщество, joint-stock company; public company.

а́кция *n.* **1,** share of stock. **2,** *pl., fig.* stock: Его́ а́кции повыша́ются, his stock is rising. **3,** action.

алба́нец [*gen.* **-нца**] *n.m.* [*fem.* **-нка**] Albanian. **—алба́нский,** *adj.* Albanian.

а́лгебра *n.* algebra. **—алгебраи́ческий,** *adj.* algebraic.

алгори́тм *n.* algorithm.

алеба́рда *n.* halberd.

алеба́стр *n.* alabaster. **—алеба́стровый,** *adj.* alabaster.

александри́т *n.* alexandrite.

але́ть *v.impfv.* [*pfv.* **заале́ть**] **1,** to turn red; turn scarlet; blush. **2,** [*impfv. only*] (*of anything red*) to glow; gleam.

алжи́рец [*gen.* **-рца**] *n.m.* [*fem.* **-рка**] Algerian. **—алжи́рский,** *adj.* Algerian.

а́либи *n.neut. indecl.* alibi.

алиме́нты [*gen.* **тов**] *n.pl.* alimony. **—алиме́нтный,** *adj.* alimony (*attrib.*).

алкало́ид *n.* alkaloid.

алка́ть *v.impfv.* [*pres.* **а́лчу, а́лчешь** *or* **алка́ю, алка́ешь**] (*with gen.*) *obs.* to crave; hunger (for).

алка́ш [*gen.* **-каша́**] *n., colloq.* drunkard.

алкоголи́зм *n.* alcoholism. **—алкого́лик,** *n.* alcoholic.

алкого́ль *n.* alcohol. **—алкого́льный,** *adj.* alcohol (*attrib.*).

алла́х *n.* Allah.

аллего́рия *n.* allegory. **—аллегори́ческий,** *adj.* allegorical.

аллегре́тто *adv. & n. indecl.* allegretto.

алле́гро *adv. & n. indecl.* allegro.

аллерге́н *n.* allergen.

аллерги́я *n.* allergy. **—аллерги́ческий,** *adj.* allergic. **—аллерго́лог,** *n.* allergist.

алле́я *n.* tree-lined walk.

аллига́тор *n.* alligator.

аллилу́йя *interj.* hallelujah!

аллитера́ция *n.* alliteration.

алло́ *interj., used when answering the telephone,* hello!

аллопа́тия *n.* allopathy. **—аллопа́т,** *n.* allopath. **—аллопати́ческий,** *adj.* allopathic.

аллю́вий *n.* alluvium. **—аллювиа́льный,** *adj.* alluvial.

аллю́р *n.* gait (*of a horse*).

алма́з *n.* diamond. **—алма́зный,** *adj.* diamond.

ало́э *n.neut. indecl.* **1,** aloe (*plant*). **2,** aloes (*drug*).

алта́ец [*gen.* **-а́йца**] *n.m.* [*fem.* **-а́йка**] Altai (*one of a people inhabiting southern Siberia*).

алта́йский *adj.* **1,** Altai. **2,** Altaic.

алта́рь [*gen.* **алтаря́**] *n.m.* altar.

алте́й *n.* marsh mallow.

алты́н [*gen. pl.* **алты́н** *or* **алты́нов**] *n.* old Russian coin worth three kopecks; altyn.

алфави́т *n.* alphabet. —**алфави́тный,** *adj.* alphabetical.

алхи́мия *n.* alchemy. —**алхи́мик,** *n.* alchemist.

а́лчный *adj.* greedy. —**а́лчность,** *n.f.* greed.

а́лый *adj.* scarlet.

алыча́ *n.* a variety of plum.

альбатро́с *n.* albatross.

альбини́зм *n.* albinism. —**альбино́с,** *n.* albino.

альбо́м *n.* album.

альбуми́н *n.* albumin.

альвео́ла *n.* alveola. —**альвеоля́рный,** *adj.* alveolar.

алько́в *n.* alcove.

альмана́х *n.* literary miscellany.

альпака́ *n.m. or neut. indecl.* alpaca.

альпи́йский *adj.* Alpine.

альпини́зм *n.* mountain climbing. —**альпини́ст,** *n.* mountain climber. —**альпини́стский,** *adj.* for mountain climbers.

альт [*gen.* **альта́**] *n.* **1,** alto (*voice or singer*). **2,** viola.

альтернати́ва (тэ) *n.* alternative. —**альтернати́вный,** *adj.* alternative; alternate.

альтерна́тор (тэ) *n.* alternator.

альтиме́тр *n.* altimeter.

альто́вый *adj.* alto.

альтруи́зм *n.* altruism. —**альтруи́ст,** *n.* altruist. —**альтруисти́ческий,** *adj.* altruistic.

а́льфа *n.* alpha. —**а́льфа-лучи́,** alpha rays. —**а́льфа-части́ца,** alpha particle.

алья́нс *n.* alliance.

алюми́ний *n.* aluminum. —**алюми́ниевый,** *adj.* aluminum.

аляпова́тый *adj.* **1,** crude; crudely made. **2,** ugly.

аля́скинский *adj.* Alaskan.

амазо́нка [*gen. pl.* **-нок**] *n.* **1,** *myth.* Amazon. **2,** horsewoman. **3,** *obs.* riding habit.

амальга́ма *n.* **1,** amalgam. **2,** *fig.* amalgamation; mixture; blend.

амальгама́ция *n., chem.* amalgamation.

амальгами́ровать *v.impfv. & pfv.* [*pres.* **-рую, -руешь**] **1,** to amalgamate; alloy with mercury. **2,** to coat with an amalgam.

амара́нт *n.* amaranth.

амари́ллис *n.* amaryllis.

амба́р *n.* **1,** barn; granary. **2,** storehouse; warehouse. —**амба́рный,** *adj.* barn (*attrib.*).

амбицио́зный *adj.* haughty; conceited.

амби́ция *n.* **1,** arrogance; conceit. **2,** *pl.* ambitions. —**уда́риться в амби́цию,** to take umbrage; get into a huff.

а́мбра *n.* ambergris.

амбразу́ра *n.* embrasure; loophole.

амбро́зия *n.* **1,** ambrosia. **2,** ragweed.

амбулато́рия *n.* outpatient clinic; dispensary.

амбулато́рный *adj.* dispensary (*attrib.*). —**амбулато́рный больно́й,** outpatient.

амёба *n.m. or f.* ameba.

америка́нец [*gen.* **-нца**] *n.m.* [*fem.* **-нка**] American.

америка́нский *adj.* American.

америций *n.* americium.

амети́ст *n.* amethyst. —**амети́стовый,** *adj.* amethyst.

аминокислота́ [*pl.* **-ло́ты**] *n.* amino acid.

ами́нь *particle & interj.* amen!

аммиа́к *n.* ammonia.

аммиа́чный *adj.* ammonia (*attrib.*); ammonium (*attrib.*). —**аммиа́чная сели́тра,** ammonium nitrate.

аммо́ний *n.* ammonium. —**аммо́ниевый,** *adj.* ammonium (*attrib.*).

амнези́я *n.* amnesia.

амнисти́ровать *v.impfv. & pfv.* [*pres.* **-рую, -руешь**] to grant amnesty to.

амни́стия *n.* amnesty.

амора́льный *adj.* amoral; immoral. —**амора́льность,** *n.f.* amorality; immorality.

амортиза́тор *n.* shock absorber.

амортизацио́нный *adj.* **1,** shock-absorbing. **2,** *finance* amortization (*attrib.*). —**амортизацио́нный фонд,** sinking fund.

амортиза́ция *n.* **1,** amortization; depreciation. **2,** shock absorption.

амортизи́ровать *v.impfv. & pfv.* [*pres.* **-рую, -руешь**] **1,** to soften; cushion (blows, shocks, etc.). **2,** to amortize.

амо́рфный *adj.* amorphous.

ампе́р [*gen. pl.* **ампе́р**] *n.* ampere. —**ампермéтр,** *n.* ammeter.

амплиту́да *n., physics* amplitude.

амплуа́ *n.neut. indecl., theat.* (one's) kind of role.

а́мпула *n.* ampule.

ампута́ция *n.* amputation.

ампути́ровать *v.impfv. & pfv.* [*pres.* **-рую, -руешь**] to amputate.

амуле́т *n.* amulet; charm.

аму́р *n.* **1,** Cupid. **2,** *pl., obs., colloq.* love affairs.

амфи́бия *n.* **1,** amphibian. **2,** amphibious plane or vehicle.

амфитеа́тр *n.* **1,** amphitheater. **2,** *theat.* raised back rows of the orchestra.

ан *conj. & particle, colloq.* but; on the contrary: ан нет, but no.

анагра́мма *n.* anagram.

анако́нда *n.* anaconda.

ана́лиз *n.* **1,** analysis. **2,** *med.* test: ана́лиз кро́ви, blood test.

анализи́ровать *v.impfv. & pfv.* [*pfv. also* **проанали́зировать**; *pres.* **-рую, -руешь**] to analyze.

анали́тик *n.* analyst. —**аналити́ческий,** *adj.* analytic; analytical.

ана́лог *n.* analogue.

аналоги́чный *adj.* analogous.

анало́гия *n.* analogy.

анало́й *n.* lectern (*in a church*).

ана́льный *adj.* anal.

анана́с *n.* pineapple. —**анана́сный; анана́совый,** *adj.* pineapple.

ана́пест *n.* anapest.

анархи́зм *n.* anarchism. —**анархи́ст,** *n.* anarchist. —**анархи́стский,** *adj.* anarchist (*attrib.*). —**анар-**

хи́ческий, *adj.* anarchistic. —**анархи́чный,** *adj., col-loq.* chaotic.

ана́рхия *n.* **1,** anarchy. **2,** *fig., colloq.* anarchy; chaos.

ана́том *n.* anatomist.

анатоми́ровать *v.impfv. & pfv.* [*pres.* **-рую, -руешь**] to anatomize; dissect.

анато́мия *n.* anatomy. —**анатоми́ческий,** *adj.* anatomical.

ана́фема *n.* anathema.

анахрони́зм *n.* anachronism. —**анахрони́ческий,** *adj.* anachronistic.

анаэро́б *n.* anaerobe. —**анаэро́бный,** *adj.* anaerobic.

анга́р *n.* hangar.

а́нгел *n.* angel. —**а́нгельский,** *adj.* angelic.

анги́на *n.* angina.

англизи́ровать *v.impfv. & pfv.* [*pres.* **-рую, -руешь**] to Anglicize.

англи́йский *adj.* **1,** English. **2,** British. —**англи́йская була́вка,** safety pin. —**англи́йская ми́ля,** statute mile. —**англи́йская соль,** Epsom salt(s).

англика́нский *adj.* Anglican.

англици́зм *n.* Anglicism.

англича́нин [*pl.* **-ча́не, -ча́н**] *n.* **1,** Englishman. **2,** *pl.* the English; the British.

англича́нка [*gen. pl.* **-нок**] *n.* Englishwoman.

англосаксо́нский *adj.* Anglo-Saxon.

англофи́л *n.* Anglophile.

англоязы́чный *adj.* **1,** English-speaking. **2,** English-language.

анда́нте (тэ) *adv. & n.neut. indecl.* andante.

аневри́зма *n.* aneurysm.

анекдо́т *n.* **1,** anecdote; joke. **2,** amusing incident; funny thing.

анекдоти́ческий *adj.* **1,** anecdotal. **2,** [*also,* **анекдоти́чный**] improbable; incredible.

анеми́я *n.* anemia. —**анеми́чный,** *adj.* anemic.

анемо́метр *n.* anemometer.

анемо́н *n.* anemone. *Also,* **анемо́на.**

анеро́ид *n.* aneroid barometer.

анестезио́лог (нэстэ) *n.* anesthesiologist.

анестези́ровать (нэстэ) *v. impfv. & pfv.* [*pres.* **-рую, -руешь**] to anesthetize.

анестези́рующий (нэстэ) *adj.* anesthetic. —**анестези́рующее сре́дство,** anesthetic.

анестези́я (нэстэ) *n.* anesthesia.

анили́н *n.* aniline. —**анили́новый,** *adj.* aniline.

аними́зм *n.* animism. —**аними́ст,** *n.* animist. —**анимисти́ческий,** *adj.* animistic.

ани́с *n.* anise.

ани́совка *n.* anisette.

ани́совый *adj.* anise.

анке́та *n.* **1,** questionnaire; form; blank. **2,** *colloq.* survey.

анке́тный *adj.* questionnaire (*attrib.*). —**анке́тные да́нные,** biographical data.

анкла́в *n.* enclave.

анна́лы [*gen.* **лов**] *n.pl.* annals.

аннекси́ровать *v.impfv. & pfv.* [*pres.* **-рую, -руешь**] to annex.

анне́ксия *n.* annexation.

аннота́ция *n.* annotation.

аннули́рование *n.* annulment; cancellation; abrogation.

аннули́ровать *v.impfv. & pfv.* [*pres.* **-рую, -руешь**] to annul; cancel; abrogate.

ано́д *n.* anode.

анома́лия *n.* anomaly. —**анома́льный,** *adj.* anomalous.

анони́м *n.* **1,** anonymous author. **2,** anonymous work; anonymous letter.

анони́мка [*gen. pl.* **-мок**] *n., colloq.* anonymous letter.

анони́мный *adj.* anonymous. —**анони́мно,** *adv.* anonymously. —**анони́мность,** *n.f.* anonymity.

ано́нс *n.* announcement; notice (*of a performance*).

анонси́ровать *v.impfv. & pfv.* [*pres.* **-рую, -руешь**] to announce; advertise (a performance).

анорма́льный *adj.* abnormal.

анофе́лес *n.* anopheles.

анса́мбль *n.m.* ensemble.

антагони́зм *n.* antagonism. —**антагони́ст,** *n.* antagonist. —**антагонисти́ческий,** *adj.* antagonistic.

антаркти́ческий *adj.* antarctic.

анте́нна (тэ) *n.* antenna.

антиамерикани́зм *n.* anti-Americanism. —**антиамерика́нский,** *adj.* anti-American.

антибио́тик *n.* antibiotic.

антивещество́ *n.* antimatter.

антивое́нный *adj.* antiwar.

антиге́н *n.* antigen.

антидемократи́ческий *adj.* undemocratic.

антидепресса́нт (дэ) *n.* anti-depressant.

антиква́р *n.* antique dealer; antiquary. —**антиква́рный,** *adj.* antique.

антикоагуля́нт *n.* anticoagulant.

антикоммуни́зм *n.* anticommunism. —**антикоммуни́ст,** *n.* anticommunist. —**антикоммунисти́ческий,** *adj.* anticommunist.

антило́па *n.* antelope.

антиобледени́тель *n.m.* deicer.

антиобще́ственный *adj.* antisocial; harmful to society.

антипати́чный *adj.* unpleasant; disagreeable; antipathetic.

антипа́тия *n.* antipathy; aversion.

антипо́ды *n.pl.* [*sing.* **антипо́д**] **1,** antipodes. **2,** *fig.* (*of people*) opposites.

антиправи́тельственный *adj.* antigovernment.

антираке́та *n.* anti-missile missile; anti-ballistic missile.

антирелигио́зный *adj.* antireligious.

антисанита́рный *adj.* unsanitary.

антисемити́зм *n.* anti-Semitism. —**антисеми́т,** *n.* anti-Semite. —**антисеми́тский,** *adj.* anti-Semitic.

антисе́птик (сэ) *n.* antiseptic.

антисе́птика (сэ) *n.* **1,** antisepsis. **2,** antiseptics. —**антисепти́ческий,** *adj.* antiseptic.

антите́за (тэ) *n.* antithesis; opposite.

антите́зис (тэ) *n., logic* antithesis.

антите́ло [*pl.* **-тела́**] *n.* antibody.

антитети́ческий (тэ) *adj.* antithetical.

антитокси́н *n.* antitoxin. —**антитокси́ческий,** *adj.* antitoxic.

антифри́з *n.* antifreeze.

анти́христ *n.* Antichrist.

анти́чный *adj.* ancient. —**анти́чность,** *n.f.* antiquity.

антоло́гия *n.* anthology.

анто́ним *n.* antonym.

анто́новка *n.* a variety of apple.

антра́кт *n.* **1,** *theat.* intermission. **2,** musical interlude.

антраци́т *n.* anthracite. —**антраци́тный; антраци́товый,** *adj.* anthracite.

антреко́т *n.* rib steak.

антрепренёр *n.* **1,** impresario. **2,** *obs.* entrepreneur.

антресо́ли [*gen.* -лей] *n.pl.* **1,** attic. **2,** mezzanine.

антропо́ид *n.* anthropoid.

антрополо́гия *n.* anthropology. —**антропо́лог,** *n.* anthropologist. —**антропологи́ческий,** *adj.* anthropological.

антропоморфи́зм *n.* anthropomorphism. —**антропоморфи́ческий,** *adj.* anthropomorphic.

анфа́с *adv.* full-face: сня́ться анфа́с, to be photographed full-face.

анфила́да *n.* suite of rooms.

анча́р *n.* upas (*tree*).

анчо́ус *n.* anchovy.

аншла́г *n.,* *theat.* "sold out" sign. —**идти́** (*or* проходи́ть) **с аншла́гом,** to be sold out; play to packed houses.

аню́тин *adj., in* **аню́тины гла́зки,** pansy.

ао́рта *n.* aorta.

апартаме́нт *also,* **апарта́мент** *n., usu. pl.* luxurious living quarters.

апартеи́д (тэ) *n.* apartheid.

апати́чный *adj.* apathetic.

апа́тия *n.* apathy.

апелли́ровать *v.impfv. & pfv.* [*pres.* -рую, -руешь] **1,** *law* to appeal. **2,** (*with* к) to appeal (to).

апелляцио́нный *adj., law* of appeal; appellate.

апелля́ция *n.* **1,** *law* appeal. **2,** (*with* к) plea; appeal.

апельси́н *n.* **1,** orange. **2,** orange tree. —**апельси́нный; апельси́новый,** *adj.* orange (*attrib.*).

аперити́в *n.* aperitif.

апорту́ра *n.* aperture.

аплоди́ровать *v.impfv.* [*pres.* -рую, -руешь] (*with dat.*) to applaud.

аплодисме́нты [*gen.* -тов] *n.pl.* applause.

апло́мб *n.* self-assurance; aplomb.

апоге́й *n.* **1,** *astron.* apogee. **2,** *fig.* high point; pinnacle; acme.

апока́липсис *n.* **1,** apocalypse. **2,** *cap.* (book of) Revelation. —**апокалипти́ческий; апокалипси́ческий,** *adj.* apocalyptic.

апо́крифы [*gen.* фов] *n.pl.* Apocrypha. —**апокрифи́ческий,** *adj.* Apocryphal.

аполити́чный *adj.* apolitical. —**аполити́чность,** *n.f.* indifference to politics.

Аполло́н *n.* Apollo.

апологе́т *n.* apologist.

апологе́тика *n.* apologetics.

аполо́гия *n.* apologia.

апоплекси́ческий *adj.* apoplectic.

апопле́ксия *also,* **апоплекси́я** *n.* apoplexy; apoplectic stroke.

апостерио́ри (тэ) *adv.* a posteriori. —**апостерио́рный,** *adj.* a posteriori.

апо́стол *n.* apostle; disciple. —**апо́стольский,** *adj.* apostolic.

апостро́ф *n.* apostrophe.

апофео́з *n.* apotheosis.

аппара́т *n.* **1,** apparatus; device. **2,** *physiol.* system: дыха́тельный аппара́т, respiratory system. **3,** administrative machinery: госуда́рственный аппара́т, machinery of government. Аппара́т управле́ния, administrative apparatus. **4,** staff; personnel: аппара́т министе́рства, staff of the ministry. —**лета́тельный аппара́т,** aircraft. —**фотографи́ческий аппара́т,** camera.

аппарату́ра *n.* apparatus; equipment.

аппара́тчик *n.* **1,** maintenance man. **2,** party functionary; apparatchik.

аппе́ндикс *n., anat.* appendix. —**аппендици́т,** *n.* appendicitis.

апперко́т *n., boxing* uppercut.

апперце́пция *n., psychol.* apperception.

аппети́т *n.* appetite. —**прия́тного аппети́та!,** bon appétit!

аппети́тный *adj.* appetizing.

аппликату́ра *n., music* fingering.

апплика́ция *n.* appliqué work.

апре́ль *n.m.* April. —**апре́льский,** *adj.* April (*attrib.*).

априо́ри *adv.* a priori. —**априо́рный,** *adj.* a priori.

апроба́ция *n.* approbation; approval.

апроби́ровать *v.impfv. & pfv.* [*pres.* -рую, -руешь] to approve.

апси́да *n., archit.* apse; apsis.

апте́ка *n.* drugstore; pharmacy. —**как в апте́ке,** *colloq.* exactly.

апте́карский *adj.* pharmaceutical.

апте́карь *n.m.* pharmacist; druggist.

апте́чка [*gen. pl.* -чек] *n.* **1,** medicine chest; medicine cabinet. **2,** first-aid kit. **3,** *colloq.* small drugstore.

апте́чный *adj.* of or for drugs. —**апте́чный шкаф,** medicine chest; medicine cabinet.

ар *n.* are (*100 sq. meters*).

а́ра *n.* macaw.

ара́б *n.m.* [*fem.* **ара́бка**] Arab.

арабе́ска [*gen. pl.* -сок] *n.* arabesque. *Also,* **арабе́ск.**

ара́бский *adj.* **1,** Arab. **2,** Arabic.

арави́йский *adj.* Arabian.

араме́йский *adj.* Aramaic.

аранжи́ровать *v.impfv. & pfv.* [*pres.* -рую, -руешь] *music* to arrange.

аранжиро́вка *n., music* arrangement.

ара́п *n.* **1,** *obs.* Negro. **2,** *colloq.* cheat; crook.

ара́пник *n.* hunting whip.

а́рара *n.* macaw.

ара́хис *n.* **1,** peanut plant. **2,** peanuts. —**ара́хисовый,** *adj.* peanut (*attrib.*).

арба́ [*pl.* а́рбы *or* арбы́, арб, а́рбам *or* арба́м] *n.* a kind of cart used in the Crimea and the Caucasus.

арби́тр *n.* **1,** arbitrator; arbiter. **2,** *sports* referee; umpire.

арбитра́ж *n.* arbitration. —**арбитра́жный,** *adj.* of arbitration: арбитра́жный суд, court of arbitration.

арбу́з *n.* watermelon. —**арбу́зный,** *adj.* watermelon (*attrib.*).

аргенти́нец [*gen.* **-нца**] *n.m.* [*fem.* **-нка**] Argentinean. —**аргенти́нский,** *adj.* Argentinean; Argentine.

арго́ *n. indecl.* jargon; argo; cant.

арго́н *n.* argon.

аргуме́нт *n.* argument.

аргумента́ция *n.* argumentation; line of reasoning.

аргументи́ровать *v.impfv. & pfv.* [*pres.* **-рую, -руешь**] to argue; adduce arguments to support.

ареа́л *n.* geographic range *or* extent.

аре́на *n.* **1,** arena. **2,** (*with gen.*) the scene (of). **3,** *fig.* arena: полити́ческая аре́на, the political arena.

аре́нда *n.* **1,** rental. **2,** rent. **3,** leasing; leaseholding. Срок аре́нды, lease. —**брать в аре́нду,** to take a lease on; rent. —**сдава́ть в аре́нду,** to rent out.

аренда́тор *n.* renter; tenant; lessee; leaseholder.

аре́ндный *adj.* rent (*attrib.*); rental (*attrib.*): аре́ндная пла́та, rent. —**аре́ндный догово́р,** lease.

арендова́ть *v.impfv. & pfv.* [*pres.* **-ду́ю, -ду́ешь**] to rent; take a lease on.

ареопа́г *n.* supreme council.

аре́ст *n.* **1,** arrest; custody: брать под аре́ст, to place under arrest; take into custody. **2,** seizure; sequestration. Налага́ть аре́ст на, to seize; sequester; impound.

аресто́ванный *n., decl. as an adj.* prisoner.

арестова́ть [*infl.* **-ту́ю, -ту́ешь**] *v., pfv. of* **аресто́вывать.**

аресто́вывать *v.impfv.* [*pfv.* **арестова́ть**] **1,** to arrest. **2,** to seize; sequester; impound.

ари́ец [*gen.* **ари́йца**] *n.m.* [*fem.* **ари́йка**] Aryan. —**ари́йский,** *adj.* Aryan.

аристокра́т *n.* aristocrat. —**аристократи́ческий; аристократи́чный,** *adj.* aristocratic. —**аристокра́тия,** *n.* aristocracy.

аритми́я *n.* arrhythmia.

арифме́тика *n.* arithmetic. —**арифмети́ческий,** *adj.* arithmetic; arithmetical.

арифмо́метр *n.* calculating machine; calculator.

а́рия *n.* aria.

а́рка [*gen. pl.* **а́рок**] *n.* arch.

арка́да *n., archit.* arcade.

арка́н *n.* lasso.

арка́нить *v.impfv.* [*pfv.* **заарка́нить**] to lasso.

аркти́ческий *adj.* arctic.

арлеки́н *n.* harlequin.

арма́да *n.* armada.

армату́ра *n.* **1,** steel framework. **2,** fittings; fixtures. **3,** armature.

арме́ец [*gen.* **-е́йца**] *n., colloq.* army man; serviceman.

арме́йский *adj.* army (*attrib.*).

а́рмия *n.* army.

армяни́н [*pl.* **-мя́не, -мя́н**] *n.m.* [*fem.* **-мя́нка**] Armenian. —**армя́нский,** *adj.* Armenian.

а́рника *n.* arnica.

арома́т *n.* aroma; fragrance. —**арома́тный; аромати́чный; аромати́ческий,** *adj.* aromatic; fragrant.

а́рочный *adj.* arched: а́рочный мост , arched bridge.

арпе́джио *adv. & n. indecl.* arpeggio.

арсена́л *n.* **1,** arsenal; armory. **2,** *fig.* (*with gen.*) fund (of); store (of).

арта́читься *v.r.impfv.* to balk.

артезиа́нский *adj.* artesian: артезиа́нский коло́дец, artesian well.

арте́ль *n.f.* workers' cooperative; artel. —**арте́льный,** *adj.* artel (*attrib.*). —**арте́льщик,** *n., obs.* member of an artel.

артериа́льный *adj.* arterial.

артериосклеро́з *n.* arteriosclerosis.

арте́рия *n.* **1,** *anat.* artery. **2,** main route; artery. —**во́дная арте́рия,** waterway.

арти́кль *n.m., gram.* article.

артикули́ровать *v.impfv. & pfv.* [*pres.* **-рую, -руешь**] to articulate.

артикуля́ция *n.* articulation.

артилле́рия *n.* artillery. —**артиллери́йский,** *adj.* artillery (*attrib.*); gunnery (*attrib.*); ordnance (*attrib.*). —**артиллери́ст,** *n.* artilleryman; gunner.

арти́ст *n.m.* [*fem.* **-ти́стка**] performing artist; performer.

артисти́зм *n.* artistry.

артисти́ческий *adj.* **1,** artist's; performer's. **2,** artistic; masterly; masterful.

артисти́чность *n.f.* artistic talent; artistry.

артисти́чный *adj.* artistic.

арти́стка [*gen. pl.* **-сток**] *n., fem. of* **арти́ст.**

артишо́к *n.* artichoke.

артри́т *n.* arthritis.

а́рфа *n.* harp. —**арфи́ст; арфи́стка,** *n.* harpist.

архаи́зм *n.* archaism.

архаи́ческий *adj.* archaic. *Also,* **архаи́чный.**

арха́нгел *n.* archangel.

археоло́гия *n.* archeology. —**архео́лог,** *n.* archeologist. —**археологи́ческий,** *adj.* archeological.

архи́в *n.* archives. —**сдать в архи́в,** to put away for good; consign to oblivion.

архива́риус *n.* archivist.

архи́вный *adj.* archival.

архидья́кон *n.* archdeacon.

архиепи́скоп *n.* archbishop.

архиере́й *n., Orth. Ch.* bishop; archbishop; metropolitan.

архимандри́т *n., Orth. Ch.* archimandrite.

архипела́г *n.* archipelago.

архите́ктор *n.* architect. —**архите́кторский,** *adj.* architect's.

архитекту́ра *n.* architecture. —**архитекту́рный,** *adj.* architectural.

арши́н *n.* **1,** [*gen. pl.* **арши́н**] old Russian unit of length equal to approx. 28 inches; arshin. **2,** [*gen. pl.* **арши́нов**] ruler measuring an arshin in length. —**как арши́н проглоти́л,** ramrod straight. —**ме́рить на свой арши́н,** to measure by one's own yardstick.

арши́нный *adj.* **1,** of the length of an arshin. **2,** (*of writing, headlines, etc.*) huge.

арьерга́рд *n.* rear guard. —**арьерга́рдный,** *adj.* rearguard (*attrib.*).

ас *n.* ace (pilot).

асбе́ст *n.* asbestos. —**асбе́стовый,** *adj.* asbestos.

асе́птика (сэ) *n.* asepsis. —**асепти́ческий,** *adj.* aseptic.

асимметри́я *n.* asymmetry. —**асимметри́ческий**; **асимметри́чный**, *adj.* asymmetric; asymmetrical.

аске́т *n.* ascetic. —**аскети́зм**, *n.* asceticism. —**аске-ти́ческий**, *adj.* ascetic.

аскорби́новый *adj., in* **аскорби́новая кислота́**, ascorbic acid.

аспе́кт *n.* aspect; viewpoint; perspective.

а́спид *n.* **1**, asp (*snake*). **2**, *obs.* slate.

а́спидный *adj.* **1**, slate. **2**, slate-black. —**а́спидный сла́нец**, slate.

аспира́нт *n.* graduate student.

аспиранту́ра *n.* postgraduate studies. Занима́ться *or* учи́ться в аспиранту́ре, to go to graduate school.

аспири́н *n.* aspirin.

ассамбле́я *n.* assembly.

ассениза́ция *n.* sewage disposal.

ассигнова́ние *n.* **1**, allocation; appropriation. **2**, allocated sum; appropriation.

ассигнова́ть *v.impfv. & pfv.* [*pres.* **-ну́ю, -ну́ешь**] to allocate; appropriate (funds).

ассимили́ровать *v.impfv. & pfv.* [*pres.* **-рую, -руешь**] to assimilate. —**ассимили́роваться**, *refl.* to assimilate; become assimilated.

ассимиля́ция *n.* assimilation.

ассири́ец [*gen.* **-и́йца**] *n.m.* [*fem.* **-и́йка**] Assyrian. —**ассири́йский**, *adj.* Assyrian.

ассисте́нт *n.* **1**, assistant. **2**, lecturer; assistant professor.

ассисти́ровать *v.impfv.* [*pres.* **-рую, -руешь**] (*with dat.*) to assist.

ассона́нс *n.* assonance.

ассорти́ *n.neut. indecl.* assortment (*of things to eat*).

ассортиме́нт *n.* selection; assortment.

ассоциа́ция *n.* **1**, association; society. **2**, association (*in one's mind*).

ассоции́рованный *adj.* **1**, associated. **2**, associate: ассоции́рованный член, associate member.

ассоции́ровать *v.impfv. & pfv.* [*pres.* **-рую, -руешь**] to associate (*in one's mind*); make an association between.

аста́т *n.* astatine.

астеро́ид (тэ) *n.* asteroid.

астигмати́зм *n.* astigmatism. —**астигмати́ческий**, *adj.* astigmatic.

а́стма *n.* asthma. —**астма́тик**, *n., colloq.* asthmatic. —**астмати́ческий**, *adj.* asthmatic.

а́стра *n.* aster.

астроло́гия *n.* astrology. —**астро́лог**, *n.* astrologer. —**астрологи́ческий**, *adj.* astrological.

астроля́бия *n.* astrolabe.

астронавига́ция *n.* celestial navigation.

астроно́мия *n.* astronomy. —**астроно́м**, *n.* astronomer. —**астрономи́ческий**, *adj.* astronomic(al).

астрофи́зика *n.* astrophysics. —**астрофи́зик**, *adj.* astrophysicist. —**астрофизи́ческий**, *adj.* astrophysical.

асфа́льт *n.* asphalt.

асфальти́ровать *v.impfv. & pfv.* [*pres.* **-рую, -руешь**] to asphalt.

асфа́льтовый *adj.* asphalt.

асфи́ксия *also,* **асфикси́я** *n.* asphyxia; asphyxiation.

атави́зм *n.* atavism. —**атависти́ческий**, *adj.* atavistic.

ата́ка *n.* attack; assault.

атакова́ть *v.impfv. & pfv.* [*pres.* **-ку́ю, -ку́ешь**] to attack.

атакси́я *n.* ataxia.

атама́н *n.* Cossack chieftain; ataman.

атеи́зм (тэ) *n.* atheism. —**атеи́ст**, *n.* atheist. —**атеисти́ческий**, *adj.* atheistic.

ателье́ (тэ) *n.neut. indecl.* **1**, studio (*of an artist, photographer, etc.*). **2**, dress shop; tailor shop. **3**, repair shop. —**ателье́ мод**, fashion house.

атипи́чный *adj.* atypical.

атланти́ческий *adj.* Atlantic.

а́тлас *n.* atlas.

атла́с *n.* satin. —**атла́сный**, *adj.* satin.

атле́т *n.* athlete.

атле́тика *n.* athletics. —**лёгкая атле́тика**, track and field. —**тяжёлая атле́тика**, weightlifting.

атлети́ческий *adj.* athletic.

атмосфе́ра *n.* **1**, atmosphere. **2**, *fig.* atmosphere; climate. —**атмосфе́рный**, *adj.* atmospheric.

ато́лл *n.* atoll.

а́том *n.* atom.

а́томный *adj.* **1**, atomic. **2**, nuclear. —**а́томная бо́мба**, atomic bomb. —**а́томная эне́ргия**, **1**, atomic energy. **2**, nuclear power. —**а́томная электроста́н-ция**, nuclear power plant.

атона́льный *adj.* atonal. —**атона́льность**, *n.f.* atonality.

атрибу́т *n.* **1**, attribute; characteristic. **2**, *gram.* modifier; qualifier; attribute; attributive. —**атрибути́вный**, *adj.* attributive.

атропи́н *n.* atropine.

атрофи́рованный *adj.* atrophied.

атрофи́роваться *v.r.impfv. & pfv.* [*pres.* **-руется**] to atrophy; become atrophied.

атрофи́я *n.* atrophy.

атташе́ *n.m. indecl.* attaché.

аттеста́т *n.* certificate; diploma. —**аттеста́т зре́-лости**, secondary school diploma.

аттеста́ция *n.* **1**, certification: аттеста́ция учителе́й, certification of teachers. **2**, written recommendation; character reference. —**аттестацио́нный**, *adj.* certification (*attrib.*).

аттестова́ть *v.impfv. & pfv.* [*pres.* **-ту́ю, -ту́ешь**] **1**, to give (someone) a character reference. **2**, to give; award (someone) a certain rank. **3**, to grade (a pupil).

аттракцио́н *n.* **1**, number; act. **2**, *pl.* amusements; attractions (*in a park*).

ату́ *interj., used in hunting with hounds,* tallyho!; halloo! —**ату́ его́!**, sic 'im!

ау́ *interj., shouted to another from a distance,* hello there!

аудие́нция *n.* audience; formal interview.

аудито́рия *n.* **1**, auditorium; lecture hall. **2**, audience.

ау́кать *v.impfv.* [*pfv.* **ау́кнуть**] *colloq.* to shout "ау́!" —**ау́каться**, *refl., colloq.* to exchange shouts of "ау́!"

аукцио́н *n.* auction. —**аукционе́р**; **аукциони́ст**, *n.* auctioneer. —**аукцио́нный**, *adj.* auction (*attrib.*).

ау́л *n.* village in the Caucasus or Central Asia; aul.

аутенти́чный (тэ) *adj.* authentic; genuine. —**аутенти́чность,** *n.f.* authenticity.

аутса́йдер (дэ) *n., sports* outsider; long shot.

афа́зия *also,* **афази́я** *n.* aphasia.

афга́нец [*gen.* -нца] *n.m.* [*fem.* -нка] Afghan. —**афга́нский,** *adj.* Afghan; Afghanistani.

афе́лий *n.* aphelion.

афе́ра *n.* swindle; fraud. —**афери́ст,** *n.* swindler; crook.

афи́нский *adj.* Athenian.

афи́ша *n.* poster; bill.

афиши́ровать *v.impfv. & pfv.* [*pres.* -ру́ю, -ру́ешь] to flaunt; parade; advertise.

афори́зм *n.* aphorism. —**афористи́ческий; афористи́чный,** *adj.* aphoristic.

африка́анс *n.* Afrikaans.

африка́нер *n.* Afrikaner.

африка́нец [*gen.* -нца] *n.m.* [*fem.* -нка] African. —**африка́нский,** *adj.* African.

афро́нт *n., obs.* affront; insult.

аффе́кт *n.* fit of passion; burst of frenzy.

аффекта́ция *n.* affectation.

аффекти́рованный *adj.* affected.

ах *interj.* ah!; oh!

а́хать *v.impfv.* [*pfv.* а́хнуть] to shout "**ах!**"

ахилле́сов *adj., in* **ахилле́сова пята́,** Achilles' heel; **ахилле́сово сухожи́лие,** Achilles' tendon.

ахине́я *n., colloq.* nonsense: **нести́ ахине́ю,** to talk nonsense.

а́хнуть *v., pfv. of* **а́хать.**

а́ховый *adj., colloq.* **1,** rotten; lousy. **2,** unbelievable. **3,** reckless; wild.

ахтерште́вень (тэ) [*gen.* -вня] *n.m.* sternpost.

ахти́ *interj., obs.* oh! —**не ахти́ как,** *colloq.* not particularly. —**не ахти́ како́й,** *colloq.* no great shakes; nothing to rave about.

ацета́т *n.* acetate.

ацетиле́н *n.* acetylene. —**ацетиле́новый,** *adj.* acetylene.

ацето́н *n.* acetone.

ацте́к *n.* Aztec. —**ацте́кский,** *adj.* Aztec.

аэра́рий *n.* terrace for sunbathing.

аэра́ция *n.* aeration.

аэро́бика *n.* aerobics.

аэровокза́л *n.* air terminal.

аэродина́мика *n.* aerodynamics.

аэродинами́ческий *adj.* aerodynamic. —**аэродинами́ческая труба́,** wind tunnel.

аэродро́м *n.* airdrome; airfield.

аэрозо́ль *n.m.* aerosol. —**аэрозо́льный,** *adj.* aerosol (*attrib.*).

аэрона́вт *n.* balloonist; aeronaut. —**аэрона́втика,** *n.* aeronautics.

аэропла́н *n., obs.* airplane. —**аэропла́нный,** *adj., obs.* airplane (*attrib.*).

аэропо́рт [*2nd loc.* аэропорту́] *n.* airport.

аэросни́мок [*gen.* -мка] *n.* aerial photograph.

аэроста́т *n.* balloon; aerostat. —**аэроста́тика,** *n.* aerostatics.

аэрофотоаппара́т *n.* aerial camera.

аэрофотосъёмка *n.* aerial photography; aerial survey.

аятолла́ *n.m.* ayatollah.

Б

Б, б *n.neut.* second letter of the Russian alphabet.

б *particle* = **бы.**

ба *interj., colloq., expressing surprise,* well!

ба́ба *n.* **1,** *colloq.* woman. **2,** *colloq.* milksop; sissy. **3,** tall round cake. —**ро́мовая ба́ба,** baba au rhum. —**снежная ба́ба,** snowman.

бабёнка [*gen. pl.* -нок] *n., colloq.* young woman.

ба́бий [*fem.* -бья] *adj., colloq.* woman's. —**ба́бье ле́то,** Indian summer. —**ба́бьи ска́зки,** old wives' tales. —**ба́бье ца́рство,** petticoat government.

ба́бка [*gen. pl.* ба́бок] *n.* **1,** *colloq.* grandmother. **2,** *colloq.* old woman. **3,** [*often* **повива́льная ба́бка**] *obs.* midwife. **4,** *anat.* pastern. —**подби́ть ба́бки,** to total everything up.

ба́бник *n., colloq.* ladies' man; womanizer.

ба́бочка [*gen. pl.* -чек] *n.* **1,** butterfly. **2,** moth. **3,** [*also,* **га́лстук-ба́бочка**] *colloq.* bow tie.

ба́бушка [*gen. pl.* -шек] *n.* grandmother.

бава́рский *adj.* Bavarian.

бага́ж [*gen.* -гажа́] *n.* baggage; luggage. —**сдать ве́щи в бага́ж,** to check one's luggage through.

бага́жник *n.* **1,** luggage rack. **2,** trunk (*of an automobile*).

бага́жный *adj.* baggage (*attrib.*).

баго́р [*gen.* багра́] *n.* hook; boat hook. —**рыболо́вный баго́р,** gaff.

багрове́ть *v.impfv.* [*pfv.* побагрове́ть] to turn crimson; flush.

багро́вый *adj.* crimson.

багря́нец [*gen.* -нца] *n.* crimson.

бадминто́н *n.* badminton.

бадья́ *n.* bucket; pail.

ба́за *n.* **1,** base. **2,** basis; foundation. **3,** depot. **4,** camp; lodge; center; facility: тури́стская ба́за, tourist center; лы́жная ба́за, ski lodge. **—ба́за да́нных,** data base.

база́льт *n.* basalt. **—база́льтовый,** *adj.* basalt.

база́р *n.* **1,** market; marketplace; bazaar. **2,** sale; fair; bazaar. **3,** *colloq.* clamor; hullabaloo. **—пти́чий база́р,** seashore colony of birds.

база́рный *adj.* market (*attrib.*); of the marketplace.

базе́дов (зэ) *adj., in* **базе́дова боле́знь,** exophthalmic goiter.

базили́к *n.* basil.

базили́ка *also,* **бази́лика** *n.* basilica.

бази́рование *n., mil.* basing. Назе́много бази́рования, land-based.

бази́ровать *v.impfv.* [*pres.* **-рую, -руешь**] to base. **—бази́роваться,** *refl.* (*with* **на** + *prepl.*) to be based (on).

ба́зис *n.* base; basis.

ба́зисный *adj.* base: ба́зисная цена́, base price.

ба́зовый *adj.* base (*attrib.*); of a base.

бай-бай *interj.* bye-bye.

байба́к [*gen.* **-бака́**] *n.* a species of marmot; bobac.

байда́рка [*gen. pl.* **-рок**] *n.* kayak; canoe.

ба́йка *n.* **1,** baize; flannel. **2,** [*gen. pl.* **ба́ек**] *colloq.* fable; myth. **—ба́йковый,** *adj.* baize; flannel.

бак *n.* **1,** tank; cistern. Бензи́новый бак, gasoline tank. Му́сорный бак, garbage can. **2,** forecastle.

бакала́вр *n.* bachelor (*holder of a bachelor's degree*). **—сте́пень бакала́вра,** bachelor's degree; baccalaureate.

бакале́я *n.* groceries. **—бакале́йный,** *adj.* grocery (*attrib.*). **—бакале́йщик,** *n.* grocer.

бакели́т *n.* bakelite.

ба́кен *n.* buoy.

бакенба́рды [*gen.* **-ба́рд**] *n.pl.* whiskers.

ба́ки [*gen.* **бак**] *n.pl.* = бакенба́рды.

баккара́ *n.neut. indecl.* Baccarat glass. **—***n.fem. indecl.* baccarat (*card game*).

бакла́га *n.* flask; canteen.

баклажа́н *n.* eggplant. **—баклажа́нный,** *adj.* eggplant (*attrib.*).

бакла́н *n.* cormorant (*bird*).

баклу́ши *n.pl., in* **бить баклу́ши,** to twiddle one's thumbs.

бактериа́льный *adj.* bacterial; bacteria (*attrib.*).

бактериоло́гия *n.* bacteriology. **—бактерио́лог,** *n.* bacteriologist. **—бактериологи́ческий,** *adj.* bacteriological.

бакте́рия *n.* bacterium.

бал [*2nd loc.* **балу́;** *pl.* **балы́**] *n.* ball; formal dance. **—ко́нчен бал,** *colloq.* it's all over. **—пра́вить бал,** *colloq.* to run the show.

балабо́лка [*gen. pl.* **-лок**] *n.m. & f., colloq.* chatterbox.

балага́н *n.* **1,** carnival booth. **2,** side show. **3,** *fig.* farce.

балага́нить *v.impfv., colloq.* to play the buffoon; clown (around).

балага́нный *adj.* farcical.

балагу́р *n., colloq.* joker; jester.

балагу́рить *v.impfv., colloq.* to jest; joke.

балагу́рство *n., colloq.* witty talk; joking.

балала́ечник *n.* balalaika player.

балала́йка [*gen. pl.* **-ла́ек**] *n.* balalaika.

баламу́тить *v.impfv.* [*pfv.* **взбаламу́тить;** *pres.* **-чу, -тишь**] *colloq.* to agitate; disturb.

бала́нс *n.* **1,** balance; equilibrium. **2,** *econ.; finance* balance: платёжный/торго́вый бала́нс, balance of payments/trade. **—подводи́ть бала́нс, 1,** to balance the books. **2,** *fig.* to strike a balance.

балансёр *n.* balancer; tightrope walker.

баланси́р *n.* **1,** balancing pole. **2,** *mech.* balance beam. **3,** balance wheel.

баланси́ровать *v.impfv.* [*pfv.* **сбаланси́ровать;** *pres.* **-рую, -руешь**] **1,** [*impfv. only*] to balance oneself; remain balanced. **2,** [*impfv. only*] (*with instr.*) to balance (something precariously). **3,** to balance; bring into balance. **4,** *bookkeeping* to balance.

бала́нсовый *adj.* balance (*attrib.*): бала́нсовый отчёт, balance sheet.

балахо́н *n.* long loose robe or gown.

балбе́с *n., colloq.* booby; nitwit.

балда́ *n.m. & f., colloq.* blockhead.

балдахи́н *n.* canopy.

балери́на *n.* ballerina.

бале́т *n.* ballet.

балетме́йстер *n.* ballet master.

бале́тный *adj.* ballet (*attrib.*).

балетома́н *n.* ballet lover.

ба́лка [*gen. pl.* **ба́лок**] *n.* **1,** beam; girder. **2,** ravine; gully.

балка́нский *adj.* Balkan.

балка́р [*gen. pl.* **-ка́р**] *n.m.* [*fem.* **-ка́рка**] Balkar (*one of a people inhabiting the Caucasus*). *Also,* **балка́рец** [*gen.* **-рца**].

балка́рский *adj.* Balkan.

балко́н *n.* balcony.

балл *n.* **1,** unit of measure of the intensity of winds, earthquakes, etc. **2,** mark; grade (*in school*). **3,** *sports* point.

балла́да *n.* **1,** ballad. **2,** *music* ballade.

балла́ст *n.* ballast.

балли́стика *n.* ballistics. **—баллисти́ческий,** *adj.* ballistic.

балло́н *n.* **1,** bottle. **2,** rubber tire.

баллоти́ровать *v.impfv.* [*pres.* **-рую, -руешь**] to vote on; vote for. **—баллоти́роваться,** *refl.* (*with* **в** *or* **на** + *acc.*) to run (for); be a candidate (for).

баллотиро́вка *n.* voting; balloting.

бало́ванный *adj., colloq.* spoiled; pampered.

балова́ть *v.impfv.* [*pfv.* **избалова́ть;** *pres.* **-лу́ю, -лу́ешь**] to spoil; pamper. **—балова́ться,** *refl.* [*impfv. only*] *colloq.* **1,** to be naughty; be mischievous. **2,** (*with* **с** + *instr.*) to play with (something dangerous). **3,** (*with instr.*) to dabble (in); indulge (in).

ба́ловень [*gen.* **-вня**] *n.m.* **1,** pet; favorite. **2,** mischievous child. **—ба́ловень судьбы́,** minion of fortune.

баловни́к [*gen.* **-ника́**] *n., colloq.* naughty child; mischievous child.

баловство́ *n., colloq.* **1,** spoiling. **2,** mischief.

балти́йский *adj.* Baltic.

ба́льза *n.* **1,** balsa (*tree*). **2,** balsa wood.

бальза́м *n.* **1,** balsam. **2,** *fig.* balm.

бальзами́ровать *v.impfv. & pfv.* [*pfv. also* набаль-зами́ровать; *pres.* -ру́ю, -ру́ешь] to embalm.

бальзамиро́вщик *n.* embalmer.

ба́льный *adj.* of or for a ball; ballroom (*attrib.*).

балюстра́да *n.* balustrade.

баля́сина *n.* baluster.

баля́сы *n.pl., in* баля́сы точи́ть, *colloq.* to joke; jest; talk nonsense.

бамбу́к *n.* bamboo. —бамбу́ковый, *adj.* bamboo.

ба́мия *n.* okra; gumbo.

ба́мпер *n.* bumper.

бана́льность *n.f.* **1,** banality. **2,** platitude.

бана́льный *adj.* trite; banal.

бана́н *n.* banana. —бана́новый, *adj.* banana (*attrib.*).

ба́нда *n.* gang; band.

банда́ж [*gen.* -дажа́] *n.* **1,** abdominal support: грыже-во́й банда́ж, truss. **2,** *mech.* tire; rim.

бандеро́ль *n.f.* **1,** wrapping for mailing printed matter. **2,** printed matter sent through the mail: отправля́ть бандеро́лью, to send as printed matter.

ба́нджо *n. indecl.* banjo.

банди́т *n.* bandit; thug. —бандити́зм, *n.* banditry. —банди́тский, *adj.* of or typical of bandits; bandit-like.

банк *n.* **1,** bank. **2,** faro (*card game*). —банк да́нных, data bank. —банк кро́ви, blood bank.

ба́нка [*gen. pl.* ба́нок] *n.* **1,** jar; can. **2,** *usu. pl.* cupping glass. **3,** shoal; sandbank. —у́стричная ба́нка, oyster bed.

банке́т *n.* banquet. —банке́тный, *adj.* banquet (*attrib.*).

банки́р *n.* banker. —банки́рский, *adj.* banking (*attrib.*).

банкно́т [*gen. pl.* банкно́т *or* банкно́тов] *n.* bank note.

ба́нковский *adj.* bank (*attrib.*); banking (*attrib.*). —ба́нковская кни́жка, bankbook.

ба́нковый *adj.* bank (*attrib.*); banking (*attrib.*).

банкомёт *n.* banker (*in a game*).

банкро́т *n.* one who is bankrupt. —банкро́тство, *n.* bankruptcy.

ба́нный *adj.* bath (*attrib.*): ба́нное полоте́нце, bath towel.

бант *n.* bow: завяза́ть ба́нтом, to tie in a bow.

ба́нтик *n.* small bow.

ба́нщик *n.* bathhouse attendant.

банья́н *also,* баниа́н *n.* banyan.

ба́ня *n.* **1,** public bath. **2,** *colloq.* steam bath. **3,** *colloq.* tongue-lashing; dressing-down. —крова́вая ба́ня, blood bath.

баоба́б *n.* baobab.

бапти́ст *n.* Baptist. —бапти́стский, *adj.* Baptist.

баптисте́рий (тэ) *n.* baptistery.

бар *n.* **1,** bar; barroom. **2,** bar (*unit of pressure*).

бараба́н *n.* **1,** drum. **2,** cylinder (*of a revolver*).

бараба́нить *v.impfv.* **1,** to drum: бараба́нить па́льцами по́ столу, to drum on the table. **2,** (*of rain*) to patter.

бараба́нный *adj.* drum (*attrib.*); of drums: бараба́нный бой, drumbeat. —бараба́нная перепо́нка, eardrum.

бараба́нщик *n.* drummer.

барабу́лька [*gen. pl.* -лек] *n.* red mullet.

бара́к *n.* hut.

бара́н *n.* **1,** ram. **2,** (wild) sheep. —сне́жный бара́н, bighorn sheep.

бара́ний [*fem.* -нья] *adj.* **1,** sheep's; sheep (*attrib.*); ram's; ram (*attrib.*). **2,** sheepskin. **3,** mutton (*attrib.*). —согну́ть *or* скрути́ть в бара́ний рог, to bend to one's will.

бара́нина *n.* **1,** mutton. **2,** lamb.

бара́нка [*gen. pl.* -нок] *n.* **1,** bagel. **2,** *colloq.* steering wheel.

барахло́ *n., colloq.* **1,** old things; old clothes. **2,** junk; trash.

бара́хтаться *v.r.impfv.* to flounder; thrash around.

бара́чный *adj.* like barracks.

бара́шек [*gen.* -шка] *n.* **1,** lamb. **2,** lambskin. **3,** *mech.* thumbscrew. **4,** *pl.* fleecy clouds. **5,** whitecaps (*on the sea*).

бара́шковый *adj.* lamb (*attrib.*); lambskin (*attrib.*).

барбари́с *n.* **1,** barberries. **2,** a (single) barberry.

барбитура́т *n.* barbiturate.

барбо́с *n.* watchdog.

барви́нок [*gen.* -нка] *n.* periwinkle.

бард *n.* bard.

барелье́ф *n.* bas-relief. —барелье́фный, *adj.* bas-relief (*attrib.*).

ба́ржа *also,* баржа́ *n.* barge.

ба́рий *n.* barium.

ба́рин *n., pre-rev.* gentleman; nobleman; aristocrat. —жить ба́рином, to live like a king.

бари́т *n.* barite; heavy spar.

барито́н *n.* baritone.

баритона́льный *adj.* baritone. —баритона́льный бас, bass baritone.

барито́нный *adj.* baritone.

барк *n.* bark (*sailing vessel*).

ба́рка [*gen. pl.* ба́рок] *n.* barge.

баркаро́ла *n.* barcarole.

барка́с *n.* **1,** large rowboat. **2,** harbor vessel; launch.

ба́рмен (мэ) *n.* barman; bartender.

баро́кко *n. indecl.* baroque.

баро́метр *n.* barometer. —барометри́ческий, *adj.* barometric.

баро́н *n.* baron.

бароне́сса (нэ) *n.* baroness.

бароне́т (нэ) *n.* baronet.

баро́нство *n.* barony. —баро́нский, *adj.* baron's; baronial.

баро́чный *adj.* baroque.

барраку́да *n.* barracuda.

ба́ррель *n.m.* barrel (*measure*).

баррика́да *n.* barricade.

баррикади́ровать *v.impfv* [*pfv.* забаррикади́ро-вать; *pres.* -ру́ю, -ру́ешь] to barricade.

барс *n.* snow leopard.

ба́рский *adj.* **1,** gentleman's; master's, **2,** haughty; supercilious.

бáрственный *adj.* lordly.

бáрство *n., pre-rev.* **1,** gentry; nobility. **2,** haughtiness. **3,** idle luxury.

барсýк [*gen.* **-сукá**] *n.* badger.

бáртер (тэ) *n.* barter.

бархáн *n.* sand dune.

бáрхат *n.* velvet.

бархати́стый *adj.* velvety.

бáрхатка [*gen. pl.* **-ток**] *n.* velvet ribbon.

бáрхатный *adj.* **1,** velvet. **2,** (*of sounds*) mellow. —**бáрхатный сезóн,** warm months of early autumn in the south of Russia.

бáрхатцы [*gen.* **-цев**] *n.pl.* (French *or* African) marigold.

бáрыня *n., pre-rev.* wife of a **бáрин.**

барýш [*gen.* **-рышá**] *n., usu. pl., colloq.* profit.

бары́шник *n., obs.* **1,** horsetrader. **2,** profiteer. —**бары́шничество,** *n., obs.* profiteering.

бáрышня [*gen. pl.* **-шень**] *n., pre-rev.* **1,** unmarried daughter of a nobleman. **2,** young lady; miss.

барьéр *n.* **1,** barrier; bar. **2,** *sports* hurdle. —**барьéрный,** *adj.* hurdle (*attrib.*): барьéрный бег, hurdle race; hurdles.

бас [*pl.* **басы́**] *n., music* bass.

баси́стый *adj., colloq.* deep; low (*in sound*); bass.

баси́ть *v.impfv.* [*pres.* **башý, баси́шь**] *colloq.* to speak (*or* sing) in a bass voice.

баск *n.m.* [*fem.* **-кóнка**] Basque.

баскетбóл *n.* basketball. —**баскетболи́ст,** *n.* basketball player. —**баскетбóльный,** *adj.* basketball (*attrib.*).

бáскский *adj.* Basque.

баснопи́сец [*gen.* **-сца**] *n.* fabulist.

баснослóвный *adj.* **1,** fabled; legendary. **2,** fabulous; fantastic.

бáсня [*gen. pl.* **бáсен**] *n.* fable.

басóвый *adj., music* bass.

бассéйн *n.* **1,** pool: бассéйн для плáвания, swimming pool. **2,** *geol.* basin: бассéйн реки́, river basin. Донéцкий бассéйн, the Donetsk Basin. —**ýгольный бассéйн,** coal field.

бáста *interj., colloq.* enough!; that'll do!

бастиóн *n.* bastion.

бастовáть *v.impfv.* [*pres.* **-тýю, -тýешь**] to strike; be on strike; go on strike.

батали́ст *n.* painter of battle scenes.

батáлия *n.* **1,** *obs.* battle; fray. **2,** *colloq.* row; ruckus.

батальóн *n.* battalion. —**батальóнный,** *adj.* battalion (*attrib.*).

батарéйка [*gen. pl.* **-реек**] *n.* small battery.

батарéйный *adj.* **1,** battery (*attrib.*); battery-operated. **2,** *mil.* battery (*attrib.*).

батарéя *n.* **1,** *electricity* battery. **2,** *mil.* battery. —**батарéя отоплéния,** radiator.

батáт *n.* sweet potato; yam.

бáтенька *n.m., obs., familiar form of address,* my friend; old boy.

бати́ст *n.* cambric; batiste. —**бати́стовый,** *adj.* made of this fabric.

батóн *n.* **1,** long loaf of bread. **2,** stick of candy.

батрáк [*gen.* **-тракá**] *n.* farm worker; farm hand. —**батрáцкий,** *adj.* farm worker's.

батрáчество *n.* **1,** farm work. **2,** farm laborers; farm hands.

батрáчить *v.impfv.* to work as a farm laborer.

батýт *n.* trampoline.

бáтюшка *n.m.* **1,** *obs.* father. **2,** (*used in addressing a priest*) father. **3,** *obs., colloq.* old boy!; my dear fellow! **4,** *colloq.* father's name; patronymic. —**бáтюшки (мои́)!,** good gracious!; dear me!

баýл *n.* steamer trunk.

бах *interj.* bang!

бахвáл *n., colloq.* braggart.

бахвáлиться *v.r.impfv., colloq.* to brag.

бахвáльство *n., colloq.* bragging; boasting.

бахромá *n.* fringe. —**бахрóмчатый,** *adj.* fringed.

бахчá *n.* melon field.

бац *interj.* bang!; smack!; crack!

баци́лла *n.* bacillus.

бачóк [*gen.* **бачкá**] *n., colloq.* (small) tank. —**мýсорный бачóк,** garbage can.

бáшенка [*gen. pl.* **-нок**] *n.* small tower; turret.

бáшенный *adj.* tower (*attrib.*).

башкá *n., colloq.* head; noggin.

башки́р [*gen. pl.* **-ки́р**] *n.m.* [*fem.* **-ки́рка**] Bashkir (*one of a people inhabiting central European Russia*). —**башки́рский,** *adj.* Bashkir.

башмáк [*gen.* **-макá**] *n.* shoe. —**под башмакóм у,** under the thumb of.

башмáчник *n., obs.* shoemaker; cobbler.

башмáчный *adj.* shoe (*attrib.*).

бáшня [*gen. pl.* **бáшен**] *n.* tower. —**оруди́йная бáшня,** turret (*for a gun*).

баю́кать *v.impfv.* [*pfv.* **убаю́кать**] to lull/sing/rock to sleep.

баян *n.* accordion.

бдéние *n.* vigil; watch.

бди́тельный *adj.* vigilant; watchful. —**бди́тельность,** *n.f.* vigilance.

бег *n.* **1,** run; running. **2,** race. —**бег на мéсте,** *sports* running in place. —**в бегáх,** on the run. —**на бегý,** on the double.

бегá [*gen.* **бегóв**] *n.pl.* harness racing; harness races.

бéгать *v.impfv.* **1,** *indeterm. of* **бежáть. 2,** to jog. **3,** to move rapidly; flit; dart. **4,** (*with* **от**) *colloq.* to avoid; get away from. **5,** (*with* **за** + *instr.*) *colloq.* to chase (after).

бегемóт *n.* **1,** hippopotamus. **2,** behemoth.

беглéц [*gen.* **-лецá**] *n.m.* [*fem.* **-ля́нка**] fugitive; escaped convict.

бéгло *adv.* **1,** fluently. **2,** with facility. **3,** in a cursory manner.

бéглость *n.f.* **1,** fluency. **2,** facility.

бéглый *adj.* **1,** fluent. **2,** facile. **3,** cursory. **4,** fugitive; runaway. **5,** *phonet.* (*of a vowel*) fleeting. **6,** *in* бéглый огóнь, rapid fire. —*n.* fugitive.

бегля́нка [*gen. pl.* **-нок**] *n., fem. of* **беглéц.**

беговóй *adj.* running (*attrib.*); racing (*attrib.*); race (*attrib.*). —**беговáя дорóжка,** running track. —**беговáя лóшадь,** racehorse.

бегóм *adv.* running; on the double.

бего́ния *n.* begonia.

беготня́ *n., colloq.* running about; scurrying about.

бе́гство *n.* **1,** flight: обраща́ть в бе́гство, to put to flight. **2,** escape.

бегу́н [*gen.* **-гуна́**] *n.m.* [*fem.* **-гу́нья**] *sports* runner.

беда́ [*pl.* **бе́ды**] *n.* **1,** trouble; misfortune. Поки́нуть (кого́-нибудь) в беде́, to leave (someone) stranded; leave in the lurch. **2,** *pl.* ills; woes. —**беда́ в том, что...**, the trouble is... —**беда́ как,** *colloq.* very much. —**в то́м-то и беда́,** that's just the trouble. —**как на беду́,** as luck would have it. —**на беду́,** unfortunately. —**на свою́ беду́,** to one's cost. —**не беда́,** it doesn't matter; no harm done. —**что за беда́!,** what does it matter?

бедла́м *n.* bedlam; chaos.

бедне́ть *v.impfv.* [*pfv.* **обедне́ть**] to become poor.

бе́дно *adv.* **1,** in poor circumstances: Они́ живу́т ужа́сно бе́дно, they live in utter poverty. **2,** shabbily: бе́дно оде́тый, shabbily dressed.

бе́дность *n.f.* poverty.

беднота́ *n.* **1,** the poor. **2,** *colloq.* poverty.

бе́дный *adj.* [*short form* **бе́ден, бедна́, бе́дно, бе́дны** *or* **бедны́**] **1,** poor. **2,** meager. **3,** (*of language, writing, etc.*) insipid. **4,** poor (*unfortunate*): Бе́дный Са́ша!, poor Sasha!

бедня́га *n.m. & f., colloq.* poor fellow; poor devil. *Also,* **бедня́жка.**

бедня́к [*gen.* **-няка́**] *n.* poor person; pauper.

бедо́вый *adj., colloq.* **1,** daring. **2,** mischievous.

бедоку́р *n.m.* [*fem.* **-ку́рка**] *colloq.* mischief-maker.

бедоку́рить *v.impfv.* [*pfv.* **набедоку́рить**] *colloq.* to make mischief.

бедола́га *n.m. & f., colloq.* poor fellow.

бе́дренный *adj.* hip (*attrib.*); thigh (*attrib.*). —**бе́дренная кость,** thighbone; femur.

бедро́ [*pl.* **бёдра, бёдер**] *n.* hip; thigh.

бе́дственный *adj.* calamitous; disastrous.

бе́дствие *n.* calamity; disaster. —**сигна́л бе́дствия,** distress signal.

бе́дствовать *v.impfv.* [*pres.* **-ствую, ствуешь**] to live in poverty.

бедуи́н *n.* Bedouin.

беж *adj. indecl.* beige: пла́тье цве́та беж, beige dress.

бежа́ть *v.impfv.* [*pfv.* **побежа́ть**; *pres.* **бегу́, бежи́шь, ...бегу́т**] **1,** to run. **2,** to race. **3,** *fig.* (*of time*) to fly; (*of water*) to flow. —*v.impfv. & pfv.* to escape; flee: бежа́ть из тюрьмы́, to escape from prison; бежа́ть из страны́, to flee the country. *See also* **бе́гать.**

бе́жевый *adj., colloq.* beige.

бе́женец [*gen.* **-нца**] *n.m.* [*fem.* **-нка**] refugee.

без *also, before* **весь** *and* **вся́кий, безо** *prep., with gen.* **1,** without: идти́ без шля́пы, to go without a hat. **2,** *used to express minutes before the hour,* to; before; of: без десяти́ семь, ten minutes to seven; без че́тверти три, a quarter to three. —**и без того́,** already: и без того́ сло́жное положе́ние, an already complicated situation.

без- *also,* **бес-, безъ-** *prefix* not; without; lacking; *often equivalent to English* **un-; in-; ir-; im-; il-; -less:** безалкого́льный, nonalcoholic; бесце́льный, aimless.

безала́берный *adj.* disorderly; slipshod.

безалкого́льный *adj.* nonalcoholic.

безапелляцио́нный *adj.* **1,** *law* not subject to appeal. **2,** categorical; peremptory.

беза́томный *adj.* atom-free.

безбе́дный *adj.* materially secure; comfortable. —**безбе́дно,** *adv.* comfortably: жить безбе́дно, to live comfortably.

безбиле́тный *adj.* having no ticket.

безбо́жие *n.* atheism. —**безбо́жник,** *n.* atheist.

безбо́жный *adj.* **1,** *obs.* godless. **2,** *colloq.* shameless; outrageous. —**безбо́жно,** *adv., colloq.* outrageously; something awful.

безболе́зненный *adj.* painless. —**безболе́зненно,** *adv.* painlessly.

безборо́дый *adj.* beardless.

безбоя́зненный *adj.* fearless; intrepid.

безбра́чие *n.* celibacy. —**безбра́чный,** *adj.* celibate.

безбре́жный *adj.* boundless; limitless.

безве́стный *adj.* unknown; obscure. —**безве́стность,** *n.f.* obscurity.

безве́тренный *adj.* **1,** windless. **2,** still; calm.

безве́трие *n.* absence of wind.

безви́нный *adj.* innocent; guiltless.

безвку́сие *n.* poor taste; lack of taste; tastelessness. *Also, colloq.* **безвку́сица.**

безвку́сный *adj.* **1,** tasteless. **2,** in poor taste. **3,** lacking good taste. —**безвку́сно,** *adv.* without taste.

безвла́стие *n.* anarchy.

безво́дный *adj.* arid; waterless. —**безво́дье,** *n.* lack (*or* shortage) of water.

безвозвра́тный *adj.* **1,** irretrievable. **2,** not requiring repayment: безвозвра́тная ссу́да, outright grant. —**безвозвра́тно,** *adv.* for good; forever.

безвозду́шный *adj.* airless. —**безвозду́шное простра́нство,** vacuum.

безвозме́здный *adj.* **1,** free (*of charge*). **2,** (*of labor*) unpaid. —**безвозме́здно,** *adv.* free of charge; without pay; without compensation.

безво́лие *n.* lack of will.

безволо́сый *adj.* having no hair.

безво́льный *adj.* weak-willed.

безвре́дный *adj.* harmless; innocuous.

безвре́менный *adj.* (*of someone's death*) untimely.

безвы́ездно *adv.* **1,** without a break. **2,** all one's life.

безвы́ездный *adj.* (*of a stay or residence*) permanent.

безвы́лазно *adv., colloq.* never going out: безвы́лазно сиде́ть до́ма, to sit home all the time (without ever going out).

безвы́ходный *adj.* hopeless; untenable. —**безвы́ходность,** *n.f.* hopelessness.

безгла́зый *adj.* **1,** having no eyes. **2,** one-eyed.

безгла́сный *adj.* **1,** *obs.* mute. **2,** *fig.* speechless; having no voice.

безголо́вый *adj.* **1,** headless. **2,** *colloq.* brainless; scatterbrained.

безголо́сый *adj.* **1,** voiceless; without a voice. **2,** having a poor voice.

безгра́мотный *adj.* **1,** illiterate. **2,** ungrammatical; full of mistakes. —**безгра́мотно,** *adv.* like an illiterate person. —**безгра́мотность,** *n.f.* illiteracy.

безграни́чный *adj.* boundless; limitless; infinite.
—**безграни́чно,** *adv.* to an unlimited degree.

безгре́шный *adj.* without sin.

безда́рность *n.f.* **1,** lack of talent. **2,** *fig.* person with no talent.

безда́рный *adj.* **1,** lacking (*or* without) talent. **2,** incompetent; inept. **3,** without merit; with no redeeming feature.

безде́йственный *adj.* inactive; idle.

безде́йствие *n.* inaction; inactivity; idleness.

безде́йствовать *v.impfv.* [*pres.* -ствую, -ствуешь] **1,** to do nothing; take no action. **2,** to be idle; be inoperative.

безде́лица *n., colloq.* trifle.

безделу́шка [*gen. pl.* -шек] *n.* trinket; knickknack.

безде́лье *n.* idleness. —**от безде́лья,** having nothing better to do.

безде́льник *n., colloq.* idler; loafer.

безде́льничать *v.impfv.* to idle; loaf; do nothing.

безде́нежный *adj.* **1,** not involving cash. **2,** *colloq.* penniless.

безде́нежье *n.* lack of money.

безде́тный *adj.* childless. —**безде́тность,** *n.f.* childlessness.

безде́ятельный *adj.* inactive; lethargic. —**безде́ятельность,** *n.f.* inactivity; lethargy.

бе́здна *n.* **1,** chasm; abyss. **2,** *colloq.* huge amount; endless number.

бездоказа́тельный *adj.* unsubstantiated; unsupported.

бездо́мный *adj.* homeless; stray. —**бездо́мные,** *n.pl.* homeless people; the homeless.

бездо́нный *adj.* bottomless: бездо́нная про́пасть, bottomless pit.

бездоро́жье *n.* **1,** absence of passable roads; bad roads. **2,** time of year when roads are impassable.

безду́мный *adj.* thoughtless; unthinking.

безду́мье *n.* inability to think clearly; daze.

бездухо́вность *n.f.* intellectual poverty/barrenness/squalor.

безду́шие *n.* heartlessness; callousness.

безду́шный *adj.* **1,** *obs.* dead; lifeless. **2,** *fig.* heartless; callous; without a soul. **3,** *fig.* (*of a performance*) uninspired.

бездыха́нный *adj.* lifeless.

безжа́лостный *adj.* ruthless; merciless; pitiless. —**безжа́лостно,** *adv.* ruthlessly; mercilessly. —**безжа́лостность,** *n.f.* ruthlessness.

безжи́зненный *adj.* **1,** dead; lifeless. **2,** *fig.* without expression; blank.

беззабо́тно *adv.* in a carefree manner; without a care.

беззабо́тность *n.f.* **1,** carefree manner. **2,** lack of concern; unconcern.

беззабо́тный *adj.* **1,** carefree; happy-go-lucky. **2,** casual; unconcerned.

беззаве́тный *adj.* selfless.

беззако́ние *n.* **1,** lawlessness. **2,** unlawful act.

беззако́нный *adj.* lawless; unlawful.

беззасте́нчивый *adj.* shameless; brazen.

беззащи́тный *adj.* defenseless; unprotected.

беззвёздный *adj.* starless.

беззву́чный *adj.* soundless; silent.

безземе́лье *n.* lack of land. —**безземе́льный,** *adj.* landless.

беззло́бие *n.* good nature. —**беззло́бный,** *adj.* good-natured.

беззубцо́вый *adj.* (*of postage stamps*) imperforate.

беззу́бый *adj.* toothless.

безле́сный *adj.* treeless.

безле́сье *n.* lack of forests.

безли́кий *adj.* faceless.

безли́чный *adj.* **1,** faceless. **2,** impersonal.

безлю́дный *adj.* **1,** uninhabited; sparsely populated. **2,** (*of streets, public places, etc.*) empty; deserted.

безлю́дье *n.* absence of people.

безме́н *n.* steelyard.

безме́рный *adj.* boundless; immeasurable. —**безме́рно,** *adv.* beyond measure; extraordinarily.

безмо́зглый *adj., colloq.* brainless; witless.

безмо́лвие *n.* silence.

безмо́лвный *adj.* **1,** silent; hushed. **2,** mute; speechless.

безмо́лвствовать *v.impfv.* [*pres.* -ствую, -ствуешь] to be silent; keep silent.

безмяте́жный *adj.* serene; tranquil; undisturbed. —**безмяте́жность,** *n.f.* serenity; tranquillity.

безнадёжный *adj.* hopeless. —**безнадёжно,** *adv.* hopelessly. —**безнадёжность,** *n.f.* hopelessness.

безнадзо́рный *adj.* unsupervised; neglected.

безнака́занный *adj.* unpunished. —**безнака́занно,** *adv.* with impunity. —**безнака́занность,** *n.f.* impunity.

безнали́чный *adj.* not involving cash.

безнача́лие *n.* anarchy.

безно́гий *adj.* **1,** legless. **2,** having only one leg.

безнра́вственный *adj.* immoral. —**безнра́вственность,** *n.f.* immorality.

безоби́дный *adj.* inoffensive; innocuous; harmless.

безо́блачный *adj.* **1,** cloudless. **2,** *fig.* serene.

безобра́зие *n.* **1,** ugliness. **2,** outrage; scandal; disgrace.

безобра́зить *v.impfv.* [*pfv.* обезобра́зить; *pres.* -жу, -зишь] to make unattractive; mar the appearance of.

безобра́зник *n., colloq.* **1,** hooligan; rowdy. **2,** naughty child.

безобра́зничать *v.impfv., colloq.* to carry on; behave disgracefully.

безобра́зный *adj.* **1,** *obs.* formless; shapeless. **2,** (*of writing*) lacking imagery.

безобра́зный *adj.* **1,** ugly; hideous; deformed. **2,** outrageous; scandalous; disgraceful.

безогля́дный *adj.* impetuous; rash. —**безогля́дно,** *adv.* rashly; without considering the consequences.

безогово́рочный *adj.* unconditional; unreserved; unqualified.

безопа́сно *adv.* safely. —*adj., used predicatively,* safe: Здесь безопа́сно, it is safe here.

безопа́сность *n.f.* safety; security. В безопа́сности, safe. —**Сове́т Безопа́сности,** Security Council. —**те́хника безопа́сности,** accident prevention; safety procedures.

безопа́сный *adj.* **1,** safe; secure. **2,** safety (*attrib.*); security (*attrib.*): безопа́сная бри́тва, safety razor.

безору́жный *adj.* **1,** unarmed. **2,** *fig.* defenseless.

безоснова́тельный *adj.* groundless; baseless.

безостано́вочный *adj.* **1,** ceaseless; uninterrupted. **2,** nonstop. **—безостано́вочно,** *adv.* nonstop.

безотве́тный *adj.* **1,** unrequited. **2,** giving no answer; silent. **3,** meek.

безотве́тственный *adj.* irresponsible. **—безотве́тственно,** *adv.* irresponsibly. **—безотве́тственность,** *n.f.* irresponsibility.

безотка́зный *adj., colloq.* **1,** ever-willing. **2,** (*of the functioning of a machine*) smooth; steady. **—безотка́зно,** *adv., colloq.* smoothly; perfectly.

безотка́тный *adj.* recoilless.

безотлага́тельный *adj.* urgent. **—безотлага́тельно,** *adv.* urgently.

безотлу́чный *adj.* **1,** ever-present. **2,** continual.

безотноси́тельно *adv.* (*with* **к**) irrespective of; regardless of; without regard to.

безотра́дный *adj.* bleak; dismal; cheerless.

безотчётный *adj.* **1,** instinctive; unconscious. **2,** not accountable; not subject to control.

безоши́бочный *adj.* **1,** without error; perfect. **2,** unerring; infallible.

безрабо́тица *n.* unemployment.

безрабо́тный *adj.* unemployed. **—***n.* unemployed person.

безра́достный *adj.* joyless; cheerless.

безразде́льно *adv.* completely. Руководи́ть безразде́льно, to be completely in charge.

безразде́льный *adj.* undivided; absolute; complete.

безразли́чие *n.* indifference.

безразли́чно *adv.* with indifference. **—***adj., used predicatively,* immaterial: Мне э́то безразли́чно, it's immaterial to me.

безразли́чный *adj.* indifferent.

безразме́рный *adj., colloq.* (*of socks, stockings, etc.*) stretch.

безрассу́дный *adj.* rash; reckless; foolhardy. **—безрассу́дно,** *adv.* rashly; recklessly.

безрассу́дство *n.* **1,** recklessness; foolhardiness. **2,** rash act; reckless act.

безрезульта́тный *adj.* futile; unsuccessful. **—безрезульта́тно,** *adv.* without result(s); in vain.

безро́гий *adj.* hornless.

безро́дный *adj.* having no relatives; without kith or kin.

безро́потный *adj.* uncomplaining; mild-mannered. **—безро́потно,** *adv.* without complaining; without a murmur.

безрука́вка [*gen. pl.* **-вок**] *n.* sleeveless jacket. **—безрука́вный,** *adj.* sleeveless.

безру́кий *adj.* **1,** lacking one or both arms; lacking one or both hands. **2,** *colloq.* unhandy; clumsy.

безуда́рный *adj., phonet.* unaccented; unstressed.

безуде́ржный *adj.* unrestrained; unchecked; uncontrollable. Безуде́ржная инфля́ция, rampant (*or* runaway) inflation.

безукори́зненно *adv.* flawlessly; perfectly. **—безукори́зненно чи́стый,** spotlessly clean.

безукори́зненный *adj.* irreproachable; unimpeachable; flawless; impeccable.

безу́мец [*gen.* **-мца**] *n.* madman; lunatic.

безу́мие *n.* **1,** *obs.* madness; insanity. **2,** madness; insanity; lunacy; folly. **—до безу́мия,** to distraction.

безу́мно *adv.* **1,** madly. **2,** *colloq.* extremely. Безу́мно уста́л, terribly tired. Сто́ить безу́мно до́рого, to be ridiculously expensive.

безу́мный *adj.* **1,** *obs.* mad; insane. **2,** mad; crazy. Безу́мный посту́пок, act of folly. **3,** *colloq.* extreme.

безумо́лчный *adj.* (*of noise*) incessant.

безу́мство *n.* madness; folly.

безу́мствовать *v.impfv.* [*pres.* **-ствую, -ствуешь**] to rant; rave; behave like a madman.

безупре́чный *adj.* irreproachable; unimpeachable; flawless; impeccable. **—безупре́чно,** *adv.* flawlessly; perfectly.

безусло́вно *adv.* **1,** absolutely; positively. **2,** certainly; undoubtedly; of course.

безусло́вный *adj.* absolute; unconditional.

безуспе́шный *adj.* unsuccessful; unavailing. **—безуспе́шно,** *adv.* without success; unsuccessfully.

безуста́нный *adj.* **1,** tireless; untiring. **2,** ceaseless; unending.

безу́сый *adj.* **1,** having no mustache. **2,** *fig.* callow; beardless.

безуте́шный *adj.* inconsolable.

безуча́стие *n.* indifference; apathy.

безуча́стный *adj.* indifferent; unmoved; apathetic. **—безуча́стность,** *n.f.* indifference; apathy.

безъя́дерный *adj.* nuclear-free.

безызве́стный *adj.* obscure; unknown. **—безызве́стность,** *n.f.* obscurity.

безымя́нный *adj.* nameless; anonymous. **—безымя́нный па́лец,** ring finger; fourth finger.

безынициати́вный *adj.* lacking initiative; unenterprising.

безыску́сный *adj.* **1,** simple; unpretentious. **2,** unsophisticated.

безыску́сственный *adj.* artless; ingenuous.

безысхо́дный *adj.* **1,** hopeless. **2,** endless. **—безысхо́дность,** *n.f.* hopelessness.

бейсбо́л *n.* baseball. **—бейсбо́льный,** *adj.* baseball (*attrib.*).

бека́р *n., music* natural sign; natural: ля-бека́р, A-natural.

бека́с *n.* snipe.

беко́н *n.* bacon.

белена́ *n.* henbane.

беле́ние *n.* bleaching.

белёный *adj.* bleached.

белёсый *adj.* whitish; off-white.

беле́ть *v.impfv.* [*pfv.* **побеле́ть**] **1,** to turn white. **2,** [*impfv. only*] (*of anything white*) to be visible; appear; shine; gleam.

белиберда́ *n., colloq.* nonsense; rubbish.

белизна́ *n.* whiteness.

бели́ла [*gen.* **бели́л**] *n.pl.* **1,** whiting. **2,** ceruse (*cosmetic*). **—свинцо́вые бели́ла,** white lead; ceruse. **—ци́нковые бели́ла,** zinc white

бели́льный *adj.* bleaching (*attrib.*).

бели́ть *v.impfv.* [*pres.* **белю́, бе́лишь** *or* **бели́шь**] **1,**

[*pfv.* **побели́ть**] to whitewash; whiten. **2,** [*pfv.* **на-бели́ть**] to white (one's face) with ceruse. **3,** [*pfv.* **вы́белить**] to bleach. —**бели́ться,** *refl.* [*pfv.* **на-бели́ться**] to put on white make-up; whiten one's face with ceruse.

бе́личий [*fem.* **-чья**] *adj.* squirrel (*attrib.*); squirrel's.

бе́лка [*gen. pl.* **бе́лок**] *n.* squirrel. —**верте́ться как бе́лка в колесе́,** to be on a treadmill; go around in circles.

белко́вый *adj.* protein (*attrib.*).

белладо́нна *n.* belladonna.

беллетри́стика *n.* fiction. —**беллетри́ст,** *n.* fiction writer. —**беллетристи́ческий,** *adj.* fictional.

белобры́сый *adj., colloq.* towheaded.

белова́тый *adj.* whitish; off-white.

белови́к [*gen.* **-вика́**] *n.* clean copy.

белово́й *adj.* (*of a copy, manuscript, etc.*) clean; in final form.

беловоло́сый *adj.* white-haired.

белогварде́ец [*gen.* **-е́йца**] *n.* White Guard; counter-revolutionary. —**белогварде́йский,** *adj.* White-Guard (*attrib.*).

белоголо́вый *adj.* white-haired.

бело́к [*gen.* **белка́**] *n.* **1,** white of an egg; egg white; albumen. **2,** protein. **3,** white of the eye.

белокро́вие *n.* leukemia.

белоку́рый *adj.* blond; fair-haired.

белоли́цый *adj.* white-faced.

белору́с *n.m.* [*fem.* **-ру́ска**] Belorussian. —**белору́сский,** *adj.* Belorussian.

белору́чка [*gen. pl.* **-чек**] *n.m. & f., colloq.* one who disdains manual labor; one not wishing to dirty his hands.

белосне́жный *adj.* snow-white.

белошве́йка [*gen. pl.* **-шве́ек**] *n.* seamstress.

белу́га *n.* white sturgeon; beluga. —**реве́ть белу́гой,** to howl like a stuck pig.

белу́ха *n.* white whale; beluga.

бе́лый *adj.* white. —*n.* **1,** white man; white. **2,** *neut.* white (clothes): оде́т(а) в бе́лое, dressed in white. **3,** *pl.* whites (*in the Russian Civil War*). **4,** *pl., chess* white: игра́ть бе́лыми, to be white; play the white pieces. —**бе́лая воро́на,** rara avis. —**бе́лый медве́дь,** polar bear. —**бе́лые пя́тна,** unexplored areas; blank spots. —**бе́лая сова́,** snowy owl. —**бе́лые стихи́,** blank verse.

бельги́ец [*gen.* **-и́йца**] *n.m.* [*fem.* **-и́йка**] Belgian. —**бельги́йский,** *adj.* Belgian.

бельё *n.* **1,** linen: столо́вое бельё, table linen. **2,** laun-dry; wash: гря́зное бельё, dirty clothes/linen/laundry. —**да́мское бельё,** lingerie. —**ни́жнее бельё,** under-wear.

бельево́й *adj.* **1,** linen (*attrib.*). **2,** lingerie (*attrib.*).

бельме́с *n., colloq., in* не знать (*or* не понима́ть) ни бельме́са о, not to know the first thing about.

бельмо́ *n.* walleye. —**бельмо́ на глазу́,** thorn in one's side.

бельэта́ж *n.* **1,** second floor. **2,** *theat.* mezzanine.

беля́к [*gen.* **-яка́**] *n.* **1,** white hare. **2,** *pl.* whitecaps.

бемо́ль *n.m., music* flat; flat sign: си-бемо́ль, B-flat.

бенга́лец [*gen.* **-льца**] *n.m.* [*fem.* **-лка**] Bengali. —**бенга́льский,** *adj.* Bengali.

бенефи́с *n., theat.* benefit performance.

бензи́н *n.* **1,** benzine. **2,** gasoline. —**бензи́новый,** *adj.* gasoline (*attrib.*).

бензиноме́р *n.* gasoline gauge; fuel gauge.

бензоба́к *n.* gas tank.

бензово́з *n.* gasoline truck.

бензозапра́вочный *adj., in* бензозапра́вочная коло́нка, gasoline pump; бензозапра́вочная ста́нция, gas station; service station.

бензои́н *n.* benzoin.

бензоколо́нка [*gen. pl.* **-нок**] *n.* **1,** gas (*or* gasoline) pump. **2,** *colloq.* gas station.

бензо́л *n.* benzene; benzol.

бенуа́р *n., theat.* boxes (*at orchestra level*).

бе́рег [*2nd loc.* **берегу́**; *pl.* **берега́**] *n.* **1,** coast: плыть вдоль бе́рега, to sail along the coast. **2,** bank (*of a river*): вы́йти из берего́в, to overflow its banks, **3,** shore: достига́ть бе́рега, to reach the shore. Сойти́ на бе́рег, to go ashore. —**бе́рег мо́ря,** seashore.

берегово́й *adj.* coastal; shore (*attrib.*). —**берегова́я ли́ния,** coastline. —**берегова́я охра́на,** coast guard.

береди́ть *v.impfv.* [*pfv.* **разбереди́ть**; *pres.* **-жу́, -ди́шь**] to irritate; aggravate (a wound). —**береди́ть ста́рые ра́ны,** to reopen old wounds.

бережли́вость *n.f.* **1,** thrift. **2,** *obs.* care.

бережли́вый *adj.* **1,** thrifty; economical. **2,** = бе́реж-ный.

бе́режный *adj.* **1,** careful; gentle. **2,** solicitous; consid-erate. —**бе́режно,** *adv.* carefully; gently. —**бе́реж-ность,** *n.f.* care.

берёза *n.* birch.

березня́к [*gen.* **-няка́**] *n.* birch forest.

берёзовый *adj.* birch (*attrib.*).

бере́йтор *n.* riding master.

бере́менеть *v.impfv.* [*pfv.* **забере́менеть**] to become pregnant.

бере́менная *adj.* pregnant. —*n.* pregnant woman.

бере́менность *n.f.* pregnancy.

берёста *n.* birch bark.

берестяно́й *adj.* birch-bark (*attrib.*). Also, **берёсто-вый.**

бере́т *n.* beret.

бере́чь *v.impfv.* [*pres.* **берегу́, бережёшь, ...берегу́т**; *past* **берёг, берегла́, берегло́, берегли́**] **1,** to save; keep. **2,** to save; conserve. **3,** to take care of; guard; protect. —**бере́чься,** *refl.* (*with gen.*) to watch out (for); beware (of); guard (against).

бе́ри-бе́ри *n.f. indecl.* beriberi.

бери́лл *n.* beryl.

бери́ллий *n.* beryllium.

берке́лий *n.* berkelium. Also, **бе́рклий.**

бе́ркут *n.* golden eagle.

берло́га *n.* den; lair (*of a bear*).

берцо́вый *adj., in* больша́я берцо́вая кость, shin-bone; tibia; ма́лая берцо́вая кость, fibula.

бес *n.* demon; devil; evil spirit. —**рассыпа́ться ме́л-ким бе́сом пе́ред,** *colloq.* to curry favor with; play up to.

бес- *prefix, var. of* **без-** (*used before voiceless consonants*).

бесе́да *n.* **1,** conversation; talk; chat. **2,** discussion. **3,** interview.

бесе́дка [*gen. pl.* **-док**] *n.* summerhouse.

бесе́довать *v.impfv.* [*pres.* **-дую, -дуешь**] to talk; chat; converse.

бесёнок [*gen.* **-нка**; *pl.* **бесеня́та, -ня́т**] *n., colloq.* imp; little devil.

беси́ть *v.impfv.* [*pfv.* **взбеси́ть**; *pres.* **бешу́, бе́сишь**] to enrage; infuriate. —**беси́ться,** *refl.* **1,** to become enraged. **2,** (*of animals*) to become rabid.

беска́мерный *adj.* (*of a tire*) tubeless.

бескла́ссовый *adj.* classless.

бескозы́рка [*gen. pl.* **-рок**] *n.* peakless cap.

бескомпроми́ссный *adj.* uncompromising.

бесконе́чно *adv.* infinitely; endlessly. —**бесконе́чно ма́лый,** infinitesimal.

бесконе́чность *n.f.* infinity. —**до бесконе́чности,** endlessly; ad infinitum.

бесконе́чный *adj.* **1,** endless; interminable. **2,** infinite.

бесконтро́льный *adj.* uncontrolled; unsupervised. —**бесконтро́льно,** *adv.* uncontrolled; without control.

бескоры́стие *n.* unselfishness. —**бескоры́стный,** *adj.* unselfish; disinterested.

беско́стный *adj.* boneless.

бескра́йний *adj.* endless; boundless.

бескри́зисный *adj.* crisis-free.

бескро́вный *adj.* **1,** pallid; anemic. **2,** bloodless; without bloodshed. **3,** *obs.* homeless.

бескры́лый *adj.* **1,** wingless; flightless. **2,** *fig.* uninspired.

бескульту́рье *n., colloq.* lack of culture.

беснова́тый *adj., obs.* mad; deranged.

беснова́ться *v.r.impfv.* [*pres.* **-ну́юсь, -ну́ешься**] to rant; rage.

бесо́вский *adj.* diabolical; devilish.

беспа́лый *adj.* **1,** having no fingers. **2,** having no toes.

беспа́мятный *adj., colloq.* forgetful.

беспа́мятство *n.* unconsciousness.

беспардо́нный *adj., colloq.* brazen; insolent.

беспарти́йный *adj.* non-party. —*n.* non-party member.

беспереб́о́йный *adj.* uninterrupted; regular; smooth. —**бесперебо́йно,** *adv.* without interruption; without a hitch.

беспереса́дочный *adj.* through; without transfer to another vehicle: беспереса́дочное сообще́ние, through connection.

бесперспекти́вный *adj.* having no prospects.

беспе́чно *adv.* in a carefree manner; without a care.

беспе́чность *n.f.* **1,** lack of concern; unconcern. **2,** carefree manner.

беспе́чный *adj.* **1,** carefree; happy-go-lucky. **2,** casual; unconcerned.

беспило́тный *adj.* not piloted; (*of a spacecraft*) unmanned.

беспи́сьменный *adj.* **1,** having no written language. **2,** (*of a language*) unwritten.

беспла́новый *adj.* unplanned.

беспла́тный *adj.* free (of charge): беспла́тное

обуче́ние, free tuition. —**беспла́тно,** *adv.* free of charge; gratis.

бесплацка́ртный *adj.* **1,** (*of a car on a train*) unreserved; with unreserved seats. **2,** (*of a passenger*) having no reserved seat.

беспло́дие *n.* **1,** sterility; infertility. **2,** barrenness; infertility (*of soil*).

беспло́дность *n.f.* **1,** barrenness; infertility (*of soil*). **2,** futility.

беспло́дный *adj.* **1,** barren; sterile; infertile. **2,** futile; fruitless.

беспло́тный *adj.* incorporeal.

бесповоро́тный *adj.* irrevocable.

беспод́о́бный *adj., colloq.* incomparable; matchless; peerless.

беспозвоно́чный *adj.* invertebrate. —**беспозвоно́чные,** *n.pl.* invertebrates.

беспоко́ить *v.impfv.* **1,** to worry; trouble; disturb. **2,** to bother; disturb. —**беспоко́иться,** *refl.* **1,** to worry. **2,** to trouble oneself; bother.

беспоко́йно *adv.* **1,** anxiously. **2,** unevenly; fitfully.

беспоко́йный *adj.* **1,** worried; troubled; anxious; uneasy. **2,** worrisome; disturbing. **3,** restless.

беспоко́йство *n.* **1,** worry; anxiety; uneasiness; concern. **2,** trouble; disturbance; bother.

бесполе́зно *adv.* uselessly. —*adj., used predicatively,* useless: Спо́рить с ним бесполе́зно, it's useless to argue with him.

бесполе́зность *n.f.* uselessness.

бесполе́зный *adj.* **1,** useless. **2,** futile.

беспо́лый *adj.* sexless; asexual.

беспо́мощный *adj.* **1,** helpless. **2,** utterly without merit; hopeless. —**беспо́мощность,** *n.f.* helplessness.

беспоро́чный *adj.* faultless; irreproachable.

беспоря́док [*gen.* **-дка**] *n.* **1,** disorder; disarray; confusion. **2,** *pl.* disorders; disturbances; riots.

беспоря́дочный *adj.* **1,** disorderly; untidy. **2,** unsystematic; disorganized. —**беспоря́дочно,** *adv.* in a disorderly manner; haphazardly.

беспоса́дочный *adj.* (*of a flight*) nonstop.

беспо́чвенный *adj.* groundless; unfounded.

беспо́шлинный *adj.* duty-free. —**беспо́шлинно,** *adv.* duty-free.

беспоща́дный *adj.* merciless. —**беспоща́дно,** *adv.* mercilessly.

беспра́вие *n.* absence of rights.

беспра́вный *adj.* without rights.

беспреде́л *n., colloq.* unbridled freedom; license.

беспреде́льный *adj.* boundless; limitless; infinite.

беспредме́тный *adj.* pointless; aimless.

беспрекосло́вный *adj.* unquestioning; absolute; implicit. —**беспрекосло́вно,** *adv.* unhesitatingly; unfailingly.

беспрепя́тственный *adj.* unhindered; unimpeded. —**беспрепя́тственно,** *adv.* without hindrance; unimpeded.

беспреры́вный *adj.* continuous; uninterrupted. —**беспреры́вно,** *adv.* continuously.

беспреста́нный *adj.* continual; incessant. —**беспреста́нно,** *adv.* continually; incessantly.

беспрецеде́нтный *adj.* unprecedented.

беспри́быльный *adj.* unprofitable; unremunerative.

бесприда́нница *n., obs.* girl without a dowry.

беспризо́рничать *n.* street urchin; waif.

беспризо́рничать *v.impfv., colloq.* to live on the streets; be a waif.

беспризо́рный *adj.* **1,** neglected; uncared-for. **2,** homeless; stray. —*n.* = **беспризо́рник.**

беспримерный *adj.* unexampled; unparalleled.

беспринци́пный *adj.* unprincipled; unscrupulous.

беспристра́стие *n.* impartiality. —**беспристра́стный,** *adj.* impartial; unbiased.

беспричи́нный *adj.* lacking any visible cause; groundless. —**беспричи́нно,** *adv.* for no (apparent) reason.

бесприю́тный *adj.* homeless; lacking a roof over one's head.

беспробу́дный *adj.* **1,** (*of sleep*) deep. **2,** *colloq.* (*of drinking*) unrestrained.

беспро́волочный *adj.* wireless: беспро́волочный телегра́ф, wireless.

беспро́игрышный *adj.* risk-free; safe.

беспросве́тный *adj.* **1,** pitch black; pitch dark. **2,** (*of darkness*) total. **3,** *fig.* hopeless; unrelieved.

беспроце́нтный *adj.* interest-free.

беспу́тный *adj.* dissolute. —**беспу́тство,** *n.* dissoluteness.

бессвя́зный *adj.* rambling; disconnected; incoherent; disjointed. —**бессвя́зность,** *n.f.* incoherence.

бессеме́йный *adj.* having no family.

бессемя́нный *adj.* seedless.

бессерде́чие *n.* heartlessness; callousness. *Also,* **бессерде́чность,** *n.f.*

бессерде́чный *adj.* heartless; callous.

бесси́лие *n.* **1,** weakness; debility. **2,** helplessness; impotence. —полово́е бесси́лие, *med.* impotence.

бесси́льный *adj.* **1,** weak; feeble. **2,** powerless; helpless; impotent.

бессисте́мный *adj.* unsystematic.

бессла́вие *n.* ignominy. —**бессла́вный,** *adj.* inglorious; ignominious.

бессле́дный *adj.* (*of the disappearance of someone or something*) complete. —**бессле́дно,** *adv.* without a trace; completely.

бессло́весный *adj.* **1,** mute; dumb. **2,** quiet; meek. —бессло́весная роль, non-speaking part.

бессме́нный *adj.* **1,** permanent. **2,** continuous.

бессме́ртие *n.* immortality.

бессме́ртный *adj.* immortal.

бессмы́сленно *adv.* senselessly. —*adj., used predicatively,* making no sense: Сде́лать э́то — соверше́нно бессмы́сленно, it makes no sense whatever to do that.

бессмы́сленность *n.f.* senselessness.

бессмы́сленный *adj.* **1,** having no meaning; meaningless. **2,** pointless. **3,** senseless; irrational; wanton. **4,** (*of a look*) blank; vacant.

бессмы́слица *n., colloq.* foolishness; nonsense.

бессо́вестный *adj.* unscrupulous; unconscionable.

бессодержа́тельный *adj.* empty; shallow; insipid; vapid; dull.

бессозна́тельный *adj.* **1,** unconscious. **2,** involuntary; instinctive.

бессо́нница *n.* insomnia.

бессо́нный *adj.* sleepless.

бесспо́рный *adj.* indisputable; incontrovertible. —**бесспо́рно,** *adv.* unquestionably; without question.

бессро́чный *adj.* for an indefinite period; for an unlimited time; open-ended; (*of a contract or treaty*) of unlimited duration.

бесстра́стие *n.* impassivity. —**бесстра́стный,** *adj.* impassive.

бесстра́шие *n.* fearlessness. —**бесстра́шный,** *adj.* fearless; intrepid.

бессты́дник *n.m.* [*fem.* **-ница**] *colloq.* shameless person.

бессты́дный *adj.* shameless; brazen. —**бессты́дно,** *adv.* shamelessly; brazenly.

бессты́дство *n.* **1,** shamelessness. **2,** audacity.

бессчётный *adj.* countless; innumerable.

беста́ктность *n.f.* **1,** tactlessness. **2,** indiscretion: соверши́ть беста́ктность, to commit an indiscretion.

беста́ктный *adj.* tactless.

бестала́нный *adj.* lacking talent; untalented.

бестеле́сный *adj.* incorporeal.

бе́стия *n., colloq.* rogue; knave. —хи́трая *or* продувна́я бе́стия, sly devil.

бестолко́вый *adj.* **1,** obtuse; stupid. **2,** incoherent; confused.

бестсе́ллер (сэ) *n.* best seller.

бесфо́рменный *adj.* formless; shapeless; amorphous.

бесхара́ктерный *adj.* lacking in character; weak-willed.

бесхи́тростный *adj.* artless; ingenuous.

бесхо́зный *adj., colloq.* = **бесхозя́йный.**

бесхозя́йный *adj.* without an owner; ownerless.

бесхозя́йственный *adj.* **1,** incompetent; inefficient. **2,** uneconomical; wasteful. —**бесхозя́йственность,** *n.f.* mismanagement.

бесхребе́тный *adj.* spineless; weak-willed.

бесцве́тный *adj.* **1,** colorless. **2,** *fig.* colorless; insipid; dull; drab. —**бесцве́тность,** *n.f.* dullness; drabness; monotony.

бесце́льный *adj.* **1,** aimless. **2,** pointless. —**бесце́льно,** *adv.* aimlessly.

бесце́нный *adj.* priceless; invaluable.

бесце́нок *n., colloq., in* за бесце́нок, for next to nothing; for a song.

бесцеремо́нный *adj.* unceremonious; familiar. —**бесцеремо́нно,** *adv.* unceremoniously; without ceremony. —**бесцеремо́нность,** *n.f.* familiarity.

бесчелове́чный *adj.* inhuman; inhumane. —**бесчелове́чность,** *n.f.* inhumanity.

бесче́стить *v.impfv.* [*pfv.* **обесче́стить;** *pres.* **-щу, -стишь**] to disgrace; dishonor.

бесче́стный *adj.* dishonorable. —**бесче́стье,** *n.* disgrace; dishonor.

бесчи́нство *n.* outrage.

бесчи́нствовать *v.impfv.* [*pres.* **-ствую, -ствуешь**] to run wild; go on a rampage; commit outrages.

бесчи́сленный *adj.* innumerable; countless.

бесчу́вственный *adj.* **1,** insensible; unconscious. **2,** insensitive; unfeeling.

бесчу́вствие *n.* **1,** insensibility; unconsciousness. **2,** insensitivity; indifference.

бесшаба́шный *adj., colloq.* reckless; devil-may-care.

бесшо́вный *adj.* (*of pipes*) seamless.

бесшу́мный *adj.* noiseless. —**бесшу́мно,** *adv.* noiselessly; without making a sound.

бе́та (бэ) *n.* beta. —**бе́та-лучи́,** beta rays. —**бе́та-части́ца,** beta particle.

бе́тель *also,* **бете́ль** *n.m.* betel.

бето́н *n.* concrete.

бетони́ровать *v.impfv. & pfv.* [*pfv. also* **забетони́ровать;** *pres.* **-ру́ю, -руешь**] to pave with concrete.

бето́нный *adj.* concrete.

бефстро́ганов *n. indecl.* beef stroganoff.

бечева́ *n.* towline; towrope.

бечёвка [*gen. pl.* **-вок**] *n.* string; twine.

бечевни́к [*gen.* **-ника́**] *n.* towpath. *Also,* **бече́вник.**

бечево́й *adj.* towing (*attrib.*); tow (*attrib.*).

бе́шенство *n.* **1,** rabies; hydrophobia. **2,** rage; fury.

бе́шеный *adj.* **1,** (*of an animal*) rabid; mad. **2,** (*of a person*) violent; tempestuous. —**бе́шеные де́ньги, 1,** exorbitant price: плати́ть бе́шеные де́ньги, to pay through the nose. **2,** quick (*or* easy) money. —**бе́шеные це́ны,** *colloq.* crazy prices.

бзик *n., colloq.* quirk.

библе́йский *adj.* Biblical.

библиогра́фия *n.* bibliography. —**библио́граф,** *n.* bibliographer. —**библиографи́ческий,** *adj.* bibliographic.

библиоте́ка *n.* library.

библиоте́карь *n.m.* [*fem.* **-арша**] librarian.

библиотекове́дение *n.* library science.

библиоте́чный *adj.* library (*attrib.*). —**библиоте́чное де́ло,** librarianship.

библиофи́л *n.* bibliophile.

би́блия *n.* the Bible; bible.

бива́к *also,* **бивуа́к** *n.* bivouac. —**жить (как) на бива́ках,** to camp out.

би́вень [*gen.* **би́вня**] *n.m.* tusk.

бивуа́к *n.* = **бива́к.**

бигуди́ *n.pl. indecl.* (hair) curlers.

бидо́н *n.* large can: бидо́н для молока́, milk can.

бие́ние *n.* beating (*of the heart or pulse*).

бижуте́рия (тэ) *n.* costume jewelry.

биза́нь *n.f.* mizzen (*sail*).

би́знес (нэ) *n.* business. —**бизнесме́н,** *n.* businessman.

бизо́н *n.* bison.

биле́т *n.* **1,** ticket. **2,** membership card; identity card. **3,** [*also,* **экзаменацио́нный биле́т**] card selected at random during an oral examination containing questions to be answered. **4,** *finance* note: креди́тный биле́т, bank note; казначе́йский биле́т, treasury note.

билетёр *n.m.* [*fem.* **-тёрша**] ticket collector; usher.

биле́тный *adj.* ticket (*attrib.*).

биллио́н *n.* billion.

билль *n.m.* bill (*draft of a proposed law*). —**билль о права́х,** Bill of Rights.

би́ло *n.* striking part (*of various mechanisms*).

билья́рд *n.* **1,** billiards. **2,** billiard table; pool table. —**билья́рдная,** *n.* billiard room; pool hall. —**билья́рдный,** *adj.* billiard (*attrib.*).

биметалли́зм *n.* bimetallism. —**биметалли́ческий,** *adj.* bimetallic.

бина́рный *adj.* binary.

бино́кль *n.m.* binoculars. —**полево́й бино́кль,** field glasses. —**театра́льный бино́кль,** opera glasses.

бино́м *n., math.* binomial.

бинт [*gen.* **бинта́**] *n.* bandage.

бинтова́ть *v.impfv.* [*pfv.* **забинтова́ть;** *pres.* **-ту́ю, -ту́ешь**] to bandage.

биогра́фия *n.* biography. —**био́граф,** *n.* biographer. —**биографи́ческий,** *adj.* biographical.

биоло́гия *n.* biology. —**био́лог,** *n.* biologist. —**биологи́ческий,** *adj.* biological.

био́ника *n.* bionics.

биопси́я *n.* biopsy.

биофи́зика *n.* biophysics.

биохи́мия *n.* biochemistry. —**биохи́мик,** *n.* biochemist. —**биохими́ческий,** *adj.* biochemical.

бипла́н *n.* biplane.

би́ржа *n.* exchange; market: фо́ндовая би́ржа, stock exchange; stock market. —**би́ржа труда́, 1,** state employment agency. **2,** labor exchange.

биржеви́к [*gen.* **-вика́**] *n.* trader in stocks.

биржево́й *adj.* stock (*attrib.*); stock market (*attrib.*).

би́рка [*gen. pl.* **би́рок**] *n.* **1,** tally (*notched stick*). **2,** tag; marker; label.

бирма́нец [*gen.* **-нца**] *n.* Burmese (man): Он бирма́нец, he is Burmese. —**бирма́нка,** *n.* Burmese woman. —**бирма́нский,** *adj.* Burmese.

бирюза́ *n.* turquoise. —**бирюзо́вый,** *adj.* turquoise.

бирю́к [*gen.* **-юка́**] *n.* lone wolf (*lit. & fig.*). —**бирюко́м смотре́ть,** to look sullen; scowl.

бирю́льки [*gen.* **-лек**] *n.pl.* jackstraws. —**игра́ть в бирю́льки, 1,** to play jackstraws. **2,** *fig.* to trifle away one's time.

бис *interj.* encore! —**испо́лнить (что́-нибудь) на бис,** to perform (something) as an encore.

би́сер *n.* beads. —**мета́ть би́сер пе́ред сви́ньями,** to cast pearls before swine.

би́серина *n., colloq.* bead. *Also,* **би́серинка.**

би́серный *adj.* **1,** bead (*attrib.*); beaded. **2,** (*of handwriting*) tiny; minute.

биси́ровать *v.impfv. & pfv.* [*pres.* **-рую, -руешь**] to give an encore.

бискви́т *n.* sponge cake.

бита́ *n.* bat (*used in various games*).

би́тва *n.* battle.

битко́м *adv., in* **битко́м наби́ть,** to pack; jam; fill to capacity.

бито́к [*gen.* **битка́**] *n.* meatball. *Also* **бито́чек** [*gen.* **-чка**].

биту́м *also* **би́тум** *n.* bitumen. —**битумино́зный; биту́мный,** *adj.* bituminous.

би́тый *adj.* **1,** beaten. **2,** damaged. **3,** broken. —**би́тая пти́ца,** freshly killed poultry. —**би́тый час,** a whole hour.

бить *v.impfv.* [*pres.* **бью, бьёшь**] **1,** to beat; strike; hit. **2,** [*pfv.* **поби́ть**] to beat; thrash; give a beating to. **3,** (*with* **в** + *acc.*) to beat (a drum); strike (a bell); clap (one's hands). **4,** (*with* **по** *or* **о**) to bang (on); beat (against). **5,** [*pfv.* **разби́ть**] to break; shatter; smash. **6,** [*pfv.* **поби́ть**] to defeat; conquer; subdue. **7,** [*pfv.* **проби́ть**] (*of clocks*) to strike; chime; (*of drums*) to beat. **8,** [*pfv.* **проби́ть**] to sound (an alarm, retreat, etc.). **9,** to kill; shoot (game). **10,** to shoot; (*with* **из**) fire (a weapon); (*with* **по**) fire (at). **11,** to gush; spurt; (*of a fountain*) to play. **12,** (*with* **на** + *acc.*) (*of a gun*) to have a range of. —**бить в глаза́, 1,** (*of light or the sun*) to be blinding. **2,** *fig.* to be striking; catch the eye. —**бить в цель,** to hit the mark. —**бить ключо́м,** *see* **ключ.** —**бить ми́мо це́ли,** to be wide of the mark. —**бить по рука́м,** to strike a bargain; make a deal.

битьё *n.* **1,** *colloq.* beating; thrashing. **2,** breaking; smashing. —**ма́льчик для битья́,** whipping boy.

би́ться *v.r.impfv.* [*pres.* **бьюсь, бьёшься**] **1,** to fight. **2,** *fig.* (*with* **над**) to struggle (with *or* over); wrestle (with). **3,** (*with* **о** + *acc.*) to beat (against); strike (against); batter. **4,** (*with instr.*) to beat; bang (*repeatedly*): **би́ться голово́й об сте́ну,** to beat/bang one's head against the wall. **5,** (*of the heart, pulse, etc.*) to beat; pulsate. **6,** to writhe; toss about; thrash about. **7,** to be fragile; be breakable. —**би́ться об закла́д,** to bet; wager. —**би́ться как ры́ба об лёд,** to struggle to keep body and soul together.

битю́г [*gen.* **-тюга́**] *n.* a type of dray horse.

бифока́льный *adj.* bifocal. —**бифока́льные очки́,** bifocals.

бифште́кс (тэ) *n.* steak; beefsteak.

бихевиори́зм *n.* behaviorism.

би́цепс *n.* biceps.

бич [*gen.* **бича́**] *n.* **1,** whip; lash. **2,** *fig.* (*with gen.*) scourge (of).

бичева́ние *n.* flagellation.

бичева́ть *v.impfv.* [*pres.* **-чу́ю, -чу́ешь**] **1,** to whip; flog; flagellate. **2,** *fig.* to castigate; excoriate.

бишь *particle, colloq.,* used when one has forgotten *something:* О чём бишь мы говори́ли?, what is it we were talking about? —**то бишь,** *colloq.* or rather.

бла́го[1] *n.* **1,** good: на бла́го челове́чества, for the good of mankind. **2,** *pl.* benefits; blessings. —**жела́ю вам всех благ,** I wish you all the best. —**ни за каки́е бла́га,** not for anything in the world. —**счита́ть за бла́го** (+ *inf.*), to think it best/wise to...

бла́го[2] *conj., colloq.* since; inasmuch as.

бла́говест *n., obs.* ringing of church bells; call to prayer.

бла́говестить *v.impfv.* [*pres.* **-щу, -стишь**] *obs.* to ring church bells.

благове́щение *n., relig.* Annunciation. —**благове́щенский,** *adj.* Annunciation (*attrib.*): Благове́щенский собо́р, Cathedral of the Annunciation (*in the Kremlin*).

благови́дный *adj.* **1,** *obs.* attractive; good-looking. **2,** proper; suitable. **3,** (*of an excuse*) plausible; specious.

благоволе́ние *n., obs.* favor; good graces.

благоволи́ть *v.impfv.* **1,** (*with* **к**) to like; regard with favor; be favorably disposed (toward). **2,** (*with inf.*) *obs.* to be so kind as to: благоволи́те отве́тить, kindly favor us with a reply.

благовоспи́танный *adj.* well-mannered; well-bred.

благогове́йный *adj.* reverent.

благогове́ние *n.* (*with* **пе́ред**) reverence (for); veneration (of).

благогове́ть *v.impfv.* (*with* **пе́ред**) to revere; venerate.

благодаре́ние *n., obs.* expression of thanks; thanksgiving.

благодари́ть *v.impfv.* [*pfv.* **поблагодари́ть**] to thank. —**благодарю́ вас!,** thank you! —**благодари́ть судьбу́,** to thank one's lucky stars.

благода́рность *n.f.* **1,** gratitude. **2,** (expression of) thanks. **3,** *mil.* citation; commendation. —**не сто́ит благода́рности,** don't mention it!

благода́рный *adj.* [*short form* **-рен, -рна**] **1,** grateful; thankful; appreciative. **2,** worthy; worthwhile.

благода́рственный *adj., obs.* of thanks; of gratitude.

благодаря́ *prep., with dat.* thanks to; owing to. —**благодаря́ тому́, что...,** owing to (*or* due to) the fact that...

благода́тный *adj.* **1,** welcome. **2,** fertile; abundant.

благода́ть *n.f.* **1,** *obs.* blessing; divine gift. **2,** abundance; plenty. **3,** *colloq.* a delight.

благоде́нствие *n.* well-being; prosperity.

благоде́нствовать *v.impfv.* [*pres.* **-ствую, -ствуешь**] to prosper; thrive.

благоде́тель *n.m., obs.* benefactor.

благоде́тельный *adj.* **1,** beneficial. **2,** *obs.* benevolent.

благодея́ние *n.* good deed.

благоду́шествовать *v.impfv.* [*pres.* **-ствую, -ствуешь**] to relax; take life easy.

благоду́шие *n.* **1,** good nature. **2,** good humor; happy frame of mind.

благоду́шный *adj.* **1,** good-natured. **2,** in a good mood; in a happy frame of mind.

благожела́тельный *adj.* **1,** good-natured; kindly. **2,** favorable. —**благожела́тельность,** *n.f.* good will; benevolence.

благозву́чие *n.* harmony; euphony. *Also,* **благозву́чность,** *n.f.*

благозву́чный *adj.* euphonious; harmonious; melodious.

благо́й *adj., obs.* good. —**крича́ть благи́м ма́том,** *colloq.* to yell one's head off.

благонадёжный *adj., obs.* reliable; trustworthy. —**благонадёжность,** *n.f., obs.* reliability; trustworthiness.

благонаме́ренный *adj., obs.* well-intentioned; well-meaning.

благообра́зный *adj.* good-looking; handsome.

благополу́чие *n.* well-being; welfare.

благополу́чный *adj.* successful; happy; satisfactory. —**благополу́чно,** *adv.* all right; safely; without mishap.

благопристо́йный *adj.* proper; decorous; seemly.

благоприя́тный *adj.* favorable; auspicious.

благоприя́тствовать *v.impfv.* [*pres.* **-ствую, -ствуешь**] (*with dat.*) to favor; work to the advantage of.

благоразу́мие *n.* prudence; discretion; good sense.

благоразу́мный *adj.* **1,** reasonable; prudent; judicious; discreet. **2,** (*of advice*) sensible. —**благоразу́мно,** *adv.* prudently; judiciously; wisely.

благоро́дный *adj.* noble. —**благоро́дные мета́ллы**, precious metals. —**благоро́дный оле́нь**, red deer.

благоро́дство *n.* nobility.

благоскло́нный *adj.* [*short form* **-о́нен, -о́нна**] **1**, favorable; kindly. **2**, (*with* **к**) kind (to). —**благоскло́нно**, *adv.* with favor; favorably. —**благоскло́нность**, *n.f.* favor; good graces.

благослове́ние *n.* blessing.

благослове́нный *adj., poetic* blessed.

благословля́ть *v.impfv.* [*pfv.* **благослови́ть**] to bless. —**благословля́ть судьбу́**, to thank one's lucky stars.

благосостоя́ние *n.* well-being; welfare.

бла́гостный *adj.* serene.

благотвори́тель *n.m.* philanthropist.

благотвори́тельность *n.f.* charity; philanthropy.

благотвори́тельный *adj.* charitable; philanthropic. Благотвори́тельный конце́рт, benefit concert.

благотво́рный *adj.* beneficial; wholesome; salutary.

благоустро́енный *adj.* well-designed; well-equipped; with all the modern conveniences.

благоустро́йство *n.* providing of public services and amenities.

благоуха́ние *n.* fragrance; sweet smell; redolence. —**благоуха́нный**, *adj.* fragrant; sweet-smelling; redolent.

благоуха́ть *v.impfv.* to smell sweet; be fragrant.

благочести́вый *adj.* pious; devout. —**благоче́стие**, *n.* piety.

блаже́нный *adj.* **1**, blissful. **2**, blessed. **3**, *colloq.* wacky. —**блаже́нной па́мяти**, of blessed memory. —**в блаже́нном неве́дении**, in blissful ignorance.

блаже́нство *n.* bliss.

блаже́нствовать *v.impfv.* [*pres.* **-ствую, -ствуешь**] to be blissfully happy; be in a state of bliss.

блажь *n.f., colloq.* whim; fancy.

бланк *n.* form; blank.

блат *n.* **1**, thieves' cant. **2**, *colloq.* pull; connections; influence: по бла́ту, by pulling strings.

блатно́й *adj., colloq.* thieves': блатно́й язы́к, thieves' cant.

бледне́ть *v.impfv.* [*pfv.* **побледне́ть**] **1**, to turn pale; turn white. **2**, [*impfv. only*] *fig.* (*with* **перед**) to pale (before); suffer in comparison (with).

бледно- *prefix, used with colors,* pale: бледно-зелё́ный, pale green.

бле́дность *n.f.* pallor.

бле́дный *adj.* [*short form* **бле́ден, бледна́, бле́дно, бледны́** *or* **бле́дны**] **1**, pale. **2**, *fig.* dull; colorless; insipid.

бле́йзер (зэ) *n.* blazer.

блёклый *adj.* faded; withered.

блёкнуть *v.impfv.* [*pfv.* **поблёкнуть**; *past* **блёк** *or* **блёкнул, блёкла**] **1**, to fade. **2**, to wither.

блеск *n.* **1**, brilliance; luster. **2**, *fig.* magnificence; splendor: во всём бле́ске, in all its splendor. **3**, (*with gen.*) brilliance (*of wit, talent, etc.*). —**с бле́ском**, with flying colors.

блесна́ [*pl.* **блёсны, блёсен**] *n.* spoon bait.

блесну́ть *v.pfv.* **1**, *pfv. of* **блесте́ть**. **2**, to flash across one's mind: У меня́ блесну́ла мысль, the thought flashed across my mind.

блесте́ть *v.impfv.* [*pfv.* **блесну́ть**; *pres.* **блещу́, блести́шь** *or* **бле́щешь**] **1**, to shine; sparkle; glitter; gleam. **2**, *fig.* (*with instr.*) be blessed (with): Он не бле́щет умо́м, he is not blessed with a great mind; he is no genius.

блёстки *n.pl.* [*sing.* **блёстка**] **1**, spangles; sequins. **2**, *fig.* (*with gen.*) flashes (*of wit, talent, etc.*).

блестя́щий *adj.* **1**, shining; sparkling. **2**, *fig.* brilliant. —**блестя́ще**, *adv.* brilliantly.

блеф *n.* bluff.

блефова́ть *v.impfv.* [*pres.* **-фу́ю, -фу́ешь**] *colloq.* to bluff.

бле́яние *n.* bleat; bleating.

бле́ять *v.impfv.* [*pres.* **бле́ет**] to bleat.

ближа́йший *adj.* **1**, nearest. **2**, next: в ближа́йшие дни, in the next few days. **3**, immediate: ближа́йший нача́льник, immediate superior. **4**, more exact: при ближа́йшем рассмотре́нии, on closer examination. **5**, *in* ближа́йший ро́дственник, nearest relative; next of kin. —**в ближа́йшем бу́дущем; в ближа́йшее вре́мя**, in the near (*or* immediate) future.

бли́же *adj., comp. of* **бли́зкий**.

ближневосто́чный *adj.* Middle East (*attrib.*); Middle Eastern.

бли́жний *adj.* near; nearby. —*n., obs.* neighbor; fellow human being. —**бли́жний бой**, close combat. —**Бли́жний Восто́к**, Middle East. —**бли́жний свет**, low beams (*on a car*).

близ *prep., with gen.* near; close to.

бли́зиться *v.r.impfv.* to approach; draw near.

бли́зкий *adj.* [*short form* **бли́зок, близка́, бли́зко, бли́зки** *or* **близки́**; *comp.* **бли́же**] **1**, nearby. На бли́зком расстоя́нии, at close range. **2**, near (*in time*); imminent: Побе́да близка́, victory is near. **3**, close; intimate: бли́зкий друг, close friend. Я с ним не́ был бли́зок, I was not close to him. **4**, *fig.* (*with* **к**) close (to): бли́зок к по́длиннику, close to the original. —**бли́зкие**, *n.pl.* one's relatives.

бли́зко *adv.* near; close; nearby. —*adj., used predicatively,* nearby; close to here: По́чта совсе́м бли́зко, the post office is right nearby. —**бли́зко от** *or* **к**, near; close to.

близлежа́щий *adj.* nearby; neighboring.

близне́ц [*gen.* **-неца́**] *n.* **1**, twin. **2**, *pl., cap.* Gemini.

близору́кий *adj.* **1**, nearsighted; myopic. **2**, *fig.* shortsighted.

близору́кость *n.f.* **1**, nearsightedness; myopia. **2**, *fig.* shortsightedness.

бли́зость *n.f.* **1**, nearness; closeness; proximity. **2**, closeness of relations.

блик *n.* patch of light.

блин [*gen.* **блина́**] *n.* pancake.

блинда́ж [*gen.* **-дажа́**] *n., mil.* dugout; bunker.

бли́нчатый *adj.* pancake (*attrib.*).

бли́нчик *n.* small pancake.

блиста́тельный *adj.* brilliant; glittering; resplendent.

блиста́ть *v.impfv.* to shine; sparkle; glitter. —**блиста́ть свои́м отсу́тствием**, to be conspicuous by one's absence.

блиц *n.* flash bulb.

блок *n.* **1,** block (*pulley*). **2,** block (*of cement, marble, etc.*). **3,** *mech.* block: блок цили́ндров, cylinder block. **4,** *mech.* unit: блок пита́ния, power supply unit. **5,** prefabricated building unit; block. **6,** (political) bloc. **7,** carton (of cigarettes). **8,** *sports* (body) block. **9,** *philately* block; souvenir sheet.

блока́да *n.* blockade.

блокга́уз *n., mil.* blockhouse.

блоки́ровать *v.impfv. & pfv.* [*pfv. also* **заблоки́ровать**; *pres.* **-рую, -руешь**] **1,** to block. **2,** to blockade. **3,** *sports* to block. —**блоки́роваться,** *refl.* (*with* **с** + *instr.*) to form an alliance (with).

блокно́т *n.* writing pad; note pad; tablet.

блонди́н *n.* blond (man). —**блонди́нка,** *n.* [*gen. pl.* **-нок**] blonde.

блоха́ [*pl.* **бло́хи, блох, блоха́м**] *n.* flea. —**кака́я блоха́ его́ укуси́ла?,** what's eating him?

блоши́ный *adj.* flea (*attrib.*). —**блоши́ный уку́с,** fleabite.

бло́шки [*gen.* **-шек**] *n.pl.* tiddlywinks.

блуд *n., obs.* lechery; debauchery.

блуди́ть *v.impfv.* [*pres.* **блужу́, блу́дишь**] *colloq.* to wander.

блу́дный *adj.,* в блу́дный сын, prodigal son.

блужда́ние *n., often pl.* wanderings.

блужда́ть *v.impfv.* to roam; wander. —**блужда́ть в потёмках,** to feel one's way.

блужда́ющий *adj.* roaming; wandering. —**блужда́ющие огни́,** will-o'-the-wisp.

блу́за *n.* **1,** smock. **2,** *obs.* blouse.

блу́зка [*gen. pl.* **-зок**] *n.* (lady's) blouse.

блю́дечко [*gen. pl.* **-чек**] *n.* saucer.

блю́до *n.* **1,** platter. **2,** dish; food: моё люби́мое блю́до, my favorite dish/food. **3,** course: второ́е блю́до, main course; entrée. Обе́д из трёх блюд, three-course dinner.

блю́дце [*gen. pl.* **-дец**] *n.* **1,** saucer. **2,** *colloq.* dish antenna.

блюз *n., music* blues.

блюсти́ *v.impfv.* [*pfv.* **соблюсти́**; *pres.* **блюду́, блюдёшь**; *past* **блюл, блюла́, блюло́**] **1,** to guard; watch over. **2,** to maintain; keep. **3,** to observe; abide by.

блюсти́тель *n.m.* keeper; guardian. —**блюсти́тель поря́дка,** keeper of order; guardian of the law.

бля́ха *n.* name plate; badge. *Also,* **бля́шка.**

боа́ *n.m. indecl.* boa constrictor. —*n.neut. indecl., obs.* boa (*lady's scarf*).

боб [*gen.* **боба́**] *n.* bean. —**гада́ть на боба́х,** to make wild guesses. —**оста́ться на боба́х,** *colloq.* to be left with nothing.

бобёр [*gen.* **бобра́**] *n.* beaver fur.

бобо́вый *adj.* **1,** bean (*attrib.*). **2,** leguminous.

бобр [*gen.* **бобра́**] *n.* beaver.

бо́брик *n.* castor (*cloth*).

бобро́вый *adj.* beaver (*attrib.*).

бо́бслей *n.* bobsled.

бобы́ль [*gen.* **-быля́**] *n.m.* **1,** *obs.* poor landless peasant. **2,** *colloq.* lonely unmarried man.

бог [*pl.* **бо́ги, бого́в, бога́м**] *n., often cap.* God; god. —**бог его́ зна́ет!,** God knows! —**бог с** (+ *instr.*), to

hell with...; forget about... —**дай бог!,** God grant. —**ей бо́гу!,** really!; truly! —**не дай бог!,** God forbid!; heaven forbid! —**ра́ди бо́га!,** for God's sake!; for goodness' sake!; for heaven's sake! —**сла́ва бо́гу!,** thank God!; thank goodness!; thank heaven!

богаде́льня [*gen. pl.* **-лен**] *n.* poorhouse; almshouse.

богате́ть *v.impfv.* [*pfv.* **разбогате́ть**] to get rich.

бога́то *adv.* lavishly; in lavish style.

бога́тство *n.* **1,** wealth; riches. **2,** richness. **3,** *pl.* (natural) resources. **4,** *fig.* (*with gen.*) wealth (of); profusion (of).

бога́тый *adj.* [*comp.* **бога́че**] **1,** rich; wealthy. **2,** abundant. **3,** (*of a collection*) large; (*of a choice*) wide; (*of experience*) broad; (*of one's imagination*) fertile. **4,** luxurious; sumptuous. —*n.* rich man. —**чем бога́ты, тем и ра́ды,** you are welcome to what we have.

богаты́рский *adj.* of or like a **богаты́рь** (*see entry below*). —**богаты́рское сложе́ние,** powerful physique. —**богаты́рское здоро́вье,** robust health.

богаты́рь [*gen.* **-тыря́**] *n.m.* **1,** Russian epic hero. **2,** *fig.* big strapping man.

бога́ч [*gen.* **-гача́**] *n.* rich man.

бога́че *adj., comp. of* **бога́тый.**

боге́ма *n.* **1,** Bohemians. **2,** *colloq.* Bohemian way of life. —**боге́мный,** *adj., colloq.* Bohemian.

боге́мский *adj.* of or from Bohemia; Bohemian.

боги́ня *n.* goddess.

богобоя́зненный *adj.* god-fearing.

богома́терь *n.f., usu. cap.* Mother of God (*the Virgin Mary*). —**собо́р богома́тери,** Cathedral of Notre Dame.

богомо́л *n.* **1,** pilgrim. **2,** *zool.* (praying) mantis.

богомо́лец [*gen.* **-льца**] *n.m.* [*fem.* **-лка**] **1,** devout person. **2,** pilgrim. —**богомо́лье,** *n.* pilgrimage. —**богомо́льный,** *adj.* devout.

богоро́дица *n., usu. cap.* the Virgin Mary.

богосло́вие *n.* theology. —**богосло́в,** *n.* theologian. —**богосло́вский,** *adj.* theological.

богослуже́ние *n.* religious service.

боготвори́ть *v.impfv.* to worship; idolize.

богоху́льство *n.* blasphemy. —**богоху́льный,** *adj.* blasphemous.

богоху́льствовать *v.impfv.* [*pres.* **-ствую, -ствуешь**] to blaspheme; engage in blasphemy.

богоявле́ние *n., usu. cap.* Epiphany.

бода́ть *v.impfv.* to butt. —**бода́ться,** *refl.* **1,** to butt (*generally*). **2,** to butt each other.

бодли́вый *adj.* (*of an animal*) that butts a lot.

бодри́ть *v.impfv.* **1,** to invigorate. **2,** to be invigorating. —**бодри́ться,** *refl.* to try to keep one's spirits up.

бо́дрость *n.f.* **1,** vigor. **2,** cheerfulness; good spirits.

бо́дрствовать *v.impfv.* [*pres.* **-ствую, -ствуешь**] to stay awake; keep vigil.

бо́дрый *adj.* **1,** cheerful; buoyant; jaunty. **2,** vigorous; sprightly; hale and hearty. **3,** awake: совсе́м бо́дрый, wide-awake.

бодря́щий *adj.* invigorating; bracing.

боеви́к [*gen.* **-вика́**] *n.* **1,** militant. **2,** *colloq.* hit (*movie*).

боеви́тость *n.f.* fighting spirit; enthusiasm. —**боеви́тый,** *adj.* active; energetic; lively; enthusiastic.

боево́й adj. **1,** combat (attrib.); battle (attrib.); fighting. Боевы́е де́йствия, combat operations. **2,** mil. live: боевы́е патро́ны, live ammunition. **3,** militant; belligerent. **4,** urgent. —**боева́я голо́вка; боева́я часть,** warhead. —**боево́й поря́док,** order of battle.

боеголо́вка [gen. pl. **-вок**] n. warhead.

боегото́вность n.f. combat readiness.

боеприпа́сы [gen. **-сов**] n.pl. **1,** ammunition. **2,** munitions.

боеспосо́бность n.f., mil. fighting efficiency; combat effectiveness. —**боеспосо́бный,** adj. fit for combat.

бое́ц [gen. **бойца́**] n. soldier; fighting man.

божба́ n. swearing.

бо́же n., vocative case of **бог.** —interj. God! —**бо́же мой!,** God!; my God!

боже́ственный adj. **1,** divine. **2,** colloq. divine; idyllic; sublime. —**боже́ственность,** n.f. divinity.

божество́ n. deity.

бо́жий [fem. **-жья**] adj. **1,** God's. **2,** divine. —**бо́жья коро́вка,** ladybug; ladybird. —**ка́ждый бо́жий день,** every blessed day. —**я́сный как бо́жий день,** as clear as day.

божи́ться v.r.impfv. [pfv. **побожи́ться**] to swear.

божо́к [gen. **божка́**] n. **1,** figurine or statuette of a god. **2,** idol; one who is idolized.

бой [2nd loc. **бою́**; pl. **бои́, боёв, боя́м**] n. **1,** combat; battle: поги́бнуть в бою́, to be killed in combat/battle/action. **2,** fight: кула́чный бой, fistfight; бой быко́в, bullfight. Без бо́я, without a fight. **3,** pl. fighting: тяжёлые бои́, heavy fighting. **4,** breaking; breakage. **5,** striking (of a clock); beating (of drums). **6,** killing; slaughter (of fish, whales, etc.). —**взять с бо́ю,** to take by force. —**дать бой** (+ dat.), to do battle (with).

бо́йкий adj. [short form **бо́ек, бойка́, бо́йко, бо́йки;** comp. **бо́йче**] **1,** sharp; clever; lively; brisk. **2,** lively. **3,** glib; facile.

бойко́т n. boycott.

бойкоти́ровать v.impfv. & pfv. [pres. **-рую, -руешь**] to boycott.

бо́йница n. embrasure.

бо́йня [gen. pl. **бо́ен**] n. **1,** slaughterhouse. **2,** massacre; slaughter; carnage.

бок [2nd loc. **боку́**; pl. **бока́**] n. side. —**бок о́ бок,** side by side. —**под бо́ком, 1,** nearby; close at hand. **2,** (with у) colloq. right next to. —**с бо́ку на́ бок,** from side to side. See also **бо́ком.**

бока́л n. wineglass; goblet.

боково́й adj. side (attrib.); lateral. Боковая у́лица, side street. Боково́й ве́тер, crosswind. —**отпра́виться на боковую,** colloq. to turn in; hit the hay.

бо́ком adv. sideways. —**вы́йти бо́ком** (+ dat.), colloq. to turn out badly (for); backfire (on).

бокс n. boxing.

боксёр n. **1,** boxer (fighter). **2,** boxer (dog). —**боксёрский,** adj. boxing (attrib.).

бокси́ровать v.impfv. [pres. **-рую, -руешь**] sports to box.

бокси́т n. bauxite. —**бокси́товый,** adj. bauxite (attrib.).

болва́н n. **1,** colloq. dolt; blockhead. **2,** [also, **болва́нка**] block (for shaping hats). **3,** cards dummy.

болга́рин [pl. **-га́ры, -га́р**] n.m. [fem. **-га́рка**] Bulgarian. —**болга́рский,** adj. Bulgarian.

болево́й adj. painful. —**болева́я то́чка, 1,** sore spot. **2,** fig. trouble spot.

бо́лее adv. **1,** more: я бо́лее чем дово́лен, I am more than satisfed. Бо́лее полуго́да тому́ наза́д, more than half a year ago. **2,** used in forming compound comparatives, more: бо́лее интере́сный, more interesting. —**бо́лее и́ли ме́нее,** more or less. —**бо́лее того́,** what is more. —**всё бо́лее** (+ adj.), more and more; increasingly. —**тем бо́лее, 1,** all the more; the more so. **2,** (in neg. sentences) much less. —**тем бо́лее, что...,** especially since; all the more so because...

боле́зненно adv. **1,** painfully. **2,** with difficulty; hard.

боле́зненность n.f. **1,** sickliness. **2,** morbidity.

боле́зненный adj. **1,** sickly. **2,** painful; causing pain. **3,** of pain: боле́зненный крик, a cry of pain. **4,** abnormal; morbid: боле́зненное любопы́тство, morbid curiosity.

боле́знь n.f. illness; disease. —**боле́зни ро́ста,** growing pains. —**морска́я боле́знь,** seasickness. —**о́тпуск по боле́зни,** sick leave. —**со́нная боле́знь,** sleeping sickness.

боле́льщик n., colloq., sports fan.

бо́лен see **больно́й.**

боле́ть[1] v.impfv. [pres. **боле́ю, боле́ешь**] **1,** to be ill. Боле́ть ко́рью, to have the measles. **2,** (with за + acc. or о) colloq. to agonize (over). **3,** (with за + acc.) colloq. to be a fan of; root (for). —**боле́ть душо́й** (with за + acc. or о), to feel for; grieve for.

боле́ть[2] v.impfv. [pres. **боли́т, боля́т**] to ache; hurt: У меня́ боли́т голова́, I have a headache. —**у меня́ душа́ боли́т за** (+ acc.), my heart aches for...

болеутоля́ющий adj. pain-relieving; analgesic. —**болеутоля́ющее сре́дство,** analgesic.

болиго́лов n. (poison) hemlock.

боли́д n. fireball (meteor).

боло́нка [gen. pl. **-нок**] n. small white poodle.

боло́тистый adj. swampy; marshy.

боло́тный adj. marsh (attrib.). —**боло́тная пти́ца,** wading bird.

боло́то n. swamp; marsh. —**торфяно́е боло́то,** peat bog.

болт [gen. **болта́**] n., mech. bolt.

болта́нка n., aero., colloq. bumpiness; turbulence.

болта́ть v.impfv. **1,** colloq. to talk; chatter. **2,** [pfv. **взболта́ть**] to shake; stir (a liquid). **3,** (with instr.) to dangle; swing. **4,** in болта́ть языко́м, colloq. to babble; prattle. —**болта́ться,** refl. **1,** to dangle. **2,** colloq. to hang around; loiter.

болтли́вый adj. talkative; loquacious; garrulous. —**болтли́вость,** n.f. loquaciousness.

болтовня́ n., colloq. chatter.

болту́н [gen. **-туна́**] n.m. [fem. **-ту́нья**] chatterbox.

болту́нья n. **1,** fem. of **болту́н. 2,** in яи́чница-болту́нья, scrambled eggs.

боль n.f. pain; ache. —**до бо́ли, 1,** till it hurt(s). **2,** painfully. —**с бо́лью в се́рдце,** with a heavy heart.

больни́ца n. hospital.

больни́чный *adj.* hospital (*attrib.*). —**больни́чный лист** *or* **листо́к,** medical/doctor's certificate (*certifying inability to work*). Он на больни́чном (листе́), he is on sick leave.

бо́льно *adv.* **1,** badly: бо́льно ушиби́ться, to hurt oneself badly. **2,** *colloq.* terribly; a bit too. —*adj., used predicatively* (*with dat.*) painful: Мне бо́льно, it is painful; it hurts. Мне бо́льно ви́деть..., it pains me to see... —**сде́лать бо́льно** (+ *dat.*), to hurt.

больно́й *adj.* [*short form* бо́лен, больна́] **1,** sick; ill. **2,** sore: больно́й зуб, a sore tooth. **3,** bad: больно́е се́рдце, a bad heart. **4,** (*with instr.*) suffering (from): лю́ди, больны́е диабе́том, people with (*or* suffering from) diabetes. —*n.* patient; sick person. —**больно́й вопро́с,** sore subject. —**больно́е ме́сто,** tender spot.

бо́льше *adj., comp. of* большо́й, bigger; larger; greater. —*adv., comp. of* мно́го, more. —**бо́льше всего́,** most of all. —**бо́льше не,** no more; anymore; any longer. —**бо́льше нигде́,** nowhere else. —**бо́льше никогда́,** never again. —**бо́льше никого́,** no one else. —**бо́льше ничего́,** nothing else. —**бо́льше того́,** what is more.

большеви́к [*gen.* -вика́] *n.* Bolshevik. —**большеви́стский,** *adj.* Bolshevik (*attrib.*).

бо́льший *adj., used only as a modifier, comp. of* большо́й *and* вели́кий, larger; greater. —**бо́льшая часть** (+ *gen.*), most (of). —**бо́льшей ча́стью; по бо́льшей ча́сти,** for the most part; mostly. —**са́мое бо́льшее, 1,** at (the) most. **2,** (*fol. by* что) the most (that).

большинство́ *n.* **1,** majority. **2,** (*with gen. or* из) most: в большинстве́ слу́чаев, in most cases; большинство́ из нас, most of us. —**в большинстве́; в большинстве́ своём,** for the most part; mainly.

большо́й *adj.* [*comp.* бо́льше *and* бо́льший] **1,** big; large. **2,** (*of a book, article, etc.*) long. **3,** great: большо́е откры́тие, great discovery. **4,** *colloq.* grownup. **5,** *cap.* Greater: Большо́й Нью-Йо́рк, Greater New York. —*n., usu. pl., colloq.* grownup. —**больша́я бу́ква,** capital letter. —**большо́й па́лец,** thumb. —**большо́е (вам) спаси́бо!,** thank you very much! *See also* бо́льше *and* бо́льший.

большу́щий *adj., colloq.* huge; tremendous.

боля́чка [*gen. pl.* -чек] *n., colloq.* sore.

бо́мба *n.* bomb.

бомбарди́р *n.* bombardier.

бомбардирова́ть *v.impfv.* [*pres.* -ру́ю, -ру́ешь] to bombard; bomb.

бомбардиро́вка *n.* bombardment; bombing.

бомбардиро́вочный *adj.* bombing (*attrib.*). —**бомбардиро́вочный прице́л,** bombsight.

бомбардиро́вщик *n.* bomber.

бомбёжка *n., colloq.* bombing.

бомби́ть *v.impfv.* [*pres.* -блю́, -би́шь] *colloq.* to bomb.

бо́мбовый *adj.* bomb (*attrib.*).

бомбодержа́тель *n.m.* bomb rack.

бомбомета́ние *n.* bombing.

бомбоубе́жище *n.* bomb shelter; air-raid shelter.

бо́ндарь *n.m.* cooper. *Also,* бонда́рь [*gen.* -даря́].

бо́нза *n.m., colloq.* bigwig; member of the elite.

бор[1] [*2nd loc.* бору́; *pl.* боры́] *n.* pine forest.

бор[2] *n.* boron.

бордо́ *n. indecl.* claret (*wine*). —*adj. indecl.* wine-colored; claret; maroon. —**бордо́вый,** *adj.* = бордо́.

бордю́р *n.* border; trimming.

боре́ц [*gen.* -рца́] *n.* **1,** (*often with* за + *acc.*) fighter (for). **2,** wrestler.

борза́я *n., decl. as an adj.* **1,** borzoi; Russian wolfhound. **2,** greyhound; whippet.

бо́рзый *adj., archaic* (*of a horse*) fleet; swift.

бормаши́на *n.* (dentist's) drill.

бормота́нье *also,* бормота́ние *n.* muttering; mumbling.

бормота́ть *v.impfv.* [*pfv.* пробормота́ть; *pres.* -мочу́, -мо́чешь] to mutter; mumble.

бо́рный *adj.* boric: бо́рная кислота́, boric acid.

бо́ров *n.* **1,** [*pl.* бо́ровы, -во́в] gelded hog. **2,** [*pl.* борова́, -во́в] chimney flue.

борода́ [*acc.* бо́роду; *pl.* бо́роды, боро́д, -да́м] *n.* **1,** beard. **2,** wattle (*of a bird*).

борода́вка [*gen. pl.* -вок] *n.* wart.

борода́вочник *n.* wart hog.

борода́вчатый *adj.* covered with warts.

борода́тый *adj.* bearded.

борода́ч [*gen.* -дача́] *n.* **1,** *colloq.* man with a beard. **2,** bearded vulture.

боро́дка [*gen. pl.* -док] *n.* small beard. —**козли́ная боро́дка,** goatee.

борозда́ [*acc.* бо́розду *or* борозду́; *pl.* бо́розды, боро́зд, -да́м] *n.* furrow.

борозди́ть *v.impfv.* [*pfv.* изборозди́ть; *pres.* -зжу́, -зди́шь] **1,** to furrow. **2,** *in* борозди́ть моря́ *or* океа́ны, to ply the seas. **3,** *in* борозди́ть не́бо, to pierce the sky.

борона́ [*acc.* бо́рону; *pl.* бо́роны, боро́н, -на́м] *n.* harrow.

борони́ть *v.impfv.* [*pfv.* взборони́ть] to harrow. *Also,* боронова́ть [*pres.* -ну́ю, -ну́ешь].

боро́ться *v.r.impfv.* [*pres.* борю́сь, бо́решься] **1,** to fight; struggle. **2,** (*with* с + *instr.*) to combat; fight; battle. **3,** to wrestle.

борт [*2nd loc.* борту́; *pl.* борта́] *n.* **1,** side (*of a ship*). **2,** breast (*of a coat*). **3,** cushion (*of a billiard table*). —**за́ борт; за бо́ртом,** overboard. —**на бо́рт; на́ борт; на борту́,** aboard; on board. —**оста́вить/ оста́ться за бо́ртом,** to leave/ be left/ out in the cold. —**челове́к за бо́ртом!,** man overboard!

бортмеха́ник *n.* flight engineer.

бортово́й *adj.* **1,** on-board. **2,** side (*attrib.*). —**бортово́й журна́л,** ship's log. —**бортова́я ка́чка,** rolling (*of a ship*). —**бортово́й самопи́сец,** flight recorder.

бортпроводни́к [*gen.* -ника́] *n.* steward. —**бортпроводни́ца,** *n.* stewardess.

борщ [*gen.* борща́] *n.* borscht.

борьба́ *n.* **1,** struggle; fight. **2,** wrestling. —**япо́нская борьба́,** jujitsu.

босико́м *adv., colloq.* barefoot; in one's bare feet.

босни́йский *adj.* Bosnian.

босо́й *adj.* **1,** barefoot. **2,** (*of feet*) bare. —**(надева́ть** ту́фли) **на босу́ но́гу,** (to put on one's shoes) without socks.

босоно́гий *adj.* barefoot.

босоно́жка [*gen. pl.* **-жек**] *n.* **1,** barefoot girl or woman. **2,** *usu. pl.* sandals.

босс *n.* boss.

бося́к [*gen.* **-сяка́**] *n.* vagabond; tramp.

бот *n.* **1,** boat. **2,** boot.

бота́ника *n.* botany. —**бота́ник,** *n.* botanist. —**бота́ни́ческий,** *adj.* botanical.

ботва́ *n.* vegetable tops.

ботви́нья *n.* cold soup make of kvass, cooked vegetables and fish.

бо́тик *n.* **1,** small boat. **2,** lady's boot.

боти́нок [*gen.* **-нка;** *gen. pl.* **-нок**] *n.* shoe.

бо́цман *n.* boatswain.

боча́р [*gen.* **-чара́**] *n.* cooper.

бо́чка [*gen. pl.* **бо́чек**] *n.* barrel; keg; cask. —**де́ньги на бо́чку,** cash on the barrel.

бочко́м *adv.* sideways.

бочо́нок [*gen.* **-нка**] *n.* small barrel; keg.

боязли́вый *adj.* timid; timorous. —**боязли́вость,** *n.f.* timidity.

боя́зно *adj., used predicatively (with dat.) colloq.* afraid.

боя́знь *n.f.* fear; dread.

боя́рин [*pl.* **боя́ре, боя́р**] *n., hist.* boyar. —**боя́рский,** *adj.* boyar (*attrib.*); boyars'. —**боя́рство,** *n.* the boyars.

боя́рышник *n.* hawthorn.

боя́ться *v.r.impfv.* [*pres.* **бою́сь, бои́шься**] **1,** (*with gen.*) to be afraid of; fear. **2,** (*with inf. or a dependent clause*) to be afraid; fear: **боя́ться выходи́ть/простуди́ться,** to be afraid to go out; be afraid of catching cold. **Бою́сь, что...,** I'm afraid/ I fear/ that... **3,** (*with за + acc.*) to fear for; be worried about. **4,** (*with gen.*) to be sensitive to; be easily damaged by. —**бою́сь сказа́ть,** I would not want to say; I cannot say for sure.

бра *n.neut. indecl.* candlestick or lamp bracket mounted on a wall.

брава́да *n.* bravado.

брави́ровать *v.impfv.* [*pres.* **-рую, -руешь**] (*with instr.*) **1,** to flaunt; parade. **2,** to brave; defy.

брави́ссимо *interj.* bravissimo!

бра́во *interj.* bravo!

брав́урный *adj.* (*of a work of music*) stirring. —**брав́урная му́зыка,** bravura.

бра́вый *adj.* dashing.

бра́га *n.* home-brewed beer.

бразды́ *n.pl., obs.* bridle; bit. —**бразды́ правле́ния,** the reins of government.

брази́лец [*gen.* **-льца**] *n.m.* [*fem.* **-лья́нка**] Brazilian. —**брази́льский,** *adj.* Brazilian.

брак *n.* **1,** marriage. **2,** defect; flaw. **3,** defective merchandise.

брако́ванный *adj.* (*of merchandise*) defective.

бракова́ть *v.impfv.* [*pfv.* **забракова́ть;** *pres.* **-ку́ю, -ку́ешь**] to reject as defective.

брако́вщик *n.* quality control inspector.

бракоде́л *n.* slipshod worker.

браконье́р *n.* poacher. —**браконье́рство,** *n.* poaching.

бракоразво́дный *adj.* divorce (*attrib.*).

бракосочета́ние *n.* wedding ceremony. —**дворе́ц бракосочета́ния,** wedding palace.

брами́н *n.* = **брахма́н.**

бра́мсель *n.m.* topgallant sail.

брам-сте́ньга *n.* topgallant mast.

брандспо́йт *n.* **1,** nozzle (*of a fire hose*). **2,** portable pump.

брани́ть *v.impfv.* to scold; berate. —**брани́ться,** *refl.* **1,** to quarrel. **2,** to swear; curse.

бра́нный *adj.* **1,** abusive: **бра́нное сло́во,** swearword. **2,** *archaic* martial.

брань *n.f.* **1,** swearing; profanity. **2,** *archaic* battle.

брасле́т *n.* bracelet.

брасс *n., swimming* breast stroke.

брат [*pl.* **бра́тья, бра́тьев**] *n.* brother.

брата́ние *n.* fraternization.

брата́ться *v.r.impfv.* [*pfv.* **побрата́ться**] to fraternize.

бра́тец [*gen.* **-тца**] *n.* **1,** *dim., endearing form of* **брат. 2,** *in direct address,* old man; old chap.

брати́шка [*gen. pl.* **-шек**] *n.m., dim. of* **брат.**

бра́тия *n.* fraternity: **литерату́рная бра́тия,** literary fraternity.

братоуби́йство *n.* fratricide. —**братоуби́йственный,** *adj.* fratricidal.

бра́тский *adj.* brotherly; fraternal. —**бра́тская моги́ла,** common grave.

бра́тство *n.* brotherhood; fraternity.

брать *v.impfv.* [*pfv.* **взять;** *pres.* **беру́, берёшь;** *past fem.* **брала́**] **1,** to take. **2,** to borrow. **3,** to buy; get. **4,** to levy; exact. **5,** to charge (a certain price). **6,** to clear (a hurdle, height, etc.). **7,** (*with instr.*) to succeed (by means of). **8,** *colloq.* to work; be effective: Нож не берёт, the knife doesn't cut. —**брать в долг,** to borrow. —**брать верх,** *see* **верх.** —**брать в ру́ки,** to take (someone) in hand. —**брать в свои́ ру́ки,** to take into one's own hands; take over. —**брать за́ сердце** (*or* **за́ душу**), to touch someone's heart. —**брать курс на,** to head for. —**брать на себя́,** to take upon oneself; assume. —**брать но́ту,** to strike *or* hit a note. —**брать приме́р с** (+ *gen.*), to follow someone's example. —**брать своё,** *see* **свой.** —**брать себя́ в ру́ки,** to pull oneself together. —**брать сло́во с** (+ *gen.*), to make someone promise. —**брать с собо́й,** to take along; bring along. *See also* **взять.**

бра́ться *v.r.impfv.* [*pfv.* **взя́ться;** *pres.* **беру́сь, берёшься;** *past* **бра́лся, брала́сь, брало́сь** *or* **бра́лось, брали́сь** *or* **бра́лись**] **1,** (*with за + acc.*) to take hold of; grasp. **2,** (*with за + acc.*) to begin; take up; undertake. **3,** (*with inf.*) to take it upon oneself (to); dare (to); presume (to). **4,** to come (from): Отку́да же они́ беру́тся?, where on earth do they come from? —**бра́ться за́ руки,** to join hands. —**бра́ться за ору́жие,** to take up arms. —**бра́ться за ум,** *colloq.* to come to one's senses. *See also* **взя́ться.**

брахма́н *also,* **брами́н** *n.* Brahman. —**брахмани́зм;** **брамани́зм,** *n.* Brahmanism.

бра́чный *adj.* marriage (*attrib.*); marital; matrimonial; conjugal; nuptial. —**бра́чный пери́од,** mating period; mating season.

бра́шпиль *n.m.* windlass.

бреве́нчатый *adj.* log (*attrib.*); made of logs.

бревно́ [*pl.* **брёвна, брёвен**] *n.* log.

бред [*2nd loc.* **бреду́**] *n.* **1**, delirium: быть в бреду́, to be delirious; rave. **2**, ravings. **3**, *colloq.* madness; lunacy.

бре́день [*gen.* **-дня**] *n.m.* dragnet.

бре́дить *v.impfv.* [*pres.* **бре́жу, бре́дишь**] **1**, to be delirious; rave. **2**, (*with instr.*) *colloq.* to be crazy (about); be mad (about).

бре́дни [*gen.* **-ней**] *n.pl.* ravings; wild fantasy.

бредово́й *also*, **бредо́вый** *adj.* **1**, delirious. **2**, (*of an idea, plan, etc.*) mad; insane; wild.

бре́згать *v.impfv.* [*pfv.* **побре́згать**] (*with instr. or inf.*) **1**, to be squeamish about; have an aversion to. **2**, to disdain; shrink from: Он не бре́згает никаки́ми сре́дствами, he will use any methods; he will stop at nothing.

брезгли́вый *adj.* squeamish. —**брезгли́вость,** *n.f.* squeamishness.

брезе́нт *n.* tarpaulin. —**брезе́нтовый,** *adj.* tarpaulin (*attrib.*).

бре́зжить *v.impfv.* **1**, to glimmer; gleam faintly. **2**, *impers.* to dawn; get light. *Also*, **бре́зжиться,** *refl.*

брело́к *n.* charm (*on a chain or bracelet*).

бре́мя [*gen., dat. & prepl.* **бре́мени**; *instr.* **бре́менем**] *n.neut.* burden.

бре́нный *adj., obs.* perishable. —**бре́нные оста́нки,** mortal remains.

бренча́ть *v.impfv.* [*pres.* **-чу́, -чи́шь**] **1**, *v.i.* (*of inanimate objects*) to jingle; clink. **2**, *v.t.* (*with instr.*) to jingle; clink (something). **3**, (*with* **на** + *prepl.*) *colloq.* to strum.

брести́ *v.impfv.* [*pres.* **бреду́, бредёшь**; *past* **брёл, брела́, брело́, брели́**] to trudge along; drag oneself along.

брете́лька (тэ) [*gen. pl.* **-лек**] *n.* strap (*of an undergarment*). *Also*, **брете́ль,** *n.f.*

бреха́ть *v.impfv.* [*pfv.* **брехну́ть**; *pres.* **брешу́, бре́шешь**] *colloq.* **1**, to bark. **2**, to tell lies.

брехня́ *n., colloq.* lies.

брехун́ [*gen.* **-хуна́**] *n.m.* [*fem.* **-ху́нья**] *colloq.* liar.

брешь *n.f.* breach; gap.

бре́ющий *pres. active part. of* **брить.** —*adj., in* **бре́ющий полёт,** low-altitude flight.

бриг *n.* brig (*ship*).

брига́да *n.* **1**, *mil.* brigade. **2**, team; crew; brigade (*of workers*).

бригади́р *n.* foreman.

брига́дный *adj.* team (*attrib.*). —**брига́дный генера́л,** brigadier general.

бридж *n., cards* bridge.

бри́джи [*gen.* **-жей**] *n.pl.* breeches.

бриз *n.* sea breeze.

брике́т *n.* briquette.

бриллиа́нт *also*, **брилья́нт** *n.* (cut) diamond. —**бриллиа́нтовый; брилья́нтовый,** *adj.* diamond.

брита́нский *adj.* British.

бри́тва *n.* razor.

бри́твенный *adj.* shaving (*attrib.*): бри́твенные принадле́жности, shaving equipment.

бри́тый *adj.* **1**, shaved. **2**, clean-shaven.

брить *v.impfv.* [*pfv.* **побри́ть**; *pres.* **бре́ю, бре́ешь**] to shave.

бритьё *n.* shaving; shave.

бри́ться *v.r.impfv.* [*pfv.* **побри́ться**; *pres.* **бре́юсь, бре́ешься**] **1**, to shave (oneself). **2**, to get a shave.

бри́финг *n.* briefing.

бри́чка [*gen. pl.* **-чек**] *n.* light car or carriage.

бровь [*pl.* **бро́ви, -ве́й, -вя́м**] *n.f.* eyebrow. —**попа́сть не в бровь, а в глаз,** to hit the nail on the head.

брод *n.* ford.

броди́льный *adj.* fermenting (*attrib.*).

броди́ть *v.impfv.* [*pres.* **брожу́, бро́дишь**] **1**, to wander; roam. **2**, to ferment.

бродя́га *n.m.* tramp; vagrant; vagabond; hobo.

бродя́жничать *v.impfv.* **1**, to lead the life of a tramp. **2**, *colloq.* to wander; roam. *Also*, **бродя́жить.**

бродя́жничество *n.* **1**, vagrancy. **2**, *colloq.* wandering about.

бродя́чий *adj.* **1**, wandering; itinerant. **2**, (*of a dog or cat*) stray. **3**, nomadic.

броже́ние *n.* **1**, fermentation. **2**, *fig.* ferment.

бро́кколи *n.f. indecl.* broccoli.

бром *n.* **1**, bromine. **2**, *med.* bromide. —**броми́д,** *n.,* *chem.* bromide. —**бро́мистый,** *adj.* bromide: бро́мистый ка́лий, potassium bromide.

бронеавтомоби́ль *n.m.* armored car.

бронебо́йный *adj.* armor-piercing.

броневи́к [*gen.* **-вика́**] *n.* = **бронеавтомоби́ль.**

бронево́й *adj.* armored. —**бронева́я плита́; бронево́й лист,** armor plate; armor plating.

бронежиле́т *n.* bulletproof vest.

бронемаши́на *n.* armored car.

бронено́сец [*gen.* **-сца**] *n.* **1**, *hist.* battleship. **2**, armadillo.

бронено́сный *adj.* (*of a ship*) armored: бронено́сный кре́йсер, armored cruiser.

бронепо́езд *n.* armored train.

бронета́нковый *adj.* armored: бронета́нковые войска́, armored troops.

бронетранспортёр *n.* armored personnel carrier.

бро́нза *n.* bronze.

бронзирова́ть *v.impfv. & pfv.* [*pres.* **-ру́ю, -ру́ешь**] to bronze.

бро́нзовый *adj.* **1**, bronze; made of bronze. **2**, bronze (*in color*). —**бро́нзовый век,** the Bronze Age.

брони́рованный *adj.* armored. —**брони́рованный кула́к,** mailed fist.

брони́ровать *v.impfv. & pfv.* [*pfv. also* **заброни́ровать**; *pres.* **-рую, -руешь**] to reserve; book.

бронирова́ть *v.impfv. &. pfv.* [*pfv. also* **забронирова́ть**; *pres.* **-ру́ю, -ру́ешь**] to armor; cover with armor.

бронтоза́вр *n.* brontosaurus.

бро́нхи *n.pl.* [*sing.* **бронх**] bronchi; bronchial tubes. —**бронхиа́льный,** *adj.* bronchial.

бронхи́т *n.* bronchitis.

бро́ня *n.* reservation (*advance order*).

броня́ *n.* armor.

броса́ть *v.impfv.* [*pfv.* **бро́сить**] **1**, to throw; toss. **2**, to cast (a shadow, glance, etc.). **3**, to throw away; toss out. **4,** to abandon; forsake; desert. **5,** to give up; quit: брóсить курúть, to give up/quit smoking; брóсить шкóлу, to quit school. **6,** *impers.* to careen: Машúну бросáло из стороны́ в стóрону, the car careened from side to side. **7,** *impers., expressing a strong physical reaction:* Егó брóсило в пот, he broke out in a sweat; меня́ брóсило в дрожь, I began to tremble/shiver. —**бросáть жрéбий,** to cast lots; decide something by chance. —**бросáть орýжие,** to throw down one's weapons. —**брóсить трýбку,** to hang up (the phone). —**бросáть я́корь,** to cast *or* drop anchor. —**брóсь!; брóсьте!, 1,** stop!; stop it! **2,** come on!; don't be silly!

бросáться *v.r.impfv.* [*pfv.* **брóситься**] **1,** to rush; dash. **2,** to jump; plunge. **3,** (*with* в *or* на + *acc.*) to flop (into *or* onto). **4,** (*with* под + *acc.*) to throw oneself under (a moving vehicle). **5,** (*with inf.*) to hasten (to). **6,** [*impfv. only*] (*with instr.*) to throw (something) at each other. —**бросáться в глазá,** to be striking; catch the eye. —**бросáться деньгáми,** to toss money around. —**брóситься на колéни,** to fall to one's knees. —**бросáться словáми,** to make irresponsible statements.

брóсить [*infl.* **брóшу, брóсишь**] *v., pfv. of* **бросáть.** —**брóситься,** *refl., pfv. of* **бросáться.**

брóский *adj., colloq.* **1,** garish; loud. **2,** striking.

брóсовый *adj., colloq.* **1,** cheap; trashy; worthless. **2,** throwaway; disposable. —**брóсовые цéны,** below cost; giveaway prices.

бросóк [*gen.* **-скá**] *n.* **1,** throw. **2,** *sports* shot. **3,** spurt; burst of speed.

брошь *n.f.* brooch. *Also,* **брóшка.**

брошюрá (шу) *n.* pamphlet; brochure.

брус [*pl.* **брýсья, брýсьев**] *n.* **1,** beam. **2,** *pl., sports* bars: параллéльные брýсья, parallel bars.

бруснúка *n.* **1,** cowberries. **2,** a (single) cowberry.

брусóк [*gen.* **-скá**] *n.* **1,** bar. **2,** whetstone.

брýствер *n.* breastwork; parapet.

брусчáтка *n.* **1,** paving stones; paving blocks. **2,** *colloq.* paved road.

брусчáтый *adj.* made of paving blocks.

брýтто *adj. & adv. indecl.* gross: вес брýтто, gross weight; ценá брýтто, gross price.

брыжи [*gen.* **-жéй**] *n.pl., obs.* frilled collar; ruff.

брызгать *v.impfv.* [*pfv.* **брызнуть**; *pres.* **брызжу, брызжешь** *or* **брызгаю, брызгаешь**] **1,** (*with instr.*) to sprinkle; splash (a liquid). Брызгать слюнóй, to foam at the mouth; sputter. **2,** to sprinkle (something with a liquid). **3,** to spurt; gush; shoot forth; shoot out. —**брызгаться,** *refl.* [*impfv. only*] **1,** (*with instr.*) to sprinkle; splash (a liquid); spray oneself (with a liquid). **2,** to splash each other.

брызги [*gen.* **брызг**] *n.pl.* spray.

брызговúк [*gen.* **-викá**] *n.* mudguard.

брызнуть *v., pfv. of* **брызгать.**

брыкáть *v.impfv.* [*pfv.* **брыкнýть**] to kick. *Also,* **брыкáться,** *refl.*

брынза *n.* cheese made from sheep's milk.

брюзгá *n.m. & f.* grouch.

брюзглúвый *adj.* grouchy; grumpy.

брюзжáть *v.impfv.* [*pres.* **-зжý, -зжúшь**] to grumble; grouch.

брюква *n.* rutabaga.

брюки [*gen.* **брюк**] *n.pl.* pants; trousers; slacks.

брюнéт *n.m.* [*fem.* **-нéтка**] brunette.

брюссéльский (сэ) *adj., in* брюссéльская капýста, Brussels sprouts.

брюхо *n.* **1,** belly (*of an animal*). **2,** *colloq.* paunch; potbelly.

брюшúна *n.* peritoneum. —**воспалéние брюшúны,** peritonitis.

брюшкó [*pl.* **-кú, -кóв**] *n., colloq.* paunch; potbelly.

брюшнóй *adj.* abdominal. —**брюшнóй тиф,** typhoid.

брякать *v.impfv.* [*pfv.* **брякнуть**] **1,** *v.i.* to rattle; clang; clatter; jingle. **2,** *v.t.* (*with instr.*) to rattle; jingle. **3,** *colloq.* to slam down. **4,** *colloq.* to blurt out. —**брякаться,** *refl., colloq.* to fall heavily; come crashing down.

бряцáние *n.* clank; jingling; jangling. —**бряцáние орýжием,** saber rattling.

бряцáть *v.impfv.* **1,** *v.i.* to clank; jingle; jangle. **2,** *v.t.* (*with instr.*) to jingle; jangle. —**бряцáть орýжием,** to brandish weapons; indulge in saber rattling.

бýбен [*gen.* **бýбна**] *n.* tambourine.

бубенцы *n.pl.* [*sing.* **бубенéц**] small bells; sleigh bells.

бубéнчики *n.pl.* [*sing.* **бубéнчик**] = бубенцы.

бýблик *n.* thick bagel.

бубнúть *v.impfv.* [*pfv.* **пробубнúть**] *colloq.* **1,** to mumble; mutter. **2,** [*impfv. only*] to drone (on and on).

бубнóвый *adj., cards* of diamonds: бубнóвый корóль, king of diamonds.

бýбны [*gen.* **бубён** *or* **бýбен;** *dat.* **бубнáм** *or* **бýбнам**] *n.pl., cards* diamonds.

бубóн *n.* bubo.

бубóнный *adj.* bubonic. —**бубóнная чумá,** bubonic plague.

бугóр [*gen.* **бугрá**] *n.* **1,** mound; knoll. **2,** bump; lump.

бугорóк [*gen.* **-ркá**] *n.* **1,** *dim. of* бугóр. **2,** protuberance. **3,** *med.* tubercle.

бугóрчатый *adj.* **1,** covered with lumps. **2,** tuberous.

бугрúстый *adj.* **1,** hilly; uneven. **2,** bumpy.

буддúзм *n.* Buddhism. —**буддúйский,** *adj.* Buddhist.

буддúст *n.m.* [*fem.* **-дúстка**] *n.* Buddhist.

бýдет *v., 3rd person sing. of* **быть.** —*interj., colloq.* enough!; that'll do! —**что бýдет, то бýдет,** what will be will be.

будúльник *n.* alarm clock.

будúть *v.impfv.* [*pres.* **бужý, бýдишь**] **1,** [*pfv.* **разбудúть**] to wake; wake up; waken; awaken. **2,** [*pfv.* **пробудúть**] *fig.* to awaken; arouse.

бýдка [*gen. pl.* **бýдок**] *n.* booth. —**карáульная бýдка,** sentry box. —**телефóнная бýдка,** telephone booth.

бýдни [*gen.* **-ней**] *n.pl.* **1,** weekdays. **2,** everyday life. **3,** *fig.* humdrum existence.

бýдний *adj., in* бýдний день, weekday.

бýдничный *also,* **бýднишний** *adj.* **1,** = бýдний. **2,** everyday; ordinary. **3,** *fig.* humdrum; routine.

будорáжить *v.impfv.* [*pfv.* **взбудорáжить**] *colloq.* to stir up; rouse; excite.

бýдто *conj.* **1,** that (*implying doubt as to the truth of a statement*): Говоря́т, бýдто онá зáмужем, they say she's married. **2,** [*also,* **как бу́дто**] as if: как бу́дто по волшебству́, as if by magic. У вас тако́й вид, бу́дто вы не по́няли, you look as if you did not understand. —*particle, colloq.* [*also,* **как бу́дто**] apparently: Дождь как бу́дто ко́нчился, the rain appears to have stopped.

будуа́р *n.* boudoir.

бу́дучи *verbal adverb of* **быть**, being: бу́дучи в Ми́нске, being in Minsk; while in Minsk; бу́дучи в опа́сности, when in danger.

бу́дущее *n., decl. as an adj.* the future.

бу́дущий *adj.* **1,** future. **2,** next: в бу́дущем году́, next year.

бу́дущность *n.f.* future.

будь *v., imperative of* **быть**. ♦*Also, in contrary-to-fact constructions,* were: будь он сейча́с жив, were he alive today; будь я на её ме́сте, if I were in her place. —**будь то...,** be it... —**бу́дь, что бу́дет,** come what may. —**не будь** (+ *gen.*), were it not for...

бу́ер [*pl.* буера́] *n.* iceboat.

бужени́на *n.* boiled pork.

бузина́ *n.* elder (*shrub*).

буй [*pl.* буи́, буёв, буя́м] *n.* buoy.

бу́йвол *n.* buffalo. —**бу́йволовый,** *adj.* buffalo (*attrib.*).

бу́йный *adj.* **1,** wild; boisterous; unruly; rambunctious. **2,** (*of an emotion*) violent; uncontrollable. **3,** (*of natural phenomena*) violent; stormy. **4,** (*of vegetation*) lush; luxuriant.

бу́йство *n.* unruly behavior.

бу́йствовать *v.impfv.* [*pres.* **-ствую, -ствуешь**] to run wild; run riot; go on a rampage; run amuck.

бук *n.* beech (tree).

бу́ка *n.m. & f., colloq.* **1,** bogeyman. **2,** surly, unfriendly person. —**смотре́ть бу́кой,** to look surly.

бука́шка [*gen. pl.* **-шек**] *n.* insect; bug.

бу́ква *n.* **1,** letter (*of the alphabet*). **2,** *fig.* (*with gen.*) the letter (of): бу́ква зако́на, the letter of the law. —**бу́ква в бу́кву,** word for word; literally.

буква́льный *adj.* literal. —**буква́льно,** *adv.* literally.

буква́рь [*gen.* **-варя́**] *n.m.* primer; book of ABC's.

бу́квенный *adj.* letter (*attrib.*).

буквое́д *n.* pedant. —**буквое́дство,** *n.* pedantry.

буке́т *n.* bouquet. —**буке́тик,** *n.* small bouquet.

букини́ст *n.* secondhand book dealer. —**букинисти́ческий,** *adj.* secondhand-book (*attrib.*).

букле́т *n.* booklet.

букме́кер *n.* bookmaker.

бу́ковый *adj.* **1,** beech (*attrib.*). **2,** beechwood (*attrib.*).

букси́р *n.* **1,** tugboat. **2,** towline; towrope. Тяну́ть *or* тащи́ть на букси́ре, to tow. —**брать на букси́р,** to take in tow (*lit. & fig.*).

букси́ровать *v.impfv.* [*pres.* **-рую, -руешь**] to tow.

букси́ровка *n.* towing.

буксова́ть *v.impfv.* [*pres.* **-су́ет**] (*of wheels*) to spin around (*without gaining traction*).

булава́ *n.* mace (*weapon*).

була́вка [*gen. pl.* **-вок**] *n.* pin. —**англи́йская була́вка,** safety pin. —**де́ньги на була́вки,** pin money.

була́вочный *adj.* pin (*attrib.*).

бу́лка [*gen. pl.* **бу́лок**] *n.* roll; bun.

бу́лла *n.* (papal) bull.

бу́лочка [*gen. pl.* **-чек**] *n.* small roll; bun.

бу́лочная *n., decl. as an adj.* bakery.

бу́лочник *n.* baker.

бултых *interj., colloq.* plop!; splash!

бултыха́ться *v.r.impfv.* [*pfv.* **булты́хнуться** *or* **бултыхну́ться**] *colloq.* **1,** to plunge; plop (*into water*). **2,** [*impfv. only*] to flop about; thrash about.

булы́жник *n.* cobblestone. —**булы́жный,** *adj.* cobbled; cobblestone (*attrib.*).

бульва́р *n.* public walk; promenade; mall.

бульва́рный *adj.* **1,** of a **бульва́р. 2,** *fig.* (*of literature, a newspaper, etc.*) trashy.

бульдо́г *n.* bulldog.

бульдо́зер *n.* bulldozer.

бу́льканье *n.* gurgling; gurgle.

бу́лькать *v.impfv.* to gurgle.

бульо́н *n.* clear soup; broth; consommé; bouillon.

бум *n.* **1,** *econ.* boom. **2,** (media) sensation. —*interj.* boom!

бума́га *n.* **1,** paper. **2,** *pl.* papers; documents. **3,** *archaic* cotton. —**газе́тная бума́га,** newsprint. —**це́нные бума́ги,** securities.

бума́жка [*gen. pl.* **-жек**] *n.* **1,** piece of paper. **2,** *colloq.* bill; bank note: бума́жка в пять до́лларов, five-dollar bill.

бума́жник *n.* wallet; billfold.

бума́жный *adj.* **1,** paper. **2,** cotton.

бумера́нг *n.* boomerang.

бу́нкер [*pl.* бункера́ *or* бу́нкеры] *n.* **1,** bunker; storage bin; hopper. **2,** bunker; underground shelter.

бунт *n.* **1,** [*gen.* бу́нта; *pl.* бу́нты] riot; uprising; rebellion; mutiny. **2,** [*gen.* бунта́; *pl.* бунты́] bundle; bale.

бунта́рский *adj.* rebellious; mutinous. —**бунта́рство,** *n.* rebelliousness.

бунта́рь [*gen.* **-таря́**] *n.m.* **1,** rioter. **2,** rebel.

бунтова́ть *v.impfv.* [*pres.* **-ту́ю, -ту́ешь**] **1,** to rebel; revolt; mutiny. **2,** [*pfv.* **взбунтова́ть**] to incite to rebellion.

бунтовщи́к [*gen.* **-щика́**] *n.* rioter; rebel.

бур *n.* **1,** drill; auger. **2,** Boer.

бура́ *n.* borax.

бура́в [*gen.* **-рава́**] *n.* auger; gimlet.

бура́вить *v.impfv.* [*pfv.* **пробура́вить**; *pres.* **-влю, -вишь**] to bore; drill.

бура́вчик *n.* auger; gimlet.

бура́к [*gen.* **-рака́**] *n., colloq.* beet.

бура́н *n.* blizzard.

бургоми́стр *n.* burgomaster.

бурда́ *n., colloq.* slop.

бурдю́к [*gen.* **-дюка́**] *n.* wineskin.

буреве́стник *n.* petrel (*bird*).

бурело́м *n.* fallen trees.

буре́ние *n.* drilling.

буре́ть *v.impfv.* [*pfv.* **побуре́ть**] to become brown; turn brown.

буржуа́ *n.m. indecl.* bourgeois.

буржуази́я *n.* bourgeoisie. —**буржуа́зный,** *adj.* bourgeois.

бури́льный *adj.* drilling (*attrib.*); boring (*attrib.*).

бури́ть *v.impfv.* [*pfv.* **пробури́ть**] **1**, to bore; drill; drill through. **2**, [*impfv. only*] to drill for (oil).

бу́рка [*gen. pl.* **бу́рок**] *n.* **1**, felt cloak (*worn in the Caucasus*). **2**, *usu. pl.* felt boot with a leather sole.

бу́ркать *v.impfv.* [*pfv.* **бу́ркнуть**] *colloq.* to mutter; growl.

бурла́к [*gen.* **-лака́**] *n.* bargeman.

бурле́ск *n.* burlesque. *Also,* **бурле́ска**.

бурли́вый *adj.* turbulent.

бурли́ть *v.impfv.* to seethe; bubble.

бу́рный *adj.* **1**, (*of the sea*) stormy; (*of a river*) turbulent. **2**, (*of a discussion or debate*) stormy; (*of applause*) tumultuous. **3**, (*of passions, one's temperament, etc.*) violent. **4**, (*of time, a day, etc.*) hectic; (*of activity*) frantic; furious. **5**, (*of growth, development, etc.*) rapid.

буровой *adj.* drilling (*attrib.*). —**бурова́я вы́шка,** oil rig; oil derrick; drilling rig.

бу́рский *adj.* Boer.

буру́н [*gen.* **-руна́**] *n.* breaker (*wave*).

бурунду́к [*gen.* **-дука́**] *n.* chipmunk.

бурча́ть *v.impfv.* [*pfv.* **пробурча́ть**; *pres.* **-чу́, -чи́шь**] *colloq.* **1**, to mumble; mutter. **2**, (*of one's stomach*) to rumble.

бу́рый *adj.* brown.

бурья́н *n.* (tall) weeds.

бу́ря *n.* storm. —**бу́ря в стака́не воды́,** tempest in a teapot.

буря́т [*gen. pl.* **буря́т**] *n.m.* [*fem.* **-ря́тка**] Buryat (*one of a people inhabiting southern Siberia*). —**буря́тский,** *adj.* Buryat.

бу́сина *n.* bead. *Also,* **бу́синка**.

буссо́ль *n.f.* surveyor's compass.

бу́сы [*gen.* **бус**] *n.pl.* beads.

бута́н *n.* butane.

бутафо́рия *n., theat.* properties; stage props. —**бутафо́р,** *n.* property man. —**бутафо́рский,** *adj.* of or for stage props.

бутербро́д (тэ) *n.* sandwich.

бути́л *n.* butyl.

бутиле́н *n.* butylene.

буто́н *n.* bud.

бутонье́рка [*gen. pl.* **-рок**] *n.* boutonniere.

бу́тсы [*gen.* **бутс** *or* **бу́тсов**] *n.pl.* soccer shoes (*with cleats*).

буту́з *n., colloq.* roly-poly child.

буты́лка [*gen. pl.* **-лок**] *n.* bottle. —**буты́лочка,** *n.* small bottle.

буты́лочный *adj.* **1**, bottle (*attrib.*). **2**, bottled. —**буты́лочный цвет,** bottle green.

буты́ль *n.f.* large bottle.

бу́фер [*pl.* **буфера́**] *n.* **1**, bumper. **2**, *fig.* buffer. —**бу́ферный,** *adj.* buffer (*attrib.*).

буфе́т *n.* **1**, buffet; sideboard. **2**, snack bar.

буфе́тный *adj.* **1**, of a buffet. **2**, of a snack bar.

буфе́тчик *n.m.* [*fem.* **-чица**] person who works behind a counter.

буффо́н *n.* buffoon. —**буффона́да,** *n.* buffoonery.

буха́нка [*gen. pl.* **-нок**] *n.* loaf of bread.

бу́хать *v.impfv.* [*pfv.* **бу́хнуть**] *colloq.* **1**, (*of a door, gate,*

etc.) to bang; (*of guns*) to rumble. **2**, to drop (something) with a thud. **3**, to throw oneself; plop. **4**, to blurt out. —**бу́хаться,** *refl., colloq.* to throw oneself; plop.

бухга́лтер *n.* bookkeeper; accountant.

бухгалте́рия *n.* **1**, bookkeeping; accounting. **2**, bookkeeping department; accounting department.

бухга́лтерский *adj.* bookkeeping (*attrib.*); accounting (*attrib.*). —**бухга́лтерский учёт,** bookkeeping.

бу́хнуть[1] *v.impfv.* [*pfv.* **разбу́хнуть**; *past* **бух, бу́хла**] to swell; swell up.

бу́хнуть[2] [*past* **бу́хнул**] *v., pfv. of* **бу́хать**. —**бу́хнуться,** *refl., pfv. of* **бу́хаться**.

бу́хта *n.* small bay.

бу́хточка [*gen. pl.* **-чек**] *n.* cove; inlet.

бу́ча *n., colloq.* row; fracas.

бушева́ть *v.impfv.* [*pres.* **-шу́ю, -шу́ешь**] (*of a fire, storm, etc.*) to rage.

бу́шель *n.m.* bushel.

бушла́т *n.* pea jacket.

бу́шприт *also,* **бушпри́т** *n.* bowsprit.

буя́н *n.* rowdy; ruffian; roughneck.

буя́нить *v.impfv.* to run wild; run riot; go on a rampage; run amuck.

бы *also,* **б** *particle, used only with the inf. or past tense of a verb,* **1**, would; should: Я бы хоте́л(а) спроси́ть..., I would/should like to ask... Я бы сказа́л(а) вам е́сли бы вы спроси́ли, I would have told you if you had asked. **2**, *used to express a polite suggestion:* Ты бы бро́сил кури́ть, you should give up smoking. Вам лу́чше бы пойти́ самому́, you had better go yourself. **3**, *used to express a wish:* Был бы он здесь!, if only he were here! Побо́льше бы нам таки́х люде́й, we should have (*or* could use) more people like that.

быва́ло *particle, colloq.* would (often): Он, быва́ло, ча́сто заходи́л к нам, he would often come to see us.

быва́лый *adj.* **1**, *obs.* former; olden; bygone. **2**, *colloq.* experienced; worldly-wise. —**э́то де́ло быва́лое,** it's nothing new; it has happened before.

быва́ть *v.impfv.* **1**, to be (*regularly or customarily*): Он быва́ет в магази́не ка́ждый день, he is in the store every day. Он ча́сто быва́ет у нас, he is often over at our house. **2**, to happen: как э́то ча́сто быва́ет, as often happens. **3**, to take place; be held: Заседа́ния быва́ют раз в ме́сяц, meetings are held once a month. —**как ни в чём не быва́ло,** as if nothing happened.

бы́вший *adj.* former; ex-.

бык [*gen.* **быка́**] *n.* **1**, bull. **2**, pier (*of a bridge*). —**бой быко́в,** bullfight; bullfighting. —**взять быка́ за рога́,** to take the bull by the horns.

были́на *n.* Russian epic poem.

были́нка [*gen. pl.* **-нок**] *n.* blade of grass.

бы́ло *particle* (*without stress*) just about to; on the point of: Он встал бы́ло из-за стола́, когда́..., he was about to get up from the table when...

было́й *adj.* bygone: в были́е времена́, in bygone days. —**было́е,** *n.* the past.

быль *n.f.* **1**, *archaic* fact; event. **2**, true story.

быльё *n., obs.* grass. —**быльём поросло́,** lost in oblivion.

быстрина́ [*pl.* **-стри́ны**] *n.* rapids.

бы́стро *adv.* fast; quickly; rapidly.

быстроде́йствующий *adj.* **1,** (*of a machine, computer, etc.*) high-speed. **2,** (*of a medicine or drug*) quick-acting; fast-acting.

быстроно́гий *adj.* fleet-footed.

быстрораствори́мый *adj.* dissolving quickly. —**быстрораствори́мый ко́фе,** instant coffee.

быстрота́ *n.* speed; rapidity.

быстрохо́дный *adj.* fast-moving; high-speed.

бы́стрый *adj.* fast; quick; rapid; swift.

быт [*2nd loc.* **быту́**] *n.* **1,** way of life; life. **2,** daily life.

бытие́ *n.* **1,** being; existence. **2,** *cap., Bib.* Genesis: Кни́га Бытия́, the book of Genesis.

бы́тность *n.f., in* **в бы́тность (мою́, его́,** *etc.*), during one's stay (in); (*with instr.*) when one was (in a certain capacity).

бытова́ть *v.impfv.* [*pres.* **-ту́ет**] to exist.

бытово́й *adj.* **1,** pert. to everyday life; everyday. **2,** of or depicting everyday life.

быть *v., used only in the future* [**бу́ду, бу́дешь**] *and the past* [**был, была́, бы́ло, бы́ли;** *neg.* **не́ был, не была́, не́ было, не́ были**] to be. —**не́ было** (*with gen.*), expressing the absence of something in the past: Там никого́ не́ было, there was no one there. —**была́ не была́!,** come what may; whatever the risk. —**как бы то ни́ было,** be that as it may. —**как быть?,** what are we to do?; what is to be done? —**так и быть,** so be it. *See also* **бу́дет, будь, было.**

бытьё *n., archaic* life; existence.

бы́чий [*fem.* **-чья**] *adj.* ox (*attrib.*); bovine.

бычо́к [*gen.* **бычка́**] *n.* **1,** young bull; young ox. **2,** goby (*fish*). **3,** *colloq.* cigarette butt.

бювар *n.* letter case with leaves of blotting paper.

бюдже́т *n.* budget. —**бюдже́тный,** *adj.* budget (*attrib.*); budgetary.

бюллете́нь *n.m.* **1,** bulletin. **2,** ballot. **3,** *colloq.* doctor's certificate (*stating that one is ill*).

бю́ргер *n.* burgher.

бюро́ *n. indecl.* **1,** office; bureau. **2,** writing desk. —**бюро́ нахо́док,** lost and found department. —**бюро́ путеше́ствий,** travel agency. —**похоро́нное бюро́,** funeral home; funeral parlor; mortuary. —**спра́вочное бюро́,** information office.

бюрокра́т *n.* bureaucrat.

бюрократи́зм *n.* **1,** bureaucracy. **2,** red tape.

бюрокра́тия *n.* bureaucracy. —**бюрократи́ческий,** *adj.* bureaucratic.

бюст *n.* **1,** *sculpture* bust. **2,** bosom; bust.

бюстга́льтер (тэ) *n.* brassiere.

бязь *n.f.* heavy cloth; sheeting.

В

В, в *n.neut.* third letter of the Russian alphabet.

в *also,* **во** *prep.* **A,** *with acc.* **1,** to: ходи́ть в шко́лу, to go to school; е́хать в Нью-Йо́рк, go to New York. **2,** into: попа́сть в лову́шку, to fall into a trap; вложи́ть письмо́ в конве́рт, to put the letter into an envelope. **3,** for (*a destination*): уйти́ в шко́лу, to leave for school; уе́хать в Евро́пу, leave for Europe. **4,** (*with certain nouns*) through: смотре́ть в телеско́п, to look through a telescope; проходи́ть в дверь, to fit through the door. **5,** (*with certain nouns*) under: рассма́тривать что́-нибудь в микроско́п/ в лу́пу/, to examine something under a microscope/ magnifying glass/. **6,** in (*a certain amount of time, emphasizing rapidity*): оде́ться в одну́ мину́ту, to get dressed in one minute. **7,** (*with nouns indicating a certain time*) in; on; at: в ми́рное вре́мя, in peacetime; в то вре́мя, at that time; в э́тот /в тот/ день/год, on that day; in that year; в после́дние дни, in recent days. **8,** (*with the time of day*) at: в три часа́, at three o'clock; в де́сять мину́т шесто́го, at 5:10. **9,** (*with days of the week*) on: в сре́ду, on Wednesday. **10,** а; per: два ра́за в неде́лю, twice a week. **11,** (*with a number +* **раз**) *indicating a difference by multiples:* в два ра́за бо́льше, twice as much; в ты́сячу раз ху́же, a thousand times worse. **12,** in the amount of: ски́дка в де́сять проце́нтов, а 10% discount; заём в три́ста до́лларов, a $300 loan. **13,** (*with various nouns fol. by the gen.*) in ... of: в честь/па́мять/похвалу́ (+ *gen.*): in honor/memory/ praise of. **14,** as; by way of: приводи́ть (что́-нибудь) в приме́р/ в дока́зательство/, to cite (something) as an example/ by way of evidence/. **15,** in (*a certain color*): кра́сить что́-нибудь в зелёный цвет, to paint something green; укра́шенный в я́ркие цвета́, decorated in bright colors. **16,** *indicating the design on a material:* ткань в поло́ску, striped fabric; пла́тье в горо́шек, polka-dot dress. **17,** (*with pl. nouns*) *indicating a new or temporary status:* кандида́т в президе́нты, candidate for president; производи́ть в полко́вники, to promote to colonel. **В,** *with prepl.* **1,** in; at: в шко́ле, in/at school; в ко́мнате, in the room;

в Аме́рике, in America. **2,** on (*a mode of transportation*): ме́сто в по́езде, seat on a train; засну́ть в самолёте, to fall asleep on the plane. **3,** (*with months, years, centuries*) in: в апре́ле, in April; в 1941-ом году́, in 1941; в семна́дцатом ве́ке, in the 17th century. **4,** at a distance of: в двух киломе́трах от гости́ницы, two kilometers from the hotel.

в- *also,* **во-, въ-** *prefix* **1,** *indicating motion into:* входи́ть, to enter; вкла́дывать, to insert. **2,** (*with -ся*) *indicating intensity of an action:* вчи́тываться, to read carefully; вслу́шаться, to listen carefully.

ва-ба́нк *adv., in* **идти́ ва-ба́нк,** to go for broke; shoot the works.

вавило́нский *adj.* Babylonian. **—вавило́нская ба́шня,** Tower of Babel. **—вавило́нское столпотворе́ние,** *see* **столпотворе́ние.**

ва́га *n.* lever; crowbar.

ваго́н *n.* **1,** (railroad) car; (trolley) car. **2,** (*with gen.*) carload (of). **—ваго́н-платфо́рма,** railroad flatcar. **—ваго́н-рестора́н,** dining car; diner.

вагоне́тка [*gen. pl.* **-ток**] *n.* trolley; truck; car. **—подвесна́я вагоне́тка,** cable car.

ваго́нный *adj.* car (*attrib.*); wagon (*attrib.*).

вагоновожа́тый *n., decl. as an adj.* motorman (*on a streetcar*).

важне́йший *adj.* most important; paramount.

важне́цкий *adj., colloq.* excellent; first-rate.

ва́жничать *v.impfv., colloq.* to act important; give oneself airs.

ва́жно *adv.* proudly; with an air of importance. **—***adj., used predicatively,* important: Э́то не ва́жно, it's not important; мне ва́жно знать, it is important for me to know.

ва́жность *n.f.* **1,** importance. **2,** self-importance; pomposity.

ва́жный *adj.* [*short form* **ва́жен, важна́, ва́жно, ва́жны** *or* **важны́**] **1,** important. **2,** self-important; pompous.

ва́за *n.* vase; bowl.

вазели́н *n.* vaseline.

вазо́н *n.* flowerpot.

ва́зочка [*gen. pl.* **-чек**] *n.* small bowl.

вака́нсия *n.* vacancy; opening. **—вака́нтный,** *adj.* vacant; unfilled.

ва́кса *n.* black shoe polish.

ва́ксить *v.impfv.* [*pfv.* **нава́ксить;** *pres.* **ва́кшу, ва́ксишь**] *colloq.* to shine; polish (shoes).

вакуо́ль *n.f.* vacuole.

ва́куум *n.* vacuum. **—ва́куум-насо́с,** vacuum pump.

вакци́на *n.* vaccine. **—вакцина́ция,** *n.* vaccination.

вакцини́ровать *v.impfv. & pfv.* [*pres.* **-рую, -руешь**] to vaccinate.

вал [*2nd loc.* **валу́;** *pl.* **валы́**] *n.* **1,** earthen wall; bank; embankment. **2,** large wave; billow. **3,** shaft: коле́нчатый вал, crankshaft. **—крепостно́й вал,** rampart. **—огнево́й вал,** covering fire; barrage.

валёж *n.* windfallen branches.

валёк [*gen.* **-лька́**] *n.* **1,** roller. **2,** swingletree.

ва́ленок [*gen.* **-нка;** *gen. pl.* **-нок**] *n.* felt boot.

вале́нтность *n.f.* valence.

валерья́на *also,* **валериа́на** *n.* valerian. **—валерья́нка,** *n., colloq.* valerian drops. **—валерья́новый,** *adj.* valerian.

вале́т *n., cards* jack.

ва́лик *n.* **1,** roller. **2,** platen (*on a typewriter*). **3,** bolster (*pillow*).

вали́ть[1] *v.impfv.* [*pfv.* **свали́ть;** *pres.* **валю́, ва́лишь**] **1,** [*pfv. also* **повали́ть**] to knock down; topple; fell. **2,** (*with* в *or* на + *acc.*) to throw (into); toss (into); dump (into *or* on): вали́ть (что́-нибудь) в ку́чу, to toss (something) into a pile. **3,** (*with* на + *acc.*) *colloq.* to blame: вали́ть всё на, to blame everything on. **—вали́ть с больно́й головы́ на здоро́вую,** to lay the blame at someone else's doorstep.

вали́ть[2] *v.impfv.* [*pres.* **вали́т**] **1,** *colloq.* (*of people*) to flock; stream. **2,** (*of snow*) to fall heavily; (*of smoke*) to pour out.

вали́ться *v.r.impfv.* [*pfv.* **повали́ться** *or* **свали́ться;** *pres.* **валю́сь, ва́лишься**] **1,** to fall; collapse. **2,** to topple over. **—вали́ться с ног,** to be exhausted; be falling off one's feet.

ва́лка *n.* chopping down; felling (*of trees*).

ва́лкий *adj.* [*short form* **ва́лок, валка́, ва́лко, ва́лки**] unsteady; shaky; wobbly. **—ни ша́тко ни ва́лко,** fair to middling; so-so.

валли́ец [*gen.* **-и́йца**] *n.* Welshman. **—валли́йский,** *adj.* Welsh.

валово́й *adj., econ.* gross: валово́й дохо́д, gross income.

вало́м *adv., colloq., in* **вало́м вали́ть,** to flock; stream.

валто́рна *n.* French horn.

валу́н [*gen.* **-луна́**] *n.* boulder.

ва́льдшнеп (нэ) *n.* woodcock.

вальс *n.* waltz.

вальси́ровать *v.impfv.* [*pres.* **-рую, -руешь**] to waltz.

вальцева́ть *v.impfv.* [*pres.* **-цую, -цуешь**] to roll; mill (metal).

вальцо́вка *n.* rolling; milling. **—вальцо́вый,** *adj.* rolling: вальцо́вая ме́льница, rolling mill.

валья́жный *adj.* imposing; handsome.

валю́та *n.* currency.

валю́тный *adj.* currency (*attrib.*); hard currency (*attrib.*). **—валю́тный курс,** exchange rate; rate of exchange.

валя́льщик *n.* fuller (*of cloth*).

ва́ляный *adj.* (*of boots*) made of felt.

валя́ть *v.impfv.* **1,** (*with* по) to drag (along *or* through). **2,** [*pfv.* **повала́ть**] *cooking* to roll (*e.g.* in bread crumbs). **3,** [*pfv.* **сваля́ть**] to full (cloth). **4,** *impers.* (*of a ship*) to be tossed from side to side. **5,** *in* **валя́ть дурака́,** to play the fool. **—валя́ться,** *refl.* [*pfv.* **повала́ться**] **1,** to roll; wallow. **2,** [*impfv. only*] *colloq.* to lie (scattered) about. **3,** *colloq.* to lie around; lounge; loll.

вам *pron., dat. of* **вы.**

ва́ми *pron., instr. of* **вы.**

вампи́р *n.* **1,** vampire. **2,** vampire bat.

вана́дий *n.* vanadium.

ванда́л *n.* vandal. **—вандали́зм,** *n.* vandalism.

вани́ль *n.f.* vanilla. **—вани́льный,** *adj.* vanilla.

ва́нна *n.* **1,** bath. **2,** bathtub.

ва́нная *n., decl. as an adj.* bathroom.

ва́нночка [*gen. pl.* **-чек**] *n., dim. of* **ва́нна** (bath). —**глазна́я ва́нночка,** eyecup.

ва́нный *adj.* bath (*attrib.*): **ва́нная ко́мната,** bathroom.

ва́нька-вста́нька *n.m.* self-righting toy doll.

вар *n.* pitch. —**сапо́жный вар,** cobbler's wax.

вара́н *n.* monitor lizard.

ва́рвар *n.* barbarian. —**варвари́зм,** *n.* (literary) barbarism. —**ва́рварский,** *adj.* barbarian; barbarous; barbaric. —**ва́рварство,** *n.* barbarity.

ва́режка [*gen. pl.* **-жек**] *n.* mitten.

варене́ц [*gen.* **-нца́**] *n.* fermented boiled milk.

варе́ние *n.* boiling.

варе́ник *n.* dumpling filled with cheese or fruit.

варёный *adj.* boiled.

варе́нье *n.* jam.

вариа́нт *n.* **1,** version. **2,** possibility; alternative.

вариа́ция *n.* variation.

варико́зный *adj.* varicose.

вари́ть *v.impfv.* [*pfv.* **свари́ть;** *pres.* **варю́, ва́ришь**] **1,** to boil; cook. **2,** to make (coffee, soup, etc.); brew (beer). **3,** to weld (metals). —**вари́ться,** *refl.* to boil; be boiling; cook; be cooking; *pfv.* be cooked.

ва́рка *n.* boiling.

варьете́ (тэ) *n.neut. indecl.* variety show; floor show.

варьи́ровать *v.impfv.* [*pres.* **-рую, -руешь**] to vary; modify. —**варьи́роваться,** *refl.* to vary.

варя́г *n.* Varangian. —**варя́жский,** *adj.* Varangian.

вас *pron., gen., acc. & prepl. of* **вы.**

василёк [*gen.* **-лька́**] *n.* cornflower.

васса́л *n.* vassal. —**васса́льный,** *adj.* vassal (*attrib.*).

ва́та *n.* **1,** absorbent cotton. **2,** wadding; padding; stuffing. **3,** *in certain combinations,* wool: **минера́льная ва́та,** mineral wool; **стекловата,** glass wool.

вата́га *n., colloq.* crowd; throng; gang.

ватерли́ния (тэ) *n.* waterline.

ватерпа́с (тэ) *n.* spirit level.

ватерпо́ло (тэ) *n. indecl.* water polo.

Ватика́н *n.* Vatican.

вати́н *n.* batting (*sewn into a garment for extra warmth*).

ва́тник *n., colloq.* quilted jacket.

ва́тный *adj.* **1,** made of absorbent cotton. **2,** padded; quilted.

ватру́шка [*gen. pl.* **-шек**] *n.* pastry containing cheese or jam.

ватт [*gen. pl.* **ватт**] *n.* watt.

ва́учер *n.* voucher.

ва́фля [*gen. pl.* **-фель**] *n.* waffle. —**ва́фельница,** *n.* waffle iron. —**ва́фельный,** *adj.* made of waffles.

ва́хта *n., naut.* watch: **стоя́ть на ва́хте,** to stand watch.

ва́хтенный *adj., naut.* watch (*attrib.*). —**ва́хтенный журна́л,** (ship's) log.

вахтёр *n.* (security) guard.

ваш [*fem.* **ва́ша;** *neut.* **ва́ше;** *pl.* **ва́ши;** *gen.* **ва́шего, ва́шей, ва́ших;** *acc. fem.* **ва́шу;** *dat.* **ва́шему, ва́шей, ва́шим;** *instr.* **ва́шим, ва́шей, ва́шими;** *prepl.* **ва́шем, ва́шей, ва́ших**] *poss. adj. & pron.* your; yours.

вая́ние *n.* sculpture. —**вая́тель,** *n.m.* sculptor.

вая́ть *v.impfv.* [*pfv.* **извая́ть**] to sculpt; chisel; carve; model.

вбега́ть *v.impfv.* [*pfv.* **вбежа́ть**] **1,** to run in. **2,** (*with* **в** + *acc.*) to run into. **3,** (*with* **на** + *acc.*) to run up (a hill, stairs, etc.).

вбежа́ть [*infl. like* **бежа́ть**] *v., pfv. of* **вбега́ть.**

вбива́ть *v.impfv.* [*pfv.* **вбить**] to hammer in; drive in. **Вбива́ть клин ме́жду,** to drive a wedge between. —**вбива́ть в го́лову** (+ *dat.*), to get it through someone's head. —**вбива́ть себе́ в го́лову,** to get it into one's head.

вбира́ть *v.impfv.* [*pfv.* **вобра́ть**] (*often with* **в себя́**) to absorb; take in; draw in.

вбить [*infl.* **вобью́, вобьёшь**] *v., pfv. of* **вбива́ть.**

вблизи́ *adv.* **1,** near; nearby; close by. **2,** up close. —*prep., with gen.* near. —**вблизи́ от,** not far from.

вбок *adv.* to the side; to one side.

вброд *adv.* by wading: **переходи́ть вброд,** to wade across; ford.

ввали́вать *v.impfv.* [*pfv.* **ввали́ть**] (*with* **в** + *acc.*) *colloq.* to throw (into); toss (into); —**ввали́ваться,** *refl.* **1,** (*of one's cheeks or eyes*) to become sunken; become hollow. **2,** (*with* **в** + *acc.*) *colloq.* to fall into; plunge into. **3,** (*with* **в** + *acc.*) *colloq.* to burst into.

ввали́ть [*infl.* **ввалю́, вва́лишь**] *v., pfv. of* **ввали́вать.** —**ввали́ться,** *refl., pfv. of* **ввали́ваться.**

введе́ние *n.* introduction. —**введе́ние в до́лжность,** induction (into office).

ввезти́ [*infl. like* **везти́**] *v., pfv. of* **ввози́ть.**

ввек *adv., colloq.* never.

вверга́ть *v.impfv.* [*pfv.* **вве́ргнуть**] **1,** *obs.* to hurl; toss. **2,** *fig.* to plunge; throw (into despair, confusion, etc.).

вве́ргнуть [*past* **вверг, вве́ргла**] *v., pfv. of* **вверга́ть.**

вве́рить *v., pfv. of* **вверя́ть.** —**вве́риться,** *refl., pfv. of* **вверя́ться.**

вверты́вать *v.impfv.* [*pfv.* **вверну́ть**] **1,** to screw in. **2,** *colloq.* to interject; interpose; put in (a word, remark, etc.).

вверх *adv., expressing motion or direction,* up; upward(s). —**вверх дном; вверх нога́ми,** upside down; topsy-turvy. —**вверх по,** up: **вверх по тече́нию,** upstream.

вверху́ *adv., expressing location* **1,** above; overhead. **2,** at the top. —*prep., with gen.* at the top of.

вверя́ть *v.impfv.* [*pfv.* **вве́рить**] to entrust; confide. —**вверя́ться,** *refl.* (*with dat.*) to entrust oneself to; place oneself in the hands of.

ввести́ [*infl. like* **вести́**] *v., pfv. of* **вводи́ть.**

ввиду́ *prep., with gen.* in view of.

вви́нчивать *v.impfv.* [*pfv.* **ввинти́ть**] to screw in. —**вви́нчиваться,** *refl.* to screw in.

ввод *n.* **1,** *mech.* lead-in. **2,** bringing in(to). **3,** putting into: **ввод в де́йствие,** putting into operation. **4,** input.

вводи́ть *v.impfv.* [*pfv.* **ввести́;** *pres.* **ввожу́, вво́дишь**] **1,** to bring in; bring into. **2,** to lead in; lead into. *Also fig.:* **вводи́ть в собла́зн,** to lead into temptation. **3,** to introduce; institute; initiate. **4,** to include; bring in to. **5,** to impose (restrictions, a tax, etc.). **6,** *med.* to inject. —**вводи́ть в бой,** to commit to battle. —**вводи́ть в де́йствие, 1,** to put into effect. **2,** to put into operation.

—вводи́ть в курс де́ла, to brief; bring up to date. —вводи́ть в расхо́д, to put to expense. —вводи́ть в строй, to put into service; put into operation.

вво́дный *adj.* introductory. —вво́дное сло́во, *gram.* parenthetic word; introductory particle.

ввоз *n.* 1, importing; importation. 2, total imports.

ввози́ть *v.impfv.* [*pfv.* ввезти́; *pres.* вжу́, вво́зишь] 1, to import. 2, (*with* в + *acc.*) to wheel into; convey into; transport into. 3, (*with* на + *acc.*) convey up; convey to the top of.

вво́зный *adj.* 1, import (*attrib.*). 2, imported.

вво́лю *adv., colloq.* = вдо́воль.

ввысь *adv.* upward; high into the air.

ввяза́ть [*infl.* ввяжу́, ввя́жешь] *v., pfv. of* ввя́зывать. —ввяза́ться, *refl., pfv. of* ввя́зываться.

ввя́зывать *v.impfv.* [*pfv.* ввяза́ть] (*with* в + *acc.*) 1, to sew in. 2, *colloq.* to involve in; get (someone) mixed up in. —ввя́зываться, *refl.* (*with* в + *acc.*) *colloq.* to meddle (in); get mixed up (in); become involved (in). Ввя́зываться в разгово́р, to break into a conversation.

вгиба́ть *v.impfv.* [*pfv.* вогну́ть] to bend inwards; curve inwards.

вглубь *adv.* deep inside; deep into the interior. —*prep.*, *with gen.* deep into; far into.

вгляде́ться [*infl.* -жу́сь, -ди́шься] *v.r., pfv. of* вгля́дываться.

вгля́дываться *v.r.impfv.* [*pfv.* вгляде́ться] (*with* в + *acc.*) 1, to look closely (at); take a good look (at). 2, to peer (into).

вгоня́ть *v.impfv.* [*pfv.* вогна́ть] (*with* в + *acc.*) 1, to drive into; herd into. 2, *colloq.* to hammer in; drive in. —вгоня́ть в кра́ску, to make (someone) blush. —вгоня́ть в пот, to make (someone) sweat (*from hard work*).

вдава́ться *v.r.impfv.* [*pfv.* вда́ться; *pres.* вдаю́сь, вдаёшься] (*with* в + *acc.*) 1, to protrude into; jut out into. 2, *fig.* to sink into; lapse into. 3, *fig.* to go into; delve into. —вдава́ться в кра́йности, to go to extremes. —вдава́ться в подро́бности, to go into detail.

вдави́ть [*infl.* вдавлю́, вда́вишь] *v., pfv. of* вда́вливать.

вда́вливать *v.impfv.* [*pfv.* вдави́ть] 1, to press in; force in. 2, to batter in; dent.

вда́лбливать *v.impfv.* [*pfv.* вдолби́ть] *colloq.* to drum in; drill in: вдолби́ть что́-нибудь в го́лову (+ *dat.*), to drum/drill something into someone's head.

вдалеке́ *adv.* in the distance. —вдалеке́ от, far from; a long way from.

вдали́ *adv.* in the distance. —вдали́ от, far from; a long way from.

вдаль *adv.* into the distance.

вда́ться [*infl. like* да́ться] *v.r., pfv. of* вдава́ться.

вдвига́ть *v.impfv.* [*pfv.* вдви́нуть] (*with* в + *acc.*) to push into; thrust into.

вдво́е *adv.* 1, twice as; twice the; double the: вдво́е бо́льше, twice as much (*or* as big); double *or* twice the amount (*or* size). 2, (in) half: вдво́е ме́ньше, half as much (*or* as many); half the size. Вдво́е сократи́ть, to reduce in half; halve. Сложи́ть вдво́е, to fold in half (*or* in two).

вдвоём *adv.* 1, two together: они́ вдвоём, the two of

them together. 2, together with one another. 3, (*with* с) together with.

вдвойне́ *adv.* 1, double; twice as much. 2, (*with adjectives*) doubly.

вдева́ть *v.impfv.* [*pfv.* вдеть] (*with* в + *acc.*) to put in; put into. —вдева́ть ни́тку в иго́лку, to thread a needle.

вде́лывать *v.impfv.* [*pfv.* вде́лать] (*with* в + *acc.*) 1, to set (a gem, stone, etc.) into. 2, to embed (in).

вдёргивать *v.impfv.* [*pfv.* вдёрнуть] to draw through; thread.

вде́сятеро *adv.* ten times; tenfold.

вдесятеро́м *adv.* ten together: они́ вдесятеро́м, the ten of them.

вдеть [*infl.* вде́ну, вде́нешь] *v., pfv. of* вдева́ть.

вдоба́вок *adv., colloq.* besides; in addition; to boot.

вдова́ [*pl.* вдо́вы] *n.* widow.

вдове́ть *v.impfv.* to be a widow *or* widower.

вдове́ц [*gen.* -вца́] *n.* widower.

вдо́воль *adv., colloq.* 1, in abundance; as much as one could wish for. 2, to one's heart's content: нае́сться вдо́воль, to eat one's fill.

вдовство́ *n.* widowhood.

вдо́вствовать *v.impfv.* [*pres.* -ствую, -ствуешь] to become a widow *or* widower. —вдо́вствующая короле́ва, dowager queen.

вдо́вый *adj.* widowed.

вдого́нку *adv., colloq.* after; in pursuit of: бро́ситься вдого́нку за (+ *instr.*), to take off after. Кри́кнуть вдого́нку (+ *dat.*), to call after (someone).

вдолби́ть [*infl.* -блю́, -би́шь] *v., pfv. of* вда́лбливать.

вдоль *prep., with gen.* along: идти́ вдоль доро́ги, to walk along (the side of) the road. —*adv.* lengthwise. —вдоль и поперёк, 1, far and wide. 2, *colloq.* thoroughly; inside out; backwards and forwards.

вдо́сталь *adv., colloq.* 1, in abundance; as much as one could wish for. 2, to one's heart's content.

вдох *n.* (a single) breath.

вдохнове́ние *n.* inspiration. —вдохнове́нно, *adv.* with inspiration; in an inspired manner. —вдохнове́нный, *adj.* inspired.

вдохнови́тель *n.m.* moving spirit; inspiration.

вдохновля́ть *v.impfv.* [*pfv.* вдохнови́ть] to inspire.

вдохну́ть *v.pfv.* 1, *pfv. of* вдыха́ть. 2, (*with* в + *acc.*) to breathe (into): вдохну́ть но́вую жизнь в (+ *acc.*), to breathe new life into.

вдре́безги *adv.* 1, to pieces; to smithereens. 2, *colloq.* completely; utterly: вдре́безги пьян, dead drunk.

вдруг *adv.* 1, suddenly; all of a sudden. 2, *colloq.* together; at once: Не говори́те все вдруг, don't talk all at once. 3, *colloq.* suppose...?; what if...?

вдува́ть *v.impfv.* [*pfv.* вдуть] (*with* в + *acc.*) to blow (*e.g.* air) into (something).

вду́маться *v.r., pfv. of* вду́мываться.

вду́мчивый *adj.* thoughtful; pensive.

вду́мываться *v.r.impfv.* [*pfv.* вду́маться] 1, to reflect; ponder. 2, (*with* в + *acc.*) to consider; go into.

вдуть [*infl.* вду́ю, вду́ешь] *v., pfv. of* вдува́ть.

вдыха́ние *n.* inhalation.

вдыха́тельный *adj.* 1, respiratory. 2, intake (*attrib.*): вдыха́тельный кла́пан, intake valve.

вдыха́ть *v.impfv.* [*pfv.* **вдохну́ть**] to inhale; breathe in. *See also* **вдохну́ть**.

вегетариа́нец [*gen.* **-нца**] *n.* vegetarian. —**вегетариа́нский**, *adj.* vegetarian.

вегета́ция *n.* (process of) vegetation.

ве́дать *v.impfv.* **1**, (*with instr.*) to manage; be in charge of. **2**, *obs.* to know.

ве́дение *n.* authority; jurisdiction.

веде́ние *n.* (*with gen.*) keeping (of); conduct (of); handling (of); management (of).

ве́домо *n.*, *in* **с/без ве́дома** (+ *gen.*), with/without the knowledge of.

ве́домость [*pl.* **ве́домости, -сте́й, -стя́м**] *n.f.* **1**, register; roll. **2**, *pl.* official bulletin. —**платёжная ве́домость**, payroll.

ве́домственный *adj.* departmental.

ве́домство *n.* (government) department.

ведо́мый *pres. passive part. of* **вести́**. —**ведо́мый самолёт**, supporting aircraft.

ведро́ [*pl.* **вёдра, вёдер**] *n.* bucket; pail. —**дождь льёт как из ведра́**, it is raining cats and dogs.

веду́щий *adj.* **1**, lead: веду́щий самолёт, lead aircraft. **2**, *fig.* leading: веду́щая роль, leading role. **3**, *mech.* drive (*attrib.*); driving: веду́щее колесо́, driving wheel. —*n., radio & TV* **1**, moderator. **2**, anchorman.

ведь *particle* **1**, why; after all; you know: Ведь э́то всем изве́стно, why everyone knows that! Он ведь ребёнок, after all, he is only a child. **2**, isn't that so?: Ведь он до́ма?, he is home, isn't he?

ве́дьма *n.* witch; hag.

ве́ер [*pl.* **веера́**] *n.* fan.

веерообра́зный *adj.* fan-shaped.

ве́жливый *adj.* polite; courteous. —**ве́жливо**, *adv.* politely; courteously. —**ве́жливость**, *n.f.* politeness; courtesy.

везде́ *adv.* everywhere. —**везде́, где...**, everywhere; wherever. —**везде́ и всю́ду**, absolutely everywhere.

вездесу́щий *adj.* omnipresent; ubiquitous.

вездехо́д *n.* cross-country vehicle; land rover. —**вездехо́дный**, *adj.* cross-country.

везе́ние *n.*, *colloq.* luck.

везти́ *v.impfv.* [*pfv.* **повезти́**; *pres.* **везу́, везёшь**; *past* **вёз, везла́, везло́, везли́**] **1**, to carry; take; convey (*in a vehicle*). **2**, *impers.* (*with dat.*) *colloq.* to be lucky; have luck: Ему́ всегда́ везёт, he is always lucky. Вам повезло́, что..., you are lucky that...

везу́чий *adj.*, *colloq.* lucky.

век [*pl.* **века́**] *n.* **1**, century. **2**, age: ка́менный век, the Stone Age; сре́дние века́, the Middle Ages. **3**, *colloq.* life; lifetime: Я мно́го повида́л(а) на своём веку́, I have seen a lot in my life/lifetime. —**во ве́ки веко́в**, *archaic* for all time; for all eternity. — **в ко́и-то ве́ки**; **в ко́и ве́ки**, once in a blue moon. —**испоко́н веко́в**, since time immemorial. —**на ве́ки ве́чные**, forever.

ве́ко [*pl.* **ве́ки, век**] *n.* eyelid.

веково́й *adj.* age-old.

ве́ксель [*pl.* **векселя́**] *n.m.* promissory note; bill of exchange.

ве́ктор *n.* vector. —**ве́кторный**, *adj.* vector (*attrib.*).

веле́невый *adj.* (*of paper*) vellum.

веле́ние *n.* command; dictate: веле́ния со́вести, the dictates of one's conscience.

веле́ть *v.impfv. & pfv.* [*pres.* **велю́, вели́шь**] (*with dat.*) **1**, to order; tell. **2**, *used negatively*, not to allow; forbid.

велика́н *n.* giant.

вели́кий *adj.* **1**, great. **2**, [*short form* — **вели́к, велика́, велико́, велики́** — *only*] (*of clothes*) too big; too large: Боти́нки мне велики́, the shoes are big on me; the shoes are too big for me. —**от ма́ла до вели́ка**, young and old alike.

великоду́шие *n.* magnanimity. —**великоду́шный**, *adj.* magnanimous.

великоле́пие *n.* magnificence; splendor.

великоле́пно *adv.* **1**, magnificently. **2**, marvelously. **3**, *as an interj.* splendid!

великоле́пный *adj.* **1**, magnificent; splendid. **2**, *colloq.* wonderful; marvelous.

великопо́стный *adj.* Lenten.

велича́вый *adj.* stately; majestic.

велича́йший *adj.*, *superl. of* **вели́кий**, greatest; utmost: де́ло велича́йшей ва́жности, a matter of the greatest/utmost importance.

велича́ть *v.impfv.* **1**, to call (*by a certain name*). **2**, *obs.* to extol; sing the praises of.

вели́чественный *adj.* majestic; stately.

вели́чество *n.* Majesty: его́ вели́чество, His Majesty.

вели́чие *n.* greatness; grandeur. —**ма́ния вели́чия**, megalomania; delusions of grandeur.

величина́ [*pl.* **-чи́ны**] *n.* **1**, size. **2**, *math.* value; quantity. **3**, magnitude (*of a star*). **4**, *fig.* eminent figure.

велого́нка [*gen. pl.* **-нок**] *n.* bicycle race. —**велого́нщик**, *n.* bicycle racer.

велодро́м *n.* velodrome.

велосипе́д *n.* bicycle. —**велосипеди́ст**, *n.* cyclist. —**велосипе́дный**, *adj.* bicycle (*attrib.*).

вельве́т *n.* velveteen. —**вельве́товый**, *adj.* velveteen.

вельмо́жа *n.m.* **1**, *archaic* aristocrat. **2**, *ironic* bigwig.

велю́р *n.* velour. —**велю́ровый**, *adj.* velour.

веля́рный *adj.* velar.

ве́на *n.* vein.

венге́рка [*gen. pl.* **-рок**] *n.* **1**, Hungarian woman. **2**, Hungarian dance. **3**, Hungarian-style jacket.

венге́рский *adj.* Hungarian.

венгр *n.m.* [*fem.* **венге́рка**] Hungarian.

Вене́ра *n.* Venus.

венери́ческий *adj.* venereal.

венесу́эльский *adj.* Venezuelan.

вене́ц [*gen.* **венца́**] *n.* **1**, crown. **2**, *poetic* wreath. **3**, *astron.* corona. **4**, row of crossbeams. —**идти́ под вене́ц**, *obs.* to wed.

венециа́нский *adj.* Venetian.

вене́чный *adj.*, *anat.* coronary.

ве́нзель [*pl.* **вензеля́**] *n.m.* monogram.

ве́ник *n.* broom made of twigs.

вено́зный *adj.* venous.

вено́к [*gen.* **венка́**] *n.* wreath.

ве́нский *adj.* of Vienna; Viennese.

вентили́ровать *v.impfv.* [*pfv.* **провентили́ровать**; *pres.* **-рую, -руешь**] to ventilate.

ве́нтиль *n.m.* valve.

вентиля́тор *n.* fan; blower.

вентиля́ция *n.* ventilation.

венча́льный *adj.* wedding (*attrib.*).

венча́ние *n.* **1,** (religious) wedding ceremony. **2,** [*also,* венча́ние на ца́рство] coronation.

венча́ть *v.impfv.* **1,** [*pfv.* увенча́ть] to crown. **2,** [*pfv.* повенча́ть *or* обвенча́ть] to marry. —венча́ться, *refl.* **1,** to be crowned. **2,** to be married.

ве́нчик *n.* **1,** *dim. of* вене́ц. **2,** corolla.

вепрь *n.m.* wild boar.

ве́ра *n.* faith; belief. —дава́ть ве́ру (+ *dat.*), to give credence to. —принима́ть на ве́ру, to take on faith. —служи́ть ве́рой и пра́вдой, to serve faithfully.

вера́нда *n.* veranda.

ве́рба *n.* pussy willow.

вербе́на *n.* verbena.

верблю́д *n.* camel.

верблю́жий [*fem.* -жья] *adj.* **1,** camel (*attrib.*). **2,** camel's-hair.

ве́рбный *adj.* pussy-willlow (*attrib.*). —ве́рбное воскресе́нье, Palm Sunday.

вербова́ть *v.impfv.* [*pfv.* завербова́ть; *pres.* -бу́ю, -бу́ешь] to recruit. —вербова́ться, *refl.* to enlist.

вербо́вка *n.* recruitment. —вербо́вщик, *n.* recruiter.

ве́рбовый *adj.* pussy-willow (*attrib.*).

верди́кт *n.* verdict.

верёвка [*gen. pl.* -вок] *n.* rope; cord; string; line: верёвка для белья́, clothesline. —вить верёвки из, to twist around one's little finger.

верёвочный *adj.* rope (*attrib.*); string (*attrib.*).

верени́ца *n.* file; row; line.

ве́реск *n.* heather.

веретено́ [*pl.* -тёна, -тён] *n.* spindle.

вереща́ть *v.impfv.* [*pres.* -щу́, -щи́шь] to chirp.

верзи́ла *n.m. & f., colloq.* tall, ungainly person.

вери́ги *n.pl.* [*sing.* вери́га] chains worn by religious ascetics.

вери́тельный *adj., in* вери́тельные гра́моты, credentials (*of a diplomat*).

ве́рить *v.impfv.* [*pfv.* пове́рить] **1,** (*with dat.*) to believe. **2,** (*with* в + *acc.*) to believe in. **3,** [*impfv. only*] to believe (in God). **4,** *in* ве́рить (+ *dat.*) на́ слово, to take at one's word; take one's word for it. —ве́риться, *refl.* [*impfv. only*] *impers.* **1,** to be believed; be believable: Не ве́рится, it is not to be believed; ка́к-то не ве́рится, somehow it does not ring true. **2,** (*with dat.*) to believe: Мне не ве́рится, I can't believe it.

вермише́ль *n.f.* vermicelli.

ве́рмут *n.* vermouth.

верне́е *adj., comp. of* ве́рный. —*particle* or rather; or to be more precise.

верниса́ж *n.* **1,** opening day (*of an art exhibit*). **2,** preview; advance showing (*of an art exhibit*).

ве́рно *adv.* **1,** faithfully. **2,** correctly. —*adj., used predicatively* **1,** true: Э́то не ве́рно, that is not true. **2,** correct; right: соверше́нно ве́рно, absolutely right. —*particle, colloq.* probably; most likely.

ве́рность *n.f.* **1,** fidelity; faithfulness. **2,** loyalty; allegiance. **3,** correctness; accuracy.

верну́ть *v., pfv. of* возвраща́ть. —верну́ться, *refl., pfv. of* возвраща́ться.

ве́рный *adj.* [*short form* ве́рен, верна́, ве́рно, верны́] **1,** faithful; loyal; true. **2,** correct; right; true. **3,** reliable; sure; safe. **4,** sure; certain; inevitable. *See also* верне́е.

ве́рование *n.* **1,** belief; conviction. **2,** *pl.* religious beliefs.

ве́ровать *v.impfv.* [*pres.* -рую, -руешь] **1,** (*with* в + *acc.*) to believe (in). **2,** to believe in God.

вероисповéдание *n.* faith; religion; creed; denomination.

вероло́мный *adj.* perfidious. —вероло́мство, *n.* perfidy.

вероуче́ние *n., relig.* teachings; dogma.

вероя́тно *adv.* probably.

вероя́тность *n.f.* probability; likelihood. —по всей вероя́тности, in all probability.

вероя́тный *adj.* probably; likely.

ве́рсия *n.* version.

верста́ [*pl.* вёрсты] *n.* old Russian unit of length equal to approx. one kilometer; verst. В трёх верста́х (*with different stress*) от, three versts from. —за версту́, from far off.

верста́к [*gen.* -стака́] *n.* carpenter's bench.

верста́ть *v.impfv.* [*pfv.* сверста́ть] *printing* to make up; make into pages.

вёрстка *n., printing* **1,** page make-up. **2,** page proofs.

верстово́й *adj., in* верстово́й столб, milepost; milestone.

ве́ртел [*pl.* вертела́] *n.* spit; skewer.

верте́п *n.* den (*of criminals, vice, etc.*).

верте́ть *v.impfv.* [*pres.* верчу́, ве́ртишь] **1,** to turn; spin. **2,** to twirl. **3,** (*with instr.*) to shake (one's head); wag (one's tail). **4,** (*with instr.*) *colloq.* to boss around; twist around one's little finger. —как ни верти́, no matter what you do; like it or not.

верте́ться *v.r.impfv.* [*pres.* верчу́сь, ве́ртишься] **1,** to turn; spin; revolve; rotate. **2,** to fidget. **3,** *colloq.* to hang around. **4,** *fig.* (*with* о́коло *or* вокру́г) *colloq.* to revolve (around); center (around). **5,** *colloq.* to beat around the bush. —верте́ться на языке́ *or* на ко́нчике языка́, to be on the tip of one's tongue. —верте́ться пе́ред глаза́ми *or* на глаза́х (*with* у), to pester. —верте́ться под нога́ми (*with* у), to be (*or* keep getting) in someone's way. —как ни верти́сь, = как ни верти́.

вертика́ль *n.f.* **1,** vertical line. **2,** *chess* file.

вертика́льный *adj.* vertical. —вертика́льно, *adv.* vertically.

вёрткий *adj., colloq.* agile; nimble; spry.

вертлю́г [*gen.* -люга́] *n.* swivel.

вертля́вый *adj., colloq.* fidgety; frisky.

вертодро́м *n.* heliport.

вертолёт *n.* helicopter.

верту́шка [*gen. pl.* -шек] *n., colloq.* **1,** any of a number of revolving devices — *e.g.* revolving door; revolving bookcase, etc. **2,** private telephone. **3,** flighty woman.

ве́рующий *n., decl. as an adj.* believer.

верфь *n.f.* shipyard.

верх [*2nd loc.* **верху́**; *pl.* **верхи́**] *n.* **1**, top. **2**, folding top (*of a carriage, automobile, etc.*). **3**, right side (*of material*); outer side (*of a garment*). **4**, *pl., colloq.* the leadership; the upper strata. **5**, (*with gen.*) the height (of); the acme (of). **6**, *pl., music* upper register; high notes. **7**, *pl.* superficial aspects: скользи́ть по верха́м, to skim the surface. —**брать** *or* **одержа́ть верх**, **1**, to prevail; gain the upper hand; come out on top. **2**, (*with* над) to prevail over; get the better (*or* best) of. —**встре́ча в верха́х**, summit meeting; summit conference. *See also* **ве́рхом** *and* **верхо́м**.

ве́рхний *adj.* upper; top. —**ве́рхняя оде́жда; ве́рхнее пла́тье**, outer clothing; outdoor clothes.

верхо́вный *adj.* supreme.

верхово́д *n., colloq.* boss.

верхово́дить *v.impfv.* [*pres.* **-во́жу, -во́дишь**] *colloq.* to be the boss; (*with instr.*) boss around.

верхово́й *adj.* **1**, of or pert. to horseback riding: верхова́я езда́, horseback riding; верхова́я ло́шадь, riding horse; saddle horse. **2**, up-river: верховы́е сёла, towns located up-river. —*n.* horseman; rider.

верхо́вье *n.* upper reaches (*of a river*); headwaters.

верхогля́д *n., colloq.* superficial person. —**верхогля́дство**, *n., colloq.* superficiality.

верхола́з *n.* steeplejack.

ве́рхом *adv.* **1**, along the top; taking the high ground. **2**, to the brim; to overflowing.

верхо́м *adv.* (on) horseback: е́здить верхо́м, to ride horseback; ride a horse; ката́ться верхо́м, to go (horseback) riding. —**верхо́м на** (+ *prepl.*), astride.

верху́шка [*gen. pl.* **-шек**] *n.* **1**, peak; top. **2**, *colloq.* the leaders; the elite.

ве́рша *n.* creel.

верши́на *n.* **1**, top; peak; summit. **2**, *math.* apex (*of a triangle*); vertex (*of an angle*). **3**, *fig.* (*with gen.*) the acme (of); the pinnacle (of).

верши́ть *v.impfv.* **1**, to decide. **2**, (*with instr.*) to direct; control.

вершо́к [*gen.* **-шка́**] *n.* old Russian unit of length equal to approx. 1 3/4 inches.

вес *n.* weight. —**держа́ть(ся) на весу́**, to hold/remain suspended in midair. —**на вес зо́лота**, worth its weight in gold. *See also* **веси́**.

веселе́ть *v.impfv.* [*pfv.* **повеселе́ть**] to cheer up; become cheerful.

весели́ть *v.impfv.* **1**, to gladden; cheer. **2**, to amuse. —**весели́ться**, *refl.* to enjoy oneself; make merry; have fun.

ве́село *adv.* gaily; merrily. —*adj., used predicatively,* gay; merry: На вечери́нке бы́ло о́чень ве́село, at the party everyone was having a good time.

весёлость *n.f.* gaiety; cheerfulness.

весёлый *adj.* [*short form* **ве́сел, весела́, ве́село, ве́селы** *or* **веселы́**] gay; merry; cheerful.

весе́лье *n.* gaiety; merriment.

весе́льный *adj., in* **весе́льная ло́дка**, rowboat.

весельча́к [*gen.* **-чака́**] *n., colloq.* jolly fellow.

веселя́щий *adj., in* **веселя́щий газ**, laughing gas.

весе́нний *adj.* spring (*attrib.*). —**весе́ннее равноде́нствие**, vernal equinox.

ве́сить *v.impfv.* [*pres.* **ве́шу, ве́сишь**] to weigh (so many pounds).

ве́ский *adj.* weighty.

весло́ [*pl.* **вёсла, вёсел**] *n.* oar; paddle.

весна́ [*pl.* **вёсны, вёсен**] *n.* spring (*season*).

весно́й *also,* **весно́ю**, *adv.* in (the) spring.

весну́шка [*gen. pl.* **-шек**] *n.* freckle. —**весну́шчатый**, *adj.* freckled; freckle-faced.

весо́мый *adj.* **1**, having weight; not weightless. **2**, *fig.* weighty.

вест *n., naut.* **1**, west. **2**, west wind.

ве́стерн (тэ) *n.* western (*movie*).

вести́ *v.impfv.* [*pres.* **веду́, ведёшь**; *past* **вёл, вела́, вело́, вели́**] **1**, [*pfv.* **повести́**] to lead; take (someone somewhere). **2**, (*of a road, path, etc.*) to lead (somewhere). **3**, to drive; steer; pilot; fly. **4**, to conduct (a meeting, lesson, seminar, negotiations, trade, etc.). **5**, to teach (a course, class, etc.). **6**, to carry on (a conversation, correspondence, etc.). **7**, to keep (a diary, the books, etc.). **8**, to wage (war, a struggle, etc.). **9**, to plead (a case). **10**, to lead (a certain kind of life). **11**, [*pfv.* **повести́**] (*with* к) to lead (to a certain result). **12**, (*with instr. and* по) to pass; run (something over something). —**вести́ ого́нь (по)**, to fire (on). —**вести́ себя́**, to behave. *See also* **води́ть**.

вестибю́ль *n.m.* lobby; foyer.

вести́сь *v.r.impfv.* [*pres.* **ведётся**; *past* **вёлся, вела́сь, вело́сь, вели́сь**] **1**, to be conducted; be carried out. **2**, *impers., colloq.* to be the custom: Так у нас не ведётся, this is not the way we do things.

ве́стник *n.* **1**, messenger; herald. **2**, bulletin (*title of a publication*).

вестово́й *n., decl. as an adj., obs.* orderly.

ве́сточка [*gen. pl.* **-чек**] *n., dim. of* **весть**. —**пришли́те мне ве́сточку**, drop me a line.

весть[1] [*pl.* **ве́сти, весте́й, вестя́м**] *n.f.* (piece of) news. —**пропа́сть без вести**, to be missing (in action).

весть[2] *v., obs. 3rd person sing. of* **ве́дать**. —**бог весть**, God knows! —**не бог весть**, not particularly: не бог весть как далеко́, not particularly far; не бог весть кака́я кру́пная фигу́ра, not a particularly prominent figure.

веси́ [*gen.* **весо́в**] *n.pl.* **1**, scale(s). **2**, *cap.* Libra.

весь[1] [*fem.* **вся**; *neut.* **всё**; *pl.* **все**; *gen.* **всего́, всей, всех**; *acc. fem.* **всю**; *dat.* **всему́, всей, всем**; *instr.* **всем, всей, все́ми**; *prepl.* **всём, всей, всех**] *adj.* all; the whole: весь день, all day; весь мир, the whole world; всё вре́мя, all the time; все стра́ны, all nations. —**весь в** (+ *acc.*), the image of: Он весь в отца́, he is the image of his father. *See also* **всё, все, всего́**.

весь[2] *n.f., obs.* village; town. Города́ и ве́си, cities and towns.

весьма́ *adv.* highly; extremely.

ветви́стый *adj.* having many branches.

ветвь [*pl.* **ве́тви, ветве́й, ветвя́м**] *n.f.* branch; limb.

ве́тер [*gen.* **ве́тра**; *2nd loc.* **ветру́**] *n.* wind. —**броса́ть** *or* **пуска́ть** (*e.g.* **де́ньги**) **на ве́тер**, to toss to the winds; squander. —**бросáть словá на вéтер,** to waste words. —**держáть нос по вéрту,** to follow the prevailing winds. —**ищи́ вéтра в пóле,** you'll never find it (him, her, etc.). —**кудá** or **откýда вéтер дýет,** which way the wind blows. —**у негó вéтер в головé,** he hasn't got a brain in his head.

ветерáн adj. veteran.

ветеринáр n. veterinarian. —**ветеринáрия,** n. veterinary medicine. —**ветеринáрный,** adj. veterinary.

ветерóк [gen. **-ркá**] n. breeze.

вéтка [gen. pl. **вéток**] n. **1,** branch; twig. **2,** R.R. branch line.

ветлá [pl. **вётлы, вётел**] n. white willow.

вéто n. indecl. veto.

вéточка [gen. pl. **-чек**] n. twig; sprig.

вéтошь n.f. tattered clothes; rags.

вéтреник n., colloq. frivolous person; flighty person; scatterbrain.

вéтреница n. **1,** fem. of **вéтреник. 2,** anemone.

вéтрено adv. frivolously. —adj., used predicatively, windy: Сегóдня вéтрено, it is windy today.

вéтреный adj. **1,** windy. **2,** colloq. frivolous.

ветровóй adj. wind (attrib.). —**ветровóе стеклó,** windshield.

ветромéр n. anemometer.

ветря́нка n., colloq. chicken pox.

ветряно́й adj. wind (attrib.). —**ветряна́я мéльница,** windmill.

вéтряный adj. wind (attrib.). —**вéтряная óспа,** chicken pox.

вéтхий adj. ramshackle; dilapidated. —**Вéтхий завéт,** Old Testament.

ветхозавéтный adj. Old Testament (attrib.).

вéтхость n.f. disrepair; decay: приходи́ть в вéтхость, to fall into disrepair.

ветчинá n. ham.

ветшáть v.impfv. [pfv. **обветшáть**] to deteriorate; become dilapidated; fall into decay.

вéха n. **1,** stake. **2,** signpost. **3,** usu. pl., fig. landmark; milestone.

вéче [gen. **вéча**] n., hist. popular assembly in old Russia; veche.

вéчер [pl. **вечерá**] n. **1,** evening. **2,** (evening) party; soirée. See also **вéчером.**

вечерéть v.impfv., impers. to grow dark: Вечерéет, dusk is falling; evening is coming on.

вечери́нка [gen. pl. **-нок**] n. (evening) party.

вечéрний adj. evening (attrib.). —**вечéрняя шкóла,** night school.

вечéрня n. vespers.

вéчером adv. in the evening. —**вчерá вéчером,** last evening; last night. —**зáвтра вéчером,** tomorrow evening; tomorrow night. —**сегóдня вéчером,** this evening; tonight.

вéчеря n., in **тáйная вéчеря,** the Last Supper.

вéчно adv. **1,** eternally; forever. **2,** colloq. constantly; always; forever.

вечнозелёный adj. evergreen.

вéчность n.f. **1,** eternity. **2,** in цéлая вéчность, ages: Не ви́дел(а) вас цéлую вéчность, I haven't seen you

for ages. —**кáнуть в вéчность,** to sink into oblivion. —**отойти́ в вéчность,** to pass into eternity.

вéчный adj. **1,** eternal; everlasting; perpetual. **2,** colloq. endless; constant; continual. —**вéчная пáмять** (+ dat.), may his (her) memory live forever. —**вéчное перó,** obs. fountain pen. —**на вéки вéчные,** forever. —**на вéчные временá,** for all time. —**заснýть вéчным сном,** to go to one's eternal rest.

вéшалка [gen. pl. **-лок**] n. **1,** rack. **2,** hanger. **3,** colloq. cloakroom.

вéшать v.impfv. [pfv. **повéсить**] **1,** to hang; hang up. **2,** to hang (execute). **3,** in **вéшать нос** or **гóлову,** to be/become discouraged; lose heart. **4,** [pfv. **свéшать**] to weigh. —**вéшаться,** refl. **1,** to hang oneself. **2,** in **вéшаться на шéю** (+ dat.), to throw oneself at.

вещáние n. **1,** broadcasting. **2,** prophesying. **3,** prophecy.

вещáть v.impfv. **1,** obs. to prophesy. **2,** colloq. to preach; expound. **3,** to broadcast.

вещевóй adj. clothing (attrib.). —**вещевóй мешóк,** knapsack. —**вещевóй склад,** warehouse.

вещéственный adj. material. —**вещéственные доказáтельства,** material evidence.

веществó n. **1,** matter; substance. **2,** agent: токси́ческое веществó, toxic agent. **3,** in взры́вчатое веществó, explosive; пита́тельное веществó, nutrient; растворя́ющее веществó, solvent; сма́зочное веществó, lubricant. —**обмéн вещéств,** metabolism.

вéщий adj., obs. **1,** wise. **2,** prophetic.

вéщица n. **1,** dim. of **вещь. 2,** knickknack.

вещь [pl. **вéщи, вещéй, вещáм**] n.f. **1,** thing. **2,** pl. things; belongings; clothes. **3,** work; piece (of art, literature, music, etc.): три вéщи Прокóфьева, three works by Prokofiev.

вéялка [gen. pl. **-лок**] n. winnowing machine.

вéяние n. **1,** winnowing. **2,** blowing (of the wind). **3,** sign; portent. **4,** fig. trend.

вéять v.impfv. [pres. **вéю, вéешь**] **1,** to blow gently. **2,** fig. (with instr.) to be in the air: Вéет весно́й, spring is in the air. **3,** to wave; flutter. **4,** v.t. [pfv. **провéять**] to winnow.

вживáться v.r.impfv. [pfv. **вжи́ться**] (with в + acc.) to get used to. —**вживáться в свою́ роль,** to get the feel of a part.

вживи́ть [infl. **-влю́, -ви́шь**] v., pfv. of **вживля́ть.**

вживлéние n., med. implantation.

вживля́ть v.impfv. [pfv. **вживи́ть**] med. to implant.

вжи́ться [infl. like **жить**; past вжи́лся, вжила́сь, вжило́сь or вжи́лось, вжили́сь or вжи́лись] v.r., pfv. of **вживáться.**

взад adv., colloq. back. —**взад и вперёд,** back and forth; to and fro; up and down.

взаи́мно adv. mutually.

взаи́мность n.f. mutuality; reciprocity. —**без взаи́мности,** without requital. —**отвечáть кому́-нибудь взаи́мностью,** to reciprocate someone's feelings.

взаи́мный adj. mutual; reciprocal.

взаимовы́годный adj. mutually beneficial or advantageous.

взаимодéйствие n. **1,** interaction; interplay. **2,** mil. cooperation; coordination.

взаимоде́йствовать *v.impfv.* [*pres.* **-ствую, -ствуешь**] **1,** to interact. **2,** *mil.* to cooperate.

взаимозави́симый *adj.* interdependent. —**взаимозави́симость,** *n.f.* interdependence.

взаимозаменя́емый *adj.* interchangeable.

взаимоотноше́ние *n.* relation; interrelation.

взаимопо́мощь *n.f.* mutual aid; mutual assistance.

взаимопонима́ние *n.* mutual understanding.

взаимосвя́занный *adj.* interconnected; interrelated.

взаимосвя́зь *n.f.* interconnection.

взаймы́ *adv.* on loan. —**дава́ть взаймы́,** to lend; loan. —**брать** *or* **получа́ть взаймы́,** to borrow.

взаме́н *adv.* **1,** instead. **2,** in return; in exchange. —*prep., with gen.* **1,** in return for; in exchange for. **2,** in place of.

взаперти́ *adv.* **1,** locked up; under lock and key. **2,** *fig.* in seclusion.

вза́пуски *adv., colloq.* racing (with) one another: бе́гать вза́пуски, to race each other.

взахлёб *adv., colloq.* avidly; with gusto. Жить взахлёб, to live life to the fullest.

взба́дривать *v.impfv.* [*pfv.* **взбодри́ть**] *colloq.* **1,** to invigorate. **2,** to cheer up.

взбаламу́тить *v., pfv. of* **баламу́тить.**

взба́лмошный *adj., colloq.* eccentric; erratic; unbalanced.

взба́лтывать *v.impfv.* [*pfv.* **взболта́ть**] to shake (up).

взбега́ть *v.impfv.* [*pfv.* **взбежа́ть**] (*with* **на** + *acc. or* **по**) to run up.

взбежа́ть [*infl. like* **бежа́ть**] *v., pfv. of* **взбега́ть.**

взбелени́ться *v.r.pfv., colloq.* to fly into a rage.

взбеси́ть *v., pfv. of* **беси́ть.** —**взбеси́ться,** *refl., pfv. of* **беси́ться.**

взбива́ть *v.impfv.* [*pfv.* **взбить**] **1,** to fluff (up). **2,** to whip (cream); beat (egg whites); churn up (water).

взбира́ться *v.r.impfv.* [*pfv.* **взобра́ться**] (*with* **на** + *acc. or* **по**) to climb; climb up.

взби́тый *adj.* beaten; whipped: взби́тые сли́вки, whipped cream.

взбить [*infl.* **взобью́, взобьёшь**] *v., pfv. of* **взбива́ть.**

взбодри́ть *v., pfv. of* **взба́дривать.**

взболта́ть *v., pfv. of* **болта́ть** (*in sense #2*) *and* **взба́лтывать.**

взборони́ть *v., pfv. of* **борони́ть.**

взбреда́ть *v.impfv.* [*pfv.* **взбрести́**] (*with* **на** + *acc.*) *colloq.* to mount with difficulty. —**взбрести́ в го́лову** *or* **на ум** (+ *dat.*), to come into one's head.

взбрести́ [*infl. like* **брести́**] *v., pfv. of* **взбреда́ть.**

взбудора́жить *v., pfv. of* **будора́жить.**

взбунтова́ть *v., pfv. of* **бунтова́ть** (*in sense #2*). —**взбунтова́ться,** *refl.* to rebel; revolt.

взбуха́ть *v.impfv.* [*pfv.* **взбу́хнуть**] to swell out; bulge.

взбу́хнуть [*past* взбух, взбу́хла] *v., pfv. of* **взбуха́ть.**

взбу́чка *n., colloq.* **1,** beating; thrashing. **2,** scolding; dressing-down.

взва́ливать *v.impfv.* [*pfv.* **взвали́ть**] (*with* **на** + *acc.*) **1,** to load (onto). **2,** *fig.* to load (work on someone). **3,** *fig.* to lay; place (blame).

взвали́ть [*infl.* **взвалю́, взва́лишь**] *v., pfv. of* **взва́ливать.**

взве́сить [*infl.* **-шу, -сишь**] *v., pfv. of* **взве́шивать.** —**взве́ситься,** *refl., pfv. of* **взве́шиваться.**

взвести́ [*infl. like* **вести́**] *v., pfv. of* **взводи́ть.**

взве́шенный *adj.* carefully thought out; carefully weighed.

взве́шивать *v.impfv.* [*pfv.* **взве́сить**] **1,** to weigh. **2,** *fig.* to weigh; ponder. —**взве́шиваться,** *refl.* to weigh oneself.

взвива́ть *v.impfv.* [*pfv.* **взви́ть**] to blow up; swirl. —**взвива́ться,** *refl.* **1,** to shoot up; soar. **2,** [*also,* **взвива́ться на дыбы́**] (*of a horse*) to rear. **3,** (*of a flag, curtain, etc.*) to go up.

взви́зг *n., colloq.* screech; yelp.

взви́згивать *v.impfv.* [*pfv.* **взви́згнуть**] to screech; yelp.

взви́нчивать *v.impfv.* [*pfv.* **взвинти́ть**] *colloq.* **1,** to upset; agitate. Взви́нчивать себя́, to get oneself all worked up. **2,** to jack up; drive up (prices).

взви́ть [*infl.* **взовью́, взовьёшь**] *v., pfv. of* **взвива́ть.** —**взви́ться,** *refl., pfv. of* **взвива́ться.**

взвод *n.* **1,** platoon. **2,** cocking recess (*of a firearm*): на боево́м взво́де, cocked; ready to fire; на предохрани́тельном взво́де, at half cock. —**на взво́де,** *colloq.* tipsy.

взводи́ть *v.impfv.* [*pfv.* **взвести́;** *pres.* **-вожу́, -во́дишь**] **1,** to lead up. **2,** to level (an accusation). **3,** *in* взводи́ть куро́к, to cock a gun.

взво́дный *adj.* platoon (*attrib.*). —*n.* platoon leader.

взволно́ванный *adj.* agitated; anxious; uneasy.

взволнова́ть *v., pfv. of* **волнова́ть.** —**взволнова́ться,** *refl., pfv. of* **волнова́ться.**

взвы́ть *v.pfv.* [*infl.* **взво́ю, взво́ешь**] to howl.

взгляд *n.* **1,** look; glance. **2,** opinion; view: на мой взгляд, in my opinion. —**на пе́рвый взгляд,** at first glance; on the face of it. —**с пе́рвого взгля́да, 1,** at first glance. **2,** at a glance; from the first.

взгля́дывать *v.impfv.* [*pfv.* **взгляну́ть**] (*with* **на** + *acc.*) to glance (at); take a look (at).

взго́рье *n., colloq.* hill.

взгроможда́ть *v.impfv.* [*pfv.* **взгромозди́ть**] (*with* **на** + *acc.*) *colloq.* to pile (onto); load (onto); hoist (onto). —**взгроможда́ться,** *refl.* (*with* **на** + *acc.*) *colloq.* to clamber up (on).

взгрустну́ть *v.pfv., colloq.* to feel somewhat depressed; have a touch of melancholy.

вздёргивать *v.impfv.* [*pfv.* **вздёрнуть**] *colloq.* **1,** to raise; hoist up; jerk up. **2,** to execute by hanging; string up.

вздёрнутый *adj., in* вздёрнутый нос, snub nose.

вздёрнуть *v., pfv. of* **вздёргивать.**

вздор *n.* nonsense.

вздо́рить *v.impfv.* [*pfv.* **повздо́рить**] *colloq.* to argue; squabble; bicker.

вздо́рный *adj., colloq.* **1,** absurd; preposterous. **2,** quarrelsome; cantankerous.

вздорожа́ть *v., pfv. of* **дорожа́ть.**

вздох *n.* deep breath; sigh.

вздохну́ть *v.pfv.* **1,** *pfv. of* **вздыха́ть. 2,** *colloq.* to take a short rest; take a breath.

вздра́гивать *v.impfv.* [*pfv.* **вздро́гнуть**] to give a start; jump; wince.

вздремну́ть *v.pfv., colloq.* to take a nap.

вздро́гнуть *v., pfv. of* вздра́гивать.

вздува́ть *v.impfv.* [*pfv.* **вздуть**] **1,** to blow up (*into the air*). **2,** to bloat. **3,** *impers.* to be swollen: У него́ вздуло щёку, his cheek is swollen. **4,** *fig., colloq.* to inflate (prices). —**вздува́ться,** *refl.* to swell up; puff up.

вздумать *v.pfv., colloq.* to take it into one's head (to). —**вздуматься,** *refl., impers.* (*with dat.*) *colloq.* = **вздумать:** Мне вздумалось (+ *inf.*), I took it into my head to...

взду́тие *n.* swelling.

взду́тый *adj.* **1,** swollen. **2,** *fig.* inflated.

вздуть [*infl.* **взду́ю, взду́ешь**] *v., pfv. of* **вздува́ть.** —**взду́ться,** *refl., pfv. of* **вздува́ться.**

вздыбливаться *v.r.impfv.* [*pfv.* **вздыбиться**] (*of a horse*) to rear.

вздыма́ть *v.impfv.* to raise. —**вздыма́ться,** *refl.* **1,** to rise. **2,** (*of one's chest*) to heave.

вздыха́ть *v.impfv.* [*pfv.* **вздохну́ть**] **1,** to sigh. **2,** [*impfv. only*] (*with* **по** + *prepl. or* **о**) to yearn (for); pine (for).

взима́ть *v.impfv.* to levy; collect. Взима́ть пла́ту, to charge (money); charge a fee.

взира́ть *v.impfv.* to look; gaze.

взла́мывать *v.impfv.* [*pfv.* **взлома́ть**] to break open; force open.

взлеза́ть *v.impfv.* [*pfv.* **взлезть**] to climb up.

взлезть [*infl. like* **лезть**] *v., pfv. of* **взлеза́ть.**

взлёт *n.* **1,** upward flight. **2,** *aero.* takeoff. **3,** *fig.* (*with gen.*) upsurge (of).

взлета́ть *v.impfv.* [*pfv.* **взлете́ть**] **1,** to fly up; soar. **2,** (*of an airplane*) to take off. —**взлете́ть на во́здух,** to go up in smoke.

взлете́ть [*infl.* **-чу́, -ти́шь**] *v., pfv. of* **взлета́ть.**

взлётный *adj.* take-off (*attrib.*). —**взлётно-поса́дочная полоса́,** runway; landing strip.

взлом *n.* breaking in. —**кра́жа со взло́мом,** burglary.

взлома́ть *v., pfv. of* **взла́мывать.**

взло́мщик *n.* burglar.

взлохма́тить [*infl.* **-чу, -тишь**] *v., pfv. of* **взлохма́чивать.**

взлохма́ченный *adj.* **1,** (*of hair*) disheveled. **2,** (*of a dog*) shaggy.

взлохма́чивать *v.impfv.* [*pfv.* **взлохма́тить**] to muss; tousle.

взмах *n.* wave; sweep (*of the hand*); stroke (*of an oar*); flap (*of wings*); snip (*of scissors*).

взма́хивать *v.impfv.* [*pfv.* **взмахну́ть**] (*with instr.*) to flap; wave.

взметну́ть *v.pfv.* **1,** to throw up into the air; send flying. **2,** (*with instr.*) to flap (one's wings); throw up (one's hands). —**взметну́ться,** *refl.* to shoot up; fly up into the air.

взмоли́ться *v.r.pfv.* [*infl.* **взмолю́сь, взмо́лишься**] to implore; (*with* **о**) beg (for).

взмо́рье *n.* seashore.

взмыва́ть *v.impfv.* [*pfv.* **взмыть**] to soar.

взмы́ленный *adj.* (*of a horse*) foaming.

взмыть [*infl.* **взмо́ю, взмо́ешь**] *v., pfv. of* **взмыва́ть.**

взнос *n.* **1,** deposit; payment. **2,** fee; dues.

взну́здывать *v.impfv.* [*pfv.* **взнузда́ть**] to bridle (a horse).

взобра́ться [*infl.* **взберу́сь, взберёшься;** *past tense stress as in* **бра́ться**] *v.r., pfv. of* **взбира́ться.**

взойти́ [*infl.* **взойду́, взойдёшь;** *past* **взошёл, взошла́, взошло́, взошли́**] *v., pfv. of* **всходи́ть** *and* **восходи́ть.**

взор *n.* look; glance; gaze.

взорва́ть [*infl. like* **рвать**] *v., pfv. of* **взрыва́ть**[1]. —**взорва́ться,** *refl.* [*past tense stress as in* **рва́ться**] *pfv. of* **взрыва́ться.**

взрасти́ть [*infl.* **-щу́, -сти́шь**] *v., pfv. of* **взра́щивать.**

взра́щивать *v.impfv.* [*pfv.* **взрасти́ть**] **1,** to grow; cultivate. **2,** to raise; rear; bring up.

взреве́ть *v.pfv.* [*infl.* **-ву́, -вёшь**] to roar; let out a roar.

взросле́ть *v.impfv.* to grow up; become an adult.

взро́слый *adj.* adult; grown. —*n.* adult; grownup.

взрыв *n.* **1,** explosion; blast. **2,** *fig.* (*with gen.*) burst (of); outburst (of): взрыв аплодисме́нтов, burst of applause. —**демографи́ческий взрыв,** population explosion.

взрыва́тель *n.m.* fuse.

взрыва́ть[1] *v.impfv.* [*pfv.* **взорва́ть**] **1,** to blow up (a bridge, building, etc.); set off; detonate (a bomb). **2,** *fig., colloq.* to infuriate; send into a rage. —**взрыва́ться,** *refl.* **1,** to explode; burst; blow up; (*of a bomb, grenade, etc.*) go off. **2,** *fig., colloq.* to blow up; become infuriated.

взрыва́ть[2] *v.impfv.* [*pfv.* **взрыть**] to dig; dig up.

взрывно́й *adj.* **1,** explosive: взрывно́е устро́йство, explosive device. **2,** blasting (*attrib.*): взрывны́е рабо́ты, blasting operations.

взрывоопа́сный *adj.* explosive; dangerous.

взрывча́тка *n., colloq.* explosives.

взры́вчатый *adj.* explosive. —**взры́вчатое вещество́,** explosive.

взрыть [*infl.* **взро́ю, взро́ешь**] *v., pfv. of* **взрыва́ть**[2].

взрыхли́ть *v., pfv. of* **рыхли́ть** *and* **взрыхля́ть.**

взрыхля́ть *v.impfv.* [*pfv.* **взрыхли́ть**] to loosen; turn up (soil, dirt, etc.).

взъеда́ться *v.r.impfv.* [*pfv.* **взъе́сться**] *colloq.* **1,** to rant and rave. **2,** (*with* **на** + *acc.*) to lace into.

взъезжа́ть *v.impfv.* [*pfv.* **взъе́хать**] (*with* **на** + *acc.*) to drive up; ascend.

взъеро́шенный *adj.* disheveled.

взъеро́шить *v., pfv. of* **еро́шить.**

взъе́сться [*infl. like* **есть**] *v.r., pfv. of* **взъеда́ться.**

взъе́хать [*infl.* **взъе́ду, взъе́дешь**] *v., pfv. of* **взъезжа́ть.**

взыва́ть *v.impfv.* [*pfv.* **воззва́ть**] **1,** [*impfv. only*] to shout; call. **2,** to appeal.

взыгра́ть *v.pfv.* **1,** to become playful; act up. **2,** (*of the sea*) to become choppy. —**се́рдце во мне взыгра́ло,** my heart leaped for joy.

взыска́ние *n.* penalty.

взыска́тельный *adj.* exacting; demanding.

взыска́ть [*infl.* **взыщу́, взы́щешь**] *v., pfv. of* **взы́скивать.**

взы́скивать *v.impfv.* [*pfv.* **взыска́ть**] **1,** to exact; force payment of. **2,** to recover (a debt). **3,** (*with* **с** + *gen.*) to call to account; make answer. —**не взыщи́те!**, don't be too strict; don't expect too much.

взя́тие *n.* taking; capture; seizure.

взя́тка [*gen. pl.* **-ток**] *n.* **1,** bribe. **2,** *cards* trick.

взя́точник *n.* bribe taker. —**взя́точничество,** *n.* bribery.

взять *v.pfv.* [*infl.* **возьму́, возьмёшь;** *past fem.* **взяла́**] **1,** *pfv. of* **брать. 2,** to seize; arrest. **3,** (*with* **и, да** *or* **да и**) *denoting a sudden unexpected action:* Он взял и ушёл, he up and left; он взял и жени́лся, he went and got married. —**с чего́ вы взя́ли, что...?**, where did you get the idea that...?

взя́ться [*infl.* **возьму́сь, возьмёшься;** *past* **взя́лся, взяла́сь, взяло́сь** *or* **взя́лось, взяли́сь** *or* **взя́лись**] *v.r., pfv. of* **бра́ться. —отку́да ни возьми́сь,** from out of nowhere; from out of the blue.

виаду́к *n.* viaduct.

вибра́тор *n.* vibrator.

вибра́ция *n.* **1,** vibration. **2,** *music* tremolo.

вибри́ровать *v.impfv.* [*pres.* **-рует**] to vibrate.

виве́рра *n.* civet.

вивисе́кция *n.* vivisection.

вигва́м *n.* wigwam.

виго́нь *n.f.* vicuna. —**виго́невый,** *adj.* vicuna.

вид *n.* **1,** look; appearance. В тако́м ви́де, looking like that. **2,** (*with* **в** + *an adj.*) state; condition: в пья́ном ви́де, drunk; in a drunken state. **3,** view: вид на мо́ре, view of the sea. **4,** sight: в виду́ (+ *gen.*), in *or* within sight of; при ви́де (+ *gen.*), at the sight of. **5,** *pl.* prospects. **6,** kind; sort. **7,** form: в ви́де (+ *gen.*), in the form of; в его́ ны́нешнем ви́де, in its present form. **8,** species. **9,** *gram.* aspect. **10,** *mil.* branch (of the armed forces). —**для ви́да,** for appearance's sake. —**из ви́да; и́з виду,** from view. —**на вид; по ви́ду; с ви́ду,** in appearance. —**на виду́,** in the public eye. —**ни под каки́м ви́дом,** under no circumstances. —**под ви́дом** (+ *gen.*), under the guise of. —**у всех на виду́,** on view; in full view of everyone. —**де́лать вид,** to pretend; give the appearance of; make it look as if. —**име́ть в виду́, 1,** to have in mind. **2,** to bear in mind; keep in mind. —**име́ть ви́ды на** (+ *acc.*), **1,** to have an eye on; have designs on. **2,** to count on. —**име́ться в виду́,** to be meant. —**поста́вить на вид** (+ *dat.*), to reprimand (someone).

ви́данный *adj., in* ви́данное ли э́то де́ло?, *colloq.* did you ever see such a thing?

вида́ть[1] *v.impfv.* [*pfv.* **повида́ть**] *colloq.* **1,** to see. **2,** *in* вида́ть ви́ды, to have seen a lot; have been through a lot. Вида́вшие ви́ды сви́тер, a sweater that has seen better days. —**вида́ться,** *refl.* (*with* **с** + *instr.*) to see; visit.

вида́ть[2] *particle, colloq.* apparently; it seems.

ви́дение *n.* sight; vision.

виде́ние *n.* apparition; vision.

видеоза́пись *n.f.* videotape.

видеокассе́та *n.* video cassette.

видеомагнитофо́н *n.* video cassette recorder; VCR.

ви́деть *v.impfv.* [*pfv.* **уви́деть;** *pres.* **ви́жу, ви́дишь**] to see. —**ви́деться,** *refl.* **1,** [*impfv. only*] to be visible. **2,** (*with* **с** + *instr.*) to see; meet with. **3,** to see each other.

4, [*impfv. only*] *impers.* (*with dat.*) to see: мне ви́делось (+ *nom.*), I saw... Как вам ви́дится э́та пробле́ма сейча́с?, how do you see this problem now? **5,** [*impfv. only*] (*with instr.*) to be seen (as); be regarded (as): Он ви́дится им спаси́телем, they see him as a savior.

ви́димо *adv.* apparently; evidently.

ви́димость *n.f.* **1,** visibility. **2,** semblance; appearance. —**по всей ви́димости,** from all appearances.

ви́димый *adj.* **1,** visible. **2,** apparent; evident. **3,** *colloq.* seeming; apparent.

видне́ться *v.r.impfv.* to be seen; be visible.

ви́дно *adj., used predicatively* **1,** visible: Моста́ ещё не ви́дно, the bridge is not visible yet. **2,** clear; obvious: Ви́дно, что он не придёт, it is clear/obvious that he is not coming. —*adv., colloq.* apparently; evidently.

ви́дный *adj.* [*short form* **ви́ден, видна́, ви́дно, ви́дны** *or* **видны́**] **1,** visible; in sight. **2,** noticeable; conspicuous. **3,** prominent.

видово́й *adj.* **1,** *biol.* pert. to a species. **2,** *gram.* aspectual. —**видово́й фильм,** travel film.

видоизмене́ние *n.* **1,** modification; alteration. **2,** type; variety.

видоизменя́ть *v.impfv.* [*pfv.* **видоизмени́ть**] to modify; alter. —**видоизменя́ться,** *refl.* to change; undergo a change.

видоиска́тель *n.m., photog.* view finder.

ви́за *n.* visa.

визави́ *adv.* face to face. —*n.m. & f. indecl.* person opposite; person facing.

византи́йский *adj.* Byzantine.

визг *n.* squeal; screech; yelp.

визгли́вый *adj.* **1,** shrill. **2,** squealing; screeching.

визжа́ть *v.impfv.* [*pfv.* **ви́згнуть;** *pres.* **визжу́, визжи́шь**] to squeal; screech; yelp.

визи́р *n.* **1,** sight (*sighting device*). **2,** *photog.* view finder.

визи́ровать *v.impfv. & pfv.* [*pres.* **-рую, -руешь**] **1,** [*pfv. also* **завизи́ровать**) to enter a visa in (a passport). **2,** to sight; aim.

визи́рь *n.m.* vizier.

визи́т *n.* visit; call. —**визитёр,** *n., obs.* visitor; caller.

визи́тка [*gen. pl.* **-ток**] *n.* morning coat.

визи́тный *adj.* of or for visiting. —**визи́тная ка́рточка,** business card; calling card.

ви́ка *n.* vetch.

вика́рий *n.* vicar.

ви́кинг *n.* viking.

вико́нт *n.* viscount.

виктори́на *n.* quiz.

ви́лка [*gen. pl.* **ви́лок**] *n.* **1,** fork. **2,** plug (*for a socket*).

ви́лла *n.* villa.

ви́ллис *n.* jeep.

вило́к [*gen. pl.* **вилка́**] *n., colloq.* head of cabbage.

ви́лы [*gen. pl.* **вил**] *n.pl.* pitchfork. —**ви́лами на воде́ пи́сано,** it remains to be seen; it is anyone's guess.

виля́ть *v.impfv.* [*pfv.* **вильну́ть**] **1,** (*with instr.*) to wag (one's tail). **2,** (*of one's tail*) to wag. **3,** to weave; zigzag. **4,** *colloq.* to equivocate.

вина́ *n*. **1,** fault; blame. Всему́ вино́й (+ *nom.*), it's all the fault of.... Не по мое́й вине́, through no fault of mine. **2,** guilt. **3,** misdeed; transgression: загла́живать вину́, to redress a wrong. —**ста́вить (что́-нибудь) в вину́** (+ *dat.*), to hold something against someone.

винегре́т *n*. **1,** Russian salad. **2,** *fig., colloq.* hodge-podge; potpourri.

вини́л *n*. vinyl.

вини́тельный *adj., in* **вини́тельный паде́ж,** accusative case.

вини́ть *v.impfv.* to blame: вини́ть кого́-нибудь в оши́бке, to blame someone for a mistake; blame a mistake on someone.

виннока́менный *adj.* tartaric.

ви́нный *adj.* wine (*attrib.*). —**ви́нный ка́мень,** tartar; cream of tartar. —**ви́нная кислота́,** tartaric acid. —**ви́нный спирт,** ethyl alcohol. —**ви́нная я́года,** fig.

вино́ [*pl.* **ви́на**] *n*. wine.

винова́тый *adj.* **1,** guilty; at fault; to blame: Я винова́т, it's my fault. **2,** (*of a look or expression*) guilty; apologetic. —**винова́т!,** I'm sorry!; I beg your pardon!

вино́вник *n*. **1,** culprit; guilty party. **2,** (*with gen.*) perpetrator (of); cause (of). —**вино́вник торжества́,** guest of honor; hero of the occasion.

вино́вность *n.f.* guilt; culpability.

вино́вный *adj.* [*short form* **-вен, -вна**] guilty.

виногра́д *n*. grapes. —**виногра́дарство,** *n*. viniculture; viticulture. —**виногра́дина,** *n*. a (single) grape. —**виногра́дник,** *n*. vineyard.

виногра́дный *adj.* grape (*attrib.*). —**виногра́дный са́хар,** grape sugar.

виноде́л *n*. winemaker; winegrower. —**виноде́лие,** *n*. winemaking; winegrowing. —**виноде́льческий,** *adj.* winemaking (*attrib.*); winegrowing (*attrib.*).

виноку́р *n*. distiller. —**винокуре́ние,** *n*. distilling. —**виноку́ренный,** *adj.* distilling (*attrib.*).

винт [*gen.* **винта́**] *n*. **1,** screw. **2,** propeller.

ви́нтик *n., dim. of* **винт.** —**у него́ ви́нтика не хвата́ет,** he has a screw loose.

винто́вка [*gen. pl.* **-вок**] *n*. rifle.

винтово́й *adj.* **1,** spiral: винтова́я ле́стница, spiral staircase. **2,** propeller-driven.

винто́вочный *adj.* rifle (*attrib.*).

винтообра́зный *adj.* spiral.

винье́тка [*gen. pl.* **-ток**] *n*. vignette.

вио́ла *n*. **1,** viol. **2,** viola.

виолончели́ст *n*. cellist.

виолонче́ль *n.f.* cello.

вира́ж *n*. **1,** [*gen.* **-ража́**] turn. **2,** [*gen.* **-ража**] *photog.* toning agent.

виртуо́з *n*. virtuoso.

виртуо́зный *adj.* masterful; masterly. —**виртуо́зно,** *adv.* masterfully. —**виртуо́зность,** *n.f.* virtuosity.

вируле́нтный *adj.* virulent; deadly. —**вируле́нтность,** *n.f.* virulence.

ви́рус *n*. virus. —**ви́русный,** *adj.* viral.

ви́рши [*gen.* **-шей**] *n.pl.* poetry; doggerel.

ви́селица *n*. gallows.

висе́ть *v.impfv.* [*pres.* **виси́т, вися́т**] to hang; be hanging. —**висе́ть в во́здухе,** to be up in the air; be undecided.

ви́ски *n.neut. indecl.* whiskey.

виско́за *n*. **1,** viscose. **2,** rayon. —**виско́зный,** *adj.* viscose.

вислоу́хий *adj.* lop-eared.

ви́смут *n*. bismuth.

ви́снуть *v.impfv.* [*past* **вис** *or* **ви́снул, ви́сла**] *colloq.* **1,** to hang. **2,** to droop.

висо́к [*gen.* **виска́**] *n., anat.* temple.

високо́сный *adj., in* **високо́сный год,** leap year.

вист *n*. whist.

висю́лька [*gen. pl.* **-лек**] *n., colloq.* pendant.

вися́чий *adj.* hanging; suspended. —**вися́чий замо́к,** padlock. —**вися́чий мост,** suspension bridge.

витами́н *n*. vitamin. —**витами́нный,** *adj.* vitamin (*attrib.*). —**витамино́зный,** *adj.* rich in vitamins.

вита́ть *v.impfv.* **1,** *obs.* to be; live. **2,** (*with* **над**) to hang (over); hover (over). —**вита́ть в облака́х,** to be up in the clouds.

витиева́тый *adj.* (*of speech or writing*) flowery.

вито́й *adj.* **1,** twisted: вита́я бу́лка, twist (*of bread*). **2,** winding; spiral.

вито́к [*gen.* **витка́**] *n*. **1,** turn; loop; coil. **2,** strand. **3,** circuit; orbit (*of a planet by a space vehicle*). **4,** *fig.* round (*e.g. of the arms race*).

витра́ж [*gen.* **-ража́**] *n*. stained-glass window.

витри́на *n*. **1,** store window. **2,** showcase.

вить *v.impfv.* [*pfv.* **свить**; *pres.* **вью, вьёшь**; *past fem.* **вила́**] **1,** to make (*by twisting*). **2,** to build (a nest). —**ви́ться,** *refl.* [*past* **ви́лся, вила́сь, вило́сь, вили́сь**] [*impfv. only*] **1,** (*of hair*) to curl; (*of vines*) to twine. **2,** (*of a road*) to wind; (*of a snake*) to twist. **3,** (*of a bird*) to hover; (*of dust*) to swirl.

ви́тязь *n.m., obs., folk poetry* warrior; hero.

вихля́ть *v.impfv., colloq.* to sway; wobble. *Also* **вихля́ться,** *refl.*

вихо́р [*gen.* **вихра́**] *n*. **1,** tuft (*of hair*). **2,** forelock.

вихра́стый *adj., colloq.* shaggy.

вихрь *n.m.* **1,** whirlwind. **2,** vortex. **3,** *in* снѣжный вихрь, snowstorm; песча́ный вихрь, sandstorm. **4,** *fig.* maelstrom.

ви́це- *prefix* vice-: ви́це-президе́нт, vice-president; ви́це-адмира́л, vice-admiral. —**ви́це-коро́ль,** viceroy.

вишнёвка *n*. cherry brandy.

вишнёвый *adj.* **1,** cherry (*attrib.*). **2,** cherry-colored; cerise.

ви́шня [*gen. pl.* **ви́шен**] *n*. **1,** cherries. **2,** a (single) cherry. **3,** cherry tree.

вка́лывать *v.impfv.* [*pfv.* **вколо́ть**] (*with* **в** + *acc.*) to stick in; stick into.

вка́пывать *v.impfv.* [*pfv.* **вкопа́ть**] (*with* **в** + *acc.*) to implant; set (in the ground).

вкати́ть [*infl.* **вкачу́, вка́тишь**] *v., pfv. of* **вка́тывать.** —**вкати́ться,** *refl., pfv. of* **вка́тываться.**

вка́тывать *v.impfv.* [*pfv.* **вкати́ть**] **1,** (*with* **в** + *acc.*) to roll into; wheel into. **2,** *colloq.* to give; administer. —**вка́тываться,** *refl.* (*with* **в** + *acc.*) to roll into.

вклад *n*. **1,** deposit. **2,** investment. **3,** *fig.* contribution.

вкла́дка [*gen. pl.* **-док**] *n*. supplement; insert (*in a publication*).

вкладно́й *adj.* **1,** deposit (*attrib.*). **2,** deposited. —**вкладно́й лист,** page insert.

вкла́дчик *n.* **1,** depositor. **2,** investor.

вкла́дывание *n.* inserting; insertion.

вкла́дывать *v.impfv.* [*pfv.* **вложи́ть**] (*with* **в** + *acc.*) **1,** to put into; insert. **2,** to invest (money) in. **3,** *fig.* to put (effort, one's heart, etc.) into.

вкла́дыш *n.* insert.

вкле́ивать *v.impfv.* [*pfv.* **вкле́ить**] (*with* **в** + *acc.*) to paste in.

вкле́йка *n.* **1,** pasting in. **2,** [*gen. pl.* **вкле́ек**] inset.

вкли́нивать *v.impfv.* [*pfv.* **вкли́нить** *or* **вклини́ть**] (*with* **в** + *acc.*) to wedge (into). —**вкли́ниваться,** *refl.* **1,** to be wedged in. **2,** (*with* **в** + *acc.*) to drive a wedge (into).

включа́ть *v.impfv.* [*pfv.* **включи́ть**] **1,** to include. **2,** to turn on; switch on. —**включа́ться,** *refl.* (*with* **в** + *acc.*) **1,** to be included (in). **2,** to join in; enter.

включа́я *prep.,* *with acc.* including.

включе́ние *n.* **1,** inclusion. **2,** turning on; switching on.

включи́тельно *adv.* inclusive.

включи́ть *v., pfv. of* **включа́ть.** —**включи́ться,** *refl., pfv. of* **включа́ться.**

вкола́чивать *v.impfv.* [*pfv.* **вколоти́ть**] *colloq.* to hammer in; drive in.

вколоти́ть [*infl.* **-лочу́, -ло́тишь**] *v., pfv. of* **вкола́чивать.**

вколо́ть [*infl.* **вколю́, вко́лешь**] *v., pfv. of* **вка́лывать.**

вконе́ц *adv., colloq.* completely; entirely; utterly.

вкопа́ть *v., pfv. of* **вка́пывать.** —**как вко́панный,** dead in one's tracks.

вкореня́ть *v.impfv.* [*pfv.* **вкорени́ть**] to implant; inculcate. —**вкореня́ться,** *refl.* to take root.

вкось *adv.* at an angle; diagonally; catty-corner.

вкра́дчивый *adj.* ingratiating.

вкра́дываться *v.r.impfv.* [*pfv.* **вкра́сться**] (*with* **в** + *acc.*) **1,** to creep in(to); steal in(to). **2,** (*of errors, misprints, etc.*) to creep in. —**вкра́дываться в дове́рие к,** to worm one's way into the confidence of.

вкра́пить *v.pfv.* [*infl.* **-плю, -пишь**] to sprinkle (*usu. fig.*): В докла́д бы́ли вкра́плены анекдо́ты, the report was sprinkled with (*or* contained numerous) anecdotes.

вкра́сться [*infl. like* **кра́сться**] *v.r., pfv. of* **вкра́дываться.**

вкра́тце *adv.* in brief; briefly.

вкривь *adv., colloq.* aslant. —**вкривь и вкось,** every which way; helter-skelter.

вкругову́ю *adv., colloq.* around; in a circle.

вкруту́ю *adv., in* **яйцо́ вкруту́ю,** hard-boiled egg.

вку́пе *adv., obs.* together.

вкус *n.* taste. —**быть по вку́су** (+ *dat.*); **быть в (чьём-нибудь) вку́се,** to be to someone's taste. —**со вку́сом,** tastefully.

вкуси́ть [*infl.* **вкушу́, вку́сишь**] *v., pfv. of* **вкуша́ть.**

вку́сно *adv.* (*with verbs of eating, cooking, etc.*) well: вку́сно есть, to eat well; вку́сно гото́вить, be a good cook. —*adj., used predicatively,* tasty; delicious: Óчень вку́сно!, delicious!

вку́сный *adj.* tasty; delicious; good.

вкусово́й *adj.* taste (*attrib.*); gustatory.

вкуша́ть *v.impfv.* [*pfv.* **вкуси́ть**] to taste; savor.

вла́га *n.* moisture.

влага́лище *n.* vagina. —**влага́лищный,** *adj.* vaginal.

владе́лец [*gen.* **-льца**] *n.m.* [*fem.* **-лица**] owner.

владе́ние *n.* **1,** (*with instr.*) ownership; possession: владе́ние иму́ществом, ownership of property. **2,** (*with instr.*) mastery; command (*of a language*). **3,** *obs.* property; holdings. **4,** *pl.* territories; possessions.

владе́ть *v.impfv.* (*with instr.*) **1,** to own. **2,** to control (a territory). **3,** to hold (an audience, someone's attention, etc.). **4,** to know how to use; handle (a tool, weapon, etc.) with great skill. **5,** to speak; be fluent in (a foreign language). **6,** (*usu. neg.*) (not) have the use of (a part of one's body). —**владе́ть собо́й,** to control oneself; keep one's temper.

влады́ка *n.m.* ruler; sovereign. —**влады́чество,** *n.* dominion; sway.

вла́жность *n.f.* **1,** humidity. **2,** moisture; dampness.

вла́жный *adj.* **1,** humid. **2,** moist; damp.

вла́мываться *v.r.impfv.* [*pfv.* **вломи́ться**] (*with* **в** + *acc.*) **1,** to burst into. **2,** to break into.

вла́ствовать *v.impfv.* [*pres.* **-ствую, -ствуешь**] (*with* **над**) to rule; wield power (over).

властели́н *n.* **1,** absolute ruler. **2,** *fig.* (*with gen.*) master (of).

власти́тель *n.m., obs.* ruler. —**власти́тель дум,** major figure; major influence.

вла́стный *adj.* **1,** [*short form —* **вла́стен, вла́стна** *— only*] having power; (*with inf.*) having the power to; (*with* **над**) having power (*or* control) over. **2,** overpowering. **3,** overbearing; domineering. **4,** (*of one's tone of voice*) peremptory.

властолюби́вый *adj.* power-seeking; power-hungry. —**властолю́бие,** *n.* love of power.

власть *n.f.* **1,** power. **2,** rule: сове́тская власть, Soviet rule; the Soviet regime. **3,** branch (*of government*). **4,** (*in certain contexts*) government: гла́вная обя́занность вла́сти, the chief responsibility of the government. **5,** *pl.* [*gen.* **-сте́й, -стя́м**] the authorities. —**ва́ша власть,** *colloq.* as you wish; please yourself. —**во вла́сти** (+ *gen.*), **1,** at the mercy of. **2,** in the thrall of.

власяни́ца *n.* hair shirt.

влачи́ть *v.impfv.* **1,** *obs.* to drag. **2,** *fig.* to lead; live: влачи́ть жа́лкое существова́ние, to lead a miserable existence.

вле́во *adv.* to the left.

влеза́ть *v.impfv.* [*pfv.* **влезть**] **1,** (*with* **на** + *acc.*) to climb (a tree, wall, etc.); climb onto. **2,** (*with* **в** + *acc.*) to climb into; get into (a car, bathtub, etc.). **3,** (*with* **в** *or* **на** + *acc.*) *colloq.* to fit (into); fit (onto). —**влезть в дове́рие к,** to gain the confidence of. —**влезть в долги́,** to get into debt. —**влезть в ду́шу** (*with gen., dat. or* **к**) **1,** to win over; gain the confidence of. **2,** to intrude into the personal life of.

влезть [*infl. like* **лезть**] *v., pfv. of* **влеза́ть.**

влеко́мый *pres. passive part. of* **влечь.**

влепи́ть [*infl.* **влеплю́, вле́пишь**] *v., pfv. of* **влепля́ть.**

влепля́ть *v.impfv.* [*pfv.* **влепи́ть**] **1,** to inlay. **2,** *colloq.* to give; let one have: влепи́ть пощёчину (+ *dat.*), to give someone a slap in the face.

влета́ть *v.impfv.* [*pfv.* **влете́ть**] (*with* в + *acc.*) **1,** to fly into. **2,** *colloq.* to burst into; dash into. **3,** *impers.* (*with dat.*) *colloq.* to get into trouble: Ему́ опя́ть влете́ло, he is in trouble again. —**влета́ть в копе́ечку,** to cost a fortune.

влете́ть [*infl.* **-чу́, -ти́шь**] *v., pfv. of* **влета́ть.**

влече́ние *n.* (*with* к) **1,** bent (for); penchant (for). **2,** attraction (toward). **3,** desire (for); lust (for): половое влече́ние, sexual desire/drive/appetite.

влечь *v.impfv.* [*pfv.* **повле́чь**; *pres.* **влеку́, влечёшь, ...влеку́т;** *past* **влёк, влекла́, влекло́, влекли́**] **1,** to draw; drag. **2,** to attract. —**влечь за собо́й, 1,** to involve; entail. **2,** to lead to; bring in its wake.

влива́ние *n.* injection; infusion.

влива́ть *v.impfv.* [*pfv.* **влить**] (*with* в + *acc.*) **1,** to pour in; pour into. **2,** *fig.* to infuse; instill. —**влива́ться,** *refl.* (*with* в + *acc.*) **1,** to flow into. **2,** to become a part of; join.

влипа́ть *v.impfv.* [*pfv.* **вли́пнуть**] (*with* в + *acc.*) **1,** to stick (to); get stuck (to); get stuck (in). **2,** *colloq.* to get into (trouble, a mess, etc.).

вли́пнуть [*past* **влип, вли́пла**] *v., pfv. of* **влипа́ть.**

влито́й *adj., in* **сиде́ть как влито́й,** to fit like a glove.

влить [*infl.* **волью́, вольёшь;** *past fem.* **влила́**] *v., pfv. of* **влива́ть.** —**вли́ться,** *refl., pfv. of* **влива́ться.**

влия́ние *n.* **1,** influence. **2,** effect. —**под влия́нием мину́ты,** on the spur of the moment.

влия́тельный *adj.* influential.

влия́ть *v.impfv.* [*pfv.* **повлия́ть**] (*with* на + *acc.*) to influence; affect; have an effect upon.

вложе́ние *n.* **1,** enclosure. **2,** investment.

вложи́ть [*infl.* **вложу́, вло́жишь**] *v., pfv. of* **вкла́дывать.**

вломи́ться [*infl.* **вломлю́сь, вло́мишься**] *v.r., pfv. of* **вла́мываться.**

влюби́ть [*infl.* **влюблю́, влю́бишь**] *v., pfv. of* **влюбля́ть.** —**влюби́ться,** *refl., pfv. of* **влюбля́ться.**

влюблённый *adj.* **1,** (*with* в + *acc.*) in love (with). **2,** loving; amorous. —*n., usu. pl.* lover(s).

влюбля́ть *v.impfv.* [*pfv.* **влюби́ть**] (*with* в + *acc.*) to make (someone) fall in love (with). —**влюбля́ться,** *refl.* (*with* в + *acc.*) to fall in love (with).

влю́бчивый *adj.* amorous. —**влю́бчивость,** *n.f.* amorousness.

вмени́ть [*infl.* **вменю́, вмени́шь**] *v., pfv. of* **вменя́ть.**

вменя́емый *adj., law* of sound mind. —**вменя́емость,** *n.f., law* soundness of mind.

вменя́ть *v.impfv.* [*pfv.* **вмени́ть**] (*with dat. and* в + *acc.*) to regard; consider: вменя́ть что́-нибудь в недоста́ток (+ *dat.*), to regard something as a shortcoming of. —**вменя́ть (что́-нибудь) в вину́** (+ *dat.*), to blame (something) on; accuse of. —**вменя́ть** (+ *dat.*) **в обя́занность** (+ *inf.*), to assign (someone) the task of...; make it someone's responsibility to...

вме́сте *adv.* together. —**вме́сте с,** together with; along with. —**вме́сте с тем,** at the same time.

вмести́лище *n.* container; receptacle.

вмести́мость *n.f.* capacity.

вмести́тельный *adj.* spacious; roomy. —**вмести́тельность,** *n.f.* spaciousness; roominess.

вмести́ть [*infl.* **-щу́, -сти́шь**] *v., pfv. of* **вмеща́ть.** —**вмести́ться,** *refl., pfv. of* **вмеща́ться.**

вме́сто *prep., with gen.* instead of; in place of: вме́сто меня́, instead of me; in my place. Вме́сто того́, что́бы оста́ться здесь, instead of remaining here.

вмеша́тельство *n.* (*with* в + *acc.*) interference (in); intervention (in); meddling (in).

вме́шиваться *v.r.impfv.* [*pfv.* **вмеша́ться**] (*with* в + *acc.*) to interfere (in); intervene (in); meddle (in). Вме́шиваться в разгово́р, to break into a conversation.

вмеща́ть *v.impfv.* [*pfv.* **вмести́ть**] **1,** to hold; seat; accommodate; have a capacity of. **2,** (*with* в + *acc.*) to fit (into); get (into). —**вмеща́ться,** *refl.* (*with* в + *acc.*) to fit (into); go (into).

вмиг *adv.* in an instant; in a flash.

вмина́ть *v.impfv.* [*pfv.* **вмять**] **1,** to press in. **2,** to dent.

вмя́тина *n.* dent.

вмять [*infl.* **вомну́, вомнёшь**] *v., pfv. of* **вмина́ть.**

внаём *also,* **внаймы́** *adv., in* **брать внаём,** to rent; hire; **сдава́ть** *or* **отдава́ть внаём,** to rent (out).

внаки́дку *adv.* over one's shoulders: носи́ть пальто́ внаки́дку, to wear a coat over one's shoulders.

внакла́де *adv., colloq., in* **оста́ться внакла́де,** to be the loser; end up losing.

внакла́дку *adv., in* **пить чай внакла́дку,** to drink tea with sugar.

внача́ле *adv.* at first; in the beginning.

вне *prep., with gen.* **1,** outside: вне го́рода, outside the city. **2,** out of: вне о́череди, out of turn. **3,** *in* вне сомне́ния, beyond doubt; вне подозре́ний, above suspicion. —**вне себя́ (от),** beside oneself (with joy, grief, etc.). —**челове́к вне зако́на,** outlaw.

внебра́чный *adj.* **1,** extramarital. **2,** (*of a child*) illegitimate.

вневре́менный *adj.* timeless.

внедре́ние *n.* introduction; incorporation; adoption.

внедря́ть *v.impfv.* [*pfv.* **внедри́ть**] **1,** (*with* в + *acc.*) to instill (in); inculcate (in). **2,** to introduce: внедря́ть но́вую те́хнику, to introduce new equipment. —**внедря́ться,** *refl.* (*with* в + *acc.*) to take root (in).

внеза́пно *adv.* suddenly.

внеза́пность *n.f.* **1,** suddenness. **2,** *mil.* (element of) surprise.

внеза́пный *adj.* **1,** sudden. **2,** *mil.* surprise: внеза́пное нападе́ние, surprise attack.

внеземно́й *adj.* extraterrestrial.

внекла́ссный *adj.* extracurricular.

внеочередно́й *adj.* **1,** out of turn; out of order. **2,** (*of a meeting, session, etc.*) extraordinary; special.

внесе́ние *n.* **1,** bringing in; carrying in. **2,** entering; insertion. **3,** putting forward; submission.

внести́ [*infl. like* **нести́**] *v., pfv. of* **вноси́ть.**

вне́шне *adv.* outwardly; on the surface.

внешнеполити́ческий *adj.* of or pert. to foreign policy.

внешнеторго́вый *adj.* trade (*attrib.*).

вне́шний *adj.* **1,** outward; outer; outside; external. **2,** foreign: вне́шняя поли́тика, foreign policy.

вне́шность *n.f.* appearance; exterior.

внешта́тный *adj.* not on the permanent staff.

вниз *adv., expressing motion or direction* **1,** down;

downward. **2,** downstairs. —**вниз голово́й,** headfirst. —**вниз по,** down: вниз по тече́нию, downstream.

внизу́ *adv., expressing location* **1,** below. **2,** downstairs. —*prep., with gen.* at the bottom of.

вника́ть *v.impfv.* [*pfv.* **вни́кнуть**] (*with* в + *acc.*) to go deeply into; delve into; probe.

вни́кнуть [*past* вник *or* вни́кнул, вни́кла] *v., pfv. of* **вника́ть.**

внима́ние *n.* **1,** attention: обраща́ть внима́ние на, to pay attention to. **2,** kindness; consideration. —**принима́ть во внима́ние,** to consider; take into account; take account of.

внима́тельно *adv.* **1,** attentively; closely; carefully. **2,** with consideration.

внима́тельность *n.f.* **1,** attentiveness. **2,** kindness; consideration.

внима́тельный *adj.* **1,** attentive. **2,** considerate; thoughtful.

внима́ть *v.impfv.* [*pfv.* **внять**] *poetic* (*with dat.*) to hearken (to); heed.

вничью́ *adv., sports; games* in a draw; in a tie: зако́нчиться вничью́, to end in a draw/tie. Сыгра́ть вничью́, to play to a draw/tie.

вно́ве *adv., used predicatively, colloq.* new; unfamiliar.

вновь *adv.* **1,** once again; once more. **2,** newly.

вноси́ть *v.impfv.* [*pfv.* **внести́**; *pres.* вношу́, вно́сишь] **1,** to bring in; carry in. **2,** to make (changes, corrections, etc.). **3,** to cause; create: вноси́ть разла́д в семью́, to cause dissension in the family. **4,** to enter (on a list); insert (in a document). **5,** to put forward; submit (a proposal); introduce (a bill). **6,** to pay. Вноси́ть пла́ту, to make a payment. **7,** to contribute (one's share). Вноси́ть свой вклад (*with* в + *acc.*), to make one's contribution (to).

внук *n.* grandson; grandchild.

вну́тренний *adj.* **1,** internal; inner; interior; inside. **2,** domestic (*as opposed to foreign*). **3,** *in* вну́треннее мо́ре, inland sea. —**вну́тренне,** *adv.* inwardly.

вну́тренность *n.f.* **1,** interior; inside. **2,** *pl.* internal organs; innards.

внутри́ *adv.* inside. —*prep., with gen.* inside; within.

внутриве́нный *adj.* intravenous.

внутрь *adv., expressing direction,* inside. Принима́ть лека́рство внутрь, to take medicine internally. —*prep., with gen.* inside.

внуча́та [*gen.* -ча́т] *n.pl., colloq.* grandchildren.

внуча́тый *adj., in* **внуча́тый племя́нник,** grandnephew; **внуча́тая племя́нница,** grandniece. *Also,* **внуча́тный.**

вну́чка [*gen. pl.* -чек] *n.* granddaughter.

внуша́ть *v.impfv.* [*pfv.* **внуши́ть**] **1,** to instill (respect, confidence, etc.); arouse (fear, envy, etc.): внуша́ть кому́-нибудь страх, to arouse fear in someone. **2,** (*with a dependent clause*) to convince; bring home to: Он нам внуши́л (*or* внуши́л нам мысль), что..., he convinced us (of the fact) that...

внуше́ние *n.* **1,** *psychol.* suggestion. **2,** hypnosis. **3,** reprimand.

внуши́тельный *adj.* imposing; impressive.

внуши́ть *v., pfv. of* **внуша́ть.**

вня́тный *adj.* **1,** distinct; clear. **2,** intelligible.

внять *v.pfv., used only in the past tense* [*fem.* вняла́] *pfv. of* **внима́ть.**

во *prep.* = **в** (*used before certain words beginning with two consonants*): во вре́мя; во вто́рник; во мно́гом; во мне́ниях; во Влади́мир; Во Льво́ве; во Фра́нции; во вся́ком слу́чае.

вобра́ть [*infl.* вберу́, вберёшь; *past fem.* вобрала́] *v., pfv. of* **вбира́ть.**

вове́к *also,* **вове́ки** *adv.* **1,** forever. **2,** (*with a neg. verb*) never.

вовлека́ть *v.impfv.* [*pfv.* **вовле́чь**] (*with* в + *acc.*) to draw (into); involve (in).

вовлече́ние *n.* involvement (*act of involving*).

вовлечённость *n.f.* involvement (*being involved*).

вовле́чь [*infl. like* **влечь**] *v., pfv. of* **вовлека́ть.**

вовне́ *adv.* outside; without.

во́время *adv.* in time; on time. —**не во́время,** at the wrong time.

во́все *adv., colloq.* **1,** completely. **2,** (*fol. by* **не** + *verb or adj.*) not at all; not the least bit. —**во́все нет!,** not at all!

вовсю́ *adv., colloq.* **1,** with all one's might; as fast (*or* as hard) as one can. **2,** to the utmost; to the full.

во-вторы́х secondly; in the second place.

вогна́ть [*infl.* вгоню́, вго́нишь; *past fem.* вогнала́] *v., pfv. of* **вгоня́ть.**

во́гнутый *adj.* concave. —**во́гнутость,** *n.f.* concavity.

вогну́ть *v., pfv. of* **вгиба́ть.**

вода́ [*acc.* во́ду; *pl.* во́ды] *n.* water. —**держа́ться на воде́,** to remain afloat.

водворя́ть *v.impfv.* [*pfv.* **водвори́ть**] **1,** to settle; install (people somewhere). **2,** to put back (in its former place). **3,** *fig.* to establish; restore. —**водворя́ться,** *refl.* **1,** to settle. **2,** *fig.* to be established; set in.

водеви́ль *n.m.* vaudeville.

води́тель *n.m.* driver (*of a vehicle*).

води́тельский *adj.* driver (*attrib.*); driver's. —**води́тельские права́,** driver's license.

води́тельство *n., obs.* leadership.

води́ть *v.impfv.* [*pres.* вожу́, во́дишь] **1,** *indeterm. of* **вести́. 2,** to keep (animals, birds, etc.). —**води́ть дру́жбу с,** to keep up a friendship with. —**води́ть компа́нию с,** to keep company with.

води́ться *v.r.impfv.* [*pres.* вожу́сь, во́дишься] **1,** (*of animals, birds, etc.*) to be found (*in a certain area*). **2,** (*with* с + *instr.*) *colloq.* to associate (with); consort (with); hang around (with). **3,** (*with* за + *instr.*) (*of traits of character*) to be noticed; be observed: За ним никаки́х стра́нностей не води́лось, no peculiarities were observed in his behavior. **4,** *colloq.* (*with* у) to be in one's possession: У него́ всегда́ води́лись де́ньги, he always had plenty of money. —**как во́дится,** as usual.

во́дка *n.* vodka.

воднолы́жный *adj., in* **воднолы́жный спорт,** waterskiing.

во́дный *adj.* water (*attrib.*).

водобоя́знь *n.f.* rabies; hydrophobia.

водово́з *n.* water carrier.

водоворо́т *n.* **1,** whirlpool; eddy. **2,** *fig.* vortex; maelstrom.

водоём *n.* **1,** reservoir. **2,** body of water.

водоизмеще́ние *n., naut.* displacement; tonnage.

водока́чка [*gen. pl.* **-чек**] *n.* pumping station.

водола́з *n.* **1,** diver. **2,** Newfoundland dog. —водола́зный, *adj.* diving (*attrib.*).

Водоле́й *n.* Aquarius.

водоме́р *n.* water meter.

водомёт *n.* water cannon.

водонапо́рный *adj., in* водонапо́рная ба́шня, water tower.

водонепроница́емый *adj.* waterproof; watertight.

водоно́с *n.* water carrier.

водоотво́д *n.* drainage system. —водоотво́дный, *adj.* drain (*attrib.*); drainage (*attrib.*).

водоотта́лкивающий *adj.* water-repellent.

водопа́д *n.* waterfall.

водопла́вающий *adj., in* водопла́вающая пти́ца, water bird; waterfowl.

водопо́й *n.* **1,** watering place. **2,** watering (*of livestock*).

водопрово́д *n.* indoor plumbing; running water.

водопрово́дный *adj.* pert. to the carrying or supplying of water: водопрово́дная магистра́ль, water main. —водопрово́дная вода́, tap water.

водопрово́дчик *n.* plumber.

водоразбо́рный *adj., in* водоразбо́рная коло́нка; водоразбо́рный кран, fire hydrant.

водоразде́л *n.* watershed.

водоро́д *n.* hydrogen.

водоро́дный *adj.* hydrogen (*attrib.*). —водоро́дная бо́мба, hydrogen bomb.

во́доросль *n.f.* algae; seaweed. *Often,* морска́я во́доросль.

водосви́нка [*gen. pl.* **-нок**] *n.* capybara.

водосли́в *n.* spillway.

водосто́к *n.* drain; gutter.

водосто́чный *adj., in* водосто́чный жёлоб *and* водосто́чная кана́ва, gutter; водосто́чная труба́, drainpipe.

водохрани́лище *n.* reservoir.

во́дочный *adj.* vodka (*attrib.*).

водружа́ть *v.impfv.* [*pfv.* водрузи́ть] to place firmly; plant; implant.

водяни́стый *adj.* **1,** watery. **2,** *fig.* colorless; insipid.

водя́нка *n.* dropsy.

водяно́й *adj.* water (*attrib.*); aquatic. —*n.* water sprite. —водяно́й знак, watermark. —водяно́е колесо́, water wheel. —водяна́я ли́лия, water lily.

воева́ть *v.impfv.* [*pres.* вою́ю, вою́ешь] **1,** (*with* с + *instr. or* про́тив) to be at war (with); fight (against). **2,** (*of a soldier*) to fight; see action.

воево́да *n.m., hist.* military governor in Old Russia (*from the 16th to the end of the 18th century*).

воеди́но *adv.* into one; together.

военача́льник *n.* commander (*of a large military or naval unit*).

вое́нно-возду́шный *adj., in* вое́нно-возду́шные си́лы, air force.

вое́нно-морско́й *adj., in* вое́нно-морско́й флот, navy.

военнообя́занный *n., decl. as an adj.* person subject to call-up; person subject to the draft.

военнопле́нный *n., decl. as an adj.* prisoner of war.

военнослу́жащий *n., decl. as an adj.* soldier; serviceman.

вое́нный *adj.* **1,** war (*attrib.*): вое́нное вре́мя, wartime. **2,** military. —*n.* military man; serviceman. —вое́нные де́йствия, military action; military operations; hostilities. —вое́нный заво́д, munitions factory. —вое́нное положе́ние, martial law. —вое́нная промы́шленность, the armaments industry. —вое́нный суд, court-martial.

вое́нщина *n.* the military; militarists.

вожа́к [*gen.* **-жака́**] *n.* **1,** leader. **2,** guide.

вожа́тый *n., decl. as an adj.* **1,** *obs.* guide. **2,** young pioneer leader. **3,** streetcar driver.

вожделе́ние *n.* **1,** longing; craving. **2,** desire; lust.

вожделе́нный *adj.* longed-for; coveted; ardently desired; eagerly sought after.

вожде́ние *n.* driving; steering; piloting; flying.

вождь [*gen.* **вождя́**] *n.m.* leader.

во́жжи [*gen.* **вожже́й**] *n.pl.* [*sing.* вожжа́] reins.

воз [*2nd loc.* возу́; *pl.* возы́] *n.* **1,** cart. **2,** cartload. —а воз и ны́не там, things are right where they started. —что с во́зу упа́ло, то пропа́ло, there's no use crying over spilt milk.

воз- *also,* вос- *prefix* **1,** *indicating upward direction:* возводи́ть, to erect; elevate; raise. **2,** *indicating repetition of an action:* воссоединя́ть, to reunite; воспроизводи́ть, to reproduce.

возбраня́ть *v.impfv.* [*pfv.* возбрани́ть] *obs.* to forbid. —возбраня́ться, *refl.* [*impfv. only*] *obs.* to be forbidden.

возбуди́мый *adj.* excitable. —возбуди́мость, *n.f.* excitability.

возбуди́тель *n.m.* agent; cause; stimulus.

возбуди́ть [*infl.* **-жу́, -ди́шь**] *v., pfv. of* возбужда́ть. —возбуди́ться, *refl., pfv. of* возбужда́ться.

возбужда́ть *v.impfv.* [*pfv.* возбуди́ть] **1,** to arouse (curiosity, suspicion, pity, envy, etc.); raise (hopes, doubts, etc.); stimulate; whet (one's appetite). **2,** to excite; arouse (a person, audience, etc.). **3,** to agitate; upset. **4,** to raise (a question); bring; file (a lawsuit). —возбужда́ться, *refl.* **1,** to be aroused. **2,** to get excited.

возбужда́ющий *adj.* rousing; stirring. —возбужда́ющее сре́дство, stimulant.

возбужде́ние *n.* **1,** excitation; stimulation. **2,** excitement.

возбуждённый *adj.* excited.

возведе́ние *n.* **1,** erection. **2,** leveling (*of an accusation*). **3,** *math.* raising (*to a certain power*).

возвели́чивать *v.impfv.* [*pfv.* возвели́чить] to exalt.

возвести́ [*infl. like* вести́] *v., pfv. of* возводи́ть.

возвеща́ть *v.impfv.* [*pfv.* возвести́ть] **1,** (*with* о) to announce. **2,** to herald; usher in.

возводи́ть *v.impfv.* [*pfv.* возвести́; *pres.* -вожу́, -во́дишь] **1,** to erect. **2,** to elevate (to a certain rank): возводи́ть на престо́л, to raise to the throne. **3,** to level (an accusation). **4,** (*with* к) to trace back (to a time in the past). **5,** *math.* to raise (to a certain power).

возврáт *n.* **1,** return. **2,** recurrence. **3,** repayment.

возвратúть [*infl.* -щý, -тúшь] *v., pfv. of* возвращáть. **—возвратúться,** *refl., pfv. of* возвращáться.

возврáтный *adj.* **1,** return (*attrib.*): на возврáтном путú, on the way back. **2,** *gram.* reflexive: возврáтный глагóл, reflexive verb. **—возврáтный тиф,** relapsing fever.

возвращáть *v.impfv.* [*pfv.* вернýть *and* возвратúть] **1,** to return; give back. **2,** to repay (a debt, loan, etc.). **3,** to restore. **4,** to recover; regain; get back. **—возвращáться,** *refl.* to return; come back; go back.

возвращéние *n.* **1,** return: по возвращéнии домóй, on returning home. **2,** return; giving back. **3,** repayment.

возвышáть *v.impfv.* [*pfv.* возвы́сить] **1,** *obs.* to raise. **2,** to elevate; promote. **3,** to raise (one's voice). **4,** [*impfv. only*] to uplift; ennoble. **—возвышáться,** *refl.* **1,** to rise. **2,** [*impfv. only*] (*with* над) to tower (over *or* above).

возвышéние *n.* **1,** rise; rising. **2,** platform; dais. **3,** elevation; hill.

возвы́шенность *n.f.* **1,** height; hill. **2,** loftiness.

возвы́шенный *adj.* **1,** high; elevated. **2,** *fig.* lofty.

возглавля́ть *v.impfv.* [*pfv.* возглáвить] to head; lead; be the head of.

вóзглас *n.* shout; cry; exclamation.

возглашáть *v.impfv.* [*pfv.* возгласúть] to proclaim.

возгóнка *n., chem.* sublimation.

возгоня́ть *v.impfv., chem.* to sublimate.

возгорáться *v.r.impfv.* [*pfv.* возгорéться] **1,** to flare up. **2,** *fig.* (*with instr.*) to be stirred (with); be inflamed (with).

возгордúться *v.r.pfv.* [*infl.* -жýсь, -дúшься] (*with instr.*) to get a swelled head (over).

возгорéться *v.r., pfv. of* возгорáться.

воздавáть *v.impfv.* [*pfv.* воздáть; *pres.* -даю́, даёшь] **1,** to render. **2,** (*with instr.*) to repay (with). **—воздавáть дóлжное,** *see* дóлжное. **—воздавáть пóчести,** *see* пóчести.

воздáть [*infl. like* дать; *past* воздáл, -далá, -дáло, -дáли] *v., pfv. of* воздавáть.

воздвигáть *v.impfv.* [*pfv.* воздвúгнуть] to erect.

воздвúгнуть [*past* -двúг *or* -двúгнул, -двúгла] *v., pfv. of* воздвигáть.

воздéйствие *n.* influence; effect; impact.

воздéйствовать *v.impfv. & pfv.* [*pres.* -ствую, -ствуешь] (*with* на + *acc.*) to influence; bring pressure to bear (on).

воздéлывать *v.impfv.* [*pfv.* воздéлать] **1,** to till; cultivate. **2,** to grow.

воздержáвшийся *n., decl. as an adj.* abstention: при двух воздержáвшихся, with two abstentions.

воздержáние *n.* **1,** (*with* от) abstention; abstinence. **2,** (*with* в + *prepl.*) moderation; temperance.

воздéржанность *n.f.* moderation; temperance. **—воздéржанный,** *adj.* observing moderation.

воздержáться [*infl.* -держýсь, -дéржишься] *v.r., pfv. of* воздéрживаться.

воздéрживаться *v.r.impfv.* [*pfv.* воздержáться] (*with* от) **1,** to refrain (from). **2,** to abstain (from).

воздéть *v.pfv.* [*infl.* -дéну, -дéнешь], *in* воздéть рýки, *obs.* to lift up (*or* raise) one's hands.

вóздух *n.* air. **—как вóздух,** (*with words indicating need or necessity*) in order to survive; desperately. **—на вóздух** (*with verbs of motion*), outdoors. **—на (открытом) вóздухе,** outdoors; out of doors.

воздухоплáвание *n.* aeronautics. **—воздухоплáватель,** *n.m.* aeronaut. **—воздухоплáвательный,** *adj.* aeronautic; aeronautical.

воздýшно-десáнтный *adj., mil.* airborne: воздýшно-десáнтные войскá, airborne troops.

воздýшный *adj.* **1,** air (*attrib.*); aerial. **2,** airy. **—воздýшный шар,** balloon.

воззвáние *n.* appeal.

воззвáть [*infl. like* звать] *v., pfv. of* взывáть.

воззрéние *n.* outlook; view.

воззрúться *v.r.pfv.* (*with* на + *acc.*) *colloq.* to stare (at).

возúть *v.impfv.* [*pres.* вожý, вóзишь] *indeterm. of* везтú. **—возúться,** *refl.* **1,** to play; romp; frolic. **2,** *colloq.* to putter (about). **3,** (*with* с + *instr.*) *colloq.* to fiddle (with); tinker (with).

возлагáть *v.impfv.* [*pfv.* возложúть] (*with* на + *acc.*) **1,** to place (on); lay (on): возложúть венóк на могúлу, to place/lay a wreath on a grave. **2,** to give; assign; turn over (work, a task, etc.) to. **3,** to place; pin (hopes, blame, responsibility, etc.) on.

вóзле *prep., with gen.* **1,** by; near. **2,** beside; alongside; next to. **—*adv.* nearby.

возлия́ние *n.* libation.

возложúть [*infl.* -ложý, -лóжишь] *v., pfv. of* возлагáть.

возлю́бленный *n., decl. as an adj.* loved one; sweetheart.

возмéздие *n.* retribution.

возмещáть *v.impfv.* [*pfv.* возместúть] **1,** to compensate for; pay (damages). **2,** (*with dat.*) to compensate; reimburse: возмещáть комý-нибудь расхóды, to reimburse someone for his expenses. **3,** to compensate for; make up for.

возмещéние *n.* compensation; reimbursement: возмещéние убы́тков, compensation for damages; restitution; redress.

возмóжно *adv.* **1,** possibly. **2,** (*with comp. adjectives & adverbs*) as ... as possible: возмóжно скорéе, as soon as possible. **—*adj., used predicatively,* possible: Это вполнé возмóжно, it/that is entirely possible.

возмóжность *n.f.* **1,** possibility. **2,** opportunity; chance. **3,** *pl.* means; resources. **4,** *pl., mil.* capabilities. **—до послéдней возмóжности,** to the utmost. **—по (мéре) возмóжности,** as far as possible. **—по возмóжности** (+ *adj.*), as ... as possible.

возмóжный *adj.* possible. **—дéлать всё возмóжное,** to do everything possible; do everything in one's power; do one's utmost.

возмужáлый *adj.* mature; virile. **—возмужáлость,** *n.f.* maturity; virility; manhood.

возмужáть *v.pfv.* (*of a young boy or girl*) to mature; develop.

возмутúтельно *adv.* outrageously. **—*adj., used predicatively,* outrageous: Это возмутúтельно!, it's outrageous!; it's an outrage!

возмутúтельный *adj.* outrageous; disgraceful.

возмуща́ть *v.impfv.* [*pfv.* **возмути́ть**] to rouse the indignation of; outrage. —**возмуща́ться,** *refl.* to be indignant; be outraged.

возмуще́ние *n.* indignation; outrage.

возмущённый *adj.* indignant; outraged.

вознагражда́ть *v.impfv.* [*pfv.* **вознагради́ть**] **1,** to reward. **2,** to compensate; remunerate; recompense.

вознагражде́ние *n.* **1,** reward. **2,** compensation; remuneration; recompense.

вознаме́риться *v.r.pfv.* (*with inf.*) to decide (to); get the idea (of); take it into one's head (to).

возненави́деть *v.pfv.* [*infl.* **-ви́жу, -ви́дишь**] to have a deep hatred of.

вознесе́ние *n., relig.* **1,** the Ascension. **2,** Ascension Day.

вознести́ [*infl. like* **нести́**] *v., pfv. of* **возноси́ть.** —**вознести́сь,** *refl., pfv. of* **возноси́ться.**

возника́ть *v.impfv.* [*pfv.* **возни́кнуть**] to arise; spring up; crop up.

возникнове́ние *n.* origin; rise; beginning. Возникнове́ние войны́, outbreak of war.

возни́кнуть [*past* **-ни́к, -ни́кла**] *v., pfv. of* **возника́ть.**

возни́ца *n.m.* coachman.

возноси́ть *v.impfv.* [*pfv.* **вознести́;** *pres.* **-ношу́, -но́сишь**] **1,** to raise; lift up. **2,** to offer up (a prayer). —**возноси́ться,** *refl.* to rise; ascend; go up.

возня́ *n., colloq.* **1,** bustle; scurrying. **2,** trouble; bother. —**мыши́ная возня́,** petty cares.

возоблада́ть *v.pfv.* (*with* **над**) to prevail (over).

возобнови́ть [*infl.* **-влю́, -ви́шь**] *v., pfv. of* **возобновля́ть.** —**возобнови́ться,** *refl., pfv. of* **возобновля́ться.**

возобновле́ние *n.* renewal; resumption.

возобновля́ть *v.impfv.* [*pfv.* **возобнови́ть**] to renew; resume. Возобнови́ть де́ло, to reopen a case. —**возобновля́ться,** *refl.* to start again; resume.

возомни́ть *v.pfv.* (*usu. with* **себя́** *and instr.*) *colloq.* to imagine oneself to be. —**возомни́ть о себе́,** to get a swelled head.

возража́ть *v.impfv.* [*pfv.* **возрази́ть**] **1,** to object; have an objection. **2,** (*with* **про́тив**) to object to; oppose. **3,** (*with dat.*) to challenge; take issue with.

возраже́ние *n.* objection.

возрази́ть [*infl.* **-жу́, -зи́шь**] *v., pfv. of* **возража́ть.**

во́зраст *n.* age.

возраста́ние *n.* growth; increase.

возраста́ть *v.impfv.* [*pfv.* **возрасти́**] **1,** *obs.* to grow. **2,** to increase.

возрасти́ [*infl. like* **расти́**] *v., pfv. of* **возраста́ть.**

возрастно́й *adj.* age (*attrib.*).

возрожда́ть *v.impfv.* [*pfv.* **возроди́ть**] to revive; restore. —**возрожда́ться,** *refl.* **1,** to be revived. **2,** to be reborn.

возрожде́ние *n.* **1,** revival. **2,** rebirth; renaissance. **3,** the Renaissance.

во́зчик *n.* carter.

возыме́ть *v.pfv.* **1,** *obs.* to acquire; achieve. **2,** to develop (a feeling, liking, etc.). —**возыме́ть де́йствие,** to have an effect; achieve the desired effect. —**возыме́ть обра́тное де́йствие,** to have the reverse effect.

во́ин *n.* warrior; soldier.

во́инский *adj.* military. —**во́инская пови́нность,** *see* **пови́нность.** —**во́инский эшело́н,** troop train.

во́инственный *adj.* militant; warlike; belligerent; bellicose. —**во́инственность,** *n.f.* militancy; belligerence; bellicosity.

во́инство *n.* army; forces.

во́инствующий *adj.* militant.

вои́стину *adv., archaic* truly; verily.

вой *n.* howl; howling; wail; wailing.

во́йлок *n.* felt. —**во́йлочный,** *adj.* felt.

война́ [*pl.* **во́йны**] *n.* war. —**идти́/пойти́ войно́й на** (+ *acc.*), to go to war against. —**пойти́** *or* **уйти́ на войну́,** to go off to war.

войска́ [*gen.* **войск**] *n., pl. of* **во́йско,** troops.

во́йско *n.* army.

войсково́й *adj.* troop (*attrib.*).

войти́ [*infl.* **войду́, войдёшь;** *past* **вошёл, вошла́, вошло́, вошли́**] *v., pfv. of* **входи́ть.**

вокали́ст *n.* voice teacher.

вока́льный *adj.* vocal.

вокза́л *n.* (railroad) station. —**вокза́льный,** *adj.* station (*attrib.*).

вокру́г *prep., with gen.* **1,** around: сиде́ть вокру́г костра́, to sit around the fire. **2,** *fig.* over: спор/стра́сти вокру́г..., arguments/passions over... —*adv.* around; about. —**ходи́ть вокру́г да о́коло,** to beat around the bush.

вол [*gen.* **вола́**] *n.* ox.

вола́н *n.* **1,** flounce (*on a dress*). **2,** shuttlecock.

волды́рь [*gen.* **-дыря́**] *n.m.* blister.

волево́й *adj.* **1,** volitional. **2,** strong-willed.

волеизъявле́ние *n.* expression of one's will.

волейбо́л *n.* volleyball. —**волейболи́ст,** *n.* volleyball player. —**волейбо́льный,** *adj.* volleyball (*attrib.*).

во́лей-нево́лей *adv.* having no other choice; perforce; willy-nilly.

волк [*pl.* **во́лки, волко́в, волка́м**] *n.* wolf. —**волк в ове́чьей шку́ре,** wolf in sheep's clothing. —**во́лком смотре́ть,** to scowl; glower. —**морско́й волк,** *colloq.* old sailor; sea dog.

волкода́в *n.* wolfhound.

волна́ [*pl.* **во́лны, волн, волна́м** *or* **во́лнам**] *n.* wave.

волне́ние *n.* **1,** rough seas; choppy seas. **2,** agitation; nervousness. **3,** *pl.* unrest; disturbances (*civil, political, etc.*).

волни́стый *adj.* **1,** wavy. **2,** rolling; undulating.

волнова́ть *v.impfv.* [*pfv.* **взволнова́ть;** *pres.* **-ну́ю, -ну́ешь**] **1,** to agitate; ruffle. **2,** to excite; stir. **3,** to disturb; upset. —**волнова́ться,** *refl.* **1,** (*of the sea*) to be agitated; be choppy. **2,** to be excited. **3,** to be disturbed; be nervous; be upset.

волноло́м *n.* breakwater.

волнообра́зный *adj.* wavy; undulating.

волноре́з *n.* breakwater.

волну́ющии *adj.* **1,** stirring; exciting; thrilling. **2,** disturbing; troubling; upsetting.

воло́вий [*fem.* **-вья**] *adj.* ox (*attrib.*).

во́лок *n.* (place of) portage. —**тащи́ть** *or* **тяну́ть (что-нибудь) во́локом,** to carry overland (*between rivers*).

волоки́та *n.f.* red tape. —*n.m.*, *obs.* ladies' man.

волокни́стый *adj.* fibrous; stringy.

волокно́ [*pl.* -о́кна, -о́кон] *n.* fiber; filament.

волоко́нный *adj.*, *in* **волоко́нная о́птика**, fiber optics.

волонтёр *n.*, *obs.* volunteer.

во́лос [*pl.* во́лосы, воло́с, -са́м] *n.* **1**, a single hair. **2**, *pl.* hair. —**ни на́ волос**, not in the least; not a bit.

волоса́тый *adj.* hairy.

волосо́к [*gen.* -ска́] *n.* **1**, *dim. of* во́лос. **2**, filament (*of a bulb*); hairspring (*of a watch*). —**висе́ть на волоске́**, to hang by a thread. —**на волосо́к (волоске́) от**, within a hairbreadth of.

во́лость [*pl.* во́лости, -сте́й, -стя́м] *n.f.*, *obs.* small administrative district.

волосяно́й *adj.* **1**, hair (*attrib.*). **2**, made of horsehair.

волочи́ть *v.impfv.* [*pres.* -лочу́, -ло́чишь *or* -лочи́шь] to drag. —**волочи́ться**, *refl.* **1**, to drag; trail. **2**, to drag oneself along; shuffle along.

воло́чь *v.impfv.* [*pres.* -локу́, -лочёшь, ...-локу́т; *past* воло́к, волокла́, волокло́, волокли́] *colloq.* = **волочи́ть**. —**воло́чься**, *refl.* = **волочи́ться**.

волхв [*gen.* волхва́] *n.* **1**, sorcerer. **2**, *pl.* the Magi.

волча́нка *n.* lupus (*skin disease*).

во́лчий [*fem.* -чья] *adj.* wolf (*attrib.*); wolf's. —**во́лчий аппети́т**, voracious appetite. —**во́лчья пасть**, cleft palate.

волчо́к [*gen.* -чка́] *n.* top (*toy*).

волчо́нок [*gen.* -нка; *pl.* -ча́та, -ча́т] *n.* wolf cub.

волше́бник *n.* magician; wizard; sorcerer.

волше́бный *adj.* **1**, magic; magical. **2**, *fig.* enchanting; captivating. —**волше́бная ска́зка**, fairy tale.

волшебство́ *n.* magic.

волы́нка *n.* **1**, bagpipe; bagpipes. **2**, *colloq.* delay; dawdling; procrastination. —**волы́нщик**, *n.* piper.

вольго́тный *adj.*, *colloq.* free; free and easy. —**вольго́тно**, *adv.* in freedom.

вольера *also,* **вольер** *n.* enclosure (*for animals or birds*).

во́льничать *v.impfv.*, *colloq.* to take liberties.

во́льно *adv.* **1**, freely. **2**, *mil.* at ease. —*interj.*, *mil.* at ease!; as you were!

вольноду́мец [*gen.* -мца] *n.*, *obs.* freethinker. —**вольноду́мный**, *adj.*, *obs.* freethinking. —**вольноду́мство**, *n.*, *obs.* free thought.

вольнолюби́вый *adj.* freedom-loving.

вольнонаёмный *adj.* **1**, hired. **2**, civilian. —*n.* civilian (*employed by the military*).

вольнослу́шатель *n.m.*, *obs.* non-matriculated student.

во́льность *n.f.* **1**, *obs.* freedom; liberty; license. **2**, undue familiarity; *pl.* liberties. —**поэти́ческая во́льность**, poetic license.

во́льный *adj.* **1**, free. **2**, unrestricted. **3**, unduly familiar. **4**, [*short form* — во́лен, вольна́, во́льно, вольны́ — *only*] (*with inf.*) free (to); at liberty (to).

вольт [*gen. pl.* вольт] *n.* volt.

вольта́ж [*gen.* -тажа́] *n.* voltage.

вольтме́тр *n.* voltmeter.

вольфра́м *n.* tungsten. —**вольфра́мовый**, *adj.* tungsten.

во́ля *n.* **1**, will. **2**, freedom. **3**, *hist.* emancipation. —**во́лею суде́б**, by the will of fate. —**во́ля ва́ша**, as you please. —**дава́ть во́лю** (+ *dat.*), to give free rein to. —**дать себе́ во́лю**, to let oneself go. —**до́брая во́ля**, good will. —**на во́ле**, **1**, free. **2**, (*of animals*) in the wild. —**отпуска́ть на во́лю**, to set free. —**по до́брой во́ле**, of one's own free will. —**после́дняя во́ля**, last will and testament. —**си́ла во́ли**, will power.

вон *adv.*, *colloq.* out; away: Он вы́шел вон, he went out; пошёл вон!, away with you! У меня́ э́то из ума́ вон, it completely slipped my mind. —*particle* there; over there: вон там, over there. Вон он идёт, there he goes. —*interj.* be off!; get out!

вонза́ть *v.impfv.* [*pfv.* вонзи́ть] (*with* в + *acc.*) to plunge (into); thrust (into). —**вонза́ться**, *refl.* (*with* в + *acc.*) to pierce; enter.

вонзи́ть [*infl.* вонжу́, вонзи́шь] *v.*, *pfv. of* вонза́ть. —**вонзи́ться**, *refl.*, *pfv. of* вонза́ться.

вонь *n.f.*, *colloq.* stench.

воню́чий *adj.*, *colloq.* stinking.

воню́чка [*gen. pl.* -чек] *n.* skunk.

воня́ть *v.impfv.*, *colloq.* **1**, to stink. *Also impers.* В по́гребе отврати́тельно воня́ет, there is a revolting odor in the basement. **2**, (*with instr.*) to reek (of).

вообража́емый *adj.* imaginary.

вообража́ть *v.impfv.* [*pfv.* вообрази́ть] to imagine. —**вообража́ть о себе́**, to think a great deal of oneself.

воображе́ние *n.* imagination.

вообрази́мый *adj.* imaginable.

вообрази́ть [*infl.* -жу́, -зи́шь] *v.*, *pfv. of* вообража́ть.

вообще́ *adv.* **1**, in general. **2**, always: Он вообще́ тако́й, he is always like that. **3**, at all: е́сли э́то вообще́ возмо́жно, if it's at all possible. Он придёт о́чень по́здно — е́сли придёт вообще́, he will come very late, if he comes at all. —**вообще́ говоря́**, generally speaking.

воодушеви́ть [*infl.* -влю́, -ви́шь] *v.*, *pfv. of* воодушевля́ть.

воодушевле́ние *n.* enthusiasm; animation.

воодушевлённый *adj.* animated; enthusiastic.

воодушевля́ть *v.impfv.* [*pfv.* воодушеви́ть] to inspire; fill with enthusiasm.

вооружа́ть *v.impfv.* [*pfv.* вооружи́ть] **1**, to arm. **2**, to equip; supply. **3**, (*with* про́тив) to set against. —**вооружа́ться**, *refl.* to arm (oneself).

вооруже́ние *n.* **1**, arming; armament. **2**, *often pl.* armaments; weapons; arms: го́нка вооруже́ний, arms race. —**брать** *or* **принима́ть (что́-нибудь) на вооруже́ние**, **1**, to place in service. **2**, *fig.* to add to one's arsenal. —**снима́ть (что́-нибудь) с вооруже́ния**, to retire from service; take out of service.

вооружённый *adj.* armed. —**вооружённые си́лы**, armed forces.

вооружи́ть *v.*, *pfv. of* вооружа́ть. —**вооружи́ться**, *refl.*, *pfv. of* вооружа́ться.

воо́чию *adv.* **1**, with one's own eyes: воо́чию убеди́ться, to see for oneself. **2**, clearly; graphically.

во-пе́рвых in the first place; to begin with.

вопи́ть *v.impfv.* [*pres.* воплю́, вопи́шь] *colloq.* to cry out; howl; wail.

вопию́щий *adj.* **1,** outrageous; appalling. Вопию́щая несправедли́вость, crying injustice. **2,** glaring; flagrant. —гла́с вопию́щего в пусты́не, voice in the wilderness.

воплоща́ть *v.impfv.* [*pfv.* **воплоти́ть**] to embody; personify. —воплоща́ть в жизнь, to make a reality of.

воплоще́ние *n.* embodiment. —воплоще́ние здоро́вья, the picture of health.

вопль *n.m.* cry; howl; wail.

вопреки́ *prep., with dat.* contrary to; against; in defiance of.

вопро́с *n.* **1,** question. **2,** problem; matter. **3,** issue. —под вопро́сом, open to question; undecided. —ста́вить под вопро́с, to question; call into question.

вопроси́тельный *adj.* **1,** questioning; inquiring. **2,** *gram.* interrogative. —вопроси́тельный знак, question mark.

вопроси́ть [*infl.* **-шу́, -си́шь**] *v., pfv. of* **вопроша́ть**.

вопро́сник *n.* questionnaire.

вопроша́ть *v.impfv.* [*pfv.* **вопроси́ть**] to ask; inquire.

вор [*pl.* **во́ры, воро́в, вора́м**] *n.* thief. —карма́нный вор, pickpocket. —магази́нный вор, shoplifter.

во́рвань *n.f.* blubber.

ворва́ться [*infl. like* **рва́ться**] *v.r., pfv. of* **врыва́ться**.

вори́шка [*gen. pl.* **-шек**] *n.m.* petty thief.

воркова́ть *v.impfv.* [*pres.* **-ку́ю, -ку́ешь**] **1,** to coo. **2,** *fig.* to bill and coo.

воркотня́ *n., colloq.* grumbling; griping.

воробе́й [*gen.* **-бья́**] *n.* sparrow. —стре́ляный воробе́й, *colloq.* old hand.

воробьи́ный *adj.* sparrow's.

воро́ванный *adj.* stolen.

ворова́тый *adj.* **1,** thievish. **2,** furtive.

ворова́ть *v.impfv.* [*pres.* **-ру́ю, -ру́ешь**] to steal.

воро́вка [*gen. pl.* **-вок**] *n., fem. of* **вор**.

воровски́ *adv., colloq.* **1,** dishonestly. **2,** furtively.

воровско́й *adj.* thieves'.

воровство́ *n.* stealing; theft; larceny.

ворожба́ *n.* fortunetelling. —ворожея́, *n.* fortuneteller.

ворожи́ть *v.impfv.* [*pfv.* **поворожи́ть**] to tell fortunes.

во́рон *n.* raven.

воро́на *n.* crow.

воро́ний [*fem.* **-нья**] *adj.* **1,** crow's. **2,** of crows: воро́нья ста́я, flock of crows.

伏орони́ть *v.impfv.* to burnish.

воро́нка [*gen. pl.* **-нок**] *n.* **1,** funnel. **2,** bomb crater.

вороно́й *adj. (of a horse)* black. —*n.* black horse.

во́рот *n.* **1,** collar. **2,** neck *(of a garment)*. **3,** winch. —схвати́ть за́ ворот, to seize by the collar; seize by the scruff of one's neck.

воро́та [*gen.* **воро́т**] *n.pl.* **1,** gate. **2,** *sports* goal; net. —от воро́т поворо́т, pointblank refusal.

вороти́ла *n.m., colloq.* bigwig.

вороти́ть *v.pfv.* [*infl.* **-рочу́, -ро́тишь**] *colloq.* to bring back. —вороти́ться, *refl., colloq.* to return; come back.

воротни́к [*gen.* **-ника́**] *n.* collar.

воротничо́к [*gen.* **-чка́**] *n., dim. of* **воротни́к**.

во́рох [*pl.* **вороха́** *or* **во́рохи**] *n.* pile; heap.

воро́чать *v.impfv.* **1,** to move; shift; roll; turn. **2,** *(with instr.) colloq.* to boss; manage; manipulate. —воро́чаться, *refl., colloq.* to turn from side to side; toss and turn.

вороши́ть *v.impfv., colloq.* **1,** to pitch (hay). **2,** *(of the wind)* to stir; scatter. **3,** *fig.* to dig up; rake up (the past or past events). —вороши́ться, *refl., colloq.* to stir; move about.

ворс *n.* nap; pile *(on cloth)*.

ворси́нка [*gen. pl.* **-нок**] *n.* hair; fiber.

ворча́ние *n.* **1,** growling. **2,** *colloq.* grumbling; griping.

ворча́ть *v.impfv.* [*pres.* **-чу́, -чи́шь**] **1,** *(with* на + *acc.)* to growl (at). **2,** *colloq.* to grumble; gripe.

ворчли́вый *adj.* grumbling; grouchy; grumpy; surly.

ворчу́н [*gen.* **-чуна́**] *n.m.* [*fem.* **-чу́нья**] *colloq.* grumbler; griper.

вос- *prefix, var. of* **воз-** *(used before voiceless consonants)*.

восвоя́си *adv., colloq.* home: пойти́ восвоя́си, to go home.

восемна́дцать *numeral* eighteen. —восемна́дцатый, *ordinal numeral* eighteenth.

во́семь [*gen., dat. & prepl.* **восьми́;** *instr.* **восьмью́** *or* **восемью́**] *numeral* eight.

во́семьдесят [*gen., dat. & prepl.* **восьми́десяти;** *instr.* **восьмью́десятью** *or* **восемью́десятью**] *numeral* eighty.

восемьсо́т [*gen.* **восьмисо́т;** *dat.* **восьмиста́м;** *instr.* **восьмьюста́ми** *or* **восемьюста́ми;** *prepl.* **восьмиста́х**] *numeral* eight hundred.

во́семью *adv.* eight times: во́семью де́сять — во́семьдесят, eight times ten is eighty.

воск *n.* wax.

воскли́кнуть *v., pfv. of* **восклица́ть**.

восклица́ние *n.* exclamation.

восклица́тельный *adj.* exclamatory; exclamation *(attrib.).* —восклица́тельный знак, exclamation point.

восклица́ть *v.impfv.* [*pfv.* **воскли́кнуть**] to exclaim.

восково́й *adj.* **1,** wax *(attrib.).* **2,** waxy; waxen.

воскреса́ть *v.impfv.* [*pfv.* **воскре́снуть**] **1,** to rise from the dead; come back to life. **2,** to regain one's strength; revive. —воскреса́ть в па́мяти, to come back to mind.

воскресе́ние *n.* **1,** resurrection. **2,** *fig.* revival.

воскресе́нье *n.* Sunday.

воскреси́ть [*infl.* **-шу́, -си́шь**] *v., pfv. of* **воскреша́ть**.

воскре́снуть [*past* **-кре́с, -кре́сла**] *v., pfv. of* **воскреса́ть**.

воскре́сный *adj.* Sunday *(attrib.).*

воскреша́ть *v.impfv.* [*pfv.* **воскреси́ть**] **1,** to resurrect; raise from the dead; bring back to life. **2,** to revive; resurrect (a custom, hopes, etc.). **3,** to invigorate; perk up. **4,** *in* воскреша́ть в па́мяти, to (re)call to mind.

воскреше́ние *n.* **1,** raising from the dead. **2,** *fig.* revival.

воспале́ние *n.* inflammation. —воспале́ние лёгких, pneumonia. —воспале́ние не́рвов, neuritis.

воспалённый *adj.* inflamed.

воспали́тельный *adj.* inflammatory; inflammation *(attrib.).*

воспаля́ть *v.impfv.* [*pfv.* **воспали́ть**] *obs.* to inflame. —воспаля́ться, *refl., obs.* to become inflamed.

воспевáть *v.impfv.* [*pfv.* **воспéть**] to praise; extol (*in verse or song*).

воспéть [*infl.* **-пою́, -поёшь**] *v., pfv. of* **воспевáть**.

воспитáние *n.* **1,** raising; rearing; bringing up. **2,** upbringing. **3,** education. **4,** (good) breeding. **5,** fostering; cultivating.

воспи́танник *n.* **1,** pupil. **2,** adopted child; ward. **3,** (*with gen.*) graduate (of); alumnus (of).

воспи́танность *n.f.* (good) breeding.

воспи́танный *adj.* well-bred; well-mannered.

воспитáтель *n.m.* educator; teacher; mentor. —**воспитáтельница,** *n.* teacher; governess.

воспитáтельный *adj.* educational. —**воспитáтельный дом,** pre-rev. foundling home.

воспи́тывать *v.impfv.* [*pfv.* **воспитáть**] **1,** to raise; rear; bring up. **2,** to educate; train. **3,** to foster; cultivate.

воспламенéние *n.* **1,** combustion. **2,** ignition.

воспламени́ть *v., pfv. of* **воспламеня́ть.** —**воспламени́ться,** *refl., pfv. of* **воспламеня́ться.**

воспламеня́емость *n.f.* inflammability.

воспламеня́ть *v.impfv.* [*pfv.* **воспламени́ть**] **1,** to ignite; kindle. **2,** *fig.* to rouse; fire (up). —**воспламеня́ться,** *refl.* **1,** to flare up; burst into flames. **2,** *fig.* to get worked up. Воспламеня́ться гнéвом, to flare up; become enraged.

восполня́ть *v.impfv.* [*pfv.* **воспóлнить**] to fill (a gap); make up for (a deficiency).

воспóльзоваться *v.r., pfv. of* **пóльзоваться.**

воспоминáние *n.* **1,** memory; recollection. **2,** *pl.* memoirs; reminiscences.

воспрепя́тствовать *v., pfv. of* **препя́тствовать.**

воспрети́ть [*infl.* **-щу́, -ти́шь**] *v., pfv. of* **воспреща́ть.**

воспреща́ть *v.impfv.* [*pfv.* **воспрети́ть**] **1,** to prohibit; forbid. **2,** *mil.* to interdict. —**воспреща́ться,** *refl.* [*impfv. only*] to be prohibited; be forbidden.

воспрещéние *n.* **1,** prohibition. **2,** *mil.* interdiction.

восприи́мчивость *n.f.* **1,** receptivity. **2,** susceptibility.

восприи́мчивый *adj.* **1,** keen. **2,** (*with* **к**) receptive (to). **3,** (*with* **к**) susceptible (to).

воспринимáть *v.impfv.* [*pfv.* **восприня́ть**] **1,** to perceive. **2,** to take in; assimilate; absorb (*mentally*). **3,** (*with* **как**) to take (as). **4,** to react to (*in a certain way*): воспринимáть чтó-нибудь с востóргом/негодовáнием, to react to something with delight/indignation.

восприня́ть [*infl. like* **приня́ть**] *v., pfv. of* **воспринимáть.**

восприя́тие *n.* perception.

воспроизведéние *n.* reproduction.

воспроизвести́ [*infl. like* **вести́**] *v., pfv. of* **воспроизводи́ть.**

воспроизводи́тельный *adj.* reproductive.

воспроизводи́ть *v.impfv.* [*pfv.* **воспроизвести́**; *pres.* **-вожу́, -вóдишь**] **1,** to reproduce. **2,** to re-create. **3,** to recall.

воспроти́виться *v.r., pfv. of* **проти́виться.**

воспря́нуть *v.pfv.* **1,** to jump up; leap up. **2,** [*also,* **воспря́нуть ду́хом**] to perk up; come alive. —**воспря́нуть ото снá,** to awake from one's slumber.

воссоединéние *n.* reunification.

воссоединя́ть *v.impfv.* [*pfv.* **воссоедини́ть**] to reunite. —**воссоединя́ться,** *refl.* to be reunited.

воссоздавáть *v.impfv.* [*pfv.* **воссоздáть**; *pres.* **-даю́, -даёшь**] **1,** to re-create. **2,** to (mentally) reconstruct.

воссоздáть [*infl. like* **дáть**; *past* **-дáл, -далá, -дáло**] *v., pfv. of* **воссоздавáть.**

восставáть *v.impfv.* [*pfv.* **воссáть**; *pres.* **-стаю́, -стаёшь**] (*with* **прóтив**) to rebel (against); revolt (against); rise up (against).

восстанáвливать *v.impfv.* [*pfv.* **восстанови́ть**] **1,** to restore; re-establish. **2,** to recover; regain (one's health, strength, etc.). **3,** (*with* **прóтив**) to set against. —**восстанови́ть в (прéжней) дóлжности,** to reinstate; give someone his/her job back. —**восстанови́ть (когó-нибудь) в правáх,** to restore someone's rights. —**восстанови́ть прóтив себя́,** to antagonize.

восстáние *n.* revolt; rebellion; uprising; insurrection.

восстанови́тельный *adj.* of restoration. —**восстанови́тельный пер́иод,** period of reconstruction. —**восстанови́тельный ремóнт,** renovation; overhaul.

восстанови́ть [*infl.* **-новлю́, -нóвишь**] *v., pfv. of* **восстанáвливать.**

восстановлéние *n.* **1,** restoration. **2,** recovery (*of one's health*).

воссáть [*infl.* **-стáну, -стáнешь**] *v., pfv. of* **восставáть.**

востóк *n.* **1,** east. **2,** *cap.* the East.

востоковéд *n.* Orientalist. —**востоковéдение,** *n.* Oriental studies.

востóрг *n.* ecstasy: быть в востóрге (от), to be in ecstasy (over); be ecstatic (about).

восторгáть *v.impfv.* to delight; enchant; enrapture. —**восторгáться,** *refl.* (*with instr.*) to be in ecstasy (over); be enthusiastic (about); be enchanted (with).

востóрженность *n.f.* ecstasy; delight.

востóрженный *adj.* ecstatic; enthusiastic; rapturous.

восторжествовáть *v., pfv. of* **торжествовáть.**

востóчный *adj.* **1,** eastern; East; easterly. **2,** oriental.

вострéбование *n.* claiming. —**до вострéбования,** general delivery.

вострéбовать *v.pfv.* [*infl.* **-бую, -буешь**] to claim.

вострó *adv., in* держáть у́хо вострó, *colloq.* to be on one's guard.

восхвалéние *n.* **1,** extolling. **2,** acclaim.

восхвали́ть [*infl.* **-хвалю́, -хвáлишь**] *v., pfv. of* **восхваля́ть.**

восхваля́ть *v.impfv.* [*pfv.* **восхвали́ть**] to laud; extol; eulogize.

восхити́тельный *adj.* delightful; captivating; enchanting.

восхити́ть [*infl.* **-щу́, -ти́шь**] *v., pfv. of* **восхища́ть.** —**восхити́ться,** *refl., pfv. of* **восхища́ться.**

восхища́ть *v.impfv.* [*pfv.* **восхити́ть**] to delight; captivate; enchant. —**восхища́ться,** *refl.* (*with instr.*) to be captivated (by); be enchanted (with).

восхищéние *n.* delight; enchantment; admiration.

восхищённый *adj.* delighted; of delight. —**восхищённо,** *adv.* in *or* with delight.

восхóд *n.* rise (*of the sun or moon*): восхóд сóлнца, sunrise.

восходи́ть *v.impfv.* [*pfv.* **взойти́**; *pres.* **-хожу́, -хо́дишь**] **1,** = **всходи́ть**. **2,** [*impfv. only*] (*with* **к**) to go back to; date back to.

восходя́щий *adj.* rising; ascending. —**восходя́щая звезда́,** *fig.* rising star.

восхожде́ние *n.* ascent.

восше́ствие *n., obs.* ascent. —**восше́ствие на престо́л,** accession to the throne.

восьма́я *n., decl. as an adj.* eighth: **одна́ восьма́я,** one-eighth.

восьме́рка *n.* **1,** the numeral 8. **2,** *colloq.* anything numbered 8. **3,** figure eight (*in skating, flying, etc.*). **4,** *cards* eight.

во́сьмеро *collective numeral* eight.

восьмигра́нник *n.* octahedron. —**восьмигра́нный,** *adj.* octahedral.

восьмидеся́тый *ordinal numeral* eightieth.

восьмиле́тний *adj.* **1,** eight-year (*attrib.*). **2,** eight-year-old.

восьмисо́тый *ordinal numeral* eight-hundredth.

восьмиуго́льник *n.* octagon. —**восьмиуго́льный,** *adj.* octagonal.

восьмичасово́й *adj.* eight-hour (*attrib.*).

восьмо́й *ordinal numeral* eighth.

восьму́шка [*gen. pl.* **-шек**] *n.* **1,** *obs.* eighth of a pound. **2,** octavo.

вот *particle* **1,** here (is): Вот ва́ша кни́га, here is your book; вот он идёт, here he comes. А вот и звоно́к!, there's the bell! **2,** (*with* **где, как, что**) this is; that is: Вот где я живу́, this is where I live. Вот в чём вопро́с, that is the question! **3,** *used for emphasis:* вот э́то на́до посмотре́ть!, you really must see it! —**вот так!; вот что!,** really!; you don't say! —**вот так так!,** well, I never!; well, I'll be! —**вот тебе́ и...,** so much for... —**вот тебе́ и раз!,** how do you like that!; what do you know! —**вот э́то да!,** now that's something like it!

вот-во́т *adv., colloq., used with the future tense of verbs,* (just) about to: Он вот-во́т уйдёт, he is (just) about to leave. Вот-во́т пойдёт дождь, it's about to rain.

воткну́ть *v., pfv. of* **втыка́ть**.

во́тум *n.* vote. —**во́тум (не)дове́рия,** vote of (no) confidence.

во́тчина *n., hist.* ancestral lands; estate.

воцари́ться *v.r.impfv.* [*pfv.* **воцари́ться**] **1,** *obs.* to ascend the throne. **2,** *fig.* to set in; be established: Воцари́лась тишина́, silence reigned.

вошь [*gen., dat. & prepl.* **вши;** *instr.* **во́шью**] *n.f.* louse.

вощанка *n.* wax paper.

вощёный *adj.* waxed.

вощи́ть *v.impfv.* [*pfv.* **навощи́ть**] to wax.

вою́ющий *adj.* warring; belligerent.

воя́ка *n.m., colloq., ironic* warrior.

впада́ть *v.impfv.* [*pfv.* **впасть**] **1,** [*impfv. only*] (*with* **в** + *acc.*) to flow (into); empty (into). **2,** to become hollow; become sunken. **3,** *fig.* (*with* **в** + *acc.*) to fall (into); sink (into); lapse (into). Впада́ть в па́нику, to panic.

впаде́ние *n.* **1,** emptying (*of a river into a larger body of water*). **2,** confluence: при впаде́нии (*or* у впа-де́ния) реки́ Оки́ в Во́лгу, at the confluence of the Oka and the Volga; where the Oka flows into the Volga.

впа́дина *n.* **1,** hollow; depression; cavity. **2,** *anat.* socket: глазна́я впа́дина, eye socket.

впа́лый *adj.* hollow; sunken.

впасть [*infl. like* **пасть**] *v., pfv. of* **впада́ть**.

впервы́е *adv.* first; for the first time.

вперева́лку *adv., colloq., in* ходи́ть вперева́лку, to waddle.

вперёд *adv.* **1,** forward; ahead. **2,** *colloq.* henceforth; from now on. **3,** *colloq.* ahead of time; beforehand; in advance.

впереди́ *adv.* **1,** in front; ahead. **2,** ahead; yet to occur: Что нас ждёт впереди́?, what lies ahead for us? Развя́зка ещё впереди́, the climax is yet to come. —*prep., with gen.* in front of; ahead of.

вперемежку *adv., colloq.* alternately.

вперемешку *adv., colloq.* pell-mell; every which way.

впечатле́ние *n.* impression.

впечатли́тельный *adj.* impressionable.

впечатля́ющий *adj.* impressive.

впива́ть *v.impfv.* [*pfv.* **впить**] to absorb; imbibe.

впива́ться *v.impfv.* [*pfv.* **впи́ться**] (*with* **в** + *acc.*) **1,** to pierce; cut into. **2,** (*of an insect or certain animals*) to sink its teeth into; bite into. **3,** *fig.* to fix one's gaze (on).

вписа́ть [*infl.* впишу́, впи́шешь] *v., pfv. of* **впи́сывать**. —**вписа́ться,** *refl., pfv. of* **впи́сываться**.

впи́сывать *v.impfv.* [*pfv.* **вписа́ть**] (*with* **в** + *acc.*) **1,** to write in; enter; insert. **2,** *math.* to inscribe. —**впи́сываться,** *refl.* (*with* **в** + *acc.*) *colloq.* **1,** to enroll (in); join. **2,** to fit in (with); blend in (with).

впи́тывать *v.impfv.* [*pfv.* **впита́ть**] to absorb; soak up.

впить [*infl.* вопью́, вопьёшь; *past fem.* впила́] *v., pfv. of* **впива́ть**. —**впи́ться,** *refl.* [*past* впи́лся, впила́сь, впило́сь, впили́сь *or* впи́лись] *pfv. of* **впива́ться**.

впи́хивать *v.impfv.* [*pfv.* **впихну́ть**] *colloq.* **1,** to stuff in; cram in; force in. **2,** to push in; shove in.

вплавь *adv.* by swimming.

вплести́ [*infl. like* **плести́**] *v., pfv. of* **вплета́ть**.

вплета́ть *v.impfv.* [*pfv.* **вплести́**] (*with* **в** + *acc.*) to plait (into).

вплотну́ю *adv.* **1,** closely; tightly. **2,** (*with* **к**) right up to; right up against. **3,** *fig., colloq.* in earnest.

вплоть *adv., usu. in* вплоть до (+ *gen.*), **1,** right up to. **2,** down to.

вплыва́ть *v.impfv.* [*pfv.* **вплыть**] (*with* **в** + *acc.*) **1,** to swim into. **2,** to sail into.

вплыть [*infl. like* **плыть**] *v., pfv. of* **вплыва́ть**.

впова́лку *adv., colloq.* side by side: лежа́ть/спать впова́лку, to lie/sleep side by side.

вполго́лоса *adv.* in a low voice; under one's breath; in an undertone.

вполза́ть *v.impfv.* [*pfv.* **вползти́**] **1,** (*with* **в** + *acc.*) to crawl into; creep into. **2,** (*with* **на** + *acc.*) to crawl up; creep up.

вползти́ [*infl. like* **ползти́**] *v., pfv. of* **вполза́ть**.

вполне́ *adv.* fully; entirely; completely; quite.

вполоборо́та *adv.* (*with* **к**) half-turned (toward).

вполу́ха *adv., colloq.* with half an ear.

впопа́д *adv., colloq.* to the point.

впопыха́х *adv.* **1,** hastily; hurriedly. **2,** in one's haste.

впо́ру *adv., colloq.* **1,** of the right size: Пла́тье вам впо́ру, the dress is the right size for you. **2,** (*with dat. and inf.*) all one can do is...

впорхну́ть *v.pfv.* to fly in; flit in.

впосле́дствии *adv.* afterwards; subsequently; later on.

впотьма́х *adv.* in the dark.

впра́вду *adv., colloq.* really.

впра́ве *adv.* having a right: Она́ впра́ве горди́ться, she has a right to be proud.

впра́вить [*infl.* -влю, -вишь] *v., pfv. of* вправля́ть.

вправля́ть *v.impfv.* [*pfv.* впра́вить] **1,** to set (a bone, joint, etc.). **2,** (*with* в + *acc.*) *colloq.* to tuck into.

впра́во *adv.* to the right.

впредь *adv.* hereafter; henceforth; from now on. —впредь до, until; pending.

вприку́ску *adv., in* пить чай вприку́ску, to drink tea holding a lump of sugar in one's mouth.

вприпры́жку *adv., in* бежа́ть вприпры́жку, to skip along.

вприся́дку *adv.* in a squatting position (*while dancing*).

впритьк *adv.* (*with* к) *colloq.* flush (against).

впро́голодь *adv.* hungry: жить *or* пита́ться впро́голодь, to go hungry.

впрок *adv.* **1,** in store; for future use: заготовля́ть впрок, to store up; stock up on. **2,** (*usu. with* идти́) to one's advantage: Это вам не пойдёт впрок, it won't do you any good. Ему́ всё (идёт) впрок, everything goes right for him.

впроса́к *adv. in* попа́сть впроса́к, *colloq.* to commit a gaffe; put one's foot in it.

впросо́нках *adv., colloq.* while half-asleep.

впро́чем *conj.* **1,** however; but; though. **2,** but then; but then again.

впры́гивать *v.impfv.* [*pfv.* впры́гнуть] **1,** (*with* в + *acc.*) to jump into. **2,** (*with* на + *acc.*) to jump onto.

впры́скивание *n.* injection.

впры́скивать *v.impfv.* [*pfv.* впры́снуть] to inject.

впряга́ть *v.impfv.* [*pfv.* впрячь] (*with* в + *acc.*) to harness (to); hitch (to).

впряму́ю *adv., colloq.* directly.

впрямь *adv., colloq.* really; indeed.

впрячь [*infl.* впрягу́, впряжёшь, ...впрягу́т; *past* впряг, впрягла́, впрягло́, впрягли́] *v., pfv. of* впряга́ть.

впуск *n.* **1,** admission; admittance. **2,** intake.

впуска́ть *v.impfv.* [*pfv.* впусти́ть] to admit; let in.

впусти́ть [*infl.* впущу́, впу́стишь] *v., pfv. of* впуска́ть.

впусту́ю *adv., colloq.* in vain; for nothing.

впу́тать *v., pfv. of* пу́тать (*in sense #6*) *and* впу́тывать. —впу́таться, *refl., pfv. of* пу́таться (*in sense #4*) *and* впу́тываться.

впу́тывать *v.impfv.* [*pfv.* впу́тать] (*with* в + *acc.*) *colloq.* to involve (in); get (someone) mixed up (in). —впу́тываться, *refl.* (*with* в + *acc.*) *colloq.* to get mixed up (in).

впя́теро *adv.* five times: впя́теро бо́льше, five times as much (*or* as big).

впятеро́м *adv.* five together: они́ впятеро́м, the five of them.

враг [*gen.* врага́] *n.* enemy.

вражда́ *n.* hostility; animosity; enmity.

вражде́бный *adj.* hostile. —вражде́бно, *adv.* with hostility; with animosity. —вражде́бность, *n.f.* hostility; animosity.

враждова́ть *v.impfv.* [*pres.* -ду́ю, -ду́ешь] (*with* с + *instr.*) to feud (with); be at odds (with).

вра́жеский *adj.* enemy (*attrib.*); hostile.

вразби́вку *adv., colloq.* at random; in no particular order.

вразбро́д *adv., colloq.* **1,** separately; not together. **2,** without coordination.

вразбро́с *adv., colloq.* scattered about; every which way.

вразва́лку *adv., colloq., in* ходи́ть вразва́лку, to waddle.

вразнобо́й *adv., colloq.* without coordination; haphazardly.

вразно́с *adv., colloq., in* торгова́ть *or* продава́ть вразно́с, to peddle.

вразре́з *adv., in* идти́ вразре́з с (+ *instr.*), to run counter to; go against.

вразуми́тельный *adj.* clear; intelligible; understandable.

вразумля́ть *v.impfv.* [*pfv.* вразуми́ть] to make (someone) understand; bring to one's senses.

вра́ки [*gen.* врак] *n.pl., colloq.* **1,** nonsense. **2,** lies.

враль [*gen.* враля́] *n.m., colloq.* **1,** liar. **2,** chatterbox.

враньё *n., colloq.* **1,** lying. **2,** lies.

врасплóх *adv., in* заста́ть *or* засти́гнуть врасплóх, to take by surprise; catch off guard; catch unawares.

врассыпну́ю *adv.* in all directions; helter-skelter; every which way.

враста́ть *v.impfv.* [*pfv.* врасти́] (*with* в + *acc.*) **1,** to grow into. **2,** to sink into (the ground).

врасти́ [*infl. like* расти́] *v., pfv. of* враста́ть.

врастя́жку *adv., colloq.* **1,** flat; stretched out. **2,** in a drawl.

врата́рь [*gen.* -таря́] *n.m.* **1,** *obs.* gatekeeper. **2,** *sports* goalkeeper; goalie.

врать *v.impfv.* [*pfv.* совра́ть; *pres.* вру, врёшь; *past fem.* врала́] *colloq.* to lie; tell lies.

врач [*gen.* врача́] *n.* doctor; physician. —зубно́й врач, dentist.

враче́бный *adj.* medical.

враща́тельный *adj.* rotary.

враща́ть *v.impfv.* to rotate; turn (*trans. verb*). —враща́ть глаза́ми, to roll one's eyes.

враща́ться *v.r.impfv.* **1,** to revolve; rotate; turn (*intrans.*). **2,** *fig.* (*with* вокру́г) (*of a conversation*) to revolve (around); center (around). **3,** (*with* в + *prepl.*) *fig.* to move (*in certain circles*); (*with* среди́) mingle (with *or* among).

враща́ющийся *adj.* revolving.

враще́ние *n.* rotation.

вред [*gen.* вреда́] *n.* harm; injury; damage. —во вред (+ *dat.*), to the detriment of.

вреди́тель *n.m.* **1,** pest; *pl.* vermin. **2,** economic saboteur. —вреди́тельство, *n.* economic sabotage.

вреди́ть *v.impfv.* [*pfv.* повреди́ть; *pres.* врежу́, вреди́шь] (*with dat.*) to harm; damage; be injurious to.

вре́дно *adv.* in a harmful manner: вре́дно де́йствовать на, to have a harmful effect on. —*adj., used predicatively,* harmful; bad: вре́дно для зре́ния, bad for one's eyesight.

вре́дный *adj.* [*short form* вре́ден, вредна́, вре́дно, вре́дны *or* вредны́] harmful; damaging; detrimental; injurious; deleterious. Вре́дная привы́чка, pernicious habit. Вре́дные испаре́ния, noxious fumes.

вредоно́сный *adj.* harmful.

вре́зать [*infl.* вре́жу, вре́жешь] *v., pfv. of* вреза́ть *and* вре́зывать. —**вре́заться,** *refl., pfv. of* вреза́ться *and* вре́зываться.

вреза́ть *v.impfv.* [*pfv.* вре́зать] (*with* в + *acc.*) **1,** to insert; set; install (*by cutting into something*): вре́зать замо́к в дверь, to install a lock in a door. **2,** *fig.* to etch (in one's memory). —**вреза́ться,** *refl.* (*with* в + *acc.*) **1,** to cut into. **2,** (*of a vehicle, airplane, etc.*) to crash (into); slam (into); plunge (into). **3,** *fig.* to be etched (in one's memory).

вре́зывать *v.impfv.* = вреза́ть. —**вре́зываться,** *refl.* = вреза́ться.

вре́менно *adv.* temporarily.

временно́й *adj.* time (*attrib.*); temporal.

вре́менный *adj.* **1,** temporary. **2,** provisional. **3,** (*of an agreement*) interim.

вре́мя [*gen., dat. & prepl.* вре́мени; *instr.* вре́менем; *pl.* времена́, времён, времена́м] *n.neut.* **1,** time. **2,** *gram.* tense. **3,** *in* вре́мя го́да, season. —**во вре́мя** (+ *gen.*), during. —**во времена́** (+ *gen.*), in (someone's) time. —**во все времена́,** at all times. —**в** (*or* **за**) **после́днее вре́мя,** recently; of late. —**времена́ми,** at times; now and then. —**вре́мя от вре́мени,** from time to time. —**в своё вре́мя, 1,** in one's time; in one's day. **2,** in due time; in due course. —**всё вре́мя,** all the time. —**в ско́ром вре́мени,** before long; shortly. —**в то вре́мя как,** while; whereas. —**в то же вре́мя,** at the same time. —**на вре́мя,** for a while; for a time. —**на вре́мя** (+ *gen.*), for the duration of. —**одно́ вре́мя,** at one time. —**пе́рвое вре́мя,** at first. —**по времена́м,** from time to time. —**ско́лько вре́мени?, 1,** how long? **2,** what time?: ско́лько вре́мени сейча́с (*or* у вас)?, what time is it/ have you got/? —**со вре́менем,** in time; over time. —**со вре́мени** (+ *gen.*), since. —**тем вре́менем,** meanwhile.

время́нка [*gen. pl.* -нок] *n., colloq.* temporary structure.

времяпрепровожде́ние *n.* way of spending time; pastime. *Also,* **времяпровожде́ние.**

вро́вень *adv.* (*with* с + *instr.*) on a level (with); even (with); flush (with).

вро́де *prep., with gen.* **1,** like; not unlike. **2,** a sort of. —*particle, colloq.* **1,** (*with nouns*) such as; like. **2,** (*often fol. by* бы] (*with verbs*) seems to (have); (*with adjectives*) seems to be.

врождённый *adj.* innate; inborn; inherent; congenital. —**врождённый дефе́кт,** birth defect.

врозь *adv.* apart: жить врозь, to live apart.

вро́сший *adj.* ingrown.

вруба́ть *v.impfv.* [*pfv.* вруби́ть] (*with* в + *acc.*) to place; set (in an opening that has been cut out). —**вруба́ться,** *refl.* (*with* в + *acc.*) to cut one's way (into *or* through).

вруби́ть [*infl.* врублю́, вру́бишь] *v., pfv. of* вруба́ть. —**вруби́ться,** *refl., pfv. of* вруба́ться.

врукопа́шную *adv.* in hand-to-hand combat: би́ться врукопа́шную, to engage in hand-to-hand combat.

врун [*gen.* вруна́] *n.m.* [*fem.* вру́нья] *colloq.* liar.

вруча́ть *v.impfv.* [*pfv.* вручи́ть] **1,** to hand; deliver (a note, protest, etc.). **2,** to present (an award, diploma, one's credentials, etc.). **3,** to serve (a legal document). **4,** *fig.* to entrust.

вруче́ние *n.* presentation; presenting.

вручи́ть *v., pfv. of* вруча́ть.

вручну́ю *adv.* by hand; manually.

врыва́ть *v.impfv.* [*pfv.* врыть] (*with* в + *acc.*) to implant; set (in the ground).

врыва́ться *v.r.impfv.* [*pfv.* ворва́ться] (*with* в + *acc.*) **1,** to burst into. **2,** to break into.

врыть [*infl.* вро́ю, вро́ешь] *v., pfv. of* врыва́ть.

вряд ли *particle* hardly; it is unlikely; I doubt whether...: Вряд ли он придёт, I doubt whether he is coming.

всади́ть [*infl.* всажу́, вса́дишь] *v., pfv. of* вса́живать.

вса́дник *n.* rider; horseman.

вса́живать *v.impfv.* [*pfv.* всади́ть] (*with* в + *acc.*) **1,** to plunge (a knife) into; put (a bullet) in. **2,** *colloq.* to sink (money) into.

вса́сывание *n.* **1,** suction. **2,** absorption.

вса́сывать *v.impfv.* [*pfv.* всоса́ть] to suck in; absorb. —**вса́сываться,** *refl.* (*with* в + *acc.*) **1,** to be absorbed (in). **2,** to be sucked into (a swamp, morass, etc.).

все *adj., pl. of* весь. —*pron.* everybody; everyone. —**все и вся,** *colloq.* [*acc.* всех и вся] everybody and everything. *See also* весь.

всё *adj., neut. of* весь, all: всё вре́мя, all the time. —*pron.* everything; all: Э́то всё, that's all; всё в поря́дке, everything is all right —*adv., colloq.* **1,** constantly; all the time: Телефо́н всё звони́т, the telephone keeps ringing (all the time). **2,** still: Ем ме́ньше, чем други́е, а всё полне́ю, I eat less than other people and I still put on weight. **3,** (*with comp. adjectives and some verbs*) more and more; -er and -er: всё лу́чше и лу́чше, better and better; всё бо́лее интере́сный, more and more interesting. Он всё слабе́ет, he keeps getting weaker and weaker. Всё увели́чивающаяся сто́имость (+ *gen.*), the ever increasing cost of... —**всё ещё;** still; all the same. —**всё же,** still; all the same. —**всё и вся,** *colloq.* [*gen.* всего́ и вся] absolutely everything. —**всё равно́,** *see* равно́. —**при всём том,** for all that. *See also* весь.

всеве́дение *n.* omniscience.

всеве́дущий *adj.* omniscient.

всевла́стие *n.* absolute power. —**всевла́стный,** *adj.* all-powerful.

всевозмо́жный *adj.* all sorts of; all kinds of; every possible.

всевы́шний *n., usu. cap., decl. as an adj.* the Almighty.

всегда́ *adv.* always. —**как всегда́,** as always; as usual.

всегда́шний *adj., colloq.* regular; usual; customary.

всего́ *adj., gen. of* весь. —*adv.* **1,** in all. **2,** only. —*interj.* so long! —**всего́ хоро́шего!; всего́ до́брого!,** all the best! —**всего́-на́всего,** only; nothing but.

всёдозво́ленность *n.f.* absence of all restraint; license; permissiveness.

всезна́йка [*gen. pl.* **-зна́ек**] *n.m. & f., colloq.* know-it-all.

вселе́ние *n.* moving in: вселе́ние в но́вый дом, moving into a new house.

вселе́нная *n., decl. as an adj.* universe.

вселе́нский *adj.* ecumenical.

вселя́ть *v.impfv.* [*pfv.* **всели́ть**] (*with* в + *acc.*) **1,** to move; settle (people) into. **2,** *fig.* to instill (hope, confidence, etc.) into; strike (fear) into. **—вселя́ться,** *refl.* **1,** to move in; (*with* в + *acc.*) move into; settle into. **2,** *fig.* (*with* в + *acc.*) (*of an emotion*) to fill; seize.

всеме́рный *adj.* all possible: всеме́рная подде́ржка, all possible support. **—всеме́рно,** *adv.* in every (possible) way.

всеми́рный *adj.* world (*attrib.*); worldwide; universal. **—всеми́рная вы́ставка,** world's fair.

всемогу́щество *n.* omnipotence. **—всемогу́щий,** *adj.* all-powerful; almighty; omnipotent.

всенаро́дный *adj.* nationwide; national.

всено́щная *n., decl. as an adj.* vespers.

всеобщий *adj.* universal; general.

всеобъе́млющий *adj.* all-embracing; comprehensive.

всеору́жие *n., in* во всеору́жии, fully armed. **—во всеору́жии зна́ний,** fully versed in one's subject.

всепобежда́ющий *adj.* all-conquering.

всепоглоща́ющий *adj.* all-consuming.

всеросси́йский *adj.* all-Russian.

всерьёз *adv., colloq.* seriously; in earnest. **—принима́ть всерьёз,** to take seriously.

всеси́льный *adj.* all-powerful; omnipotent.

всесторо́нний *adj.* all-round; thorough; comprehensive. **—всесторо́нне,** *adv.* thoroughly; in every way.

всё-таки *conj.* still; all the same.

всеуслы́шание *n., in* во всеуслы́шание, publicly; for all to hear.

всецело *adv.* completely; entirely.

всея́дный *adj.* omnivorous.

вска́кивать *v.impfv.* [*pfv.* **вскочи́ть**] **1,** (*with* в *or* на + *acc.*) to jump on *or* onto: вскочи́ть в по́езд/ на ло́шадь/, to jump on/onto a train/horse. Вскочи́ть на́ ноги, to leap (*or* spring) to one's feet. **2,** to jump up; leap up: вскочи́ть со сту́ла, to leap up from one's chair. Вскочи́ть с посте́ли, to leap out of bed. **3,** *colloq.* (*of a bruise, bump, blister, etc.*) to appear.

вска́пывать *v.impfv.* [*pfv.* **вскопа́ть**] to dig; dig up.

вскара́бкиваться *v.r.impfv.* [*pfv.* **вскара́бкаться**] (*with* на + *acc.*) to climb (onto); scramble (up); clamber (up).

вска́рмливать *v.impfv.* [*pfv.* **вскорми́ть**] to raise (animals, birds, etc.). **—вскорми́ть и вспои́ть,** to raise; nurture (a child).

вскачь *adv.* at a gallop.

вски́дывать *v.impfv.* [*pfv.* **вски́нуть**] **1,** to throw up; toss up. **2,** (*with* на + *acc.*) to toss (onto). **—вски́нуть глаза́,** to look up suddenly. **—вски́нуть го́лову,** to toss one's head.

вски́дываться *v.r.impfv.* [*pfv.* **вски́нуться**] *colloq.* **1,**

to jump up. **2,** *fig.* (*with* на + *acc.*) *colloq.* to jump on; berate.

вскипа́ть *v.impfv.* [*pfv.* **вскипе́ть**] **1,** to boil up; come to a boil. **2,** (*of emotions*) to well up; flare up. **3,** [*also,* **вскипе́ть гне́вом**] to fly into a rage.

вскипе́ть [*infl.* **-плю́, -пи́шь**] *v., pfv. of* вскипа́ть.

вскипяти́ть *v., pfv. of* кипяти́ть. **—вскипяти́ться,** *refl., pfv. of* кипяти́ться.

всклоко́ченный *adj., colloq.* disheveled.

всколыхну́ть *v.pfv.* **1,** to stir. **2,** *fig.* to stir up; agitate.

вскользь *adv.* casually; in passing: упомяну́ть вскользь, to mention in passing.

вскопа́ть *v., pfv. of* вска́пывать.

вско́ре *adv.* soon; shortly; presently.

вскорми́ть [*infl.* **вскормлю́, вско́рмишь**] *v., pfv. of* вска́рмливать.

вскочи́ть [*infl.* **вскочу́, вско́чишь**] *v., pfv. of* вска́кивать.

вскри́кивать *v.impfv.* [*pfv.* **вскри́кнуть**] to cry out; scream; shriek.

вскрича́ть *v.pfv.* [*infl.* **-чу́, -чи́шь**] to exclaim; cry.

вскружи́ть *v.pfv., in* вскружи́ть го́лову (+ *dat.*), to turn someone's head; go to one's head.

вскрыва́ть *v.impfv.* [*pfv.* **вскрыть**] **1,** to open up; unseal. **2,** to expose; uncover; reveal. **3,** *med.* to cut open; lance. **4,** *med.* to dissect; perform an autopsy on. **—вскрыва́ться,** *refl.* **1,** to be revealed; come to light. **2,** (*of a river*) to become free of ice.

вскры́тие *n.* **1,** opening; unsealing. **2,** revelation; disclosure. **3,** thawing; breaking up (*of a frozen river*). **4,** *med.* autopsy; dissection. **5,** *med.* cutting open; lancing.

вскрыть [*infl.* **вскро́ю, вскро́ешь**] *v., pfv. of* вскрыва́ть. **—вскры́ться,** *refl., pfv. of* вскрыва́ться.

власть *adv., colloq.* to one's heart's content.

вслед *adv.* behind: идти́ вслед, to follow after; walk behind. **—***prep., with dat.* after; following. Смотре́ть вслед (+ *dat.*), to follow with one's eyes. **—вслед за** (+ *instr.*), **1,** after; in pursuit of. **2,** right after; on the heels of. **—вслед за тем,** after that.

всле́дствие *prep., with gen.* as a result of; on account of; owing to.

вслепу́ю *adv., colloq.* blind; blindly; blindfolded.

вслух *adv.* aloud; out loud.

вслу́шиваться *v.r.impfv.* [*pfv.* **вслу́шаться**] (*with* в + *acc.*) to listen carefully (to); strain one's ears to hear.

всма́триваться *v.r.impfv.* [*pfv.* **всмотре́ться**] (*with* в + *acc.*) to peer into; take a good look at.

всмотре́ться [*infl.* **всмотрю́сь, всмо́тришься**] *v.r., pfv. of* всма́триваться.

всмя́тку *adv., in* яйцо́ всмя́тку, soft-boiled egg.

всо́вывать *v.impfv.* [*pfv.* **всу́нуть**] (*with* в + *acc.*) to stick (into); slip (into); thrust (into).

всоса́ть [*infl.* **-су́, -сёшь**] *v., pfv. of* вса́сывать. **—всоса́ться,** *refl., pfv. of* вса́сываться.

вспа́ивать *v.impfv.* [*pfv.* **вспои́ть**] *colloq.* to raise; rear; bring up.

вспа́рывать *v.impfv.* [*pfv.* **вспоро́ть**] *colloq.* to cut open; rip open.

вспаха́ть [*infl.* **вспашу́, вспа́шешь**] *v., pfv. of* паха́ть *and* вспа́хивать.

вспа́хивать *v.impfv.* [*pfv.* **вспаха́ть**] to plow.

вспа́шка *n.* plowing.

вспе́нить *v., pfv. of* **пе́нить**. —**вспе́ниться**, *refl., pfv. of* **пе́ниться**.

всплакну́ть *v.pfv., colloq.* to have a little cry; shed a few tears.

всплеск *n.* **1,** splash; splashing. **2,** *fig.* (*with gen.*) outburst (of); outbreak (of); surge (in).

всплёскивать *v.impfv.* [*pfv.* **всплесну́ть**] to splash. —**всплёскивать рука́ми**, to throw up one's hands (*in astonishment, dismay, etc.*).

всплыва́ть *v.impfv.* [*pfv.* **всплыть**] **1,** [*often with* **на пове́рхность**] to rise/float/come to the surface; (*of a submarine*) to surface. **2,** *fig.* to come to light.

всплыть [*infl. like* **плыть**] *v., pfv. of* **всплыва́ть**.

вспои́ть *v., pfv. of* **вспа́ивать**.

всполоши́ть *v.pfv., colloq.* to startle; alarm. —**всполоши́ться**, *refl., colloq.* to be startled; be alarmed.

вспомина́ть *v.impfv.* [*pfv.* **вспо́мнить**] **1,** to remember; recall; recollect. **2,** [*impfv. only*] to try to remember. **3,** [*impfv. only*] to recall; reminisce about. —**вспомина́ться**, *refl.* (*with dat.*) to come back to someone; come back to (one's mind).

вспомога́тельный *adj.* **1,** auxiliary; subsidiary. Вспомога́тельная роль, supporting role. **2,** *gram.* auxiliary: вспомога́тельный глаго́л, auxiliary verb.

вспоро́ть [*infl.* **вспорю́, вспо́решь**] *v., pfv. of* **вспа́рывать**.

вспорхну́ть *v.pfv.* to take wing.

вспоте́ть *v.pfv.* **1,** *pfv of* **поте́ть**. **2,** to become fogged; fog up.

вспры́гивать *v.impfv.* [*pfv.* **вспры́гнуть**] (*with* **на** + *acc.*) to jump onto; jump up on.

вспры́скивание *n.* sprinkling.

вспры́скивать *v.impfv.* [*pfv.* **вспры́снуть**] to sprinkle.

вспу́гивать *v.impfv.* [*pfv.* **вспугну́ть**] to frighten away; scare away.

вспуха́ть *v.impfv.* [*pfv.* **вспу́хнуть**] to swell up.

вспу́хнуть [*past* **вспух, вспу́хла**] *v., pfv. of* **пу́хнуть** *and* **вспуха́ть**.

вспу́чивать *v.impfv.* [*pfv.* **вспу́чить**] *colloq.* **1,** to cause to bulge. **2,** *impers.* to distend: У него́ вспу́чило живо́т, his stomach is distended. —**вспу́чиваться**, *refl., colloq.* to bulge; swell; distend.

вспыли́ть *v.pfv., colloq.* to flare up; fly into a rage.

вспы́льчивый *adj.* hot-tempered; quick-tempered; irascible. —**вспы́льчивость**, *n.f.* hot temper; irascibility.

вспы́хивать *v.impfv.* [*pfv.* **вспы́хнуть**] **1,** to blaze up; suddenly catch fire. Вспы́хнуть пла́менем, to burst into flames. **2,** (*of fire, war, panic, etc.*) to break out. **3,** to blush; flush. **4,** to flare up (*in anger*).

вспы́шка [*gen. pl.* **-шек**] *n.* **1,** flash. **2,** *fig.* (*with gen.*) burst (of); outburst (of); outbreak (of). **3,** (angry) outburst. **4,** *photog.* flash gun.

вспять *adv.* back; in the opposite direction.

встава́ние *n.* standing up; rising.

встава́ть *v.impfv.* [*pfv.* **встать**; *pres.* **встаю́, встаёшь**] **1,** to stand up; get up; rise. **2,** to stand (*in a certain place*). **3,** (*of the sun*) to rise. **4,** *fig.* (*of a question,*

difficulty, etc.) to arise; come up. **5,** *colloq.* (*of a machine or device*) to stop working. —**встать на защи́ту** (+ *gen.*), to rise to the defense of. —**встать на путь** (+ *gen.*), to embark on the path of. —**встать на сто́рону** (+ *gen.*), to side with; take the side of.

вста́вить [*infl.* **-влю, -вишь**] *v., pfv. of* **вставля́ть**.

вста́вка [*gen. pl.* **-вок**] *n.* **1,** mounting; setting. **2,** an insertion. **3,** inset; front (*of a dress*).

вставля́ть *v.impfv.* [*pfv.* **вста́вить**] **1,** to put in; insert. **2,** to interject; interpose; put in (a word, remark, etc.).

вставно́й *adj.* that can be inserted and later removed. —**вставны́е зу́бы**, false teeth. —**вставны́е ра́мы**, storm windows.

встарь *adv.* in the old days; in olden times.

встать [*infl.* **вста́ну, вста́нешь**] *v., pfv. of* **встава́ть**.

встра́ивать *v.impfv.* [*pfv.* **встро́ить**] to build in.

встрево́женный *adj.* alarmed.

встрево́жить *v., pfv. of* **трево́жить**. —**встрево́житься**, *refl., pfv. of* **трево́житься**.

встрёпанный *adj., colloq.* disheveled.

встрепену́ться *v.r.pfv.* **1,** (*of a bird*) to ruffle its feathers. **2,** to give a start (and be aroused). **3,** (*of the heart*) to palpitate; begin to beat faster.

встре́тить [*infl.* **-чу, -тишь**] *v., pfv. of* **встреча́ть**. —**встре́титься**, *refl., pfv. of* **встреча́ться**.

встре́ча *n.* **1,** meeting; encounter. **2,** appointment; engagement. **3,** welcome; reception. **4,** *sports* match; contest. **5,** *in* встре́ча Но́вого го́да, New Year's Eve party. —**до (ско́рой) встре́чи!**, see you soon! До встре́чи в два часа́!, see you at two o'clock!

встреча́ть *v.impfv.* [*pfv.* **встре́тить**] **1,** to meet. **2,** to encounter; meet with; be met with. **3,** to greet; welcome; receive. **4,** to celebrate (a holiday, esp. New Year's Eve). —**встреча́ться**, *refl.* **1,** to meet (each other). **2,** (*with* **с** + *instr.*) to meet; get together (with). **3,** [*impfv. only*] (*with* **с** + *instr.*) to go out with; date; see. **4,** (*with dat.*) to meet; encounter; run into; come across: Ему́ встре́тился ста́рый знако́мый, he ran into an old acquaintance. **5,** (*with* **с** + *instr.*) to meet; encounter; run into (difficulties, obstacles, etc.). **6,** to be found; occur.

встре́чный *adj.* **1,** oncoming; approaching. **2,** counter-: встре́чный уда́р, counterblow. —*n.* passer-by. —**встре́чный ве́тер**, head wind. —**ка́ждый встре́чный и попере́чный**, *adj.* any (*or* every) Tom, Dick, or Harry. —**пе́рвый встре́чный**, the first person to come along; anyone.

встря́ска *n., colloq.* **1,** shaking. **2,** shock. **3,** dressing-down.

встря́хивать *v.impfv.* [*pfv.* **встряхну́ть**] to shake; shake out; shake up. —**встря́хиваться**, *refl.* **1,** to shake oneself off. **2,** *fig., colloq.* to cheer up; pull oneself together.

вступа́ть *v.impfv.* [*pfv.* **вступи́ть**] (*with* **в** + *acc.*) **1,** to enter; enter into: вступи́ть в но́вую э́ру, to enter a new era; вступи́ть в разгово́р, to enter into a conversation. **2,** to join: вступи́ть в па́ртию, to join the party. —**вступи́ть в брак**, to marry; get married. —**вступи́ть в де́йствие, 1,** to go into operation. **2,** to come into play. —**вступи́ть в до́лжность**, to take *or* assume office. —**вступи́ть в свои́ права́,** to come into one's own. —**вступи́ть в си́лу,** to go into effect. —**вступи́ть в строй,** to go into operation. —**вступи́ть на престо́л,** to assume *or* ascend the throne.

вступа́ться *v.r.impfv.* [*pfv.* **вступи́ться**] (*with* за + *acc.*) to come to the defense of; stand up for; stick up for.

вступи́тельный *adj.* **1,** introductory; opening. **2,** entrance (*attrib.*): вступи́тельный экза́мен, entrance examination.

вступи́ть [*infl.* **вступлю́, всту́пишь**] *v., pfv. of* **вступа́ть.** —**вступи́ться,** *refl., pfv. of* **вступа́ться.**

вступле́ние *n.* **1,** (*with* в + *acc.*) entry (*into a place*); joining (*an organization*); taking (*office*). **2,** introduction (*to a book, musical work, etc.*).

всуе́ *adv., obs.* in vain.

всу́нуть *v., pfv. of* **всо́вывать.**

всухомя́тку *adv., colloq., in* **есть всухомя́тку,** to eat food dry (*without an accompanying beverage*).

всуху́ю *adv., colloq.* **1,** without grease. **2,** without having anything to drink. **3,** *sports* being shut out: проигра́ть всуху́ю, to be shut out.

всучивать *v.impfv.* [*pfv.* **всучи́ть**] (*with dat.*) *colloq.* to foist (on); palm off (on). *Also,* **всуча́ть.**

всучи́ть [*infl.* **всучу́, всу́чишь**] *v., pfv. of* **всу́чивать** *and* **всуча́ть.**

всхли́пывать *v.impfv.* [*pfv.* **всхли́пнуть**] to sniffle (*when crying*).

всходи́ть *v.impfv.* [*pfv.* **взойти́**; *pres.* **всхожу́, всхо́дишь**] **1,** (*with* на + *acc. or* по) to go up; mount; ascend; climb. **2,** (*of the sun, moon, etc.*) to rise. **3,** (*of plants, crops, etc.*) to sprout; come up.

всхо́ды [*gen.* **-дов**] *n.pl.* shoots; sprouts.

всхра́пывать *v.impfv.* to snore.

всы́пать [*infl.* **всы́плю, всы́плешь**] *v., pfv. of* **всыпа́ть.**

всыпа́ть *v.impfv.* [*pfv.* **всы́пать**] **1,** (*with* в + *acc.*) to pour into. **2,** (*with dat.*) *colloq.* to give (someone) a good licking. —**всы́пать** (+ *dat.*) **по пе́рвое число́,** *colloq.* **1,** to chew out. **2,** to rout.

всю́ду *adv.* everywhere.

вся *adj., fem. of* **весь.**

вся́кий *adj.* **1,** any. **2,** all sorts of; all kinds of. —*n.* anyone; anybody. —**во вся́ком слу́чае,** in any case; at any rate. —**на вся́кий слу́чай,** just in case.

вся́кое *n., decl. as an adj.* anything: Вся́кое мо́жет случи́ться, anything can happen.

вся́чески *adv., colloq.* in every way.

вся́ческий *adj., colloq.* of every kind; of all kinds.

вся́чина *n., colloq., in* **вся́кая вся́чина,** all sorts of things.

вта́йне *adv.* secretly; in secret.

вта́лкивать *v.impfv.* [*pfv.* **втолкну́ть**] (*with* в + *acc.*) to push in; shove in; force in.

вта́птывать *v.impfv.* [*pfv.* **втопта́ть**] (*with* в + *acc.*) trample into. —**втопта́ть в грязь,** to drag through the mud; vilify.

вта́скивать *v.impfv.* [*pfv.* **втащи́ть**] **1,** (*with* в + *acc.*) to drag in. **2,** (*with* на + *acc.*) to drag up.

втащи́ть [*infl.* **втащу́, вта́щишь**] *v., pfv. of* **вта́скивать.**

втека́ть *v.impfv.* [*pfv.* **втечь**] (*with* в + *acc.*) to flow into.

втере́ть [*infl.* **вотру́, вотрёшь;** *past* **втёр, втёрла**] *v., pfv. of* **втира́ть.** —**втере́ться,** *refl., pfv. of* **втира́ться.**

втира́ние *n.* **1,** rubbing in. **2,** liniment.

втира́ть *v.impfv.* [*pfv.* **втере́ть**] **1,** (*with* в + *acc.*) to rub in. **2,** *in* втира́ть очки́ (+ *dat.*), to pull the wool over someone's eyes. —**втира́ться,** *refl.* **1,** to be absorbed through rubbing. **2,** (*with* в + *acc.*) *colloq.* to make one's way (through); force one's way (into). **3,** *fig.* (*with* в + *acc.*) to worm one's way (into): втира́ться в дове́рие к, to worm one's way into the confidence of.

вти́скивать *v.impfv.* [*pfv.* **вти́снуть**] (*with* в + *acc.*) to squeeze (into); stuff (into); cram (into). —**вти́скиваться,** *refl.* (*with* в + *acc.*) *colloq.* **1,** to fit (into). **2,** to squeeze (into); crowd (into); jam (into).

втихомо́лку *adv., colloq.* secretly; stealthily; on the sly.

втолкну́ть *v., pfv. of* **вта́лкивать.**

втолкова́ть [*infl.* **-ку́ю, -ку́ешь**] *v., pfv. of* **втолко́вывать.**

втолко́вывать *v.impfv.* [*pfv.* **втолкова́ть**] (*with dat.*) *colloq.* to make (someone) understand; drive home the point (to).

втопта́ть [*infl.* **втопчу́, вто́пчешь**] *v., pfv. of* **вта́птывать.**

вторга́ться *v.r.impfv.* [*pfv.* **вто́ргнуться**] (*with* в + *acc.*) **1,** to invade. **2,** *fig.* to intrude (into). **3,** *fig.* to encroach (upon).

вто́ргнуться [*past* **вто́ргся** *or* **вто́ргнулся, вто́рглась**] *v.r., pfv. of* **вторга́ться.**

вторже́ние *n.* **1,** invasion. **2,** intrusion.

вто́рить *v.impfv.* (*with dat.*) **1,** *music* to sing second part (to). **2,** to echo; repeat.

вторично *adv.* a second time; for a second time.

втори́чный *adj.* **1,** second. **2,** secondary.

вто́рник *n.* Tuesday.

второго́дник *n.* pupil left back in school.

второе *n., decl. as an adj.* **1,** (*with dates*) second: Сего́дня — второе апре́ля, today is April 2nd. **2,** main course; entrée.

Второзако́ние *n.* Deuteronomy.

второ́й *ordinal numeral & adj.* second. —**из вторы́х рук,** second hand; through an intermediary. *See also* **второе.**

второкла́ссник *n.* second-grade pupil.

второку́рсник *n.* second-year student; sophomore.

второпя́х *adv.* **1,** hastily; hurriedly. **2,** in one's haste.

второразря́дный *adj.* second-rate.

второсо́ртный *adj.* second-rate.

второстепе́нный *adj.* **1,** secondary. **2,** minor.

в-тре́тьих thirdly; in the third place.

втри́дорога *adv., colloq.* triple the price; three times as much. —**плати́ть втри́дорога,** to pay through the nose.

втро́е *adv.* **1,** three times; triple: втро́е бо́льше, three times as much (*or* as big). **2,** in three: сложи́ть втро́е, to fold in three.

втроём *adv.* three together: они́ втроём, the three of them.

втройне́ *adv.* triple; three times as much.

втýлка [*gen. pl.* **-лок**] *n.* **1,** *mech.* bushing. **2,** plug; stopper.

втýне *adv., obs.* for nothing; in vain.

втыкáть *v.impfv.* [*pfv.* **воткнýть**] (*with* в + *acc.*) to drive in; drive into; stick in; stick into.

втя́гивать *v.impfv.* [*pfv.* **втянýть**] **1,** to pull into; drag into. **2,** (*with* на + *acc.*) to pull onto; drag onto. **3,** to breathe in; draw in: втянýть в себя́ вóздух, to breathe in; inhale. **4,** to pull in; draw in (one's stomach). **5,** *fig., colloq.* to draw into (a conversation, argument, war, etc.). —**втя́гиваться,** *refl., colloq.* **1,** (*of one's cheeks*) to become drawn. **2,** (*with* в + *acc.*) to be drawn into. **3,** (*with* в + *acc.*) to get used to; come to enjoy.

втянýть [*infl.* **втяну́, втя́нешь**] *v., pfv. of* **втя́гивать.** —**втянýться,** *refl., pfv. of* **втя́гиваться.**

вуáль *n.f.* veil.

вуз *n., abbr. of* **вы́сшее уче́бное заведе́ние,** institution of higher learning.

вýзовец [*gen.* **-вца**] *n.m.* [*fem.* **-вка**] *colloq.* student in a вуз.

вулка́н *n.* volcano.

вулканиза́ция *n.* vulcanization.

вулканизи́ровать *v.impfv. & pfv.* [*pres.* **-рую, -руешь**] to vulcanize.

вулкани́ческий *adj.* volcanic.

вульгаризи́ровать *v.impfv. & pfv.* [*pres.* **-рую, -руешь**] to vulgarize.

вульгари́зм *n.* vulgarism.

вульга́рный *adj.* vulgar. —**вульга́рность,** *n.f.* vulgarity.

вундерки́нд (дэ) *n.* child prodigy.

вурдала́к *n., folklore* vampire.

вход *n.* **1,** entry. **2,** admission; admittance. **3,** entrance.

входи́ть *v.impfv.* [*pfv.* **войти́;** *pres.* **вхожу́, вхóдишь**] **1,** to enter; come in; go in; walk in. **2,** (*with* в + *acc.*) to enter; come into; go into; walk into. **3,** (*with* в + *acc.*) to fit into. **4,** (*with* в + *acc.*) to be a part of; belong to; be a member of: В коми́ссию вхóдят две же́нщины, the commission includes two women. **5,** (*with* в + *acc.*) to go into; be included in (a book, report, program, etc.). —**входи́ть во вкус** (+ *gen.*), to begin to enjoy. —**входи́ть в дове́рие к,** to gain the confidence of. —**входи́ть в исто́рию,** to go down in history. —**входи́ть в привы́чку,** to become a habit. —**входи́ть в роль,** to grow into a role. —**входи́ть в дóлю/мóду/обихóд/ посло́вицу/соста́в,** *see entry under noun.*

входнóй *adj.* entrance (*attrib.*); admission (*attrib.*): входна́я пла́та, admission/entrance fee.

входя́щий *adj.* incoming.

вхожде́ние *n.* (*with* в + *acc.*) entering.

вхóжий *adj., colloq.* having entrée: Он вхож в лу́чшие дома́, he has entrée into the best homes.

вхолостýю *adv., in* **рабóтать вхолостýю,** (*of a motor*) to idle.

вцепи́ться [*infl.* **вцеплю́сь, вце́пишься**] *v.r., pfv. of* **вцепля́ться.**

вцепля́ться *v.r.impfv.* [*pfv.* **вцепи́ться**] (*with* в + *acc.*) to seize; grab hold of.

вчера́ *adv.* yesterday.

вчера́шний *adj.* yesterday's; of yesterday. —**вчера́шний день,** yesterday.

вчерне́ *adv.* in the rough: Докла́д напи́сан вчерне́, the report is written in the rough.

вче́тверо *adv.* **1,** four times; quadruple: вче́тверо бóльше, four times as much (*or* as big). **2,** in four; in quarters: слóженный вче́тверо, folded in four/ in quarters/.

вчетверóм *adv.* four together: они́ вчетверóм, the four of them.

в-четвёртых in the fourth place.

вчи́тываться *v.r.impfv.* [*pfv.* **вчита́ться**] (*with* в + *acc.*) *colloq.* **1,** to read carefully. **2,** to be thoroughly familiar with (*by reading*).

вшива́ть *v.impfv.* [*pfv.* **вшить**] (*with* в + *acc.*) to sew in; sew into.

вшивнóй *adj.* sewn in.

вши́вый *adj.* infested with lice.

вширь *adv.* **1,** in breadth. **2,** over a great distance.

вшить [*infl.* **вошью́, вошьёшь**] *v., pfv. of* **вшива́ть.**

въеда́ться *v.r.impfv.* [*pfv.* **въе́сться**] (*with* в + *acc.*) **1,** to eat into. **2,** (*of something sharp*) to sink into. **3,** *fig.* to be embedded; be etched (in one's consciousness, memory, etc.).

въе́дливый *adj., colloq.* **1,** corrosive. **2,** *fig.* (*of one's eyes, a glance, etc.*) piercing. **3,** *fig.* fussy.

въезд *n.* **1,** entry. **2,** entrance. —**въезднóй,** *adj.* entry (*attrib.*); entrance (*attrib.*).

въезжа́ть *v.impfv.* [*pfv.* **въе́хать**] **1,** (*with* в + *acc.*) to enter (*in a conveyance*); drive into. **2,** (*with* на + *acc.*) to drive onto. **3,** (*with* на + *acc.*) to drive up. **4,** (*with* в + *acc.*) to move in; move into (a house, apartment, etc.).

въе́сться [*infl. like* **есть**] *v.r., pfv. of* **въеда́ться.**

въе́хать [*infl.* **въе́ду, въе́дешь**] *v., pfv. of* **въезжа́ть.**

вы [*gen., acc. & prepl.* **вас;** *dat.* **вам;** *instr.* **ва́ми**] *pers. pron., 2nd person pl. and polite 2nd person sing.* you. —**быть с** (+ *instr.*) **на вы,** to address each other as «вы» (*as opposed to* «ты»).

вы- *prefix* **1,** *indicating motion to the outside:* вы́бежать, to run out. **2,** *indicating thoroughness of an action or process:* вы́мокнуть, to get soaked. **3,** *indicating attainment of a goal:* вы́требовать: to demand and obtain. **4,** (*with* -**ся**) *indicating indulgence to the point of complete satisfaction:* вы́спаться, to have a good sleep; вы́плакаться, have a good cry.

вы́балтывать *v.impfv.* [*pfv.* **вы́болтать**] *colloq.* to blab; let out: вы́болтать секре́т, to spill the beans; let the cat out of the bag.

выбега́ть *v.impfv.* [*pfv.* **вы́бежать**] to run out.

вы́бежать [*infl.* **вы́бегу, вы́бежишь, ...вы́бегут**] *v., pfv. of* **выбега́ть.**

вы́белить *v., pfv. of* **бели́ть** (*in sense #3*).

выбива́ть *v.impfv.* [*pfv.* **вы́бить**] **1,** to knock out. **2,** to drive out; dislodge (an enemy). **3,** to beat (a carpet). **4,** to strike (a medal); hammer out (metals). **5,** *in* выбива́ть чек, to get a receipt (*from the cashier in a store, which is then used to claim one's purchase*). —**выбива́ть из равнове́сия,** to throw off balance.

выбива́ться *v.r.impfv.* [*pfv.* **вы́биться**] **1,** *colloq.* to get out; work one's way out. **2,** to come out; appear. —**вы́биться из гра́фика** *or* **из расписа́ния,** to be behind schedule; be thrown off schedule. —**вы́биться из сил,** to be exhausted.

выбира́ть *v.impfv.* [*pfv.* **вы́брать**] **1,** to choose; select. **2,** to elect. **3,** to take out; remove (all of something). **4,** to haul in (a net); pull up (an anchor). **5,** *colloq.* to find (time, a spare moment, etc.). —**выбира́ться,** *refl.* **1,** to be chosen. **2,** (*with* из) *colloq.* to get out (of); find one's way out (of). **3,** *colloq.* to move (*change one's residence*). **4,** (*with* в + *acc.*) *colloq.* to find time to go to.

вы́бить [*infl.* **вы́бью, вы́бьешь**] *v., pfv. of* **выбива́ть.** —**вы́биться,** *refl., pfv. of* **выбива́ться.**

вы́боина *n.* **1,** dent; hole. **2,** pothole.

вы́болтать *v., pfv. of* **выба́лтывать.**

вы́бор *n.* **1,** choice. **2,** assortment. —**без вы́бора,** indiscriminately. —**на вы́бор** (*with* **предлага́ть**), one's choice; of one's choice. —**с вы́бором,** selectively. *See also* **вы́боры.**

вы́борка [*gen. pl.* **-рок**] *n.* **1,** sample; sampling: случа́йная вы́борка, random sample/sampling. **2,** *usu. pl.* excerpts; extracts. —**произво́льная вы́борка,** random access.

вы́борность *n.f.* election; electing.

вы́борный *adj.* **1,** election (*attrib.*). **2,** elective; electoral. **3,** elected. —*n.* elected representative.

вы́борочно *adv.* selectively.

вы́борочный *adj.* selective. —**вы́борочная прове́рка,** spot check.

вы́борщик *n.* elector.

вы́боры [*gen.* **-ров**] *n.pl.* elections.

вы́бранить *v.pfv., colloq.* to chew out; give (someone) the devil.

выбра́сывание *n.* throwing out; ejection.

выбра́сывать *v.impfv.* [*pfv.* **вы́бросить**] **1,** to throw out: вы́бросить чтó-нибудь в окнó *or* из окнá, to throw something out the window. **2,** to throw away; throw out; discard. **3,** to discharge (into the atmosphere). **4,** to hoist (a flag). **5,** *colloq.* to find. **6,** *colloq.* to proclaim (a slogan). —**выбра́сывать из головы́,** to put out of one's head *or* mind; dismiss from one's mind. —**выбра́сывать на бе́рег,** to wash ashore. —**выбра́сывать на ры́нок,** to dump on the market. —**выбра́сывать на у́лицу,** to put out (*or* turn out) on the street.

выбра́сываться *v.r.impfv.* [*pfv.* **вы́броситься**] to jump out. —**вы́броситься с парашю́том,** to bail out.

вы́брать [*infl.* **вы́беру, вы́берешь**] *v., pfv. of* **выбира́ть.** —**вы́браться,** *refl.* **1,** *pfv. of* **выбира́ться. 2,** *colloq.* (*of time*) to become available.

выбрива́ть *v.impfv.* [*pfv.* **вы́брить**] to shave. Гла́дко вы́бритый, clean-shaven. —**выбрива́ться,** *refl.* to shave (oneself).

вы́брить [*infl.* **вы́брею, вы́бреешь**] *v., pfv. of* **выбрива́ть.** —**вы́бриться,** *refl., pfv. of* **выбрива́ться.**

вы́брос *n.* **1,** ejection. **2,** *pl.* emissions.

вы́бросить [*infl.* **-шу, -сишь**] *v., pfv. of* **выбра́сывать.** —**вы́броситься,** *refl., pfv. of* **выбра́сываться.**

выбыва́ть *v.impfv.* [*pfv.* **вы́быть**] **1,** to leave; depart. **2,** (*with* из) to withdraw; quit; drop out (of). —**выбыва́ть из стро́я, 1,** to quit the ranks. **2,** to be put out of action.

вы́быть [*infl.* **вы́буду, вы́будешь**] *v., pfv. of* **выбыва́ть.**

выва́ливать *v.impfv.* [*pfv.* **вы́валить**] *colloq.* to throw out; dump out. —**выва́ливаться,** *refl., colloq.* to fall out.

выва́ривать *v.impfv.* [*pfv.* **вы́варить**] **1,** to remove by boiling. **2,** to overcook.

выве́дывать *v.impfv.* [*pfv.* **вы́ведать**] *colloq.* to worm (out); wangle; ferret out (a secret, information, etc.).

вы́везти [*infl.* **вы́везу, вы́везешь;** *past* **вы́вез, вы́везла**] *v., pfv. of* **вывози́ть.**

вы́верить *v., pfv. of* **выверя́ть.**

вы́верка *n., colloq.* adjustment.

вы́вернуть *v., pfv. of* **вывёртывать.** —**вы́вернуться,** *refl., pfv. of* **вывёртываться.**

вы́верт *n., colloq.* **1,** turn; twist. **2,** quirk; eccentricity; idiosyncrasy.

вывёртывать *v.impfv.* [*pfv.* **вы́вернуть**] **1,** to unscrew. **2,** to turn inside out. **3,** *colloq.* to twist; wrench. —**вывёртываться,** *refl.* **1,** *colloq.* to come unscrewed. **2,** to be turned inside out. **3,** to wriggle out; slip away.

выверя́ть *v.impfv.* [*pfv.* **вы́верить**] **1,** to adjust. **2,** to check.

вы́весить [*infl.* **-шу, -сишь**] *v., pfv. of* **выве́шивать.**

вы́веска [*gen. pl.* **-сок**] *n.* sign; signboard.

вы́вести [*infl.* **вы́веду, вы́ведешь;** *past* **вы́вел, вы́вела**] *v., pfv. of* **выводи́ть.** —**вы́вестись,** *refl., pfv. of* **выводи́ться.**

выве́тривание *n.* **1,** ventilating; ventilation. **2,** erosion; decay.

выве́тривать *v.impfv.* [*pfv.* **вы́ветрить**] **1,** to get rid of (an odor) by ventilation. **2,** to erode; wear away. —**выве́триваться,** *refl.* **1,** (*of something in the air*) to disappear; be blown away. **2,** to erode; become eroded.

выве́шивать *v.impfv.* [*pfv.* **вы́весить**] **1,** to hang out. **2,** to put up; post. **3,** to weigh.

выви́нчивать *v.impfv.* [*pfv.* **вы́винтить**] to unscrew. —**выви́нчиваться,** *refl.* to come unscrewed.

вы́вих *n., med.* dislocation.

вы́вихнуть *v.pfv., med.* to dislocate.

вы́вод *n.* **1,** conclusion. **2,** withdrawal. **3,** derivation.

выводи́ть *v.impfv.* [*pfv.* **вы́вести;** *pres.* **-вожу́, -во́дишь**] **1,** to bring out; take out; lead out. **2,** to bring out; get out (of an awkward situation, crisis, etc.). **3,** to withdraw (troops). **4,** to remove; drop (from a committee, team, etc.); eliminate (from a contest). **5,** to conclude; deduce; infer. **6,** to derive (a formula); draw (a conclusion). **7,** to grow; raise. **8,** to hatch. **9,** to construct; put up. **10,** to draw carefully; trace. **11,** to give (a grade). **12,** to remove; take out (a stain). **13,** to exterminate (insects). —**выводи́ть из равнове́сия, 1,** to throw off balance. **2,** to disconcert; rattle. —**выводи́ть из себя́,** to drive (someone) crazy. —**выводи́ть из стро́я,** to put out of operation; put out of commission. —**выводи́ть из терпе́ния,** to make (someone) lose patience. —**выводи́ть на чи́стую во́ду,** to bring out into the open. —**выводи́ть на орби́ту,** to put into orbit.

выводи́ться *v.r.impfv.* [*pfv.* **вы́вестись;** *pres.* **-вожу́сь, -во́дишься**] **1,** to disappear; become extinct. **2,** (*of a stain*) to come out. **3,** to hatch; be hatched; be born.

выводно́й *adj.* **1,** discharge (*attrib.*). **2,** *anat.* excretory.

вы́водок [*gen.* **-дка**] *n.* brood; litter.

вы́воз *n.* **1,** removal. **2,** exporting. **3,** exports.

вывози́ть *v.impfv.* [*pfv.* **вы́везти;** *pres.* **-вожу́, -во́зишь**] **1,** to take out; take away; cart out; cart away. **2,** to take; bring; deliver. **3,** to bring back (a souvenir). **4,** to export. **5,** *colloq.* to save; rescue.

вы́возка *n.* carting out; removal.

вывозно́й *adj.* export (*attrib.*).

вывола́кивать *v.impfv.* [*pfv.* **вы́волочь**] *colloq.* to drag out.

вы́волочка *n., colloq.* **1,** beating; whipping. **2,** rebuke; dressing-down.

вы́волочь [*infl.* **-локу, -лочешь, ...-локут;** *past* **вы́волок, вы́волокла**] *v., pfv. of* **вывола́кивать.**

выбора́чивать *v.impfv.* [*pfv.* **вы́воротить**] *colloq.* **1,** to pull up; uproot. **2,** to wrench; twist. **3,** to turn inside out.

вы́воротить [*infl.* **-чу, -тишь**] *v., pfv. of* **выбора́чивать.**

выга́дывать *v.impfv.* [*pfv.* **вы́гадать**] **1,** to gain. **2,** to save (time, money, etc.).

вы́гиб *n.* bend; curve.

выгиба́ть *v.impfv.* [*pfv.* **вы́гнуть**] to bend; arch. **—выгиба́ться,** *refl.* to bend; curve.

вы́гладить *v., pfv. of* **гла́дить** (*in sense #1*).

вы́глядеть *v.impfv.* [*pres.* **-жу, -дишь**] (*with an adv. or instr. case*): to look: Она́ хорошо́ вы́глядит, she looks well. Он вы́глядит здоро́вым/старико́м, he looks healthy/ like an old man/. Вы́глядеть на свой во́зраст, to look one's age.

вы́гля́дывать *v.impfv.* [*pfv.* **вы́глянуть**] **1,** to look out. **2,** to appear; come into view.

вы́гнать [*infl.* **вы́гоню, вы́гонишь**] *v., pfv. of* **выгоня́ть.**

вы́гнутый *adj.* curved; bent.

вы́гнуть *v., pfv. of* **выгиба́ть. —вы́гнуться,** *refl., pfv. of* **выгиба́ться.**

выгова́ривать *v.impfv.* [*pfv.* **вы́говорить**] **1,** to pronounce; enunciate; articulate. **2,** (*with* **себе́**) *colloq.* to win; gain; elicit; secure (for oneself). **3,** [*impfv. only*] (*with dat.*) *colloq.* to scold; berate.

вы́говор *n.* **1,** pronunciation. **2,** reprimand; rebuke.

вы́говорить *v., pfv. of* **выгова́ривать. —вы́говориться,** *refl., colloq.* to speak one's mind; sound off.

вы́года *n.* **1,** profit; gain. **2,** benefit; advantage.

вы́годно *adv.* **1,** at a profit. **2,** to advantage; favorably. **—***adj., used predicatively* **1,** profitable. **2,** advantageous: Кому́ э́то вы́годно?, whom is this good for?; who stands to gain from this?

вы́годный *adj.* **1,** profitable. **2,** favorable; advantageous.

вы́гон *n.* pasture.

выгоня́ть *v.impfv.* [*pfv.* **вы́гнать**] **1,** to drive out; chase out. **2,** to send (cattle) out to pasture. **3,** *colloq.* to expel. **4,** *in* выгоня́ть с рабо́ты, *colloq.* to fire; give (someone) the sack. **5,** to force (plants).

выгора́живать *v.impfv.* [*pfv.* **вы́городить**] **1,** to fence off. **2,** *colloq.* to shield (from blame, responsibility, etc.).

выгора́ть *v.impfv.* [*pfv.* **вы́гореть**] **1,** to burn down. **2,** to fade (*from the sun*). **3,** *colloq.* to work out; pan out.

вы́городить [*infl.* **-жу, -дишь**] *v., pfv. of* **выгора́живать.**

вы́гравировать *v., pfv. of* **гравирова́ть.**

выгреба́ть *v.impfv.* [*pfv.* **вы́грести**] **1,** *v.t.* to rake out; shovel out. **2,** *v.i.* to row: выгреба́ть к бе́регу, to row toward shore.

выгребно́й *adj. , in* **выгребна́я я́ма,** cesspool.

вы́грести [*infl.* **вы́гребу, вы́гребешь;** *past* **вы́греб, вы́гребла**] *v., pfv. of* **выгреба́ть.**

выгружа́ть *v.impfv.* [*pfv.* **вы́грузить**] to unload (cargo). **—выгружа́ться,** *refl.* to disembark.

вы́грузка *n.* unloading.

выгрыза́ть *v.impfv.* [*pfv.* **вы́грызть**] **1,** to gnaw away. **2,** to gnaw (a hole).

вы́грызть [*infl.* **вы́грызу, вы́грызешь;** *past* **вы́грыз, вы́грызла**] *v., pfv. of* **выгрыза́ть.**

выгу́ливать *v.impfv.* [*pfv.* **вы́гулять**] to walk (a dog).

выдава́ть *v.impfv.* [*pfv.* **вы́дать;** *pres.* **-даю́, -даёшь**] **1,** to give out; issue. **2,** to extradite; hand over. **3,** to give away; betray. Вы́дать себя́, to give oneself away. **4,** to produce. **5,** (*with* **за** + *acc.*) to pass (someone or something) off as; (*with* **себя́** *and* **за** + *acc.*) pose as; pass oneself off as. **—выдава́ться,** *refl.* **1,** to stick out; jut out; protrude. **2,** to stand out; be distinguished. **3,** to become available: Наконе́ц, у меня́ вы́далась свобо́дная мину́та, at last I have a free moment. **4,** to turn out to be: Вы́дался хоро́ший денёк, it turned out to be a nice day.

вы́давить [*infl.* **-влю, -вишь**] *v., pfv. of* **выда́вливать.**

выда́вливать *v.impfv.* [*pfv.* **вы́давить**] **1,** to press out; squeeze out. **2,** to break; knock out (*e.g.* a pane of glass). **3,** *fig.* to force (a smile, laugh, utterance, etc.). Вы́давить из себя́ сло́во, to manage to utter a word.

выда́лбливать *v.impfv.* [*pfv.* **вы́долбить**] to hollow out.

вы́дать [*infl. like* **дать;** *past* **вы́дал, вы́дала**] *v., pfv. of* **выдава́ть. —вы́даться,** *refl., pfv. of* **выдава́ться.**

вы́дача *n.* **1,** giving out; issuance. **2,** extradition. **—«вы́дача багажа́»,** "Baggage claim".

выдаю́щийся *adj.* outstanding; distinguished; eminent; illustrious.

выдвига́ть *v.impfv.* [*pfv.* **вы́двинуть**] **1,** to pull out; draw out; move out. **2,** to open; pull out; pull open (a drawer). **3,** to advance; put forward (an idea, hypothesis, etc.); raise (a question, objection, etc.); set; lay down (conditions); bring; level (an accusation). **4,** to nominate. **5,** to promote. **—выдвига́ться,** *refl.* **1,** to advance; move forward. **2,** to rise (in rank); work one's way up. **3,** [*impfv. only*] (*of a drawer*) to slide.

выдвиже́нец [*gen.* **-нца**] *n.m.* [*fem.* **-нка**] worker promoted to a position of responsibility.

выдвиже́ние *n.* **1,** moving forward. **2,** nomination. **3,** promotion.

выдвижно́й *adj.* sliding.

вы́двинуть *v., pfv. of* **выдвига́ть. —вы́двинуться,** *refl., pfv. of* **выдвига́ться.**

выдворя́ть *v.impfv.* [*pfv.* **вы́дворить**] **1,** to expel (from a country). **2,** *colloq.* to throw out; kick out.

вы́делать *v., pfv. of* **выде́лывать.**

выделе́ние *n.* **1,** allocation; allotment; apportionment. **2,** excretion; secretion; discharge. **3,** *pl.* (bodily) secretions.

выдели́тельный *adj.* excretory; secretory.

вы́делить *v., pfv. of* **выделя́ть**. —**вы́делиться**, *refl., pfv. of* **выделя́ться**.

вы́делка *n.* **1,** making; manufacture. **2,** currying. **3,** workmanship.

выде́лывать *v.impfv.* [*pfv.* **вы́делать**] **1,** to manufacture; make; fashion. **2,** to curry; dress (leather, hides, etc.). **3,** [*impfv. only*] *colloq.* to perform (a dance, stunt, etc.). **4,** [*impfv. only*] *colloq.* to do: Что он там выде́лывает?, what is he up to?

выделя́ть *v.impfv.* [*pfv.* **вы́делить**] **1,** to single out. **2,** to set apart. **3,** to allot; allocate; apportion; earmark. **4,** (*in writing or printing*) to set off (with commas, in italics, etc.). **5,** to give off; discharge; excrete; secrete. —**выделя́ться**, *refl.* **1,** to stand out. **2,** to ooze; exude. **3,** to take one's inheritance and separate from the family.

выдёргивать *v.impfv.* [*pfv.* **вы́дернуть**] to pull out.

вы́держанность *n.f.* **1,** consistency. **2,** steadfastness. **3,** self-control.

вы́держанный *adj.* **1,** consistent. **2,** steadfast. **3,** (*of a style of writing*) restrained; subdued. **4,** self-controlled; self-possessed. **5,** (*of wine, cheese, etc.*) aged; mellowed.

вы́держать [*infl.* **вы́держу, вы́держишь**] *v., pfv. of* **выде́рживать**.

выде́рживать *v.impfv.* [*pfv.* **вы́держать**] **1,** to bear; support. **2,** to endure; withstand; survive. **3,** *v.i.* to hold out; last. **4,** *v.i.* (*usu. neg.*) to be (un)able to control oneself (*or* contain oneself). Он не вы́держал, he couldn't stand it any longer. Она́ не вы́держала и запла́кала, she broke down and cried. **5,** to maintain; keep up; stay within. **6,** to pass (an examination). **7,** to phrase (*in a certain way*): заявле́ние вы́держано в споко́йных тона́х, the statement is phrased in mild tones. **8,** (*of a book*) to go through (a certain number of editions). **9,** to age (wine, cheese, etc.). —**выде́рживать роль**, to keep playing a role. —**выде́рживать хара́ктер**, to stand firm. —**не выде́рживать кри́тики**, not stand up (to criticism); not hold water.

вы́держка *n.* **1,** composure; self-control. **2,** fortitude. **3,** extract; excerpt. **4,** *photog.* exposure. —**на вы́держку**, picked at random.

вы́дернуть *v., pfv. of* **выдёргивать**.

выдира́ть *v.impfv.* [*pfv.* **вы́драть**] *colloq.* to tear out.

вы́долбить [*infl.* **-блю, -бишь**] *v., pfv. of* **выда́лбливать**.

вы́дох *n.* an outward breath; exhalation.

вы́дохнуть [*past* **-нул, -нула**] *v., pfv. of* **выдыха́ть**. —**вы́дохнуться**, *refl.* [*past* **-дохся, -дохлась**] *pfv. of* **выдыха́ться**.

вы́дра *n.* otter.

вы́драть [*infl.* **вы́деру, вы́дерешь**] *v., pfv. of* **драть** (*in sense #3*) *and* **выдира́ть**.

вы́дрессировать *v., pfv. of* **дрессирова́ть**.

вы́дубить *v., pfv. of* **дуби́ть**.

выдува́ть *v.impfv.* [*pfv.* **вы́дуть**] to blow out.

вы́думанный *adj.* fictitious; made-up.

вы́думать *v., pfv. of* **выду́мывать**.

вы́думка [*gen. pl.* **-мок**] *n.* **1,** *colloq.* inventiveness; imagination. **2,** invention. **3,** falsehood; fabrication.

вы́думщик *n., colloq.* **1,** one who thinks up something. **2,** one who makes things up.

выду́мывать *v.impfv.* [*pfv.* **вы́думать**] **1,** to think up; invent. **2,** to make up; concoct.

вы́дуть [*infl.* **вы́дую, вы́дуешь**] *v., pfv. of* **выдува́ть**.

выдыха́ние *n.* exhalation.

выдыха́ть *v.impfv.* [*pfv.* **вы́дохнуть**] to exhale; breathe out. —**выдыха́ться**, *refl.* **1,** to lose its fragrance/taste/ zest. **2,** *fig., colloq.* to become exhausted. **3,** *fig., colloq.* to fizzle; bog down; peter out.

выеда́ть *v.impfv.* [*pfv.* **вы́есть**] to eat away; corrode. —**вы́еденного яйца́ не сто́ит**, not worth a hill of beans.

вы́езд *n.* **1,** departure. **2,** exit; road leading out. **3,** horse and carriage. —**на вы́езде**, *sports* on the road.

вы́ездить [*infl.* **вы́езжу, вы́ездишь**] *v., pfv. of* **выезжа́ть** (*in sense #4*).

выездно́й *adj.* **1,** exit (*attrib.*). **2,** (*of a horse*) for riding.

выезжа́ть *v.impfv.* [*pfv.* **вы́ехать**] **1,** to drive out; depart; leave (*by conveyance*). **2,** to move out. **3,** (*with* на + *prepl.*) *colloq.* to exploit; make capital of. **4,** [*pfv.* **вы́ездить**] to break in (a horse).

вы́емка *n.* **1,** taking out; removing. **2,** [*gen. pl.* **-мок**] hollow; depression. —**вы́емка пи́сем**, collection (*of mail*).

вы́есть [*infl. like* **есть**] *v., pfv. of* **выеда́ть**.

вы́ехать [*infl.* **вы́еду, вы́едешь**] *v., pfv. of* **выезжа́ть**.

вы́жать [*infl.* **вы́жму, вы́жмешь**] *v., pfv. of* **выжима́ть**.

вы́ждать [*infl.* **вы́жду, вы́ждешь**] *v., pfv. of* **выжида́ть**.

вы́жечь [*infl.* **вы́жгу, вы́жжешь, ...вы́жгут**; *past* **вы́жег, вы́жгла**] *v., pfv. of* **выжига́ть**.

вы́жженный *past passive part. of* **вы́жечь**. —**страте́гия вы́жженной земли́**, scorched-earth policy.

выжива́ние *n.* survival. —**выжива́ние наибо́лее приспосо́бленных**, survival of the fittest.

выжива́ть *v.impfv.* [*pfv.* **вы́жить**] **1,** *v.i.* to survive; live; pull through. **2,** *v.t., colloq.* to drive out (by making life impossible). —**вы́жить из ума́**, to lose possession of one's faculties.

выжига́ние *n.* **1,** burning out. **2,** pyrography. **3,** cauterization.

выжига́ть *v.impfv.* [*pfv.* **вы́жечь**] **1,** to burn down; burn out. **2,** to burn in; trace by burning. **3,** to cauterize.

выжида́ние *n.* **1,** waiting. **2,** expectancy: с выжида́нием, expectantly.

выжида́тельный *adj.* waiting; temporizing. Выжида́тельная пози́ция, wait-and-see attitude.

выжида́ть *v.impfv.* [*pfv.* **вы́ждать**] **1,** to wait for (the right moment): выжида́ть удо́бный слу́чай, to wait for an opportunity. **2,** to wait out; wait till the end of. **3,** *v.i.* to bide one's time; sit tight.

выжима́ть *v.impfv.* [*pfv.* **вы́жать**] **1,** to squeeze out. **2,** to wring out. —**мо́крый, хоть вы́жми** (*or* вы́жима́й), wringing/dripping/soaking/sopping wet.

вы́жить [*infl.* **вы́живу, вы́живешь**] *v., pfv. of* **выжива́ть**.

вы́звать [*infl.* вы́зову, вы́зовешь] *v., pfv. of* вызыва́ть. —**вы́зваться,** *refl., pfv. of* вызыва́ться.

вызволя́ть *v.impfv.* [*pfv.* вы́зволить] *colloq.* to help out (of trouble); get out (of a place).

выздора́вливать *v.impfv.* [*pfv.* вы́здороветь] to get well; recover; recuperate.

вы́здороветь [*infl.* -вею, -веешь] *v., pfv. of* выздора́вливать.

выздоровле́ние *n.* recovery.

вы́зов *n.* **1,** call: вы́зов по телефо́ну, telephone call. **2,** summons. **3,** challenge. **4,** invitation; affidavit (*from someone abroad to a person wishing to emigrate*). —**бро́сить вы́зов** (+ *dat.*), to challenge; defy.

вы́золотить *v., pfv. of* золоти́ть.

вы́золоченный *adj.* gilded; gilt.

вызрева́ть *v.impfv.* [*pfv.* вы́зреть] to ripen.

вызу́бривать *v.impfv.* [*pfv* вы́зубрить] **1,** to notch; make notches in. **2,** *colloq.* to learn by rote.

вызыва́ть *v.impfv.* [*pfv.* вы́звать] **1,** to call. **2,** to summon. **3,** to challenge. **4,** to cause. **5,** to arouse; evoke (an emotion). **6,** *in* вызыва́ть к жи́зни, to give rise to. —**вызыва́ться,** *refl.* to volunteer.

вызыва́ющий *adj.* defiant; provocative.

выи́грывать *v.impfv.* [*pfv.* вы́играть] **1,** to win. **2,** (*with* у) to defeat; beat. **3,** to gain.

вы́игрыш *n.* **1,** winnings. **2,** win; winning: игра́ть на вы́игрыш, to play to win; play for a win. **3,** gain; advantage. —**быть в вы́игрыше,** to be winning; be ahead of the game.

вы́игрышный *adj.* **1,** winning. **2,** advantageous.

вы́искать [*infl.* вы́ищу, вы́ищешь] *v., pfv. of* выи́скивать. —**вы́искаться,** *refl., pfv. of* выи́скиваться.

выи́скивать *v.impfv.* [*pfv.* вы́искать] *colloq.* **1,** to find; locate; turn up. **2,** [*impfv. only*] to try to find; look for; seek. —**выи́скиваться,** *refl., colloq.* to turn up; appear.

вы́йти [*infl.* вы́йду, вы́йдешь; *past* вы́шел, вы́шла, вы́шло, вы́шли] *v., pfv. of* выходи́ть.

вы́казать [*infl.* вы́кажу, вы́кажешь] *v., pfv. of* выка́зывать.

выка́зывать *v.impfv.* [*pfv.* вы́казать] *colloq.* to show; display; evince.

выка́лывать *v.impfv.* [*pfv.* вы́колоть] to put out; gouge out (someone's eye). —**темно́, хоть глаз вы́коли,** so dark you can't see your hand in front of your face.

выка́пывать *v.impfv.* [*pfv.* вы́копать] **1,** to dig (a hole, well, etc.). **2,** to dig up; dig out. **3,** to exhume; disinter. **4,** *fig.* to unearth.

выкара́бкиваться *v.r.impfv.* [*pfv.* вы́карабкаться] *colloq.* **1,** (*with* из *if noun follows*) to scramble out (of); extricate oneself (from). **2,** *fig.* (*with* из) to work one's way out of. **3,** (*of someone who is or was seriously ill*) to pull through.

выка́рмливать *v.impfv.* [*pfv.* вы́кормить] to bring up; rear.

вы́катать *v., pfv. of* ката́ть (*in sense #4*).

вы́катить [*infl.* -чу, -тишь] *v., pfv. of* выка́тывать. —**вы́катиться,** *refl., pfv. of* выка́тываться.

выка́тывать *v.impfv.* [*pfv.* вы́катить] to roll out; wheel out. —**выка́тываться,** *refl.* to roll out.

выка́чивать *v.impfv.* [*pfv.* вы́качать] to pump; pump out.

выка́шивать *v.impfv.* [*pfv.* вы́косить] **1,** to clear of grass. **2,** *fig.* to cut down; mow down (*i.e.* kill).

выка́шливать *v.impfv.* [*pfv.* вы́кашлять] *colloq.* to cough up. —**выка́шливаться,** *refl., colloq.* to clear one's throat.

выки́дывать *v.impfv.* [*pfv.* вы́кинуть] **1,** to throw out. **2,** to delete. **3,** to raise; hoist (a flag). **4,** *colloq.* to do; perform (a funny thing, a trick, etc.).

вы́кидыш *n.* **1,** miscarriage. **2,** abortion. **3,** stillborn fetus.

вы́кинуть *v.pfv.* **1,** *pfv. of* выки́дывать. **2,** *colloq.* to have a miscarriage.

выкипа́ть *v.impfv.* [*pfv.* вы́кипеть] to boil away.

вы́кладка [*gen. pl.* -док] *n.* **1,** *colloq.* laying out; spreading out. **2,** *usu. pl.* calculations. **3,** *mil.* kit: с по́лной вы́кладкой, with full kit.

выкла́дывать *v.impfv.* [*pfv.* вы́ложить] **1,** to lay out; spread out. **2,** *fig., colloq.* to tell; reveal; lay bare. **3,** (*with instr.*) to face (with); line (with); pave (with). —**выкла́дываться,** *refl., colloq.* to go all out. Он осо́бенно не выкла́дывался, he did not try especially hard.

вы́клевать [*infl.* вы́клюю, вы́клюешь] *v., pfv. of* выклёвывать.

выклёвывать *v.impfv.* [*pfv.* вы́клевать] to peck out.

выклика́ть *v.impfv.* [*pfv.* вы́кликнуть] to call out by name.

выключа́тель *n.m.* switch (*for turning something on or off*).

выключа́ть *v.impfv.* [*pfv.* вы́ключить] **1,** to turn off; switch off; shut off (a device); turn out (the light). **2,** (*with* из) to remove (from).

выкля́нчивать *v.impfv.* [*pfv.* вы́клянчить] *colloq.* to coax out of.

вы́ковать [*infl.* вы́кую, вы́куешь] *v., pfv. of* выко́вывать.

выко́вывать *v.impfv.* [*pfv.* вы́ковать] to forge.

выкола́чивать *v.impfv.* [*pfv.* вы́колотить] **1,** to knock out; beat out; hammer out. **2,** to beat (*in order to clean*). **3,** *colloq.* to extort; wring out.

вы́колоть [*infl.* вы́колю, вы́колешь] *v., pfv. of* выка́лывать.

вы́копать *v., pfv. of* копа́ть *and* выка́пывать.

вы́кормить [*infl.* -млю, -мишь] *v., pfv. of* выка́рмливать.

вы́корчевать [*infl.* -чую, -чуешь] *v., pfv. of* выкорчёвывать.

выкорчёвывать *v.impfv.* [*pfv.* вы́корчевать] **1,** to uproot. **2,** to root out; eradicate.

вы́косить [*infl.* -шу, -сишь] *v., pfv. of* выка́шивать.

выкра́дывать *v.impfv.* [*pfv.* вы́красть] to steal.

выкра́ивать *v.impfv.* [*pfv.* вы́кроить] **1,** to cut out the material for: вы́кроить пла́тье, to cut out (the material for) a dress. **2,** *fig., colloq.* to scrape up (money); find (time).

вы́красить [*infl.* -шу, -сишь] *v., pfv. of* выкра́шивать.

вы́красть [*infl.* вы́краду, вы́крадешь; *past* вы́крал, вы́крала] *v., pfv. of* выкра́дывать.

выкра́шивать *v.impfv.* [*pfv.* **вы́красить**] to paint; dye.

вы́крик *n.* shout; cry; yell.

выкри́кивать *v.impfv.* [*pfv.* **вы́крикнуть**] **1**, *v.i.* to cry out; shout; yell. **2**, *v.t.* to shout (an order, slogan, etc.).

вы́кроить *v., pfv. of* **выкра́ивать**.

вы́кройка [*gen. pl.* **-кроек**] *n.* pattern (*for sewing*).

выкрута́сы [*gen.* **-та́с**] *n.pl., colloq.* **1**, twists and turns (*of the body*). **2**, *fig.* flourishes.

вы́крутить [*infl.* **-чу, -тишь**] *v., pfv. of* **выкру́чивать**. —**вы́крутиться**, *refl., pfv. of* **выкру́чиваться**.

выкру́чивать *v.impfv.* [*pfv.* **вы́крутить**] *colloq.* **1**, to unscrew. **2**, to twist: выкрутить кому́-нибудь ру́ку, to twist someone's arm. —**выкру́чиваться**, *refl., colloq.* **1**, to come unscrewed. **2**, (*with* из) to work one's way out (of); wiggle out (of a situation). **3**, to manage; muddle through.

вы́куп *n.* **1**, redeeming; redemption. **2**, ransom.

вы́купать *v., pfv. of* **купа́ть**. —**вы́купаться**, *refl., pfv. of* **купа́ться**.

выкупа́ть *v.impfv.* [*pfv.* **вы́купить**] **1**, to redeem. **2**, to ransom. **3**, *colloq.* to buy; acquire. Вы́купить у кого́-нибудь его́ до́лю, to buy out someone.

выку́ривать *v.impfv.* [*pfv.* **вы́курить**] **1**, to finish smoking; smoke completely. **2**, to smoke out; flush out.

выла́вливать *v.impfv.* [*pfv.* **вы́ловить**] to fish out.

вы́лазка [*gen. pl.* **-зок**] *n.* **1**, *mil.* sortie; sally. **2**, *colloq.* excursion; outing.

выла́кать *v., pfv. of* **лака́ть**.

выла́мывать *v.impfv.* [*pfv.* **вы́ломать**] to break open; break down (a door).

вы́лежать *v.pfv.* [*infl.* **вы́лежу, вы́лежишь**] *colloq.* (*of a sick person*) to remain in bed (for a certain length of time). —**вы́лежаться**, *refl.* **1**, *colloq.* to have a complete rest. **2**, to ripen; mature.

вылеза́ть *v.impfv.* [*pfv.* **вы́лезть** *or* **вы́лезти**] **1**, to climb out; crawl out; get out. **2**, (*of hair*) to fall out.

вы́лезть *also,* **вы́лезти** [*infl. like* **лезть**] *v., pfv. of* **вылеза́ть**.

вы́лепить *v., pfv. of* **лепи́ть** (*in sense* #1).

вы́лет *n.* **1**, flight. **2**, takeoff. **3**, *mil.* mission.

вылета́ть *v.impfv.* [*pfv.* **вы́лететь**] **1**, to fly out. **2**, to leave; depart (*by plane*). **3**, (*of a plane*) to leave; take off. **4**, *fig.* to dash out; rush out. **5**, *colloq.* to be fired (from a job); be eliminated (from a tournament). —**вы́лететь из головы́**, to slip one's mind; go right out of one's mind.

вы́лететь [*infl.* **-чу, -тишь**] *v., pfv. of* **вылета́ть**.

выле́чивать *v.impfv.* [*pfv.* **вы́лечить**] (*with* от) to cure (of). —**выле́чиваться**, *refl.* (*with* от) to be cured (of).

вылива́ть *v.impfv.* [*pfv.* **вы́лить**] **1**, to pour out. **2**, *fig.* to vent (feelings). **3**, to cast; mold. —**вылива́ться, 1**, to run out; flow out. **2**, *fig.* (*with* в + *acc.*) to take the form of; develop into; end up being.

вы́лизать [*infl.* **вы́лижу, вы́лижешь**] *v., pfv. of* **вы́ли́зывать**.

вы́ли́зывать *v.impfv.* [*pfv.* **вы́лизать**] to lick clean.

вы́линять *v., pfv. of* **линя́ть** (*in sense* #2).

вы́литый *adj., colloq., in* **вы́литый оте́ц** *and* **вы́литая мать**, the very image of one's father *or* mother.

вы́лить [*infl.* **вы́лью, вы́льешь**] *v., pfv. of* **вылива́ть**. —**вы́литься**, *refl., pfv. of* **вылива́ться**.

вы́ловить [*infl.* **-влю, -вишь**] *v., pfv. of* **выла́вливать**.

вы́ложить *v., pfv. of* **выкла́дывать**. —**вы́ложиться**, *refl., pfv. of* **выкла́дываться**.

вы́ломать *v., pfv. of* **выла́мывать**.

вы́лощить *v.pfv.* to polish.

вылупля́ться *v.r.impfv.* [*pfv.* **вы́лупиться**] to hatch.

вы́мазать [*infl.* **вы́мажу, вы́мажешь**] *v., pfv. of* **ма́зать** (*in senses* #2 *and* #4) *and* **выма́зывать**. —**вы́мазаться**, *refl., pfv. of* **ма́заться** (*in sense* #2).

выма́зывать *v.impfv.* [*pfv.* **вы́мазать**] **1**, (*with instr.*) to coat (with); cover (with). **2**, *colloq.* to get dirty.

выма́ливать *v.impfv.* [*pfv.* **вы́молить**] **1**, [*impfv. only*] to beg for; plead for. **2**, to get by begging or pleading.

выма́нивать *v.impfv.* [*pfv.* **вы́манить**] *colloq.* **1**, (*with* из) to lure out of. **2**, (*with* у) to coax out of. **3**, (*with* у) to cheat out of.

вы́марать *v., pfv. of* **мара́ть** (*in sense* #3) *and* **выма́рывать**.

выма́рывать *v.impfv.* [*pfv.* **вы́марать**] *colloq.* **1**, to soil; dirty. **2**, to cross out.

выма́тывать *v.impfv.* [*pfv.* **вы́мотать**] *colloq.* to exhaust; drain; use up.

выма́хивать *v.impfv.* [*pfv.* **вы́махать**] *colloq.* to grow very rapidly; shoot up.

выма́чивать *v.impfv.* [*pfv.* **вы́мочить**] **1**, (*of rain*) to soak; drench. **2**, to soak; steep.

выма́щивать *v.impfv.* [*pfv.* **вы́мостить**] to pave.

выме́нивать *v.impfv.* [*pfv.* **вы́менять**] to exchange; swap.

вы́мереть [*infl.* **вы́мрет**; *past* **вы́мер, вы́мерла**] *v., pfv. of* **вымира́ть**.

вымерза́ть *v.impfv.* [*pfv.* **вы́мерзнуть**] **1**, to freeze; be destroyed by frost. **2**, to freeze solid.

вы́мерзнуть [*past* **вы́мерз, вы́мерзла**] *v., pfv. of* **вымерза́ть**.

вы́мерить *v., pfv. of* **вымеря́ть** *and* **выме́ривать**.

вы́мерший *adj.* extinct.

вымеря́ть *v.impfv.* [*pfv.* **вы́мерить**] to measure. *Also,* **выме́ривать**.

вы́мести [*infl.* **вы́мету, вы́метешь**; *past* **вы́мел, вы́мела**] *v., pfv. of* **вымета́ть**.

вы́местить [*infl.* **-щу, -стишь**] *v., pfv. of* **вымеща́ть**.

вы́метать *v.pfv.* **1**, [*infl.* **-мечу, -мечешь**], *in* вы́метать икру́, to spawn. **2**, [*infl.* **-таю, -таешь**] *pfv. of* **вымётывать**.

вымета́ть *v.impfv.* [*pfv.* **вы́мести**] **1**, to sweep up; sweep out (refuse). **2**, to sweep (a surface).

вымётывать *v.impfv.* [*pfv.* **вы́метать**] to make (buttonholes).

вымеща́ть *v.impfv.* [*pfv.* **вы́местить**] **1**, (*with dat. and* за + *acc.*) to get even with (someone for something). **2**, to vent (one's feelings): вымеща́ть свою́ доса́ду на ко́м-нибудь, to take out one's annoyance on someone.

вымира́ние *n.* extinction.

вымира́ть *v.impfv.* [*pfv.* **вы́мереть**] **1**, to die out; become extinct. **2**, to become depopulated; become desolate.

вымога́тель *n.m.* extortionist. —**вымога́тельство**, *n.* extortion.

вымога́ть *v.impfv.* to extort.

вы́мокнуть *v.pfv.* [*past* вы́мок, вы́мокла] to get drenched; get soaked.

вы́молвить *v.pfv.* [*infl.* -влю, -вишь] *colloq.* to utter.

вы́молить *v., pfv. of* выма́ливать.

вымора́живать *v.impfv.* [*pfv.* вы́морозить] **1,** to air out. **2,** to kill by freezing.

вы́морить *v., pfv. of* мори́ть (*in sense #1*).

вы́морозить [*infl.* -жу, -зишь] *v., pfv. of* вымора́живать.

вы́мостить [*infl.* -щу, -стишь] *v., pfv. of* мости́ть *and* выма́щивать.

вы́мотать *v., pfv. of* выма́тывать.

вы́мочить *v., pfv. of* выма́чивать.

вы́мпел *n.* pennant.

вы́мученный *adj., colloq.* labored; forced; unnatural.

выму́чивать *v.impfv.* [*pfv.* вы́мучить] **1,** *obs.* to force; wrest; wring. **2,** *colloq.* to produce only with great effort.

вы́муштровать *v., pfv. of* муштрова́ть.

вымыва́ть *v.impfv.* [*pfv.* вы́мыть] to wash. —**вымыва́ться,** *refl.* to wash oneself; get washed.

вы́мысел [*gen.* -сла] *n.* **1,** fantasy. **2,** untruth; falsehood; fabrication; fiction.

вы́мыть [*infl.* вы́мою, вы́моешь] *v., pfv. of* мыть *and* вымыва́ть. —**вы́мыться,** *refl., pfv. of* мы́ться *and* вымыва́ться.

вы́мышленный *adj.* fictitious; imaginary.

вы́мя [*gen., dat. & prepl.* вы́мени; *instr.* вы́менем; *pl.* вымена́, вымён, вымена́м] *n.neut.* udder.

вына́шивать *v.impfv.* [*pfv.* вы́носить] **1,** to carry; be pregnant with. **2,** to nurture (an idea); hatch (plans). **3,** *colloq.* to wear out.

вынесе́ние *n.* handing down (*of a verdict, sentence, etc.*).

вы́нести [*infl.* вы́несу, вы́несешь; *past* вы́нес, вы́несла] *v., pfv. of* выноси́ть. —**вы́нестись,** *refl., pfv. of* выноси́ться.

вынима́ть *v.impfv.* [*pfv.* вы́нуть] to take out. —**вынь да поло́жь,** *colloq.* here and now; on the spot.

вы́нос *n.* **1,** carrying out. На вы́нос, (*of food*) to take out; "to go". **2,** funeral procession. —**вы́нос зна́мени,** trooping of the colors.

вы́носить [*infl.* вы́ношу, вы́носишь] *v., pfv. of* вына́шивать.

выноси́ть *v.impfv.* [*pfv.* вы́нести; *pres.* выношу́, выно́сишь] **1,** to carry out; take out; bring out. **2,** to carry away; carry off. **3,** to get; come away with. **4,** to pass; render; issue; pronounce; hand down (a decision, sentence, verdict, resolution, reprimand, etc.). **5,** (*with* на + *acc.*) to submit (for a discussion, vote, etc.). **6,** to stand; bear; endure: Я его́ не выношу́, I can't stand him; я не выношу́ жару́, I can't stand the heat. **7,** *in* выноси́ть на бе́рег, to wash ashore. **8,** *in* выноси́ть благода́рность (+ *dat.*), to thank; extend one's thanks to. **9,** *in* выноси́ть зна́мя, to troop the colors. —**выноси́ться,** *refl.* to dash out; dart out.

выно́сливый *adj.* sturdy; hardy; possessing great powers of endurance. —**выно́сливость,** *n.f.* endurance; staying power.

вы́нудить [*infl.* -жу, -дишь] *v., pfv. of* вынужда́ть.

вынужда́ть *v.impfv.* [*pfv.* вы́нудить] **1,** to force; compel. **2,** to extract (a promise, confession, etc.).

вы́нужденный *adj.* forced: вы́нужденная поса́дка, forced landing; emergency landing.

вы́нуть *v., pfv. of* вынима́ть.

вы́нырнуть *v.pfv.* **1,** to come to the surface. **2,** *fig., colloq.* to emerge.

выню́хивать *v.impfv.* [*pfv.* вы́нюхать] *colloq.* to sniff out; ferret out; uncover.

выня́нчивать *v.impfv.* [*pfv.* вы́нянчить] to bring up; raise; nurse.

вы́пад *n.* **1,** *sports* lunge; thrust. **2,** (verbal) attack.

выпада́ть *v.impfv.* [*pfv.* вы́пасть] **1,** to fall out. **2,** (*of rain, snow, etc.*) to fall. **3,** (*with dat.*) to fall to; befall. Выпада́ть на до́лю (+ *dat.*), to fall to someone's lot. **4,** to turn out to be: День вы́пал хоро́ший, it turned out to be a nice day.

выпаде́ние *n.* **1,** falling out (*of hair, teeth, etc.*). **2,** falling (*of rain, snow, etc.*). **3,** *med.* prolapse.

выпа́ливать *v.impfv.* [*pfv.* вы́палить] *colloq.* **1,** to fire; shoot. **2,** *fig.* to blurt out.

вы́палить *v., pfv. of* пали́ть (*in sense #4*) *and* выпа́ливать.

выпа́ривать *v.impfv.* [*pfv.* вы́парить] to steam; steam-clean.

выпа́рывать *v.impfv.* [*pfv.* вы́пороть] to rip out.

вы́пасть [*infl.* вы́паду, вы́падешь; *past* вы́пал, вы́пала] *v., pfv. of* выпада́ть.

вы́пачкать *v.pfv., colloq.* to soil; get (something) dirty. —**вы́пачкаться,** *refl., colloq.* to get (oneself) dirty.

выпека́ть *v.impfv.* [*pfv.* вы́печь] to bake.

вы́переть [*infl.* вы́пру, вы́прешь; *past* вы́пер, вы́перла] *v., pfv. of* выпира́ть.

вы́пестовать *v., pfv. of* пе́стовать.

вы́печка *n.* **1,** baking. **2,** batch (*of baked goods*).

вы́печь [*infl.* вы́пеку, вы́печешь, …вы́пекут; *past* вы́пек, вы́пекла] *v., pfv. of* выпека́ть.

выпива́ть *v.impfv., colloq.* to drink; like to drink; drink a lot.

вы́пивка *n., colloq.* **1,** drinking spree; binge. **2,** drinks.

выпи́ливать *v.impfv.* [*pfv.* вы́пилить] to cut; cut out (*with a saw*).

выпира́ть *v.impfv.* [*pfv.* вы́переть] *colloq.* **1,** *v.t.* to push out; shove out; force out. **2,** *v.i.* [*impfv. only*] to stick out; jut out; protrude.

вы́писать [*infl.* вы́пишу, вы́пишешь] *v., pfv. of* выпи́сывать. —**вы́писаться,** *refl., pfv. of* выпи́сываться.

вы́писка *n.* **1,** writing out; copying out. **2,** (*with gen.*) subscription (to). **3,** discharge; release. **4,** [*gen. pl.* -сок] excerpt.

выпи́сывать *v.impfv.* [*pfv.* вы́писать] **1,** to write out; make out (a bill, receipt, etc.). **2,** to copy out. **3,** to write *or* draw carefully. **4,** to order (*by mail*). **5,** to subscribe to. **6,** to send for (*in writing*); summon; call home. **7,** to discharge. —**выпи́сываться,** *refl.* (*with* из) **1,** to check out (of a hotel). **2,** to be discharged (from a hospital).

вы́пить [*infl.* вы́пью, вы́пьешь] *v., pfv. of* пить.

выпи́хивать *v.impfv.* [*pfv.* вы́пихнуть] *colloq.* to push out; shove out.

вы́плавить [*infl.* -влю, -вишь] *v., pfv. of* выплавля́ть.

вы́плавка *n.* 1, smelting. 2, smelted metal; output of smelted metal.

выплавля́ть *v.impfv.* [*pfv.* вы́плавить] to smelt.

вы́плакать *v.pfv.* [*infl.* вы́плачу, вы́плачешь] 1, to cry out; alleviate (sorrow, disappointment, etc.) by crying. 2, *colloq.* to obtain by crying. 3, *in* вы́плакать все глаза́, to cry one's eyes out. —вы́плакаться, *refl.* to have a good cry.

вы́плата *n.* payment.

вы́платить [*infl.* -чу, -тишь] *v., pfv. of* выпла́чивать.

выпла́чивать *v.impfv.* [*pfv.* вы́платить] 1, to pay out; disburse. 2, to pay; pay off; pay in full.

выплёвывать *v.impfv.* [*pfv.* вы́плюнуть] to spit out.

выплёскивать *v.impfv.* [*pfv.* вы́плеснуть] to splash out. —выплёскиваться, *refl.* 1, (*of water*) to splash out. 2, (*of a fish*) to jump out. 3, *in* вы́плеснуться на пове́рхность, to come to the surface.

выплыва́ть *v.impfv.* [*pfv.* вы́плыть] 1, to swim out. 2, to sail out. 3, to come to the surface. 4, *fig.* to emerge; come up; come to light.

вы́плыть [*infl.* вы́плыву, вы́плывешь] *v., pfv. of* вы́плыва́ть.

вы́плюнуть *v., pfv. of* выплёвывать.

выпола́скивать *v.impfv.* [*pfv.* вы́полоскать] to rinse; rinse out.

выполза́ть *v.impfv.* [*pfv.* вы́ползти] to crawl out; creep out.

вы́ползти [*infl.* вы́ползу, вы́ползешь; *past* вы́полз, вы́ползла] *v., pfv. of* выполза́ть.

выполне́ние *n.* 1, fulfillment; execution. 2, discharge; performance (*of one's duties*).

выполни́мый *adj.* feasible.

выполня́ть *v.impfv.* [*pfv.* вы́полнить] 1, to fulfill; carry out; execute. 2, discharge; perform (one's duties). 3, to fill (an order).

вы́полоскать [*infl.* -лощу, -лощешь] *v., pfv. of* полоска́ть *and* выпола́скивать.

вы́полоть [*infl.* вы́полю, вы́полешь] *v., pfv. of* поло́ть.

вы́пороть [*infl.* вы́порю, вы́порешь] *v., pfv. of* поро́ть (*in sense #1*) *and* выпа́рывать.

вы́порхнуть *v.pfv.* 1, to fly out; flit out. 2, *colloq.* to dash out; dart out.

вы́потрошить *v., pfv. of* потроши́ть.

вы́править [*infl.* -влю, -вишь] *v., pfv. of* выправля́ть. —вы́правиться, *refl., pfv. of* выправля́ться.

вы́правка *n.* bearing; carriage.

выправля́ть *v.impfv.* [*pfv.* вы́править] 1, to straighten; straighten out. 2, *fig.* to straighten out (matters, a situation etc.). 3, to correct; make corrections in (a manuscript, proofs, etc.). —выправля́ться, *refl.* to get straightened out; straighten oneself out.

выпра́стывать *v.impfv.* [*pfv.* вы́простать] *colloq.* 1, to extricate (a part of one's body). 2, to empty.

выпра́шивать *v.impfv.* [*pfv.* вы́просить] 1, to obtain by persistent asking; coax out of; wheedle. 2, [*impfv. only*] to try hard to get; keep asking for.

выпрова́живать *v.impfv.* [*pfv.* вы́проводить] *colloq.* to send on one's way; send packing.

вы́просить [*infl.* -шу, -сишь] *v., pfv. of* выпра́шивать.

вы́простать *v., pfv. of* выпра́стывать.

выпры́гивать *v.impfv.* [*pfv.* вы́прыгнуть] 1, to jump out; leap out. 2, to jump off (a moving bus, streetcar, etc.).

выпряга́ть *v.impfv.* [*pfv.* вы́прячь] to unharness.

выпрямля́ть *v.impfv.* [*pfv.* вы́прямить] to straighten. —выпрямля́ться, *refl.* to stand erect; straighten up.

вы́прячь [*infl.* вы́прягу, вы́пряжешь, ...вы́прягут; *past* вы́пряг, вы́прягла] *v., pfv. of* выпряга́ть.

вы́пуклость *n.f.* 1, convexity. 2, bulge; protuberance.

вы́пуклый *adj.* 1, convex. 2, prominent; bulging. 3, embossed; raised. 4, *fig.* vivid; distinct.

вы́пуск *n.* 1, issue; issuance. 2, output. 3, an issue; number; installment; edition. 4, graduates; graduating class.

выпуска́ть *v.impfv.* [*pfv.* вы́пустить] 1, to let out. 2, to release; set free. 3, to produce; turn out. 4, to publish; put out. 5, to issue (stamps, money, etc.). 6, to graduate; turn out. 7, to delete. 8, to put out; let stick out. 9, to let out (clothing). 10, to fire (a bullet, shell, etc.). —выпуска́ть в свет, to bring out; publish. — выпуска́ть из рук, 1, to let go of. 2, *fig.* to let slip; miss.

выпускни́к [*gen.* -ника́] *n.* 1, senior. 2, graduate.

выпускно́й *adj.* 1, *mech.* exhaust (*attrib.*). 2, graduation (*attrib.*). Выпускно́й экза́мен, examination taken before graduating.

вы́пустить [*infl.* -щу, -стишь] *v., pfv. of* выпуска́ть.

выпу́тывать *v.impfv.* [*pfv.* вы́путать] to extricate; disentangle. —выпу́тыватся, *refl.* 1, to extricate oneself; disentangle oneself. 2, (*with* из) to work one's way out; wiggle out (of a situation).

вы́пучить *v.pfv., in* вы́пучить глаза́, *colloq.* to stare wide-eyed.

вы́пушка [*gen. pl.* -шек] *n.* edging; piping.

выпы́тывать *v.impfv.* [*pfv.* вы́пытать] *colloq.* 1, to elicit; find out (information, a secret, etc.). 2, [*impfv. only*] to try to get (information); try to find out (a secret).

выпь *n.f.* bittern.

выпя́чивать *v.impfv.* [*pfv.* вы́пятить] *colloq.* 1, to stick out; throw out (one's stomach, chest, etc.). 2, *fig.* to emphasize; play up. —выпя́чиваться, *refl., colloq.* to stick out; jut out; protrude.

выраба́тывать *v.impfv.* [*pfv.* вы́работать] 1, to make; produce; manufacture. 2, to work out; draw up. 3, to develop. 4, *colloq.* to earn. —выраба́тываться, *refl.* to develop. У него́ вы́работалась привы́чка (+ *inf.*), he has developed the habit of...

вы́работка *n.* 1, making; manufacture. 2, production; output. 3, working out; drawing up. 4, *colloq.* workmanship.

выра́внивание *n.* 1, smoothing; leveling. 2, alignment.

выра́внивать *v.impfv.* [*pfv.* вы́ровнять] 1, to even; level; smooth out. 2, to align; dress (a file, column, etc.). 3, to straighten out (an airplane). 4, *in* вы́ровнять шаг, to get in step; regain one's stride. —выра́вниваться, *refl.* 1, to even out. 2, to line up; dress. 3, to develop (*physically*). 4, to improve; get better.

выража́ть *v.impfv.* [*pfv.* вы́разить] to express. *See also* вы́раженный.

выража́ться *v.r.impfv.* [*pfv.* **вы́разиться**] **1,** to be expressed. **2,** to express oneself. Е́сли мо́жно так вы́разиться, if I (one) may say so. **3,** (*with* **в** + *prepl.*) to manifest itself (in). **4,** *in* выража́ться в су́мме (+ *gen.*), to amount to; come to. **5,** [*impfv. only*] *colloq.* to use foul language. —**мя́гко выража́ясь,** to put it mildly.

выраже́ние *n.* **1,** expression; act of expressing. **2,** expression (*on one's face*). **3,** expression; feeling: чита́ть с выраже́нием, to read with expression. **4,** expression; phrase: идиомати́ческое выраже́ние, idiomatic expression. —**в де́нежном выраже́нии,** in terms of money; in dollars and cents.

вы́раженный *adj., usu. preceded by an adverb,* pronounced; marked. —**я́рко вы́раженная фо́рма боле́зни,** acute form of a disease.

вырази́тель *n.m.* exponent; spokesman.

вырази́тельный *adj.* expressive. —**вырази́тельность,** *n.f.* expressiveness.

вы́разить [*infl.* **-жу, -зишь**] *v., pfv. of* **выража́ть.** —**вы́разиться,** *refl., pfv. of* **выража́ться.**

выраста́ть *v.impfv.* [*pfv.* **вы́расти**] **1,** to grow. **2,** to grow up. **3,** (*with* **в** + *acc.*) to grow into; develop (into). **4,** to increase; grow. **5,** (*with* **из**) *colloq.* to outgrow; grow out of. **6,** to appear; loom up. —**вы́расти в (чьи́х-нибудь) глаза́х,** to go up in someone's estimation.

вы́расти [*infl.* **вы́расту, вы́растешь;** *past* **вы́рос, вы́росла**] *v., pfv. of* **расти́** *and* **выраста́ть.**

вы́растить [*infl.* **-щу, -стишь**] *v., pfv. of* **расти́ть** *and* **выра́щивать.**

выра́щивать *v.impfv.* [*pfv.* **вы́растить**] **1,** to raise; grow; cultivate (plants). **2,** to raise; breed (animals).

вы́рвать *v.pfv.* [*infl.* **вы́рву, вы́рвешь**] **1,** *pfv. of* **вырыва́ть. 2,** *pfv. of* **рвать** (*in sense #8*). —**вы́рваться,** *refl., pfv. of* **вырыва́ться.**

вы́рез *n.* cut; cut-out section: пла́тье с ни́зким/больши́м/глубо́ким вы́резом, low-cut (*or* low-necked) dress. —**треуго́льный вы́рез,** V-neck.

вы́резать [*infl.* **вы́режу, вы́режешь**] *v., pfv. of* **выреза́ть** *and* **вырезывать.**

выреза́ть *v.impfv.* [*pfv.* **вы́резать**] **1,** to cut out; clip out. **2,** *med.* to cut out; excise. **3,** to carve; engrave. **4,** to massacre; slaughter. *Also,* **вырезывать.**

вы́резка [*gen. pl.* **-зок**] *n.* **1,** cutting out. **2,** clipping (*from a newspaper, magazine, etc.*). **3,** fillet; tenderloin (*of beef*).

вырезно́й *adj.* **1,** carved. **2,** to be cut out: вырезны́е карти́нки, pictures to be cut out.

вырезывать *v.impfv.* = **выреза́ть.**

вы́рисовать [*infl.* **-сую, -суешь**] *v., pfv. of* **вырисо́вывать.** —**вы́рисоваться,** *refl., pfv. of* **вырисо́вываться.**

вырисо́вывать *v.impfv.* [*pfv.* **вы́рисовать**] to draw carefully; draw in great detail. —**вырисо́вываться,** *refl.* to loom; appear; be etched (*against a background*).

вы́ровнять *v., pfv. of* **выра́внивать.** —**вы́ровняться,** *refl., pfv. of* **выра́вниваться.**

вы́родиться *v.r., pfv. of* **вырожда́ться.**

вы́родок [*gen.* **-дка**] *n., colloq.* outcast.

вырожда́ться *v.r.impfv.* [*pfv.* **вы́родиться**] to degenerate.

вырожде́нец [*gen.* **-нца**] *n.* degenerate. —**вырожде́ние,** *n.* degeneration; degeneracy. —**вырожде́нческий,** *adj.* degenerative.

вы́ронить *v.pfv.* **1,** to drop. **2,** *fig., colloq.* to utter.

выруба́ть *v.impfv.* [*pfv.* **вы́рубить**] **1,** to chop down; cut down. **2,** to cut out; hack out. **3,** to carve; carve out.

вы́рубка *n.* **1,** chopping down; cutting down. **2,** clearing; glade.

вы́ругать *v., pfv. of* **руга́ть.** —**вы́ругаться,** *refl., colloq.* to swear; curse.

выру́ливать *v.impfv.* [*pfv.* **вы́рулить**] *aero.* to taxi.

выруча́ть *v.impfv.* [*pfv.* **вы́ручить**] **1,** to rescue; help out; come to the aid of. **2,** to make (money, a profit, etc.).

вы́ручка *n.* **1,** rescue: прийти́ на вы́ручку (+ *dat.*), to come to the rescue of. **2,** receipts; proceeds; takings; take.

вырыва́ть *v.impfv.* [*pfv.* **вы́рвать**] **1,** to tear out. **2,** to pull up (*from the ground*). **3,** to pull; extract (a tooth). **4,** to grab; snatch; wrest (something from someone). **5,** *fig.* to wring (a confession); wrest (a concession, the initiative, etc.). **6,** *in* вырыва́ть из конте́кста, to take (*or* lift) out of context. **7,** [*pfv.* **вы́рыть**] to dig; dig up; exhume; unearth.

вырыва́ться *v.r.impfv.* [*pfv.* **вы́рваться**] **1,** to break away; break out; break loose. **2,** (*of pages*) to come out; come loose. **3,** to shoot forward; shoot ahead. **4,** (*of fire*) to shoot up; shoot out. **5,** (*of a sigh, groan, etc.*) to escape.

вы́рыть [*infl.* **вы́рою, вы́роешь**] *v., pfv. of* **рыть** *and* **вырыва́ть** (*in sense #7*).

выряжа́ть *v.impfv.* [*pfv.* **вы́рядить**] *colloq.* to dress up. —**выряжа́ться,** *refl., colloq.* to get dressed up.

вы́садить [*infl.* **вы́сажу, вы́садишь**] *v., pfv. of* **выса́живать.** —**вы́садиться,** *refl., pfv. of* **выса́живаться.**

вы́садка *n.* **1,** debarkation; disembarkation. **2,** *mil.* [*also,* **вы́садка деса́нта**] landing. **3,** transplanting.

выса́живать *v.impfv.* [*pfv.* **вы́садить**] **1,** to drop off; let off; discharge (a passenger). **2,** to help out; help off (of *or* from a vehicle). **3,** to make (a passenger) get off; put off. **4,** to land (troops); put ashore. Вы́садить челове́ка на Луну́, to land/place/put a man on the moon. **5,** to transplant. —**выса́живаться,** *refl.* to get off; disembark.

выса́сывать *v.impfv.* [*pfv.* **вы́сосать**] to suck out. —**вы́сосать из па́льца,** to fabricate; concoct.

высве́рливать *v.impfv.* [*pfv.* **вы́сверлить**] to drill; bore.

высве́чивать *v.impfv.* [*pfv.* **вы́светить**] **1,** to light up. **2,** to highlight.

высвобожда́ть *v.impfv.* [*pfv.* **вы́свободить**] **1,** to free; disentangle. **2,** to free; free up; release; make available.

высева́ть *v.impfv.* [*pfv.* **вы́сеять**] to sow.

высека́ть *v.impfv.* [*pfv.* **вы́сечь**] **1,** to carve; carve out; hew. **2,** to strike; ignite (a fire, spark, etc.).

выселе́ние *n.* **1,** eviction. **2,** emptying (*of a town*).

выселя́ть *v.impfv.* [*pfv.* **вы́селить**] **1,** to evict. **2,** to forcibly evict the population of; empty (a town). —**выселя́ться,** *refl.* to move.

вы́сечь [*infl.* **вы́секу, вы́сечешь;** *past* **вы́сек, вы́секла**] *v., pfv. of* **сечь** (*in sense #3*) *and* **высека́ть.**

вы́сеять [*infl.* **вы́сею, вы́сеешь**] *v., pfv. of* **высева́ть.**

выси́живать *v.impfv.* [*pfv.* **вы́сидеть**] **1,** *colloq.* to sit; stay (for a certain length of time). **2,** *in* вы́сидеть до конца́ (+ *gen.*), to sit (something) out to the end; sit through. **3,** to hatch.

вы́ситься *v.r.impfv.* to tower; rise; loom.

выска́бливать *v.impfv.* [*pfv.* **вы́скоблить**] **1,** to scrape off; scrape clean. **2,** to scrape out; erase.

вы́сказать [*infl.* **вы́скажу, вы́скажешь**] *v., pfv. of* **выска́зывать.** —**вы́сказаться,** *refl., pfv. of* **выска́зываться.**

выска́зывание *n.* **1,** expression; utterance. **2,** statement; pronouncement. **3,** *logic* proposition.

выска́зывать *v.impfv.* [*pfv.* **вы́сказать**] to express. —**выска́зываться,** *refl.* **1,** to state one's opinion; have one's say. **2,** (*with* **за** *or* **про́тив**) to come out (in favor of *or* against).

выска́кивать *v.impfv.* [*pfv.* **вы́скочить**] **1,** to jump out. **2,** to jump off (a moving streetcar, bus, etc.). **3,** *colloq.* to dart out. **4,** *colloq.* to fall out; slip out. **5,** (*of a sore, boil, etc.*) to appear. —**вы́скочить из головы́,** to slip one's mind; go right out of one's mind.

выска́льзывать *v.impfv.* [*pfv.* **вы́скользнуть**] **1,** to slip out. **2,** to sneak out.

вы́скоблить *v., pfv. of* **выска́бливать.**

вы́скользнуть *v., pfv. of* **выска́льзывать.**

вы́скочить *v., pfv. of* **выска́кивать.**

вы́скочка *n.m. & f., colloq.* upstart.

вы́слать [*infl.* **вы́шлю, вы́шлешь**] *v., pfv. of* **высыла́ть.**

вы́следить *v.pfv.* [*infl.* **-жу, -дишь**] **1,** *pfv. of* **высле́живать. 2,** to track down; hunt down.

высле́живать *v.impfv.* [*pfv.* **вы́следить**] to follow; trail; track; shadow; stalk.

вы́слуга *n., in* **за вы́слугу лет,** by virtue of long service.

выслу́живать *v.impfv.* [*pfv.* **вы́служить**] to qualify for; receive (*through service*). —**выслу́живаться,** *refl.* (*with* **пе́ред**) to curry favor (with).

вы́служить *v.pfv.* **1,** *pfv. of* **выслу́живать. 2,** *colloq.* to serve (a certain length of time). —**вы́служиться,** *refl., pfv. of* **выслу́живаться.**

вы́слушать *v., pfv. of* **выслу́шивать.**

выслу́шивание *n.* auscultation.

выслу́шивать *v.impfv.* [*pfv.* **вы́слушать**] **1,** to listen (to); hear out. **2,** *med.* to listen to; examine.

высма́тривать *v.impfv.* [*pfv.* **вы́смотреть**] **1,** [*usu. pfv.*] to spot; spy; detect. **2,** [*impfv. only*] (*often with* **стать**] to try to spot. **3,** *colloq.* (*with* **всё** *or* **все**) to look over; examine. **4,** [*impfv. only*] *colloq.* to look out.

высме́ивать *v.impfv.* [*pfv.* **вы́смеять**] to mock; deride; ridicule; make fun of.

вы́смеять [*infl.* **вы́смею, вы́смеешь**] *v., pfv. of* **высме́ивать.**

вы́смолить *v., pfv. of* **смоли́ть.**

вы́сморкать *v., pfv. of* **сморка́ть.** —**вы́сморкаться,** *refl., pfv. of* **сморка́ться.**

вы́смотреть [*infl.* **-трю, -тришь**] *v., pfv. of* **высма́тривать.**

высо́вывать *v.impfv.* [*pfv.* **вы́сунуть**] to stick out. —**высо́вываться,** *refl.* **1,** to stick out; jut out. **2,** to lean out.

высо́кий *adj.* [*short form* **высо́к, высока́, высоко́** *or* **высо́ко, высоки́** *or* **высо́ки;** *comp.* **вы́ше**] **1,** high. **2,** tall. **3,** *fig.* lofty; elevated. **4,** high; high-pitched. **5,** (*of a guest*) distinguished; honored.

высоко́ *also,* **высо́ко** *adv.* high: держа́ть го́лову высоко́, to hold one's head high. —*adj., used predicatively* **1,** high: Окна́ бы́ли высоко́ от земли́, the windows were high off the ground. **2,** too high: Это мне высоко́, it is too high for me.

высокока́чественный *adj.* high-quality; quality (*attrib.*).

высокоме́рие *n.* haughtiness; arrogance.

высокоме́рный *adj.* haughty; arrogant; supercilious.

высокоопла́чиваемый *adj.* high-paid; highly paid.

высокопа́рный *adj.* high-flown; bombastic; grandiloquent. —**высокопа́рность,** *n.f.* grandiloquence; bombast.

высокопоста́вленный *adj.* high-ranking; senior: высокопоста́вленный чино́вник, senior official. Высокопоста́вленное лицо́, V.I.P.

высокора́звитый *adj.* highly-developed.

вы́сосать [*infl.* **вы́сосу, вы́сосешь**] *v., pfv. of* **выса́сывать.**

высота́ [*pl.* **высо́ты**] *n.* **1,** height. **2,** altitude. **3,** height(s): кома́ндные высо́ты, commanding heights. **4,** *music* pitch. —**быть на высоте́ (положе́ния),** to be equal to (*or* rise to) the occasion. —**на до́лжной высоте́,** up to the mark; up to par.

высо́тный *adj.* **1,** (*of a flight*) high-altitude. **2,** (*of a building*) very tall.

высотоме́р *n.* altimeter.

вы́сохнуть [*past* **вы́сох, вы́сохла**] *v., pfv. of* **со́хнуть** *and* **высыха́ть.**

высоча́йший *adj.* **1,** *superl. of* **высо́кий. 2,** *pre-rev.* royal; imperial.

высоче́нный *adj., colloq.* very high; very tall.

высо́чество *n.* Highness (title).

вы́спаться [*infl.* **вы́сплюсь, вы́спишься**] *v.r., pfv. of* **высыпа́ться** (*in sense #2*).

выспра́шивать *v.impfv.* [*pfv.* **вы́спросить**] *colloq.* **1,** (*with acc. or* **у**) to ply with questions; pump. **2,** to find out (*by asking a lot of questions*).

вы́спренний *adj.* high-flown.

вы́спросить [*infl.* **-шу, -сишь**] *v., pfv. of* **выспра́шивать.**

вы́ставить [*infl.* **-влю, -вишь**] *v., pfv. of* **выставля́ть.** —**вы́ставиться,** *refl., pfv. of* **выставля́ться.**

вы́ставка [*gen. pl.* **-вок**] *n.* **1,** exhibition; show. **2,** display. —**всеми́рная вы́ставка,** world's fair.

выставля́ть *v.impfv.* [*pfv.* **вы́ставить**] **1,** to put out; move out. **2,** to put forward; stick out. **3,** to exhibit; display. **4,** to lay out (food). **5,** *colloq.* to send out; order out. **6,** to post (a guard). **7,** to put forth (demands, arguments, etc.). **8,** *in* выставля́ть (чью-нибудь) кандидату́ру, to nominate; выставля́ть свою́ кандидату́ру, to announce one's candidacy. **9,** to put down; enter (grades, a date, etc.). **10,** *colloq.* to present (in a certain light). —**выставля́ть на свет,** to expose to the light. —**выставля́ть себя́** (+ *instr.*), *colloq.* to make oneself out to be.

выставля́ться *v.r.impfv.* [*pfv.* **вы́ставиться**] *colloq.* **1,** to stick out; lean out. **2,** *fig.* to show off.

вы́ставочный *adj.* exhibition (*attrib.*).

выста́вать *v.impfv.* [*pfv.* **вы́стоять**] **1,** to stand; remain standing. **2,** *fig.* to hold out. Кре́пость вы́стояла, the fortress held. —**выста́иваться,** *refl.* (*of wine*) to mature.

выстега́ть *v., pfv. of* **стега́ть** (*in sense #1*).

выстила́ть *v.impfv.* [*pfv.* **вы́стлать**] **1,** to cover. **2,** to pave.

выстира́ть *v., pfv. of* **стира́ть** (*in sense #4*).

вы́стлать [*infl.* **вы́стелю, вы́стелешь**] *v., pfv. of* **выстила́ть.**

вы́стоять [*infl.* **вы́стою, вы́стоишь**] *v., pfv. of* **выста́ивать.** —**вы́стояться,** *refl., pfv. of* **выста́иваться.**

вы́страдать *v.pfv.* **1,** to suffer; endure; have been (*or* gone) through. **2,** to deserve; earn (*after long suffering*).

выстра́ивать *v.impfv.* [*pfv.* **вы́строить**] *mil.* to form up. —**выстра́иваться,** *refl.* **1,** *mil.* to form; line up. **2,** (*of a line*) to form.

вы́стрел *n.* shot: произвести́ вы́стрел, to fire a shot. —**без вы́стрела,** without firing a shot. —**на вы́стрел,** within gunshot.

вы́стрелить *v.pfv.* **1,** *pfv. of* **стреля́ть. 2,** (*of a gun*) to discharge; go off.

выстрига́ть *v.impfv.* [*pfv.* **вы́стричь**] **1,** to cut off. **2,** to cut (one's hair in a certain style).

вы́стричь [*infl.* **вы́стригу, вы́стрижешь;** *past* **вы́стриг, вы́стригла**] *v., pfv. of* **выстрига́ть.**

вы́строгать *v., pfv. of* **строга́ть.**

вы́строить *v.pfv.* **1,** *pfv. of* **выстра́ивать. 2,** to build. —**вы́строиться,** *refl.* **1,** *pfv. of* **выстра́иваться. 2,** to be built; go up.

вы́стукивать *v.impfv.* [*pfv.* **вы́стукать**] *colloq.* to tap out.

вы́ступ *n.* **1,** projection. **2,** ledge.

выступа́ть *v.impfv.* [*pfv.* **вы́ступить**] **1,** to come forward; step forward. **2,** to appear (publicly): выступа́ть на сце́не, to appear on stage; выступа́ть по телеви́дению, appear on television; выступа́ть на собра́нии, address a meeting; выступа́ть на соревнова́ниях, to appear (*or* take part) in a competition; выступа́ть с ре́чью, to give *or* deliver a speech. **3,** (*with* **за** + *acc.*) to come out in favor of; favor; advocate; (*with* **про́тив**) to come out against; oppose. **4,** to appear (*on one's face or body*). **5,** [*impfv. only*] to jut out. **6,** [*impfv. only*] to strut; swagger.

вы́ступить [*infl.* **-плю, -пишь**] *v., pfv. of* **выступа́ть.**

выступле́ние *n.* **1,** performance; appearance. **2,** speech; address. **3,** campaign (*on behalf of a political cause*).

вы́сунуть *v., pfv. of* **высо́вывать.** —**вы́сунуться,** *refl., pfv. of* **высо́вываться.**

высу́шивать *v.impfv.* [*pfv.* **вы́сушить**] **1,** to dry; dry out. **2,** to parch. —**высу́шиваться,** *refl.* to dry out; become dry.

вы́сушить *v., pfv. of* **суши́ть** *and* **высу́шивать.** —**вы́сушиться,** *refl., pfv. of* **суши́ться** *and* **высу́шиваться.**

высчи́тывать *v.impfv.* [*pfv.* **вы́считать**] to calculate; compute.

вы́сший *adj., used only as a modifier* **1,** highest: вы́сшего ка́чества, of the highest quality. **2,** higher: вы́сшее уче́бное заведе́ние, institution of higher learning. **3,** *with certain nouns,* high: вы́сшее кома́ндование, high command; вы́сшая то́чка, the high point; climax. —**в вы́сшей сте́пени** (+ *adj.*), extraordinarily; most. —**вы́сшая ме́ра наказа́ния,** the supreme penalty.

высыла́ть *v.impfv.* [*pfv.* **вы́слать**] **1,** to send (out); mail (out). **2,** to send out; order out. **3,** to banish; exile; deport.

вы́сылка *n.* **1,** sending; dispatch. **2,** banishment; deportation.

вы́сыпать [*infl.* **вы́сыплю, вы́сыплешь**] *v., pfv. of* **высыпа́ть.** —**вы́сыпаться,** *refl., pfv. of* **высыпа́ться** (*in sense #1*).

высыпа́ть *v.impfv.* [*pfv.* **вы́сыпать**] **1,** *v.t.* to pour (out of, into, onto, etc.). **2,** *colloq.* (*of many people*) to pour out; throng. **3,** *impers.* to break out (*in a rash*): У него́ вы́сыпало на лице́, his face is broken out.

высыпа́ться *v.r.impfv.* **1,** [*pfv.* **вы́сыпаться**] to pour out; spill out. **2,** [*pfv.* **вы́спаться**] to have a good (night's) sleep.

высыха́ть *v.impfv.* [*pfv.* **вы́сохнуть**] **1,** to dry out; dry up. **2,** to wither. **3,** to waste away.

высь *n.f.* **1,** height. **2,** *pl.* mountain tops.

выта́лкивать *v.impfv.* [*pfv.* **вы́толкнуть**] to push out; throw out.

выта́пливать *v.impfv.* [*pfv.* **вы́топить**] **1,** *colloq.* to heat. **2,** to melt.

выта́птывать *v.impfv.* [*pfv.* **вы́топтать**] to trample down.

вы́таращить *v., pfv. of* **тара́щить.**

выта́скивать *v.impfv.* [*pfv.* **вы́тащить**] **1,** to pull out. **2,** to drag out. **3,** to pull out; extract; remove. **4,** to haul in (*a fish*). **5,** *colloq.* to drag (someone) somewhere against his will.

вы́тачать *v., pfv. of* **тача́ть.**

выта́чивать *v.impfv.* [*pfv.* **вы́точить**] to make; fashion (*in a lathe*).

вы́тачка [*gen. pl.* **-чек**] *n.* tuck (*on a garment*).

вы́тащить *v., pfv. of* **тащи́ть** (*in senses #3, 4, 5*) *and* **выта́скивать.**

вы́твердить *v., pfv. of* **тверди́ть** (*in sense #2*).

вытворя́ть *v.impfv.* [*pfv.* **вы́творить**] *colloq.* to do (something odd or foolish).

вытека́ть *v.impfv.* [*pfv.* **вы́течь**] **1,** to flow out; run out; leak out. **2,** [*impfv. only*] to follow; result; ensue.

вытека́ющий *adj.* resulting.

вы́тереть [*infl.* **вы́тру, вы́трешь;** *past* **вы́тер, вы́терла**] *v., pfv. of* **вытира́ть.** —**вы́тереться,** *refl., pfv. of* **вытира́ться.**

вы́терпеть *v.pfv.* [*infl.* **-плю, -пишь**] **1,** to endure. **2,** (*usu. neg.*) to stand it: Наконе́ц он не вы́терпел, finally he could stand it no longer.

вы́тертый *adj., colloq.* threadbare.

вы́тесать [*infl.* **вы́тешу, вы́тешешь**] *v., pfv. of* **вытёсывать.**

вытесне́ние *n.* ouster; exclusion.

вытесня́ть v.impfv. [pfv. **вы́теснить**] **1,** to crowd out; force out; oust. **2,** to replace; displace; supplant.

вытёсывать v.impfv. [pfv. **вы́тесать**] to hew.

вы́течь [infl. **вы́течет** and **вы́текут**; past **вы́тек, вы́текла**] v., pfv. of **вытека́ть**.

вытира́ть v.impfv. [pfv. **вы́тереть**] **1,** to wipe. **2,** to dry. **3,** to wipe away. **4,** colloq. to wear thin (by frequent rubbing). —**вытира́ться**, refl. **1,** to dry oneself. **2,** colloq. to wear thin.

вытисня́ть v.impfv. [pfv. **вы́тиснить**] to imprint.

вы́ткать v.pfv. [infl. **вы́тку, вы́ткешь**] to weave.

вы́толкнуть v., pfv. of **выта́лкивать**.

вы́топить [infl. **вы́топлю, вы́топишь**] v., pfv. of **выта́пливать**.

вы́топтать [infl. **вы́топчу, вы́топчешь**] v., pfv. of **выта́птывать**.

вы́торговать [infl. **-гую, -гуешь**] v., pfv. of **вытрго́вывать**.

выторго́вывать v.impfv. [pfv. **вы́торговать**] colloq. **1,** to make; earn; net; clear. **2,** to get (a reduction in price) by bargaining.

вы́точить v., pfv. of **точи́ть** (in sense #2) and **выта́чивать**.

вы́травить [infl. **-влю, -вишь**] v., pfv. of **трави́ть** (in senses #1, 4, 5), **вытравля́ть** and **вытра́вливать**.

вытра́вливать v. = **вытравля́ть**.

вытравля́ть v.impfv. [pfv. **вы́травить**] **1,** to remove (using a chemical substance). **2,** to etch. **3,** to exterminate. **4,** (of cattle) to trample down. —**вы́травить (что́-нибудь) из па́мяти** (+ gen.), to blot out someone's memory.

вы́требовать v.pfv. [infl. **-бую, -буешь**] **1,** to demand and obtain. **2,** to summon; send for.

вытрезви́тель n.m. sobering-up station.

вытрезвля́ть v.impfv. [pfv. **вы́трезвить**] to sober; sober up. —**вытрезвля́ться**, refl. to sober up; become sober.

вытряса́ть v.impfv. [pfv. **вы́трясти**] to shake out.

вы́трясти [infl. **вы́трясу, вы́трясешь**; past **вы́тряс, вы́трясла**] v., pfv. of **трясти́** (in sense #2) and **вытряса́ть**.

вытря́хивать v.impfv. [pfv. **вы́тряхнуть**] to shake out.

выть v.impfv. [pres. **вою, во́ешь**] to howl; wail.

вытьё n., colloq. howling; wailing.

вытя́гивать v.impfv. [pfv. **вы́тянуть**] **1,** to stretch. Вытя́гивать ше́ю, to crane one's neck. **2,** to pull out. **3,** to draw out (air, smoke, etc.). **4,** fig. to draw out; elicit: Из него́ ни сло́ва не вы́тянешь, you can't get a word out of him. **5,** colloq. to take out. **6,** v.i., colloq. to hold out; last. —**вытя́гиваться**, refl. **1,** to stretch; expand. **2,** to stretch; extend. **3,** to stretch out. **4,** colloq. to straighten up; stand up straight. **5,** colloq. to grow; shoot up. **6,** (of one's face) to fall.

вытяже́ние n. **1,** stretching. **2,** med. traction.

вы́тяжка n. **1,** stretching. **2,** drawing out. **3,** chem. extract.

вытяжно́й adj. exhaust (attrib.): вытяжно́й вентиля́тор, exhaust fan. —**вытяжно́й трос**, ripcord.

вы́тянутый adj. **1,** outstretched. **2,** elongated. —**вы́тянутое лицо́**, long face.

вы́тянуть v., pfv. of **вытя́гивать**. —**вы́тянуться**, refl., pfv. of **вытя́гиваться**.

выу́живать v.impfv. [pfv. **вы́удить**] **1,** to hook; catch (a fish). **2,** colloq. to coax out; worm out.

вы́тюжить v., pfv. of **утюжить**.

выу́ченик n. (with gen.) colloq. pupil (of).

выу́чивать v.impfv. [pfv. **вы́учить**] **1,** to learn. **2,** to teach. —**выу́чиваться**, refl. (with dat.) to learn.

вы́учить [infl. **вы́учу, вы́учишь**] v., pfv. of **учи́ть** and **выу́чивать**. —**вы́учиться**, refl., pfv. of **учи́ться** (in sense #2) and **выу́чиваться**.

вы́учка n. **1,** colloq. training. **2,** skill; ability.

выха́живать v.impfv. [pfv. **вы́ходить**] colloq. **1,** to nurse back to health. **2,** to bring up; raise.

выхва́тывать v.impfv. [pfv. **вы́хватить**] **1,** to grab; snatch. **2,** to pull out; whip out. **3,** to pick out (at random).

вы́хлоп n., mech. exhaust. —**выхлопно́й**, adj. exhaust (attrib.).

вы́хлопотать v.pfv. [infl. **-почу, -почешь**] to manage to obtain (after much effort).

вы́ход n. **1,** going out; coming out; emergence. **2,** theat. entrance (onstage). **3,** withdrawal. **4,** secession. **5,** exit. **6,** outlet: вы́ход к мо́рю, outlet to the sea. Иска́ть вы́ход свои́м чу́вствам, to seek an outlet for one's emotions. **7,** fig. way out. **8,** appearance (in print); publication. **9,** output; yield. —**дать вы́ход** (+ dat.), to give vent to.

вы́ходец [gen. **-дца**] n. (with из) **1,** person originally from; émigré (from). **2,** person originally of a different social class. —**вы́ходец с того́ све́та**, apparition.

вы́ходить v.pfv. [infl. **вы́хожу, вы́ходишь**] **1,** pfv. of **выха́живать**. **2,** to walk all over or around.

выходи́ть v.impfv. [pfv. **вы́йти**; pres. **выхожу́, выхо́дишь**] **1,** (with из) to go out (of); come out (of); walk out (of); get out (of); emerge (from); (with в or на + acc.) to go out; walk out (into or onto). **2,** (with из) to leave: выходи́ть из ко́мнаты/ из войны́/, to leave the room/war. **3,** to get off (at a certain stop); (with из) to get off (a bus, plane, etc.). **4,** (with в or на + acc.) (with certain nouns) to go into; enter: выходи́ть на орби́ту, to go into orbit; выходи́ть на полити́ческую аре́ну, to enter the political arena. Выходи́ть в эфи́р, to go on the air. Вы́йти в фина́л, to advance to the finals. **5,** (with из) to withdraw (from); drop out (of). Выходи́ть из па́ртии, to leave (or quit) the party. Выходи́ть из соста́ва (+ gen.), to secede (from). **6,** [often **выходи́ть в свет**] to appear; come out; be published. Выходи́ть из печа́ти, to come off the press. **7,** (with из) to go out of (style, use, etc.). **8,** (with instr.) to come out; emerge: выходи́ть победи́телем, to emerge the victor. **9,** (of a photograph or subject) to come out. **10,** (with из) to come of: Из э́того ничего́ не вы́йдет, nothing will come of it. **11,** (of something unfortunate) to occur. **12,** to work out: Де́ло не вы́шло, things didn't work out. **13,** to turn out. Вы́шло, что..., it turned out that... **14,** (with из) to make: Из него́ вы́йдет хоро́ший врач, he will make a good doctor. **15,** to run out; be used up: У нас вы́шел бензи́н, we ran out of gas. **16,** [impfv. only] (*with* в *or* на + *acc.*) to look out on; face. —**выходи́ть в мо́ре, 1,** to go to sea. **2,** to put out to sea. —**выходи́ть из берего́в,** to overflow its banks. —**выходи́ть из-под контро́ля,** to get out of control. —**выходи́ть из себя́,** to lose one's temper. —**выходи́ть из терпе́ния,** to lose patience. —**выходи́ть на рабо́ту, 1,** to return to work. **2,** to report for work.

вы́ходка [*gen. pl.* **-док**] *n.* trick; prank; escapade.

выходно́й *adj.* **1,** serving as an exit. **2,** worn on social occasions: выходно́е пла́тье, party dress; cocktail dress. —*n., colloq.* day off. —**выходно́й день,** day off. —**выходно́е посо́бие,** severance pay. —**выходна́я роль,** bit part.

выхола́щивать *v.impfv.* [*pfv.* **вы́холостить**] **1,** to castrate. **2,** *fig.* to emasculate.

вы́холенный *adj.* well-groomed; trim; dapper.

вы́холить *v.pfv.* to groom.

вы́холостить [*infl.* **-щу, -стишь**] *v., pfv. of* холости́ть *and* выхола́щивать.

вы́хухоль *n.m. & f.* desman.

выцара́пывать *v.impfv.* [*pfv.* **вы́царапать**] **1,** to scratch out. **2,** *colloq.* to get; obtain; wangle.

вы́цвести [*infl.* **вы́цветет;** *past* **вы́цвел, вы́цвела**] *v., pfv. of* выцвета́ть.

выцвета́ть *v.impfv.* [*pfv.* **вы́цвести**] to fade.

вы́цветший *adj.* faded.

вычека́нивать *v.impfv.* [*pfv.* **вы́чеканить**] to mint.

вычёркивание *n.* deleting; deletion.

вычёркивать *v.impfv.* [*pfv.* **вы́черкнуть**] to cross out; cross off; delete. —**вы́черкнуть из па́мяти,** to erase from one's memory. —**вы́черкнуть из свое́й жи́зни,** to put out of one's life.

вычёрпывать *v.impfv.* [*pfv.* **вы́черпать**] to scoop out; bail out.

вычёрчивать *v.impfv.* [*pfv.* **вы́чертить**] to draw; trace.

вы́чесать [*infl.* **вы́чешу, вы́чешешь**] *v., pfv. of* вычёсывать.

вы́честь [*infl.* **вы́чту, вы́чтешь;** *past* **вы́чел, вы́чла**] *v., pfv. of* вычита́ть.

вычёсывать *v.impfv.* [*pfv.* **вы́чесать**] to comb out.

вы́чет *n.* deduction. —**за вы́четом** (+ *gen.*), less; minus; after deducting.

вычисле́ние *n.* calculation; computation.

вычисли́тель *n.m.* **1,** calculator. **2,** computer. **3,** computer specialist.

вычисли́тельный *adj.* **1,** computing. **2,** computer (*attrib.*). —**вычисли́тельная маши́на,** computer.

вычисля́ть *v.impfv.* [*pfv.* **вы́числить**] to calculate; compute.

вы́чистить [*infl.* **-щу, -стишь**] *v., pfv. of* чи́стить *and* вычища́ть.

вычита́емое *n., decl. as an adj.* subtrahend.

вычита́ние *n.* subtraction.

вы́читать *v., pfv. of* вычи́тывать.

вычита́ть *v.impfv.* [*pfv.* **вы́честь**] **1,** to subtract. **2,** to deduct.

вычи́тывать *v.impfv.* [*pfv.* **вы́читать**] **1,** *colloq.* to learn; find out (*by reading*). **2,** to read; proofread.

вычища́ть *v.impfv.* [*pfv.* **вы́чистить**] to clean; clean out.

вы́чурный *adj.* fancy; elaborate; ornate.

вышвы́ривать *v.impfv.* [*pfv.* **вы́швырнуть**] *colloq.* to throw out; toss out; hurl out.

вы́ше *adj., comp. of* высо́кий. —*adv.* **1,** *comp. of* высоко́. **2,** above. —*prep., with gen.* **1,** above; over. **2,** beyond: вы́ше моего́ понима́ния, beyond my comprehension.

вышеприведённый *adj.* cited above.

вышеска́занный *adj.* aforesaid.

вышестоя́щий *adj.* higher: вышестоя́щий о́рган, higher body.

вышеука́занный *adj.* foregoing; aforesaid.

вышеупомя́нутый *adj.* above-mentioned; aforementioned. —**вышеупомя́нутое,** *n.* the above.

вышиба́ла *n.m., colloq.* bouncer.

вышиба́ть *v.impfv.* [*pfv.* **вы́шибить**] *colloq.* **1,** to knock out; dislodge. **2,** to throw out; kick out.

вы́шибить [*infl.* **вы́шибу, вы́шибешь;** *past* **вы́шиб, вы́шибла**] *v., pfv. of* вышиба́ть.

вышива́ние *n.* embroidery.

вышива́ть *v.impfv.* [*pfv.* **вы́шить**] to embroider.

вы́шивка *n.* embroidery.

вышина́ *n.* height. **в вышине́, 1,** on high. **2,** in the sky.

вы́шитый *adj.* embroidered.

вы́шить [*infl.* **вы́шью, вы́шьешь**] *v., pfv. of* вышива́ть.

вы́шка [*gen. pl.* **вы́шек**] *n.* tower. —**бурова́я вы́шка,** drilling rig. —**нефтяна́я вы́шка,** oil rig; oil derrick.

вы́школить *v., pfv. of* шко́лить.

вы́шмыгнуть *v.pfv., colloq.* to dart out; slip out.

выштукату́ривать *v.impfv.* [*pfv.* **вы́штукатурить**] to plaster; stucco.

вышу́чивать *v.impfv.* [*pfv.* **вы́шутить**] to make fun of; ridicule.

вы́щербленный *adj., colloq.* jagged; pockmarked.

вы́щипать [*infl.* **вы́щиплю, вы́щиплешь**] *v., pfv. of* выщи́пывать.

выщи́пывать *v.impfv.* [*pfv.* **вы́щипать**] to pull out; pluck.

вы́явить [*infl.* **-влю, -вишь**] *v., pfv. of* выявля́ть.

выявле́ние *n.* **1,** revelation. **2,** discovery.

выявля́ть *v.impfv.* [*pfv.* **вы́явить**] **1,** to reveal; display. **2,** to discover; bring to light.

выясне́ние *n.* **1,** clarification. **2,** determination.

выясня́ть *v.impfv.* [*pfv.* **вы́яснить**] **1,** to clarify; clear up. **2,** to find out; determine; ascertain. —**выясня́ться,** *refl.* **1,** to be discovered; become clear. **2,** to turn out: Вы́яснилось, что..., it turned out that...

вьетна́мец [*gen.* **-мца**] *n.m.* [*fem.* **-мка**] Vietnamese. —**вьетна́мский,** *adj.* Vietnamese.

вью́га *n.* snowstorm; blizzard.

вьюк *n.* pack; load.

вьюно́к [*gen.* **-нка́**] *n.* bindweed.

вьюро́к [*gen.* **-рка́**] *n.* **1,** brambling. **2,** (*in combinations*) finch: го́рный вьюро́к, rosy finch.

вью́чить *v.impfv.* [*pfv.* **навью́чить**] to load (an animal).

вью́чный *adj.* pack (*attrib.*): вью́чное живо́тное, pack animal; beast of burden. —**вью́чное седло́,** packsaddle. —**вью́чная тропа́,** bridle path.

вью́шка [*gen. pl.* **-шек**] *n.* damper.

вью́щийся *adj.* **1,** (*of hair*) curly. **2,** (*of a plant*) climbing.

вя́жущий *adj.* astringent.

вяз *n.* elm.

вязáльный *adj.* knitting (*attrib.*): вязáльная спúца, knitting needle.

вязáние *n.* **1,** binding; tying. **2,** knitting; crocheting.

вязáнка [*gen. pl.* **-нок**] *n.* bundle (*of wood, straw, etc.*).

вязаный *adj.* knitted.

вязáть *v.impfv.* [*pfv.* **связáть**; *pres.* **вяжý, вяжешь**] **1,** to bind: вязáть снопы́, to bind sheaves. **2,** to tie. **3,** to knit; crochet. **4,** [*impfv. only*] *impers.* to be astringent: У меня́ вя́жет во рту, my mouth feels drawn. —**вязáться**, *refl.* [*impfv. only*] **1,** (*with* **с** + *instr.*) to accord (with); tally (with); square (with). **2,** (*usu. neg.*) (not) work out well: Дéло не вя́жется, things are not working out well.

вя́зка *n.* **1,** binding; tying. **2,** knitting; crocheting. **3,** *colloq.* bunch.

вя́зкий *adj.* [*short form* **вя́зок, вязкá, вя́зко, вя́зки;** *comp.* **вя́зче**] **1,** sticky; viscous. **2,** muddy; swampy. —**вя́зкость**, *n.f.* viscosity.

вя́знуть *v.impfv.* [*pfv.* **завя́знуть** *or* **увя́знуть;** *past* **вяз** *or* **вя́знул, вя́зла**] to get stuck.

вя́леный *adj.* dried; cured by drying.

вя́лить *v.impfv.* [*pfv.* **провя́лить**] to cure (meat) by drying.

вя́лый *adj.* **1,** faded; withered. **2,** flabby; limp. **3,** sluggish; listless. —**вя́ло**, *adv.* sluggishly; listlessly. —**вя́лость**, *n.f.* sluggishness; languor; lethargy.

вя́нуть *v.impfv.* [*pfv.* **завя́нуть** *or* **увя́нуть;** *past* **вял** *or* **вя́нул, вя́ла**] **1,** to wilt; wither. **2,** (*of a person*) to fade; decline. —**ýши вя́нут,** one gets sick of hearing it.

вя́щий *adj.*, *obs.* greater: для вя́щей убедúтельности, in order to be more convincing.

Г

Г, г *n.neut.* fourth letter of the Russian alphabet.

габардúн *n.* gabardine. —**габардúновый**, *adj.* gabardine.

габарúт *n.* size; dimensions.

гавáйский *adj.* Hawaiian.

гáвань *n.f.* harbor.

гáга *n.* eider.

гагáра *n.* loon (*bird*).

гагáрка [*gen. pl.* **-рок**] *n.* auk.

гагáт *n.* jet (*mineral*).

гагáчий [*fem.* **-чья**] *adj.* eider (*attrib.*). —**гагáчий пух,** eider down.

гад *n.* **1,** reptile. **2,** *colloq.* skunk; rat; louse.

гадáлка [*gen. pl.* **-лок**] *n.* fortuneteller.

гадáние *n.* **1,** fortunetelling. **2,** guessing; guesswork; conjecture.

гадáтельный *adj.* doubtful; problematic; hypothetical; conjectural.

гадáть *v.impfv.* **1,** to guess; speculate; conjecture. **2,** to tell fortunes. Гадáть на кáртах, to do card reading.

гáдина *n.*, *colloq.* = гад.

гáдкий *adj.* [*comp.* **гáже**] nasty; foul; vile. —**гáдкий утёнок,** ugly duckling.

гадлúвый *adj.* of disgust; of revulsion: гадлúвое чýвство, feeling of disgust/revulsion. —**гадлúвость**, *n.f.* disgust; revulsion.

гадолúний *n.* gadolinium.

гáдость *n.f.* **1,** filth; muck. **2,** dirty trick; foul deed. **3,** *pl.* ugly/nasty remarks.

гадю́ка *n.* adder; viper.

гáечный *adj.*, *in* гáечный ключ, wrench.

газ *n.* **1,** gas: природный газ, natural gas. **2,** *pl.* fumes: выхлопны́е гáзы, exhaust fumes. **3,** *in* угáрный газ, carbon monoxide; углекúслый газ, carbon dioxide. **4,** *pl.* gas (*in one's stomach*). **5,** gauze (*fabric*). —**дать газ,** *colloq.* to step on the gas. —**сбáвить газ,** *colloq.* to slow down.

газéль *n.f.* gazelle.

газéта *n.* newspaper.

газéтный *adj.* newspaper (*attrib.*). —**газéтная бумáга,** newsprint. —**газéтный киóск,** newsstand.

газéтчик *n.* **1,** news vendor; newsboy. **2,** *colloq.* newsman; journalist.

газирóванный *adj.* carbonated.

газúровать *v.impfv.* [*pres.* **-рую, -руешь**] to carbonate. *Also,* **газировáть** [*pres.* **-рую́, -ру́ешь**].

гáзовый *adj.* **1,** gas (*attrib.*): гáзовый счётчик, gas meter. **2,** made of gauze.

газолúн *n.* gasoline.

газомéр *n.* gas meter.

газóн *n.* lawn. —**газонокосúлка**, *n.* lawn mower.

газообрáзный *adj.* gaseous.

газопровóд *n.* gas pipeline.

гаитя́нин [*pl.* **-тя́не, -тя́н**] *n.m.* [*fem.* **-тя́нка**] Haitian. —**гаитя́нский**, *adj.* Haitian.

гáичка [*gen. pl.* **-чек**] *n.* chickadee.

гáйка [*gen. pl.* **гáек**] *n.* nut (*for a bolt*).

гак *n.*, *colloq.*, *in* с гáком, a little over; a little more than.

галáктика *n.* galaxy. —**галактúческий**, *adj.* galactic.

галантерéя *n.* **1,** dry goods; haberdashery. **2,** *colloq.* dry goods store; haberdashery. —**галантерéйный**, *adj.* haberdashery (*attrib.*); haberdasher's. —**галантерéй-щик**, *n.* haberdasher.

галáнтный *adj.* gallant (*toward women*); chivalrous. —**галáнтность**, *n.f.* gallantry; chivalry.

галдёж [*gen.* -**дежá**] *n.*, *colloq.* uproar; hubbub.

галдéть *v.impfv.* [*pres.* -**дúшь**; *1st pers. sing. not used*] *colloq.* to make a racket.

галенúт *n.* galena.

галéра *n.* galley (*ship*).

галерéя *n.* gallery.

галёрка [*gen. pl.* -**рок**] *n.*, *colloq.*, gallery (*in a theater*).

галéта *n.* cracker; biscuit.

гáлечный *adj.* pebble (*attrib.*).

галиматья́ *n.*, *colloq.* nonsense; rubbish.

галифé (фэ) *n.pl. or neut.* riding breeches.

гáлка [*gen. pl.* **гáлок**] *n.* jackdaw. —**считáть гáлок**, **1**, to gape. **2**, to loaf.

галл *n.*, *bot.* gall.

гáллий *n.* gallium.

галлицúзм *n.* Gallicism.

галлóн *n.* gallon.

гáлльский *adj.* Gallic.

галлюцинáция *n.* hallucination.

галогéн *n.* halogen.

галóп *n.* gallop. —**галóпом**, *adv.* at a gallop.

галопúровать *v.impfv.* [*pres.* -**рую**, -**руешь**] to gallop.

гáлочка [*gen. pl.* -**чек**] *n.*, *colloq.* mark; check; tick.

галóши *n.pl.* [*sing.* **галóша**] rubbers; overshoes; galoshes.

галс *n.*, *naut.* tack.

гáлстук *n.* tie; necktie.

галýн [*gen.* -**лунá**] *n.* galloon.

галýшки *n.pl.* [*sing.* **галýшка**] dumplings.

гальванизúровать *v.impfv. & pfv.* [*pres.* -**рую**, -**руешь**] to galvanize.

гальванúческий *adj.* galvanic.

гáлька [*gen. pl.* **гáлек**] *n.* **1**, pebble. **2**, pebbles.

гам *n.*, *colloq.* racket; din; hubbub.

гамáк [*gen.* **гамакá**] *n.* hammock.

гамáши [*gen.* **гамáш**] *n.pl.* leggings.

гамбúт *n.* gambit.

гамéта *n.* gamete.

гáмма *n.* **1**, *music* scale. **2**, *fig.* (*with gen.*) gamut (of); range (of). —**гáмма-глобулúн**, gamma globulin. —**гáмма-лучú**, gamma rays.

гáнглий *n.* ganglion.

гангрéна *n.* gangrene. —**гангренóзный**, *adj.* gangrenous.

гáнгстер *n.* gangster.

гандбóл *n.* team handball.

гандикáп *n.*, *sports* handicap.

гантéль (тэ) *n.f.*, *often pl.* dumbbell.

гарáж [*gen.* **гаражá**] *n.* garage.

гарáнт *n.* guarantor.

гарантúровать *v.impfv. & pfv.* [*pres.* -**рую**, -**руешь**] to guarantee.

гарáнтия *n.* **1**, guarantee. **2**, safeguard.

гардéния *n.* gardenia.

гардерóб *n.* **1**, cloakroom. **2**, wardrobe.

гардерóбщик *n.m.* [*fem.* -**щица**] cloakroom attendant.

гардúна *n.* window curtain.

гаревóй *also*, **гáревый** *adj.* cinder (*attrib.*). Гáревая дорóжка, cinder path *or* track.

гарéм *n.* harem.

гáркать *v.impfv.* [*pfv.* **гáркнуть**] *colloq.* to shout; bark.

гармонизúровать *v.impfv. & pfv.* [*pres.* -**рую**, -**руешь**] *music* to harmonize. *Also*, **гармонизовáть** [*pres.* -**зýю**, -**зýешь**].

гармóника *n.* accordion. —**губнáя гармóника**, harmonica.

гармонúровать *v.impfv.* [*pres.* -**рую**, -**руешь**] (*with* **с** + *instr.*) to harmonize (with); go well (with).

гармонúст *n.* accordionist.

гармонúческий *adj.* **1**, harmonic. **2**, harmonious.

гармонúчный *adj.* harmonious.

гармóния *n.* harmony.

гармóнь *n.f.*, *colloq.* = **гармóника**. *Also*, **гармóшка**.

гарнизóн *n.* garrison.

гарнúр *n.* garnish; trimmings.

гарнúровать *v.impfv. & pfv.* [*pres.* -**рую**, -**руешь**] to garnish.

гарнитýр *n.* **1**, complete set. **2**, suite (*of furniture*).

гарпýн [*gen.* -**пунá**] *n.* harpoon.

гарпýнить *v.impfv.* to harpoon.

гáрус *n.* worsted. —**гáрусный**, *adj.* worsted.

гарцевáть *v.impfv.* [*pres.* -**цýю**, -**цýешь**] to prance (*on a horse*).

гáршнеп (нэ) *n.* jacksnipe.

гарь *n.f.* **1**, something burning: Пáхнет гáрью, there is a smell of something burning. **2**, cinders.

гасúть *v.impfv.* [*pfv.* **погасúть**; *pres.* **гашý**, **гáсишь**] **1**, to extinguish; put out. **2**, to turn off; turn out (the lights). **3**, to cancel (a stamp); liquidate (a debt). **4**, *fig.* to suppress; stifle. **5**, to slake (lime).

гáснуть *v.impfv.* [*pfv.* **погáснуть** *or* **угáснуть**; *past* **гас** *or* **гáснул**, **гáсла**] **1**, (*of a light, fire, etc.*) to go out; (*of a TV set*) go off. **2**, (*of emotions*) to fade; wane. **3**, (*of a person*) to be failing; sink.

гастрúт *n.* gastritis.

гастролёр *n.* guest performer.

гастролúровать *v.impfv.* [*pres.* -**рую**, -**руешь**] (*of a performer*) to tour; be on tour.

гастрóль *n.f.*, *usu. pl.* tour: выезжáть на гастрóли, to go on tour. —**гастрóльный**, *adj.* touring; on tour.

гастронóм *n.* **1**, gourmet. **2**, grocery store; delicatessen. —**гастрономúческий**, *adj.* gastronomic.

гастронóмия *n.* **1**, gastronomy. **2**, groceries.

гать *n.f.* road of logs laid across a marshy area.

гáубица *n.* howitzer.

гауптвáхта *n.*, *mil.* guardhouse; stockade.

гáфний *n.* hafnium.

гашéние *n.* **1**, extinguishing; extinction. **2**, cancellation (*on a postage stamp*).

гашёный *adj.* **1**, (*of a postage stamp*) used; canceled. **2**, *in* гашёная úзвесть, slaked lime.

гашéтка [*gen. pl.* -**ток**] *n.* trigger.

гашúш *n.* hashish.

гвалт *n.*, *colloq.* racket; hubbub.

гвардеец [*gen.* -дейца] *n.* guardsman. —**гвардейский,** *adj.* guards (*attrib.*); of guards.

гвардия *n.* Guards: Красная гвардия, Red Guards. —национальная гвардия, National Guard (*of the U.S.*). —старая гвардия, the old guard.

гвоздевой *adj.* 1, nail (*attrib.*). 2, feature: гвоздевой номер программы, feature item on the program.

гвоздик *n.* small nail; tack.

гвоздика *n.* 1, pink (*flower*); carnation. 2, cloves. —турецкая *or* бородатая гвоздика, sweet william.

гвоздичный *adj.* clove (*attrib.*). —**гвоздичный перец,** allspice; pimento.

гвоздь [*gen.* -здя; *pl.* гвозди, -дей, -дям] *n.m.* 1, nail. 2, *colloq.* highlight; hit.

где *adv.* 1, *interr.* where?: Где вы живёте?, where do you live? 2, *rel.* where: Я не знаю, где он сейчас, I don't know where he is right now. —**где бы ни,** wherever; no matter where. —**где бы то ни было,** anywhere.

где-либо *adv.* = где-нибудь.

где-нибудь *adv.* somewhere; anywhere.

где-то *adv.* somewhere; someplace.

гегемония *n.* hegemony.

гедонизм *n.* hedonism. —**гедонист,** *n.* hedonist. —**гедонистический,** *adj.* hedonistic.

гей *interj., colloq.* 1, hey! 2, gidd(y)ap!

гейзер *n.* geyser.

гейша *n.* geisha.

гектар *n.* hectare.

гелий *n.* helium.

гелиограф *n.* heliograph.

гелиотроп *n.* heliotrope.

гемоглобин *n.* hemoglobin.

геморрой *n.* hemorrhoids; piles.

гемофилия *n.* hemophilia.

ген *n.* gene.

генеалогия *n.* genealogy. —**генеалогический,** *adj.* genealogical.

генезис (нэ) *n.* genesis; origin.

генерал *n.* general. —**генерал-майор,** major general (*equivalent to U.S. brigadier general*). —**генерал-лейтенант,** lieutenant general (*equivalent to U.S. major general*). —**генерал-полковник,** colonel general (*equivalent to U.S. lieutenant general*). —**генерал армии,** general of the army (*equivalent to U.S. full general*).

генералиссимус *n.* generalissimo.

генералитет *n.* the generals.

генеральный *adj.* general. —**Генеральная Ассамблея,** General Assembly. —**генеральный план,** master plan. —**генеральный прокурор,** prosecutor general. —**генеральная репетиция,** dress rehearsal. —**генеральный секретарь,** 1, secretary-general (*of the United Nations, NATO, etc.*). 2, general secretary (*of a communist party*). —**генеральное сражение,** decisive battle; pitched battle. —**генеральный штаб,** general staff.

генеральский *adj.* of or for a general; general's.

генератор *n.* generator; oscillator.

генетика (нэ) *n.* genetics. —**генетик,** *n.* geneticist. —**генетический,** *adj.* genetic.

гениальный *adj.* 1, of genius. 2, ingenious. —**гениальность,** *n.f.* genius.

гений *n.* genius.

генный *adj., in* генная инженерия, genetic engineering.

геноцид *n.* genocide.

география *n.* geography. —**географ,** *n.* geographer. —**географический,** *adj.* geographic.

геодезия (дэ) *n.* geodesy. —**геодезический,** *adj.* geodetic.

геология *n.* geology. —**геолог,** *n.* geologist. —**геологический,** *adj.* geological.

геометрия *n.* geometry. —**геометрический,** *adj.* geometric; geometrical.

геополитика *n.* geopolitics. —**геополитический,** *adj.* geopolitical.

георгин *n.* dahlia. *Also,* **георгина.**

геотермальный *adj.* geothermal. *Also,* **геотермический.**

геофизика *n.* geophysics. —**геофизический,** *adj.* geophysical.

геоцентрический *adj.* geocentric.

гепард *n.* cheetah.

гепатит *n.* hepatitis.

геральдика *n.* heraldry. —**геральдический,** *adj.* heraldic.

герань *n.f.* geranium.

герб [*gen.* герба] *n.* coat of arms.

гербарий *n.* herbarium.

гербицид *n.* herbicide; weed-killer.

гербовый *adj.* bearing the coat of arms.

гериатрия *n.* geriatics. —**гериатрический,** *adj.* geriatric.

Геркулес *n.* 1, Hercules. 2, *l.c.* oatmeal.

германец [*gen.* -нца] *n.m.* [*fem.* -нка] German.

германий *n.* germanium.

германский *adj.* 1, German. 2, Germanic.

гермафродит *n.* hermaphrodite.

герметический *adj.* airtight; pressurized. —**герметически,** *adv.* hermetically.

героизм *n.* heroism. —**героика,** *n.* heroic spirit.

героин *n.* heroin.

героиня *n.* heroine.

героический *adj.* heroic. —**героически,** *adv.* heroically.

герой *n.* hero. —**отрицательный герой,** villain (*of a story*).

геройский *adj.* heroic. —**геройски,** *adv.* heroically.

геройство *n.f.* heroism.

герольд *n., hist.* herald.

геронтология *n.* gerontology.

герундий *n.* gerund.

герц [*gen. pl.* герц] *n., electricity* cycle per second.

герцог *n.* duke. —**герцогиня,** *n.* duchess. —**герцогский,** *adj.* ducal.

герцогство *n.* 1, dukedom. 2, duchy.

гетман *n., hist.* Ukrainian Cossack leader in the 17th and 18th centuries; hetman.

гетры *n.pl.* [*sing.* гетра] gaiters; spats.

гетто *n. indecl.* ghetto.

гиацинт *n.* hyacinth.

гиббон *n.* gibbon.

ги́бель *n.f.* **1,** destruction; death. **2,** wreck; crash. **3,** ruin; ruination; downfall.

ги́бельный *adj.* disastrous; ruinous; fatal.

гиби́скус *n.* hibiscus.

ги́бкий *adj.* [*comp.* **ги́бче**] **1,** flexible. **2,** supple. —**ги́бкий диск,** floppy disk.

ги́бкость *n.f.* flexibility.

ги́блый *adj.,* *colloq.* hopeless; worthless. —**ги́блое де́ло,** hopeless case; lost cause.

ги́бнуть *v.impfv.* [*pfv.* **поги́бнуть;** *past* **гиб** *or* **ги́бнул, ги́бла**] to be killed; perish.

гибри́д *n.* hybrid. —**гибри́дный,** *adj.* hybrid.

гига́нт *n.* giant. —**гига́нтский,** *adj.* giant; gigantic.

гигие́на *n.* hygiene. —**гигиени́ческий,** *adj.* of or pert. to hygiene; hygienic. —**гигиени́чный,** *adj.* hygienic; clean; sanitary.

гид *n.* **1,** guide (*person*). **2,** *obs.* guidebook.

ги́дра *n.* hydra.

гидра́влика *n.* hydraulics. —**гидравли́ческий,** *adj.* hydraulic.

гидра́нт *n.* (fire) hydrant.

гидра́т *n.* hydrate.

гидродина́мика *n.* hydrodynamics.

гидро́лиз *n.* hydrolysis.

гидроло́гия *n.* hydrology.

гидролока́тор *n.* sonar (*device*). —**гирдолока́ция,** *n.* sonar (*method*).

гидро́метр *n.* hydrometer.

гидроо́кись *n.f.* hydroxide.

гидропла́н *n.* seaplane.

гидросамолёт *n.* seaplane.

гидроста́тика *n.* hydrostatics.

гидроэлектри́ческий *adj.* hydroelectric.

гидроэлектроста́нция *n.* hydroelectric station.

гие́на *n.* hyena.

ги́кать *v.impfv.* [*pfv.* **ги́кнуть**] *colloq.* to shout; whoop.

гико́ри *n.m. indecl.* hickory.

ги́льдия *n.,* *hist.* guild.

ги́льза *n.* **1,** shell; cartridge case. **2,** cigarette wrapper.

гильоти́на *n.* guillotine.

гильотини́ровать *v.impfv. & pfv.* [*pres.* **-рую, -руешь**] to guillotine.

гимн *n.* hymn. —**госуда́рственный гимн,** national anthem.

гимна́зия *n.,* pre-rev. high school. —**гимнази́ст,** *n.,* pre-rev. high school student.

гимна́ст *n.* gymnast.

гимнастёрка [*gen. pl.* **-рок**] *n.* soldier's blouse.

гимна́стика *n.* gymnastics.

гимнасти́ческий *adj.* gymnastic. —**гимнасти́ческий зал,** gymnasium.

гимна́стка [*gen. pl.* **-ток**] *n.* (female) gymnast.

гинеколо́гия *n.* gynecology. —**гинеко́лог,** *n.* gynecologist. —**гинекологи́ческий,** *adj.* gynecological.

гине́я *n.* guinea.

гипе́рбола *n.* **1,** hyperbola. **2,** hyperbole. —**гиперболи́ческий,** *adj.* hyperbolic.

гиперинфля́ция *n.* hyperinflation.

гипертони́я *n.* hypertension; high blood pressure. —**гипертони́ческий,** *adj.* hypertension (*attrib.*).

гипно́з *n.* hypnosis. —**гипнотизёр,** *n.* hypnotist.

гипнотизи́ровать *v.impfv.* [*pfv.* **загипнотизи́ровать;** *pres.* **-рую, -руешь**] to hypnotize.

гипноти́зм *n.* hypnotism. —**гипноти́ческий,** *adj.* hypnotic.

гипо́теза *n.* hypothesis.

гипотену́за *n.* hypotenuse.

гипотети́ческий *also,* **гипотети́чный** *adj.* hypothetical.

гипо́физ *also,* **гипофи́з** *n.* pituitary gland.

гиппопота́м *n.* hippopotamus.

гипс *n.* **1,** gypsum. **2,** plaster of Paris. **3,** cast. —**ги́псовый,** *adj.* gypsum (*attrib.*); plaster.

гиреви́к [*gen.* **-вика́**] *n.* weightlifter.

гирля́нда *n.* garland.

гироко́мпас *n.* gyrocompass.

гироско́п *n.* gyroscope.

ги́ря *n.* **1,** weight. **2,** *sports* weight; dumbbell.

гистоло́гия *n.* histology.

гита́ра *n.* guitar. —**гитари́ст,** *n.* guitarist.

ги́чка [*gen. pl.* **ги́чек**] *n.* gig (*boat*).

глава́ [*pl.* **гла́вы**] *n.* **1,** *m. or f.* (*with gen.*) head (of): **глава́ семьи́,** head of the family. **2,** chapter. **3,** cupola; dome. **4,** *poetic* = **голова́.** —**во главе́** (+ *gen.*), at the head of. —**во главе́ с** (+ *instr.*), headed by. —**ста́вить во главу́ угла́,** to put at the top of the list; give top priority to; consider paramount.

глава́рь [*gen.* **-варя́**] *n.m.* leader; ringleader.

главе́нство *n.* supremacy.

главе́нствовать *v.impfv.* [*pres.* **-ствую, -ствуешь**] **1,** to be dominant; be the boss. **2,** (*with* **над**) to dominate; hold sway over.

главнокома́ндующий *n., decl. as an adj.* commander in chief.

гла́вный *adj.* **1,** main; chief; principal. **2,** head; chief. —**гла́вное,** *n.* the main thing. —**гла́вным о́бразом,** mainly; chiefly; for the most part.

глаго́л *n.* verb.

глаго́лица *n.* one of the two original Slavonic alphabets; Glagolitic alphabet.

глаго́льный *adj.* verbal.

глади́атор *n.* gladiator.

глади́льный *adj.* ironing (*attrib.*): **глади́льная доска́,** ironing board.

гладио́лус *n.* gladiolus.

гла́дить *v.impfv.* [*pres.* **гла́жу, гла́дишь**] **1,** [*pfv.* **вы́гладить**] to iron; press. **2,** [*pfv.* **погла́дить**] to stroke; pet; pat. —**гла́дить по голо́вке,** to give (someone) a pat on the back.

гла́дкий *adj.* [*short form* **гла́док, гладка́, гла́дко, гла́дки;** *comp.* **гла́же**] **1,** smooth. **2,** (*of material*) plain. —**гла́дко,** *adv.* smoothly.

гладкоство́льный *adj.* smoothbore.

гла́дкость *n.f.* smoothness.

гладь *n.f.* **1,** smooth surface. **2,** satin stitch.

гла́же *adj., comp. of* **гла́дкий.**

гла́женье *n.* ironing; pressing.

глаз [*2nd loc.* **глазу́;** *pl.* **глаза́, глаз**] *n.* eye. —**в глаза́ не ви́деть,** to have never seen (someone or something). —**в глаза́х** (+ *gen.*), in the eyes of. —**за**

глаза́, **1,** behind one's back. **2,** sight unseen. **3,** quite enough; more than enough. —**на глаз,** by eye. —**на глаза́х** (+ *gen. or* у), in full view of; before the very eyes of. —**с гла́зу на глаз,** alone with one another; in private. —**с глаз доло́й, из се́рдца вон,** out of sight, out of mind.

глаза́стый *adj., colloq.* **1,** big-eyed. **2,** sharp-eyed.

глазе́ть *v.impfv., colloq.* to stare; gawk; gape.

глази́рованный *adj.* **1,** glazed. **2,** with icing.

глазирова́ть *v.impfv. & pfv.* [*pres.* -ру́ю, -ру́ешь] **1,** to put icing on. **2,** to give a glossy finish to.

глазни́к [*gen.* -ника́] *n., colloq.* eye doctor.

глазни́ца *n.* eye socket.

глазно́й *adj.* eye (*attrib.*).

глазо́к [*gen.* -зка́] *n.* **1,** [*pl.* гла́зки] *dim. of* глаз. **2,** [*pl.* глазки́] *colloq.* peephole. —**де́лать** *or* **стро́ить гла́зки** (+ *dat.*), to make eyes (at). —**на глазо́к,** by eye. —**одни́м глазко́м,** with half an eye.

глазоме́р *n.* **1,** measurement with the naked eye. На глазоме́р; по глазоме́ру, by eye. **2,** ability to so measure.

глазу́нья *n.* fried eggs. *Also,* яи́чница-глазу́нья.

глазурова́ть *v.impfv. & pfv.* [*pres.* -ру́ю, -ру́ешь] to glaze (pottery).

глазу́рь *n.f.* **1,** glaze (*on pottery*). **2,** icing.

гла́нды *n.pl.* [*sing.* гла́нда] **1,** tonsils. **2,** *colloq.* swollen glands.

глас *n., archaic* voice. —**глас вопию́щего в пусты́не,** voice in the wilderness.

гласи́ть *v.impfv.* (*of a text, saying, etc.*) to read; say; go: как гласи́т погово́рка, as the saying goes.

гла́сно *adv.* publicly; openly.

гла́сность *n.f.* **1,** publicity. **2,** openness. —**предава́ть (что́-нибудь) гла́сности,** to make public; publicize.

гла́сный *adj.* **1,** vowel (*attrib.*). **2,** open; public. —*n.* vowel.

глауко́ма *n.* glaucoma.

глаша́тай *n.* **1,** town crier. **2,** (*with gen.*) apostle (of).

гле́тчер *n.* glacier.

гликоге́н *n.* glycogen.

гли́на *n.* clay.

гли́нистый *adj.* clay (*attrib.*); clayey. —**гли́нистый сла́нец,** shale.

глиноби́тный *adj.* clay (*attrib.*); mud (*attrib.*); adobe (*attrib.*).

гли́няный *adj.* **1,** clay (*attrib.*). **2,** earthenware (*attrib.*). —**гли́няная посу́да,** pottery.

гли́ссер *n.* hydroplane (*boat*).

глист [*gen.* глиста́] *n.* (intestinal) worm.

глицери́н *n.* glycerine. —**глицери́новый,** *adj.* glycerine (*attrib.*).

глици́ния *n.* wisteria.

глоба́льный *adj.* global.

гло́бус *n.* globe.

глода́ть *v.impfv.* [*pres.* гложу́, гло́жешь] **1,** to gnaw. **2,** *fig.* (*of emotions*) to gnaw at; oppress. Что вас гло́жет?, what's eating you?

глокси́ния *n.* gloxinia.

гло́сса *n.* gloss (*commentary*).

глосса́рий *n.* glossary.

глота́ние *n.* swallowing.

глота́ть *v.impfv.* [*pfv.* глотну́ть] **1,** to swallow. **2,** *colloq.* to gulp down. **3,** *fig.* to devour (books). **4,** *in* глота́ть слёзы, to choke back the tears.

гло́тка [*gen. pl.* -ток] *n.* **1,** gullet. **2,** *colloq.* throat. —**во всю гло́тку,** at the top of one's lungs.

глотну́ть *v., pfv. of* глота́ть.

глото́к [*gen.* -тка́] *n.* **1,** swallow; gulp. **2,** mouthful. —**как глото́к све́жего во́здуха,** like a breath of fresh air.

гло́хнуть *v.impfv.* [*past* глох *or* гло́хнул, гло́хла] **1,** [*pfv.* огло́хнуть] to become deaf. **2,** [*pfv.* загло́хнуть] (*of sounds*) to become inaudible; (*of an engine*) to stall; (*of feelings*) to wane. **3,** [*pfv.* загло́хнуть] to become overgrown (*or* choked) with weeds.

глу́бже *adj., comp. of* глубо́кий.

глубина́ [*pl.* -би́ны] *n.* **1,** depth. **2,** *pl.* depths: морски́е глуби́ны, ocean depths. **3,** innermost *or* farthermost point. В глубине́ ле́са, in the deepest part of the forest; в глубине́ сце́ны, at the back of the stage. —**в глубине́ души́,** in one's heart; deep down.

глуби́нка *n., colloq.* interior (*of a country*).

глуби́нный *adj.* **1,** deep; deep-water (*attrib.*). **2,** remote; out-of-the-way. —**глуби́нная бо́мба,** depth charge.

глубо́кий *adj.* [*short form* -бо́к, -бока́, -боко́ *or* -бо́ко, -боки́ *or* -бо́ки; *comp.* глу́бже] **1,** deep. **2,** profound. **3,** in-depth; thorough. —**глубо́кой но́чью,** in the dead of night. —**глубо́кий о́бморок,** dead faint. —**глубо́кая о́сень,** late autumn. —**глубо́кая ста́рость,** extreme old age.

глубоко́ *adv.* deeply; profoundly. —*adj., used predicatively,* deep: Здесь глубоко́, it is deep here.

глубоково́дный *adj.* deep-water; deep-sea.

глубокомы́сленный *adj.* profound. —**глубокомы́слие,** *n.* depth of thought; profundity.

глубокоуважа́емый *adj., used in salutations,* honored; dear.

глубь *n.f.* depth; depths. —**в глубь** (+ *gen.*), deep into; far into.

глуми́ться *v.r.impfv.* [*pres.* -млю́сь, -ми́шься] (*with* над) to mock; deride.

глумле́ние *n.* mocking; derision.

глумли́вый *adj.* mocking; derisive.

глупе́ть *v.impfv.* [*pfv.* поглупе́ть] to become foolish; become stupid.

глупе́ц [*gen.* -пца́] *n.* dolt; oaf; dunce.

глупи́ть *v.impfv.* [*pres.* -плю́, -пи́шь] *colloq.* to be foolish; behave foolishly.

глу́по *adv.* foolishly; stupidly. —*adj., used predicatively,* foolish; silly: Глу́по волнова́ться из-за э́того, it is silly to get upset over that.

глупова́тый *adj.* dull; not very bright.

глу́пость *n.f.* **1,** foolishness; stupidity. **2,** foolish act; foolish thing. **3,** *usu. pl., colloq.* nonsense.

глу́пый *adj.* foolish; dumb; silly; stupid.

глупы́ш [*gen.* -пыша́] *n.* **1,** fulmar (*bird*). **2,** *colloq.* silly person.

глуха́рь [*gen.* -харя́] *n.m.* **1,** wood grouse. **2,** *colloq.* deaf person.

глу́хо *adv.* **1,** softly. **2,** vaguely. **3,** thickly. **4,** *colloq.* tight(ly). —*adj., used predicatively,* quiet: В лесу́ бы́ло глу́хо, it was quiet in the woods.

глухо́й *adj.* **1,** deaf. **2,** (*of a sound*) muted; muffled; hollow. **3,** *phonet.* voiceless. **4,** closed up; having no openings. Глуха́я стена́, blank wall. **5,** latent; suppressed. **6,** (*of a forest*) dense. **7,** remote; desolate. Глуха́я у́лица, lonely street. **8,** *in* глуха́я о́сень, late autumn; глуха́я ночь, the dead of night. —*n.* deaf person.

глухома́нь *n.f.* remote corner; out-of-the-way place.

глухонемо́й *adj.* deaf-and-dumb. —*n.* deaf-mute.

глухота́ *n.* deafness.

глуши́тель *n.m.* muffler; silencer.

глуши́ть *v.impfv.* [*pfv.* **заглуши́ть**] **1,** to muffle; drown out. **2,** to deaden (pain). **3,** (*of weeds*) to choke. **4,** to turn off (the motor). **5,** to jam (a radio broadcast). **6,** *fig.* to stifle; suppress. **7,** *colloq.* [*pfv.* **оглуши́ть**] to stun (*with a blow*).

глушь [*gen., dat. & prepl.* **глуши́**; *instr.* **глу́шью**] *n.f.* **1,** wilderness; wilds. **2,** out-of-the-way place.

глы́ба *n.* **1,** block (*of ice, granite, etc.*). **2,** clod (*of earth*).

глюко́за *n.* glucose.

гляде́ть *v.impfv.* [*pfv.* **погляде́ть**; *pres.* **гляжу́, гляди́шь**] **1,** to look. **2,** (*with* **на** + *acc.*) to look at. **3,** [*impfv. only*] (*with* **на** + *acc.*) to look out on. **4,** (*with* **за** + *instr.*) *colloq.* to look after; keep an eye on. **5,** [*impfv. only*] *colloq.* (*with an adv.*) to look; appear; (*with instr.*) look like. —**гля́дя по** (+ *dat.*), depending on. —**идти́ куда́ глаза́ глядя́т**, to wander aimlessly; follow one's nose. —**как** (*or* **сло́вно**) **в во́ду гляде́л**, as if he had inside information; as if he were clairvoyant. —**того́ и гляди́**, one would expect (at any moment).

гляде́ться *v.r.impfv.* [*pfv.* **погляде́ться**; *pres.* **-жу́сь, -ди́шься**] to look at oneself: гляде́ться в зе́ркало, to look at oneself in the mirror.

гля́нец [*gen.* **-нца**] *n.* luster; gloss.

гля́нуть *v.pfv.* (*with* **на** + *acc.*) to glance (at).

гля́нцевый *adj.* glossy; lustrous. *Also,* **глянцеви́тый.**

гм *interj.* ahem!; hm!

гнать *v.impfv.* [*pres.* **гоню́, го́нишь**; *past fem.* **гнала́**] **1,** to drive (cattle). **2,** to urge on; ride *or* drive hard. **3,** *v.i.* to race; tear along. **4,** to hunt; chase (an animal). **5,** (*of the wind*) to blow (leaves, snow, etc.). **6,** to drive out. **7,** *colloq.* to drive (a car, truck, etc.). **8,** to distill. —**гна́ться**, *refl.* [*past* **гна́лся, гнала́сь, гнало́сь** *or* **гна́лось, гнали́сь** *or* **гна́лись**] (*with* **за** + *instr.*) to chase; pursue.

гнев *n.* anger. —**гне́вный**, *adj.* angry; irate.

гнедо́й *adj.* (*of a horse*) bay.

гнезди́ться *v.r.impfv.* **1,** to nest. **2,** *fig.* to be lodged.

гнездо́ [*pl.* **гнёзда**] *n.* **1,** nest. **2,** socket. **3,** mortise.

гнёздышко [*pl.* **-шки, -шек**] *n., dim. of* **гнездо́.**

гнейс *n.* gneiss.

гнести́ *v.impfv.* [*pres.* **гнету́, гнетёшь**; *not used in the past*] to weigh on; oppress.

гнёт *n.* **1,** burden; weight; yoke. **2,** oppression.

гнету́щий *adj.* oppressive.

гни́да *n.* nit.

гние́ние *n.* rotting; decay.

гнило́й *adj.* **1,** rotten; decayed. **2,** (*of weather*) damp; muggy.

гни́лостный *adj.* putrid.

гни́лость *n.f.* rottenness.

гниль *n.f.* **1,** something rotten or decayed. **2,** mold. **3,** rot (*plant disease*).

гнить *v.impfv.* [*pfv.* **сгнить**; *pres.* **гнию́, гниёшь**; *past fem.* **гнила́**] to rot; decay.

гное́ние *n.* festering.

гнои́ть *v.impfv.* [*pfv.* **сгнои́ть**] **1,** to let rot; leave to rot. **2,** to cause to rot. —**гнои́ться**, *refl.* [*impfv. only*] to fester.

гной *n.* pus.

гнойни́к [*gen.* **-ника́**] *n.* abscess.

гнойничо́к [*gen.* **-чка́**] *n.* pustule.

гно́йный *adj.* festering.

гном *n.* gnome.

гну *n.m. indecl.* gnu.

гнус *n.* bloodsucking insects (*mosquitoes, gnats, etc.*).

гнуса́вить *v.impfv.* [*pres.* **-влю, -вишь**] to speak with a nasal twang.

гнуса́вый *adj.* **1,** (*of one's voice*) nasal. **2,** (*of a person*) speaking with a nasal twang.

гну́сность *n.f.* **1,** heinousness; infamy. **2,** heinous act; rotten thing.

гну́сный *adj.* vile; heinous; odious; infamous.

гнуть *v.impfv.* [*pfv.* **согну́ть**] **1,** to bend. **2,** [*impfv. only*] *colloq.* to drive at: Куда́ ты гнёшь?, what are you driving at? —**гнуть свою́ ли́нию**, to press one's point; insist on having one's way. —**гнуть спи́ну, 1,** to break one's back (*i.e.* work hard). **2,** (*with* **перед**) to kowtow (to).

гну́ться *v.r.impfv.* [*pfv.* **согну́ться**] to bend.

гнуша́ться *v.r.impfv.* [*pfv.* **погнуша́ться**] **1,** (*with gen. or instr.*) to disdain; have an aversion to. **2,** (*with instr.*) to disdain (to); be averse (to).

гобеле́н *n.* tapestry.

гобо́й *n.* oboe. —**гобои́ст,** *n.* oboist.

гове́ть *v.impfv.* to prepare for Communion (*by worship or fasting*).

го́вор *n.* **1,** sound of voices. **2,** manner of speaking; accent. **3,** dialect.

говори́ть *v.impfv.* [*pfv.* **сказа́ть**] **1,** [*impfv. only*] to speak; talk: говори́ть гро́мким го́лосом, to speak/talk in a loud voice. Говори́ть по-ру́сски, to speak Russian. **2,** to say; tell. Говори́ть пра́вду, to tell the truth. Он говори́т, что о́чень за́нят, he says he's very busy. **3,** to make; deliver (a speech, sermon, etc.). **4,** [*impfv. only*] (*with* **о**) to indicate; suggest: говори́ть о мно́гом, to say a lot; speak volumes. —**говори́т само́ за себя́**, to speak for itself. —**да что вы гово́рите!**, you don't say! —**и не говори́те!**, you can say that again! —**как говоря́т**, as they say. —**не говоря́ уже́ о**, not to mention; to say nothing of. —**не́чего и говори́ть**, it goes without saying. —**ничего́ не говори́ть** (+ *dat.*), to mean nothing to; be totally unfamiliar to. —**об э́том и говори́ть не́чего**, it is not even worth talking about; it/that is out of the question. —**что и говори́ть**, to be sure; it cannot be denied. *See also* **сказа́ть**.

говори́ться *v.r.impfv.* to be said; be stated. В зако́не говори́тся..., the law states... В телегра́мме говори́тся..., the telegram reads... —**как говори́тся**, as the saying goes; as they say.

говорли́вый *adj.* talkative; garrulous; loquacious. —**говорли́вость,** *n.f.* loquaciousness.

говору́н [*gen.* -руна́] *n.m.* [*fem.* -ру́нья] *colloq.* habitual talker; chatterbox.

говя́дина *n.* beef.

говя́жий [*fem.* -жья] *adj.* beef (*attrib.*).

го́голь *n.m.* goldeneye (*duck*). —**ходи́ть го́голем**, to strut.

го́гот *n.* cackle (*of a goose*).

гогота́нье *n.* cackling (*of geese*).

гогота́ть *v.impfv.* [*pres.* **гогочу́, гого́чешь**] (*of geese*) to cackle.

год [*2nd loc.* году́; *nom. pl.* **го́ды** and *sometimes* года́; *gen. pl.* **лет** and *sometimes* годо́в; *other pl. forms* **года́м, года́ми, года́х**] *n.* year. —**без году неде́ля**, *colloq.* a very short time; only a few days. —**быть в года́х**, to be getting on in years. —**в мои́ го́ды**, at my age. —**год от году; год от го́да**, with each passing year. —**из го́да в год**, year after year; year in and year out. —**не по года́м**, beyond one's years: у́мный не по года́м, smart beyond one's years. —**с года́ми**, over the years. —**с Но́вым го́дом!**, Happy New Year! *See also* **лета́**.

годи́ться *v.r.impfv.* [*pres.* **гожу́сь, годи́шься**] 1, to do; be all right; fill the bill. 2, (*with* **на** + *acc.*) to be good (for); do (for). 3, (*with* **в** + *nom. pl.*) to be qualified to be: Он не годи́тся в учителя́, he is not qualified to be a teacher. 4, (*with* **в** + *nom. pl.*) to be old enough to be: Я вам в отцы́ гожу́сь, I am old enough to be your father. —**никуда́ не годи́ться**, to be of no use; be no good at all.

годи́чный *adj.* 1, a year's; lasting a year. 2, annual; yearly.

го́дность *n.f.* fitness; suitability.

го́дный *adj.* [*short form* **го́ден, годна́, го́дно, го́дны** *or* годны́] (*with* **к** *or* **для**) fit (for *or* to); suitable (for).

годова́лый *adj.* year-old.

годово́й *adj.* annual; yearly.

годовщи́на *n.* anniversary.

гол [*pl.* **голы́**] *n., sports* goal.

Голго́фа *n.* Calvary.

голени́ще *n.* boot top.

го́лень *n.f.* shin.

голла́ндец [*gen.* -дца] *n.* 1, Dutchman. 2, *pl.* the Dutch.

голла́ндка [*gen. pl.* -док] *n.* Dutchwoman; Dutch girl.

голла́ндский *adj.* Dutch. —**голла́ндская печь**, tiled stove.

голова́ [*acc.* го́лову; *pl.* го́ловы, голо́в, -ва́м] *n.* head. —**в пе́рвую го́лову**, *colloq.* first of all. —**голова́ в го́лову**, neck and neck. —**на́ голову вы́ше** (+ *gen.*), head and shoulders above. —**над голово́й**, overhead. —**на све́жую го́лову**, with a fresh mind. —**на свою́ го́лову**, to one's detriment; to one's

cost. —**поста́вить с ног на́ голову**, to stand (*e.g.* the truth) on its head. —**с голово́й, 1**, smart; bright; clever. **2**, *in* окуну́ться *or* уйти́ с голово́й в (+ *acc.*), to plunge into; become completely absorbed in. —**с головы́**, a/per head. —**с головы́ до ног**, from head to toe. —**че́рез го́лову** (+ *gen.*), over the head of; without letting someone know.

голова́стик *n.* tadpole.

голове́шка [*gen. pl.* -шек] *n.* smoldering piece of wood.

голо́вка [*gen. pl.* -вок] *n.* 1, *dim. of* голова́. 2, head (*of a pin, match, etc.*). 3, *colloq.* the people on top; the brass. —**боева́я голо́вка**, warhead.

головно́й *adj.* 1, head (*attrib.*). 2, *mil.* leading; advance. 3, (*of an institution*) leading. —**головно́й мозг**, cerebrum.

головня́ [*gen. pl.* -не́й] *n.* 1, charred log. 2, smut (*plant disease*).

головокруже́ние *n.* dizziness. —**головокружи́тельный,** *adj.* dizzying; causing one's head to spin.

головоло́мка [*gen. pl.* -мок] *n.* puzzle; conundrum; brain-twister. —**головоло́мный,** *adj.* baffling.

головомо́йка *n., colloq.* scolding; dressing-down.

головоре́з *n., colloq.* 1, daredevil. 2, bandit; cutthroat; desperado.

голо́вушка [*gen. pl.* -шек] *n., colloq., dim. of* голова́. —**бе́дная моя́ голо́вушка!**, woe is me!

геоло́гра́фия *n.* holography.

го́лод *n.* 1, hunger. 2, starvation. 3, famine. 4, *fig.* acute shortage: бума́жный го́лод, acute shortage of paper.

голода́ние *n.* starvation.

голода́ть *v.impfv.* to starve; go hungry.

голода́ющий *adj.* starving; hungry. —*n.* starving person; hungry person.

голо́дный *adj.* [*short form* **го́лоден, -дна́, го́лодны**] 1, hungry. 2, hunger (*attrib.*): голо́дные бо́ли, hunger pangs. Голо́дный бунт, food riot. 3, *colloq.* (*of a meal*) meager. Голо́дная дие́та, starvation diet. —*n.* hungry person. —**умира́ть голо́дной сме́ртью**, to die of hunger/starvation; starve to death.

голодо́вка *n.* 1, *colloq.* starvation. 2, hunger strike.

гололе́дица *n.* 1, icy surface. 2, icy conditions.

го́лос [*pl.* голоса́] *n.* 1, voice. 2, vote. —**в го́лос**, loudly; for all to hear. —**во весь го́лос, 1**, at the top of one's lungs. **2**, *fig.* loud and clear. —**в оди́н го́лос**, with one voice.

голоси́стый *adj.* having a loud voice.

голоси́ть *v.impfv.* [*pres.* -шу́, -си́шь] *colloq.* to wail.

голосло́вно *adv.* without (furnishing) any evidence.

голосло́вный *adj.* groundless; unfounded; unsubstantiated. —**чтобы не быть голосло́вным**, by way of evidence; to back up my statement.

голосова́ние *n.* voting; vote. Та́йное голосова́ние, secret ballot. —**ста́вить** (*e.g.* **вопро́с**) **на голосова́ние**, to put to the vote.

голосова́ть *v.impfv.* [*pfv.* **проголосова́ть**; *pres.* -су́ю, -су́ешь] 1, (*with* **за** *or* **про́тив**) to vote (for *or* against). 2, (*with a dir. obj.*) to vote on. 3, *colloq.* to hitchhike; thumb a ride.

голосово́й *adj.* vocal.

голубе́ть *v.impfv.* [*pfv.* **поголубе́ть**] **1**, to turn blue; become blue. **2**, [*impfv. only*] (*of anything blue*) to shine; gleam.

голубизна́ *n.* bright blue color.

голуби́ный *adj.* pigeon (*attrib.*).

голу́бка [*gen. pl.* **-бок**] *n.* **1**, female pigeon. **2**, (*in direct address*) darling; sweetheart.

голубова́тый *adj.* bluish.

голубо́й *adj.* **1**, light blue; sky-blue. **2**, *colloq.* homosexual; gay. —*n.*, *colloq.* homosexual; gay.

голубо́к [*gen.* **-бка́**] *n.*, *dim. of* **го́лубь.**

голубцы́ *n.pl.* [*sing.* **голубе́ц**] stuffed cabbage.

голу́бчик *n.*, *used in direct address,* my dear fellow; my friend.

го́лубь [*pl.* **го́луби, -бе́й, -бя́м**] *n.m.* pigeon; dove.

голубя́тник *n.* pigeon lover.

голубя́тня [*gen. pl.* **-тен**] *n.* dovecote; pigeon house.

го́лый *adj.* naked; bare. —**на го́лое те́ло**, next to the skin.

голы́ш [*gen.* **голыша́**] *n.* **1**, *colloq.* naked child. **2**, *obs.* pauper. **3**, pebble.

голышо́м *adv.*, *colloq.* stark naked; in the nude.

голь *n.f.*, *obs.* **1**, the poor. **2**, wasteland. —**голь на вы́думки хитра́**, necessity is the mother of invention.

го́льмий *n.* holmium.

гольф *n.* golf.

голья́н *n.* minnow.

гомеопа́тия *n.* homeopathy. —**гомеопа́т,** *n.* homeopath. —**гомеопати́ческий,** *adj.* homeopathic.

гомогенизи́ровать *v.impfv. & pfv.* [*pres* **-рую, -руешь**] to homogenize.

гомоге́нный *adj.* homogenous.

го́мон *n.*, *colloq.* hum (*of voices*); hubbub.

гомосексуали́зм *n.* homosexuality. —**гомосексуали́ст,** *n.* homosexual. —**гомосексуа́льный,** *adj.* homosexual.

гонг *n.* gong.

гондо́ла *n.* gondola. —**гондолье́р,** *n.* gondolier.

гоне́ние *n.* persecution.

гоне́ц [*gen.* **гонца́**] *n.* messenger.

гони́тель *n.m.* persecutor.

го́нка [*gen. pl.* **го́нок**] *n.* **1**, *usu. pl.* race: автомоби́льные го́нки, automobile race. **2**, *colloq.* rush; hurry. **3**, *obs.* dressing-down. —**го́нка вооруже́ний,** arms race.

гоноко́кк *n.* gonococcus.

го́нор *n.* arrogance; conceit.

гонора́р *n.* fee; royalty; honorarium.

гоноре́я *n.* gonorrhea.

го́ночный *adj.* racing (*attrib.*).

гонт *n.* shingles (*for roofing*).

гонча́р [*gen.* **-чара́**] *n.* potter. —**гонча́рный,** *adj.* pottery (*attrib.*); potter's.

го́нчая *n.*, *decl. as an adj.* hound; beagle.

го́нщик *n.* racing driver.

гоня́ть *v.impfv.*, *indeterm. of* **гнать.** —**гоня́ться,** *refl.*, *indeterm. of* **гна́ться.**

гопа́к [*gen.* **гопака́**] *n.* gopak (*Ukrainian dance*).

гора́ [*acc.* **го́ру**; *pl.* **го́ры, гор, гора́м**] *n.* **1**, mountain. **2**, (*with prepositions*) hill: кати́ться с горы́, to roll down the hill. **3**, *in* **америка́нские го́ры,** roller coaster. —**в го́ру,** uphill. —**гора́ с плеч,** a load off one's shoulders. —**идти́ в го́ру,** to come up in the world. —**наде́яться на кого́-нибудь как на ка́менную го́ру,** to rely fully on; put implicit faith in. —**не за гора́ми,** not far off. —**под гору,** downhill. —**стоя́ть за кого́-нибудь горо́й,** to be solidly behind (someone).

гора́зд *adj.* (*with* **на** + *acc. or* **в** + *prepl.*) *colloq.* good (at). —**кто во что гора́зд,** each in his own way.

гора́здо *adv.*, used only with comparative adjectives, much; far: гора́здо лу́чше, much better.

горб [*gen.* **горба́**; *2nd loc.* **горбу́**] *n.* hump.

горба́тый *adj.* **1**, hunchbacked; humpbacked. **2**, (*of one's nose*) hooked. —*n.* hunchback; humpback.

горби́на *n.* bump; rise.

горби́нка *n.*, *in* нос с горби́нкой, hooked nose.

го́рбить *v.impfv.* [*pfv.* **сго́рбить**; *pres.* **-блю, -бишь**] to hunch. —**го́рбиться,** *refl.* to hunch one's back; be hunched over.

горбу́н [*gen.* **-буна́**] *n.m.* [*fem.* **-бу́нья**] hunchback; humpback.

горбу́шка [*gen. pl.* **-шек**] *n.* end crust.

гордели́вый *adj.* proud; haughty.

горде́ц [*gen.* **-деца́**] *n.* proud man; haughty man.

го́рдиев *adj.*, *in* го́рдиев у́зел, Gordian knot.

горди́ться *v.r.impfv.* [*pres.* **-жу́сь, -ди́шься**] (*with instr.*) to be proud (of).

го́рдо *adv.* proudly.

го́рдость *n.f.* pride.

го́рдый *adj.* proud.

го́ре *n.* **1**, grief; sorrow. Уби́тый го́рем, grief-stricken. **2**, misfortune. **3**, (*with dat.*) woe (to): го́ре тому́, кто..., woe to him who... Го́ре мне!, woe is me! —**на своё го́ре,** to one's grief; to one's sorrow.

горева́ть *v.impfv.* [*pres.* **горю́ю, горю́ешь**] to mourn; grieve.

горе́лка [*gen. pl.* **-лок**] *n.* **1**, burner: га́зовая горе́лка, gas burner. **2**, torch: сва́рочная горе́лка, welding torch.

горе́лки [*gen.* **-лок**] *n.pl.* children's game similar to tag.

горе́лый *adj.* burnt. —**горе́лое,** *n.* something burning. Па́хнет горе́лым, there is a smell of something burning.

горемы́ка *n.m. & f.*, *colloq.* hapless creature; unlucky soul.

горемы́чный *adj.*, *colloq.* hapless.

горе́ние *n.* **1**, burning; combustion. **2**, *fig.* ardor; enthusiasm.

го́рестный *adj.* sorrowful; mournful.

го́ресть *n.f.* **1**, sorrow; grief. **2**, *pl.* misfortunes; sorrows.

горе́ть *v.impfv.* [*pres.* **горю́, гори́шь**] **1**, to burn; be on fire. **2**, (*of light, a lamp, etc.*) to be on; be burning. **3**, to shine; sparkle. **4**, *fig.* (*with instr.*) to burn; seethe (with an emotion).

го́рец [*gen.* **го́рца**] *n.* mountaineer; highlander.

гореча́вка *n.* gentian.

го́речь *n.f.* **1**, bitter taste. **2**, something bitter. **3**, *fig.* bitterness.

горже́т *n.* fur neckpiece. *Also,* **горже́тка.**

горизо́нт *n.* horizon.

горизонта́ль *n.f.* **1**, horizontal line; horizontal. **2**, contour line.

горизонта́льный *adj.* horizontal. —**горизонта́льно,** *adv.* horizontally.

гори́лла *n.* gorilla.

гори́стый *adj.* mountainous.

горихво́стка [*gen. pl.* **-ток**] *n.* redstart.

го́рка [*gen. pl.* **го́рок**] *n.* **1**, hill; hillock. **2**, (glass) cabinet. **3**, *aero.* vertical climb. **4**, sliding board.

го́ркнуть *v.impfv.* [*pfv.* **прого́ркнуть;** *past* **го́ркнул** *or* **го́рк, го́ркла**] to turn rancid.

горла́нить *v.impfv., colloq.* to bellow.

го́рлица *n.* turtledove. *Also,* **го́рлинка.**

го́рло *n.* **1**, throat. **2**, neck (*of a bottle*). —**во всё го́рло,** at the top of one's lungs. —**по го́рло** (*usu. with* **за́нят, рабо́ты**), up to one's eyeballs. —**попа́сть не в то го́рло,** (*of food*) to go down the wrong way.

горлово́й *adj.* **1**, throat (*attrib.*). **2**, guttural.

го́рлышко [*pl.* **-шки, -шек**] *n., dim. of* **го́рло.**

горля́нка *n.* calabash; gourd.

гормо́н *n.* hormone.

горн *n.* **1**, furnace; forge. **2**, bugle.

горни́ло *n.* crucible.

горни́ст *n.* bugler.

го́рничная *n., decl. as an adj.* maid; housemaid; chambermaid.

горнодобыва́ющий *adj.* mining (*attrib.*).

горнопромы́шленный *adj.* mining (*attrib.*).

горнорабо́чий *n., decl. as an adj.* miner.

горноста́й *n.* ermine. —**горноста́евый,** *adj.* ermine.

го́рный *adj.* **1**, mountain (*attrib.*). **2**, mountainous. **3**, mining (*attrib.*). **4**, mineral (*attrib.*). —**го́рное де́ло,** mining. —**го́рная поро́да,** *geol.* rock. —**го́рное со́лнце,** artificial sunlight. —**го́рный хруста́ль,** rock crystal.

горня́к [*gen.* **-няка́**] *n.* **1**, miner. **2**, mining engineer. **3**, mining student.

го́род [*pl.* **города́**] *n.* city; town. —**за́ город,** to the country; out of town. —**за́ городом,** outside the city; out of town; in the country.

городи́ть *v.impfv.* [*pres.* **-рожу́, -ро́дишь** *or* **-роди́шь**] *colloq.* to talk (nonsense). —**огоро́д городи́ть,** to start something.

городки́ [*gen.* **-ко́в**] *n.pl.* game similar to skittles.

городо́к [*gen.* **-дка́**] *n.* **1**, small town. **2**, premises of an institution: **медици́нский городо́к,** medical center; **вое́нный городо́к,** military post; **университе́тский городо́к,** campus.

городско́й *adj.* city (*attrib.*); town (*attrib.*); municipal; urban.

горожа́нин [*pl.* **-жа́не, -жа́н**] *n.* city dweller; townsman.

гороско́п *n.* horoscope.

горо́х *n.* peas. —**как об сте́нку горо́х,** like talking to a stone wall.

горо́ховый *adj.* **1**, pea (*attrib.*). **2**, of the color of peas; green. —**шут горо́ховый; чу́чело горо́ховое,** buffoon.

горо́шек [*gen.* **-шка**] *n.* **1**, *dim. of* **горо́х. 2**, polka dots. —**души́стый горо́шек,** sweet peas.

горо́шина *n.* pea.

горсове́т *n.* municipal council (*contr. of* **городско́й сове́т**).

го́рстка [*gen. pl.* **-сток**] *n., colloq.* handful.

го́рсточка [*gen. pl.* **-чек**] *n.* handful.

горсть [*pl.* **го́рсти, -сте́й, -стя́м**] *n.f.* **1**, hollow of the hand. **2**, (*with gen.*) handful (of).

горта́нный *adj.* **1**, laryngeal. **2**, guttural.

горта́нь *n.f.* larynx.

горте́нзия (тэ) *n.* hydrangea.

го́рче *adj., comp. of* **го́рький** (*in sense #1*).

горчи́ть *v.impfv.* to taste bitter; have a bitter taste.

горчи́ца *n.* mustard. —**горчи́чник,** *n.* mustard plaster. —**горчи́чница,** *n.* mustard pot. —**горчи́чный,** *adj.* mustard (*attrib.*).

го́рше *adj., comp. of* **го́рький** (*in sense #2*).

горше́чник *n.* master potter.

горше́чный *adj.* **1**, pottery (*attrib.*); potter's. **2**, (*of plants*) potted.

горшо́к [*gen.* **-шка́**] *n.* (earthenware) pot. —**ночно́й горшо́к,** chamber pot.

го́рькая *n., decl. as an adj.* **1**, vodka. **2**, bitters.

го́рький *adj.* [*short form* **го́рек, горька́, го́рько, го́рьки**] **1**, [*comp.* **го́рче**] bitter; bitter-tasting. **2**, [*comp.* **го́рше**] *fig.* bitter; unhappy. —**го́рький пья́ница,** heavy drinker. —**пить го́рькую,** to drink hard; hit the bottle.

го́рько *adv.* bitterly. —*adj., used predicatively* **1**, bitter: У меня́ го́рько во рту, I have a bitter taste in my mouth. **2**, (*with inf.*) distressing: Мне го́рько слы́шать таки́е слова́, it distresses me to hear such words.

горю́чее *n., decl. as an adj.* (motor) fuel. —**горю́честь,** *n.f.* combustibility. —**горю́чий,** *adj.* combustible; inflammable.

горя́чий *adj.* [*short form* **горя́ч, -ча́, -чо́, -чи́**] **1**, hot. **2**, ardent; passionate. **3**, heated; intense. **4**, warm; hearty. **5**, hot-tempered. **6**, busy; hectic. —**по горя́чим следа́м, 1**, hot on the trail. **2**, without delay. —**под горя́чую ру́ку,** in the heat of the moment; in a fit of anger. —**попа́сть под горя́чую ру́ку** (+ *dat. or gen.*), to run into someone when he is hopping mad.

горячи́ть *v.impfv.* [*pfv.* **разгорячи́ть**] **1**, to heat; make hot. **2**, excite; arouse. —**горячи́ться,** *refl.* to become excited; get hot under the collar.

горя́чка *n., colloq.* **1**, fever. **2**, fever; panic: биржева́я горя́чка, speculative fever. **3**, bustle; rush. **4**, *m. & f.* hothead.

горя́чность *n.f.* **1**, ardor; fervor. **2**, hot temper.

горячо́ *adv.* **1**, hotly; heatedly. **2**, ardently; fervently. —*adj., used predicatively,* hot: Куй желе́зо, пока́ горячо́, strike while the iron is hot.

госба́нк *n.* State Bank (*contr. of* **Госуда́рственный банк**).

госпитализа́ция *n.* hospitalization.

госпитализи́ровать *v.impfv. & pfv.* [*pres.* **-рую, -руешь**] to hospitalize.

го́спиталь *n.m.* (military) hospital. —**госпита́льный,** *adj.* hospital (*attrib.*).

госпо́день [*fem.* -дня; *neut.* -дне] *adj.* the Lord's; God's. —**гроб госпо́день**, the Holy Sepulcher. —**ле́та госпо́дня**, (*with dates*) of the year of our Lord. —**моли́тва госпо́дня**, the Lord's Prayer. —**наказа́ние госпо́дне**, God's punishment.

го́споди *interj.* good Lord!; good heavens! —**го́споди поми́луйте!**, Lord have mercy!

господи́н [*pl.* господа́, госпо́д, -да́м] *n.* 1, master. 2, gentleman. 3, (*in direct address to foreigners*) Mister; Mr.

госпо́дство *n.* 1, domination; dominion. 2, dominance; supremacy.

госпо́дствовать *v.impfv.* [*pres.* -ствую, -ствуешь] 1, (*with* над, в *or* на) to dominate. 2, to predominate. 3, (*with* над) to dominate; tower over.

госпо́дствующий *adj.* 1, ruling; dominant. 2, prevailing.

госпо́дь [*gen.* го́спода] *n.m.*, *often cap.* Lord; God. *See also* го́споди.

госпожа́ *n.*, *fem. of* господи́н, Mrs.; madam.

гостево́й *adj.* guest (*attrib.*); for guests.

гостеприи́мный *adj.* hospitable. —**гостеприи́мство**, *n.* hospitality.

гости́ная *n.*, *decl. as an adj.*, living room; drawing room; sitting room; parlor.

гости́ница *n.* hotel.

гости́ный *adj.*, *in* гости́ный двор, *pre-rev.* arcade.

гости́ть *v.impfv.* [*pres.* гощу́, гости́шь] (*with* у) to be a guest (of); stay (with).

гость [*pl.* го́сти, госте́й, гостя́м] *n.m.* [*fem.* го́стья] guest. —**быть в гостя́х** (*with* у), to be a guest (of); be visiting. —**идти́ в го́сти**, to go visiting. —**прийти́ в го́сти к**, to come to visit (someone).

госуда́рственность *n.f.* statehood; nationhood.

госуда́рственный *adj.* 1, state (*attrib.*); government (*attrib.*). 2, national: госуда́рственный гимн, national anthem. —**госуда́рственные дела́**, affairs of state. —**госуда́рственный де́ятель**, statesman. —**госуда́рственная изме́на**, high treason. —**госуда́рственный переворо́т**, coup d'état. —**госуда́рственное пра́во**, public law; constitutional law. —**госуда́рственный слу́жащий**, civil servant. —**госуда́рственная слу́жба**, government service; civil service. —**госуда́рственный язы́к**, official language.

госуда́рство *n.* 1, state. 2, the State.

госуда́рь *n.m.* 1, sovereign. 2, (*in direct address*) Your Majesty; Sire.

гот *n.* Goth. —**го́тика**, *n.* Gothic architecture. —**готи́ческий**, *adj.* Gothic.

гото́вить *v.impfv.* [*pfv.* пригото́вить; *pres.* -влю, -вишь] 1, to prepare. 2, to cook. 3, [*impfv. only*] to train. —**гото́виться**, *refl.* 1, (*with* к) to prepare (for); get ready (for). 2, [*impfv. only*] to be in the offing.

гото́вность *n.f.* 1, readiness; preparedness. 2, readiness; willingness. С гото́вностью, willingly.

гото́вый *adj.* 1, ready. 2, prepared. 3, willing. 4, (*with inf.*) about (to); on the verge of. 5, (*of goods*) finished; (*of clothes*) ready-made; ready-to-wear; (*of a dish*) ready to serve.

го́тский *adj.* Gothic: го́тский язы́к, Gothic.

го́фер *n.* gopher.

гофрирова́ть *v.impfv. & pfv.* [*pres.* -ру́ю, -ру́ешь] 1, to corrugate. 2, to emboss.

граб *n.* hornbeam.

грабёж [*gen.* -бежа́] *n.* 1, robbery. 2, looting; plundering; pillage. —**грабёж на большо́й доро́ге**, highway robbery.

граби́тель *n.m.* 1, robber. 2, looter.

граби́тельский *adj.* 1, predatory. 2, (*of prices*) exorbitant; prohibitive.

гра́бить *v.impfv.* [*pfv.* огра́бить; *pres.* -блю, -бишь] 1, to rob. 2, to sack; plunder; pillage.

гра́бли [*gen.* -бель *or* -блей] *n.pl.* rake.

гравёр *n.* engraver; etcher.

гра́вий *n.* gravel.

гравирова́льный *adj.* engraving (*attrib.*).

гравирова́ние *n.* engraving.

гравирова́ть *v.impfv.* [*pfv.* вы́гравировать; *pres.* -ру́ю, -ру́ешь] to engrave; etch.

гравиро́вка *n.* engraving.

гравита́ция *n.* gravitation. —**гравитацио́нный**, *adj.* gravitational.

гравю́ра *n.* engraving; etching; print. —**гравю́ра на де́реве**, woodcut.

град *n.* 1, hail: Идёт град, it is hailing. 2, *fig.* hail; flurry; shower; volley: град пуль, hail of bullets. 3, *archaic* city.

града́ция *n.* gradation.

гради́ент *n.*, *physics* gradient.

гра́дина *n.*, *colloq.* hailstone.

гра́дом *adv.* thick and fast.

градострои́тельство *n.* town planning; urban planning; urban development.

градуи́ровать *v.impfv. & pfv.* [*pres.* -ру́ю, -ру́ешь] to calibrate. —**градуи́рованная шкала́**, graduated scale.

гра́дус *n.* degree: со́рок гра́дусов, forty degrees. —**под гра́дусом**, *colloq.* under the influence; tipsy.

гра́дусник *n.*, *colloq.* thermometer.

граждани́н [*pl.* гра́ждане, гра́ждан] *n.* 1, citizen. 2, man.

гражда́нка [*gen. pl.* -нок] *n.* 1, (female) citizen. 2, *colloq.* civilian life.

гражда́нский *adj.* 1, civil: гражда́нская война́, civil war. 2, civilian: гражда́нская оде́жда, civilian clothes. Гражда́нское лицо́, civilian. 3, civic: гражда́нский долг, civic duty.

гражда́нственность *n.f.* sense of civic duty.

гражда́нство *n.* citizenship. —**получи́ть права́ гражда́нства**, 1, to be granted citizenship. 2, *fig.* to gain acceptance; win recognition.

грамза́пись *n.f.* recording.

грамм *n.* gram.

грамма́тика *n.* grammar. —**граммати́ст**, *n.* grammarian. —**граммати́ческий**, *adj.* grammatical.

граммофо́н *n.* phonograph. —**граммофо́нный**, *adj.* phonograph (*attrib.*).

гра́мота *n.* 1, ability to read and write. 2, document; deed. —**вери́тельные гра́моты**, credentials. —**почётная гра́мота**, diploma. —**ратификацио́нные гра́моты**, instruments of ratification.

грáмотно *adv.* **1,** grammatically. **2,** competently.

грáмотность *n.f.* **1,** literacy. **2,** grammatical correctness. **3,** knowledgeability.

грáмотный *adj.* **1,** literate; educated. **2,** grammatically correct. **3,** knowledgeable; competent.

граммпластúнка [*gen. pl.* **-нок**] *n.* phonograph record (*contr. of* граммофóнная пластúнка).

гран [*gen. pl.* **гран**] *n.* grain (*unit of weight*).

гранáт *n.* **1,** pomegranate. **2,** garnet.

гранáта *n.* grenade. —**гранáтный,** *adj.* grenade (*attrib.*).

гранáтовый *adj.* **1,** pomegranate (*attrib.*). **2,** garnet (*attrib.*).

гранатомёт *n.* grenade launcher.

грандиóзный *adj.* grandiose; vast; huge; immense. —**грандиóзность,** *n.f.* grandeur; immensity.

гранёный *adj.* (*of glass, gems, etc.*) cut.

гранúльный *adj.* lapidary. —**гранúльщик,** *n.* lapidary; diamond cutter.

гранúт *n.* granite. —**гранúтный,** *adj.* granite (*attrib.*).

гранúть *v.impfv.* to cut (glass, gems, etc.).

гранúца *n.* **1,** border; boundary; frontier. **2,** *usu. pl.* limits; bounds: не знать гранúц, to know no bounds. —**за гранúцей,** abroad (*location*). —**за гранúцу,** abroad (*direction*). —**из-за гранúцы,** from abroad.

гранúчить *v.impfv.* (*with* **с** + *instr.*) **1,** to border (on). **2,** *fig.* to border (on); verge (on): гранúчить с безýмием, to border/verge on insanity.

грáнка [*gen. pl.* **-нок**] *n.* (galley) proof.

гранулúровать *v.impfv. & pfv.* [*pres.* **-рую, -руешь**] to granulate.

грануляция *n.* granulation.

грань *n.f.* **1,** boundary. **2,** verge; brink: на грáни вымирáния, on the verge of extinction. **3,** side; surface (*of a geometric figure*). **4,** line (*i.e.* distinction): провестú грань мéжду, to draw a line/distinction between. **5,** facet (*of a gem*).

граф *n.* count; earl.

графá *n.* column (*of a page*).

грáфик *n.* **1,** chart; graph. **2,** schedule; timetable. **3,** graphic artist.

грáфика *n.* graphic arts.

графúн *n.* carafe; decanter.

графúня *n.* countess.

графúт *n.* **1,** graphite. **2,** lead (*for a pencil*). —**графúтовый,** *adj.* graphite (*attrib.*).

графúть *v.impfv.* [*pfv.* **разграфúть;** *pres.* **-флю́, -фúшь**] to rule (paper).

графúческий *adj.* graphic.

графлёный *adj.* (*of paper*) ruled.

грáфство *n.* county; shire.

граффúти *n.pl. indecl.* graffiti.

грациóзный *adj.* graceful. —**грациóзно,** *adv.* gracefully. —**грациóзность,** *n.f.* gracefulness.

грáция *n.* grace.

грач [*gen.* **грачá**] *n.* rook (*bird*).

гребёнка [*gen. pl.* **-нок**] *n.* comb. —**стричь когó-нибудь под гребёнку,** to crop someone's hair. —**стричь под однý гребёнку,** to lump together.

грéбень [*gen.* **-бня**] *n.m.* **1,** comb. **2,** comb (*of fowl*);

crest (*of a bird*). **3,** crest (*of a wave, mountain, etc.*). **4,** ridge (*of a roof*). **5,** ridge (*of plowed land*).

гребéц [*gen.* **-бцá**] *n.* rower; oarsman.

гребешóк [*gen.* **-шкá**] *n.* **1,** *dim. of* грéбень. **2,** scallop. —**петýший гребешóк,** cockscomb (*plant*).

грéбля *n.* rowing.

гребнóй *adj.* rowing (*attrib.*). —**гребнóй винт,** screw propeller. —**гребнóе колесó,** paddle wheel. —**гребнáя лóдка** *or* шлю́пка, rowboat.

гребóк [*gen.* **-бкá**] *n.* **1,** stroke (*of an oar*). **2,** paddle.

грёза *n.* dream; vision. —**мир грёз; цáрство грёз,** dreamworld; dreamland.

грéзить *v.impfv.* [*pres.* **грéжу, грéзишь**] to dream; daydream. —**грéзиться,** *refl.* [*pfv.* **пригрéзиться**] (*with dat.*) to appear in one's dreams: Онá емý чáсто грéзилась, he often dreamt about her.

грéйдер (дэ) *n.* **1,** *mech.* grader. **2,** *colloq.* graded road.

грéйпфрут *n.* grapefruit.

грек *n.m.* [*fem.* **гречáнка**] Greek.

грéлка [*gen. pl.* **-лок**] *n.* hot-water bottle. —**электрúческая грéлка,** heating pad.

гремéть *v.impfv.* [*pres.* **-млю́, -мúшь**] **1,** to thunder; rumble. **2,** to ring out; resound. **3,** to clank; rattle; jingle. **4,** (*with instr.*) to rattle; jingle. **5,** *fig.* to be famous.

гремýчий *adj.* **1,** thundering. **2,** rattling. —**гремýчая змея,** rattlesnake. —**гремýчая ртуть,** fulminate of mercury.

гренадéр [*gen. pl.* **-дéр**] *n.* grenadier.

гренкú *n.pl.* [*sing.* **гренóк**] croutons.

грестú *v.impfv.* [*pres.* **гребý, гребёшь;** *past* **грёб, греблá, греблó, греблú**] **1,** to row; paddle. **2,** to rake.

греть *v.impfv.* **1,** to warm. **2,** to provide warmth; keep (someone) warm: Сóлнце грéет, the sun is warm; шýба грéет, the coat keeps one warm. **3,** to heat; heat up. —**греть рýки,** to reap a profit; (*with* **на** + *prepl.*) to exploit; capitalize on.

грéться *v.r.impfv.* **1,** to warm oneself. **2,** to warm up; get warm. **3,** to bask (in the sun).

грех [*gen.* **грехá**] *n.* sin. —**как на грех,** as luck would have it. —**нéчего/чегó/что грехá таúть,** we might as well admit it; let's face it. —**от грехá подáльше,** out of harm's way. —**с грехóм пополáм,** barely; by the skin of one's teeth.

грéцкий *adj., in* **грéцкий орéх,** walnut.

гречáнка [*gen. pl.* **-нок**] *n.* Greek woman.

грéческий *adj.* Greek.

гречúха *n.* buckwheat.

грéчневый *adj.* buckwheat (*attrib.*).

грешúть *v.impfv.* **1,** [*pfv.* **согрешúть**] to sin. **2,** [*pfv.* **погрешúть**] (*with* **прóтив**) to go against: грешúть прóтив лóгики, to go against logic.

грéшник, *n.* sinner.

грешнó *adj., used predicatively with inf.,* it's a sin (to); it is wrong (to).

грéшный *adj.* [*short form* **грéшен, грешнá, грéшно, грешны**] **1,** sinful. **2,** [*short form only*] *colloq.* guilty. —**грéшным дéлом,** *colloq.* I must admit; sad to say.

грешóк [*gen.* **-шкá**] *n.* sin; peccadillo.

гриб [*gen.* **грибá**] *n.* mushroom.

грибкóвый *adj.* fungous; fungus (*attrib.*).

грибно́й *adj.* mushroom (*attrib.*). —**грибно́й дождь,** rain that falls while the sun in shining.

грибо́к [*gen.* -бка́] *n.* **1,** *dim. of* **гриб. 2,** fungus.

гри́ва *n.* mane.

гри́венник *n.,* *colloq.* ten-kopeck piece.

григориа́нский *adj.* Gregorian. —**григориа́нский календа́рь,** Gregorian calendar.

гри́зли *n.m. indecl.* grizzly bear.

грим *n.* make-up; grease paint.

грима́са *n.* grimace.

грима́сничать *v.impfv.* to make faces; grimace.

гримёр *n.* make-up artist.

гримирова́ть *v.impfv.* [*pres.* -ру́ю, -ру́ешь] *theat.* **1,** [*pfv.* **нагримирова́ть**] to make up; put make-up on. **2,** [*pfv.* **загримирова́ть**] (*with instr. or* под + *acc.*) to make (someone) up to look like. —**гримирова́ться,** *refl.* **1,** [*pfv.* **нагримирова́ться**] to put on one's make-up. **2,** [*pfv.* **загримирова́ться**] (*with instr. or* под + *acc.*) to make oneself up (as).

грипп *n.* grippe; influenza.

гриф *n.* **1,** vulture. **2,** *myth.* griffin. **3,** *music* finger board. **4,** rubber stamp. **5,** security classification (*stamped on a document*).

гри́фель *n.m.* slate pencil.

гри́фельный *adj.* slate (*attrib.*). —**гри́фельная доска́,** writing slate.

грифо́н *n.* **1,** *myth.* griffin. **2,** griffon (*dog*).

гроб [*2nd loc.* **гробу́;** *pl.* **гробы́**] *n.* coffin; casket. —**до гро́ба; по гроб жи́зни,** till the end of one's days; to one's dying day.

гробни́ца *n.* tomb.

гробово́й *adj.* **1,** coffin (*attrib.*). **2,** deathly; funereal: гробово́е молча́ние, deathly silence. —**до гробово́й доски́,** to the end of one's days.

гробовщи́к [*gen.* -щика́] *n.* coffin maker.

грог *n.* grog.

гроза́ [*pl.* **гро́зы**] *n.* storm; thunderstorm.

гроздь [*pl.* **гро́зди, -де́й, -дя́м** *or* **гро́здья, -дьев, -дьям**] *n.f.* cluster; bunch.

грози́ть *v.impfv.* [*pres.* **грожу́, грози́шь**] (*with dat.*) to threaten. Грози́ть кулако́м (+ *dat.*), to shake one's fist at. Ему́ грози́т пожи́зненное тюре́мное заключе́ние, he faces life imprisonment. —**грози́ться,** *refl.,* *colloq.* to threaten (to).

гро́зный *adj.* **1,** threatening; menacing. **2,** fearsome; awesome; dread. —**Ива́н Гро́зный,** Ivan the Terrible.

грозово́й *adj.* storm (*attrib.*). —**грозова́я ту́ча,** storm cloud; thundercloud.

гром *n.* thunder. —**гром среди́ я́сного не́ба,** bolt from the blue.

грома́да *n.* huge mass; hulk: грома́да горы́, the great hulk of a mountain.

грома́дный *adj.* huge; enormous; tremendous; immense.

громи́ла *n.m.,* *colloq.* **1,** burglar. **2,** thug.

громи́ть *v.impfv.* [*pfv.* **разгроми́ть;** *pres.* -млю́, -ми́шь] **1,** to smash; wreck. **2,** to rout; crush. **3,** *colloq.* to assail; fulminate against.

гро́мкий *adj.* [*short form* **гро́мок, громка́, гро́мко, гро́мки;** *compr.* **гро́мче**] **1,** loud. **2,** famous; notori-

ous. **3,** high-sounding; fine-sounding. —**гро́мко,** *adv.* loud; loudly.

громкоговори́тель *n.m.* loudspeaker.

гро́мкость *n.f.* loudness; volume.

громово́й *adj.* **1,** thunder (*attrib.*). **2,** thunderous; booming. **3,** devastating; crushing.

громогла́сный *adj.* **1,** loud. **2,** loud-voiced.

громозди́ть *v.impfv.* [*pfv.* **нагромозди́ть;** *pres.* -зжу́, -зди́шь] to pile up. —**громозди́ться,** *refl.* [*impfv. only*] **1,** to tower; rise. **2,** (*with* на + *acc.*) *colloq.* to climb up on.

гро́моздкий *adj.* bulky; cumbersome; unwieldy.

громоотво́д *n.* lightning rod.

громоподо́бный *adj.* thunderous.

гро́мче *adj.,* *comp. of* **гро́мкий.**

громыха́ние *n.,* *colloq.* rumble; rumbling.

громыха́ть *v.impfv.,* *colloq.* to rumble; clatter.

гросс *n.* gross (*12 dozen*).

гроссбу́х *also,* **гро́ссбух** *n.* ledger.

гроссме́йстер *n.,* *chess* grandmaster.

грот *n.* **1,** grotto. **2,** mainsail.

гроте́ск (тэ) *n.,* *art* grotesque style. —**гроте́сковый,** *adj.,* *art* grotesque.

грот-ма́чта *n.* mainmast.

гро́хать *v.impfv.* [*pfv.* **гро́хнуть**] *colloq.* **1,** to come crashing down. **2,** to drop. **3,** to bang down; slam down.

гро́хнуть *v.,* *pfv. of* **гро́хать.** —**гро́хнуться,** *refl.,* *colloq.* to fall with a bang; come crashing down.

гро́хот *n.* **1,** crash; din. **2,** screen; sieve.

грохота́ть *v.impfv.* [*pres.* -хочу́, -хо́чешь] **1,** to rumble. **2,** *colloq.* to howl (*with laughter*).

грош [*gen.* **гроша́**] *n.* **1,** *pre-rev.* half a kopeck. **2,** *colloq.* penny; red cent; *pl.* pittance. —**грош цена́** (+ *dat.*); **не гроша́ не сто́ит; гроша́ ме́дного** (*or* **ло́маного**) **не сто́ит,** worthless; not worth two cents. —**за гроши́,** for a song. —**не име́ть ни гроша́ за душо́й,** not to have a penny/cent to one's name. —**ни в грош не ста́вить, 1,** not to give a damn (*or* care a whit) about. **2,** to take no account of. —**ни за грош,** for nothing; completely in vain. —**ни на грош** (+ *gen.*), not a bit (*or* drop) of (*some admirable quality*).

грошо́вый *adj.,* *colloq.* **1,** cheap (*in quality*). **2,** petty; paltry; insignificant.

грубе́ть *v.impfv.* [*pfv.* **огрубе́ть**] to become rough; become coarse.

груби́ть *v.impfv.* [*pfv.* **нагруби́ть;** *pres.* -блю́, -би́шь] (*with dat.*) **1,** to make rude or offensive remarks (to); be insulting (to). **2,** to talk back (to); answer back. *Also,* **грубия́нить** [*pfv.* **нагрубия́нить**].

грубия́н *n.,* *colloq.* rude person; boor.

гру́бо *adv.* **1,** roughly. **2,** crudely. **3,** rudely. **4,** *in* гру́бо ошиби́ться, to make a gross mistake. —**гру́бо говоря́, 1,** roughly speaking. **2,** to put it rather crudely.

гру́бость *n.f.* **1,** rudeness. **2,** coarseness; crudity. **3,** rude remark; coarse remark.

гру́бый *adj.* **1,** rough. **2,** coarse; rude; crude. Гру́бая си́ла, brute force. **3,** gross; flagrant.

гру́да *n.* heap; pile.

груди́на *n.* breastbone; sternum.

груди́нка *n.* brisket. —**копчёная груди́нка**, bacon.

грудни́ца *n.* mastitis.

грудно́й *adj.* **1,** chest (*attrib.*); thoracic; pectoral. **2,** (*of an infant*) suckling. —**грудна́я жа́ба**, angina pectoris. —**грудна́я железа́**, mammary gland. —**грудна́я кле́тка**, thorax.

грудобрю́шный *adj., in* **грудобрю́шная прегра́да**, *anat.* diaphragm.

грудь [*gen.* гру́ди *or* груди́; *2nd loc.* груди́; *pl.* гру́ди, -де́й, -дя́м] *n.f.* **1,** chest. **2,** breast. —**отнима́ть от груди́,** to wean. —**стоя́ть** *or* **встать гру́дью за** (+ *acc.*), to stand firmly behind.

гружёный *adj.* loaded.

груз *n.* **1,** load. **2,** freight; cargo. —**поле́зный груз,** payload.

груздь [*gen.* -зда́; *pl.* гру́зди, -де́й, -дя́м] *n.m.* a variety of mushroom.

грузи́ло *n., fishing* sinker.

грузи́н [*gen. pl.* грузи́н] *n.m.* [*fem.* -зи́нка] Georgian. —**грузи́нский,** *adj.* Georgian.

грузи́ть *v.impfv.* [*pres.* гружу́, гру́зишь *or* грузи́шь] **1,** [*pfv.* нагрузи́ть *or* загрузи́ть] to load (a vehicle, vessel, etc.). **2,** [*pfv.* погрузи́ть] to load (cargo). —**грузи́ться,** *refl.* [*pfv.* погрузи́ться] **1,** to take on cargo. **2,** (*of many people*) to pile; load (into *or* onto).

гру́зный *adj.* **1,** heavy; weighty. **2,** stout; corpulent.

грузови́к [*gen.* -вика́] *n.* truck.

грузово́й *adj.* freight (*attrib.*); cargo (*attrib.*).

грузоотправи́тель *n.m.* shipper.

грузоподъёмный *adj., in* **грузоподъёмный кран,** loading crane.

гру́зчик *n.* longshoreman; stevedore.

грунт *n.* **1,** soil; ground. **2,** *painting* ground; priming.

грунтово́й *adj., in* **грунтова́я доро́га,** dirt road; **грунтовы́е во́ды,** ground water.

гру́ппа *n.* **1,** group. **2,** team; party: **поиско́вая гру́ппа,** search party; **инспекцио́нная гру́ппа,** inspection team. —**гру́ппа кро́ви,** blood type.

группирова́ть *v.impfv.* [*pfv.* сгруппирова́ть; *pres.* -ру́ю, -ру́ешь] to group; classify. —**группирова́ться,** *refl.* to group; form groups.

группиро́вка [*gen. pl.* -вок] *n.* **1,** grouping; classification. **2,** group; grouping.

группово́й *adj.* group (*attrib.*).

грусти́ть *v.impfv.* [*pres.* грущу́, -сти́шь] **1,** to be melancholy. **2,** (*with* по *or* о) to yearn for; mourn the loss of.

гру́стно *adv.* sadly. —*adj., used predicatively with dat.,* sad: Ему́ гру́стно, he is sad; мне ста́ло гру́стно, I felt sad.

гру́стный *adj.* sad; melancholy.

грусть *n.f.* melancholy; sadness.

гру́ша *n.* **1,** pear. **2,** pear tree. —**земляна́я гру́ша,** Jerusalem artichoke.

гру́шевый *also,* **грушо́вый** *adj.* pear (*attrib.*).

гры́жа *n.* hernia; rupture.

грыжево́й *also,* **гры́жевый** *adj.* of or for a hernia; hernial. —**грыжево́й банда́ж,** truss.

грызня́ *n., colloq.* **1,** fight (*between animals*). **2,** *fig.* squabbling; bickering.

грызть *v.impfv.* [*pres.* грызу́, грызёшь; *past* грыз, гры́зла] **1,** to gnaw. **2,** to nibble (at). **3,** *colloq.* to nag; badger. **4,** to torment; beset. —**гры́зться,** *refl.* **1,** (*of animals*) to fight. **2,** *colloq.* to squabble; bicker.

грызу́н [*gen.* -зуна́] *n.* rodent.

гряда́ [*pl.* гря́ды, гряд, гряда́м] *n.* **1,** ridge (*of mountains*). **2,** bed (*for flowers or vegetables*). **3,** row; series. **4,** bank (*of clouds*).

гря́дка [*gen. pl.* -док] *n.* bed (*for flowers, vegetables, etc.*).

гряду́щий *adj.* coming; future. —**на сон гряду́щий,** *colloq.* at bedtime.

грязево́й *adj.* mud (*attrib.*).

грязни́ть *v.impfv.* [*pfv.* загрязни́ть] **1,** to soil; dirty. **2,** [*impfv. only*] to sully; besmirch. —**грязни́ться,** *refl.* to get dirty.

гря́зно *adv.* sloppily. —*adj., used predicatively* **1,** dirty; messy: Здесь гря́зно, it is dirty/messy in here. **2,** muddy.

грязну́ля *n.m. & f., colloq.* slob. *Also,* **грязну́ха.**

гря́зный *adj.* [*short form* гря́зен, грязна́, гря́зно, грязны́] dirty; filthy; muddy.

грязь [*2nd loc.* грязи́] *n.f.* **1,** mud. **2,** dirt; filth. **3,** *pl.* mud; mud baths. —**броса́ть** *or* **забра́сывать гря́зью** (+ *acc.*), to throw mud at.

гря́нуть *v.pfv.* **1,** to sound; ring out. **2,** to break out; erupt.

гуа́но *n. indecl.* guano.

гуа́шь *n.f.* gouache.

губа́ [*pl.* гу́бы, губ, губа́м] *n.* **1,** lip. **2,** inlet; bay (*in northern Russia*). —**у вас гу́ба** (*with different stress*) **не ду́ра,** *colloq.* you know how to pick ’em!

губа́стый *adj., colloq.* thick-lipped.

губерна́тор *n.* governor. —**губерна́торский,** *adj.* governor’s; gubernatorial. —**губерна́торство,** *n.* governorship.

губе́рния *n., pre-rev.* province.

губи́тельный *adj.* disastrous; devastating; pernicious; ruinous.

губи́ть *v.impfv.* [*pfv.* погуби́ть; *pres.* гублю́, гу́бишь] **1,** to ruin. **2,** to destroy; kill.

гу́бка [*gen. pl.* гу́бок] *n.* **1,** *dim. of* губа́. **2,** sponge.

губно́й *adj.* **1,** lip (*attrib.*). **2,** *phonet.* labial. —**губна́я пома́да,** lipstick.

гу́бчатый *adj.* spongy. —**гу́бчатая рези́на,** foam rubber.

губерна́нтка [*gen. pl.* -ток] *n.* governess.

гуверне́р *n.* tutor.

гугено́т *n.m.* [*fem.* -но́тка] Huguenot.

гугу́ *adv., in* **ни гугу́,** silent; mum. —**ни гугу́!,** mum’s the word!

гуде́ние *n.* **1,** buzzing; droning; hum. **2,** honking (*of horns*).

гуде́ть *v.impfv.* [*pres.* гужу́, гуди́шь] **1,** to buzz; hum; drone. **2,** (*of a horn or factory whistle*) to sound; blow. **3,** *colloq.* to blow the horn (*of a car*). **4,** *colloq.* to ache.

гудо́к [*gen.* гудка́] *n.* **1,** (car) horn; (factory) whistle. **2,** hoot; toot; honk.

гудро́н *n.* tar; artificial asphalt.

гу́кать *v.impfv., colloq.* to hoot.

гул *n.* hum; rumble; drone; din.

гу́лкий *adj.* **1,** resounding; booming. **2,** resonant.

гу́льден (дэ) *n.* guilder (*monetary unit of the Netherlands*).

гуля́ка *n.m. & f., colloq.* playboy; reveler.

гуля́нье *n.* **1,** walking; strolling. **2,** outdoor party. **3,** festival; celebration.

гуля́ть *v.impfv.* **1,** to walk; stroll. **2,** *colloq.* to make merry; live it up. **3,** *colloq.* to be off from work; have the day off. **4,** (*with* с + *instr.*) *colloq.* to run around (with); take up (with). —води́ть гуля́ть, to take for a walk. —идти́ гуля́ть, to go for a walk.

гуля́ш [*gen.* -яша́] *n.* goulash.

гумани́зм *n.* humanism. —гумани́ст, *n.* humanist. —гуманисти́ческий, *adj.* humanistic.

гуманита́рный *adj.* humanitarian. —гуманита́рные нау́ки, liberal arts; the humanities.

гума́нный *adj.* humane; humanitarian. —гума́нно, *adv.* humanely. —гума́нность, *n.f.* humaneness; humanity.

гу́мми *n.neut. indecl.* gum.

гуммиара́бик *n.* gum arabic.

гумно́ [*pl.* гу́мна, гу́мен *or* гумён] *n.* threshing floor.

гу́мус *n.* humus.

гунн *n., hist.* Hun.

гурма́н *n.* gourmet.

гурт [*gen.* гурта́] *n.* herd; flock.

гуртовщи́к [*gen.* -щика́] *n.* herdsman; drover.

гурто́м *adv., colloq.* **1,** wholesale; in bulk. **2,** in a group; as one group.

гурьба́ *n., colloq.* crowd; throng.

гуса́к [*gen.* -сака́] *n.* gander.

гуса́р [*gen. pl.* гуса́р] *n.* hussar.

гу́сеница *n.* **1,** caterpillar. **2,** *mech.* caterpillar track.

гу́сеничный *adj.* **1,** caterpillar (*attrib.*). **2,** (*of a vehicle*) tracked.

гусёнок [*gen.* -нка; *pl.* гуся́та, гуся́т] *n.* gosling.

гуси́ный *adj.* goose (*attrib.*). —гуси́ная ко́жа, goose flesh; goose pimples. —гуси́ный шаг, goose step.

гу́сли [*gen.* -лей] *n.pl.* old Russian stringed instrument; gusli.

густе́ть *v.impfv.* [*pfv.* загусте́ть *or* погусте́ть] to thicken.

гу́сто *adv.* **1,** densely. **2,** *colloq.* in abundance. —то гу́сто, то пу́сто, it's feast or famine.

густо́й *adj.* [*comp.* гу́ще] **1,** thick; dense. **2,** (*of a sound, voice, etc.*) deep; rich.

густонаселённый *adj.* densely populated.

густота́ *n.* **1,** thickness; density. **2,** richness (*of color, sound, voice, etc.*).

гусы́ня *n.* female goose.

гусь [*pl.* гу́си, гусе́й, гуся́м] *n.m.* goose. —как с гу́ся вода́, like water off a duck's back.

гусько́м *adv.* (in) single file.

гуся́тина *n.* goose (*prepared as food*).

гуся́тник *n.* goose pen.

гутали́н *n.* shoe polish.

гуттапе́рча *n.* gutta-percha.

гу́ща *n.* **1,** dregs; grounds; lees. **2,** (*with gen.*) the thick of: в гу́ще ле́са, in the thick of the forest. —гада́ть на кофе́йной гу́ще, to guess in the dark.

гэ́льский *adj.* Gaelic.

Д, д *n.neut.* fifth letter of the Russian alphabet.

да *particle* **1,** yes. **2,** right?; isn't that so? **3,** really?; indeed? **4,** *used for emphasis:* Да замолчи́те же!, do be quiet! **5,** let; may: да бу́дет изве́стно, что..., let it be known that... Да испо́лнится ва́ше жела́ние!, may your wish be fulfilled! —*conj.* **1,** and: хлеб да вода́, bread and water. **2,** but: Я и пошёл бы, да не могу́, I would like to go, but I can't. —да и, and; and besides. —да ещё, and besides; and what is more. —да и то, and even; at that: то́лько одна́ руба́шка, да и то потрёпанная, only one shirt and a tattered one at that. —да и то́лько, and nothing else: Он смея́лся, да и то́лько, all he did was laugh; he just laughed and laughed.

да́бы *conj., archaic* in order to; in order that.

дава́й *also,* дава́йте *verbal particle* **1,** *fol. by inf. or 1st person pl.* let's: Дава́й чита́ть вме́сте, let's read together; дава́йте ся́дем на авто́бус, let's take the bus. **2,** start!; go ahead!: Ну, дава́йте!, O.K., go ahead!

дава́ть *v.impfv.* [*pfv.* дать; *pres.* даю́, даёшь] **1,** to give. **2,** to let: Дай ему́ говори́ть, let him speak. **3,** *with certain nouns, to make:* дава́ть обеща́ние/рекоменда́цию, to make a promise/recommendation. **4,** to yield; produce (results). **5,** *in* дать звоно́к, to ring the bell; дать свисто́к, to blow a whistle. **6,** *in* дать течь, to spring a leak; дать тре́щину, to crack; дать осе́чку, to misfire. **7,** *in* дать телегра́мму, to send a telegram. **8,** (*with dat.*) *colloq.* to hit; strike; clip: дать кому́-нибудь в зу́бы, to give someone a smack in the teeth. —**дать знать** (+ *dat.*), to let (someone) know. —**дать поня́ть,** to give to understand. Дать я́сно поня́ть, что..., to make it clear that... —**дать себя́ знать** *or* чу́вствовать, to make itself felt. —**ни дать ни взять,** exactly like.

давáтся *v.r.impfv.* [*pfv.* **дáться**; *pres.* **даю́сь, даёшься**] *colloq.* **1,** (*with* **в** + *acc.*) to allow oneself (to be): не давáться в оби́ду, not to allow oneself to be pushed around. **2,** (*usually with* легкó *and dat.*) to come easy to: Языки́ ему́ легкó даю́тся, languages come easy to him.

дави́льный *adj.* for pressing: дави́льный пресс, wine press.

дави́льня [*gen. pl.* **-лен**] *n.* wine press.

дави́ть *v.impfv.* [*pres.* **давлю́, дáвишь**] **1,** (*with acc. or* **на** + *acc.*) to press down on; weigh down on. **2,** (*with* **на** + *acc.*) to press hard on (a button). **3,** to squeeze. **4,** to pinch; be tight. **5,** [*pfv.* **раздави́ть**] to crush. **6,** [*pfv.* **раздави́ть** *or* **задави́ть**] to run over; kill. **7,** [*pfv.* **задави́ть**] *fig.* to suppress; stifle. **8,** (*of a feeling*) to oppress. —**дави́ться,** *refl.* [*pfv.* **подави́ться**] to choke.

дáвка *n.* crowding together; crush; jam.

давлéние *n.* pressure.

дáвний *adj.* **1,** old; olden; ancient. **2,** long-standing; of long standing. —**с дáвних пор,** for a long time; for ages.

давни́шний *adj., colloq.* = **дáвний.**

давнó *adv.* **1,** long ago; a long time ago: Э́то случи́лось давнó, that happened a long time ago. **2,** a long time (*up to and including the present moment*): Вы давнó ждёте?, have you been waiting long? —**давны́м-давнó,** *colloq.* long long ago; ages ago.

давнопрошéдший *adj.* of long ago; that happened long ago. —**давнопрошéдшее врéмя,** *gram.* pluperfect tense.

дáвность *n.f.* **1,** distance back in time: собы́тия сорокалéтней дáвности, events which took place forty years ago. Э́та газéта трёхнедéльной дáвности, this newspaper is three weeks old. **2,** long history; long standing. **3,** *law* prescription. —**срок дáвности,** statute of limitations.

дáже *particle* even.

дáктиль *n.m.* dactyl. —**дактили́ческий,** *adj.* dactylic.

дáлее *adv.* farther; further. —**и так дáлее,** and so on; and so forth; et cetera. —**не дáлее как, 1,** no farther than. **2,** as recently as.

далёкий *adj.* [*short form* **далёк, далекá, далекó, далеки́**; *comp.* **дáльше**] **1,** far; far away; faraway; distant. **2,** (*of a distance, journey, etc.*) long. **3,** [*short form only*] (*with* **от**) *fig.* far (from): Он не далёк от и́стины, he is not far from the truth; he is not far wrong. **4,** (*with* **не** *and preceded by an adverb*) *colloq.* (not) bright: Он не сли́шком далёк, he is not too bright.

далекó *adv.* far: остáвить далекó позади́, to leave far behind. Он пойдёт далекó, he will go far. —*adj.,* used predicatively, far; far away: Москвá далекó, Moscow is far away. Тудá ещё далекó, it is still a long way to there. —**далекó до,** far beneath; not in

the same class as: Ему́ далекó до неё, he can't compare to her. —**далекó за** (+ *acc.*), well past: далекó зá полночь, well past midnight. —**далекó иду́щий,** far-reaching. —**далекó не,** far from; by no means: далекó не увéрен, far from/ by no means/ certain.

даль [*2nd loc.* **дали́**] *n.f.* **1,** distance: в таку́ю даль, such a great distance. **2,** expanse: бесконéчная даль, endless expanse.

дальневостóчный *adj.* Far Eastern.

дальнéйший *adj.* further. —**в дальнéйшем, 1,** in the future; hereafter. **2,** subsequently; thereafter. **3,** hereinafter.

дáльний *adj.* **1,** far; far-off; distant. **2,** (*of a trip, distance, etc.*) long. **3,** *in* дáльний рóдственник, distant relative. —**без дáльних слов,** without wasting words; wasting no time on talk; without further ado. —**Дáльний Востóк,** Far East. —**дáльнего дéйствия,** *mil.* long-range. —**дáльний свет,** high beams.

дальнобóйный *adj., mil.* long-range.

дальнови́дный *adj.* farsighted; having or showing foresight. —**дальнови́дность,** *n.f.* foresight.

дальнозóркий *adj., med.* farsighted. —**дальнозóркость,** *n.f., med.* farsightedness.

дальномéр *n.* range finder.

дáльность *n.f.* **1,** distance. **2,** range. —**за дáльностью расстоя́ния,** because of the great distance.

дальтони́зм *n.* colorblindness. —**дальтóник,** *n., colloq.* colorblind person.

дáльше *adj., comp. of* **далёкий** *and* **далекó.** —*adv.* **1,** *comp. of* **далекó. 2,** then; next: А что случи́лось дáльше?, and what happened next? **3,** further; on: Читáйте дáльше!, read on! **4,** continue!; go on! **5,** any longer: Молчáть дáльше бы́ло нельзя́, it was impossible to remain silent any longer. —*prep., with gen.* beyond: Егó нé было слы́шно дáльше трéтьего ря́да, he could not be heard beyond the third row. —**дáльше — бóльше,** but there is more to come. —**éсли так пойдёт дáльше,** at this rate; if things go on like this.

дáма *n.* **1,** lady. **2,** *cards* queen. **3,** partner (*in dancing*).

дамáн *n.* hyrax.

дáмба *n.* dike; levee.

дáмка [*gen. pl.* **дáмок**] *n., checkers* king.

дамóклов *adj., in* **дамóклов меч,** sword of Damocles.

дáмский *adj.* lady's; ladies'.

дáнность *n.f.* a given.

дáнные *n.pl., decl. as an adj.* **1,** data. **2,** gifts; talent; ability.

дáнный *adj.* this; the given; the present. —**в дáнный момéнт,** at the (present) moment. —**на дáнный момéнт,** as of the moment; to date. —**в дáнном слу́чае,** in the present case.

данти́ст *n., obs.* dentist.

дань *n.f.* **1,** *hist.* tribute (*exacted from the population*). **2,** *fig.* tribute; due: отдавáть *or* плати́ть дань (+ *dat.*), to give someone (*or* something) his/its due.

дар [*pl.* **дары́**] *n.* **1,** gift. **2,** gift; talent: дар красноречия, the gift of eloquence. —**дар слóва** *or* **рéчи, 1,** one's ability to speak. **2,** gift of gab.

дарёный *adj., colloq.* received as a gift. —**дарёному**

коню́ в зу́бы не смо́трят, don't look a gift horse in the mouth.

дари́ть v.impfv. [pfv. подари́ть; pres. дарю́, да́ришь] to give (as a gift); donate.

дармое́д n., colloq. sponger; parasite.

дарова́ние n. 1, gift; talent. 2, talented person.

дарова́ть v.impfv. & pfv. [pres. -ру́ю, -ру́ешь] obs. to grant; bestow.

дарови́тый adj. gifted.

дарово́й adj., colloq. free; given away free.

да́ром adv. 1, gratis; free of charge. 2, colloq. for next to nothing; for a song. 3, in vain; for nothing; to no purpose. —пропада́ть да́ром, to go to waste; go for naught. —не пройти́ да́ром, 1, (with dat.) to have serious consequences for: Э́то ему́ да́ром не пройдёт, he won't get away with that. 2, (with для) (of a lesson) not to be lost upon.

да́рственный adj. 1, obs. received as a gift. 2, confirming a gift. —да́рственная на́дпись, inscription (on a gift, esp. a book).

да́та n. date: да́та рожде́ния, date of birth.

да́тельный adj., in да́тельный паде́ж, dative case.

дати́ровать v.impfv. & pfv. [pres. -рую, -руешь] to date.

да́тский adj. Danish. —да́тский дог, Great Dane.

датча́нин [pl. -ча́не, -ча́н] n.m. [fem. -ча́нка] Dane.

да́тчик n. sensor: теплово́й да́тчик, heat sensor.

дать [infl. дам, дашь, даст, дади́м, дади́те, даду́т; pres. fem. дала́] v., pfv. of дава́ть. —да́ться, refl. [past да́лся, дала́сь, дало́сь or да́лось, дали́сь or да́лись] pfv. of дава́ться.

да́ча n. 1, country house; summer cottage; dacha. 2, the country: жить на да́че, to live in the country. 3, giving: да́ча ло́жных показа́ний, giving false evidence.

да́чник n. person spending the summer in the country.

да́чный adj. 1, of or pert. to a dacha. 2, suburban. 3, in да́чный сезо́н, summer season.

два [fem. две; gen. & prepl. двух; dat. двум; instr. двумя́] numeral two. —два-три [fem. две-три], a couple; two or three.

двадцатиле́тие n. 1, twentieth anniversary; twentieth birthday. 2, twenty-year period.

двадцатиле́тний adj. 1, twenty-year (attrib.). 2, twenty-year-old.

двадцатипятиле́тие n. 1, twenty-fifth anniversary; twenty-fifth birthday. 2, twenty-five-year period.

двадцатипятиле́тний adj. 1, twenty-five-year (attrib.). 2, twenty-five-year-old.

двадца́тый ordinal numeral twentieth.

два́дцать [gen., dat. & prepl. -цати́; instr. -цатью́] numeral twenty.

два́жды adv. twice; two times. —как два́жды два четы́ре, as plain as day.

две numeral, fem. of два.

двенадцатипе́рстный adj., in двенадцатипе́рстная кишка́, duodenum.

двена́дцатый ordinal numeral twelfth.

двена́дцать [gen., dat. & prepl. -цати; instr. -цатью] numeral twelve.

две́рка [gen. pl. -рок] n., dim. of дверь.

дверно́й adj. door (attrib.).

две́рца [gen. pl. -рец] n. small door.

дверь [2nd loc. двери́; pl. две́ри, -ре́й, -ря́м, дверя́ми or дверьми́, -ря́х] n.f. door. —в дверя́х, in the doorway. —за дверь, out the door. —за две́рью, outside the door. —при закры́тых дверя́х, behind closed doors.

две́сти [gen. двухсо́т; dat. двумста́м; instr. двумя-ста́ми; prepl. двухста́х] numeral two hundred.

дви́гатель n.m. motor; engine.

дви́гательный adj. motive. —дви́гательный нерв, motor nerve.

дви́гать v.impfv. [pfv. дви́нуть; pres. дви́гаю, дви́гаешь or дви́жу, дви́жешь] 1, to move (something). 2, (with instr.) to move (a part of one's body). 3, [impfv. only] to drive: Мото́р дви́гает колесо́, a motor drives the wheel. 4, fig. to promote; further; advance. —дви́гаться, refl. 1, to move. 2, to stir; budge. 3, colloq. to start out.

движе́ние n. 1, motion; movement. Ве́чное движе́ние, perpetual motion. Лежа́ть без движе́ния, to lie motionless. 2, traffic. 3, fig. movement: партиза́нское движе́ние, guerrilla movement; движе́ние за гражда́нские права́, the civil rights movement. —реакти́вное движе́ние, jet propulsion.

дви́жимость n.f., law movable property; personal property.

дви́жимый adj. movable. —дви́жимое иму́щество, = дви́жимость.

дви́жущий adj. 1, in дви́жущая си́ла, motive force. 2, in дви́жущие си́лы (+ gen.), fig. the driving force (behind); the forces that drive.

дви́нуть v., pfv. of дви́гать. —дви́нуться, refl., pfv. of дви́гаться.

дво́е [gen. & prepl. двои́х; dat. двои́м; instr. двои́ми] collective numeral two.

двоебра́чие n. bigamy.

двоевла́стие n. diarchy.

двоеже́нец [gen. -нца] n. bigamist. —двоеже́нство, n. bigamy.

двоето́чие n. colon (punctuation mark).

двои́ться v.r.impfv. 1, to divide in two. 2, impers. to see double: У меня́ двои́тся в глаза́х, I am seeing double.

дво́йка n. 1, the numeral 2. 2, colloq. anything numbered 2. 3, a grade of "two", signifying "poor". 4, cards two; deuce.

двойни́к [gen. -ника́] n. 1, (a person's) double. 2, colloq. twin.

двойно́й adj. double; dual.

дво́йня [gen. pl. дво́ен] n. (set of) twins.

дво́йственность n.f. 1, duality. 2, ambivalence. 3, duplicity.

дво́йственный adj. 1, dual. 2, bipartite. 3, ambivalent. 4, two-faced.

двор [gen. двора́] n. 1, court (of a sovereign). 2, yard; courtyard. 3, peasant homestead. 4, in моне́тный двор, mint. —на дворе́, out of doors; outside. —не ко двору́, not right; ill-suited. —прийти́сь ко двору́ (+ dat.), to fit in (with).

дворе́ц [gen. -рца́] n. palace. —дворе́ц съе́здов, the Palace of Congresses (in the Kremlin).

дворе́цкий *n., decl. as an adj.* butler.

дво́рник *n.* **1,** caretaker. **2,** *colloq.* windshield wiper.

дво́рницкая *n., decl. as an adj., obs.* caretaker's house *or* quarters.

дворня́га *n., colloq.* mongrel. *Also,* **дворня́жка.**

дворо́вый *adj.* yard (*attrib.*). —**дворо́вая соба́ка,** watchdog.

дворцо́вый *adj.* palace (*attrib.*).

дворяни́н [*pl.* **-я́не, -я́н**] *n.m.* [*fem.* **-я́нка**] nobleman; noble. —**дворя́нский,** *adj.* nobleman's. —**дворя́нство,** *n.* the nobility; the gentry.

двою́родный *adj., denoting relationships of cousins:* двою́родный брат; двою́родная сестра́, first cousin. Двою́родный дя́дя; двою́родная тётка, cousin of one's father or mother. Двою́родный племя́нник; двою́родная племя́нница, child of one's first cousin.
♦*Also denoting other relationships:* двою́родная ба́бушка, great-aunt; двою́родный де́душка, great-uncle. Двою́родный внук, grandnephew; двою́родная вну́чка, grandniece.

двоя́кий *adj.* double; dual.

двоя́ко *adv.* in two ways.

двубо́ртный *adj.* double-breasted.

двугла́вый *adj.* two-headed. —**двугла́вая мы́шца,** biceps.

двугла́сный *adj., in* **двугла́сный звук,** diphthong. —*n.* diphthong.

двугра́нный *adj.* dihedral.

двугри́венный *n., decl. as an adj., colloq.* twenty-kopeck piece.

двудо́льный *adj.* dicotyledonous.

двузна́чный *adj.* two-digit.

двуко́лка [*gen. pl.* **-лок**] *n.* two-wheeled cart.

двукра́тный *adj.* **1,** twofold; double. **2,** second. **3,** two-time (*attrib.*).

двули́кий *adj.* **1,** having a dual nature. **2,** two-faced; duplicitous; double-dealing.

двули́чие *n.* duplicity. *Also,* **двули́чность,** *n.f.*

двули́чный *adj.* two-faced; duplicitous; double-dealing.

двуно́гий *adj.* two-legged.

двуо́кись *n.f.* dioxide. —**двуо́кись се́ры,** sulfur dioxide.

двупо́лый *adj.* bisexual.

двуру́шник *n.* double-dealer. —**двуру́шнический,** *adj.* double-dealing. —**двуру́шничество,** *n.* double-dealing.

двуска́тный *adj., in* **двуска́тная кры́ша,** gable roof.

двусло́жный *adj.* two-syllable. *Also,* **двухсло́жный.**

двусмы́сленность *n.f.* **1,** ambiguity. **2,** double entendre.

двусмы́сленный *adj.* **1,** ambiguous. **2,** suggestive.

двуспа́льный *adj.* (*of a bed*) double. *Also,* **двухспа́льный.**

двуство́лка *also,* **двухство́лка** [*gen. pl.* **-вок**] *n., colloq.* double-barreled gun. —**двуство́льный,** *adj.* double-barreled.

двуство́рчатый *adj.* **1,** bivalve. **2,** (*of doors*) folding. *Also,* **двухство́рчатый.**

двусторо́нний *adj.* **1,** two-sided. **2,** bilateral; bipartite. **3,** two-way. **4,** (*of a garment*) reversible.

двуугле́кислый *adj., chem.* bicarbonate (of): двуугле́ки́слый на́трий, sodium bicarbonate; двуугле́ки́слая со́да, bicarbonate of soda.

двухвале́нтный *adj.* bivalent.

двухгоди́чный *adj.* two-year (*attrib.*).

двухдне́вный *adj.* two-day (*attrib.*).

двухкварти́рный *adj., in* **двухкварти́рный дом,** duplex.

двухколёсный *adj.* two-wheel(ed).

двухко́мнатный *adj.* two-room.

двухле́тний *adj.* **1,** two-year (*attrib.*). **2,** two-year-old. **3,** *bot.* biennial.

двухме́стный *adj.* accommodating two persons; for two.

двухме́сячник *n.* bimonthly (*publication*).

двухме́сячный *adj.* **1,** two-month (*attrib.*). **2,** two-month-old. **3,** bimonthly.

двухмото́рный *adj.* twin-engine.

двухнеде́льник *n.* biweekly (*publication*).

двухнеде́льный *adj.* **1,** two-week (*attrib.*). **2,** two-week-old. **3,** (*of a publication*) biweekly; fortnightly.

двухпала́тный *adj.* bicameral.

двухпарти́йный *adj.* **1,** two-party (*attrib.*). **2,** bipartisan.

двухсотле́тие *n.* bicentennial; bicentenary. —**двухсотле́тний,** *adj.* bicentennial.

двухсо́тый *ordinal numeral* two-hundredth.

двухто́мник *n., colloq.* two-volume work.

двухто́мный *adj.* two-volume.

двухфо́кусный *adj.* bifocal.

двухчасово́й *adj.* **1,** two-hour (*attrib.*). **2,** *colloq.* two-o'clock (*attrib.*).

двухъя́русный *adj.* **1,** two-tier. **2,** (*of a bridge*) double-decker.

двухэта́жный *adj.* **1,** two-story. **2,** (*of a bus*) double-decker.

двучле́н *n.* binomial. —**двучле́нный,** *adj.* binomial.

двуязы́чие *n.* bilingualism. —**двуязы́чный,** *adj.* bilingual.

двуяйцо́вый *adj., in* **двуяйцо́вые близнецы́,** fraternal twins.

дебарка́дер (дэ, дэ) *n.* pier; wharf; landing stage.

дебати́ровать *v.impfv.* [*pres.* **-рую, -руешь**] to debate.

деба́ты [*gen.* **-тов**] *n.pl.* debate; discussion.

дебе́лый *adj.* plump; buxom.

де́бет *n.* debit.

дебетова́ть *v.impfv. & pfv.* [*pres.* **-ту́ю, -ту́ешь**] to debit.

дебо́ш *n.* row; fracas; brawl.

дебоши́рить *v.impfv.* to carry on; run wild; kick up a row.

де́бри [*gen.* **-рей**] *n.pl.* **1,** jungle; wilderness; wilds. **2,** backwoods; sticks. **3,** maze; labyrinth.

дебю́т *n.* **1,** debut. **2,** *chess* opening.

дебюта́нт *n.m.* [*fem.* **-та́нтка**] person making his or her debut.

дебюти́ровать *v.impfv. & pfv.* [*pres.* **-рую, -руешь**] to make one's debut.

де́ва *n.* **1,** *archaic* maid; maiden. **2,** *relig.* the virgin. **3,** *cap.* Virgo. —**ста́рая де́ва,** old maid.

девальва́ция (дэ) *n.* devaluation.

девальви́ровать (дэ) *v.impfv. & pfv.* [*pres.* **-рую, -руешь**] to devalue.

дева́ть *v.impfv.* [*pfv.* **деть**] *colloq.* to put; do with: Куда́ я дел мои́ очки́?, where did I put my glasses?;

what did I do with my glasses? —**дева́ться**, *refl., colloq.* **1,** (*usu. with* куда́) to get (to); disappear (to): Куда́ де́лась моя́ шля́па?, where has my hat gotten/disappeared to? **2,** (*with* куда́ *or* не́куда) to go; hide: Мне не́куда дева́ться, I have no place to go/hide.

де́верь [*pl.* **деверья́, -ре́й**] *n.m.* brother-in-law (*husband's brother*).

деви́з *n.* motto.

деви́ца *also,* **де́вица** *n., obs., poetic* maiden; damsel.

деви́ческий *adj.* = **де́вичий.** —**деви́чество,** *n.* girlhood; maidenhood.

де́вичий *also,* **деви́чий** [*fem.* **-чья**] *adj.* girlish; maidenly. —**де́вичья фами́лия,** maiden name.

де́вка [*gen. pl.* **де́вок**] *n., colloq.* girl; wench.

де́вочка [*gen. pl.* **-чек**] *n.* (little) girl.

де́вственник *n.m.* [*fem.* **-ница**] virgin.

де́вственный *adj.* **1,** virgin; virginal. **2,** (*of a forest*) virgin; primeval. —**де́вственность,** *n.f.* virginity.

де́вушка [*gen. pl.* **-шек**] *n.* (teenage) girl; young lady.

девчо́нка [*gen. pl.* **-нок**] *n., colloq.* girl.

девяно́сто [*gen., dat., instr.* & *prepl.* **девяно́ста**] *numeral* ninety. —**девяно́стый,** *ordinal numeral* ninetieth.

девя́тая *n., decl. as an adj.,* ninth: одна́ девя́тая, one-ninth.

де́вятеро *collective numeral* nine.

девятиле́тний *adj.* **1,** nine-year (*attrib.*). **2,** nine-year-old.

девятисо́тый *ordinal numeral* nine-hundredth.

девя́тка *n.* **1,** the numeral 9. **2,** *colloq.* anything numbered 9. **3,** *cards* nine.

девятна́дцатый *ordinal numeral* nineteenth.

девятна́дцать *numeral* nineteen.

девя́тый *ordinal numeral* ninth.

де́вять [*gen., dat.* & *prepl.* **девяти́;** *instr.* **девятью́**] *numeral* nine.

девятьсо́т [*gen.* **девятисо́т;** *dat.* **девятиста́м;** *instr.* **девятьюста́ми;** *prepl.* **девятиста́х**] *numeral* nine hundred.

де́вятью *adv.* nine times: де́вятью де́сять — девяно́сто, nine times ten is ninety.

дегаза́ция (дэ) *n.* decontamination.

дегази́ровать (дэ) *v.impfv.* & *pfv.* [*pres.* **-рую, -руешь**] to decontaminate.

дегенера́т *n.* degenerate.

дегенерати́вный *adj.* degenerative.

дегенера́ция *n.* degeneration.

дёготь [*gen.* **дёгтя**] *n.m.* tar. —**ло́жка дёгтя в бо́чке мёда,** fly in the ointment.

деграда́ция (дэ) *n.* degeneration.

дегради́ровать (дэ) *v.impfv.* & *pfv.* [*pres.* **-рую, -руешь**] to degenerate; deteriorate; decline.

дегтя́рный *adj.* tar (*attrib.*).

дегуста́тор (дэ) *n.* taster. —**дегуста́ция,** *n.* tasting: дегуста́ция вина́, wine tasting.

дед *n.* grandfather. —**дед-моро́з,** Santa Claus; Grandfather Frost.

де́дов *adj.* belonging to one's grandfather; grandfather's.

де́довский *adj.* **1,** grandfather's. **2,** old-fashioned.

дедовщи́на *n., mil., colloq.* hazing.

деду́кция *n., logic* deduction. —**дедукти́вный,** *adj., logic* deductive.

де́душка [*gen. pl.* **-шек**] *n.* grandfather.

дееприча́стие *n.* verbal adverb.

дееспосо́бность *n.f.* **1,** efficiency; energy; vitality. **2,** *law* competence.

дееспосо́бный *adj.* **1,** able to function. **2,** effective. **3,** *law* competent.

дежу́рить *v.impfv.* **1,** to be on duty. **2,** to keep vigil.

дежу́рный *adj.* **1,** on duty: дежу́рный офице́р, duty officer; officer of the day. **2,** (*of a store*) open extra hours. **3,** *fig.* standard; stock. —*n.* person on duty. —**дежу́рное блю́до,** plat du jour.

дежу́рство *n.* **1,** duty: ночно́е дежу́рство, night duty. **2,** *mil.* alert: боево́е дежу́рство, combat alert.

дезерти́р *n.* deserter.

дезерти́ровать *v.impfv.* & *pfv.* [*pres.* **-рую, -руешь**] *mil.* to desert.

дезерти́рство *n., mil.* desertion.

дезинфе́кция *n.* disinfection.

дезинфици́ровать *v.impfv.* & *pfv.* [*pres.* **-рую, -руешь**] to disinfect.

дезинформа́ция (дэ) *n.* disinformation.

дезинформи́ровать (дэ) *v.impfv.* & *pfv.* [*pres.* **-рую, -руешь**] to misinform.

дезодора́нт (дэ) *n.* deodorant.

дезорганиза́ция *n.* disorganization; disruption.

дезorganiзова́ть *v.impfv.* & *pfv.* [*pres.* **-зу́ю, -зу́ешь**] to disorganize; disrupt.

дезориента́ция *n.* disorientation.

дезориенти́ровать *v.impfv.* & *pfv.* [*pres.* **-рую, -руешь**] to disorient.

деи́зм (дэ) *n.* deism. —**деи́ст,** *n.* deist. —**деисти́ческий,** *adj.* deistic.

де́йственный *adj.* effective; efficacious. —**де́йственность,** *n.f.* effectiveness; efficacy.

де́йствие *n.* **1,** *usu. pl.* action: бы́стрые де́йствия, quick action. **2,** *pl.* acts: незако́нные де́йствия, illegal acts. **3,** operation: вводи́ть в де́йствие, to put into operation. Приводи́ть в де́йствие, to start (*e.g.* a machine) going. **4,** effect: оказа́ть де́йствие на, to have an effect on. **5,** (legal) force; effect: вводи́ть зако́н в де́йствие, to put a law into effect; invoke a law. Продли́ть де́йствие догово́ра, to extend a treaty. **6,** action (*of a novel, film, etc.*): Де́йствие происхо́дит в Чика́го, the action takes place in Chicago; the scene is laid in Chicago. **7,** act (*of a play*). —**вое́нные де́йствия,** military action; military operations; hostilities. —**свобо́да де́йствий,** freedom of action. —**срок де́йствия,** *see* **срок.**

действи́тельно *adv.* really; actually; truly; indeed.

действи́тельность *n.f.* **1,** reality: в действи́тельности, in reality. **2,** validity.

действи́тельный *adj.* **1,** real; actual; true. **2,** [*short form* **-лен, -льна**] valid. **3,** effective. **4,** *mil.* active: действи́тельная слу́жба, active service. —**действи́тельный зало́г,** *gram.* active voice. —**действи́тельное число́,** real number. —**действи́тельный член,** full member.

де́йствовать *v.impfv.* [*pres.* -ствую, -ствуешь] 1, to act. 2, to operate; function; work. 3, to be in effect; be in force. 4, (*with instr.*) *colloq.* to use; employ; operate; handle. 5, [*pfv.* поде́йствовать] to take effect; work; (*with* на + *acc.*) have an effect (on). Де́йствовать на (+ *acc.*) отрезвля́юще, to have a sobering effect on. —де́йствовать на не́рвы (+ *dat.*), to get on someone's nerves.

де́йствующий *adj.* active; operating; functioning. —де́йствующая а́рмия, army in the field; front-line army. —де́йствующее лицо́, character (*in a play or story*).

дейте́рий (дэ, тэ) *n.* deuterium.

де́ка (дэ) *n., music* sounding board.

декабри́ст *n., hist.* Decembrist. —декабри́стский, *adj.* Decembrist.

дека́брь [*gen.* -бря́] *n.m.* December. —дека́брьский, *adj.* December (*attrib.*).

дека́да *n.* ten days; ten-day period.

декаде́нт *n.* decadent. —декаде́нтский, *adj.* decadent. —декаде́нство, *n.* decadence.

дека́дный *adj.* ten-day (*attrib.*).

дека́н *n.* dean (*at a university*). —декана́т, *n.* dean's office.

деклама́тор *n.* declaimer; reciter.

деклама́ция *n.* declamation; recitation. —деклама-цио́нный, *adj.* declamatory.

деклами́ровать *v.impfv.* [*pfv.* продеклами́ровать; *pres.* -рую, -руешь] to recite; declaim.

деклерати́вный *adj.* 1, declarative. 2, solemn.

деклара́ция *n.* (solemn) declaration.

деклари́ровать *v.impfv. & pfv.* [*pres.* -рую, -руешь] 1, to declare (income, goods at customs, etc.). 2, to proclaim.

деколониза́ция *n.* decolonization.

декольте́ (дэ, тэ) *n.neut. indecl.* décolletage. —*adj. indecl.* low-necked; décolleté. —декольти́рованный, *adj.* = деколльте́.

декомпре́ссия *n.* decompression.

декорати́вный *adj.* 1, decorative; ornamental. 2, picturesque.

декора́тор *n.* 1, stage designer. 2, interior decorator.

декора́ция *n., usu. pl.* 1, *theat.* scenery; stage set. 2, *fig.* trappings; window dressing. —переме́на декора́ций, 1, *theat.* change of scenery. 2, *fig.* change in the situation.

декори́ровать *v.impfv. & pfv.* [*pres.* -рую, -руешь] to decorate.

деко́рум (дэ) *n.* decorum.

декре́т *n.* decree.

декре́тный *adj.* established by decree. —декре́тный о́тпуск, maternity leave.

декстро́за (дэ) *n.* dextrose.

де́ланный *adj.* affected; unnatural. —де́ланность, *n.f.* affectation.

де́лать *v.impfv.* [*pfv.* сде́лать] 1, to do. 2, to make. 3, *rendered by various English verbs depending on the noun:* де́лать шаг, to take a step; де́лать пода́рок, to give a present; де́лать опера́цию, to perform an operation; де́лать уко́л, to give an injection; де́лать предупрежде́ние, to give a warning; де́лать ком-плиме́нт, to pay a compliment; де́лать зака́з, to place an order; де́лать долги́ to incur debts; де́лать ски́дку, to give a discount; де́лать вы́вод, to draw a conclusion; де́лать на́дпись, to write an inscription; де́лать упо́р, to lay *or* place (the) emphasis. —де́латься, *refl.* 1, [*impfv. only*] to be done (*in a certain way*). 2, [*impfv. only*] (*with* из) to be made (of *or* from). 3, (*with instr.*) to become. 4, to happen; take place; be going on.

делега́т *n.* delegate.

делега́ция *n.* delegation.

делеги́ровать *v.impfv. & pfv.* [*pres.* -рую, -руешь] to send as a delegate.

делёж [*gen.* дележа́] *n., colloq.* dividing up; parceling out. Also, деле́жка.

деле́ние *n.* 1, division. 2, fission. 3, *math.* division. 4, unit; point; notch (*on a scale, thermometer, etc.*).

деле́ц [*gen.* дельца́] *n.* shrewd businessman; smart operator.

деликате́с *n.* delicacy (*choice item of food*).

делика́тничать *v.impfv., colloq.* to be overly delicate; (*with* с + *instr.*) treat with kid gloves.

делика́тный *adj.* 1, polite; tactful. 2, *colloq.* delicate; ticklish. 3, *colloq.* frail; delicate. —делика́тность, *n.f.* delicacy; tact.

дели́мое *n., decl. as an adj., math.* dividend.

дели́мый *adj.* divisible. —дели́мость, *n.f.* divisibility.

дели́тель *n.m., math.* divisor.

дели́ть *v.impfv.* [*pfv.* раздели́ть *or* подели́ть; *pres.* делю́, де́лишь] 1, to divide. 2, to share. —дели́ться, *refl.* 1, [*pfv.* раздели́ться] to divide; be divided. 2, [*impfv. only*] (*with* на + *acc.*) *math.* to be divisible (by). 3, [*pfv.* подели́ться] (*with instr.*) to share: дели́ться с ке́м-нибудь куско́м хле́ба, to share a piece of bread with someone. 4, [*pfv.* подели́ться] (*with* с + *instr.*) to confide in.

дели́шко [*pl.* -шки, -шек] *n., colloq., dim. of* де́ло: Как ва́ши дели́шки?, how are you getting along?

де́ло [*pl.* дела́, дел, дела́м] *n.* 1, matter; affair; business. 2, deed; act. 3, cause: де́ло ми́ра, the cause of peace. 4, *law* case. 5, file. 6, *pl., colloq.* things; matters: Как дела́?, how are things? 7, *in* го́рное де́ло, mining; печа́тное де́ло, printing; переплётное де́ло, bookbinding, etc. Вое́нное де́ло, military science. —в са́мом де́ле, really; truly; indeed. —в то́м-то и де́ло, that's just the point. —в чём де́ло?, what's the matter? —говори́ть де́ло, to talk sense. —де́ло бы́ло в (+ *prepl.*), it happened in... —де́ло в том, что..., the point is... —де́ло рук (+ *gen.*), one's doing; the work of; one's handiwork. —име́ть де́ло с, to deal with. —ме́жду де́лом, in between times; at odd moments. —на де́ле, in practice. —на са́мом де́ле, actually; in point of fact. —не в э́том де́ло, that is not the point. —не у дел, out of work. —нет де́ла (+ *dat.*) до, not to care about. —пе́рвым де́лом, *colloq.* first of all. —сде́лать своё де́ло, 1, to do one's job; do one's part. 2, to do its work; have its effect. —то и де́ло, continually; constantly.

делови́тый *adj.* businesslike. —делови́тость, *n.f.* businesslike manner; efficiency.

делово́й *adj.* **1,** business (*attrib.*). **2,** businesslike. —**деловы́е ка́чества,** professional qualities.

делопроизво́дство *n.* office work; paper work.

де́льный *adj.* **1,** able; efficient. **2,** (*of advice, an idea, etc.*) practical; sensible; sound.

де́льта (дэ) *n.* delta.

дельтови́дный (дэ) *adj.* deltoid.

дельфи́н *n.* dolphin.

демаго́г *n.* demagogue. —**демагоги́ческий,** *adj.* demagogic. —**демаго́гия,** *n.* demagoguery; demagogy.

демаркацио́нный *adj.,* *in* **демаркацио́нная ли́ния,** line of demarcation.

демарка́ция *n.* demarcation.

дема́рш (дэ) *n.* démarche.

демилитариза́ция (дэ) *n.* demilitarization.

демилитаризова́ть (дэ) *v.impfv. & pfv.* [*pres.* -зу́ю, -зу́ешь] to demilitarize.

демисезо́нный *adj.* (*of a coat*) worn in the spring or fall.

демобилиза́ция *n.* demobilization.

демобилизова́ть *v.impfv. & pfv.* [*pres.* -зу́ю, -зу́ешь] *mil.* **1,** to demobilize. **2,** to discharge. —**демобилизова́ться,** *refl.* to be discharged; receive one's discharge.

демогра́фия (дэ) *n.* demography. —**демо́граф,** *n.* demographer. —**демографи́ческий,** *adj.* demographic.

демокра́т *n.* democrat.

демократиза́ция *n.* democratization.

демократизи́ровать *v.impfv. & pfv.* [*pres.* -рую, -руешь] to democratize.

демокра́тия *n.* democracy. —**демократи́ческий,** *adj.* democratic.

де́мон *n.* demon. —**демони́ческий,** *adj.* demonic; demoniac.

демонстра́нт *n.* demonstrator (*one who takes part in a demonstration*).

демонстрати́вно *adv.* in a pointed or emphatic manner: демонстрати́вно вы́йти из за́ла, to walk *or* stalk out of the hall.

демонстрати́вный *adj.* **1,** pointed; emphatic. **2,** employing visual aids. **3,** *mil.* diversionary.

демонстра́тор *n.* demonstrator (*one who demonstrates something*).

демонстраци́онный *adj.* used for demonstrations.

демонстра́ция *n.* **1,** demonstration; march. **2,** demonstration; show. **3,** *mil.* diversionary action.

демонстри́ровать *v.impfv. & pfv.* [*pres.* -рую, -руешь] **1,** to demonstrate; participate in a demonstration. **2,** to demonstrate; show.

демонта́ж (дэ) *n.* dismantling.

демонти́ровать (дэ) *v.impfv. & pfv.* [*pres.* -рую, -руешь] to dismantle.

деморализа́ция (дэ) *n.* demoralization.

деморализова́ть (дэ) *v.impfv. & pfv.* [*pres.* -зу́ю, -зу́ешь] to demoralize.

де́мпинг (дэ) *n.,* *econ.* dumping.

денатура́т (дэ) *n.* denatured alcohol.

денатури́ровать (дэ) *v.impfv. & pfv.* [*pres.* -рую, -руешь] to denature (alcohol).

де́нди (дэ) *n.m. indecl.* dandy.

дендра́рий (дэ) *n.* arboretum.

дендри́т (дэ) *n.* dendrite.

де́нежный *adj.* **1,** monetary; money (*attrib.*). **2,** *colloq.* affluent; well-to-do.

денёк [*gen.* денька́] *n.,* *dim. of* **день.** Вы́дался хоро́ший денёк, it turned out to be a nice day.

де́нно *adv., colloq., in* **де́нно и но́щно ,** day and night.

денонси́ровать (дэ) *v.impfv. & pfv.* [*pres.* -рую, -руешь] to repudiate; renounce (a treaty, agreement, etc.).

денти́н (дэ) *n.* dentine.

денщи́к [*gen.* -щика́] *n., mil.,* pre-rev. orderly.

день [*gen.* дня] *n.m.* day. —**день деньско́й,** *colloq.* all day long. —**день ото дня,** day by day; with each passing day. —**изо дня в день,** day after day; day in and day out. —**на днях, 1,** the other day. **2,** one of these days; some day soon. —**по сей день,** to this day. —**со дня на́ день, 1,** any day (now). **2,** from day to day; from one day to the next. —**средь бе́ла дня,** in broad daylight. —**что ни день,** practically every day; hardly a day passes when one does not...

де́ньги [*gen.* де́нег; *other forms* деньга́м, -га́ми, -га́х] *n.pl.* money. —**быть при деньга́х,** to be in the chips. —**быть не при деньга́х,** to be short of cash.

департа́мент *n.* (governmental) department.

депе́ша *n.* **1,** dispatch. **2,** *obs.* telegram.

депо́ *n. indecl., R.R.* repair shop. —**парово́зное депо́,** roundhouse. —**пожа́рное депо́,** firehouse; fire station.

депози́т *n., finance* deposit. —**депози́тор,** *n.* depositor.

депоне́нт *n., finance* depositor.

депони́ровать *v.impfv. & pfv.* [*pres.* -рую, -руешь] *finance* to deposit.

депорта́ция *n.* deportation.

депорти́ровать *v.impfv. & pfv.* [*pres.* -рую, -руешь] to deport.

депре́ссия (дэ) *n.* **1,** *med.* depression. **2,** *econ.* depression.

депута́т *n.* deputy (*in a legislative body*). —**пала́та депута́тов,** Chamber of Deputies.

депута́ция *n.* deputation.

де́рби (дэ) *n.neut. indecl., horse racing* derby.

де́рбник *n.* merlin (*bird*).

де́рвиш *n.* dervish.

дёргать *v.impfv.* [*pfv.* **дёрнуть**] **1,** to pull; jerk; yank; tug at. **2,** (*with instr.*) to jerk (a part of one's body). **3,** [*impfv. only*] *impers.* to twitch: Его́ всего́ дёргает, he is twitching all over. **4,** [*impfv. only*] *colloq.* to pull out; extract. **5,** [*impfv. only*] *colloq.* to harass. —**дёргаться,** *refl.* **1,** to quiver. **2,** to twitch. *See also* **дёрнуть** *and* **дёрнуться.**

дерга́ч [*gen.* -гача́] *n.* corn crake (*bird*).

деревене́ть *v.impfv.* [*pfv.* **одеревене́ть**] to become stiff; become numb.

дереве́нский *adj.* **1,** village (*attrib.*). **2,** country (*attrib.*); rural.

дереве́нщина *n.m. & f., colloq.* country bumpkin; hick; yokel.

дере́вня [*pl.* дере́вни, -ве́нь, -вня́м] *n.* **1,** village. **2,** the country (*as opposed to the city*).

де́рево *n.* **1,** [*pl.* дере́вья, дере́вьев, дере́вьям] tree. **2,** wood. —**за дере́вьями ле́са не ви́деть,** (one) cannot see the forest for the trees.

дереообде́лочник *n.* woodworker. —**дереообде́лочный,** *adj.* woodworking.

дереву́шка [*gen. pl.* **-шек**] *n.* small village; hamlet.

де́ревце *also,* **деревцо́** [*pl.* **-вца́, -ве́ц, -вца́м**] *n.* sapling.

деревяни́стый *adj.* woody.

деревя́нный *adj.* **1,** wooden; wood. **2,** *fig.* wooden; dull.

деревя́шка [*gen. pl.* **-шек**] *n.* **1,** piece of wood. **2,** *colloq.* wooden leg; peg leg.

держа́ва *n.* power: мирова́я держа́ва, a world power.

держа́лка [*gen. pl.* **-лок**] *n., colloq.* handle.

держа́тель *n.m.* holder (*person or device*).

держа́ть *v.impfv.* [*pres.* **держу́, де́ржишь**] **1,** to hold. **2,** to keep. **3,** to support; hold up. —**держа́ть курс** *or* **путь на** (+ *acc.*), to head for. —**держа́ть отве́т за** (+ *acc.*), to answer for; be responsible for. —**держа́ть пари́,** to bet. —**держа́ть речь,** to make a speech. —**держа́ть себя́,** to behave. —**держа́ть чью-нибудь сто́рону,** to take someone's side. —**держа́ть экза́мен,** to take an examination. —**держи́те во́ра!,** stop thief!

держа́ться *v.r.impfv.* [*pres.* **держу́сь, де́ржишься**] **1,** (*with* **за** + *acc.*) to hold on to. Держа́ться за́ руки, to hold hands. **2,** (*with* **на** + *prepl.*) to be held up (by); be supported (by). **3,** to stay; remain: держа́ться на воде́, to remain afloat. **4,** to behave. **5,** (*with gen.*) to keep to: держа́ться пра́вой стороны́, to keep to the right. **6,** (*with gen.*) to stick to (the rules, subject, etc.). **7,** to hold together; remain in one piece. **8,** to hold out; stand firm. **9,** to last; persist. **10,** (*of food*) to keep. —**держа́ться бе́рега,** to stick close to the shore; hug the shore. —**держа́ться вме́сте,** to stick together. —**держа́ться пря́мо,** to stand up straight.

держимо́рда *n.m., colloq.* bully; tyrant.

дерза́ние *n.* **1,** daring. **2,** *pl.* bold initiatives.

дерза́ть *v.impfv.* [*pfv.* **дерзну́ть**] **1,** [*impfv. only*] to be daring. **2,** to dare.

дерзи́ть *v.impfv.* [*pfv.* **надерзи́ть**] (*with dat.*) *colloq.* to be rude (to); be insolent (to).

де́рзкий *adj.* [*short form* **де́рзок, дерзка́, де́рзко, де́рзки**] **1,** impudent; impertinent; insolent. **2,** daring; bold; audacious.

дерзнове́нный *adj.* **1,** *obs.* impudent; insolent. **2,** daring; audacious.

дерзну́ть *v., pfv. of* **дерза́ть** (*in sense #2*).

де́рзость *n.f.* **1,** impudence; impertinence; insolence. **2,** daring; audacity.

дерива́т (дэ) *n., chem.* derivative.

дермати́н *n.* leatherette.

дерматоло́гия *n.* dermatology. —**дермато́лог,** *n.* dermatologist.

дёрн *n.* turf; sod.

дёрнуть *v.pfv.* **1,** *pfv. of* **дёргать. 2,** to lurch forward. —**дёрнуться,** *refl.* **1,** *pfv. of* **дёргаться. 2,** to lurch forward. **3,** to lunge.

де́ррик (дэ) *n.* derrick. *Also,* **де́ррик-кра́н.**

дерю́га *n.* sackcloth; burlap. —**дерю́жный,** *adj.* burlap.

деса́нт *n., mil.* **1,** landing (*of troops*). Морско́й деса́нт, amphibious landing. **2,** landing party.

деса́нтник *n.* member of a landing party; commando.

деса́нтный *adj., mil.* landing (*attrib.*); assault (*attrib.*). —**морско́й деса́нтный,** amphibious.

десегрега́ция (дэ) *n.* desegregation.

десегреги́ровать (дэ) *v.impfv. & pfv.* [*pres.* **-рую, -руешь**] to desegregate.

десе́рт *n.* dessert. —**десе́ртный,** *adj.* dessert (*attrib.*).

де́скать *particle, colloq.* they say; he/she says.

десна́ [*pl.* **дёсны, дёсен**] *n.* gum (*in the mouth*).

десни́ца *n., poetic* right hand.

де́спот *n.* despot. —**despotíзм,** *n.* despotism. —**despotíческий; despotíчный,** *adj.* despotic. —**despotíя,** *n.* despotism.

дестабилиза́ция (дэ) *n.* destabilization.

дестабилизи́ровать (дэ) *v.impfv. & pfv.* [*pres.* **-рую, -руешь**] to destabilize.

десть [*pl.* **де́сти, десте́й, деетя́м**] *n.f.* unit of quantity for sheets of paper: ру́сская десть, quire; метри́ческая десть, fifty sheets.

деся́тая *n., decl. as an adj.* tenth: одна́ деся́тая, one-tenth.

десятери́чный *adj., in* **и десятери́чное,** name of the letter i of the Russian alphabet, in use prior to 1918.

де́сятеро *collective numeral* ten.

десятибо́рье *n., sports* decathlon.

десятигра́нник *n.* decahedron. —**десятигра́нный,** *adj.* decahedral.

десятидне́вный *adj.* ten-day (*attrib.*).

десятикра́тный *adj.* tenfold.

десятиле́тие *n.* **1,** tenth anniversary; tenth birthday. **2,** decade.

десятиле́тка [*gen. pl.* **-ток**] *n.* ten-year secondary school.

десятиле́тний *adj.* **1,** ten-year (*attrib.*). **2,** ten-year-old.

десяти́на *n.* **1,** *hist.* tithe. **2,** old Russian measure equal to approx. 2.7 acres.

десятирублёвка [*gen. pl.* **-вок**] *n., colloq.* ten-ruble note.

десятиуго́льник *n.* decagon.

десяти́чный *adj.* decimal (*attrib.*).

деся́тка *n.* **1,** the numeral 10. **2,** *colloq.* anything numbered 10. **3,** *colloq.* group of ten. **4,** *cards* ten. **5,** *colloq.* ten-ruble note.

деся́тник *n.* foreman.

деся́ток [*gen.* **-тка**] *n.* (*with gen. pl.*) **1,** ten: деся́ток я́блок, ten apples. **2,** decade (*of one's life*): Ему́ идёт шесто́й деся́ток, he is in his sixties. **3,** *pl.* tens of; dozens of: деся́тки раз, dozens of times; деся́тки ты́сяч рубле́й, tens of thousands of rubles.

деся́тый *ordinal numeral* tenth. —**де́ло деся́тое,** *colloq.* a minor matter.

де́сять [*gen., dat. & prepl.* **десяти́**; *instr.* **десятью́**] *numeral* ten.

де́сятью *adv.* ten times: де́сятью де́сять — сто, ten times ten is a hundred.

детализа́ция *n.* working out in detail.

детализи́ровать *v.impfv. & pfv.* [*pres.* **-рую, -руешь**] to work out in detail.

дета́ль *n.f.* **1,** detail. **2,** part; component.

дета́льный *adj.* detailed. —**дета́льно,** *adv.* in detail.

детвора́ *n., colloq.* children; kids.

детдо́м *n.* children's home (*contr. of* **де́тский дом**).

детекти́в (дэ, тэ) *n.* **1,** detective. **2,** detective story. —**детекти́вный,** *adj.* detective (*attrib.*).

детéктор (дэ, тэ) *n.* detector. —**детéктор лжи**, lie detector.

детёныш *n.* young animal; cub; calf.

детерминизм (дэ, тэ) *n.* determinism.

дéти [*gen.* детéй; *dat.* дéтям; *instr.* детьми; *prepl.* дéтях] *n.pl.* children.

детишки [*gen.* **-шек**] *n.pl.*, *colloq.* children; kids.

дéтище *n.* **1**, *obs.* child; offspring. **2**, *fig.* brainchild.

детонáтор *n.* detonator.

детонáция *n.* detonation.

детонировать *v.impfv.* [*pres.* **-рую, -руешь**] **1**, to detonate; go off. **2**, to be out of tune; be off key.

детородный *adj.* **1**, genital. **2**, childbearing (*attrib.*).

деторождéние *n.* **1**, childbearing. **2**, procreation.

детоубийство *n.* infanticide.

детсáд *n.* kindergarten; nursery school (*contr. of* дéтский сад).

дéтская *n., decl. as an adj.* nursery room for children.

дéтский *adj.* **1**, children's; child's. **2**, childish; childlike. **3**, baby (*attrib.*). —**дéтский дом**, children's home. —**дéтская коляска**, baby carriage. —**дéтское мéсто**, placenta. —**дéтская престýпность**, juvenile delinquency. —**дéтская психолóгия**, child psychology. —**дéтский сад**, kindergarten. —**дéтская смéртность**, infant mortality. —**дéтский труд**, child labor.

дéтство *n.* childhood. —**впадáть в дéтство**, to be in one's second childhood; be in one's dotage.

деть [*infl.* дéну, дéнешь] *v., pfv. of* девáть. —**дéться**, *refl., pfv. of* девáться.

де-фáкто (дэ) *adv.* de facto.

дефéкт *n.* defect: дефéкт рéчи, speech defect.

дефективный *adj.* having a physical or mental defect or abnormality; physically or mentally abnormal.

дефéктный *adj.* defective; faulty.

дефис *n.* hyphen.

дефицит *n.* **1**, deficit. **2**, shortage: дефицит в тóпливе, fuel shortage.

дефицитный *adj.* **1**, operating at a loss; unprofitable. **2**, (*of goods*) scarce; in short supply.

дефляция (дэ) *n., econ.* deflation.

деформáция (дэ) *n.* deformation.

деформировать (дэ) *v.impfv. & pfv.* [*pres.* **-рую, -руешь**] to change the shape of.

децентрализáция (дэ) *n.* decentralization.

децентрализовáть (дэ) *v.impfv. & pfv.* [*pres.* **-зую, -зуешь**] to decentralize.

децибéл (дэ) *n.* decibel.

децигрáмм (дэ) *n.* decigram.

децилитр (дэ) *n.* deciliter.

децимéтр (дэ) *n.* decimeter.

дешевéть *v.impfv.* [*pfv.* **подешевéть**] to go down in price; become cheaper.

дешевизна *n.* (*with gen.*) low cost (of); low prices (for).

дешёвка *n., colloq.* **1**, low price. **2**, something low in price. —**по дешёвке**, dirt-cheap.

дешéвле *adj., comp. of* дешёвый.

дёшево *adv.* cheap; cheaply. —**дёшево и сердито**, cheap but good; good, and inexpensive as well. —**дёшево отдéлаться**, to get off cheap.

дешёвый *adj.* [*short form* дёшев, дешевá, дёшево, дёшевы; *comp.* дешéвле] **1**, inexpensive; cheap. **2**, (*of a price*) low. **3**, *fig.* cheap; worthless; vulgar.

дешифрировать (дэ) *v.impfv. & pfv.* [*pres.* **-рую, -руешь**] to decipher. *Also*, дешифровáть [*pres.* **-рую, -руешь**].

дешифрóвка (дэ) *n.* decipherment; deciphering.

де-юре (дэ) *adv.* de jure.

деяние *n.* deed; act.

деятель *n.m.* figure: общéственный деятель, public figure. —**госудáрственный деятель**, statesman. —**политический деятель**, politician.

деятельность *n.f.* **1**, activity; activities. **2**, functioning; action.

деятельный *adj.* active.

джаз *n.* jazz. —**джáзовый**, *adj.* jazz.

джем *n.* jam.

джéмпер *n.* pullover; sweater.

джентльмéн *n.* gentleman.

джентльмéнский *adj.* gentlemanly. —**джентльмéнское соглашéние**, gentlemen's agreement.

джига *n.* jig (*dance*).

джигит *n.* skillful horseman.

джин *n.* **1**, gin. **2**, [*also*, джинн] genie.

джинсы [*gen.* **-сов**] *n.pl.* jeans.

джип *n.* jeep.

джиу-джитсу *n.neut. indecl.* jujitsu.

джóкер *n., cards* joker.

джóнка [*gen. pl.* **-нок**] *n.* junk (*boat*).

джóуль *n.m.* joule.

джýнгли [*gen.* **-лей**] *n.pl.* jungle.

джут *n.* jute. —**джýтовый**, *adj.* jute.

дзюдó *n. indecl.* judo.

диабéт *n.* diabetes. —**диабéтик**, *n.* diabetic. —**диабетический**, *adj.* diabetic.

диáгноз *n.* diagnosis.

диагнóст *n.* diagnostician.

диагнóстика *n.* **1**, diagnostics. **2**, diagnosing; diagnosis.

диагностический *adj.* diagnostic.

диагонáль *n.f.* diagonal. —**диагонáльный**, *adj.* diagonal.

диагрáмма *n.* diagram; chart; graph.

диадéма (дэ) *n.* diadem.

диакритический *adj.* diacritical.

диалéкт *n.* dialect.

диалéктика *n.* dialectics. —**диалектический**, *adj.* dialectical.

диалéктный *adj.* dialectal.

диалóг *n.* dialogue.

диáметр *n.* diameter.

диаметрáльно *adv.* diametrically: диаметрáльно противопóложный, diametrically opposite. —**диаметрáльный**, *adj.* diametrical.

диапазóн *n.* **1**, *music* range. **2**, *radio* band. **3**, *fig.* range; scope.

диапозитив *n., photog.* slide; transparency.

диатермия (тэ) *n.* diathermy.

диатонический *adj.* diatonic.

диафрáгма *n., anat.; optics; photog.* diaphragm.

дивáн *n.* sofa; couch. —**дивáнный**, *adj.* sofa (*attrib.*); couch (*attrib.*).

диверса́нт *n.* saboteur.

диверсио́нный *adj.* **1,** *mil.* diversionary. **2,** of sabotage.

диверсифика́ция *n.* diversification.

диве́рсия *n.* **1,** *obs., mil.* diversion. **2,** sabotage.

дивиде́нд *n.* dividend.

дивизио́н *n.* (artillery) battalion.

дивизио́нный *adj., mil.* division (*attrib.*); divisional.

дивизия *n., mil.* division.

диви́ть *v.impfv.* [*pres.* **дивлю́, диви́шь**] *colloq.* to surprise; startle. —**диви́ться,** *refl.* [*pfv.* **подиви́ться**] (*with dat.*) *colloq.* to wonder (at); marvel (at).

ди́вный *adj.* **1,** wonderful; marvelous. **2,** *obs.* amazing; remarkable.

ди́во *n.* wonder: Ди́во, что..., it's a wonder that... —**ди́ву дава́ться,** to wonder; marvel. —**на ди́во,** wonderfully; marvelously.

дида́ктика *n.* didactics. —**дидакти́ческий,** *adj.* didactic.

дие́з *n., music* sharp; sharp sign: соль-дие́з, G-sharp.

дие́та *n.* diet.

диете́тика (тэ) *n.* dietetics; nutrition. —**диетети́ческий,** *adj.* dietetic.

диети́ческий *adj.* dietary.

диетоло́гия *n.* dietetics; nutrition. —**дието́лог,** *n.* dietitian.

диза́йн *n.* (industrial) design.

ди́зель *n.m.* diesel engine. —**ди́зельный,** *adj.* diesel.

дизентери́я *n.* dysentery.

дика́рь [*gen.* **-каря́**] *n.m.* [*fem.* **-ка́рка**] **1,** savage. **2,** *colloq.* unsociable person; loner.

ди́кий *adj.* **1,** wild. **2,** absurd; preposterous. **3,** shy; retiring. —**ди́кое мя́со,** proud flesh. —**ди́кое я́блоко,** crab apple.

ди́ко *adv.* **1,** wild: расти́ ди́ко, to grow wild. **2,** wildly. —*adj., used predicatively* **1,** desolate: Вокру́г бы́ло ди́ко, it was desolate all around. **2,** absurd: Ди́ко да́же ду́мать об э́том, it is absurd even to think about it.

дикобра́з *n.* porcupine.

дико́вина *also,* **дико́винка** *n., colloq.* strange thing; wonder; novelty. —**быть в дико́вин(к)у** (+ *dat.*), to be amazing to.

дико́винный *adj., colloq.* odd; strange; bizarre.

дикорасту́щий *adj.* wild; growing wild.

ди́кость *n.f.* **1,** wild state; uncivilized state. **2,** savagery. **3,** lack of sociability. **4,** *colloq.* folly.

дикта́нт *n.* dictation (*classroom exercise*).

дикта́т *n.* diktat.

дикта́тор *n.* dictator. —**дикта́торский,** *adj.* dictatorial.

дикта́торство *n.* **1,** dictatorship. **2,** *colloq.* dictatorial manner.

диктату́ра *n.* dictatorship.

диктова́ть *v.impfv.* [*pfv.* **продиктова́ть;** *pres.* **-ту́ю, -ту́ешь**] **1,** to dictate. **2,** *usu. passive,* to prompt: Реше́ние диктова́лось (*or* бы́ло продикто́вано) двумя́ фа́кторами, the decision was prompted by two factors.

дикто́вка *n.* dictation: писа́ть под дикто́вку, to take dictation. —**под дикто́вку** (+ *gen.*), at the urging of; at the behest of.

ди́ктор *n.* (radio) announcer.

диктофо́н *n.* dictaphone.

ди́кция *n.* diction; enunciation.

диле́мма *n.* dilemma.

дилета́нт *n.* amateur; dilettante. —**дилетанти́зм; дилета́нтство,** *n.* dilettantism. —**дилета́нтский,** *adj.* amateurish.

дилижа́нс *n.* stagecoach.

диминуэ́ндо *adv.* diminuendo.

ди́на *n.* dyne.

динами́зм *n.* dynamism.

дина́мик *n.* loudspeaker.

дина́мика *n.* dynamics.

динами́т *n.* dynamite. —**динами́тный,** *adj.* dynamite (*attrib.*).

динами́ческий *adj.* **1,** of dynamics. **2,** dynamic.

динами́чный *adj.* dynamic. —**динами́чность,** *n.f.* dynamic quality.

дина́мо *n. indecl.* dynamo.

динамо́метр *n.* dynamometer.

дина́стия *n.* dynasty. —**династи́ческий,** *adj.* dynastic.

диноза́вр *n.* dinosaur.

дио́д *n.* diode.

дипло́м *n.* diploma; degree.

диплома́т *n.* diplomat.

дипломати́ческий *adj.* **1,** diplomatic. **2,** *fig.* diplomatic; tactful.

дипломати́чный *adj.* diplomatic; tactful. —**дипломати́чность,** *n.f.* diplomacy; tact.

диплома́тия *n.* diplomacy.

диплома́рованный *adj.* having a degree: дипломи́рованный инжене́р, person with a degree in engineering.

дипло́мный *adj.* done toward a degree: дипло́мный прое́кт, project for one's degree.

директи́ва *n.* directive. —**директи́вный,** *adj.* containing instructions.

дире́ктор [*pl.* **директора́**] *n.* **1,** director; manager. **2,** principal (*of a school*).

директора́т *n.* board of directors; directorate.

дире́кторский *adj.* director's; directorial.

дире́кция *n.* **1,** (top) management. **2,** director's office.

дирижа́бль *n.m.* dirigible.

дирижёр *n., music* conductor. —**дирижёрский,** *adj.* conductor's.

дирижи́ровать *v.impfv.* [*pres.* **-рую, -руешь**] *music* (*with instr.*) to conduct; direct.

дисбала́нс *n.* imbalance.

дисгармони́ровать *v.impfv.* [*pres.* **-рую, -руешь**] (*with* **с**) to clash (with).

дисгармо́ния *n.* disharmony.

диск *n.* **1,** disk. **2,** dial (*of a telephone*). **3,** turntable (*of a phonograph*). **4,** *sports* discus.

ди́скант *n.* **1,** high-pitched voice of a young boy. **2,** *music* treble. —**диска́нтовый,** *adj.* treble.

дисквалифика́ция *n.* disqualification.

дисквалифици́ровать *v.impfv. & pfv.* [*pres.* **-рую, -руешь**] to disqualify.

ди́сковый *adj.* disk-shaped. —**ди́сковая борона́,** disk harrow. —**ди́сковый то́рмоз,** disk brake.

дискообра́зный *adj.* disk-shaped. —**дискообра́зная анте́нна,** dish antenna.

дискредити́ровать *v.impfv. & pfv.* [*pres.* **-рую, -руешь**] to discredit.

дискрецио́нный *adj.* discretionary.

дискримина́ция *n.* discrimination. —**дискримина-цио́нный,** *adj.* discriminatory.

дискримини́ровать *v.impfv. & pfv.* [*pres.* **-рую, -руешь**] to discriminate (against).

дискуссио́нный *adj.* **1,** discussion (*attrib.*): в дискуссио́нном поря́дке, as a basis for discussion. **2,** debatable; controversial.

диску́ссия *n.* discussion; debate.

дискути́ровать *v.impfv.* [*pres.* **-рую, -руешь**] to discuss; debate.

дислока́ция *n., mil.* deployment; disposition (*of troops*).

дислоци́ровать *v.impfv. & pfv.* [*pres.* **-рую, -руешь**] *mil.* to deploy (troops).

диспансе́р (сэ) *n.* sanitarium; health center.

диспепси́я *n.* dyspepsia.

диспе́рсия *n., physics* dispersion.

диспе́тчер *n.* **1,** traffic manager. **2,** air traffic controller.

диспе́тчерская *n., decl. as an adj.* control tower. *Also,* **диспе́тчерская вы́шка.**

диспро́зий *n.* dysprosium.

диспропо́рция *n.* disproportion.

ди́спут *n.* (public) debate.

диссерта́ция *n.* dissertation; thesis.

диссиде́нт *n.* dissident.

диссона́нс *n.* **1,** *music* dissonance; discord. **2,** *fig.* disharmony; incongruity.

дистанцио́нный *adj.* controlled from a distance. —**дистанцио́нное управле́ние,** remote control.

диста́нция *n.* distance. —**сойти́ с диста́нции,** to fail to go the distance; drop out of a race.

дистилли́ровать *v.impfv. & pfv.* [*pres.* **-рую, -руешь**] to distill.

дистилля́ция *n.* distillation.

дистрофи́я *n.* dystrophy.

дисципли́на *n.* **1,** discipline. **2,** discipline (*branch of knowledge*).

дисциплина́рный *adj.* disciplinary. —**дисциплина́р-ное взыска́ние,** summary punishment.

дисциплини́ровать *v.impfv. & pfv.* [*pres.* **-рую, -ру-ешь**] to discipline.

дитя́ [*acc.* **дитя́;** *other cases rarely used*] *n.neut.* child.

дифира́мб *n., in* **петь дифира́мбы** (+ *dat.*), to sing the praises of.

дифтери́я *also,* **дифтери́т** *n.* diphtheria. —**дифте-ри́йный,** *adj.* diphtheria (*attrib.*); diphtherial.

дифто́нг *n.* diphthong.

диффама́ция *n.* defamation.

дифференциа́л *n., math., mech.* differential. —**диф-ференциа́льный,** *adj.* differential.

дифференциа́ция *n.* differentiation.

дифференци́ровать *v.impfv. & pfv.* [*pres.* **-рую, -руешь**] to differentiate.

диффу́зия *n.* diffusion.

дича́ть *v.impfv.* [*pfv.* **одича́ть**] **1,** to become wild. **2,** to become shy; become unsociable.

дичи́ться *v.r.impfv., colloq.* **1,** to be shy; avoid people. **2,** (*with gen.*) to avoid.

дичь *n.f.* **1,** game (*animals, birds, etc.*): кру́пная дичь, big game. **2,** *colloq.* wilderness. **3,** *colloq.* nonsense.

длина́ *n.* length. —**в длину́,** lengthwise. —**длина́ волны́,** wavelength.

длинново́лновый *adj.* long-wave.

длинноволо́сый *adj.* long-haired.

длинноно́гий *adj.* long-legged.

длиннота́ [*pl.* **длинно́ты**] *n.* **1,** *obs.* (great) length. **2,** *pl.* long drawn-out passages.

дли́нный *adj.* [*short form* **дли́нен, длинна́, дли́нно, дли́нны**] long. Рукава́ длинны́ (*with different stress*), the sleeves are too long.

дли́тельность *n.f.* length; duration.

дли́тельный *adj.* long; lengthy; protracted; prolonged. —**това́ры дли́тельного по́льзования,** durable goods.

дли́ться *v.r.impfv.* [*pfv.* **продли́ться**] to last.

для *prep., with gen.* for: кни́га для дете́й, a book for children. Корзи́на для бума́ги, wastebasket. Хорошо́ вы́глядеть для своего́ во́зраста, to look well for one's age. ♦*In certain combinations,* to: ва́жен для меня́, important to me; опа́сность для о́бщества, a danger to society; прие́млемый для всех, acceptable to all; закры́т для судохо́дства, closed to navigation. Выкра́ивать вре́мя для посеще́ния теа́тра, to find time to attend the theater. —**для того́, чтобы,** *see* **чтобы.**

днева́льный *n., decl. as an adj., mil.* man on duty.

днева́ть *v.impfv.* [*pres.* **дню́ю, дню́ешь**] to spend the day (*in a certain place*). —**днева́ть и ночева́ть,** to spend all one's time; "live" (*in a certain place*).

дневни́к [*gen.* **-ника́**] *n.* diary.

дневно́й *adj.* **1,** day (*attrib.*). **2,** daytime (*attrib.*). **3,** a day's; one day's.

днём *adv.* during the day; in the daytime.

дни́ще *n.* bottom (*of a vessel or barrel*).

дно *n.* bottom. Морско́е дно, ocean floor; seabed. —**вверх дном,** upside down; topsy-turvy. —**идти́ ко дну,** (*of a ship*) to sink; go down; go to the bottom. —**пить до дна,** to empty one's glass. —**пуска́ть ко дну,** to sink; send to the bottom.

до[1] *prep., with gen.* **1,** to; up to; as far as: дойти́ до ста́нции, to walk as far as the station; довести́ (кого́-нибудь) до отча́яния, to drive (someone) to despair. От Балти́йского до Чёрного мо́ря, from the Baltic to the Black Sea. **2,** before: до войны́, before the war. **3,** until: рабо́тать до двух часо́в но́чи, to work until two o'clock in the morning. **4,** to the point of: рабо́тать до изнеможе́ния, to work to the point of exhaustion. Изна́шивать пальто́ до дыр, to wear a coat to shreds. **5,** up to; as many as: Зал вмеща́ет до ты́сячи челове́к, the hall accommodates up to a thousand people. —**до сих/тех пор; до тех пор пока́ (не),** *see* **пора́.** —**до того́** (+ *adj.*), so: до того́ слаб, что..., so weak that... —**до того́, что,** until. —**не до,** not in the mood for: Ему́ не до шу́ток, he is not in the mood for jokes. Мне бы́ло не до того́, чтобы торгова́ться, I was not in a mood (*or* not of a mind) to bargain. —**что до,** as for.

до[2] *n.neut., music* do; C.

до- *prefix* **1,** *indicating action or motion up to a point:* дойти́ до моста́, to walk as far as the bridge. **2,** *indi-*

cating completion of an action: договори́ть, to finish speaking. **3,** *indicating something additional:* дополучи́ть, to receive in addition. **4,** (*with* **-ся**) *indicating attainment after persistent effort:* дозвони́ться, to ring until someone answers. **5,** (*with* **-ся**) *indicating an action to some extreme:* докрича́ться до хрипоты́, to shout oneself hoarse. **6,** *with adjectives,* pre-: дошко́льный, preschool. **7,** *with adverbs,* completely: до́суха, completely dry.

доба́вить [*infl.* **-влю, -вишь**] *v., pfv. of* **добавля́ть.**

доба́вка *n., colloq.* **1,** addition. **2,** second helping (*of something*). **3,** additive.

добавле́ние *n.* **1,** addition (*act of adding*). **2,** an addition: примеча́ния и добавле́ния, notes and additions. —**в добавле́ние к,** in addition to.

добавля́ть *v.impfv.* [*pfv.* **доба́вить**] to add.

доба́вочный *adj.* **1,** additional; extra. **2,** (*with telephone numbers*) extension: доба́вочный со́рок два, extension 42. —**доба́вочный нало́г,** surtax.

добега́ть *v.impfv.* [*pfv.* **добежа́ть**] (*with* **до**) to run to; run up to; run as far as.

добежа́ть [*infl. like* **бежа́ть**] *v., pfv. of* **добега́ть.**

добела́ *adv.* **1,** until something is spotlessly clean. **2,** *in* **раскаля́ть добела́,** to make white-hot; **раскалённый добела́,** white-hot.

добива́ть *v.impfv.* [*pfv.* **доби́ть**] **1,** to kill; finish off; deal the finishing blow to. **2,** to crush; rout; smite. **3,** (*with* **до**) to beat to a certain point or state.

добива́ться *v.r.impfv.* [*pfv.* **доби́ться**] (*with gen.*) **1,** to achieve; obtain; gain; get. **2,** [*impfv. only*] to seek; strive for. —**доби́ться своего́,** to gain one's objective; get one's way.

добира́ться *v.r.impfv.* [*pfv.* **добра́ться**] (*with* **до**) *colloq.* **1,** to reach; get to. **2,** to get one's hands on (someone).

доби́ть [*infl.* **добью, добьёшь**] *v., pfv. of* **добива́ть.** —**доби́ться,** *refl., pfv. of* **добива́ться.**

до́блестный *adj.* valiant; valorous.

до́блесть *n.f.* valor.

добра́сывать *v.impfv.* [*pfv.* **добро́сить**] (*with* **до**) to throw as far as.

добра́ться [*infl. like* **бра́ться**] *v.r., pfv. of* **добира́ться.**

добра́чный *adj.* before one is/was married; premarital.

добрести́ *v.pfv.* [*infl. like* **брести́**] (*with* **до**) to manage to reach; finally make it to.

добре́ть *v.impfv.* **1,** [*pfv.* **подобре́ть**] to become kind; become kinder. **2,** [*pfv.* **раздобре́ть**] *colloq.* to get fat; put on weight.

добро́ *n.* **1,** good: добро́ и зло, good and evil. Отлича́ть добро́ от зла, to tell right from wrong. Де́лать добро́, to do good; (*fol. by dat.*) be good to. Жела́ть кому́-нибудь добра́, to wish someone well. Это не к добру́, it's a bad sign (*or* omen). **2,** *colloq.* goods; property. —*adv., colloq.* good; all right. —**дать добро́ на** (+ *acc.*), to give the go-ahead for. —**добро́ бы,** *colloq.* it would be all right if; it would be one thing if. —**добро́ пожа́ловать!,** welcome! —**от добра́ добра́ не и́щут,** to know when one is well off; let well enough alone; not trifle with a good thing.

доброво́лец [*gen.* **-льца**] *n.* volunteer.

доброво́льный *adj.* voluntary. —**доброво́льно,** *adv.* voluntarily.

доброво́льческий *adj.* volunteer (*attrib.*).

доброде́тель *n.f.* virtue. —**доброде́тельный,** *adj.* virtuous.

доброду́шие *n.* good nature. —**доброду́шный,** *adj.* good-natured.

доброжела́тель *n.m.* well-wisher.

доброжела́тельный *adj.* **1,** good-natured; friendly. **2,** benevolent. —**доброжела́тельность,** *n.f.* benevolence.

доброжела́тельство *n.* good will.

доброка́чественный *adj.* **1,** of good quality. **2,** *med.* benign; not malignant.

добро́м *adv., colloq.* willingly; of one's own free will.

добросерде́чие *n.* kindheartedness. —**добросерде́чный,** *adj.* kindhearted; good-hearted.

добро́сить [*infl.* **-шу, -сишь**] *v., pfv. of* **добра́сывать.**

добросо́вестный *adj.* conscientious. —**добросо́вестность,** *n.f.* conscientiousness.

добрососе́дский *adj.* neighborly; good-neighbor.

доброта́ *n.* kindness.

добро́тный *adj.* of high quality; sound; durable.

до́брый *adj.* [*short form* **добр, добра́, добро́, добры́**] **1,** kind. **2,** good: до́брое де́ло, good deed; до́брая во́ля, good will. **3,** *in greetings,* good: До́брое у́тро!, good morning!; до́брый ве́чер!, good evening! **4,** *colloq.* a good; at least: до́брый час, a good hour. —**бу́дьте добры́** (+ *imperative*), would you be so kind as to... —**в до́брый час!,** the best of luck (in your new venture)! —**всего́ до́брого!,** all the best! —**чего́ до́брого,** for all one knows.

добря́к [*gen.* **-бряка́**] *n., colloq.* good-natured person; good soul.

добуди́ться *v.r.pfv.* [*infl.* **-бужу́сь, -бу́дишься**] (*with gen.*) *colloq.* to succeed in waking (someone) up.

добыва́ть *v.impfv.* [*pfv.* **добы́ть**] **1,** to obtain. **2,** to extract; mine. **3,** to capture; bag (*when hunting*).

добы́ть [*infl. like* **быть;** *past* **добы́л, добыла́, добы́ло, добы́ли**] *v., pfv. of* **добыва́ть.**

добы́ча *n.* **1,** (*with gen.*) extraction (of); mining (of). Добы́ча не́фти, oil production. **2,** anything mined from the earth. **3,** booty; loot; plunder; spoils. **4,** prey.

дова́ривать *v.impfv.* [*pfv.* **довари́ть**] to finish cooking; finish making.

довари́ть [*infl.* **-варю́, -ва́ришь**] *v., pfv. of* **дова́ривать.**

довезти́ [*infl. like* **везти́**] *v., pfv. of* **довози́ть.**

дове́ренность *n.f.* power of attorney. —**по дове́ренности,** by proxy.

дове́ренный *adj.* authorized. Дове́ренное лицо́, one's personal representative. —*n.* proxy; agent.

дове́рие *n.* trust; confidence.

довери́тельный *adj.* **1,** trusting. **2,** *obs.* secret; confidential.

дове́рить *v., pfv. of* **доверя́ть.** —**дове́риться,** *refl., pfv. of* **доверя́ться.**

до́верху *adv.* to the top; to the brim. —**сни́зу до́верху,** from top to bottom.

дове́рчивый *adj.* trusting. —**дове́рчивость,** *n.f.* trusting nature.

доверша́ть *v.impfv.* [*pfv.* доверши́ть] to complete.

доверше́ние *n.* completion. —в доверше́ние всего́, to top it off.

доверши́ть *v., pfv. of* доверша́ть.

доверя́ть *v.impfv.* [*pfv.* дове́рить] 1, [*impfv. only*] (*with dat.*) to trust. 2, to entrust; confide. —доверя́ться, *refl.* (*with dat.*) to trust (in).

дове́сок [*gen.* -ска] *n.* makeweight.

довести́ [*infl. like* вести́] *v., pfv. of* доводи́ть. —довести́сь, *refl., pfv. of* доводи́ться.

довле́ть *v.impfv.* 1, *obs.* to suffice. 2, (*with* над) to hold sway over (*a usage generally considered incorrect*).

до́вод *n.* argument: до́воды за и про́тив, the arguments for and against; the pros and cons.

доводи́ть *v.impfv.* [*pfv.* довести́; *pres.* -вожу́, -во́дишь] (*with* до) 1, to take to; bring to; accompany to. 2, to extend (a road, pipeline, etc.) to *or* as far as. 3, *fig.* to drive; carry; reduce (*to a certain point or state*): доводи́ть до отча́яния, to drive to despair; доводи́ть до кра́йности, to carry to an extreme; доводи́ть до нищеты́, to reduce to poverty. 4, to convey (news, information, etc.). —доводи́ть до конца́, to see through to the end. —доводи́ть до (чьего́-нибудь) све́дения, *see* све́дение.

доводи́ться *v.r.impfv.* [*pfv.* довести́сь; *pres.* -вожу́сь, -во́дишься] 1, *impers.* (*with dat. and inf.*) *colloq.* to happen (to); have occasion (to): Нам не довело́сь встре́титься, we did not have occasion to meet. 2, [*impfv. only*] (*with dat. and instr.*) *colloq.* to be related in a certain way: Он дово́дится мне дя́дей, he is my uncle.

довое́нный *adj.* prewar.

довози́ть *v.impfv.* [*pfv.* довезти́; *pres.* -вожу́, -во́зишь] (*with* до) to take to; bring to.

дово́льно *adv.* 1, rather; fairly; pretty: дово́льно ча́сто, fairly often. 2, enough: Дово́льно крича́ть!, enough shouting! С меня́ дово́льно, I've had enough. 3, contentedly.

дово́льный *adj.* 1, [*short form* -лен, -льна] (*with instr.*) pleased (with); satisfied (with); contented (with). 2, contented: дово́льный вид, contented look.

дово́льствие *n., mil.* allowance.

дово́льство *n.* 1, satisfaction; contentment. 2, *colloq.* comfortable circumstances.

дово́льствоваться *v.r.impfv.* [*pfv.* удово́льствоваться; *pres.* -ствуюсь, -ствуешься] (*with instr.*) to be content (with); be satisfied (with); settle for.

дог *n.* mastiff. —да́тский дог, Great Dane.

догада́ться *v.r., pfv. of* дога́дываться.

дога́дка [*gen. pl.* -док] *n.* 1, guess; conjecture. 2, *pl.* guesswork. —стро́ить дога́дки, to conjecture; speculate. —теря́ться в дога́дках, to be at a loss.

дога́дливый *adj.* bright; clever; quick-witted.

дога́дываться *v.r.impfv.* [*pfv.* догада́ться] 1, (*with* о *or a dependent clause*) to guess. 2, (*with a dependent clause*) to figure out. 3, (*with inf.*) to have the good sense (to).

до́гма *n.* dogma. —догмати́зм, *n.* dogmatism. —догма́тик, *n.* dogmatist. —догмати́ческий, *adj.* dogmatic.

догна́ть [*infl.* -гоню́, -го́нишь; *past fem.* догнала́] *v., pfv. of* догоня́ть.

догова́ривать *v.impfv.* [*pfv.* договори́ть] to finish speaking; have one's say. —догова́риваться, *refl.* 1, to arrange; make arrangements. Договори́лись!, it's all arranged/settled. 2, (*with inf.*) to agree (to); arrange (to); (*with* о) agree (on). 3, (*with* до) to talk to some extreme: договори́ться до хрипоты́, to talk oneself hoarse. Догова́риваться до того́, что..., to go so far as to say.

догово́р *also,* до́говор *n.* 1, treaty. 2, contract. —аре́ндный догово́р, lease.

договорённость *n.f.* agreement; understanding.

договори́ть *v., pfv. of* догова́ривать. —договори́ться, *refl., pfv. of* догова́риваться.

договóрный *adj.* 1, treaty (*attrib.*). 2, contractual.

догола́ *adv.* (*with verbs of undressing*) naked; to the skin.

догоня́ть *v.impfv.* [*pfv.* догна́ть] 1, to overtake; catch up with. 2, [*impfv. only*] to gain on.

догора́ть *v.impfv.* [*pfv.* догоре́ть] to burn down; burn out.

додава́ть *v.impfv.* [*pfv.* дода́ть; *pres.* -даю́, -даёшь] to pay the remainder: Он додаст вам де́сять рубле́й, he will pay you the remaining ten rubles.

дода́ть [*infl. like* дать; *past* до́дал, додала́, до́дало, до́дали] *v., pfv. of* додава́ть.

доде́лывать *v.impfv.* [*pfv.* доде́лать] to finish; complete.

доду́мываться *v.r.impfv.* [*pfv.* доду́маться] (*with* до) to think of; hit upon; come up with (an idea, solution, etc.).

доеда́ть *v.impfv.* [*pfv.* дое́сть] to finish eating; eat up.

доезжа́ть *v.impfv.* [*pfv.* дое́хать] (*with* до) 1, to reach; arrive at. 2, to go/drive/ride as far as.

дое́ние *n.* milking.

дое́сть [*infl. like* есть] *v., pfv. of* доеда́ть.

дое́хать [*infl.* дое́ду, дое́дешь] *v., pfv. of* доезжа́ть.

дож *n.* doge.

дожда́ться *v.r.pfv.* [*infl. like* ждать] 1, to wait (*as long as necessary*): Я не могу́ дожда́ться, I can't wait. 2, (*with gen.*) to wait (*until someone comes or something happens*): дожда́ться врача́, to wait till the doctor comes. Я е́ле дожда́лся вас, I wasn't going to wait for you much longer. Он не дожда́лся нас, he did not wait for us; he left before we came. —ждать не дожда́ться (+ *gen.*), one can hardly wait (for).

дождева́льный *adj.* sprinkling (*attrib.*); sprinkler (*attrib.*): дождева́льная устано́вка, sprinkler system.

дождева́ние *n.* sprinkling (*of a lawn, crops, etc.*).

дождеви́к [*gen.* -вика́] *n., colloq.* raincoat.

дождево́й *adj.* rain (*attrib.*): дождева́я вода́, rain water.

до́ждик *n.* light rain; shower.

дождли́вый *adj.* rainy.

дождь [*gen.* дождя́] *n.m.* rain. —идёт дождь, it is raining.

дожива́ть *v.impfv.* [*pfv.* дожи́ть] 1, (*with* до) to live to; live to see. 2, [*impfv. only*] to live out: дожива́ть после́дние дни, to be living out one's last days; be nearing the end of one's life. 3, *colloq.* to spend the rest of: дожи́ть ле́то на да́че, to spend the rest of the summer at one's dacha.

дожи́ть [*infl.* **доживу́, доживёшь;** *past* **до́жил, дожила́, до́жило, до́жили**] *v., pfv. of* **дожива́ть.**

до́за *n.* dose.

дозапра́вить [*infl.* -**влю, -вишь**] *v., pfv. of* **дозаправля́ть.** —**дозапра́виться,** *refl., pfv. of* **дозаправля́ться.**

дозапра́вка *n.* refueling.

дозаправля́ть *v.impfv.* [*pfv.* **дозапра́вить**] to refuel (a plane). —**дозаправля́ться,** *refl.* (*of a plane*) to refuel.

дозва́ться *v.r.pfv.* [*infl. like* **звать**] (*with gen.*) *colloq.* (*usu. neg.*) to reach on the telephone: Его́ ника́к не дозовёшься, you can't reach/get him on the phone.

дозво́ленный *adj.* permitted; permissible.

дозволя́ть *v.impfv.* [*pfv.* **дозво́лить**] *obs.* to permit; allow.

дозвони́ться *v.r.pfv.* (*with* до *or* к) *colloq.* to ring until one receives an answer; reach (*by telephone*).

дозвуково́й *adj.* subsonic.

дозиро́вка *n.* dosage.

дознава́ться *v.r.impfv.* [*pfv.* **дозна́ться;** *pres.* -**знаю́сь, -знаёшься**] *colloq.* **1,** to find out. **2,** [*impfv. only*] to inquire.

дозна́ние *n., law* inquest; inquiry.

дозна́ться [*infl.* -**знаю́сь, -знаёшься**] *v.r., pfv. of* **дознава́ться.**

дозо́р *n.* patrol. —**дозо́рный,** *adj.* patrol (*attrib.*).

дозрева́ть *v.impfv.* [*pfv.* **дозре́ть**] to become fully ripe.

доигра́ть *v., pfv. of* **доигрывать.**

дои́грывание *n., chess* resumption of play (*after an adjournment*).

дои́грывать *v.impfv.* [*pfv.* **доигра́ть**] to finish playing; play to the end.

дои́льный *adj.* used for milking: дои́льная маши́на, milking machine.

доиска́ться [*infl.* -**ищу́сь, -и́щешься**] *v.r., pfv. of* **дои́скиваться.**

дои́скиваться *v.r.impfv.* [*pfv.* **доиска́ться**] (*with gen.*) *colloq.* **1,** to find (*after searching*). **2,** [*impfv. only*] to try to find; search for (something) until it is found. **3,** [*impfv. only*] to inquire into; try to find out; seek.

доисторический *adj.* prehistoric.

дои́ть *v.impfv.* [*pfv.* **подои́ть;** *pres.* **дою́, дои́шь** *or* **до́ишь**] to milk. —**дои́ться,** *refl.* [*impfv. only*] to give milk.

до́йка *n.* milking.

до́йный *adj.* milch.

дойти́ [*infl.* **дойду́, дойдёшь;** *past* **дошёл, дошла́, дошло́, дошли́**] *v., pfv. of* **доходи́ть.**

док *n.* dock.

доказа́тельный *adj.* demonstrative; conclusive.

доказа́тельство *n.* proof; evidence.

доказа́ть [*infl.* -**кажу́, -ка́жешь**] *v., pfv. of* **дока́зывать.**

доказу́емый *adj.* demonstrable.

дока́зывать *v.impfv.* [*pfv.* **доказа́ть**] **1,** to prove. **2,** [*impfv. only*] to try to prove; argue.

дока́нчивать *v.impfv.* [*pfv.* **доко́нчить**] **1,** to finish. **2,** *colloq.* to finish off (*i.e.* eating or drinking).

дока́пывать *v.impfv.* [*pfv.* **докопа́ть**] to finish digging. —**дока́пываться,** *refl.* (*with* до) **1,** to dig as far

as. **2,** *fig., colloq.* to get to: докопа́ться до и́стины, to get to the truth.

докати́ться [*infl.* -**качу́сь, -ка́тишься**] *v.r., pfv. of* **дока́тываться.**

дока́тываться *v.r.impfv.* [*pfv.* **докати́ться**] **1,** (*with* до) to roll to; roll as far as. **2,** (*with* до) to reach. **3,** *colloq.* (*of loud noises*) to thunder; resound. **4,** (*with* до) *fig., colloq.* to sink to.

до́кер *n.* dock worker; longshoreman.

докла́д *n.* **1,** report. **2,** lecture; talk; paper. **3,** announcement (*of a visitor*): входи́ть без докла́да, to walk in unannounced.

докладно́й *adj., in* докладна́я запи́ска, report; memorandum.

докла́дчик *n.* person delivering a report, talk or paper; speaker.

докла́дывать *v.impfv.* [*pfv.* **доложи́ть**] **1,** (*with acc. or* о) to report (on). **2,** (*with* о) to announce (a visitor). **3,** *colloq.* to add.

доко́ле *adv., obs.* **1,** how long? **2,** as long as.

докона́ть *v.pfv., colloq.* to finish; be the end of.

доко́нчить *v., pfv. of* **дока́нчивать.**

докопа́ть *v., pfv. of* **дока́пывать.** —**докопа́ться,** *refl., pfv. of* **дока́пываться.**

докраснá *also,* **до́красна** *adv.* **1,** until something is red. **2,** *in* раскаля́ть докрасна́, to make red-hot; **раскалённый докрасна́,** red-hot.

докрича́ться *v.r.pfv.* [*infl.* -**чу́сь, -чи́шься**] **1,** *colloq.* to shout until one is heard. **2,** (*with* до) to shout to some extreme: докрича́ться до хрипоты́, to shout oneself hoarse.

до́ктор [*pl.* **доктора́**] *n.* **1,** doctor (*holder of a doctoral degree*): до́ктор нау́к, Doctor of Science. **2,** *colloq.* doctor; physician. —**до́кторский,** *adj.* doctor's; doctoral.

доктора́нт *n.* person pursuing a doctoral degree.

доктри́на *n.* doctrine.

доктринёр *n.* doctrinaire. —**доктринёрский,** *adj.* doctrinaire.

докуме́нт *n.* document. —**документа́льный,** *adj.* documentary. —**документа́ция,** *n.* documentation.

документи́ровать *v.impfv. & pfv.* [*pres.* -**рую, -руешь**] to document.

докупа́ть *v.impfv.* [*pfv.* **докупи́ть**] to buy in addition.

докупи́ть [*infl.* -**куплю́, -ку́пишь**] *v., pfv. of* **докупа́ть.**

доку́ривать *v.impfv.* [*pfv.* **докури́ть**] to finish smoking. Докури́ть сигаре́ту, to finish one's cigarette.

докури́ть [*infl.* -**курю́, -ку́ришь**] *v., pfv. of* **доку́ривать.**

докуча́ть *v.impfv.* (*with dat.*) *colloq.* to bother; annoy; pester.

доку́чливый *adj., colloq.* annoying; bothersome.

дол *n., poetic* valley; vale; dale.

долби́ть *v.impfv.* [*pres.* -**блю́, -би́шь**] **1,** [*pfv.* **продолби́ть**] to gouge; hollow out. **2,** *colloq.* to bang repeatedly. **3,** *colloq.* to memorize; learn by rote.

долг *n.* **1,** duty. **2,** [*2nd loc.* долгу́; *pl.* долги́] debt. —**в долгу́** *or* **пе́ред,** indebted to; in someone's debt. —**брать в долг,** to borrow. —**дава́ть в долг,** to lend. —**долг платежо́м кра́сен,** one good turn deserves another. —**не остава́ться в долгу́,** to reply in kind;

(one was) not to be outdone. —отда́ть после́дний долг (+ *dat.*), to pay one's last respects to. —по до́лгу слу́жбы, in one's official capacity.

до́лгий *adj.* [*comp.* до́льше *and* до́лее] long (*in time*). —до́лгие го́ды, many long years.

до́лго *adv.* long; (for) a long time. —как до́лго?, how long?

долгове́чный *adj.* long-lasting; long-lived. —долгове́чность, *n.f.* longevity.

долгово́й *adj.* of or for a debt. —долгово́е обяза́тельство, promissory note. —долгова́я тюрьма́; долгова́я я́ма, debtor's prison.

долговре́менный *adj.* of long duration; lasting a long time.

долговя́зый *adj., colloq.* lanky; gangling.

долгожда́нный *adj.* long-awaited.

долгоигра́ющий *adj., in* долгоигра́ющая пласти́нка, long-playing record.

долголе́тие *n.* longevity. —долголе́тний, *adj.* of many years.

долгоно́жка [*gen. pl.* -жек] *n.* crane fly.

долгоно́сик *n.* weevil. —хло́пковый долгоно́сик, boll weevil.

долгосро́чный *adj.* long-range; long-term.

долгота́ *n.* 1, length: долгота́ дня, the length of a day. 2, [*pl.* -го́ты] longitude.

до́лее *adj., comp. of* до́лгий. —*adv., comp. of* до́лго.

долеза́ть *v.impfv.* [*pfv.* доле́зть] (*with* до) 1, to climb as far as. 2, to reach by climbing.

доле́зть [*infl. like* лезть] *v., pfv. of* долеза́ть.

долета́ть *v.impfv.* [*pfv.* долете́ть] (*with* до) 1, to fly as far as. 2, to reach by flying. 3, (*of sounds, news, etc.*) to reach.

долете́ть [*infl.* -чу́, -ти́шь] *v., pfv. of* долета́ть.

до́лжен *adj., used predicatively* [*fem.* -жна́; *neut.* -жно́; *pl.* -жны́] 1, must; have to: Я до́лжен (должна́) предупреди́ть вас, I must warn you. 2, should; ought to: Она́ должна́ ско́ро прийти́, she should be here soon. Я не до́лжен был э́того сде́лать, I shouldn't have done it. 3, due to; supposed to; scheduled to: По́езд до́лжен прибы́ть в семь часо́в, the train is due/scheduled to arrive at seven o'clock. 4, in debt; indebted: остава́ться до́лжен (+ *dat.*), to remain in debt (to). Он мне до́лжен ты́сячу рубле́й, he owes me 1,000 rubles. —должно́ быть, probably; must: Он, должно́ быть, уже́ ушёл, he must have left already.

должни́к [*gen.* -ника́] *n.* debtor.

до́лжное *n., decl as an adj.* one's due. —отдава́ть *or* воздава́ть до́лжное (+ *dat.*), 1, to give someone his/her due; give someone credit. 2, to pay tribute to. —принима́ть как до́лжное, to take as a matter of course; take for granted.

должностно́й *adj.* official. —должностно́е лицо́, official; officeholder. —должностно́е преступле́ние, malfeasance in office.

до́лжность [*infl.* до́лжности, -сте́й, -стя́м] *n.f.* post; position; office.

до́лжный *adj.* due; proper. —до́лжным о́бразом, properly. —на до́лжной высоте́, up to the mark. *See also* до́лжное.

долива́ть *v.impfv.* [*pfv.* доли́ть] 1, to fill (*by pouring*). 2, (*with gen.*) to pour more (of).

доли́на *n.* valley.

доли́ть [*infl.* долью́, дольёшь; *past* до́лил *or* доли́л, долила́, до́лило *or* доли́ло, до́лили *or* доли́ли] *v., pfv. of* долива́ть.

до́ллар *n.* dollar. —до́лларовый, *adj.* dollar (*attrib.*).

доложи́ть [*infl.* доложу́, доло́жишь] *v., pfv. of* докла́дывать.

долой *adv.* 1, (*with acc.*) down with...! 2, off: Ша́пки доло́й!, hats off! —с глаз мои́х доло́й!, out of my sight! —с плеч доло́й, (a load) off one's shoulders.

доломи́т *n.* dolomite.

долото́ [*pl.* доло́та] *n.* chisel.

до́лька [*gen. pl.* -лек] *n.* 1, lobule. 2, section (*of a citrus fruit*).

до́льше *adj., comp. of* до́лгий. —*adv., comp. of* до́лго.

до́ля [*pl.* до́ли, доле́й, доля́м] *n.* 1, share; portion. 2, lot: вы́пасть на до́лю (+ *dat.*), to fall to someone's lot. 3, *anat.* lobe. 4, *in* до́ля и́стины, grain of truth. —войти́ в до́лю с, to go shares with.

дом [*pl.* дома́] *n.* 1, house; home. 2, building. —из до́ма, from home. —и́з дому, out of the house. —на́ дом, to one's home: брать рабо́ту на́ дом, to take work home. —на дому́, at home (*as opposed to one's place of work*). *See also* до́ма *and* домо́й.

до́ма *adv.* at home. —бу́дьте как до́ма, make yourself at home. —у него́ не все до́ма, *colloq.* he is not all there.

дома́шние *n.pl., decl. as an adj.* members of one's family.

дома́шний *adj.* 1, home (*attrib.*); house (*attrib.*); household (*attrib.*). 2, domestic. 3, homemade; (*of a meal*) home-cooked. —дома́шнее зада́ние, homework. —дома́шняя пти́ца, poultry. —дома́шняя хозя́йка, housewife. —дома́шнее хозя́йство, housekeeping.

до́менный *adj., in* до́менная печь, blast furnace.

до́мик *n.* small house; small cottage. Охо́тничий до́мик, hunting lodge.

домина́нта *n.* dominant idea; main thrust.

доминио́н *n.* dominion.

домини́ровать *v.impfv.* [*pres.* -рую, -руешь] 1, to predominate; be (pre)dominant. 2, (*with* над) to dominate; tower over.

домини́рующий *adj.* dominant.

домино́ *n.indecl.* 1, domino (*costume*). 2, dominoes (*game*).

доми́шко [*pl.* -шки, -шек] *n.m.* 1, tiny house. 2, shack; hovel.

домкра́т *n.* jack (*for lifting*).

до́мна [*gen. pl.* до́мен] *n.* blast furnace.

домови́тый *adj.* 1, thrifty; economical. 2, capable; efficient.

домовладе́лец [*gen.* -льца] *n.* homeowner.

домово́дство *n.* 1, housekeeping. 2, home economics.

домово́й *n., decl. as an adj.* elf; goblin.

домо́вый *adj.* house (*attrib.*). —домо́вая кни́га, register of tenants.

домога́тельство *n.* 1, solicitation. 2, *pl.* advances; overtures.

домога́ться *v.r.impfv.* (*with gen.*) to seek; strive to obtain.

домо́й *adv.* home: идти́ домо́й, to go home.

доморо́щенный *adj.* **1,** homebred. **2,** *fig.* homespun; half-baked.

домосе́д *n.* stay-at-home; homebody.

домотка́ный *adj.* homespun.

домоуправле́ние *n.* **1,** building management. **2,** *colloq.* building manager's office.

домохозя́йка [*gen. pl.* **-я́ек**] *n.* housewife.

домоча́дцы [*gen.* **-цев**] *n.pl., obs.* household.

до́мра *n.* old Russian musical instrument resembling a mandolin.

домрабо́тница *n.* maid; housemaid.

домча́ть *v.pfv.* [*infl.* **-чу́, -чи́шь**] *colloq.* to deliver in a hurry; rush; whisk. —**домча́ться,** *refl.* (*with* до) *colloq.* to race (to); rush (to); dash (to).

до́мысел [*gen.* **-сла**] *n.* conjecture; supposition.

донага́ *adv., colloq.* (*with verbs of undressing*) naked; to the skin.

дона́шивать *v.impfv.* [*pfv.* **доноси́ть**] **1,** to wear out. **2,** to carry (a baby) to full term.

доне́льзя *adv., colloq.* completely; utterly: доне́льзя уста́л, utterly exhausted.

донесе́ние *n.* message; dispatch.

донести́ [*infl. like* **нести́**] *v., pfv. of* **доноси́ть**[1]. —**донести́сь,** *refl., pfv. of* **доноси́ться.**

до́низу *adv.* to the bottom. —**све́рху до́низу,** from top to bottom.

донима́ть *v.impfv.* [*pfv.* **доня́ть**] *colloq.* to pester; harass; beset.

донкихо́тский *adj.* quixotic.

до́нный *adj.* bottom (*attrib.*).

до́нор *n.* blood donor.

доно́с *n.* denunciation; accusation; report to the authorities.

доноси́ть[1] *v.impfv.* [*pfv.* **донести́**] **1,** (*with* до) to carry (to); deliver (to). **2,** to report. **3,** (*with* на + *acc.*) to inform on; squeal on. —**доноси́ться,** *refl.* **1,** to be heard; be sensed. **2,** (*with* до) to reach.

доноси́ть[2] [*infl.* **-ношу́, -носишь**] *v., pfv. of* **дона́шивать.**

доно́счик *n.* informer; stool pigeon.

донско́й *adj.* of the Don River. —**донско́й каза́к,** Don Cossack.

доны́не *adv., poetic* to this day.

доня́ть [*infl. like* **поня́ть**] *v., pfv. of* **донима́ть.**

допека́ть *v.impfv.* [*pfv.* **допе́чь**] **1,** to finish baking. **2,** *colloq.* to plague.

допе́чь [*infl. like* **печь**] *v., pfv. of* **допека́ть.**

допива́ть *v.impfv.* [*pfv.* **допи́ть**] to drink (up); finish drinking. —**допива́ться,** *refl.* (*with* до) *colloq.* to drink oneself into a state of...

до́пинг *n.* drug (*administered to athletes, racehorses, etc.*).

дописа́ть [*infl.* **-пишу́, -пишешь**] *v., pfv. of* **допи́сывать.**

допи́сывать *v.impfv.* [*pfv.* **дописа́ть**] **1,** to finish writing. **2,** (*with* до) to write as far as. **3,** to write additionally; add (*by writing*).

допи́ть [*infl.* **допью́, допьёшь;** *past* **до́пил** *or* **допи́л,**

допила́, до́пило *or* **допи́ло, до́пили** *or* **допи́ли**] *v., pfv. of* **допива́ть.** —**допи́ться,** *refl.* [*past* **допи́лся, допила́сь, допило́сь** *or* **допи́лось допили́сь** *or* **допи́лись**] *pfv. of* **допива́ться.**

допла́та *n.* additional charge; surcharge.

доплати́ть [*infl.* **-плачу́, -пла́тишь**] *v., pfv. of* **допла́чивать.**

допла́чивать *v.impfv.* [*pfv.* **доплати́ть**] **1,** to pay in addition; pay the remainder: доплати́ть сто рубле́й, to pay an additional (*or* the remaining) 100 rubles. **2,** to pay in full.

доплести́сь [*infl. like* **плести́сь**] *v.r., pfv. of* **доплета́ться.**

доплета́ться *v.r.impfv.* [*pfv.* **доплести́сь**] (*with* до) *colloq.* to drag oneself (to).

доплыва́ть *v.impfv.* [*pfv.* **доплы́ть**] (*with* до) to swim as far as.

доплы́ть [*infl. like* **плыть**] *v., pfv. of* **доплыва́ть.**

допо́длинный *adj., colloq.* true; authentic. —**допо́длинно,** *adv., colloq.* for certain.

допоздна́ *adv., colloq.* till late at night.

доползать *v.impfv.* [*pfv.* **доползти́**] (*with* до) to crawl up to; crawl as far as.

доползти́ [*infl. like* **ползти́**] *v., pfv. of* **доползать.**

дополна́ *adv., colloq.* to the brim.

дополне́ние *n.* **1,** addition. **2,** supplement; addendum; annex. **3,** *gram.* object. —**в дополне́ние к,** in addition to.

дополни́тельно *adv.* in addition.

дополни́тельный *adj.* **1,** additional; supplementary. **2,** (*of colors*) complementary. —**дополни́тельное вре́мя,** *sports* overtime.

дополня́ть *v.impfv.* [*pfv.* **допо́лнить**] **1,** to expand; enlarge (something written). **2,** to amplify; add to (a statement). —**дополня́ть друг дру́га,** to complement each other.

дополуча́ть *v.impfv.* [*pfv.* **дополучи́ть**] to receive in addition; receive the remaining.

дополучи́ть [*infl.* **-лучу́, -лу́чишь**] *v., pfv. of* **дополуча́ть.**

допото́пный *adj.* antediluvian.

допра́шивать *v.impfv.* [*pfv.* **допроси́ть**] to interrogate; question.

допро́с *n.* interrogation; questioning. —**перекрёстный допро́с,** cross-examination.

допроси́ть [*infl.* **-прошу́, -про́сишь**] *v., pfv. of* **допра́шивать.**

до́пуск *n.* **1,** admission; admittance. **2,** (security) clearance. **3,** *mech.* tolerance.

допуска́ть *v.impfv.* [*pfv.* **допусти́ть**] **1,** to admit; let in; allow in; (*with* к) allow to see (someone). **2,** to allow; permit; tolerate. **3,** to commit (an error, indiscretion, etc.). **4,** to assume: допу́стим, let us assume. **5,** to grant; concede. **6,** (*used negatively*) to prevent (something from happening).

допусти́мый *adj.* **1,** permissible. **2,** conceivable; possible.

допусти́ть [*infl.* **-пущу́, -пу́стишь**] *v., pfv. of* **допуска́ть.**

допуще́ние *n.* **1,** admission. **2,** assumption.

допы́тываться *v.r.impfv.* [*pfv.* **допыта́ться**] *colloq.* **1,** to find out. **2,** [*impfv. only*] to try to find out.

допьяна́ *also,* **до́пьяна** *adv., colloq.* till one is completely drunk.

дораба́тывать *v.impfv.* [*pfv.* **дорабо́тать**] **1,** *v.t.* to finish; put the finishing touches on. **2,** *v.i.* (*with* до) to work until. —**дораба́тываться,** *refl.* (*with* до) *colloq.* to work to some extreme: дорабо́таться до изнеможе́ния, to work to the point of exhaustion.

дораста́ть *v.impfv.* [*pfv.* **дорасти́**] (*with* до) **1,** to grow (to a certain height). **2,** to reach the age of. **3,** (*with* не) not be old enough: Он ещё не доро́с, чтобы (+ *inf.*), he is not old enough to...

дорасти́ [*infl. like* **расти́**] *v., pfv. of* **дораста́ть.**

дореволюцио́нный *adj.* prerevolutionary.

доро́га *n.* **1,** road. **2,** way: всю доро́гу, the whole way. **3,** trip: уста́ть с доро́ги, to be tired from the trip. —**по** (*or* **в**) **доро́ге,** on the way; en route. —**дать доро́гу** (+ *dat.*), to make way for. —**идти́ свое́й доро́гой,** to go one's own way. —**стать поперёк доро́ги** (+ *dat.*), to stand in someone's way. —**туда́ ему́ и доро́га,** it serves him right.

до́рого *adv.* **1,** a lot (of money): заплати́ть/брать до́рого, to pay/charge a lot of money. **2,** dearly: Э́то ему́ до́рого обошло́сь, it cost him dearly. —*adj., used predicatively* **1,** expensive: Э́то не до́рого, that's not expensive. **2,** dear; precious: Вре́мя бы́ло до́рого, time was precious.

дорогови́зна *n.* **1,** high prices. **2,** (*with gen.*) high cost (of).

дорого́й *adj.* [*short form* **до́рог, дорога́, до́рого, до́роги;** *comp.* **доро́же**] **1,** dear: дорого́й друг, a dear friend. Дорого́й Ива́н Серге́евич!, Dear Ivan Sergeyevich. **2,** expensive. **3,** (*of a price*) high. **4,** precious. —*n.* dear; my dear.

дорогостоя́щий *adj.* high-priced; expensive; costly.

доро́дный *adj.* stout; corpulent. —**доро́дность,** *n.f.*; **доро́дство,** *n.* corpulence.

дорожа́ть *v.impfv.* [*pfv.* **вздорожа́ть** *or* **подорожа́ть**] to go up in price; become more expensive.

доро́же *adj., comp. of* **дорого́й.**

дорожи́ть *v.impfv.* (*with instr.*) to value; prize; treasure.

доро́жка [*gen. pl.* -**жек**] *n.* **1,** path; walk. **2,** track: бегова́я доро́жка, running track. **3,** lane (*on a running track*). **4,** strip of carpet. —**звукова́я доро́жка,** sound track.

доро́жный *adj.* **1,** road (*attrib.*): доро́жный знак, road sign. **2,** travel (*attrib.*); traveling (*attrib.*).

дортуа́р *n., obs.* dormitory.

доса́да *n.* annoyance; vexation. —**кака́я доса́да!,** how annoying!

досади́ть [*infl.* -**жу́,** -**ди́шь**] *v., pfv. of* **досажда́ть.**

доса́дный *adj.* expressing annoyance; of annoyance.

доса́дный *adj.* **1,** annoying; maddening. **2,** regrettable. —**доса́дно,** *adj., used predicatively,* annoying: как доса́дно!, how annoying!

доса́довать *v.impfv.* [*pres.* -**дую,** -**дуешь**] (*with* на + *acc.*) to be annoyed (with).

досажда́ть *v.impfv.* [*pfv.* **досади́ть**] (*with dat.*) to annoy; vex.

досе́ле *adv., obs.* hitherto.

досиде́ть [*infl.* -**жу́,** -**ди́шь**] *v., pfv. of* **доси́живать.**

доси́живать *v.impfv.* [*pfv.* **досиде́ть**] (*with* до) to sit (until); stay (until).

доска́ [*acc.* **до́ску;** *pl.* **до́ски, досо́к, доска́м**] *n.* **1,** board. **2,** blackboard. **3,** plaque. **4,** *in* гладѝльная доска́, ironing board; доска́ объявле́ний, bulletin board; ша́хматная доска́, chessboard; прибо́рная доска́, instrument panel. —**от доски́ до доски́,** from cover to cover. —**ста́вить на одну́ до́ску,** to equate; place on a par.

досказа́ть *v.pfv.* [*infl.* -**скажу́,** -**ска́жешь**] **1,** to finish telling. **2,** (*with* до) to tell as far as.

доскона́льный *adj.* thorough. —**доскона́льно,** *adv.* thoroughly. —**доскона́льность,** *n.f.* thoroughness.

досла́ть [*infl.* **дошлю́, дошлёшь**] *v., pfv. of* **досыла́ть.**

досло́вный *adj.* literal; verbatim. —**досло́вно,** *adv.* literally; verbatim; word for word.

дослу́живать *v.impfv.* [*pfv* **дослужи́ть**] (*with* до) to serve (until). —**дослу́живаться,** *refl.* (*with* до) to serve (until one reaches a certain rank): дослужи́ться до майо́ра, to rise to the rank of major.

дослужи́ть [*infl.* -**служу́,** -**слу́жишь**] *v., pfv. of* **дослу́живать.** —**дослужи́ться,** *refl., pfv. of* **дослу́живаться.**

дослу́шать *v.pfv.* to listen (to something) till the end.

досма́тривать *v.impfv.* [*pfv.* **досмотре́ть**] **1,** to watch to the end. **2,** to watch (until): досмотре́ть пье́су до тре́тьего де́йствия, to watch a play till the third act.

досмо́тр *n.* examination; inspection: тамо́женный досмо́тр, customs inspection.

досмотре́ть [*infl.* -**смотрю́,** -**смо́тришь**] *v., pfv. of* **досма́тривать.**

досмо́трщик *n.* customs inspector.

доспа́ть [*infl. like* **спать**] *v., pfv. of* **досыпа́ть.**

доспева́ть *v.impfv.* [*pfv.* **доспе́ть**] to become fully ripe.

доспе́хи [*gen.* -**хов**] *n.pl.* armor.

досро́чно *adv.* ahead of schedule. —**досро́чный,** *adj.* ahead of schedule; early.

достава́ть *v.impfv.* [*pfv.* **доста́ть;** *pres.* -**стаю́,** -**стаёшь**] **1,** (*with* до) to reach; be able to touch. **2,** to take (*from a certain place*): доста́ть кни́гу с по́лки, to take a book from the shelf. **3,** to obtain; get. **4,** *impers.* (*with gen.*) *colloq.* to suffice: Де́нег у нас доста́нет, we have enough money. —**достава́ться,** *refl.* (*with dat.*) **1,** to pass into the possession of. **2,** to fall to one's lot. **3,** *impers., colloq.* to get it; catch it; catch hell.

доста́вить [*infl.* -**влю,** -**вишь**] *v., pfv. of* **доставля́ть.**

доста́вка *n.* delivery.

доставля́ть *v.impfv.* [*pfv.* **доста́вить**] **1,** to deliver. **2,** to give; provide; afford (pleasure, an opportunity, etc.). **3,** to give; cause (trouble, anxiety, etc.).

доста́ток [*gen.* -**тка**] *n.* **1,** circumstances; means: лю́ди сре́днего доста́тка, people of moderate means. **2,** comfortable circumstances. **3,** *colloq.* sufficiency; plenty. **4,** *pl., colloq.* income.

доста́точно *adv.* enough; sufficiently: доста́точно широ́кий, wide enough. —*adj.* **1,** (*with gen.*) enough; sufficient: доста́точно сил, enough strength. **2,** (*with* *inf.*) it is sufficient to: доста́точно сказа́ть, suffice it to say. —*interj.* enough!

доста́точность *n.f.* sufficiency.

доста́точный *adj.* sufficient; ample.

доста́ть [*infl.* -ста́ну, -ста́нешь] *v., pfv. of* достава́ть. —**доста́ться**, *refl., pfv. of* достава́ться.

достига́ть *v.impfv.* [*pfv.* дости́гнуть *or* дости́чь] (*with gen.*) **1**, to reach. **2**, to achieve; attain.

дости́гнуть [*past* дости́г, дости́гла] *v., pfv. of* достига́ть.

достиже́ние *n.* achievement. По достиже́нии (+ *gen.*), on reaching (a certain age).

достижи́мый *adj.* attainable.

дости́чь [*infl. like* дости́гнуть] *v., pfv. of* достига́ть.

достове́рно *adv.* for certain; for sure.

достове́рность *n.f.* **1**, reliability. **2**, authenticity.

достове́рный *adj.* (*of information or a source*) reliable.

досто́инство *n.* **1**, dignity. **2**, merit; virtue; advantage. **3**, value; denomination (*of a bill or coin*). —**оцени́ть по досто́инству**, *see* оце́нивать.

досто́йно *adv.* **1**, in a worthy *or* fitting manner. **2**, *obs.* with dignity.

досто́йный *adj.* [*short form* досто́ин, досто́йна] **1**, (*with gen.*) worthy (of); deserving (of). **2**, deserved; well-deserved. **3**, fitting; worthy.

достопримеча́тельность *n.f.* sight; point of interest.

достопримеча́тельный *adj.* noteworthy.

достоя́ние *n.* **1**, property. **2**, *fig.* common property: стать достоя́нием наро́да, to become the common property of the people.

достра́ивать *v.impfv.* [*pfv.* достро́ить] to finish building.

до́ступ *n.* access.

досту́пность *n.f.* **1**, accessibility. **2**, availability.

досту́пный *adj.* **1**, accessible. **3**, (*of a person*) approachable. **4**, available. **4**, easily understood; understandable. **5**, (*of prices*) moderate; reasonable.

достуча́ться *v.r.pfv.* [*infl.* -чу́сь, -чи́шься] *colloq.* to knock until someone answers.

досу́г *n.* leisure. —**на досу́ге**, in one's spare time.

досу́жий *adj., colloq.* **1**, (*of time*) leisure. **2**, idle.

до́суха *adv.* dry; until thoroughly dry.

досчи́тывать *v.impfv.* [*pfv.* досчита́ть] **1**, to finish counting. **2**, (*with* до) to count to. —**досчи́тываться**, *refl.* (*with gen.*) *usu. neg.* to fail to count. Не досчита́ться одного́ ребёнка, to find one child missing (*after making a count*).

досыла́ть *v.impfv.* [*pfv.* досла́ть] to send in addition; send the remainder.

досыпа́ть *v.impfv.* [*pfv.* доспа́ть] *colloq.* **1**, to get enough sleep. **2**, (*with* до) to sleep until. **3**, to sleep the whole of: доспа́ть ночь, to sleep the whole night.

до́сыта *also,* **досы́та** *adv.* **1**, one's fill: нае́сться до́сыта, to eat one's fill. **2**, to one's heart's content.

досье́ *n.neut. indecl.* dossier.

досю́да *adv., colloq.* up to here; up to this point.

досяга́емость *n.f.* range; reach: вне досяга́емости, out of range.

дот *n.* pillbox (*abbr. of* долговре́менная огнева́я то́чка).

дота́скивать *v.impfv.* [*pfv.* дотащи́ть] (*with* до) to drag to; drag as far as. —**дота́скиваться**, *refl.* (*with* до) *colloq.* to drag oneself to.

дота́ция *n.* subsidy; grant.

дотащи́ть [*infl.* -тащу́, -та́щишь] *v., pfv. of* дота́скивать. —**дотащи́ться**, *refl., pfv. of* дота́скиваться.

дотемна́ *adv.* until dark; until nightfall.

дотла́ *adv.* to the ground: сгоре́ть дотла́, to burn to the ground.

дото́ле *adv., obs.* up to that time; until then.

дото́шный *adj., colloq.* meticulous.

дотра́гиваться *v.r.impfv.* [*pfv.* дотро́нуться] (*with* до) to touch.

дотя́гивать *v.impfv.* [*pfv.* дотяну́ть] (*with* до) **1**, to drag as far as. **2**, to stretch as far as. **3**, *colloq.* to bring in (a disabled ship, aircraft, etc.). **4**, *colloq.* to make it (to a place). **5**, *colloq.* to live until; hold out until. —**дотя́гиваться**, *refl.* (*with* до) **1**, to reach; be able to touch. **2**, *colloq.* to stretch; extend (as far as). **3**, *colloq.* to make it (to a place).

дотяну́ть [*infl.* -тяну́, -тя́нешь] *v., pfv. of* дотя́гивать. —**дотяну́ться**, *refl., pfv. of* дотя́гиваться.

доу́чивать *v.impfv.* [*pfv.* доучи́ть] **1**, to finish teaching; (*with* до) teach up to. **2**, to finish learning; (*with* до) learn up to. —**доу́чиваться**, *refl.* **1**, to finish one's studies. **2**, (*with* до) to study up to a certain grade: доучи́ться до восьмо́го кла́сса, to go through eighth grade.

доучи́ть [*infl.* доучу́, доу́чишь] *v., pfv. of* доу́чивать. —**доучи́ться**, *refl., pfv. of* доу́чиваться.

дофи́н *n.* dauphin.

доха́ [*pl.* до́хи] *n.* heavy fur coat (*with fur both outside and inside*).

до́хлый *adj.* **1**, (*of animals, insects, fish, etc.*) dead. **2**, *colloq.* (*of a person*) sickly.

дохля́тина *n., colloq.* carrion.

до́хнуть *v.impfv.* [*pfv.* подо́хнуть *or* сдо́хнуть; *past* дох *or* до́хнул, до́хла] (*of animals*) to die.

дохну́ть *v.pfv.* to breathe; take a breath.

дохо́д *n.* income; revenue.

доходи́ть *v.impfv.* [*pfv.* дойти́; *pres.* -хожу́, -хо́дишь] (*with* до) **1**, to walk as far as. **2**, to reach. **3**, to extend (to). **4**, (*of legends, ancient writings, etc.*) to come down (to). **5**, *colloq.* (*of a speech, play, etc.*) to come across (to). **6**, to reach the point of: дойти́ до отча́яния, to be on the point of despair; become desperate. Де́ло дошло́ до того́, что..., things got to the point where... —**дойти́ свои́м умо́м**, to figure it out by oneself. —**ру́ки не дохо́дят**, there is no time.

дохо́дный *adj.* profitable; remunerative; lucrative. —**дохо́дность**, *n.f.* profitability.

дохо́дчивый *adj.* lucid; easy to understand.

доце́нт *n.* associate professor.

дочерний *adj.* **1**, one's daughter's. **2**, (*of a company*) subsidiary.

до́чиста *adv.* clean; till something is spotless. —**всё до́чиста**, absolutely everything; so that nothing is left.

дочи́тывать *v.impfv.* [*pfv.* дочита́ть] **1**, to finish reading. **2**, (*with* до) to read as far as.

до́чка [*gen. pl.* -чек] *n., dim. of* дочь.

дочь [*gen., dat. & prepl.* до́чери; *instr.* до́черью; *pl.* до́чери, -ре́й, -ря́м, -рьми́, -ря́х] *n.f.* daughter.

дошко́льник *n.* child of preschool age. —**дошко́льный,** *adj.* preschool.

до́шлый *adj., colloq.* clever; shrewd.

доща́тый *adj.* made of boards or planks.

дощёчка [*gen. pl.* -чек] *n.* **1,** small board. **2,** name-plate; plaque.

доя́рка [*gen. pl.* -рок] *n.* milkmaid.

дра́га *n.* dredge.

драгоце́нность *n.f.* **1,** jewel; gem. **2,** *pl.* jewelry. **3,** *pl.* valuables.

драгоце́нный *adj.* precious. —**драгоце́нный ка́мень, 1,** precious stone; gemstone. **2,** jewel; gem.

драгу́н [*gen. pl.* -гу́н] *n.* dragoon.

драже́ *n.neut. indecl.* drops (*candy*).

дразни́ть *v.impfv.* [*pres.* дразню́, дра́знишь] **1,** to tease. **2,** to whet; arouse (one's appetite, curiosity, etc.).

дра́ить *v.impfv.* to scrub; swab.

дра́ка *n.* fight: затея́ть дра́ку, to start a fight. —**дойти́ до дра́ки,** to come to blows.

драко́н *n.* dragon.

драко́новский *adj.* draconian: драко́новские ме́ры, draconian measures.

дра́ма *n.* drama.

драматизи́ровать *v.impfv. & pfv.* [*pres.* -рую, -руешь] to dramatize.

драмати́зм *n.* dramatic effect; drama.

драмати́ческий *adj.* dramatic.

драмату́рг *n.* playwright.

драматурги́я *n.* **1,** dramaturgy. **2,** plays; works.

драмкружо́к [*gen.* -жка́] *n.* dramatic circle (*contr. of* драмати́ческий кружо́к).

драндуле́т *n., colloq.* jalopy.

дра́нка [*gen. pl.* -нок] *n.* **1,** lath. **2,** shingle.

дра́ный *adj., colloq.* ragged; tattered.

драп *n.* heavy woolen cloth.

драпирова́ть *v.impfv.* [*pfv.* задрапирова́ть; *pres.* -ру́ю, -ру́ешь] to drape.

драпиро́вка [*gen. pl.* -вок] *n.* drapery.

драпиро́вщик *n.* upholsterer.

дра́повый *adj.* made of heavy woolen cloth.

драть *v.impfv.* [*pres.* деру́, дерёшь; *past fem.* драла́] **1,** *colloq.* to tear to pieces. **2,** to strip off. **3,** [*pfv.* вы́драть] to whip; thrash; flog. **4,** (*of an animal*) to tear to pieces; kill. **5,** *colloq.* to irritate; sting; burn. **6,** [*pfv.* содра́ть] *colloq.* to charge (an exorbitant price): драть вдво́е доро́же, чем..., to charge twice as much as. —**дра́ться,** *refl.* [*past* дра́лся, драла́сь, драло́сь *or* дра́лось, драли́сь *or* дра́лись] to fight.

дра́хма *n.* drachma (*monetary unit of Greece*).

драчли́вый *adj.* pugnacious; combative. —**драчли́вость,** *n.f.* pugnacity.

драчу́н [*gen.* -чуна́] *n., colloq.* scrapper; brawler.

дребеде́нь *n.f., colloq.* **1,** nonsense. **2,** junk.

дребезжа́ние *n.* rattling; rattle.

дребезжа́ть *v.impfv.* [*pres.* -жи́т] **1,** to rattle. **2,** to jingle.

древеси́на *n.* **1,** wood. **2,** timber.

древе́сница *n.* tree frog.

древе́сный *adj.* **1,** arboreal. **2,** wood (*attrib.*). —дре-ве́сная ма́сса, wood pulp. —**древе́сный спирт,** wood alcohol. —**древе́сный у́голь,** charcoal.

дре́вко [*pl.* -вки, -вков] *n.* **1,** pole; staff (*for a flag or banner*). **2,** shaft (*of a spear*).

древнеангли́йский *adj.* Old English.

древнегре́ческий *adj.* ancient Greek.

древнееврейский *adj.* Hebrew.

древнеру́сский *adj.* Old Russian.

дре́вний *adj.* ancient. —**дре́вние,** *n.pl.* the ancients.

дре́вность *n.f.* **1,** antiquity; ancient times. **2,** *pl.* antiquities.

дре́во [*pl.* древеса́, древе́с, древеса́м] *n., archaic & poetic* tree.

дредно́ут *n.* dreadnought.

дрези́на *n., R.R.* handcar.

дрейф *n., naut.* drift. —**лежа́ть в дре́йфе,** *naut.* to lie to. —**лечь в дрейф,** *naut.* to heave to.

дре́йфить *v.impfv.* [*pfv.* сдре́йфить; *pres.* -флю, -фишь] *colloq.* to get cold feet.

дрейфова́ть *v.impfv.* [*pres.* -фу́ет] *naut.* to drift; be adrift.

дрель *n.f.* drill (*tool*).

дрема́ть *v.impfv.* [*pres.* дремлю́, дре́млешь] to doze; slumber.

дремо́та *n.* drowsiness.

дремо́тный *adj.* drowsy.

дрему́чий *adj.* (*of a forest*) thick; dense.

дрена́ж *n.* drainage. —**дрена́жный,** *adj.* drainage (*attrib.*); drain (*attrib.*).

дрени́ровать *v.impfv. & pfv.* [*pres.* -рую, -руешь] to drain.

дрессиро́ванный *adj.* (*of an animal*) trained.

дрессирова́ть *v.impfv.* [*pfv.* вы́дрессировать; *pres.* -ру́ю, -ру́ешь] to train (animals).

дрессиро́вка *n.* training (*of animals*). —**дрессиро́вщик,** *n.* animal trainer.

дроби́лка [*gen. pl.* -лок] *n.* crusher; crushing machine.

дроби́льный *adj.* crushing (*attrib.*). —**дроби́льная маши́на,** = дроби́лка.

дроби́на *n.* pellet. *Also,* дроби́нка.

дроби́ть *v.impfv.* [*pfv.* раздроби́ть; *pres.* -блю́, -би́шь] **1,** to crush; shatter; splinter. **2,** to divide up; split up; fragment. —**дроби́ться,** *refl.* **1,** to break into pieces; splinter. **2,** to split up.

дробле́ние *n.* **1,** crushing; grinding. **2,** splitting up; fragmentation.

дроблёный *adj.* crushed.

дро́бный *adj.* **1,** separate; fragmented. **2,** (*of sounds*) rhythmic; steady. **3,** *math.* fractional.

дробови́к [*gen.* -вика́] *n.* shotgun.

дробь *n.f.* **1,** shot: кру́пная дробь, buckshot. **2,** steady sound; beating; patter. Бараба́нная дробь, drumbeat. **3,** [*pl.* дро́би, -бе́й] *math.* fraction. **4,** oblique stroke; slash: пять дробь шесть, 5/6.

дрова́ [*gen.* дров] *n.pl.* firewood.

дро́вни [*gen.* -ней] *n.pl.* sledge.

дровосе́к *n., obs.* woodcutter.

дровяно́й *adj.* wood (*attrib.*): дровяно́й сара́й, woodshed.

дро́ги [*gen.* дрог] *n.pl.* wagon; cart. —**похоро́нные дро́ги,** hearse.

дро́гнуть[1] *v.impfv.* [*past* дрог, дро́гла] to freeze; be chilled to the bone.

дро́гнуть[2] *v.pfv.* [*past* дро́гнул] **1,** to shake; tremble; quiver. **2,** to waver; falter; flinch.

дрожа́ние *n.* trembling; shivering; shaking.

дрожа́ть *v.impfv.* [*pres.* -жу́, -жи́шь] **1,** to tremble; shiver; shake. **2,** *fig.* (*with* пе́ред) to live in fear of; be deathly afraid of. **3,** *fig.* (*with* над) to begrudge: дрожа́ть над ка́ждой копе́йкой, to begrudge every penny.

дро́жжи [*gen.* -жже́й] *n.pl.* yeast. —**дрожжево́й,** *adj.* of yeast.

дро́жки [*gen.* -жек] *n.pl.* open carriage; droshky.

дрожь *n.f.* tremor; trembling. —**меня́ бро́сило в дрожь,** I began to tremble/shiver.

дрозд [*gen.* дрозда́] *n.* thrush. —**белозо́бый дрозд,** ring ouzel. —**чёрный дрозд,** blackbird.

дромаде́р (дэ) *n.* dromedary.

дро́ссель *n.m.* throttle; choke.

дро́тик *n.* javelin.

дрофа́ [*pl.* дро́фы] *n.* bustard.

друг [*pl.* друзья́, друзе́й, друзья́м] *n.* friend. —**друг дру́га, 1,** each other; one another. **2,** each other's; one another's. —**друг за дру́гом,** one after another; one after the other. —**друг с дру́гом,** with each other.

друго́й *adj.* **1,** other; another: друго́е де́ло, another matter; други́е стра́ны, other countries. **2,** a different: друго́й подхо́д, a different approach. **3,** else: кто́-то друго́й, someone else; что́-то друго́е, something else. —*n.* **1,** the other (one). **2,** another person. **3,** *neut.* another thing; something else. **4,** *pl.* others. —**на друго́й день,** the next day. —**тот и́ли друго́й,** one ... or another. —**и тот и друго́й,** both. —**ни тот ни друго́й,** neither (one).

дру́жба *n.* friendship.

дружелю́бие *n.* friendliness. —**дружелю́бный,** *adj.* friendly; amicable.

дру́жеский *adj.* friendly; amicable.

дру́жественный *adj.* friendly; amicable.

дружи́на *n.* **1,** *hist.* military retinue of a medieval Russian prince. **2,** *pre-rev.* militia unit; detachment. **3,** squad; brigade.

дружи́ть *v.impfv.* [*pres.* дружу́, дру́жишь *or* дружи́шь] (*with* с + *instr.*) to be friends (with). —**дружи́ться,** *refl.* [*pfv.* подружи́ться] (*with* с + *instr.*) to become friends (with); become friendly (with).

дру́жно *adv.* **1,** in harmony. **2,** (all) together; in concert.

дру́жный *adj.* [*short form* дру́жен, дружна́, дру́жны] **1,** friendly. **2,** [*short form only*] friendly; friends: Он дру́жен с мои́м сы́ном, he is friendly with my son; he and my son are friends. **3,** harmonious. **4,** on the part of everyone; concerted: дру́жные уси́лия, concerted efforts.

дружо́к [*gen.* -жка́] *n., colloq.* **1,** friend; pal. **2,** (*in direct address*) my dear; sweetheart.

дры́гать *v.impfv.* (*with instr.*) *colloq.* to kick (one's feet).

дря́блый *adj.* flabby; flacid. —**дря́блость,** *n.f.* flabbiness.

дря́зги [*gen.* дрязг] *n.pl., colloq.* petty quarrels; squabbles.

дрянно́й *adj., colloq.* miserable; rotten; lousy.

дрянь *n.f., colloq.* **1,** rubbish; trash. **2,** nonsense. **3,** good-for-nothing. **4,** something that is no good: Де́ло дрянь, things are lousy.

дряхле́ть *v.impfv.* [*pfv.* одряхле́ть] to become decrepit; become enfeebled.

дря́хлый *adj.* decrepit; enfeebled. —**дря́хлость,** *n.f.* decrepitude.

дуали́зм *n.* dualism. —**дуалисти́ческий,** *adj.* dualistic.

дуб [*pl.* дубы́] *n.* oak (tree & wood).

дуба́сить *v.impfv.* [*pres.* -шу, -сишь] *colloq.* **1,** to beat; thrash. **2,** (*with* по *or* в) to bang on.

дуби́льный *adj.* tanning (*attrib.*). —**дуби́льная кислота́,** tannic acid.

дуби́льня [*gen. pl.* -лен] *n.* tannery.

дуби́льщик *n.* tanner.

дуби́на *n.* club; cudgel; nightstick; billy club; bludgeon; truncheon. *Also,* дуби́нка.

дуби́ть *v.impfv.* [*pfv.* вы́дубить; *pres.* дублю́, дуби́шь] to tan (leather).

дубле́ние *n.* tanning.

дублёнка [*gen. pl.* -нок] *n., colloq.* sheepskin coat.

дублёный *adj.* tanned. Дублёный полушу́бок, sheepskin coat.

дублёр *n.* **1,** backup man. **2,** *theat.* understudy. **3,** *motion pictures* one who dubs in a part.

дубле́т *n.* duplicate.

дублика́т *n.* duplicate. —**дублика́тный,** *adj.* duplicate.

дубли́рование *n.* **1,** duplication. **2,** understudying. **3,** dubbing.

дубли́ровать *v.impfv.* [*pres.* -рую, -руешь] **1,** to duplicate. **2,** to understudy. **3,** to dub.

дубня́к [*gen.* -няка́] *n.* oak forest.

дубова́тый *adj., colloq.* clumsy; coarse.

дубо́вый *adj.* oak (*attrib.*).

дубо́к [*gen.* дубка́] *n.* young oak.

дубоно́с *n.* grosbeak.

дубра́ва *n.* oak forest.

дуга́ [*pl.* ду́ги] *n.* **1,** arc. **2,** shaft bow (*of a harness*).

дугообра́зный *adj.* arched.

дуде́ть *v.impfv.* [*pres.* дуди́шь, дуди́т; *1st pers. sing. not used*] *colloq.* **1,** *in* дуде́ть в ду́дку, to play a fife. **2,** to drone (on and on). —**дуде́ть в одну́ ду́дку,** *colloq.* to keep saying the same thing; harp on the same string.

ду́дка [*gen. pl.* ду́док] *n.* fife. —**пляса́ть под чью́-нибудь ду́дку,** to dance to someone's tune.

ду́дник *n.* angelica.

ду́жка [*gen. pl.* ду́жек] *n.* **1,** hoop. **2,** handle.

дука́т *n.* ducat.

ду́ло *n.* muzzle (*of a gun*). —**под ду́лом пистоле́та,** at gunpoint.

ду́ма *n.* **1,** thought. **2,** Duma (*legislature*).

ду́мать *v.impfv.* [*pfv.* поду́мать] **1,** to think. Ду́маю, что нет, I don't think so. Не ду́маю!, I hardly think so; I doubt it. Я ду́маю!, I should think so! Я так и ду́мал!, I thought so! **2,** (*with inf.*) to think (of); plan (to): Когда́ вы ду́маете взять о́тпуск?, when are you thinking of taking a vacation?; when do you plan to take a vacation? Она́ и не ду́мает выходи́ть за́муж, she has no thought of getting married. **3,** (*with* **о**) to think of (*i.e.* care about; concern oneself about): ду́мать о после́дствиях, to think of the consequences. —**мно́го ду́мать о себе́,** to have an exalted opinion of oneself. —**не до́лго ду́мая,** without a moment's hesitation.

ду́маться *v.r.impf., impers.* (*with dat.*) to seem: Мне ду́мается, it seems to me; I think.

ду́мка [*gen. pl.* ду́мок] *n., colloq.* small pillow.

дунове́ние *n.* puff; breath (*of wind, air, etc.*). Заду́ть све́чи одни́м дунове́нием, to blow the candles out with one blow.

ду́нуть *v.pfv.* to blow.

ду́пель [*pl.* дупеля́] *n.m.* great snipe (*bird*).

дуплёт *n., billiards* bank shot.

дупли́стый *adj.* (*of a tree*) hollow.

дупло́ [*pl.* ду́пла, ду́пел] *n.* **1,** hollow (*in a tree*). **2,** cavity (*in a tooth*).

дура́к [*gen.* дурака́] *n.m.* [*fem.* ду́ра] fool. —**оста́вить в дурака́х,** to dupe; take in. —**оста́ться в дурака́х,** to make a fool of oneself; look like a fool.

дурале́й *n., colloq.* fool; jerk; dope.

дура́цкий *adj., colloq.* **1,** fool's. **2,** ridiculous; idiotic.

дура́чество *n., colloq.* **1,** prank. **2,** *pl.* horseplay; tomfoolery.

дура́чить *v.impfv.* [*pfv.* одура́чить] to fool; make a fool of. —**дура́читься,** *refl.* [*impfv. only*] to fool around.

дурачо́к [*gen.* -чка́] *n., colloq.* **1,** little fool. **2,** idiot.

дура́шливый *adj., colloq.* **1,** silly. **2,** mischievous.

ду́рень [*gen.* ду́рня] *n.m., colloq.* dope; dolt.

дуре́ть *v.impfv.* [*pfv.* одуре́ть] *colloq.* to go crazy; lose one's wits.

дури́ть *v.impfv., colloq.* to play around; horse around. —**дури́ть го́лову** (+ *dat.*), to confuse; mix up.

дурма́н *n.* **1,** thorn apple; jimsonweed. **2,** narcotic; drug.

дурма́нить *v.impfv.* [*pfv.* одурма́нить] to cloud (someone's) mind *or* senses; leave in a daze; befuddle.

дурне́ть *v.impfv.* [*pfv.* подурне́ть] to lose one's beauty; become less attractive.

ду́рно *adv.* badly; bad. —*adj., used predicatively,* faint; ill: Мне ду́рно, I feel faint.

дурно́й *adj.* **1,** bad. **2,** evil; wicked. —**ду́рен** (дурна́) собо́й, homely; unattractive.

дурнота́ *n.* (feeling of) faintness: чу́вствовать дурноту́, to feel faint.

дурну́шка [*gen. pl.* -шек] *n., colloq.* plain girl; homely girl.

дуршла́г *n.* colander.

дурь *n.f., colloq.* foolishness; nonsense.

ду́тый *adj.* **1,** hollow. **2,** inflated; exaggerated.

дуть *v.impfv.* [*pfv.* поду́ть; *pres.* ду́ю, ду́ешь] **1,** (*of the wind*) to blow. **2,** *impers.* to be drafty: Здесь ду́ет, it is drafty in here. **3,** (*of a person*) to blow: дуть на горя́чий чай, to blow on the hot tea.

дутьё *n.* **1,** blowing. **2,** blast.

ду́ться *v.r.impfv.* [*pres.* ду́юсь, ду́ешься] *colloq.* to pout; sulk.

дух *n.* **1,** spirit. **2,** spirits: поднима́ть дух (+ *gen.*), to lift the spirits of... Быть в ду́хе, to be in good spirits; быть не в ду́хе, be out of sorts. **3,** *in certain set ex-*

pressions, breath: перевести́ дух, to catch one's breath. От э́того дух захва́тывает, it takes one's breath away. **4,** *in certain set expressions,* courage: собра́ться с ду́хом, to summon up one's courage. **5,** *in certain set expressions,* heart: па́дать ду́хом, to lose heart. У него́ не хвата́ет ду́ху (+ *inf.*), he doesn't have the heart to... **6,** *in certain set expressions,* mind: прису́тствие ду́ха, presence of mind; расположе́ние ду́ха, frame of mind. —**во весь дух,** full tilt. —**в том же ду́хе,** in the same vein; along the same lines. —**еди́ным** *or* **одни́м ду́хом, 1,** all at once. **2,** in an instant. —**что есть ду́ху, 1,** full tilt. **2,** at the top of one's lungs. —**что́-то в э́том ду́хе,** something of the sort.

духи́ [*gen.* духо́в] *n.pl.* perfume.

ду́хов *adj., in* ду́хов день, Whitmonday.

духове́нство *n.* clergy.

духо́вка [*gen. pl.* -вок] *n.* oven.

духовни́к [*gen.* -ника́] *n.* confessor.

духо́вность *n.f.* spirituality.

духо́вный *adj.* **1,** spiritual. **2,** ecclesiastical. **3,** (*of a seminary, academy, etc.*) theological. —**духо́вное завеща́ние,** last will and testament. —**духо́вное о́ко,** mind's eye.

духово́й *adj.* **1,** *music,* духово́й инструме́нт, wind instrument; духово́й орке́стр, brass band. **2,** operated by heat: духова́я печь, oven. —**духово́е ружьё, 1,** air gun. **2,** blowgun.

духота́ *n.* **1,** stuffiness; closeness. **2,** sweltering heat.

душ *n.* **1,** shower. **2,** douche.

душа́ [*acc.* ду́шу; *pl.* ду́ши, душ, ду́шам] *n.* soul. —**в душе́, 1,** inwardly; in one's heart. **2,** at heart. —**всей душо́й,** with all one's heart. —**для души́,** for one's own pleasure. —**душа́ в ду́шу,** in perfect harmony. —**душа́ о́бщества,** the life of the party. —**душо́й и те́лом,** heart and soul. —**за душо́й,** to one's name. —**на ду́шу населе́ния,** per capita. —**ни души́,** not a soul. —**от всей души́,** from the bottom of one's heart. —**от души́, 1,** straight from the heart. **2,** (*with verbs of laughing*) heartily. —**по душе́** (+ *dat.*), to one's liking. —**разгово́р по душа́м** (*with different stress*), heart-to-heart talk. —**с душо́й,** with feeling. —**ско́лько душе́ уго́дно,** to one's heart's content. —**стоя́ть над чьей-нибудь душо́й,** to stand over; breathe down someone's neck.

душева́я *n., decl. as an adj.,* shower room.

душевнобольно́й *adj.* mentally ill. —*n.* mental patient; mental case.

душе́вно *adv.* **1,** mentally. **2,** sincerely.

душе́вный *adj.* **1,** mental; emotional: душе́вное состоя́ние, emotional state; state of mind; душе́вная боле́знь, mental illness. **2,** sincere; heartfelt.

душево́й *adj.* **1,** per capita. **2,** shower (*attrib.*).

душегу́б *n., obs., colloq.* killer; murderer.

душегу́бка [*gen. pl.* -бок] *n.* **1,** canoe. **2,** mobile gas chamber.

ду́шенька *n.f.* (*used in direct address*) dear; darling; sweetheart.

душеприка́зчик *n., obs.* executor (*of a will*).

душераздира́ющий *adj.* ` heart-rending; harrowing; bloodcurdling.

ду́шечка *n.* = ду́шенька.

души́стый *adj.* fragrant; aromatic; sweet-smelling. —души́стый горо́шек, sweet peas. —души́стый пе́рец, allspice; pimento.

души́ть *v.impfv.* [*pfv.* задуши́ть; *pres.* душу́, ду́шишь] 1, to strangle. 2, to smother. 3, *fig.* to stifle. 4, [*impfv. only*] to choke: Его́ ду́шит ка́шель, he is choking from a cough. 5, [*pfv.* надуши́ть] to perfume. —души́ться, *refl.* [*pfv.* надуши́ться] to use perfume; put on perfume.

ду́шка [*gen. pl.* ду́шек] *n.m. & f., colloq.* 1, dear person; lovely person. 2, dear; darling.

ду́шно *adj., used predicatively,* stuffy: Здесь ду́шно, it is stuffy in here; мне ду́шно, I am suffocating.

ду́шный *adj.* stuffy; close.

душо́к [*gen.* душка́] *n., colloq.* 1, smell of something beginning to decay. 2, *fig.* taint; tinge.

дуэ́ль *n.f.* duel. —дуэли́ст; дуэля́нт, *n.* duelist.

дуэ́т *n.* duet.

ды́ба *n.* rack (*instrument of torture*).

ды́бом *adv., in* станови́ться/стать ды́бом, (*of hair*) to stand on end.

дыбы́ *adv., in* станови́ться на дыбы́, 1, (*of a horse*) to rear. 2, to stand straight up in the air. 3, *fig.* to kick up one's heels.

ды́лда *n.m. & f., colloq.* tall, ungainly person.

дым [*2nd loc.* дыму́] *n.* smoke.

дыми́ть *v.impfv.* [*pfv.* надыми́ть] 1, to smoke; give off smoke. 2, [*impfv. only*] (*with instr.*) to smoke (a cigarette, cigar, etc.). —дыми́ться, *refl.* [*impfv. only*] to give off smoke.

ды́мка *n.* haze.

ды́мный *adj.* smoky.

дымово́й *adj.* smoke (*attrib.*). —дымова́я заве́са, smoke screen. —дымова́я труба́, chimney; smokestack.

дымо́к [*gen.* дымка́] *n.* thin column of smoke.

дымохо́д *n.* flue; stovepipe.

ды́мчатый *adj.* smoke-colored; smoky. Ды́мчатые очки́, tinted glasses.

ды́нный *adj.* melon (*attrib.*). —ды́нное де́рево, papaya.

ды́ня *n.* melon.

дыра́ [*pl.* ды́ры] *n.* 1, hole. 2, *colloq.* out-of-the-way place. —заткну́ть дыру́, to plug a gap.

ды́рка [*gen. pl.* ды́рок] *n.* (small) hole.

дыроко́л *n., colloq.* punch; hole punch.

дыря́вый *adj.* having a hole; full of holes. —дыря́вая па́мять, memory like a sieve.

дыха́ние *n.* breath; breathing; respiration. —второе дыха́ние, second wind.

дыха́тельный *adj.* respiratory. —дыха́тельное го́рло, windpipe. —дыха́тельные пути́, respiratory tract.

дыша́ть *v.impfv.* [*pres.* дышу́, ды́шишь] to breathe: дыша́ть све́жим во́здухом, to breathe fresh air. —е́ле дыша́ть, to be hardly breathing; be scarcely alive.

ды́шло *n.* pole; beam; shaft (*on a carriage*).

дья́вол *n.* devil. —дья́вольский, *adj.* devilish; diabolical.

дья́кон *n.* deacon.

дю́жий *adj., colloq.* hefty; robust; strapping.

дю́жина *n.* dozen.

дю́жинный *adj.* ordinary; run-of-the-mill.

дюйм *n.* inch. —дюймо́вый, *adj.* one-inch; inch-long.

дю́на *n.* dune.

дюра́ль *n.m.* duralumin. —дюра́левый, *adj.* of duralumin.

дюралюми́ний *n.* duralumin. —дюралюми́ниевый, *adj.* of duralumin.

дя́гиль *n.m.* angelica.

дя́денька *n.m., colloq.* uncle. *Also,* дя́дюшка.

дя́дя [*gen. pl.* дя́дей] *n.m.* uncle.

дя́тел [*gen.* дя́тла] *n.* woodpecker.

Е

Е, е *n.neut.* sixth letter of the Russian alphabet.

Ё, ё *n.neut.* not considered a separate letter of the Russian alphabet. Usually written Е and е except in dictionaries and textbooks.

ева́нгелие *n.* gospel. —евангели́ст, *n., Bib.* Evangelist. —евангели́ческий, *adj.* evangelical. —ева́нгельский, *adj.* in *or* of the gospel.

евге́ника *n.* eugenics. —евгени́ческий, *adj.* eugenic.

е́внух *n.* eunuch.

евразийский *adj.* Eurasian.

евре́й *n.m.* [*fem.* евре́йка] Jew. —евре́йский, *adj.* Jewish; Hebrew. —евре́йство, *n.* Jewry.

европе́ец [*gen.* -е́йца] *n.m.* [*fem.* -е́йка] European. —европе́йский, *adj.* European.

европеоид *n.* Caucasoid; Caucasian. —европеоидный, *adj.* Caucasoid; Caucasian.

евро́пий *n.* europium.

евста́хиев *adj., in* евста́хиева труба́, Eustachian tube.

евхари́стия *n.* Eucharist.

е́герь [*pl.* егеря́] *n.m.* professional hunter.

еги́петский *adj.* Egyptian.

египтоло́гия *n.* Egyptology. —**египто́лог,** *n.* Egyptologist.

египтя́нин [*pl.* **-тя́не, -тя́н**] *n.m.* [*fem.* **-тя́нка**] Egyptian.

его́ (vo) *pron., gen. & acc. of* **он** *and* **оно́.** —*poss. adj. & pron.* his; its.

егоза́ *n.m. & f., colloq.* fidgety person; fidget.

егози́ть *v.impfv.* [*pres.* **-жу́, -зи́шь**] *colloq.* **1,** to fidget. **2,** (*with* **пе́ред**) to fawn (upon).

егозли́вый *adj., colloq.* fidgety.

еда́ *n.* **1,** meal. **2,** food.

едва́ *adv.* **1,** hardly; scarcely. **2,** just; barely. —**едва́..., как...,** hardly/scarcely.., when...: Он едва́ ко́нчил говори́ть, как..., he had hardly finished speaking, when... —**едва́ ли,** hardly; it is unlikely (that). —**едва́ ли не,** nearly; almost; practically: едва́ ли не ка́ждый день, nearly every day. —**едва́ не,** almost; nearly: Он едва́ не утону́л, he nearly drowned.

едине́ние *n.* unity.

едини́ца *n.* **1,** the numeral 1. **2,** a grade of "one", signifying "very poor". **3,** unit. **4,** *pl.* (only) a few individuals.

едини́чный *adj.* individual; isolated; unique.

едино- *prefix* **1,** one; single: единобо́жие, monotheism. **2,** same; of the same: единове́рный, of the same religion.

единобо́жие *n.* monotheism.

единобо́рство *n.* single combat.

единобра́чие *n.* monogamy. —**единобра́чный,** *adj.* monogamous.

единове́рец [*gen.* **-рца**] *n.* coreligionist.

единове́рный *adj.* of the same religion; of the same faith.

единовла́стие *n.* autocracy; absolute rule. —**единовла́стный,** *adj.* autocratic; having absolute power.

единовре́менный *adj.* one-time; given only once. —**единовре́менно,** *adv.* all at once; in a lump sum.

единогла́сие *n.* unanimity.

единогла́сный *adj.* unanimous. —**единогла́сно,** *adv.* unanimously.

единоду́шие *n.* unanimity.

единоду́шный *adj.* unanimous. —**единоду́шно,** *adv.* unanimously.

единокро́вный *adj., obs.* **1,** having the same father. **2,** kindred; consanguineous.

единоли́чно *adv.* on one's own; single-handedly.

единоли́чный *adj.* **1,** individual. **2,** one-man.

единомы́слие *n.* harmony of views; agreement.

единомы́шленник *n.* **1,** person holding similar views; like-minded person. **2,** confederate; accomplice.

единообра́зие *n.* uniformity. —**единообра́зный,** *adj.* uniform.

единоро́г *n.* unicorn.

единоутро́бный *adj.,* having the same mother.

еди́нственно *adv.* only; solely. —**еди́нственно, что...,** the only thing that...: Еди́нственно, что я могу́ сказа́ть, the only thing I can say is...; all I can say is...

еди́нственный *adj.* only; sole. —*n., fol. by* **кто,** the only one (who); the only person (who). —**еди́нственный в своём ро́де,** unique; the only one of its kind. —**еди́нственное число́,** *gram.* the singular.

еди́нство *n.* unity.

еди́ный *adj.* **1,** (*with* **ни** *or* **без**) (not) a single. **2,** united; unified. **3,** single; common. —**все до еди́ного,** everyone without exception; one and all.

е́дкий *adj.* **1,** caustic; corrosive. **2,** acrid; pungent. **3,** *fig.* cutting; sarcastic.

е́дкость *n.f.* **1,** corrosiveness; causticity. **2,** *fig.* cutting remark.

едо́к [*gen.* **едока́**] *n.* **1,** mouth to feed: пять едоко́в в семье́, five mouths to feed. **2,** *colloq.* eater: хоро́ший едо́к, good eater.

её *pron., gen. & acc. of* **она́.** —*poss. adj. & pron.* her; hers; its.

ёж [*gen.* **ежа́**] *n.* hedgehog. —**морско́й ёж,** sea urchin.

еже- *prefix* -ly; once a: ежеме́сячный, monthly; ежеме́сячно, once a month.

ежеви́ка *n.* **1,** blackberries. **2,** a (single) blackberry. **3,** blackberry bush.

ежего́дник *n.* yearbook; annual.

ежего́дный *adj.* annual; yearly. —**ежего́дно,** *adv.* annually.

ежедне́вный *adj.* daily. —**ежедне́вно,** *adv.* daily.

е́жели *conj., obs., colloq.* = **е́сли.**

ежеме́сячник *n.* monthly publication; monthly.

ежеме́сячный *adj.* monthly. —**ежеме́сячно,** *adv.* monthly; once a month.

ежемину́тный *adj.* **1,** occurring once a minute. **2,** constant; incessant.

еженеде́льник *n.* weekly publication; weekly.

еженеде́льный *adj.* weekly. —**еженеде́льно,** *adv.* weekly; once a week.

ежено́щный *adj.* nightly. —**ежено́щно,** *adv.* nightly.

ежеча́сный *adj.* hourly.

ёжик *n., dim. of* **ёж.** —**ёжиком,** *adv.* in a crew cut: постри́чься ёжиком, to get a crew cut.

ёжиться *v.r.impfv.* [*pfv.* **съёжиться**] **1,** to huddle up (*from the cold*). **2,** *fig., colloq.* to hesitate; vacillate.

ежо́вый *adj.* hedgehog (*attrib.*). —**держа́ть в ежо́вых рукави́цах,** to rule with an iron hand.

езда́ *n.* ride; riding; drive; driving: два часа́ езды́, a two-hour ride/drive.

е́здить *v.impfv.* [*pres.* **е́зжу, е́здишь**] **1,** *indeterm. of* **е́хать. 2,** to ride: е́здить на велосипе́де, to ride a bicycle. Е́здить верхо́м, to ride a horse; ride horseback.

ездово́й *adj.* **1,** for riding. **2,** *in* ездова́я соба́ка, draft dog; harness dog. —*n., mil.* driver (*of a team of horses*).

ездо́к [*gen.* **ездока́**] *n.* rider; horseman. —**туда́ я бо́льше не ездо́к,** you won't catch me going there again.

е́зженый *adj., colloq.* (*of a road*) well-worn; well-trodden.

ей *pron., dat. & instr. of* **она́.**

ей-бо́гу *interj., colloq.* really; really and truly.

ёкать *v.impfv.* [*pfv.* **ёкнуть**] (*of one's heart*) to skip a beat: У меня́ се́рдце ёкнуло, my heart skipped a beat.

е́ле *adv.* **1,** hardly; scarcely. **2,** just; barely. *Also,* **е́ле-е́ле.**

еле́й *n.* **1,** holy oil; unction. **2,** *fig.* balm; solace.

елéйный *adj.* unctuous.

ёлка [*gen. pl.* **ёлок**] *n.* **1,** spruce. **2,** Christmas tree. **3,** children's New Year's party.

елóвый *adj.* spruce (*attrib.*).

елóзить *v.impfv.* [*pres.* **-жу, -зишь**] *colloq.* to crawl; crawl around.

ёлочка [*gen. pl.* **-чек**] *n., dim. of* **ёлка.** —**ёлочкой; в ёлочку,** herringbone style.

ёлочный *adj.* of or for a Christmas tree.

ель *n.f.* spruce.

éльник *n.* spruce grove.

ёмкий *adj.* capacious. —**ёмкость,** *n.f.* capacity; cubic content.

емý *pron., dat. of* **он** *and* **онó.**

енóт *n.* raccoon. —**енóтовый,** *adj.* raccoon (*attrib.*).

епáрхия *n.* diocese.

епúскоп *n.* bishop. —**епископáльный,** *adj.* Episcopalian. —**епúскопский,** *adj.* Episcopal.

ералáш *n., colloq.* muddle; jumble.

éресь *n.f.* heresy.

еретúк [*gen.* **-тикá**] *n.m.* [*fem.* **-тúчка**] heretic. —**еретúческий,** *adj.* heretical.

ёрзать *v.impfv., colloq.* to fidget.

ермóлка [*gen. pl.* **-лок**] *n.* skullcap.

ерóшить *v.impfv.* [*pfv.* **взъерóшить**] *colloq.* to muss; tousle.

ерундá *n., colloq.* **1,** nonsense. **2,** trifling amount: Пять рублéй — ерундá, five rubles is nothing. **3,** a cinch; a snap; child's play.

ерундóвый *adj., colloq.* **1,** nonsensical. **2,** trifling; petty.

ёрш [*gen.* **ершá**] *n.* **1,** ruff (*fish*). **2,** brush; lamp brush. **3,** *colloq.* highly intoxicating mixture of beer and vodka.

ершúстый *adj., colloq.* **1,** (*of hair*) sticking out. **2,** *fig.* (*of a person or his character*) prickly; difficult.

ершúться *v.r.impfv., colloq.* **1,** (*of one's hair*) to bristle. **2,** *fig.* to flare up; fly into a rage.

есаýл *n., hist.* Cossack captain.

éсли *conj.* **1,** if: éсли не бýдет дождя́, if it doesn't rain. **2,** when (*considering that*): Зачéм убеждáть егó, éсли он и слýшать не хóчет?, why try to persuade him when he won't even listen? **3,** whereas: éсли в 1980..., то сегóдня..., whereas in 1980..., today... —**éсли бы,** (*in contrary-to-fact sentences*) if; had: éсли бы я был там, if I had been there; had I been there. —**éсли бы не,** if it were not for; were it not for. —**éсли бы тóлько,** if only. —**éсли не...,** **1,** if not... **2,** unless. —**éсли тóлько,** only if; provided; on condition that.

естéственник *n.* naturalist.

естéственно *adv.* **1,** naturally. **2,** naturally; of course. —*adj., used predicatively,* natural: Естéственно полагáть, что..., it is natural to suppose that...

естéственный *adj.* natural.

естествó *n.* essence.

естествовéд *n., obs.* naturalist.

естествовéдение *n., obs.* = **естествознáние.**

естествознáние *n.* nature study.

естествоиспытáтель *n.m.* naturalist.

есть[1] *v.impfv.* [*pres.* **ем, ешь, ест, едúм, едúте, едя́т**] **1,** [*pfv.* **съесть**] to eat. **2,** [*pfv.* **поéсть**] to eat; have something to eat.

есть[2] *v., 3rd person sing. pres. of* **быть. 1,** (he, she, it) is: Закóн есть закóн, the law is the law. Рáзница мáленькая, но всё-таки есть, the difference is small but it exists nevertheless. **2,** there is; there are: Есть лю́ди, котóрые..., there are people who... **3,** (*with* **у**) *indicating possession:* У вас есть спúчка?, do you have a match? —*interj., mil.; naval* yes, sir!; aye aye, sir! —**есть когдá!,** *colloq.* there is still time. —**есть такóе дéло!,** *colloq.* agreed! —**ни на есть, 1,** any at all: кто ни на есть, anyone at all. **2,** (*with superl. adjectives*) the most: сáмый ни на есть обыкновéнный человéк, the most ordinary kind of person. —**так и есть,** and so it is.

ефрéйтор *n., mil.* private first class.

éхать *v.impfv.* [*pfv.* **поéхать;** *pres.* **éду, éдешь**] to go (*by riding*); ride; drive. *See also* **éздить.**

ехúдна *n.* **1,** spiny anteater; echidna. **2,** *colloq.* vicious person; viper.

ехúдный *adj.* malicious.

ехúдство *n.* malice; spite.

ещё *adv.* **1,** still: Ещё рáно, it is still early. **2,** yet: Я ещё не ел, I haven't eaten yet. **3,** else: Кудá вы ещё éздили?, where else did you go? **4,** also; besides; in addition: А ещё мы бы́ли в зоопáрке, we were also at the zoo. Сомнéние вознúкло ещё и потомý, что..., doubts also arose because... **5,** more: Хотúте ещё хлéба?, would you like some more bread? **6,** another: Хотúте ещё чáшку чáю?, would you like another cup of tea? **7,** (*before comp. adjectives*) still; even: ещё бóльше, still more; even greater. **8,** as long ago as; as far back as: Москвá былá оснóвана ещё в двенáдцатом вéке, Moscow was founded as far back as the 12th century. **9,** as recently as: ещё в 1980-ом годý, as recently as 1980. **10,** as early as: ещё в бýдущем годý, as early as next year. —**всё ещё,** still; all the same. —**ещё бы!,** and how!; I should say so!; you can say that again! —**ещё раз,** again; once again. —**нет ещё,** not yet. —**никогдá ещё,** never before.

éю *pron., instr. of* **онá.**

Ж

Ж, ж *n.neut.* seventh letter of the Russian alphabet.

ж *conj. & particle* = **же**.

жа́ба *n.* **1,** toad. **2,** *obs.* angina. —**грудна́я жа́ба,** angina pectoris.

жа́бры *n.pl.* [*sing.* **жа́бра**] gills.

жа́воронок [*gen.* **-нка**] *n.* lark. —**полево́й жа́воронок,** skylark.

жа́дничать *v.impfv., colloq.* to be greedy; be stingy.

жа́дно *adv.* **1,** greedily. **2,** avidly; eagerly.

жа́дность *n.f.* **1,** greed; avarice. **2,** stinginess. —**с жа́дностью,** eagerly; avidly.

жа́дный *adj.* [*short form* **жа́ден, жадна́, жа́дно, жа́дны** *or* **жадны́**] **1,** greedy. **2,** (*with* **на, до, к**) hungry (for). **3,** (*of desire, curiosity, etc.*) avid. **4,** stingy.

жа́жда *n.* **1,** thirst. **2,** (*with gen.*) thirst (for); craving (for).

жа́ждать *v.impfv.* [*pres.* **жа́жду, жа́ждешь**] **1,** (*with gen.*) to thirst for; crave. **2,** (*with inf.*) to long (to); be dying (to).

жа́ждущий *adj.* thirsty.

жаке́т *n.* woman's jacket. *Also,* **жаке́тка.**

жале́ть *v.impfv.* [*pfv.* **пожале́ть**] **1,** to feel sorry for; pity. **2,** to regret. **3,** to spare. **4,** to begrudge.

жа́лить *v.impfv.* [*pfv.* **ужа́лить**] to sting.

жа́лкий *adj.* [*short form* **жа́лок, жалка́, жа́лко, жа́лки**] **1,** pitiful; pathetic. **2,** wretched; miserable.

жа́лко *adv.* pitifully; pathetically. —*adj., used predicatively* = **жаль.**

жа́ло *n.* stinger.

жа́лоба *n.* complaint. —**кассацио́нная** *or* **апелляцио́нная жа́лоба,** *law* appeal.

жа́лобный *adj.* plaintive; mournful. —**жа́лобная кни́га,** complaints book.

жа́лобщик *n.* person registering a complaint.

жа́лованье *n.* wage(s); salary.

жа́ловать *v.impfv.* [*pfv.* **пожа́ловать**; *pres.* **-лую, -луешь**] **1,** *obs.* to grant; confer; award; bestow. **2,** [*impfv. only*] *colloq.* to like; favor. **3,** (*with* **к**) *obs.* to visit. —**добро́ пожа́ловать!,** welcome!

жа́ловаться *v.r.impfv.* [*pfv.* **пожа́ловаться**; *pres.* **-луюсь, -луешься**] **1,** (*with* **на** + *acc.*) to complain (about). **2,** (*with* **в** + *acc.*) to register a complaint (with). **3,** (*with* **на** + *acc.*) to report (someone).

жа́лостливый *adj., colloq.* **1,** compassionate; sympathetic. **2,** sad; mournful.

жа́лостный *adj., colloq.* **1,** plaintive. **2,** compassionate; sympathetic.

жа́лость *n.f.* pity.

жаль *predicate* **1,** it is a pity; it is a shame: Жаль сиде́ть до́ма сего́дня, it's a pity/shame to have to sit home today. **2,** (*with dat.*) feeling sorry for: Мне жаль его́, I feel sorry for him. **3,** (*with dat.*) sorry about: Мне жаль вас беспоко́ить, I am sorry to bother you. **4,** (*with dat. & inf.*) to hate to: мне жаль тра́тить де́ньги на э́то, I hate to spend money for that. **5,** (*with* **не** + *dat. & gen.*) to begrudge; (not) to mind: Ему́ не́ было жаль тако́й небольшо́й су́ммы, he didn't begrudge (*or* didn't mind spending) such a small amount. На хоро́ший това́р де́нег не жаль, people don't mind spending money for good merchandise.

жалюзи́ *n.pl. indecl.* jalousie. —**подъёмные жалюзи́,** Venetian blinds.

жанда́рм *n.* gendarme. —**жандарме́рия,** *n.* gendarmerie.

жанр *n.* **1,** genre. **2,** genre painting. —**жа́нровый,** *adj.* genre (*attrib.*): жа́нровая жи́вопись, genre painting.

жар *n.* **1,** heat. **2,** fever; high temperature. **3,** *fig.* ardor; fervor. **4,** *colloq.* embers. —**в жару́,** running a high fever. —**зада́ть жа́ру** (+ *dat.*), to rake (someone) over the coals.

жара́ *n.* heat.

жарго́н *n.* jargon; slang. —**жарго́нный,** *adj.* slang.

жа́реный *adj.* fried; roast; broiled.

жа́рить *v.impfv.* [*pfv.* **зажа́рить** *or* **изжа́рить**] **1,** to fry; roast; broil. **2,** [*impfv. only*] *colloq.* (*of the sun*) to beat down (on). —**жа́риться,** *refl.* **1,** (*of meat, coffee, etc.*) to fry; roast. **2,** [*impfv. only*] *colloq.* to bake (in the sun).

жа́ркий *adj.* [*comp.* **жа́рче**] **1,** hot. **2,** *fig.* heated; passionate; intense.

жа́рко *adj., used predicatively,* hot: Сего́дня жа́рко, it is hot today; мне жа́рко, I am hot.

жарко́е *n., decl. as an adj.* roast meat.

жаро́вня [*gen. pl.* **-вен**] *n.* roasting pan; brazier.

жар-пти́ца *n.* firebird.

жа́рче *adj., comp. of* **жа́ркий** *and* **жа́рко.**

жасми́н *n.* jasmine. —**жасми́нный; жасми́новый,** *adj.* jasmine.

жа́тва *n.* **1,** harvesting; reaping. **2,** harvest. **3,** harvest time.

жа́твенный *adj.* harvesting (*attrib.*). —**жа́твенная маши́на,** harvester; reaper.

жа́тка [*gen. pl.* **жа́ток**] *n.* harvester; reaper.

жать¹ *v.impfv.* [*pres.* **жму, жмёшь**] **1,** to squeeze; press. **2,** [*pfv.* **пожа́ть**] (*with* **ру́ку** + *dat.*), to shake (someone's hand). **3,** (*of clothes, shoes, etc.*) to pinch; be tight.

жать² *v.impfv.* [*pfv.* **сжать**; *pres.* **жну, жнёшь**] to reap.

жа́ться *v.r.impfv.* [*pres.* **жмусь, жмёшься**] **1,** to huddle up. **2,** (*with* **к**) to press close against. **3,** to crowd together; squeeze together. **4,** *colloq.* to hesitate; vacillate. **5,** *colloq.* to economize; watch one's pennies.

жбан *n.* jug.

жва́чка *n.* **1,** cud. **2,** *colloq.* chewing gum.

жва́чный *adj. & n.* ruminant.

жгут [*gen.* **жгута́**] *n.* **1,** twisted strand; braid. **2,** tourniquet.

жгу́чий *adj.* burning.

ждать *v.impfv.* [*pfv.* **подожда́ть**; *pres.* **жду, ждёшь**; *past fem.* **ждала́**] **1,** to wait; wait for; await. **2,** [*impfv. only*] to expect. —**того́ и жди,** at any moment.

же *also,* **ж** *conj., expressing contrast:* Я уезжа́ю, он же остаётся, I am leaving but he is staying. —*particle* **1,** *used for emphasis:* Говори́те же!, speak up! Отку́да же я зна́ю?, how should I know? Вам лу́чше слу́шаться его́, он же ваш оте́ц, you had better obey him — after all, he is your father. **2,** *expressing sameness or identity:* тот же; тако́й же, the same; так же, in the same way; тогда́ же, at the same time; там же, in the same place.

жева́ние *n.* chewing; mastication.

жёваный *adj.* **1,** chewed. **2,** *colloq.* crumpled.

жева́тельный *adj.* chewing (*attrib.*): жева́тельный таба́к, chewing tobacco. —**жева́тельная рези́нка,** chewing gum.

жева́ть *v.impfv.* [*pres.* **жую́, жуёшь**] to chew.

жезл [*gen.* **жезла́**] *n.* rod; staff (*carried as a symbol of authority*).

жела́ние *n.* wish; desire. —**при всём моём жела́нии,** much as I would like to.

жела́нный *adj.* **1,** desired. **2,** welcome. **3,** *obs.* dearest.

жела́тельно *adj., used predicatively,* desirable: Жела́тельно, чтобы..., it is desirable that...

жела́тельный *adj.* **1,** desirable. **2,** desired. —**жела́тельность,** *n.f.* desirability.

желати́н *n.* gelatin. —**желати́новый,** *adj.* gelatinous; gelatin (*attrib.*).

жела́ть *v.impfv.* [*pfv.* **пожела́ть**] **1,** (*with gen.*) to wish for; desire. **2,** (*with inf.*) to wish (to); (*with* **чтобы**) wish (that). **3,** (*with dat. & gen.*) to wish (someone something): Жела́ю вам всего́ хоро́шего, I wish you the best of everything. —**оставля́ть жела́ть лу́чшего,** to leave something to be desired. —**сам того́ не жела́я,** willy-nilly; though that was not one's intention.

жела́ющие *n.pl., decl. as an adj.* those wishing; those who wish.

желва́к [*gen.* **-вака́**] *n.* lump; tumor.

желе́ *n.neut. indecl.* jelly.

железа́ [*pl.* **же́лезы, желёз, железа́м**] *n.* gland.

желе́зистый *adj.* **1,** glandular. **2,** containing iron; ferrous.

желе́зка [*gen. pl.* **-зок**] *n.* **1,** *colloq.* piece of iron; iron bar. **2,** *obs., colloq.* railroad.

желёзка [*gen. pl.* **-зок**] *n.* glandule.

железнодоро́жник *n.* railway worker.

железнодоро́жный *adj.* railroad (*attrib.*); railway (*attrib.*).

желе́зный *adj.* iron. —**желе́зный блеск,** hematite. —**желе́зный век,** the Iron Age. —**желе́зная доро́га,** railroad.

железня́к [*gen.* **-няка́**] *n.* iron ore. —**бу́рый железня́к,** limonite. —**кра́сный железня́к,** hematite. —**хро́мистый железня́к,** chromite.

желе́зо *n.* iron.

железобето́н *n.* reinforced concrete. —**железобето́нный,** *adj.* of reinforced concrete.

жёлоб [*pl.* **желоба́**] *n.* chute. —**водосто́чный жёлоб,** gutter.

желобо́к [*gen.* **-бка́**] *n.* groove.

желте́ть *v.impfv.* [*pfv.* **пожелте́ть**] **1,** to become yellow; turn yellow. **2,** (*of leaves*) to turn. **3,** [*impfv. only*] (*of anything yellow*) to appear; gleam.

желтизна́ *n.* yellow color; yellow hue.

желтова́тый *adj.* **1,** yellowish. **2,** sallow.

желто́к [*gen.* **-тка́**] *n.* yolk.

желторо́тый *adj.* **1,** yellow-beaked. **2,** *colloq.* immature; inexperienced; green.

желтофио́ль *n.f.* wallflower.

желту́ха *n.* (yellow) jaundice.

жёлтый *adj.* yellow.

желудёвый *adj.* acorn (*attrib.*).

желу́док [*gen.* **-дка**] *n.* stomach. —**му́скульный желу́док,** gizzard.

желу́дочек [*gen.* **-чка**] *n.* ventricle.

желу́дочный *adj.* stomach (*attrib.*); gastric.

жёлудь [*pl.* **жёлуди, желудёй, желудя́м**] *n.m.* acorn.

жёлчный *adj.* **1,** bilious. **2,** ill-tempered; peevish. —**жёлчные ка́мни,** gallstones. —**жёлчный прото́к,** bile duct. —**жёлчный пузы́рь,** gall bladder.

жёлчь *n.f.* **1,** bile. **2,** *fig.* bitterness; rancor.

жема́ниться *v.r.impfv., colloq.* to put on airs.

жема́нный *adj.* unnatural; affected. —**жема́нство,** *n.* affectation.

же́мчуг [*pl.* **жемчуга́**] *n.* pearl; pearls.

жемчу́жина *n.* a (single) pearl. —**жемчу́жница,** *n.* pearl oyster. —**жемчу́жный,** *adj.* pearl (*attrib.*); pearly.

жена́ [*pl.* **жёны**] *n.* wife.

жена́тый *adj.* (*with* **на** + *prepl.*) (*of a man*) married (to): Вы жена́ты?, are you married? Он жена́т на англича́нке, he is married to an Englishwoman.

жени́ть *v.impfv. & pfv.* [*pres.* **женю́, же́нишь**] to marry off (a son). —**жени́ться,** *refl.* (*with* **на** + *prepl.*) (*of a man*) to marry; get married (to).

жени́тьба *n.* marriage (*of a man*).

жени́х [*gen.* **жениха́**] *n.* **1,** fiancé. **2,** groom; bridegroom. **3,** eligible bachelor. **4,** suitor.

женолю́б *n.* ladies' man; womanizer. —**женолюби́вый,** *adj.* having a fondness for women. —**женолю́бие,** *n.* fondness for women.

женоненави́стник *n.* woman-hater; misogynist. —**женоненави́стничество,** *n.* misogyny.

женоподо́бный *adj.* effeminate.

же́нский *adj.* **1,** feminine; female. **2,** woman's; women's; ladies'.

же́нственный *adj.* feminine; womanly. —**же́нственность,** *n.f.* femininity.

же́нщина *n.* woman.

женьше́нь *n.m.* ginseng.

жердь [*pl.* **же́рди, жердéй, жердя́м**] *n.f.* pole; long stick.

жеребёнок [*pl.* **-нка**; *pl.* **-бя́та, -бя́т**] *n.* **1,** colt. **2,** foal.

жеребе́ц [*gen.* **-бца́**] *n.* stallion.

жереби́ться *v.r.impfv.* [*pfv.* **ожереби́ться**] to foal.

жеребьёвка *n.* casting of lots.

жерло́ [*pl.* **жёрла**] *n.* **1,** mouth (*of a volcano*). **2,** muzzle (*of a gun*).

жёрнов [*pl.* **жернова́**] *n.* millstone.

же́ртва *n.* **1,** victim: пасть же́ртвой (+ *gen.*), to fall victim to. **2,** *pl.* casualties: больши́е челове́ческие же́ртвы, heavy casualites. Жертв не́ было, there were no casualties. **3,** sacrifice: идти́ на же́ртвы, to make sacrifices. Принести́ (что́-нибудь) в же́ртву, to sacrifice (something).

же́ртвенник *n.* altar.

же́ртвенность *n.f.* self-sacrifice.

же́ртвенный *adj.* **1,** sacrificial. **2,** selfless.

же́ртвователь *n.m.* contributor; donor.

же́ртвовать *v.impfv.* [*pfv.* **поже́ртвовать**; *pres.* **-твую, -твуешь**] **1,** (*with instr.*) to sacrifice. **2,** to contribute; donate.

жертвоприноше́ние *n.* sacrifice; (burnt) offering.

жест *n.* gesture. Он же́стом предложи́л мне войти́, he motioned to me to come in. —**язы́к же́стов,** sign language.

жестикули́ровать *v.impfv.* [*pres.* **-рую, -руешь**] to gesticulate.

жестикуля́ция *n.* gesticulation.

жёсткий *adj.* [*short form* **жёсток, жестка́, жёстко, жёстки**; *comp.* **жёстче**] **1,** hard. **2,** tough. **3,** stiff; rigid. **4,** harsh. **5,** *fig.* rigid; strict. —**жёсткий ваго́н,** coach with hard (unupholstered) seats.

жёстко *adv.* **1,** harshly. **2,** abruptly. **3,** decisively. —*adj., used predicatively,* hard: Мне жёстко сиде́ть, this seat is too hard for me.

жёсткость *n.f.* **1,** hardness; toughness. **2,** stiffness; rigidity.

жесто́кий *adj.* [*short form* **жесто́к, -тока́, -то́ко, -то́ки**] **1,** cruel; brutal. **2,** bitter; fierce. **3,** severe; harsh.

жесто́ко *adv.* **1,** cruelly; brutally. **2,** severely; harshly.

жестокосе́рдие *n.* hardheartedness. —**жестокосе́рдный,** *adj.* hardhearted.

жесто́кость *n.f.* **1,** cruelty; brutality. **2,** *pl.* cruel acts. **3,** severity.

жёстче *adj., comp. of* **жёсткий.**

жесть *n.f.* tin.

жестя́нка [*gen. pl.* **-нок**] *n.* tin can.

жестяно́й *adj.* tin.

жестя́нщик *n.* tinsmith.

жето́н *n.* **1,** token; counter. **2,** badge; medal.

жечь *v.impfv.* [*pfv.* **сжечь**; *pres.* **жгу, жжёчь, ... жгут**; *past* **жёг, жгла, жгло, жгли**] **1,** to burn.

2, to burn down. **3,** [*impfv. only*] to burn; sting. —**же́чься,** *refl.* [*impfv. only*] *colloq.* **1,** (*of an object*) to get very hot; burn. **2,** to sting. **3,** to burn oneself.

жже́ние *n.* burning sensation.

жжёнка *n.* hot beverage made of rum or brandy with burnt sugar and spices.

жжёный *adj.* burnt.

живе́й *interj.* hurry!; speed it up!

живе́ц [*gen.* **живца́**] *n.* small fish used for bait.

живи́тельный *adj.* **1,** life-giving. **2,** invigorating; bracing.

живи́ца *n.* oleoresin.

жи́вность *n.f., colloq.* **1,** living things. **2,** poultry; livestock.

жи́во *adv.* **1,** vividly. **2,** keenly. **3,** with great animation. **4,** *colloq.* quickly. **5,** *colloq.* (*as an exclamation*) look alive!; look lively!

живодёр *n., colloq.* hustler.

живо́й *adj.* [*short form* **жив, жива́, жи́во, жи́вы**] **1,** living; alive; live. **2,** lively; active. **3,** vivacious; animated. **4,** (*of life*) real. **5,** vivid; expressive. **6,** (*of flowers*) real; natural. **7,** (*of a wound*) raw. —**в живы́х,** alive; living. Оста́ться в живы́х, to survive. —**жива́я си́ла,** (the strength of) men and animals (*as opposed to that of machines*). **2,** kinetic energy. —**задева́ть за живо́е,** to cut to the quick. —**на живу́ю ру́ку,** hastily; on the run.

жи́вокость *n.f.* delphinium; larkspur.

живопи́сец [*gen.* **-сца**] *n.* painter.

живопи́сный *adj.* picturesque.

жи́вопись *n.f.* **1,** painting (*as an art*). **2,** paintings. Коллекционе́р жи́вописи, art collector.

живородя́щий *adj.* viviparous.

жи́вость *n.f.* **1,** liveliness; vivacity. **2,** vividness; intensity. —**жи́вость ума́,** quickness of mind; mental alertness.

живо́т [*gen.* **живота́**] *n.* **1,** stomach; belly; abdomen. **2,** *obs.* life. —**надрыва́ть живо́т** (**со́ смеху**), to laugh oneself silly; be in stitches.

животво́рный *adj.* life-giving. *Also,* **животворя́щий.**

живо́тик *n., colloq.* tummy.

животново́дство *n.* livestock breeding; cattle raising; animal husbandry.

живо́тное *n., decl. as an adj.* animal.

живо́тный *adj.* **1,** animal (*attrib.*). **2,** *fig.* bestial.

животрепе́щущий *adj.* timely; vital.

живу́честь *n.f.* ability to survive; hardiness.

живу́чий *adj.* **1,** hardy. **2,** *fig.* hard to get rid of: Предрассу́дки живу́чи, prejudices die hard.

жи́вчик *n.* **1,** *colloq.* lively person. **2,** *colloq.* noticeable pulsation of an artery in one's temple. **3,** sperm cell.

живьём *adv., colloq.* alive: брать кого́-нибудь живьём, to take someone alive.

жид [*gen.* **жида́**] *n.* Jew (*derogatory term*).

жи́дкий *adj.* [*comp.* **жи́же**] **1,** liquid; fluid. **2,** thin; watery; weak. **3,** (*of hair, a beard, etc.*) thin; scanty. **4,** (*of metal, lava, etc.*) molten. **5,** *colloq.* puny.

жи́дкость *n.f.* liquid; fluid.

жи́жа *n.* liquid; wash; swill. *Also,* **жи́жица.**

жи́же *adj., comp. of* **жи́дкий.**

жи́зненно *adv.* **1,** true to life. **2,** vitally.

жи́зненность *n.f.* **1,** vitality. **2,** closeness to life. **3,** life-like quality.

жи́зненный *adj.* **1,** of life. **2,** lifelike. **3,** vital. —**жи́зненный у́ровень,** standard of living.

жизнеописа́ние *n.* biography.

жизнера́достный *adj.* buoyant; bubbling with life. —**жизнера́достность,** *n.f.* zest for life.

жизнеспосо́бный *adj.* viable. —**жизнеспосо́бность,** *n.f.* viability.

жизнь *n.f.* life. —**в жи́зни не** (+ *verb*), never in one's life. —**как жизнь?,** *colloq.* how are you?; how are things?; how is life (treating you)? —**на всю жизнь,** for life. —**не на жизнь, а на́ смерть,** to the death. —**не от хоро́шей жи́зни,** not because he/she wanted to; not out of the goodness of his/her heart. —**никогда́ в жи́зни,** never. —**при жи́зни,** in/during one's lifetime.

жиклёр *n.* jet; nozzle.

жи́ла *n.* **1,** *anat.* vein. **2,** tendon; sinew. **3,** *mining* lode; vein. —**тяну́ть жи́лы из,** to work to the bone.

жиле́т *n.* vest. —**спаса́тельный жиле́т,** life jacket.

жиле́тка [*gen. pl.* **-ток**] *n., colloq.* vest.

жиле́тный *adj.* vest (*attrib.*).

жиле́ц [*gen.* **жильца́**] *n.* tenant; lodger. —**не жиле́ц на бе́лом све́те,** not long for this world.

жи́листый *adj.* **1,** sinewy; wiry. **2,** (*of meat*) stringy.

жили́ще *n.* dwelling; abode; living quarters. Пра́во на жили́ще, right to housing.

жили́щный *adj.* housing (*attrib.*).

жи́лка [*gen. pl.* **жи́лок**] *n.* **1,** vein. **2,** *fig.* bent; streak: артисти́ческая жи́лка, artistic bent; романти́ческая жи́лка, romantic streak.

жило́й *adj.* **1,** living (*attrib.*); dwelling (*attrib.*): жило́е помеще́ние, living quarters; жила́я пло́щадь, floorspace. **2,** residential: жилы́е райо́ны, residential areas; жило́й дом, apartment house. **3,** *in* жило́й вид, lived-in look.

жилпло́щадь *n.f.* floorspace (*contr. of* **жила́я пло́щадь**).

жильё *n.* **1,** inhabited area; place where people live. **2,** habitation: неприго́дный для жилья́, unfit for habitation. Кварти́ра для жилья́, apartment in which to live. **3,** housing: нехва́тка жилья́, shortage of housing.

жим *n., weightlifting* press.

жи́молость *n.f.* honeysuckle.

жир [*2nd loc.* **жиру́**; *pl.* **жиры́**] *n.* fat; grease. —**кито́вый жир,** whale oil. —**ры́бий жир,** cod-liver oil.

жира́ф *n.* giraffe. *Also,* **жира́фа.**

жире́ть *v.impfv.* [*pfv.* **ожире́ть** *or* **разжире́ть**] to get fat.

жи́рно *adv.* **1,** with a lot of butter or fat. Есть жи́рно, to eat a lot of rich (*or* fatty) food. **2,** *colloq.* too much.

жи́рность *n.f.* fat content.

жи́рный *adj.* **1,** fatty. **2,** (*of foods*) fattening; rich. **3,** greasy; oily. **4,** fat; plump. **5,** (*of a line*) thick; (*of type*) boldface; bold-faced. —**жи́рное пятно́,** grease spot.

жи́ро *n. indecl.* endorsement (*on a check*).

жирови́к [*gen.* **-вика́**] *n.* fatty tumor.

жирово́й *adj.* fatty.

жите́йский *adj.* worldly; mundane.

жи́тель *n.m.* inhabitant; resident.

жи́тельство *n.* residence. —**вид на жи́тельство,** residence permit.

жи́тница *n.* **1,** *obs.* granary. **2,** grain-producing region; granary; breadbasket.

жи́то *n., regional* grain; rye; barley.

жить *v.impfv.* [*pres.* **живу́, живёшь**; *past fem.* **жила́**] to live. —**жил-был,** once upon a time there lived... —**как живёшь?; как живёте?,** how are you?; how are things?; how are you getting along?

житьё *n., colloq.* **1,** life; existence. **2,** habitation; occupancy. —**житьё-бытьё,** *n., colloq.* life; the way one lives. —**нет житья́** (+ *dat.*) **от...,** there is no living with ... (around).

жи́ться *v.r.impfv.* [*pres.* **живётся**; *past* **жило́сь**] *colloq., used impersonally with the dat. case,* to live: Им непло́хо живётся, they don't live badly. —**как вам живётся?,** how are you getting along?; how is life treating you?

жму́рить *v.impfv.* [*pfv.* **зажму́рить**], *in* **жму́рить глаза́,** to squint. —**жму́риться,** *refl.* to squint.

жму́рки [*gen.* **-рок**] *n.pl.* blindman's bluff.

жне́йка [*gen. pl.* **жне́ек**] *n.* harvester; reaper.

жнец [*gen.* **жнеца́**] *n.m.* [*fem.* **жни́ца**] harvest hand.

жнивьё *n.* stubs of cut grain; stubble.

жоке́й *n.* jockey.

жонглёр *n.* juggler. —**жонглёрство,** *n.* juggling (*lit. & fig.*).

жонгли́ровать *v.impfv.* [*pres.* **-рую, -руешь**] (*with instr.*) to juggle (*lit. & fig.*).

жонки́ль *n.f.* jonquil.

жрать *v.impfv.* [*pfv.* **сожра́ть**; *pres.* **жру, жрёшь**; *past fem.* **жрала́**] *vulg.* to eat; gobble up.

жре́бий *n.* **1,** lot: по жре́бию, by lot. **2,** lots: броса́ть/тяну́ть жре́бий, to cast/draw lots. —**жре́бий бро́шен,** the die is cast.

жрец [*gen.* **жреца́**] *n.* pagan priest.

жу́желица *n.* ground beetle.

жужжа́ние *n.* hum; buzz.

жужжа́ть *v.impfv.* [*pres.* **жужжу́, жужжи́шь**] to hum; buzz; drone.

жуи́р *n.* playboy.

жук [*gen.* **жука́**] *n.* beetle. —**ма́йский жук,** cockchafer.

жу́лик *n.* crook; swindler; cheat. —**жуликова́тый,** *adj., colloq.* crooked.

жу́льничать *v.impfv., colloq.* to cheat.

жу́льнический *adj., colloq.* crooked; underhanded. —**жу́льничество,** *n., colloq.* cheating; chicanery.

жу́пел *n.* bugaboo; bugbear.

журавли́ный *adj.* of a crane; of cranes. —**журавли́ные но́ги,** spindlelegs.

жура́вль [*gen.* **-вля́**] *n.m.* **1,** crane (*bird*). **2,** well sweep.

жури́ть *v.impfv.* [*pfv.* **пожури́ть**] *colloq.* to chide.

журна́л *n.* **1,** magazine; journal. **2,** log: ва́хтенный журна́л, ship's log.

журнали́ст *n.* journalist; newspaperman.

журнали́стика *n.* **1,** journalism. **2,** periodic literature.

журнали́стский *adj.* journalist's; journalistic.

журна́льный *adj.* magazine (*attrib.*).

журча́ние *n.* babble; babbling (*of a stream, brook, etc.*).

журча́ть *v.impfv.* [*pres.* **-чи́т**] **1,** (*of water*) to rumble; (*of a brook*) to babble. **2,** (*of a speech, conversation, etc.*) to drone on.

жу́ткий *adj.* [*short form* жу́ток, жутка́, жу́тко, жу́тки] frightful; ghastly; gruesome; grim.

жу́тко *adv.* **1,** frighteningly. **2,** *colloq.* terribly. —*adj., used predicatively* **1,** terrified: Мне бы́ло жу́тко, I was terrified. **2,** frightening: Но́чью в лесу́ бы́ло жу́тко, it was frightening in the woods at night.

жуть *n.f., colloq.* horror. —**до жу́ти** (+ *adj.*), extraordinarily.

жу́хлый *adj.* **1,** withered; dried up. **2,** (*of colors*) faded.

жу́хнуть *v.impfv.* [*pfv.* **пожу́хнуть** *or* **зажу́хнуть**; *past* жу́хнул *or* жух, жу́хла] **1,** to wither; dry up. **2,** (*of colors*) to fade.

жучо́к [*gen.* жучка́] *n., dim. of* жук.

жюри́ (жу) *n.neut. indecl.* **1,** judges; jury (*in a contest*). **2,** *law* jury: большо́е жюри́, grand jury.

З

З, з *n.neut.* eighth letter of the Russian alphabet.

за *prep.* **A,** *with acc.* **1,** behind (*with verbs of motion*): Со́лнце зашло́ за ту́чи, the sun went behind the clouds. **2,** beyond (*with verbs of motion*): вы́йти за преде́лы (+ *gen.*), to go beyond the bounds of... **3,** (*with certain nouns*) out (of): выходи́ть за дверь, to walk out the door; вы́бросить что́-нибудь за окно́, throw something out the window. **4,** past; over: Ему́ за со́рок, he is past/over forty. Далеко́ за́ полночь, past *or* beyond midnight. **5,** (*with verbs and nouns expressing, fear, joy, struggle, death, forgiveness, gratitude, payment, reward, and many others*) for: награ́да за му́жество, an award for bravery; боя́ться за свою́ жизнь, to fear for one's life; боро́ться за незави́симость, fight for independence; умере́ть за ро́дину, die for one's country. **6,** for; in exchange for: купи́ть кни́гу за шесть до́лларов, to buy a book for six dollars; меня́ть фра́нки на до́ллары, to exchange francs for dollars. **7,** for; in place of: расписа́ться за председа́теля, to sign for the chairman. **8,** for; in favor of: голосова́ть за кандида́та, to vote for a candidate. **9,** during; in: за э́то вре́мя, during that time. За всю исто́рию страны́, in the entire history of the country. Получи́ть три письма́ за одну́ неде́лю; to receive three letters in one week. **10,** (*indicating how long it takes to accomplish a task*) in: покры́ть расстоя́ние за три часа́, to cover the distance in three hours. **11,** (*with* до) before: за час до его́ отъе́зда, an hour before his departure. **12,** *indicating distance*: за пять миль отсю́да, five miles from here; за мно́го миль, for many miles; for miles around. Шум был слы́шен за ми́лю, the noise could be heard a mile away. **13,** (*with verbs of sitting*) at; to: сесть за стол, to sit down at the table. **14,** (*with verbs of taking, grasping, holding*) by; on to: взять за́ руку, to take by the hand; держа́ться за пери́ла, hold on to the banister. **15,** (*in toasts*) to: За ва́ше здоро́вье!, to your health!; за новобра́чных!, to the newlyweds! **B,** *with instr.* **1,** behind: за мое́й спино́й, behind my back. **2,** beyond; outside: за преде́лами го́рода, outside the city; beyond the city limits. За две́рью, outside the door. За окно́м, outside the window. **3,** (*following*) after: оди́н за други́м, one after the other. **4,** for; to fetch: идти́ за сигаре́тами, to go for some cigarettes; заходи́ть за това́рищем, call for one's friend. О́чередь за моро́женым, the line for/ to buy/ ice cream. **5,** after; in pursuit of: бежа́ть за ке́м-нибудь, to run after someone. **6,** at; occupied with; doing something: обсужда́ть вопро́с за обе́дом, to discuss a question at (*or* over) dinner; проводи́ть вре́мя за чте́нием, spend time reading. Пить вино́ за обе́дом, to drink wine with dinner. **7,** (*with verbs of sitting*) at: сиде́ть за столо́м, to be sitting at the table. **8,** (*with verbs of watching, caring, etc.*) for; after: присма́тривать за детьми́, to look after the children. **9,** owing to; for: за неимéнием ули́к, for lack of evidence. **10,** *indicating someone's turn:* Сло́во за ва́ми, you have the floor; вы́бор остаётся за ни́ми, the choice is theirs; де́ло за ва́ми, it's up to you.

за- *prefix* **1,** *indicating the beginning of an action:* засмея́ться, to (begin to) laugh. **2,** *indicating motion behind or beyond:* заходи́ть, to go behind. **3,** *indicating action taken en route:* заходи́ть к кому́-нибудь, to drop in on someone. **4,** (*with* **-ся**) *indicating absorption to the point of forgetfulness:* засмотре́ться, to be lost in contemplation. **5,** (*with nouns and adjectives*) outside of: за́городный, out-of-town. **6,** (*with proper nouns and adjectives*) Trans-: Закавка́зье, Transcaucasia.

заале́ть *v., pfv. of* **але́ть**.

заарка́нить *v., pfv. of* **арка́нить.**

заатланти́ческий *adj.* transatlantic; located across the Atlantic.

заба́ва *n.* **1,** amusement; fun. **2,** pastime.

забавля́ть *v.impfv.* to amuse; entertain. —**забавля́ться,** *refl.* to amuse oneself.

заба́вник *n., colloq.* funny person; amusing fellow.

заба́вно *adv.* in an amusing way. —*adj., used predicatively,* funny; amusing: Заба́вно!, that's funny! Мне заба́вно, что..., I find it funny/amusing that...

заба́вный *adj.* funny; amusing.

забаллоти́ровать *v.pfv.* [*infl.* -**рую, -руешь**] to fail to elect; reject; blackball.

забаррикади́ровать *v., pfv. of* **баррикади́ровать.**

забастова́ть *v.pfv.* [*infl.* -**сту́ю, -сту́ешь**] to strike; go on strike.

забасто́вка [*gen. pl.* -**вок**] *n.* strike. —**забасто́вочный,** *adj.* strike (*attrib.*).

забасто́вщик *n.* striker.

забве́ние *n.* **1,** oblivion: предава́ть забве́нию, to consign to oblivion. **2,** (*with gen.*) neglect (of); disregard (of).

забе́г *n., sports* race; dash; heat.

забега́ловка *n., colloq.* eating house.

забе́гать *v.pfv.* to start running. —**забе́гаться,** *refl., colloq.* to run oneself ragged.

забега́ть *v.impfv.* [*pfv.* **забежа́ть**] **1,** (*with* в *or* на + *acc.*) to run into. **2,** (*with* к) *colloq.* to drop in on. **3,** to run (far) away. —**забега́ть вперёд, 1,** to run ahead. **2,** to anticipate events; act in advance.

забежа́ть [*infl. like* **бежа́ть**] *v., pfv. of* **забега́ть.**

забели́ть *v.pfv.* [*infl.* -**белю́, -бе́лишь** *or* -**бели́шь**] **1,** to whiten; paint white. **2,** *colloq.* to add milk or sour cream to.

забере́менеть *v., pfv. of* **забере́менеть.**

забеспоко́иться *v.r.pfv.* to become anxious; become uneasy; begin to worry.

забетони́ровать *v., pfv. of* **бетони́ровать.**

забива́ть *v.impfv.* [*pfv.* **заби́ть**] **1,** to drive in; hammer in. **2,** to nail up; nail down. **3,** to seal up; board up. **4,** to block up; clog; (*of weeds*) choke. **5,** (*usu. passive*) to jam: заби́т бе́женцами, jammed with refugees. **6,** to beat to death; beat into submission. **7,** *fig.* to grind down; wear down. **8,** to slaughter (cattle). **9,** *sports* to drive in (a ball); score (a goal). **10,** *colloq.* to excel; outdo. —**забива́ть чью-нибудь го́лову** (+ *instr.*), to fill *or* stuff someone's head (with). *See also* **заби́ть.**

забива́ться *v.r.impfv.* [*pfv.* **заби́ться**] **1,** to hide; huddle. **2,** to become blocked; become clogged.

забинтова́ть *v., pfv. of* **бинтова́ть.**

забира́ть *v.impfv.* [*pfv.* **забра́ть**] **1,** to take. **2,** to take away. **3,** to pick up; collect. **4,** to arrest. **5,** to take in; shorten. **6,** *colloq.* (*of a feeling*) to come over (someone). **7,** to seal up; close up. **8,** to bear: забра́ть впра́во, to bear (to the) right. **9,** *in* забира́ть в ру́ки, to take (someone) in hand.

забира́ться *v.r.impfv.* [*pfv.* **забра́ться**] **1,** (*with* на, в *or* под + *acc.*) to climb. **2,** (*with* в + *acc.*) to get into; steal into. **3,** to get to: Куда́ он забра́лся?, where has he gotten to? **4,** to hide.

заби́тый *adj.* downtrodden; cowed.

заби́ть *v.pfv.* [*infl.* **забью́, забьёшь**] **1,** *pfv. of* **забива́ть. 2,** (*with* в + *acc.*) to begin to strike. **3,** (*with instr.*) to begin to bang; begin to pound (one's fists, feet, etc.). **4,** to sound (an alarm, retreat, etc.). **5,** (*of a musical instrument, firearm, etc.*) to sound. **6,** to begin to spurt; begin to gush. —**заби́ться,** *refl., pfv. of* **забива́ться.**

забия́ка *n.m. & f., colloq.* roughneck; bully.

заблаговре́менно *adv.* beforehand; in advance; ahead of time.

заблагорассу́диться *v.r.pfv., impers.* (*with dat.*) to see fit: Я сде́лаю, что мне заблагорассу́дится, I shall do as I see fit.

заблесте́ть *v.pfv.* [*infl. like* **блесте́ть**] to begin to shine; begin to sparkle.

заблоки́ровать *v., pfv. of* **блоки́ровать.**

заблуди́ться *v.r.pfv.* [*infl.* -**блужу́сь, -блу́дишься**] to lose one's way; get lost. —**заблуди́ться в трёх со́снах,** to be confounded by the simplest problem.

заблу́дший *adj.* **1,** lost; stray. **2,** *fig.* wayward; gone astray. —**заблу́дшая овца́,** lost sheep.

заблужда́ться *v.r.impfv.* to be mistaken.

заблужде́ние *n.* error; misapprehension; misconception; delusion. —**вводи́ть в заблужде́ние,** to mislead; delude; lead astray.

забода́ть *v.pfv.* to gore.

забо́й *n.* slaughter; slaughtering (*of cattle*).

заболева́емость *n.f.* incidence; prevalence; rate; number of cases (*of a disease*).

заболева́ние *n.* illness; disease.

заболева́ть *v.impfv.* [*pfv.* **заболе́ть**] to become ill; fall ill; be taken ill.

заболе́ть *v.pfv.* **1,** [*infl.* -**е́ю, -е́ешь**] *pfv. of* **заболева́ть. 2,** [*infl.* -**и́т**] to begin to hurt; begin to ache.

за́болонь *n.f.* alburnum; sapwood.

заболо́ченный *adj.* swampy; marshy.

заболта́ться *v.r.pfv., colloq.* to become engrossed in conversation.

забо́р *n.* fence.

забо́ристый *adj., colloq.* **1,** strong; pungent. **2,** racy; risqué.

забо́рный *adj.* **1,** fence (*attrib.*). **2,** coarse; vulgar.

забо́та *n.* **1,** care; concern: забо́та о челове́ке, concern for people. **2,** care; worry: без забо́т, without a care.

забо́тить *v.impfv.* [*pres.* -**чу, -тишь**] to worry; trouble; concern.

забо́титься *v.r.impfv.* [*pfv.* **позабо́титься**; *pres.* -**чусь, -тишься**] (*with* о) **1,** to take care of; care for; look after. **2,** to care about; be concerned about. **3,** [*usu. pfv.*] to take care of; attend to; see to (a matter). Позабо́титься о том, чтобы..., to see to it that...

забо́тливый *adj.* thoughtful; solicitous; considerate. —**забо́тливость,** *n.f.* thoughtfulness; solicitude.

забракова́ть *v., pfv. of* **бракова́ть.**

забра́ло *n.* visor (*of a helmet*). —**с откры́тым забра́лом,** openly; frankly; boldly.

забра́сывать¹ *v.impfv.* [*pfv.* **заброса́ть**] (*with instr.*) **1,** to fill (with). **2,** to pelt (with): заброса́ть кого-нибудь камня́ми, to throw stones at. **3,** *fig.* to shower (with); bombard (with); pepper (with): заброса́ть кого-нибудь вопро́сами, to shower/bombard/pepper with questions.

забра́сывать² *v.impfv.* [*pfv.* **забро́сить**] **1,** to throw (*with force or over a distance*). **2,** to throw; toss (a part of one's body): забро́сить го́лову наза́д, to toss one's head back. **3,** to neglect. **4,** to give up; drop; abandon. **5,** *colloq.* to deliver; drop off.

забра́ть [*infl.* **-беру́, -берёшь;** *past fem.* **-брала́**] *v., pfv. of* забира́ть. —**забра́ться,** *refl.* [*past tense stress as in* бра́ться] *pfv. of* забира́ться.

забрести́ *v.pfv.* [*infl. like* брести́] *colloq.* **1,** (*with* в + *acc.*) to wander into. **2,** to wander off.

заброни́рованный *adj.* reserved.

заброни́ровать *v., pfv. of* брони́ровать.

забронирова́ть *v., pfv. of* бронирова́ть.

забро́с *n., colloq.* neglect: быть в забро́се, to be in a state of neglect.

заброса́ть *v., pfv. of* забра́сывать¹.

забро́сить [*infl.* **-шу, -сишь**] *v., pfv. of* забра́сывать².

забро́шенность *n.f.* **1,** neglect. **2,** desolation.

забро́шенный *adj.* **1,** neglected. **2,** deserted; desolate.

забры́згивать *v.impfv.* [*pfv.* **забры́згать**] (*with instr.*) to splash (with); spatter (with); splatter (with). —**забры́згиваться,** *refl.* to be *or* get splashed.

забыва́ть *v.impfv.* [*pfv.* **забы́ть**] **1,** to forget: He забу́дьте!, don't forget! **2,** to leave (*accidentally*): забы́ть зо́нтик на рабо́те, to leave one's umbrella at work. —**забыва́ться,** *refl.* **1,** to doze off. **2,** to be lost in thought. **3,** to forget oneself. **4,** to be forgotten.

забы́вчивый *adj.* forgetful. —**забы́вчивость,** *n.f.* forgetfulness.

забы́тый *adj.* forgotten.

забы́ть [*infl.* **-бу́ду, -бу́дешь**] *v., pfv. of* забыва́ть. —**забы́ться,** *refl., pfv. of* забыва́ться.

забытьё [*prepl.* **в забытьи́**] *n.* **1,** drowsiness. **2,** semiconsciousness. **3,** (state of) distraction.

зава́л *n.* **1,** pile; accumulation: сне́жный зава́л, snowdrift. **2,** obstruction; barrier.

зава́ливать *v.impfv.* [*pfv.* **завали́ть**] **1,** to block up. **2,** (*with instr.*) *colloq.* to pile high (with); *fig.* overload (with); flood (with); swamp (with). —**зава́ливаться,** *refl.* **1,** to fall. **2,** *colloq.* to fall down; come tumbling down; collapse. **3,** *colloq.* to tilt to one side. **4,** *colloq.* to lie down; flop down.

завали́ть [*infl.* **-валю́, -ва́лишь**] *v., pfv. of* зава́ливать. —**завали́ться,** *refl., pfv. of* зава́ливаться.

за́валь *n.f., colloq.* unsold or unsalable merchandise; junk.

заваля́ться *v.r.pfv., colloq.* to lie unused; lie unsold; lie unattended to.

заваля́щий *adj., colloq.* useless; worthless.

зава́ривать *v.impfv.* [*pfv.* **завари́ть**] to make; brew (coffee, tea, etc.). —**завари́ть ка́шу,** to stir up trouble.

зава́риваться *v.r.impfv.* [*pfv.* **завари́ться**] (*of tea, coffee, etc.*) **1,** to brew; be brewing. **2,** [*usu. pfv.*] to be brewed; be ready (to be served).

завари́ть [*infl.* **-варю́, -ва́ришь**] *v., pfv. of* зава́ривать. —**завари́ться,** *refl., pfv. of* зава́риваться.

заварно́й *adj.* boiled. —**заварно́й крем,** custard. —**заварно́е пиро́жное,** pastry filled with custard.

завару́ха *n., colloq.* turmoil; commotion.

заведе́ние *n.* institution; establishment. —**вы́сшее уче́бное заведе́ние,** institution of higher learning.

заведённый *adj.* established: заведённый поря́док, established procedure. —**как заведённый,** nonstop; without letup.

заве́дование *n.* (*with instr.*) management (of); being head (of).

заве́довать *v.impfv.* [*pres.* **-дую, -дуешь**] (*with instr.*) to manage; be in charge of; be head of.

заве́домо *adv.* **1,** obviously; known to be. **2,** knowingly; wittingly.

заве́домый *adj.* **1,** notorious. **2,** obvious.

заве́дующий *n., decl. as an adj.* (*with instr.*) manager (of); head (of).

завезти́ [*infl. like* везти́] *v., pfv. of* завози́ть.

завербова́ть *v., pfv. of* вербова́ть. —**завербова́ться,** *refl., pfv. of* вербова́ться.

заве́рение *n.* assurance.

заве́рить *v., pfv. of* заверя́ть.

заверну́ть *v., pfv. of* завёртывать. —**заверну́ться,** *refl., pfv. of* завёртываться.

заверте́ть *v.pfv.* [*infl.* **-верчу́, -ве́ртишь**] **1,** (*with instr.*) to spin around; set spinning. **2,** *fig., colloq.* to captivate; carry away. —**заверте́ться,** *refl.* **1,** to begin to spin; begin to whirl. **2,** *fig., colloq.* to be in a whirl.

завёртывать *v.impfv.* [*pfv.* **заверну́ть**] **1,** to wrap; wrap up. Заверну́ть что-нибудь в бума́гу, to wrap something in paper. **2,** *v.i.* to turn: заверну́ть за́ угол, to turn the corner. **3,** to turn up; roll up; tuck up. **4,** to screw tight; tighten. **5,** *colloq.* to turn off. **6,** (*with* к) *colloq.* to drop in (on). —**завёртываться,** *refl.* **1,** (*with* в + *acc.*) to wrap oneself (in). **2,** to be turned up; be folded *or* rolled back.

заверша́ть *v.impfv.* [*pfv.* **заверши́ть**] to complete. —**заверша́ться,** *refl.* **1,** to be completed. **2,** (*with instr.*) to conclude (with); end (with).

заверша́ющий *adj.* concluding; final. —**заверша́ющий уда́р,** crowning blow.

заверше́ние *n.* completion.

заверши́ть *v., pfv. of* заверша́ть. —**заверши́ться,** *refl., pfv. of* заверша́ться.

заверя́ть *v.impfv.* [*pfv.* **заве́рить**] **1,** to assure. **2,** to witness; certify.

заве́са *n.* **1,** curtain. **2,** *fig.* veil; screen. —**дымова́я заве́са,** smoke screen.

заве́сить [*infl.* **-шу, -сишь**] *v., pfv. of* заве́шивать (*in sense #1*).

завести́ [*infl. like* вести́] *v., pfv. of* заводи́ть. —**завести́сь,** *refl., pfv. of* заводи́ться.

заве́т *n.* **1,** precept. **2,** *relig.* covenant. **3,** *obs.* vow. —**Ве́тхий заве́т,** Old Testament. —**Но́вый заве́т,** New Testament.

заве́тный *adj.* **1,** (*of a dream, desire, etc.*) fondest; lifelong. **2,** secret; hidden.

заве́шивать *v.impfv.* **1,** [*pfv.* **заве́сить**] to cover; curtain off. **2,** [*pfv.* **заве́шать**] to hang with: Сте́ны бы́ли заве́шаны карти́нами, the walls were hung with paintings.

завеща́ние *n.* will. —**духо́вное завеща́ние,** last will and testament.

завеща́тель *n.m.* testator. —**завеща́тельница**, *n.* testatrix.

завеща́ть *v.impfv. & pfv.* to bequeath; will; leave.

завзя́тый *adj., colloq.* **1**, inveterate. **2**, avid; ardent.

завива́ть *v.impfv.* [*pfv.* **зави́ть**] to curl; wave. —**завива́ться**, *refl.* **1**, (*of hair*) to curl; become curly. **2**, to have one's hair curled.

зави́вка [*gen. pl.* **-вок**] *n.* wave. —**шестиме́сячная зави́вка**, permanent wave.

зави́деть *v.pfv.* [*infl.* **-жу, -дишь**] *colloq.* to catch sight of (*from afar*).

зави́дно *adj., used predicatively* (*with dat.*) envious: Ему́ зави́дно смотре́ть на неё, he is envious when he looks at her.

зави́дный *adj.* enviable.

зави́довать *v.impfv.* [*pfv.* **позави́довать**; *pres.* **-дую, -дуешь**] (*with dat.*) to envy; be jealous of.

завиду́щий *adj., colloq.* envious; covetous.

завизи́ровать *v., pfv. of* визи́ровать.

завинти́ть [*infl.* **-чу́, -ти́шь**] *v., pfv. of* зави́нчивать. —**завинти́ться**, *refl., pfv. of* зави́нчиваться.

зави́нчивать *v.impfv.* [*pfv.* **завинти́ть**] to tighten (a screw, nut, etc.). —**зави́нчиваться**, *refl.* (*of a nut or lid*) to screw on.

завира́ться *v.r.impfv.* [*pfv.* **завра́ться**] *colloq.* to become tangled in lies.

зави́сеть *v.impfv.* [*pres.* **-шу, -сишь**] (*with* от) to depend (on). —**по не зави́сящим от нас обстоя́тельствам**, due to circumstances beyond our control.

зави́симость *n.f.* dependence. —**в зави́симости от**, depending on. —**вне зави́симости от**, regardless of.

зави́симый *adj.* dependent.

зави́стливый *adj.* envious.

зави́стник *n.* envious person.

за́висть *n.f.* envy. —**на за́висть**, such as to make others envious.

завито́й *adj.* (*of hair*) curled; waved.

завито́к [*gen.* **-тка́**] *n.* **1**, lock; ringlet. **2**, flourish (*in handwriting or oratory*).

завиту́шка [*gen. pl.* **-шек**] *n., colloq.* = завито́к.

зави́ть [*infl. like* вить] *v., pfv. of* завива́ть. —**зави́ться**, *refl., pfv. of* завива́ться.

завихре́ние *n.* **1**, eddy. **2**, swirl (*of dust*).

завко́м *n.* factory committee (*contr. of* заводско́й комите́т).

завладева́ть *v.impfv.* [*pfv.* **завладе́ть**] (*with instr.*) **1**, to seize; take possession of; capture. **2**, *fig.* to grip: завладе́ть чьи́м-нибудь внима́нием, to grip someone's attention. **3**, *fig.* to captivate.

завлека́тельный *adj.* enticing; alluring.

завлека́ть *v.impfv.* [*pfv.* **завле́чь**] **1**, to entice; lure. **2**, to captivate; enthrall.

завле́чь [*infl. like* влечь] *v., pfv. of* завлека́ть.

заво́д *n.* **1**, factory; plant; mill; works. ♦*Rendered variously with specific adjectives:* лите́йный заво́д, foundry; пивова́ренный заво́д, brewery; са́харный заво́д, sugar refinery; ко́нный заво́д, stud farm. **2**, winding mechanism.

заводи́ть *v.impfv.* [*pfv.* **завести́**; *pres.* **-вожу́, -во́дишь**] **1**, (*with various prepositions*) to take; bring;

lead (to, into, behind, etc.). **2**, *colloq.* to drop (someone) off (somewhere). **3**, to take out of one's way; take far away: Куда́ ты нас завёл?, where have you taken us? **4**, to start; launch. **5**, to introduce; institute. **6**, to strike up (a conversation, acquaintance, etc.). **7**, to get; acquire. **8**, to wind (a watch); start (a car or motor). —**заводи́ться**, *refl.* **1**, to appear; turn up. **2**, to be established; start up. **3**, (*of an engine*) to start. **4**, *colloq.* to get worked up.

заводно́й *adj.* **1**, operated by winding; mechanical. **2**, serving to wind; winding: заводна́я рукоя́тка, hand crank.

заво́дский *also,* **заводско́й** *adj.* factory (*attrib.*).

заво́дчик *n.* factory owner.

за́водь *n.f.* inlet; creek. Ти́хая за́водь, quiet backwater.

завоева́ние *n.* **1**, conquest. **2**, *pl.* conquests. **3**, *pl.* achievements.

завоева́тель *n.m.* conqueror.

завоева́ть [*infl.* **-вою́ю, -вою́ешь**] *v., pfv. of* завоёвывать.

завоёвывать *v.impfv.* [*pfv.* **завоева́ть**] **1**, to conquer. **2**, to gain; win.

заво́з *n.* delivery.

завози́ть *v.impfv.* [*pfv.* **завезти́**; *pres.* **-вожу́, -во́зишь**] **1**, to deliver; drop off. **2**, to take far away; take out of one's way. **3**, to bring into (a country).

завола́кивать *v.impfv.* [*pfv.* **заволо́чь**] to cloud; obscure: Ту́чи заволокли́ со́лнце, clouds obscured the sun. *Also impers.:* Её глаза́ заволокло́ слеза́ми, her eyes were clouded with tears.

заволнова́ться *v.r.pfv.* [*infl.* **-ну́юсь, -ну́ешься**] to become agitated.

заволо́чь [*infl. like* воло́чь] *v., pfv. of* завола́кивать.

завора́живать *v.impfv.* [*pfv.* **заворожи́ть**] **1**, to bewitch; cast a spell over. **2**, *fig.* to captivate.

завора́чивать *v.impfv.* [*pfv.* **завороти́ть**] *colloq.* **1**, *v.i.* to turn; make a turn. **2**, *v.t.* to turn around; turn back. **3**, to turn up (an edge, sleeve, etc.). **4**, to drop in. **5**, [*impfv. only*] (*with instr.*) to be in charge of.

заворожённый *adj.* spellbound; bewitched.

заворожи́ть *v., pfv. of* завора́живать.

заворо́т *n., colloq.* **1**, sharp turn. **2**, bend (*in a road, river, etc.*).

завороти́ть [*infl.* **-рочу́, -ро́тишь**] *v., pfv. of* завора́чивать.

завра́ться [*infl. like* врать] *v.r., pfv. of* завира́ться.

завсегда́тай *n.* habitué.

за́втра *adv.* tomorrow.

за́втрак *n.* **1**, breakfast. **2**, lunch. **3**, luncheon.

за́втракать *v.impfv.* [*pfv.* **поза́втракать**] to have breakfast; have lunch.

за́втрашний *adj.* tomorrow's. —**за́втрашний день**, **1**, tomorrow. **2**, the future.

завуали́ровать *v.pfv.* [*infl.* **-рую, -руешь**] to veil; conceal.

за́вуч *n., colloq.* director of studies (*contr. of* заве́дующий уче́бной ча́стью).

завхо́з *n., colloq.* steward; household manager (*contr. of* заве́дующий хозя́йством).

завыва́ть *v.impfv.* to howl; wail.

завыша́ть *v.impfv.* [*pfv.* **завы́сить**] to overstate; inflate (figures); set (goals, norms, etc.) too high.

завяза́ть[1] [*infl.* **-вяжу́, -вя́жешь**] *v., pfv. of* **завя́зывать**. —**завяза́ться**, *refl., pfv. of* **завя́зываться**.

завяза́ть[2] *v.impfv.* [*pfv.* **завя́знуть**; *pres.* **-за́ю, -за́ешь**] **1,** to get stuck. **2,** *fig.* (*with* **в** + *prepl.*) *colloq.* to become mired (in).

завя́зка [*gen. pl.* **-зок**] *n.* **1,** string; lace; band. **2,** beginning; starting point.

завя́знуть [*past* **завя́з, завя́зла**] *v., pfv. of* **вя́знуть** *and* **завяза́ть**[2].

завя́зывать *v.impfv.* [*pfv.* **завяза́ть**] **1,** to tie; tie up. **2,** to bind; bind up. **3,** *in* **завяза́ть глаза́** (+ *dat.*), to blindfold. **4,** to start; strike up (a conversation, acquaintance, etc.). —**завя́зываться**, *refl.* **1,** to be tied; tie. **2,** to begin; develop; spring up.

за́вязь *n.f., bot.* ovary.

завя́нуть [*past* **завя́л, завя́ла**] *v., pfv. of* **вя́нуть**.

загада́ть *v., pfv. of* **зага́дывать**.

зага́дить [*infl.* **-жу, -дишь**] *v., pfv. of* **зага́живать**.

зага́дка [*gen. pl.* **-док**] *n.* **1,** riddle; puzzle. **2,** mystery; enigma.

зага́дочный *adj.* enigmatic; mysterious.

зага́дывать *v.impfv.* [*pfv.* **загада́ть**] **1,** to pose (a riddle). **2,** to think of; pick (*as part of a riddle*). **3,** *colloq.* to think ahead; look ahead.

зага́женный *adj., colloq.* filthy.

зага́живать *v.impfv.* [*pfv.* **зага́дить**] *colloq.* to foul; dirty; pollute.

зага́р *n.* sunburn; suntan.

загаси́ть *v.pfv.* [*infl.* **-гашу́, -га́сишь**] *colloq.* to put out; extinguish.

загво́здка [*gen. pl.* **-док**] *n., colloq.* hitch; catch; snag; rub.

заги́б *n.* **1,** bend. **2,** crease (*in a page*). **3,** *fig.* deviation.

загиба́ть *v.impfv.* [*pfv.* **загну́ть**] **1,** to turn up; turn down; fold down; fold over. **2,** *v.i., colloq.* to turn: загну́ть за́ угол, to turn the corner. **3,** *colloq.* to utter; come out with. —**загиба́ться**, *refl.* **1,** to turn up. **2,** to bend. **3,** *colloq.* to die; kick the bucket.

загипнотизи́ровать *v., pfv. of* **гипнотизи́ровать**.

загла́вие *n.* title.

загла́вный *adj.* title (*attrib.*). —**загла́вная бу́ква**, capital letter. —**загла́вный лист**, title page. —**загла́вная роль**, title role.

загла́дить [*infl.* **-жу, -дишь**] *v., pfv. of* **загла́живать**.

загла́живать *v.impfv.* [*pfv.* **загла́дить**] **1,** to smooth out; iron out. **2,** *fig.* to redress; make amends for.

загла́зно *adv., colloq.* **1,** behind one's back. **2,** sight unseen.

загла́зный *adj., colloq.* said or done behind one's back.

загло́хнуть [*past* **загло́х, загло́хла**] *v., pfv. of* **гло́хнуть** (*in senses #2 and #3*).

заглуша́ть *v.impfv.* [*pfv.* **заглуши́ть**] **1,** to muffle; drown out (sound); jam (radio broadcasts). **2,** (*of weeds*) to choke. **4,** *fig.* to stifle.

заглуше́ние *n.* jamming (*of radio broadcasts*).

заглуши́ть *v., pfv. of* **глуши́ть** *and* **заглуша́ть**.

загляде́нье *n., colloq.* lovely sight; sight for sore eyes.

загляде́ться [*infl.* **-жу́сь, -ди́шься**] *v.r., pfv. of* **загля́дываться**.

загля́дывать *v.impfv.* [*pfv.* **загляну́ть**] **1,** (*with various prepositions*) to look; peep (into, under, over, behind, etc.). **2,** (*with* **в** + *acc.*) to glance at; glance over (a book, newspaper, etc.); look (in a dictionary). **3,** *colloq.* to drop in; drop by; (*with* **к**) drop in on; look in on. —**загля́дывать вперёд**, to look ahead.

загля́дываться *v.r.impfv.* [*pfv.* **загляде́ться**] (*with* **на** + *acc.*) to stare at (longingly); eye.

загляну́ть [*infl.* **-гляну́, -гля́нешь**] *v., pfv. of* **загля́дывать**.

загна́ивать *v.impfv* [*pfv.* **загнои́ть**] *colloq.* to allow to fester; allow to rot. —**загна́иваться**, *refl.* to fester.

за́гнанный *adj.* **1,** (*of an animal*) exhausted (*from being chased*). **2,** *fig.* downtrodden; persecuted.

загна́ть [*infl.* **-гоню́, -го́нишь**; *past fem.* **загнала́**] *v., pfv. of* **загоня́ть**.

загнива́ние *n.* **1,** rotting. **2,** *fig.* decay.

загнива́ть *v.impfv.* [*pfv.* **загни́ть**] to rot; decay.

загни́ть [*infl. like* **гнить**] *v., pfv. of* **загнива́ть**.

загнои́ть *v., pfv. of* **загна́ивать**. —**загнои́ться**, *refl., pfv. of* **загна́иваться**.

загну́ть *v., pfv. of* **загиба́ть**. —**загну́ться**, *refl., pfv. of* **загиба́ться**.

загова́ривать *v.impfv.* [*pfv.* **заговори́ть**] **1,** [*impfv. only*] (*with* **с** + *instr.*) to start a conversation (with). **2,** *colloq.* to talk (someone's) head off. **3,** to cast a spell over. **4,** *in* **загова́ривать зу́бы** (+ *dat.*), *colloq.* to fool (someone) with fine words. —**загова́риваться**, *refl.* **1,** [*impfv. only*] to ramble (*when speaking*). **2,** to become engrossed in conversation.

за́говор *n.* **1,** plot; conspiracy. **2,** incantation.

заговори́ть *v.pfv.* **1,** *pfv. of* **загова́ривать**. **2,** to learn to speak. **3,** to begin to speak. —**заговори́ться**, *refl., pfv. of* **загова́риваться** (*in sense #2*).

загово́рщик *n.* conspirator; plotter. —**загово́рщический**, *adj.* conspiratorial.

за́годя *adv., colloq.* ahead of time; in advance.

заголо́вок [*gen.* **-вка**] *n.* **1,** headline. **2,** heading.

заго́н *n.* **1,** pen (*for cattle*). **2,** herding; rounding up. **3,** strip of land. —**быть в заго́не**, to be neglected; be in a state of neglect.

загоня́ть *v.impfv.* [*pfv.* **загна́ть**] **1,** (*with* **в** + *acc.*) to herd into; drive into. **2,** *colloq.* to drive in; hammer in. **3,** to drive away. **4,** (*of adverse conditions*) to drive (someone somewhere). **5,** to drive to exhaustion. **6,** to bring (an animal) to bay. —**загоня́ть в у́гол**, to drive or back into a corner.

загора́живать *v.impfv.* [*pfv.* **загороди́ть**] **1,** to enclose; fence in. **2,** to bar; block; obstruct. **3,** to block; obscure. **4,** to shield. —**загора́живаться**, *refl.* **1,** to fence oneself in. **2,** to shield oneself.

загора́ть *v.impfv.* [*pfv.* **загоре́ть**] **1,** to become (*or* get) sunburned. **2,** [*impfv. only*] to sun-bathe. —**загора́ться**, *refl.* **1,** to catch fire. **2,** (*of one's eyes*) to light up; (*of one's face*) to be flushed. **3,** (*of an argument, fight, etc.*) to break out. **4,** (*with instr.*) to be consumed with (an emotion, idea, etc.). **5,** *impers.* (*with dat.*) *colloq.* to have a burning desire.

загоре́лый *adj.* sunburned; suntanned.

загоре́ть [*infl.* -горю́, -гори́шь] *v., pfv. of* загора́ть. —**загоре́ться,** *refl., pfv. of* загора́ться.

загороди́ть [*infl.* -рожу́, -ро́дишь *or* -роди́шь] *v., pfv. of* загора́живать. —**загороди́ться,** *refl., pfv. of* загора́живаться.

загоро́дка [*gen. pl.* -док] *n., colloq.* **1,** fence. **2,** partition. **3,** enclosure.

за́городный *adj.* out-of-town; country (*attrib.*).

загости́ться *v.r.pfv.* [*infl.* -щу́сь, -сти́шься] *colloq.* to overstay one's welcome.

загота́вливать *v.impfv.* = заготовля́ть.

загото́вительный *adj.* purchasing (*attrib.*); procurement (*attrib.*).

загото́вить [*infl.* -влю, -вишь] *v., pfv. of* заготовля́ть *and* загота́вливать.

загото́вка [*gen. pl.* -вок] *n.* **1,** storing up; stocking up. **2,** *often pl.* purchase(s) by the state.

заготовля́ть *v.impfv.* [*pfv.* загото́вить] **1,** to prepare in advance. **2,** (*often fol. by* впрок) to store up; stock up on.

загради́тель *n.m.* minelayer. *Also,* ми́нный загради́тель.

загради́тельный *adj., mil.* protecting; covering. —**загради́тельный ого́нь,** covering fire; barrage.

загради́ть [*infl.* -жу́, -ди́шь] *v., pfv. of* заграждать.

заграждать *v.impfv.* [*pfv.* загради́ть] to bar; block; obstruct.

загражде́ние *n.* obstacle; barrier; obstruction.

заграни́ца *n., colloq.* foreign countries. —**по заграни́цам,** abroad.

заграни́чный *adj.* foreign.

загреба́ть *v.impfv.* [*pfv.* загрести́] **1,** to rake together; rake up. **2,** *in* загреба́ть жар, to bank the fire (*in a furnace*). **3,** *colloq.* to rake in (money). —**чужи́ми рука́ми жар загреба́ть,** to make someone else do one's dirty work.

загреме́ть *v.pfv.* [*infl.* -млю́, -ми́шь] **1,** to begin to sound, clank, thunder, etc.; resound. **2,** (*with instr.*) to rattle. **3,** *colloq.* to come crashing down.

загрести́ [*infl. like* грести́] *v., pfv. of* загреба́ть.

загри́вок [*gen.* -вка] *n.* **1,** withers. **2,** *colloq.* nape of the neck.

загримирова́ть *v., pfv. of* гримирова́ть (*in sense #2*). —**загримирова́ться,** *refl., pfv. of* гримирова́ться (*in sense #2*).

загро́бный *adj.* occurring after death: загро́бный мир, the next world; загро́бная жизнь, life after death; afterlife.

загроможда́ть *v.impfv.* [*pfv.* загромозди́ть] to clutter (up); jam.

загромозди́ть [*infl.* -зжу́, -зди́шь] *v., pfv. of* загроможда́ть.

загрубе́лый *adj.* calloused.

загрубе́ть *v.pfv.* **1,** to become calloused. **2,** *fig.* to become callous.

загружа́ть *v.impfv.* [*pfv.* загрузи́ть] **1,** to load (a vehicle, vessel, etc.). **2,** *fig.* to assign a full load of work to (someone); fill out (a period of time) with work. —**загружа́ться,** *refl.* to load up.

загрузи́ть [*infl.* -гружу́, -гру́зишь *or* -грузи́шь] *v., pfv. of* грузи́ть (*in sense #1*) *and* загружа́ть. —**загрузи́ться,** *refl., pfv. of* загружа́ться.

загру́зка *n.* **1,** loading. **2,** *colloq.* workload; capacity.

загрусти́ть *v.pfv.* [*infl.* -щу́, -сти́шь] to become sad.

загрыза́ть *v.impfv.* [*pfv.* загры́зть] **1,** to kill; bite to death; tear to pieces. **2,** *colloq.* to nag; hound; badger.

загры́зть [*infl. like* грызть] *v., pfv. of* загрыза́ть.

загрязне́ние *n.* **1,** soiling. **2,** pollution; contamination.

загрязни́ть *v., pfv. of* грязни́ть *and* загрязня́ть. —**загрязни́ться,** *refl., pfv. of* грязни́ться *and* загрязня́ться.

загрязня́ть *v.impfv.* [*pfv.* загрязни́ть] **1,** to soil; dirty. **2,** to pollute; contaminate. —**загрязня́ться,** *refl.* to get dirty.

загс *n.* civilian registry office (*abbr. of* за́пись а́ктов гражда́нского состоя́ния).

загуби́ть *v.pfv.* [*infl.* -гублю́, -гу́бишь] *colloq.* **1,** to ruin. **2,** to squander.

загуля́ть *v.pfv., colloq.* to go on a spree. —**загуля́ться,** *refl., colloq.* **1,** to walk for too long a time. **2,** to carouse till one forgets the time.

загусте́ть *v., pfv. of* густе́ть.

зад [*2nd loc.* заду́; *pl.* зады́] *n.* **1,** back; rear. **2,** behind; backside. **3,** rump; buttocks. **4,** *pl., colloq.* old stuff: повторя́ть зады́, to repeat old stuff; say what has been said many times before. *See also* за́дом.

зада́бривать *v.impfv.* [*pfv.* задо́брить] **1,** to bring around; win over. **2,** to cajole; coax.

задава́ть *v.impfv.* [*pfv.* зада́ть; *pres.* задаю́, задаёшь] **1,** to ask (a question); pose (a problem). **2,** to assign (a lesson, task, etc.). **3,** to set (the tone, pace, fashion, etc.). **4,** *colloq.* to give; throw (a party, banquet, etc.). **5,** *colloq.* to give; administer (a scolding, punishment, etc.). —**задава́ться,** *refl.* **1,** *in* задава́ться це́лью (+ *inf.*), to set as one's goal. **2,** *in* зада́ться вопро́сом, to ask oneself a question. **3,** *colloq.* (*usu. neg.*) (not) turn out well. **4,** [*impfv. only*] *colloq.* to put on airs.

задави́ть *v., pfv. of* дави́ть (*in senses #6 & #7*).

зада́ние *n.* task; assignment. —**дома́шнее зада́ние,** homework.

зада́ривать *v.impfv.* [*pfv.* задари́ть] **1,** to lavish gifts upon. **2,** *obs.* to bribe; "buy off".

задари́ть [*infl.* -дарю́, -да́ришь] *v., pfv. of* зада́ривать.

зада́ром *adv., colloq.* = да́ром.

зада́ток [*gen.* -тка] *n.* **1,** deposit; down payment. **2,** *pl.* makings: зада́тки хоро́шего писа́теля, the makings of a good writer.

зада́ть [*infl. like* дать; *past* за́дал, задала́, за́дало, за́дали] *v., pfv. of* задава́ть. —**зада́ться,** *refl.* [*past* зада́лся, задала́сь, задало́сь, задали́сь] *pfv. of* задава́ться.

зада́ча *n.* **1,** task. **2,** (arithmetical) problem.

зада́чник *n.* book of arithmetical problems.

задвига́ть *v.impfv.* [*pfv.* задви́нуть] **1,** to push; slide (in, under, *or* behind). **2,** to close; slide shut. **3,** to close off. **4,** to draw (a curtain). **5,** to bolt (a door). —**задвига́ться,** *refl.* **1,** to slide into place. **2,** [*impfv. only*] to be movable; slide.

задви́жка [*gen. pl.* -**жек**] *n.* bolt; catch (*for a door, gate, etc.*).

задвижно́й *adj.* sliding.

задви́нуть *v., pfv. of* задвига́ть. —задви́нуться, *refl., pfv. of* задвига́ться.

задво́рки [*gen.* -**рок**] *n.pl.* area behind a house. —**на задво́рках,** in the background.

задева́ть *v.impfv.* [*pfv.* заде́ть] **1,** to brush against; graze. **2,** *v.i.* (*with* за + *acc.*) to catch (on); snag (on). **3,** to affect. **4,** to touch; affect (*emotionally*). **5,** to arouse; whet (one's curiosity); hurt; wound (one's pride). **6,** *colloq.* to hurt; offend. —**задева́ть за живо́е,** to cut to the quick.

заде́йствовать *v.pfv.* [*infl.* -**ствую, -ствуешь**] **1,** *v.i.* to begin to operate; go into operation. **2,** *v.t.* to activate; put into operation.

заде́л *n., colloq.* **1,** work already completed. **2,** reserve; margin.

заде́лывать *v.impfv.* [*pfv.* заде́лать] to close; seal up; stop up (a hole, crack, breach, etc.).

задёргать *v.pfv.* **1,** (*with instr.*) to tug at; give a tug. **2,** *colloq.* to wear out (a horse) by continually tugging at the reins. **3,** *colloq.* to harass.

задёргивать *v.impfv.* [*pfv.* задёрнуть] **1,** to draw (a curtain). **2,** to cover with a curtain.

задеревене́лый *adj., colloq.* stiff; numb.

задеревене́ть *v.pfv., colloq.* to become numb; become stiff.

задержа́ние *n.* **1,** detention; arrest. **2,** retention (*of moisture, urine, etc.*).

задержа́ть [*infl.* -**держу́, -де́ржишь**] *v., pfv. of* заде́рживать. —задержа́ться, *refl., pfv. of* заде́рживаться.

заде́рживать *v.impfv.* [*pfv.* задержа́ть] **1,** to delay; detain; hold up. **2,** to withhold; hold back. **3,** to arrest; detain. **4,** to retain (moisture). —заде́рживаться, *refl.* **1,** to be delayed. **2,** to linger.

заде́ржка [*gen. pl.* -**жек**] *n.* delay. —**без заде́ржек,** without interruption.

задёрнуть *v., pfv. of* задёргивать.

заде́ть [*infl.* -**де́ну, -де́нешь**] *v., pfv. of* задева́ть.

задира́ *n.m. & f., colloq.* roughneck; bully.

задира́ть *v.impfv.* [*pfv.* задра́ть] *colloq.* **1,** to lift up; stick up (one's head, legs, etc.). **2,** to pull up; lift up (one's shirt, dress, etc.). **3,** to tear (the skin); break (a nail). **4,** [*impfv. only*] to tease; pick on. **5,** *in* задира́ть нос, to turn up one's nose; put on airs. —задира́ться, *refl.* [*impfv. only*] *colloq.* to pick a fight. *See also* задра́ть.

задири́стый *adj., colloq.* **1,** pugnacious. **2,** sprightly.

задненёбный *adj.* velar.

заднепрохо́дный *adj.* anal. —**заднепрохо́дное отве́рстие,** anus.

за́дний *adj.* rear; back; hind. —**без за́дних ног,** unable to move. —**за́дняя мысль,** ulterior motive. —**за́дний план,** background. —**за́дний прохо́д,** anus. —**за́дним умо́м кре́пок,** wise after the event. —**за́дний ход,** backward motion; reverse motion: дать за́дний ход, to go into reverse; back up; *fig.* reverse oneself. —**за́дним число́м, 1,** later; after-

wards. **2,** after the fact; in hindsight; in retrospect. —**поме́тить за́дним число́м,** to backdate; predate.

за́дник *n.* **1,** back (*of a shoe*). **2,** *theat.* backdrop.

задо́брить *v., pfv. of* задабривать.

задо́к [*gen.* задка́] *n.* back (*of a vehicle, piece of furniture, or shoe*).

задо́лго *adv.* [*usu.* задо́лго до] long before.

задолжа́ть *v.pfv., colloq.* **1,** to borrow. **2,** to owe. **3,** to be in debt.

задо́лженность *n.f.* indebtedness; debts.

за́дом *adv.* **1,** backward; backwards. **2,** (*with* к) with one's back to. —**бить за́дом,** (*of a horse*) to kick. —**за́дом наперёд,** *see* наперёд.

задо́р *n.* ardor; zeal; fervor.

задо́ринка *n., in* ни/без сучка́, ни/без задо́ринки, without a hitch.

задо́рный *adj.* **1,** ardent; passionate. **2,** lively; sprightly.

задохну́ться *v.r., pfv. of* задыха́ться.

задра́ивать *v.impfv.* [*pfv.* задра́ить] to batten down.

задрапирова́ть *v., pfv. of* драпирова́ть.

задра́ть *v.pfv.* [*infl. like* драть] **1,** *pfv. of* задира́ть. **2,** to tear to pieces; kill. **3,** to whip; flog.

задрема́ть *v.pfv.* [*infl.* -дремлю́, -дре́млешь] to doze off.

задрожа́ть *v.pfv.* [*infl.* -жу́, -жи́шь] to begin to tremble; begin to shiver.

задува́ть *v.impfv.* [*pfv.* заду́ть] **1,** (*of the wind*) to begin to blow. **2,** [*impfv. only*] (*of the wind*) (*with a prep.*) A, *v.i.* to blow (into, through, etc.). B, *v.t.* to blow (something somewhere). **3,** to blow out (a candle).

заду́мать *v., pfv. of* заду́мывать. —заду́маться, *refl., pfv. of* заду́мываться.

заду́мчивый *adj.* thoughtful; pensive. —**заду́мчивость,** *n.f.* pensiveness; deep thought.

заду́мывать *v.impfv.* [*pfv.* заду́мать] **1,** to plan; conceive. **2,** to decide on; (*with inf.*) decide to. **3,** to think of; choose (*e.g.* a number in a game). —заду́мываться, *refl.* **1,** (*with* над *or* о) to ponder; meditate (over). **2,** to be lost in thought. **3,** to hesitate: не заду́мываясь, without a moment's hesitation.

заду́ть [*infl.* заду́ю, заду́ешь] *v., pfv. of* задува́ть.

задуше́вный *adj.* **1,** sincere; heartfelt. **2,** intimate; innermost.

задуши́ть *v., pfv. of* души́ть.

задыми́ть *v.pfv.* [*infl.* -млю́, -ми́шь] **1,** *v.i.* to begin to emit smoke. **2,** *v.t.* to blacken with smoke.

задымлённый *adj.* smoky; smoke-filled.

задыха́ться *v.r.impfv.* [*pfv.* задохну́ться] **1,** to gasp for breath; pant. **2,** to choke (*with anger, tears, etc.*). **3,** to suffocate.

заеда́ть *v.impfv.* [*pfv.* зае́сть] **1,** to chew to death; nibble to death. **2,** to take away the taste of (something) by eating something else: зае́сть лека́рство са́харом, to take sugar with the medicine. **3,** *fig.* to torment; harass. **4,** *fig.* to corrupt. **5,** *impers.* to stick; jam: Ключ в замке́ зае́ло, the key stuck in the lock.

зае́зд *n.* **1,** visit; call. **2,** horse race.

зае́здить *v.pfv.* [*infl.* -е́зжу, -е́здишь] *colloq.* to overwork; wear out.

заезжа́ть *v.impfv.* [*pfv.* зае́хать] **1,** (*with* в + *acc. or* к) to stop in at; drop in on. **2,** (*with* в *or* на + *acc.*) to drive to; drive into. **3,** (*with* **за** + *instr.*) to pick up; call for. **4,** to approach (from a certain direction).

заéзженный *adj., colloq.* **1,** (*of a horse*) worn out. **2,** *fig.* hackneyed; trite.

заéзжий *adj.* visiting; touring. —*n.* person passing through.

заём [*gen.* за́йма] *n.* loan. —**заёмщик,** *n.* borrower.

заéсть [*infl. like* **есть**] *v., pfv. of* **заеда́ть.**

заéхать [*infl.* заéду, заéдешь] *v., pfv. of* **заезжа́ть.**

зажа́рить *v., pfv. of* **жа́рить.** —**зажа́риться,** *refl., pfv. of* **жа́риться.**

зажа́ть [*infl.* зажму́, зажмёшь] *v., pfv. of* **зажима́ть.**

зажда́ться *v.r.pfv.* [*infl. like* **ждать**] (*with gen.*) *colloq.* to get tired of waiting (for).

зажéчь [*infl. like* **жечь**] *v., pfv. of* **зажига́ть.** —**зажéчься,** *refl., pfv. of* **зажига́ться.**

зажжённый *adj.* lighted.

зажива́ть *v.impfv.* [*pfv.* **зажи́ть**] to heal. —**зажива́ться,** *refl., colloq.* to live too long.

заживля́ть *v.impfv.* [*pfv.* **заживи́ть**] *colloq.* to heal (a wound). —**заживля́ться,** *refl., colloq.* (*of a wound*) to heal.

за́живо *adv., used only with certain verbs,* alive: хорони́ть за́живо, to bury alive: сгорéть за́живо, to be burned alive; be burned to death.

зажига́лка [*gen. pl.* **-лок**] *n.* cigarette lighter.

зажига́ние *n.* **1,** lighting; act of lighting. **2,** *mech.* ignition.

зажига́тельный *adj.* **1,** incendiary. **2,** *fig.* fiery; inflammatory; incendiary.

зажига́ть *v.impfv.* [*pfv.* **зажéчь**] **1,** to light (a lamp *or* match); turn on (a light). **2,** *fig.* to fire up. **3,** *fig.* to kindle; spark; ignite (emotions). —**зажига́ться,** *refl.* **1,** (*of a match*) to light; (*of lights*) go on; (*of stars*) come out. **2,** (*with instr.*) (*of one's eyes*) to light up; blaze (with an emotion). **3,** (*of emotions*) to be aroused.

зажи́м *n.* **1,** clamp. **2,** *electricity* terminal. **3,** *fig.* stifling; suppression.

зажима́ть *v.impfv.* [*pfv.* **зажа́ть**] **1,** to squeeze; clutch; grip. **2,** to stop up; block up; plug up. **3,** to hold (one's nose); cover (one's ears). **4,** to hem in. **5,** *fig., colloq.* to stifle; suppress.

зажи́точный *adj.* prosperous; affluent; well-to-do. —**зажи́точность,** *n.f.* prosperity; affluence.

зажи́ть *v.pfv.* [*infl.* живу́, -живёшь; *past* за́жил, зажила́, за́жило, за́жили] **1,** *pfv. of* **зажива́ть. 2,** to begin to live: зажи́ть споко́йной жи́знью, to begin to live a quiet life. —**зажи́ться,** *refl.* [*past* зажи́лся, -ла́сь, -ло́сь, -ли́сь] *pfv. of* **зажива́ться.**

зажму́рить *v., pfv. of* **жму́рить.** —**зажму́риться,** *refl., pfv. of* **жму́риться.**

зажу́хнуть *v., pfv. of* **жу́хнуть.**

зазва́ть [*infl. like* **звать**] *v., pfv. of* **зазыва́ть.**

зазвони́ть *v.pfv.* to begin to ring.

здра́вный *adj., in* **здра́вный тост,** toast to someone's health.

зазева́ться *v.r.pfv.* (*with* **на** + *acc.*) *colloq.* to stare (at); gape (at).

зазеленéть *v.pfv.* to turn green.

землéние *n., electricity* ground connection.

заземля́ть *v.impfv.* [*pfv.* **заземли́ть**] *electricity* to ground.

зазимова́ть *v.pfv.* [*infl.* **-му́ю, -му́ешь**] to winter; spend the winter.

зазнава́ться *v.r.impfv.* [*pfv.* **зазна́ться**; *pres.* **-знаю́сь, -знаёшься**] *colloq.* to get a swelled head.

зазна́йка [*gen. pl.* **-áек**] *n.m. & f., colloq.* conceited person; person with a swelled head.

зазна́йство *n., colloq.* conceit.

зазна́ться *v.r., pfv. of* **зазнава́ться.**

зазно́ба *n., colloq.* ladylove.

зазо́р *n., mech.* clearance.

зазо́рный *adj., colloq.* shameful.

зазрéние *n., in* **без зазрéния со́вести,** without any pangs of conscience; without compunction.

зазу́бренный *adj.* **1,** jagged; notched. **2,** *bot.* serrate(d). **3,** *colloq.* memorized; rote.

зазу́бривать *v.impfv.* [*pfv.* **зазубри́ть**] **1,** to notch; make notches in. **2,** *colloq.* to learn by rote.

зазу́брина *n.* notch.

зазубри́ть *v., pfv. of* **зубри́ть** *and* **зазу́бривать.**

зазыва́ть *v.impfv.* [*pfv.* **зазва́ть**] *colloq.* to invite repeatedly; urge to come.

заигра́ть *v.pfv.* **1,** *pfv. of* **заи́грывать. 2,** to begin to play.

заи́грывание *n.* flirting; *pl.* advances.

заи́грывать *v.impfv.* [*pfv.* **заигра́ть**] **1,** to wear out (cards, records, etc.) by playing. **2,** to make trite by repetition; play to death. **3,** [*impfv. only*] (*with* **с** + *instr.*) *colloq.* to flirt (with); play up to. —**заи́грываться,** *refl.* to become absorbed in playing.

заи́ка *n.m. & f.* stutterer.

заика́ние *n.* stutter; stuttering.

заика́ться *v.r.impfv.* [*pfv.* **заикну́ться**] **1,** [*impfv. only*] to stammer; stutter. **2,** (*with* **о**) *colloq.* to mention; breathe a word of.

заимода́вец [*gen.* **-вца**] *n., obs.* moneylender.

заи́мствование *n.* borrowing.

заи́мствовать *v.impfv. & pfv.* [*pfv. also* **позаи́мствовать**; *pres.* **-ствую, -ствуешь**] to borrow; adopt; incorporate.

заи́ндеветь *v., pfv. of* **и́ндеветь.**

заинтересо́ванный *adj.* **1,** (*with* **в** + *prepl.*) interested (in). **2,** interested; concerned: заинтересо́ванные сто́роны, the interested parties; the parties concerned.

заинтересова́ть *v.pfv.* [*infl.* **-су́ю, -су́ешь**] to interest; arouse the interest of. —**заинтересова́ться,** *refl.* (*with instr.*) to become interested (in).

заинтригова́ть *v., pfv. of* **интригова́ть.**

заи́скивать *v.impfv.* (*with* **пéред**) to try to ingratiate oneself (with); curry favor (with).

заи́скивающий *adj.* ingratiating.

зайти́ [*infl.* зайду́, зайдёшь; *past* зашёл, зашла́, зашло́, зашли́] *v., pfv. of* **заходи́ть.**

за́йчик *n.* **1,** *dim. of* за́яц. **2,** *colloq.* spot of reflected light.

закабаля́ть *v.impfv.* [*pfv.* **закабали́ть**] to enslave.

закавка́зский *adj.* Transcaucasian.

закавы́ка *n., colloq.* **1,** curlicue. **2,** hitch; snag. **3,** innuendo. *Also,* **закавы́чка.**

закады́чный *adj.*, *in* **закады́чный друг**, *colloq.* bosom friend.

зака́з *n.* order. —**на зака́з**, (made to) order.

заказа́ть [*infl.* **-кажу́, -ка́жешь**] *v.*, *pfv. of* **зака́зывать.**

заказно́й *adj.*, *in* **заказно́е письмо́**, registered letter.

зака́зчик *n.* customer.

зака́зывать *v.impfv.* [*pfv.* **заказа́ть**] to order; place an order for.

зака́л *n.* **1**, tempering; hardening. **2**, toughness. **3**, *fig.* cast; stamp; breed: **челове́к ста́рого зака́ла**, man of the old school.

закалённый *adj.* tempered; hardened. —**закалённый в боя́х**, battle-hardened.

закали́ть *v.*, *pfv. of* **закаля́ть.** —**закали́ться**, *refl.*, *pfv. of* **закаля́ться.**

зака́лка *n.* **1**, tempering; hardening. **2**, *fig.* toughness.

зака́лывать *v.impfv.* [*pfv.* **заколо́ть**] **1**, to stab to death. **2**, to slaughter (an animal). **3**, to fasten with a pin.

закаля́ть *v.impfv.* [*pfv.* **закали́ть**] **1**, to temper; harden. **2**, *fig.* to steel; inure. —**закаля́ться**, *refl.* **1**, to harden; become hard. **2**, *fig.* to be toughened; become inured.

зака́нчивать *v.impfv.* [*pfv.* **зако́нчить**] to finish; end. —**зака́нчиваться**, *refl.* to end; be over.

зака́пать *v.pfv.* **1**, to spot; stain. **2**, to begin to drip.

зака́пывать *v.impfv.* [*pfv.* **закопа́ть**] **1**, to bury. **2**, to fill in (a hole).

зака́рмливать *v.impfv.* [*pfv.* **закорми́ть**] to overfeed; stuff.

зака́т *n.* **1**, sunset. **2**, *fig.* end. —**на зака́те дней**, in the twilight of one's life.

заката́ть *v.*, *pfv. of* **зака́тывать**[1].

закати́ть [*infl.* **-качу́, -ка́тишь**] *v.*, *pfv. of* **зака́тывать**[2]. —**закати́ться**, *refl.*, *pfv. of* **зака́тываться.**

зака́тывать[1] *v.impfv.* [*pfv.* **заката́ть**] **1**, (*with* **в** + *acc.*) to roll (in); roll up (in). **2**, *colloq.* to roll up (one's sleeves).

зака́тывать[2] *v.impfv.* [*pfv.* **закати́ть**] **1**, (*with various prepositions*) to roll; wheel (into, under, behind, etc.). **2**, *colloq.* to cause; create (a scandal); make (a scene). —**закати́ть глаза́**, to roll up one's eyes. —**закати́ть исте́рику**, *colloq.* to go into hysterics.

зака́тываться *v.r.impfv.* [*pfv.* **закати́ться**] **1**, (*with various prepositions*) to roll (into, under, behind, etc.). **2**, (*of the sun*) to set; go down. **3**, *fig.* (*of one's life, an era, etc.*) to come to an end. —**закати́ться сме́хом**, to go into gales of laughter.

закача́ть *v.pfv.* **1**, to rock to sleep. **2**, *impers.* to feel sick; feel nauseous (*from rocking or swaying*): **Меня́ закача́ло**, I feel sick. **3**, to begin to shake.

зака́шлять *v.pfv.* to begin to cough. —**зака́шляться**, *refl.* to have a fit of coughing.

зака́яться *v.r.pfv.* [*infl.* **-ка́юсь, -ка́ешься**] (*with inf.*) *colloq.* to swear off; swear never to do again.

заква́сить [*infl.* **-шу, -сишь**] *v.*, *pfv. of* **заква́шивать.**

заква́ска *n.* **1**, leaven; ferment. **2**, *fig.* mold: **одно́й заква́ски**, of the same mold. **3**, *fig.* stuff: **У него́ хоро́шая заква́ска**, he is made of good stuff.

заква́шивать *v.impfv.* [*pfv.* **заква́сить**] to leaven; ferment.

заки́дывать[1] *v.impfv.* [*pfv.* **закида́ть**] = **забра́сывать**[1]. —**ша́пками закида́ем**, *colloq.* we'll win easily; we've got it won.

заки́дывать[2] *v.impfv.* [*pfv.* **заки́нуть**] = **забра́сывать**[2]. —**заки́нуть но́гу на́ ногу**, to cross one's legs. —**заки́нуть слове́чко за** (+ *acc.*), to put in a word for. —**заки́нуть у́дочку**, to drop a hint; put out a feeler.

закипа́ть *v.impfv.* [*pfv.* **закипе́ть**] **1**, to begin to boil; simmer. **2**, *fig.* (*with instr.*) to be seething (with). **3**, *fig.* to become agitated; become wrought up. **4**, *fig.* to get rolling; move into high gear.

закиса́ть *v.impfv.* [*pfv.* **заки́снуть**] **1**, to turn sour. **2**, *fig.*, *colloq.* to become apathetic; become listless.

заки́снуть [*past* **заки́с, заки́сла**] *v.*, *pfv. of* **закиса́ть.**

за́кись *n.f.* protoxide. ♦*In compounds* -ous oxide: **за́кись желе́за**, ferrous oxide.

закла́д *n.*, *obs.* **1**, pawning: **в закла́де**, in hock. **2**, bet; wager. —**би́ться** *or* **поби́ться об закла́д**, to bet; wager.

закла́дка [*gen. pl.* **-док**] *n.* **1**, laying. **2**, bookmark.

закладна́я *n.*, *decl. as an adj.* mortgage.

закла́дывать *v.impfv.* [*pfv.* **заложи́ть**] **1**, to put; place (*usually deep into something*). **2**, (*with* **за** + *acc.*) to put behind; place behind. **3**, to lay (mines, a foundation, etc.). **4**, to mark (a place in a book). **5**, to pawn; mortgage. **6**, to harness. **7**, (*with instr.*) to load (with); pile (with). **8**, to stop up; block. *See also* **заложи́ть.**

закла́ние *n.*, *obs.* slaughter.

заклева́ть [*infl.* **-клюю́, -клюёшь**] *v.*, *pfv. of* **заклёвывать.**

заклёвывать *v.impfv.* [*pfv.* **заклева́ть**] **1**, to peck to death. **2**, *fig.*, *colloq.* to nag; harass.

закле́ивать *v.impfv.* [*pfv.* **закле́ить**] **1**, to seal up; to seal (an envelope). —**закле́иваться**, *refl.* to stick: **Конве́рт не закле́ивается**, the envelope doesn't stick.

заклейми́ть *v.*, *pfv. of* **клейми́ть.**

заклепа́ть *v.*, *pfv. of* **заклёпывать.**

заклёпка [*gen. pl.* **-пок**] *n.* rivet.

заклёпывать *v.impfv.* [*pfv.* **заклепа́ть**] to rivet.

заклина́ние *n.* **1**, incantation. **2**, entreaty.

заклина́тель *n.m.* conjurer. —**заклина́тель змей**, snake charmer.

заклина́ть *v.impfv.* **1**, to bewitch; cast a spell over. **2**, to entreat; implore.

закли́нивать *v.impfv.* [*pfv.* **заклини́ть**] **1**, to wedge. **2**, to jam (a device, machine, etc.). **3**, *impers.* to jam; become jammed: **Дверь заклини́ло**, the door jammed. —**закли́ниваться**, *refl.* **1**, to become wedged. **2**, to jam; become jammed.

заключа́ть *v.impfv.* [*pfv.* **заключи́ть**] **1**, to conclude; close; end. **2**, to conclude (a deal, peace, etc.); sign (a treaty, agreement, etc.); make (a bet); form (an alliance). **3**, to enclose: **заключи́ть в ско́бки**, to enclose in brackets. **4**, [*impfv. only*] (*often with* **в себе́**) to contain. **5**, to conclude; infer; gather. **6**, to imprison; confine; incarcerate. —**заключа́ться**, *refl.* [*impfv. only*] **1**, to conclude; close; end. **2**, (*of an agreement*) to be concluded; be signed. **3**, to be enclosed. **4**, (*with* **в** + *prepl.*) to be; consist of; lie in.

заключéние *n.* **1,** conclusion: прийти́ к заключéнию, to come to/ arrive at/ a conclusion. **2,** conclusion; end. **3,** signing (*of a treaty, agreement, etc.*). **4,** imprisonment; confinement. —**в заключéние,** in conclusion; in closing.

заключённый *n., decl. as an adj.* prisoner.

заключи́тельный *adj.* concluding; closing; final.

заключи́ть *v., pfv. of* заключáть.

закля́тие *n., obs.* **1,** incantation. **2,** oath; pledge.

закля́тый *adj.* (*of an enemy*) sworn: закля́тый враг, sworn enemy; archenemy.

закова́ть [*infl.* закую́, закуёшь] *v., pfv. of* закóвывать.

закóвывать *v.impfv.* [*pfv.* закова́ть] to chain; shackle. Закова́ть когó-нибудь в цéпи, to put someone in chains.

заковы́ристый *adj., colloq.* **1,** complex; involved. **2,** intricate; elaborate; fancy.

закоди́ровать *v., pfv. of* коди́ровать.

заколáчивать *v.impfv.* [*pfv.* заколоти́ть] *colloq.* **1,** to board up; seal up. **2,** to hammer in; drive in. **3,** to beat up; beat the life out of.

заколдóванный *adj.* charmed; bewitched; enchanted. —**заколдóванный круг,** vicious circle.

заколдова́ть [*infl.* -ду́ю, -ду́ешь] *v., pfv. of* заколдóвывать.

заколдóвывать *v.impfv.* [*pfv.* заколдова́ть] **1,** to cast a spell over. **2,** *fig.* to bewitch; charm.

закóлка [*gen. pl.* -лок] *n., colloq.* **1,** bobby pin. **2,** tiepin.

заколоти́ть *v.pfv.* [*infl.* -лочу́, -лóтишь] **1,** *pfv. of* заколáчивать. **2,** to begin to knock.

заколóть [*infl.* -колю́, -кóлешь] *v., pfv. of* колóть (*in sense #5*) *and* закáлывать.

закóн *n.* law. —**объяви́ть вне закóна,** to outlaw.

закóнник *n., colloq.* **1,** expert in law. **2,** one who strictly observes the law.

закóнно *adv.* legally.

законнорождённый *adj.* (*of a child*) legitimate.

закóнность *n.f.* legality; legitimacy.

закóнный *adj.* **1,** legal; lawful; legitimate. **2,** legitimate; justifiable. **3,** rightful.

законовéд *n.* specialist in law; jurist. —**законовéдение,** *n.* jurisprudence.

законода́тель *n.m.* **1,** legislator; lawmaker. **2,** arbiter: законода́тель мод, arbiter of fashion.

законода́тельный *adj.* legislative. —**законода́тельство,** *n.* legislation.

закономéрно *adv.* naturally.

закономéрность *n.f.* regularity; pattern; law.

закономéрный *adj.* natural; logical.

законопáтить *v., pfv. of* конопáтить.

законоположéние *n.* statute.

законопослу́шный *adj.* law-abiding.

законопроéкт *n.* (legislative) bill.

законсерви́ровать *v., pfv. of* консерви́ровать.

законтрактова́ть *v., pfv. of* контрактова́ть.

закóнченность *n.f.* completeness.

закóнченный *adj.* **1,** complete; finished. **2,** (*of an artist, musician, etc.*) finished; accomplished; consummate.

закóнчить *v., pfv. of* закáнчивать. —**закóнчиться,** *refl., pfv. of* закáнчиваться.

закопа́ть *v., pfv. of* закáпывать.

закоптéлый *adj.* sooty.

закоптéть *v.pfv., colloq.* to become covered with soot.

закопти́ть *v., pfv. of* копти́ть (*in sense #1*). —**закопти́ться,** *refl.* to become covered with soot.

закопчённый *adj.* sooty; covered with soot.

закоренéлый *adj.* **1,** chronic; ingrained; deep-rooted. **2,** inveterate; hardened; confirmed.

закоренéть *v.pfv.* **1,** to become ingrained. **2,** (*with* в + *prepl.*) to become steeped in (prejudice, sin, etc.).

закóрки *n.pl., colloq., in* на закóрки; на закóрках, on one's back; on one's shoulders; piggyback.

закорми́ть [*infl.* -кормлю́, -кóрмишь] *v., pfv. of* закáрмливать.

закорю́чка [*gen. pl.* -чек] *n., colloq.* **1,** hook; curlicue; squiggle. **2,** trick; ploy. **3,** hitch; snag.

закоснéлый *adj.* **1,** inveterate; confirmed. **2,** ingrained; deep-seated.

закоснéть *v., pfv. of* коснéть.

закостенéлый *adj.* numb; stiff.

закостенéть *v.pfv.* to become numb; become stiff.

закоу́лок [*gen.* -лка] *n.* **1,** back street. **2,** nook: все закоу́лки, every nook and cranny.

закоченéлый *adj.* frozen stiff; numb.

закоченéть *v., pfv. of* коченéть.

закра́дываться *v.r.impfv.* [*pfv.* закра́сться] (*of feelings, doubts, etc.*) to creep in.

закра́сить [*infl.* -шу, -сишь] *v., pfv. of* закра́шивать.

закра́сться [*infl. like* кра́сться] *v.r., pfv. of* закра́дываться.

закра́шивать *v.impfv.* [*pfv.* закра́сить] to paint over; cover over.

закрепи́тель *n.m., photog.* fixing agent.

закрепи́ть [*infl.* -плю́, -пи́шь] *v., pfv. of* закрепля́ть. —**закрепи́ться,** *refl., pfv. of* закрепля́ться.

закреплéние *n.* **1,** fastening; securing. **2,** consolidation. **3,** *photog.* fixing.

закрепля́ть *v.impfv.* [*pfv.* закрепи́ть] **1,** to fasten; secure. **2,** to consolidate. **3,** (*with* за + *instr.*) to assign (to); set aside (for). Закрепи́ть за собóй (+ *acc.*), to get; obtain; secure for oneself. **4,** *photog.* to fix. —**закрепля́ться,** *refl.* **1,** to hold firm. **2,** *mil.* to dig in. **3,** *fig.* to become firm; become deeply rooted.

закрепоща́ть *v.impfv.* [*pfv.* закрепости́ть] to enslave.

закрепощéние *n.* enslavement.

закрича́ть *v.pfv.* [*infl.* -чу́, -чи́шь] to cry out; shout; scream; yell.

закрóйщик *n.* cutter (*of cloth*).

за́кром [*pl.* закрома́] *n.* (grain) bin.

закруглéние *n.* **1,** rounding; curving. **2,** curve.

закругля́ть *v.impfv.* [*pfv.* закругли́ть] to round off.

закружи́ть *v.pfv.* [*infl.* -кружу́, -кру́жишь *or* -кружи́шь] **1,** to begin to twirl/swirl/whirl; set spinning. **2,** to make dizzy. —**закружи́ться,** *refl.* **1,** to begin to whirl/swirl. **2,** to be dizzy; be in a whirl.

закрути́ть [*infl.* -кручу́, -кру́тишь] *v., pfv. of* крути́ть (*in sense #1*) *and* закру́чивать. —**закрути́ться,** *refl., pfv. of* закру́чиваться.

закру́чивать *v.impfv.* [*pfv.* **закрути́ть**] **1**, to twist. **2**, to twirl (one's mustache). **3**, (*with* **на** + *acc.*) to wind (around *or* onto). —**закру́чиваться**, *refl.* to become twisted.

закрыва́ть *v.impfv.* [*pfv.* **закры́ть**] **1**, to close; shut. **2**, to lock. **3**, to cover. **4**, to block. **5**, to turn off; shut off (water, gas, etc.). **6**, to close down. **7**, to adjourn (a meeting). —**закрыва́ться**, *refl.* **1**, to close; shut; be closed; be shut. **2**, to lock: Чемода́н закрыва́ется на ключ, the suitcase locks with a key. **3**, to cover oneself. **4**, (*of a meeting*) to adjourn.

закры́лок [*gen.* **-лка**] *n.* flap (*of an airplane wing*).

закры́тие *n.* **1**, closing; shutting. **2**, close; end.

закры́тый *adj.* closed. —**в закры́том помеще́нии**, indoors. —**закры́тый бассе́йи**, indoor pool. —**закры́тое голосова́ние**, secret ballot. —**закры́тое мо́ре**, inland sea. —**закры́тое пла́тье**, high-necked dress.

закры́ть [*infl.* **-кро́ю, -кро́ешь**] *v., pfv. of* **закрыва́ть**. —**закры́ться**, *refl., pfv. of* **закрыва́ться**.

закули́сный *adj.* occurring behind the scenes; backstage; offstage.

закупа́ть *v.impfv.* [*pfv.* **закупи́ть**] to buy up.

закупи́ть [*infl.* **-куплю́, -ку́пишь**] *v., pfv. of* **закупа́ть**.

заку́пка *n.* purchase.

заку́поривать *v.impfv.* [*pfv.* **заку́порить**] **1**, to plug up; stop up; cork. **2**, to block; obstruct.

заку́порка *n.* **1**, plugging up; stopping up. **2**, *med.* embolism; thrombosis; occlusion.

заку́почный *adj.* purchase (*attrib.*); purchasing.

заку́пщик *n.* (wholesale) buyer.

заку́ривать *v.impfv.* [*pfv.* **закури́ть**] **1**, *v.t.* to light (a cigarette, cigar, etc.). **2**, *v.i.* to light up; light a cigarette.

закури́ть [*infl.* **-курю́, -ку́ришь**] **1**, *pfv. of* **заку́ривать**. **2**, to begin to smoke; take up smoking.

закуси́ть [*infl.* **-кушу́, -ку́сишь**] *v., pfv. of* **заку́сывать**.

заку́ска [*gen. pl.* **-сок**] *n.* **1**, snack; bite. **2**, hors d'oeuvre; appetizer.

заку́сочная *n., decl. as an adj.* snack bar.

заку́сывать *v.impfv.* [*pfv.* **закуси́ть**] **1**, to have a snack; have a bite to eat. **2**, (*with instr.*) to have (with); eat *or* drink (with): закуси́ть во́дку селёдкой, to have some vodka with one's herring. **3**, to bite. —**закуси́ть губу́** *or* **гу́бы**, to bite one's lip. —**закуси́ть язы́к**, to hold one's tongue. —**закуси́ть удила́**, to take the bit in one's teeth.

заку́тать *v., pfv. of* **ку́тать** *and* **заку́тывать**. —**заку́таться**, *refl., pfv. of* **ку́таться** *and* **заку́тываться**.

заку́тывать *v.impfv.* [*pfv.* **заку́тать**] **1**, to bundle (someone) up; dress (someone) warmly. **2**, (*with instr. or* **в** + *acc.*) to wrap (in); bundle (in). —**заку́тываться**, *refl.* (*with instr. or* **в** + *acc.*) to wrap/bundle oneself (in).

зал *n.* hall. —**а́ктовый зал**, assembly hall; (school) auditorium. —**гимнасти́ческий зал**, gymnasium. —**зал ожида́ния**, waiting room. —**зал (заседа́ний) суда́**, courtroom. —**зри́тельный зал**, auditorium. —**по́лный зал**, full house; packed house. —**спорти́вный зал**, gymnasium. —**чита́льный зал**, reading room.

за́ла *n., obs.* = зал.

зала́дить *v.pfv.* [*infl.* **-жу, -дишь**] *colloq.* **1**, to keep re-

peating. **2**, (*with inf.*) to take to (doing something). —**зала́дить одно́ и то же**, to harp on the same string.

зала́мывать *v.impfv.* [*pfv.* **заломи́ть**] **1**, to break (*by bending*). **2**, *colloq.* to charge (an exorbitant price). —**зала́мывать ру́ки**, to bend one's arms (back *or* behind one's back). —**зала́мывать ша́пку**, to cock one's hat.

залата́ть *v., pfv. of* **лата́ть**.

зала́ять *v.pfv.* [*infl.* **-ла́ю, -ла́ешь**] to begin to bark.

залега́ть *v.impfv.* [*pfv.* **зале́чь**] **1**, to lie down (*for a long rest*). **2**, to lie low. **3**, to lie; be located (*in a low place*). **4**, *fig.* to become ingrained.

заледене́лый *adj.* **1**, covered with ice; icy. **2**, frozen; icy.

заледене́ть *v., pfv. of* **ледене́ть**.

залежа́лый *adj., colloq.* **1**, lying unused *or* unsold; shopworn. **2**, stale.

залёживаться *v.r.impfv.* [*pfv.* **залежа́ться**] **1**, to lie around (unused *or* unsold). **2**, to become stale.

за́лежный *adj.* (*of land*) long fallow.

за́лежь *n.f.* **1**, (mineral) deposit. **2**, *pl.* accumulation. **3**, fallow land. **4**, *colloq.* unsold or unsalable merchandise.

залеза́ть *v.impfv.* [*pfv.* **зале́зть**] **1**, (*with various prepositions*) to climb (into, onto, under, etc.). **2**, (*with* **в** + *acc.*) *colloq.* to get into. —**зале́зть в долги́**, to get into debt. —**зале́зть в ду́шу**, *see* **влезть в ду́шу**. —**зале́зть в карма́н** (+ *dat.*), to pick someone's pocket; rob.

зале́зть [*infl. like* **лезть**] *v., pfv. of* **залеза́ть**.

залени́ться *v.r.pfv.* [*infl.* **-леню́сь, -ле́нишься**] *colloq.* to become lazy.

залепи́ть [*infl.* **-леплю́, -ле́пишь**] *v., pfv. of* **залепля́ть**.

залепля́ть *v.impfv.* [*pfv.* **залепи́ть**] **1**, to seal up. **2**, to cover; plaster.

залета́ть *v.impfv.* [*pfv.* **залете́ть**] **1**, (*with* **в** + *acc.*) to fly into. **2**, (*with* **в** + *acc.*) to stop briefly (in); land briefly (in). **3**, (*with* **за** + *acc.*) to fly over; fly beyond.

залете́ть [*infl.* **-чу́, -ти́шь**] *v., pfv. of* **залета́ть**.

залётный *adj.* stray: залётная пу́ля, stray bullet. —**залётная пти́ца**, migratory bird.

зале́чивать *v.impfv.* [*pfv.* **залечи́ть**] **1**, to heal (a wound, sore, etc.). **2**, *colloq.* to doctor (someone) to death. —**зале́чиваться**, *refl.* (*of a wound*) to heal.

залечи́ть [*infl.* **-лечу́, -ле́чишь**] *v., pfv. of* **зале́чивать**. —**залечи́ться**, *refl., pfv. of* **зале́чиваться**.

зале́чь [*infl. like* **лечь**] *v., pfv. of* **залега́ть**.

зали́в *n.* bay; gulf.

залива́ть *v.impfv.* [*pfv.* **зали́ть**] **1**, (*of water, a river, etc.*) to flood. **2**, to stain (*by spilling something*): зали́ть ска́терть вино́м, to spill wine on the tablecloth. **3**, to douse (a fire). **4**, (*with instr.*) to cover (with); pave (with). **5**, *colloq.* to pour in; put in (gas, oil, etc.). **6**, *fig.* (*with instr.*) to suffuse (in); bathe (in): зали́тый со́лнцем, bathed in sunlight. —**залива́ться**, *refl.* **1**, (*with instr.*) to be filled; be covered (with a liquid). **2**, *fig.* (*with instr.*) to burst into; break into (tears, laughter, song, etc.). **3**, (*with* **в** + *acc.*) (*of liquids*) to run into; get into.

заливно́е *n., decl. as an adj.* aspic.

заливно́й *adj.* **1**, flood (*attrib.*): заливны́е по́ймы, flood plains. **2**, jellied: заливна́я осетри́на, jellied sturgeon.

зализа́ть [*infl.* -лижу́, -ли́жешь] *v., pfv. of* **зали́зывать**.

зали́зывать *v.impfv.* [*pfv.* **зализа́ть**] **1,** to lick (a wound). **2,** *colloq.* to slick down (one's hair).

зали́ть [*infl.* залью́, зальёшь; *past* за́лил *or* зали́л, залила́, за́лило *or* зали́ло, за́лили *or* зали́ли] *v., pfv. of* **залива́ть**. —**зали́ться,** *refl.* [*past* зали́лся, залила́сь, зали́лось *or* залило́сь, зали́лись *or* залили́сь] *pfv. of* **залива́ться**.

залихва́тский *adj., colloq.* rollicking; devil-may-care.

зало́г *n.* **1,** pawning: отдава́ть в зало́г, to pawn. **2,** deposit; security: Оста́вить что́-нибудь в зало́г, to leave something as security. **3,** bail: отпуска́ть под зало́г, to release on bail. **4,** (*with gen.*) token (of). **5,** (*with gen.*) guarantee (of); key (to). **6,** *gram.* voice.

зало́говый *adj.* pawn (*attrib.*); mortgage (*attrib.*): зало́говая квита́нция, pawn ticket.

залогода́тель *n.m.* one who pawns or mortgages something.

залогодержа́тель *n.m.* pawnbroker.

заложи́ть *v.pfv.* [*infl.* -ложу́, -ло́жишь] **1,** *pfv. of* **закла́дывать**. **2,** *colloq.* to mislay. **3,** *impers.* (*with dat.*) *colloq., indicating a stuffy or heavy feeling:* Мне заложи́ло нос, my nose is stuffed up; мне заложи́ло грудь, I feel a heaviness in my chest.

зало́жник *n.* hostage.

заломи́ть [*infl.* -ломлю́, -ло́мишь] *v., pfv. of* **зала́мывать**.

залп *n.* volley; salvo.

за́лпом *adv.* **1,** in one volley. **2,** *colloq.* without stopping; without pausing for breath; (*with verbs of drinking*) in one gulp; (*with verbs of reading*) in one stretch.

залуча́ть *v.impfv.* [*pfv.* **залучи́ть**] *colloq.* to entice; lure.

залюбова́ться *v.r.pfv.* [*infl.* -бу́юсь, -бу́ешься] (*with instr.*) to gaze with admiration (at); be lost in contemplation (of).

заля́пывать *v.impfv.* [*pfv.* **заля́пать**] *colloq.* to splash; spatter.

зама́зать [*infl.* -ма́жу, -ма́жешь] *v., pfv. of* **зама́зывать**.

зама́зка *n.* putty.

зама́зывать *v.impfv.* [*pfv.* **зама́зать**] **1,** to paint over. **2,** *fig., colloq.* to cover up; conceal. **3,** to seal up; putty. **4,** to smear; soil; dirty.

зама́лчивать *v.impfv.* [*pfv.* **замолча́ть**] *colloq.* to keep (something) quiet; keep quiet about; hush up.

зама́нивание *n.* enticing; enticement.

зама́нивать *v.impfv.* [*pfv.* **замани́ть**] to entice; lure.

замани́ть [*infl.* -маню́, -ма́нишь] *v., pfv. of* **зама́нивать**.

зама́нчивый *adj.* tempting; enticing; alluring.

замара́ть *v., pfv. of* **мара́ть** (*in sense #1*). —**замара́ться,** *refl., pfv. of* **мара́ться**.

замара́шка [*gen. pl.* -шек] *n., colloq.* slob.

замаринова́ть *v., pfv. of* **маринова́ть**.

замаскиро́ванный *adj.* **1,** masked. **2,** disguised; camouflaged.

замаскирова́ть *v., pfv. of* **маскирова́ть**. —**замаскирова́ться,** *refl., pfv. of* **маскирова́ться**.

зама́сливать *v.impfv.* [*pfv.* **зама́слить**] **1,** to spill oil or grease on. **2,** to treat with oil. **3,** *fig., colloq.* to butter up. —**зама́сливаться,** *refl.* to become soiled with oil *or* grease.

зама́тывать *v.impfv.* [*pfv.* **замота́ть**] *colloq.* **1,** to wind around *or* onto. **2,** (*with instr.*) to wrap (in *or* with). **3,** to wear out; tire out. —**зама́тываться,** *refl., colloq.* **1,** (*with вокру́г*) to be wound around. **2,** (*with instr.*) to wrap oneself (in). **3,** to be worn out.

замаха́ть *v.pfv.* [*infl.* -машу́, -ма́шешь] (*with instr.*) to begin to wave. Замаха́ть на кого́-нибудь рука́ми, to wave one's hands at someone (*to signal disagreement or disapproval*); wave away.

зама́хиваться *v.r.impfv.* [*pfv.* **замахну́ться**] **1,** (*with instr. and* на + *acc.*) to threaten (with); brandish; wave: замахну́ться ножо́м на кого́-нибудь, to threaten someone with a knife. **2,** (*with* на + *acc.*) to decide upon; embark upon. **3,** (*with* на + *acc.*) to make a grab for.

зама́чивать *v.impfv.* [*pfv.* **замочи́ть**] **1,** to get (something) wet. **2,** to soak.

зама́шка [*gen. pl.* -шек] *n., colloq.* **1,** habit; custom. **2,** *pl.* ways; manner: аристократи́ческие зама́шки, aristocratic manner. Дикта́торские зама́шки, dictatorial tendencies.

зама́щивать *v.impfv.* [*pfv.* **замости́ть**] to pave.

замедле́ние *n.* **1,** slowing down; deceleration. **2,** *obs.* delay.

заме́дленный *adj.* **1,** slow; slowed; slowed-down. **2,** slow-motion. —**заме́дленного де́йствия,** delayed-action (*attrib.*): бо́мба заме́дленного де́йствия, time bomb.

замедля́ть *v.impfv.* [*pfv.* **заме́длить**] **1,** to slow down. **2,** to delay. **3,** (*with inf. or* с + *instr.*) to be slow (in); be long (in). —**замедля́ться,** *refl.* to slow down; become slower.

заме́на *n.* **1,** substitution; replacement. **2,** substitute.

замени́мый *adj.* replaceable.

замени́тель *n.m.* substitute: замени́тель ко́жи, leather substitute.

замени́ть [*infl.* заменю́, заме́нишь] *v., pfv. of* **заменя́ть**.

заменя́ть *v.impfv.* [*pfv.* **замени́ть**] **1,** (*with instr. or* на + *acc.*) to replace (with). **2,** to replace; take the place of; substitute for.

замере́ть [*infl.* замру́, замрёшь; *past* за́мер, замерла́, за́мерло, за́мерли] *v., pfv. of* **замира́ть**.

замерза́ние *n.* freezing.

замерза́ть *v.impfv.* [*pfv.* **замёрзнуть**] **1,** to freeze; become frozen. **2,** (*of a person*) to be freezing (cold); be frozen. **3,** to freeze to death; perish from the frost.

замёрзнуть [*past* замёрз, замёрзла] *v., pfv. of* **мёрзнуть** *and* **замерза́ть**.

за́мертво *adv.* unconscious; in a dead faint.

замеси́ть [*infl.* -мешу́, -ме́сишь] *v., pfv. of* **заме́шивать** (*in sense #2*).

замести́ [*infl. like* мести́] *v., pfv. of* **замета́ть**[1].

замести́тель *n.m.* **1,** substitute; replacement. **2,** deputy: замести́тель дире́ктора, deputy director.

замести́ть [*infl.* -щу́, -сти́шь] *v., pfv. of* **замеща́ть**.

заметáть¹ *v.impfv.* [*pfv.* **заместú**] **1**, (*with* в + *acc.*) to sweep; sweep into. **2**, (*of snow*) to cover. *Also impers.:* Дорóгу замелó снéгом, the road is covered/blocked with snow. —**заметáть следы́**, to cover up one's tracks; cover up the traces.

заметáть² *v., pfv. of* **замётывать**.

заметáться *v.r.pfv.* [*infl.* -мечу́сь, -мéчешься] **1**, to begin rushing about. **2**, to begin tossing about (*in bed*). **3**, to become confused; become flustered.

замéтить [*infl.* -чу, -тишь] *v., pfv. of* **замечáть**.

замéтка [*gen. pl.* -ток] *n.* **1**, mark. **2**, note: путевы́е замéтки, travel notes. **3**, notice; item (*in a newspaper*). —**брать на замéтку**, to take/make note of.

замéтно *adv.* noticeably; visibly: Он замéтно постарéл, he has aged visibly. —*adj., used predicatively,* noticeable: Это едвá замéтно, it is hardly noticeable.

замéтный *adj.* noticeable; visible; appreciable; marked.

замётывать *v.impfv.* [*pfv.* **заметáть**] to baste.

замечáние *n.* **1**, remark; observation; comment. **2**, reprimand; rebuke.

замечáтельно *adv.* **1**, remarkably. **2**, marvelously. —*adj., used predicatively,* wonderful; marvelous: Это замечáтельно, that's wonderful.

замечáтельный *adj.* remarkable; wonderful; marvelous.

замечáть *v.impfv.* [*pfv.* **замéтить**] **1**, to notice. **2**, to note; make note of. **3**, to remark; comment; observe.

замечтáться *v.r.pfv.* to fall to thinking; lapse into daydreaming.

замешáтельство *n.* confusion; embarrassment.

замешáть *v., pfv. of* **замéшивать** (*in sense #1*). —**замешáться**, *refl., pfv. of* **замéшиваться**.

замéшивать *v.impfv.* **1**, [*pfv.* **замешáть**] (*with* в + *acc.*) to mix up (in); implicate (in). **2**, [*pfv.* **замесú ть**] to knead. —**замéшиваться**, *refl.* [*pfv.* **замешáться**] **1**, to get lost: замешáться в толпé/толпу́, to get lost in a crowd. **2**, (*with* в + *acc.*) to get mixed up (in); become implicated (in).

замéшкаться *v.r.pfv., colloq.* to tarry; linger.

замещáть *v.impfv.* [*pfv.* **заместú ть**] **1**, to replace. **2**, to fill (a position). **3**, [*impfv. only*] to substitute for; fill in for.

замещéние *n.* **1**, substitution; replacement. **2**, filling (*of a position*).

замини́ровать *v., pfv. of* **мини́ровать**.

зами́нка [*gen. pl.* -нок] *n., colloq.* **1**, hitch; delay. **2**, hesitation (*in speech*).

замирáние *n.* dying down. —**с замирáнием сéрдца**, with a sinking heart; with one's heart in one's mouth.

замирáть *v.impfv.* [*pfv.* **замерéть**] **1**, to freeze; stand motionless. **2**, *fig.* to come to a standstill. **3**, (*of a sound*) to die down. **4**, (*of one's heart*) to sink. **5**, [*impfv. only*] (*of one's voice*) to falter.

зáмкнутый *adj.* **1**, withdrawn; tight-lipped; close-mouthed. **2**, exclusive. **3**, secluded. **4**, *electricity* closed: зáмкнутая цепь, closed circuit.

замкну́ть *v., pfv. of* **замыкáть**. —**замкну́ться**, *refl., pfv. of* **замыкáться**.

замоги́льный *adj.* **1**, *obs.* occurring after death. **2**, *colloq.* (*of a voice*) sepulchral.

зáмок [*gen.* зáмка] *n.* castle.

замóк [*gen.* замкá] *n.* lock. —**за семью́ замкáми**, **1**, guarded day and night. **2**, a deep dark secret. —**под замкóм**, under lock and key.

замóлвить *v.pfv.* [*infl.* -влю, -вишь] *colloq., in* **замóлвить слóво** (*or* **словéчко**) **за** (+ *acc.*), to put in a word for.

замолкáть *v.impfv.* [*pfv.* **замóлкнуть**] **1**, to fall silent. **2**, (*of noise, sounds, conversation, etc.*) to die away; stop; cease.

замóлкнуть [*past* замóлк, замóлкла] *v., pfv. of* **замолкáть**.

замолчáть *v.pfv.* [*infl.* -чу́, -чи́шь] **1**, to stop talking; fall silent. **2**, *pfv. of* **замáлчивать**.

заморáживание *n.* freezing.

заморáживать *v.impfv.* [*pfv.* **заморóзить**] to freeze.

замори́ть *v.pfv., colloq.* **1**, *pfv. of* **мори́ть** (*in sense #2*). **2**, *v.t.* to starve. **3**, to assuage (one's hunger, appetite, etc.). —**замори́ть червякá**, *colloq.* to have a bite to eat.

заморóженный *adj.* **1**, frozen. **2**, icy; iced-up. **3**, *fig.* (*of a person, one's face, etc.*) cold; icy.

заморóзить [*infl.* -жу, -зишь] *v., pfv. of* **заморáживать**.

зáморозки [*gen.* -ков] *n.pl.* light frost (*in spring or autumn*).

замóрский *adj., obs.* foreign; from overseas.

замóрыш *n., colloq.* puny creature; starveling.

замости́ть [*infl.* -щу́, -сти́шь] *v., pfv. of* **замáщивать**.

замотáть *v.pfv.* **1**, *pfv. of* **замáтывать**. **2**, (*with instr.*) to shake (one's head); wag (one's tail). —**замотáться**, *refl., pfv. of* **замáтываться**.

замочи́ть [*infl.* -мочу́, -мóчишь] *v., pfv. of* **мочи́ть** *and* **замáчивать**.

замóчный *adj.* of a lock. —**замóчная сквáжина**, keyhole.

замполи́т *n.* deputy chief for political indoctrination; political officer (*contr. of* **замести́тель команди́ра по полити́ческой чáсти**).

зáмуж *adv.* **1**, *in* **выходи́ть зáмуж за** (+ *acc.*), (*of a woman*) to marry; get married (to). **2**, *in* **выдавáть** (+ *acc.*) **зáмуж за** (+ *acc.*), to marry off (a daughter) to.

зáмужем *adv.* (*with* за + *instr.*) (*of a woman*) married (to).

замýжество *n.* marriage (*of a woman*).

замýжняя *adj.* (*of a woman*) married.

замуровáть [*infl.* -рý ю, -рý ешь] *v., pfv. of* **замурóвывать**.

замурóвывать *v.impfv.* [*pfv.* **замуровáть**] to wall up.

замусóливать *v.impfv.* [*pfv.* **замусóлить**] *colloq.* to soil.

замýсорить *v.pfv.* to litter; leave trash all over.

замути́ть *v., pfv. of* **мути́ть** (*in sense #1*). —**замути́ться**, *refl., pfv. of* **мути́ться** (*in sense #1*).

замýчить *v.pfv.* **1**, to torture to death. **2**, to torment; rack; wear out. —**замýчиться**, *refl.* to be exhausted.

зáмша *n.* suede; chamois. —**зáмшевый**, *adj.* suede.

замшéлый *adj.* moss-grown.

замывáть *v.impfv.* [*pfv.* **замы́ть**] to wash out; wash away.

замы́зганный *adj., colloq.* **1**, worn out; tattered. **2**, dilapidated; run-down. **3**, dirty; filthy.

замыка́ние *n.* locking; closing. —**коро́ткое замыка́ние,** short circuit.

замыка́ть *v.impfv.* [*pfv.* **замкну́ть**] **1,** *obs.* to lock. **2,** to close. **3,** to ring; surround. **4,** [*impfv. only*] *in* **замыка́ть ше́ствие,** to bring up the rear. —**замыка́ться,** *refl.* **1,** *obs.* to lock; be locked. **2,** *obs.* (*with* в + *prepl.*) to lock oneself in. **3,** to close. **4,** (*with* в + *acc. or prepl.*) to withdraw (into): замыка́ться в себе́, to withdraw into oneself.

за́мысел [*gen.* **-сла**] *n.* **1,** design; intention. **2,** idea; conception.

замы́слить *v., pfv. of* **замышля́ть.**

замылова́тый *adj.* **1,** intricate; ingenious. **2,** abstruse; recondite. **3,** elaborate; fancy.

замы́ть [*infl.* **замо́ю, замо́ешь**] *v., pfv. of* **замыва́ть.**

замышля́ть *v.impfv.* [*pfv.* **замы́слить**] to plan; plot.

замя́ть *v.pfv.* [*infl.* **замну́, замнёшь**] *colloq.* **1,** to crush. **2,** to hush up; suppress. —**замя́ться,** *refl., colloq.* **1,** to become flustered. **2,** to stumble (*in speech*).

за́навес *n.* curtain. —**под за́навес,** *colloq.* toward the end.

занаве́сить [*infl.* **-шу, -сишь**] *v., pfv. of* **занаве́шивать.**

занаве́ска [*gen. pl.* **-сок**] *n.* (window) curtain.

занаве́шивать *v.impfv.* [*pfv.* **занаве́сить**] to curtain.

зана́шивать *v.impfv.* [*pfv.* **заноси́ть**] to wear too long; wear without changing.

занемо́чь *v.pfv.* [*infl. like* **мочь**] *obs.* to be taken ill.

занесе́ние *n.* entering; recording.

занести́ [*infl. like* **нести́**] *v., pfv. of* **заноси́ть**[1]. —**занести́сь,** *refl., pfv. of* **заноси́ться.**

занижа́ть *v.impfv.* [*pfv.* **зани́зить**] to understate (figures).

занима́тельный *adj.* entertaining; diverting.

занима́ть *v.impfv.* [*pfv.* **заня́ть**] **1,** to occupy (a room, apartment, etc.); take up (space, room, etc.). **2,** to take; take up (time). **3,** to occupy; hold (a post or position). **4,** to engage (someone's attention). **5,** to entertain; keep amused. **6,** to employ; engage. **7,** *mil.* to occupy. **8,** to borrow.

занима́ться *v.r.impfv.* [*pfv.* **заня́ться**] **1,** (*with instr.*) to be occupied (with); be engaged (in); be busy (doing something). **2,** (*with instr.*) to go in for; take up. **3,** (*with instr.*) to take care of; attend to; see to. **4,** [*impfv. only*] to study: Он меша́ет мне занима́ться, he is preventing me from studying. **5,** [*impfv. only*] (*with instr.*) to study (a certain subject). **6,** [*impfv. only*] (*with* с + *instr.*) to give special instruction to. **7,** to catch fire.

за́ново *adv.* all over again; anew.

зано́за *n.* splinter.

зано́зистый *adj., colloq.* **1,** rough; jagged. **2,** *fig.* abrasive.

занози́ть *v.pfv.* [*infl.* **-жу́, -зи́шь**] (*usu. with* **себе́**) to get a splinter in: занози́ть себе́ па́лец, to get a splinter in one's finger.

зано́с *n.* drift: сне́жный зано́с, snowdrift.

заноси́ть[1] *v.impfv.* [*pfv.* **занести́**; *pres.* **-ношу́, -но́сишь**] **1,** to bring; carry. **2,** to drop off; deliver (*on one's way*). **3,** (*with* в + *acc.*) to enter (on a list, in the minutes, etc.). **4,** to raise (*in order to strike with or put somewhere*). **5,** *impers.* to become covered with; be

blocked by: Доро́гу занесло́ сне́гом, the road is covered with/ blocked by/ snow. Нас занесло́ сне́гом, we were snowed in; we were snowbound. **6,** *impers.* to skid: Маши́ну занесло́, the car skidded. —**заноси́ться,** *refl., colloq.* **1,** to get carried away. **2,** to get a swelled head.

заноси́ть[2] [*infl.* **-ношу́, -но́сишь**] *v., pfv. of* **зана́шивать.**

зано́счивый *adj.* arrogant. —**зано́счивость,** *n.f.* arrogance.

заночева́ть *v.pfv.* [*infl.* **-чу́ю -чу́ешь**] to spend the night.

зано́шенный *adj.* worn; threadbare.

зану́дный *adj., colloq.* irksome; pestiferous. *Also,* **зану́дливый.**

занумерова́ть *v., pfv. of* **нумерова́ть.**

заня́тие *n.* **1,** occupation (*act of occupying*). **2,** occupation; work. **3,** (*with instr.*) study (of); pursuit (of); engaging (in). **4,** *pl.* studies; classes; lessons. **5,** pastime.

заня́тный *adj., colloq.* amusing; entertaining.

занято́й *adj.* busy.

за́нятость *n.f.* **1,** being busy; pressure of work. **2,** *econ.* employment: по́лная за́нятость, full employment.

за́нятый *adj.* [*short form* **за́нят, занята́, за́нято, за́няты**] **1,** busy. **2,** occupied. Это ме́сто за́нято?, is this seat taken?

заня́ть [*infl.* **займу́, займёшь**; *past* **за́нял, заняла́, за́няло, за́няли**] *v., pfv. of* **занима́ть.** —**заня́ться,** *refl.* [*past* **заня́лся, заняла́сь, заняло́сь, заняли́сь**] *pfv. of* **занима́ться.**

заодно́ *adv.* **1,** jointly; together; in concert. **2,** *colloq.* at the same time. —**быть заодно́ с,** to be in agreement with; be at one with.

заокеа́нский *adj.* located across the ocean; transoceanic.

заострённый *adj.* sharp; pointed.

заостря́ть *v.impfv.* [*pfv.* **заостри́ть**] **1,** to sharpen. **2,** *fig.* to emphasize; point up. **3,** *fig.* to make more pointed. **4,** *in* заостря́ть внима́ние, to focus attention. —**заостря́ться,** *refl.* **1,** to come to a point; taper off. **2,** *fig.* to become more acute.

зао́чник *n.* student taking correspondence courses.

зао́чно *adv.* **1,** in absentia: суди́ться зао́чно, to be tried in absentia. **2,** by correspondence.

зао́чный *adj.* **1,** in absentia. **2,** by correspondence: зао́чные ку́рсы, correspondence courses.

за́пад *n.* **1,** west. **2,** *cap.* the West.

запада́ть *v.impfv.* [*pfv.* **запа́сть**] **1,** to become hollow; become sunken. **2,** (*of piano keys*) to stick. **3,** (*with* в + *acc.*) *colloq.* to fall into. **4,** *fig.* (*with* в + *acc.*) to be etched in (one's memory): Карти́на запа́ла мне в ду́шу, the picture is etched in my memory.

за́падный *adj.* **1,** western; Western; West. **2,** westerly.

западня́ [*gen. pl.* **-не́й**] *n.* trap.

запа́здывание *n.* **1,** tardiness; lateness. **2,** time lag.

запа́здывать *v.impfv.* [*pfv.* **запозда́ть**] to be late.

запа́ивать *v.impfv.* [*pfv.* **запая́ть**] to solder.

запа́йка *n.* soldering.

запакова́ть [*infl.* **-ку́ю, -ку́ешь**] *v., pfv. of* **запако́вывать.**

запако́вывать *v.impfv.* [*pfv.* **запакова́ть**] to pack; pack up.

запа́л *n.* **1,** primer; fuse. **2,** *colloq.* ardor. **3,** heaves (*disease of horses*).

запали́ть *v.pfv.*, *colloq.* to set fire to.

запа́льный *adj.*, *in* **запа́льная свеча́**, spark plug.

запа́льчивый *adj.* hot-tempered; quick-tempered; explosive. —**запа́льчивость**, *n.f.* quick temper.

запанибра́та *adv.*, *colloq.* as equals; on equal terms.

запа́ривать *v.impfv.* [*pfv.* **запа́рить**] to steam.

запарши́веть *v.*, *pfv. of* **парши́веть**.

запа́рывать *v.impfv.* [*pfv.* **запоро́ть**] **1,** to whip to death; flog to death. **2,** *colloq.* to spoil; mess up.

запа́с *n.* **1,** supply; stock; reserve; stockpile. Запа́с зна́ний, fund of knowledge. Запа́с слов, stock of words; vocabulary. Запа́с про́чности, margin of safety. **2,** *mil.* reserve. **3,** *colloq.* hem. —**про запа́с**, as a reserve; in case of need. Держа́ть *or* оставля́ть про запа́с, to hold/keep in reserve.

запаса́ть *v.impfv.* [*pfv.* **запасти́**] to store up. —**запаса́ться**, *refl.* (*with instr.*) **1,** to stock up on. **2,** *in* запаса́ться терпéнием, to steel oneself.

запа́сливый *adj.* provident.

запа́сник *n.* **1,** *mil.*, *colloq.* reservist. **2,** storeroom (*of a museum*).

запасно́й *adj.* spare; reserve. —**запасно́й игро́к**, *sports* reserve; utility player. —*n.*, *mil.* reservist.

запа́сный *adj.* = **запасно́й**. —**запа́сный вы́ход**, emergency exit. —**запа́сный путь**, sidetrack; siding.

запасти́ [*infl. like* **пасти́**] *v.*, *pfv. of* **запаса́ть**. —**запасти́сь**, *refl.*, *pfv. of* **запаса́ться**.

запа́сть [*infl. like* **пасть**] *v.*, *pfv. of* **запада́ть**.

за́пах *n.* smell; odor.

запаха́ть [*infl.* **-пашу́, -па́шешь**] *v.*, *pfv. of* **запа́хивать** (*in sense #1*).

запа́хивать *v.impfv.* **1,** [*pfv.* **запаха́ть**] to plow. **2,** [*pfv.* **запахну́ть**] to wrap around oneself. —**запа́хиваться**, *refl.* [*pfv.* **запахну́ться**] (*with в + acc.*) to wrap oneself tighter (in).

запа́хнуть *v.pfv.* [*past* **запа́х, запа́хла**] to begin to smell.

запахну́ть *v.*, *pfv. of* **запа́хивать** (*in sense #2*). —**запахну́ться**, *refl.*, *pfv. of* **запа́хиваться**.

запа́чкать *v.*, *pfv. of* **па́чкать**. —**запа́чкаться**, *refl.*, *pfv. of* **па́чкаться**.

запашо́к [*gen.* **-шка́**] *n.*, *colloq.* faint smell; faint odor.

запая́ть *v.*, *pfv. of* **запа́ивать**.

запева́ла *n.m. & f.* **1,** leading singer in a choir. **2,** *fig.* guiding spirit.

запева́ть *v.impfv.* to be the first to sing; lead the singing.

запека́нка *n.* **1,** baked pudding. **2,** spiced brandy.

запека́ть *v.impfv.* [*pfv.* **запе́чь**] to bake. —**запека́ться**, *refl.* **1,** to bake; be baked. **2,** to clot; coagulate. **3,** (*of lips*) to become parched.

запелена́ть *v.*, *pfv. of* **пелена́ть**.

запе́ниться *v.r.pfv.* to begin to foam.

запере́ть [*infl.* **запру́, запрёшь**; *past* **за́пер, заперла́, за́перло, за́перли**] *v.*, *pfv. of* **запира́ть**. —**запере́ться**, *refl.* [*past* **заперся́** *or* **за́перся, заперла́сь,**

заперло́сь *or* **за́перлось, заперли́сь** *or* **за́перлись**] *pfv. of* **запира́ться**.

запе́ть *v.pfv.* [*infl.* **запою́, запоёшь**] to begin to sing; break (*or* burst) into song. —**запе́ть друго́е**; **запе́ть на друго́й лад**, to change one's tune; sing a different tune.

запеча́тать *v.*, *pfv. of* **запеча́тывать**.

запечатлева́ть *v.impfv.* [*pfv.* **запечатлéть**] **1,** to set down; record; capture (*in writing, painting, on film, etc.*). **2,** to etch (*in one's memory*). **3,** to mark; commemorate. —**запечатлева́ться**, *refl.* to be etched (in one's memory).

запеча́тывать *v.impfv.* [*pfv.* **запеча́тать**] to seal.

запе́чь [*infl. like* **печь**] *v.*, *pfv. of* **запека́ть**. —**запе́чься**, *refl.*, *pfv. of* **запека́ться**.

запива́ть *v.impfv.* [*pfv.* **запи́ть**] **1,** (*with instr.*) to wash down (with). **2,** *colloq.* to go on a drinking spree.

запина́ться *v.r.impfv.* [*pfv.* **запну́ться**] **1,** (*with за или о + acc.*) to stumble (on). **2,** to stumble (*in speech*).

запи́нка *n.* stumbling (*in speech*): без запи́нки, without stumbling once.

запира́тельство *n.* refusal to confess one's guilt.

запира́ть *v.impfv.* [*pfv.* **запере́ть**] **1,** to lock (a door, room, etc.). **2,** to lock; lock up; lock in (someone *or* something). **3,** to block. —**запира́ться**, *refl.* **1,** to lock oneself in. **2,** (*of a door, lock, etc.*) to lock. **3,** [*impfv. only*] *colloq.* to refuse to admit one's guilt.

записа́ть [*infl.* **-пишу́, -пи́шешь**] *v.*, *pfv. of* **записы́вать**. —**записа́ться**, *refl.*, *pfv. of* **запи́сываться**.

запи́ска [*gen. pl.* **-сок**] *n.* **1,** note; short letter: оставля́ть запи́ску, to leave a note. **2,** memorandum. **3,** *pl.* notes.

записно́й *adj.* **1,** intended for notes: записна́я кни́жка, notebook; address book. **2,** *colloq.* a true; real; out-and-out.

запи́сывание *n.* writing down; recording.

запи́сывать *v.impfv.* [*pfv.* **записа́ть**] **1,** to write down; record. **2,** to take notes of. **3,** (*with в + acc.*) to enter (in); enroll (in). **4,** (*with на + acc.*) to record (on film, tape, a phonograph record, etc.). —**запи́сываться**, *refl.* **1,** (*with в or на + acc.*) to sign up for; enroll in; join. **2,** (*with к*) to make an appointment (with).

за́пись *n.f.* **1,** writing down; recording. **2,** registration. **3,** entry; notation. **4,** recording (*on a record, tape, etc.*). **5,** *pl.* notes.

запи́ть *v.pfv.* [*infl. like* **пить**] **1,** [*past* **за́пил, запила́, за́пило, запи́ли**] *pfv. of* **запива́ть** (*in sense #1*). **2,** [*past* **запи́л, запила́, запи́ло, запи́ли**] *pfv. of* **запива́ть** (*in sense #2*).

запи́хивать *v.impfv.* [*pfv.* **запиха́ть** *or* **запихну́ть**] (*with в + acc.*) *colloq.* to stuff (into); cram (into).

запла́канный *adj.* full of tears; tear-stained.

запла́кать *v.pfv.* [*infl.* **-пла́чу, -пла́чешь**] to begin to cry.

заплани́ровать *v.*, *pfv. of* **плани́ровать** (*in sense #1*).

запла́та *n.* patch.

заплати́ть *v.*, *pfv. of* **плати́ть**.

заплева́ть [*infl.* **-плюю́, -плюёшь**] *v.*, *pfv. of* **заплёвывать**.

заплёвывать *v.impfv.* [*pfv.* **заплева́ть**] to spit on.

заплéсневелый *adj.* moldy; mildewed.

заплéсневеть *v., pfv. of* **плéсневеть**.

заплестú [*infl. like* **плестú**] *v., pfv. of* **заплета́ть**.

заплета́ть *v.impfv.* [*pfv* **заплестú**] to braid; plait. —**заплета́ться,** *refl.* [*impfv. only*] **1,** (*of one's legs*) to wobble. **2,** (*with* **язы́к**): У него́ язы́к заплета́ется, his speech is slurred.

заплéчный *adj.* worn over the shoulder: заплéчный мешо́к, knapsack. —**ма́стер заплéчных дел,** *obs.* executioner.

запломбирова́ть *v., pfv. of* **пломбирова́ть**.

заплута́ться *v.r.pfv., colloq.* to lose one's way.

заплы́в *n., swimming* heat; lap.

заплыва́ть *v.impfv.* [*pfv.* **заплы́ть**] **1,** to swim (*to a distant point*). **2,** (*with* **в** + *acc.*) to swim into; (*of a ship*) sail into; steam into. **3,** to be swollen; be bloated.

заплы́ть [*infl. like* **плыть**] *v., pfv. of* **заплыва́ть**.

запну́ться *v.r., pfv. of* **запина́ться**.

заповéдник *n.* reserve; preserve.

заповéдный *adj.* **1,** closed; off-limits. **2,** secret. **3,** cherished.

за́поведь *n.f.* **1,** *relig.* commandment. **2,** precept. —**за́поведи блажéнства,** the Beatitudes.

заподо́зрить *v.pfv.* (*with* **в** + *prepl.*) to (begin to) suspect (of).

запоéм *adv., colloq.* avidly; nonstop: чита́ть запоéм, to read avidly; пить запоéм, to drink like a fish.

запозда́лый *adj.* belated; tardy.

запозда́ние *n.* lateness; tardiness.

запозда́ть *v., pfv. of* **запа́здывать**.

запо́й *n.* **1,** addiction to alcohol. **2,** drinking bout.

заполза́ть *v.impfv.* [*pfv.* **заползти́**] (*with various prepositions*) to crawl (into, under, behind, etc.).

заползти́ [*infl. like* **ползти́**] *v., pfv. of* **заполза́ть**.

заполня́ть *v.impfv.* [*pfv.* **запо́лнить**] **1,** to fill. **2,** to fill out (a form); fill in (a blank space).

заполучи́ть *v.pfv.* [*infl.* -лучу́, -лу́чишь] *colloq.* **1,** to obtain; get. **2,** to catch (an illness).

запомина́ть *v.impfv.* [*pfv.* **запо́мнить**] **1,** to remember; make it a point to remember. **2,** to memorize. —**запомина́ться,** *refl.* (*with dat.*) to remain in one's memory.

за́понка [*gen. pl.* -**нок**] *n.* cuff link; stud.

запо́р *n.* **1,** lock; bolt. **2,** constipation.

запоро́ть [*infl.* -**порю́**, -**по́решь**] *v., pfv. of* **запа́рывать**.

запороши́ть *v.pfv.* (*of snow, dust, etc.*) to cover lightly.

запотева́ть *v.impfv.* [*pfv.* **запотéть**] to become misty; steam up.

запотéлый *adj.* steamed up; misted up.

запотéть *v., pfv. of* **потéть** (*in sense #2*) *and* **запотева́ть**.

запра́вила *n.m., colloq.* **1,** boss; bigwig. **2,** ringleader; instigator.

запра́вить [*infl.* -**влю**, -**вишь**] *v., pfv. of* **заправля́ть**. —**запра́виться,** *refl., pfv. of* **заправля́ться**.

запра́вка *n.* **1,** seasoning. **2,** refueling.

заправля́ть *v.impfv.* [*pfv.* **запра́вить**] **1,** to tuck in; tuck under. **2,** (*with instr.*) to season (with). **3,** to put fuel in; put gas in. **4,** to load (film). **5,** [*impfv. only*] (*with instr.*) *colloq.* to boss; run. —**заправля́ться,**

refl. **1,** to buy gas(oline): Мне на́до запра́виться, I have to get some gas. **2,** (*with instr.*) to take on (fuel, food, water, etc.). Заправля́ться горю́чим, to refuel.

запра́вочный *adj.* (re)fueling (*attrib.*): запра́вочная ста́нция, filling station.

запра́вский *adj., colloq.* real; true; regular.

запра́шивать *v.impfv.* [*pfv.* **запроси́ть**] **1,** (*with* **о**) to inquire (about). **2,** to charge (a high price).

запрéт *n.* prohibition; ban. —**под запрéтом,** prohibited; banned.

запрети́тельный *adj.* prohibitive.

запрети́ть [*infl.* -**щу́**, -**ти́шь**] *v., pfv. of* **запреща́ть**.

запрéтный *adj.* forbidden. —**запрéтная зо́на,** forbidden zone; restricted area.

запреща́ть *v.impfv.* [*pfv.* **запрети́ть**] **1,** (*with dat.*) to forbid (someone to do something). **2,** to forbid; prohibit; ban; outlaw. **3,** to suppress (a publication). —**запреща́ться,** *refl.* [*impfv. only*] to be forbidden; be prohibited.

запрещéние *n.* prohibition; banning; ban.

заприхо́довать *v., pfv. of* **прихо́довать**.

запрограмми́ровать *v., pfv. of* **программи́ровать**.

запроки́дывать *v.impfv.* [*pfv.* **запроки́нуть**] *colloq.* to throw back (one's head).

запропасти́ться *v.r.pfv.* [*infl.* -**щу́сь**, -**сти́шься**] *colloq.* to disappear.

запро́с *n.* **1,** inquiry. **2,** demand. **3,** *pl.* needs; requirements. **4,** *pl.* aspirations; pretensions. **5,** *colloq.* overcharging.

запроси́ть [*infl.* -**прошу́**, -**про́сишь**] *v., pfv. of* **запра́шивать**.

за́просто *adv., colloq.* without ceremony; on an informal basis.

запру́да *n.* **1,** weir; dam. **2,** pond; reservoir (*formed by dammed-up water*).

запруди́ть [*infl.* -**пружу́**, -**пру́дишь** *or* -**пруди́шь**] *v., pfv. of* **пруди́ть** *and* **запру́живать**.

запру́живать *v.impfv.* [*pfv.* **запруди́ть**] **1,** to dam up. **2,** to jam; pack; throng.

запряга́ть *v.impfv.* [*pfv.* **запря́чь**] (*with* **в** + *acc.*) to harness (to); hitch up (to). —**запряга́ться,** *refl.* (*with* **в** + *acc.*) *colloq.* to get down to; buckle down to (work).

запря́жка *n.* **1,** harnessing. **2,** team of horses in harness.

запря́тать [*infl.* -**пря́чу**, -**пря́чешь**] *v., pfv. of* **запря́тывать**.

запря́тывать *v.impfv.* [*pfv.* **запря́тать**] *colloq.* to hide away; secrete.

запря́чь [*infl.* -**прягу́**, -**пряжёшь**, ...-**прягу́т**; *past* -**пря́г**, -**прягла́**, -**прягло́**, -**прягли́**] *v., pfv. of* **запряга́ть**. —**запря́чься,** *refl., pfv. of* **запряга́ться**.

запу́гивание *n.* intimidation.

запу́гивать *v.impfv.* [*pfv.* **запуга́ть**] to intimidate; cow; browbeat.

за́пуск *n.* **1,** starting. **2,** launching; launch.

запуска́ть *v.impfv.* [*pfv.* **запусти́ть**] **1,** to launch; send up (a rocket, satellite, balloon, etc.); fly (a kite). **2,** (*usu. with instr.*) *colloq.* to throw; hurl: запусти́ть ка́мнем в кого́-нибудь, to throw a stone at someone. **3,** to start; start up (a machine, motor, etc.). **4,** (*with* **в**

+ *acc.*) *colloq.* to thrust (into); plunge (into). **5,** to neglect.

запустёлый *adj., obs.* neglected; deserted; abandoned.

запустёние *n.* **1,** desolation. **2,** (state of) neglect.

запустить [*infl.* -пущу́, -пу́стишь] *v., pfv. of* запуска́ть.

запу́танность *n.f.* confusion.

запу́танный *adj.* **1,** tangled. **2,** *fig.* intricate; involved: запу́танный вопро́с, knotty problem.

запу́тать *v., pfv. of* пу́тать (*in senses #1 & #5*) *and* запу́тывать. —запу́таться, *refl., pfv. of* пу́таться (*in senses #1 & #2*) *and* запу́тываться.

запу́тывать *v.impfv.* [*pfv.* запу́тать] **1,** to tangle. **2,** to muddle; complicate. **3,** *colloq.* to confuse; mix up. **4,** (*with* в + *acc.*) *colloq.* to involve (in); embroil (in). —запу́тываться, *refl.* **1,** to become (en)tangled. **2,** *colloq.* to become confused; get mixed up.

запуши́ть *v.pfv.* (*of snow, frost, etc.*) to cover lightly.

запу́щенный *adj.* **1,** neglected; run-down. **2,** (*of an illness*) not treated in time. —запу́щенность, *n.f.* neglect.

запыла́ть *v.pfv.* to flare up; burst into flame.

запылённый *adj.* covered with dust.

запыли́ть *v.pfv.* to cover with dust. —запыли́ться, *refl., pfv. of* пыли́ться.

запыха́ться *v.r.impfv. & pfv., colloq.* to be out of breath; pant.

запя́стье *n.* **1,** wrist. **2,** *obs.* bracelet.

запята́я *n., decl. as an adj.* comma. —то́чка с запято́й, semicolon.

запятна́ть *v., pfv. of* пятна́ть.

зараба́тывать *v.impfv.* [*pfv.* зарабо́тать] to earn. Хорошо́ зараба́тывать, to earn good money. Зараба́тывать на жизнь, to earn a living; earn one's livelihood. —зараба́тываться, *refl., colloq.* to overwork.

зарабо́тать *v.pfv.* **1,** *pfv. of* зараба́тывать. **2,** to start working. —зарабо́таться, *refl., pfv. of* зараба́тываться.

за́работный *adj., in* за́работная пла́та, wages; pay; salary.

за́работок [*gen.* -тка] *n.* earnings; wages; pay.

зара́внивать *v.impfv.* [*pfv.* заровня́ть] to fill; even up (a hole).

заража́ть *v.impfv.* [*pfv.* зарази́ть] **1,** to infect. **2,** to contaminate; pollute. **3,** *fig.* (*with instr.*) to infect (with); inspire (with). —заража́ться, *refl.* (*with instr.*) to become infected (with); catch.

зараже́ние *n.* infection. —зараже́ние кро́ви, blood poisoning.

зара́з *adv., colloq.* all at once; at one sitting; in one fell swoop.

зара́за *n.* infection.

зарази́тельный *adj.* infectious; contagious.

зарази́ть [*infl.* -жу́, -зи́шь] *v., pfv. of* заража́ть. —зарази́ться, *refl., pfv. of* заража́ться.

зара́зный *adj.* infectious; contagious; communicable.

зара́нее *adv.* beforehand; in advance.

зарапортова́ться *v.r.pfv.* [*infl.* -ту́юсь, -ту́ешься] *colloq.* to talk too much; run off at the mouth.

зараста́ть *v.impfv.* [*pfv.* зарасти́] **1,** (*with instr.*) to be overgrown (with). **2,** *colloq.* (*of a wound*) to heal.

зарасти́ [*infl. like* расти́] *v., pfv. of* зараста́ть.

зарва́ться [*infl. like* рва́ться] *v.r., pfv. of* зарыва́ться (*in sense #2*).

зарде́ться *v.r.pfv.* to flush with color; blush.

за́рево *n.* glow.

зарегистри́ровать *v., pfv. of* регистри́ровать. —зарегистри́роваться, *refl., pfv. of* регистри́роваться.

заре́з *n., in* до заре́зу, urgently; desperately.

заре́зать *v., pfv. of* ре́зать (*in sense #5*). —заре́заться, *refl., colloq.* to cut one's throat.

зарезерви́ровать *v., pfv. of* резерви́ровать.

зарека́ться *v.r.impfv.* [*pfv.* заре́чься] (*with inf.*) to swear off.

зарекомендова́ть *v.pfv.* [*infl.* -ду́ю, -ду́ешь] (*with* себя́ *and instr. or* как) to prove to be. —хорошо́ себя́ зарекомендова́ть, to make a good showing; give a good account of oneself.

заре́чный *adj.* located on the other side of the river.

заре́чье *n.* area on the other side of a river.

заре́чься [*infl. like* отре́чься] *v.r., pfv. of* зарека́ться.

заржа́веть *v., pfv. of* ржа́веть.

заржа́вленный *adj.* rusty.

зарисова́ть [*infl.* -су́ю, -су́ешь] *v., pfv. of* зарисо́вывать.

зарисо́вка [*gen. pl.* -вок] *n.* **1,** sketching. **2,** sketch.

зарисо́вывать *v.impfv.* [*pfv.* зарисова́ть] to sketch.

за́риться *v.r.impfv.* [*pfv.* поза́риться] (*with* на + *acc.*) *colloq.* to covet.

зарни́ца *n.* summer lightning; heat lightning.

заровня́ть *v., pfv. of* зара́внивать.

зароди́ть [*infl.* -жу́, -ди́шь] *v., pfv. of* зарожда́ть. —зароди́ться, *refl., pfv. of* зарожда́ться.

заро́дыш *n.* embryo; fetus. —в заро́дыше, in its initial stages. —подавля́ть в заро́дыше, to nip in the bud.

заро́дышевый *adj.* embryonic.

зарожда́ть *v.impfv.* [*pfv.* зароди́ть] to generate; engender. —зарожда́ться, *refl.* to arise; originate; come into being.

зарожде́ние *n.* **1,** generation; engendering. **2,** *fig.* origin.

заро́к *n.* pledge; vow; resolution.

зарони́ть *v.pfv.* [*infl.* -роню́, -ро́нишь] **1,** *colloq.* to drop. **2,** *fig.* to arouse; inspire (feelings, thoughts, etc.).

за́росль *n.f., usu. pl.* undergrowth; brushwood.

зарпла́та *n.* wages; pay; salary (*contr. of* за́работная пла́та).

заруба́ть *v.impfv.* [*pfv.* заруби́ть] **1,** to slash to death; hack to death. **2,** to notch; make a notch in. —заруби́те себе́ на носу́, remember for the next time; don't you dare forget.

зарубе́жный *adj.* foreign.

зарубе́жье *n.* foreign countries. —бли́жнее зарубе́жье, neighboring countries (*esp. former Soviet republics*).

заруби́ть [*infl.* -рублю́, -ру́бишь] *v., pfv. of* заруба́ть.

зару́бка [*gen. pl.* -бок] *n.* notch.

зарубцева́ться *v.r., pfv. of* рубцева́ться.

зарумя́нить *v., pfv. of* **румя́нить** (*in sense #2*). **—зарумя́ниться**, *refl., pfv. of* **румя́ниться** (*in sense #2*).

заручи́ться *v.r.pfv.* (*with instr.*) to enlist; secure; obtain (one's support, services, etc.).

зару́чка *n., colloq.* influence; pull.

зарыва́ть *v.impfv.* [*pfv.* **зары́ть**] to bury. **—зарыва́ться**, *refl.* **1**, [*pfv.* **зары́ться**] to bury oneself. Зары́ться голово́й в поду́шку, to bury one's head in a pillow. **2**, [*pfv.* **зарва́ться**] *colloq.* to go too far; go to extremes; overdo things.

зары́ть [*infl.* **заро́ю, заро́ешь**] *v., pfv. of* **зарыва́ть**. **—зары́ться**, *refl., pfv. of* **зарыва́ться** (*in sense #1*).

заря́ *n.* **1**, glow on the horizon before sunrise or after sunset. **2**, (*often with* **у́тренняя**) dawn; daybreak: на заре́, at dawn. **3**, (*often with* **вече́рняя**) dusk; nightfall. **4**, *fig.* dawn; beginning. **5**, [*acc.* **зо́рю**] *mil.* reveille; taps. **—ни свет ни заря́**, before dawn; at the crack of dawn. **—от зари́ до зари́**, **1**, from dawn to dusk. **2**, from night to morn.

заря́д *n.* **1**, (powder) charge. **2**, *electricity* charge. **3**, cartridge. **4**, warhead. **5**, *fig.* (*with gen.*) fund; supply; store.

заряди́ть *v.pfv.* [*infl.* **-ряжу́, -ряди́шь** *or* **-ря́дишь**] **1**, *pfv. of* **заряжа́ть**. **2**, *colloq.* to keep repeating. **3**, *colloq.* (*of rain*) to keep coming down.

заря́дка *n.* **1**, loading (*of a gun*); charging (*of a battery*). **2**, exercise(s); calisthenics.

заря́дный *adj.* charging (*attrrib.*): заря́дный агрега́т, battery charger. **—заря́дный я́щик**, caisson; ammunition wagon.

заряжа́ние *n.* loading (*of a gun or camera*); charging (*of a battery*).

заряжа́ть *v.impfv.* [*pfv.* **заряди́ть**] to load (a gun, camera, etc.); charge (a battery).

заря́женный *also,* **заряжённый** *adj.* **1**, (*of a gun*) loaded. **2**, charged: заря́женные части́цы, charged particles.

заря́нка [*gen. pl.* **-нок**] *n.* robin.

заса́да *n.* ambush.

засади́ть [*infl.* **-сажу́, -са́дишь**] *v., pfv. of* **заса́живать**.

заса́живать *v.impfv.* [*pfv.* **засади́ть**] **1**, to plant: заса́живать сад цвета́ми, to plant a garden with flowers. **2**, *colloq.* to confine; keep confined (at home, in/to prison, etc.). **3**, (*with за + acc.*) *colloq.* to sit (someone) down (to): заса́живать кого́-нибудь за кни́гу, to sit someone down to a book. **4**, (*with в + acc.*) *colloq.* to stick; thrust; plunge (something into something). **—заса́живаться**, *refl.* [*impfv. only*] (*with за + acc.*) *colloq.* to sit down (to).

заса́ливать *v.impfv.* **1**, [*pfv.* **заса́лить**] to soil; get grease on. **2**, [*pfv.* **засоли́ть**] to salt; pickle. **—заса́ливаться**, *refl.* [*pfv.* **заса́литься**] to be soiled from grease.

заса́сывать *v.impfv.* [*pfv.* **засоса́ть**] to suck in; swallow up.

заса́харенный *adj.* candied.

засвети́ть *v.pfv..* [*infl.* **-свечу́, -све́тишь**] **1**, to light (a candle, lamp, etc.). **2**, *photog.* to spoil (a roll of film) by exposing it to light. **—засвети́ться**, *refl.* **1**, to (begin to) shine; sparkle. **2**, (*of one's eyes*) to light up. **3**, (*of film*) to be spoiled by exposure to light.

за́светло *adv.* before dark.

засвиде́тельствовать *v.pfv.* [*infl.* **-ствую, -ствуешь**] **1**, to attest (to). **2**, to certify; notarize. **—засвиде́тельствовать почте́ние** (+ *dat.*), *obs.* to pay one's respects to.

засе́в *n.* **1**, sowing. **2**, sown area.

засева́ть *v.impfv.* [*pfv.* **засе́ять**] to sow (a field).

заседа́ние *n.* session; meeting.

заседа́тель *n.m.* **1**, *in* наро́дный заседа́тель, people's representative (*one of two who, together with a judge, preside over a trial*). **2**, *in* прися́жный заседа́тель, juror (*in Western countries*).

заседа́ть *v.impfv.* to be in session; meet.

засе́ивать *v.impfv.* = **засева́ть**.

засе́ка *n.* barricade of felled trees.

засека́ть *v.impfv.* [*pfv.* **засе́чь**] **1**, to notch. **2**, to locate; plot (*on a map*). **3**, *colloq.* to spot; detect; discover. **4**, to whip brutally; flog to death. *See also* **засе́чь**.

засекре́тить [*infl.* **-чу, -тишь**] *v., pfv. of* **засекре́чивать**.

засекре́ченный *adj.* **1**, secret. **2**, (*of documents*) classified.

засекре́чивать *v.impfv.* [*pfv.* **засекре́тить**] **1**, to classify (as secret). **2**, *colloq.* to give (someone) access to classified documents; clear.

заселе́ние *n.* **1**, occupancy (*of a building*). **2**, settlement (*of an area*).

заселя́ть *v.impfv.* [*pfv.* **засели́ть**] **1**, to put tenants in (a building). **2**, to settle (an area).

засе́сть *v.pfv.* [*infl.* **зася́ду, зася́дешь**; *past* **засе́л, засе́ла**] *colloq.* **1**, (*with за + acc.*) to sit down (to); settle down (to): засе́сть за рабо́ту, to sit down to work. **2**, to ensconce oneself. **3**, (*with в + prepl.*) (*of a bullet*) to lodge (in).

засе́чка [*gen. pl.* **-чек**] *n.* notch.

засе́чь *v.pfv.* [*infl. like* **сечь**] **1**, [*past* **засе́к, -секла́, -секло́, -секли́**] *pfv. of* **засека́ть** (*in senses #1-3*). **2**, [*past* **засе́к, -се́кла, -се́кло, -се́кли**] *pfv. of* **засека́ть** (*in sense #4*). **—засе́чь вре́мя** [*past fem.* **-секла́**], to note the time.

засе́ять [*infl.* **засе́ю, засе́ешь**] *v., pfv. of* **засева́ть** *and* **засе́ивать**.

засиди́ться [*infl.* **-жу́сь, -ди́шься**] *v.r., pfv. of* **заси́живаться**.

заси́живаться *v.r.impfv.* [*pfv.* **засиде́ться**] *colloq.* **1**, to sit a long time; sit up late. **2**, *fig.* to remain for a long time.

заси́лье *n.* domination; dominance.

засия́ть *v.pfv.* **1**, to begin to shine. **2**, (*of something bright*) to appear.

заска́кивать *v.impfv.* [*pfv.* **заскочи́ть**] *colloq.* **1**, (*with various prepositions*) to jump (onto, behind, etc.). **2**, (*with в + acc.*) to get into; break into. **3**, (*with в + acc.*) to drop in at; drop in on.

заско́к *n., colloq.* quirk; idiosyncrasy.

заскору́злый *adj.* **1**, hardened; calloused. **2**, *fig.* callous.

заскочи́ть [*infl.* **-скочу́, -ско́чишь**] *v., pfv. of* **заска́кивать**.

засла́ть [*infl.* **зашлю́, зашлёшь**] *v., pfv. of* **засыла́ть**.

засло́н *n.* **1**, barrier; screen. **2**, *mil.* covering force.

заслони́ть *v., pfv. of* **заслоня́ть**.

засло́нка [*gen. pl.* **-нок**] *n.* **1**, oven door. **2**, damper.

заслоня́ть *v.impfv.* [*pfv.* **заслони́ть**] **1**, to shield. **2**, *fig.* to overshadow. —**заслоня́ть свет** (+ *dat.*), to stand in someone's light.

заслу́га *n.* **1**, *usu. pl.* services; contribution; accomplishments; achievements. **2**, merit; virtue. —**по заслу́гам**, according to one's deserts; as one deserves. —**получи́ть по заслу́гам**, to get what one deserves; get one's just deserts/reward. —**ста́вить что́-нибудь в заслу́гу** (+ *dat.*), to give (someone) credit for something.

заслу́женно *adv.* deservedly.

заслу́женный *adj.* **1**, deserved; well-earned. **2**, distinguished. **3**, (*in titles*) Honored.

заслу́живать *v.impfv.* (*with gen.*) to deserve; merit; be worthy of.

заслужи́ть *v.pfv.* [*infl.* **-служу́, -слу́жишь**] to deserve; earn; win; gain.

заслу́шивать *v.impfv.* [*pfv.* **заслу́шать**] to listen to; hear (a report, speech, etc.). —**заслу́шиваться**, *refl.* (*with gen.*) to listen (to) with rapt attention.

заслы́шать *v.pfv.* [*infl.* **-шу, -шишь**] to hear; catch the sound of.

засма́тривать *v.impfv.* (*with* **в** + *acc.*) *colloq.* to peep into; peer into.

засма́триваться *v.r.impfv.* [*pfv.* **засмотре́ться**] (*with* **на** + *acc.*) **1**, to be lost in contemplation of. **2**, [*impfv. only*] *colloq.* to stare at; eye.

засмея́ться *v.r.pfv.* [*infl.* **-смею́сь, -смеёшься**] to laugh; begin to laugh.

засмотре́ться [*infl.* **-смотрю́сь, -смо́тришься**] *v.r., pfv. of* **засма́триваться**.

заснеженный *also,* **заснежённый** *adj.* snow-clad; snow-covered.

засну́ть *v., pfv. of* **засыпа́ть**[1].

засня́ть *v.pfv.* [*infl. like* **снять**] to photograph; film; shoot.

засо́в *n.* bolt; bar.

засо́вывать *v.impfv.* [*pfv.* **засу́нуть**] **1**, to stick; thrust. **2**, *colloq.* to put (somewhere and be unable to find).

засо́л *n.* salting; pickling.

засоли́ть [*infl.* **-солю́, -со́лишь** *or* **-соли́шь**] *v., pfv. of* **заса́ливать** (*in sense #2*).

засоре́ние *n.* clogging up. —**засоре́ние желу́дка**, constipation.

засоря́ть *v.impfv.* [*pfv.* **засори́ть**] **1**, to litter. **2**, to clog (up). **3**, *in* засори́ть себе́ глаз, to get something in one's eye. **4**, to choke (with weeds). **5**, to clutter. —**засоря́ться**, *refl.* to become clogged.

засоса́ть [*infl.* **-сосу́, -сосёшь**] *v., pfv. of* **заса́сывать**.

засо́хнуть [*past* **засо́х, засо́хла**] *v., pfv. of* **засыха́ть**.

за́спанный *adj.* sleepy; sleepy-eyed.

заспа́ться *v.r.impfv.* [*infl. like* **спать**] *colloq.* to oversleep.

заста́ва *n.* **1**, gate; gates (*to a city*). **2**, *mil.* security detachment. Пограни́чная заста́ва, border post.

застава́ть *v.impfv.* [*pfv.* **заста́ть**; *pres.* **застаю́, застаёшь**] to find; catch (*at a certain moment*): заста́ть кого́-нибудь до́ма/ за обе́дом/ бесе́дующим с ке́м-нибудь/, to find someone at home/ at dinner/

talking to someone/. Заста́ть кого́-нибудь врасплóх, to catch someone unawares. Война́ заста́ла его́ в Герма́нии, the war found him in Germany; at the outbreak of war he was in Germany.

заста́вить [*infl.* **-влю, -вишь**] *v., pfv. of* **заставля́ть**.

заста́вка [*gen. pl.* **-вок**] *n.* drawing at the top of a text.

заставля́ть *v.impfv.* [*pfv.* **заста́вить**] **1**, to make; force; compel. **2**, to induce; make; get. **3**, to cram; jam; clutter. **4**, to block off; close off.

заста́иваться *v.r.impfv.* [*pfv.* **застоя́ться**] **1**, to stand too long. **2**, to become stale; become stagnant.

застаре́лый *adj.* chronic; inveterate.

заста́ть [*infl.* **-ста́ну, -ста́нешь**] *v., pfv. of* **застава́ть**.

застёгивать *v.impfv.* [*pfv.* **застегну́ть**] to button (up); fasten; hook. —**застёгиваться**, *refl.* **1**, to button; hook. **2**, to button oneself up.

застёжка [*gen. pl.* **-жек**] *n.* clasp; fastener. —**застёжка-мо́лния**, zipper.

застекля́ть *v.impfv.* [*pfv.* **застекли́ть**] to glaze; fit with glass.

застенографи́ровать *v., pfv. of* **стенографи́ровать**.

засте́нок [*gen.* **-нка**] *n.* **1**, *hist.* torture chamber. **2**, prison (*tsarist, fascist, Nazi, etc.*).

засте́нчивый *adj.* shy; timid; bashful; diffident. —**засте́нчивость**, *n.f.* shyness; timidity; bashfulness; diffidence.

застига́ть *v.impfv.* [*pfv.* **засти́гнуть** *or* **засти́чь**] to catch (unawares); take by surprise.

засти́гнуть [*past* **засти́г, засти́гла**] *v., pfv. of* **застига́ть**.

застила́ть *v.impfv.* [*pfv.* **застла́ть**] **1**, to cover. **2**, to cloud; obscure.

засти́рывать *v.impfv.* [*pfv.* **застира́ть**] *colloq.* **1**, to wash out (a spot, stain, etc.). **2**, to ruin in the wash.

засти́чь [*infl. like* **засти́гнуть**] *v., pfv. of* **застига́ть**.

застла́ть [*infl.* **-стелю́, -сте́лешь**] *v., pfv. of* **застила́ть**.

засто́й *n.* **1**, standing still; immobility. **2**, *fig.* stagnation. —**засто́й кро́ви**, *med.* congestion.

засто́йный *adj.* stagnant.

засто́лье *n., colloq.* meal; repast.

засто́льный *adj.* occurring at the table: засто́льная бесе́да, table talk. —**засто́льная пе́сня**, drinking song.

застопо́рить *v., pfv. of* **сто́порить**. —**застопо́риться**, *refl., pfv. of* **сто́пориться**.

застоя́ться *v.r., pfv. of* **заста́иваться**.

застра́ивать *v.impfv.* [*pfv.* **застро́ить**] to build up (an area).

застрахова́ть [*infl.* **-ху́ю, -ху́ешь**] *v., pfv. of* **страхова́ть** *and* **застрахо́вывать**. —**застрахова́ться**, *refl., pfv. of* **страхова́ться** *and* **застрахо́вываться**.

застрахо́вывать *v.impfv.* [*pfv.* **застрахова́ть**] to insure. —**застрахо́вываться**, *refl.* to insure oneself; take out insurance.

застра́чивать *v.impfv.* [*pfv.* **застрочи́ть**] to sew up; stitch up.

застра́щивать *v.impfv.* [*pfv.* **застраща́ть**] *colloq.* to intimidate; frighten.

застрева́ть *v.impfv.* [*pfv.* **застря́ть**] to stick; get stuck.

застрели́ть *v.pfv.* [*infl.* -стрелю́, -стре́лишь] to shoot; kill. —**застрели́ться,** *refl.* to shoot oneself; kill oneself.

застре́льщик *n.* leader; initiator; pioneer.

застро́ить *v., pfv. of* **застра́ивать.**

застро́йка *n.* building up; development. —**застро́йщик,** *n.* builder; developer.

застрочи́ть *v.pfv.* [*infl.* -строчу́, -строчи́шь *or* -стро́чишь] 1, *pfv. of* **застра́чивать.** 2, *colloq.* (*of a machine gun*) to blaze away.

застря́ть [*infl.* -стря́ну, -стря́нешь] *v., pfv. of* застрева́ть.

застуди́ться *v.r.pfv.* [*infl.* -стужу́сь, -сту́дишься] *colloq.* to catch cold.

за́ступ *n.* spade.

заступа́ться *v.r.impfv.* [*pfv.* **заступи́ться**] (*with* за + *acc.*) to come to the defense of; stand up for; stick up for.

заступи́ться [*infl.* -ступлю́сь, -сту́пишься] *v.r., pfv. of* **заступа́ться.**

засту́пник *n.* defender; intercessor. —**засту́пничество,** *n.* intercession.

застыва́ть *v.impfv.* [*pfv.* **засты́ть**] 1, to thicken; harden; congeal. 2, *colloq.* to freeze; be frozen. 3, *fig.* to freeze: засты́ть от у́жаса, to freeze in horror.

застыди́ть *v.pfv.* [*infl.* -жу́, -ди́шь] *colloq.* to shame. —**застыди́ться,** *refl.* to become embarrassed.

засты́ть [*infl.* -сты́ну, -сты́нешь] *v., pfv. of* **стыть** (*in sense #2*) *and* **застыва́ть.**

засу́нуть *v., pfv. of* **засо́вывать.**

за́суха *n.* drought.

засухоусто́йчивый *adj.* drought-resistant.

засу́чивать *v.impfv.* [*pfv.* **засучи́ть**] to roll up (one's sleeves).

засучи́ть [*infl.* -сучу́, -су́чишь] *v., pfv. of* **засу́чивать.**

засу́шивать *v.impfv.* [*pfv.* **засуши́ть**] to dry; press (flowers).

засуши́ть [*infl.* -сушу́, -су́шишь] *v., pfv. of* **засу́шивать.**

засу́шливый *adj.* drought-afflicted; arid.

засчи́тывать *v.impfv.* [*pfv.* **засчита́ть**] (*with* в + *acc.*) to count (toward); apply (toward). —**засчи́тываться,** *refl.* [*impfv. only*] (*with* в + *acc.*) to count (toward); be counted (toward).

засыла́ть *v.impfv.* [*pfv.* **засла́ть**] *colloq.* 1, to send out (*on a secret mission*). 2, to send (*far away or to the wrong place*).

засыпа́ть [*infl.* -сы́плю, -сы́плешь] *v., pfv. of* засыпа́ть². —**засыпа́ться,** *refl., pfv. of* засыпа́ться².

засыпа́ть¹ *v.impfv.* [*pfv.* **засну́ть**] to fall asleep.

засыпа́ть² *v.impfv.* [*pfv.* **засы́пать**] (*with instr.*) 1, to fill up (with dirt, sand, etc.). 2, to cover; strew (with dust, papers, etc.). 3, *fig.* to shower; deluge; bombard (with questions, gifts, etc.). —**засыпа́ться,** *refl.* 1, (*with* в + *acc.*) (*of sand, snow, etc.*) to get into. 2, (*with instr.*) to be covered (with).

засыха́ть *v.impfv.* [*pfv.* **засо́хнуть**] 1, to dry up. 2, to wither.

зата́ивать *v.impfv.* [*pfv.* **затаи́ть**] 1, *colloq.* to hide; conceal. 2, to bear; harbor; nurse (a grudge). 3, to hold (one's breath): затаи́в дыха́ние; с затаённым дыха́нием, with bated breath. —**зата́иваться,** *refl., colloq.* to hide.

зата́лкивать *v.impfv.* [*pfv.* **затолкну́ть**] *colloq.* (*with various prepositions*) to push; shove (into, under, etc.).

зата́пливать *v.impfv.* [*pfv.* **затопи́ть**] to light (a stove).

зата́птывать *v.impfv.* [*pfv.* **затопта́ть**] 1, to trample down; trample upon. 2, (*with* в + *acc.*) to press into (the ground). 3, to stamp out (a fire, cigarette, etc.). 4, *colloq.* to leave footmarks on; track up. —**зата́птывать в грязь,** to drag through the mud.

зата́сканный *adj., colloq.* 1, worn; worn out; threadbare. 2, *fig.* trite; hackneyed.

затаска́ть *v., pfv. of* **зата́скивать** (*in sense #2*).

зата́скивать *v.impfv.* 1, [*pfv.* **затащи́ть**] to drag away; drag off. 2, [*pfv.* **затаска́ть**] *colloq.* to wear out; *fig.* make trite.

зата́чивать *v.impfv.* [*pfv.* **заточи́ть**] to sharpen.

затащи́ть [*infl.* -тащу́, -та́щишь] *v., pfv. of* **зата́скивать** (*in sense #1*).

затвердева́ть *v.impfv.* [*pfv.* **затверде́ть**] to harden; become hard.

затверде́лый *adj.* hardened.

затверде́ние *n.* 1, hardening. 2, hard lump.

затверде́ть *v., pfv. of* **тверде́ть** *and* **затвердева́ть.**

затверди́ть *v., pfv. of* **тверди́ть** (*in sense #2*).

затво́р *n.* 1, *colloq.* bolt (*of a door*). 2, bolt (*of a gun*); shutter (*of a camera*).

затвори́ть [*infl.* -творю́, -тво́ришь] *v., pfv. of* затворя́ть. —**затвори́ться,** *refl., pfv. of* **затворя́ться.**

затво́рник *n.* hermit; recluse. —**затво́рнический,** *adj.* of a hermit; solitary. —**затво́рничество,** *n.* solitary life.

затворя́ть *v.impfv.* [*pfv.* **затвори́ть**] to close; shut. —**затворя́ться,** *refl.* 1, to close; be closed. 2, to shut oneself in.

затева́ть *v.impfv.* [*pfv.* **зате́ять**] *colloq.* 1, to start; undertake; launch. 2, (*with inf.*) to decide (to); make up one's mind (to). 3, *in* затева́ть недо́брое, to be up to something; be up to no good. —**затева́ться,** *refl., colloq.* 1, to start. 2, [*impfv. only*] to be afoot.

зате́йливый *adj.* 1, elaborate; fancy. 2, intricate. 3, clever; ingenious.

зате́йник *n.* 1, amusing fellow; jokester. 2, organizer of social activities; social director.

затека́ть *v.impfv.* [*pfv.* **зате́чь**] 1, (*with* в + *acc.*) to leak (into); get (into). 2, to swell; swell up. 3, to become numb.

зате́м *adv.* 1, then; next. 2, that is why. —**зате́м, что́бы,** in order to.

затемне́ние *n.* 1, darkening. 2, blackout. 3, *fig.* obscuring.

затемни́ть *v., pfv. of* **затемня́ть.**

за́темно *adv., colloq.* 1, before dawn; before daybreak; before daylight. 2, after dark.

затемня́ть *v.impfv.* [*pfv.* **затемни́ть**] 1, to darken; black out. 2, *fig.* to obscure; cloud; blur.

затеня́ть *v.impfv.* [*pfv.* **затени́ть**] to shade; shield.

затере́ть [*infl. like* **тере́ть**] *v., pfv. of* **затира́ть.**

затеря́нный *adj.* lost; forgotten.

затеря́ть *v.pfv., colloq.* to lose; mislay. —**затеря́ться,** *refl., colloq.* 1, to be lost. 2, to disappear.

затеса́ться *v.r.pfv.* [*infl.* -тешу́сь, -те́шешься] (*with* в *or* на + *acc.*) *colloq.* to get into; worm one's way into.

зате́чь [*infl. like* течь] *v., pfv. of* затека́ть.

зате́я *n.* **1,** undertaking; venture. **2,** game; amusement. —**без зате́й** [*often* по́просту, **без зате́й**] simply; without fanfare.

зате́ять [*infl.* зате́ю, зате́ешь] *v., pfv. of* затева́ть. —**зате́яться,** *refl., pfv. of* затева́ться.

затира́ть *v.impfv.* [*pfv.* затере́ть] **1,** to rub out; efface. **2,** to hem in; trap; hold fast. —**затёртый льда́ми,** icebound.

зати́скивать *v.impfv.* [*pfv.* зати́снуть] *colloq.* to squeeze in.

затиха́ть *v.impfv.* [*pfv.* зати́хнуть] to subside; abate; die down.

зати́хнуть [*past* зати́х, зати́хла] *v., pfv. of* затиха́ть.

зати́шье *n.* calm; lull. —**зати́шье пе́ред грозо́й,** the calm before the storm.

заткну́ть *v., pfv. of* затыка́ть. —**заткну́ться,** *refl., colloq.* to shut up; keep one's mouth shut. Заткни́сь!, shut up!

затмева́ть *v.impfv.* [*pfv.* затми́ть] **1,** to obscure. **2,** *fig.* to eclipse; overshadow.

затме́ние *n.* eclipse.

затми́ть *v., pfv. of* затмева́ть.

зато́ *conj.* but; but then; but on the other hand.

затолка́ть *v.pfv.* **1,** to push; shove. **2,** to jostle; elbow.

затолкну́ть *v., pfv. of* зата́лкивать.

зато́н *n.* inlet; creek.

затону́ть *v.pfv.* [*infl.* -тону́, -то́нешь] to sink.

затопи́ть [*infl.* -топлю́, -то́пишь] *v., pfv. of* зата́пливать *and* затопля́ть. —**затопи́ться,** *pfv. of* затопля́ться.

затопле́ние *n.* **1,** sinking. **2,** flooding.

затопля́ть *v.impfv.* [*pfv.* затопи́ть] **1,** to flood; inundate. **2,** to sink. —**затопля́ться,** *refl.* to be flooded.

затопта́ть [*infl.* -топчу́, -то́пчешь] *v., pfv. of* зата́птывать.

зато́р *n.* jam (*of people, traffic, etc.*).

затормози́ть *v., pfv. of* тормози́ть.

заточа́ть *v.impfv.* [*pfv.* заточи́ть] *obs.* to imprison; incarcerate.

заточе́ние *n., obs.* imprisonment; incarceration.

заточи́ть *v.pfv.* **1,** [*infl.* -точу́, -то́чишь] *pfv. of* зата́чивать. **2,** [*infl.* -точу́, -точи́шь] *pfv. of* заточа́ть.

затрави́ть *v., pfv. of* трави́ть (*in sense #3*).

затра́вленный *adj.* **1,** (*of an animal*) hunted; trapped. **2,** *fig.* hounded; harassed.

затра́гивать *v.impfv.* [*pfv.* затро́нуть] **1,** (*of a bullet*) to touch; graze. **2,** to affect. **3,** *fig.* to wound (someone's pride). **4,** to touch upon; broach.

затрапе́зный *adj., colloq.* **1,** (*of clothes*) everyday. **2,** shabby; run-down.

затра́та *n*., **1,** expenditure. **2,** *usu. pl.* expenses.

затра́тить [*infl.* -чу, -тишь] *v., pfv. of* затра́чивать.

затра́чивать *v.impfv.* [*pfv.* затра́тить] to spend; expend.

затре́бовать *v.pfv.* [*infl.* -бую, -буешь] to request; demand; require; order.

затрёпанный *adj., colloq.* **1,** worn; frayed; shabby. **2,** *fig.* trite.

затрепа́ть *v.pfv.* [*infl.* -треплю́, -тре́плешь] *colloq.* to wear out.

затре́щина *n., colloq.* box on the ears.

затро́нуть *v., pfv. of* затра́гивать.

затрудне́ние *n.* **1,** difficulty. **2,** predicament.

затруднённый *adj.* difficult; labored.

затрудни́тельный *adj.* difficult; awkward; embarrassing.

затрудня́ть *v.impfv.* [*pfv.* затрудни́ть] **1,** to bother; trouble; inconvenience. **2,** to hamper; make difficult. —**затрудня́ться,** *refl.* (*with inf.*) to have difficulty; find it difficult (to).

затума́нивать *v.impfv.* [*pfv.* затума́нить] to cloud; obscure. —**затума́ниваться,** *refl.* **1,** to cloud up; become clouded. **2,** (*of the senses*) to become muddled.

затума́нить *v., pfv. of* тума́нить *and* затума́нивать. —**затума́ниться,** *refl., pfv. of* тума́ниться *and* затума́ниваться.

затупи́ть *v., pfv. of* тупи́ть. —**затупи́ться,** *refl., pfv. of* тупи́ться.

затуха́ть *v.impfv.* [*pfv.* зату́хнуть] *colloq.* **1,** (*of something burning*) to go out. **2,** *fig.* to subside; wane.

зату́хнуть [*past* зату́х, зату́хла] *v., pfv. of* затуха́ть.

затушева́ть [*infl.* -шу́ю, -шу́ешь] *v., pfv. of* тушева́ть *and* затушёвывать.

затушёвывать *v.impfv.* [*pfv.* затушева́ть] **1,** to shade; add shading to. **2,** *fig.* to gloss over; obscure.

затуши́ть *v.pfv.* [*infl.* -тушу́, -ту́шишь] *colloq.* **1,** to put out; extinguish. **2,** to suppress.

за́тхлый *adj.* musty.

затыка́ть *v.impfv.* [*pfv.* заткну́ть] **1,** to stop up; plug up; cork up. **2,** to stick; thrust. —**заткну́ть за́ пояс,** *colloq.* outdo; outshine; put to shame.

заты́лок [*gen.* -лка] *n.* back of the head. —**в заты́лок,** single file; one behind the other.

заты́лочный *adj.* occipital.

заты́чка [*gen. pl.* -чек] *n., colloq.* stopper; plug.

затя́гивать *v.impfv.* [*pfv.* затяну́ть] **1,** to tighten; pull tight; draw tight. **2,** (*with instr.*) to cover (with); clothe (in). ◆*Also impers. and therefore intransitive:* Не́бо затяну́ло, the sky (has) clouded over; ра́ну затяну́ло, the wound has healed over. **3,** to delay; drag out. **4,** to suck in. **5,** (*with* в + *acc.*) to draw (into); involve (in). **6,** *colloq.* to strike up (a song). —**затя́гиваться,** *refl.* **1,** to tighten something around oneself: затяну́ться по́ясом, to tighten one's belt. **2,** to tighten; become tight. **3,** (*of a wound*) to heal over. **4,** (*of the sky*) to become clouded; be obscured; (*with instr.*) be covered (with). **5,** to drag out; drag on; last a long time. **6,** to inhale (*when smoking*).

затя́жка [*gen. pl.* -жек] *n.* **1,** tightening; drawing. **2,** delay; dragging out. **3,** puff; drag (*on a cigarette*).

затяжно́й *adj.* lengthy; protracted.

затяну́ть [*infl.* -тяну́, -тя́нешь] *v., pfv. of* затя́гивать. —**затяну́ться,** *refl., pfv. of* затя́гиваться.

зау́мный *adj.* abstruse; esoteric; arcane.

зауны́вный *adj.* mournful; plaintive.

заупоко́йный *adj.* for the repose of the dead. Заупоко́йная слу́жба, funeral service.

заупря́миться *v.r.pfv.* [*infl.* -млю́сь, -мишься] to balk.

заура́дный *adj.* ordinary; mediocre.

заусе́ница *n.* **1,** hangnail. **2,** burr (*on metal*).

зау́треня *n.* matins; Morning Prayer.

зау́ченный *adj.* rote; mechanical.

зау́чивать *v.impfv.* [*pfv.* **заучи́ть**] to memorize; learn by heart. —**зау́чиваться,** *refl., colloq.* to study too much; study too hard.

заучи́ть [*infl.* заучу́, зау́чишь] *v., pfv. of* **зау́чивать.** —**заучи́ться,** *refl., pfv. of* **зау́чиваться.**

зауша́тельский *adj.* vicious; abusive. —**зауша́тельство,** *n.* vicious criticism; abuse.

зафикси́ровать *v., pfv. of* **фикси́ровать.**

зафрахтова́ть *v., pfv. of* **фрахтова́ть.**

заха́живать *v.impfv., colloq.* to drop in; stop in.

захва́ливать *v.impfv.* [*pfv.* **захвали́ть**] *colloq.* to praise excessively.

захвали́ть [*infl.* -хвалю́, -хва́лишь] *v., pfv. of* **захва́ливать.**

захва́т *n.* **1,** seizure; capture. **2,** *wrestling* hold.

захва́танный *adj., colloq.* soiled by fingering; full of finger marks.

захвата́ть *v., pfv. of* **захва́тывать** (*in sense #6*).

захвати́ть [*infl.* -хвачу́, -хва́тишь] *v., pfv. of* **захва́тывать.**

захва́тнический *adj.* (*of a policy*) expansionist; (*of wars*) of conquest.

захва́тчик *n.* invader.

захва́тывать *v.impfv.* [*pfv.* **захвати́ть**] **1,** to seize; capture. **2,** (*often with* **с собо́й**) to take (along); bring (along). **3,** to carry away; thrill; engross. **4,** *colloq.* to catch; take by surprise. **5,** *colloq.* to stop; check (in time). **6,** [*pfv.* **захвата́ть**] *colloq.* to soil (*by fingering*). —**от э́того дух захва́тывает,** it takes one's breath away.

захва́тывающий *adj.* exciting; thrilling; gripping; engrossing; absorbing.

захвора́ть *v.pfv., colloq.* **1,** to be taken ill. **2,** (*with instr.*) to come down with.

захире́ть *v., pfv. of* **хире́ть.**

захламля́ть *v.impfv.* [*pfv.* **захлами́ть**] *colloq.* to litter; leave trash all over.

захлёбываться *v.r.impfv.* [*pfv.* **захлебну́ться**] **1,** to choke. **2,** *fig.* (*with* **от**) to be breathless (with an emotion). **3,** to bog down; peter out. **4,** (*of an engine*) to stall.

захлёстывать *v.impfv.* [*pfv.* **захлестну́ть**] **1,** (*with* **за** + *acc.*) to wind around. **2,** (*with instr.*) to secure (with a rope, lasso, etc.). **3,** (*of water*) to sweep over. **4,** (*of a feeling*) to come over.

захло́пывать *v.impfv.* [*pfv.* **захло́пнуть**] to slam; slam shut. —**захло́пываться,** *refl.* (*of a door*) to slam shut; close with a bang.

захмеле́ть *v., pfv. of* **хмеле́ть.**

захо́д *n.* stop; call. Порт захо́да, port of call. —**захо́д со́лнца,** sunset.

заходи́ть[1] *v.impfv.* [*pfv.* **зайти́**; *pres.* -хожу́, -хо́дишь] **1,** (*with* **в** or **на** + *acc.*) to stop (in) at; (*of a ship*) to call at. **2,** (*with* **к**) to call on; drop in on; **3,** (*with* **в** + *acc.*) to go into; get into. **4,** (*with* **за** + *instr.*) to call for; pick up. **5,** (*with* **за** + *acc.*) to go behind. **6,**

to go (far). **7,** (*with* **в** + *acc.*) to get to; find oneself (*in a certain place*). **8,** (*of the sun*) to set. **9,** (*with* **о**) (*of an argument*) to arise (over); (*of a conversation*) to turn (to).

заходи́ть[2] *v.pfv.* [*infl.* -хожу́, -хо́дишь] **1,** to begin to walk. **2,** to circulate. **3,** (*of an object*) to begin to shake.

заходи́ться *v.r.impfv.* [*pfv.* **зайти́сь**; *pres.* -хожу́сь, -хо́дишься] *colloq.* **1,** to become numb (*from the cold*). **2,** (*of one's heart*) to stop beating momentarily.

захолу́стный *adj.* remote; out-of-the-way.

захолу́стье *n.* out-of-the-way place.

захороне́ние *n.* **1,** burial. **2,** burial place.

захорони́ть *v.pfv.* [*infl.* -роню́, -ро́нишь] to bury.

захоте́ть *v.pfv.* [*infl. like* **хоте́ть**] to want. —**захоте́ться,** *refl., impers.* (*with dat.*) to want.

захуда́лый *adj.* **1,** impoverished. **2,** shabby; run-down.

зацвести́ [*infl. like* **цвести́**] *v., pfv. of* **зацвета́ть.**

зацвета́ть *v.impfv.* [*pfv.* **зацвести́**] **1,** to begin to bloom; begin to blossom. **2,** to become filled with algae. **3,** *colloq.* to become mildewed.

зацелова́ть *v.pfv.* [*infl.* -лу́ю, -лу́ешь] *colloq.* to smother with kisses.

зацепи́ть [*infl.* -цеплю́, -це́пишь] *v., pfv. of* **зацепля́ть.** —**зацепи́ться,** *refl., pfv. of* **зацепля́ться.**

заце́пка [*gen. pl.* -пок] *n., colloq.* **1,** hook; peg. **2,** pull; influence; connections. **3,** hitch; catch; snag.

зацепля́ть *v.impfv.* [*pfv.* **зацепи́ть**] **1,** to hook. **2,** (*with instr. and* **за** + *acc.*) to catch (on); snag (on). —**зацепля́ться,** *refl.* (*with* **за** + *acc.*) to catch (on); get caught (on).

зачаро́ванный *adj.* **1,** enchanted. **2,** bewitched. **3,** spellbound.

зачарова́ть [*infl.* -ру́ю, -ру́ешь] *v., pfv. of* **зачаро́вывать.**

зачаро́вывать *v.impfv.* [*pfv.* **зачарова́ть**] to bewitch; charm; enchant; captivate.

зачасти́ть *v.pfv.* [*infl.* -щу́, -сти́шь] *colloq.* **1,** to increase in intensity. **2,** to begin to speak rapidly. **3,** (*with* **к**) to begin to visit frequently.

зачасту́ю *adv., colloq.* often; frequently.

зача́тие *n., physiol.* conception.

зача́ток [*gen.* -тка] *n.* **1,** embryo. **2,** *usu. pl.* beginning; early stages.

зача́точный *adj.* rudimentary; embryonic.

зача́ть *v.pfv.* [*infl.* зачну́, зачнёшь; *past fem.* зачала́] to conceive (a child).

зача́хнуть *v., pfv. of* **ча́хнуть.**

зачём *adv.* **1,** why?; what for? **2,** why; what ... for: Он забы́л, зачём пришёл, he forgot what he came for.

зачём-то *adv.* for some reason or other.

зачёркивать *v.impfv.* [*pfv.* **зачеркну́ть**] to cross out.

зачерни́ть *v., pfv. of* **черни́ть** (*in sense #1*).

заче́рпывать *v.impfv.* [*pfv.* **зачерпну́ть**] to scoop up; ladle.

зачерстве́лый *adj.* **1,** stale; hard. **2,** *fig.* callous.

зачерстве́ть *v., pfv. of* **черстве́ть** (*in sense #1*).

зачеса́ть *v.pfv.* [*infl.* -чешу́, -че́шешь] **1,** *pfv. of* **зачёсывать. 2,** to scratch; begin to scratch (an itch). —**зачеса́ться,** *refl.* to itch; begin to itch.

зачесть [*infl.* зачту́, зачтёшь; *past* зачёл, зачла́] *v., pfv. of* зачи́тывать[2]. —**зачесться**, *refl., pfv. of* зачи́тываться.

зачёсывать *v.impfv.* [*pfv.* зачеса́ть] to comb.

зачёт *n.* test (*in school*).

зачётный *adj.* 1, test (*attrib.*). 2, record (*attrib.*): зачётная кни́жка, (student's) record book.

зачина́тель *n.m.* founder; initiator; pioneer.

зачини́ть *v.pfv.* [*infl.* -чиню́, -чи́нишь] 1, *colloq.* to mend; repair. 2, to sharpen (a pencil).

зачи́нщик *n.* instigator; ringleader.

зачисле́ние *n.* enrollment.

зачисля́ть *v.impfv.* [*pfv.* зачи́слить] 1, to enroll; take in (a student); hire; take on (an employee). 2, to enter; record. —**зачисля́ться**, *refl.* to enroll; join.

зачита́ть *v., pfv. of* зачи́тывать[1]. —**зачита́ться**, *refl., pfv. of* зачи́тываться.

зачи́тывать[1] *v.impfv.* [*pfv.* зачита́ть] 1, to read out. 2, *colloq.* to read (a book) until it is tattered. 3, *colloq.* to fail to return (a borrowed book). —**зачи́тываться**, *refl. (with instr.) colloq.* to become engrossed in reading (a book, novel, etc.).

зачи́тывать[2] *v.impfv.* [*pfv.* зачесть] 1, (*with* в + *acc.*) to apply (toward). 2, to accept; pass (academic work). —**зачи́тываться**, *refl.* to be counted.

зашага́ть *v.pfv.* to begin to walk; set out on foot.

зашевели́ть *v.pfv.* (*with acc. or instr.*) to (begin to) stir. —**зашевели́ться**, *refl.* 1, to move slightly; begin to stir. 2, *colloq.* to begin to take action; begin to move.

зашиба́ть *v.impfv.* [*pfv.* зашиби́ть] *colloq.* 1, to injure; hurt (*by striking*). 2, to earn (money). 3, [*impfv. only*] to have too much to drink.

зашиби́ть [*infl.* -бу́, -бёшь; *past* заши́б, заши́бла] *v., pfv. of* зашиба́ть.

зашива́ть *v.impfv.* [*pfv.* заши́ть] to sew up; mend.

заши́ть [*infl.* зашью́, зашьёшь] *v., pfv. of* зашива́ть.

зашифрова́ть *v., pfv. of* шифрова́ть.

зашнурова́ть *v., pfv. of* шнурова́ть.

зашпаклева́ть *v., pfv. of* шпаклева́ть.

зашпи́ливать *v.impfv.* [*pfv.* зашпи́лить] to pin; fasten with a pin.

заштемпелева́ть *v., pfv. of* штемпелева́ть.

заштопать *v., pfv. of* штопать.

зашто́ривать *v.impfv.* [*pfv.* зашто́рить] *colloq.* to draw the blinds on (windows).

заштрихова́ть *v., pfv. of* штрихова́ть.

защёлка [*gen. pl.* -лок] *n.* latch; catch.

защёлкивать *v.impfv.* [*pfv.* защёлкнуть] to snap; snap shut. —**защёлкиваться**, *refl. (of a lock, latch, etc.)* to snap shut.

защеми́ть *v.pfv.* [*infl.* -млю́, -ми́шь] 1, *pfv. of* защемля́ть. 2, (*of one's heart*) to ache.

защемля́ть *v.impfv.* [*pfv.* защеми́ть] 1, to squeeze; crush. 2, *colloq.* to catch; jam.

защи́та *n.* defense; protection. —брать (кого́-нибудь) под защи́ту, to take under one's wing.

защити́тельный *adj., in* защити́тельная речь, speech for the defense.

защити́ть [*infl.* -щу́, -ти́шь] *v., pfv. of* защища́ть. —**защити́ться**, *refl., pfv. of* защища́ться.

защи́тник *n.* 1, defender; protector. 2, defense attorney. 3, *sports* defenseman; back.

защи́тный *adj.* protective. —**защи́тная окра́ска**, protective coloration. —**защи́тный цвет**, khaki.

защища́ть *v.impfv.* [*pfv.* защити́ть] 1, to defend. 2, to protect; shield. —**защища́ться**, *refl.* to defend oneself; protect oneself.

заяви́ть [*infl.* заявлю́, зая́вишь] *v., pfv. of* заявля́ть.

зая́вка [*gen. pl.* -вок] *n.* 1, claim. 2, application. 3, order; requisition.

заявле́ние *n.* 1, announcement; statement. 2, application.

заявля́ть *v.impfv.* [*pfv.* заяви́ть] 1, (*with* о) to announce: заяви́ть о своём реше́нии, to announce one's decision. 2, (*with a dependent clause*) to state (that) ...; declare (that)... 3, to file; lodge (a protest, complaint, etc.). 4, to report: заяви́ть о происше́ствии в мили́цию, to report an incident to the police. —**заяви́ть о себе́**, to make one's presence felt.

заявля́ться *v.r.impfv.* [*pfv.* заяви́ться] *colloq.* to show up; turn up.

зая́длый *adj., colloq.* inveterate; avid.

за́яц [*gen.* за́йца] *n.* 1, hare. 2, *colloq.* stowaway: е́хать за́йцем, to stow away.

за́ячий [*fem.* -чья] *adj.* hare (*attrib.*). —**за́ячья губа́**, harelip.

зва́ние *n.* 1, rank: во́инское зва́ние, military rank. 2, title: зва́ние чемпио́на, championship title.

зва́ный *adj.* 1, invited: зва́ный гость, invited guest. 2, with invited guests, зва́ный обе́д, dinner party.

зва́тельный *adj., in* зва́тельный паде́ж, vocative case.

звать *v.impfv.* [*pfv.* позва́ть; *pres.* зову́, зовёшь; *past fem.* звала́] 1, to call. 2, to invite. 3, [*impfv. only*] to name; call: Как вас зову́т?, what is your name? Меня́ зову́т Ири́на, my name is Irina. —**зва́ться**, *refl.* [*past* зва́лся, звала́сь, звало́сь *or* зва́лось, звали́сь *or* зва́лись] [*impfv. only*] to be called.

звезда́ [*pl.* звёзды] *n.* star. —**морска́я звезда́**, starfish. —**но́вая звезда́**, nova.

звёздный *adj.* 1, star (*attrib.*); stellar. 2, starry. —**звёздный час**, one's finest hour; one's crowning moment.

звездочёт *n., obs.* astrologer.

звёздочка [*gen. pl.* -чек] *n.* 1, little star. 2, asterisk.

звене́ть *v.impfv.* [*pres.* звеню́, звени́шь] 1, *v.i.* to ring; jingle: колоко́льчики звеня́т, sleighbells are ringing. 2, *v.t.* (*with instr.*) to jingle: Звене́ть моне́тами, to jingle coins.

звено́ [*pl.* зве́нья, зве́ньев] *n.* 1, link. 2, unit; section (*of a device or structure*). 3, team; group; unit. 4, flight (*of aircraft*). 5, *mil.* level; echelon.

зверёк [*gen.* -рька́] *n.* small animal.

зверёныш *n., colloq.* cub.

звере́ть *v.impfv.* [*pfv.* озвере́ть] to become like an animal.

звери́нец [*gen.* -нца] *n., obs., colloq.* menagerie.

звери́ный *adj.* 1, animal (*attrib.*). 2, brutal; savage.

зверобо́й *n.* 1, hunter (*of aquatic mammals*). 2, St.-John's-wort.

зверолóв *n.* trapper.

звéрский *adj.* **1,** brutal; savage. **2,** *colloq.* beastly; frightful. —**звéрски,** *adv.* brutally.

звéрство *n.* **1,** brutality; bestiality. **2,** *usu. pl.* atrocities.

зверь [*pl.* **звéри, зверéй, зверя́м**] *n.m.* (wild) animal; beast. —**смотрéть звéрем,** to glare; glower.

зверьё *n., colloq.* wild animals.

звон *n.* **1,** ringing; pealing; tolling. **2,** clinking; jingling; tinkling. —**похорóнный звон,** knell.

звонáрь [*gen.* **-наря́**] *n.m.* bell ringer.

звони́ть *v.impfv.* [*pfv.* **позвони́ть**] **1,** (*of a bell, phone, alarm clock, etc.*) to ring. **2,** (*with* **в** + *acc.*) to ring: звони́ть в кóлокол, to ring a bell. **3,** (*with dat.*) to call; phone: Я вам позвоню́, I'll call/phone you. Звони́ть в аптéку/ на вокзáл/, to phone the drug store/station/.

звóнкий *adj.* **1,** clear; ringing; resounding. **2,** *phonet.* voiced. —**звóнкая монéта,** specie; coin. —**звóнкая фрáза,** high-sounding phrase.

звóнница *n.* bell tower; belfry.

звонóк [*gen.* **-нкá**] *n.* **1,** bell. **2,** ring. Звонóк в дверь, ring of a doorbell. **3,** *colloq.* phone call.

звук *n.* sound.

звуковóй *adj.* **1,** sound (*attrib.*): звуковóй барьéр, sound barrier. —**звуковáя дорóжка,** sound track. —**звуковóй фильм,** talking film.

звукозáпись *n.f.* sound recording.

звуконепроницáемый *adj.* soundproof.

звукоoperáтор *n.* soundman.

звукоподражáние *n.* onomatopoeia.

звукоусилéние *n.* amplification. —**систéма звукоусилéния,** amplification system; public-address system.

звучáние *n.* **1,** sound. **2,** *fig.* significance: пьéса огрóмного звучáния, play of enormous significance.

звучáть *v.impfv.* [*pfv.* **прозвучáть;** *pres.* **-чý, -чи́шь**] to sound; be heard.

звýчный *adj.* **1,** ringing; resounding. **2,** resonant.

звя́канье *n.* tinkling; jingling; jangling.

звя́кать *v.impfv.* [*pfv.* **звя́кнуть**] to tinkle; jingle; jangle.

зги *n., in* **ни зги не ви́дно,** it is pitch-dark.

здáние *n.* building.

здесь *adv.* here.

здéшний *adj., colloq.* of this place; local. Я не здéшний, I am not from around here.

здорóваться *v.r.impfv.* [*pfv.* **поздорóваться**] (*with* **с** + *instr.*) to say hello (to); greet.

здоровéнный *adj., colloq.* **1,** robust; healthy. **2,** huge.

здоровéть *v.impfv.* [*pfv.* **поздоровéть**] *colloq.* to grow healthy; grow stronger.

здóрово *adv., colloq.* **1,** very; awfully; terribly. **2,** marvelously; splendidly. —*adj., used predicatively,* nice; wonderful: Как здóрово бы́ло бы (+ *inf.*), how nice/wonderful it would be to...

здорóво *adv. & adj.* healthy: вы́глядеть здорóво, to look healthy. —(за) **здорóво живёшь,** *colloq.* for no reason at all; just like that.

здорóвый *adj.* **1,** healthy. **2,** (*of food*) wholesome. —**бýдьте здорóвы!, 1,** stay well! **2,** (*after a sneeze*)

God bless you! —**жив и здорóв,** alive and well; safe and sound.

здорóвье *n.* health. —**за вáше здорóвье!,** to your health!; to good health! —**как вáше здорóвье?,** how are you? —**на здорóвье,** help yourself; take as much as you like.

здоровя́к [*gen.* **-вякá**] *n., colloq.* healthy person; robust person.

здрáвица *n.* toast to one's health.

здрáвница *n.* health resort; sanatorium.

здрáво *adv.* **1,** soundly. **2,** sensibly.

здравомы́слящий *adj.* sensible; of sound judgment.

здравоохранéние *n.* public health. —**Всеми́рная организáция здравоохранéния,** World Health Organization.

здрáвствовать *v.impfv.* [*pres.* **-ствую, -ствуешь**] to be well; be healthy; thrive. —**здрáвствуйте!,** *interj.* hello! —**да здрáвствует** (+ *nom.*), long live...!

здрáвый *adj.* sensible; sound. —**в здрáвом умé,** of sound mind; sane. Никтó в здрáвом умé, no one in his right mind. —**здрáвый смысл,** common sense.

зéбра *n.* zebra.

зéбу *n.m. indecl.* zebu.

зев *n.* pharynx. —**льви́ный зев,** snapdragon.

зевáка *n.m. & f., colloq.* idle onlooker.

зевáть *v.impfv.* **1,** [*pfv.* **зевнýть**] to yawn. **2,** [*impfv. only*] *colloq.* to gape. **3,** [*pfv.* **прозевáть**] *colloq.* to miss one's chance; let an opportunity slip by.

зевóк [*gen.* **зевкá**] *n.* yawn.

зевóта *n.* yawning.

Зевс *n.* Zeus.

зеленéть *v.impfv.* [*pfv.* **позеленéть**] **1,** to become green; turn green. **2,** [*impfv. only*] (*of anything green*) to loom; appear.

зеленщи́к [*gen.* **-щикá**] *n.* greengrocer.

зелёный *adj.* green. —**зелёная скýка** *or* **тоскá,** utter boredom. —**зелёная ýлица,** the green light.

зéлень *n.f.* **1,** greenery; verdure. **2,** greens; vegetables.

зéлье *n., obs.* **1,** poison. **2,** potion: любóвное зéлье, love potion.

земéльный *adj.* land (*attrib.*).

землевéдение *n.* physical geography.

землевладéлец [*gen.* **-льца**] *n.* landowner. —**землевладéльческий,** *adj.* landowner's. —**землевладéние,** *n.* ownership of land.

земледéлец [*gen.* **-льца**] *n.* farmer.

земледéлие *n.* farming. —**земледéльческий,** *adj.* farming (*attrib.*).

землекóп *n.* digger.

землемéр *n., obs.* surveyor. —**землемéрный,** *adj.* surveying (*attrib.*).

землерóйка [*gen. pl.* **-рóек**] *n.* shrew.

землерóйный *adj.* excavation (*attrib.*). —**землерóйная маши́на,** steam shovel.

землетрясéние *n.* earthquake.

земли́стый *adj.* **1,** earthy. **2,** (*of one's complexion*) sallow.

земля́ [*acc.* **зéмлю;** *pl.* **зéмли, земéль, зéмлям**] *n.* **1,** land; ground; earth. **2,** dirt. **3,** *cap.* the earth.

земля́к [*gen.* **-лякá**] *n.m.* [*fem.* **-ля́чка**] compatriot; fellow countryman.

земляни́ка *n.* **1,** (wild) strawberries. **2,** a (single) strawberry. —**земляни́чный,** *adj.* strawberry (*attrib.*).

земля́нка [*gen. pl.* **-нок**] *n.* dugout; mud hut.

земляно́й *adj.* earthen. —**земляна́я гру́ша,** Jerusalem artichoke. —**земляно́й оре́х,** peanut. —**земляно́й червь,** earthworm.

земля́чество *n.* community; colony (of fellow countrymen).

земново́дный *adj.* amphibious. —**земново́дные,** *n.pl.* amphibia; amphibians.

земно́й *adj.* **1,** of the earth; the earth's; terrestrial. **2,** earthly; mundane.

зе́мский *adj., hist.* **1,** national; people's: зе́мский собо́р, zemski sobor (*legislative assembly in old Russia*). **2,** of or pert. of the zemstvos.

зе́мство *n., hist.* zemstvo (*local assembly in 19th-century Russia*).

зени́т *n.* zenith.

зени́тка [*gen. pl.* **-ток**] *n., colloq.* antiaircraft gun.

зени́тный *adj.* **1,** *astron.* zenith (*attrib.*). **2,** *mil.* antiaircraft.

зени́ца *n., obs.* pupil of the eye. —**бере́чь как зени́цу о́ка,** to guard like the apple of one's eye.

зе́ркало [*pl.* **зеркала́, зерка́л**] *n.* mirror.

зерка́льный *adj.* **1,** mirror (*attrib.*). **2,** having a mirror; with a mirror. **3,** mirror-like. **4,** (*of a telescope*) reflecting; (*of a camera*) reflex. —**зерка́льное стекло́,** plate glass.

зе́ркальце [*gen. pl.* **-лец**] *n.* small mirror.

зерни́стый *adj.* **1,** grainy. **2,** granular. —**зерни́стая икра́,** soft caviar.

зерно́ [*pl.* **зёрна, зёрен**] *n.* **1,** grain: произво́дство зерна́, grain production. **2,** *fig.* grain; kernel: зерно́ и́стины, grain/kernel of truth. —**жемчу́жное зерно́,** a pearl. —**кофе́йные зёрна,** coffee beans.

зерново́й *adj.* grain (*attrib.*); cereal (*attrib.*).

зернохрани́лище *n.* granary.

зёрнышко [*gen. pl.* **-шек**] *n.* grain; granule.

зефи́р *n.* **1,** *obs.* zephyr (*gentle breeze*). **2,** zephyr (*lightweight cloth*). **3,** a kind of candy; marshmallow.

зигза́г *n.* zigzag. —**зигзагообра́зный,** *adj.* zigzag.

зиго́та *n.* zygote.

зи́ждиться *v.r.impfv.* [*pres.* **зи́ждется**] (*with* **на** + *prepl.*) to be based (upon).

зима́ [*acc.* **зи́му;** *pl.* **зи́мы**] *n.* winter.

зи́мний *adj.* **1,** winter (*attrib.*). **2,** wintry.

зимова́ть *v.impfv.* [*pfv.* **прозимова́ть;** *pres.* **-му́ю, -му́ешь**] to spend the winter.

зимо́вка *n.* **1,** wintering; spending the winter. **2,** winter camp; winter quarters.

зимо́вье *n.* winter camp; winter quarters.

зимо́й *adv.* in (the) winter. *Also,* **зимо́ю.**

зиморо́док [*gen.* **-дка**] *n.* halcyon; kingfisher.

зимосто́йкий *adj.* winter (*attrib.*); winter-hardy.

зипу́н [*gen.* **зипуна́**] *n.* homespun peasant's coat worn in old Russia.

зия́ние *n., ling.* hiatus.

зия́ть *v.impfv.* (*of a wound, abyss, etc.*) to gape; yawn.

зла́ки *n.pl.* [*sing.* **злак**] cereals. —**зла́ковый,** *adj.* cereal (*attrib.*).

зла́то *n., poetic* gold.

злЕ́йший *adj.* worst; bitterest.

злить *v.impfv.* [*pfv.* **обозли́ть** *or* **разозли́ть**] to anger. —**зли́ться,** *refl.* to become angry.

зло[1] [*gen. pl.* **зол;** *other pl. forms not used*] *n.* **1,** evil. Из двух зол выбира́ть ме́ньшее, to choose the lesser of two evils. **2,** wrong: отлича́ть добро́ от зла, to tell right from wrong. **3,** harm. **4,** *colloq.* spite; malice. Со зла, out of spite. Не держа́ть зла на (+ *acc.*), to bear someone no ill will. —**употребля́ть во зло,** to take unfair advantage of.

зло[2] *adv.* **1,** maliciously. Зло подшути́ть над, to make malicious fun of. **2,** with anger or hostility. Зло посмотре́ть на кого́-нибудь, to give someone a mean look. **3,** violently.

зло́ба *n.* **1,** spite; malice; rancor; ill will. **2,** grudge: таи́ть зло́бу, to bear a grudge. —**зло́ба дня,** topic of the day.

зло́бный *adj.* malicious; vicious; spiteful. —**зло́бно,** *adv.* maliciously.

злободне́вный *adj.* (*of a question, issue, etc.*) timely; vital.

зло́бствовать *v.impfv.* [*pres.* **-ствую, -ствуешь**] (*with* **на** + *acc.*) to bear ill will (toward).

злове́щий *adj.* ominous; sinister.

злово́ние *n.* stench. —**злово́нный,** *adj.* stinking; fetid.

зловре́дный *adj.* harmful; pernicious.

злоде́й *n.* villain.

злоде́йский *adj.* vicious; heinous.

злоде́йство *n.* **1,** villainy. **2,** evil deed.

злодея́ние *n.* evil deed; crime; outrage.

злой *adj.* [*short form* **зол, зла, зло, злы**] **1,** (*of a person*) mean; nasty. **2,** cross; ill-tempered. **3,** [*short form only*] (*with* **на** + *acc.*) angry (at); cross (with). **4,** evil; wicked. **5,** (*of an act, trick, etc.*) mean; malicious. **6,** (*of animals*) mean; ferocious. **7,** biting; acerbic. **8,** nasty; painful.

злока́чественный *adj., med.* malignant. —**злока́чественное малокро́вие,** pernicious anemia.

злоключе́ние *n.* misadventure; mishap.

злонаме́ренный *adj.* **1,** having evil intentions. **2,** (*of an act*) malicious.

злопа́мятный *adj.* slow to forgive; harboring lingering resentment.

злополу́чный *adj.* ill-fated; ill-starred; hapless.

злопыха́тель *n.m.* malicious critic; mudslinger. —**злопыха́тельский,** *adj.* malicious. —**злопыха́тельство,** *n.* maliciousness.

злора́дный *adj.* gloating.

злора́дство *n.* malicious pleasure.

злора́дствовать *v.impfv.* [*pres.* **-ствую, -ствуешь**] to gloat.

злосло́вие *n.* malicious gossip.

злосло́вить *v.impfv.* [*pres.* **-влю, -вишь**] to utter malicious gossip.

зло́стный *adj.* **1,** malicious. **2,** (*of an offender, defaulter, etc.*) persistent; habitual.

злость *n.f.* **1,** malice. **2,** rage; fury.

злосча́стный *adj., obs.* ill-fated; ill-starred.

зло́тый *n., decl. as an adj.* zloty (*monetary unit of Poland*).

злоупотреби́ть [*infl.* -блю́, -би́шь] *v.*, *pfv.* of **зло-употребля́ть**.

злоупотребле́ние *n.* **1,** (*with instr.*) misuse (of); abuse (of): злоупотребле́ние вла́стью, abuse of power. **2,** abuse; instance of wrongdoing.

злоупотребля́ть *v.impfv.* [*pfv.* **злоупотреби́ть**] (*with instr.*) to misuse; abuse. Я не хочу́ злоупотребля́ть ва́шим вре́менем, I don't want to take too much of your time.

злю́ка *n.m. & f.*, *colloq.* ill-tempered person; grouch.

злю́щий *adj.*, *colloq.* extremely mean, malicious or vicious.

змееви́дный *adj.* like a serpent; serpentine.

змеи́ный *adj.* snake (*attrib.*); snake's.

змеи́ться *v.r.impfv.* to wind; snake.

змей [*gen. & acc.* **змея́**] *n.* **1,** dragon. **2,** kite.

змея́ [*pl.* зме́и, змей, зме́ям] *n.* snake.

знава́ть *v.impfv.*, *colloq.*, *used only in the past tense,* to have known; have seen: знава́ть лу́чшие времена́, to have known better times; to have seen better days.

знак *n.* **1,** sign: доро́жный знак, road sign. Знак уваже́ния, sign of respect. **2,** signal. **3,** mark; point: зна́ки препина́ния, punctuation marks; восклица́тельный знак, exclamation point. **4,** *in* де́нежный знак, (piece of) paper money. **5,** *in* фи́рменный знак, trademark; водяно́й знак, watermark. **6,** *in* погра-ни́чный *or* межево́й знак, boundary marker. **7,** *in* номерно́й знак, license plate. **—в знак** (+ *gen.*), as a sign, token or gesture of. **—под зна́ком** (+ *gen.*), under the banner of.

знако́мить *v.impfv.* [*pfv.* **познако́мить**; *pres.* **-млю, -мишь**] (*with* **с** + *instr.*) **1,** to introduce (to). **2,** to acquaint (with); familiarize (with). **—знако́миться,** *refl.* (*with* **с** + *instr.*) **1,** to make the acquaintance (of); become acquainted (with). **2,** to familiarize oneself (with); become familiar (with).

знако́мство *n.* **1,** acquaintance. **2,** (circle of) acquaintances. **3,** familiarity; knowledge.

знако́мый *adj.* **1,** acquainted: Вы знако́мы?, are you acquainted?; do you know each other? **2,** familiar: знако́мый звук, familiar sound. Я знако́м с э́тим вопро́сом, I am familiar with this matter. **—n.** acquaintance.

знамена́тель *n.m.* denominator. **—приводи́ть к одному́** (*or* **к о́бщему**) **знамена́телю,** to reduce to a common denominator.

знамена́тельный *adj.* **1,** momentous; memorable. **2,** significant; revealing.

знаме́ние *n.*, *obs.* sign. **—знаме́ние вре́мени,** sign of the times. **—кре́стное знаме́ние,** sign of the cross.

знамени́тость *n.f.* **1,** fame; eminence; celebrity. **2,** a celebrity.

знамени́тый *adj.* famous; celebrated.

знаменова́ть *v.impfv.* [*pfv.* **ознаменова́ть**; *pres.* **-ну́ю, -ну́ешь**] (*often with* **собо́й**) to mark; signify; represent.

знамено́сец [*gen.* **-сца**] *n.* standard-bearer.

зна́мя [*gen.*, *dat. & prepl.* зна́мени; *instr.* зна́менем; *pl.* знамёна, знамён] *n.neut.* banner.

зна́ние *n.*, *often pl.* knowledge. **—со зна́нием де́ла, 1,** knowledgeably. **2,** with great skill.

зна́тный *adj.* **1,** from among the nobility or elite. **2,** prominent; noted: зна́тные лю́ди, notables. **3,** *colloq.* sizable. **4,** *colloq.* splendid.

знато́к [*gen.* **-тока́**] *n.* expert; connoisseur.

знать[1] *v.impfv.* to know. **—как зна́ешь,** as you wish. **—как знать?,** how is one to know? **—кто его́ зна́ет?,** who knows? **—то и знай,** *colloq.* continually.

знать[2] *n.f.* aristocracy; nobility.

зна́ться *v.r.impfv.* (*with* **с** + *instr.*) *colloq.* to associate (with); have to do with.

зна́харь *n.m.* [*fem.* зна́харка] medicine man; witch doctor; quack. **—зна́харство,** *n.* quackery.

знача́щий *adj.* meaningful; significant.

значе́ние *n.* **1,** meaning; sense: двойно́е значе́ние, dual meaning. **2,** significance; importance: не име́ть значе́ния, to be of no significance. Име́ть большо́е значе́ние для, to be of great importance to. **3,** value: коне́чное значе́ние, finite value.

зна́чимый *adj.* significant. **—зна́чимость,** *n.f.* significance.

зна́чит *particle*, *colloq.* so; then.

значи́тельно *adv.* considerably; significantly; substantially.

значи́тельность *n.f.* significance; importance.

значи́тельный *adj.* **1,** considerable. **2,** significant.

зна́чить *v.impfv.* to mean; signify. **—зна́читься,** *refl.* to be listed.

значо́к [*gen.* **-чка́**] *n.* **1,** badge. **2,** mark.

зна́ющий *adj.* knowledgeable.

зноби́ть *v.impfv.*, *impers.* to have a chill; be chilled: Меня́ зноби́т, I have a chill.

зной *n.* intense heat.

зно́йный *adj.* burning hot; sultry.

зоб *n.* **1,** craw; crop (*of a bird*). **2,** *med.* goiter.

зо́бный *adj.*, *in* зо́бная железа́, thymus.

зов *n.* **1,** call. **2,** *colloq.* invitation.

зодиа́к *n.* zodiac.

зо́дчество *n.* architecture. **—зо́дческий,** *adj.* architectural.

зо́дчий *n.*, *decl. as an adj.* architect.

зол *adj.*, *short form masc. of* **злой**. **—n.**, *gen. pl. of* **зло**.

зола́ *n.* **1,** ashes. **2,** ash: вулкани́ческая зола́, volcanic ash.

золо́вка [*gen. pl.* **-вок**] *n.* sister-in-law (*husband's sister*).

золота́рник *n.* goldenrod.

золоти́стый *adj.* golden.

золоти́ть *v.impfv.* [*pfv.* **позолоти́ть** *or* **вы́золотить**; *pres.* **-чу́, -ти́шь**] to gild. **—золоти́ть пилю́лю,** to sweeten the pill.

золотни́к [*gen.* **-ника́**] *n.* old Russian measure of weight equal to about 1/6 of an ounce. **—мал золотни́к, да до́рог,** good things come in small packages.

зо́лото *n.* gold. **—на вес зо́лота,** worth its weight in gold.

золотоиска́тель *n.m.* prospector (*for gold*).

золото́й *adj.* gold; golden. **—золоты́х дел ма́стер,** goldsmith. **—золото́е дно,** gold mine (*fig.*). **—золото́й дождь,** windfall. **—золото́й мешо́к,** rich man; moneybags. **—золото́й песо́к,** gold dust.

золотоно́сный *adj.* containing gold.

золоту́ха *n., obs.* scrofula.

золоче́ние *n.* gilding.

золочёный *adj.* gilded; gilt.

Зо́лушка *n.* Cinderella.

зо́на *n.* zone. —**зона́льный,** *adj.* zone (*attrib.*); zonal.

зонд *n.* **1,** *med.* probing device: желу́дочный зонд, stomach pump. **2,** weather balloon. —**косми́ческий зонд,** space probe.

зонда́ж *n.* sounding out.

зонди́ровать *v.impfv.* [*pres.* **-рую, -руешь**] **1,** to probe; sound. **2,** *fig.* to sound out. —**зонди́ровать по́чву,** to see which way the land lies; test the waters.

зонт [*gen.* **зонта́**] *n.* **1,** umbrella. **2,** awning.

зо́нтик *n.* umbrella.

зооло́гия *n.* zoology. —**зоо́лог,** *n.* zoologist. —**зоологи́ческий,** *adj.* zoological.

зоомагази́н *n.* pet store.

зоопа́рк *n.* zoo.

зо́ркий *adj.* **1,** sharp-eyed. Зо́ркий глаз, keen eye. **2,** *fig.* perceptive. —**зо́рко,** *adv.* with a watchful eye.

зо́ркость *n.f.* **1,** keen vision. **2,** perspicacity; acumen.

зра́зы [*gen.* **зраз**] *n.pl.* meat patties stuffed with rice, kasha, etc.

зрачо́к [*gen.* **-чка́**] *n.* pupil (*of the eye*).

зре́лище *n.* **1,** sight; spectacle. **2,** show.

зре́лость *n.f.* **1,** ripeness. **2,** maturity. —**полова́я зре́лость,** puberty.

зре́лый *adj.* **1,** ripe. **2,** mature.

зре́ние *n.* sight; eyesight; vision. —**по́ле зре́ния,** field of vision. —**то́чка зре́ния,** point of view; viewpoint. —**у́гол зре́ния,** viewpoint; standpoint.

зреть[1] *v.impfv.* [*pfv.* **созре́ть;** *pres.* **зре́ю, зре́ешь**] **1,** to ripen. **2,** to mature.

зреть[2] *v.impfv.* [*pfv.* **узре́ть;** *pres.* **зрю, зришь**] *archaic* to behold.

зри́мый *adj.* visible.

зри́тель *n.m.* **1,** spectator. **2,** *pl.* audience.

зри́тельный *adj.* **1,** visual. **2,** optic. —**зри́тельный зал,** auditorium.

зря *adv., colloq.* in vain; for nothing; to no purpose. —**почём зря,** *colloq.* for all one is worth.

зря́чий *adj.* able to see; sighted. —*n.* sighted person.

зря́шный *adj., colloq.* **1,** useless. **2,** (*of a person*) good-for-nothing.

зуб *n.* **1,** [*pl.* **зу́бы, зубо́в, зуба́м**] tooth. **2,** [*pl.* **зу́бья, зу́бьев**] tooth (*of a saw, gear, etc.*). —**име́ть зуб на** *or* **про́тив,** to have a grudge against. —**класть зу́бы на по́лку,** to stint oneself; tighten one's belt. —**не по зуба́м** (+ *dat.*), *colloq.* too much for; beyond one.

зуба́стый *adj., colloq.* **1,** having large teeth; toothy. **2,** sharp-tongued.

зубе́ц [*gen.* **зубца́**] *n.* tooth; cog; prong; sprocket.

зуби́ло *n.* cutting tool; chisel.

зубно́й *adj.* tooth (*attrib.*); dental. —**зубно́й врач,** dentist. —**зубна́я па́ста,** toothpaste. —**зубна́я щётка,** toothbrush.

зубоврачёбный *adj.* of or pert. to dentistry; dental.

зубо́к [*gen.* **зубка́**] *n., colloq., dim. of* зуб. —**на зубо́к,** *colloq.* **1,** as a present for a newborn child. **2,** (*with verbs of knowing or learning*) thoroughly; inside out. —**попа́сть на зубо́к** (+ *dat.*), to be subjected to (someone's) criticism or ridicule; be the target of someone's tongue.

зубоска́л *n., colloq.* joker; kidder. —**зубоска́льство,** *n., colloq.* scoffing; kidding.

зуботы́чина *n., colloq.* smack in the teeth.

зубочи́стка [*gen. pl.* **-ток**] *n.* toothpick.

зубр *n.* European bison.

зубрёжка *n., colloq.* cramming.

зубри́ла *n.m. & f., colloq.* crammer; grind. *Also,* зубри́лка.

зубри́ть *v.impfv.* [*pfv.* **зазубри́ть;** *pres.* **зубрю́, зубри́шь** *or* **зу́бришь**] **1,** to notch; make notches in. **2,** *colloq.* to cram (*study hard*). **3,** *colloq.* to learn by rote.

зубцо́вка *n.* perforation (*on stamps*). —**зубцо́вый,** *adj.* perforate; perforated.

зубча́тый *adj.* **1,** toothed. **2,** jagged. **3,** (*of a wall or fortress*) crenelated. —**зубча́тое колесо́,** cogwheel. —**зубча́тая ре́йка,** rack (*for a pinion*).

зуд *n.* itch.

зуде́ть[1] *v.impfv.* [*pres.* **зуди́т**] *colloq.* to itch.

зуде́ть[2] *v.impfv.* [*pres.* **зужу́, зуди́шь**] *colloq.* **1,** to hum; buzz. **2,** to nag.

зуёк [*gen.* **зуйка́**] *n.* plover.

зулу́с *n.m.* [*fem.* **-ка**] Zulu. —**зулу́сский,** *adj.* Zulu.

зу́ммер *n.* buzzer.

зы́бкий *adj.* **1,** unsteady; unstable. **2,** shifting; rippling. **3,** *fig.* vacillating.

зыбу́чий *adj.* shifting: зыбу́чие пески́, shifting sands.

зыбь *n.f.* rippling; undulating (*of water*). —**лёгкая зыбь,** ripples. —**мёртвая зыбь,** groundswell.

зы́чный *adj.* loud; resounding.

зюйд *n., naut.* **1,** south. **2,** south wind.

зя́бкий *adj., colloq.* sensitive to cold.

зя́бко *adv., colloq.* from *or* against the cold: зя́бко ку́таться, to bundle up against the cold. —*adj., colloq., used predicatively,* cold: Мне зя́бко, I am cold.

зя́блик *n.* chaffinch.

зя́бнуть *v.impfv.* [*past* **зяб, зя́бла**] to suffer from the cold; feel the cold.

зябь *n.f.* **1,** autumn plowing. **2,** land plowed in autumn for spring sowing.

зять [*pl.* **зятья́, зятьёв**] *n.m.* **1,** son-in-law. **2,** brother-in-law (*sister's husband or husband's sister's husband*).

И

И, и *n.neut.* ninth letter of the Russian alphabet.

и *conj.* **1,** and: причи́на и сле́дствие, cause and effect. **2,** *used for emphasis:* Вы себе́ и предста́вить не мо́жете!, you just can't imagine! **3,** also; as well: Мы опозда́ли и на второ́й по́езд, we missed the second train as well. Он понима́л и друго́е, he understood something else as well. **4,** (*with negatives*) either: Э́то не легко́ и для меня́, it is not easy for me either. **5,** even: Он и спаси́бо не сказа́л, he didn't even say thank you. **—и … и,** both: и мужчи́ны и же́нщины, both men and women.

ибери́йский *adj.* Iberian.

и́бис *n.* ibis.

и́бо *conj.* for; as.

и́ва *n.* willow. **—плаку́чая и́ва,** weeping willow.

ива́новский *adj., in* во всю ива́новскую, at the top of one's lungs.

ивня́к [*gen.* **-няка́**] *n.* **1,** willow bed. **2,** willow branches.

и́вовый *adj.* willow (*attrib.*).

и́волга *n.* European oriole.

иври́т *n.* (modern) Hebrew.

игла́ [*pl.* и́глы, игл] *n.* **1,** needle. **2,** quill (*of an animal*).

игли́стый *adj.* covered with needles or quills.

иглова́тый *adj.* **1,** needle-like. **2,** *colloq.* prickly.

иглови́дный *adj.* needle-shaped. *Also,* **иглообра́зный.**

иглотерапи́я *n.* acupuncture. *Also,* **иглоука́лывание.**

и́глу *n.neut. indecl.* igloo.

игнори́ровать *v.impfv. & pfv.* [*pres.* **-рую, -руешь**] to ignore; disregard.

и́го *n.* yoke (*of oppression*).

иго́лка [*gen. pl.* **-лок**] *n.* needle. **—быть** *or* **сиде́ть как на иго́лках,** to be on pins and needles; be on tenterhooks.

иго́лочка [*gen. pl.* **-чек**] *n., dim. of* игла́ *and* иго́лка. **—с иго́лочки,** brand-new. **—оде́т с иго́лочки,** impeccably dressed.

иго́лочный *adj.* needle (*attrib.*).

иго́льник *n.* needle cushion; needle case.

иго́льный *adj.* of a needle; needle (*attrib.*): иго́льное ушко́, eye of a needle.

иго́льчатый *adj.* needle-shaped.

иго́рный *adj.* gambling (*attrib.*); gaming (*attrib.*).

игра́ [*pl.* и́гры, игр] *n.* **1,** game: аза́ртная игра́, game of chance. **2,** play; playing: игра́ в ка́рты, cardplaying; игра́ на роя́ле, playing (of) the piano. Гру́бая

игра́, rough play. **3,** performance; acting. **—вне игры́,** *sports* **1,** out of play. **2,** out of bounds. **—игра́ воображе́ния,** figment of the imagination. **—игра́ слов,** play on words. **—игра́ судьбы́** *or* **слу́чая,** quirk of fate. **—игра́ ума́,** battle of wits.

игра́льный *adj.* playing (*attrib.*): игра́льные ка́рты, playing cards. **—игра́льные ко́сти,** dice.

игра́ть *v.impfv.* [*pfv.* **сыгра́ть**] **1,** to play. **2,** (*with* в + *acc.*) to play (a game). **3,** (*with* на + *prepl.*) to play (a musical instrument) **4,** to act; perform. **5,** [*impfv. only*] (*with instr.*) to play (with); fiddle (with); twiddle **6,** [*impfv. only*] (*with instr.*) to play (with); toy (with); trifle (with). **7,** (*with* в + *acc.*) to dabble (in). **8,** [*impfv. only*] (*of beverages*) to sparkle. **9,** (*with instr.*) *chess* to move (a pawn or piece). **—игра́ть глаза́ми,** to ogle. **—игра́ть на́ руку** (+ *dat.*), to play into the hands of. *See also* **сыгра́ть.**

игра́ючи *adv., colloq.* effortlessly; as if it were child's play.

и́грек *n.* the letter y.

игри́вый *adj.* playful. **—игри́вость,** *n.f.* playfulness.

игри́стый *adj.* (*of wine, champagne, etc.*) sparkling.

игрово́й *adj.* **1,** playing (*attrib.*). **2,** acting (*attrib.*). **3,** (*of a film, play, etc.*) full of action.

игро́к [*gen.* **игрока́**] *n.* **1,** player. **2,** gambler.

игру́шечный *adj.* **1,** toy (*attrib.*). **2,** miniature.

игру́шка [*gen. pl.* **-шек**] *n.* **1,** toy. **2,** *fig.* plaything.

игуа́на *n.* iguana.

игу́мен *n.* abbot; father superior (*of a Russian Orthodox monastery*). **—игу́менья,** *n.* abbess; mother superior (*of a Russian Orthodox convent*).

идеа́л *n.* ideal.

идеализи́ровать *v.impfv. & pfv.* [*pres.* **-рую, -руешь**] to idealize.

идеали́зм *n.* idealism. **—идеали́ст,** *n.* idealist. **—идеалисти́ческий,** *adj.* idealistic.

идеа́льный *adj.* **1,** ideal; sublime. **2,** ideal; perfect.

иде́йность *n.f.* **1,** ideological content. **2,** progressive character. **3,** high-mindedness.

иде́йный *adj.* **1,** ideological. **2,** progressive; high-minded. **3,** *in* иде́йный за́мысел, the basic idea; the point (*of a novel, play, etc.*).

иденти́чный (дэ) *adj.* identical. **—иденти́чность,** *n.f.* identity.

идеогра́мма *n.* ideogram; ideograph.

идео́лог *n.* **1,** ideologist. **2,** ideologue.

идеоло́гия *n.* ideology. **—идеологи́ческий,** *adj.* ideological.

иде́я *n.* idea.

иди́ллия *n.* idyll. **—идилли́ческий,** *adj.* idyllic.

идио́ма *n.* idiom. **—идиомати́ческий,** *adj.* idiomatic.

идио́т *n.* idiot; imbecile. **—идиоти́зм,** *n.* idiocy; imbecility. **—идио́тский,** *adj.* idiotic; imbecilic. **—идио́тство,** *n., colloq.* idiocy; nonsense.

и́диш *n.* Yiddish.

и́дол *n.* idol. **—(сиде́ть** *or* **стоя́ть) и́долом,** motionless; like a statue.

идолопокло́нник *n.* idolater. **—идолопокло́ннический,** *adj.* idolatrous. **—идолопокло́нство,** *n.* idolatry.

идти́ *v.impfv.* [*pfv.* **пойти́**; *pres.* **иду́, идёшь**; *past* **шёл, шла, шло, шли**] **1,** to go: Куда́ вы идёте?, where are you going? **2,** [*impfv. only*] to walk: Почему́ вы так ме́дленно идёте?, why are you walking so slowly? **3,** [*impfv. only*] to come: Вот они́ иду́т, here they come. Когда́ он шёл с рабо́ты, while he was coming home from work. **4,** to come out: Дым идёт из трубы́, smoke is coming out of the chimney. **5,** (*with* **за** + *instr.*) to follow: Иди́те за мной!, follow me! **6,** (*with* **в** *or* **на** + *acc.*) *colloq.* to go into; go onto: Гвоздь не идёт в сте́ну, the nail will not go into the wall; боти́нок не идёт на́ ногу, the shoe will not go onto my foot. **7,** [*impfv. only*] (*of a road, mountain range, etc.*) to run; stretch; extend. **8,** to go; proceed; progress: Рабо́та идёт хорошо́, the work is going well. **9,** [*impfv. only*] to be in progress: Иду́т экза́мены, exams are in progress. **10,** (*with* **на** + *acc.*) to be used for; go into the making of: Де́рево идёт на изготовле́ние бума́ги, wood is used in making paper. **11,** (*of time*) to pass; go by: Вре́мя бы́стро идёт, time passes quickly. **12,** (*of rain, snow, etc.*): Идёт дождь, it is raining. **13,** (*of mail*) to take a certain amount of time to arrive: Пи́сьма сюда́ иду́т о́чень до́лго, the mail takes a long time to get here. **14,** (*of a device*) to work: Мои́ часы́ не иду́т, my watch is not working. Мои́ часы́ хорошо́ иду́т, my watch keeps good time. **15,** (*of a film or play*) to be playing. **16,** (*with dat.*) to become: Шля́па вам идёт, the hat is becoming on you; (*with* **к**) to go (well) with: Га́лстук не идёт к ва́шему костю́му, the tie doesn't go with your suit. **17,** *colloq.* to sell: Това́р хорошо́ идёт, the merchandise is selling well. **18,** (*with* **на** + *acc.*) to make; take (*with certain nouns*): идти́ на усту́пки/же́ртвы, to make concessions/sacrifices; идти́ на риск, to take a risk. Идти́ на компроми́сс, to compromise. Идти́ на все усло́вия, to be prepared to accept all the conditions. Идти́ на хи́трость, to resort to guile. Идти́ на всё, to go to any length. **19,** *cards* to play; lead: идти́ с туза́, to play/lead an ace; идти́ ко́зырем, to play/lead a trump. **20,** (*with instr.*) *chess* to move: идти́ пе́шкой, to move a pawn. *See also* **ходи́ть** *and* **пойти́.**

и́ды [*gen.* **ид**] *n.pl.* ides: и́ды ма́рта, the ides of March.

Иего́ва *n.* Jehovah.

иезуи́т *n.* Jesuit. **—иезуи́тский,** *adj.* Jesuit.

ие́на *n.* yen (*monetary unit of Japan*).

иера́рхия *n.* hierarchy. **—иерархи́ческий,** *adj.* hierarchical.

иеро́глифы *n.pl.* [*sing.* **иеро́глиф**] (Egyptian) hieroglyph(ic)s; (Chinese) characters. **—иероглифи́ческий,** *adj.* hieroglyphic.

иждиве́нец [*gen.* **-нца**] *n.m.* [*fem.* **-нка**] dependent.

иждиве́ние *n.* maintenance; support. **—на иждиве́нии кого́-нибудь,** dependent on someone for support.

и́же *pron., in* **и и́же с ним** *or* **с ни́ми,** and others like him/them; and others of his/their ilk.

из *also,* **изо** *prep., with gen.* **1,** from: письмо́ из до́ма, a letter from home. Прие́хать из Пари́жа, to arrive from Paris. Из достове́рных исто́чников, from reliable sources. **2,** out of: вы́йти из ко́мнаты, to go out of the room. Выпуска́ть пти́цу из кле́тки, to let the bird out of the cage. **3,** of; made of: стол из де́рева, a table made of wood. **4,** of; consisting of: буке́т из роз, a bouquet of roses. **5,** of; out of (*a group*): оди́н из них, one of them. В девяно́ста девяти́ слу́чаях из ста, in 99 cases out of 100. **6,** (*with emotions*) out of: из жа́лости, out of pity.

из- *also,* **ис-, изо-, изъ-** *prefix* **1,** out of; ex-: извлека́ть, to extract; исключа́ть, to exclude. **2,** covering a surface: исписа́ть лист бума́ги, to fill up a sheet of paper with writing. **3,** entirely; all over: изъе́здить всю страну́, to travel all over the country. **4,** thoroughly; severely: измока́ть, to get soaked; исцара́пывать, to scratch severely. **5,** (*with* **-ся**) to the point of exhaustion: избе́гаться, to run oneself ragged.

изба́ [*pl.* **и́збы**] *n.* peasant's hut; log cabin.

изба́витель *n.m.* deliverer; savior; redeemer.

изба́вить [*infl.* **-влю, -вишь**] *v., pfv. of* **избавля́ть.** **—изба́виться,** *refl., pfv. of* **избавля́ться.**

избавле́ние *n.* deliverance.

избавля́ть *v.impfv.* [*pfv.* **изба́вить**] (*with* **от**) to save (from); rescue (from); deliver (from); spare. **—избавля́ться,** *refl.* (*with* **от**) **1,** to get rid of; rid oneself of. **2,** to avoid; escape.

избало́ванный *adj.* spoiled.

избалова́ть [*infl.* **-лу́ю, -лу́ешь**] *v., pfv. of* **балова́ть** *and* **избало́вывать.** **—избалова́ться,** *refl., pfv. of* **избало́вываться.**

избало́вывать *v.impfv.* [*pfv.* **избалова́ть**] to spoil; pamper. **—избало́вываться,** *refl.* to become spoiled.

избе́гать *v.pfv., colloq.* to run all over (a place).

избега́ть *v.impfv.* [*pfv.* **избежа́ть** *or* **избе́гнуть**] (*with gen.*) to avoid; evade.

избе́гаться *v.r.pfv., colloq.* to run oneself ragged.

избе́гнуть [*past* **избе́г** *or* **избе́гнул, избе́гла**] *v., pfv. of* **избега́ть.**

избежа́ние *n., in* **во избежа́ние** (+ *gen.*), in order to avoid.

избежа́ть [*infl. like* **бежа́ть**] *v., pfv. of* **избега́ть.**

избива́ть *v.impfv.* [*pfv.* **изби́ть**] **1,** to beat up. **2,** *obs.* to slaughter; massacre.

избие́ние *n.* **1,** beating. **2,** slaughter; massacre. **3,** *law* assault and battery.

избира́тель *n.m.* voter.

избира́тельный *adj.* **1,** electoral; election (*attrib.*). **2,** selective. **—избира́тельный бюллете́нь,** ballot. **—избира́тельный нало́г,** poll tax. **—избира́тельное пра́во,** suffrage. **—избира́тельный пункт,** polling place. —**избира́тельная у́рна; избира́тельный я́щик,** ballot box. —**избира́тельный уча́сток, 1,** voting/election district/precinct. **2,** polling place.

избира́ть *v.impfv.* [*pfv.* **избра́ть**] **1,** to select. **2,** to elect. —**избира́ться,** *refl.* [*impfv. only*] to be elected.

изби́тый *adj.* **1,** beaten up. **2,** *fig.* (*of a road, path, etc.*) well-trodden. **3,** *fig.* trite; hackneyed. —**изби́тая и́стина,** truism.

изби́ть [*infl.* **изобью́, изобьёшь**] *v., pfv. of* **избива́ть.**

изборозди́ть *v., pfv. of* **борозди́ть.**

избра́ние *n.* election.

избра́нник *n.* chosen one.

и́збранные *n.pl., decl. as an adj.* select people.

и́збранный *adj.* **1,** elected. **2,** select. —**и́збранные сочине́ния,** selected works.

избра́ть [*infl.* **-беру́, -берёшь;** *past fem.* **-брала́**] *v., pfv. of* **избира́ть.**

избу́шка [*gen. pl.* **-шек**] *n.* hut; log cabin.

избы́ток [*gen.* **-тка**] *n.* **1,** surplus; excess. **2,** abundance. —**в избы́тке; с избы́тком,** in abundance.

избы́точный *adj.* **1,** surplus; excess. **2,** redundant. —**избы́точность,** *n.f.* redundancy.

изва́яние *n.* piece of sculpture; sculptured figure.

изваять *v., pfv. of* **вая́ть.**

изве́дывать *v.impfv.* [*pfv.* **изве́дать**] to experience.

и́зверг *n.* fiend; monster.

изверга́ть *v.impfv.* [*pfv.* **изве́ргнуть**] to spew forth. —**изверга́ться,** *refl.* **1,** (*of a volcano*) to erupt. **2,** (*of lava*) to spew forth.

изве́ргнуть [*past* **изве́рг** *or* **изве́ргнул, изве́ргла**] *v., pfv. of* **изверга́ть.** —**изве́ргнуться,** *refl., pfv. of* **изверга́ться.**

изверже́ние *n.* **1,** eruption. **2,** ejection; expulsion. **3,** *fig.* outpouring; torrent (*of words, abuse, etc.*).

изве́рженный *adj., geol.* igneous.

изве́риться *v.r.pfv.* (*with* **в** + *prepl. or acc.*) to lose faith (in); lose confidence (in).

изверну́ться *v.r., pfv. of* **изворачиваться.**

извести́ [*infl. like* **вести́**] *v., pfv. of* **изводи́ть.** —**извести́сь,** *refl., pfv. of* **изводи́ться.**

изве́стие *n.* **1,** piece of news. **2,** *pl.* news.

извести́ть [*infl.* **-щу́, -сти́шь**] *v., pfv. of* **извеща́ть.**

извёстка *n., colloq.* = **и́звесть.**

известко́вый *adj.* lime. —**известко́вая вода́,** lime-water.

изве́стно *adj., used predicatively,* known: **как изве́стно,** as is known. **Изве́стно, что...,** it is known that... **Наско́лько мне изве́стно,** as far as I know. —**одному́ бо́гу изве́стно,** God alone knows.

изве́стность *n.f.* **1,** fame; notoriety; renown. **2,** *colloq.* a celebrity. —**ста́вить в изве́стность,** to inform; notify.

изве́стный *adj.* [*short form* **-стен, -стна**] **1,** known. **2,** well-known. **3,** notorious. **4,** a certain: **в** *or* **до изве́стной сте́пени,** to a certain extent. —**изве́стное де́ло,** naturally; of course.

известня́к [*gen.* **-няка́**] *n.* limestone. —**известня-ко́вый,** *adj.* limestone.

и́звесть *n.f.* lime. —**хло́рная и́звесть,** bleaching powder.

изве́чный *adj.* primeval; age-old; ancient.

извеща́ть *v.impfv.* [*pfv.* **извести́ть**] to inform; notify.

извеще́ние *n.* notice; notification.

изви́в *n.* bend (*in a river*); curve (*in a road*).

извива́ться *v.r.impfv.* **1,** to wriggle; squirm. **2,** (*of a river, road, etc.*) to wind; meander.

изви́лина *n.* bend (*in a river*); curve (*in a road*).

изви́листый *adj.* winding.

извине́ние *n.* **1,** apology. **2,** pardon: **проси́ть извине́ния у,** to beg someone's pardon. **3,** excuse: **Это не извине́ние,** that's no excuse.

извини́тельный *adj.* **1,** pardonable; excusable. **2,** of apology: **извини́тельное письмо́,** letter of apology. **3,** apologetic.

извиня́ть *v.impfv.* [*pfv.* **извини́ть**] to excuse; pardon: **Извини́те!,** excuse me!; pardon me! —**извиня́ться,** *refl.* (*with* **пе́ред**) to apologize (to).

извиня́ющийся *adj.* apologetic.

извлека́ть *v.impfv.* [*pfv.* **извле́чь**] **1,** to extract. **Извлека́ть пострада́вших из обло́мков,** to remove/free/extricate/pull victims from the wreckage. **2,** to derive: **извлека́ть по́льзу из,** to derive benefit from. **Извлека́ть уро́к из,** to draw/derive/learn a lesson from.

извлече́ние *n.* **1,** extraction. **2,** excerpt; extract.

извле́чь [*infl. like* **влечь**] *v., pfv. of* **извлека́ть.**

извне́ *adv.* from without; from the outside.

изводи́ть *v.impfv.* [*pfv.* **извести́;** *pres.* **-вожу́, -во́дишь**] *colloq.* **1,** to use up; waste; exhaust. **2,** to destroy; exterminate. **3,** to torment; exasperate. —**изводи́ться,** *refl., colloq.* **1,** to tire oneself out. **2,** to eat one's heart out. **3,** to waste away. **4,** to be used up.

изво́з *n.* private taxi service (*transporting passengers for pay in one's own car*).

изво́зчик *n.* **1,** driver; coachman (*of a hired carriage*). **2,** carriage for hire.

изво́лить *v.impfv., obs.* to wish; desire. —**изво́льте,** (*with inf.*) please; be so kind as to.

извора́чиваться *v.r.impfv.* [*pfv.* **изверну́ться**] **1,** to twist and turn. **2,** *fig., colloq.* to use cunning; resort to trickery.

изворо́т *n.* **1,** *obs.* bend. **2,** *usu. pl.* twist. **3,** *fig.* trick.

изворо́тливый *adj.* **1,** (*of a person*) shifty; clever; resourceful. **2,** (*of an animal*) elusive; slippery.

извраща́ть *v.impfv.* [*pfv.* **изврати́ть**] **1,** to distort; misrepresent. **2,** to corrupt; pervert.

извраще́ние *n.* **1,** distortion; misrepresentation. **2,** corruption; perversion.

извращённый *adj.* perverted. —**извращённость,** *n.f.* perversity.

изги́б *n.* bend; curve.

изгиба́ть *v.impfv.* [*pfv.* **изогну́ть**] to bend. —**изгиба́ться,** *refl.* **1,** to bend; become bent. **2,** to bend over. **3,** (*of a road, path, river, etc.*) to curve; wind.

изгла́живать *v.impfv.* [*pfv.* **изгла́дить**] to efface; blot out; erase.

изгна́ние *n.* **1,** banishment; expulsion; ostracism. **2,** exile: **жить в изгна́нии,** to live in exile. —**изгна́нник,** *n.* exile; outcast.

изгна́ть [*infl.* **-гоню́, -го́нишь;** *past fem.* **-гнала́**] *v., pfv. of* **изгоня́ть.**

изго́й *n.* outcast.

изголо́вье *n.* **1,** head of a bed. **2,** something that serves as a pillow.

изголода́ться *v.r.pfv.* **1,** to starve; be starving. **2,** (*with* **по** + *dat.*) to yearn (for).

изгоня́ть *v.impfv.* [*pfv.* **изгна́ть**] to drive out; banish; exile; ostracize.

и́згородь *n.f.* fence. —**жива́я и́згородь,** hedge.

изгота́вливать *v.* = **изготовля́ть.**

изгото́вить [*infl.* **-влю, -вишь**] *v., pfv. of* **изготовля́ть** *and* **изгота́вливать.**

изгото́вка *n., in* **на изгото́вку,** (*of a gun*) at the ready.

изготовле́ние *n.* manufacture.

изготовля́ть *v.impfv.* [*pfv.* **изгото́вить**] to make; manufacture.

издава́ть *v.impfv.* [*pfv.* **изда́ть**; *pres.* **-даю́, -даёшь**] **1,** to publish. **2,** to issue; promulgate. **3,** to emit; utter. **4,** to emit; give off (an odor).

и́здавна *adv.* **1,** since olden times; since days of yore. **2,** for a very long time; for as long as one can remember.

издалека́ *also,* **издалёка** *adv.* from afar.

и́здали *adv.* from a distance; from afar.

изда́ние *n.* **1,** issuance; promulgation. **2,** publication. **3,** a publication. Периоди́ческие изда́ния, periodicals. **4,** edition.

изда́тель *n.m.* publisher. —**изда́тельский,** *adj.* publishing (*attrib.*).—**изда́тельство,** *n.* publishing house.

изда́ть [*infl. like* **дать;** *past* **изда́л, издала́, изда́ло, изда́ли**] *v., pfv. of* **издава́ть.**

издева́тельский *adj.* mocking; derisive.

издева́тельство *n.* (*usu. with* **над**) **1,** mockery; derision. **2,** harassment; persecution; violation of one's dignity. **3,** *usu. pl.* malicious insults.

издева́ться *v.r.impfv.* (*with* **над**) **1,** to mock; taunt. **2,** to harass.

издёвка [*gen. pl.* **-вок**] *n., colloq.* **1,** gibe. **2,** mockery. Говори́ть с издёвкой, to speak in a mocking tone.

изде́лие *n.* **1,** make; manufacture. **2,** product; manufactured article. **3,** *pl.* goods: ко́жаные изде́лия, leather goods.

издёрганный *adj., colloq.* harried. Издёрганные не́рвы, jangled nerves.

издёргать *v.pfv., colloq.* to harry; harass; unnerve. —**издёргаться,** *refl., colloq.* to be unnerved.

издержа́ть [*infl.* **-держу́, -де́ржишь**] *v., pfv. of* **изде́рживать.** —**издержа́ться,** *refl., pfv. of* **изде́рживаться.**

изде́рживать *v.impfv.* [*pfv.* **издержа́ть**] to spend; expend. —**изде́рживаться,** *refl., colloq.* to spend all one's money.

изде́ржки [*gen.* **-жек**] *n.pl.* expenses; costs.

издо́льщик *n.* sharecropper. *Also,* **издо́льник.**

издо́хнуть [*past* **издо́х, издо́хла**] *v., pfv. of* **издыха́ть.**

издре́вле *adv.* from time immemorial.

издыха́ние *n.* last breath; dying gasp. —**до после́днего издыха́ния,** to one's last breath; to the death. —**при после́днем издыха́нии,** breathing one's last; near death.

издыха́ть *v.impfv.* [*pfv.* **издо́хнуть**] (*of animals*) to die.

изжа́рить *v., pfv. of* **жа́рить.** —**изжа́риться,** *refl., pfv. of* **жа́риться.**

изжива́ть *v.impfv.* [*pfv.* **изжи́ть**] to rid oneself of; eliminate. —**изжи́ть себя́,** to become obsolete.

изжи́ть [*infl.* **-живу́, -живёшь;** *past fem.* **-жила́**] *v., pfv. of* **изжива́ть.**

изжо́га *n.* heartburn.

из-за *prep., with gen.* **1,** from behind: вы́лететь из-за куста́, to dart out from behind a bush. ♦*With certain nouns,* from: встать из-за стола́, to get up from the table; верну́ться из-за грани́цы, to return from abroad. **2,** because of; on account of: Из-за него́ я опозда́л на рабо́ту, because of him I was late for work. **3,** (*with certain verbs*) over: спо́рить из-за де́нег, to argue over money; торгова́ться из-за ка́ждой копе́йки, to haggle over every penny.

иззя́бнуть *v.pfv.* [*past* **иззя́б, иззя́бла**] *colloq.* to be chilled to the bone.

излага́ть *v.impfv.* [*pfv.* **изложи́ть**] to state; set forth; expound.

изла́мывать *v.impfv.* [*pfv.* **изломáть**] **1,** to smash; shatter. **2,** *colloq.* to cripple. **3,** to ruin. —**изла́мываться,** *refl.* to be broken; be smashed.

излени́ться *v.r.pfv.* [*infl* **-еню́сь, -е́нишься**] *colloq.* to become incorrigibly lazy.

излёт *n., in* **на излёте,** (*of a bullet*) spent.

излече́ние *n.* **1,** medical treatment. **2,** recovery.

изле́чивать *v.impfv.* [*pfv.* **излечи́ть**] to cure. —**изле́чиваться,** *refl.* (*with* **от**) to be cured (of).

излечи́мый *adj.* curable.

излечи́ть [*infl.* **-лечу́, -ле́чишь**] *v., pfv. of* **изле́чивать.** —**излечи́ться,** *refl., pfv. of* **изле́чиваться.**

излива́ть *v.impfv.* [*pfv.* **изли́ть**] **1,** *obs.* to pour out. **2,** *fig.* to pour out; give vent to. **3,** *in* излива́ть ду́шу, to pour out one's heart *or* soul. —**излива́ться,** *refl.* to give vent to one's feelings.

изли́ть [*infl.* **изолью́, изольёшь;** *past fem.* **излила́**] *v., pfv. of* **излива́ть.** —**изли́ться,** *refl., pfv. of* **излива́ться.**

изли́шек [*gen.* **-шка**] *n.* **1,** surplus. **2,** excess. —**с изли́шком,** with something to spare.

изли́шество *n.* **1,** *obs.* excess; overabundance. **2,** excess; immoderation; *pl.* excesses. —**до изли́шества,** to excess.

изли́шне *adv.* excessively. —*adj., used predicatively,* superfluous; unnecessary: Изли́шне сказа́ть, что..., it is superfluous/unnecessary to say that...

изли́шний *adj.* **1,** excessive. **2,** superfluous; unnecessary.

излия́ние *n., usu. pl.* outpouring (*of emotion*).

излови́ть *v.pfv.* [*infl.* **-ловлю́, -ло́вишь**] *colloq.* to catch.

изловчи́ться *v.r.pfv.* (*with inf.*) *colloq.* to manage (to); succeed (in); contrive (to).

изложе́ние *n.* exposition; presentation.

изложи́ть [*infl.* **-ложу́, -ло́жишь**] *v., pfv. of* **излага́ть.**

изло́м *n.* **1,** break; fracture. **2,** sharp turn; sharp curve.

изло́манный *adj.* **1,** broken; smashed. **2,** crooked; winding. **3,** *fig.* warped; perverted.

изломáть *v., pfv. of* **изла́мывать.** —**изломáться,** *refl., pfv. of* **изла́мываться.**

излуча́ть *v.impfv.* to radiate. —**излуча́ться,** *refl.* to radiate; emanate.

излуче́ние *n.* radiation.

излу́чина *n.* bend; curve.

излю́бленный *adj.* favorite; pet.

изма́зать [*infl.* -ма́жу, -ма́жешь] *v., pfv. of* изма́зывать. —изма́заться, *refl., pfv. of* изма́зываться.

изма́зывать *v.impfv.* [*pfv.* изма́зать] *colloq.* to smear; get dirty. —изма́зываться, *refl.* (*with instr.*) *colloq.* to get (dirt, paint, ink, etc.) all over oneself.

изма́тывать *v.impfv.* [*pfv.* измота́ть] *colloq.* **1,** to exhaust; wear out. **2,** *mil.* to harass. —изма́тываться, *refl., colloq.* to be exhausted; be worn out.

изма́яться *v.r.pfv., colloq.* to be exhausted.

измельча́ть[1] *v., pfv. of* мельча́ть.

измельча́ть[2] *v.impfv.* [*pfv.* измельчи́ть] to grind; reduce to fine particles.

изме́на *n.* **1,** treason. **2,** betrayal. **3,** infidelity.

измене́ние *n.* change; alteration.

измени́ть [*infl.* -меню́, -ме́нишь] *v., pfv. of* изменя́ть. —измени́ться, *refl., pfv. of* изменя́ться.

изме́нник *n.* traitor. —изме́ннический, *adj.* traitorous.

изме́нчивый *adj.* changeable; fickle. —изме́нчивость, *n.f.* changeability.

изменя́ть *v.impfv.* [*pfv.* измени́ть] **1,** to change; alter. **2,** (*with dat.*) to betray; be unfaithful to. **3,** (*with dat.*) to fail: Си́лы ему́ измени́ли, his strength failed him.

изменя́ться *v.r.impfv.* [*pfv.* измени́ться] to change: Времена́ измени́лись, times have changed. —измени́ться в лице́, to change the expression on one's face.

измере́ние *n.* **1,** measurement; measuring. **2,** taking (*of temperature*). **3,** dimension.

измери́мый *adj.* measurable.

измери́тель *n.m.* **1,** measuring device; gauge. **2,** indicator; index. —измери́тельный, *adj.* (for) measuring.

измеря́ть *v.impfv.* [*pfv.* изме́рить] to measure. —измеря́ть температу́ру, **1,** (*with dat.*) to take someone's temperature. **2,** (*with gen.*) to measure the temperature of (*e.g.* water).

измождённый *adj.* haggard; gaunt; drawn; emaciated.

измока́ть *v.impfv.* [*pfv.* измо́кнуть] *colloq.* to get drenched; get soaked.

измо́кнуть [*past* измо́к, измо́кла] *v., pfv. of* измока́ть.

измо́р *n., in* взять изма́ром, **1,** to starve into submission. **2,** *fig.* to wear down; wear down the resistance of.

измори́ть *v.pfv., colloq.* to wear out; exhaust.

и́зморозь *n.f.* frost; hoarfrost.

и́зморось *n.f.* drizzle.

измота́ть *v., pfv. of* изма́тывать. —измота́ться, *refl., pfv. of* изма́тываться.

измоча́ливать *v.impfv.* [*pfv.* измоча́лить] *colloq.* **1,** to reduce to shreds. **2,** to wear out; exhaust completely.

изму́ченный *adj.* worn out; exhausted.

изму́чить *v.pfv.* **1,** to wear out; exhaust. **2,** to torment; rack. —изму́читься, *refl.* to be worn out; be exhausted.

измыва́ться *v.r.impfv.* (*with* над) *colloq.* **1,** to make fun of; poke fun at. **2,** to harass.

измы́слить *v., pfv. of* измышля́ть.

измышле́ние *n.* fabrication; falsehood; invention.

измышля́ть *v.impfv.* [*pfv.* измы́слить] **1,** to invent; fabricate. **2,** to think up; devise.

измя́тый *adj.* **1,** rumpled; crumpled; creased. **2,** battered. **3,** haggard.

измя́ть *v.pfv.* [*infl.* изомну́, изомнёшь] **1,** *pfv. of* мять (*in sense #2*). **2,** to batter. —измя́ться, *refl., pfv. of* мя́ться (*in sense #1*).

изна́нка *n.* **1,** wrong side; reverse side. **2,** *fig.* seamy side.

изнаси́лование *n.* rape.

изнаси́ловать *v., pfv. of* наси́ловать.

изнача́льный *adj.* **1,** primordial. **2,** original. —изнача́льно, *adv.* from the very beginning.

изна́шивание *n.* wearing out.

изна́шивать *v.impfv.* [*pfv.* износи́ть] to wear out (clothing, machinery, etc.). —изна́шиваться, *refl.* to wear out; be worn out.

изнёженный *adj.* soft; spoiled.

изнёживать *v.impfv.* [*pfv.* изне́жить] to spoil; pamper.

изнемога́ть *v.impfv.* [*pfv.* изнемо́чь] to be exhausted; be worn out.

изнеможе́ние *n.* utter exhaustion.

изнеможённый *adj.* utterly exhausted.

изнемо́чь [*infl. like* мочь] *v., pfv. of* изнемога́ть.

изне́рвничаться *v.r.pfv., colloq.* to be a nervous wreck.

изно́с *n.* wear; wear and tear. Мора́льный изно́с, obsolescence. —нет изно́су (+ *dat.*), immune to wear: Э́тим боти́нкам нет изно́су, these shoes will never wear out.

износи́ть [*infl.* -ношу́, -но́сишь] *v., pfv. of* изна́шивать. —износи́ться, *refl., pfv. of* изна́шиваться.

изно́шенный *adj.* worn out; threadbare.

изнуре́ние *n.* exhaustion.

изнури́тельный *adj.* **1,** exhausting; grueling. **2,** enervating; debilitating.

изнуря́ть *v.impfv.* [*pfv.* изнури́ть] to exhaust.

изнутри́ *adv.* **1,** from inside; from within. **2,** on the inside.

изныва́ть *v.impfv.* [*pfv.* изны́ть] **1,** to languish. **2,** to wilt (from the heat). **3,** to be dying (of thirst, boredom, etc.).

изны́ть [*infl.* изно́ю, изно́ешь] *v., pfv. of* изныва́ть.

изо *prep.* = из (*used before certain words beginning with two consonants*): изо рта; изо дня в день; изо всех сил.

изоба́ра *n.* isobar.

изоби́лие *n.* abundance; plenty; profusion. —рог изоби́лия, horn of plenty; cornucopia.

изоби́ловать *v.impfv.* [*pres.* -лует] (*with instr.*) to abound (in).

изоби́льный *adj.* abundant.

изоблича́ть *v.impfv.* [*pfv.* изобличи́ть] **1,** to expose; catch: изоблича́ть кого́-нибудь во лжи, to catch someone in a lie. **2,** [*impfv. only*] to show; reveal. **3,** [*impfv. only*] to reveal; give away: Акце́нт изоблича́л в нём иностра́нца, his accent gave him away as a foreigner.

изобличе́ние *n.* exposure.

изобличи́тель *n.m.* exposer. —изобличи́тельный, *adj.* incriminating.

изобличи́ть *v., pfv. of* изоблича́ть.

изобража́ть *v.impfv.* [*pfv.* изобрази́ть] to depict; portray; represent. —изобража́ть из себя́ (+ *acc.*), *colloq.* to make oneself out to be.

изображе́ние *n.* **1,** portrayal; representation. **2,** image; picture.

изобрази́тельный *adj.* graphic. —**изобрази́тельные иску́сства**, fine arts.

изобрази́ть [*infl.* -жу́, -зи́шь] *v., pfv. of* **изобража́ть**.

изобрести́ [*infl.* -брету́, -брете́шь; *past* -брёл, -брела́, -брело́] *v., pfv. of* **изобрета́ть**.

изобрета́тель *n.m.* inventor.

изобрета́тельный *adj.* inventive. —**изобрета́тельность**, *n.f.* inventiveness.

изобрета́ть *v.impfv.* [*pfv.* **изобрести́**] to invent.

изобрете́ние *n.* invention.

изо́гнутый *adj.* bent; curved.

изогну́ть *v., pfv. of* **изгиба́ть**. —**изогну́ться**, *refl., pfv. of* **изгиба́ться**.

изо́дранный *adj., colloq.* tattered.

изодра́ть *v.pfv.* [*infl.* издеру́, издерёшь; *past fem.* изодрала́] *colloq.* to tatter; tear to shreds.

изойти́ [*infl.* изойду́, изойдёшь; *past* изошёл, изошла́] *v., pfv. of* **исходи́ть**[1] (*in sense #4*).

изолга́ться *v.r.pfv.* [*infl. like* **лгать**] to become a habitual liar.

изоли́рованный *adj.* isolated; separate. —**изоли́рованно**, *adv.* in isolation.

изоли́ровать *v.impfv. & pfv.* [*pres.* -рую, -руешь] 1, to isolate. 2, to quarantine. 3, to insulate.

изоля́тор *n.* 1, insulator. 2, isolation ward. 3, solitary confinement cell.

изоляциони́зм *n.* isolationism. —**изоляциони́ст**, *n.* isolationist. —**изоляциони́стский**, *adj.* isolationist.

изоляцио́нный *adj.* 1, isolation (*attrib.*). 2, quarantine (*attrib.*). 3, insulation (*attrib.*). —**изоляцио́нная ле́нта**, friction tape.

изоля́ция *n.* 1, isolation. 2, quarantine. 3, insulation.

изоме́р *n.* isomer.

изо́рванный *adj.* torn; tattered.

изорва́ть *v.pfv.* [*infl.* -рву́, -рвёшь; *past fem.* -рвала́] 1, to tear up; tear to shreds. 2, to tear in many places. —**изорва́ться**, *refl.* to be torn to shreds; be full of holes.

изото́п *n.* isotope.

изощре́ние *n.* refinement; perfection.

изощрённый *adj.* 1, keen; acute. 2, perfected to a high degree.

изощря́ть *v.impfv.* [*pfv.* **изощри́ть**] to sharpen (one's hearing, mind, etc.); refine; cultivate (one's tastes); perfect (one's skills). —**изощря́ться**, *refl.* 1, to become refined. 2, (*with* в + *prepl.*) to excel (in); be a master of. 3, [*impfv. only*] to try hard; make a great effort.

из-под *prep., with gen.* 1, from under: вы́лезть из-под стола́, to crawl out from under the table. Из-под са́мого но́са, from under one's very nose. Вода́ из-под кра́на, water from the tap; tap water. 2, from somewhere near (a certain city). 3, (*of a container*) for holding: буты́лка из-под вина́, wine bottle. 4, *in various expressions:* вы́йти из-под контро́ля, to get out of control; освободи́ть из-под стра́жи, to release from custody.

изразе́ц [*gen.* -зца́] *n.* (glazed) tile. —**изразцо́вый**, *adj.* tile (*attrib.*); tiled.

изра́ильский *adj.* Israeli.

израильтя́нин [*pl.* -тя́не, -тя́н] *n.m.* [*fem.* -тя́нка] 1, *hist.* Israelite. 2, Israeli.

изра́нить *v.pfv.* to wound severely; wound in many places.

израсхо́довать *v., pfv. of* **расхо́довать**. —**израсхо́доваться**, *refl.* to be used up; be consumed.

и́зредка *adv.* now and then; from time to time.

изре́занный *adj.* 1, cut up; sliced up. 2, (*of a coastline*) irregular; indented; jagged. 3, (*of a region*) rugged.

изре́зать [*infl.* -ре́жу, -ре́жешь] *v., pfv. of* **изре́зывать**.

изре́зывать *v.impfv.* [*pfv.* **изре́зать**] 1, to cut up; cut into small pieces. 2, to gash; slash. 3, to cut across; crisscross.

изрека́ть *v.impfv.* [*pfv.* **изре́чь**] *obs.* to state; utter.

изрече́ние *n.* saying; maxim; adage; dictum.

изре́чь [*infl.* -реку́, -рече́шь, ...-реку́т; *past* -рёк, -рекла́, -рекло́] *v., pfv. of* **изрека́ть**.

изреше́чивать *v.impfv.* [*pfv.* **изрешети́ть**] to riddle (with bullets, shrapnel, etc.).

изрисова́ть *v.pfv.* [*infl.* -су́ю, -су́ешь] to cover with drawings.

изруби́ть *v.pfv.* [*infl.* -рублю́, -ру́бишь] 1, to chop up; hack to pieces. 2, to massacre (*by sword*).

изруга́ть *v.pfv., colloq.* to curse (someone) roundly; heap abuse on.

изрыва́ть *v.impfv.* [*pfv.* **изры́ть**] to dig up; dig holes in; dig holes all over.

изрыга́ть *v.impfv.* [*pfv.* **изрыгну́ть**] 1, to belch up; regurgitate. 2, to belch forth (flames, smoke, etc.). 3, to spew forth (profanities).

изры́тый *adj.* 1, dug up; full of holes or ruts. 2, rough; bumpy; uneven. —**изры́тый о́спой**, pockmarked.

изры́ть [*infl.* изро́ю, изро́ешь] *v., pfv. of* **изрыва́ть**.

изря́дно *adv., colloq.* 1, quite a lot. 2, (*with adjectives*) rather; pretty. 3, excellently; extremely well.

изря́дный *adj., colloq.* quite a; a pretty fair; a handsome; a goodly.

изуве́р *n.* 1, fanatic. 2, fiend; monster.

изуве́рский *adj.* 1, fanatical. 2, savage; barbaric.

изуве́рство *n.* 1, fanaticism. 2, barbarity.

изуве́чивать *v.impfv.* [*pfv.* **изуве́чить**] to mutilate; maim.

изуве́чить *v., pfv. of* **уве́чить** *and* **изуве́чивать**.

изукра́шивать *v.impfv.* [*pfv.* **изукра́сить**] to decorate lavishly; bedeck.

изуми́тельно *adv.* 1, amazingly. 2, marvelously.

изуми́тельный *adj.* 1, amazing; astonishing. 2, wonderful; marvelous.

изуми́ть [*infl.* -млю́, -ми́шь] *v., pfv. of* **изумля́ть**. —**изуми́ться**, *refl., pfv. of* **изумля́ться**.

изумле́ние *n.* amazement; astonishment.

изумлённый *adj.* amazed. —**изумлённо**, *adv.* in amazement.

изумля́ть *v.impfv.* [*pfv.* **изуми́ть**] to amaze; astonish. —**изумля́ться**, *refl.* (*with dat.*) to be amazed (at); be astonished (at).

изумру́д *n.* emerald. —**изумру́дный**, *adj.* emerald.

изуро́дованный *adj.* disfigured.

изуро́довать *v., pfv. of* **уро́довать.**

изуча́ть *v.impfv.* [*pfv.* **изучи́ть**] to study.

изуче́ние *n.* study; studying.

изучи́ть *v.pfv.* [*infl.* **изучу́, изу́чишь**] **1,** *pfv. of* **изуча́ть. 2,** to learn. **3,** to get to know.

изъеда́ть *v.impfv.* [*pfv.* **изъе́сть**] **1,** to eat away. Изъе́денный мо́лью, moth-eaten. **2,** to eat into.

изъе́здить *v.pfv.* [*infl.* **-е́зжу, -е́здишь**] to travel all over (an area).

изъе́сть [*infl. like* **есть**] *v., pfv. of* **изъеда́ть.**

изъяви́тельный *adj., in* **изъяви́тельное наклоне́ние,** *gram.* indicative mood.

изъяви́ть [*infl.* **-явлю́, -я́вишь**] *v., pfv. of* **изъявля́ть.**

изъявле́ние *n.* expression; declaration.

изъявля́ть *v.impfv.* [*pfv.* **изъяви́ть**] to express.

изъязви́ть [*infl.* **-влю́, -ви́шь**] *v., pfv. of* **изъязвля́ть.** —**изъязви́ться,** *refl., pfv. of* **изъязвля́ться.**

изъязвле́ние *n.* ulceration.

изъязвля́ть *v.impfv.* [*pfv.* **изъязви́ть**] to ulcerate. —**изъязвля́ться,** *refl.* to ulcerate; become ulcerated.

изъя́н *n.* defect; flaw.

изъясня́ться *v.r.impfv.* [*pfv.* **изъясни́ться**] **1,** *obs.* to express oneself. **2,** [*impfv. only*] to speak.

изъя́тие *n.* **1,** withdrawal; removal. **2,** seizure; confiscation. **3,** exception.

изъя́ть [*infl.* **изыму́, изы́мешь**] *v., pfv. of* **изыма́ть.**

изыма́ть *v.impfv.* [*pfv.* **изъя́ть**] **1,** to withdraw; remove. **2,** to seize; confiscate.

изыска́ние *n.* **1,** seeking. **2,** *usu. pl.* research. **3,** *usu. pl.* surveying; prospecting.

изы́сканный *adj.* refined; exquisite. —**изы́сканность,** *n.f.* refinement.

изыска́тель *n.m.* prospector.

изыска́ть [*infl.* **изыщу́, изы́щешь**] *v., pfv. of* **изы́скивать.**

изы́скивать *v.impfv.* [*pfv.* **изыска́ть**] **1,** to find; obtain. **2,** [*impfv. only*] to seek; look for.

изю́бр *also,* **изю́брь** *n.m.* a variety of red deer; Altai wapiti.

изю́м *n.* raisins. —**не фунт изю́ма,** nothing to sneeze at.

изю́мина *n.* a (single) raisin.

изю́минка [*gen. pl.* **-нок**] *n.* **1,** a (single) raisin. **2,** *fig.* spark; sparkle (*in a person*).

изя́щество *n.* elegance; grace.

изя́щно *adv.* elegantly.

изя́щный *adj.* elegant; graceful. —**изя́щные иску́сства,** fine arts.

Иису́с *n.* Jesus.

ика́ть *v.impfv.* [*pfv.* **икну́ть**] to hiccup.

ико́на *n.* icon. —**ико́нный,** *adj.* icon (*attrib.*).

иконобо́рец [*gen.* **-рца**] *n.* iconoclast. —**иконобо́р-(че)ство,** *n.* iconoclasm. —**иконобо́рческий,** *adj.* iconoclastic.

иконопи́сец [*gen.* **-сца**] *n.* icon painter. —**и́конопись,** *n.f.* icon painting.

иконоста́с *n.* iconostasis.

ико́та *n.* hiccups.

икра́ *n.* **1,** fish eggs. **2,** caviar. **3,** [*pl.* **и́кры**] calf (*of the leg*).

икромета́ние *n.* spawning.

икс *n.* the letter x.

ил *n.* silt.

и́ли *conj.* or. —**и́ли ..., и́ли ...,** either ..., or ...

и́листый *adj.* silty; slimy; muddy.

иллюзиони́ст *n.* magician.

иллю́зия *n.* illusion.

иллюзо́рный *adj.* illusory.

иллюмина́тор *n.* **1,** porthole (*on a ship*). **2,** window (*on an airplane*).

иллюмина́ция *n.* illumination; decorative lighting.

иллюминова́ть *v.impfv. & pfv.* [*pres.* **-ну́ю, -ну́ешь**] to decorate with lights. *Also,* **иллюмини́ровать** [*pres.* **-рую, -руешь**].

иллюстра́ция *n.* illustration. —**иллюстрати́вный,** *adj.* illustrative. —**иллюстра́тор,** *n.* illustrator.

иллюстри́ровать *v.impfv. & pfv.* [*pfv. also* **проиллюстри́ровать;** *pres.* **-рую, -руешь**] to illustrate.

и́лька [*gen. pl.* **и́лек**] *n.* fisher (*animal*).

ильм *n.* elm.

им *pron.* **1,** *instr. of* **он** *and* **оно́. 2,** *dat. of* **они́.**

имби́рь [*gen.* **-ря́**] *n.m.* ginger. —**имби́рный,** *adj.* ginger.

име́ние *n.* estate.

имени́ны [*gen.* **-ни́н**] *n.pl.* name day; one's saint's day. —**имени́нник,** *n.* person celebrating his/her name day. —**имени́нный,** *adj.* of or pert. to one's name day.

имени́тельный *adj., in* **имени́тельный паде́ж,** nominative case.

имени́тый *adj.* prominent; distinguished; eminent.

и́менно *particle* **1,** just; exactly; precisely. Вот и́менно!, exactly!; precisely! **2,** [*often* **а и́менно**] namely; to wit.

именно́й *adj.* inscribed with the owner's name. —**именно́й спи́сок,** roll; list of names.

имено́ванный *adj., in* **имено́ванное число́,** *math.* concrete number.

именова́ть *v.impfv.* [*pfv.* **наименова́ть;** *pres.* **-ну́ю, -ну́ешь**] to name. —**именова́ться,** *refl.* [*impfv. only*] to be called.

име́ть *v.impfv.* **1,** to have: име́ть возмо́жность (+ *inf.*), to have the opportunity to. **2,** *rendered by various English verbs according to the noun:* име́ть вес, to carry weight; име́ть успе́х, to be successful; име́ть схо́дство с, to bear a resemblance to; не име́ть смы́сла, to make no sense; не име́ть значе́ния, to be of no significance. —**ничего́ не име́ть про́тив,** to have no objection.

име́ться *v.r.impfv.* to be; exist; be available. В го́роде име́ется мно́го кни́жных магази́нов, there are many bookstores in town. Возраже́ний не име́ется, there are no objections.

име́ющийся *adj.* available; on hand.

и́ми *pron., instr. of* **они́.**

и́мидж *n.* (public) image.

имита́тор *n.* imitator; mimic.

имита́ция *n.* **1,** imitation; mimicry. **2,** imitation; fake.

имити́ровать *v.impfv.* [*pres.* **-рую, -руешь**] to imitate.

иммигра́нт *n.m.* [*fem.* **-ка**] immigrant.

иммигра́ция *n.* **1,** immigration. **2,** immigrants. —**иммиграцио́нный,** *adj.* immigration (*attrib.*).

иммигри́ровать *v.impfv. & pfv.* [*pres.* **-ру́ю, -ру́ешь**] to immigrate.

иммобилизова́ть *v.impfv.* [*pres.* **-зу́ю, -зу́ешь**] *med.* to immobilize.

иммуниза́ция *n.* immunization.

иммунизи́ровать *v.impfv. & pfv.* [*pres.* **-ру́ю, -ру́ешь**] to immunize.

иммуните́т *n.* immunity.

имму́нный *adj.* immune. —**имму́нная систе́ма,** immune system.

императи́в *n.* **1,** imperative. **2,** *gram.* imperative (mood).

императи́вный *adj.* **1,** imperative; obligatory. **2,** imperious; peremptory.

импера́тор *n.* emperor. —**импера́торский,** *adj.* emperor's; imperial.

императри́ца *n.* empress.

империали́зм *n.* imperialism. —**империали́ст,** *n.* imperialist. —**империалисти́ческий,** *adj.* imperialist; imperialistic.

импе́рия *n.* empire. —**импе́рский,** *adj.* imperial.

импи́чмент *n.* impeachment.

имплата́ция *n.* implantation.

импоза́нтный *adj.* imposing; impressive.

импони́ровать *v.impfv.* [*pres.* **-ру́ю, -ру́ешь**] (with dat.) to impress; make an impression on.

и́мпорт *n.* **1,** import; importation. **2,** imports. —**импортёр,** *n.* importer.

импорти́ровать *v.impfv. & pfv.* [*pres.* **-ру́ю, -ру́ешь**] to import.

и́мпортный *adj.* **1,** import (*attrib.*). **2,** imported.

импоте́нт *n.* man who is impotent. —**импоте́нтный,** *adj.* impotent. —**импоте́нция,** *n.* impotence.

импреса́рио *n.m. indecl.* impresario.

импрессиони́зм *n.* impressionism. —**импрессиони́ст,** *n.* impressionist. —**импрессионисти́ческий;** **импрессиони́стский,** *adj.* impressionist(ic).

импровиза́ция *n.* improvisation. —**импровиза́тор,** *n.* improviser.

импровизи́рованный *adj.* improvised; extemporaneous; impromptu.

импровизи́ровать *v.impfv. & pfv.* [*pres.* **-ру́ю, -ру́ешь**] to improvise.

и́мпульс *n.* impulse; impetus. —**импульси́вный,** *adj.* impulsive.

иму́щественный *adj.* property (*attrib.*).

иму́щество *n.* **1,** property. **2,** *mil.* equipment. **3,** *colloq.* belongings. —**недви́жимое иму́щество,** real estate.

иму́щий *adj.* propertied. —**власть иму́щие,** those in power; the powers that be.

и́мя [*gen., dat. & prepl.* **и́мени;** *instr.* **и́менем;** *pl.* **имена́, имён, имена́м**] *n.neut.* **1,** name; first name. **2,** name; reputation: сде́лать себе́ и́мя, to make a name for oneself. **3,** *noun:* и́мя со́бственное, proper noun. **4,** *in* и́мя существи́тельное, noun; и́мя прилага́тельное, adjective; и́мя числи́тельное, numeral. —**во и́мя** (+ *gen.*), in the name of; for the sake of. —**на и́мя** (+ *gen.*), **1,** in the name of. **2,** addressed to. —**от и́мени** (+ *gen.*), on behalf of. —**по и́мени, 1,** by name. **2,** (*fol. by a name*) by the name of. —**и́менем** (+ *gen.*), in the name of: и́менем зако́на, in the name

of the law. —**и́мени** (+ *gen.*), named in honor of: институ́т и́мени Па́влова, the Pavlov Institute.

имяре́к *n.* so-and-so.

инакомы́слие *n.* dissent; dissidence. —**инакомы́слящий,** *adj. & n.* dissident.

инаугура́ция *n.* inauguration.

ина́че *also,* **и́наче** *adv.* differently; otherwise. Сде́лать что́-нибудь ина́че, to do something differently. Вы́шло ина́че, it turned out otherwise. —*conj., colloq.* or; or else; otherwise. Спеши́те, ина́че вы опозда́ете, hurry, or you'll be late. —**ина́че говоря́,** in other words. —**так и́ли ина́че,** somehow or other; one way or another.

инвали́д *n.* invalid; disabled person. —**инвали́дность,** *n.f.* disability.

инвали́дный *adj.* invalid (*attrib.*); invalid's. —**инвали́дная коля́ска,** wheelchair.

инвалю́та *n., colloq.* foreign currency (*contr. of* иностра́нная валю́та).

инвентариза́ция *n.* (taking) of inventory.

инвентаризи́ровать *v.impfv. & pfv.* [*pres.* **-ру́ю, -ру́ешь**] to take inventory of. *Also,* **инвентаризова́ть** [*pres.* **-зу́ю, -зу́ешь**].

инвента́рный *adj.* inventory (*attrib.*).

инвента́рь [*gen.* **-таря́**] *n.m.* inventory. —**живо́й инвента́рь,** livestock. —**мёртвый инвента́рь,** farm tools and equipment.

инве́рсия *n., gram.; chem.; meteorol.* inversion.

инвести́тор *n.* investor. —**инвести́тура,** *n.* investiture. —**инвести́ция,** *n.* investment. —**инве́стор,** *n.* investor.

ингаля́тор *n., med.* inhaler.

ингредие́нт *n.* ingredient.

ингу́ш [*gen.* **-гуша́**] *n.m.* [*fem.* **-гу́шка**] Ingush (*one of a people inhabiting the Caucasus*).

и́ндеветь *v.impfv.* [*pfv.* **зайи́ндеветь**] to become covered with frost.

инде́ец [*gen.* **-де́йца**] *n.m.* [*fem.* **-диа́нка**] American Indian.

инде́йка [*gen. pl.* **-де́ек**] *n.* turkey.

инде́йский *adj.* (American) Indian.

и́ндекс (дэ) *n.* index: и́ндекс цен, price index.

индиа́нка [*gen. pl.* **-нок**] *n.* **1,** Indian woman; woman of India. **2,** American Indian woman; squaw.

индиви́д *n.* individual.

индивидуали́зм *n.* individualism. —**индивидуали́ст,** *n.* individualist.

индивидуа́льный *adj.* individual. —**индивидуа́льность,** *n.f.* individuality.

индивиду́ум *n.* individual.

инди́го *n. indecl.* indigo.

инди́ец [*gen.* **-ди́йца**] *n.m.* [*fem.* **-диа́нка**] *n.* Indian; native of India.

и́ндий *n.* indium.

инди́йский *adj.* Indian; of India.

индика́тор *n.* indicator.

индиффере́нтный *adj.* indifferent. —**индиффере́нтность,** *n.f.* indifference.

индоевропе́йский *adj.* Indo-European.

индонези́ец [*gen.* **-ийца**] *n.m.* [*fem.* **-ийка**] Indonesian. —**индонези́йский,** *adj.* Indonesian.

индоссамéнт *n., finance* endorsement.
индоссировать *v.impfv. & pfv.* [*pres.* **-рую, -руешь**] *finance* to endorse.
индуизм *n.* Hinduism.
индуктивный *adj.* inductive.
индуктор *n.* inductor.
индукционный *adj.* induction (*attrib.*): индукционная катушка, induction coil.
индукция *n., logic; electricity* induction.
индус *n.m.* [*fem.* **-дуска**] Hindu. —**индусский**, *adj.* Hindu.
индустриализация *n.* industrialization.
индустриализировать *v.impfv. & pfv.* [*pres.* **-рую, -руешь**] to industrialize.
индустриальный *adj.* 1, industrial. 2, industrialized.
индустрия *also,* **индустрия** *n.* industry.
индюк *n.* [*gen.* **-дюка**] *n.* turkey cock.
индюшка *n.* [*gen. pl.* **-шек**] *n., colloq.* turkey.
иней *n.* frost; hoarfrost.
инертный *adj.* 1, *chem.* inert. 2, inert; sluggish. —**инертность**, *n.f.* inertia; sluggishness.
инерция *n.* 1, inertia. 2, momentum. 3, *fig.* inertia; sluggishness.
инженер *n.* engineer. —**инженер-механик**, mechanical engineer. —**инженер-строитель**, civil engineer. —**инженер-химик**, chemical engineer. —**инженер-электрик**, electrical engineer.
инженерия *n., obs.* engineering. —**генная инженерия**, genetic engineering.
инженерный *adj.* 1, engineering (*attrib.*). Инженерное дело, engineering. 2, *mil.* engineer (*attrib.*): инженерные войска, engineer troops.
инжир *n.* 1, fig. 2, fig tree.
инициалы [*gen.* **-лов**] *n.pl.* initials.
инициатива *n.* initiative. —**инициативный**, *adj.* with initiative; possessing initiative.
инициатор *n.* initiator.
инквизиция *n.* inquisition. —**инквизитор**, *n.* inquisitor.
инкогнито *adv.* incognito.
инкорпорация *n.* incorporation.
инкорпорировать *v.impfv. & pfv.* [*pres.* **-рую, -руешь**] to incorporate.
инкриминировать *v.impfv. & pfv.* [*pres.* **-рую, -руешь**] to charge; impute: инкриминировать кому-нибудь кражу, to charge someone with theft; impute a theft to someone.
инкрустация *n.* inlaid work; inlay.
инкрустировать *v.impfv. & pfv.* [*pres.* **-рую, -руешь**] to inlay; encrust.
инкубатор *n.* incubator.
инкубация *n.* incubation. —**инкубационный**, *adj.* incubation (*attrib.*).
иногда *adv.* sometimes.
иногородный *adj.* from another city; out-of-town.
иноземец [*gen.* **-мца**] *n.m.* [*fem.* **-мка**] *obs.* foreigner. —**иноземный**, *adj.* foreign.
иной *adj.* 1, other; another. 2, else: никто иной, no one else. 3, some; certain. —**иной раз**, sometimes. —**не кто иной, как**, none other than. —**не что иное, как**, nothing but; nothing less than. —**тот или иной**, some ... or other; one ... or another.

инок *n., obs.* monk.
инородный *adj.* foreign: инородное тело, foreign body.
иносказание *n.* allegory. —**иносказательный**, *adj.* allegorical.
иностранец [*gen.* **-нца**] *n.m.* [*fem.* **-нка**] 1, foreigner. 2, *law* alien.
иностранный *adj.* foreign.
иноходец [*gen.* **-дца**] *n.* pacer (*horse*).
иноходь *n.f.* amble; pace: идти иноходью, to amble; pace.
иноязычный *adj.* 1, speaking another language. 2, belonging to another language family; foreign.
инсектицид *n.* insecticide.
инсинуация *n.* insinuation; innuendo.
инспектировать *v.impfv.* [*pres.* **-рую, -руешь**] to inspect.
инспектор [*pl.* **инспектора**] *n.* inspector. —**инспекторский**, *adj.* inspector's.
инспекция *n.* 1, inspection. 2, inspection board. —**инспекционный**, *adj.* inspection (*attrib.*).
инспирировать *v.impfv. & pfv.* [*pres.* **-рую, -руешь**] 1, to influence. 2, to inspire; incite; instigate.
инстанция *n.* 1, level of authority; echelon. 2, *law* instance: суд первой инстанции, court of the first instance. —**командные инстанции**, *mil.* chain of command.
инстинкт *n.* instinct.
инстинктивный *adj.* instinctive. —**инстинктивно**, *adv.* instinctively.
институт *n.* 1, institute. 2, institution: институт брака, the institution of marriage.
инструктаж *n.* 1, instructing. 2, instructions; *mil.* briefing.
инструктивный *adj.* instructional.
инструктирование *n.* instructing; instruction.
инструктировать *v.impfv. & pfv.* [*pres.* **-рую, -руешь**] 1, to instruct. 2, to brief.
инструктор *n.* instructor.
инструкция *n.* instructions; directions.
инструмент *n.* 1, tool; instrument. 2, *music* instrument.
инструменталист *n.* instrumentalist.
инструментальный *adj.* 1, tool (*attrib.*); used in making tools. 2, *music* instrumental.
инструментальщик *n.* toolmaker.
инструментарий *n.* tools; instruments.
инструментовать *v.impfv. & pfv.* [*pres.* **-тую, -туешь**] to orchestrate.
инструментовка *n.* orchestration.
инсулин *n.* insulin.
инсульт *n., med.* stroke.
инсценировать *v.impfv. & pfv.* [*pres.* **-рую, -руешь**] 1, to stage; adapt for the stage. 2, *fig.* to feign.
инсценировка *n.* staging.
интеграл (тэ) *n., math.* integral.
интегральный (тэ) *adj.* 1, *math.* integral. 2, *electronics* integrated: интегральная схема, integrated circuit.
интеграция (тэ) *n.* integration. *Also,* **интегрирование**.
интегрировать (тэ) *v.impfv. & pfv.* [*pres.* **-рую, -руешь**] to integrate.

интелле́кт *n.* intellect.

интеллектуа́л *n.* intellectual. —**интеллектуа́льный,** *adj.* intellectual.

интеллиге́нт *n.* intellectual.

интеллиге́нтный *adj.* cultured; educated.

интеллиге́нция *n.* intelligentsia.

интенда́нт *n., mil.* quartermaster. —**интенда́нтство,** *n.* quartermaster corps; commissariat.

интенси́вный (тэ) *adj.* intensive. —**интенси́вность,** *n.f.* intensity.

интерва́л *n.* interval; space. —**че́рез два интерва́ла,** double-spaced.

интерве́нция *n.* intervention.

интервью́ (тэ) *n.neut. indecl.* interview. —**интервьюе́р,** *n.* interviewer.

интервьюи́ровать (тэ) *v.impfv. & pfv.* [*pres.* **-рую, -руешь**] to interview.

интере́с *n.* **1,** interest: интере́с к иску́сству, an interest in art. **2,** *pl.* interests: жи́зненные интере́сы, vital interests. —**в интере́сах** (+ *gen.*), in the interest of; for the sake of.

интере́сно *adv.* in an interesting manner. —*adj., used predicatively* **1,** interesting: Интере́сно знать, кто э́то сказа́л, it would be interesting to know who said that. **2,** (*with dat.*) interested: е́сли вам интере́сно знать, if it is of any interest to you; in case you're interested. **3,** I wonder: Интере́сно, куда́ он пошёл, I wonder where he went.

интере́сный *adj.* [*short form* **-сен, -сна**] **1,** interesting. **2,** *colloq.* attractive; good-looking; cute. —**в инте́ресном положе́нии,** in the family way.

интересова́ть *v.impfv.* [*pres.* **-су́ю, -су́ешь**] to interest. —**интересова́ться,** *refl.* (*with instr.*) to be interested (in).

интерлю́дия (тэ) *n., music* interlude.

интерме́ццо (тэ) *n. indecl.* intermezzo.

инте́рн (тэ) *n.* intern.

интерна́т (тэ) *n.* dormitory. —**шко́ла-интерна́т,** boarding school.

Интернациона́л (тэ) *n.* **1,** international (*socialist organization*). **2,** the Internationale (*revolutionary hymn*).

интернационали́зм (тэ) *n.* internationalism.

интернациона́льный (тэ) *adj.* international.

интерни́рование (тэ) *n.* internment.

интерни́ровать (тэ) *v.impfv. & pfv.* [*pres.* **-рую, -руешь**] to intern.

интерполи́ровать (тэ) *v.impfv. & pfv.* [*pres.* **-рую, -руешь**] to interpolate.

интерполя́ция (тэ) *n.* interpolation.

интерпрета́тор (тэ) *n.* interpreter.

интерпрета́ция (тэ) *n.* interpretation.

интерпрети́ровать (тэ) *v.impfv. & pfv.* [*pres.* **-рую, -руешь**] to interpret.

интерье́р (тэ) *n.* interior (*of a building*).

инти́мный *adj.* intimate. —**инти́мно,** *adv.* intimately. —**инти́мность,** *n.f.* intimacy.

интона́ция *n.* intonation.

интри́га *n.* **1,** intrigue. **2,** plot (*of a novel*). **3,** *obs.* love affair.

интрига́н *n.* schemer.

интригова́ть *v.impfv.* [*pfv.* **заинтригова́ть;** *pres.* **-гу́ю, -гу́ешь**] **1,** to intrigue; fascinate. **2,** [*impfv. only*] to engage in intrigue; scheme.

интригу́ющий *adj.* **1,** intriguing. **2,** engaging in intrigue; scheming.

интроду́кция *n., music* introduction.

интроспе́кция *n.* introspection. —**интроспекти́вный,** *adj.* introspective.

интуити́вный *adj.* intuitive. —**интуити́вно,** *adv.* intuitively.

интуи́ция *n.* intuition.

инфа́ркт *n.* heart attack.

инфе́кция *n.* infection. —**инфекцио́нный,** *adj.* infectious.

инфинити́в *n.* infinitive.

инфля́ция *n.* inflation. —**инфляцио́нный,** *adj.* inflation (*attrib.*); inflationary.

информа́нт *n.* informant.

информа́тика *n.* information science.

информа́тор *n.* informant.

информа́ция *n.* information. —**информацио́нный,** *adj.* information (*attrib.*).

информи́ровать *v.impfv. & pfv.* [*pfv. also* **проинформи́ровать;** *pres.* **-рую, -руешь**] to inform.

инфракра́сный *adj.* infrared.

инфраструкту́ра *n.* infrastructure.

инциде́нт *n.* incident.

инъе́кция *n.* injection.

ио́н *n.* ion.

иониза́ция *n.* ionization.

ионизи́ровать *v.impfv. & pfv.* [*pres.* **-рую, -руешь**] to ionize. *Also,* **ионизова́ть** [*pres.* **-зу́ю, -зу́ешь**].

ио́нный *adj.* ionic; ion (*attrib.*).

ионосфе́ра *n.* ionosphere.

иорда́нский *adj.* Jordanian.

ипоме́я *n.* morning-glory.

ипоста́сь *n.f.* role; capacity.

ипоте́ка *n.* mortgage.

ипохо́ндрия *n.* hypochondria. —**ипохо́ндрик,** *n.* hypochondriac.

ипподро́м *n.* racetrack.

ипри́т *n.* mustard gas.

ира́кский *adj.* Iraqi.

ира́нец [*gen.* **-нца**] *n.m.* [*fem.* **-нка**] Iranian. —**ира́нский,** *adj.* Iranian.

ири́дий *n.* iridium.

и́рис *n.* iris (*flower*).

ири́с *n.* taffy.

ирла́ндец [*gen.* **-дца**] *n.m.* [*fem.* **-дка**] Irishman. —**ирла́ндский,** *adj.* Irish.

иронизи́ровать *v.impfv.* [*pres.* **-рую, -руешь**] **1,** to be ironic or sarcastic; remark ironically or sarcastically. **2,** (*with* **над**) to speak sarcastically (of).

ирони́ческий *adj.* ironic; ironical. —**ирони́чески,** *adv.* ironically.

иро́ния *n.* irony. —**по иро́нии судьбы́,** by an irony of fate; ironically.

иррадиа́ция *n.* irradiation.

иррациона́льный *adj., math.* irrational.

ирригáция *n.* irrigation. —**ирригацио́нный,** *adj.* irrigation (*attrib.*).

ис- *prefix, var. of* **из-** (*used before voiceless consonants*).

иск *n.* suit; lawsuit.

искажáть *v.impfv.* [*pfv.* **исказить**] **1,** to distort; contort. **2,** to distort; misrepresent.

искажéние *n.* distortion.

исказить [*infl.* **-жу́, -зи́шь**] *v., pfv. of* **искажáть.**

искалéчить *v., pfv. of* **калéчить.**

искáлывать *v.impfv.* [*pfv.* **исколо́ть**] to prick all over.

искáние *n., often pl.* search; quest.

искáпывать *v.impfv.* [*pfv.* **ископáть**] to dig up; dig holes in; dig holes all over.

искáтель *n.m.* seeker. —**искáтель приключéний,** adventure-seeker; adventurer.

искáть *v.impfv.* [*pres.* **ищу́, и́щешь**] **1,** (*with acc.*) to look for; search for. **2,** (*with gen. or acc.*) to seek; try to obtain.

исключáть *v.impfv.* [*pfv.* **исключи́ть**] **1,** to expel; dismiss; remove. **2,** to eliminate. **3,** to exclude; preclude; rule out. Это исключено́, that is out of the question. **4,** to delete; drop; strike off *or* from. —**взаи́мно исключáть друг дру́га,** to be mutually exclusive.

исключáя *prep., with acc.* except; excepting; excluding; barring.

исключéние *n.* **1,** exception: за исключéнием (+ *gen.*), with the exception of. **2,** elimination; exclusion. **3,** expulsion.

исключи́тельно *adv.* **1,** exceptionally. **2,** exclusively; only; solely.

исключи́тельность *n.f.* **1,** exceptional nature. **2,** exclusivity: рáсовая исключи́тельность, racial exclusivity.

исключи́тельный *adj.* **1,** exceptional. **2,** extraordinary. **3,** exclusive.

исключи́ть *v., pfv. of* **исключáть.**

исковéркать *v., pfv. of* **ковéркать.**

исколеси́ть *v.pfv.* [*infl.* **-шу́, -си́шь**] *colloq.* to travel all over (an area).

исколоти́ть *v.pfv.* [*infl.* **-лочу́, -ло́тишь**] *colloq.* to beat up.

исколо́ть [*infl.* **-колю́, -ко́лешь**] *v., pfv. of* **искáлывать.**

иско́мый *adj.* **1,** sought after. **2,** *math.* sought; to be found. —**иско́мое,** *n., math.* unknown.

искони́ *adv.* from time immemorial.

иско́нный *adj.* **1,** age-old; long-standing. **2,** native; indigenous.

ископáемое *n., decl. as an adj.* fossil. —**полéзные ископáемые,** minerals.

ископáемый *adj.* **1,** extracted from the earth. **2,** fossil (*attrib.*); fossilized.

ископáть *v., pfv. of* **искáпывать.**

искорёженный *adj.* twisted (*out of shape*).

искорёжить *v., pfv. of* **корёжить.**

искоренéние *n.* eradication; rooting out.

искореня́ть *v.impfv.* [*pfv.* **искорени́ть**] to eradicate; stamp out; root out.

и́скорка [*gen. pl.* **-рок**] *n., dim. of* **и́скра.**

и́скоса *adv.* askance; out of the corner of one's eye.

и́скра *n.* **1,** spark. **2,** *fig.* (*with gen.*) ray; glimmer (*of hope*); seed (*of doubt, suspicion, etc.*). —**у него́ и́скры из глаз посы́пались,** he saw stars.

и́скренний *adj.* sincere. —**и́скренне; и́скренно,** *adv.* sincerely. —**и́скренность,** *n.f.* sincerity.

искриви́ть [*infl.* **-влю́ -ви́шь**] *v., pfv. of* **искривля́ть.**

искривлéние *n.* curvature.

искривля́ть *v.impfv.* [*pfv.* **искриви́ть**] **1,** to bend out of shape. **2,** to contort.

и́скристый *also,* **искри́стый** *adj.* sparkling.

искри́ть *v.impfv.* to spark.

и́скриться *also,* **искри́ться** *v.r.impfv.* to sparkle.

искромётный *adj.* sparkling; flashing; dazzling.

искромсáть *v., pfv. of* **кромсáть.**

искроши́ть *v., pfv. of* **кроши́ть.** —**искроши́ться,** *refl., pfv. of* **кроши́ться.**

искупáть *v.impfv.* [*pfv.* **искупи́ть**] **1,** to atone for; expiate. **2,** to make up for; make amends for.

искупáться *v.r.pfv., colloq.* **1,** to take a bath. **2,** to go for a swim.

искупи́тельный *adj.* expiatory.

искупи́ть [*infl.* **-куплю́, -ку́пишь**] *v., pfv. of* **искупáть.**

искуплéние *n.* (*with gen.*) expiation (of); atonement (for).

иску́с *also,* **и́скус** *n.* **1,** ordeal. **2,** test.

искусáть *v.pfv.* to sting; bite (*in many places*).

искуси́тель *n.m.* tempter.

искуси́ть [*infl.* **-кушу́, -куси́шь**] *v., pfv. of* **искушáть.** —**искуси́ться,** *refl.* (*with* **в** + *prepl.*) *obs.* to become experienced (in); become an expert (at).

иску́сник *n., colloq.* master craftsman; past master.

иску́сный *adj.* skillful. —**иску́сно,** *adv.* skillfully.

иску́сственный *adj.* **1,** artificial; synthetic; man-made. **2,** artificial; unnatural; affected. —**иску́сственно,** *adv.* artificially. —**иску́сственность,** *n.f.* artificiality.

иску́сство *n.* **1,** art: изя́щные иску́сства, fine arts; произведéние иску́сства, work of art; иску́сство шитья́, the art of sewing. **2,** skill: с больши́м иску́сством, with great skill.

искусствовéд *n.* art critic. —**искусствовéдение,** *n.* art criticism; study of art.

искушáть *v.impfv.* [*pfv.* **искуси́ть**] to tempt. —**искушáть судьбу́,** to tempt fate; press *or* stretch one's luck.

искушéние *n.* temptation.

искушённый *adj.* experienced; knowledgeable; (*with* **в** + *prepl.*) versed (in).

ислáм *n.* Islam.

ислáндец [*gen.* **-дца**] *n.m.* [*fem.* **-дка**] *n.* Icelander. —**ислáндский,** *adj.* Icelandic.

испáнец [*gen.* **-нца**] *n.m.* [*fem.* **-нка**] Spaniard.

испáнка [*gen. pl.* **-нок**] *n.* **1,** Spanish woman. **2,** *colloq.* influenza; flu.

испáнский *adj.* Spanish.

испарéние *n.* **1,** evaporation. **2,** *pl.* fumes.

испáрина *n.* perspiration.

испари́тель *n.m.* vaporizer.

испаря́ть *v.impfv.* [*pfv.* **испари́ть**] to evaporate; convert to vapor. —**испаря́ться,** *refl.* **1,** to evaporate; turn into vapor. **2,** *colloq.* to vanish; evaporate.

испа́чкать *v., pfv. of* па́чкать. —испа́чкаться, *refl., pfv. of* па́чкаться.

испепеля́ть *v.impfv.* [*pfv.* испепели́ть] to incinerate; reduce to ashes.

испестря́ть *v.impfv.* [*pfv.* испестри́ть] to make colorful.

испе́чь *v., pfv. of* печь. —испе́чься, *refl., pfv. of* пе́чься (*in sense #1*).

испещря́ть *v.impfv.* [*pfv.* испещри́ть] 1, to dot with color. 2, to mark up.

исписа́ть [*infl.* -пишу́, -пи́шешь] *v., pfv. of* испи́сывать. —исписа́ться, *refl., pfv. of* испи́сываться.

испи́сывать *v.impfv.* [*pfv.* исписа́ть] 1, to cover with writing. 2, to use up (paper, a pencil, etc.). —испи́сываться, *refl.* 1, (*of a pencil*) to be used up; be worn to a stump. 2, *colloq.* (*of a writer*) to lose one's creativity; become stale.

испито́й *adj., colloq.* haggard; gaunt; drawn.

исповеда́льня [*gen. pl.* -лен] *n.* confessional.

испове́дание *n.* 1, profession (*of a certain faith*). 2, espousal. 3, faith; creed.

испове́дник *n.* confessor.

испове́довать *v.impfv. & pfv.* [*pres.* -дую, -дуешь] 1, to hear the confession of. 2, to confess. 3, to practice; profess (a certain religion). 4, to espouse (an idea, principle, etc.). —испове́доваться, *refl.* to confess; confess one's sins.

и́споведь *n.f.* confession.

и́сподволь *adv., colloq.* gradually; slowly; little by little.

исподло́бья *adv., in* смотре́ть исподло́бья (на), to glower (at).

исподтишка́ *adv., colloq.* secretly; stealthily; on the sly.

испоко́н *adv., in* испоко́н веко́в (*or* ве́ку), since time immemorial.

исполи́н *n.* giant. —исполи́нский, *adj.* giant; gigantic.

исполко́м *n.* executive committee (*contr. of* исполни́тельный комите́т).

исполне́ние *n.* 1, execution; fulfillment; performance. 2, performance; rendition. —приводи́ть в исполне́ние, to carry out.

испо́лненный *adj.* (*with gen.*) full (of).

исполни́мый *adj.* feasible.

исполни́тель *n.m.* 1, executor. 2, performer. —соста́в исполни́телей, cast. —суде́бный исполни́тель, bailiff.

исполни́тельный *adj.* 1, executive. 2, efficient; industrious. —исполни́тельный комите́т, executive committee. —исполни́тельный лист, writ.

исполня́ть *v.impfv.* [*pfv.* испо́лнить] 1, to fulfill (a wish); comply with (a request); carry out; execute (an order); perform (duties). 2, to perform (a song, dance, role, etc.). —исполня́ющие обя́занности (+ *gen.*), acting: исполня́ющие обя́занности дире́ктора, acting director.

исполня́ться *v.r.impfv.* [*pfv.* испо́лниться] 1, to be fulfilled. 2, (*of an anniversary*) to occur. 3, *impers.* (*with dat.*) *indicating attainment of a certain age:* За́втра мне испо́лнится два́дцать оди́н год, tomorrow I will be twenty-one.

исполосова́ть *v., pfv. of* полосова́ть.

испо́льзование *n.* utilization; use.

испо́льзовать *v.impfv. & pfv.* [*pres.* -зую, -зуешь] to use; utilize; make use of; exploit.

испо́льщик *n.* sharecropper.

испо́ртить *v., pfv. of* по́ртить. —испо́ртиться, *refl., pfv. of* по́ртиться.

испо́рченный *adj.* 1, spoiled; rotten; tainted. 2, damaged. 3, depraved; perverted.

исправи́мый *adj.* 1, reparable; rectifiable; remediable. 2, repairable.

исправи́тельный *adj.* corrective; remedial. —исправи́тельный дом, reformatory; reform school; house of correction.

испра́вить [*infl.* -влю, -вишь] *v., pfv. of* исправля́ть. —испра́виться, *refl., pfv. of* исправля́ться.

исправле́ние *n.* 1, repairing. 2, correcting. 3, a correction.

исправля́ть *v.impfv.* [*pfv.* испра́вить] 1, to correct. Испра́вленное изда́ние, revised edition. 2, to repair. 3, to reform. —исправля́ться, *refl.* to reform; mend one's ways.

испра́вность *n.f.* good condition; good working order.

испра́вный *adj.* 1, in good condition; in good working order. 2, conscientious; industrious.

испражне́ние *n.* 1, defecation. 2, *pl.* excrement; feces; stool.

испражня́ться *v.r.impfv.* [*pfv.* испражни́ться] to defecate.

испра́шивать *v.impfv.* [*pfv.* испроси́ть] *obs.* to solicit; formally request.

испро́бовать *v.pfv.* [*infl.* -бую, -буешь] 1, to test; try out. 2, to experience.

испроси́ть [*infl.* -прошу́, -про́сишь] *obs.* 1, *pfv. of* испра́шивать. 2, to obtain; receive (*by asking*).

испу́г *n.* fright.

испу́ганный *adj.* frightened; scared.

испуга́ть *v., pfv. of* пуга́ть. —испуга́ться, *refl., pfv. of* пуга́ться.

испуска́ние *n.* emission.

испуска́ть *v.impfv.* [*pfv.* испусти́ть] 1, to emit; give off. 2, to emit; utter. —испусти́ть дух *or* после́дний вздох, to breathe one's last.

испусти́ть [*infl.* -пущу́, -пу́стишь] *v., pfv. of* испуска́ть.

испыта́ние *n.* 1, trial; test. 2, examination. 3, trial; ordeal.

испы́танный *adj.* tried; tested; proven.

испыта́тель *n.m.* tester. —лётчик-испыта́тель, test pilot.

испыта́тельный *adj.* test (*attrib.*); trial (*attrib.*).

испыта́ть *v., pfv. of* испы́тывать.

испыту́ющий *adj.* searching; penetrating.

испы́тывать *v.impfv.* [*pfv.* испыта́ть] 1, to test; try out. 2, to experience; feel. 3, to try; tax (someone's patience). 4, *in* испы́тывать судьбу́, to tempt fate; press *or* stretch one's luck.

иссека́ть *v.impfv.* [*pfv.* иссе́чь] 1, to carve (*in stone, marble, etc.*). 2, *med.* to excise. 3, to slash in many places. 4, *obs.* to flog.

иссече́ние *n., med.* excision.

иссе́чь *v.pfv.* [*infl. like* сечь] 1, [*past* -сёк, -секла́,

-секлó] *pfv. of* **иссекáть** (*in senses #1 & #2*). **2,** [*past* **-сéк, -сéкла, -сéкло]** *pfv. of* **иссекáть** (*in senses #3 & #4*).

исслéдование *n.* **1,** research. **2,** a study (*piece of research*). **3,** exploration.

исслéдователь *n.m.* **1,** researcher. **2,** explorer.

исслéдовательский *adj.* research (*attrib.*).

исслéдовать *v.impfv. & pfv.* [*pres.* **-дую, -дуешь]** **1,** to explore. **2,** to examine. **3,** to study; do research in.

иссóп *n.* hyssop.

иссóхнуть [*past* **иссóх, иссóхла]** *v., pfv. of* **иссыхáть.**

и́сстари *adv.* since ancient times.

исстрадáться *v.r.pfv.* to be worn out with suffering.

исступлéние *n.* frenzy.

исступлённый *adj.* frenzied.

иссушáть *v.impfv.* [*pfv.* **иссушить]** **1,** to dry thoroughly; dry completely. **2,** *fig.* to drain; exhaust (someone).

иссушить [*infl.* **-сушу́, -су́шишь]** *v., pfv. of* **иссушáть.**

иссыхáть *v.impfv.* [*pfv.* **иссóхнуть]** **1,** to dry up. **2,** *fig.* to shrink away to nothing.

иссякáть *v.impfv.* [*pfv.* **исся́кнуть]** **1,** to dry up; run dry. **2,** to give out; run out; be used up; be exhausted.

исся́кнуть [*past* **исся́к, исся́кла]** *v., pfv. of* **иссякáть.**

истáпливать *v.impfv.* [*pfv.* **истопить]** **1,** to heat; heat up (a stove). **2,** *colloq.* to use; consume (firewood). **3,** *colloq.* to melt completely; melt all of.

истáптывать *v.impfv.* [*pfv.* **истоптáть]** **1,** to trample. **2,** *colloq.* to track up (a clean floor). **3,** *colloq.* to wear out (shoes).

истáскивать *v.impfv.* [*pfv.* **истаскáть]** *colloq.* to wear out (clothes, shoes, etc.).

истáчивать *v.impfv.* [*pfv.* **источить]** **1,** to wear down (*by repeated rubbing*). **2,** to eat away.

истекáть *v.impfv.* [*pfv.* **истéчь]** **1,** *obs.* to flow out. **2,** *in* истекáть крóвью, to bleed profusely; истéчь крóвью, to bleed to death. **3,** (*of time*) to elapse; expire; run out; be up. **4,** [*impfv. only*] (*with* **от** *or* **из**) to emanate (from); stem (from).

истéкший *adj.* past: за истéкший год, during the past year.

истерéть [*infl.* **изотру́, изотрёшь**; *past* **истёр, истёрла]** *v., pfv. of* **истирáть. —истерéться,** *refl., pfv. of* **истирáться.**

истéрзанный *adj.* **1,** slashed to bits. **2,** bedraggled. **3,** tormented.

истерзáть *v.pfv.* **1,** to tear to pieces. **2,** *fig.* to beset; torment; wrack.

истéрик *n., colloq.* person often going into fits of hysteria.

истéрика *n.* hysterics.

истери́ческий *adj.* hysterical.

истери́чка [*gen. pl.* **-чек]** *n., colloq.* hysterical woman.

истери́чный *adj.* hysterical.

истери́я *n.* hysteria.

истёртый *adj., colloq.* **1,** worn out; worn down. **2,** *fig.* trite; overused.

истéц [*gen.* **истцá]** *n.* plaintiff.

истечéние *n.* **1,** outflow. **2,** expiration.

истéчь [*infl. like* **течь]** *v., pfv. of* **истекáть.**

и́стина *n.* truth.

и́стинный *adj.* true; veritable. **—и́стинно,** *adv.* truly.

истирáть *v.impfv.* [*pfv.* **истерéть]** **1,** to grate; shred. **2,** to wear away (a surface); wear out (clothes or furniture); wear down (an eraser). **—истирáться,** *refl.* **1,** to be worn out. **2,** *obs.* to be effaced.

истлевáть *v.impfv.* [*pfv.* **истлéть]** **1,** to rot; decay. **2,** to burn to ashes.

и́стовый *adj., obs.* **1,** real; true. **2,** energetic; vigorous. **3,** proper; sedate.

истóк *n.* **1,** source (*of a river*); *pl.* headwaters. **2,** *usu. pl.* source; origin.

истолковáние *n.* interpretation.

истолковáтель *n.m.* interpreter; commentator.

истолковáть [*infl.* **-ку́ю, -ку́ешь]** *v., pfv. of* **истолкóвывать.**

истолкóвывать *v.impfv.* [*pfv.* **истолковáть]** to interpret; construe.

истолóчь *v.pfv.* [*infl. like* **толóчь]** to pound; crush; pulverize.

истóма *n.* lassitude; languor.

истомить [*infl.* **-млю́, -ми́шь]** *v., pfv. of* **истомля́ть. —истоми́ться,** *refl., pfv. of* **истомля́ться.**

истомля́ть *v.impfv.* [*pfv.* **истомить]** to tire; weary; fatigue; exhaust. **—истомля́ться,** *refl.* to be exhausted.

истóмный *adj.* tiring; tedious.

истончи́ть *v.pfv.* to make very thin. **—истончи́ться,** *refl.* to become very thin; wear thin.

истопи́ть [*infl.* **-топлю́, -тóпишь]** *v., pfv. of* **истáпливать.**

истопни́к [*gen.* **-никá]** *n.* boilerman; stoker.

истоптáть [*infl.* **-топчу́, -тóпчешь]** *v., pfv. of* **истáптывать.**

исторгáть *v.impfv.* [*pfv.* **истóргнуть]** **1,** to banish. **2,** to wrest; grab. **3,** to rescue; deliver. **4,** to elicit; evoke. **5,** to extract; extort.

истóргнуть [*past* **истóрг** *or* **истóргнул, истóргла]** *v., pfv. of* **исторгáть.**

истори́зм *n.* historical method.

истóрик *n.* historian.

историогрáфия *n.* historiography. **—историóграф,** *n.* historiographer.

истори́ческий *adj.* **1,** historical. **2,** historic. **3,** of history. **—истори́чески,** *adv.* historically.

истóрия *n.* **1,** history. **2,** story. **3,** *colloq.* incident; untoward event: попáсть *or* влипнуть в истóрию, to get into an unpleasant situation. **—истóрия болéзни,** case history.

истосковáться *v.r.pfv.* [*infl.* **-ку́юсь, -ку́ешься]** (*with* **по** + *dat.*) *colloq.* to miss greatly; yearn for.

источáть *v.impfv.* **1,** *obs.* to shed (tears). **2,** to give off; emit.

источи́ть [*infl.* **-точу́, -тóчишь]** *v., pfv. of* **истáчивать.**

истóчник *n.* **1,** spring. **2,** source.

истóшный *adj., colloq.* heart-rending; bloodcurdling.

истощáть *v.impfv.* [*pfv.* **истощи́ть]** **1,** to exhaust; tire out. **2,** to exhaust; deplete; use up. **—истощáться,** *refl.* **1,** to be exhausted (*physically*). **2,** to be exhausted; be used up; run out.

истощéние *n.* **1,** exhaustion: нéрвное истощéние, nervous exhaustion. **2,** exhaustion; depletion. **—войнá на истощéние,** war of attrition.

истощённый *adj.* **1,** exhausted. **2,** emaciated.

истощи́ть *v., pfv. of* **истоща́ть.** —**истощи́ться,** *refl., pfv. of* **истоща́ться.**

истра́тить *v., pfv. of* **тра́тить.** —**истра́титься,** *refl., pfv. of* **тра́титься.**

истреби́тель *n.m.* **1,** (*with gen.*) destroyer (of). **2,** fighter plane; fighter.

истреби́тельный *adj.* **1,** destructive. Истреби́тельная война́, war of annihilation. **2,** *aero.* fighter (*attrib.*).

истреби́ть [*infl.* -блю́, -би́шь] *v., pfv. of* **истребля́ть.**

истребле́ние *n.* destruction; extermination.

истребля́ть *v.impfv.* [*pfv.* **истреби́ть**] to destroy; annihilate; exterminate; wipe out.

истрёпанный *adj., colloq.* **1,** torn; tattered. **2,** *fig.* exhausted; worn down.

истрепа́ть [*infl.* -треплю́, -тре́плешь] *v., pfv. of* **трепа́ть** (*in sense #4*) *and* **истрёпывать.** —**истрепа́ться,** *refl., pfv. of* **трепа́ться** (*in sense #2*) *and* **истрёпываться.**

истрёпывать *v.impfv.* [*pfv.* **истрепа́ть**] *colloq.* **1,** to wear out. **2,** *fig.* to exhaust; wear down. —**истрёпываться,** *refl., colloq.* to be worn out.

истука́н *n.* idol. —(сиде́ть *or* стоя́ть) истука́ном, motionless; like a statue.

иступи́ть *v., pfv. of* **тупи́ть.** —**иступи́ться,** *refl., pfv. of* **тупи́ться.**

и́стый *adj.* true; real.

исте́блишмент *n.* (the) establishment.

истяза́ние *n.* torture. —**истяза́тель,** *n.m.* torturer.

истяза́ть *v.impfv.* to torture.

исхо́д *n.* **1,** end; close. **2,** outcome. **3,** way out (*of a situation*). **4,** outlet (*for one's emotions*). **5,** *Bib.* exodus; *cap.* (book of) Exodus. —на исхо́де, **1,** drawing to a close. **2,** (*with gen.*) at the end (of). **3,** running low; running out.

исходи́ть[1] *v.impfv.* [*pres.* -хожу́, -хо́дишь] **1,** (*with* из *or* от) (*of smoke, an odor, etc.*) to come (from); issue (from). **2,** (*with* из *or* от) to originate (from); emanate (from). **3,** (*with* из) to proceed on (an assumption, premise, etc.). **4,** [*pfv.* **изойти́**] (*with instr.*) *colloq.* to be drained of (tears, blood, etc.).

исходи́ть[2] *v.pfv.* [*infl.* -хожу́, -хо́дишь] *colloq.* to walk all over (a place).

исхо́дный *adj.* initial; starting.

исходя́щий *adj.* (*of mail, documents, etc.*) outgoing.

исхуда́лый *adj.* emaciated; haggard; gaunt.

исхуда́ть *v.pfv.* to become emaciated.

исцара́пывать *v.impfv.* [*pfv.* **исцара́пать**] to scratch severely; scratch in many places.

исцеле́ние *n.* **1,** cure; healing. **2,** recovery. —**исцели́тель,** *n.m.* healer.

исцеля́ть *v.impfv.* [*pfv.* **исцели́ть**] to cure; heal.

исча́дие *n., obs.* child; offspring. —**исча́дие а́да,** the devil incarnate.

исча́хнуть *v.pfv.* [*past* исча́х, исча́хла] to waste away.

исчеза́ть *v.impfv.* [*pfv.* **исче́знуть**] to disappear; vanish.

исчезнове́ние *n.* disappearance.

исче́знуть [*past* исче́з, исче́зла] *v., pfv. of* **исчеза́ть.**

исчёркивать *v.impfv.* [*pfv.* **исчерка́ть** *or* **исчёркать**] *colloq.* **1,** to mark up completely (*with corrections*). **2,** to scribble all over.

исче́рпывать *v.impfv.* [*pfv.* **исче́рпать**] **1,** to exhaust. **2,** to settle; close (a matter).

исче́рпывающий *adj.* exhaustive.

исчерти́ть [*infl.* -черчу́, -че́ртишь] *v., pfv. of* **исче́рчивать.**

исче́рчивать *v.impfv.* [*pfv.* **исчерти́ть**] to cover with lines.

исчисле́ние *n.* **1,** calculation. **2,** calculus.

исчисля́ть *v.impfv.* [*pfv.* **исчи́слить**] to calculate; estimate. —**исчисля́ться,** *refl.* [*impfv. only*] (*with instr. or* в + *acc.*) to number in; amount to.

ита́к *conj.* so; and so; thus.

италья́нец [*gen.* -нца] *n.m.* [*fem.* -нка] Italian.

италья́нский *adj.* Italian. —**италья́нская забасто́вка,** sit-down strike.

и т.д. *abbr. of* **и так да́лее,** and so forth; et cetera.

ито́г *n.* **1,** sum; total. **2,** result. —**в ито́ге,** as a result. —**в коне́чном ито́ге,** in the final analysis. —**подводи́ть ито́г(и),** *see* **подводи́ть.**

итого́ *adv.* **1,** in all; altogether. **2,** (*at the bottom of a column of figures*) total.

ито́говый *adj.* **1,** total. **2,** final; closing; concluding.

итте́рбий *n.* ytterbium.

и́ттрий *n.* yttrium.

Иу́да *n.* Judas.

иудаи́зм *n.* Judaism.

иуде́й *n.* Jew. —**иуде́йский,** *adj.* Judaic. —**иуде́йство,** *n.* Judaism.

их *pron., gen. & acc. of* **они́.** —*poss. adj. & pron.* their; theirs.

ихневмо́н *n.* ichneumon.

и́хний *adj., colloq.* their; theirs.

ихтиоло́гия *n.* ichthyology.

иша́к [*gen.* **ишака́**] *n.* donkey.

ишеми́я *n.* ischemia.

и́шиас *n.* sciatica.

ишь *particle, colloq.* see!; look!; oh! —**ишь ты, 1,** = ишь. **2,** oh, come on!; what you are talking about!

ище́йка [*gen. pl.* **ище́ек**] *n.* **1,** bloodhound. **2,** *colloq.* sleuth.

ию́ль *n.m.* July. —**ию́льский,** *adj.* July (*attrib.*).

ию́нь *n.m.* June. —**ию́ньский,** *adj.* June (*attrib.*).

Й

Й, й *n.neut., called* **и кра́ткое,** tenth letter of the Russian alphabet.
йе́менский *adj.* Yemeni; Yemenite.
йог *n.* yogi. —**йо́га,** *n.* yoga.
йогу́рт *n.* yogurt.

йод *n.* iodine.
йо́дистый *adj.* **1,** containing iodine. **2,** iodide (of): йо́дистый ка́лий, potassium iodide.
йо́дный *adj.* iodine (*attrib.*).
йо́та *n.* iota. —**ни на йо́ту,** not a bit; not one iota.

К

К, к *n.neut.* eleventh letter of the Russian alphabet.
к *also,* **ко** *prep., with dat.* **1,** to; toward: идти́ к доске́, to go to the blackboard; идти́ к до́му, to walk toward the house. К ве́черу, toward evening. Подходи́ть к концу́, to draw to a close. **2,** to; to the home or place of business of: идти́ к врачу́, to go to the doctor. Он ча́сто приходи́л к нам, he often came to visit us. **3,** (*with emotions*) of; for; toward: любо́вь к ро́дине, love of one's country; жа́лость к пострада́вшим, pity for the victims; мои́ чу́вства к ней, my feelings toward her. **4,** (*in introductory expressions*) to: к моему́ удивле́нию, to my surprise. К сча́стью, fortunately; к сожале́нию, unfortunately. **5,** (*with expressions of time*) by: к тому́ вре́мени, by that time; by then; к концу́ ве́ка, by the end of the century. —**к тому́ же,** moreover; besides. —**к чему́?,** what for?; why?
-ка *particle, colloq., used to lessen the force of a suggestion, request, command, etc.:* ну́-ка, well?; встава́й-ка!, get up, now!; закро́й-ка окно́!, close the window, will you?
каба́к [*gen.* -бака́] *n.* **1,** *pre-rev.* tavern. **2,** *colloq.* mess.
кабала́ *n.* servitude; bondage.
каба́льный *adj.* **1,** serving to enslave. **2,** (*of a treaty, provisions, etc.*) one-sided.
каба́н [*gen.* -бана́] *n.* **1,** wild boar. **2,** male hog.
кабарга́ [*gen. pl.* -ро́г] *n.* musk deer.

кабарди́нец [*gen.* -нца] *n.m.* [*fem.* -нка] Kabardian (*one of a people inhabiting the Caucasus*). —**кабарди́нский,** *adj.* Kabardian.
кабаре́ (рэ) *n.neut. indecl.* cabaret.
кабачо́к [*gen.* -чка́] *n.* **1,** cheap restaurant. **2,** squash (*vegetable*).
ка́бель *n.m.* cable. —**ка́бельный,** *adj.* cable (*attrib.*).
кабеста́н *n.* capstan.
каби́на *n.* **1,** booth; cubicle. **2,** cab (*of a truck*). **3,** *aero.* cabin; cockpit.
кабине́т *n.* **1,** private office; study. **2,** (specially equipped) room: рентге́новский кабине́т, X-ray room. Космети́ческий кабине́т, beauty parlor. **3,** set of office furniture. **4,** private room in a restaurant. **5,** *polit.* cabinet.
кабине́тный *adj.* office (*attrib.*). —**кабине́тный роя́ль,** baby grand piano. —**кабине́тный страте́г,** armchair strategist.
каби́нка [*gen. pl.* -нок] *n., dim. of* каби́на.
каблогра́мма *n.* cablegram.
каблу́к [*gen.* -блука́] *n.* heel (*of a shoe*). —**под каблуко́м** у, under the thumb of.
каблучо́к [*gen.* -чка́] *n., dim. of* каблу́к.
кабриоле́т *n.* cabriolet; gig.
кабы́ *conj., colloq.* **1,** if. **2,** if only. —**е́сли бы да кабы́ (то во рту росли́ б грибы́),** if wishes were horses (beggars would ride).

кавалéр *n.* **1,** escort; dancing partner. **2,** holder (*of an order or award*). **3,** *colloq.* admirer.

кавалéрия *n.* cavalry. —**кавалерúйский,** *adj.* cavalry (*attrib.*). —**кавалерúст,** *n.* cavalryman.

кавалькáда *n.* cavalcade.

кавардáк [*gen.* -дакá] *n., colloq.* confusion; disorder; mess.

кáверза *n., colloq.* **1,** intrigue; chicanery. **2,** mean trick.

кáверзный *adj., colloq.* **1,** (*of a problem or question*) tricky. **2,** scheming.

кавéрна *n., med.* cavity.

кавкáзец [*gen.* -зца] *n.m.* [*fem.* -зка] native of the Caucasus. —**кавкáзский,** *adj.* Caucasian; Caucasus (*attrib.*).

кавы́чки [*gen.* -чек] *n.pl.* quotation marks.

кадéнция (дэ) *n., music* **1,** cadence. **2,** cadenza.

кадéт *n.* **1,** *pre-rev.* (military) cadet. **2,** *hist.* member of the Constitutional Democrat party; Cadet.

кадéтский *adj.* **1,** *pre-rev.* cadet (*attrib.*). **2,** *hist.* of or pert. to the Constitutional Democrats.

кадúло *n.* censer.

кáдка [*gen. pl.* кáдок] *n.* tub.

кáдмий *n.* cadmium.

кадр *n., motion pictures* **1,** frame. **2,** shot; scene.

кадрúль *n.f.* quadrille.

кáдровый *adj.* **1,** (*of a worker*) trained; skilled. **2,** *mil.* regular; career.

кáдры [*gen.* -ров] *n.pl.* **1,** personnel. **2,** cadres.

кады́к [*gen.* -дыкá] *n.* Adam's apple.

каёмка [*gen. pl.* -мок] *n.* border; edging.

каждоднéвный *adj.* daily; everyday.

кáждый *adj.* every; each: кáждый день, every day. —*indef. pron.* **1,** each; each one: кáждый из вас, each (one) of you. **2,** everyone; everybody. **3,** anyone; anybody. —**кáждому своё,** to each his own.

кáжущийся *adj.* apparent; seeming.

казáк [*gen.* -закá] *n.* Cossack.

казáрка [*gen. pl.* -рок] *n.* brant goose. —**белощёкая казáрка,** barnacle goose —**канáдская казáрка,** Canada goose.

казáрма *n.* **1,** *usu. pl.* barracks. **2,** *colloq.* ugly building. —**казáрменный,** *adj.* barracks (*attrib.*).

казáть *v.impfv.* [*pres.* кажý, кáжешь] *obs.* to show. —**не казáть глаз** *or* нóса (*with* в + *acc.*), not to show one's face (somewhere).

казáться *v.r.impfv.* [*pfv.* показáться; *pres.* кажýсь, кáжешься] (*with instr.*) to seem: казáться стрáнным, to seem strange. *Also impers.:* Кáжется, it seems. Мне кáжется, что..., it seems to me that... Вам э́то тóлько кáжется/показáлось, you're just imagining it; you just imagined it. —**казáлось бы, 1,** it would seem; one would think. **2,** seemingly.

казáх *n.m.* [*fem.* -зáшка] Kazakh (*one of a people living mainly in Kazakhstan*). —**казáхский,** *adj.* Kazakh.

казáцкий *adj.* Cossack (*attrib.*).

казáчество *n.* the Cossacks.

казáчий [*fem.* -чья] *adj.* Cossack (*attrib.*).

казачóк [*gen.* -чкá] *n.* **1,** a lively Ukrainian dance. **2,** *obs.* boy servant; page.

казеúн *n.* casein.

каземáт *n.* **1,** casemate. **2,** solitary confinement cell (*in a fortress*).

казённый *adj.* **1,** public; belonging to, issued by, or paid for by the government. Казённые дéньги, public funds. На казённый счёт, at government expense. **2,** *fig.* bureaucratic; formal. —**казённая часть,** breech (*of a firearm*).

казинó *n. indecl.* casino.

казнá *n., obs.* **1,** treasury. **2,** the State. **3,** money.

казначéй *n.* **1,** treasurer. **2,** purser; paymaster. —**казначéйский,** *adj.* treasury (*attrib.*): казначéйский билéт, treasury note. —**казначéйство,** *n.* treasury.

казнúть *v.impfv. & pfv.* to execute; put to death. —**казнúться,** *refl.* to suffer acute remorse; blame oneself bitterly.

казнокрáд *n.* embezzler of public funds.

казнь *n.f.* execution. —**смéртная казнь,** the death penalty; capital punishment.

казуúстика *n.* casuistry. —**казуúст,** *n.* casuist. —**казуистúческий,** *adj.* casuistic.

кáзус *n.* **1,** complex legal case. **2,** *colloq.* incident.

кáзусный *adj.* involved; complex.

кáйзер (зэ) *n.* Kaiser.

кайлó [*pl.* кáйла] *n.* pick; hack. *Also,* кайлá.

каймá [*gen. pl.* каём] *n.* border; edging.

кáйра *n.* murre (*bird*).

как *adv.* **1,** how: Как делá?, how are things?; как красúво!, how beautiful! Я забы́л, как тудá пройтú, I forgot how to get there. **2,** *in certain expressions,* what?: Как вáше úмя?, what is your name?; как э́то называ́ется?, what is this called?; как вы дýмаете?, what do you think? —*conj.* **1,** as; like: как обы́чно, as usual; бéлый как снег, white as snow; рабóтать как вол, to work like a horse. **2,** *following verbs of perceiving:* Я вúдел, как он ушёл, I saw him leave. **3,** *when preceded and followed by the same word,* like any other: гóрод как гóрод, a city like any other city. —**а как же, 1,** (*as an exclamation*) of course!; do you really have to ask? **2,** (*fol. by nom. case*) what about...?; how about...? —**как бы, 1,** as if. **2,** seeming to. **3,** a sort of. —**как бы не,** that (something might happen). —**как бы не так!,** *colloq.* no chance!; no way! —**как бы то ни было,** *see* быть. —**как быть?,** *see* быть. —**как же!,** why, of course! —**как не,** but; besides: Кто мóжет э́то сдéлать, как не вы?, who else can do it but/besides you? **2,** if not: Кто, как не мы?, who, if not us? —**как ни, 1,** (*with verbs*) however; no matter how: Как он ни стара́лся, no matter how he tried. **2,** (*with adjectives*) as ... as one is: как он ни умён, он не мог..., as smart as he is, he could not... —**как раз,** *see* раз. —**как ..., так и** ..., both ..., and ... —**как тóлько,** as soon as.

какадý *n.m. indecl.* cockatoo.

какáо *n. indecl.* **1,** cacao. **2,** cocoa.

кáк-либо *adv.* somehow.

кáк-нибудь *adv.* **1,** somehow. **2,** *colloq.* haphazardly; any which way. **3,** *colloq.* sometime; someday.

как-никáк *adv., colloq.* **1,** despite all; still and all. **2,** after all; in the end.

какóв [*fem.* каковá; *neut.* каковó; *pl.* каковы́] *pron.*

1, *interr.* what is?; what are?: Каковы́ фа́кты?, what are the facts? **2,** *interr.* what is ... like?; what kind of ... is ...?: Каќов он?, what is he like?; каков он собо́й?, what does he look like? **3,** *rel.* what kind of; the sort of: Я тебе́ расскажу́, каковы́ э́ти лю́ди, I'll tell you what kind of people they are. Каково́ бы́ло моё удивле́ние, когда́..., you can imagine my surprise when... **4,** *rel.* such as: каќов он есть, such as he is. —**каќов ..., таќов и ...,** like ..., like ...: каков оте́ц, таков и сын, like father, like son.

каково́ *pron., neut. of* **каќов.** —*interr. & rel. adv., colloq.* how: Каково́ ей живётся?, how is she getting along?

каково́й *rel. pron., obs.* which.

каќой *adj.* **1,** which?; what?: В каку́ю сто́рону он пошёл?, which way did he go? До како́й сте́пени?, to what extent? **2,** what is ...?: Како́й счёт?, what's the score? Како́е сего́дня число́?, what is today's date? **3,** what sort of; what kind of: Кака́я сего́дня пого́да?, what sort of weather is it today?; what is the weather like today? **4,** *in exclamations,* what...!: Како́е чу́дное ме́сто!, what a delightful place! —*rel. pron.* such as; the kind of: Он не тако́й знато́к, каќой ты ду́мал, he is not the expert you thought he was. —**каќой бы (ни),** whatever; whichever. —**каќой бы то ни́ было,** any whatsoever. —**ни** (+ *preposition*) **каќой,** not any; no: ни под каки́м ви́дом, under no circumstances. Он не отвеча́л ни на каки́е вопро́сы, he did not answer any questions.

каќой-либо *adj.* = **каќой-нибудь.**

каќой-нибудь *adj.* **1,** some; a: Да́йте мне каќой-нибудь приме́р, give me an example. **2,** (*with numerals*) *colloq.* about; some.

каќой-то *adj.* **1,** some: Вас спра́шивает каќой-то челове́к, some man is asking for you. **2,** a kind of; a sort of. —**каки́м-то о́бразом,** somehow.

какофо́ния *n.* cacophony. —**какофони́ческий,** *adj.* cacophonous.

ка́к-то *adv.* **1,** somehow. **2,** *colloq.* once; one day. **3,** *colloq.* I wonder how. **4,** *colloq.* namely. —**ка́к-то раз,** once.

ка́ктус *n.* cactus.

кал *n.* excrement; feces.

каламбу́р *n.* pun. —**каламбури́ст,** *n.* punster.

каламбу́рить *v.impfv.* to pun; make puns.

кала́н *n.* sea otter.

кала́ндр *n.* calender.

каланча́ *n.* **1,** watchtower (*of a fire station*). **2,** *colloq.* beanpole (*tall person*).

кала́ч [*gen.* -лача́] *n.* a kind of roll with a distinctive shape. —**тёртый кала́ч,** old hand; person who has been around.

кала́чик *n., dim. of* кала́ч. —**сверну́ться кала́чиком,** to curl up into a ball.

калейдоско́п *n.* kaleidoscope. —**калейдоскопи́ческий,** *adj.* kaleidoscopic.

кале́ка *n.m. & f.* cripple.

календа́рь [*gen.* -даря́] *n.m.* calendar. —**календа́рный,** *adj.* calendar (*attrib.*).

кале́ние *n.* incandescence. —**бе́лое кале́ние,** white heat. —**довести́ до бе́лого кале́ния,** to drive (someone) into a rage.

калёный *adj.* **1,** red-hot. **2,** (*of nuts*) roasted.

кале́чить *v.impfv.* [*pfv.* искале́чить] **1,** to maim; cripple. **2,** *fig.* to pervert; warp.

кали́бр *n.* **1,** caliber (*of a gun or bullet*). **2,** gauge.

калиброва́ние *n.* calibration.

калиброва́ть *v.impfv.* [*pres.* -ру́ю, -ру́ешь] to calibrate.

ка́лий *n.* potassium. —**ка́лиевый; кали́йный,** *adj.* potassium (*attrib.*).

кали́льный *adj.* used for heating or smelting metals. —**кали́льная се́тка,** (incandescent) mantle.

кали́на *n.* viburnum.

кали́тка [*gen. pl.* -ток] *n.* gate in a fence.

кали́ть *v.impfv.* **1,** to make red-hot. **2,** to roast.

кали́ф *n.* caliph.

калифо́рний *n.* californium.

каллигра́фия *n.* calligraphy. —**каллиграфи́ческий,** *adj.* calligraphic.

калмы́к *n.m.* [*fem.* -мы́чка] Kalmyk; Kalmuck (*one of a people inhabiting the Volga delta*). —**калмы́цкий,** *adj.* Kalmyk; Kalmuck.

калори́йность *n.f.* caloric content.

калори́метр *n.* calorimeter.

калори́фер *n.* radiator; heater.

кало́рия *n.* calorie.

кало́ши *n.pl.* [*sing.* кало́ша] rubbers. —**сесть в кало́шу,** *colloq.* to make a fool of oneself; put one's foot in it.

калу́жница *n.* marsh marigold.

ка́лька [*gen. pl.* ка́лек] *n.* **1,** [*usu.* бума́жная ка́лька] tracing paper. **2,** a tracing. **3,** *ling.* loan translation; calque.

кальки́ровать *v.impfv.* [*pfv.* скальки́ровать; *pres.* -рую, -руешь] to trace.

калькули́ровать *v.impfv.* [*pfv.* скалькули́ровать; *pres.* -рую, -руешь] to calculate.

калькуля́тор *n.* calculator.

кальма́р *n.* squid.

кальсо́ны [*gen.* -со́н] *n.pl.* men's drawers; long underpants.

ка́льций *n.* calcium. —**ка́льциевый,** *adj.* calcium (*attrib.*).

каля́кать *v.impfv., colloq.* to chatter.

кама́ринская *n., decl. as an adj.* Russian folk dance; kamarinskaia.

ка́мбала *n.* flounder; plaice; sole.

ка́мбий *n.* cambium.

камбоджи́йский *adj.* Cambodian.

ка́мбуз *n.* **1,** ship's galley. **2,** ship's boiler.

камво́льный *adj.* worsted.

каме́дь *n.f.* gum.

камелёк [*gen.* -лька́] *n.* small fireplace.

каме́лия *n.* camellia.

камене́ть *v.impfv.* [*pfv.* окамене́ть] **1,** to turn to stone; become petrified; petrify. **2,** to stiffen; freeze. **3,** *fig.* to harden; become callous.

камени́стый *adj.* stony; rocky.

каменноуго́льный *also,* **каменноу́гольный,** *adj.* coal (*attrib.*).

ка́менный *adj.* **1,** stony. **2,** *fig.* of stone; stony: ка́менное се́рдце, heart of stone. —**ка́менный век,** the Stone Age. —**ка́менная соль,** rock salt. —**ка́менный у́голь,** (anthracite or bituminous) coal.

каменоло́мня [*gen. pl.* **-мен**] *n.* quarry.

каменотёс *n.* stonemason.

ка́менщик *n.* mason; bricklayer.

ка́мень [*gen.* **ка́мня;** *pl.* **ка́мни, -не́й, -ня́м**] *n.m.* **1,** stone (*substance*). **2,** a stone; a rock. —**ка́мня на ка́мне не оста́вить,** not to leave a stone standing.

ка́мера *n.* **1,** chamber. **2,** cell (*of a prison*). **3,** inner tube. **4,** camera. —**ка́мера хране́ния (багажа́),** baggage room.

камерге́р *n.* chamberlain.

камерди́нер *n.* valet.

камери́стка [*gen. pl.* **-ток**] *n.* lady's maid.

ка́мерный *adj.* **1,** *mech.* having chambers. **2,** *music* chamber (*attrib.*): ка́мерная му́зыка, chamber music.

камерто́н *n.* tuning fork.

ка́мешек [*gen.* **-шка**] *n.* small stone; pebble. —**броса́ть ка́мешки в чей-нибудь огоро́д,** to make snide remarks about someone.

каме́я *n.* cameo.

ками́н *n.* fireplace. —**электри́ческий ками́н,** electric heater.

ками́нный *adj.* fireplace (*attrib.*). —**ками́нная по́лка,** mantel; mantelpiece. —**ками́нная решётка,** fire screen. —**ками́нные щипцы́,** fire irons.

камнедроби́лка [*gen. pl.* **-лок**] *n.* stone crusher; rock crusher.

камнело́мка *n.* saxifrage.

камнере́з *n.* stonecutter.

камо́рка [*gen. pl.* **-рок**] *n.* tiny room; closet.

кампа́ния *n.* campaign.

камуфли́ровать *v.impfv. & pfv.* [*pres.* **-рую, -руешь**] to camouflage.

камуфля́ж *n.* camouflage.

ка́мушек [*gen.* **-шка**] *n.* = **ка́мешек.**

камфара́ *also,* **ка́мфора** *n.* camphor. —**камфа́рный; ка́мфорный,** *adj.* camphor.

камы́ш [*gen.* **-ша́**] *n.* rush; cane; reed. —**камышо́вый,** *adj.* made of rush/cane/reed.

кана́ва *n.* ditch. —**сто́чная** *or* **водосто́чная кана́ва,** gutter.

кана́дец [*gen.* **-дца**] *n.m.* [*fem.* **-дка**] Canadian. —**кана́дский,** *adj.* Canadian.

кана́л *n.* **1,** canal. **2,** *anat.* duct. **3,** bore (*of a firearm*). **4,** *television* channel. **5,** *fig.* channel: дипломати́ческие кана́лы, diplomatic channels.

канализа́ция *n.* sewage system. —**канализацио́нный,** *adj.* sewage (*attrib.*).

канаре́ечный *adj.* **1,** canary (*attrib.*). **2,** canary-yellow.

канаре́йка [*gen. pl.* **-ре́ек**] *n.* canary.

кана́т *n.* **1,** rope. **2,** tightrope. **3,** cable.

кана́тный *adj.* **1,** rope (*attrib.*); cable (*attrib.*). **2,** funicular.

канатохо́дец [*gen.* **-дца**] *n.* tightrope walker.

канва́ *n.* **1,** canvas (*for needlework*). **2,** *fig.* outline.

кандалы́ [*gen.* **-ло́в**] *n.pl.* shackles; fetters; irons.

канделя́бр *n.* candelabrum.

кандида́т *n.* **1,** candidate. **2,** holder of an academic degree roughly equivalent to a master's degree; candidate: кандида́т нау́к, candidate of science. —**кандида́т в чле́ны** (+ *gen.*), candidate (*or* alternate) member (of).

кандида́тский *adj.* candidate's.

кандидату́ра *n.* candidacy. —**выдвига́ть** *or* **выставля́ть чью-нибудь кандидату́ру,** to nominate someone. —**выдвига́ть** *or* **выставля́ть свою́ кандидату́ру,** to announce one's candidacy; run.

кани́кулы [*gen.* **-кул**] *n.pl.* vacation (*from school*). —**каникуля́рный,** *adj.* vacation (*attrib.*).

кани́стра *n.* fuel can.

каните́литься *v.r.impfv.* [*pfv.* **проканите́литься**] *colloq.* to dawdle.

каните́ль *n.f.* **1,** gold or silver thread. **2,** *colloq.* long drawn-out affair; waste of time. —**каните́льный,** *adj., colloq.* long drawn-out.

канифо́ль *n.f.* rosin.

канка́н *n.* cancan.

канниба́л *n.* cannibal. —**каннибали́зм,** *n.* cannibalism. —**канниба́льский,** *adj.* cannibalistic. —**канниба́льство,** *n.* cannibalism.

кано́ист *n.* canoeist.

кано́н *n.* canon.

канона́да *n.* cannonade.

каноне́рка [*gen. pl.* **-рок**] *n.* gunboat. —**каноне́рский,** *adj., in* каноне́рская ло́дка, gunboat.

канонизи́ровать *v.impfv.* [*pres.* **-рую, -руешь**] to canonize.

кано́ник *n.* canon (*clergyman*).

канони́ческий *adj.* canonical. —**канони́ческое пра́во,** canon law.

кано́э *n.neut. indecl.* canoe.

кант *n.* edging; piping.

кантал́упа *n.* cantaloupe.

канта́та *n.* cantata.

кантова́ть *v.impfv.* [*pfv.* **окантова́ть;** *pres.* **-ту́ю, -ту́ешь**] **1,** to trim with piping. **2,** to mount (a picture). **3,** [*impfv. only*] to invert; turn over: «не кантова́ть», "do not invert".

канто́н *n.* canton. —**кантона́льный,** *adj.* cantonal.

ка́нтор *n.* cantor.

кану́н *n.* eve. —**в кану́н** (+ *gen.*), on the eve of.

ка́нуть *v.pfv.* **1,** *obs.* to drip; drop. **2,** to sink. **3,** to disappear; fade from memory. —**как в во́ду ка́нуть,** to vanish into thin air. —**ка́нуть в ве́чность** *или* **в Ле́ту,** to sink into oblivion.

канцеляри́ст *n.* **1,** clerk. **2,** *fig.* bureaucrat.

канцеля́рия *n.* **1,** office. **2,** chancellery.

канцеля́рский *adj.* **1,** office (*attrib.*). **2,** *fig.* (*of language*) bureaucratic.

канцеля́рщина *n., colloq.* **1,** routine office work. **2,** bureaucracy; red tape.

канцероге́н *n.* carcinogen. —**канцероге́нный,** *adj.* carcinogenic.

ка́нцлер *n.* chancellor.

каньо́н *n.* canyon.

каню́к [*gen.* **-нюка́**] *n.* buzzard.

каоли́н *n.* kaolin.

ка́панье *n.* dripping; drip.

ка́пать *v.impfv.* [*pfv.* **ка́пнуть**] **1,** to drip; fall in drops. Из кра́на ка́пает, the faucet is dripping. **2,** to pour a drop at a time. **3,** to drip; spill: ка́пать себе́ на га́лстук, to spill something on one's tie; ка́пать вино́м на ска́терть, to drip wine on the tablecloth. —**над на́ми не ка́плет** (*old conjugation*), there's no rush.

капе́лла *n.* **1,** choir. **2,** (Catholic) chapel.

капелла́н *n.* chaplain.

ка́пелька [*gen. pl.* **-лек**] *n.* **1,** droplet. **2,** *fig.* drop; grain; ounce; particle; modicum. Име́йте ка́пельку терпе́ния, have a little patience. —**до ка́пельки, 1,** to the last drop. **2,** completely; absolutely. —**ни ка́пельки,** not a bit; not the least bit.

ка́пельку *adv., colloq.* a little: Подожди́те ка́пельку, wait just a moment.

капельме́йстер *n.* conductor of a military band; bandmaster.

ка́пельница *n.* dropper; eye dropper; medicine dropper.

ка́персы [*gen.* **-сов**] *n.pl.* capers (*condiment*).

капилля́р *n.* capillary. —**капилля́рный,** *adj.* capillary.

капита́л *n.* capital.

капитализа́ция *n., econ.* capitalization.

капитализи́ровать *v.impfv. & pfv.* [*pres.* **-рую, -руешь**] to capitalize; convert into capital.

капитали́зм *n.* capitalism. —**капитали́ст,** *n.* capitalist. —**капиталисти́ческий,** *adj.* capitalist.

капиталовложе́ния *n.pl.* [*sing.* **-ние**] capital investment.

капита́льный *adj.* **1,** *econ.* capital (*attrib.*). **2,** major: капита́льный ремо́нт, major repairs; major renovation.

капита́н *n.* **1,** captain (*army rank*). **2,** captain (*of a ship*). **3,** *sports* captain (*of a team*). —**капита́н пе́рвого ра́нга,** *naval* captain. —**капита́н второ́го ра́нга,** *naval* commander. —**капита́н тре́тьего ра́нга,** *naval* lieutenant commander.

капита́нский *adj.* captain's.

капито́лий *n.* capitol.

капитули́ровать *v.impfv. & pfv.* [*pres.* **-рую, -руешь**] to capitulate.

капитуля́ция *n.* surrender; capitulation.

ка́пище *n.* pagan temple.

капка́н *n.* trap; snare.

каплу́н [*gen.* **-луна́**] *n.* capon.

ка́пля [*gen. pl.* **-пель**] *n.* **1,** drop: ка́пля воды́, a drop of water. Ка́пли по́та, beads of perspiration. **2,** *pl.* drops: глазны́е ка́пли, eye drops. —**ка́пля в мо́ре,** drop in the bucket. —**ка́пля за ка́плей; ка́пля по ка́пле,** bit by bit. —**ни ка́пли,** not a bit. —**по ка́пле,** a drop at a time. —**после́дняя ка́пля,** the last straw. —**похо́жи как две ка́пли воды́,** like two peas in a pod.

ка́пнуть *v., pfv. of* **ка́пать.**

капо́к [*gen.* **капка́**] *n.* kapok.

ка́пор *n.* bonnet.

капо́т *n.* **1,** *obs.* housecoat. **2,** *mech.* hood. **3,** *aero.* cowling.

капра́л *n.* corporal.

капри́з *n.* whim; caprice.

капри́зничать *v.impfv.* to be capricious.

капри́зный *adj.* capricious.

капро́н *n.* kapron (*a kind of nylon*). —**капро́новый,** *adj.* kapron.

ка́псула *n.* **1,** capsule. **2,** space capsule.

ка́псюль *n.m.* percussion cap; primer.

капу́ста *n.* cabbage. —**брюссе́льская капу́ста,** Brussels sprouts. —**ки́слая** *or* **ква́шеная капу́ста,** sauerkraut. —**морска́я капу́ста,** sea kale. —**спа́ржевая капу́ста,** broccoli. —**цветна́я капу́ста,** cauliflower.

капу́стник *n.* **1,** *colloq.* cabbage patch. **2,** series of skits.

капу́стница *n.* cabbage butterfly.

капу́стный *adj.* cabbage (*attrib.*).

капу́т *adv.* (*with dat.*) *colloq.* done for: Ему́ капу́т, he's done for.

капуци́н *n.* **1,** Capuchin (*monk*). **2,** capuchin (*monkey*).

капюшо́н *n.* hood.

ка́ра *n.* punishment; retribution.

караби́н *n.* carbine.

кара́бкаться *v.r.impfv.* to clamber; scramble.

карава́й *n.* round loaf of bread.

карава́н *n.* **1,** caravan. **2,** convoy (*of ships*).

караве́лла *n.* caravel.

карака́тица *n.* cuttlefish.

кара́ковый *adj.* (*of a horse*) dark bay.

кара́куль *n.m.* Persian lamb; astrakhan; caracul. —**кара́кулевый,** *adj.* Persian lamb (*attrib.*).

караку́льский *adj., in* **караку́льская овца́,** caracul sheep.

каракульча́ *n.* broadtail.

кара́куля *n., usu. pl.* scrawl; scribble.

карамбо́ль *n.m., billiards* carom (*shot*).

караме́ль *n.f.* **1,** caramels. **2,** a (single) caramel.

караме́лька [*gen. pl.* **-лек**] *n., colloq.* a (single) caramel.

караме́льный *adj.* caramel.

каранда́ш [*gen.* **-даша́**] *n.* pencil. —**каранда́шный,** *adj.* pencil (*attrib.*).

каранти́н *n.* quarantine. —**каранти́нный,** *adj.* quarantine (*attrib.*).

карапу́з *n., colloq.* small (often chubby) child.

кара́сь [*gen.* **-ся́**] *n.m.* European carp.

кара́т *n.* carat.

кара́тель *n.m.* member of a punitive expedition.

кара́тельный *adj.* punitive.

кара́ть *v.impfv.* [*pfv.* **покара́ть**] to punish. —**кара́ться,** *refl.* [*impfv. only*] (*with instr.*) to be punishable (by).

карате́ *n.neut. indecl.* karate.

карау́л *n.* **1,** guard: почётный карау́л, honor guard. **2,** guard duty; sentry duty. Стоя́ть в карау́ле, to stand guard. Нести́ карау́л, to be on guard duty. —**взять на карау́л,** to present arms. —**взять под карау́л,** to take into custody.

карау́лить *v.impfv.* **1,** to guard; watch over. **2,** *colloq.* to watch for; lie in wait for.

карау́льный *adj.* guard (*attrib.*); sentry (*attrib.*). —*n.* sentry. —**карау́льная,** *n.* guardhouse.

карау́льщик *n., colloq.* watchman.

кара́чки *n.pl., colloq., in* **на кара́чки** *and* **на кара́чках,** on one's hands and knees; on all fours.

карби́д *n.* carbide.

карбо́лка *n., colloq.* carbolic acid.

карбо́ловый *adj.* carbolic.

карбона́т *n.* carbonate.

карбору́нд *n.* carborundum.

карбу́нкул *n.* carbuncle.

карбюра́тор *n.* carburetor.

карга́ *n., colloq.* hag.

кардина́л *n.* **1,** cardinal (*prelate*). **2,** cardinal (*bird*).

кардина́льный *adj.* cardinal; fundamental.

кардиогра́мма *n.* cardiogram.

кардио́граф *n.* cardiograph.

кардиоло́гия *n.* cardiology. —**кардио́лог,** *n.* cardiologist.

каре́та *n.* coach; carriage. —**каре́та ско́рой по́мощи,** *obs.* ambulance.

каре́тка [*gen. pl.* -ток] *n.* **1,** *dim. of* **каре́та. 2,** carriage (*of a typewriter*).

каре́тный *adj.* of or for a coach. —**каре́тный сара́й,** coach house.

кариати́да *n.* caryatid.

кари́бский *adj.* Caribbean.

ка́риес *n.* caries. —**ка́риес зубо́в,** tooth decay.

ка́рий *adj.* (*of one's eyes*) brown.

карикату́ра *n.* **1,** cartoon. **2,** caricature. —**карикату́рист,** *n.* cartoonist.

карикату́рный *adj.* **1,** of or like a cartoon. **2,** *fig.* grotesque; ludicrous.

карильо́н *n.* carillon.

карио́з *n.* = **ка́риес.** —**карио́зный,** *adj.* carious.

ка́рканье *n.* caw; cawing.

карка́с *n.* frame; framework. —**карка́сный,** *adj.* frame (*attrib.*): карка́сный дом, frame house.

ка́ркать *v.impfv.* [*pfv.* ка́ркнуть] (*of a bird*) to caw.

ка́рлик *n.m.* [*fem.* -лица] midget; dwarf. —**ка́рликовый,** *adj.* midget; tiny.

карма́н *n.* pocket. —**бить** *or* **ударя́ть по карма́ну,** to put a hole in one's pocketbook. —**э́то мне не по карма́ну,** I can't afford it.

карма́нник *n., colloq.* pickpocket.

карма́нный *adj.* pocket (*attrib.*). —**карма́нный вор,** pickpocket.

карми́н *n.* carmine. —**карми́нный; карми́новый,** *adj.* carmine.

карнава́л *n.* carnival.

карни́з *n.* cornice.

карп *n.* carp.

ка́рта *n.* **1,** map. **2,** playing card. **3,** *in* ка́рта вин, wine list. —**его́ ка́рта би́та,** his game is up. —**(с)пу́тать чьи́-нибудь ка́рты,** to upset someone's plans. —**(с)пу́тать все ка́рты,** to upset the applecart. —**ста́вить (что́-нибудь) на ка́рту,** to stake. Поста́влен на ка́рту, at stake.

карта́вить *v.impfv.* [*pres.* -влю, -вишь] to have difficulty pronouncing the letters "L" and "R".

карта́вость *n.f.* improper pronunciation of the letters "L" and "R"; burr.

картёжник *n., colloq.* avid cardplayer.

картёжный *adj., colloq.* of or pert. to card playing.

карте́ль (тэ) *n.m.* cartel.

ка́ртер (тэ) *n.* crankcase.

карте́чь *n.f.* **1,** canister shot. **2,** buckshot.

карти́на *n.* **1,** picture. **2,** painting. **3,** scene. **4,** *theat.* scene (*part of an act of a play*). **5,** *colloq.* movie.

карти́нка [*gen. pl.* -нок] *n., dim. of* **карти́на.** —**мо́дная карти́нка,** fashion plate. —**составна́я карти́нка,** jigsaw puzzle.

карти́нный *adj.* **1,** picture (*attrib.*). **2,** picturesque. —**карти́нная галере́я,** art gallery; art museum.

карто́граф *n.* cartographer.

картографи́ровать *v.impfv.* [*pres.* -рую, -руешь] to map; draw a map of.

картогра́фия *n.* cartography. —**картографи́ческий,** *adj.* cartographic.

карто́н *n.* cardboard.

картона́ж *n.* article made of cardboard. —**картона́жный,** *adj.* cardboard.

карто́нка [*gen. pl.* -нок] *n.* cardboard box; carton. —**карто́нка для шля́пы,** hatbox; bandbox.

карто́нный *adj.* cardboard.

картоте́ка *n.* card index; card file. —**картоте́чный,** *adj.* of or for a card file.

карто́фелина *n., colloq.* a (single) potato.

карто́фель *n.m.* potatoes.

карто́фельный *adj.* potato (*attrib.*). —**карто́фельный жук,** potato beetle (*or* bug). —**карто́фельное пюре́,** mashed potatoes.

ка́рточка [*gen. pl.* -чек] *n.* **1,** card: визи́тная ка́рточка, business card. **2,** small photograph. **3,** *in* ка́рточка вин, wine list. —**выдава́ться по ка́рточкам,** to be rationed.

ка́рточный *adj.* card (*attrib.*). —**ка́рточный до́мик,** house of cards. —**ка́рточная систе́ма,** rationing.

карто́шка [*gen. pl.* -шек] *n., colloq.* **1,** potatoes. **2,** a (single) potato.

карту́з [*gen.* -туза́] *n.* peaked cap.

карусе́ль *n.f.* merry-go-round; carousel.

ка́рцер *n.* prison cell (usu. dark and cold) used for special punishment.

карциноге́н *n.* carcinogen.

карье́р *n.* **1,** full gallop. **2,** quarry. —**с ме́ста в карье́р,** right away; at once.

карье́ра *n.* career. —**бы́стро сде́лать карье́ру,** to rise (very) rapidly.

карьери́ст *n.* careerist.

каса́ние *n.* touch; contact.

каса́тельная *n., decl. as an adj., geom.* tangent.

каса́тельно *prep., with gen.* regarding; concerning.

каса́тельство *n.* relation; connection. Име́ть каса́тельство к, to have a connection with; relate to.

каса́тик *n.* iris (*flower*).

каса́тка [*gen. pl.* -ток] *n.* barn swallow.

каса́ться *v.r.impfv.* [*pfv.* косну́ться] (*with gen.*) **1,** to touch. **2,** to touch upon. **3,** to concern; have to do with. —**что каса́ется** (+ *gen.*), as to; as for; as far as ... is concerned.

каса́ющийся *prep., with gen.* regarding; concerning.

ка́ска [*gen. pl.* ка́сок] *n.* helmet.

каска́д *n.* cascade.

каскадёр *n.* stunt man.

ка́сса *n.* **1,** cashier's office; cashier's desk: плати́ть в ка́ссу, to pay the cashier. **2,** box office; ticket office. **3,** cash register. **4,** cash box; till. **5,** ticket machine (*on a bus or trolley*). **6,** typography case (*for holding type*). —несгора́емая ка́сса, safe. —сберега́тельная ка́сса, savings bank.

кассацио́нный *adj., law* appeal (*attrib.*); of appeal. —кассацио́нная жа́лоба, appeal.

касса́ция *n., law* appeal.

кассе́та *n.* cassette.

Кассиопе́я *n.* Cassiopeia.

касси́р *n.m.* [*fem.* **-и́рша**] **1,** cashier. **2,** (bank) teller. **3,** ticket seller.

касси́ровать *v.impfv. & pfv.* [*pres.* **-рую, -руешь**] *law* to annul; set aside.

ка́ссовый *adj.* **1,** cash (*attrib.*): ка́ссовая кни́га, cash-book. **2,** box-office (*attrib.*).

ка́ста *n.* caste.

кастанье́ты *n.pl.* [*sing.* **-нье́та**] castanets.

кастеля́нша *n.* woman in charge of linen (*in a hotel, hospital, etc.*).

кастет *n.* brass knuckles.

касти́льский *adj.* Castilian.

ка́стовый *adj.* caste (*attrib.*).

касто́р *n.* castor (*heavy woolen cloth*).

касто́рка *n., colloq.* castor oil.

касто́ровый *adj.* **1,** made of castor or beaver fur. **2,** *in* касто́ровое ма́сло, castor oil.

кастра́т *n.* castrated man or boy. —кастра́ция, *n.* castration.

кастри́ровать *v.impfv. & pfv.* [*pres.* **-рую, -руешь**] to castrate.

кастрю́ля *n.* pot; saucepan. *Also,* кастрю́лька.

катава́сия *n., colloq.* tumult; commotion.

катакли́зм *n.* cataclysm.

катако́мбы *n.pl.* [*sing.* **-ко́мба**] catacombs.

катала́нский *adj.* Catalan.

катале́псия *n.* catalepsy. —каталепти́ческий; каталепси́ческий, *adj.* cataleptic.

ката́лиз *n.* catalysis.

катализа́тор *n.* catalyst. —каталити́ческий, *adj.* catalytic.

катало́г *n.* catalogue.

каталогиза́тор *n.* cataloguer.

каталогизи́ровать *v.impfv. & pfv.* [*pres.* **-рую, -руешь**] to catalogue.

катало́жная *n., decl. as an adj.* catalogue room (*in a library*).

катало́жный *adj.* catalogue (*attrib.*). —катало́жная ка́рточка, index card.

катало́нский *adj.* Catalan.

ката́ние *n.* **1,** rolling. **2,** riding; driving. —ката́ние на велосипе́де/конька́х/ло́дке, bicycling/skating/boating. —фигу́рное ката́ние, figure skating.

ката́нье *n., in* не мытьём, так ка́таньем, by hook or by crook.

катапу́льта *n.* catapult.

катапульти́ровать *v.impfv. & pfv.* [*pres.* **-рую, -руешь**] to eject (*from an aircraft*). —катапульти́роваться, *refl.* to be ejected (*from an aircraft*).

катапульти́руемый *adj., in* катапульти́руемое кре́сло, *aero.* ejection seat.

ката́р *n.* catarrh.

катара́кт *n.* cataract (*waterfall*).

катара́кта *n.* cataract (*of the eye*).

катастро́фа *n.* **1,** catastrophe; disaster; calamity. **2,** accident; crash. —катастрофи́ческий, *adj.* catastrophic; disastrous.

ката́ть *v.impfv.* **1,** *indeterm. of* кати́ть. **2,** [*pfv.* **поката́ть**] to take for a ride or drive. **3,** to roll (dough); make (little balls). **4,** [*pfv.* **вы́катать**] to mangle; press in a mangle.

ката́ться *v.r.impfv.* **1,** *indeterm. of* кати́ться. **2,** [*pfv.* **поката́ться**] to ride; go riding: ката́ться на маши́не, to go for a drive; ката́ться верхо́м, to go horseback riding; ката́ться на велосипе́де, to go bicycle riding; ката́ться на са́нках, to go sleigh riding. Ката́ться на конька́х *or* на ро́ликах, to go skating. Ката́ться на ло́дке, to go boating. —ката́ться как сыр в ма́сле, to be in clover. —ката́ться со́ смеху, to roar with laughter.

катафа́лк *n.* **1,** hearse. **2,** bier; catafalque.

категори́ческий *adj.* categorical. —категори́чески, *adv.* categorically.

катего́рия *n.* category.

ка́тер [*pl.* **катера́**] *n.* cutter; launch. ♦*In combinations,* boat: сторожево́й ка́тер, patrol boat; торпе́дный ка́тер, PT boat.

кате́тер (тэтэ) *n.* catheter.

катехи́зис *n.* catechism.

кати́ть *v.impfv.* [*pfv.* **покати́ть**; *pres.* **качу́, ка́тишь**] **1,** to roll; wheel. **2,** *v.i., colloq.* (*of a vehicle*) to roll along. **3,** to stir; cause to move slightly. —кати́ться, *refl.* **1,** to roll. **2,** (*of a vehicle*) to roll along. **3,** to slide down. **4,** to flow; stream. **5,** (*of a sound*) to roll; resound. *See also* ката́ть *and* ката́ться.

като́д *n.* cathode. —като́дный, *adj.* cathode (*attrib.*): като́дные лучи́, cathode rays.

като́к [*gen.* **катка́**] *n.* **1,** skating rink. **2,** roller: парово́й като́к, steamroller. **3,** mangle; rolling press.

като́лик *n.m.* [*fem.* **-ли́чка**] Catholic. —католици́зм, *n.* Catholicism. —католи́ческий, *adj.* Catholic. —католи́чество, *n.* Catholicism.

ка́торга *n.* penal servitude; hard labor.

ка́торжник *n.* convict.

ка́торжный *adj.* **1,** *in* ка́торжные рабо́ты, penal servitude; hard labor. **2,** *fig.* onerous; unbearable; backbreaking.

кату́шка [*gen. pl.* **-шек**] *n.* **1,** spool; reel; bobbin. **2,** *electricity* coil. —на по́лную кату́шку, *colloq.* **1,** full force. **2,** to the full.

катю́ша *n.* rocket launcher mounted on a vehicle; Katyusha.

кау́рый *adj.* (*of a horse*) light chestnut.

каусти́ческий *adj.* caustic.

каучу́к *n.* rubber. —каучу́ковый, *adj.* rubber. —каучуконо́с, *n.* rubber plant.

кафе́ *n.neut. indecl.* café.

ка́федра *n.* **1,** pulpit; rostrum. **2,** department (*of a university*). **3,** chair; professorship.

кафедра́льный *adj.*, *in* **кафедра́льный собо́р,** cathedral.

ка́фель *n.m.* (glazed) tile. —**ка́фельный,** *adj.* tiled; tile (*attrib.*).

кафете́рий (тэ) *n.* cafeteria.

кафта́н *n.* caftan.

кача́лка [*gen. pl.* -**лок**] *n.* rocking chair.

кача́ние *n.* **1,** rocking; swinging. **2,** pumping.

кача́ть *v.impfv.* [*pfv.* **качну́ть**] **1,** to rock; swing. **2,** to sway; cause to sway. **3,** (*of waves*) to toss (a ship). **4,** *impers.* (*of a boat*) to toss; pitch; roll: Ло́дку кача́ет, the boat is tossing. **5,** *in* кача́ть голово́й, to shake one's head. **6,** to pump. —**кача́ться,** *refl.* **1,** to swing; rock; sway. **2,** (*of a boat*) to toss; pitch. **3,** to reel; stagger. **4,** *in* кача́ться на каче́лях, to ride a swing.

каче́ли [*gen.* -**лей**] *n.pl.* (child's) swing.

ка́чественный *adj.* **1,** qualitative. **2,** high-quality; high-grade.

ка́чество *n.* quality. —**в ка́честве** (+ *gen.*), as; by way of; in the capacity of.

ка́чка *n.* tossing; pitching; rolling (*of a ship*). —**борто-ва́я ка́чка,** rolling. —**килева́я ка́чка,** pitching.

качну́ть *v.*, *pfv. of* **кача́ть.** —**качну́ться,** *refl.*, *pfv. of* **кача́ться.**

качу́рка [*gen. pl.* -**рок**] *n.* petrel.

ка́ша *n.* cooked cereal; porridge; kasha. —**ма́нная ка́ша,** cereal made from farina. —**овся́ная ка́ша,** oatmeal.

кашало́т *n.* sperm whale.

кашева́р *n.*, *mil.* cook.

ка́шель [*gen.* **ка́шля**] *n.m.* cough.

кашеми́р *n.* cashmere. —**кашеми́ровый,** *adj.* cashmere.

каши́ца *also,* **ка́шица** *n.* gruel.

ка́шка *n.* pap.

ка́шлять *v.impfv.* [*pfv.* **ка́шлянуть**] to cough.

кашне́ (нэ) *n.neut. indecl.* muffler; scarf.

кашта́н *n.* **1,** chestnut. **2,** chestnut tree.

кашта́новый *adj.* **1,** (of) chestnut. **2,** chestnut-colored; brown.

каю́та *n.* cabin; stateroom.

ка́ющийся *adj.* repentant; penitent.

кая́к *n.* kayak.

ка́яться *v.r.impfv.* [*pfv.* **пока́яться;** *pres.* **ка́юсь, ка́ешься**] **1,** to repent; be sorry. Ка́яться в свои́х греха́х, to repent one's sins. **2,** to confess. Публи́чно ка́яться, to publicly recant.

квадра́нт *n.* quadrant.

квадра́т *n.* **1,** square (*figure*). **2,** *math.* square (*second power*): возводи́ть в квадра́т, to square.

квадра́тный *adj.* **1,** square. **2,** quadratic. —**квад-ра́тный ко́рень,** square root. —**квадра́тные ско́бки,** brackets.

квадрату́ра *n.* squaring. —**квадрату́ра кру́га,** squaring the circle.

квадрильо́н *also,* **квадриллио́н** *n.* quadrillion.

кваза́р *n.* quasar.

ква́канье *n.* croaking.

ква́кать *v.impfv.* [*pfv.* **ква́кнуть**] to croak.

ква́кер *n.* Quaker. —**ква́керский,** *adj.* Quaker.

ква́кша *n.* tree frog.

квалификацио́нный *adj.*, *sports* qualifying.

квалифика́ция *n.* qualification; skill.

квалифици́рованный *adj.* skilled.

квалифици́ровать *v.impfv. & pfv.* [*pres.* -**рую, -руешь**] to characterize; categorize.

квант *n.*, *physics* quantum. —**ква́нтовый,** *adj.* quantum (*attrib.*).

ква́рта *n.* **1,** quart. **2,** *music* fourth.

кварта́л *n.* **1,** quarter; section (*of a city*). **2,** block (*in a city*). **3,** quarter (*of a year*). —**кварта́льный,** *adj.* quarterly.

кварте́т *n.* quartet.

кварти́ра *n.* **1,** apartment. **2,** *pl.*, *mil.* quarters; billets. —**квартира́нт,** *n.* lodger; tenant.

квартирме́йстер *n.* quartermaster.

кварти́рный *adj.* housing (*attrib.*); billeting (*attrib.*). —**кварти́рная пла́та,** rent.

квартирова́ть *v.impfv.* [*pres.* -**ру́ю, -ру́ешь**] **1,** to lodge; live. **2,** *mil.* to be quartered; be billeted.

квартпла́та *n.*, *colloq.* rent (*contr. of* **кварти́рная пла́та**).

кварц *n.* quartz. —**ква́рцевый,** *adj.* quartz.

кварци́т *n.* quartzite.

квас *n.* kvass (*fermented drink*).

ква́сить *v.impfv.* [*pres.* -**шу, -сишь**] to make sour.

квасно́й *adj.* kvass (*attrib.*).

квасцы́ [*gen.* -**цо́в**] *n.pl.* alum.

ква́шеный *adj.* sour. —**ква́шеная капу́ста,** sauerkraut.

квашня́ [*gen. pl.* -**не́й**] *n.* kneading trough.

кве́рху *adv.* up; upward(s). —**лицо́м кве́рху,** face up; right side up.

квинте́т *n.* quintet.

квинтэссе́нция *n.* quintessence.

квит *also,* **кви́ты** *adj.*, *colloq.* all even: Мы (с ва́ми) кви́ты, we are all even.

квита́нция *n.* **1,** receipt. **2,** sales slip. **3,** claim check: бага́жная квита́нция, baggage (claim) check.

кво́рум *n.* quorum.

кво́та *n.* quota.

КГБ *abbr. of* **Комите́т госуда́рственной безопа́с-ности,** Committee of State Security; the KGB.

кегельба́н *n.* bowling alley.

ке́гля [*gen. pl.* -**лей**] *n.* **1,** bowling pin. **2,** *pl.* bowling (*game*).

кедр *n.* cedar. —**кедро́вый,** *adj.* cedar.

ке́ды [*gen.* **ке́дов** *or* **кед**] *n.pl.* sneakers.

кекс *n.* fruit cake.

келе́йный *adj.* **1,** like that in a monastic cell. **2,** *fig.* secret; private. —**келе́йно,** *adv.* in secret.

ке́льнер *n.* waiter, esp. in Germany. —**ке́льнерша,** *n.* waitress.

кельт *n.* Celt. —**ке́льтский,** *adj.* Celtic.

ке́лья [*gen. pl.* **ке́лий**] *n.* monastic cell.

кем *pron.*, *instr. of* **кто.**

ке́мпинг (кэ) *n.* campsite.

кенгуру́ *n.m. indecl.* kangaroo.

кента́вр *n.* centaur.

ке́пка [*gen. pl.* **ке́пок**] *n.* cap.

кера́мика *n.* ceramics. —**керами́ческий,** *adj.* ceramic.

керога́з *n.* kerosene stove.

кероси́н *n.* kerosene.

кероси́нка [*gen. pl.* **-нок**] *n.* kerosene stove.

кероси́новый *adj.* kerosene (*attrib.*).

ке́сарев *adj., in* **ке́сарево сече́ние,** Caesarean section.

кессо́н *n.* caisson.

кессо́нный *adj.* caisson (*attrib.*). —**кессо́нная боле́знь,** the bends.

ке́та *n.* Siberian salmon.

кетгу́т *n.* catgut.

ке́товый *adj., in* **ке́товая икра́,** red caviar.

ке́тчуп *n.* ketchup.

кефа́ль *n.f.* (gray) mullet.

кефи́р *n.* drink made of fermented milk; kefir.

киберне́тика (нэ) *n.* cybernetics.

киби́тка [*gen. pl.* **-ток**] *n.* **1,** covered wagon. **2,** nomad's tent. **3,** mud house (*in Central Asia*).

кива́ть *v.impfv.* [*pfv.* **кивну́ть**] **1,** (*with instr.*) to nod (one's head). **2,** (*with dat.*) to nod (to). **3,** (*with* на + *acc.*) to nod (at); nod in the direction of. **4,** (*with* на + *acc.*) *colloq.* to try to put the blame on.

ки́ви-ки́ви *n.f. or neut. indecl.* kiwi.

кивну́ть *v., pfv. of* **кива́ть.**

киво́к [*gen.* **кивка́**] *n.* nod.

кида́ть *v.impfv.* [*pfv.* **ки́нуть**] **1,** to throw; toss; cast. **2,** *in* **куда́ ни кинь гла́зом,** wherever you look. —**кида́ться,** *refl.* **1,** to throw oneself; rush; dash. **2,** [*impfv. only*] (*with instr.*) to throw (something) at each other.

киевля́нин [*pl.* **-ля́не, -ля́н**] *n.m.* [*fem.* **-ля́нка**] native of Kiev.

кизи́л *n.* dogwood. *Also,* **кизи́ль,** *n.m.* [*gen.* **кизиля́**].

кий [*gen.* **кия́** *or* **ки́я;** *pl.* **кии́, кие́в**] *n.* billiard cue.

кики́мора *n., folklore* female hobgoblin.

килево́й *adj., in* **килева́я ка́чка,** pitching (*of a ship*).

кило́ *n. indecl., colloq.* = **килогра́мм.**

килова́тт [*gen. pl.* **-ва́тт**] *n.* kilowatt. —**килова́тт-ча́с,** *n.* kilowatt-hour.

килоге́рц [*gen. pl.* **-ге́рц**] *n.* kilocycle.

килогра́мм *n.* kilogram.

киломе́тр *n.* kilometer.

килото́нна *n.* kiloton.

киль *n.m.* keel.

кильва́тер (тэ) *n., naut.* wake.

ки́лька [*gen. pl.* **ки́лек**] *n.* sprat.

кимоно́ *n. indecl.* kimono.

кинемато́граф *n., obs.* **1,** motion-picture camera; movie camera. **2,** movie theater.

кинематогра́фия *n.* cinematography.

кинеско́п *n.* kinescope; picture tube.

кине́тика (нэ) *n.* kinetics. —**кинети́ческий,** *adj.* kinetic.

кинжа́л *n.* dagger.

кино́ *n. indecl.* **1,** motion pictures; movies; the cinema. Немо́е кино́, silent pictures. Ходи́ть в кино́, to go to the movies. **2,** movie theater.

киноактёр *n.* movie actor. —**киноактри́са,** *n.* movie actress.

киноаппара́т *n.* motion-picture camera; movie camera.

киноарти́ст *n.* movie actor. —**киноарти́стка,** *n.* movie actress.

ки́новарь *n.f.* cinnabar; vermilion.

киножурна́л *n.* short subject.

кинозвезда́ [*pl.* **кинозвёзды**] *n., colloq.* movie star.

кинока́мера *n.* movie camera.

кинокарти́на *n., colloq.* movie; film.

кинокри́тик *n.* film critic.

киноле́нта *n.* reel of film.

киномеха́ник *n.* projectionist.

кинооператор *n.* cameraman.

киноплёнка *n.* movie film.

кинопрое́ктор *n.* movie projector.

кинорежиссёр *n.* film director.

киносту́дия *n.* movie studio.

кинотеа́тр *n.* movie theater.

кинофестива́ль *n.m.* film festival.

кинофи́льм *n.* film; movie.

кинохро́ника *n.* newsreel.

ки́нуть *v., pfv. of* **кида́ть.** —**ки́нуться,** *refl., pfv. of* **кида́ться.**

кио́ск *n.* kiosk; booth; stand.

кио́т *n.* icon case.

ки́па *n.* **1,** pile; stack. **2,** bale (*measure*).

кипари́с *n.* cypress. —**кипари́сный; кипари́совый,** *adj.* cypress (*attrib.*).

кипе́ние *n.* boiling. —**то́чка кипе́ния,** boiling point.

кипе́ть *v.impfv.* [*pres.* **-плю́, -пи́шь**] **1,** to boil. **2,** to seethe. **3,** (*of emotions*) to boil; rage. **4,** (*of activity*) to be in full swing. **5,** (*with instr.*) to boil; seethe; burn (with anger, indignation, etc.).

кипре́й *n.* willow herb.

кипу́честь *n.f.* ebullience; effervescence.

кипу́чий *adj.* **1,** seething. **2,** ebullient; effervescent. **3,** frenetic.

кипяти́ть *v.impfv.* [*pfv.* **вскипяти́ть;** *pres.* **-чу́, -ти́шь**] to boil (water, milk, etc.). —**кипяти́ться,** *refl.* **1,** to boil. **2,** *colloq.* to get excited; flare up.

кипято́к [*gen.* **-тка́**] *n.* **1,** boiling water. **2,** *colloq.* hothead.

кипяче́ние *n.* boiling.

кипячёный *adj.* boiled.

кира́са *n.* cuirass.

кирги́з *n.m.* [*fem.* **-ка**] Kyrgyz. —**кирги́зский,** *adj.* Kyrgyz.

кири́ллица *n.* the Cyrillic alphabet.

ки́рка [*gen. pl.* **ки́рок**] *n.* Protestant church.

кирка́ [*pl.* **ки́рки, ки́рок**] *n.* pick (*tool*).

кирпи́ч [*gen.* **-пича́**] *n.* brick.

кирпи́чный *adj.* **1,** brick (*attrib.*). **2,** brick-red.

ки́са *n., colloq.* pussy cat.

кисе́йный *adj.* muslin.

кисе́ль [*gen.* **-селя́**] *n.m.* dessert made of fruit, berries and potato- (or corn-) starch and served with milk.

кисе́т *n.* tobacco pouch.

кисея́ *n.* muslin.

ки́ска [*gen. pl.* **ки́сок**] *n.* pussy cat.

кисли́ца *n.* wood sorrel.

кислоро́д *n.* oxygen. —**кислоро́дный,** *adj.* oxygen (*attrib.*).

ки́сло-сла́дкий *adj.* sweet-and-sour.

кислота́ *n.* **1,** [*pl.* **кисло́ты**] acid: се́рная кислота́, sulfuric acid. **2,** acidity.

кисло́тный *adj.* acid (*attrib.*). —кисло́тность, *n.f.* acidity.

ки́слый *adj.* [*short form* ки́сел, кисла́, ки́сло, ки́слы] **1,** sour. **2,** acid. **3,** *fig., colloq.* sour: в ки́слом настрое́нии, in a sour mood. —ки́слая капу́ста, sauerkraut.

ки́снуть *v.impfv.* [*pfv.* проки́снуть; *past* кис *or* ки́снул, ки́сла] **1,** to turn sour. **2,** *fig., colloq.* (*of a person*) A, to stagnate; vegetate. B, to mope.

киста́ *n.* cyst.

кисте́нь [*gen.* -теня́] *n.m.* slung shot.

ки́сточка [*gen. pl.* -чек] *n., dim. of* кисть. —ки́сточка для бритья́, shaving brush.

кисть [*pl.* ки́сти, -сте́й, -стя́м] *n.f.* **1,** hand. **2,** cluster; bunch. **3,** *bot.* raceme. **4,** tassel. **5,** [*usu.* маля́рная кисть] paintbrush. **6,** painting; brushwork.

кит [*gen.* кита́] *n.* whale.

кита́ец [*gen.* -а́йца] *n.* Chinese (man): Он кита́ец, he is Chinese.

кита́йский *adj.* Chinese.

китая́нка [*gen. pl.* -нок] *n.* Chinese woman; Chinese girl.

ки́тель [*pl.* кителя́] *n.m.* tunic.

китобо́ец [*gen.* -бо́йца] *n.* whaling ship.

китобо́й *n.* **1,** whaler (*person*). **2,** whaling ship. —китобо́йный, *adj.* whaling (*attrib.*).

кито́вый *adj.* whale (*attrib.*). —кито́вый жир, whale oil. —кито́вый ус, whalebone.

кичи́ться *v.r.impfv.* **1,** to boast; sing one's own praises. **2,** (*with instr.*) to brag about; trumpet.

кичли́вый *adj.* conceited; arrogant. —кичли́вость, *n.f.* conceit.

кише́ть *v.impfv.* [*pres.* киши́т] **1,** to swarm. **2,** (*with instr.*) to swarm (with); teem (with).

кише́чник *n.* bowels; intestines.

кише́чный *adj.* intestinal.

кишка́ [*gen. pl.* кишо́к] *n.* **1,** intestine. **2,** hose. —пряма́я кишка́, rectum. —слепа́я кишка́, cecum.

кишмя́ *adv., in* кишмя́ кише́ть, to swarm.

клавеси́н *n.* harpsichord.

клавиату́ра *n.* keyboard.

клавико́рды [*gen.* -дов] *n.pl.* clavichord.

кла́виша *n.* key (*of a piano, organ, typewriter, etc.*).

кла́вишный *adj.* **1,** driven by keys: кла́вишный перфора́тор, key punch. **2,** keyboard (*attrib.*).

клад *n.* **1,** buried treasure. **2,** *colloq.* treasure.

кла́дбище *n.* cemetery; graveyard. —кла́дбищенский, *adj.* cemetery (*attrib.*).

кла́дезь *n.m., archaic* = коло́дец. —кла́дезь прему́дрости, fountain of information.

кла́дка *n.* laying (*of stone or brick*). —ка́менная кла́дка, stonework; masonry. —кирпи́чная кла́дка, brickwork.

кладова́я *n., decl. as an adj.* pantry; larder; storeroom.

кладо́вка [*gen. pl.* -вок] *n., colloq.* small pantry.

кладовщи́к [*gen.* -щика́] *n.* storekeeper; keeper of supplies.

кладь *n.f.* load. —ручна́я кладь, hand luggage.

кла́ка *n.* claque. —клакёр, *n.* claqueur.

кла́ксон *n.* horn (*of a car*).

клан *n.* clan.

кла́няться *v.r.impfv.* [*pfv.* поклони́ться] **1,** to bow. **2,** (*with dat.*) to give one's regards (to). **3,** (*with dat. or* пе́ред) to beg (someone); lower oneself before.

кла́пан *n.* **1,** valve. **2,** flap (*of a pocket*).

кларне́т *n.* clarinet. —кларнети́ст, *n.* clarinetist.

класс *n.* **1,** (social) class: рабо́чий класс, the working class. **2,** class (*category*). **3,** class (*mode of travel*): е́хать пе́рвым кла́ссом, to travel first class. **4,** class; classroom: идти/войти́ в класс, to go to/ enter the/ class. Класс ожи́вился, the class came alive. **5,** grade: Он в тре́тьем кла́ссе, he is in the third grade.

кла́ссик *n.* **1,** classical writer. **2,** classicist.

кла́ссика *n.* the classics.

классифика́ция *n.* classification.

классифици́ровать *v.impfv. & pfv.* [*pres.* -рую, -руешь] to classify.

классици́зм *n.* classicism.

класси́ческий *adj.* **1,** classical. **2,** classic: класси́ческий приме́р, classic example.

кла́ссный *adj.* **1,** class (*attrib.*); classroom (*attrib.*). **2,** *sports* first-class; top-level. —кла́ссный ваго́н, railway passenger car. —кла́ссная доска́, blackboard.

кла́ссовый *adj.* class (*attrib.*): кла́ссовая борьба́, class struggle.

кла́ссы [*gen.* -сов] *n.pl.* hopscotch.

класть *v.impfv.* [*pfv.* положи́ть; *pres.* кладу́, кладёшь; *past* клал, кла́ла, кла́ло, кла́ли] **1,** to lay; put; place. **2,** to apply (*to a surface*). **3,** *in* класть тру́бку, to put down (the receiver); hang up. **4,** to put; deposit (money in a bank). **5,** to put (work, effort, etc.) into. **6,** [*impfv. only*] to build; erect. **7,** [*impfv. only*] to lay (eggs). **8,** *colloq.* to set aside; lay aside; put aside. —класть не на ме́сто, to put in the wrong place; misplace. —класть но́гу на́ ногу, to cross one's legs. *See also* положи́ть.

клаустрофо́бия *n.* claustrophobia.

клева́ть *v.impfv.* [*pfv.* клю́нуть; *pres.* клюю́, клюёшь] **1,** to peck. **2,** to bite; take the bait. —клева́ть но́сом, to nod; be drowsy. —у него́ де́нег ку́ры не клю́ют, he has money to burn.

кле́вер *n.* clover. —кле́верный, *adj.* of clover.

клевета́ *n.* slander; libel.

клевета́ть *v.impfv.* [*pfv.* наклевета́ть; *pres.* -вещу́, -ве́щешь] (*with на + acc.*) to slander.

клеветни́к [*gen.* -ника́] *n.* slanderer.

клеветни́ческий *adj.* slanderous; libelous.

клево́к [*gen.* -вка́] *n.* peck.

кле́врет *n.* follower; supporter; minion.

клеёнка *n.* oilcloth. —клеёнчатый, *adj.* oilcloth (*attrib.*).

кле́ить *v.impfv.* [*pfv.* скле́ить] **1,** to glue; paste. **2,** to hang (wallpaper). **3,** to make (*by gluing or pasting something together*). —кле́иться, *refl.* **1,** *colloq.* to get sticky. **2,** to stick. **3,** *colloq.* (*usu. neg.*) to go well: Де́ло не кле́ится, things are not going well.

клей *n.* [*2nd loc.* на клею́] *n.* glue. —пти́чий клей, birdlime. —ры́бий клей, isinglass.

кле́йкий *adj.* sticky; gummy.

клейкови́на *n.* gluten.

клёйкость *n.f.* stickiness.

клейми́ть *v.impfv.* [*pfv.* заклейми́ть; *pres.* -млю́, -ми́шь] **1,** to stamp; mark. **2,** to brand (cattle). **3,** *fig.* to brand; stigmatize.

клеймо́ [*pl.* клёйма, клейм] *n.* **1,** mark; stamp. **2,** brand (*on cattle*). **3,** branding iron. —клеймо́ позо́ра, stigma.

клёйстер *n.* paste.

клёкот *n.* screech.

клекота́ть *v.impfv.* [*pres.* -ко́чет] (*of a bird*) to screech.

клён *n.* maple (tree). —клено́вый, *adj.* maple.

клепа́льщик *n.* riveter.

клепа́ть *v.impfv.* to rivet.

клёпка [*gen. pl.* -пок] *n.* **1,** riveting. **2,** barrel stave.

клептома́н *n.* kleptomaniac. —клептома́ния, *n.* kleptomania.

клерк *n.* clerk.

клёст [*gen.* клеста́] *n.* crossbill.

клётка [*gen. pl.* -ток] *n.* **1,** cage. **2,** *biol.* cell. **3,** check; square. Ткань в клётку, checked material. Бума́га в клётку, graph paper. **4,** square (*on a chessboard*). —грудна́я клётка, thorax. —лёстничная клётка, stairwell.

клёточка [*gen. pl.* -чек] *n., dim. of* клётка.

клёточный *adj.* cellular.

клету́шка [*gen. pl.* -шек] *n., colloq.* tiny room; cubicle.

клетча́тка *n.* cellulose.

клётчатый *adj.* checked.

клёцки [*gen.* -цек] *n.pl.* [*sing.* клёцка] dumplings.

клёш *n.* flare (*in a skirt or trousers*): ю́бка клёш, flared skirt; брю́ки клёш, bell-bottom trousers.

клешня́ [*gen. pl.* -нёй] *n.* claw; nipper; pincers (*of a crab or lobster*).

клещ [*gen.* клеща́] *n.* tick; mite.

клещи́ [*gen.* -щёй] *n.pl.* pliers; tongs; pincers.

клещи́ [*gen.* -щёй] *n.pl.* **1,** = клёщи. **2,** *mil.* pincers movement.

кли́вер [*pl.* кливера́] *n., naut.* jib.

клиёнт *n.* client; customer.

клиенту́ра *n.* clientele.

кли́зма *n.* enema.

клик *n.* cry; call.

кли́ка *n.* clique.

кли́кать *v.impfv.* [*pfv.* кли́кнуть; *pres.* кли́чу, кли́чешь] *colloq.* to call; hail.

кли́макс *n.* menopause. *Also,* климактёрий.

кли́мат *n.* climate. —климати́ческий, *adj.* climatic.

клин [*pl.* кли́нья, кли́ньев] *n.* **1,** wedge. **2,** gore; gusset. —свет не кли́ном сошёлся на (+ *prepl.*), he/she/it is not the only one in the world; there are other fish in the sea.

кли́ника *n.* clinic. —клини́ческий, *adj.* clinical.

клинови́дный *adj.* wedge-shaped.

клино́к [*gen.* -нка́] *n.* blade (*of a sword, knife, etc.*).

клинообра́зный *adj.* wedge-shaped.

кли́нопись *n.f.* cuneiform.

кли́пер [*pl.* клипера́] *n., naut.* clipper.

клипс *n.* earring (*for an unpierced ear*).

кли́рос *n.* choir (*part of a church*).

кли́тор *n.* clitoris.

клич *n.* call; appeal. —боево́й клич, war cry; battle cry.

кли́чка [*gen. pl.* -чек] *n.* **1,** name of a household pet. **2,** nickname.

клише́ *n.neut. indecl.* cliché.

клоа́ка *n.* **1,** sewer; cesspool. **2,** *fig.* foul place; sewer.

клок [*gen.* клока́; *pl.* кло́чья, кло́чьев *or* клоки́, клоко́в] *n.* **1,** shred. **2,** tuft (*of hair*); wisp (*of hay*).

клокота́ть *v.impfv.* [*pres.* -кочу́, -ко́чешь] **1,** (*of liquids*) to bubble. **2,** *fig.* (*of emotions*) to bubble; seethe.

клони́ть *v.impfv.* [*pres.* клоню́, кло́нишь] **1,** to incline; bend. *Also impers.:* Ло́дку клони́ло на́ бок, the boat was listing. **2,** (*of sleep*) to overcome. *Also impers.:* Его́ кло́нит ко сну, he is drowsy. **3,** *fig.* (*with* к) to incline (toward); predispose (toward). **4,** *fig.* to guide; steer (a conversation, affair, etc.). **5,** (*with* к) *colloq.* to get at; drive at: К чему́ ты кло́нишь?, what are you getting/driving at? —клони́ться, *refl.* **1,** to bow; bend. **2,** (*with* к) to be nearing. День клони́лся к ве́черу, day was drawing toward evening. Де́ло кло́нится к развя́зке, matters are reaching a climax. **3,** *fig.* (*with* к) to be leading (to): К чему́ всё э́то кло́нится?, what is all this leading to?

клоп [*gen.* клопа́] *n.* bedbug.

кло́ун *n.* clown.

кло́унский *adj.* **1,** clown (*attrib.*); clown's. **2,** clownish.

клохта́нье *n.* cluck; clucking.

клохта́ть *v.impfv.* [*pres.* клохчу́, кло́хчешь] to cluck.

клочо́к [*gen.* -чка́] *n.* **1,** scrap (*of paper*). **2,** shred. **3,** wisp (*of hay*). **4,** small plot; patch. **5,** patch (*of fog, blue sky, etc.*).

клуб *n.* **1,** [*pl.* клу́бы] club. **2,** [*pl.* клубы́] puff (*of smoke*); *pl.* clouds (*of smoke, dust, etc.*).

клу́бень [*gen.* -бня] *n.m.* tuber.

клуби́ть *v.impfv.* to swirl; blow into the air. —клуби́ться, *refl.* **1,** to swirl (*in the wind*). **2,** (*of smoke*) to curl.

клубнево́й *adj.* tuberous.

клубни́ка *n.* **1,** strawberries. **2,** a (single) strawberry. —клубни́чный, *adj.* strawberry (*attrib.*).

клу́бный *adj.* club (*attrib.*).

клубо́к [*gen.* -бка́] *n.* **1,** ball (*of thread or yarn*). **2,** *fig.* (*with gen.*) tangle (of); web (of). —клубо́к в го́рле, lump in one's throat.

клу́мба *n.* flower bed.

клык [*gen.* клыка́] *n.* **1,** fang. **2,** tusk. **3,** canine tooth; cuspid.

клюв *n.* beak; bill.

клюка́ *n.* cane; walking stick.

клю́ква *n.* **1,** cranberries. **2,** a (single) cranberry. **3,** cranberry bush. —клю́квенный, *adj.* cranberry (*attrib.*).

клю́нуть *v., pfv. of* клева́ть.

ключ [*gen.* ключа́] *n.* **1,** key: ключ от ко́мнаты, the key to the room. **2,** [*also,* га́ечный ключ] wrench: францу́зский ключ, monkey wrench. **3,** *music* clef; key. **4,** (*with* к) key (*solution*): ключ к та́йне, the key to the mystery. **5,** spring: го́рные ключи́, mountain springs. —бить ключо́м, **1,** to spurt; spout. **2,** *fig.* to throb; be bursting (with life, energy, etc.).

ключевóй *adj.* **1,** key (*attrib.*). **2,** *fig.* key; vital. **3,** coming from underground springs: ключева́я вода́, spring water.

клю́чик *n., dim. of* ключ.

ключи́ца *n.* collarbone; clavicle.

клю́шка [*gen. pl.* -шек] *n.* **1,** hockey stick. **2,** golf club.

кля́кса *n.* inkblot.

кля́нчить *v.impfv., colloq.* to beg; pester.

кляп *n.* gag.

клясть *v.impfv.* [*pres.* кляну́, клянёшь; *past* клял, кляла́, кля́ло, кля́ли] to curse. —**кля́сться,** *refl.* [*pfv.* покля́сться] to swear; vow. Я торже́ственно кляну́сь, I solemnly swear. Кля́сться в ве́рности, to swear allegiance.

кля́тва *n.* oath; vow. —**взять с кого́-нибудь кля́тву,** to make someone swear. —**дава́ть кля́тву,** to take an oath; swear.

кля́твенный *adj.* (*of a promise, oath, etc.*) solemn; sworn.

клятвопреступле́ние *n.* perjury. —**клятвопресту́пник,** *n.* perjurer.

кля́уза *n.* **1,** *colloq.* petty lie; piece of malicious gossip. **2,** *obs.* petty lawsuit.

кля́узничать *v.impfv., colloq.* to tell petty lies; spread malicious gossip.

кля́ча *n.* old horse; nag; jade.

кни́га *n.* book.

кни́жка [*gen. pl.* -жек] *n., dim. of* кни́га. —**сберега́тельная кни́жка,** bankbook; passbook. —**записна́я кни́жка,** notebook. —**трудова́я кни́жка,** work-record book. —**че́ковая кни́жка,** checkbook.

кни́жник *n.* **1,** *colloq.* lover of books; bibliophile. **2,** *colloq.* one who has only book knowledge. **3,** *colloq.* bookseller. **4,** *Bib.* scribe.

кни́жный *adj.* **1,** book (*attrib.*): кни́жный магази́н, bookstore. **2,** *fig.* bookish.

кни́зу *adv.* down; downward(s).

кни́ксен (сэ) *n.* curtsy.

кно́пка [*gen. pl.* -пок] *n.* **1,** button; push button. **2,** thumbtack. **3,** snap; snap fastener. —**кно́почный,** *adj.* push-button (*attrib.*).

кнут [*gen.* кнута́] *n.* whip; knout.

кнутови́ще *n.* whip handle.

княги́ня *n.* princess (*prince's wife*).

кня́жеский *adj.* **1,** prince's. **2,** princely.

кня́жество *n.* principality. —**вели́кое кня́жество,** grand duchy.

кня́жить *v.impfv.* to reign (*as prince*).

княжна́ [*gen. pl.* -жо́н] *n.* princess (*prince's daughter*).

князь [*pl.* князья́, -зе́й, -зья́м] *n.m., pre-rev.* prince. —**вели́кий князь,** grand duke.

ко *prep.* = **к** (*used before certain words beginning with two consonants*): ко мне; ко дну; ко вре́мени.

коагуля́нт *n.* coagulant. —**коагуля́ция,** *n.* coagulation.

коаксиа́льный *adj., in* коаксиа́льный ка́бель, coaxial cable.

коа́ла *n.* koala.

коали́ция *n.* coalition. —**коалицио́нный,** *adj.* coalition (*attrib.*).

ко́бальт *n.* cobalt. —**ко́бальтовый,** *adj.* cobalt.

кобе́ль [*gen.* -беля́] *n.m.* male dog.

ко́бра *n.* cobra.

кобура́ *n.* holster.

кобы́ла *n.* **1,** mare. **2,** *gymnastics* horse.

кобы́лка [*gen. pl.* -лок] *n.* **1,** filly. **2,** bridge (*of a stringed instrument*).

ко́ваный *adj.* **1,** forged; hammered. **2,** *fig.* terse; crisp.

кова́рный *adj.* insidious; treacherous. —**кова́рство,** *n.* treachery.

кова́ть *v.impfv.* [*pres.* кую́, куёшь] **1,** to forge. **2,** to shoe (a horse). **3,** *fig.* to forge; carve out (a victory). —**куй желе́зо, пока́ горячо́,** strike while the iron is hot.

ковбо́й *n.* cowboy.

ковбо́йка [*gen. pl.* -бо́ек] *n., colloq.* man's checked shirt.

ковбо́йский *adj.* cowboy (*attrib.*); cowboy's.

ковёр [*gen.* ковра́] *n.* carpet; rug. —**вызыва́ть на ковёр,** *colloq.* to call on the carpet.

кове́ркать *v.impfv.* [*pfv.* искове́ркать] **1,** to break; damage; wreck; mangle. **2,** to warp; distort. **3,** to mispronounce (a word, name, etc.); murder; butcher (a language).

ко́вка *n.* **1,** forging. **2,** shoeing.

ко́вкий *adj.* [*short form* ко́вок, ко́вка *or* ковка́, ко́вко, ко́вки] malleable; ductile. —**ко́вкость,** *n.f.* malleability.

коври́га *n.* large round loaf of bread.

коври́жка [*gen. pl.* -жек] *n.* **1,** *dim. of* коври́га. **2,** honey cake; gingerbread. —**ни за каки́е коври́жки,** *colloq.* not for anything in the world.

ко́врик *n.* **1,** small rug. **2,** mat.

ковро́вый *adj.* carpet (*attrib.*); rug (*attrib.*).

ковче́г *n.* ark: Но́ев ковче́г, Noah's ark. —**ковче́г заве́та,** ark of the covenant.

ковш [*gen.* ковша́] *n.* scoop; dipper.

ковы́ль [*gen.* ковыля́] *n.m.* feather grass.

ковыля́ть *v.impfv., colloq.* **1,** to hobble. **2,** (*of a child*) to toddle.

ковыря́ть *v.impfv., colloq.* **1,** to dig up (earth, soil, etc.). **2,** (*with* в + *prepl.*) to pick (one's teeth, nose, etc.). —**ковыря́ться,** *refl.* (*with* в + *prepl.*) *colloq.* to putter (in); poke about (in).

когда́ *adv.* when?: Когда́ ты бу́дешь гото́в?, when will you be ready? —*conj.* **1,** when: когда́ я был (была́) в Москве́, when I was in Moscow. Быва́ли дни, когда́..., there were days when... Быва́ли слу́чаи, когда́..., there have been cases where/ in which/... **2,** while; as: когда́ мы обе́дали, while/as we were having dinner. —**вот когда́...,** that was when... —**есть когда́!,** *colloq.* there is no time. —**когда́ бы ни,** whenever; no matter when. —**когда́ бы то ни́ было,** at any time. —**когда́ как; как когда́,** *colloq.* it depends. —**тепе́рь, когда́...,** now that... —**тогда́, когда́...,** when...

когда́-либо *adv.* **1,** sometime. **2,** ever: бо́льше чем когда́-либо ра́ньше, more than ever before.

когда́-нибудь *adv.* **1,** sometime; someday. **2,** (*in interr. sentences*) ever: Вы когда́-нибудь быва́ли там?, have you ever been there?

когда́-то *adv.* **1,** at one time; once. **2,** sometime; someday.

кого́ (во) *pron., gen. & acc. of* кто.

ко́готь [ко́гтя; *pl.* ко́гти, -те́й, -тя́м] *n.m.* claw. —в когтя́х сме́рти, in the jaws of death. —пока́зывать ко́гти, to show one's teeth. —попа́сть в ко́гти (*with gen., dat. or* к), to fall into the clutches of.

когти́стый *adj.* having sharp claws.

когти́ть *v.impfv.* to claw.

код *n.* code.

коде́ин *n.* codeine.

ко́декс (дэ) *n.* code (*of law, principles, etc.*).

коди́ровать *v.impfv. & pfv.* [*pfv. also* закоди́ровать; *pres.* -рую, -руешь] to encode.

кодифика́ция *n.* codification.

кодифици́ровать *v.impfv. & pfv.* [*pres.* -рую, -руешь] to codify.

ко́довый *adj.* code (*attrib.*).

ко́е-где́ *adv.* in some places; here and there.

ко́е-ка́к *adv.* **1,** carelessly; any which way. **2,** somehow; with great difficulty.

ко́е-како́й *adj.* some.

ко́е-когда́ *adv.* now and then.

ко́е-кто́ *indef. pron.* someone; some people.

ко́е-куда́ *adv.* somewhere.

ко́е-что́ *indef. pron.* something.

ко́жа *n.* **1,** skin. **2,** leather. —гуси́ная ко́жа, goose flesh; goose pimples. —ко́жа да ко́сти, (he's all) skin and bones.

ко́жаный *adj.* leather.

коже́венный *adj.* leather (*attrib.*). —коже́венный заво́д, tannery.

коже́вник *n.* currier.

кожими́т *n.* imitation leather.

ко́жица *n.* **1,** thin skin (*e.g. of a sausage*). **2,** skin; peel; rind.

ко́жный *adj.* skin (*attrib.*).

кожура́ *n.* rind; skin; peel.

кожу́х [*gen.* -жуха́] *n.* **1,** sheepskin coat. **2,** housing; casing.

коза́ [*pl.* ко́зы] *n.* (nanny) goat.

козёл [*gen.* козла́] *n.* goat; billy goat. —козёл отпуще́ния, scapegoat.

козеро́г *n.* **1,** ibex. **2,** *cap.* Capricorn: тро́пик Козеро́га, Tropic of Capricorn.

ко́зий [*fem.* -зья] *adj.* goat (*attrib.*); goat's.

козлёнок [*gen.* -нка; *pl.* -ля́та, -ля́т] *n.* young goat; kid.

ко́злик *n., dim. of* козёл.

козли́ный *adj.* **1,** goat (*attrib.*); goat's. **2,** goatskin (*attrib.*). —козли́ная боро́дка, goatee.

козло́вый *adj.* goatskin (*attrib.*).

ко́злы [*gen.* ко́зел] *n.pl.* **1,** coachman's seat. **2,** trestle. **3,** sawhorse.

козля́тина *n.* goat meat.

ко́зни [*gen.* -ней] *n.pl.* intrigues; machinations.

козодо́й *n.* goatsucker (*bird*).

ко́зочка [*gen. pl.* -чек] *n., dim. of* коза́.

козырёк [*gen.* -рька́] *n.* **1,** peak (*of a cap*). **2,** visor. —взять *or* сде́лать под козырёк, to salute.

козырно́й *also,* ко́зырный *adj.* trump (*attrib.*); of trump: козырно́й/ко́зырный туз, ace of trump.

козырну́ть *v., pfv. of* козыря́ть.

ко́зырь [*pl.* ко́зыри, -ре́й, -ря́м] *n.m.* **1,** trump. **2,** *fig.* trump card. —пусти́ть в ход после́дний ко́зырь, to play one's trump card.

козыря́ть *v.impfv.* [*pfv.* козырну́ть] *colloq.* **1,** to play a trump. **2,** (*with instr.*) to flaunt. **3,** to salute.

козя́вка [*gen. pl.* -вок] *n., colloq.* insect; bug.

кой *adj., archaic* = како́й *and* кото́рый. —в ко́и ве́ки, once in a blue moon. —ни в ко́ем слу́чае, under no circumstances.

ко́йка [*gen. pl.* ко́ек] *n.* **1,** berth; bunk. **2,** hospital bed. —подвесна́я ко́йка, hammock.

койо́т *n.* coyote.

кок *n.* **1,** cook (*on board a ship*). **2,** forelock.

ко́ка *n.* coca.

кока́ин *n.* cocaine.

кока́рда *n.* cockade.

коке́тка [*gen. pl.* -ток] *n.* **1,** coquette; flirt. **2,** yoke (*of a dress*).

коке́тливый *adj.* **1,** coquettish; flirtatious. **2,** attractive; fetching.

коке́тничать *v.impfv.* **1,** to flirt. **2,** (*with instr.*) to flaunt.

коке́тство *n.* coquetry; flirting.

кокк *n.* coccus.

коклю́ш *n.* whooping cough.

ко́кон *n.* cocoon.

коко́с *n.* **1,** coconut. **2,** coconut palm; coconut tree. —коко́совый, *adj.* coconut (*attrib.*).

коко́тка [*gen. pl.* -ток] *n.* kept woman.

коко́шник *n.* woman's headdress worn in old Russia.

кокс *n.* coke. —ко́ксовый; коксова́льный, *adj.* coke (*attrib.*). —коксу́ющийся, *adj., in* коксу́ющийся у́голь, coking coal.

кокте́йль (тэ) *n.m.* cocktail. —моло́чный кокте́йль, milk shake.

кол [*gen.* кола́; *2nd loc.* на колу́] *n.* **1,** [*pl.* ко́лья, ко́льев] stake; picket. Посади́ть на́ кол, to impale on a stake. **2,** [*pl.* колы́, коло́в] *colloq.* one (*lowest grade in school*). —ему́ хоть кол на голове́ теши́, *colloq.* you can beat him over the head; you can talk to him till you're blue in the face. —ни кола́ ни двора́, penniless; without a roof over one's head.

ко́лба *n.* flask; retort.

колбаса́ [*pl.* -ба́сы] *n.* sausage. —ли́верная колбаса́, liverwurst.

колба́сник *n.* sausage maker.

колба́сный *adj.* sausage (*attrib.*).

колго́тки [*gen.* -ток] *n.pl.* pantyhose.

колдо́бина *n., colloq.* rut; pothole.

колдова́ть *v.impfv.* [*pres.* -ду́ю, -ду́ешь] to practice witchcraft.

колдовско́й *adj.* **1,** of witchcraft. **2,** *fig.* magical; mysterious.

колдовство́ *n.* sorcery; witchcraft.

колду́н [*gen.* -дуна́] *n.* sorcerer. —колду́нья, *n.* sorceress.

колеба́ние *n.* **1,** swaying. **2,** oscillation; vibration. **3,** fluctuation; variation. **4,** *often pl.* hesitation; hesitancy; vacillation: без колеба́ний, without hesitation.

колеба́ть *v.impfv.* [*pfv.* поколеба́ть; *pres.* -ле́блю, -ле́блешь] **1,** [*impf. only*] to sway; cause to sway. **2,** to shake; weaken. **3,** to cause to waver. —колеба́ться, *refl.* **1,** to sway; swing to and fro. **2,** to oscillate. **3,** to fluctuate; vary. **4,** to hesitate; waver; vacillate. **5,** to be shaken; be weakened.

коле́нка [*gen. pl.* -нок] *n., colloq.* knee.

коленко́р *n.* buckram. —э́то совсе́м друго́й коленко́р, that's a horse of a different color.

коле́нный *adj.* knee (*attrib.*). —коле́нная ча́шка *or* ча́шечка, kneecap.

коле́но *n.* **1,** [*pl.* коле́ни, коле́ней *or* коле́н] knee. На коле́нях, A, on one's knees. B, on one's lap. **2,** [*pl.* коле́нья, коле́ньев] A, bend (*in a pipe, duct, etc.*). B, section (*of a pipe, duct, etc.*). **3,** [*pl.* коле́на, коле́н] *music* part; *dance* figure. **4,** [*pl.* коле́на, коле́н] generation. Брат (сестра́) во второ́м коле́не, cousin twice removed. **5,** [*pl.* коле́на, коле́н] *Bib.* tribe: коле́на Изра́илевы, the tribes of Israel. —ему́ мо́ре по коле́но, *colloq.* he couldn't care less.

коле́нчатый *adj.* consisting of several branches. —коле́нчатый вал, crankshaft.

колёсико *n.* **1,** *dim. of* колесо́. **2,** caster.

колеси́ть *v.impfv.* [*pres.* -шу́, -си́шь] *colloq.* **1,** to travel in a roundabout way. **2,** to travel about (a place); travel all over.

колесни́ца *n.* chariot. —погреба́льная колесни́ца, hearse.

колёсный *adj.* **1,** wheel (*attrib.*). **2,** wheeled. —колёсный ма́стер, wheelwright.

колесо́ [*pl.* колёса] *n.* wheel. —вставля́ть па́лки в колёса, **1,** to throw a monkey wrench into the works. **2,** (*with dat.*) to put a spoke in someone's wheel.

колесова́ть *v.impfv. & pfv.* [*pres.* -су́ю, -су́ешь] to break on the wheel.

коле́чко [*pl.* -чки, -чек] *n.* small ring.

колея́ *n.* **1,** rut. **2,** *R.R.* track; gauge. **3,** *fig.* normal routine: войти́ в колею́, to settle into one's normal routine. —вы́бить из колеи́, to unsettle; throw off stride.

ко́ли *also,* коли́ *and* коль *conj., obs.* if.

коли́бри *n.m. or f. indecl.* hummingbird.

колизе́й *n.* coliseum.

ко́лики [*gen.* ко́лик] *n.pl.* colic.

коли́т *n.* colitis.

коли́чественный *adj.* quantitative. —коли́чественное числи́тельное, cardinal number.

коли́чество *n.* quantity; amount; number.

ко́лкий *adj.* **1,** prickly. **2,** *fig.* biting; mordant; caustic.

ко́лкость *n.f.* **1,** causticity. **2,** caustic remark.

коллаборациони́ст *n.* collaborator.

колле́га *n.m. & f.* **1,** colleague. **2,** counterpart.

коллегиа́льный *adj.* collective; joint.

колле́гия *n.* **1,** collegium; college. **2,** board: редакцио́нная колле́гия, editorial board. **3,** *in* суде́йская колле́гия, panel of judges.

колле́дж *n.* college.

коллекти́в *n.* collective; team; body; group.

коллективиза́ция *n.* collectivization.

коллективизи́ровать *v.impfv. & pfv.* [*pres.* -рую, -руешь] to collectivize.

коллективи́зм *n.* collectivism.

коллекти́вный *adj.* collective. —коллекти́вное хозя́йство, collective farm(ing).

коллекционе́р *n.* collector.

коллекциони́ровать *v.impfv.* [*pres.* -рую, -руешь] to collect.

колле́кция *n.* collection.

ко́лли *n.m. indecl.* collie.

колло́дий *n.* collodion. *Also,* колло́диум.

колло́ид *n.* colloid. —колло́идный, *adj.* colloidal.

колло́квиум *n.* **1,** oral examination. **2,** colloquium.

колобро́дить *v.impfv.* [*pres.* -жу, -дишь] *colloq.* **1,** to wander; drift; loiter. **2,** to carouse; live it up.

коловоро́т *n.* drill brace.

коло́да *n.* **1,** log. **2,** chopping block. **3,** deck (*of cards*). —че́рез пень коло́ду, in a slipshod manner.

коло́дезный *adj.* well (*attrib.*): коло́дезная вода́, well water.

коло́дец [*gen.* -дца] *n.* well.

коло́дка [*gen. pl.* -док] *n.* **1,** shoetree. **2,** last (*for a shoe*). **3,** shoe (*of a brake*). **4,** *pl.* stocks (*instrument of punishment*).

коло́к [*gen.* колка́] *n.* peg (*of a musical instrument*).

ко́локол [*pl.* колокола́] *n.* bell. —во все колокола́, *colloq.* for all to hear.

колоко́льный *adj.* of bells: колоко́льный звон, ringing *or* tolling of bells.

колоко́льня [*gen. pl.* -лен] *n.* bell tower. —смотре́ть (на что́-нибудь) со свое́й колоко́льни, to look at (solely) from one's own point of view.

колоко́льчик *n.* **1,** small bell. **2,** bluebell; bellflower; campanula.

колониали́зм *n.* colonialism.

колониа́льный *adj.* colonial.

колониза́тор *n.* **1,** colonialist; colonizer. **2,** colonist. —колониза́ция, *n.* colonization.

колонизи́ровать *v.impfv. & pfv.* [*pres.* -рую, -руешь] to colonize. *Also,* колонизова́ть [*pres.* -зу́ю, -зу́ешь].

колони́ст *n.* colonist; settler.

коло́ния *n.* colony.

коло́нка [*gen. pl.* -нок] *n.* **1,** *dim. of* коло́нна. **2,** column (*of print, figures, etc.*). **3,** any of a number of devices dispensing liquid: бензи́новая коло́нка, gasoline pump; водоразбо́рная коло́нка, hydrant; пожа́рная коло́нка, fire hydrant. —бензозапра́вочная коло́нка, **1,** gasoline pump. **2,** gas station. —рулева́я коло́нка, steering column.

коло́нна *n.* **1,** column; pillar. **2,** column (*of print, figures, etc.*). **3,** column; file: коло́нна демонстра́нтов, column of demonstrators (*or* marchers). **4,** *mil.* column: коло́нна та́нков, column of tanks; armored column. **5,** convoy.

колонна́да *n.* colonnade.

коло́нный *adj.* columned.

колоно́к [*gen.* -нка́] *n.* kolinsky (*Russian mink*).

колонти́тул *n., printing* running head.

колорату́ра *n.* coloratura. —колорату́рный, *adj.* coloratura.

колори́т *n.* coloring; color. —ме́стный колори́т, local color.

колори́тный *adj.* colorful.

ко́лос [*pl.* **коло́сья, коло́сьев**] *n.* ear (*of a cereal plant*).

колосовы́е *n.pl., decl. as an adj.* cereal.

коло́сс *n.* colossus.

колосса́льный *adj.* colossal; huge; tremendous.

колоти́ть *v.impfv.* [*pres.* **-лочу́, -ло́тишь**] **1,** (*with* в + *acc. or* по) to strike; bang; pound. **2,** *colloq.* to beat; whip; thrash. **3,** *colloq.* to break; smash. —**колоти́ться,** *refl.* **1,** (*with* о + *acc.*) *colloq.* to beat (against); strike (against). **2,** (*of the heart*) to thump; pound.

колоту́шка [*gen. pl.* **-шек**] *n.* **1,** wooden hammer; mallet. **2,** watchman's stick.

ко́лотый *adj.* (*of wood*) chopped. —**ко́лотая ра́на,** stab wound. —**ко́лотый са́хар,** lump sugar.

коло́ть *v.impfv.* [*pfv.* **кольну́ть**; *pres.* **колю́, ко́лешь**] **1,** to prick. **2,** to stab. **3,** *impers.* to cause a sharp pain: У меня́ ко́лет в боку́, I have a sharp pain in my side. **4,** [*pfv.* **расколо́ть**] to crack (nuts); chop (wood). **5,** [*pfv.* **заколо́ть**] to slaughter (an animal). **6,** *fig.* to taunt. —**коло́ться,** *refl.* [*impfv. only*] **1,** to be prickly. **2,** to split; break apart. **3,** to slash each other.

колпа́к [*gen.* **-пака́**] *n.* **1,** tall pointed cap. **2,** cone-shaped cover. **3,** hubcap. **4,** cowl.

колпачо́к [*gen.* **-чка́**] *n.* **1,** *dim. of* колпа́к. **2,** cap: буты́лочный колпачо́к, bottle cap.

ко́лпица *n.* spoonbill.

колумби́йский *adj.* **1,** Colombian. **2,** Columbia (*attrib.*): колумби́йский университе́т, Columbia University.

колу́н [*gen.* **-луна́**] *n.* heavy ax.

колхо́з *n.* collective farm (*contr. of* коллекти́вное хозя́йство). —**колхо́зник,** *n.* collective farmer; member of a collective farm. —**колхо́зный,** *adj.* of or pert. to a collective farm.

колча́н *n.* quiver.

колчеда́н *n.* pyrites.

колчено́гий *adj., colloq.* having one leg shorter than the other.

колыбе́ль *n.f.* cradle.

колыбе́льный *adj.* cradle (*attrib.*). —**колыбе́льная пе́сня,** lullaby.

колыма́га *n.* **1,** old-fashioned coach. **2,** *colloq.* rattle-trap; jalopy.

колыха́ние *n.* swaying.

колыха́ть *v.impfv.* [*pfv.* **колыхну́ть**; *pres.* **колы́шу, колы́шешь**] to sway; cause to sway. —**колыха́ться,** *refl.* to sway; wave; flutter.

ко́лышек [*gen.* **-шка**] *n.* peg.

коль *conj.* = **ко́ли.** —**коль ско́ро, 1,** since. **2,** as soon as.

кольдкре́м *n.* cold cream.

колье́ *n.neut. indecl.* necklace.

кольну́ть *v., pfv. of* коло́ть.

кольра́би *n.f. indecl.* kohlrabi.

кольцево́й *adj.* circular. —**кольцева́я доро́га,** ring road; beltway.

кольцо́ [*pl.* **ко́льца, коле́ц, ко́льцам**] *n.* ring.

ко́льчатый *adj.* **1,** made of rings. **2,** ring-shaped.

кольчу́га *n.* coat; chain mail.

колю́чий *adj.* **1,** prickly. **2,** itchy. **3,** biting; cutting; sarcastic. —**колю́чая про́волока,** barbed wire.

колю́чка [*gen. pl.* **-чек**] *n.* thorn; prickle.

ко́люшка [*gen. pl.* **-шек**] *n.* stickleback.

ко́лющий *adj.* stabbing: ко́лющая боль, stabbing pain.

коля́дка [*gen. pl.* **-док**] *n.* Christmas carol.

коля́ска [*gen. pl.* **-сок**] *n.* **1,** carriage. **2,** sidecar. —**де́тская коля́ска,** baby carriage. —**инвали́дная коля́ска,** wheelchair.

ком[1] [*pl.* **ко́мья, ко́мьев**] *n.* lump; clod. Сне́жный ком, snowball. —**ком в го́рле,** lump in one's throat.

ком[2] *pron., prepl. of* кто.

ко́ма *n.* coma.

кома́нда *n.* **1,** command; order. **2,** command: под кома́ндой (+ *gen.*), under the command of. **3,** crew (*of a ship*). **4,** *sports* team. **5,** *mil.* party; team. —**пожа́рная кома́нда,** fire brigade. —**спаса́тельная кома́нда,** rescue party.

команди́р *n.* **1,** commander. **2,** (ship's) captain.

командиро́ванный *adj.* on an assignment or business trip. —*n.* person on an assignment or business trip.

командирова́ть *v.impfv. & pfv.* [*pres.* **-ру́ю, -ру́ешь**] to send on an assignment; dispatch.

командиро́вка [*gen. pl.* **-вок**] *n.* assignment; business trip.

командиро́вочный *adj.* connected with an assignment or business trip. —**командиро́вочные,** *n.pl., colloq.* travel allowance.

кома́ндный *adj.* **1,** command (*attrib.*). Кома́ндные инста́нции, chain of command. **2,** team (*attrib.*). **3,** *fig.* commanding: кома́ндная высота́, commanding heights.

кома́ндование *n.* **1,** command: принима́ть кома́ндование, to assume command. **2,** command; commanding officers: вы́сшее кома́ндование, high command.

кома́ндовать *v.impfv.* [*pres.* **-дую, -дуешь**] **1,** to command; give orders. **2,** (*with instr.*) to command; be in command of. **3,** (*with* над) *colloq.* to boss around; order about.

кома́ндующий *n., decl. as an adj.* commander.

кома́р [*gen.* **-мара́**] *n.* mosquito. —**комари́ный,** *adj.* mosquito (*attrib.*).

комато́зный *adj.* comatose.

комба́йн *n.* combine; harvester.

комбина́т *n.* **1,** integrated plant. **2,** center: комбина́т бытово́го обслу́живания, service center; уче́бный комбина́т, training center.

комбина́ция *n.* **1,** combination. **2,** *sports* maneuver. **3,** *fig.* scheme. **4,** (lady's) slip.

комбинезо́н *n.* overalls.

комбини́ровать *v.impfv.* [*pfv.* **скомбини́ровать**; *pres.* **-рую, -руешь**] to combine.

комеди́йный *adj.* comedy (*attrib.*). —**комеди́йный актёр,** comedian.

коме́дия *n.* comedy. —**разы́грывать** *or* **лома́ть коме́дию,** to put on an act.

ко́мель [*gen.* **ко́мля**] *n.m.* thick end; stump; base.

коменда́нт *n.* **1,** commandant. **2,** superintendent.

коменда́нтский *adj., in* **коменда́нтский час,** curfew.

комендату́ра *n.* commandant's headquarters.

коме́та *n.* comet.

коми́зм *n.* comedy; humor.

ко́мик *n.* comedian; comic actor.

ко́микс *n., usu. pl.* comics.

комисса́р *n.* **1,** commissar. **2,** commissioner. —**комиссариа́т,** *n.* commissariat.

комиссионе́р *n.* broker; agent.

комиссио́нный *adj.* commission (*attrib.*). —**комиссио́нные,** *n.pl.* commission; fee.

коми́ссия *n.* **1,** commission; committee; board. **2,** *comm.* commission: взима́ть коми́ссию, to charge a commission. Брать *or* принима́ть ве́щи на коми́ссию, to accept items for sale on a commission basis.

комите́т *n.* committee.

коми́ческий *adj.* **1,** comic. **2,** comical.

коми́чный *adj.* comical; funny.

ко́мкать *v.impfv.* [*pfv.* **ско́мкать**] **1,** to crumple. **2,** *colloq.* to rush through; cut short.

комкова́тый *adj.* bumpy; uneven.

коммента́рий *n.* **1,** commentary. **2,** *pl.* comment: никаки́х коммента́риев, no comment.

коммента́тор *n.* commentator.

комменти́ровать *v.impfv. & pfv.* [*pfv. also* **прокомменти́ровать;** *pres.* **-ру́ю, -ру́ешь**] **1,** to annotate. **2,** to comment on.

коммерса́нт *n.* merchant; businessman.

комме́рция *n.* commerce. —**комме́рческий,** *adj.* commercial.

коммивояжёр *n.* traveling salesman.

комму́на *n.* commune.

коммуна́льный *adj.* **1,** public; municipal. **2,** (*of an apartment*) communal.

коммуни́зм *n.* communism.

коммуника́бельный *adj.* communicative; approachable; easy to talk to.

коммуника́ция *n., mil., often pl.* communications. —**коммуникацио́нный,** *adj.* of communications.

коммуни́ст *n.* communist. —**коммунисти́ческий,** *adj.* communist.

коммута́тор *n.* switchboard.

коммюнике́ *n.neut. indecl.* communiqué.

ко́мната *n.* room.

ко́мнатный *adj.* **1,** room (*attrib.*). **2,** indoor: ко́мнатные расте́ния, indoor plants; ко́мнатные и́гры, indoor games; parlor games. —**ко́мнатная му́ха,** housefly. —**ко́мнатная соба́чка,** lap dog.

комо́д *n.* bureau; dresser.

комо́к [*gen.* **комка́**] *n.* lump. —**комо́к в го́рле,** lump in one's throat. —**комо́к не́рвов,** bundle of nerves.

комо́лый *adj.* hornless.

компа́ктный *adj.* compact; solid.

компане́йский *adj., colloq.* social; companionable; outgoing.

компа́ния *n.* **1,** company: води́ть компа́нию с, to keep company with. Он тебе́ не компа́ния, he is not the proper company for you. **2,** group: отдели́ться от компа́нии, to become separated from the group. Пойти́ всей компа́нией, to go in a group. **3,** *comm.* company: нефтяна́я компа́ния, oil company.

компаньо́н *n.* **1,** (male) companion. **2,** partner. —**компаньо́нка,** *n.* (female) companion.

компа́ртия *n.* Communist Party (*contr. of* **коммунисти́ческая па́ртия**).

ко́мпас *n.* compass. —**ко́мпасный,** *adj.* compass (*attrib.*).

компе́ндиум *also,* **компе́ндий** *n.* compendium.

компенса́ция *n.* compensation. —**компенсацио́нный,** *adj.* compensatory.

компенси́ровать *v.impfv. & pfv.* [*pres.* **-ру́ю, -ру́ешь**] **1,** to compensate. **2,** to compensate for; make up for; offset.

компете́нтность *n.f.* competence.

компете́нтный *adj.* **1,** competent; qualified. **2,** competent; having jurisdiction.

компете́нция *n.* jurisdiction.

компили́ровать *v.impfv.* [*pfv.* **скомпили́ровать;** *pres.* **-ру́ю, -ру́ешь**] to compile.

компиля́ция *n.* compilation. —**компиля́тор,** *n.* compiler.

ко́мплекс *n.* **1,** complex. **2,** series. **3,** system. **4,** *psychoanalysis* complex: ко́мплекс неполноце́нности, inferiority complex.

ко́мплексный *adj.* **1,** complex; composite; multiple. **2,** integrated. **3,** all-round; comprehensive. —**ко́мплексное соглаше́ние,** package deal.

компле́кт *n.* **1,** (complete) set. **2,** complement (*of personnel*). —**компле́ктный,** *adj.* (*of a set*) complete.

комплектова́ние *n.* **1,** bringing up to full strength. **2,** acquisition (*of books for a library*).

комплектова́ть *v.impfv.* [*pfv.* **укомплектова́ть;** *pres.* **-ту́ю, -ту́ешь**] **1,** to complete (a set); acquire a complete set of. **2,** to bring up to full strength.

компле́кция *n.* build; figure; frame.

комплиме́нт *n.* compliment.

компози́тор *n.* composer.

компози́ция *n.* composition.

компоне́нт *n.* component.

компонова́ть *v.impfv.* [*pfv.* **скомпонова́ть;** *pres.* **-ну́ю, -ну́ешь**] to arrange; put together.

компоно́вка *n.* arrangement; layout.

компо́ст *n.* compost.

компо́стер *n.* punch (*for punching tickets*).

компости́ровать *v.impfv.* [*pfv.* **прокомпости́ровать;** *pres.* **-ру́ю, -ру́ешь**] to punch (a ticket).

компо́т *n.* fruit compote; stewed fruit.

компре́сс *n.* compress.

компре́ссор *n.* compressor.

компрома́ция *n.* compromising (*of someone or something*).

компроме́ти́ровать *v.impfv.* [*pfv.* **скомпромети́ровать;** *pres.* **-ру́ю, -ру́ешь**] to compromise; place in a compromising position.

компромети́рующий *adj.* compromising.

компроми́сс *n.* compromise. —**компроми́ссный,** *adj.* compromise (*attrib.*).

компью́тер (тэ) *n.* computer.

комсомо́л *n.* Komsomol; Communist Youth League (*contr. of* **Коммунисти́ческий Сою́з Молодёжи**).

комсомо́лец [*gen.* **-льца**] *n.m.* [*fem.* **-лка**] member of the Komsomol.

комсомо́льский *adj.* Komsomol (*attrib.*).

кому́ *pron., dat. of* **кто**.

комфо́рт *n.* comfort.

комфорта́бельный *adj.* comfortable.

кон [*2nd loc.* **кону́**; *pl.* **коны́**] *n.* kitty (*in a game*). —**ста́вить на́ кон**, **1**, to put (money) in the kitty. **2**, *fig.* to put (one's life) on the line.

конве́йер *n.* conveyor. —**сбо́рочный конве́йер**, assembly line.

конве́йерный *adj.* conveyor (*attrib.*): конве́йерная ле́нта, conveyor belt.

конве́нт *n., hist.* convention.

конве́нция *n.* convention; compact.

конве́рсия *n., econ.* conversion.

конве́рт *n.* envelope.

конве́ртер (тэ) *n.* converter.

конверти́ровать *v.impfv. & pfv.* [*pres.* **-рую, -руешь**] *finance* to convert.

конверти́руемый *adj., finance* convertible.

конве́ртор *n.* = **конве́ртер**.

конвои́р *n.* **1**, armed guard; escort. **2**, escort (*for ships*).

конвои́ровать *v.impfv.* [*pres.* **-рую, -руешь**] *mil.* to escort.

конво́й *n.* (armed) escort; под конво́ем, under escort; under guard.

конво́йный *adj.* escort (*attrib.*). —*n.* armed guard; escort.

конву́льсия *n.* convulsion. —**конвульси́вный**, *adj.* convulsive.

конгломера́т *n.* **1**, conglomeration. **2**, conglomerate.

конголе́зский *adj.* Congolese.

конгре́сс *n.* **1**, congress: Ве́нский конгре́сс, Congress of Vienna. **2**, Congress (*of the U.S.*). —**конгрессме́н**, *n.* (U.S.) congressman.

конгру́энтный *adj., math.* congruent. —**конгруэ́нция**, *n., math.* congruence.

конденса́тор (дэ) *n.* **1**, *chem.* condenser. **2**, *electricity* capacitor; condenser.

конденса́ция (дэ) *n., physics* condensation. —**конденсацио́нный**, *adj.* obtained by condensation.

конденси́ровать (дэ) *v.impfv. & pfv.* [*pres.* **-рую, -руешь**] *physics* to condense.

конди́тер *n.* pastry cook; pastry chef; confectioner.

конди́терская *n., decl. as an adj.* pastry shop; confectionery. —**конди́терский**, *adj.* pastry (*attrib.*); confectionery (*attrib.*).

кондиционе́р *n.* air conditioner.

кондициони́рование *n.* conditioning. —**кондициони́рование во́здуха**, air conditioning.

кондициони́ровать *v.impfv. & pfv.* [*pres.* **-рую, -руешь**] to air-condition.

кондоми́ниум *n.* condominium.

ко́ндор *n.* condor.

кондотье́р *n.* soldier of fortune.

конду́ктор [*pl.* **кондуктора́**] *n.* conductor (*on a train, bus, etc.*). —**конду́кторский**, *adj.* conductor's.

конево́дство *n.* horse breeding. —**конево́д**, *n.* horse breeder. —**конево́дческий**, *adj.* of or pert. to breeding horses: конево́дческая фе́рма, stud farm.

конёк [*gen.* **конька́**] *n.* **1**, *dim. of* **конь**. **2**, *pl.* skates (*esp.* ice skates). **3**, ridge (*of a roof*). **4**, carved horse's head used as a decoration for a roof. **5**, *fig.* one's chief

interest; one's favorite topic of conversation. —**морско́й конёк**, sea horse.

коне́ц [*gen.* **конца́**] *n.* end. —**без конца́**, endlessly. —**в конце́ концо́в**, in the end; after all; when all is said and done. —**в оди́н коне́ц**, (*of a trip*) one-way. —**до конца́**, **1**, to the end. **2**, completely; totally. —**и де́ло с концо́м**, *colloq.* and that will be the end of it. —**и концы́ в во́ду**, and no one will know the difference; and none will be the wiser. —**из конца́ в коне́ц**, from end to end. —**на худо́й коне́ц**, *colloq.* if worst comes to worst. —**со всех концо́в** (+ *gen.*), from every corner of.

коне́чно *adv.* of course; certainly.

коне́чность *n.f.* extremity (*of the body*).

коне́чный *adj.* **1**, final; last. **2**, ultimate; eventual. **3**, finite. **4**, *in* коне́чный проду́кт, end product. —**в коне́чном ито́ге** *or* счёте, ultimately; in the final analysis.

кони́на *n.* horsemeat.

кони́ческий *adj.* conic; conical.

ко́нка [*gen. pl.* **ко́нок**] *n.* horsecar.

конкла́в *n., relig.* conclave.

конкорда́т *n.* concordat.

конкретизи́ровать *v.impfv. & pfv.* [*pres.* **-рую, -руешь**] to make specific; spell out.

конкре́тный *adj.* concrete; specific.

конкуре́нт *n.* (business) competitor.

конкурентоспосо́бный *adj.* able to compete; competitive. —**конкурентоспосо́бность**, *n.f.* competitiveness.

конкуре́нция *n.* (business) competition.

конкури́ровать *v.impfv.* [*pres.* **-рую, -руешь**] to compete.

ко́нкурс *n.* competition; contest. —**ко́нкурсный**, *adj.* competitive.

ко́нник *n.* cavalryman.

ко́нница *n.* cavalry.

коннозаво́дство *n.* horse breeding.

ко́нный *adj.* **1**, horse (*attrib.*). **2**, horse-drawn. **3**, mounted. **4**, (*of a statue*) equestrian. —**ко́нный двор**, stable. —**ко́нный заво́д**, stud farm.

конова́л *n.* horse doctor.

ко́новязь *n.f.* hitching post.

конокра́д *n.* horse thief. —**конокра́дство**, *n.* horse stealing.

конопа́тить *v.impfv.* [*pfv.* **законопа́тить**; *pres.* **-чу, -тишь**] to caulk.

конопля́ *n.* hemp.

конопля́нка [*gen. pl.* **-нок**] *n.* linnet.

конопля́ный *adj.* hemp (*attrib.*).

коносаме́нт *n.* bill of lading.

консе́нсус (сэ) *n.* consensus.

консерва́нт *n.* preservative.

консервати́вный *adj.* conservative. —**консервати́зм**, *n.* conservatism. —**консерва́тор**, *n.* conservative.

консервато́рия *n.* conservatory (*of music*).

консерва́ция *n.* **1**, temporary closing. **2**, mothballing.

консерви́рование *n.* preserving (*of meat, fruit, etc.*).

консерви́ровать *v.impfv. & pfv.* [*pfv. also* **законсерви́ровать**; *pres.* **-рую, -руешь**] **1**, to can; preserve. **2**, to halt temporarily; close down temporarily. **3**, to mothball.

консе́рвный *adj.* canning (*attrib.*). —**консе́рвная ба́нка,** tin can. —**консе́рвный нож,** can opener. —**консе́рвная фа́брика,** cannery.

консе́рвы [*gen.* **-вов**] *n.pl.* canned food; canned goods: мясны́е консе́рвы, canned meat; овощны́е консе́рвы, canned vegetables.

конси́лиум *n.* consultation (*between doctors*).

консисте́нция *n.* consistency (*firmness*).

ко́нский *adj.* horse (*attrib.*). —**ко́нский во́лос,** horsehair.

консолида́ция *n.* consolidation.

консо́ль *n.f.* **1,** console (*bracket*). **2,** pedestal; stand. **3,** cantilever. —**консо́льный,** *adj.* cantilever (*attrib.*): консо́льный мост, cantilever bridge.

консона́нс *n.* consonance.

консо́рциум *n.* consortium.

конспе́кт *n.* synopsis; outline; abstract.

конспекти́вный *adj.* concise; brief.

конспекти́ровать *v.impfv.* [*pfv.* **проконспекти́ровать;** *pres.* **-рую, -руешь**] to abstract; make an abstract of.

конспирати́вный *adj.* secret. —**конспира́тор,** *n.* conspirator. —**конспира́ция,** *n.* secrecy.

конста́нта *n., physics; math.* constant.

констата́ция *n.* **1,** statement. **2,** establishment; certification.

констати́ровать *v.impfv. & pfv.* [*pres.* **-рую, -руешь**] to establish; certify.

консте́бль (тэ) *n.m.* constable.

конституцио́нный *adj.* constitutional. —**конституцио́нность,** *n.f.* constitutionality.

конститу́ция *n.* constitution.

конструи́ровать *v.impfv.* [*pfv.* **сконструи́ровать;** *pres.* **-рую, -руешь**] **1,** to construct; design. **2,** to organize.

констру́кти́вный *adj.* **1,** structural. **2,** *fig.* constructive.

констру́ктор *n.* designer.

констру́кторский *adj.* design (*attrib.*). —**констру́кторское бюро́,** design office (*in a factory*).

констру́кция *n.* **1,** construction; design. **2,** a structure. **3,** *gram.* construction.

ко́нсул *n.* consul. —**ко́нсульский,** *adj.* consular.

ко́нсульство *n.* consulate.

консульта́нт *n.* **1,** consultant. **2,** consulting physician.

консультати́вный *adj.* consultative; advisory.

консульта́ция *n.* **1,** consultation. **2,** expert advice; expert opinion. **3,** guidance center; clinic.

консульти́ровать *v.impfv.* [*pfv.* **проконсульти́ровать;** *pres.* **-рую, -руешь**] **1,** to advise; give advice to. **2,** [*impfv. only*] (*with* **с** + *instr.*) to consult. —**консульти́роваться,** *refl.* (*with* **с** + *instr.*) to consult.

конта́кт *n.* contact.

контакти́ровать *v.impfv.* [*pres.* **-рую, -руешь**] (*with* **с** + *instr.*) to contact; make *or* establish contact (with). *Also,* **контакти́роваться,** *refl.*

конта́ктный *adj.* **1,** contact (*attrib.*). **2,** *colloq.* easy to talk to; outgoing. —**конта́ктные ли́нзы,** contact lenses.

конте́йнер (тэ) *n.* container (*for shipping goods*). —**конте́йнерный,** *adj.* container (*attrib.*).

конте́кст *n.* context: вырыва́ть из конте́кста, to take out of context.

континге́нт *n.* **1,** contingent. **2,** quota.

контине́нт *n.* continent. —**континента́льный,** *adj.* continental.

конто́ра *n.* office.

конто́рка [*gen. pl.* **-рок**] *n.* **1,** small office. **2,** high old-fashioned writing desk.

конто́рский *adj.* office (*attrib.*).

ко́нтра *n., colloq.* **1,** rebel; counterrevolutionary. **2,** *pl.* quarrel; falling-out. —**быть в ко́нтрах (с),** to be on the outs (with).

контраба́нда *n.* **1,** smuggling. **2,** contraband goods. —**контрабанди́ст,** *n.* smuggler. —**контраба́ндный,** *adj.* contraband; smuggled.

контраба́с *n.* bass viol; double bass; contrabass.

контраге́нт *n.* party to a contract; contractor.

контр-адмира́л *n.* rear admiral.

контра́кт *n.* contract.

контрактова́ть *v.impfv.* [*pfv.* **законтрактова́ть;** *pres.* **-ту́ю, -ту́ешь**] to contract (for).

контра́льто *n.neut. indecl.* contralto (*voice*). —*n.f. indecl.* contralto (*singer*). —**контра́льтовый,** *adj.* contralto.

контрама́рка [*gen. pl.* **-рок**] *n.* free pass; complimentary ticket.

контрапу́нкт *n., music* counterpoint. —**контрапункти́ческий,** *adj.* contrapuntal.

контра́ст *n.* contrast.

контрасти́ровать *v.impfv.* [*pres.* **-рую, -руешь**] to contrast; form a contrast.

контра́стный *adj.* contrasting.

контрата́ка *n.* counterattack.

контратакова́ть *v.impfv. & pfv.* [*pres.* **-ку́ю, -ку́ешь**] to counterattack.

контрафаго́т *n.* double bassoon; contrabassoon.

контрибу́ция *n.* war indemnity.

контрме́ра *n.* countermeasure.

контрнаступле́ние *n.* counteroffensive.

контролёр *n.* **1,** controller. **2,** inspector; examiner. **3,** ticket collector. —**фина́нсовый контролёр,** auditor.

контроли́ровать *v.impfv.* [*pfv.* **проконтроли́ровать;** *pres.* **-рую, -руешь**] **1,** to check; monitor. **2,** [*impfv. only*] to control.

контро́ль *n.m.* **1,** control. **2,** inspection; verification; monitoring.

контро́льный *adj.* **1,** control (*attrib.*). **2,** check (*attrib.*): контро́льный пункт, checkpoint. **3,** monitoring: контро́льный аппара́т *or* прибо́р, monitoring device. —**контро́льный о́пыт,** control experiment. —**контро́льный паке́т (а́кций),** controlling interest (*in a company*). —**контро́льная рабо́та,** test; quiz (*in school*). —**контро́льные ци́фры,** control figures (*in a planned economy*).

контрпредложе́ние *n.* counteroffer; counterproposal.

контрразве́дка *n.* counterintelligence; counterespionage. —**контрразве́дчик,** *n.* counterintelligence agent.

контрреволю́ция *n.* counterrevolution. —**контрреволюционе́р,** *n.* counterrevolutionary. —**контрреволюцио́нный,** *adj.* counterrevolutionary.

контруда́р *n.* counterblow; counterstroke.

контрфо́рс *n.* buttress.

конту́зить *v.impfv.* [*pres.* **-жу, -зишь**] to contuse.

контузия *n.* contusion.

контур *n.* **1,** contour. **2,** *electricity* circuit. **—контурный,** *adj.* contour (*attrib.*).

конура *n.* **1,** kennel; doghouse. **2,** *colloq.* hovel; dump.

конус *n., geom.* cone.

конусообразный *adj.* cone-shaped.

конфедерация (дэ) *n.* confederation; confederacy. **—конфедеративный,** *adj.* confederate.

конферансье *n.m. indecl.* master of ceremonies.

конференц-зал *n.* conference hall.

конференция *n.* conference.

конфета *also,* **конфетка** *n.* **1,** piece of candy. **2,** *pl.* candy. **—конфетный,** *adj.* candy (*attrib.*).

конфетти *n.neut. indecl.* confetti.

конфигурация *n.* configuration.

конфиденциальный *adj.* confidential. **—конфиденциально,** *adv.* confidentially.

конфирмация *n., relig.* confirmation.

конфирмовать *v.impfv. & pfv.* [*pres.* **-мую, -муешь**] *relig.* to confirm.

конфискация *n.* confiscation.

конфисковать *v.impfv. & pfv.* [*pres.* **-кую, -куешь**] to confiscate.

конфликт *n.* conflict.

конфликтовать *v.impfv.* [*pres.* **-тую, -туешь**] (*with* **с** + *instr.*) *colloq.* to come into conflict (with); clash (with).

конфорка [*gen. pl.* **-рок**] *n.* burner (*on a stove*).

конформизм *n.* conformism.

конфронтация *n.* confrontation.

конфуз *n.* embarrassment.

конфузить *v.impfv.* [*pfv.* **сконфузить;** *pres.* **-жу, -зишь**] to embarrass. **—конфузиться,** *refl.* **1,** to be embarrassed. **2,** (*with gen.*) to be shy (in the presence of).

конфузливый *adj.* bashful; shy.

конфузный *adj., colloq.* embarrassing; awkward.

концентрат *n.* concentrate.

концентрационный *adj., in* **концентрационный лагерь,** concentration camp.

концентрация *n.* concentration.

концентрировать *v.impfv.* [*pfv.* **сконцентрировать;** *pres.* **-рую, -руешь**] to concentrate. **—концентрироваться,** *refl.* **1,** to concentrate; mass. **2,** [*impfv. only*] (*with* **на** + *prepl.*) to concentrate (on).

концентрический *adj.* concentric.

концепция *n.* conception.

концерн *n.* (business) concern.

концерт *n.* **1,** concert; recital. **2,** concerto.

концертант *n.m.* [*fem.* **-тантка**] concert performer.

концертино *n. indecl.* concertina.

концертировать *v.impfv.* [*pres.* **-рую, -руешь**] to give concerts.

концертмейстер *n.* concertmaster.

концертный *adj.* concert (*attrib.*).

концессия *n., comm.* concession. **—концессионер,** *n.* concessionaire.

концлагерь [*pl.* **концлагеря**] *n.m.* concentration camp (*contr. of* **концентрационный лагерь**).

кончать *v.impfv.* [*pfv.* **кончить**] **1,** to finish. **2,** to close; conclude. **3,** to stop. **4,** to graduate from. **5,** *in*

плохо кончить, to end up badly; come to a bad end. **—кончаться,** *refl.* **1,** to end; come to an end; be over. **2,** to be used up; run out.

конченый *adj.* **1,** settled. **2,** *colloq.* done for: со мной кончено, I'm done for. **3,** *colloq.* all over: между ними всё кончено, it's all over between them. **—конченый человек,** failure; ne'er-do-well.

кончик *n.* tip; point.

кончина *n.* death; passing; demise.

кончить *v., pfv. of* **кончать. —кончиться,** *refl., pfv. of* **кончаться.**

конъюнктивит *n.* conjunctivitis.

конъюнктура *n.* **1,** situation; state of affairs. **2,** *econ.* conditions: рыночная конъюнктура, market conditions.

конъюнктурный *adj.* temporary; of the moment: конъюнктурные соображения, considerations of the moment.

конь [*gen.* **коня;** *pl.* **кони, коней, коням**] *n.m.* **1,** horse. **2,** *chess* knight. **3,** *gymnastics* horse. **—конькачалка,** hobbyhorse.

коньки *n.pl. See* **конёк.**

конькобежец [*gen.* **-жца**] *n.* skater. **—конькобежный,** *adj.* skating.

коньяк [*gen.* **-яка**] *n.* cognac; brandy.

конюх *n.* stableboy; stable hand; groom.

конюшня [*gen. pl.* **-шен**] *n.* stable.

кооператив *n.* **1,** cooperative. **2,** cooperative store. **—кооперативный,** *adj.* cooperative.

кооператор *n.* member of a cooperative.

кооперация *n.* **1,** *econ.* cooperation. **2,** cooperative.

координата *n.* **1,** *math.* coordinate. **2,** *pl., colloq.* whereabouts.

координатор *n.* coordinator.

координационный *adj.* coordinating.

координация *n.* coordination.

координировать *v.impfv. & pfv.* [*pres.* **-рую, -руешь**] to coordinate.

копал *n.* copal.

копание *n.* digging.

копатель *n.m., obs.* digger.

копать *v.impfv.* [*pfv.* **выкопать**] **1,** to dig. **2,** to dig; dig up; dig out. **—копаться,** *refl.* [*impfv. only*] (*with* **в** + *prepl.*) **1,** to dig (in the sand, dirt, etc.). **2,** to rummage through. **3,** to delve (into); probe. **4,** (*with* **с** + *instr.*) *colloq.* to dawdle (over).

копеечка [*gen. pl.* **-чек**] *n., dim. of* **копейка. —обойтись** *or* **влететь в копеечку,** to cost a pretty penny.

копеечный *adj.* **1,** worth one kopeck; one-kopeck (*attrib.*). **2,** (*of expenses*) minor; trifling. **3,** *fig.* petty.

копейка [*gen. pl.* **-пеек**] *n.* **1,** kopeck. **2,** *in idiomatic expressions,* penny: копейка в копейку, penny for penny; до последней копейки, to the last penny. **—без копейки,** penniless.

копёр [*gen.* **копра**] *n.* pile driver.

копи [*gen.* **копей**] *n.pl.* mines.

копилка [*gen. pl.* **-лок**] *n.* money box; piggy bank.

копирка *n., colloq.* carbon paper.

копировальный *adj.* copying (*attrib.*). **—копировальная бумага,** carbon paper.

копи́рование *n.* copying.

копи́ровать *v.impfv.* [*pfv.* **скопи́ровать**; *pres.* **-рую, -руешь**] **1,** to copy; make a copy of. **2,** to copy; imitate.

копиро́вка *n., colloq.* copying. **—копиро́вщик,** *n.* copier; copyist.

копи́ть *v.impfv.* [*pfv.* **накопи́ть**; *pres.* **коплю́, ко́пишь**] to accumulate; amass. **—копи́ться,** *refl.* to accumulate; pile up.

ко́пия *n.* **1,** copy. **2,** (*with gen.*) *colloq.* the image of: то́чная (*or* жива́я) ко́пия своего́ отца́, the living image of his father.

копна́ [*pl.* **ко́пны, копён, копна́м**] *n.* **1,** haycock. **2,** shock (*of hair*).

ко́поть *n.f.* soot.

копоши́ться *v.r.impfv.* **1,** (*of insects*) to swarm about; (*of fish*) to swim about. **2,** (*of a person*) to putter about.

ко́пра *n.* copra.

копте́ть *v.impfv.* [*pres.* **-чу́, -ти́шь**] *colloq.* **1,** to vegetate; stagnate. **2,** (*with* над) to pore over.

копти́лка [*gen. pl.* **-лок**] *n.* wick lamp.

копти́льня [*gen. pl.* **-лен**] *n.* smokehouse.

копти́ть *v.impfv.* [*pfv.* **закопти́ть**; *pres.* **-чу́, -ти́шь**] **1,** to smoke (ham, fish, glass, etc.). **2,** [*impfv. only*] (*of a lamp, candle, etc.*) to smoke; emit smoke. **—копти́ть не́бо,** to sit around doing nothing.

ко́птский *adj.* Coptic.

копу́н [*gen.* **-пуна́**] *n., colloq.* procrastinator; dawdler.

копу́ша *n.m. & f., colloq.* = копу́н.

копче́ние *n.* smoking (*of meat*).

копчёности *n.pl.* [*sing.* **-ность**] smoked products.

копчёный *adj.* smoked.

ко́пчик *n.* coccux.

копы́тный *adj.* **1,** hoof (*attrib.*). **2,** hoofed; ungulate.

копы́то *n.* hoof.

копьё [*pl.* **ко́пья, ко́пий**] *n.* spear. **—лома́ть ко́пья,** to fight; do battle; cross swords.

кора́ *n.* **1,** bark. **2,** *bot.* cortex. **3,** crust: земна́я кора́, the earth's crust. **—кора́ головно́го мо́зга,** *anat.* cortex.

корабе́льный *adj.* ship (*attrib.*); ship's.

кораблевожде́ние *n.* navigation.

кораблекруше́ние *n.* shipwreck.

кораблестрое́ние *n.* shipbuilding. **—кораблестрои́тель,** *n.m.* shipbuilder.

кора́блик *n.* **1,** *dim. of* кора́бль. **2,** nautilus.

кора́бль [*gen.* **-бля́**] *n.m.* **1,** ship. **2,** *archit.* nave. **—косми́ческий кора́бль,** spaceship.

кора́лл *n.* coral. **—кора́лловый,** *adj.* coral.

кора́н *n.* the Koran.

корве́т *n.* corvette.

кордебале́т (дэ) *n.* corps de ballet.

кордо́н *n.* **1,** cordon. **2,** post; station.

коре́ец [*gen.* **-е́йца**] *n.* Korean (man): Он коре́ец, he is Korean.

корёжить *v.impfv.* [*pfv.* **искорёжить**] *colloq., usu. impers.* **1,** to warp; bend; twist: Фане́ру корёжило, the plywood has become warped. **2,** [*impfv. only*] to writhe: Его́ корёжило от бо́ли, he was writhing in pain.

коре́йка *n.* brisket (*of pork or veal*).

коре́йский *adj.* Korean.

корена́стый *adj.* stocky; thickset; heavyset.

корени́ться *v.r.impfv.* (*with* в + *prepl.*) to be rooted (in).

коренни́к [*gen.* **-ника́**] *n.* wheel horse.

коренно́й *adj.* **1,** native; indigenous. **2,** fundamental; radical. **3,** vital. **—коренно́й зуб,** molar. **—коренна́я ло́шадь,** = коренни́к. **—коренны́м о́бразом,** radically.

ко́рень [*gen.* **ко́рня;** *pl.* **ко́рни, -не́й, -ня́м**] *n.m.* root. **—в ко́рне,** radically. **—вырыва́ть с ко́рнем,** to uproot. **—знак ко́рня,** *math.* radical sign. **—ко́рень зла,** the root of all evil. **—на корню́, 1,** (*of timber, crops, etc.*) standing; not (yet) cut down. **2,** *fig.* while still in its infancy. **—пресека́ть в ко́рне,** to nip in the bud. **—пуска́ть ко́рни, 1,** to develop roots; put down roots. **2,** to take root. **—смотре́ть в ко́рень** (+ *gen.*), to get to the root (*or* heart) of. **—уходи́ть свои́ми корня́ми в** (+ *acc.*), to have its roots in.

коре́нья [*gen.* **-ньев**] *n.pl., cooking* roots.

ко́реш *n., colloq.* pal; chum.

корешо́к [*gen.* **-шка́**] *n.* **1,** *dim. of* ко́рень. **2,** spine (*of a book*). **3,** counterfoil; stub.

коре́янка [*gen. pl.* **-нок**] *n.* Korean woman.

ко́ржик *n.* cookie.

корзи́на *n.* basket. **—корзи́на для бума́ги,** wastebasket.

корзи́нка [*gen. pl.* **-нок**] *n.* small basket.

кориа́ндр *n.* coriander. **—кориа́ндровый,** *adj.* coriander (*attrib.*).

коридо́р *n.* corridor; hall.

коридо́рный *adj.* corridor (*attrib.*); hall (*attrib.*). **—***n.* bellboy.

кори́нка *n.* currants (*seedless raisins*).

кори́нфский *adj.* Corinthian.

кори́ть *v.impfv., colloq.* to scold; rebuke; upbraid.

корифе́й *n.* leading light; luminary.

кори́ца *n.* cinnamon.

кори́чневый *adj.* brown.

ко́рка *n.* **1,** crust. **2,** rind; peel. **—от ко́рки до ко́рки,** from cover to cover.

корм [*pl.* **корма́**] *n.* **1,** forage; feed; fodder. **2,** feeding. **—пти́чий корм,** birdseed.

корма́ *n., naut.* stern.

кормёжка *n., colloq.* feeding.

корми́лец [*gen.* **-льца**] *n.* breadwinner.

корми́лица *n.* **1,** wet nurse. **2,** (female) breadwinner.

корми́ло *n., archaic* helm. **—стоя́ть у корми́ла вла́сти,** to be at the helm of state.

корми́ть *v.impfv.* [*pfv.* **накорми́ть** *or* **покорми́ть**; *pres.* **кормлю́, ко́рмишь**] **1,** to feed. **2,** to suckle; nurse. **3,** [*pfv.* **прокорми́ть**] to feed; keep (*i.e.* a family) fed. **—корми́ться,** *refl.* [*impfv. only*] **1,** (*of animals*) to feed; (*with instr.*) feed on. **2,** (*with instr.*) (*of people*) to live (by); support oneself (by); feed oneself (by).

кормле́ние *n.* **1,** feeding. **2,** suckling; nursing.

кормово́й *adj.* **1,** *naut.* stern (*attrib.*). **2,** fodder (*attrib.*); forage (*attrib.*). **—кормово́е зерно́,** feed grain.

корму́шка [*gen. pl.* **-шек**] *n.* feeding trough.

ко́рмчий *n., decl. as an adj.* helmsman.

корневи́ще *n.* rhizome.

корнево́й *adj.* root (*attrib.*).

корне́т *n.* cornet.

корнишо́н *n.* gherkin.

ко́роб [*pl.* коро́ба] *n.* basket. —**це́лый ко́роб новосте́й,** all sorts of news; loads of news.

коробе́йник *n.* peddler.

коро́бить *v.impfv.* [*pfv.* покоро́бить] 1, to warp: Жар коро́бил де́рево, the heat warped the wood. *Also impers. & intrans.* До́ски покоро́било, the boards have warped. 2, *fig., colloq.* to irk; grate on: Его́ э́то покоро́било, it irked/ grated on/ him. —**коро́биться,** *refl.* to warp; curl; buckle.

коро́бка [*gen. pl.* -бок] *n.* 1, box. 2, frame (*of a building, door, etc.*). —**коро́бка переда́ч** *or* **скоросте́й,** gearbox. —**черепна́я коро́бка,** cranium.

коро́бление *n.* warping.

коробо́к [*gen.* -бка́] *n.* small box.

коро́бочка [*gen. pl.* -чек] *n.* 1, small box. 2, *bot.* boll.

коро́ва *n.* cow. Ста́до коро́в, herd of cattle. —**морска́я коро́ва,** sea cow.

коро́вий [*fem.* -вья] *adj.* cow (*attrib.*); cow's. —**коро́вья о́спа,** cowpox.

коро́вка [*gen. pl.* -вок] *n., dim. of* коро́ва. —**бо́жья коро́вка,** ladybug; ladybird.

коро́вник *n.* cowshed.

короле́ва *n.* queen.

короле́вский *adj.* 1, king's; queen's. 2, royal. 3, *chess* king's.

короле́вство *n.* kingdom.

королёк [*gen.* -лька́] *n.* 1, kinglet (*bird*). 2, blood orange.

коро́ль [*gen.* короля́] *n.m.* 1, king. 2, *cards; chess* king.

коромы́сло [*gen. pl.* -сел] *n.* yoke (*for carrying buckets*).

коро́на *n.* 1, crown. 2, *astron.* corona.

корона́ция *n.* coronation.

коро́нка [*gen. pl.* -нок] *n.* 1, *dim. of* коро́на. 2, crown (*of or for a tooth*).

коро́нный *adj.* crown (*attrib.*). —**коро́нная коло́ния,** crown colony. —**коро́нный но́мер, 1,** best-known number (*of a performer*). 2, *colloq.* one's usual trick: Э́то его́ коро́нный но́мер, that's his usual trick; he's always doing that. —**коро́нная роль,** best-known role (*of an actor*).

коронова́ть *v.impfv. & pfv.* [*pres.* -ну́ю, -ну́ешь] to crown.

коро́ста *n.* sores; pustules.

коросте́ль [*gen.* -стеля́] *n.m.* corn crake (*bird*).

корота́ть *v.impfv.* [*pfv.* скорота́ть] *colloq.* to while away (the time).

коро́тенький *adj., colloq.* short.

коро́ткий *adj.* [*short form* ко́роток, коротка́, ко́ротко, коротки́ *or* ко́ротки; *comp.* коро́че] short.

ко́ротко *adv.* 1, short. 2, briefly. 3, intimately.

короткво́лновый *adj.* short-wave.

короткометра́жный *adj., in* **короткометра́жный фильм,** short.

коро́ткость *n.f.* 1, shortness. 2, intimacy; familiarity.

короты́ш [*gen.* -тыша́] *n., colloq.* shrimp; runt. *Also,* **короты́шка.**

коро́че *adj., comp. of* коро́ткий. —**коро́че говоря́,** in short.

корпе́ть *v.impfv.* [*pres.* -плю́, -пи́шь] (*with* над) *colloq.* to slave (over); pore (over).

ко́рпия *n.* lint (*for surgical dressings*).

корпора́ция *n.* corporation. —**корпорати́вный,** *adj.* corporate; corporative.

ко́рпус *n.* 1, [*pl.* -ы] body; trunk; torso. 2, [*pl.* -а́] body; casing; frame. 3, [*pl.* -а́] hull (*of a ship*). 4, [*pl.* -а́] building (*one of several in a complex*). 5, [*no pl.*] corps: дипломати́ческий ко́рпус, diplomatic corps. 6, [*pl.* -а́] *mil.* corps. 7, [*pl.* -ы] horse racing length. —**ко́рпусный; корпусно́й,** *adj.* corps (*attrib.*).

корректи́в *n.* correction; modification; change.

корректи́вный *adj.* remedial: корректи́вное чте́ние, remedial reading.

корректи́ровать *v.impfv.* [*pfv.* прокорректи́ровать; *pres.* -рую, -руешь] 1, to correct; adjust. 2, to proofread.

корректиро́вщик *n., mil.* 1, spotter. 2, spotter plane.

корре́ктный *adj.* correct; proper. —**корре́ктность,** *n.f.* proper behavior.

корре́ктор *n.* proofreader.

корректу́ра *n.* 1, proofreading. 2, correction. 3, proofs. —**держа́ть** *or* **пра́вить корректу́ру,** to do proofreading; read proofs; proofread.

корреспонде́нт *n.* correspondent. —**корреспонде́нтский,** *adj.* correspondent's; press (*attrib.*).

корреспонде́нция *n.* 1, correspondence; mail. 2, report; dispatch.

корро́зия *n.* corrosion.

коррумпи́рованный *adj.* corrupt.

корру́пция *n.* corruption.

корса́ж *n.* bodice.

корса́р *n.* corsair.

корсе́т *n.* corset.

корсика́нский *adj.* Corsican.

корт *n.* tennis court.

корте́ж (тэ) *n.* 1, cortege; procession. 2, motorcade.

кортизо́н *n.* cortisone.

ко́ртик *n.* dagger.

ко́рточки *n.pl., in* **сиде́ть на ко́рточках; сесть** (*or* **присе́сть) на ко́рточки,** to squat.

кору́нд *n.* corundum.

корчева́ть *v.impfv.* [*pres.* -чу́ю, -чу́ешь] to uproot; tear up by the roots.

ко́рчи [*gen.* -чей] *n.pl.* [*sing.* ко́рча] *colloq.* cramps; convulsions.

ко́рчить *v.impfv.* [*pfv.* ско́рчить] 1, *impers.* to writhe: Его́ ко́рчило от бо́ли, he was writhing in pain. 2, [*impfv. only*] (*with* из себя́ + *acc.*) *colloq.* to pose (as): ко́рчить из себя́ знатока́ му́зыки, to pose as an expert on music. 3, *in* ко́рчить ро́жи *or* грима́сы, to make faces. —**ко́рчиться,** *refl.* to writhe.

корчма́ [*gen. pl.* -чём] *n., pre-rev.* tavern; inn.

ко́ршун *n.* kite (*bird*).

коры́стный *adj.* mercenary; selfish.

корыстолюби́вый *adj.* mercenary. —**корыстолю́бие,** *n.* self-interest.

коры́сть *n.f.* 1, profit; advantage; gain. 2, self-interest.

коры́то *n.* washtub; trough. —**оста́ться** *or* **оказа́ться у разби́того коры́та**, to be left with nothing.

корь *n.f.* measles.

ко́рюшка [*gen. pl.* -**шек**] *n.* smelt (*fish*).

коря́вый *adj.* 1, twisted; gnarled. 2, *colloq.* clumsy; maladroit. 3, *colloq.* pockmarked.

коря́га *n.* snag (*tree or branch lying in the water*).

коса́ [*acc.* ко́су *or* косу́; *pl.* ко́сы] *n.* 1, scythe. 2, braid; plait. 3, spit (*of land*). —**нашла́ коса́ на ка́мень**, stone cutting stone; a clash of wills.

коса́рь [*gen.* -**ря́**] *n.m.* 1, one who mows grass, chops hay, etc. 2, chopping knife.

коса́тка [*gen. pl.* -**ток**] *n.* killer whale.

ко́свенно *adv.* indirectly; obliquely.

ко́свенный *adj.* indirect; oblique. —**ко́свенные ули́ки**, circumstantial evidence.

косе́канс (сэ) *n.* cosecant.

косе́ц [*gen.* косца́] *n.* one who mows grass, cuts hay, etc.

коси́лка [*gen. pl.* -**лок**] *n.* mower.

ко́синус *n.* cosine.

коси́ть[1] *v.impfv.* [*pfv.* скоси́ть; *pres.* кошу́, ко́сишь] 1, to mow; cut. 2, *fig.* to mow down; wipe out; decimate.

коси́ть[2] *v.impfv.* [*pfv.* скоси́ть; *pres.* кошу́, коси́шь] 1, to twist; contort. 2, (*with acc. or instr.*) to cock (one's eye). 3, *v.i.* [*impfv. only*] to be cross-eyed; (*of one's eyes*) be crossed. —**коси́ться**, *refl.* [*pfv.* покоси́ться] 1, to slant. 2, (*with* на + *acc.*) to cast a sidelong glance (at). 3, [*impfv. only*] (*with* на + *acc.*) to look askance (at).

коси́чка [*gen. pl.* -**чек**] *n.* pigtail.

косма́тый *adj.* shaggy.

косме́тика *n.* 1, make-up; cosmetics. 2, cosmetology.

косме́тический *adj.* cosmetic. —**космети́ческий кабине́т**, beauty parlor.

косме́ти́чка [*gen. pl.* -**чек**] *n., colloq.* beautician.

косми́ческий *adj.* 1, space (*attrib.*): косми́ческий кора́бль, spaceship. Косми́ческое простра́нство, (outer) space. 2, cosmic.

космого́ния *n.* cosmogony.

космодро́м *n.* space center.

космоло́гия *n.* cosmology.

космона́вт *n.* cosmonaut; astronaut; spaceman.

космополи́т *n.* cosmopolite; cosmopolitan. —**космополити́зм**, *n.* cosmopolitanism. —**космополити́ческий**, *adj.* cosmopolitan.

ко́смос *n.* (outer) space; the cosmos.

ко́смы [*gen.* косм] *n.pl., colloq.* long disheveled locks of hair.

косне́ть *v.impfv.* [*pfv.* закосне́ть] 1, to stagnate. 2, *fig.* (*with* в + *prepl.*) to wallow (in). 3, (*of the tongue*) to become stiff.

ко́сность *n.f.* lethargy; indolence; resistance to change.

косноязы́чие *n.* tongue-tie. —**косноязы́чный**, *adj.* tongue-tied.

косну́ться *v.r., pfv. of* каса́ться.

ко́сный *adj.* negative; unreceptive to new ideas.

ко́со *adv.* obliquely; aslant; askew. —**смотре́ть ко́со**, to look askance.

кособо́кий *adj.* lopsided; crooked.

косоворо́тка [*gen. pl.* -**ток**] *n.* man's blouse (*with the collar fastening at the side*).

косогла́зие *n.* squint; cross-eye; strabismus. —**косогла́зый**, *adj.* cross-eyed.

косого́р *n.* 1, hillside. 2, slope.

косо́й *adj.* 1, slanting; oblique. 2, (*of a person*) cross-eyed; (*of eyes*) slanting. 3, crooked. —**косо́й взгляд**, 1, glance to one side. 2, suspicious look. —**косо́й па́рус**, fore-and-aft sail.

косола́пый *adj.* 1, pigeon-toed. 2, *colloq.* clumsy; awkward.

костёл *n.* Roman Catholic church, esp. in Poland.

костене́ть *v.impfv.* [*pfv.* **окостене́ть**] 1, to becme numb (*from the cold*). 2, (*of a corpse*) to become stiff; ossify.

костёр [*gen.* -**тра́**] *n.* fire; campfire; bonfire. —**погреба́льный костёр**, funeral pyre.

кости́стый *adj.* bony (*full of bones*).

кости́ть *v.impfv.* [*pres.* -**щу́**, -**сти́шь**] *colloq.* to curse out.

костля́вый *adj.* bony (*skinny*).

ко́стный *adj.* bone (*attrib.*). —**ко́стный мозг**, marrow.

костое́да *n.* bone decay; caries.

ко́сточка [*gen. pl.* -**чек**] *n.* 1, *dim. of* кость. 2, pit; stone (*of a fruit*). 3, stay (*for a collar, corset, etc.*).

косты́ль [*gen.* -**ля́**] *n.m.* 1, crutch. 2, large nail; spike.

кость [*pl.* ко́сти, косте́й, костя́м] *n.f.* 1, bone. 2, *pl.* dice. 3, *in* слоно́вая кость, ivory. —**до мо́зга косте́й**, to the bone; through and through: продро́гнуть до мо́зга косте́й, to be chilled to the bone. —**лечь костьми́**, to be killed (*in battle*). —**промо́кнуть до косте́й**, to be soaked to the skin. —**язы́к без косте́й**, loose tongue.

костю́м *n.* 1, suit. 2, outfit; attire. 3, costume.

костюме́р *n.m.* [*fem.* -**ме́рша**] costume designer.

костюмиро́ванный *adj.* costumed. —**костюмиро́ванный бал**, costume party; masquerade.

костю́мный *adj.* of or for a suit.

костя́к [*gen.* -**яка́**] *n.* 1, skeleton. 2, *fig.* backbone.

костяно́й *adj.* made of bone; bone (*attrib.*). —**костяна́я мука́**, bone meal.

костя́шка [*gen. pl.* -**шек**] *n., colloq.* 1, knuckle. 2, ball; bead; button.

косу́ля *n.* roe deer.

косы́нка [*gen. pl.* -**нок**] *n.* triangular kerchief or scarf.

косьба́ *n.* mowing.

коса́к [*gen.* -**яка́**] *n.* 1, doorpost; jamb. 2, school (*of fish*); flock (*of birds*); herd (*of horses*).

косяко́м *adv., colloq.* at an angle.

кот [*gen.* кота́] *n.* 1, male cat; tomcat. 2, *in* морско́й кот, stingray. —**кот напла́кал**, *colloq.* practically none: Де́нег у меня́ кот напла́кал, I have practically no money. —**купи́ть кота́ в мешке́**, to buy a pig in a poke.

кота́нгенс *n.* cotangent.

котёл [*gen.* котла́] *n.* 1, caldron. 2, boiler.

котело́к [*gen.* -**лка́**] *n.* 1, pot. 2, mess tin. 3, bowler (*hat*); derby.

коте́льная *n., decl. as an adj.* boiler room.

коте́льный *adj.* boiler (*attrib.*). —**коте́льное желе́зо**;

коте́льный лист, boiler plate. —коте́льное отделе́ние, boiler room.

котёнок [*gen.* -нка; *pl.* -тя́та, -тя́т] *n.* kitten.

ко́тик *n.* 1, *dim. of* кот. 2, [*also,* морско́й ко́тик] fur seal. 3, sealskin. —ко́тиковый, *adj.* sealskin.

котильо́н *n.* cotillion.

коти́ровать *v.impfv. & pfv.* [*pres.* -ру́ю, -ру́ешь] *finance* 1, to set the price of. 2, to quote.

котиро́вка *n., finance* quotation.

коти́ться *v.r.impfv.* [*pfv.* окоти́ться] to have kittens.

котле́та *n.* chop; cutlet: свина́я котле́та, pork chop; теля́чья котле́та, veal cutlet. —отбивна́я котле́та, chop; cutlet. —ру́бленая котле́та, hamburger. —ры́бная котле́та, fish cake.

котлова́н *n.* foundation pit.

котлови́на *n.* hollow; depression.

кото́мка [*gen. pl.* -мок] *n.* knapsack; shoulder pack.

кото́рый *pron.* 1, *interr.* what?; which?: в кото́ром часу́?, at what time? Кото́рый из них ста́рше?, which (one) of them is older? 2, *rel.* who; that; which: челове́к, кото́рый то́лько что ушёл, the man who just left. Кни́га, кото́рую вы мне одолжи́ли, the book that/which you lent me. 3, (*gen. case*) whose: челове́к, и́мя кото́рого изве́стно всем, a man whose name is known to everyone. 4, (*with expressions of time*) *colloq.* quite a few: уже́ кото́рые су́тки подря́д, for quite a few days now. —в кото́рый раз, once again; for the umpteenth time. —кото́рый раз?, how many times?: Кото́рый раз я тебе́ говорю́?, how many times have I told you?

котте́дж (тэ) *n.* cottage.

ко́фе *n.m. indecl.* coffee.

кофева́рка [*gen. pl.* -рок] *n.* coffee maker.

кофеи́н *n.* caffeine.

кофе́йник *n.* coffeepot.

кофе́йница *n.* coffee mill.

кофе́йный *adj.* 1, coffee (*attrib.*). 2, coffee-colored.

кофе́йня [*gen. pl.* -фе́ен] *n., obs.* coffee house.

кофемо́лка [*gen. pl.* -лок] *n.* coffee grinder.

ко́фта *n.* woman's jacket.

ко́фточка [*gen. pl.* -чек] *n.* blouse.

коча́н [*gen.* кочана́ *or* кочна́] *n.* head of cabbage.

кочева́ть *v.impfv.* [*pres.* -чу́ю, -чу́ешь] 1, to lead a nomadic life; be a nomad. 2, (*of animals, birds, etc.*) to migrate.

коче́вник *n.* nomad.

кочево́й *adj.* nomadic; nomad's.

коче́вье *n.* 1, migration. 2, nomads' encampment. 3, territory where nomads roam.

кочега́р *n.* stoker; fireman (*on a locomotive*).

кочене́ть *v.impfv.* [*pfv.* окочене́ть *or* закочене́ть] to become numb (*from the cold*).

кочерга́ [*gen. pl.* -рёг] *n.* poker (*for a fire*).

кочеры́жка [*gen. pl.* -жек] *n.* cabbage stump.

ко́чка [*gen. pl.* ко́чек] *n.* hummock.

коша́чий [*fem.* -чья] *adj.* cat (*attrib.*); cat's; feline.

кошелёк [*gen.* -лька́] *n.* purse.

коше́лка [*gen. pl.* -лок] *n., colloq.* basket.

кошени́ль *n.f.* cochineal.

коше́рный *adj.* kosher.

ко́шечка [*gen. pl.* -чек] *n.* pussy cat.

ко́шка [*gen. pl.* ко́шек] *n.* 1, cat. 2, *pl.* cat-o'-nine-tails. 3, grapnel; grappling iron. 4, *pl.* climbing irons. —жить как ко́шка с соба́кой, to be at each other's throat. —ме́жду ни́ми пробежа́ла чёрная ко́шка, they have had a falling-out; something has come between them. —у него́ ко́шки скребу́т на се́рдце, he has a sense of great uneasiness.

ко́шки-мы́шки *n.* cat-and-mouse game.

кошма́р *n.* nightmare. —кошма́рный, *adj.* nightmarish.

Коще́й *n., folklore,* a bony old man who knows the secret of eternal life.

кощу́нство *n.* sacrilege; blasphemy. —кощу́нственный, *adj.* sacrilegious; blasphemous.

кощу́нствовать *v.impfv.* [*pres.* -ствую, -ствуешь] to blaspheme; commit a sacrilege.

коэффицие́нт *n.* coefficient; factor; ratio. —коэффицие́нт поле́зного де́йствия, efficiency (*of a machine in transmitting energy*).

краб *n.* crab. —кра́бовый, *adj.* crab (*attrib.*).

кра́ги [*gen.* краг] *n.pl.* leggings; puttees.

кра́деное *n., decl. as an adj.* stolen goods; loot.

кра́деный *adj.* stolen.

кра́дучись *adv.* stealthily.

кра́дущийся *adj.* stealthy; furtive.

краеве́дение *n.* the study of a particular region. —краеве́дческий, *adj., in* краеве́дческий музе́й, regional museum.

краево́й *adj.* of or pert. to a край; regional.

краеуго́льный *adj., in* краеуго́льный ка́мень, cornerstone.

кра́ешек [*gen.* -шка] *n., colloq.* edge.

кра́жа *n.* theft; larceny. —кра́жа со взло́мом, burglary.

край [*2nd loc.* краю́; *pl.* края́, краёв] *n.* 1, edge; rim; brim; brink. На краю́ про́пасти, on the edge/brink of the precipice. По́лный до краёв, full to the brim. 2, land; country; *pl.* places; parts: в э́тих края́х, in these places/parts. 3, [*loc.* кра́е] large administrative division of Russia; krai: в Краснода́рском кра́е, in Krasnodar krai. —кра́ем гла́за, out of the corner of one's eye. —кра́ем у́ха, 1, (*with* слу́шать) with half an ear. 2, (*with* слы́шать) to happen to hear. —на край све́та (*or* земли́), to the ends of the earth. —че́рез край, 1, over the edge: ли́ться че́рез край, to overflow. 2, *fig.* in abundance. 3, *in* хвати́ть че́рез край, *see* хвати́ть. 4, *in* хлебну́ть че́рез край, *colloq.* to have had a bit too much to drink.

кра́йне *adv.* extremely.

кра́йний *adj.* 1, extreme. 2, last: кра́йняя ко́мната спра́ва, the last room on the right. 3, *fig.* (*of surprise, exhaustion, etc.*) complete; utter. 4, *fig.* dire. 5, *in* кра́йний срок, deadline. 6, *in* кра́йний Се́вер, the Far North. 7, *in* кра́йняя цена́, lowest price; rock-bottom price. —в кра́йнем слу́чае, if worst comes to worst; as a last resort. —по кра́йней ме́ре, at least.

кра́йность *n.f.* 1, extreme. 2, extreme situation. —до кра́йности, to an extreme.

крамо́ла *n., obs.* uprising; revolt. —крамо́льный, *adj., obs.* seditious; rebellious.

кран *n.* **1,** faucet; spigot; tap. **2,** [*also,* **подъёмный кран**] crane. —**водоразбо́рный кран,** hydrant. —**пожа́рный кран,** fire hydrant.

крано́вщи́к [*gen.* -**щика́**] *n.* crane operator.

крап *n.* spots; specks.

кра́пать *v.impfv.* [*pres.* **кра́плет** *or* **кра́пает**] (*of rain*) to drizzle; fall in drops.

крапи́ва *n.* nettle.

крапи́вник *n.* wren.

крапи́вница *n.* hives.

кра́пинка [*gen. pl.* -**нок**] *n.* spot; speckle. —**в кра́пинку,** spotted; speckled. *Also,* **кра́пина.**

краплёный *adj.* (*of cards*) marked.

кра́пчатый *adj.* spotted; speckled.

краса́ *n.* **1,** *archaic* beauty. **2,** (*with gen.*) the pride (of).

краса́вец [*gen.* -**вца**] *n.* **1,** very handsome man. **2,** a beauty.

краса́вица *n.* **1,** beautiful woman. **2,** a beauty.

краси́вый *adj.* beautiful; handsome; good-looking. —**краси́во,** *adv.* beautifully.

краси́льный *adj.* dye (*attrib.*); dyeing (*attrib.*).

краси́льня [*gen. pl.* -**лен**] *n.* dye works. —**краси́льщик,** *n.* dyer.

краси́тель *n.m.* dye.

кра́сить *v.impfv.* [*pfv.* **покра́сить**; *pres.* -**шу, -сишь**] **1,** to paint. **2,** to dye. **3,** [*impfv. only*] to become; make (someone) look pretty. —**кра́ситься,** *refl.* [*pfv.* **накра́ситься**] *colloq.* to put on make-up.

кра́ска [*gen. pl.* -**сок**] *n.* **1,** paint. **2,** dye. **3,** *pl.* colors. **4,** flush (*of anger, embarrassment, etc.*). —**ма́сляная кра́ска,** oil (*for painting*). —**типогра́фская кра́ска,** printer's ink.

краскопу́льт *n.* spray gun; airbrush.

красне́ть *v.impfv.* [*pfv.* **покрасне́ть**] **1,** to turn red; redden; flush. **2,** to blush. **3,** [*impfv. only*] (*of anything red*) to appear prominently; shine; gleam.

краснобай *n.* windbag; big talker.

краснова́тый *adj.* reddish.

красногварде́ец [*gen.* -**е́йца**] *n.* Red Guard. —**красногварде́йский,** *adj.* Red Guard (*attrib.*).

красноко́жий *adj.* red-skinned. —*n.* redskin; American Indian.

краснолесье *n.* pine forest.

краснолицый *adj.* ruddy-faced.

красноречи́вый *adj.* eloquent.

красноре́чие *n.* eloquence.

краснота́ *n.* redness.

краснота́л *n.* red willow.

красну́ха *n.* German measles; rubella.

кра́сный *adj.* [*short form* **кра́сен, красна́, красно́** *or* **кра́сно, красны́** *or* **кра́сны**] **1,** red. **2,** *obs., poetic* beautiful. —*n.* **1,** the red one. **2,** *pl.* reds (*communists*). —**кра́сное де́рево,** mahogany. —**кра́сная строка́,** new paragraph. —**кра́сный уголо́к,** recreation and reading room.

красова́ться *v.r.impfv.* [*pres.* -**су́юсь, -су́ешься**] **1,** to stand out (in all its splendor). **2,** to show off.

красота́ *n.* **1,** beauty. **2,** [*pl.* -**со́ты**] beauty: **красо́ты приро́ды,** the beauties of nature.

красо́тка [*gen. pl.* -**ток**] *n., colloq.* beautiful girl; beauty.

кра́сочный *adj.* **1,** paint (*attrib.*); dye (*attrib.*). **2,** colorful.

красть *v.impfv.* [*pfv.* **укра́сть**; *pres.* **краду́, крадёшь;** *past* **крал, кра́ла, кра́ло, кра́ли**] to steal. —**кра́сться,** *refl.* [*impfv. only*] to sneak; creep; steal.

кра́сящий *adj.* dye (*attrib.*); dyeing (*attrib.*). —**кра́сящее вещество́,** dyestuff.

крат *n., in* **во́ сто крат,** a hundred times; a hundredfold.

кра́тер *n.* crater.

кра́ткий *adj.* [*short form* **кра́ток, кратка́, кра́тко, кра́тки**] short; brief; concise. —**в кра́тких слова́х,** briefly; in a few words.

кра́тко *adv.* briefly.

кратковре́менный *adj.* brief; of short duration.

краткосро́чный *adj.* short-term.

кра́ткость *n.f.* brevity. —**для кра́ткости,** for short.

кра́тный *adj.* (*of a number*) divisible by another number. —**кра́тное,** *n.* multiple.

кратча́йший *adj., superl. of* **кра́ткий.**

крах *n.* **1,** (*financial*) crash. **Крах ба́нка,** bank failure. **2,** *fig.* collapse.

крахма́л *n.* starch. —**крахма́листый,** *adj.* starchy.

крахма́лить *v.impfv.* [*pfv.* **накрахма́лить**] to starch.

крахма́льный *adj.* starched.

кра́чка [*gen. pl.* -**чек**] *n.* tern.

кра́ше *adj., colloq.* more beautiful.

кра́шение *n.* dyeing.

кра́шеный *adj.* **1,** painted. **2,** dyed. **3,** wearing make-up; made up.

краю́ха *n., colloq.* hunk (*of bread*).

креве́тка [*gen. pl.* -**ток**] *n.* shrimp.

кре́дит *n., bookkeeping* credit.

креди́т *n.* credit: **в креди́т,** on credit. —**креди́тный,** *adj.* credit (*attrib.*).

кредитова́ть *v.impfv. & pfv.* [*pres.* -**ту́ю, -ту́ешь**] **1,** to extend credit (to). **2,** to extend credit for; finance.

кредито́р *n.* creditor.

кредитоспосо́бный *adj.* [*short form masc.* -**бен**] creditworthy.

кре́до *n. indecl.* credo.

кре́йсер *n.* cruiser.

кре́йсерский *adj.* cruiser (*attrib.*). —**кре́йсерская ско́рость,** cruising speed.

крейси́ровать *v.impfv.* [*pres.* -**рую, -руешь**] to cruise.

крем *n.* **1,** cream; lotion. **2,** cream (*used in desserts*). —**заварно́й крем,** custard. —**сапо́жный крем,** shoe polish.

кремато́рий *n.* crematorium.

крема́ция *n.* cremation.

креме́нь [*gen.* -**мня́**] *n.m.* flint.

креми́ровать *v.impfv. & pfv.* [*pres.* -**рую, -руешь**] to cremate.

кремлёвский *adj.* of the Kremlin; Kremlin (*attrib.*).

Кремль [*gen.* -**мля́**] *n.m.* **1,** the Kremlin (*in Moscow*). **2,** *l.c.* fortress or citadel in old Russian towns; kremlin.

кремнёвый *adj.* made of flint; flint (*attrib.*).

кремнезём *n.* silica.

кре́мниевый *adj.* silicic: **кре́мниевая кислота́,** silicic acid.

кре́мний *n.* silicon.

кремни́стый *adj.* **1,** siliceous. **2,** stony.

кре́мовый *adj.* **1,** cream (*attrib.*). **2,** cream-colored.

крен *n.*, *naut.* list. **2,** *aero.* bank. **3,** *fig.* shift: взять крен впра́во, to shift to the right (*politically*).

кре́ндель [*pl.* **кре́ндели, -лей, -ля́м**] *n.m.* pretzel. —**выпи́сывать кренделя́** (*with different stress*), to stagger; reel.

крени́ть *v.impfv.* [*pfv.* **накрени́ть**] to tip; tilt. —**крени́ться**, *refl.* to tilt; list.

креозо́т *n.* creosote.

крео́л *n.* Creole. —**крео́льский**, *adj.* Creole.

креп *n.* crepe.

крепи́тельный *adj.* **1,** *obs.* invigorating; refreshing. **2,** *med.* binding.

крепи́ть *v.impfv.* [*pres.* **-плю́, -пи́шь**] **1,** to fasten. **2,** to strengthen. **3,** to constipate. *Also impers.:* Его́ крепи́т, he is constipated. —**крепи́ться**, *refl.* to hold out; stand firm; bear up.

кре́пкий *adj.* [*short form* **кре́пок, крепка́, кре́пко, кре́пки** *or* **крепки́**; *comp.* **кре́пче**] **1,** strong; durable. **2,** strong; sturdy; robust. **3,** (*of a handshake*) firm. **4,** (*of tea, cigarettes, an odor, etc.*) strong. **5,** (*of frost*) hard. **6,** (*of sleep*) sound.

кре́пко *adv.* **1,** firmly. **2,** sturdily: кре́пко сложён-ный, sturdily built. **3,** tight(ly): держа́ться кре́пко, to hold tight. —**кре́пко спать, 1,** to be sound *or* fast asleep. **2,** to be a sound sleeper.

крепколо́бый *adj.*, *colloq.* stubborn; pigheaded.

крепле́ние *n.* **1,** strengthening; fastening. **2,** mount; mounting. —**у́зел крепле́ния дви́гателя**, engine mount.

кре́пнуть *v.impfv.* [*pfv.* **окре́пнуть**; *past* **креп** *or* **кре́пнул, кре́пла**] to grow stronger; regain one's strength.

кре́повый *adj.* crepe.

крепостни́чество *n.* serfdom.

крепостно́й *adj.* **1,** serf (*attrib.*): крепостно́е пра́во, serfdom. **2,** of a fortress. —*n.* serf. —**крепостно́й вал**, rampart. —**крепостно́й ров**, moat.

кре́пость *n.f.* **1,** strength. **2,** [*pl.* **кре́пости, -сте́й, -стя́м**] fortress.

крепча́ть *v.impfv.* **1,** to increase in intensity; (*of the wind*) blow harder. **2,** *colloq.* (*of a person*) to grow stronger; gain strength.

кре́пче *adj.*, *comp. of* **кре́пкий**.

крепы́ш [*gen.* **-пыша́**] *n.*, *colloq.* robust man; sturdy youngster.

кре́сло [*gen. pl.* **-сел**] *n.* armchair; easy chair.

кресс *n.* cress. —**водяно́й кресс,** watercress. —**кресс-сала́т**, *n.* garden cress.

крест [*gen.* **креста́**] *n.* **1,** cross. **2,** the sign of the cross. —**ста́вить крест на** (+ *prepl.*), to give up on; give up as hopeless.

крестец́ [*gen.* **-тца́**] *n.* **1,** *anat.* sacrum. **2,** rump (*of an animal*).

кре́сти [*gen.* **-те́й**] *n.pl.*, *colloq.*, *cards* clubs.

кре́стик *n.* **1,** *dim. of* **крест**. **2,** *printing* dagger.

крести́льный *adj.* baptismal.

крести́ны [*gen.* **-ти́н**] *n.pl.* christening.

крести́ть *v.impfv.* [*pres.* **крещу́, кре́стишь**] **1,** [*pfv.* **окрести́ть**] to baptize; christen. **2,** [*impfv. only*] to be a godfather *or* godmother to. **3,** [*pfv.* **перекрести́ть**] to make the sign of the cross over. —**крести́ться, refl. 1,** [*pfv.* **окрести́ться**] to be baptized. **2,** [*pfv.* **перекрести́ться**] to cross oneself.

крест-на́крест *adv.* crosswise; crisscross.

крёстная *n.*, decl. as an adj., colloq. godmother.

крёстник *n.* godson; godchild. —**крёстница**, *n.* goddaughter; godchild.

крёстный *adj.*, *in* **1, крёстное зна́мение**, the sign of the cross. **2, крёстный ход**, religious procession.

крёстный *adj.*, *in* **крёстный оте́ц**, godfather; **крёстная мать**, godmother; **крёстный сын**, godson; **крёстная дочь**, goddaughter. —*n.*, *colloq.* godfather.

крестови́на *n.* crosspiece.

кресто́вый *adj.*, *in* **кресто́вый похо́д**, *hist.* crusade.

крестоно́сец [*gen.* **-сца**] *n.*, *hist.* crusader.

крестообра́зный *adj.* in the shape of a cross; cruciform. —**крестообра́зно**, *adv.* crosswise.

крестья́нин [*pl.* **-я́не, -я́н**] *n.m.* [*fem.* **-я́нка**] peasant. —**крестья́нский**, *adj.* peasant (*attrib.*). —**крестья́нство**, *n.* peasantry.

крети́н *n.* cretin. —**кретини́зм**, *n.* cretinism.

крето́н *n.* cretonne. —**крето́нный**; **крето́новый**, *adj.* cretonne.

кре́чет *n.* gyrfalcon.

креще́ндо *adv. & n. indecl.* crescendo.

креще́ние *n.* **1,** baptism; christening. **2,** Epiphany. —**боево́е креще́ние**, baptism of fire.

крещёный *adj.* baptized.

крива́я *n.*, decl. as an adj., math. curve.

кривизна́ *n.* **1,** curvature. **2,** crookedness.

криви́ть *v.impfv.* [*pfv.* **покриви́ть** *or* **скриви́ть**; *pres.* **-влю́, -ви́шь**] **1,** to bend out of shape. **2,** to twist; contort (one's face, mouth, etc.); curl (one's lip). **3,** *in* **(по)криви́ть душо́й**, to play the hypocrite; dissemble. —**криви́ться**, *refl.* **1,** to become bent; get out of shape. **2,** *colloq.* to make a face; grimace.

кривля́ка *n.m. & f.*, *colloq.* affected person.

кривля́нье *n.* affectation; artificiality.

кривля́ться *v.r.impfv.* **1,** to make faces. **2,** to put on airs.

кри́во *adv.* **1,** in a crooked line. **2,** askew; awry.

кривобо́кий *adj.* lopsided.

криво́й *adj.* **1,** crooked. **2,** curved. **3,** *colloq.* one-eyed; blind in one eye. —**криво́е зе́ркало**, distorting mirror. —**кривы́е пути́**, crooked ways. —**крива́я улы́бка**, wry smile.

криволине́йный *adj.* curvilinear.

кривоно́гий *adj.* bowlegged; bandy-legged; knock-kneed.

кривото́лки [*gen.* **-ков**] *n.pl.* false rumors; idle gossip; loose talk.

кривоши́п *n.*, *mech.* crank.

криз *n.*, *med.* crisis: гипертони́ческий криз, hypertension crisis.

кри́зис *n.* crisis. —**кри́зисный**, *adj.* crisis (*attrib.*); critical.

крик *n.* cry; shout; scream; yell. Крик ра́дости, a cry of joy. Крик о по́мощи, a cry/shout for help. —**после́дний крик мо́ды**, the latest thing in fashion.

кри́кет *n., sports* cricket.

крикли́вый *adj.* **1,** loud; noisy. **2,** *fig.* loud; flashy; garish.

кри́кнуть *v., pfv. of* крича́ть.

крику́н [*gen.* -куна́] *n.m.* [*fem.* -ку́нья] *colloq.* noisy person; loudmouth.

кримина́л *n., colloq.* **1,** a crime. **2,** improper behavior.

криминали́ст *n.* specialist on crime or criminal law. —**криминали́стика,** *n.* crime detection. —**криминалисти́ческий,** *adj.* of or pert. to crime detection.

кримина́льный *adj.* criminal.

криминоло́гия *n.* criminology. —**кримино́лог,** *n.* criminologist.

кри́нка [*gen. pl.* -нок] *n.* = кры́нка.

кринoли́н *n.* hoop skirt.

криптогра́мма *n.* cryptogram.

криптогра́фия *n.* cryptography. —**криптографи́ческий,** *adj.* cryptographic.

крипто́н *n.* krypton.

криста́лл *n.* crystal.

кристаллиза́ция *n.* crystallization.

кристаллизова́ть *v.impfv. & pfv.* [*pres.* -зу́ю, -зу́ешь] to crystallize. —**кристаллизова́ться,** *refl.* to crystallize; take shape.

кристалли́ческий *adj.* crystalline.

криста́льный *adj.* **1,** crystal-clear. **2,** pure; perfect. —**криста́льно,** *adv., in* криста́льно чи́стый, crystal-clear.

крите́рий *n.* criterion.

кри́тик *n.* critic.

кри́тика *n.* criticism.

критика́н *n.* faultfinder. —**критика́нство,** *n.* carping; faultfinding.

критикова́ть *v.impfv.* [*pres.* -ку́ю, -ку́ешь] to criticize.

крити́ческий *adj.* **1,** critical; containing criticism. **2,** critical; crucial. **3,** critical; extremely serious.

крича́ть *v.impfv.* [*pfv.* кри́кнуть; *pres.* -чу́, -чи́шь] to shout; yell; scream; cry. Крича́ть о по́мощи, to shout *or* cry for help. Крича́ть от бо́ли, to cry out in pain. Крича́ть кому́-нибудь, to shout to someone. Крича́ть на кого́-нибудь, to shout at someone.

крича́щий *adj.* loud; flashy; garish.

кров *n.* shelter. —**оста́ться без кро́ва,** to be left without a roof over one's head.

крова́вый *adj.* **1,** bloody. **2,** blood-red. **3,** (*of meat*) rare; underdone. —**крова́вая ба́ня,** bloodbath. —**крова́вое пятно́,** bloodstain.

крова́тка [*gen. pl.* -ток] *n.* small bed; child's bed.

крова́ть *n.f.* bed. —**де́тская крова́ть,** crib.

кро́вельный *adj.* roofing (*attrib.*).

кро́вельщик *n.* roofer.

кровено́сный *adj.* of the circulatory system. —**кровено́сная систе́ма,** circulatory system. —**кровено́сный сосу́д,** blood vessel.

крови́нка [*gen. pl.* -нок] *n., colloq.* drop of blood. —**ни крови́нки в лице́,** white as a sheet.

кро́вля [*gen. pl.* -вель] *n.* **1,** roof. **2,** roofing.

кро́вно *adv.* **1,** by blood: кро́вно свя́занный, bound by ties of blood. **2,** vitally: кро́вно заинтересо́ванный, vitally interested. **3,** grievously: кро́вно оби́деть кого́-нибудь, to grievously offend someone.

кро́вный *adj.* **1,** blood (*attrib.*); related by blood. **2,** thoroughbred. **3,** *fig.* vital. —**кро́вный враг,** mortal enemy. —**кро́вные де́ньги,** hard-earned money. —**кро́вная месть,** vendetta. —**кро́вная оби́да,** grievous insult.

кровожа́дный *adj.* bloodthirsty.

кровоизлия́ние *n.* hemorrhage.

кровообраще́ние *n.* circulation (*of the blood*).

кровооостана́вливающий *adj.* styptic. —**кровооостана́вливающее сре́дство,** styptic agent.

кровопи́йца *n.m. & f.* bloodsucker.

кровоподтёк *n.* bruise.

кровопроли́тие *n.* bloodshed. —**кровопроли́тный,** *adj.* (*of a battle, conflict, etc.*) bloody.

кровопуска́ние *n.* bloodletting; phlebotomy.

кровосмеше́ние *n.* incest. —**кровосмеси́тельный,** *adj.* incestuous.

кровосо́с *n.* vampire bat.

кровотече́ние *n.* bleeding; hemorrhaging.

кровоточи́вость *n.f.* **1,** bleeding: кровоточи́вость дёсен, bleeding gums. **2,** hemophilia.

кровоточи́ть *v.impfv.* to bleed.

кровь [*2nd loc.* крови́] *n.f.* blood. —**в кровь** (*with verbs of beating*) till one bleeds. —**в крови́,** bloody; covered with blood. —**кровь с молоко́м,** the picture of health. —**с кро́вью,** (*of meat*) rare. —э́то у него́ в крови́, it's in his blood.

кровяно́й *adj.* blood (*attrib.*). —**кровяно́е давле́ние,** blood pressure. —**кровяны́е ша́рики,** corpuscles.

крои́ть *v.impfv.* **1,** [*pfv.* раскрои́ть] to cut out (material for a garment). **2,** [*pfv.* скрои́ть] to cut; make (a garment).

кро́йка *n.* cutting.

кроке́т *n.* croquet.

крокоди́л *adj.* crocodile. —**крокоди́лов,** *adj., in* крокоди́ловы слёзы, crocodile tears. —**крокоди́ловый,** *adj.* made of crocodile skin; crocodile (*attrib.*).

кро́кус *n.* crocus.

кро́лик *n.* rabbit. —**кро́личий,** *adj.* [*fem.* -чья] rabbit (*attrib.*); rabbit's.

кроль *n.m., swimming* crawl.

кро́ме *prep., with gen.* **1,** except (for); but. **2,** besides; in addition to. —**кро́ме как,** except. —**кро́ме того́,** besides; moreover; furthermore; in addition.

кроме́шный *adj., in* ад кроме́шный, sheer hell; тьма кроме́шная, absolute darkness.

кро́мка [*gen. pl.* -мок] *n.* **1,** selvage. **2,** edge.

кромса́ть *v.impfv.* [*pfv.* искромса́ть] *colloq.* to cut (unevenly); cut up.

кро́на *n.* **1,** crown (*of a tree*). **2,** crown (*monetary unit*).

кронци́ркуль *n.m.* calipers.

кро́ншнеп (нэ) *n.* curlew (*bird*).

кронште́йн (тэ) *n.* bracket; holder.

кропи́ть *v.impfv.* [*pfv.* окропи́ть; *pres.* -плю́, -пи́шь] **1,** to sprinkle. **2,** [*impfv. only*] (*of rain*) to fall lightly.

кропотли́вый *adj.* laborious; painstaking.

кросс *n.* cross-country race.

кроссво́рд *n.* crossword puzzle.

кроссо́вки [*gen.* -вок] *n.pl.* [*sing.* кроссо́вка] sneakers.

крот [*gen.* крота́] *n.* **1,** mole. **2,** moleskin.

кро́ткий *adj.* [*short form* кро́ток, кротка́, кро́тко, кро́тки] meek.

крото́вый *adj.* **1,** mole (*attrib.*); mole's. **2,** moleskin.

кро́тость *n.f.* meekness.

кроха́ [*acc.* кро́ху; *pl.* кро́хи, крох, кроха́м] *n.* **1,** *obs.* crumb. **2,** *pl., fig.* crumbs: кро́хи зна́ний, crumbs of knowledge.

кроха́ль [*gen.* -халя́] *n.m.* merganser.

крохобо́р *n.* quibbler. —**крохобо́рство,** *n.* quibbling.

кро́хотный *adj., colloq.* tiny. *Also,* **кро́шечный.**

кроши́ть *v.impfv.* [*pfv.* искроши́ть *or* раскроши́ть; *pres.* крошу́, кро́шишь] **1,** to chop up. **2,** to crumble. **3,** [*pfv.* накроши́ть] to spill crumbs. —**кроши́ться,** *refl.* to crumble; disintegrate.

кро́шка [*gen. pl.* -шек] *n.* crumb. —**ни кро́шки,** not a bit.

круг [*loc.* кру́ге *or* кругу́; *pl.* круги́] *n.* **1,** circle. **2,** *fig.* (*with gen.*) circle (*of people*); sphere; range (*of activities*). **3,** *pl., fig.* circles: деловы́е круги́, business circles; пра́вящие круги́, ruling circles. **4,** detour: сде́лать круг, to make a detour. **5,** *pl.* ripples (*on water*). **6,** *sports* lap. **7,** *in.* гонча́рный круг, potter's wheel; поворо́тный круг, *R.R.* turntable; спаса́тельный круг, life buoy. —**на круги́ своя́,** back to where one was. *See also* **кру́гом** *and* **круго́м.**

кру́гленький *adj.* **1,** round. **2,** chubby; plump. —**кру́гленькая су́мма,** a tidy sum.

кругле́ть *v.impfv.* [*pfv.* округле́ть] *colloq.* to become round.

круглоли́цый *adj.* round-faced.

круглосу́точный *adj.* twenty-four-hour (*attrib.*); round-the-clock.

кру́глый *adj.* **1,** round. **2,** (*with periods of time*) throughout: кру́глые су́тки, day and night; round the clock; кру́глый год, the year round. **3,** *colloq.* utter. —**де́лать кру́глые глаза́,** to goggle. —**кру́глый** (*or* кру́глая) **сирота́,** child who has lost both parents. —**кру́глым счётом; в кру́глых ци́фрах,** in round figures *or* numbers.

кругово́й *adj.* circular. —**кругова́я доро́га,** roundabout route. —**кругова́я пору́ка,** *see* пору́ка. —**кругова́я систе́ма,** *sports* round robin. —**кругова́я ча́ша,** loving cup.

круговоро́т *n.* **1,** rotation. **2,** *fig.* constant flow (*of events, life, etc.*).

кругозо́р *n.* **1,** range of vision. **2,** *fig.* outlook; range of interests.

кру́гом *adv., in* у меня́ голова́ идёт кру́гом, my head is in a whirl.

круго́м *adv.* **1,** around. **2,** *colloq.* entirely. —*prep., with gen., colloq.* around. —*interj., mil.* about face!

кругообра́зный *adj.* circular.

кругосве́тный *adj.* round-the-world.

кружевно́й *adj.* lace (*attrib.*).

кру́жево [*often pl.* кружева́, кру́жев, кружева́м] *n.* lace.

круже́ние *n.* whirling; swirling.

кружи́ть *v.impfv.* [*pres.* кружу́, кру́жишь *or* кру-жи́шь] **1,** *v.t.* to twirl; whirl; swirl. **2,** *v.i.* (*of a bird,*

plane, *etc.*) to circle. **3,** to wander. —**кружи́ть го́-лову** (+ *dat.*), **1,** to make (someone) dizzy. **2,** [*pfv.* вскружи́ть] to turn someone's head; go to one's head.

кружи́ться *v.r.impfv.* [*pres.* кружу́сь, кру́жишься *or* кружи́шься] **1,** to spin; whirl; go round: У меня́ кру́жится голова́, my head is spinning. **2,** (*of dust, snow, etc.*) to swirl. **3,** *colloq.* to wander.

кру́жка [*gen. pl.* -жек] *n.* **1,** mug; tankard. **2,** poorbox.

кру́жный *adj., colloq.* roundabout; circuitous.

кружо́к [*gen.* -жка́] *n.* **1,** *dim. of* круг. **2,** circle; group; club.

круи́з *n.* cruise.

круп *n.* **1,** *med.* croup. **2,** croup (*of a horse*).

крупа́ *n.* **1,** groats. **2,** sleet. —**гре́чневая крупа́,** buck-wheat. —**ма́нная крупа́,** farina. —**овся́ная крупа́,** oatmeal. —**перло́вая крупа́,** pearl barley.

крупи́нка [*gen. pl.* -нок] *n.* grain.

крупи́ца *n.* **1,** grain. **2,** *fig.* grain; ounce; particle.

кру́пно *adv.* **1,** into large pieces. **2,** with large strides or strokes. **3,** using strong language: кру́пно поговори́ть с, to use strong language with; have words with. **4,** *in* ему́ кру́пно повезло́, he had tremendous luck.

крупномасшта́бный *adj.* large-scale.

кру́пный *adj.* **1,** large. **2,** major; prominent. **3,** (*of sand*) coarse. —**кру́пный план,** close-up. —**кру́пный разгово́р,** sharp words; sharp exchange.

крупча́тый *adj.* grainy; coarse.

крупье́ *n.m. indecl.* croupier.

крупяно́й *adj.* groats (*attrib.*).

крутизна́ *n.* **1,** steepness. **2,** steep slope.

крути́ть *v.impfv.* [*pres.* кручу́, кру́тишь] **1,** [*pfv.* за-крути́ть] to turn; twist; twirl. **2,** [*pfv.* скрути́ть] to twist (cloth, rope, etc.); roll (a cigarette). **3,** [*impfv. only*] to whirl; swirl (dust, snow, etc.). **4,** *v.i.* [*impfv. only*] (*of a snowstorm*) to swirl. —**крути́ться,** *refl.* [*impfv. only*] **1,** to turn; spin; gyrate; whirl. **2,** *fig., colloq.* to hang around.

кру́то *adv.* **1,** steeply. **2,** abruptly; sharply. **3,** tightly. **4,** harshly.

круто́й *adj.* [*comp.* кру́че] **1,** steep. **2,** sharp; abrupt. **3,** drastic. **4,** stern. **5,** (*of foods*) thick. —**круто́е яйцо́,** hard-boiled egg.

кру́тость *n.f.* **1,** steepness; slope. **2,** sternness.

кру́ча *n.* steep slope.

кру́че *adj., comp. of* **круто́й.**

круче́ние *n.* **1,** twisting. **2,** torsion.

кручи́на *n., poetic* sorrow; grief.

круше́ние *n.* **1,** crash; wreck. **2,** *fig.* downfall; collapse.

круши́на *n.* buckthorn.

круши́ть *v.impfv.* to destroy; shatter; smite.

крыжо́вник *n.* **1,** gooseberries. **2,** (a single) goose-berry. **3,** gooseberry shrub.

крыла́тый *adj.* winged. —**крыла́тая раке́та,** cruise missile. —**крыла́тые слова́,** pithy saying; popular expression.

крыле́чко [*pl.* -чки, -чек] *n., dim. of* крыльцо́.

крыло́ [*pl.* кры́лья, кры́льев] *n.* **1,** wing. **2,** fender. **3,** blade; vein. —**взять под своё крыло́,** to take under one's wing.

кры́лышко [*pl.* **-шки, -шек**] *n., dim. of* **крыло́.** —взять под своё кры́лышко, to take under one's wing.

крыльцо́ [*pl.* **кры́льца, крыле́ц, крыльца́м**] *n.* porch.

кры́мский *adj.* Crimean.

кры́нка [*gen. pl.* **-нок**] *n.* milk jug.

кры́са *n.* rat. —**крыси́ный,** *adj.* rat (*attrib.*).

крысоло́вка [*gen. pl.* **-вок**] *n.* rattrap.

кры́тый *adj.* covered; sheltered.

крыть *v.impfv.* [*pfv.* **покры́ть;** *pres.* **кро́ю, кро́ешь**] to cover. —**кры́ться,** *refl.* [*impfv. only*] to lie (beneath the surface): Что за э́тим кро́ется?, what's behind it all?

кры́ша *n.* roof. —**застеклённая кры́ша,** skylight.

кры́шка [*gen. pl.* **-шек**] *n.* **1,** lid; cover. **2,** (*for a lens*) cap.

крюк [*gen.* **крюка́;** *pl:* **крю́чья, крю́чьев** *or* **крюки́, крюко́в**] *n.* **1,** hook. **2,** *colloq.* detour.

крючкова́тый *adj.* hooked.

крючкотво́рство *n., obs.* pettifoggery; chicanery.

крючо́к [*gen.* **-чка́**] *n.* **1,** hook. **2,** curlicue. **3,** *in* рыбо́ловный крючо́к, fishhook; спусково́й крючо́к, trigger. —**попа́сться на крючо́к,** to swallow *or* take the bait.

крюшо́н *n.* punch made of white wine, liqueur and fruit.

кря́ду *adv., colloq.* in a row; running.

кряж *n.* **1,** ridge (*of mountains*). **2,** block; stump (*of wood*).

кря́жистый *adj.* **1,** (*of a tree*) sturdy. **2,** *fig.* stocky; thickset.

кря́канье *n.* **1,** quacking. **2,** grunting.

кря́кать *v.impfv.* [*pfv.* **кря́кнуть**] **1,** to quack. **2,** *colloq.* to grunt.

кря́ква *n.* wild duck; mallard.

кря́кнуть *v., pfv. of* **кря́кать.**

кряхте́ть *v.impfv.* [*pres.* **-хчу́, -хти́шь**] *colloq.* to groan.

ксено́н *n.* xenon.

ксероко́пия *n.* Xerox copy.

ксилогра́фия *n.* wood engraving.

ксилофо́н *n.* xylophone.

кста́ти *adv.* **1,** incidentally; by the way. **2,** timely; apropos; to the point. **3,** at the same time; while you're at it. —**приходи́ться кста́ти,** to come in handy.

кто [*gen. & acc.* **кого́;** *dat.* **кому́;** *instr.* **кем;** *prepl.* **ком**] *pron.* **1,** *interr.* who?; whom?: Кто зна́ет?, who knows? Кого́ вы име́ете в виду́?, whom do you have in mind? **2,** *rel.* who; whom: Те, кто жела́ет идти́..., those who wish to go; those wishing to go. Вся́кий, кто знако́м с..., anyone who is acquainted with... Он тот, кого́ никто́ не лю́бит, he is the one (whom) no one likes. Пе́рвым, кого́ я ви́дел, the first person I saw. **3,** *rel.* he who; whoever: Кто не с на́ми, тот про́тив нас, he who is not with us is against us. **4,** *indef., colloq.* anyone; someone: е́сли кто спро́сит, if anyone asks. Он ре́дко кого́ хва́лит, he seldom praises anyone. **5,** *indef.* (*when repeated*) some: Кто возража́л, а кто нет, some (people) objected, some did not. —**кто бы ни,** whoever: кто бы ни́ был там,

whoever is there. Кто бы то ни́ был, whoever it may be. —**кто где,** in various places. —**кто как,** in various ways. —**кто как мог,** each person in whatever way he could. —**кто-кто, а...,** maybe no one else does/did, but... —**кто куда́,** in various directions.

кто́-либо *indef. pron.* = **кто́-нибудь.**

кто́-нибудь *indef. pron.* someone; somebody; anyone; anybody.

кто́-то *indef. pron.* someone; somebody.

куб [*pl.* **кубы́**] *n.* **1,** cube (*figure*). **2,** *math.* cube (*third power*). **3,** *colloq.* cubic meter. **4,** boiler. —**перего́нный куб,** still (*for distilling liquids*).

ку́барем *adv., colloq. in* кати́ться ку́барем, to roll head over heels.

куба́рь [*gen.* **-баря́**] *n.m.* peg top.

кубату́ра *n.* cubic capacity.

куби́зм *n., art* cubism.

ку́бик *n.* **1,** small cube: ку́бик льда, ice cube. **2,** *pl.* (children's) blocks. **3,** *colloq.* cubic centimeter.

куби́нец [*gen.* **-нца**] *n.m.* [*fem.* **-нка**] Cuban. —**куби́нский,** *adj.* Cuban.

куби́ческий *adj.* cubic. —**куби́ческий ко́рень,** cube root.

ку́бовый *adj.* deep blue.

ку́бок [*gen.* **ку́бка**] *n.* **1,** goblet. **2,** *sports* cup: переходя́щий ку́бок, challenge cup.

кубоме́тр *n.* cubic meter.

ку́брик *n., naut.* crew's quarters.

кубы́шка [*gen. pl.* **-шек**] *n.* **1,** money box. **2,** *colloq.* plump woman.

кува́лда *n.* sledgehammer.

куве́йтский *adj.* Kuwaiti.

кувши́н *n.* pitcher; jug.

кувши́нка [*gen. pl.* **-нок**] *n.* water lily.

кувырка́ться *v.r.impfv.* [*pfv.* **кувыркну́ться** *or* **кувырну́ться**] to somersault; turn somersaults; tumble.

кувырко́м *adv., colloq.* head over heels.

кугуа́р *n.* cougar.

куда́ *adv.* **1,** *interr.* (*used with verbs of motion*) where?; which way?: Куда́ ты идёшь?, where are you going? Куда́ мне э́то положи́ть?, where should I put it? **2,** *rel.* (*used with verbs of motion*) where; to which: Я не зна́ю, куда́ мы идём, I don't know where we're going. Го́род, куда́ его́ сосла́ли, the city to which he was exiled. **3,** *colloq.* what for?: Куда́ вам сто́лько де́нег?, what do you need all that money for? **4,** *colloq.* much; much more: куда́ лу́чше, much better. —**куда́ (бы) ни,** wherever. —**куда́ бы то ни́ было,** anywhere. —**куда́ ни шло,** all right; very well.

куда́-либо *adv.* = **куда́-нибудь.**

куда́-нибудь *adv.* somewhere; anywhere.

куда́-то *adv.* somewhere; to some place.

куда́хтанье *n.* cackle.

куда́хтать *v.impfv.* [*pres.* **-хчу, -хчешь**] to cackle.

куде́ль *n.f.* tow (*fiber*).

куде́сник *n.* sorcerer.

кудла́тый *adj., colloq.* shaggy.

ку́дри [*gen.* **кудре́й**] *n.pl.* curls.

кудря́вый *adj.* **1,** (*of hair*) curly. **2,** curly-headed. **3,** leafy; lush. **4,** *fig.* (*of handwriting, a drawing, etc.*) full of flourishes; (*of writing*) flowery.

кудря́шки *n.pl.* [*sing.* -шка] ringlets (*of hair*).

кузе́н (зэ) *n.* (male) cousin.

кузи́на *n.* (female) cousin.

кузне́ц [*gen.* -неца́] *n.* blacksmith.

кузне́чик *n.* grasshopper.

кузне́чный *adj.* blacksmith's.

ку́зница *n.* blacksmith's shop; smithy; forge.

ку́зов [*pl.* кузова́] *n.* **1,** basket. **2,** body (*of a car or carriage*).

кукаре́канье *n.* crowing (*of a rooster*).

кукаре́кать *v.impfv.* (*of a rooster*) to crow.

ку́киш *n., colloq.* fig (*insulting gesture*).

ку́кла [*gen. pl.* ку́кол] *n.* **1,** doll. **2,** puppet.

кукова́ть *v.impfv.* [*pres.* -ку́ет] to cuckoo; cry "cuckoo".

ку́колка [*gen. pl.* -лок] *n.* **1,** *dim. of* ку́кла. **2,** *zool.* chrysalis; pupa.

ку́коль *n.m.* cockle (*weed*).

ку́кольный *adj.* **1,** doll (*attrib.*). **2,** puppet (*attrib.*).

ку́кситься *v.r.impfv.* [*pres.* -шусь, -сишься] *colloq.* to sulk; mope.

кукуру́за *n.* corn. —**кукуру́зный,** *adj.* corn (*attrib.*).

куку́шка [*gen. pl.* -шек] *n.* cuckoo.

кула́к [*gen.* кулака́] *n.* **1,** fist. **2,** kulak. **3,** *mech.* cam. —**держа́ть в кулаке́; зажима́ть в кула́к,** to keep under one's thumb. —**смея́ться в кула́к,** to laugh up one's sleeve. —**собра́ть во́лю в кула́к,** to summon up all one's will.

кула́цкий *adj.* of the kulaks; kulak (*attrib.*).

кула́чество *n.* the kulaks.

кула́чки *n.pl., in* **би́ться** *or* **дра́ться на кула́чках,** to engage in fisticuffs; spar.

кулачко́вый *adj., in* **кулачко́вый вал,** camshaft.

кула́чный *adj.* with fists: кула́чный бой, fisticuffs.

кулачо́к [*gen.* -чка́] *n.* **1,** *dim. of* кула́к. **2,** *mech.* cam.

кулебя́ка *n.* pie with meat, fish, or cabbage filling.

кулёк [*gen.* кулька́] *n.* small bag.

ку́ли *n.m. indecl.* coolie.

кули́к [*gen.* кулика́] *n.* snipe.

кулина́рия *n.* **1,** (the art of) cooking; cookery. **2,** delicatessen: отде́л кулина́рии, delicatessen department. —**кулина́рный,** *adj.* culinary.

кули́сы *n.pl.* [*sing.* кули́са] *theat.* wings. —**за кули́сами,** backstage; behind the scenes; in the wings.

кули́ч [*gen.* кулича́] *n.* Easter cake.

кули́чки *n.pl., in* **у чёрта на кули́чках,** in the middle of nowhere; at the ends of the earth.

куло́н *n.* **1,** pendant. **2,** coulomb (*unit of electricity*).

кулуа́ры [*gen.* -ров] *n.pl.* corridors. —**кулуа́рный,** *adj.* in the corridors: кулуа́рные разгово́ры, talk in the corridors.

куль [*gen.* куля́] *n.m.* sack.

кульмина́ция *n.* culmination. —**кульминацио́нный,** *adj.* climactic: кульминацио́нный пункт; кульминацио́нный моме́нт, climax; culmination.

культ *n.* cult.

культиви́ровать *v.impfv.* [*pres.* -рую, -руешь] to cultivate. —**культиви́рованный же́мчуг,** cultured pearls.

культу́ра *n.* **1,** culture. **2,** (*with gen.*) standard (of): level (of). **3,** (*with gen.*) *agric.* cultivation (of). **4,**

crop: кормовы́е культу́ры, forage crops. **5,** *bacteriology* culture. —**физи́ческая культу́ра,** physical training; physical education.

культу́рность *n.f.* level of culture; high degree of culture.

культу́рный *adj.* **1,** cultural. **2,** cultured; cultivated; educated.

культя́ *n.* stump (*of an amputated limb*).

кум [*pl.* кумовья́, кумовьёв] *n.* **1,** godfather of one's child. **2,** father of one's godchild.

кума́ *n.* **1,** godmother of one's child. **2,** mother of one's godchild.

куманика́ *n.* bramble (*shrub*).

кума́ч [*gen.* -мача́] *n.* bright red cotton cloth. —**кума́чный,** *adj.* made of this material.

куми́р *n.* idol.

кумовство́ *n., colloq.* nepotism.

кумуляти́вный *adj.* cumulative.

ку́мушка [*gen. pl.* -шек] *n.* **1,** *dim. of* кума́. **2,** gossipmonger.

кумы́к *n.m.* [*fem.* -мы́чка] Kumyk (*one of a people inhabiting the Caucasus*). —**кумы́кский,** *adj.* Kumyk.

кумы́с *n.* fermented mare's milk; kumiss.

кунжу́т *n.* sesame. —**кунжу́тный,** *adj.* sesame (*attrib.*).

куни́ца *n.* marten.

ку́па *n.* clump (*of trees, bushes, etc.*).

купа́льник *n., colloq.* bathing suit.

купа́льный *adj.* bathing (*attrib.*): купа́льный костю́м, bathing suit.

купа́льня [*gen. pl.* -лен] *n.* bathhouse.

купа́льщик *n.* bather.

купа́ние *n.* bathing.

купа́ть *v.impfv.* [*pfv.* вы́купать] to bathe; give a bath to. —**купа́ться,** *refl.* **1,** to bathe; take a bath. **2,** to go bathing; go swimming. **3,** [*impfv. only*] (*with* **в** + *prepl.*) A, to sink (into). B, to revel (in); bask (in). C, to have more of than one knows what to do with: купа́ться в зо́лоте, to be rolling in money.

купе́ (пэ) *n.neut. indecl.* compartment (*on a train*).

купе́йный *adj.* (*of a railroad car*) consisting of compartments.

купе́ль *n.f.* font; baptistery.

купе́ц [*gen.* купца́] *n.* merchant. —**купе́ческий,** *adj.* merchants'. —**купе́чество,** *n.* the merchants (*as an economic class*).

Купидо́н *n.* Cupid.

купи́рованный *adj.* = купе́йный.

купи́ть [*infl.* куплю́, ку́пишь] *v., pfv. of* покупа́ть.

купле́т *n.* **1,** verse; stanza. **2,** *pl.* satirical songs.

ку́пля *n.* purchase.

ку́пол [*pl.* купола́] *n.* dome; cupola.

купо́н *n.* coupon.

купоро́с *n.* vitriol. —**желе́зный купоро́с,** green vitriol; ferrous sulfate. —**ме́дный купоро́с,** blue vitriol; copper sulfate. —**ци́нковый купоро́с,** white vitriol; zinc sulfate.

купчи́ха *n.* **1,** woman merchant. **2,** merchant's wife.

купю́ра *n.* **1,** cut; deletion. **2,** bill (*paper money*).

курага́ *n.* dried apricots.

кура́житься *v.r.impfv., colloq.* **1,** to swagger; boast. **2,** (*with* **над**) to lord it over. **3,** to act coy.

куранты [*gen.* **-тов**] *n.pl.* chimes.

курган *n.* burial mound.

кургузый *adj., colloq.* **1,** with a short tail. **2,** (*of a garment*) tight-fitting; too short.

курд *n.m.* [*fem.* **-дянка**] *n.* Kurd. —**курдский,** *adj.* Kurdish.

курево *n., colloq.* something to smoke.

курение *n.* **1,** smoking. **2,** incense.

курилка [*gen. pl.* **-лок**] *n., colloq.* smoking room. —**жив курилка!,** there's life in the old boy yet!

курильница *n.* censer.

курильня [*gen. pl.* **-лен**] *n.* place where narcotics are smoked: **курильня опиума,** opium den.

курильщик *n.* smoker; one who smokes.

куриный *adj.* chicken (*attrib.*); chicken's; hen's. —**куриная слепота,** night blindness.

курировать *v.impfv.* [*pres.* **-рую, -руешь**] to be in charge of; monitor; oversee; supervise.

курительный *adj.* smoking (*attrib.*).

курить *v.impfv.* [*pres.* **курю, куришь**] **1,** to smoke. **2,** *in* **курить ладаном,** to burn incense. —**куриться,** *refl.* to smoke; give off smoke.

курица [*pl.* **куры, кур**] *n.* hen; chicken. —**мокрая курица,** milksop.

курия *n.* curia.

куркума *n.* turmeric.

курносый *adj.* **1,** *in* **курносый нос,** pug nose. **2,** pug-nosed; snub-nosed.

куроводство *n.* poultry breeding.

курок [*gen.* **курка**] *n.* cock; hammer (*of a firearm*). —**спускать курок,** to pull the trigger.

куропатка [*gen. pl.* **-ток**] *n.* partridge. —**белая куропатка,** ptarmigan.

курорт *n.* resort. —**курортник,** *n., colloq.* person staying at a resort. —**курортный,** *adj.* resort (*attrib.*).

курослеп *n.* buttercup.

курочка [*gen. pl.* **-чек**] *n.* **1,** pullet. **2,** crake. —**водяная курочка,** gallinule.

курс *n.* **1,** course: **изменить курс,** to change course. Брать курс на (+ *acc.*), to head for. **2,** policy: **курс на индустриализацию,** policy of industrialization. **3,** course (*of instruction*): (про)слушать курс, to take a course. Курс лекций, series of lectures. Курс обучения, curriculum. **4,** year (*of study at a university*): на третьем курсе, in one's third year. **5,** rate: курс валюты, rate of exchange. Курс доллара, the value of the dollar. **6,** *in* курс лечения, treatment: проходить курс лечения, to undergo treatment. —**быть в курсе** (+ *gen.*), to be up on. —**в курсе дела,** up on things; aware of what is going on. —**вводить (кого-нибудь) в курс (дела),** to bring someone up to date. —**держать (кого-нибудь) в курсе,** to keep someone informed (*or* posted).

курсант *n.* **1,** student. **2,** cadet.

курсив *n.* italics. —**курсивный,** *adj.* italic.

курсировать *v.impfv.* [*pres.* **-рую, -руешь**] to ply; travel back and forth.

курсовка *n.* document entitling the bearer to treatment and meals (but not accommodations) at a sanitarium.

курсовой *adj.* course (*attrib.*). —**курсовая работа,** term paper. —**курсовой экзамен,** examination given at the end of a course or at the end of a year.

куртизанка [*gen. pl.* **-нок**] *n.* courtesan.

куртка [*gen. pl.* **-ток**] *n.* (man's) jacket; lumber jacket.

курчавый *adj.* **1,** (*of hair*) curly. **2,** curly-headed.

куры *n., pl. of* **курица.**

курьёз *n.* funny thing; queer thing. —**курьёзный,** *adj.* strange; odd; queer; curious.

курьер *n.* **1,** courier. **2,** messenger; errand boy.

курьерский *adj.* courier's. —**курьерский поезд,** express train.

курятина *n., colloq.* chicken (*used as food*).

курятник *n.* henhouse; chicken coop.

курящий *adj., decl. as an adj.* smoker. Я не курящий, I don't smoke. —**вагон для курящих,** smoking car.

кусать *v.impfv.* [*pfv.* **укусить**] to bite. —**кусаться,** *refl.* [*impfv. only*] **1,** to bite; have a tendency to bite. **2,** to bite each other.

кусачки [*gen.* **-чек**] *n.pl.* cutting pliers; wire cutter.

кусковой *adj.* lump (*attrib.*): кусковой сахар, lump sugar.

кусок [*gen.* **куска**] *n.* **1,** piece; bit. **2,** slice (*of bread*); lump (*of sugar*); bar (*of soap*).

кусочек [*gen.* **-чка**] *n., dim. of* **кусок.** —**лакомый кусочек,** tasty morsel.

куст [*gen.* **куста**] *n.* bush; shrub.

кустарник *n.* bushes; shrubs; shrubbery.

кустарный *adj.* **1,** handicraft (*attrib.*). **2,** *fig.* crude; primitive.

кустарь [*gen.* **-старя**] *n.m.* handicraftsman.

кутать *v.impfv.* [*pfv.* **закутать**] to wrap; bundle. —**кутаться,** *refl.* (*with* в + *acc.*) to wrap/bundle oneself (in).

кутёж [*gen.* **-тежа**] *n.* drinking spree.

кутерьма *n., colloq.* commotion.

кутила *n.m., colloq.* reveler; carouser.

кутить *v.impfv.* [*pres.* **кучу, кутишь**] to carouse.

кутузка [*gen. pl.* **-зок**] *n., colloq.* jail; hoosegow.

кухарка [*gen. pl.* **-рок**] *n.* cook.

кухня [*gen. pl.* **-хонь**] *n.* **1,** kitchen. **2,** cooking; cuisine. —**кухонный,** *adj.* kitchen (*attrib.*).

куцый *adj.* **1,** (*of a tail*) short. **2,** short-tailed. **3,** (*of clothes*) skimpy. **4,** *fig.* limited; reduced; incomplete.

куча *n.* **1,** pile; heap. **2,** (*with gen.*) *colloq.* heaps (of); lots (of). —**валить в одну кучу,** to lump together.

кучевой *adj.* (*of clouds*) cumulous.

кучер [*pl.* **кучера**] *n.* coachman.

кучка [*gen. pl.* **кучек**] *n.* **1,** *dim. of* **куча.** **2,** small group; small circle (*of people*).

куш *n.* **1,** bet (*in a card game*). **2,** *colloq.* large sum of money. —**сорвать куш,** to clean up; make a killing.

кушак [*gen.* **-шака**] *n.* sash.

кушанье *n.* food.

кушать *v.impfv.* [*pfv.* **покушать**] to eat.

кушетка [*gen. pl.* **-ток**] *n.* couch.

куща [*gen. pl.* **кущ** *or* **кущей**] *n., obs.* tent; hut. —**праздник кущей,** Feast of Tabernacles.

кш *interj.* shoo! *Also,* **кыш.**

кювет *n.* ditch (*along the side of the road*).

кюрий *n.* curium.

Л

Л, л *n.neut.* twelfth letter of the Russian alphabet.

лабири́нт *n.* labyrinth; maze.

лабора́нт *n.* laboratory assistant.

лаборато́рия *n.* laboratory. **—лаборато́рный,** *adj.* laboratory (*attrib.*).

ла́ва *n.* lava.

лава́нда *n.* lavender. **—лава́ндовый,** *adj.* lavender (*attrib.*).

лави́на *n.* avalanche.

лави́ровать *v.impfv.* [*pres.* **-рую, -руешь**] **1,** *naut.* to tack with the wind. **2,** *fig.* to maneuver.

ла́вка [*gen. pl.* **ла́вок**] *n.* **1,** bench. **2,** store; shop.

ла́вочка [*gen. pl.* **-чек**] *n.* **1,** small bench. **2,** small shop; small store. **—закры́ть ла́вочку,** to close up shop.

ла́вочник *n., obs.* shopkeeper.

лавр *n.* **1,** laurel. **2,** laurel wreath. **3,** *pl., fig.* laurels: почива́ть на ла́врах, to rest on one's laurels.

ла́вра *n.* large monastery: Печёрская ла́вра, Monastery of the Caves (*in Kiev*).

лавро́вый *also,* **ла́вровый** *adj.* laurel (*attrib.*). **—лавро́вый лист,** bay leaf.

лавса́н *n.* polyester fiber similar to dacron; lavsan.

ла́герный *adj.* camp (*attrib.*).

ла́герь *n.m.* **1,** [*pl.* **лагеря́**] camp. **2,** [*pl.* **ла́гери**] *fig.* camp; side; faction.

лагу́на *n.* lagoon.

лад [*2nd loc.* **ладу́**; *pl.* **лады́**] *n.* **1,** *colloq.* harmony (*between people*). **2,** way; manner: на ста́рый лад, the old way; на ру́сский лад, in the Russian manner. **3,** *fig.* mood; frame of mind: настро́ить кого́-нибудь на весёлый лад, to put someone in a happy frame of mind. **4,** *fig.* basis; footing: перестро́ить на вое́нный лад, to place on a war footing. **5,** *music* key; tone. **6,** *usu. pl.* fret (*of a stringed instrument*); key (*of an accordion*). **—в лад, 1,** in harmony; in tune. **2,** (*with dat.*) in time to. **3,** (*with* **с** + *instr.*) in harmony (with); in keeping (with); consistent (with). **—в ладу́; в лада́х,** on good terms. **—на все лады́,** thoroughly; from all angles. **—не в ладу́; не в лада́х,** not getting along; on the outs. **—де́ло идёт/пошло́ на лад,** *colloq.* things are going well; things have taken a turn for the better. **—запе́ть на друго́й лад,** to change one's tune; sing a different tune.

ла́дан *n.* **1,** incense. **2,** *in* ро́сный ла́дан, benzoin.

—дыша́ть на ла́дан, to be near death; have one foot in the grave. **—как чёрт ла́дана,** (*with verbs of shunning, fearing, etc.*) like the plague.

ла́данка [*gen. pl.* **-нок**] *n.* amulet.

ла́дить *v.impfv.* [*pres.* **ла́жу, ла́дишь**] (*with* **с** + *instr.*) to get along (with); be on good terms (with). **—ла́диться,** *refl.* to get on well; proceed satisfactorily: Де́ло не ла́дится, things are not working out well. Что́-то не ла́дится с телеви́зором, something is wrong with the television.

ла́дно *particle, colloq.* all right; O.K. **—adv., colloq. 1,** harmoniously. **2,** well.

ла́дный *adj., colloq.* **1,** graceful. **2,** harmonious. **3,** well-built; well-made.

ладо́нь *n.f.* palm of the hand. **—ви́дно как на ладо́ни,** clearly visible.

ладо́ши *n.pl., in* хло́пать *or* бить в ладо́ши, to clap one's hands.

ладья́ [*gen. pl.* **-де́й**] *n., chess* rook; castle.

лаз *n.* manhole.

ла́занье *n.* climbing.

лазаре́т *n.* **1,** field hospital. **2,** infirmary.

лазе́йка [*gen. pl.* **-зе́ек**] *n.* **1,** small opening. **2,** *fig.* loophole: оста́вить себе́ лазе́йку, to leave oneself a loophole.

ла́зер *n.* laser. **—ла́зерный,** *adj.* (*attrib.*).

ла́зить *v.impfv.* [*pres.* **ла́жу, ла́зишь**] *indeterm. of* **лезть.**

лазу́рный *adj.* light-blue; azure. **—Лазу́рный бе́рег,** Côte d'Azur.

лазу́рь *n.f.* light blue; azure. **—берли́нская лазу́рь,** Prussian blue.

лазу́тчик *n., obs.* **1,** scout. **2,** spy.

лай *n.* bark; barking.

ла́йка [*gen. pl.* **ла́ек**] *n.* **1,** husky (*dog*). **2,** kidskin. **—ла́йковый,** *adj.* kid (*attrib.*); kidskin (*attrib.*): ла́йковые перча́тки, kid gloves.

лайм *n.* lime (*fruit & tree*).

ла́йнер *n.* ocean liner. **—возду́шный ла́йнер,** airliner.

лак *n.* lacquer; varnish; polish. **—лак для воло́с,** hair spray. **—лак для ногте́й,** nail polish.

лака́ть *v.impfv.* [*pfv.* **вы́лакать**] to lap; lap up.

лаке́й *n.* **1,** footman. **2,** *fig.* lackey.

лаке́йский *adj.* **1,** of a footman. **2,** *fig.* servile.

лакиро́ванный *adj.* **1,** lacquered. Лакиро́ванные

изде́лия, lacquerware. **2,** gleaming; lustrous. —**лакиро́ванная ко́жа,** patent leather. —**лакиро́ванные ту́фли,** patent-leather shoes.

лакирова́ть *v.impfv.* [*pfv.* **отлакирова́ть**; *pres.* **-ру́ю, -ру́ешь**] **1,** to lacquer; varnish. **2,** [*impfv. only*] *fig.* to varnish; embellish.

лакиро́вка *n.* lacquering; varnishing.

ла́кмус *n.* litmus. —**ла́кмусовый,** *adj.* litmus (*attrib.*): ла́кмусовая бума́га, litmus paper.

ла́ковый *adj.* **1,** lacquer (*attrib.*). **2,** lacquered.

ла́комиться *v.r.impfv.* [*pfv.* **пола́комиться**; *pres.* **-млюсь, -мишься**] (*with instr.*) to feast (on).

ла́комка [*gen. pl.* **-мок**] *n.m. & f.*, *colloq.* person with a sweet tooth.

ла́комство *n.* **1,** *usu. pl.* sweets. **2,** delicacy.

ла́комый *adj.* **1,** tasty; luscious. **2,** [*short form only*] (*with* до) *colloq.* fond (of); having a weakness (for). —**ла́комый кусо́чек,** tasty morsel.

лакони́зм *n.* terseness; brevity.

лакони́ческий *adj.* laconic.

лакони́чный *adj.* laconic. —**лакони́чность,** *n.f.* terseness; brevity.

лакри́ца *n.* licorice. *Also,* **лакри́чник.**

лакри́чный *adj.* licorice.

лакта́ция *n.* lactation.

лакто́за *n.* lactose.

лакфио́ль *n.f.* wallflower.

ла́ма[1] *n.* llama.

ла́ма[2] *n.* lama. —**ламаи́зм,** *n.* Lamaism. —**ламаи́стский,** *adj.* Lamaist.

ламанти́н *n.* manatee.

ла́мпа *n.* **1,** lamp. **2,** *radio* tube: электро́нная ла́мпа, vacuum tube. —**ла́мпа дневно́го све́та,** daylight lamp.

лампа́да *n.* icon lamp.

лампа́с *n.* stripe (*on the side of uniform trousers*).

ла́мповый *adj.* lamp (*attrib.*).

ла́мпочка [*gen. pl.* **-чек**] *n.* **1,** *dim. of* ла́мпа. **2,** (electric light) bulb. —**э́то ему́ до ла́мпочки,** *colloq.* he couldn't care less.

ланге́т *n.* sliced steak.

лангу́ст *also,* **лангу́ста** *n.* spiny lobster.

ландша́фт *n.* landscape.

ла́ндыш *n.* lily of the valley.

ланоли́н *n.* lanolin.

ланта́н *n.* lanthanum.

ланце́т *n.* lancet.

лань *n.f.* fallow deer.

лао́сский *adj.* Laotian.

ла́па *n.* **1,** paw. **2,** claw (*of a hammer*); fluke (*of an anchor*). —**попа́сть в ла́пы** (*with gen., dat. or* к), to fall into the clutches of.

ла́пка [*gen. pl.* **ла́пок**] *n.* **1,** paw. **2,** *in* гуси́ные ла́пки, crow's-feet (*near the eye*). —**ходи́ть на за́дних ла́пках пе́ред,** to kowtow to; bow and scrape to.

ла́поть [*gen.* **ла́птя**; *pl.* ла́пти, лаптей, лаптя́м] *n.m.* sandal made of bark.

лапта́ *n.* **1,** Russian game, somewhat like baseball. **2,** wooden bat used in this game.

лапша́ *n.* **1,** noodles. **2,** noodle soup.

лапше́вник *n.* noodle pudding.

ла́рго *n.neut. & adv., music* largo.

ларёк [*gen.* **ларька́**] *n.* stall; booth.

ларе́ц [*gen.* **ларца́**] *n.* small box or case (*for valuables*).

ларинги́т *n.* laryngitis.

ла́рчик *n.* small box. —**а ла́рчик про́сто открыва́лся,** the explanation was quite simple.

ларь [*gen.* **ларя́**] *n.m.* bin.

ла́ска *n.* **1,** [*gen. pl.* **ласк**] caress. **2,** [*sing. only*] kindness. **3,** [*gen. pl.* **ла́сок**] weasel.

ласка́тельный *adj.* **1,** tender. **2,** *gram.* of endearment: ласка́тельное и́мя, endearing form of a name.

ласка́ть *v.impfv.* **1,** to caress; fondle; pet. **2,** *fig.* to please; delight (the senses). —**ласка́ться,** *refl.* (*with* к) **1,** to show affection (for *or* towards). **2,** *obs.* to play up to.

ла́сковый *adj.* **1,** affectionate; tender. **2,** (*of a breeze, sound, etc.*) gentle.

лассо́ *n. indecl.* lasso; lariat.

ласт *n.* flipper (*of a seal, walrus, etc.*).

ла́стик *n.* **1,** lasting. **2,** *colloq.* eraser.

ла́сточка [*gen. pl.* **-чек**] *n.* swallow (*bird*). —**пе́рвая ла́сточка,** first sign. —**прыжо́к в во́ду ла́сточкой,** swan dive.

ла́сточкин *adj.* of a swallow: ла́сточкино гнездо́, swallows' nest. —**ла́сточкин хвост,** dovetail.

лата́ть *v.impfv.* [*pfv.* **залата́ть**] *colloq.* to patch; patch up.

латви́йский *adj.* Latvian.

ла́текс *n.* latex.

лате́нтный *adj.* latent.

латиноамерика́нский *adj.* Latin American.

лати́нский *adj.* **1,** Latin. **2,** (*of the alphabet, characters, etc.*) Roman.

ла́тный *adj.* armor (*attrib.*). —**ла́тные доспе́хи,** suit of armor.

лату́к *n.* lettuce.

лату́нь *n.f.* brass. —**лату́нный,** *adj.* brass.

ла́ты [*gen.* **лат**] *n.pl.* armor.

латы́нь *n.f., colloq.* Latin.

латы́ш [*gen.* **-тыша́**] *n.m.* [*fem.* **-ты́шка**] Latvian; Lett. —**латы́шский,** *adj.* Latvian; Lettish.

лауреа́т *n.* laureate. Лауреа́т Но́белевской пре́мии, Nobel Prize winner.

лафе́т *n.* gun carriage.

ла́цкан *n.* lapel.

лачу́га *n.* shanty; shack; hovel.

ла́ять *v.impfv.* [*pres.* **ла́ю, ла́ешь**] to bark.

лга́ть *v.impfv.* [*pfv.* **солга́ть**; *pres.* **лгу, лжёшь, ...лгут**; *past fem.* лгала́] to lie; tell lies.

лгун [*gen.* **лгуна́**] *n.m.* [*fem.* **лгу́нья**] liar.

лебеди́ный *adj.* **1,** swan (*attrib.*); swan's. **2,** like that of a swan; graceful. —**лебеди́ная пе́сня,** swan song.

лебёдка [*gen. pl.* **-док**] *n.* **1,** female swan. **2,** *mech.* winch.

ле́бедь [*pl.* **ле́беди, -дей, -дям**] *n.m.* swan.

лебези́ть *v.impfv.* [*pres.* **-жу́, -зи́шь**] (*with* пе́ред) *colloq.* to be obsequious (to); kowtow (to).

лебя́жий [*fem.* **-жья**] *adj.* swan (*attrib.*); swan's.

лев [*gen.* **льва**] *n.* **1**, lion. **2**, *cap.* Leo. **—морско́й лев,** sea lion.

лева́к [*gen.* **-вака́**] *n., colloq.* leftist.

лева́цкий *adj., colloq.* leftist.

леве́ть *v.impfv.* [*pfv.* **полеве́ть**] to move to the left (*politically*).

левиафа́н *n.* leviathan.

Леви́т *n.* Leviticus.

левко́й *n.* gillyflower.

левре́тка [*gen. pl.* **-ток**] *n.* Italian greyhound.

левша́ *n.m. & f.* left-handed person.

ле́вый *adj.* **1**, left; left-hand. **2**, *polit.* left; left-wing. **3**, (*of a side of material*) wrong. **4**, *naut.* port. —*n.* left-winger; leftist. **—встать с ле́вой ноги́,** to get up on the wrong side of the bed.

лега́вый *adj., in* **лега́вая соба́ка,** pointer; setter.

легализа́ция *n.* legalization.

легализи́ровать *v.impfv. & pfv.* [*pres.* **-рую, -руешь**] to legalize. *Also,* **легализова́ть** [*pres.* **-зу́ю, зу́ешь**].

лега́льный *adj.* legal. **—лега́льно,** *adv.* legally. **—лега́льность,** *n.f.* legality.

лега́то *n.neut. & adj., music* legato.

леге́нда *n.* legend. **—легенда́рный,** *adj.* legendary.

легио́н *n.* legion. **—легионе́р,** *n.* legionnaire.

легислату́ра *n.* legislature.

лёгкий *adj.* [*short form* **лёгок, легка́, легко́, легки́;** *comp.* **ле́гче**] **1**, light (*in weight*). **2**, easy. **3**, not severe; light; slight; mild. **4**, graceful; light. **5**, (*of a breeze, nudge, etc.*) slight; gentle. **6**, (*of foods*) light; soft; bland; (*of a meal*) light. **7**, (*of music, reading, etc.*) light. **8**, easygoing. **9**, (*of behavior*) lax; loose. **10**, (*of industry, artillery, etc.*) light. **—лёгкая атле́тика,** track and field. **—лёгкая фигу́ра,** *chess* minor piece. **—лёгок на подъём,** always ready and willing. **—лёгок (легка́) на поми́не!,** talk of the devil! **—с лёгкой руки́** (+ *gen.*), thanks to; at the initiative of. **—у него́ лёгкая рука́,** he brings luck; he has a magic touch. *See also* **ле́гче.**

легко́ *adv.* **1**, easily. **2**, lightly. **3**, slightly: **легко́ ра́неный,** slightly wounded. **—***adj., used predicatively,* easy: Легко́ ошиба́ться, it is easy to make a mistake.

легкоатле́т *n.* (track and field) athlete; one taking part in any track or field event. **—легкоатлети́ческий,** *adj.* track-and-field.

легкове́рие *n.* credulity; gullibility. **—легкове́рный,** *adj.* credulous; gullible.

легкове́с *n., sports* lightweight.

легкове́сный *adj.* **1**, lightweight. **2**, *fig.* frivolous.

легково́й *adj., in* **легково́й автомоби́ль,** passenger car.

лёгкое *n., decl. as an adj.* lung.

легкомы́сленный *adj.* frivolous; flighty. **—легкомы́слие,** *n.* frivolity.

лёгкость *n.f.* **1**, lightness. **2**, ease; facility.

лёгочный *adj.* lung (*attrib.*); pulmonary.

легча́ть *v.impfv.* [*pfv.* **полегча́ть**] *colloq.* **1**, to abate; moderate. **2**, *impers.* (*with dat.*) to feel better.

ле́гче *adj., comp. of* **лёгкий. —ле́гче на поворо́тах!,** *colloq.* take it easy!; watch what you're say-

ing! **—ста́ло ле́гче** (*with dat.*), one is feeling better. **—час о́т часу не ле́гче!,** things are getting worse by the minute.

лёд [*gen.* **льда**; *2nd loc.* **льду**] *n.* ice.

леденѐть *v.impfv.* [*pfv.* **оледене́ть** *or* **заледене́ть**] **1**, to turn to ice; be covered with ice. **2**, to become numb.

ледене́ц [*gen.* **-нца́**] *n.* piece of hard candy.

ледени́ть *v.impfv.* to (cause to) turn to ice; freeze. **—леденя́щий кровь** (+ *noun*), chilling.

леденя́щий *adj.* **1**, icy. **2**, *fig.* (*of fear, horror, etc.*) numbing.

ледери́н *n.* leatherette.

ле́ди *n.f. indecl.* lady.

ле́дник *n.* **1**, ice house; ice cellar. **2**, icebox; refrigerator.

ледни́к [*gen.* **-ника́**] *n.* glacier.

леднико́вый *adj.* glacial. **—леднико́вый пери́од,** glacial epoch; glacial period; ice age.

ледо́вый *adj.* **1**, ice (*attrib.*). **2**, (*of a voyage*) made through icy regions. **—ледо́вое побо́ище,** *see* **побо́ище.**

ледоко́л *n.* icebreaker (*ship*).

ледоста́в *n.* freeze-up (*of a river*).

ледохо́д *n.* drifting of ice.

леды́шка [*gen. pl.* **-шек**] *n., colloq.* piece of ice.

ледяно́й *adj.* **1**, ice (*attrib.*). **2**, icy; ice-cold. **3**, *fig.* icy: ледяно́й взгляд, icy look; icy stare.

лёжа *adv.* in a reclining position; lying down.

лежа́лый *adj.* stale; old.

лежа́нка [*gen. pl.* **-нок**] *n.* sleeping ledge over a Russian chimney stove.

лежа́ть *v.impfv.* [*pres.* **лежу́, лежи́шь**] **1**, to lie. **2**, to be; be situated; lie. **3**, *colloq.* be ill; be in bed; be laid up. **4**, (*of responsibility, duties, etc.*) to lie; rest. **—лежа́ть на боку́,** *colloq.* to loaf. **—всё, что пло́хо лежи́т,** everything in sight; everything that is not tied down. **—у него́ душа́ не лежи́т к э́тому,** his heart isn't in it; he has no appetite for it.

лежа́чий *adj.* **1**, lying; recumbent. **2**, *colloq.* confined to bed. **—***n., in* **бить лежа́чего,** to strike a man when he is down.

ле́жбище *n.* breeding ground (*of seals, walruses, etc.*).

лежебо́ка *n.m. & f., colloq.* loafer; lazybones.

лежмя́ *adv., in* **лежмя́ лежа́ть,** to lie prostrate.

ле́звие *n.* blade (*of a knife, ax, etc.*). **—ле́звие бри́твы,** razor blade.

лезги́н [*gen. pl.* **-ги́н**] *n.m.* [*fem.* **-ги́нка**] Lezgin (*one of a people inhabiting the Caucasus*).

лезть *v.impfv.* [*pfv.* **поле́зть;** *pres.* **ле́зу, ле́зешь;** *past* **лез, ле́зла**] **1**, (*with various prepositions*) to climb (into, onto, over, under, etc.). Лезть на де́рево, to climb a tree. **2**, (*with* в + *acc.*) to sneak (into). **3**, (*with* в + *acc.*) *colloq.* to reach (into). **4**, [*impfv. only*] *usu. neg.* A, (*with* в + *acc.*) (not) to fit *or* go (into): Кни́га не ле́зет в портфе́ль, the book won't fit/go into the briefcase. B, (*with dat. or* на + *acc.*) (not) to go on; (not) fit: Ту́фли мне не ле́зут, I can't get these shoes on; пиджа́к на него́ не ле́зет, the suit jacket doesn't fit him. **5**, (*of hair, fur, etc.*) to fall out. **—лезть в буты́лку,** *colloq.* to fly off the handle. **—лезть в го́лову,** (*of thoughts*) to pop into one's head. **—лезть**

в дра́ку, to be spoiling for a fight. —**лезть в ду́шу** (+ *dat.*), to worm one's way into someone's confidence. —**лезть в карма́н** (+ *dat.*), to pick someone's pocket. —**лезть в пе́тлю,** to risk one's neck. —**лезть из ко́жи вон,** to try in every way; go to great lengths. —**лезть на глаза́** (+ *dat.*), *colloq.* to (try to) catch someone's eye. —**лезть (поле́зть) на лоб,** (*of one's eyes*) to pop out of one's head. —**лезть на́ стену,** *colloq.* to fly off the handle; hit the ceiling. —**лезть не в своё де́ло,** to poke one's nose into someone else's affairs. —**не лезть в карма́н за сло́вом,** never to be at a loss for words. —**не лезть ни в каки́е воро́та,** to be completely unacceptable.

лейбори́ст *n.* Labourite. —**лейбори́стский,** *adj.* Labour (*attrib.*).

ле́йка [*gen. pl.* ле́ек] *n.* **1,** watering can; sprinkling can. **2,** *colloq.* funnel.

лейко́з *n.* leukemia. *Also,* **лейкеми́я.**

лейкопла́стырь *n.m.* band-aid.

лейкоци́т *n.* leukocyte.

лейтена́нт *n.* lieutenant. —**мла́дший лейтена́нт,** second lieutenant. —**ста́рший лейтена́нт,** first lieutenant.

лейтмоти́в *n.* leitmotif.

лека́ло *n.* French curve.

лека́рственный *adj.* medicinal.

лека́рство *n.* medicine.

ле́карь [*pl.* ле́кари, -ре́й, -ря́м] *n.m., obs.* doctor.

ле́ксика *n.* vocabulary; lexicon.

лексикогра́фия *n.* lexicography. —**лексико́граф,** *n.* lexicographer. —**лексикографи́ческий,** *adj.* lexicographic.

лексико́н *n.* lexicon (*wordbook*).

лекси́ческий *adj.* lexical.

ле́ктор *n.* lecturer.

ле́кция *n.* lecture. —**лекцио́нный,** *adj.* lecture (*attrib.*).

леле́ять *v.impfv.* [*pres.* леле́ю, леле́ешь] **1,** to care for lovingly. **2,** *fig.* to cherish; nurture (a dream, hope, etc.).

ле́мех *also,* **леме́х** [*pl.* лемеха́] *n.* plowshare.

ле́мминг *n.* lemming.

лему́р *n.* lemur.

лён [*gen.* льна] *n.* flax.

лени́вец [*gen.* -вца] *n.* **1,** lazy person. **2,** *zool.* sloth.

лени́вый *adj.* **1,** lazy. **2,** sluggish.

ле́нинец [*gen.* -нца] *n.* Leninist. —**ленини́зм,** *n.* Leninism. —**ле́нинский,** *adj.* Leninist.

лени́ться *v.r.impfv.* [*pres.* леню́сь, ле́нишься] **1,** to be lazy. **2,** (*with inf.*) to be too lazy (to).

ле́ность *n.* laziness.

ле́нта *n.* **1,** ribbon. **2,** tape. **3,** band. **4,** film. —**конве́йерная ле́нта,** conveyor belt. —**патро́нная ле́нта,** cartridge belt; ammunition belt.

ле́нто *n.neut. & adv., music* lento.

ле́нточный *adj.* tape (*attrib.*); band (*attrib.*). —**ле́нточная пила́,** band saw. —**ле́нточный транспортёр,** conveyor belt. —**ле́нточный червь,** tapeworm.

лентя́й *n.m.* [*fem.* -тя́йка] lazy person; lazybones.

лентя́йничать *v.impfv., colloq.* to loaf; idle.

ленца́ *n., colloq.* lazy streak: челове́к с ленцо́й, person with a lazy streak.

ленч *n.* lunch.

лень *n.f.* laziness. —*predicate* (*with dat.*) *colloq.* too lazy: Мне лень идти́, I am too lazy to go; I don't feel like going.

леопа́рд *n.* leopard. —**леопа́рдовый,** *adj.* leopard (*attrib.*); leopard's.

лепесто́к [*gen.* -стка́] *n.* petal.

ле́пет *n.* babble; prattle.

лепета́ние *n.* babbling; prattling.

лепета́ть *v.impfv.* [*pres.* лепечу́, лепе́чешь] to babble; prattle.

лепёшка [*gen. pl.* -шек] *n.* **1,** small cake; crumpet. **2,** tablet; lozenge. **3,** (*with gen.*) clod (*of dirt*).

лепи́ть *v.impfv.* [*pres.* леплю́, ле́пишь] **1,** [*pfv.* вы́лепить] to model; fashion; sculpture. **2,** [*pfv.* слепи́ть] to make; build (a nest, hive, etc.). —**лепи́ться,** *refl.* [*impfv. only*] to nestle.

ле́пка *n.* modeling.

лепно́й *adj.* sculptured. —**лепно́е украше́ние,** molding.

ле́пта *n.* small contribution; mite: вноси́ть свою́ ле́пту, to contribute one's (small) share; do one's bit.

лес [*2nd loc.* лесу́; *pl.* леса́] *n.* **1,** forest; woods. **2,** timber; lumber. —**быть как в лесу́,** to be all at sea.

леса́[1] *also,* **ле́са** [*pl.* лёсы] *n.* fishing line.

леса́[2] [*gen.* лесо́в] *n.pl.* scaffolding.

лесбия́нка [*gen. pl.* -нок] *n.* lesbian. —**лесби́йский,** *adj.* lesbian.

ле́сенка [*gen. pl.* -нок] *n.* **1,** small ladder. **2,** small staircase; short flight of stairs.

леси́стый *adj.* wooded.

ле́ска [*gen. pl.* ле́сок] *n.* fishing line.

лесни́к [*gen.* -ника́] *n.* forest ranger.

лесни́чество *n.* forest district.

лесни́чий *n., decl. as an adj.* forester.

лесно́й *adj.* **1,** forest (*attrib.*). **2,** timber (*attrib.*); lumber (*attrib.*). **3,** of forestry. —**лесна́я земляни́ка,** wild strawberries. —**лесно́й оре́х,** hazelnut.

лесово́д *n.* specialist in forestry. —**лесово́дство,** *n.* forestry.

лесозаво́д *n.* lumber mill.

лесоматериа́л *n., usu. pl.* timber; lumber.

лесопа́рк *n.* wooded park.

лесопи́лка [*gen. pl.* -лок] *n., colloq.* sawmill.

лесопи́льный *adj.* sawing; saw (*attrib.*). —**лесопи́льный заво́д,** sawmill.

лесору́б *n.* woodcutter; lumberjack.

ле́стница *n.* **1,** stairs; staircase; stairway. **2,** ladder. —**пожа́рная ле́стница,** fire escape.

ле́стничный *adj.* stair (*attrib.*).

ле́стно *adv.* in flattering terms. —*adj., used predicatively,* flattering: Мне бы́ло ле́стно, что..., it was flattering to me that...; I was flattered that...

ле́стный *adj.* flattering; complimentary.

лесть *n.f.* flattery.

лёт *n.* flight; flying. —**на лету́,** in midair; on the fly; on the wing. —**лови́ть на лету́,** *fig.* to be quick to grasp.

Ле́та *n., in* ка́нуть в Ле́ту, to sink into oblivion.

лета́ [*gen.* лет] *n.pl.* years: пять лет, five years. Мне два́дцать лет, I am twenty years old. —**быть в лета́х,** to be getting on in years. —**мно́гая ле́та** (*with* *different stress*), here's to long life! —**одни́х лет**, the same age. —**с де́тских** (*or* **с ма́лых**) **лет**, since childhood. —**ско́лько вам лет?**, how old are you? —**сре́дних лет**, middle-aged.

летарги́я *n.* lethargy. —**летарги́ческий**, *adj.* lethargic.

лета́тельный *adj.* flying (*attrib.*). —**лета́тельный аппара́т**, aircraft.

лета́ть *v.impfv.*, indeterm. *of* **лете́ть**.

лета́ющий *adj.* flying.

лете́ть *v.impfv.* [*pfv.* **полете́ть**; *pres.* **лечу́, лети́шь**] to fly. —**лете́ть вверх**, *colloq.* to soar. —**лете́ть вниз**, *colloq.* to plummet.

ле́тний *adj.* summer (*attrib.*).

лётный *adj.* flying (*attrib.*). —**лётная полоса́**, runway; landing strip. —**лётное по́ле**, airfield. —**лётный соста́в**, flight personnel.

ле́то *n.* summer.

летоисчисле́ние *n.* method of numbering the years.

ле́том *adv.* in (the) summer.

летопи́сец [*gen.* **-сца**] *n.* chronicler.

ле́топись *n.f.* chronicle.

летосчисле́ние *n.* = **летоисчисле́ние**.

лету́н [*gen.* **-туна́**] *n.*, *colloq.* **1,** flier. **2,** person continually changing jobs.

лету́честь *n.f.* volatility.

лету́чий *adj.* **1,** flying. **2,** fleeting; momentary. **3,** *chem.* volatile. —**лету́чая мышь**, *zool.* bat. —**лету́чая ры́ба**, flying fish.

лету́чка [*gen. pl.* **-чек**] *n.*, *colloq.* **1,** leaflet. **2,** quick meeting. **3,** mobile unit.

лётчик *n.* pilot. —**лётчик-испыта́тель**, test pilot. —**лётчик-истреби́тель**, fighter-pilot.

летя́га *n.* flying squirrel.

лече́бница *n.* (special) hospital.

лече́бный *adj.* **1,** medical. **2,** medicinal; curative.

лече́ние *n.* (medical) treatment.

лечи́ть *v.impfv.* [*pres.* **лечу́, ле́чишь**] to treat (*medically*). —**лечи́ться**, *refl.* **1,** to undergo (medical) treatment. **2,** to treat oneself.

лечь [*infl.* **ля́гу, ля́жешь, ...ля́гут**; *past* **лёг, легла́, легло́, легли́**] *v., pfv. of* **ложи́ться**.

ле́ший *n., decl. as an adj.* wood goblin.

лещ [*gen.* **леща́**] *n.* bream (*fish*).

лещи́на *n.* hazel (*tree*).

лженау́ка *n.* pseudoscience. —**лженау́чный**, *adj.* pseudoscientific.

лжесвиде́тель *n.m.* false witness; perjurer. —**лжесвиде́тельство**, *n.* false evidence; perjury.

лжесвиде́тельствовать *v.impfv.* [*pres.* **-ствую, -ствуешь**] to give false evidence; commit perjury; perjure oneself.

лжец [*gen.* **лжеца́**] *n.* liar.

лжи́вый *adj.* lying; untruthful; false. —**лжи́вость**, *n.f.* falsity.

ли *conj.* if; whether: Я не зна́ю, смогу́ ли я пойти́, I don't know if I'll be able to go. Он попро́бовал, хорошо́ ли вино́, he tasted the wine to see if it was good. —*interr. particle:* Есть ли у вас спи́чка?, do you have a match?; have you a match? Нра́вится ли вам э́то?, do you like it?

либера́л *n.* liberal. —**либерали́зм**, *n.* liberalism.

либера́льничать *v.impfv.*, *colloq.* to be overly tolerant.

либера́льный *adj.* liberal.

ли́бо *conj.* or. —**ли́бо..., ли́бо...**, either..., or...

либре́тто *n. indecl.* libretto. —**либретти́ст**, *n.* librettist.

лива́нский *adj.* Lebanese.

ли́вень [*gen.* **ли́вня**] *n.m.* rainstorm; downpour; cloudburst; thundershower.

ли́вер *n.* giblets.

ли́верный *adj.*, *in* **ли́верная колбаса́**, liverwurst.

ливи́йский *adj.* Libyan.

ливмя́ *adv.*, *colloq.*, *in* **ливмя́ лить**, (*of rain*) to come down in torrents.

ливре́я *n.* livery. —**ливре́йный**, *adj.* livery (*attrib.*); liveried; in livery.

ли́га *n.* **1,** league: Ли́га на́ций, League of Nations. **2,** *music* slur.

лигату́ра *n.* ligature.

лигни́т *n.* lignite.

лигрои́н *n.* naphtha.

ли́дер *n.* leader.

ли́дерство *n.* **1,** leadership. **2,** lead (*in a race, contest, election, etc.*).

лиди́ровать *v.impfv. & pfv.* [*pres.* **-рую, -руешь**] to lead; be in the lead (*in a race, contest, election, etc.*).

лиза́ние *n.* licking.

лиза́ть *v.impfv.* [*pfv.* **лизну́ть**; *pres.* **лижу́, ли́жешь**] to lick.

лизоблю́д *n.*, *colloq.* bootlicker.

лик *n.* **1,** *archaic* face; countenance. **2,** face (*of the moon, sun, etc.*). **3,** *eccles.* assembly. —**причисля́ть к ли́ку святы́х**, to canonize; beatify.

ликвида́ция *n.* **1,** liquidation. **2,** elimination.

ликвиди́ровать *v.impfv. & pfv.* [*pres.* **-рую, -руешь**] **1,** to liquidate. **2,** to eliminate. —**ликвиди́роваться**, *refl.* to be liquidated.

ликви́дный *adj.*, *finance* liquid: ликви́дные сре́дства, liquid assets. —**ликви́дность**, *n.f.* liquidity.

ликёр *n.* liqueur; cordial.

ликова́ние *n.* rejoicing; jubilation; exultation.

ликова́ть *v.impfv.* [*pres.* **-ку́ю, -ку́ешь**] to rejoice; exult.

лику́ющий *adj.* jubilant; exultant.

ли́лия *n.* lily. —**водяна́я ли́лия**, water lily.

лилове́ть *v.impfv.* to turn purple.

лило́вый *adj.* purple.

лима́н *n.* estuary.

лими́т *n.* limit; quota.

лимити́ровать *v.impfv. & pfv.* [*pres.* **-рую, -руешь**] to limit.

лимо́н *n.* **1,** lemon. **2,** lemon tree.

лимона́д *n.* **1,** lemonade. **2,** carbonated fruit drink; squash.

лимо́нный *adj.* lemon. —**лимо́нная кислота́**, citric acid.

ли́мский *adj.*, *in* **ли́мская фасо́ль**, lima bean(s).

лимузи́н *n.* limousine.

ли́мфа *n.* lymph. —**лимфати́ческий**, *adj.* lymph (*attrib.*); lymphatic.

лингви́ст *n.* linguist. —**лингви́стика**, *n.* linguistics. —**лингвисти́ческий**, *adj.* linguistic.

линéйка [*gen. pl.* **-нéек**] *n.* **1,** ruled line (*on paper*). В линéйку, (*of paper*) lined; ruled. **2,** ruler; straight edge. **3,** line; file: вы́строиться в линéйку, to form a line. **4,** line-up; assembly (*in a camp*). —**логарифми́ческая линéйка,** slide rule.

линéйный *adj.* linear. —**линéйный корáбль,** battleship.

ли́нза *n.* lens.

ли́ния *n.* **1,** line. **2,** (*with* на + *acc.*) policy (of). —**по ли́нии** (+ *gen.*), through; under the auspices of.

линкóр *n.* battleship (*contr. of* **линéйный корáбль**).

линóванный *adj.* lined; ruled.

линовáть *v.impfv.* [*pfv.* **налиновáть**; *pres.* **-нýю, -нýешь**] to rule; draw lines on.

линóлеум *n.* linoleum.

линоти́п *n.* linotype.

линчевáние *n.* lynching.

линчевáть *v.impfv. & pfv.* [*pres.* **-чýю, -чýешь**] to lynch.

ли́нька *n.* molting.

линю́чий *adj., colloq.* (*of material*) that fades easily.

линя́лый *adj., colloq.* faded; discolored.

линя́ть *v.impfv.* **1,** [*pfv.* **полиня́ть**] (*of material*) to fade; (*of colors*) to run. **2,** [*pfv.* **вы́линять**] (*of animals*) to shed hair; (*of birds*) to molt.

ли́па *n.* **1,** linden tree; lime tree. **2,** *colloq.* forgery.

ли́пка [*gen. pl.* **ли́пок**] *n.* young linden tree. —**ободрáть (когó-нибудь) как ли́пку,** *colloq.* to rob someone blind.

ли́пкий *adj.* sticky; adhesive. —**ли́пкий плáстырь,** sticking plaster.

ли́пнуть *v.impfv.* [*past* **лип** *or* **ли́пнул, ли́пла**] (*with* **к**) to stick (to).

ли́повый *adj.* **1,** linden (*attrib.*); lime (*attrib.*). **2,** *colloq.* false; fake; phony.

липýчий *adj., colloq.* sticky.

липýчка *n., colloq.* **1,** sticky paper: липýчка от мух, flypaper. **2,** sticking plaster.

ли́ра *n.* **1,** lyre. **2,** lira (*monetary unit of Italy and Turkey*).

лири́зм *n.* lyricism.

ли́рик *n.* lyric poet.

ли́рика *n.* **1,** lyric poetry. **2,** lyric poem. —**лири́ческий,** *adj.* lyric; lyrical.

лисá [*pl.* **ли́сы**] *n.* fox.

ли́сий [*fem.* **-сья**] *adj.* **1,** fox (*attrib.*). **2,** *fig.* foxy.

лиси́ца *n.* fox. —**морскáя лиси́ца,** thresher shark.

лиси́чка [*gen. pl.* **-чек**] *n.* a kind of edible mushroom; chanterelle.

лист [*gen.* **листá**] *n.* **1,** [*pl.* **ли́стья, ли́стьев**] leaf. **2,** [*pl.* **листы́, листóв**] sheet (*of paper, metal, etc.*). **3,** [*pl.* **листы́, листóв**] any of various official documents: опрóсный лист, questionnaire; исполни́тельный лист, writ. —**с листá,** from sight: читáть с листá, to sight-read. Перевóд с листá, sight translation.

листáть *v.impfv., colloq.* to leaf through.

листвá *n.* foliage.

ли́ственница *n.* larch (*tree*).

ли́ственный *adj.* leafy; leaf-bearing.

листóвка [*gen. pl.* **-вок**] *n.* leaflet.

листовóй *adj.* **1,** sheet (*attrib.*): листовóй метáлл, sheet metal. **2,** leaf (*attrib.*).

листóк [*gen.* **-сткá**] *n.* **1,** leaf. **2,** sheet (*of paper*).

листопáд *n.* falling of leaves. —**листопáдный,** *adj.* deciduous.

литáвры *n.pl.* [*sing.* **литáвра**] kettledrums.

литáния *n.* litany.

литéйный *adj.* founding; casting. —**литéйный завóд,** foundry.

литéйщик *n.* founder; caster.

литерáтор *n.* man of letters.

литератýра *n.* literature. —**литератýрный,** *adj.* literary.

ли́терный *adj.* **1,** designated by a letter. **2,** (*of a seat*) reserved.

ли́тий *n.* lithium.

литóвец [*gen.* **-вца**] *n.m.* [*fem.* **-вка**] *n.* Lithuanian. —**литóвский,** *adj.* Lithuanian.

литóграф *n.* lithographer.

литографи́ровать *v.impfv. & pfv.* [*pres.* **-рую, -руешь**] to lithograph.

литогрáфия *n.* **1,** lithography. **2,** lithograph. —**литогрáфский,** *adj.* lithographic.

литóй *adj.* (*of metals*) cast.

литори́на *n.* periwinkle (*mollusk*).

литосфéра *n.* lithosphere.

литр *n.* liter. —**литрóвый,** *adj.* with a capacity of one liter.

литурги́я *n.* liturgy. —**литурги́ческий,** *adj.* liturgical.

лить *v.impfv.* [*pres.* **лью, льёшь**; *past fem.* **лилá**] **1,** to pour. **2,** to emit (sound, light, etc.). **3,** to shed (tears, blood, etc.). **4,** to cast; form; make. **5,** *v.i., colloq.* (*of liquids*) to flow; stream; run; (*of rain*) to come down.

литьё *n.* **1,** casting (*process*). **2,** castings.

ли́ться *v.r.impfv.* [*pres.* **льюсь, льёшься**; *past* **ли́лся, лилáсь, ли́лось** *or* **лилóсь, ли́лись** *or* **лили́сь**] to flow; stream; pour.

лиф *n.* bodice.

лифт *n.* elevator.

лифтёр *n.* elevator operator. —**лифтёрша,** *n., colloq.* (female) elevator operator.

ли́фчик *n.* underbodice.

лихáч [*gen.* **-хачá**] *n.* **1,** daredevil. **2,** reckless driver. **3,** *obs.* coachman (*equipped with a good horse and carriage*).

лихáчество *n.* recklessness; foolhardiness.

лихвá *n., obs.* interest (*on a loan*). —**с лихвóй,** with something to spare: окупáться с лихвóй, to more than pay for itself. Возмещáться с лихвóй, to be more than made up for (by).

ли́хо *n., colloq.* evil; misfortune. —*adv., colloq.* **1,** dashingly; jauntily. **2,** *colloq.* at a brisk pace. —**не поминáйте ли́хом,** don't think badly of me. —**почём фунт ли́ха,** what misfortune is all about.

лихóй *adj.* **1,** *obs.* evil; hard. **2,** *colloq.* daring; dashing; jaunty. **3,** *colloq.* rapid; fast; brisk. **4,** *colloq.* deft. —**лихá бедá начáло,** the hard part is getting started.

лихолéтье *n., obs.* turmoil; upheaval.

лихорáдить *v.impfv., impers.* to have a fever: Егó лихорáдит, he has a fever; he is feverish.

лихора́дка *n.* fever: сенна́я лихора́дка, hay fever; жёлтая лихора́дка, yellow fever. —золота́я лихора́дка, gold rush.

лихора́дочный *adj.* feverish.

ли́хость *n.f.* daring; audacity; bravado.

ли́хтер *n., naut.* lighter.

лицево́й *adj.* **1,** facial. **2,** *in* лицева́я сторона́, the right side (*of material, a coin, etc.*). —лицева́я ру́копись, illuminated manuscript. —лицево́й счёт, personal account.

лицезре́ть *v.impfv.* [*pres.* -зрю́, -зри́шь] *obs.* to behold.

лице́й *n.* lycée.

лицеме́р *n.* hypocrite.

лицеме́рие *n.* hypocrisy.

лицеме́рить *v.impfv.* to be hypocritical; play the hypocrite.

лицеме́рный *adj.* hypocritical.

лице́нзия *n.* (commercial) license.

лицо́ [*pl.* ли́ца] *n.* **1,** face. **2,** person; individual; personage. Официа́льное *or* должностно́е лицо́, official. **3,** face; right side (*of an object, fabric, etc.*). **4,** *gram.* person. —в (чьём-нибудь) лице́, in; in the person of: ве́рный друг в его́ лице́, a true friend in him. —в лицо́ (+ *dat.*), **1,** in one's face. **2,** to one's face. —знать в лицо́, to know (someone) by sight. —к лицу́ (+ *dat.*), becoming: Пла́тье вам к лицу́, the dress is becoming on you. —лицо́м к, facing. —лицо́м кве́рху, face up; right side up. —лицо́м к лицу́, face to face. —на нём (ней) нет лица́, he (she) looks awful. —на одно́ лицо́, all alike; exactly alike. —от лица́ (+ *gen.*), on behalf of. —пе́ред лицо́м (+ *gen.*), in the face of. —показа́ть своё настоя́щее лицо́, to show one's true colors. —показа́ть това́р лицо́м, to show something in its best light; put one's best foot forward. —с лица́ земли́, from the face of the earth. —смотре́ть (+ *dat.*) в лицо́, **1,** to look (someone) in the face. **2,** *fig.* to face (squarely): смотре́ть фа́ктам в лицо́, to face the facts.

ли́чико *n., dim. of* лицо́.

личи́на *n.* mask.

личи́нка *n.* **1,** larva. **2,** maggot. —личи́ночный, *adj.* larval.

ли́чно *adv.* **1,** personally. **2,** in person.

лично́й *adj.* face (*attrib.*).

ли́чность *n.f.* **1,** person; figure; individual; character. **2,** personality. **3,** identity. —переходи́ть на ли́чности, to get personal.

ли́чный *adj.* **1,** personal. **2,** private. —ли́чный соста́в, personnel; staff.

лиша́й [*gen.* лишая́] *n.* **1,** [*also,* лиша́йник] lichen. **2,** *med.* herpes. —опоя́сывающий лиша́й, shingles. —стригу́щий лиша́й, ringworm.

лиша́ть *v.impfv.* [*pfv.* лиши́ть] (*with gen.*) to deprive (of); rob (of). —лиша́ть (кого́-нибудь) жи́зни, to kill (someone); take someone's life. —лиши́ть (кого́-нибудь) насле́дства, to disinherit (someone).

лиша́ться *v.r.impfv.* [*pfv.* лиши́ться] (*with gen.*) to be deprived of; lose.

лише́ние *n.* **1,** deprivation. **2,** *pl.* privations; hardships.

лишённый *adj.* [*short form* лишён, лишена́, лишено́, лишены́] (*with gen.*) **1,** lacking; without. **2,** devoid (of); void (of).

лиши́ть *v., pfv. of* лиша́ть. —лиши́ться, *refl., pfv. of* лиша́ться.

ли́шнее *n., decl. as an adj.* too much: брать ли́шнее, to overcharge. Вы́пить ли́шнего, to have too much to drink. —с ли́шним, *colloq.* a little over: три до́ллара с ли́шним, three dollars and change.

ли́шний *adj.* **1,** superfluous; excess. **2,** spare; extra. —ли́шний раз, once again; once more. —не ли́шнее (+ *inf.*), it would not be a bad idea (to).

лишь *adv.* only. —лишь бы, **1,** if only. **2,** as long as. —лишь то́лько, as soon as.

лоб [*gen.* лба; *2nd loc.* лбу] *n.* forehead; brow. —в лоб, frontally; head-on. —на лбу напи́сано (*with* у), it's written all over his/her face. —пусти́ть себе́ пу́лю в лоб, to blow one's brains out. —столкну́ть (+ *acc.*) лба́ми, to set against each other; bring into conflict; set at loggerheads. —что в лоб, что по́ лбу, it's as broad as it is long.

ло́бби *n.neut. indecl., polit.* lobby. —лобби́зм, *n.* lobbying. —лобби́ст, *n.* lobbyist.

лобза́ть *v.impfv., archaic* to kiss.

ло́бзик *n.* fret saw.

ло́бный *adj., anat.* frontal. —ло́бное ме́сто, *hist.* place of execution (*in a public square*).

лобово́й *adj.* **1,** *mil.* frontal. **2,** front. **3,** *fig.* (*of a question*) direct.

лоботря́с *n., colloq.* lazybones; loafer.

лобыза́ть *v.impfv.* = лобза́ть.

лов *n.* catch (*of fish*).

ловела́с *n.* ladies' man.

лове́ц [*gen.* ловца́] *n.* **1,** fisherman. **2,** hunter.

лови́ть *v.impfv.* [*pfv.* пойма́ть; *pres.* ловлю́, ло́вишь] **1,** to (try to) catch. **2,** *colloq.* to pick up (a radio signal). —лови́ть ка́ждое сло́во, to devour (*or* hang on) every word. —лови́ть (кого́-нибудь) на сло́ве, to take (someone) at his word. —лови́ть моме́нт *or* слу́чай, to seize the opportunity. —лови́ть ры́бу в му́тной воде́, to fish in troubled waters. —лови́ть себя́ на (+ *prepl.*), to catch oneself doing something. Лови́ть себя́ на мы́сли, что..., to find oneself thinking that... —лови́ть чей-нибудь взгляд, to catch someone's eye.

ловка́ч [*gen.* -кача́] *n., colloq.* clever fellow.

ло́вкий *adj.* [*short form* ло́вок, ловка́, ло́вко, ло́вки; *comp.* ло́вче] **1,** adroit; dexterous; deft. **2,** *colloq.* clever; resourceful.

ло́вко *adv.* **1,** adroitly. **2,** *colloq.* well: ло́вко сде́лано!, well done!

ло́вкость *n.f.* **1,** adroitness; dexterity. **2,** *colloq.* ingenuity; resourcefulness. —ло́вкость рук, sleight of hand; legerdemain.

ло́вля *n.* catching (*of fish*); trapping (*of animals*). —ры́бная ло́вля, fishing.

лову́шка [*gen. pl.* -шек] *n.* trap.

ло́вчий *adj.* hunting (*attrib.*).

лог [*2nd loc.* ло́ге *or* логу́; *pl.* лога́] *n.* ravine.

логари́фм *n.* logarithm. —логарифми́ческий, *adj.* logarithmic.

ло́гик *n.* logician.

ло́гика *n.* logic.

логи́ческий *adj.* logical. —логи́чески, *adv.* logically.

логи́чный *adj.* logical. —логи́чно, *adv.* logically. —логи́чность, *n.f.* logic.

ло́говище *n.* lair; den. *Also,* ло́гово.

логопе́дия *n.* speech therapy. —логопе́д, *n.* speech therapist.

ло́дка [*gen. pl.* ло́док] *n.* boat: па́русная ло́дка, sailboat; мото́рная ло́дка, motorboat; гребна́я ло́дка, rowboat. —подво́дная ло́дка, submarine.

ло́дочка [*gen. pl.* -чек] *n.* 1, small boat. 2, pump (*shoe*).

ло́дочник *n.* boatman.

ло́дочный *adj.* boat (*attrib.*); boating (*attrib.*).

лоды́жка [*gen. pl.* -жек] *n.* ankle.

ло́дырничать *v.impfv., colloq.* to loaf.

ло́дырь *n.m., colloq.* loafer; idler.

ло́жа *n.* 1, *theat.* box. 2, *obs.* (masonic) lodge. 3, rifle stock.

ложби́на *n.* hollow; depression.

ло́же *n.* 1, *archaic; poetic* bed. 2, river bed.

ло́жечка [*gen. pl.* -чек] *n., dim. of* ло́жка. —под ло́жечкой, in the pit of one's stomach.

ложи́ться *v.r.impfv.* [*pfv.* лечь] 1, to lie down. 2, to go to bed; go to sleep. 3, (*with* в + *acc.*) to get into (bed); go into; enter (a hospital). 4, (*with* на + *acc.*) (*of snow, frost, fog, etc.*) to lie (on); cover. 5, (*of shadows, light, etc.*) to fall. 6, (*with* на + *acc.*) *fig.* (*of responsibility, suspicion, etc.*) to lie (on); fall (on). —лечь в моги́лу *or* в гроб, to die. —лечь в осно́ву (+ *gen.*), to underlie. —лечь на курс, (*of an aircraft or ship*) to embark (*or* set off) on a certain course. —лечь/ложи́ться спать, to go to bed; go to sleep.

ло́жка [*gen. pl.* ло́жек] *n.* 1, spoon. 2, spoonful. 3, ladle: разлива́тельная ло́жка, soup ladle. —че́рез час по ча́йной ло́жке, in dribs and drabs.

ло́жно *adv.* 1, falsely; wrongfully. 2, incorrectly; wrongly.

ло́жность *n.f.* falsity.

ло́жный *adj.* 1, false. 2, erroneous; fallacious. —быть на ло́жном пути́, to be on the wrong track. —поста́вить в ло́жное положе́ние, to put (someone) in a false position.

ложь [*gen., dat. & prep.* лжи; *instr.* ло́жью] *n.f.* 1, lie; falsehood. 2, lying; lies.

лоза́ [*pl.* ло́зы] *n.* 1, vine: виногра́дная лоза́, grapevine. 2, rod (*used for punishment*). 3, willow.

лозня́к [*gen.* -няка́] *n.* willow shrub.

ло́зунг *n.* slogan.

локализа́ция *n.* localization.

локализова́ть *v.impfv. & pfv.* [*pres.* -зу́ю, -зу́ешь] to localize. —локализова́ться, *refl.* to become localized.

лока́льный *adj.* local.

лока́тор *n.* locator; detector; radar.

лока́ут *n.* lockout.

локомоти́в *n.* locomotive.

ло́кон *n.* lock; curl.

ло́коть [*gen.* ло́ктя; *pl.* ло́кти, -те́й, -тя́м] *n.m.* 1, elbow. Толкну́ть ло́ктем, to nudge. 2, elbow (*of a garment*): потёртый на локтя́х, worn at the elbows. 3,

cubit (*ancient measure*). —бли́зок ло́коть, да не уку́сишь, so near and yet so far. —чу́вство ло́ктя, feeling of comradeship.

локтево́й *adj.* elbow (*attrib.*). —локтева́я кость, funny bone.

лом *n.* 1, [*pl.* ло́мы, ломо́в, лома́м] crowbar. 2, scrap: желе́зный лом, scrap iron.

лома́ка *n.m. & f., colloq.* person who puts on airs.

ло́маный *adj.* broken.

лома́ть *v.impfv.* [*pfv.* слома́ть] 1, to break. 2, to fracture. 3, to tear down. 4, [*impfv. only*] to quarry. 5, to break down (old beliefs, customs, etc.). 6, to ruin; wreck. —лома́ть себе́ го́лову, to rack one's brains. —лома́ть себе́ ру́ки, to wring one's hands. —лома́ть себя́; лома́ть свой хара́ктер, to change one's ways. —лома́ть спи́ну, to break one's back (*fig.*).

лома́ться *v.r.impfv.* [*pfv.* слома́ться] 1, to break. 2, (*of a device, vehicle, etc.*) to be broken; break down. 3, [*impfv. only*] to be breakable. 4, [*impfv. only*] (*of one's voice*) to break; crack; (*of a young man's voice*) to change. 5, (*of something well-established*) to break down; collapse; crumble. 6, [*pfv.* полома́ться] to be coy; put on airs.

ломба́рд *n.* pawnshop; hockshop. —ломба́рдный, *adj.* of or pert. to a pawnshop: ломба́рдная квита́нция, pawn ticket.

ло́мберный *adj., in* ло́мберный стол, card table.

ломи́ть *v.impfv.* [*pres.* ломлю́, ло́мишь] 1, *colloq.* to break. 2, *impers.* to ache: У меня́ ло́мит спи́ну, my back aches; I have a pain in my back. —ломи́ться, *refl.* 1, *obs.* to break; snap. 2, (*with* от) to be loaded (with); be crammed (with). 3, (*with* в + *acc.*) *colloq.* to break through; force one's way into. 4, *in* ломи́ться в откры́тую дверь, to belabor the obvious.

ло́мка *n.* breaking; breakup.

ло́мкий *adj.* fragile; brittle. —ло́мкость, *n.f.* fragility.

ломови́к [*gen.* -вика́] *n., colloq.* carter.

ломово́й *adj.* dray (*attrib.*): ломова́я ло́шадь, dray horse. —*n.* [*also,* ломово́й изво́зчик] carter.

ломоно́с *n.* clematis.

ломо́та *n.* dull ache (*in the joints, muscles, etc.*).

ломо́ть [*gen.* ломтя́] *n.m.* hunk; chunk (*of bread, meat, etc.*).

ло́мтик *n.* slice (*of bread*).

лонжеро́н *n., aero.* spar.

ло́но *n., poetic* bosom. —на ло́не приро́ды, in the lap of nature.

ло́пасть [*pl.* ло́пасти, -сте́й, -стя́м] *n.f.* blade (*of an oar, propeller, etc.*).

лопа́та *n.* shovel; spade.

лопа́тка [*gen. pl.* -ток] *n.* 1, small shovel; trowel. 2, blade. 3, shoulder blade. 4, chuck (*cut of beef*). —бежа́ть во все лопа́тки, *colloq.* to run for all one is worth. —положи́ть на о́бе лопа́тки, 1, *wrestling* to pin down. 2, *fig.* to beat; get the best (*or* better) of.

лопа́ть *v.impfv.* [*pfv.* сло́пать] *colloq.* to eat; gobble.

ло́паться *v.r.impfv.* [*pfv.* ло́пнуть] 1, to burst; break; snap. 2, (*of one's patience*) to be at an end. 3, *colloq.* to fail; go broke. —ло́паться от за́висти, *colloq.* to be green with envy.

лопота́ть *v.impfv.* [*pres.* **лопочу́, лопо́чешь**] *colloq.* to mumble; mutter.

лопоу́хий *adj.* lop-eared.

лопу́х [*gen.* **-пуха́**] *n.* burdock.

лорд *n.* lord. —**пала́та ло́рдов,** House of Lords.

лорне́т *n.* lorgnette.

лоси́на *n.* **1,** elk skin. **2,** elk meat. **3,** *pl.* buckskin breeches.

лоси́ный *adj.* **1,** elk (*attrib.*); elk's. **2,** made of elk skin.

лоск *n.* **1,** luster; gloss; sheen. **2,** *fig.* polish; refinement.

лоску́т [*gen.* **-кута́;** *pl.* **-куты́, -куто́в** *or* **-ку́тья, -ку́тьев**] *n.* shred; scrap of cloth.

лоску́тный *adj.* made of patches; patchwork (*attrib.*): лоску́тное одея́ло, patchwork quilt.

лосни́ться *v.r.impfv.* to be glossy; shine.

лосня́щийся *adj.* (*of cloth*) shiny (*from long wear*).

лососёвый *adj.* salmon (*attrib.*).

лососи́на *n.* salmon (*prepared as food*).

лосо́сь *also,* **ло́сось** *n.m.* salmon.

лось [*pl.* **ло́си, лосе́й, лося́м**] *n.m.* elk; moose.

лосьо́н *n.* skin lotion.

лот *n.* **1,** *naut.* plumb line. **2,** old Russian unit of weight equal to 12.8 grams (*less than half an ounce*).

лотере́я *n.* lottery; raffle. —**лотере́йный,** *adj.* lottery (*attrib.*).

лото́ *n. indecl.* lotto; bingo.

лото́к [*gen.* **лотка́**] *n.* **1,** tray (*of a street peddler*). **2,** chute. Ме́льничный лото́к, millrace. —**торгова́ть с лотка́,** to peddle one's wares.

ло́тос *n.* lotus.

лото́чник *n.* street vendor.

лоха́нь *n.f.* washtub. *Also,* **лоха́нка.**

лохма́тый *adj.* **1,** shaggy. **2,** disheveled.

лохмо́тья [*gen.* **-тьев**] *n.pl.* tatters.

ло́ция *n.* book of navigational information for a certain body of water.

ло́цман *n.* **1,** harbor pilot. **2,** pilot fish.

лошади́ный *adj.* horse (*attrib.*). —**лошади́ная си́ла,** horsepower.

лоша́дка [*gen. pl.* **-док**] *n., dim. of* **ло́шадь.**

ло́шадь [*pl.* **ло́шади, -де́й, -дя́м, -дьми́, -дя́х**] *n.f.* horse.

лоша́к [*gen.* **-шака́**] *n.* hinny.

лощёный *adj.* **1,** glossy. **2,** *fig.* polished.

лощи́на *n.* hollow; glen; dell.

лощи́ть *v.impfv.* [*pfv.* **налощи́ть**] to buff; polish.

лоя́льный *adj.* loyal. —**лоя́льность,** *n.f.* loyalty.

луб *n.* bast.

лубо́к [*gen.* **лубка́**] *n.* **1,** strip of bast. **2,** splint. **3,** print; wood block; woodcut.

лубяно́й *adj.* bast (*attrib.*).

луг [*2nd loc.* **лугу́;** *pl.* **луга́**] *n.* meadow.

лугови́на *n., colloq.* small meadow.

лугово́й *adj.* meadow (*attrib.*).

луди́льщик *n.* tinsmith.

луди́ть *v.impfv.* [*pfv.* **полуди́ть;** *pres.* **лужу́, лу́дишь** *or* **луди́шь**] to tin; tin-plate.

лу́жа *n.* puddle. —**сесть в лу́жу,** *colloq.* to make a fool of oneself; put one's foot in it.

лужа́йка [*gen. pl.* **-жа́ек**] *n.* **1,** lawn. **2,** clearing (*in the woods*); glade.

лужёный *adj.* tin-plated.

лу́жица *n., dim. of* **лу́жа.**

лужо́к [*gen.* **лужка́**] *n., dim. of* **луг.**

лу́за *n.* pocket (*of a billiard table*). —**лу́зный,** *adj., in* лу́зный билья́рд, pocket billiards.

луизиа́нский мох Spanish moss.

лук *n.* **1,** onions. **2,** bow (*for shooting arrows*).

лука́ [*pl.* **лу́ки**] *n.* **1,** bend (*in a road or river*). **2,** pommel (*of a saddle*).

лука́вить *v.impfv.* [*pres.* **-влю, -вишь**] to dissemble.

лука́вство *n.* trickery; guile.

лука́вый *adj.* crafty; cunning.

лу́ковица *n.* **1,** an onion. **2,** *bot.* bulb. **3,** onion dome (*of a Russian church*). —**лу́ковичный,** *adj.* bulbous.

лу́ковый *adj.* onion (*attrib.*).

луко́шко [*pl.* **-шки, -шек**] *n.* basket.

лук-поре́й *n.* leek.

луна́ [*pl.* **лу́ны**] *n.* moon.

лу́на-па́рк *n.* amusement park.

луна́-ры́ба *n.* sunfish.

лунати́зм *n.* sleepwalking; somnambulism. —**луна́тик,** *n.* sleepwalker; somnambulist.

лу́нка [*gen. pl.* **лу́нок**] *n.* **1,** small hole. **2,** alveolus.

лу́нный *adj.* **1,** moon (*attrib.*); lunar. **2,** moonlit. —**лу́нный ка́мень,** moonstone.

лунь [*gen.* **луня́**] *n.m.* harrier (*bird*). —**седо́й** *or* **бе́лый как лунь,** his/her hair is completely white.

лу́па *n.* magnifying glass.

лупи́ть *v.impfv.* [*pres.* **луплю́, лу́пишь**] *colloq.* **1,** [*pfv.* **облупи́ть**] to peel off the skin or bark from; shell (an egg). **2,** [*pfv.* **слупи́ть**] to peel off; strip off (skin, bark, etc.). **3,** [*pfv.* **слупи́ть**] to charge (an exorbitant price) **4,** [*pfv.* **отлупи́ть**] to beat; thrash. **5,** *in* лупи́ть глаза́ на (+ *acc.*), to stare wide-eyed at. —**лупи́ться,** *refl.* [*pfv.* **облупи́ться**] *colloq.* **1,** to peel off; come off. **2,** (*of one's face*) to peel.

луфа́рь [*gen.* **-фаря́**] *n.m.* bluefish.

луч [*gen.* **луча́**] *n.* **1,** ray; beam. Луч луны́, moonbeam. Рентге́новы лучи́, X-rays. **2,** *fig.* ray (*e.g. of hope*).

лучево́й *adj.* radial. —**лучева́я боле́знь,** radiation sickness. —**лучева́я терапи́я,** radiation therapy.

лучеза́рный *adj.* radiant; effulgent.

лучеиспуска́ние *n.* radiation.

лучи́на *n.* thin stick; sliver (*of kindling wood*).

лучи́стый *adj.* radiant.

лучи́ться *v.r.impfv.* **1,** to shine; sparkle. **2,** *fig.* (*with instr.*) to radiate.

лучко́вый *adj., in* лучко́вая пила́, whipsaw.

лу́чник *n.* archer.

лу́чше *adj. & adv., comp. of* **хоро́ший** *and* **хорошо́,** better. —**лу́чше всего́,** best of all. —**тем лу́чше,** so much the better.

лу́чшее *n., decl. as an adj.* something better: Я ожида́л лу́чшего, I expected something better. —**жела́ю вам (са́мого) лу́чшего,** I wish you all the best. —**оставля́ть жела́ть мно́го лу́чшего,** to leave much to be desired. —**переме́на к лу́чшему,** change for the better.

лу́чший *adj., used only as a modifier, comp. and superl. of* **хоро́ший, 1,** (a) better: лу́чший спо́соб, a better method. **2,** [*also,* **са́мый лу́чший**] (the) best. **—в лу́чшем слу́чае,** at best. **—измени́ться в лу́чшую сто́рону,** to change for the better.

лущёный *adj.* hulled; shelled.

лущи́ть *v.impfv.* [*pfv.* **облущи́ть**] to shell; husk; hull.

лы́жа *n.* ski. Ходи́ть на лы́жах, to ski. **—лы́жник,** *n.* skier. **—лы́жный,** *adj.* ski (*attrib.*); skiing (*attrib.*).

лыжня́ [*gen. pl.* **лыжне́й**] *n.* track left by skis.

лы́ко *n.* bast. **—не лы́ком шит,** *colloq.* no slouch.

лы́ковый *adj.* made of bast.

лысе́ть *v.impfv.* [*pfv.* **облысе́ть** *or* **полысе́ть**] to become bald.

лы́сина *n.* bald spot.

лысу́ха *n.* coot.

лы́сый *adj.* bald.

ль *conj.* = ли.

львёнок [*gen.* **-нка;** *pl.* **льва́та; львя́т**] *n.* lion cub.

льви́ный *adj.* lion's. **—льви́ная до́ля,** the lion's share. **—льви́ный зев; льви́ная пасть,** snapdragon.

льви́ца *n.* lioness.

льго́та *n.* privilege; benefit; perquisite.

льго́тный *adj.* **1,** favorable; preferential: на льго́тных усло́виях, on favorable terms. **2,** (*of a price, fare, etc.*) reduced; (*of a ticket*) cut-rate. **—льго́тный срок,** grace period. Три́дцать льго́тных дней, 30-day grace period.

льди́на *n.* block of ice. **—плаву́чая льди́на,** ice field.

льнуть *v.impfv.* [*pfv.* **прильну́ть**] (*with* **к**) **1,** to stick (to); cling (to). **2,** [*impfv. only*] *fig.* to feel drawn toward. **3,** [*impfv. only*] *fig.* to play up to; cultivate.

льняно́й *adj.* **1,** flax (*attrib.*). **2,** linen (*attrib.*). **3,** (*of hair*) flaxen. **—льняно́е ма́сло,** linseed oil.

льстец [*gen.* **льстеца́**] *n.* flatterer.

льсти́вый *adj.* flattering; ingratiating.

льсти́ть *v.impfv.* [*pfv.* **польсти́ть;** *pres.* **льщу, льсти́шь**] (*with dat.*) to flatter.

любвеоби́льный *adj.* loving; full of love.

любе́зничать *v.impfv.* (*with* **с** + *instr.*) *colloq.* to exchange pleasantries with; say nice things to.

любе́зно *adv.* kindly; graciously. **—***adj., used predicatively,* kind; gracious: о́чень любе́зно с ва́шей стороны́, very kind/gracious of you.

любе́зность *n.f.* **1,** courtesy; graciousness. **2,** *pl.* kind words; compliments. **3,** favor; kindness; good turn. **—не откажи́те в любе́зности (и)** (+ *imperative*), would you be so kind as to...

любе́зный *adj.* [*short form* **-зен, -зна**] kind; gracious. **—бу́дьте любе́зны** (+ *imperative*), be so kind as to...

люби́мец [*gen.* **-мца**] *n.m.* [*fem.* **-мица**] favorite; pet.

люби́мчик *n., colloq.* favorite; pet.

люби́мый *adj.* **1,** favorite; pet. **2,** beloved. **—***n.* darling; beloved.

люби́тель *n.m.* **1,** lover: люби́тель му́зыки, lover of music. **2,** amateur; dilettante. **—люби́тельский,** *adj.* amateur.

люби́ть *v.impfv.* [*pres.* **люблю́, лю́бишь**] **1,** to love. **2,** to like; be fond of.

лю́бо *predicate, used with inf., colloq.* it is a pleasure (to).

любова́ться *v.r.impfv.* [*pfv.* **полюбова́ться;** *pres.* **-бу́юсь, -бу́ешься**] (*with instr. or* **на** + *acc.*) to admire; watch with pleasure.

любо́вник *n.* lover; paramour.

любо́вница *n.* lover; mistress.

любо́вный *adj.* **1,** love (*attrib.*). **2,** loving; tender. **3,** amorous. **—любо́вно,** *adv.* lovingly.

любо́вь [*gen., dat. & prep.* **любви́;** *instr.* **любо́вью**] *n.f.* love.

любозна́тельный *adj.* curious; inquisitive; thirsty for knowledge. **—любозна́тельность,** *n.f.* (intellectual) curiosity; inquisitiveness.

любо́й *adj.* **1,** any: в любо́е вре́мя, (at) any time; любо́й цено́й, at any price. **2,** either: в любо́м слу́чае, in either case; either way. **—***n.* **1,** anyone; anybody. **2,** either one.

любопы́тно *adv.* curiously; with curiosity. **—***adj., used predicatively,* curious: Мне любопы́тно знать, куда́ они́ пое́хали, I am curious to know where they went.

любопы́тный *adj.* curious. **—любопы́тство,** *n.* curiosity.

любопы́тствовать *v.impfv.* [*pfv.* **полюбопы́тствовать;** *pres.* **-ствую, -ствуешь**] to be curious.

лю́бящий *adj.* loving.

люд *n., colloq.* people.

лю́ди [*gen.* **люде́й;** *dat.* **лю́дям;** *instr.* **людьми́;** *prepl.* **лю́дях**] *n.pl.* people. **—вы́вести в лю́ди,** to put (someone) on his feet. **—вы́йти** *or* **выбиться в лю́ди,** to be successful in life. **—на лю́дях; на́ люди,** in public. **—пойти́** *or* **уйти́ в лю́ди,** to start out in life; go out and earn a living.

лю́дный *adj.* **1,** populous. **2,** crowded.

людое́д *n.* cannibal. **—людое́дский,** *adj.* cannibalistic. **—людое́дство,** *n.* cannibalism.

людска́я *n., decl. as an adj.* servants' quarters.

людско́й *adj.* human.

люк *n.* hatch; manhole; trap door. **—светово́й люк,** skylight.

люкс *adj. indecl.* de luxe: гости́ница-люкс, de luxe hotel.

лю́лька [*gen. pl.* **лю́лек**] *n.* cradle.

люмба́го *n. indecl.* lumbago.

люмина́л *n.* phenobarbital.

люминесце́нтный *adj.* luminescent. **—люминесце́нтная ла́мпа,** fluorescent lamp.

люминесце́нция *n.* luminescence.

лю́стра *n.* chandelier.

лютера́нин [*pl.* **-ра́не, -ра́н**] *n.m.* [*fem.* **-ра́нка**] Lutheran. **—лютера́нский,** *adj.* Lutheran. **—лютера́нство,** *n.* Lutheranism.

люте́ций (тэ) *n.* lutetium.

лю́тик *n.* buttercup.

лю́тня [*gen. pl.* **лю́тен**] *n.* lute.

лю́тость *n.f.* ferocity.

лю́тый *adj.* **1,** fierce; ferocious. **2,** (*of cold, hatred, etc.*) bitter. **3,** (*of pain*) excruciating.

люце́рна *n.* alfalfa.

ля *n.neut., music* la; A.

ляга́ть *v.impfv.* [*pfv.* **лягну́ть**] (*of a horse*) to kick. *Also,* **ляга́ться,** *refl.* [*impfv. only*].

лягу́шечий *also,* **лягуша́чий** [*fem.* **-чья**] *adj.* frog's; frogs'.

лягу́шка [*gen. pl.* **-шек**] *n.* frog.

ля́жка [*gen. pl.* **ля́жек**] *n., colloq.* thigh; haunch.

лязг *n.* clang; clank.

ля́згать *v.impfv.* [*pfv.* **ля́згнуть**] **1**, to clang; clank; make a clanking sound. **2**, (*with instr.*) to rattle; clank.

лякро́сс *n.* lacrosse.

ля́мка [*gen. pl.* **ля́мок**] *n.* shoulder strap. —**тяну́ть ля́мку**, *colloq.* to slave; toil.

ля́пис *n.* silver nitrate.

ля́пис-лазу́рь *n.f.* lapis lazuli.

ля́пнуть *v.pfv., colloq.* to blurt out.

ля́псус *n.* blunder.

M

M, м *n.neut.* thirteenth letter of the Russian alphabet.

мавзоле́й *n.* mausoleum.

мавр *n.* Moor. —**маврита́нский,** *adj.* Moorish.

маг *n.* magician; wizard.

магази́н *n.* **1**, store; shop. **2**, magazine (*of a firearm, camera, etc.*).

магази́нный *adj.* **1**, store (*attrib.*); shop (*attrib.*). **2**, (*of a firearm*) repeating: магази́нная винто́вка, repeating rifle. —**магази́нный вор,** shoplifter.

магара́джа *n.m.* maharajah.

маги́стр *n.* **1**, holder of a master's degree. **2**, master's degree. **3**, grandmaster (*of a monastic or knightly order*).

магистра́ль *n.f.* **1**, highway; thoroughfare. **2**, *R.R.* main line. **3**, main: га́зовая магистра́ль, gas main. —**магистра́льный,** *adj.* main; arterial.

магистра́т *n.* city council. —**магистрату́ра,** *n.* magistracy.

маги́ческий *adj.* magic; magical.

ма́гия *n.* magic.

магна́т *n.* magnate; tycoon.

магне́зия *n.* magnesia.

магнети́зм *n.* **1**, magnetism. **2**, magnetics.

магнети́т *n.* magnetite.

магнети́ческий *adj.* magnetic.

магне́то *n. indecl.* magneto.

магнетро́н *n.* magnetron.

ма́гниевый *adj.* magnesium (*attrib.*).

ма́гний *n.* magnesium.

магни́т *n.* magnet. —**магни́тный,** *adj.* magnetic.

магнитофо́н *n.* tape recorder. —**магнитофо́нный,** *adj.* of a tape recorder: магнитофо́нная за́пись, tape recording.

магно́лия *n.* magnolia.

магомета́нин [*pl.* **-та́не, -та́н**] *n.m.* [*fem.* **-та́нка**] Mohammedan. —**магомета́нский,** *adj.* Mohammedan. —**магомета́нство,** *n.* Mohammedanism.

мада́м *n.f. indecl.* madam.

мадемуазе́ль (дмуазэ́) *n.f. indecl.* mademoiselle.

маде́ра *n.* Madeira wine.

мадо́нна *n.* madonna.

мадрига́л *n.* madrigal.

мадья́р *n.m.* [*fem.* **-ка**] Magyar. —**мадья́рский,** *adj.* Magyar.

маёвка [*gen. pl.* **-вок**] *n.* **1**, illegal May-day meeting (*in pre-rev. Russia*). **2**, spring outing; picnic.

мажо́р *n.* **1**, *music* major key: тона́льность до мажо́р, key of C major. **2**, *colloq.* good spirits; high spirits.

мажордо́м *n.* majordomo.

мажо́рный *adj.* **1**, *music* major. **2**, *fig., colloq.* buoyant; exuberant.

ма́занка [*gen. pl.* **-нок**] *n.* clay-walled hut.

ма́зать *v.impfv.* [*pres.* **ма́жу, ма́жешь**] **1**, [*pfv.* **нама́зать** *or* **пома́зать**] (*with instr.*) to smear (with): ма́зать хлеб ма́слом, to smear butter on bread; butter one's bread. **2**, [*pfv.* **вы́мазать**] (*with instr.*) to coat (with): ма́зать сте́ны кра́ской, to paint the walls. **3**, [*pfv.* **нама́зать**] *colloq.* to paint (one's lips); put make-up on (one's face). **4**, [*pfv.* **вы́мазать**] *colloq.* to soil. **5**, [*pfv.* **нама́зать**] *colloq.* to paint poorly; daub. **6**, [*pfv.* **прома́зать**] *colloq.* to miss (*in shooting or games*). —**одни́м ми́ром ма́заны**, alike; one and the same.

ма́заться *v.r.impfv.* [*pres.* **ма́жусь, ма́жешься**] **1**, [*pfv.* **нама́заться**] to put on make-up; (*with instr.*) to put on (salve, make-up, etc.). **2**, [*pfv.* **вы́мазаться**] *colloq.* to soil; become soiled; get dirty.

мазня́ *n., colloq.* poor painting.

мазо́к [*gen.* **мазка́**] *n.* **1**, dab; stroke (*with a paintbrush*). **2**, *med.* smear.

мазохи́зм *n.* masochism. —**мазохи́ст,** *n.* masochist. —**мазохи́стский,** *adj.* masochistic.

мазу́рка *n.* mazurka.

мазу́т *n.* fuel oil.

мазь *n.f.* **1**, ointment; salve. **2**, grease. **3**, *in* сапо́жная мазь, shoe polish. —**де́ло на мази́,** *colloq.* things are moving right along.

маи́с *n.* maize.

май *n.* May.

ма́йка [*gen. pl.* **ма́ек**] *n.* T-shirt.

майонéз *n.* mayonnaise.

майóр *n.* major.

майорáн *n.* marjoram.

майóрский *adj.* major's.

мáйский *adj.* May (*attrib.*).

мак *n.* **1,** poppy. **2,** poppy seeds.

макáка *n.* macaque.

макарóны [*gen.* -рóн] *n.pl.* macaroni.

макáть *v.impfv.* [*pfv.* макнýть] to dip; dunk.

македóнский *adj.* Macedonian.

макéт *n.* **1,** model; mock-up. **2,** *printing* dummy.

макиавéллевский *adj.* Machiavellian.

макинтóш *n.* mackintosh.

мáклер *n.* stockbroker. —мáклерский, *adj.* of a broker; brokerage (*attrib.*). —мáклерство, *n.* brokerage.

макнýть *v.*, *pfv. of* макáть.

мáковка [*gen. pl.* -вок] *n.* **1,** poppy head. **2,** dome; cupola (*of a church*). **3,** *colloq.* top.

мáковый *adj.* poppy (*attrib.*).

макрéль *n.f.* mackerel.

макрокóсм *n.* macrocosm.

максимáльный *adj.* maximum. —максимáльно, *adv.* to the maximum.

мáксимум *n.* maximum. —*adv.* a maximum of; at (the) most.

макулатýра *n.* **1,** pages spoiled in printing. **2,** literary trash.

макýшка [*gen. pl.* -шек] *n.* **1,** top. **2,** crown of the head.

малáга *n.* Malaga wine.

малáец [*gen.* -áйца] *n.m.* [*fem.* -áйка] Malay. —малáйский, *adj.* Malay.

малахи́т *n.* malachite. —малахи́товый, *adj.* malachite.

малевáть *v.impfv.* [*pfv.* намалевáть; *pres.* -люю, -люешь] *colloq.* to paint.

малéйший *adj.*, *superl. of* мáлый, the least; the slightest; the faintest. —ни в малéйшей стéпени, not in the least.

малёк [*gen.* -лькá] *n.* young fish; newly-hatched fish.

мáленький *adj.* [*comp.* мéньше] little; small. —*n.* the little one; the baby. *See also* мéньше.

малéнько *adv.*, *colloq.* a little; a bit; somewhat.

мали́на *n.* **1,** raspberries. **2,** a (single) raspberry.

мали́новка [*gen. pl.* -вок] *n.* robin (redbreast).

мали́новый *adj.* **1,** raspberry (*attrib.*). **2,** crimson.

мáло *adv.* **1,** little; not much: мáло сдéлать, to do little; not do much; мáло врéмени, little time; not much time. **2,** few; not many: мáло нарóду, few people; not many people. **3,** hardly: мáло кто, hardly anyone; мáло что, hardly anything. **4,** (*with* ли) many; lots of; all kinds of: мáло ли что, all kinds of things; anything. Да мáло ли что ещё?, and goodness knows what else! —мáло (ли) что (+ *past tense verb*), what of it!; what if I (you, etc.) did...? —мáло тогó, moreover. —мáло тогó, что..., not only...; it is not enough that... —этого мáло, that's only a small part of it. *See also* мáлый.

маловáжный *adj.* of little importance; of little significance.

маловáто *adv.*, *colloq.* not quite enough.

маловéр *n.* skeptic.

маловероя́тный *adj.* not likely; unlikely; improbable. —маловероя́тность, *n.f.* improbability.

маловóдный *adj.* **1,** shallow. **2,** arid.

маловóдье *n.* **1,** shortage of water. **2,** low level of water (*in a river, lake, etc.*).

малогабари́тный *adj.* small-size; compact.

малогрáмотный *adj.* semiliterate.

малодостýпный *adj.* **1,** inaccessible. **2,** *fig.* esoteric.

малодýшие *n.* faintheartedness; cowardice. —малодýшный, *adj.* fainthearted; craven; cowardly.

малозамéтный *adj.* **1,** hardly noticeable. **2,** ordinary; undistinguished.

малознакóмый *adj.* unfamiliar.

малоизвéстный *adj.* little-known.

малоимýщий *adj.* poor; underprivileged.

малоинтерéсный *adj.* of little interest; uninteresting.

малокали́берный *adj.* (*of a firearm*) small-caliber; small-bore.

малокрóвие *n.* anemia. —малокрóвный, *adj.* anemic.

малолéтний *adj.* underage; juvenile. —*n.* juvenile. —малолéтство, *n.* childhood.

малолитрáжный *adj.* (*of a car*) fuel-efficient.

малолю́дный *adj.* **1,** sparsely populated. **2,** with few people to be seen. **3,** (*of a meeting*) poorly attended.

мало-мáльски *adv.*, *colloq.* the least bit; the slightest bit: Кáждый, кто мало-мáльски знакóм с..., anyone who is the least acquainted with...

маломóщный *adj.* not powerful; low-powered.

малонадёжный *adj.* not very reliable.

малонаселённый *adj.* sparsely populated.

мáло-помáлу *adv.*, *colloq.* little by little; bit by bit.

малопоня́тный *adj.* difficult to understand.

малоприбыльный *adj.* showing little profit.

малорáзвитый *adj.* **1,** undeveloped; underdeveloped. **2,** limited (*in intellect*).

малорóслый *adj.* undersized.

малосвéдущий *adj.* poorly informed.

малосемéйный *adj.* having a small family.

малоси́льный *adj.* **1,** weak. **2,** low-powered.

малосодержáтельный *adj.* containing little of interest; lacking substance.

малосóльный *adj.* lightly salted.

мáлость *n.f.* **1,** *obs.* small size. **2,** tiny bit. **3,** *colloq.* trifle. —*adv.*, *colloq.* a little; a bit.

малотирáжный *adj.* **1,** having a small circulation. **2,** (*of an edition*) limited.

малоупотреби́тельный *adj.* little used; rarely used.

малоцéнный *adj.* of little value.

малочи́сленный *adj.* small in number; not numerous. —малочи́сленность, *n.f.* small number.

мáлый *adj.* **1,** small. **2,** [*short form only* — мал, малá, мало́, малы́] (too) small: Боти́нки мне малы́, the shoes are too small on me. —*n.* **1,** *colloq.* fellow; chap; guy: дóбрый мáлый, a decent fellow. **2,** *neut.* little: довóльствоваться мáлым, to be satisfied with little. **3,** *pl.* little ones; children. —без мáла; без мáлого, *colloq.* almost; nearly. —за мáлым дéло стáло; дéло остаётся за мáлым, only one small matter is holding things up. —от мáла до велика, young and old alike. —са́мое ма́лое, **1,** the least. **2,** at (the) least. —с ма́лых лет, since childhood.

малы́ш [*gen.* **малыша́**] *n.* small child; tot.

ма́льва *n.* mallow.

мальто́за *n.* maltose.

ма́льчик *n.* boy.

мальчи́шеский *adj.* **1,** boy's. **2,** childish. —**мальчи́шество,** *n.* childish behavior.

мальчи́шка [*gen. pl.* **-шек**] *n.m., colloq.* (little) boy.

мальчуга́н *n., colloq.* little boy; little fellow.

малю́сенький *adj., colloq.* tiny; wee; minuscule.

малю́тка [*gen. pl.* **-ток**] *n.m. & f.* little one.

маля́р [*gen.* **маляра́**] *n.* house painter.

маляри́йный *adj.* malarial.

маля́рия *n.* malaria.

маля́рный *adj.* painting (*attrib.*); paint (*attrib.*). —**маля́рная кисть,** paintbrush. —**маля́рный цех,** paint shop (*in a factory*).

ма́ма *n.* mama; mommy.

мамалы́га *n.* hominy.

мама́ша *n., colloq.* = **ма́ма.**

ма́менька *n., obs.* = **ма́ма.**

ма́менькин *adj., colloq.* mother's. —**ма́менькин сыно́к,** mother's boy; mama's boy.

ма́мин *adj.* mother's.

ма́монт *n.* mammoth.

ма́мочка *n.* mother dear.

мана́тки [*gen.* **-ток**] *n.pl., colloq.* (one's) things; belongings.

мангани́т *n.* manganite.

ма́нго *n. indecl.* **1,** mango. **2,** mango tree.

мангу́ста *n.* mongoose.

мандари́н *n.* **1,** tangerine; mandarin. **2,** mandarin (*Chinese official*). —**мандари́нный; мандари́новый,** *adj.* tangerine (*attrib.*). —**мандари́нский,** Mandarin: мандари́нский язы́к, Mandarin.

манда́т *n.* **1,** mandate. **2,** warrant.

манда́тный *adj.* mandate (*attrib.*); mandated. —**манда́тная коми́ссия,** credentials committee.

мандоли́на *n.* mandolin.

мандраго́ра *n.* mandrake.

мандри́л *n.* mandrill.

манёвр *n.* **1,** maneuver. **2,** *pl., mil.* maneuvers: быть на манёврах, to be on maneuvers.

манёвренность *n.f.* **1,** *mil.* mobility; **2,** maneuverability.

манёвренный *adj.* **1,** *mil.* mobile: манёвренная война́, mobile warfare. **2,** maneuverable.

маневри́ровать *v.impfv.* [*pres.* **-рую, -руешь**] **1,** to maneuver. **2,** *fig.* (*with instr.*) to manipulate.

мане́ж *n.* **1,** riding academy; riding school. **2,** circus arena; ring. **3,** playpen.

манеке́н *n.* mannequin; dummy.

манеке́нщик *n.m.* [*fem.* **-щица**] model.

мане́р *n., colloq.* manner; way. Ка́ждый на свой мане́р, each in his own way. —**на мане́р** (+ *gen.*), in the manner of. На ру́сский мане́р, in the Russian manner; Russian-style.

мане́ра *n.* **1,** manner. **2,** *pl.* manners.

мане́рный *adj.* affected; mannered. —**мане́рность,** *n.f.* affectation.

манже́та *n.* cuff.

маниака́льный *adj.* maniacal; manic. —**маниака́льно-депресси́вный,** *adj.* manic-depressive.

маникю́р *n.* manicure. —**маникю́рный,** *adj.* manicure (*attrib.*). —**маникю́рша,** *n.* manicurist.

манио́ка *n.* manioc; cassava.

манипули́ровать *v.impfv.* [*pres.* **-рую, -руешь**] (*with instr.*) to manipulate.

манипуля́тор *n.* manipulator.

манипуля́ция *n.* manipulation.

мани́ть *v.impfv.* [*pfv.* **помани́ть;** *pres.* **маню́, ма́нишь**] **1,** to beckon. **2,** *fig.* to draw; attract: Его́ ма́нит мо́ре, he feels drawn to the sea.

манифе́ст *n.* manifesto.

манифеста́ция *n.* demonstration; march.

мани́шка [*gen. pl.* **-шек**] *n.* shirt front; dickey.

ма́ния *n.* mania. —**ма́ния вели́чия,** delusions of grandeur; megalomania. —**ма́ния пресле́дования,** persecution complex.

манки́ровать *v.impfv. & pfv.* [*pres.* **-рую, -руешь**] **1,** (*with instr.*) to neglect. **2,** *obs.* to be absent.

ма́нна *n.* manna.

ма́нный *adj.* **1,** *in* **ма́нная крупа́,** farina. **2,** *in* **ма́нная ка́ша,** cereal made from farina.

манове́ние *n., obs.* wave (*of the hand*); nod (*of the head*). —**как по манове́нию волше́бного жезла́,** instantly; as if by magic.

мано́метр *n.* pressure gauge; manometer. —**манометри́ческий,** *adj.* manometric.

манса́рда *n.* garret.

манса́рдный *adj.* of a garret; garret (*attrib.*). —**манса́рдная кры́ша,** mansard roof.

манти́лья *n.* mantilla.

ма́нтия *n.* mantle; cloak; robe; gown.

манто́ *n. indecl.* (woman's) fur coat.

мануфакту́ра *n.* **1,** *hist.* manufacturing. **2,** *obs.* textile mill. **3,** textiles; soft goods.

мануфакту́рный *adj.* **1,** manufacturing (*attrib.*). **2,** textile (*attrib.*); soft-goods (*attrib.*).

маньчжу́р *n.* Manchu. —**маньчжу́рский,** *adj.* Manchu.

манья́к *n.* maniac.

маня́щий *adj.* alluring.

ма́ори *n.m. & f. indecl.* Maori.

марабу́ *n.m. indecl.* marabou.

мара́зм *n.* marasmus. —**ста́рческий мара́зм,** senility.

мара́л *n.* a variety of red deer; maral.

мара́нье *n., colloq.* **1,** soiling. **2,** scribble; scrawl.

мараски́н *n.* maraschino.

мара́ть *v.impfv., colloq.* **1,** [*pfv.* **замара́ть**] to soil; dirty. **2,** [*pfv.* **намара́ть**] to scribble. **3,** [*pfv.* **вы́марать**] to cross out. —**мара́ться,** *refl.* [*pfv.* **замара́ться**] *colloq.* to get oneself dirty.

марафо́нский *adj., in* **марафо́нский бег,** marathon (race).

ма́рганец [*gen.* **-нца**] *n.* manganese. —**ма́рганцевый,** *adj.* manganese (*attrib.*).

маргари́н *n.* margarine.

маргари́тка [*gen. pl.* **-ток**] *n.* daisy; English daisy.

маргина́лии *n.pl.* [*sing.* **маргина́лия**] marginalia.

ма́рево *n.* **1,** mirage. **2,** haze.

маре́на *n.* madder (*plant*).

мари́ец [*gen.* **-и́йца**] *n.m.* [*fem.* **-и́йка**] Mari (*one of a people inhabiting central European Russia*). —**мари́йский,** *adj.* Mari.

мари́на *n.* seascape.

марина́д *n.* marinade.

марини́ст *n.* painter of seascapes.

марино́ванный *adj.* pickled; marinated.

маринова́ть *v.impfv.* [*pfv.* **замаринова́ть;** *pres.* **-ну́ю, -ну́ешь**] **1,** to pickle; marinate. **2,** *colloq.* to delay; shelve; put off.

марионе́тка [*gen. pl.* **-ток**] *n.* **1,** puppet; marionette. **2,** *fig.* puppet. —**марионе́точный,** *adj., fig.* puppet (*attrib.*): марионе́точное прави́тельство, puppet government.

марихуа́на *n.* marijuana.

ма́рка [*gen. pl.* **ма́рок**] *n.* **1,** (postage) stamp. **2,** make; model; brand. **3,** mark: фабри́чная ма́рка, trademark. **4,** counter; token (*used as payment*). **5,** chip (*used in games*). **6,** mark (*German monetary unit*). **7,** *fig.* reputation: держа́ть ма́рку, to uphold one's reputation. —**вы́сшей ма́рки, 1,** of the highest quality. **2,** (*of a type of person*) of the worst type. —**под ма́ркой** (+ *gen.*), under the guise of.

марки́з *n.* marquis.

марки́за *n.* **1,** marquise; marchioness. **2,** sun blind.

ма́ркий *adj.* [*short form masc.* **ма́рок**] that soils easily.

маркирова́ть *v.impfv. & pfv.* [*pres.* **-ру́ю, -ру́ешь**] to mark.

маркси́зм *n.* Marxism. —**маркси́ст,** *n.* Marxist. —**маркси́стский,** *adj.* Marxist; Marxian.

ма́рля *n.* **1,** gauze. **2,** cheesecloth. —**ма́рлевый,** *adj.* gauze (*attrib.*).

мармела́д *n.* fruit jellies (*candy*).

мароде́р *n.* **1,** marauder. **2,** *colloq.* profiteer. —**мароде́рский,** *adj.* marauding. —**мароде́рство,** *n.* marauding.

мароде́рствовать *v.impfv.* [*pres.* **-ствую, -ствуешь**] to maraud.

ма́рочный *adj., in* **ма́рочные ви́на,** fine wines; vintage wines.

Марс *n.* Mars.

марса́ла *n.* Marsala wine.

ма́рсель *n.m.* topsail.

Марсельє́за *n.* Marseillaise.

марсиа́нин [*pl.* **-а́не, -а́н**] *n.* Martian. —**марсиа́нский,** *adj.* Martian.

март *n.* March (*month*).

марте́н (тэ) *n.* open-hearth furnace. —**марте́новский,** *adj.* open-hearth (*attrib.*): марте́новская печь, open-hearth furnace.

ма́ртовский *adj.* March (*attrib.*).

марты́шка [*gen. pl.* **-шек**] *n.* marmoset.

марципа́н *n.* marchpane; marzipan.

марш *n.* **1,** march. **2,** flight of stairs. —*interj.* **1,** (*as a military command*) forward march! **2,** *colloq.* [*often* **марш отсю́да**] off with you!; get going!

ма́ршал *n.* marshal. —**ма́ршальский,** *adj.* marshal's.

марширова́ть *v.impfv.* [*pres.* **-ру́ю, -ру́ешь**] to march.

марширо́вка *n.* marching. —**марширо́вочный,** *adj.* marching (*attrib.*).

маршру́т *n.* route; itinerary. —**маршру́т ожида́ния,** holding pattern.

ма́ска [*gen. pl.* **ма́сок**] *n.* **1,** mask. **2,** *fig.* mask; guise.

маскара́д *n.* masquerade. —**маскара́дный,** *adj.* masquerade (*attrib.*).

маскирова́ть *v.impfv.* [*pfv.* **замаскирова́ть;** *pres.* **-ру́ю, -ру́ешь**] **1,** to disguise. **2,** *fig.* to mask; conceal. **3,** to camouflage. —**маскирова́ться,** *refl.* **1,** to put on a mask. **2,** (*with instr.*) to dress up (as); come disguised (as). **3,** to camouflage oneself.

маскиро́вка *n.* **1,** masking; disguising; camouflaging. **2,** *mil.* camouflage.

маскиро́вочный *adj.* camouflage (*attrib.*).

ма́сленица *n.* Shrovetide; Mardi gras.

маслёнка [*gen. pl.* **-нок**] *n.* **1,** butter dish. **2,** lubricator; oilcan.

маслёнок [*gen.* **-нка**] *n.* a variety of edible mushroom.

ма́сленый *adj.* **1,** buttered. **2,** oily. **3,** *fig.* unctuous.

масли́на *n.* **1,** olive. **2,** olive tree.

ма́слить *v.impfv.* [*pfv.* **нама́слить**] *colloq.* **1,** to butter. **2,** to put butter in. **3,** to grease. **4,** to put oil in; oil.

масли́чный *adj.* yielding edible oil; oil-bearing. —**масли́чное се́мя,** oilseed.

масли́чный *adj.* olive (*attrib.*).

ма́сло *n.* **1,** butter. **2,** oil. **3,** *art* oil; oils: писа́ть ма́слом, to paint in oils. —**всё идёт как по ма́слу,** everything is hunky-dory. —**подлива́ть ма́сла в ого́нь,** to add fuel to the fire.

маслобо́йка [*gen. pl.* **-бо́ек**] *n.* churn.

маслобо́йня [*gen. pl.* **-бо́ен**] *n.* creamery.

маслоде́лие *n.* butter making. —**маслоде́льный,** *adj.* butter-making.

маслозаво́д *n.* creamery

масляни́стый *adj.* oily.

ма́сляный *adj.* oil (*attrib.*); grease (*attrib.*).

масо́н *n.* Mason; Freemason. —**масо́нский,** *adj.* Masonic; Mason's; Freemason's. —**масо́нство,** *n.* Masonry; Freemasonry.

ма́сса *n.* **1,** mass. **2,** *pl.* the masses. **3,** pulp: древе́сная ма́сса, wood pulp. **4,** (*with gen.*) *colloq.* a lot (of); heaps (of). —**в (о́бщей) ма́ссе; в ма́ссе свое́й,** on the whole; for the most part. —**основна́я ма́сса** (+ *gen.*), the bulk (of).

масса́ж *n.* massage. —**массажи́ст,** *n.* masseur. —**массажи́стка,** *n.* masseuse.

масси́в *n.* **1,** mountain range. **2,** tract of land. —**жило́й** *or* **жили́щный масси́в,** housing development.

масси́вный *adj.* massive.

масси́ровать *v.impfv. & pfv.* [*pres.* **-рую, -руешь**] **1,** to massage. **2,** *mil.* to mass. —**масси́роваться,** *refl., mil.* to mass.

массо́вка [*gen. pl.* **-вок**] *n., colloq.* **1,** secret meeting. **2,** group excursion. **3,** *theat.; motion pictures* crowd scene.

ма́ссовый *adj.* **1,** mass (*attrib.*). **2,** for the masses; popular. —**ма́ссовое произво́дство,** mass production. —**ма́ссовые сре́дства информа́ции,** the (mass) media. —**ма́ссовый чита́тель,** the general reader.

мáстер [*pl.* **мастерá**] *n.* **1,** master: мáстер своегó дéла, master of one's trade; мáстер расскáза, master storyteller. **2,** craftsman; technician. Сапóжный мáстер, shoemaker; оружéйный мáстер, gunsmith; золотых дел мáстер, goldsmith. Мáстер по ремóнту (+ *gen.*), repairman (*TV, washing machine, etc.*). **3,** foreman. —**мáстер на все рýки,** jack-of-all-trades.

мастери́ть *v.impfv.* [*pfv.* **смастери́ть**] *colloq.* to make; fashion; build.

мастерóк [*gen.* **-ркá**] *n.* trowel (*used by a plasterer or bricklayer*).

мастерскáя *n., decl. as an adj.* **1,** shop; repair shop; workshop: пошивóчная мастерскáя, tailor's *or* dressmaker's shop; обувнáя мастерскáя, shoe repair shop; железнодорóжные мастерски́е, railroad workshops. **2,** shop (*in a factory*). **3,** (artist's) studio.

мастерски́ *adv.* in masterful fashion; like an expert.

мастерскóй *adj.* masterly; masterful.

мастерствó *n.* **1,** skill. **2,** handicraft; trade.

масти́ка *n.* **1,** mastic. **2,** floor polish. —**масти́ковый,** *adj.* mastic.

масти́т *n.* mastitis.

масти́тый *adj.* venerable.

мастодóнт *n.* mastodon.

мастурбáция *n.* masturbation.

мастурби́ровать *v.impfv. & pfv.* [*pres.* **-рую, -руешь**] to masturbate.

масть [*pl.* **мáсти, мастéй, мастя́м**] *n.f.* **1,** color (*of an animal*). **2,** *cards* suit. —**всех мастéй,** of every stripe. —**ходи́ть в масть,** to follow suit.

масштáб *n.* **1,** scale (*of a map*). **2,** *fig.* scale: в большóм масштáбе, on a large scale.

масштáбный *adj.* large-scale.

мат *n.* **1,** *chess* mate; checkmate. **2,** floor mat. **3,** *obs.* mat (*dull surface*). **4,** obscene language. —**кричáть благи́м мáтом,** *colloq.* to yell one's head off.

матемáтика *n.* mathematics. —**матемáтик,** *n.* mathematician. —**математи́ческий,** *adj.* mathematical.

матереуби́йство *n.* matricide.

материáл *n.* **1,** material: строи́тельные материáлы, building materials; материáл для кни́ги, material for a book. **2,** *pl.* documents; record (*of a conference, law case, etc.*). **3,** (newspaper or magazine) article. **4,** material; fabric.

материали́зм *n.* materialism.

материализовáть *v.impfv. & pfv.* [*pres.* **-зýю, -зýешь**] to give material form to. —**материализовáться,** *refl.* to assume material form.

материали́ст *n.* materialist. —**материалисти́ческий,** *adj.* materialistic.

материáльно *adv.* materially.

материáльный *adj.* **1,** material. **2,** financial: материáльные затруднéния, financial difficulties. —**материáльная часть,** matériel.

матери́к [*gen.* **-рикá**] *n.* continent; mainland.

материкóвый *adj.* continental. —**материкóвая порóда,** bedrock.

матери́нский *adj.* maternal.

матери́нство *n.* motherhood; maternity.

матéрия *n.* **1,** matter. **2,** material; fabric. **3,** *colloq.* subject; topic.

матéрный *adj., colloq.* obscene.

матéрчатый *adj.* cloth (*attrib.*); made of cloth.

матёрый *adj.* **1,** (*of an animal*) full-grown. **2,** *colloq.* experienced; veteran. **3,** inveterate.

мáтка [*gen. pl.* **мáток**] *n.* **1,** uterus; womb. **2,** female (*of animals*). **3,** queen bee.

мáтовый *adj.* **1,** mat; dull. Мáтовое стеклó, frosted glass. **2,** *chess* mating: мáтовая сеть, mating net.

мáточный *adj.* uterine.

матрáс *also*, **матрáц** *n.* mattress. —**матрáсный,** *adj.* mattress (*attrib.*).

матрёшка [*gen. pl.* **-шек**] *n.* set of nesting dolls.

матриархáльный *adj.* matriarchal. —**матриархáт,** *n.* matriarchy.

матримониáльный *adj., obs.* matrimonial.

мáтрица *n.* matrix.

матрóна *n.* matron.

матрóс *n.* sailor; seaman.

матрóска [*gen. pl.* **-сок**] *n.* sailor's jacket.

матрóсский *adj.* sailor's; sailor (*attrib.*).

мáтушка [*gen. pl.* **-шек**] *n., archaic* mother.

матч *n.* **1,** match. **2,** game. —**матч-ревáнш,** return match.

мать [*gen., dat. & prep.* **мáтери**; *instr.* **мáтерью**; *pl.* **мáтери, -рéй, -ря́м**] *n.f.* mother.

мáузер (зэ) *n.* Mauser.

мáфия *n.* Mafia.

мах *n., colloq.* stroke. —**дать мáху,** to commit a blunder. —**одни́м мáхом, 1,** with one stroke; in one fell swoop. **2,** at a single bound. —**с мáху, 1,** with all one's might. **2,** rashly; without thinking.

махаóн *n.* swallowtail (*butterfly*).

махáть *v.impfv.* [*pfv.* **махнýть**; *pres.* **машý, мáшешь**] (*with instr.*) **1,** to wave: махáть платкóм, to wave a handkerchief. Махáть (*or* махáть рукóй) (+ *dat.*), to wave to. **2,** to wag (one's tail); flap (one's wings). —**махнýть рукóй на** (+ *acc.*), to give up on; give up as hopeless.

махи́на *n., colloq.* large cumbersome object.

махинáция *n.* machination.

махнýть *v., pfv. of* **махáть.**

махови́к [*gen.* **-викá**] *n.* flywheel.

маховóй *adj., in* **маховóе колесó,** flywheel.

махóрка *n.* **1,** a kind of low-grade tobacco. **2,** the plant from which it comes.

махрóвый *adj.* **1,** made of terry cloth: махрóвая ткань, terry cloth. Махрóвое полотéнце, Turkish towel. **2,** *bot.* double: махрóвая рóза, double rose. **3,** *fig.* blatant; out-and-out. **4,** *fig.* rabid; fanatical.

мацá *n.* matzo.

мáчеха *n.* stepmother.

мáчта *n.* mast (*of a ship*).

маши́на *n.* **1,** machine: стирáльная маши́на, washing machine; швéйная маши́на, sewing machine. **2,** car. **3,** vehicle: боевáя маши́на, combat vehicle. **4,** engine: паровáя маши́на, steam engine.

машинáльный *adj.* mechanical; automatic; subconscious.

машиниза́ция *n.* mechanization.

машинизи́ровать *v.impfv. & pfv.* [*pres.* **-рую, -руешь**] to mechanize.

машини́ст *n.* **1,** machinist. **2,** engineer; motorman. **3,** operator.

машини́стка [*gen. pl.* **-ток**] *n.* (woman) typist.

маши́нка [*gen. pl.* **-нок**] *n.* **1,** machine. **2,** device. —пи́шущая маши́нка, typewriter.

маши́нный *adj.* machine (*attrib.*). —маши́нное отделе́ние, engine room.

машинопи́сный *adj.* typewritten.

маши́нопись *n.f.* typing.

машинострое́ние *n.* **1,** machine building. **2,** mechanical engineering. —машинострои́тельный, *adj.* machine-building.

маэ́стро *n.m. indecl.* maestro.

мая́к [*gen.* **маяка́**] *n.* lighthouse.

ма́ятник *n.* **1,** pendulum. **2,** balance wheel.

ма́яться *v.r.impfv., colloq.* **1,** to toil; slave. **2,** to suffer.

мая́чить *v.impfv., colloq.* **1,** to loom up; appear in the distance. **2,** *fig.* to be in prospect.

мгла *n.* **1,** haze. **2,** gloom; darkness. —мгли́стый, *adj.* hazy.

мгнове́ние *n.* instant; moment. —в мгнове́ние о́ка, in the twinkling of an eye.

мгнове́нный *adj.* **1,** instantaneous. **2,** momentary. —мгнове́нно, *adv.* instantly.

ме́бель *n.f.* furniture. —ме́бельный, *adj.* furniture (*attrib.*). —ме́бельщик, *n.* furniture maker.

меблиро́ванный *adj.* furnished.

меблирова́ть *v.impfv. & pfv.* [*pres.* **-ру́ю, -ру́ешь**] to furnish.

меблиро́вка *n.* **1,** furnishing. **2,** furniture; furnishings.

мегава́тт [*gen. pl.* **-ва́тт**] *n.* megawatt.

мегаге́рц [*gen. pl.* **-ге́рц**] *n.* megacycle.

мегали́т *n.* megalith.

мегато́нна *n.* megaton.

мегафо́н *n.* megaphone.

меге́ра *n., colloq.* shrew; termagant; virago.

мёд [*2nd loc.* **меду́**] *n.* **1,** honey. **2,** mead.

медали́ст *n.m.* [*fem.* **-ли́стка**] medal winner; medalist.

меда́ль *n.f.* medal. —оборо́тная сторона́ меда́ли, the other side of the coin.

медальо́н *n.* medallion; locket.

медбра́т *n.* male nurse (*contr. of* медици́нский брат).

медве́дица *n.* female bear. —Больша́я Медве́дица, Big Dipper; Ursa Major. —Ма́лая Медве́дица, Little Dipper; Ursa Minor.

медве́дь *n.m.* bear. Бе́лый *or* поля́рный медве́дь, polar bear. —медве́дь наступи́л на́ ухо (+ *dat.*), one has no ear for music; one has a tin ear. —смотре́ть медве́дем, to glower.

медве́жий [*fem.* **-жья**] *adj.* **1,** bear (*attrib.*); bear's. **2,** bearskin. **3,** bear-like. Медве́жья фигу́ра, hulking figure. —медве́жий у́гол, godforsaken place. —медве́жья услу́га, a well-meaning gesture that backfires.

медвежо́нок [*gen.* **-нка**; *pl.* **-жа́та, -жа́т**] *n.* bear cub.

медвя́ный *adj.* smelling of honey. —медвя́ная роса́, honeydew.

медиа́на *n.* median.

ме́дик *n.* **1,** *obs.* physician; doctor. **2,** *colloq.* medical student.

медикаме́нты [*gen.* **-тов**] *n.pl.* medicines.

ме́диум *n.* medium; spiritualist.

медици́на *n.* medicine (*the science*).

медици́нский *adj.* medical. —медици́нский осмо́тр, physical examination. —медици́нская сестра́, (hospital) nurse.

ме́дленный *adj.* slow. —ме́дленно, *adv.* slowly. —ме́дленность, *n.f.* slowness.

медли́тельный *adj.* slow; slow-moving; sluggish. —медли́тельность, *n.f.* slowness; sluggishness.

ме́длить *v.impfv.* to be slow; delay; tarry.

ме́дник *n.* coppersmith.

ме́дный *adj.* copper. —ме́дный лоб, *colloq.* blockhead.

медо́вый *adj.* **1,** honey (*attrib.*). **2,** sweet-smelling. **3,** *fig.* honeyed; sugary. —медо́вый ме́сяц, honeymoon.

медоно́сный *adj.* yielding or producing honey. —медоно́сная пчела́, honeybee.

медосмо́тр *n.* physical examination (*contr. of* медици́нский осмо́тр).

медпу́нкт *n.* first-aid station (*contr. of* медици́нский пункт).

медсестра́ [*infl.* **-сестры, -сестёр, -сёстрам**] *n.* (hospital) nurse (*contr. of* медици́нская сестра́).

меду́за *n.* jellyfish; medusa.

медь *n.f.* copper.

медя́к [*gen.* **-дяка́**] *n., colloq.* copper coin.

медя́нка *n.* **1,** a species of non-poisonous snake. **2,** verdigris.

меж *prep.* = ме́жду.

межа́ [*pl.* **ме́жи, меж, межа́м**] *n.* boundary (*between property*).

междоме́тие *n., gram.* interjection.

междоусо́бие *also,* междоусо́бица *n.* civil strife. —междоусо́бный, *adj.* internecine.

ме́жду *prep., with instr.* **1,** between: ме́жду окно́м и две́рью, between the window and the door; ме́жду пятью́ и шестью́ часа́ми, between five and six o'clock. **2,** among: ме́жду собо́й, among oneselves. ♦*Also with gen. in certain set expressions:* чита́ть ме́жду строк, to read between the lines. —ме́жду на́ми, between you and me; confidentially. —ме́жду про́чим, incidentally; by the way. —ме́жду тем, **1,** meanwhile; in the meantime. **2,** but. —ме́жду тем как, while; whereas.

междугоро́дный *adj.* **1,** intercity; interurban. **2,** (*of a phone call*) long-distance.

междунаро́дный *adj.* international.

междуца́рствие *n.* interregnum.

межева́ние *n.* surveying.

межева́ть *v.impfv.* [*pres.* **-жу́ю, -жу́ешь**] to survey; set boundaries to.

межево́й *adj.* **1,** boundary (*attrib.*): межево́й знак, boundary marker. **2,** surveying (*attrib.*).

ме́жень *n.f.* lowest water level (*of a river or lake*).

межеу́мок [*gen.* **-мка**] *n.* **1,** something impossible to categorize; something belonging to no category. **2,** *col-*

loq. nonentity; nobody. —**межеу́мочный,** *adj.* hard to categorize; ill-defined.

межзвёздный *adj.* interstellar.

межконтинента́льный *adj.* intercontinental.

межнациона́льный *adj.* between (*or* among) nationalities; interethnic.

межплане́тный *adj.* interplanetary.

межсезо́нье *n.* off-season.

мезозо́йский *adj.* Mesozoic.

мезо́н *n.* meson.

мезони́н *n.* attic.

мексика́нец [*gen.* -нца] *n.m.* [*fem.* -нка] Mexican. —**мексика́нский,** *adj.* Mexican.

мел *n.* chalk.

меланхо́лия *n.* 1, melancholy. 2, *med.* melancholia. —**меланхо́лик,** *n.* person suffering from melancholia. —**меланхоли́ческий; меланхоли́чный,** *adj.* melancholic; melancholy.

меле́ть *v.impfv.* [*pfv.* обмеле́ть] to become shallow.

мелиора́ция *n.* land reclamation.

ме́лкий *adj.* [*short form* ме́лок, мелка́, ме́лко, ме́лки; *comp.* ме́льче; *superl.* мельча́йший] 1, small; minute. 2, (*of rain, sand, etc.*) fine. 3, shallow. 4, minor; trivial; petty. 5, petty; small-minded. —**ме́лкая буржуази́я,** petite bourgeoisie. —**ме́лкие де́ньги,** small change. —**ме́лкая кра́жа,** petty larceny. —**ме́лкая таре́лка,** (flat) plate; dinner plate.

ме́лко *adv.* fine; into fine particles.

мелкобуржуа́зный *adj.* petit-bourgeois.

мелково́дный *adj.* shallow.

мелково́дье *n.* shallow water.

мелкозерни́стый *adj.* fine-grained.

мелкота́ *n., colloq.* 1, small size. 2, small fry.

меловой *adj.* 1, chalk (*attrib.*); chalky. 2, *geol.* cretaceous. —**мелова́я бума́га,** coated paper.

мело́дика *n.* melodics.

мелоди́ческий *adj.* 1, melodic. 2, melodious.

мелоди́чный *adj.* melodious. —**мелоди́чность,** *n.f.* melodiousness.

мело́дия *n.* melody.

мелодра́ма *n.* melodrama. —**мелодрамати́ческий,** *adj.* melodramatic.

мело́к [*gen.* мелка́] *n.* piece of chalk. —**игра́ть на мело́к,** *cards* to play on credit.

멜ома́н *n.* music lover.

ме́лочный *also,* **мелочно́й** *adj.* petty; picayune. —**ме́лочность,** *n.f.* pettiness.

ме́лочь [*pl.* ме́лочи, -че́й, -ча́м] *n.f.* 1, small things; small items. 2, (small) change. 3, trifle.

мель [*2nd loc.* мели́] *n.f.* 1, shoal. 2, *in* песча́ная мель, sandbank. —**на мели́, 1,** aground. 2, *fig.* high and dry; on the rocks. —**сесть на мель,** to run aground.

мелька́ть *v.impfv.* [*pfv.* мелькну́ть] 1, to flash; flash by: У меня́ мелькну́ла мысль, the thought flashed across my mind. 2, (*of stars*) to glimmer.

ме́льком *adv.* 1, for a moment; briefly; quickly: ви́деть ме́льком, to catch a glimpse of; слы́шать ме́льком, to chance to hear. 2, cursorily; perfunctorily.

ме́льник *n.* miller.

ме́льница *n.* mill. —**лить во́ду на чью́-нибудь ме́льницу,** to be grist for (*or* bring grist to) someone's mill.

ме́льничный *adj.* mill (*attrib.*). —**ме́льничный лото́к,** millrace.

мельтеши́ть *v.impfv., colloq.* to flash before one's eyes.

мельхио́р *n.* nickel silver.

мельча́ть *v.impfv.* [*pfv.* измельча́ть] 1, to become smaller. 2, to become shallow. 3, *fig.* to deteriorate; degenerate.

ме́льче *adj., comp. of* **ме́лкий.**

мельчи́ть *v.impfv.* to crush; grind.

мелюзга́ *n., colloq.* small fry.

мембра́на *n.* diaphragm (*in an earphone, microphone, etc.*).

мемора́ндум *n.* memorandum.

мемориа́л *n.* memorial. —**мемориа́льный,** *adj.* memorial.

мемуа́ры [*gen.* -ров] *n.pl.* memoirs.

менделе́вий *n.* mendelevium.

ме́нее *adv., used in forming compound comparatives,* less: ме́нее интере́сный, less interesting. —**не ме́нее** (+ *gen.*), no less than; at least. —**бо́лее и́ли ме́нее,** more or less. —**тем не ме́нее,** nevertheless.

менестре́ль *n.m.* minstrel; troubadour.

мензу́рка [*gen. pl.* -рок] *n.* measuring glass; beaker.

менинги́т *n.* meningitis.

меновой *adj.* of exchange: менова́я едини́ца, unit of exchange. —**менова́я торго́вля,** barter.

менструа́ция *n.* menstruation. —**менструа́льный,** *adj.* menstrual.

менструи́ровать *v.impfv.* [*pres.* -ру́ю, -ру́ешь] to menstruate.

менталите́т *n.* mentality. *Also,* **мента́льность,** *n.f.*

менто́л *n.* menthol. —**менто́ловый,** *adj.* menthol (*attrib.*); mentholated.

ме́нтор *n., obs.* mentor.

менуэ́т *n.* minuet.

ме́ньше *adj., comp. of* **ма́лый** *and* **ма́ленький,** smaller. —*adv., comp. of* **ма́ло,** less. —**ме́ньше всего́,** least of all.

меньшеви́к [*gen.* -вика́] *n.* Menshevik. —**меньшеви́стский,** *adj.* Menshevik (*attrib.*).

ме́ньший *adj., used only as a modifier, comp. of* **ма́лый** *and* **ма́ленький,** smaller; lesser. —*n.* the smaller one. Ме́ньшее из двух зол, the lesser of two evils. —**по ме́ньшей ме́ре, 1,** at least. 2, to say the least. —**са́мое ме́ньшее, 1,** the least. 2, at the least.

меньшинство́ *n.* minority.

меню́ *n.neut. indecl.* menu.

меня́ *pron., gen. & acc. of* **я.**

меня́ла *n.m.* moneychanger.

меня́ть *v.impfv.* [*pfv.* поменя́ть] 1, to change. 2, to exchange. 3, to disguise (one's voice). —**меня́ться,** *refl.* 1, [*impfv. only*] to change. 2, (*with instr.*) to exchange; trade: меня́ться роля́ми, to exchange roles; меня́ться места́ми, to trade places.

ме́ра *n.* 1, measure: ме́ра жи́дкости, liquid measure. 2, extent; degree; measure: в большо́й ме́ре, to a great extent/degree; in large measure. 3, measure (*action*): круты́е мéры, drastic measures. —**в мéру, 1,** in the right amount; in moderation. **2,** (*fol. by an adj.*) moderately; rather. **3,** (*with gen.*) to the extent of. —**в пóлной мéре,** fully; in full measure. —**знать мéру,** to know one's limits; know when to stop. —**не в мéру,** excessively. —**по крáйней мéре,** at least. —**по мéньшей мéре, 1,** at least. **2,** to say the least. —**по мéре** (+ *gen.*), in proportion to; to the extent of: по мéре возмóжности, to the fullest extent possible. Заменя́ть ковры́ нóвыми по мéре изнóса, to replace the carpets as they wear out. —**по мéре тогó, как,** as. —**сверх мéры; чéрез мéру,** excessively. —**чу́вство мéры,** sense of proportion.

мéргель *n.m., geol.* marl.

мерéжка *n.* openwork.

мерéнга *n.* meringue.

мерéть *v.impfv.* [*pres.* мрёт, мрут; *past* мёр, мёрла] *colloq.* to die (*in large numbers*).

мерéщиться *v.r.impfv.* [*pfv.* померéщиться] *colloq.* **1,** to seem: Ему́ мерéщилось, что..., it seemed to him that... **2,** to imagine: Э́то вам тóлько померéщилось, you just imagined it.

мерзáвец [*gen.* -вца] *n.* scoundrel.

мéрзкий *adj.* [*short form* мéрзок, мерзкá, мéрзко, мéрзки] **1,** loathsome; vile. **2,** *colloq.* rotten; foul.

мерзлотá *n.* frozen earth. —**вéчная мерзлотá,** permafrost.

мёрзлый *adj.* frozen.

мёрзнуть *v.impfv.* [*pfv.* замёрзнуть; *past* мёрз, мёрзла] **1,** to freeze; become frozen. **2,** (*of a person*) to be freezing (cold); be frozen. **3,** to freeze to death; perish from the frost.

мéрзость *n.f.* vile thing; abomination.

меридиáн *n.* meridian.

мери́ло *n.* standard; criterion; yardstick; gauge.

мéрин *n.* gelding. —**врать как си́вый мéрин,** to be a habitual liar.

меринóс *n.* **1,** merino sheep. **2,** merino wool. —**мери-нóсовый,** *adj.* merino.

мéрить *v.impfv.* **1,** to measure. **2,** to try on. **3,** *in* мéрить (когó-нибудь) глазáми *or* взгля́дом, to look over carefully; give someone the eye. —**мé-риться,** *refl.* [*pfv.* помéриться] (*with instr.*) to measure: мéриться си́лами с, to measure one's strength against. Мéриться рóстом с, to see who (*or* which one) is taller.

мéрка [*gen. pl.* мéрок] *n.* **1,** measurements. **2,** measuring rod; yardstick. **3,** *fig.* yardstick; criterion. Двойнáя мéрка, double standard. —**по мéрке,** to measure.

меркантили́зм *n.* mercantilism. —**мерканти́льный,** *adj.* mercantile.

мéркнуть *v.impfv.* [*pfv.* помéркнуть; *past* мéркнул *or* мерк, мéркла] **1,** to grow dim. **2,** *fig.* to fade; wane. **3,** (*impfv. only*) (*with* пéред) to pale (before).

Мерку́рий *n.* Mercury (*the planet*).

мерлу́шка [*gen. pl.* -шек] *n.* lambskin. —**мерлу́шко-вый,** *adj.* lambskin (*attrib.*).

мéрный *adj.* measured; rhythmical.

мероприя́тие *n.* measure; step.

мéртвенный *adj.* **1,** lifeless; dead. **2,** *fig.* deathly.

мертвéть *v.impfv.* [*pfv.* омертвéть *or* помертвéть] **1,** to become numb. **2,** *fig.* to be paralyzed (*with fear, terror, etc.*).

мертвéц [*gen. & acc.* -вецá] *n.* dead person.

мертвéцкая *n., decl. as an adj., colloq.* morgue (*attached to a hospital*).

мертвéцки *adv., colloq., in* мертвéцки пьян, dead drunk; **спать мертвéцки,** to be dead to the world.

мертвечи́на *n.* carrion.

мертви́ть *v.impfv.* [*pres.* -влю́, -ви́шь] **1,** to kill; destroy. **2,** *fig.* to deaden.

мертворождённый *adj.* stillborn.

мёртвый *adj.* dead. —*n.* **1,** dead person. **2,** *pl.* the dead. —**мёртвая бу́ква,** dead letter. —**мёртвый груз,** dead weight. —**мёртвый сезóн,** off-season. —**мёртвая тишинá,** deathly silence. —**мёртвая тóчка,** dead center: сдви́нуть(ся) с мёртвой тóчки, to move off dead center. На мёртвой тóчке, deadlocked; at a standstill. —**мёртвый язы́к,** dead *or* extinct language. —**ни жив ни мёртв,** in a state of shock. —**спать мёртвым сном,** to be dead to the world.

мерцáние *n.* glimmer; twinkling; flickering.

мерцáть *v.impfv.* to twinkle; flicker; glimmer; shimmer.

мéсиво *n., colloq.* **1,** liquid refuse. **2,** mash (*fed to livestock*).

меси́ть *v.impfv.* [*pres.* мешу́, мéсишь] to knead. —**меси́ть грязь,** to slosh through the mud.

мéсса *n., relig.* Mass.

мессия *n.* Messiah. —**мессиáнский,** *adj.* Messianic.

местéчко [*pl.* -чки, -чек] *n.* **1,** *dim. of* мéсто. **2,** small town. —**тёплое местéчко,** soft job.

мести́ *v.impfv.* [*pres.* мету́, метёшь; *past* мёл, мелá, мелó, мели́] **1,** to sweep. **2,** to scatter; swirl. **3,** (*of a snowstorm*) to be raging. **4,** *impers.* to be snowing: Сегóдня си́льно метёт, it is snowing hard today.

мéстность *n.f.* **1,** area; region: сéльская/болóтистая мéстность, rural/marshy area. **2,** country; terrain: холми́стая мéстность, hilly country; пересечённая мéстность, rugged terrain.

мéстный *adj.* local. —**мéстный падéж,** locative case.

мéсто [*pl.* местá] *n.* **1,** place. **2,** (*with gen.*) site (of); scene (of). **3,** space; room. **4,** seat; place. **5,** (*with gen.*) part; place (*of/in a book, story, etc.*). **6,** berth. **7,** job; position. **8,** piece (*of luggage*). **9,** *pl.* provinces; outlying areas. **10,** *in* óбщее мéсто, platitude. —**всё стáло** (*or* встáло) **на свои́ местá,** everything fell into place. —**знать своё мéсто,** to know one's place. —**имéть мéсто, 1,** to take place. **2,** to exist; be found. —**класть не на мéсто,** to misplace. —**местáми,** in places; in spots; here and there. —**на вáшем мéсте,** in your place; if I were you. —**на мéсте, 1,** in place: стоя́ть на мéсте, to stand in place; stand still. **2,** on the spot: уби́ть когó-нибудь на мéсте, to kill someone on the spot. —**на своём мéсте,** in one's proper place; doing what one should be doing. —**не к мéсту,** inappropriate; out of place. —**не мéсто, 1,** (*with dat.*) not to belong: Здесь вам не мéсто, you don't belong here. **2,** not the place to: Здесь не мéсто говори́ть об э́том, this is not the place to talk about it. —**не находи́ть себé мéста,** to be unable to sit still (*because of nervous agitation*). —**не оста́вить живо́го ме́ста на** (+ *prepl.*), to beat to a pulp. —**ни с ме́ста, 1,** (*as a command*) don't move!; stay put! **2,** making no progress; getting nowhere. —**поста́вить кого́-нибудь на (своё) ме́сто,** to put someone in his place.

местожи́тельство *n.* (place of) residence.

местоиме́ние *n.* pronoun. —**местоиме́нный,** *adj.* pronominal.

местонахожде́ние *n.* location; whereabouts.

местоположе́ние *n.* location; site.

местопребыва́ние *n.* residence; abode. —**местопребыва́ние прави́тельства,** the seat of government.

месторожде́ние *n.* **1,** deposit. Месторожде́ние не́фти, oil field. **2,** *obs.* [*now* **ме́сто рожде́ния**] place of birth.

месть *n.f.* revenge; vengeance. —**кро́вная месть,** vendetta.

ме́сяц *n.* **1,** month. **2,** moon. —**медо́вый ме́сяц,** honeymoon.

ме́сячник *n.* month (*devoted to a special cause*): ме́сячник де́тской кни́ги, children's book month.

ме́сячный *adj.* **1,** lasting a month; a month's. **2,** monthly.

ме́та *n.* **1,** mark. **2,** *obs.* target.

мета́лл *n.* metal. —**металли́ст,** *n.* metalworker. —**металли́ческий,** *adj.* metal (*attrib.*); metallic.

металло́ид *n.* metalloid.

металлоиска́тель *n.m.* metal detector.

металлоло́м *n.* scrap metal.

металлоно́сный *adj.* metalliferous.

металлообраба́тывающий *adj.* metal-working.

металлоплави́льный *adj.* smelting (*attrib.*).

металлу́ргия *also,* **металлурги́я** *n.* metallurgy. —**металлу́рг,** *n.* metallurgist. —**металлурги́ческий,** *adj.* metallurgic.

метаморфо́з *n., biol.* metamorphosis. —**метаморфо́за,** *n., fig.* metamorphosis; complete transformation.

мета́н *n.* methane.

мета́ние *n.* **1,** throwing: мета́ние ди́ска, discus throw. **2,** *in* мета́ние икры́, spawning.

метано́л *n.* methanol.

метаста́з *n.* metastasis.

мета́тель *n.m., sports* thrower: мета́тель ди́ска, discus thrower.

мета́тельный *adj.* to be thrown or launched: мета́тельный снаря́д, missile; projectile.

мета́ть[1] *v.impfv.* [*pfv.* метну́ть; *pres.* мечу́, ме́чешь] to throw; hurl; fling; cast. —**мета́ть банк,** *cards* to keep the bank. —**мета́ть гро́мы и мо́лнии,** to fulminate; rant and rave. —**мета́ть икру́,** to spawn. —**мета́ть се́но,** to pitch hay.

мета́ть[2] *v.impfv.* [*pfv.* смета́ть; *pres.* мета́ю, мета́ешь] to baste. —**мета́ть пе́тли,** to make buttonholes.

мета́ться *v.r.impfv.* [*pres.* мечу́сь, ме́чешься] **1,** to rush about; bustle about. **2,** to toss about (*in bed*); toss (*in one's sleep*).

метафи́зика *n.* metaphysics. —**метафи́зик,** *n.* metaphysician; metaphysicist. —**метафизи́ческий,** *adj.* metaphysical.

мета́фора *n.* metaphor. —**метафори́ческий,** *adj.* metaphorical.

мете́лица *n.* = **мете́ль.**

метёлка [*gen. pl.* **-лок**] *n.* **1,** whisk broom. **2,** *bot.* panicle.

мете́ль *n.f.* snowstorm; blizzard.

метео́р *n.* meteor.

метеори́зм *n., med.* flatulence.

метеори́т *n.* meteorite.

метео́рный *adj.* meteor (*attrib.*); meteoric.

метеороло́гия *n.* meteorology. —**метеоро́лог,** *n.* meteorologist. —**метеорологи́ческий,** *adj.* meteorological.

метеоспу́тник *n.* weather satellite.

метиза́ция *n.* crossbreeding.

мети́л *n.* methyl.

метиле́н *n.* methylene.

мети́ловый *adj.* methyl (*attrib.*).

мети́с *n.* **1,** mongrel. **2,** mestizo.

ме́тить *v.impfv.* [*pres.* ме́чу, ме́тишь] **1,** [*pfv.* **наме́тить** *or* **поме́тить**] **1,** to mark. **2,** (*with* **в** + *acc.*) to aim (at). **3,** (*with* **в** + *nom. pl. or* **на** + *acc.*) *colloq.* to aim (to become); aspire (to). Он ме́тит на ва́ше ме́сто, he has his eye on your job.

ме́тка [*gen. pl.* **ме́ток**] *n.* **1,** marking. **2,** mark. **3,** name tape containing one's initials.

ме́ткий *adj.* [*short form* **ме́ток, метка́, ме́тко, ме́тки**] **1,** (*of a marksman, weapon, etc.*) accurate. **2,** (*of a blow, bullet, etc.*) well-aimed. **3,** (*of one's eye*) keen. **4,** *fig.* (*of a comment, remark, etc.*) pointed; apt.

ме́ткость *n.f.* **1,** accuracy; marksmanship. **2,** keenness (*of eyesight*).

метла́ [*pl.* **мётлы, мётел**] *n.* broom.

метну́ть *v., pfv. of* **мета́ть**[1].

ме́тод *n.* method.

методи́зм *n.* Methodism.

мето́дика *n.* methods.

методи́ст *n.* **1,** Methodist. **2,** specialist on the methodology of teaching. —**методи́стский,** *adj.* Methodist.

методи́ческий *adj.* **1,** [*also,* **методи́чный**] methodical; systematic. **2,** pert. to the methodology of teaching.

методоло́гия *n.* methodology. —**методологи́ческий,** *adj.* methodological.

метр *n.* **1,** meter (*unit of length*). **2,** measuring rod *or* tape (*one meter in length*). **3,** *pros.* meter.

метра́ж [*gen.* **-ажа́**] *n.* **1,** length (*in meters*). **2,** *motion pictures* footage. **3,** area (*in square meters*).

метранпа́ж *n., printing* make-up man.

метрдоте́ль (тэ) *n.m.* maître d'hotel; headwaiter.

ме́трика *n.* **1,** birth certificate. **2,** *pros.* metrics.

метри́ческий *adj.* **1,** metric: метри́ческая систе́ма мер, metric system. **2,** pert. to the registration of births, marriages and deaths: метри́ческое свиде́тельство, birth certificate.

метро́ *n. indecl.* subway.

метроно́м *n.* metronome.

метрополите́н (тэ) *n.* subway.

метропо́лия *n.* parent state; home country (*of an empire*).

ме́тчик *n.* marker; one who marks.

мех *n.* **1**, [*pl.* меха́] fur. **2**, [*pl.* мехи́] skin (*vessel*); wineskin. —**на меху́**, fur-lined. *See also* **мехи́**.

механиза́тор *n.* **1**, specialist in mechanization. **2**, farm-machine operator.

механиза́ция *n.* mechanization.

механизи́ровать *v.impfv. & pfv.* [*pres.* -ру́ю, -ру́ешь] to mechanize.

механи́зм *n.* mechanism.

меха́ник *n.* **1**, mechanical engineer. **2**, mechanic.

меха́ника *n.* mechanics.

механи́ческий *adj.* **1**, mechanical. **2**, power-driven; power (*attrib.*). **3**, *fig.* mechanical; automatic. —**механи́ческий цех**; **механи́ческая мастерска́я**, machine shop.

мехи́ [*gen.* мехо́в] *n.pl.* bellows.

меховой *adj.* fur.

меховщи́к [*gen.* -щика́] *n.* furrier.

мецена́т *n.* patron of the arts.

ме́ццо-сопра́но *n.neut. indecl.* mezzo-soprano (*voice*). —*n.f. indecl.* mezzo-soprano (*singer*).

меч [*gen.* меча́] *n.* sword.

ме́ченый *adj.* marked.

мече́ть *n.f.* mosque.

меч-ры́ба *n.* swordfish.

мечта́ *n.* **1**, dream: заве́тная мечта́, lifelong dream. **2**, ambition. **3**, daydreaming: предава́ться мечта́м, to give way to daydreaming.

мечта́ние *n.* daydreaming; reverie.

мечта́тель *n.m.* dreamer; visionary.

мечта́тельный *adj.* **1**, given to dreaming. **2**, dreamy. **3**, visionary. —**мечта́тельность**, *n.f.* reverie.

мечта́ть *v.impfv.* **1**, to dream. **2**, to daydream.

меша́лка [*gen. pl.* -лок] *n.* mixer.

мешани́на *n.*, *colloq.* mishmash; hodgepodge.

меша́ть *v.impfv.* [*pfv.* помеша́ть] **1**, (*with dat.*) to bother; disturb; hinder; impede; prevent. **2**, to hurt; do harm: Не меша́ло бы (+ *inf.*), it wouldn't hurt to... **3**, to stir. **4**, [*pfv.* смеша́ть] to mix; blend. —**меша́ться**, *refl.* [*pfv.* смеша́ться] **1**, to mix; blend; mingle. **2**, to become confused. **3**, [*impfv. only*] (*with* в + *acc.*) *colloq.* to interfere (in). **4**, [*impfv. only*] *colloq.* to be a hindrance; get in the way.

ме́шкать *v.impfv.*, *colloq.* to tarry; dally; dawdle.

мешкова́тый *adj.* **1**, (*of clothing*) baggy. **2**, clumsy; awkward.

мешкови́на *n.* sacking; sackcloth.

ме́шкотный *adj.*, *colloq.* **1**, sluggish. **2**, laborious.

мешо́к [*gen.* мешка́] *n.* bag; sack. —**де́нежный мешо́к**, moneybags; rich man. —**мешки́ под глаза́ми**, bags under one's eyes. —**сиде́ть мешко́м**, (*of a garment*) to be too big; be baggy.

мешо́чек [*gen.* -чка] *n.* **1**, *dim. of* мешо́к. **2**, sac. —**яйцо́ в мешо́чек**, medium-boiled egg.

меща́ни́н [*pl.* -ща́не, -ща́н] *n.m.* [*fem.* -ща́нка] **1**, petit bourgeois. **2**, *fig.* person of narrow or petty interests.

меща́нский *adj.* **1**, petit-bourgeois. **2**, *fig.* narrow-minded.

меща́нство *n.* **1**, lower middle class; petite bourgeoisie. **2**, *fig.* narrow-mindedness.

мзда *n.*, *obs.* **1**, payment. **2**, bribe.

ми *n.neut.*, *music* mi; E.

миа́змы *n.pl.* [*sing.* миа́зма] miasma.

миг *n.* moment; instant. —**в оди́н миг**, in a flash; in a jiffy.

мига́лка [*gen. pl.* -лок] *n.* blinking light; blinker; flasher.

мига́ние *n.* **1**, wink (*of the eye*). **2**, blinking (*of a light*).

мига́ть *v.impfv.* [*pfv.* мигну́ть] **1**, to blink. **2**, (*with instr.*) to blink (one's eyes). **3**, (*with dat.*) to wink (at). **4**, to twinkle; flicker.

ми́гом *adv.*, *colloq.* in a flash; in a jiffy.

мигра́ция *n.* migration.

мигре́нь *n.f.* migraine.

мигри́ровать *v.impfv.* [*pres.* -ру́ю, -ру́ешь] to migrate.

ми́дия *n.* mussel.

мизансце́на *n.*, *theat.* staging.

мизантро́пия *n.* misanthropy. —**мизантро́п**, *n.* misanthrope. —**мизантропи́ческий**, *adj.* misanthropic.

мизе́рный *adj.* **1**, wretched. **2**, paltry; meager; measly.

мизи́нец [*gen.* -нца] *n.* **1**, little finger. **2**, little toe.

микро́б *n.* microbe; germ.

микробиоло́гия *n.* microbiology. —**микробио́лог**, *n.* microbiologist.

микроко́см *n.* microcosm.

микро́метр *n.* micrometer.

микро́н [*gen. pl.* -кро́н] *n.* micron.

микроорганизм *n.* microorganism.

микроско́п *n.* microscope. —**микроскопи́ческий**, *adj.* microscopic.

микросхе́ма *n.* microcircuit.

микрофи́льм *n.* microfilm.

микрофо́н *n.* microphone.

микроэлектро́ника *n.* microelectronics.

ми́ксер (сэ) *n.* mixer.

миксту́ра *n.* (liquid) medicine.

ми́лая *n.*, *decl. as an adj.* sweetheart; darling.

ми́ленький *adj.*, *colloq.* **1**, pretty; cute. **2**, dear; sweet. **3**, (*in direct address*) darling.

милитариза́ция *n.* militarization.

милитаризи́ровать *v.impfv. & pfv.* [*pres.* -ру́ю, -ру́ешь] to militarize. *Also*, **милитаризова́ть** [*pres.* -зу́ю, -зу́ешь].

милитари́зм *n.* militarism. —**милитари́ст**, *n.* militarist. —**милитаристи́ческий**, *adj.* militaristic.

милице́йский *adj.* **1**, militia (*attrib.*). **2**, police (*attrib.*).

милиционе́р *n.* **1**, policeman. **2**, militiaman.

мили́ция *n.* **1**, the police. **2**, militia.

миллиа́рд *n.* (*U.S.*) billion; (*Brit.*) milliard. —**миллиарде́р**, (дэ) *n.* multimillionaire.

миллиа́рдный *ordinal numeral* billionth. —*adj.* **1**, containing or consisting of billions. **2**, worth billions.

миллигра́мм *n.* milligram.

миллиме́тр *n.* millimeter.

миллио́н *n.* million. —**миллионе́р**, *n.* millioniare.

миллио́нный *ordinal numeral* millionth. —*adj.* **1**, containing or consisting of millions. **2**, worth millions.

ми́ло *adv.* **1**, nicely. **2**, prettily. —*adj.*, *used predicatively*, nice; kind: Как ми́ло, что вы пришли́, how nice/kind of you to come!

ми́ловать *v.impfv.* [*pres.* -лую, -луешь] *obs.* to show mercy to; pardon.

милови́дный *adj.* pretty; good-looking.

милосе́рдие *n.* **1,** mercy. **2,** clemency. —**милосе́рдный,** *adj.* merciful; charitable.

ми́лостивый *adj.,* *obs.* kind; gracious.

ми́лостыня *n.* alms.

ми́лость *n.f.* **1,** favor; good graces: быть в ми́лости у, to be in the good graces of. **2,** favor; good turn: сде́лать ми́лость (+ *dat.*), to do (someone) a favor. **3,** mercy. —**ми́лости про́сим!,** you are always welcome! —**по ми́лости** (+ *gen.*), **1,** thanks to. **2,** through the fault of. —**сдава́ться на ми́лость** (+ *gen.*), to surrender unconditionally to. —**скажи́(те) на ми́лость, 1,** would you please tell (*or* mind telling) me. **2,** you don't say! —**смени́ть гнев на ми́лость,** to cease being angry; turn around and be nice.

ми́лый *adj.* **1,** nice; sweet. **2,** dear: ми́лый друг, dear friend. —*n.* darling; sweetheart.

ми́ля *n.* mile.

мим *n.* mime (*farce performed in ancient times*).

ми́мика *n.* **1,** facial expressions. **2,** mimicry.

мимикри́я *n.,* *biol.* mimicry.

мими́ст *n.* mimic. —**мими́ческий,** *adj.* mimic.

ми́мо *prep.,* *with gen.* past; by: проходи́ть ми́мо до́ма, to walk past/by the house. —*adv.* past; by: Солда́ты прошли́ ми́мо, the soldiers walked past (*or* passed by). —**ми́мо це́ли,** wide of the mark.

мимоéздом *adv., colloq.* passing by; passing through.

мимо́за *n.* mimosa.

мимолётный *adj.* passing; fleeting.

мимохо́дом *adv.* **1,** while passing by; on the way. **2,** *colloq.* in passing: упомяну́ть мимохо́дом, to mention in passing.

ми́на *n.* **1,** *mil.* mine. **2,** mortar shell. **3,** facial expression; countenance. —**де́лать хоро́шую (весёлую) ми́ну при плохо́й игре́,** to put up a bold front. —**подкла́дывать** *or* **подводи́ть ми́ну** (+ *dat.* or with под + *acc.*), to play a dirty trick on.

минаре́т *n.* minaret.

миндалеви́дный *adj.* almond-shaped. —**миндалеви́дная железа́,** tonsil.

минда́лина *n.* tonsil.

минда́ль [*gen.* **-даля́**] *n.m.* **1,** almonds. **2,** almond tree. —**минда́льный,** *adj.* almond (*attrib.*).

минёр *n.* specialist in mine-laying.

минера́л *n.* mineral.

минерало́гия *n.* mineralogy. —**минерало́г,** *n.* mineralogist. —**минералоги́ческий,** *adj.* mineralogical.

минера́льный *adj.* mineral.

миниатю́ра *n.* miniature.

миниатюриза́ция *n.* miniaturization.

миниатю́рный *adj.* **1,** miniature. **2,** tiny.

минима́льный *adj.* minimum; minimal.

ми́нимум *n.* minimum. —*adv.* a minimum of; at least.

мини́ровать *v.impf. & pf.* [*pfv. also* **замини́ровать;** *pres.* **-рую, -руешь**] *mil.* to mine.

министе́рский *adj.* ministerial.

министе́рство *n.* **1,** ministry. **2,** (*in the U.S.*) department.

мини́стр *n.* minister. —**мини́стр иностра́нных дел,** foreign minister. —**мини́стр торго́вли,** trade minister; (*in the U.S.*) Secretary of Commerce. —**мини́стр фина́нсов,** finance minister; (*in the U.S.*) Secretary of the Treasury. —**мини́стр юсти́ции,** Minister of Justice; (*in the U.S.*) Attorney General.

ми́нный *adj.,* *mil.* mine (*attrib.*). —**ми́нное по́ле,** minefield. —**ми́нный по́рох,** blasting powder.

минова́ть *v.pfv.* [*infl.* **-ну́ю, -ну́ешь**] **1,** [*also impfv.*] *v.t.* to pass; pass by. **2,** *v.i.* to pass; be over. **3,** (*usu. neg.*) to avoid; escape. —**мину́я подро́бности,** omitting details.

мино́га *n.* lamprey.

миноиска́тель *n.m.* mine detector.

миномёт *n.,* *mil.* mortar. —**миномётный,** *adj.* mortar (*attrib.*).

миноно́сец [*gen.* **-сца**] *n.* torpedo boat. —**эска́дренный миноно́сец,** destroyer.

мино́р *n.* **1,** *music* minor key: сона́та си мино́р, sonata in B minor. **2,** *colloq.* melancholy; the blues; the dumps: быть в мино́ре, to be in the dumps.

мино́рный *adj.* **1,** *music* minor. **2,** *colloq.* melancholy; gloomy.

мину́вший *adj.* past; bygone.

ми́нус *n.* **1,** minus sign. **2,** *fig., colloq.* minus; drawback. —*adv.* minus: пять ми́нус два равно́ трём, five minus two equals three. Ми́нус де́сять гра́дусов, ten degrees below freezing.

ми́нусовый *adj.* (*of temperature*) subzero.

мину́та *n.* **1,** minute. **2,** moment: незабыва́емая мину́та, unforgettable moment. —**мину́та в мину́ту,** on the dot. —**с мину́ты на мину́ту,** any minute.

мину́тка [*gen. pl.* **-ток**] *n., dim. of* **мину́та.**

мину́тный *adj.* **1,** minute (*attrib.*): мину́тная стре́лка, minute hand. **2,** lasting a moment; momentary.

мину́точка [*gen. pl.* **-чек**] *n., colloq., dim. of* **мину́тка.**

мину́ть *v.pfv.* [*infl.* **ми́нет**] **1,** [*past* **мину́л**] to pass. **2,** [*past* **ми́нуло**] *impers.* (*with dat.*) *indicating attainment of a certain age:* Ему́ ми́нуло со́рок лет, he has turned forty.

миопи́я *n.* myopia.

мир[1] [*pl.* **миры́**] *n.* **1,** world. **2,** *hist.* village commune; mir. —**не от ми́ра сего́,** (*of a person*) from (*or* living in) a different world. —**пусти́ть по́ миру,** to bankrupt; make a beggar out of (someone). —**ходи́ть по́ миру,** to live by begging.

мир[2] *n.* peace: мир во всём ми́ре, peace throughout the world. —**отпусти́ть с ми́ром,** to let off (unpunished); let go in peace.

мира́ж *n.* mirage.

мириа́ды [*gen.* **-а́д**] *n.pl.* myriads.

мири́ть *v.impfv.* [*pfv.* **помири́ть** *or* **примири́ть**] to reconcile. —**мири́ться,** *refl.* **1,** [*pfv.* **помири́ться**] become reconciled (*after a quarrel*); make up. **2,** [*pfv.* **примири́ться**] (*with* с + *instr.*) to reconcile oneself (to); resign oneself (to); (learn to) accept.

ми́рный *adj.* **1,** peace (*attrib.*). **2,** peaceful. —**ми́рно,** *adv.* peacefully.

мирова́я *n., decl. as an adj., colloq.* amicable agreement: пойти́ на мирову́ю, to reach an amicable agreement.

мировоззре́ние *n.* world outlook; world view.

мирово́й *adj.* **1,** world (*attrib.*). Втора́я мирова́я война́, World War II. **2,** *law* of arbitration: мирово́й суд, court of arbitration. Мировóй судьЯ, justice of the peace.

мирозда́ние *n.* the universe.

миролюби́вый *adj.* peace-loving; peaceful. —**миролю́-бие,** *n.* peaceful nature.

миропома́зание *n.* anointing; unction.

миротво́рец [*gen.* **-рца**] *n.* peacemaker.

ми́рра *n.* myrrh.

мирско́й *adj.* **1,** worldly; mundane. **2,** secular; lay. **3,** *hist.* pert. to a **мир.**

мирт *n.* myrtle. —**ми́ртовый,** *adj.* myrtle.

миря́нин [*pl.* **-я́не, -я́н**] *n.* **1,** *obs.* layman. **2,** *hist.* member of a **мир.**

ми́ска [*gen. pl.* **ми́сок**] *n.* bowl; tureen.

мисс *n.f. indecl.* miss; Miss.

миссионе́р *n.* missionary. —**миссионе́рский,** *adj.* missionary. —**миссионе́рство,** *n.* missionary work.

ми́ссис *n.f. indecl.* Mrs.

ми́ссия *n.* **1,** mission (*assignment*). **2,** delegation; mission. **3,** legation; diplomatic mission. **4,** *relig.* mission.

ми́стер *n.* mister; Mr.

ми́стик *n.* mystic.

ми́стика *n.* mysticism.

мистифика́ция *n.* hoax; practical joke.

мистици́зм *n.* mysticism.

мисти́ческий *adj.* mystical.

ми́тинг *n.* mass meeting; rally.

митингова́ть *v.impfv.* [*pres.* **-гу́ю, -гу́ешь**] to hold a rally.

митка́ль [*gen.* **-каля́**] *n.m.* calico (*plain unfinished cloth*). —**миткалёвый; митка́левый,** *adj.* calico.

митóз *n.* mitosis.

ми́тра *n.* miter (*worn by a bishop*).

митрополи́т *n.,* Orth. Ch. metropolitan.

ми́ттельшпиль (тэ) *n.m., chess* middle game.

миф *n.* myth. —**мифи́ческий,** *adj.* mythical.

мифоло́гия *n.* mythology. —**мифологи́ческий,** *adj.* mythological.

ми́чман *n., naval* warrant officer.

мише́нь *n.f.* target. —**я́блоко мише́ни,** bull's-eye.

ми́шка [*gen. pl.* **ми́шек**] *n.m.* teddy bear.

мишура́ *n.* **1,** tinsel. **2,** *fig.* ostentation; show; window dressing.

мишу́рный *adj.* **1,** tinsel (*attrib.*). **2,** *fig.* showy; tawdry; ostentatious; meretricious.

младе́нец [*gen.* **-нца**] *n.* infant; baby.

младе́нческий *adj.* **1,** of an infant; infant (*attrib.*). **2,** infantile.

младе́нчество *n.* infancy.

младо́й *adj., archaic* young. —**стар и млад,** young and old (alike).

младопи́сьменный *adj.* (*of a language*) recently reduced to writing; recently given an alphabet.

мла́дший *adj., used only as a modifier* **1,** younger. **2,** youngest. **3,** junior. —**мла́дший лейтена́нт,** second lieutenant.

млекопита́ющее *n., decl. as an adj.* mammal.

млеть *v.impfv.* **1,** (*with* **от**) to be overcome (*with an emotion*). **2,** to languish. **3,** *colloq.* to become numb.

мле́чный *adj., archaic* = **молóчный.** —**Мле́чный Путь,** the Milky Way.

мне *pron., dat. & prepl. of* **я.**

мнемо́ника *n.* mnemonics. —**мнемони́ческий,** *adj.* mnemonic.

мне́ние *n.* opinion. —**быть высо́кого мне́ния о,** to have a high opinion of. —**быть одного́ мне́ния,** to be of one mind. —**по моему́ мне́нию,** in my opinion. —**я того́ мне́ния, что...,** I am of the opinion that...

мни́мый *adj.* **1,** imaginary. **2,** false; feigned.

мни́тельный *adj.* **1,** forever worrying about one's health. **2,** suspicious; distrustful.

мнить *v.impfv., obs.* to imagine. —**мнить себя́** (+ *instr.*), to imagine oneself to be; see oneself as; fancy oneself as; like to think of oneself as. —**мно́го** (*or* **высоко́**) **мнить о себе́,** to have a high opinion of oneself.

мно́гие *adj.* many: мно́гие дома́, many houses; во мно́гих отноше́ниях, in many respects. —*indef. pron.* many; many people: Мно́гие счита́ют, что..., many people believe that...

мно́го *adv.* much; a lot; a great deal: Я мно́го о вас слы́шал(а), I've heard a lot about you. Ви́деть и слы́шать мно́го, to see and hear a great deal. —*adj. (with gen.)* many; much; a lot of; a great deal of: мно́го раз, many times; мно́го рабо́ты, a lot of work. —**ни мно́го ни ма́ло,** as much as; as many as; no less than. *See also* **мно́гое.**

многобо́жие *n.* polytheism.

многобра́чие *n.* polygamy. —**многобра́чный,** *adj.* polygamous.

многова́то *adv., colloq.* a bit too much.

многовеково́й *adj.* **1,** centuries-old. **2,** that lasted for centuries.

многогра́нник *n.* polyhedron.

многогра́нный *adj.* **1,** polyhedral; many-sided. **2,** *fig.* multifaceted.

многоде́тный *adj.* **1,** having many children. **2,** (*of a family*) large.

мно́гое [*gen.* **мно́гого;** *dat.* **мно́гому;** *instr.* **мно́гим;** *prepl.* **мно́гом**] *n., decl. as an adj.* much; a great deal: Óпыт нас у́чит мно́гому, experience teaches us a great deal. Я мно́гим вам обя́зан, I am much indebted to you. —**во мно́гом,** in many respects; largely; in large part.

многоже́нец [*gen.* **-нца**] *n.* polygamist. —**многоже́нство,** *n.* polygamy.

многозначи́тельный *adj.* **1,** significant. **2,** (*of a look, smile, etc.*) knowing.

многокварти́рный *adj., in* **многокварти́рный дом,** apartment house.

многокра́сочный *adj.* multicolored; polychromatic.

многокра́тный *adj.* **1,** repeated; frequent. **2,** *gram.* frequentative: многокра́тный вид, frequentative aspect. —**многокра́тно,** *adv.* repeatedly.

многоле́тний *adj.* **1,** of many years. **2,** long-lived. **3,** *bot.* perennial.

многолю́дный *adj.* **1,** populous. **2,** crowded.

многомиллио́нный *adj.* consisting of many millions.

многому́жие *n.* polyandry.

многонациона́льный *adj.* multinational.

многоно́жка [*gen. pl.* **-жек**] *n.* myriapod; centipede; millipede;

многообеща́ющий *adj.* promising; up-and-coming.

многообра́зие *n.* variety; diversity. —**многообра́зный,** *adj.* varied; diverse.

многопарти́йный *adj.* multiparty.

многопло́дный *adj., in* многопло́дные ро́ды, multiple births.

многоречи́вый *adj.* loquacious; verbose; long-winded.

многосеме́йный *adj.* having a large family.

многосери́йный *adj.* serial.

многосло́вие *n.* verbosity. —**многосло́вный,** *adj.* long-winded; verbose.

многосло́жный *adj.* polysyllabic.

многосторо́нний *adj.* **1,** multilateral. **2,** *fig.* versatile. —**многосторо́нность,** *n.f.* versatility.

многострада́льный *adj.* long-suffering.

многоступе́нчатый *adj.* multistage.

многотира́жка [*gen. pl.* -жек] *n., colloq.* company newspaper; house organ.

многотира́жный *adj.* (*of a publication*) having a large circulation.

многото́мный *adj.* multivolume.

многото́чие *n.* suspension points (...).

многоуважа́емый *adj.* (*in salutations of letters*) dear: Многоуважа́емый Ива́н Петро́вич, Dear Ivan Petrovich.

многоуго́льник *n.* polygon. —**многоуго́льный,** *adj.* polygonal.

многоцве́тный *adj.* multicolored; polychromatic.

многочи́сленность *n.f.* **1,** great number. **2,** large size (*of a family, army, etc.*).

многочи́сленный *adj.* **1,** numerous. **2,** consisting of many people; large.

многочле́н *n.* polynomial. —**многочле́нный,** *adj.* polynomial.

многоэта́жный *adj.* multistoried.

многоязы́чный *adj.* multilingual; polyglot.

мно́жественность *n.f.* multiplicity.

мно́жественный *adj.* plural. —**мно́жественное число́,** *gram.* the plural.

мно́жество *n.* **1,** (*with gen.*) a great number (of); a multitude (of). **2,** *math.* set: тео́рия мно́жеств, theory of sets. —**во мно́жестве,** in great numbers.

мно́жимое *n., decl. as an adj., math.* multiplicand.

мно́житель *n.m., math.* **1,** multiplier. **2,** factor.

мно́жительный *adj.* for making copies: мно́жительная маши́на, duplicating machine; duplicator.

мно́жить *v.impfv.* [*pfv.* помно́жить *or* умно́жить] **1,** *math.* to multiply. **2,** *fig.* to increase; augment. —**мно́житься,** *refl.* [*pfv.* умно́житься] to multiply; increase in number.

мной *also,* мно́ю *pron., instr. of* я.

мобилиза́ция *n.* mobilization. —**мобилизацио́нный,** *adj.* mobilization (*attrib.*).

мобилизова́ть *v.impfv.* [*pres.* -зу́ю, -зу́ешь] **1,** to mobilize. **2,** to call up; call to active duty. **3,** *fig.* to mobilize; muster; rally. —**мобилизова́ться,** *refl.* **1,** to mobilize; be mobilized. **2,** *fig.* to brace oneself; buckle down.

моби́льный *adj.* mobile. —**моби́льность,** *n.f.* mobility.

моги́ла *n.* grave. —**своди́ть в моги́лу,** to be the death

of. —**стоя́ть одно́й ного́й в моги́ле,** to have one foot in the grave.

моги́льный *adj.* **1,** grave (*attrib.*); burial (*attrib.*). **2,** deathly; sepulchral. —**моги́льная плита́,** gravestone.

моги́льщик *n.* gravedigger.

мого́л *n.* Mogul.

могу́чий *adj.* powerful; mighty.

могу́щественный *adj.* powerful; mighty.

могу́щество *n.* power; might.

мо́да *n.* fashion; style; vogue: быть в мо́де, to be in fashion/style/vogue. —**войти́ в мо́ду,** to come into fashion. —**вы́йти из мо́ды,** to go out of style.

мода́льный *adj.* modal.

модели́ровать (дэ) *v.impfv. & pfv.* [*pres.* -рую, -руешь] to design (clothes).

моде́ль (дэ) *n.f.* model.

модельер (дэ) *n.* designer (*of clothes*).

моде́льный (дэ) *adj.* **1,** model (*attrib.*); pattern (*attrib.*): моде́льный цех, pattern shop. **2,** fashionable.

моде́льщик (дэ) *n.* modeler.

моде́м (дэ) *n.* modem.

моде́рн (дэ) *n.* modernist style. —*adj. indecl.* modern: та́нец моде́рн, modern dance.

модерниза́ция (дэ) *n.* modernization.

модернизи́ровать (дэ) *v.impfv. & pfv.* [*pres.* -рую, -руешь] to modernize.

модерни́зм (дэ) *n.* modernism. —**модерни́ст,** *n.* modernist. —**модерни́стский,** *adj.* modernistic.

моди́стка [*gen. pl.* -ток] *n.* milliner.

модифика́ция *n.* modification.

модифици́ровать *v.impfv. & pfv.* [*pres.* -рую, -руешь] to modify.

мо́дник *n.m.* [*fem.* -ница] *colloq.* fashion plate.

мо́дничать *v.impfv., colloq.* to dress fashionably; dress in the latest fashions.

мо́дно *adv.* stylishly; fashionably. —*adj., used predicatively,* fashionable: стать мо́дно, to become fashionable.

мо́дный *adj.* **1,** fashionable; stylish. **2,** fashion (*attrib.*): мо́дный журна́л, fashion magazine.

модули́ровать *v.impfv.* [*pres.* -рую, -руешь] to modulate.

мо́дуль *n.m.* module; modulus.

модуля́тор *n.* modulator.

модуля́ция *n.* modulation. —**часто́тная модуля́ция,** frequency modulation.

моёвка [*gen. pl.* -вок] *n.* kittiwake.

можжеве́льник *n.* juniper. —**можжеве́ловый,** *adj.* juniper (*attrib.*).

мо́жно *predicate* may; can; it is permitted: Мо́жно войти́?, may I come in? Здесь мо́жно кури́ть, you may smoke here; you are allowed to smoke here. —**как мо́жно** (+ *comp.*), as ... as possible: как мо́жно бо́льше, as much as possible; как мо́жно скоре́е, as soon as possible.

моза́ика *n.* mosaic; inlay. —**моза́ичный,** *adj.* mosaic; inlaid.

мозг [*2nd loc.* мозгу́; *pl.* мозги́] *n.* **1,** brain. **2,** *pl.* brains (*food*). —**головно́й мозг,** cerebrum. —**ко́стный мозг,** marrow. —**продолгова́тый мозг,** medulla oblongata. —**спинно́й мозг,** spinal cord.

мозгови́тый *adj.*, *colloq.* brainy.

мозгово́й *adj.* brain (*attrib.*); cerebral.

мозжечо́к [*gen.* **-чка́**] *n.* cerebellum.

мозо́листый *adj.* calloused.

мозо́лить *v.impfv.* [*pfv.* **намозо́лить**] to get calluses on. —**мозо́лить глаза́** (+ *dat.*), *colloq.* **1**, to offend the eye (of). **2**, to be a nuisance to.

мозо́ль *n.f.* callus; corn. —**мозо́льный**, *adj.* for removing corns: мозо́льный пла́стырь, corn plaster.

мой [*fem.* **моя́**; *neut.* **моё**; *pl.* **мои́**; *gen.* **моего́, мое́й, мои́х**; *acc. fem.* **мою́**; *dat.* **моему́, мое́й, мои́м**; *instr.* **мои́м, мое́й, мои́ми**; *prepl.* **моём, мое́й, мои́х**] *poss. adj. & pron.* my; mine.

мо́йка *n.* **1**, *colloq.* washing. **2**, [*gen. pl.* **мо́ек**] washer (*machine*).

мо́йщик *n.* washer (*one who washes*).

мокаси́н [*gen. pl.* **-си́н**] *n.* moccasin.

мокаси́новый *adj.*, *in* **мокаси́новая змея́**, moccasin (*snake*).

мо́кко *n. indecl.* mocha.

мо́кнуть *v.impfv.* [*past* **мок** *or* **мо́кнул, мо́кла**] **1**, to become wet; get wet. **2**, to soak.

мокри́ца *n.* wood louse.

мокрова́тый *adj.* moist; damp.

мокро́та *n.* phlegm.

мокрота́ *n.*, *colloq.* **1**, dampness; humidity. **2**, light rain; wet snow.

мо́крый *adj.* wet. —**у неё глаза́ на мо́кром ме́сте**, she is easily moved to tears.

мол[1] *n.* breakwater; jetty.

мол[2] *particle*, *colloq.* he says; they say.

молва́ *n.* rumors; talk.

мо́лвить *v.impfv. & pfv.* [*pres.* **-влю, -вишь**] *obs.*, *poetic* to say.

молдова́нин [*pl.* **-ва́не, -ва́н**] *n.m.* [*fem.* **-ва́нка**] Moldovan. —**молда́вский**, *adj.* Moldovan.

моле́бен [*gen.* **-бна**] *n.* short church service.

моле́кула *n.* molecule. —**молекуля́рный**, *adj.* molecular.

моле́льня [*gen. pl.* **-лен**] *n.* prayer house; meeting house.

моле́ние *n.* **1**, prayer service: соверши́ть моле́ние, to hold a prayer service. **2**, entreaty; supplication.

молески́н *n.* moleskin (*cloth*). —**молески́новый**, *adj.* moleskin.

молибде́н (дэ) *n.* molybdenum. —**молибде́новый**, *adj.* molybdic.

моли́тва *n.* prayer. —**моли́твенник**, *n.* prayer book. —**моли́твенный**, *adj.* of prayer.

моли́ть *v.impfv.* [*pres.* **молю́, мо́лишь**] **1**, to entreat; beseech. **2**, (*with* **о**) to beg (for); plead (for). —**моли́ться**, *refl.* **1**, [*pfv.* **помоли́ться**] to pray. **2**, (*with* **на** + *acc.*) *colloq.* to idolize.

моллю́ск *n.* mollusk; shellfish.

молниено́сный *adj.* quick as lightning; lightning fast. —**молниено́сная война́**, blitzkrieg.

молниеотво́д *n.* lightning rod.

мо́лния *n.* **1**, lightning. **2**, [*also*, **застёжка-мо́лния**] zipper. **3**, express telegram. **4**, special edition (*of a newspaper*).

молодёжный *adj.* youth (*attrib.*).

молодёжь *n.f.* youth; young people.

моло́денький *adj.* young; very young.

молоде́ть *v.impfv.* [*pfv.* **помолоде́ть**] to get younger; become young again.

молоде́ц [*gen.* **-дца́**] *n.* good boy; fine fellow. —*interj.* well done!

молоде́цкий *adj.* bold; dashing.

молоде́чество *n.* daring; bravado.

молоди́ть *v.impfv.* [*pres.* **-жу́, -ди́шь**] to make (someone) look younger; give a youthful appearance to.

молодня́к [*gen.* **-няка́**] *n.* **1**, young animals. **2**, young forest. **3**, *colloq.* youth; the younger generation.

молодожёны [*gen.* **-жёнов**] *n.pl.* newlyweds.

молодо́й *adj.* [*short form* **мо́лод, молода́, мо́лодо, мо́лоды**; *compr.* **моло́же**] **1**, young. **2**, (*of qualities or emotions*) youthful: молодо́й задо́р, youthful enthusiasm. **3**, (*of potatoes, wine, etc.*) new. —**молоды́е**, *n.pl.* **1**, young people. **2**, young couple; newlyweds. **3**, (*of animals*) newly-born; (their) young.

мо́лодость *n.f.* youth. —**втора́я мо́лодость**, new lease on life. —**не пе́рвой мо́лодости**, getting on in years; no spring chicken. —**по мо́лодости лет**, through inexperience.

молодцева́тый *adj.* dashing.

моло́дчик *n.*, *colloq.* punk; thug.

молодчи́на *n.m.*, *colloq.* = **молоде́ц**.

моложа́вый *adj.* young-looking; youthful.

моло́же *adj.*, *comp. of* **молодо́й**.

моло́ки [*gen.* **моло́к**] *n.pl.* milt; soft roe.

молоко́ *n.* milk. —**кровь с молоко́м**, the picture of health.

молокосо́с *n.*, *colloq.* greenhorn; neophyte.

мо́лот *n.* (large) hammer; sledgehammer.

молоти́лка [*gen. pl.* **-лок**] *n.* thresher; threshing machine.

молоти́льщик *n.* thresher (*one who threshes*).

молоти́ть *v.impfv.* [*pfv.* **смолоти́ть**; *pres.* **-лочу́, -ло́тишь**] **1**, to thresh. **2**, *colloq.* to thrash.

молото́к [*gen.* **-тка́**] *n.* hammer. —**продава́ть с молотка́**, to auction (off).

мо́лот-ры́ба *n.* hammerhead (*fish*).

мо́лотый *adj.* ground.

моло́ть *v.impfv.* [*pfv.* **смоло́ть**; *pres.* **мелю́, ме́лешь**] **1**, to grind. **2**, [*impfv. only*] *colloq.* to talk (nonsense).

молотьба́ *n.* **1**, threshing. **2**, threshing season.

моло́чная *n.*, *decl. as an adj.* dairy.

моло́чник *n.* **1**, milk pitcher. **2**, milkman; dairyman.

моло́чница *n.* **1**, dairymaid. **2**, thrush (*disease*).

моло́чный *adj.* **1**, milk (*attrib.*). **2**, dairy (*attrib.*). **3**, milky. **4**, suckling. **5**, lactic. —**моло́чные же́лезы**, mammary glands. —**моло́чный зуб**, baby tooth. —**моло́чная коро́ва**, milch cow. —**моло́чный са́хар**, milk sugar; lactose. —**моло́чный скот**, dairy cattle.

молча́ *adv.* silently; in silence.

молчали́вый *adj.* **1**, taciturn; reticent. **2**, tacit. —**молчали́вость**, *n.f.* taciturnity; reticence.

молча́ние *n.* silence. —**обойти́ что-нибудь молча́нием**, to pass over in silence. —**храни́ть молча́ние**, to maintain silence; keep *or* remain silent.

молча́ть *v.impfv.* [*pres.* **-чу́, -чи́шь**] to be quiet; keep quiet; be silent.

молчо́к [*gen.* **-чка́**] *n., colloq.* silence; no answer; not a word.

моль *n.f.* moth; clothes moth.

мольба́ *n.* entreaty; supplication.

мольбе́рт *n.* easel.

моля́щийся *n., decl. as an adj.* worshiper.

моме́нт *n.* **1,** moment; instant: в да́нный моме́нт, at the present moment. **2,** feature; element; factor; aspect.

момента́льно *adv.* instantly; instantaneously; immediately. —**момента́льный,** *adj.* instantaneous.

мона́рх *n.* monarch. —**монархи́зм,** *n.* monarchism. —**монархи́ст,** *n.* monarchist. —**монархи́ческий,** *adj.* monarchist; monarchical. —**мона́рхия,** *n.* monarchy.

монасты́рь [*gen.* **-ря́**] *n.m.* monastery; convent; cloister. —**монасты́рский,** *adj.* of a monastery; monasterial.

мона́х *n.* monk. —**постри́чься в мона́хи,** to take the monastic vows.

мона́хиня *n.* nun. —**постри́чься в мона́хини,** to take the veil.

мона́шенка [*gen. pl.* **-нок**] *n., colloq.* nun.

мона́шеский *adj.* monastic.

мона́шество *n.* **1,** monasticism; monkhood. Приня́ть мона́шество, to take the monastic vows; become a monk *or* nun. **2,** monks.

монго́л *n.m.* [*fem.* **-го́лка**] Mongol. —**монго́льский,** *adj.* Mongol; Mongolian.

моне́та *n.* coin. Ме́лкая *or* разме́нная моне́та, small change. —**плати́ть той же моне́той,** to repay in kind. —**принима́ть за чи́стую моне́ту,** to take in good faith; take at face value.

моне́тный *adj.* monetary. —**моне́тный двор,** mint.

мони́зм *n.* monism. —**монисти́ческий,** *adj.* monistic.

мони́сто *n.* necklace (*of beads or coins*).

монито́р *n.* television monitor.

монога́мия *n.* monogamy. —**монога́мный,** *adj.* monogamous.

моногра́мма *n.* monogram.

моногра́фия *n.* monograph. —**монографи́ческий,** *adj.* monographic.

моно́кль *n.m.* monocle.

моноли́т *n.* monolith.

моноли́тный *adj.* monolithic. —**моноли́тность,** *n.f.* monolithic nature.

моноло́г *n.* monologue; soliloquy.

мононуклео́з *n.* mononucleosis.

монопла́н *n.* monoplane.

монополиза́ция *n.* monopolization.

монополизи́ровать *v.impfv. & pfv.* [*pres.* **-рую, -руешь**] to monopolize.

монополи́ст *n.* monopolist. —**монополисти́ческий,** *adj.* monopolistic.

монопо́лия *n.* monopoly.

монопо́льный *adj.* **1,** monopoly (*attrib.*). **2,** exclusive.

моноспекта́кль *n.m.* one-man (*or* one-woman) show.

монотеи́зм (тэ) *n.* monotheism. —**монотеисти́ческий,** *adj.* monotheistic.

моноти́п *n.* monotype.

моното́нный *adj.* **1,** monotone. **2,** monotonous. —**моното́нность,** *n.f.* monotony.

монохромати́ческий *adj.* monochromatic.

монсенье́р *n.* Monsignor.

монта́ж [*gen.* **-жа́**] *n.* **1,** assembling; installing (*of machinery*). **2,** editing (*of a film or literary work*); arrangement (*of a musical composition*). **3,** montage.

монта́жник *n.* fitter.

монтёр *n.* **1,** fitter. **2,** electrician.

монти́ровать *v.impfv.* [*pfv.* **смонти́ровать;** *pres.* **-рую, -руешь**] **1,** to assemble. **2,** to edit (a film).

монуме́нт *n.* monument. —**монумента́льный,** *adj.* monumental.

мопе́д *n.* motorbike; moped.

мопс *n.* pug (*dog*).

морализи́ровать *v.impfv.* [*pres.* **-рую, -руешь**] to moralize.

морали́ст *n.* moralist.

мора́ль *n.f.* **1,** morals; morality. **2,** moral; moral lesson. **3,** *colloq.* moralizing. —**чита́ть мора́ль** (+ *dat.*), to lecture; preach to.

мора́льно *adv.* morally. —**мора́льно устарева́ть,** to become obsolescent.

мора́льный *adj.* moral. —**мора́льный дух; мора́льное состоя́ние,** morale. —**мора́льный изно́с,** obsolescence. —**мора́льный уще́рб,** psychological damage.

морато́рий *n.* moratorium.

морг *n.* morgue.

морганати́ческий *adj.* morganatic.

морга́ть *v.impfv.* [*pfv.* **моргну́ть**] **1,** to blink. **2,** (*with instr.*) to blink (one's eyes). **3,** (*with dat.*) to wink (at). **4,** to twinkle; flicker. —**гла́зом не моргну́в,** without batting an eye.

мо́рда *n.* **1,** snout; muzzle. **2,** *colloq.* face; mug.

мордви́н *n.m.* [*fem.* **-ви́нка**] Mordvin (*one of a people inhabiting central European Russia*). —**мордо́вский,** *adj.* Mordvinian; Mordovian.

мо́ре [*pl.* **моря́, море́й**] *n.* sea. —**за мо́ре** (*or* **за́ море**); **за мо́рем** (*or* **за́ морем**), overseas. —**на мо́ре; на́ море, 1,** at sea. **2,** at the seashore. —**плыть по мо́рю** *or* **по́ морю,** to sail the seas. —**у мо́ря,** at the seashore.

море́на *n.* moraine.

морёный *adj.* stained: морёный дуб, stained oak.

морепла́вание *n.* navigation. —**морепла́ватель,** *n.m.* navigator.

морехо́д *n.* = морепла́ватель.

морехо́дный *adj.* **1,** nautical; navigational. **2,** seaworthy.

морж [*gen.* **моржа́**] *n.* walrus.

Мо́рзе (зэ) *n. indecl.,* in а́збука Мо́рзе, Morse code.

мори́лка *n.* stain (*for wood*).

мори́ть *v.impfv.* **1,** [*pfv.* **вы́морить**] to exterminate; poison (insects, rodents, etc.). **2,** [*pfv.* **замори́ть**] *colloq.* to wear out; exhaust. **3,** [*impfv. only*] to stain (wood). —**мори́ть го́лодом,** to starve.

морко́вь *n.f.* **1,** carrots. **2,** a (single) carrot. —**морко́вный,** *adj.* carrot (*attrib.*).

мормо́н *n.* Mormon. —**мормо́нский,** *adj.* Mormon.

моро́женое *n., decl. as an adj.* ice cream.

моро́женщик *n.* ice-cream vendor.

моро́женый *adj.* frozen.

моро́з *n.* **1,** frost: де́сять гра́дусов моро́за, ten degrees of frost. **2,** freezing weather.

морóзец [*gen.* **-зца**] *n., colloq.* slight frost.

морозúлка [*gen. pl.* **-лок**] *n.* freezing compartment; freezer. *Also,* **морозúльник**.

морóзить *v.impfv.* [*pres.* **-жу, -зишь**] **1,** to freeze. **2,** *impers.* to be freezing: На дворé морóзит, it is freezing outside.

морóзный *adj.* frosty; freezing.

морозостóйкий *adj.* frost-resistant; hardy.

моросúть *v.impfv.* to drizzle.

морóчить *v.impfv.* [*pfv.* **обморóчить**] *colloq.* to trick; fool. —**морóчить гóлову** (+ *dat.*), to mislead; deceive.

морóшка *n.* **1,** cloudberries. **2,** a (single) cloudberry.

морс *n.* fruit drink.

морскóй *adj.* **1,** sea (*attrib.*); maritime; marine; nautical. **2,** naval. —**морскáя болéзнь**, seasickness. —**морскóе млекопитáющее**, aquatic mammal. —**морскáя пехóта**, the marines. —**морскóй флот**, navy.

мортúра *n., mil.* mortar.

морфéма *n.* morpheme.

мóрфий *n.* morphine.

морфинúст *n.* morphine addict.

морфолóгия *n.* morphology. —**морфологúческий**, *adj.* morphological.

морщúна *n.* wrinkle.

морщúнистый *adj.* wrinkled. Морщúнистый лоб, furrowed brow.

мóрщить *v.impfv.* **1,** [*pfv.* **намóрщить**] to knit (one's brow). **2,** [*pfv.* **смóрщить**] to purse (one's lips); wrinkle (one's nose).

морщúть *v.impfv., colloq.* (*of material*) to become creased; pucker.

мóрщиться *v.r.impfv.* [*pfv.* **смóрщиться** *or* **намóрщиться**] **1,** (*of one's skin*) to become wrinkled; (*of one's brow*) to become furrowed. **2,** to make a face; wince.

моряк *n.* [*gen.* **-якá**] *n.* sailor; seaman.

москатéль *n.f.* paint supplies. —**москатéльный**, *adj.* pert. to paint supplies: москатéльный магазúн, store selling paint supplies.

москвúч [*gen.* **-вичá**] *n.* Muscovite; native of Moscow.

москúт *n.* sand fly.

москóвский *adj.* Moscow (*attrib.*).

мост [*gen.* **мостá** *or* **мóста**; *2nd loc.* **мостý**; *pl.* **мосты**] *n.* bridge.

мóстик *n.* **1,** small bridge; footbridge. **2,** bridge (*of a ship*).

мостúть *v.impfv.* [*pfv.* **выúмостить**; *pres.* **мощý, мостúшь**] to pave.

мосткú [*gen.* **-кóв**] *n.pl.* **1,** planked walkway. **2,** wooden platform (*extending out over water*).

мостовáя *n., decl. as an adj.* roadway.

мостовóй *adj.* bridge (*attrib.*).

мосьé *n.m. indecl.* monsieur.

мóська *n., colloq.* pug (*dog*).

мот *n., colloq.* spendthrift.

мотáльный *adj., colloq.* winding.

мотáть *v.impfv.* **1,** [*pfv.* **намотáть**] to wind. **2,** [*pfv.* **мотнýть**] (*with instr.*) *colloq.* to shake (one's head). —**мотáть себé на ус**, *colloq.* to make a mental note of.

мотáться *v.r.impfv., colloq.* **1,** to dangle; bob. **2,** to fuss; rush about. **3,** to wander; knock about.

мотéль (тэ) *n.m.* motel.

мотúв *n.* **1,** motive; reason. **2,** motif; theme. **3,** tune; melody.

мотивúровать *v.impfv. & pfv.* [*pres.* **-рую, -руешь**] to explain; justify; give reasons for; show just cause for.

мотивирóвка *n.* reasons; justification.

мотнýть *v., pfv. of* **мотáть** (*in sense #2*).

мотобóл *n.* football (soccer) played on motorcycles.

мотовствó *n.* extravagance; prodigality.

мотогóнки [*gen.* **-нок**] *n.pl.* motorcycle races; motorcycle racing.

мотóк [*gen.* **моткá**] *n.* skein; hank (*of thread*).

мотопехóта *n.* motorized infantry.

мотопилá *n.* power saw.

мотóр *n.* motor; engine.

моторизóванный *adj.* motorized.

мотóрный *adj.* motor (*attrib.*).

моторóллер *n.* motor scooter.

мотострелкóвый *adj., mil.* motorized rifle (*attrib.*).

мотоцúкл *also,* **мотоциклéт**, *n.* motorcycle. —**мотоциклúст**, *n.* motorcyclist.

мотыúга *n.* hoe.

мотыúжить *v.impfv.* to hoe.

мотылёк [*gen.* **-лькá**] *n.* moth.

мох [*gen.* **мха** *or* **мóха**] *n.* moss.

мохéр *n.* mohair. —**мохéровый**, *adj.* mohair.

мохнáтый *adj.* shaggy; hairy.

моциóн *n.* walking (*as a form of exercise*); walk; constitutional.

мочá *n.* urine.

мочáлка [*gen. pl.* **-лок**] *n.* piece of bast used as a bath sponge.

мочáло *n.* bast.

мочевúна *n.* urea.

мочевóй *adj.* **1,** urinary. **2,** uric. —**мочевáя кислотá**, uric acid. —**мочевóй песóк**, *med.* gravel.

мочегóнный *adj.* diuretic. —**мочегóнное срéдство**, diuretic.

мочеиспускáние *n.* urination.

мочеиспускáтельный *adj.* urinary. —**мочеиспускáтельный канáл**, urethra.

мочёный *adj.* (*of foods*) soaked.

мочúть *v.impfv.* [*pfv.* **намочúть** *or* **замочúть**; *pres.* **мочý, мóчишь**] **1,** to wet. **2,** to get (something wet). **3,** to soak. —**мочúться**, *refl.* [*pfv.* **помочúться**] to urinate.

мóчка [*gen. pl.* **-чек**] *n.* **1,** wetting; soaking. **2,** ear lobe.

мочь[1] *v.impfv.* [*pfv.* **смочь**; *pres.* **могý, мóжешь, ...мóгут**; *past* **мог, моглá, моглó, моглú**] **1,** to be able: Я не могý прийтú сегóдня, I am unable to come today; I can't come today. **2,** may; (*with* **бы**) might: Вы мóжете тепéрь идтú, you may go now. Вы моглú бы предложúть свою пóмощь, you might have offered to help. —**мóжет быть**, perhaps; maybe. —**мочь не** (+ *inf.*), **1,** (*present tense*) one need not. **2,** (*present tense*) one may not. **3,** (*past tense*) one didn't have to. —**не мóжет быть!**, impossible!; it can't be! —**не мочь не** (+ *inf.*), **1,** one can't help: Я не могý не ду́мать об э́том, I can't help thinking about it. **2,** must: Он не мо́жет не знать об э́том, he must know about it.

мочь² *n.f., colloq.* power; might. —**во всю мочь; изо всей мо́чи; что есть мо́чи, 1,** with all one's might. **2,** for all one is worth. **3,** at the top of one's lungs.

моше́нник *n.* swindler.

моше́нничать *v.impfv.* [*pfv.* **смоше́нничать**] to engage in fraud.

моше́ннический *adj.* fraudulent. —**моше́нничество,** *n.* swindle; swindling; fraud.

мо́шка [*gen. pl.* **мо́шек**] *n.* gnat; midge. —**мошкара́,** *n.* gnats.

мошо́нка *n.* scrotum.

моще́ние *n.* paving.

мощёный *adj.* paved.

мо́щи [*gen.* **мощей**] *n.pl.* earthly remains (*of a saint*).

мо́щность *n.f.* **1,** power. **2,** output; capacity: рабо́тать на по́лную мо́щность, to operate at full capacity.

мо́щный *adj.* powerful.

мощь *n.f.* power; might. Огнева́я мощь, firepower. —**во всю мощь; на по́лную мощь,** full force.

мо́ющий *adj., in* мо́ющее сре́дство, cleanser; detergent.

мразь *n.f., colloq.* scum; dregs.

мрак *n.* darkness; gloom. —**покры́т мра́ком неизве́стности,** shrouded in secrecy.

мракобе́с *n.* obscurantist. —**мракобе́сие,** *n.* obscurantism.

мра́мор *n.* marble. —**мра́морный,** *adj.* marble.

мрачне́ть *v.impfv.* [*pfv.* **помрачне́ть**] to grow dark; become gloomy.

мра́чность *n.f.* **1,** gloominess; dreariness. **2,** moroseness.

мра́чный *adj.* **1,** gloomy; dismal; dreary; bleak. **2,** somber; morose; glum.

мсти́тель *n.m.* avenger.

мсти́тельный *adj.* vindictive. —**мсти́тельность,** *n.f.* vindictiveness.

мстить *v.impfv.* [*pfv.* **отомсти́ть;** *pres.* **мщу, мстишь**] **1,** (*with dat.*) to take revenge on. **2,** (*with* **за** + *acc.*) to avenge.

муар *n.* moire. —**муа́ровый,** *adj.* moiré.

мудрено́ *adj., used predicatively,* difficult; next to impossible: Мудрено́ поня́ть его́, there is no making him out. —**не мудрено́,** it is no wonder.

мудрёный *adj., colloq.* **1,** difficult; hard to understand; esoteric. **2,** (*of a task*) difficult; formidable. **3,** intricate; fancy. **4,** odd; queer.

мудре́ц [*gen.* **-реца́**] *n.* wise man; sage.

мудри́ть *v.impfv., colloq.* to make matters unnecessarily complicated.

му́дрость *n.f.* wisdom.

му́дрствовать *v.impfv.* [*pres.* **-ствую, -ствуешь**] *colloq.* to philosophize. —**не му́дрствуя лука́во,** without equivocation; without beating around the bush.

му́дрый *adj.* wise.

муж [*pl.* **мужья́, муже́й, мужья́м**] *n.* husband.

мужа́ть *v.impfv.* to mature; become a man. —**мужа́ться,** *refl.* (*usu. imperative*) to be brave.

мужеподо́бный *adj.* mannish.

му́жественно *adv.* bravely; courageously.

му́жественность *n.f.* **1,** courageousness. **2,** manliness; masculinity.

му́жественный *adj.* **1,** brave; courageous. **2,** manly.

му́жество *n.* courage.

мужи́к [*gen.* **-жика́**] *n., pre-rev.* Russian peasant; muzhik.

мужско́й *adj.* **1,** masculine; male. **2,** man's; men's.

мужчи́на *n.m.* man.

му́за *n.* muse.

музе́й *n.* museum.

музе́йный *adj.* museum (*attrib.*). —**музе́йная ре́дкость,** museum piece.

му́зыка *n.* music. —**испо́ртить всю му́зыку,** *colloq.* to upset the applecart.

музыка́льный *adj.* **1,** music (*attrib.*). **2,** musical. —**музыка́льный ве́чер,** musicale. —**музыка́льный слух,** ear for music. —**музыка́льная шкату́лка; музыка́льный я́щик,** music box.

музыка́нт *n.* musician.

музыкове́д *n.* musicologist. —**музыкове́дение,** *n.* musicology.

му́ка *n.* **1,** torment; torture; agony. **2,** *pl.* pangs; throes.

мука́ *n.* **1,** flour. **2,** meal.

мукомо́льный *adj.* flour-milling (*attrib.*).

мул *n.* mule.

мула́т *n.m.* [*fem.* **-ка**] mulatto.

мулла́ *n.* mullah.

мультимиллионе́р *n.* multimillionaire.

мультипликацио́нный *adj., in* **мультиплика-цио́нный фильм,** (animated) cartoon.

мультиплика́ция *n.* making of animated cartoons.

мультфи́льм *n.* (animated) cartoon.

му́льча *n.* mulch.

му́мия *n.* mummy.

мунди́р *n.* uniform dress coat. —**карто́фель в мунди́ре,** potatoes boiled in their skins.

мундштук [*gen.* **-штука́**] *n.* **1,** mouthpiece. **2,** cigarette holder; cigar holder.

муниципалите́т *n.* municipality.

муниципа́льный *adj.* municipal.

мура́ *n., colloq.* rubbish; nonsense.

мураве́й [*gen.* **-вья́**] *n.* ant.

мураве́йник *n.* anthill.

мураве́д *n.* anteater.

муравьи́ный *adj.* **1,** ant (*attrib.*); ants'. **2,** *chem.* formic.

мура́шки *n.pl., colloq., in* мура́шки бе́гают (забе́-гали, попо́лзли) по спине́ (*with* **у**), to get the creeps; get chills up and down one's spine.

муре́на *n.* moray (eel).

мурлы́канье *n.* purr; purring.

мурлы́кать *v.impfv.* [*pres.* **-лы́чу, -лы́чешь**] **1,** to purr. **2,** *colloq.* to hum.

муска́т *n.* **1,** nutmeg. **2,** muscat (*grape*). **3,** muscatel (*wine*). —**муска́тник,** *n.* nutmeg (*tree*).

муска́тный *adj.* nutmeg. —**муска́тное вино́,** muscatel wine. —**муска́тный оре́х,** nutmeg. —**муска́тный цвет,** mace (*spice*).

му́скул *n.* muscle. —**мускулату́ра,** *n.* muscles; musculature. —**му́скулистый,** *adj.* muscular; brawny. —**му́скульный,** *adj.* muscle (*attrib.*); muscular.

му́скус *n.* musk. —**му́скусный,** *adj.* musk (*attrib.*).

мусли́н *n.* muslin. —**мусли́новый,** *adj.* muslin.

му́слить *v.impfv., colloq.* to moisten with saliva. *Also,* **мусо́лить.**

му́сор *n.* garbage; rubbish; refuse; trash.

му́сорный *adj.* garbage (*attrib.*); rubbish (*attrib.*); refuse (*attrib.*); trash (*attrib.*). —**му́сорный я́щик,** garbage can; trash can.

мусоропрово́д *n.* garbage chute; refuse chute.

мусоросжига́тельный *adj., in* **мусоросжига́тельная печь,** incinerator.

му́сорщик *n.* garbage collector.

мусс *n.* mousse.

мусси́ровать *v.impfv.* [*pres.* -ру́ю, -ру́ешь] **1,** to spread; fan (rumors, fears, etc.). **2,** to exaggerate; blow up; overstate. **3,** to write a great deal about; cover extensively.

муссо́н *n.* monsoon.

муста́нг *n.* mustang.

мусульма́нин [*pl.* -ма́не, -ма́н] *n.m.* [*fem.* -ма́нка] Moslem. —**мусульма́нский,** *adj.* Moslem. —**мусульма́нство,** *n.* Mohammedanism; Islam.

мута́ция *n.* mutation.

мути́ть *v.impfv.* [*pres.* мучу́, му́тишь *or* мути́шь] **1,** [*pfv.* замути́ть] to make turbid; muddy (water). **2,** [*pfv.* помути́ть] to dull; cloud (the senses). **3,** *in* **мути́ть во́ду,** *colloq.* to muddy the waters. **4,** *impers., colloq.* to feel nauseous: Его́ мути́т, he feels nauseous. —**мути́ться,** *refl.* **1,** [*pfv.* замути́ться] to become cloudy. **2,** [*pfv.* помути́ться] (*of the senses*) to become dulled.

мутне́ть *v.impfv.* [*pfv.* помутне́ть] to become cloudy; become muddy.

му́тность *n.f.* turbidity.

му́тный *adj.* **1,** turbid; murky. **2,** clouded; misty. **3,** dull; dim. **4,** (*of the senses*) dulled. —**лови́ть ры́бу в му́тной воде́,** to fish in troubled waters.

муто́вка [*gen. pl.* -вок] *n.* **1,** *bot.* whorl. **2,** stick for churning or whipping.

му́торный *adj., colloq.* dull; dreary; tedious.

муть *n.f.* **1,** dregs; lees. **2,** haze; mist.

му́фта *n.* **1,** muff. **2,** *mech.* coupling; clutch.

му́фтий *adj.* mufti (*interpreter of Moslem law*).

му́ха *n.* fly (*insect*). —**де́лать из му́хи слона́,** to make a mountain out of a molehill. —**кака́я му́ха его́ укуси́ла?,** what's gotten into him?; what's eating him? —**он и му́хи не оби́дит,** he wouldn't hurt a fly. —**слы́шно, как му́ха пролети́т,** you could have heard a pin drop.

мухоло́вка [*gen. pl.* -вок] *n.* **1,** flytrap; flycatcher. **2,** flycatcher (*bird*). **3,** flytrap (*plant*).

мухомо́р *n.* a variety of poisonous mushroom; fly agaric.

муче́ние *n.* torment; torture.

му́ченик *n.* martyr. —**му́ченический,** *adj.* martyr's. —**му́ченичество,** *n.* martyrdom.

мучи́тель *n.m.* tormentor.

мучи́тельно *adv.* **1,** painfully. **2,** terribly. —*adj., used predicatively,* agonizing: Мучи́тельно смотре́ть на них, it is an agony/ordeal to look at them.

мучи́тельный *adj.* **1,** painful; agonizing; excruciating. **2,** of anguish; anguished.

му́чить *v.impfv.* [*pres.* му́чу, му́чишь *or* му́чаю, му́чаешь] to torment; plague. Их му́чила жа́жда, they were dying of thirst. Меня́ му́чит неизве́стность, the suspense is killing me. Меня́ му́чит любопы́тство, I am dying of curiosity. —**му́читься,** *refl.* **1,** to suffer. **2,** (*with instr.*) to be plagued (with); be beset (with). **3,** (*with* с + *instr. or* над) *colloq.* to struggle (with *or* over)

мучни́стый *adj.* **1,** farinaceous. **2,** mealy. —**мучни́стая роса́,** mildew.

мучно́е *n., decl. as an adj.* starchy foods.

мучно́й *adj.* flour (*attrib.*).

му́шка [*gen. pl.* му́шек] *n.* **1,** *dim. of* му́ха. **2,** beauty spot. **3,** front sight (*on a firearm*). —**взять на му́шку,** to draw a bead on.

мушке́т *n.* musket. —**мушкетёр,** *n.* musketeer.

мушмула́ *n.* medlar.

муштра́ *n.* **1,** drill; drilling. **2,** strict discipline; regimentation.

муштрова́ть *v.impfv.* [*pfv.* вы́муштровать; *pres.* -тру́ю, -тру́ешь] to drill.

муштро́вка *n.* drilling.

муэдзи́н *n.* muezzin.

мчать *v.impfv.* [*pfv.* помча́ть; *pres.* мчу, мчишь] to rush; whisk. —**мча́ться,** *refl.* to race; speed along; tear along.

мши́стый *adj.* mossy.

мще́ние *n.* revenge; vengeance.

мы [*gen., acc. & prepl.* нас; *dat.* нам; *instr.* на́ми] *pers. pron., 1st person pl.* **1,** we. **2,** (*with* с + *instr.*) and I: мы с вами, you and I.

мы́каться *v.r.impfv., colloq.* to wander; knock about.

мы́лить *v.impfv.* [*pfv.* намы́лить] to soap; lather. —**мы́литься,** *refl.* to soap oneself.

мы́лкий *adj.* (*of soap*) soft; easily lathering.

мы́ло *n.* soap.

мылова́рение *n.* soap making.

мылова́ренный *adj., in* **мылова́ренный заво́д,** soap works.

мы́льница *n.* soap dish.

мы́льный *adj.* **1,** soap (*attrib.*). **2,** soapy.

мыльня́нка *n.* soapwort.

мыс *n., geog.* cape.

мы́сленный *adj.* mental. —**мы́сленно,** *adv.* mentally; in one's mind.

мысли́мый *adj.* conceivable.

мысли́тель *n.m.* thinker.

мы́слить *v.impfv.* to think; reason.

мысль *n.f.* **1,** thought. **2,** idea. —**за́дняя мысль,** ulterior motive. —**о́браз мы́слей,** way of thinking. —**ход мы́слей,** train of thought.

мы́слящий *adj.* thinking; capable of thinking.

мыта́рить *v.impfv., colloq.* to torment. —**мыта́риться,** *refl., colloq.* to suffer; have a hard time of it; go through hell.

мыта́рство *n., usu. pl.* ordeal; tribulation.

мыть *v.impfv.* [*pfv.* помы́ть *or* вы́мыть; *pres.* мо́ю, мо́ешь] to wash.

мытьё *n.* washing.

мы́ться *v.r.impfv.* [*pfv.* помы́ться *or* вы́мыться; *pres.* мо́юсь, мо́ешься] to wash; wash oneself.

мыча́ние *n.* **1,** moo; mooing. **2,** *colloq.* mumbling.

мыча́ть *v.impfv.* [*pres.* **-чу́, -чи́шь**] **1,** to moo; bellow. **2,** *colloq.* to mumble.

мышело́вка [*gen. pl.* **-вок**] *n.* mousetrap.

мы́шечный *adj.* muscle (*attrib.*); muscular.

мыши́ный *adj.* **1,** mouse (*attrib.*). **2,** like that of a mouse. —**мыши́ная возня́,** fuss over nothing. —**мыши́ный хво́стик,** pigtail.

мы́шка [*gen. pl.* **мы́шек**] *n.* **1,** *dim. of* мышь. **2,** *in* под мы́шкой *and* под мы́шку, under one's arm: нести́ под мы́шкой, to carry under one's arm. —**игра́ в ко́шки-мы́шки,** cat-and-mouse game.

мышле́ние *also,* **мы́шление** *n.* thinking; thought.

мышо́нок [*gen.* **-нка**; *pl.* **-ша́та, -ша́т**] *n.* baby mouse.

мы́шца *n.* muscle.

мышь [*pl.* **мы́ши, мыше́й, мыша́м**] *n.f.* mouse. —**лету́чая мышь,** bat.

мышья́к [*gen.* **-яка́**] *n.* arsenic. —**мышьяко́вый,** *adj.* arsenic (*attrib.*).

мэр *n.* mayor.

мэ́рия *n.* **1,** city administration. **2,** mayor's office; city hall.

мю́зикл *n.* musical.

мю́зик-хо́лл *n.* music hall.

мя́гкий *adj.* [*short form* **мя́гок, мягка́, мя́гко, мя́гки;** *comp.* **мя́гче**] **1,** soft. **2,** mild. **3,** gentle. **4,** (*of punishment, a sentence, etc.*) light. —**мя́гкий ваго́н,** coach with soft (upholstered) seats. —**мя́гкий знак,** soft sign (ь).

мя́гко *adv.* **1,** softly. **2,** mildly. —**мя́гко выража́ясь,** to put it mildly.

мягкосерде́чие *n.* softheartedness; tenderheartedness. *Also,* **мягкосерде́чность,** *n.f.*

мягкосерде́чный *adj.* softhearted; tenderhearted.

мя́гкость *n.f.* softness; mildness; gentleness.

мягкоте́лый *adj.* **1,** flabby; soft. **2,** *fig.* spineless.

мя́гче *adj., comp. of* **мя́гкий.**

мягчи́ть *v.impfv.* to soften (the skin).

мяки́на *n.* chaff. —**его́ на мяки́не не проведёшь,** you can't fool him.

мя́киш *n.* the soft part of bread.

мя́кнуть *v.impfv.* [*pfv.* **размя́кнуть;** *past* **мяк, мя́кла**] *colloq.* **1,** to become soft; become flabby. **2,** to go limp.

мя́коть *n.f.* **1,** flesh. **2,** pulp (*of fruit*).

мя́млить *v.impfv.* [*pfv.* **промя́млить**] *colloq.* **1,** to mumble. **2,** [*impfv. only*] to procrastinate. —**тяну́ть и мя́млить,** to hem and haw.

мя́мля *n.m. & f., colloq.* wishy-washy person.

мяси́стый *adj.* meaty; fleshy.

мясна́я *n., decl. as an adj., colloq.* butcher shop.

мясни́к [*gen.* **-ника́**] *n.* butcher.

мясно́й *adj.* meat (*attrib.*); beef (*attrib.*). —**мясна́я ла́вка,** butcher shop.

мя́со *n.* **1,** meat. **2,** flesh. —**сла́дкое мя́со,** sweetbread.

мясокомбина́т *n.* meat-packing plant.

мясору́бка [*gen. pl.* **-бок**] *n.* meat grinder.

мя́та *n., bot.* mint.

мяте́ж [*gen.* **-тежа́**] *n.* mutiny; revolt; rebellion. —**мяте́жник,** *n.* mutineer; rebel; insurgent.

мяте́жный *adj.* **1,** mutinous; rebellious. **2,** stormy; restless.

мя́тный *adj.* **1,** mint (*attrib.*). **2,** mint-flavored; peppermint.

мя́тый *adj.* crushed; crumpled; creased.

мять *v.impfv.* [*pres.* **мну, мнёшь**] **1,** [*pfv.* **размя́ть**] to knead; work (clay, leather, etc.). **2,** [*pfvs.* **измя́ть, помя́ть, смя́ть**] to rumple; crease; wrinkle; crush. **3,** [*pfv.* **смя́ть**] to crush; crumble. **4,** [*pfv.* **помя́ть**] to dent. **5,** [*pfv.* **помя́ть**] *colloq.* to press; squeeze. —**мя́ться,** *refl.* **1,** [*pfv.* **из-, по-, с-**] to wrinkle; crease; become rumpled. **2,** [*pfv.* **по-**] *colloq.* to hesitate; waver.

мяу́канье *n.* meow; meowing.

мяу́кать *v.impfv.* to meow.

мяч [*gen.* **мяча́**] *n.* ball.

мя́чик *n., dim. of* мяч.

Н

Н, н *n.neut.* fourteenth letter of the Russian alphabet.

на¹ *prep.* **A,** *with acc.* **1,** on; onto: сесть на зе́млю, to sit (down) on the ground; положи́ть кни́гу на стол, to put the book on the table; нагрузи́ть ме́бель на грузови́к, to load the furniture onto a truck. **2,** to (*used in place of* в *before certain nouns denoting a large building, an open place, an event, or direction*): идти́ на по́чту, на вокза́л, на фа́брику, на пло́щадь, на рабо́ту, на собра́ние, to go to the post office, station, factory, square, work, meeting. ♦*Also after certain nouns related to traveling:* по́езд на Москву́, the train to Moscow; сле́дующий рейс на Ри́гу, the next flight to Riga. **3,** for: уро́к на за́втра, the lesson for tomorrow; обе́д на двои́х, dinner for two. ♦*Also indicating the amount of time the result of an action lasts:* Он прие́хал на три дня, he has come to stay for three days. **4,** (*with certain nouns*) into: дели́ть на ча́сти, to divide into parts; переводи́ть на ру́сский язы́к, to translate into Russian. **5,** *indicating the degree of difference, as in comparisons:* Он на три го́да ста́рше меня́, he is three years older than I. Населе́ние увели́чилось на два миллио́на, the population increased by two million. **6,** by: продава́ть на фунт, to sell by the pound; шесть ме́тров на три, six by three meters; помно́жить семь на пять, to multiply seven by five. **7,** (*with dates*) as of: на пе́рвое ию́ля 1990, as of July 1, 1990. **8,** worth of: на рубль ма́рок, a ruble's worth of stamps. **B,** *with prepl.* **1,** on: Они́ сиде́ли на скаме́йке, they were sitting on a bench. Кни́га лежи́т на столе́, the book is (lying) on the table. **2,** in; at (*used in place of* **в** *as above*): на пло́щади, in the square; на конце́рте, at the concert. **3,** (*in certain time expressions*) in; at: на рассве́те, at dawn; на э́той неде́ле, this week; на шесто́м ме́сяце бере́менности, in her sixth month of pregnancy; на шестьдеся́т второ́м году́ жи́зни, at the age of 62. **4,** (*with modes of travel*) by: е́хать на по́езде, to go by train.

на² *particle, colloq.* here!: На, возьми́те!, here, take it! Да́йте мне, пожа́луйста, кни́гу! На!, Give me the book, please! Here! —**вот тебе́ и на́!**, look (*or* see) what happened!

на- *prefix* **1,** on; onto: наплева́ть, to spit on. **2,** *indicating accidental meeting or collision:* нае́хать, to run over; run down. **3,** (*with pfv. verbs only*) a quantity of: накупи́ть, to buy a quantity of. **4,** (*with* **-ся**) to one's heart's content: наигра́ться, to play to one's heart's content.

набавля́ть *v.impfv.* [*pfv.* **наба́вить**] **1,** to add on (a certain amount to the price of something). **2,** to raise (a price).

набалда́шник *n.* handle; knob (*of a walking stick*).

набальзами́ровать *v., pfv. of* **бальзами́ровать**.

наба́т *n.* alarm: бить (в) наба́т, to sound the alarm.

наба́тный *adj.* alarm (*attrib.*): наба́тный ко́локол, alarm bell.

набе́г *n.* raid; foray; incursion.

набега́ть *v.impfv.* [*pfv.* **набежа́ть**] **1,** (*with* **на** + *acc.*) to run into; smash into; dash against. **2,** (*of wind*) to blow up; (*of clouds*) to gather. **3,** (*with* **на** + *acc.*) (*of waves*) to sweep over; wash over. **4,** *colloq.* to appear suddenly; turn up suddenly. **5,** *colloq.* (*of many people*) to come running; congregate. **6,** *colloq.* to accumulate; pile up.

набе́гаться *v.r.pfv., colloq.* **1,** to run to one's heart's content. **2,** to tire oneself out by running.

набедоку́рить *v., pfv. of* **бедоку́рить**.

набе́дренный *adj., in* **набе́дренная повя́зка**, loincloth.

набежа́ть [*infl. like* **бежа́ть**] *v., pfv. of* **набега́ть**.

набекре́нь *adv.* cocked; at an angle; on one side.

набели́ть *v., pfv. of* **бели́ть** (*in sense #2*). —**набели́ться**, *refl., pfv. of* **бели́ться**.

на́бело *adv.* (*of something written*) in final form; without corrections or erasures.

на́бережная *n., decl. as an adj.* embankment.

набива́ть *v.impfv.* [*pfv.* **наби́ть**] **1,** to stuff; fill; cram; pack. **2,** to nail; attach. **3,** *colloq.* to give; cause (a

bump, bruise, swelling, etc.). **4,** *textiles* to print. —**наби́ть карма́н** *or* **мошну́**, *colloq.* to get rich. —**наби́ть ру́ку на** (+ *prepl.*), *colloq.* to become experienced at. —**наби́ть це́ну**, to jack up the price. —**наби́ть себе́ це́ну**, to build oneself up. *See also* **наби́ть**.

набива́ться *v.r.impfv.* [*pfv.* **наби́ться**] **1,** (*with* **в** + *acc.*) to crowd into. **2,** (*with instr.*) to be crammed (with); be jammed (with). **3,** *colloq.* to force; impose (oneself): набива́ться в друзья́, to force one's friendship on someone; набива́ться в го́сти, invite oneself somewhere.

наби́вка *n.* **1,** (act of) stuffing. **2,** stuffing; filling; packing; padding. **3,** *textiles* printing. —**наби́вка чу́чел**, taxidermy.

набивно́й *adj.* (*of fabric*) printed.

наби́вщик *n.* one who stuffs anything. —**наби́вщик чу́чел**, taxidermist.

набира́ть *v.impfv.* [*pfv.* **набра́ть**] **1,** (*with gen. or acc.*) to gather; collect (a quantity of something). **2,** (*with gen.*) *colloq.* to draw in; take in (water, air, etc.). **3,** to gain (strength, experience, altitude, etc.); gather; pick up (speed). **4,** to recruit; enlist. **5,** to form; assemble; put together (a group, team, etc.). **6,** to dial (a telephone number). **7,** *sports* to score (points). **8,** *printing* to compose; set in type.

набира́ться *v.r.impfv.* [*pfv.* **набра́ться**] **1,** (*of many people*) to gather. **2,** (*of dust, water, etc.*) to collect; accumulate. **3,** (*of work, debts, etc.*) to pile up; accumulate. **4,** (*with gen.*) to amount to; add up to. **5,** (*with gen.*) to summon up; muster (courage, strength, patience, etc.). **6,** (*with gen.*) to experience (fear, grief, etc.). **7,** (*with gen.*) *colloq.* to pick up; acquire. **8,** *colloq.* to get drunk. —**набра́ться ума́**, to get smart.

наби́тый *adj.* stuffed; tightly packed; crammed. —**наби́тый дура́к**, *colloq.* utter fool.

наби́ть *v.pfv.* [*infl.* **набью́, набьёшь**] **1,** *pfv. of* **набива́ть**. **2,** (*with gen.*) to drive in (a quantity of something, esp. nails). **3,** *colloq.* to shoot; kill; bag (a number of animals or birds). **4,** (*with gen.*) *colloq.* to break; smash (a number of things). —**наби́ться**, *refl., pfv. of* **набива́ться**.

наблюда́тель *n.m.* observer.

наблюда́тельность *n.f.* keenness of observation; powers of observation.

наблюда́тельный *adj.* **1,** observant. **2,** observation (*attrib.*): наблюда́тельный пост, observation post.

наблюда́ть *v.impfv.* (*with* **за** + *instr.*) **1,** (*also with acc.*) to observe; watch. **2,** to look after; keep an eye on. **3,** to monitor; supervise. **4,** to see that (order, cleanliness, etc.) is maintained. —**наблюда́ться**, *refl.* to exist; be seen: Наблюда́ются определённые тру́дности, certain difficulties exist (*or* are to be seen).

наблюде́ние *n.* **1,** observation. **2,** supervision. **3,** surveillance. —**вести́ наблюде́ние**, to keep a lookout.

на́божный *adj.* pious; devout. —**на́божность**, *n.f.* piety.

наби́йка [*gen. pl.* **-бо́ек**] *n.* **1,** printed fabric. **2,** lift; tap (*on a heel*).

на́бок *adv.* to one side.

наболе́вший *adj.* painful; sore. —**наболе́вший во-про́с,** sore subject; sore point.

наболе́ть *v.pfv.* [*infl.* **-боли́т**] to become painful.

наболта́ть *v.pfv.* (*with gen. or acc.*) *colloq.* to talk (a lot of).

набо́р *n.* **1,** registration; enrollment (*of students*); hiring; taking on (*of workers*). **2,** set; collection. **3,** *printing* composition. —**набо́р высоты́,** *aero.* climb. —**набо́р слов,** gibberish.

набо́рный *adj.* typesetting (*attrib.*); composition (*attrib.*).

набо́рщик *n.* typesetter; compositor.

набра́сывать[1] *v.impfv.* [*pfv.* **наброса́ть**] **1,** to toss (a quantity of something). **2,** to sketch; outline. **3,** to jot down; dash off.

набра́сывать[2] *v.impfv.* [*pfv.* **набро́сить**] to throw on; throw over: набро́сить что́-нибудь на́ пол/ на пле́чи/, to throw something on the floor/ over one's shoulders/. —**набра́сываться,** *refl.* (*with* на + *acc.*) **1,** to attack; pounce on. **2,** *colloq.* to jump on; jump down someone's throat.

набра́ть [*infl.* **-беру́, -берёшь**; *past fem.* **-брала́**] *v., pfv. of* **набира́ть.** —**набра́ться,** *refl.* [*past tense stress as in* **бра́ться**] *pfv. of* **набира́ться.**

набрести́ *v.pfv.* [*infl. like* **брести́**] **1,** (*with* на + *acc.*) to come upon; wander upon; *fig.* hit upon (an idea). **2,** *impers.* to gather (*in large numbers*): Набрело́ мно́го наро́ду, a large crowd gathered.

наброса́ть *v., pfv. of* **набра́сывать**[1].

набро́сить [*infl.* **-шу, -сишь**] *v., pfv. of* **набра́сы-вать**[2]. —**набро́ситься,** *refl., pfv. of* **набра́сываться.**

набро́сок [*gen.* **-ска**] *n.* sketch; draft; outline.

набры́згать *v.pfv.* (*with instr. or gen.*) to spill; splash.

набрю́шник *n.* abdominal band.

набря́кнуть *v.pfv.* [*past* **-бря́к, -бря́кла**] *colloq.* to swell up; become swollen.

набуха́ть *v.impfv.* [*pfv.* **набу́хнуть**] to swell.

набу́хнуть [*past* **набу́х, набу́хла**] *v., pfv. of* **набуха́ть.**

нава́га *n.* a variety of codfish found in northern waters.

наважде́ние *n.* delusion; hallucination.

навакси́ть *v., pfv. of* **ва́ксить.**

нава́ливать *v.impfv.* [*pfv.* **навали́ть**] **1,** (*with* на + *acc.*) to load (on); pile (on). **2,** to toss into a pile; pile up. **3,** *impers.* (*of snow*) to pile up. —**нава́ливаться,** *refl.* (*with* на + *acc.*) **1,** to lean heavily on; put all one's weight on. **2,** *colloq.* to attack; pounce on; tear into.

навали́ть [*infl.* **-валю́, -ва́лишь**] *v., pfv. of* **нава́ли-вать.** —**навали́ться,** *refl., pfv. of* **нава́ливаться.**

нава́лом *adv., colloq.* **1,** in a pile; in a heap. **2,** (*with gen.*) piles of; tons of: Рабо́ты у меня́ нава́лом, I have piles/tons of work.

нава́р *n.* fat (*forming on the surface of soup*).

нава́ривать *v.impfv.* [*pfv.* **навари́ть**] to weld on.

нава́ристый *adj.* (*of soup*) rich; concentrated.

навари́ть *v.pfv.* [*infl.* **-варю́, -ва́ришь**] **1,** *pfv. of* **нава́ривать. 2,** to cook (a quantity of something).

наварно́й *adj.* welded; welded on.

навева́ть *v.impfv.* [*pfv.* **наве́ять**] **1,** (*of the wind*) to bring on; waft. **2,** *fig.* to bring on; induce.

наве́даться *v.r., pfv. of* **наве́дываться.**

наведе́ние *n.* **1,** aiming (*of a gun*). **2,** applying; appli-cation (*of a polish*). **3,** *aerospace* guidance. **4,** *in* наве-де́ние спра́вок, making of inquiries.

наве́дываться *v.r.impfv.* [*pfv.* **наве́даться**] (*with* к) *colloq.* to drop in on; call on.

навезти́ *v.pfv.* [*infl. like* **везти́**] to bring (a quantity of something).

наве́к *also,* **наве́ки** *adv.* forever.

навербова́ть *v.pfv.* [*infl.* **-бу́ю, -бу́ешь**] to recruit (a quantity of people).

наве́рно *adv.* **1,** probably; most likely. **2,** *obs.* certainly; for sure. *Also,* **наве́рное.**

наверну́ть *v., pfv. of* **наве́ртывать.** —**наверну́ться,** *refl., pfv. of* **наве́ртываться.**

наверняка́ *adv., colloq.* **1,** for sure. **2,** when one is sure of success.

наверста́ть *v.impfv.* [*pfv.* **наверста́ть**] to make up for: наверста́ть поте́рянное вре́мя, to make up for lost time.

наверте́ть *v.pfv.* [*infl.* **-верчу́, -ве́ртишь**] **1,** *pfv. of* **наве́ртывать** (*in sense #1*). **2,** (*with gen.*) to make (*by spinning or drilling*).

наве́ртывать *v.impfv.* [*pfv.* **наверну́ть**] (*with* на + *acc.*) **1,** [*pfv. also* **наверте́ть**] to wind onto; wind around. **2,** to screw onto. —**наве́ртываться,** *refl.* [*pfv.* **наверну́ться**] (*of tears*) to well up: У неё (*or* на её глаза́) наверну́лись слёзы, tears came to her eyes.

наве́рх *adv., expressing motion or direction* **1,** up; upward(s). **2,** upstairs.

наверху́ *adv., expressing location* **1,** above. **2,** upstairs.

наве́с *n.* **1,** awning. **2,** *fig.* cover: под наве́сом (+ *gen.*), under a cover of.

навеселе́ *adv., colloq.* tipsy; high.

наве́сить [*infl.* **-шу, -сишь**] *v., pfv. of* **наве́шивать.**

навесно́й *adj.* hanging.

навести́ [*infl. like* **вести́**] *v., pfv. of* **наводи́ть.**

навести́ть [*infl.* **-щу́, -сти́шь**] *v., pfv. of* **навеща́ть.**

наве́т *n., obs.* slander; calumny.

наве́тренный *adj.* windward.

наве́чно *adv.* forever; for all time.

наве́шать *v.pfv.* **1,** to hang up; hang out (a quantity of something). **2,** to weigh; weigh out (a quantity of something).

наве́шивать *v.impfv.* [*pfv.* **наве́сить**] to hang; install by hanging.

навеща́ть *v.impfv.* [*pfv.* **навести́ть**] to visit.

наве́ять *v.pfv.* [*infl.* **-ве́ю, -ве́ешь**] **1,** *pfv. of* **навева́ть. 2,** to winnow (a quantity of something).

на́взничь *adv.* flat on one's back: упа́сть на́взничь, to fall flat on one's back.

навзры́д *adv., in* пла́кать навзры́д, to sob uncontrol-lably.

навига́тор *n.* navigator.

навига́ция *n.* navigation. —**навигацио́нный,** *adj.* navigation (*attrib.*); navigational.

навида́ться *v.r.pfv.* (*with gen.*) *colloq.* to have seen a lot (*or* enough) of.

нави́нчивать *v.impfv.* [*pfv.* **навинти́ть**] to screw on. —**нави́нчиваться,** *refl.* (*of an object*) to screw on.

нависа́ть *v.impfv.* [*pfv.* **нави́снуть**] **1,** (*with* на + *acc.*

or **над**) to hang over; overhang. **2,** *fig.* (*with* **над**) (*of a danger, threat, etc.*) to hang over.

нави́снуть [*past* **нави́с, нави́сла**] *v., pfv. of* **нависа́ть**.

нави́сший *adv.* overhanging. —**с нави́сшими бровя́ми,** beetle-browed.

навлека́ть *v.impfv.* [*pfv.* **навле́чь**] (*with* **на** + *acc.*) to bring (trouble, shame, etc.) on *or* upon; (*with* **на себя́**) to incur.

навле́чь [*infl. like* **вле́чь**] *v., pfv. of* **навлека́ть**.

наводи́ть *v.impfv.* [*pfv.* **навести́**; *pres.* **-вожу́, -во́дишь**] **1,** (*with* **на** + *acc.*) to lead (to); guide (to). **2,** to aim; point; train; direct. **3,** to cause; arouse; inspire (sadness, fear, boredom, melancholy, etc.). **4,** to apply; apply a coat of. —**наводи́ть блеск** *or* **лоск на** (+ *acc.*), to give a luster (*or* sheen) to. —**наводи́ть (на себя́) красоту́,** to make oneself beautiful. —**наводи́ть кри́тику на** (+ *acc.*), to level criticism at. —**наводи́ть мост,** to throw up a bridge. —**наводи́ть на мысль,** to suggest a thought. —**наводи́ть (кого́-нибудь) на размышле́ния,** to set (someone) to thinking (*or* pondering). —**наводи́ть (кого́-нибудь) на след** (+ *gen.*), to put (someone) on the track (of). —**наводи́ть (кого́-нибудь) на ум,** to bring to one's senses; bring to reason. —**наводи́ть поря́док,** to establish *or* restore order. —**наводи́ть спра́вки,** to make inquiries. —**наводи́ть чистоту́ в** (+ *prepl.*), to bring an air of cleanliness to.

наво́дка *n.* **1,** aiming (*of a weapon*). **2,** application (*of a coat or layer of something*). **3,** throwing up (*of a bridge*). **4,** *in* **наво́дка на ре́зкость,** focusing.

наводне́ние *n.* flood.

наводня́ть *v.impfv.* [*pfv.* **наводни́ть**] **1,** *obs.* to flood; inundate. **2,** *fig.* to flood: **наводня́ть ры́нок,** to flood the market.

наво́дчик *n.* **1,** *mil.* one who aims a gun. **2,** inside man (*in a robbery*).

наводя́щий *adj., in* **наводя́щий вопро́с,** leading question.

наво́з *n.* dung; manure.

наво́зить *v.impfv.* [*pfv.* **унаво́зить**; *pres.* **-во́жу, -во́зишь**] to treat with manure.

навози́ть *v.pfv.* [*infl.* **-вожу́, -во́зишь**] to bring in (a supply of something).

наво́зник *n.* dung beetle.

наво́зный *adj.* manure (*attrib.*); dung (*attrib.*). —**наво́зный жук,** dung beetle.

на́волочка [*gen. pl.* **-чек**] *n.* pillowcase.

навора́чивать *v.impfv.* [*pfv.* **навороти́ть**] *colloq.* **1,** to pile up. **2,** [*impfv. only*] (*with* **на** + *acc.*) to wind (onto).

наворова́ть *v.pfv.* [*infl.* **-ру́ю, -ру́ешь**] to steal (a quantity of something).

навороти́ть [*infl.* **-рочу́, -ро́тишь**] *v., pfv. of* **навора́чивать**.

навостри́ть *v.pfv., colloq.* to sharpen. —**навостри́ть лы́жи,** *colloq.* to take to one's heels. —**навостри́ть у́ши,** *colloq.* to prick up one's ears.

навостри́ться *v.r.pfv.* (*with* **в** + *prepl. or inf.*) *colloq.* to become good (at); become adept (at).

навощи́ть *v., pfv. of* **вощи́ть**.

навра́ть *v.pfv.* [*infl. like* **врать**] *colloq.* **1,** to tell lies. **2,** (*with* **на** + *acc.*) to tell lies about. **3,** (*with* **в** + *prepl.*) to make a mistake (in).

навреди́ть *v.pfv.* [*infl.* **-жу́, -ди́шь**] (*with dat.*) to harm; do a great deal of harm to.

навря́д ли *particle, colloq.* = **вряд ли.**

навсегда́ *adv.* forever; for good. —**раз (и) навсегда́,** once and for all.

навстре́чу *adv.* in someone's direction. —*prep., with dat.* toward; to meet: **вы́йти навстре́чу гостя́м,** to go out to meet the guests. —**идти́ навстре́чу** (+ *dat.*), to meet halfway; cooperate with; accommodate.

на́выворот *adv., colloq.* **1,** inside out. **2,** *fig.* upside down; backwards: **Всё получи́лось на́выворот,** everything turned out backwards.

на́вык *n.* skill: **на́выки чте́ния/письма́,** reading/writing skills.

навы́кат *also,* **навы́кате** *adv., in* **глаза́ навы́кат(е),** bulging eyes.

навы́лет *adv.* (*of a bullet, wound, etc.*) going right through (one's body).

навы́нос *adv., colloq.* for consumption off the premises.

навы́пуск *adv., in* **брю́ки навы́пуск,** trousers worn over one's boots; **руба́шка навы́пуск,** shirt worn loose (*or* not tucked in).

навы́рез *adv., in* **купи́ть арбу́з навы́рез,** to buy watermelon with the right to sample a piece.

навы́тяжку *adv., in* **стоя́ть навы́тяжку,** to stand at attention.

навяза́ть[1] *v.impfv.* [*pfv.* **навя́знуть**; *pres.* **-за́ю, -за́ешь**] to stick; get stuck. —**навя́знуть у** (+ *gen.*) **в зуба́х,** *colloq.* to bore to death; make sick and tired.

навяза́ть[2] *v.pfv.* [*infl.* **-вяжу́, -вя́жешь**] **1,** *pfv. of* **навя́зывать. 2,** to knit (a quantity of something). —**навяза́ться,** *refl., pfv. of* **навя́зываться.**

навя́знуть [*past* **навя́з, навя́зла**] *v., pfv. of* **навяза́ть**[1].

навя́зчивый *adj.* **1,** obtrusive; irksome; pesky. **2,** (*of an idea, thought, etc.*) fixed; obsessive. **3,** (*of a melody*) haunting.

навя́зывать *v.impfv.* [*pfv.* **навяза́ть**] **1,** (*with* **на** + *acc.*) to tie (to); attach (to); fasten (to). **2,** (*with dat.*) to impose (upon); force (upon); foist (upon): **навяза́ть свою́ во́лю кому́-нибудь,** to impose one's will on someone. —**навя́зываться,** *refl.* to intrude; obtrude.

нага́йка [*gen. pl.* **-га́ек**] *n.* whip.

нага́н *n.* revolver.

нага́р *n.* snuff (*of a candle*).

нагиба́ть *v.impfv.* [*pfv.* **нагну́ть**] to bend. —**нагиба́ться,** *refl.* to bend over; bend down; stoop.

нагишо́м *adv., colloq.* stark naked.

нагла́живать *v.impfv.* [*pfv.* **нагла́дить**] *colloq.* **1,** to iron. **2,** to smooth out.

нагла́зник *n.* **1,** eyeshade. **2,** blinker; blinder.

нагле́ть *v.impfv.* [*pfv.* **обнагле́ть**] to become (more) brazen.

наглёц [*gen.* **-леца́**] *n.* insolent person; impudent person.

на́глость *n.f.* **1,** insolence; impudence; impertinence. **2,** effrontery; audacity; gall.

наглота́ться *v.r.pfv.* (*with gen.*) to swallow (a quantity of something).

на́глухо *adv.* (*with verbs of closing*) tightly; tight.

на́глый *adj.* insolent; impudent; impertinent.

нагляде́ться *v.r.pfv.* [*infl.* -жу́сь, -ди́шься] (*with* на + *acc.*) to see a lot (of); see enough (of).

нагля́дно *adv.* graphically.

нагля́дность *n.f.* **1,** clarity. Для нагля́дности, for clarity; for visual effect; to demonstrate one's point. **2,** use of visual aids.

нагля́дный *adj.* **1,** graphic: нагля́дный приме́р, graphic example. **2,** employing visual aids: нагля́дное обуче́ние, instruction using visual aids. —**нагля́дные посо́бия**, visual aids. —**нагля́дный уро́к**, object lesson.

нагна́ть [*infl.* -гоню́, -го́нишь; *past fem.* нагнала́] *v., pfv. of* **нагоня́ть**.

нагнести́ [*infl.* -гнету́, -гнетёшь; *not used in the past tense*] *v., pfv. of* **нагнета́ть**.

нагнета́тель *n.m.* supercharger.

нагнета́ть *v.impfv.* [*pfv.* **нагнести́**] **1,** to force; pump (liquid, air, etc.). **2,** *fig.* to heat up; inflame (passions, a situation, etc.); build up; heighten (tension).

нагное́ние *n.* festering; suppuration.

нагнои́ться *v.r.pfv.* to fester.

нагну́ть *v., pfv. of* **нагиба́ть**. —**нагну́ться**, *refl., pfv. of* **нагиба́ться**.

нагова́ривать *v.impfv.* [*pfv.* **наговори́ть**] **1,** (*with* на + *acc.*) *colloq.* to slander. **2,** *in* нагова́ривать пласти́нку, to record one's voice. —**нагова́риваться**, *refl.* to have a long talk; say all that one wishes to say.

наговор *n., colloq.* slander; calumny.

наговори́ть *v.pfv.* **1,** *pfv. of* **нагова́ривать**. **2,** to say; utter (a lot of things). —**наговори́ться**, *refl., pfv. of* **нагова́риваться**.

наго́й *adj.* naked; nude; bare.

на́голо *adv., in* стричь на́голо, to cut off all of someone's hair; shave someone's head.

наголо́ *adv.* (*of a sword, saber, etc.*) drawn.

на́голову *adv., in* разби́ть на́голову, to rout; defeat utterly.

наголода́ться *v.r.pfv., colloq.* to go hungry; be half-starved.

нагоня́й *n., colloq.* scolding; bawling out; dressing-down; tongue-lashing.

нагоня́ть *v.impfv.* [*pfv.* **нагна́ть**] **1,** to overtake; catch up to. **2,** to make up for. **3,** to drive together; gather together. **4,** *colloq.* to cause; arouse; evoke (fear, boredom, drowsiness, etc.). Нагоня́ть стра́ху на (+ *acc.*), to strike fear into the heart of.

нагора́ть *v.impfv.* [*pfv.* **нагоре́ть**] **1,** (*of a candle*) to be covered with snuff. **2,** *impers., colloq.* (*of fuel or electricity*) to be consumed. **3,** *impers.* (*with dat.*) *colloq.* to get it; catch it; catch hell.

нагоре́ть [*infl.* -горю́, -гори́шь] *v., pfv. of* **нагора́ть**.

наго́рный *adj.* **1,** situated in the mountains; mountain (*attrib.*). **2,** (*of a river bank*) high. —**Наго́рная про́поведь**, the Sermon on the Mount.

нагороди́ть *v.pfv.* [*infl.* -рожу́, -ро́дишь *or* -роди́шь] **1,** to erect; put up. **2,** *colloq.* to heap up. **3,** *colloq.* to talk (nonsense).

наго́рье *n.* highland; upland.

нагота́ *n.* nakedness; nudity.

нагото́ве *adv.* in readiness.

нагото́вить *v.pfv.* [*infl.* -влю, -вишь] *colloq.* **1,** to lay in (a supply of something). **2,** to cook (a large quantity of something).

награ́бить *v.pfv.* [*infl.* -блю, -бишь] to rob (a quantity of something); amass by robbing.

награ́да *n.* **1,** reward. **2,** award; decoration.

награди́ть [*infl.* -жу́, -ди́шь] *v., pfv. of* **награжда́ть**.

наградно́й *adj.* award (*attrib.*); of awards. —**наградны́е**, *n.pl.* monetary award; bonus.

награжда́ть *v.impfv.* [*pfv.* **награди́ть**] **1,** to reward; decorate: награжда́ть кого́-нибудь за хра́брость, to reward/decorate someone for (his/her) bravery. **2,** to award: награжда́ть кого́-нибудь меда́лью, to award a medal to someone. **3,** *fig.* to endow.

награжде́ние *n.* **1,** rewarding; awarding. **2,** reward; award.

награждённый *n., decl. as an adj.* recipient of an award.

нагре́в *n.* **1,** heating. **2,** (amount of) heat.

нагрева́ние *n.* heating.

нагрева́тель *n.m.* heater. —**нагрева́тельный**, *adj.* heating (*attrib.*).

нагрева́ть *v.impfv.* [*pfv.* **нагре́ть**] **1,** to warm; heat. **2,** *in* нагре́ть ру́ки, to line one's pocket; feather one's nest. —**нагрева́ться**, *refl.* to become warm; get warm.

нагре́тый *adj.* hot: нагре́тый во́здух, hot air.

нагримирова́ть *v., pfv. of* **гримирова́ть** (*in sense #1*). —**нагримирова́ться**, *refl., pfv. of* **гримирова́ться** (*in sense #1*).

нагроможда́ть *v.impfv.* [*pfv.* **нагромозди́ть**] to pile up. —**нагроможда́ться**, *refl.,* to pile up; accumulate.

нагроможде́ние *n.* **1,** piling up. **2,** disorderly pile; accumulation.

нагромозди́ть [*infl.* -зжу́, -зди́шь] *v., pfv. of* **громозди́ть** *and* **нагроможда́ть**. —**нагромозди́ться**, *refl., pfv. of* **нагроможда́ться**.

нагруби́ть *v., pfv. of* **груби́ть**.

нагрубия́нить *v., pfv. of* **грубия́нить**.

нагру́дник *n.* **1,** bib. **2,** breastplate.

нагру́дный *adj.* breast (*attrib.*); worn over the breast.

нагружа́ть *v.impfv.* [*pfv.* **нагрузи́ть**] **1,** to load (a vehicle, vessel, etc.). **2,** (*with* на + *acc.*) to load (something) onto. **3,** *fig., colloq.* to burden. —**нагружа́ться**, *refl.* (*with instr.*) to load up (with); take on.

нагрузи́ть [*infl.* -гружу́, -гру́зишь *or* -грузи́шь] *v., pfv. of* **грузи́ть** (*in sense #1*) *and* **нагружа́ть**. —**нагрузи́ться**, *refl., pfv. of* **нагружа́ться**.

нагру́зка [*gen. pl.* -зок] *n.* **1,** loading. **2,** load. **3,** workload. —**поле́зная нагру́зка**, payload. —**преподава́тельская нагру́зка**, teaching load.

нагря́нуть *v.pfv.* **1,** to turn up unexpectedly; (*with* к) drop in on without warning; descend on. **2,** to occur suddenly. **3,** (*with* в *or* на + *acc.*) to swoop down on; raid.

нагу́ливать *v.impfv.* [*pfv.* **нагуля́ть**] *colloq.* to develop; work up (*as a result of walking*): нагуля́ть аппети́т, to work up an appetite.

нагуля́ть *v., pfv. of* **нагу́ливать.** —**нагуля́ться,** *refl.* to have had a long walk; have walked enough.

над *also,* **надо** *prep., with instr.* **1,** over: кры́ша над голово́й, a roof over one's head; побе́да над враго́м, victory over the enemy. **2,** above: над у́ровнем мо́ря, above sea level. **3,** *used with certain verbs and nouns:* рабо́тать над, to work on; смея́ться над, to laugh at. Суд над ке́м-нибудь, the trial of someone. Контро́ль над вооруже́ниями, arms control.

над- *also,* **надо-** *prefix* **1,** adding on: надстра́ивать, to build on; надставля́ть, to lengthen. **2,** supervision: надзира́ть; надсма́тривать, to supervise. **3,** *indicating partial or superficial action:* надрыва́ть, to tear slightly; надкуси́ть, to take a bite of.

надава́ть *v.pfv.* [*infl.* -да́ю, -дае́шь] *colloq.* to give (a quantity of something).

надави́ть [*infl.* -давлю́, -да́вишь] *v., pfv. of* **нада́вливать.**

нада́вливать *v.impfv.* [*pfv.* **надави́ть**] (*with acc. or* на + *acc.*) to press (on).

надари́ть *v.pfv.* [*infl.* -дарю́, -да́ришь] *colloq.* to give (a quantity of gifts).

надба́вить [*infl.* -влю, -вишь] *v., pfv. of* **надбавля́ть.**

надба́вка *n., colloq.* **1,** increase. **2,** raise (*in pay*).

надбавля́ть *v.impfv.* = **набавля́ть.**

надбива́ть *v.impfv.* [*pfv.* **надби́ть**] *colloq.* to chip (a glass, cup, etc.).

надби́ть [*infl.* **надобью́, надобье́шь**] *v., pfv. of* **надбива́ть.**

надвига́ть *v.impfv.* [*pfv.* **надви́нуть**] (*with* на + *acc.*) to pull; pull down (over one's ears, forehead, etc.). —**надвига́ться,** *refl.* **1,** to approach; come on. **2,** to be impending; be imminent.

надвига́ющийся *adj.* imminent; impending.

надви́нуть *v., pfv. of* **надвига́ть.** —**надви́нуться,** *refl., pfv. of* **надвига́ться.**

надво́дный *adj.* surface (*attrib.*): надво́дный кора́бль, surface vessel. —**надво́дная часть,** topsides.

на́двое *adv.* in two; in half. —**ба́бушка на́двое сказа́ла,** it (*or* that) remains to be seen.

надво́рный *adj.* situated outside: надво́рная постро́йка, outbuilding.

надгорта́нник *n.* epiglottis.

надгро́бие *n.* **1,** tombstone; gravestone. **2,** *obs.* epitaph.

надгро́бный *adj.* **1,** grave (*attrib.*); tomb (*attrib.*): надгро́бный ка́мень; надгро́бная плита́, tombstone; gravestone. Надгро́бная на́дпись, epitaph. **2,** graveside (*attrib.*): надгро́бная речь, graveside speech.

надгрыза́ть *v.impfv.* [*pfv.* **надгры́зть**] to nibble at; nibble on.

надгры́зть [*infl. like* **грызть**] *v., pfv. of* **надгрыза́ть.**

надева́ние *n.* putting on; donning.

надева́ть *v.impfv.* [*pfv.* **наде́ть**] **1,** to put on. **2,** to wear: Что мне наде́ть?, what should I wear?

надёжда *n.* hope.

надёжный *adj.* **1,** reliable; dependable; trustworthy. **2,** safe: в надёжных рука́х, in safe hands. **3,** firm; steady. —**надёжность,** *n.f.* reliability; dependability.

наде́л *n., hist.* parcel of land (*given to a peasant*).

наде́лать *v.pfv.* **1,** to make (a quantity of something). **2,** (*with gen.*) to do (damage); make (mistakes); cause

(trouble); pile up (debts). —**что ты наде́лал?,** what have you done?

наделе́ние *n.* allotment.

наделя́ть *v.impfv.* [*pfv.* **надели́ть**] (*with instr.*) **1,** to allot; provide (with): наделя́ть крестья́н землёй, to allot land to the peasants. **2,** *fig.* to endow (with).

надёргать *v.pfv.* (*with gen.*) *colloq.* to draw; cull (from various sources).

надерзи́ть *v., pfv. of* **дерзи́ть.**

наде́ть [*infl.* **наде́ну, наде́нешь**] *v., pfv. of* **надева́ть.**

наде́яться *v.r.impfv.* [*pres.* **наде́юсь, наде́ешься**] **1,** to hope; (*with* на + *acc.*) to hope for. **2,** (*with* на + *acc.*) to rely on; count on.

надзе́мный *adj.* above-ground; overhead; elevated.

надзира́тель *n.m.* **1,** supervisor; overseer. **2,** (prison) guard. —**надзира́тельский,** *adj.* supervisory.

надзира́ть *v.impfv.* (*with* за + *instr.*) **1,** to supervise; oversee. **2,** to look after; keep an eye on. **3,** to see that (something) is maintained.

надзо́р *n.* **1,** supervision; oversight. **2,** surveillance.

надиви́ться *v.r.pfv., colloq., in* **не мочь надиви́ться,** to not but wonder; not get over; never cease to be amazed.

нади́р *n., astron.* nadir.

надка́лывать *v.impfv.* [*pfv.* **надколо́ть**] to split (slightly).

надколо́ть [*infl.* -колю́, -ко́лешь] *v., pfv. of* **надка́лывать.**

надкуси́ть [*infl.* -кушу́, -ку́сишь] *v., pfv. of* **надку́сывать.**

надку́сывать *v.impfv.* [*pfv.* **надкуси́ть**] to bite into; take a bite (out) of.

надла́мывать *v.impfv.* [*pfv.* **надломи́ть**] **1,** to break partly; crack. **2,** *fig.* to undermine (one's health, strength, etc.). —**надла́мываться,** *refl.* **1,** to crack. **2,** to break down.

надлежа́ть *v.impfv.* [*pres.* -**жи́т**] *impers.* to be required: Э́то надлежи́т сде́лать в ука́занный срок, this must (*or* is to) be done within the period indicated. Вам надлежи́т яви́ться в де́вять часо́в, you are to report at nine o'clock.

надлежа́щий *adj.* proper; appropriate. —**надлежа́щим о́бразом,** properly.

надло́м *n.* **1,** break; crack. **2,** *fig.* breakdown.

надломи́ть [*infl.* -ломлю́, -ло́мишь] *v., pfv. of* **надла́мывать.** —**надломи́ться,** *refl., pfv. of* **надла́мываться.**

надло́мленный *adj.* **1,** broken; cracked. **2,** *fig.* shattered; broken (*in spirit*).

надме́нный *adj.* haughty; arrogant; supercilious. —**надме́нность,** *n.f.* haughtiness; arrogance.

надо *prep.* = **над** (*used mainly in the combination* **надо мной**).

на́до *adv.* (one) must; (one) has to: На́до соблюда́ть пра́вила, one must observe the rules; мне на́до идти́, I have to go. —**не на́до, 1,** (one) must not: Не на́до так говори́ть, you must not talk like that. **2,** (one) does not have to; (one) need not: Не на́до боя́ться, you need not be afraid. **3,** *as an exclamation,* don't!; don't do that! —**так ему́ и на́до,** it serves him right.

на́добно *adv., obs.* = на́до.

на́добность *n.f.* necessity; need.

на́добный *adj., obs.* necessary; needed.

надое́да *n.m. & f., colloq.* pest; nuisance. *Also,* надое́дала.

надоеда́ть *v.impfv.* [*pfv.* надое́сть] (*with dat.*) 1, to pester; bother. 2, to bore. 3, *impers.* to be tired of; be sick of: Мне надое́ло безде́льничать, I am tired of doing nothing. Мне надое́ла холо́дная пого́да, I am sick of this cold weather.

надое́дливый *adj.* 1, annoying; irksome. 2, tiresome; boring.

надое́сть [*infl. like* есть] *v., pfv. of* надоеда́ть.

надои́ть *v.pfv.* [*infl.* -дою́, -до́ишь *or* -дои́шь] to draw (a quantity of milk).

надо́й *n.* yield (*of milk*).

на́долба *n.* 1, post; stake. 2, *pl., mil.* anti-tank obstacles.

надо́лго *adv.* for a long time (*subsequent to the action expressed by the verb*): Он уе́хал надо́лго, he went away (*or* has gone away) for a long time. Я не надо́лго, I won't be (*or* stay) long.

надо́мник *n.* person who works at home.

надорва́ть [*infl.* -рву́, -рвёшь; *past fem.* -рвала́] *v., pfv. of* надрыва́ть. —надорва́ться, *refl.* [*infl. like* рва́ться] 1, *pfv. of* надрыва́ться. 2, *colloq.* to strain oneself. 3, *fig.* to break down; crack up.

надоу́мить *v.pfv.* [*infl.* -млю, -мишь] *colloq.* to suggest; give someone the idea (to *or* that): надоу́мить кого́-нибудь уйти́, to suggest to someone that he leave.

надпа́рывать *v.impfv.* [*pfv.* надпоро́ть] to rip partly open; remove a few stitches from.

надпи́ливать *v.impfv.* [*pfv.* надпили́ть] to saw a little; saw partially.

надпили́ть [*infl.* -пилю́, -пи́лишь] *v., pfv. of* надпи́ливать.

надписа́ть [*infl.* -пишу́, -пи́шешь] *v., pfv. of* надпи́сывать.

надпи́сывать *v.impfv.* [*pfv.* надписа́ть] 1, to inscribe; autograph. 2, *obs.* to address (a letter).

на́дпись *n.f.* inscription. —надгро́бная на́дпись, epitaph.

надпоро́ть [*infl.* -порю́, -по́решь] *v., pfv. of* надпа́рывать.

надпо́чечник *n.* adrenal gland.

надпо́чечный *adj.* adrenal.

надра́ть *v.pfv.* [*infl.* -деру́, -дерёшь; *past fem.* -драла́] to tear off (a quantity of something). —надра́ть у́ши (+ *dat.*), *colloq.* to pull someone's ears.

надре́з *n.* cut; incision.

надре́зать [*infl.* -ре́жу, -ре́жешь] *v., pfv. of* надреза́ть.

надреза́ть *v.impfv.* [*pfv.* надре́зать] to cut slightly; make an incision in. *Also,* надре́зывать.

надруга́тельство *n.* an outrage.

надруга́ться *v.r.pfv.* (*with над*) to commit an outrage (against).

надры́в *n.* 1, (slight) tear. 2, *fig.* great effort. 3, *fig.* breakdown. 4, *fig.* emotional outburst.

надрыва́ть *v.impfv.* [*pfv.* надорва́ть] 1, to tear slightly. 2, to strain; overtax. —надрыва́ться, *refl.* 1, to have a slight tear; be slightly torn. 2, [*impfv. only*] to overexert oneself. 3, [*impfv. only*] to yell at the top of one's lungs. 4, [*impfv. only*] (*with* от) to suffer grievously. 5, *in* се́рдце надрыва́ется, one's heart aches.

надры́вный *adj.* heart-rending; (*of laughter*) hysterical.

надса́да *n., colloq.* strain; great effort.

надса́дный *adj.* 1, (*of a cough*) hacking; (*of a cry*) shrill; piercing. 2, exhausting; backbreaking.

надсма́тривать *v.impfv.* (*with над or за* + *instr.*) to supervise; oversee; watch over.

надсмо́тр *n.* supervision.

надсмо́трщик *n.* overseer; supervisor.

надста́вить [*infl.* -влю, -вишь] *v., pfv. of* надставля́ть.

надста́вка [*gen. pl.* -вок] *n.* 1, lengthening. 2, extra piece.

надставля́ть *v.impfv.* [*pfv.* надста́вить] to lengthen (a garment).

надстра́ивать *v.impfv.* [*pfv.* надстро́ить] 1, to build on (*at the top*). 2, to increase the height of; make taller.

надстро́йка [*gen. pl.* -стро́ек] *n.* 1, building on(to). 2, superstructure.

надстро́чный *adj.* written above the line. —надстро́чный знак, superscript.

надтре́снутый *adj.* cracked.

надува́ла *n.m. & f., colloq.* swindler; cheat.

надува́ние *n.* inflating; blowing up.

надува́тельство *n., colloq.* cheating; trickery; deceit. —надува́тельский, *adj., colloq.* deceitful; underhanded.

надува́ть *v.impfv.* [*pfv.* наду́ть] 1, to inflate; blow up. 2, to puff up. 3, *colloq.* to swindle; cheat; dupe. —надува́ть гу́бы, to pout; show displeasure. *See also* наду́ть.

надува́ться *v.r.impfv.* [*pfv.* наду́ться] 1, to inflate; be inflatable; become inflated. 2, to puff up one's cheeks. 3, *colloq.* to swell; become swollen. 4, *fig., colloq.* to get a swelled head. 5, *fig., colloq.* to pout; sulk.

надувно́й *adj.* inflatable.

наду́манный *adj.* farfetched; artificial; forced.

наду́мать *v.pfv., colloq.* 1, to decide. 2, to think up; devise.

наду́тый *adj.* 1, inflated. 2, swollen. 3, *colloq.* haughty; puffed up. 4, (*of a style of writing*) pompous. 5, *colloq.* peeved.

наду́ть *v.pfv.* [*infl.* наду́ю, наду́ешь] 1, *pfv. of* надува́ть. 2, *impers., colloq.* to be affected (*by sitting in a draft*): мне наду́ло (в) ше́ю, I have a stiff neck. —наду́ться, *refl., pfv. of* надува́ться.

надуши́ть *v., pfv. of* души́ть (*in sense #5*). —надуши́ться, *refl., pfv. of* души́ться.

надшива́ть *v.impfv.* [*pfv.* надши́ть] 1, to lengthen (*by sewing*). 2, (*with* к *or* на) to sew onto.

надши́ть [*infl.* надошью́, надошьёшь] *v., pfv. of* надшива́ть.

надыми́ть *v., pfv. of* дыми́ть.

наеда́ться *v.r.impfv.* [*pfv.* нае́сться] 1, to eat one's fill. 2, (*with gen. or instr.*) to eat one's fill of: Он не мог нае́сться моро́женого, he couldn't get enough ice cream to eat. —**нае́сться до отва́ла, 1,** to gorge oneself. **2,** to be ready to burst.

наедине́ *adv.* **1,** in private; privately. **2,** (*with* **с** + *instr.*) alone (with).

нае́зд *n.* quick visit: Он быва́ет там то́лько нае́здом (*or* нае́здами), he goes there only on quick visits.

нае́здить *v.pfv.* [*infl.* **-е́зжу, -е́здишь**] **1,** *pfv. of* **наезжа́ть** (*in sense #3*) *and* **нае́зживать. 2,** to travel (a certain distance *or* amount of time).

нае́здник *n.* horseman; rider. —**нае́здничество,** *n.* horsemanship.

наезжа́ть *v.impfv.* **1,** [*pfv.* **нае́хать**] (*with* **на** + *acc.*) to run into; strike: На него́ нае́хала маши́на, he was struck by a car. **2,** [*pfv.* **нае́хать**] *colloq.* to arrive in large numbers. **3,** [*pfv.* **нае́здить**] to smooth down (a road). **4,** [*impfv. only*] (*with* **в** + *acc.*) *colloq.* to make periodic visits (to).

нае́зженный *adj.* (*of a road*) worn; well-trodden.

нае́зживать *v.impfv.* [*pfv.* **нае́здить**] to smooth down (a road).

наём [*gen.* **на́йма**] *n.* **1,** hiring. **2,** renting. —**рабо́-тать по на́йму,** to work as a hired hand.

наёмник *n.* **1,** hireling. **2,** mercenary (*soldier*).

наёмный *adj.* **1,** hired. **2,** mercenary.

нае́сться [*infl. like* **есть**] *v.r., pfv. of* **наеда́ться.**

нае́хать [*infl.* **нае́ду, нае́дешь**] *v., pfv. of* **наезжа́ть.**

нажа́рить *v.pfv.* to roast; fry (a quantity of something).

нажа́тие *n.* pressing; a press.

нажа́ть[1] *v.pfv.* [*infl.* **нажму́, нажмёшь**] **1,** *pfv. of* **нажима́ть. 2,** to squeeze (a quantity of something).

нажа́ть[2] *v.pfv.* [*infl.* **нажну́, нажнёшь**] to harvest (a quantity of something).

нажда́к [*gen.* **-дака́**] *n.* emery.

нажда́чный *adj.* emery (*attrib.*). —**нажда́чная бума́га,** sandpaper.

нажечь *v.pfv.* [*infl. like* **жечь**] to burn (a quantity of something).

нажи́ва *n.* **1,** *colloq.* making money. **2,** bait.

нажива́ть *v.impfv.* [*pfv.* **нажи́ть**] **1,** to make; amass (a fortune). **2,** to contract (a disease). **3,** (*with gen.*) to make (troubles, enemies, etc.) for oneself. —**нажива́ться,** *refl.* (*with* **на** + *prepl.*). to get rich (on).

наживи́ть [*infl.* **-влю́, -ви́шь**] *v., pfv. of* **наживля́ть.**

нажи́вка *n.* bait.

наживля́ть *v.impfv.* [*pfv.* **наживи́ть**] to bait (a fishhook).

наживно́й *adj., in* **де́ло наживно́е,** something easily acquired; something that is not hard to get.

нажи́м *n.* **1,** pressure. **2,** emphasis (*when speaking*). **3,** exaggerated gesture. **4,** thickened lines (*when writing*).

нажима́ть *v.impfv.* [*pfv.* **нажа́ть**] **1,** (*with acc. or* **на** + *acc.*) to press (on). **2,** (*with* **на** + *acc.*) *colloq.* to put pressure on.

нажи́ть [*infl.* **наживу́, наживёшь;** *past* **на́жил, нажила́, на́жило, на́жили**] *v., pfv. of* **нажива́ть.** —**нажи́ться,** *refl.* [*past* **нажи́лся, нажила́сь, нажило́сь** *or* **нажи́лось, нажили́сь** *or* **нажи́лись**] *pfv. of* **нажива́ться.**

наза́втра *adv., colloq.* the next day.

наза́д *adv.* back; backwards. —*interj.* stand back! —**тому́ наза́д,** ago.

назва́нивать *v.impfv., colloq.* to make a lot of phone calls; call all around.

назва́ние *n.* **1,** name (*of a city, place, organization, etc.*). **2,** title (*of a book, film, etc.*).

назва́ть [*infl.* **назову́, назовёшь;** *past fem.* **назвала́**] *v., pfv. of* **называ́ть.** —**назва́ться,** *refl.* [*past tense stress as in* **зва́ться**] *pfv. of* **называ́ться.**

назе́мный *adj.* ground (*attrib.*); surface (*attrib.*); overland.

на́земь *adv.* to the ground.

назида́ние *n.* edification: в назида́ние (+ *dat.*), for the edification of.

назида́тельный *adj.* **1,** edifying; instructive. **2,** didactic: назида́тельный тон, didactic tone.

назло́ *also,* **на́зло** *adv.* for spite; out of spite. —*prep., with dat.* to spite (someone). —**как назло́,** as luck would have it.

назнача́ть *v.impfv.* [*pfv.* **назна́чить**] **1,** to set; schedule. **2,** to appoint; name. **3,** to assign. **4,** to designate; earmark. **5,** to award; grant. **6,** *colloq.* to prescribe. —**назнача́ться,** *refl.* [*impfv. only*] **1,** to be scheduled. **2,** to be appointed. **3,** to be assigned.

назначе́ние *n.* **1,** setting (*of a date*). **2,** awarding (*of a pension or scholarship*). **3,** appointment; assignment. **4,** function; purpose. **5,** prescribing (*of medicine*).

назна́чить *v., pfv. of* **назнача́ть.**

назо́йливый *adj.* obtrusive; officious.

назрева́ть *v.impfv.* [*pfv.* **назре́ть**] **1,** to ripen; mature. **2,** to become imminent; come to a head. Это назрева́ло давно́, it was building up for a long time.

назре́вший *adj.* urgent.

назре́ть *v., pfv. of* **назрева́ть.**

назубо́к *adv., colloq.* (*with verbs of knowing, learning, etc.*) thoroughly; by heart.

называ́емый *adj., in* **так называ́емый,** the so-called.

называ́ть *v.impfv.* [*pfv.* **назва́ть**] **1,** to name. Назва́ть имена́, to name names. Назови́те ва́шу це́ну, name your price. **2,** to call: назва́ть кого́-нибудь лжецо́м, to call someone a liar. **3,** *in* назва́ть себя́, to identify oneself; give one's name. —**называ́ть ве́щи свои́ми имена́ми,** to call a spade a spade.

называ́ться *v.r.impfv.* [*pfv.* **назва́ться**] **1,** to call oneself. **2,** [*impfv. only*] to be called. **3,** to identify oneself; give one's name. **4,** *colloq.* to invite oneself. —**что называ́ется,** as they say.

наибо́лее *adv., used in forming compound superlatives,* the most: наибо́лее уда́чный спо́соб, the most successful method.

наибо́льший *adj.* the greatest; the largest.

наи́вный *adj.* naïve. —**наи́вность,** *n.f.* naïveté.

наивы́сший *adj.* the highest; the greatest.

наи́гранный *adj.* affected; artificial.

наигра́ть *v., pfv. of* **наи́грывать.** —**наигра́ться,** *refl.* to play to one's heart's content; play as much as one wishes.

наи́грывать *v.impfv.* [*pfv.* **наигра́ть**] **1,** *colloq.* to play (a number of songs or works of music). **2,** *colloq.* to win (money) in a game. **3,** to make (a record); record. **4,** [*impfv. only*] to play softly.

наизна́нку *adv.* inside out.

наизу́сть *adv.* by heart.

наилу́чший *adj.* the best: наилу́чшим о́бразом, in the best possible manner. —**наилу́чшие пожела́ния,** best wishes.

наиме́нее *adv., used in forming compound superlatives,* the least: наиме́нее вероя́тный слу́чай, the least probable case.

наименова́ние *n.* name; appellation.

наименова́ть *v., pfv. of* **именова́ть.**

наиме́ньший *adj.* the least; the least amount.

наискосо́к *adv., colloq.* = **на́искось.**

на́искось *adv.* at an angle; diagonally; catty-corner.

на́йтие *n., obs.* inspiration. —**по на́йтию,** instinctively; intuitively.

наиху́дший *adj.* the worst.

найдёныш *n.* foundling.

найми́т *n.* hireling.

найти́ [*infl.* **найду́, найдёшь;** *past* **нашёл, нашла́, нашло́, нашли́**] *v., pfv. of* **находи́ть.** —**найти́сь,** *refl., pfv. of* **находи́ться.**

нака́з *n.* **1,** *obs.* order; instructions. **2,** mandate (*from the voters*). **3,** *hist.* set of instructions issued by Catherine II.

наказа́ние *n.* punishment.

наказа́ть [*infl.* **-кажу́, -ка́жешь**] *v., pfv. of* **нака́зывать.**

наказу́емый *adj., law* punishable.

нака́зывать *v.impfv.* [*pfv.* **наказа́ть**] to punish.

нака́л *n.* **1,** incandescence. **2,** *fig.* fever pitch. —**бе́лый/кра́сный нака́л,** white/red heat.

накалённый *adj.* **1,** burning hot; incandescent, **2,** *fig.* tense; charged; explosive.

нака́ливание *n., in* **ла́мпа нака́ливания,** incandescent lamp.

нака́ливать *v.impfv.* [*pfv.* **накали́ть**] **1,** to make red hot. **2,** *fig.* to inflame. —**нака́ливаться,** *refl.* **1,** to become red hot. **2,** *fig.* to become heated; become inflamed. Накали́ться до преде́ла, to reach a fever pitch.

накали́ть *v., pfv. of* **нака́ливать** *and* **накаля́ть.** —**накали́ться,** *refl., pfv. of* **нака́ливаться** *and* **накаля́ться.**

нака́лывать *v.impfv.* [*pfv.* **наколо́ть**] **1,** to prick. **2,** (*with* **на** + *acc.*) to pin on. —**нака́лываться,** *refl.* to prick oneself.

накаля́ть *v.impfv.* = **нака́ливать.** —**накаля́ться,** *refl.* = **нака́ливаться.**

накану́не *adv.* the day before. —*prep., with gen.* on the eve of.

нака́пливать *v.impfv.* = **накопля́ть.** —**нака́пливаться,** *refl.* = **накопля́ться.**

наката́ть *v.pfv.* **1,** *pfv. of* **нака́тывать** (*in sense #1*). **2,** to roll (a quantity of something). **3,** to make (a quantity of something) by rolling.

накати́ть [*infl.* **-качу́, -ка́тишь**] *v., pfv. of* **нака́тывать** (*in sense #2*).

нака́тывать *v.impfv.* **1,** [*pfv.* **наката́ть**] to wear down; smooth down (a road). **2,** [*pfv.* **накати́ть**] (*with* **на** + *acc.*) to roll (something) onto.

нака́чивать *v.impfv.* [*pfv.* **накача́ть**] **1,** to pump. **2,** to pump up; inflate.

наки́дка [*gen. pl.* **-док**] *n.* **1,** cape. **2,** pillow cover. **3,** *colloq.* extra charge.

наки́дывать *v.impfv.* [*pfv.* **наки́нуть**] **1,** to throw on; throw over. **2,** *colloq.* to add on (a certain amount). —**наки́дываться,** *refl.* (*with* **на** + *acc.*) to attack; pounce (on).

накипа́ть *v.impfv.* [*pfv.* **накипе́ть**] **1,** (*of scum*) to form. **2,** *fig.* (*of feelings*) to build up.

на́кипь *n.f.* scum.

накла́д *n. in* **в накла́де,** *see* **внакла́де.**

накла́дка [*gen. pl.* **-док**] *n.* **1,** hairpiece; wig. **2,** protective plate, pad or strip. —**тормозна́я накла́дка,** brake lining.

накладна́я *n., decl. as an adj.* invoice; bill of lading.

накла́дно *adv.* (*with dat. and inf.*) *colloq.* not to one's advantage; a losing proposition.

накладно́й *adj.* **1,** superimposed. **2,** (*of hair, a beard, etc.*) false. —**накладно́е зо́лото,** gold plate. —**накладно́й карма́н,** patch pocket. —**накладны́е расхо́ды,** overhead (costs). —**накладно́е серебро́,** silver plate.

накла́дывать *v.impfv.* [*pfv.* **наложи́ть**] **1,** to lay on; lay over; superimpose. **2,** to apply; put on (face cream, a bandage, etc.); put in (stitches). **3,** to load (with); pack (with). **4,** to load; pack; pile (a quantity of something). —**накла́дывать на себя́ ру́ки,** *obs.* to kill oneself; commit suicide. —**накла́дывать свой отпеча́ток на** (+ *acc.*), to leave its mark upon. —**накла́дывать себе́ на таре́лку** (+ *gen.*), to help oneself to.

наклевета́ть *v., pfv. of* **клевета́ть.**

накле́ивать *v.impfv.* [*pfv.* **накле́ить**] **1,** to glue on; paste on; affix. **2,** to paste up; post (a notice).

накле́йка [*gen. pl.* **-кле́ек**] *n.* **1,** pasting on; gluing on. **2,** sticker; label. **3,** hinge (*for a postage stamp*).

накли́кать [*infl.* **-кли́чу, -кли́чешь**] *v., pfv. of* **наклика́ть.**

наклика́ть *v.impfv.* [*pfv.* **накли́кать**] *colloq.* to invite; court; bring on (trouble, disaster, etc.).

накло́н *n.* **1,** inclination. **2,** slope; incline.

наклоне́ние *n.* **1,** inclination. **2,** *gram.* mood.

наклони́ть [*infl.* **-клоню́, -кло́нишь**] *v., pfv. of* **наклоня́ть.** —**наклони́ться,** *refl., pfv. of* **наклоня́ться.**

накло́нность *n.f.* inclination; tendency; leaning; propensity.

накло́нный *adj.* inclined; sloping; slanting.

наклоня́ть *v.impfv.* [*pfv.* **наклони́ть**] to incline; lean; tilt; bow. —**наклоня́ться,** *refl.* to bend over; lean over.

накова́льня [*gen. pl.* **-лен**] *n.* anvil. —**ме́жду мо́лотом и накова́льней,** between the devil and the deep blue sea.

нако́жный *adj.* appearing on the skin: нако́жная сыпь, skin rash.

наколе́нник *n.* kneepad.

наколо́ть *v.pfv.* [*infl.* **-колю́, -ко́лешь**] **1,** *pfv. of* **нака́лывать.** **2,** to chop; split (a quantity of wood). **3,** to slaughter; kill (a quantity of animals, fish, etc.). —**наколо́ться,** *refl., pfv. of* **нака́лываться.**

накома́рник *n.* mosquito netting.

наконе́ц *adv.* at last; finally. —**наконе́ц-то!**, at last!; at long last!

наконе́чник *n.* tip.

накопа́ть *v.pfv.* **1,** to dig. **2,** to dig (a quantity of something).

накопи́ть [*infl.* -коплю́, -ко́пишь] *v., pfv. of* копи́ть, накопля́ть *and* нака́пливать. —**накопи́ться**, *refl., pfv. of* копи́ться, накопля́ться *and* нака́пливаться.

накопле́ние *n.* **1,** accumulation. **2,** *pl.* savings.

накопля́ть *v.impfv.* [*pfv.* накопи́ть] **1,** to accumulate; amass. **2,** to stockpile. —**накопля́ться**, *refl.* to accumulate; pile up; build up.

накорми́ть *v., pfv. of* корми́ть.

накоротке́ *adv., colloq.* **1,** from close up; at close range. **2,** for a short time; for a moment. **3,** (*with* с + *instr.*) on friendly terms (with).

накра́пывать *v.impfv.* (*of rain*) to fall lightly. *Also impers.:* Ста́ло накра́пывать, it began to drizzle.

накра́сить *v.pfv.* [*infl.* -шу, -сишь] **1,** *pfv. of* накра́шивать. **2,** to paint (a quantity of something). —**накра́ситься**, *refl., pfv. of* кра́ситься *and* накра́шиваться.

накра́сть *v.pfv.* [*infl. like* красть] to steal (a quantity of something).

накрахма́лить *v., pfv. of* крахма́лить.

накра́шивать *v.impfv.* [*pfv.* накра́сить] to paint (one's lips, face, etc.). —**накра́шиваться**, *refl., colloq.* to put on make-up.

накрени́ть *v., pfv. of* крени́ть *and* накреня́ть. —**накрени́ться**, *refl., pfv. of* крени́ться *and* накреня́ться.

накреня́ть *v.impfv.* [*pfv.* накрени́ть] **1,** *v.t.* to tip; tilt. **2,** *v.i., impers.* to tilt to one side: дом/ло́дку накрени́ло, the house/boat tilted to one side. —**накреня́ться**, *refl.* to list; tilt to one side.

на́крепко *adv.* **1,** firmly; fast. **2,** *colloq.* categorically. —**кре́пко-на́крепко**, *intensive form of* кре́пко: кре́пко-на́крепко засну́ть, to fall fast asleep.

на́крест *adv.* crosswise. *Also,* крест-на́крест.

накрича́ть *v.pfv.* [*infl.* -чу́, -чи́шь] to shout; (*with* на + *acc.*) shout at.

накрои́ть *v.pfv.* to cut out (a quantity of something).

накроши́ть *v.pfv.* [*infl.* -крошу́, -кро́шишь] **1,** to chop up (a quantity of something). **2,** to crumble (a quantity of bread). **3,** *pfv. of* кроши́ть (*in sense #3*).

накрути́ть [*infl.* -кручу́, -кру́тишь] *v., pfv. of* накру́чивать.

накру́чивать *v.impfv.* [*pfv.* накрути́ть] (*with* на + *acc.*) to wind (onto); wind (around).

накрыва́ть *v.impfv.* [*pfv.* накры́ть] **1,** to cover. **2,** *in* накрыва́ть (на) стол, to set the table; накрыва́ть за́втрак/обе́д/у́жин, to set the table for breakfast/dinner/supper. **3,** *colloq.* to catch in the act. **4,** *mil.* to hit; destroy. —**накрыва́ться**, *refl.* (*with instr.*) to cover oneself (with).

накры́ть [*infl.* накро́ю, накро́ешь] *v., pfv. of* накрыва́ть. —**накры́ться**, *refl., pfv. of* накрыва́ться.

накупи́ть *v.pfv.* [*infl.* -куплю́, -ку́пишь] to buy (a quantity of something).

накури́ть *v.pfv.* [*infl.* -курю́, -ку́ришь] to fill (a room) with smoke. —**накури́ться**, *refl.* to smoke to one's heart's content.

налага́ть *v.impfv.* [*pfv.* наложи́ть] to impose (a fine, penalty, duty, ban, etc.). —**налага́ть аре́ст на**, to seize; sequester; impound.

нала́дить [*infl.* -жу, -дишь] *v., pfv. of* нала́живать. —**нала́диться**, *refl., pfv. of* нала́живаться.

нала́дчик *n.* adjuster.

нала́женный *adj.* well-ordered.

нала́живание *n.* adjustment; setting right.

нала́живать *v.impfv.* [*pfv.* нала́дить] **1,** to adjust; repair; put right. **2,** to organize; establish. **3,** to normalize; smooth out (relations). —**нала́живаться**, *refl.* to settle down; take shape; work out. Сно́ва нала́живаться, to return to normal.

налакирова́ть *v.pfv.* [*infl.* -ру́ю, -ру́ешь] to varnish; lacquer.

налга́ть *v.pfv.* [*infl. like* лгать] **1,** to lie; tell lies. **2,** (*with* на + *acc.*) to tell lies about; slander.

нале́во *adv.* to the left; on the left.

налега́ть *v.impfv.* [*pfv.* нале́чь] (*with* на + *acc.*) **1,** to lean (on); put one's weight on. **2,** to wield (*vigorously*); ply (*with energy*). **3,** *colloq.* to apply oneself (to).

налегке́ *adv.* **1,** with little or no baggage or cargo: путеше́ствовать налегке́, to travel light. **2,** lightly dressed.

налеза́ть *v.impfv.* [*pfv.* нале́зть] *colloq.* **1,** to come swarming in. **2,** (*with* на + *acc.*) (*of clothes*) to go on.

нале́зть [*infl. like* лезть] *v., pfv. of* налеза́ть.

налепи́ть *v.pfv.* [*infl.* -леплю́, -ле́пишь] **1,** *pfv. of* налепля́ть. **2,** to make (a quantity of something by modeling).

налепля́ть *v.impfv.* [*pfv.* налепи́ть] *colloq.* to stick on; paste on.

налёт *n.* **1,** raid. **2,** holdup. **3,** thin layer; thin coating. Зубно́й налёт, plaque. **4,** *fig.* touch; tinge. —**с налёта, 1,** on the run; at full speed. **2,** in a flash; with only a moment's thought.

налета́ть[1] *v.impfv.* [*pfv.* налете́ть] **1,** (*with* на + *acc.*) to fly into; fly onto; swoop down on; pounce on. **2,** (*with* на + *acc.*) to run into; smash into; strike. **3,** (*of a storm*) to blow up.

налета́ть[2] *v.pfv.* to fly (a certain distance *or* amount of time).

налете́ть *v.pfv.* [*infl.* -чу́, -ти́шь] **1,** *pfv. of* налета́ть[1]. **2,** to fly in (*in large numbers*).

налётчик *n.* robber; assailant.

нале́чь [*infl. like* лечь] *v., pfv. of* налега́ть.

налива́ть *v.impfv.* [*pfv.* нали́ть] **1,** to pour. **2,** (*with gen. or acc.*) to spill. —**налива́ться**, *refl.* **1,** (*with* в + *acc.*) (*of liquids*) to flow into; get into. **2,** (*with instr.*) to become filled (with). **3,** (*of fruits*) to ripen. **4,** *in* нали́ться кро́вью, to become bloodshot.

нали́вка *n.* fruit liqueur.

наливно́й *adj.* **1,** liquid: наливно́й груз, liquid cargo. **2,** designed to carry liquids: наливно́е су́дно, tanker. **3,** fully ripe; juicy.

нали́м *n.* burbot (*fish*).

налинова́ть *v., pfv. of* линова́ть.

налипа́ть *v.impfv.* [*pfv.* **нали́пнуть**] (*with* **на** + *acc.*) (*of dirt, leaves, etc.*) to stick (to); collect (on).

нали́пнуть [*past* **нали́п, нали́пла**] *v., pfv. of* **налипа́ть.**

нали́ть [*infl.* **налью́, нальёшь;** *past* **на́лил** *or* **нали́л, налила́, на́лило** *or* **нали́ло, на́лили** *or* **нали́ли**] *v., pfv. of* **налива́ть.** —**нали́ться,** *refl.* [*past tense stress as in* **ли́ться**] *pfv. of* **налива́ться.**

налицо́ *adv.* present; on hand.

нали́чествовать *v.impfv.* [*pres.* **-ствует**] to be present.

нали́чие *n.* presence; existence; availability. —**быть в нали́чии,** to be available; be on hand.

нали́чность *n.f.* **1,** cash on hand. **2,** = **нали́чие.**

нали́чный *adj.* available; on hand. —**нали́чные,** *n.pl.* [*also,* **нали́чные де́ньги**] cash.

налови́ть *v.pfv.* [*infl.* **-ловлю́, -ло́вишь**] to catch (a quantity of something).

наловчи́ться *v.r.pfv.* (*with inf. or* **в** + *prepl.*) *colloq.* to become proficient (at); become adept (at); get the hang of.

нало́г *n.* tax. —**нало́говый,** *adj.* tax (*attrib.*).

налогообложе́ние *n.* taxation.

налогоплате́льщик *n.* taxpayer.

наложе́ние *n.* **1,** application (*of a bandage, cream, etc.*). **2,** imposition (*of a fine, tax, etc.*).

нало́женный *adj., in* **нало́женным платежо́м,** C.O.D.

наложи́ть [*infl.* **-ложу́, -ло́жишь**] *v., pfv. of* **накла́дывать** *and* **налага́ть.**

нало́жница *n., obs.* concubine.

налома́ть *v.pfv.* to break (a quantity of something). —**налома́ть дров,** *colloq.* to commit a series of blunders.

налощи́ть *v., pfv. of* **лощи́ть.**

налущи́ть *v.pfv.* to shell; husk (a quantity of something).

налюбова́ться *v.r.pfv.* [*infl.* **-бу́юсь, -бу́ешься**] (*with* **на** + *acc.*) to gaze at to one's heart's content: Не могу́ налюбова́ться на э́ту карти́ну, I never get tired of looking at that picture.

нам *pron., dat. of* **мы.**

намагни́чивать *v.impfv.* [*pfv.* **намагни́тить**] to magnetize.

нама́зать *v., pfv. of* **ма́зать** (*in senses #1, 3 & 5*). —**нама́заться,** *refl., pfv. of* **ма́заться** (*in sense #1*).

намалева́ть *v., pfv. of* **малева́ть.**

намара́ть *v., pfv. of* **мара́ть** (*in sense #2*).

нама́слить *v., pfv. of* **ма́слить.**

нама́тывать *v.impfv.* [*pfv.* **намота́ть**] (*with* **на** + *acc.*) to wind onto; wind around. —**намота́ть себе́ на ус,** *colloq.* to make a mental note of.

нама́чивать *v.impfv.* [*pfv.* **намочи́ть**] **1,** to wet; moisten. **2,** to soak. **3,** (*with* **на** + *prepl.*) *colloq.* to make a puddle (on).

наме́дни *adv., colloq.* recently; the other day.

намёк *n.* hint.

намека́ть *v.impfv.* [*pfv.* **намекну́ть**] **1,** (*with* **на** + *acc.*) to hint (at); allude (to). **2,** to suggest; infer; intimate (that).

наменя́ть *v.pfv.* **1,** to obtain (a quantity of something) by exchanging. **2,** to change (a quantity of money).

намерева́ться *v.r.impfv.* to intend.

наме́рен *adj., used predicatively,* intending: Что вы наме́рены сде́лать?, what do you intend to do?

наме́рение *n.* intention.

наме́ренный *adj.* intentional; deliberate. —**наме́ренно,** *adv.* intentionally; deliberately.

намерза́ть *v.impfv.* [*pfv.* **намёрзнуть**] (*with* **на** + *prepl.*) (*of a layer of ice*) to form (on).

намёрзнуть [*past* **намёрз, намёрзла**] *v., pfv. of* **намерза́ть.**

на́мертво *adv., colloq.* firmly; fast.

намести́ [*infl. like* **мести́**] *v., pfv. of* **намета́ть**[1].

наме́стник *n., obs.* **1,** deputy. **2,** provincial governor.

намета́ть[1] *v.impfv.* [*pfv.* **намести́**] **1,** to sweep together (a quantity of something). **2,** (*of a storm, the wind, etc.*) to form (snowdrifts); drift (the snow). **3,** *impers.* to drift; pile up: намело́ мно́го сне́гу, large snowdrifts formed.

намета́ть[2] *v., pfv. of* **намётывать.**

наме́тить [*infl.* **-чу, -тишь**] *v., pfv. of* **ме́тить** (*in sense #1*) *and* **намеча́ть.** —**наме́титься,** *refl., pfv. of* **намеча́ться.**

намётка [*gen. pl.* **-ток**] *n.* **1,** basting. **2,** basting thread. **3,** rough draft; outline.

намётывать *v.impfv.* [*pfv.* **намета́ть**] **1,** to pile up (a quantity of something). **2,** *colloq.* (*with* **глаз** *or* **ру́ку**) to train: намётанный глаз, trained eye. Намета́ть ру́ку на (+ *prepl.*), to become proficient at. **3,** to baste.

намеча́ть *v.impfv.* [*pfv.* **наме́тить**] **1,** to mark. **2,** to plan; map out; outline. **3,** to set; schedule. —**намеча́ться,** *refl.* **1,** to appear; be visible. **2,** *fig.* to emerge; take shape. **3,** [*impfv. only*] to be planned; be scheduled.

на́ми *pron., instr. of* **мы.**

намно́го *adv.* **1,** (*with comp. adjectives*) much; far. **2,** (*with verbs*) greatly; considerably.

намозо́лить *v., pfv. of* **мозо́лить.**

намока́ть *v.impfv.* [*pfv.* **намо́кнуть**] to get wet; get soaked.

намо́кнуть [*past* **намо́к, намо́кла**] *v., pfv. of* **намока́ть.**

намоло́ть *v.pfv.* [*infl.* **-мелю́, -ме́лешь**] to grind (a quantity of something).

намо́рдник *n.* muzzle.

намо́рщить *v., pfv. of* **мо́рщить** (*in sense #1*). —**намо́рщиться,** *refl., pfv. of* **мо́рщиться.**

намота́ть *v.pfv.* **1,** *pfv. of* **мота́ть** (*in sense #1*) *and* **нама́тывать. 2,** to wind (a quantity of something).

намочи́ть [*infl.* **-мочу́, -мо́чишь**] *v., pfv. of* **мочи́ть** *and* **нама́чивать.**

наму́читься *v.r.pfv., colloq.* **1,** to suffer; go through hell. **2,** (*with* **с** + *instr.*) to have a hell of a time with.

намы́ливать *v.impfv.* [*pfv.* **намы́лить**] **1,** to soap; lather. **2,** *in* **намы́лить го́лову** (+ *dat.*), *colloq.* to chew someone out. —**намы́ливаться,** *refl.* to soap oneself.

намы́лить *v., pfv. of* **мы́лить** *and* **намы́ливать.** —**намы́литься,** *refl., pfv. of* **мы́литься** *and* **намы́ливаться.**

намя́ть *v.pfv.* [*infl.* **намну́, намнёшь**] *colloq.* **1,** to trample down; flatten. **2,** to irritate; chafe. —**намя́ть**

бока́ *or* ше́ю (+ *dat.*), *colloq.* to administer a beating to; beat up.

нанесе́ние *n.* **1,** inflicting; causing. **2,** drawing; plotting. **3,** applying; laying.

нанести́ [*infl. like* нести́] *v., pfv. of* наноси́ть.

наниза́ть [*infl.* -нижу́, -ни́жешь] *v., pfv. of* низа́ть *and* нани́зывать.

нани́зывать *v.impfv.* [*pfv.* наниза́ть] to string; thread.

нанима́тель *n.m.* **1,** tenant. **2,** employer.

нанима́ть *v.impfv.* [*pfv.* наня́ть] **1,** to hire; engage; employ. **2,** to hire; rent. —нанима́ться, *refl.* to take a job; hire oneself out.

на́ново *adv., colloq.* anew; over again.

нано́с *n.* alluvium.

наноси́ть *v.impfv.* [*pfv.* нанести́; *pres.* -ношу́, -но́сишь] **1,** to inflict: нанести́ кому́-нибудь уда́р/пораже́ние, to inflict a blow/defeat on someone. Наноси́ть уще́рб (+ *dat.*), to cause *or* do damage (to). **2,** to drift; pile up (snow, sand, etc.); (*of water*) wash up. **3,** to draw; plot (*on a map*). **4,** to apply a layer of. **5,** *impers.* to strike; run into: Ло́дку нанесло́ на ка́мень, the boat struck a rock. **6,** *in* наноси́ть визи́т (+ *dat.*), to pay a visit on.

нано́сный *adj.* **1,** alluvial. **2,** *fig.* alien; external.

наня́ть [*infl.* найму́, наймёшь; *past* на́нял, наняла́, на́няло, на́няли] *v., pfv. of* нанима́ть. —наня́ться, *refl.* [*past* наня́лся *or* наня́лся, наняла́сь, наня́лось, наняли́сь] *pfv. of* нанима́ться.

наоборо́т *adv.* **1,** backwards. **2,** the other way round. **3,** (*with* и *or* и́ли) vice versa. **4,** on the contrary. **5,** conversely.

наобу́м *adv., colloq.* **1,** without thinking. **2,** at random.

наотма́шь *adv.* **1,** (*with verbs of striking, throwing, etc.*) with a full sweep of one's arm. **2,** (*of one's arms*) stretched out; fully extended.

наотре́з *adv.* flatly; pointblank.

напа́дать *v.pfv.* to fall (*in large quantities*).

напада́ть *v.impfv.* [*pfv.* напа́сть] (*with* на + *acc.*) **1,** to attack. **2,** to run across; come across; come upon. Напа́сть на след (+ *gen.*), to come upon (*or* pick up) the trail (of). **3,** to come up with; hit upon (an idea). **4,** *colloq.* to attack; assail; jump on. **5,** (*of a feeling*) to come over.

напада́ющий *n., decl. as an adj.* **1,** attacker; assailant. **2,** *sports* forward (*offensive player*).

нападе́ние *n.* attack. Нападе́ние на самолёт, hijacking (of an airplane).

напа́дки [*gen.* -док] *n.pl.* (verbal) attacks.

напа́ивать *v.impfv.* [*pfv.* напои́ть] **1,** to give (someone) something to drink. **2,** to make drunk. **3,** [*pfv.* напая́ть] to solder on.

напа́лм *n.* napalm. —напа́лмовый, *adj.* napalm.

напа́рник *n., colloq.* partner; buddy; mate.

напа́рывать *v.impfv.* [*pfv.* напоро́ть] to cut: напоро́ть но́гу на гвоздь, to cut one's foot on a nail. —напа́рываться, *refl.* (*with* на + *acc.*) *colloq.* **1,** to cut oneself (on). **2,** to run into; encounter.

напа́сть[1] *v.pfv.* [*infl.* нападу́, нападёшь; *past* напа́л, напа́ла] **1,** *pfv. of* напада́ть. **2,** to fall (*in large quantities*).

напа́сть[2] *n.f., colloq.* misfortune.

напая́ть *v., pfv. of* напа́ивать (*in sense #3*).

напе́в *n.* tune; melody; air.

напева́ть *v.impfv.* [*pfv.* напе́ть] **1,** to sing. **2,** to record; make (a record). **3,** [*impfv. only*] to hum.

напе́вный *adj.* melodious.

наперебо́й *adv.* **1,** interrupting each other. **2,** vying with one another; trying to outdo one another.

напереве́с *adv.* (*of a weapon*) tilted forward.

наперегонки́ *also,* наперего́нки *adv., colloq.* racing one another: бежа́ть наперегонки́, to race each other.

наперёд *adv., colloq.* **1,** forward. **2,** in advance. —за́дом наперёд, backwards: наде́ть шля́пу за́дом наперёд, to put one's hat on backwards.

напереко́р *prep., with dat.* contrary to; in defiance of.

напере́з *prep., with dat.* so as to cut across the path of; so as to intercept; so as to head off.

наперерыв *adv.* = наперебо́й.

напере́ть [*infl.* напру́, напрёшь; *past* напёр, напёрла] *v., pfv. of* напира́ть.

наперечёт *adv.* **1,** (*with verbs of knowing*) inside out; like a book; (*with* все) every single one. **2,** few and far between.

напе́рсник *n., obs.* confidant.

напе́рсный *adj., in* напе́рсный крест, pectoral cross.

напёрсток [*gen.* -стка] *n.* thimble.

наперстя́нка *n.* foxglove; digitalis.

напе́ть [*infl.* напою́, напоёшь] *v., pfv. of* напева́ть.

напеча́тать *v., pfv. of* печа́тать. —напеча́таться, *refl., pfv. of* печа́таться.

напе́чь *v.pfv.* [*infl. like* печь] to bake (a quantity of something).

напива́ться *v.r.impfv.* [*pfv.* напи́ться] **1,** to drink one's fill. **2,** (*with gen.*) to have a drink of. **3,** to get drunk. **4,** (*with* до) to drink oneself into a state of...

напили́ть *v.pfv.* [*infl.* -пилю́, -пи́лишь] to saw (a quantity of something).

напи́лок [*gen.* -лка] *n., colloq.* = напи́льник.

напи́льник *n.* file (*tool*).

напира́ть *v.impfv.* [*pfv.* напере́ть] *colloq.* **1,** to press forward. **2,** (*with* на + *acc.*) to press against. **3,** [*impfv. only*] (*with* на + *acc.*) to stress; emphasize.

написа́ние *n.* **1,** writing. **2,** spelling.

написа́ть *v., pfv. of* писа́ть.

напита́ть *v.pfv.* **1,** *pfv. of* напи́тывать. **2,** *colloq.* to feed.

напи́ток [*gen.* -тка] *n.* drink; beverage.

напи́тывать *v.impfv.* [*pfv.* напита́ть] to saturate.

напи́ться [*infl.* -пью́сь, -пьёшься; *past* -пи́лся, -пила́сь, -пило́сь *or* -пи́лось, -пили́сь *or* -пи́лись] *v.r., pfv. of* напива́ться.

напи́хивать *v.impfv.* [*pfv.* напиха́ть] *colloq.* to stuff; cram.

напи́чкать *v., pfv. of* пи́чкать.

наплавно́й *adj., in* наплавно́й мост, floating bridge.

напла́каться *v.pfv.* [*infl.* -пла́чу, -пла́чешь], *in* напла́кать себе́ глаза́, to have red eyes from crying. —напла́каться, *refl.* **1,** to have a good cry. **2,** (*with* с + *instr.*) *colloq.* to have trouble (with).

напластова́ние *n., geol.* bedding; stratification.

наплева́тельский *adj., colloq.* couldn't-care-less: наплева́тельское отноше́ние, couldn't-care-less attitude.

наплева́ть *v.pfv.* [*infl.* **-плюю́, -плюёшь**] (*with* **на** + *acc.*) **1,** to spit on. **2,** *colloq.* not to give a damn: Ему́ наплева́ть на э́то, he doesn't give a damn about it.

наплести́ *v.pfv.* [*infl. like* **плести́**] **1,** to weave (a quantity of something). **2,** *colloq.* to talk a lot of (nonsense).

напле́чный *adj.* worn on the shoulders.

наплы́в *n.* **1,** influx. **2,** excrescence (*on trees*).

напова́л *adv., in* **уби́ть напова́л,** to kill outright; kill on the spot.

наподо́бие *prep., with gen.* like; resembling.

напои́ть [*infl.* **напою́, напо́ишь** *or* **напои́шь**] *v., pfv. of* **пои́ть** *and* **напа́ивать.**

напока́з *adv.* **1,** on display. **2,** for show. —**выставля́ть напока́з, 1,** to put on display. **2,** to show off; flaunt.

наполза́ть *v.impfv.* [*pfv.* **наползти́**] *colloq.* (*with* **на** + *acc.*) to crawl onto.

наползти́ [*infl. like* **ползти́**] *v., pfv. of* **наполза́ть.**

наполне́ние *n.* (act of) filling.

наполни́тель *n.m.* filler.

наполня́ть *v.impfv.* [*pfv.* **напо́лнить**] to fill. —**наполня́ться,** *refl.* to be filled; become filled.

наполови́ну *adv.* **1,** half: наполови́ну пусто́й, half-empty. **2,** in half; by half: уменьша́ть наполови́ну, to reduce in/by half.

напо́льный *adj.* floor (*attrib.*).

напома́дить *v., pfv. of* **пома́дить.** —**напома́диться,** *refl., pfv. of* **пома́диться.**

напомина́ние *n.* **1,** reminder. **2,** mention: при напомина́нии о..., at the mention of...

напомина́ть *v.impfv.* [*pfv.* **напо́мнить**] **1,** (*with dat.*) to remind: напо́мните кому́-нибудь о встре́че, to remind someone about an appointment. Вы напомина́ете мне моего́ му́жа, you remind me of my husband. **2,** (*with acc. or* **о** + *prepl.*) to bring back memories of. **3,** (*with* **о**) to mention; bring up; (*with* **что**) recall (that...). **4,** [*impfv. only*] to resemble: Фо́рма ку́пола напомина́ет лу́ковицу, the shape of the dome resembles an onion. **5,** [*impfv. only*] to be reminiscent of.

напо́р *n.* pressure.

напо́ристый *adj.* assertive; aggressive. —**напо́ристость,** *n.f.* assertiveness; aggressiveness.

напо́рный *adj.* pressure (*attrib.*).

напоро́ть *v.pfv.* [*infl.* **-порю́, -по́решь**] **1,** *pfv. of* **напа́рывать. 2,** (*with gen. or acc.*) *colloq.* to talk a lot of (nonsense). —**напоро́ться,** *refl., pfv. of* **напа́рываться.**

напо́ртить *v.pfv.* [*infl.* **-чу, -тишь**] *colloq.* **1,** to damage (a quantity of something). **2,** (*with dat.*) to harm.

напосле́док *adv., colloq.* **1,** finally; at last; in the end. **2,** in conclusion. **3,** for last.

напра́вить [*infl.* **-влю, -вишь**] *v., pfv. of* **направля́ть.** —**напра́виться,** *refl., pfv. of* **направля́ться.**

направле́ние *n.* **1,** direction. **2,** trend. **3,** assignment. **4,** order; permit. **5,** *mil.* axis.

напра́вленность *n.f.* direction; orientation.

напра́вленный *adj.* **1,** purposeful. **2,** *radio* directional.

направля́ть *v.impfv.* [*pfv.* **напра́вить**] **1,** to direct; aim (a blow); point (a weapon); direct (one's gaze). **2,** to direct (efforts, energies, criticism, attention, etc.). **3,** to send; assign. **4,** to send; refer (to a doctor, lawyer, etc.). **5,** to guide; steer. **6,** to send; address; dispatch (a letter, greetings, etc.). **7,** *in* направля́ть свои́ шаги́ *or* стопы́, to make *or* wend one's way; head for. —**направля́ться,** *refl.* (*with* **в, на,** *or* **к**) **1,** to head for; make for. **2,** [*impfv. only*] to be headed for; be bound for.

напра́во *adv.* to the right; on the right.

напрактикова́ться *v.r.pfv.* [*infl.* **-ку́юсь, -ку́ешься**] (*with* **в** + *prepl.*) *colloq.* to become proficient (at); get the knack (of).

напра́слина *n., colloq.* false charge; false allegation.

напра́сно *adv.* **1,** in vain; for nothing. Вы напра́сно ждёте её, you're wasting your time waiting for her. **2,** for no reason: Вы напра́сно обвиня́ете его́, you have no reason to accuse him.

напра́сный *adj.* **1,** vain; futile. **2,** (*of fears, anxiety, etc.*) needless; groundless.

напра́шиваться *v.r.impfv.* [*pfv.* **напроси́ться**] *colloq.* **1,** (*with* **в** *or* **на** + *acc.*) to invite oneself (to); (try to) get invited (to). Напра́шиваться в го́сти, to (try to) get oneself invited. Напроси́ться на сва́дьбу, to wangle an invitation to a wedding. Напроси́ться в командиро́вку, to wangle a business trip. **2,** (*with* **на** + *acc.*) to ask for; look for; invite (trouble); fish for (a compliment). **3,** [*impfv. only*] to come to mind; suggest itself.

наприме́р *adv.* for example; for instance.

напрока́зить *v., pfv. of* **прока́зить.**

напрока́зничать *v., pfv. of* **прока́зничать.**

напрока́т *adv.* on a rental basis. —**брать напрока́т,** to rent; hire. —**дава́ть** *or* **отдава́ть напрока́т,** to rent; rent out. —**сдава́ться напрока́т,** to be for hire.

напролёт *adv., colloq.* through; long; straight: всю ночь напролёт, the whole day through/long; весь день напролёт, all day long; два дня напролёт, two days straight.

напроло́м *adv., colloq.* full speed ahead (*regardless of obstacles*).

напропалу́ю *adv., colloq.* headlong; for all one is worth.

напроро́чить *v., pfv. of* **проро́чить.**

напроси́ться [*infl.* **-прошу́сь, -про́сишься**] *v.r., pfv. of* **напра́шиваться.**

напро́тив *adv.* **1,** opposite. **2,** across the street. **3,** on the contrary. **4,** on the other hand; by contrast. —*prep., with gen.* opposite; facing.

на́прочь *adv., colloq.* completely.

напру́живать *v.impfv.* [*pfv.* **напру́жить**] *colloq.* to strain; make taut. —**напру́живаться,** *refl., colloq.* to strain oneself.

напряга́ть *v.impfv.* [*pfv.* **напря́чь**] to strain; exert. —**напряга́ться,** *refl.* **1,** to become taut. **2,** to strain oneself; exert oneself.

напряже́ние *n.* **1,** straining; exertion. **2,** tension; strain; stress. **3,** *electricity* tension; voltage.

напряжённо *adv.* **1,** intently. **2,** intensely.

напряжённость *n.f.* tension: междунаро́дная напряжённость, international tension.

напряжённый *adj.* **1,** tense; strained. **2,** intense; strenuous. **3,** (*of attention*) rapt.

напрями́к *adv., colloq.* **1,** straight; in a straight line. **2,** *fig.* to the point; pointblank.

напряму́ю *adv.* **1,** = **напрями́к. 2,** directly.

напря́чь [*infl.* -прягу́, -пряжёшь, ...-прягу́т; *past* -пря́г, -прягла́, -прягло́, -прягли́] *v., pfv. of* **напряга́ть.** —**напря́чься,** *refl., pfv. of* **напряга́ться.**

напуга́ть *v.pfv.* to frighten; scare. —**напуга́ться,** *refl.* to become frightened; become scared.

напу́дрить *v., pfv. of* **пу́дрить.** —**напу́дриться,** *refl., pfv. of* **пу́дриться.**

напу́льсник *n.* wristband.

напуска́ть *v.impfv.* [*pfv.* **напусти́ть**] **1,** to let in. **2,** (*with* **на** + *acc.*) *colloq.* to sic (an animal) on. **3,** (*with* **на** + *acc.*) *colloq.* to strike (fear, terror, etc.) into. **4,** (*with* **на себя́**) *colloq.* to affect; assume an air of. **5,** *in* **напуска́ть тума́ну,** to confuse the issue. —**напуска́ться,** *refl.* (*with* **на** + *acc.*) *colloq.* to attack; pounce on.

напускно́й *adj.* affected; assumed.

напусти́ть [*infl.* -пущу́, -пу́стишь] *v., pfv. of* **напуска́ть.** —**напусти́ться,** *refl., pfv. of* **напуска́ться.**

напу́тать *v.pfv., colloq.* **1,** to make a mess of; botch. **2,** (*with* **в** + *prepl.*) to get (something) wrong; get (something) mixed up.

напу́тственный *adj.* parting; farewell.

напу́тствие *n.* parting words.

напу́тствовать *v.impfv. & pfv.* [*pres.* -ствую, -ствуешь] (*with instr.*) to say (*when parting*).

напуха́ть *v.impfv.* [*pfv.* **напу́хнуть**] *colloq.* to swell up; become swollen.

напу́хнуть [*past* напу́х, напу́хла] *v., pfv. of* **напуха́ть.**

напыжиться *v.r., pfv. of* **пыжиться.**

напыли́ть *v., pfv. of* **пыли́ть** (*in sense #1*).

напы́щенность *n.f.* **1,** pomposity. **2,** bombast.

напы́щенный *adj.* **1,** pompous. **2,** bombastic; high-flown.

напя́ливать *v.impfv.* [*pfv.* **напя́лить**] **1,** to stretch (material) on a frame. **2,** *colloq.* to pull on (an item of clothing that is too small).

нарабо́тать *v.pfv., colloq.* **1,** to produce (a quantity of something). **2,** to earn (a sum of money). —**нарабо́таться,** *refl., colloq.* to do a lot of work; do enough work.

наравне́ *adv.* (*with* **с** + *instr.*) **1,** even (with); on a level (with). **2,** equally (with); on a par (with); on an equal footing (with).

нараспа́шку *adv., colloq.* unbuttoned; unfastened. —**душа́ нараспа́шку,** open-hearted; not one to hold back.

нараспе́в *adv.* in a singsong voice.

нараста́ние *n.* growth; expansion.

нараста́ть *v.impfv.* [*pfv.* **нарасти́**] **1,** (*with* **на** + *prepl.*) to grow (on); form (on). **2,** to grow; expand. **3,** to increase; build up; mount. **4,** (*of debts*) to pile up; (*of interest*) to accrue.

нарасти́ [*infl. like* **расти́**] *v., pfv. of* **нараста́ть.**

нарасти́ть [*infl.* -щу́, -сти́шь] *v., pfv. of* **нара́щивать.**

нарасхва́т *adv., colloq.* like hot cakes: раскупа́ться нарасхва́т, to sell (*or* go) like hot cakes.

нара́щивание *n.* increase; build-up.

нара́щивать *v.impfv.* [*pfv.* **нарасти́ть**] **1,** [*impfv. only*] to increase; augment; step up; build up. **2,** *colloq.* to grow; develop (muscles, corns, etc.). **3,** to lengthen; extend. **4,** *colloq.* to accumulate; pile up (interest, debts, etc.).

нарва́л *n.* narwhal.

нарва́ть *v.pfv.* [*infl.* нарву́, нарвёшь; *past fem.* нарвала́] **1,** *pfv. of* **нарыва́ть. 2,** to pick (a quantity of something). **3,** to tear (a quantity of something). —**нарва́ться,** *refl.* [*past tense stress as in* **рва́ться**] *pfv. of* **нарыва́ться.**

нард *n.* nard; spikenard.

наре́зать [*infl.* -ре́жу, -ре́жешь] *v., pfv. of* **нареза́ть.**

нареза́ть *v.impfv.* [*pfv.* **наре́зать**] **1,** to cut; slice. **2,** to thread (a screw); rifle (a gun barrel).

наре́зка *n.* **1,** cutting; slicing. **2,** thread (*of a screw*).

нарека́ние *n.* censure; reprimand.

нарека́ть *v.impfv.* [*pfv.* **наре́чь**] *obs.* to name.

наре́чие *n.* **1,** adverb. **2,** dialect. —**наре́чный,** *adj.* adverbial.

наре́чь [*infl.* -реку́, -речёшь, ...-реку́т; *past* -рёк, -рекла́, -рекло́, -рекли́] *v., pfv. of* **нарека́ть.**

нарза́н *n.* a kind of mineral water; narzan.

нарисова́ть *v., pfv. of* **рисова́ть.**

нарица́тельный *adj., in* **и́мя нарица́тельное,** common noun.

наркоби́знес (нэ) *n., colloq.* drug dealing. —**деле́ц наркоби́знеса,** drug dealer.

нарко́з *n.* **1,** anesthesia. **2,** anesthetic.

наркома́н *n.* drug addict. —**наркома́ния,** *n.* drug addiction.

наркотизи́ровать *v.impfv. & pfv.* [*pres.* -рую, -руешь] to anesthetize.

нарко́тик *n.* narcotic; drug.

наркоти́ческий *adj.* narcotic. —**наркоти́ческие сре́дства,** narcotics; drugs.

наро́д *n.* **1,** a people: ру́сский наро́д, the Russian people. **2,** the (common) people: челове́к из наро́да, a man of the people. **3,** people: мно́го наро́ду, a lot of people.

народи́ть *v.pfv.* [*infl.* -жу́, -ди́шь] *colloq.* to give birth to (a number of children). —**народи́ться,** *refl., pfv. of* **нарожда́ться.**

наро́дник *n., hist.* Narodnik; Populist. —**наро́днический,** *adj.* Populist. —**наро́дничество,** *n.* Populism.

наро́дность *n.f.* **1,** nationality; people. **2,** national character; national roots.

наро́дный *adj.* **1,** people's. **2,** national. **3,** folk-: наро́дная пе́сня, folk song.

народовла́стие *n.* government by the people.

народонаселе́ние *n.* population.

нарожда́ться *v.r.impfv.* [*pfv.* **народи́ться**] **1,** (*of a number of people*) to be born. **2,** *fig.* to arise; come into being.

наро́ст *n.* growth; tumor.

нарочи́тый *adj.* **1,** deliberate; intentional. **2,** feigned; affected. —**нарочи́то,** *adv.* deliberately; intentionally.

наро́чно *adv.* **1,** deliberately; on purpose. **2,** (*with* для) specially (for); expressly (for). **3,** for spite; just to be contrary. **4,** *colloq.* for fun. —**как наро́чно,** as luck would have it.

на́рочный *n., decl. as an adj.* special messenger; courier.

на́рты [*gen.* нарт] *n.pl.* dog sled; reindeer sled.

наруби́ть *v.pfv.* [*infl.* -рублю́, -ру́бишь] to chop (a quantity of something).

нару́жно *adv.* outwardly.

нару́жное *n., decl. as an adj.* medicine to be taken externally.

нару́жность *n.f.* **1,** appearance; looks. **2,** exterior.

нару́жный *adj.* **1,** external; outward. **2,** (*of a wall*) outside. **3,** outward: нару́жное споко́йствие, outward calm. **4,** (*of medicine*) to be taken externally.

нару́жу *adv.* outside; outward(s); out. —**весь нару́жу,** (*of a person*) completely open about everything. —**вы́вести нару́жу,** to bring out into the open; bring to light. —**вы́йти нару́жу,** to come to the surface; come to light.

нарука́вник *n.* sleeve cover; sleeve protector.

нарука́вный *adj.* worn on the sleeve: нарука́вная повя́зка, armband.

нарумя́нить *v., pfv. of* румя́нить. —**нарумя́ниться,** *refl., pfv. of* румя́ниться (*in sense #1*).

нару́чники *n.pl.* [*sing.* нару́чник] handcuffs; manacles.

нару́чный *adj.* worn on the arm. —**нару́чные часы́,** wrist watch.

наруша́ть *v.impfv.* [*pfv.* нару́шить] **1,** to violate; break. **2,** to disturb; disrupt; upset.

наруше́ние *n.* **1,** violation; breach; infringement. Наруше́ние до́лга, dereliction of duty. **2,** disturbance; disruption.

наруши́тель *n.m.* violator.

нару́шить *v., pfv. of* наруша́ть.

нарци́сс *n.* narcissus; daffodil.

на́ры [*gen.* нар] *n.pl.* plank bed.

нары́в *n.* abscess; boil.

нарыва́ть *v.impfv.* [*pfv.* нарва́ть] to become infected and swollen. —**нарыва́ться,** *refl.* (*with* на + *acc.*) *colloq.* to run into; bump into.

нары́ть *v.pfv.* [*infl.* наро́ю, наро́ешь] to dig (a quantity of something).

наря́д *n.* **1,** dress; attire; apparel. **2,** order; warrant. **3,** *mil.* detail. **4,** *mil.* duty. —**наря́д дежу́рств;** лист наря́дов, duty roster.

наряди́ть [*infl.* -ряжу́, -ряди́шь *or* -ря́дишь] *v., pfv. of* наряжа́ть. —**наряди́ться,** *refl., pfv. of* наряжа́ться.

наря́дный *adj.* **1,** well-dressed. **2,** (*of an item of clothing*) good-looking; smart.

наряду́ *adv.* (*with* с + *instr.*) **1,** along (with); side by side (with). **2,** on a level (with); on a par (with). —**наряду́ с э́тим,** at the same time.

наряжа́ть *v.impfv.* [*pfv.* наряди́ть] **1,** to dress; dress up. **2,** to order; assign; detail. —**наряжа́ться,** *refl.* **1,** to dress up; get dressed up. **2,** (*with instr.*) to get dressed up (as).

нас *pron., gen. & prepl. of* мы.

насади́ть *v.pfv.* [*infl.* -сажу́, -са́дишь] **1,** *pfv. of* **наса́живать. 2,** to plant (a quantity of something).

наса́дка [*gen. pl.* -док] *n.* **1,** putting on. **2,** attachment (*for a camera or other device*). **3,** bait.

насажа́ть *v.pfv.* = насади́ть (*in sense #2*).

насажда́ть *v.impfv.* to implant; instill.

насажде́ние *n.* **1,** planting. **2,** *fig.* implanting. **3,** *usu. pl.* plantings (*trees, plants, etc.*).

наса́живать *v.impfv.* [*pfv.* насади́ть] **1,** to plant. **2,** (*with* на + *acc.*) to put; fix; stick; fasten (onto a hook, spit, etc.). **3,** *colloq.* to put on; slip over.

наса́ливать *v.impfv.* [*pfv.* насоли́ть] **1,** to salt; pickle. **2,** (*with dat.*) *colloq.* to hurt; injure; spite.

наса́харивать *v.impfv.* [*pfv.* наса́харить] *colloq.* to put sugar into.

насви́стывать *v.impfv.* to whistle.

наседа́ть *v.impfv.* [*pfv.* насе́сть] **1,** (*of dust*) to settle; collect. **2,** (*with* на + *acc.*) *colloq.* to pounce on; *fig.* press; put pressure on (someone).

насе́дка [*gen. pl.* -док] *n.* brood hen.

насека́ть *v.impfv.* [*pfv.* насе́чь] to carve (*on a surface*).

насеко́мое *n., decl. as an adj.* insect.

населе́ние *n.* population.

населённость *n.f.* population density.

населённый *adj.* populated.

населя́ть *v.impfv.* [*pfv.* насели́ть] **1,** to populate; settle. **2,** [*impfv. only*] to inhabit.

насе́ст *n.* roost; perch.

насе́сть *v.pfv.* [*infl. like* сесть] **1,** *pfv. of* наседа́ть. **2,** (*of many people*) to sit down.

насе́чка [*gen. pl.* -чек] *n.* **1,** notch; groove. **2,** inlay.

насе́чь [*infl. like* сечь; *past* -сёк, -секла́, -секло́, -секли́] *v.pfv.* **1,** *pfv. of* насека́ть. **2,** *colloq.* to chop (a quantity of something).

насе́ять *v.pfv.* [*infl.* насе́ю, насе́ешь] to sow (a quantity of something).

насиде́ть [*infl.* -жу́, -ди́шь] *v., pfv. of* наси́живать. —**насиде́ться,** *refl., colloq.* to sit a long time; sit long enough.

наси́женный *adj., in* наси́женное ме́сто, place where one has always lived; one's home of many years.

наси́живать *v.impfv.* [*pfv.* насиде́ть] to hatch (an egg).

наси́лие *n.* violence.

наси́ловать *v.impfv.* [*pfv.* изнаси́ловать; *pres.* -лую, -луешь] **1,** to force; coerce. **2,** to rape.

наси́лу *adv., colloq.* barely; with great difficulty.

наси́льник *n.* **1,** tyrant; oppressor. **2,** rapist.

наси́льно *adv.* by force; forcibly.

наси́льственный *adj.* forcible; violent. —**наси́льственно,** *adv.* forcibly.

наска́кивать *v.impfv.* [*pfv.* наскочи́ть] **1,** (*with* на + *acc.*) to run into; collide (with); strike. **2,** to pounce on. **3,** *fig., colloq.* to jump on; assail.

насканда́лить *v., pfv. of* сканда́лить (*in sense #1*).

наскво́зь *adv.* **1,** through; right through. **2,** *fig.* through and through; to the core. —**ви́деть наскво́зь,** to see through (someone).

наско́к *n., colloq.* **1,** lunge; attack. —**с наско́ку, 1,** with a swoop; by swooping down. **2,** on impulse; on the spur of the moment.

наско́лько *adv.* **1,** (*with adjectives and adverbs*) how: Наско́лько э́то ве́рно?, how true is this? **2,** as far as: наско́лько я зна́ю, as far as I know.

на́скоро *adv., colloq.* hastily; hurriedly.

наскочи́ть [*infl.* -скочу́, -ско́чишь] *v., pfv. of* **наска́кивать.**

наскрести́ *v.pfv.* [*infl. like* **скрести́**] to scrape up; scrape together (*lit. & fig.*).

наску́чить *v.pfv.* (*with dat.*) *colloq.* to bore.

наслажда́ться *v.r.impfv.* [*pfv.* **наслади́ться**] (*with instr.*) to enjoy; take pleasure in.

наслажде́ние *n.* delight; pleasure; enjoyment.

насла́иваться *v.r.impfv.* [*pfv.* **наслои́ться**] to accumulate; pile up.

насла́ть *v.pfv.* [*infl.* **нашлю́, нашлёшь**] **1,** *pfv. of* **насыла́ть. 2,** to send (a quantity of something).

насле́дие *n.* legacy; heritage.

наследи́ть *v., pfv. of* **следи́ть** (*in sense #6*).

насле́дник *n.* heir. —**насле́дница,** *n.* heiress.

насле́дный *adj., in* **насле́дный принц/князь,** crown prince.

насле́дование *n.* inheritance. —**пра́во насле́дования,** succession.

насле́довать *v.impfv. & pfv.* [*pfv. also* **унасле́довать;** *pres.* -дую, -дуешь] **1,** to inherit. **2,** (*with dat.*) to succeed (someone) to the throne.

насле́дственность *n.f.* heredity.

насле́дственный *adj.* hereditary; inherited.

насле́дство *n.* **1,** inheritance. **2,** heritage. —**получи́ть (что-нибудь) в насле́дство** *or* **по насле́дству,** to inherit.

наслое́ние *n.* **1,** stratification. **2,** layer.

наслои́ться *v.r., pfv. of* **насла́иваться.**

наслу́шаться *v.r.pfv.* (*with gen.*) **1,** to hear a lot of. **2,** to hear enough of.

наслы́шан *adj.* (*with* **о**) *colloq.* familar (with): челове́к, о кото́ром мно́гие из нас наслы́шаны, a person with whom many of us are familiar.

наслы́шаться *v.r. pfv.* [*infl.* -шусь, -шишься] (*with* **о**) *colloq.* to hear enough (about).

насма́рку *adv., colloq., in* **идти́/пойти́ насма́рку,** to go awry; go down the drain.

на́смерть *adv.* **1,** to death; mortally. Разби́ться на́смерть, to be killed (*in a crash, fall, etc.*). **2,** to the death: сража́ться на́смерть, to fight to the death. **3,** *fig., colloq.* to an extreme degree: испуга́ть на́смерть, to frighten to death; ненави́деть на́смерть, to hate with a passion.

насмеха́ться *v.r.impfv.* (*with* **над**) to mock; ridicule; deride.

насмеши́ть *v., pfv. of* **смеши́ть.**

насме́шка [*gen. pl.* -шек] *n.* **1,** taunt; jibe. **2,** *usu. pl.* ridicule; derision.

насме́шливый *adj.* **1,** (*of a person*) sarcastic. **2,** mocking; derisive.

насме́шник *n.* sarcastic person.

насме́шничать *v.impfv., colloq.* to scoff; sneer; (*with* **над**) scoff at; deride.

насмея́ться *v.r.pfv.* [*infl.* -смею́сь, -смеёшься] **1,** *colloq.* to have a lot of laughs. **2,** (*with* **над**) to laugh at; make fun of; deride.

на́сморк *n.* (head) cold.

насмотре́ться *v.r.pfv.* [*infl.* -смотрю́сь, -смо́тришь-ся] **1,** (*with gen.*) to see a lot of. **2,** (*with* **на** + *acc.*) to see enough of: Не могу́ насмотре́ться на э́то, I can't see enough of it.

насовсе́м *adv., colloq.* for good.

насоли́ть [*infl. like* **соли́ть**] *v., pfv. of* **наса́ливать.**

насори́ть *v., pfv. of* **сори́ть.**

насо́с *n.* pump.

насо́сный *adj.* pump (*attrib.*) pumping.

на́спех *adv.* hastily; hurriedly; in a hurry.

наспле́тничать *v., pfv. of* **спле́тничать.**

наст *n.* frozen crust on snow.

настава́ть *v.impfv.* [*pfv.* **наста́ть;** *pres.* -стаёт] (*of time, a season, etc.*) to come.

настави́тельный *adj.* didactic.

наста́вить *v.pfv.* [*infl.* -влю, -вишь] **1,** *pfv. of* **наставля́ть. 2,** to place (a quantity of something).

наставле́ние *n.* **1,** instructions. **2,** admonition. **3,** *mil.* manual.

наставля́ть *v.impfv.* [*pfv.* **наста́вить**] **1,** to lengthen. **2,** to aim; point. **3,** to teach; enlighten. —**наставля́ть нос** (+ *dat.*), to fool; dupe.

наста́вник *n.* teacher; tutor; mentor.

наста́ивать *v.impfv.* [*pfv.* **настоя́ть**] (*with* **на** + *prepl.*) to insist (on). —**наста́ивать на своём,** to insist on having one's own way. —**настоя́ть на своём,** to have one's own way.

наста́ть [*infl.* -ста́нет] *v., pfv. of* **настава́ть.**

на́стежь *adv.* **1,** (*with verbs of opening*) wide. **2,** wide open.

насте́нный *adj.* wall (*attrib.*).

настига́ть *v.impfv.* [*pfv.* **насти́гнуть** *or* **насти́чь**] to overtake; catch up to.

насти́гнуть [*past* насти́г, насти́гла] *v., pfv. of* **настига́ть.**

насти́л *n.* flooring.

настила́ть *v.impfv.* [*pfv.* **настла́ть**] **1,** to lay (straw, matting, etc.) over a surface. **2,** to lay (a floor, carpet, etc.).

насти́лка *n., colloq.* flooring.

насти́чь [*infl. like* **насти́гнуть**] *v., pfv. of* **настига́ть.**

настла́ть [*infl.* -стелю́, -сте́лешь] *v., pfv. of* **настила́ть.**

насто́й *n.* (liquid) extract.

насто́йка *n.* **1,** (fruit) brandy: вишнёвая насто́йка, cherry brandy. **2,** tincture: насто́йка йо́да, tincture of iodine.

насто́йчивый *adj.* persistent; insistent. —**насто́йчивость,** *n.f.* persistence; perseverance.

насто́лько *adv.* **1,** (*with adjectives*) so: Э́то бы́ло насто́лько невероя́тно, что..., it was so unbelievable that... **2,** (*with verbs*) so much: Он насто́лько вы́рос, что..., he has grown so much that... —**насто́лько..., наско́лько,** as..., as: Она́ насто́лько умна́, наско́лько краси́ва, she is as intelligent as she is beautiful.

насто́льный *adj.* **1,** table (*attrib.*); desk (*attrib.*). **2,** *fig.* continually referred to: насто́льная кни́га, book of ready reference; one's "bible". —**насто́льная игра́,** board game. —**насто́льный те́ннис,** table tennis.

настора́живать *v.impfv.* [*pfv.* **насторожи́ть**] **1,** to make (someone) apprehensive; put on one's guard. **2,** *in* **насторожи́ть у́ши,** to prick up one's ears. **3,** *v.i.* to be cause for concern. —**насторожи́ться,** *refl.* to prick up one's ears; become alert.

насторожé *adv.* on the alert; on the lookout; on one's guard.

насторо́женный *also,* **насторожённый** *adj.* **1,** watchful; wary. **2,** guarded. —**насторо́женно; насторожённо,** *adv.* warily. —**насторо́женность; насторожённость,** *n.f.* wariness.

насторожи́ть *v.,* *pfv. of* **настора́живать.** —**насторожи́ться,** *refl., pfv. of* **настора́живаться.**

настоя́ние *n.* insistence.

настоя́тель *n.m.* **1,** abbot; prior. **2,** dean (*of a cathedral*). —**настоя́тельница,** *n.* mother superior.

настоя́тельно *adv.* **1,** insistently; persistently. **2,** urgently.

настоя́тельность *n.f.* **1,** persistence. **2,** urgency.

настоя́тельный *adj.* **1,** insistent; persistent. **2,** vital; urgent.

настоя́ть [*infl.* -**сто́ю,** -**стои́шь**] *v., pfv. of* **наста́ивать.**

настоя́щее *n., decl. as an adj.* **1,** the present. **2,** *instr.* hereby: Настоя́щим удостоверя́ется что..., this is to certify that...

настоя́щий *adj.* **1,** present: в настоя́щее вре́мя, at the present time. **2,** the present; this. **3,** real; true; genuine. —**настоя́щее вре́мя,** *gram.* present tense.

настрада́ться *v.r.pfv.* to suffer much.

настра́ивать *v.impfv.* [*pfv.* **настро́ить**] **1,** to tune (a musical instrument); tune in (a radio). **2,** to adjust (a device). **3,** to put (someone) in a certain mood: настро́ить кого́-нибудь на весёлый лад, to put someone in a happy frame of mind. ♦*Often passive.* Он пло́хо настро́ен, he is in a bad mood. Я настро́ен(а) пойти́ в кино́, I am in the mood to go to a movie. **4,** to influence; dispose: настро́ить кого́-нибудь в по́льзу (*or* про́тив) чего́-нибудь, to influence someone in favor of (*or* against) something. Настро́ить (кого́-нибудь) в свою́ по́льзу, to win over. Настро́ить (кого́-нибудь) про́тив себя́, to antagonize. Настро́ить сы́на про́тив отца́, to turn a son against his father. Он настро́ен про́тив меня́, he has something against me. Я настро́ен(а) оптимисти́чески/скепти́чески, I am optimistic/skeptical. —**настра́иваться,** *refl.* **1,** (*with* на + *acc.*) to tune in (a program, station, etc.). **2,** (*with* к *or* про́тив) to feel disposed (in a certain way toward or against). **3,** (*with inf.*) to make up one's mind to; (*with* на + *acc.*) decide upon.

настреля́ть *v.pfv.* to shoot (a quantity of something).

на́строго *adv., colloq.* strictly.

настро́ение *n.* **1,** mood; frame of mind. У меня́ нет настро́ения (+ *inf.*), I am not in the mood to... **2,** *pl.* attitudes; sentiments.

настро́енность *n.f.* mood; attitude.

настро́ить *v.pfv.* **1,** *pfv. of* **настра́ивать. 2,** to build (a quantity of something). —**настро́иться,** *refl., pfv. of* **настра́иваться.**

настро́й *n., colloq.* mood.

настро́йка *n.* tuning.

настро́йщик *n.* tuner.

настрочи́ть *v., pfv. of* **строчи́ть** (*in sense #2*).

настря́пать *v.pfv.* to cook; whip up (a quantity of something).

наступа́тельный *adj., mil.* offensive.

наступа́ть *v.impfv.* [*pfv.* **наступи́ть**] **1,** (*with* на + *acc.*) to step on; tread on. **2,** [*impfv. only*] to attack; go on the offensive; (*with* на + *acc.*) attack; advance on or against. **3,** [*impfv. only*] (*with* на + *acc.*) to harass; press. **4,** [*impfv. only*] (*of natural phenomena*) to advance. **5,** (*of time, a season, etc.*) to come.

наступи́ть [*infl.* -**ступлю́,** -**сту́пишь**] *v., pfv. of* **наступа́ть.**

наступле́ние *n.* **1,** *mil.* offensive. **2,** coming (*of a season, time, etc.*). Наступле́ние ста́рости, the onset of old age. До наступле́ния темноты́, before nightfall.

насту́рция *n.* nasturtium.

насты́рный *adj., colloq.* pushy; pesky.

насу́пить *v.pfv.* [*infl.* -**су́плю,** -**су́пишь**], *in* насу́пить бро́ви, to frown. —**насу́питься,** *refl.* to scowl; frown.

насу́пленный *adj.* glum; morose. —**насу́пленные бро́ви,** frown.

на́сухо *adv.* dry: вы́тереть на́сухо, to wipe dry.

насуши́ть *v.pfv.* [*infl.* -**сушу́,** -**су́шишь**] to dry (a quantity of something).

насу́щный *adj.* **1,** vital. **2,** urgent. —**насу́щный хлеб,** daily bread.

насчёт *prep., with gen.* about; regarding; concerning. —**как насчёт** (+ *gen.*), how about...?; what about...?

насчи́тывать *v.impfv.* [*pfv.* **насчита́ть**] **1,** to count: Я насчита́л бо́лее двадцати́ повреждённых домо́в, I counted more than twenty damaged houses. **2,** [*impfv. only*] to number; consist of: А́рмия насчи́тывала сто ты́сяч солда́т, the army numbered/ consisted of/ 100,000 soldiers. Исто́рия Кита́я насчи́тывает 4,5 ты́сячи лет, the history of China goes back 4,500 years. —**насчи́тываться,** *refl.* [*impfv. only*] to number: насчи́тываться со́тнями, to number in the hundreds. ♦*Also impers.:* В го́роде насчи́тывается три́ста ты́сяч жи́телей, the city's inhabitants number 300,000; the city has a population of 300,000. Эскимо́сов в Росси́и насчи́тывается всего́ ты́сяча, Eskimos in Russia number only a thousand.

насыла́ть *v.impfv.* [*pfv.* **насла́ть**] (*of divine powers*) to send down; inflict (destruction, a calamity, etc.).

насыпа́ть [*infl.* -**сы́плю,** -**сы́плешь**] *v., pfv. of* **насыпа́ть.**

насыпа́ть *v.impfv.* [*pfv.* **насы́пать**] **1,** to sprinkle; spread. **2,** to pour (a dry substance): насыпа́ть муки́ в мешо́к, to pour flour into a sack. **3,** to fill: насыпа́ть мешо́к муко́й, to fill a sack with flour. **4,** to build (*out of dirt, sand, etc.*).

на́сыпь *n.f.* embankment: железнодоро́жная на́сыпь, railway embankment.

насы́тить [*infl.* -**сы́щу,** -**сы́тишь**] *v., pfv. of* **насыща́ть.** —**насы́титься,** *refl., pfv. of* **насыща́ться.**

насыща́ть *v.impfv.* [*pfv.* **насы́тить**] **1,** to satiate; sate. **2,** to saturate. **3,** *fig.* to satisfy (a desire, curiosity, etc.). —**насыща́ться,** *refl.* **1,** to be full; be sated. **2,** to be saturated.

насыще́ние *n.* **1,** satiation. **2,** saturation.

насы́щенный *adj.* **1,** saturated. **2,** (*of a schedule or itinerary*) full; busy; tight.

ната́лкивать *v.impfv.* [*pfv.* натолкну́ть] **1,** *colloq.* to push into/against/onto: натолкну́ть кого́-нибудь на стол, to push someone into/against the table. **2,** *fig.* to lead (to): ната́лкивать кого́-нибудь на мысль, to lead someone to think; give someone an idea. —ната́лкиваться, *refl.* (*with* на + *acc.*) **1,** to run into; bump into; strike. **2,** *fig.* to run into; encounter. **3,** *fig.* to run across; come across.

ната́птывать *v.impfv.* [*pfv.* натопта́ть] (*with* на + *prepl.*) *colloq.* to track up.

натаска́ть *v.pfv.* **1,** *pfv. of* ната́скивать. **2,** to bring, drag, store, or steal (a quantity of something). **3,** *colloq.* to cull; drag up (from various sources).

ната́скивать *v.impfv.* [*pfv.* натаска́ть] **1,** to train (a dog). **2,** *colloq.* to coach; teach (*quickly or superficially*). **3,** [*pfv.* натащи́ть] *colloq.* to pull on (an item of clothing); pull over.

натащи́ть *v.pfv.* [*infl.* -тащу́, -та́щишь] **1,** *pfv. of* ната́скивать (*in sense #3*). **2,** = натаска́ть (*in sense #2*).

натвори́ть *v.pfv.*, *colloq.* to do (something harmful): Что ты натвори́л?, what have you done?

на́те *particle, colloq.* here is; here you are.

натека́ть *v.impfv.* [*pfv.* нате́чь] (*of water*) to accumulate.

нате́льный *adj.* worn next to the skin: нате́льное бельё, underwear.

натере́ть *v.pfv.* [*infl.* натру́, натрёшь; *past* натёр, натёрла] **1,** *pfv. of* натира́ть. **2,** to grate (a quantity of something). —натере́ться, *refl., pfv. of* натира́ться.

натерпе́ться *v.r.pfv.* [*infl.* -терплю́сь, -те́рпишься] *colloq.* **1,** to suffer greatly. **2,** (*with gen.*) to suffer (a great deal of). —натерпе́ться стра́ху, to have a terrible fright.

нате́чь [*infl. like* течь] *v., pfv. of* натека́ть.

нате́шиться *v.r.pfv., colloq.* **1,** to enjoy oneself to the full. **2,** (*with* над) to have a good laugh (over).

натира́ть *v.impfv.* [*pfv.* натере́ть] **1,** to rub: натира́ть спи́ну спи́ртом, to rub one's back with alcohol. **2,** to polish. **3,** to rub sore; irritate. Натере́ть себе́ мозо́ль, to get a corn. —натира́ться, *refl.* (*with instr.*) to rub oneself (with).

на́тиск *n.* onslaught; charge.

натка́ть *v.pfv.* [*infl. like* ткать] to weave (a quantity of something).

наткну́ться *v.r., pfv. of* натыка́ться.

натолкну́ть *v., pfv. of* ната́лкивать. —натолкну́ться, *refl., pfv. of* ната́лкиваться.

натоло́чь *v.pfv.* [*infl. like* толо́чь] to pound; crush (a quantity of something).

натопи́ть *v.pfv.* [*infl.* -топлю́, -то́пишь] **1,** to heat well. **2,** to melt (a quantity of something).

натопта́ть [*infl.* -топчу́, -то́пчешь] *v., pfv. of* ната́птывать.

наторе́ть *v.pfv.* (*with* в + *prepl.*) *colloq.* to become adept (at).

наточи́ть *v., pfv. of* точи́ть (*in sense #1*).

натоща́к *adv.* on an empty stomach.

натр *n., in* е́дкий натр, caustic soda.

натрави́ть [*infl.* -травлю́, -тра́вишь] *v., pfv. of* натра́вливать.

натра́вливать *v.impfv.* [*pfv.* натрави́ть] (*with* на + *acc.*) **1,** to sic (a dog on). **2,** *colloq.* to set (people against each other).

натрениро́ванный *adj.* trained.

натренирова́ть *v., pfv. of* тренирова́ть. —натренирова́ться, *refl., pfv. of* тренирова́ться.

на́триевый *adj.* sodium (*attrib.*). —на́триевая ла́мпа, sodium-vapor lamp. —на́триевая сели́тра, sodium nitrate.

на́трий *n.* sodium.

на́трое *adv.* in three; into three parts.

натруди́ть *v.pfv.* [*infl.* -тружу́, -тру́дишь *or* труди́шь] *colloq.* to overexert; wear out (a part of one's body).

нату́га *n., colloq.* strain; exertion.

нату́го *adv., colloq.* very tightly.

нату́живать *v.impfv.* [*pfv.* нату́жить] *colloq.* to strain; stretch; exert. —нату́живаться, *refl., colloq.* to make a supreme effort; bear down.

нату́жный *adj., colloq.* **1,** strenuous. **2,** strained. —нату́жно, *adv., colloq.* with great effort.

нату́ра *n.* **1,** nature; temperament; disposition. **2,** *art* real life: писа́ть с нату́ры, to paint from real life. **3,** model (*one who poses*). **4,** *motion pictures* location: на нату́ре, on location. —нату́рой, in kind: получа́ть жа́лованье нату́рой, to receive one's wages in kind.

натурализа́ция *n.* naturalization.

натурали́зм *n.* naturalism.

натурализова́ть *v.impfv. & pfv.* [*pres.* -зу́ю, -зу́ешь] to naturalize (*confer citizenship upon*). —натурализова́ться, *refl.* to become naturalized.

натурали́ст *n.* naturalist. —натуралисти́ческий, *adj.* naturalist (*attrib.*); naturalistic.

натура́льный *adj.* **1,** natural (*in various meanings*). **2,** (*of a product, material, etc.*) natural; real. **3,** (*of a person, gesture, etc.*) natural; genuine. —в натура́льную величину́, life-size.

нату́рщик *n.m.* [*fem.* -щица] model (*one who poses*).

натыка́ть *v.pfv., colloq.* to stick in (a quantity of something).

натыка́ться *v.r.impfv.* [*pfv.* наткну́ться] (*with* на + *acc.*) *colloq.* **1,** to run into; run against (a sharp object). **2,** to come upon; come across; run across; run into; encounter.

натюрмо́рт *n.* still life.

натя́гивать *v.impfv.* [*pfv.* натяну́ть] **1,** to draw (a bow, reins, etc.). **2,** to draw tight; tighten. **3,** to pull on; slip on. **4,** to pull over: натяну́ть ша́пку на́ уши, to pull one's cap down over one's ears. —натя́гиваться, *refl.* to become taut.

натяже́ние *n.* pull; tension.

натя́жка *n.* **1,** stretching. **2,** *fig.* stretching of a point: с натя́жкой, by stretching a point.

натя́нутость *n.f.* tension; strain.

натя́нутый *adj.* **1,** strained. **2,** unnatural; forced.

натяну́ть [*infl.* -тяну́, -тя́нешь] *v., pfv. of* натя́гивать. —натяну́ться, *refl., pfv. of* натя́гиваться.

науга́д *adv.* **1,** at random. **2,** by guesswork.

науго́льник *n.* bevel; bevel square.

науда́чу *adv.* at random.

науди́ть *v.pfv.* [*infl.* **-ужу́, -у́дишь**] to catch (a quantity of fish).

нау́ка *n.* **1,** science. **2,** *colloq.* lesson: Э́то тебе́ нау́ка!, let that be a lesson to you!

нау́ськивать *v.impfv.* [*pfv.* **нау́ськать**] *colloq.* **1,** to sic (a dog). **2,** to egg on; incite.

наутёк *adv., colloq., in* **пусти́ться** *or* **бро́ситься наутёк**, to take to one's heels.

наутофо́н *n.* foghorn.

нау́тро *adv.* the next morning.

научи́ть *v., pfv. of* **учи́ть** (*in sense #1*). —**научи́ться**, *refl., pfv. of* **учи́ться** (*in sense #2*).

нау́чный *adj.* scientific. —**нау́чно**, *adv.* scientifically.

нау́шник *n.* **1,** earlap; earmuff. **2,** earphone; headphone. **3,** *colloq.* informer; tattletale.

нау́шничать *v.impfv., colloq.* **1,** to spread malicious gossip. **2,** (*with* **на** + *acc.*) to say nasty things (about).

нау́шничество *n., colloq.* malicious gossip.

наущéние *n., in* **по наущéнию** (+ *gen.*), at the urging of.

нафтали́н *n.* naphthalene.

нафто́л *n.* naphthol.

наха́л *n.m.* [*fem.* **-ка**] insolent person.

наха́льничать *v.impfv., colloq.* to be insolent; behave insolently.

наха́льный *adj.* impudent; insolent; impertinent.

наха́льство *n.* **1,** impudence; insolence; impertinence. **2,** effrontery; gall.

нахва́ливать *v.impfv.* [*pfv.* **нахвали́ть**] *colloq.* to extol.

нахвали́ть [*infl.* **-хвалю́, -хва́лишь**] *v., pfv. of* **нахва́ливать**. —**нахвали́ться**, *refl.* (*with instr.*) to praise sufficiently: Не могу́ им нахвали́ться, I cannot praise him too highly.

нахвата́ть *v.pfv., colloq.* to acquire; pick up (a quantity of something). —**нахвата́ться**, *refl.* (*with gen.*) *colloq.* to pick up (bits of knowledge, a few words of a language, etc.).

нахлéбник *n.* **1,** parasite; hanger-on. **2,** *obs.* boarder.

нахлеста́ть [*infl.* **-хлещу́, -хлéщешь**] *v., pfv. of* **нахлёстывать**.

нахлёстывать *v.impfv.* [*pfv.* **нахлеста́ть**] *colloq.* to whip; flog.

нахлобу́чивать *v.impfv.* [*pfv.* **нахлобу́чить**] *colloq.* to pull down (a hat) over one's eyes, ears, etc.

нахлобу́чка [*gen. pl.* **-чек**] *n., colloq.* scolding; bawling out; dressing-down.

нахлы́нуть *v.pfv.* **1,** (*of liquids*) to stream; flow; gush. **2,** (*of people*) to rush; throng; surge. **3,** *fig.* (*of thoughts*) to spring to mind.

нахму́ренный *adj.* **1,** frowning. **2,** gloomy.

нахму́рить *v., pfv. of* **хму́рить**. —**нахму́риться**, *refl., pfv. of* **хму́риться**.

находи́ть *v.impfv.* [*pfv.* **найти́**; *pres.* **-хожу́, -хо́дишь**] **1,** to find: найти́ свой портфе́ль, to find one's briefcase. Находи́ть до́вод убеди́тельным, to find an argument convincing. **2,** to derive; gain (pleasure, satisfaction, etc.). **3,** (*with* **на** + *acc.*) to strike; run into. **4,** (*with* **на** + *acc.*) to come upon. **5,** (*with* **на** + *acc.*) (*of emotions*) to come over. **6,** (*of clouds, twilight, etc.*) to gather. **7,** (*with* **на** + *acc.*) (*of clouds*) to cover; obscure. **8,** *impers.* (*of a crowd*) to gather: Нашло́ мно́го

наро́ду, a large crowd gathered. **9,** *in* найти́ свою́ смерть, to meet one's death (*or* end). —**находи́ться**, *refl.* **1,** [*impfv. only*] to be; be found; be located. **2,** to be found; turn up. **3,** to be ready with an answer; come up with a quick answer. Я не нашёлся, что отве́тить, I was at a loss as to how to answer.

нахо́дка [*gen. pl.* **-док**] *n.* a find.

нахо́дчивый *adj.* resourceful. —**нахо́дчивость**, *n.f.* resourcefulness.

нахождéние *n.* **1,** finding. **2,** being (somewhere).

нахо́хлиться *v.r., pfv. of* **хо́хлиться**.

нахохота́ться *v.r.pfv.* [*infl.* **-хочу́сь, -хо́чешься**] *colloq.* to have a good laugh.

нахра́пистый *adj., colloq.* brash.

нахра́пом *adv., colloq.* brazenly.

нацара́пать *v., pfv. of* **цара́пать** (*in sense #2*).

нацеди́ть *v.pfv.* [*infl.* **-цежу́, -це́дишь**] to strain (a quantity of something).

наце́ленность *n.f.* **1,** purposefulness. **2,** (*with* **на** + *acc.*) tendency (toward); propensity (for).

наце́ливать *v.impfv.* [*pfv.* **наце́лить**] to aim (a weapon). —**наце́ливаться**, *refl.* **1,** to take aim. **2,** (*with inf.*) to get ready (to).

на́цело *adv., colloq.* totally; entirely; completely.

наце́нивать *v.impfv.* [*pfv.* **нацени́ть**] to mark up; raise the price of.

нацени́ть [*infl.* **-ценю́, -це́нишь**] *v., pfv. of* **наце́нивать**.

наце́нка *n.* markup; increase in price.

нацепи́ть [*infl.* **-цеплю́, -це́пишь**] *v., pfv. of* **нацепля́ть**.

нацепля́ть *v.impfv.* [*pfv.* **нацепи́ть**] (*with* **на** + *acc.*) to fasten to; hook onto; pin to.

наци́зм *n.* Nazism.

национализа́ция *n.* nationalization.

национализи́ровать *v.impfv.* [*pres.* **-рую, -руешь**] to nationalize.

национали́зм *n.* nationalism. —**национали́ст**, *n.* nationalist. —**националисти́ческий**, *adj.* nationalist (*attrib.*); nationalistic.

национа́льность *n.f.* nationality.

национа́льный *adj.* national.

наци́ст *n.* Nazi. —**наци́стский**, *adj.* Nazi.

на́ция *n.* nation.

нача́ть *v., pfv. of* **чади́ть**.

нача́ло *n.* **1,** beginning: с са́мого нача́ла, from the very beginning; from the outset. В нача́ле семидеся́тых годо́в, in the early 1970s. В нача́ле девя́того, between 8 and 8:30. **2,** origin; source. Вести́ своё нача́ло от *or* к, to have its origin in. **3,** *pl.* basis: на доброво́льных нача́лах, on a voluntary basis. **4,** *pl.* rudiments: нача́ла хи́мии, rudiments of chemistry. —**брать нача́ло**, to originate; (*of a river*) rise. —**дать нача́ло** (+ *dat.*), to give rise to. —**для нача́ла**, to start with; for starters. —**под нача́лом** (+ *gen. or* **у**), under the direction of. Име́ть под свои́м нача́лом, to have (working) under (one). —**положи́ть нача́ло** (+ *dat.*), **1,** to begin; initiate. **2,** to mark the beginning of. —**по нача́лу**, at first.

нача́льник *n.* chief; head; boss; superior. —**нача́льник ста́нции**, stationmaster. —**нача́льник шта́ба**, chief of staff.

нача́льный *adj.* **1,** first; initial. **2,** (*of education, a school, etc.*) elementary; primary.

нача́льственный *adj.* overbearing; domineering.

нача́льство *n.* **1,** the authorities. **2,** command; direction. **3,** *colloq.* boss; chief.

нача́льствование *n.* command.

нача́льствовать *v.impfv.* [*pres.* **-ствую, -ствуешь**] (*with* **над**) to be in command (of); be in charge (of).

нача́тки *n.pl.* [*sing.* **нача́ток**] rudiments.

нача́ть [*infl.* **начну́, начнёшь;** *past* **на́чал, начала́, на́чало, на́чали**] *v., pfv. of* **начина́ть.** —**нача́ться,** *refl.* [*past* **начался́, началась́, начало́сь, начали́сь**] *pfv. of* **начина́ться.**

начеку́ *adv.* on one's guard; on the alert.

начерни́ть *v., pfv. of* **черни́ть** (*in sense #1*).

на́черно *adv.* in the rough: писа́ть (что-нибудь) на́черно, to make a rough draft of.

начерта́ние *n.* **1,** tracing. **2,** outline.

начерта́тельный *adj., in* **начерта́тельная геоме́трия,** descriptive geometry.

начерта́ть *v.pfv.* **1,** to trace; inscribe. **2,** *fig.* to set forth; outline.

начерти́ть *v., pfv. of* **черти́ть.**

начёс *n.* nap (*on cloth*).

начётчик *n.* pedant.

начина́ние *n.* project; undertaking.

начина́тельный *adj., gram.* inceptive: начина́тельный глаго́л, inceptive verb (*e.g.* забе́гать, to begin to run).

начина́ть *v.impfv.* [*pfv.* **нача́ть**] **1,** to begin; start (something). **2,** (*with inf.*) to begin (to); start (to). —**начина́ться,** *refl.* (*of something*) to begin; start.

начина́ющий *adj.* beginning. —*n.* beginner.

начина́я *prep.* (*with* **с** + *gen.*) beginning (with).

начини́ть *v.pfv.* **1,** [*infl.* **-чиню́, -чини́шь**] *pfv. of* **начиня́ть. 2,** [*infl.* **-чиню́, -чи́нишь**] to mend (a quantity of something); sharpen (a quantity of pencils).

начи́нка *n.* stuffing; filling.

начиня́ть *v.impfv.* [*pfv.* **начини́ть**] to stuff.

начи́стить *v.pfv.* [*infl.* **-чи́щу, -чи́стишь**] **1,** *pfv. of* **начища́ть. 2,** to peel (a quantity of something).

на́чисто *adv.* **1,** clean: на́чисто вы́бритый, clean-shaven. Переписа́ть (что-нибудь) на́чисто, to make a clean copy of. **2,** *colloq.* completely; utterly. **3,** *colloq.* openly; candidly.

начистоту́ *adv.* frankly; without equivocation; straight from the shoulder.

начи́танный *adj.* well-read. —**начи́танность,** *n.f.* erudition.

начита́ть *v.pfv., colloq.* to read (a quantity of something). —**начита́ться,** *refl.* (*with gen.*) to read a great deal of.

начища́ть *v.impfv.* [*pfv.* **начи́стить**] *colloq.* to polish; shine.

наша́лить *v.pfv.* to be naughty; act up.

нашаты́рный *adj., in* **нашаты́рный спирт,** liquid ammonia.

нашаты́рь [*gen.* **-тыря́**] *n.m.* ammonium chloride.

нашепта́ть *v.pfv.* [*infl.* **-шепчу́, -ше́пчешь**] **1,** to whisper. **2,** (*with dat.*) to whisper in someone's ear.

наше́ствие *n.* invasion.

нашива́ть *v.impfv.* [*pfv.* **наши́ть**] to sew on.

наши́вка [*gen. pl.* **-вок**] *n., mil.* stripe; chevron.

нашивно́й *adj.* sewn-on.

наши́ть *v.pfv.* [*infl.* **нашью́, нашьёшь**] **1,** *pfv. of* **нашива́ть. 2,** to sew (a quantity of something).

нашигова́ть *v., pfv. of* **шпигова́ть.**

нашпи́ливать *v.impfv.* [*pfv.* **нашпи́лить**] **1,** to place (*or* stick) on a pin. **2,** to pin on.

нашуме́вший *adj.* sensational; much talked about; having caused quite a stir.

нашуме́ть *v.pfv.* [*infl.* **-млю́, -ми́шь**] **1,** to make a lot of noise. **2,** *fig.* to cause a sensation.

нащипа́ть *v.pfv.* [*infl.* **-щиплю́, -щи́плешь**] **1,** to pluck; pick (a quantity of something). **2,** *colloq.* to pinch.

нащу́пывать *v.impfv.* [*pfv.* **нащу́пать**] **1,** [*impfv. only*] to grope for; fumble for; feel about for. **2,** to feel (someone's pulse). **3,** to find; come upon (*after groping*). **4,** *fig.* to find; discover; detect. —**нащу́пывать по́чву,** to get the lay of the land; sound out the possibilities.

наэлектризова́ть *v., pfv. of* **электризова́ть.**

нася́бедничать *v., pfv. of* **я́бедничать.**

наяву́ *adv.* while awake; not in one's dreams.

не *neg. particle* **1,** not: Э́то не ве́рно, that is not true; лифт не рабо́тает, the elevator is not working. **2,** *inserted between such words as* ничего́, никто́, никогда́, *etc. and a verb following:* Никто́ не зна́ет, no one knows. Мы почти́ никогда́ не ви́дим её, we almost never see her. **3,** (*with imperatives*) don't: Не забу́дьте!, don't forget! **4,** *used in polite questions and requests:* Вы не ска́жете как (+ *inf.*), could you tell me how to...? Вы случа́йно не ви́дели куда́...?, did you happen to see where...? **5,** *occurring as a separate word when* не́чего, не́кого *and their oblique case forms are separated to permit the insertion of a preposition in between:* Ему́ не́ с кем игра́ть he has no one to play with. Разгова́ривать бы́ло не́ о чем, there was nothing to talk about. Де́ньги есть, а истра́тить их не́ на что, people have money, but there is nothing to spend it on. **6,** (*with past tense verbal adverbs*) without: гла́зом не моргну́в, without batting an eye. Ни с кем не простя́сь, without saying goodbye to anyone. **7,** (*with inf.*) will never; would never: Его́ не узна́ть, you would never recognize him. —**не́ за что!,** not at all!; don't mention it! —**не то, что** *or* **чтобы...,** it is not that...

неаккура́тность *n.f.* **1,** lack of punctuality. **2,** carelessness. **3,** sloppiness.

неаккура́тный *adj.* **1,** not punctual. **2,** careless; sloppy; inefficient. **3,** untidy.

неандерта́лец [*gen.* **-льца**] *n.* Neanderthal man. —**неандерта́льский,** *adj.* Neanderthal.

неаппети́тный *adj.* unappetizing.

небезопа́сный *adj.* somewhat dangerous; unsafe.

небезоснова́тельный *adj.* not without foundation.

небезразли́чный *adj.* **1,** not indifferent; interested. **2,** (*with dat. or* для) of interest (to).

небезызве́стный *adj.* not unknown; rather well-known.

небезынтере́сный *adj.* rather interesting.

небелёный *adj.* unbleached.

небе́сный *adj.* heavenly; celestial.

неблагови́дный *adj.* unseemly; improper.

неблагода́рный *adj.* **1,** ungrateful. **2,** thankless. —**неблагода́рность,** *n.f.* ingratitude.

неблагожела́тельный *adj.* unfriendly; hostile. —**неблагожела́тельность,** *n.f.* ill will.

неблагозву́чие *n.* dissonance; disharmony. —**неблагозву́чный,** *adj.* dissonant; discordant.

неблагонадёжный *adj.* (politically) unreliable.

неблагополу́чие *n.* trouble; troubles.

неблагополу́чный *adj.* unhappy; unfortunate. —**неблагополу́чно,** *adv.* badly; in an unhappy way.

неблагопристо́йный *adj.* improper; indecent.

неблагоприя́тный *adj.* unfavorable.

неблагоразу́мие *n.* imprudence. —**неблагоразу́мный,** *adj.* imprudent; unwise; ill-advised.

неблагоро́дный *adj.* ignoble. —**неблагоро́дные мета́ллы,** base metals.

неблагоскло́нный *adj.* ill-disposed; unfavorably disposed. —**неблагоскло́нность,** *n.f.* unfavorable attitude.

неблагоустро́енный *adj.* lacking amenities or conveniences.

неблестя́щий *adj.* not outstanding; mediocre.

нёбный *adj.* palatal. —**нёбная занаве́ска,** *anat.* uvula.

не́бо [*pl.* небеса́, небе́с, небеса́м] *n.* sky; heaven. —**ме́жду не́бом и землёй,** without a roof over one's head. —**на седьмо́м не́бе,** in seventh heaven. —**под откры́тым не́бом,** in the open air. —**попа́сть па́льцем в не́бо,** to be wide of the mark. —**превозноси́ть до небе́с,** to praise to the skies. —**хвата́ть звёзды с не́ба,** (*often used negatively*) to be a genius; be a whiz.

нёбо *n.* palate; roof of the mouth.

небога́тый *adj.* **1,** not rich; of modest means. **2,** modest; unpretentious. **3,** meager; scanty.

небоеспосо́бный *adj.* unfit for (military) action; disabled.

небольшо́й *adj.* **1,** small; not large; not great. **2,** (*of time, distance, etc.*) short. —**с небольши́м,** a little over; a little past: в три с небольши́м, a little after three.

небосво́д *n.* firmament.

небоскло́н *n.* lower part of the sky near the horizon.

небоскрёб *n.* skyscraper.

небо́сь *particle, colloq.* in all probability; most likely.

небре́жно *adv.* **1,** carelessly. **2,** casually.

небре́жность *n.f.* carelessness; negligence.

небре́жный *adj.* **1,** careless; negligent. **2,** sloppy; slipshod. **3,** casual.

небри́тый *adj.* unshaven.

небыва́ло *adv.* extraordinarily. Небыва́ло высо́кий урожа́й, record harvest.

небыва́лый *adj.* **1,** unprecedented; unheard-of. Небыва́лый урожа́й, bumper harvest. **2,** fantastic; unreal.

небыли́ца *n.* tall story; cock-and-bull story.

небытие́ *n.* nonexistence.

небью́щийся *adj.* unbreakable; nonbreakable; shatterproof.

нева́жно *adv.* **1,** not well; poorly. **2,** *as an exclamation,* never mind!; it doesn't matter!

нева́жный *adj.* **1,** unimportant. **2,** *colloq.* poor; not so good.

невдалеке́ *adv.* not far away; not far off.

невдомёк *adv., with dat., colloq.* having no idea: Мне невдомёк, I had no idea; it never occurred to me.

неве́дение *n.* ignorance. —**держа́ть в неве́дении,** to keep in the dark.

неве́домо *adv., colloq.* there is no telling; there is no way of knowing.

неве́домый *adj.* **1,** unknown. **2,** mysterious.

неве́жа *n.m. & f.* boor; lout.

неве́жда *n.m. & f.* ignoramus.

неве́жественный *adj.* ignorant.

неве́жество *n.* ignorance.

неве́жливый *adj.* impolite; discourteous; rude. —**неве́жливость,** *n.f.* impoliteness; rudeness.

невезе́ние *n., colloq.* bad luck.

невезу́чий *adj., colloq.* unlucky.

невели́кий *adj., usu. used in short form* [*fem.* -лика́; *neut.* -лико́ *or* -ли́ко; *pl.* -ли́ки *or* -ли́ки] **1,** small; not large. Невели́к ро́стом, short (*in height*). **2,** not great; slight; insignificant.

неве́рие *n.* **1,** disbelief. **2,** lack of faith.

неве́рно *adv.* **1,** incorrectly. **2,** with an uncertain gait.

неве́рность *n.f.* **1,** error; fallacy. **2,** infidelity.

неве́рный *adj.* **1,** incorrect; wrong; erroneous. **2,** unfaithful; untrue. **3,** unsteady; faltering. **4,** *in* неве́рная но́та, false note. —*n.* infidel.

невероя́тно *adv.* incredibly; unbelievably.

невероя́тность *n.f.* **1,** unbelievability. **2,** *pl.* unbelievable stories. —**до невероя́тности,** unbelievably; incredibly; to an incredible degree.

невероя́тный *adj.* incredible; unbelievable.

неве́рующий *adj.* nonbelieving; irreligious. —*n.* nonbeliever.

невесёлый *adj.* **1,** melancholy; sad; blue. **2,** (*of a place or situation*) unhappy; depressing.

невесо́мый *adj.* weightless. —**невесо́мость,** *n.f.* weightlessness.

неве́ста *n.* **1,** fiancée. **2,** bride.

неве́стка [*gen. pl.* -ток] *n.* **1,** daughter-in-law. **2,** sister-in-law (*brother's wife or spouse's brother's wife*).

неве́сть *adv., colloq.* heaven knows; God knows.

невеще́ственный *adj.* immaterial.

невзви́деть *v.pfv., in* све́та невзви́деть, *colloq.* **1,** to be stupefied (*from shock or surprise*). **2,** to see stars (*from pain*).

невзго́да *n.* adversity; misfortune.

невзира́я на (*with acc.*) in spite of; regardless of. —**невзира́я на ли́ца,** without consideration of the persons involved.

невзлюби́ть *v.pfv.* [*infl.* -люблю́, -лю́бишь] to dislike; take a disliking to.

невзнача́й *adv., colloq.* **1,** by chance; accidentally. **2,** unintentionally; inadvertently.

невзнóс *n.* nonpayment of dues.

невзря́чный *adj.* ugly; homely; unattractive.

невзыска́тельный *adj.* undemanding.

не́видаль *n.f., colloq.* wonder; something to marvel at. —**вот** (*or* **э́ка**) **не́видаль!**, what's all the fuss?

неви́данный *adj.* not seen before; unprecedented.

невиди́мка [*gen. pl.* -**мок**] *n.m. & f.* invisible man or creature. —*n.f.* invisible hairpin.

неви́димый *adj.* invisible.

неви́дный *adj.* **1,** invisible. **2,** *colloq.* insignificant. **3,** *colloq.* unattractive.

неви́дящий *adj.* **1,** unseeing; sightless; blind. **2,** (*of a look*) blank; absent; vacant.

неви́нность *n.f.* **1,** innocence. **2,** virginity.

неви́нный *adj.* **1,** innocent; guiltless. **2,** innocent; naïve; ingenuous. **3,** innocent; innocuous; harmless. **4,** innocent; virginal.

невино́вность *n.f.* innocence.

невино́вный *adj.* [*short form* -**вен**, -**вна**] innocent; not guilty.

невку́сный *adj.* tasteless; unpalatable.

невменя́емый *adj.*, not responsible for one's actions; *law* insane. —**невменя́емость**, *n.f.* non-responsibility for one's actions; *law* insanity.

невмеша́тельство *n.* noninterference; nonintervention.

невмоготу́ *adv., colloq.* too much; more than one can bear.

невнима́ние *n.* **1,** inattention. **2,** lack of consideration.

невнима́тельность *n.f.* **1,** carelessness. **2,** lack of consideration.

невнима́тельный *adj.* **1,** inattentive. **2,** careless. **3,** inconsiderate; thoughtless.

невнуши́тельный *adj.* unimpressive.

невня́тица *n., colloq.* babble.

невня́тный *adj.* indistinct; scarcely audible.

не́вод [*pl.* невода́] *n.* large fishing net.

невозвра́тный *adj.* **1,** irretrievable. **2,** (*of a loss*) irreparable.

невозвраще́нец [*gen.* -**нца**] *n.* defector. Стать невозвраще́нцем, to defect.

невозде́ланный *adj.* untilled; uncultivated.

невоздержа́ние *n.* intemperance; immoderation.

невозде́ржанный *also,* **невозде́ржный** *adj.* intemperate; immoderate. —**невозде́ржанность**; **невозде́ржность**, *n.f.* intemperance; immoderation.

невозмо́жно *adj.*, used predicatively, impossible: Э́то практи́чески невозмо́жно, it is practically impossible.

невозмо́жное *n.*, decl. as an adj. the impossible.

невозмо́жность *n.f.* impossibility. —**до невозмо́жности**, to the extreme.

невозмо́жный *adj.* impossible.

невозмути́мый *adj.* **1,** imperturbable; unflappable. **2,** (*of calm, quiet, etc.*) perfect; undisturbed. —**невозмути́мость**, *n.f.* imperturbability; coolness.

невознагради́мый *adj.* **1,** irreparable. **2,** that can never be repaid.

небо́лить *v.impfv., colloq.* to force; compel.

небо́льник *n.* slave. —**небо́льничество**, *n.* slavery. —**небо́льничий**, *adj.* [*fem.* -**чья**] slave (*attrib.*).

нево́льно *adv.* **1,** unintentionally; unwittingly. **2,** instinctively.

нево́льный *adj.* **1,** unintentional; involuntary. **2,** involuntary; forced.

нево́ля *n.* **1,** slavery. **2,** captivity: размножа́ться в нево́ле, to breed in captivity. **3,** *colloq.* necessity.

необрази́мый *adj.* inconceivable; unimaginable.

невооружённый *adj.* unarmed. —**невооружённым гла́зом**, with the naked (*or* unaided) eye.

невоспе́тый *adj.* unsung.

невоспи́танный *adj.* ill-bred; ill-mannered. —**невоспи́танность**, *n.f.* lack of upbringing.

невоспламеня́емый *adj.* incombustible; nonflammable.

невосполни́мый *adj.* irreparable.

невосприи́мчивый *adj.* **1,** slow to absorb or learn. **2,** (*with* **к**) immune (to). —**невосприи́мчивость**, *n.f.* immunity.

невостре́бованный *adj.* unclaimed.

невою́ющий *adj.* nonbelligerent.

невпопа́д *adv., colloq.* not to the point: Он отвеча́л невпопа́д, his answers were not to the point.

невпроворо́т *adv.* (*with gen.*) *colloq.* a tremendous amount (of); an enormous number (of). Рабо́ты невпроворо́т, up to one's ears in work.

невразуми́тельный *adj.* unintelligible.

невралги́я *n.* neuralgia. —**невралги́ческий**, *adj.* neuralgic.

неврастени́я *n.* nervous breakdown; nervous exhaustion; neurasthenia.

невреди́мый *adj.* unharmed; safe. —**цел и невреди́м**, safe and sound.

невре́дный *adj.* harmless.

неври́т *n.* neuritis.

невро́з *n.* neurosis.

невроло́гия *n.* neurology. —**невро́лог**, *n.* neurologist. —**неврологи́ческий**, *adj.* neurological.

невропато́лог *n.* neurologist.

невроти́ческий *adj.* neurotic.

невы́года *n.* **1,** disadvantage. **2,** loss.

невы́годно *adv.* **1,** not to one's advantage. **2,** at a loss. —*adj., used predicatively,* disadvantageous; not a good idea.

невы́годный *adj.* **1,** unprofitable. **2,** unfavorable; disadvantageous.

невы́держанный *adj.* **1,** lacking self-control. **2,** uneven. **3,** (*of wine, cheese, etc.*) not aged; new. —**невы́держанность**, *n.f.* lack of self-control.

невыла́зный *adj., colloq.* **1,** impassable. **2,** offering no way out.

невыноси́мый *adj.* unbearable; unendurable; insufferable. —**невыноси́мо**, *adv.* unbearably.

невыполне́ние *n.* nonfulfillment; failure to carry out.

невы́полненный *adj.* unfulfilled.

невыполни́мый *adj.* impracticable; unfeasible. —**невыполни́мость**, *n.f.* impracticability.

невырази́мый *adj.* inexpressible. —**невырази́мые**, *n.pl., jocular* unmentionables.

невырази́тельный *adj.* inexpressive; unexpressive; expressionless. —**невырази́тельность**, *n.f.* lack of expression.

невы́сказанный *adj.* unexpressed; unspoken.

невысо́кий *adj.* low. —**невысо́кого ка́чества,** low-grade; of poor quality.

невы́ход *n.* failure to appear.

невы́ясненный *adj.* unexplained; not clear.

не́га *n.* **1,** comfort; contentment; ease. **2,** bliss.

негати́в *n., photog.* negative.

негати́вный *adj.* negative.

негашёный *adj.* **1,** (*of stamps*) uncanceled; unused. **2,** *in* негашёная и́звесть, quicklime.

не́где *adv., used with inf.* nowhere; no place: Мне не́где сесть, I have no place to sit.

неги́бкий *adj.* stiff; rigid; inflexible. —**неги́бкость,** *n.f.* stiffness.

неглиже́ *n.neut. indecl.* negligee.

неглубо́кий *adj.* **1,** shallow. **2,** (*of sleep*) light. **3,** *fig.* shallow; superficial.

неглу́пый *adj.* **1,** quite intelligent. **2,** (*of advice*) sound; sensible.

негну́щийся *adj.* stiff.

него́ (vo) *pron., var. of* его́, *used after prepositions.*

него́дник *n., colloq.* **1,** good-for-nothing. **2,** brat.

него́дность *n.f.* **1,** lack of fitness. **2,** uselessness. —**приходи́ть в него́дность, 1,** to fall into disrepair. **2,** to become unusable.

него́дный *adj.* **1,** unfit. **2,** *colloq.* worthless; good-for-nothing.

негодова́ние *n.* indignation.

негодова́ть *v.impfv.* [*pres.* -ду́ю, -ду́ешь] to be indignant.

негоду́ющий *adj.* indignant.

негодя́й *n.* scoundrel.

него́жий *adj., colloq.* improper; unseemly. Него́же (+ *inf.*), it is unseemly to.

негостеприи́мный *adj.* inhospitable.

негото́вый *adj.* unready.

негр *n.* Negro; black.

негра́мотный *adj.* **1,** illiterate. **2,** full of errors (*in grammar, spelling, etc.*). —*n.* illiterate. —**негра́мотно,** *adv.* making many mistakes in grammar or spelling. —**негра́мотность,** *n.f.* illiteracy.

негритёнок [*gen.* -нка; *pl.* -тя́та, -тя́т] *n.* Negro child; black child.

негритя́нка [*gen. pl.* -нок] *n.* Negro woman; black woman.

негритя́нский *adj.* Negro; black.

негро́идный *adj.* Negroid.

негро́мкий *adj.* low; not loud. —**негро́мко,** *adv.* in a low voice.

негума́нный *adj.* inhumane.

неда́вний *adj.* recent. —**до неда́внего вре́мени,** until recently. —**с неда́вних пор,** lately; of late.

неда́вно *adv.* recently; not long ago.

недалёкий *adj.* **1,** nearby; not far off. **2,** near (*in time*). В недалёком про́шлом, in the recent past. **3,** not very bright.

недалеко́ *also,* **недалёко** *adv.* not far. —*adj., used predicatively,* not far: По́чта недалеко́ от вокза́ла, the post office is not far from the station. Недалеко́ то вре́мя, когда́..., the time is not far off when.

недальнови́дный *adj.* shortsighted. —**недальнови́дность,** *n.f.* shortsightedness.

неда́ром *adv.* **1,** for a reason; with good reason. **2,** not in vain; not for nothing.

недви́жимость *n.f.* real estate.

недви́жимый *also,* **недви́жимый** *adj.* immovable. —**недви́жимое иму́щество,** real estate.

недвусмы́сленный *adj.* unequivocal; unambiguous. —**недвусмы́сленно,** *adv.* unequivocally.

недееспосо́бный *adj.* **1,** unable to function. **2,** *law* incompetent. —**недееспосо́бность,** *n.f., law* incompetence.

недействи́тельный *adj.* **1,** *obs.* ineffective; ineffectual. **2,** invalid; null and void.

неделика́тный *adj.* indelicate; indiscreet. —**неделика́тность,** *n.f.* indelicacy.

недели́мый *adj.* **1,** indivisible. **2,** (*of numbers*) prime. —**недели́мость,** *n.f.* indivisibility.

неде́льный *adj.* a week's.

неде́ля *n.* week.

недемократи́ческий *adj.* undemocratic.

недержа́ние *n., med.* incontinence.

недёшево *adv., colloq.* not cheap: сто́ить недёшево, to be quite expensive.

недипломати́чный *adj.* undiplomatic.

недисциплини́рованный *adj.* undisciplined.

недобо́р *n.* shortage; shortfall.

недоброжела́тель *n.m.* ill-wisher.

недоброжела́тельный *adj.* unfriendly; hostile. —**недоброжела́тельность,** *n.f.;* **недоброжела́тельство,** *n.neut.* ill will.

недоброка́чественный *adj.* poor-quality; low-grade; inferior; shoddy. —**недоброка́чественность,** *n.f.* poor quality.

недобросо́вестность *n.f.* **1,** lack of conscientiousness. **2,** lack of integrity; bad faith.

недобросо́вестный *adj.* **1,** not conscientious; lackadaisical. **2,** unscrupulous.

недо́брый *adj.* **1,** unkind; unfriendly; hostile. **2,** evil; bad. —**недо́брое,** *n.* trouble: чу́ять недо́брое, to sense trouble; smell a rat.

недова́ривать *v.impfv.* [*pfv.* **недовари́ть**] to undercook.

недовари́ть [*infl.* -варю́, -ва́ришь] *v., pfv. of* **недова́ривать.**

недове́рие *n.* **1,** (*with* к) distrust (of); mistrust (of). **2,** (*with* к) lack of confidence (in). **3,** incredulity. —**во́тум недове́рия,** vote of no confidence.

недове́рчивый *adj.* **1,** distrustful; mistrustful. **2,** incredulous. —**недове́рчивость,** *n.f.* distrust; mistrust.

недово́льный *adj.* [*short form* -лен, -льна] dissatisfied; discontented; displeased. —*n.* malcontent.

недово́льство *n.* dissatisfaction; discontent; displeasure.

недовыполне́ние *n.* failure to fulfill completely; underfulfillment.

недовыполня́ть *v.impfv.* [*pfv.* **недовы́полнить**] to fail to fulfill completely.

недога́дливый *adj.* slow to grasp things; dull; dense.

недогляде́ть *v.pfv.* [*infl.* -жу́, -ди́шь] *colloq.* **1,** to overlook. **2,** (*with* за + *instr.*) to fail to look after.

недогова́ривать *v.impfv.* [*pfv.* **недоговори́ть**] **1,** *v.t.*

to hold back; leave unsaid. **2,** *v.i.* to hold something back; not tell the whole story.

недоговорённость *n.f.* **1,** lack of agreement; lack of coordination. **2,** failure to tell all.

недоговори́ть *v., pfv. of* **недогова́ривать.**

недодава́ть *v.impfv.* [*pfv.* **недода́ть;** *pres.* **-даю́, -даёшь**] to give less than the required amount: Он мне недо́дал три рубля́, he gave me three rubles less than he was supposed to.

недода́ть [*infl. like* **дать;** *past* **недо́дал, недодала́, недо́дало, недо́дали**] *v., pfv. of* **недодава́ть.**

недоде́ланный *adj.* unfinished.

недоде́лать *v.pfv.* to fail to do; fail to finish.

недоде́лка [*gen. pl.* **-лок**] *n., colloq.* defect; imperfection.

недодержа́ть [*infl.* **-держу́, -де́ржишь**] *v., pfv. of* **недоде́рживать.**

недоде́рживать *v.impfv.* [*pfv.* **недодержа́ть**] *photog.* to underexpose.

недоде́ржка *n., photog.* underexposure.

недоеда́ние *n.* malnutrition.

недоеда́ть *v.impfv.* to be underfed; be undernourished.

недожа́ривать *v.impfv.* [*pfv.* **недожа́рить**] to undercook.

недозво́ленный *adj.* unauthorized; unlawful; illicit.

недозре́лый *adj.* **1,** not fully ripe. **2,** *fig.* immature.

недои́мка [*gen. pl.* **-мок**] *n.* arrears; back rent; back taxes. —**недои́мщик,** *n.* person in arrears.

недока́занный *adj.* unproved; unproven.

недоказу́емый *adj.* that cannot be proved.

недолга́ *adv., in* (**вот**) **и вся недолга́,** *colloq.* and that's (all there is to) it!

недо́лгий *adj.* short; brief.

недо́лго *adv.* not long. Дли́ться недо́лго, not last (for) long. —**недо́лго ду́мая,** without pausing to think. —**недо́лго и** (+ *inf.*), *colloq.* easily: Недо́лго и тону́ть, one could easily drown.

недолгове́чный *adj.* short-lived; ephemeral.

недолю́бливать *v.impfv.* to have little liking for; not particularly like.

недомога́ние *n.* indisposition.

недомога́ть *v.impfv.* to be unwell; be ailing; be indisposed.

недомо́лвка [*gen. pl.* **-вок**] *n.* allusion; innuendo.

недомы́слие *n.* failure to think things through.

недоно́сок [*gen.* **-ска**] *n.* prematurely born baby.

недоно́шенный *adj.* born prematurely.

недооце́нивать *v.impfv.* [*pfv.* **недооцени́ть**] to underestimate.

недооцени́ть [*infl.* **-ценю́, -це́нишь**] *v., pfv. of* **недооце́нивать.**

недооце́нка *n.* underestimation.

недопечённый *adj.* half-baked.

недоплати́ть [*infl.* **-плачу́, -пла́тишь**] *v., pfv. of* **недопла́чивать.**

недопла́чивать *v.impfv.* [*pfv.* **недоплати́ть**] to underpay: недоплати́ть пять рубле́й, to underpay by five rubles.

недополуча́ть *v.impfv.* [*pfv.* **недополучи́ть**] to receive less that one should: недополучи́ть де́сять рубле́й, to receive ten rubles less than one was supposed to.

недополучи́ть [*infl.* **-лучу́, -лу́чишь**] *v., pfv. of* **недополуча́ть.**

недопонима́ть *v.impfv.* [*pfv.* **недопоня́ть**] *colloq.* to fail to understand completely.

недопоня́ть [*infl. like* **поня́ть**] *v., pfv. of* **недопонима́ть.**

недопроизво́дство *n.* underproduction.

недопусти́мый *adj.* impermissible; intolerable.

недопуще́ние *n.* **1,** prohibition. **2,** prevention. **3,** refusal to admit or allow in.

недораба́тывать *v.impfv.* [*pfv.* **недорабо́тать**] **1,** *v.i.* to work less than the required time. **2,** *v.t.* to fail to complete.

недора́звитый *adj.* underdeveloped.

недоразуме́ние *n.* misunderstanding.

недо́рого *adv.* inexpensively; for a reasonable price.

недорого́й *adj.* inexpensive.

недоро́д *n.* poor harvest; crop failure.

не́доросль *n.m.* ignorant young man.

недоро́сток [*gen.* **-стка**] *n., colloq.* shrimp; runt.

недоска́занный *adj.* not fully expressed; incomplete.

недослы́шать *v.impfv. & pfv.* [*infl.* **-шу, -шишь**] **1,** [*pfv.*] to fail to hear entirely. **2,** [*impfv.*] *colloq.* to be somewhat hard of hearing.

недосмо́тр *n.* oversight.

недосмотре́ть *v.pfv.* [*infl.* **-смотрю́, -смо́тришь**] *colloq.* **1,** to overlook. **2,** (*with* **за** + *instr.*) to fail to look after.

недоспа́ть [*infl. like* **спать**] *v., pfv. of* **недосыпа́ть.**

недоспе́лый *adj.* not fully ripe.

недостава́ть *v.impfv.* [*pfv.* **недоста́ть;** *pres.* **-стаёт**] *impers.* (*with gen.*) **1,** to be insufficient; be lacking: Чего́ вам недостаёт?, what are you lacking? Нам недостаёт де́нег, we are short of money. **2,** [*impfv. only*] to be missing: Недостаёт двух страни́ц, two pages are missing. **3,** [*impfv. only*] to be missed: Нам вас недостава́ло, we missed you.

недоста́ток [*gen.* **-тка**] *n.* **1,** shortage; scarcity; deficiency; lack. **2,** defect; shortcoming; drawback; failing; deficiency.

недоста́точно *adv.* (*fol. by an adj.*) not ... enough; insufficiently. —*adj., used predicatively,* not enough; insufficient: Пять рубле́й недоста́точно, five rubles is not enough.

недоста́точность *n.f.* insufficiency; deficiency; inadequacy.

недоста́точный *adj.* insufficient; inadequate.

недоста́ть [*infl.* **-ста́нет**] *v., pfv. of* **недостава́ть.**

недоста́ча *n., colloq.* shortage.

недостаю́щий *adj.* missing: недостаю́щее звено́, missing link.

недостижи́мый *adj.* unattainable.

недостове́рный *adj.* of doubtful authenticity; unreliable.

недосто́йно *adv.* badly; improperly. —*adj., used predicatively* (*with gen.*) unworthy of; beneath: Э́то его́ недосто́йно, it is unworthy of him; it is beneath him.

недосто́йный *adj.* [*short form* **-сто́ин, -сто́йна**] **1,** unworthy: Он её недосто́ин, he is unworthy of her. **2,** undignified. **3,** dishonorable.

недостро́енный *adj.* (*of something being built*) unfinished.

недосту́пный *adj.* **1,** inaccessible. **2,** unattainable. **3,** distant; unapproachable. **4,** beyond one's comprehension. **5,** beyond one's means; more than one can afford. —**недосту́пность,** *n.f.* inaccessibility.

недосу́г *n., colloq.,* used impersonally with dat. lack of (leisure) time: Мне недосу́г, I haven't the time.

недосчи́тываться *v.r.impfv.* [*pfv.* **недосчита́ться**] **1,** (*with gen.*) to be short; find missing (*when counting*). **2,** (*with subject in gen.*) to be short; be missing.

недосыпа́ние *n.* lack of sleep.

недосыпа́ть *v.impfv.* [*pfv.* **недоспа́ть**] not get enough sleep.

недосяга́емый *adj.* **1,** unattainable. **2,** inaccessible.

недотёпа *n.m. & f., colloq.* maladroit person; clod.

недотро́га *n.* touch-me-not (*flower*). —*n.m. & f., colloq.* touchy person.

недоу́здок [*gen.* **-дка**] *n.* halter (*for a horse*).

недоумева́ть *v.impfv.* to be puzzled; be perplexed; be bewildered.

недоумева́ющий *adj.* puzzled; perplexed; bewildered.

недоуме́ние *n.* bewilderment; perplexity.

недоуме́нный *adj.* **1,** puzzled; perplexed; bewildered. **2,** puzzling; perplexing; baffling. —**недоуме́нно,** *adv.* in bewilderment.

недоу́чка [*gen. pl.* **-чек**] *n.m. & f., colloq.* person with little education.

недочёт *n.* **1,** shortage; deficit. **2,** defect; shortcoming.

не́дра [*gen.* **недр**] *n.pl.* **1,** area under ground: разве́дка недр, underground exploration. Не́дра земли́, interior of the earth; bowels of the earth. Бога́тства недр, mineral wealth; mineral resources. **2,** *fig.* innermost depths.

недре́млющий *adj.* vigilant; watchful.

не́друг *n.* enemy; foe.

недружелю́бие *n.* unfriendliness. —**недружелю́бный,** *adj.* unfriendly.

неду́г *n.* ailment.

недурно́й *adj.* **1,** not bad. **2,** *in* недурён (недурна́) собо́й, not bad-looking. —**неду́рно,** *adv.* rather well.

недю́жинный *adj.* exceptional; outstanding.

неё *pron., var. of* её, *used after prepositions.*

невре́й *n.* non-Jew; gentile. —**невре́йский,** *adj.* non-Jewish; gentile.

неедногла́сный *adj.* not unanimous. —**неедногла́сное реше́ние,** *boxing* split decision.

неесте́ственный *adj.* unnatural.

нежда́нный *adj., colloq.* unexpected.

нежела́ние *n.* unwillingness; reluctance; disinclination.

нежела́нный *adj.* unwanted.

нежела́тельный *adj.* undesirable.

не́жели *conj., archaic* than.

нежена́тый *adj.* (*of a man*) unmarried; single.

не́женка [*gen. pl.* **-нок**] *n.m. & f., colloq.* sissy.

неживо́й *adj.* **1,** lifeless; dead. **2,** inorganic. **3,** listless; apathetic. **4,** (*of light*) faint.

нежи́зненный *adj.* **1,** unrealistic; impractical. **2,** unreal; weird.

нежило́й *adj.* **1,** unoccupied; vacant; unlived-in. **2,** unfit for occupation.

нежи́рный *adj.* not fatty; lean.

не́жить *v.impfv.* to pamper; coddle. —**не́житься,** *refl.* **1,** to lounge around; loll. **2,** to luxuriate; bask (in the sun).

не́жничать *v.impfv., colloq.* to be overly gentle.

не́жно *adv.* **1,** tenderly. **2,** gently.

не́жность *n.f.* **1,** tenderness; gentleness. **2,** *pl., colloq.* tender words.

не́жный *adj.* tender; gentle; delicate.

незабве́нный *adj.* unforgettable.

незаброни́рованный *adj.* unreserved: незаброни́рованное ме́сто, unreserved seat.

незабу́дка [*gen. pl.* **-док**] *n.* forget-me-not.

незабыва́емый *adj.* unforgettable.

незавершённый *adj.* uncompleted; unfinished.

незави́дный *adj.* unenviable.

незави́симо *adv.* independently. —**незави́симо от,** regardless of; irrespective of.

незави́симость *n.f.* independence.

незави́симый *adj.* independent.

незави́сящий *adj., in* по незави́сящим от (+ *gen.*) обстоя́тельствам, due to circumstances beyond (one's) control.

незада́ча *n., colloq.* bad luck.

незада́чливый *adj., colloq.* unlucky; luckless.

незадо́лго *adv.* (*with* до) shortly (before); not long (before).

незаинтересо́ванный *adj.* disinterested.

незако́нно *adv.* unlawfully; illegally.

незаконнорождённый *adj.* (*of a child*) illegitimate.

незако́нный *adj.* unlawful; illegal; illegitimate; illicit. —**незако́нность,** *n.f.* illegality.

незако́нченный *adj.* unfinished.

незамедли́тельный *adj.* immediate.

незамени́мый *adj.* irreplaceable; indispensable.

незаме́тно *adv.* **1,** without being seen. **2,** *fig.* imperceptibly; unnoticed: пройти́ незаме́тно, to pass unnoticed. —*adj., used predicatively* **1,** not noticeable: Незаме́тно, чтобы..., it is not noticeable that...; you cannot tell that... **2,** (*with* для) unnoticed (by); without (someone) noticing it. Незаме́тно для себя́, without realizing it.

незаме́тный *adj.* **1,** imperceptible. **2,** inconspicuous. **3,** insignificant.

незаме́ченный *adj.* unnoticed.

незаму́жняя *adj.* (*of a woman*) unmarried; single.

незамыслова́тый *adj., colloq.* simple; unimaginative.

неза́нятый *adj.* **1,** (*of a building, house, etc.*) unoccupied. **2,** not busy; not occupied.

незапа́мятный *adj.* immemorial. —**в незапа́мятные времена́,** in ancient times. —**с незапа́мятных времён,** since time immemorial.

неза́пертый *adj.* unlocked.

незаплани́рованный *adj.* unplanned.

незапя́тнанный *adj.* unblemished; unsullied; untarnished.

незара́зный *adj.* noncontagious.

незаря́женный *also,* **незаряжённый** *adj.* **1,** (*of a rifle, pistol, etc.*) unloaded. **2,** (*of a battery*) not charged.

незаселённый *adj.* unsettled.

незаслу́женный *adj.* undeserved.

незастрахо́ванный *adj.* uninsured.

незатейливый *adj.* simple; unpretentious.

незаурядный *adj.* exceptional; outstanding.

незачем *adv.* (*with inf.*) *colloq.* there is no need (to); there is no reason (to); there is no point (in). Мне незачем туда идти, there is no reason for me to go there. Мне незачем жить, I have nothing to live for; I have no reason to live.

незащищённый *adj.* unprotected; undefended.

незваный *adj.* uninvited.

нездешний *adj.* **1**, *colloq.* not of this place: Я нездешний, I am not from around here. **2**, *obs.* unearthly; supernatural.

нездоровиться *v.r.impfv., impers.* (*with dat.*) to feel ill: Мне нездоровится, I feel ill; I am not feeling well.

нездоровый *adj.* **1**, unwell. **2**, unhealthy; unwholesome.

нездоровье *n.* **1**, ill health. **2**, ailment.

неземной *adj.* unearthly.

незлой *adj.* kind; good-natured.

незлопамятный *adj.* forgiving; not one to bear a grudge.

незнакомец [*gen.* **-мца**] *n.m.* [*fem.* **-мка**] stranger.

незнакомство *n.* lack of familiarity; unfamiliarity.

незнакомый *adj.* **1**, unfamiliar; unknown. **2**, (*with* **с** + *instr.*) unacquainted (with). —*n., colloq.* stranger.

незнание *n.* ignorance.

незначащий *adj.* insignificant.

незначительный *adj.* **1**, insignificant; very slight; negligible. **2**, insignificant; minor; trivial. —**незначительность,** *n.f.* insignificance.

незрелый *adj.* **1**, unripe; green. **2**, *fig.* immature. —**незрелость,** *n.f.* immaturity.

незримый *adj.* invisible.

незрячий *adj.* unseeing; sightless; blind.

незыблемый *adj.* **1**, firm; solid. **2**, *fig.* steadfast; unwavering; unshakable.

неизбежный *adj.* inevitable; unavoidable. —**неизбежно,** *adv.* inevitably. —**неизбежность,** *n.f.* inevitability.

неизбывный *adj.* unending; permanent; constant.

неизведанный *adj.* **1**, unexplored. **2**, never before experienced.

неизвестно *adj., used predicatively,* unknown; not known: Кто он такой — неизвестно, who he is is not known.

неизвестность *n.f.* **1**, lack of information; uncertainty. Быть в неизвестности (о), to be unaware (of); have no knowledge (of). **2**, obscurity: жить в неизвестности, to live in obscurity.

неизвестный *adj.* unknown. —*n.* **1**, unknown person. **2**, *neut., math.* unknown.

неизгладимый *adj.* indelible.

неизданный *adj.* unpublished.

неизлечимый *adj.* incurable.

неизменный *adj.* **1**, invariable; unchanging. **2**, unfailing; devoted. —**неизменно,** *adv.* invariably.

неизменяемый *adj.* unalterable; unchanging; fixed.

неизмеримый *adj.* immeasurable; unfathomable. —**неизмеримо,** *adv.* immeasurably; infinitely.

неизъяснимый *adj.* **1**, unexplainable; inexplicable. **2**, inexpressible; indescribable.

неимение *n., in* **за неимением** (+ *gen.*), owing to the lack of; for want of. За неимением лучшего, for want of anything better.

неимоверный *adj.* incredible; fantastic. —**неимоверно,** *adv.* unbelievably; fantastically.

неимущий *adj.* poor; indigent; needy.

неинтеллигентный *adj.* not cultured; unsophisticated.

неинтересный *adj.* uninteresting.

неискоренимый *adj.* ineradicable.

неискренний *adj.* insincere. —**неискренность,** *n.f.* insincerity.

неискушённый *adj.* unsophisticated; inexperienced.

неисповедимый *adj.* inscrutable.

неисполнение *n.* nonperformance; failure to carry out; failure to obey.

неисполнимый *adj.* **1**, impossible to carry out; impracticable. **2**, impossible to perform. **3**, unrealizable. Неисполнимая мечта, impossible dream. —**неисполнимость,** *n.f.* impracticability.

неиспользованный *adj.* unused.

неиспорченный *adj.* **1**, unspoiled. **2**, innocent; pure.

неисправимый *adj.* **1**, incorrigible. **2**, irreparable.

неисправность *n.f.* **1**, disrepair. **2**, failure; malfunction(ing). **3**, carelessness.

неисправный *adj.* **1**, defective; faulty; out of order. **2**, careless.

неиспытанный *adj.* **1**, untried; untested. **2**, never before experienced.

неисследованный *adj.* unexplored; uncharted.

неиссякаемый *adj.* inexhaustible.

неистовство *n.* **1**, fury; rage. **2**, *usu. pl.* atrocities.

неистовствовать *v.impfv.* [*pres.* **-ствую, -ствуешь**] **1**, to rage; rave. **2**, (*of a storm, the sea, etc.*) to rage. **3**, to run wild; go on a rampage.

неистовый *adj.* **1**, violent. **2**, (*of a noise*) thundering.

неистощимый *adj.* inexhaustible.

неисцелимый *adj.* incurable.

неисчерпаемый *adj.* inexhaustible.

неисчислимый *adj.* countless; incalculable; innumerable.

ней *pron., var. of* **ей,** *used after prepositions.*

нейлон *n.* nylon. —**нейлоновый,** *adj.* nylon.

нейрон *n.* neuron.

нейрохирургия *n.* neurosurgery. —**нейрохирург,** *n.* neurosurgeon.

нейтрализация *n.* neutralization.

нейтрализовать *v.impfv. & pfv.* [*pres.* **-зую, -зуешь**] to neutralize.

нейтралитет *n.* neutrality.

нейтральный *adj.* neutral.

нейтрон *n.* neutron. —**нейтронный,** *adj.* neutron (*attrib.*): нейтронная бомба, neutron bomb.

неказистый *adj., colloq.* homely; unattractive.

неквалифицированный *adj.* unskilled.

некий [*gen. masc. & neut.* **некоего**; *gen. fem.* **некоей** *or* **некой**] *indef. pron.* **1**, a certain: некое беспокойство, a certain anxiety. **2**, a certain; someone named: Вас спрашивал некий Иванов someone named Ivanov was asking for you.

некогда *adv.* **1**, no time: Мне некогда, I have no time. **2**, once; formerly; at one time.

не́кого *indef. pron., gen. & acc.* [*dat.* **не́кому**; *instr.* **не́кем**; *prepl.* **не́** (+ *prep.*) **ком**] *used with inf.,* there is no one; there is nobody (*as the obj. of a verb*): Не́кого посла́ть за посы́лкой, there is no one to send to pick up the package. Мне не́кого спроси́ть, there is no one I can ask. *See also* **не́кому**.

неколеби́мый *adj.* = **непоколеби́мый**.

некомпете́нтный *adj.* incompetent.

не́кому *indef. pron.* **1,** *dat. of* **не́кого**. **2,** there is no one (*as the subject of a verb*): не́кому его́ замени́ть, there is no one to replace him.

неконституцио́нный *adj.* unconstitutional.

неконтроли́руемый *adj.* uncontrolled.

некороно́ванный *adj.* uncrowned.

некорре́ктный *adj.* improper; indecorous.

не́которые *indef. pron.* some; some people; certain people. **—не́которые из,** some of.

не́который *adj.* **1,** *pl.* some; certain: не́которые лю́ди, some/certain people. **2,** some; a certain amount of: не́которое сомне́ние, some doubt. В/до не́которой сте́пени, to a certain extent. **—не́которое вре́мя,** for some time; (for) a while. **— с не́которых пор,** for some time now.

некраси́вый *adj.* **1,** ugly; unattractive. **2,** *colloq.* improper; not nice: Э́то некраси́во, that's not nice.

некра́шеный *adj.* unpainted.

некре́пкий *adj.* **1,** not strong; not firm; flimsy. **2,** not robust. **3,** weak; diluted.

некрити́ческий *adj.* uncritical.

некро́з *n.* necrosis.

некроло́г *n.* obituary.

некста́ти *adv.* **1,** at the wrong time; at an inopportune moment. **2,** out of place; inappropriate.

некта́р *n.* nectar.

не́кто *indef. pron.* **1,** someone; somebody. **2,** a certain: Вас спра́шивал не́кто Ива́нов, someone named Ivanov was asking for you.

не́куда *adv.* **1,** (*used with inf.*) nowhere; no place: Мне е́хать не́куда, I have nowhere to go. **2,** (*used with comp. adjectives*) *colloq.* as can be: про́ще не́куда, as simple as can be; it couldn't be simpler.

некульту́рный *adj.* **1,** uncivilized; uncultured. **2,** (*of plants*) uncultivated. **—некульту́рность,** *n.f.* lack of culture; lack of refinement.

некуря́щий *adj.* who does not smoke. **—***n.* nonsmoker.

нела́дно *adv.* badly. **—***adj., used predicatively,* wrong: Чтó-то с ним нела́дно, something is wrong with him.

нела́дный *adj., colloq.* **1,** wrong: Чтó-то нела́дное происхо́дит, something wrong is going on. **2,** ungainly. **—нела́дное,** *n.* something wrong: чу́вствовать нела́дное, to sense that something is wrong.

нелады́ [*gen.* **-до́в**] *n.pl., colloq.* disagreements; friction; failure to get along: У них нелады́, they are not getting along.

нелакиро́ванный *adj.* not lacquered; unvarnished.

нела́сковый *adj.* cold; unfriendly.

нелега́льный *adj.* illegal. **—нелега́льно,** *adv.* illegally. **—нелега́льность,** *n.f.* illegality.

нелёгкий *adj.* **1,** not easy; hard; difficult. **2,** heavy; not light.

нелегко́ *adv.* not easily: Языки́ даю́тся ему́ нелегко́, languages do not come easily to him.

неле́пость *n.f.* **1,** absurdity (*of something*). **2,** nonsense.

неле́пый *adj.* ridiculous; absurd.

неле́стный *adj.* unflattering; uncomplimentary.

нелётный *adj.* non-flying; unsuitable for flying.

нелино́ванный *adj.* (*of paper*) unlined; unruled.

нелицеприя́тный *adj.* **1,** impartial; unbiased. **2,** unfavorable; unflattering.

нели́шний *adj.* not out of place; useful. **—нели́шне,** *adj., used predicatively,* useful; worthwhile: нели́шне отме́тить, что..., it is worth noting that...

нело́вкий *adj.* **1,** awkward; clumsy. **2,** *fig.* awkward; uncomfortable; embarrassing: нело́вкое молча́ние, awkward silence.

нело́вко *adv.* awkwardly. **—***adj., used predicatively,* awkward; ill at ease: чу́вствовать себя́ нело́вко, to feel awkward/uncomfortable/ ill at ease/.

нело́вкость *n.f.* **1,** awkwardness. **2,** (an) indiscretion. **3,** (sense of) awkwardness; embarrassment.

нелоги́чный *adj.* illogical. **—нелоги́чно,** *adv.* illogically.

нелоя́льный *adj.* disloyal. **—нелоя́льность,** *n.f.* disloyalty.

нельзя́ *adv.* **1,** it is impossible; one cannot: Нельзя́ сказа́ть, it is impossible to say; one cannot say. **2,** it is forbidden; one may not: Нельзя́ кури́ть, smoking is forbidden. **—как нельзя́ лу́чше,** perfectly. **—нельзя́ ли...,** can't you...?; couldn't you?: нельзя́ ли поти́ше?, can't/couldn't you be a little more quiet?

нелюбе́зный *adj.* ungracious.

нелюби́мый *adj.* unloved.

нелюбо́вь [*infl. like* **любо́вь**] *n.f.* dislike.

нелюди́м *n.m.* [*fem.* **-ка**] unsociable person.

нелюди́мый *adj.* unsociable. **—нелюди́мость,** *n.f.* unsociability.

нём *pron., prepl. of* **он** *and* **оно́**.

нема́ло *adv.* **1,** (*with gen.*) quite a bit of; quite a few. **2,** (*with verbs*) quite; quite a bit; quite a lot.

немалова́жный *adj.* of no small importance; not unimportant.

нема́лый *adj.* considerable.

немеблиро́ванный *adj.* unfurnished.

неме́дленный *adj.* immediate. **—неме́дленно,** *adv.* immediately; at once.

неме́для *adv.* immediately; at once.

Немези́да *n.* **1,** Nemesis (*Greek goddess*). **2,** (one's) nemesis.

неме́ркнущий *adj.* **1,** never fading. **2,** *fig.* undying.

неме́ть *v.impfv.* [*pfv.* **онеме́ть**] **1,** to be speechless; be dumbfounded. **2,** to become numb.

не́мец [*gen.* **не́мца**] *n.m.* [*fem.* **не́мка**] German. **—неме́цкий,** *adj.* German.

немилосе́рдный *adj.* merciless; unmerciful. **—немилосе́рдно,** *adv.* mercilessly.

немилостивый *adj., obs.* **1,** ungracious. **2,** unmerciful.

неми́лость *n.f.* disfavor; disgrace.

немину́емый *adj.* inevitable; unavoidable. **—немину́емо,** *adv.* inevitably; unavoidably.

не́мка [*gen. pl.* **не́мок**] *n.* German woman.

немно́гие *adj.* a few: в немно́гих слова́х, in a few words. *—indef. pron.* **1,** few people; not many people. **2,** the few: немно́гие, кто..., the few who... **—немно́гим,** *adv., used with comp. adjectives,* a little.

немно́го *adv.* **1,** a little; a bit of. **2,** little; not much. **3,** a little; rather; somewhat.

немно́гое *n., in* **то немно́гое, что...,** the little that...; what little...

немногосло́вный *adj.* of few words; laconic.

немногочи́сленный *adj.* **1,** small (*in number of people, members, etc.*). **2,** *pl.* the few: немногочи́сленные доброво́льцы, the few volunteers.

немно́жко *adv., colloq.* = **немно́го.**

немну́щийся *adj.* (*of fabric*) crease-resistant.

немо́й *adj.* **1,** dumb; mute. **2,** (*of a film*) silent. *—n.* mute.

немолодо́й *adj.* not young.

немота́ *n.* inability to speak.

не́мочь *n.f., colloq.* sickness; illness.

немощёный *adj.* unpaved.

не́мощный *adj.* [*short form* **-щен, -щна**] feeble; infirm.

не́мощь *n.f.* infirmity.

нему́ *pron., var. of* **ему́,** *used after prepositions.*

немудрено́ *adv.* no wonder: Немудрено́, что он не отве́тил, no wonder he didn't answer.

немудрёный *adj., colloq.* simple; plain.

нему́дрый *adj.* **1,** not very bright. **2,** *colloq.* = **немудрёный.**

немы́слимый *adj.* unthinkable.

ненаблюда́тельный *adj.* unobservant.

ненави́деть *v.impfv.* [*pres.* **-ви́жу, -ви́дишь**] to hate; detest.

ненави́стник *n.* person who hates. **—ненави́стничество,** *n.* hostile attitude.

ненави́стный *adj.* hated; hateful; abhorrent.

не́нависть *n.f.* hatred; hate.

ненагля́дный *adj.* beloved.

ненадёжный *adj.* unreliable. **—ненадёжность,** *n.f.* unreliability.

ненадобность *n.f.* lack of need (for). **—за ненадобностью,** for lack of use. **—за ненадобностью** (+ *gen.*), there being no need (for).

ненадо́лго *adv.* for a short time; for a short while (*subsequent to the action expressed by the verb*): Я уезжа́ю ненадо́лго, I am going away for a short time/while. Пра́вило отмени́ли, но ненадо́лго, the rule was rescinded, but not for long.

ненáзванный *adj.* unnamed.

ненаказу́емый *adj.* not punishable by law.

ненаме́ренный *adj.* unintentional. **—ненаме́ренно,** *adv.* unintentionally.

ненападе́ние *n.* nonaggression.

ненаро́ком *adv., colloq.* by chance: Он ненаро́ком зашёл, he just happened to drop in.

ненáстный *adj.* inclement.

ненáстье *n.* inclement weather.

ненасы́тный *adj.* insatiable.

ненасы́щенный *adj.* unsaturated.

ненатура́льный *adj.* **1,** artificial. **2,** unnatural.

ненау́чный *adj.* unscientific.

не́нец [*gen.* **не́нца**] *n.m.* [*fem.* **не́нка**] Nenets (*one of a people inhabiting northernmost Russia*). **—не́нецкий,** *adj.* Nenets.

ненорма́льный *adj.* abnormal. **—ненорма́льно,** *adv.* abnormally. **—ненорма́льность,** *n.f.* abnormality.

нену́жность *n.f.* **1,** uselessness. **2,** *usu. pl., colloq.* useless things.

нену́жный *adj.* unneeded; needless; unnecessary.

необду́манный *adj.* not thought out; rash.

необескура́женный *adj.* not discouraged; undismayed.

необеспе́ченный *adj.* **1,** without means; unprovided for. **2,** *finance* unsecured.

необеспоко́енный *adj.* unworried; undisturbed.

необжи́тый *also,* **необжито́й** *adj.* uninhabited; un-lived-in.

необита́емый *adj.* uninhabited.

необнару́женный *adj.* undetected.

необозри́мый *adj.* boundless; vast. **—необозри́мость,** *n.f.* vastness.

необосно́ванный *adj.* **1,** groundless; unfounded. **2,** unsound.

необрабо́танный *adj.* **1,** uncultivated; untilled. **2,** crude; rough; unfinished.

необразо́ванный *adj.* uneducated. **—необразо́ванность,** *n.f.* lack of education.

необрати́мый *adj.* irreversible.

необу́зданный *adj.* unrestrained; unbridled.

необу́ченный *adj.* untrained.

необходи́мо *adj., used predicatively,* necessary; essential; imperative: Необходи́мо де́йствовать без промедле́ния, it is essential/imperative that we act without delay. Необходи́мо приня́ть сро́чные ме́ры, urgent measures must be taken.

необходи́мое *n., decl. as an adj.* necessities; essentials: всё необходи́мое, all the necessities; everything one needs; са́мое необходи́мое, the basic necessities.

необходи́мость *n.f.* necessity; need. **—по необходи́мости,** out of necessity. **—при** (*or* **в слу́чае**) **необходи́мости,** when (*or* if) necessary. **—предме́ты пе́рвой необходи́мости,** the basic necessities.

необходи́мый *adj.* necessary; essential. *See also* **необходи́мое.**

необщи́тельный *adj.* unsociable; antisocial. **—необщи́тельность,** *n.f.* unsociability.

необъекти́вный *adj.* not objective; biased. **—необъекти́вность,** *n.f.* lack of objectivity.

необъя́вленный *adj.* (*of a war*) undeclared.

необъясни́мый *adj.* inexplicable; unexplainable; unaccountable.

необъя́тный *adj.* boundless; vast.

необыкнове́нный *adj.* unusual; uncommon; extraordinary. **—необыкнове́нно,** *adv.* unusually; uncommonly.

необыча́йность *n.f.* **1,** (*with gen.*) extraordinary nature (of). **2,** extraordinary event.

необыча́йный *adj.* extraordinary; exceptional.

необы́чный *adj.* unusual. **—необы́чно,** *adv.* unusually.

необяза́тельный *adj.* **1,** optional; not obligatory. **2,** (*of a person*) not obliging.

неогля́дный *adj.* boundless; vast.

неограни́ченный *adj.* unlimited.

неодина́ковый *adj.* different; dissimilar.

неоднокра́тно *adv.* repeatedly; more than once. **—неоднокра́тный,** *adj.* repeated.

неоднора́дный *adj.* **1,** heterogeneous. **2,** dissimilar. **—неоднора́дность,** *n.f.* heterogeneity.

неодобре́ние *n.* disapproval.

неодобри́тельный *adj.* disapproving. **—неодобри́тельно,** *adv.* in disapproval.

неодоли́мый *adj.* **1,** (*of a force, urge, etc.*) irresistible. **2,** *obs.* invincible.

неодушевлённый *adj.* inanimate.

неожи́данно *adv.* unexpectedly.

неожи́данность *n.f.* **1,** suddenness. **2,** unexpected development; surprise: Кака́я прия́тная неожи́данность!, what a pleasant surprise!

неожи́данный *adj.* unexpected.

неоклассици́зм *n.* neoclassicism. **—неокласси́ческий,** *adj.* neoclassical.

неоконча́тельный *adj.* not final.

неоко́нченный *adj.* unfinished.

неолити́ческий *adj.* neolithic.

неологи́зм *n.* neologism.

нео́н *n.* neon. **—нео́новый,** *adj.* neon.

неопа́сный *adj.* not dangerous.

неопера́бельный *adj., med.* inoperable.

неопери́вшийся *adj.* **1,** unfledged. **2,** *fig., colloq.* callow.

неопису́емый *adj.* indescribable.

неопла́тный *adj.* **1,** that cannot be repaid. В неопла́тном долгу́ у (*or* пе́ред), eternally indebted to; forever in one's debt. **2,** unable to pay one's debts.

неопла́ченный *adj.* unpaid.

неопо́знанный *adj.* unidentified.

неопра́вданный *adj.* **1,** unjustified; unwarranted. **2,** unfounded.

неопределённо *adv.* vaguely.

неопределённость *n.f.* **1,** vagueness. **2,** uncertainty.

неопределённый *adj.* **1,** indefinite; uncertain; indeterminate. **2,** vague; unclear. **—неопределённая фо́рма глаго́ла,** infinitive.

неопредели́мый *adj.* indefinable.

неопровержи́мый *adj.* irrefutable; incontrovertible; conclusive. **—неопровержи́мо,** *adv.* conclusively.

неопря́тный *adj.* untidy. **—неопря́тность,** *n.f.* untidiness.

неопублико́ванный *adj.* unpublished.

нео́пытный *adj.* inexperienced. **—нео́пытность,** *n.f.* inexperience; lack of experience.

неорганизо́ванный *adj.* unorganized; disorganized. **—неорганизо́ванность,** *n.f.* lack of organization; disorganization.

неоргани́ческий *adj.* inorganic.

неосведомлённый *adj.* uninformed. **—неосведомлённость,** *n.f.* lack of information; ignorance.

неосвещённый *adj.* unlighted; unlit.

неосла́бно *adv.* without letup.

неосла́бный *adj.* unflagging; unremitting. С неосла́бным внима́нием, with rapt attention. *Also,* **неослабева́ющий.**

неосмотри́тельный *adj.* imprudent. **—неосмотри́тельность,** *n.f.* imprudence.

неоснова́тельный *adj.* **1,** groundless; unfounded. **2,** *colloq.* frivolous; superficial; shallow.

неосо́знанный *adj.* subconscious.

неоспори́мый *adj.* indisputable; incontestable; unchallengeable; undeniable.

неосторо́жно *adv.* carelessly.

неосторо́жность *n.f.* carelessness: по неосторо́жности, through carelessness. Име́ть неосторо́жность (+ *inf.*), to be incautious enough to...

неосторо́жный *adj.* careless; incautious.

неосуществи́мый *adj.* impracticable; infeasible. **—неосуществи́мость,** *n.f.* impracticability.

неосяза́емый *adj.* intangible.

неота́пливаемый *adj.* unheated.

неотврати́мый *adj.* inevitable. **—неотврати́мость,** *n.f.* inevitability.

неотвя́зный *adj.* **1,** (*of a thought, question, etc.*) nagging. **2,** (*of a person*) bothersome; annoying. *Also,* **неотвя́зчивый.**

неотдели́мый *adj.* inseparable. **—неотдели́мость,** *n.f.* inseparability.

неотёсанный *adj., colloq.* crude; uncouth.

неотзы́вчивый *adj.* unresponsive.

неоткры́тый *adj.* unopened.

нео́ткуда *adv., used with inf.* there is no place (from): Мне нео́ткуда э́то доста́ть, there is no place I can get it from. Узна́ть об э́том мне бы́ло нео́ткуда, there was no place I could find out about it.

неотло́жка *n., colloq.* ambulance (service): вы́звать неотло́жку, to call an ambulance.

неотло́жный *adj.* urgent. **—неотло́жность,** *n.f.* urgency.

неотлу́чный *adj.* always present; ever-present. **—неотлу́чно,** *adv.* constantly.

неотполиро́ванный *adj.* unpolished.

неотрази́мый *adj.* irresistible. **—неотрази́мость,** *n.f.* irresistibility.

неотрепети́рованный *adj.* unrehearsed.

неотсту́пный *adj.* relentless. **—неотсту́пно,** *adv.* relentlessly.

неотчётливый *adj.* indistinct. **—неотчётливость,** *n.f.* indistinctness.

неотшлифо́ванный *adj.* unpolished.

неотъе́млемый *adj.* inalienable. **—неотъе́млемая часть,** integral part.

неофи́т *n.* neophyte.

неофициа́льный *adj.* unofficial.

неохо́та *n.* reluctance; unwillingness. **—мне неохо́та** (+ *inf.*), I don't feel like...; I don't care to...

неохо́тно *adv.* reluctantly. **—неохо́тный,** *adj.* reluctant.

неоцени́мый *adj.* inestimable; invaluable.

неочи́щенный *adj.* unrefined; crude.

неощути́мый *adj.* imperceptible. *Also,* **неощути́тельный.**

непа́рный *adj.* odd (*one of an incomplete pair*). **—непа́рный шелкопря́д,** gypsy moth.

непарти́йный *adj.* **1,** non-party; not belonging to the party. **2,** not befitting a member of the party.

непатриоти́ческий *adj.* unpatriotic. *Also,* **непатри-**
оти́чный.

непереводи́мый *adj.* untranslatable.

непередава́емый *adj.* indescribable; inexpressible.

непереноси́мый *adj.* unbearable.

непереходный *adj.* (*of a verb*) intransitive.

неперспекти́вный *adj.* having poor prospects; unpromising.

непеча́тный *adj., colloq.* unprintable (*i.e.* obscene).

непи́саный *adj.* unwritten.

неплатёж [*gen.* **-тежа́**] *n.* nonpayment.

неплатёжеспосо́бный *adj.* insolvent. —**неплатёже-**
спосо́бность, *n.f.* insolvency.

неплате́льщик *n.* person who has not paid.

неплодоро́дный *adj.* barren; infertile. —**неплодо-**
ро́дность, *n.f.* barrenness; infertililty.

непло́тный *adj.* not dense; thin. —**непло́тно,** *adv.* not
tightly: непло́тно закры́тый, not closed tightly.

непло́хо *adv.* quite well; rather well. —*adj., used pred-*
icatively, not bad: Э́то непло́хо, that's not bad.

неплохо́й *adj.* not (a) bad.

непобеди́мый *adj.* invincible; unconquerable. —**не-**
победи́мость, *n.f.* invincibility.

непова́дно *adv., colloq., in* **чтобы непова́дно бы́ло**
(+ *dat.*), so that he/she won't do it again. Чтобы
други́м непова́дно бы́ло, so as to serve as a lesson
(*or* deterrent) to others.

неповинный *adj.* innocent.

неповинове́ние *n.* disobedience; insubordination.

неповоро́тливый *adj.* awkward; clumsy. —**непово-**
ро́тливость, *n.f.* awkwardness; clumsiness.

неповреждённый *adj.* undamaged.

неповтори́мый *adj.* inimitable; unique. —**неповто-**
ри́мость, *n.f.* uniqueness.

непого́да *n.* bad weather.

непого́жий *adj., colloq.* overcast; dreary.

непогреши́мый *adj.* infallible. —**непогреши́мость,**
n.f. infallibility.

неподалёку *adv.* **1,** not far away; not far off. **2,** (*with*
от) not far (from).

непода́тливый *adj.* unyielding; intractable.

неподви́жный *adj.* **1,** motionless; stationary; immobile. **2,** (*of a look, stare, etc.*) fixed. —**неподви́жно,**
adv. motionless. —**неподви́жность,** *n.f.* immobility.

неподгото́вленный *adj.* **1,** unprepared. **2,** untrained.

неподде́льный *adj.* **1,** genuine; authentic. **2,** genuine;
unfeigned; sincere.

неподку́пный *adj.* incorruptible. —**неподку́пность,**
n.f. incorruptibility.

неподоба́ющий *adj.* **1,** improper; unseemly. **2,** (*with*
dat.) not worthy of; beneath (someone).

неподпи́санный *adj.* unsigned.

неподража́емый *adj.* inimitable.

неподтверждённый *adj.* unconfirmed.

неподходя́щий *adj.* unsuitable; inappropriate.

неподчине́ние *n.* insubordination. —**неподчине́ние**
суде́бному постановле́нию, contempt of court.

непозволи́тельный *adj.* impermissible.

непоколеби́мый *adj.* unshakable; unwavering; steadfast. —**непоколеби́мость,** *n.f.* steadfastness.

непоко́рный *adj.* rebellious; recalcitrant; unruly. —**не-**
поко́рность, *n.f.* rebelliousness; recalcitrance.

непокры́тый *adj.* uncovered.

непола́дки *n.pl.* [*sing.* **-дка**] *colloq.* **1,** defects; bugs. **2,**
arguments; squabbles.

неполити́чный *adj., colloq.* impolitic; tactless.

неполноправный *adj.* not enjoying full rights.

неполнота́ *n.* incompleteness.

неполноце́нность *n.f.* inferiority.

неполноце́нный *adj.* inferior. —**у́мственно непол-**
ноце́нный, *adj.* mentally defective.

непо́лный *adj.* **1,** (*of a container*) partially filled; not
completely full. **2,** incomplete. —**рабо́тать непо́л-**
ный день, to work part-time.

неполо́женный *adj.* the wrong: в неполо́женном
ме́сте, in the wrong place; not where one is (*or* was)
supposed to.

непоме́рный *adj.* excessive; inordinate; exorbitant.

непонима́ние *n.* lack of understanding; failure to understand; incomprehension.

непоня́тливый *adj.* slow to grasp things; slow-witted;
dull; dense.

непоня́тно *adv.* incomprehensibly. —*adj., used predica-*
tively, incomprehensible; impossible to understand: Мне
непоня́тно, как э́то случи́лось, it is incomprehensible
to me (*or* I cannot understand) how it happened.

непоня́тный *adj.* incomprehensible; unintelligible.
—**непоня́тность,** *n.f.* incomprehensibility; unintelligibility.

непопада́ние *n.* miss (*in shooting*).

непоправи́мый *adj.* irreparable; irretrievable.

непопуля́рный *adj.* [*short form masc.* **-рен**] unpopular. —**непопуля́рность,** *n.f.* unpopularity.

непоро́чность *n.f.* innocence; purity; chastity.

непоро́чный *adj.* innocent; pure; chaste. —**непоро́ч-**
ное зача́тие, the Immaculate Conception.

непо́ртящийся *adj.* nonperishable.

непоря́док [*gen.* **-дка**] *n.* **1,** disorder. **2,** *pl.* failings;
mix-ups.

непоря́дочный *adj.* dishonorable.

непосвящённый *adj.* uninitiated.

непосе́да *n.m. & f., colloq.* fidgety person; fidget.

непосе́дливый *adj.* restless; fidgety. —**непосе́д-**
ливость, *n.f.* restlessness.

непосеще́ние *n.* (*with gen.*) failure to attend.

непоси́льный *adj.* exhausting; backbreaking.

непосле́довательный *adj.* inconsistent. —**непо-**
сле́довательность, *n.f.* inconsistency.

непослуша́ние *n.* disobedience.

непослу́шный *adj.* disobedient.

непосре́дственный *adj.* **1,** immediate; direct. **2,** natural;
spontaneous. —**непосре́дственно,** *adv.* immediately;
directly. —**непосре́дственность,** *n.f.* spontaneity.

непостижи́мость *n.f.* incomprehensibility.

непостижи́мый *adj.* incomprehensible. —**уму́ непо-**
стижи́мо, beyond all comprehension.

непостоя́нный *adj.* **1,** inconstant; changeable; fickle.
2, nonpermanent: непостоя́нные чле́ны Сове́та Без-
опа́сности, nonpermanent members of the Security
Council. —**непостоя́нство,** *n.* inconstancy.

непоти́зм *n.* nepotism.

непотопля́емый *adj.* unsinkable.

непотре́бный *adj., obs.* indecent; obscene.

непохо́жий *adj.* (*with* **на** + *acc.*) unlike; different (from).

непоча́тый *adj.* untouched; unopened; unused. —**непоча́тый край** (+ *gen.*), no end (of); tons (of).

непочте́ние *n.* disrespect.

непочти́тельный *adj.* disrespectful; irreverent. —**непочти́тельность,** *n.f.* disrespect; irreverence.

непра́вда *n.* **1,** untruth; falsehood; lie. **2,** deception; trickery. —*interj.* not so! —**все́ми пра́вдами и непра́вдами,** by hook or by crook.

неправдоподо́бие *n.* improbability; unlikelihood.

неправдоподо́бный *adj.* **1,** improbable; unlikely. **2,** implausible.

непра́ведный *adj., obs.* unjust; unfair.

непра́вильно *adv.* incorrectly. —*adj., used predicatively,* incorrect: Бы́ло бы непра́вильно (+ *inf.*), it would be incorrect to...

непра́вильность *n.f.* **1,** error; fallacy. **2,** irregularity.

непра́вильный *adj.* **1,** wrong; incorrect. **2,** irregular. **3,** (*of a fraction*) improper.

неправоме́рный *adj.* illegal.

неправомо́чный *adj.* lacking the necessary authority.

неправота́ *n.* error.

непра́вый *adj.* [*short form* **непра́в, неправа́, непра́во, непра́вы**] *usu. used predicatively,* wrong: Она́ была́ неправа́, she was wrong.

непракти́чный *adj.* impractical. —**непракти́чность,** *n.f.* impracticality.

непревзойдённый *adj.* unsurpassed; unexcelled.

непредви́денный *adj.* unforeseen.

непреднаме́ренный *adj.* unintentional; unpremeditated.

непредприи́мчивый *adj.* unenterprising.

непредсказу́емый *adj.* unpredictable.

непредубеждённый *adj.* unbiased; unprejudiced.

непредумы́шленный *adj.* unpremeditated. —**непредумы́шленное уби́йство,** manslaughter.

непредусмотри́тельный *adj.* lacking foresight; improvident. —**непредусмотри́тельность,** *n.f.* lack of foresight; improvidence.

непрекло́нный *adj.* inflexible; intransigent; adamant. —**непрекло́нность,** *n.f.* inflexibility; intransigence.

непрело́жный *adj.* immutable.

непреме́нно *adv.* **1,** absolutely; definitely; without fail. **2,** sure; bound: Он непреме́нно опозда́ет, he is sure/bound to be late. —**непреме́нный,** *adj.* absolutely necessary; essential.

непреобори́мый *adj.* irresistible.

непреодоли́мый *adj.* **1,** insurmountable; insuperable. **2,** irresistible.

непререка́емый *adj.* unquestionable; indisputable.

непреры́вный *adj.* continuous; uninterrupted. —**непреры́вно,** *adv.* continuously. —**непреры́вность,** *n.f.* continuity.

непреста́нный *adj.* incessant; continual. —**непреста́нно,** *adv.* incessantly; continually.

непреходя́щий *adj.* lasting; enduring.

неприве́тливый *adj.* **1,** unfriendly; ungracious. **2,** un-inviting; forbidding. —**неприве́тливость,** *n.f.* unfriend-liness; ungraciousness.

непривлека́тельный *adj.* unattractive.

непривы́чка *n.* not being used to something: с непривы́чки (+ **к** *or inf.*), not being used to...

непривы́чно *adv.* unusually. —*adj., used predicatively* (*with dat.*) unaccustomed; not used to: (Мне) непривы́чно по́здно ложи́ться, I am not used to going to bed late.

непривы́чный *adj.* **1,** strange; unfamiliar. **2,** (*with* **к**) unaccustomed (to). **3,** inexperienced; untrained.

непригля́дный *adj.* unattractive; unsightly.

неприго́дность *n.f.* **1,** (*with* **к**) unsuitability (for). **2,** uselessness.

неприго́дный *adj.* **1,** (*with* **к**) unfit (for); unsuited (for). **2,** unusable; useless.

неприе́млемый *adj.* unacceptable. —**неприе́млемость,** *n.f.* unacceptability.

непризна́ние *n.* **1,** failure (*or* refusal) to recognize; nonrecognition. **2,** failure (*or* refusal) to admit.

непри́знанный *adj.* unrecognized.

неприкаса́емые *n.pl., decl. as an adj.* untouchables (*in India*).

неприка́янный *adj., colloq.* aimless; not knowing what to do with oneself.

неприкоснове́нность *n.f.* **1,** inviolability: неприкоснове́нность жили́ща, inviolability of the home. **2,** original state: сохраня́ться в неприкоснове́нности, to be preserved intact. **3,** *law* immunity: дипломати́ческая неприкоснове́нность, diplomatic immunity.

неприкоснове́нный *adj.* **1,** saved for an emergency: неприкоснове́нный запа́с, emergency reserve. **2,** in its original state. **3,** inviolable.

неприкра́шенный *adj.* plain; unadorned; unvarnished: неприкра́шенная пра́вда, the unvarnished truth.

неприкреплённый *adj.* unattached.

неприкры́тый *adj.* **1,** uncovered; unprotected; unde-fended. **2,** *fig.* naked; barefaced; undisguised.

неприли́чие *n.* impropriety; indecency. Груб до неприли́чия, rude to the point of indecency; scan-dalously rude.

неприли́чный *adj.* improper; indecent. —**неприли́чно,** *adv.* improperly; indecently.

неприменение *n.* nonuse: неприменение си́лы, non-use of force.

непримени́мый *adj.* not applicable; inapplicable.

непримé́тный *adj.* **1,** imperceptible. **2,** not noteworthy; ordinary.

непримеча́тельный *adj.* ordinary; undistinguished.

непримири́мость *n.f.* **1,** irreconcilability. **2,** (*with* **к**) implacable attitude (toward); refusal to tolerate.

непримири́мый *adj.* **1,** irreconcilable. **2,** implacable.

непринуждённый *adj.* natural; casual; relaxed; non-chalant. —**непринуждённость,** *n.f.* ease; abandon; nonchalance.

неприсоедине́ние *n.* nonalignment. —**неприсоедини́вшийся,** *adj.* nonaligned.

неприспосо́бленный *adj.* unable to adjust easily; mal-adjusted. —**неприспосо́бленность,** *n.f.* inability to adjust; maladjustment.

непристо́йность *n.f.* **1,** obscenity. **2,** *often pl.* an obscenity.

непристо́йный *adj.* obscene.

непристу́пный *adj.* **1,** impregnable; unassailable. **2,** *fig.* (*of a person*) unapproachable.

непритво́рный *adj.* unfeigned; genuine.

непритяза́тельный *adj.* unpretentious; unassuming.

неприхотли́вый *adj.* unpretentious; simple; plain.

неприча́стность *n.f.* (*with* к) noninvolvement (in).

неприча́стный *adj.* [*short form* -стен, -стна] (*with* к) not implicated (in); not involved (in).

неприя́зненный *adj.* hostile; unfriendly.

неприя́знь *n.f.* hostility; enmity.

неприя́тель *n.m.* enemy. —**неприя́тельский,** *adj.* enemy (*attrib.*).

неприя́тие *n.* refusal to accept.

неприя́тно *adj., used predicatively,* unpleasant: Мне неприя́тно слы́шать э́то, it is unpleasant to hear it; I am sorry to hear it.

неприя́тность *n.f.* **1,** unpleasantness. **2,** *pl.* trouble.

неприя́тный *adj.* unpleasant; disagreeable.

непробива́емый *adj.* impenetrable.

непробу́дный *adj.* **1,** (*of sleep*) deep. **2,** *colloq.* (*of drinking*) unrestrained; (*of a drinker*) chronic.

непрове́ренный *adj.* unverified.

непроводни́к [*gen.* -ника́] *n., physics* nonconductor.

непрогля́дный *adj.* **1,** pitch-dark. **2,** (*of darkness, fog, etc.*) impenetrable.

непро́данный *adj.* unsold.

непродолжи́тельный *adj.* short; of short duration. —**непродолжи́тельность,** *n.f.* shortness; short duration.

непродукти́вный *adj.* unproductive. —**непродукти́вность,** *n.f.* unproductiveness.

непроду́манный *adj.* not thought through.

непрое́зжий *adj.* impassable.

непрозра́чный *adj.* opaque. —**непрозра́чность,** *n.f.* opacity; opaqueness.

непроизводи́тельный *adj.* **1,** unproductive. **2,** nonproductive. —**непроизводи́тельность,** *n.f.* unproductiveness.

непроизво́льный *adj.* involuntary.

непроизноси́мый *adj.* unpronounceable.

непрола́зный *adj., colloq.* impassable.

непромока́емый *adj.* waterproof. —**непромока́емый плащ,** raincoat.

непроница́емый *adj.* impenetrable. —**непроница́емость,** *n.f.* impenetrability.

непропорциона́льный *adj.* disproportionate. —**непропорциона́льно,** *adv.* disproportionately. —**непропорциона́льность,** *n.f.* disproportion.

непросвещённый *adj.* unenlightened.

непрости́тельный *adj.* unforgivable; inexcusable; unpardonable.

непроходи́мость *n.f.* **1,** impassability; impenetrability. **2,** *med.* obstruction; blockage.

непроходи́мый *adj.* **1,** impassable; impenetrable. **2,** *colloq.* utter.

непро́чный *adj.* **1,** not durable; flimsy. **2,** *fig.* tenuous. —**непро́чность,** *n.f.* flimsiness.

непро́шеный *adj.* **1,** uninvited. **2,** unsought; unsolicited.

непрямо́й *adj.* **1,** indirect. **2,** devious; evasive.

Непту́н *n.* Neptune.

непту́ний *n.* neptunium.

непутёвый *adj., colloq.* shiftless; good-for-nothing.

непью́щий *adj.* who does not drink. —*n.* teetotaler.

неработоспосо́бный *adj.* disabled; incapacitated.

нерабо́чий *adj.* **1,** nonworking. **2,** off: нерабо́чий день, day off; нерабо́чее вре́мя, time off. **3,** *colloq.* not conducive to work.

нера́венство *n.* inequality.

неравноду́шный *adj.* [*short form* -шен, -шна] (*with* к) not indifferent (to).

неравноме́рный *adj.* uneven. —**неравноме́рно,** *adv.* unevenly. —**неравноме́рность,** *n.f.* unevenness.

неравнопра́вие *n.* lack of equal rights; inequality.

неравнопра́вный *adj.* **1,** not enjoying equal rights. **2,** inequitable.

нера́вный *adj.* unequal.

нераде́ние *n., obs.* = **неради́вость.**

неради́вый *adj.* lackadaisical. —**неради́вость,** *n.f.* lackadaisical attitude.

неразбери́ха *n., colloq.* confusion; chaos; disorder.

неразбо́рчивость *n.f.* **1,** illegibility. **2,** lack of discrimination.

неразбо́рчивый *adj.* **1,** illegible. **2,** not fussy; undiscriminating. —**неразбо́рчивый в сре́дствах,** unscrupulous.

неразве́данный *adj.* unexplored; untapped.

неразвито́й *adj.* [*short form* нера́звит, -вита́, нера́звито, нера́звиты] **1,** undeveloped. **2,** backward; retarded. —**нера́звитость,** *n.f.* backwardness; retardation.

неразга́данный *adj.* unsolved.

неразгово́рчивый *adj.* taciturn; uncommunicative. —**неразгово́рчивость,** *n.f.* taciturnity.

неразд̇ели́мый *adj.* indivisible.

неразде́льный *adj.* **1,** (*of property*) commonly held. **2,** indivisible; inseparable.

неразличи́мый *adj.* **1,** indistinguishable. **2,** indiscernible.

неразлу́чный *adj.* inseparable. —**неразлу́чность,** *n.f.* inseparability.

неразре́занный *adj.* uncut.

неразрешённый *adj.* **1,** unsolved; unresolved. **2,** forbidden; prohibited.

неразреши́мый *adj.* insoluble.

неразруши́мый *adj.* indestructible.

неразры́вный *adj.* indissoluble. —**неразры́вно,** *adv.* indissolubly; inextricably.

неразу́мный *adj.* **1,** unreasonable; irrational. **2,** unwise; injudicious. —**неразу́мность,** *n.f.* unreasonableness; irrationality.

нераска́явшийся *adj.* unrepentant; impenitent.

нераскры́тый *adj.* (*of a crime or mystery*) unsolved.

нерасположе́ние *n.* (*with* к) **1,** dislike (of). **2,** disinclination (to *or* toward).

нераспоряди́тельный *adj.* lacking administrative ability; incompetent. —**нераспоряди́тельность,** *n.f.* incompetence.

нераспространéние *n.* nonproliferation.

нерасскáзанный *adj.* untold.

нерассудúтельный *adj.* irrational; lacking common sense. —**нерассудúтельность,** *n.f.* irrationality; lack of common sense.

нерастворúмый *adj.* insoluble; indissoluble.

нерасторжúмый *adj.* indissoluble.

нерасторóпный *adj.* sluggish; inert.

нерасчётливость *n.f.* **1,** extravagance. **2,** lack of foresight; improvidence.

нерасчётливый *adj.* **1,** extravagant; wasteful. **2,** shortsighted; improvident.

нерационáльный *adj.* inefficient.

нерв *n.* nerve.

нервúровать *v.impfv.* [*pres.* **-рую, -руешь**] to make nervous; unnerve.

нервúческий *adj.* nervous.

нéрвничать *v.impfv.* to be nervous; become fidgety.

нервнобольнóй *adj.* suffering from a nervous disorder. —*n.* person suffering from a nervous disorder.

нéрвность *n.f.* nervousness.

нéрвный *adj.* **1,** nerve (*attrib.*): нéрвные клéтки, nerve cells. **2,** nervous. **3,** irritable; high-strung. **4,** trying (on one's nerves). —**нéрвная систéма,** nervous system.

нервóзный *adj.* nervous; high-strung. —**нервóзность,** *n.f.* nervousness.

нереáльный *adj.* **1,** unreal. **2,** unrealistic; impractical.

нерегуля́рный *adj.* irregular. —**нерегуля́рность,** *n.f.* irregularity.

нерéдкий *adj.* not infrequent; not uncommon.

нерéдко *adv.* quite often.

нерентáбельный *adj.* unprofitable.

нéрест *n.* spawning. —**нерестúлище,** *n.* spawning ground.

нерешённый *adj.* unresolved; unsolved.

нерешúмость *n.f.* indecision: быть в нерешúмости, to be undecided.

нерешúтельно *adv.* hesitantly.

нерешúтельность *n.f.* **1,** indecisiveness. **2,** indecision: быть в нерешúтельности, to be undecided.

нерешúтельный *adj.* indecisive; irresolute; hesitant.

нержавéющий *adj.* rust-resistant. —**нержавéющая сталь,** stainless steel.

неритмúчный *adj.* irregular; uneven.

нерóбкий *adj.* not timid; brave. —**нерóбкого деся́тка,** not easily intimidated; not easily pushed around.

нерóвно *adv.* unevenly. —**нерóвность,** *n.f.* unevenness.

нерóвный *adj.* [*short form* **нерóвен, -внá, нерóвно, нерóвны**] **1,** uneven. **2,** crooked. **3,** (*of one's pulse, breathing, etc.*) irregular. **4,** *fig.* erratic. —**нерóвен час,** *colloq.* I wouldn't be surprised if...

нерóвня *also,* **неровня́** *n.m. & f., colloq.* person not the equal of another.

нéрпа *n.* ringed seal.

нерукотвóрный *adj.* not created by human hands.

нерýсский *adj.* non-Russian.

нерушúмый *adj.* inviolable; indissoluble. —**нерушú-мость,** *n.f.* inviolability.

неря́ха *n.m. & f.* slovenly person; slob.

неря́шливость *n.f.* sloppiness; slovenliness. *Also,* **неря́шество.**

неря́шливый *adj.* **1,** sloppy; slovenly. **2,** slipshod.

несбалансúрованный *adj.* unbalanced.

несбы́точный *adj.* unrealizable; vain.

несварéние *n., in* **несварéние желу́дка,** indigestion.

несвéдущий *adj.* **1,** ignorant; uninformed. **2,** (*with* **в** + *prepl.*) unfamiliar (with); unversed (in).

несвéжий *adj.* **1,** not fresh; stale; spoiled. **2,** worn; dirty; soiled. **3,** worn; tired; drawn.

несвобóдный *adj.* **1,** not free. **2,** married.

несвоеврéменно *adv.* **1,** at an inopportune time. **2,** too late.

несвоеврéменный *adj.* **1,** inopportune; ill-timed; untimely. **2,** tardy; belated.

несвя́зный *adj.* rambling; disconnected; incoherent; disjointed. —**несвя́зность,** *n.f.* incoherence.

несгибáемый *adj.* unbending; inflexible.

несговóрчивый *adj.* uncooperative; intractable.

несгорáемый *adj.* fireproof; incombustible; noninflammable. —**несгорáемый шкаф,** safe. —**несгорáемый я́щик,** strongbox.

несдéржанный *adj.* **1,** broken; unkept. **2,** unrestrained; violent.

несдобровáть *v.pfv., used in inf. only with dat. case:* Ему́ несдобровáть, he is in for trouble.

несекрéтный *adj.* **1,** not secret. **2,** unclassified.

несéние *n.* performance; execution; carrying out.

несерьёзный *adj.* **1,** not serious. **2,** casual; lackadaisical. **3,** trivial; unimportant.

несессéр (нэ-сэ-сэр) *n.* traveling case; toilet case.

несимметрúчный *adj.* asymmetrical. —**несимметрúчность,** *n.f.* asymmetry.

несказáнный *adj.* indescribable; unspeakable. —**несказáнно,** *adv.* extraordinarily; more than one can say.

несклáдица *n., colloq.* incoherent talk; nonsense; prattle.

несклáдный *adj.* **1,** awkward; ungainly. **2,** incoherent. **3,** discordant. **4,** absurd.

несклоня́емый *adj., gram.* indeclinable.

нéсколько *adj.* a few; some; several: нéсколько люде́й, a few people; в нéскольких словáх, in a few words. —*adv.* somewhat: нéсколько удивлён, somewhat surprised.

несконча́емый *adj.* endless; unending; interminable.

нескрóмность *n.f.* **1,** immodesty. **2,** indiscretion.

нескрóмный *adj.* **1,** immodest. **2,** indiscreet. **3,** indecent.

нескрывáемый *adj.* unconcealed; undisguised.

неслáженный *adj.* uncoordinated; disorganized.

неслóжный *adj.* uncomplicated; simple.

неслы́ханный *adj.* unheard-of.

неслы́шный *adj.* inaudible.

несмéлый *adj.* timid; diffident.

несменя́емость *n.f.* irremovability from office; tenure.

несменя́емый *adj.* **1,** ever-present; never removed. **2,** (*of a position*) permanent; (*of a person*) having tenure.

несмéтный *adj.* countless; incalculable.

несмолкáемый *adj.* (*of a noise or sound*) incessant.

несмотря́ на (*with acc.*) in spite of; despite. —**несмотря́ ни на что,** in spite of everything; despite all.

несмывáемый *adj.* indelible.

несмышлёный *adj., colloq.* slow to grasp things; slow-witted; dense; dull.

несно́сный *adj.* unbearable; unendurable.

несоблюде́ние *n.* failure to observe.

несовершенноле́тие *n.* minority (*being under legal age*).

несовершенноле́тний *adj.* under legal age. —*n.* minor.

несовершённый *adj.* **1,** imperfect. **2,** *gram.* imperfective: несоверше́нный вид, imperfective aspect.

несоверше́нство *n.* **1,** lack of perfection. **2,** *usu. pl.* imperfection.

несовмести́мый *adj.* incompatible. —**несовмести́мость,** *n.f.* incompatibility.

несогла́сие *n.* **1,** disagreement; difference of opinion. **2,** discord. **3,** refusal.

несогла́сный *adj.* **1,** in disagreement. **2,** (*with* с + *instr.*) inconsistent (with). **3,** uncoordinated. **4,** discordant.

несогласо́ванный *adj.* uncoordinated. —**несогласо́ванность,** *n.f.* lack of coordination.

несозна́тельный *adj.* **1,** thoughtless; irresponsible. **2,** lacking political consciousness.

несоизмери́мый *adj.* incommensurable. —**несоизмери́мость,** *n.f.* incommensurability.

несокращённый *adj.* unabridged.

несокруши́мый *adj.* indestructible; unshakable.

несо́лоно *adv., in* **несо́лоно хлеба́вши,** having accomplished nothing.

несомне́нно *adv.* undoubtedly; doubtlessly; indubitably. —*adj., used predicatively,* certain: Одно́ несомне́нно, one thing is certain.

несомне́нный *adj.* undoubted; indubitable; unquestioned.

несообрази́тельный *adj.* slow-witted; slow to grasp things; dull; dense.

несообра́зный *adj.* **1,** incongruous. **2,** absurd. —**несообра́зность,** *n.f.* incongruity; absurdity.

несоотве́тствие *n.* discrepancy; disparity.

несоразме́рно *adv.* disproportionately. —**несоразме́рно с** (+ *instr.*), out of proportion to.

несоразме́рность *n.f.* disproportion.

несоразме́рный *adj.* (*with* с + *instr.*) disproportionate (to); incommensurate (with).

несостоя́тельность *n.f.* **1,** insolvency; bankruptcy. **2,** helplessness. **3,** fallacy.

несостоя́тельный *adj.* **1,** of modest means. **2,** insolvent; bankrupt. **3,** powerless; helpless. **4,** unsound; untenable.

несочу́вствующий *adj.* unsympathetic.

неспе́лый *adj.* unripe.

неспе́шный *adj.* unhurried.

неспоко́йно *adv.* anxiously. —*adj., used predicatively,* uneasy: На душе́ у него́ неспоко́йно, he feels uneasy.

неспоко́йный *adj.* **1,** restless. **2,** anxious; uneasy. **3,** unsettled. **4,** (*of the sea*) rough; choppy.

неспорти́вный *adj.* unsportsmanlike.

неспосо́бность *n.f.* inability.

неспосо́бный *adj.* [*short form* **-бен, -бна**] **1,** not bright. **2,** (*with* к) having no aptitude (for). **3,** (*with* к *or* на) incapable (of).

несправедли́во *adv.* **1,** unjustly; unfairly. **2,** incorrectly; erroneously.

несправедли́вость *n.f.* injustice; unfairness.

несправедли́вый *adj.* **1,** unjust; unfair. **2,** incorrect.

неспровоци́рованный *adj.* unprovoked.

непроста́ *adv., colloq.* for a (definite) reason. Это неспроста́, there is a reason for this.

несравне́нно *adv.* **1,** incomparably. **2,** (*with comparisons*) far; infinitely.

несравне́нный *adj.* incomparable; matchless; peerless.

несравни́мый *adj.* incomparable.

нестаби́льный *adj.* unstable. —**нестаби́льность,** *n.f.* instability.

нестерпи́мый *adj.* unbearable; unendurable.

нестеснённый *adj.* uninhibited.

нести́ *v.impfv.* [*pfv.* **понести́**; *pres.* **несу́, несёшь**; *past* **нёс, несла́, несло́, несли́**] **1,** to carry. **2,** to carry swiftly; whisk. **3,** (*of the current, wind, etc.*) to carry; propel; sweep. **4,** to suffer; sustain; incur. **5,** [*impfv. only*] to bear (responsibility). **6,** [*impfv. only*] to perform (duties, military service, etc.). Нести́ дежу́рство, to be on duty. Нести́ карау́л, to be on guard duty. **7,** [*impfv. only*] to bring (death, freedom, ruin, etc.). **8,** *colloq.* to talk (nonsense). **9,** *impers.* (*with instr.*) *colloq.* to blow: От окна́ несёт хо́лодом, there is a draft from the window. **10,** *impers.* (*with instr.*) to reek (of): От него́ несёт во́дкой, he reeks of vodka. **11,** [*pfv.* **снести́**] to lay (eggs). —**нести́сь,** *refl.* **1,** to race; tear along. **2,** *colloq.* to rush; dash. **3,** to float; drift (*on water or through the air*). **4,** to be heard. **5,** [*pfv.* **снести́сь**] to lay eggs. *See also* **носи́ть** *and* **носи́ться.**

несто́йкий *adj.* **1,** unstable. **2,** (*of an odor*) slight; (*of perfume*) weak.

несто́ящий *adj., colloq.* worthless; good-for-nothing.

нестро́гий *adj.* not strict; lenient.

нестроево́й *adj.* **1,** unfit for building purposes. **2,** *mil.* noncombatant. —*n., mil.* noncombatant.

нестро́йный *adj.* **1,** ungraceful; ungainly. **2,** irregular; disorderly. **3,** discordant.

несть *predicate, obs.* there is no... —**несть конца́** *or* **числа́** (+ *dat.*), there is no end of...

несудохо́дный *adj.* unnavigable.

несура́зица *n., colloq.* nonsense.

несура́зность *n.f., colloq.* **1,** absurdity. **2,** nonsense. **3,** awkwardness.

несура́зный *adj., colloq.* **1,** ridiculous; absurd. **2,** awkward; ungainly.

несусве́тный *adj., colloq.* **1,** idiotic; inane. **2,** utter; absolute; unmitigated. **3,** not of this world; not to be believed; unbearable.

несу́шка [*gen. pl.* **-шек**] *n.* hen that lays eggs; layer.

несуще́ственный *adj.* minor; unimportant; inconsequential.

несуществу́ющий *adj.* nonexistent.

несхо́дный *adj.* different; dissimilar; disparate. —**несхо́дство,** *n.* difference; dissimilarity; disparity.

несхо́жесть *n.f., colloq.* difference; dissimilarity.

несхо́жий *adj., colloq.* different; dissimilar.

несчастли́вец [*gen.* **-вца**] *n.m.* [*fem.* **-вица**] *colloq.* unlucky person.

несчастли́вый *adj.* **1,** unhappy. **2,** unlucky; unfortunate.

несча́стный *adj.* **1,** unhappy. **2,** unfortunate. —*n.* poor fellow. —**несча́стный слу́чай,** accident; mishap.

несча́стье *n.* misfortune. —**к несча́стью,** unfortunately.

несчётный *adj.* countless; innumerable.

несъедо́бный *adj.* inedible; uneatable.

нет *neg. particle* **1,** no. **2,** not: нет ещё, not yet; почему́ нет?, why not? Вы идёте и́ли нет?, are you going or not? Я иду́, а он нет, I am going but he isn't. **3,** (*with gen.*) *indicating the absence of something:* Нет вре́мени, there is no time. Его́ нет, he is not here. Здесь никого́ нет, there is no one here. У меня́ нет спи́чек, I don't have any matches. —**нет и нет; нет как нет** (*with gen.*), no sign of (someone). —**нет-нет да и,** once in a while. —**своди́ть на нет,** to negate; nullify. —**своди́ться** *or* **сходи́ть на нет,** to come to naught.

нетакти́чный *adj.* tactless. —**нетакти́чность,** *n.f.* tactlessness.

нетала́нтливый *adj.* untalented; lacking talent.

нетвёрдо *adv.* not firmly: нетвёрдо держа́ться на нога́х, to be unsteady on one's feet.

нетвёрдый *adj.* **1,** not hard; soft. **2,** unsteady; shaky. **3,** irresolute; uncertain.

нетерпели́вый *adj.* impatient. —**нетерпели́во,** *adv.* impatiently. —**нетерпели́вость,** *n.f.* impatience.

нетерпе́ние *n.* impatience. —**ждать с нетерпе́нием, 1,** to wait impatiently; anxiously await. **2,** to look forward to.

нетерпи́мость *n.f.* intolerance.

нетерпи́мый *adj.* **1,** intolerable. **2,** intolerant.

нетипи́чный *adj.* not typical.

нетле́нный *adj.* **1,** imperishable. **2,** *fig.* eternal; immortal.

нето́пленый *adj.* unheated.

нетопы́рь [*gen.* **-пыря́**] *n.m.* pipistrelle (*bat*).

неторопли́вый *adj.* leisurely; unhurried. —**неторопли́во,** *adv.* leisurely.

нето́чность *n.f.* **1,** inaccuracy. **2,** *usu. pl.* inaccuracies.

нето́чный *adj.* inaccurate; inexact; imprecise.

нетре́бовательный *adj.* not demanding; undemanding.

нетре́звый *adj.* not sober; drunk: в нетре́звом ви́де, in a drunken state; while intoxicated.

нетро́нутый *adj.* **1,** untouched. **2,** *fig.* pure; unsullied; virginal.

нетру́дный *adj.* [*short form* **нетру́ден, нетрудна́, нетру́дно, нетру́дны**] not difficult.

нетрудово́й *adj.* **1,** nonworking. **2,** unearned.

нетрудоспосо́бность *n.f.* disability.

нетрудоспосо́бный *adj.* disabled; incapacitated.

не́тто (нэ) *adj. & adv., indecl.* net: вес не́тто, net weight; цена́ не́тто, net price.

не́ту *particle, colloq.* = **нет.**

неубеди́тельный *adj.* unconvincing; unpersuasive.

неу́бранный *adj.* **1,** (*of a room*) not straightened up; (*of a bed*) not made; (*of dishes*) not taken away. **2,** (*of crops*) not gathered; not harvested.

неуваже́ние *n.* disrespect; lack of respect.

неуважи́тельный *adj.* **1,** (*of a reason or excuse*) invalid. **2,** *colloq.* disrespectful.

неуве́ренность *n.f.* uncertainty; lack of confidence. —**неуве́ренность в себе́,** lack of self-confidence.

неуве́ренный *adj.* uncertain. —**неуве́ренный в себе́,** lacking self-confidence.

неувяда́емый *adj.* **1,** *obs.* never fading. **2,** *fig.* undying. *Also,* **неувяда́ющий.**

неувя́зка [*gen. pl.* **-зок**] *n., colloq.* mix-up; slip-up; hitch.

неугаси́мый *adj.* **1,** unquenchable. **2,** *fig.* undying.

неуго́дный *adj.* [*short form* **-ден, -дна**] undesirable; objectionable.

неугомо́нный *adj., colloq.* **1,** indefatigable; always on the go. **2,** (*of a sound or noise*) incessant.

неуда́вшийся *adj.* unsuccessful.

неуда́ча *n.* failure; setback.

неуда́чливый *adj.* unlucky.

неуда́чник *n.* unlucky person; failure.

неуда́чно *adv.* **1,** unsuccessfully. **2,** poorly; badly.

неуда́чный *adj.* **1,** unsuccessful. **2,** unfortunate; having turned out badly.

неудержи́мый *adj.* irrepressible; uncontrollable.

неудиви́тельно *adj., used predicatively,* not surprising: Неудиви́тельно, что..., it is not surprising that...

неудиви́тельный *adj.* not surprising.

неудо́бно *adv.* uncomfortably. —*adj., used predicatively,* **1,** uncomfortable: Мне неудо́бно так сиде́ть, I am uncomfortable sitting this way. **2,** inconvenient. **3,** awkward.

неудо́бный *adj.* [*short form* **-бен, -бна**] **1,** uncomfortable. **2,** inconvenient. **3,** awkward.

неудобовари́мый *adj.* indigestible.

неудобопроизноси́мый *adj.* difficult to pronounce; unpronounceable.

неудобочита́емый *adj.* difficult to read.

неудо́бство *n.* **1,** inconvenience; discomfort. **2,** awkwardness; embarrassment.

неудовлетворе́ние *n.* dissatisfaction.

неудовлетворённость *n.f.* dissatisfaction.

неудовлетворённый *adj.* **1,** (*of a desire, requirement, etc.*) unsatisfied. **2,** (*of a person*) dissatisfied.

неудовлетвори́тельно *adv.* **1,** unsatisfactorily. **2,** (*as a school grade*) "unsatisfactory".

неудовлетвори́тельный *adj.* unsatisfactory.

неудово́льствие *n.* displeasure.

неуёмный *adj., colloq.* **1,** irrepressible; indefatigable. **2,** (*of an emotion*) uncontrollable.

неуже́ли *interr. particle* really?; is it possible?: Неуже́ли вы ду́маете, что...?, do you really think that...?

неужи́вчивый *adj.* hard to get along with.

неу́жто *adv., colloq.* = **неуже́ли.**

неузнава́емо *adv.* beyond recognition.

неузнава́емость *n.f., in* **до неузнава́емости,** beyond recognition.

неузнава́емый *adj.* unrecognizable.

неука́занный *adj.* **1,** not indicated; unspecified. **2,** *obs.* not permitted.

неукло́нный *adj.* **1,** steady: неукло́нный рост, steady growth. **2,** steadfast; unwavering. —**неукло́нно,** *adv.* steadily; progressively.

неуклю́жий *adj.* awkward; clumsy. —**неуклю́же,** *adv.* awkwardly; clumsily. —**неуклю́жесть,** *n.f.* awkwardness; clumsiness.

неукосни́тельный *adj.* strict; rigorous; unfailing. **—неукосни́тельно,** *adv.* unfailingly.

неукроти́мый *adj.* **1,** untamable. **2,** uncontrollable. **3,** indomitable.

неулови́мый *adj.* **1,** elusive. **2,** barely audible or visible. **—неулови́мость,** *n.f.* elusiveness.

неулы́бчивый *adj., colloq.* unsmiling.

неуме́лый *adj.* clumsy; inept.

неуме́ние *n.* inability; lack of ability; ineptitude.

неуме́ренный *adj.* **1,** immoderate. **2,** intemperate. **—неуме́ренность,** *n.f.* immoderation.

неуме́стность *n.f.* **1,** impropriety. **2,** irrelevance.

неуме́стный *adj.* **1,** inappropriate; out of place; uncalled-for. **2,** irrelevant.

неу́мный *adj.* **1,** unintelligent. **2,** unwise.

неумоли́мый *adj.* **1,** implacable. **2,** inexorable.

неумолка́емый *adj. (of a sound or noise)* incessant.

неумо́лчный *adj.* = **неумолка́емый.**

неумы́шленный *adj.* unintentional.

неупла́та *n.* failure to pay; nonpayment.

неупла́ченный *adj.* unpaid; outstanding.

неупотреби́тельный *adj.* not in use.

неуправля́емый *adj.* **1,** unmanageable. **2,** ungovernable.

неуравнове́шенный *adj.* unbalanced; (emotionally) unstable. **—неуравнове́шенность,** *n.f.* (mental) instability.

неурегули́рованный *adj. (of questions, issues, etc.)* unsettled; outstanding.

неурожа́й *n.* crop failure; poor harvest. **—неурожа́йный,** *adj., in* **неурожа́йный год,** poor harvest year.

неуро́чный *adj.* untimely; inopportune.

неуря́дица *n., colloq.* **1,** confusion; disorder. **2,** squabbling; squabbles.

неуси́дчивый *adj.* **1,** restless. **2,** not diligent; not persevering.

неуспева́емость *n.f.* poor progress *(among pupils)*; poor grades; pupils' failure.

неуспева́ющий *adj. (of a student)* poor; not making satisfactory progress.

неуспе́х *n.* failure.

неуспе́шный *adj.* unsuccessful.

неуста́нный *adj.* **1,** untiring; tireless. **2,** unceasing; ceaseless.

неусто́йка *n.* **1,** *law* forfeit. **2,** *colloq.* failure.

неусто́йчивость *n.f.* instability.

неусто́йчивый *adj.* **1,** shaky; unstable; unsteady. **2,** fluctuating; variable; changeable.

неустрани́мый *adj.* **1,** irremovable. **2,** insurmountable. **3,** inevitable.

неустраши́мый *adj.* fearless; intrepid. **—неустраши́мость,** *n.f.* fearlessness; intrepidity.

неустро́енный *adj.* **1,** unsettled. **2,** poorly organized. **3,** not provided for. **—неустро́енность,** *n.f.* unsettled state.

неустро́йство *n.* disorder.

неусту́пчивый *adj.* unyielding; uncompromising. **—неусту́пчивость,** *n.f.* obstinacy; unwillingness to compromise.

неусы́пный *adj.* unyielding; tireless. **2,** unflagging; unremitting.

неутеши́тельный *adj.* unencouraging; inauspicious.

неуте́шный *adj.* inconsolable; disconsolate.

неутоли́мый *adj.* unquenchable.

неутоми́мый *adj.* indefatigable; tireless. **—неутоми́мость,** *n.f.* indefatigability.

неухо́женный *adj., colloq.* unkempt.

неу́ч *n., colloq.* ignoramus.

неучти́вый *adj.* impolite; discourteous. **—неучти́вость,** *n.f.* impoliteness; discourtesy.

неую́тный *adj.* lacking in comforts. **—неую́тно,** *adj., used predicatively,* uncomfortable: чу́вствовать себя́ неую́тно, to feel uncomfortable.

неуязви́мый *adj.* invulnerable. **—неуязви́мость,** *n.f.* invulnerability.

нефри́т *n.* **1,** nephritis. **2,** nephrite; jade.

нефтеналивно́й *adj.* carrying oil: нефтеналивно́е су́дно, oil tanker.

нефтено́сный *adj.* containing oil; yielding oil: нефтено́сный сла́нец, oil shale.

нефтеперего́нный *adj., in* **нефтеперего́нный заво́д,** oil refinery.

нефтепрово́д *n.* oil pipeline.

нефтехими́ческий *adj.* petrochemical.

нефтехрани́лище *n.* oil storage tank.

нефть *n.f.* oil; petroleum.

нефтяно́й *adj.* oil *(attrib.)*; petroleum *(attrib.)*.

нехаракте́рный *adj.* not typical; uncharacteristic.

нехва́тка [*gen. pl.* **-ток**] *n., colloq.* shortage.

нехи́трый *adj.* **1,** without guile; ingenuous. **2,** *colloq.* simple; unpretentious.

неходово́й *adj.* **1,** not in working order; out of commission. **2,** *(of merchandise)* unsalable; unwanted.

нехо́женый *adj., colloq.* untrodden.

нехоро́ший *adj.* bad. **—нехоро́ш собо́й,** ugly; unattractive.

нехорошо́ *adv.* badly. **—***adj., used predicatively* **1,** not good; bad: Нехорошо́, что..., it's not good that... **2,** ill: Ему́ ста́ло нехорошо́, he began to feel ill.

не́хотя *adv.* **1,** unwillingly; reluctantly. **2,** accidentally; inadvertently.

нецелесообра́зный *adj.* **1,** inadvisable. **2,** pointless.

нецензу́рный *adj.* unprintable; obscene.

нецеремо́нный *adj.* unceremonious.

нецивилизо́ванный *adj.* uncivilized.

неча́янный *adj.* **1,** unexpected; chance. **2,** accidental; inadvertent. **—неча́янно,** *adv.* accidentally; inadvertently; by chance.

не́чего *indef. pron., gen. & acc.* [*dat.* **не́чему;** *instr.* **не́чем;** *prepl.* **не́** (+ *prep.*) **чем**] *used with the inf.* there is nothing: Не́чего чита́ть, there is nothing to read. Мне не́чего сказа́ть, I have nothing to say. Об э́том не́чего и ду́мать, that is out of the question. Удивля́ться тут не́чему, there is nothing surprising about this. Им не́чем с на́ми торгова́ть, they have nothing to sell us. Разгова́ривать бы́ло не́ о чем, there was nothing to talk about. **—***adv., colloq., used with the inf.* **1,** there is no need: Не́чего беспоко́иться, there is no need to worry. **2,** there is no point; it is no use: Не́чего жа́ловаться, there is no point *(or* it's no use)* complaining. **—не́чего и говори́ть, об э́том и говори́ть не́чего,** *see* говори́ть. **—не́чего**

сказа́ть, **1,** of course; to be sure. **2,** I must say! **—от не́чего де́лать,** having nothing better to do.

нечелове́ческий adj. **1,** inhuman. **2,** superhuman.

нечёсаный adj. unkempt.

нечести́вый adj., obs. wicked; unholy.

нече́стный adj. dishonest. **—нече́стно,** adv. dishonestly. **—нече́стность,** n.f. dishonesty.

не́чет n., colloq. odd number.

нечёткий adj. **1,** unclear; indistinct; illegible. **2,** careless; slipshod.

нечётный adj. (of a number) odd.

нечистокро́вный adj. half-blooded.

нечистопло́тный adj. **1,** dirty; sloppy. **2,** fig. unscrupulous; shady.

нечистота́ [pl. **-то́ты**] n. **1,** uncleanliness. **2,** pl. sewage. **3,** pl. impurities.

нечи́стый adj. **1,** unclean; dirty. **2,** impure; adulterated. **3,** (of sounds or speech) unclear. **4,** in нечи́стая со́весть, guilty conscience. **5,** fig. dishonest; shady. **—на́ руку нечи́ст,** light-fingered.

не́чисть n.f., colloq. **1,** evil spirits. **2,** fig. scum.

нечленоразде́льный adj. inarticulate; unintelligible.

не́что indef. pron. something.

нечувстви́тельный adj. insensitive. **—нечувстви́-тельность,** n.f. insensitivity.

нечу́ткий adj. **1,** insensitive; not keen; dull. **2,** insensitive; not caring; indifferent.

нешу́точный adj., colloq. not to be taken lightly: нешу́точное де́ло, no laughing matter.

неща́дный adj. merciless. **—неща́дно,** adv. mercilessly.

неэконо́мный adj. uneconomical.

неэкспони́рованный adj. (of film) unexposed.

неэтили́рованный adj. (of gasoline) unleaded.

неэти́чный adj. unethical.

неэффекти́вность n.f. **1,** inefficacy. **2,** inefficiency.

неэффекти́вный adj. **1,** ineffective. **2,** inefficient.

нея́вка n. failure to appear.

нея́ркий adj. **1,** dim; faint. **2,** pale; subdued.

нея́сно adv. **1,** dimly; faintly. **2,** in an unclear manner. **—**adj., used predicatively, unclear: Ещё нея́сно, что бу́дет, it is still unclear what will happen.

нея́сность n.f. **1,** lack of clarity; vagueness. **2,** unclear point; ambiguity.

нея́сный adj. [short form **нея́сен, неясна́, нея́сно, нея́сны**] **1,** unclear; vague. **2,** indistinct. **3,** (of sounds) faint; indistinct.

нея́сыть n.f. tawny owl.

ни neg. particle **1,** not a: На не́бе ни обла́чка, there is not a cloud in the sky. ♦ Often used with оди́н: Он не сказа́л ни одного́ сло́ва, he did not say a single word. **2,** occurring as a separate word when никто́, ничто́, никако́й and their oblique case forms are broken up to permit the insertion of a preposition in between: ни за что на све́те, not for anything in the world. Я ни с кем не встре́тился, I did not meet anyone. Он не отвеча́л ни на каки́е вопро́сы, he did not answer any questions. **—**indef. particle, equivalent to English -ever: что ни or что бы ни, whatever; где ни or где бы ни, wherever. Кто бы он ни́ был, whoever he is.

Куда́ ни посмо́тришь, wherever you look. **—ни... ни,** neither...nor: ни за ни про́тив, neither for nor against; ни тот ни друго́й, neither one.

ни́ва n. **1,** field of grain. **2,** fig. field (of endeavor): на ни́ве просвеще́ния, in the field of education.

нивели́р n. level (instrument).

нивели́ровать v.impfv. & pfv. [pres. **-рую, -руешь**] to level.

нивелиро́вка n. leveling.

нивя́ник n. (oxeye) daisy.

нигде́ adv. nowhere: Его́ нигде́ нет, he is nowhere to be found; he is not to be found anywhere.

нигери́йский adj. Nigerian.

нигили́зм n. nihilism. **—нигили́ст,** n. nihilist. **—нигилисти́ческий,** adj. nihilistic.

нидерла́ндец [gen. **-дца**] n. Dutchman. **—нидерла́ндский,** adj. Dutch; Netherlands (attrib.).

ни́же adj., comp. of **ни́зкий.** **—**adv. below. **—**prep., with gen. **1,** below: ни́же нуля́, below zero. **2,** beneath: ни́же его́ досто́инства, beneath his dignity.

нижеподписа́вшийся n., decl. as an adj. the undersigned.

нижесле́дующий adj. the following.

нижестоя́щий adj. (of an organization, governmental body, etc.) lower-level.

ни́жний adj. **1,** lower. **2,** bottom. **—ни́жнее бельё,** underwear. **—ни́жняя руба́шка,** undershirt. **—ни́жний эта́ж,** ground floor.

низ [2nd loc. низу́; pl. низы́] n. **1,** bottom. **2,** pl., music low notes. **3,** pl., colloq. lower classes; lower strata.

низа́ть v.impfv. [pfv. **наниза́ть;** pres. **нижу́, ни́жешь**] to string; thread.

низверга́ть v.impfv. [pfv. **низве́ргнуть**] **1,** to throw (down); plunge. **2,** fig. to overthrow; bring down. **—низверга́ться,** refl. (of water) to come rushing down; cascade down.

низве́ргнуть [past низве́рг, низве́ргла] v., pfv. of низверга́ть. **—низве́ргнуться,** refl., pfv. of низверга́ться.

низверже́ние n. overthrow.

низвести́ [infl. like вести́] v., pfv. of низводи́ть.

низводи́ть v.impfv. [pfv. **низвести́;** pres. **-вожу́, -во́дишь**] **1,** to bring down. **2,** fig. (with до) to reduce (to).

низи́на n. low-lying area. **—низи́нный,** adj. low-lying.

ни́зкий adj. [short form ни́зок, низка́, ни́зко, ни́зки; comp. ни́же] **1,** low. **2,** (of quality) poor. **3,** base; despicable. **4,** (of a sound, voice, etc.) deep. **—ни́зкого ро́ста,** short (in height).

ни́зко adv. **1,** low: поклони́ться ни́зко, to bow low. **2,** despicably.

низкооплачиваемый adj. **1,** low-paid. **2,** low-paying.

низкопокло́нник n. sycophant.

низкопокло́нничать v.impfv. (with пе́ред) to grovel (before); kowtow (to); bow and scrape (before).

низкопокло́нство n. servility.

низкопро́бный adj. **1,** (of gold or silver) base-alloy; low-grade. **2,** fig. low-grade; second-rate.

низкоро́слый adj. undersized.

низкосо́ртный adj. poor-quality; low-grade.

низлага́ть *v.impfv.* [*pfv.* **низложи́ть**] to overthrow; depose; bring down.

низложе́ние *n.* overthrow.

низложи́ть [*infl.* -ложу́, -ло́жишь] *v., pfv. of* **низлага́ть.**

ни́зменность *n.f.* **1,** lowland. **2,** baseness; meanness.

ни́зменный *adj.* **1,** *geol.* low-lying. **2,** base; mean.

низово́й *adj.* **1,** low; close to the ground. **2,** located downstream. **3,** local; at the local level.

низо́вье *n.* lower reaches (*of a river*).

ни́зом *adv.* along the bottom; along the lower route.

ни́зость *n.f.* baseness; meanness.

ни́зший *adj., superl. of* **ни́зкий,** lowest. —**ни́зшее образова́ние,** elementary education.

ника́к *adv.* (in) no way; (not) at all. Я ника́к не мог откры́ть дверь, there was no way I could open the door; I simply could not open the door. Ника́к не могу́ вспо́мнить, I simply (*or* just) can't remember. Это ника́к не помо́жет, that won't help at all. Ника́к не могу́ с э́тим согласи́ться, I can't agree with that at all. —**ника́к нельзя́,** absolutely impossible.

никако́й *adj.* not any; no: Не мо́жет быть никако́го сомне́ния, there can be no doubt. Никаки́х извине́ний!, no apologies!

ни́келевый *adj.* nickel.

никелирова́ть *v.impfv. & pfv.* [*pres.* -ру́ю, -ру́ешь] to plate with nickel; nickel-plate.

никелиро́вка *n.* **1,** nickel-plating. **2,** nickel plate.

ни́кель *n.m.* nickel.

нике́м *indef. pron., instr. of* **никто́.**

ни́кнуть *v.impfv.* [*pfv.* **пони́кнуть;** *past* ник *or* ни́кнул, ни́кла] to droop.

никогда́ *adv.* never. —**бо́льше никогда́,** never again. —**как никогда́,** more than ever; as never before. —**никогда́ ещё,** never before.

никого́ *indef. pron., gen. & acc. of* **никто́.**

нико́й *adj., in* **нико́им о́бразом** *and* **ни в ко́ем слу́чае,** under no circumstances.

никому́ *indef. pron., dat. of* **никто́.**

никоти́н *n.* nicotine. —**никоти́нный; никоти́новый,** *adj.* nicotine (*attrib.*).

никто́ *indef. pron.* [*gen. & acc.* **никого́;** *dat.* **никому́;** *instr.* **нике́м;** *prepl.* **ни** (+ *prep.*) **ком**] no one; nobody.

никуда́ *adv.* nowhere. Я никуда́ не пошёл, I didn't go anywhere. —**никуда́ не годи́ться,** to be of no use; be no good at all.

никуды́шный *adj., colloq.* useless; worthless; good-for-nothing.

никчёмный *adj., colloq.* useless; worthless; good-for-nothing. —**никчёмность,** *n.f., colloq.* uselessness; worthlessness.

ним *pron., var. of* **им,** *used after prepositions.*

нима́ло *adv.* not at all; not in the least; not a bit.

нимб *n.* nimbus.

ни́ми *pron., var. of* **и́ми,** *used after prepositions.*

ни́мфа *n.* nymph.

нимфома́ния *n.* nymphomania. —**нимфома́нка,** *n.* nymphomaniac.

нио́бий *n.* niobium.

ниоди́мий *n.* neodymium.

ниотку́да *adv.* from nowhere; not from anywhere.

нипочём *adv., colloq.* **1,** (*with dat.*) it is nothing (for someone): Ему́ нипочём пройти́ два́дцать киломе́тров, it is nothing for him to walk twenty kilometers. **2,** dirt-cheap.

ни́ппель [*pl.* **ниппеля́**] *n.m.* nipple (*threaded pipe*).

нирва́на *n.* nirvana.

ниско́лько *adv.* not at all; not a bit; not in the least.

ниспада́ть *v.impfv.* to hang down.

ниспроверга́ть *v.impfv.* [*pfv.* **ниспрове́ргнуть**] to overthrow.

ниспрове́ргнуть [*past* -ве́рг, -ве́ргла] *v., pfv. of* **ниспроверга́ть.**

ниспроверже́ние *n.* overthrow.

нисходя́щий *adj.* descending.

ни́тка [*gen. pl.* -ток] *n.* **1,** thread. **2,** string (*of pearls, beads, etc.*). —**до ни́тки, 1,** (*with* всё) down to the last penny. **2,** (*with the verb* промо́кнуть) to the skin. —**на живу́ю ни́тку,** hastily; crudely. —**шит бе́лыми ни́тками,** transparent; poorly disguised.

ни́точка [*gen. pl.* -чек] *n., dim. of* **ни́тка.** —**висе́ть** *or* **держа́ться на ни́точке,** to hang by a thread. —**ходи́ть по ни́точке, 1,** to toe the line. **2,** (*with* у) to meekly obey.

ни́точный *adj.* of or for thread.

нитра́т *n.* nitrate. —**нитра́тный,** *adj.* containing nitrate; nitrate (*attrib.*).

нитри́т *n.* nitrite.

нитроглицери́н *n.* nitroglycerin(e).

нить *n.f.* **1,** thread. **2,** filament. **3,** suture. —**потеря́ть нить разгово́ра,** to lose the thread of the conversation. —**проходи́ть кра́сной ни́тью** (*with* в + *prepl. or* че́рез), to be the dominant theme of; run through.

ни́тяный *adj.* made of thread.

них *pron., var. of* **их,** *used after prepositions.*

ниц *adv.* with one's face touching the ground. —**пасть ниц,** to prostrate oneself.

ничего́ *indef. pron., gen. of* **ничто́,** nothing: ничего́ осо́бенного, nothing special. Ничего́ не зна́чить, not mean anything. Я ничего́ не ви́дел, I didn't see anything. —*adv. & adj., colloq.* [*also,* **ничего́ себе́**] not bad; pretty good; pretty well. —**ничего́!,** no matter!; it doesn't matter!; never mind!

ничегонеде́лание *n., colloq.* idleness.

ниче́й *indef. pron.* [*infl. like* **чей**] nobody's; no one's. —**ничья́ земля́,** no man's land. *See also* **ничья́.**

ниче́йный *adj.* **1,** *sports; games* drawn; tied. **2,** *colloq.* no man's: ниче́йная земля́, no man's land.

ниче́м *indef. pron., instr. of* **ничто́.**

ничему́ *indef. pron., dat. of* **ничто́.**

ничко́м *adv.* prone; face down.

ничто́ *indef. pron.* [*gen. & acc.* **ничего́;** *dat.* **ничему́;** *instr.* **ниче́м;** *prepl.* **ни** (+ *prep.*) **чём**] nothing. *See also* **ничего́.** —*n.* nonentity; nobody.

ничто́же *adv., in* **ничто́же сумня́шеся,** *colloq.* without a moment's hesitation; just like that.

ничто́жество *n.* **1,** insignificance. **2,** nonentity; nobody.

ничто́жно *adv., in* **ничто́жно ма́ло,** extremely little; almost nothing.

ничто́жность *n.f.* **1,** insignificance. **2,** nonentity; nobody.

ничто́жный *adj.* **1,** (*of an amount*) insignificant; infinitesimal; paltry. **2,** insignificant; meaningless. **3,** (*of a person*) worthless; good-for-nothing.

ничу́ть *adv., colloq.* not at all; not the least; not a bit. —**ничу́ть не быва́ло,** *colloq.* **1,** not at all; not in the least. **2,** but it was not that way; but that was not the case.

ничья́ [*gen., dat., instr. & prepl.* **ничье́й;** *acc.* **ничью́**] *n., sports; games* tie; draw.

ни́ша *n.* niche; recess; alcove.

нища́ть *v.impfv.* [*pfv.* **обнища́ть**] to become impoverished.

ни́щенка [*gen. pl.* **-нок**] *n.* beggar (woman).

ни́щенский *adj.* **1,** beggarly. **2,** *fig.* paltry.

ни́щенство *n.* **1,** begging. **2,** poverty; destitution.

ни́щенствовать *v.impfv.* [*pres.* **-ствую, -ствуешь**] **1,** to beg; go begging. **2,** to live in poverty.

нищета́ *n.* poverty.

ни́щий *adj.* destitute; poverty-stricken. —*n.* beggar.

но *conj.* but.

Но́белевский *adj.,* in **Но́белевская пре́мия,** Nobel Prize.

нобе́лий *n.* nobelium.

нова́тор *n.* innovator. —**нова́торский,** *adj.* innovative. —**нова́торство,** *n.* innovation.

нове́йший *adj., superl. of* **но́вый,** newest; latest.

нове́лла *n.* short story; novella.

новелли́ст *n.* short story writer.

но́венький *adj.* new; brand-new. —*n., colloq.* **1,** newcomer. **2,** freshman. —**что но́венького?,** *colloq.* what's new?

новизна́ *n.* novelty; newness.

нови́нка [*gen. pl.* **-нок**] *n.* something new: кни́жные нови́нки, new books. —**э́то мне в нови́нку,** it is new to me; it is something I've never done before.

новичо́к [*gen.* **-чка́**] *n.* **1,** novice. **2,** new boy *or* girl (*in school*).

новобра́нец [*gen.* **-нца**] *n.* recruit.

новобра́чный *n., decl. as an adj.* newlywed.

нововведе́ние *n.* innovation.

нового́дний *adj.* New Year's.

новогре́ческий *adj.* Modern Greek.

новозаве́тный *adj.* New Testament (*attrib.*).

новозела́ндец [*gen.* **-дца**] *n.m.* [*fem.* **-дка**] New Zealander. —**новозела́ндский,** *adj.* New Zealand (*attrib.*).

новоиспечённый *adj., colloq.* **1,** newly made. **2,** newly appointed.

новокаи́н *n.* novocaine. —**новокаи́новый,** *adj.* novocaine (*attrib.*).

новолу́ние *n.* new moon.

новомо́дный *adj.* **1,** in the latest style. **2,** (*of words*) currently fashionable.

новообразова́ние *n.* **1,** new formation. **2,** *med.* growth; neoplasm. **3,** newly coined word.

новообращённый *adj.* newly converted (*to another religion*). —*n.* neophyte; convert; proselyte.

новоприбы́вший *adj.* newly arrived; recently arrived. —*n.* newcomer.

новорождённый *adj.* newborn. —*n.* newborn baby.

новосёл *n.* **1,** new settler. **2,** new tenant.

новосе́лье *n.* **1,** new home. **2,** housewarming.

новостро́йка [*gen. pl.* **-стро́ек**] *n.* **1,** new building. **2,** construction project.

но́вость [*pl.* **но́вости, -сте́й, -стя́м**] *n.f.* **1,** news. **2,** a novelty; something new. **3,** newness.

новоя́вленный *adj.* newly emerged.

но́вшество *n.* innovation; novelty.

но́вый *adj.* [*short form* **нов, нова́, но́во, но́вы**] **1,** new. **2,** (*of history, languages, etc.*) modern. —**Но́вый год,** the New Year. —**Но́вый свет,** the New World. —**но́вый стиль,** New Style (*of dates*). —**что но́вого?,** what's new?

новь *n.f.* virgin soil.

нога́ [*acc.* **но́гу;** *pl.* **но́ги, ног, нога́м**] *n.* **1,** leg. **2,** foot. —**быть без ног,** to be falling off one's feet. —**вверх нога́ми,** upside-down; topsy-turvy. —**идти́ в но́гу,** to keep in step. —**идти́ в но́гу с,** to keep up with; keep pace with. —**идти́ нога́ за́ ногу,** to amble along. —**к ноге́!,** *mil.* order arms! —**на дру́жеской** (*or* **на коро́ткой**) **ноге́ с,** on friendly terms with. —**на нога́х, 1,** on one's feet. **2,** awake; up. **3,** on the go. **4,** up and about. —**на ра́вной ноге́ с,** on an equal footing with. —**ни ного́й,** never going to: Мы туда́ ни ного́й, we never set foot in there. —**одна́ нога́ здесь, друга́я там,** be quick about it! —**со всех ног,** as fast as one's legs would carry one. —**с головы́ до ног,** from head to toe. —**ста́вить** (**что-нибудь**) **с ног на́ голову,** to turn (*e.g. an argument*) on its head.

нога́ец [*gen.* **-а́йца**] *n.m.* [*fem.* **-га́йка**] Nogai (*one of a people inhabiting the Caucasus*). —**нога́йский,** *adj.* Nogai.

ноготки́ [*gen.* **-ко́в**] *n.pl.* marigold.

но́готь [*gen.* **но́гтя;** *pl.* **но́гти, ногте́й, ногтя́м**] *n.m.* nail; finger nail; toenail. —**до конца́ ногте́й,** to the tips of one's toes.

нож [*gen.* **ножа́**] *n.* knife. —**быть на ножа́х,** to be at swords' points. —**нож в спи́ну,** stab in the back.

ножево́й *also,* **ножо́вый** *adj.* knife (*attrib.*). —**ножево́й това́р; ножевы́е изде́лия,** cutlery.

но́жик *n.* small knife.

но́жка [*gen. pl.* **но́жек**] *n.* **1,** *dim. of* **нога́. 2,** leg (*of a chair, table, etc.*). **3,** stem (*of a wineglass*). **4,** stem (*of a mushroom*). —**подставля́ть но́жку,** *see* **подставля́ть.**

но́жницы [*gen.* **-ниц**] *n.pl.* **1,** scissors. **2,** shears.

ножно́й *adj.* **1,** foot (*attrib.*). **2,** operated with the foot.

но́жны [*gen.* **но́жен**] *n.pl.* scabbard; sheath. *Also,* **ножны́** [*gen.* **ножо́н**].

ножо́вка [*gen. pl.* **-вок**] *n.* handsaw; hacksaw.

ноздрева́тый *adj.* porous.

ноздря́ [*pl.* **но́здри, -дре́й, -дря́м**] *n.* nostril.

нока́ут *n., boxing* knockout.

нокаути́ровать *v.impfv. & pfv.* [*pres.* **-рую, -руешь**] *boxing* to knock out.

нокда́ун *n., boxing* knockdown.

нокто́рн *n.* nocturne.

нолево́й *adj.* = **нулево́й.**

ноль [*gen.* **ноля́**] *n.m.* = **нуль.**

номенклату́ра *n.* **1,** nomenclature. **2,** the privileged class; the elite. —**номенклату́рный,** *adj.* **1,** (*of a post*) reserved for the privileged class. **2,** (*of a person*) belonging to the privileged class.

но́мер [*pl.* **номера́**] *n.* **1,** number. **2,** issue (*of a newspaper*). **3,** size (*of an article of clothing*). **4,** hotel room. **5,** number; item; act (*on a program*). **6,** *colloq.* trick; ploy: Но́мер не прошёл, the ploy didn't work.

номерно́й *adj.* containing a number: номерно́й знак, license plate. —*n.* room attendant (*in a hotel*).

номеро́к [*gen.* **-рка́**] *n.* **1,** small room (*in a hotel*). **2,** check; ticket.

номина́л *n., finance* par; face value.

номина́льный *adj.* nominal; titular.

нора́ [*pl.* **но́ры**] *n.* hole; burrow (*of an animal*).

норве́жец [*gen.* **-жца**] *n.m.* [*fem.* **-жка**] Norwegian. —**норве́жский,** *adj.* Norwegian.

норд *n., naut.* **1,** north. **2,** north wind.

норд-ве́ст *n., naut.* **1,** northwest. **2,** northwester (*wind*).

но́рдовый *adj., naut.* north.

норд-о́ст *n., naut.* **1,** northeast. **2,** northeaster (*wind*).

но́рка [*gen. pl.* **но́рок**] *n.* **1,** *dim. of* нора́. **2,** mink. —**но́рковый,** *adj.* mink (*attrib.*).

но́рма *n.* **1,** norm; standard. **2,** quota. **3,** rate. —**войти́ в но́рму,** to return to normal.

нормализа́ция *n.* normalization.

нормализова́ть *v.impfv. & pfv.* [*pres.* **-зу́ю, -зу́ешь**] **1,** to standardize. **2,** to normalize. —**нормализова́ться,** *refl.* to become normal; return to normal.

норма́ль *n.f., math.* normal.

норма́льно *adv.* normally. —*adj., used predicatively, colloq.* all right; O.K.: Всё норма́льно, everything is all right/O.K. —**норма́льность,** *n.f.* normalcy. —**норма́льный,** *adj.* normal.

норма́ндский *adj.* Norman: Норма́ндское завоева́ние Англии, the Norman Conquest.

норма́нн *n.* Norseman. —**норма́ннский,** *adj.* Norse.

нормати́в *n.* norm. —**нормати́вный,** *adj.* normative.

нормирова́ние *n.* **1,** standardization; setting of norms. **2,** rationing.

нормирова́ть *v.impfv. & pfv.* [*pres.* **-ру́ю, -ру́ешь**] **1,** to standardize; set. **2,** to ration.

но́ров *n., colloq.* character; temperament; disposition. —**с но́ровом,** (*of a person*) stubborn; strong-willed; (*of a horse*) restive; balky.

норови́стый *adj., colloq.* (*of a horse*) restive; balky.

норови́ть *v.impfv.* [*pres.* **-влю́, -ви́шь**] *colloq.* to try (to).

нос [*2nd loc.* **носу́**; *pl.* **носы́**] *n.* **1,** nose. **2,** *naut.* prow; bow. **3,** *geol.* point. —**води́ть за́ нос,** to lead (someone) on; string (someone) along; take in. —**из-под са́мого но́са,** from under one's very nose. —**на носу́,** near at hand; just around the corner: Весна́ на носу́, spring is just around the corner. —**под нос,** under one's breath. —**под (са́мым) но́сом; по́д носом,** under one's very nose. —**оста́вить с но́сом,** *colloq.* to leave (someone) holding the bag. —**оста́ться с но́сом,** *colloq.* to be left holding the bag. —**с но́са; с но́су,** *colloq.* apiece; a head.

носа́тый *adj., colloq.* big-nosed.

но́сик *n.* **1,** *dim. of* нос. **2,** spout (*on a teapot, watering can, etc.*).

носи́лки [*gen.* **-лок**] *n.pl.* stretcher; litter.

носи́льщик *n.* porter.

носи́тель *n.m.* **1,** transmitter (*e.g. of new ideas*). **2,** speaker (*of a certain language*). **3,** carrier (*of a disease*).

носи́ть *v.impfv.* [*pres.* **ношу́, но́сишь**] **1,** *indeterm. of* нести́. Носи́ть ору́жие, to bear arms. **2,** to wear. **3,** *fig.* to bear (traces, characteristics, etc.). **4,** to hold (a certain rank). —**носи́ть на рука́х,** to dote on.

носи́ться *v.r.impfv.* [*pres.* **ношу́сь, но́сишься**] **1,** *indeterm. of* нести́сь. **2,** to rush about; dash about. **3,** (*of clothing*) to wear: Это пла́тье хорошо́ но́сится, this dress wears well. **4,** (*with* с + *instr.*) *colloq.* to be obsessed with (an idea); be all *or* much involved with.

но́ска *n.* **1,** carrying. **2,** wearing; wear: от до́лгой но́ски, from long wear. **3,** laying (*of eggs*).

но́ский *adj.* **1,** *colloq.* giving long wear; durable. **2,** producing eggs in large quantities: но́ская ку́рица, a good layer.

носово́й *adj.* nose (*attrib.*); nasal. —**носово́й ко́нус,** nose cone. —**носово́й плато́к,** handkerchief.

носо́к [*gen.* **носка́**] *n.* **1,** sock. **2,** toe (*of a shoe*).

носоро́г *n.* rhinoceros.

ностальги́я *n.* nostalgia. —**ностальги́ческий,** *adj.* nostalgic.

носу́ха *n.* coati.

но́та *n.* **1,** *music* note. **2,** *pl.* music: игра́ть по но́там, to play from music. **3,** *dipl.* note. —**разы́грывать (что́-нибудь) как по но́там,** to perform (*or* carry out) with precision.

нота́риус *n.* notary public. —**нотариа́льный,** *adj.* notary (*attrib.*).

нота́ция *n.* **1,** notation. **2,** admonition; talking-to: чита́ть кому́-нибудь нота́цию, to give someone a talking-to.

но́тка [*gen. pl.* **но́ток**] *n.* faint note; trace; hint; suggestion.

но́тный *adj.* music (*attrib.*): но́тный пюпи́тр, music stand. —**но́тный стан,** *music* staff.

нотоно́сец [*gen.* **-сца**] *n., music* staff.

ночева́ть *v.impfv. & pfv.* [*pres.* **-чу́ю, -чу́ешь**] to spend the night.

ночёвка *n., colloq.* spending the night.

ночле́г *n.* **1,** place to spend the night. **2,** spending the night: останови́ться на ночле́г, to stop for the night; spend the night.

ночле́жка [*gen. pl.* **-жек**] *n., colloq.* = **ночле́жный дом.**

ночле́жный *adj., in* **ночле́жный дом,** flophouse.

ночни́к [*gen.* **-ника́**] *n.* night light.

ночно́й *adj.* night (*attrib.*). —**ночно́й горшо́к,** chamber pot. —**ночно́й сто́лик,** night table.

ночь [*pl.* **но́чи, ноче́й, ноча́м**] *n.f.* night. —**на́ ночь, 1,** for the night; overnight. Закрыва́ть две́ри на ночь, to lock the doors at night. **2,** before going to bed. —**по ноча́м,** at night. —**споко́йной но́чи!,** good night!

но́чью *adv.* at night.

но́ша *n.* **1,** load. **2,** *fig.* burden.

ноше́ние *n.* **1,** carrying; bearing. **2,** wearing.

но́щно *adv., in* **де́нно и но́щно,** *colloq.* day and night.

нóющий *adj. of* (*a pain*) nagging.

ноЯбрь [*gen.* **-брЯ**] *n.m.* November. —**ноЯбрьский,** *adj.* November (*attrib.*).

нрав *n.* disposition; temperament. —**быть** (*or* **приходи́ться**) **по нрáву** (+ *dat.*), to please: Всё ему́ не по нрáву, nothing pleases him. *See also* **нрáвы.**

нрáвиться *v.r.impfv.* [*pfv.* **понрáвиться**; *pres.* **-влюсь, -вишься**] (*with dat.*) to please; be to the liking of: Онá мне нрáвится, I like her; пьéса мне не понрáвилась, I did not like (*or* enjoy) the play.

нравоучéние *n.* moral admonition. Он всем читáет нравоучéния, he lectures everyone.

нравоучи́тельный *adj.* moralizing; moralistic.

нрáвственно *adv.* morally.

нрáвственность *n.f.* **1,** morality. **2,** morals.

нрáвственный *adj.* moral.

нрáвы [*gen.* **нрáвов**] *n.pl.* customs; ways; way of life. —**комéдия нрáвов,** comedy of manners.

ну *interj., colloq.* well; well then; why; now: Ну, я пошёл, well, I'm off; ну, конéчно!, why of course! —**а ну** (+ *gen.*), to hell with... —**да ну?,** you don't say so! —**ну и...,** what...!: Ну и погóда!, what weather! —**ну и ну!,** well, I never!; well I'll be (damned)! —**ну и что?,** well, what of it?; so what?

нугá *n.* nougat.

нýдный *adj., colloq.* **1,** boring; tiresome. **2,** inane.

нуждá [*pl.* **нýжды**] *n.* **1,** (dire) need. Жить в нуждé, to live in poverty. **2,** need; necessity: в слýчае нужды́, in case of need; if need be. **3,** *pl.* needs: нýжды насе-лéния, the needs of the populace.

нуждáться *v.r.impfv.* **1,** to be in need; be poor. **2,** (*with* **в** + *prepl.*) to need; be in need of.

нуждáющийся *adj.* needy.

нýжно *adv.* **1,** (one) must; (one) has to; (one) needs to: Это нýжно сдéлать сейчáс, this must be done at once; мне нýжно идти́, I have to go. **2,** needed: Для чегó это вам нýжно?, what do you need this for?

нýжный *adj.* [*short form* **нýжен, нужнá, нýжно, нужны́**] **1,** necessary: нýжные дáнные, the necessary data. Находи́ть нýжным (+ *inf.*), to find it necessary to. **2,** needed: Я здесь не нýжен (нужнá), I am not needed here. **3,** (*with dat.*) one needs: Емý нýжен óтдых, he needs rest; мне нужны́ дéньги, I need money.

нý-ка *interj., colloq.* well?; well then?; how about it?

нулевóй *adj.* zero (*attrib.*).

нуль [*gen.* **нуля́**] *n.m.* **1,** zero; naught. **2,** (*of a person*) a nothing; a nobody. —**с нуля́,** from scratch; from the ground up. —**своди́ть к нулю́,** to negate; nullify. —**своди́ться к нулю́,** to come to naught.

нумерáтор *n.* numbering machine.

нумерáция *n.* numeration; numbering.

нумерóванный *adj.* numbered. —**нумерóванное мéсто,** reserved seat.

нумеровáть *v.impfv.* [*pfv.* **занумеровáть** *or* **пронумеровáть**; *pres.* **-рýю, -рýешь**] to number.

нумизмáтика *n.* numismatics. —**нумизмáт,** *n.* numismatist. —**нумизмати́ческий,** *adj.* numismatic.

нýнций *n.* nuncio.

нут *n.* chickpea.

нýтрия *n.* coypu; nutria.

нутрó *n., colloq.* **1,** insides; innards. **2,** interior. **3,** essence. **4,** instinct. Нутрóм чýвствовать, что..., to sense instinctively that... —**не по нутрý** (+ *dat.*), not to one's liking.

ны́не *adv.* now.

ны́нешний *adj., colloq.* present.

ны́нче *adv., colloq.* now; nowadays. —**не ны́нче зáвтра,** any day now.

нырнýть *v., pfv. of* **ныря́ть.**

нырóк [*gen.* **ныркá**] *n.* **1,** *colloq.* dive. **2,** pochard (*duck*).

ныря́льщик *n.* diver.

ныря́ть *v.impfv.* [*pfv.* **нырнýть**] **1,** to dive. **2,** (*of a road*) to dip. **3,** *fig., colloq.* to disappear (into, behind, etc.). **4,** *boxing* to duck.

ны́тик *n., colloq.* whiner.

ныть *v.impfv.* [*pres.* **нóю, нóешь**] **1,** to ache. **2,** *colloq.* to whine.

нытьё *n.* **1,** whining; complaining. **2,** dull pain.

ньюфáундленд *n.* Newfoundland (*dog*).

нэп *n., abbr. of* **нóвая экономи́ческая поли́тика,** New Economic Policy (1921–27); N.E.P.

нюáнс *n.* nuance.

ню́ни *n.pl., in* **распускáть ню́ни,** *colloq.* **1,** to start crying. **2,** to whine; start whining.

ню́ня *n.m. & f., colloq.* crybaby; whiner.

нюх *n., colloq.* **1,** sense of smell (*of an animal*). **2,** *fig.* (keen) sense: имéть нюх на, to have a nose for.

ню́хательный *adj.* for smelling; to be smelled: ню́хательная соль, smelling salts. —**ню́хательный табáк,** snuff.

ню́хать *v.impfv.* [*pfv.* **поню́хать**] to smell; sniff; take a whiff of.

ня́нчить *v.impfv.* to nurse; take care of. —**ня́нчиться,** *refl.* (*with* **с** + *instr.*) **1,** to nurse; take care of. **2,** *colloq.* to fuss with.

ня́нька [*gen. pl.* **ня́нек**] *n., colloq.* = **ня́ня.**

ня́ня *n.* **1,** nurse; nursemaid. **2,** *colloq.* nurse's aide.

O

O, o *n.neut.* fifteenth letter of the Russian alphabet.

o[1] *also,* **об** *and* **обо** *prep.* **А,** *with prepl.* about: говори́ть о поли́тике, to talk about politics; кни́га о Че́хове, a book about Chekhov. ♦*Also:* on; of; for: ле́кция о гипно́зе, a lecture on hypnosis; догово́р о дру́жбе, a treaty of friendship; крик о по́мощи, a cry for help. Проси́ть о по́мощи, to ask for help. Он ду́мает то́лько о себе́, he thinks only of himself. **В,** *with acc.* **1,** on; against (*involving contact or collision*): опира́ться о сте́ну, to lean against the wall; порва́ть рука́в о гвоздь, to tear one's sleeve on a nail. Во́лны бью́тся о бе́рег, the waves are beating against the shore. **2,** *in* бок о́ бок, side by side; рука́ о́б руку, hand in hand.

o[2] *interj.* oh!

o- *also,* **об-, обо-, объ-** *prefix* **1,** *indicating motion around:* обходи́ть, to walk around; оплыва́ть, to swim around. **2,** *indicating action affecting everyone present:* обноси́ть, to serve (everyone present). **3,** *indicating the gaining of an advantage:* обы́грывать, to beat; defeat; обсчи́тывать, to shortchange. **4,** (*with* **-ся**) *indicating a mistake or misstep:* ослы́шаться, to hear incorrectly; оступи́ться, to stumble. **5,** (*with* **-ся**) *indicating excess:* объеда́ться, to overeat.

оа́зис *n.* oasis.

об *prep.* = **o** (*used when the word following begins with a vowel*): об э́том, об Аме́рике. ♦*Also with certain other nouns in the acc. case:* рука́ о́б руку, уда́риться о́б стену, би́ться об закла́д.

о́ба [*fem.* **о́бе**; *gen. & prepl.* **обо́их, обе́их**; *dat.* **обо́им, обе́им**; *instr.* **обо́ими, обе́ими**] *numeral* (*nominative forms govern gen. sing.*) both: о́ба ма́льчика, both boys; о́бе де́вочки, both girls; о́ба колеса́, both wheels; обе́ими рука́ми, with both hands. —**гляде́ть** *or* **смотре́ть в о́ба, 1,** to be on one's guard. **2,** (*with* **в/на** + *acc. or* **за** + *instr.*) to keep a watchful eye on. *See also* **обо́его**.

обагря́ть *v.impfv.* [*pfv.* **обагри́ть**] to give a reddish or purplish hue to. —**обагря́ть кро́вью,** to stain with blood.

обалде́лый *adj., colloq.* dazed; groggy.

обалде́ть *v.pfv., colloq.* **1,** to lose one's wits. **2,** to be dumbfounded.

обанкро́титься *v.r.pfv.* [*infl.* **-чусь, -тишься**] to go bankrupt.

обая́ние *n.* charm; attraction.

обая́тельный *adj.* charming; enchanting.

обва́л *n.* **1,** collapse; cave-in. **2,** landslide.

обва́ливать *v.impfv.* **1,** [*pfv.* **обвали́ть**] to cause to collapse; bring down. **2,** [*pfv.* **обваля́ть**] to roll (in flour, bread crumbs, etc.). —**обва́ливаться,** *refl.* [*pfv.* **обвали́ться**] to collapse; cave in; come tumbling down.

обвали́ть [*infl.* **-валю́, -ва́лишь**] *v., pfv. of* **обва́ливать** (*in sense #1*). —**обвали́ться,** *refl., pfv. of* **обва́ливаться**.

обваля́ть *v., pfv. of* **обва́ливать** (*in sense #2*).

обва́ривать *v.impfv.* [*pfv.* **обвари́ть**] **1,** to pour boiling water over. **2,** to scald. —**обва́риваться,** to scald oneself.

обвари́ть [*infl.* **-варю́, -ва́ришь**] *v., pfv. of* **обва́ривать**. —**обвари́ться,** *refl., pfv. of* **обва́риваться**.

обвева́ть *v.impfv.* [*pfv.* **обве́ять**] (*of the wind*) to blow upon; fan.

обвенча́ть *v., pfv. of* **венча́ть** (*in sense #2*). —**обвенча́ться,** *refl., pfv. of* **венча́ться** (*in sense #2*).

обвёртывать *v.impfv.* [*pfv.* **обверну́ть**] to wrap; bundle.

обве́сить [*infl.* **-шу, -сишь**] *v., pfv. of* **обве́шивать** (*in sense #1*).

обвести́ [*infl. like* **вести́**] *v., pfv. of* **обводи́ть**.

обве́тренный *adj.* **1,** weather-beaten; weather-worn. **2,** (*of one's hands, lips, etc.*) chapped.

обве́трить *v.pfv., usu. in the past passive part.,* to chap. —**обве́триться,** *refl.* **1,** to become weather-beaten. **2,** to become chapped.

обветша́лый *adj.* ramshackle; dilapidated.

обветша́ть *v., pfv. of* **ветша́ть**.

обве́шивать *v.impfv.* **1,** [*pfv.* **обве́сить**] to cheat in weighing. **2,** [*pfv.* **обве́шать**] to hang (with); cover (with).

обве́ять [*infl.* **обве́ю, обве́ешь**] *v., pfv. of* **обвева́ть**.

обвива́ть *v.impfv.* [*pfv.* **обви́ть**] to wind around. —**обвива́ться,** *refl.* (*with* **вокру́г**) to wind (around); twine (around); coil (around).

обвине́ние *n.* **1,** accusation; charge. **2,** *law* the prosecution.

обвини́тель *n.m.* **1,** accuser. **2,** prosecutor.

обвини́тельный *adj.* of accusation; accusatory. —**обвини́тельный акт; обвини́тельное заключе́ние,** (bill of) indictment. —**обвини́тельный пригово́р,** verdict of "guilty".

обвини́ть *v., pfv. of* **обвиня́ть**.

обвиня́емый *n., decl. as an adj.* the accused; defendant.

обвиня́ть *v.impfv.* [*pfv.* **обвини́ть**] (*with* **в** + *prepl.*) to accuse (of); charge (with). —**обвиня́ться,** *refl.* [*impfv. only*] (*with* **в** + *prepl.*) to be accused (of); be charged (with).

обвиса́ть *v.impfv.* [*pfv.* **обви́снуть**] to hang down; droop.

обви́слый *adj., colloq.* drooping.

обви́снуть [*past* **обви́с, обви́сла**] *v., pfv. of* **обвиса́ть.**

обви́ть [*infl.* **обовью́, обовьёшь;** *past fem.* **обвила́**] *v., pfv. of* **обвива́ть.** —**обви́ться,** *refl.* [*past* **обви́лся, обвила́сь, обвило́сь** *or* **обви́лось, обвили́сь** *or* **обви́лись**] *pfv. of* **обвива́ться.**

обводи́ть *v.impfv.* [*pfv.* **обвести́;** *pres.* **-вожу́, -во́дишь**] **1,** (*with* **вокру́г**) to lead around; walk around; take around. **2,** to enclose; surround; ring. **3,** to circle; draw a line around. —**обводи́ть (что́-нибудь) взгля́дом** *or* **глаза́ми,** to cast one's eyes over. Обвести́ горизо́нт взгля́дом, to scan the horizon. —**обводи́ть (кого́-нибудь) вокру́г па́льца,** to dupe; hoodwink.

обвола́кивать *v.impfv.* [*pfv.* **обволо́чь**] (*of smoke, clouds, etc.*) to envelop.

обволо́чь [*infl. like* **воло́чь**] *v., pfv. of* **обвола́кивать.**

обвора́живать *v.impfv.* [*pfv.* **обворожи́ть**] to charm; captivate; enchant; bewitch.

обворова́ть [*infl.* **-ру́ю, -ру́ешь**] *v., pfv. of* **обворо́вывать.**

обворо́вывать *v.impfv.* [*pfv.* **обворова́ть**] *colloq.* to rob.

обворожи́тельный *adj.* charming; enchanting; bewitching.

обворожи́ть *v., pfv. of* **обвора́живать.**

обвяза́ть [*infl.* **-вяжу́, -вя́жешь**] *v., pfv. of* **обвя́зывать.** —**обвяза́ться,** *refl., pfv. of* **обвя́зываться.**

обвя́зывать *v.impfv.* [*pfv.* **обвяза́ть**] to tie around: обвяза́ть го́лову платко́м, to tie a kerchief around one's head. —**обвя́зываться,** *refl.* (*with instr.*) to tie (something) around oneself.

обгова́ривать *v.impfv.* [*pfv.* **обговори́ть**] *colloq.* to discuss; talk over.

обго́н *n.* passing: Обго́н запрещён!, no passing!

обгоня́ть *v.impfv.* [*pfv.* **обогна́ть**] **1,** to pass (*on the road, in a race, etc.*). **2,** *fig.* to outstrip; outpace; excel.

обгора́ть *v.impfv.* [*pfv.* **обгоре́ть**] **1,** to be partially burned. **2,** *colloq.* to get a bad sunburn.

обгоре́лый *adj.* charred; burnt.

обгоре́ть *v., pfv. of* **обгора́ть.**

обгрыза́ть *v.impfv.* [*pfv.* **обгры́зть**] to nibble (at).

обгры́зть [*infl. like* **грызть**] *v., pfv. of* **обгрыза́ть.**

обдава́ть *v.impfv.* [*pfv.* **обда́ть;** *pres.* **-даю́, -даёшь**] **1,** to douse (with water); splash (with mud). **2,** *impers.* to be seized with; be filled with: Меня́ о́бдало хо́лодом, I suddenly felt very cold.

обда́ть [*infl. like* **дать;** *past* **о́бдал, обдала́, о́бдало, о́бдали**] *v., pfv. of* **обдава́ть.**

обде́лать *v., pfv. of* **обде́лывать.**

обдели́ть [*infl.* **-делю́, -де́лишь**] *v., pfv. of* **обделя́ть.**

обде́лывать *v.impfv.* [*pfv.* **обде́лать**] *colloq.* **1,** to finish; dress. **2,** to set (a precious stone). **3,** to arrange; manage; handle.

обделя́ть *v.impfv.* [*pfv.* **обдели́ть**] **1,** to cheat (someone) out of his/her rightful share; give (someone) less

than his/her due. **2,** to deprive (of). Не обделён че́м-нибудь, not lacking in something.

обдира́ть *v.impfv.* [*pfv.* **ободра́ть**] **1,** to skin; flay. **2,** *colloq.* to lacerate. **3,** *colloq.* to wear out. **4,** *colloq.* to rob; fleece.

обдува́ть *v.impfv.* [*pfv.* **обду́ть**] **1,** (*of the wind*) to blow on. **2,** to blow off (dust, ashes, etc.). **3,** *colloq.* to swindle; dupe.

обду́манный *adj.* **1,** considered; carefully thought out. **2,** deliberate.

обду́мывать *v.impfv.* [*pfv.* **обду́мать**] to think over; consider carefully.

обдуря́ть *v.impfv.* [*pfv.* **обдури́ть**] *colloq.* to trick; make a fool of.

обду́ть [*infl.* **-ду́ю, -ду́ешь**] *v., pfv. of* **обдува́ть.**

о́бе *numeral, fem. of* **о́ба.**

обе́гать *v., pfv. of* **обега́ть** (*in sense #2*).

обега́ть *v.impfv.* [*pfv.* **обежа́ть**] **1,** (*with acc. or* **вокру́г**) to run around. **2,** [*pfv. also* **обе́гать**] to run all over; make the rounds of. —**обежа́ть (что́-нибудь) глаза́ми** *or* **взгля́дом,** to look over; glance over.

обе́д *n.* midday meal; dinner; lunch.

обе́дать *v.impfv.* [*pfv.* **пообе́дать**] to have dinner; have lunch.

обе́денный *adj.* dinner (*attrib.*); lunch (*attrib.*).

обедне́вший *adj.* impoverished.

обедне́ние *n.* impoverishment.

обедне́ть *v., pfv. of* **бедне́ть.**

обедни́ть *v., pfv. of* **обедня́ть.**

обе́дня [*gen. pl.* **-ден**] *n., relig.* Mass.

обедня́ть *v.impfv.* [*pfv.* **обедни́ть**] to impoverish.

обежа́ть [*infl. like* **бежа́ть**] *v., pfv. of* **обега́ть** (*in sense #1*).

обезбо́ливать *v.impfv.* [*pfv.* **обезбо́лить**] to anesthetize.

обезбо́ливающий *adj.* anesthetic. —**обезбо́ливающее сре́дство,** anesthetic.

обезбо́лить *v., pfv. of* **обезбо́ливать.**

обезво́дить [*infl.* **-во́жу, -во́дишь**] *v., pfv. of* **обезво́живать.**

обезво́живание *n.* dehydration.

обезво́живать *v.impfv.* [*pfv.* **обезво́дить**] to dehydrate.

обезвре́живать *v.impfv.* [*pfv.* **обезвре́дить**] **1,** to render harmless. **2,** to defuse (a bomb); deactivate (a mine).

обезгла́вить [*infl.* **-влю, -вишь**] *v., pfv. of* **обезгла́вливать.**

обезгла́вливание *n.* beheading; decapitation.

обезгла́вливать *v.impfv.* [*pfv.* **обезгла́вить**] to behead; decapitate.

обезде́нежеть *v.pfv., colloq.* to run short of money; run out of money.

обездо́ленный *adj.* indigent; destitute.

обездо́ливать *v.impfv.* [*pfv.* **обездо́лить**] to leave destitute.

обезжи́ривать *v.impfv.* [*pfv.* **обезжи́рить**] to remove the fat from.

обеззара́живание *n.* disinfection; decontamination.

обеззара́живать *v.impfv.* [*pfv.* **обеззара́зить**] to disinfect; decontaminate.

обезземе́ливать *v.impfv.* [*pfv.* **обезземе́лить**] to dispossess of one's land.

обезле́сение *n.* deforestation.

обезле́сить *v.pfv.* to deforest.

обезли́чивать *v.impfv.* [*pfv.* **обезли́чить**] to rob of one's individuality; depersonalize.

обезлю́деть *v.pfv.* to become depopulated.

обезлю́дить *v.pfv.* to depopulate.

обезобра́живать *v.impfv.* [*pfv.* **обезобра́зить**] to make unattractive; mar the appearance of; disfigure.

обезобра́зить [*infl.* **-жу, -зишь**] *v., pfv. of* **безобра́зить** *and* **обезобра́живать**.

обезопа́сить *v.pfv.* [*infl.* **-шу, -сишь**] to secure.

обезору́живать *v.impfv.* [*pfv.* **обезору́жить**] to disarm.

обезу́меть *v.pfv.* to lose one's senses; lose one's head. Обезу́меть от стра́ха, to become crazed with fear.

обезья́на *n.* monkey; ape.

обезья́ний [*fem.* **-нья**] *adj.* **1,** monkey (*attrib.*). **2,** apelike.

обезья́нничать *v.impfv., colloq.* to ape; imitate.

обезьяноподо́бный *adj.* ape-like.

обезьяночелове́к [*pl.* **обезьянолю́ди**] *n.* ape-man.

обели́ск *n.* obelisk.

обеля́ть *v.impfv.* [*pfv.* **обели́ть**] *colloq.* to vindicate; clear of a charge; prove the innocence of. **—обели́ть себя́,** to prove (*or* establish) one's innocence.

оберега́ть *v.impfv.* [*pfv.* **обере́чь**] to guard; protect.

обере́чь [*infl. like* **бере́чь**] *v., pfv. of* **оберега́ть**.

оберну́ть *v., pfv. of* **обёртывать** *and* **обора́чивать**. **—оберну́ться,** *refl., pfv. of* **обёртываться** *and* **обора́чиваться**.

обёртка [*gen. pl.* **-ток**] *n.* **1,** wrapping; wrapper. **2,** cover (*for a book*).

оберто́н *n., music* overtone.

обёрточный *adj.* for wrapping: обёрточная бума́га, wrapping paper.

обёртывание *n., med.* pack.

обёртывать *v.impfv.* [*pfv.* **оберну́ть**] **1,** (*with* **вокру́г**) to wrap (around). **2,** (*with instr. or* **в** *+ acc.*) to wrap (in). **3,** *in* оберну́ть кого́-нибудь вокру́г па́льца, to dupe; hoodwink. **—обёртываться,** *refl.* = **обора́чиваться**.

обескро́вливать *v.impfv.* [*pfv.* **обескро́вить**] **1,** to drain of blood; bleed white. **2,** *fig.* to rob of vitality.

обескура́женность *n.f., colloq.* discouragement.

обескура́женный *adj.* discouraged.

обескура́живать *v.impfv.* [*pfv.* **обескура́жить**] to discourage; dishearten.

обеспа́мятеть *v.pfv., colloq.* **1,** to lose one's memory. **2,** to lose consciousness. **3,** to lose one's senses.

обеспе́чение *n.* **1,** (*with instr.*) providing (with); supplying (with). **2,** ensuring; securing. **3,** (financial) security. **4,** security; guarantee.

обеспе́ченность *n.f.* **1,** (*with instr.*) supply: обеспе́ченность уче́бниками, supply of textbooks. **2,** (financial) security; material well-being.

обеспе́ченный *adj.* well-to-do.

обеспе́чивать *v.impfv.* [*pfv.* **обеспе́чить**] **1,** to ensure; assure; secure. **2,** (*with instr.*) to provide (with); supply (with). **3,** to provide for; support. **4,** (*with* **от**) *obs.* to protect (from).

обеспоко́енный *adj.* worried; concerned. **—обеспоко́енность,** *n.f.* worry; concern.

обеспоко́ить *v.pfv.* to worry; trouble; disturb. **—обеспоко́иться,** *refl.* to be worried; be disturbed.

обесси́леть *v.pfv.* to lose one's strength; become weak.

обесси́ливать *v.impfv.* [*pfv.* **обесси́лить**] to weaken; debilitate; rob of one's strength.

обессла́вить *v.pfv.* [*infl.* **-влю, -вишь**] to disgrace.

обессме́ртить *v.pfv.* [*infl.* **-рчу, -ртишь**] to immortalize.

обесцве́тить [*infl.* **-чу, -тишь**] *v., pfv. of* **обесцве́чивать**.

обесцве́чивание *n.* discoloration.

обесцве́чивать *v.impfv.* [*pfv.* **обесцве́тить**] to discolor.

обесце́нение *n.* depreciation. *Also,* **обесце́нивание**.

обесце́нивать *v.impfv.* [*pfv.* **обесце́нить**] to cheapen; lessen the value of. **—обесце́ниваться,** *refl.* to depreciate; decrease in value.

обесче́стить *v., pfv. of* **бесче́стить**.

обе́т *n.* vow; pledge.

обетова́нный *adj., in* земля́ обетова́нная, the Promised Land.

обеща́ние *n.* promise.

обеща́ть *v.impfv. & pfv.* **1,** (*with dat.*) to promise. **2,** *impers.* to promise: День обеща́ет быть хоро́шим, the day promises to be nice; it promises to be a nice day.

обжа́лование *n., law* appeal.

обжа́ловать *v.pfv.* [*infl.* **-лую, -луешь**] to appeal (a verdict, decision, etc.).

обже́чь [*infl.* **обожгу́, обожжёшь, ...обожгу́т;** *past* **обжёг, обожгла́**] *v., pfv. of* **обжига́ть**. **—обже́чься,** *refl., pfv. of* **обжига́ться**.

обжива́ть *v.impfv.* [*pfv.* **обжи́ть**] *colloq.* to make habitable. **—обжива́ться,** *refl., colloq.* to make oneself at home; feel at home.

обжига́тельный *adj.* used for burning or baking. **—обжига́тельная печь,** kiln.

обжига́ть *v.impfv.* [*pfv.* **обже́чь**] **1,** to burn. **2,** to bake (pottery, bricks, etc.). **—обжига́ться,** *refl.* **1,** to burn oneself. **2,** *fig.* to get burned; burn one's fingers.

обжито́й *adj.* **1,** (*of a region*) settled; inhabited. **2,** (*of a house*) lived-in; livable. Име́ть обжито́й вид, to have a lived-in look.

обжи́ть [*infl.* **-живу́, -живёшь;** *past* **о́бжил, обжила́, о́бжило, о́бжили**] *v., pfv. of* **обжива́ть**. **—обжи́ться,** *refl.* [*past* **обжи́лся, -ла́сь, -ло́сь, -ли́сь**] *pfv. of* **обжива́ться**.

обжо́ра *n.m. & f., colloq.* glutton. **—обжо́рливый,** *adj., colloq.* gluttonous. **—обжо́рство,** *n., colloq.* gluttony.

обжу́ливать *v.impfv.* [*pfv.* **обжу́лить**] *colloq.* to swindle; cheat; gyp.

обзавести́сь [*infl. like* **вести́**] *v.r., pfv. of* **обзаводи́ться**.

обзаводи́ться *v.r.impfv.* [*pfv.* **обзавести́сь;** *pres.* **-вожу́сь, -во́дишься**] (*with instr.*) *colloq.* **1,** to acquire; provide oneself with. **2,** to make (friends); start (a family). **—обзаводи́ться хозя́йством,** to set up house.

обзва́нивать *v.impfv.* [*pfv.* **обзвони́ть**] *colloq.* to call; telephone; call around to (many people).

обзо́р *n.* **1,** observation. **2,** survey; roundup. **3,** field of vision.

обзо́рный *adj.* giving an overall view. —**обзо́рный курс,** survey course.

обзыва́ть *v.impfv.* [*pfv.* **обозва́ть**] *colloq.* to call (someone something insulting): обозва́ть кого́-нибудь глупцо́м, to call someone a dunce.

обива́ть *v.impfv.* [*pfv.* **оби́ть**] **1,** to chip. **2,** *colloq.* to hurt; injure (one's arms or legs). **3,** to knock off; shake off. **4,** to upholster; cover. **5,** *colloq.* to wear out; wear thin. —**обива́ть (все) поро́ги,** to knock on every door.

оби́вка *n.* **1,** upholstering. **2,** upholstery.

оби́да *n.* **1,** offense; insult. **2,** offense; resentment. —**быть в оби́де на** (+ *acc.*), to be offended (*or* angry) with. —**не в оби́ду будь ска́зано,** no offense meant. —**не дать (кого́-нибудь) в оби́ду,** to allow no harm to come to. —**не дава́ться в оби́ду,** not to allow oneself to be pushed around.

оби́деть [*infl.* **оби́жу, оби́дишь**] *v., pfv. of* **обижа́ть.** —**оби́деться,** *refl., pfv. of* **обижа́ться.**

оби́дно *adj., used predicatively* **1,** (*with dat.*) offended; annoyed: Ему́ бы́ло оби́дно, что..., he was offended/annoyed that... **2,** unfortunate; distressing: Оби́дно э́то слы́шать, I am sorry to hear it. Оби́дно, что вы опозда́ли, it's a pity that you were late.

оби́дный *adj.* **1,** insulting; offensive. **2,** *colloq.* annoying.

оби́дчивый *adj.* touchy; sensitive. —**оби́дчивость,** *n.f.* touchiness.

оби́дчик *n., colloq.* person who has offended someone.

обижа́ть *v.impfv.* [*pfv.* **оби́деть**] **1,** to offend; hurt the feelings of. **2,** *colloq.* to defraud; victimize. **3,** *colloq.* to be stingy toward: Приро́да не оби́дела его́ тала́нтом, nature endowed him with great talent. —**обижа́ться,** *refl.* (*with* **на** + *acc.*) to take offense (at); be offended (by); be hurt (by); resent.

оби́женный *adj.* **1,** offended: Вы оби́жены на меня́?, are you offended/angry/annoyed with me? **2,** (*of a look*) resentful.

оби́лие *n.* abundance; plenty.

оби́льный *adj.* abundant; plentiful; bountiful. —**оби́льно,** *adv.* abundantly.

обиня́к (*gen.* **-няка́**) *n., in* говори́ть обиняка́ми, to equivocate; beat around the bush; говори́ть без обиняко́в, to speak straight to the point.

обира́ть *v.impfv.* [*pfv.* **обобра́ть**] *colloq.* **1,** to gather; pick. **2,** to rob; fleece.

обита́емый *adj.* inhabited.

обита́тель *n.m.* inhabitant.

обита́ть *v.impfv.* (*with* **в** + *prepl.*) to dwell (in); inhabit.

оби́тель *n.f., obs.* monastery.

оби́тый *adj.* upholstered.

оби́ть [*infl.* **обобью́, обобьёшь**] *v., pfv. of* **обива́ть.**

обихо́д *n.* **1,** everyday life; day-to-day existence. **2,** use: входи́ть в обихо́д, to come into use. —**предме́ты дома́шнего обихо́да,** (everyday) household items.

обихо́дный *adj.* everyday.

обка́пывать *v.impfv., colloq.* **1,** [*pfv.* **обка́пать**] to stain (*by spilling drops of something on*). **2,** [*pfv.* **обкопа́ть**] to dig around.

обка́рмливать *v.impfv.* [*pfv.* **обкорми́ть**] to give (someone) too much to eat; stuff.

обка́тывать *v.impfv.* [*pfv.* **обката́ть**] **1,** to make round or smooth by rolling. **2,** *colloq.* to roll (in flour, bread crumbs, etc.). **3,** to wear smooth. **4,** to break in (a car, motor, etc.).

обкла́дывать *v.impfv.* [*pfv.* **обложи́ть**] **1,** to surround (*by laying objects around*). **2,** to face (*with stone, marble, etc.*). **3,** (*of clouds*) to cover. *Also impers.:* не́бо обложи́ло ту́чами, the sky is overcast. **4,** to surround; lay siege to. **5,** *impers.* to become coated: У меня́ обложи́ло язы́к, my tongue is coated. —**обкла́дываться,** *refl.* (*with instr.*) to surround oneself (with).

обко́м *n.* regional committee (*contr. of* **областно́й комите́т**).

обкопа́ть *v., pfv. of* **обка́пывать** (*in sense #2*).

обкорми́ть [*infl.* **-кормлю́, -ко́рмишь**] *v., pfv. of* **обка́рмливать.**

обкорна́ть *v.pfv., colloq.* to trim.

обкра́дывать *v.impfv.* [*pfv.* **обокра́сть**] to rob.

обку́ривать *v.impfv.* [*pfv.* **обкури́ть**] **1,** to break in (a pipe). **2,** (*usu. passive*) *colloq.* to stain by exposure to smoke.

обкури́ть [*infl.* **-курю́, -ку́ришь**] *v., pfv. of* **обку́ривать.**

обку́сывать *v.impfv.* [*pfv.* **обкуса́ть**] to bite around the edges of; nibble.

обла́ва *n.* **1,** hunt (*involving surrounding, driving out, and shooting animals*). **2,** (police) raid; roundup; dragnet.

облага́ть *v.impfv.* [*pfv.* **обложи́ть**] to assess; tax. Облага́ть кого́-нибудь нало́гом, to impose a tax on.

облагора́живать *v.impfv.* [*pfv.* **облагоро́дить**] **1,** to ennoble. **2,** to refine.

облада́ние *n.* possession. —**облада́тель,** *n.m.* possessor.

облада́ть *v.impfv.* (*with instr.*) to possess; have.

обла́зить *v.pfv.* [*infl.* **-ла́жу, -ла́зишь**] *colloq.* (*usu. with* **все**) **1,** to climb all over; climb all of. **2,** to travel all over.

о́блако [*pl.* облака́, облако́в] *n.* cloud.

обла́мывать *v.impfv.* [*pfv.* **обломо́ть** *or* **обломи́ть**] to break off.

обла́пить *v.pfv.* [*infl.* **-плю, -пишь**] *colloq.* (*of an animal*) to grab in its paws.

облапо́шивать *v.impfv.* [*pfv.* **облапо́шить**] *colloq.* to swindle; dupe.

обласка́ть *v.pfv.* to show kindness toward.

областно́й *adj.* of an oblast; regional; provincial.

о́бласть [*pl.* **о́бласти, -сте́й, -стя́м**] *n.f.* **1,** oblast: моско́вская о́бласть, Moscow oblast. **2,** area; region. **3,** *fig.* field; sphere; domain.

обла́тка (*gen. pl.* **-ток**) *n.* **1,** capsule; tablet. **2,** *relig.* wafer.

облача́ть *v.impfv.* [*pfv.* **облачи́ть**] **1,** to robe; clothe (a clergyman). **2,** *colloq.* to dress up; deck out.

облаче́ние *n.* **1,** *relig.* vestment(s). **2,** clothes.

облачи́ть *v., pfv. of* **облача́ть.**

о́блачко [*pl.* облачка́, -ко́в] *n., dim. of* **о́блако.**

о́блачность *n.f.* cloudiness.

о́блачный *adj.* **1,** cloud (*attrib.*): о́блачный покро́в, cloud cover. **2,** cloudy.

обла́ять *v.pfv.* [*infl.* **обла́ю, обла́ешь**] *colloq.* to bark furiously at.

облега́ть *v.impfv.* [*pfv.* **обле́чь**] **1,** to envelop; shroud. **2,** [*impfv. only*] (*of clothes*) to fit snugly; cling to.

облегча́ть *v.impfv.* [*pfv.* **облегчи́ть**] **1,** to lighten. **2,** to ease; facilitate. **3,** to ease; relieve; alleviate. —облегча́ться, *refl.* **1,** to lighten; become lighter. **2,** to become easier. **3,** to be relieved.

облегче́ние *n.* **1,** lightening. **2,** facilitating. **3,** (feeling of) relief.

облегчённый *adj.* **1,** made lighter. **2,** of relief: облегчённый вздох, sigh of relief. —облегчённо, *adv.* with (a sense of) relief.

облегчи́ть *v., pfv. of* облегча́ть. —облегчи́ться, *refl., pfv. of* облегча́ться.

обледене́лый *adj.* ice-covered; ice-coated.

обледене́ние *n.* icing up; icing over.

обледене́ть *v.pfv.* to ice up; be coated with ice.

облеза́ть *v.impfv.* [*pfv.* **обле́зть**] *colloq.* **1,** to lose one's fur; become mangy. **2,** (*of something painted*) to peel. **3,** (*of paint, varnish, etc.*) to peel off.

обле́злый *adj., colloq.* **1,** (*of an animal*) mangy. **2,** with the paint having worn off; shabby.

обле́зть [*infl. like* **лезть**] *v., pfv. of* облеза́ть.

облека́ть *v.impfv.* [*pfv.* **обле́чь**] **1,** *obs.* to clothe. **2,** to envelop; shroud. **3,** to vest (with power, authority, etc.). **4,** (*with* **в** + *acc.*) to express; couch (in certain language).

облени́ваться *v.r.impfv.* [*pfv.* **облени́ться**] to become lazy.

облени́ться [*infl.* **-еню́сь, -е́нишься**] *v.r., pfv. of* облени́ваться.

облепи́ть [*infl.* **-леплю́, -ле́пишь**] *v., pfv. of* облепля́ть.

облепля́ть *v.impfv.* [*pfv.* **облепи́ть**] **1,** to stick to; cling to. **2,** to cover; plaster. **3,** *fig., colloq.* to swarm around.

облета́ть[1] *v.impfv.* [*pfv.* **облете́ть**] **1,** (*with acc. or* **вокру́г**) to fly around. **2,** to fly all over. **3,** *fig.* to spread all over: весть облете́ла весь го́род, the news spread all over town. **4,** (*of leaves*) to fall.

облета́ть[2] *v.pfv.* **1,** to fly all over. **2,** to test-fly.

облете́ть [*infl.* **-чу́, -ти́шь**] *v., pfv. of* облета́ть[1].

обле́чь *v.pfv.* **1,** [*infl. like* **лечь**] *pfv. of* облега́ть. **2,** [*infl. like* **течь**] *pfv. of* облека́ть.

облива́ние *n.* **1,** dousing (*with water*). **2,** douche.

облива́ть *v.impfv.* [*pfv.* **обли́ть**] **1,** to pour or spill water over; douse. **2,** (*usu. passive*) to soak; drench; bathe (with tears, sweat, etc.). **3,** to soil; stain (*by spilling something on*): облива́ть ска́терть су́пом, to spill soup all over the tablecloth. —облива́ть (кого́-нибудь) гря́зью *or* помо́ями, to vilify; drag through the mud.

облива́ться *v.r.impfv.* [*pfv.* **обли́ться**] (*with instr.*) **1,** to douse oneself (with); pour over oneself. **2,** to spill over oneself. **3,** to be covered (with blood); be drowning (in tears); be drenched (with perspiration). **4,** *fig.* to be filled (with light, an emotion, etc.). —у меня́ се́рдце кро́вью облива́ется, I am sick at heart.

облига́ция *n., finance* bond.

облиза́ть [*infl.* **-лижу́, -ли́жешь**] *v., pfv. of* обли́зывать. —облиза́ться, *refl., pfv. of* обли́зываться.

обли́зывать *v.impfv.* [*pfv.* **облиза́ть**] **1,** to lick. **2,** *in* па́льчики обли́жешь, you'll love it! —обли́зываться, *refl.* **1,** to lick oneself. **2,** [*impfv. only*] to lick one's lips; *fig.* lick one's chops.

о́блик *n.* **1,** look; appearance. **2,** *fig.* character; make-up.

об線я́ть *v.pfv., colloq.* to fade.

обли́ть [*infl.* **оболью́, обольёшь;** *past* **о́блил** *or* **обли́л, облила́, о́блило** *or* **обли́ло, о́блили** *or* **обли́ли**] *v., pfv. of* облива́ть. —обли́ться, *refl.* [*past* **обли́лся, облила́сь, облило́сь** *or* **обли́лось, обли́лись** *or* **обли́лись**] *pfv. of* облива́ться.

облицева́ть [*infl.* **-цу́ю, -цу́ешь**] *v., pfv. of* облицо́вывать.

облицо́вка *n.* facing; revetment.

облицо́вывать *v.impfv.* [*pfv.* **облицева́ть**] to face (*with stone, marble, etc.*).

облича́ть *v.impfv.* [*pfv.* **обличи́ть**] **1,** to expose (wrongs, misdeeds, a guilty party, etc.). **2,** [*impfv. only*] to reveal; indicate: Всё облича́ет в нём вое́нного, everything points to his being a military man.

обличе́ние *n.* **1,** accusation. **2,** exposure.

обличи́тель *n.m.* exposer. —обличи́тельный, *adj.* serving to expose something.

обличи́ть *v., pfv. of* облича́ть.

обли́чье *n., colloq.* look; appearance.

облобыза́ть *v.pfv., obs.* to kiss.

обложе́ние *n.* **1,** levying: обложе́ние нало́гами, levying of taxes. **2,** *obs.* siege.

обложи́ть [*infl.* **-ложу́, -ло́жишь**] *v., pfv. of* обкла́дывать *and* облага́ть. —обложи́ться, *refl., pfv. of* обкла́дываться.

обло́жка [*gen. pl.* **-жек**] *n.* **1,** cover (*of a book or magazine*). В бума́жной обло́жке, in paperback. **2,** folder (*for papers*); case (*for documents*).

обложно́й *adj., in* обложно́й дождь, *colloq.* steady downpour.

облока́чиваться *v.r.impfv.* [*pfv.* **облокоти́ться**] (*with* **на** *or* **о** + *acc.*) to lean one's elbows (on *or* against).

облокоти́ться [*infl.* **-кочу́сь, -ко́тишься** *or* **-коти́шься**] *v.r., pfv. of* облока́чиваться.

облома́ть *v., pfv. of* обла́мывать.

обломи́ть [*infl.* **-ломлю́, -ло́мишь**] *v., pfv. of* обла́мывать.

обло́мовщина *n.* lethargy; apathy; sluggishness (*after Oblomov, central character of the novel of the same name by Goncharov*).

обло́мок [*gen.* **-мка**] *n.* **1,** fragment. **2,** *pl.* wreckage; rubble; debris.

облупи́ть [*infl.* **-луплю́, -лу́пишь**] *v., pfv. of* лупи́ть (*in sense #1*) *and* облу́пливать. —облупи́ться, *refl., pfv. of* лупи́ться *and* облу́пливаться.

облу́пливать *v.impfv.* [*pfv.* **облупи́ть**] *colloq.* **1,** to peel; shell. **2,** *fig.* to swindle; fleece. —облу́пливаться, *refl.* **1,** (*of paint, plaster, etc.*) to come off; peel off. **2,** (*of a wall or part of one's body*) to peel.

облуча́ть *v.impfv.* [*pfv.* **облучи́ть**] to treat with rays; expose to rays.

облуче́ние *n.* irradiation; exposure to radiation; radiation treatment.

облучи́ть *v., pfv. of* **облуча́ть.**

облучо́к [*gen.* **-чка́**] *n.* coachman's seat.

облущи́ть *v., pfv. of* **лущи́ть.**

облысе́лый *adj.* bald.

облысе́ть *v., pfv. of* **лысе́ть.**

облюбова́ть *v.pfv.* [*infl.* **-бу́ю, -бу́ешь**] to choose; select; settle on.

обма́зать [*infl.* **-ма́жу, -ма́жешь**] *v., pfv. of* **обма́зывать.**

обма́зывать *v.impfv.* [*pfv.* **обма́зать**] **1,** to coat (with). **2,** to smear (with).

обма́кивать *v.impfv.* [*pfv.* **обмакну́ть**] to dip.

обма́н *n.* **1,** deception; deceit; fraud. **2,** illusion; delusion. —**обма́н зре́ния, опти́ческий обма́н,** optical illusion.

обма́нка *n.,* *in* **рогова́я обма́нка,** hornblende; **смоляна́я обма́нка,** pitchblende.

обма́нный *adj.* fraudulent; dishonest; deceitful; underhanded.

обману́ть [*infl.* **обману́, обма́нешь**] *v., pfv. of* **обма́нывать.** —**обману́ться,** *refl., pfv. of* **обма́нываться.**

обма́нчивый *adj.* **1,** deceptive. **2,** illusory.

обма́нщик *n.* one who deceives; faker; cheat.

обма́нывать *v.impfv.* [*pfv.* **обману́ть**] **1,** to deceive. **2,** to trick; cheat. **3,** to disappoint; let down. **4,** to betray (someone's trust); fail to live up to (hopes, expectations, etc.). **5,** to be unfaithful to (one's spouse). **6,** to seduce. **7,** *in* **обма́нывать себя́,** to delude oneself. —**обма́нываться,** *refl.* **1,** to be deceived. **2,** to be mistaken.

обма́тывать *v.impfv.* [*pfv.* **обмота́ть**] to wind around; wrap around. —**обма́тываться,** *refl.* **1,** (*with instr.*) to wrap oneself in. **2,** (*with* **вокру́г**) to wrap around; be wrapped around.

обма́хивать *v.impfv.* [*pfv.* **обмахну́ть**] **1,** to fan. **2,** to brush off. **3,** to brush away. —**обма́хиваться,** *refl.* to fan oneself.

обма́чивать *v.impfv.* [*pfv.* **обмочи́ть**] to wet; moisten.

обмеле́ть *v., pfv. of* **меле́ть.**

обме́н *n.* exchange. —**обме́н веще́ств,** metabolism.

обме́нивать *v.impfv.* [*pfv.* **обменя́ть**] to exchange; trade; swap (*one thing for another*). —**обме́ниваться,** *refl.* (*with instr.*) **1,** to exchange; trade (*similar things*): обме́ниваться места́ми, to exchange/trade places. Обме́ниваться впечатле́ниями, to compare notes. **2,** to take (something belonging to someone else) by mistake: обменя́ться зо́нтиками, to take someone's umbrella by mistake.

обмени́ть *v.pfv.* [*infl.* **-меню́, -ме́нишь**] = **обменя́ть.**

обме́нный *adj.* exchange (*attrib.*).

обменя́ть *v., pfv. of* **обме́нивать.** —**обменя́ться,** *refl., pfv. of* **обме́ниваться.**

обме́р *n.* **1,** measurement. **2,** *colloq.* dishonesty in measuring.

обмере́ть [*infl.* **обомру́, обомрёшь;** *past* **о́бмер, обмерла́, о́бмерло, о́бмерли**] *v., pfv. of* **обмира́ть.**

обме́ривать *v.impfv.* [*pfv.* **обме́рить**] **1,** to measure. **2,** *colloq.* to cheat in measuring.

обмести́ [*infl. like* **мести́**] *v., pfv. of* **обмета́ть.**

обмета́ть *v.impfv.* [*pfv.* **обмести́**] to sweep off; dust off; brush off.

обмина́ть *v.impfv.* [*pfv.* **обмя́ть**] to press down; trample down.

обмира́ть *v.impfv.* [*pfv.* **обмере́ть**] *colloq.* **1,** to faint. **2,** to go numb (*from fear, shock, etc.*). **3,** (*of one's heart*) to skip a beat.

обмозгова́ть [*infl.* **-гу́ю, -гу́ешь**] *v., pfv. of* **обмозго́вывать.**

обмозго́вывать *v.impfv.* [*pfv.* **обмозгова́ть**] *colloq.* to think over; mull over.

обмола́чивать *v.impfv.* [*pfv.* **обмолоти́ть**] to thresh.

обмо́лвиться *v.r.pfv.* [*infl.* **-влюсь, -вишься**] *colloq.* **1,** to make a slip of the tongue. **2,** (*with instr.*) to utter. **3,** (*with* **о** *or a dependent clause*) to mention; (*used negatively*) not utter a word (about).

обмо́лвка [*gen. pl.* **-вок**] *n.* slip of the tongue.

обмолоти́ть [*infl.* **-лочу́, -ло́тишь**] *v., pfv. of* **обмола́чивать.**

обмора́живать *v.impfv.* [*pfv.* **обморо́зить**] to get (a part of one's body) frostbitten: Я обморо́зил себе́ ру́ки, my hands are frostbitten. —**обмора́живаться,** *refl.* to suffer frostbite.

обморо́жение *also,* **обмороже́ние** *n.* frostbite.

обморо́женный *adj.* frostbitten.

обморо́зить [*infl.* **-жу, -зишь**] *v., pfv. of* **обмора́живать.** —**обморо́зиться,** *refl., pfv. of* **обмора́живаться.**

о́бморок *n.* fainting spell. —**упа́сть в о́бморок,** to faint.

обморо́чить *v., pfv. of* **моро́чить.**

о́бморочный *adj., in* о́бморочное состоя́ние, unconscious state.

обмота́ть *v., pfv. of* **обма́тывать.** —**обмота́ться,** *refl., pfv. of* **обма́тываться.**

обмо́тки [*gen.* **-ток**] *n.pl.* puttees.

обмочи́ть [*infl.* **-мочу́, -мо́чишь**] *v., pfv. of* **обма́чивать.**

обмундирова́ние *n.* **1,** fitting out (*with uniforms*). **2,** uniform.

обмундирова́ть *v.pfv.* [*infl.* **-ру́ю, -ру́ешь**] to fit out (*with uniforms*).

обмундиро́вка *n., colloq.* = **обмундирова́ние.**

обмыва́ть *v.impfv.* [*pfv.* **обмы́ть**] to wash; bathe. —**обмыва́ться,** *refl.* to bathe (oneself).

обмы́лок [*gen.* **-лка**] *n., colloq.* remaining piece of a bar of soap.

обмы́ть [*infl.* **обмо́ю, обмо́ешь**] *v., pfv. of* **обмыва́ть.** —**обмы́ться,** *refl., pfv. of* **обмыва́ться.**

обмяка́ть *v.impfv.* [*pfv.* **обмя́кнуть**] *colloq.* **1,** to become soft. **2,** *fig.* to become flabby.

обмя́кнуть [*past* **обмя́к, обмя́кла**] *v., pfv. of* **обмяка́ть.**

обмя́ть [*infl.* **обомну́, обомнёшь**] *v., pfv. of* **обмина́ть.**

обнагле́ть *v., pfv. of* **нагле́ть.**

обнадёживать *v.impfv.* [*pfv.* **обнадёжить**] to reassure; give hope to; raise the hopes of.

обнажа́ть *v.impfv.* [*pfv.* **обнажи́ть**] **1,** to bare; expose; uncover. **2,** to denude. **3,** to draw; unsheathe (a sword). **4,** *fig.* to reveal; lay bare. **5,** *mil.* to expose. —**обнажа́ться,** *refl.* **1,** to take off all one's clothes. **2,** to be exposed. **3,** to be denuded.

обнажённый *adj.* bare; naked; nude.

обнажи́ть *v., pfv. of* **обнажа́ть.** —**обнажи́ться,** *refl., pfv. of* **обнажа́ться.**

обнаро́дование *n.* promulgation; publication.

обнаро́довать *v.pfv.* [*infl.* -дую, -дуешь] to promulgate; publish; release; make public.

обнару́жение *also,* **обнаруже́ние** *n.* **1,** discovery; detection. **2,** revelation; disclosure.

обнару́живать *v.impfv.* [*pfv.* **обнару́жить**] **1,** to reveal; display; show. **2,** to discover; detect. —**обнару́живаться,** *refl.* **1,** to be found; turn up; come to light. **2,** to be revealed. **3,** to reveal itself.

обна́шивать *v.impfv.* [*pfv.* **обноси́ть**] *colloq.* **1,** to wear in; break in (new clothes). **2,** to wear out (clothes). —**обна́шиваться,** *refl., colloq.* **1,** (*of new clothes*) to become broken in. **2,** (*of clothes*) to wear out.

обнести́ [*infl. like* **нести́**] *v., pfv. of* **обноси́ть**[1].

обнима́ть *v.impfv.* [*pfv.* **обня́ть**] **1,** to embrace; hug. **2,** *fig.* to engulf; envelop. **3,** *fig.* to take in; embrace. —**обнима́ться,** *refl.* (*of two people*) to embrace; hug. Он обня́лся с ней, they embraced.

обни́мка *n., colloq., in* **в обни́мку,** in each other's arms.

обнища́лый *adj.* impoverished; destitute.

обнища́ние *n.* impoverishment.

обнища́ть *v., pfv. of* **нища́ть.**

обно́ва *n., colloq.* = **обно́вка.**

обнови́ть [*infl.* -влю́, -ви́шь] *v., pfv. of* **обновля́ть.** —**обнови́ться,** *refl., pfv. of* **обновля́ться.**

обно́вка [*gen. pl.* -вок] *n., colloq.* article of clothing just bought; new acquisition; new outfit.

обновле́ние *n.* **1,** renovation. **2,** renewal. **3,** replenishment.

обновля́ть *v.impfv.* [*pfv.* **обнови́ть**] **1,** to renovate; refurbish; revamp. **2,** to renew; revitalize. **3,** to replenish. **4,** *colloq.* to wear for the first time. —**обновля́ться,** *refl.* **1,** to revive. **2,** to be revitalized. **3,** to be replenished.

обноси́ть[1] *v.impfv.* [*pfv.* **обнести́**; *pres.* -ношу́, -но́сишь] **1,** to carry around. **2,** to enclose; surround (with a fence, wall, etc.). **3,** to serve (everyone): обноси́ть госте́й шампа́нским, to serve champagne to all the guests. **4,** to pass by (*while serving*); not serve.

обноси́ть[2] [*infl.* -ношу́, -но́сишь] *v., pfv. of* **обна́шивать.** —**обноси́ться,** *refl.* **1,** *pfv. of* **обна́шиваться. 2,** to wear out all one's clothes.

обно́ски [*gen.* -ков] *n.pl., colloq.* old clothes.

обня́ть [*infl.* **обниму́, обни́мешь**; *past* о́бнял, обняла́, о́бняло, о́бняли] *v., pfv. of* **обнима́ть.** —**обня́ться,** *refl.* [*past* обня́лся *or* обнялся́, обня́лась, обня́лось *or* обняло́сь, обняли́сь *or* обня́лись] *pfv. of* **обнима́ться.**

обо *prep.* = **о** (*used before* мне, всем, всей *and* всех).

обобра́ть [*infl.* оберу́, обере́шь; *past fem.* обобрала́] *v., pfv. of* **обира́ть.**

обобща́ть *v.impfv.* [*pfv.* **обобщи́ть**] **1,** *v.t.* to summarize; synthesize. **2,** *v.i.* to generalize.

обобще́ние *n.* **1,** summarizing; synthesizing. **2,** generalization.

обобществи́ть [*infl.* -влю́, -ви́шь] *v., pfv. of* **обобществля́ть.**

обобществле́ние *n.* socialization; collectivization.

обобществля́ть *v.impfv.* [*pfv.* **обобществи́ть**] to socialize; collectivize.

обобщи́ть *v., pfv. of* **обобща́ть.**

обогаща́ть *v.impfv.* [*pfv.* **обогати́ть**] to enrich. —**обогаща́ться,** *refl.* **1,** to get rich; enrich oneself. **2,** *fig.* to be enriched.

обогаще́ние *n.* enrichment.

обогна́ть [*infl.* обгоню́, обго́нишь; *past fem.* обогнала́] *v., pfv. of* **обгоня́ть.**

обогну́ть *v., pfv. of* **огиба́ть.**

обоготворе́ние *n.* deification.

обоготворя́ть *v.impfv.* [*pfv.* **обоготвори́ть**] to deify.

обогрева́ние *n.* heating.

обогрева́тель *n.m.* **1,** heater. **2,** defroster.

обогрева́ть *v.impfv.* [*pfv.* **обогре́ть**] to warm; heat. —**обогрева́ться,** *refl.* to warm up; get warm.

о́бод [*pl.* обо́дья, обо́дьев] *n.* rim (*of a wheel*).

ободо́к [*gen.* -дка́] *n.* **1,** thin rim; ring. **2,** band.

ободо́чный *adj., in* ободо́чная кишка́, *anat.* colon.

ободра́нец [*gen.* -нца] *n., colloq.* ragamuffin.

обо́дранный *adj., colloq.* **1,** ragged; torn; tattered. **2,** (*of a person*) in rags. **3,** (*of one's hands, face, etc.*) cut up; scratched up. **4,** dilapidated; run-down.

ободра́ть [*infl.* обдеру́, обдерёшь; *past fem.* ободрала́] *v., pfv. of* **обдира́ть.**

ободре́ние *n.* encouragement; reassurance.

ободри́тельный *adj.* encouraging; reassuring.

ободря́ть *v.impfv.* [*pfv.* **ободри́ть**] to cheer up; hearten; encourage; reassure. —**ободря́ться,** *refl.* to cheer up; take heart.

обо́его *numeral, obs.* of both. —ли́ца обо́его по́ла, people of both sexes.

обожа́ние *n.* adoration.

обожа́тель *n.m., colloq.* worshiper; admirer.

обожа́ть *v.impfv.* to adore; worship.

обожда́ть *v.pfv.* [*infl. like* **ждать**] *colloq.* to wait; wait a while.

обожестви́ть [*infl.* -влю́, -ви́шь] *v., pfv. of* **обожествля́ть.**

обожествле́ние *n.* deification.

обожествля́ть *v.impfv.* [*pfv.* **обожестви́ть**] to deify.

обо́з *n.* line; string; column (*of wagons, sleds, etc.*). —в обо́зе, in the rear; at the tail end.

обозва́ть [*infl.* обзову́, обзовёшь; *past fem.* обозвала́] *v., pfv. of* **обзыва́ть.**

обозли́ть *v., pfv. of* **злить.** —**обозли́ться,** *refl., pfv. of* **зли́ться.**

обозна́ться *v.r.pfv., colloq.* to mistake someone for someone else.

обознача́ть *v.impfv.* [*pfv.* **обозна́чить**] **1,** to mark; indicate; designate. **2,** [*impfv. only*] to mean; signify; denote. —**обознача́ться,** *refl.* **1,** to appear; become visible. **2,** to be felt; be sensed. **3,** to become clear.

обозначе́ние *n.* **1,** indication. **2,** symbol; designation.

обозна́чить *v.pfv.* **1,** *pfv. of* **обознача́ть. 2,** to highlight; accentuate (*visually*). —**обозна́читься,** *refl., pfv. of* **обознача́ться.**

обозрева́тель *n.m.* commentator; columnist.

обозрева́ть *v.impfv.* [*pfv.* **обозре́ть**] **1**, to look around; survey; view. **2**, *fig.* to review; survey.

обозре́ние *n.* **1**, viewing. **2**, review; survey. **3**, review (*publication*). **4**, *theat.* revue.

обозре́ть [*infl.* -**зрю́**, -**зри́шь**] *v.*, *pfv. of* **обозрева́ть**.

обозри́мый *adj.* visible. —**в обозри́мом бу́дущем**, in the foreseeable future.

обо́и [*gen.* **обо́ев**] *n.pl.* wallpaper.

обо́йма *n.* cartridge clip.

обо́йный *adj.* wallpaper (*attrib.*).

обойти́ [*infl.* **обойду́**, **обойдёшь**; *past* **обошёл**, **обошла́**, **обошло́**, **обошли́**] *v.*, *pfv. of* **обходи́ть**. —**обойти́сь**, *refl.*, *pfv. of* **обходи́ться**.

обо́йщик *n.* **1**, upholsterer. **2**, paperhanger.

о́бок *adv.*, *colloq.* alongside. —*prep.*, *with gen.*, *colloq.* alongside.

обокра́сть [*infl.* **обкраду́**, **обкрадёшь**; *past* **обокра́л**, **обокра́ла**] *v.*, *pfv. of* **обкра́дывать**.

оболва́нить *v.pfv.*, *colloq.* to dupe; make a fool of.

оболга́ть *v.pfv.* [*infl. like* **лгать**] to slander.

оболо́чка [*gen. pl.* -**чек**] *n.* **1**, shell (*of a fruit or seed*). **2**, *anat.* membrane: сли́зистая оболо́чка, mucous membrane. **3**, *fig.* shell: вне́шняя оболо́чка, one's outer shell. —**ра́дужная оболо́чка**, iris. —**рогова́я оболо́чка**, cornea. —**се́тчатая оболо́чка**, retina.

обо́лтус *n.*, *colloq.* blockhead; dunce; oaf.

обольсти́тель *n.m.* seducer. —**обольсти́тельный**, *adj.* seductive.

обольсти́ть [*infl.* -**льщу́**, -**льсти́шь**] *v.*, *pfv. of* **обольща́ть**. —**обольсти́ться**, *refl.*, *pfv. of* **обольща́ться**.

обольща́ть *v.impfv.* [*pfv.* **обольсти́ть**] **1**, to entice; beguile. **2**, to seduce. —**обольща́ться**, *refl.* (*with instr.*) **1**, [*impfv. only*] to be deluded (by). **2**, to let (success, fame, etc.) go to one's head.

обольще́ние *n.* **1**, seduction. **2**, lure; temptation. **3**, delusion.

обомле́ть *v.pfv.*, *colloq.* to be stunned; freeze (*in shock, surprise, etc.*).

обомше́лый *adj.* moss-grown.

обоня́ние *n.* sense of smell. —**обоня́тельный**, *adj.* olfactory.

обоня́ть *v.impfv.* to smell (something).

обора́чивать *v.impfv.* [*pfv.* **оберну́ть**] **1**, to turn: оберну́ть лицо́ к, to turn one's face toward. **2**, to turn over; invert. —**обора́чиваться**, *refl.* **1**, to turn around; look around. **2**, *fig.* to turn out; work out. **3**, *fig.* (*with instr.*) to bring on; result in; cause. **4**, (*with instr. or* **в** + *acc.*) to turn into; become. **5**, *colloq.* to return; get back; be back. **6**, *colloq.* to manage; get by.

оборва́нец [*gen.* -**нца**] *n.*, *colloq.* vagabond; hobo.

обо́рванный *adj.* ragged; torn; tattered.

оборва́ть [*infl.* -**рву́**, -**рвёшь**; *past fem.* **оборвала́**] *v.*, *pfv. of* **обрыва́ть**. —**оборва́ться**, *refl.* [*past tense stress as in* **рва́ться**] *pfv. of* **обрыва́ться**.

обо́рвыш *n.*, *colloq.* ragamuffin.

обо́рка [*gen. pl.* -**рок**] *n.* frill; flounce; ruffle.

оборо́на *n.* **1**, defense. **2**, defensive: быть в оборо́не, to be on the defensive. **3**, defenses.

оборони́тельный *adj.* defensive.

оборони́ть *v.*, *pfv. of* **обороня́ть**. —**оборони́ться**, *refl.*, *pfv. of* **обороня́ться**.

оборо́нный *adj.* defense (*attrib.*).

обороня́ть *v.impfv.* [*pfv.* **оборони́ть**] to defend. —**обороня́ться**, *refl.* to defend oneself.

оборо́т *n.* **1**, revolution: сто оборо́тов в мину́ту, 100 r.p.m. **2**, *fig.* turn: оборо́т ре́чи, turn of speech. Приня́ть дурно́й оборо́т, to take a bad turn; take a turn for the worse. **3**, use; circulation: пуска́ть в оборо́т, to put into circulation. **4**, back; reverse side: Смотри́ на оборо́те, please turn over. **5**, *finance* turnover. —**брать в оборо́т**, **1**, to take in hand. **2**, to take to task.

о́боротень [*gen.* -**тня**] *n.m.* werewolf.

оборо́тливый *adj.*, *colloq.* clever; resourceful. *Also,* **оборо́тистый**.

оборо́тный *adj.* **1**, *finance* circulating; negotiable. Оборо́тный капита́л, working capital. **2**, (*of a side*) back; reverse. —**оборо́тная сторона́ меда́ли**, the other side of the coin.

обору́дование *n.* **1**, equipping. **2**, equipment.

обору́довать *v.impfv. & pfv.* [*pres.* -**дую**, -**дуешь**] to equip.

обоснова́ние *n.* **1**, substantiation. **2**, basis; grounds.

обосно́ванный *adj.* sound; well-founded. —**обосно́ванность**, *n.f.* validity.

обоснова́ть [*infl.* -**ную́**, -**нуёшь**] *v.*, *pfv. of* **обосно́вывать**. —**обоснова́ться**, *refl.*, *pfv. of* **обосно́вываться**.

обосно́вывать *v.impfv.* [*pfv.* **обоснова́ть**] to substantiate. —**обосно́вываться**, *refl.* **1**, to be substantiated. **2**, *colloq.* to settle (*in a certain place*).

обосо́бить [*infl.* -**блю**, -**бишь**] *v.*, *pfv. of* **обособля́ть**. —**обосо́биться**, *refl.*, *pfv. of* **обособля́ться**.

обособле́ние *n.* isolation.

обосо́бленно *adv.* apart; in isolation.

обосо́бленность *n.f.* isolation.

обосо́бленный *adj.* **1**, isolated; separate. **2**, solitary.

обособля́ть *v.impfv.* [*pfv.* **обосо́бить**] to isolate. —**обособля́ться**, *refl.* to stand apart; remain aloof.

обостре́ние *n.* **1**, intensification. **2**, aggravation; exacerbation.

обострённый *adj.* **1**, (*of facial features*) sharp; pointed. **2**, (*of the senses*) unusually keen. **3**, (*of relations*) strained.

обостря́ть *v.impfv.* [*pfv.* **обостри́ть**] **1**, to intensify; increase; heighten. **2**, to aggravate; exacerbate; strain. —**обостря́ться**, *refl.* **1**, to become more acute. **2**, (*of the senses*) to become keener. **3**, (*of pain*) to become more intense. **4**, (*of relations*) to be strained; worsen.

обо́чина *n.* **1**, side of a road; shoulder. **2**, curb. **3**, *fig.* sidelines.

обою́дный *adj.* mutual; reciprocal. —**обою́дно**, *adv.* mutually. —**обою́дность**, *n.f.* mutuality; reciprocity.

обоюдоо́стрый *adj.* double-edged.

обраба́тывать *v.impfv.* [*pfv.* **обрабо́тать**] **1**, to work; treat; process. **2**, to till; cultivate. **3**, to put in final form; refine; polish. **4**, *colloq.* to work on; work over (someone); indoctrinate.

обрабо́тка *n.* **1**, working; treatment; processing. Обрабо́тка да́нных, data processing. **2**, tillage; cultivation. **3**, refinement. **4**, *colloq.* indoctrination. —**брать**

в обрабо́тку, to work on (someone); twist someone's arm.

обра́довать *v., pfv. of* **ра́довать.** —**обра́доваться,** *refl., pfv. of* **ра́доваться.**

о́браз *n.* **1,** appearance; form. В о́бразе (+ *gen.*), in the form of. **2,** image. **3,** (*with gen.*) way; mode; manner: о́браз жи́зни, way of life; о́браз мы́слей, way of thinking. О́браз де́йствий, course of action. О́браз правле́ния, form of government. **4,** *used in forming adverbial expressions:* до́лжным о́бразом, properly; коренны́м о́бразом, radically; суще́ственным о́бразом, substantially. **5,** [*pl.* **образа́**] icon. —**гла́вным о́бразом,** chiefly; mainly; for the most part. —**каки́м о́бразом?,** how?; in what way? —**каки́м-то о́бразом,** somehow. —**не́которым о́бразом,** of sorts; after a fashion. —**нико́им о́бразом,** under no circumstances. —**ра́вным о́бразом,** by the same token. —**таки́м о́бразом, 1,** this way; like this. **2,** thus.

образе́ц [*gen.* **зца́**] *n.* **1,** sample; specimen. Образе́ц обо́ев, wallpaper sample. **2,** model: образе́ц самоотве́рженности, a model of selflessness. **3,** pattern.

о́бразно *adv.* **1,** graphically. **2,** using imagery. —**о́бразно говоря́,** figuratively speaking.

о́бразность *n.f.* **1,** imagery. **2,** graphic nature.

о́бразный *adj.* **1,** using imagery. **2,** (*of language, words, etc.*) graphic; colorful.

образова́ние *n.* **1,** formation. **2,** education.

образо́ванный *adj.* educated; cultured; cultivated.

образова́тельный *adj.* educational.

образова́ть *v.pfv. & impfv.* [*pres.* **-зу́ю, -зу́ешь**] to form. —**образова́ться,** *refl.* **1,** to form; appear; come into being. **2,** *colloq.* to be all right: Всё образу́ется, everything will be all right.

образо́вывать *v.impfv.* = **образова́ть.** —**образо́вываться,** *refl.* = **образова́ться.**

образу́мить *v.pfv.* [*infl.* **-млю, -мишь**] to bring to one's senses; bring to reason. —**образу́миться,** *refl.* to come to one's senses.

образцо́вый *adj.* model; exemplary.

обра́зчик *n.* **1,** sample. **2,** *fig.* (*with gen.*) *colloq.* sample (of); example (of).

обра́мить [*infl.* **-млю, -мишь**] *v., pfv. of* **обрамля́ть.**

обрамле́ние *n.* **1,** framing. **2,** setting; background.

обрамля́ть *v.impfv.* [*pfv.* **обра́мить**] to frame.

обраста́ть *v.impfv.* [*pfv.* **обрасти́**] (*with instr.*) **1,** to become overgrown (with). **2,** *colloq.* to be covered (with a layer of). **3,** *colloq.* to be made larger by the addition of.

обрасти́ [*infl. like* **расти́**] *v., pfv. of* **обраста́ть.**

обрати́мость *n.f.* **1,** reversibility. **2,** convertibility.

обрати́мый *adj.* **1,** reversible. **2,** convertible.

обрати́ть [*infl.* **-щу́, -ти́шь**] *v., pfv. of* **обраща́ть.** —**обрати́ться,** *refl., pfv. of* **обраща́ться.**

обра́тно *adv.* **1,** back: получи́ть де́ньги обра́тно, to get one's money back. **2,** *colloq.* conversely; vice versa; the other way round. **3,** *in* обра́тно пропорциона́льный (+ *dat.*), inversely proportional (to). —**биле́т туда́ и обра́тно,** round-trip ticket. —**пое́здка туда́ и обра́тно,** round trip.

обра́тное *n., decl. as an adj.* the opposite; the reverse.

обра́тный *adj.* **1,** reverse: обра́тная сторона́, the reverse side; the back. **2,** opposite: в обра́тном направле́нии, in the opposite direction. **3,** return (*attrib.*): обра́тный а́дрес/биле́т/путь, return address/ticket/trip. С обра́тной по́чтой, by return mail. На обра́тном пути́, on the way back. **4,** *math.* inverse. —**обра́тная связь,** feedback.

обраща́ть *v.impfv.* [*pfv.* **обрати́ть**] **1,** to turn; direct: обраща́ть глаза́ на (+ *acc.*) to turn one's eyes toward. **2,** to turn; point (a weapon): обрати́ть ору́жие про́тив, to turn one's guns on; point a gun at. **3,** (*with* **в** + *acc.*) to turn (into); convert (to *or* into): обрати́ть что́-нибудь в шу́тку, to turn something into a joke; обрати́ть во́ду в пар, to convert water to steam. **4,** (*with* **в** + *acc.*) to convert (someone to another religion). —**обраща́ть внима́ние на** (+ *acc.*), to pay attention to. —**обрати́ть чьё-нибудь внима́ние на** (+ *acc.*), to draw *or* call someone's attention to. —**обрати́ть в бе́гство,** to put to flight. —**обрати́ть в прах,** to reduce to dust (*or* ashes). —**обрати́ть в свою́ по́льзу,** to turn to one's advantage.

обраща́ться *v.r.impfv.* [*pfv.* **обрати́ться**] **1,** (*with* **к**) to apply (to); appeal (to); address. **2,** (*with* **к**) to turn to; consult; go to; see. Обрати́ться к кому́-нибудь за по́мощью, to turn to someone for help. Обрати́ться к врачу́, to see a doctor. Обрати́ться к словарю́, to refer to a dictionary. **3,** (*with* **в** + *acc.*) to turn into; become. **4,** (*with* **в** + *acc.*) to convert (to another religion). **5,** [*impfv. only*] (*of blood, money, etc.*) to circulate. **6,** [*impfv. only*] (*with* **с** + *instr.*) to treat; handle (*in a certain way*). **7,** [*impfv. only*] (*with* **с** + *instr.*) to handle; operate. —**обраща́ться в бе́гство,** to take flight.

обраще́ние *n.* **1,** (*with* **к**) turning (toward). **2,** conversion. **3,** appeal. **4,** form of address: обраще́ние на «ты», familiar form of address. **5,** (*with* **с** + *instr.*) treatment (of); handling (of). **6,** circulation.

обре́з *n.* **1,** edge. **2,** sawed-off rifle. —**в обре́з,** *colloq.* barely enough: У меня́ вре́мени в обре́з, I barely have enough time; I am pressed for time.

обре́зание *n.* circumcision.

обреза́ние *n.* cutting; trimming.

обре́зать [*infl.* **-ре́жу, -ре́жешь**] *v., pfv. of* **обреза́ть** *and* **обре́зывать.** —**обре́заться,** *refl., pfv. of* **обреза́ться.**

обреза́ть *v.impfv.* [*pfv.* **обре́зать**] **1,** to trim; clip; prune. **2,** to cut (*accidentally*). **3,** *fig., colloq.* to cut short; interrupt. **4,** to circumcise. —**обреза́ться,** *refl., colloq.* to cut oneself.

обре́зок [*gen.* **-зка**] *n., usu. pl.* scraps (*of meat, paper, etc.*).

обре́зывать *v.impfv.* = **обреза́ть.**

обрека́ть *v.impfv.* [*pfv.* **обре́чь**] (*with* **на** + *acc.*) to doom (to).

обремени́тельный *adj.* burdensome; onerous.

обременя́ть *v.impfv.* [*pfv.* **обремени́ть**] to burden.

обрести́ [*infl.* **обрету́, обрете́шь;** *past* **обрёл, обрела́, обрело́, обрели́**] *v., pfv. of* **обрета́ть.**

обрета́ть *v.impfv.* [*pfv.* **обрести́**] **1,** to find. **2,** to gain.

обречённый *adj.* doomed. —**обречённость,** *n.f.* (impending) doom.

обре́чь [*infl.* -реку́, -речёшь, ...-реку́т; *past* -рёк, -рекла́, -рекло́, -рекли́] *v., pfv. of* обрека́ть.

обрисова́ть [*infl.* -су́ю, -су́ешь] *v., pfv. of* обрисо́вывать. —обрисова́ться, *refl., pfv. of* обрисо́вываться.

обрисо́вывать *v.impfv.* [*pfv.* обрисова́ть] 1, to draw a line around. 2, *fig.* to describe; portray. —обрисо́вываться, *refl.* 1, to appear (in outline). 2, *fig.* to become clear.

обри́ть *v.pfv.* [*infl.* обре́ю, обре́ешь] to shave; shave off. —обри́ться, *refl.* to shave one's head; shave off one's beard, mustache, etc.

обро́к *n., hist.* tax paid by a peasant to the state for the use of land allotted to him; obrok.

оброни́ть *v.pfv.* [*infl.* -роню́, -ро́нишь] *colloq.* 1, to drop. 2, to let (a remark) drop.

обруба́ть *v.impfv.* [*pfv.* обруби́ть] 1, to chop off; lop off. 2, to chop off the end of.

обруби́ть [*infl.* -рублю́, -ру́бишь] *v., pfv. of* обруба́ть.

обру́бок [*gen.* -бка] *n.* stump.

обруга́ть *v.pfv.* 1, to curse out; call names. 2, *colloq.* to criticize; attack; pan.

обрусе́ть *v.pfv.* to become Russified.

о́бруч [*pl.* о́бручи, -че́й, -ча́м] *n.* hoop. —обруча́льный *adj.* engagement (*attrib.*). —обруча́льное кольцо́, engagement ring; wedding ring.

обруча́ть *v.impfv.* [*pfv.* обручи́ть] to betroth; affiance. —обруча́ться, *refl.* (*with* с + *instr.*) to become engaged (to).

обруче́ние *n.* engagement; betrothal.

обручи́ть *v., pfv. of* обруча́ть. —обручи́ться, *refl., pfv. of* обруча́ться.

обру́шивать *v.impfv.* [*pfv.* обру́шить] 1, to bring down; send crashing to the ground. 2, (*with* на + *acc.*) to bring down (on); rain (blows, bombs, etc.); hurl (epithets) at. —обру́шиваться, *refl.* 1, to collapse; come tumbling down. 2, (*with* на + *acc.*) (*of the elements*) to pound; batter. 3, (*with* на + *acc.*) to befall. 4, (*with* на + *acc.*) to attack; pounce on. 5, (*with* на + *acc.*) to assail (*verbally*).

обры́в *n.* cliff; precipice.

обрыва́ть *v.impfv.* [*pfv.* оборва́ть] 1, to tear off; pluck. 2, to break; snap. 3, *fig.* to cut short; interrupt. —обрыва́ться, *refl.* 1, to break; snap. 2, to slip; fall. 3, *fig.* to stop suddenly; be suddenly cut short.

обры́вистый *adj.* steep; precipitous.

обры́вок [*gen.* -вка] *n.* 1, scrap. 2, *usu. pl.* snatches (*of a song, conversation, etc.*).

обры́вочный *adj.* (*of thoughts, phrases, etc.*) disjointed.

обры́згивать *v.impfv.* [*pfv.* обры́згать] 1, to spatter; splash. 2, to sprinkle. —обры́згиваться, *refl.* 1, to become spattered. 2, (*with instr.*) to sprinkle oneself (with).

обры́скать *v.pfv., colloq.* to roam: обры́скать свет, to roam the world.

обрю́зглый *adj.* flabby.

обрю́згнуть *v.pfv.* [*past* обрю́зг, обрю́згла] to become flabby.

обрю́згший *adj.* flabby.

обря́д *n.* rite; ceremony. —обря́довый, *adj.* ritual; ceremonial.

обсади́ть [*infl.* -сажу́, -са́дишь] *v., pfv. of* обса́живать.

обса́живать *v.impfv.* [*pfv.* обсади́ть] to plant around; plant along: обса́живать доро́гу дере́вьями, to plant trees along a road.

обсервато́рия *n.* observatory.

обсе́сть [*infl.* обся́ду, обся́дешь; *past* обсе́л, обсе́ла] *colloq.* to sit around.

обскака́ть [*infl.* обскачу́, обска́чешь] *v., pfv. of* обска́кивать.

обска́кивать *v.impfv.* [*pfv.* обскака́ть] 1, to gallop around. 2, (*of a horse*) to outrun. 3, *fig., colloq.* to overtake.

обскура́нт *n.* obscurant. —обскуранти́зм, *n.* obscurantism.

обсле́дование *n.* 1, inspection. 2, *med.* checkup. 3, survey.

обсле́довать *v.impfv. & pfv.* [*pres.* -дую, -дуешь] 1, to inspect. 2, to examine (a patient).

обслу́га *n., colloq.* service personnel.

обслу́живание *n.* 1, service. 2, servicing; maintenance. 3, *in* медици́нское обслу́живание, medical care.

обслу́живать *v.impfv.* [*pfv.* обслужи́ть] 1, to serve. 2, to wait on. 3, to service. 4, [*impfv. only*] to operate (a machine).

обслужи́ть [*infl.* -служу́, -слу́жишь] *v., pfv. of* обслу́живать.

обсо́хнуть [*past* обсо́х, обсо́хла] *v., pfv. of* обсыха́ть.

обста́вить [*infl.* -влю, -вишь] *v., pfv. of* обставля́ть.

обставля́ть *v.impfv.* [*pfv.* обста́вить] 1, to surround (with). 2, to furnish (a home, room, etc.). 3, *fig.* to arrange; organize.

обстано́вка [*gen. pl.* -вок] *n.* 1, situation: междунаро́дная обстано́вка, the international situation. 2, *fig.* atmosphere; environment; setting: в дру́жественной обстано́вке, in a friendly atmosphere; в здоро́вой обстано́вке, in a wholesome environment. 3, furniture. 4, *theat.* set. —переме́на обстано́вки, change of scenery (*fig.*).

обсти́рывать *v.impfv.* [*pfv.* обстира́ть] *colloq.* to do all the washing for.

обстоя́тельный *adj.* 1, thorough; detailed. 2, *colloq.* steady; reliable.

обстоя́тельство *n.* circumstance.

обстоя́ть *v.impfv.* [*pres.* -стои́т] to be; stand: Как обстои́т де́ло с (+ *instr.*), how do matters stand with...? Вот как обстои́т де́ло, this is the way things stand; this is the way it is.

обстра́ивать *v.impfv.* [*pfv.* обстро́ить] *colloq.* 1, to surround (with buildings); line (with buildings). 2, to build; build up. —обстра́иваться, *refl., colloq.* 1, to build a house for oneself. 2, to be built up.

обстре́л *n.* fire; firing; shelling: попа́сть под обстре́л, to come under fire. Артиллери́йский обстре́л, artillery bombardment. —взять под обстре́л, to rake over the coals.

обстре́ливать *v.impfv.* [*pfv.* обстреля́ть] to fire upon; shell.

обстре́лянный *adj.* battle-hardened.

обстреля́ть *v., pfv. of* **обстре́ливать.**

обстро́ить *v., pfv. of* **обстра́ивать.** —**обстро́иться,** *refl., pfv. of* **обстра́иваться.**

обструкциони́зм *n.* obstructionism. —**обструкциони́ст,** *n.* obstructionist. —**обструкцио́нный,** *adj.* obstructionist.

обстру́кция *n.* obstruction; delaying tactics.

обступа́ть *v.impf.* [*pfv.* **обступи́ть**] to surround; crowd around; cluster around.

обступи́ть [*infl.* -ступлю́, -сту́пишь] *v., pfv. of* **обступа́ть.**

обсуди́ть [*infl.* -сужу́, -су́дишь] *v., pfv. of* **обсужда́ть.**

обсужда́ть *v.impf.* [*pfv.* **обсуди́ть**] to discuss.

обсужде́ние *n.* discussion.

обсу́шивать *v.impf.* [*pfv.* **обсуши́ть**] to dry; dry out. —**обсу́шиваться,** *refl.* to dry oneself; get dry.

обсуши́ть [*infl.* -сушу́, -су́шишь] *v., pfv. of* **обсу́шивать.** —**обсуши́ться,** *refl., pfv. of* **обсу́шиваться.**

обсчи́тывать *v.impf.* [*pfv.* **обсчита́ть**] to short-change. —**обсчи́тываться,** *refl.* to make an error in counting; miscount.

обсы́пать [*infl.* -сы́плю, -сы́плешь] *v., pfv. of* **обсыпа́ть.**

обсыпа́ть *v.impf.* [*pfv.* **обсы́пать**] to sprinkle (with).

обсыха́ть *v.impf.* [*pfv.* **обсо́хнуть**] to dry; dry off. —**у него́ молоко́ на губа́х не обсо́хло,** he is still wet behind the ears.

обта́чивать *v.impf.* [*pfv.* **обточи́ть**] to grind smooth.

обтека́емый *adj.* streamlined.

обтека́ть *v.impf.* [*pfv.* **обте́чь**] **1,** to flow around. **2,** to bypass; skirt.

обтере́ть [*infl.* оботру́, оботрёшь; *past* обтёр, обтёрла] *v., pfv. of* **обтира́ть.** —**обтере́ться,** *refl., pfv. of* **обтира́ться.**

обтеса́ть [*infl.* -тешу́, -те́шешь] *v., pfv. of* **обтёсывать.**

обтёсывать *v.impf.* [*pfv.* **обтеса́ть**] **1,** to trim; rough-hew. **2,** *fig., colloq.* to teach (someone) good manners.

обте́чь [*infl. like* те́чь] *v., pfv. of* **обтека́ть.**

обтира́ние *n.* rubdown.

обтира́ть *v.impf.* [*pfv.* **обтере́ть**] **1,** to wipe. **2,** to wipe away. **3,** to rub (with). —**обтира́ться,** *refl.* **1,** to dry oneself. **2,** to sponge oneself down. **3,** *colloq.* to wear thin.

обточи́ть [*infl.* -точу́, -то́чишь] *v., pfv. of* **обта́чивать.**

обтрёпанный *adj.* **1,** frayed; tattered. **2,** shabbily dressed.

обтрепа́ть *v.pfv.* [*infl.* -треплю́, -тре́плешь] to fray. —**обтрепа́ться,** *refl.* to fray; become frayed.

обтя́гивать *v.impf.* [*pfv.* **обтяну́ть**] **1,** to cover; upholster. **2,** (*of clothes*) to fit tightly; hug. —**обтя́гиваться,** *refl., colloq.* **1,** to become covered. **2,** (*of one's face*) to become drawn.

обтя́жка *n.* **1,** covering. **2,** cover. —**в обтя́жку,** tight-fitting; close-fitting.

обтяну́ть [*infl.* -тяну́, -тя́нешь] *v., pfv. of* **обтя́гивать.** —**обтяну́ться,** *refl., pfv. of* **обтя́гиваться.**

обува́ть *v.impf.* [*pfv.* **обу́ть**] **1,** to put on (someone's) shoes. **2,** *colloq.* to put on (one's shoes). **3,** to provide with shoes. —**обува́ться,** *refl.* to put on one's shoes.

обувно́й *adj.* shoe (*attrib.*).

о́бувь *n.f.* shoes; footwear.

обу́гливать *v.impf.* [*pfv.* **обу́глить**] to char.

обу́за *n.* **1,** heavy responsibility. **2,** burden.

обузда́ние *n.* restraining; curbing.

обу́здывать *v.impf.* [*pfv.* **обузда́ть**] **1,** to bridle (a horse). **2,** *fig.* to restrain; curb.

обурева́ть *v.impf.* (*of fears, doubts, etc.*) to seize; grip.

обусло́вливать *v.impf.* [*pfv.* **обусло́вить**] **1,** to condition; make conditional. **2,** to cause; occasion. —**обусло́вливаться,** *refl.* (*with instr.*) **1,** to be conditional (upon); be determined (by). **2,** to be the result (of); be due (to).

обустра́ивать *v.impf.* [*pfv.* **обустро́ить**] **1,** to equip. **2,** *fig.* to revitalize.

обу́ть [*infl.* обу́ю, обу́ешь] *v., pfv. of* **обува́ть.** —**обу́ться,** *refl., pfv. of* **обува́ться.**

о́бух *n.* butt (*of an ax*). —**бить/ударя́ть кого́-нибудь как о́бухом по голове́,** to hit someone like a thunderbolt. *Also,* **обу́х** [*gen.* обуха́].

обуча́ть *v.impf.* [*pfv.* **обучи́ть**] to teach; instruct; train: обуча́ть кого́-нибудь ремеслу́, to teach someone a trade. —**обуча́ться,** *refl.* **1,** (*with dat.*) to learn: обуча́ться ремеслу́, to learn a trade. **2,** [*impfv. only*] to study (in a certain institution).

обуче́ние *n.* **1,** (*with gen.*) teaching; training (*of people*). Обуче́ние взро́слых, adult education. Беспла́тное обуче́ние, free tuition. **2,** (*with dat.*) teaching (*of a subject*); instruction (in): обуче́ние ремеслу́, teaching of a trade.

обучи́ть [*infl.* обучу́, обу́чишь] *v., pfv. of* **обуча́ть.** —**обучи́ться,** *refl., pfv. of* **обуча́ться.**

обуя́ть *v.pfv.* (*of a feeling or physical state*) to seize; come over.

обха́живать *v.impf., colloq.* **1,** to play up to; cultivate. **2,** to take care of; care for.

обхва́т *n.* **1,** circumference; girth: метр в обхва́те, a meter in circumference. **2,** circumference equal to a span of the arm: дуб в три обхва́та, an oak tree three spans in circumference.

обхвати́ть [*infl.* -хвачу́, -хва́тишь] *v., pfv. of* **обхва́тывать.**

обхва́тывать *v.impf.* [*pfv.* **обхвати́ть**] **1,** to put one's arms around. **2,** *fig.* to take in; embrace; encompass.

обхо́д *n.* **1,** going around. **2,** detour; bypass. **3,** rounds; beat: идти́ в обхо́д, to make one's rounds. **4,** *mil.* flanking movement. —**в обхо́д** (+ *gen.*), skirting; bypassing.

обходи́тельный *adj.* polite; courteous. —**обходи́тельность,** *n.f.* politeness.

обходи́ть *v.impf.* [*pfv.* **обойти́;** *pres.* обхожу́, обхо́дишь] **1,** to go around; walk around. **2,** *mil.* to outflank. **3,** to walk around; bypass; avoid. **4,** to pass over; ignore. **5,** to circumvent; get around (a law, rule, etc.). **6,** to pass over; fail to promote. **7,** *colloq.* to pass; outpace. **8,** (*with* весь) to walk all over. **9,** (*with* все) to make the rounds of; go to every one of. **10,** to spread all over: Но́вость обошла́ весь го́род, the news spread all over town. —**обходи́ться,** *refl.* **1,** (*with* с + *instr.*) to treat (*someone in a certain way*). **2,** *colloq.* to cost: обойти́сь кому́-нибудь в пятьдеся́т до́лларов, to cost someone fifty dollars. **3,** *colloq.* to get along; manage; (*with instr.*) manage (on *or* with); get along (on). Обходи́ться без маши́ны, to manage/ get along/ without a car. **4,** *colloq.* to turn out; work out.

обхо́дный *adj.* **1,** roundabout; circuitous: обхо́дным путём, by a roundabout way; by a circuitous route. **2,** *mil.* outflanking: обхо́дное движе́ние, outflanking movement.

обхо́дчик *n.* inspector. —**путево́й обхо́дчик,** *R.R.* trackwalker.

обхожде́ние *n.* (*with* с + *instr.*) **1,** behavior (toward); manner (toward). **2,** treatment (of).

обче́сться *v.r.pfv.* [*infl.* обочту́сь, обочтёшься; *past* обчёлся, обочла́сь] *colloq.* = обсчита́ться. —**раз-два и обчёлся,** you can count them on the fingers of your hand.

обчи́стить [*infl.* -чи́щу, -чи́стишь] *v., pfv. of* обчи-ща́ть.

обчища́ть *v.impfv.* [*pfv.* обчи́стить] *colloq.* **1,** to clean. **2,** (*in gambling*) to clean out; take to the cleaners.

обша́ривать *v.impfv.* [*pfv.* обша́рить] *colloq.* to rummage; ransack.

обша́рпанный *adj., colloq.* dilapidated; run-down.

обшива́ть *v.impfv.* [*pfv.* обши́ть] **1,** (*with instr.*) to edge (with); border (with); trim (with). **2,** (*with instr.*) to plank (with boards). **3,** *colloq.* to sew all the clothes for.

обши́вка *n.* **1,** edging; bordering; trimming. **2,** plating; sheeting; planking.

обши́рный *adj.* vast; extensive. —**обши́рность,** *n.f.* huge size; magnitude.

обши́ть [*infl.* обошью́, обошьёшь] *v., pfv. of* обшива́ть.

обшла́г [*gen. sing. & nom. pl.* обшлага́] *n.* cuff.

обща́ться *v.r.impfv.* (*with* с + *instr.*) to associate (with); consort (with); socialize (with); mingle (with).

общедосту́пный *adj.* **1,** available to all. **2,** understandable to all; popular. **3,** (*of prices*) moderate; reasonable.

общежи́тие *n.* **1,** dormitory. **2,** society; everyday life.

общеизве́стный *adj.* generally known; known to all. Общеизве́стно, что..., it is common knowledge that...

общенаро́дный *adj.* national; of all the people.

обще́ние *n.* association; contact; intercourse.

общеобразова́тельный *adj.* (*of a school, subject, etc.*) general; not specialized.

общепри́нятый *adj.* generally accepted; conventional.

обще́ственник *n.* person active in public life.

обще́ственность *n.f.* **1,** the public. **2,** public opinion.

обще́ственный *adj.* public; social.

о́бщество *n.* **1,** society. **2,** company: в о́бществе друзе́й, in the company of friends. **3,** a society: литерату́рное о́бщество, literary society.

о́бщий *adj.* **1,** general; common. **2,** mutual. **3,** total; overall. —**в о́бщем,** in general; on the whole. —**в о́бщем и це́лом,** on the whole; all in all. —**о́бщее ме́сто,** platitude. —**о́бщая су́мма; о́бщий ито́г,** sum total; grand total. —**не име́ть ничего́ о́бщего с,** to have nothing in common with.

общи́на *also,* **общи́на** *n.* **1,** community. **2,** commune.

общи́нный *adj.* communal.

общипа́ть [*infl.* -щиплю́, -щи́плешь] *v., pfv. of* щипа́ть (*in sense #4*) *and* общи́пывать.

общи́пывать *v.impfv.* [*pfv.* общипа́ть] to pluck.

общи́тельный *adj.* sociable; gregarious. —**общи́тельность,** *n.f.* sociability.

о́бщность *n.f.* commonality: о́бщность интере́сов, commonality of interests.

объего́ривать *v.impfv.* [*pfv.* объего́рить] *colloq.* to swindle; cheat; gyp.

объеда́ть *v.impfv.* [*pfv.* объе́сть] **1,** to eat around; nibble at. **2,** *colloq.* to eat out of house and home. —**объеда́ться,** *refl.* **1,** to overeat. **2,** (*with instr. or gen.*) to eat too much of.

объеде́ние *n.* **1,** overeating. **2,** *colloq.* something delicious; something out of this world.

объедине́ние *n.* **1,** unification. **2,** amalgamation; merger. **3,** union; association. **4,** *mil.* large formation (*front, army, etc.*).

объединённый *adj.* **1,** united: Объединённые На́ции, United Nations. **2,** joint: объединённый комите́т, joint committee.

объединя́ть *v.impfv.* [*pfv.* объедини́ть] **1,** to unite; unify. **2,** to combine (into one); merge; amalgamate. **3,** to join; combine (forces, efforts, etc.). —**объединя́ться,** *refl.* to unite; combine; amalgamate.

объе́дки [*gen.* -ков] *n.pl., colloq.* leftover scraps of food.

объе́зд *n.* **1,** traveling around. **2,** detour: е́хать в объе́зд, to make a detour.

объе́здить [*infl.* -е́зжу, -е́здишь] *v., pfv. of* объезжа́ть.

объе́здка *n.* breaking in (*of a horse*).

объе́здчик *n.* warden; ranger.

объезжа́ть *v.impfv.* **1,** [*pfv.* объе́хать] to go around; drive around; detour around. **2,** [*pfv.* объе́хать *or* объе́здить] to drive all over; travel throughout (a city, region, etc.). **3,** [*pfv.* объе́здить] to break in (a horse).

объе́кт *n.* **1,** object. **2,** establishment; installation. **3,** *mil.* objective; target.

объекти́в *n.* lens.

объекти́вный *adj.* objective. —**объекти́вно,** *adv.* objectively. —**объекти́вность,** *n.f.* objectivity.

объе́ктный *adj., in* объе́ктный паде́ж, objective case.

объём *n.* **1,** volume (*of a geometric figure, trade, etc.*). **2,** *fig.* scope; range. —**во всём объёме; в по́лном объёме,** fully.

объёмистый *adj., colloq.* bulky; voluminous.

объёмный *adj.* **1,** by volume; volumetric. **2,** (*of an image, film, etc.*) three-dimensional.

объе́сть [*infl. like* есть] *v., pfv. of* объеда́ть. —**объе́сться,** *refl., pfv. of* объеда́ться.

объе́хать [*infl.* объе́ду, объе́дешь] *v., pfv. of* объезжа́ть.

объяви́ть [*infl.* объявлю́, объя́вишь] *v., pfv. of* объявля́ть. —**объяви́ться,** *refl., pfv. of* объявля́ться.

объявле́ние *n.* **1,** declaration: объявле́ние войны́, declaration of war. **2,** announcement: объявле́ние о собра́нии, announcement of a meeting. **3,** advertisement. —**доска́ объявле́ний,** bulletin board.

объявля́ть *v.impfv.* [*pfv.* объяви́ть] **1,** to declare: объяви́ть войну́ (+ *dat.*), to declare war on. **2,** (*with* *acc.* or **o** + *prepl.*) to announce. —**объявля́ться**, *refl.* **1**, to turn up; show up. **2**, (*with instr.*) *colloq.* to declare oneself to be.

объясне́ние *n.* **1**, explanation. **2**, face-to-face meeting (*to settle something*). **3**, *in* объясне́ние в любви́, declaration of love.

объясни́мый *adj.* explainable; explicable.

объясни́тельный *adj.* explanatory.

объясня́ть *v.impf.* [*pfv.* **объясни́ть**] to explain. —**объясня́ться**, *refl.* **1**, (*with* с + *instr.*) to have a talk (with); have it out with. **2**, *obs.* to explain oneself; explain one's behavior. **3**, to become clear. **4**, [*impfv. only*] to express oneself; make oneself understood. **5**, [*impfv. only*] (*with instr.*) to be explained (by); be accounted for (by): Чем э́то объясня́ется?, how do you account for this?; what is the reason for this? Э́тим объясня́ется его́ стра́нное поведе́ние, this accounts for his strange behavior. **6**, *in* объясни́ться в любви́ (+ *dat.*), to make a declaration of love (to).

объя́тие *n.*, *usu. pl.* embrace. —**с распростёртыми объя́тиями**, with open arms.

объя́ть *v.pfv.* [*infl.* **обойму́, обоймёшь**; *past* **объя́л, объя́ла**] **1**, to embrace. **2**, to engulf; envelop. **3**, (*of an emotion*) to fill; seize; come over.

обыва́тель *n.m.* **1**, *obs.* inhabitant; resident. **2**, the average person; the ordinary person. —**обыва́тельский**, *adj.* narrow; narrow-minded.

обы́грывать *v.impf.* [*pfv.* **обыгра́ть**] **1**, to beat; defeat (*in a game*). **2**, *colloq.* to take advantage of; use to good advantage. **3**, *colloq.* to break in (a musical instrument).

обы́денный *adj.* ordinary; everyday.

обыкнове́ние *n.* habit. —**по обыкнове́нию**, as usual; as is his/her custom (*or* wont).

обыкнове́нно *adv.* usually.

обыкнове́нный *adj.* **1**, usual; customary. **2**, ordinary.

о́быск *n.* search (*of a person, premises, etc.*).

обыска́ть [*infl.* **обыщу́, обы́щешь**] *v., pfv. of* **обы́скивать**.

обы́скивать *v.impf.* [*pfv.* **обыска́ть**] to search; conduct a search of.

обы́чай *n.* custom.

обы́чно *adv.* usually; generally; ordinarily; customarily; normally. —**как обы́чно**, as usual.

обы́чный *adj.* **1**, usual; customary. Ра́ньше обы́чного, earlier than usual. **2**, ordinary. **3**, (*of weapons*) conventional. —**обы́чное пра́во**, common law.

обя́занность *n.f.* duty; responsibility.

обя́занный *adj.* **1**, (*with inf.*) obliged (to); required (to). **2**, (*with dat.*) obliged (to); indebted (to); obligated (to). Я ей мно́гим обя́зан(а), I am much indebted to her. Я обя́зан(а) ему́ жи́знью, I owe my life to him.

обяза́тельно *adv.* **1**, without fail. **2**, necessarily. **3**, *as an interj.* of course!; absolutely!

обяза́тельный *adj.* **1**, compulsory; obligatory; mandatory. **2**, (*of a condition, prerequisite, etc.*) essential. **3**, (*with* для) binding (on). **4**, obliging; accommodating.

обяза́тельство *n.* obligation; commitment. —**долгово́е обяза́тельство**, promissory note.

обяза́ть [*infl.* **обяжу́, обя́жешь**] *v., pfv. of* **обя́зывать**. —**обяза́ться**, *refl., pfv. of* **обя́зываться**.

обя́зывать *v.impf.* [*pfv.* **обяза́ть**; *pres.* **-зываю, -зываешь** *or* **-зу́ю, -зу́ешь**] **1**, to oblige; obligate; bind; commit. Э́то вас ни к чему́ не обя́зывает, this does not obligate/commit/bind you to anything. **2**, to oblige; do (someone) a favor: Вы меня́ э́тим о́чень обя́жете, you will be doing me a big favor. —**обя́зываться**, *refl.* (*with inf.*) to pledge (to); undertake (to).

ова́л *n.* oval. —**ова́льный**, *adj.* oval.

ова́ция *n.* ovation: устро́ить кому́-нибудь ова́цию, to give someone an ovation.

овдове́ть *v.pfv.* to become a widow *or* widower.

овева́ть *v.impf.* [*pfv.* **ове́ять**] **1**, (*of the wind*) to blow upon; fan. **2**, *fig.* to pervade; infuse.

ове́н [*gen.* **овна́**; *pl.* **о́вны**] *n.* **1**, *obs.* ram. **2**, *cap.* Aries.

овёс [*gen.* **овса́**] *n.* oats.

ове́чий [*fem.* **-чья**] *adj.* sheep (*attrib.*); sheep's. —**волк в ове́чьей шку́ре**, wolf in sheep's clothing.

ове́чка [*gen. pl.* **-чек**] *n., dim. of* **овца́**.

ове́ять [*infl.* **ове́ю, ове́ешь**] *v., pfv. of* **овева́ть**.

овладева́ть *v.impf.* [*pfv.* **овладе́ть**] (*with instr.*) **1**, to seize; capture. **2**, to control; dominate. **3**, (*of emotions*) to seize; grip; come over. **4**, to master (a subject, theory, technique, etc.). —**овладе́ть собо́й**, to compose oneself; regain one's composure.

овладе́ние *n.* **1**, capture. **2**, mastery.

овладе́ть *v., pfv. of* **овладева́ть**.

о́вод [*pl.* **о́воды** *or* **овода́**] *n.* gadfly.

о́вощи [*gen.* **овоще́й**] *n.pl.* [*sing.* **о́вощ**] vegetables.

овощно́й *adj.* vegetable (*attrib.*).

овра́г *n.* ravine.

овся́нка [*gen. pl.* **-нок**] *n.* **1**, oatmeal. **2**, bunting (*bird*). —**обыкнове́нная овся́нка**, yellowhammer. —**садо́вая овся́нка**, ortolan.

овся́ный *also,* **овся́ной** *adj.* oat (*attrib.*). —**овся́ная ка́ша**; овся́ная крупа́, oatmeal.

овуля́ция *n.* ovulation.

овца́ [*pl.* **о́вцы, ове́ц, о́вцам**] *n.* **1**, sheep. **2**, ewe.

овцебы́к *n.* musk ox.

овцево́д *n.* sheep farmer. —**овцево́дство**, *n.* sheep raising. —**овцево́дческий**, *adj.* pert. to the raising of sheep: овцево́дческая фе́рма, sheep farm.

овча́рка [*gen. pl.* **-рок**] *n.* sheep dog. —**неме́цкая овча́рка**, German shepherd.

овча́рня [*gen. pl.* **-рен**] *n.* sheepfold.

овчина́ *also,* **овчи́нка** *n.* sheepskin. —**овчи́нный**, *adj.* sheepskin.

ога́рок [*gen.* **-рка**] *n.* candle end.

огиба́ть *v.impf.* [*pfv.* **обогну́ть**] **1**, to bend around; wind around. **2**, to go round; go around; skirt.

оглавле́ние *n.* table of contents.

огласи́ть [*infl.* **-шу́, -си́шь**] *v., pfv. of* **оглаша́ть**. —**огласи́ться**, *refl., pfv. of* **оглаша́ться**.

огла́ска *n.* publicity.

оглаша́ть *v.impf.* [*pfv.* **огласи́ть**] **1**, to announce; read out. **2**, *obs.* to divulge; make public. **3**, to fill (the air, room, etc.) with a certain sound. —**оглаша́ться**, *refl.* (*with instr.*) to be filled (with); resound (with).

оглаше́ние *n.* publication. —**не подлежа́ть оглаше́нию**, not to be subject to publication; not to be released into the public domain.

оглóбля [*gen. pl.* **-бель**] *n.* shaft (*for harnessing a horse to a carriage*).

оглóхнуть [*past* **оглóх, оглóхла**] *v., pfv. of* **глóхнуть** (*in sense #1*).

оглушáть *v.impfv.* [*pfv.* **оглуши́ть**] **1,** to deafen. **2,** to stun.

оглуши́тельный *adj.* deafening.

оглуши́ть *v., pfv. of* **глуши́ть** (*in sense #7*) *and* **оглушáть**.

оглядéть [*infl.* **-жý, -ди́шь**] *v., pfv. of* **оглядывать**. —**оглядéться, 1,** *pfv. of* **оглядываться** (*in sense #1*). **2,** *fig.* to get used to one's surroundings.

оглядка *n., colloq.* looking back. —**без оглядки, 1,** (*with verbs of running*) without looking back; like a jack rabbit. **2,** without second thoughts; without looking back. —**с оглядкой,** with caution; cautiously; looking over one's shoulder.

оглядывать *v.impfv.* [*pfv.* **оглядéть** *or* **оглянýть**] to look over; examine. —**оглядываться,** *refl.* **1,** [*pfv.* **оглядéться**] (*often with* **вокрýг** *or* **кругóм**) to look around. **2,** [*pfv.* **оглянýться**] to look back; turn around and look.

оглянýть [*infl.* **оглянý, оглянешь**] *v., pfv. of* **оглядывать**. —**оглянýться,** *refl., pfv. of* **оглядываться** (*in sense #2*).

огневóй *adj.* **1,** fire (*attrib.*): **огневáя мощь,** firepower. **2,** fiery. **3,** fiery red. —**огневóй вал,** covering fire; barrage. —**огневáя пози́ция,** *mil.* emplacement.

огнемёт *n.* flame thrower.

óгненный *adj.* **1,** fiery; in flames. **2,** fiery red. **3,** *fig.* fiery; impassioned.

огнеопáсный *adj.* flammable; inflammable.

огнестóйкий *adj.* fireproof.

огнестрéльный *adj., in* **огнестрéльное орýжие,** firearm; firearms; **огнестрéльная рáна,** gunshot wound.

огнетуши́тель *n.m.* fire extinguisher.

огнеупóрный *adj.* heat-resistant; refractory.

огó *interj.* oho!

оговáривать *v.impfv.* [*pfv.* **оговори́ть**] **1,** to agree upon in advance. **2,** to spell out; specify; stipulate. **3,** *colloq.* to slander. —**оговáриваться,** *refl.* **1,** to point out in advance. **2,** to qualify one's statement. **3,** make a slip of the tongue.

оговóр *n.* slander.

оговори́ть *v., pfv. of* **оговáривать**. —**оговори́ться,** *refl., pfv. of* **оговáриваться**.

оговóрка [*gen. pl.* **-рок**] *n.* **1,** reservation; stipulation; proviso; qualification. **2,** slip of the tongue.

оголённый *adj.* bare; nude.

оголи́ть *v., pfv. of* **оголять**. —**оголи́ться,** *refl., pfv. of* **оголяться**.

оголтéлый *adj., colloq.* mad; rabid; fanatical.

оголять *v.impfv.* [*pfv.* **оголи́ть**] **1,** to bare; expose. **2,** to denude. **3,** to draw; unsheathe (a sword). **4,** *mil.* to expose. —**оголяться,** *refl.* to be exposed.

огонёк [*gen.* **-нька́**] *n.* **1,** (point of) light: **огоньки́ гóрода,** the lights of a city. **2,** *fig.* zest; verve. —**зайти́ на огонёк** (*with* **к**), to drop in (on).

огóнь [*gen.* **огня**] *n.m.* **1,** fire. **2,** *usu. pl.* (point of) light: **огни́ гóрода,** the lights of a city. **3,** fire (*from*

a gun): **пулемётный огóнь,** machine-gun fire. Открыть огóнь (по), to open fire (on). —**в огнé,** on fire; aflame; ablaze. —**днём с огнём (не найти́, не сыскáть,** *etc.*), seldom seen anywhere; not to be found anywhere. —**игрáть с огнём,** to play with fire. —**идти́/пойти́ в огóнь и в вóду за** (+ *acc. or instr.*), to be willing to do anything for. —**мéжду двух огнéй,** between the devil and the deep blue sea. —**пройти́ огóнь и вóду,** to have been through the mill.

огорáживать *v.impfv.* [*pfv.* **огороди́ть**] to fence in; enclose.

огорóд *n.* vegetable garden. —**бросáть кáмень** (*or* **кáмешек**) **в чéй-нибудь огорóд,** to make a disparaging (*or* slighting) remark about.

огороди́ть [*infl.* **-рожý, -рóдишь** *or* **-роди́шь**] *v., pfv. of* **огорáживать**.

огорóдник *n.* truck farmer. —**огорóдничество,** *n.* truck farming.

огорóдный *adj.* garden (*attrib.*).

огорóшить *v.pfv., colloq.* to take aback.

огорчáть *v.impfv.* [*pfv.* **огорчи́ть**] to distress; upset. —**огорчáться,** *refl.* to be distressed.

огорчéние *n.* distress; chagrin. —**огорчи́тельный,** *adj.* distressing.

огорчи́ть *v., pfv. of* **огорчáть**. —**огорчи́ться,** *refl., pfv. of* **огорчáться**.

огрáбить *v., pfv. of* **грáбить**.

ограблéние *n.* robbery.

огрáда *n.* fence.

огради́ть [*infl.* **-жý, -ди́шь**] *v., pfv. of* **ограждáть**.

ограждáть *v.impfv.* [*pfv.* **огради́ть**] **1,** *obs.* to fence in. **2,** to protect; shield.

ограждéние *n.* **1,** fencing in. **2,** protection. **3,** fence; barrier.

ограничéние *n.* limitation; restriction; curb.

ограни́ченность *n.f.* **1,** limited nature. **2,** limited intellect.

ограни́ченный *adj.* **1,** limited. **2,** (*of a person*) of limited intellect.

ограни́чивать *v.impfv.* [*pfv.* **ограни́чить**] to limit; restrict; confine. —**ограни́чиваться,** *refl.* (*with instr.*) **1,** to limit/restrict/confine oneself (to). **2,** to be limited (to).

ограничи́тельный *adj.* **1,** restrictive. **2,** *fig.* narrow: **ограничи́тельное толковáние,** narrow interpretation.

ограни́чить *v., pfv. of* **ограни́чивать**. —**ограни́читься,** *refl., pfv. of* **ограни́чиваться**.

огрéть *v.pfv., colloq.* to smack; whack.

огрéх *n., colloq.* fault; shortcoming; imperfection.

огрóмный *adj.* enormous; huge; tremendous; immense.

огрубéлый *adj.* rough; coarse; callous(ed).

огрубéть *v., pfv. of* **грубéть**.

огрызáть *v.impfv.* [*pfv.* **огрызть**] *colloq.* to nibble at. —**огрызáться,** *refl.* [*pfv.* **огрызнýться**] **1,** (*with* **на** + *acc.*) (*of a dog*) to snap (at). **2,** *colloq.* to snap; retort sharply.

огрызок [*gen.* **-зка**] *n.* **1,** leftover bit (*of an apple, piece of meat, etc.*). **2,** stub (*of a pencil*).

огрызть [*infl. like* **грызть**] *v., pfv. of* **огрызáть**.

огýлом *adv., colloq.* **1,** indiscriminately; wholesale. **2,** in one lot; in a lump. **3,** all together; en masse.

огу́льно *adv.* **1,** indiscriminately; wholesale. **2,** without grounds; unfairly.

огу́льный *adj.* **1,** *colloq.* indiscriminate; wholesale; sweeping. **2,** unfounded; groundless.

огуре́ц [*gen.* -рца́] *n.* cucumber. —огуре́чный, *adj.* cucumber (*attrib.*).

о́да *n.* ode.

ода́лживать *v.impfv.* [*pfv.* одолжи́ть] to lend.

одарённость *n.f.* gifts; talents; endowments.

одарённый *adj.* gifted.

одаря́ть *v.impfv.* [*pfv.* одари́ть] **1,** to give gifts (to many people). Одаря́ть дете́й игру́шками, to give the children toys as gifts. **2,** (*with instr.*) to endow (with). *Also,* ода́ривать.

одева́ть *v.impfv.* [*pfv.* оде́ть] to dress; clothe. —одева́ться, *refl.* to dress; get dressed.

оде́жда *n.* clothes; clothing.

одеколо́н *n.* eau de Cologne.

оделя́ть *v.impfv.* [*pfv.* одели́ть] (*with instr.*) to present (with): оделя́ть дете́й сластя́ми, to present sweets to the children.

одёр [*gen.* одра́] *n., colloq.* old horse; jade.

одёргивать *v.impfv.* [*pfv.* одёрнуть] **1,** to pull down; straighten (an article of clothing). **2,** *colloq.* to restrain; rein in.

одеревене́лый *adj.* **1,** stiff; numb. **2,** *fig.* lifeless.

одеревене́ть *v.pfv.* **1,** *pfv. of* деревене́ть. **2,** *fig.* to become indifferent; become apathetic.

оде́рживать *v.impfv.* [*pfv.* одержа́ть] to score (a victory). —одержа́ть верх, *see* верх.

одержа́ть [*infl.* одержу́, оде́ржишь] *v., pfv. of* оде́рживать.

одержи́мость *n.f.* obsession; preoccupation.

одержи́мый *adj.* (*with instr.*) obsessed (by); possessed (by).

одёрнуть *v., pfv. of* одёргивать.

оде́ть [*infl.* оде́ну, оде́нешь] *v., pfv. of* одева́ть. —оде́ться, *refl., pfv. of* одева́ться.

одея́ло *n.* blanket; cover.

одея́ние *n., obs.* clothing; raiment.

оди́н [*fem.* одна́; *neut.* одно́; *pl.* одни́; *gen.* одного́, одно́й, одни́х; *acc. fem.* одну́; *dat.* одному́, одно́й, одни́м; *instr.* одни́м, одно́й, одни́ми; *prepl.* одно́м, одно́й, одни́х] *numeral* one: оди́н биле́т, one ticket; одна́ ко́мната, one room; одни́ часы́, one watch. —*pron.* **1,** one: оди́н из са́мых лу́чших, one of the best. Оди́н друго́го удиви́тельнее, one more surprising than the next. **2,** *pl.* some: Одни́ бо́льше, чем други́е, some are larger than others. Одни́ счита́ют, что..., други́е..., some (people) believe that..., (while) others... —*adj.* **1,** a; a certain: Я прочёл э́то в одно́й газе́те, I read that in a (certain) newspaper. **2,** alone; by oneself: Вы оди́н (одна́)?, are you alone? Он живёт оди́н, he lives alone. **3,** only: В це́ркви бы́ли одни́ стару́шки, there were only old women in the church. Он мне доставля́ет одни́ неприя́тности, he gives me nothing but trouble. Одни́х слов недоста́точно, words alone are not enough. **4,** the same: Они́ живу́т в одно́м до́ме, they live in the same house; они́ одни́х лет, they are the same age.

—все до одного́, every last man/one; down to the last man. —все как оди́н, to a man; one and all. —не оди́н, more than one. —ни оди́н, not a single: Ни оди́н член не возража́л, not a single member objected. Он не сказа́л ни одного́ сло́ва, he did not say a single word. —оди́н за други́м, one by one; one after the other. —оди́н и тот же, the same. —оди́н на оди́н, one on one; face to face. —оди́н то́лько, alone: в одно́й то́лько Фра́нции, in France alone. —по одному́, one by one; one at a time. *See also* одно́.

одина́ково *adv.* **1,** identically; alike. **2,** equally.

одина́ковый *adj.* identical. Они́ одина́кового ро́ста; они́ одина́ковы по ро́сту, they are of identical height; they are identical in height. —в одина́ковой ме́ре, in equal measure.

одина́рный *adj.* single.

оди́ннадцатый *ordinal numeral* eleventh.

оди́ннадцать [*gen., dat. & prepl.* -цати; *instr.* -цатью] *numeral* eleven.

одино́кий *adj.* **1,** lone; solitary. **2,** lonely; lonesome. **3,** single; unmarried. —*n.* single person; unmarried person.

одино́ко *adv.* **1,** alone. **2,** lonely: чу́вствовать себя́ одино́ко, to feel lonely.

одино́чество *n.* solitude; loneliness. —в одино́честве, alone; by oneself.

одино́чка [*gen. pl.* -чек] *n.m. & f.* lone person; person on his/her own. ♦ *Often in compounds:* мать-одино́чка, unwed mother; single mother. —*n.f., colloq.* solitary (confinement) cell. —в одино́чку, alone; by oneself; on one's own. —одино́чкой, alone. —по одино́чке, one by one.

одино́чный *adj.* **1,** lone; solitary. **2,** for one person; single. —одино́чный бой, single combat. —одино́чное заключе́ние, solitary confinement. —одино́чный полёт, solo flight.

одио́зный *adj.* odious; offensive.

одиссе́я *n.* odyssey.

одича́лый *adj.* (*of an animal, plant, etc.*) wild.

одича́ть *v., pfv. of* дича́ть.

одна́жды *adv.* **1,** once. **2,** once; one day; once upon a time.

одна́ко *adv.* however; but.

одно́ *numeral, neut. of* оди́н. —*pron.* one thing: Одно́ несомне́нно, one thing is certain. —одно́ и то же, the same thing.

однобо́кий *adj.* **1,** lopsided. **2,** *fig.* one-sided.

однобо́ртный *adj.* single-breasted.

одновреме́нно *also,* одновре́менно, *adv.* simultaneously; at the same time.

одновреме́нность *also,* одновре́менность, *n.f.* simultaneity.

одновреме́нный *also,* одновре́менный *adj.* simultaneous.

одногла́зый *adj.* one-eyed.

одногоди́чный *adj.* one-year.

одного́док [*gen.* -дка] *n.m.* [*fem.* -дка] *colloq.* = одноле́ток.

однодне́вный *adj.* one-day.

однозна́чный *adj.* **1,** synonymous. **2,** having only one meaning. **3,** (*of a number*) one-digit. **4,** *fig.* unequivocal;

unambiguous; straightforward; explicit. —**однозна́чно,** *adv.* unequivocally; unambiguously.

одноимённый *adj.* of the same name.

однока́шник *n., colloq.* fellow student.

однокла́ссник *n.* classmate.

однокле́точный *adj.* one-celled.

одноколе́йный *adj.* single-track.

одноко́лка [*gen. pl.* **-лок**] *n.* gig.

однокóмнатный *adj.* one-room.

однокра́тный *adj.* one-time. —**однокра́тный глаго́л,** semelfactive verb (*e.g.* кри́кнуть).

однокýрсник *n.* person enrolled in the same course; classmate.

однолéтний *adj.* **1,** *obs.* one-year-old. **2,** *bot.* annual.

однолéток [*gen.* **-тка**] *n.m.* [*fem.* **-тка**] *colloq.* contemporary; person the same age.

одномéстный *adj.* having one seat; having room for one; single-seat.

одномотóрный *adj.* single-engine.

однонóгий *adj.* one-legged.

однообрáзие *n.* monotony. —**однообрáзный,** *adj.* monotonous.

однопалáтный *adj.* unicameral.

однополчáнин [*pl.* **-чáне, -чáн**] *n.* fellow soldier; comrade in arms (*from the same unit*).

однопóлый *adj.* unisexual.

однорáзовый *adj.* for one-time use only; disposable. —**однорáзового употреблéния,** = **однорáзовый.**

однорéльсовый *adj.* single-rail. —**однорéльсовая желéзная дорóга,** monorail.

однорóдный *adj.* **1,** homogeneous. **2,** similar; uniform. —**однорóдность,** *n.f.* homogeneity.

однорýкий *adj.* one-armed.

односельчáнин [*pl.* **-чáне, -чáн**] *n.m.* [*fem.* **-чáнка**] person from the same village.

однослóжный *adj.* **1,** one-syllable; monosyllabic. **2,** *fig.* one-syllable; terse.

односпáльный *adj., in* **односпáльная кровáть,** single bed.

односторо́нний *adj.* **1,** one-sided. **2,** unilateral. **3,** (*of movement, traffic, etc.*) one-way. —**в односторо́ннем поря́дке,** unilaterally.

однотúпный *adj.* of the same type.

однотóмный *adj.* one-volume.

однотóнный *adj.* **1,** monotone. **2,** single-colored. **3,** (*of a color*) solid.

однофамúлец [*gen.* **-льца**] *n.m.* [*fem.* **-лица**] person with the same (last) name.

одноцвéтный *adj.* one-color; plain.

одночáсье *n., in* **в одночáсье,** *colloq.* in an instant.

одноэтáжный *adj.* one-story.

одобрéние *n.* approval.

одобрúтельный *adj.* approving; of approval. —**одобрúтельно,** *adv.* approvingly.

одобря́ть *v.impfv.* [*pfv.* **одóбрить**] to approve (of).

одолевáть *v.impfv.* [*pfv.* **одолéть**] **1,** to overcome; overpower. **2,** to overcome; conquer (a feeling). **3,** (*of a feeling*) to come over; overcome. **4,** to master. **5,** *colloq.* to get through (a book, course, etc.). **6,** *colloq.* to give (someone) no peace.

одолжáть *v.impfv.* [*pfv.* **одолжúть**] **1,** to lend; loan. **2,** *obs.* to oblige; do (someone) a favor.

одолжéние *n.* favor: сдéлать одолжéние (+ *dat.*), to do someone a favor.

одолжúть *v., pfv. of* **одолжáть** *and* **одáлживать.**

одомáшнивание *n.* domestication. *Also,* **одомáшнение.**

одомáшнивать *v.impfv.* [*pfv.* **одомáшнить**] to domesticate.

одóметр *n.* odometer.

одонтолóгия *n.* odontology.

одр [*gen.* **одрá**] *n., obs.* bed. —**на смéртном одрé,** on one's deathbed.

одряхлéвший *adj.* decrepit; enfeebled.

одряхлéние *n.* declining vigor; decrepitude.

одряхлéть *v., pfv. of* **дряхлéть.**

одувáнчик *n.* dandelion.

одýмываться *v.r.impfv.* [*pfv.* **одýматься**] **1,** to change one's mind; think better of it. **2,** *colloq.* to collect oneself; come to one's senses.

одурáчить *v., pfv. of* **дурáчить.**

одурéлый *adj., colloq.* dazed; groggy.

одурéние *n., colloq.* stupor: пить до одурéния, to drink oneself into a stupor.

одурéть *v., pfv. of* **дурéть.**

одурмáнивать *v.impfv.* [*pfv.* **одурмáнить**] to cloud (someone's) mind *or* senses; leave in a daze; befuddle.

одурмáнить *v., pfv. of* **дурмáнить** *and* **одурмáнивать.**

óдурь *n.f., colloq.* daze; trance; stupor.

одуря́ть *v.impfv., colloq.* to cloud (someone's) mind *or* senses; leave in a daze; befuddle.

одутловáтый *adj.* puffy.

одухотворя́ть *v.impfv.* [*pfv.* **одухотворúть**] **1,** to ascribe intelligent powers to. **2,** to animate; inspire.

одушевúть [*infl.* **-влю́, -вúшь**] *v., pfv. of* **одушевля́ть.**

одушевлéние *n.* animation.

одушевлённый *adj.* **1,** animate. **2,** animated.

одушевля́ть *v.impfv.* [*pfv.* **одушевúть**] to animate.

оды́шка *n.* shortness of breath.

ожеребúться *v.r., pfv. of* **жеребúться.**

ожерéлье *n.* necklace.

ожесточáть *v.impfv.* [*pfv.* **ожесточúть**] **1,** to harden. **2,** to embitter.

ожесточéние *n.* **1,** bitterness. **2,** zeal; fervor; intensity.

ожесточённый *adj.* bitter; fierce.

ожесточúть *v., pfv. of* **ожесточáть.**

оживáть *v.impfv.* [*pfv.* **ожúть**] **1,** to come back to life. **2,** *fig.* to perk up; come alive.

оживúть [*infl.* **-влю́, -вúшь**] *v., pfv. of* **оживля́ть.** —**оживúться,** *refl., pfv. of* **оживля́ться.**

оживлéние *n.* **1,** revival; resuscitation. **2,** animation.

оживлённый *adj.* **1,** animated; lively. **2,** (*of a street*) busy; (*of trade*) brisk. —**оживлённо,** *adv.* with great animation.

оживля́ть *v.impfv.* [*pfv.* **оживúть**] **1,** to bring back to life. **2,** to revive; resuscitate. **3,** to invigorate; revitalize. **4,** *fig.* to liven up; enliven; brighten. —**оживля́ться,** *refl.* **1,** to become animated. **2,** to perk up; come alive.

ожидáние *n.* **1,** waiting; wait. **2,** expectation: сверх вся́кого ожидáния, beyond all expectations. —**в ожидáнии** (+ *gen.*), while awaiting; pending.

ожида́ть *v.impfv.* (*with gen.*) **1,** to expect. **2,** to wait for; await. Вас ожида́ет разочарова́ние, you are in for a disappointment.

ожире́ние *n.* obesity.

ожире́ть *v., pfv. of* жире́ть.

ожи́ть [*infl.* оживу́, оживёшь; *past* о́жил, ожила́, о́жило, о́жили] *v., pfv. of* ожива́ть.

ожо́г *n.* burn.

озабо́тить [*infl.* -чу, -тишь] *v., pfv. of* озабо́чивать. —**озабо́титься,** *refl., pfv. of* озабо́чиваться.

озабо́ченность *n.f.* anxiety; concern; apprehension.

озабо́ченный *adj.* anxious; concerned; worried; apprehensive.

озабо́чивать *v.impfv.* [*pfv.* озабо́тить] to cause (someone) anxiety. —**озабо́чиваться,** *refl.* (*with instr.*) to see to; attend to.

озагла́вливать *v.impfv.* [*pfv.* озагла́вить] to entitle.

озада́ченный *adj.* puzzled; perplexed; baffled. —**озада́ченность,** *n.f.* puzzlement; perplexity; bafflement.

озада́чивать *v.impfv.* [*pfv.* озада́чить] to perplex; baffle; confound; bewilder; take aback.

озаре́ние *n.* **1,** light. **2,** *fig.* sudden insight.

озаря́ть *v.impfv.* [*pfv.* озари́ть] **1,** to light up. **2,** *fig.* (*of a thought or idea*) to strike; dawn upon. *Also impers.:* Меня́ озари́ла мысль; меня́ озари́ло, the thought struck me. —**озаря́ться,** *refl.* to light up.

озвере́лый *adj.* crazed.

озвере́ние *n.* brutality; ferocity.

озвере́ть *v., pfv. of* звере́ть.

оздорови́тельный *adj.* health (*attrib.*); sanitary (*attrib.*).

оздорови́ть [*infl.* -влю́, -ви́шь] *v., pfv. of* оздоровля́ть.

оздоровле́ние *n.* **1,** making healthier. **2,** *fig.* improvement.

оздоровля́ть *v.impfv.* [*pfv.* оздорови́ть] **1,** to make healthy; make healthier. **2,** *fig.* to improve.

озелене́ние *n.* planting of trees and shrubs.

озеленя́ть *v.impfv.* [*pfv.* озелени́ть] to plant trees and shrubs (in).

о́земь *adv., colloq.* to the ground.

озёрный *adj.* of a lake; lake (*attrib.*).

о́зеро [*pl.* озёра, озёр] *n.* lake.

ози́мый *adj.* (*of crops*) winter. —**ози́мые,** *n.pl.* winter crops.

о́зимь *n.f.* winter crop(s).

озира́ть *v.impfv.* to look over. —**озира́ться,** *refl.* to look around.

озло́бить [*infl.* -блю, -бишь] *v., pfv. of* озлобля́ть. —**озло́биться,** *refl., pfv. of* озлобля́ться.

озлобле́ние *n.* bitterness; animosity.

озлобля́ть *v.impfv.* [*pfv.* озло́бить] to embitter. —**озлобля́ться,** *refl.* to become embittered.

ознако́мить [*infl.* -млю, -мишь] *v., pfv. of* ознако́мля́ть. —**ознако́миться,** *refl., pfv. of* ознако́мля́ться.

ознакомле́ние *n.* **1,** acquainting; familiarizing. **2,** acquaintance; familiarization.

ознакомля́ть *v.impfv.* [*pfv.* ознако́мить] (*with* с + *instr.*) to acquaint (with); familiarize (with). —**ознакомля́ться,** *refl.* (*with* с + *instr.*) to familiarize oneself (with); become familiar (with).

ознаменова́ние *n., in* в ознаменова́ние (+ *gen.*), in honor of; to mark; in commemoration of.

ознаменова́ть *v.pfv.* [*infl.* -ну́ю, -ну́ешь] **1,** *pfv. of* знаменова́ть. **2,** to mark; be a feature of. **3,** to celebrate; observe; commemorate.

означа́ть *v.impfv.* to mean; signify; denote.

озно́б *n.* shivering; chill.

озокери́т *n.* ozocerite.

озолоти́ть *v.pfv.* [*infl.* -чу́, -ти́шь] **1,** to give a golden color to. **2,** *colloq.* to shower with money, gifts, etc.

озо́н *n.* ozone. —**озо́новый,** *adj.* ozone (*attrib.*).

озорни́к [*gen.* -ника́] *n., colloq.* mischief-maker.

озорнича́ть *v.impfv., colloq.* to be naughty; make mischief.

озорно́й *adj., colloq.* mischievous.

озорство́ *n., colloq.* mischief.

озя́бнуть *v.pfv.* [*past* озя́б, озя́бла] to be cold; freeze.

ой *interj.* **1,** oh!; o! **2,** ouch!

оказа́ние *n.* rendering; providing; giving.

оказа́ть [*infl.* окажу́, ока́жешь] *v., pfv. of* ока́зывать. —**оказа́ться,** *refl., pfv. of* ока́зываться.

ока́зия *n.* **1,** *obs.* opportunity. **2,** *colloq.* unexpected event.

ока́зывать *v.impfv.* [*pfv.* оказа́ть] **1,** to render; provide (assistance, support, etc.). **2,** to do (a favor); render (a service). **3,** to give; accord (preference, a welcome, reception, etc.). **4,** to exert; apply; bring to bear; put (pressure). **5,** to exert; have (an influence, effect, etc.). **6,** show; accord (respect); place (trust); extend (hospitality). **7,** to put up; offer (resistance).

ока́зываться *v.r.impfv.* [*pfv.* оказа́ться] **1,** to find oneself (in a certain place). **2,** *impers.* to turn out: Оказа́лось, что..., it turned out that... **3,** to turn out to be: оказа́ться самозва́нцем, to turn out to be an impostor; оказа́ться безуспе́шным, turn out to be/ prove/ unsuccessful. Он оказа́лся прав, he turned out to be right. Мой бума́жник оказа́лся под крова́тью, my wallet turned out to be under the bed. Его́ оказа́лось легко́ уговори́ть, persuading him turned out to be easy. **4,** to be: оказа́ться в большинстве́, to be in the majority. **5,** *impers.* (*with* не) *indicating the absence of something*: В холоди́льнике проду́ктов не оказа́лось, there was no food in the refrigerator.

окаймля́ть *v.impfv.* [*pfv.* окайми́ть] to border; edge.

ока́лина *n.* dross.

окамене́лость *n.f.* fossil.

окамене́лый *adj.* **1,** petrified. **2,** *fig.* stony; impassive.

окамене́ть *v., pfv. of* камене́ть.

окантова́ть *v., pfv. of* кантова́ть.

ока́нчивать *v.impfv.* [*pfv.* око́нчить] **1,** to finish; end; complete. **2,** to graduate (from). —**ока́нчиваться,** *refl.* **1,** to finish; end; be over. **2,** [*impfv. only*] (*with instr.*) to end (in); terminate (in).

о́канье *n.* pronunciation of unstressed Russian o as o rather than a.

ока́пи *n.m. indecl.* okapi.

ока́пывать *v.impfv.* [*pfv.* окопа́ть] **1,** to dig around. **2,** to dig a ditch around. —**ока́пываться,** *refl.* to dig in; entrench oneself.

окари́на *n.* ocarina.

окати́ть [*infl.* окачу́, ока́тишь] *v.*, *pfv. of* ока́чивать.

о́кать *v.impfv.* to pronounce unstressed Russian о as о rather than а.

ока́чивать *v.impfv.* [*pfv.* окати́ть] (*with instr.*) to douse (with). —**окати́ть кого́-нибудь холо́дной водо́й**, to dampen someone's enthusiasm.

океа́н *n.* ocean.

океаногра́фия *n.* oceanography. —**океано́граф**, *n.* oceanographer. —**океанографи́ческий**, *adj.* oceanographic.

океа́нский *adj.* ocean (*attrib.*); oceanic.

оки́дывать *v.impfv.* [*pfv.* оки́нуть], *in* оки́дывать (что́-нибудь) взгля́дом, to cast one's eyes over. Оки́нуть горизо́нт взгля́дом, to scan the horizon.

о́кисел [*gen.* -сла] *n.* oxide.

окисле́ние *n.* oxidation.

окисля́ть *v.impfv.* [*pfv.* окисли́ть] to oxidize. —**окисля́ться**, *refl.* to oxidize; become oxidized.

о́кись *n.f.* oxide: о́кись желе́за, ferric oxide.

окклульти́зм *n.* occultism. —**окку́льтный**, *adj.* occult.

оккупа́нт *n.* invader.

оккупацио́нный *adj.* occupying; of occupation: оккупацио́нная а́рмия, army of occupation.

оккупа́ция *n.* (military) occupation.

оккупи́ровать *v.impfv. & pfv.* [*pres.* -рую, -руешь] *mil.* to occupy.

окла́д *n.* salary; wages; rate of pay.

окла́дистый *adj.* (*of a beard*) wide.

оклевета́ть *v.pfv.* [*infl.* -вещу́, -ве́щешь] to slander; smear.

окле́ивать *v.impfv.* [*pfv.* окле́ить] to cover by pasting something on: окле́ивать ко́мнату обо́ями, to paper a room.

о́клик *n.* 1, call. 2, challenge (*of a sentry*).

оклика́ть *v.impfv.* [*pfv.* окли́кнуть] 1, to call to; hail. 2, (*of a sentry*) to challenge.

окно́ [*pl.* о́кна, о́кон, о́кнам] *n.* window. —**на окно́; на окне́**, on the window sill.

о́ко [*pl.* о́чи, оче́й, оча́м] *n.*, *archaic* eye. —**о́ко за о́ко, зуб за зуб**, an eye for an eye, a tooth for a tooth.

окова́ть [*infl.* окую́, окуёшь] *v.*, *pfv. of* око́вывать.

око́вы [*gen.* око́в] *n.pl.* shackles; fetters.

око́вывать *v.impfv.* [*pfv.* окова́ть] 1, to bind (with metal). 2, *fig.* to shackle.

окола́чиваться *v.r.impfv.*, *colloq.* to knock about; hang around.

околдова́ть [*infl.* -ду́ю, -ду́ешь] *v.*, *pfv. of* околдо́вывать.

околдо́вывать *v.impfv.* [*pfv.* околдова́ть] to bewitch; cast a spell over.

околева́ть *v.impfv.* [*pfv.* околе́ть] (*of animals*) to die.

околёсица *n.*, *colloq.* nonsense.

околе́ть *v.*, *pfv. of* околева́ть.

око́лица *n.* 1, fence surrounding a village. 2, outskirts of a village.

околи́чности *n.pl.* [*sing.* околи́чность] *obs.* circumlocution. —**без околи́чностей**, plainly; to the point.

о́коло *prep.*, *with gen.* 1, near; close to. 2, about; approximately: о́коло десяти́ киломе́тров, about ten

kilometers. —*adv.* around; about: Никого́ нет о́коло, there is no one around/about. —**ходи́ть вокру́г да о́коло**, to beat around the bush.

околопло́дник *n.* pericarp.

околосерде́чный *adj.*, *in* околосерде́чная су́мка, pericardium.

околото́к [*gen.* -тка] *n.*, *obs.* neighborhood; district.

околощитови́дный *adj.*, *in* околощитови́дная железа́, parathyroid gland.

околпа́чивать *v.impfv.* [*pfv.* околпа́чить] *colloq.* to fool; dupe; make a fool of.

око́лыш *n.* hatband.

око́льный *adj.* roundabout; circuitous: око́льным путём, by a roundabout way; by a circuitous route.

оконе́чность *n.f.* extremity (*of an island or continent*).

око́нный *adj.* window (*attrib.*).

оконча́ние *n.* 1, completion; termination. 2, end. 3, graduation. 4, *gram.* ending. 5, concluding installment: оконча́ние в сле́дующем но́мере, to be concluded in the next issue.

оконча́тельно *adv.* 1, definitively. 2, utterly; completely. 3, permanently; for good.

оконча́тельность *n.f.* finality.

оконча́тельный *adj.* final; definitive.

око́нчить *v.*, *pfv. of* ока́нчивать. —**око́нчиться**, *refl.*, *pfv. of* ока́нчиваться.

око́п *n.*, *mil.* trench; foxhole.

окопа́ть *v.*, *pfv. of* ока́пывать. —**окопа́ться**, *refl.*, *pfv. of* ока́пываться.

око́пный *adj.* trench (*attrib.*). —**око́пная война́**, trench warfare.

окорна́ть *v.pfv.*, *colloq.* to trim.

о́корок [*pl.* окорока́] *n.* ham; leg of veal; leg of mutton.

окостене́лый *adj.* 1, ossified. 2, numb; stiff.

окостене́ние *n.* ossification.

окостене́ть *v.*, *pfv. of* костене́ть.

окоти́ться *v.r.*, *pfv. of* коти́ться.

окочене́лый *adj.* 1, numb (*from the cold*). 2, (*of a corpse*) stiff.

окочене́ние *n.* rigidity. —**тру́пное окочене́ние**, rigor mortis.

окочене́ть *v.*, *pfv. of* кочене́ть.

око́шко [*pl.* -шки, -шек] *n.* 1, small window. 2, window (*for a cashier, bank teller, etc.*).

о́кра *n.* okra; gumbo.

окра́ина *n.* 1, outskirts (*of a city*). 2, *pl.* border districts (*of a country*).

окра́инный *adj.* outlying.

окра́сить [*infl.* -шу, -сишь] *v.*, *pfv. of* окра́шивать.

окра́ска *n.* 1, painting. 2, color; coloring; coloration. 3, *fig.* coloration; complexion. —**защи́тная** *or* **покрови́тельственная окра́ска**, protective coloration.

окра́шивать *v.impfv.* [*pfv.* окра́сить] 1, to paint. 2, to dye. 3, to color.

окре́пнуть [*past* окре́п, окре́пла] *v.*, *pfv. of* кре́пнуть.

окрести́ть *v.pfv.* [*infl.* окрещу́, окре́стишь] 1, *pfv. of* крести́ть (*in sense #1*). 2, *colloq.* to nickname; dub. —**окрести́ться**, *refl.*, *pfv. of* крести́ться (*in sense #1*).

окре́стность *n.f.*, *usu. pl.* environs; suburbs.

окрéстный *adj.* **1,** neighboring; adjacent. **2,** local; living nearby.

óкрик *n.* shout; cry.

окрѝкнуть *v.pfv.* to shout to; call to.

окровáвить *v.pfv.* [*infl.* **-влю, -вишь**] to stain with blood.

окровáвленный *adj.* bloodstained.

окропѝть [*infl.* **-плю́, -пи́шь**] *v., pfv. of* кропи́ть *and* окропля́ть.

окропля́ть *v.impfv.* [*pfv.* **окропи́ть**] to sprinkle; besprinkle.

окрóшка *n.* **1,** cold soup made from kvass with meat and vegetables. **2,** *colloq.* hodgepodge.

óкруг [*pl.* **округá**] *n.* district.

окрýга *n., colloq.* neighborhood.

округлéть *v.pfv., colloq.* **1,** *pfv. of* круглéть. **2,** to get fat; put on weight.

округли́ть *v., pfv. of* округля́ть. —округли́ться, *refl., pfv. of* округля́ться.

окрýглый *adj.* round; rounded.

округля́ть *v.impfv.* [*pfv.* **округли́ть**] **1,** to round; make round. **2,** to round off. **3,** *in* округля́ть глазá, to stare wide-eyed. **4,** *colloq.* to enlarge (one's holdings). —округля́ться, *refl.* **1,** to become round. **2,** to fill out.

окружáть *v.impfv.* [*pfv.* **окружи́ть**] **1,** to surround; encircle. **2,** to gather round. **3,** to lavish: окружáть когó-нибудь забóтой, to lavish care on someone.

окружáющий *adj.* surrounding. —окружáющее, *n.neut.* one's surroundings: всё окружáющее, everything around one. —окружáющие, *n.pl.* those around one.

окружéние *n.* **1,** encirclement. **2,** surroundings; environment. **3,** entourage. —в окружéнии (+ *gen.*), accompanied by; surrounded by; in the midst of.

окружи́ть *v., pfv. of* окружáть.

окружнóй *adj.* district (*attrib.*). —окружнáя желéзная дорóга, suburban railway (*circling a city*). —окружнóй суд, circuit court.

окрýжность *n.f.* circumference.

окрути́ть [*infl.* **окручý, окрýтишь**] *v., pfv. of* окрýчивать.

окрýчивать *v.impfv.* [*pfv.* **окрути́ть**] *colloq.* to wind around: окрути́ть прóволоку лéнтой, to wind tape around a wire.

окрыля́ть *v.impfv.* [*pfv.* **окрыли́ть**] to inspire.

окры́ситься *v.r.pfv.* (*with* **на** + *acc.*) *colloq.* to snap (at).

октáва *n.* octave.

октáн *n.* octane.

октéт *n.* octet.

октя́брь [*gen.* **-бря́**] *n.m.* **1,** October. **2,** *cap.* the October Revolution (*of 1917*).

октя́брьский *adj.* **1,** October (*attrib.*). **2,** of or pert. to the October Revolution.

окули́ст *n.* oculist.

окуля́р *n.* eyepiece.

окунáть *v.impfv.* [*pfv.* **окуну́ть**] (*with* **в** + *acc.*) to dip (something into a liquid). —окунáться, *refl.* (*with* **в** + *acc.*) **1,** to dip (into). **2,** *fig.* to be plunged into (darkness). **3,** *fig.* to be absorbed (in); be engrossed (in).

óкунь [*pl.* **óкуни, окунéй, окуня́м**] *n.m.* perch; bass (*fish*).

окупáть *v.impfv.* [*pfv.* **окупи́ть**] to cover (a cost); cover the cost of. —окупáться, *refl.* **1,** to pay; pay off; pay for itself. **2,** *fig.* to be justified; be worth it.

окупи́ть [*infl.* **окуплю́, окýпишь**] *v., pfv. of* окупáть. —окупи́ться, *refl., pfv. of* окупáться.

окýривание *n.* fumigation.

окýривать *v.impfv.* [*pfv.* **окури́ть**] to fumigate.

окури́ть [*infl.* **окурю́, окýришь**] *v., pfv. of* окýривать.

окýрок [*gen.* **-рка**] *n.* cigarette butt; cigar stub.

окýтывать *v.impfv.* [*pfv.* **окýтать**] **1,** to wrap (*snugly*). **2,** *fig.* to envelop; shroud.

олáдья [*gen. pl.* **-дий**] *n.* pancake; fritter.

олеáндр *n.* oleander. —олеáндровый, *adj.* oleander (*attrib.*).

оледенéлый *adj.* frozen.

оледенéть *v., pfv. of* леденéть.

оленебы́к [*gen.* **-бы́ка**] *n.* eland (*antelope*).

оленевóд *n.* reindeer breeder. —оленевóдство, *n.* reindeer breeding. —оленевóдческий, *adj.* reindeer-breeding (*attrib.*).

олéний [*fem.* **-нья**] *adj.* **1,** deer (*attrib.*); deer's; reindeer (*attrib.*). **2,** deerskin. —олéньи рогá, antlers.

олéнина *n.* venison.

оленýха *n.* doe (*female deer*).

олéнь *n.m.* deer. —благорóдный олéнь, red deer. —сéверный олéнь, reindeer.

оли́ва *n.* **1,** olive. **2,** olive tree. *Also,* оли́вка.

оли́вковый *adj.* **1,** olive (*attrib.*). **2,** olive-green.

олигáрх *n.* oligarch. —олигархи́ческий, *adj.* oligarchic. —олигáрхия, *n.* oligarchy.

олимпиáда *n.* **1,** Olympiad. **2,** Olympics.

олимпи́йский *adj.* Olympian; Olympic. —Олимпи́йские и́гры, Olympic games.

оли́фа *n.* drying oil.

олицетворéние *n.* personification; embodiment.

олицетворя́ть *v.impfv.* [*pfv.* **олицетвори́ть**] to personify; embody.

óлово *n.* tin. —оловя́нный, *adj.* tin.

óлух *n., colloq.* oaf; dolt; blockhead.

олýша *n.* gannet (*bird*).

ольхá [*pl.* **óльхи**] *n.* alder. —ольхóвый, *adj.* alder (*attrib.*).

оля́пка [*gen. pl.* **-пок**] *n.* water ouzel; dipper.

ом *n.* ohm.

омáр *n.* lobster.

омéга *n.* omega.

омéла *n.* mistletoe.

омерзéние *n.* loathing.

омерзи́тельный *adj.* loathsome; disgusting; revolting.

омертвéлый *adj.* **1,** (*of tissues, cells, etc.*) dead. **2,** *fig.* stiff; numb. **3,** *fig.* deserted; lifeless.

омертвéть *v., pfv. of* мертвéть.

омёт *n.* stack of straw.

омлéт *n.* omelet.

óмнибус *n., obs.* horse-drawn coach (*carrying paying passengers*).

омовéние *n.* ablution.

омолáживать *v.impfv.* [*pfv.* **омолоди́ть**] to rejuvenate.

омоложéние *n.* rejuvenation.

омóним *n.* homonym.

омрача́ть *v.impfv.* [*pfv.* **омрачи́ть**] **1,** *obs.* to darken. **2,** to mar; spoil; dampen.

о́мут *n.* **1,** deep place in a river or lake. **2,** whirlpool. **3,** *fig.* maelstrom.

омыва́ть *v.impfv.* [*pfv.* **омы́ть**] **1,** to wash. **2,** [*impfv. only*] (*of waves, the sea, etc.*) to wash (the shore).

омы́ть [*infl.* **омо́ю, омо́ешь**] *v., pfv. of* **омыва́ть.**

он [*gen. & acc.* **его́**; *dat.* **ему́**; *instr.* **им**; *prepl.* **нём**] *pers. pron., 3rd person sing. masc.* he; (*of inanimate objects*) it.

она́ [*gen. & acc.* **её**; *dat.* **ей**; *instr.* **е́ю**; *prepl.* **ней**] *pers. pron., 3rd person sing. fem.* she; (*of inanimate objects*) it.

она́гр *n.* onager.

онани́зм *n.* masturbation.

онани́ровать *v.impfv.* [*pres.* **-рую, -руешь**] to masturbate.

онда́тра *n.* muskrat.

онемéлый *adj.* **1,** dumb; mute. **2,** numb; stiff.

онемéние *n.* **1,** inability to speak. **2,** numbness.

онемéть *v., pfv. of* **немéть.**

онёры *n.pl.* [*sing* **онéра**] *cards* honors.

они́ [*gen. & acc.* **их**; *dat.* **им**; *instr.* **и́ми**; *prepl.* **них**] *pers. pron., 3rd person pl.* they.

о́никс *n.* onyx. **—о́никсовый,** *adj.* onyx.

онколóгия *n.* oncology.

о́но *see* **о́ный.**

оно́ [*infl. like* **он**] *pers. pron., 3rd person sing. neut.* it. **—вот оно́ что!,** so *that's* it!

онтолóгия *n.* ontology. **—онтологи́ческий,** *adj.* ontological.

ону́ча [*gen. pl.* **ону́ч**] *n.* piece of cloth wrapped around the foot and worn instead of a stocking.

о́ный *adj., obs.* that. **—во врéмя о́но,** long ago; way back when.

опада́ть *v.impfv.* [*pfv.* **опа́сть**] **1,** (*of leaves*) to fall; (*of fruit or petals*) to fall off. **2,** (*of wind*) to subside. **3,** (*of a swelling*) to go down. **4,** *colloq.* (*of one's face or cheeks*) to become sunken.

опа́здывать *v.impfv.* [*pfv.* **опозда́ть**] to be late: опозда́ть в шкóлу/ на рабóту/ к обéду/, to be late for school/work/dinner. Опозда́ть с отвéтом, to be late in answering. Опозда́ть пода́ть заявлéние, to be late in submitting one's application. Опозда́ть на полчаса́, to be half an hour late.

опа́ивать *v.impfv.* [*pfv.* **опои́ть**] **1,** to give (an animal) too much to drink. **2,** to make (someone) drunk. **3,** *obs.* to poison.

опа́л *n.* opal.

опа́ла *n.* disgrace: быть в опа́ле, to be in disgrace.

опа́ливать *v.impfv.* [*pfv.* **опали́ть**] **1,** to scorch; sear. **2,** to singe (feathers, a chicken, etc.).

опали́ть *v., pfv. of* **пали́ть** (*in sense #1*), **опаля́ть** *and* **опа́ливать.**

опа́ловый *adj.* opal; opaline.

опа́льный *adj.* disgraced; in disgrace.

опаля́ть *v.* = **опа́ливать.**

опа́ра *n.* leavened dough.

опарши́веть *v., pfv. of* **парши́веть.**

опаса́ться *v.r.impfv.* **1,** (*with gen.*) to fear. **2,** (*with gen. or inf.*) to avoid; refrain from.

опасéние *n.* fear; apprehension.

опа́ска *n., colloq., in* **с опа́ской,** cautiously; **без опа́ски,** without fear.

опа́сливый *adj., colloq.* cautious; fearful.

опа́сно *adv.* dangerously. —*adj., used predicatively,* dangerous: По э́той доро́ге опа́сно éхать, it is dangerous to drive on this road.

опа́сность *n.f.* danger.

опа́сный *adj.* dangerous. **—опа́сная бри́тва,** straight razor.

опа́сть [*infl. like* **пасть**] *v., pfv. of* **опада́ть.**

опаха́ло *n.* large fan.

опéка *n.* guardianship; tutelage. **—Междунаро́дная опéка,** International Trusteeship. **—Совéт по Опéке,** Trusteeship Council (*of the United Nations*).

опекáемый *n., decl. as an adj.* ward.

опекáть *v.impfv.* **1,** to be the guardian of. **2,** *fig.* to watch over.

опеку́н [*gen.* **-куна́**] *n.* guardian. **—опеку́нский,** *adj.* of a guardian; guardian's; tutelary. **—опеку́нство,** *n.* guardianship.

о́пера *n.* opera.

операти́вный *adj.* **1,** operative; surgical: операти́вное вмеша́тельство, surgical intervention. **2,** *mil.* operations (*attrib.*). **3,** effective; efficient. **4,** prompt; expeditious.

опера́тор *n.* **1,** operator (*of a machine*). **2,** cameraman. **3,** *obs.* surgeon.

операцио́нный *adj.* **1,** *med.* operating. **2,** *mil.* operations (*attrib.*). **—операцио́нная,** *n.* operating room.

опера́ция *n., med.; mil.; finance* operation.

опережа́ть *v.impfv.* [*pfv.* **опереди́ть**] **1,** to pass; get ahead of; outdistance; leave behind. **2,** [*impfv. only*] to lead; be ahead of: опережа́ть (кого́-нибудь) на де́сять очко́в, to lead (someone) by ten points. **3,** to do something ahead of (someone); beat (someone) to it. **4,** to surpass; excel. **—опереди́ть свой век,** to be ahead of one's time.

оперéние *n.* plumage. **—хвостово́е оперéние,** *aero.* tail assembly.

оперённый *adj.* feathered.

оперéтта *n.* operetta; musical comedy. **—оперéточный,** *adj.* of operetta; musical-comedy.

оперéть [*infl.* **обопру́, обопрёшь**; *past* **опёр, оперла́** *or* **опёрла, опёрло, опёрли**] *v., pfv. of* **опира́ть. —оперéться,** *refl.* [*past* **опёрся, оперла́сь, оперло́сь** *or* **опёрлось, оперли́сь** *or* **опёрлись**] *pfv. of* **опира́ться.**

опери́ровать *v.impfv.* [*pres.* **-рую, -руешь**] **1,** to operate on. **2,** *mil.* to operate. **3,** (*with instr.*) to use.

опери́ться *v.r., pfv. of* **оперя́ться.**

о́перный *adj.* opera (*attrib.*); operatic.

оперя́ться *v.r.impfv.* [*pfv.* **опери́ться**] **1,** (*of a bird*) to become fully fledged. **2,** *fig.* to become independent; stand on one's own feet.

опеча́ленный *adj.* sad; sorrowful.

опеча́лить *v., pfv. of* **печа́лить. —опеча́литься,** *refl., pfv. of* **печа́литься.**

опеча́тать *v., pfv. of* **опеча́тывать.**

опеча́тка [*gen. pl.* **-ток**] *n.* misprint.

опеча́тывать *v.impfv.* [*pfv.* опеча́тать] to seal up.

опе́шить *v.pfv., colloq.* to be taken aback.

опива́ться *v.r.impfv.* [*pfv.* опи́ться] *colloq.* to drink to excess; have too much to drink; (*with instr.*) drink too much (of); have too much (of something) to drink.

о́пий *n.* opium. —о́пийный, *adj.* opium (*attrib.*).

опи́ливать *v.impfv.* [*pfv.* опили́ть] to saw.

опили́ть [*infl.* опилю́, опи́лишь] *v., pfv. of* опи́ливать.

опи́лки [*gen.* -лок] *n.pl.* **1,** filings. **2,** sawdust.

опира́ть *v.impfv.* [*pfv.* опере́ть] (*with* на *or* о + *acc.*) to lean (something) on *or* against. —опира́ться, *refl.* (*with* на *or* о + *acc.*) **1,** to lean on; lean against. **2,** *fig.* to lean on; rely on; depend on.

описа́ние *n.* description. —описа́тельный, *adj.* descriptive.

описа́ть [*infl.* опишу́, опи́шешь] *v., pfv. of* опи́сывать. —описа́ться, *refl.* to make a slip of the pen.

опи́ска [*gen. pl.* -сок] *n.* slip of the pen.

опи́сывать *v.impfv.* [*pfv.* описа́ть] **1,** to describe. **2,** to take inventory of. **3,** *math.* circumscribe. **4,** to make; move in; describe (a circle, arc, etc.).

о́пись *n.f.* inventory.

опи́ться [*infl.* обопью́сь, обопьёшься; *past* опи́лся, опила́сь, опило́сь *or* опи́лось, опили́сь *or* опи́лись] *v.r., pfv. of* опива́ться.

о́пиум *n.* opium. —о́пиумный, *adj.* opium (*attrib.*).

опла́кать [*infl.* опла́чу, опла́чешь] *v., pfv. of* опла́кивать.

опла́кивать *v.impfv.* [*pfv.* опла́кать] **1,** to mourn; mourn the loss of. **2,** to bemoan (one's fate); bewail (one's misfortune).

опла́та *n.* pay; payment. Он на почасово́й опла́те, he is paid by the hour.

оплати́ть [*infl.* оплачу́, опла́тишь] *v., pfv. of* опла́чивать.

опла́чиваемый *adj.* paid: опла́чиваемый о́тпуск, paid vacation.

опла́чивать *v.impfv.* [*pfv.* оплати́ть] **1,** to pay. **2,** to pay for.

оплева́ть [*infl.* оплюю́, оплюёшь] *v., pfv. of* оплёвывать.

оплёвывать *v.impfv.* [*pfv.* оплева́ть] *colloq.* to spit on (*lit. & fig.*).

оплести́ [*infl. like* плести́] *v., pfv. of* оплета́ть.

оплета́ть *v.impfv.* [*pfv.* оплести́] to entwine; string: оплести́ и́згородь колю́чей про́волокой, to entwine/string a fence with barbed wire.

оплеу́ха *n., colloq.* slap in the face.

оплеши́веть *v., pfv. of* плеши́веть.

оплодотворе́ние *n.* fertilization; impregnation; insemination.

оплодотворя́ть *v.impfv.* [*pfv.* оплодотвори́ть] to fertilize; impregnate.

опло́т *n.* bulwark; bastion.

оплоша́ть *v.pfv., colloq.* to make a blunder; slip up.

опло́шность *n.f.* mistake; blunder.

оплыва́ть *v.impfv.* [*pfv.* оплы́ть] **1,** to swim around; sail around. **2,** to swell up; become swollen. **3,** (*of a candle*) to drip.

оплы́ть [*infl. like* плыть] *v., pfv. of* оплыва́ть.

оповеща́ть *v.impfv.* [*pfv.* оповести́ть] to notify; inform.

оповеще́ние *n.* notification.

опо́ек [*gen.* опо́йка] *n.* calfskin.

опозда́ние *n.* **1,** lateness; tardiness. Нача́ть собра́ние с опозда́нием, to start the meeting late. **2,** delay.

опозда́ть *v., pfv. of* опа́здывать.

опознава́тельный *adj.* identification (*attrib.*); identifying. —опознава́тельный знак, **1,** identification mark. **2,** landmark.

опознава́ть *v.impfv.* [*pfv.* опозна́ть; *pres.* -знаю́, -знаёшь] to identify.

опозна́ние *n.* identification.

опозна́ть [*infl.* -зна́ю, -зна́ешь] *v., pfv. of* опознава́ть.

опозо́рить *v., pfv. of* позо́рить. —опозо́риться, *refl., pfv. of* позо́риться.

опои́ть [*infl.* опою́, опо́ишь *or* опои́шь] *v., pfv. of* опа́ивать.

опо́йковый *adj.* calfskin (*attrib.*).

опола́скивать *v.impfv.* [*pfv.* ополосну́ть] to rinse.

ополза́ть *v.impfv.* [*pfv.* оползти́] **1,** to crawl around. **2,** (*of the ground or a building*) to slip; sink.

о́ползень [*gen.* -зня] *n.m.* landslide; mudslide.

оползти́ [*infl. like* ползти́] *v., pfv. of* ополза́ть.

ополосну́ть *v., pfv. of* опола́скивать.

ополча́ться *v.r.impfv.* [*pfv.* ополчи́ться] (*with* на + *acc. or* про́тив) **1,** to take up arms (against). **2,** *fig.* to assail; sail into.

ополче́нец [*gen.* -нца] *n.* militiaman.

ополче́ние *n.* militia.

ополчи́ться *v.r., pfv. of* ополча́ться.

опо́мниться *v.r.pfv.* **1,** to regain consciousness. **2,** to come to one's senses.

опо́р *n., in* во весь опо́р, at top speed; full tilt.

опо́ра *n.* **1,** support. **2,** *fig.* basis. —то́чка опо́ры, **1,** fulcrum. **2,** foothold: найти́ то́чку опо́ры, to gain a foothold.

опора́жнивать *v.impfv.* [*pfv.* опоро́жнить *or* опорожни́ть] to empty. —опора́жниваться, *refl.* to empty; become empty.

опо́рки *n.pl.* [*sing.* опо́рок] worn-out shoes.

опо́рный *adj.* supporting: опо́рная коло́нна, supporting column. —опо́рный пункт, *mil.* strong point.

опоро́жнить *also,* опорожни́ть *v., pfv. of* опора́жнивать *and* опорожня́ть. —опоро́жниться, *refl., pfv. of* опора́жниваться *and* опорожня́ться.

опорожня́ть *v.* = опора́жнивать. —опорожня́ться, *refl.* = опора́жниваться.

опоро́с *n.* farrow.

опоро́чить *v., pfv. of* поро́чить.

опо́ссум *n.* opossum.

опосты́леть *v.pfv.* (*with dat.*) *colloq.* to become hateful (to).

опохмеля́ться *v.r.impfv.* [*pfv.* опохмели́ться] *colloq.* to take a drink in order to cure a hangover.

опочи́ть *v.* [*infl.* -чи́ю, -чи́ешь] *obs.* **1,** to go to sleep. **2,** to die.

опошля́ть *v.impfv.* [*pfv.* опо́шлить] **1,** to vulgarize; debase. **2,** to make trite by overuse.

опоя́сать [*infl.* опоя́шу, опоя́шешь] *v., pfv. of* опоя́сывать. —опоя́саться, *refl., pfv. of* опоя́сываться.

опоя́сывать *v.impfv.* [*pfv.* **опоя́сать**] **1,** to gird. **2,** to circle; girdle. —**опоя́сываться,** *refl.* **1,** [*also,* опоя́сываться ремнём] to put on one's belt. **2,** *fig.* (*with instr.*) to be encircled (by); be surrounded (by).

оппози́ция *n.* opposition. —**оппозицио́нный,** *adj.* opposition (*attrib.*).

оппоне́нт *n.* opponent (*in a debate or argument*).

оппони́ровать *v.impfv.* [*pres.* **-рую, -руешь**] (*with dat.*) to oppose (*in a discussion, debate, etc.*).

оппортуни́зм *n.* opportunism. —**оппортуни́ст,** *n.* opportunist. —**оппортунисти́ческий,** *adj.* opportunistic.

опра́ва *n.* **1,** mount; setting. **2,** frame; rim (*for eyeglasses*).

оправда́ние *n.* **1,** justification. **2,** excuse. **3,** *law* acquittal.

оправда́тельный *adj.,* *in* **оправда́тельный пригово́р,** verdict of "not guilty".

опра́вдывать *v.impfv.* [*pfv.* **оправда́ть**] **1,** to justify. **2,** to excuse. **3,** to acquit. **4,** to live up to (expectations). **5,** *in* **оправда́ть себя́,** to prove its worth; prove worthwhile. —**опра́вдываться,** *refl.* **1,** to justify oneself; justify one's actions. **2,** to justify itself; be justified. **3,** to (try to) prove one's innocence. **4,** to prove to be correct. **5,** to be realized; materialize; come true.

опра́вить [*infl.* **-влю, -вишь**] *v., pfv. of* **оправля́ть.** —**опра́виться,** *refl., pfv. of* **оправля́ться.**

опра́вка [*gen. pl.* **-вок**] *n.* mandrel.

оправля́ть *v.impfv.* [*pfv.* **опра́вить**] **1,** to straighten; adjust. **2,** to mount; set in a mount. —**оправля́ться,** *refl.* **1,** to straighten one's clothes; tidy oneself up. **2,** to recover; get well.

опра́шивать *v.impfv.* [*pfv.* **опроси́ть**] **1,** to poll; canvass. **2,** to question (many people). **3,** to quiz (a class).

определе́ние *n.* **1,** determination. **2,** definition. **3,** *gram.* attribute; modifier.

определённо *adv.* definitely.

определённость *n.f.* **1,** certainty. **2,** precision. —**со всей определённостью, 1,** as clearly as possible; unequivocally. **2,** with absolute certainty.

определённый *adj.* **1,** definite. **2,** certain: при определённых усло́виях, under certain conditions.

определи́тель *n.m.* **1,** determining factor. **2,** guide to identifying something. **3,** *math.* determinant.

определя́ть *v.impfv.* [*pfv.* **определи́ть**] **1,** to determine. **2,** to define. **3,** to fix; set. **4,** to diagnose (an illness). —**определя́ться,** *refl.* **1,** to be determined. **2,** to be formed; take shape. **3,** to determine one's position.

опресне́ние *n.* desalinization; desalination.

опресня́ть *v.impfv.* [*pfv.* **опресни́ть**] to desalinate.

опри́чнина *n., hist.* oprichnina (*period of terror during the reign of Tsar Ivan IV; also those charged with carrying it out*).

опро́бовать *v.pfv.* [*infl.* **-бую, -буешь**] to test.

опроверга́ть *v.impfv.* [*pfv.* **опрове́ргнуть**] **1,** to refute; rebut; disprove. **2,** to deny.

опрове́ргнуть [*past* **-ве́рг, -ве́ргла**] *v., pfv. of* **опроверга́ть.**

опроверже́ние *n.* **1,** refutation; rebuttal. **2,** denial. **3,** disclaimer; retraction.

опроки́дывать *v.impfv.* [*pfv.* **опроки́нуть**] to overturn; upset; tip over; knock over; topple. —**опроки́ды-**

ваться, *refl.* **1,** to overturn; fall over; tip over; topple over. **2,** (*of a boat*) to capsize.

опроме́тчивый *adj.* rash; impetuous. —**опроме́тчиво,** *adv.* rashly; impetuously. —**опроме́тчивость,** *n.f.* rashness; impetuosity.

о́прометью *adv.* headlong.

опро́с *n.* **1,** questioning. **2,** poll; survey. **3,** quiz (*in school*).

опроси́ть [*infl.* **опрошу́, опро́сишь**] *v., pfv. of* **опра́шивать.**

опро́сный *adj., in* **опро́сный лист,** questionnaire.

опроста́ть *v.pfv., colloq.* to empty; empty the contents of.

опростоволо́ситься *v.r.pfv.* [*infl.* **-шусь, -сишься**] *colloq.* to make a fool of oneself.

опротестова́ть *v.pfv.* [*infl.* **-ту́ю, -ту́ешь**] *law* to appeal; protest; contest.

опроти́веть *v.pfv.* (*with dat.*) to become loathsome (to).

опры́скивать *v.impfv.* [*pfv.* **опры́скать**] **1,** to sprinkle. **2,** to spray.

опря́тный *adj.* neat; tidy. —**опря́тно,** *adv.* neatly. —**опря́тность,** *n.f.* neatness; tidiness.

о́птик *n.* optician; optometrist. —**о́птика,** *n.* optics.

оптима́льный *adj.* optimum.

оптими́зм *n.* optimism. —**оптими́ст,** *n.* optimist.

оптимисти́чески *adv.* optimistically. Я настро́ен оптимисти́чески, I am optimistic.

оптимисти́ческий *adj.* optimistic.

о́птимум *n.* optimum.

опти́ческий *adj.* optical.

оптови́к [*gen.* **-вика́**] *n.* wholesaler. —**опто́вый,** *adj.* wholesale. —**о́птом,** *adv.* wholesale.

опубликова́ние *n.* **1,** publication. **2,** promulgation.

опубликова́ть *v.pfv.* [*infl.* **-ку́ю, -ку́ешь**] **1,** *pfv. of* **публикова́ть. 2,** to promulgate.

опу́нция *n.* prickly pear.

о́пус *n.* opus.

опуска́ть *v.impfv.* [*pfv.* **опусти́ть**] **1,** to lower; let down. **2,** (*with* **в** + *acc.*) to put (into); drop; deposit: опусти́ть письмо́ в почто́вый я́щик, to deposit a letter in the mailbox; mail a letter. **3,** to turn down (a collar). **4,** to omit; leave out. —**как в во́ду опу́щенный,** dejected; crestfallen. —**опуска́ть ру́ки,** to become disheartened; lose heart.

опуска́ться *v.r.impfv.* [*pfv.* **опусти́ться**] **1,** to go down; descend; sink. Опусти́ться на одно́ коле́но, to get down on one knee. **2,** (*of a bird or aircraft*) to land. **3,** *fig.* to go downhill; go to seed.

опусте́лый *adj.* deserted.

опусте́ть *v., pfv. of* **пусте́ть.**

опусти́ть [*infl.* **опущу́, опу́стишь**] *v., pfv. of* **опуска́ть.** —**опусти́ться,** *refl., pfv. of* **опуска́ться.**

опустоша́ть *v.impfv.* [*pfv.* **опустоши́ть**] to devastate; ravage; lay waste.

опустоше́ние *n.* devastation.

опустоши́тельный *adj.* devastating.

опустоши́ть *v.pfv.* [*infl.* **-шу́, -ши́шь**] *pfv. of* **опустоша́ть.**

опу́тывать *v.impfv.* [*pfv.* **опу́тать**] **1,** to wind around; tie around: опу́тать что́-нибудь верёвкой, to tie/wind a string around something. **2,** *fig.* to entangle.

опуха́ние *n.* swelling.

опуха́ть *v.impfv.* [*pfv.* **опу́хнуть**] to swell (up); become swollen.

опу́хлый *adj., colloq.* swollen.

опу́хнуть [*past* опу́х, опу́хла] *v., pfv. of* опуха́ть.

о́пухоль *n.f.* **1**, swelling. **2**, tumor.

опуша́ть *v.impfv.* [*pfv.* **опуши́ть**] **1**, to trim with fur. **2**, (*with instr.*) to cover with (fur, snow, frost, etc.).

опу́шка [*gen. pl.* -шек] *n.* **1**, edge of a forest. **2**, fur trimming.

опуще́ние *n.* **1**, lowering. **2**, descent; coming down. **3**, omission. **4**, *med.* prolapse.

опыле́ние *n.* pollination.

опы́ливать *v.impfv.* [*pfv.* опыли́ть] to dust (crops).

опыли́ть *v., pfv. of* опыля́ть *and* опы́ливать.

опыля́ть *v.impfv.* [*pfv.* опыли́ть] to pollinate.

о́пыт *n.* **1**, experience. **2**, experiment.

о́пытный *adj.* **1**, experienced. **2**, experimental.

опьяне́лый *adj., colloq.* intoxicated.

опьяне́ние *n.* intoxication.

опьяне́ть *v., pfv. of* пьяне́ть.

опьяни́ть *v., pfv. of* пьяни́ть *and* опьяня́ть.

опьяня́ть *v.impfv.* [*pfv.* опьяни́ть] to intoxicate; make drunk.

опя́ть *adv.* again. —опя́ть-таки, **1**, again. **2**, and what is more.

ора́ва *n., colloq.* **1**, crowd; mob. **2**, throng; horde.

ора́кул *n.* oracle.

ора́ло *n., obs.* plow. —перекова́ть мечи́ на ора́ла, to beat swords into plowshares.

орангута́нг *n.* orangutan.

ора́нжевый *adj.* orange.

оранжере́я *n.* hothouse; greenhouse. —оранжере́й-ный, *adj.* hothouse (*attrib.*).

ора́тор *n.* speaker; orator.

орато́рия *n.* oratorio.

ора́торский *adj.* oratorical. —ора́торское иску́с-ство, oratory; public speaking.

ора́торствовать *v.impfv.* [*pres.* -ствую, -ствуешь] *colloq.* to orate; perorate.

ора́ть *v.impfv.* [*pres.* ору́, орёшь] *colloq.* to yell; scream.

орби́та *n.* **1**, orbit: быть на орби́те, to be in orbit. **2**, eye socket. —орбита́льный, *adj.* orbital; orbiting.

орга́зм *n.* orgasm.

о́рган *n.* **1**, *physiol.* organ: о́рганы ре́чи, organs of speech. **2**, (governmental) organ; body: о́рганы вла́сти, organs of power; законода́тельный о́рган, legislative body. **3**, organ; publication.

орга́н *n.* organ (*musical instrument*).

организа́тор *n.* organizer. —организа́торский, *adj.* organizational.

организацио́нный *adj.* organizational.

организа́ция *n.* **1**, organization. **2**, an organization.

органи́зм *n.* **1**, organism. **2**, (one's) body; one's system. **3**, constitution; physique.

организо́ванный *adj.* organized; well-organized. —орга-низо́ванно, *adv.* in an organized manner. —органи-зо́ванность, *n.f.* (good) organization.

организова́ть *v.impfv. & pfv.* [*pres.* -зу́ю, -зу́ешь] to organize. —организова́ться, *refl.* **1**, to be organized. **2**, to organize; get organized.

органи́ст *n.* organist.

органи́ческий *adj.* organic.

орга́нный *adj., music* organ (*attrib.*).

о́ргия *n.* orgy.

орда́ [*pl.* о́рды] *n.* horde. —Золота́я орда́, the Golden Horde.

о́рден *n.* **1**, [*pl.* ордена́] order (*medal*): о́рден Кра́сного Зна́мени, Order of the Red Banner. **2**, [*pl.* о́рдены] order (*society*): масо́нский о́рден, the Masonic Order.

орденоно́сец [*gen.* -сца] *n.* holder of an order.

о́рденский *adj.* of or pert. to an order. —о́рденская ле́нта, *mil.* ribbon. —о́рденская пла́нка, bar of ribbons.

о́рдер [*pl.* ордера́] *n.* **1**, warrant; order; writ. **2**, voucher.

ордина́рец [*gen.* -рца] *n., mil.* orderly.

ордина́рный *adj.* ordinary.

ордина́та *n., geom.* ordinate.

орёл [*gen.* орла́] *n.* eagle. —орёл и́ли ре́шка?, heads or tails?

орео́л *n.* **1**, halo. **2**, *fig.* aura.

оре́х *n.* **1**, nut. **2**, walnut (*tree & wood*). —доста́ться на оре́хи (+ *dat.*), *colloq.* to get it hot; get it good. —разде́лывать под оре́х, **1**, to rake over the coals. **2**, to rout.

оре́ховый *adj.* **1**, nut (*attrib.*). **2**, walnut (*attrib.*).

оре́шек [*gen.* -шка] *n., dim. of* оре́х. —бу́ковый оре́шек, beechnut. —черни́льный оре́шек, gallnut.

оре́шник *n.* hazel (*tree*).

оригина́л *n.* **1**, original: чита́ть в оригина́ле, to read in the original. **2**, *colloq.* a character; queer duck; one of a kind.

оригина́льничать *v.impfv., colloq.* to try to be clever.

оригина́льный *adj.* original. —оригина́льность, *n.f.* originality.

ориента́ция *n.* orientation; getting one's bearings.

ориенти́р *n.* landmark; reference point.

ориенти́ровать *v.impfv. & pfv.* [*pres.* -рую, -руешь] to orient. —ориенти́роваться, *refl.* **1**, [*pfv. also* сориенти́роваться] to orient oneself; get one's bearings. Хорошо́/пло́хо ориенти́роваться, to have a good/poor sense of direction. **2**, (*with* на + *acc.*) to be oriented (toward); direct one's efforts (toward).

ориентиро́вка *n.* orientation; getting one's bearings. —чу́вство ориентиро́вки, sense of direction.

ориентиро́вочно *adv.* **1**, approximately. **2**, tentatively.

ориентиро́вочный *adj.* **1**, reference (*attrib.*): ориенти-ро́вочный пункт, reference point. **2**, preliminary; tentative. **3**, approximate.

Орио́н *n.* Orion.

орке́стр *n.* **1**, orchestra. **2**, orchestra pit.

оркестрова́ть *v.impfv. & pfv.* [*pres.* -ру́ю, -ру́ешь] to orchestrate.

оркестро́вка *n.* orchestration.

оркестро́вый *adj.* orchestral.

орла́н *n.* sea eagle; bald eagle.

орлёнок [*gen.* -нка; *pl.* орля́та, орля́т] *n.* eaglet.

орли́ный *adj.* eagle (*attrib.*). —орли́ный нос, aquiline nose.

орна́мент *n.* ornamental design; decorative pattern.

орнитоло́гия *n.* ornithology. —**орнито́лог**, *n.* ornithologist. —**орнитологи́ческий**, *adj.* ornithological.

оробе́лый *adj.* frightened; timid.

оробе́ть *v.pfv.* to become shy; lose one's nerve.

ороси́тельный *adj.* irrigation (*attrib.*).

ороси́ть [*infl.* -шу́, -си́шь] *v., pfv. of* ороша́ть.

ороша́ть *v.impfv.* [*pfv.* ороси́ть] to irrigate.

ороше́ние *n.* irrigation.

ортодо́кс *n.* **1,** person of orthodox views. **2,** Orthodox Jew.

ортодокса́льный *adj.* orthodox. —**ортодо́ксия**, *n.* orthodoxy.

ортодонти́я *n.* orthodontia.

ортопе́дия *n.* orthopedics. —**ортопе́д**, *n.* orthopedist. —**ортопеди́ческий**, *adj.* orthopedic.

ору́дие *n.* **1,** instrument; implement. Ору́дие пы́тки, instrument of torture. Ору́дие уби́йства, the murder weapon. **2,** *fig.* instrument; tool: ору́дия произво́дства, instruments/tools of production. **3,** *fig.* tool: ору́дие в рука́х (+ *gen.*), a tool in the hands of. **4,** *mil.* gun: зени́тное ору́дие, antiaircraft gun.

оруди́йный *adj., mil.* gun (*attrib.*). —**оруди́йный ого́нь**, gunfire.

ору́довать *v.impfv.* [*pres.* -дую, -дуешь] *colloq.* **1,** (*with instr.*) to handle; wield (an instrument). **2,** (*with instr.*) to be in charge of; boss. **3,** to be active; operate.

оруже́йник *n.* gunsmith.

оруже́йный *adj.* gun (*attrib.*); arms (*attrib.*); weapons (*attrib.*). —**оруже́йный ма́стер**, gunsmith. —**Оруже́йная пала́та**, the Armory (*in the Kremlin*).

ору́жие *n.* **1,** weapon. Огнестре́льное ору́жие, firearm. **2,** weapons; arms: я́дерное ору́жие, nuclear weapons. Това́рищ по ору́жию, comrade in arms. Си́лой ору́жия, by force of arms. Бра́ться за ору́жие, to take up arms. —**бить (кого́-нибудь) его́ же ору́жием**, to beat (someone) at his own game.

орфогра́фия *n.* orthography; spelling. —**орфографи́ческий**, *adj.* orthographic; spelling (*attrib.*).

орхиде́я (дэ) *n.* orchid.

оса́ [*pl.* о́сы] *n.* wasp.

оса́да *n.* siege. —**в оса́де**, under siege.

осади́ть [*infl.* осажу́, оса́дишь] *v., pfv. of* осажда́ть *and* оса́живать.

оса́дка *n.* **1,** sinking; settling. **2,** draft (*of a sailing vessel*).

оса́дный *adj.* siege (*attrib.*). —**оса́дное положе́ние**, state of siege.

оса́док [*gen.* -дка] *n.* **1,** sediment. **2,** *fig.* aftertaste. **3,** *pl.* precipitation. —**радиоакти́вные оса́дки**, (radioactive) fallout.

оса́дочный *adj.* sedimentary.

осажда́ть *v.impfv.* [*pfv.* осади́ть] **1,** to lay siege to; besiege. **2,** *fig.* to besiege (with questions, requests, etc.).

оса́живать *v.impfv.* [*pfv.* осади́ть] **1,** to rein in (a horse). **2,** *v.i.* (*of an animal*) to stop short and retreat. **3,** to force back. **4,** to pull down. **5,** *fig., colloq.* to restrain; rein in. **6,** *fig., colloq.* to order (someone) to stop speaking; cut short.

оса́нистый *adj.* imposing; stately.

оса́нка *n.* carriage; bearing.

оса́нна *n.* hosanna.

осва́ивать *v.impfv.* [*pfv.* осво́ить] **1,** to master. **2,** to settle; open up; develop (new territory). —**осва́иваться**, *refl.* **1,** to (come to) feel at home. **2,** (*with* с + *instr.*) to get used to; adjust (to). **3,** (*with* с + *instr.*) to familiarize oneself (with).

осведоми́тель *n.m.* informer; informant. —**осведоми́тельный**, *adj.* pert. to information; information (*attrib.*).

осве́домить [*infl.* -млю, -мишь] *v., pfv. of* осведомля́ть. —**осве́домиться**, *refl., pfv. of* осведомля́ться.

осведомле́ние *n.* notification.

осведомлённость *n.f.* **1,** (*with* о) knowledge (of). **2,** knowledgeability.

осведомлённый *adj.* well-informed; knowledgeable.

осведомля́ть *v.impfv.* [*pfv.* осве́домить] to inform; notify. —**осведомля́ться**, *refl.* (*with* о) to inquire (about).

освежа́ть *v.impfv.* [*pfv.* освежи́ть] **1,** to refresh; freshen up. Освежа́ть в па́мяти что́-нибудь, to refresh one's (*or* someone's) memory about something. **2,** to brush up (one's knowledge of a subject). **3,** to touch up; brighten (the colors in a painting). —**освежа́ться**, *refl.* **1,** to be refreshed. **2,** to freshen up.

освежа́ющий *adj.* refreshing.

освежева́ть *v., pfv. of* свежева́ть.

освеже́ние *n.* refreshment.

освежи́тельный *adj.* refreshing.

освежи́ть *v., pfv. of* освежа́ть. —**освежи́ться**, *refl., pfv. of* освежа́ться.

освети́тельный *adj.* lighting (*attrib.*); illuminating.

освети́ть [*infl.* -щу́, -ти́шь] *v., pfv. of* освеща́ть. —**освети́ться**, *refl., pfv. of* освеща́ться.

освеща́ть *v.impfv.* [*pfv.* освети́ть] **1,** to light up; illuminate. **2,** *fig.* to elucidate; shed light on. **3,** to cover (a newspaper story). —**освеща́ться**, *refl.* to light up.

освеще́ние *n.* **1,** lighting; illumination. **2,** *fig.* interpretation. **3,** *fig.* coverage (*in the press*).

освещённость *n.f.* luminosity.

освиде́тельствование *n.* examination.

освиде́тельствовать *v.pfv.* [*infl.* -ствую, -ствуешь] to examine.

освиста́ть [*infl.* освищу́, освищешь] *v., pfv. of* осви́стывать.

осви́стывать *v.impfv.* [*pfv.* освиста́ть] to hiss (a speaker or performer).

освободи́тель *n.m.* liberator; emancipator.

освободи́тельный *adj.* liberation (*attrib.*): освободи́тельное движе́ние, liberation movement.

освободи́ть [*infl.* -жу́, -ди́шь] *v., pfv. of* освобожда́ть. —**освободи́ться**, *refl., pfv. of* освобожда́ться.

освобожда́ть *v.impfv.* [*pfv.* освободи́ть] **1,** to free; liberate. **2,** (*with* из) to release (from). **3,** (*with* от) to excuse (from); exempt (from). **4,** (*with* от) to relieve; dismiss (of *or* from a position, duties, etc.); remove (from office). **5,** to vacate. **6,** to clear; empty. —**освобожда́ться**, *refl.* **1,** to be freed; be released. **2,** to free oneself; get free. **3,** to be cleared; be vacated.

освобожде́ние *n.* **1,** liberation. **2,** release. **3,** exemption. **4,** evacuation.

освое́ние *n.* **1,** mastering; mastery. **2,** settling; development (*of new territory*).

осво́ить *v., pfv. of* осва́ивать. —**осво́иться,** *refl., pfv. of* осва́иваться.

освяща́ть *v.impfv.* [*pfv.* освяти́ть] to sanctify; hallow; consecrate. —**освящённый века́ми,** time-honored.

освяще́ние *n.* sanctification; consecration.

осево́й *adj.* axial. —**осева́я ли́ния,** center line (*in a road*).

оседа́ть *v.impfv.* [*pfv.* осе́сть] **1,** to settle; sink. **2,** to settle; establish residence.

оседла́ть *v.pfv.* **1,** *pfv. of* седла́ть. **2,** *colloq.* to sit astride; straddle. **3,** *fig.* to get control of; dominate.

осе́длость *n.f.* settled way of life. —**черта́ осе́длости,** the Pale of Settlement; the Jewish Pale.

осе́длый *adj.* settled: осе́длый о́браз жи́зни, settled way of life.

осека́ться *v.r.impfv.* [*pfv.* осе́чься] **1,** *obs.* (*of a gun*) to misfire. **2,** *colloq.* to stop short (*in speaking*); (*of one's voice*) break off. **3,** *colloq.* to suffer a setback.

осёл [*gen.* осла́] *n.* donkey; ass.

осело́к [*gen.* -лка́] *n.* **1,** whetstone. **2,** *fig.* touchstone.

осемене́ние *n.* insemination.

осени́ть *v., pfv. of* осеня́ть.

осе́нний *adj.* autumn (*attrib.*); fall (*attrib.*).

о́сень *n.f.* autumn; fall.

о́сенью *adv.* in autumn; in (the) fall.

осеня́ть *v.impfv.* [*pfv.* осени́ть] **1,** to shade. **2,** (*of a thought*) to strike: Меня́ осени́ло; меня́ осени́ла мысль, the thought struck me; it dawned on me. —**осеня́ть (кого́-нибудь) кресто́м,** to make the sign of the cross over; bless.

осе́сть [*infl.* ося́ду, ося́дешь; *past* осе́л, осе́ла] *v., pfv. of* оседа́ть.

осети́н [*gen. pl.* -ти́н] *n.m.* [*fem.* -ти́нка] Ossetian (*one of a people living on either side of the Russian-Georgian border*). —**осети́нский,** *adj.* Ossetian.

осётр [*gen.* осетра́] *n.* sturgeon. —**осетри́на,** *n.* sturgeon (*prepared as food*). —**осетро́вый,** *adj.* sturgeon (*attrib.*).

осе́чка [*gen. pl.* -чек] *n.* misfire. —**дать осе́чку,** to misfire.

осе́чься [*infl. like* се́чься; *past* осе́кся, осе́клась] *v.r., pfv. of* осека́ться.

оси́ливать *v.impfv.* [*pfv.* оси́лить] **1,** to overpower. **2,** *fig.* to overcome (a feeling, emotion, etc.). **3,** to manage; handle. **4,** *colloq.* to master (a subject); get through (a book).

оси́на *n.* aspen. —**оси́нник,** *n.* aspen grove.

оси́новый *adj.* aspen (*attrib.*). —**дрожа́ть как оси́новый лист,** to shake like a leaf.

оси́ный *adj.* wasp's. —**оси́ное гнездо́,** hornets' nest.

оси́плый *adj.* hoarse; husky.

оси́пнуть *v.pfv.* [*past* оси́п, оси́пла] to become hoarse.

осироте́лый *adj.* orphan (*attrib.*); orphaned.

осироте́ть *v., pfv. of* сироте́ть.

оска́л *n., in* оска́л зубо́в, bared teeth.

оска́лить *v.pfv., in* оска́лить зу́бы, to bare one's teeth; show one's teeth. —**оска́литься,** *refl.* = оска́лить зу́бы.

осканда́литься *v.r., pfv. of* сканда́литься.

оскверне́ние *n.* desecration; defilement.

оскверня́ть *v.impfv.* [*pfv.* оскверни́ть] to desecrate; defile; profane.

оскла́биться *v.r.pfv.* [*infl.* -блюсь, -бишься] to grin.

оско́лок [*gen.* -лка] *n.* splinter; fragment.

оско́лочный *adj.* **1,** fragmentation (*attrib.*): оско́лочная бо́мба, fragmentation bomb. **2,** shrapnel (*attrib.*): оско́лочная ра́на, shrapnel wound.

оско́мина *n.* soreness of the mouth. —**набива́ть оско́мину** (+ *dat.*), **1,** to make one's mouth sore. **2,** *fig.* to bore to death.

оскопля́ть *v.impfv.* [*pfv.* оскопи́ть] to castrate.

оскорби́тельный *adj.* insulting; offensive; abusive.

оскорби́ть [*infl.* -блю́, -би́шь] *v., pfv. of* оскорбля́ть. —**оскорби́ться,** *refl., pfv. of* оскорбля́ться.

оскорбле́ние *n.* insult; affront. —**оскорбле́ние де́йствием,** assault and battery. —**оскорбле́ние суда́,** contempt of court.

оскорбля́ть *v.impfv.* [*pfv.* оскорби́ть] to insult; offend. —**оскорбля́ться,** *refl.* to take offense; be (*or* feel) insulted.

оскуде́ние *n.* impoverishment.

оскуде́ть *v., pfv. of* скуде́ть.

ослабева́ть *v.impfv.* [*pfv.* ослабе́ть] **1,** to weaken; grow weak. **2,** to slacken. **3,** to loosen; come loose.

ослабе́лый *adj., colloq.* weakened; enfeebled.

ослабе́ть *v., pfv. of* слабе́ть *and* ослабева́ть.

осла́бить [*infl.* -блю, -бишь] *v., pfv. of* ослабля́ть.

ослабле́ние *n.* **1,** weakening. **2,** relaxation; slackening.

ослабля́ть *v.impfv.* [*pfv.* осла́бить] **1,** to weaken. **2,** to relax; slacken; lessen. **3,** to loosen.

осла́бнуть *v.pfv.* [*past* осла́б, осла́бла] = ослабе́ть.

осла́вить *v.pfv.* [*infl.* -влю, -вишь] *colloq.* to malign; defame. —**осла́виться,** *refl., colloq.* to get a bad reputation.

ослепи́тельный *adj.* blinding; dazzling.

ослепи́ть [*infl.* -плю́, -пи́шь] *v., pfv. of* ослепля́ть.

ослепле́ние *n.* **1,** (act of) blinding. **2,** *fig.* blindness.

ослепля́ть *v.impfv.* [*pfv.* ослепи́ть] **1,** to blind. **2,** *fig.* to dazzle.

осле́пнуть [*past* осле́п, осле́пла] *v., pfv. of* сле́пнуть.

о́слик *n.* small donkey; burro.

осли́ный *adj.* donkey's.

осли́ца *n.* female donkey.

осложне́ние *n.* complication.

осложня́ть *v.impfv.* [*pfv.* осложни́ть] to complicate. —**осложня́ться,** *refl.* **1,** to become complicated. **2,** (*with instr.*) to be complicated (by).

ослуша́ние *n.* disobedience.

ослу́шаться *v.r.pfv.* (*with gen.*) *colloq.* to disobey.

ослы́шаться *v.r.pfv.* [*infl.* -шусь, -шишься] to hear incorrectly.

ослы́шка *n., colloq.* something heard incorrectly.

осма́тривать *v.impfv.* [*pfv.* осмотре́ть] **1,** to examine; inspect. **2,** to visit (a museum, exhibition, etc.); see (the sights). —**осма́триваться,** *refl.* to look around.

осме́ивать *v.impfv.* [*pfv.* осмея́ть] to ridicule; deride.

осмеле́ть *v., pfv. of* смеле́ть.

осме́ливаться *v.r.impfv.* [*pfv.* **осме́литься**] (*with inf.*) to dare; venture: Осме́люсь сказа́ть, I dare say; I venture to say.

осмея́ние *n.* ridicule; derision; mockery.

осмея́ть [*infl.* **осмею́, осмеёшь**] *v., pfv. of* **осме́ивать**.

о́смий *n.* osmium.

о́смос *n.* osmosis.

осмо́тр *n.* examination; inspection; checkup.

осмотре́ть [*infl.* **осмотрю́, осмо́тришь**] *v., pfv. of* **осма́тривать**. —**осмотре́ться**, *refl., pfv. of* **осма́триваться**.

осмотри́тельный *adj.* wary; circumspect. —**осмотри́тельность,** *n.f.* circumspection.

осмо́трщик *n.* inspector.

осмысле́ние *n.* comprehension.

осмы́сленный *adj.* **1,** intelligent (*able to reason*). **2,** conscious.

осмы́сливать *v.impfv.* [*pfv.* **осмы́слить**] **1,** to comprehend; grasp. **2,** to interpret. *Also,* **осмысля́ть**.

оснасти́ть [*infl.* **-щу́, -сти́шь**] *v., pfv. of* **оснаща́ть**.

осна́стка *n.* **1,** fitting out. **2,** *naut.* rig; rigging.

оснаща́ть *v.impfv.* [*pfv.* **оснасти́ть**] to equip; fit out.

оснаще́ние *n.* **1,** equipping; fitting out. **2,** equipment.

оснащённость *n.f.* level of equipment.

осне́женный *also,* **оснежённый** *adj.* snow-covered.

осно́ва *n.* **1,** base. **2,** *fig.* basis. **3,** *pl.* fundamentals. **4,** *textiles* warp. **5,** *ling.* stem. —**класть (что́-нибудь) в осно́ву; брать** *or* **принима́ть (что́-нибудь) за осно́ву,** to take as a starting point. —**лежа́ть в осно́ве; лечь в осно́ву** (+ *gen.*), **1,** to form the basis of. **2,** to underlie. —**осно́ва осно́в** (+ *gen.*), the cornerstone (of).

основа́ние *n.* **1,** founding. **2,** foundation; base. **3,** *fig.* basis. **4,** reason; grounds; cause. Име́ть основа́ния ду́мать, что..., to have reason to think that... На како́м основа́нии?, on what grounds? Нет основа́ний для трево́ги, there is no cause for alarm. **5,** *chem.; math.* base. —**до основа́ния,** to the ground; to its foundations: разру́шить (что́-нибудь) до основа́ния, to raze to the ground. —**на основа́нии** (+ *gen.*), on the basis of; on the strength of.

основа́тель *n.m.* founder.

основа́тельно *adv.* thoroughly; soundly.

основа́тельность *n.f.* **1,** soundness. **2,** thoroughness.

основа́тельный *adj.* **1,** sound; well-founded. **2,** sound; firm; stable. **3,** (*of a person*) solid; dependable. **4,** thorough. **5,** *colloq.* sizable.

основа́ть [*infl.* **-ную́, -нуёшь**] *v., pfv. of* **осно́вывать**. —**основа́ться**, *refl., pfv. of* **осно́вываться**.

основно́й *adj.* **1,** basic; fundamental; primary. **2,** main; principal; primary. —**в основно́м,** mainly; for the most part; in the main. —**основна́я часть** *or* **ма́сса** (+ *gen.*), the bulk (of).

основополага́ющий *adj.* fundamental.

основополо́жник *n.* founder (*of a school of thought*).

осно́вывать *v.impfv.* [*pfv.* **основа́ть**] **1,** to found. **2,** (*with* **на** + *prepl.*) to base (on). Э́то обвине́ние ни на чём не осно́вано, the charge is completely baseless. —**осно́вываться**, *refl.* **1,** [*impfv. only*] (*with* **на** + *prepl.*) to be based (on). **2,** to be formed. **3,** to settle down.

осо́ба *n.f.* person.

осо́бенно *adv.* especially; particularly.

осо́бенность *n.f.* particular feature; distinctive feature. —**в осо́бенности,** in particular.

осо́бенный *adj.* special; particular; peculiar. —**ничего́ осо́бенного,** nothing special; nothing in particular; nothing much.

особня́к [*gen.* **-няка́**] *n.* private house; mansion.

особняко́м *adv.* apart; by oneself. —**держа́ться особняко́м,** to remain aloof.

осо́бо *adv.* **1,** separately; apart. **2,** especially; particularly.

осо́бый *adj.* **1,** special; particular: осо́бый тип/ме́тод, special type/method. **2,** special; separate: осо́бая ко́мната, special/separate room.

о́собь *n.f.* **1,** individual. **2,** specimen.

осознава́ть *v.impfv.* [*pfv.* **осозна́ть**; *pres.* **-знаю́, -знаёшь**] to realize; become aware of.

осозна́ние *n.* realization; awareness.

осо́знанный *adj.* conscious; deliberate. —**осо́знанно,** *adv.* consciously; deliberately.

осозна́ть [*infl.* **-зна́ю, -зна́ешь**] *v., pfv. of* **осознава́ть**.

осо́ка *n.* sedge.

осоко́рь *n.m.* black poplar.

осоловёлый *adj., colloq.* bleary-eyed.

о́спа *n.* **1,** pox. **2,** smallpox. **3,** *colloq.* pockmarks: изры́тый о́спой, pockmarked. —**ве́тряная о́спа,** chicken pox. —**коро́вья о́спа,** cowpox. —**чёрная о́спа,** (black) smallpox.

оспа́ривать *v.impfv.* [*pfv.* **оспо́рить**] **1,** to challenge; dispute; contest. **2,** [*impfv. only*] to contend for; contest (a championship, prize, etc.).

о́спенный *adj.* smallpox (*attrib.*).

о́спина *n.* pockmark.

оспоприва́ние *n.* vaccination.

оспо́рить *v., pfv. of* **оспа́ривать**.

осрами́ть *v., pfv. of* **срами́ть**. —**осрами́ться**, *refl., pfv. of* **срами́ться**.

ост *n., naut.* **1,** east. **2,** east wind.

остава́ться *v.r.impfv.* [*pfv.* **оста́ться**; *pres.* **остаю́сь, остаёшься**] **1,** to remain; stay. **2,** to be left; remain: Ско́лько вре́мени оста́лось?, how much time is left?; how much time remains? Оста́ться сирото́й, to be left an orphan. Дверь оста́лась неза́пертой, the door was left unlocked. Остаётся то́лько доба́вить, что..., it remains only to add that... **3,** *impers.* (*with dat.*) to have: Ему́ оста́лось недо́лго жить, he hasn't long to live. Нам не остаётся ничего́ друго́го, как..., we have no choice but to... —**остава́ться на второ́й год,** to be left back (*in school*).

оста́вить [*infl.* **-влю, -вишь**] *v., pfv. of* **оставля́ть**.

оставля́ть *v.impfv.* [*pfv.* **оста́вить**] **1,** to leave: оставля́ть кому́-нибудь запи́ску, to leave a note for someone. Оставля́ть кого́-нибудь в беде́, to leave someone stranded/ in the lurch/. **2,** to leave; abandon (one's spouse, family, etc.). **3,** to give up (hope). **4,** (*usu. with* **себе́**) to keep: Оста́вьте себе́ сда́чу!, keep the change! —**оста́вьте!,** stop it! —**оставля́ть без внима́ния,** to disregard; take no notice of. —**оставля́ть жела́ть мно́го лу́чшего,** to leave much to be desired. —**оставля́ть за собо́й, 1,** to keep for oneself; retain. **2,** to reserve: оставля́ть за собо́й пра́во, to reserve the right. —**оставля́ть на второ́й год,** to leave back (*in school*). —**оставля́ть по́сле себя́,** to leave; leave behind (*at one's death*). —**оставля́ть по́сле уро́ков,** to keep in after school.

остально́е *n., decl. as an adj.* the rest.

остально́й *adj.* the other; the remaining; the rest. —**в остально́м; во всём остально́м,** in all other respects. —**всё остально́е,** everything else.

остальны́е *n.pl., decl. as an adj.* the others; the rest.

остана́вливать *v.impfv.* [*pfv.* останови́ть] **1,** to stop; bring (something moving) to a stop. **2,** to stop; halt: останови́ть рабо́ту, to stop/halt work. —**остана́вливать взгляд на** (+ *prepl.*), to rest one's gaze on. —**остана́вливать свой вы́бор на** (+ *prepl.*), to choose; opt for.

остана́вливаться *v.r.impfv.* [*pfv.* останови́ться] **1,** to stop; come to a stop. **2,** to stay (at a hotel, with friends, etc.). **3,** (*with* на + *prepl.*) to dwell on (a subject, details, etc.). **4,** (*with* на + *prepl.*) to settle on; decide on. **5,** *fig.* (*with* пе́ред) to stop (at): ни пе́ред чем не останови́ться, to stop at nothing; не останови́ться пе́ред са́мыми кра́йними ме́рами, not hesitate to use the most extreme measures.

оста́нки [*gen.* **-ков**] *n.pl.* remains (*of a human being*). —**бре́нные оста́нки,** mortal remains.

останови́ть [*infl.* **-новлю́, -но́вишь**] *v., pfv. of* **остана́вливать.** —**останови́ться,** *refl., pfv. of* **остана́вливаться.**

остано́вка [*gen. pl.* **-вок**] *n.* **1,** stop; stopping. **2,** stop; stay. **3,** stop (*of or for a vehicle*): сле́дующая остано́вка, the next stop; авто́бусная остано́вка, bus stop. —**остано́вка се́рдца,** cardiac arrest.

оста́ток [*gen.* **-тка**] *n.* **1,** remainder; rest. **2,** *pl.* remains; vestiges. **3,** *pl.* leftovers; leavings. **4,** residue. **5,** *math.* remainder.

оста́точный *adj.* **1,** remaining. **2,** vestigial. **3,** residual.

оста́ться [*infl.* **оста́нусь, оста́нешься**] *v.r., pfv. of* **остава́ться.**

остекле́ть *v., pfv. of* **стекле́ть.**

остеоло́гия (тэ) *n.* osteology. —**остео́лог,** *n.* osteologist.

остеопоро́з *n.* osteoporosis.

остепени́ть *v.pfv.* to steady (someone) down. —**остепени́ться,** *refl.* to steady down; have sown one's wild oats.

остервене́лый *adj.* frenzied. —**остервене́ние,** *n.* frenzy.

остервене́ть *v.pfv.* to become enraged.

остервени́ть *v.pfv.* to enrage. —**остервени́ться,** *refl.* = **остервене́ть.**

остерега́ть *v.impfv.* [*pfv.* остере́чь] (*with* от) to warn (against); caution (against). —**остерега́ться,** *refl.* **1,** to be careful. **2,** (*with gen.*) to beware (of); be wary (of); guard against. **3,** (*with gen. or inf.*) to avoid.

остере́чь [*infl. like* стере́чь] *v., pfv. of* **остерега́ть.** —**остере́чься,** *refl., pfv. of* **остерега́ться.**

о́стов *n.* **1,** frame; framework. **2,** *anat.* skeleton.

остолбене́лый *adj., colloq.* stupefied; dumbfounded. —**остолбене́ние,** *n.* stupefaction; stupor.

остолбене́ть *v., pfv. of* **столбене́ть.**

остоло́п *n., colloq.* blockhead; bonehead.

осторо́жничать *v.impfv., colloq.* to be overly cautious.

осторо́жно *adv.* carefully; cautiously. —*interj.* careful!; be careful!; look out!; watch out!; watch it!

осторо́жность *n.f.* care; caution.

осторо́жный *adj.* [*short form* **-жен, -жна**] careful; cautious.

осточерте́ть *v.pfv.* (*with dat.*) *colloq.* to make sick and tired: Э́то мне осточерте́ло, I am sick and tired of it; I am fed up with it.

остраки́зм *n.* ostracism.

остра́стка *n., colloq.* warning: для остра́стки, as a warning.

острига́ть *v.impfv.* = **стричь.** —**острига́ться,** *refl.* = **стри́чься.**

острие́ *n.* **1,** (sharp) point. **2,** cutting edge. **3,** *fig.* (*with gen.*) cutting edge (*of a joke, criticism, etc.*).

остри́ть *v.impfv.* **1,** to sharpen. **2,** to make jokes; crack jokes.

остри́чь [*infl. like* стричь] *v., pfv. of* стричь *and* острига́ть. —**остри́чься,** *refl., pfv. of* стри́чься *and* острига́ться.

о́стро *adv.* **1,** (*with verbs of sharpening*) to a fine point. **2,** *fig.* sharply: о́стро критикова́ть, to sharply criticize. О́стро па́хнуть, to have a pungent odor. О́стро нужда́ться в (+ *prepl.*), to be in dire need of.

о́стров [*pl.* острова́] *n.* island.

островитя́нин [*pl.* **-тя́не, -тя́н**] *n.m.* [*fem.* **-тя́нка**] islander.

островно́й *adj.* island (*attrib.*); insular.

острово́к [*gen.* **-вка́**] *n.* small island.

остро́г *n., obs.* jail.

острога́ *n.* spear; harpoon: бить ры́бу острого́й, to spear a fish.

острогла́зый *adj., colloq.* sharp-eyed.

острогу́бцы [*gen.* **-цев**] *n.pl.* cutting pliers.

остроконе́чный *adj.* pointed; coming to a point.

остроли́ст *n.* holly.

остро́та *n.* witticism; quip; wisecrack.

острота́ *n.* sharpness; keenness; pungency.

остроу́мие *n.* wit.

остроу́мно *adv.* **1,** with great wit. **2,** cleverly.

остроу́мный *adj.* **1,** witty. **2,** clever; ingenious.

о́стрый *adj.* **1,** sharp. **2,** acute. **3,** keen. **4,** pungent. **5,** (*of criticism*) harsh; severe. **6,** (*of a situation, moment, etc.*) critical. —**о́стрый на язы́к,** sharp-tongued.

остря́к [*gen.* **-ряка́**] *n.* witty person; wit.

остуди́ть [*infl.* **остужу́, осту́дишь**] *v., pfv. of* студи́ть *and* остужа́ть.

остужа́ть *v.impfv.* [*pfv.* остуди́ть] to cool; chill.

оступа́ться *v.r.impfv.* [*pfv.* оступи́ться] to stumble.

оступи́ться [*infl.* **-ступлю́сь, -сту́пишься**] *v.r., pfv. of* оступа́ться.

остыва́ть *v.impfv.* [*pfv.* осты́ть] **1,** to get cold. **2,** *fig.* to cool off; calm down. **3,** (*with* к) to grow cool (toward). **4,** (*of strong emotions*) to cool.

осты́ть [*infl.* **осты́ну, осты́нешь**] *v., pfv. of* стыть (*in senses #1 & #3*) *and* остыва́ть.

осуди́ть [*infl.* **осужу́, осу́дишь**] *v., pfv. of* осужда́ть.

осужда́ть *v.impfv.* [*pfv.* **осуди́ть**] **1,** to condemn; denounce. **2,** to convict. **3,** to sentence.

осужде́ние *n.* **1,** condemnation; denunciation; censure. **2,** conviction.

осуждённый *n., decl. as an adj.* convict.

осу́нуться *v.r.pfv.* to become drawn in the face.

осуша́ть *v.impfv.* [*pfv.* **осуши́ть**] **1,** to dry. **2,** to drain (a swamp, glass of wine, etc.). —**осуша́ть свои́ слёзы,** to stop crying. —**осуша́ть слёзы** (+ *dat.*), to console.

осуше́ние *n.* drainage. —**осуши́тельный,** *adj.* drainage (*attrib.*).

осуши́ть [*infl.* **осушу́, осу́шишь**] *v., pfv. of* **осуша́ть.**

осуществи́мый *adj.* feasible; practicable. —**осуществи́мость,** *n.f.* feasibility; practicability.

осуществи́ть [*infl.* **-влю́, -ви́шь**] *v., pfv. of* **осуществля́ть.** —**осуществи́ться,** *refl., pfv. of* **осуществля́ться.**

осуществле́ние *n.* realization; fulfillment; implementation.

осуществля́ть *v.impfv.* [*pfv.* **осуществи́ть**] **1,** to carry out; implement. **2,** to accomplish; realize. **3,** to exercise (leadership, a right, etc.). —**осуществля́ться,** *refl.* to be realized; come true.

осцилло́граф *n.* oscillograph.

осциллоско́п *n.* oscilloscope.

осцилля́тор *n.* oscillator.

осчастли́вить *v.pfv.* [*infl.* **-влю, -вишь**] to make happy.

осы́пать [*infl.* **осы́плю, осы́плешь**] *v., pfv. of* **осыпа́ть.** —**осы́паться,** *refl., pfv. of* **осыпа́ться.**

осыпа́ть *v.impfv.* [*pfv.* **осы́пать**] (*with instr.*) **1,** to sprinkle (with); strew (with). **2,** *fig.* to shower (with praise, gifts, etc.); rain (blows) on; hurl (insults) at; heap (ridicule) upon. —**осыпа́ться,** *refl.* **1,** (*of plaster*) to peel off. **2,** to crumble. **3,** (*of leaves*) to fall. **4,** (*with instr.*) to be strewn (with).

ось [*pl.* **о́си, осе́й, ося́м**] *n.f.* **1,** axis. **2,** axle.

осьмино́г *n.* octopus.

осяза́емый *adj.* tangible; palpable.

осяза́ние *n.* touch: чу́вство осяза́ния, sense of touch.

осяза́тельный *adj.* **1,** tactile. **2,** tangible.

осяза́ть *v.impfv.* **1,** to feel. **2,** *fig.* to perceive; sense.

от *also,* **ото** *prep., with gen.* **1,** from: письмо́ от А́ни, a letter from Anya; от Москвы́ до Санкт-Петербу́рга, from Moscow to St. Petersburg; счита́ть от одного́ до десяти́, to count from one to ten. Отходи́ть от стола́, to walk away from the table. **2,** *indicating cause:* дрожа́ть от хо́лода, to tremble from the cold; дрожа́ть от стра́ха, to tremble with fear; умере́ть от ра́ка, to die of cancer. **3,** to; belonging to: ключ от ко́мнаты, the key to the room; пу́говица от пальто́, a button to a coat. **4,** of (*a certain date*): ва́ше письмо́ от седьмо́го ма́рта, your letter of March 7. **5,** for (*an illness*): что́-нибудь от ка́шля, something for a cough; лечи́ть больно́го от я́звы, to treat a patient for an ulcer. **6,** to protect against: сре́дство от насеко́мых, insect repellent; липу́чая бума́га от мух, flypaper.

от- *also,* **ото-, отъ-** *prefix* **1,** *indicating motion away, aside or back:* отходи́ть, to walk away; step back;

отта́лкивать, to push away; push aside. **2,** *indicating taking, carrying, delivering, etc. to a certain place:* отвезти́ (кого́-нибудь) куда́-нибудь, to drive someone somewhere. **3,** *indicating separation, detachment, etc.:* отделя́ть, to separate; отреза́ть, to cut off. **4,** *indicating unfastening, unhooking, etc.:* отстёгивать, to unfasten; отпряга́ть, to unharness; отку́поривать, to uncork. **5,** *indicating response, return, etc.:* отвеча́ть, to answer; отклика́ться, to respond; отдава́ть, to give back; отпла́чивать, to pay back. **6,** *indicating rejection, refusal, etc.:* отка́зываться, to refuse; отверга́ть, to reject; отрека́ться, to renounce. **7,** *indicating completion of an action:* отобе́дать, to be finished with dinner; отде́лывать, to put into final form.

ота́пливать *v.impfv.* [*pfv.* **отопи́ть**] to heat (a building, room, etc.). —**ота́пливаться,** *refl.* [*impfv. only*] to be heated.

ота́ра *n.* flock (*of sheep*).

отбавля́ть *v.impfv.* [*pfv.* **отба́вить**] (*with gen.*) to pour off (a certain amount of). —**хоть отбавля́й,** more than enough; enough and then some.

отбараба́нить *v.pfv., colloq.* **1,** to stop drumming. **2,** to bang out (*on a musical instrument*). **3,** to rattle off (a speech, answers, etc.).

отбега́ть *v.impfv.* [*pfv.* **отбежа́ть**] to run away; run back.

отбежа́ть [*infl. like* **бежа́ть**] *v., pfv. of* **отбега́ть.**

отбе́ливать *v.impfv.* [*pfv.* **отбели́ть**] to bleach.

отбели́ть [*infl.* **-белю́, -бе́лишь** *or* **-бели́шь**] *v., pfv. of* **отбе́ливать.**

отбива́ть *v.impfv.* [*pfv.* **отби́ть**] **1,** to break off. **2,** to beat off; repel; repulse (an attack); beat back (an attacker); parry; deflect (a blow). **3,** to recapture; retake. **4,** *colloq.* to take away; remove (a taste, odor, desire, etc.). **5,** to hurt; injure. **6,** to sharpen; hone. **7,** to beat (time). **8,** *sports* to return (a ball). —**отбива́ться,** *refl.* **1,** to be broken off. **2,** to defend oneself; fight back; (*with* **от**) fight off. **3,** to fall behind; (*with* **от**) stray (from). **4,** (*with* **от**) *colloq.* to drift away from; get away from. **5,** *in* **отби́ться от рук,** to get out of hand.

отбивно́й *adj., in* отбивна́я котле́та, chop; cutlet. Бара́нья/свина́я отбивна́я, lamp/pork chop. Теля́чья отбивна́я, veal chop; veal cutlet.

отбира́ть *v.impfv.* [*pfv.* **отобра́ть**] **1,** to take away; take (from): отбира́ть конфе́ты у ребёнка, to take candy (away) from a child. **2,** to select.

отби́ть [*infl.* **отобью́, отобьёшь**] *v., pfv. of* **отбива́ть.** —**отби́ться,** *refl., pfv. of* **отбива́ться.**

отблагодари́ть *v.pfv.* **1,** to thank. **2,** to show one's appreciation to.

о́тблеск *n.* **1,** reflection. **2,** *fig.* (*with gen.*) spark (of); trace (of).

отбо́й *n.* **1,** *mil.* retreat: дава́ть *or* бить отбо́й, to sound retreat. **2,** the all-clear signal. —**бить отбо́й, 1,** to beat a retreat. **2,** *fig.* to back down. —**дать отбо́й,** to ring off; hang up (the receiver). —**отбо́ю нет от,** no end of: У меня́ нет отбо́ю от предложе́ний, I've had no end of offers.

отбо́йный *adj., in* **отбо́йный молото́к,** mechanical pick; **пневмати́ческий отбо́йный молото́к,** jackhammer.

отбо́р *n.* selection.

отбо́рный *adj.* **1,** select; choice. Отбо́рные войска́, crack troops. **2,** *colloq.* (*of swearwords*) choice; unprintable.

отбо́рочный *adj.* **1,** selection (*attrib.*). **2,** *sports* qualifying: отбо́рочные соревнова́ния, qualifying rounds, heats, etc.

отбоя́риваться *v.r.impfv.* [*pfv.* **отбоя́риться**] (*with* **от**) *colloq.* to get out of; avoid.

отбра́сывать *v.impfv.* [*pfv.* **отбро́сить**] **1,** to throw aside; cast aside. **2,** *mil.* to throw back; hurl back. **3,** to cast (light, a shadow, etc.). **4,** *fig.* to reject; dismiss (an idea, theory, etc.); cast aside (thoughts, doubts, etc.).

отбро́сить [*infl.* **-шу, -сишь**] *v., pfv. of* **отбра́сывать.**

отбро́сы [*gen.* **-сов**] *n.pl.* refuse; garbage.

отбыва́ть *v.impfv.* [*pfv.* **отбы́ть**] **1,** *v.i.* to leave; depart. **2,** *v.t.* to serve; serve out (time, a sentence, etc.).

отбы́тие *n.* **1,** departure. **2,** serving; completion (*of a sentence, term, etc.*).

отбы́ть [*infl.* **-бу́ду, -бу́дешь;** *past* **о́тбыл, отбыла́, о́тбыло, о́тбыли**] *v., pfv. of* **отбыва́ть.**

отва́га *n.* courage; bravery.

отва́живать *v.impfv.* [*pfv.* **отва́дить**] (*with* **от**) *colloq.* **1,** to break (someone) of the habit (of). **2,** to drive off; scare off. —**отва́живаться,** *refl.* **1,** [*pfv.* **отва́диться**] (*with* **от**) *colloq.* to break the habit of; get out of the habit of. **2,** [*pfv.* **отва́житься**] to dare; venture.

отва́жный *adj.* courageous; brave. —**отва́жно,** *adv.* courageously; bravely.

отва́л *n.* **1,** casting off (*of a boat*). **2,** heap; dump: отва́л шла́ка, slag heap. —**до отва́ла,** to the bursting point.

отва́ливать *v.impfv.* [*pfv.* **отвали́ть**] **1,** to push aside. **2,** *v.i.* (*of a boat*) to cast off. **3,** *colloq.* to hand out (money). —**отва́ливаться,** *refl.* **1,** to fall off; come off. **2,** *colloq.* to lean back.

отвали́ть [*infl.* **-валю́, -ва́лишь**] *v., pfv. of* **отва́ливать.** —**отвали́ться,** *refl., pfv. of* **отва́ливаться.**

отва́льная *n., decl. as an adj., colloq.* farewell party.

отва́р *n.* decoction. —**мясно́й отва́р,** stock. —**ри́совый отва́р,** rice water.

отва́ривать *v.impfv.* [*pfv.* **отвари́ть**] to boil.

отвари́ть [*infl.* **-варю́, -ва́ришь**] *v., pfv. of* **отва́ривать.**

отварно́й *adj.* boiled.

отве́дывать *v.impfv.* [*pfv.* **отве́дать**] **1,** to try; taste. **2,** to taste; experience.

отвезти́ [*infl. like* **везти́**] *v., pfv. of* **отвози́ть.**

отверга́ть *v.impfv.* [*pfv.* **отве́ргнуть**] to reject; turn down.

отве́ргнуть [*past* **отве́рг, отве́ргла**] *v., pfv. of* **отверга́ть.**

отвердева́ть *v.impfv.* [*pfv.* **отверде́ть**] to harden; solidify.

отверде́лый *adj.* hard; hardened.

отверде́ть *v., pfv. of* **отвердева́ть.**

отве́рженный *adj. & n.* outcast.

отверну́ть *v., pfv. of* **отвёртывать** *and* **отвора́чивать.** —**отверну́ться,** *refl., pfv. of* **отвёртываться** *and* **отвора́чиваться.**

отве́рстие *n.* **1,** opening; hole. **2,** aperture. **3,** slot (*for a coin*). **4,** orifice.

отверте́ться [*infl.* **-верчу́сь, -ве́ртишься**] *v.r., pfv. of* **отвёртываться** (*in sense #3*).

отвёртка [*gen. pl.* **-ток**] *n.* screwdriver.

отвёртывать *v.impfv.* [*pfv.* **отверну́ть**] **1,** = отвора́чивать. **2,** to turn on (a faucet). **3,** to unscrew; screw off. —**отвёртываться,** *refl.* **1,** = отвора́чиваться. **2,** to come unscrewed. **3,** [*pfv.* **отверте́ться**] (*with* **от**) *colloq.* to get out of; avoid; evade.

отве́с *n.* **1,** plumb. **2,** sheer cliff.

отве́сить [*infl.* **-шу, -сишь**] *v., pfv. of* **отве́шивать.**

отве́сный *adj.* sheer; vertical; perpendicular. —**отве́сная скала́,** cliff.

отвести́ [*infl. like* **вести́**] *v., pfv. of* **отводи́ть.**

отве́т *n.* answer; reply: в отве́т на (+ *acc.*), in answer/reply to. —**без отве́та,** unanswered: оста́вить/оста́ться без отве́та, to leave/go unanswered. —**(быть) в отве́те за** (+ *acc.*), to be responsible for.

ответви́ться *v.r., pfv. of* **ответвля́ться.**

ответвле́ние *n.* branch; offshoot.

ответвля́ться *v.r.impfv.* [*pfv.* **ответви́ться**] to branch off.

отве́тить [*infl.* **-чу, -тишь**] *v., pfv. of* **отвеча́ть.**

отве́тный *adj.* **1,** return (*attrib.*): отве́тный визи́т, return visit. **2,** in reply: отве́тная речь, speech in reply. **3,** retaliatory.

отве́тственность *n.f.* responsibility: нести́ отве́тственность за (+ *acc.*), to bear the responsibility for.

отве́тственный *adj.* **1,** responsible: отве́тственный за рабо́ту, responsible for the work. **2,** senior: отве́тственный рабо́тник, senior official. **3,** crucial: отве́тственный моме́нт, crucial moment. —**отве́тственный реда́ктор,** managing editor.

отве́тчик *n.* **1,** *law* defendant. **2,** *colloq.* person responsible. **3,** answering machine.

отвеча́ть *v.impfv.* [*pfv.* **отве́тить**] **1,** (*with dat.*) to answer; reply (to) (a person); (*with* **на** + *acc.*) (a question, letter, etc.). **2,** (*with* **на** + *acc.*) to respond to (a request, appeal, etc.). **3,** (*with* **на** + *acc.*) to return; reciprocate: отвеча́ть на ого́нь проти́вника, to return the enemy's fire. **4,** [*impfv. only*] (*with* **за** + *acc.*) to answer (for); be responsible (for). **5,** [*pfv. only*] (*with* **за** + *acc.*) to pay for: Вы за э́то отве́тите!, you'll pay for this! **6,** [*impfv. only*] (*with dat.*) to meet; answer (needs, requirements, etc.). **7,** *in* отвеча́ть уро́к, to recite one's lesson.

отве́шивать *v.impfv.* [*pfv.* **отве́сить**] **1,** to weigh out. **2,** *colloq.* to deal; dish out (a blow). **3,** *in* отве́шивать покло́н, to make a bow.

отви́ливать *v.impfv.* [*pfv.* **отвильну́ть**] (*with* **от**) *colloq.* to avoid; dodge.

отви́нчивать *v.impfv.* [*pfv.* **отвинти́ть**] to unscrew; screw off.

отвиса́ть *v.impfv.* [*pfv.* **отви́снуть**] to hang down; sag; droop.

отви́слый *adj.* loose-hanging; flaccid.

отви́снуть [*past* **отви́с, отви́сла**] *v., pfv. of* **отви-са́ть.**

отвлека́ть *v.impfv.* [*pfv.* **отвле́чь**] to distract; divert. —**отвлека́ться,** *refl.* **1,** to be distracted. **2,** (*with* **от**) to digress (from).

отвлека́ющий *adj., mil.* diversionary.

отвлече́ние *n.* **1,** distraction; diversion. **2,** abstraction.

отвлечённый *adj.* abstract. —**отвлечённо,** *adv.* in an abstract manner; in the abstract.

отвле́чь [*infl. like* **влечь**] *v., pfv. of* **отвлека́ть.** —**отвле́чься,** *refl., pfv. of* **отвлека́ться.**

отво́д *n.* **1,** taking; delivering. **2,** draining off (*of water*). **3,** allocation (*of land*). **4,** diversion: для отво́да глаз, to divert attention. **5,** rejection (*of a candidate*); challenge (*to a witness*).

отводи́ть *v.impfv.* [*pfv.* **отвести́;** *pres.* **-вожу́, -во́дишь**] **1,** to take (someone on foot to a certain place): отводи́ть ребёнка в шко́лу, to take a child to school. **2,** to lead away; take away. **3,** to draw aside. **4,** *mil.* to pull back (troops). **5,** to deflect; ward off. **6,** to drain; drain off (water). **7,** to allot; allocate; allow; assign. Отвести́ роль кому́-нибудь, to assign a part to someone. Отводи́ть вре́мя на вопро́сы, to allow time for questions. **8,** (*with* **под** + *acc. or* **для**) to set aside; designate (for a certain purpose): отвести́ уча́сток под сад, to set aside a plot for a garden; отвести́ поме-ще́ние для мастерско́й, to designate the premises to be a workshop. **9,** to reject. —**отводи́ть глаза́,** to avert (*or* turn away) one's eyes. —**отводи́ть глаза́** (+ *dat.*), to mislead; delude; lead astray. —**отводи́ть ду́шу,** to let out one's feelings; unburden oneself; (*with* **на** + *prepl.*) take out one's anger on.

отво́дный *adj.* drainage (*attrib.*); drain (*attrib.*).

отвоева́ть *v.pfv.* [*infl.* **-вою́ю, -вою́ешь**] **1,** *pfv. of* **отвоёвывать. 2,** *colloq.* to fight (*for a certain length of time*). **3,** *colloq.* to finish fighting.

отвоёвывать *v.impfv.* [*pfv.* **отвоева́ть**] to win back (*in war*); retake.

отвози́ть *v.impfv.* [*pfv.* **отвезти́;** *pres.* **-вожу́, -во́зишь**] **1,** to take; drive (someone to a certain place). **2,** to take away; cart away.

отвора́чивать *v.impfv.* [*pfv.* **отверну́ть**] **1,** to turn away; turn aside. **2,** to turn down; fold down. **3,** *v.i., colloq.* to turn; make a turn. —**отвора́чиваться,** *refl.* (*with* **от**) to turn away (from); turn one's back (on).

отвори́ть [*infl.* **отворю́, отво́ришь**] *v., pfv. of* **отворя́ть.** —**отвори́ться,** *refl., pfv. of* **отворя́ться.**

отворо́т *n.* **1,** lapel. **2,** cuff.

отворя́ть *v.impfv.* [*pfv.* **отвори́ть**] to open. —**от-воря́ться,** *refl.* to open; come open; be opened.

отврати́тельный *adj.* **1,** disgusting. **2,** *colloq.* miserable; rotten.

отвраща́ть *v.impfv.* [*pfv.* **отврати́ть**] **1,** *obs.* to turn away. **2,** to avert; ward off.

отвраще́ние *n.* disgust; repugnance; loathing; aversion.

отвыка́ть *v.impfv.* [*pfv.* **отвы́кнуть**] (*with* **от**) **1,** to become unaccustomed to. **2,** to get out of the habit of. **3,** to become estranged (from).

отвы́кнуть [*past* **отвы́к, отвы́кла**] *v., pfv. of* **от-выка́ть.**

отвяза́ть [*infl.* **-вяжу́, -вя́жешь**] *v., pfv. of* **отвя́зы-вать.** —**отвяза́ться,** *refl., pfv. of* **отвя́зываться.**

отвя́зывать *v.impfv.* [*pfv.* **отвяза́ть**] to untie; unfasten. —**отвя́зываться,** *refl.* **1,** to come untied; come loose. **2,** to break loose. **3,** (*with* **от**) *colloq.* to get rid of; rid oneself of; shake off. **4,** (*with* **от**) *colloq.* to leave alone; leave in peace.

отгада́ть *v., pfv. of* **отга́дывать.**

отга́дка [*gen. pl.* **-док**] *n.* answer; solution (*to a riddle*).

отга́дчик *n., colloq.* guesser.

отга́дывать *v.impfv.* [*pfv.* **отгада́ть**] **1,** to guess (*correctly*). **2,** to solve (a riddle).

отгиба́ть *v.impfv.* [*pfv.* **отогну́ть**] **1,** to unbend; straighten. **2,** to turn down; turn back.

отглаго́льный *adj., gram.* verbal: отглаго́льное су-ществи́тельное, verbal noun.

отгла́живать *v.impfv.* [*pfv.* **отгла́дить**] to iron; press.

отгова́ривать *v.impfv.* [*pfv.* **отговори́ть**] (*with inf. or* **от**) **1,** to dissuade; talk out of. **2,** [*impfv. only*] to try to dissuade; try to talk out of. —**отгова́риваться,** *refl.* **1,** to beg off (*by giving excuses*). **2,** (*with instr.*) to cite; plead (illness, ignorance, etc.).

отгово́рка [*gen. pl.* **-рок**] *n.* excuse.

отголо́сок [*gen.* **-ска**] *n.* **1,** echo. **2,** faint sound. **3,** *fig.* sympathetic response. **4,** *pl.* repercussions; aftereffects; aftermath.

отгоня́ть *v.impfv.* [*pfv.* **отогна́ть**] to drive away; chase away; drive off.

отгора́живать *v.impfv.* [*pfv.* **отгороди́ть**] **1,** to fence off; partition off. **2,** *fig.* to shut off; isolate. —**от-гора́живаться,** *refl.* **1,** to be fenced off. **2,** to fence oneself off. **3,** *fig.* (*with* **от**) to shut (*or* cut) oneself off (from).

отгоре́ть *v.impfv.* [*pfv.* **отгоре́ть**] **1,** to burn down; die out. **2,** to fall off; break off (*after burning*).

отгоре́ть [*infl.* **-горю́, -гори́шь**] *v., pfv. of* **отгора́ть.**

отгороди́ть [*infl.* **-рожу́, -ро́дишь** *or* **-роди́шь**] *v., pfv. of* **отгора́живать.** —**отгороди́ться,** *refl., pfv. of* **отгора́живаться.**

отгреба́ть *v.impfv.* [*pfv.* **отгрести́**] **1,** *v.t.* to rake away. **2,** *v.i.* to row away.

отгреме́ть *v.pfv.* [*infl.* **-ми́т**] to die down; fall silent.

отгрести́ [*infl. like* **грести́**] *v., pfv. of* **отгреба́ть.**

отгружа́ть *v.impfv.* [*pfv.* **отгрузи́ть**] to ship.

отгрузи́ть [*infl.* **-гружу́, -гру́зишь** *or* **-грузи́шь**] *v., pfv. of* **отгружа́ть.**

отгру́зка *n.* shipment.

отгрыза́ть *v.impfv.* [*pfv.* **отгры́зть**] to bite off; gnaw off.

отгры́зть [*infl. like* **грызть**] *v., pfv. of* **отгрыза́ть.**

отгу́л *n.* compensatory leave.

отгу́ливать *v.impfv.* [*pfv.* **отгуля́ть**] *colloq.* to take (time) off; take compensatory leave: отгу́ливать два дня, to take two days off; take two days compensatory leave.

отгуля́ть *v.pfv., colloq.* **1,** *pfv. of* **отгу́ливать. 2,** to reach the end of (one's vacation). **3,** to celebrate (a holiday, wedding, etc.). **4,** to finish celebrating.

отдава́ть *v.impfv.* [*pfv.* **отда́ть;** *pres.* **отдаю́, отда-ёшь**] **1,** to give back; return. **2,** to repay (a debt). **3,** to hand over; turn over. **4,** to devote: отдава́ть жизнь теа́тру, to devote one's life to the theater. **5,** (*with* **в** + *acc.*) to have (cleaned, repaired, etc.): отда́ть (что́-нибудь) в чи́стку/ремо́нт, to have something cleaned/repaired. **6,** (*with various nouns*) to give: отда́ть прика́з, to give an order; отда́ть предпочте́ние (+ *dat.*), to give preference (to); отда́ть жизнь за (+ *acc.*), to give one's life (for). Всё отда́м, что́бы..., I'd give anything to... **7,** to place (in school). **8,** *colloq.* to sell (something cheap): Я отда́м вам э́то за де́сять до́лларов, I'll let you have it for ten dollars. **9,** *v.i.* (*of a gun*) to recoil. **10,** *v.i.* [*impfv. only*] (*with instr.*) to taste of; smell of; smack of. —**отдава́ть в зало́г,** to pawn. —**отдава́ть до́лжное,** *see* **до́лжное.** —**отдава́ть (кого́-нибудь) под суд,** to prosecute; bring to trial. —**отдава́ть после́дний долг** (+ *dat.*), to pay one's last respects to. —**отдава́ть свой го́лос** (+ *dat.*), to cast one's vote (for). —**отдава́ть себе́ отчёт,** *see* **отчёт.** —**отдава́ть честь** (+ *dat.*), *mil.* to salute.

отдава́ться *v.r.impfv.* [*pfv.* **отда́ться;** *pres.* **-даю́сь, -даёшься**] **1,** (*with dat.*) to give oneself up (to). **2,** (*with dat.*) (*of a woman*) to give in (to). **3,** (*with dat.*) to devote oneself (to). **4,** (*of a sound*) to resound; reverberate. Отдава́ться э́хом, to echo. **5,** (*of pain*) to be felt. Боль отдаётся в се́рдце, my heart aches. В моём се́рдце отдава́лось бо́лью, I felt sick at heart.

отдави́ть *v.pfv.* [*infl.* **-давлю́, -да́вишь**], *in* отдави́ть но́гу (+ *dat.*), to step on someone's foot (*or* toe).

отдале́ние *n.* **1,** removal. **2,** estrangement. **3,** distance. —**в отдале́нии,** in the distance. —**на отдале́нии,** at a distance.

отдалённость *n.f.* **1,** remoteness. **2,** distance.

отдалённый *adj.* remote; distant. —**места́ не столь отдалённые,** place of exile (*in tsarist times*).

отдаля́ть *v.impfv.* [*pfv.* **отдали́ть**] **1,** to remove; move away. **2,** to postpone; put off. **3,** to estrange; alienate. —**отдаля́ться,** *refl.* (*with* **от**) **1,** to drift away (from). **2,** to digress (from).

отда́ние *n., in* **отда́ние че́сти,** salute.

отда́ривать *v.impfv.* [*pfv.* **отдари́ть**] *colloq.* to give (a gift) in return.

отда́ть [*infl. like* **дать;** *past* **о́тдал, отдала́, о́тдало, о́тдали**] *v., pfv. of* **отдава́ть.** —**отда́ться,** *refl.* [*past tense stress as in* **да́ться**] *pfv. of* **отдава́ться.**

отда́ча *n.* **1,** return; returning. **2,** paying back (*a debt*). **3,** return (*on an investment*). **4,** giving (*of an order*). **5,** recoil; kick (*of a gun*). —**без отда́чи,** with no intention of returning it. —**с по́лной отда́чей,** giving one's all.

отде́л *n.* **1,** section. **2,** department: отде́л зака́зов, order department. **3,** *mil.* branch.

отде́лать *v., pfv. of* **отде́лывать.** —**отде́латься,** *refl., pfv. of* **отде́лываться.**

отделе́ние *n.* **1,** separation. **2,** department; section; division; branch. Почто́вое отделе́ние, local post office. **3,** compartment; section. **4,** part (*of a concert, performance, etc.*). **5,** *mil.* squad. —**коте́льное отделе́ние,** boiler room. —**маши́нное отделе́ние,** engine room. —**роди́льное отделе́ние,** maternity ward.

отдели́ть [*infl.* **-делю́, -де́лишь**] *v., pfv. of* **отделя́ть.** —**отдели́ться,** *refl., pfv. of* **отделя́ться.**

отде́лка *n.* **1,** decorating. **2,** finishing. Оконча́тельная отде́лка, finishing touches. **3,** finish; surface: ме́дная отде́лка, copper finish. **4,** trimming; trim.

отде́лывать *v.impfv.* [*pfv.* **отде́лать**] **1,** to put into final form. **2,** to decorate; trim. **3,** to finish (a surface). **4,** *colloq.* to rebuke; bawl out. —**отде́лываться,** *refl., colloq.* **1,** (*with* **от**) to finish; be done with; get out of the way. **2,** (*with* **от**) to get rid of. **3,** (*with* **от**) to shake off (a feeling). **4,** (*with instr. or an adv.*) to get off (with): отде́латься штра́фом, to get off with a fine; дёшево отде́латься, to get off cheap.

отде́льно *adv.* **1,** separately; apart. **2,** individually.

отде́льность *n.f., in* **в** *or* **по отде́льности,** individually; separately.

отде́льный *adj.* **1,** separate. **2,** individual.

отделя́ть *v.impfv.* [*pfv.* **отдели́ть**] **1,** to separate. **2,** [*impfv. only*] to divide; serve as the boundary between. —**отделя́ться,** *refl.* (*with* **от**) **1,** to become separated (from). **2,** to come off. **3,** to move away (from).

отдёргивать *v.impfv.* [*pfv.* **отдёрнуть**] **1,** to pull back; draw back. **2,** to pull aside; draw aside.

отдира́ть *v.impfv.* [*pfv.* **отодра́ть**] to tear off; rip off.

отдохну́ть *v., pfv. of* **отдыха́ть.**

отдува́ть *v.impfv.* [*pfv.* **отду́ть**] to blow away: отдува́ть пар, to blow away the steam. —**отдува́ться,** *refl.* **1,** to become puffed up. **2,** (*of one's pockets*) to bulge. **3,** [*impfv. only*] to pant; puff. **4,** [*impfv. only*] (*with* **за** + *acc.*) *colloq.* to take the rap (for).

отду́мывать *v.impfv.* [*pfv.* **отду́мать**] (*with inf.*) *colloq.* to change one's mind (about).

отду́ть [*infl.* **-ду́ю, -ду́ешь**] *v., pfv. of* **отдува́ть.** —**отду́ться,** *refl., pfv. of* **отдува́ться.**

отду́шина *n.* **1,** (air) vent. **2,** *fig.* outlet (*for one's emotions*).

о́тдых *n.* rest. —**дом о́тдыха,** rest home.

отдыха́ть *v.impfv.* [*pfv.* **отдохну́ть**] **1,** to rest. **2,** to be on vacation; take a vacation.

отдыша́ться *v.r.pfv.* [*infl.* **-дышу́сь, -ды́шишься**] to catch one's breath.

отёк *n., med.* edema.

отека́ть *v.impfv.* [*pfv.* **оте́чь**] **1,** to swell up; become swollen. **2,** to become numb. **3,** (*of a candle*) to drip.

отели́ться *v.r., pfv. of* **тели́ться.**

оте́ль (тэ) *n.m.* hotel.

отепля́ть *v.impfv.* [*pfv.* **отепли́ть**] to winterize.

оте́ц [*gen.* **отца́**] *n.* father. —**оте́ческий,** *adj.* fatherly; paternal.

оте́чественый *adj.* **1,** native. **2,** domestically produced. —**Вели́кая Оте́чественная война́,** the Great Patriotic War (*World War II*).

оте́чество *n.* native land; homeland; fatherland.

оте́чь [*infl. like* **течь**] *v., pfv. of* **отека́ть.**

отжа́ть [*infl.* **отожму́, отожмёшь**] *v., pfv. of* **отжима́ть.**

отже́чь [*infl.* **отожгу́, отожжёшь, ...отожгу́т;** *past* **отжёг, отожгла́**] *v., pfv. of* **отжига́ть.**

отжива́ть *v.impfv.* [*pfv.* **отжи́ть**] to die out; become a thing of the past. *See also* **отжи́ть.**

отжи́вший *adj.* **1,** having lived out one's life. **2,** out-of-date; obsolete.

отжига́ть *v.impfv.* [*pfv.* **отже́чь**] to anneal.

отжима́ть *v.impfv.* [*pfv.* **отжа́ть**] **1**, to wring out. **2**, to squeeze out (liquid). **3**, *colloq.* to push back; force back.

отжи́ть *v.pfv.* [*infl.* -**живу́, -живёшь;** *past* **о́тжил, отжила́, о́тжило, о́тжили**] **1**, *pfv. of* **отжива́ть. 2**, to have lived one's life. —**отжи́ть свой век,** to become a thing of the past; have had one's day.

отзвони́ть *v.pfv.* **1**, (*of a clock*) to strike (a certain hour). **2**, to stop ringing.

о́тзвук *n.* **1**, echo. **2**, faint sound. **3**, *fig.* sympathetic response. **4**, *pl.* reverberations.

о́тзыв *n.* **1**, review; comment: получи́ть благоприя́тные о́тзывы, to receive favorable reviews/notices/comment. **2**, (character) reference. **3**, *fig.* responsive chord. **4**, reply (*to a password*).

отзы́в *n.* recall (*of an ambassador, representative, etc.*).

отзыва́ть *v.impfv.* [*pfv.* **отозва́ть**] **1**, to take aside. **2**, to recall (an ambassador). **3**, *v.i.* [*impfv. only*] (*with instr.*) `colloq.` to have the taste of; smell faintly of. —**отзыва́ться,** *refl.* **1**, to answer. **2**, (*with* на + *acc.*) to respond to (an appeal, request, etc.). **3**, to reverberate. **4**, (*with* на + *prepl.*) to affect; have an effect on. **5**, (*with* о) to speak (well, badly, etc.) of; comment (favorably, negatively, etc.) on.

отзы́вчивый *adj.* responsive; kindhearted; sympathetic. —**отзы́вчивость,** *n.f.* sympathy; kindheartedness; empathy.

отка́з *n.* **1**, refusal. Получи́ть отка́з, to be turned down. **2**, repudiation; renunciation; disavowal. **3**, failure; breakdown: де́йствовать без отка́за, to work perfectly. —**наби́тый до отка́за,** chock-full; filled to the brim.

отказа́ть [*infl.* -**кажу́, -ка́жешь**] *v., pfv. of* **отка́зывать.** —**отказа́ться,** *refl., pfv. of* **отка́зываться.**

отка́зывать *v.impfv.* [*pfv.* **отказа́ть**] **1**, to say no: Он не уме́ет отка́зывать, he doesn't know how to say no. **2**, (*with dat.*) to turn (someone) down: Ему́ отказа́ли, they turned him down; he was turned down. **3**, (*with dat. and* в + *prepl.*) to refuse; deny: отка́зывать кому́-нибудь в по́мощи, to refuse help to someone; отка́зывать себе́ в са́мом необходи́мом, to deny oneself (even) the barest necessities. Ему́ нельзя́ отказа́ть в остроу́мии, you can't say he is not clever. **4**, to fail to operate; fail.

отка́зываться *v.r.impfv.* [*pfv.* **отказа́ться**] **1**, (*with inf.*) to refuse (to). **2**, (*with* от) to turn down; decline. Не откажу́сь от (*or with inf.*), I wouldn't mind... **3**, (*with* от) to abandon; give up; relinquish. **4**, (*with* от) to retract; renounce; repudiate; disavow; disown. —**отказа́ться служи́ть** *or* **рабо́тать,** (*of one's heart, a machine, etc.*) to fail.

отка́лывать *v.impfv.* [*pfv.* **отколо́ть**] **1**, to chop off; break off. **2**, to unpin. —**отка́лываться,** *refl.* **1**, to break off; break away. **2**, (*with* от) *fig.* to break away (from); cut oneself off (from). **3**, to come unpinned.

отка́пывать *v.impfv.* [*pfv.* **откопа́ть**] **1**, to dig up; disinter; exhume. **2**, *fig., colloq.* to dig up; unearth.

отка́рмливать *v.impfv.* [*pfv.* **откорми́ть**] to fatten up.

отка́т *n.* recoil (*of an artillery gun*).

откати́ть [*infl.* -**качу́, -ка́тишь**] *v., pfv. of* **отка́тывать.** —**откати́ться,** *refl., pfv. of* **отка́тываться.**

отка́тывать *v.impfv.* [*pfv.* **откати́ть**] to roll (away, aside, or back). —**отка́тываться,** *refl.* **1**, to roll away; roll back. **2**, (*of troops*) to retreat; fall back. **3**, (*of an artillery gun*) to recoil.

отка́чивать *v.impfv.* [*pfv.* **откача́ть**] **1**, to pump out. **2**, to give artificial respiration to.

откачну́ться *v.r.pfv., colloq.* **1**, to swing to one side. **2**, to reel back; slump back.

отка́шливаться *v.r.impfv.* [*pfv.* **отка́шляться**] to clear one's throat.

откидно́й *adj.* folding; collapsible.

отки́дывать *v.impfv.* [*pfv.* **отки́нуть**] **1**, to cast aside; throw aside; toss aside. **2**, (*with* наза́д) to throw back. **3**, to fold back; fold aside; raise; open. —**отки́дываться,** *refl.* to lean back; settle back.

откла́дывание *n., chess* adjournment.

откла́дывать *v.impfv.* [*pfv.* **отложи́ть**] **1**, to lay aside; put aside; set aside. **2**, to postpone; put off. **3**, to adjourn. **4**, to unhitch; unharness.

откла́ниваться *v.r.impfv.* [*pfv.* **откла́няться**] *obs.* to depart; take one's leave.

откле́ивать *v.impfv.* [*pfv.* **откле́ить**] to peel off (something that is stuck). —**откле́иваться,** *refl.* to come unstuck; come off.

о́тклик *n.* **1**, response. **2**, echo. **3**, *pl.* reaction; comments. **4**, *fig.* responsive chord.

откли́каться *v.r.impfv.* [*pfv.* **откли́кнуться**] **1**, to answer; reply. **2**, (*with* на + *acc.*) to respond (to). **3**, [*impfv. only*], *in* откли́каться э́хом, to echo.

отклоне́ние *n.* **1**, rejection; denial. **2**, deviation; departure; digression. **3**, deflection.

отклони́ть [*infl.* -**клоню́, -кло́нишь**] *v., pfv. of* **отклоня́ть.** —**отклони́ться,** *refl., pfv. of* **отклоня́ться.**

отклоня́ть *v.impfv.* [*pfv.* **отклони́ть**] **1**, to deflect. **2**, to reject; turn down; decline. **3**, to dissuade; talk out of. —**отклоня́ться,** *refl.* (*with* от) to deviate (from); digress (from); stray (from).

отключа́ть *v.impfv.* [*pfv.* **отключи́ть**] to unplug; disconnect; cut off; shut off. —**отключа́ться,** *refl.* to become disconnected.

откозыря́ть *v.pfv.* (*with dat.*) *colloq.* to salute.

отколоти́ть *v.pfv.* [*infl.* -**лочу́, -ло́тишь**] *colloq.* **1**, to knock off; hammer off. **2**, to beat up.

отколо́ть [*infl.* -**колю́, -ко́лешь**] *v., pfv. of* **отка́лывать.** —**отколо́ться,** *refl., pfv. of* **отка́лываться.**

откомандирова́ть [*infl.* -**ру́ю, -ру́ешь**] *v., pfv. of* **откомандиро́вывать.**

откомандиро́вывать *v.impfv.* [*pfv.* **откомандирова́ть**] **1**, to send (*on an assignment*). **2**, to assign; transfer.

откопа́ть *v., pfv. of* **отка́пывать.**

откорми́ть [*infl.* -**кормлю́, -ко́рмишь**] *v., pfv. of* **отка́рмливать.**

отко́с *n.* slope; side (*of a hill, embankment, etc.*): свали́ться под отко́с, to go/ tumble over/ plunge down/ an embankment. Пусти́ть *or* толка́ть по́езд под отко́с, to derail a train. —**пойти́ под отко́с,** to fall apart; go to pieces.

открепля́ть *v.impfv.* [*pfv.* **открепи́ть**] **1,** to unfasten. **2,** to strike off the list.

откре́щиваться *v.r.impfv.* (*with* **от**) *colloq.* **1,** to try to avoid; shun. **2,** to disavow; disown.

открове́ние *n.* revelation.

открове́нничать *v.impfv.* (*with* **с** + *instr.*) *colloq.* to be frank (with); open up (to).

открове́нно *adv.* frankly. **—открове́нно говоря́,** frankly (speaking); to be perfectly frank.

открове́нность *n.f.* frankness; candor.

открове́нный *adj.* [*short form* **-нен, -нна**] **1,** frank; candid; outspoken. **2,** undisguised; unconcealed. **3,** *colloq.* (*of a woman's garment*) revealing.

открути́ть [*infl.* **-кручу́, -кру́тишь**] *v., pfv. of* **откру́чивать**.

откру́чивать *v.impfv.* [*pfv.* **открути́ть**] to untwist; unscrew.

открыва́лка [*gen. pl.* **-лок**] *n., colloq.* opener: открыва́лка для буты́лок/консе́рвов, bottle/can opener.

открыва́тель *n.m.* discoverer.

открыва́ть *v.impfv.* [*pfv.* **откры́ть**] **1,** to open. **2,** to uncover; reveal. **3,** to unveil; dedicate (a monument). **4,** to discover. **5,** to reveal (a secret). **6,** to begin; launch. **7,** *colloq.* to turn on (water, gas, a faucet, etc.). **8,** *in* откры́ть счёт, to score first; be the first to score. **—открыва́ться,** *refl.* **1,** to open; be opened. **2,** (*with* **пе́ред**) to open up before one's eyes. **3,** *fig.* to be revealed; come to light. **4,** (*with dat.*) to open up to; confide in.

откры́тие *n.* **1,** opening. **2,** unveiling; dedication (*of a monument*). **3,** discovery.

откры́тка [*gen. pl.* **-ток**] *n.* postcard.

откры́то *adv.* openly.

откры́тость *n.f.* openness.

откры́тый *adj.* **1,** open: Окно́ откры́то, the window is open; бассе́йн откры́т, the swimming pool is open. Откры́тый автомоби́ль, open car; convertible. Откры́тое письмо́, open letter. **2,** outdoor: откры́тый бассе́йн, outdoor swimming pool. **3,** (*of a dress*) low-cut. **—в откры́тую,** openly.

откры́ть [*infl.* **-кро́ю, -кро́ешь**] *v., pfv. of* **открыва́ть. —откры́ться,** *refl., pfv. of* **открыва́ться.**

отку́да *adv.* **1,** from where: Отку́да вы?, where are you from? Он верну́лся туда́, отку́да он пришёл, he returned to the place from whence he came. **2,** from what source?; how?: Отку́да вы э́то зна́ете?, how do you (happen) to know that? Отку́да же я зна́ю?, how should I know? **—откуда́ ни возьми́сь,** from out of nowhere; from out of the blue.

отку́да-либо *adv.* = **отку́да-нибудь.**

отку́да-нибудь *adv.* from somewhere or other.

отку́да-то *adv.* from somewhere.

о́ткуп *n.* tax farming. **—брать на о́ткуп,** to acquire exclusive rights to. **—отдава́ть на о́ткуп,** to farm out.

откупа́ть *v.impfv.* [*pfv.* **откупи́ть**] *obs.* to buy up. **—откупа́ться,** *refl.* (*with* **от**) *colloq.* to buy off; pay off.

откупи́ть [*infl.* **-куплю́, -ку́пишь**] *v., pfv. of* **откупа́ть. —откупи́ться,** *refl., pfv. of* **откупа́ться.**

отку́поривать *v.impfv.* [*pfv.* **отку́порить**] to uncork; open.

откуси́ть [*infl.* **-кушу́, -ку́сишь**] *v., pfv. of* **отку́сывать.**

отку́сывать *v.impfv.* [*pfv.* **откуси́ть**] to bite off.

отлага́тельство *n.* delay. **—не терпе́ть отлага́тельства,** to brook no delay.

отла́дить [*infl.* **-жу, -дишь**] *v., pfv. of* **отла́живать.**

отла́женный *adj.* smoothly functioning; well-oiled.

отла́живать *v.impfv.* [*pfv.* **отла́дить**] to adjust; put in good working order.

отлакирова́ть *v., pfv. of* **лакирова́ть.**

отла́мывать *v.impfv.* [*pfv.* **отлома́ть** *or* **отломи́ть**] to break off. **—отла́мываться,** *refl.* to break off; fall off; come off.

отлега́ть *v.impfv.* [*pfv.* **отле́чь**] (*of a pain, feeling, etc.*) to pass. **—у меня́ отлегло́ от се́рдца,** I felt relieved.

отлежа́ть [*infl.* **-лежу́, -лежи́шь**] *v., pfv. of* **отлёживать. —отлежа́ться,** *refl., pfv. of* **отлёживаться.**

отлёживать *v.impfv.* [*pfv.* **отлежа́ть**] to cause to become numb: Я отлежа́л(а) но́гу, my foot is asleep. **—отлёживаться,** *refl., colloq.* **1,** to recover (*after spending time in bed*). **2,** [*impfv. only*] to lie low.

отлёт *n.* departure (*by flying*). **—на отлёте, 1,** off at a distance. **2,** away from everything. **3,** about to leave. **—держа́ть (что́-нибудь) на отлёте,** to hold in one's outstretched hand.

отлета́ть *v.impfv.* [*pfv.* **отлете́ть**] **1,** to fly away; fly off. **2,** to be thrown (*from a blow or jolt*). **3,** to rebound; ricochet. **4,** *colloq.* to come off; come loose.

отлете́ть [*infl.* **-чу́, -ти́шь**] *v., pfv. of* **отлета́ть.**

отле́чь [*infl. like* **лечь**] *v., pfv. of* **отлега́ть.**

отли́в *n.* **1,** ebb; ebb tide. **2,** *fig.* ebb; decline; falling off. **3,** tint; fleck (*of color*). **—прили́в и отли́в,** ebb and flow of the tides. **—прили́вы и отли́вы,** tide; tides.

отлива́ть *v.impfv.* [*pfv.* **отли́ть**] **1,** to pour off. **2,** to pump out. **3,** to cast: отли́ть ста́тую из бро́нзы, to cast a statue in bronze. **4,** *v.i.* (*of a liquid*) to flow; rush: Кровь отлила́ от его́ лица́, the blood rushed from his face (*i.e.* he turned pale). **5,** *colloq.* to revive (*by throwing water on*). **6,** *v.i.* [*impfv. only*] (*with instr.*) to be streaked with (a certain color).

отли́вка *n.* casting.

отлипа́ть *v.impfv.* [*pfv.* **отли́пнуть**] *colloq.* to come unstuck.

отли́пнуть [*past* **отли́п, отли́пла**] *v., pfv. of* **отлипа́ть.**

отли́ть [*infl.* **отолью́, отольёшь;** *past* **о́тлил** *or* **отли́л, отлила́, о́тлило** *or* **отли́ло, о́тлили** *or* **отли́ли**] *v., pfv. of* **отлива́ть.**

отлича́ть *v.impfv.* [*pfv.* **отличи́ть**] **1,** to distinguish; tell (from): отлича́ть фиоле́товый цвет от лило́вого, to distinguish violet from purple. **2,** [*impfv. only*] to distinguish; set apart: что отлича́ет его́ от други́х — э́то... what sets him apart from the others is... **3,** [*impfv. only*] to single out. **4,** to reward; honor. **—отлича́ться,** *refl.* **1,** to stand out. **2,** to distinguish oneself; excel. **3,** [*impfv. only*] (*with* **от**) to differ (from). **4,** [*impfv. only*] (*with instr.*) to be remarkable (for); be notable (for): Он не отлича́ется умо́м, he is not particularly bright.

отли́чие *n.* **1,** difference; distinction. **2,** distinguished service. **3,** honors; distinction: око́нчить шко́лу с отли́чием, to graduate with honors. **4,** *in* знак отли́чия, *mil.* medal; decoration. **—в отли́чие от,** unlike; as opposed to; in contrast to; as distinct from.

отличи́тельный *adj.* distinguishing; distinctive.

отличи́ть *v., pfv. of* **отлича́ть. —отличи́ться,** *refl., pfv. of* **отлича́ться.**

отли́чник *n.* **1,** A-student. **2,** outstanding worker.

отли́чно *adv.* excellently; very well. **—adj.,** *used predicatively,* excellent. **—n.** a grade of A (*in school*): сдать экза́мен на отли́чно, to get an A on an examination.

отли́чный *adj.* **1,** excellent. **2,** (*with* **от**) different (from).

отло́гий *adj.* not steep; gently sloping.

отложе́ние *n.* **1,** *geol.* sediment. **2,** deposit: жировы́е отложе́ния, fatty deposits.

отложи́ть [*infl.* -ложу́, -ло́жишь] *v., pfv. of* **откла́дывать.**

отложно́й *adj.* (*of a collar*) turndown.

отлома́ть *v., pfv. of* **отла́мывать. —отлома́ться,** *refl., pfv. of* **отла́мываться.**

отломи́ть [*infl.* -ломлю́, -ло́мишь] *v., pfv. of* **отла́мывать. —отломи́ться,** *refl., pfv. of* **отла́мываться.**

отлупи́ть *v., pfv. of* **лупи́ть** (*in sense #4*).

отлуча́ть *v.impfv.* [*pfv.* **отлучи́ть**] **1,** *obs.* to remove; separate. **2,** *in* отлуча́ть от це́ркви, to excommunicate. **—отлуча́ться,** *refl.* to go away; leave; absent oneself.

отлуче́ние *n.* **1,** *obs.* separation. **2,** *in* отлуче́ние от це́ркви, excommunication.

отлучи́ть *v., pfv. of* **отлуча́ть. —отлучи́ться,** *refl., pfv. of* **отлуча́ться.**

отлу́чка *n.* absence: быть в отлу́чке, to be absent; be away. **—самово́льная отлу́чка,** absence without leave.

отлы́нивать *v.impfv.* (*with* **от**) *colloq.* to shirk.

отма́лчиваться *v.r.impfv.* [*pfv.* **отмолча́ться**] *colloq.* to keep silent; say nothing.

отма́тывать *v.impfv.* [*pfv.* **отмота́ть**] to wind off.

отмаха́ть [*infl.* -маха́ю, -маха́ешь] *v., pfv. of* **отма́хивать** (*in sense #2*).

отма́хивать *v.impfv.* **1,** [*pfv.* **отмахну́ть**] to brush away; chase away. **2,** [*pfv.* **отмаха́ть**] *colloq.* to cover (a certain distance). **—отма́хиваться,** *refl.* [*pfv.* **отмахну́ться**] **1,** to wave one's hand (*in disagreement or to object*). **2,** (*with* **от**) to brush away; brush off; chase away. **3,** *fig.* (*with* **от**) to brush aside; wave aside; dismiss.

отма́чивать *v.impfv.* [*pfv.* **отмочи́ть**] to soak off.

отмежева́ть [*infl.* -жу́ю, -жу́ешь] *v., pfv. of* **отмежёвывать. —отмежева́ться,** *refl., pfv. of* **отмежёвываться.**

отмежёвывать *v.impfv.* [*pfv.* **отмежева́ть**] to mark off; delimit. **—отмежёвываться,** *refl.* (*with* **от**) to dissociate oneself (from); distance oneself (from).

о́тмель *n.f.* shoal. **—песча́ная о́тмель,** sandbank. sand bar.

отме́на *n.* **1,** abolition. **2,** cancellation. **3,** repeal.

отмени́ть [*infl.* -меню́, -ме́нишь] *v., pfv. of* **отменя́ть.**

отме́нный *adj.* excellent; splendid.

отменя́ть *v.impfv.* [*pfv.* **отмени́ть**] **1,** to abolish. **2,** to cancel. **3,** to repeal; rescind; annul.

отмере́ть [*infl.* **отомрёт;** *past* о́тмер, отмерла́, о́тмерло, о́тмерли] *v., pfv. of* **отмира́ть.**

отмерза́ть *v.impfv.* [*pfv.* **отмёрзнуть**] **1,** to perish from the frost. **2,** *colloq.* (*of one's hands, ears, etc.*) to be frozen.

отмёрзнуть [*past* -мёрз, -мёрзла] *v., pfv. of* **отмерза́ть.**

отме́ривать *v.impfv.* [*pfv.* **отме́рить**] to measure off. *Also,* **отмеря́ть.**

отмести́ [*infl. like* мести́] *v., pfv. of* **отмета́ть.**

отме́стка *n., colloq.* revenge. **—в отме́стку,** in revenge; in retaliation.

отмета́ть *v.impfv.* [*pfv.* **отмести́**] **1,** to sweep away; sweep off. **2,** *fig.* to wave aside; brush aside; sweep aside.

отме́тина *n.* **1,** mark. **2,** spot of color (*on an animal or bird*).

отме́тить [*infl.* -чу, -тишь] *v., pfv. of* **отмеча́ть. —отме́титься,** *refl., pfv. of* **отмеча́ться.**

отме́тка [*gen. pl.* -ток] *n.* **1,** mark; note. **2,** grade; mark (*in school*).

отмеча́ть *v.impfv.* [*pfv.* **отме́тить**] **1,** to mark. **2,** to note; take note of. **3,** to mark; celebrate; commemorate. **—отмеча́ться,** *refl.* **1,** to register. **2,** *colloq.* to sign out. **3,** [*impfv. only*] to be noticed. **4,** to be noted.

отмира́ть *v.impfv.* [*pfv.* **отмере́ть**] **1,** to die; die off. **2,** *fig.* to die out; disappear.

отмока́ть *v.impfv.* [*pfv.* **отмо́кнуть**] **1,** to get wet. **2,** to come off (*as a result of being wet*).

отмо́кнуть [*past* отмо́к, отмо́кла] *v., pfv. of* **отмока́ть.**

отмолча́ться [*infl.* -чу́сь, -чи́шься] *v.r., pfv. of* **отма́лчиваться.**

отмора́живать *v.impfv.* [*pfv.* **отморо́зить**] (*with* **себе́**) to get (a part of one's body) frostbitten: Он отморо́зил себе́ нос, his nose was frostbitten.

отморо́жение *n.* frostbite.

отморо́зить [*infl.* -жу, -зишь] *v., pfv. of* **отмора́живать.**

отмота́ть *v., pfv. of* **отма́тывать.**

отмочи́ть [*infl.* -мочу́, -мо́чишь] *v., pfv. of* **отма́чивать.**

отмыва́ть *v.impfv.* [*pfv.* **отмы́ть**] **1,** to wash off. **2,** wash; wash clean. **—отмыва́ться,** *refl.* **1,** to wash oneself off. **2,** to become clean. **3,** to come off; come out (*when something is washed*).

отмыка́ть *v.impfv.* [*pfv.* **отомкну́ть**] *colloq.* to unlock.

отмы́ть [*infl.* отмо́ю, отмо́ешь] *v., pfv. of* **отмыва́ть. —отмы́ться,** *refl., pfv. of* **отмыва́ться.**

отмы́чка [*gen. pl.* -чек] *n.* **1,** master key; skeleton key. **2,** jimmy.

отне́киваться *v.r.impfv., colloq.* to decline (by making excuses).

отнести́ [*infl. like* нести́] *v., pfv. of* **относи́ть. —отнести́сь,** *refl., pfv. of* **относи́ться.**

отнима́ть *v.impfv.* [*pfv.* **отня́ть**] **1,** to take away. **2,** to withdraw; remove (one's hand). **3,** to rob of (hope, faith, etc.). **4,** to take (a certain amount of time, effort, etc.). **5,** *colloq.* to amputate. **6,** *colloq.* to subtract; take away. —**отнима́ться,** *refl. (of a part of one's body)* to become paralyzed.

относи́тельно *adv.* relatively. —*prep., with gen.* regarding; concerning.

относи́тельность *n.f.* relativity. —**тео́рия относи́тельности,** theory of relativity.

относи́тельный *adj.* relative. —**относи́тельное местоиме́ние,** relative pronoun.

относи́ть *v.impfv.* [*pfv.* **отнести́;** *pres.* **-ношу́, -но́сишь**] **1,** to take; carry; deliver (to a certain place or person). **2,** (*with* **от** *or* **с**) to carry away (from); move away (from). **3,** (*of the wind, current, etc.*) to sweep (to, toward, away, etc.). **4,** (*with* **к**) consider (among); place (among); place (in a certain category). Относи́ть на счёт (+ *gen.*), to attribute to; put down to. Относи́ть что́-нибудь к пятна́дцатому ве́ку, to place something in the 15th century.

относи́ться *v.r.impfv.* [*pfv.* **отнести́сь;** *pres.* **-ношу́сь, -но́сишься**] (*with* **к**) **1,** to behave (toward); act (toward); treat. **2,** to react (toward); have a certain attitude (toward). **3,** [*impfv. only*] to belong to; be among. К э́той катего́рии отно́сятся..., this category includes... **4,** [*impfv. only*] to apply to; pertain to: Э́то не отно́сится к вам, this does not apply to you. Э́то не отно́сится к де́лу, that is beside the point. **5,** [*impfv. only*] to date (from).

отноше́ние *n.* **1,** (*with* **к**) attitude (toward). **2,** (*with* **к**) relation; relationship; connection: не име́ть никако́го отноше́ния к, bear no relation(ship) to; have no connection with; have nothing to do with. **3,** *pl.* relations: междунаро́дные отноше́ния, international relations. Быть в хоро́ших отноше́ниях с, to be on good terms with. **4,** respect; regard; connection: в э́том отноше́нии, in this connection; во мно́гих отноше́ниях, in many respects. **5,** ratio. **6,** memorandum. —**в отноше́нии** (+ *gen.*); **по отноше́нию к,** with respect to; with regard to.

отны́не *adv.* hereafter; henceforth; from now on.

отню́дь *adv.* [*usu.* **отню́дь не**] by no means; in no way.

отня́тие *n.* **1,** taking away; seizure. **2,** *colloq.* amputation.

отня́ть [*infl.* **отниму́, отни́мешь;** *past* **о́тнял, отняла́, о́тняло, о́тняли**] *v., pfv. of* **отнима́ть.** —**отня́ться,** *refl.* [*past* **отня́лся, -ла́сь, -ло́сь, -ли́сь**] *pfv. of* **отнима́ться.**

ото *prep.* = **от** (*used before certain words beginning with two consonants; e.g.* день ото дня).

отобе́дать *v.pfv.* to have finished dinner.

отобража́ть *v.impfv.* [*pfv.* **отобрази́ть**] to reflect; depict; represent.

отображе́ние *n.* reflection; representation.

отобрази́ть [*infl.* **-жу́, -зи́шь**] *v., pfv. of* **отобража́ть.**

отобра́ть [*infl.* **отберу́, отберёшь;** *past fem.* **отобрала́**] *v., pfv. of* **отбира́ть.**

отова́ривать *v.impfv.* [*pfv.* **отова́рить**] to redeem; exchange for merchandise.

отовсю́ду *adv.* from everywhere.

отогна́ть [*infl.* **отгоню́, отго́нишь;** *past fem.* **отогнала́**] *v., pfv. of* **отгоня́ть.**

отогну́ть *v., pfv. of* **отгиба́ть.**

отогрева́ть *v.impfv.* [*pfv.* **отогре́ть**] to warm. —**отогрева́ться,** *refl.* to warm oneself; warm up; get warm.

отодвига́ть *v.impfv.* [*pfv.* **отодви́нуть**] **1,** to move aside; move away. **2,** *colloq.* to put off; postpone. **3,** to relegate: отодвига́ть на за́дний план, to relegate to the background. —**отодвига́ться,** *refl.* **1,** to move aside; step aside. **2,** to move back; draw back. **3** *colloq.* to be postponed; be put off.

отодра́ть [*infl.* **отдеру́, отдерёшь;** *past fem.* **отодрала́**] *v., pfv. of* **отдира́ть.**

отождествля́ть *also,* **отожествля́ть** *v.impfv.* [*pfv.* **отождестви́ть** *or* **отожестви́ть**] **1,** to equate. **2,** (*with* **с** + *instr.*) to identify (something with something). Отождествля́ть себя с, to identify with.

отозва́ть [*infl.* **отзову́, отзовёшь;** *past fem.* **отозвала́**] *v., pfv. of* **отзыва́ть.** —**отозва́ться,** *refl.* [*past tense stress as in* зва́ться] *pfv. of* **отзыва́ться.**

отойти́ [*infl.* **отойду́, отойдёшь;** *past* **отошёл, отошла́, отошло́, отошли́**] *v., pfv. of* **отходи́ть.**

отомкну́ть *v., pfv. of* **отмыка́ть.**

отомсти́ть *v., pfv. of* **мстить.**

отопи́тельный *adj.* heating (*attrib.*). Отопи́тельный сезо́н, season when heat is required.

отопи́ть [*infl.* **отоплю́, ото́пишь**] *v., pfv. of* **ота́пливать.**

отопле́ние *n.* heating.

ото́рванность *n.f.* isolation; being cut off.

оторва́ть [*infl.* **оторву́, оторвёшь;** *past fem.* **оторвала́**] *v., pfv. of* **отрыва́ть.** —**оторва́ться,** *refl.* [*past tense stress as in* рва́ться] *pfv. of* **отрыва́ться.**

оторопе́лый *adj., colloq.* dazed; dumbfounded.

оторопе́ть *v.pfv., colloq.* to be struck dumb; be dumbfounded.

о́торопь *n.f., colloq.* confusion; panic; fright.

оторо́чка *n.* edging; trimming.

отосла́ть [*infl.* **отошлю́, отошлёшь**] *v., pfv. of* **отсыла́ть.**

отоспа́ться [*infl.* **-сплю́сь, -спи́шься**] *v.r., pfv. of* **отсыпа́ться.**

отоща́лый *adj., colloq.* emaciated.

отоща́ть *v., pfv. of* **тоща́ть.**

отпада́ть *v.impfv.* [*pfv.* **отпа́сть**] **1,** to fall off; come off; peel off. **2,** (*with* **от**) to drop out of (an organization). **3,** to cease to have significance; be no longer relevant. **4,** (*of a feeling*) to pass.

отпари́ровать *v.pfv.* [*infl.* **-рую, -руешь**] **1,** to parry (a blow). **2,** *fig.* to rebut (attacks, an argument, etc.). **3,** to retort.

отпа́рывать *v.impfv.* [*pfv.* **отпоро́ть**] to snip off; rip off. —**отпа́рываться,** *refl.* to come off; tear off.

отпа́сть [*infl. like* **пасть**] *v., pfv. of* **отпада́ть.**

отпева́ние *n.* (religious) funeral service.

отпева́ть *v.impfv.* [*pfv.* **отпе́ть**] to hold a funeral service for. *See also* **отпе́ть.**

отпере́ть [*infl.* **отопру́, отопрёшь;** *past* **о́тпер, отперла́, о́тперло, о́тперли**] *v., pfv. of* **отпира́ть.** —**отпере́ться,** *refl.* [*past* **отперся́, -ла́сь, -ло́сь, -ли́сь**] *pfv. of* **отпира́ться.**

отпётый *adj., colloq.* incorrigible.

отпе́ть *v.pfv.* [*infl.* **отпою́, отпоёшь**] **1,** *pfv. of* **отпева́ть. 2,** to sing; chant (a song, prayer, etc.). **3,** to stop singing; finish singing.

отпеча́тать *v., pfv. of* **отпеча́тывать.** —**отпеча́таться,** *refl., pfv. of* **отпеча́тываться.**

отпеча́ток [*gen.* **-тка**] *n.* **1,** print; imprint: отпеча́ток па́льца, fingerprint. **2,** *fig.* imprint; mark: накла́дывать свой отпеча́ток на (+ *acc.*), to leave its mark on.

отпеча́тывать *v.impfv.* [*pfv.* **отпеча́тать**] **1,** to print; run off. **2,** to type (something) on a typewriter. **3,** *photog.* to print. **4,** to make (fingerprints or footprints): отпеча́тать следы́ на песке́, to make footprints in the sand.

отпива́ть *v.impfv.* [*pfv.* **отпи́ть**] to take a sip of.

отпи́ливать *v.impfv.* [*pfv.* **отпили́ть**] to saw off.

отпили́ть [*infl.* **-пилю́, -пи́лишь**] *v., pfv. of* **отпи́ливать.**

отпира́тельство *n.* persistent denial; refusal to confess.

отпира́ть *v.impfv.* [*pfv.* **отпере́ть**] to unlock. —**отпира́ться,** *refl.* **1,** to unlock; come unlocked. **2,** *colloq.* to deny; (*with* **от**) disavow.

отписа́ть [*infl.* **-пишу́, -пи́шешь**] *v., pfv. of* **отпи́сывать.** —**отписа́ться,** *refl., pfv. of* **отпи́сываться.**

отпи́ска [*gen. pl.* **-сок**] *n.* noncommittal answer; answer that is not really an answer.

отпи́сывать *v.impfv.* [*pfv.* **отписа́ть**] *obs.* **1,** to confiscate. **2,** to bequeath. —**отпи́сываться,** *refl., colloq.* to write a purely formal reply.

отпи́ть *v.pfv.* [*infl.* **отопью́, отопьёшь; past** о́тпил, отпила́, о́тпило, о́тпили] **1,** *pfv. of* **отпива́ть. 2,** *colloq.* to finish drinking.

отпи́хивать *v.impfv.* [*pfv.* **отпихну́ть**] *colloq.* to push away; push aside; shove aside.

отпла́та *n.* repayment. —**в отпла́ту за,** in repayment for; in return for.

отплати́ть [*infl.* **-плачу́, -пла́тишь**] *v., pfv. of* **отпла́чивать.**

отпла́чивать *v.impfv.* [*pfv.* **отплати́ть**] (*with dat.*) to pay back; repay (someone).

отплёвывать *v.impfv.* [*pfv.* **отплю́нуть**] *colloq.* **1,** *v.t.* to spit out. **2,** *v.i.* to spit (a certain distance). —**отплёвываться,** *refl.* [*impfv. only*] to spit (*in disgust*).

отплыва́ть *v.impfv.* [*pfv.* **отплы́ть**] **1,** to swim away; (*with* **от**) swim a certain distance (from). **2,** (*of a ship*) to set sail; depart. **3,** to float away; float off. **4,** *fig.* to slip away.

отплы́тие *n.* sailing; departure.

отплы́ть [*infl. like* **плыть**] *v., pfv. of* **отплыва́ть.**

отплю́нуть *v., pfv. of* **отплёвывать.**

о́тповедь *n.f.* rebuke.

отполза́ть *v.impfv.* [*pfv.* **отползти́**] to crawl away.

отползти́ [*infl. like* **ползти́**] *v., pfv. of* **отполза́ть.**

отполирова́ть *v., pfv. of* **полирова́ть.**

отпо́р *n.* rebuff.

отпоро́ть [*infl.* **-порю́, -по́решь**] *v., pfv. of* **отпа́рывать.** —**отпоро́ться,** *refl., pfv. of* **отпа́рываться.**

отправи́тель *n.m.* sender.

отпра́вить [*infl.* **-влю, -вишь**] *v., pfv. of* **отправля́ть.** —**отпра́виться,** *refl., pfv. of* **отправля́ться.**

отпра́вка *n.* **1,** dispatch; shipment. **2,** departure.

отправле́ние *n.* **1,** sending; dispatch. **2,** departure. **3,** item of mail. **4,** exercise; performance; discharge. **5,** *pl.* functions (*of the body*). —**то́чка отправле́ния,** point of departure.

отправля́ть *v.impfv.* [*pfv.* **отпра́вить**] **1,** to send; dispatch. **2,** [*impfv. only*] to discharge; perform. Отправля́ть правосу́дие, to administer justice. —**отправля́ться,** *refl.* **1,** [*often* отправля́ться в путь] to leave; start out; set out. **2,** [*impfv. only*] (*with* **от**) to proceed from (*in one's thinking*).

отправно́й *adj.* **1,** dispatch (*attrib.*); shipping (*attrib.*). **2,** initial. —**отправно́й пункт; отправна́я то́чка,** starting point.

отпра́здновать *v., pfv. of* **пра́здновать.**

отпра́шиваться *v.r.impfv.* [*pfv.* **отпроси́ться**] **1,** [*usu. impfv.*] to request permission to be absent. **2,** [*usu. pfv.*] to obtain permission to be absent: отпроси́ться на одну́ неде́лю, to (ask for and) get a week off.

отпроси́ться [*infl.* **-прошу́сь, -про́сишься**] *v.r., pfv. of* **отпра́шиваться.**

отпры́гивать *v.impfv.* [*pfv.* **отпры́гнуть**] to jump back; jump aside.

о́тпрыск *n.* **1,** *bot.* shoot. **2,** *fig., obs.* offspring; scion.

отпряга́ть *v.impfv.* [*pfv.* **отпря́чь**] to unharness.

отпря́нуть *v.pfv.* to jump back; draw back; recoil.

отпря́чь [*infl.* **-прягу́, -пряжёшь, ...-прягу́т; past** -пря́г, -прягла́, -прягло́, -прягли́] *v., pfv. of* **отпряга́ть.**

отпу́гивать *v.impfv.* [*pfv.* **отпугну́ть**] to frighten away; frighten off.

о́тпуск [*pl.* **отпуска́**] *n.* **1,** vacation: в о́тпуске (*or colloquially* в отпуску́), on vacation. **2,** leave: о́тпуск по боле́зни, sick leave.

отпуска́ть *v.impfv.* [*pfv.* **отпусти́ть**] **1,** to let go of. **2,** to let go; release (a prisoner, animal, bird, etc.). **3,** to let; allow (someone) to go (somewhere). **4,** (*with* **с** + *gen.*) to excuse (from class, a meeting, etc.). **5,** to dismiss (pupils, a class, etc.). **6,** to loosen; slacken. **7,** to release (a brake). **8,** *v.i., colloq.* (*of pain*) to lessen; ease. **9,** to grow (a beard, mustache, etc.); let (one's hair, nails, etc.) grow. **10,** to allot; allocate. **11,** *obs.* to remit (a sin). **12,** *colloq.* to utter (a remark); crack (a joke).

отпускни́к [*gen.* **-ника́**] *n.* person on vacation; person on leave.

отпускно́й *adj.* **1,** vacation (*attrib.*). **2,** *in* отпускна́я цена́, selling price. —**отпускны́е,** *n.pl., colloq.* vacation pay.

отпусти́ть [*infl.* **-пущу́, -пу́стишь**] *v., pfv. of* **отпуска́ть.**

отпуще́ние *n.* **1,** *obs.* remission (*of sins*). **2,** *in* отпуще́ние на во́лю, emancipation. —**козёл отпуще́ния,** scapegoat.

отраба́тывать *v.impfv.* [*pfv.* **отрабо́тать**] **1,** to work off (a debt); make up (time not worked). **2,** to perfect; polish.

отрабо́танный *adj.* exhaust (*attrib.*); waste (*attrib.*). Отрабо́танное то́пливо, spent fuel. *Also,* **отрабо́тавший.**

отрабо́тать *v.pfv.* **1,** *pfv. of* **отраба́тывать. 2,** to work (*for a certain length of time*). **3,** *colloq.* to finish working; stop working.

отра́ва *n.* poison.

отрави́ть [*infl.* **отравлю́, отра́вишь**] *v., pfv. of* **отравля́ть. —отрави́ться,** *refl., pfv. of* **отравля́ться.**

отравле́ние *n.* poisoning. **—отравле́ние свинцо́м,** lead poisoning.

отравля́ть *v.impfv.* [*pfv.* **отрави́ть**] **1,** to poison. **2,** *fig.* to spoil; ruin. **—отравля́ться,** *refl.* **1,** to poison oneself; take poison. **2,** to be poisoned; suffer poisoning.

отравля́ющий *adj., in* **отравля́ющее вещество́,** toxic agent; poison gas.

отра́да *n.* joy; delight.

отра́дный *adj.* pleasing; gratifying. Отра́дно, что..., it is gratifying that...

отража́тель *n.m.* reflector.

отража́ть *v.impfv.* [*pfv.* **отрази́ть**] **1,** to reflect. **2,** to repulse; repel. **3,** to parry; ward off. **—отража́ться,** *refl.* **1,** to be reflected. **2,** (*with* **на** + *prepl.*) to affect; have an effect upon.

отраже́ние *n.* **1,** reflection. **2,** repulsing; repelling.

отрази́ть [*infl.* **-жу́, -зи́шь**] *v., pfv. of* **отража́ть. —отрази́ться,** *refl., pfv. of* **отража́ться.**

отрапортова́ть *v.pfv.* [*infl.* **-ту́ю, -ту́ешь**] to report.

отраслево́й *adj.* of a particular branch or field. **—отраслева́я библиогра́фия,** bibliography by subject.

о́трасль *n.f.* branch; field.

отраста́ть *v.impfv.* [*pfv.* **отрасти́**] (*of hair, nails, etc.*) to grow.

отрасти́ [*infl. like* **расти́**] *v., pfv. of* **отраста́ть.**

отрасти́ть [*infl.* **-щу́, -сти́шь**] *v., pfv. of* **отра́щивать.**

отра́щивать *v.impfv.* [*pfv.* **отрасти́ть**] **1,** to let (one's hair, nails, etc.) grow. **2,** to grow (a beard); develop (a paunch).

отреаги́ровать *v.pfv.* [*infl.* **-рую, -руешь**] to react.

отре́бье *n.* rabble. **—отре́бье о́бщества,** the dregs of society.

отрегули́ровать *v., pfv. of* **регули́ровать** (*in sense #2*).

отредакти́ровать *v., pfv. of* **редакти́ровать.**

отре́з *n.* **1,** cut. **2,** length (*of material*). **3,** perforated line (*for tearing off something*).

отре́зать [*infl.* **-ре́жу, -ре́жешь**] *v., pfv. of* **отреза́ть** *and* **отрезывать.**

отреза́ть *v.impfv.* [*pfv.* **отре́зать**] **1,** to cut off; slice off. **2,** to cut off; block (a road, access, etc.). **3,** to cut off; isolate: отре́занный от вне́шнего ми́ра, cut off from the outside world. **4,** *colloq.* to snap back (*when answering*). *Also,* **отре́зывать.**

отрезве́ть *v., pfv. of* **трезве́ть.**

отрезви́ть [*infl.* **-влю́, -ви́шь**] *v., pfv. of* **отрезвля́ть. —отрезви́ться,** *refl., pfv. of* **отрезвля́ться.**

отрезвля́ть *v.impfv.* [*pfv.* **отрезви́ть**] to sober; sober up. **—отрезвля́ться,** *refl.* to sober up; become sober.

отрезно́й *adj.* **1,** to be torn off. **2,** detachable.

отре́зок [*gen.* **-зка**] *n.* **1,** piece; length (*of material*). **2,** segment; section; part. Отре́зок вре́мени, stretch/ span/space of time.

отре́зывать *v.impfv.* = **отреза́ть.**

отрека́ться *v.r.impfv.* [*pfv.* **отре́чься**] (*with* **от**) to renounce; disavow; repudiate. Отрека́ться от престо́ла, to renounce the throne; abdicate.

отрекомендова́ть *v.pfv.* [*infl.* **-ду́ю, -ду́ешь**] **1,** to introduce. **2,** to comment (favorably or unfavorably upon); characterize (in a certain way). **3,** *obs.* to recommend. **—отрекомендова́ться,** *refl.* to introduce oneself.

отремонти́ровать *v., pfv. of* **ремонти́ровать.**

отре́пье *n., often pl., colloq.* rags; tatters.

отрече́ние *n.* (*with* **от**) renunciation; disavowal; repudiation. Отрече́ние от престо́ла, abdication.

отре́чься [*infl.* **-реку́сь, -рече́шься, ...-реку́тся;** *past* **-рёкся, -рекла́сь, -рекло́сь, -рекли́сь**] *v.r., pfv. of* **отрека́ться.**

отреша́ть *v.impfv.* [*pfv.* **отреши́ть**] to remove; dismiss; suspend. **—отреша́ться,** *refl.* (*with* **от**) **1,** to rid oneself of; get away from. **2,** to renounce.

отреше́ние *n.* removal: отреше́ние от до́лжности, removal from office.

отрешённый *adj.* **1,** aloof; isolated. **2,** (*of a look*) blank; distracted. **—отрешённость,** *n.f.* aloofness; isolation.

отреши́ть *v., pfv. of* **отреша́ть. —отреши́ться,** *refl., pfv. of* **отреша́ться.**

отрица́ние *n.* **1,** denial. **2,** negation. **3,** *gram.* negative.

отрица́тельно *adv.* **1,** negatively. **2,** in the negative. **3,** adversely.

отрица́тельный *adj.* negative.

отрица́ть *v.impfv.* to deny.

отро́г *n.* spur (*of a mountain range*).

о́троду *adv.* (*with* **не**) *colloq.* never in one's life; never in all one's born days. *Also,* **отродя́сь.**

отро́сток [*gen.* **-стка**] *n.* **1,** shoot; sprout. **2,** *anat.* outgrowth.

о́трочеcкий *adj.* adolescent. **—о́трочество,** *n.* adolescence.

отруба́ть *v.impfv.* [*pfv.* **отруби́ть**] to chop off.

о́труби [*gen.* **-бе́й**] *n.pl.* bran.

отруби́ть *v.pfv.* [*infl.* **-рублю́, -ру́бишь**] **1,** *pfv. of* **отруба́ть. 2,** *colloq.* to snap back (*in answering*).

отру́гиваться *v.r.impfv., colloq.* to reply in kind; use the same foul language as the other person.

отры́в *n.* **1,** tearing off. **2,** break; hiatus. **3,** alienation; isolation. **—в отры́ве от,** isolated from; cut off from. **—отры́в от земли́,** takeoff; liftoff.

отрыва́ть *v.impfv.* [*pfv.* **оторва́ть**] **1,** to tear off. **2,** (*with* **от**) to tear away (from): Я не мог оторва́ть от э́того мы́слей, I couldn't stop thinking about it. Я не могла́ оторва́ть от э́того глаз, I couldn't take my eyes off it. **3,** to cut off; isolate. **4,** [*pfv.* **отры́ть**] to dig up; unearth.

отрыва́ться *v.r.impfv.* [*pfv.* **оторва́ться**] **1,** to come off; be torn off. **2,** (*with* **от**) to break away (from); give (someone) the slip. **3,** *in* оторва́ться от земли́, (*of a plane*) to take off; (*of a spacecraft*) to lift off. **4,** (*with* **от**) to tear oneself away (from work, a book, etc.). **5,** (*with* **от**) to lose touch (with); lose contact (with). **—не отрыва́ясь,** without a break; without letup.

отры́вистый *adj.* **1,** (*of sounds*) staccato. **2,** (*of speech*) uneven; disjointed.

отрывно́й *adj.* **1,** that can be torn off. **2,** with sheets that can be torn off.

отры́вок [*gen.* **-вка**] *n.* **1,** passage; excerpt. **2,** fragment; snatch: отры́вки разгово́ра, snatches of a conversation.

отры́вочный *adj.* **1,** fragmentary. **2,** disjointed.

отры́гивать *v.impfv.* [*pfv.* **отрыгну́ть**] to belch up.

отры́жка *n.* **1,** belch. **2,** *fig.*, *colloq.* vestige.

отры́ть [*infl.* **отро́ю, отро́ешь**] *v., pfv. of* **отрыва́ть** (*in sense #4*).

отря́д *n.* **1,** *mil.* detachment. **2,** group: пионе́рский отря́д, (young) pioneer group. **3,** *zool.* order.

отряжа́ть *v.impfv.* [*pfv.* **отряди́ть**] **1,** to dispatch; send (*on a certain assignment*). **2,** *mil.* to assign; detail.

отряса́ть *v.impfv.* [*pfv.* **отрясти́**] to shake off. —**отрясти́ прах от свои́х ног,** to shake the dust from one's feet.

отрясти́ [*infl. like* **трясти́**] *v., pfv. of* **отряса́ть**.

отря́хивать *v.impfv.* [*pfv.* **отряхну́ть**] to shake off.

отсади́ть [*infl.* **-сажу́, -са́дишь**] *v., pfv. of* **отса́живать**.

отса́живать *v.impfv.* [*pfv.* **отсади́ть**] to seat apart from the others (*or* from each other). —**отса́живаться,** *refl.* [*pfv.* **отсе́сть**] (*with* **от**) to take a seat farther away (from).

отсалютова́ть *v.pfv.* [*infl.* **-ту́ю, -ту́ешь**] to salute; fire a salute.

отса́сывать *v.impfv.* [*pfv.* **отсоса́ть**] to draw off; draw out; suck out.

отсве́т *also,* **о́тсвет** *n.* reflection.

отсве́чивать *v.impfv.* to shine; gleam (*by reflecting light*).

отсебя́тина *n., colloq.* words of one's own.

отсе́в *n.* **1,** sifting out; weeding out. **2,** *fig.* dropping out: проце́нт отсе́ва, dropout rate.

отсе́ивать *v.impfv.* [*pfv.* **отсе́ять**] **1,** to sift out. **2,** *fig.* to weed out; filter out; winnow out. —**отсе́иваться,** *refl.* to drop out.

отсе́к *n.* **1,** compartment. **2,** bay (*in an aircraft or spacecraft*): бо́мбовый отсе́к, bomb bay; грузово́й отсе́к, cargo bay. **3,** (space) module.

отсека́ть *v.impfv.* [*pfv.* **отсе́чь**] to chop off.

отсе́сть [*infl. like* **сесть**] *v., pfv. of* **отса́живаться**.

отсече́ние *n.* chopping off. —**дать го́лову** (*or* **ру́ку**) **на отсече́ние,** to stake one's life on it.

отсе́чь [*infl. like* **сечь**; *past* **-сёк, -секла́, -секло́, -секли́**] *v., pfv. of* **отсека́ть**.

отсе́ять [*infl.* **отсе́ю, отсе́ешь**] *v., pfv. of* **отсе́ивать**.

отсиде́ть [*infl.* **-жу́, -ди́шь**] *v., pfv. of* **отси́живать**. —**отсиде́ться,** *refl., pfv. of* **отси́живаться**.

отси́живать *v.impfv.* [*pfv.* **отсиде́ть**] **1,** to make numb (*by sitting*): Я отсиде́л себе́ но́гу, my foot is asleep. **2,** *colloq.* to sit through: отсиде́ть весь спекта́кль, to sit through the entire performance. **3,** to serve out; finish serving (*a prison term*). —**отси́живаться,** *refl., colloq.* to take cover. **2,** to sit it out.

отска́бливать *v.impfv.* [*pfv.* **отскобли́ть**] to scrape off.

отска́кивать *v.impfv.* [*pfv.* **отскочи́ть**] **1,** to jump back; jump aside; jump out of the way. **2,** to rebound; (*with* **от**) bounce off. **3,** *colloq.* to come off; fly off.

отскобли́ть [*infl.* **-скоблю́, -ско́блишь** *or* **-скобли́шь**] *v., pfv. of* **отска́бливать**.

отско́к *n.* bounce; rebound.

отскочи́ть [*infl.* **-скочу́, -ско́чишь**] *v., pfv. of* **отска́кивать**.

отсла́ивать *v.impfv.* [*pfv.* **отслои́ть**] to remove layer by layer. —**отсла́иваться,** *refl.* to come off in layers.

отсло́йка *n., in* отсло́йка сетча́тки; отсло́йка се́тчатой оболо́чки, detached retina.

отслужи́ть *v.pfv.* [*infl.* **-служу́, -слу́жишь**] **1,** to serve out; finish serving. **2,** to be worn out (*from use*). **3,** to conduct (a service, mass, etc.).

отсове́товать *v.pfv.* [*infl.* **-тую, -туешь**] (*with dat. & inf.*) to dissuade (from); talk out of.

отсоединя́ть *v.impfv.* [*pfv.* **отсоедини́ть**] *electricity* to disconnect.

отсоса́ [*infl.* **-сосу́, -сосёшь**] *v., pfv. of* **отса́сывать**.

отсо́хнуть [*past* **отсо́х, отсо́хла**] *v., pfv. of* **отсыха́ть**.

отсро́чивать *v.impfv.* [*pfv.* **отсро́чить**] **1,** to postpone; defer. **2,** *colloq.* to extend (a passport, license, etc.).

отсро́чка [*gen. pl.* **-чек**] *n.* postponement; deferment; delay.

отстава́ние *n.* lag; lagging behind.

отстава́ть *v.impfv.* [*pfv.* **отста́ть**; *pres.* **отстаю́, отстаёшь**] **1,** (*with* **от**) to lag behind; be behind; fall behind. **2,** (*of a clock or watch*) to be slow. **3,** to come off; peel off. **4,** (*with* **от**) *colloq.* to lose touch (with). **5,** (*with* **от**) *colloq.* to leave alone; leave in peace. —**отстава́ть от жи́зни** (*or* **от вре́мени**), to be behind the times. —**отстава́ть от по́езда,** to fail to get back on a train in time.

отста́вить [*infl.* **-влю, -вишь**] *v., pfv. of* **отставля́ть**.

отста́вка *n.* **1,** resignation. **2,** retirement. —**в отста́вке,** retired. —**уйти́** *or* **вы́йти в отста́вку, 1,** to resign. **2,** to retire. —**уво́лить в отста́вку,** to send (*or* force) into retirement.

отставля́ть *v.impfv.* [*pfv.* **отста́вить**] **1,** to move aside. **2,** *obs.* to discharge; dismiss. —**отста́вить!,** *mil.* as you were!

отставно́й *adj.* retired.

отста́ивать *v.impfv.* [*pfv.* **отстоя́ть**] **1,** to defend. **2,** *fig.* to uphold (a principle); assert; stand up for (one's rights). —**отста́иваться,** *refl.* **1,** (*of a liquid*) to settle. **2,** *fig.* to take definite shape. **3,** *colloq.* to wait motionlessly (*in anticipation of something*). See also **отстоя́ть**.

отста́лость *n.f.* backwardness. —**у́мственная отста́лость,** mental retardation.

отста́лый *adj.* **1,** backward. **2,** retarded.

отста́ть [*infl.* **-ста́ну, -ста́нешь**] *v., pfv. of* **отстава́ть**.

отстега́ть *v., pfv. of* **стега́ть** (*in sense #2*).

отстёгивать *v.impfv.* [*pfv.* **отстегну́ть**] to unfasten; undo. —**отстёгиваться,** *refl.* to come unfastened; come undone.

отсти́рывать *v.impfv.* [*pfv.* **отстира́ть**] to wash off; wash out. —**отсти́рываться,** *refl.* to come out in the wash.

отстоя́ть[1] *v.pfv.* [*infl.* **-стою́, -стои́шь**] **1,** *pfv. of* **отста́ивать**. **2,** to retain; hold onto (a title, position, etc.). **3,** to stand through: отстоя́ть весь конце́рт, to stand through the entire concert. —**отстоя́ться**, *refl.*, *pfv. of* **отста́иваться**.

отстоя́ть² *v.impfv.* [*pres.* **-стою́, -стои́шь**] (*with* **на** *and* **от**) to be; be located (a certain distance from): отстоя́ть на оди́н киломе́тр от вокза́ла, to be (located) one kilometer from the station.

отстра́ивать *v.impfv.* [*pfv.* **отстро́ить**] **1**, to build; finish building. **2**, to rebuild (*after a disaster*).

отстране́ние *n.* removal; dismissal.

отстраня́ть *v.impfv.* [*pfv.* **отстрани́ть**] **1**, to push aside. **2**, to remove; dismiss; suspend. —**отстраня́ться**, *refl.* **1**, to step aside. **2**, (*with* **от**) to avoid; dodge. **3**, (*with* **от**) to keep away (from); remain aloof (from).

отстре́ливать *v.impfv.* **1**, [*pfv.* **отстрели́ть**] to shoot off (an arm, leg, etc.). **2**, [*pfv.* **отстреля́ть**] to kill; shoot. —**отстре́ливаться** [*pfv.* **отстреля́ться**] to shoot back; fire back; (*with* **от**) fire back on.

отстрели́ть [*infl.* **-стрелю́, -стре́лишь**] *v.*, *pfv. of* **отстре́ливать** (*in sense #1*).

отстреля́ть *v.*, *pfv. of* **отстре́ливать** (*in sense #2*). —**отстреля́ться**, *refl.*, *pfv. of* **отстре́ливаться**.

отстрига́ть *v.impfv.* [*pfv.* **отстри́чь**] to cut off (someone's hair).

отстри́чь [*infl. like* **стричь**] *v.*, *pfv. of* **отстрига́ть**.

отстро́ить *v.*, *pfv. of* **отстра́ивать**.

о́тступ *n.* indention; indentation (*in writing or printing*).

отступа́ть *v.impfv.* [*pfv.* **отступи́ть**] **1**, to step back. **2**, to recede. **3**, to retreat. **4**, to back down. **5**, (*with* **пе́ред**) to shrink (from); retreat in the face of. **6**, (*with* **от**) to give up (one's views). **7**, (*with* **от**) to deviate (from); depart (from); digress (from). **8**, to indent. —**отступа́ться**, *refl.* (*with* **от**) **1**, to retreat from (principles, beliefs, etc.). **2**, to back down on (a demand); go back on (one's word). **3**, to give up; relinquish (a right). **4**, to cease to have anything to do with; turn one's back on.

отступи́ть [*infl.* **-ступлю́, -сту́пишь**] *v.*, *pfv. of* **отступа́ть**. —**отступи́ться**, *refl.*, *pfv. of* **отступа́ться**.

отступле́ние *n.* **1**, retreat. **2**, deviation; departure. **3**, digression.

отсту́пник *n.* apostate. —**отсту́пнический**, *adj.* apostate. —**отсту́пничество**, *n.* apostasy.

отступно́е *n.*, *decl. as an adj.* indemnity; compensation.

отступя́ *adv.* away; off: немно́го отступя́, a short distance away.

отсу́тствие *n.* **1**, absence: в моё отсу́тствие, in my absence. **2**, lack.

отсу́тствовать *v.impfv.* [*pres* **-ствую, -ствуешь**] **1**, to be absent: отсу́тствовать на собра́нии, to be absent from the meeting. **2**, to be lacking: ули́ки отсу́тствуют, evidence is lacking.

отсу́тствующий *adj.* **1**, absent. **2**, (*of a look*) absent; blank; vacant. —*n.* absentee.

отсчёт *n.* **1**, counting out; marking off. **2**, reading (*on an instrument*). —**обра́тный отсчёт вре́мени**, countdown. —**то́чка отсчёта**, reference point.

отсчи́тывать *v.impfv.* [*pfv.* **отсчита́ть**] **1**, to count out: отсчита́ть ты́сячу рубле́й, to count out 1,000 rubles. **2**, to mark off; count off: отсчита́ть де́сять шаго́в, to mark off ten paces.

отсыла́ть *v.impfv.* [*pfv.* **отосла́ть**] **1**, to send off. **2**, to send away; dismiss. **3**, (*with* **к**) to refer (someone) to.

отсы́лка *n.* **1**, sending; dispatch. **2**, reference.

отсыпа́ть [*infl.* **-сы́плю, -сы́плешь**] *v.*, *pfv. of* **отсыпа́ть**.

отсыпа́ть *v.impfv.* [*pfv.* **отсы́пать**] (*usu. with gen.*) to pour out (a quantity or portion of something).

отсыпа́ться *v.r.impfv.* [*pfv.* **отоспа́ться**] to catch up on one's sleep.

отсыре́лый *adj.* damp; soggy.

отсыре́ть *v.*, *pfv. of* **сыре́ть**.

отсыха́ть *v.impfv.* [*pfv.* **отсо́хнуть**] to wither.

отсю́да *adv.* **1**, from here. **2**, hence. Отсю́да сле́дует, что..., from this it follows that...

отта́ивать *v.impfv.* [*pfv.* **отта́ять**] *v.t. & i.* to thaw; thaw out. —**отта́ивать чьё-нибудь се́рдце**, to melt someone's heart.

отта́лкивать *v.impfv.* [*pfv.* **оттолкну́ть**] **1**, to push back; push away; push aside. **2**, to repel; antagonize; alienate. —**отта́лкиваться**, *refl.* (*with* **от**) **1**, to push off: оттолкну́ться от бе́рега, to push off from the shore. Оттолкну́ться рука́ми от стола́, to push oneself away from the table. **2**, *fig.* to take as a starting point.

отта́лкивающий *adj.* repulsive; repellent.

отта́скивать *v.impfv.* [*pfv.* **оттащи́ть**] **1**, to pull aside; drag aside. **2**, to pull away.

отта́чивать *v.impfv.* [*pfv.* **отточи́ть**] **1**, to sharpen; hone. **2**, *fig.* to polish; perfect.

оттащи́ть [*infl.* **-тащу́, -та́щишь**] *v.*, *pfv. of* **отта́скивать**.

отта́ять [*infl.* **отта́ю, отта́ешь**] *v.*, *pfv. of* **отта́ивать**.

оттека́ть *v.impfv.* [*pfv.* **отте́чь**] to flow off; run off.

оттени́ть *v.*, *pfv. of* **оттеня́ть**.

отте́нок [*gen.* **-нка**] *n.* **1**, shade; hue. **2**, *fig.* shade; nuance (*of meaning*). **3**, (*with gen.*) trace (of); touch (of); tinge (of).

оттеня́ть *v.impfv.* [*pfv.* **оттени́ть**] **1**, to shade; shade in. **2**, *fig.* to highlight; set off.

о́ттепель *n.f.* thaw.

оттере́ть [*infl.* **ототру́, ототрёшь**; *past* **оттёр, оттёрла**] *v.*, *pfv. of* **оттира́ть**.

оттесня́ть *v.impfv.* [*pfv.* **оттесни́ть**] **1**, to drive back; push back; force back. **2**, *fig.* to force out; crowd out.

отте́чь [*infl. like* **течь**] *v.*, *pfv. of* **оттека́ть**.

оттира́ть *v.impfv.* [*pfv.* **оттере́ть**] **1**, to rub off; rub out. **2**, to rub (one's hands, ears, etc.) until the feeling returns. **3**, *colloq.* to push aside; force aside.

о́ттиск *n.* **1**, imprint; print; impression. **2**, print; proof. **3**, reprint.

отти́скивать *v.impfv.* [*pfv.* **отти́снуть**] **1**, *colloq.* to push back. **2**, to imprint.

оттого́ *adv.* (*often* **оттого́ и**) that is why; which is why. —**оттого́ что,** because.

отто́к *n.* outflow.

оттолкну́ть *v.*, *pfv. of* **отта́лкивать**. —**оттолкну́ться**, *refl.*, *pfv. of* **отта́лкиваться**.

оттома́нка [*gen. pl.* **-нок**] *n.* ottoman.

оттома́нский *adj.* Ottoman.

оттопы́ренный *adj.* protruding; prominent.

оттопы́ривать *v.impfv.* [*pfv.* оттопы́рить] *colloq.* to stick out. —оттопы́риваться, *refl., colloq.* to stick out; bulge; protrude.

отторга́ть *v.impfv.* [*pfv.* отто́ргнуть] 1, to tear away; forcibly separate: отто́ргнутый от семьи́, separated from one's family. 2, to annex (territory). 3, *med.* to reject.

отто́ргнуть [*past* отто́рг *or* отто́ргнул, отто́ргла] *v., pfv. of* отторга́ть.

отторже́ние *n.* 1, forcible separation. 2, annexation. 3, *med.* rejection.

отточи́ть [*infl.* -точу́, -то́чишь] *v., pfv. of* отта́чивать.

отту́да *adv.* from there.

оттузи́ть *v., pfv. of* тузи́ть.

оття́гивать *v.impfv.* [*pfv.* оттяну́ть] 1, to draw aside; pull aside. 2, *mil.* to draw off. 3, to weigh down. 4, to delay; put off. —оття́гивать вре́мя, to play for time; stall for time.

отта́жка [*gen. pl.* -жек] *n., colloq.* (deliberate) delay.

оттяну́ть [*infl.* -тяну́, -тя́нешь] *v., pfv. of* оття́гивать.

отума́нивать *v.impfv.* [*pfv.* отума́нить] 1, to blur; dim; obscure. 2, to dull; cloud (the senses).

отупе́лый *adj., colloq.* dazed.

отупе́ние *n.* daze; stupor; torpor.

отупе́ть *v.pfv.* to become dazed.

отупи́ть [*infl.* отуплю́, оту́пишь] *v., pfv. of* отупля́ть.

отупля́ть *v.impfv.* [*pfv.* отупи́ть] to dull the mind of.

отутю́живать *v.impfv.* [*pfv.* отутю́жить] to iron; press.

отуча́ть *v.impfv.* [*pfv.* отучи́ть] (*with* от *or inf.*) to break (someone) of the habit of; train not to; wean away from. —отуча́ться, *refl.* (*with* от *or inf.*) to break oneself of (a habit); break the habit of.

отучи́ть [*infl.* отучу́, оту́чишь] *v., pfv. of* отуча́ть. —отучи́ться, *refl., pfv. of* отуча́ться.

отха́живать *v.impfv.* [*pfv.* отходи́ть] *colloq.* to nurse back to health.

отха́ркивать *v.impfv.* [*pfv.* отха́ркнуть] to cough up. —отха́ркиваться, *refl.* to clear one's throat.

отхвати́ть [*infl.* -хвачу́, -хва́тишь] *v., pfv. of* отхва́тывать.

отхва́тывать *v.impfv.* [*pfv.* отхвати́ть] *colloq.* to cut off; slice off; snip off.

отхлёбывать *v.impfv.* [*pfv.* отхлебну́ть] *colloq.* 1, to take a sip of. 2, (*with* из) to sip (from).

отхлеста́ть *v.pfv.* [*infl.* -хлещу́, -хле́щешь] *colloq.* to give (someone) a lashing; horsewhip.

отхлы́нуть *v.pfv.* to surge back.

отхо́д *n.* 1, departure. 2, *mil.* withdrawal. 3, *fig.* departure; deviation; retreat. 4, *pl.* waste; waste matter.

отходи́ть[1] *v.impfv.* [*pfv.* отойти́; *pres.* -хожу́, -хо́дишь] 1, to walk away (from); move away (from). 2, (*of a train*) to leave; depart. 3, *mil.* to withdraw; fall back. 4, (*with* от) to deviate (from); depart (from); digress (from). 5, (*with* от) to drift away (from). 6, to come off; peel off; (*of a stain*) come out. 7, to recover; come round. 8, to calm down. 9, (*with* к) (*of territory, property, etc.*) to pass (to). 10, *obs.* to pass; come to an end. —отойти́ в про́шлое *or* в исто́рию, to pass into history; become a thing of the past. —отойти́ от дел, to give up one's duties; retire.

отходи́ть[2] [*infl.* -хожу́, -хо́дишь] *v., pfv. of* отха́живать.

отхо́дная *n., decl. as an adj.* prayer said for a dying person.

отхо́дчивый *adj.* quick to forgive; not such as to harbor a grudge.

отхо́жий *adj.,* in отхо́жее ме́сто, outhouse; latrine.

отцвести́ [*infl. like* цвести́] *v., pfv. of* отцвета́ть.

отцвета́ть *v.impfv.* [*pfv.* отцвести́] 1, to cease to bloom. 2, *fig.* to lose its bloom; fade.

отцепи́ть [*infl.* -цеплю́, -це́пишь] *v., pfv. of* отцепля́ть. —отцепи́ться, *refl., pfv. of* отцепля́ться.

отцепля́ть *v.impfv.* [*pfv.* отцепи́ть] to unhook; uncouple. —отцепля́ться, *refl.* 1, to become unhooked; come uncoupled. 2, (*with* от) *colloq.* to leave (someone) alone; stop bothering.

отцеуби́йство *n.* patricide.

отцо́вский *adj.* 1, one's father's. 2, paternal. —отцо́вство, *n.* paternity; fatherhood.

отча́иваться *v.r.impfv.* [*pfv.* отча́яться] (*with inf. or* в + *prepl.*) to despair (of).

отча́ливать *v.impfv.* [*pfv.* отча́лить] (*of a boat*) to cast off.

отча́сти *adv.* partly; in part.

отча́яние *n.* despair.

отча́янно *adv.* 1, desperately. 2, *colloq.* frightfully.

отча́янный *adj.* 1, desperate. 2, *colloq.* reckless. 3, *colloq.* frightful; awful.

отча́яться [*infl.* -ча́юсь, -ча́ешься] *v.r., pfv. of* отча́иваться.

о́тче *n., vocative case of* оте́ц. —О́тче наш, Our Father (*prayer*).

отчего́ *adv.* why. —*conj.* and as a result; and because of that.

отчего́-нибудь *adv.* for some reason or other. *Also,* отчего́-либо.

отчего́-то *adv.* for some unknown reason.

отчека́нить *v., pfv. of* чека́нить.

отчёркивать *v.impfv.* [*pfv.* отчеркну́ть] to mark; mark off.

о́тчество *n.* patronymic (name).

отчёт *n.* account; report. —отдава́ть себе́ отчёт в (+ *prepl.*), to realize; be aware of.

отчётливый *adj.* distinct; clear. —отчётливо, *adv.* distinctly; clearly.

отчётность *n.f.* 1, accounting; bookkeeping. 2, accounts; records. —прове́рка отчётности, audit; auditing.

отчётный *adj.* 1, of or pert. to a report. Отчётный докла́д, report. 2, covered in a report: отчётный пери́од, the period covered.

отчи́зна *n., archaic* native land; fatherland.

о́тчий *adj., obs.* one's father's.

о́тчим *n.* stepfather.

отчисле́ние *n.* 1, deduction. 2, *pl.* money deducted; deductions. 3, dismissal.

отчисля́ть *v.impfv.* [*pfv.* отчи́слить] 1, to deduct. 2, to dismiss.

отчи́стить [*infl.* -щу, -стишь] *v., pfv. of* **отчища́ть**.

отчи́тывать *v.impfv.* [*pfv.* **отчита́ть**] *colloq.* to bawl out; give (someone) a talking-to. —**отчи́тываться**, *refl.* **1,** to give a report; (*with* в + *acc.*) to give an account (of). **2,** (*with* пе́ред) to report (to); be accountable (to). **3,** (*with* в + *prepl.*) to account for; give an accounting of.

отчища́ть *v.impfv.* [*pfv.* **отчи́стить**] **1,** to clean; scour. **2,** to remove (a stain, rust, etc.).

отчужда́ть *v.impfv.* [*pfv.* **отчуди́ть**] to alienate; estrange.

отчужде́ние *n.* alienation; estrangement; disaffection.

отчуждённость *n.f.* coolness; aloofness; distance (*in relations between people*).

отшага́ть *v.pfv., colloq.* to walk (a certain distance).

отшагну́ть *v.pfv., colloq.* to step aside; step back.

отша́тываться *v.r.impfv.* [*pfv.* **отшатну́ться**], **1,** to jump back; recoil. **2,** *fig.* (*with* от) to turn one's back on.

отшвы́ривать *v.impfv.* [*pfv.* **отшвырну́ть**] *colloq.* to throw away; fling away.

отше́льник *n.* hermit; recluse. —**отше́льнический**, *adj.* (like that) of a hermit; solitary. —**отше́льничество,** *n.* life of a hermit; solitary life.

отши́б *n., in* **на отши́бе, 1,** at a distance. **2,** alone; by oneself. **3,** (*with* от) apart (from); aloof (from).

отшиба́ть *v.impfv.* [*pfv.* **отшиби́ть**] *colloq.* **1,** to hurt: отшиби́ть себе́ но́гу, to hurt one's leg. **2,** *impers.* to lose (one's appetite, memory, etc.): У меня́ отши́бло аппети́т, I've lost my appetite.

отшиби́ть [*infl.* -бу́, -бёшь; *past* отши́б, отши́бла] *v., pfv. of* **отшиба́ть**.

отшлёпать *v.pfv., colloq.* to spank.

отшлифова́ть *v., pfv. of* **шлифова́ть**.

отшути́ться [*infl.* -шучу́сь, -шу́тишься] *v.r., pfv. of* **отшу́чиваться**.

отшу́чиваться *v.r.impfv.* [*pfv.* **отшути́ться**] *colloq.* to reply with a joke; come back with a joke.

отщепе́нец [*gen. pl.* -нца] *n.* renegade.

отщепля́ть *v.impfv.* [*pfv.* **отщепи́ть**] to split off (a piece of wood). —**отщепля́ться,** *refl.* to chip off; be chipped off.

отщи́пывать *v.impfv.* [*pfv.* **отщипну́ть**] to pinch off (*usu.* a piece of bread).

отъеда́ть *v.impfv.* [*pfv.* **отъе́сть**] to bite off. —**отъеда́ться,** *refl.* to put on weight from good food.

отъе́зд *n.* departure. —**быть в отъе́зде,** to be away; be out of town.

отъезжа́ть *v.impfv.* [*pfv.* **отъе́хать**] **1,** to drive away; drive off; ride away; ride off. **2,** (*with* наза́д) to back up.

отъе́сть [*infl. like* есть] *v., pfv. of* **отъеда́ть**. —**отъе́сться,** *refl., pfv. of* **отъеда́ться**.

отъе́хать [*infl.* -е́ду, -е́ду] *v., pfv. of* **отъезжа́ть**.

отъя́вленный *adj.* arrant; unmitigated; out-and-out.

оты́грывать *v.impfv.* [*pfv.* **отыгра́ть**] to win back. —**оты́грываться,** *refl.* **1,** to recoup one's losses. **2,** *fig.* to wiggle out of a situation.

отыска́ть [*infl.* отыщу́, оты́щешь] *v., pfv. of* **оты́скивать**. —**отыска́ться,** *refl., pfv. of* **оты́скиваться**.

оты́скивать *v.impfv.* [*pfv.* **отыска́ть**] **1,** to find. **2,** [*impfv. only*] to look for; search for; try to find. —**оты́скиваться,** *refl.* to be found; turn up.

отягоща́ть *v.impfv.* [*pfv.* **отяготи́ть**] to weigh down; burden.

отягча́ть *v.impfv.* [*pfv.* **отягчи́ть**] **1,** to weigh down; burden. **2,** *fig.* to aggravate: отягча́ющие вину́ обсто-я́тельства, aggravating circumstances.

отяжеле́ть *v.pfv.* to grow heavy; become heavy.

отяжеля́ть *v.impfv.* [*pfv.* **отяжели́ть**] **1,** to make heavy. **2,** to weigh down.

офице́р *n.* officer. —**офице́рский,** *adj.* officer (*attrib.*); officer's; officers'.

офице́рство *n.* **1,** the officers. **2,** officer's rank; commission.

официа́льный *adj.* **1,** official. **2,** *fig.* formal. —**официа́льно,** *adv.* officially.

официа́нт *n.* waiter.

официа́нтка [*gen. pl.* -ток] *n.* waitress.

официо́з *n.* semi-official publication.

официо́зный *adj.* semi-official.

офо́рмитель *n.m.* **1,** designer. **2,** stage designer.

офо́рмить [*infl.* -млю, -мишь] *v., pfv. of* **оформля́ть**. —**офо́рмиться,** *refl., pfv. of* **оформля́ться**.

оформле́ние *n.* **1,** design. **2,** legalization. **3,** processing (*of documents*). **4,** enrollment.

оформля́ть *v.impfv.* [*pfv.* **офо́рмить**] **1,** to design; arrange; lay out. **2,** to legalize; formalize; make legal; make official. **3,** to process; validate (documents). **4,** to enroll; register. Оформля́ть на рабо́ту, to put on the payroll. —**оформля́ться,** *refl.* **1,** to take shape; (*with* в + *acc.*) take the form of. **2,** to go through the formalities; complete the paperwork.

офо́рт *n.* etching.

офсе́т *n.* offset. —**офсе́тный,** *adj.* offset (*attrib.*): офсе́тная печа́ть, offset printing.

офтальмоло́гия *n.* ophthalmology. —**офтальмо́лог,** *n.* ophthalmologist.

ох *interj.* oh!; ah!

оха́ивать *v.impfv.* [*pfv.* **оха́ять**] *colloq.* to disparage; run down.

о́ханье *n.* moaning; groaning.

оха́пка [*gen. pl.* -пок] *n.* armful. —**в оха́пку; в оха́пке,** in one's arms.

охарактеризова́ть *v.pfv.* [*infl.* -зу́ю, -зу́ешь] to characterize; describe.

о́хать *v.impfv.* [*pfv.* **о́хнуть**] to moan; groan.

оха́ять [*infl.* оха́ю, оха́ешь] *v., pfv. of* **оха́ивать**.

охва́т *n.* **1,** encompassing. **2,** scope; range. **3,** *mil.* envelopment.

охвати́ть [*infl.* охвачу́, охва́тишь] *v., pfv. of* **охва́тывать**.

охва́тывать *v.impfv.* [*pfv.* **охвати́ть**] **1,** (*usu. with* рука́ми) to put one's arms around; embrace. **2,** to engulf; envelop: Пла́мя охвати́ло зда́ние, flames engulfed the building. **3,** (*of emotions, feelings, etc.*) to seize; grip. **4,** *fig.* to take in; include; embrace; encompass. —**охвати́ть (что́-нибудь) взгля́дом,** to take in; survey. —**охвати́ть (что́-нибудь) умо́м,** to grasp; encompass in one's mind.

охладева́ть *v.impfv.* [*pfv.* **охладе́ть**] **1,** (*with* к) to grow cold (toward). **2,** (*of feelings*) to die down.

охлажда́ть *v.impfv.* [*pfv.* **охлади́ть**] **1,** to cool; chill.

2, *fig.* to calm down. **3,** *fig.* to dampen (one's ardor, enthusiasm, etc.). **—охлажда́ться,** *refl.* to cool; cool off; cool down.

охлажде́ние *n.* **1,** cooling. **2,** *fig.* coolness (*toward someone*).

охмеле́ть *v., pfv. of* **хмеле́ть.**

охмуря́ть *v.impfv.* [*pfv.* **охмури́ть**] *colloq.* to trick.

о́хнуть *v., pfv. of* **о́хать.**

охо́та *n.* **1,** hunt; hunting: идти́ на охо́ту, to go hunting. **2,** wish; desire. Мне (не) охо́та (+ *inf.*), I (don't) feel like (reading, walking, etc.). **—что за охо́та; охо́та вам** (+ *inf.*), *colloq.* why do you want to...?; why bother...?; what's the use of...?

охо́титься *v.r.impfv.* [*pres.* **-чусь, -тишься**] (*with* **на** + *acc. or* **за** + *instr.*) to hunt; go hunting (for).

охо́тник *n.* **1,** hunter. **2,** volunteer. **3,** (*with* **до**) enthusiast: охо́тник до ша́хмат, chess enthusiast.

охо́тничий [*fem.* **-чья**] *adj.* hunting (*attrib.*). **—охо́тничий до́мик,** hunting lodge. **—охо́тничий расска́з,** fish story. **—охо́тничья соба́ка,** hunting dog; hound.

охо́тно *adv.* gladly; willingly.

о́хра *n.* ocher.

охра́на *n.* **1,** guarding; protection. Быть под охра́ной, to be under guard. Брать под охра́ну, to place under protection. **2,** guard; guards.

охране́ние *n.* safeguarding; protection.

охрани́ть *v., pfv. of* **охраня́ть.**

охра́нка *n., colloq.* secret police in tsarist Russia.

охра́нник *n.* guard.

охра́нный *adj.* safe-conduct: охра́нная гра́мота; охра́нный лист, safe-conduct pass.

охраня́ть *v.impfv.* [*pfv.* **охрани́ть**] **1,** to guard. **2,** to protect. **3,** *fig.* to safeguard.

охри́плый *adj., colloq.* hoarse. *Also,* **охри́пший.**

охри́пнуть *v.pfv.* [*past* **охри́п, охри́пла**] to become hoarse.

оцара́пать *v.pfv.* to scratch.

оцело́т *n.* ocelot.

оце́нивать *v.impfv.* [*pfv.* **оцени́ть**] **1,** to appraise; assess; evaluate. **2,** to estimate. **—оцени́ть по досто́инству, 1,** to assess properly. **2,** to appreciate; recognize the value of.

оцени́ть [*infl.* **оценю́, оце́нишь**] *v., pfv. of* **оце́нивать.**

оце́нка [*gen. pl.* **-нок**] *n.* **1,** assessment; appraisal; evaluation. **2,** estimate. **3,** grade; mark.

оце́нщик *n.* appraiser.

оцепене́лый *adj.* dazed; stunned.

оцепене́ние *n.* stupor; torpor.

оцепене́ть *v., pfv. of* **цепене́ть.**

оцепле́ние *n.* **1,** cordoning off. **2,** cordon.

оцепля́ть *v.impfv.* [*pfv.* **оцепи́ть**] to surround; seal off; cordon off.

оча́г [*gen.* **очага́**] *n.* **1,** hearth; fireside. **2,** *mil.* pocket (*of resistance*). **3,** *fig.* center; hotbed; breeding ground.

очарова́ние *n.* charm; fascination; enchantment.

очаро́ванный *adj.* **1,** charmed. **2,** spellbound.

очарова́тельный *adj.* charming.

очарова́ть [*infl.* **-ру́ю, -ру́ешь**] *v., pfv. of* **очаро́вывать.**

очаро́вывать *v.impfv.* [*pfv.* **очарова́ть**] to charm; captivate.

очеви́дец [*gen.* **-дца**] *n.* eyewitness.

очеви́дно *adv.* **1,** obviously. **2,** evidently. **—adj., used predicatively,** obvious: Бы́ло очеви́дно, что..., it was obvious that...

очеви́дный *adj.* [*short form* **-ден, -дна**] obvious.

очелове́чивать *v.impfv.* [*pfv.* **очелове́чить**] to humanize.

о́чень *adv.* **1,** very. **2,** (*before verbs*) very much. **—о́чень и о́чень** (+ *adj. or verb*), enormously.

очерви́веть *v., pfv. of* **черви́веть.**

очередно́й *adj.* **1,** next; immediate; at hand. **2,** regular; regularly scheduled. **3,** ordinary; routine; just another. **—в очередно́й раз,** once again.

очерёдность *n.f.* (prescribed) order; order of priority.

о́чередь [*pl.* **о́череди, -де́й, -дя́м**] *n.f.* **1,** turn: по о́череди, in turn; taking turns. Ждать свое́й о́череди, to wait one's turn. **2,** line: о́чередь за биле́тами, the line for tickets. Стоя́ть в о́череди, to stand in line. Пройти́ без (*or* вне) о́череди, to go to the head of the line; not have to wait on line. **3,** waiting list: о́чередь на жильё, waiting list for housing. Быть на о́череди, to be on the waiting list. **4,** burst of fire: пулемётная о́чередь, burst of machine-gun fire. **—в пе́рвую о́чередь,** first of all. **—в свою́ о́чередь,** for one's part: я, в свою́ о́чередь, for my part. **—на о́череди,** next in line; next to come. **—не в после́днюю о́чередь,** in no small measure.

о́черк *n.* essay. **—очерки́ст,** *n.* essayist.

очерни́ть *v., pfv. of* **черни́ть** (*in sense #2*).

очерстве́лый *adj.* callous.

очерстве́ть *v., pfv. of* **черстве́ть** (*in sense #2*).

очерствля́ть *v.impfv.* [*pfv.* **очерстви́ть**] to harden (someone's heart).

очерта́ние *n., usu. pl.* outline; contour.

очерти́ть [*infl.* **очерчу́, оче́ртишь**] *v., pfv. of* **оче́рчивать.**

оче́рчивать *v.impfv.* [*pfv.* **очерти́ть**] **1,** to draw a line around. **2,** *fig.* to describe; outline; sketch. **—очертя́ го́лову,** headlong; rashly.

очёски [*gen.* **-ков**] *n.pl.* combings.

очини́ть [*infl.* **очиню́, очи́нишь**] *v., pfv. of* **чини́ть** (*in sense #2*).

очисти́тельный *adj.* cleansing. **—очисти́тельный заво́д,** refinery.

очи́стить *v.pfv.* [*infl.* **-щу, -стишь**] **1,** *pfv. of* **чи́стить** (*in sense #5*) *and* **очища́ть. 2,** *colloq.* to clean out; rob. **—очи́ститься,** *refl., pfv. of* **очища́ться.**

очи́стка *n.* **1,** cleaning; cleanup. **2,** clearing. **3,** purification. **—для очи́стки со́вести,** to clear one's conscience.

очи́стки [*gen.* **-ков**] *n.pl.* peelings: карто́фельные очи́стки, potato peelings; potato skins.

очистно́й *also,* **очи́стный** *adj.* cleanup (*attrib.*).

очища́ть *v.impfv.* [*pfv.* **очи́стить**] **1,** to clean. **2,** to purify; refine. **3,** to cleanse; purge. **4,** to clear out. **5,** (*with* **от**) to clear (of unwanted objects, persons, etc.). **6,** to clear; vacate (a building). **—очища́ться,** *refl.* **1,** to clear; clear up. **2,** (*with* **от**) to become clear (of).

очищéние *n.* **1,** clearing. **2,** cleansing. **3,** purification.

очки́ [*gen.* очкóв] *n.pl.* glasses; eyeglasses.

очкó [*pl.* очки́, очкóв] *n.* **1,** point (*scored in a game*). **2,** pip (*on a playing card, die, domino, etc.*). **3,** *colloq.* blackjack (*game*). **4,** small opening; mesh.

очковтирáтельство *n., colloq.* fakery.

очкóвый *adj., sports* based on points scored. —очкó-вая змея́, cobra.

очну́ться *v.r.pfv.* **1,** to awaken. **2,** to regain consciousness.

óчный *adj.* **1,** *in* óчное обучéние, classroom instruction (*as opposed to correspondence courses*). **2,** *in* óч-ная стáвка, simultaneous questioning of witnesses or defendants (*in order to resolve contradictions*). **3,** *in* óчный цвет, pimpernel.

очумéть *v.pfv., colloq.* to lose one's head.

очути́ться *v.r.pfv.* [*infl.* очу́тишься; *1st person sing. not used*] to find oneself; wind up; end up (*in a certain place*).

очу́хаться *v.r.pfv., colloq.* to come to; regain consciousness.

ошалéть *v., pfv. of* шалéть.

ошарáшивать *v.impfv.* [*pfv.* ошарáшить] *colloq.* to dumbfound; flabbergast.

ошéйник *n.* collar (*for a dog*).

ошеломи́тельный *adj.* stunning; staggering.

ошеломля́ть *v.impfv.* [*pfv.* ошеломи́ть] to stun; stagger.

ошельмовáть *v., pfv. of* шельмовáть.

ошибáться *v.r.impfv.* [*pfv.* ошиби́ться] **1,** to make a mistake. **2,** to be mistaken; be wrong.

ошиби́ться [*infl.* -бу́сь, -бёшься; *past* оши́бся, оши́блась] *v.r., pfv. of* ошибáться.

оши́бка [*gen. pl.* -бок] *n.* mistake; error.

оши́бочно *adv.* **1,** erroneously; mistakenly. **2,** by mistake.

оши́бочность *n.f.* fallaciousness.

оши́бочный *adj.* erroneous; mistaken; fallacious.

оши́кать *v.pfv., colloq.* to hiss; boo (a performer, play, etc.).

ошпáривать *v.impfv.* [*pfv.* ошпáрить] *colloq.* to scald. —ошпáриваться, *refl., colloq.* to scald oneself.

ошпáрить *v., pfv. of* шпáрить *and* ошпáривать. —ошпáриться, *refl., pfv. of* ошпáриваться.

оштрафовáть *v., pfv. of* штрафовáть.

оштукату́рить *v., pfv. of* штукату́рить.

ощени́ться *v.r., pfv. of* щени́ться.

ощети́ниться *v.r., pfv. of* щети́ниться.

ощипáть [*infl.* ощиплю́, ощи́плешь] *v., pfv. of* щи-пáть (*in sense #4*) *and* ощи́пывать.

ощи́пывать *v.impfv.* [*pfv.* ощипáть] **1,** to pluck. **2,** to pick (clean).

ощу́пывать *v.impfv.* [*pfv.* ощу́пать] to feel (*with one's fingers*).

óщупь *n.f., in* на óщупь, **1,** to the touch. **2,** by touch. —идти́ на óщупь, to feel one's way.

óщупью *adv.* by groping one's way: идти́ óщупью, to grope one's way; искáть óщупью, to grope for.

ощути́мый *adj.* **1,** perceptible; tangible; palpable. **2,** noticeable; marked; appreciable. *Also,* ощути́тельный.

ощущáть *v.impfv.* [*pfv.* ощути́ть] to feel; sense. —ощущáться, *refl.* [*impfv. only*] to be felt; be sensed.

ощущéние *n.* sensation; feeling. Си́льные *or* óстрые ощущéния, excitement; thrills.

оягни́ться *v.r., pfv. of* ягни́ться.

П

П, п *n.neut.* sixteenth letter of the Russian alphabet.

па *n.neut. indecl.* step (*in dancing*).

пáва *n.* peahen.

павиáн *n.* baboon.

павильóн *n.* **1,** pavilion. **2,** film studio.

павли́н *n.* peacock. —павли́ний, *adj.* [*fem.* -нья] peacock (*attrib.*).

пáводок [*gen.* -дка] *n.* high water; flood.

пáвший *adj.* fallen.

пагинáция *n.* pagination.

пáгода *n.* pagoda.

пáгуба *n., obs.* ruin; downfall.

пáгубный *adj.* ruinous; pernicious; disastrous.

пáдаль *n.f.* carrion.

пáдать *v.impfv.* [*pfv.* упáсть *or* пасть] **1,** to fall: упáсть на зéмлю, to fall to the ground; пасть в бою́, to fall in battle. Ли́стья пáдают, the leaves are falling. **2,** [*usu. pfv.*] (*of an airplane*) to crash. **3,** to decline; go down; fall: Цéны пáдают, prices are going down. —пáдать ду́хом, to lose heart. —пáдать в óбморок, to faint.

пáдающий *adj.* falling. —пáдающая звездá, shooting star. —пáдающий мóлот, triphammer.

падéж [*gen.* -дежá] *n., gram.* case.

падёж [*gen.* -дежá] *n.* murrain.

падéжный *adj., gram.* case (*attrib.*).

падéние *n.* **1,** fall. **2,** drop; decline. **3,** downfall. **4,** *physics* incidence.

пáдкий *adj.* [*short form* пáдок, пáдка] (*with* на + *acc. or* до) having a weakness (for); susceptible (to): пáдкий на лесть, susceptible to flattery.

пáдуб *n.* holly.

па́дучий *adj.*, *obs.* falling. —па́дучая боле́знь, *obs.* epilepsy.

па́дчерица *n.* stepdaughter.

па́дший *adj.* fallen. —па́дшая же́нщина, fallen woman.

паёк [*gen.* пайка́] *n.* ration. —на голо́дном пайке́, on starvation rations.

паж [*gen.* пажа́] *n.* page; attendant.

паз [*2nd loc.* пазу́; *pl.* пазы́] *n.* 1, crack; crevice. 2, slot; groove; mortise.

па́зуха *n.* 1, bosom. 2, *anat.* sinus. 3, *bot.* axil. —держа́ть ка́мень за па́зухой, to bear a grudge.

па́инька [*gen. pl.* -нек] *n.m. & f., colloq.* good child.

пай [*pl.* паи́] *n.* share.

па́йка *n.* soldering.

па́йщик *n.* shareholder.

пакга́уз *n.* warehouse.

паке́т *n.* 1, package. 2, packet. 3, paper bag.

пакетбо́т *n.* packet (*steamship*).

паке́тик *n.* 1, small package. 2, paper bag.

пакиста́нец [*gen.* -нца] *n.m.* [*fem.* -нка] Pakistani. —пакиста́нский, *adj.* Pakistani.

па́кля *n.* oakum; tow.

пакова́ть *v.impfv.* [*pfv.* упакова́ть; *pres.* -ку́ю, -ку́ешь] to pack (things).

па́костить *v.impfv.* [*pres.* -щу, -стишь] *colloq.* 1, to soil; dirty. 2, to spoil. 3, (*with dat.*) to play dirty tricks on; do nasty things to.

па́костный *adj., colloq.* nasty; foul; vile.

па́кость *n.f., colloq.* 1, dirty trick; mean trick. 2, dirty word; obscenity.

пакт *n.* pact: пакт о ненападе́нии, nonaggression pact.

паланти́н *n.* (fur) stole.

пала́та *n.* 1, house; chamber (*of a legislature*): пала́та представи́телей/о́бщин/ло́рдов, House of Representatives/Commons/Lords. Пала́та депута́тов, Chamber of Deputies. 2, bureau; chamber: торго́вая пала́та, chamber of commerce; пала́та мер и весо́в, Bureau of Weights and Measures. 3, ward (*of a hospital*). —у него́ ума́ пала́та, he is as smart as they come.

палатализа́ция *n., phonet.* palatalization.

палатализова́ть *v.impfv. & pfv.* [*pres.* -зу́ю, -зу́ешь] *phonet.* to palatalize.

пала́тальный *adj., phonet.* palatal.

пала́тка [*gen. pl.* -ток] *n.* 1, tent. 2, stall; booth.

пала́точный *adj.* tent (*attrib.*).

пала́ч [*gen.* -лача́] *n.* 1, executioner; hangman. 2, *fig.* butcher.

пала́ш [*gen.* -лаша́] *n.* broadsword.

па́левый *adj.* pale yellow; straw-colored.

палёный *adj.* singed; scorched.

палеоазиа́тский *adj.* Paleo-Asiatic.

палеогра́фия *n.* paleography. —палео́граф, *n.* paleographer. —палеографи́ческий, *adj.* paleographic.

палеозо́йский *adj.* Paleozoic.

палеолити́ческий *adj.* paleolithic.

палеонтоло́гия *n.* paleontology. —палеонто́лог, *n.* paleontologist. —палеонтологи́ческий, *adj.* paleontological.

палести́нец [*gen.* -нца] *n.m.* [*fem.* -нка] Palestinian. —палести́нский, *adj.* Palestinian.

па́лец [*gen.* па́льца] *n.* 1, finger. Большо́й па́лец, thumb. 2, *in* па́лец ноги́; па́лец на ноге́, toe. —знать (что́-нибудь) как свои́ пять па́льцев, to know like the back of one's hand. —па́лец о па́лец не уда́рить; па́льцем не шевельну́ть, not to lift a finger. —па́льца в рот не клади́ (+ *dat.*), *colloq.* watch out for...!; be on your guard against...! —пока́зывать *or* ука́зывать па́льцем на (+ *acc.*), to point one's finger at. —попа́сть па́льцем в не́бо, to be wide of the mark. —смотре́ть сквозь па́льцы на (+ *acc.*), to wink at; deliberately overlook; look the other way at; turn a blind eye to.

палиса́д *n.* palisade.

палиса́дник *n.* small garden.

палиса́ндр *n.* rosewood. —палиса́ндровый, *adj.* rosewood (*attrib.*).

пали́тра *n.* palette.

пали́ть *v.impfv.* 1, [*pfv.* опали́ть] to singe (an animal). 2, [*pfv.* спали́ть] to singe; scorch (*accidentally*). 3, [*impfv. only*] (*of the sun*) to beat down. 4, [*pfv.* вы́палить] *colloq.* to fire; shoot.

па́лка [*gen. pl.* па́лок] *n.* 1, stick. 2, cane; walking stick. —из-под па́лки, under compulsion. —па́лка о двух конца́х, double-edged sword.

палла́дий *n.* palladium.

паллиати́в *n.* palliative. —паллиати́вный, *adj.* palliative.

пало́мник *n.* pilgrim.

пало́мничать *v.impfv.* to go on a pilgrimage.

пало́мничество *n.* pilgrimage. —пало́мнический, *adj.* pilgrim (*attrib.*); pilgrims'.

па́лочка [*gen. pl.* -чек] *n.* 1, small stick: бараба́нная па́лочка, drumstick. 2, baton; wand. 3, bacillus.

па́лочный *adj.* with or using a stick. —па́лочная дисципли́на, discipline enforced with the rod.

па́лтус *n.* halibut.

па́луба *n.* deck (*of a ship*). —па́лубный, *adj.* deck (*attrib.*).

пальба́ *n., colloq.* firing: откры́ть пальбу́, to open fire.

па́льма *n.* palm (tree). —па́льма пе́рвенства, the crown; the chief laurels.

па́льмовый *adj.* palm (*attrib.*).

пальто́ *n.indecl.* overcoat.

па́льчик *n., dim. of* па́лец.

паля́щий *adj.* burning; scorching; searing.

пампа́сы [*gen.* -сов] *n.pl.* pampas.

памфле́т *n.* (political) pamphlet. —памфлети́ст, *n.* pamphleteer.

па́мятка [*gen. pl.* -ток] *n.* 1, book of instructions; book of rules. 2, *colloq.* reminder; memento.

па́мятливый *adj., colloq.* having a retentive memory. —па́мятливость, *n.f., colloq.* retentive memory.

па́мятник *n.* monument; memorial. —надгро́бный па́мятник, monument; (large) tombstone.

па́мятный *adj.* [*short form* -тен, -тна] 1, memorable. 2, (*with dat.*) well remembered (by): Мно́гим па́мятен (+ *nom.*), many people remember well... 3, serving as a reminder: па́мятная кни́жка, memorandum book; notebook. 4, memorial; commemorative: па́мятная доска́, memorial plaque; па́мятная ма́рка, commemorative stamp. —па́мятная запи́ска, memorandum; aide-mémoire. —па́мятный пода́рок, memento.

па́мятовать *v.impfv., in* **па́мятуя о,** remembering; recalling.

па́мять *n.f.* memory. —**без па́мяти, 1,** unconscious. **2,** (*with verbs of running or racing*) madly; for all one is worth. **3,** (*with* **от**) madly in love (with). **4,** (*with* **люби́ть**) to distraction. —**в па́мять** (+ *gen.*), in memory of. —**на (чье́й-нибудь) па́мяти,** in (*or* within) someone's memory. У всех на па́мяти (+ *nom.*), everyone remembers... —**на па́мять, 1,** by heart. **2,** from memory. **3,** for memory's sake; as a keepsake; as a souvenir. —**па́мяти** (+ *dat.*), in memory of. —**по па́мяти,** from memory. —**по ста́рой па́мяти, 1,** by force of habit. **2,** for old times' sake. —**приходи́ть на па́мять** (+ *dat.*), to come to mind.

пана́ма *n.* Panama hat.

пана́мский *adj.* Panamanian.

панаце́я *n.* panacea.

па́нда *n.* panda.

пандеми́я (дэ) *n.* pandemic.

панеги́рик *n.* panegyric; eulogy. —**панегири́ст,** *n.* panegyrist.

пане́ль *n.f.* **1,** pavement; sidewalk. **2,** paneling; panel; wainscot.

панибра́тский *adj., colloq.* overly familiar. —**панибра́тство,** *n., colloq.* undue familiarity.

па́ника *n.* panic.

паникёр *n.* alarmist; scaremonger.

паникова́ть *v.impfv.* [*pres.* **-ку́ю, -ку́ешь**] *colloq.* to panic.

панихи́да *n.* funeral service; requiem.

пани́чески *adv.* **1,** in panic. **2,** *in* пани́чески боя́ться, to be deathly afraid.

пани́ческий *adj.* **1,** of panic: в пани́ческом состоя́нии, in a state of panic. Пани́ческий страх, utter panic. **2,** panicky; panic-stricken. **3,** causing panic; alarming.

панно́ *n.indecl., art* panel.

пано́птикум *n.* wax museum.

панора́ма *n.* panorama; panoramic view. —**панора́мный,** *adj.* panoramic.

пансио́н *n.* **1,** boarding house. **2,** room and board: жить на пансио́не, to receive room and board. **3,** *pre-rev.* boarding school.

пансиона́т *n.* (resort) hotel.

пансионе́р *n.* **1,** *pre-rev.* boarding school student. **2,** boarder; roomer.

пантало́ны [*gen.* **-ло́н**] *n.pl.* **1,** *obs.* pants. **2,** (woman's) drawers.

панталы́к *n., colloq., in* сбить с панталы́ку, to confuse; сби́ться с панталы́ку, to become confused.

пантеи́зм (тэ) *n.* pantheism. —**пантеи́ст,** *n.* pantheist. —**пантеисти́ческий,** *adj.* pantheistic.

пантео́н (тэ) *n.* pantheon.

панте́ра *n.* panther.

пантоми́ма *n.* pantomime. —**пантоми́мный; пантомими́ческий,** *adj.* pantomime.

панхромати́ческий *adj.* panchromatic.

па́нцирный *adj.* **1,** clad in armor. **2,** *zool.* testaceous. —**па́нцирная се́тка,** series of interlocking rings.

па́нцирь *n.m.* **1,** armor; coat of mail. **2,** shell (*of a turtle*); armor (*of an armadillo*).

па́па *n.m.* **1,** papa; daddy. **2,** Pope.

папа́ха *n.* tall fur hat.

папа́ша *n.m., colloq.* daddy.

па́перть *n.f.* portico of a church.

папильо́тка [*gen. pl.* **-ток**] *n.* (hair) curler.

папиро́са *n.* cigarette.

папиро́сница *n.* cigarette case.

папиро́сный *adj.* cigarette (*attrib.*). —**папиро́сная бума́га,** tissue paper.

папи́рус *n.* papyrus.

па́пка [*gen. pl.* **па́пок**] *n.* **1,** (cardboard) folder. **2,** file.

па́поротник *n.* fern.

па́прика *n.* paprika.

па́пский *adj.* papal. —**па́пство,** *n.* papacy.

па́пула *n.* papule.

папье́-маше́ *n.neut. indecl.* papier-mâché.

пар[1] [*2nd loc.* **пару́;** *pl.* **пары́**] *n., often. pl.* **1,** steam. **2,** vapor. —**на всех пара́х, 1,** under a full head of steam. **2,** *fig.* at top speed.

пар[2] [*2nd loc.* **пару́;** *pl.* **пары́**] *n.* fallow land: лежа́ть под па́ром, to lie fallow.

па́ра *n.* **1,** pair: па́ра чуло́к, pair of stockings. **2,** (married) couple: счастли́вая па́ра, happy couple. **3,** (*with gen. or* **к**) mate (*other of a pair*): Эта перча́тка — па́ра (к) уте́рянной, this glove is the mate to the one that was lost. **4,** (*with dat.*) *colloq.* suitable mate (for); good mate (for); good match (for): Он ей не па́ра, he is not a good match for her. **5,** (*with gen. pl.*) *colloq.* a few: Мо́жно попроси́ть вас на па́ру слов?, may I have a few words (*or* a word) with you? **6,** man's suit. **7,** *pl., tennis* doubles: мужски́е па́ры, men's doubles. —**в па́ре; на па́ру,** together; jointly. —**стать** *or* **встать в па́ры,** to line up in pairs. —**ходи́ть** *or* **гуля́ть па́рами,** to walk in pairs.

пара́бола *n.* parabola. —**параболи́ческий,** *adj.* parabolic.

пара́граф *n.* paragraph.

пара́д *n.* parade.

паради́гма *n.* paradigm.

пара́дность *n.f.* ostentation.

пара́дный *adj.* **1,** parade (*attrib.*). **2,** (*of clothes*) formal; dress. **3,** gala; festive. **4,** (*of an entrance, staircase, etc.*) main; front. —**пара́дное,** *n.* front door.

парадо́кс *n.* paradox. —**парадокса́льный,** *adj.* paradoxical.

парази́т *n.* **1,** *biol.* parasite. **2,** *fig.* parasite; sponger. —**паразити́зм,** *n.* parasitism. —**паразити́ческий; парази́тный,** *adj.* parasitic.

парализова́ть *v.impfv. & pfv.* [*pres.* **-зу́ю, -зу́ешь**] to paralyze.

парали́тик *n.* paralytic. —**паралити́ческий,** *adj.* paralytic.

парали́ч [*gen.* **-лича́**] *n.* **1,** paralysis. **2,** palsy. —**парали́чный,** *adj.* paralytic.

паралла́кс *n.* parallax.

параллелепи́пед *n.* parallelepiped.

параллели́зм *n.* parallelism.

параллелогра́мм *n.* parallelogram.

паралле́ль *n.f.* parallel.

параллéльно *adv.* **1,** parallel (to each other). **2,** (*with dat.*) parallel to: параллéльно дорóге, parallel to the road. **3,** *fig.* (*with* **c** + *instr.*) parallel (to): параллéльно с э́тим, parallel to this. **4,** *fig.* at the same time.

параллéльный *adj.* parallel.

парáметр *n.* parameter.

парамéция *n.* paramecium.

паранóик *n.*, *colloq.* paranoiac. —**параноúческий**, *adj.* paranoid.

паранóйя *n.* paranoia.

парапéт *n.* parapet.

параплеги́я *n.* paraplegia.

парапсихолóгия *n.* parapsychology. —**парапсихó-лог**, *n.* parapsychologist.

парати́ф *n.* paratyphoid (fever).

парафи́н *n.* paraffin. —**парафи́новый**, *adj.* paraffin.

парафи́ровать *v.impfv. & pfv.* [*pres.* **-рую, -руешь**] to initial (a treaty, document, etc.).

парашю́т (шу) *n.* parachute. Вы́броситься с парашю́том, to bail out. —**парашюти́зм**, *n.* parachute jumping (*as a sport*). —**парашюти́ст**, *n.* parachutist; parachute jumper; paratrooper. —**парашю́тный**, *adj.* parachute (*attrib.*).

паращитови́дный *adj.*, *in* **паращитови́дная железá**, parathyroid gland.

парéз (рэ) *n.* paresis.

пáреный *adj.* stewed. —**дешéвле пáреной рéпы**, *colloq.* dirt-cheap.

пáрень [*gen.* **пáрня**; *pl.* **пáрни, -нéй, -ня́м**] *n.m.*, *colloq.* fellow; lad; chap; guy.

пари́ *n.neut. indecl.* bet; wager.

парижáнин [*pl.* **-жáне, -жáн**] *n.m.* [*fem.* **-жáнка**] Parisian.

пари́жский *adj.* of Paris; Parisian.

пари́к [*gen.* **-рикá**] *n.* wig.

парикмáхер *n.* barber; hairdresser. —**парикмáхерская**, *n.*, *decl. as an adj.* barbershop.

пари́льня [*gen. pl.* **-лен**] *n.* steam room.

пари́ровать *v.impfv & pfv.* [*pres.* **-рую, -руешь**] **1,** to parry; ward off. **2,** to parry; counter.

паритéт *n.* parity. —**паритéтный**, *adj.* equal.

пáрить *v.impfv.* **1,** to steam. **2,** to stew. **3,** *impers.* to be sultry: Сегóдня пáрит, it is sultry today. —**пáриться**, *refl.* **1,** to steam; sweat (*in a bath*). **2,** (*of food*) to stew.

пари́ть *v.impfv.* to soar; glide.

пáрия *n.* pariah; outcast.

парк *n.* **1,** park. **2,** depot; yard. **3,** fleet; stock: автомоби́льный парк США, the total number of cars in the U.S.

пáрка [*gen. pl.* **пáрок**] *n.* parka.

паркéт *n.* parquetry; parquet. —**паркéтный**, *adj.* parquet.

парлáмент *n.* parliament. —**парламентари́зм**, *n.* parliamentarianism. —**парламентáрий**, *n.* member of parliament. —**парламентáрный**, *adj.* parliamentary.

парламентёр *n.* bearer of a flag of truce.

парламентёрский *adj.*, *in* **парламентёрский флаг**, flag of truce.

парлáментский *adj.* parliamentary.

парни́к [*gen.* **-никá**] *n.* hotbed.

парникóвый *adj.* hotbed (*attrib.*); hothouse (*attrib.*): Парникóвые растéния, hothouse plants.

парни́шка [*gen. pl.* **-шек**] *n.m.*, *colloq.* lad; boy.

парнóй *adj.* **1,** (*of milk*) fresh from the cow; (*of meat*) from a freshly killed animal. **2,** *colloq.* stuffy; sultry.

пáрный *adj.* **1,** being one (or the other) of a pair. **2,** arranged or done in pairs. —**пáрная игрá**, *tennis* doubles.

паровóз *n.* locomotive.

паровóзный *adj.* locomotive (*attrib.*). —**паровóзное депó**, roundhouse.

паровóй *adj.* **1,** steam (*attrib.*); steam-driven: паровáя маши́на, steam engine. **2,** (*of food*) steamed. **3,** (*of land*) fallow.

пароди́ровать *v.impfv. & pfv.* [*pres.* **-рую, -руешь**] to parody.

пароди́ст *n.* parodist.

парóдия *n.* **1,** parody. **2,** *fig.* (*with* **на** + *acc.*) parody (of); travesty (of); mockery (of).

пароксúзм *n.* paroxysm.

парóль *n.m.* password.

парóм *n.* ferry. —**парóмный**, *adj.* ferry (*attrib.*). —**парóмщик**, *n.* ferryman.

парообрáзный *adj.* vaporous.

парообразовáние *n.* vaporization; generation of steam.

парохóд *n.* ship; steamship. —**парохóдный**, *adj.* steamship (*attrib.*). —**парохóдство**, *n.* steamship line; steamship company.

пáрочка [*gen. pl.* **-чек**] *n.*, *colloq.* **1,** pair. **2,** couple.

пáрта *n.* school desk.

партеногенéз (тэ, нэ) *n.* parthenogenesis.

партéр (тэ) *n.*, *theat.* orchestra.

партизáн [*gen. pl.* **-зáн**] *n.* partisan; guerrilla. —**партизáнский**, *adj.* guerrilla (*attrib.*). —**партизáнство**, *n.* guerrilla activity.

парти́йность *n.f.* **1,** party membership. **2,** party spirit. **3,** reflection of party principles (*in literature, art, etc.*).

парти́йный *adj.* party (*attrib.*); Party (*attrib.*).

партиту́ра *n.*, *music* score.

пáртия *n.* **1,** (political) party. **2,** party; team; group. **3,** batch; lot; shipment; consignment. **4,** game. **5,** *music* part. **6,** *obs.* suitable mate; match.

партнёр *n.m.* [*fem.* **-нёрша**] **1,** partner. **2,** player. **3,** (one's) opponent (*in a game*). —**партнёрство**, *n.* partnership.

пáрус [*pl.* **парусá**] *n.* sail. —**на всех парусáх**, (at) full speed.

паруси́на *n.* canvas. —**паруси́новый**, *adj.* canvas.

пáрусник *n.* **1,** sailing vessel. **2,** sailfish. **3,** swallow-tail (*butterfly*).

пáрусный *adj.* sail (*attrib.*): пáрусная лóдка, sailboat.

Парфенóн *n.* Parthenon.

парфюмéрия *n.* perfumes. —**парфюмéр**, *n.* perfumer. —**парфюмéрный**, *adj.* perfume (*attrib.*).

парчá *n.* brocade. —**парчóвый**, *adj.* brocade; brocaded.

паршá *n.* mange.

парши́веть *v.impfv.* [*pfv.* **запарши́веть** *or* **опарши́веть**] *colloq.* to become mangy.

парши́вый *adj.* **1,** mangy. **2,** *colloq.* rotten; lousy. —**парши́вая овцá**, black sheep.

пас *n., cards; sports* pass. —*predicate, colloq.* over one's head: В э́том де́ле я пас, this is way over my head; this is beyond me.

па́сека *n.* apiary. —**па́сечник,** *n.* beekeeper.

па́сквиль *n.m.* scurrilous piece of writing; libel; slander; hatchet job.

паску́дный *adj., colloq.* foul; vile.

паслён *n.* nightshade.

па́смурный *adj.* **1,** overcast; dreary; dismal. **2,** gloomy; sullen; morose.

пасова́ть *v.impfv.* [*pfv.* **спасова́ть;** *pres.* **-су́ю, -су́ешь**] **1,** *cards* to pass. **2,** [*impfv. only*] *sports* to pass (a ball, puck, etc.). **3,** *fig.* (*with* **пе́ред**) to shrink (from); retreat in the face of.

паспарту́ *n.neut. indecl.* mount (*for a picture or photograph*).

па́спорт [*pl.* **паспорта́**] *n.* passport. —**па́спортный,** *adj.* passport (*attrib.*).

пасса́ж *n.* **1,** arcade. **2,** *obs.* passage (*in a written text*). **3,** *music* passage.

пассажи́р *n.* passenger. —**пассажи́рский,** *adj.* passenger (*attrib.*).

пасса́т *n.* trade wind.

пасси́в *n.* **1,** *comm.* liabilities. **2,** *gram.* passive voice.

пасси́вный *adj.* **1,** passive. **2,** *econ.* adverse; unfavorable. —**пасси́вность,** *n.f.* passivity.

па́ссия *n., obs.* passion; flame.

па́ста *n.* paste. —**зубна́я па́ста,** toothpaste.

па́стбище *n.* pasture. —**па́стбищный,** *adj.* pasture (*attrib.*); grazing (*attrib.*).

па́ства *n.* flock; congregation; parishioners.

пасте́ль (тэ) *n.f.* pastel. —**пасте́льный,** *adj.* pastel.

пастериза́ция (тэ) *n.* pasteurization.

пастеризова́ть (тэ) *v.impfv. & pfv.* [*pres.* **-зу́ю, -зу́ешь**] to pasteurize.

пастерна́к *n.* parsnip.

пасти́ *v.impfv.* [*pres.* **пасу́, пасёшь;** *past* **пас, пасла́, пасло́, пасли́**] to tend; graze; herd.

пастила́ [*pl.* **пасти́лы**] *n.* a confection made of fruit, sugar and egg whites.

пасти́сь *v.r.impfv.* [*pres.* **пасётся;** *past* **пасся, пасла́сь, пасло́сь, пасли́сь**] (*of cattle*) to graze.

па́стор *n.* pastor; minister.

пастора́ль *n.f.* **1,** pastoral. **2,** pastorale. —**пастора́льный,** *adj.* pastoral.

па́сторский *adj.* of a pastor; pastoral.

пасту́х [*gen.* **-стуха́**] *n.* shepherd.

пасту́шеский *adj.* **1,** shepherd's. **2,** *obs.* pastoral.

пасту́ший [*fem.* **-шья**] *adj.* shepherd's.

пастушо́к [*gen.* **-шка́**] *n.* **1,** young shepherd. **2,** swain. **3,** rail (*bird*).

па́стырь *n.m.* **1,** *poetic* shepherd. **2,** pastor. —**па́стырский,** *adj.* of a pastor; pastoral.

пасть[1] [*infl.* **паду́, падёшь;** *past* **пал, па́ла, па́ло, па́ли**] *v., pfv.* of **па́дать.**

пасть[2] *n.f.* mouth (*of an animal*). —**во́лчья пасть,** cleft palate.

пастьба́ *n.* pasturage.

па́сха *n.* **1,** Easter. **2,** Passover. **3,** traditional Easter dish made of cottage cheese and other ingredients.

пасха́льный *adj.* **1,** Easter (*attrib.*). **2,** Passover (*attrib.*). **3,** paschal.

па́сынок [*gen.* **-нка**] *n.* stepchild; stepson.

пасья́нс *n., cards* solitaire.

пат *n., chess* stalemate.

пате́нт *n.* patent. —**пате́нтный,** *adj.* patent (*attrib.*).

патенто́ванный *adj.* **1,** patent (*attrib.*). **2,** patented.

патентова́ть *v.impfv. & pfv.* [*pres.* **-ту́ю, -ту́ешь**] to patent; take out a patent on.

патети́ческий (тэ) *adj.* passionate; impassioned; emotional. —**патети́чески,** *adv.* with emotion.

патефо́н *n.* small portable phonograph. —**патефо́нный,** *adj.* phonograph (*attrib.*).

па́тио *n. indecl.* patio.

па́тлы [*gen.* **патл**] *n.pl., colloq.* long disheveled locks of hair.

па́тока *n.* molasses; treacle.

патоло́гия *n.* pathology. —**пато́лог,** *n.* pathologist. —**патологи́ческий,** *adj.* pathological.

па́точный *adj.* **1,** made of molasses. **2,** *fig.* sugary; saccharine.

патриа́рх *n.* patriarch. —**патриарха́льный,** *adj.* patriarchal. —**патриарха́т,** *n.* patriarchy. —**патриа́рхия,** *n.* patriarchate.

патрио́т *n.* **1,** patriot. **2,** *fig.* supporter; booster. —**патриоти́зм,** *n.* patriotism. —**патриоти́ческий,** *adj.* patriotic.

патри́ций *n.* patrician.

патро́н *n.* **1,** *obs.* patron. **2,** cartridge. **3,** *mech.* chuck. **4,** socket (*for a bulb*).

патро́нник *n.* chamber (*of a gun*).

патро́нный *adj.* cartridge (*attrib.*). —**патро́нная ле́нта,** cartridge belt; ammunition belt.

патронта́ш *n.* cartridge belt; ammunition belt.

патрули́ровать *v.impfv.* [*pres.* **-рую, -руешь**] to patrol.

патру́ль [*gen.* **-руля́**] *n.m.* patrol.

патру́льный *adj.* patrol (*attrib.*). —*n.* man on patrol.

па́уза *n.* **1,** pause. **2,** *music* rest.

пау́к [*gen.* **паука́**] *n.* spider.

паути́на *n.* **1,** spider web; cobweb. **2,** *fig.* web (*of lies, intrigue, etc.*).

па́фос *n.* fervor; zeal.

пах [*2nd loc.* **паху́**] *n.* groin.

па́харь *n.m.* plowman.

паха́ть *v.impfv.* [*pfv.* **вспаха́ть;** *pres.* **пашу́, па́шешь**] to plow.

па́хнуть *v.impfv.* [*past* **пах** or **па́хнул, па́хла**] **1,** (*with an adv.*) to smell (good, bad, nice, etc.). От него́ пло́хо па́хнет, he smells bad; there is a bad odor about him. **2,** (*with instr.*) to smell (of). От него́ па́хнет перега́ром, he smells of alcohol. **3,** (*with instr.*) to smack (of). **4,** (*with instr.*) to be in the air: Па́хнет весно́й, spring is in the air.

пахну́ть *v.pfv., colloq., usu. impers.* (*of air, a fragrance, etc.*) to blow in: со двора́ пахну́ло хо́лодом, a gust of cold air blew in from the yard.

па́хота *n.* **1,** plowing. **2,** plowed land.

па́хотный *adj.* arable.

па́хта *n.* buttermilk.

па́хтать *v.impfv.* to churn.

пахучий *adj.* **1,** strong-smelling. **2,** sweet-smelling; fragrant.

пацан [*gen.* **-цана**] *n., colloq.* boy; lad; kid.

пациент *n.m.* [*fem.* **-ка**] patient.

пацифизм *n.* pacifism. —**пацифист**, *n.* pacifist. —**пацифистский**, *adj.* pacifist.

паче *adv., obs.* more. —**паче того**; **тем паче,** the more so; all the more. —**паче чаяния,** contrary to (or beyond one's) expectations.

пачка [*gen. pl.* **пачек**] *n.* **1,** pack; bundle; batch. **2,** tutu.

пачкать *v.impfv.* [*pfv.* **запачкать** *or* **испачкать**] **1,** to soil; dirty; stain. **2,** [*impfv. only*] *colloq.* to daub. —**пачкаться,** *refl.* to become dirty; become soiled.

пачкотня *n., colloq.* poorly painted picture; daub.

пачкун [*gen.* **-куна**] *n., colloq.* **1,** slovenly person. **2,** poor painter.

паша [*gen. pl.* **пашей**] *n.m.* pasha.

пашня [*gen. pl.* **пашен**] *n.* plowed land; land under cultivation.

паштет *n.* pâté.

паюсный *adj., in* **паюсная икра,** pressed caviar.

паяльник *n.* soldering iron.

паяльный *adj.* soldering (*attrib.*). —**паяльная лампа,** blowtorch. —**паяльная трубка,** blowpipe.

паяльщик *n.* solderer.

паяние *n.* soldering.

паясничать *v.impfv., colloq.* to clown around.

паять *v.impfv.* to solder.

паяц *n.* clown; buffoon.

певец [*gen.* **певца**] *n.* singer.

певица *n.* (female) singer.

певун [*gen.* **-вуна**] *n.m.* [*fem.* **-вунья**] *colloq.* person who likes to sing.

певучий *adj.* melodious. —**певучесть,** *n.f.* melodiousness.

певчий *adj., in* **певчая птица,** songbird. —*n.* chorister; choirboy.

пеганка [*gen. pl.* **-нок**] *n.* sheldrake.

Пегас *n.* Pegasus.

пегий *adj.* piebald.

педагог *n.* teacher; pedagogue. —**педагогика,** *n.* pedagogy. —**педагогический,** *adj.* pedagogical.

педаль *n.f.* pedal.

педант *n.* pedant. —**педантизм,** *n.* pedantry. —**педантичный,** *adj.* pedantic.

педерастия *n.* sodomy.

педиатрия *n.* pediatrics. —**педиатр,** *n.* pediatrician. —**педиатрический,** *adj.* pediatric.

педикюр *n.* pedicure; chiropody. —**педикюрша,** *n.* (woman) chiropodist.

педометр *n.* pedometer.

пезета *n.* = **песета.**

пезо *n. indecl.* peso.

пейзаж *n.* **1,** landscape; scenery. **2,** landscape painting. —**пейзажист,** *n.* landscape painter. —**пейзажный,** *adj.* landscape (*attrib.*).

пекан *n.* pecan.

пекари *n.m. indecl.* peccary.

пекарный *adj.* baking (*attrib.*).

пекарня [*gen. pl.* **-рен**] *n.* bakery.

пекарь [*pl.* **пекаря** *or* **пекари**] *n.m.* baker. —**пекарский,** *adj.* baker's.

пеклеванный *adj.* (*of flour*) fine; finely ground. —**пеклеванный хлеб,** fine rye bread.

пекло *n., colloq.* **1,** intense heat. **2,** hell. **3,** *fig.* (*with gen.*) the heat (of); the thick (of).

пелена [*gen. pl.* **пелён**] *n.* cover; veil; shroud (*of clouds, fog, snow, smoke, etc.*).

пеленать *v.impfv.* [*pfv.* **спеленать** *or* **запеленать**] to diaper; swaddle.

пеленг *n., navigation* bearing.

пеленгатор *n.* direction finder.

пеленговать *v.impfv. & pfv.* [*pres.* **-гую, -гуешь**] to take a bearing on.

пелёнка [*gen. pl.* **-нок**] *n.* diaper. —**с пелёнок,** from the cradle.

пелерина *n.* cape.

пеликан *n.* pelican.

пеллагра *n.* pellagra.

пельмени *n.pl.* [*sing.* **пельмень,** *m.*] meat dumplings.

пемза *n.* pumice; pumice stone.

пена *n.* **1,** foam. **2,** lather; suds: **мыльная пена,** soapsuds. **3,** scum. —**с пеной у рта,** passionately; vehemently; with fervor.

пенал *n.* pencil case.

пенёк [*gen.* **пенька**] *n.* stump (*of a tree*).

пение *n.* singing.

пенистый *adj.* foamy.

пенить *v.impfv.* [*pfv.* **вспенить**] to froth; cause to foam. —**пениться,** *refl.* to froth; foam.

пенициллин *n.* penicillin.

пенка *n.* **1,** skin (*forming on milk*). **2,** [*also,* **морская пенка**] meerschaum. —**пенковый,** *adj.* meerschaum.

пенни *n.neut. indecl.* penny (*in Great Britain*).

пенный *adj.* foamy. —**пенный огнетушитель,** foam fire extinguisher.

пенопласт *n.* foam plastic; expanded plastic.

пенс *n.* penny (*in Great Britain*); *pl.* pence.

пенсионер *n.* pensioner; retiree.

пенсионный *adj.* pension (*attrib.*). —**пенсионный возраст,** retirement age.

пенсия *n.* pension. **Выйти** *or* **уйти на пенсию,** to retire (*on a pension*).

пенсне (нэ) *n.neut. indecl.* pince-nez.

Пентагон *n.* the Pentagon.

пентаметр *n.* pentameter.

пень [*gen.* **пня**] *n.m.* stump (*of a tree*). —**стоять как пень,** to stand (there) like a dummy.

пенька *n.* hemp. —**пеньковый,** *adj.* hemp (*attrib.*).

пеньюар *n.* peignoir.

пеня *n.* fine; penalty.

пенять *v.impfv.* [*pfv.* **попенять**] *colloq.* **1,** [*impfv. only*] (*with* **на** + *acc.*) to blame. **2,** (*with dat.*) to scold; chide.

пеон *n.* peon. —**пеонаж,** *n.* peonage.

пепел [*gen.* **пепла**] *n.* **1,** ashes. **2,** (volcanic) ash.

пепелище *n.* site of a fire.

пепельница *n.* ashtray.

пепельный *adj.* ash-colored.

пепсин *n.* pepsin.

пептóн *n.* peptone.

первéйший *adj., colloq.* **1,** primary. **2,** the very best.

пéрвенец [*gen.* **-нца**] *n.* first-born.

пéрвенство *n.* **1,** championship. **2,** primacy.

пéрвенствовать *v.impfv.* [*pres.* **-ствую, -ствуешь**] **1,** to come in first; finish first. **2,** (*with* **над**) to take precedence (over). **3,** (*with* **мéжду** *or* **среди́**) to stand out (among); dominate.

перви́чный *adj.* primary; initial.

первобы́тный *adj.* **1,** primitive. **2,** primeval; pristine.

пéрвое *n., decl. as an adj.* **1,** the first thing: пéрвое, что нáдо сдéлать, the first thing to be done. **2,** (*with dates*) first: Сегóдня — пéрвое мáрта, today is March 1st. **3,** first course.

первоздáнный *adj.* primordial; primeval.

первоистóчник *n.* original source; primary source.

первоклáссный *adj.* first-class; first-rate.

первокýрсник *n.* freshman.

первомáйский *adj.* May Day (*attrib.*).

первоначáльный *adj.* **1,** original. **2,** initial; primary. **3,** elementary. —**первоначáльно,** *adv.* originally.

первообрáз *n.* prototype.

первооткрывáтель *n.m.* discoverer.

первоочереднóй *adj.* primary; of the highest priority.

первопрохóдец [*gen.* **-дца**] *n.* **1,** earliest explorer. **2,** pioneer.

перворазря́дный *adj.* first-rate; first-class.

перворóдный *adj.* **1,** *obs.* first-born. **2,** *fig.* pristine. —**перворóдный грех,** original sin.

перворóдство *n.* primogeniture.

первосвящéнник *n.* high priest.

первосóртный *adj.* **1,** of the highest quality. **2,** *colloq.* first-rate; first-class.

первостатéйный *adj., colloq.* first-rate; first-class.

первостепéнный *adj.* paramount; overriding.

первоцвéт *n.* primrose.

пéрвый *ordinal numeral & adj.* first: пéрвая страни́ца, the first page. —*n.* **1,** the first. **2,** the former. —**в пéрвую óчередь,** first of all. —**из пéрвых рук,** first-hand. —**пéрвое врéмя; в пéрвое врéмя; на пéрвых порáх,** at first; in the beginning. —**пéрвым дéлом; пéрвым дóлгом,** *colloq.* first thing; first of all. *See also* **пéрвое.**

пергáмент *n.* parchment. —**пергáментный,** *adj.* parchment.

пере- *prefix* **1,** *indicating motion over or across:* перейти́ (чéрез) ýлицу, to cross the street; перелетéть чéрез забóр, to fly over the fence. **2,** *indicating motion to another place:* перелéчь на другóй дивáн, to lie on another couch; перевéсить карти́ну на другýю стéну, to hang the picture on another wall. **3,** *indicating repetition of an action:* перечитáть, to reread; перепродáть, to resell. **4,** *indicating excess:* перéесть, to overeat; переплати́ть, to overpay. **5,** (*with pfv. verbs only*) *colloq., indicating thoroughness or completeness of an action:* переискáть, to search everywhere; перемóкнуть, to get completely drenched. **6,** (*with pfv. verbs only*) *colloq., indicating outdoing someone:* перепи́ть, to outdrink; перехитри́ть, to outwit. **7,** (*with pfv. verbs only*) *colloq., used when the subject is all or many:* Все цветы́ перемёрзли, all the flowers perished from the frost. **8,** (*with pfv. verbs only*) *colloq., used when the object is all or many:* перекупáть всех детéй, to bathe all the children; перемéрить мнóго шляп, to try on many hats. **9,** (*with* **-ся**) *indicating reciprocity or exchange:* перепи́сываться, to correspond; перемúгиваться, to wink at each other.

переадресовáть [*infl.* **-сýю, -сýешь**] *v., pfv. of* **переадрéсовывать.**

переадрéсовывать *v.impfv.* [*pfv.* **переадресовáть**] to readdress; forward.

перебази́ровать *v.pfv.* [*infl.* **-рую, -руешь**] to shift; transfer; relocate.

перебáрщивать *v.impfv.* [*pfv.* **переборщи́ть**] *colloq.* to overdo it; go too far.

перебегáть *v.impfv.* [*pfv.* **перебежáть**] **1,** (*with acc. or* **чéрез**) to run across. **2,** to run from one place to another. **3,** to defect. —**перебегáть дорóгу** (+ *dat.*), to stand in someone's way.

перебежáть [*infl. like* **бежáть**] *v., pfv. of* **перебегáть.**

перебéжка [*gen. pl.* **-жек**] *n.* **1,** run; rush; dash. **2,** defection. **3,** *sports* rerunning (*of a race*).

перебéжчик *n.* defector; turncoat.

перебéливать *v.impfv.* [*pfv.* **перебели́ть**] **1,** to repaint; give (something) a fresh coat of white paint. **2,** to make a clean copy of; put in final form.

перебели́ть [*infl.* **-белю́, -бéлишь** *or* **-бели́шь**] *v., pfv. of* **перебéливать.**

перебеси́ться *v.r.pfv.* [*infl.* **-бешýсь, -бéсишься**] **1,** (*of dogs*) to become rabid. **2,** *colloq.* to settle down (*after leading a wild life*).

перебивáть *v.impfv.* [*pfv.* **переби́ть**] **1,** to interrupt. **2,** to drown out. **3,** to reupholster. **4,** *colloq.* to snatch up (*ahead of someone else*). —**перебивáться,** *refl.* **1,** to be smashed; be shattered. **2,** *colloq.* to manage; get along; make ends meet.

перебинтовáть *v.pfv.* [*infl.* **-тýю, -тýешь**] **1,** to rebandage; change the bandage on. **2,** to bandage all of; bandage entirely.

перебирáть *v.impfv.* [*pfv.* **перебрáть**] **1,** to sort out. **2,** to go through; run through. **3,** to run one's fingers over. **4,** [*often,* **перебирáть в пáмяти**] to review in one's mind. **5,** *printing* to reset. —**перебирáться,** *refl., colloq.* **1,** to cross; get across. **2,** to move (*change residence*).

переби́ть *v.pfv.* [*infl.* **-бью́, -бьёшь**] **1,** *pfv. of* **перебивáть. 2,** to slaughter; massacre. **3,** to break; fracture. **4,** to break (all of something). —**переби́ться,** *refl., pfv., of* **перебивáться.**

перебóй *n.* **1,** irregularity: пульс с перебóями, irregular pulse. **2,** (temporary) interruption; stoppage.

переболéть[1] *v.pfv.* [*infl.* **-лéю, -лéешь**] (*with instr.*) **1,** to have had (a certain illness or many illnesses). **2,** (*of many people*) to come down with (a certain illness).

переболéть[2] *v.pfv.* [*infl.* **-ли́т**] *fig.* (*of one's heart*) to ache: Сéрдце переболéло (*or* душá переболéла) за тебя́, my heart ached for you.

перебóр *n., colloq.* excess.

перебóрка [*gen. pl.* **-рок**] *n.* **1,** sorting out. **2,** partition. **3,** *naut.* bulkhead.

переборо́ть *v.pfv.* [*infl.* **-борю́, -бо́решь**] to overcome. —**переборо́ть себя́,** to keep control of oneself.

переборщи́ть *v., pfv. of* **перебо́рщивать.**

перебра́ниваться *v.r.impfv., colloq.* to exchange angry words.

перебра́нка [*gen. pl.* **-нок**] *n., colloq.* squabble; altercation.

перебра́сывать *v.impfv.* [*pfv.* **перебро́сить**] **1,** to throw over: **перебро́сить шарф че́рез плечо́,** to throw a scarf over one's shoulder. **2,** to throw across: **перебро́сить мост че́рез ре́ку,** to throw a bridge across a river. **3,** to transfer. **4,** *mil.* to transport; airlift. —**перебра́сываться,** *refl.* **1,** (*with* **че́рез**) to dash across. **2,** to spread. **3,** (*with instr.*) to toss back and forth; throw at each other. **4,** *fig.* (*with instr.*) to exchange (words, comments, etc.).

перебра́ть [*infl. like* **брать**] *v., pfv. of* **перебира́ть.** —**перебра́ться,** *refl.* [*past tense stress as in* **бра́ться**] *pfv. of* **перебира́ться.**

переброди́ть *v.pfv.* [*infl.* **-брожу́, -бро́дишь**] **1,** to have fermented. **2,** *fig., colloq.* to mature; mellow.

перебро́сить [*infl.* **-бро́шу, -бро́сишь**] *v., pfv. of* **перебра́сывать.** —**перебро́ситься,** *refl., pfv. of* **перебра́сываться.**

перебро́ска *n.* transfer.

перебыва́ть *v.pfv., used mainly in the past tense* **1,** to have been (in all or many places). **2,** (*with* **у**) to visit; go see (all or many people). **3,** (*of all or many people*) to have been (somewhere).

перева́л *n.* **1,** crossing: **перева́л че́рез го́ры,** crossing of mountains. **2,** mountain pass.

перева́ливать *v.impfv.* [*pfv.* **перевали́ть**] **1,** to turn over on one's/its side. **2,** *colloq.* to shift; transfer (something heavy); load onto something else. **3,** (*with acc. or* **че́рез**) to cross; traverse. **4,** (*with* **за** + *acc.*) *colloq.* to exceed; (*of a person*) be past a certain age: **Ему́ перевали́ло за со́рок,** he is past forty. —**перева́ливаться,** *refl.* **1,** to roll over. **2,** [*impfv. only*] to waddle.

перевали́ть [*infl.* **-валю́, -ва́лишь**] *v., pfv. of* **перева́ливать.** —**перевали́ться,** *refl., pfv. of* **перева́ливаться.**

перева́лка *n.* **1,** transfer of cargo; transshipment. **2,** transshipment point. **3,** *colloq.* waddle. —**перева́лочный,** *adj.* transfer (*attrib.*); transshipment (*attrib.*).

перева́ривать *v.impfv.* [*pfv.* **перевари́ть**] **1,** to recook. **2,** to overcook. **3,** to digest. **4,** *fig., colloq.* to put up with; stomach. —**перева́риваться,** *refl.* to be overcooked; be overdone.

перевари́ть [*infl.* **-варю́, -ва́ришь**] *v., pfv. of* **перева́риваться.** —**перевари́ться,** *refl., pfv. of* **перева́риваться.**

перевезти́ [*infl. like* **везти́**] *v., pfv. of* **перевози́ть.**

перевёрнутый *adj.* inverted.

переверну́ть *v., pfv. of* **перевёртывать** *and* **перевора́чивать.** —**переверну́ться,** *refl., pfv. of* **перевёртываться** *and* **перевора́чиваться.**

переверте́ть [*infl.* **-верчу́, -ве́ртишь**] *v., pfv. of* **перевёртывать** (*in sense #7*).

перевёртывание *n.* inversion.

перевёртывать *v.impfv.* [*pfv.* **переверну́ть**] **1,** to turn over; invert. **2,** *colloq.* to overturn; upset. **3,** to turn (a page). **4,** *colloq.* to turn (everything) upside down (*when searching for something*). **5,** *fig., colloq.* to change completely; transform. **6,** *fig., colloq.* to shake; stagger; stun. **7,** [*pfv.* **переверте́ть**] to overwind. —**перевёртываться,** *refl.* **1,** to turn over. **2,** to capsize. **3,** *fig.* to change completely.

переве́с *n.* **1,** superiority; preponderance. **2,** advantage; edge. **3,** *colloq.* excess weight.

переве́сить [*infl.* **-шу, -сишь**] *v., pfv. of* **переве́шивать.** —**переве́ситься,** *refl., pfv. of* **переве́шиваться.**

перевести́ [*infl. like* **вести́**] *v., pfv. of* **переводи́ть.** —**перевести́сь,** *refl., pfv. of* **переводи́ться.**

переве́шивать *v.impfv.* [*pfv.* **переве́сить**] **1,** to move by hanging elsewhere. **2,** to weigh again. **3,** *fig.* to outweigh. **4,** *v.i., colloq.* to prevail. —**переве́шиваться,** *refl.* (*with* **в, на** *or* **че́рез**) to hang over; lean over.

перевива́ть *v.impfv.* [*pfv.* **переви́ть**] to interweave; intertwine.

перевида́ть *v.pfv., colloq.* to have seen (everything or many things).

перевира́ть *v.impfv.* [*pfv.* **переврать**] *colloq.* to garble; misquote.

переви́ть [*infl. like* **вить**] *v., pfv. of* **перевива́ть.**

перево́д *n.* **1,** transfer. **2,** translation. **3,** remittance: **де́нежный перево́д,** money order. **4,** conversion (*to a different unit of measurement*).

переводи́ть *v.impfv.* [*pfv.* **перевести́**; *pres.* **-вожу́, -во́дишь**] **1,** (*with* **че́рез**) to lead across; take across. **2,** to transfer; reassign. **3,** to shift. **4,** to translate. **5,** to convert (to a different unit of measurement). **6,** (*with* **вперёд** *or* **наза́д**) to set (a clock) ahead *or* back. **7,** to remit (money). **8,** *colloq.* to exterminate. **9,** *colloq.* to waste. **10,** *in* **перевести́ дух** *or* **дыха́ние,** to catch one's breath. —**переводи́ться,** *refl.* **1,** to transfer; switch; shift. **2,** *colloq.* to disappear; cease to exist. **3,** *colloq.* to be in short supply; be spent: **У него́ де́ньги никогда́ не перево́дятся,** he is never lacking for money.

переводно́й *adj.* **1,** of or for a money order. **2,** *in* **переводна́я бума́га,** carbon paper; **переводна́я карти́нка,** decal. **3,** [*also,* **перево́дный**] (*of literature*) translated; in translation.

перево́дческий *adj.* of translating; of a translator.

перево́дчик *n.m.* [*fem.* **-чица**] translator; interpreter.

перево́з *n.* **1,** transportation. **2,** ferrying station.

перевози́ть *v.impfv.* [*pfv.* **перевезти́**; *pres.* **-вожу́, -во́зишь**] **1,** to transport; carry; convey. **2,** (*with* **че́рез**) to take across; transport across; ferry across.

перево́зка *n.* transportation. —**возду́шная перево́зка,** airlift.

перево́зочный *adj., in* **перево́зочные сре́дства,** means of conveyance.

перево́зчик *n.* **1,** ferryman. **2,** *colloq.* mover. **3,** sandpiper.

перевооружа́ть *v.impfv.* [*pfv.* **перевооружи́ть**] to rearm (*supply with new arms*). —**перевооружа́ться,** *refl.* to rearm (*acquire new arms*).

перевооруже́ние *n.* rearmament.

перевооружи́ть v., pfv. of **перевооружа́ть**. —**перевооружи́ться**, refl., pfv. of **перевооружа́ться**.

перевоплоща́ть v.impfv. [pfv. **перевоплоти́ть**] to reincarnate.

перевоплоще́ние n. reincarnaton.

перевора́чивать v.impfv. = **перевёртывать**. —**перевора́чиваться**, refl. = **перевёртываться**.

переворо́т n. revolution; upheaval; coup. —**госуда́рственный переворо́т**, coup d'état.

перевороши́ть v.pfv., colloq. **1**, to toss (hay). **2**, to mess up; disarrange. **3**, to turn over in one's mind. **4**, fig. to alter completely; transform; turn upside down.

перевоспита́ние n. re-education.

перевоспи́тывать v.impfv. [pfv. **перевоспита́ть**] to re-educate.

перевра́ть [infl. like врать] v., pfv. of **перевира́ть**.

перевы́боры [gen. -ров] n.pl. **1**, election(s). **2**, new election(s).

перевыполне́ние n. overfulfillment.

перевыполня́ть v.impfv. [pfv. **перевы́полнить**] to exceed; overfulfill.

перевяза́ть [infl. -вяжу́, -вя́жешь] v., pfv. of **перевя́зывать**. —**перевяза́ться**, refl., pfv. of **перевя́зываться**.

перевя́зка n. **1**, tying up. **2**, bandaging; dressing. **3**, colloq. bandage.

перевя́зочный adj. for the dressing of wounds: перевя́зочный пункт, place where wounds are dressed.

перевя́зывать v.impfv. [pfv. **перевяза́ть**] **1**, to tie; tie up. **2**, to bandage. **3**, to retie. **4**, to rebandage. **5**, to knit again. —**перевя́зываться**, refl. to bandage oneself.

пе́ревязь n.f. **1**, mil. shoulder belt. **2**, med. sling.

перега́р n., colloq. smell of alcohol.

переги́б n. **1**, bend. **2**, fig. excess; extreme.

перегиба́ть v.impfv. [pfv. **перегну́ть**] **1**, to bend. **2**, in перегну́ть па́лку, to go too far; go overboard. —**перегиба́ться**, refl. to bend over; lean over.

перегласо́вка n., phonet. mutation.

перегля́дываться v.r.impfv. [pfv. **перегляну́ться**] to exchange glances.

перегляну́ться [infl. -гляну́сь, -гля́нешься] v.r., pfv. of **перегля́дываться**.

перегна́ть [infl. -гоню́, -го́нишь; past fem. перегнала́] v., pfv. of **перегоня́ть**.

перегнива́ть v.impfv. [pfv. **перегни́ть**] to rot through.

перегни́ть [infl. like гнить] v., pfv. of **перегнива́ть**.

перегно́й n. humus.

перегну́ть v., pfv. of **перегиба́ть**. —**перегну́ться**, refl., pfv. of **перегиба́ться**.

перегова́риваться v.r.impfv. to exchange a few words (with).

переговори́ть v.pfv. **1**, to talk; have a talk. **2**, colloq. to outtalk; talk down.

перегово́ры [gen. -ров] n.pl. **1**, negotiations. **2**, talks. —**стол перегово́ров**, conference table; negotiating table; bargaining table.

перего́н n. **1**, driving (of cattle). **2**, space between two stations. **3**, stage; leg (of a journey).

перего́нка n. distillation.

перего́нный adj. of or for distilling. —**перего́нный заво́д**, distillery. —**перего́нный куб**, still.

перегоня́ть v.impfv. [pfv. **перегна́ть**] **1**, to outdistance; outrun. **2**, fig. to outstrip; surpass; leave behind. **3**, to drive (to another place). **4**, to distill.

перегора́живать v.impfv. [pfv. **перегороди́ть**] **1**, to partition. **2**, colloq. to block: перегора́живать путь or доро́гу (+ dat.), to block someone's way.

перегора́ть v.impfv. [pfv. **перегоре́ть**] **1**, (of a bulb, fuse, etc.) to burn out. **2**, to be burned down to nothing. **3**, (of a fire) to burn itself out. **4**, fig. (of emotions) to die down.

перегороди́ть [infl. -рожу́, -ро́дишь or -роди́шь] v., pfv. of **перегора́живать**.

перегоро́дка [gen. pl. -док] n. **1**, partition. **2**, fig. barrier.

перегре́в n. overheating. Also, **перегрева́ние**.

перегрева́ть v.impfv. [pfv. **перегре́ть**] to overheat. —**перегрева́ться**, refl. **1**, to overheat; become overheated. **2**, to get too much sun.

перегружа́ть v.impfv. [pfv. **перегрузи́ть**] **1**, to load from one place to another. **2**, to overload; overburden. —**перегружа́ться**, refl. to be overloaded.

перегрузи́ть [infl. -гружу́, -гру́зишь or -грузи́шь] v., pfv. of **перегружа́ть**. —**перегрузи́ться**, refl., pfv. of **перегружа́ться**.

перегру́зка n. **1**, transfer of cargo; transshipment. **2**, overloading. —**перегру́зочный**, adj. transfer (attrib.); transshipment (attrib.).

перегруппирова́ть [infl. -ру́ю, -ру́ешь] v., pfv. of **перегруппиро́вывать**. —**перегруппирова́ться**, refl., pfv. of **перегруппиро́вываться**.

перегруппиро́вка n. regrouping.

перегруппиро́вывать v.impfv. [pfv. **перегруппирова́ть**] to regroup (one's forces). —**перегруппиро́вываться**, refl. (of forces) to regroup.

перегрыза́ть v.impfv. [pfv. **перегры́зть**] to gnaw through. —**перегрыза́ться**, refl., colloq. **1**, (of animals) to fight; scrap. **2**, (of people) to squabble.

перегры́зть [infl. like грызть] v., pfv. of **перегрыза́ть**. —**перегры́зться**, refl., pfv. of **перегрыза́ться**.

пе́ред prep., with instr. **1**, in front of; before: сиде́ть пе́ред зе́ркалом, to sit in front of the mirror; предста́ть пе́ред судо́м, to appear before the court. **2**, before (in time): пе́ред обе́дом, before dinner. **3**, compared to: Э́то ничто́ пе́ред..., that's nothing compared to... —**пе́ред тем, как**, before: пе́ред тем, как вы́йти и́з дому, before leaving the house; пе́ред тем, как он вы́шел и́з дому, before he left the house.

пе́рёд [gen. пе́реда; pl. переда́] n. front.

передава́ть v.impfv. [pfv. **переда́ть**; pres. -даю́, -даёшь] **1**, to hand (something to someone); hand over; pass. **2**, to convey (a thought, news, regards, etc.). Переда́йте ему́ (от меня́) приве́т, give him my regards. Переда́йте ей, что..., tell her that... **3**, to refer; turn over (a matter). **4**, to turn over; hand over; transfer (power, property, etc.). **5**, to transmit; pass on (an infection). **6**, sports to pass (the ball, puck, baton, etc.). **7**, to transmit (over the airwaves). Передава́ть по ра́дио, to broadcast; передава́ть по телеви́дению, to televise. **8**, colloq. to overpay. —**передава́ться**, refl. **1**, to be passed; be transmitted. **2**, to be handed down (to another generation).

передáточный *adj.* transmission (*attrib.*); gear (*attrib.*): передáточный ремéнь, transmission belt; передáточное числó, gear ratio.

передáтчик *n.* **1,** transmitter. **2,** messenger.

передáть [*infl. like* **дать**; *past* пéредал *or* передáл, передалá, пéредало *or* передáло, пéредали *or* передáли] *v., pfv. of* **передавáть**. —**передáться**, *refl.* [*past tense stress as in* **дáться**] *pfv. of* **передавáться**.

передáча *n.* **1,** transmission. **2,** transfer. **3,** broadcast. **4,** *mech.* transmission; gear; drive. **5,** parcel (*for a hospital patient, prisoner, etc.*). **6,** *sports* pass.

передвигáть *v.impfv.* [*pfv.* **передви́нуть**] to move; shift (from one place to another). —**передвигáться**, *refl.* **1,** to move. **2,** [*impfv. only*] to move about; walk.

передвижéние *n.* **1,** movement; transportation. **2,** movement; locomotion. —**срéдства передвижéния**, means of conveyance.

передви́жка *n., colloq.* movement. —**библиотéка-передви́жка**, mobile library; bookmobile.

передвижнóй *adj.* **1,** movable. **2,** traveling; mobile.

передви́нуть *v., pfv. of* **передвигáть**. —**передви́нуться**, *refl., pfv. of* **передвигáться**.

переде́л *n.* **1,** dividing up; carving up. **2,** redistribution (*of land*).

переде́лать *v.pfv.* **1,** *pfv. of* **переде́лывать**. **2,** *colloq.* to do (all or everything).

переде́ли́ть [*infl.* -делю́, -де́лишь] *v., pfv. of* **переделя́ть**.

переде́лка *n.* **1,** alteration (*of a garment*). **2,** adaptation (*of a book, play, etc.*). **3,** *colloq.* fix; mess; jam: попáсть в переде́лку, to get into a mess.

переде́лывать *v.impfv.* [*pfv.* **переде́лать**] **1,** to alter (a garment). **2,** to redo; do over. **3,** to remake; make into something else.

переделя́ть *v.impfv.* [*pfv.* **передели́ть**] to redistribute.

передёргивать *v.impfv.* [*pfv.* **передёрнуть**] **1,** to pull aside; yank aside. **2,** *impers.* to wince: Егó передёрнуло от э́тих слов, he winced on hearing those words. **3,** *colloq.* to cheat (at cards); juggle (facts).

передержáть [*infl.* -держу́, -де́ржишь] *v., pfv. of* **передéрживать**.

передéрживать *v.impfv.* [*pfv.* **передержáть**] **1,** to keep in too long. **2,** *photog.* to overexpose. **3,** to retake (an examination).

передéржка [*gen. pl.* -жек] *n.* **1,** *photog.* overexposure. **2,** *colloq.* misstatement; distortion of the facts.

передёрнуть *v., pfv. of* **передёргивать**.

передислоци́ровать *v.impfv. & pfv.* [*pres.* -ру́ю, -ру́ешь] *mil.* to redeploy.

перéдний *adj.* front. —**перéдний план**, foreground. —**перéдний приво́д**, front-wheel drive.

перéдник *n.* apron.

перéдняя *n., decl. as an adj.* vestibule; hall.

передо *prep.* = **пéред** (*used mainly in the combination* **передо мной**).

передовáя *n., decl. as an adj.* **1,** feature article; lead article. **2,** *mil.* front line.

передоверя́ть *v.impfv.* [*pfv.* **передовéрить**] to transfer (legal title, power of attorney, etc.).

передови́к [*gen.* -вика́] *n.* outstanding worker.

передови́ца *n., colloq.* = **передовáя статья́**.

передовóй *adj.* **1,** forward. Передовóй отря́д, advance guard. **2,** advanced. **3,** progressive. —**передовáя статья́**, feature article; lead article.

передо́к [*gen.* -дка́] *n.* **1,** front (*of a vehicle*). **2,** vamp (*of a shoe*).

передо́хнуть *v.pfv.* [*past* -до́х, -до́хла] *colloq.* (*of many animals*) to die.

передохну́ть *v.pfv.* **1,** to take a breath. **2,** *colloq.* to pause for breath; take a short rest.

передрáзнивать *v.impfv.* [*pfv.* **передразни́ть**] to mimic; imitate.

передразни́ть [*infl.* -дразню́, -дра́знишь] *v., pfv. of* **передрáзнивать**.

передра́ться *v.r.pfv.* [*infl. like* **дрáться**] (*of many people*) to fight; scrap.

передро́гнуть *v.pfv.* [*past* -дро́г, -дро́гла] *colloq.* to be chilled (*or* frozen) to the bone.

передря́га *n., colloq.* scrape; row: попáсть в передря́гу, to get into a scrape.

переду́мывать *v.impfv.* [*pfv.* **переду́мать**] **1,** to change one's mind. **2,** (*with acc. or* **о**) *colloq.* to think over carefully.

переды́шка [*gen. pl.* -шек] *n.* breathing spell; breathing space; breather; respite.

переедáть *v.impfv.* [*pfv.* **перее́сть**] **1,** to overeat. **2,** to corrode; eat away.

перее́зд *n.* **1,** (act of) crossing. **2,** crossing (*place to cross*). **3,** moving; move (*to another residence*).

переезжáть *v.impfv.* [*pfv.* **перее́хать**] **1,** (*with acc. or* **че́рез**) to cross. **2,** to move (to another residence). **3,** *colloq.* to run over.

перее́сть [*infl. like* **есть**] *v., pfv. of* **переедáть**.

перее́хать [*infl.* -е́ду, -е́дешь] *v., pfv. of* **переезжáть**.

пережáривать *v.impfv.* [*pfv.* **пережáрить**] to overcook; overdo.

переждáть [*infl. like* **ждать**] *v., pfv. of* **пережидáть**.

пережевáть [*infl.* -жую́, -жуёшь] *v., pfv. of* **пережёвывать**.

пережёвывание *n.* chewing.

пережёвывать *v.impfv.* [*pfv.* **пережевáть**] **1,** to chew. **2,** [*impfv. only*] *fig.* to keep repeating.

пережени́ть *v.pfv.* [*infl.* -женю́, -же́нишь] to marry off (many or all of one's sons). —**пережени́ться**, *refl.* (*of many men*) to get married.

переже́чь *v.pfv.* [*infl. like* **жечь**] **1,** *pfv. of* **пережигáть**. **2,** to burn (all or much of something).

пережива́ние *n., usu. pl.* **1,** (emotional) experiences. **2,** sufferings; tribulations.

пережива́ть *v.impfv.* [*pfv.* **пережи́ть**] **1,** to go through; experience. **2,** to survive. **3,** outlive. **4,** [*impfv. only*] (*with an adv.*) *colloq.* to take; feel: о́чень (*or* тяжело́) пережива́ть что-нибудь, to take something hard. **5,** *v.i.* [*impfv. only*] *colloq.* to be upset.

пережигáть *v.impfv.* [*pfv.* **переже́чь**] **1,** to heat to excess. **2,** to burn out (a bulb); blow (a fuse). **3,** *colloq.* to burn too much (fuel, electricity, etc.).

пережидáть *v.impfv.* [*pfv.* **переждáть**] to wait out; wait till (something) is over.

пережитóе *n., decl. as an adj.* past experiences; what one has experienced or gone through.

пережи́ток [*gen.* **-тка**] *n.* vestige; remnant; survival.

пережи́ть [*infl. like* **жить**; *past* пе́режил *or* пережи́л, пережила́, пе́режило *or* пережи́ло, пе́режили *or* пережи́ли] *v., pfv. of* **пережива́ть**.

перезабы́ть *v.pfv.* [*infl.* **-бу́ду, -бу́дешь**] *colloq.* to forget (much or everything).

перезаключа́ть *v.impfv.* [*pfv.* **перезаключи́ть**] to renew (a treaty, contract, etc.).

перезаряди́ть [*infl.* **-ряжу́, -ря́дишь** *or* **-ряди́шь**] *v., pfv. of* **перезаряжа́ть**.

перезаряжа́ть *v.impfv.* [*pfv.* **перезаряди́ть**] **1,** to recharge. **2,** to overcharge. **3,** to reload.

перезахороне́ние *n.* reburial.

перезахорони́ть *v.pfv.* [*infl.* **-роню́, -ро́нишь**] to rebury.

перезва́нивать *v.impfv.* [*pfv.* **перезвони́ть**] **1,** to call back; call again. **2,** [*impfv. only*] (*of bells*) to chime. —**перезва́ниваться**, *refl.* to call each other.

перезво́н *n.* ringing of bells.

перезвони́ть *v., pfv. of* **перезва́нивать**. —**перезвони́ться**, *refl., pfv. of* **перезва́ниваться**.

перезимова́ть *v.pfv.* [*infl.* **-му́ю, -му́ешь**] to winter; spend the winter.

перезрева́ть *v.impfv.* [*pfv.* **перезре́ть**] to become overripe.

перезре́лый *adj.* overripe.

перезре́ть *v., pfv. of* **перезрева́ть**.

переигра́ть *v.pfv.* **1,** *pfv. of* **переи́грывать**. **2,** to play; perform (all or many of something).

переи́грывать *v.impfv.* [*pfv.* **переигра́ть**] **1,** to replay. **2,** *colloq.* to outplay. **3,** *theat., colloq.* to overplay (a part); overact.

переизбира́ть *v.impfv.* [*pfv.* **переизбра́ть**] **1,** to re-elect. **2,** *colloq.* to replace (with someone else).

переизбра́ние *n.* re-election.

переизбра́ть [*infl. like* **брать**] *v., pfv. of* **переизбира́ть**.

переиздава́ть *v.impfv.* [*pfv.* **переизда́ть**; *pres.* **-даю́, -даёшь**] to republish; reissue.

переизда́ние *n.* **1,** republication. **2,** new edition; reissue.

переизда́ть [*infl. like* **дать**] *v., pfv. of* **переиздава́ть**.

переименова́ть *v.pfv.* [*infl.* **-ну́ю, -ну́ешь**] to rename.

переи́мчивый *adj., colloq.* imitative.

переина́чивать *v.impfv.* [*pfv.* **переина́чить**] *colloq.* to modify; alter.

перейти́ [*infl.* **перейду́, перейдёшь**; *past* перешёл, перешла́, перешло́, перешли́] *v., pfv. of* **переходи́ть**.

перека́лывать *v.impfv.* [*pfv.* **переколо́ть**] to pin (somewhere else). *See also* **переколо́ть**.

перека́пывать *v.impfv.* [*pfv.* **перекопа́ть**] **1,** to dig (all of something). **2,** to dig again. **3,** to dig a ditch across.

перека́рмливать *v.impfv.* [*pfv.* **перекорми́ть**] to overfeed.

перека́т *n.* **1,** *usu. pl.* sharp sound; crack (*of shots being fired*); clap (*of thunder*). **2,** sandbank; shoal.

перекати́-по́ле *n.* tumbleweed.

перекати́ть [*infl.* **-качу́, -ка́тишь**] *v., pfv. of* **перека́тывать**. —**перекати́ться**, *refl., pfv. of* **перека́тываться**.

перека́тывать *v.impfv.* [*pfv.* **перекати́ть**] to roll (from one place to another). —**перека́тываться**, *refl.* to roll (over, across, etc.).

перека́шивать *v.impfv.* [*pfv.* **перекоси́ть**] *usu. impers.* to distort; warp; twist: (Лицо́) его́ перекоси́ло, his face became distorted. —**перека́шиваться**, *refl.* **1,** to become warped. **2,** (*of one's face*) to become distorted.

переквалифика́ция *n.* retraining.

переквалифици́ровать *v.impfv. & pfv.* [*pres.* **-рую, -руешь**] to retrain. —**переквалифици́роваться**, *refl.* to be retrained; learn a new trade.

переки́дывать *v.impfv.* [*pfv.* **переки́нуть**] = **переброса́сывать**. —**переки́дываться**, *refl.* = **переброса́сываться**.

перекипа́ть *v.impfv.* [*pfv.* **перекипе́ть**] **1,** (*of water, coffee, etc.*) to boil too long. **2,** *fig., colloq.* to cool off; calm down.

пе́рекис *n.f.* peroxide: пе́рекись водоро́да, hydrogen peroxide.

перекла́дина *n.* **1,** crossbeam; crossbar; transom. **2,** *sports* horizontal bar.

перекла́дывать *v.impfv.* [*pfv.* **переложи́ть**] **1,** to move (from one place to another). **2,** *fig.* to shift (a job, responsibility, etc.). **3,** (*with instr.*) to pack (with); interlay (with). **4,** to pile up again. **5,** *music; lit.* to rearrange; (*with* **в** *or* **на** + *acc.*) set (to music); put (into verse). **6,** *colloq.* to put too much (salt, sugar, etc.).

перекле́ивать *v.impfv.* [*pfv.* **перекле́ить**] **1,** to glue again; paste again. **2,** to glue; paste (somewhere else).

переклика́ть *v.impfv., colloq.* to call the roll. —**перекли́ка́ться**, *refl.* **1,** to call; shout (to one another). **2,** *fig.* (*with* **с** + *instr.*) to have certain things in common (with).

перекли́чка *n.* roll call: де́лать перекли́чку, to call the roll.

переключа́тель *n.m.* switch: переключа́тель све́та, light switch.

переключа́ть *v.impfv.* [*pfv.* **переключи́ть**] to switch; shift. —**переключа́ться**, *refl.* (*with* **на** + *acc.*) to switch (to); shift (to).

переключе́ние *n.* switch; switching over; changeover.

переключи́ть *v., pfv. of* **переключа́ть**. —**переключи́ться**, *refl., pfv. of* **переключа́ться**.

перекова́ть [*infl.* **-кую́, -куёшь**] *v., pfv. of* **переко́вывать**.

переко́вывать *v.impfv.* [*pfv.* **перекова́ть**] **1,** to reforge. **2,** *fig.* to remold. **3,** to make a new shoe for (a horse). —**перекова́ть мечи́ на ора́ла**, to beat swords into plowshares.

переколо́ть *v.pfv.* [*infl.* **-колю́, -ко́лешь**] **1,** *pfv. of* **перека́лывать**. **2,** to prick in many places. **3,** to slaughter; massacre. **4,** to chop (all or much of something).

переконструи́ровать *v.impfv. & pfv.* [*pres.* **-рую, -руешь**] to redesign.

перекопа́ть *v., pfv. of* **перека́пывать**.

перекорми́ть [*infl.* **-кормлю́, -ко́рмишь**] *v., pfv. of* **перека́рмливать**.

переко́ры [*gen.* **-ров**] *n.pl., colloq.* squabble.

переко́с *n.* **1,** warp; warping. **2,** *fig.* defect.

перекоси́ть[1] [*infl.* **-кошу́, -коси́шь**] *v., pfv. of* **перека́шивать**. —**перекоси́ться**, *refl., pfv. of* **перека́шиваться**.

перекоси́ть² *v.pfv.* [*infl.* **-кошу́, -ко́сишь**] **1,** to mow (all or much of). **2,** *colloq.* to mow down (*i.e.* kill).

перекочева́ть [*infl.* **-чу́ю, -чу́ешь**] *v., pfv. of* **перекочёвывать.**

перекочёвывать *v.impfv.* [*pfv.* **перекочева́ть**] to wander; migrate (from one place to another).

переко́шенный *adj.* **1,** crooked; lopsided. **2,** (*of one's face*) twisted; distorted.

перекра́ивать *v.impfv.* [*pfv.* **перекрои́ть**] **1,** to cut again. **2,** *fig., colloq.* to refashion; reshape; revise; revamp. Перекра́ивать ка́рту ми́ра, to recarve the map of the world.

перекра́сить *v.pfv.* [*infl.* **-шу, -сишь**] **1,** *pfv. of* **перекра́шивать. 2,** to paint (all or many things). —**перекра́ситься,** *refl., pfv. of* **перекра́шиваться.**

перекра́шивать *v.impfv.* [*pfv.* **перекра́сить**] to paint (something) in a different color; repaint. —**перекра́шиваться,** *refl.* **1,** to change color. **2,** *fig., colloq.* to hide one's true colors.

перекрести́ть [*infl.* **-крещу́, -кре́стишь**] *v., pfv. of* **крести́ть** (*in sense #3*) *and* **перекре́щивать.** —**перекрести́ться,** *refl., pfv. of* **крести́ться** (*in sense #2*) *and* **перекре́щиваться.**

перекрёстный *adj.* cross-. —**перекрёстный допро́с,** cross-examination. —**перекрёстный ого́нь,** crossfire. —**перекрёстная ссы́лка,** cross-reference.

перекрёсток [*gen.* **-стка**] *n.* intersection; crossing. —**крича́ть на всех перекрёстках,** to shout from the rooftops.

перекре́щивать *v.impfv.* [*pfv.* **перекрести́ть**] **1,** to lie across; crisscross. **2,** *colloq.* to rename; rechristen. —**перекре́щиваться,** *refl.* to intersect; crisscross.

перекрича́ть *v.pfv.* [*infl.* **-чу́, -чи́шь**] to shout down.

перекрои́ть *v., pfv. of* **перекра́ивать.**

перекрути́ть [*infl.* **-кручу́, -кру́тишь**] *v., pfv. of* **перекру́чивать.**

перекру́чивать [*pfv.* **перекрути́ть**] *colloq.* **1,** to twist. **2,** to twist too far; turn too far.

перекрыва́ть *v.impfv.* [*pfv.* **перекры́ть**] **1,** to cover again; re-cover. **2,** to cut off (water, steam, etc.); close off (pipes). **3,** to block (a road); dam (a river). **4,** *colloq.* to exceed.

перекры́ть [*infl.* **-кро́ю, -кро́ешь**] *v., pfv. of* **перекрыва́ть.**

перекувырну́ть *v.pfv., colloq.* to upset; tip over. —**перекувырну́ться,** *refl., colloq.* **1,** to tip over; topple over. **2,** to turn a somersault (*in the air*).

перекупа́ть¹ *v.impfv.* [*pfv.* **перекупи́ть**] *colloq.* **1,** to buy by outbidding someone else. **2,** to buy back.

перекупа́ть² *v.pfv., colloq.* **1,** to bathe too long. **2,** to bathe (all or many people). —**перекупа́ться,** *refl., colloq.* to bathe too long; stay in the water too long.

перекупи́ть *v.pfv.* [*infl.* **-куплю́, -ку́пишь**] **1,** *pfv. of* **перекупа́ть¹. 2,** to buy (all of something).

перекупщик *n.* one who buys for resale; dealer.

перекур *n., colloq.* smoke break.

переку́ривать *v.impfv.* [*pfv.* **перекури́ть**] *colloq.* to take a smoke break.

перекури́ть *v.pfv.* [*infl.* **-курю́, -ку́ришь**] **1,** *pfv. of* **переку́ривать. 2,** to smoke all of. **3,** to smoke many kinds of.

перекуси́ть *v.pfv.* [*infl.* **-кушу́, -ку́сишь**] **1,** to bite in half. **2,** to bite through. **3,** *colloq.* to have a bite of (something); have a bite to eat.

перела́мывать *v.impfv.* [*pfv.* **переломи́ть**] **1,** to break in two; fracture. **2,** to alter; transform. **3,** *colloq.* to overcome; conquer (a feeling). —**перела́мываться,** *refl.* to be broken in two; be fractured.

перележа́ть *v.pfv.* [*infl.* **-жу́, -жи́шь**] *colloq.* to lie too long (*e.g.* in the sun).

перелеза́ть *v.impfv.* [*pfv.* **переле́зть**] (*with acc. or* **че́рез**) to climb over.

переле́зть [*infl.* like **лезть**] *v., pfv. of* **перелеза́ть.**

переле́ска *n.* hepatica.

переле́сок [*gen.* **-ска**] *n.* coppice; copse.

перелёт *n.* **1,** (long) flight. **2,** migration (*of birds*). **3,** overshooting (*of a target*).

перелета́ть *v.impfv.* [*pfv.* **перелете́ть**] **1,** to fly over; fly across. **2,** to fly (from one place to another).

перелете́ть [*infl.* **-чу́, -ти́шь**] *v., pfv. of* **перелета́ть.**

перелётный *adj.* (*of a bird*) migratory.

переле́чь *v.pfv.* [*infl.* like **лечь**] to lie down (somewhere else).

перели́в *n.* **1,** flowing. **2,** *usu. pl.* play (*of colors*). **3,** *usu. pl.* modulation.

перелива́ние *n.* **1,** pouring (*from one container to another*). **2,** transfusion: перелива́ние кро́ви, blood transfusion.

перелива́ть *v.impfv.* [*pfv.* **перели́ть**] **1,** to pour (from one vessel to another). **2,** *in* перелива́ть кровь (+ *dat.*), to give a blood transfusion (to). **3,** to recast. **4,** [*impfv. only*] to gleam; glisten. —**перелива́ться,** *refl.* **1,** to flow (from one place to another). **2,** to overflow. **3,** [*impfv. only*] to gleam; glisten. **4,** [*impfv. only*] (*of sounds*) to modulate.

перели́вчатый *adj.* **1,** (*of colors*) iridescent. **2,** (*of a voice*) lilting.

перели́стывать *v.impfv.* [*pfv.* **перелиста́ть**] to leaf through.

перели́ть [*infl.* like **лить**] *v., pfv. of* **перелива́ть.** —**перели́ться,** *refl., pfv. of* **перелива́ться.**

перелицева́ть [*infl.* **-цу́ю, -цу́ешь**] *v., pfv. of* **перелицо́вывать.**

перелицо́вывать *v.impfv.* [*pfv.* **перелицева́ть**] **1,** to alter (a garment) by turning it inside out. **2,** *fig., colloq.* to give a new face to.

перелови́ть *v.pfv.* [*infl.* **-ловлю́, -ло́вишь**] to catch (all or many of something).

переложе́ние *n.* **1,** (*with* **в** *or* **на** + *acc.*) setting (to music); turning into (verse). **2,** *music* arrangement; transposition.

переложи́ть [*infl.* **-ложу́, -ло́жишь**] *v., pfv. of* **перекла́дывать.**

перело́м *n.* **1,** break; fracture. **2,** *fig.* critical period; turning point. **3,** *fig.* sudden change; radical change.

перелома́ть *v.pfv.* to break (all or many things). —**перелома́ться,** *refl.* (*of many things*) to be broken.

переломи́ть [*infl.* **-ломлю́, -ло́мишь**] *v., pfv. of* **перела́мывать.** —**переломи́ться,** *refl., pfv. of* **перела́мываться.**

перело́мный *adj.* critical; crucial.

перема́зать *v.pfv.* [*infl.* -ма́жу, -ма́жешь] *colloq.* to smear; make dirty. —**перема́заться**, *refl.*, *colloq.* to get all dirty.

перема́лывать *v.impfv.* [*pfv.* перемоло́ть] *colloq.* to wipe out.

перема́нивать *v.impfv.* [*pfv.* перемани́ть] to entice; win over.

перемани́ть [*infl.* -маню́, -ма́нишь] *v., pfv. of* **перема́нивать**.

перема́тывать *v.impfv.* [*pfv.* перемота́ть] **1,** to wind (onto something else). **2,** to rewind.

перема́хивать *v.impfv.* [*pfv.* перемахну́ть] *colloq.* to jump over.

перемежа́ть *v.impfv.* to alternate: перемежа́ть рабо́ту (с) о́тдыхом, to alternate rest and work. —**перемежа́ться**, *refl.* to alternate.

перемежа́ющийся *adj.* intermittent.

переме́на *n.* **1,** change. **2,** recess; break (*between classes*).

перемени́ть *v.pfv.* [*infl.* -меню́, -ме́нишь] to change. —**перемени́ться**, *refl.* **1,** to change. **2,** (*with* к) to change one's attitude (toward); act differently (toward). **3,** (*with instr.*) to change; exchange; trade.

переме́нный *adj.* variable. —**переме́нная величина́**, *math.* variable. —**переме́нный ток**, alternating current. —**с переме́нным успе́хом**, with varying (degrees of) success.

переме́нчивый *adj., colloq.* changeable.

перемерза́ть *v.impfv.* [*pfv.* перемёрзнуть] **1,** to freeze up; freeze solid. **2,** *colloq.* to freeze; be frozen.

перемёрзнуть *v.pfv.* [*past* -мёрз, -мёрзла] **1,** *pfv. of* **перемерза́ть**. **2,** (*of all of something, usu. plants*) to perish from the frost.

переме́ривать *v.impfv.* [*pfv.* переме́рить] **1,** to re-measure. **2,** to try on again.

переме́рить *v.pfv.* **1,** *pfv. of* **переме́ривать**. **2,** to measure (all or many things). **3,** to try on (all or many things).

перемести́ть [*infl.* -щу́, -сти́шь] *v., pfv. of* **переме-ща́ть**. —**перемести́ться**, *refl., pfv. of* **переме-ща́ться**.

переме́тить *v.pfv.* [*infl.* -чу, -тишь] **1,** *pfv. of* **переме-ча́ть**. **2,** to mark (all or many things).

переметну́ться *v.r.pfv., colloq.* **1,** to jump across; dart across. **2,** to defect (to the enemy).

переме́тный *adj., in* **переме́тная сума́**, saddlebag.

перемеча́ть *v.impfv.* [*pfv.* переме́тить] to mark again.

переме́шивать *v.impfv.* [*pfv.* перемеша́ть] **1,** to mix. **2,** to stir. **3,** to mix up; disarrange. **4,** *colloq.* to mix up; confuse. —**переме́шиваться**, *refl.* **1,** (*with* с + *instr.*) to mix (with); blend (with). **2,** to get mixed up.

перемеща́ть *v.impfv.* [*pfv.* перемести́ть] to move; shift; transfer. —**перемеща́ться**, *refl.* to move; shift.

перемеще́ние *n.* **1,** shift; movement. **2,** displacement. **3,** transfer. **4,** *pl.* changes; shifts (*of personnel*).

перемещённый *adj., in* **перемещённые ли́ца**, displaced persons.

переми́гиваться *v.r.impfv.* [*pfv.* перемигну́ться] to wink at each other.

перемина́ться *v.r.impfv., colloq.* (*often with* с ноги́ на́ ногу) to shift from foot to foot (*in anxiety*).

переми́рие *n.* truce; armistice.

перемога́ть *v.impfv., colloq.* to fight off (drowsiness, an illness, etc.). —**перемога́ться**, *refl., colloq.* to try to fight off an illness.

перемо́кнуть *v.pfv.* [*past* -мо́к, -мо́кла] *colloq.* to get drenched.

перемо́лвить *v.pfv.* [*infl.* -влю, -вишь] *colloq., in* перемо́лвить сло́во с (+ *instr.*), to have a word with. —**перемо́лвиться**, *refl.* (*with* с + *instr.*) *colloq.* to have a word with.

перемоло́ть *v.pfv.* [*infl.* -мелю́, -ме́лешь] **1,** *pfv. of* **перема́лывать**. **2,** to grind (all or much of).

перемоло́ться *v.r.pfv.* [*infl.* -ме́лется] to be ground. —**переме́лется — мука́ бу́дет**, everything will be all right in the end.

перемота́ть *v., pfv. of* **перема́тывать**.

перемыва́ть *v.impfv.* [*pfv.* перемы́ть] to wash again. —**перемыва́ть ко́сточки** (+ *dat.*), to say malicious things about.

перемы́ть [*infl.* -мо́ю, -мо́ешь] **1,** *pfv. of* **перемы-ва́ть**. **2,** to wash (all or many of something).

перемы́чка [*gen. pl.* -чек] *n.* **1,** crosspiece. **2,** lintel. **3,** bulkhead.

перенапряга́ть *v.impfv.* [*pfv.* перенапря́чь] to over-exert.

перенапряже́ние *n.* overexertion.

перенапря́чь [*infl. like* напря́чь] *v., pfv. of* **перена-пряга́ть**.

перенаселе́ние *n.* overpopulation. *Also,* **перенасе-лённость**, *n.f.*

перенаселённый *adj.* overpopulated.

перенаселя́ть *v.impfv.* [*pfv.* перенасели́ть] to over-populate.

перенесе́ние *n.* **1,** moving; shifting; transferring. **2,** postponement; putting off. **3,** enduring.

перенести́ [*infl. like* нести́] *v., pfv. of* **переноси́ть**. —**перенести́сь**, *refl., pfv. of* **переноси́ться**.

перенима́ть *v.impfv.* [*pfv.* переня́ть] **1,** to adopt; copy. **2,** *colloq.* to grab; snatch.

перено́с *n.* **1,** moving; transporting; transferring. **2,** postponement. **3,** *in* перено́с сло́ва, dividing a word at the end of a line; word division. **4,** hyphen (*at the end of a line*).

переноси́ть *v.impfv.* [*pfv.* перенести́; *pres.* -ношу́, -но́сишь] **1,** (*with* че́рез) to carry across. **2,** to carry from one place to another. **3,** to move; shift; transfer. **4,** to postpone; put off. **5,** to endure; bear; stand: переноси́ть жару́, to endure/stand the heat. Я не переношу́ его́, I can't stand him. **6,** to come through (an illness, operation, etc.). **7,** *in* переноси́ть сло́во, to carry part of a word over to the next line. —**пере-носи́ться**, *refl.* **1,** *colloq.* to dash from one place to another; (*with* че́рез) dash across. **2,** (*of thoughts, attention, etc.*) to shift. **3,** to shift one's thoughts; turn one's thoughts.

перено́сица *n.* bridge of the nose.

перено́сный *adj.* **1,** portable. **2,** figurative: в пере-но́сном смы́сле, in the figurative sense.

перено́счик *n.* **1,** carrier. **2,** carrier (*of a disease*). **3,** *obs.* spreader of gossip.

переночева́ть *v.pfv.* [*infl.* -чу́ю, -чу́ешь] to spend the night.

перенумерова́ть *v.pfv.* [*infl.* -ру́ю, -ру́ешь] **1,** to renumber. **2,** to number (all or many of something).

переня́ть [*infl.* перейму́, переймёшь; *past* пе́ренял *or* переня́л, переняла́, пе́реняло *or* переня́ло, пе́реняли *or* переня́ли] *v., pfv. of* перенима́ть.

переобору́дование *n.* re-equipping.

переобору́довать *v.impfv. & pfv.* [*pres.* -дую, -дуешь] to re-equip.

переобременя́ть *v.impfv.* [*pfv.* переобремени́ть] to overburden.

переобува́ть *v.impfv.* [*pfv.* переобу́ть] to change (someone's) shoes: переобу́ть ребёнка, to change a child's shoes. Переобу́ть боти́нки, to change (one's) shoes. —**переобува́ться,** *refl.* **1,** to change (one's) shoes. **2,** (*with в + acc.*) to change into (different shoes). **3,** to put one's shoes back on.

переобу́ть [*infl.* -бу́ю, -бу́ешь] *v., pfv. of* переобува́ть. —**переобу́ться,** *refl., pfv. of* переобува́ться.

переодева́ть *v.impfv.* [*pfv.* переоде́ть] **1,** to change (someone's) clothes. **2,** *colloq.* to change (an article of clothing). **3,** (*with instr. or в + acc.*) to dress (someone) up (as); disguise (as). —**переодева́ться,** *refl.* **1,** to change clothes. **2,** (*with в + acc.*) to change (into). **3,** (*with instr. or в + acc.*) to dress up (as); disguise oneself (as).

переоде́ть [*infl.* -де́ну, -де́нешь] *v., pfv. of* переодева́ть. —**переоде́ться,** *refl., pfv. of* переодева́ться.

переосмы́сливать *v.impfv.* [*pfv.* переосмы́слить] to reinterpret.

переоце́нивать *v.impfv.* [*pfv.* переоцени́ть] **1,** to reappraise; reassess. **2,** to overestimate; overrate.

переоцени́ть [*infl.* -еню́, -е́нишь] *v., pfv. of* переоце́нивать.

переоце́нка *n.* **1,** reappraisal; reassessment. **2,** overestimation.

перепа́д *n.* **1,** difference; differential. **2,** *colloq.* drop; dip.

перепада́ть *v.impfv.* [*pfv.* перепа́сть] **1,** (*of rain, snow, etc.*) to fall intermittently. **2,** (*with dat.*) *colloq.* to come one's way.

перепа́ивать *v.impfv.* [*pfv.* перепои́ть] **1,** to give (an animal) too much to drink. **2,** *colloq.* to make (a person) drunk.

перепа́лка [*gen. pl.* -лок] *n., colloq.* **1,** exchange of gunfire. **2,** squabble; wrangle.

перепа́сть [*infl. like* пасть] *v., pfv. of* перепада́ть.

перепа́чкать *v.pfv.* to get (something) all dirty. —**перепа́чкаться,** *refl.* to get (oneself) all dirty.

перепе́в *n.* **1,** hum. **2,** *fig.* repetition; rehash.

перепева́ть *v.impfv.* to repeat; parrot; echo.

пе́репел [*pl.* перепела́] *n.* quail.

перепёлка [*gen. pl.* -лок] *n.* female quail.

перепеля́тник *n.* sparrow hawk.

перепе́рчивать *v.impfv.* [*pfv.* перепе́рчить] to put too much pepper in.

перепеча́тать *v., pfv. of* перепеча́тывать.

перепеча́тка [*gen. pl.* -ток] *n.* **1,** (act of) reprinting. **2,** reprint.

перепеча́тывать *v.impfv.* [*pfv.* перепеча́тать] **1,** to reprint. **2,** to retype.

перепива́ть *v.impfv.* [*pfv.* перепи́ть] *colloq.* **1,** to have too much to drink. **2,** to outdrink. —**перепива́ться,** *refl., colloq.* to get completely drunk.

перепи́ливать *v.impfv.* [*pfv.* перепили́ть] to saw in two.

перепили́ть *v.pfv.* [*infl.* -пилю́, -пи́лишь] **1,** *pfv. of* перепи́ливать. **2,** to saw (all of something).

переписа́ть [*infl.* -пишу́, -пи́шешь] *v., pfv. of* переписывать.

перепи́ска *n.* **1,** copying. **2,** correspondence. Быть в перепи́ске с, to correspond with.

перепи́счик *n.* copier; copyist.

перепи́сывать *v.impfv.* [*pfv.* переписа́ть] **1,** to rewrite. **2,** to copy; copy over. **3,** to make a list of. —**перепи́сываться,** *refl.* [*impfv. only*] to correspond (*by mail*).

пе́репись *n.f.* census.

перепи́ть [*infl. like* пи́ть] *v., pfv. of* перепива́ть. —**перепи́ться,** *refl.* [*past* перепи́лся, перепила́сь, перепило́сь *or* перепи́лось, перепили́сь *or* перепи́лись] *pfv. of* перепива́ться.

переплавля́ть *v.impfv.* [*pfv.* перепла́вить] **1,** (*with в or на + acc.*) to melt down (into something else). **2,** to float; transport by floating downstream.

перепла́та *n., colloq.* overpayment.

перепла́тить [*infl.* -плачу́, -пла́тишь] *v., pfv. of* перепла́чивать.

перепла́чивать *v.impfv.* [*pfv.* переплати́ть] to overpay.

переплёвывать *v.impfv.* [*pfv.* переплю́нуть] *colloq.* **1,** (*with че́рез*) to spit over. **2,** to outdo.

переплести́ [*infl. like* плести́] *v., pfv. of* переплета́ть. —**переплести́сь,** *refl., pfv. of* переплета́ться.

переплёт *n.* **1,** cover; binding (*of a book*). **2,** sash: око́нный переплёт, window sash. **3,** *colloq.* mess; jam: попа́сть в переплёт, to get into a mess.

переплета́ть *v.impfv.* [*pfv.* переплести́] **1,** to bind (a book). **2,** to interlace; interweave; intertwine. **3,** to lock together; interlock (one's fingers, arms, etc.). **4,** to braid again. —**переплета́ться,** *refl.* **1,** to become intertwined. **2,** *fig.* to be intertwined; be interwoven.

переплете́ние *n.* **1,** interlacing; interweaving. **2,** *textiles* weave; texture.

переплётная *n., decl. as an adj.* bindery.

переплётный *adj.* bookbinding (*attrib.*). —**переплётное де́ло,** bookbinding.

переплётчик *n.* bookbinder.

переплыва́ть *v.impfv.* [*pfv.* переплы́ть] (*with acc. or че́рез*) **1,** to swim across. **2,** to sail across.

переплы́ть [*infl. like* плы́ть] *v., pfv. of* переплыва́ть.

переплю́нуть *v., pfv. of* переплёвывать.

переподгота́вливать *v.impfv.* [*pfv.* переподгото́вить] to provide with additional training; give (someone) a refresher course.

переподгото́вка *n.* additional training; refresher course.

перепои́ть *v.pfv.* [*infl.* -пою́, -по́ишь *or* -пои́шь] **1,** *pfv. of* перепа́ивать. **2,** to give (everyone or many people) something to drink.

перепо́лзать *v.impfv.* [*pfv.* переползти́] (*with acc. or че́рез*) to crawl across; creep across.

переползти́ [*infl. like* ползти́] *v., pfv. of* перепо́лзать.

переполне́ние *n.* **1,** overfilling. **2,** overcrowding.

перепо́лненный *adj.* crowded; jammed; packed.

переполня́ть *v.impfv.* [*pfv.* **перепо́лнить**] **1,** to overfill. **2,** to overcrowd. **3,** *fig.* to overwhelm (with emotion). —**переполня́ться,** *refl.* **1,** to be filled to overflowing; overflow. **2,** be crowded/packed/jammed.

переполо́х *n.* **1,** alarm; panic. **2,** turmoil; commotion.

переполоши́ть *v.pfv., colloq.* to throw into a panic. —**переполоши́ться,** *refl., colloq.* to be thrown into a panic.

перепо́нка [*gen. pl.* **-нок**] *n.* **1,** membrane. **2,** *zool.* web. —**бараба́нная перепо́нка,** eardrum.

перепо́нчатый *adj., zool.* webbed: перепо́нчатые ла́пы, webbed feet.

перепоруча́ть *v.impfv.* [*pfv.* **перепоручи́ть**] to turn over; hand over; entrust.

перепоручи́ть [*infl.* **-ручу́, -ру́чишь**] *v., pfv. of* **перепоруча́ть.**

перепра́ва *n.* **1,** crossing (*of a river*). **2,** place to cross (a river).

переправля́ть *v.impfv.* [*pfv.* **перепра́вить**] **1,** to carry across; ferry across. **2,** to forward. **3,** *colloq.* to correct. —**переправля́ться,** *refl.* to cross; make one's way across.

перепрева́ть *v.impfv.* [*pfv.* **перепре́ть**] **1,** to rot. **2,** (*of food*) to be overcooked.

перепре́лый *adj.* rotten.

перепре́ть *v., pfv. of* **перепрева́ть.**

перепро́бовать *v.pfv.* [*infl.* **-бую, -буешь**] to try; taste (all or many of something).

перепродава́ть *v.impfv.* [*pfv.* **перепрода́ть;** *pres.* **-даю́, -даёшь**] to resell.

перепрода́жа *n.* resale.

перепрода́ть [*infl. like* **прода́ть**] *v., pfv. of* **перепродава́ть.**

перепроизво́дство *n.* overproduction.

перепры́гивать *v.impfv.* [*pfv.* **перепры́гнуть**] **1,** (*with acc. or* **че́рез**) to jump over; jump across. **2,** to jump from place to place; jump from one thing to another.

перепу́г *n., colloq.* fright.

перепуга́ть *v.pfv.* to frighten; scare. —**перепуга́ться,** *refl.* to be frightened; be terrified.

перепу́тать *v., pfv. of* **пу́тать** (*in senses #2 & #4*) *and* **перепу́тывать.** —**перепу́таться,** *refl., pfv. of* **перепу́тываться.**

перепу́тывать *v.impfv.* [*pfv.* **перепу́тать**] **1,** to tangle. **2,** to mix up; disarrange. **3,** to confuse; get (two or more things) mixed up. —**перепу́тываться,** *refl.* **1,** to become (en)tangled. **2,** to get mixed up. **3,** to get confused.

перепу́тье *n.* crossroads. —**на перепу́тье,** at the crossroads.

перераба́тывать *v.impfv.* [*pfv.* **перерабо́тать**] **1,** to process; refine. **2,** (*with* **в** *or* **на** + *acc.*) to make (into); convert (into). **3,** to rework; revise. **4,** to work overtime. **5,** *colloq.* to overwork; tire oneself out.

перерабо́тка *n.* **1,** processing; refining. **2,** reworking. **3,** *colloq.* overtime work.

перераспределе́ние *n.* redistribution.

перераспределя́ть *v.impfv.* [*pfv.* **перераспредели́ть**] to redistribute.

перераста́ние *n.* **1,** outgrowing. **2,** (*with* **в** + *acc.*) development (into); *mil.* escalation (into).

перераста́ть *v.impfv.* [*pfv.* **перерасти́**] **1,** to outgrow. **2,** (*with* **в** + *acc.*) to develop (into); evolve (into).

перерасти́ [*infl. like* **расти́**] *v., pfv. of* **перераста́ть.**

перерасхо́д *n.* overexpenditure.

перерасхо́довать *v.impfv. & pfv.* [*pres.* **-дую, -дуешь**] to use too much (of).

перерва́ть [*infl. like* **рвать**] *v., pfv. of* **перерыва́ть** (*in sense #1*).

перере́зать *v.pfv.* [*infl.* **-ре́жу, -ре́жешь**] **1,** *pfv. of* **перереза́ть. 2,** *colloq.* to kill (all or many of something).

перереза́ть *v.impfv.* [*pfv.* **перере́зать**] **1,** to cut (*usu. in two*). **2,** to cut off (a road, army, etc.).

перереша́ть *v.impfv.* [*pfv.* **перереши́ть**] *colloq.* **1,** to change one's mind. **2,** to solve in a different manner.

перерисова́ть [*infl.* **-су́ю, -су́ешь**] *v., pfv. of* **перерисо́вывать.**

перерисо́вывать *v.impfv.* [*pfv.* **перерисова́ть**] to draw again; make a copy of.

перерожда́ть *v.impfv.* [*pfv.* **перероди́ть**] to regenerate; make a new person of. —**перерожда́ться,** *refl.* **1,** *colloq.* to be reborn. **2,** to be (completely) regenerated; become a new person. **3,** to degenerate. **4,** (*with* **в** + *acc.*) to turn into.

перерожде́ние *n.* **1,** regeneration. **2,** degeneration.

перерос́ток [*gen.* **-стка**] *n.* youngster who is slow to develop (*and is therefore older than his classmates*).

переруба́ть *v.impfv.* [*pfv.* **переруби́ть**] to cut in two; chop in two.

переруби́ть *v.pfv.* [*infl.* **-рублю́, -ру́бишь**] **1,** *pfv. of* **переруба́ть. 2,** to chop down (all or many of something).

переруга́ть *v.pfv., colloq.* to swear at (everyone). —**переруга́ться,** *refl., colloq.* to swear at each other; cuss each other out.

переру́гиваться *v.r.impfv., colloq.* to swear at each other; swear back and forth.

переры́в *n.* recess; break. —**с переры́вами,** intermittently; off and on.

перерыва́ть *v.impfv.* **1,** [*pfv.* **перерва́ть**] to break; snap. **2,** [*pfv.* **переры́ть**] to dig up; *fig.* rummage through.

переры́ть [*infl.* **-ро́ю, -ро́ешь**] *v., pfv. of* **перерыва́ть** (*in sense #2*).

переряди́ть [*infl.* **-ряжу́, -ря́дишь**] *v., pfv. of* **переряжа́ть.** —**переряди́ться,** *refl., pfv. of* **переряжа́ться.**

переряжа́ть *v.impfv.* [*pfv.* **переряди́ть**] (*with instr. or* **в** + *acc.*) *colloq.* to dress (someone) up (as); disguise (as). —**переряжа́ться,** *refl., colloq.* **1,** to disguise oneself. **2,** (*with instr. or* **в** + *acc.*) to dress up (as); disguise oneself (as).

пересади́ть [*infl.* **-сажу́, -са́дишь**] *v., pfv. of* **переса́живать.**

переса́дка [*gen. pl.* **-док**] *n.* **1,** change (*of trains, planes, etc.*). **2,** transplant; graft; transplantation.

переса́дочный *adj.* transfer (*attrib.*); transit.

переса́живать *v.impfv.* [*pfv.* **пересади́ть**] **1,** to seat somewhere else; move to another seat. **2,** to transplant; graft. —**переса́живаться,** *refl.* [*pfv.* **пересе́сть**] **1,** to change one's seat. **2,** to change trains; change planes.

переса́ливать *v.impfv.* [*pfv.* **пересоли́ть**] **1,** to put too much salt in. **2,** *fig., colloq.* to go too far; overdo it.

пересдава́ть *v.impfv.* [*pfv.* **пересда́ть**; *pres.* **-сдаю́, -сдаёшь**] **1,** to rent again; sublet. **2,** *cards* to deal again. **3,** *colloq.* to retake (an examination).

пересда́ть [*infl. like* **сдать**] *v., pfv. of* **пересдава́ть**.

пересека́ть *v.impfv.* [*pfv.* **пересе́чь**] **1,** to cross; cut across; traverse. **2,** to cross; extend across; cut across; intersect. **3,** *in* пересека́ть путь *or* доро́гу (+ *dat.*), to block someone's way; bar the way (to). —**пересека́ться,** *refl.* to cross (each other); intersect.

пересе́ленец [*gen.* **-нца**] *n.* **1,** migrant. **2,** settler.

переселе́ние *n.* **1,** migration; transmigration. **2,** moving; resettlement. —**переселе́ние душ,** *relig.* transmigration.

переселя́ть *v.impfv.* [*pfv.* **пересели́ть**] to move; resettle. —**переселя́ться,** *refl.* **1,** to migrate. **2,** to move; relocate.

пересе́сть [*infl. like* **сесть**] *v., pfv. of* **переса́живаться**.

пересече́ние *n.* **1,** crossing. **2,** intersection.

пересечённый *adj.* (*of terrain*) rough; broken; rugged.

пересе́чь [*infl. like* **сечь**; *past* **-сёк, -секла́, -секло́, -секли́**] *v., pfv. of* **пересека́ть.** —**пересе́чься,** *refl., pfv. of* **пересека́ться.**

переси́живать *v.impfv.* [*pfv.* **пересиде́ть**] *colloq.* **1,** to sit longer than; stay longer than. **2,** to sit too long; stay too long. **3,** to sit out; wait out.

переси́ливать *v.impfv.* [*pfv.* **переси́лить**] **1,** to overpower. **2,** *fig.* to overcome; master.

переска́з *n.* **1,** retelling. **2,** exposition.

пересказа́ть [*infl.* **-скажу́, -ска́жешь**] **1,** *pfv. of* **переска́зывать. 2,** to tell (all or many of something).

переска́зывать *v.impfv.* [*pfv.* **пересказа́ть**] to retell.

переска́кивать *v.impfv.* [*pfv.* **перескочи́ть**] **1,** (*with acc. or* че́рез) to jump over; jump across. **2,** to jump from place to place; jump from one thing to another. **3,** *fig., colloq.* to skip over (*when reading or telling something*).

перескочи́ть [*infl.* **-скочу́, -ско́чишь**] *v., pfv. of* **переска́кивать.**

пересла́ть [*infl.* **-шлю́, -шлёшь**] *v., pfv. of* **пересыла́ть.**

пересма́тривать *v.impfv.* [*pfv.* **пересмотре́ть**] **1,** to look over; go over again. **2,** to re-examine; reconsider; review. **3,** to revise.

пересме́иваться *v.r.impfv., colloq.* to look at each other and giggle.

пересме́шник *n.* **1,** mockingbird. **2,** *colloq.* one who likes to tease.

пересмо́тр *n.* **1,** reconsideration; review. **2,** revision.

пересмотре́ть [*infl.* **-смотрю́, -смо́тришь**] *v., pfv. of* **пересма́тривать.**

пересыма́ть *v.impfv.* [*pfv.* **пересня́ть**] **1,** to make a copy of (a photograph). **2,** to reshoot (a film, scene, etc.).

пересня́ть [*infl. like* **снять**] *v., pfv. of* **пересыма́ть.**

пересоздава́ть *v.impfv.* [*pfv.* **пересозда́ть**; *pres.* **-даю́, -даёшь**] to re-create.

пересозда́ть [*infl. like* **дать**] *v., pfv. of* **пересоздава́ть.**

пересо́л *n.* excess of salt.

пересоли́ть [*infl.* **-солю́, -со́лишь** *or* **-соли́шь**] *v., pfv. of* **переса́ливать.**

пересо́хнуть [*past* **-со́х, -со́хла**] *v., pfv. of* **пересыха́ть.**

переспа́ть *v.pfv.* [*infl. like* **спать**] *colloq.* **1,** to oversleep. **2,** to spend the night (somewhere).

переспева́ть *v.impfv.* [*pfv.* **переспе́ть**] to become overripe.

переспе́лый *adj.* overripe.

переспе́ть *v., pfv. of* **переспева́ть.**

переспо́рить *v.pfv.* to win an argument from; get the better of in an argument.

переспра́шивать *v.impfv.* [*pfv.* **переспроси́ть**] to ask again.

переспроси́ть *v.pfv.* [*infl.* **-спрошу́, -спро́сишь**] **1,** *pfv. of* **переспра́шивать. 2,** *colloq.* to ask (many people or everyone).

пересо́рить *v.pfv., colloq.* to cause a quarrel between. —**пересо́риться,** *refl.* **1,** to quarrel with each other. **2,** to quarrel (with many people).

перестава́ть *v.impfv.* [*pfv.* **переста́ть**; *pres.* **-стаю́, -стаёшь**] to stop; cease.

переста́вить [*infl.* **-влю, -вишь**] *v., pfv. of* **переставля́ть.**

переставля́ть *v.impfv.* [*pfv.* **переста́вить**] **1,** to move (from one place to another). **2,** to rearrange; transpose. —**переставля́ть но́ги,** to plod along. —**е́ле переставля́ть но́ги,** to be scarcely able to walk.

переста́ивать *v.impfv.* [*pfv.* **перестоя́ть**] **1,** to be left standing too long (and turn sour). **2,** *colloq.* to wait out; wait until something passes.

перестано́вка [*gen. pl.* **-вок**] *n.* **1,** rearrangement; transposition. **2,** *often. pl.* reshuffle (*of personnel*). **3,** *math.* permutation.

перестара́ться *v.r.pfv., colloq.* to try too hard; overdo it.

переста́ть [*infl.* **-ста́ну, -ста́нешь**] *v., pfv. of* **перестава́ть.**

перестила́ть *v.impfv.* [*pfv.* **перестла́ть**] **1,** to remake (a bed). **2,** to re-lay (a floor).

перестира́ть *v.pfv. of* **перести́рывать. 2,** to wash; launder (all of something).

перести́рывать *v.impfv.* [*pfv.* **перестира́ть**] to wash again; launder again.

перестла́ть [*infl.* **-стелю́, -сте́лешь**] *v., pfv. of* **перестила́ть.**

перестоя́ть [*infl.* **-стою́, -стои́шь**] *v., pfv. of* **переста́ивать.**

перестрада́ть *v.pfv.* **1,** to suffer a great deal. **2,** to suffer through; go through.

перестра́ивать *v.impfv.* [*pfv.* **перестро́ить**] **1,** to rebuild; reconstruct. **2,** to rearrange; revise. **3,** to reorganize; restructure. **4,** to switch (to a different channel or station). **5,** *mil.* to re-form. —**перестра́иваться,** *refl.* **1,** to change one's methods of work. **2,** *mil.* to re-form.

перестрахова́ть [*infl.* **-ху́ю, -ху́ешь**] *v., pfv. of* **перестрахо́вывать.** —**перестрахова́ться,** *refl., pfv. of* **перестрахо́вываться.**

перестрахо́вка *n.* **1,** reinsurance. **2,** *colloq.* excessive caution. —**для перестрахо́вки,** to be on the safe side.

перестрахо́вщик *n., colloq.* person who never takes any chances.

перестрахо́вывать *v.impfv.* [*pfv.* **перестрахова́ть**] to reinsure. —**перестрахо́вываться,** *refl.* **1,** to reinsure oneself. **2,** *fig., colloq.* to play safe; make extra sure.

перестре́ливаться *v.r.impfv.* to exchange shots; exchange gunfire.

перестре́лка [*gen. pl.* -лок] *n.* exchange of gunfire.

перестреля́ть *v.pfv.* **1,** to shoot (all or many of something). **2,** *colloq.* to use up (*in shooting*).

перестро́ить *v., pfv. of* **перестра́ивать**. —**перестро́иться,** *refl., pfv. of* **перестра́иваться**.

перестро́йка *n.* **1,** rebuilding; reconstruction. **2,** revision. **3,** reorganization; restructuring.

пересту́киваться *v.r.impfv.* (*of prisoners*) to communicate with each other by tapping.

переступа́ть *v.impfv.* [*pfv.* **переступи́ть**] **1,** (*with acc. or* **че́рез**) to step over; step across. **2,** step; walk. **3,** *fig.* to overstep; transgress. —**переступа́ть нога́ми, 1,** to take steps. **2,** to shift from foot to foot. —**переступа́ть с ноги́ на́ ногу,** to shift from foot to foot.

переступи́ть [*infl.* -ступлю́, -сту́пишь] *v., pfv. of* **переступа́ть**.

пересу́д *n., colloq.* retrial.

пересу́ды [*gen.* -до́в] *n.pl., colloq.* gossip.

пересу́шивать *v.impfv.* [*pfv.* **пересуши́ть**] **1,** to dry again. **2,** to dry too much.

пересуши́ть *v.pfv.* [*infl.* -сушу́, -су́шишь] **1,** *pfv. of* **пересу́шивать**. **2,** to dry (all of something).

пересчёт *n.* recount; recounting.

пересчи́тывать *v.impfv.* [*pfv.* **пересчита́ть**] **1,** to count. **2,** to recount.

пересыла́ть *v.impfv.* [*pfv.* **пересла́ть**] to send; remit; forward by mail.

пересы́лка *n.* **1,** sending; forwarding. **2,** remittance (*of money*). **3,** postage: плати́ть за пересы́лку, to pay the postage.

пересы́льный *adj.* transit: пересы́льная тюрьма́, transit prison.

пересы́пать [*infl.* -сы́плю, -сы́плешь] *v., pfv. of* **пересыпа́ть**.

пересыпа́ть *v.impfv.* [*pfv.* **пересы́пать**] **1,** to pour (into another container). **2,** (*with instr.*) to sprinkle (with); *fig.* intersperse (with). **3,** *colloq.* to pour too much.

пересыха́ть *v.impfv.* [*pfv.* **пересо́хнуть**] to dry up; become parched. *Also impers.:* У меня́ в го́рле пересо́хло, my throat is parched.

перета́пливать *v.impfv.* [*pfv.* **перетопи́ть**] **1,** to light (a stove) again. **2,** to melt; melt down.

перетаска́ть *v.pfv., colloq.* **1,** to carry; haul (from one place to another). **2,** to carry off; steal.

перета́скивать *v.impfv.* [*pfv.* **перетащи́ть**] **1,** to drag over; drag across. **2,** to drag (from one place to another); move (something heavy).

перетасова́ть [*infl.* -су́ю, -су́ешь] *v., pfv. of* **перетасо́вывать**.

перетасо́вка *n.* shake-up; shuffle; reshuffle.

перетасо́вывать *v.impfv.* [*pfv.* **перетасова́ть**] **1,** to shuffle (cards). **2,** *fig., colloq.* to shuffle; reshuffle; move around.

перетащи́ть [*infl.* -тащу́, -та́щишь] *v., pfv. of* **перета́скивать**.

перетере́ть *v.pfv.* [*infl. like* **тере́ть**] **1,** *pfv. of* **перетира́ть**. **2,** to wipe (all of something). —**перетере́ться,** *refl., pfv. of* **перетира́ться**.

перетерпе́ть *v.pfv.* [*infl.* -терплю́, -те́рпишь] *colloq.* to suffer; endure.

перетира́ть *v.impfv.* [*pfv.* **перетере́ть**] **1,** to break; wear through (a rope). **2,** to grind; grate. —**перетира́ться,** *refl.* (*of a rope*) to wear through.

перето́лки [*gen.* -ков] *n.pl., colloq.* gossip.

перетолкова́ть *v.pfv.* [*infl.* -ку́ю, -ку́ешь] **1,** *pfv. of* **перетолко́вывать**. **2,** *colloq.* to talk (with many people); talk over (many things).

перетолко́вывать *v.impfv.* [*pfv.* **перетолкова́ть**] to misinterpret; misconstrue.

перетопи́ть [*infl.* -топлю́, -то́пишь] *v., pfv. of* **перета́пливать**.

перетряса́ть *v.impfv.* [*pfv.* **перетрясти́**] **1,** to shake out. **2,** to rummage through.

перетрясти́ [*infl. like* **трясти́**] *v., pfv. of* **перетряса́ть**.

перетря́хивать *v.impfv.* [*pfv.* **перетряхну́ть**] to shake out.

пере́ть *v.impfv.* [*pres.* **пру, прёшь;** *past* **пёр, пёрла**] *colloq.* **1,** to go; make one's way. **2,** to force one's way. **3,** to come out; stream out. **4,** to haul.

перетя́гивание *n., in* **перетя́гивание кана́та,** tug of war.

перетя́гивать *v.impfv.* [*pfv.* **перетяну́ть**] **1,** to pull (from one place to another). **2,** *v.i., colloq.* to make it (to a certain place). **3,** (*with instr.*) to tie tightly (with). **4,** to retighten. **5,** *v.i.* to weigh more. —**перетя́гивать весы́** *or* **ча́шу весо́в,** to tip the scales. —**перетя́гивать на свою́ сто́рону,** to win over to one's side.

перетя́гиваться *v.r.impfv.* [*pfv.* **перетяну́ться**] (*with instr.*) to tie (something) tightly around one's waist.

перетяну́ть [*infl.* -тяну́, -тя́нешь] *v., pfv. of* **перетя́гивать**. —**перетяну́ться,** *refl., pfv. of* **перетя́гиваться**.

переубежда́ть *v.impfv.* [*pfv.* **переубеди́ть**] to change (someone's mind); make (someone) change his mind. —**переубежда́ться,** *refl.* to change one's mind.

переу́лок [*gen.* -лка] *n.* side street.

переустра́ивать *v.impfv.* [*pfv.* **переустро́ить**] **1,** to reconstruct. **2,** to reorganize.

переустро́йство *n.* **1,** reconstruction. **2,** reorganization.

переутоми́ть [*infl.* -млю́, -ми́шь] *v., pfv. of* **переутомля́ть**. —**переутоми́ться,** *refl., pfv. of* **переутомля́ться**.

переутомле́ние *n.* exhaustion; fatigue; overwork.

переутомля́ть *v.impfv.* [*pfv.* **переутоми́ть**] to tire out; wear out. —**переутомля́ться,** *refl.* to tire oneself out; wear oneself out.

переуче́сть [*infl. like* **уче́сть**] *v., pfv. of* **переучи́тывать**.

переучёт *n.* stocktaking; inventory.

переу́чивать *v.impfv.* [*pfv.* **переучи́ть**] **1,** to teach again; retrain. **2,** to study again; study a second time. —**переу́чиваться,** *refl.* **1,** to be retrained; undergo retraining. **2,** (*with dat.*) to relearn.

переучи́тывать *v.impfv.* [*pfv.* **переуче́сть**] to take stock of; take inventory of.

переучи́ть [*infl.* -учу́, -у́чишь] *v., pfv. of* **переу́чивать**. —**переучи́ться,** *refl., pfv. of* **переу́чиваться**.

переформирова́ть *v.pfv.* [*infl.* -ру́ю, -ру́ешь] **1,** *mil.* to re-form; reorganize. **2,** *fig.* to reshape.

перефрази́ровать *v.impfv. & pfv.* [*pres.* -ру́ю, -ру́ешь] to reword; rephrase; paraphrase.

перефразиро́вка *n.* paraphrase.

перехва́ливать *v.impfv.* [*pfv.* **перехвали́ть**] to praise excessively; give undue praise to.

перехвали́ть [*infl.* -хвалю́, -хва́лишь] *v., pfv. of* **перехва́ливать.**

перехва́т *n., colloq.* interception. —**перехва́т теле-фо́нных сообще́ний,** wiretapping.

перехвати́ть [*infl.* -хвачу́, -хва́тишь] *v., pfv. of* **перехва́тывать.**

перехва́тчик *n.* one who intercepts something. —**ис-треби́тель-перехва́тчик,** *aero.* interceptor.

перехва́тывать *v.impfv.* [*pfv.* **перехвати́ть**] **1,** to intercept. **2,** to grab. **3,** to tie around: перехвати́ть но́гу жгуто́м, to tie a tourniquet around one's leg. **4,** to interrupt momentarily; cut off (one's breathing, ability to speak, etc.). **5,** *colloq.* to borrow for a short time, **6,** *v.i., colloq.* to have a quick bite to eat. **7,** *v.i., colloq.* to go too far; overdo it.

перехитри́ть *v.pfv.* to outwit; outsmart; outfox.

перехлёстывать *v.impfv.* [*pfv.* **перехлестну́ть**] (*with* **че́рез**) (*of water*) to sweep over.

перехо́д *n.* **1,** (act of) crossing. **2,** crossing (*place to cross*). **3,** passage; passageway. **4,** *mil.* day's march. **5,** shift; switch. **6,** transition. **7,** conversion (*to another religion*).

переходи́ть *v.impfv.* [*pfv.* **перейти́;** *pres.* -хожу́, -хо́дишь] **1,** (*with acc. or* **че́рез**) to cross. **2,** to go; walk; move; pass (from one place to another). **3,** to shift; switch; move. **4,** to pass (to); be passed (to); pass (into the hands of). **5,** (*with* **в** + *acc.*) to turn into. **6,** (*with* **в** + *acc.*) to adopt; be converted to (another religion).

перехо́дный *adj.* **1,** connecting. **2,** transitional. **3,** (*of a grade*) passing. **4,** (*of a verb*) transitive.

переходя́щий *adj.* **1,** transitory. **2,** *finance* carried over to the following year. —**переходя́щие дожди́,** intermittent showers. —**переходя́щий ку́бок,** *sports* challenge cup.

перехорони́ть *v.pfv.* [*infl.* -роню́, -ро́нишь] to rebury.

пе́рец [*gen.* пе́рца] *n.* pepper. —**души́стый** *or* **гвозди́чный пе́рец,** allspice.

перецара́пать *v.pfv.* to scratch severely. —**переца-ра́паться,** *refl.* **1,** to scratch each other. **2,** *colloq.* to scratch oneself.

пе́речень [*gen.* -чня] *n.m.* list; enumeration; inventory.

перечёркивать *v.impfv.* [*pfv.* **перечеркну́ть**] **1,** to cross out. **2,** *fig.* to cancel; nullify; erase; undo.

перечерти́ть [*infl.* -черчу́, -че́ртишь] *v., pfv. of* **пере-че́рчивать.**

перече́рчивать *v.impfv.* [*pfv.* **перечерти́ть**] **1,** to draw again. **2,** to copy.

перече́сть *v.pfv.* [*infl.* -чту́, -чтёшь; *past* -чёл, -чла́, -чло́, -чли] *colloq.* = **перечита́ть** *and* **пересчита́ть.**

перечини́ть *v.pfv.* [*infl.* -чиню́, -чи́нишь] **1,** to repair; mend (all or many of something). **2,** to repair again; mend again.

перечисле́ние *n.* **1,** enumeration. **2,** transfer.

перечисля́ть *v.impfv.* [*pfv.* **перечи́слить**] **1,** to enumerate. **2,** to transfer.

перечита́ть *v.pfv.* **1,** *pfv. of* **перечи́тывать. 2,** to read (all or many of something).

перечи́тывать *v.impfv.* [*pfv.* **перечита́ть**] to reread.

перечи́ть *v.impfv.* (*with dat.*) *colloq.* to contradict.

пе́речница *n.* pepper shaker.

пе́речный *adj.* pepper (*attrib.*).

перечу́вствовать *v.pfv.* [*infl.* -ствую, -ствуешь] to experience; live through; go through (a lot).

переша́гивать *v.impfv.* [*pfv.* **перешагну́ть**] **1,** (*with acc. or* **че́рез**) to step over. **2,** *fig.* to overcome. **3,** (*with* **за** + *acc.*) to be past (a certain age).

переше́ек [*gen.* -ше́йка] *n.* isthmus; neck of land.

перешёптываться *v.r.impfv.* to whisper to each other.

перешиба́ть *v.impfv.* [*pfv.* **перешиби́ть**] *colloq.* to break; fracture.

перешиби́ть [*infl.* -бу́, -бёшь; *past* -ши́б, -ши́бла] *v., pfv. of* **перешиба́ть.**

перешива́ть *v.impfv.* [*pfv.* **переши́ть**] to alter (*by sewing*).

переши́ть [*infl.* -шью́, -шьёшь] *v., pfv. of* **перешива́ть.**

перещеголя́ть *v.pfv., colloq.* to outdo; surpass.

переэкзаменова́ть *v.pfv.* [*infl.* -ну́ю, -ну́ешь] to give (someone) a second examination. —**переэкзамен-ова́ться,** *refl.* to take an examination for the second time.

переэкзамено́вка *n.* repeat examination (*for one who has failed the first tiime*).

периге́й *n.* perigee.

периге́лий *n.* perihelion.

перика́рд *n.* pericardium.

пери́ла [*gen.* пери́л] *n.pl.* banister; railing.

пери́метр *n.* perimeter.

пери́на *n.* feather bed.

пери́од *n.* **1,** period (*of time*). **2,** (historical) period: послевое́нный пери́од, the postwar period. **3,** *geol.* age; period; epoch: леднико́вый пери́од, ice age; glacial epoch; glacial period.

перио́дика *n.* periodicals.

периоди́ческий *adj.* **1,** [*also,* **периоди́чный**] peri-odic. **2,** (*of a publication*) periodical. **3,** (*of a decimal*) repeating. —**периоди́чески,** *adv.* periodically.

перипети́я *n., usu. pl.* vicissitudes; ups and downs.

периско́п *n.* periscope.

периста́льтика *n.* peristalsis. —**перистальти́че-ский,** *adj.* peristaltic.

перисти́ль *n.m.* peristyle.

пе́ристый *adj.* **1,** feathered. **2,** *bot.* pinnate. **3,** (*of clouds*) fleecy.

перитони́т *n.* peritonitis.

перифери́йный *adj.* provincial.

перифери́ческий *adj.* peripheral.

перифери́я *n.* **1,** periphery. **2,** outlying districts; the provinces.

перифра́за *also,* **перифра́з** *n.* periphrasis.

пёрка [*gen. pl.* пёрок] *n.* drill bit.

перка́ль *n.m. or f.* percale. —**перка́левый,** *adj.* percale.

перку́ссия *n., med.* percussion.

перл *n.* **1,** *obs.* pearl. **2,** *fig.* pearl; gem.

перламу́тр *n.* mother-of-pearl. —**перламу́тровый,** *adj.* mother-of-pearl (*attrib.*).

пе́рлинь *also,* перли́нь *n.m.* hawser.

пе́рловый *adj., obs.* made of pearls; pearl (*attrib.*).

перло́вый *adj.* 1, *in* перло́вая крупа́, pearl barley. 2, made of pearl barley.

перлюстра́ция *n.* secret opening of mail.

пермане́нт *n.* permanent wave.

пермане́нтный *adj.* permanent.

пе́рмский *adj.* Permian.

перна́тый *adj.* feathered. —перна́тые, *n.pl.* birds.

перо́ [*pl.* пе́рья, пе́рьев] *n.* 1, feather. 2, (quill) pen. —взя́ться за перо́, to take pen in hand. —вы́йти из-под пера́ (+ *gen.*), to emerge from the pen of.

перочи́нный *adj., in* перочи́нный нож (но́жик), penknife.

перпендикуля́р *n.* perpendicular. —перпендикуля́рный, *adj.* perpendicular.

перро́н *n.* platform (*in a railway station*).

перс *n.m.* [*fem.* персия́нка] Persian. —перси́дский, *adj.* Persian.

пе́рсик *n.* 1, peach. 2, peach tree. —пе́рсиковый, *adj.* peach (*attrib.*).

персо́на *n.* person. —со́бственной персо́ной, in person.

персона́ж *n.* character (*in a play or story*).

персона́л *n.* personnel.

персона́льный *adj.* personal.

перспекти́ва *n.* 1, perspective. 2, vista; view. 3, prospect: в перспекти́ве, in prospect. 4, *pl.* prospects; outlook. —в бли́жней (*or* краткосро́чной) перспекти́ве, in the short run; in the near term. —в бо́лее отдалённой перспекти́ве, in the more distant future.

перспекти́вный *adj.* 1, long-term; long-range. 2, having good prospects; promising. 3, *art* perspective.

перст [*gen.* перста́] *n., obs.* finger. —оди́н как перст, all alone in the world.

пе́рстень [*gen.* -стня] *n.m.* ring set with a stone.

пертурба́ция *n., astron. & fig.* perturbation.

перуа́нский *adj.* Peruvian.

перфе́кт (пэ, фэ) *n., gram.* perfect; the perfect tense.

перфока́рта *n.* punch card.

перфора́тор *n.* 1, perforator. 2, punch: кла́вишный перфора́тор, key punch. 3, drill.

перфора́ция *n.* perforation.

перфори́ровать *v.impfv. & pfv.* [*pres.* -рую, -руешь] to perforate.

перха́ть *v.impfv., colloq.* to cough (*in order to clear one's throat*).

перхо́та *n., colloq.* tickling sensation in one's throat.

пе́рхоть *n.f.* dandruff.

перцо́вка *n.* pepper brandy.

перцо́вый *adj.* pepper (*attrib.*).

перча́тка [*gen. pl.* -ток] *n.* glove. —бро́сить перча́тку, to throw down the gauntlet.

пе́рчить *v.impfv.* to put pepper in *or* on.

перши́ть *v.impfv., impers., colloq.* to have a tickling sensation in one's throat: У меня́ перши́т в го́рле, I have a tickling sensation in my throat; my throat tickles.

пёрышко [*gen. pl.* -шек] *n.* small feather.

пёс [*gen.* пса] *n.* dog.

пе́сенка [*gen. pl.* -нок] *n., dim. of* пе́сня. —его́ пе́сенка спе́та, he is done for; he has had it.

пе́сенник *n.* 1, member of a chorus. 2, songwriter. 3, songbook.

песе́та *n.* peseta (*monetary unit of Spain*).

песе́ц [*gen.* песца́] *n.* polar fox.

песка́рь [*gen.* -каря́] *n.m.* gudgeon (*fish*).

песнопе́ние *n.* 1, religious song; hymn; chant. 2, *obs.* poem; poetry.

песнь *n.f.* 1, *obs.* song. 2, canto. —Песнь Пе́сней, Song of Songs.

пе́сня [*gen. pl.* пе́сен] *n.* song. —до́лгая пе́сня, a long story. —ста́рая пе́сня, the same old story. —тяну́ть всё ту же пе́сню, to harp on the same string.

пе́со *n.indecl.* peso (*monetary unit of a number of Latin American countries*).

песо́к [*gen.* песка́] *n.* sand. —золото́й песо́к, gold dust. —са́харный песо́к, granulated sugar.

песо́чник *n.* sandpiper.

песо́чница *n.* sandbox.

песо́чный *adj.* 1, sand (*attrib.*). 2, *colloq.* sand-colored; sandy. 3, (*of pastry*) short: песо́чный торт, shortcake. —песо́чные часы́, hourglass.

пессими́зм *n.* pessimism. —пессими́ст, *n.* pessimist. —пессимисти́ческий, *adj.* pessimistic.

пест [*gen.* песта́] *n.* pestle.

пе́стик *n.* 1, *dim. of* пест. 2, *bot.* pistil.

пестици́д *n.* pesticide.

пе́стовать *v.impfv.* [*pfv.* вы́пестовать; *pres.* -тую, -туешь] 1, *obs.* to nurse. 2, *fig.* to nurture.

пестре́ть[1] *v.impfv.* [*pres.* -ре́ет] 1, (*of something brightly colored or multicolored*) to appear; strike the eye. 2, (*with instr.*) to be bright (with); be gay (with).

пестре́ть[2] *v.impfv.* [*pres.* -ри́т] 1, to be all over (a surface). 2, (*with instr.*) to abound (in); be filled (with); be replete (with).

пестри́ть *v.impfv.* 1, to make colorful. 2, (*with instr.*) to sprinkle (with); intersperse (with). 3, *impers.* to be dazzled: У меня́ пестри́ло в глаза́х, I was dazzled.

пестрота́ *n.* 1, diversity of colors. 2, *fig.* diversity; diverse nature.

пёстрый *adj.* 1, multicolored; motley. 2, *fig.* mixed; diverse; motley; heterogeneous.

песча́ник *n.* sandstone.

песча́нка [*gen. pl.* -нок] *n.* 1, gerbil. 2, sanderling.

песча́ный *adj.* 1, sand (*attrib.*): песча́ная о́тмель, sandbank. 2, sandy.

песчи́нка [*gen. pl.* -нок] *n.* grain of sand.

пета́рда *n.* 1, petard. 2, firecracker.

пе́телька [*gen. pl.* -лек] *n.* 1, *dim. of* пе́тля. 2, eyelet.

пети́ция *n.* petition.

петли́стый *adj.* winding.

петли́ца *n.* 1, buttonhole (*in a lapel*). 2, colored patch or stripe (*on a uniform*).

пе́тля [*gen. pl.* -тель] *n.* 1, loop. 2, noose. 3, buttonhole. 4, stitch (*in knitting*): спусти́ть пе́тлю, to drop a stitch. 5, hinge (*of a door*). 6, *aero.* [*often* мёртвая пе́тля] loop: де́лать мёртвую пе́тлю, to loop the loop. —лезть в пе́тлю, to risk one's neck.

петля́ть *v.impfv., colloq.* 1, to weave; zigzag. 2, *fig.* to equivocate; prevaricate.

петру́шка *n.f.* parsley. —*n.m.* **1,** puppet show. **2,** chief character in this show.

пету́ния *also,* **пету́нья** *n.* petunia.

пету́х [*gen.* **-туха́**] *n.* rooster; cock. —**встава́ть с петуха́ми,** to get up at the crack of dawn. —**пусти́ть кра́сного петуха́,** to start a fire.

пету́ший [*fem.* **-шья**] *adj.* rooster's; cock's. —**пету́ший гребешо́к,** cockscomb (*plant*).

петуши́ный *adj.* rooster (*attrib.*); cock (*attrib.*). —**петуши́ный бой,** cockfight; cockfighting. —**петуши́ный гре́бень,** cockscomb.

петуши́ться *v.r.impf., colloq.* to get on one's high horse.

петушо́к [*gen.* **-шка́**] *n.* cockerel.

петь *v.impf.* [*pfv.* **спеть** *or* **пропе́ть**; *pres.* **пою́, поёшь**] to sing.

пехо́та *n.* infantry. —**морска́я пехо́та,** the marines.

пехоти́нец [*gen.* **-нца**] *n.* infantryman; foot soldier. —**морско́й пехоти́нец,** marine.

пехо́тный *adj.* infantry (*attrib.*).

печа́лить *v.impf.* [*pfv.* **опеча́лить**] to sadden. —**печа́литься,** *refl.* to be sad; be saddened; grieve.

печа́ль *n.f.* sorrow; sadness.

печа́льно *adv.* sadly. —**печа́льно знамени́тый,** notorious; infamous.

печа́льный *adj.* [*short form* **-лен, -льна**] sad.

печа́тание *n.* printing.

печа́тать *v.impf.* [*pfv.* **напеча́тать**] **1,** to print. **2,** *in* печа́тать на маши́нке, to type. **3,** to publish. **4,** to have (something) published. —**печа́таться,** *refl.* **1,** to be printed; (*of a book*) be in print. **2,** to have something published.

печа́тка [*gen. pl.* **-ток**] *n.* signet.

печа́тник *n.* printer.

печа́тно *adv.* in print; in the press.

печа́тный *adj.* **1,** printing (*attrib.*): печа́тный стано́к, printing press. **2,** printed. **3,** published. —**печа́тные бу́квы,** block letters. —**печа́тный лист,** signature (*of 16 pages*). —**печа́тное сло́во,** the printed word.

печа́ть *n.f.* **1,** seal; stamp. **2,** type; print. **3,** the press: освеща́ться в печа́ти, to be covered in the press. —**быть в печа́ти,** to be on the presses. —**выходи́ть из печа́ти,** to come off the presses; come out.

пече́ние *n.* baking.

печёнка *n.* liver (*meat*).

печёночник *n.* liverwort.

печёночница *n.* hepatica.

печёночный *adj.* liver (*attrib.*); hepatic.

печёный *adj.* baked.

пе́чень *n.f., anat.* liver.

пече́нье *n.* pastry; cookies.

пе́чка [*gen. pl.* **пе́чек**] *n.* stove. —**танцева́ть от пе́чки,** to start over from the beginning.

печно́й *adj.* stove (*attrib.*).

печу́рка [*gen. pl.* **-рок**] *n.* small portable stove.

печь[1] *v.impf.* [*pfv.* **испе́чь**; *pres.* **пеку́, печёшь, ...пеку́т**; *past* **пёк, пекла́, пекло́, пекли́**] **1,** to bake. **2,** [*impf. only*] (*of the sun*) to beat down. —**пе́чься,** *refl.* **1,** to bake; be baked. **2,** [*impf. only*] (*with* о) to care (about).

печь[2] [*2nd loc.* **в печи́**; *pl.* **пе́чи, пече́й, печа́м**] *n.f.* **1,** stove; oven. **2,** furnace: до́менная печь, blast furnace. —**обжига́тельная печь,** kiln.

пешехо́д *n.* pedestrian. —**пешехо́дный,** *adj.* pedestrian (*attrib.*).

пе́ший *adj.* traveling on foot.

пе́шка [*gen. pl.* **пе́шек**] *n., chess & fig.* pawn.

пешко́м *adv.* on foot.

пеще́ра *n.* cave; cavern.

пеще́рный *adj.* cave (*attrib.*): пеще́рный челове́к, cave man.

пиани́но *n. indecl.* upright piano.

пиани́ссимо *adv. & n. indecl.* pianissimo.

пиани́ст *n.m.* [*fem.* **-ни́стка**] *n.* pianist.

пиа́но *adv., music* piano; soft.

пиано́ла *n.* player piano.

пиа́стр *n.* piaster (*monetary unit of several Middle Eastern countries*).

пивна́я *n., decl. as an adj.* tavern; saloon; pub.

пивно́й *adj.* beer (*attrib.*).

пи́во *n.* beer.

пивова́р *n.* brewer. —**пивоваре́ние,** *n.* brewing. —**пивова́ренный,** *adj.* brewing (*attrib.*): пивова́ренный заво́д, brewery.

пи́галица *n.* lapwing; pewit.

пигме́й *n.* pygmy.

пигме́нт *n.* pigment. —**пигмента́ция,** *n.* pigmentation. —**пигме́нтный,** *adj.* pigmented.

пиджа́к [*gen.* **-жака́**] *n.* (man's) suit jacket; coat.

пиетет *n.* reverence.

пижа́ма *n.* pajamas.

пижо́н *n., colloq.* fop; dandy.

пик *n.* **1,** peak (*of a mountain*). **2,** peak time (*of work, traffic, etc.*). —**часы́ пик,** rush hours.

пи́ка *n.* lance; pike. —**в пи́ку** (+ *dat.*), in order to spite someone.

пика́нтный *adj.* **1,** piquant; pungent. **2,** *fig.* spicy. —**пика́нтность,** *n.f.* piquancy.

пика́п *n.* pickup truck.

пике́ *n.neut. indecl.* **1,** piqué. **2,** *aero.* dive. —**пике́йный,** *adj.* piqué.

пике́т *n.* **1,** picket line. **2,** *mil.* picket. **3,** bench mark. **4,** piquet (*card game*).

пикети́ровать *v.impf.* [*pres.* **-рую, -руешь**] to picket.

пике́тчик *n.* picket (*one who pickets*).

пи́ки [*gen.* **пик**] *n.pl., cards* spades.

пики́рование *n., aero.* diving.

пики́ровать *v.impf. & pfv.* [*pres.* **-рую, -руешь**] *aero.* to dive; go into a dive.

пики́роваться *v.r.impf.* [*pres.* **-руюсь, -руешься**] to squabble; bicker; trade insults.

пикиро́вка *n.* squabbling; bickering.

пикиро́вщик *n.* dive bomber.

пики́рующий *adj., in* пики́рующий бомбардиро́вщик, dive bomber.

пи́кколо *n.indecl.* piccolo.

пикни́к [*gen.* **-ника́**] *n.* picnic.

пи́кнуть *v.pfv., colloq., usu. used negatively,* to object: Он и пи́кнуть не успе́л, before he had a chance to say "no".

пи́ковый *adj.* **1,** *cards* of spades: пи́ковая да́ма, queen of spades. **2,** *colloq.* awkward; sticky: пи́ковое положе́ние, awkward/sticky situation. —**оставаться при пи́ковом интере́се,** to be left holding the bag.

пиктогра́мма *n.* pictograph. —**пиктогра́фия,** *n.* pictography. —**пиктографи́ческий,** *adj.* pictographic.

пи́кули [*gen.* -**лей**] *n.pl.* pickles.

пи́кша *n.* haddock.

пила́ [*pl.* пи́лы] *n.* saw.

пила́в *n.* pilaf.

пила́-рыба *n.* sawfish.

пилёный *adj.* sawed. —**пилёный са́хар,** lump sugar.

пилигри́м *n., obs.* pilgrim.

пили́кать *v.impfv., colloq.* to scrape (on a musical instrument).

пили́ть *v.impfv.* [*pres.* пилю́, пи́лишь] **1,** to saw. **2,** *fig.* to nag.

пи́лка [*gen. pl.* пи́лок] *n.* **1,** sawing. **2,** small handsaw. **3,** nail file.

пи́ллерс *n., naut.* stanchion.

пиломатериа́лы [*gen.* -**лов**] *n.pl.* lumber.

пило́н *n.* pylon.

пило́т *n.* pilot. —**пилота́ж,** *n.* piloting; flying.

пилоти́ровать *v.impfv.* [*pres.* -**рую, -руешь**] to pilot.

пилоти́руемый *adj.* piloted; (*of a spacecraft*) manned.

пило́тка [*gen. pl.* -**ток**] *n., mil.* overseas cap.

пи́льщик *n.* sawyer; woodcutter.

пилю́ля *n.* pill.

пиля́стра *also,* **пиля́стр** *n.* pilaster.

пина́ть *v.impfv.* [*pfv.* пнуть] (*usu. with* ного́й) *colloq.* to kick.

пингви́н *n.* penguin.

пинг-по́нг *n.* ping-pong.

пи́ния *n.* stone pine.

пино́к [*gen.* пинка́] *n., colloq.* kick.

пи́нта *n.* pint.

пинце́т *n.* tweezers.

пио́н *n.* peony.

пионе́р *n.* pioneer. —**пионе́рский,** *adj.* pioneer (*attrib.*).

пиоре́я *n.* pyorrhea.

пипе́тка [*gen. pl.* -**ток**] *n.* eye dropper; medicine dropper.

пир [*2nd loc.* пиру́; *pl.* пиры́] *n.* feast; banquet. —**пир горо́й; пир на весь мир,** lavish banquet; sumptuous feast.

пирами́да *n.* pyramid. —**пирамида́льный,** *adj.* pyramidal.

пира́т *n.* pirate. —**пира́тский,** *adj.* pirate (*attrib.*); piratical. —**пира́тство,** *n.* piracy.

пири́т *n.* pyrite.

пирова́ть *v.impfv.* [*pres.* -**рую, -руешь**] to feast; have a feast.

пиро́г [*gen.* -**рога́**] *n.* pie.

пиро́жное *n., decl. as an adj.* pastry.

пирожо́к [*gen.* -**жка́**] *n.* small pie; patty.

пирома́ния *n.* pyromania.

пироте́хника *n.* pyrotechnics.

пи́рров *adj., in* **пи́ррова побе́да,** Pyrrhic victory.

пирс *n.* pier.

пиру́шка [*gen. pl.* -**шек**] *n., colloq.* lively party.

пируэ́т *n.* pirouette.

пи́ршество *n.* sumptuous feast.

писа́ка *n.m. & f., colloq.* poor writer; hack writer; scribbler.

писа́ние *n.* writing. —**свяще́нное писа́ние,** Holy Scripture; Holy Writ.

пи́саный *adj.* written. —**пи́саная краса́вица,** a picture of beauty.

пи́сарь [*pl.* писаря́] *n.m., usu. mil.* clerk.

писа́тель *n.m.* [*fem.* -**ница**] writer. —**писа́тельский,** *adj.* writer's. —**писа́тельство,** *n., colloq.* writing; being a writer.

писа́ть *v.impfv.* [*pfv.* написа́ть; *pres.* пишу́, пи́шешь] **1,** to write. **2,** to paint. **3,** *in* писа́ть на маши́нке, to type. —**писа́ться,** *refl.* [*impfv. only*] **1,** to be spelled: Как пи́шется э́то сло́во?, how is this word spelled? **2,** *impers.* (*with dat.*) to feel like writing: Мне сего́дня не пи́шется, I don't feel like writing today; I can't get myself to do any writing today.

писе́ц [*gen.* писца́] *n.* scribe.

писк *n.* peep; cheep.

пискли́вый *adj.* (*of one's voice*) squeaky.

пи́скнуть *v., pfv. of* **пища́ть.**

писсуа́р *n.* urinal.

пистоле́т *n.* pistol; gun. —**пистоле́т-пулемёт,** submachine gun.

пистоле́тный *adj.* pistol (*attrib.*).

писто́н *n.* **1,** percussion cap. **2,** *music* piston.

пису́лька [*gen. pl.* -**лек**] *n., colloq.* short letter; note.

писчебума́жный *adj.* stationery (*attrib.*).

пи́счий *adj.* writing (*attrib.*): пи́счая бума́га, writing paper.

письмена́ [*gen.* -**мён**] *n.pl.* characters; letters.

пи́сьменно *adv.* in writing.

пи́сьменность *n.f.* **1,** written language; system of writing. **2,** literature; literary texts (*of an ancient people*).

пи́сьменный *adj.* **1,** writing (*attrib.*): пи́сьменный стол, desk. **2,** written: пи́сьменная про́сьба, written request.

письмо́ [*pl.* пи́сьма, пи́сем] *n.* **1,** letter: писа́ть письмо́, to write a letter. **2,** writing: чте́ние и письмо́, reading and writing. **3,** script: ара́бское письмо́, the Arabic script.

письмоно́сец [*gen.* -**сца**] *n.* mailman.

пита́ние *n.* **1,** feeding. **2,** food: де́тское пита́ние, baby food. **3,** nourishment; nutrition. **4,** power supply.

пита́тельный *adj.* **1,** nourishing; nutritious. **2,** feeding (*attrib.*). —**пита́тельное вещество́,** nutrient. —**пита́тельный крем,** skin cream. —**пита́тельная среда́,** culture medium.

пита́ть *v.impfv.* **1,** to feed; nourish. **2,** to supply (with energy). **3,** *fig.* to harbor (a feeling); have a feeling of. —**пита́ться,** *refl.* **1,** to eat; take one's meals. **2,** (*with instr.*) (*of a person*) to live (on); (*of an animal*) to feed (on).

пито́мец [*gen.* -**мца**] *n.m.* [*fem.* -**мица**] **1,** charge; ward. **2,** pupil. **3,** graduate; alumnus.

пито́мник *n.* **1,** nursery (*for plants*). **2,** farm (*for breeding and raising animals*).

пито́н *n.* python.

пить *v.impfv.* [*pfv.* **вы́пить**; *pres.* **пью, пьёшь**; *past fem.* **пила́**] to drink. Я хочу́ пить, I am thirsty. —**как пить дать**, *colloq.* for sure.

питьё *n.* **1**, drinking: го́дный для питья́, fit to drink. **2**, drink; beverage.

питьево́й *adj.* drinking (*attrib.*): питьева́я вода́, drinking water. —**питьева́я со́да**, baking soda; bicarbonate of soda.

пифаго́ров *adj.*, *in* **пифаго́рова теоре́ма**, Pythagorean theorem.

пиха́ть *v.impfv.* [*pfv.* **пихну́ть**] *colloq.* **1**, to push; shove. **2**, (*with* в + *acc.*) to stuff (into); cram (into).

пи́хта *n.* fir. —**пи́хтовый**, *adj.* fir (*attrib.*).

пи́цца *n.* pizza.

пиццика́то *adv. & n. indecl.* pizzicato.

пи́чкать *v.impfv.* [*pfv.* **напи́чкать**] (*with instr.*) *colloq.* **1**, to stuff (with food, drink, medicine, etc.). (На)пи́чкать (кого́-нибудь) нарко́тиками, to drug (someone). **2**, to cram (with); saturate (with).

пичу́га *n.*, *colloq.* small bird. *Also,* **пичу́жка**.

пиччика́то *adv. & n. indecl.* pizzicato.

пи́шущий *adj.*, *in* **пи́шущая маши́нка**, typewriter.

пи́ща *n.* food. —**пи́ща для ума́** (*or* для размышле́ния), food for thought.

пища́ль *n.f.* arquebus; harquebus.

пища́ть *v.impfv.* [*pfv.* **пи́скнуть**; *pres.* **пищу́, пищи́шь**] to peep; cheep.

пищеваре́ние *n.* digestion. —**расстро́йство пищеваре́ния**, indigestion.

пищевари́тельный *adj.* digestive. —**пищевари́тельный кана́л**, alimentary canal.

пищево́д *n.* gullet; esophagus.

пищево́й *adj.* food (*attrib.*).

пищу́ха *n.* **1**, pika (*animal*). **2**, creeper (*bird*).

пия́вка [*gen. pl.* **-вок**] *n.* leech.

плав *n.*, *in* **на плаву́**, afloat.

пла́вание *n.* **1**, swimming. **2**, sailing; navigation. **3**, voyage.

пла́вательный *adj.* swimming (*attrib.*).

пла́вать *v.impfv.* **1**, *indeterm. of* **плыть**. **2**, to float (*not sink*). **3**, *colloq.* to flounder; be at sea.

пла́вающий *adj.* **1**, swimming. **2**, floating. **3**, (*of a vehicle*) amphibious.

пла́вень [*gen.* **-вня**] *n.m.*, *metall.* flux.

плавико́вый *adj.*, *in* **плавико́вая кислота́**, hydrofluoric acid; **плавико́вый шпат**, fluorspar; fluorite.

плави́льный *adj.* melting (*attrib.*); smelting (*attrib.*). —**плави́льный котёл**, melting pot.

плави́льня [*gen. pl.* **-лен**] *n.* smelting plant. —**плави́льщик**, *n.* smelter.

пла́вить *v.impfv.* [*pres* **-влю, -вишь**] to melt; smelt. —**пла́виться**, to melt.

пла́вка *n.* melting; smelting.

пла́вки [*gen.* **-вок**] *n.pl.* swimming trunks.

пла́вкий *adj.* capable of being melted.

плавле́ние *n.* melting. —**то́чка плавле́ния**, melting point.

плавни́к [*gen.* **-ника́**] *n.* **1**, fin (*of a fish*). **2**, driftwood.

пла́вный *adj.* **1**, (*of movements*) smooth; graceful. **2**, (*of sounds or speech*) smooth; fluent. —**пла́вность**, *n.f.* smoothness.

плаву́нчик *n.* phalarope.

плаву́честь *n.f.* buoyancy.

плаву́чий *adj.* **1**, floating. **2**, buoyant. —**плаву́чая ба́за**, *naut.* tender. —**плаву́чая льди́на**, ice floe; ice field.

плагиа́т *n.* plagiarism. —**плагиа́тор**, *n.* plagiarist.

пла́зма *n.* plasma.

плака́т *n.* poster; placard.

пла́кать *v.impfv.* [*pres.* **пла́чу, пла́чешь**] to cry; weep. —**пла́каться**, *refl.* (*with* на + *acc.*) *colloq.* to cry (about); bemoan.

пла́кса *n.m. & f.*, *colloq.* crybaby.

плакси́вый *adj.*, *colloq.* whining.

плаку́чий *adj.* **1**, *obs.* whining. **2**, (*of trees*) weeping: плаку́чая и́ва, weeping willow.

пламене́ть *v.impfv.* to blaze; flame.

пла́менный *adj.* **1**, flaming; fiery. **2**, *fig.* fiery; ardent.

пла́мя [*gen., dat. & prepl.* **пла́мени**; *instr.* **пла́менем**] *n.neut.* flame; blaze.

план *n.* **1**, plan. **2**, diagram; map: план кварти́ры, floor plan of an apartment; план го́рода, city map. **3**, *fig.* aspect; context. —**за́дний план**, background. —**кру́пный план**, close-up. —**пере́дний план**, foreground. —**уче́бный план**, curriculum.

планёр *n.*, *aero.* glider. —**планери́зм**, *n.* gliding. —**планери́ст**, *n.* glider pilot. —**планёрный**, *adj.* gliding (*attrib.*).

плане́та *n.* planet.

планета́рий *n.* planetarium.

плане́тный *adj.* planetary.

планиме́трия *n.* plane geometry.

плани́рование *n.* **1**, planning. **2**, *aero.* gliding; glide.

плани́ровать *v.impfv.* [*pfv.* **сплани́ровать**; *pres.* **-рую, -руешь**] **1**, [*pfv. also* **заплани́ровать**] to plan. **2**, *aero.* to glide; glide down.

планирова́ть *v.impfv.* [*pfv.* **распланирова́ть**; *pres.* **-ру́ю, -ру́ешь**] to lay out.

плани́ровка *n.* **1**, planning. **2**, laying out. **3**, layout; design.

планиро́вщик *n.* planner; one who lays out a city, town, etc.

пла́нка [*gen. pl.* **-нок**] *n.* **1**, plank; strip. **2**, bar; crossbar (*used in high jumping*). —**о́рденская пла́нка**, bar of ribbons.

планкто́н *n.* plankton.

планови́к [*gen.* **-вика́**] *n.* (economic) planner.

пла́новый *adj.* **1**, planned: пла́новое хозя́йство, planned economy. **2**, planning (*attrib.*): пла́новый отде́л, planning department.

планоме́рный *adj.* planned; systematic.

планта́тор *n.* plantation owner; planter.

планта́ция *n.* plantation.

планше́т *n.* map case.

планши́р *n.* gunwale.

пласт [*gen.* **пласта́**] *n.* **1**, layer. **2**, *geol.* stratum. —**лежа́ть пласто́м**, (*of a sick person*) to be flat on one's back.

пла́стик *n.* plastic.

пла́стика *n.* **1**, plastic arts. **2**, grace of movement.

пла́стиковый *adj.* plastic. —**пла́стиковая бо́мба**, plastic bomb.

пластили́н *n.* plasticine.

пласти́на *n.* plate.

пласти́нка [*gen. pl.* -нок] *n.* **1,** metal plate. **2,** phonograph record. **3,** photographic plate. **4,** blade *(of a leaf).* —кровяны́е пласти́нки, platelets.

пласти́ческий *adj.* **1,** plastic. **2,** *(of movements of the body)* rhythmical; graceful.

пластма́сса *n.* plastic. —пластма́ссовый, *adj.* plastic.

пла́стырь *n.m.* plaster *(applied to a sore or wound).*

пла́та *n.* **1,** pay; payment. **2,** fee; charge: входна́я пла́та, admission fee/charge. Пла́та за обуче́ние, tuition. —за́работная пла́та, pay; wages; salary. —кварти́рная пла́та, rent.

плата́н *n.* plane tree.

платёж [*gen.* -тежа́] *n.* payment. —нало́женным платежо́м, C.O.D.

платёжеспосо́бный *adj.* solvent. —платёжеспосо́бность, *n.f.* solvency.

платёжный *adj.* pay *(attrib.);* payment *(attrib.).* —платёжный бала́нс, balance of payments. —платёжная ве́домость, payroll.

плате́льщик *n.* payer.

пла́тина *n.* platinum. —пла́тиновый, *adj.* platinum.

плати́ть *v.impf.* [*pfv.* заплати́ть; *pres.* плачу́, пла́тишь] to pay: плати́ть кому́-нибудь за (+ *acc.*), to pay someone for (something). —плати́ться, *refl.* [*pfv.* поплати́ться] to pay; pay the penalty: поплати́ться жи́знью за (+ *acc.*), to pay for (something) with one's life.

пла́тный *adj.* **1,** requiring payment. Пла́тный мост, toll bridge. **2,** paying. **3,** paid.

плато́ *n. indecl.* plateau.

плато́к [*gen.* -тка́] *n.* kerchief. —носово́й плато́к, handkerchief. —ше́йный плато́к, neckerchief.

платони́ческий *adj.* platonic.

платфо́рма *n.* **1,** platform. **2,** flatcar. **3,** (political) platform.

пла́тье *n.* **1,** [*gen. pl.* -тьев] dress; gown. **2,** clothes; clothing.

платяно́й *adj.* clothes *(attrib.).* —платяно́й шкаф, wardrobe.

плафо́н *n.* **1,** decorated ceiling. **2,** shade *(for a lamp suspended from a ceiling).*

пла́ха *n.* **1,** block; log. **2,** execution block.

плац [*2nd loc.* плацу́] *n.* parade ground.

плацда́рм *n.* **1,** bridgehead; beachhead. **2,** springboard; jumping-off place; staging area.

плаце́нта *n.* placenta.

плацка́рта *n.* reserved seat ticket *(for a train).* —плацка́ртный, *adj.* reserved.

плач *n.* weeping; crying.

плаче́вный *adj.* **1,** mournful; sad. **2,** deplorable; pathetic; sorry.

пла́шка [*gen. pl.* -шек] *n.* flat board.

плашмя́ *adv.* flat: лежа́ть плашмя́, to lie flat.

плащ [*gen.* плаща́] *n.* **1,** cloak. **2,** raincoat.

плебе́й *n.* plebeian. —плебе́йский, *adj.* plebeian.

плебисци́т *n.* plebiscite.

плебс *n.* the common people; hoi polloi.

плева́ *n.* membrane. —де́вственная плева́, hymen.

плева́тельница *n.* spittoon; cuspidor.

плева́ть *v.impfv.* [*pfv.* плю́нуть; *pres.* плюю́, плюёшь] **1,** to spit. **2,** (*with* на + *acc.*) *colloq.* to ignore; shrug off; brush off. **3,** (*with inf.*) *colloq.* not to give a damn: Ему́ наплева́ть на э́то, he doesn't give a damn about it. —плева́ться, *refl.* [*impfv. only*] *colloq.* = плева́ть.

пле́вел [*gen. pl.* пле́вел] *n.* **1,** ryegrass; darnel. **2,** *fig.* weed *(undesirable element).*

плево́к [*gen.* -вка́] *n.* spit; spittle; sputum.

пле́вра *n.* pleura. —плевра́льный, *adj.* pleural.

плеври́т *n.* pleurisy.

плёвый *adj., colloq.* **1,** miserable; rotten. **2,** trifling; insignificant.

плед *n.* lap robe; steamer rug.

плексигла́с *n.* plexiglass.

плектр *n.* plectrum.

племенно́й *adj.* **1,** tribal. **2,** pedigreed. **3,** breeding *(attrib.);* stud *(attrib.).* —племенна́я кобы́ла, brood mare.

пле́мя [*gen., dat. & instr.* пле́мени; *instr.* пле́менем; *pl.* племена́, племён, племена́м] *n.neut.* tribe.

племя́нник *n.* nephew.

племя́нница *n.* niece.

плен [*2nd loc.* плену́] *n.* captivity. —брать/взять в плен, to take (someone) prisoner; capture; take captive. —держа́ть в плену́, to hold prisoner; hold captive. —попа́сть в плен (к), to be taken prisoner (by). —сдава́ться в плен, to give oneself up.

плена́рный *adj.* plenary.

плене́ние *n.* **1,** taking prisoner; capture. **2,** captivity.

плени́тельный *adj.* captivating; enchanting.

плени́ть *v.pfv.* **1,** *pfv. of* пленя́ть. **2,** *obs.* to take prisoner. —плени́ться, *refl., pfv. of* пленя́ться.

плёнка [*gen. pl.* -нок] *n.* **1,** thin layer *(of ice, dust, fat, etc.).* **2,** *photog.* film. **3,** tape: записа́ть на плёнку, to tape; tape-record. **4,** pellicle.

пле́нник *n.* prisoner; captive.

пле́нный *adj.* captive. —*n.* prisoner; captive.

плёночный *adj.* film *(attrib.).* —плёночный фотоаппара́т, roll-film camera.

пле́нум *n.* plenum; plenary session.

пленя́ть *v.impfv.* [*pfv.* плени́ть] to captivate; enchant. —пленя́ться, *refl.* (*with instr.*) to be captivated (by); be fascinated (with).

плёс *n.* stretch; section *(of a river).*

пле́сень *n.f.* mold.

плеск *n.* **1,** splash; splashing. **2,** lapping *(of waves).*

плеска́ть *v.impfv.* [*pfv.* плесну́ть; *pres.* плещу́, пле́щешь] **1,** *v.i.* *(of water or other liquids)* to splash. **2,** *v.t.* to splash: плеска́ть во́ду *(or* водо́й*)* на́ пол, to splash water on the floor. **3,** *v.i.* *(of waves)* to lap (against something). —плеска́ться, *refl.* [*impfv. only*] **1,** to splash. **2,** to spill.

пле́сневеть *v.impfv.* [*pfv.* запле́сневеть] to grow moldy.

плесну́ть *v., pfv. of* плеска́ть.

плести́ *v.impfv.* [*pfv.* сплести́; *pres.* плету́, плетёшь; *past* плёл, плела́, плело́, плели́] **1,** to weave; braid; plait. **2,** *colloq.* to weave (intrigues); spin (a tale); utter (nonsense). —плести́сь, *refl.* [*impfv. only*] *colloq.* to plod along; trudge along.

плете́ние *n.* **1,** weaving. **2,** weave. **3,** wickerwork.

плетёнка [*gen. pl.* **-нок**] *n., colloq.* **1,** wicker basket. **2,** wicker enclosure. **3,** twist (*of bread*).

плетёный *adj.* wicker (*attrib.*); wattled.

плете́нь [*gen.* **-тня́**] *n.m.* wattle fence. —**навести́ тень на плете́нь,** to confuse the issue.

плётка [*gen. pl.* **-ток**] *n.* lash.

плеть [*pl.* **пле́ти, плете́й, плетя́м**] *n.f.* lash.

плечево́й *adj.* shoulder (*attrib.*).

пле́чико [*pl.* **-ки, -ков**] *n.* **1,** *dim. of* плечо́. **2,** shoulder strap. **3,** *pl.* clothes hanger; coat hanger.

плечи́стый *adj.* broad-shouldered.

плечо́ [*pl.* **пле́чи, плеч, плеча́м**] *n.* shoulder. —**выноси́ть на свои́х плеча́х,** to carry on one's shoulders. —**за плеча́ми, 1,** behind one. **2,** close at hand. —**го́лову с плеч!,** off with his head! —**име́ть го́лову на плеча́х,** to have a good head on one's shoulders. —**не по плечу́** (+ *dat.*), *colloq.* too much for; beyond one. —**плечо́м к плечу́,** shoulder to shoulder. —**с плеч доло́й,** off one's back; over and done with.

плеши́веть *v.impfv.* [*pfv.* **оплеши́веть**] to grow bald.

плеши́вый *adj.* bald. —**плеши́вость,** *n.f.* baldness.

плешь *n.f.* bald spot.

плея́да *n.* brilliant assemblage; galaxy. —**Плея́ды,** *n.pl., astron.* Pleiades.

пли́нтус *n.* plinth.

плис *n.* velveteen. —**пли́совый,** *adj.* velveteen.

плиссе́ (сэ) *n.neut. indecl.* accordion pleats. —*adj. indecl.* with accordion pleats.

плисси́рованный *adj.* pleated.

плисси́ровать *v.impfv.* [*pres.* **-ру́ю, -ру́ешь**] to pleat; make pleats in.

плита́ [*pl.* **пли́ты**] *n.* **1,** slab. **2,** flagstone. **3,** (electric) stove; range. —**броневая плита́,** armor plating. —**моги́льная плита́,** gravestone. —**надгро́бная плита́,** tombstone.

пли́тка [*gen. pl.* **-ток**] *n.* **1,** thin slab; tile. **2,** bar (*of chocolate*). **3,** small stove.

плитня́к [*gen.* **-няка́**] *n.* flagstone. —**плитняко́вый,** *adj.* flagstone.

пли́точный *adj.* tiled: пли́точный пол, tiled floor.

плов *n.* pilaf.

пловец [*gen.* **-вца́**] *n.m.* [*fem.* **пловчи́ха**] swimmer.

плод [*gen.* **плода́**] *n.* **1,** fruit. **2,** fetus. **3,** *fig.* fruit; product: плоды́ на́ших трудо́в, the fruits of our labor. —**плод воображе́ния,** product (*or* figment) of the imagination.

плоди́ть *v.impfv.* [*pfv.* **расплоди́ть;** *pres.* **-жу́, -ди́шь**] **1,** to produce; bring forth. **2,** *fig.* to generate; engender. —**плоди́ться,** *refl.* to propagate; multiply; breed.

пло́дный *adj.* **1,** of a fruit. **2,** producing fruit. **3,** fertilized. **4,** fetal.

плодови́тый *adj.* **1,** (*of animals*) prolific; fertile; fecund. **2,** *fig.* (*of a writer, composer, etc.*) prolific. —**плодови́тость,** *n.f.* fertility.

плодово́дство *n.* fruit growing.

плодо́вый *adj.* **1,** fruit (*attrib.*). **2,** fruit-bearing.

плодоноси́ть *v.impfv.* [*pres.* **-но́сит**] to bear fruit.

плодоно́сный *adj.* fruit-bearing.

плодоро́дие *n.* fertility.

плодоро́дный *adj.* fertile.

плодотво́рный *adj.* fruitful; productive.

пло́мба *n.* **1,** seal (*for a door or package*). **2,** filling (*for a tooth*).

пломби́р *n.* ice cream topped with fruit.

пломбирова́ть *v.impfv.* [*pfv.* **запломбирова́ть;** *pres.* **-ру́ю, -ру́ешь**] **1,** to seal. **2,** to fill (a tooth).

пло́ский *adj.* [*short form* **пло́сок, плоска́, пло́ско, пло́ски;** *comp.* **пло́ще**] **1,** flat. **2,** *fig.* flat; vapid; banal. —**пло́ская стопа́,** flatfoot. —**пло́ский червь,** flatworm.

плоского́рье *n.* plateau; tableland.

плоскогру́дый *adj.* flat-chested.

плоскогу́бцы [*gen.* **-цев**] *n.pl.* pliers.

плоскодо́нка [*gen. pl.* **-нок**] *n., colloq.* flat-bottomed boat.

плоскодо́нный *adj.* flat-bottomed.

плоскосто́пие *n.* flatfoot; fallen arches.

пло́скость [*pl.* **пло́скости, -сте́й, -стя́м**] *n.f.* **1,** flatness. **2,** plane. **3,** *fig.* plane; level. **4,** *fig.* platitude; banality.

плот [*gen.* **плота́;** *2nd loc.* **плоту́**] *n.* raft.

плотва́ *n.* roach (*fish*).

плоти́на *n.* dam.

пло́тник *n.* carpenter.

пло́тничать *v.impfv.* to work as a carpenter.

пло́тничество *n.* carpentry.

пло́тничий [*fem.* **-чья**] *adj.* carpenter's (*attrib.*). *Also,* **пло́тничный.**

пло́тно *adv.* **1,** tight; tightly. **2,** densely. **3,** *in* пое́сть пло́тно, to eat heartily.

пло́тность *n.f.* **1,** density. **2,** solidity.

пло́тный *adj.* [*short form* **пло́тен, плотна́, пло́тно, пло́тны**] **1,** dense; compact. **2,** (*of material*) closely woven. **3,** *colloq.* stocky; solidly built. **4,** *colloq.* (*of a meal*) hearty.

плотоя́дный *adj.* carniverous. —**плотоя́дное живо́тное,** carnivore.

пло́тский *adj., obs.* carnal.

плоть *n.f.* **1,** flesh. **2,** *in* кра́йняя плоть, *anat.* foreskin. —**во плоти́,** in the flesh. —**плоть и кровь моя́,** my own flesh and blood. —**плоть от пло́ти** (+ *gen.*), the flesh and blood of. —**плоть от пло́ти мое́й,** flesh of my flesh.

пло́хо *adv.* badly; poorly. Пло́хо па́хнуть, to smell bad. —*adj., used predicatively* **1,** bad: Э́то пло́хо, that's bad. **2,** (*with dat.*) ill; not well: Ему́ пло́хо, he is not well. **3,** (*with dat.*) in a bad way: Ей пло́хо, she is in a bad way.

плохо́й *adj.* [*short form* **плох, плоха́, пло́хо, пло́хи** *or* **плохи́;** *comp.* **ху́же**] bad; poor.

плоша́ть *v.impfv.* (*usu. used negatively*) *colloq.* to make a mistake.

площа́дка [*gen. pl.* **-док**] *n.* **1,** ground; site; area: площа́дка для игр, playground; строи́тельная площа́дка, construction site; съёмочная площа́дка, (movie) set; поса́дочная площа́дка, landing field; пусковая *or* ста́ртовая площа́дка, launch(ing) pad. **2,** *sports* field; court: спорти́вная площа́дка, athletic field; playing field; баскетбо́льная площа́дка, basketball court. **3,** landing (*of a staircase*). **4,** platform (*of a railway car or streetcar*).

площадно́й *adj.* coarse; crude; vulgar; of the gutter.

пло́щадь [*pl.* **пло́щади, -де́й, -дя́м**] *n.f.* **1,** area: пло́щадь треуго́льника, the area of a triangle. **2,** space: жила́я пло́щадь, living space. **3,** square: Кра́сная пло́щадь, Red Square.

плуг [*pl.* **плуги́**] *n.* plow.

плу́нжер *n.* plunger.

плут [*gen.* **плута́**] *n.* cheat; swindler.

плута́ть *v.impfv., colloq.* to stray; wander.

плути́шка [*gen. pl.* **-шек**] *n.m.* imp; rascal.

плу́тни [*gen.* **-ней**] *n.pl., colloq.* tricks.

плутова́тый *adj.* crafty; cunning.

плутова́ть *v.impfv.* [*pfv.* **сплутова́ть**; *pres.* **-ту́ю, -ту́ешь**] *colloq.* to cheat.

плуто́вско́й *adj.* **1,** crooked; underhanded. **2,** (*of one's face, eyes, etc.*) roguish. **3,** *lit.* picaresque.

плутовство́ *n.* **1,** cheating. **2,** trickery.

плутокра́т *n.* plutocrat. **—плутократи́ческий,** *adj.* plutocratic. **—плутокра́тия,** *n.* plutocracy.

Плуто́н *n.* Pluto (*the planet*).

плуто́ний *n.* plutonium.

плыть *v.impfv.* [*pfv.* **поплы́ть**; *pres.* **плыву́, плывёшь**; *past fem.* **плыла́**] **1,** to swim. **2,** to sail. **3,** to float. **—плыть сто́я,** to tread water. *See also* **пла́вать.**

плюга́вый *adj., colloq.* **1,** ugly; miserable-looking. **2,** *fig.* trivial; piddling.

плюма́ж *n.* plume (*on a hat*).

плю́нуть *v., pfv. of* **плева́ть.**

плюрали́зм *n.* pluralism.

плюс *n.* **1,** plus sign. **2,** *fig., colloq.* plus; advantage: плю́сы и ми́нусы, pluses and minuses. **—adv.** plus: два плюс три равно́ пяти́, two plus three equals five. Плюс пять гра́дусов, five degrees above freezing.

плюсна́ [*pl.* **плю́сны, плю́сен**] *n.* metatarsus. **—плюсневой,** *adj.* metatarsal.

плю́хаться *v.r.impfv.* [*pfv.* **плю́хнуться**] (*with* **в** *or* **на** + *acc.*) *colloq.* to flop (into *or* onto).

плюш *n.* plush (*fabric*). **—плю́шевый,** *adj.* plush.

плю́шка [*gen. pl.* **-шек**] *n.* sweet bun; roll.

плющ [*gen.* **плюща́**] *n.* ivy. **—плющево́й,** *adj.* ivy (*attrib.*).

пляж *n.* beach. **—пля́жный,** *adj.* beach (*attrib.*).

пляс *n., colloq.* dance.

пляса́ть *v.impfv.* [*pfv.* **спляса́ть**; *pres.* **пляшу́, пля́шешь**] colloq. to dance.

пля́ска [*gen. pl.* **-сок**] *n.* dance. **—пля́ска свято́го Ви́тта; ви́ттова пля́ска,** St. Vitus' dance.

плясово́й *adj.* dance (*attrib.*); dancing. **—плясова́я,** *n.* dance tune.

плясу́н [*gen.* **-суна́**] *n.m.* [*fem.* **-су́нья**] *colloq.* dancer.

пневмати́ческий *adj.* pneumatic.

пнуть *v., pfv. of* **пина́ть.**

по *prep.* **A,** *with dat.* **1,** along; over: идти́ по у́лице, to walk along the street; пробежа́ть па́льцами по клавиату́ре, to run one's fingers over the keyboard. Съе́хать по пери́лам, to slide down the banister. По пути́ домо́й, on the way home. **2,** about; around; across; through: ходи́ть по ко́мнате, to pace about the room; промча́ться по не́бу; to flash across the sky; лета́ть по во́здуху, to fly through the air; е́здить по стране́, to travel around/through a country; идти́ по ваго́нам метро́, to walk through the subway cars. **3,** in *or* to various places: ходи́ть по магази́нам, to go shopping; размести́ть това́ры по по́лкам, to arrange the merchandise on the shelves. **4,** over (the radio). По телеви́зору, on television. **5,** by: по оши́бке, by mistake; по желе́зной доро́ге, by rail; по профе́ссии, by profession. **6,** through; due to; on account of: по недоразуме́нию, through a misunderstanding; не по мое́й вине́, through no fault of mine; отсу́тствовать по боле́зни, to be absent on account of illness. **7,** by; according to: по мои́м часа́м, according to (*or* by) my watch; игра́ть по пра́вилам, to play by (*or* according to) the rules; **8,** on (*in the field of*): кни́га по иску́сству, a book on art; art book. Конфере́нция по разоруже́нию, a conference on disarmament; disarmament conference. Чемпио́н по бо́ксу, boxing champion. **9,** to; for the purpose of: кампа́ния по привлече́нию тури́стов, a campaign to attract tourists; опера́ция по удале́нию пу́ли, an operation to remove a bullet. **10,** (*with verbs of striking*) on: уда́рить кулако́м по́ столу, to bang one's fist on the table. **11,** (*with pl. nouns only*) *used in expressions of time,* each; every; on: по вечера́м, each evening; in the evening; evenings. По среда́м, on Wednesdays. **B,** *with acc.* **1,** through: с ию́ля по сентя́брь, from July through September; с шесто́й страни́цы по восьму́ю, from pages 6 through 8. По сей день, to this day. **2,** up to; down to (*on one's body*): ко́сы по по́яс, braids down to one's waist. Грязь была́ по коле́но, the mud was knee-deep. **3,** on (*a side or direction*): по ту (*or* другу́ю) сто́рону (+ *gen.*), on the other side of; по о́бе сторо́ны (+ *gen.*), on both sides of; по ра́зные сто́роны (+ *gen.*), on opposite (*or* different) sides of. По пра́вую ру́ку от меня́, to the right of me. **4,** *obs.* for; to fetch: идти́ по́ воду, to go for water; ходи́ть по грибы́, to go picking mushrooms. **C,** *with prepl.* on; upon; after: по сме́рти отца́, on the death of his father; по оконча́нии университе́та, upon graduation from the university. **D,** *with dat. or acc.* **1,** each; apiece: Де́ти получи́ли по я́блоку, each child received an apple. Чле́ны получи́ли по два биле́та, each member received two tickets. Я купи́л четы́ре я́блока по рублю́, I bought four apples at one ruble each. **2,** by; in: по одному́, one by one; по́ двое, two by two; in twos. Ночева́ть по́ трое в ко́мнате, to sleep three to a room. **—по мне,** as far as I am concerned.

по- *prefix* **1,** *used to form the perfective aspect:* побледне́ть, *pfv. of* бледне́ть. **2,** *indicating the beginning of an action:* побежа́ть, to begin to run. **3,** *indicating action of short duration:* почита́ть, to read for a while. **4,** (*with* **-ива** *or* **-ыва** *verbs*) *indicating action performed intermittently:* попи́сывать, to write from time to time. **5,** (*with comp. adjectives*) a little: погро́мче, a little louder. **6,** *in various combinations:* по-мо́ему, in my opinion; по-ра́зному, in different ways; говори́ть по-ру́сски, to speak Russian. **7,** (*with intervals of time*) by the...: поде́нно, by the day; поме́сячно, by the month.

побагрове́ть *v., pfv. of* **багрове́ть**.

поба́иваться *v.r.impfv.* (*with gen. or inf.*) *colloq.* to be somewhat afraid.

поба́ливать *v.impfv., colloq.* to ache a little; ache on and off; ache now and then.

побасёнка [*gen. pl.* -**нок**] *n., colloq.* little story.

побе́г *n.* 1, escape. 2, *bot.* sprout; shoot.

побе́гать *v.pfv.* to do a little running.

побегу́шки *n.pl., in* **быть на побегу́шках**, *colloq.* 1, to run errands. 2, (*with* у) to be at someone's beck and call.

побе́да *n.* victory.

победи́тель *n.m.* [*fem.* -**ница**] victor; winner. —**кома́нда-победи́тельница**, the winning team.

победи́ть [*infl.* -**ди́шь, -ди́т**; *1st person sing. not used*] *v., pfv. of* **побежда́ть**.

побе́дный *adj.* 1, victory (*attrib.*); of victory. 2, victorious; triumphant. —**довести́ до побе́дного конца́**, to see through to victory; see through to a successful conclusion.

победоно́сный *adj.* victorious; triumphant.

побежа́ть *v.pfv.* [*infl. like* **бежа́ть**] 1, *pfv. of* **бежа́ть**. 2, to begin to run.

побежда́ть *v.impfv.* [*pfv.* **победи́ть**] 1, to defeat; conquer; vanquish. 2, *v.i.* to triumph; win. 3, *fig.* to conquer; overcome.

побеле́ть *v., pfv. of* **беле́ть**.

побели́ть *v., pfv. of* **бели́ть** (*in sense #1*).

побе́лка *n.* whitewashing.

побере́жье *n.* coast; seacoast.

побере́чь *v.pfv.* [*infl. like* **бере́чь**] 1, to save; preserve. 2, to take care of. 3, to watch; look after. —**побере́чься**, *refl.* to take care of oneself.

побесе́довать *v.pfv.* [*infl.* -**дую, -дуешь**] to have a chat.

побеспоко́ить *v.pfv.* to trouble; disturb. —**побеспоко́иться**, *refl.* 1, to trouble oneself. 2, to be concerned.

побира́ться *v.r.impfv., colloq.* to beg; live by begging.

поби́ть *v.pfv.* [*infl.* **побью, побьёшь**] 1, *pfv. of* **бить** (*in senses #2 & #6*). 2, to beat up. 3, to kill; slaughter; destroy. 4, (*of rain, hail, etc.*) to beat down; flatten; (*of frost*) to nip. 5, *sports* to break (a record). —**поби́ться**, *refl.* 1, to break; be broken. 2, (*of fruit*) to be bruised; be damaged. 3, *in* **поби́ться об закла́д**, to bet; wager.

поблагодари́ть *v., pfv. of* **благодари́ть**.

побла́жка [*gen. pl.* -**жек**] *n., colloq.* 1, indulgence. 2, concession. —**дава́ть побла́жку** (+ *dat.*), to be lenient with.

побледне́ть *v., pfv. of* **бледне́ть**.

побле́клый *adj.* faded.

побле́кнуть [*past* -**блёк, -блёкла**] *v., pfv. of* **блёкнуть**.

побли́зости *adv.* nearby. —**побли́зости от**, near.

побожи́ться *v.r., pfv. of* **божи́ться**.

побо́и [*gen.* -**бо́ев**] *n.pl.* beating.

побо́ище *n.* 1, *obs.* bloody battle. 2, *colloq.* brawl. —**ледо́вое побо́ище**, Battle on the Ice (*famous battle fought on the ice of Lake Peipus in 1242*).

поболта́ть *v.pfv., colloq.* 1, to have a chat. 2, to shake; agitate. 3, (*with instr.*) to dangle.

побо́льше *adj.* a little larger. —*adv.* a little more.

побо́рник *n.* champion; defender.

поборо́ть *v.pfv.* [*infl.* -**борю́, -бо́решь**] 1, to defeat; conquer. 2, *fig.* to overcome (a feeling). —**поборо́ть себя́**, to control oneself.

побо́ры [*gen.* -**ров**] *n.pl.* 1, bribery. 2, extortion.

побо́чный *adj.* 1, occurring or done on the side; secondary; incidental: побо́чный проду́кт, by-product; побо́чные эффе́кты, side effects; побо́чная рабо́та, sideline. 2, *obs.* illegitimate.

побоя́ться *v.r.pfv.* [*infl.* -**бою́сь, -бои́шься**] (*with gen. or inf.*) to be afraid.

побрани́ть *v.pfv.* to scold slightly; chide. —**побрани́ться**, *refl.* to have a quarrel.

побрата́ться *v.r., pfv. of* **брата́ться**.

побра́ть *v.pfv.* [*infl. like* **брать**] *colloq.* to take (all or many of something). —**чёрт побери́!**, 1, what the hell! 2, doggone it!; shucks!

побре́згать *v., pfv. of* **бре́згать**.

побрести́ *v.pfv.* [*infl. like* **брести́**] to trudge.

побри́ть *v., pfv. of* **брить**. —**побри́ться**, *refl., pfv. of* **бри́ться**.

поброди́ть *v.pfv.* [*infl.* -**брожу́, -бро́дишь**] *colloq.* to wander (*for a while*).

поброса́ть *v.pfv.* 1, to throw; toss. 2, to forsake; desert.

побря́кивать *v.impfv.* (*with instr.*) *colloq.* to rattle.

побряку́шка [*gen. pl.* -**шек**] *n., colloq.* 1, trinket. 2, (child's) rattle.

побуди́тельный *adj.* serving to cause or induce. —**побуди́тельная причи́на**, motive; incentive.

побуди́ть [*infl.* -**жу́, -ди́шь**] *v., pfv. of* **побужда́ть**.

побу́дка *n.* reveille.

побужда́ть *v.impfv.* [*pfv.* **побуди́ть**] to impel; induce; prompt; motivate.

побужде́ние *n.* 1, urge: внеза́пное побужде́ние, a sudden urge. 2, motive; reason: из коры́стных побужде́ний, for selfish motives/reasons. 3, initiative: по со́бственному побужде́нию, on one's own initiative; on one's own.

побуре́ть *v., pfv. of* **буре́ть**.

побыва́ть *v.pfv.* 1, (*with* в *or* на + *prepl.*) to visit; have been to (a place or many places). 2, (*with* у) to visit; go see (a person).

побы́вка *n., colloq.* 1, short visit; stay. 2, *mil.* furlough; leave.

побы́ть *v.pfv.* [*infl.* -**бу́ду, -бу́дешь**; *past* по́был, побыла́, по́было, по́были] to stay (somewhere).

пова́дить *v.pfv.* [*infl.* -**ва́жу, -ва́дишь**] *colloq.* to train. —**пова́диться**, *refl., colloq.* 1, (*with inf.*) to get into the habit of. 2, (*with a prep.*) to go all the time (to); drop in on constantly.

пова́дка [*gen. pl.* -**док**] *n., colloq.* 1, habit; mannerism. 2, *pl.* manner; ways.

пова́дно *adv., colloq., in* чтобы не́ было (+ *dat.*) пова́дно (+ *inf.*), so as to be certain that one will not do it again.

повали́ть[1] [*infl.* -**валю́, -ва́лишь**] *v., pfv. of* **вали́ть**[1] (*in sense #1*). —**повали́ться**, *refl., pfv. of* **вали́ться**.

повали́ть[2] *v.pfv.* [*infl.* ва́лит] *colloq.* 1, to flock; throng. 2, (*of snow*) to begin to fall heavily; (*of smoke*) to begin to pour out.

пова́льный *adj.* general; mass.

повалять *v., pfv. of* **валять** (*in sense #2*). —**повал-**
я́ться, *refl., pfv. of* **валя́ться.**

пова́нивать *v.impfv., colloq.* to smell slightly.

по́вар [*pl.* **повара́**] *n.* cook.

пова́ренный *adj.* culinary. —**пова́ренная кни́га,** cookbook. —**пова́ренная соль,** common salt; table salt.

поварёшка [*gen. pl.* **-шек**] *n., colloq.* ladle.

по-ва́шему *adv.* **1,** in your opinion. **2,** as you wish:
Пусть бу́дет по-ва́шему, have it your way.

пове́дать *v.pfv.* **1,** to tell. **2,** to announce.

поведе́ние *n.* behavior; conduct.

повезти́ *v., pfv. of* **везти́.**

повелева́ть *v.impfv.* [*pfv.* **повеле́ть**] **1,** (*with dat.*) to
order; command. **2,** [*impfv. only*] (*with instr.*) to rule;
rule over.

повеле́ние *n.* command.

повеле́ть [*infl.* **-велю́, -вели́шь**] *v., pfv. of* **повелева́ть.**

повели́тель *n.m.* **1,** sovereign; ruler. **2,** *colloq.* lord and
master.

повели́тельный *adj.* imperious; peremptory. —**пове-**
ли́тельное наклоне́ние, *gram.* imperative mood.

повенча́ть *v., pfv. of* **венча́ть** (*in sense #2*). —**по-**
венча́ться, *refl., pfv. of* **венча́ться** (*in sense #2*).

поверга́ть *v.impfv.* [*pfv.* **пове́ргнуть**] **1,** *obs.* to knock
down; topple. **2,** *obs.* to defeat. **3,** (*with* **в** + *acc.*) to
plunge (into a state, mood, etc.).

пове́ргнуть [*past* **-ве́рг, -ве́ргла**] *v., pfv. of* **поверга́ть.**

пове́ренный *n., decl. as an adj.* **1,** attorney. **2,** confidant. —**пове́ренный в дела́х,** chargé d'affaires.

пове́рженный *past passive part. of* **пове́ргнуть.**
—*adj.* fallen; toppled.

пове́рить *v., pfv. of* **ве́рить** *and* **поверя́ть.**

пове́рка *n.* **1,** check. **2,** roll call. —**на пове́рку,** in
actual fact; in reality.

поверну́ть *v., pfv. of* **повёртывать** *and* **повора́чи-**
вать. —**поверну́ться,** *refl., pfv. of* **повёртываться**
and **повора́чиваться.**

поверте́ть *v.pfv.* [*infl.* **-верчу́, -ве́ртишь**] **1,** to turn
slightly. **2,** to turn this way and that. —**поверте́ться,**
refl. to turn; turn this way and that.

повёртывать *v.* = **повора́чивать.** —**повёрты-**
ваться, *refl.* = **повора́чиваться.**

пове́рх *prep., with gen.* over: наде́ть сви́тер пове́рх
пла́тья, to wear a sweater over one's dress. Смотре́ть
на кого́-нибудь пове́рх очко́в, to look at someone
over one's glasses. —*adv.* above; overhead.

пове́рхностный *adj.* **1,** surface (*attrib.*). **2,** superficial.
—**пове́рхностно,** *adv.* superficially. —**пове́рхност-**
ность, *n.f.* superficiality.

пове́рхность *n.f.* surface. Держа́ться на пове́рх-
ности, to keep from sinking; keep afloat; keep one's
head above water.

по́верху *adv., colloq.* on top; on the surface.

пове́рье *n.* popular belief; superstition.

поверя́ть *v.impfv.* [*pfv.* **пове́рить**] **1,** to confide; entrust. **2,** *obs.* to check; verify.

пове́са *n.m.* playboy.

повеселе́ть *v., pfv. of* **веселе́ть.**

повесели́ть *v.pfv.* to amuse; entertain. —**повесе-**
ли́ться, *refl.* to have fun.

пове́сить [*infl.* **-ве́шу, -ве́сишь**] *v., pfv. of* **ве́шать.**
—**пове́ситься,** *refl., pfv. of* **ве́шаться.**

повествова́ние *n.* narration; narrative.

повествова́тельный *adj.* **1,** narrative. **2,** *gram.* declarative.

повествова́ть *v.impfv.* [*pres.* **-ству́ю, -ству́ешь**] to
tell; relate; narrate.

повести́ *v.pfv.* [*infl. like* **вести́**] **1,** *pfv. of* **вести́** (*in
senses #1 & #11*) *and* **поводи́ть**[1]. **2,** to begin; start;
launch. **3,** to manage; handle. —**повести́ себя́,** to
behave (*in a certain way*).

повести́сь *v.r.pfv.* [*infl. like* **вести́сь**] **1,** to begin (to be
conducted): повели́сь перегово́ры, negotiations have
begun. **2,** *impers.* to be the custom: И́сстари повело́сь
(+ *inf.*), since ancient times it has been the custom to...
3, (*with* **с** + *instr.*) *colloq.* to take up with (someone).

пове́стка [*gen. pl.* **-сток**] *n.* notice; notification.
—**пове́стка в суд,** summons; subpoena. —**пове́стка**
дня, agenda.

по́весть [*pl.* **по́вести, -сте́й, -стя́м**] *n.f.* story; tale.

пове́трие *n.* **1,** *obs.* epidemic. **2,** *colloq.* rage; craze; fad.

пове́шение *n.* hanging (*method of execution*).

пове́ять *v.pfv.* [*infl.* **пове́ю, пове́ешь**] **1,** to begin to
blow. **2,** *impers.* (*with instr.*) to be in the air: Пове́яло
весно́й, spring was in the air; пове́яло прохла́дой,
there was a coolness in the air.

повздо́рить *v., pfv. of* **вздо́рить.**

повзросле́ть *v.pfv.* to grow up; become an adult.

повива́льный *adj., in* **повива́льная ба́бка,** *obs.* midwife.

повида́ть *v., pfv. of* **вида́ть.** —**повида́ться,** *refl., pfv.*
of **вида́ться.**

по-ви́димому *adv.* apparently; evidently.

пови́дло *n.* jam.

пови́нная *n., decl. as an adj.* admission; confession (*of
guilt*). —**прийти́** (*or* **яви́ться**) **с пови́нной,** to give
oneself up; turn oneself in. —**принести́ пови́нную,**
to confess one's guilt.

пови́нность *n.f.* obligation; duty. —**во́инская по-**
ви́нность, compulsory military service; military conscription; the draft.

пови́нный *adj.* [*short form* **пови́нен, -нна, -нно,**
-нны] (*with* **в** + *prepl.*) guilty (of). *See also* **пови́нная.**

повинова́ться *v.r.impfv. & pfv.* [*pres.* **-ну́юсь, -ну́ешься**]
(*with dat.*) to obey.

повинове́ние *n.* obedience.

повиса́ть *v.impfv.* [*pfv.* **пови́снуть**] **1,** to hang; remain
suspended. **2,** (*with* **на** + *prepl.*) to hang on to; cling
to. **3,** to hang down; droop. —**повиса́ть** (**пови́снуть**)
в во́здухе, 1, to remain poised in midair. **2,** *fig.* to be
left hanging. **3,** *fig.* to elicit no response; go unanswered. **4,** *fig.* to be up in the air.

пови́снуть [*past* **пови́с, пови́сла**] *v., pfv. of* **повиса́ть.**

повиту́ха *n., obs., colloq.* midwife.

повле́чь *v.pfv.* [*infl. like* **влечь**] **1,** *pfv. of* **влечь. 2,** to
cause; lead to; result in.

повлия́ть *v., pfv. of* **влия́ть.**

по́вод[1] *n.* grounds; cause; reason. —**по по́воду** (+ *gen.*),
regarding; with regard to. —**по э́тому по́воду,** in this
connection. —**дать по́вод к** *or* **для,** to give rise to.
—**послужи́ть по́водом для,** to bring about; bring on.

по́вод² *n*. [*2nd loc.* поводу́; *pl.* пово́дья, пово́дьев] *n*. rein. —**быть** *or* **идти́ на поводу́ у,** to be under the thumb of. —**вести́ на поводу́,** to lead by the nose.

поводи́ть¹ *v.impfv*. [*pfv.* повести́; *pres.* -вожу́, -во́дишь] (*with instr.*) **1,** to move; wiggle: Он и бро́вью не повёл, he didn't bat an eye. **2,** to run along the surface of something: поводи́ть па́льцами по мате́рии, to run one's fingers over the material. —**поводи́ть глаза́ми,** to look; look around. —**поводи́ть но́сом,** to sniff the air.

поводи́ть² *v.pfv*. [*infl.* -вожу́, -во́дишь] to lead (a person); walk (a horse).

поводо́к [*gen.* -дка́] *n*. leash.

поводы́рь [*gen.* дыря́] *n.m.* **1,** one who leads a blind person. **2,** *obs.* guide. —**соба́ка поводы́рь,** Seeing Eye dog.

повози́ть *v.pfv*. [*infl.* -вожу́, -во́зишь] to take for a ride; take for a drive.

пово́зка [*gen. pl.* -зок] *n*. wagon.

пово́йник *n*. kerchief worn around the head by married peasant women in old Russia.

поволо́ка *n., in* глаза́ с поволо́кой, languishing eyes.

повора́чивать *v.impfv*. [*pfv.* поверну́ть] **1,** *v.t.* to turn: поверну́ть кран, to turn the faucet. **2,** *v.i.* to turn: поверну́ть напра́во, to turn right. —**куда́** (*or* **как) ни поверни́,** any way you look at it.

повора́чиваться *v.r.impfv*. [*pfv.* поверну́ться] **1,** to turn: Он поверну́лся ко мне, he turned toward me; ключ не повора́чивается, the key won't turn. **2,** [*often with* круго́м] to turn around. **3,** *fig.* to turn out. —**поверну́ться спино́й к,** to turn one's back on (*figuratively*). —**у меня́ язы́к не поверну́лся,** I couldn't bring myself (to tell him, say it, etc.).

поворожи́ть *v., pfv. of* ворожи́ть.

поворо́т *n*. **1,** turn: поворо́т напра́во, right turn; круто́й поворо́т, sharp turn. **2,** bend; turn (*in a road*). **3,** *fig.* turn; change: поворо́т к лу́чшему, turn/change for the better.

поворо́тливость *n.f.* **1,** agility. **2,** maneuverability.

поворо́тливый *adj*. **1,** nimble; agile. **2,** *colloq.* clever. **3,** (*of a vehicle*) maneuverable.

поворо́тный *adj*. **1,** rotary; turning; swivel (*attrib.*): поворо́тный круг, turntable; поворо́тное сиде́нье, swivel seat. **2,** *fig.* turning; decisive: поворо́тный пункт, turning point.

повреди́ть [*infl.* -жу́, -ди́шь] *v., pfv. of* вреди́ть *and* поврежда́ть. —**повреди́ться,** *refl., pfv. of* поврежда́ться.

поврежда́ть *v.impfv*. [*pfv.* повреди́ть] to hurt; injure; damage. —**поврежда́ться,** *refl.* to be damaged. Повреди́ться в уме́, to be mentally unbalanced.

поврежде́ние *n*. **1,** damage. **2,** injury.

повремени́ть *v.pfv., colloq.* **1,** (*with* с + *instr.*) to delay; hold off (doing something). **2,** to wait.

повреме́нный *adj*. **1,** (*of a publication*) periodic. **2,** (*of work, pay, etc.*) by the hour, day, week, etc.

повседне́вный *adj*. daily; day-to-day; everyday.

повсеме́стный *adj*. general; to be found everywhere. —**повсеме́стно,** *adv.* everywhere.

повста́нец [*gen.* -нца] *n*. rebel; insurgent. —**повста́нческий,** *adj.* rebel (*attrib.*); insurgent.

повстреча́ть *v.pfv., colloq.* to run into; meet. —**повстреча́ться,** *refl.* (*with dat. or* с + *instr.*) *colloq.* to run into; come across. Нам повстреча́лся (+ *nom.*), we ran into...; we came across...

повсю́ду *adv.* everywhere.

повто́р *n., colloq.* repetition.

повторе́ние *n*. **1,** repetition. **2,** recurrence. **3,** review (*of a lesson*).

повтори́тельный *adj*. repeat (*attrib.*). —**повтори́тельный курс,** refresher course.

повтори́ть *v., pfv. of* повторя́ть. —**повтори́ться,** *refl., pfv. of* повторя́ться.

повто́рный *adj*. **1,** a second; repeat (*attrib.*). **2,** (*of an election*) runoff. —**повто́рно,** *adv.* for the second time; once again.

повторя́ть *v.impfv*. [*pfv.* повтори́ть] **1,** to repeat. **2,** to review; go over. **3,** to copy; reproduce. **4,** to equal; tie (a record). —**повторя́ться,** *refl.* **1,** to happen again. **2,** to sound again; be heard again. **3,** to repeat itself. **4,** [*impfv. only*] to repeat oneself.

повыша́ть *v.impfv*. [*pfv.* повы́сить] **1,** to raise. **2,** to increase; heighten. **3,** to improve; enhance. **4,** to promote; give a promotion to. —**повыша́ться,** *refl.* **1,** to rise. **2,** to increase. **3,** to be promoted.

повыше́ние *n*. **1,** rise; increase. Повыше́ние зарпла́ты, pay raise. **2,** *in* повыше́ние по слу́жбе, promotion.

повы́шенный *adj*. increased; heightened. Повы́шенная температу́ра, a (slight) temperature.

повяза́ [*infl.* -вяжу́, -вя́жешь] *v., pfv. of* повя́зывать. —**повяза́ться,** *refl., pfv. of* повя́зываться.

повя́зка [*gen. pl.* -зок] *n*. **1,** band. Нарука́вная повя́зка, armband. Набе́дренная повя́зка, loincloth. **2,** bandage. Повя́зка на глазу́, eye patch.

повя́зывать *v.impfv*. [*pfv.* повяза́ть] to tie. —**повя́зываться,** *refl.* (*with instr.*) to tie (something) around oneself.

пога́нить *v.impfv., colloq.* **1,** to soil; get dirty. **2,** *fig.* to defile.

пога́нка [*gen. pl.* -нок] *n*. **1,** toadstool. **2,** grebe (*bird*).

пога́ный *adj*. **1,** (*of food*) inedible; impure. **2,** *colloq.* foul; vile. —**пога́ное ведро́,** garbage pail.

погаса́ть *v.impfv*. [*pfv.* пога́снуть] **1,** (*of lights, a fire, etc.*) to go out. **2,** *fig.* to dim; fade.

погаси́ть [*infl.* -гашу́, -га́сишь] *v., pfv. of* гаси́ть *and* погаша́ть.

пога́снуть [*past* пога́с, пога́сла] *v., pfv. of* га́снуть *and* погаса́ть.

погаша́ть *v.impfv*. [*pfv.* погаси́ть] **1,** to cancel (a stamp). **2,** to pay off (a debt, loan, etc.).

погаше́ние *n*. **1,** cancellation (*of a stamp*). **2,** paying off.

погиба́ть *v.impfv*. [*pfv.* поги́бнуть] **1,** to be killed. **2,** (*of a ship or plane*) to go down.

поги́бель *n.f., obs.* **1,** death. **2,** ruin; ruination. —**гнуть (согну́ть) в три поги́бели,** to tyrannize; browbeat. —**гну́ться (согну́ться) в три поги́бели,** to bend down very low.

поги́бнуть [*past* поги́б, поги́бла] *v., pfv. of* ги́бнуть *and* погиба́ть.

погла́дить *v., pfv. of* гла́дить (*in sense #2*).

погла́живать *v.impfv*. to stroke from time to time.

поглоща́ть *v.impfv.* [*pfv.* поглоти́ть] **1**, to absorb; soak up. **2**, to consume; use up. **3**, to engulf. **4**, *fig.* to absorb; engross. **5**, [*impfv. only*] *fig.* to devour (books, stories, etc.).

поглоще́ние *n.* absorption.

поглупе́ть *v., pfv. of* глупе́ть.

погляде́ть *v., pfv. of* гляде́ть. —погляде́ться, *refl., pfv. of* гляде́ться.

погля́дывать *v.impfv.* **1**, to glance from time to time. **2**, (*with* за + *instr.*) *colloq.* to keep an eye on.

погна́ть *v.pfv.* [*infl.* -гоню́, -го́нишь; *past fem.* погнала́] to drive. —погна́ться, *refl.* [*past tense stress as in* гна́ться] (*with* за + *instr.*) to chase after; take off after.

по́гнутый *adj.* slightly bent.

погну́ть *v.pfv.* to bend. —погну́ться, *refl.* to bend; become bent.

погнуша́ться *v.r., pfv. of* гнуша́ться.

погова́ривать *v.impfv., colloq.* to talk: Погова́ривают, что..., there is talk that..., ; it is rumored that...

поговори́ть *v.pfv.* to have a talk.

погово́рка [*gen. pl.* -рок] *n.* saying.

пого́да *n.* weather. —де́лать пого́ду, to make the difference. —ждать у мо́ря пого́ды, to wait for a miracle to happen.

погоди́ть *v.pfv.* [*infl.* -жу́, -ди́шь] *colloq.* to wait a while. —немно́го погодя́, a little while later.

пого́дный *adj.* **1**, yearly. **2**, weather (*attrib.*).

пого́док [*gen.* -дка] *n.* one of a pair of siblings a year apart in age: Ива́н и О́льга пого́дки, Ivan and Olga are a year apart in age.

пого́жий *adj.* (*of the weather*) fine: пого́жий день, a fine day.

поголо́вно *adv.* to a man: все поголо́вно, everyone to a man.

поголо́вный *adj.* general; total; all-inclusive.

поголо́вье *n.* total number (*of livestock, horses, sheep, etc.*).

поголубе́ть *v., pfv. of* голубе́ть.

пого́н *n., mil.* shoulder strap.

пого́нный *adj.* (*of measures*) linear.

пого́нщик *n.* cattle driver; drover. Пого́нщик му́лов, muleteer.

пого́ня *n.* **1**, pursuit; chase. **2**, pursuers. **3**, *fig.* pursuit: пого́ня за сча́стьем, pursuit of happiness.

погоня́ть *v.impfv.* **1**, to drive on; urge on (animals). **2**, *colloq.* to hurry; rush (someone).

погоре́лец [*gen.* -льца] *n.* person made homeless by a fire.

погоре́ть *v.pfv.* [*infl.* -рю́, -ри́шь] **1**, *colloq.* (*of many things*) to be burned. **2**, *colloq.* to burn down. **3**, to burn for a while. **4**, *colloq.* to be parched. **5**, *colloq.* to lose everything in a fire.

погорячи́ться *v.r.pfv.* **1**, to get worked up; get carried away. **2**, to be hasty; act hastily.

пого́ст *n.* village cemetery.

погости́ть *v.pfv.* [*infl.* -щу́, -сти́шь] (*with* у) to stay for a while (at the home of).

пограни́чник *n.* border guard.

пограни́чный *adj.* border (*attrib.*); boundary (*attrib.*); frontier (*attrib.*).

по́греб [*pl.* погреба́] *n.* cellar. —порохово́й по́греб, **1**, powder magazine. **2**, *fig.* powder keg.

погреба́льный *adj.* funeral (*attrib.*).

погреба́ть *v.impfv.* [*pfv.* погрести́] to bury; inter.

погребе́ние *n.* burial.

погрему́шка [*gen. pl.* -шек] *n.* (child's) rattle.

погрести́ *v.pfv.* [*infl. like* грести́] **1**, *pfv. of* погреба́ть. **2**, to row (*for a while*).

погре́ть *v.pfv.* to warm (*for a while*). —погре́ться, *refl.* to warm oneself (*for a while*); warm up a little.

погреши́ть *v., pfv. of* греши́ть (*in sense #2*).

погре́шность *n.f.* error.

погрози́ть *v.pfv.* [*infl.* -жу́, -зи́шь] to make a threatening gesture: погрози́ть па́льцем (+ *dat.*), to shake one's finger at.

погро́м *n.* **1**, pogrom. **2**, massacre.

погро́мный *adj.* (*of an article, speech, etc.*) vicious; rabble-rousing.

погро́мщик *n.* one taking part in a pogrom; thug.

погружа́ть *v.impfv.* [*pfv.* погрузи́ть] **1**, to dip; immerse. **2**, *fig.* to plunge: Го́род был погружён в темноту́, the city was plunged into darkness. **3**, *fig.* to absorb; engross: весь погружён в рабо́ту, completely absorbed in one's work; погружён в размышле́ния, lost in thought. —погружа́ться, *refl.* (*with* в + *acc.*) **1**, to sink (into); be submerged (in). **2**, (*of many people*) to pile; load (into *or* onto). **3**, *fig.* to be plunged into (darkness); become absorbed in (one's work); be lost in (thought).

погруже́ние *n.* immersion; submersion.

погрузи́ть [*infl.* -гружу́, -гру́зишь *or* -грузи́шь] *v., pfv. of* грузи́ть (*in sense #2*) *and* погружа́ть. —погрузи́ться, *refl., pfv. of* грузи́ться *and* погружа́ться.

погру́зка *n.* loading. —погру́зочный, *adj.* loading (*attrib.*).

погряза́ть *v.impfv.* [*pfv.* погря́знуть] (*with* в + *prepl.*) to become mired (in); get bogged down (in).

погря́знуть *v.pfv.* [*past* -гря́з, -гря́зла] **1**, *pfv. of* погряза́ть. **2**, *fig.* (*with* в + *prepl.*) to wallow (in).

погуби́ть *v., pfv. of* губи́ть.

погу́дка [*gen.* -док] *n., colloq.* **1**, tune; melody. **2**, story; tale. —ста́рая погу́дка на но́вый лад, the same old story with a new twist.

погу́ливать *v.impfv., colloq.* **1**, to stroll; walk up and down. **2**, to carouse (*from time to time*).

погуля́ть *v.pfv.* to go for a walk; take a walk.

погусте́ть *v., pfv. of* густе́ть.

под *also*, подо *prep.* **A**, *with instr.* **1**, under (*with verbs of location*): быть под водо́й, to be under water; сиде́ть под де́ревом, to be sitting under a tree. **2**, (*in various figurative senses*) under: под прися́гой, under oath; под чужи́м и́менем, under an assumed name. **3**, in the environs of (a city): жить под Москво́й, to live in the environs of Moscow. **B**, *with acc.* **1**, under (*with verbs of motion*): Мяч закати́лся под дива́н, the ball rolled under the couch; поста́вьте чемода́н под крова́ть, put the suitcase under the bed. **2**, (*with numbers denoting age*) under; not yet: Ему́ под со́рок, he is under/ not yet/ forty. **3**, (*with certain nouns*) toward:

под ве́чер, toward evening. **4,** (*in certain combinations*) down: по́д гору, downhill; свали́ться под откóс, to plunge down an embankment. **5,** to the sound of: танцева́ть под му́зыку, to dance to the music. **6,** for use as: отвести́ уча́сток под сад, to designate a plot as a garden; дóмик, обору́дованный под шкóлу, a small house equipped for use as a school. **7,** in imitation: мéбель под крáсное дéрево, furniture in imitation mahogany. **C,** *with acc. or instr.* (*of a container*) used to hold: бáнка под варéнье *or* под варéньем, jelly jar.

под- *also,* **подо-, подъ-** *prefix* **1,** *indicating motion upward or from under:* подбрáсывать, to toss up; подпирáть, to prop up. **2,** *indicating motion under:* подлéзть под дивáн, to crawl under the couch. **3,** *indicating motion toward:* подходи́ть, to approach. **4,** *indicating action to a slight degree:* поджáрить, to fry lightly; подмёрзнуть, to be slightly frozen. **5,** *indicating the adding of something:* подливáть сли́вок в кóфе, to add some cream to the coffee. **6,** *indicating stealth:* подслу́шивать, to eavesdrop. **7,** joining in; going along: подпевáть, to join in singing. **8,** (*with nouns*) under-; sub-: подпóлье, underground; подразделéние, subdivision. **9,** (*with adjectives*) on the outskirts of: подмоскóвный, on the outskirts of Moscow.

подавáльщик *n.* waiter; server. —**подавáльщица,** *n.* waitress.

подавáть *v.impfv.* [*pfv.* **подáть;** *pres.* **-даю́, -даёшь**] **1,** (*with certain nouns*) to give: подáть совéт/сигнáл/ комáнду, to give advice/ a signal/ a command/. **2,** to serve (food, a meal, etc.). **3,** *v.i.* to give alms. **4,** to bring; deliver (a vehicle). **5,** to hand in; submit; file; lodge; register. **6,** to help on with: подáть комý-нибудь пальтó, to help someone on with his (her) coat. **7,** *tennis* to serve. —**подавáть в отстáвку,** to submit (*or* tender) one's resignation. —**подавáть в суд, 1,** to sue; go to court. **2,** (*with* на + *acc.*) to bring (*or* file) suit against. —**подавáть гóлос, 1,** to announce one's presence. **2,** to cast one's vote. —**подавáть мысль,** to suggest an idea. —**подавáть надéжду, 1,** to offer hope. **2,** to give (*or* show) promise. —**подавáть примéр,** to set an example. —**подавáть при́знаки жи́зни,** to show signs of life. —**подавáть ру́ку,** to offer (*or* extend) one's hand. —**не подавáть ви́ду,** not to show; not let on. —**рукóй подáть,** a stone's throw (from).

подавáться *v.r.impfv.* [*pfv.* **подáться;** *pres.* **-даю́сь, -даёшься**] **1,** to be served. **2,** to move. **3,** *colloq.* to yield; give way. **4,** (*with* в *or* на + *acc.*) *colloq.* to leave (for); set out (for).

подави́ть [*infl.* **-давлю́, -дáвишь**] *v., pfv. of* **подавля́ть.** —**подави́ться,** *refl., pfv. of* **дави́ться.**

подавлéние *n.* suppression.

подáвленность *n.f.* depression; despondency.

подáвленный *adj.* **1,** (*of a sound*) muffled. **2,** (*of a feeling*) suppressed. **3,** depressed; despondent.

подавля́ть *v.impfv.* [*pfv.* **подави́ть**] **1,** to press down; weigh down. **2,** to suppress; put down; crush. **3,** to suppress; repress (a feeling, laugh, etc.). **4,** *usu. passive* to depress; dispirit. **5,** to overwhelm.

подавля́ющий *adj.* **1,** overwhelming: подавля́ющее большинствó, the overwhelming (*or* vast) majority. **2,** depressing.

подáвно *adv.* [*usu.* **и подáвно**] *colloq.* even more (so): Веснóй там жáрко, а лéтом и подáвно, it's hot there in spring and even more so in summer.

подáгра *n.* gout.

подáльше *adv., colloq.* **1,** a little farther away. **2,** as far away as possible. Держáться подáльше от, to keep away from. —**от грехá подáльше,** out of harm's way.

подари́ть *v., pfv. of* **дари́ть.**

подáрок [*gen.* **-рка**] *n.* gift; present. Получи́ть чтó-нибудь в подáрок, to receive something as a gift.

подáрочный *adj.* for a gift.

подáтель *n.m.* bearer.

подáтливый *adj.* **1,** pliable; malleable. **2,** *fig.* amenable; agreeable.

пóдать *n.f.,* pre-rev. tax. —**податнóй,** *adj.* tax (*attrib.*).

подáть [*infl. like* **дать;** *past* **пóдал** *or* **подáл, подалá, пóдало** *or* **подáло, пóдали** *or* **подáли**] *v., pfv. of* **подавáть.** —**подáться,** *refl.* [*past tense stress as in* **дáться**] *pfv. of* **подавáться.**

подáча *n.* **1,** giving; presenting; handing in. **2,** supply; delivery. **3,** *tennis* serve; service.

подáчка [*gen. pl.* **-чек**] *n., colloq.* handout; sop.

подая́ние *n.* alms.

подбавля́ть *v.impfv.* [*pfv.* **подбáвить**] (*with gen.*) to add a little (of something).

подбáдривать *v.impfv.* [*pfv.* **подбодри́ть**] to cheer up; hearten. —**подбáдриваться,** *refl.* to cheer up; take heart.

подбегáть *v.impfv.* [*pfv.* **подбежáть**] (*with* к) to come running (up to).

подбежáть [*infl. like* **бежáть**] *v., pfv. of* **подбегáть.**

подбивáть *v.impfv.* [*pfv.* **подби́ть**] **1,** to nail on. **2,** to line (a garment). **3,** *mil.* to cripple; knock out. **4,** *colloq.* to trip up; knock over. **5,** *colloq.* to incite; put up to. —**подби́ть бáбки,** to total everything up. —**подби́ть глаз** (+ *dat.*), to give (someone) a black eye.

подбирáть *v.impfv.* [*pfv.* **подобрáть**] **1,** to pick up. **2,** to tuck up. **3,** to draw up (the edge of a garment); put up (one's hair). **4,** to draw in (reins, one's stomach, etc.). **5,** to purse (one's lips). **6,** to select; choose. —**подбирáться,** *refl.* **1,** to be selected; be chosen. **2,** (*with* к) to sneak up to *or* on. **3,** (*with* под + *acc.*) *colloq.* to crawl under. **4,** *colloq.* to draw oneself up; straighten up. **5,** *colloq.* to draw oneself in; huddle up.

подби́ть [*infl.* **подобью́, подобьёшь**] *v., pfv. of* **подбивáть.**

подбодри́ть *v., pfv. of* **подбáдривать** *and* **подбодря́ть.** —**подбодри́ться,** *refl., pfv. of* **подбáдриваться** *and* **подбодря́ться.**

подбодря́ть *v.* = **подбáдривать.** —**подбодря́ться,** *refl.* = **подбáдриваться.**

подбóр *n.* **1,** selection; selecting. **2,** selection; collection; assortment. —**как на подбóр,** choice: я́блоки как на подбóр, choice apples.

подбóрка *n.* **1,** selection. **2,** group of related articles under a single heading in a newspaper.

подборóдок [*gen.* **-дка**] *n.* chin.

подбоче́ниться *v.r.pfv., colloq.* to place one's hands on one's hips. Стоя́ть подбоче́нившись, to stand with one's hands on one's hips.

подбра́сывать *v.impfv.* [*pfv.* **подбро́сить**] 1, to throw up; toss up. 2, (*with* под + *acc.*) to throw under; toss under. 3, to throw in; throw on (more of something). 4, to slip; place surreptitiously. 5, to abandon (a child). 6, *colloq.* to pick up (a passenger). 7, to shake; toss up and down. *Also impers.*: маши́ну/пассажи́ров си́льно подбра́сывало, the car/passengers was/were tossed all around (*or* kept bouncing up and down).

подбро́сить [*infl.* -шу, -сишь] *v., pfv. of* **подбра́сывать**.

подва́л *n.* basement. —**подва́льный,** *adj.* basement (*attrib.*).

подведе́ние *n.* laying (*of a foundation*). —**подведе́ние ито́гов** (+ *gen.*), summing up.

подве́домственный *adj.* (*with dat.*) under one's jurisdiction; subordinate (to).

подвезти́ [*infl. like* везти́] *v., pfv. of* **подвози́ть**.

подвене́чный *adj.* wedding (*attrib.*); bridal.

подверга́ть *v.impfv.* [*pfv.* **подве́ргнуть**] (*with dat.*) to subject (to); expose (to). Подверга́ть кри́тике, to criticize. Подверга́ть сомне́нию, to question; challenge. —**подверга́ться,** *refl.* (*with dat.*) to be subjected (to); be exposed (to); undergo.

подве́ргнуть [*past* -ве́рг, -ве́ргла] *v., pfv. of* **подверга́ть**. —**подве́ргнуться,** *refl., pfv. of* **подверга́ться**.

подве́рженный *adj.* (*with dat.*) subject (to); liable (to); prone (to); susceptible (to). —**подве́рженность,** *n.f.* susceptibility.

подвёртывать *v.impfv.* [*pfv.* **подверну́ть**] 1, to turn up; fold up; roll up. 2, to tuck in; (*with* под) tuck under. 3, to sprain; twist: подверну́ть но́гу, to sprain/ twist/turn one's ankle. 4, to tighten; screw tight. —**подвёртываться,** *refl.* 1, to be turned inward. 2, [*often with* по́д руку] *colloq.* to turn up; show up; appear.

подве́сить [*infl.* -шу, -сишь] *v., pfv. of* **подве́шивать**.

подве́ска [*gen. pl.* -сок] *n.* 1, hanging up. 2, *mech.* suspension. 3, pendant.

подвесно́й *adj.* hanging; suspended. —**подвесна́я кана́тная доро́га**, (aerial) tramway. —**подвесно́й мост**, suspension bridge. —**подвесно́й мото́р**, outboard motor.

подвести́ [*infl. like* вести́] *v., pfv. of* **подводи́ть**.

подве́тренный *adj.* leeward.

подве́шивать *v.impfv.* [*pfv.* **подве́сить**] to hang; suspend. —**в подве́шенном состоя́нии**, in a state of limbo. —**у него́ язы́к хорошо́ подве́шен**, he is a glib talker.

подвива́ть *v.impfv.* [*pfv.* **подви́ть**] to curl slightly.

по́двиг *n.* feat; exploit.

подви́гать *v.pfv.* (*with instr.*) to move (a part of one's body) slightly; wiggle. —**подви́гаться,** *refl.* to move a little.

подвига́ть *v.impfv.* [*pfv.* **подви́нуть**] 1, to move. 2, *fig., colloq.* to give a push to; get (something) moving. —**подвига́ться,** *refl.* 1, to move. 2, to move over. 3, to edge (toward, forward, etc.). 4, *fig.* to make progress.

подви́д *n.* subspecies.

подви́жник *n.* 1, religious ascetic. 2, (*with gen.*) devotee (of); champion (of).

подвижно́й *adj.* mobile. —**подвижны́е и́гры,** outdoor games. —**подвижно́й соста́в**, rolling stock.

подви́жность *n.f.* 1, mobility. 2, liveliness.

подви́жный *adj.* lively; active; quick. —**подви́жное ударе́ние,** shifting stress.

подвиза́ться *v.r.impfv.* to work (in a certain field): подвиза́ться на своём по́прище, to ply one's trade.

подвинти́ть [*infl.* -чу́, -ти́шь] *v., pfv. of* **подви́нчивать**.

подви́нуть *v., pfv. of* **подвига́ть**. —**подви́нуться,** *refl., pfv. of* **подвига́ться**.

подви́нчивать *v.impfv.* [*pfv.* **подвинти́ть**] to tighten; screw tight.

подви́ть [*infl.* подовью́, подовьёшь; *past fem.* подвила́] *v., pfv. of* **подвива́ть**.

подвла́стный *adj.* [*short form* -стен, -стна] (*with dat.*) subject (to); under the control (of).

подво́да *n.* cart; wagon.

подводи́ть *v.impfv.* [*pfv.* **подвести́**; *pres.* -вожу́, -во́дишь] 1, (*with* к) to lead up to; bring to. 2, *mil.* to bring up (reserves). 3, to extend: подводи́ть доро́гу к реке́, to extend the road to the river. 4, (*with* под + *acc.*) to place under; place beneath (*for support*); lay (a foundation, mine, etc.) under. 5, (*with* под + *acc.*) to place; subsume (in a certain category). 6, to adjust (a clock). 7, to touch up (*with make-up*): подвести́ бро́ви, to pencil one's eyebrows. 8, *colloq.* to let (someone) down; disappoint. —**подводи́ть бала́нс**, to strike a balance. —**подводи́ть ито́г** *or* **ито́ги,** 1, to tally the results; total everything up. 2, (*with dat.*) to add up; total. 3, to sum up; (*with gen. or dat.*) sum up the results of. —**подводи́ть к концу́,** to complete; finish. —**подводи́ть черту́ под** (+ *instr.*), to wind up; conclude. —**у меня́ живо́т подвело́,** I have an empty feeling in my stomach.

подво́дный *adj.* 1, underwater. 2, submarine (*attrib.*). —**подво́дный ка́мень**, 1, reef. 2, *fig.* pitfall. —**подво́дное крыло́,** hydrofoil. —**подво́дная ло́дка,** submarine. —**подво́дная скала́,** reef. —**подво́дное тече́ние,** undercurrent; undertow.

подво́з *n.* supply; delivery; transport.

подвози́ть *v.impfv.* [*pfv.* **подвезти́**; *pres.* -вожу́, -во́зишь] 1, to transport; bring; deliver. 2, to pick up along the way; give (someone) a lift.

подворо́тня [*gen. pl.* -тен] *n.* 1, space beneath a gate. 2, board covering this space.

подво́х *n., colloq.* (dirty or sneaky) trick.

подвы́пивший *adj., colloq.* tipsy; high; tight.

подвяза́ть [*infl.* -вяжу́, -вя́жешь] *v., pfv. of* **подвя́зывать**. —**подвяза́ться,** *refl., pfv. of* **подвя́зываться**.

подвя́зка [*gen. pl.* -зок] *n.* garter.

подвя́зывать *v.impfv.* [*pfv.* **подвяза́ть**] 1, to tie up (*so as not to fall or come loose*). 2, to tie around oneself. —**подвя́зываться,** *refl.* (*with instr.*) to tie (something) around oneself.

подгада́ть *v.impfv.* [*pfv.* **подгада́ть**] *colloq.* to arrive in time; time it right.

подгиба́ть *v.impfv.* [*pfv.* **подогну́ть**] 1, to fold over; bend over. 2, to tuck in; (*with* под) tuck under: подгиба́ть но́ги под себя́, to tuck one's legs under one.

3, to bend (one's knees). —**подгиба́ться**, *refl.* 1, to be turned up; be folded over. 2, (*of one's legs or knees*) to give way.

подгляде́ть *v.pfv.* [*infl.* -жу́, -ди́шь] 1, *pfv.* of **подгля́дывать.** 2, to catch sight of; spot; detect.

подгля́дывать *v.impfv.* [*pfv.* **подгляде́ть**] 1, to peek. 2, (*with* в + *acc.*) to peep through. 3, (*with* за + *instr.*) to peep at.

подгнива́ть *v.impfv.* [*pfv.* **подгни́ть**] 1, to rot from under; rot on the bottom. 2, to rot slightly.

подгни́ть [*infl. like* гни́ть] *v., pfv.* of **подгнива́ть.**

подгова́ривать *v.impfv.* [*pfv.* **подговори́ть**] (*with inf. or* на + *acc.*) to incite (to); put up to.

подголо́вник *n.* headrest.

подголо́сок [*gen.* -ска] *n.* 1, *music* second part; supporting voice. 2, *fig., colloq.* yes man.

подгоня́ть *v.impfv.* [*pfv.* **подогна́ть**] 1, to drive; steer (to a certain place). 2, to drive on; urge on. 3, to adjust; fit; tailor. 4, *colloq.* to time; schedule.

подгора́ть *v.impfv.* [*pfv.* **подгоре́ть**] (*of food*) to be slightly burnt.

подгоре́лый *adj.* slightly burnt.

подгоре́ть [*infl.* -ри́т] *v., pfv.* of **подгора́ть.**

подгота́вливать *v.impfv.* [*pfv.* **подгото́вить**] 1, to prepare. 2, to train. —**подгота́вливаться**, *refl.* (*with* к) to prepare (for); get ready (for).

подготови́тельный *adj.* preparatory.

подгото́вить [*infl.* -влю, -вишь] *v., pfv.* of **подгота́вливать** *and* **подготовля́ть.** —**подгото́виться**, *refl., pfv.* of **подгота́вливаться** *and* **подготовля́ться.**

подгото́вка *n.* 1, preparation. 2, training. 3, grounding; background.

подгото́вленность *n.f.* preparedness.

подготовля́ть *v.impfv.* = **подгота́вливать.** —**подготовля́ться**, *refl.* = **подгота́вливаться.**

подгреба́ть *v.impfv.* [*pfv.* **подгрести́**] 1, to rake up; rake together; (*with* под + *acc.*) rake under. 2, (*with* к) to row toward.

подгрести́ [*infl. like* грести́] *v., pfv.* of **подгреба́ть.**

подгру́док [*gen.* -дка] *n.* dewlap; jowl.

подгру́ппа *n.* subgroup.

подгу́зник *n.* diaper.

подгуля́ть *v.pfv., colloq.* to have a little too much to drink.

поддава́ть *v.impfv.* [*pfv.* **подда́ть**; *pres.* поддаю́, поддаёшь] 1, to kick (*from below*). 2, (*with gen.*) *colloq.* to increase; step up. 3, *colloq.* (*in certain games*) to give away (a card, piece, etc.). —**поддава́ться**, *refl.* 1, (*with dat.*) to give in (to); yield (to); succumb (to). 2, (*of a door*) to give way. 3, [*impfv. only*] (*with dat.*) to respond (to treatment); lend itself (to translation); (*with* не) defy (description).

поддавки́ [*gen.* -ко́в] *n.pl.* giveaway checkers.

подда́кивать *v.impfv.* [*pfv.* **подда́кнуть**] (*with dat.*) *colloq.* to say yes (to); agree (with); nod assent (to).

по́дданный *n., decl. as an adj.* subject; citizen: англи́йский по́дданный, British subject; америка́нский по́дданный, American citizen.

по́дданство *n.* citizenship.

подда́ть [*infl. like* **да́ть**; *past* по́ддал *or* подда́л, поддала́, по́ддало *or* подда́ло, по́ддали *or* подда́ли] *v., pfv.* of **поддава́ть.** —**подда́ться**, *refl.* [*past tense stress as in* да́ться] *pfv.* of **поддава́ться.**

поддева́ть *v.impfv.* [*pfv.* **подде́ть**] 1, to raise slightly (*from underneath*). 2, to hook; snag. 3, (*with* под + *acc.*) *colloq.* to put on (under); wear (underneath). 4, *fig., colloq.* to needle; twit (someone). 5, *fig., colloq.* to trick; cheat (someone).

подде́вка [*gen. pl.* -вок] *n.* man's long coat with a fitted waist.

подде́лать *v., pfv.* of **подде́лывать.** —**подде́латься**, *refl., pfv.* of **подде́лываться.**

подде́лка [*gen. pl.* -лок] *n.* forgery.

подде́лыватель *n.m.* forger; counterfeiter.

подде́лывать *v.impfv.* [*pfv.* **подде́лать**] 1, to forge. 2, to counterfeit. —**подде́лываться**, *refl.* 1, (*with* под + *acc.*) to imitate; pose (as). 2, (*with* к) *colloq.* to ingratiate oneself (with); play up to.

подде́льный *adj.* 1, forged; counterfeit. 2, artificial; imitation (*attrib.*). 3, false; affected; put on.

поддержа́ние *n.* maintenance.

поддержа́ть [*infl.* поддержу́, подде́ржишь] *v., pfv.* of **подде́рживать.**

подде́рживать *v.impfv.* [*pfv.* **поддержа́ть**] 1, to support; hold up. 2, to support; back: подде́рживать кандида́та, to support a candidate. Подде́рживать предложе́ние, to support a proposal; second a motion. 3, to maintain (order, discipline, cleanliness, etc.). 4, to keep up (a correspondence, conversation, etc.).

подде́ржка *n.* support.

подде́ть [*infl.* подде́ну, подде́нешь] *v., pfv.* of **поддева́ть.**

поддра́знивать *v.impfv.* [*pfv.* **поддразни́ть**] to tease.

поддразни́ть [*infl.* -дразню́, -дра́знишь] *v., pfv.* of **поддра́знивать.**

поддува́ло *n.* ash pit (*of a furnace*).

поддува́ть *v.impfv., impers.* to blow slightly: От окна́ поддува́ет, there is a slight draft from the window.

подде́йствовать *v., pfv.* of **де́йствовать** (*in sense #5*).

поде́лать *v.pfv., colloq.* to do. —**ничего́ не поде́лаешь**, there is nothing you can do about it.

поде́латься *v.r.pfv., colloq.* 1, (*with instr.*) (*of many people*) to become. 2, to happen.

подели́ть *v., pfv.* of **дели́ть.** —**подели́ться**, *refl., pfv.* of **дели́ться** (*in senses #2 & #3*).

поде́лка [*gen. pl.* -лок] *n.* 1, *usu. pl.* odd jobs. 2, homemade article.

поде́лом *adv., colloq.* deservedly; properly. —**ему́/ей поде́лом**, it serves him/her right.

поде́лывать *v.impfv., colloq., in* что (вы) поде́лываете?, how are you doing?; how are you getting along?

поде́льник *n., colloq.* associate; collaborator.

подёнка [*gen. pl.* -нок] *n.* mayfly.

подённый *adj.* by the day. —*n.* dayworker; day laborer. —**подённо**, *adv.* by the day. —**подённая**, *n., colloq.* daywork.

подёнщик *n.m.* [*fem.* -щица] dayworker; day laborer. —**подёнщина**, *n.* daywork.

подёргать *v.pfv.* (*with acc. or* **за** + *acc.*) to pull at (*a number of times*).

подёргивание *n.* (nervous) twitch.

подёргивать *v.impfv.* (*with acc. or* **за** + *acc.*) to pull (at). **2,** (*with instr.*) to twitch. *Also impers.:* Его подёргивало, he was twitching. —**подёргиваться,** *refl.* to twitch.

поде́ржанный *adj.* secondhand; used.

подержа́ть *v.pfv.* [*infl.* -держу́, -де́ржишь] **1,** to hold (*for a while*). **2,** (to keep (*for a while*). —**подержа́ться,** *refl.* **1,** (*with* **за** + *acc.*) to hold onto (*for a while*). **2,** to hold out (*for a while*).

подёрнуть *v.pfv.* **1,** to cover (with a thin layer of something). **2,** to shroud; envelop.

подешеве́ть *v., pfv. of* **дешеве́ть.**

поджа́ривать *v.impfv.* [*pfv.* **поджа́рить**] **1,** to roast; broil; fry (*lightly*). **2,** to toast (bread).

поджа́ристый *adj.* brown; nice and brown.

поджа́рить *v., pfv. of* **поджа́ривать.**

поджа́рый *adj., colloq.* lean; wiry.

поджа́ть [*infl.* **подожму́, подожмёшь**] *v., pfv. of* **поджима́ть.**

поджелу́дочный *adj.* pancreatic. —**поджелу́дочная железа́,** pancreas.

поджёчь [*infl.* **подожгу́, подожжёшь, ...подожгу́т;** *past* **поджёг, подожгла́, подожгло́, подожгли́**] *v., pfv. of* **поджига́ть.**

поджига́тель *n.m.* **1,** arsonist. **2,** *fig.* instigator. —**поджига́тель войны́,** warmonger.

поджига́ть *v.impfv.* [*pfv.* **поджёчь**] **1,** to set fire to; set on fire. **2,** *colloq.* to burn (food) slightly.

поджида́ть *v.impfv.* (*with gen.*) to wait for; await.

поджи́лки [*gen.* -**лок**] *n.pl., colloq.* tendons of the knee. —**у меня́ поджи́лки затрясли́сь,** my knees were shaking; I was quaking in my boots.

поджима́ть *v.impfv.* [*pfv.* **поджа́ть**] to draw up (one's legs); purse (one's lips); put (one's tail) between one's legs.

поджо́г *n.* arson.

подзабы́ть *v.pfv.* [*infl.* -**бу́ду, -бу́дешь**] *colloq.* to forget (some of). Я подзабы́л свой неме́цкий, my German is a bit rusty.

подзаголо́вок [*gen.* -**вка**] *n.* subtitle; subheading.

подзадо́ривать *v.impfv.* [*pfv.* **подзадо́рить**] *colloq.* to goad; egg on.

подзаты́льник *n., colloq.* blow on the back of the head.

подзащи́тный *n., decl. as an adj., law* client.

подземе́лье *n.* underground cave, cell or vault.

подзе́мка *n., colloq.* subway.

подзе́мный *adj.* underground; subterranean. —**подзе́мный толчо́к,** earth tremor.

подзерка́льник *n.* pier table.

подзо́л *n.* podzol.

подзо́рный *adj., in* **подзо́рная труба́,** spyglass.

подзыва́ть *v.impfv.* [*pfv.* **подозва́ть**] to call to; beckon.

поди́ *v., imperative of* **пойти́,** *colloq.:* поди́ прочь!, go away! —*particle, colloq., used with the familiar imperative of perfective verbs, suggesting that it is useless or pointless to do so:* Поди́ поспо́рь с ним!, go argue with him!; just try arguing with him!

подиви́ться *v.r., pfv. of* **диви́ться.**

подира́ть *v.impfv., usu. in* **подира́ть по ко́же,** to go up and down one's spine. —**моро́з по ко́же подира́ет** (*with* **у**), to get the creeps (*or* shivers); get chills up and down one's spine.

по́диум *also,* **по́дий** *n.* podium.

подка́лывать *v.impfv.* [*pfv.* **подколо́ть**] **1,** to pin up. **2,** (*with* **к**) to append (to). **3,** *colloq.* to needle; twit. **4,** (*with gen.*) to chop up some more of.

подка́пывать *v.impfv.* [*pfv.* **подкопа́ть**] **1,** to dig under. **2,** *fig., colloq.* to undermine. —**подка́пываться,** *refl.* (*with* **под** + *acc.*) **1,** to dig under; tunnel under. **2,** *fig., colloq.* to undercut (someone).

подкара́уливать *v.impfv.* [*pfv.* **подкара́улить**] *colloq.* **1,** to spot; catch. **2,** [*impfv. only*] to watch for; be on the lookout for.

подка́рмливать *v.impfv.* [*pfv.* **подкорми́ть**] *colloq.* **1,** to feed. **2,** to fatten up.

подкати́ть [*infl.* -**качу́, -ка́тишь**] *v., pfv. of* **подка́тывать.** —**подкати́ться,** *refl., pfv. of* **подка́тываться.**

подка́тывать *v.impfv.* [*pfv.* **подкати́ть**] (*with* **к**) **1,** to roll (a ball, barrel, etc.) up to; drive (a vehicle) up to. **2,** *v.i., colloq.* to roll up to; pull up to. **3,** *v.i., colloq.* to form: У меня́ ком подкати́л к го́рлу (*or impers.* у меня́ подкати́ло к го́рлу), I felt a lump in my throat. Тошнота́ подкати́ла к го́рлу, I felt nauseous. —**подка́тываться,** *refl.* **1,** (*with* **к**) to roll over (to). **2,** (*with* **под** + *acc.*) to roll under. **3,** (*with* **к**) *colloq.* to roll up; pull up to. **4,** (*with* **к**) *colloq.* to come running up to.

подка́шивать *v.impfv.* [*pfv.* **подкоси́ть**] **1,** to cut; trim (grass). **2,** to knock off one's feet; (*of a bullet*) cut down. **3,** *fig.* to demoralize. —**подка́шиваться,** *refl.* (*of one's legs*) to buckle; give way.

подки́дывать *v.impfv.* [*pfv.* **подки́нуть**] **1,** to throw up; toss up. **2,** to slip; place surreptitiously. **3,** to abandon (a child).

подки́дыш *n.* abandoned child; foundling.

подки́нуть *v., pfv. of* **подки́дывать.**

подкла́дка [*gen. pl.* -**док**] *n.* lining.

подкладно́й *adj.* placed underneath. —**подкладно́е су́дно,** bedpan.

подкла́дывать *v.impfv.* [*pfv.* **подложи́ть**] **1,** (*with* **под** + *acc.*) to place under; lay under. **2,** (*with gen.*) to add; put some more: подкла́дывать дров в ого́нь, to add wood to the fire. **3,** to put furtively; slip; stick; plant. **4,** (*with* **под** + *acc.*) *colloq.* to line: подкла́дывать шёлк под пальто́, to line a coat with silk. —**подложи́ть свинью́** (+ *dat.*), to play a dirty trick on.

подкла́сс *n.* subclass.

подкле́ивать *v.impfv.* [*pfv.* **подкле́ить**] **1,** (*with* **под** + *acc.*) to glue under; paste under. **2,** to glue up; paste up.

подключа́ть *v.impfv.* [*pfv.* **подключи́ть**] to connect; hook up. —**подключа́ться,** *refl.* **1,** to be connected. **2,** (*with* **к**) *colloq.* to join.

подко́ва *n.* horseshoe.

подкова́ть [*infl.* -**кую́, -куёшь**] *v., pfv. of* **подко́вывать.**

подко́вывать *v.impfv.* [*pfv.* **подкова́ть**] **1,** to shoe (a horse). **2,** *fig., colloq.* to train; ground: хорошо́ подко́ван в фи́зике, well-grounded in physics.

подко́жный *adj.* hypodermic.

подколо́дный *adj.*, *in* подколо́дная змея́, *colloq.* snake in the grass.

подколо́ть [*infl.* -колю́, -ко́лешь] *v.*, *pfv. of* подка́лывать.

подкоми́ссия *n.* subcommittee.

подкомите́т *n.* subcommittee.

подконтро́льный *adj.* (*with dat.*) under the control (of).

подко́п *n.* **1**, undermining. **2**, underground passage; tunnel. **3**, *pl.*, *colloq.* schemes; machinations. —вести́ подко́п под (+ *acc.*), to undercut.

подкопа́ть *v.*, *pfv. of* подка́пывать. —подкопа́ться, *refl.*, *pfv. of* подка́пываться.

подкорми́ть [*infl.* -кормлю́, -ко́рмишь] *v.*, *pfv. of* подка́рмливать.

подко́с *n.* strut; cross brace.

подкоси́ть [*infl.* -кошу́, -ко́сишь] *v.*, *pfv. of* подка́шивать. —подкоси́ться, *refl.*, *pfv. of* подка́шиваться.

подкра́дываться *v.r.impfv.* [*pfv.* подкра́сться] (*with* к) to sneak up to *or* on; steal up to.

подкра́сить [*infl.* -кра́шу, -кра́сишь] *v.*, *pfv. of* подкра́шивать. —подкра́ситься, *refl.*, *pfv. of* подкра́шиваться.

подкра́сться [*infl. like* кра́сться] *v.r.*, *pfv. of* подкра́дываться.

подкра́шивать *v.impfv.* [*pfv.* подкра́сить] to touch up. —подкра́шиваться, *refl.*, *colloq.* to put on some make-up.

подкрепи́ть [*infl.* -плю́, -пи́шь] *v.*, *pfv. of* подкрепля́ть.

подкрепле́ние *n.* **1**, reinforcement. **2**, *pl.*, *mil.* reinforcements. **3**, *colloq.* sustenance. —в подкрепле́ние (+ *gen.*), to support (an argument, assertion, etc.).

подкрепля́ть *v.impfv.* [*pfv.* подкрепи́ть] **1**, to reinforce. **2**, to fortify (with food, drink, etc.). **3**, *fig.* to support; bolster. —подкрепля́ться, *refl.* to fortify oneself (*with food or drink*).

по́дкуп *n.* **1**, bribery. **2**, graft.

подкупа́ть *v.impfv.* [*pfv.* подкупи́ть] **1**, to bribe. **2**, *fig.* to win over. **3**, (*with gen.*) *colloq.* to buy an additional quantity of.

подкупа́ющий *adj.* winning; appealing; engaging.

подкупи́ть [*infl.* -куплю́, -ку́пишь] *v.*, *pfv. of* подкупа́ть.

подла́живаться *v.r.impfv.* [*pfv.* подла́диться] *colloq.* **1**, (*with* под + *acc. or* к) to adapt (to); adjust (to). **2**, (*with* к) to try to please; play up to.

подла́мывать *v.impfv.* [*pfv.* подломи́ть] to break (*at the base*). —подла́мываться, *refl.* **1**, to give way; cave in; collapse. **2**, (*of one's legs, knees, etc.*) to give way; buckle.

по́дле *prep.*, *with gen.* beside; alongside of; near. —*adv.* alongside; nearby.

подлежа́ть *v.impfv.* [*pres.* -жу́, -жи́шь] (*with dat.*) to be subject (to); be liable (to).

подлежа́щее *n.*, *decl. as an adj.*, *gram.* subject.

подлежа́щий *adj.* (*with dat.*) subject (to); liable (to).

подлеза́ть *v.impfv.* [*pfv.* подле́зть] (*with* под + *acc.*) to crawl under.

подле́зть [*infl. like* лезть] *v.*, *pfv. of* подлеза́ть.

подле́сок [*gen.* -ска] *n.* underbrush; undergrowth.

подлета́ть *v.impfv.* [*pfv.* подлете́ть] (*with* к) **1**, to fly up to. **2**, *colloq.* to rush up to.

подлете́ть [*infl.* -чу́, -ти́шь] *v.*, *pfv. of* подлета́ть.

подле́ц [*gen.* -леца́] *n.* scoundrel.

подлива́ть *v.impfv.* [*pfv.* подли́ть] (*with gen.*) to add a little more (*by pouring*). —подлива́ть ма́сла в ого́нь, to add fuel to the fire; pour oil on the flames.

подли́вка *n.* sauce; gravy.

подли́за *n.m. & f.*, *colloq.* bootlicker.

подли́зываться *v.r.impfv.* [*pfv.* подлиза́ться] (*with* к) *colloq.* to lick (someone's) boots.

по́длинник *n.* original: чита́ть в по́длиннике, to read in the original.

по́длинный *adj.* **1**, original. **2**, genuine; authentic. **3**, true; real. —по́длинно, *adv.* truly; really. —по́длинность, *n.f.* authenticity.

подли́ть [*infl.* подолью́, подольёшь; *past fem.* подлила́] *v.*, *pfv. of* подлива́ть.

по́дличать *v.impfv.* **1**, to be mean; do mean things. **2**, to be servile; (*with* пе́ред) cater to; play up to.

по́дло *adv.* despicably.

подло́г *n.* forgery.

подло́дка [*gen. pl.* -док] *n.*, *colloq.* submarine (*contr. of* подво́дная ло́дка).

подложи́ть [*infl.* -ложу́, -ло́жишь] *v.*, *pfv. of* подкла́дывать.

подло́жный *adj.* forged; counterfeit.

подлоко́тник *n.* armrest.

подломи́ть [*infl.* -ломлю́, -ло́мишь] *v.*, *pfv. of* подла́мывать. —подломи́ться, *refl.*, *pfv. of* подла́мываться.

по́длость *n.f.* **1**, meanness; baseness. **2**, mean trick; dirty trick.

по́длый *adj.* mean; base; miserable; despicable.

подма́зать [*infl.* -ма́жу, -ма́жешь] *v.*, *pfv. of* подма́зывать. —подма́заться, *refl.*, *pfv. of* подма́зываться.

подма́зывать *v.impfv.* [*pfv.* подма́зать] **1**, to grease. **2**, *colloq.* to grease the palm of. —подма́зываться, *refl.*, *colloq.* **1**, to put on some make-up. **2**, (*with* к) to play up to; curry favor with.

подманда́тный *adj.*, *in* подманда́тная террито́рия, mandated territory.

подмасте́рье [*gen. pl.* -рьев] *n.m.* apprentice.

подма́хивать *v.impfv.* [*pfv.* подмахну́ть] *colloq.* to sign hurriedly; sign without reading.

подма́чивать *v.impfv.* [*pfv.* подмочи́ть] **1**, to wet slightly. **2**, (*usu. passive*) *colloq.* to tarnish (someone's reputation).

подме́на *also*, подме́н *n.* (improper or illegal) substitution.

подмени́ть [*infl.* -меню́, -ме́нишь] *v.*, *pfv. of* подменя́ть.

подменя́ть *v.impfv.* [*pfv.* подмени́ть] **1**, to remove (stealthily) and replace with something else: подменя́ть чей-нибудь экзаменацио́нный биле́т свои́м, to replace someone's exam paper with one's own; substitute one's own exam paper for someone else's. Кто́-то подмени́л мне шля́пу, someone took my hat (instead of his own). **2**, to replace; take the place of (*for a short time*).

подмерза́ть *v.impfv.* [*pfv.* **подмёрзнуть**] to freeze slightly; become slightly frozen.

подмёрзнуть [*past* -мёрз, -мёрзла] *v.*, *pfv. of* **подмерза́ть**.

подмести́ [*infl. like* **мести́**] *v.*, *pfv. of* **подмета́ть**.

подмета́льщик *n.m.* [*fem.* -щица] sweeper.

подмета́ть *v.impfv.* [*pfv.* **подмести́**] to sweep.

подме́тить [*infl.* -чу, -тишь] *v.*, *pfv. of* **подмеча́ть**.

подмётка [*gen. pl.* -ток] *n.* sole (*of a shoe*). —в подмётки не годи́ться (+ *dat.*), to be unable to hold a candle to.

подмётный *adj.*, in **подмётное письмо́**, *obs.* anonymous letter.

подмеча́ть *v.impfv.* [*pfv.* **подме́тить**] to notice; spot; detect.

подме́шивать *v.impfv.* [*pfv.* **подмеша́ть**] (*with gen.*) to add a little (*by mixing*).

подми́гивать *v.impfv.* [*pfv.* **подмигну́ть**] (*with dat.*) to wink (at).

подмина́ть *v.impfv.* [*pfv.* **подмя́ть**] to crush. —**подмина́ть/подмя́ть под себя́, 1,** to pin down. **2,** *fig.* to trample upon; trample down.

подмо́га *n.*, *colloq.* help.

подмока́ть *v.impfv.* [*pfv.* **подмо́кнуть**] to get slightly wet.

подмо́кнуть [*past* -мо́к, -мо́кла] *v.*, *pfv. of* **подмока́ть**.

подмора́живать *v.impfv.* [*pfv.* **подморо́зить**] **1,** to freeze slightly; put in the refrigerator for a while. **2,** *impers.* to experience a bit of frost: Но́чью подморо́зило, there was some frost during the night.

подмоско́вный *adj.* located near (*or* on the outskirts of) Moscow.

подмо́стки [*gen.* -ков] *n.pl.* **1,** scaffold. **2,** the stage: на подмо́стках, on the stage; before the footlights.

подмо́ченный *adj.* **1,** slightly wet. **2,** *colloq.* (*of one's reputation*) slightly tarnished.

подмочи́ть [*infl.* -мочу́, -мо́чишь] *v.*, *pfv. of* **подма́чивать**.

подмыва́ть *v.impfv.* [*pfv.* **подмы́ть**] **1,** to wash (*from underneath*). **2,** to wash away. **3,** [*impfv. only*] *impers.*, *colloq.* to be dying to: меня́ так и подмыва́ет сказа́ть ей, I am dying to tell her.

подмы́ть [*infl.* -мо́ю, -мо́ешь] *v.*, *pfv. of* **подмыва́ть**.

подмы́шка [*gen. pl.* -шек] *n.* armpit.

подмы́шник *n.* (perspiration) shield (*sewn to the armhole of a dress*).

подмя́ть [*infl.* подомну́, подомнёшь] *v.*, *pfv. of* **подмина́ть**.

поднадзо́рный *adj.* under surveillance. —*n.* person under surveillance.

поднаторе́ть *v.pfv.* (*with* в + *prepl.*) *colloq.* to become adept in.

поднату́живаться *v.r.impfv.* [*pfv.* **поднату́житься**] *colloq.* to make an extra effort; try a little harder.

поднебе́сье *n.* the heavens; the skies.

поднево́льный *adj.* **1,** dependent; subject. **2,** (*of labor*) forced.

поднесе́ние *n.* **1,** giving (*of a gift*). **2,** *obs.* gift.

поднести́ [*infl. like* **нести́**] *v.*, *pfv. of* **подноси́ть**.

поднима́ть *v.impfv.* [*pfv.* **подня́ть**] **1,** to raise; lift. **2,** to pick up. **3,** to take up; carry up. **4,** to turn up (one's collar). **5,** *fig.* to rouse: поднима́ть на борьбу́, to rouse to action. **6,** *fig.* (*with various nouns*) to raise (a question, fuss, alarm, standard of living, etc.); increase (productivity); enhance (someone's prestige). **7,** to plow up: поднима́ть целину́, to plow up (*or* turn up) virgin soil. —**поднима́ть дух** *or* **настрое́ние** (+ *gen.*), to lift someone's spirits. —**поднима́ть на во́здух**, to blow up; blow sky-high. —**поднима́ть на́ ноги**, to arouse. —**поднима́ть на́ смех**, to hold up to ridicule. —**поднима́ть ру́ку на** (+ *acc.*), to raise a hand against.

поднима́ться *v.r.impfv.* [*pfv.* **подня́ться**] **1,** to go up; rise. **2,** (*with* по) to go up; climb; ascend; mount (stairs, a ramp, etc.). **3,** (*with* на + *acc.*) to climb up to (the roof, a certain floor, etc.). **4,** *fig.* to arise; break out; develop. —**рука́ не поднима́ется** (*with* у *and inf.*), one cannot bring oneself (to).

подновля́ть *v.impfv.* [*pfv.* **поднови́ть**] to freshen up; touch up.

подного́тная *n.*, *decl. as an adj.*, *colloq.*, in **вся подного́тная**, inside information; all there is to know.

подно́жие *n.* **1,** foot (*of a mountain*). **2,** pedestal.

подно́жка [*gen. pl.* -жек] *n.* running board. —**дава́ть** *or* **подставля́ть подно́жку** (+ *dat.*), **1,** to trip (someone). **2,** *fig.* to pull a fast one on.

подно́жный *adj.* situated or placed under one's feet. —**подно́жный корм**, pasturage.

подно́с *n.* tray.

подноси́ть *v.impfv.* [*pfv.* **поднести́**; *pres.* -ношу́, -но́сишь] **1,** (*with* в, на *or* к) to bring (to); carry (to). **2,** (*with* к) to hold up (to); lift up (to). **3,** to give; present (a gift).

подно́счик *n.* **1,** *mil.* carrier; handler. **2,** server of drinks (*in a tavern*).

подноше́ние *n.* **1,** giving; presenting. **2,** gift; present.

подны́ривать *v.impfv.* [*pfv.* **поднырну́ть**] (*with* под + *acc.*) to dive under.

подня́тие *n.* raising; lifting. —**подня́тием рук**, by a show of hands.

подня́ть [*infl.* подниму́, подни́мешь; *past* по́днял, подняла́, по́дняло, по́дняли] *v.*, *pfv. of* **поднима́ть**. —**подня́ться**, *refl.* [*past* подня́лся *or* подня́лся, подняла́сь, подняло́сь *or* подня́лось, подняли́сь *or* подня́лись] *pfv. of* **поднима́ться**.

подо *prep.* = **под**.

подоба́ть *v.impfv.* (*with dat.*) to befit; become.

подоба́ющий *adj.* **1,** proper; appropriate; fitting. **2,** (*with dat.*) befitting; appropriate (to); worthy (of).

подо́бие *n.* (*with gen.*) something resembling; semblance (of); likeness (of). Вы́глядеть не́ким подо́бием (+ *gen.*), to look something like...

подо́бно *prep.*, *adv.* like: Подо́бно отцу́, он..., like his father, he... —**подо́бно тому́, как**, just as.

подо́бный *adj.* [*short form* -бен, -бна] **1,** (*with dat.*) similar (to); like. Не име́ть себе́ подо́бных, to be one of a kind. **2,** such. **3,** *geom.* (*of figures*) similar. —**и тому́ подо́бное**, and so on; and so forth; and the like; et cetera. —**не́что подо́бное** (+ *dat.*), something resembling/ on the order of/ akin to/. —**ничегó по-дóбного,** nothing of the sort; nothing of the kind.

подобострáстие *n.* obsequiousness; servility. —**подобострáстный,** *adj.* obsequious; servile.

подóбранный *adj.* **1,** precise; efficient. **2,** neat; tidy.

подобрáть [*infl.* **подберý, подберёшь;** *past fem.* **подобралá**] *v., pfv. of* **подбирáть.** —**подобрáться,** *refl.* [*past tense stress as in* **брáться**] *refl., pfv. of* **подбирáться.**

подобрéть *v., pfv. of* **добрéть** (*in sense #1*).

подогнáть [*infl.* **подгоню, подгóнишь;** *past fem.* **подогналá**] *v., pfv. of* **подгоня́ть.**

подогнýть *v., pfv. of* **подгибáть.** —**подогнýться,** *refl., pfv. of* **подгибáться.**

подогревáть *v.impfv.* [*pfv.* **подогрéть**] **1,** to warm up. **2,** to reheat; warm over. **3,** *fig., colloq.* to rouse.

пододвигáть *v.impfv.* [*pfv.* **пододви́нуть**] (*with* **к**) to move up (to); move closer (to). —**пододвигáться,** *refl.* (*with* **к**) to move over (to); move closer (to).

пододея́льник *n.* blanket cover.

подождáть *v., pfv. of* **ждать.**

подозвáть [*infl.* **подзовý, подзовёшь;** *past fem.* **подозвалá**] *v., pfv. of* **подзывáть.**

подозревáемый *adj.* suspect(ed); under suspicion. —*n.* suspect.

подозревáть *v.impfv.* (*with* **в** + *prepl.*) to suspect (of). Я стал подозревáть, когдá..., I became suspicious when...

подозрéние *n.* suspicion.

подозри́тельный *adj.* suspicious. —**подозри́тельно,** *adv.* suspiciously. —**подозри́тельность,** *n.f.* suspiciousness; suspicion.

подои́ть *v., pfv. of* **дои́ть.**

подóйник *n.* milk pail.

подойти́ [*infl.* **подойдý, подойдёшь;** *past* **подошёл, подошлá, подошлó, подошли́**] *v., pfv. of* **подходи́ть.**

подокóнник *n.* window sill.

подóл *n.* lap (*of a skirt*).

подóлгу *adv.* for a long time; for hours on end.

подольщáться *v.r.impfv.* [*pfv.* **подольсти́ться**] (*with* **к**) to ingratiate oneself (with).

подóнки [*gen.* **-ков**] *n.pl.* dregs; residue. —**подóнки óбщества,** dregs of society.

подопéчный *adj.* under the care of a guardian. —*n.* ward; charge. —**подопéчная террито́рия,** trust territory.

подоплёка *n.* underlying cause; underlying basis.

подóпытный *adj.* experimental; used for experimental purposes. —**подóпытный крóлик,** guinea pig.

подорвáть [*infl.* **-рвý, -рвёшь;** *past fem.* **подорвалá**] *v., pfv. of* **подрывáть.**

подорожáть *v., pfv. of* **дорожáть.**

подорóжник *n.* plantain.

подорóжный *adj.* situated along a road; roadside (*attrib.*).

подослáть [*infl.* **-шлю, -шлёшь**] *v., pfv. of* **подсылáть.**

подоснóва *n.* true cause; underlying cause.

подоспéть *v.pfv., colloq.* **1,** (*of time*) to come. **2,** to arrive in time; come at the right time. Подоспéть на пóмощь (+ *dat.*), to arrive in time to help (someone).

подостлáть [*infl.* **подстелю, подстéлешь**] *v., pfv. of* **подстилáть.**

подоткнýть *v., pfv. of* **подтыкáть.**

ПОДОТЧЁТНОСТЬ *n.f.* accountability.

подотчётный *adj.* [*short form* **-тен, -тна**] **1,** (*of money*) on account. **2,** (*with dat.*) accountable (to).

подóхнуть [*past* **подóх, подóхла**] *v., pfv. of* **дóхнуть.**

подохóдный *adj., in* **подохóдный налóг,** income tax.

подóшва *n.* **1,** sole (*of a shoe*). **2,** *colloq.* sole (*of the foot*). **3,** foot (*of a mountain*).

подпадáть *v.impfv.* [*pfv.* **подпáсть**] (*with* **под** + *acc.*) **1,** to fall under; come under (the power, influence, etc. of someone). **2,** to fall into; come under (a certain category).

подпáивать *v.impfv.* [*pfv.* **подпои́ть**] *colloq.* to give (someone) too much to drink; intentionally make (someone) drunk.

подпáливать *v.impfv.* [*pfv.* **подпали́ть**] *colloq.* **1,** to singe; scorch. **2,** to set fire to; set on fire.

подпáлина *n.* **1,** *colloq.* burn mark. **2,** spot; dapple.

подпали́ть *v., pfv. of* **подпáливать.**

подпáсок [*gen.* **-ска**] *n.* shepherd boy.

подпáсть [*infl. like* **пасть**] *v., pfv. of* **подпадáть.**

подпевáла *n.m. & f., colloq.* lackey; yes man.

подпевáть *v.impfv.* **1,** to sing along; join in singing. **2,** (*with dat.*) to sing along with. **3,** *fig.* (*with dat.*) *colloq.* to echo; parrot.

подперéть [*infl.* **подопрý, подопрёшь;** *past* **подпёр, подпёрла**] *v., pfv. of* **подпирáть.** —**подперéться,** *refl., pfv. of* **подпирáться.**

подпи́ливать *v.impfv.* [*pfv.* **подпили́ть**] **1,** to saw at the base of. **2,** to shorten (*by sawing*).

подпили́ть [*infl.* **-пилю, -пи́лишь**] *v., pfv. of* **подпи́ливать.**

подпирáть *v.impfv.* [*pfv.* **подперéть**] to prop up. —**подпирáться,** *refl., colloq.* to prop oneself up.

подписáние *n.* signing.

подписáть [*infl.* **-пишý, -пи́шешь**] *v., pfv. of* **подпи́сывать.** —**подписáться,** *refl., pfv. of* **подпи́сываться.**

подпи́ска [*gen. pl.* **-сок**] *n.* **1,** subscription. **2,** signed statement; written pledge.

подписнóй *adj.* subscription (*attrib.*).

подпи́счик *n.* subscriber.

подпи́сывать *v.impfv.* [*pfv.* **подписáть**] **1,** to sign. **2,** to write at the bottom; add at the end. **3,** (*with* **на** + *acc.*) to take out a subscription for (someone) to (a publication). —**подпи́сываться,** *refl.* **1,** to sign one's name; (*with* **под** + *acc.*) to sign. **2,** (*with* **на** + *acc.*) to subscribe to (a publication). **3,** (*with* **под** + *instr.*) to subscribe to; agree with.

пóдпись *n.f.* **1,** signature. За пóдписью (+ *gen.*), over the signature of; signed by. **2,** caption.

подплывáть *v.impfv.* [*pfv.* **подплы́ть**] (*with* **к**) **1,** to swim up to. **2,** to sail up to.

подплы́ть [*infl. like* **плыть**] *v., pfv. of* **подплывáть.**

подпои́ть [*infl.* **-пою, -пóишь** *or* **-пои́шь**] *v., pfv. of* **подпáивать.**

подползáть *v.impfv.* [*pfv.* **подползти́**] **1,** (*with* **к**) to crawl up to; creep up to. **2,** (*with* **под** + *acc.*) to crawl under; creep under.

подползти́ [*infl. like* **ползти́**] *v., pfv. of* **подполза́ть.**

подполко́вник *n.* lieutenant colonel.

подпо́лье *n.* **1,** cellar. **2,** *fig.* underground: уйти́ в подпо́лье, to go underground. —**подпо́льный,** *adj.* underground (*attrib.*). —**подпо́льщик,** *n.* member of the underground.

подпо́ра *n.* prop; support. *Also,* **подпо́рка.**

подпо́рный *adj.* supporting. —**подпо́рная сте́нка,** retaining wall.

подпо́ртить *v.pfv.* [*infl.* **-чу, -тишь**] *colloq.* to spoil slightly.

подпору́чик *n., pre-rev.* second lieutenant.

подпо́чва *n.* subsoil.

подпоя́сать [*infl.* **-поя́шу, -поя́шешь**] *v., pfv. of* **подпоя́сывать.** —**подпоя́саться,** *refl., pfv. of* **подпоя́сываться.**

подпоя́сывать *v.impfv.* [*pfv.* **подпоя́сать**] to put a belt on; tie a belt around. —**подпоя́сываться,** *refl.* to put one's belt on.

подпра́вить [*infl.* **-влю, -вишь**] *v., pfv. of* **подправля́ть.**

подправля́ть *v.impfv.* [*pfv.* **подпра́вить**] to fix up; straighten; put right.

подпру́га *n.* girth; bellyband; surcingle.

подпры́гивать *v.impfv.* [*pfv.* **подпры́гнуть**] **1,** to jump up and down. **2,** to bounce up and down; bob up and down.

подпуска́ть *v.impfv.* [*pfv.* **подпусти́ть**] to allow to approach; allow to come near.

подпусти́ть [*infl.* **-пущу́, -пу́стишь**] *v., pfv. of* **подпуска́ть.**

подраба́тывать *v.impfv.* [*pfv.* **подрабо́тать**] *colloq.* **1,** to earn on the side. **2,** to work up; work out.

подра́внивать *v.impfv.* [*pfv.* **подровня́ть**] **1,** to level; make even. **2,** to trim (one's hair, beard, etc.).

подра́гивать *v.impfv., colloq.* **1,** to quiver. **2,** (*with instr.*) to shake (a part of one's body).

подража́ние *n.* imitation. —**подража́тель,** *n.m.* imitator. —**подража́тельный,** *adj.* imitative.

подража́ть *v.impfv.* (*with dat.*) to imitate.

подразделе́ние *n.* **1,** subdivision. **2,** *mil.* subunit.

подразделя́ть *v.impfv.* [*pfv.* **подраздели́ть**] to subdivide. —**подразделя́ться,** *refl.* to subdivide; be subdivided.

подразумева́ть *v.impfv.* to mean; have in mind. Под э́тим он подразумева́ет, что..., by this he means that... —**подразумева́ться,** *refl.* to be meant; be understood.

подраста́ть *v.impfv.* [*pfv.* **подрасти́**] to grow; grow up. —**подраста́ющее поколе́ние,** the rising generation.

подрасти́ [*infl. like* **расти́**] *v., pfv. of* **подраста́ть.**

подра́ться *v.r.pfv.* [*infl. like* **дра́ться**] to fight; get into a fight.

подре́зать [*infl.* **-ре́жу, -ре́жешь**] *v., pfv. of* **подреза́ть.**

подреза́ть *v.impfv.* [*pfv.* **подре́зать**] **1,** to cut; trim; clip; prune. **2,** *colloq.* to cut off (*on the road or highway*). —**подре́зать кры́лья** (+ *dat.*), to clip someone's wings.

подрисова́ть [*infl.* **-су́ю, -су́ешь**] *v., pfv. of* **подрисо́вывать.**

подрисо́вывать *v.impfv.* [*pfv.* **подрисова́ть**] **1,** to touch up. **2,** to paint in.

подро́бно *adv.* in detail.

подро́бность *n.f.* detail.

подро́бный *adj.* detailed.

подровня́ть *v., pfv. of* **подра́внивать.**

подро́стковый *adj.* adolescent.

подро́сток [*gen.* **-стка**] *n.* adolescent; teenager.

подруба́ть *v.impfv.* [*pfv.* **подруби́ть**] **1,** to chop (*at the base*). **2,** to hem.

подруби́ть [*infl.* **-рублю́, -ру́бишь**] *v., pfv. of* **подруба́ть.**

подру́га *n.* (female) friend.

подружи́ть *v.pfv.* [*infl.* **-дружу́, -дру́жишь** *or* **-дру́жишь**] to make (two people) friends; bring together. —**подружи́ться,** *refl., pfv. of* **дружи́ться.**

подру́ливать *v.impfv.* [*pfv.* **подрули́ть**] *aero.* (*with* **к**) to taxi up to.

подрумя́нивать *v.impfv.* [*pfv.* **подрумя́нить**] **1,** to redden; flush. **2,** to put some rouge on (something). **3,** to brown; toast. —**подрумя́ниваться,** *refl.* **1,** to flush; become flushed. **2,** to put on some rouge. **3,** (*of food*) to become nice and brown.

подру́чный *adj.* **1,** on hand; handy. **2,** improvised; makeshift. **3,** assistant. —*n.* assistant.

подры́в *n.* **1,** blowing up. **2,** *fig.* undermining.

подрыва́ть *v.impfv.* [*pfv.* **подорва́ть**] **1,** to blow up. **2,** *fig.* to undermine; subvert. **3,** [*pfv.* **подры́ть**] to dig under; dig the ground from under.

подрывни́к [*gen.* **-ника́**] *n.* demolition expert.

подрывно́й *adj.* **1,** demolition (*attrib.*); blasting (*attrib.*). **2,** *fig.* subversive.

подры́ть [*infl.* **-ро́ю, -ро́ешь**] *v., pfv. of* **подрыва́ть** (*in sense #3*).

подря́д *n.* contract. —*adv.* in a row; in succession.

подряди́ть [*infl.* **-ряжу́, -ря́дишь** *or* **-ряди́шь**] *v., pfv. of* **подряжа́ть.**

подря́дный *adj.* contract (*attrib.*); done on contract.

подря́дчик *n.* contractor.

подряжа́ть *v.impfv.* [*pfv.* **подряди́ть**] *colloq.* to hire.

подсади́ть [*infl.* **-сажу́, -са́дишь**] *v., pfv. of* **подса́живать.**

подса́живать *v.impfv.* [*pfv.* **подсади́ть**] **1,** (*with* **в** *or* **на** + *acc.*) to help (someone) into *or* onto. **2,** (*with* **к**) to seat next to. **3,** (*with gen.*) to plant (an additional quantity of). —**подса́живаться,** *refl.* [*pfv.* **подсе́сть**] (*with* **к**) to sit down near; take a seat near.

подса́ливать *v.impfv.* [*pfv.* **подсоли́ть**] to salt lightly; add a little salt to.

подсвети́ть [*infl.* **-свечу́, -све́тишь**] *v., pfv. of* **подсве́чивать.**

подсве́тка *n.* illumination; lighting.

подсве́чивать *v.impfv.* [*pfv.* **подсвети́ть**] to illuminate (from below); light up.

подсве́чник *n.* candlestick.

подсе́ять *v.impfv.* [*pfv.* **подсе́ять**] (*with gen.*) to sow (an additional quantity of).

подсека́ть *v.impfv.* [*pfv.* **подсе́чь**] to chop off; chop down (*at the base*).

подсе́сть [*infl. like* **сесть**] *v., pfv. of* **подса́живаться.**

подсе́чь [*infl. like* **сечь**; *past* -сёк, -секла́, -секло́, -секли́] *v., pfv. of* **подсека́ть**.

подсе́ять [*infl.* -се́ю, -се́ешь] *v., pfv. of* **подсева́ть**.

подси́живать *v.impfv.* [*pfv.* **подсиде́ть**] *colloq.* **1,** to lie in wait for. **2,** to plot against; scheme against.

подси́нивать *v.impfv.* [*pfv.* **подсини́ть**] **1,** to color blue. **2,** to rinse in bluing; blue.

подсини́ть *v., pfv. of* **сини́ть** *and* **подси́нивать**.

подска́бливать *v.impfv.* [*pfv.* **подскобли́ть**] to scrape off.

подсказа́ть [*infl.* -скажу́, -ска́жешь] *v., pfv. of* **подска́зывать**.

подска́зка *n.* prompting. —**с подска́зки** (+ *gen.*), prompted by; with prompting from.

подска́зывать *v.impfv.* [*pfv.* **подсказа́ть**] **1,** (*with dat.*) to prompt. Не подска́зывать!, no prompting! **2,** to suggest (an idea, solution, etc.). Ло́гика подска́зывает, что..., logic suggests that...

подскака́ть [*infl.* -скачу́, -ска́чешь] *v., pfv. of* **подска́кивать** (*in sense #4*).

подска́кивать *v.impfv.* [*pfv.* **подскочи́ть**] **1,** to jump up. **2,** *colloq.* (*of prices, temperature, etc.*) to shoot up; soar; skyrocket. **3,** (*with* **к**) to run up to; come running up to. **4,** [*pfv.* **подскака́ть**] (*with* **к**) to come galloping up to.

подскобли́ть [*infl.* -скоблю́, -скобли́шь *or* -скобли́шь] *v., pfv. of* **подска́бливать**.

подскочи́ть [*infl.* -скочу́, -ско́чишь] *v., pfv. of* **подска́кивать**.

подсла́щивать *v.impfv.* [*pfv.* **подсласти́ть**] to sweeten.

подсле́дственный *adj.* under investigation. —*n.* person under investigation.

подслепова́тый *adj.* having poor vision.

подслу́живаться *v.r.impfv.* [*pfv.* **подслужи́ться**] (*with* **к**) *colloq.* to curry favor (with); play up to.

подслужи́ться [*infl.* -служу́сь, -слу́жишься] *v.r., pfv. of* **подслу́живаться**.

подслу́шать *v., pfv. of* **подслу́шивать**.

подслу́шивание *n.* eavesdropping. —**пункт** *or* **пост подслу́шивания**, listening post.

подслу́шивать *v.impfv.* [*pfv.* **подслу́шать**] **1,** to overhear. **2,** [*impfv. only*] to eavesdrop.

подсма́тривать *v.impfv.* [*pfv.* **подсмотре́ть**] **1,** to watch secretly. **2,** (*with* **в** + *acc.*) to peep through. **3,** (*with* **за** + *instr.*) to spy on. *See also* **подсмотре́ть**.

подсме́иваться *v.r.impfv.* (*with* **над**) to make fun of.

подсмотре́ть *v.pfv.* [*infl.* -смотрю́, -смо́тришь] **1,** *pfv. of* **подсма́тривать**. **2,** to catch sight of; spy; detect.

подсне́жник *n.* snowdrop.

подсо́бный *adj.* auxiliary; subsidiary; accessory; additional.

подсо́вывать *v.impfv.* [*pfv.* **подсу́нуть**] **1,** (*with* **под** + *acc.*) to put under; shove under. **2,** *colloq.* to slip; put furtively. **3,** *colloq.* to palm off.

подсозна́ние *n.* the subconscious. —**подсозна́тельный**, *adj.* subconscious.

подсоли́ть [*infl.* -солю́, -со́лишь *or* -соли́шь] *v., pfv. of* **подса́ливать**.

подсо́лнечник *n.* sunflower. —**подсо́лнечный,** *adj.* sunflower (*attrib.*).

подсо́лнух *n., colloq.* **1,** sunflower. **2,** *usu. pl.* sunflower seeds.

подсо́хнуть [*past* -со́х, -со́хла] *v., pfv. of* **подсыха́ть**.

подспо́рье *n., colloq.* help; support.

подспу́дный *adj.* hidden; secret; latent. —**подспу́дно**, *adv.* secretly.

подста́вить [*infl.* -влю, -вишь] *v., pfv. of* **подставля́ть**.

подста́вка [*gen. pl.* -вок] *n.* stand; support.

подставля́ть *v.impfv.* [*pfv.* **подста́вить**] **1,** (*with* **под** + *acc.*) to place under. **2,** (*with* **к**) to place near (to). Подста́вить стул (+ *dat.*), to pull up a chair for. **3,** (*with dat.*) to turn toward: подставля́ть лицо́ со́лнцу, to turn one's face toward the sun. **4,** to expose; leave vulnerable. **5,** to substitute. —**подставля́ть другу́ю щёку,** to turn the other cheek. —**подставля́ть но́жку** (+ *dat.*), **1,** to trip (someone). **2,** *fig.* to pull a fast one on.

подставно́й *adj.* **1,** placed near or under. **2,** *fig.* false. Подставна́я организа́ция, front organization. —**подставно́е лицо́,** dummy; front.

подстака́нник *n.* glass holder (*for use when drinking*).

подстано́вка *n., math.* substitution.

подста́нция *n.* substation.

подстёгивать *v.impfv.* [*pfv.* **подстегну́ть**] **1,** *colloq.* to fasten (on). **2,** to urge on; whip (a horse). **3,** *fig., colloq.* to spur on.

подстерега́ть *v.impfv.* [*pfv.* **подстере́чь**] **1,** to be on the watch for; be on the lookout for; lie in wait for. **2,** [*impfv. only*] (*of danger*) to lurk.

подстере́чь [*infl. like* **стере́чь**] *v., pfv. of* **подстерега́ть**.

подстила́ть *v.impfv.* [*pfv.* **подостла́ть**] (*with* **под** + *acc.*) to lay under; spread under.

подсти́лка [*gen. pl.* -лок] *n.* bedding.

подстра́ивать *v.impfv.* [*pfv.* **подстро́ить**] **1,** (*with* **к**) to build on to. **2,** *colloq.* to cook up. **3,** *in* подстро́ить шу́тку/по́длость/па́кость (+ *dat.*), to play a dirty trick on. —**подстра́иваться,** *refl., colloq.* **1,** to line up; form a line. **2,** (*with* **к**) to join. **3,** (*with* **под** + *acc.*) to adjust (to).

подстрека́тель *n.m.* instigator. —**подстрека́тельство,** *n.* instigation; incitement.

подстрека́ть *v.impfv.* [*pfv.* **подстрекну́ть**] **1,** to incite; goad; egg on. **2,** to arouse (a feeling).

подстре́ливать *v.impfv.* [*pfv.* **подстрели́ть**] to wound (an animal); wing (a bird).

подстрели́ть [*infl.* -стрелю́, -стре́лишь] *v., pfv. of* **подстре́ливать**.

подстрига́ть *v.impfv.* [*pfv.* **подстри́чь**] to clip; trim; crop. —**подстрига́ться,** *refl.* to get a haircut; get a trim.

подстри́чь [*infl. like* **стричь**] *v., pfv. of* **подстрига́ть**.

подстро́ить *v., pfv. of* **подстра́ивать**. —**подстро́иться,** *refl., pfv. of* **подстра́иваться**.

подстро́чник *n.* word-for-word translation.

подстро́чный *adj.* **1,** (*of a translation*) word-for-word. **2,** placed under a line or at the bottom of a page: подстро́чное примеча́ние, footnote.

по́дступ *n.* (*with* **к**) **1,** approach: К ним нет по́дступа, there is no approaching him. **2,** *pl.* approaches (to a city, fortress, etc.).

подступа́ть *v.impfv.* [*pfv.* подступи́ть] **1,** (*with* к) to approach. **2,** [*often with* к го́рлу *or* к се́рдцу] (*of emotions, tears, etc.*) to come; come over; (*of a lump*) to form. —подступа́ться, *refl.* (*with* к) to get close (to); get near.

подступи́ть [*infl.* -ступлю́, -сту́пишь] *v., pfv. of* подступа́ть. —подступи́ться, *refl., pfv. of* подступа́ться.

подсуди́мый *n., decl. as an adj.* defendant.

подсу́дность *n.f.* jurisdiction.

подсу́дный *adj.* **1,** subject to legal action. **2,** (*with dat.*) within the jurisdiction (of).

подсу́мок [*gen.* -мка] *n.* cartridge pouch.

подсу́нуть *v., pfv. of* подсо́вывать.

подсу́шивать *v.impfv.* [*pfv.* подсуши́ть] to dry (something) a little.

подсуши́ть [*infl.* -сушу́, -су́шишь] *v., pfv. of* подсу́шивать.

подсчёт *n.* **1,** count(ing). **2,** *pl.* calculations.

подсчи́тывать *v.impfv.* [*pfv.* подсчита́ть] to count up; calculate; compute.

подсыла́ть *v.impfv.* [*pfv.* подосла́ть] to send on a secret mission.

подсыпа́ть [*infl.* -сы́плю, -сы́плешь] *v., pfv. of* подсыпа́ть.

подсыпа́ть *v.impfv.* [*pfv.* подсы́пать] (*with gen. or acc.*) to add a little (of something) by sprinkling.

подсыха́ть *v.impfv.* [*pfv.* подсо́хнуть] to dry out a little.

подта́ивать *v.impfv.* [*pfv.* подта́ять] to melt a little; melt slightly.

подта́лкивать *v.impfv.* [*pfv.* подтолкну́ть] **1,** to push slightly; shove slightly; nudge. **2,** *fig.* to prompt; encourage; egg on.

подта́пливать *v.impfv.* [*pfv.* подтопи́ть] *colloq.* to heat slightly; warm slightly.

подта́скивать *v.impfv.* [*pfv.* подтащи́ть] (*with* к) to pull up to; drag up to.

подтасова́ть [*infl.* -су́ю, -су́ешь] *v., pfv. of* подтасо́вывать.

подтасо́вка *n.* **1,** dishonest shuffling (*of cards*). **2,** *fig.* juggling (*of facts*).

подтасо́вывать *v.impfv.* [*pfv.* подтасова́ть] **1,** to shuffle (cards) dishonestly. **2,** *fig.* to juggle (facts).

подта́чивать *v.impfv.* [*pfv.* подточи́ть] **1,** to sharpen. **2,** to eat away; corrode. **3,** *fig.* to undermine; sap.

подта́шнивать *v.impfv., impers.* to become slightly nauseous.

подтащи́ть [*infl.* -тащу́, -та́щишь] *v., pfv. of* подта́скивать.

подта́ять [*infl.* -та́ет] *v., pfv. of* подта́ивать.

подтверди́ть [*infl.* -жу́, -ди́шь] *v., pfv. of* подтвержда́ть. —подтверди́ться, *refl., pfv. of* подтвержда́ться.

подтвержда́ть *v.impfv.* [*pfv.* подтверди́ть] to confirm; corroborate; bear out. Подтвержда́ть получе́ние (+ *gen.*), to acknowledge receipt of. —подтвержда́ться, *refl.* to be borne out; prove correct.

подтвержде́ние *n.* confirmation; corroboration.

подтёк *n.* **1,** streak. **2,** bruise.

подтека́ть *v.impfv.* [*pfv.* подте́чь] **1,** (*with* под + *acc.*) to flow under; run under. **2,** (*of a container*) to leak.

подте́кст *n.* underlying theme.

подтере́ть [*infl.* подотру́, подотрёшь; *past* подтёр, -тёрла] *v., pfv. of* подтира́ть.

подте́чь [*infl. like* течь] *v., pfv. of* подтека́ть.

подтира́ть *v.impfv.* [*pfv.* подтере́ть] to wipe up.

подтолкну́ть *v., pfv. of* подта́лкивать.

подтопи́ть [*infl.* -топлю́, -то́пишь] *v., pfv. of* подта́пливать.

подточи́ть [*infl.* -точу́, -то́чишь] *v., pfv. of* подта́чивать.

подтру́нивание *n.* teasing; joshing.

подтру́нивать *v.impfv.* [*pfv.* подтруни́ть] (*with* над) to poke fun at; tease; kid.

подтыка́ть *v.impfv.* [*pfv.* подоткну́ть] to tuck in; tuck under.

подтя́гивать *v.impfv.* [*pfv.* подтяну́ть] **1,** to tighten; pull tight. **2,** to pull up. **3,** (*with* к) to pull up to; drag to. **4,** (*with* под + *acc.*) to pull under; drag under. **5,** *mil.* to bring up (troops, equipment, etc.); (*with* к) move up (to); move closer (to). **6,** *fig., colloq.* to get after; clamp down on. **7,** *fig., colloq.* to bring (a poor student) up to the level of the rest. **8,** *v.i.* to join in singing. —подтя́гиваться, *refl.* **1,** to tighten one's belt. **2,** to pull oneself up. **3,** (*of troops*) to move up. **4,** *fig., colloq.* to catch up with the rest.

подтя́жка [*gen. pl.* -жек] *n.* suspender.

подтя́нутый *adj.* smart; neat; fresh.

подтяну́ть [*infl.* -тяну́, -тя́нешь] *v., pfv. of* подтя́гивать. —подтяну́ться, *refl., pfv. of* подтя́гиваться.

поду́мать *v.pfv.* **1,** *pfv. of* ду́мать. **2,** to think for a moment. —и не поду́маю!, I wouldn't dream of it! —поду́мать то́лько!, just think!; just imagine!

поду́мывать *v.impfv.* (*with inf. or* о) *colloq.* to think of or about; consider (doing something).

подурне́ть *v., pfv. of* дурне́ть.

поду́ть *v.pfv.* **1,** *pfv. of* дуть. **2,** to begin to blow.

поду́чивать *v.impfv.* [*pfv.* подучи́ть] *colloq.* **1,** to teach. **2,** to learn. **3,** to egg on. —поду́чиваться, *refl.* (*with dat. or inf.*) *colloq.* to learn.

подучи́ть [*infl.* -учу́, -у́чишь] *v., pfv. of* поду́чивать. —подучи́ться, *refl., pfv. of* поду́чиваться.

поду́шечка [*gen. pl.* -чек] *n., dim. of* поду́шка. —поду́шечка для була́вок, pincushion.

подуши́ть *v.pfv.* [*infl.* -душу́, -ду́шишь] to perfume; put some perfume on. —подуши́ться, *refl.* to put on some perfume.

поду́шка [*gen. pl.* -шек] *n.* pillow; cushion. —поду́шка для штемпеле́й, stamp pad; ink pad.

поду́шный *adj., in* поду́шный нало́г; поду́шная по́дать, poll tax; tax per head.

подфа́рник *n.* parking light.

подхали́м *n.* toady; sycophant.

подхали́мничать *v.impfv., colloq.* **1,** to be servile; bow and scrape. **2,** (*with* пе́ред) to curry favor with; play up to.

подхали́мство *n.* toadyism.

подхва́т *n., in* на подхва́те, *colloq.* ready to carry out any assignment.

подхвати́ть [*infl.* -хвачу́, -хва́тишь] *v., pfv. of* подхва́тывать.

подхва́тывать *v.impfv.* [*pfv.* **подхвати́ть**] **1**, to catch; grasp; snatch. **2**, *colloq.* to catch; pick up (an illness). **3**, to pick up (information, an expression, etc.). **4**, to join in (singing, a conversation, etc.).

подхлёстывать *v.impfv.* [*pfv.* **подхлестну́ть**] **1**, to whip; urge on (a horse). **2**, *fig., colloq.* to urge on; spur; stimulate.

подхо́д *n.* approach. —**на подхо́де**, approaching; coming soon; on the way; not far off.

подходи́ть *v.impfv.* [*pfv.* **подойти́**; *pres.* **-хожу́, -хо́дишь**] **1**, (*with* к) to approach; come up to; walk up to. **2**, to approach; come near. **3**, to do; be suitable. **4**, (*with dat.*) to suit; fit; be right for. Подходи́ть на роль (+ *gen.*), to fit the part of. **5**, (*with dat.*) (*of an article of clothing*) to fit (someone). **6**, (*with* к) (*of an article of clothing*) to go (well) with; (*of a key*) to fit (a lock). **7**, (*with* под + *acc.*) to fit; fall within (a definition, category, etc.).

подходя́щий *adj.* suitable; proper; appropriate; right.

подцепи́ть [*infl.* **-цеплю́, -це́пишь**] *v., pfv. of* **подцепля́ть**.

подцепля́ть *v.impfv.* [*pfv.* **подцепи́ть**] *colloq.* **1**, to hook on; couple. **2**, *fig.* to get; acquire; catch.

подча́с *adv.* sometimes; at times.

подчёркивать *v.impfv.* [*pfv.* **подчеркну́ть**] **1**, to underline. **2**, to emphasize; stress.

подчёркнуто *adv.* **1**, with emphasis. **2**, pointedly. —**подчёркнутый**, *adj.* pointed; emphatic.

подчеркну́ть *v., pfv. of* **подчёркивать**.

подчине́ние *n.* **1**, subjugation. **2**, submission. **3**, subordination: быть в подчине́нии у, to be subordinate to. **4**, jurisdiction: переда́ть *or* перевести́ в подчине́ние (+ *gen.*), to place under.

подчинённость *n.f.* subordination.

подчинённый *adj.* **1**, subordinate. **2**, subject. —*n.* subordinate.

подчиня́ть *v.impfv.* [*pfv.* **подчини́ть**] **1**, to subjugate; subdue. **2**, (*with dat.*) to subordinate (to); subject (to). **3**, (*with dat.*) to place under the command or jurisdiction of. —**подчиня́ться**, *refl.* (*with dat.*) to submit (to); yield (to); obey.

подчи́стить [*infl.* **-щу, -стишь**] *v., pfv. of* **подчища́ть**.

подчи́стка *n.* **1**, cleaning up. **2**, *colloq.* erasure.

подчисту́ю *adv., colloq.* completely; leaving nothing behind.

подчи́тчик *n.* [*usu.* **корре́ктор-подчи́тчик**] copyholder.

подчища́ть *v.impfv.* [*pfv.* **подчи́стить**] **1**, to clean up. **2**, to erase; rub out.

подшива́ть *v.impfv.* [*pfv.* **подши́ть**] **1**, to sew under; sew on. **2**, to sew a hem in. **3**, to sole (a shoe). **4**, to file (newspapers, documents, etc.).

подши́вка [*gen. pl.* **-вок**] *n.* **1**, hemming. **2**, soling (*of shoes*). **3**, filing. **4**, *colloq.* file: газе́тная подши́вка, newspaper file.

подши́пник *n., mech.* bearing: ша́риковый подши́пник, ball bearing.

подши́ть [*infl.* **подошью́, подошьёшь**] *v., pfv. of* **подшива́ть**.

подшта́нники [*gen.* **-ков**] *n.pl., colloq.* men's drawers.

подшути́ть [*infl.* **-шучу́, -шу́тишь**] *v., pfv. of* **подшу́чивать**.

подшу́чивать *v.impfv.* [*pfv.* **подшути́ть**] (*with* над) **1**, to make fun of. **2**, to play a trick on.

подъе́зд *n.* **1**, approach. **2**, entrance; doorway.

подъездно́й *adj.* of approach. —**подъездна́я доро́га**, access road. —**подъездно́й путь**, *R.R.* siding.

подъезжа́ть *v.impfv.* [*pfv.* **подъе́хать**] (*with* к) to drive up to; ride up to; draw up to; pull up to.

подъём *n.* **1**, raising; lifting. **2**, *aero.* ascent; climb. **3**, slope; ascent; upgrade. **4**, *fig.* rise; upsurge. Быть на подъёме, to be on the rise. **5**, enthusiasm. **6**, instep. **7**, reveille. —**лёгок на подъём**, always ready to get up and go. —**тяжёл на подъём**, hard to get moving.

подъёмник *n.* hoist.

подъёмный *adj.* lifting (*attrib.*). —**подъёмные де́ньги**, moving (*or* relocation) money. —**подъёмный кран**, crane. —**подъёмный мост**, drawbridge. —**подъёмная си́ла**, **1**, lifting capacity. **2**, *aero.* lift. —**подъёмные**, *n.pl.* = подъёмные де́ньги.

подъе́хать [*infl.* **подъе́ду, подъе́дешь**] *v., pfv. of* **подъезжа́ть**.

поды́грывать *v.impfv.* [*pfv.* **подыгра́ть**] (*with dat.*) *colloq.* **1**, to accompany (*on a musical instrument*). **2**, to play up to. —**поды́грываться**, *refl.* (*with* к) *colloq.* to play up to.

подыма́ть *v.* = поднима́ть.

подыска́ть [*infl.* **подыщу́, поды́щешь**] *v., pfv. of* **поды́скивать**.

поды́скивать *v.impfv.* [*pfv.* **подыска́ть**] **1**, to find. **2**, [*impfv. only*] to look for; seek; try to find.

подыто́живать *v.impfv.* [*pfv.* **подыто́жить**] **1**, to add up; total. **2**, to sum up.

подыша́ть *v.pfv.* [*infl.* **-дышу́, -ды́шишь**] (*with instr.*) to breathe; take a breath of.

поеда́ть *v.impfv.* [*pfv.* **пое́сть**] **1**, to eat up. **2**, (*of insects, rodents, etc.*) to eat; devour.

поеди́нок [*gen.* **-нка**] *n.* duel.

поедо́м *also*, **пое́дом** *adv., colloq., in* есть (кого́-ни́будь) поедо́м, to make someone's life miserable (*by nagging*).

по́езд [*pl.* **поезда́**] *n.* train.

пое́здить *v.pfv.* [*infl.* **-е́зжу, -е́здишь**] to do some traveling.

пое́здка [*gen. pl.* **-док**] *n.* trip.

поездно́й *adj.* train (*attrib.*).

пое́сть [*infl. like* есть] *v., pfv. of* есть (*in sense #2*) *and* поеда́ть.

пое́хать *v.pfv.* [*infl.* **пое́ду, пое́дешь**] **1**, *pfv. of* е́хать. **2**, (*of a vehicle*) to start moving. —**пое́хали!**, let's go!; let's get started!; let's be off!

пожале́ть *v., pfv. of* жале́ть.

пожа́ловать *v., pfv. of* жа́ловать. —**пожа́ловаться**, *refl., pfv. of* жа́ловаться.

пожа́луй *particle* **1**, possibly; probably: Пожа́луй, вы пра́вы, you may be right; you are probably right. **2**, well, all right! (*indicating reluctant consent*).

пожа́луйте *v., imperative of* пожа́ловать, **1**, please come!; come in please! **2**, give me...!; let me have...!; your ... please!

пожа́луйста *particle* **1**, please! **2**, you're welcome!; don't mention it! **3**, certainly!; by all means!

пожа́р *n.* a fire: лесно́й пожа́р, forest fire.

пожа́рище *n.* scene of a fire; burned-out area.

пожа́рник *n.* fireman.

пожа́рный *adj.* fire (*attrib.*). Пожа́рная ле́стница, fire escape. Пожа́рная маши́на, fire engine. —*n.* fireman. —в пожа́рном поря́дке, *colloq.* hastily; in great haste; on the run. —на вся́кий пожа́рный слу́чай, *colloq.* so as to be prepared for any emergency.

пожа́тие *n.* handshake.

пожа́ть *v.pfv.* **1**, [*infl.* -жму́, -жмёшь] *pfv. of* жать¹ (*in sense #2*) *and* пожима́ть. **2**, [*infl.* -жну́, -жнёшь] *pfv. of* пожина́ть.

пожева́ть *v.pfv.* [*infl.* -жую́, -жуёшь] to chew.

пожела́ние *n.* wish: наилу́чшие пожела́ния, best wishes.

пожела́ть *v., pfv. of* жела́ть.

пожелте́лый *adj.* yellowed. *Also,* пожелте́вший.

пожелте́ть *v., pfv. of* желте́ть.

пожени́ться *v.r.pfv.* [*infl.* -же́нится] (*of two people*) to get married.

поже́ртвование *n.* contribution; donation.

поже́ртвовать *v., pfv. of* же́ртвовать.

пожи́ва *n., colloq.* easy money.

пожива́ть *v.impfv., in* как вы пожива́ете?, how are you?; how are you getting along?

поживи́ться *v.r.pfv.* [*infl.* -влю́сь, -ви́шься] *colloq.* **1**, (*with instr.*) to make money (out of *or* off of). **2**, (*with* за счёт + *gen.*), to profit (at the expense of).

пожи́зненный *adj.* life (*attrib.*); for life; lifetime (*attrib.*): пожи́зненное заключе́ние, life imprisonment. —пожи́зненно, *adv.* for life: назнача́ться пожи́зненно, to be appointed for life.

пожило́й *adj.* getting on in years.

пожима́ние *n.* shaking (of hands); shrug (of the shoulders).

пожима́ть *v.impfv.* [*pfv.* пожа́ть] **1**, *in* пожима́ть ру́ку (+ *dat.*), to shake someone's hand. **2**, *in* пожима́ть плеча́ми, to shrug one's shoulders.

пожина́ть *v.impfv.* [*pfv.* пожа́ть] **1**, *obs.* to reap. **2**, *fig.* to reap; gain: пожина́ть плоды́ (+ *gen.*), to reap the fruits (*or* benefits) of.

пожира́ть *v.impfv.* [*pfv.* пожра́ть] **1**, to devour; consume. **2**, *colloq.* to eat; gobble.

пожи́тки [*gen.* -ков] *n.pl., colloq.* belongings.

пожи́ть *v.pfv.* [*infl.* -живу́, -живёшь; *past* по́жил, пожила́, по́жило, по́жили] **1**, to live for a while. **2**, *colloq.* to live it up. —поживём — уви́дим, we'll see what happens.

пожра́ть [*infl. like* жрать] *v., pfv. of* пожира́ть.

пожури́ть *v., pfv. of* жури́ть.

пожу́хлый *adj.* withered; dried up.

пожу́хнуть *v., pfv. of* жу́хнуть.

по́за *n.* **1**, pose. Стать в по́зу, to strike a pose. **2**, *fig.* affectation; pretense.

позаба́вить *v.pfv.* [*infl.* -влю, -вишь] to amuse; entertain. —позаба́виться, *refl., colloq.* to have a little fun.

позабо́титься *v.r., pfv. of* забо́титься.

позабыва́ть *v.impfv.* [*pfv.* позабы́ть] *colloq.* to forget all about; completely forget.

позабы́ть [*infl.* -бу́ду, -бу́дешь] *v., pfv. of* позабыва́ть.

позави́довать *v., pfv. of* зави́довать.

поза́втракать *v., pfv. of* за́втракать.

позавчера́ *adv.* the day before yesterday. —позавчера́ ве́чером, the night before last.

позади́ *adv.* behind. —*prep., with gen.* behind.

позаи́мствовать *v., pfv. of* заи́мствовать.

позапро́шлый *adj.* before last: позапро́шлый год, the year before last.

поза́риться *v.r., pfv. of* за́риться.

позва́ть *v., pfv. of* звать.

позволе́ние *n.* permission. —с позволе́ния сказа́ть, **1**, if I may say so. **2**, if you could call it that.

позволи́тельный *adj.* permissible.

позволя́ть *v.impfv.* [*pfv.* позво́лить] (*with dat.*) **1**, to allow; permit. **2**, to enable; make it possible for. **3**, (*used negatively*) to prevent (someone from doing something). —позво́льте, **1**, (*with inf.*) allow me to... **2**, excuse me!; I beg your pardon! —позво́лить себе́, **1**, (*with inf.*) to venture (to); take the liberty of. **2**, to allow oneself; be able to afford: Не могу́ себе́ э́того позво́лить, I can't afford it.

позвони́ть *v., pfv. of* звони́ть.

позвоно́к [*gen.* -нка́] *n.* vertebra.

позвоно́чник *n.* spine; backbone.

позвоно́чный *adj.* vertebrate; vertebral. Позвоно́чный столб, spinal column. —позвоно́чные, *n.pl.* vertebrates.

по́здний *adj.* late. —до по́здней но́чи, till late at night.

по́здно *adv.* late. —*adj., used predicatively,* late: Уже́ по́здно, it is already late.

поздоро́ваться *v.r., pfv. of* здоро́ваться.

поздорове́ть *v., pfv. of* здорове́ть.

поздоро́виться *v.r.pfv., colloq., impers., used negatively with dat.* to be bad for: Ему́ не поздоро́вится от э́того, it will be bad for him; he will come out the worse for it.

поздрави́тельный *adj.* congratulatory.

поздра́вить [*infl.* -влю, -вишь] *v., pfv. of* поздравля́ть.

поздравле́ние *n.* congratulation. Прими́те мой поздравле́ния, (please) accept my congratulations.

поздравля́ть *v.impfv.* [*pfv.* поздра́вить] **1**, to congratulate. **2**, (*on holidays, birthdays, etc.*) to wish a happy...: поздра́вить кого́-нибудь с Но́вым го́дом, to wish someone a happy New Year.

позелене́ть *v., pfv. of* зелене́ть.

позёр *n.* play-actor. —позёрство, *n.* play-acting.

по́зже *adv., comp. of* по́здно, later.

пози́ровать *v.impfv.* [*pres.* -рую, -руешь] to pose.

позити́в *n., photog.* positive.

позитиви́зм *n.* positivism.

позити́вный *adj.* positive.

позитро́н *n.* positron.

позицио́нный *adj.* positional.

пози́ция *n.* **1**, position. **2**, *fig.* position; viewpoint: изложи́ть свою́ пози́цию, to state one's position. —сдать пози́ции, to yield; give ground. —уси́лить чьи́-нибудь пози́ции, to strengthen someone's hand.

познава́тельный *adj.* cognitive.

познава́ть *v.impfv.* [*pfv.* **позна́ть**; *pres.* **-знаю́, -знаёшь**] **1,** to get to know. **2,** to experience. **—познава́ться,** *refl.* [*impfv. only*] to become known; become recognized (*for what one is*).

познако́мить *v., pfv. of* **знако́мить. —познако́миться,** *refl., pfv. of* **знако́миться.**

позна́ние *n.* **1,** cognition. **2,** *pl.* knowledge. **—тео́рия позна́ния,** epistemology.

позна́ть [*infl.* **-зна́ю, -зна́ешь**] *v., pfv. of* **познава́ть.**

позоло́та *n.* gilding; gilt.

позолоти́ть *v., pfv. of* **золоти́ть.**

позоло́ченный *adj.* gilded; gilt.

позо́р *n.* shame; disgrace.

позо́рить *v.impfv.* [*pfv.* **опозо́рить**] to disgrace. **—позо́риться,** *refl.* to disgrace oneself.

позо́рище *n., colloq.* shameful event; disgrace; scandal.

позо́рный *adj.* **1,** disgraceful; shameful. **2,** ignominious. **—позо́рный столб,** pillory.

позуме́нт *n.* galloon; braid.

позы́в *n.* desire; urge.

позывно́й *adj., in* **позывно́й сигна́л,** call sign. **—позывны́е,** *n.pl.* call sign.

поигра́ть *v.pfv.* to play (*for a while*).

поимённо *adv.* by name.

поимённый *adj.* of names: **поимённый спи́сок,** list of names. **—поимённое голосова́ние,** roll-call vote.

поименова́ть *v.pfv.* [*infl.* **-ну́ю, -ну́ешь**] **1,** to call; name. **2,** to mention; list.

пои́мка *n.* catching; capture.

поинтересова́ться *v.r.pfv.* [*infl.* **-су́юсь, -су́ешься**] **1,** (*with instr.*) to show an interest (in). **2,** to inquire; ask.

по́иск *n., often pl.* **1,** search; quest. **2,** retrieval (*of information*). **3,** *mil.* reconnaissance raid. **—в по́исках** (+ *gen.*), in search of. **—пойти́** *or* **отпра́виться на по́иски** (+ *gen.*), to set out in search of.

поиска́ть *v.pfv.* [*infl.* **поищу́, пои́щешь**] **1,** *v.t.* to look for. **2,** *v.i.* to look: я поищу́, I'll look. Пощи́те в шкафу́, look in the closet.

поиско́вый *also,* **по́исковый** *adj.* **1,** search (*attrib.*): поиско́вая гру́ппа, search party. **2,** exploring; prospecting.

пои́стине *adv.* truly; indeed.

пои́ть *v.impfv.* [*pfv.* **напои́ть**; *pres.* **пою́, по́ишь** *or* **пои́шь**] **1,** to give (someone) something to drink. Пои́ть кого́-нибудь ча́ем, to serve someone tea. **2,** to water (cattle).

по́йло *n.* mash; swill.

по́йма *n.* flood plain.

пойма́ть *v., pfv. of* **лови́ть.**

по́йнтер [*pl.* **пойнтера́**] *n.* pointer (*dog*).

пойти́ *v.pfv.* [*infl.* **пойду́, пойдёшь**; *past* **пошёл, пошла́, пошло́, пошли́**] **1,** *pfv. of* **идти́. 2,** to begin to walk; set out. **3,** (*of a vehicle*) to start moving. **4,** (*of rain, snow, etc.*) to begin to fall: Пошёл дождь, it began to rain. **5,** (*of a liquid*) to begin to flow. **6,** (*with* **на** + *acc.*) to do; take the step of; resort to: Он не пойдёт на э́то, he won't do (something like) that. Пойти́ на круты́е ме́ры, to resort to drastic measures. **7,** (*with inf.*) *colloq.* to begin (to). **8,** *past tense only,*

giving imperative meaning, go!; leave!; go away! Пошёл вон!, away with you!; be off! **9,** *past tense only* (*with* **в** + *acc.*) to resemble; take after (one's father or mother). **—я пошёл,** *colloq.* I'm leaving; I'm off. **—е́сли (уж) на то пошло́,** for that matter; if it comes to that. *See also* **поди́.**

пока́ *adv.* for the time being; for the present; for the moment; for now. **—***conj.* **1,** while: пока́ я ждал, while I was waiting. **2,** as long as: пока́ я бу́ду жив, as long as I live. **3,** (*with* **не** *and future tense of verb*) until: пока́ она́ не придёт, until she comes. **4,** (*with* **не** *and past tense of verb*) before: пока́ (я) не забы́л, before I forget. Пока́ не по́здно, before it is too late. **—***interj.* [*also,* **ну, пока́**] *colloq.* so long! **—пока́ ещё; пока́ что, 1,** for the time being; for the present. **2,** so far; thus far; as yet.

пока́з *n.* showing; demonstration.

показа́ние *n.* **1,** *usu. pl.* evidence; testimony: дава́ть показа́ния, to give evidence; снима́ть показа́ния с (+ *gen.*), to take down someone's testimony. **2,** deposition; affidavit. **3,** *usu. pl.* reading (*on an instrument*): снима́ть показа́ния счётчика, to read a meter.

показа́тель *n.m.* **1,** index; indicator. Показа́тель у́мственных спосо́бностей, intelligence quotient; IQ. **2,** *pl.* figures. **3,** *math.* exponent.

показа́тельный *adj.* **1,** indicative; significant; revealing. **2,** model (*attrib.*); demonstration (*attrib.*). **—показа́тельный суд,** show trial.

показа́ть [*infl.* **-кажу́, -ка́жешь**] *v., pfv. of* **пока́зывать. —показа́ться,** *refl.* **1,** *pfv. of* **каза́ться. 2,** *pfv. of* **пока́зываться.**

показно́й *adj.* **1,** for show; done for effect. **2,** ostentatious. Показна́я ро́скошь, ostentation.

показу́ха *n., colloq.* show; window dressing.

пока́зывать *v.impfv.* [*pfv.* **показа́ть**] **1,** to show: Покажи́те мне письмо́, show me the letter. Показа́ть кому́-нибудь го́род, to show someone the city; show someone around town. Показа́ть кому́-нибудь как по́льзоваться фотоаппара́том, to show someone how to use the camera. **2,** (*with* **на** + *acc.*) to point to; point at. **3,** (*of a clock, meter, thermometer, etc.*) to show; register; read. **4,** to show; display (a quality, emotion, etc.). **5,** to show; demonstrate; make clear. **6,** to stick out (one's tongue); turn (one's back); thumb (one's nose). **7,** *sports* to achieve (a certain result). **8,** to perform (a trick, play, etc.). **9,** to testify; (*with* **на** + *acc.*) testify against. **10,** (*with dat.*) *colloq.* to show; teach (someone) a lesson. **—не пока́зывать ви́ду,** not to show; not let on. **—показа́ть (кого́-нибудь) врачу́,** to take *or* bring (someone) to a doctor. **—показа́ть (кому́-нибудь) на дверь,** to show (someone) the door (*i.e.* order out). **—показа́ть приме́р** (+ *dat.*), to serve as an example to. **—показа́ть себя́, 1,** to prove oneself; show one's worth. **2,** (*with instr.*) to prove to be; show oneself to be.

пока́зываться *v.r.impfv.* [*pfv.* **показа́ться**] **1,** to appear; come into view. **2,** to show up; turn up. Показа́ться врачу́, to see a doctor. Я не могу́ показа́ться, I am not fit to be seen. **—пока́зываться на глаза́** (+ *dat.*), to show one's face (to); allow oneself to be seen (by). **—пока́зываться на глаза́х у,** (*of tears*) to come to one's eyes.

покáлывать *v.impfv., colloq.* **1,** to prick. **2,** *impers.* to have an intermittent pain: У меня́ покáлывает в боку́, I have an intermittent pain in my side.

покáмест *adv. & conj., colloq.* = **покá.**

покарáть *v., pfv. of* **карáть.**

покатáть *v., pfv. of* **катáть** (*in sense #2*). —**покатáться,** *refl., pfv. of* **катáться** (*in sense #2*).

покати́ть *v., pfv. of* **кати́ть.** —**покати́ться,** *refl.* **1,** *pfv. of* **кати́ться. 2,** *in* покати́ться сó смеху, *colloq.* to roar with laughter.

покáтость *n.f.* slope; incline.

покáтываться *v.r.impfv., colloq., in* покáтываться сó смеху, to roar with laughter.

покáтый *adj.* sloping; slanting. Покáтый лоб, receding forehead.

покачáть *v.pfv.* **1,** to rock; swing. **2,** *in* покачáть головóй, to shake one's head. —**покачáться,** *refl.* **1,** to rock. **2,** to swing back and forth. **3,** *in* покачáться на качéлях, to ride a swing.

покáчивать *v.impfv.* **1,** to rock slightly. **2,** (*with instr.*) to shake (one's head) slightly. **3,** *impers.* to toss: Парохóд стáло покáчивать, the ship began to toss. —**покáчиваться,** *refl.* **1,** to rock back and forth. Покáчиваться на волнáх, to bob on the waves. **2,** to rock oneself. **3,** *in* идти́ покáчиваясь, to walk unsteadily.

покачну́ть *v.pfv.* **1,** to shake. **2,** to tip; tilt. —**покачну́ться,** *refl.* **1,** to sway. **2,** to lurch. **3,** *colloq.* to tilt. **4,** *fig., colloq.* to take a turn for the worse.

покáшливать *v.impfv.* to have a slight cough; cough intermittently.

покáшлять *v.pfv.* to cough (*momentarily*).

покая́ние *n.* **1,** repentance; penitence. **2,** (religious) confession. **3,** penance.

покая́нный *adj.* of repentance; repentant; penitent.

покая́ться *v.r., pfv. of* **кáяться.**

поквартáльный *adj.* quarterly. —**поквартáльно,** *adv.* quarterly.

поквитáться *v.r.pfv.* (*with* с + *instr.*) *colloq.* to get even (with); settle scores (with).

пóкер *n.* poker (*card game*).

покидáть *v.impfv.* [*pfv.* **поки́нуть**] to leave; desert; abandon; forsake.

покладáя *verbal adv., in* рабóтать не поклáдая рук, to work untiringly.

поклáдистый *adj.* amenable; agreeable.

поклáжа *n., colloq.* **1,** load. **2,** baggage; luggage.

поклёп *n., colloq.* slander; calumny.

поклóн *n.* **1,** bow. **2,** regards; greetings; best wishes. —идти́ на поклóн к, to go begging to.

поклонéние *n.* (*with dat.*) worship (of): поклонéние и́долам, worship of idols.

поклони́ться [*infl.* -клоню́сь, -клóнишься] *v.r., pfv. of* **клáняться.**

поклóнник *n.* **1,** admirer. **2,** devotee. **3,** suitor. **4,** *relig.* worshiper.

поклоня́ться *v.r.impfv.* (*with dat.*) to worship.

покля́сться *v.r., pfv. of* **кля́сться.**

покóиться *v.r.impfv.* **1,** (*with* на + *prepl.*) to rest (on). **2,** (*of a dead person*) to lie; repose. Здесь покóится прах (+ *gen.*), here lies...

покóй *n.* **1,** peace (of mind); оставля́ть в покóе, to leave in peace. **2,** quiet. **3,** rest: в состоя́нии покóя, in a state of rest. **4,** *in idioms,* retirement: уйти́ на покóй, to retire; отпрáвить на покóй, to send into retirement. **5,** room; apartment. Приёмный покóй, reception office (*in a hospital*). Королéвские покóи, the royal apartments.

покóйник *n.m.* [*fem.* -ница] the deceased.

покóйницкая *n., decl. as an adj.* morgue.

покóйный *adj.* **1,** calm; tranquil; serene. **2,** deceased; (*before a name*) the late. —*n.* the deceased.

поколебáть *v., pfv. of* **колебáть.** —**поколебáться,** *refl., pfv. of* **колебáться.**

поколéние *n.* generation.

поколоти́ть *v.pfv.* [*infl.* -лочу́, -лóтишь] *colloq.* **1,** to beat; whip; thrash. **2,** (*with* в + *acc. or* по) to bang (on).

поколóть *v.pfv.* [*infl.* -колю́, -кóлешь] **1,** to prick. **2,** to slaughter. **3,** to chop (all or a quantity of something).

покóнчить *v.pfv.* (*with* с + *instr.*) **1,** to finish. **2,** to put an end to; do away with. —**покóнчить жизнь самоуби́йством; покóнчить с собóй,** to commit suicide. —**покóнчить счёты с** (*with instr.*), to break off with.

покорéние *n.* conquest.

покори́тель *n.m.* conqueror. —**покори́тель сердéц,** lady-killer.

покори́ть *v., pfv. of* **покоря́ть.** —**покори́ться,** *refl., pfv. of* **покоря́ться.**

покорми́ть *v., pfv. of* **корми́ть.**

покóрный *adj.* **1,** submissive; obedient. **2,** humble: покóрная прóсьба, humble request. —**покóрно,** *adv.* humbly. —**покóрность,** *n.f.* submissiveness.

покорóбить *v., pfv. of* **корóбить.** —**покорóбиться,** *refl., pfv. of* **корóбиться.**

покоря́ть *v.impfv.* [*pfv.* **покори́ть**] **1,** to conquer; subdue. **2,** *fig.* to captivate. Покоря́ть сéрдце (+ *gen.*), to win *or* capture the heart of. —**покоря́ться,** *refl.* (*with dat.*) **1,** to submit (to). **2,** to resign oneself (to).

покóс *n.* **1,** mowing. **2,** meadow.

покоси́ть[1] *v.pfv.* [*infl.* -кошу́, -кóсишь] *colloq.* to mow; cut.

покоси́ть[2] *v.pfv.* [*infl.* -кошу́, -коси́шь] **1,** to tilt. **2,** (*with acc. or instr.*) to cock (one's eye). —**покоси́ться,** *refl., pfv. of* **коси́ться.**

покрáсить *v., pfv. of* **крáсить.**

покраснéть *v., pfv. of* **краснéть.**

покриви́ть *v., pfv. of* **криви́ть.** —**покриви́ться,** *refl., pfv. of* **криви́ться.**

покри́кивать *v.impfv., colloq.* to shout.

покрóв *n.* **1,** cover; covering. **2,** *fig.* cover; cloak; mantle: под покрóвом нóчи, under cover of night. —**кóжный покрóв,** skin. —**ледникóвый покрóв,** icecap. —**облачный покрóв,** cloud cover. —**пóчвенный покрóв,** topsoil. —**снéжный покрóв,** blanket of snow.

покрови́тель *n.m.* patron; protector; sponsor.

покрови́тельственный *adj.* **1,** protective. **2,** patronizing. —**покрови́тельственная окрáска,** protective coloration. —**покрови́тельственный тари́ф,** protective tariff.

покрови́тельство *n.* patronage; sponsorship. Под покрови́тельством (+ *gen.*), under the auspices of.

покрови́тельствовать *v.impfv.* [*pres.* **-ствую, -ствуешь**] (*with dat.*) to patronize; sponsor.

покро́й *n.* cut (*of a garment*). —все на оди́н покро́й, all alike.

покроши́ть *v.pfv.* [*infl.* **-крошу́, -кро́шишь**] **1,** to chop up. **2,** to crumble.

покружи́ть *v.pfv.* [*infl.* **-кружу́, -кру́жишь** *or* **-кружи́шь**] **1,** *v.t.* to spin around. **2,** *v.i.* to wander (*for a while*). **3,** *v.i.* (*of an aircraft*) to circle several times. —покружи́ться, *refl.* **1,** to spin around. **2,** to wander (*for a while*). **3,** (*of a bird*) to circle.

покрути́ть *v.pfv.* [*infl.* **-кручу́, -кру́тишь**] **1,** (*with acc.*) to twist. **2,** (*with instr.*) to shake (one's head).

покрыва́ло *n.* **1,** cloth cover. **2,** bedspread; counterpane. **3,** covering; layer: нефтяно́е покрыва́ло, oil slick.

покрыва́ть *v.impfv.* [*pfv.* **покры́ть**] **1,** to cover. **2,** to coat (with paint, lacquer, etc.). **3,** to hide; cover up; shield. **4,** to cover; defray (expenses, losses, etc.). **5,** to drown out. —покрыва́ться, *refl.* **1,** to cover oneself up. **2,** (*with instr.*) to be covered (with).

покры́тие *n.* **1,** (act of) covering. **2,** covering; coating; surface. **3,** covering; defrayal (*of expenses*).

покры́ть [*infl.* **-кро́ю, -кро́ешь**] *v., pfv. of* **крыть** *and* **покрыва́ть.** —покры́ться, *refl., pfv. of* **покрыва́ться.**

покры́шка [*gen. pl.* **-шек**] *n.* **1,** tire. **2,** *colloq.* cover; lid.

поку́да *adv. & conj., colloq.* = **пока́.**

покупа́тель *n.m.* **1,** buyer; purchaser. **2,** customer.

покупа́тельный *adj.* buying (*attrib.*); purchasing (*attrib.*): покупа́тельная спосо́бность, purchasing power.

покупа́ть *v.impfv.* [*pfv.* **купи́ть**] to buy.

поку́пка [*gen. pl.* **-пок**] *n.* **1,** purchase; (act of) purchasing. **2,** a purchase: де́лать поку́пки, to go shopping. Вы́годная поку́пка, a good buy.

покупно́й *adj.* purchased; bought. —покупна́я цена́, purchase price.

покури́ть *v.impfv.* [*infl.* **-курю́, -ку́ришь**] to have a smoke.

покуса́ть *v.pfv.* to bite; sting.

покуси́ться [*infl.* **-шу́сь, -си́шься**] *v.r., pfv. of* **покуша́ться.**

поку́шать *v., pfv. of* **ку́шать.**

покуша́ться *v.r.impfv.* [*pfv.* **покуси́ться**] (*with* **на** + *acc.*) **1,** to make an attempt upon: покуси́ться на чью-нибудь жизнь, to make an attempt on someone's life. **2,** to encroach (upon).

покуше́ние *n.* (*with* **на** + *acc.*) **1,** attempted assassination of; attempt on the life of. Покуше́ние на уби́йство, attempted murder. **2,** encroachment (on).

пол *n.* **1,** [*2nd loc.* полу́; *pl.* полы́, поло́в] floor. **2,** [*pl.* по́лы, поло́в] sex.

пол- *prefix* **1,** half: полчаса́, half an hour. **2,** *colloq.* (*in telling time*) half (*before the next hour*): полшесто́го, half-past five.

пола́ [*pl.* по́лы] *n.* **1,** flap (*of a garment*). **2,** flap; fold (*of a tent*). —из-под полы́, (*of a purchase, sale, etc.*) under the table; under the counter.

полага́ть *v.impfv.* **1,** to think; believe; suppose. На́до полага́ть, one may assume; it may be assumed. **2,** to consider; regard.

полага́ться *v.r.impfv.* **1,** to be prescribed. За вход полага́ется пла́та, there is an admission charge; you have to pay to get in. За э́то полага́ется сме́ртная казнь, it carries the death penalty. **2,** *impers.* to be proper; be in order; be expected. Как полага́ется, as it should be; as expected. Не полага́ется, not supposed to; not the thing to do. **3,** (*with dat.*) to be due (someone); be payable to. **4,** [*pfv.* **положи́ться**] (*with* **на** + *acc.*) to rely on.

пола́дить *v.pfv.* [*infl.* **-ла́жу, -ла́дишь**] *colloq.* **1,** to reach an agreement. **2,** to get along.

пола́комиться *v.r., pfv. of* **ла́комиться.**

полбеды́ *n.f., colloq., in* **э́то ещё полбеды́,** it's not so terrible; it's no calamity.

полве́ка [*gen.* **полуве́ка**] *n.m.* half a century. В тече́ние полуве́ка, for half a century.

полго́да [*gen.* **полуго́да**] *n.m.* half a year. Бо́льше полуго́да, more than half a year.

по́лдень [*gen.* **полу́дня**] *n.m.* noon. —полдне́вный, *adj.* noon (*attrib.*); midday (*attrib.*).

по́лдник *n.* mid-afternoon snack.

полдоро́ги *n.f.* halfway point: на полдоро́ге, halfway; at the halfway point.

по́ле [*pl.* **поля́, поле́й, поля́м**] *n.* **1,** field. **2,** *fig.* field (*of activity*). **3,** background (*of a painting*). **4,** *chess* square. **5,** *pl.* brim (*of a hat*). **6,** *pl.* margin. —по́ле би́твы; по́ле бо́я; по́ле сраже́ния, battlefield. —по́ле зре́ния, field of vision.

полеве́ть *v., pfv. of* **леве́ть.**

полёвка [*gen. pl.* **-вок**] *n.* vole.

полево́дство *n.* field crop farming.

полево́й *adj.* field (*attrib.*). —полева́я мышь, field mouse. —полевы́е цветы́, wildflowers.

полего́ньку *adv., colloq.* slowly; little by little.

полегча́ть *v., pfv. of* **легча́ть.**

полежа́ть *v.pfv.* [*infl.* **-лежу́, -лежи́шь**] to lie for a while; lie down for a while.

поле́зно *adj., used predicatively* **1,** useful. **2,** healthy; good: По́сле обе́да поле́зно отдохну́ть, it is good to rest after dinner.

поле́зность *n.f.* usefulness.

поле́зный *adj.* [*short form* **-зен, -зна**] **1,** useful; helpful. Чем могу́ быть поле́зен (поле́зна)?, what can I do for you?; how may I help you? **2,** wholesome. **3,** good (for): поле́зный для здоро́вья, good for one's health.

поле́зть *v.pfv.* [*infl. like* **лезть**] **1,** *pfv. of* **лезть. 2,** to begin to climb.

полемизи́ровать *v.impfv.* [*pres.* **-рую, -руешь**] to engage in polemics.

поле́мика *n.* polemics. —полеми́ст, *n.* polemicist. —полеми́ческий, *adj.* polemic(al).

полени́ться *v.r.pfv.* [*infl.* **-леню́сь, -ле́нишься**] (*with inf.*) to be too lazy (to).

поле́нница *n.* stack of logs; stack of firewood.

поле́но [*pl.* **поле́нья, поле́ньев**] *n.* log (*for burning*).

поле́сье *n.* marshy woodlands.

полёт *n.* **1,** flight. **2,** *usu. pl.* flying. —полёт фанта́зии, flight of fantasy. —страх пе́ред полётами, fear of flying.

полета́ть *v.pfv.* to fly (*for a while*).

полете́ть *v.pfv.* [*infl.* -чу́, -ти́шь] **1,** *pfv. of* лете́ть. **2,** to begin to fly; take off. **3,** *colloq.* to fall. **4,** *fig., colloq.* to lose one's job; be fired.

полётный *adj.* flight (*attrib.*); flying.

полечи́ть *v.pfv.* [*infl.* -лечу́, -ле́чишь] to treat (*for a while*). —полечи́ться, *refl.* to be treated; get some treatment.

поле́чь *v.pfv.* [*infl. like* лечь] (*of all or many people*) **1,** *colloq.* to lie down. **2,** to be killed (*in battle*).

по́лзать *v.impfv., indeterm. of* ползти́.

ползко́м *adv.* by crawling; on all fours.

ползти́ *v.impfv.* [*pfv.* поползти́; *pres.* ползу́, ползёшь; *past* полз, ползла́, ползло́, ползли́] **1,** to crawl. **2,** to creep (along). **3,** to trickle. **4,** *colloq.* (*of rumors*) to circulate. **5,** *colloq.* (*of fabric*) to come apart.

ползу́н [*gen.* -зуна́] *n., colloq.* baby still in the crawling stage.

ползуно́к [*gen.* -нка́] *n., colloq.* **1,** = ползу́н. **2,** *pl.* crawlers (*baby's garment*).

ползу́чий *adj.* (*of a plant*) creeping: ползу́чее расте́ние, creeper.

полиа́ндрия *n.* polyandry.

полива́льный *adj.* watering (*attrib.*). —полива́льная маши́на, water truck.

полива́ть *v.impfv.* [*pfv.* поли́ть] **1,** to water; pour *or* spray water on; hose. **2,** to moisten (food); baste. **3,** to spray (with bullets, gunfire, etc.). —полива́ться, *refl.* (*with instr.*) to pour (water) on oneself.

поли́вка *n.* watering (*of plants*).

поли́вочный *adj.* watering (*attrib.*).

полига́мия *n.* polygamy. —полигами́ческий; полига́мный, *adj.* polygamous.

полигло́т *n.* polyglot.

полиго́н *n.* **1,** firing range. **2,** training ground. —испыта́тельный полиго́н, proving ground.

полиграфи́я *n.* printing. —полиграфи́ческий, *adj.* printing (*attrib.*).

поликли́ника *n.* polyclinic.

полиме́р *n.* polymer. —полиме́рный, *adj.* polymeric.

полинези́ец [*gen.* -и́йца] *n.m.* [*fem.* -и́йка] Polynesian. —полинези́йский, *adj.* Polynesian.

полиня́лый *adj.* faded.

полиня́ть *v., pfv. of* линя́ть (*in sense #1*).

полиомиели́т *n.* poliomyelitis.

поли́п *n.* polyp.

полирова́льный *adj.* polishing (*attrib.*). —полирова́льная маши́на, buffing machine.

полиро́ванный *adj.* polished.

полирова́ть *v.impfv.* [*pfv.* отполирова́ть; *pres.* -ру́ю, -ру́ешь] to polish.

полиро́вка *n.* **1,** polishing. **2,** polish; gloss; finish. —полиро́вочный, *adj.* polishing (*attrib.*). —полиро́вщик, *n.* polisher.

по́лис *n., in* страхово́й по́лис, insurance policy.

полисме́н *n.* policeman (*in the U.S. or Great Britain*).

полиста́ть *v.pfv.* to flip through.

полистиро́л *n.* polystyrene.

политбюро́ *n.indecl.* Politburo.

политеи́зм (тэ) *n.* polytheism. —политеи́ст, *n.* polytheist. —политеисти́ческий, *adj.* polytheistic.

полите́хникум *n.* polytechnic school.

политехни́ческий *adj.* polytechnic.

политзаключённый *n., decl. as an adj.* political prisoner.

политиза́ция *n.* politicization.

политизи́ровать *v.impfv. & pfv.* [*pres.* -рую, -руешь] to politicize.

поли́тик *n.* politician.

поли́тика *n.* **1,** policy. **2,** politics.

полити́кан *n.* (unscrupulous) politician.

полити́ческий *adj.* political. —полити́ческий де́ятель, political figure; politician.

полити́чный *adj., colloq.* politic; diplomatic.

политу́ра *n.* polish; varnish.

поли́ть *v.pfv.* [*infl.* полью́, польёшь; *past* по́лил *or* поли́л, полила́, по́лило *or* поли́ло, по́лили *or* поли́ли] **1,** *pfv. of* полива́ть. **2,** (*of rain*) to begin to come down. —поли́ться, *refl.* [*past* поли́лся, полила́сь, полило́сь *or* поли́лось, полили́сь *or* поли́лись] **1,** *pfv. of* полива́ться. **2,** to begin to flow.

полице́йский *adj.* police (*attrib.*). —*n.* policeman.

поли́ция *n.* police.

поли́чное *n., decl. as an adj., in* с поли́чным, red-handed: пойма́ть/попа́сться с поли́чным, to catch/ be caught/ red-handed.

полиэтиле́н *n.* polyethylene. —полиэтиле́новый, *adj.* polyethylene.

полиэфи́р *n.* polyester. —полиэфи́рный, *adj.* polyester.

полк [*gen.* полка́; *2nd loc.* полку́] *n.* regiment. —на́шего полку́ при́было, our numbers have grown.

по́лка [*gen. pl.* по́лок] *n.* **1,** shelf. **2,** berth.

полко́вник *n.* colonel.

полково́дец [*gen.* -дца] *n.* military leader.

полково́й *adj.* regimental.

полне́йший *adj.* sheer; utter.

полне́ть *v.impfv.* [*pfv.* пополне́ть] to put on weight; get fat.

полни́ть *v.impfv., colloq.* to make (someone) look fat.

по́лно *predicate, colloq.* **1,** enough!; stop! **2,** don't be silly!

полно́ *adv., colloq.* **1,** filled; packed: В за́ле бы́ло полно́ наро́да, the hall was packed with people. **2,** (*with gen.*) plenty of; more than enough: Кандида́тов полно́, there are plenty of candidates. У меня́ полно́ рабо́ты, I am up to my ears in work.

полнове́сный *adj.* **1,** full-weight. **2,** heavy; weighty.

полновла́стие *n.* full power; absolute power. —полновла́стный, *adj.* having full or absolute power.

полново́дный *adj.* (*of a river or lake*) at a high level.

полново́дье *n.* high water.

полногру́дый *adj.* buxom.

полнокро́вие *n., med.* plethora.

полнокро́вный *adj.* full-blooded; red-blooded.

полнолу́ние *n.* full moon.

полнометра́жный *adj.* (*of a film*) feature-length.

полномо́чие *n.* authority; power. Превыша́ть свои́ полномо́чия, to exceed one's authority/powers. —**срок полномо́чий,** term of office.

полномо́чный *adj.* plenipotentiary: полномо́чный посо́л, ambassador plenipotentiary. —**полномо́чный представи́тель,** authorized representative.

полнопра́вие *n.* full rights; equality. —**полнопра́вный,** *adj.* having full rights: полнопра́вный член, full member.

по́лностью *adv.* **1,** in full. **2,** fully; completely.

полнота́ *n.* **1,** fullness; completeness. Полнота́ вла́сти, full power. **2,** obesity; corpulence. —**для полноты́ карти́ны,** to complete the picture. —**от полноты́ се́рдца,** out of the fullness of one's heart. —**со всей полното́й; во всей полноте́,** in its entirety.

полноце́нный *adj.* **1,** worth its full value. **2,** *fig.* full-fledged.

по́лночь [*gen.* полу́ночи *or* по́лночи] *n.f.* midnight. —**полно́чный,** *adj.* midnight (*attrib.*).

по́лный *adj.* [*short form* по́лон, полна́, по́лно *or* полно́, по́лны *or* полны́] **1,** full. **2,** complete; total. **3,** fat; stout. **4,** *in* по́лные близнецы́, identical twins. —**в по́лной ме́ре,** fully; in full measure.

полны́м-полно́ *adv.* (*with gen.*) *colloq.* full (of); packed (with); jammed (with).

по́ло *n. indecl.* polo. —**во́дное по́ло,** water polo.

поло́ва *n.* chaff.

полови́к [*gen.* -вика́] *n.* floor mat; doormat.

полови́на *n.* **1,** half. **2,** (*in telling time*) half (*before the next hour*): полови́на тре́тьего, half-past two.

полови́нный *adj.* half; half a; a half: полови́нная до́ля, a half share. —**полови́нная но́та,** half note. —**в полови́нном соста́ве,** at half strength.

полови́нчатый *adj.* halfway; indecisive.

полови́ца *n.* floorboard.

поло́вник *n., colloq.* ladle.

полово́дье *n.* high water (*resulting from the melting of snow*).

полово́й *adj.* **1,** sexual; sex (*attrib.*). **2,** floor (*attrib.*).

по́лог *n.* **1,** canopy. **2,** *fig.* cover.

поло́гий *adj.* not steep; gently sloping.

положе́ние *n.* **1,** position: сидя́чее положе́ние, sitting position. Ста́вить кого́-нибудь в нело́вкое положе́ние, to put someone in an awkward position. **2,** situation: отча́янное положе́ние, desperate situation. **3,** status. **4,** statute; regulations. **5,** tenet; thesis; proposition. **6,** provision. —**в (интере́сном) положе́нии,** pregnant. —**вое́нное положе́ние,** martial law. —**положе́ние веще́й; положе́ние дел,** state of affairs. —**входи́ть в чьё-нибудь положе́ние,** to put oneself in someone's place; empathize with.

поло́женный *adj.* **1,** agreed-upon; prescribed. Ра́ньше поло́женного сро́ка, ahead of the agreed-upon time. **2,** (*with dat.*) due; befitting: Ему́ во́зданы все по́чести, поло́женные главе́ госуда́рства, he was accorded all the honors befitting a head of state.

поло́жено *short form neut. of* **поло́женный** *colloq.* (one) should; (one) is supposed to. В э́тот день не поло́жено ни есть, ни пить, on that day one is not supposed to (*or* one does not) eat or drink. Вам поло́жено слу́шаться, you are supposed to obey. —**как поло́жено,** as one should; as it should be; as prescribed.

положи́тельно *adv.* **1,** positively: положи́тельно заряжённое ядро́, a positively charged nucleus. **2,** positively; favorably. **3,** positively; absolutely: положи́тельно некраси́в, positively ugly; положи́тельно ничего́, absolutely nothing.

положи́тельный *adj.* **1,** positive. **2,** affirmative. **3,** businesslike; practical. **4,** definite. **5,** *colloq.* absolute; utter.

положи́ть [*infl.* -ложу́, -ло́жишь] *v., pfv. of* **класть.** —**поло́жим,** let us say; let us assume. —**положи́ть коне́ц** (+ *dat.*), to put an end to. —**положи́ть нача́ло,** *see* нача́ло. —**положи́ть слова́ на му́зыку,** to set words to music.

положи́ться [*infl.* -ложу́сь, -ло́жишься] *v.r., pfv. of* **полага́ться** (*in sense #4*).

по́лоз [*pl.* поло́зья, поло́зьев] *n.* runner (*of a sleigh*).

полома́ть *v.pfv.* to break. —**полома́ться,** *refl.* **1,** to break; break down. **2,** *pfv. of* лома́ться (*in sense #6*).

поло́мка [*gen. pl.* -мок] *n.* **1,** breakage. **2,** breakdown (*of a machine*). **3,** broken part.

поломо́йка [*gen. pl.* -мо́ек] *n., colloq.* woman who washes floors.

полоне́з *n.* polonaise.

поло́ний *n.* polonium.

полони́ть *v.pfv., archaic* to take prisoner.

полоса́ [*acc.* полосу́ *or* по́лосу; *pl.* по́лосы, поло́с, полоса́м] *n.* **1,** strip (*of metal, paper, etc.*). **2,** stripe (*in a design*). **3,** strip (*of land*); lane (*of a highway*). **4,** belt; region; zone. **5,** page (*of a newspaper*). **6,** band (*of frequencies, the spectrum, etc.*). **7,** welt (*from a blow*). **8,** (*with gen.*) period (of); spell (of): полоса́ хоро́шей пого́ды, spell of good weather. —**лётная полоса́; взлётно-поса́дочная полоса́,** runway; landing strip.

полоса́тик *n.* rorqual (*whale*).

полоса́тый *adj.* striped.

поло́ска [*gen. pl.* -сок] *n., dim. of* **полоса́.** —**в поло́ску,** striped. В (чёрную, си́нюю, *etc.*) поло́ску, with (black, blue, etc.) stripes.

полоска́ние *n.* **1,** rinsing; gargling. **2,** mouthwash.

полоска́тельница *n.* slop basin.

полоска́ть *v.impfv.* [*pfv.* прополоска́ть *or* вы́полоскать; *pres.* -лощу́, -ло́щешь] **1,** to rinse. **2,** *in* полоска́ть го́рло, to gargle. —**полоска́ться,** *refl.* [*impfv. only*] **1,** to splash about (*in water*). **2,** (*of a flag, sail, etc.*) to flutter; flap.

полосова́ть *v.impfv.* [*pfv.* исполосова́ть; *pres.* -су́ю, -су́ешь] *colloq.* **1,** to leave streaks on. **2,** to flog; lash.

по́лость [*pl.* по́лости, -сте́й, -стя́м] *n.f.* **1,** cavity. **2,** lap robe.

полоте́нце [*gen. pl.* -нец] *n.* towel.

полотёр *n.* floor polisher (*person or device*).

поло́тнище *n.* **1,** width (*of cloth*): простыня́ в два поло́тнища, a sheet of two widths. **2,** leaf (*of a door, gate, etc.*).

полотно́ [*pl.* поло́тна, поло́тен] *n.* **1,** linen. **2,** canvas; painting. **3,** roadbed. **4,** blade (*of a saw, ax, etc.*). —**бе́лый/бле́дный как полотно́,** white/pale as a sheet.

полотня́ный *adj.* linen.

поло́ть *v.impfv.* [*pfv.* вы́полоть; *pres.* полю́, по́лешь] **1,** to weed (a garden). **2,** to pull up (weeds).

полоу́мие *n., colloq.* madness. **—полоу́мный,** *adj., colloq.* mad; crazy.

по́лочка [*gen. pl.* -чек] *n.* small shelf.

полпо́рции *n.f.* half-portion.

полпре́д *n.* plenipotentiary (*contr. of* полномо́чный представи́тель).

полпути́ *n.m.* halfway point: на полпути́, halfway; at the halfway point; midway.

полсло́ва [*gen.* полсло́ва *or* полусло́ва] *n.neut.* **1,** a (brief) word: Мо́жно вас на полсло́ва?, may I have a word with you? **2,** a word half uttered: останови́ться на полусло́ве, to stop short (*when speaking*); прерва́ть на полусло́ве, to cut (someone) short. **—ни полсло́ва,** not a single word.

полста́вки *n.f., in* **на полста́вки,** part-time.

полти́на *n., colloq., in* **с полти́ной,** ...and fifty kopecks (*or* cents); and a half.

полти́нник *n., colloq.* fifty kopecks; fifty-kopeck coin.

полтора́ [*fem.* полторы́; *gen., dat., instr. & prepl.* полу́тора] *numeral* one and a half. В полтора́ ра́за бо́льше, one and a half times (*or* half again) as many/much.

полтора́ста [*gen., dat., instr. & prepl.* полу́тораста] *numeral* one hundred and fifty.

полуавтомати́ческий *adj.* semiautomatic.

полубессозна́тельный *adj.* semiconscious.

полубо́г *n.* demigod.

полуботи́нок [*gen.* -нка; *gen. pl.* -нок] *n.* shoe.

полувое́нный *adj.* paramilitary.

полуго́дие *n.* half a year; half of a calendar year. **—полугоди́чный; полугодово́й,** *adj.* half-year (*attrib.*); six-month (*attrib.*). **—полугодова́лый,** *adj.* six-month-old.

полуголо́дный *adj.* half-starved.

полугра́мотный *adj.* semiliterate.

полу́денный *adj.* noon (*attrib.*); midday (*attrib.*).

полуди́ть *v., pfv. of* луди́ть.

полуживо́й *adj.* more dead than alive.

полузабытьё [*2nd loc.* -тьи́] *n.* (state of) semi-consciousness.

полузащи́тник *n., sports* halfback.

полукро́вка [*gen. pl.* -вок] *n.* half-breed.

полукро́вный *adj.* half-blooded.

полукру́г *n.* semicircle. **—полукру́глый,** *adj.* semicircular.

полулежа́ть *v.impfv.* [*pres.* -лежу́, -лежи́шь] to recline.

полуме́ра *n.* half-measure.

полумёртвый *adj.* half-dead; more dead than alive.

полуме́сяц *n.* half-moon.

полуме́сячный *adj.* half a month's.

полумра́к *n.m.* semidarkness.

полуно́чник *n., colloq.* night owl.

полуно́чничать *v.impfv., colloq.* to stay up most of the night; burn the midnight oil.

полу́ночный *also,* полуно́чный *adj.* midnight (*attrib.*).

полуоборо́т *n.* half-turn.

полуо́стров [*pl.* полуострова́] *n.* peninsula. **—полуостровно́й,** *adj.* peninsular.

полуотво́ренный *adj.* half-open; ajar. *Also,* полуоткры́тый.

полупра́вда *n.* half-truth.

полуприце́п *n.* semitrailer.

полупроводни́к [*gen.* -ника́] *n.* semiconductor.

полупрозра́чный *adj.* translucent.

полупусто́й *adj.* half-empty.

полуразру́шенный *adj.* tumble-down; ramshackle.

полураспа́д *n., in* пери́од полураспа́да, half-life.

полусве́т *n.* dim light.

полусме́рть *n.f., in* до полусме́рти, (half to) death: испуга́ть до полусме́рти, to frighten (half) to death. **—изби́ть до полусме́рти,** to beat within an inch of one's life.

полусозна́тельный *adj.* semiconscious.

полусо́н [*gen.* -сна́] *n.* state of being half-asleep: в полусне́, half-asleep. **—полусо́нный,** *adj.* half-asleep.

полусредневе́с *n.* welterweight (*boxer*).

полусре́дний *adj., in* полусре́дний вес, *boxing* welterweight (*category*).

полуста́нок [*gen.* -нка] *n.* small station; way station.

полуте́нь [*2nd loc.* -тени́] *n.f.* penumbra.

полуто́н *n.* **1,** *music* half tone. **2,** *art* halftone.

полутьма́ *n.* semidarkness.

полуфабрика́т *n.* **1,** semi-finished product. **2,** *pl.* partially prepared food.

полуфина́л *n.* semifinal; semifinals. **—полуфинали́ст,** *n.* semifinalist. **—полуфина́льный,** *adj.* semifinal.

получасово́й *adj.* half-hour (*attrib.*).

получа́тель *n.m.* recipient.

получа́ть *v.impfv.* [*pfv.* получи́ть] **1,** to receive; get. **2,** to obtain. **3,** to gain. **4,** *colloq.* to catch; get (a cold, illness, etc.). **—получа́ться,** *refl.* **1,** to be received; be obtained. **2,** to come about; result. **3,** to come out; turn out. **4,** to work out: Де́ло не получи́лось, things didn't work out.

получе́ние *n.* **1,** receiving; receipt. **2,** obtaining.

получи́ть [*infl.* -лучу́, -лу́чишь] *v., pfv. of* получа́ть. **—получи́ться,** *refl., pfv. of* получа́ться.

полу́чка *n., colloq.* **1,** (act of) receiving; receipt. **2,** sum (*of money*). **3,** pay; paycheck.

полуша́рие *n.* hemisphere.

полу́шка [*gen. pl.* -шек] *n., pre-rev.* old coin worth 1/4 of a kopeck. **—ни полу́шки,** not a penny; not a plug nickel.

полушу́бок [*gen.* -бка] *n.* short sheepskin coat.

полушутя́ *adv.* half in jest.

полцены́ *n.f.* half-price: купи́ть за полцены́, to buy at half-price.

полчаса́ [*gen.* полчаса́] *n.m.* half an hour. Ка́ждые полчаса́, every half-hour.

по́лчище *n.* **1,** horde. **2,** *fig.* swarm.

по́лый *adj.* hollow. **—по́лая вода́,** floodwaters.

по́лымя *n.neut., in* из огня́ да в по́лымя, out of the frying pan into the fire.

полы́нный *adj.* wormwood (*attrib.*). **—полы́нная во́дка,** absinthe.

полы́нь *n.f.* wormwood; sagebrush.

полынья́ [*gen. pl.* **-не́й**] *n.* unfrozen patch of water in the ice; polynya.

полысе́ть *v., pfv. of* **лысе́ть**.

полыха́ть *v.impfv.* to blaze.

по́льза *n.* use; benefit; good. Кака́я от э́того по́льза?, what good will it do? **—в по́льзу** (+ *gen.*), **1,** in favor of. **2,** for; for the sake of; on behalf of. **—быть** *or* идти́ **на по́льзу** (+ *dat.*), to do (someone) good; be good for. **—говори́ть в чью́-нибудь по́льзу**, to be a point in someone's favor. **—обрати́ть в свою́ по́льзу**, to turn to one's advantage. **—с по́льзой**, to advantage.

по́льзование *n.* (*with instr.*) **1,** use (of). **2,** enjoyment (of).

по́льзователь *n.m.* user.

по́льзоваться *v.r.impfv.* [*pfv.* **воспо́льзоваться**; *pres.* **-зуюсь, -зуешься**] (*with instr.*) **1,** to use; make use of; take advantage of. **2,** [*impfv. only*] to enjoy (an advantage, good health, etc.).

по́лька [*gen. pl.* **по́лек**] *n.* **1,** Polish woman. **2,** polka (*dance*).

по́льский *adj.* Polish.

польсти́ть *v., pfv. of* **льстить**.

полюби́ть *v.pfv.* [*infl.* **-люблю́, -лю́бишь**] **1,** to come to love; fall in love with. **2,** to come to like; grow fond of. **—полюби́ться**, *refl.* (*with dat.*) *colloq.* to catch the fancy of.

полюбова́ться *v.r., pfv. of* **любова́ться**.

полюбо́вный *adj.* (*of an agreement, settlement, etc.*) amicable. **—полюбо́вно**, *adv.* amicably.

полюбопы́тствовать *v., pfv. of* **любопы́тствовать**.

по́люс *n.* pole: Се́верный по́люс, North Pole; Ю́жный по́люс, South Pole. Они́ — два по́люса, they are poles apart.

поля́к *n.* Pole.

поля́на *n.* clearing (*in the woods*); glade.

поляриза́ция *n.* polarization.

поляризова́ть *v.impfv. & pfv.* [*pres.* **-зу́ю, -зу́ешь**] to polarize.

поля́рность *n.f.* polarity.

поля́рный *adj.* polar. **—Поля́рная звезда́**, the North Star. **—Поля́рный круг**, the Arctic *or* Antarctic Circle.

пома́да *n.* pomade. **—губна́я пома́да**, lipstick.

пома́дить *v.impfv.* [*pfv.* **напома́дить**; *pres.* **-жу, -дишь**] **1,** to pomade (one's hair). **2,** to paint (one's lips). **—пома́диться**, *refl.* **1,** to pomade one's hair. **2,** to put on lipstick.

пома́дка *n.* fruit candy.

пома́зание *n., relig.* anointment.

пома́зать [*infl.* **-ма́жу, -ма́жешь**] *v., pfv. of* **ма́зать** (*in sense #1*) *and* **пома́зывать**.

помазо́к [*gen.* **-зка́**] *n.* small brush; shaving brush.

пома́зывать *v.impfv.* [*pfv.* **пома́зать**] to anoint.

помале́ньку *adv., colloq.* **1,** little by little; a little at a time. **2,** at a leisurely pace; without hurrying. **3,** tolerable; all right.

пома́лкивать *v.impfv., colloq.* to keep quiet; hold one's tongue.

помани́ть *v., pfv. of* **мани́ть**.

пома́рка [*gen. pl.* **-рок**] *n.* pencil mark; correction.

помаха́ть *v.pfv.* [*infl.* **-машу́, -ма́шешь**] **1,** (*with dat.*) to wave (to). **2,** (*with instr.*) to wave (something).

пома́хивать *v.impfv.* (*with instr.*) **1,** to wave (*back and forth*). **2,** to wag; swish (one's tail).

поме́длить *v.pfv.* (*with inf. or* **с** + *instr.*) to delay; be slow.

помело́ *n.* broom (*for cleaning out stoves and chimneys*).

поме́ньше *adj.* a little smaller. **—adv.** a little less.

поменя́ть *v., pfv. of* **меня́ть**. **—поменя́ться**, *refl., pfv. of* **меня́ться**.

помера́нец [*gen.* **-нца**] *n.* wild bitter orange. **—помера́нцевый**, *adj.* orange (*attrib.*).

помере́ть [*infl.* **помру́, помрёшь**; *past* **по́мер, померла́, по́мерло, по́мерли**] *v., pfv. of* **помира́ть**.

помере́щиться *v.r., pfv. of* **мере́щиться**.

помёрзнуть *v.pfv.* [*past* **-мёрз, -мёрзла**] *colloq.* to perish from the frost.

поме́рить *v.pfv.* to try on. **—поме́риться**, *refl., pfv. of* **ме́риться**.

поме́ркнуть *v., pfv. of* **ме́ркнуть**.

помертве́лый *adj.* **1,** deathly pale. **2,** lifeless.

помертве́ть *v., pfv. of* **мертве́ть**.

помести́тельный *adj.* spacious; roomy. **—помести́тельность**, *n.f.* spaciousness; roominess.

помести́ть [*infl.* **-щу́, -сти́шь**] *v., pfv. of* **помеща́ть**. **—помести́ться**, *refl., pfv. of* **помеща́ться**.

поме́стный *adj.* **1,** estate (*attrib.*). **2,** landed: поме́стное дворя́нство, landed aristocracy.

поме́стье *n.* estate; manor.

по́месь *n.f.* **1,** hybrid; cross. **2,** *colloq.* mixture (*of two different elements*).

поме́сячный *adj.* monthly. **—поме́сячно**, *adv.* monthly; each month; by the month.

помёт *n.* **1,** dung; droppings. **2,** litter; brood.

поме́та *n.* mark; note.

поме́тить [*infl.* **-чу, -тишь**] *v., pfv. of* **ме́тить** (*in sense #1*) *and* **помеча́ть**.

поме́тка [*gen. pl.* **-ток**] *n.* mark; note.

поме́ха *n.* **1,** hindrance; obstacle. **2,** *pl.* static; interference.

помеча́ть *v.impfv.* [*pfv.* **поме́тить**] **1,** to mark. **2,** to date; write the date on.

поме́шанный *adj.* **1,** mad; crazy; insane. **2,** (*with на* + *prepl.*) *colloq.* addicted (to); hooked (on). **—n.** madman; lunatic.

помеша́тельство *n.* madness; insanity.

помеша́ть *v., pfv. of* **меша́ть**. **—помеша́ться**, *refl.* **1,** to go mad; go crazy. **2,** (*with на* + *prepl.*) *colloq.* to develop a passion (for); become a nut (about).

поме́шивать *v.impfv.* to stir a bit; stir slowly.

помеща́ть *v.impfv.* [*pfv.* **помести́ть**] **1,** to place; put. **2,** to house; lodge; accommodate. **3,** to invest. **4,** to publish (*in a newspaper, magazine, etc.*); (*of a publication*) to carry. **—помеща́ться**, *refl.* **1,** [*impfv. only*] to be; be placed; be situated. **2,** to be housed; be lodged. **3,** to fit: помеща́ться за столо́м, to fit around the table.

помеще́ние *n.* **1,** placing; placement. **2,** quarters; accommodations; housing. Жило́е помеще́ние, living quarters. **3,** premises.

помéщик *n.* landowner.

помéщичий [*fem.* -чья] *adj.* 1, of or pert. to a landowner. 2, manorial. —помéщичий дом, manor house.

помидóр *n.* tomato. —помидóрный, *adj.* tomato (*attrib.*).

поми́лование *n.* 1, pardon; forgiveness. 2, clemency; a pardon.

поми́ловать *v.pfv.* [*infl.* -лую, -луешь] to pardon. —Гóсподи, поми́луй!, Lord have mercy!

поми́мо *prep.,* with *gen.* 1, besides; apart from; aside from. 2, without the knowledge of. —поми́мо всегó прóчего, in addition to/ apart from/ everything else; all else aside.

поми́н *n., obs.* mention. —и в поми́не нет (*preceded by gen.*), there is not a trace of; (something is) not to be found anywhere. —и поми́ну нет (*preceded by о* + *prepl.*), there is no trace/mention/question of; (something is) out of the question. —лёгок (легкá) на поми́не, talk of the devil.

помина́ть *v.impfv.* [*pfv.* помяну́ть] 1, to remember; recall. 2, (*with* о) to mention. 3, to pray for. 4, to give (*or* attend) a funeral repast in memory of. —помина́ть добрóм *or* дóбрым слóвом (+ *acc.*), to speak well of. —помяни́те моё слóво, mark my words! —не помина́й (меня́) ли́хом, don't think ill of me. —помина́й как зва́ли, he (she, it) disappeared without a trace.

поми́нки [*gen.* -нок] *n.pl.* funeral repast.

помину́тный *adj.* 1, by the minute. 2, continual; constant. —помину́тно, *adv.* constantly; continually.

помира́ть *v.impfv.* [*pfv.* померéть] *colloq.* to die. —помира́ть сó смеху, *colloq.* to die laughing.

помири́ть *v., pfv. of* мири́ть. —помири́ться, *refl., pfv. of* мири́ться.

пóмнить *v.impfv.* 1, to remember. 2, *in* не пóмнить себя́, to get carried away; lose control of oneself; (*with* от) be beside oneself (with). —пóмниться, *refl.* 1, (*with dat.*) to remember: Мне пóмнится, I remember; I seem to remember. 2, *impers., colloq.* to remember (*said of oneself*): как пóмнится, as I recall.

помнóгу *adv., colloq.* 1, a lot. 2, (*with gen.*) many.

помножа́ть *v.impfv.* [*pfv.* помнóжить] 1, *math.* to multiply. 2, *fig.* to increase; augment.

помнóжить *v., pfv. of* мнóжить *and* помножа́ть.

помога́ть *v.impfv.* [*pfv.* помóчь] (*with dat.*) to help.

по-мóему *adv.* in my opinion.

помóи [*gen.* -мóев] *n.pl.* kitchen waste; dirty dishwater. —облива́ть (когó-нибудь) помóями, to vilify; drag through the mud.

помóйка [*gen. pl.* -мóек] *n., colloq.* garbage pit.

помóйный *adj.* garbage (*attrib.*): помóйное ведрó, garbage pail. —помóйная я́ма, cesspool.

помóл *n.* 1, grinding. 2, grind: мéлкого помóла, finely ground; fine-ground.

помóлвить *v.pfv.* [*infl.* -влю, -вишь] (*with* с + *instr.*) to betroth (to).

помóлвка *n.* engagement; betrothal.

помоли́ться *v.r., pfv. of* моли́ться (*in sense #1*).

помолодéть *v., pfv. of* молодéть.

помолча́ть *v.pfv.* [*infl.* -чу́, -чи́шь] to be silent (*for a while*).

помóрник *n.* jaeger (*bird*). —большóй помóрник, skua.

помóрщиться *v.r.pfv.* to make a face; wince; grimace.

помóрье *n.* coastal region.

помóст *n.* 1, platform; dais. 2, scaffold. 3, wooden roadway.

пóмочи [*gen.* -чéй] *n.pl.* suspenders. —быть *or* ходи́ть на помоча́х у (+ *gen.*), to be tied to someone's apron strings. —води́ть на помоча́х, to keep on a leash (*fig.*).

помочи́ть *v.pfv.* [*infl.* -мочу́, -мóчишь] to moisten slightly. —помочи́ться, *refl., pfv. of* мочи́ться.

помóчь [*infl. like* мочь] *v., pfv. of* помога́ть.

помóщник *n.m.* [*fem.* -ница] assistant; helper. Помóщник дирéктора, assistant director.

пóмощь *n.f.* help; aid; assistance. —на пóмощь!, help! —при пóмощи; с пóмощью (+ *gen.*), with the help (*or* aid) of; by means of.

пóмпа *n.* 1, pump. 2, pomp.

помпéзный *adj.* lavish; extravagant. —помпéзность, *n.f.* pagentry; pomp.

помпóн *n.* pompon.

помрача́ть *v.impfv.* [*pfv.* помрачи́ть] to dull; cloud (one's mind, senses, etc.).

помрачнéть *v., pfv. of* мрачнéть.

помути́ть *v., pfv. of* мути́ть (*in sense #2*). —помути́ться, *refl., pfv. of* мути́ться (*in sense #2*).

помутнéние *n.* clouding; dimming.

помутнéть *v., pfv. of* мутнéть.

помучить *v.pfv.* to tease; torment; make suffer. —помучиться, *refl.* to suffer.

помча́ть *v., pfv. of* мчать. —помча́ться, *refl., pfv. of* мча́ться.

помыка́ть *v.impfv.* (*with instr.*) *colloq.* to order about.

пóмысел [*gen.* -сла] *n.* thought; idea; intention. —у (+ *gen.*) пóмыслов (*or* в пóмыслах) нет (*with inf. or* о), he/she has no thought of ...

помы́слить *v., pfv. of* помышля́ть.

помы́ть *v., pfv. of* мыть. —помы́ться, *refl., pfv. of* мы́ться.

помышля́ть *v.impfv.* [*pfv.* помы́слить] (*with* о) to think (about); contemplate.

помяну́ть [*infl.* -мяну́, -мя́нешь] *v., pfv. of* помина́ть.

помя́тый *adj.* 1, rumpled; creased. 2, *colloq.* haggard.

помя́ть *v., pfv. of* мять (*in senses #2, 4, 5*). —помя́ться, *refl., pfv. of* мя́ться.

понадéяться *v.r.pfv.* [*infl.* -дéюсь, -дéешься] (*with* на + *acc.*) to count on.

понáдобиться *v.r.pfv.* [*infl.* -блюсь, -бишься] (*with dat.*) 1, to be needed: Éсли вам э́то когдá-нибудь понáдобится, if you ever have need of it. 2, to be necessary.

понапрáсну *adv., colloq.* 1, in vain. 2, for no reason; for nothing.

понаслы́шке *adv., colloq.* through hearsay.

понача́лу *adv., colloq.* at first.

по-нáшему *adv.* in our opinion.

поневóле *adv.* against one's will; willy-nilly.

понедéльник *n.* Monday.

понедéльный *adj.* weekly. —понедéльно, *adv.*

понемно́гу *adv.* **1,** a little at a time. **2,** little by little.

понести́ *v.pfv.* [*infl.* like **нести́**] **1,** *pfv. of* **нести́**. **2,** (*of a horse*) to bolt. —**понести́сь**, *refl.* **1,** *pfv. of* **нести́сь**. **2,** to take off; dash off.

по́ни *n.m. indecl.* pony.

понижа́ть *v.impfv.* [*pfv.* **пони́зить**] **1,** to lower; reduce. **2,** to lower (one's voice). **3,** to demote. —**понижа́ться**, *refl.* to go down; drop; decline.

пониже́ние *n.* **1,** lowering; reduction. **2,** drop; decline; fall. **3,** *in* пониже́ние в до́лжности (*or* по слу́жбе), demotion.

пони́зить [*infl.* **-жу, -зишь**] *v., pfv. of* **понижа́ть**. —**пони́зиться**, *refl., pfv. of* **понижа́ться**.

по́низу *adv.* low; close to the ground.

поника́ть *v.impfv.* [*pfv.* **пони́кнуть**] **1,** to droop. **2,** *in* поника́ть голово́й, to hang one's head.

пони́кнуть [*past* пони́к, пони́кла] *v., pfv. of* **ни́кнуть** *and* **поника́ть**.

понима́ние *n.* **1,** understanding; comprehension. **2,** interpretation.

понима́ть *v.impfv.* [*pfv.* **поня́ть**] **1,** to understand: понима́ть по-ру́сски, to understand Russian. Поня́ть намёк, to take a hint. **2,** to realize: Он сра́зу по́нял, что..., he immediately realized that... **3,** [*impfv. only*] (*with acc. or* в + *prepl.*) to have an understanding of: know something about: Я ничего́ не понима́ю в спо́рте, I know nothing about sports.

поножо́вщина *n., colloq.* fight involving the use of knives.

понома́рь [*gen.* **-маря́**] *n.m.* sexton.

поно́с *n.* diarrhea.

поноси́ть[1] *v.impfv.* [*pres.* **-ношу́, -но́сишь**] to vilify; revile; defame.

поноси́ть[2] *v.pfv.* [*infl.* **-ношу́, -но́сишь**] **1,** to carry (*for a while*). **2,** to wear (*for a while*).

поноше́ние *n.* **1,** vilification; defamation. **2,** *usu. pl.* verbal abuse. **3,** *obs.* disgrace.

поно́шенный *adj.* **1,** worn; shabby; threadbare. **2,** *colloq.* somewhat the worse for wear.

понра́виться *v.r., pfv. of* **нра́виться**.

понтифика́т *n.* pontificate.

понто́н *n.* pontoon. —**понто́нный**, *adj.* pontoon (*attrib.*): понто́нный мост, pontoon bridge.

понужда́ть *v.impfv.* [*pfv.* **пону́дить**] to force; compel.

понужде́ние *n.* compulsion.

понука́ть *v.impfv.* **1,** to urge on (an animal). **2,** *colloq.* to hurry; rush.

пону́рить *v.pfv.* to hang (one's head). —**пону́риться**, *refl.* to hang one's head; look despondent.

пону́рый *adj.* **1,** downcast; despondent. **2,** bowed; bent.

по́нчик *n.* doughnut.

по́нчо *n. indecl.* poncho.

поны́не *adv.* until now.

поню́хать *v., pfv. of* **ню́хать**.

поню́шка [*gen. pl.* **-шек**] *n., colloq.* pinch (*of tobacco*). —**ни за поню́шку табаку́**, *colloq.* for no reason whatever; for no purpose; needlessly.

поня́тие *n.* concept; notion; idea.

поня́тливый *adj.* bright; clever; sharp.

поня́тно *adv.* **1,** clearly; intelligibly. **2,** *colloq.* naturally; understandably. —*adj., used predicatively* **1,** understandable: Э́то поня́тно, that is understandable. Всем поня́тно, что..., everyone understands that... **2,** obvious: Соверше́нно поня́тно что..., it is quite obvious that... —*predicate* **1,** I understand. **2,** *colloq., used interrogatively,* do you understand?; is that understood?

поня́тность *n.f.* intelligibility.

поня́тный *adj.* [*short form* **-тен, -тна**] **1,** understandable; comprehensible; intelligible. **2,** understandable; justified; justifiable. —**поня́тное де́ло**, *colloq.* naturally; understandably.

понято́й *n., decl. as an adj.* witness (*present during a search or when something is being counted*).

поня́ть [*infl.* **пойму́, поймёшь**; *past* по́нял, поняла́, по́няло, по́няли] *v., pfv. of* **понима́ть**.

пообе́дать *v., pfv. of* **обе́дать**.

пообеща́ть *v.pfv.* to promise.

по́одаль *adv.* at a distance: держа́ться поо́даль, to keep one's distance.

поодино́чке *adv.* one at a time; one by one.

поочерёдный *adj.* alternating; done in turn. —**поочерёдно**, *adv.* in turn.

поощре́ние *n.* encouragement.

поощри́тельный *adj.* serving to encourage: поощри́тельная улы́бка, a smile of encouragement. Поощри́тельная пре́мия, incentive bonus.

поощря́ть *v.impfv.* [*pfv.* **поощри́ть**] to encourage; stimulate.

поп [*gen.* **попа́**] *n., colloq.* priest. —**ста́вить на попа́**, *colloq.* to stand on end.

попада́ние *n.* hit: прямо́е попада́ние, direct hit.

попада́ть *v.impfv.* [*pfv.* **попа́сть**] **1,** (*with* в *or* на + *acc.*) to get (to a place). **2,** (*with* в + *acc.*) to get into (a building, situation, trouble, accident, etc.). **3,** (*with* в + *acc.*) to end up (in); wind up (in). **4,** (*with* в + *acc.*) to fall into (a trap, someone's clutches, etc.). **5,** (*with* в *or* под + *acc.*) to get caught in: попа́сть в мете́ль, to get caught in a snowstorm; попа́сть под дождь, to get caught in the rain. **6,** (*with* на + *acc.*) to catch; make; be on time for (a train, bus, etc.). **7,** (*with* под + *acc.*) to be run over (by). **8,** (*with* в *or* на + *acc.*) to get into; be accepted by: попа́сть в институ́т, to get into the institute; попа́сть на рабо́ту, to land a job. **9,** (*with* в + *acc.*) (*of a missile*) to hit; strike: попа́сть в цель, to hit/strike the target. Пу́ля попа́ла ему́ в грудь, the bullet struck him in the chest. Попа́сть мячо́м в прохо́жего, to strike a passer-by with a ball. **10,** (*with instr. and* в + *acc.*) to get (something into a small opening): попа́сть ключо́м в замо́к, to get the key into the lock. **11,** (*with* под + *acc.*) to come under (suspicion, someone's influence, etc.). **12,** (*with* в + *nom. pl.*) to become: попа́сть в лётчики, to become a pilot. **13,** *impers.* (*with dat.*) *colloq.* to get a scolding; catch it: Мне попадёт от отца́, I'll catch it from my father. —**попа́сть в плен**, to be taken prisoner. —**попа́сть в ру́ки** (+ *gen. or dat.*), **1,** to fall into the hands of (*e.g.* the enemy). **2,** to come into the hands of; come into the possession of. Мне попа́л(а) в ру́ки (+ *nom.*), I came across... —**попа́сть ного́й в** (+ *acc.*)

to step in (a puddle, mud, etc.). —**попáсть под огóнь проти́вника,** to come under enemy fire. —**попáсть пóд руку** (+ *dat.*), to turn up (*by chance*): всё, что ему́ попадáло пóд руку, everything (*or* whatever) he could get his hands on. —**попáсть под суд,** to be put on trial; be brought to trial. —**где попáло; куда́ попáло,** anywhere; wherever one happens to be. —**как попáло,** helter-skelter; in a hit or miss fashion. —**кто попáло,** anyone; the first one who comes along. —**что попáло,** anything; anything that comes along.

попадáться *v.r.impfv.* [*pfv.* попáсться] **1,** to be caught; get caught: попáсться на кра́же, to be/get caught stealing. **2,** (*with dat.*) *colloq.* to come across: Мне попáлась интерéсная кни́га, I came across an interesting book. —**пéрвый попáвшийся,** the first one to come along. —**попáсться в ру́ки,** = попáсть в ру́ки. —**попáсться на глаза́** (+ *dat.*), to catch someone's eye. —**попáсться на у́дочку,** to swallow the bait. —**попáсться пóд руку,** = попáсть пóд руку.

попадья́ [*gen. pl.* -дéй] *n., colloq.* priest's wife.
попáрно *adv.* in pairs; by two.
попáсть [*infl. like* пасть] *v., pfv. of* попадáть. —**попáсться,** *refl., pfv. of* попадáться.
попáхивать *v.impfv., colloq.* **1,** (*of spoiled food*) to smell. **2,** (*with instr.*) to smell (of).
попеня́ть *v., pfv. of* пеня́ть.
поперёк *adv.* across. —*prep., with gen.* across; athwart. —**знать вдоль и поперёк,** to know inside out. —**стать поперёк гóрла** (+ *dat.*), to stick in someone's throat. —**стоя́ть поперёк дорóги** (+ *dat.*), to stand in someone's way.
поперемéнно *adv.* alternately; in turn.
попере́чина *n.* crossbeam; crossbar; crosspiece.
попере́чник *n.* diameter.
попере́чный *adj.* transverse; cross-: попере́чный разре́з; попере́чное сечéние, cross section. Попере́чная пила́, cross-cut saw. —**ка́ждый встрéчный и попере́чный,** any (*or* every) Tom, Dick, or Harry.
поперхну́ться *v.r.pfv.* (*with instr.*) to choke (on).
попечéние *n.* care; charge: быть на попечéнии (+ *gen.*), to be in the care/charge of; имéть (+ *acc.*) на попечéнии, to have charge of.
попечи́тель *n.m.* guardian; trustee. —**попечи́тельство,** *n.* guardianship; trusteeship.
попива́ть *v.impfv., colloq.* **1,** *v.t.* to drink (something) slowly. **2,** *v.i.* to drink from time to time.
попира́ть *v.impfv.* [*pfv.* попра́ть] to trample upon; violate; flout.
пописа́ть *v.pfv.* [*infl.* -пишу́, -пи́шешь] to write (*for a while*).
попи́сывать *v.impfv., colloq.* to write occasionally; write from time to time.
попи́ть *v.pfv.* [*infl.* попью́, попьёшь; *past* пóпил, попила́, пóпило *or* попи́ло, пóпили *or* попи́ли] *colloq.* **1,** (*with gen.*) to have a drink of. **2,** to have something to drink.
поплáвать *v.pfv.* to go for a swim; have a swim.
поплавóк [*gen.* -вка́] *n.* **1,** float (*marker*). **2,** fishing float; bob. **3,** *colloq.* floating restaurant.

поплáкать *v.pfv.* [*infl.* -плáчу, -плáчешь] to have a brief cry; shed a few tears.
поплати́ться *v.r., pfv. of* плати́ться.
поплести́сь *v.r.pfv.* [*infl. like* плести́сь] to trudge along.
попли́н *n.* poplin. —**попли́новый,** *adj.* poplin.
поплы́ть *v.pfv.* [*infl. like* плыть] **1,** *pfv. of* плыть. **2,** to begin to swim. **3,** to begin to drift.
попляса́ть *v.pfv.* [*infl.* -пляшу́, -пля́шешь] *colloq.* to dance (*for a while*).
попóвич *n., colloq.* priest's son.
попóвна [*gen. pl.* -вен] *n., colloq.* priest's daughter.
попóвник *n.* (oxeye) daisy.
попóзже *adv.* a little later.
попóйка [*gen. pl.* -óек] *n., colloq.* drinking bout.
пополáм *adv.* **1,** in half; in two. **2,** half and half: снег пополáм с дождём, half snow, half rain.
пóлзень [*gen.* -зня] *n.m.* nuthatch (*bird*).
поползновéние *n.* impulse; inclination.
поползти́ *v.pfv.* [*infl. like* ползти́] **1,** *pfv. of* ползти́. **2,** to begin to crawl.
пополнéние *n.* **1,** replenishment. **2,** *mil., often pl.* reinforcements; additional personnel.
пополнéть *v., pfv. of* полнéть.
пополня́ть *v.impfv.* [*pfv.* попóлнить] **1,** to replenish (a supply of something). **2,** to supply with more of something. **3,** *fig.* to expand; broaden; enlarge. **4,** *mil.* to reinforce; beef up.
пополу́дни *adv.* in the afternoon; p.m.
попóмнить *v.pfv., colloq.* to remember. —**попóмните моё слóво,** mark my words!
попóна *n.* horsecloth.
попóртить *v.pfv.* [*infl.* -чу, -тишь] *colloq.* to damage slightly.
попóтчевать *v., pfv. of* пóтчевать.
поправéть *v., pfv. of* правéть.
поправи́мый *adj.* **1,** (*of an error*) rectifiable. **2,** (*of a situation*) not beyond repair; not hopeless.
попрáвить [*infl.* -влю, -вишь] *v., pfv. of* поправля́ть. —**попрáвиться,** *refl., pfv. of* поправля́ться.
попрáвка [*gen. pl.* -вок] *n.* **1,** correction. **2,** amendment. **3,** repair. **4,** adjustment. **5,** recovery: У негó дéло идёт на попрáвку, he is on the road to recovery; he is on the mend.
поправлéние *n.* **1,** correcting; correction. **2,** adjustment. **3,** straightening out; putting right.
поправля́ть *v.impfv.* [*pfv.* попрáвить] **1,** to correct. **2,** to repair; fix; mend. **3,** to straighten; adjust; set right; put right. **4,** to improve (one's health). —**поправля́ться,** *refl.* **1,** to correct oneself. **2,** to improve; get better. **3,** to get well; recover. **4,** to put on weight.
попрáть *v., used only in the past tense, pfv. of* попира́ть.
по-прéжнему *adv.* as before.
попрёк *n., colloq.* critical remark. Вéчные попрёки, endless nagging.
попрека́ть *v.impfv.* [*pfv.* попрекну́ть] *colloq.* to reproach.
пóприще *n.* field (of endeavor); profession: нау́чное пóприще, the scientific field; педагоги́ческое пóприще, the teaching profession.
попрóбовать *v., pfv. of* прóбовать.

попроси́ть *v., pfv. of* **проси́ть.** —**попроси́ться,** *refl., pfv. of* **проси́ться.**

по́просту *adv.* simply. —**по́просту говоря́,** to put it bluntly; in plain words.

попроша́йка [*gen. pl.* **-ша́ек**] *n.m. & f., colloq.* beggar.

попроша́йничать *v.impfv., colloq.* to beg.

попроша́йничество *n., colloq.* begging.

попроща́ться *v.r., pfv. of* **проща́ться.**

попры́гать *v.pfv.* **1,** to jump. **2,** to hop.

попры́гивать *v.impfv., colloq.* to hop about; hop around.

попрыгу́н *n.m.* [*fem.* **-гу́нья**] *colloq.* fidgety person; fidget.

попря́тать *v.pfv.* [*infl.* **-пря́чу, -пря́чешь**] *colloq.* to hide (all or many of something). —**попря́таться,** *refl., colloq.* (*of all or many of something*) to hide.

попуга́й *n.* parrot.

попуга́ть *v.pfv.* to frighten a little; scare.

попу́дрить *v.pfv.* to powder. —**попу́дриться,** *refl.* to powder one's nose.

попули́ст *n.* populist. —**попули́стский,** *adj.* populist.

популяриза́ция *n.* popularization.

популяризи́ровать *v.impfv. & pfv.* [*pres.* **-рую, -руешь**] to popularize. *Also,* **популяризова́ть** [*pres.* **-зу́ю, -зу́ешь**].

популя́рно *adv.* in understandable terms; in a way that is easy to understand.

популя́рность *n.f.* popularity.

популя́рный *adj.* [*short form* **-рен, -рна**] **1,** popular. **2,** written or set forth in understandable terms.

попурри́ *n.neut. indecl., music* medley.

попусти́тельство *n.* **1,** (*with dat.*) tolerance (of); permissive attitude (toward). **2,** connivance.

попусти́тельствовать *v.impfv.* [*pres.* **-ствую, -ству-ешь**] (*with dat.*) to permit; tolerate; put up with; do nothing about.

по́пусту *adv., colloq.* to no purpose; for nothing. *Also,* **по-пусто́му.**

попу́тно *adv.* **1,** at the same time; while one is (*or* was) at it. **2,** in passing: попу́тно отме́тить, to mention in passing.

попу́тный *adj.* **1,** going the same way. Попу́тная маши́на, passing car. **2,** situated along the way: попу́тная ста́нция, way station. **3,** *fig.* passing: попу́тное замеча́ние, passing remark. —**попу́тный ве́тер,** favorable wind; tail wind.

попу́тчик *n.* **1,** traveling companion. **2,** *polit.* fellow traveler.

попыта́ть *v.pfv., colloq.* to try: попыта́ть сча́стья, to try one's luck. —**попыта́ться,** *refl., pfv. of* **пыта́ться.**

попы́тка [*gen. pl.* **-ток**] *n.* attempt; try.

попы́хивать *v.impfv., colloq.* **1,** to give off occasional puffs of smoke. **2,** (*with instr.*) to puff on (a cigar, pipe, etc.).

попя́титься *v.r., pfv. of* **пя́титься.**

попя́тный *adj., obs.* backward; reverse. —**идти́ на попя́тный** *or* **попя́тную,** *colloq.* to go back on one's word.

по́ра *n.* pore.

пора́ [*acc.* **по́ру**] *n.* **1,** time. **2,** *impers.* it is time: Нам пора́ домо́й, it is time for us to be going home; it is

time we were going home. —**в (са́мую) по́ру,** at (just) the right time. —**в ту по́ру,** then; at that time. —**в э́ту по́ру,** now; at this time. —**до каки́х пор?,** until when?; how long (*in the future*)? —**до поры́ до вре́мени,** for the time being. —**до сих пор,** up to now; until now. —**до тех пор,** until then. —**до тех пор пока́,** as long as. —**до тех пор пока́ не,** until the time when. —**на пе́рвых пора́х,** at first. —**с да́вних пор,** for a long time. —**с каки́х пор?,** since when? —**с неда́вних пор,** lately; of late. —**с не́которых пор,** for some time now. —**с тех пор,** since then. —**с тех пор, как,** since.

порабо́тать *v.pfv.* to do some work.

пораоти́тель *n.m.* enslaver; oppressor.

порабоща́ть *v.impfv.* [*pfv.* **пораоти́ть**] to enslave.

порабоще́ние *n.* enslavement.

поравня́ть *v.pfv., colloq.* to make equal; place on an equal footing. —**поравня́ться,** *refl.* (*with* **с** + *instr.*) to pull alongside (of); draw abreast (of); draw even (with).

пора́довать *v.pfv.* [*infl.* **-дую, -дуешь**] to gladden; make happy. —**пора́доваться,** *refl.* to be glad; be happy.

поража́ть *v.impfv.* [*pfv.* **порази́ть**] **1,** to strike; smite. **2,** to hit (a target). **3,** (*of a disease*) to strike; affect. **4,** to defeat; rout. **5,** to strike; amaze. **6,** *v.i.* (*with instr.*) to be striking (for). Поража́ть свое́й красото́й, to be strikingly beautiful. —**поража́ться,** *refl.* to be struck; be amazed.

пораже́нец [*gen.* **-нца**] *n.* defeatist.

пораже́ние *n.* **1,** defeat. **2,** damage; destruction. **3,** *med.* lesion. —**пораже́ние в права́х,** loss (*or* deprivation) of rights.

пораже́нчество *n.* defeatism. —**пораже́нческий,** *adj.* defeatist.

порази́тельный *adj.* striking; astonishing. —**порази́тельно,** *adv.* strikingly.

порази́ть [*infl.* **-жу́, -зи́шь**] *v., pfv. of* **поража́ть.** —**порази́ться,** *refl., pfv. of* **поража́ться.**

поразмы́слить *v.pfv., colloq.* to ponder.

по-ра́зному *adv.* differently; in different ways.

пора́нить *v.pfv.* to wound; injure. —**пора́ниться,** *refl.* to injure oneself; hurt oneself.

пора́ньше *adv.* a little earlier.

пораски́нуть *v.pfv., colloq., in* пораски́нуть умо́м, to think it over.

пораста́ть *v.impfv.* [*pfv.* **порасти́**] (*with instr.*) to become overgrown (with).

порасти́ [*infl. like* **расти́**] *v., pfv. of* **пораста́ть.**

по́рванный *adj.* torn.

порва́ть [*infl.* **порву́, порвёшь;** *past fem.* **порвала́**] *v., pfv. of* **рвать** *and* **порыва́ть.** —**порва́ться,** *refl.* [*past tense stress as in* **рва́ться**] **1,** *pfv. of* **рва́ться** *and* **порыва́ться** (*in sense #1*). **2,** to break; snap.

пореде́ть *v., pfv. of* **реде́ть.**

поре́з *n.* cut.

поре́зать *v.pfv.* [*infl.* **-ре́жу, -ре́жешь**] **1,** to cut (accidentally). **2,** to slice. —**поре́заться,** *refl.* to cut oneself.

поре́й *n.* leek.

порекомендова́ть *v., pfv. of* **рекомендова́ть.**

по́ристый *adj.* porous. —**по́ристость,** *n.f.* porosity.

порица́ние *n.* condemnation; censure.

порица́ть *v.impfv.* to condemn; censure.

по́рка *n.* **1,** unstitching. **2,** *colloq.* whipping; thrashing; flogging.

порногра́фия *n.* pornography. —**порнографи́ческий,** *adj.* pornographic.

по́ровну *adv.* equally; in equal parts.

поро́г *n.* **1,** threshold; doorstep. **2,** *usu. pl.* rapids (*of a river*). —**на поро́ге, 1,** at hand; just around the corner. **2,** (*with gen.*) on the threshold of; on the brink of. —**обива́ть (все) поро́ги,** to knock on every door.

поро́да *n.* **1,** breed; strain. **2,** *fig.* breed; type (*of person*). —**го́рная поро́да,** *geol.* rock.

поро́дистый *adj.* thoroughbred; pedigreed.

породи́ть [*infl.* -жу́, -ди́шь] *v., pfv. of* **порожда́ть.**

породни́ть *v., pfv. of* **родни́ть.** —**породни́ться,** *refl., pfv. of* **родни́ться.**

порожда́ть *v.impfv.* [*pfv.* **породи́ть**] **1,** *obs.* to give birth to; beget. **2,** to give rise to; generate; engender.

порожде́ние *n.* product; result.

поро́жистый *adj.* (*of a river*) full of rapids.

поро́жний *adj., colloq.* empty. —**перелива́ть из пусто́го в поро́жнее,** to engage in idle chatter.

порожня́к [*gen.* -няка́] *n., colloq.* empty trains; empty cars. —**порожняко́м,** *adv., colloq.* empty; without cargo; without passengers.

по́рознь *adv.* separately; apart.

порозове́ть *v., pfv. of* **розове́ть.**

поро́й *adv.* at times; occasionally; now and then.

поро́к *n.* **1,** vice. **2,** defect.

поросёнок [*gen.* -нка; *pl.* -ся́та, -ся́т] *n.* piglet; suckling pig.

по́росль *n.f.* **1,** sprouts; shoots. **2,** thicket. **3,** *colloq.* growth of hair.

порося́тина *n.* suckling pig (*served as food*).

поро́ть *v.impfv.* [*pres.* **порю́, по́решь**] **1,** [*pfv.* **вы́пороть**] *colloq.* to whip; flog. **2,** [*pfv.* **распоро́ть**] to unstitch. **3,** [*impfv. only*] *colloq.* to talk (nonsense).

по́рох *n.* powder; gunpowder. —**не ню́хать по́роху,** never to have been in combat. —**па́хнет по́рохом,** war is in the air. —**тра́тить по́рох да́ром,** to waste one's energies. —**у него́ по́роху не хвата́ет,** he hasn't got it in him; he is not up to it.

порохово́й *adj.* powder (*attrib.*); gunpowder (*attrib.*): порохова́я бо́чка, powder keg.

поро́чить *v.impfv.* [*pfv.* **опоро́чить**] **1,** to sully; besmirch (someone's reputation). **2,** to disparage; run down. **3,** to discredit.

поро́чность *n.f.* depravity.

поро́чный *adj.* **1,** perverted; depraved. **2,** faulty; flawed; unsound. —**поро́чный круг,** vicious circle.

поро́ша *n.* fresh snow; newly-fallen snow.

пороши́ть *v.impfv.* **1,** (*of snow*) to fall lightly. **2,** *impers.* to be snowing lightly.

порошкообра́зный *adj.* powdery.

порошо́к [*gen.* -шка́] *n.* **1,** powder. **2,** *in* моло́чный порошо́к, powdered milk; яи́чный порошо́к, powdered eggs. —**стере́ть в порошо́к,** to make mincemeat of.

порт [*2nd loc.* порту́; *pl.* по́рты, -то́в, -та́м] *n.* port.

порта́л *n.* portal.

портати́вный *adj.* portable.

портве́йн *n.* port (wine).

по́ртик *n.* portico.

по́ртить *v.impfv.* [*pfv.* **испо́ртить**; *pres.* **по́рчу, по́ртишь**] **1,** to spoil; damage; mar; impair. **2,** to corrupt. **3,** to ruin. —**по́ртить кровь** (+ *dat.*), to upset; annoy. По́ртить себе́ кровь, to worry unnecessarily.

по́ртиться *v.r.impfv.* [*pfv.* **испо́ртиться**; *pres.* **по́рчусь, по́ртишься**] **1,** to spoil; decay. **2,** to deteriorate. **3,** (*of the weather*) to turn bad.

портки́ [*gen.* **портко́в** *or* **порто́к**] *n.pl., colloq.* pants.

портмоне́ (нэ) *n.neut. indecl., obs.* purse.

портни́ха *n.* dressmaker.

портно́вский *adj.* tailor's.

портно́й *n., decl. as an adj.* tailor.

портня́жничать *v.impfv., colloq.* to be a tailor; work as a tailor.

портня́жный *adj.* tailor's. —**портня́жное де́ло,** tailoring.

портови́к [*gen.* -вика́] *n.* dock worker.

порто́вый *adj.* port (*attrib.*). —**порто́вый го́род,** seaport. —**порто́вый рабо́чий,** dock worker.

портре́т *n.* portrait. —**портрети́ст,** *n.* portrait painter. —**портре́тный,** *adj.* portrait (*attrib.*).

портсига́р *n.* cigarette case.

португа́лец [*gen.* -льца] *n.* Portuguese man. —**португа́лка,** *n.* Portuguese woman. —**португа́льский,** *adj.* Portuguese.

портула́к *n.* portulaca; purslane.

портупе́я *n.* sword belt.

портфе́ль *n.m.* **1,** briefcase; portfolio. **2,** portfolio; office: мини́стр без портфе́ля, minister without portfolio.

портше́з *n.* sedan chair.

портье́ *n.m. indecl.* desk clerk (*in a hotel*).

портье́ра *n.* heavy curtain (*for a door or window*).

портя́нка [*gen. pl.* -нок] *n.* foot wrapping (*worn in place of socks*).

поруби́ть *v.pfv.* [*infl.* -рублю́, -ру́бишь] *colloq.* **1,** to chop down. **2,** to chop.

пору́бка *n., colloq.* chopping down (*of trees*).

поруга́ние *n.* **1,** humiliation; degradation. **2,** desecration.

поруга́ть *v.pfv.* **1,** to tell off; curse out. **2,** to humiliate. **3,** to desecrate. —**поруга́ться,** *refl.* **1,** (*with* с + *instr.*) to quarrel (with); have words (with). **2,** to swear; curse.

пору́ка *n.* bail; surety; guarantee. Брать на пору́ки, to put up bail for; post bond for; bail (someone) out. Отпуска́ть на пору́ки, to release on bail. —**кругова́я пору́ка, 1,** collective responsibility. **2,** covering up for each other.

поруча́ть *v.impfv.* [*pfv.* **поручи́ть**] (*with dat.*) **1,** to instruct; charge; commission. **2,** to entrust.

поруче́ние *n.* assignment; mission; errand.

пору́чик *n., pre-rev.* lieutenant.

поручи́тель *n.m.* person who vouches for another; sponsor.

поручи́тельство *n.* **1,** statement vouching for another; reference. **2,** bail.

поручи́ть [*infl.* -ручу́, -ру́чишь] *v., pfv. of* **поруча́ть.** —**поручи́ться,** *refl., pfv. of* **руча́ться.**

по́ручни [*gen.* **-ней**] *n.pl.* handrail.

порфи́р *n.* porphyry.

порха́ть *v.impfv.* [*pfv.* **порхну́ть**] to flit.

порцио́нный *adj.* à la carte.

по́рция *n.* portion; helping.

по́рча *n.* **1,** damage; spoilage. **2,** *fig.* deterioration.

по́ршень [*gen.* **-шня**] *n.m.* piston.

поршнево́й *adj.* piston (*attrib.*).

поры́в *n.* **1,** gust (*of wind*). **2,** fit; burst (*of emotion*). **3,** impulse.

порыва́ть *v.impfv.* [*pfv.* **порва́ть**] **1,** *v.i.* (*with* **с** + *instr.*) to break (with). **2,** *v.t.* to break off; sever (ties, relations, etc.). —**порыва́ться,** *refl.* **1,** (*of ties, relations, etc.*) to be broken off. **2,** [*impfv. only*] to try to move; try to get up. **3,** [*impfv. only*] (*with inf.*) to try (to); strive (to).

поры́вистый *adj.* **1,** (*of the wind*) gusty. **2,** (*of movements*) jerky. **3,** (*of a person*) impetuous; impulsive.

порыже́ть *v., pfv. of* **рыже́ть.**

поры́ться *v.r., pfv. of* **ры́ться.**

поря́дковый *adj., in* **поря́дковое числи́тельное,** ordinal number; **поря́дковый но́мер,** serial number.

поря́дком *adv., colloq.* **1,** really; good and... **2,** thoroughly. **3,** properly.

поря́док [*gen.* **-дка**] *n.* **1,** order; sequence: по поря́дку, in order; in sequence; in succession. **2,** (proper) order: Всё в поря́дке, everything is in order; everything is all right (*or* O.K.). **3,** procedure: поря́док голосова́ния, voting procedure. **4,** order; regime: ста́рый поря́док, the old order. **5,** *mil.* order; formation. **6,** *in в* спе́шном поря́дке, in short order; в обяза́тельном поря́дке, without fail; в односторо́ннем поря́дке, unilaterally. —**в поря́дке** (+ *gen.*), as; by way of. —**в поря́дке веще́й,** in the nature of things. —**идти́ свои́м поря́дком,** to take its normal course. —**поря́дка** (+ *gen.*), on the order of; approximately.

поря́дочно *adv.* **1,** honestly. **2,** *colloq.* quite a bit; quite a while; quite a way. **3,** *colloq.* fairly well.

поря́дочность *n.f.* honesty; decency.

поря́дочный *adj.* **1,** honest; decent. **2,** fairly good; decent. **3,** considerable; sizable. **4,** utter; out-and-out.

посади́ть [*infl.* **-сажу́, -са́дишь**] *v., pfv. of* **сажа́ть.**

поса́дка *n.* **1,** (act of) planting. **2,** *pl.* plantings. **3,** boarding; embarkation. **4,** landing (*of an aircraft*). **5,** manner of sitting (*when riding*). —**поса́дка головы́,** position of the head; bearing.

поса́дочный *adj.* **1,** planting (*attrib.*). **2,** boarding (*attrib.*). **3,** landing (*attrib.*).

поса́пывать *v.impfv.* to sniff; snort.

поса́сывать *v.impfv., colloq.* to suck (on *or* at).

посва́тать *v., pfv. of* **сва́тать.** —**посва́таться,** *refl., pfv. of* **сва́таться.**

посвеже́ть *v., pfv. of* **свеже́ть.**

посвети́ть *v.pfv.* [*infl.* **-свечу́, -све́тишь**] **1,** *pfv. of* **свети́ть** (*in sense #2*). **2,** to shine (*for a while*).

посветле́ть *v., pfv. of* **светле́ть.**

по́свист *n.* whistle; whistling.

посвиста́ть *v.pfv.* [*infl.* **-свищу́, -сви́щешь**] to whistle; give a whistle. *Also,* **посвисте́ть** [*infl.* **-свищу́, -свисти́шь**].

посви́стывание *n.* whistling.

посви́стывать *v.impfv.* to whistle (*softly or from time to time*).

по-сво́ему *adv.* in one's own way.

по-сво́йски *adv., colloq.* **1,** in one's own way. **2,** as a friend.

посвяти́ть [*infl.* **-щу́, -ти́шь**] *v., pfv. of* **посвяща́ть.**

посвяща́ть *v.impfv.* [*pfv.* **посвяти́ть**] **1,** (*with dat.*) to devote (to); dedicate (to). **2,** (*with* **в** + *acc.*) to let in on: посвяти́ть кого́-нибудь в та́йну, to let someone in on a secret. Я не посвящён в его́ пла́ны, I am not in on (*or* privy to) his plans. **3,** (*with* **в** + *nom. pl.*) to ordain: посвяти́ть кого́-нибудь в свяще́нники, to ordain someone as priest.

посвяще́ние *n.* **1,** dedication. **2,** letting (someone) in on (a secret). **3,** consecration; ordination; initiation.

посе́в *n.* **1,** sowing. **2,** *usu. pl.* crops.

посевна́я *n., decl. as an adj., colloq.* sowing campaign.

посевно́й *adj.* sowing (*attrib.*). —**посевна́я пло́щадь,** area under cultivation.

поседе́лый *adj.* turned gray.

поседе́ть *v., pfv. of* **седе́ть.**

посейча́с *adv., colloq.* up to now; until now.

поселе́нец [*gen.* **-нца**] *n.* **1,** settler. **2,** *pre-rev.* exile (*person sent into exile*).

поселе́ние *n.* **1,** settling. **2,** settlement. **3,** *pre-rev.* exile.

посели́ть *v., pfv. of* **поселя́ть.** —**посели́ться,** *refl., pfv. of* **поселя́ться.**

поселко́вый *adj.* village (*attrib.*).

посёлок [*gen.* **-лка**] *n.* village; community; settlement.

поселя́ть *v.impfv.* [*pfv.* **посели́ть**] **1,** to settle. **2,** *fig.* to arouse; engender. —**поселя́ться,** *refl.* to settle; take up residence.

посему́ *adv., obs.* therefore.

посеребрённый *adj.* silver-plated.

посеребри́ть *v., pfv. of* **серебри́ть.** —**посеребри́ться,** *refl., pfv. of* **серебри́ться.**

посереди́не *adv.* in the middle. —*prep., with gen.* in the middle of.

посере́ть *v., pfv. of* **сере́ть.**

посети́тель *n.m.* **1,** visitor. **2,** one who attends something. **3,** patron (*of a restaurant*).

посети́ть [*infl.* **-щу́, -ти́шь**] *v., pfv. of* **посеща́ть.**

посе́товать *v., pfv. of* **се́товать.**

посеща́емость *n.f.* (regularity of) attendance.

посеща́ть *v.impfv.* [*pfv.* **посети́ть**] **1,** to visit. **2,** [*impfv. only*] to attend.

посеще́ние *n.* **1,** visit. **2,** attendance.

посе́ять *v., pfv. of* **се́ять.**

посиде́ть *v.pfv.* [*infl.* **-жу́, -ди́шь**] to sit (*for a while*).

поси́льный *adj.* **1,** within one's power to do. **2,** (*of help, payment, etc.*) whatever one can give. Оказа́ть поси́льную по́мощь, to provide all possible assistance.

посине́ть *v., pfv. of* **сине́ть.**

поскака́ть *v.pfv.* [*infl.* **-скачу́, -ска́чешь**] **1,** to hop off (to another place). **2,** to gallop off.

поскользну́ться *v.r.pfv.* to slip (and fall).

поско́льку *conj.* **1,** since; inasmuch as; as long as. **2,** as far as; to the extent that.

по́сконь *n.f.* male hemp. —**поско́нный,** *adj.* hemp (*attrib.*).

поскорее *adv.* **1,** quick; quickly. **2,** faster. **3,** soon: напиши́те поскоре́е!, write soon! **4,** sooner. —*interj.* quick!; step on it!

поскупи́ться *v.r., pfv. of* **скупи́ться**.

поскучне́ть *v., pfv. of* **скучне́ть**.

послабле́ние *n., often pl.* relaxation of discipline; leniency.

посла́нец [*gen.* -нца] *n.* messenger; envoy.

посла́ние *n.* message.

посла́нник *n.* envoy; minister.

по́сланный *n., decl. as an adj.* messenger; envoy.

посла́ть [*infl.* **пошлю́, пошлёшь**] *v., pfv. of* **слать** *and* **посыла́ть**.

по́сле *prep., with gen.* **1,** after: по́сле обе́да, after dinner. **2,** since: по́сле его́ возвраще́ния, since his return. —*adv.* afterward. —**по́сле того́, как,** after: по́сле того́, как он ушёл, after he left. —**по́сле того́, что,** after; in view of. —**по́сле чего́,** whereupon.

послевое́нный *adj.* postwar.

после́д *n.* afterbirth.

последи́ть *v.pfv.* [*infl.* **-жу́, -ди́шь**] (*with* **за** + *instr.*) to watch; look after.

после́дний *adj.* **1,** last. **2,** past: за после́днюю неде́лю, during the past week. **3,** recent: в *or* за после́дние го́ды, in recent years. **4,** the latest: после́дние изве́стия, the latest news. **5,** the latter. **6,** *colloq.* the lowest; the worst. —**в** *or* **за после́днее вре́мя,** recently; lately; of late. —**до после́днего,** to the last; to the utmost; to the bitter end. —**после́дними слова́ми,** in the crudest possible language.

после́дователь *n.m.* follower.

после́довательно *adv.* **1,** consecutively; in succession. **2,** consistently.

после́довательность *n.f.* **1,** succession; sequence. **2,** consistency.

после́довательный *adj.* **1,** consecutive; successive. **2,** consistent.

после́довать *v., pfv. of* **сле́довать**.

после́дствие *n.* consequence. —**оставля́ть без после́дствий,** to fail to act on; take no action on.

после́дующий *adj.* subsequent.

после́дыш *n., colloq.* **1,** youngest child in a family. **2,** *fig.* last to propound a certain (reactionary) doctrine.

послеза́втра *adv.* the day after tomorrow.

послеобе́денный *adj.* after-dinner.

послеоперацио́нный *adj.* postoperative. —**послеоперацио́нная пала́та,** recovery room.

послереволюцио́нный *adj.* post-revolutionary.

послеродово́й *adj.* postnatal.

послесло́вие *n.* epilogue; postscript; afterword.

посло́вица *n.* proverb. —**войти́ в посло́вицу,** to become proverbial.

послужи́ть *v.pfv.* [*infl.* **-служу́, -слу́жишь**] **1,** *pfv. of* **служи́ть**. **2,** to serve (*for a while*).

послужно́й *adj., in* **послужно́й спи́сок,** service record; work record.

послуша́ние *n.* obedience.

послу́шать *v., pfv. of* **слу́шать** (*in sense #2*). —**послу́шаться,** *refl., pfv. of* **слу́шаться**.

по́слушник *n., eccl.* novice.

послу́шный *adj.* [*short form* -шен, -шна] obedient.

послы́шаться *v.r., pfv. of* **слы́шаться**.

послюни́ть *v., pfv. of* **слюни́ть**.

посма́тривать *v.impfv.* to look (*or* glance) from time to time.

посме́иваться *v.r.impfv.* **1,** to chuckle. **2,** (*with* **над**) to poke fun at.

посме́нный *adj.* shift (*attrib.*): посме́нная рабо́та, shift work. —**посме́нно,** *adv.* in shifts.

посме́ртно *adv.* posthumously.

посме́ртный *adj.* posthumous. —**посме́ртная ма́ска,** death mask.

посме́ть *v., pfv. of* **сметь**.

посме́шище *n.* laughingstock. —**выставля́ть (кого́-нибудь) на посме́шище,** to make a laughingstock of.

посмея́ться *v.r.pfv.* [*infl.* -смею́сь, -смеёшься] **1,** to give a (short) laugh; have a laugh. **2,** (*with* **над**) to poke fun at.

посмотре́ть *v., pfv. of* **смотре́ть**. —**посмотре́ться,** *refl., pfv. of* **смотре́ться**.

посо́бие *n.* **1,** allowance; benefits: посо́бие по безрабо́тице, unemployment benefits. **2,** textbook. **3,** *pl.* study aids: нагля́дные посо́бия, visual aids.

посо́бник *n.* accomplice.

посо́бничество *n.* (*with dat.*) collaboration (with).

посо́веститься *v.r.pfv.* [*infl.* -щусь, -стишься] *colloq.* to be ashamed; feel ashamed.

посове́товать *v., pfv. of* **сове́товать**. —**посове́товаться,** *refl., pfv. of* **сове́товаться**.

посо́л [*gen.* **посла́**] *n.* ambassador. —**посо́л по осо́бым поруче́ниям,** ambassador-at-large.

посоли́ть *v., pfv. of* **соли́ть**.

посолове́лый *adj., colloq.* bleary-eyed.

посолове́ть *v.pfv., colloq.* to become bleary-eyed.

посо́льский *adj.* **1,** ambassadorial. **2,** embassy (*attrib.*).

посо́льство *n.* embassy.

по́сох *n.* **1,** staff; crook. **2,** crosier.

посо́хнуть *v.pfv.* [*past* посо́х, посо́хла] (*of all or many things*) to wither.

поспа́ть *v.pfv.* [*infl. like* спать] to sleep a bit; take a nap.

поспева́ть *v.impfv.* [*pfv.* поспе́ть] **1,** to ripen. **2,** *colloq.* to be finished; be ready; (*of food*) be done. **3,** (*with* **к**) *colloq.* to be on time (for); have time (to). **4,** (*with* **за** + *instr.*) *colloq.* to keep up with; keep pace with.

поспе́ть [*infl.* -спе́ю, -спе́ешь] *v., pfv. of* **спеть**[1] *and* **поспева́ть**.

поспеши́ть *v., pfv. of* **спеши́ть**.

поспе́шный *adj.* hasty; hurried. —**поспе́шно,** *adv.* hastily; hurriedly; in a hurry. —**поспе́шность,** *n.f.* haste.

поспо́рить *v., pfv. of* **спо́рить**.

посрами́ть [*infl.* -млю́, -ми́шь] *v., pfv. of* **посрамля́ть**.

посрамле́ние *n.* disgrace.

посрамля́ть *v.impfv.* [*pfv.* посрами́ть] to disgrace; put to shame.

посреди́ *prep., with gen.* in the middle of. —*adv.* in the middle.

посреди́не *adv. & prep.* = **посереди́не**.

посре́дник *n.* **1,** middleman; intermediary. **2,** mediator; go-between.

посре́дничать *v.impfv.* to mediate; serve as a go-between.

посре́днический *adj.* mediation (*attrib.*); middleman (*attrib.*); intermediary.

посре́дничество *n.* mediation.

посре́дственно *adv.* so-so; not particularly well. —*n. indecl.* "fair"; "mediocre" (*school grade*).

посре́дственность *n.f.* **1,** mediocrity. **2,** mediocre person; a mediocrity.

посре́дственный *adj.* mediocre.

посре́дство *n., in* **при посре́дстве** *and* **че́рез посре́дство** (+ *gen.*), **1,** through; by means of. **2,** through the intercession of; thanks to.

посре́дством *prep., with gen.* through; by means of.

поссо́рить *v., pfv. of* **ссо́рить.** —**поссо́риться,** *refl., pfv. of* **ссо́риться.**

пост [*gen.* **поста́**; *2nd loc.* **посту́**] *n.* **1,** post: наблюда́тельный пост, observation post. **2,** post; position: пост дире́ктора, the post/position of director. **3,** *relig.* fast. —**вели́кий пост,** Lent.

поста́вить [*infl.* **-влю, -вишь**] *v., pfv. of* **ста́вить** *and* **поставля́ть.**

поста́вка [*gen. pl.* **-вок**] *n.* delivery. Поста́вки зерна́, deliveries of grain.

поставля́ть *v.impfv.* [*pfv.* **поста́вить**] to supply.

поставщи́к [*gen.* **-щика́**] *n.* supplier.

постаме́нт *n.* pedestal; base.

постанови́ть [*infl.* **-новлю́, -но́вишь**] *v., pfv. of* **постановля́ть.**

постано́вка *n.* **1,** *theat.* production. **2,** position (*of a part of the body*). **3,** (*with gen.*) organization (of). **4,** stating; posing: постано́вка вопро́са, the way a question is put. **5,** *in* постано́вка го́лоса, voice training.

постановле́ние *n.* **1,** decision; ruling. **2,** decree; pronouncement.

постановля́ть *v.impfv.* [*pfv.* **постанови́ть**] to decide; resolve; decree.

постано́вочный *adj., theat.* production (*attrib.*).

постано́вщик *n., theat.* producer; director.

постара́ться *v.r., pfv. of* **стара́ться.**

постаре́ть *v., pfv. of* **старе́ть.**

по-ста́рому *adv.* **1,** as before. Всё по-ста́рому, everything is the same; nothing has changed. **2,** like in the old days.

посте́ль *n.f.* bed. —**посте́льный,** *adj.* bed (*attrib.*).

постепе́нный *adj.* gradual. —**постепе́нно,** *adv.* gradually.

постере́чь *v.pfv.* [*infl. like* **стере́чь**] to guard; watch (*for a while*).

постесня́ться *v.r., pfv. of* **стесня́ться** (*in sense #2*).

постига́ть *v.impfv.* [*pfv.* **пости́гнуть** *or* **пости́чь**] **1,** to comprehend; grasp. **2,** (*of misfortune*) to befall; overtake.

пости́гнуть [*past* **-сти́г, -сти́гла**] *v., pfv. of* **постига́ть.**

постиже́ние *n.* comprehension; grasp.

постижи́мый *adj.* comprehensible.

постила́ть *v.impfv.* [*pfv.* **постла́ть**] to lay (a rug, tablecloth, etc.); make (a bed).

постира́ть *v.pfv., colloq.* to wash; launder.

пости́ться *v.r.impfv.* [*pres.* **пощу́сь, пости́шься**] to fast.

пости́чь [*infl. like* **пости́гнуть**] *v., pfv. of* **постига́ть.**

постла́ть [*infl. like* **стлать**] *v., pfv. of* **стлать** *and* **постила́ть.**

по́стник *n.* person who fasts.

по́стничать *v.impfv., colloq.* to fast.

по́стный *adj.* **1,** fast (*attrib.*): по́стный день, fast day. **2,** containing no milk or meat. **3,** *colloq.* (*of meat*) lean. **4,** *fig., colloq.* dreary. **5,** *fig., colloq.* pious; sanctimonious.

постово́й *adj.* **1,** duty (*attrib.*); sentry (*attrib.*): постова́я бу́дка, sentry box. **2,** on duty: постово́й милиционе́р, policeman on duty. —*n.* man on duty.

посто́й *n.* quartering; billeting (*of troops*). —**ста́вить на посто́й,** to billet. *See also* **постоя́ть.**

посто́льку *conj., in* **посто́льку, поско́льку,** insofar as; to the extent that.

посторони́ться *v.r., pfv. of* **сторони́ться.**

посторо́нний *adj.* outside; foreign; extraneous. —*n.* stranger; outsider.

постоя́лец [*gen.* **-льца**] *n., colloq.* lodger; guest (*at a hotel or inn*).

постоя́лый *adj., in* **постоя́лый двор,** *obs.* inn; hostelry.

постоя́нно *adv.* constantly; continually.

постоя́нный *adj.* **1,** constant. **2,** permanent. **3,** regular; steady. —**постоя́нная а́рмия,** standing army. —**постоя́нная величина́,** *math.* constant. —**постоя́нный ток,** direct current.

постоя́нство *n.* constancy.

постоя́ть *v.pfv.* [*infl.* **-стою́, -стои́шь**] **1,** to stand (*for a while*). **2,** (*with* **за** + *acc.*) to stand up for. —**посто́й!; посто́йте!,** wait a minute!; stop!

пострада́вший *adj.* stricken. —*n.* victim (*of a disaster*).

пострада́ть *v.pfv.* **1,** *pfv. of* **страда́ть. 2,** to be injured; be damaged; suffer damage.

постре́л *n., colloq.* imp; rascal; brat.

постре́ливать *v.impfv.* to fire an occasional shot.

постреля́ть *v.pfv.* **1,** *v.i.* to fire a gun (*for a while*); do some shooting. **2,** *v.t., colloq.* to shoot (many of something); bag.

острига́ть *v.impfv.* [*pfv.* **постри́чь**] **1,** to cut (one's hair, beard, etc.). **2,** to give (someone) a haircut. —**острига́ться,** *refl.* **1,** to cut one's hair. **2,** to get a haircut.

постри́чь [*infl. like* **стричь**] *v., pfv. of* **острига́ть.** —**постри́чься,** *refl., pfv. of* **острига́ться.**

построе́ние *n.* **1,** building; construction. **2,** *mil.* formation. **3,** *fig.* concepts.

постро́ить *v., pfv. of* **стро́ить.** —**постро́иться,** *refl., pfv. of* **стро́иться.**

постро́йка [*gen. pl.* **-о́ек**] *n.* **1,** building; edifice. **2,** building; construction.

постро́мка [*gen. pl.* **-мок**] *n.* trace (*of a harness*).

постскри́птум *n.* postscript; P.S.

посту́кивать *v.impfv.* **1,** (*of rain*) to patter; (*of a hard object*) to bang. **2,** (*with instr.*) to tap. Посту́кивать па́льцами по́ столу, to drum (one's fingers) on the table.

постула́т *n.* postulate.

постули́ровать *v.impfv. & pfv.* [*pres.* **-рую, -руешь**] to postulate.

поступа́тельный *adj.* **1,** (*of motion*) forward. **2,** *fig.* ongoing.

поступа́ть *v.impfv.* [*pfv.* **поступи́ть**] **1,** to act. **2,** (*with* **с** + *instr.*) to treat. **3,** (*with* **в** *or* **на** + *acc.*) to join; enter; enlist (in). Поступи́ть на рабо́ту, to take a job; go to work. Поступи́ть на ку́рсы, to enroll in courses. **4,** to arrive; be received; come in. —**поступи́ть в прода́жу,** to go on sale. —**поступи́ть в произво́дство,** to go into (*or* enter) production. —**поступи́ть на ры́нок,** to come onto the market. —**поступи́ть на вооруже́ние,** to enter service.

поступа́ться *v.r.impfv.* [*pfv.* **поступи́ться**] (*with instr.*) **1,** to waive; forgo. **2,** to forsake; abandon (principles).

поступи́ть [*infl.* **-ступлю́, -сту́пишь**] *v., pfv. of* **поступа́ть.** —**поступи́ться,** *refl., pfv. of* **поступа́ться.**

поступле́ние *n.* **1,** joining; entering. **2,** receipt. **3,** coming in; arrival. **4,** *pl.* receipts; earnings.

посту́пок [*gen.* **-пка**] *n.* act; deed.

по́ступь *n.f.* walk; gait.

постуча́ть *v., pfv. of* **стуча́ть.** —**постуча́ться,** *refl., pfv. of* **стуча́ться.**

постыди́ться *v.r., pfv. of* **стыди́ться.**

посты́дный *adj.* shameful; disgraceful.

посты́лый *adj., colloq.* repellent; odious.

посу́да *n.* **1,** dishes: мыть посу́ду, to wash the dishes. **2,** ware: гли́няная посу́да, earthenware; эмали́рованная посу́да, enamelware. **3,** utensils. **4,** *colloq.* vessel; utensil.

посу́дина *n., colloq.* **1,** vessel; container. **2,** boat; tub.

посуди́ть *v.pfv.* [*infl.* **-сужу́, -су́дишь**] to judge: Посуди́те са́ми, judge for yourself.

посу́дный *adj.* for dishes; dish (*attrib.*). Посу́дный шкаф, cabinet for dishes; china closet.

посудомо́ечный *adj., in* **посудомо́ечная маши́на,** dishwasher.

посудомо́йка [*gen. pl.* **-мо́ек**] *n., colloq.* dishwasher.

посу́л *n., colloq.* promise.

посули́ть *v., pfv. of* **сули́ть.**

по́суху *adv., colloq.* over dry land.

посуши́ть *v.pfv.* [*infl.* **-сушу́, -су́шишь**] to dry (*for a while*).

посчастли́виться *v.r.pfv., impers.* (*with dat. & inf.*) to have the luck (*or* good fortune) to...

посчита́ть *v.pfv.* **1,** to count. **2,** *colloq.* to consider. **3,** *colloq.* (*with a dependent clause*) to decide (that); conclude (that). —**посчита́ться,** *refl.* **1,** *pfv. of* **счита́ться** (*in sense #1*). **2,** (*with* **с** + *instr.*) to get even (with); settle scores (with).

посыла́ть *v.impfv.* [*pfv.* **посла́ть**] to send.

посы́лка [*gen. pl.* **-лок**] *n.* **1,** package; parcel. **2,** (*act of*) sending. **3,** mailing. **4,** premise. —**быть на посы́лках,** to run errands.

посы́лочный *adj.* **1,** for a package or packages. **2,** mail-order: посы́лочная торго́вля, mail-order business.

посы́льный *n., decl. as an adj.* messenger.

посы́пать [*infl.* **-сы́плю, -сы́плешь**] *v., pfv. of* **посыпа́ть.** —**посы́паться,** *refl.* **1,** to begin to fall. **2,** (*of questions, blows, etc.*) to rain down. **3,** to pour in; stream in.

посыпа́ть *v.impfv.* [*pfv.* **посы́пать**] to sprinkle.

посяга́тельство *n.* encroachment; infringement.

посяга́ть *v.impfv.* [*pfv.* **посягну́ть**] (*with* **на** + *acc.*) to infringe (upon); encroach (upon).

пот [*2nd loc.* **поту́**] *n.* perspiration; sweat: весь в поту́, all perspired. —**в по́те лица́,** by the sweat of one's brow. —**по́том и кро́вью,** by one's own sweat and blood.

потайно́й *adj.* secret; hidden.

потака́ние *n.* (*with dat.*) *colloq.* indulgence (of); catering (to).

потака́ть *v.impfv.* (*with dat.*) *colloq.* to indulge; cater to.

потанцева́ть *v.pfv.* [*infl.* **-цу́ю, -цу́ешь**] to dance (*for a while*); have a dance: Потанцу́ем?, shall we dance?

потаску́ха *n., colloq.* strumpet; tart.

потасо́вка [*gen. pl.* **-вок**] *n., colloq.* scuffle.

пота́чка [*gen. pl.* **-чек**] *n., colloq.* favor; indulgence.

пота́ш [*gen.* **-таша́**] *n.* potash. —**пота́шный,** *adj.* potash (*attrib.*).

потащи́ть *v., pfv. of* **тащи́ть.** —**потащи́ться,** *refl., pfv. of* **тащи́ться.**

потво́рство *n.* (*with dat.*) leniency (toward); indulgence (of).

потво́рствовать *v.impfv.* [*pres.* **-ствую, -ствуешь**] (*with dat.*) to indulge; be lenient (toward); look the other way (at).

потёк *n.* streak.

потёмки [*gen.* **-мок**] *n.pl.* darkness.

потёмкинский *adj., in* **потёмкинская дере́вня,** Potemkin village.

потемне́ние *n.* darkening.

потемне́ть *v., pfv. of* **темне́ть** (*in sense #1*).

поте́ние *n.* perspiring; perspiration.

потенциа́л (тэ) *n.* potential. —**потенциа́льный,** *adj.* potential.

поте́нция (тэ) *n.* potential; talent; ability.

потепле́ние *n.* warming.

потепле́ть *v., pfv. of* **тепле́ть.**

потере́ть *v.pfv.* [*infl. like* **тере́ть**] to rub. —**потере́ться,** *refl., pfv. of* **тере́ться.**

потерпе́вший *adj., law* injured; aggrieved: потерпе́вшая сторона́, the injured/aggrieved party. —*n., law* victim: потерпе́вший от пожа́ра, victim of a fire.

потерпе́ть *v.pfv.* [*infl.* **-терплю́, -те́рпишь**] **1,** *pfv. of* **терпе́ть** (*in sense #3*). **2,** to be patient. **3,** (*usu. neg.*) to tolerate; put up with.

потёртость *n.f.* sore spot (*caused by rubbing or chafing*).

потёртый *adj.* shabby; threadbare.

потеря́ *n.* **1,** loss. **2,** waste (*of time, money, etc.*). **3,** *pl.* losses; casualties.

поте́рянный *adj.* **1,** lost. **2,** confused; bewildered. **3,** *colloq.* gone to the dogs. —**как поте́рянный,** like a lost soul.

потеря́ть *v., pfv. of* **теря́ть.** —**потеря́ться,** *refl., pfv. of* **теря́ться.**

потесни́ть *v., pfv. of* **тесни́ть** (*in sense #1*). —**потесни́ться,** *refl., pfv. of* **тесни́ться** (*in sense #2*).

поте́ть *v.impfv.* **1,** [*pfv.* **вспоте́ть**] to perspire; sweat. **2,** [*pfv.* **запоте́ть**] *colloq.* to become misty; steam up.

поте́ха *n.* **1,** fun; amusement. **2,** funny incident; funny thing. —**на поте́ху** (+ *dat.*), to amuse (someone).

поте́чь *v.pfv.* [*infl. like* **течь**] **1,** to begin to flow. **2,** to begin to leak.

потеша́ть v.impfv., colloq. to entertain; amuse. —потеша́ться, refl. 1, colloq. to amuse oneself. 2, (with над) to make fun of.

поте́шить v., pfv. of те́шить. —поте́шиться, refl., pfv. of те́шиться.

поте́шный adj., colloq. funny; amusing.

потира́ть v.impfv. to rub. —потира́ть ру́ки, to rub one's hands (with glee, worry, etc.).

потихо́ньку adv., colloq. 1, quietly; silently. 2, secretly; on the sly. 3, slowly; gradually.

потни́к [gen. -ника́] n. saddlecloth.

потни́ца n. prickly heat; heat rash.

по́тный adj. 1, sweaty; covered with perspiration. 2, steamed up; misted up.

пото́вой adj. sweat (attrib.): потовы́е же́лезы, sweat glands.

потого́нный adj. 1, inducing perspiration. 2, involving sweatshop conditions: потого́нная фа́брика, sweatshop. —потого́нное, n. something taken to induce perspiration.

пото́к n. stream; torrent; flood.

потолкова́ть v.pfv. [infl. -ку́ю, -ку́ешь] colloq. to talk (for a while); have a talk.

потоло́к [gen. -лка́] n. ceiling. —взять с потолка́, to take (e.g. facts) out of the air. —плева́ть в потоло́к, to sit around doing nothing.

потолсте́ть v., pfv. of толсте́ть.

пото́м adv. 1, then; next. 2, afterward(s); later (on). —на пото́м, for later (on).

пото́мок [gen. -мка] n. descendant; offspring.

пото́мственный adj. 1, obs. hereditary; ancestral. 2, by birth: пото́мственный дворяни́н, a nobleman by birth. Он пото́мственный актёр, he comes from a long line of actors.

пото́мство n. 1, progeny. 2, posterity.

потому́ adv. which is why. —потому́...и, that is why: Потому́ я и спра́шиваю, that is why I ask. —потому́ что, because.

потону́ть v., pfv. of тону́ть (in sense #1).

пото́п n. 1, Bib. flood. 2, colloq. flood; deluge.

потопи́ть v., pfv. of топи́ть (in sense #4).

потопле́ние n. sinking.

потопта́ть v.pfv. [infl. -топчу́, -то́пчешь] to trample down.

потора́пливать v.impfv., colloq. to hurry; urge on. —потора́пливаться, refl., colloq. to hurry: потора́пливайтесь!, hurry up!; get a move on!

поторопи́ть v., pfv. of торопи́ть. —потороп́иться, refl. 1, pfv. of торопи́ться. 2, to act too hastily.

пото́чный adj. done on an assembly line: пото́чное произво́дство, assembly-line production. —пото́чная ли́ния, production line.

потра́ва n. damage done to crops by cattle.

потрави́ть v., pfv. of трави́ть (in sense #2).

потра́тить v., pfv. of тра́тить. —потра́титься, refl., pfv. of тра́титься.

потрафля́ть v.impfv. [pfv. потра́фить] (with dat.) colloq. 1, to please. 2, to cater to.

потреби́тель n.m. consumer. —потреби́тельский, adj. consumer (attrib.); consumers'.

потреби́ть [infl. -блю́, -би́шь] v., pfv. of потребля́ть.

потребле́ние n. consumption. —това́ры широ́кого потребле́ния, consumer goods.

потребля́ть v.impfv. [pfv. потреби́ть] to consume.

потре́бность n.f. need; requirement.

потре́бный adj. necessary; required; requisite.

потре́бовать v., pfv. of тре́бовать. —потре́боваться, refl., pfv. of тре́боваться.

потрево́жить v., pfv. of трево́жить (in sense #2).

потрёпанный adj. tattered; shabby; threadbare.

потрепа́ть v.pfv. [infl. -треплю́, -тре́плешь] 1, pfv. of трепа́ть. 2, mil. to inflict heavy losses on.

потре́скаться v.r., pfv. of тре́скаться.

потре́скивать v.impfv. to crackle.

потро́гать v.pfv. to touch; feel; finger.

потроха́ [gen. -хо́в] n.pl. giblets.

потроши́ть v.impfv. [pfv. вы́потрошить] to eviscerate; disembowel.

потруди́ться v.r.pfv. [infl. -тружу́сь, -тру́дишься] 1, to work (for a while). 2, (with inf.) to bother (to); take the trouble (to).

потряса́ть v.impfv. [pfv. потрясти́] 1, to shake. 2, (with instr.) to brandish (a weapon). 3, fig. to shake; shock; stagger; stun.

потряса́ющий adj. 1, staggering; stunning. 2, tremendous; stupendous. 3, colloq. marvelous; fabulous.

потрясе́ние n. 1, shock. 2, upheaval.

потрясти́ [infl. like трясти́] v., pfv. of потряса́ть.

потря́хивать v.impfv. (with acc. or instr.) colloq. to shake slightly.

поту́ги [gen. поту́г] n.pl. 1, spasms. Родовы́е поту́ги, birth pains; labor pains. 2, fig. vain attempts.

потупля́ть v.impfv. [pfv. поту́пить] to lower (one's eyes, head, etc.). —потупля́ться, refl. to lower one's eyes; lower one's head.

потускне́лый adj. dull; tarnished.

потускне́ть v., pfv. of тускне́ть.

потусторо́нний adj., in потусторо́нний мир, the next world.

потуха́ть v.impfv. [pfv. поту́хнуть] 1, (of something burning) to go out. 2, to die out; fade away.

поту́хнуть [past поту́х, поту́хла] v., pfv. of ту́хнуть (in sense #1) and потуха́ть.

поту́хший adj. 1, dull; lifeless. 2, (of a volcano) extinct.

потучне́ть v., pfv. of тучне́ть.

потуши́ть v., pfv. of туши́ть (in sense #1).

по́тчевать v.impfv. [pfv. попо́тчевать; pres. -чую, -чуешь] (with instr.) colloq. to treat (to food, drink, etc.).

потяга́ться v.r., pfv. of тяга́ться.

потя́гивать v.impfv. 1, to pull at; tug at. 2, to draw on (a cigarette, pipe, etc.). 3, to sip. —потя́гиваться, refl. [pfv. потяну́ться] to stretch; take a stretch.

потяну́ть v., pfv. of тяну́ть (in senses #3, 4, 5). —потяну́ться, refl., pfv. of тяну́ться (in sense #3) and потя́гиваться.

поу́жинать v., pfv. of у́жинать.

поумне́ть v., pfv. of умне́ть.

поуро́чный adj. 1, of or for a lesson. 2, (of payment) by the lesson.

поутру́ adv., colloq. in the morning.

поуча́ть *v.impfv.* **1,** to teach; instruct. **2,** to preach to; lecture.

поуче́ние *n.* **1,** edification: в поуче́ние (+ *dat.*), for the edification of. **2,** sermon; homily.

поучи́тельный *adj.* instructive.

поучи́ть *v.pfv.* [*infl.* поучу́, поу́чишь] **1,** to study (*for a while*). **2,** to teach (*for a while*).

поха́бный *adj., colloq.* dirty; lewd; obscene.

поха́живать *v.impfv., colloq.* **1,** to walk back and forth; pace. **2,** (*with* к) to drop in on (*from time to time*).

похвала́ *n.* praise.

похва́ливать *v.impfv., colloq.* to praise.

похвали́ть *v., pfv. of* хвали́ть. —**похвали́ться,** *refl., pfv. of* хвали́ться.

похвальба́ *n., colloq.* boasting; bragging.

похва́льный *adj.* **1,** laudable; commendable; admirable; praiseworthy. **2,** laudatory. —**похва́льная гра́мота,** certificate of good work and conduct (*in school*).

похваля́ться *v.r.impfv.* (*with instr.*) *colloq.* to boast (about); brag (about).

похва́статься *v.r., pfv. of* хва́статься.

похе́рить *v.pfv., colloq.* **1,** to cross out. **2,** to obstruct. **3,** to eliminate.

похити́тель *n.m.* **1,** thief. **2,** kidnaper; abductor. **3,** hijacker.

похища́ть *v.impfv.* [*pfv.* похи́тить] **1,** to steal. **2,** to kidnap; abduct. **3,** to hijack.

похище́ние *n.* **1,** theft. **2,** kidnaping; abduction. **3,** hijacking.

похлёбка *n.* pottage.

похло́пать *v., pfv. of* хло́пать.

похлопота́ть *v., pfv. of* хлопота́ть.

похло́пывать *v.impfv., colloq.* **1,** to clap. **2,** to tap; pat.

похме́лье *n.* hangover.

похо́д *n.* **1,** excursion; outing; hike. Туристи́ческий похо́д, hiking expedition; walking tour. Лы́жный/ло́дочный похо́д, skiing/boat trip. **2,** march. **3,** *mil.* campaign. **4,** campaign; drive. —**кресто́вый похо́д,** *hist.* crusade.

похода́тайствовать *v., pfv. of* хода́тайствовать.

походи́ть[1] *v.impfv.* [*pres.* -хожу́, -хо́дишь] (*with* на + *acc.*) to resemble; look like; be like.

походи́ть[2] *v.pfv.* [*infl.* -хожу́, -хо́дишь] to walk; walk around (*for a while*).

похо́дка *n.* walk; gait.

похо́дный *adj., mil.* **1,** field (*attrib.*): похо́дная ку́хня, (mobile) field kitchen. **2,** march (*attrib.*); marching.

по́ходя *adv., colloq.* **1,** hastily; on the run. **2,** at the same time; while one is (was) at it. **3,** casually; without thinking twice about it.

похожде́ние *n.* adventure.

похо́жий *adj.* (*with* на + *acc.*) similar (to); like; alike. Э́то на него́ не похо́же, that's not like him. Похо́же, что бу́дет дождь, it looks like rain. —**э́то ни на что не похо́же,** it's simply intolerable.

похолода́ние *n.* drop in temperature; cold snap.

похолода́ть *v., pfv. of* холода́ть.

похолоде́ть *v., pfv. of* холоде́ть.

похорони́ть *v., pfv. of* хорони́ть.

похоро́нный *adj.* funeral (*attrib.*).

по́хороны [*gen.* -ро́н; *dat.* -рона́м] *n.pl.* funeral.

похороше́ть *v., pfv. of* хороше́ть.

похотли́вый *adj.* lustful; lewd; lascivious. —**похотли́вость,** *n.f.* lewdness; lasciviousness.

похотни́к [*gen.* -ника́] *n.* clitoris.

по́хоть *n.f.* lust.

похуде́ть *v., pfv. of* худе́ть.

поцелова́ть *v., pfv. of* целова́ть. —**поцелова́ться,** *refl., pfv. of* целова́ться.

поцелу́й *n.* kiss.

почасови́к [*gen.* -вика́] *n., colloq.* employee paid by the hour.

почасово́й *adj.* by the hour; hourly.

поча́ток [*gen.* -тка] *n.* ear (*of corn*).

по́чва *n.* **1,** soil; ground. **2,** *fig.* basis; foundation: не име́ть (под собо́й) по́чвы, to be without foundation. —**на по́чве** (+ *gen.*), due to; owing to; on account of. —**выбива́ть по́чву из-под чьи́х-нибудь ног,** to cut the ground from under someone. —**подгота́вливать по́чву для,** to prepare the ground for; pave the way for; set the stage for. —**теря́ть по́чву под нога́ми,** to feel the ground slipping from beneath one's feet.

по́чвенный *adj.* soil (*attrib.*).

почвове́д *n.* soil scientist. —**почвове́дение,** *n.* soil science.

почём *adv., colloq.* how much is?; how much are?; what is the price of? —**почём знать?,** who knows?; how is one to know? —**почём зря,** *colloq.* for all one is worth. —**почём я зна́ю?,** how should I know?

почему́ *adv.* **1,** *interr.* why? **2,** *rel.* why: Я не зна́ю, почему́ он э́то сказа́л, I don't know why he said that. —*conj.* which is why. —**вот почему́,** that is why. —**почему́ бы не** (+ *inf.*), why not...?: Почему́ бы не спроси́ть её?, why not ask her? —**почему́ нет?,** why not?

почему́-либо *adv.* for some reason or other; for any reason. *Also,* **почему́-нибудь.**

почему́-то *adv.* for some reason.

по́черк *n.* handwriting.

почерне́лый *adj.* darkened; blackened.

почерне́ть *v., pfv. of* черне́ть.

почерпну́ть *v.pfv.* **1,** *colloq.* to draw (water). **2,** *fig.* to glean; cull.

почерстве́ть *v., pfv. of* черстве́ть (*in sense #1*).

почеса́ть *v., pfv. of* чеса́ть. —**почеса́ться,** *refl., pfv. of* чеса́ться (*in sense #2*).

по́чести [*gen.* -стей] *n.pl.* honors; homage: ока́зывать *or* воздава́ть по́чести (+ *dat.*), to accord honors to; pay homage to. —**отдава́ть после́дние по́чести** (+ *dat.*), to pay one's last respects to.

почёсывать *v.impfv., colloq.* to scratch occasionally. —**почёсываться,** *refl., colloq.* to scratch oneself occasionally.

почёт *n.* honor; respect; esteem.

почётный *adj.* **1,** honored; of honor: почётное ме́сто, place of honor. **2,** honorary. **3,** honorable. —**почётный карау́л,** guard of honor; honor guard.

по́чечный *adj.* kidney (*attrib.*); renal.

почива́ть *v.impfv.* [*pfv.* **почи́ть**] *obs.* **1,** to sleep. **2,** [*impfv. only*] to lie; repose (in one's grave). —почива́ть (почи́ть) на ла́врах, to rest on one's laurels.

почи́вший *n.*, *decl. as an adj.* the deceased.

почи́н *n.* **1,** initiative. **2,** start; beginning.

починить́ *v.*, *pfv. of* **чини́ть** (*in sense #1*).

почи́нка *n.* mending; repair.

почи́стить *v.*, *pfv. of* **чи́стить.**

почита́й *adv.*, *colloq.* **1,** almost. **2,** probably.

почита́ние *n.* **1,** (*with gen.*) respect (for); honoring (of). **2,** reverence.

почита́тель *n.m.* admirer.

почита́ть[1] *v.impfv.* **1,** to respect; honor; revere. **2,** *obs.* to consider.

почита́ть[2] *v.pfv.* **1,** to read (*for a while*). **2,** *colloq.* to read (a book, article, etc.).

почи́тывать *v.impfv.*, *colloq.* to read from time to time.

почи́ть [*infl.* почи́ю, почи́ешь] *v.*, *pfv. of* почива́ть.

по́чка [*gen. pl.* по́чек] *n.* **1,** bud. **2,** kidney.

по́чта *n.* **1,** mail. **2,** post office. —дипломати́ческая по́чта, diplomatic pouch.

почтальо́н *n.* mailman; postman.

почта́мт *n.* main post office.

почте́ние *n.* **1,** respect; deference. **2,** reverence. —с почте́нием, (*at the close of a letter*) respectfully yours.

почте́нный *adj.* **1,** worthy. **2,** venerable. **3,** *colloq.* considerable.

почти́ *adv.* almost; nearly. —почти́ никогда́, almost never; hardly ever. —почти́ что = почти́.

почти́тельность *n.f.* respect; deference.

почти́тельный *adj.* respectful; reverent; deferential. —держа́ться на почти́тельном расстоя́нии, to remain at a distance; keep one's distance.

почти́ть *v.pfv.* [*infl. like* чтить] to honor.

почтме́йстер *n.*, *obs.* postmaster.

почто́вый *adj.* postal; mail (*attrib.*). —почто́вая бума́га, stationery. —почто́вый го́лубь, carrier pigeon; homing pigeon. —почто́вая ка́рточка, postcard. —почто́вая ма́рка, postage stamp. —почто́вые расхо́ды, postage. —почто́вый ште́мпель, postmark. —почто́вый я́щик, mailbox.

почу́вствовать *v.*, *pfv. of* чу́вствовать. —почу́вствоваться, *refl.*, *pfv. of* чу́вствоваться.

почу́диться *v.r.*, *pfv. of* чу́диться.

почу́ять *v.*, *pfv. of* чу́ять.

пошаба́шить *v.*, *pfv. of* шаба́шить.

поша́ливать *v.impfv.*, *colloq.* to act up.

пошатну́ть *v.pfv.* to shake. —пошатну́ться, *refl.* **1,** to stagger. **2,** to be shaken. **3,** *fig.* (*of one's health*) to be impaired.

поша́тывать *v.impfv.* **1,** to shake. **2,** *impers.* to sway; totter; wobble: Его́ поша́тывает, he is unsteady on his feet. —поша́тываться, *refl.* **1,** to sway; totter; wobble. **2,** (*of a tooth*) to be loose.

пошевели́ть *v.*, *pfv. of* шевели́ть. —пошевели́ться, *refl.*, *pfv. of* шевели́ться.

поши́б *n.*, *colloq.* manner; style. —одного́ поши́ба, two of a kind; from the same mold.

поши́вка *n.*, *colloq.* sewing.

поши́вочный *adj.*, *in* поши́вочная мастерска́я, tailor's shop; dressmaker's shop.

по́шлина *n.* duty; customs.

по́шлость *n.f.* **1,** pettiness. **2,** trite remark; banality.

по́шлый *adj.* **1,** common; petty; shallow. **2,** coarse; vulgar. **3,** banal; trite.

пошля́к [*gen.* -ляка́] *n.*, *colloq.* common *or* shallow person.

пошту́чный *adj.* by the piece. —пошту́чно, *adv.* by the piece.

пошуме́ть *v.pfv.* [*infl.* -млю́, -ми́шь] to make (some) noise.

пошути́ть *v.*, *pfv. of* шути́ть.

поща́да *n.* mercy.

пощади́ть *v.*, *pfv. of* щади́ть.

пощекота́ть *v.*, *pfv. of* щекота́ть.

пощёчина *n.* slap in the face.

пощи́пывать *v.impfv.* **1,** to pinch from time to time. **2,** *impers.* to prick; tingle: У меня́ щёки пощи́пывает, my cheeks are tingling.

пощу́пать *v.*, *pfv. of* щу́пать.

поэ́зия *n.* poetry.

поэ́ма *n.* (long) poem.

поэ́т *n.* poet.

поэта́пный *adj.* done in stages; phased. —поэта́пно, *adv.* in stages.

поэте́сса (тэ) *n.* poetess.

поэти́ческий *adj.* poetic.

поэ́тому *adv.* therefore.

появи́ться [*infl.* -явлю́сь, -я́вишься] *v.r.*, *pfv. of* появля́ться.

появле́ние *n.* appearance.

появля́ться *v.r.impfv.* [*pfv.* появи́ться] to appear.

по́яс [*pl.* пояса́] *n.* **1,** belt. **2,** waist: кла́няться в по́яс, to bow from the waist. **3,** [*pl.* по́ясы] zone: часово́й по́яс, time zone. —спаса́тельный по́яс, life belt; life preserver.

поясне́ние *n.* explanation.

поясни́тельный *adj.* explanatory.

поясни́ть *v.*, *pfv. of* поясня́ть.

поясни́ца *n.* small of the back; lower back. —поясни́чный, *adj.* lumbar.

поясно́й *adj.* **1,** belt (*attrib.*). **2,** to the waist; from the waist. **3,** zonal. —поясно́й портре́т, half-length portrait.

поясня́ть *v.impfv.* [*pfv.* поясни́ть] to explain; elucidate.

праба́бка [*gen. pl.* -бок] *n.* great-grandmother. *Also,* прабабушка.

пра́вда *n.* truth. Э́то пра́вда, that is true; that's the truth. Пра́вда ли, что...?, is it true that...? —*adv.* **1,** really; indeed. **2,** true; admittedly; to be sure. **3,** isn't that so?; don't you think so? —все́ми пра́вдами и непра́вдами, by hook or by crook. —по пра́вде говоря́; по пра́вде сказа́ть, to tell the truth.

правди́вость *n.f.* truthfulness; veracity.

правди́вый *adj.* **1,** (*of a person*) truthful. **2,** (*of a story, answer, etc.*) true; truthful.

правдоподо́бие *n.* plausibility; credibility; verisimilitude. —правдоподо́бный, *adj.* plausible; believable; credible.

пра́ведник *n.* righteous man.

пра́ведный *adj.* **1,** righteous. **2,** just. —**пра́ведность,** *n.f.* righteousness.

праве́ть *v.impfv.* [*pfv.* **поправе́ть**] *polit.* to shift to the right; become more conservative.

пра́вило *n.* **1,** rule: пра́вило орфогра́фии, spelling rule. **2,** *pl.* rules; regulations: пра́вила безопа́сности, safety rules; safety regulations. —**как пра́вило,** as a rule. —**взять себе́ за пра́вило** (+ *inf.*), to make it a rule (to).

пра́вильно *adv.* **1,** correctly. **2,** properly. **3,** regularly; evenly. —*adj., used predicatively,* right; correct: соверше́нно пра́вильно, absolutely right.

пра́вильность *n.f.* **1,** rightness; correctness. **2,** regularity.

пра́вильный *adj.* **1,** right; correct. **2,** proper. **3,** regular: пра́вильный глаго́л, regular verb; пра́вильные черты́ лица́, regular features. —**пра́вильная дробь,** proper fraction.

прави́тель *n.m.* ruler.

прави́тельство *n.* government. —**прави́тельственный,** *adj.* governmental; government (*attrib.*).

пра́вить *v.impfv.* [*pres.* **-влю, -вишь**] **1,** (*with instr.*) to rule; govern. **2,** (*with instr.*) to drive; steer. **3,** (*with acc.*) to read; correct (something written). **4,** (*with acc.*) to sharpen; hone.

пра́вка *n.* reading; correcting: пра́вка корректу́ры, proofreading.

правле́ние *n.* **1,** government; rule: о́браз правле́ния, form of government. **2,** management; board of directors.

пра́внук *n.* great-grandson.

пра́внучка [*gen. pl.* **-чек**] *n.* great-granddaughter.

пра́во [*pl.* **права́**] *n.* **1,** right: пра́во на труд, the right to work; пра́во го́лоса, the right to vote. **2,** law: уголо́вное пра́во, criminal law. Изуча́ть пра́во, to study law. **3,** *pl., colloq.* (driver's) license. —*particle, colloq.* **1,** really. **2,** believe me! —**на права́х** (+ *gen.*), as; in the capacity of. На права́х бы́вшего Москвича́, as a former Muscovite. —**по пра́ву,** rightfully; deservedly.

правове́рный *adj.* orthodox. —**правове́рные,** *n.pl.* the faithful.

правово́й *adj.* legal; of (the) law. Правово́е госуда́рство, state based on the rule of law.

правоме́рный *adj.* lawful; legitimate.

правомо́чный *adj.* **1,** authorized. **2,** correct; apposite.

правонаруше́ние *n.* offense; violation of the law. —**правонаруши́тель,** *n.m.* offender; lawbreaker; wrongdoer.

правоохране́ние *n.* law enforcement. —**правоохрани́тельный,** *adj.* law enforcement (*attrib.*).

правописа́ние *n.* orthography; spelling.

правопоря́док [*gen.* **-дка**] *n.* law and order.

правосла́вие *n.* the Orthodox faith.

правосла́вный *adj.* orthodox. —*n.* member of the Orthodox Church.

правосу́дие *n.* justice.

правота́ *n.* rightness; correctness.

пра́вый *adj.* **1,** right; right-hand. **2,** *polit.* right; right-wing. **3,** *naut.* starboard. **4,** [*short form* **прав, права́,**

пра́во, пра́вы] right; correct. **5,** (*of a cause*) just. —*n.* right-winger; rightist. —**пра́вая рука́, 1,** right hand. **2,** right-hand man.

пра́вящий *adj.* ruling: пра́вящие круги́, ruling circles.

прагмати́зм *n.* pragmatism. —**прагмати́ст,** *n.* pragmatist. —**прагмати́ческий,** *adj.* pragmatic.

пра́дед *n.* **1,** great-grandfather. **2,** *pl.* ancestors; forefathers. *Also,* **праде́душка.**

пра́зднество *n.* **1,** festival; celebration. **2,** *pl.* festivities.

пра́здник *n.* **1,** holiday: с пра́здником!, happy holiday! **2,** celebration. —**бу́дет и на на́шей у́лице пра́здник,** our day will come.

пра́здничный *adj.* **1,** holiday (*attrib.*). **2,** festive; gala.

пра́здно *adv.* idly.

пра́зднование *n.* celebration.

пра́здновать *v.impfv.* [*pfv.* **отпра́здновать**; *pres.* **-ную, -нуешь**] to celebrate.

пра́здный *adj.* idle. —**пра́здность,** *n.f.* idleness.

празеоди́м *n.* praseodymium.

пра́ктик *n.* **1,** practical worker. **2,** practical person.

пра́ктика *n.* **1,** practice: на пра́ктике, in practice. **2,** practical experience. **3,** practical work. **4,** *obs.* practice (*of a physician or lawyer*).

практика́нт *n.* person undergoing practical training; trainee.

практикова́ть *v.impfv.* [*pres.* **-ку́ю, -ку́ешь**] **1,** *v.t.* to practice. **2,** *v.i., obs.* (*of a physician, lawyer, etc.*) to practice. —**практикова́ться,** *refl.* **1,** (*with* **в** + *prepl.*) to practice. **2,** to be practiced; be done.

пра́ктикум *n.* practical work; practical training.

практи́чески *adv.* **1,** in a practical manner; practically. **2,** practically; virtually; for all practical purposes.

практи́ческий *adj.* practical: практи́ческий сове́т/о́пыт, practical advice/experience.

практи́чность *n.f.* practicality.

практи́чный *adj.* practical: практи́чный челове́к/костю́м/автомоби́ль, practical person/suit/car.

пра́отец [*gen.* **-тца**] *n., obs.* forefather; ancestor.

пра́порщик *n., mil.* **1,** warrant officer. **2,** *pre-rev.* ensign; lieutenant.

прапраба́бка [*gen. pl.* **-бок**] *n.* great-great-grandmother. *Also,* **прапраба́бушка.**

прапра́внук *n.* great-great-grandson.

прапра́внучка [*gen. pl.* **-чек**] *n.* great-great-granddaughter.

прапра́дед *n.* great-great-grandfather.

прах *n.* **1,** *poetic* dust. **2,** (earthly) remains. Здесь поко́ится прах (+ *gen.*), here lies... —**мир пра́ху его́,** may he rest in peace. —**обрати́ть** *or* **преврати́ть в прах,** to reduce to dust (*or* ashes). —**пойти́ пра́хом,** to go to the dogs.

пра́чечная *n., decl. as an adj.* laundry.

пра́чка [*gen. pl.* **-чек**] *n.* laundress.

праща́ [*gen. pl.* **-ще́й**] *n.* sling (*for hurling stones*).

пра́щур *n.* ancestor; forefather.

пре- *prefix* **1,** *indicating a high degree:* превозноси́ть, to extol; пресыща́ть, to satiate. **2,** *indicating excess:* преувели́чивать, to exaggerate. **3,** *indicating transformation,* превраща́ть, to turn into. **4,** *indicating the overcoming of something:* преодолева́ть/превозмога́ть, to overcome. **5,** (*with adjectives*) *indicating a high degree:* престаре́лый, very old.

преа́мбула *n.* preamble.

пребыва́ние *n.* **1,** (one's) stay: во вре́мя на́шего пребыва́ния в Пари́же, during our stay in Paris. **2,** tenure: пребыва́ние в до́лжности, tenure in office.

пребыва́ть *v.impfv.* **1,** to be. **2,** to live (somewhere).

превали́ровать *v.impfv.* [*pres.* -ру́ю, -ру́ешь] **1,** to predominate. **2,** (*with* **над**) to dominate; take precedence over.

превенти́вный *adj.* preventive.

превзойти́ [*infl.* -взойду́, -взойдёшь; *past* -взошёл, -взошла́] *v.,* *pfv. of* **превосходи́ть.**

превозмога́ть *v.impfv.* [*pfv.* **превозмо́чь**] to overcome.

превозмо́чь [*infl. like* мо́чь] *v., pfv. of* **превозмога́ть.**

превознести́ [*infl. like* нести́] *v., pfv. of* **превозноси́ть.**

превозноси́ть *v.impfv.* [*pfv.* **превознести́**; *pres.* -ношу́, -но́сишь] to extol. —**превозноси́ть до небе́с,** to praise to the skies.

превосходи́тельство *n.* Excellency: ва́ше превосходи́тельство, Your Excellency.

превосходи́ть *v.impfv.* [*pfv.* **превзойти́**; *pres.* -хожу́, -хо́дишь] **1,** to excel. **2,** to exceed; surpass. Превзойти́ все ожида́ния, to exceed all expectations. Превосходя́щие си́лы, superior force. —**превосходи́ть (самого́) себя́,** to outdo oneself. —**превосходи́ть чи́сленностью** *or* **чи́сленно,** to outnumber.

превосхо́дный *adj.* **1,** excellent; superb. **2,** *gram.* superlative: превосхо́дная сте́пень, superlative degree.

превосхо́дство *n.* superiority.

преврати́ть [*infl.* -щу́, -ти́шь] *v., pfv. of* **превраща́ть.** —**преврати́ться,** *refl., pfv. of* **превраща́ться.**

превра́тно *adv.* incorrectly: превра́тно истолко́вывать, to misinterpret.

превра́тность *n.f.* **1,** error; fallacy. **2,** *pl.* vicissitudes: превра́тности судьбы́, the vicissitudes of life.

превра́тный *adj.* **1,** wrong; incorrect; erroneous. **2,** (*of luck, fate, etc.*) fickle; capricious.

превраща́ть *v.impfv.* [*pfv.* **преврати́ть**] (*with* **в** + *acc.*) **1,** to turn into; convert into. **2,** to reduce (to rubble, ashes, etc.). —**превраща́ться,** *refl.* (*with* **в** + *acc.*) to turn into; turn to; become.

превраще́ние *n.* **1,** conversion. **2,** transformation.

превы́сить [*infl.* -шу, -сишь] *v., pfv. of* **превыша́ть.**

превыша́ть *v.impfv.* [*pfv.* **превы́сить**] to exceed.

превыше́ние *n.* **1,** exceeding. **2,** excess.

прегра́да *n.* obstacle; barrier.

прегради́ть [*infl.* -жу́, -ди́шь] *v., pfv. of* **прегражда́ть.**

прегражда́ть *v.impfv.* [*pfv.* **прегради́ть**] to block; bar; obstruct.

прегражде́ние *n.* blocking; barring; obstructing.

прегреше́ние *n.* sin; transgression; iniquity.

пред *prep.* = **пе́ред.**

пред- *prefix, indicating prior action:* предви́деть, to foresee; предвосхища́ть, to anticipate.

предава́ть *v.impfv.* [*pfv.* **преда́ть**; *pres.* -даю́, -даёшь] **1,** to betray. **2,** (*with dat.*) to commit (to): предава́ть (что́-нибудь) огню́, to commit to the flames.

3, *in* предава́ть гла́сности, to make public; предава́ть сме́рти, to put to death; предава́ть суду́, to prosecute; put on trial. —**предава́ться,** *refl.* (*with dat.*) to give way to; indulge in.

преда́ние *n.* **1,** legend. **2,** (*with dat.*) committing (to); putting (to).

пре́данность *n.f.* devotion; dedication.

пре́данный *adj.* devoted; dedicated. —**пре́данный вам,** yours truly.

преда́тель *n.m.* traitor.

преда́тельский *adj.* **1,** traitorous; treasonable. **2,** treacherous.

преда́тельство *n.* **1,** betrayal. **2,** treachery. **3,** treason.

преда́ть [*infl. like* да́ть; *past* пре́дал, предала́, пре́дало, пре́дали] *v., pfv. of* **предава́ть.** —**преда́ться,** *refl.* [*past tense stress as in* да́ться] *pfv. of* **предава́ться.**

предба́нник *n.* dressing room in a bathhouse.

предвари́тельно *adv.* beforehand; in advance; ahead of time.

предвари́тельный *adj.* **1,** preliminary. **2,** advance; prior.

предваря́ть *v.impfv.* [*pfv.* **предвари́ть**] **1,** to anticipate. **2,** to preface. **3,** *obs.* to warn; forewarn.

предве́стие *n.* omen; augury; portent.

предве́стник *n.* harbinger; precursor; forerunner.

предвеща́ть *v.impfv.* to portend; presage; augur. Предвеща́ть хоро́шее, to augur well; bode well.

предвзя́тость *n.f.* prejudice; bias. —**предвзя́тый,** *adj.* preconceived; biased.

предви́дение *n.* **1,** foresight. **2,** anticipation: в предви́дении (+ *gen.*), in anticipation of.

предви́деть *v.impfv.* [*pres.* -ви́жу, -ви́дишь] to foresee. —**предви́деться,** *refl.* to be expected; be anticipated; be in sight.

предвкуси́ть [*infl.* -вкушу́, -вку́сишь] *v., pfv. of* **предвкуша́ть.**

предвкуша́ть *v.impfv.* [*pfv.* **предвкуси́ть**] to anticipate with pleasure; look forward to.

предвкуше́ние *n.* **1,** foretaste. **2,** anticipation.

предводи́тель *n.m.* leader. —**предводи́тельство,** *n.* leadership.

предводи́тельствовать *v.impfv.* [*pres.* -ствую, -ствуешь] **1,** to be the leader; be in charge. **2,** (*with instr.*) to lead; command; be the leader of.

предвое́нный *adj.* prewar.

предвосхища́ть *v.impfv.* [*pfv.* **предвосхи́тить**] to anticipate.

предвосхище́ние *n.* anticipation.

предвы́борный *adj.* election (*attrib.*).

предго́рье *n.* foothill(s).

преддве́рие *n.* **1,** entrance. **2,** *fig.* (*with gen.*) period immediately preceding.

преде́л *n.* **1,** limit. **2,** *pl.* bounds: вы́йти за преде́лы (+ *gen.*), to go beyond the bounds of. **3,** (*with gen.*) height (of); acme (of); pinnacle (of): преде́л жела́ний, the pinnacle of one's desires. —**в преде́лах** (+ *gen.*), within. —**за преде́лами** (+ *gen.*), outside; beyond. —**на преде́ле,** at the breaking point.

преде́льно *adv.* completely; utterly. Преде́льно я́сно, crystal-clear.

преде́льный *adj.* **1,** boundary (*attrib.*): преде́льная ли́ния, boundary line. **2,** maximum: преде́льный во́зраст, maximum age. Преде́льный срок, time limit. **3,** *fig.* utmost: с преде́льной быстрото́й, with the utmost speed.

предержа́щий *adj.*, in вла́сти предержа́щие, *obs.* the powers that be; the authorities.

предзнаменова́ние *n.* omen; augury; portent.

предикати́в *n.*, *gram.* predicate. —**предикати́вный,** *adj.*, *gram.* predicative.

предисло́вие *n.* preface; foreword.

предлага́ть *v.impfv.* [*pfv.* **предложи́ть**] **1,** to offer. **2,** to propose. **3,** to suggest. **4,** to pose (a question, riddle, etc.); give (a problem). Предложи́ть ученика́м зада́чу, to give the pupils a problem. **5,** to order (someone to do something).

предло́г *n.* **1,** pretext; excuse. **2,** preposition.

предложе́ние *n.* **1,** offer. **2,** proposal; proposition. **3,** suggestion. **4,** motion (*made at a meeting*). **5,** *gram.* sentence; clause. **6,** *econ.* supply: спрос и предложе́ние, supply and demand.

предложи́ть [*infl.* **-ложу́, -ло́жишь**] *v.*, *pfv. of* **предлага́ть.**

предло́жный *adj.*, in **предло́жный паде́ж,** prepositional case.

предме́стье *n.* suburb.

предме́т *n.* **1,** object: неодушевлённый предме́т, inanimate object. **2,** article; item: предме́т ро́скоши, luxury item. **3,** object; target: предме́т насме́шек, object of ridicule. **4,** subject; topic. **5,** subject (*in school*). —**на предме́т** (+ *gen.*), for; for the purpose of.

предме́тный *adj.* **1,** subject (*attrib.*): предме́тный катало́г, subject catalogue. **2,** dealing with (*or* devoted to) a single subject. **3,** material; physical. —**предме́тное стекло́,** slide (*for a microscope*). —**предме́тный уро́к,** object lesson.

предмо́стный *adj.* located at the foot of a bridge. —**предмо́стное укрепле́ние,** bridgehead.

предназнача́ть *v.impfv.* [*pfv.* **предназна́чить**] (*with* **на** + *acc. or* **для**) **1,** to mean; intend; design (for). **2,** to set aside; earmark (for).

предназначе́ние *n.* **1,** mission; calling. **2,** fate; destiny.

предназна́чить *v.*, *pfv. of* **предназнача́ть.**

преднаме́ренный *adj.* premeditated; intentional; deliberate. —**преднаме́ренно,** *adv.* intentionally; deliberately. —**преднаме́ренность,** *n.f.* premeditation.

предначерта́ние *n.* **1,** prescription; requirement. **2,** mission; calling.

предначерта́ть *v.pfv.* to destine; predestine; foreordain.

предо *prep.* = **пред** *and* **пе́ред.**

пре́док [*gen.* **-дка**] *n.* ancestor; forefather.

предопределе́ние *n.* **1,** predetermination. **2,** predestination.

предопределя́ть *v.impfv.* [*pfv.* **предопредели́ть**] to predetermine; predestine; foreordain.

предоста́вить [*infl.* **-влю, -вишь**] *v.*, *pfv. of* **предоставля́ть.**

предоставле́ние *n.* granting; giving; providing; extending.

предоставля́ть *v.impfv.* [*pfv.* **предоста́вить**] **1,** to grant; give; provide; extend. **2,** to leave (*to do something*): предоставля́ть реше́ние нача́льнику, to leave the decision to the boss. Нам предоста́вили э́то сде́лать, it was left for us to do. —**предоставля́ть самому́ себе́,** to leave on one's own; leave to one's own devices; leave to fend for oneself.

предоста́точно *adv.*, *colloq.* more than enough.

предостерега́ть *v.impfv.* [*pfv.* **предостере́чь**] (*with* **от**) to warn (against); caution (against).

предостереже́ние *n.* warning; caution.

предостере́чь [*infl. like* **стере́чь**] *v.*, *pfv. of* **предостерега́ть.**

предосторо́жность *n.f.* **1,** caution; precaution. **2,** *usu. pl.* precautions. —**ме́ры предосторо́жности,** precautionary measures.

предосуди́тельный *adj.* reprehensible; blameworthy.

предотвраща́ть *v.impfv.* [*pfv.* **предотврати́ть**] to avert; prevent.

предотвраще́ние *n.* prevention; preventing; averting.

предохране́ние *n.* protection.

предохрани́тель *n.m.* safety device; safety catch; safety lock. —**пла́вкий предохрани́тель,** *electricity* fuse.

предохрани́тельный *adj.* **1,** precautionary; preventive. **2,** safety (*attrib.*): предохрани́тельный кла́пан, safety valve.

предохраня́ть *v.impfv.* [*pfv.* **предохрани́ть**] to protect.

предписа́ние *n.* order: предписа́ния врача́, doctor's orders.

предписа́ть [*infl.* **-пишу́, -пи́шешь**] *v.*, *pfv. of* **предпи́сывать.**

предпи́сывать *v.impfv.* [*pfv.* **предписа́ть**] **1,** (*with dat.*) to order; direct. **2,** to prescribe.

предпле́чье *n.* forearm.

предплюсна́ [*pl.* **-плю́сны, -плю́сен**] *n.*, *anat.* tarsus. —**предплюснево́й,** *adj.* tarsal.

предполага́емый *adj.* **1,** planned. **2,** supposed; presumed.

предполага́ть *v.impfv.* [*pfv.* **предположи́ть**] **1,** to suppose; assume; presume. **2,** [*impfv. only*] (*with inf.*) to plan (to); expect (to); intend (to). **3,** [*impfv. only*] to presuppose. —**предполага́ться,** *refl.* [*impfv. only*] **1,** to be planned. **2,** *impers.* to be assumed: Предполага́лось, что..., it was assumed that...

предполётный *adj.* preflight.

предположе́ние *n.* **1,** supposition; assumption. **2,** plan; intention.

предположи́тельно *adv.* **1,** by making an assumption; hypothetically. **2,** supposedly; presumably; probably.

предположи́тельный *adj.* hypothetical; conjectural.

предположи́ть [*infl.* **-ложу́, -ло́жишь**] *v.*, *pfv. of* **предполага́ть.**

предпосла́ть [*infl.* **-шлю́, -шлёшь**] *v.*, *pfv. of* **предпосыла́ть.**

предпосле́дний *adj.* next to last.

предпосыла́ть *v.impfv.* [*pfv.* **предпосла́ть**] (*with dat.*) to preface: предпосыла́ть расска́зу анекдо́т, to preface one's story with an anecdote. Предпосыла́ть не́сколько слов к расска́зу, to preface one's story with a few words.

предпосы́лка [*gen. pl.* -лок] *n.* **1,** prerequisite; precondition. **2,** premise.

предпоче́сть [*infl.* -чту́, -чтёшь; *pres.* -чёл, -чла́, -чло́, -чли́] *v., pfv. of* **предпочита́ть.**

предпочита́ть *v.impfv.* [*pfv.* **предпоче́сть**] to prefer.

предпочте́ние *n.* preference.

предпочти́тельный *adj.* **1,** preferable; preferred. Си́ний цвет предпочти́тельнее зелёного, blue is preferable to green. **2,** (*of a tariff*) preferential.

предприи́мчивый *adj.* enterprising. —**предприи́мчивость,** *n.f.* enterprise; initiative.

предпринима́тель *n.m.* entrepreneur; businessman.

предпринима́тельство *n.* enterprise: ча́стное предпринима́тельство, private enterprise.

предпринима́ть *v.impfv.* [*pfv.* **предприня́ть**] **1,** to undertake; launch. **2,** to make (an attempt, efforts, etc.). **3,** to take (steps, measures, action, etc.). **4,** to launch; mount (an attack, offensive, etc.).

предприня́ть [*infl. like* **приня́ть**] *v., pfv. of* **предпринима́ть.**

предприя́тие *n.* **1,** undertaking; venture. **2,** enterprise: промы́шленное предприя́тие, an industrial enterprise.

предра́ковый *adj.* precancerous.

предрасполага́ть *v.impfv.* [*pfv.* **предрасположи́ть**] (*with* **к** *or* **в по́льзу**) to predispose (toward *or* in favor of).

предрасположе́ние *n.* (*with* **к**) predisposition (to *or* toward).

предрасполо́женный *adj.* (*with* **к**) predisposed (to).

предрасположи́ть [*infl.* -ложу́, -ло́жишь] *v., pfv. of* **предрасполага́ть.**

предрассу́док [*gen.* -дка] *n.* prejudice.

предрека́ть *v.impfv.* [*pfv.* **предре́чь**] **1,** to predict. **2,** to portend.

предре́чь [*infl. like* **печь**] *v., pfv. of* **предрека́ть.**

предреша́ть *v.impfv.* [*pfv.* **предреши́ть**] **1,** to decide beforehand. **2,** to prejudge. **3,** to predetermine.

предродово́й *adj.* prenatal.

председа́тель *n.m.* **1,** chairman. **2,** (*at a formal meeting*) chairman; president: господи́н председа́тель, Mr. Chairman; Mr. President. —**председа́тельский,** *adj.* chairman's. —**председа́тельство,** *n.* chairmanship.

председа́тельствовать *v.impfv.* [*pres.* -ствую, -ствуешь] to preside.

предсе́рдие *n.* auricle (*of the heart*).

предсказа́ние *n.* prediction.

предсказа́тель *n.m.* forecaster; prognosticator.

предсказа́ть [*infl.* -скажу́, -ска́жешь] *v., pfv. of* **предска́зывать.**

предсказу́емый *adj.* predictable.

предска́зывать *v.impfv.* [*pfv.* **предсказа́ть**] to predict.

предсме́ртный *adj.* **1,** occurring just before death; death (*attrib.*). **2,** (*of words, a wish, etc.*) dying.

представи́тель *n.m.* **1,** representative. **2,** spokesman.

представи́тельный *adj.* **1,** representative. **2,** impressive; imposing.

представи́тельство *n.* **1,** representation. **2,** mission: представи́тельство США при ООН, the U.S. Mission to the UN. **3,** representative office: вое́нное представи́тельство, military representative's office.

предста́вить [*infl.* -влю, -вишь] *v., pfv. of* **представля́ть.** —**предста́виться,** *refl., pfv. of* **представля́ться.**

представле́ние *n.* **1,** presentation; submission. **2,** introduction. **3,** idea; notion. **4,** picture (*in one's mind*). **5,** performance; show. **6,** representation (*formal statement*).

представля́ть *v.impfv.* [*pfv.* **предста́вить**] **1,** to present; submit. **2,** to produce; show (a document). **3,** to introduce; present (a person). **4,** (*with* **к**) to recommend (for); nominate (for): предста́вить кого́-нибудь к награ́де, to recommend/nominate someone for an award. **5,** [*impfv. only*] to represent: представля́ть свой о́круг, to represent one's district. **6,** (*with* **себе́**) to imagine; visualize; picture. **7,** to represent; depict; portray. Представля́ть в вы́годном све́те, to present in a favorable light. **8,** to realize; appreciate; understand. **9,** [*impfv. only*] (*often with* **собо́й**) to be; pose; represent; constitute: представля́ть угро́зу, to pose a threat; представля́ть (собо́й) опа́сность (для), to pose/represent/constitute a danger (to). Представля́ть интере́с (для), to be of interest (to). Представля́ть тру́дности *or* затрудне́ния, to pose/present difficulties. Что он собо́й представля́ет?, what sort of person is he?; what is he like?

представля́ться *v.r.impfv.* [*pfv.* **предста́виться**] **1,** to introduce oneself. **2,** (*of an opportunity*) to arise; present itself. **3,** (*with dat.*) to appear (before). **4,** (*with dat.*) to seem (to). **5,** (*with instr.*) to seem like; appear to be. **6,** (*with instr.*) colloq. to pretend (to be).

предста́тельный *adj., in* **предста́тельная железа́,** prostate gland.

предста́ть *v.pfv.* [*infl.* -ста́ну, -ста́нешь] (*with* **пе́ред**) to appear (before). Предста́ть пе́ред судо́м, to appear in court; stand trial.

предстоя́ть *v.impfv.* [*pres.* -стои́т] **1,** to lie ahead; be in the offing. **2,** (*with dat.*) to be in store (for). Нам предстои́т холо́дная зима́, we are in for a cold winter. **3,** (*with dat. and inf.*) to have to: Мне предстои́т пое́хать туда́, I shall have to go there.

предстоя́щий *adj.* forthcoming; impending.

предте́ча *n.m. & f., archaic* forerunner; precursor. —**Иоа́нн Предте́ча,** John the Baptist.

предубежда́ть *v.impfv.* [*pfv.* **предубеди́ть**] *obs.* to prejudice.

предубежде́ние *n.* prejudice; bias. —**предубеждённый,** *adj.* prejudiced; biased.

предуга́дывать *v.impfv.* [*pfv.* **предугада́ть**] **1,** to guess; divine. **2,** to foresee; anticipate.

предупреди́тельность *n.f.* thoughtfulness; attentiveness.

предупреди́тельный *adj.* **1,** precautionary; preventive. **2,** warning (*attrib.*): предупреди́тельный вы́стрел, warning shot. **3,** considerate; thoughtful; attentive.

предупреди́ть [*infl.* -жу́, -ди́шь] *v., pfv. of* **предупрежда́ть.**

предупрежда́ть *v.impfv.* [*pfv.* **предупреди́ть**] **1,** to warn. **2,** to notify. **3,** to prevent. **4,** to anticipate. **5,** to beat (someone) to it.

предупрежде́ние *n.* **1,** warning. **2,** notification; notice. **3,** prevention.

предусма́тривать *v.impfv.* [*pfv.* **предусмотре́ть**] **1**, to foresee; envisage; anticipate. **2**, [*impfv. only*] to provide for; stipulate.

предусмотре́ть [*infl.* -смотрю́, -смо́тришь] *v., pfv. of* **предусма́тривать.**

предусмотри́тельный *adj.* having foresight; far-sighted. —**предусмотри́тельность,** *n.f.* foresight.

предчу́вствие *n.* presentiment; premonition; foreboding.

предчу́вствовать *v.impfv.* [*pres.* -ствую, -ствуешь] **1**, to have a premonition about. **2**, (*with* **что**) to have a feeling that...

предше́ственник *n.* **1**, predecessor. **2**, forerunner; precursor.

предше́ствовать *v.impfv.* [*pres.* -ствую, -ствуешь] (*with dat.*) to precede.

предше́ствующий *adj.* preceding; previous.

предъяви́тель *n.m.* bearer (*of a document*). —**предъяви́тель и́ска,** plaintiff.

предъяви́ть [*infl.* -явлю́, -я́вишь] *v., pfv. of* **предъявля́ть.**

предъявле́ние *n.* **1**, presentation (*of a document*). **2**, bringing (*of a suit, charges, etc.*).

предъявля́ть *v.impfv.* [*pfv.* **предъяви́ть**] **1**, to present; produce; show (a document). **2**, to bring; file (a lawsuit); bring; prefer (charges). Предъяви́ть обвине́ние (+ *dat.*), to indict; charge. **3**, to make (demands); issue (an ultimatum). **4**, to assert (one's rights). Предъявля́ть тре́бование *or* пра́во на (+ *acc.*), to lay claim to.

предыду́щий *adj.* previous; preceding. —**предыду́щее,** *n.* the foregoing.

предысто́рия *n.* **1**, prehistory. **2**, (*with gen.*) background (of).

прее́мник *n.* successor.

прее́мственность *n.f.* **1**, succession. **2**, continuity.

прее́мственный *adj.* successive.

прее́мство *n.* succession.

пре́жде *adv.* **1**, before; formerly. **2**, first. —*prep., with gen.* before; ahead of. —**пре́жде всего́,** first of all; first and foremost. —**пре́жде чем,** before.

преждевре́менный *adj.* **1**, premature. **2**, untimely. —**преждевре́менно,** *adv.* prematurely.

пре́жний *adj.* **1**, former. **2**, previous. **3**, the same (as before): оста́ться пре́жним, to remain the same. —**в пре́жнее вре́мя; в пре́жние времена́,** in former times.

презента́бельный *adj.* presentable; proper.

презервати́в *n.* condom.

президе́нт *n.* president. —**президе́нтский,** *adj.* presidential. —**президе́нтство,** *n.* presidency.

прези́диум *n.* presidium.

презира́ть *v.impfv.* [*pfv.* **презре́ть**] **1**, [*impfv. only*] to despise; disdain; scorn; hold in contempt. **2**, to disregard; scorn (danger, death, etc.).

презре́ние *n.* (*with* **к**) **1**, contempt (for); disdain (for); scorn (for). **2**, disregard (of danger, death, etc.).

презре́нный *adj.* contemptible; despicable. —**презре́нный мета́лл,** filthy lucre.

презре́ть [*infl.* -зрю́, -зри́шь] *v., pfv. of* **презира́ть** (*in sense #2*).

презри́тельный *adj.* scornful; contemptuous; disdainful.

презу́мпция *n., law* presumption: презу́мпция неви́новности, presumption of innocence.

преиму́щественно *adv.* mainly; chiefly; primarily.

преиму́щественный *adj.* **1**, primary; paramount. **2**, preferred.

преиму́щество *n.* advantage: преиму́щество пе́ред сопе́рником, advantage over one's rival. —**по преиму́ществу,** mainly; chiefly; primarily.

преиспо́дняя *n., decl. as an adj.* hell; the nether world.

преиспо́лненный *adj.* (*with gen.*) filled (with); full (of).

преисполня́ть *v.impfv.* [*pfv.* **преиспо́лнить**] **1**, to fill. **2**, *fig.* to imbue.

прейскура́нт *n.* price list; catalogue. —**прейскура́нтный,** *adj.* of a price list: прейскура́нтная цена́, list price.

преклоне́ние *n.* (*with* **пе́ред**) worship (of); admiration (of); reverence (for).

преклони́ть [*infl.* -клоню́, -кло́нишь] *v., pfv. of* **преклоня́ть.** —**преклони́ться,** *refl., pfv. of* **преклоня́ться.**

прекло́нный *adj.* (*of age*) old; advanced.

преклоня́ть *v.impfv.* [*pfv. of* **преклони́ть**] **1**, to bend (one's knees); bow (one's head). **2**, *in* преклоня́ть коле́на (*or* коле́ни) пе́ред, to kneel before; bow down to. —**преклоня́ться,** *refl.* (*with* **пе́ред**) **1**, to kneel (before); bow down (to). **2**, to worship; revere. **3**, to admire; take off one's hat to.

прекосло́вить *v.impfv.* [*pres.* -влю, -вишь] (*with dat.*) to contradict.

прекра́сно *adv.* **1**, marvelously. Она́ прекра́сно вы́глядит, she looks marvelous/wonderful. **2**, perfectly well: Я прекра́сно зна́ю, что..., I know perfectly well that... **3**, *as an interj.* wonderful!; fine!; perfect!

прекра́сное *n., decl. as an adj.* the beautiful; that which is beautiful.

прекра́сный *adj.* [*short form* -сен, -сна] **1**, beautiful. **2**, excellent; wonderful. **3**, *in* прекра́сный пол, the fair sex. —**в оди́н прекра́сный день,** one fine day. —**ра́ди чьи́х-нибудь прекра́сных глаз,** for love.

прекрати́ть [*infl.* -щу́, -ти́шь] *v., pfv. of* **прекраща́ть.** —**прекрати́ться,** *refl., pfv. of* **прекраща́ться.**

прекраща́ть *v.impfv.* [*pfv.* **прекрати́ть**] to halt; cease; terminate; suspend; discontinue. Прекрати́ть своё существова́ние, to cease to exist. —**прекраща́ться,** *refl.* to end; stop; cease.

прекраще́ние *n.* halt; cessation; suspension. —**прекраще́ние огня́,** cease-fire. —**прекраще́ние пре́ний,** cloture.

прела́т *n.* prelate.

преле́стный *adj.* charming; delightful; lovely.

пре́лесть *n.f.* **1**, charm. **2**, a delight: Пря́мо пре́лесть!, it's an absolute delight; it's simply delightful.

преломи́ть [*infl.* -ломлю́, -ло́мишь] *v., pfv. of* **преломля́ть.**

преломле́ние *n.* refraction.

преломля́ть *v.impfv.* [*pfv.* **преломи́ть**] to refract.

пре́лый *adj.* rotten.

прель *n.f.* rot; mold.

прельсти́ть [*infl.* -щу́, -сти́шь] *v., pfv. of* **прельща́ть.** —**прельсти́ться,** *refl., pfv. of* **прельща́ться.**

прельща́ть *v.impfv.* [*pfv.* **прельсти́ть**] **1**, to charm; captivate. **2**, to tempt; entice; lure. —**прельща́ться**, *refl.* (*with instr.*) to be enticed (by); fall for.

прелюбоде́й *n.* adulterer. —**прелюбоде́йка**, *n.* adulteress. —**прелюбоде́йный**, *adj.* adulterous.

прелюбоде́йствовать *v.impfv.* [*pres.* **-ствую, -ствуешь**] to commit adultery.

прелюбодея́ние *n.* adultery.

прелю́дия *n.* **1**, *music* prelude. **2**, *fig.* (*with* **к**) prelude (to).

премиа́льный *adj.* bonus (*attrib.*). —**премиа́льные**, *n.pl.* bonus money.

премину́ть *v.pfv.*, *used negatively with inf.* not to fail (to).

премиро́ванный *adj.* having won a prize; prize (*attrib.*).

премирова́ть *v.impfv. & pfv.* [*pres.* **-ру́ю, -ру́ешь**] to give a bonus to; award a prize to.

пре́мия *n.* **1**, prize. **2**, bonus. **3**, premium.

прему́дрость *n.f.* **1**, wisdom. **2**, *usu. pl.* mysteries; intricacies. —**невелика́ прему́дрость**, it's not that difficult.

прему́дрый *adj.* **1**, possessing great wisdom. **2**, abstruse; arcane.

премье́р *n.* **1**, premier. **2**, leading actor; star performer.

премье́ра *n.* première.

премье́р-мини́стр *n.* prime minister.

премье́рша *n.*, *colloq.* leading lady.

пренебрега́ть *v.impfv.* [*pfv.* **пренебре́чь**] (*with instr.*) **1**, to scorn; disdain; look down on. **2**, to disregard; ignore (rules, advice, etc.). **3**, to neglect (one's duties, health, etc.).

пренебреже́ние *n.* **1**, (*with* **к**) disdain (for). **2**, (*with* **к** *or gen.*) disregard (of *or* for). **3**, (*with instr. or gen.*) neglect (of).

пренебрежи́тельный *adj.* scornful; disdainful.

пренебре́чь [*infl.* **-брегу́, -брежёшь, ...-брегу́т**; *past* **-брёг, -брегла́, -брегло́, -брегли́**] *v.*, *pfv. of* **пренебрега́ть**.

пре́ния [*gen.* **-ний**] *n.pl.* debate.

преоблада́ние *n.* **1**, predominance. **2**, preponderance.

преоблада́ть *v.impfv.* **1**, to predominate. **2**, (*with* **над**) to prevail over.

преоблада́ющий *adj.* predominant; prevailing.

преобража́ть *v.impfv.* [*pfv.* **преобрази́ть**] **1**, to transform. **2**, to transfigure. —**преобража́ться**, to be transformed.

преображе́ние *n.* **1**, transformation. **2**, *relig.* the Transfiguration.

преобрази́ть [*infl.* **-жу́, -зи́шь**] *v.*, *pfv. of* **преобража́ть**. —**преобрази́ться**, *refl.*, *pfv. of* **преобража́ться**.

преобразова́ние *n.* **1**, transformation. **2**, *pl.* reforms.

преобразова́тель *n.m.* **1**, reformer. **2**, *electricity* transformer.

преобразова́ть [*infl.* **-зу́ю, -зу́ешь**] *v.*, *pfv. of* **преобразо́вывать**.

преобразо́вывать *v.impfv.* [*pfv.* **преобразова́ть**] **1**, to transform; reorganize; reform. **2**, *electricity; physics* to transform.

преодолева́ть *v.impfv.* [*pfv.* **преодоле́ть**] to overcome; surmount.

преодоле́ние *n.* overcoming; surmounting.

преодоле́ть *v.*, *pfv. of* **преодолева́ть**.

преодоли́мый *adj.* surmountable.

препара́т *n.* **1**, preparation; compound. **2**, *med.* drug. **3**, laboratory specimen.

препина́ние *n.*, *in* **зна́ки препина́ния**, punctuation marks.

препира́тельство *n.* squabble; hassle.

препира́ться *v.r.impfv.* to squabble; wrangle.

преподава́ние *n.* teaching.

преподава́тель *n.m.* [*fem.* **-ница**] teacher. —**преподава́тельский**, *adj.* teaching (*attrib.*).

преподава́ть *v.impfv.* [*pres.* **-даю́, -даёшь**] to teach.

препода́ть *v.pfv.* [*infl. like* **пода́ть**] to give; impart; teach.

преподнести́ [*infl. like* **нести́**] *v.*, *pfv. of* **преподноси́ть**.

преподноси́ть *v.impfv.* [*pfv.* **преподнести́**; *pres.* **-ношу́, -но́сишь**] **1**, to present (a gift, award, etc.). **2**, *colloq.* to give (a surprise, bad news, etc.). **3**, to present (facts, material, etc.).

преподноше́ние *n.* **1**, presentation. **2**, present.

преподо́бие *n.* Reverence (*title*). —**преподо́бный**, *adj.* Reverend.

препо́на *n.*, *obs.* obstacle; impediment.

препроводи́ть [*infl.* **-вожу́, -води́шь** *or* **-во́дишь**] *v.*, *pfv. of* **препровожда́ть**.

препровожда́ть *v.impfv.* [*pfv.* **препроводи́ть**] **1**, to dispatch; send off (*under guard*). **2**, to forward.

препровожде́ние *n.* **1**, sending; forwarding. **2**, passing (*of time*).

препя́тствие *n.* **1**, obstacle. **2**, *sports* obstacle; hurdle: бег/ска́чка с препя́тствиями, hurdle/steeplechase race.

препя́тствовать *v.impfv.* [*pfv.* **воспрепя́тствовать**; *pres.* **-ствую, -ствуешь**] (*with dat.*) to hinder; impede.

прерва́ть [*infl.* **-рву́, -рвёшь**; *past fem.* **прервала́**] *v.*, *pfv. of* **прерыва́ть**. —**прерва́ться**, *refl.* [*past tense stress as in* **рва́ться**] *pfv. of* **прерыва́ться**.

пререка́ние *n.*, *usu. pl.* squabble; argument.

пререка́ться *v.r.impfv.* to squabble; bicker.

пре́рия *n.* prairie.

прерогати́ва *n.* prerogative.

прерыва́ние *n.* interruption.

прерыва́тель *n.m.* circuit breaker.

прерыва́ть *v.impfv.* [*pfv.* **прерва́ть**] **1**, to interrupt. **2**, to break off; suspend. **3**, to cut off (communications). **4**, to break (the silence). —**прерыва́ться**, *refl.* **1**, to be interrupted. **2**, (*of one's voice*) to break.

преры́вистый *adj.* **1**, irregular; intermittent. **2**, (*of a line*) broken (- - -).

пресви́тер *n.* presbyter.

пресвитериа́нин [*pl.* **-иа́не, -иа́н**] *n.* Presbyterian. *Also,* **пресвитериа́нец** [*gen.* **-нца**; *fem.* **-нка**].

пресвитериа́нский *adj.* Presbyterian.

пресека́ть *v.impfv.* [*pfv.* **пресе́чь**] **1**, to put a stop to. **2**, to head off; nip: пресека́ть в ко́рне, to nip in the bud. **3**, to cut short. —**пресека́ться**, *refl.* **1**, to stop. **2**, to end. **3**, (*of one's voice*) to break.

пресе́чь [*infl. like* **сечь**; *past* **-сёк** *or* **-се́к, -секла́, -секло́, -секли́**] *v.*, *pfv. of* **пресека́ть**. —**пресе́чься**, *refl.*, *pfv. of* **пресека́ться**.

преследование *n.* **1,** pursuit. **2,** persecution. **3,** *in* судебное преследование, prosecution.

преследователь *n.m.* **1,** persecutor. **2,** pursuer.

преследовать *v.impfv.* [*pres.* -дую, -дуешь] **1,** to pursue. **2,** persecute. **3,** *fig.* (*of a thought, melody, etc.*) to haunt. **4,** (*of misfortune, bad luck, etc.*) to dog. **5,** to prosecute.

пресловутый *adj.* notorious; famous.

пресмыкаться *v.r.impfv.* (with перед) to grovel (before).

пресмыкающееся *n.,* decl. as an adj. reptile.

пресноводный *adj.* fresh-water.

пресный *adj.* **1,** (*of water*) fresh. **2,** (*of bread or dough*) unleavened. **3,** (*of food*) tasteless. **4,** *fig.* insipid; vapid.

пресс *n.* press: давильный пресс, wine press.

пресса *n.* the press.

пресс-конференция *n.* press conference; news conference.

прессование *n.* pressing.

прессовать *v.impfv.* [*pfv.* спрессовать; *pres.* -сую, -суешь] to press.

прессовка *n.* pressing.

прессовщик [*gen.* -щика] *n.* presser; pressman.

пресс-папье *n.neut. indecl.* **1,** paperweight. **2,** blotter.

преставиться *v.r.pfv.,* obs. to die; pass away.

престарелый *adj.* very old; aged. —дом для престарелых, old age home.

престиж *n.* prestige.

престижный *adj.* **1,** prestigious. **2,** of prestige: престижный вопрос, matter of prestige.

престо *n.indecl. & adj., music* presto.

престол *n.* throne. —папский престол, Holy See; Apostolic See.

престолонаследие *n.* succession (to the throne).

престольный *adj.* throne (*attrib.*).

преступать *v.impfv.* [*pfv.* преступить] to break; overstep (the law).

преступить [*infl.* -ступлю, -ступишь] *v., pfv. of* преступать.

преступление *n.* crime. Уголовное преступление, criminal offense.

преступник *n.* criminal.

преступность *n.f.* **1,** crime: рост преступности, the rise in crime. **2,** criminal nature; criminality. —детская преступность, crimes committed by minors; juvenile delinquency.

преступный *adj.* criminal.

пресыщать *v.impfv.* [*pfv* пресытить] to satiate; surfeit.

пресыщение *n.* satiation; satiety; surfeit.

претворять *v.impfv.* [*pfv.* претворить] *obs.* to change; transform. —претворять в жизнь, to make a reality of; put into practice.

претендент *n.* (*with* на + *acc.*) **1,** contender; aspirant. **2,** applicant. **3,** claimant. **4,** challenger. **5,** pretender (to the throne).

претендовать *v.impfv.* [*pres.* -дую, -дуешь] (*with* на + *acc.*) **1,** to claim; lay claim to. **2,** to seek; aspire to. **3,** to have pretensions of.

претензия *n.* **1,** claim. **2,** complaint; grievance. **3,** pretension. —быть в претензии на (+ *acc.*), to have something against; have it in for. —иметь пре-

тензию на (+ *acc.*), **1,** to have a claim on. **2,** to have a complaint about. **3,** to have pretensions of. —предъявить претензию, **1,** to file (*or* put in) a claim. **2,** to raise an objection. —с претензиями, pretentious.

претенциозый (тэ) *adj.* pretentious. —претенциозность, *n.f.* pretentiousness.

претерпевать *v.impfv.* [*pfv.* претерпеть] **1,** to suffer; endure. **2,** to undergo (changes).

претерпеть [*infl.* -терплю, -терпишь] *v., pfv. of* претерпевать.

претить *v.impfv.* (with dat.) to sicken; disgust. Мне всегда претили такие высказывания, such statements always made me sick. ♦*Also impers.:* Мне претит от этого, I'm sick of it; it makes me sick.

преткновение *n., in* камень преткновения, stumbling block.

претор *n.* praetor.

преть *v.impfv.* [*pfv.* сопреть] to rot.

преувеличение *n.* exaggeration.

преувеличивать *v.impfv.* [*pfv.* преувеличить] to exaggerate.

преуменьшать *v.impfv.* [*pfv.* преуменьшить *or* преуменьшить] **1,** to underestimate; underrate. **2,** to understate; minimize; play down.

преуменьшение *n.* underestimation.

преуменьшить *also,* преуменьшить *v., pfv. of* преуменьшать.

преуспевать *v.impfv.* [*pfv.* преуспеть] **1,** to succeed; be successful. **2,** (*with* в + *prepl.*) to excel (in). **3,** [*impfv. only*] to thrive; prosper.

преуспевающий *adj.* successful (*in business or one's profession*).

префект *n.* prefect. —префектура, *n.* prefecture.

преферанс *n.* preference (*card game*).

префикс *n.* prefix. —префиксация, *n.* prefixation.

преходящий *adj.* transient; transitory; ephemeral; momentary.

прецедент *n.* precedent.

прецедентный *adj., in* прецедентное право, case law.

при *prep., with prepl.* **1,** near; by; at: при впадении реки Оки в Волгу, where the Oka River flows into the Volga. Битва при Бородине, the Battle of Borodino. Быть при смерти, to be near death. **2,** attached to: ясли при заводе, nursery attached to a factory; указатель при книге, index to a book. **3,** in the presence of: при мне, in my presence; при свидетелях, in the presence of witnesses. **4,** during: при жизни (+ *gen.*), during the life of; при Иване Грозном, during the reign of Ivan the Terrible. **5,** under (*a ruler or regime*): при Сталине, under Stalin; жить при коммунизме, to live under communism. **6,** at; on; upon; when: при виде (+ *gen.*), at the sight of; при упоминании о, at the mention of; при переходе через улицу, when crossing the street; при их первой встрече, at their first meeting. **7,** on the person of: документы при себе, documents on one's person. **8,** having; possessing: быть при деньгах, to have plenty of money. **9,** under; in view of; given: при таких условиях, under such conditions; при таком положе́нии дел, given the situation. **10,** (*with* **всём** *or* **всей**) for all; despite: при всём том, for all that. При всём моём жела́нии, much as I would like to. —**ни при чём** (*often with* **тут**), **1,** innocent. **2,** having nothing to do with it; irrelevant. **3,** *in* оста́ться ни при чём, to be left with nothing. —**при чём тут** (+ *nom.*)?, what has this to do with...? —**при э́том,** here; in the process; in so doing.

при- *prefix* **1,** *indicating arrival:* приходи́ть, to come; прилета́ть, to arrive (*by plane*). **2,** *indicating attachment:* привя́зывать, to tie to; пришива́ть, to sew on. **3,** *indicating addition:* прибавля́ть, to add; прикупа́ть, to buy some more. **4,** *indicating partial or slight action:* приотворя́ть, to open slightly; приспуска́ть, to lower slightly.

приба́вить [*infl.* -влю, -вишь] *v., pfv. of* **прибавля́ть.** —**приба́виться,** *refl., pfv. of* **прибавля́ться.**

приба́вка [*gen. pl.* -вок] *n.* **1,** adding; addition. **2,** something added; addition. **3,** increase; raise (*in pay*).

прибавле́ние *n.* **1,** adding; addition. **2,** something added; addition. Прибавле́ние семе́йства, addition to the family. **3,** increase (*in weight*); rise (*of water*).

прибавля́ть *v.impfv.* [*pfv.* **приба́вить**] **1,** to add: прибавля́ть соль (*or* со́ли) к су́пу, to add salt to the soup; прибавля́ть не́сколько слов, to add a few words. **2,** (*with acc. or gen.*) to increase. **3,** *in* прибавля́ть в ве́се, to put on weight. **4,** *in* прибавля́ть ша́гу, to quicken one's pace. —**прибавля́ться,** *refl.* **1,** to be added. **2,** to become larger. **3,** to increase; rise.

приба́вочный *adj.* **1,** additional. **2,** *econ.* surplus: приба́вочная сто́имость, surplus value.

прибалти́йский *adj.* Baltic.

прибау́тка [*gen. pl.* -ток] *n.* humorous saying.

прибега́ть *v.impfv.* **1,** [*pfv.* **прибежа́ть**] to come running. **2,** [*pfv.* **прибе́гнуть**] (*with* к) to resort to.

прибе́гнуть [*past* прибе́г *or* прибе́гнул, прибе́гла] *v., pfv. of* **прибега́ть** (*in sense #2*).

прибедня́ться *v.r.impfv.* [*pfv.* **прибедни́ться**] *colloq.* **1,** to pretend to be poorer than one is. **2,** to play down one's achievements; be excessively modest.

прибежа́ть [*infl. like* **бежа́ть**] *v., pfv. of* **прибега́ть** (*in sense #1*).

прибе́жище *n.* refuge.

приберега́ть *v.impfv.* [*pfv.* **прибере́чь**] to put aside; hold aside.

прибере́чь [*infl. like* **бере́чь**] *v., pfv. of* **приберега́ть.**

прибива́ть *v.impfv.* [*pfv.* **приби́ть**] **1,** to nail; nail down. **2,** (*of wind, rain, etc.*) to beat down; flatten. —**приби́ть к бе́регу,** *usu. impers.* to wash ashore: Ло́дку приби́ло к бе́регу, the boat was washed ashore.

прибира́ть *v.impfv.* [*pfv.* **прибра́ть**] *colloq.* **1,** to put in order; tidy up. **2,** to put away. —**прибра́ть к рука́м, 1,** to take (someone) in hand. **2,** to take over.

приби́ть [*infl.* -бью, -бьёшь] *v., pfv. of* **прибива́ть.**

приближа́ть *v.impfv.* [*pfv.* **прибли́зить**] **1,** (*with* к) to bring (*or* place) near *or* nearer (to). **2,** *fig.* (*with* к) to bring closer (to); bring in closer harmony (with). **3,** to hasten; bring on sooner. —**приближа́ться,** *refl.* **1,** to draw near. **2,** (*with* к) to approach; near. **3,** (*with* к) to approximate.

приближе́ние *n.* **1,** bringing near. **2,** approach.

приближённый *adj.* **1,** (*of people*) close; trusted. **2,** *math.* approximate; rough. —*n.* **1,** close associate (*of a ruler or high-ranking person*). **2,** retainer.

приблизи́тельно *adv.* approximately; roughly. —**приблизи́тельный,** *adj.* approximate.

прибли́зить [*infl.* -жу, -зишь] *v., pfv. of* **приближа́ть.** —**прибли́зиться,** *refl., pfv. of* **приближа́ться.**

прибо́й *n.* surf; breakers.

прибо́р *n.* **1,** instrument; device; apparatus; appliance. **2,** set: бри́твенный прибо́р, shaving set. Черни́льный прибо́р, inkstand. **3,** (place) setting. Накры́ть стол на шесть прибо́ров, to set the table for six.

прибо́рный *adj., in* прибо́рная доска́, instrument panel; dashboard.

прибра́ть [*infl. like* **брать**] *v., pfv. of* **прибира́ть.**

прибре́жный *adj.* **1,** offshore. **2,** coastal.

прибыва́ть *v.impfv.* [*pfv.* **прибы́ть**] **1,** to arrive. **2,** to increase in size or number; grow larger: Толпа́ всё прибыва́ла, the crowd kept getting larger and larger. **3,** (*of water*) to rise; (*of the moon*) to wax.

при́быль *n.f.* **1,** profit. **2,** *colloq.* benefit; gain. **3,** increase; rise. —**пойти́ на при́быль,** (*of water*) to rise.

при́быльный *adj.* profitable; lucrative. —**при́быльность,** *n.f.* profitability.

прибы́тие *n.* arrival.

прибы́ть [*infl.* -бу́ду, -бу́дешь; *past* при́был, прибыла́, при́было, при́были] *v., pfv. of* **прибыва́ть.**

прива́л *n.* **1,** halt; rest. **2,** resting place.

прива́ливать *v.impfv.* [*pfv.* **привали́ть**] **1,** (*with* к) to lean (a heavy object) against. **2,** *colloq.* to arrive in great numbers. **3,** (*with dat.*) *colloq.* (*of luck*) to strike; descend on. —**прива́ливаться,** *refl.* (*with* к) *colloq.* to lean against.

привали́ть [*infl.* -валю́, -ва́лишь] *v., pfv. of* **прива́ливать.** —**привали́ться,** *refl., pfv. of* **прива́ливаться.**

приватиза́ция *n.* privatization.

приватизи́ровать *v.impfv. & pfv.* [*pres.* -рую, -руешь] to privatize.

прива́тный *adj., obs.* private.

приведе́ние *n.* **1,** bringing. **2,** citing; adducing. **3,** putting (in order, motion, etc.).

привезти́ [*infl. like* **везти́**] *v., pfv. of* **привози́ть.**

привере́дливый *adj., colloq.* choosy; finicky; fussy.

приве́рженец [*gen.* -нца] *n.* adherent; supporter.

приве́рженность *n.f.* **1,** adherence. **2,** devotion. —**приве́рженный,** *adj.* (*with dat. or* к) devoted (to); dedicated (to).

привёртывать *v.impfv.* [*pfv.* **приверну́ть**] **1,** to tighten (a screw). **2,** (*with* к) to screw (onto). **3,** to turn down (a flame, lamp, etc.).

приве́сить [*infl.* -шу, -сишь] *v., pfv. of* **приве́шивать.**

привести́ [*infl. like* **вести́**] *v., pfv. of* **приводи́ть.** —**привести́сь,** *refl., pfv. of* **приводи́ться.**

приве́т *n.* regards; greetings. —*interj., colloq.* hello there!; hi!

приве́тливый *adj.* friendly; amiable; affable. —**приве́тливость,** *n.f.* friendliness; amiability; affability.

приве́тственный *adj.* of welcome; welcoming.

приве́тствие *n.* greeting.

приве́тствовать *v.impfv.* [*pres.* **-ствую, -ствуешь**] **1,** to greet; welcome. **2,** to welcome; hail (a proposal, decision, etc.).

приве́шивать *v.impfv.* [*pfv.* **приве́сить**] to hang up.

привива́ть *v.impfv.* [*pfv.* **приви́ть**] **1,** to graft. **2,** (*with dat.*) to inoculate: **приви́ть кому́-нибудь холе́ру,** to inoculate someone for cholera. **Приви́ть кому́-нибудь о́спу,** to vaccinate (someone). **3,** *fig.* to instill (in): **привива́ть кому́-нибудь хоро́шие мане́ры,** to instill good manners in someone. —**привива́ться,** *refl.* **1,** (*of a vaccine*) to take. **2,** *fig.* to take root; take hold. **3,** *fig.* (*of a name, word, style, etc.*) to catch on.

приви́вка *n.* **1,** inoculation: **сде́лать приви́вку** (+ *dat.*), to inoculate. **2,** grafting. —**приви́вка о́спы,** (smallpox) vaccination.

привиде́ние *n.* ghost; apparition.

приви́деться *v.r.pfv.* (*with dat.*) *colloq.* to appear in one's dreams.

привилегиро́ванный *adj.* privileged.

привиле́гия *n.* privilege.

приви́нчивать *v.impfv.* [*pfv.* **привинти́ть**] **1,** to screw on. **2,** (*with* **к**) to screw into.

привира́ть *v.impfv.* [*pfv.* **привра́ть**] *colloq.* **1,** *v.i.* to lie. **2,** *v.t.* to make up; add (fictional details).

приви́ть [*infl. like* **вить**] *v., pfv. of* **привива́ть.** —**приви́ться,** *refl.* [*past* **-ви́лся, -вила́сь, -вило́сь, -вили́сь**] *pfv. of* **привива́ться.**

при́вкус *n.* **1,** aftertaste. **2,** taste; flavor. **3,** *fig.* touch; trace; tinge.

привлека́тельный *adj.* attractive. —**привлека́тельность,** *n.f.* attractiveness.

привлека́ть *v.impfv.* [*pfv.* **привле́чь**] **1,** to attract. **2,** to bring in; call in. **3,** to win over: **привлека́ть на свою́ сто́рону,** to win over to one's side. —**привлека́ть к отве́ту** *or* **к отве́тственности,** to bring to account; bring to justice. —**привлека́ть к суду́, 1,** to take to court; institute legal proceedings against. **2,** to arraign.

привлече́ние *n.* **1,** attracting. **2,** bringing in; calling in. —**привлече́ние к отве́тственности,** bringing to account. —**привлече́ние к суду́,** arraignment.

привле́чь [*infl. like* **влечь**] *v., pfv. of* **привлека́ть.**

привнести́ [*infl. like* **нести́**] *v., pfv. of* **привноси́ть.**

привноси́ть *v.impfv.* [*pfv.* **привнести́;** *pres.* **-вношу́, -вно́сишь**] (*with* **в** + *acc.*) to introduce (into).

приво́д *n.* **1,** (forcible) arrest. **2,** *mech.* drive.

приводи́ть *v.impfv.* [*pfv.* **привести́;** *pres.* **-вожу́, -во́дишь**] **1,** to bring (*on foot*). **2,** (*with* **к**) (*of a road, tracks, etc.*) to lead (somewhere). **3,** (*with* **к**) to lead (to a certain result). **4,** (*with* **в** + *acc.*) to bring to a certain state or condition: **приводи́ть в поря́док,** to put in order; **приводи́ть в смяте́ние,** to throw into confusion; **приводи́ть в отча́яние,** to drive to despair. **5,** to cite; adduce. **Я вам приведу́ приме́р,** I'll give you an example. —**приводи́ть в движе́ние,** to set in motion. —**приводи́ть в де́йствие,** to start (*e.g.* a machine) going. —**приводи́ть в исполне́ние,** to carry out. —**приводи́ть в себя́** (*or* **в чу́вство**), **1,** to revive; re-

suscitate; bring around. **2,** to bring back to reality (a person lost in thought). —**приводи́ть к о́бщему знамена́телю,** to reduce to a common denominator.

приводи́ться *v.r.impfv.* [*pfv.* **привести́сь;** *pres.* **-во́дится**] *impers.* (*with dat. & inf.*) *colloq.* to happen to; have occasion to: **Мне не привело́сь быть там,** I have not had occasion to be there.

приводне́ние *n.* landing on water; splashdown.

приводни́ться *v.r., pfv. of* **приводня́ться.**

приводно́й *adj., mech.* drive (*attrib*); transmission (*attrib.*): **приводно́й вал,** drive shaft; **приводно́й реме́нь,** transmission belt.

приводня́ться *v.r.impfv.* [*pfv.* **приводни́ться**] to land on water.

приво́з *n.* **1,** bringing in; delivery. **2,** *colloq.* a shipment.

привози́ть *v.impfv.* [*pfv.* **привезти́;** *pres.* **-вожу́, -во́зишь**] to bring (*by vehicle*).

привозно́й *adj.* imported. *Also,* **приво́зный.**

привола́кивать *v.impfv.* [*pfv.* **приволо́чь**] to bring; drag.

приволо́чь [*infl. like* **воло́чь**] *v., pfv. of* **привола́кивать.**

приво́лье *n.* **1,** wide open spaces. **2,** freedom to move about.

приво́льный *adj.* **1,** open; spacious. **2,** free.

привора́живать *v.impfv.* [*pfv.* **приворожи́ть**] to bewitch; charm.

привра́тник *n.* gatekeeper; doorkeeper.

привра́ть [*infl. like* **врать**] *v., pfv. of* **привира́ть.**

привска́кивать *v.impfv.* [*pfv.* **привскочи́ть**] to jump up.

привскочи́ть [*infl.* **-вско́чу, -вско́чишь**] *v., pfv. of* **привска́кивать.**

привстава́ть *v.impfv.* [*pfv.* **привста́ть;** *pres.* **-встаю́, -встаёшь**] to rise (*halfway*).

привста́ть [*infl.* **-вста́ну, -вста́нешь**] *v., pfv. of* **привстава́ть.**

привходя́щий *adj.* **1,** extraneous. **2,** (*of circumstances*) attendant.

привыка́ть *v.impfv.* [*pfv.* **привы́кнуть**] (*with* **к** *or inf.*) **1,** to be *or* get used to; grow accustomed to. **2,** to be *or* get into the habit of.

привы́кнуть [*past* **привы́к, привы́кла**] *v., pfv. of* **привыка́ть.**

привы́чка [*gen. pl.* **-чек**] *n.* habit. **Э́то вошло́ у меня́ в привы́чку,** it has become a habit with me. **Не в мои́х привы́чках по́здно ложи́ться,** I am not in the habit of going to bed late.

привы́чный *adj.* **1,** habitual; usual; customary. **2,** (*with* **к**) used to; accustomed (to). **3,** (*of a person*) of set habits. **4,** (*of an eye, hand, etc.*) practiced.

привя́занность *n.f.* (*with* **к**) (emotional) attachment (to). —**привя́занный,** *adj.* (*with* **к**) attached (to).

привяза́ть [*infl.* **-вяжу́, -вя́жешь**] *v., pfv. of* **привя́зывать.** —**привяза́ться,** *refl., pfv. of* **привя́зываться.**

привязно́й *adj.* fastened; secured. —**привязно́й реме́нь,** seat belt.

привя́зчивый *adj., colloq.* **1,** easily forming attachments. **2,** annoying; bothersome.

привя́зывать *v.impfv.* [*pfv.* **привяза́ть**] **1,** (*with* **к**) to tie (to); bind (to); attach (to). **2,** (*with* **к себе́**) to win over. —**привя́зываться,** *refl.* (*with* **к**) **1,** to become attached (to). **2,** to attach oneself (to). **3,** *colloq.* to pester.

при́вязь *n.f.* **1,** leash. **2,** tether.

пригвожда́ть *v.impfv.* [*pfv.* **пригвозди́ть**] (*with* **к**) **1,** to nail (to). **2,** *fig.* to nail (to); rivet (to); chain (to): пригвождённый к ме́сту, riveted to the spot.

пригиба́ть *v.impfv.* [*pfv.* **пригну́ть**] to bend; bend down (a tree, branch, etc.). —**пригиба́ться,** *refl.* to bend down.

пригла́живать *v.impfv.* [*pfv.* **пригла́дить**] **1,** to smooth. **2,** to slick down (one's hair).

пригласи́тельный *adj.* conveying an invitation. —**пригласи́тельный биле́т,** ticket of admission (*to invited guests only*).

пригласи́ть [*infl.* **-шу́, -си́шь**] *v., pfv. of* **приглаша́ть.**

приглаша́ть *v.impfv.* [*pfv.* **пригласи́ть**] to invite.

приглаше́ние *n.* invitation.

приглашённый *adj.* invited. —*n.* person invited; invited guest. —**приглашённый дирижёр,** guest conductor.

приглуша́ть *v.impfv.* [*pfv.* **приглуши́ть**] **1,** to muffle; deaden; absorb (sound). **2,** *fig.* to relieve (pain, boredom, etc.).

приглушённый *adj.* **1,** hushed; subdued. **2,** (*of light*) subdued.

пригляде́ть [*infl.* **-жу́, -ди́шь**] *v., pfv. of* **пригля́дывать.** —**пригляде́ться,** *refl., pfv. of* **пригля́дываться.**

пригля́дывать *v.impfv.* [*pfv.* **пригляде́ть**] *colloq.* **1,** (*with* **за** + *instr.*) to look after; keep an eye on. **2,** to spot; find. —**пригля́дываться,** *refl.* **1,** (*with* **к**) to stare (at); scrutinize. **2,** (*with* **к**) to get used to. **3,** (*with dat.*) *colloq.* to pall (on); become boring (to).

пригляну́ться *v.r.pfv.* [*infl.* **-гляну́сь, -гля́нешься**] (*with dat.*) *colloq.* to catch the fancy of.

пригна́ть [*infl.* **-гоню́, -го́нишь**; *past fem.* **пригнала́**] *v., pfv. of* **пригоня́ть.**

пригну́ть *v., pfv. of* **пригиба́ть.** —**пригну́ться,** *refl., pfv. of* **пригиба́ться.**

пригова́ривать *v.impfv.* [*pfv.* **приговори́ть**] **1,** (*with* **к**) to sentence (to); condemn (to). **2,** [*impfv. only*] *colloq.* to say; repeat (*while doing something*).

пригово́р *n.* **1,** verdict. **2,** sentence.

приговори́ть *v., pfv. of* **пригова́ривать.**

пригоди́ться *v.r.pfv.* [*infl.* **-жу́сь, -ди́шься**] (*with dat.*) to come in handy; be useful (to); stand in good stead.

приго́дный *adj.* (*with* **к** *or* **для**) fit (for); suitable (for). —**приго́дность,** *n.f.* fitness; suitability.

приго́жий *adj.* **1,** *obs.* pretty; comely. **2,** *colloq.* (*of the weather*) nice; bright; clear.

пригоня́ть *v.impfv.* [*pfv.* **пригна́ть**] **1,** to drive home; bring in (cattle). **2,** to fit; adjust.

пригора́ть *v.impfv.* [*pfv.* **пригоре́ть**] to be slightly burnt.

пригоре́лый *adj.* slightly burnt.

пригоре́ть *v., pfv. of* **пригора́ть.**

при́город *n.* suburb. —**при́городный,** *adj.* suburban.

приго́рок [*gen.* **-рка**] *n.* hillock; knoll.

при́горшня *also,* **приго́ршня** [*gen. pl.* **-шней** *or* **-шен**] *n.* **1,** hollow of the hand. **2,** handful.

приготя́вливать *v.impfv.* = **приготовля́ть.** —**приготя́вливаться,** *refl.* = **приготовля́ться.**

приготови́тельный *adj.* preparatory.

пригото́вить [*infl.* **-влю, -вишь**] *v., pfv. of* **гото́вить** *and* **приготовля́ть.** —**пригото́виться,** *refl., pfv. of* **гото́виться** *and* **приготовля́ться.**

приготовле́ние *n.* **1,** preparation. **2,** *pl.* preparations.

приготовля́ть *v.impfv.* [*pfv.* **пригото́вить**] **1,** to prepare. **2,** to cook. —**приготовля́ться,** *refl.* (*with* **к**) to prepare (for); get ready (for).

пригрева́ть *v.impfv.* [*pfv.* **пригре́ть**] **1,** to warm. **2,** *fig., colloq.* to give shelter to.

пригре́зиться *v.r., pfv. of* **гре́зиться.**

пригре́ть *v., pfv. of* **пригрева́ть.**

пригрози́ть *v.pfv.* [*infl.* **-жу́, -зи́шь**] (*with dat.*) to threaten.

пригу́бить *v.pfv.* [*infl.* **-блю, -бишь**] to take a sip of; taste.

придава́ть *v.impfv.* [*pfv.* **прида́ть**; *pres.* **-даю́, -даёшь**] **1,** to give; impart. **2,** to attach (significance, importance, etc.). **3,** *mil.* to assign; attach (to a certain unit).

придави́ть [*infl.* **-давлю́, -да́вишь**] *v., pfv. of* **прида́вливать.**

прида́вливать *v.impfv.* [*pfv.* **придави́ть**] **1,** to press down upon; weigh down. **2,** (*with* **к**) to press (something) against (something).

прида́ние *n.* **1,** giving; imparting. **2,** *mil.* assigning; attaching.

прида́ное *n., decl. as an adj.* **1,** dowry. **2,** trousseau. **3,** layette.

прида́ток [*gen.* **-тка**] *n.* appendage; adjunct.

прида́точный *adj., in* **прида́точное предложе́ние,** dependent clause; subordinate clause.

прида́ть [*infl. like* **дать**; *past* **при́дал** *or* **прида́л, придала́, при́дало** *or* **прида́ло, при́дали** *or* **прида́ли**] *v., pfv. of* **придава́ть.**

прида́ча *n.* **1,** giving; imparting. **2,** *mil.* assigning; attaching. **3,** addition. —**в прида́чу,** besides; in addition; to boot; into the bargain.

придвига́ть *v.impfv.* [*pfv.* **придви́нуть**] (*with* **к**) to move (something) toward; move (something) closer to. —**придвига́ться,** *refl.* (*with* **к**) to move closer (to).

придво́рный *adj.* court (*attrib.*). —*n.* courtier.

приде́лывать *v.impfv.* [*pfv.* **приде́лать**] (*with* **к**) to attach (to); fasten (to).

придержа́ть [*infl.* **-держу́, -де́ржишь**] *v., pfv. of* **приде́рживать.**

приде́рживать *v.impfv.* [*pfv.* **придержа́ть**] **1,** to hold; hold still; hold in place. **2,** *colloq.* to hold back; withhold. **3,** *in* **придержа́ть язы́к,** to hold one's tongue. —**приде́рживаться,** *refl.* [*impfv. only*] **1,** (*with* **за** + *acc.*) to hold on to. **2,** (*with gen.*) to keep to; stick to: приде́рживаться пра́вой стороны́, to keep/stick to the right. **3,** *fig.* (*with gen.*) to stick to; adhere to (a subject, opinion, etc.); abide by (an agreement).

приди́ра *n.m. & f., colloq.* faultfinder; quibbler.

придира́ться *v.r.impfv.* [*pfv.* **придра́ться**] (*with* **к**) to find fault (with); carp (at); pick on.

приди́рка [*gen. pl.* **-рок**] *n.* cavil; quibble.

приди́рчивый *adj.* captious; carping; hypercritical.

придоро́жный *adj.* roadside; wayside.

придра́ться [*infl. like* дра́ться] *v.r., pfv. of* придира́ться.

приду́мывать *v.impfv.* [*pfv.* приду́мать] to think of; think up; devise.

придуркова́тый *adj., colloq.* dumb; stupid.

при́дурь *n.f., colloq., in* с при́дурью, slightly touched in the head.

придуши́ть *v.pfv.* [*infl.* -ду́шу, -ду́шишь] *colloq.* to strangle; choke.

придыха́ние *n., phonet.* aspiration. —придыха́тельный, *adj.* aspirate.

приеда́ться *v.r.impfv.* [*pfv.* прие́сться] (*with dat.*) *colloq.* to pall (on); become boring (to).

прие́зд *n.* arrival. —с прие́здом!, welcome!

приезжа́ть *v.impfv.* [*pfv.* прие́хать] to come (*by vehicle*); arrive.

прие́зжий *adj.* 1, newly arrived. 2, visiting; touring. —*n.* newcomer; visitor.

прие́м *n.* 1, receiving. 2, admission. 3, reception; welcome. 4, reception (*social gathering*). 5, dose. 6, method; technique. 7, trick; ploy. 8, *radio; television* reception. —в оди́н прие́м, 1, in one gulp. 2, in one sitting.

прие́млемый *adj.* acceptable.

прие́мная *n., decl. as an adj.* waiting room.

прие́мник *n.* (radio) receiver.

прие́мный *adj.* 1, receiving (*attrib.*); reception (*attrib.*). Прие́мные часы́, office hours. 2, admission (*attrib.*). Прие́мная коми́ссия, selection committee. 3, (*of a parent*) foster; adoptive; (*of a child*) adopted.

прие́мыш *n., colloq.* adopted child.

прие́сться [*infl. like* есть] *v.r., pfv. of* приеда́ться.

прие́хать [*infl.* -е́ду, -е́дешь] *v., pfv. of* приезжа́ть.

прижа́ть [*infl.* -жму́, -жмёшь] *v., pfv. of* прижима́ть. —прижа́ться, *refl., pfv. of* прижима́ться.

приже́чь [*infl. like* жечь] *v., pfv. of* прижига́ть.

прижива́льщик *n.m.* [*fem.* -ва́лка] sponger; hanger-on.

прижива́ться *v.r.impfv.* [*pfv.* прижи́ться] to become acclimated.

прижига́ние *n.* cauterization.

прижига́ть *v.impfv.* [*pfv.* приже́чь] to cauterize.

прижи́зненный *adj.* occurring in one's lifetime; occurring before one's death.

прижима́ть *v.impfv.* [*pfv.* прижа́ть] 1, (*with* к) to press (to *or* against). 2, (*with* к) to pin (to): прижима́ть к земле́, to pin to the ground; pin down. Прижима́ть к стене́, to pin (*or* drive) against the wall; *fig.* drive into a corner. 3, *fig., colloq.* to put pressure on. —прижима́ться, *refl.* (*with* к) to snuggle up to; cuddle up to; nestle close to.

прижи́мистый *adj., colloq.* tight-fisted.

прижи́ться [*infl. like* жить; *past* прижи́лся, прижила́сь, прижило́сь *or* прижи́лось, прижили́сь *or* прижи́лись] *v.r., pfv. of* прижива́ться.

приз [*pl.* призы́] *n.* prize.

призаду́мываться *v.r.impfv.* [*pfv.* призаду́маться] to become thoughtful; become pensive.

признима́ть *v.impfv.* [*pfv.* призаня́ть] *colloq.* to borrow.

призаня́ть [*infl. like* заня́ть] *v., pfv. of* признима́ть.

призва́ние *n.* vocation; calling.

призва́ть [*infl. like* звать] *v., pfv. of* призыва́ть.

призе́мистый *adj.* stocky; thickset; heavyset; squat.

приземле́ние *n.* landing.

приземлённый *adj.* practical; utilitarian.

приземля́ть *v.impfv.* [*pfv.* приземли́ть] to land (a plane). —приземля́ться, *refl.* to land; touch down.

призёр *n.* prizewinner.

при́зма *n.* prism. —призмати́ческий, *adj.* prismatic.

признава́ть *v.impfv.* [*pfv.* призна́ть; *pres.* -зна́ю, -знаёшь] 1, to recognize: призна́ть прави́тельство, to recognize a government. Призна́ть за рабо́чими пра́во забасто́вки, to recognize the workers' right to strike. 2, to admit; acknowledge. Призна́ть себя́ побеждённым, to admit defeat. Я признаю́, что..., I admit that..., Призна́ть себя́ вино́вным, to plead guilty. 3, to declare; pronounce; find: Его́ призна́ли вино́вным/душевнобольны́м, he was found guilty; he was declared insane. 4, *colloq.* to recognize (someone): Я вас сра́зу не призна́л, I didn't recognize you at first. Призна́ть в ко́м-нибудь ста́рую знако́мую, to recognize someone as an old acquaintance.

признава́ться *v.r.impfv.* [*pfv.* призна́ться; *pres.* -зна́юсь, -знаёшься] 1, (*with* в + *prepl.*) to confess (to): призна́ться в преступле́нии, to confess to a crime. Призна́ться во всём, to come clean. 2, (*with* в + *prepl.*) to admit: призна́ться в свои́х оши́бках, to admit one's mistakes. 3, to confess (that). Признаю́сь, о нём не слы́шал, I confess (*or* I must admit) I never heard of him. 4, *in* призна́ться в любви́, to make a declaration of love. *See also* призна́ться.

при́знак *n.* sign; indication; symptom.

призна́ние *n.* 1, confession; admission; acknowledgment. 2, recognition: получи́ть призна́ние, to receive recognition. Призна́ние прав меньши́нств, recognition of the rights of minorities. 3, *in* призна́ние в любви́, declaration of love.

при́знанный *adj.* recognized; acknowledged.

призна́тельный *adj.* [*short form* -лен, -льна] grateful; appreciative. —призна́тельность, *n.f.* gratitude; appreciation.

призна́ть [*infl.* -зна́ю, -зна́ешь] *v., pfv. of* признава́ть. —призна́ться, *refl.* 1, *pfv. of* признава́ться. 2, I must confess. 3, admittedly.

призово́й *adj.* prize (*attrib.*).

при́зрак *n.* specter; ghost; apparition.

при́зрачный *adj.* 1, ghostly; eerie. 2, unreal; illusory.

призы́в *n.* 1, appeal; call. 2, slogan. 3, *mil.* call-up.

призыва́ть *v.impfv.* [*pfv.* призва́ть] 1, (*with inf.*) to call upon (to); urge (to). 2, (*with* на + *acc. or* к) to call (for); appeal (for). 3, *mil.* to call up; draft. 4, *past passive part. only,* A, to destine: Он при́зван быть врачо́м, he is destined to be a doctor. B, to intend: Рабо́та при́звана воспи́тывать люде́й, the work is intended to educate people. —призыва́ть к отве́ту, to call to account. —призыва́ть к поря́дку, to call to order.

призывни́к [*gen.* -ника́] *n.* draftee; inductee; conscript.

призывно́й *adj.* of or pert. to the military draft: призывно́й во́зраст, draft age; призывно́й пункт, draft board; induction center; призывна́я коми́ссия, selective service commission.

при́иск *n., often pl.* mine: алма́зные при́иски, diamond mines.

прииска́ть [*infl.* -ищу́, -и́щешь] *v., pfv. of* **прии́скивать**.

прии́скивать *v.impfv.* [*pfv.* **прииска́ть**] *colloq.* **1**, to find. **2**, [*impfv. only*] to look for; search for.

прийти́ [*infl.* приду́, придёшь; *past* пришёл, пришла́, пришло́, пришли́] *v., pfv. of* **приходи́ть**. —**прийти́сь**, *refl., pfv. of* **приходи́ться**.

прика́з *n.* order; command. —**по прика́зу** (+ *gen.*), by order of.

приказа́ние *n.* order; command.

приказа́ть [*infl.* -кажу́, -ка́жешь] *v., pfv. of* **прика́зывать**.

прика́зчик *n., obs.* **1**, salesman; clerk. **2**, steward (*on a large estate*).

прика́зывать *v.impfv.* [*pfv.* **приказа́ть**] (*with dat.*) to order; command. —**прика́жете**, *colloq.* (*in questions*) may I ask; pray tell me: Что прика́жете де́лать с таки́м..., what (may I ask) can you do with such a...? —**приказа́ть до́лго жить**, *colloq.* to die; depart this world.

прика́лывать *v.impfv.* [*pfv.* **приколо́ть**] **1**, (*with* к) to pin (to). **2**, *colloq.* to stab to death.

прика́нчивать *v.impfv.* [*pfv.* **прико́нчить**] *colloq.* **1**, to terminate; wind up. **2**, to finish off (a quantity of food or drink). **3**, to finish off; kill.

прикарма́нивать *v.impfv.* [*pfv.* **прикарма́нить**] *colloq.* to pocket.

прикаса́ться *v.r.impfv.* [*pfv.* **прикосну́ться**] (*with* к) to touch.

прикати́ть [*infl.* -качу́, -ка́тишь] *v., pfv. of* **прика́тывать**. —**прикати́ться**, *refl., pfv. of* **прика́тываться**.

прика́тывать *v.impfv.* [*pfv.* **прикати́ть**] **1**, *v.t.* to roll (something somewhere). **2**, *v.i., colloq.* to come rolling up; arrive. —**прика́тываться**, *refl.* (*with* к) to roll up to.

прики́дка [*gen. pl.* -док] *n., colloq.* estimate.

прики́дывать *v.impfv.* [*pfv.* **прики́нуть**] *colloq.* **1**, to add; throw in; toss in. **2**, to estimate; reckon. **3**, to try on. —**прики́дываться**, *refl.* (*with instr.*) *colloq.* to pretend (to be).

прикла́д *n.* **1**, rifle butt. **2**, *sewing* findings.

прикладно́й *adj.* applied: прикладны́е нау́ки, applied sciences.

прикла́дывать *v.impfv.* [*pfv.* **приложи́ть**] (*with* к) **1**, to put (against); place (against). **2**, to apply (to); affix (to). —**приложи́ть ру́ку, к**, **1**, to have a hand in. **2**, to put one's hand to. —**ума́ не приложу́**, I have no idea; I can't imagine; I am at a loss.

прикла́дываться *v.r.impfv.* [*pfv.* **приложи́ться**] **1**, (*with instr. and* к) to put (one's eye, ear, etc.) to. **2**, (*with* к) to kiss reverently. **3**, to take aim. —**остально́е приложится**, the rest will fall into place.

прикле́ивать *v.impfv.* [*pfv.* **прикле́ить**] (*with* к) to glue (to); paste (to). —**прикле́иваться**, *refl.* (*with* к) to stick (to).

прикле́пывать *v.impfv.* [*pfv.* **приклепа́ть**] to rivet.

приклони́ть [*infl.* -клоню́, -кло́нишь] *v., pfv. of* **приклоня́ть**.

приклоня́ть *v.impfv.* [*pfv.* **приклони́ть**] (*with* к) to bend (toward); incline (toward). —**ему́ не́где го́лову приклони́ть**, he has nowhere to lay his head (*i.e. nowhere to live*).

приключа́ться *v.r.impfv.* [*pfv.* **приключи́ться**] *colloq.* to happen; occur.

приключе́ние *n.* **1**, adventure. **2**, incident. —**приключе́нческий**, *adj.* adventure (*attrib.*).

приключи́ться *v.r., pfv. of* **приключа́ться**.

прикова́ть [*infl.* -кую́, -куёшь] *v., pfv. of* **прико́вывать**.

прико́вывать *v.impfv.* [*pfv.* **прикова́ть**] **1**, (*with* к) to chain (to). **2**, *fig.* (*with* к) to tie down; nail; rivet (to a place): прикова́ть к ме́сту, to rivet to the spot; transfix. Прикова́ть к посте́ли, to confine to bed. Прико́ванный к посте́ли, bedridden. **3**, *fig.* to fix (one's gaze); rivet (one's attention).

прико́л *n., in* **на прико́ле**, **1**, tied up; moored. **2**, idle; laid up.

прикола́чивать *v.impfv.* [*pfv.* **приколоти́ть**] to nail down; fasten with nails.

приколоти́ть [*infl.* -лочу́, -ло́тишь] *v., pfv. of* **прикола́чивать**.

приколо́ть [*infl.* -колю́, -ко́лешь] *v., pfv. of* **прика́лывать**.

прикомандирова́ть *v.pfv.* [*infl.* -ру́ю, -ру́ешь] (*with* к) to assign (to).

прико́нчить *v., pfv. of* **прика́нчивать**.

прикорну́ть *v.pfv., colloq.* to curl up; settle down (*for a nap*).

прикоснове́ние *n.* touch.

прикосну́ться *v.r., pfv. of* **прикаса́ться**.

прикра́сить [*infl.* -шу, -сишь] *v., pfv. of* **прикра́шивать**.

прикра́сы *n.pl.* [*sing.* **прикра́са**] *colloq.* embellishments (*in telling or describing something*): без прикра́с, without embellishment.

прикра́шивать *v.impfv.* [*pfv.* **прикра́сить**] to embellish; embroider; exaggerate.

прикрепи́ть [*infl.* -плю́, -пи́шь] *v., pfv. of* **прикрепля́ть**. —**прикрепи́ться**, *refl., pfv. of* **прикрепля́ться**.

прикрепле́ние *n.* **1**, fastening; attaching. **2**, assigning. **3**, registration.

прикрепля́ть *v.impfv.* [*pfv.* **пркрепи́ть**] (*with* к) **1**, to fasten (to); attach (to). **2**, to assign (to); attach (to). **3**, to register (someone somewhere). —**прикрепля́ться**, *refl.* (*with* к) **1**, to fasten (onto). **2**, to register (at).

прикри́кивать *v.impfv.* [*pfv.* **прикри́кнуть**] (*with на* + *acc.*) to shout (at).

прикрыва́ть *v.impfv.* [*pfv.* **прикры́ть**] **1**, to close (*but not tightly*). **2**, to cover (*but not completely*). **3**, to cover up; conceal. **4**, to shield; protect. **5**, *mil.* to cover. **6**, *colloq.* to close down; shut down; liquidate. —**прикрыва́ться**, *refl.* **1**, (*with instr.*) to cover *or* shield oneself (with). **2**, (*of a door, window, etc.*) to close. **3**, *fig.* (*with instr.*) to cover up one's actions (by); take refuge (in). **4**, *colloq.* to shut down; go out of business.

прикры́тие *n.* **1**, concealment. **2**, protection. **3**, cover; shelter. **4**, *mil.* cover.

прикры́ть [*infl.* -кро́ю, -кро́ешь] *v., pfv. of* **прикрыва́ть.** —**прикры́ться,** *refl., pfv. of* **прикрыва́ться.**

прикупа́ть *v.impfv.* [*pfv.* **прикупи́ть**] to buy some more of.

прикупи́ть [*infl.* -куплю́, -ку́пишь] *v., pfv. of* **прикупа́ть.**

прику́ривать *v.impfv.* [*pfv.* **прикури́ть**] **1,** to light up; light a cigarette. **2,** to get a light from another cigarette.

прикури́ть [*infl.* -курю́, -ку́ришь] *v., pfv. of* **прику́ривать.**

прику́с *n., dent.* bite.

прикуси́ть [*infl.* -кушу́, -ку́сишь] *v., pfv. of* **прику́сывать.**

прику́сывать *v.impfv.* [*pfv.* **прикуси́ть**] to bite (one's tongue, lip, etc.). —**прикуси́ть язы́к,** to bite one's tongue (*i.e. say nothing*).

прила́вок [*gen.* -вка] *n.* counter; shelf. —**из-под прила́вка,** under the counter.

прилага́тельный *adj., in* **и́мя прилага́тельное,** adjective. —**прилага́тельное,** *n., decl. as an adj.* adjective.

прилага́ть *v.impfv.* [*pfv.* **приложи́ть**] **1,** (*with* к) to attach (to); append (to); enclose (in). **2,** to apply; exert. Прилага́ть все уси́лия, to make every effort.

прила́живать *v.impfv.* [*pfv.* **прила́дить**] to fit; adjust. —**прила́живаться,** *refl.* (*with* к) *colloq.* to adapt (to); adjust (to).

приласка́ть *v.pfv.* **1,** to caress; pet. **2,** to be nice to. —**приласка́ться,** *refl.* (*with* к) **1,** to snuggle up to. **2,** to make up to.

прилега́ть *v.impfv.* (*with* к) **1,** to adjoin; lie adjacent (to). **2,** (*of clothes*) to fit; fit snugly.

прилега́ющий *adj.* adjoining; adjacent; contiguous.

прилежа́ние *n.* diligence.

приле́жный *adj.* diligent. —**приле́жно,** *adv.* diligently. —**приле́жность,** *n.f.* diligence.

прилепи́ть [*infl.* -леплю́, -ле́пишь] *v., pfv. of* **прилепля́ть.** —**прилепи́ться,** *refl., pfv. of* **прилепля́ться.**

прилепля́ть *v.impfv.* [*pfv.* **прилепи́ть**] (*with* к) **1,** to stick (to); affix (to). **2,** to fasten (to); attach (to). **3,** *colloq.* to give; pin (a nickname). —**прилепля́ться,** *refl.* (*with* к) to stick (to).

прилёт *n.* arrival (*of air passengers or birds*).

прилета́ть *v.impfv.* [*pfv.* **прилете́ть**] **1,** to come flying in; arrive by plane. **2,** (*of a plane*) to arrive.

прилете́ть [*infl.* -чу́, -ти́шь] *v., pfv. of* **прилета́ть.**

приле́чь *v.pfv.* [*infl. like* лечь] to lie down for a while.

прили́в *n.* **1,** rising tide. **2,** rush (*of blood*). **3,** *fig.* influx. **4,** *fig.* wave; surge; burst. —**прили́в и отли́в,** ebb and flow of the tides. —**прили́вы и отли́вы,** tide; tides.

прилива́ть *v.impfv.* [*pfv.* **прили́ть**] **1,** to flow. **2,** (*of blood*) to rush.

прили́вный *adj.* tidal.

прили́занный *adj., colloq.* sleek.

прилипа́ние *n.* adhesion.

прилипа́ть *v.impfv.* [*pfv.* **прили́пнуть**] (*with* к) to stick (to); adhere (to).

прили́пнуть [*past* -ли́п, -ли́пла] *v., pfv. of* **прилипа́ть.**

прили́пчивый *adj.* **1,** sticky. **2,** *fig., colloq.* catching; contagious. **3,** *fig., colloq.* bothersome; pesky.

прили́ть [*infl. like* лить] *v., pfv. of* **прилива́ть.**

прили́чие *n.* **1,** propriety; decency; decorum. **2,** *pl.* the proprieties; niceties; civilities; amenities.

прили́чно *adv.* **1,** decently; properly. **2,** *colloq.* quite well.

прили́чный *adj.* **1,** decent; proper. **2,** (*of society, company, etc.*) polite. **3,** *colloq.* decent; respectable; pretty good.

приложе́ние *n.* **1,** application. **2,** enclosure. **3,** supplement; appendix. **4,** annex (*to a treaty*). **5,** *gram.* apposition.

приложи́мый *adj.* (*with* к) applicable (to).

приложи́ть [*infl.* -ложу́, -ло́жишь] *v., pfv. of* **прилага́ть** *and* **прикла́дывать.** —**приложи́ться,** *refl., pfv. of* **прикла́дываться.**

прилуне́ние *n.* moon landing.

прилуни́ться *v.r.pfv.* to land on the moon.

прильну́ть *v., pfv. of* льнуть.

примадо́нна *n.* prima donna.

прима́нивать *v.impfv.* [*pfv.* **примани́ть**] to entice; lure.

примани́ть [*infl.* -маню́, -ма́нишь] *v., pfv. of* **прима́нивать.**

прима́нка *n.* **1,** bait; lure. **2,** *fig.* lure; enticement; inducement.

прима́с *n., eccles.* primate.

прима́т *n.* **1,** primacy. **2,** *pl., zool.* primates.

примелька́ться *v.r.pfv.* (*with dat.*) to become (overly) familiar (to): Го́род мне примелька́лся, I have seen (more than) enough of the city.

примене́ние *n.* application; use; employment. —**в примене́нии к,** as applied to.

примени́мый *adj.* applicable. —**примени́мость,** *n.f.* applicability.

примени́тельно *adv.* (*with* к) as it applies to; with reference to.

примени́ть [*infl.* -меню́, -ме́нишь] *v., pfv. of* **применя́ть.** —**примени́ться,** *refl., pfv. of* **применя́ться.**

применя́ть *v.impfv.* [*pfv.* **примени́ть**] to apply; employ; use. Применя́ть на пра́ктике, to put into practice. —**применя́ться,** *refl.* **1,** to be used. **2,** (*with* к) to adjust (to).

приме́р *n.* example. —**для приме́ра,** as an example. —**к приме́ру,** for example. —**на приме́ре** (+ *gen.*), through the example of; by using ... as an example. —**не в приме́р, 1,** (*with dat.*) unlike; as distinct from. **2,** (*with comp. adjectives*) much more; far more. —**по приме́ру** (+ *gen.*), after (*or following*) the example of.

примерза́ть *v.impfv.* [*pfv.* **примёрзнуть**] (*with* к) to freeze (to).

примёрзнуть [*past* -мёрз, -мёрзла] *v., pfv. of* **примерза́ть.**

приме́рить *v., pfv. of* **примеря́ть.**

приме́рка *n.* **1,** trying on. **2,** fitting: сде́лать приме́рку, to have a fitting.

приме́рно *adv.* **1,** in exemplary fashion. **2,** so as to set an example for others. **3,** approximately. **4,** *obs.* for example.

приме́рный *adj.* **1,** exemplary; model. **2,** (*of punishment*) serving as an example to others. **3,** approximate.

примерочная *n., decl. as an adj.* dressing room (*for trying on clothes*).

примерять *v.impfv.* [*pfv.* **примерить**] to try on.

примесь *n.f.* **1,** admixture, **2,** *fig.* touch; dash; trace.

примета *n.* **1,** mark; sign. **2,** omen. —**брать на примету,** to take note of. —**иметь на примете,** to have an eye on.

приметать *v., pfv. of* **приметывать.**

приметить [*infl.* **-чу, -тишь**] *v, pfv. of* **примечать.**

приметливый *adj., colloq.* observant.

приметный *adj.* **1,** noticeable; perceptible. **2,** conspicuous.

примётывать *v.impfv.* [*pfv.* **приметать**] to stitch; baste.

примечание *n.* note; footnote; explanatory note.

примечательный *adj.* noteworthy; notable.

примечать *v.impfv.* [*pfv.* **приметить**] *colloq.* **1,** to notice. **2,** to note; take note of; make a mental note of.

примешивать *v.impfv.* [*pfv.* **примешать**] to add (something to something) by mixing.

приминать *v.impfv.* [*pfv.* **примять**] to crush; flatten; trample down.

примирение *n.* reconciliation.

примиритель *n.m.* conciliator. —**примирительный,** *adj.* conciliatory.

примирить *v., pfv. of* **мирить** *and* **примирять.** —**примириться,** *refl., pfv. of* **мириться** *and* **примиряться.**

примирять *v.impfv.* [*pfv.* **примирить**] to reconcile. —**примиряться,** *refl.* **1,** to become reconciled (*after a quarrel*). **2,** (*with* **с** + *instr.*) to become reconciled (to); reconcile oneself (to).

примитивный *adj.* primitive.

примкнуть *v., pfv. of* **примыкать.**

примолкнуть *v.pfv.* [*past* **-молк, -молкла**] *colloq.* to fall silent.

приморский *adj.* **1,** seaside (*attrib.*). **2,** maritime. —**приморский ветер,** sea breeze.

приморье *n.* area near the seashore.

примоститься *v.r.pfv.* [*infl.* **-щусь, -стишься**] *colloq.* to settle down; perch (*in an uncomfortable place*).

примочка [*gen. pl.* **-чек**] *n.* medicinal substance. Примочка для глаз, eyewash.

примула *n.* primrose.

примус *n.* small kerosene stove.

примчаться *v.r.pfv.* [*infl.* **-мчусь, -мчишься**] to arrive on the run; come tearing along.

примыкать *v.impfv.* [*pfv.* **примкнуть**] (*with* **к**) **1,** to join; side with. **2,** [*impfv. only*] to adjoin; abut. —**примыкать/примкнуть штыки,** to fix bayonets.

примять [*infl.* **-мну, -мнёшь**] *v., pfv. of* **приминать.**

принадлежать *v.impfv.* [*pres.* **-лежу, -лежишь**] **1,** (*with dat.*) to belong to. **2,** (*with* **к**) to belong to; be a member of. —**принадлежать к числу** (+ *gen.*), to be among; number among.

принадлежность *n.f.* **1,** *pl.* accessories; articles; gear. Постельные принадлежности, bedding. Рыболовные принадлежности, fishing tackle. **2,** (*with* **к**) belonging (to); affiliation (with). **3,** characteristic; attribute.

приналечь *v.pfv.* [*infl. like* **лечь**] (*with* **на** + *acc.*) *colloq.* **1,** to lean (on). **2,** *fig.* to apply oneself (to).

принаряжать *v.impfv.* [*pfv.* **принарядить**] *colloq.* to dress up; deck out. —**принаряжаться,** *refl., colloq.* to get dressed up.

приневоливать *v.impfv.* [*pfv.* **приневолить**] *obs.* to force; make; compel.

принесение *n.* **1,** bringing. **2,** *in* принесение присяги, taking of the oath. **3,** *in* принесение поздравлений, offering of congratulations.

принести [*infl. like* **нести**] *v., pfv. of* **приносить.**

принижать *v.impfv.* [*pfv.* **принизить**] **1,** to humiliate; humble. **2,** to disparage; belittle; play down.

принижение *n.* **1,** humiliation. **2,** disparagement.

приниженный *adj.* **1,** humble. **2,** humiliating.

принизить [*infl.* **-жу, -зишь**] *v., pfv. of* **принижать.**

приникать *v.impfv.* [*pfv.* **приникнуть**] (*with* **к**) to press against; nestle close to. Приникнуть губами к, to press one's lips against.

приникнуть [*past* **-ник, -никла**] *v., pfv. of* **приникать.**

принимать *v.impfv.* [*pfv.* **принять**] **1,** to accept. **2,** to receive (a person *or* persons). **3,** to admit; allow to join. **4,** to take (food, medicine, a bath, measures, an oath, etc.). **5,** to assume; take on. **6,** to take over. **7,** to adopt (a plan, resolution, amendment, etc.); pass (a law). **8,** to adopt (a religion, citizenship, etc.). **9,** (*with* **за** + *acc.*) to take for; mistake for. **10,** to receive; pick up (a signal). **11,** to deliver (a baby). —**принимать во внимание** *or* **в расчёт** *or* **к сведению,** to take account of; take into account; take into consideration. —**принимать (близко) к сердцу,** to take to heart. —**принимать на веру,** to take on faith. —**принимать на работу,** to hire; take on. —**принимать на свой счёт,** to take personally. —**принимать решение,** to make (*or less commonly,* take) a decision. —**принимать чью-нибудь сторону,** to take someone's side. —**принимать участие** (*with* **в** + *prepl.*), to take part (in); participate (in). —**принимать экзамен,** to give an examination.

приниматься *v.r.impfv.* [*pfv.* **приняться**] **1,** (*with inf. or* **за** + *acc.*) to begin; set about. **2,** (*of a plant*) to take root; (*of a vaccine*) to take.

приноравливать *v.impfv.* [*pfv.* **приноровить**] (*with* **к**) *colloq.* **1,** to adapt (to). **2,** to time to coincide with. —**приноравливаться,** *refl.* (*with* **к**) *colloq.* **1,** to adjust (to). **2,** to get the knack of.

приносить *v.impfv.* [*pfv.* **принести**; *pres.* **-ношу, -носишь**] **1,** to bring. **2,** to yield; bear. **3,** to offer; extend (one's apologies, thanks, etc.). —**приносить вред** (+ *dat.*), to cause harm *or* damage (to). —**приносить (что-нибудь) в жертву,** to sacrifice. —**приносить жертву,** to make a sacrifice. —**приносить пользу** (+ *dat.*), to be of benefit (to); do (someone) good. —**приносить присягу,** to take the oath.

приношение *n.* offering; gift.

принтер (тэ) *n.* printer (*for a computer*).

принудительный *adj.* **1,** (*of labor*) forced. **2,** (*of measures*) coercive. —**принудительно,** *adv.* forcibly.

принудить [*infl.* **-жу, -дишь**] *v., pfv. of* **принуждать.**

принуждать *v.impfv.* [*pfv.* **принудить**] to force; compel.

принуждение *n.* compulsion; coercion; duress: по принуждению, under duress.

принуждённость *n.f.* constraint; stiffness; lack of spontaneity.

принуждённый *adj.* forced; constrained; unnatural.

принц *n.* prince.

принце́сса *n.* princess.

при́нцип *n.* principle. —**в при́нципе,** in principle. —**из при́нципа,** on principle.

принципиа́льно *adv.* **1,** in principle. **2,** as a matter of principle. **3,** fundamentally.

принципиа́льность *n.f.* adherence to principle.

принципиа́льный *adj.* **1,** of principles: принципиа́льный челове́к, man of principle. **2,** fundamental: принципиа́льная ра́зница, fundamental difference.

приню́хиваться *v.r.impfv.* [*pfv.* **приню́хаться**] (*with* к) *colloq.* **1,** to sniff. **2,** to get used to the smell of.

приня́тие *n.* **1,** acceptance. **2,** receiving. **3,** admission; admittance. **4,** taking (*of food, medicine, measures, an oath, etc.*). **5,** assumption; taking on. **6,** making (*a decision*). **7,** adoption (*of a resolution, motion, etc.*).

при́нято *short form neuter of* **при́нятый** (*past passive part. of* **приня́ть**), it is customary; it is the thing to do. Э́то не при́нято, that is (just) not done. У нас не при́нято (+ *inf.*), it is not our custom (*or* practice) to... При́нято встава́ть, когда́ он вхо́дит, it is customary to rise when he enters.

приня́ть [*infl.* приму́, при́мешь; *past* при́нял, приняла́, при́няло, при́няли] *v., pfv. of* **принима́ть.** —**приня́ться,** *refl.* [*past* принялся́, -ла́сь, -ло́сь, -ли́сь] *pfv. of* **принима́ться.**

приободря́ть *v.impfv.* [*pfv.* **приободри́ть**] to cheer up; hearten. —**приободря́ться,** *refl.* to cheer up.

приобрести́ [*infl.* -брету́, -брете́шь; *past* -брёл, -брела́, -брело́, -брели́] *v., pfv. of* **приобрета́ть.**

приобрета́ть *v.impfv.* [*pfv.* **приобрести́**] **1,** to acquire; gain. **2,** to assume; take on (importance, significance, etc.).

приобрете́ние *n.* acquisition.

приобща́ть *v.impfv.* [*pfv.* **приобщи́ть**] **1,** (*with* к) to introduce (to); acquaint (with); initiate (into). **2,** (*with* к) to attach (to); append (to). **3,** to administer the sacrament to. —**приобща́ться,** *refl.* (*with* к) to join; enter into; become a part of.

приоде́ть *v.pfv.* [*infl.* -де́ну, -де́нешь] *colloq.* to dress (someone) up. —**приоде́ться,** *refl., colloq.* to get dressed up.

прио́р *n., eccles.* prior.

приорите́т *n.* **1,** being first: Ему́ принадлежи́т приорите́т откры́тия (+ *gen.*), to him belongs the distinction of having discovered... **2,** priority; precedence.

приоса́ниваться *v.r.impfv.* [*pfv.* **приоса́ниться**] *colloq.* to assume a dignified air.

приостана́вливать *v.impfv.* [*pfv.* **приостанови́ть**] to halt; interrupt; suspend. —**приостана́вливаться,** *refl.* to stop for a moment; pause.

приостанови́ть [*infl.* -новлю́, -но́вишь] *v., pfv. of* **приостана́вливать.** —**приостанови́ться,** *refl., pfv. of* **приостана́вливаться.**

приостано́вка *n.* halt; suspension.

приостановле́ние *n.* halt; suspension. —**приостановле́ние исполне́ния пригово́ра,** stay of execution.

приотвори́ть [*infl.* -ворю́, -во́ришь] *v., pfv. of* **приотворя́ть.** —**приотвори́ться,** *refl., pfv. of* **приотворя́ться.**

приотворя́ть *v.impfv.* [*pfv.* **приотвори́ть**] *v.t.* to open slightly. —**приотворя́ться,** *refl.* (*of a door*) to open slightly.

приоткрыва́ть *v.impfv.* [*pfv.* **приоткры́ть**] *v.t.* to open slightly. Оставля́ть дверь приоткры́той, to leave the door ajar. —**приоткрыва́ться,** *refl.* (*of a door*) to open slightly.

приоткры́ть [*infl.* -кро́ю, -кро́ешь] *v., pfv. of* **приоткрыва́ть.**

приохо́тить *v.pfv.* [*infl.* -хо́чу, -хо́тишь] (*with* к) *colloq.* to instill (in someone) an appreciation (of)/ a taste (for)/ an interest (in)/: приохо́тить кого́-нибудь к чте́нию, instill in someone a taste for reading. —**приохо́титься,** *refl.* (*with* к) *colloq.* to develop a taste (for); develop an interest (in).

припада́ть *v.impfv.* [*pfv.* **припа́сть**] **1,** (*with* к) to press (oneself) close to. Припада́ть у́хом к земле́, to press one's ear to the ground. **2,** (*with* на + *acc.*) to drop (to): припа́сть на одно́ коле́но, to drop to one knee. **3,** [*impfv. only*] *colloq.* to have a slight limp; (*with* на + *acc.*) limp slightly (on).

припа́док [*gen.* -дка] *n.* fit; attack; seizure. —**серде́чный припа́док,** heart attack.

припа́дочный *adj.* **1,** of an attack or fit. **2,** *colloq.* subject to attacks. —*n.* person subject to attacks.

припа́ивать *v.impfv.* [*pfv.* **припая́ть**] (*with* к) to solder (to).

припа́йка *n.* soldering.

припа́рка [*gen. pl.* -рок] *n., usu. pl.* poultice.

припаркова́ть [*infl.* -ку́ю, -ку́ешь] *v., pfv. of* **припарко́вывать.**

припарко́вывать *v.impfv.* [*pfv.* **припаркова́ть**] *colloq.* to park (a car).

припаса́ть *v.impfv.* [*pfv.* **припасти́**] *colloq.* to store (up); lay in a supply of.

припасти́ [*infl. like* **пасти́**] *v., pfv. of* **припаса́ть.**

припа́сть [*infl. like* **пасть**] *v., pfv. of* **припада́ть.**

припа́сы [*gen.* -сов] *n.pl.* supplies. —**боевы́е** *or* **огнестре́льные припа́сы,** ammunition. —**вое́нные припа́сы,** munitions. —**съестны́е припа́сы,** provisions; rations.

припая́ть *v., pfv. of* **припа́ивать.**

припе́в *n.* refrain.

припева́ть *v.impfv., colloq.* to sing (*while doing something*).

припева́ючи *adv., colloq., in* **жить припева́ючи,** to live in clover.

припёк *n.* intense heat from the sun: на припёке, in the hot sun; right in the sun.

припека́ть *v.impfv.* (*of the sun*) to be very hot; beat down.

припере́ть [*infl. like* **пере́ть**] *v., pfv. of* **припира́ть.**

припира́ть *v.impfv.* [*pfv.* **припере́ть**] **1,** (*with* к) place (something) firmly against (something). **2,** to secure: припира́ть дверь сту́лом, to secure a door by placing a chair against it. **3,** *colloq.* to set (a door or window) ajar. —**припере́ть к стене́,** to drive against the wall; drive into a corner.

приписа́ть [*infl.* **-пишу́, -пи́шешь**] *v., pfv. of* **припи́сывать**. —**приписа́ться**, *refl., pfv. of* **приписываться**.

припи́ска [*gen. pl.* **-сок**] *n.* **1**, postscript. **2**, codicil. **3**, registration. **4**, *pl.* inflated (*or* falsified) figures.

припи́сывать *v.impfv.* [*pfv.* **приписа́ть**] **1**, to add (*to something written*). **2**, (*with* **к**) to register (at). **3**, (*with dat.*) to ascribe (to); attribute (to). **4**, (*with* **себе́**) to take credit for. —**припи́сываться**, *refl.* **1**, (*with dat.*) to be attributed (to). **2**, to register.

припла́та *n.* extra charge; surcharge.

приплати́ть [*infl.* **-плачу́, -пла́тишь**] *v., pfv. of* **припла́чивать**.

припла́чивать *v.impfv.* [*pfv.* **приплати́ть**] to pay (a certain amount) extra.

припло́д *n.* litter; offspring.

приплыва́ть *v.impfv.* [*pfv.* **приплы́ть**] (*with* **к**) to swim up to; reach by swimming.

приплы́ть [*infl. like* **плыть**] *v., pfv. of* **приплыва́ть**.

приплю́снутый *adj.* flat; flattened.

приплю́снуть *v., pfv. of* **приплю́щивать**.

приплюсова́ть [*infl.* **-су́ю, -су́ешь**] *v., pfv. of* **приплюсо́вывать**.

приплюсо́вывать *v.impfv.* [*pfv.* **приплюсова́ть**] *colloq.* to add; add in.

приплю́щивать *v.impfv.* [*pfv.* **приплю́снуть**] to flatten.

припля́сывать *v.impfv.* to dance up and down.

приподнима́ть *v.impfv.* [*pfv.* **приподня́ть**] to raise slightly; lift slightly. —**приподнима́ться**, *refl.* **1**, to raise oneself slightly. **2**, to sit up.

припо́днятый *adj.* **1**, (*of one's mood*) elated; exultant. **2**, (*of style, language, etc.*) elevated.

приподня́ть [*infl. like* **подня́ть**] *v., pfv. of* **приподнима́ть**. —**приподня́ться**, *refl., pfv. of* **приподнима́ться**.

припо́й *n.* solder.

приполза́ть *v.impfv.* [*pfv.* **приползти́**] (*with* **к**) to crawl to; reach by crawling.

приползти́ [*infl. like* **ползти́**] *v., pfv. of* **приполза́ть**.

припомина́ть *v.impfv.* [*pfv.* **припо́мнить**] to remember; recall; recollect.

припра́ва *n.* seasoning; flavoring; relish; dressing; condiment.

припра́вить [*infl.* **-влю, -вишь**] *v., pfv. of* **приправля́ть**.

приправля́ть *v.impfv.* [*pfv.* **припра́вить**] to season; flavor.

припря́тать [*infl.* **-пря́чу, -пря́чешь**] *v., pfv. of* **припря́тывать**.

припря́тывать *v.impfv.* [*pfv.* **припря́тать**] *colloq.* **1**, to put away; store. **2**, *fig.* to hide; conceal.

припу́гивать *v.impfv.* [*pfv.* **припугну́ть**] *colloq.* to frighten; scare; intimidate.

припу́дривать *v.impfv.* [*pfv.* **припу́дрить**] to powder. —**припу́дриваться**, *refl.* to powder oneself.

припуска́ть *v.impfv.* [*pfv.* **припусти́ть**] *colloq.* **1**, (*with* **к**) to allow to come near; let at. **2**, to urge on (a horse). **3**, to let out (a garment). **4**, *v.i.* to quicken one's pace. **5**, *v.i.* (*of rain*) to come down harder. —**припуска́ться**, *refl., colloq.* to quicken one's pace.

припусти́ть [*infl.* **-пущу́, -пу́стишь**] *v., pfv. of* **припуска́ть**. —**припусти́ться**, *refl., pfv. of* **припуска́ться**.

припуха́ть *v.impfv.* [*pfv.* **припу́хнуть**] to be slightly swollen.

припу́хлость *n.f.* slight swelling.

припу́хлый *adj.* slightly swollen.

припу́хнуть [*past* **-пу́х, -пу́хла**] *v., pfv. of* **припуха́ть**.

прираба́тывать *v.impfv.* [*pfv.* **прирабо́тать**] to earn (extra money).

при́работок [*gen.* **-тка**] *n.* extra money earned.

прира́внивать *v.impfv.* [*pfv.* **приравня́ть**] (*with* **к**) to equate (with).

прираста́ть *v.impfv.* [*pfv.* **прирасти́**] **1**, (*with* **к**) to grow on to. **2**, *fig.* (*with* **к**) to become rooted (to); become frozen (to). **3**, to increase; grow.

прирасти́ [*infl. like* **расти́**] *v., pfv. of* **прираста́ть**.

прираще́ние *n.* **1**, increase. **2**, increment.

приревнова́ть *v.pfv.* [*infl.* **-ну́ю, -ну́ешь**] to be jealous of.

приреза́ть [*infl.* **-ре́жу, -ре́жешь**] *v., pfv. of* **прире́зать** *and* **прире́зывать**.

приреза́ть *v.impfv.* [*pfv.* **прире́зать**] **1**, to cut the throat of. **2**, to slaughter (animals). **3**, to add on (a piece of land). *Also,* **прире́зывать**.

приро́да *n.* **1**, nature: **дары́ приро́ды**, the gifts of nature; **изуча́ть приро́ду**, to study nature. **2**, physical features; climate; environment (*of a region*): **суро́вая приро́да Сиби́ри**, the harsh climate (*or* rugged environment) of Siberia. **3**, *colloq.* (a person's) nature. **Челове́ческая приро́да**, human nature. —**в приро́де веще́й**, in the nature of things. —**от приро́ды**, from birth. —**по приро́де**, by nature.

приро́дный *adj.* **1**, natural. **2**, innate; inborn; inherent.

прирождённый *adj.* **1**, innate; inborn. **2**, (*of a person*) born: **прирождённый поэ́т**, a born poet.

приро́ст *n.* increase; growth.

прируча́ть *v.impfv.* [*pfv.* **приручи́ть**] to tame; domesticate.

прируче́ние *n.* taming; domestication.

приручённый *adj.* tame.

приручи́ть *v., pfv. of* **прируча́ть**.

приса́дка *n.* additive.

приса́живаться *v.r.impfv.* [*pfv.* **присе́сть**] to sit down; have a seat; take a seat.

приса́ливать *v.impfv.* [*pfv.* **присоли́ть**] *colloq.* to add a touch of salt to.

приса́сываться *v.r.impfv.* [*pfv.* **присоса́ться**] (*with* **к**) to adhere to (*by suction*).

присва́ивать *v.impfv.* [*pfv.* **присво́ить**] **1**, to appropriate; take for one's own. **2**, to pass off (*or* claim) as one's own. **3**, (*with dat.*) to award (a degree to); confer (a title on); give (a name to).

при́свист *n.* whistle; whistling.

присви́стывать *v.impfv.* [*pfv.* **присви́стнуть**] to whistle.

присвое́ние *n.* **1**, appropriation. **2**, conferring.

присво́ить *v., pfv. of* **присва́ивать**.

приседа́ние *n.* **1**, squat. **2**, curtsy.

приседа́ть *v.impfv.* [*pfv.* **присе́сть**] **1**, to crouch; squat. **2**, to cower (*from fear*). **3**, to curtsy.

присе́ст *n., obs.* sitting. —**в** (*or* **за**) **оди́н присе́ст**, at one sitting; at a stretch.

присе́сть [*infl.* **прися́ду, прися́дешь**; *past* **присе́л, присе́ла**] *v., pfv. of* **приса́живаться** *and* **приседа́ть**.

при́сказка [*gen. pl.* -зок] *n.* **1,** introduction; prelude. **2,** saying.

прискака́ть *v.pfv.* [*infl.* -скачу́, -ска́чешь] to arrive at a gallop.

приско́рбие *n., obs.* sorrow; regret. —к моему́ приско́рбию, to my regret.

приско́рбный *adj.* **1,** sad; sorrowful. **2,** regrettable; deplorable.

приску́чить *v.pfv., colloq.* **1,** to become boring. **2,** (*with dat.*) to bore.

присла́ть [*infl.* -шлю́, -шлёшь] *v., pfv. of* присыла́ть.

прислоня́ть *v.impfv.* [*pfv.* прислони́ть] (*with* к) **1,** to lean; rest (something) against. **2,** to place; stand (something) against. —прислоня́ться, *refl.* (*with* к) to lean against; rest against.

прислу́га *n.* **1,** *obs.* servant; maid. **2,** *obs.* servants. **3,** *mil.* crew; team.

прислу́живать *v.impfv.* **1,** to be a servant. **2,** (*with dat.*) *colloq.* to wait on. —прислу́живаться, *refl.* (*with dat. or* к) to play up to.

прислу́жник *n.* **1,** *obs.* servant. **2,** *colloq.* lackey. —прислу́жничество, *n.* servility.

прислу́шиваться *v.r.impfv.* [*pfv.* прислу́шаться] (*with* к) **1,** to listen (to). **2,** to heed. **3,** *colloq.* to get used to the sound of.

присма́тривать *v.impfv.* [*pfv.* присмотре́ть] **1,** (*with* за + *instr.*) to look after; keep an eye on. **2,** [*impfv. only*] *colloq.* to look for. —присма́триваться, *refl.* (*with* к) **1,** to look closely (at). **2,** to size up; take the measure of. **3,** to grow accustomed to.

присмире́ть *v.pfv.* to calm down; grow quiet.

присмо́тр *n.* supervision. Оставля́ть без присмо́тра, to leave unattended.

присмотре́ть *v.pfv.* [*infl.* -смотрю́, -смо́тришь] **1,** *pfv. of* присма́тривать. **2,** *colloq.* to find. —присмотре́ться, *refl., pfv. of* присма́триваться.

присни́ться *v.r., pfv. of* сни́ться.

при́сные *n.pl., decl. as an adj., colloq.* those in one's immediate circle: премьер-мини́стр и его́ при́сные, the prime minister and those around him.

присовокупля́ть *v.impfv.* [*pfv.* присовокупи́ть] **1,** (*with* к) to attach (to). **2,** (*with* к) to add (to); add on (to). **3,** *obs.* to say in addition; add.

присоедине́ние *n.* **1,** addition. **2,** joining. **3,** annexation; incorporation.

присоединя́ть *v.impfv.* [*pfv.* присоедини́ть] (*with* к) **1,** to add (something) to. **2,** to join (something) to. **3,** to annex (to); incorporate (into). —присоединя́ться, *refl.* (*with* к) **1,** to be added (to). **2,** to join. **3,** to endorse; subscribe to.

присоли́ть [*infl.* -солю́, -со́лишь *or* -соли́шь] *v., pfv. of* приса́ливать.

присоса́ться [*infl.* -сосётся] *v.r., pfv. of* приса́сываться.

присе́диться *v.r.pfv.* [*infl.* -жусь, -дишься] (*with* к) *colloq.* to sit down next to.

присо́сок [*gen.* -ска] *n., bot., zool.* sucker. *Also,* присо́ска.

присо́хнуть [*past* -сох, -со́хла] *v., pfv. of* присыха́ть.

приспе́ть *v.pfv., colloq.* (*of time*) to be ripe.

приспе́шник *n.* henchman; underling; stooge.

приспоса́бливать *v.impfv.* [*pfv.* приспосо́бить] **1,** to adapt. **2,** (*with* под + *acc.*) to convert (into). —приспоса́бливаться, *refl.* (*with* к) to adjust (to); become adjusted (to); adapt (to).

приспосо́бить [*infl.* -блю, -бишь] *v., pfv. of* приспоса́бливать *and* приспособля́ть. —приспосо́биться, *refl., pfv. of* приспоса́бливаться *and* приспособля́ться.

приспособле́ние *n.* **1,** device. **2,** adaptation; adjustment.

приспособля́емость *n.f.* adaptability.

приспособля́ть *v.impfv.* = приспоса́бливать. —приспособля́ться, *refl.* = приспоса́бливаться.

приспуска́ть *v.impfv.* [*pfv.* приспусти́ть] **1,** to lower slightly. **2,** to lower (a flag) to half-mast.

приспусти́ть [*infl.* -спущу́, -спу́стишь] *v., pfv. of* приспуска́ть.

при́став *n., pre-rev.* police officer. —суде́бный при́став, *pre-rev.* bailiff.

пристава́ние *n., usu. pl.* nagging; pestering.

пристава́ть *v.impfv.* [*pfv.* приста́ть; *pres.* -стаю́, -стаёшь] (*with* к) **1,** to stick (to); adhere (to). **2,** to accost. **3,** *colloq.* to nag; pester. **4,** *colloq.* to join. **5,** (*of a boat*) to put in (to); pull up (to). **6,** *colloq.* (*of a disease*) to be transmitted (to). *See also* приста́ть.

приста́вить [*infl.* -влю, -вишь] *v., pfv. of* приставля́ть.

приста́вка [*gen. pl.* -вок] *n.* **1,** prefix. **2,** attachment; accessory.

приставля́ть *v.impfv.* [*pfv.* приста́вить] (*with* к) **1,** to place (against); lean (against). **2,** to add on (to). **3,** to assign to look after or monitor: приста́вить контролёра к рабо́чим, to assign an inspector to monitor the workers.

приставно́й *adj.* attached.

приста́вочный *adj.* **1,** prefixed. **2,** (*of a collar, cuffs, etc.*) detachable.

при́стальный *adj.* (*of a look*) intent; (*of attention*) rapt. —при́стально, *adv.* intently.

приста́нище *n.* refuge; shelter; haven.

при́стань [*pl.* при́стани, -не́й, -ня́м] *n.f.* dock; pier; wharf.

приста́ть *v.pfv.* [*infl.* -ста́ну, -ста́нешь] **1,** *pfv. of* пристава́ть. **2,** *impers.* (*with dat.*) *colloq.* to befit; become.

пристёгивать *v.impfv.* [*pfv.* пристегну́ть] to fasten; button; hook; buckle; pin. —пристёгиваться, *refl.* to hook on.

присто́йный *adj.* proper; seemly; decorous.

пристра́ивать *v.impfv.* [*pfv.* пристро́ить] **1,** (*with* к) to build on (to); add on (to). **2,** *colloq.* to place; find a job for. —пристра́иваться, *refl., colloq.* **1,** to ensconce oneself; perch. **2,** to get a job. **3,** (*with* к) to get into formation (with).

пристра́стие *n.* (*with* к) **1,** predilection; bent. **2,** partiality; bias. —допро́с с пристра́стием, interrogation under duress; the third degree.

пристрасти́ть *v.pfv.* [*infl.* -щу́, -сти́шь] (*with* к) *colloq.* to develop (in someone) a love (of): пристрасти́ть кого́-нибудь к кни́гам, to develop in someone a love of books. —**пристрасти́ться**, *refl.* (*with* к) to develop a passion (for).

пристра́стный *adj.* **1,** partial; biased. **2,** (*with* к) partial (to); drawn (to). —**пристра́стно**, *adv.* in a biased manner. —**пристра́стность**, *n.f.* partiality; bias.

пристра́чивать *v.impfv.* [*pfv.* **пристрочи́ть**] (*with* к) to sew on (to).

пристре́ливать *v.impfv.* **1,** [*pfv.* **пристрели́ть**] to shoot; kill. **2,** [*pfv.* **пристреля́ть**] to zero in (a weapon); zero in on (a target). —**пристре́ливаться**, *refl.* [*pfv.* **пристреля́ться**] to zero in.

пристрели́ть [*infl.* **-стрелю́, -стре́лишь**] *v., pfv. of* **пристре́ливать** (*in sense #1*).

пристре́лка *n.* zeroing in (*of a weapon*); zeroing in on (*a target*).

пристреля́ть *v., pfv. of* **пристре́ливать** (*in sense #2*). —**пристреля́ться**, *refl., pfv. of* **пристре́ливаться**.

пристро́ить *v., pfv. of* **пристра́ивать**. —**пристро́иться**, *refl., pfv. of* **пристра́иваться**.

пристро́йка [*gen. pl.* **-о́ек**] *n.* annex; extension.

пристрочи́ть [*infl.* **-строчу́, -стро́чишь** *or* **-строчи́шь**] *v., pfv. of* **пристра́чивать**.

пристру́нивать *v.impfv.* [*pfv.* **пристру́нить**] *colloq.* to clamp down on; crack down on.

присту́кивать *v.impfv.* [*pfv.* **присту́кнуть**] (*with instr.*) **1,** to rap. **2,** to click (one's heels).

при́ступ *n.* **1,** fit; attack. **2,** *mil.* attack; assault. Взять при́ступом, to storm (and capture).

приступа́ть *v.impfv.* [*pfv.* **приступи́ть**] (*with* к) to proceed (to); begin; set about. —**приступа́ться**, *refl.* (*with* к) *colloq.* to approach; come near (to).

приступи́ть [*infl.* **-ступлю́, -сту́пишь**] *v., pfv. of* **приступа́ть**. —**приступи́ться**, *refl., pfv. of* **приступа́ться**.

пристыди́ть *v., pfv. of* **стыди́ть**.

присуди́ть [*infl.* **-сужу́, -су́дишь**] *v., pfv. of* **присужда́ть**.

присужда́ть *v.impfv.* [*pfv.* **присуди́ть**] **1,** to award; confer. **2,** (*with* к) to sentence (to).

присужде́ние *n.* awarding; conferring.

прису́тствие *n.* presence: в моём прису́тствии, in my presence. —**прису́тствие ду́ха**, presence of mind.

прису́тствовать *v.impfv.* [*pres.* **-ствую, -ствуешь**] to be present; attend: прису́тствовать на собра́нии, to be present at/ attend/ a meeting. Прису́тствовать в за́ле/ при разгово́ре/, to be present in the hall/ during a conversation/.

прису́тствующий *n., decl. as an adj.* person present.

прису́щий *adj.* (*with dat.*) **1,** inherent: Челове́ку прису́щ инсти́нкт самосохране́ния, the instinct of self-preservation is inherent in man. **2,** characteristic: с прису́щим ему́ доброду́шием, with his characteristic good nature.

присчи́тывать *v.impfv.* [*pfv.* **присчита́ть**] to add on.

присла́ть *v.impfv.* [*pfv.* **присла́ть**] to send.

присы́лка [*gen. pl.* **-лок**] *n.* **1,** sending. **2,** *colloq.* parcel.

присы́пать [*infl.* **-сы́плю, -сы́плешь**] *v., pfv. of* **присыпа́ть**.

присыпа́ть *v.impfv.* [*pfv.* **присы́пать**] **1,** (*with gen.*) to pour some more (of). **2,** to sprinkle (a surface): при-

сыпа́ть что́-нибудь песко́м, to sprinkle something with sand.

присы́пка *n.* **1,** sprinkling. **2,** powder: де́тская присы́пка, baby powder.

присыха́ть *v.impfv.* [*pfv.* **присо́хнуть**] (*with* к) to stick (to): adhere (*in drying*).

прися́га *n.* oath. —**дава́ть прися́гу**, to swear. —**приводи́ть (кого́-нибудь) к прися́ге**, to swear in; administer the oath to. —**приноси́ть** *or* **принима́ть прися́гу**, to take the oath.

присяга́ть *v.impfv.* [*pfv.* **присягну́ть**] **1,** to swear. **2,** (*with dat.*) to swear allegiance (to).

прися́жный *adj.* **1,** *obs.* sworn. **2,** *colloq.* inveterate; persistent. —*n.* **1,** juror. **2,** *pl.* jury.

притаи́ть *v.pfv., colloq.* **1,** to conceal. **2,** to harbor. —**притаи́ться**, *refl.* to hide.

пританцо́вывать *v.impfv.* to make dancing steps; pretend to dance.

прита́птывать *v.impfv.* [*pfv.* **притопта́ть**] to trample; trample down.

прита́скивать *v.impfv.* [*pfv.* **притащи́ть**] to bring in; drag in. —**прита́скиваться**, *refl., colloq.* to drag oneself along.

притащи́ть [*infl.* **-тащу́, -та́щишь**] *v., pfv. of* **прита́скивать**. —**притащи́ться**, *refl., pfv. of* **прита́скиваться**.

притвори́ть [*infl.* **-творю́, -тво́ришь**] *v., pfv. of* **притворя́ть**. —**притвори́ться**, *refl.* **1,** [*infl.* **-тво́рится**] *pfv. of* **притворя́ться** (*in sense #1*). **2,** [*infl.* **-творю́сь, -твори́шься**] *pfv. of* **притворя́ться** (*in sense #2*).

притво́рный *adj.* feigned; pretended. —**притво́рно**, *adv.* pretending to: притво́рно рассерди́ться, to pretend to be angry.

притво́рство *n.* sham; pretense. —**притво́рщик**, *n.* faker.

притворя́ть *v.impfv.* [*pfv.* **притвори́ть**] to close; shut. —**притворя́ться**, *refl.,* **1,** to be closed; be shut. **2,** (*with instr.*) to pretend (to be).

притека́ть *v.impfv.* [*pfv.* **прите́чь**] **1,** to leak in. **2,** *fig.* to filter in.

притерпе́ться *v.r.pfv.* [*infl.* **-терплю́сь, -те́рпишься**] (*with* к) *colloq.* to get used to; learn to live with.

притёртый *adj.* ground in; ground smooth. —**притёртое стекло́**, ground glass.

притесне́ние *n.* oppression.

притесни́тель *n.m.* oppressor.

притесня́ть *v.impfv.* [*pfv.* **притесни́ть**] to oppress; keep down.

прите́чь [*infl. like* **течь**] *v., pfv. of* **притека́ть**.

прити́скивать *v.impfv.* [*pfv.* **прити́снуть**] (*with* к) to press (something) against (something).

притиха́ть *v.impfv.* [*pfv.* **прити́хнуть**] **1,** to quiet down; (*of noise*) die down. **2,** to subside; abate.

прити́хнуть [*past* **-ти́х, -ти́хла**] *v., pfv. of* **притиха́ть**.

приткну́ть *v.pfv., colloq.* to stick; put; lay. —**приткну́ться**, *refl., colloq.* to find room for oneself; find a place to stay.

прито́к *n.* **1,** inflow (*of water, air, etc.*). **2,** *fig.* influx. **3,** *fig.* surge (*of energy, an emotion, etc.*). **4,** tributary.

при́толока *n.* lintel.

прито́м *conj.* besides; moreover; furthermore.

прито́н *n.* den: иго́рный прито́н, gambling den.

прито́пнуть *v., pfv. of* **прито́пывать.**

притопта́ть [*infl.* -топчу́, -то́пчешь] *v., pfv. of* **прита́птывать.**

прито́пывать *v.impfv.* [*pfv.* **прито́пнуть**] (*with instr.*) **1,** to stamp (one's foot). **2,** to tap (one's foot in time to music).

притормози́ть *v.pfv.* [*infl.* -жу́, -зи́шь] to slow down (*trans. & intrans.*).

при́торный *adj.* sugary; saccharine.

притра́гиваться *v.r.impfv.* [*pfv.* **притро́нуться**] (*with* **к**) to touch.

притупи́ть [*infl.* -туплю́, -ту́пишь] *v., pfv. of* **притупля́ть.** —**притупи́ться,** *refl., pfv. of* **притупля́ться.**

притупля́ть *v.impfv.* [*pfv.* **притупи́ть**] **1,** to blunt. **2,** *fig.* to dull (the mind, senses, etc.). —**притупля́ться,** *refl.* **1,** to become dull. **2,** *fig.* to fade; wane.

притуши́ть *v.pfv.* [*infl.* -тушу́, -ту́шишь] *colloq.* **1,** to put out; extinguish. **2,** to dim (lights).

при́тча *n.* **1,** parable. **2,** *in exclamations, colloq.* strange thing: Что за при́тча!, what a strange thing! —**при́тча во язы́цех,** the talk of the town.

притяга́тельный *adj.* attractive; magnetic.

притя́гивать *v.impfv.* [*pfv.* **притяну́ть**] **1,** to pull in (a boat). **2,** to attract; draw. **3,** *colloq.* to summon: притяну́ть к отве́ту, to call to account. —**притя́нутый за́ уши,** farfetched.

притяжа́тельный *adj., gram.* possessive.

притяже́ние *n.* attraction; gravitation; gravity.

притяза́ние *n.* (*with* **на** + *acc.*) **1,** claim (to). **2,** pretension (to).

притяза́тельный *adj.* demanding; exacting.

притяну́ть [*infl.* -тяну́, -тя́нешь] *v., pfv. of* **притя́гивать.**

приукра́шивать *v.impfv.* [*pfv.* **приукра́сить**] *colloq.* **1,** to decorate; spruce up; brighten up. **2,** to embellish (a story, an account, etc.). —**приукра́шиваться,** *refl., colloq.* to spruce up.

приуменьша́ть *v.impfv.* [*pfv.* **приуме́ньшить**] **1,** to reduce somewhat. **2,** to play down.

приумножа́ть *v.impfv.* [*pfv.* **приумно́жить**] to increase even further; augment.

приуны́ть *v.pfv., colloq., used only in the past tense,* to become depressed; become despondent.

приуро́чивать *v.impfv.* [*pfv.* **приуро́чить**] (*with* **к**) to time (for); time to coincide (with).

приуча́ть *v.impfv.* [*pfv.* **приучи́ть**] (*with* **к** *or inf.*) **1,** to teach (to); train (to). **2,** to inure (to). —**приуча́ться,** *refl.* (*with* **к** *or inf.*) **1,** to train oneself (to). **2,** to get used to.

приучи́ть [*infl.* -учу́, -у́чишь] *v., pfv. of* **приуча́ть.** —**приучи́ться,** *refl., pfv. of* **приуча́ться.**

прифронтово́й *adj., mil.* forward; front-line. —**прифронтова́я полоса́,** forward area.

прихва́рывать *v.impfv.* [*pfv.* **прихворну́ть**] *colloq.* to be ailing; be unwell.

прихвастну́ть *v.pfv., colloq.* to brag a little; boast a little.

прихвати́ть [*infl.* -хвачу́, -хва́тишь] *v., pfv. of* **прихва́тывать.**

прихва́тывать *v.impfv.* [*pfv.* **прихвати́ть**] **1,** to grab; grip. **2,** to take along. **3,** to tie up; fasten. **4,** *colloq.* (*of frost*) to nip; damage.

прихворну́ть *v., pfv. of* **прихва́рывать.**

при́хвостень [*gen.* -стня] *n.m., colloq.* toady; sycophant.

прихлеба́тель *n.m., colloq.* parasite; sponger.

прихлёбывать *v.impfv.* [*pfv.* **прихлебну́ть**] *colloq.* to sip.

прихло́пывать *v.impfv.* [*pfv.* **прихло́пнуть**] **1,** to slap; bang. **2,** to slam (shut). **3,** *colloq.* to catch: прихло́пнуть па́лец две́рью, to catch one's finger in a door. **4,** [*impfv. only*] to clap (*in rhythm*).

прихлы́нуть *v.pfv.* to rush; surge.

прихо́д *n.* **1,** coming; arrival. **2,** income; receipts. **3,** parish; congregation.

приходи́ть *v.impfv.* [*pfv.* **прийти́;** *pres.* **-хожу́, -хо́дишь**] **1,** to come; arrive. **2,** (*with* **к**) to come to; arrive at; reach (a decision, conclusion, agreement, etc.). **3,** (*with* **в** + *acc.*) to reach a certain state or condition: приходи́ть в у́жас, to be horrified; приходи́ть в я́рость, to become enraged; приходи́ть в упа́док, to decline; decay; приходи́ть в ве́тхость, to fall into disrepair. —**приходи́ть в го́лову** (+ *dat.*), to cross (*or* enter) one's mind; occur to. —**приходи́ть в себя́,** to regain consciousness; come to. —**приходи́ть к вла́сти,** to come to power. —**приходи́ть к концу́,** to come to an end.

приходи́ться *v.r.impfv.* [*pfv.* **прийти́сь;** *pres.* **-хожу́сь, -хо́дишься**] **1,** (*with* **по**) to fit: Сапоги́ пришли́сь по ноге́, the shoes fitted well. **2,** (*with* **по**) (*of a blow or flying object*) to land (on); fall (on). **3,** (*with* **на** + *acc.*) to fall (*on a certain date or day of the week*). **4,** *impers.* (*with dat. and inf.*) to have to: Ему́ придётся подожда́ть, he will have to wait. **5,** *impers.* (*with dat. and inf.*) to happen to; have occasion to: Мне ча́сто приходи́лось (+ *inf.*), I frequently had occasion to... Нам не пришло́сь ви́деться два́дцать лет, we did not see each other for twenty years. Удивля́ться не прихо́дится, one should not (*or there is no reason to*) be surprised. **6,** *impers.* (*with dat. and adverb*) to have a certain time of it: Ему́ пришло́сь тяжело́ *or* нелегко́, he has had a hard time of it. **7,** *impers.* (*with* **на** + *acc.*) to number; account for: На ка́ждую же́нщину приходи́лось по тро́е мужчи́н, there were three men for every woman. Че́тверть всего́ э́кспорта прихо́дится на нефть, oil accounts for one-fourth of all exports. **8,** *impers.* to be due (from): На ка́ждого пришло́сь по сто рубле́й, each person had to pay 100 rubles. С вас прихо́дится де́сять до́лларов, you owe ten dollars. **9,** [*impfv. only*] to be related in a certain way: Кем он вам прихо́дится?, how is he related to you? **10,** *in* приходи́ться по вку́су (+ *dat.*), to be to someone's taste; приходи́ться по душе́ (+ *dat.*), to suit; please; be to someone's liking. —**где придётся,** wherever one can. —**как придётся,** in whatever way one can. —**чем придётся,** with whatever happens to be on hand.

приходный *adj.* receipts (*attrib.*): приходная книга, receipts book.

приходовать *v.impfv.* [*pfv.* **заприходовать**; *pres.* -дую, -дуешь] *bookkeeping* to credit.

приходский *adj.* parish (*attrib.*). —**приходская школа**, parochial school.

прихожанин [*pl.* -жане, -жан] *n.m.* [*fem.* -жанка] parishioner.

прихожая *n., decl. as an adj.* vestibule; hall.

прихорашивать *v.impfv., colloq.* to spruce up; doll up. —**прихорашиваться**, *refl., colloq.* to spruce up.

прихотливый *adj.* **1,** (*of a person*) whimsical; capricious. **2,** (*of a design*) fancy; intricate. **3,** (*of a dream*) fanciful.

прихоть *n.f.* whim; fancy; caprice.

прихрамывать *v.impfv.* to have a slight limp.

прицел *n.* sight (*on a gun*). Бомбардировочный прицел, bombsight. —**взять на прицел**, to take aim at; draw a bead on.

прицеливание *n.* aiming (*of a weapon*).

прицеливаться *v.r.impfv.* [*pfv.* **прицелиться**] **1,** to take aim. **2,** (*with* в + *acc.*) to aim (at).

прицельный *adj.* **1,** aiming; sighting: прицельное приспособление, sighting device. **2,** aimed. Прицельное бомбометание, precision bombing.

прицениваться *v.r.impfv.* [*pfv.* **прицениться**] (*with* к) *colloq.* to ask the price of.

прицениться [*infl.* -ценюсь, -ценишься] *v.r., pfv. of* **прицениваться**.

прицеп *n.* trailer.

прицепить [*infl.* -цеплю, -цепишь] *v.. pfv. of* **прицеплять**. —**прицепиться**, *refl., pfv. of* **прицепляться**.

прицепка [*gen. pl.* -пок] *n.* **1,** hitching; hooking. **2,** *colloq.* cavil; quibble.

прицеплять *v.impfv.* [*pfv.* **прицепить**] (*with* к) **1,** to hitch (to); hook (to). **2,** *colloq.* to pin (to). —**прицепляться**, *refl.* (*with* к) **1,** to be hitched (to); hook (onto). **2,** to stick (to); cling (to). **3,** *fig., colloq.* to join. **4,** *fig., colloq.* to attach oneself to. **5,** *fig., colloq.* to pick on.

причал *n.* **1,** mooring; moorage. **2,** mooring line. **3,** berth (*at a pier*).

причаливать *v.impfv.* [*pfv.* **причалить**] **1,** *v.t.* to moor. **2,** *v.i.* (*with* к) to tie up (at).

причальный *adj.* mooring (*attrib.*): причальный канат, mooring line.

причастие *n.* **1,** *gram.* participle. **2,** *relig.* communion; Eucharist.

причастить [*infl.* -щу, -стишь] *v., pfv. of* **причащать**. —**причаститься**, *refl., pfv. of* **причащаться**.

причастность *n.f.* involvement.

причастный *adj.* [*short form* -стен, -стна] **1,** (*with* к) involved (in); being a party (to); connected (with); concerned (with). **2,** *gram.* participial.

причащать *v.impfv.* [*pfv.* **причастить**] to give communion to. —**причаститься**, *refl.* to receive communion.

причём *conj.* **1,** in which connection. **2,** at that. ◆*Often not translated:* Супруги развелись, причём сын остался у отца, the couple was divorced, the son remaining with the father.

причесать [*infl.* -чешу, -чешешь] *v., pfv. of* **причёсы-**

вать. —**причесаться**, *refl., pfv. of* **причёсываться**.

причёска [*gen. pl.* -сок] *n.* hairdo.

причёсывать *v.impfv.* [*pfv.* **причесать**] **1,** to comb. **2,** to comb the hair of. —**причёсываться**, *refl.* **1,** to comb one's hair. **2,** to have one's hair done.

причина *n.* **1,** cause. **2,** reason: по этой причине, for this reason. —**без всякой причины**, for no reason whatever.

причиндалы [*gen.* -лов] *n.pl., colloq.* **1,** goods; possessions. **2,** attachments; appurtenances.

причинить *v., pfv. of* **причинять**.

причинный *adj.* causal; causative. —**причинность**, *n.f.* causality.

причинять *v.impfv.* [*pfv.* **причинить**] to cause: причинять вред (+ *dat.*), to cause harm (*or* damage) to.

причислять *v.impfv.* [*pfv.* **причислить**] (*with* к) **1,** to add (to). **2,** to number (among). **3,** *in* причислить к лику святых, to canonize. —**причисляться**, *refl.* (*with* к) to belong to.

причитание *n.* lamentation.

причитать *v.impfv.* to wail; moan (*in grief*).

причитаться *v.r.impfv.* **1,** (*with dat.*) to be owed (to); be due (to). **2,** (*with* с + *gen.*), to owe; be obligated to pay: С вас причитается тридцать рублей you owe thirty rubles.

причмокивать *v.impfv.* [*pfv.* **причмокнуть**] to smack one's lips. —**причмокивать губами**, = **причмокивать.**

причуда *n.* whim; fancy; caprice.

причудливый *adj.* **1,** fancy; intricate. **2,** quaint; cute. **3,** *obs.* whimsical; capricious.

пришвартовать *v., pfv. of* **швартовать**. —**пришвартоваться**, *refl., pfv. of* **швартоваться**.

пришелец [*gen.* -льца] *n.* newcomer.

пришёптывать *v.impfv.* to whisper.

пришествие *n.* coming; appearance; advent. —**до второго пришествия**, till doomsday.

пришибить *v.pfv.* [*infl.* -шибу, -шибёшь; *past* -шиб, -шибла] *colloq.* **1,** to strike dead; kill. **2,** *fig.* to depress.

пришибленный *adj., colloq.* crushed; crestfallen.

пришивать *v.impfv.* [*pfv.* **пришить**] to sew on.

пришить [*infl.* -шью, -шьёшь] *v., pfv. of* **пришивать**.

пришлый *adj.* having come from somewhere else; newly arrived.

пришпиливать *v.impfv.* [*pfv.* **пришпилить**] to pin on. **2,** (*with* к) to pin to.

пришпоривать *v.impfv.* [*pfv.* **пришпорить**] **1,** to spur (a horse). **2,** *fig., colloq.* to spur on; urge on.

прищёлкивать *v.impfv.* [*pfv.* **прищёлкнуть**] (*with instr.*) to snap; crack.

прищемлять *v.impfv.* [*pfv.* **прищемить**] to catch: прищемить палец дверью, to catch one's fingers in a door.

прищепка [*gen. pl.* -пок] *n.* clothespin.

прищуривать *v.impfv.* [*pfv.* **прищурить**] *in* прищуривать глаза, to squint. —**прищуриваться**, *refl.* to squint.

приют *n.* **1,** shelter; refuge. **2,** *pre-rev.* orphanage; foundling home.

приютить *v.pfv.* [*infl.* -чу, -тишь] to shelter; give refuge to. —**приютиться**, *refl.* to take shelter.

прия́знь *n.f.* friendship; kind feelings.

прия́тель *n.m.* [*fem.* **-ница**] friend. **—прия́тельский**, *adj.* friendly.

прия́тно *adv.* pleasantly. **—***adj., used predicatively,* pleasant; nice: Прия́тно э́то слы́шать, it is nice to hear it. Мне бу́дет прия́тно (+ *inf.*), I will be happy to...; it will be a pleasure to...

прия́тный *adj.* [*short form* **-тен, -тна**] pleasant; nice; pleasing; enjoyable.

про *prep., with acc.* about: рассказа́ть про свои́ приключе́ния, to tell about one's adventures. **—про запа́с,** *see* **запа́с. —про себя́,** to oneself: чита́ть про себя́, to read to oneself.

про- *prefix* **1,** *indicating motion through:* пробира́ться сквозь толпу́, to make one's way through a crowd. **2,** *indicating motion past:* прое́хать ми́мо ста́нции, to drive past the station. **3,** *indicating thoroughness of an action:* просу́шивать, to dry (something) thoroughly. **4,** *indicating failure, error, etc.:* проигра́ть, to lose; промахну́ться, to miss; провали́ться, to fail; просчита́ться, to miscalculate. **5,** (*with pfv. verbs only*) *indicating action performed over or throughout a certain period of time:* прожи́ть три го́да за грани́цей, to live abroad for three years; проспа́ть всё у́тро, to sleep through the entire morning. **6,** (*with adjectives*) pro-: проамерика́нский, pro-American.

проанализи́ровать *v., pfv. of* **анализи́ровать.**

про́ба *n.* **1,** test; trial. Про́ба сил, test of strength. Про́ба пера́, first published work; literary debut. Взять на про́бу, to take on trial. **2,** sample; specimen. **3,** unit of fineness of precious metals based on 1,000 parts for pure metals: зо́лото семисо́т пятидеся́той про́бы, 18-karat gold. **4,** hallmark (*of precious metals*). **—высо́кой/вы́сшей про́бы,** of a high/ the highest/ order. **—ни́зкой** *or* **ни́зшей про́бы,** of the worst type.

пробавля́ться *v.r.impfv.* (*with instr.*) *colloq.* **1,** to get along (on); subsist (on). **2,** to support oneself (by).

проба́лтывать *v.impfv.* [*pfv.* **проболта́ть**] *colloq.* to blab; blurt out; let out. **—проба́лтываться,** *refl., colloq.* to shoot off one's mouth; let the cat out of the bag; spill the beans.

пробе́г *n.* **1,** run. **2,** race. **—испыта́тельный пробе́г,** trial run. **—про́бный пробе́г,** test run; road test.

пробе́гать *v.pfv.* to run (*for a certain length of time*).

пробега́ть *v.impfv.* [*pfv.* **пробежа́ть**] **1,** to run; (*with* **по**) run along; run down; (*with* **че́рез**) run through; (*with* **ми́мо**) run past. **2,** (*with* **по**) to pass over; sweep over. **3,** (*with instr. and* **по**) to run (something over something): пробежа́ть па́льцами по клавиату́ре, to run one's fingers over the keyboard. **4,** to glance over; scan.

пробежа́ть [*infl. like* **бежа́ть**] *v., pfv. of* **пробега́ть. —пробежа́ться,** *refl.* (*with* **по**) to run about; race about.

пробе́жка [*gen. pl.* **-жек**] *n.* run.

пробе́л *n.* **1,** blank space; blank. **2,** *fig.* gap: пробе́лы в зна́ниях, gaps in one's knowledge.

пробива́ть *v.impfv.* [*pfv.* **проби́ть**] **1,** to pierce; penetrate. **2,** to break through; breach. **3,** to make (a hole); make a hole in. **4,** *colloq.* to lay (a road); clear (a

path). **—пробива́ть себе́ доро́гу, 1,** to force one's way through. **2,** *fig.* to make one's way in the world.

пробива́ться *v.r.impfv.* [*pfv.* **проби́ться**] **1,** (*with* **к, сквозь** *or* **че́рез**) to force one's way (to *or* through); break through (to). **2,** (*with* **в** + *acc. or* **сквозь**) to seep (into *or* through); filter through. **3,** (*of plants, hair, etc.*) to push through; come out; appear.

пробивно́й *adj., colloq.* aggressive; pushy.

пробира́ть *v.impfv.* [*pfv.* **пробра́ть**] *colloq.* **1,** (*of cold*) to penetrate; (*of fear*) to seize. **2,** to bawl out. **—пробира́ться,** *refl.* **1,** to make one's way. **2,** to sneak; steal (into *or* through).

проби́рка [*gen. pl.* **-рок**] *n.* test tube.

проби́рный *adj.* pert. to the analyzing of precious metals. **—проби́рный ка́мень,** touchstone.

проби́ть [*infl.* **-бью́, -бьёшь**] *v., pfv. of* **бить** (*in senses #7 & #8*) *and* **пробива́ть. —проби́ться,** *refl., pfv. of* **пробива́ться.**

про́бка [*gen. pl.* **-бок**] *n.* **1,** cork. **2,** plug; stopper. **3,** *fig.* jam; congestion. **4,** fuse. **—глуп как про́бка,** dumb as they come.

про́бковый *adj.* cork (*attrib.*). **—про́бковый по́яс,** life belt.

пробле́ма *n.* problem.

проблема́тика *n.* problems. **—проблемати́ческий; проблемати́чный,** *adj.* problematic(al).

про́блеск *n.* **1,** flash; gleam. **2,** *fig.* ray; glimmer (*of hope*).

проблужда́ть *v.pfv.* to wander (*for a certain length of time*).

про́бный *adj.* **1,** test (*attrib.*); trial (*attrib.*). **2,** sample (*attrib.*). **—про́бный ка́мень,** touchstone. **—про́бная опера́ция,** exploratory operation. **—про́бный шар,** trial balloon.

про́бовать *v.impfv.* [*pfv.* **попро́бовать;** *pres.* **-бую, -буешь**] **1,** to try. **2,** to test. **3,** to taste. Про́бовать свои́ си́лы (*or* себя́) в (+ *prepl.*), to try one's hand at. **—про́боваться,** *refl.* **1,** to be tried; be tested. **2,** (*with* **на** + *acc.*) to try out (for).

пробода́ние *n., med.* perforation. **—прободно́й,** *adj., med.* perforated: прободна́я я́зва, perforated ulcer.

пробо́ина *n.* hole; breach. Пулева́я пробо́ина, bullet hole.

пробо́й *n.* hasp.

проболе́ть *v.pfv.* **1,** [*infl.* **-е́ю, -е́ешь**] to be ill (*for a certain length of time*). **2,** [*infl.* **-ли́т**] to hurt (*for a certain length of time*).

проболта́ть *v.pfv.* **1,** *pfv. of* **проба́лтывать. 2,** (*of two people*) to talk (*for a certain length of time*). **—проболта́ться,** *refl., pfv. of* **проба́лтываться.**

пробо́р *n.* part (*in one's hair*).

пробормота́ть *v., pfv. of* **бормота́ть.**

пробо́чник *n., colloq.* corkscrew.

пробра́ть [*infl. like* **брать**] *v., pfv. of* **пробира́ть. —пробра́ться,** *refl.* [*past tense stress as in* **бра́ться**] *pfv. of* **пробира́ться.**

проброди́ть *v.pfv.* [*infl.* **-брожу́, -бро́дишь**] to wander (*for a certain length of time*).

пробубни́ть *v., pfv. of* **бубни́ть.**

пробуди́ть *v.pfv.* **1,** [*infl.* **-бужу́, -бу́дишь**] *pfv. of* **пробужда́ть** (*in sense #1*). **2,** [*infl.* **-бужу́, -буди́шь**] *pfv.*

of **буди́ть** (*in sense #2*) *and* **пробужда́ть** (*in sense #2*). —**пробуди́ться**, *refl.*, *pfv. of* **пробужда́ться**.

пробужда́ть *v.impfv.* [*pfv.* **пробуди́ть**] **1,** to wake up; awaken. **2,** *fig.* to rouse; arouse. —**пробужда́ться**, *refl.* **1,** to wake up. **2,** *fig.* to be aroused; be awakened.

пробужде́ние *n.* awakening.

пробура́вить *v.*, *pfv. of* **бура́вить**.

пробури́ть *v.*, *pfv. of* **бури́ть**.

пробурча́ть *v.*, *pfv. of* **бурча́ть**.

пробы́ть *v.pfv.* [*infl.* -**бу́ду**, -**бу́дешь**; *past* **про́был**, **пробыла́**, **про́было**, **про́были**] to stay (*for a certain length of time*); spend (*a certain amount of time*).

прова́л *n.* **1,** collapse; cave-in. **2,** depression; hole. **3,** failure. **4,** lapse: **прова́л па́мяти**, lapse of memory. **5,** exposure (*of illegal activity*).

прова́ливать *v.impfv.* [*pfv.* **провали́ть**] **1,** to cause to collapse; cause to cave in. **2,** *colloq.* to ruin; make a mess of. **3,** *colloq.* to fail (a student). **4,** to expose (illegal activity). **5,** *colloq.* to vote down; reject; defeat. —**прова́ливаться**, *refl.* **1,** (*with* **в** + *acc.*) to fall (into). **Провали́ться под лёд**, to fall through the ice. **2,** to collapse; cave in; come tumbling down. **3,** to fail; be unsuccessful; fall through. **4,** (*with* **на** + *prepl. or* **по**) to fail (an examination or subject). **5,** *colloq.* to disappear. **6,** *in* **как сквозь зе́млю провали́ться**, to vanish into thin air.

провали́ть [*infl.* -**валю́**, -**ва́лишь**] *v.*, *pfv. of* **прова́ливать**. —**провали́ться**, *refl.*, *pfv. of* **прова́ливаться**.

прованса́ль *n.m.* mayonnaise. —**капу́ста прованса́ль**, pickled cabbage with a dressing added.

прова́нский *adj.*, *in* **прова́нское ма́сло**, olive oil.

прова́ривать *v.impfv.* [*pfv.* **провари́ть**] to boil thoroughly; cook thoroughly.

провари́ть [*infl.* -**варю́**, -**ва́ришь**] *v.*, *pfv. of* **прова́ривать**.

прове́дать *v.*, *pfv. of* **прове́дывать**.

проведе́ние *n.* **1,** guiding; conducting. **2,** building; construction. **3,** installation. **4,** conducting; carrying out; holding.

прове́дывать *v.impfv.* [*pfv.* **прове́дать**] **1,** to call on; pay a visit on. **2,** *colloq.* to find out; learn.

провезти́ [*infl. like* **везти́**] *v.*, *pfv. of* **провози́ть**.

провентили́ровать *v.*, *pfv. of* **вентили́ровать**.

прове́ренный *adj.* tested; of proven ability.

прове́рить *v.*, *pfv. of* **проверя́ть**.

прове́рка [*gen. pl.* -**рок**] *n.* **1,** check; checking. **2,** verification. **3,** testing.

проверну́ть *v.*, *pfv. of* **провёртывать** *and* **провора́чивать**.

прове́рочный *adj.* **1,** control (*attrib.*). **2,** test (*attrib.*): **прове́рочная рабо́та**, test paper (*in school*).

проверте́ть [*infl.* -**верчу́**, -**ве́ртишь**] *v.*, *pfv. of* **провора́чивать** (*in sense #1*).

провёртывать *v.impfv.* [*pfv.* **проверну́ть**] *colloq.* **1,** to drill; bore (a hole). **2,** to drill a hole in.

проверя́ть *v.impfv.* [*pfv.* **прове́рить**] **1,** to check. **2,** to verify. **3,** to test. **4,** to read; correct (students' compositions, homework, etc.).

провести́ *v.pfv.* [*infl. like* **вести́**] **1,** *pfv. of* **проводи́ть**[2]. **2,** *colloq.* to trick; fool; take in.

прове́тривание *n.* ventilation.

прове́тривать *v.impfv.* [*pfv.* **прове́трить**] to air out; ventilate. —**прове́триваться**, *refl.* **1,** to be aired out. **2,** *colloq.* to get some fresh air.

прове́ять *v.*, *pfv. of* **ве́ять** (*in sense #4*).

прови́дение *n.* foresight; vision.

провиде́ние *n.*, *relig.* Providence. —**провиденци́альный**, *adj.* providential.

прови́деть *v.impfv.* [*pres.* -**ви́жу**, -**ви́дишь**] to foresee.

прови́дец [*gen.* -**дца**] *n.m.* [*fem.* -**дица**] prophet; seer.

прови́зия *n.* food; provisions.

прови́зор *n.* pharmacist.

провини́ться *v.r.pfv.* (*with* **в** + *prepl.*) to be guilty (of); do (something) wrong.

прови́нность *n.f.*, *colloq.* **1,** fault. **2,** misdeed.

провинциа́л *n.* a provincial; hick. —**провинциали́зм**, *n.* provincialism. —**провинциа́льный**, *adj.* provincial.

прови́нция *n.* **1,** province. **2,** the provinces.

провиса́ть *v.impfv.* [*pfv.* **прови́снуть**] to be weighed down; sag.

прови́снуть [*past* -**ви́с**, -**ви́сла**] *v.*, *pfv. of* **провиса́ть**.

про́вод [*pl.* **провода́**] *n.* **1,** wire. **2,** (telephone) line: **прямо́й про́вод**, direct line. **Быть на про́воде**, to be calling; be on the line.

проводи́мость *n.f.* conductivity.

проводи́ть[1] [*infl.* -**вожу́**, -**во́дишь**] *v.*, *pfv. of* **провожа́ть**.

проводи́ть[2] *v.impfv.* [*pfv.* **провести́**; *pres.* -**вожу́**, -**во́дишь**] **1,** to lead; guide; conduct; escort; take. **2,** (*with instr. and* **по**) to run (one's hand, fingers, etc.) over the surface of. **3,** to build; construct (a railroad, canal, etc.). **4,** to install (a telephone, electricity, etc.). **5,** to conduct (a meeting, investigation, etc.); perform (an operation); carry out (reforms); hold (elections). **6,** to spend (time). **Хорошо́ провести́ вре́мя**, to have a good time. **7,** to draw (a line, boundary, etc.). **8,** to make; draw (a distinction, comparison, etc.). **9,** to get (a proposal, bill, etc.) through. **10,** [*impfv. only*] to conduct (electricity, heat, etc.). —**проводи́ть в жизнь**, to put into practice; make a reality of. *See also* **провести́**.

прово́дка *n.* **1,** guiding; conducting. **2,** building; construction. **3,** installation. **4,** wiring.

проводни́к [*gen.* -**ника́**] *n.* **1,** guide. **2,** conductor (*on a train*). **3,** *physics* conductor.

про́воды [*gen.* -**дов**] *n.pl.* send-off.

провожа́тый *n.*, *decl. as an adj.* guide; escort.

провожа́ть *v.impfv.* [*pfv.* **проводи́ть**] **1,** to accompany. **2,** (*with* **в** *or* **на** + *acc.*) to see (someone) off (at). **3,** (*with* **до**) to walk to; see to: **провожа́ть (кого́-нибудь) до гости́ницы/ до две́ри/**, to walk (someone) to the hotel; see (someone) to the door. **4,** to send off (to war, the army, etc.). **5,** to follow (*with one's eyes*).

прово́з *n.* **1,** transport; delivery. **2,** smuggling in. —**пла́та за прово́з**, freight charges; carrying charges.

провозгласи́ть [*infl.* -**шу́**, -**си́шь**] *v.*, *pfv. of* **провозглаша́ть**.

провозглаша́ть *v.impfv.* [*pfv.* **провозгласи́ть**] **1,** to proclaim. **2,** to propose (a toast).

провозглаше́ние *n.* proclamation.

провози́ть¹ *v.impfv.* [*pfv.* **провезти́**; *pres.* **-вожу́, -во́зишь**] **1,** to transport; convey. **2,** to smuggle (in).

провози́ть² *v.pfv.* [*infl.* **-вожу́, -во́зишь**] to convey; carry; deliver (*for a certain length of time*). —**провози́ться**, *refl.* (*with* **с** + *instr.*) to be busy (with); concern oneself (with) (*for a certain length of time*).

провока́тор *n.* **1,** agent provocateur. **2,** instigator.

провока́ция *n.* provocation. —**провокацио́нный**, *adj.* provocative.

про́волока *n.* wire. —**колю́чая про́волока**, barbed wire.

про́волочка [*gen. pl.* **-чек**] *n.* **1,** short piece of wire. **2,** fine wire.

проволо́чка *n., colloq.* delay. Без проволо́чек, without delay.

про́волочный *adj.* wire (*attrib.*).

провоня́ть *v.pfv., colloq.* **1,** *v.i.* to smell; stink. **2,** *v.t.* to smell up; stink up.

провора́чивать *v.impfv.* **1,** [*pfv.* **проверну́ть** *or* **проверте́ть**] to drill; bore; make (a hole); drill a hole in. **2,** [*pfv.* **проверну́ть**] *colloq.* to handle; dispose of (*quickly*).

прово́рный *adj.* **1,** agile; nimble; adroit; dexterous. **2,** quick; swift; brisk.

проворова́ться *v.r.pfv.* [*infl.* **-ру́юсь, -ру́ешься**] *colloq.* to be caught stealing.

проворо́нить *v.pfv., colloq.* to miss; let slip by.

прово́рство *n.* **1,** agility; dexterity. **2,** promptness.

проворча́ть *v.pfv.* [*infl.* **-чу́, -чи́шь**] to mumble; grumble.

провоци́ровать *v.impfv. & pfv.* [*pfv. also* **спровоци́ровать**; *pres.* **-ру́ю, -ру́ешь**] to provoke.

провы́ть *v.pfv.* [*infl.* **-во́ю, -во́ешь**] to howl; wail.

провя́лить *v., pfv. of* **вя́лить**.

прога́дывать *v.impfv.* [*pfv.* **прогада́ть**] *colloq.* to miscalculate.

прога́лина *n.* **1,** clearing; glade. **2,** space; gap.

проги́б *n.* sagging; sag.

прогиба́ть *v.impfv.* [*pfv.* **прогну́ть**] to bend; weigh down; cause to sag. —**прогиба́ться**, *refl.* to bend; sag.

прогла́дить *v.pfv.* [*infl.* **-жу, -дишь**] **1,** *pfv. of* **прогла́живать**. **2,** to iron (*for a certain length of time*).

прогла́живать *v.impfv.* [*pfv.* **прогла́дить**] to iron.

прогла́тывать *v.impfv.* [*pfv.* **проглоти́ть**] **1,** to swallow. **2,** *colloq.* to gulp down. **3,** *fig., colloq.* to devour (books). —**проглоти́ть язы́к**, to keep quiet; hold one's tongue. —**язы́к прогло́тишь**, it will make your mouth water.

проглоти́ть [*infl.* **-глочу́, -гло́тишь**] *v., pfv. of* **прогла́тывать**.

прогляде́ть *v.pfv.* [*infl.* **-жу́, -ди́шь**] **1,** *pfv. of* **прогля́дывать** (*in sense #1*). **2,** to overlook. **3,** to gaze at; stare at (*for a certain length of time*).

прогля́дывать *v.impfv.* **1,** [*pfv.* **прогляде́ть**] *colloq.* to look over; skim; scan. **2,** [*pfv.* **прогляну́ть**] to appear; come partly into view; peep.

прогляну́ть [*infl.* **-гляну́, -гля́нешь**] *v., pfv. of* **прогля́дывать** (*in sense #2*).

прогна́ть [*infl.* **-гоню́, -го́нишь**; *past fem.* **прогнала́**] *v., pfv. of* **прогоня́ть**.

прогнива́ть *v.impfv.* [*pfv.* **прогни́ть**] to rot through.

прогни́ть [*infl. like* **гнить**] *v., pfv. of* **прогнива́ть**.

прогно́з *n.* prognosis; forecast.

прогнози́рование *n.* prognostication.

прогнози́ровать *v.impfv.* [*pres.* **-рую, -руешь**] to prognosticate; predict.

прогну́ть *v., pfv. of* **прогиба́ть**. —**прогну́ться**, *refl., pfv. of* **прогиба́ться**.

прогова́ривать *v.impfv.* [*pfv.* **проговори́ть**] to say; utter. —**прогова́риваться**, *refl.* to spill the beans; let the cat out of the bag.

проговори́ть *v.pfv.* **1,** *pfv. of* **прогова́ривать**. **2,** to talk; converse (*for a certain length of time*). —**проговори́ться**, *refl., pfv. of* **прогова́риваться**.

проголода́ться *v.r.pfv.* to be hungry; get hungry.

проголосова́ть *v., pfv. of* **голосова́ть**.

прого́н *n.* **1,** driving (*of animals*). **2,** girder. **3,** stairwell.

прогоня́ть *v.impfv.* [*pfv.* **прогна́ть**] **1,** to drive (animals). **2,** to drive away; chase away. **3,** *fig., colloq.* to dispel. **4,** *colloq.* to fire; dismiss.

прогора́ть *v.impfv.* [*pfv.* **прогоре́ть**] **1,** (*of wood*) to be burned completely. **2,** to be damaged (*by fire*). **3,** *fig., colloq.* to go bankrupt; go broke.

прого́рклый *adj.* rancid.

прого́ркнуть [*past* **-го́рк, -го́ркла**] *v., pfv. of* **го́ркнуть**.

програ́мма *n.* **1,** program. **2,** syllabus.

программи́рование *n.* (computer) programming. —**язы́к программи́рования**, programming language.

программи́ровать *v.impfv.* [*pfv.* **запрограмми́ровать**; *pres.* **-рую, -руешь**] to program.

программи́ст *n.* (computer) programmer.

програ́ммный *adj.* **1,** program (*attrib.*): програ́ммная му́зыка, program music. **2,** programmed. —**програ́ммное обеспе́чение**, software.

прогрева́ть *v.impfv.* [*pfv.* **прогре́ть**] to warm up; make warm. —**прогрева́ться**, *refl.* to warm up; become warm.

прогреме́ть *v.pfv.* [*infl.* **-млю́, -ми́шь**] **1,** to thunder; ring out. **2,** to roar past.

прогре́сс *n.* progress.

прогресси́вный *adj.* progressive. —**прогресси́вный подохо́дный нало́г**, progressive income tax.

прогресси́ровать *v.impfv.* [*pres.* **-рую, -руешь**] **1,** to progress; make progress. **2,** (*of an illness*) to grow progressively worse.

прогре́ссия *n., math.* progression.

прогре́ть *v., pfv. of* **прогрева́ть**. —**прогре́ться**, *refl., pfv. of* **прогрева́ться**.

прогрыза́ть *v.impfv.* [*pfv.* **прогры́зть**] to gnaw through.

прогры́зть [*infl. like* **грызть**] *v., pfv. of* **прогрыза́ть**.

прогуде́ть *v.pfv.* [*infl.* **-жу́, -ди́шь**] **1,** to buzz; hum; drone. **2,** (*of a horn or factory whistle*) to sound; blow.

прогу́л *n.* unexcused absence from work or school; truancy; *pl.* absenteeism.

прогу́ливать *v.impfv.* [*pfv.* **прогуля́ть**] **1,** to miss; fail to show up for: прогу́ливать уро́ки, to play hooky; play truant. **2,** [*impfv. only*] *colloq.* to walk; take for a walk. —**прогу́ливаться**, *refl.* to take a walk; go for a stroll.

прогу́лка [*gen. pl.* **-лок**] *n.* **1,** walk; stroll. **2,** outing; ride; drive.

прогу́лочный *adj.* excursion (*attrib.*); pleasure (*attrib.*). —**прогу́лочная па́луба,** promenade deck. —**прогу́лочный шаг,** leisurely pace.

прогу́льщик *n.* **1,** shirker. **2,** truant.

прогуля́ть *v.pfv.* **1,** *pfv. of* **прогу́ливать. 2,** to walk; stroll (*for a certain length of time*). —**прогуля́ться,** *refl., pfv. of* **прогу́ливаться.**

продава́ть *v.impfv.* [*pfv.* **прода́ть**; *pres.* -**даю́, -даёшь**] **1,** to sell. **2,** to sell out; betray. —**продава́ться,** *refl.* **1,** [*impfv. only*] to sell; be selling (*well, poorly, etc.*). **2,** [*impfv. only*] to be for sale. **3,** to sell oneself. **4,** to be a traitor; (*with dat.*) sell out to.

продаве́ц [*gen.* -**вца́**] *n.* seller; salesman; salesperson.

продави́ть [*infl.* -**давлю́, -да́вишь**] *v., pfv. of* **прода́вливать.**

прода́вливать *v.impfv.* [*pfv.* **продави́ть**] **1,** to cause to sag in the middle. **2,** to break through. **3,** to make a hole in.

продавщи́ца *n.* saleslady; salesgirl.

прода́жа *n.* sale. —**в прода́же,** in stock. —**нет в прода́же,** out of stock; not on sale; sold out.

прода́жность *n.f.* corruption; venality.

прода́жный *adj.* **1,** sale (*attrib.*); selling (*attrib.*): прода́жная цена́, selling price. **2,** for sale. **3,** corrupt; venal. —**прода́жная же́нщина,** prostitute.

прода́ть [*infl. like* **дать**; *past* **про́дал, продала́, про́дало, про́дали**] *v., pfv. of* **продава́ть.** —**прода́ться,** *refl.* [*past tense stress as in* **да́ться**] *pfv. of* **продава́ться.**

продвига́ть *v.impfv.* [*pfv.* **продви́нуть**] **1,** to move (something) forward. **2,** (*with* **к**) to move (something) toward; (*with* **че́рез**) move through. **3,** to promote; advance. **4,** *colloq.* to move along; expedite. —**продвига́ться,** *refl.* **1,** to move forward; move ahead; advance. **2,** *fig.* to advance; move up. **3,** *colloq.* to move along; make progress.

продвиже́ние *n.* **1,** advance; advancement. **2,** promotion.

продви́нутый *adj.* advanced.

продви́нуть *v., pfv. of* **продвига́ть.** —**продви́нуться,** *refl., pfv. of* **продвига́ться.**

продева́ть *v.impfv.* [*pfv.* **проде́ть**] to pass through: продева́ть ни́тку в иго́лку, to thread a needle.

прорекламировать *v., pfv. of* **деклами́ровать.**

проде́лка [*gen. pl.* -**лок**] *n.* prank; trick.

проде́лывать *v.impfv.* [*pfv.* **проде́лать**] **1,** to make a hole). **2,** to do; perform. **3,** to play (a trick).

продемонстри́ровать *v.pfv.* [*infl.* -**рую, -руешь**] to demonstrate; display; show.

продёргивать *v.impfv.* [*pfv.* **продёрнуть**] *colloq.* to pass through: продёргивать ни́тку в иго́лку, to thread a needle.

продержа́ть [*infl.* -**держу́, -де́ржишь**] to hold; keep (*for a certain length of time*). —**продержа́ться,** *refl.* **1,** to remain (*in a certain position*). **2,** to last. **3,** to hold out.

продёрнуть *v., pfv. of* **продёргивать.**

проде́ть [*infl.* -**де́ну, -де́нешь**] *v., pfv. of* **продева́ть.**

продешеви́ть [*infl.* -**влю́, -ви́шь**] to sell (something) cheap.

продиктова́ть *v., pfv. of* **диктова́ть.**

продира́ть *v.impfv.* [*pfv.* **продра́ть**] **1,** *colloq.* to tear; wear through. **2,** *in* продира́ть глаза́, to wake up; open one's eyes. —**продира́ться,** *refl., colloq.* **1,** to be torn; be worn through. **2,** to make one's way; force one's way.

продлева́ть *v.impfv.* [*pfv.* **продли́ть**] to extend; prolong.

продле́ние *n.* extension; prolongation.

продли́ть *v., pfv. of* **продлева́ть.** —**продли́ться,** *refl., pfv. of* **дли́ться.**

продово́льственный *adj.* food (*attrib.*). —**продово́льственый магази́н,** food store; grocery store. —**продово́льственные това́ры,** foodstuffs.

продово́льствие *n.* food.

продолби́ть *v., pfv. of* **долби́ть** (*in sense #1*).

продолгова́тый *adj.* oblong. —**продолгова́тый мозг,** medulla oblongata.

продолжа́тель *n.m.* continuer.

продолжа́ть *v.impfv.* [*pfv.* **продо́лжить**] **1,** [*usu. impfv.*] to continue. **2,** [*usu. pfv.*] to extend; prolong. —**продолжа́ться,** *refl.* to continue; last; go on.

продолже́ние *n.* **1,** continuation. **2,** sequel. —**в продолже́ние** (+ *gen.*), during; in the course of. —**продолже́ние сле́дует,** "to be continued" (in the next issue).

продолжи́тельность *n.f.* length; duration. —**продолжи́тельность жи́зни,** life expectancy.

продолжи́тельный *adj.* prolonged; long.

продо́лжить *v., pfv. of* **продолжа́ть.** —**продо́лжиться,** *refl., pfv. of* **продолжа́ться.**

продо́льный *adj.* **1,** longitudinal. **2,** *naut.* fore-and-aft. —**продо́льная пила́,** ripsaw.

продохну́ть *v.pfv., colloq.* to take a deep breath. —**не** (*or* **нельзя́**) **продохну́ть,** it's impossible to breathe.

продра́ть [*infl.* -**деру́, -дерёшь**; *past fem.* **продрала́**] *v., pfv. of* **продира́ть.** —**продра́ться,** *refl.* [*past tense stress as in* **дра́ться**] *pfv. of* **продира́ться.**

продро́гнуть *v.pfv.* [*past* -**дро́г, -дро́гла**] to be chilled to the bone.

продува́ть *v.impfv.* [*pfv.* **проду́ть**] **1,** to blow out; clean out by blowing. **2,** [*impfv. only*] (*of a wind, draft, etc.*) *colloq.* to blow through. **3,** *impers.* to be chilled through (*by the wind*): Меня́ продуло, I am chilled (from the wind).

продувно́й *adj., colloq.* sly; crafty.

проду́кт *n.* **1,** product. **2,** *pl.* food; food products; groceries: моло́чные проду́кты, dairy products; заморо́женные проду́кты, frozen food(s).

продукти́вный *adj.* productive. —**продукти́вность,** *n.f.* productivity.

продукто́вый *adj.* food (*attrib.*). —**продукто́вый магази́н,** grocery store.

проду́кция *n.* **1,** production; output. **2,** products.

проду́манный *adj.* considered; carefully thought out.

проду́мывать *v.impfv.* [*pfv.* **проду́мать**] to think out; think through.

проду́ть [*infl.* -**ду́ю, -ду́ешь**] *v., pfv. of* **продува́ть.**

продыря́вливать *v.impfv.* [*pfv.* **продыря́вить**] *colloq.* **1,** to make a hole in. **2,** to wear holes in.

—**продыря́вливаться**, *refl.*, *colloq.* to develop holes; become full of holes.

продю́сер (сэ) *n.* producer (*of a motion picture*).

проеда́ть *v.impf.* [*pf.* **прое́сть**] **1,** to eat through. **2,** to corrode. **3,** *colloq.* to spend (one's money) on food.

прое́зд *n.* **1,** passage; getting across: Туда́ нет прое́зда, you cannot get there; there is no way to get there. **2,** trip: де́ньги на прое́зд, money for the trip. Пла́та за прое́зд, fare. Ско́лько сто́ит прое́зд в...?, what is the fare to...? **3,** passage; passageway. **4,** street; thoroughfare.

прое́здить *v.pf.* [*infl.* **-е́зжу, -е́здишь**] **1,** to travel (*for a certain length of time*). **2,** *colloq.* to spend (a certain amount of money) on a trip.

проездно́й *adj.*, *in* **проездна́я пла́та**, fare; **проездно́й биле́т**, ticket.

прое́здом *adv.* while passing through.

проезжа́ть *v.impf.* [*pf.* **прое́хать**] **1,** to ride; drive (along, through, past, etc.). **2,** (*with* **ми́мо**) to pass (by). **3,** to go (right) past (*inadvertently*). **4,** to cover (a certain distance).

прое́зжий *adj.* **1,** passing by; passing through. **2,** (*of a road*) fit for traffic; used for traffic. —*n.* person passing through.

прое́кт *n.* **1,** project. **2,** design. **3,** draft: прое́кт резолю́ции, draft resolution.

проекти́ровать *v.impf.* [*pf.* **спроекти́ровать**; *pres.* **-рую, -руешь**] **1,** to design. **2,** [*impf. only*] to plan. **3,** *math.* to project. **4,** to project (*onto a screen*).

проектиро́вщик *n.* designer.

прое́ктный *adj.* **1,** planning (*attrib.*). **2,** planned; projected. —**прое́ктная мо́щность, 1,** planned production capacity (*of a factory*). **2,** rated capacity (*of a machine*).

прое́ктор *n.* projector.

проекцио́нный *adj.*, *in* **проекцио́нный аппара́т** *or* **фона́рь**, projector.

прое́кция *n.* projection.

проём *n.* opening (*for a door, window, etc.*). Дверно́й проём, doorway.

прое́сть [*infl. like* **есть**] *v.*, *pf. of* **проеда́ть**.

прое́хать [*infl.* **-е́ду, -е́дешь**] *v.*, *pf. of* **проезжа́ть**. —**прое́хаться**, *refl.*, *colloq.* to go for a ride; go for a drive.

прожа́ренный *adj.* (*of meat*) well-done.

прожа́ривать *v.impf.* [*pf.* **прожа́рить**] to roast thoroughly; fry thoroughly.

прожда́ть *v.pf.* [*infl. like* **ждать**] to wait (*for a certain length of time*).

прожева́ть [*infl.* **-жую́, -жуёшь**] *v.*, *pf. of* **прожёвывать**.

прожё́вывать *v.impf.* [*pf.* **прожева́ть**] to chew well; chew thoroughly.

прожё́кт *n.*, *colloq.* impractical *or* unworkable scheme.

прожектёр *n.* promoter of impractical schemes.

проже́ктор *n.* searchlight; floodlight; spotlight.

проже́чь [*infl. like* **жечь**] *v.*, *pf. of* **прожига́ть**.

прожжё́нный *adj.*, *colloq.* arch; arrant; out-and-out.

прожива́ние *n.* **1,** residing; residence. **2,** squandering.

прожива́ть *v.impf.* [*pf.* **прожи́ть**] **1,** [*impf. only*] to live; reside. **2,** to spend; run through (a sum of

money). —**прожива́ться**, *refl.*, *colloq.* to use up all one's money.

прожига́ть *v.impf.* [*pf.* **прожё́чь**] **1,** to burn: прожё́чь дыру́ в (+ *prepl.*), to burn a hole in. **2,** to burn through. —**прожига́ть жизнь**, to lead a dissolute life.

прожи́лка [*gen. pl.* **-лок**] *n.* vein; streak.

прожи́тие *n.*, *in* **на прожи́тие**, to live on: де́ньги на прожи́тие, money to live on.

прожи́точный *adj.*, *in* **прожи́точный ми́нимум,** living wage; subsistence wage.

прожи́ть *v.pf.* [*infl.* **-живу́, -живёшь;** *past* **про́жил, прожила́, про́жило, про́жили**] **1,** *pfv. of* **прожива́ть** (*in sense #2*). **2,** to live (*for a certain length of time*). **3,** to live; get along: На э́то прожи́ть невозмо́жно, you can't live on that. —**прожи́ться**, *refl.* [*past* **прожи́лся, прожила́сь, прожило́сь** *or* **прожи́лось, прожили́сь** *or* **прожи́лись**] *pfv. of* **прожива́ться**.

прожо́рливый *adj.* voracious; gluttonous.

прожужжа́ть *v.pf.* [*infl.* **-жжу́, -жжи́шь**] to buzz. —**прожужжа́ть у́ши** (+ *dat.*), to tell (someone) over and over.

про́за *n.* prose.

проза́ик *n.* writer of prose.

прозаи́ческий *adj.* **1,** prose (*attrib.*). **2,** [*also,* **прозаи́чный**] prosaic.

прозва́ние *n.* nickname.

прозва́ть [*infl. like* **звать**] *v.*, *pfv. of* **прозыва́ть**.

прозвене́ть *v.pfv.* [*infl.* **-ни́т, -ня́т**] to ring out; resound.

про́звище *n.* nickname.

прозвони́ть *v.pfv.* **1,** (*of a bell*) to ring. **2,** to announce by ringing a bell.

прозвуча́ть *v.*, *pfv. of* **звуча́ть**.

прозева́ть *v.*, *pfv. of* **зева́ть** (*in sense #3*).

прозели́т *n.* proselyte.

прозимова́ть *v.*, *pfv. of* **зимова́ть**.

прозорли́вый *adj.* sagacious; perspicacious. —**прозорли́вость,** *n.f.* sagacity; perspicacity; acumen.

прозра́чный *adj.* **1,** transparent. **2,** (*of water, air, etc.*) clear. **3,** (*of material*) very thin; gauzy. **4,** (*of a hint*) broad. —**прозра́чность,** *n.f.* transparency.

прозрева́ть *v.impf.* [*pf.* **прозре́ть**] **1,** to regain one's eyesight. **2,** *fig.* to see things clearly; see the light.

прозре́ние *n.* **1,** regaining one's eyesight. **2,** *fig.* insight; discernment.

прозре́ть [*infl.* **-зрю́, -зри́шь**] *v.*, *pfv. of* **прозрева́ть**.

прозыва́ть *v.impf.* [*pf.* **прозва́ть**] to nickname.

прозяба́ть *v.impf.* to vegetate (*lit. & fig.*).

прозя́бнуть *v.pfv.* [*past* **-зя́б, -зя́бла**] *colloq.* to be frozen; be chilled to the bone.

проигра́ть *v.pfv.* **1,** *pfv. of* **прои́грывать**. **2,** to play (*for a certain length of time*). —**проигра́ться,** *refl.*, *pfv. of* **прои́грываться**.

прои́грыватель *n.m.* record player.

прои́грывать *v.impf.* [*pf.* **проигра́ть**] **1,** to lose. **2,** to gamble away. **3,** *colloq.* to play; perform. —**прои́грываться**, *refl.* to gamble away all one's money.

про́игрыш *n.* **1,** loss; defeat. **2,** losses (*in gambling*). —**быть в про́игрыше**, to be the loser; end up losing.

про́игрышный *adj.* losing.

произведе́ние *n.* **1,** work (*of art or literature*). **2,** *math.* product.

произвести́ [*infl. like* вести́] *v., pfv. of* производи́ть.

производи́тель *n.m.* **1,** producer. **2,** sire. —**произ-води́тель рабо́т,** construction superintendent; foreman.

производи́тельный *adj.* productive. —**производи́-тельность,** *n.f.* productivity.

производи́ть *v.impfv.* [*pfv.* произвести́; *pres.* -вожу́, -во́дишь] **1,** [*usu. impfv.*] to produce; manufacture. **2,** to conduct; carry out. **3,** to produce; cause; create. **4,** to make (an impression, calculation, repairs, etc.). **5,** to fire (a shot). **6,** to produce; give birth to. Производи́ть на свет, to bring into the world. **7,** (*with* в + *nom. pl.*) to promote (to): Его́ произвели́ в капита́ны, he was promoted to captain.

произво́дный *adj.* derivative. —**произво́дная,** *n., math.* derivative. —**произво́дное,** *n., chem.* derivative.

произво́дственный *adj.* production (*attrib.*); industrial.

произво́дство *n.* **1,** production. **2,** manufacture. **3,** conducting; carrying out. **4,** promotion. **5,** *colloq.* factory: рабо́тать на произво́дстве, to work in a factory.

произво́л *n.* **1,** arbitrary rule; tyranny; despotism. **2,** arbitrariness. —**оставля́ть** *or* **бро́сить на произво́л судьбы́,** to leave to the mercy of fate.

произво́льный *adj.* **1,** arbitrary. **2,** *physiol.* voluntary. —**произво́льно,** *adv.* arbitrarily.

произнесе́ние *n.* **1,** pronouncement; pronouncing (*of a sentence*). **2,** giving (*of a speech*).

произнести́ [*infl. like* нести́] *v., pfv. of* произноси́ть.

произноси́ть *v.impfv.* [*pfv.* произнести́; *pres.* -ношу́, -но́сишь] **1,** to pronounce. **2,** to utter (a word); deliver (a speech, sermon, toast, etc.).

произноше́ние *n.* pronunciation.

произойти́ [*infl.* произойдёт; *past* произошёл, произошла́, произошло́, произошли́] *v., pfv. of* происходи́ть.

произраста́ть *v.impfv.* [*pfv.* произрасти́] to sprout; spring up.

произрасти́ [*infl. like* расти́] *v., pfv. of* произраста́ть.

проиллюстри́ровать *v., pfv. of* иллюстри́ровать.

проинформи́ровать *v., pfv. of* информи́ровать.

про́иски [*gen.* -ков] *n.pl.* intrigues; schemes; machinations.

проистека́ть *v.impfv.* [*pfv.* происте́чь] (*with* из *or* от) to arise (out of); stem (from); spring (from); result (from).

происте́чь [*infl. like* течь] *v., pfv. of* проистека́ть.

происходи́ть *v.impfv.* [*pfv.* произойти́; *pres.* -хожу́, -хо́дишь] **1,** to happen; occur; take place. **2,** (*with* от) to result (from); be the result (of). **3,** (*with* от *or* из) to be descended (from); come (from).

происхожде́ние *n.* **1,** origin. **2,** parentage; descent; extraction; ancestry. Англича́нин по происхожде́нию, of English origin; English by birth.

происше́ствие *n.* incident.

пройдо́ха *n.m. & f., colloq.* sly person; rascal.

про́йма *n.* armhole.

пройти́ [*infl.* пройду́, пройдёшь; *past* прошёл, прошла́, прошло́, прошли́] *v., pfv. of* проходи́ть. —**пройти́сь,** *refl., pfv. of* проха́живаться.

прок [*2nd gen.* про́ку] *n., colloq.* use; good: Како́й прок в э́том?; что про́ку от э́того?, what's the good of it?

прокажённый *adj.* leprous. —*n.* leper.

прока́за *n.* **1,** leprosy. **2,** prank; trick.

прока́зить *v.impfv.* [*pfv.* напрока́зить; *pres.* -жу, -зишь] *colloq.* = прока́зничать.

прока́зливый *adj., colloq.* mischievous.

прока́зник *n.* mischief-maker; prankster.

прока́зничать *v.impfv.* [*pfv.* напрока́зничать] to play pranks; horse around.

прока́лывать *v.impfv.* [*pfv.* проколо́ть] to prick; pierce; puncture.

проканите́литься *v.r., pfv. of* каните́литься.

прока́пывать *v.impfv.* [*pfv.* прокопа́ть] **1,** to dig (a canal, ditch, etc.). **2,** to dig through.

прока́т *n.* **1,** rental. **2,** rolling (*of metal*). **3,** rolled metal. Стально́й прока́т, rolled steel.

проката́ть *v., pfv. of* прока́тывать.

прокати́ть *v.pfv.* [*infl.* -качу́, -ка́тишь] **1,** to roll. **2,** to take for a ride. **3,** *v.i.* to roll by; roll past. **4,** *colloq.* to fail to elect; reject at the polls. **5,** *colloq.* to berate; roundly condemn. —**прокати́ться,** *refl.* **1,** to roll; roll along. **2,** to go for a ride. **3,** (*with* по) to sweep across; sweep over.

прока́тка *n.* rolling (*of metal*).

прока́тный *adj.* **1,** for rent; rented; rental (*attrib.*). **2,** of or pert. to the rolling of metal: прока́тный стан, rolling mill. **3,** (*of metal*) rolled.

прока́тывать *v.impfv.* [*pfv.* прокати́ть] **1,** to roll flat; press. **2,** to roll (metal).

прока́шливаться *v.r.impfv.* [*pfv.* прока́шляться] to clear one's throat.

прокипяти́ть *v.pfv.* [*infl.* -чу́, -ти́шь] to boil (thoroughly).

проки́снуть [*past* -ки́с, -ки́сла] *v., pfv. of* ки́снуть.

прокла́дка *n.* **1,** laying (*of a road, pipeline, etc.*). **2,** padding. **3,** washer; gasket.

прокла́дывать *v.impfv.* [*pfv.* проложи́ть] **1,** to lay; build (a road, pipeline, etc.). **2,** to make; form (a path, trail, etc.). **3,** (*with instr.*) to interlay (with); pack (with). —**прокла́дывать путь** *or* **доро́гу, 1,** to blaze a trail. p.g. (*with dat.*) to pave (*or* clear) the way (for). —**прокла́дывать себе́ доро́гу,** to make one's way in the world.

проклама́ция *n.* **1,** leaflet. **2,** *obs.* proclamation.

проклами́ровать *v.impfv. & pfv.* [*pres.* -рую, -руешь] to proclaim.

проклёвываться *v.r.impfv.* [*pfv.* проклю́нуться] *colloq.* **1,** (*of a chick*) to break out of its shell (and be born). **2,** *fig.* to emerge; come into being.

прокле́ивать *v.impfv.* [*pfv.* прокле́ить] to smear; cover (*with paste or glue*).

проклина́ть *v.impfv.* [*pfv.* прокля́сть] **1,** to curse; damn. Проклина́ть тот день, когда́..., to rue the day when... **2,** [*impfv. only*] *colloq.* to berate.

проклю́нуться *v.r., pfv. of* проклёвываться.

прокля́сть [*infl.* -кляну́, -кляне́шь; *past* про́клял, прокляла́, про́кляло, про́кляли] *v., pfv. of* проклина́ть.

прокля́тие *n.* 1, curse: налага́ть прокля́тие на, to place a curse on. 2, damnation; perdition. 3, curse word; swearword. —*interj.* damn it!; damn it all!

про́клятый *past passive part. of* прокля́сть: Будь я про́клят (про́клята), е́сли..., I'll be damned if...

прокля́тый *adj.* cursed; damned; accursed.

проко́л *n.* puncture.

проколо́ть [*infl.* -колю́, -ко́лешь] *v., pfv. of* прока́лывать.

прокомменти́ровать *v., pfv. of* комменти́ровать.

прокомпости́ровать *v., pfv. of* компости́ровать.

проконспекти́ровать *v., pfv. of* конспекти́ровать.

проко́нсул *n.* proconsul.

проконсульти́ровать *v., pfv. of* консульти́ровать. —проконсульти́роваться, *refl., pfv. of* консульти́роваться.

проконтроли́ровать *v., pfv. of* контроли́ровать.

прокопа́ть *v., pfv. of* прока́пывать.

прокопте́лый *adj., colloq.* sooty; covered with soot.

проко́рм *n.* nourishment; sustenance.

прокорми́ть *v., pfv. of* корми́ть (*in sense #3*). —прокорми́ться, *refl., colloq.* 1, to feed oneself; sustain oneself. 2, (*with instr.*) to subsist (on).

прокорректи́ровать *v., pfv. of* корректи́ровать.

проко́с *n.* swath.

прокра́дываться *v.r.impfv.* [*pfv.* прокра́сться] to sneak; steal; creep (into, through, etc.).

прокра́сться [*infl. like* кра́сться] *v.r., pfv. of* прокра́дываться.

прокрича́ть *v.pfv.* [*infl.* -чу́, -чи́шь] 1, to shout. 2, *fig.* to trumpet; crow.

прокурату́ра *n.* office of the public prosecutor.

прокуро́р *n.* public prosecutor. —прокуро́рский, *adj.* public prosecutor's.

прокуси́ть [*infl.* -кушу́, -ку́сишь] *v., pfv. of* проку́сывать.

проку́сывать *v.impfv.* [*pfv.* прокуси́ть] to bite through.

прокути́ть *v.pfv.* [*infl.* -кучу́, -ку́тишь] 1, *v.t.* to squander; dissipate. 2, *v.i.* to go on a binge.

прола́мывать *v.impfv.* [*pfv.* проломи́ть] 1, to break through; make a hole in. 2, to fracture (one's skull). —прола́мываться, *refl.* to break; give way.

пролега́ть *v.impfv.* (*of a road*) to lie; run; pass.

пролежа́ть *v.pfv.* [*infl.* -лежу́, -лежи́шь] to lie (*for a certain length of time*).

про́лежень [*gen.* -жня] *n.m.* bedsore.

пролеза́ть *v.impfv.* [*pfv.* проле́зть] 1, (*with* сквозь *or* че́рез) to climb through. 2, (*with* в + *acc.*) to fit through; get through; go through. 3, (*with* в + *acc.*) *colloq.* to worm one's way into.

проле́зть [*infl. like* лезть] *v., pfv. of* пролеза́ть.

проле́т *n.* 1, flight. 2, open space. 3, span (*of a bridge*). 4, *archit.* bay. 5, stairwell. 6, *colloq.* distance between two railway stations.

пролетариа́т *n.* proletariat. —пролета́рий, *n.* proletarian; worker. —пролета́рский, *adj.* proletarian.

пролета́ть *v.impfv.* [*pfv.* пролете́ть] 1, to fly; (*with* над) fly over; (*with* че́рез) fly across; (*with* ми́мо) fly past. 2, to fly (a certain distance). 3, *fig.* (*of time*) to fly by.

пролете́ть [*infl.* -чу́, -ти́шь] *v., pfv. of* пролета́ть.

проле́тка [*gen. pl.* -ток] *n.* open carriage.

проли́в *n.* strait; channel; sound.

пролива́ть *v.impfv.* [*pfv.* проли́ть] 1, to spill. 2, to shed (light, tears, blood, etc.). —пролива́ться, *refl.* to spill; be spilled.

проливно́й *adj.* (*of rain*) driving; torrential.

проли́ть [*infl.* -лью́, -лье́шь; *past* про́лил *or* проли́л, пролила́, про́лило *or* проли́ло, про́лили *or* проли́ли] *v., pfv. of* пролива́ть. —проли́ться, *refl.* [*past tense stress as in* ли́ться] *pfv. of* пролива́ться.

проло́г *n.* prologue.

проложи́ть [*infl.* -ложу́, -ло́жишь] *v., pfv. of* прокла́дывать.

проло́м *n.* break; breach.

проломи́ть [*infl.* -ломлю́, -ло́мишь] *v., pfv. of* прола́мывать. —проломи́ться, *refl., pfv. of* прола́мываться.

прома́зать [*infl.* -ма́жу, -ма́жешь] *v., pfv. of* ма́зать (*in sense #6*) *and* прома́зывать.

прома́зывать *v.impfv.* [*pfv.* прома́зать] 1, to oil; grease (*thoroughly*). 2, *colloq.* to miss (*in shooting or games*).

прома́сливать *v.impfv.* [*pfv.* прома́слить] to treat with oil.

прома́тывать *v.impfv.* [*pfv.* промота́ть] *colloq.* to squander; dissipate.

про́мах *n.* 1, miss (*in shooting*). 2, *fig.* blunder. —ма́лый не про́мах, nobody's fool.

промахну́ться *v.r.pfv.* 1, to miss (*in striking, shooting, etc.*). 2, *colloq.* to make a blunder.

прома́чивать *v.impfv.* [*pfv.* промочи́ть] to drench; soak. Промочи́ть но́ги, to get one's feet wet. —промочи́ть го́рло, to wet one's whistle.

промедле́ние *n.* delay.

проме́длить *v.pfv.* to delay; procrastinate.

проме́жность *n.f.* crotch.

промежу́ток [*gen.* -тка] *n.* 1, space (*between two objects*). 2, interval (*of time*).

промежу́точный *adj.* 1, intermediate. Промежу́точной да́льности, intermediate-range. 2, intervening; interim. —промежу́точные вы́боры, off-year elections.

промелькну́ть *v.pfv.* 1, to flash by; flash past. 2, (*of a thought*) to flash across one's mind. 3, *fig.* to appear momentarily; be faintly perceptible.

проме́нивать *v.impfv.* [*pfv.* променя́ть] to exchange; trade; barter.

промерза́ть *v.impfv.* [*pfv.* проме́рзнуть] 1, to be frozen solid. 2, to be chilled through.

проме́рзлый *adj.* frozen.

проме́рзнуть [*past* -мёрз, -мёрзла] *v., pfv. of* промерза́ть.

проме́ривать *v.impfv.* [*pfv.* проме́рить] to measure; survey.

промеря́ть *v.impfv.* = проме́ривать.

Промете́й *n.* Prometheus.

проме́тий *n.* promethium.

промешка́ть *v.pfv., colloq.* to linger; dawdle.

промо́зглый *adj.* dank; damp.

промока́тельный *adj., in* промока́тельная бума́га, blotting paper.

промока́ть *v.impfv.* [*pfv.* промо́кнуть] **1,** to get wet; get soaked; get drenched. **2,** [*impfv. only*] to be not waterproof: Плащ промока́ет, the raincoat is not waterproof. **3,** *v.t.* [*pfv.* промокну́ть] to blot; dry (ink).

промока́шка [*gen. pl.* -шек] *n., colloq.* blotter.

промо́кнуть [*past* -мо́к, -мо́кла] *v., pfv. of* промока́ть.

промокну́ть [*past* -мокну́л] *v., pfv. of* промока́ть (*in sense #3*).

промо́лвить *v.pfv.* [*infl.* -влю, -вишь] to utter; say.

промолча́ть *v.pfv.* [*infl.* -чу́, -чи́шь] to keep silent; say nothing.

проморга́ть *v.pfv., colloq.* **1,** to fail to notice. **2,** to miss; let slip by.

промота́ть *v., pfv. of* прома́тывать.

промочи́ть [*infl.* -мочу́, -мо́чишь] *v., pfv. of* прома́чивать.

промтова́рный *adj., in* промтова́рный магази́н, general store (*selling clothes, manufactured items, etc.*).

промтова́ры [*gen.* -ров] *n.pl.* manufactured goods (*contr. of* промы́шленные това́ры).

промча́ться *v.r.pfv.* [*infl.* -мчу́сь, -мчи́шься] to flash by; race by; speed by.

промыва́ть *v.impfv.* [*pfv.* промы́ть] **1,** to wash; cleanse; bathe. **2,** to pan (gold).

про́мысел [*gen.* -сла] *n.* **1,** trade: пушно́й про́мысел, fur trade. Куста́рный про́мысел, cottage industry. **2,** hunting; catching. Ры́бный про́мысел, fishing. **3,** *pl.* fields; mines: нефтяны́е про́мыслы, oil fields; соля́ны́е про́мыслы, salt mines.

про́мысл *n., relig.* Providence.

промысло́вый *adj.* **1,** commercial. **2,** sold commercially: промысло́вая пти́ца, game bird; промысло́вая ры́ба, food fish; промысло́вый зверь, animal hunted for its fur. **3,** producers': промысло́вая коопера́ция, producers' cooperative.

промы́ть [*infl.* -мо́ю, -мо́ешь] *v., pfv. of* промыва́ть.

промы́шленник *n.* manufacturer; industrialist.

промы́шленность *n.f.* industry.

промы́шленный *adj.* **1,** industrial. **2,** *in* промы́шленные това́ры, manufactured goods.

промышля́ть *v.impfv.* (*with instr.*) to earn one's living (by); make a living (from).

промя́млить *v., pfv. of* мя́млить.

прона́шивать *v.impfv.* [*pfv.* проноси́ть] to wear out (clothes). —**прона́шиваться,** *refl.* (*of clothes*) to wear out.

пронести́ [*infl. like* нести́] *v., pfv. of* проноси́ть[1]. —**пронести́сь,** *refl., pfv. of* проноси́ться.

пронза́ть *v.impfv.* [*pfv.* пронзи́ть] to pierce; impale.

пронзи́тельный *adj.* piercing.

пронзи́ть [*infl.* -нжу́, -нзи́шь] *v., pfv. of* пронза́ть.

прониза́ть [*infl.* -нижу́, -ни́жешь] *v., pfv. of* прони́зывать.

прони́зывать *v.impfv.* [*pfv.* прониза́ть] **1,** to pierce. **2,** *fig.* to penetrate; permeate.

прони́зывающий *adj.* penetrating; piercing.

проника́ть *v.impfv.* [*pfv.* прони́кнуть] (*with* в + *acc.*) **1,** to penetrate. **2,** to get into; leak (into); seep (into); filter (into). **3,** to get into; enter (*surreptitiously*). **4,** to infiltrate. **5,** *fig.* to delve into; (try to) fathom. —**проника́ться,** *refl.* (*with instr.*) to be filled (with); have a deep sense (of). Проника́ться к кому́-нибудь сочу́вствием, to feel truly sorry for someone. Они́ прони́клись взаи́мной симпа́тией, they developed a great fondness for each other.

проникнове́ние *n.* **1,** penetration; infiltration. **2,** feeling; sincerity.

проникнове́нный *adj.* heartfelt; earnest. —**проникнове́нно,** *adv.* with deep feeling; with emotion. —**проникнове́нность,** *n.f.* feeling; sincerity.

прони́кнуть [*past* -ни́к, -ни́кла] *v., pfv. of* проника́ть. —**прони́кнуться,** *refl., pfv. of* проника́ться.

пронима́ть *v.impfv.* [*pfv.* проня́ть] *colloq.* **1,** (*of cold, wind, etc.*) to penetrate. **2,** *fig.* to move; touch; affect.

проница́емый *adj.* permeable. —**проница́емость,** *n.f.* permeability.

проница́тельность *n.f.* astuteness; perspicacity; discernment; acumen; insight.

проница́тельный *adj.* **1,** astute; shrewd; penetrating; perspicacious. **2,** (*of a look*) penetrating.

проноси́ть[1] *v.impfv.* [*pfv.* пронести́; *pres.* -ношу́, -но́сишь] **1,** (*with* че́рез) to carry through; (*with* ми́мо) carry past. **3,** to carry quickly; whisk. **4,** to smuggle (something) into, past, *or* out of. **5,** *impers.* to pass: Грозу́ пронесло́, the storm has passed; the storm has blown over. —**проноси́ться,** *refl.* **1,** to rush past; flash by; sweep over. **2,** *fig.* (*of a rumor*) to start going around; (*of time*) to fly by.

проноси́ть[2] *v.pfv.* [*infl.* -ношу́, -но́сишь] **1,** *pfv. of* прона́шивать. **2,** to carry (*for a certain length of time*). **3,** to wear (*for a certain length of time*). —**проноси́ться,** *refl.* **1,** *pfv. of* прона́шиваться. **2,** (*of clothes*) to last (*a certain length of time*).

пронумерова́ть *v., pfv. of* нумерова́ть.

проны́ра *n.m. & f., colloq.* one always able to gain access; wire-puller.

проны́рливый *adj., colloq.* sneaky; slippery; able to worm one's way in.

проню́хивать *v.impfv.* [*pfv.* проню́хать] (*with acc. or* о) *colloq.* to hear about; get wind of.

проня́ть [*infl. like* поня́ть] *v., pfv. of* пронима́ть.

прообраз *n.* prototype.

пропага́нда *n.* **1,** propaganda. **2,** (*with gen.*) propagandizing (of).

пропаганди́ровать *v.impfv.* [*pres.* -рую, -руешь] to propagandize.

пропаганди́ст *n.* propagandist. —**пропаганди́стский,** *adj.* propagandistic; propaganda (*attrib.*).

пропада́ть *v.impfv.* [*pfv.* пропа́сть] **1,** to disappear; be missing: Где вы пропада́ли?; куда́ вы пропа́ли?, where did you disappear to?; where have you been? У меня́ пропа́ло зо́нтик, my umbrella has disappeared; I've lost my umbrella. **2,** to die; perish. **3,** to be wasted; go to waste. **4,** *colloq.* to be done for. —**пиши́ пропа́ло,** it's hopeless. —**пропади́ про́падом!,** *colloq.* damn it all! —**пропада́ть да́ром,** *see* да́ром.

пропа́жа *n.* **1,** disappearance; loss. **2,** lost object; missing thing.

пропа́лывать *v.impfv.* [*pfv.* **прополо́ть**] to weed.

пропа́н *n.* propane.

про́пасть [*pl.* **про́пасти, -сте́й, -стя́м**] *n.f.* **1,** abyss; chasm. Бездо́нная про́пасть, bottomless pit. **2,** *fig.* (*with* **ме́жду**) gulf (between); gap (between). **3,** (*with gen.*) *colloq.* lots of; tons of. **—на краю́ про́пасти,** on the brink of disaster.

пропа́сть [*infl. like* **пасть**] *v., pfv. of* **пропада́ть**.

пропа́хнуть *v.pfv.* [*past* **-па́х, -па́хла**] (*with instr.*) to become permeated with the smell of; reek (of).

пропа́щий *adj., colloq.* **1,** lost; gone for good. **2,** hopeless.

пропека́ть *v.impfv.* [*pfv.* **пропе́чь**] to bake thoroughly. **—пропека́ться,** *refl.* to be baked thoroughly.

пропе́ллер *n.* propeller.

пропе́ть *v.pfv.* [*infl.* **-пою́, -поёшь**] **1,** *pfv. of* **петь. 2,** to sing (*for a certain length of time*).

пропе́чь [*infl. like* **печь**] *v., pfv. of* **пропека́ть. —пропе́чься,** *refl., pfv. of* **пропека́ться**.

пропива́ть *v.impfv.* [*pfv.* **пропи́ть**] to drink away; squander by drinking.

пропи́ливать *v.impfv.* [*pfv.* **пропили́ть**] to saw through.

пропили́ть [*infl.* **-пилю́, -пи́лишь**] *v., pfv. of* **пропи́ливать**.

прописа́ть [*infl.* **-пишу́, -пи́шешь**] *v., pfv. of* **пропи́сывать. —прописа́ться,** *refl., pfv. of* **пропи́сываться**.

пропи́ска [*gen. pl.* **-сок**] *n.* **1,** registration. **2,** residence permit.

прописно́й *adj.* **1,** *in* прописна́я бу́ква, capital letter. **2,** conventional: прописна́я мора́ль, conventional morality. **—прописна́я и́стина,** truism.

пропи́сывать *v.impfv.* [*pfv.* **прописа́ть**] **1,** to prescribe (medicine). **2,** to register (someone). **—пропи́сываться,** *refl.* **1,** to register (*e.g.* at a hotel). **2,** to obtain a residence permit.

про́пись *n.f.* **1,** sample of writing (*used in school*). **2,** cliché; platitude. **—про́писью,** *adv.* written out: написа́ть число́ про́писью, to write out a number (*using letters*).

пропита́ние *n.* **1,** subsistence: сре́дства пропита́ния, means of subsistence. **2,** food; sustenance.

пропи́тывать *v.impfv.* [*pfv.* **пропита́ть**] **1,** to saturate; impregnate. **2,** *fig.* to permeate. **—пропи́тываться,** *refl.* **1,** to be saturated. **2,** *colloq.* to sustain oneself.

пропи́ть *v.pfv.* [*infl.* **-пью́, -пьёшь**; *past* **про́пил** *or* **пропи́л, пропила́, про́пило** *or* **пропи́ло, про́пили** *or* **пропи́ли**] **1,** *pfv. of* **пропива́ть. 2,** to drink (*for a certain length of time*).

пропла́вать *v.pfv.* **1,** to swim (*for a certain length of time*). **2,** to sail (*for a certain length of time*).

пропла́кать *v.pfv.* [*infl.* **-пла́чу, -пла́чешь**] to cry (*for a certain length of time*). **—пропла́кать глаза́,** *colloq.* to cry one's eyes out.

проплыва́ть *v.impfv.* [*pfv.* **проплы́ть**] **1,** to swim; sail; float; drift. **2,** (*with acc. or* **ми́мо**) to swim past; sail past. **3,** to swim; sail (a certain distance).

проплы́ть [*infl. like* **плыть**] *v., pfv. of* **проплыва́ть**.

пропове́дник *n.* **1,** preacher. **2,** *fig.* advocate; exponent; proponent.

пропове́довать *v.impfv.* [*pres.* **-дую, -дуешь**] **1,** to preach; propagate (a religion, idea, etc.). **2,** *v.i.* to preach (*deliver a sermon*).

про́поведь *n.f.* **1,** sermon. **2,** spreading; propagation.

пропо́йца *n.m. & f., colloq.* drunkard; drunk.

пропо́лза́ть *v.impfv.* [*pfv.* **проползти́**] to crawl; creep.

проползти́ [*infl. like* **ползти́**] *v., pfv. of* **пропо́лза́ть**.

пропо́лка *n.* weeding.

прополоска́ть *v., pfv. of* **полоска́ть**.

прополо́ть [*infl.* **-полю́, -по́лешь**] *v., pfv. of* **пропа́лывать**.

пропорциона́льно *adv.* **1,** proportionally; proportionately. **2,** (*with dat.*) proportionately with; in proportion to. **—пропорциона́льность,** *n.f.* proportion.

пропорциона́льный *adj.* **1,** proportional; proportionate. **2,** well-proportioned.

пропо́рция *n.* proportion.

пропоте́ть *v.pfv.* **1,** to perspire heavily. **2,** (*of an item of clothing*) to become drenched with perspiration.

про́пуск *n.* **1,** admission; admittance. **2,** passing through; letting through. **3,** omission. **4,** failure to attend; absence. **5,** blank; gap. **6,** [*pl.* **-ска́**] pass; permit. **7,** [*pl.* **-ска́**] password.

пропуска́ть *v.impfv.* [*pfv.* **пропусти́ть**] **1,** to admit; let in; let pass; let through. **2,** to pass through; run through; put through. **3,** to let in (light, water, etc.). **4,** *sports* to allow (a goal, point to be scored, etc.). **5,** to omit; leave out. **6,** to skip; pass over. **7,** to miss; fail to attend. **8,** to miss; let slip by.

пропускно́й *adj.* admission (*attrib.*). **—пропускна́я спосо́бность,** (carrying) capacity.

пропусти́ть [*infl.* **-пущу́, -пу́стишь**] *v., pfv. of* **пропуска́ть**.

прора́б *n.* construction superintendent; foreman (*contr. of* **производи́тель рабо́т**).

прораба́тывать *v.impfv.* [*pfv.* **прорабо́тать**] **1,** to work over; study carefully. **2,** *colloq.* to give (someone) a going over.

прорабо́тать *v.pfv.* **1,** *pfv. of* **прораба́тывать. 2,** to work (*for a certain length of time*).

прорабо́тка *n.* **1,** study; studying. **2,** *colloq.* public criticism; public censure.

прораста́ние *n.* germination; sprouting.

прораста́ть *v.impfv.* [*pfv.* **прорасти́**] to germinate; sprout.

прорасти́ [*infl. like* **расти́**] *v., pfv. of* **прораста́ть**.

про́рва *n., colloq.* **1,** huge amount. **2,** glutton.

прорва́ть [*infl.* **-рву́, -рвёшь**; *past fem.* **прорвала́**] *v., pfv. of* **прорыва́ть**[1]. **—прорва́ться,** *refl.* [*past tense stress as in* **рва́ться**] *pfv. of* **прорыва́ться**.

проре́з *n.* cut; slit; opening.

проре́зать [*infl.* **-ре́жу, -ре́жешь**] *v., pfv. of* **прореза́ть. —проре́заться,** *refl., pfv. of* **прореза́ться**.

прореза́ть *v.impfv.* [*pfv.* **проре́зать**] to cut; cut through. **—прореза́ться,** *refl.* (*of teeth*) to cut through: У ребёнка прореза́ются зу́бы, the child is teething.

прорези́нивать *v.impfv.* [*pfv.* **прорези́нить**] to rubberize.

про́резь *n.f.* cut; slit; opening.

прорепети́ровать *v., pfv. of* репети́ровать.

проре́ха *n.* 1, tear. 2, *fig.* deficiency; shortcoming.

прорецензи́ровать *v., pfv. of* рецензи́ровать.

проржа́веть *v.pfv.* to rust through.

прорица́ние *n.* prophecy; prediction. —прорица́-тель, *n.m.* prophet.

прорица́ть *v.impfv.* to prophesy.

проро́к *n.* prophet.

пророни́ть *v.pfv.* [*infl.* -роню́, -ро́нишь] 1, to utter: не пророни́ть ни сло́ва, not to utter a word. 2, to miss; fail to hear. —не пророни́ть (ни) слезы́ *or* слези́нки, not to shed a tear.

проро́ческий *adj.* prophetic. —проро́чество, *n.* prophecy.

проро́чить *v.impfv.* [*pfv.* напроро́чить] to prophesy.

проруба́ть *v.impfv.* [*pfv.* проруби́ть] 1, to cut through; hack through. 2, to make (an opening) by cutting through something.

проруби́ть [*infl.* -рублю́, -ру́бишь] *v., pfv. of* про-руба́ть.

про́рубь *n.f.* hole in the ice.

проры́в *n.* 1, bursting. 2, breach. 3, breakthrough. 4, *fig.* hitch; lag (*in production*).

прорыва́ть[1] *v.impfv.* [*pfv.* прорва́ть] 1, to tear. 2, to break through. 3, *impers.* to burst: Плоти́ну про-рва́ло, the dam burst. —прорыва́ться, *refl.* 1, to tear; break; burst. 2, to break through; (*with* сквозь) break through (something); (*with* к) break through (to); force one's way (to).

прорыва́ть[2] *v.impfv.* [*pfv.* проры́ть] to dig (a hole, canal, tunnel, etc.).

проры́ть [*infl.* -ро́ю, -ро́ешь] *v., pfv. of* прорыва́ть[2].

проса́ливать *v.impfv.* 1, [*pfv.* проса́лить] to grease. 2, [*pfv.* просоли́ть] to salt.

проса́чивание *n.* 1, seepage. 2, penetration; infiltration.

проса́чиваться *v.r.impfv.* [*pfv.* просочи́ться] 1, to seep. 2, (*with* в + *acc.*) to penetrate; infiltrate. 3, *fig.* (*of news, a rumor, etc.*) to leak out; (*with* в + *acc.*) fil-ter (into).

просве́рливать *v.impfv.* [*pfv.* просверли́ть] 1, to drill; bore (a hole). 2, to drill through; drill a hole in.

просверли́ть *v., pfv. of* сверли́ть (*in senses #1 & #2*) *and* просве́рливать.

просве́т *n.* 1, narrow shaft of light (*shining through an opening onto a surface*). 2, *fig.* bright spot (*in a situa-tion, one's life, etc.*). 3, open space; empty space. 4, opening; crack (*in a door or window*). 5, *mil.* stripe (*on shoulder insignia*).

просвети́тельный *adj.* educational.

просвети́ть *v.pfv.* 1, [*infl.* -свечу́, -све́тишь] *pfv. of* просве́чивать. 2, [*infl.* -свещу́, -свети́шь] *pfv. of* просвеща́ть.

просветле́ние *n.* 1, brightening (*of the sky*). 2, *fig.* lucid moment.

просветлённый *adj.* bright; clear; serene. —про-светлённый объекти́в, *photog.* coated lens.

просветле́ть *v., pfv. of* светле́ть.

просветля́ть *v.impfv.* [*pfv.* просветли́ть] 1, to brighten up. 2, to clarify. 3, to gladden.

просве́чивание *n.* X-raying; X-ray examination.

просве́чивать *v.impfv.* [*pfv.* просвети́ть] 1, (*of the sun*) to light up. 2, to X-ray. 3, [*impfv. only*] to be translucent. 4, [*impfv. only*] (*with* сквозь) to appear through; shine through.

просвеща́ть *v.impfv.* [*pfv.* просвети́ть] to enlighten.

просвеще́ние *n.* 1, enlightenment. 2, education.

просвира́ *n., Orth. Ch.* communion bread.

просви́рник *n.* mallow. *Also,* просвирня́к [*gen.* -няка́].

просвиста́ть *v.pfv.* [*infl.* -свищу́, -сви́щешь] 1, *pfv. of* просви́стывать. 2, to whistle; give a whistle. *Also,* просвисте́ть [*infl.* -свищу́, -свисти́шь].

просви́стывать *v.impfv.* [*pfv.* просвиста́ть *or* про-свисте́ть] 1, to whistle (a tune). 2, (*with* ми́мо *or* над) to whistle by; whistle past.

про́седь *n.f.* streaks of gray.

просе́ивать *v.impfv.* [*pfv.* просе́ять] to sift.

про́сека *n.* path cleared in a forest.

просёлок [*gen.* -лка] *n.* country road; byroad.

просёлочный *adj., in* просёлочная доро́га, = про-сёлок.

просе́ять [*infl.* -се́ю, -се́ешь] *v., pfv. of* просе́ивать.

просиде́ть [*infl.* -жу́, -ди́шь] *v., pfv. of* проси́жи-вать.

проси́живать *v.impfv.* [*pfv.* просиде́ть] 1, to sit (*for a certain length of time*). 2, (*with* над) to spend (a great deal of time) working on (*while seated*); labor over. 3, to spend (a certain amount of time) in prison. 4, *col-loq.* to stay (*for a certain length of time*). 5, *colloq.* to wear out the seat of; wear out by sitting on.

про́синь *n.f.* bluish tint.

проси́тель *n.m., obs.* applicant; petitioner.

проси́тельный *adj.* pleading; suppliant.

проси́ть *v.impfv.* [*pfv.* попроси́ть; *pres.* прошу́, про́сишь] 1, to ask: попроси́ть кого́-нибудь смотре́ть за детьми́, to ask someone to look after the children. 2, to ask for; request: проси́ть кни́гу, to ask for a book; проси́ть разреше́ния, to ask (for) permission; проси́ть (о) по́мощи, to ask for help. 3, to beg: проси́ть проще́ния, to beg someone's par-don. Я вас о́чень прошу́!, please!; I beg of you! 4, to invite; call; ask: Попроси́те его́ войти́, ask him to come in. Прошу́ всех к столу́!, everyone please come to the table! 5, [*impfv. only*] to ask; charge (a certain amount of money). 6, (*with* за + *acc.*) to plead for (someone). —прошу́ вас!, please go ahead!; (*when serving food*) please help yourself!; (*when offering a chair*) please have a seat!; (*when en-tering a doorway*) after you!

проси́ться *v.r.impfv.* [*pfv.* попроси́ться; *pres.* про-шу́сь, про́сишься] 1, (*with inf. or* в/на + *acc.*) to ask (for); apply (for); ask permission (to). Проси́ться обра́тно, to ask (for) permission to go back. 2, [*impfv. only*] (*with* на + *acc.*): проси́ться на язы́к, to be on the tip of one's tongue; проси́ться на карти́ну, to cry out to be painted.

просия́ть *v.pfv.* 1, (*of the sun*) to begin to shine. 2, *fig.* (*with instr.*) to beam (with joy); light up (with a smile).

проскака́ть *v.pfv.* [*infl.* -скачу́, -ска́чешь] 1, to gal-lop. 2, (*with* ми́мо) to gallop past.

проска́кивать *v.impfv.* [*pfv.* **проскочи́ть**] **1,** *v.t.* to race through; race past. Проскочи́ть светофо́р, to go through a traffic light; run a red light. **2,** (*with* **сквозь**) to get through; slip through. **3,** to slip (into a small opening). **4,** *colloq.* (*of time*) to slip by. **5,** *colloq.* (*of mistakes*) to creep in.

проска́льзывание *n.* slippage.

проска́льзывать *v.impfv.* [*pfv.* **проскользну́ть**] **1,** to slip through (a small opening). **2,** to slip; sneak (into, past, through, etc.).

просквози́ть *v.pfv., impers.* to catch a chill from sitting in a draft: Не сиди́ здесь — тебя́ просквози́т, don't sit here (in the draft) — you'll catch a chill.

просклоня́ть *v., pfv. of* **склоня́ть** (*in sense #3*).

проскользну́ть *v., pfv. of* **проска́льзывать**.

проскочи́ть [*infl.* **-скочу́, -ско́чишь**] *v., pfv. of* **проска́кивать**.

проскрипе́ть *v., pfv. of* **скрипе́ть**.

проскурня́к [*gen.* **-няка́**] *n.* mallow.

проскуча́ть *v.pfv.* to be bored (*for a certain length of time*).

просла́вить [*infl.* **-влю, -вишь**] *v., pfv. of* **прославля́ть**. —**просла́виться,** *refl., pfv. of* **прославля́ться**.

прославле́ние *n.* glorification.

просла́вленный *adj.* celebrated; renowned.

прославля́ть *v.impfv.* [*pfv.* **просла́вить**] **1,** to make famous. **2,** to glorify; celebrate (*in song, poetry, etc.*). —**прославля́ться,** *refl.* (*with instr.*) to become famous (for).

проследи́ть [*infl.* **-жу́, -ди́шь**] *v., pfv. of* **просле́живать**.

просле́довать *v.pfv.* [*infl.* **-дую, -дуешь**] to proceed.

просле́живать *v.impfv.* [*pfv.* **проследи́ть**] **1,** to follow; trail; shadow. **2,** *fig.* to trace; trace the development of. **3,** (*with* за + *instr.*) to monitor; keep tabs on. Проследи́ть за тем, что́бы..., to see (to it) that...

прослези́ться *v.r.pfv.* [*infl.* **-жу́сь, -зи́шься**] to shed a few tears.

просло́йка [*gen. pl.* **-о́ек**] *n.* **1,** layer. **2,** *fig.* social stratum.

прослужи́ть *v.pfv.* [*infl.* **-служу́, -слу́жишь**] **1,** to serve (*for a certain length of time*). **2,** (*of a product*) to last (*for a certain length of time*).

прослу́шать *v.pfv.* **1,** *pfv. of* **слу́шать** (*in sense #4*) *and* **прослу́шивать**. **2,** *colloq.* to fail to hear; fail to catch; miss.

прослу́шивать *v.impfv.* [*pfv.* **прослу́шать**] **1,** to listen to (*from beginning to end*). **2,** *med.* to examine (*by listening to*). **3,** to "bug" a room; tap (a telephone). —**прослу́шиваться,** *refl.* [*impfv. only*] **1,** to be heard. **2,** to be "bugged."

прослы́ть *v., pfv. of* **слыть**.

прослы́шать *v.pfv.* [*infl.* **-шу, -шишь**] (*with* о) *colloq.* to hear (about).

просма́тривать *v.impfv.* [*pfv.* **просмотре́ть**] **1,** to look over; glance over; scan. **2,** to examine; view. **3,** [*usu. pfv.*] to overlook; miss. —**просма́триваться,** *refl.* [*impfv. only*] to be visible.

просмо́тр *n.* **1,** examination. **2,** viewing: предвари́тельный просмо́тр, preview. **3,** oversight; error.

просмотре́ть [*infl.* **-смотрю́, -смо́тришь**] *v., pfv. of* **просма́тривать**.

просну́ться *v.r., pfv. of* **просыпа́ться**.

про́со *n.* millet.

просо́вывать *v.impfv.* [*pfv.* **просу́нуть**] to stick; thrust (into, through, etc.).

просо́дия *n.* prosody. —**просоди́ческий,** *adj.* prosodic.

просоли́ть [*infl.* **-солю́, -со́лишь** *or* **-соли́шь**] *v., pfv. of* **проса́ливать** (*in sense #2*).

просо́хнуть [*past* **-сох, -со́хла**] *v., pfv. of* **просыха́ть**.

просочи́ться *v.r., pfv. of* **проса́чиваться**.

проспа́ть *v.pfv.* [*infl. like* **спать**] **1,** *pfv. of* **просыпа́ть**[2]. **2,** to sleep (*for a certain length of time*). —**проспа́ться,** *refl., colloq.* to sleep it off.

проспе́кт *n.* **1,** broad street; avenue: Не́вский проспе́кт, the Nevsky Prospekt (*main street of St. Petersburg*). **2,** outline; prospectus. **3,** advertisement: рекла́мные проспе́кты, promotional material.

проспо́рить *v.pfv.* **1,** to lose (*in a bet*). **2,** to argue (*for a certain length of time*).

проспряга́ть *v., pfv. of* **спряга́ть**.

просро́ченный *adj.* **1,** overdue. **2,** expired.

просро́чивать *v.impfv.* [*pfv.* **просро́чить**] **1,** to be behind in. **2,** to exceed; overstep (a time limit). **3,** to allow to expire: Мой па́спорт просро́чен, my passport has expired.

просро́чка *n.* **1,** delinquency (*in paying*). **2,** expiration. **3,** *in* просро́чка вре́мени, *chess* overstepping the time limit.

проста́вить [*infl.* **-ста́влю, -ста́вишь**] *v., pfv. of* **проставля́ть**.

проставля́ть *v.impfv.* [*pfv.* **проста́вить**] to write in; fill in; enter.

проста́ивать *v.impfv.* [*pfv.* **простоя́ть**] **1,** to stand; stay (*for a certain length of time*). **2,** to stand idle; sit idle; lie idle.

проста́к [*gen.* **-стака́**] *n.* simpleton.

проста́та *n.* prostate (gland).

просте́йшие *n.pl., decl. as an adj.* protozoa.

просте́нок [*gen.* **-нка**] *n.* space between windows; pier.

простере́ть [*past* **-стёр, -стёрла**; *future rarely used*] *v., pfv. of* **простира́ть**[1]. —**простере́ться,** *refl., pfv. of* **простира́ться**.

простёртый *adj.* **1,** (*of one's hand or arm*) outstretched. **2,** stretched out on the floor or ground.

просте́цкий *adj., colloq.* **1,** simple; humble; unpretentious. **2,** direct; straightforward.

простира́ть[1] *v.impfv.* [*pfv.* **простере́ть**] to stretch out; hold out; extend. —**простира́ться,** *refl.* to extend; stretch.

простира́ть[2] *v., pfv. of* **прости́рывать**.

прости́рывать *v.impfv.* [*pfv.* **простира́ть**] *colloq.* to wash; launder.

прости́тельный *adj.* pardonable; forgivable; excusable.

проститу́тка [*gen. pl.* **-ток**] *n.* prostitute. —**проститу́ция,** *n.* prostitution.

прости́ть [*infl.* **прощу́, прости́шь**] *v., pfv. of* **проща́ть**. —**прости́ться,** *refl., pfv. of* **проща́ться**.

про́сто *adv.* simply. —*adj., used predicatively,* simple: Э́то не так про́сто, it's not so simple. Вам про́сто критикова́ть, it is easy for you to criticize. —**про́сто так, 1,** as usual; in the usual manner. **2,** for no particular reason.

простова́тый *adj., colloq.* **1,** simple-minded. **2,** naïve; ingenuous.

простоволо́сый *adj., colloq.* bareheaded.

простоду́шие *n.* simple-heartedness.

простоду́шный *adj.* **1,** simple-hearted. **2,** artless; ingenuous.

просто́й[1] *adj.* [*short form* **прост, проста́, про́сто, просты́;** *comp.* **про́ще**] **1,** simple. **2,** plain: просто́й материа́л, plain material; проста́я пи́ща, plain food. **3,** mere: просто́й сме́ртный, mere mortal. —**просты́м гла́зом,** with the naked (*or* unaided) eye. —**просто́е число́,** prime number.

просто́й[2] *n.* idle time; downtime.

простоква́ша *n.* thick sour milk; clabber.

про́сто-на́просто *adv.* simply (*used for emphasis*).

простонаро́дный *adj., obs.* of the common people. —**простонаро́дье,** *n., obs.* the common people.

простона́ть *v.pfv.* [*infl.* **-стону́, -сто́нешь**] to groan; moan.

просто́р *n.* **1,** space; expanse. **2,** range; scope; freedom.

просторе́чие *n.* vernacular; common speech. —**просторе́чный,** *adj.* vernacular.

просто́рный *adj.* **1,** spacious; roomy. **2,** (*of clothes*) loose; loose-fitting.

простосерде́чие *n.* simple-heartedness. —**простосерде́чный,** *adj.* simple-hearted.

простота́ *n.* simplicity.

простофи́ля *n.m. & f., colloq.* nincompoop.

простоя́ть *v.pfv.* **1,** *pfv. of* **проста́ивать. 2,** to remain (*for a certain length of time*).

простра́нный *adj.* **1,** vast; extensive. **2,** (*of a speech, letter, etc.*) lengthy; wordy; long-winded.

простра́нственный *adj.* spatial.

простра́нство *n.* space. —**безвозду́шное простра́нство,** vacuum. —**во́дное простра́нство,** body of water.

простра́ция *n.* prostration.

простра́чивать *v.impfv.* [*pfv.* **прострочи́ть**] to stitch.

простре́л *n.* lumbago.

простре́ливать *v.impfv.* [*pfv.* **прострели́ть**] **1,** to shoot through. **2,** [*impfv. only*] to rake (with machine-gun fire).

прострели́ть [*infl.* **-стрелю́, -стре́лишь**] *v., pfv. of* **простре́ливать.**

прострочи́ть *v., pfv. of* **строчи́ть** (*in sense #1*) *and* **простра́чивать.**

просту́да *n.* a cold.

простуди́ть [*infl.* **-стужу́, -сту́дишь**] *v., pfv. of* **простужа́ть.** —**простуди́ться,** *refl., pfv. of* **простужа́ться.**

просту́дливый *adj., colloq.* susceptible to colds; easily catching cold.

просту́дный *adj.* of or from a cold.

простужа́ть *v.impfv.* [*pfv.* **простуди́ть**] to allow to catch cold. —**простужа́ться,** *refl.* to catch cold.

просту́женный *adj.* **1,** having a cold: Я просту́жен(а), I have a cold. **2,** showing the effects of a cold.

просту́кивать *v.impfv.* [*pfv.* **просту́кать**] to tap.

проступа́ть *v.impfv.* [*pfv.* **проступи́ть**] **1,** to ooze. **2,** to appear; become faintly visible.

проступи́ть [*infl.* **-сту́пит**] *v., pfv. of* **проступа́ть.**

просту́пок [*gen.* **-пка**] *n.* **1,** misdeed; offense. **2,** *law* misdemeanor.

простуча́ть *v.pfv.* [*infl.* **-чу́, -чи́шь**] **1,** to tap out (a message). **2,** to come rolling by; come rattling by.

простыва́ть *v.impfv.* [*pfv.* **просты́ть**] *colloq.* to get cold. —**его́ и след просты́л,** there is no trace of him.

просты́нный *adj.* of or for sheets: просты́нное полотно́, sheeting.

простыня́ [*pl.* **про́стыни, -сты́нь, -стыня́м**] *n.* sheet; bed sheet.

просты́ть [*infl.* **-сты́ну, -сты́нешь**] *v., pfv. of* **простыва́ть.**

просу́нуть *v., pfv. of* **просо́вывать.**

просу́шивать *v.impfv.* [*pfv.* **просуши́ть**] to dry (thoroughly). —**просу́шиваться,** *refl.* to dry out (thoroughly).

просуши́ть [*infl.* **-сушу́, -су́шишь**] *v., pfv. of* **просу́шивать.** —**просуши́ться,** *refl., pfv. of* **просу́шиваться.**

просу́шка *n.* drying. Выве́шивать что́-нибудь для просу́шки, to hang something out to dry.

просуществова́ть *v.pfv.* [*infl.* **-ству́ю, -ству́ешь**] **1,** to exist; subsist. **2,** to last; endure.

просфора́ *n., Orth. Ch.* communion bread.

просце́ниум *n.* proscenium.

просчёт *n.* **1,** error (*in counting or calculation*). **2,** *fig.* miscalculation.

просчита́ть *v., pfv. of* **просчи́тывать.** —**просчита́ться,** *refl., pfv. of* **просчи́тываться.**

просчи́тывать *v.impfv.* [*pfv.* **просчита́ть**] **1,** to count. **2,** to miscount. —**просчи́тываться,** *refl.* **1,** to miscount. **2,** *fig.* to miscalculate.

про́сып *also,* **просы́п** *n., colloq., in* спать без про́сыпу/про́сыпа, to sleep on and on; sleep like a log.

просы́пать [*infl.* **-сы́плю, -сы́плешь**] *v., pfv. of* **просыпа́ть.**

просыпа́ть[1] *v.impfv.* [*pfv.* **просы́пать**] to spill.

просыпа́ть[2] *v.impfv.* [*pfv.* **проспа́ть**] **1,** *v.i.* to oversleep. **2,** *v.t., colloq.* to sleep through. —**просыпа́ться,** *refl.* [*pfv.* **проснýться**] to wake up.

просыха́ть *v.impfv.* [*pfv.* **просо́хнуть**] to dry out.

про́сьба *n.* request. У меня́ к вам про́сьба, I have a favor to ask of you. Про́сьба не кури́ть!, you are requested not to smoke.

прося́ной *adj.* millet (attrib.).

прося́щий *adj.* pleading; supplicating.

протагони́ст *n.* protagonist.

прота́ивать *v.impfv.* [*pfv.* **прота́ять**] **1,** *v.i.* to melt. **2,** *v.i.* to appear as the snow begins to melt. **3,** *v.t.* to melt; cause to melt.

протакти́ний *n.* protactinium.

прота́лина *n.* thawed patch; place where the snow has melted.

прота́лкивать *v.impfv.* [*pfv.* **протолкну́ть**] **1,** to push; press; force (into, through, forward, etc.). **2,** *colloq.* to expedite (a matter); give (something) a push. —**про-**

та́лкиваться, *refl.* [*pfv.* **протолка́ться** *or* **протолкну́ться**] *colloq.* to force one's way; elbow one's way.

протанцева́ть *v.pfv.* [*infl.* **-цу́ю, -цу́ешь**] **1,** to dance. **2,** to dance (*for a certain length of time*).

прота́пливать *v.impfv.* [*pfv.* **протопи́ть**] **1,** to heat properly; heat sufficiently. **2,** [*impfv. only*] to heat slightly; warm slightly.

прота́птывать *v.impfv.* [*pfv.* **протопта́ть**] **1,** to beat (a path). **2,** *colloq.* to wear holes in (a carpet, pair of socks, etc.).

протара́нить *v., pfv. of* **тара́нить.**

прота́скивать *v.impfv.* [*pfv.* **протащи́ть**] **1,** to drag. **2,** to drag through; pull through. **3,** *colloq.* to push through (a law, resolution, etc.). **4,** *colloq.* to give (someone) a going over (*in the press*).

прота́чивать *v.impfv.* [*pfv.* **проточи́ть**] to eat through; gnaw through.

протащи́ть [*infl.* **-тащу́, -та́щишь**] *v., pfv. of* **прота́скивать.**

прота́ять [*infl.* **-та́ет**] *v., pfv. of* **прота́ивать.**

протеже́ (тэ) *n.m. & f. indecl.* protégé.

проте́з (тэ) *n.* prosthesis; artificial limb. —**зубно́й проте́з,** denture.

проте́зный (тэ) *adj.* prosthetic.

протеи́н (тэ) *n.* protein. —**протеи́новый,** *adj.* protein (*attrib.*).

протека́ть *v.impfv.* [*pfv.* **проте́чь**] **1,** to flow. **2,** to leak; seep. **3,** to leak; have a leak. **4,** (*of time, life, etc.*) to pass; go by. **5,** (*of an event, illness, etc.*) to proceed. Боле́знь протека́ет норма́льно, the illness is taking its normal course.

проте́ктор *n.* **1,** *obs.* protector; patron. **2,** tread (*on tires*).

протектора́т *n.* protectorate.

протекциони́зм *n.* **1,** *econ.* protectionism. **2,** *colloq.* favoritism; cronyism.

проте́кция *n.* patronage; influence.

протере́ть [*infl. like* **тере́ть**] *v., pfv. of* **протира́ть.** —**протере́ться,** *refl., pfv. of* **протира́ться.**

протёртый *adj.* **1,** having a hole; containing holes. **2,** (*of vegetables, fruits, etc.*) strained.

проте́ст *n.* protest.

протеста́нт *n.* **1,** Protestant. **2,** protester. —**протеста́нтизм; протеста́нство,** *n.* Protestantism. —**протеста́нтский,** *adj.* Protestant.

протестова́ть *v.impfv.* [*pres.* **-ту́ю, -ту́ешь**] (*with* **про́тив**) to protest.

проте́чь [*infl. like* **течь**] *v., pfv. of* **протека́ть.**

про́тив *prep., with gen.* **1,** against: голосова́ть про́тив предложе́ния, to vote against the motion. **2,** opposite; facing. **3,** against; contrary to. **4,** against; compared to. —*predicate,* against: Я не про́тив, I am not against it. —*n., colloq.* con: все за и про́тив, all the pros and cons. —**ничего́ не име́ть про́тив,** to have no objection (to).

про́тивень [*gen.* **-вня**] *n.m.* baking sheet; roasting pan.

проти́виться *v.r.impfv.* [*pfv.* **воспроти́виться;** *pres.* **-влюсь, -вишься**] (*with dat.*) to oppose; resist.

проти́вник *n.* **1,** enemy. **2,** opponent; adversary.

проти́вно *adv.* in a disgusting way. Проти́вно па́хнуть, to have a disgusting odor. —*adj., used predicatively,* disgusting; revolting: Мне проти́вно (+ *inf.*), I find it disgusting/revolting to have to... —*prep., with dat., obs.* against; contrary to.

проти́вный *adj.* **1,** *obs.* opposite; facing. **2,** contrary. **3,** opposing. **4,** disgusting; repugnant. —**в проти́вном слу́чае,** otherwise; failing which.

противоа́томный *adj., in* **противоа́томная защи́та,** defense *or* protection against nuclear attack.

противобо́рство *n.* confrontation.

противобо́рствовать *v.impfv.* [*pres.* **-ствую, -ствуешь**] **1,** (*with dat.*) to oppose; combat. **2,** (*of two people*) to contend with each other.

противове́с *n.* counterbalance; counterweight. —**в противове́с** (+ *dat.*), in contrast to; as distinct from. —**для противове́са,** for balance.

противовозду́шный *adj., in* **противовозду́шная оборо́на,** air defense.

противога́з *n.* gas mask.

противоде́йствие *n.* opposition; counteraction.

противоде́йствовать *v.impfv.* [*pres.* **-ствую, -ствуешь**] (*with dat.*) to oppose; counteract.

противоесте́ственный *adj.* unnatural; perverted.

противозако́нный *adj.* illegal; unlawful. —**противозако́нность,** *n.f.* illegality.

противозача́точный *adj.* contraceptive. —**противозача́точные сре́дства,** contraceptives.

противолежа́щий *adj.* **1,** opposite; facing. **2,** (*of an angle*) alternate.

противоло́дочный *adj.* anti-submarine.

противопехо́тный *adj., mil.* anti-personnel.

противопожа́рный *adj.* fire-prevention (*attrib.*).

противопока́занный *adj., med.* not recommended; inadvisable.

противополо́жное *n., decl. as an adj.* the opposite.

противополо́жность *n.f.* **1,** opposite: по́лная противополо́жность, the complete opposite. **2,** contrast. Противополо́жность мне́ний, conflict of opinion. **3,** (*with* **ме́жду**) distinction (between). —**в противополо́жность** (+ *dat.*), **1,** unlike; in contrast to. **2,** as opposed to; in contradistinction to.

противополо́жный *adj.* **1,** opposite: в противополо́жном направле́нии, in the opposite direction. **2,** opposite; opposing: противополо́жные взгля́ды, opposite/opposing views.

противопоста́вить [*infl.* **-влю, -вишь**] *v., pfv. of* **противопоставля́ть.**

противопоставле́ние *n.* contrasting; setting against.

противопоставля́ть *v.impfv.* [*pfv.* **противопоста́вить**] (*with dat.*) **1,** to compare (to); contrast (with). **2,** to oppose: противопоставля́ть си́лу си́ле, to oppose force with force. **3,** to set against: противопоставля́ть себя́ наро́ду, to set oneself against the people.

противораке́тный *adj.* anti-missile.

противоречи́вый *adj.* contradictory; conflicting.

противоре́чие *n.* contradiction.

противоре́чить *v.impfv.* (*with dat.*) **1,** to contradict (someone). **2,** to contradict; be contrary to; conflict with; be at variance with.

противоспу́тниковый *adj.* anti-satellite.

противостоя́ние *n.* **1,** *astron.* opposition. **2,** *fig.* confrontation.

противостоя́ть *v.impfv.* [*pres.* -стою́, -стои́шь] (*with dat.*) **1,** to resist; withstand. **2,** to be at variance with. **3,** to stand in opposition to.

противота́нковый *adj.* antitank.

противоя́дие *n.* antidote.

протира́ть *v.impfv.* [*pfv.* **протере́ть**] **1,** to wear holes in. **2,** to wear (a hole in something). **3,** to wipe; wipe clean; rub clean. **4,** to strain; grate. —**протира́ться,** *refl.* to be worn through.

проти́скивать *v.impfv.* [*pfv.* **проти́снуть**] to force; press; squeeze (something) into *or* through. —**проти́скиваться,** *refl.* **1,** to squeeze into; squeeze through; squeeze between. **2,** to force one's way; elbow one's way.

проткну́ть *v., pfv. of* **протыка́ть**.

протодья́кон *n., Orth. Ch.* archdeacon.

прото́к *n.* **1,** river channel. **2,** *anat.* duct.

протоко́л *n.* **1,** minutes (*of a meeting*). **2,** report (*of an incident, interrogation, etc.*). **3,** protocol. —**протоко́льный,** *adj.* protocol (*attrib.*).

протолка́ться *v.r., pfv. of* **прота́лкиваться**.

протолкну́ть *v., pfv. of* **прота́лкивать**. —**протолкну́ться,** *refl., pfv. of* **прота́лкиваться**.

прото́н *n.* proton.

протопи́ть [*infl.* -топлю́, -то́пишь] *v., pfv. of* **прота́пливать**.

протопла́зма *n.* protoplasm.

протопта́ть [*infl.* -топчу́, -то́пчешь] *v., pfv. of* **прота́птывать**.

проторённый *adj.* (*of a road or path*) beaten; well-trodden.

проторя́ть *v.impfv.* [*pfv.* **протори́ть**], *usu. in* **проторить путь** *or* **доро́гу, 1,** to beat a path. **2,** *fig.* to open the way.

прототи́п *n.* prototype.

проточи́ть [*infl.* -точу́, -то́чишь] *v., pfv. of* **прота́чивать**.

прото́чный *adj.* (*of water*) running; flowing; (*of a pond*) not stagnant; fed by springs.

протра́ва *n.* mordant.

протрезви́ть [*infl.* -влю́, -ви́шь] *v., pfv. of* **протрезвля́ть**. —**протрезви́ться,** *refl., pfv. of* **протрезвля́ться**.

протрезвля́ть *v.impfv.* [*pfv.* **протрезви́ть**] to sober up; make sober. —**протрезвля́ться,** *refl.* to sober up; become sober.

протруби́ть *v., pfv. of* **труби́ть**.

протуха́ть *v.impfv.* [*pfv.* **проту́хнуть**] to spoil; rot.

проту́хнуть [*past* -ту́х, -ту́хла] *v., pfv. of* **ту́хнуть** (*in sense #2*) *and* **протуха́ть**.

проту́хший *adj.* rotten.

протыка́ть *v.impfv.* [*pfv.* **проткну́ть**] to pierce.

протя́гивать *v.impfv.* [*pfv.* **протяну́ть**] **1,** to extend; stretch (a rope, wire, etc.). **2,** to build; lay (a road, railroad, etc.) to a certain place. **3,** to stretch out; hold out; offer; extend. **4,** to sustain (a note, sound, etc.). —**протя́гиваться,** *refl.* **1,** to reach out. **2,** to stretch;

extend. **3,** *colloq.* to stretch out. **4,** *colloq.* to last; go on. *See also* **протяну́ть.**

протяже́ние *n.* length; extent. На всём протяже́нии (+ *gen.*), over the entire length of. —**на протяже́нии** (+ *gen.*), for; over a period of.

протяжённость *n.f.* length; extent.

протя́жный *adj.* (*of speech, a sound, etc.*) slow; prolonged.

протяну́ть *v.pfv.* [*infl.* -тяну́, -тя́нешь] **1,** *pfv. of* **протя́гивать**. **2,** *colloq.* to delay; drag out. **3,** *v.i., colloq.* to hold out; live a little while longer. **4,** *in* **протяну́ть но́ги,** *colloq.* to kick the bucket. —**протяну́ться,** *refl., pfv. of* **тяну́ться** (*in sense #2*) *and* **протя́гиваться**.

проучи́ть *v.pfv.* [*infl.* -учу́, -у́чишь] **1,** *colloq.* to teach (someone) a (good) lesson. **2,** to teach (*for a certain length of time*). —**проучи́ться,** *refl.* to study (*for a certain length of time*).

профа́н *n.* ignoramus.

профана́ция *n.* profanation.

профани́ровать *v.impfv. & pfv.* [*pres.* -рую, -руешь] to profane.

профессиона́л *n.* professional.

профессиона́льный *adj.* professional. —**профессиона́льная боле́знь,** occupational disease. —**профессиона́льное обуче́ние,** vocational training.

профе́ссия *n.* profession. —**челове́к свобо́дной профе́ссии,** professional man (*in private practice*).

профе́ссор [*pl.* **профессора́**] *n.* professor. Профе́ссор исто́рии, professor of history; history professor. —**профе́ссорский,** *adj.* professorial. —**профе́ссорство,** *n.* professorship.

профессу́ра *n.* **1,** professorship. **2,** professors.

профила́ктика *n.* **1,** prophylaxis. **2,** prevention; preventive measures: профила́ктика боле́зней, prevention of disease. Пожа́рная профила́ктика, fire prevention. —**профилакти́ческий,** *adj.* prophylactic.

про́филь *n.m.* **1,** profile. **2,** *fig.* type: худо́жники разли́чного про́филя, painters of various types/styles/ schools. Специали́ст широ́кого про́филя, broad specialist.

профо́рма *n.* formality. —**для профо́рмы,** as a matter of form.

профсою́з *n.* trade union (*contr. of* **профессиона́льный сою́з**). —**профсою́зный,** *adj.* trade-union (*attrib.*).

проха́живаться *v.r.impfv.* [*pfv.* **пройти́сь**] **1,** to walk; stroll. Проха́живаться по ко́мнате, to pace up and down the room. **2,** *colloq.* (*with instr. and* **по**) to run (something over something): пройти́сь щёткой по волоса́м, to run a brush over one's hair. **3,** (*with* **насчёт** *or* **по а́дресу**) *colloq.* to make slighting remarks about; take a swipe at.

прохвати́ть [*infl.* -хвачу́, -хва́тишь] *v., pfv. of* **прохва́тывать**.

прохва́тывать *v.impfv.* [*pfv.* **прохвати́ть**] *colloq.* **1,** (*of cold, wind, etc.*) to penetrate. **2,** *impers.* to get a chill: Меня́ прохвати́ло в откры́той маши́не, I got a chill in the open car.

прохво́ст *n., colloq.* scoundrel.

прохла́да *n.* cool; coolness: вече́рняя прохла́да, the cool of the evening.

прохла́дец *also,* прохла́дца *n., in* с прохла́дцем; с прохла́дцей, *colloq.* leisurely; without making much effort.

прохлади́тельный *adj.* cooling; refreshing. —прохлади́тельные напи́тки, soft drinks.

прохлади́ться [*infl.* -жу́сь, -ди́шься] *v.r., pfv. of* прохлажда́ться.

прохла́дно *adv.* coolly. —*adj., used predicatively* 1, cool: Сего́дня прохла́дно, it is cool today. 2, chilly: Мне прохла́дно, I am chilly.

прохла́дный *adj.* cool.

прохла́дца *n.* = прохла́дец.

прохлажда́ться *v.r.impfv.* [*pfv.* прохлади́ться] 1, to cool off. 2, [*impfv. only*] *colloq.* to idle; loaf.

прохо́д *n.* 1, passing. 2, passage; passageway. 3, aisle. 4, *in* за́дний прохо́д, anus. 5, *in* пра́во прохо́да, right of way. 6, *in* на прохо́де, *chess* en passant. —не дава́ть прохо́да (+ *dat.*), to give (someone) no peace. —прохо́да нет от, there is no getting away from...

проходи́мец [*gen.* -мца] *n., colloq.* scoundrel; crook; rogue.

проходи́мость *n.f.* 1, ability (of a surface) to carry traffic. 2, ability (of a vehicle) to travel cross-country.

проходи́мый *adj.* passable.

проходи́ть[1] *v.impfv.* [*pfv.* пройти́; *pres.* -хожу́, -хо́дишь] 1, to walk (along, through, past, into, etc.). 2, to pass: да́йте мне пройти́!, let me pass! 3, (*with* ми́мо) to pass (by); (*with* че́рез) to pass through. 4, to go (right) past (*inadvertently*). 5, (*with* в + *acc.*) to fit into; fit through. 6, to cover (a certain distance); traverse (a route or path); walk the length of (*e.g.* a street). 7, (*of a road, border, etc.*) to run; extend. 8, to pass; elapse; go by. 9, (*of pain, rain, a storm, etc.*) to pass; stop. 10, to take place; be held. 11, to go; proceed: Заседа́ние прошло́ хорошо́, the meeting went well. Как прошла́ пое́здка?, how was the trip? 12, to be approved; be accepted; (*of a proposal or motion*) carry; pass. 13, to undergo (treatment, training, etc.); [*pfv. only*] complete (a course); pass (a physical examination); clear (customs). 14, *colloq.* to study (a subject).

проходи́ть[2] *v.pfv.* [*infl.* -хожу́, -хо́дишь] to walk (*for a certain length of time*).

проходна́я *n., decl. as an adj.* checkpoint (*at the entrance to a factory or other building*).

проходно́й *adj.* 1, (*of a room, courtyard, etc.*) connecting; communicating. 2, *colloq.* trivial; inconsequential. —проходно́й балл, lowest passing score (*on an entrance examination*). —проходна́я бу́дка, entrance gate; checkpoint. —проходна́я пе́шка, *chess* passed pawn.

прохожде́ние *n.* 1, passing; passage. 2, performance; completion (*of military service*).

прохо́жий *adj.* 1, passing. 2, passing through; in transit. —*n.* passer-by.

прохрипе́ть *v.pfv.* [*infl.* -плю́, -пи́шь] to utter in a hoarse voice.

процвета́ние *n.* prosperity.

процвета́ть *v.impfv.* to prosper; flourish; thrive.

процеди́ть [*infl.* -цежу́, -це́дишь] *v., pfv. of* проце́живать.

процеду́ра *n.* 1, procedure. 2, *usu. pl., med.* treatment (*baths, massages, etc.*). —процеду́рный, *adj.* procedural.

проце́живать *v.impfv.* [*pfv.* процеди́ть] 1, to strain; filter. 2, *colloq.* to mutter.

проце́нт *n.* 1, percent: два́дцать проце́нтов, twenty percent. 2, percentage. 3, *often pl.* interest: сло́жные проце́нты, compound interest. Под ни́зкий проце́нт, at low interest.

проце́нтный *adj.* 1, percentage (*attrib.*). В проце́нтном отноше́нии, percentagewise. 2, interest-bearing.

проце́сс *n.* 1, process. 2, [*often* суде́бный проце́сс] A, trial. B, lawsuit. 3, *med.* condition. Проце́сс в лёгких, turberculosis of the lungs. —в проце́ссе (+ *gen.*), in the course of.

процессия *n.* procession.

процессуа́льный *adj., law* 1, procedural. 2, judicial. 3, legal.

процити́ровать *v., pfv. of* цити́ровать.

про́черк *n.* dash (*to show the absence of something*).

прочерти́ть [*infl.* -черчу́, -че́ртишь] *v., pfv. of* проче́рчивать. —прочерти́ться, *refl., pfv. of* проче́рчиваться.

проче́рчивать *v.impfv.* [*pfv.* прочерти́ть] to draw (a line). —проче́рчиваться, *refl.* to be visible; stand out.

прочеса́ть [*infl.* -чешу́, -че́шешь] *v., pfv. of* прочёсывать.

проче́сть [*infl.* -чту́, -чтёшь; *past* -чёл, -чла́, -чло́, -чли́] *v., pfv. of* чита́ть.

прочёсывать *v.impfv.* [*pfv.* прочеса́ть] 1, to comb (flax, fiber, etc.). 2, *fig., colloq.* to comb; search. 3, *mil., colloq.* to rake (with fire).

про́чий *adj.* other. —про́чие, *n.pl.* the others. —в числе́ про́чего, among other things. —и про́чее, and so on; and so forth. —ме́жду про́чим, by the way. —поми́мо всего́ про́чего, *see* поми́мо. —при про́чих ра́вных усло́виях, other things being equal. —среди́ про́чего, among other things.

прочи́стить [*infl.* -чи́щу, -чи́стишь] *v., pfv. of* прочища́ть.

прочита́ть *v.pfv.* 1, *pfv. of* чита́ть. 2, to read (*for a certain length of time*).

про́чить *v.impfv.* 1, (*with* в + *nom. pl.*) to have (someone) in mind; envision: про́чить кого́-нибудь в зятья́, to have someone in mind to be one's son-in-law. He про́чить себя́ в солда́ты, not see oneself as (*or* becoming) a soldier. 2, to predict: Ему́ про́чат блестя́щее бу́дущее, they are predicting a brilliant future for him.

прочища́ть *v.impfv.* [*pfv.* прочи́стить] 1, to clean; clean out. 2, to clear (a road, forest, etc.).

про́чно *adv.* firmly; solidly; securely.

про́чность *n.f.* 1, strength; durability. 2, soundness; solidity. —запа́с про́чности, margin of safety.

про́чный *adj.* 1, firm; durable. 2, (*of colors*) fast. 3, *fig.* (*of peace, a friendship, etc.*) lasting; enduring.

прочте́ние *n.* 1, reading. 2, reciting. 3, giving (*of lectures*).

прочу́вствованный *adj.* full of emotion; deeply felt. —**прочу́вствованно,** *adv.* with deep feeling.

прочу́вствовать *v.pfv.* [*infl.* **-ствую, -ствуешь**] **1,** to feel deeply. **2,** to experience; live through.

прочь *adv.* away; off: Ру́ки прочь!, hands off! —*interj.* begone! Прочь отсю́да!, get out of (*or* away from) here! Прочь с доро́ги!, get out of the way! —**быть не прочь** (+ *inf.*), not to mind; not be averse to.

проше́дшее *n., decl. as an adj.* the past.

проше́дший *adj.* last; past. —**проше́дшее вре́мя,** *gram.* past tense.

проше́ние *n., obs.* application; petition; formal request.

прошепта́ть *v., pfv. of* **шепта́ть.**

проше́ствие *n., in* **по проше́ствии** (+ *gen.*), with the passage (of); upon the expiration (of).

прошиба́ть *v.impfv.* [*pfv.* **прошиби́ть**] *colloq.* **1,** to break through. **2,** (*of cold, wind, etc.*) to penetrate; (*of pain, a chill, etc.*) to come over. Его́ проши́б пот, he broke into a sweat. Её прошибла́ слеза́, tears came to her eyes.

прошиби́ть [*infl.* **-бу́, -бёшь;** *past* **-ши́б, -ши́бла**] *v., pfv. of* **прошиба́ть.**

прошива́ть *v.impfv.* [*pfv.* **проши́ть**] **1,** to sew; stitch. **2,** *colloq.* to riddle (with bullets); rack (with a bomb).

проши́вка *n.* lace trim.

проши́ть [*infl.* **-шью, -шьёшь**] *v., pfv. of* **прошива́ть.**

прошлого́дний *adj.* last year's.

про́шлое *n., decl. as an adj.* the past: в про́шлом, in the past. —**отойти́** *or* **уйти́ в про́шлое,** to become a thing of the past.

про́шлый *adj.* **1,** last: в про́шлом году́, last year. **2,** past: про́шлые во́йны/оши́бки, past wars/mistakes.

прошмы́гивать *v.impfv.* [*pfv.* **прошмыгну́ть**] *colloq.* to sneak; slip (into, past, etc.).

проштра́фиться *v.r.pfv.* [*infl.* **-флюсь, -фишься**] *colloq.* to make a mistake; do something wrong.

проштуди́ровать *v., pfv. of* **штуди́ровать.**

проща́й *interj.* farewell!; adieu! *Also,* **проща́йте.**

проща́льный *adj.* parting; farewell (*attrib.*).

проща́ние *n.* parting; farewell. —**на проща́ние,** at parting.

проща́ть *v.impfv.* [*pfv.* **прости́ть**] to forgive; excuse; pardon. Прости́те!, excuse me! —**проща́ться,** *refl.* [*pfv.* **прости́ться** *or* **попроща́ться**] (with **с** + *instr.*) to say goodbye (to); bid (someone) farewell.

про́ще *adj., comp. of* **просто́й.**

проще́ние *n.* **1,** forgiveness: проси́ть проще́ния у кого́-нибудь, to ask for someone's forgiveness. **2,** pardon: Прошу́ проще́ния!, I beg your pardon!

прощу́пывать *v.impfv.* [*pfv.* **прощу́пать**] **1,** to feel. **2,** *fig.* to reconnoiter. **3,** *fig.* to size up. —**прощу́пывать по́чву,** to get the lay of the land; sound out the possibilities.

проэкзаменова́ть *v., pfv. of* **экзаменова́ть.** —**проэкзаменова́ться,** *refl., pfv. of* **экзаменова́ться.**

прояви́тель *n.m., photog.* developer.

прояви́ть [*infl.* **-явлю́, -я́вишь**] *v., pfv. of* **проявля́ть.** —**прояви́ться,** *refl., pfv. of* **проявля́ться.**

проявле́ние *n.* **1,** display; manifestation. **2,** *photog.* developing.

проявля́ть *v.impfv.* [*pfv.* **прояви́ть**] **1,** to show; display (a quality or emotion). **2,** *photog.* to develop. —**прояви́ть себя́, 1,** to show one's worth. **2,** to manifest itself. **3,** (*with instr.*) to prove to be.

проявля́ться *v.r.impfv.* [*pfv.* **прояви́ться**] to reveal itself; manifest itself.

проя́снеть *v.pfv., colloq.* (*of the sky*) to clear up.

проясне́ть *v.pfv.* **1,** to become clear. **2,** to brighten up.

проясня́ть *v.impfv.* [*pfv.* **проясни́ть**] **1,** to clear; make clear. **2,** to clear up. —**проясня́ться,** *refl.* **1,** to clear up. **2,** *fig.* to become clear. **3,** to brighten up.

пруд [*gen.* **пруда́;** *2nd loc.* **пруду́**] *n.* pond.

пруди́ть *v.impfv.* [*pfv.* **запруди́ть;** *pres.* **пружу́, пру́дишь** *or* **пруди́шь**] to dam up. —**хоть пруд пруди́,** plenty; galore.

пружи́на *n.* **1,** spring. **2,** *in* гла́вная пружи́на, mainspring. —**нажа́ть на все пружи́ны,** to pull out all the stops.

пружи́нистый *adj.* springy; resilient.

пружи́нить *v.impfv.* to be springy; be resilient. —**пружи́ниться,** *refl.* = **пружи́нить.**

пружи́нный *adj.* spring (*attrib.*): пружи́нный матра́с, spring mattress.

пруса́к [*gen.* **-сака́**] *n.* Croton bug; German cockroach.

прусса́к [*gen.* **-ссака́**] *n.* Prussian. —**пру́сский,** *adj.* Prussian.

прут [*gen.* **пру́та** *or* **прута́;** *pl.* **пру́тья, пру́тьев**] *n.* **1,** twig. **2,** rod.

пры́гание *also,* **пры́ганье** *n.* jumping.

пры́гать *v.impfv.* [*pfv.* **пры́гнуть**] **1,** to jump; leap. **2,** to bounce. —**пры́гать на одно́й ноге́,** to hop.

прыгу́н [*gen.* **-гуна́**] *n.* jumper.

прыжо́к [*gen.* **-жка́**] *n.* jump; leap. —**прыжки́ в во́ду,** diving. —**прыжо́к в во́ду,** dive. —**прыжо́к в высоту́,** high jump. —**прыжо́к в длину́,** broad jump. —**прыжо́к с ме́ста,** standing broad jump. —**прыжо́к с разбе́га,** running broad jump. —**прыжо́к с шесто́м,** pole vault. —**тройно́й прыжо́к,** hop, step and jump.

пры́скать *v.impfv.* [*pfv.* **пры́снуть**] *colloq.* **1,** (*with instr.*) to sprinkle. **2,** [*impfv. only*] (*of rain*) to fall in small drops. **3,** to dash; dart. **4,** to burst out laughing.

пры́снуть *v.pfv., colloq.* **1,** *pfv. of* **пры́скать. 2,** to spurt; gush.

пры́ткий *adj.* [*comp.* **пры́тче**] *colloq.* quick; nimble; agile.

прыть *n.f., colloq.* **1,** speed. **2,** energy; vim; pep. —**во всю прыть,** at full speed.

прыщ [*gen.* **прыща́**] *n.* pimple.

прыща́вый *adj.* pimply.

пряде́ние *n.* spinning.

пря́деный *adj.* spun.

пряди́льный *adj.* spinning (*attrib.*).

пряди́льщик *n.m.* [*fem.* **-щица**] spinner.

прядь *n.f.* strand (*of hair*).

пря́жа *n.* yarn.

пря́жка [*gen. pl.* **-жек**] *n.* buckle.

пря́лка [*gen. pl.* **-лок**] *n.* **1,** distaff. **2,** spinning wheel.

пряма́я *n., decl. as an adj.* straight line. —**по прямо́й,** as the crow flies.

прямизна́ *n.* straightness.

прямико́м *adv., colloq.* **1,** straight; in a straight line. **2,** straight to the point.

пря́мо *adv.* **1,** straight. **2,** straight ahead. **3,** right; directly. **4,** openly; frankly. Пря́мо ска́жем, to be frank; be honest. **5,** *colloq.* really; truly. **6,** *colloq.* simply; just: Я пря́мо не зна́ю, I don't know.

прямоду́шие *n.* directness; straightforwardness. —**прямоду́шный,** *adj.* direct; straightforward.

прямо́й *adj.* **1,** straight. **2,** erect; upright. **3,** direct. **4,** straightforward. **5,** *in* прямо́й у́гол, right angle. —**прямо́й расчёт** *or* смысл (+ *inf.*), *colloq.* there is every reason to...; it makes a lot of sense to... *See also* **пряма́я.**

прямолине́йный *adj.* **1,** rectilinear. **2,** *fig.* straightforward.

прямота́ *n.* directness; straightforwardness.

прямоуго́льник *n.* rectangle. —**прямоуго́льный,** *adj.* rectangular.

пря́ник *n.* cake: медо́вый пря́ник, honey cake. Имби́рный пря́ник, gingerbread. —**поли́тика кнута́ и пря́ника,** the carrot and stick.

пря́ность *n.f.* spice. —**пря́ный,** *adj.* spicy.

прясть *v.impfv.* [*pfv.* **спрясть;** *pres.* **пряду́, пря-дёшь;** *past* **прял, пряла́, пря́ло, пря́ли**] to spin (cloth, yarn, etc.).

пря́танье *n.* hiding.

пря́тать *v.impfv.* [*pfv.* **спря́тать;** *pres.* **пря́чу, пря́-чешь**] to hide; conceal. —**пря́тать концы́ в во́ду,** to cover up the traces; cover up one's tracks.

пря́таться *v.r.impfv.* [*pfv.* **спря́таться;** *pres.* **пря́-чусь, пря́чешься**] to hide; be hiding.

пря́тки [*gen.* **-ток**] *n.pl.* hide-and-seek.

пря́ха *n.* (woman) spinner.

псало́м [*gen.* **-лма́**] *n.* psalm.

псалты́рь [*gen.* **-тыря́**] *n.m.* Psalter. *Also,* **пса́л-тырь,** *n.f.*

пса́рня [*gen. pl.* **-рен**] *n.* kennel (*for hunting dogs*).

псевдони́м *n.* pseudonym; pen name.

пси́на *n., colloq.* **1,** dogmeat. **2,** smell of a dog.

псих *n., colloq.* madman; lunatic; nut.

психиа́тр *n.* psychiatrist.

психиатри́ческий *adj.* psychiatric. —**психиатри́че-ская больни́ца,** mental hospital.

психиатри́я *n.* psychiatry.

пси́хика *n.* psyche.

психи́ческий *adj.* mental. —**психи́чески,** *adv.* mentally.

психоана́лиз *n.* psychoanalysis. —**психоаналити́-ческий,** *adj.* psychoanalytic(al).

психо́з *n.* psychosis.

психоло́гия *n.* psychology. —**психо́лог,** *n.* psychologist. —**психологи́ческий,** *adj.* psychological.

психопа́т *n.* psychopath. —**психопати́ческий,** *adj.* psychopathic. —**психопа́тия,** *n.* psychopathy.

психосомати́ческий *adj.* psychosomatic.

психотерапи́я *n.* psychotherapy. —**психотерапе́вт,** *n.* psychotherapist.

психоти́ческий *adj.* psychotic.

псориа́з *n.* psoriasis.

пта́шка [*gen. pl.* **-шек**] *n., colloq.* little bird; birdie. —**ра́нняя пта́шка,** early bird.

птене́ц [*gen.* **-нца́**] *n.* baby bird; chick; nestling; fledgling.

птерода́ктиль *n.m.* pterodactyl.

пти́ца *n.* bird. —**дома́шняя пти́ца,** poultry.

птицево́д *n.* poultry farmer; poultry breeder. —**пти-цево́дство,** *n.* poultry farming; poultry breeding.

птицело́в *n.* fowler. —**птицело́вство,** *n.* fowling.

пти́чий [*fem.* **-чья**] *adj.* **1,** bird (*attrib.*); bird's. **2,** bird-like. **3,** *in* пти́чий двор, barnyard. —**вид с пти́чьего полёта,** bird's-eye view. —**ему́ то́лько пти́чьего молока́ не хвата́ет,** he has everything; he lacks for nothing. —**жить на пти́чьих права́х,** to live from hand to mouth.

пти́чка [*gen. pl.* **-чек**] *n.* **1,** *dim. of* пти́ца. **2,** check; check mark; tick [√].

пти́чник *n.* poultry yard.

пу́блика *n.* **1,** (the) public. **2,** audience. **3,** *colloq.* people.

публика́ция *n.* **1,** publication. **2,** anything published; book, article, etc.

публикова́ть *v.impfv.* [*pfv.* **опубликова́ть;** *pres.* **-ку́ю, -ку́ешь**] to publish.

публици́ст *n.* commentator; columnist; publicist.

публи́чно *adv.* publicly; in public.

публи́чный *adj.* public. —**публи́чный дом,** brothel.

пу́гало *n.* **1,** scarecrow. **2,** *fig.* bugaboo; bugbear.

пуга́ть *v.impfv.* [*pfv.* **испуга́ть**] to frighten; scare. —**пуга́ться,** *refl.* (*with gen.*) to be frightened (of); be scared (of).

пуга́ч [*gen.* **-гача́**] *n.* toy pistol.

пуга́ющий *adj.* frightening.

пугли́вый *adj.* easily frightened; fearful; timorous.

пу́говица *n.* button.

пуд [*pl.* **пуды́**] *n.* old Russian unit of weight equal to approx. 36 pounds; pood.

пу́дель *n.m.* poodle.

пу́динг *n.* pudding.

пу́дра *n.* powder. —**са́харная пу́дра,** powdered sugar.

пу́дреница *n.* (lady's) compact.

пу́дрить *v.impfv.* [*pfv.* **напу́дрить**] to powder. —**пу́-дриться,** *refl.* to powder one's face; powder one's nose.

пуза́тый *adj., colloq.* potbellied.

пу́зо *n., colloq.* belly; paunch.

пузырёк [*gen.* **-рька́**] *n.* **1,** small bottle; vial. **2,** bubble.

пузы́риться *v.r.impfv.* **1,** to bubble. **2,** *colloq.* (*of clothes*) to billow.

пузы́рь [*gen.* **-зыря́**] *n.m.* **1,** bubble. **2,** *colloq.* blister. **3,** bladder: жёлчный пузы́рь, gall bladder; мочево́й пузы́рь, urinary bladder. **4,** bag: пузы́рь со льдом, ice bag; ice pack.

пук [*pl.* **пуки́**] *n.* bunch; bundle; tuft; wisp.

пулево́й *adj.* bullet (*attrib.*).

пулемёт *n.* machine gun. —**пулемётный,** *adj.* machine-gun (*attrib.*). —**пулемётчик,** *n.* machine gunner.

пулесто́йкий *adj.* bulletproof. *Also,* **пуленепро-бива́емый; пуленепроница́емый.**

пуло́вер *n.* pullover.

пульвериза́тор *n.* atomizer; sprayer.

пу́льпа *n.* pulp (*of a tooth*).

пульс *n.* pulse.

пульса́р *n.* pulsar.

пульса́ция *n.* pulsation.

пульси́ровать *v.impfv.* [*pres.* **-рует**] to pulsate.

пульт *n.* **1,** music stand: дирижёрский пульт, conductor's stand. **2,** control panel; console.

пу́ля *n.* bullet.

пуля́рка [*gen. pl.* **-рок**] *n.* fattened chicken.

пу́ма *n.* puma.

пункт *n.* **1,** point: поворо́тный пункт, turning point. Са́мый се́верный пункт страны́, the northernmost point in the country. **2,** station; post; center: медици́нский пункт, first-aid station; наблюда́тельный пункт, observation post; призывно́й пункт, induction center. **3,** point; paragraph; item (*in a document*). **4,** *in* пу́нкты обвине́ния, counts (*of an indictment*). —**по пу́нктам; пункт за пу́нктом,** point by point.

пункти́р *n.* dotted line. —**пункти́рный,** *adj., in* **пункти́рная ли́ния,** = **пункти́р.**

пунктуа́льный *adj.* punctual. —**пунктуа́льность,** *n.f.* punctuality.

пунктуа́ция *n.* punctuation.

пу́нкция *n., med.* puncture; tapping. —**спинномозгова́я пу́нкция,** spinal tap.

пу́ночка [*gen. pl.* **-чек**] *n.* snow bunting.

пунцо́вый *adj.* crimson.

пунш *n.* punch (*drink*).

пуп [*gen.* **пупа́**] *n., colloq.* navel; bellybutton.

пупа́вка [*gen. pl.* **-вок**] *n.* camomile.

пупови́на *n.* umbilical cord.

пупо́к [*gen.* **пупка́**] *n.* navel.

пупо́чный *adj.* umbilical.

пупы́рышек [*gen.* **-шка**] *n., colloq.* pimple. —**пупы́рчатый,** *adj., colloq.* pimply.

пурга́ *n.* blizzard; snowstorm.

пури́зм *n.* purism. —**пури́ст,** *n.* purist.

пурита́нин [*pl.* **-та́не, -та́н**] *n.m.* [*fem.* **-та́нка**] **1,** *hist.* Puritan. **2,** puritan.

пурита́нский *adj.* **1,** Puritan. **2,** puritanical.

пурпу́рный *adj.* purple; crimson. *Also,* **пурпу́ровый.**

пуск *n.* **1,** starting; setting in motion. **2,** launching.

пуска́й *particle* = **пусть.**

пуска́ть *v.impfv.* [*pfv.* **пусти́ть**] **1,** to let go (of). **2,** to let (someone) go (somewhere). **3,** to let in; admit. **4,** to take in (lodgers). **5,** to start up; switch on; set in motion. **6,** (*with acc. or instr.*) to throw; toss. **7,** to fire; shoot. **8,** to blow (smoke, bubbles, etc.). **9,** (*with* в + *acc.*) to put (into production, into circulation, on sale, etc.). **10,** to sprout (buds, shoots, etc.). **11,** *colloq.* to start; set afloat (a rumor, gossip, etc.). —**пуска́ть в де́ло,** to put to use. —**пуска́ть в ход,** *see* **ход.** —**пуска́ть ко дну** *or* **на дно,** to send (a ship) to the bottom. —**пуска́ть ко́рни,** *see* **ко́рень.** —**пуска́ть кровь** (+ *dat.*), to bleed (someone). —**пуска́ть по кру́гу,** to pass around. —**пусти́ть по́ миру,** *see* **мир.** —**пуска́ть по тече́нию,** to set adrift. —**пуска́ть пыль в глаза́,** *see* **пыль.** —**пуска́ть себе́ пу́лю в лоб,** to blow one's brains out.

пуска́ться *v.r.impfv.* [*pfv.* **пусти́ться**] *colloq.* **1,** to set out; set off. **2,** to dash; race. **3,** (*with inf.*) to begin (to);

start (to). **4,** (*with* в + *acc.*) to begin; launch into; embark upon. **5,** (*with* на + *acc.*) to resort to.

пусково́й *adj.* starting (*attrib.*); launching (*attrib.*). —**пускова́я устано́вка,** launcher.

пустельга́ *n.* kestrel.

пусте́ть *v.impfv.* [*pfv.* **опусте́ть**] to become empty; become deserted.

пусти́ть [*infl.* **пущу́, пу́стишь**] *v., pfv. of* **пуска́ть.** —**пусти́ться,** *refl., pfv. of* **пуска́ться.**

пу́сто *adj., used predicatively,* empty; deserted: На у́лицах бы́ло пу́сто, the streets were empty/deserted.

пустова́ть *v.impfv.* [*pres.* **-ту́ет**] to be empty; stand empty.

пустоголо́вый *adj., colloq.* empty-headed.

пустозво́н *n., colloq.* windbag.

пусто́й *adj.* [*short form* **пуст, пуста́, пу́сто, пусты́**] **1,** empty. **2,** *fig.* (*of words, promises, etc.*) empty; hollow. **3,** *fig.* lacking depth; shallow. **4,** groundless. —**пусто́е ме́сто, 1,** blank space. **2,** a nothing; nonentity; nobody. —**пуста́я тра́та** (+ *gen.*), a waste (of). —**с пусты́ми рука́ми,** empty-handed.

пустоме́ля *n.m. & f., colloq.* windbag.

пустопоро́жний *adj.* **1,** *obs.* empty. **2,** *fig., colloq.* vapid.

пустосло́в *n., colloq.* windbag. —**пустосло́вие,** *n., colloq.* idle talk; twaddle; hot air.

пустосло́вить *v.impfv.* [*pres.* **-влю, -вишь**] *colloq.* to babble; chatter.

пустота́ [*pl.* **пусто́ты**] *n.* **1,** emptiness. **2,** vacuum. **3,** *fig.* void.

пустоте́лый *adj.* hollow.

пустоцве́т *n.* **1,** sterile flower. **2,** *fig.* person who contributes nothing to society.

пу́стошь *n.f.* uncultivated plot of land.

пусты́нник *n.* hermit.

пусты́нный *adj.* **1,** desert (*attrib.*). **2,** uninhabited; deserted. **3,** bleak; desolate. —**пусты́нно,** *adj., used predicatively,* deserted: На у́лицах пусты́нно, the streets are deserted.

пусты́ня *n.* **1,** desert. **2,** wilderness; wasteland.

пусты́рь [*gen.* **-стыря́**] *n.m.* abandoned lot; neglected plot of land.

пусты́шка [*gen. pl.* **-шек**] *n., colloq.* **1,** pacifier (*for a baby*). **2,** shallow person; person with no depth.

пусть *particle* let: Пусть он говори́т, let him speak. Пусть икс ра́вен и́греку, let x equal y. —*conj.* **1,** though: Зада́ча, пусть тру́дная, но выполни́ма, the task, though difficult, can be accomplished. **2,** granted; so what if...?: Пусть он мне помо́г, ра́зве э́то даёт ему́ пра́во (+ *inf.*), so what if he helped me? Does that give him the right to...? —**пусть бу́дет по-ва́шему,** have it your way. —**пусть бу́дет так,** so be it.

пустя́к [*gen.* **-тяка́**] *n.* **1,** trifle. **2,** *pl.* nonsense. —**па́ра пустяко́в,** child's play. —**пустяки́!,** never mind!; it's nothing!

пустяко́вый *adj., colloq.* trifling; trivial. *Also,* **пустя́чный.**

пу́таник *n., colloq.* muddle-headed person.

пу́таница *n.* mess; muddle; jumble.

пу́таный *adj.* **1,** tangled. **2,** confusing; rambling; incoherent. **3,** *colloq.* (*of a person*) confused; mixed up.

пу́тать *v.impfv.* **1,** [*pfv.* **запу́тать** *or* **спу́тать**] to tangle. **2,** [*pfv.* **спу́тать** *or* **перепу́тать**] to mix up (objects previously in order). **3,** [*impfv. only*] *v.i.* to get mixed up; get confused (*when speaking*). **4,** [*pfv.* **спу́тать** *or* **перепу́тать**] to confuse; get (two or more things) mixed up. **5,** [*pfv.* **запу́тать** *or* **спу́тать**] *colloq.* to confuse; mix (someone) up. **6,** [*pfv.* **впу́тать**] (*with* **в** + *acc.*) *colloq.* to involve (in); embroil (in). **7,** [*pfv.* **спу́тать**] to hobble; fetter (a horse).

пу́таться *v.r.impfv.* **1,** [*pfv.* **запу́таться** *or* **спу́таться**] to become tangled. **2,** [*pfv.* **запу́таться**] (*with* **в** + *prepl.*) to become entangled (in). **3,** [*pfv.* **спу́таться**] *colloq.* to become confused. **4,** [*pfv.* **впу́таться**] (*with* **в** + *acc.*) to interfere (in); meddle (in). **5,** [*pfv.* **спу́таться**] (*with* **с** + *instr.*) *colloq.* to consort (with); take up (with). —**пу́таться под нога́ми,** to be in the way; be underfoot.

путёвка [*gen. pl.* **-вок**] *n.* **1,** pass; permit; authorization. **2,** ticket for a group tour; place in a tourist group. —**путёвка в жизнь,** a start in life.

путеводи́тель *n.m.* guidebook.

путево́дный *adj.* guiding. —**путево́дная звезда́,** guiding star; lodestar. —**путево́дная нить,** clue.

путево́й *adj.* **1,** travel (*attrib.*): путевы́е заме́тки, travel notes. **2,** *R.R.* track (*attrib.*): путево́й обхо́дчик, trackman; lineman. —**путева́я ка́рта,** road map. —**путева́я ско́рость,** ground speed.

путе́ец [*gen.* **-те́йца**] *n.* railway engineer.

путём *prep.,* with *gen.* by means of; by.

путепрово́д *n.* overpass.

путеше́ственник *n.* traveler.

путеше́ствие *n.* trip; journey; voyage.

путеше́ствовать *v.impfv.* [*pres.* **-ствую, -ствуешь**] to travel.

пу́тник *n.* traveler.

пу́тный *adj., colloq.* **1,** sensible. **2,** worthwhile. —**из него́ ничего́ пу́тного не вы́йдет,** he'll never amount to anything.

путч *n.* putsch.

пу́ты [*gen.* **пут**] *n.pl.* fetters; shackles (*lit. & fig.*).

путь [*gen., dat. & prepl.* **пути́**; *instr.* **путём**; *pl.* **пути́, путе́й, путя́м**] *n.m.* **1,** way; route: на обра́тном пути́, on the way back. Око́льным путём, by a roundabout way/route. Прегради́ть путь (+ *dat.*), to block someone's way. Сби́ться с пути́, to lose one's way **2,** journey; traveling: два дня пути́, a two-day journey; two days of traveling. Отпра́виться в путь, to start out (*or* set out) on a journey. Счастли́вого пути́!, have a good trip!; bon voyage! **3,** *fig.* path: и́збранный путь, one's chosen path. **4,** *fig.* track: на ло́жном пути́, on the wrong track. **5,** way; means: каки́м путём?, in what way?; by what means? **6,** *R.R.* track: запа́сный путь, sidetrack; siding. **7,** *pl., anat.* tract: дыха́тельные пути́, respiratory tract. —**по пути́, 1,** [*also,* **в пути́**] on the way; along the way; en route. **2,** (*with dat.*) going one's way: Нам с ва́ми по пути́, I am going your way; we are going the same way. *See also* **путём.**

пуф *n.* padded stool; hassock.

пух *n.* down; fluff; fuzz. —**в пух и прах, 1,** thoroughly; utterly. **2,** (*with verbs of dressing*) in one's finest. —**ни пу́ха ни пера́!,** good luck!

пу́хлый *adj.* chubby; pudgy; plump.

пу́хнуть *v.impfv.* [*pfv.* **вспу́хнуть**; *past* **пух, пу́хла**] to swell; swell up; become swollen.

пухови́к [*gen.* **-вика́**] *n.* feather bed.

пухо́вка [*gen. pl.* **-вок**] *n.* powder puff.

пухо́вый *adj.* made of down; downy.

пучегла́зый *adj., colloq.* goggle-eyed.

пучи́на *n.* **1,** ocean depths. **2,** *fig.* (*with gen.*) the depths (of).

пучо́к [*gen.* **пучка́**] *n.* **1,** bunch (*of flowers*); tuft (*of grass*). **2,** wisp (*of hay, straw, etc.*). **3,** beam: пучо́к части́ц, particle beam. **4,** bun: носи́ть во́лосы пучко́м, to wear one's hair in a bun.

пу́шечный *adj.* gun (*attrib.*); cannon (*attrib.*). —**пу́шечное мя́со,** cannon fodder. —**пу́шечное ядро́,** cannon ball.

пуши́нка [*gen. pl.* **-нок**] *n.* **1,** bit of fluff. **2,** tiny flake (*of snow*).

пуши́стый *adj.* downy; fluffy; fuzzy.

пуши́ть *v.impfv.* [*pfv.* **распуши́ть**] to fluff (up).

пу́шка [*gen. pl.* **пу́шек**] *n.* **1,** gun. **2,** cannon. —**как из пу́шки,** punctually; right on time. —**стреля́ть из пу́шки** (*or* **из пу́шек**) **по воробья́м,** to use overkill.

пушка́рь [*gen.* **-каря́**] *n.m., obs.* gunner; artilleryman.

пушни́на *n.* fur; furs.

пушно́й *adj.* **1,** fur (*attrib.*). **2,** fur-bearing.

пушо́к [*gen.* **пушка́**] *n.* fluff.

пу́ща *n.* dense forest.

пу́ще *adv., obs.* more.

пу́щий *adj., obs.* **1,** greatest. **2,** *preceded by* **для,** greater: для пу́щей ва́жности, for greater effect.

пуэрторика́нец [*gen.* **-нца**] *n.m.* [*fem.* **-нка**] Puerto Rican. —**пуэрторика́нский,** *adj.* Puerto Rican.

пчела́ [*pl.* **пчёлы**] *n.* bee.

пчели́ный *adj.* bee (*attrib.*). —**пчели́ный воск,** beeswax.

пчелово́д *n.* beekeeper. —**пчелово́дство,** beekeeping.

пче́льник *n.* apiary.

пшени́ца *n.* wheat. —**твёрдая пшени́ца,** durum wheat.

пшени́чный *adj.* wheat (*attrib.*).

пшено́ *n.* millet.

пыж [*gen.* **пыжа́**] *n.* wad (*used in loading a firearm*).

пы́жик *n.* **1,** young reindeer. **2,** fur of young reindeer.

пы́житься *v.r.impfv.* [*pfv.* **напы́житься**] *colloq.* **1,** to make every effort; strain every nerve. **2,** to act high and mighty.

пыл [*2nd loc.* **пылу́**] *n.* ardor. —**в пылу́** (+ *gen.*), in the heat of (battle, an argument, etc.); in a moment of (anger, passion, etc.). —**с пы́лу, с жа́ру,** piping hot.

пыла́ть *v.impfv.* **1,** to flame; blaze. **2,** (*of one's face*) to glow. **3,** (*with instr.*) to be consumed with (an emotion). Пыла́ть любо́вью к, to be madly in love with.

пылесо́с *n.* vacuum cleaner.

пылесо́сить *v.impfv., colloq.* to vacuum.

пыли́нка [*gen. pl.* **-нок**] *n.* speck of dust.

пыли́ть *v.impfv.* [*pfv.* **напыли́ть**] to raise (a cloud of) dust. —**пыли́ться,** *refl.* [*pfv.* **запыли́ться**] to get dusty; gather dust.

пы́лкий *adj.* ardent; fervent; fiery. —**пы́лкость,** *n.f.* ardor; fervor.

пыль [*2nd loc.* **пыли́**] *n.f.* dust. —**пуска́ть пыль в глаза́, 1,** to put on a false front. **2,** (*with dat.*) to pull the wool over someone's eyes.

пы́льник *n.* **1,** *bot.* anther. **2,** smock to protect against dust; duster. **3,** light summer overcoat.

пы́льный *adj.* **1,** dust (*attrib.*). **2,** dusty.

пыльца́ *n.* pollen.

пыта́ть *v.impfv.* **1,** to torture. **2,** *fig.* to torment.

пыта́ться *v.r.impfv.* [*pfv.* **попыта́ться**] to attempt; try; endeavor.

пы́тка [*gen. pl.* **пы́ток**] *n.* **1,** torture. **2,** *fig.* torture; agony; sheer hell.

пытли́вый *adj.* inquisitive. —**пытли́вость,** *n.f.* inquisitiveness.

пы́хать *v.impfv.* [*pres.* **пы́шу, пы́шешь**] *colloq.* **1,** to blaze. Пы́хать жа́ром, to be burning hot. **2,** *fig.* (*with instr.*) to radiate: пы́хать сча́стьем, to radiate happiness. Он пы́шет здоро́вьем, he is the picture of health.

пыхте́ние *n.* panting; puffing.

пыхте́ть *v.impfv.* [*pres.* **пыхчу́, пыхти́шь**] to puff; pant.

пы́шка [*gen. pl.* **пы́шек**] *n.* **1,** bun. **2,** *colloq.* plump child.

пы́шность *n.f.* sumptuousness; splendor; pomp.

пы́шный *adj.* **1,** sumptuous; magnificent. **2,** fluffy. **3,** (*of vegetation*) luxuriant; lush. **4,** (*of a woman*) plump; buxom. **5,** pompous; high-flown.

пьедеста́л *n.* pedestal.

пье́са *n.* (stage) play.

пью́щий *adj.* (*of a person*) who drinks. —*n.* drinker.

пьяне́ть *v.impfv.* [*pfv.* **опьяне́ть**] to get drunk.

пьяни́ть *v.impfv.* [*pfv.* **опьяни́ть**] to intoxicate; make drunk.

пья́ница *n.m. & f.* drunkard.

пья́нка *n., colloq.* drinking bout.

пья́нство *n.* drunkenness.

пья́нствовать *v.impfv.* [*pres.* **-ствую, -ствуешь**] to drink too much; be frequently drunk.

пья́ный *adj. & n.* drunk. —**под пья́ную ру́ку,** *colloq.* while drunk.

пэр *n.* peer. —**пэ́рство,** *n.* peerage.

пюпи́тр *n.* reading desk. —**но́тный пюпи́тр,** music stand.

пюре́ (рэ) *n.neut. indecl.* purée. —**я́блочное пюре́,** applesauce. —**карто́фельное пюре́,** mashed potatoes.

пядь [*pl.* **пя́ди, пяде́й, пядя́м**] *n.f.* span (*distance from thumb to forefinger*). —**пядь земли́,** dot of land. —**не отда́ть** (*or* **не уступи́ть**) **ни пя́ди земли́,** not to yield an inch. —**будь он семи́ пяде́й во лбу,** even if he were a genius/ the smartest man in the world/.

пя́лить *v.impfv., colloq.* **1,** *in* **пя́лить глаза́ на** (+ *acc.*) to stare at. **2,** (*often with* **на себя́**) to put on (a garment) with difficulty; struggle into.

пя́льцы [*gen.* **-лец**] *n.pl.* tambour (*embroidery frame*).

пясть *n.f.* metacarpus.

пята́ [*pl.* **пя́ты, пят, пята́м**] *n.* **1,** *obs.* heel. **2,** abutment. —**до пят,** (*of a garment*) extending down to one's ankles. —**по пята́м,** on someone's heels. —**под пято́й** (+ *gen.*), under the heel of.

пята́к [*gen.* **-така́**] *n., colloq.* **1,** five-kopeck piece. **2,** (*in the U.S.*) a nickel.

пятачо́к [*gen.* **-чка́**] *n., colloq.* **1,** = пята́к. **2,** pig's snout. **3,** small area; patch.

пя́тая *n., decl. as an adj.* fifth: одна́ пя́тая, one-fifth.

пятёрка *n.* **1,** the numeral 5. **2,** *colloq.* anything numbered 5. **3,** a grade of "five", signifying "excellent". **4,** *cards* five. **5,** *colloq.* five-ruble note.

пятерня́ *n., colloq.* one's hand.

пя́теро *collective numeral* five.

пятибо́рье *n.* pentathlon.

пятигра́нник *n.* pentahedron.

пятидесятиле́тие *n.* **1,** fiftieth anniversary; fiftieth birthday. **2,** fifty-year period.

пятидесятиле́тний *adj.* **1,** fifty-year (*attrib.*). **2,** fifty-year-old.

пятидеся́тница *n.* Pentecost.

пятидеся́тый *ordinal numeral* fiftieth.

пятидне́вный *adj.* five-day (*attrib.*).

пятикни́жие *n.* the Pentateuch.

пятиконе́чный *adj.* (*of a star*) five-pointed.

пятикра́тный *adj.* fivefold.

пятиле́тие *n.* **1,** fifth anniversary; fifth birthday. **2,** five-year period.

пятиле́тка [*gen. pl.* **-ток**] *n.* Five-Year Plan.

пятиле́тний *adj.* **1,** five-year (*attrib.*). **2,** five-year-old.

пятирублёвка [*gen. pl.* **-вок**] *n., colloq.* five-ruble note.

пятисо́тый *ordinal numeral* five-hundredth.

пятисто́пный *adj.* pentameter. —**пятисто́пный стих,** pentameter. —**пятисто́пный ямб,** iambic pentameter.

пя́титься *v.r.impfv.* [*pfv.* **попя́титься**; *pres.* **пя́чусь, пя́тишься**] **1,** to back up; move backwards; walk backwards. **2,** *colloq.* to back out; (*with* **от**) go back on.

пятиуго́льник *n.* pentagon. —**пятиуго́льный,** *adj.* pentagonal.

пя́тка [*gen. pl.* **пя́ток**] *n.* heel. —**лиза́ть пя́тки** (+ *dat.*), to lick someone's boots. —**наступа́ть на пя́тки** (+ *dat.*), to be close on the heels of. —**показа́ть пя́тки,** to take to one's heels. —**у меня́ душа́ ушла́ в пя́тки,** my heart sank.

пятна́дцатый *ordinal numeral* fifteenth.

пятна́дцать [*gen., dat. & prepl.* **-цати;** *instr.* **-цатью**] *numeral* fifteen.

пятна́ть *v.impfv.* [*pfv.* **запятна́ть**] **1,** to spot; stain. **2,** *fig.* to sully; tarnish.

пятна́шки [*gen.* **-шек**] *n.pl.* tag (*game*).

пятни́стый *adj.* spotted.

пя́тница *n.* Friday.

пятно́ [*pl.* **пя́тна, пя́тен**] *n.* spot; stain; blemish.

пя́тнышко [*pl.* **-шки, -шек**] *n., dim. of* пятно́.

пято́к [*gen.* **пятка́**] *n.* (*with gen. pl.*) *colloq.* five (*similar objects*).

пя́тый *ordinal numeral* fifth.

пять [*gen., dat. & prepl.* **пяти́;** *instr.* **пятью́**] *numeral* five.

пятьдеся́т [*gen., dat. & prepl.* **пяти́десяти;** *instr.* **пятью́десятью**] *numeral* fifty.

пятьсо́т [*gen.* **пятисо́т;** *dat.* **пятиста́м;** *instr.* **пятью́ста́ми;** *prepl.* **пятиста́х**] *numeral* five hundred.

пя́тью *adv.* five times: пя́тью пять — два́дцать пять, five times five is twenty-five.

P

P, p *n.neut.* seventeenth letter of the Russian alphabet.

раб [*gen.* **раба́**] *n.m.* [*fem.* **раба́**] slave.

рабовладе́лец [*gen.* **-льца**] *n.* slaveowner. **—рабовладе́льческий,** *adj.* slave-owning.

раболе́пный *adj.* servile; obsequious. **—раболе́пие; раболе́пство,** *n.* servility.

раболе́пствовать *v.impfv.* [*pres.* **-ствую, -ствуешь**] (*with* **пе́ред**) to be servile (to); kowtow (to); grovel (before).

рабо́та *n.* **1,** work: тяжёлая рабо́та, hard work; без рабо́ты, out of work. **2,** job: меня́ть рабо́ту, to change jobs. **3,** *pl.* work; operations: строи́тельные рабо́ты, construction work; спаса́тельные рабо́ты, rescue operations. **4,** deliberations (*of a congress, committee, etc.*). **5,** work (*produced by an artist, writer, etc.*): его́ после́дняя рабо́та, his latest work. **6,** workmanship: превосхо́дной рабо́ты, of superb workmanship. **7,** *in* курсова́я рабо́та, term paper. **—брать в рабо́ту, 1,** to take in hand. **2,** to take to task. **—брать** *or* **принима́ть на рабо́ту,** to take on; hire.

рабо́тать *v.impfv.* **1,** to work. **2,** (*with instr.*) to use; handle; wield (a tool). **3,** (*of a device*) to work; function; operate. **4,** (*of a store, library, etc.*) to be open (*on a given day*). **5,** *in* рабо́тать над собо́й, to work to improve oneself. **—вре́мя рабо́тает на нас,** time is on our side.

рабо́таться *v.r.impfv., impers.* **1,** *indicating the progress of work:* Сего́дня хорошо́ рабо́тается, the work is going well today. **2,** (*with dat.*) to feel like working: Мне сего́дня не рабо́тается, I don't feel like working today; I can't get down to work today.

рабо́тник *n.* **1,** worker: отли́чный рабо́тник, excellent worker. Рабо́тник иску́сства, person who works in the arts. Нау́чный рабо́тник, person engaged in scientific research. **2,** employee; official: рабо́тник посо́льства, embassy employee/official. Руководя́щий рабо́тник, person in a supervisory position.

рабо́тница *n.* woman worker.

рабо́тный *adj., obs.* working (*attrib.*). **—рабо́тный дом,** workhouse.

работода́тель *n.m.* employer.

работорго́вец [*gen.* **-вца**] *n.* slave trader. **—работорго́вля,** *n.* slave trade.

работоспосо́бный *adj.* **1,** able-bodied. **2,** hard-working; industrious. **—работоспосо́бность,** *n.f.* ability to work; capacity for work.

работя́га *n.m. & f., colloq.* hard worker.

работя́щий *adj., colloq.* hard-working; industrious.

рабо́чий *adj.* work (*attrib.*); working; worker's. **—**n. worker; workman; *pl.* the workers. **—рабо́чий день,** workday. **—рабо́чий класс,** the working class. **—рабо́чая ло́шадь,** workhorse. **—рабо́чее ме́сто, 1,** workplace. **2,** job: сто рабо́чих мест, one hundred jobs. **—рабо́чие ру́ки,** workmen; hands. **—рабо́чая си́ла,** manpower; labor. **—рабо́чий скот,** draft animals. **—рабо́чий стол,** desk. **—рабо́чий сце́ны,** stagehand. **—в рабо́чем поря́дке,** in the course of work; (while) on the job.

ра́бский *adj.* **1,** slave (*attrib.*). **2,** servile; slavish.

ра́бство *n.* slavery; bondage; servitude.

рабы́ня *n.* slave; bondwoman.

равви́н *n.* rabbi. **—равви́нский,** *adj.* rabbinical.

ра́венство *n.* equality. **—знак ра́венства,** equal sign.

равне́ние *n., mil.* alignment.

равни́на *n.* plain.

равни́нный *adj.* **1,** of the plains. **2,** (*of terrain*) flat.

равно́ *adv.* equally. **—**adj., used predicatively (*with dat.*) equal (to): Два плюс три равно́ пяти́, two plus three equals five. **—всё равно́, 1,** it is all the same; it makes no difference. **2,** still; all the same; nevertheless. **—всё равно́, что,** just the same as. **—равно́ и; равно́ как,** as well as.

равнобе́дренный *adj., math.* isosceles.

равнове́сие *n.* balance; equilibrium. **—выводи́ть из равнове́сия, 1,** to throw (*or* knock) off balance. **2,** *fig.* to disconcert; rattle.

равноде́нствие *n.* equinox.

равноду́шие *n.* indifference.

равноду́шный *adj.* [*short form* **-шен, -шна, -шно, -шны**] (*with* **к**) indifferent (to). **—равноду́шно,** *adv.* with indifference.

равнозна́чный *adj.* equivalent.

равноме́рный *adj.* even; uniform. **—равноме́рно,** *adv.* evenly.

равнопра́вие *n.* equal rights; equality.

равнопра́вный *adj.* **1,** equal; enjoying equal rights. **2,** equitable.

равноси́льный *adj.* **1,** of equal strength. **2,** (*with dat.*) equivalent (to); tantamount (to).

равносторо́нний *adj.* equilateral.

равноуго́льный *adj.* equiangular.

равноце́нный *adj.* **1,** equal in price. **2,** of equal value.

ра́вный *adj.* [*short form* **ра́вен, равна́, равно́, равны́**] equal. —*n.* equal: пе́рвый среди́ ра́вных, first among equals. —**на ра́вной ноге́ с,** on an equal footing with. —**при про́чих ра́вных усло́виях,** other things being equal. —**ра́вным о́бразом,** by the same token.

равня́ть *v.impfv.* [*pfv.* **сравня́ть**] **1,** to make equal; equalize. **2,** [*impfv. only*] (*with* **с** + *instr.*) to equate (with). —**равня́ться,** *refl.* [*impfv. only*] **1,** (*with dat.*) to equal. **2,** (*with dat.*) to amount to; be tantamount to. **3,** (*with* **с** + *instr.*) *colloq.* to compete (with); compare (with). **4,** (*with* **по**) to emulate. **5,** *mil.* to dress.

рагу́ *n.neut. indecl.* ragout; stew.

рад *adj., used predicatively* (*with inf., dat. or* **что**) glad; pleased: О́чень рад (ра́да) познако́миться с ва́ми!, pleased to meet you! Я рад слу́чаю (+ *inf.*), I am glad (*or* pleased) to have the opportunity to...

рада́р *n.* radar. —**рада́рный,** *adj.* radar (*attrib.*).

ра́джа *n.m.* rajah.

ра́ди *prep., with gen.* for; for the sake of. —**ра́ди бо́га!,** *see* бог.

радиа́льный *adj.* radial.

радиа́тор *n.* radiator.

радиа́ция *n.* radiation.

ра́дий *n.* radium. —**ра́диевый,** *adj.* radium.

радика́л *n.* **1,** *polit.* radical. **2,** *math.* radical sign. **3,** *chem.* radical. —**радикали́зм,** *n.* radicalism.

радика́льный *adj.* **1,** *polit.* radical. **2,** radical; drastic. —**радика́льно,** *adv.* radically.

ра́дио *n. indecl.* **1,** radio: по ра́дио, on (*or* over) the radio. **2,** = радиоприёмник.

радиоакти́вный *adj.* radioactive. —**радиоакти́вность,** *n.f.* radioactivity.

радиовеща́ние *n.* broadcasting. —**радиовеща́тельный,** *adj.* broadcasting.

радиогра́мма *n.* radio message; radiogram.

радио́ла *n.* radio-phonograph.

радиоло́гия *n.* radiology. —**радио́лог,** *n.* radiologist.

радиолока́тор *n.* radar (set). —**радиолока́ция,** *n.* radar; detection by radar. —**радиолокацио́нный,** *adj.* radar (*attrib.*).

радиолюби́тель *n.m.* amateur radio operator; ham operator.

радиомая́к [*gen.* **-маяка́**] *n.* (radio) beacon.

радиопеленга́тор *n.* (radio) direction finder.

радиопереда́тчик *n.* radio transmitter.

радиопереда́ча *n.* radio broadcast; radio transmission.

радиоприёмник *n.* radio: включи́ть радиоприёмник, to turn on the radio.

радиосвя́зь *n.f.* radio communication.

радиослу́шатель *n.m.* (radio) listener.

радиоста́нция *n.* radio station.

радиотелегра́фия *n.* radiotelegraphy.

радиотелефо́н *n.* radiotelephone. —**радиотелефони́я,** *n.* radiotelephony.

радиотерапи́я *n.* radiation therapy; radiotherapy.

радиоте́хник *n.* radio mechanic. —**радиоте́хника,** *n.* radio engineering.

ради́ровать *v.impfv. & pfv.* [*pres.* **-рую, -руешь**] to radio.

ради́ст *n.* radio operator.

ра́диус *n.* radius. —**ра́диус де́йствия,** range (*of an aircraft, missile, etc.*).

ра́довать *v.impfv.* [*pfv.* **обра́довать;** *pres.* **-дую, -дуешь**] to gladden; make happy. —**ра́доваться,** *refl.* to be glad; be happy; rejoice. Ра́доваться изве́стию, to be happy about the news; rejoice over the news.

радо́н *n.* radon.

ра́достно *adv.* with joy. —*adj., used predicatively* (*with dat.*) delighted: Мне бы́ло ра́достно, что..., I was delighted that...

ра́достный *adj.* joyful; joyous. Ра́достное изве́стие, joyful news; glad tidings.

ра́дость *n.f.* joy; gladness. —**на ра́достях, 1,** in one's joy. **2,** to celebrate; to mark the (happy) occasion.

ра́дуга *n.* rainbow.

ра́дужность *n.f.* iridescence.

ра́дужный *adj.* **1,** iridescent; opalescent. **2,** *fig.* bright; rosy. **3,** (*of hopes, spirits, etc.*) high. —**ра́дужная оболо́чка,** *anat.* iris. —**ра́дужная форе́ль,** rainbow trout.

раду́шие *n.* cordiality; hospitality.

раду́шный *adj.* cordial. —**раду́шно,** *adv.* cordially.

раёк [*gen.* **райка́**] *n., colloq.* **1,** little paradise. **2,** *obs., theat.* gallery.

раж *n., colloq.* passion; frenzy. —**войти́ в раж,** to become very emotional; get all worked up.

раз [*pl.* **разы́, раз**] *n.* **1,** time: два ра́за, two times. **2,** *in counting,* one: раз, два, три, one, two, three. —*adv.* once: Раз по́здно ве́чером, once late at night. —*conj., colloq.* since; if: Раз не зна́ешь, не говори́, if you don't know, don't talk. —**в са́мый раз, 1,** the right time. **2,** the right size. —**вся́кий раз, когда́,** every time; whenever. —**ещё раз,** again; once again. —**как раз,** just; exactly; precisely: как раз то, что мне ну́жно, just what I need. —**не раз,** more than once. —**ни ра́зу,** not a single time. —**раз за ра́зом,** time after time; time and again.

раз- *also,* **рас-, разо-, разъ-,** *prefix* **1,** *indicating breaking asunder:* разбива́ть, to smash. **2,** (*with* **-ся**) *indicating dispersal:* разъезжа́ться, to depart (*in various directions*). **3,** *indicating distribution:* раздава́ть, to hand out. **4,** *indicating undoing or unfastening:* развя́зывать, to untie. **5,** *indicating reversal of action:* разлюби́ть, to cease to love. **6,** (*with* **-ся**) [*with pfv. verbs only*] *indicating warming up to one's activity:* разговори́ться, to warm to one's subject.

разбави́тель *n.m.* thinner (*e.g. of paints*).

разба́вить [*infl.* **-влю, -вишь**] *v., pfv. of* разбавля́ть.

разбавля́ть *v.impfv.* [*pfv.* **разба́вить**] to dilute.

разбаза́ривать *v.impfv.* [*pfv.* **разбаза́рить**] *colloq.* to squander.

разбалова́ться *v.r.pfv.* [*infl.* **-лу́юсь, -лу́ешься**] *colloq.* **1,** to act up; get out of hand. **2,** to become spoiled.

разба́лтывать *v.impfv.* [*pfv.* **разболта́ть**] *colloq.* **1,** to shake up; stir. **2,** to work loose; knock loose. **3,** to give away (a secret). —**разба́лтываться,** *refl., colloq.* **1,** to come loose. **2,** to get carried away (*when speaking*). **3,** *fig.* to get out of hand.

разбе́г *n.* running start (*before jumping, diving, taking off, etc.*). —**с разбе́га; с разбе́гу**, while running at top speed. —**прыжо́к с разбе́га/разбе́гу**, running broad jump.

разбега́ться *v.r.impfv.* [*pfv.* **разбежа́ться**] **1,** to scatter; disperse. **2,** to run at top speed. **3,** to make a running start. —**у меня́ глаза́ разбега́ются**, I don't know where to look first.

разбежа́ться [*infl. like* **бежа́ть**] *v.r., pfv. of* **разбега́ться**.

разбереди́ть *v., pfv. of* **береди́ть**.

разбива́ть *v.impfv.* [*pfv.* **разби́ть**] **1,** to break; smash; shatter. **2,** to hurt badly; fracture. **3,** to defeat; crush. **4,** *fig.* to shatter (hopes, illusions, etc.). **5,** *fig.* to demolish (an argument, theory, etc.). **6,** *fig.* to ruin; wreck (someone's life). **7,** *colloq.* to wear out (shoes). **8,** to divide; break up. **9,** to lay out (a garden, park, etc.). **10,** to pitch (a tent); set up (camp). *See also* **разби́тый**.

разбива́ться *v.r.impfv.* [*pfv.* **разби́ться**] **1,** to break; be broken; be smashed. **2,** to break up; split up. **3,** (*of a plane*) to crash. **4,** to be badly hurt. —**разби́ться на́смерть**, to be killed (*in a crash, fall, etc.*).

разби́вка *n.* **1,** dividing up. **2,** laying out.

разбинтова́ть [*infl.* **-ту́ю, -ту́ешь**] *v., pfv. of* **разбинто́вывать**.

разбинто́вывать *v.impfv.* [*pfv.* **разбинтова́ть**] to unbandage.

разбира́тельство *n.* investigation. —**суде́бное разбира́тельство**, trial.

разбира́ть *v.impfv.* [*pfv.* **разобра́ть**] **1,** to take apart; dismantle. **2,** to analyze; examine; look into. **3,** to sort out; go over; go through. **4,** to buy up. **5,** to make out; discern. **6,** to make out; decipher (something written). **7,** *gram.* to parse. **8,** *colloq.* (*of an emotion*) to seize; come over. **9,** [*impfv. only*] *colloq.* to stop to choose; take time to choose.

разбира́ться *v.r.impfv.* [*pfv.* **разобра́ться**] **1,** [*impfv. only*] (*with* **в** + *prepl.*) to understand; have an understanding of. **2,** (*with* **в** + *prepl.*) to figure out; gain an understanding of. **3,** (*with* **с** + *instr.*) to deal with; handle. **4,** *colloq.* to put one's things away (*after a trip*).

разбитно́й *adj., colloq.* **1,** capable; adept. **2,** sprightly; outgoing.

разби́тый *adj.* **1,** broken. **2,** battered; bruised. **3,** defeated. **4,** ruined; shattered. **5,** worn down. **6,** worn out; jaded. —**разби́т параличо́м**, paralyzed.

разби́ть [*infl.* **разобью́, разобьёшь**] *v., pfv. of* **бить** (*in sense #5*) *and* **разбива́ть**. —**разби́ться**, *refl., pfv. of* **разбива́ться**.

разбогате́ть *v., pfv. of* **богате́ть**.

разбо́й *n.* robbery. —**разбо́йник**, *n.* robber.

разбо́йничать *v.impfv.* to commit robberies.

разбо́йничий [*fem.* **-чья**] *adj.* **1,** robbers'. **2,** (*of an attack*) treacherous. *Also,* **разбо́йнический**.

разболе́ться *v.r.pfv., colloq.* **1,** [*infl.* **-е́юсь, -е́ешься**] to become seriously ill. **2,** [*infl.* **-и́тся**] to begin to hurt.

разболта́ть *v., pfv. of* **разба́лтывать**. —**разболта́ться**, *refl., pfv. of* **разба́лтываться**.

разбомби́ть *v.pfv.* [*infl.* **-блю́, -би́шь**] to destroy; wipe out (*by bombing*); bomb out.

разбо́р *n.* **1,** taking apart. **2,** analysis. **3,** investigation. **4,** sorting out. **5,** selectivity. С разбо́ром, selectively. Без разбо́ра, indiscriminately. **6,** *gram.* parsing. **7,** *colloq.* quality; caliber.

разбо́рка *n.* **1,** taking apart; dismantling. **2,** sorting out.

разбо́рный *adj.* **1,** collapsible. **2,** (*of furniture*) sectional.

разбо́рчиво *adv.* legibly.

разбо́рчивость *n.f.* **1,** discrimination. **2,** legibility.

разбо́рчивый *adj.* **1,** discriminating; particular. **2,** legible.

разбрани́ть *v.pfv., colloq.* to scold; bawl out; berate. —**разбрани́ться**, *refl.* (*with* **с** + *instr.*) *colloq.* to quarrel (with).

разбра́сывать *v.impfv.* [*pfv.* **разброса́ть**] to scatter. —**разбра́сываться**, *refl., colloq.* **1,** to stretch out. **2,** *fig.* to do too many things at once; spread oneself thin.

разбреда́ться *v.r.impfv.* [*pfv.* **разбрести́сь**] (*of many people*) to wander off (*in different directions*).

разбрести́сь [*infl. like* **брести́**] *v.r., pfv. of* **разбреда́ться**.

разбро́д *n.* **1,** confusion; disorder. **2,** discord; dissension.

разбро́санный *adj.* **1,** scattered; dispersed. **2,** *colloq.* spread out; rambling. **3,** *colloq.* disconnected; incoherent. **4,** *colloq.* spread too thin; doing too many things at once.

разброса́ть *v., pfv. of* **разбра́сывать**. —**разброса́ться**, *refl., pfv. of* **разбра́сываться**.

разбры́згиватель *n.m.* sprinkler.

разбры́згивать *v.impfv.* [*pfv.* **разбры́згать**] to splash; sprinkle; spray. —**разбры́згиваться**, *refl.* to splash; sprinkle.

разбуди́ть *v., pfv. of* **буди́ть** (*in sense #1*).

разбуха́ть *v.impfv.* [*pfv.* **разбу́хнуть**] to swell; swell up; become swollen.

разбу́хнуть [*past* **-бу́х, -бу́хла**] *v., pfv. of* **бу́хнуть**[1] *and* **разбуха́ть**.

разбушева́ться *v.r.pfv.* [*infl.* **-шу́юсь, -шу́ешься**] **1,** (*of a storm, the sea, etc.*) to rage. **2,** *colloq.* to become enraged; fly into a rage.

разва́л *n.* **1,** collapse; breakdown; breakup. **2,** outdoor secondhand market (*with merchandise displayed on the ground*).

разва́лец [*gen.* **-льца**] *n., in* **ходи́ть с разва́льцем**, *colloq.* **1,** to waddle. **2,** to shuffle along; amble along.

разва́ливать *v.impfv.* [*pfv.* **развали́ть**] **1,** to tear down. **2,** *fig.* to ruin; make a mess of. —**разва́ливаться**, *refl.* **1,** to collapse; come tumbling down. **2,** to fall apart; go to pieces. **3,** *colloq.* to sprawl out.

разва́лина *n.* **1,** *pl.* ruins. **2,** *colloq.* (physical) wreck.

развали́ть [*infl.* **-валю́, -ва́лишь**] *v., pfv. of* **разва́ливать**. —**развали́ться**, *refl., pfv. of* **разва́ливаться**.

разва́ривать *v.impfv.* [*pfv.* **развари́ть**] to boil (something) until it is soft.

развари́ть [*infl.* **-варю́, -ва́ришь**] *v., pfv. of* **разва́ривать**.

ра́зве *particle* **1,** really? **2,** (*with inf.*) perhaps one should...; shouldn't one...? **3,** (*with* **не**) isn't it...?: Ра́зве не я́сно, что..., isn't it clear that...? —*conj.* unless: ра́зве пого́да испо́ртится, unless the weather turns bad. —**ра́зве то́лько; ра́зве что, 1,** only: Туда́ хо́дят ра́зве то́лько старики́, only old people go there. За исключе́нием ра́зве что (+ *gen.*), with the sole exception of... **2,** except: ра́зве то́лько на кра́йнем се́вере, except in the extreme north. Он почти́ не постаре́л, ра́зве что стал чу́точку седе́е, he has hardly aged at all except for becoming a bit grayer.

развева́ть *v.impfv.* to blow about; cause to wave. —**развева́ться,** *refl.* to blow; flutter.

разве́дать *v., pfv. of* разве́дывать.

разведе́ние *n.* raising; breeding.

разведённый *adj.* divorced. —*n.* divorced man. —**разведённая,** *n.* divorcée.

разве́дка *n.* **1,** (gathering of) intelligence. **2,** intelligence service. **3,** reconnaissance. **4,** prospecting; exploration.

разве́дочный *adj.* **1,** exploratory. **2,** reconnaissance (*attrib.*); intelligence (*attrib.*).

разве́дчик *n.* **1,** *mil.* scout. **2,** intelligence agent. **3,** prospector. **4,** reconnaissance plane.

разве́дывательный *adj.* intelligence (*attrib.*); reconnaissance (*attrib.*).

разве́дывать *v.impfv.* [*pfv.* разве́дать] **1,** (*with* о) *colloq.* to find out (about). **2,** *mil.* to reconnoiter. **3,** to prospect; explore (a region). **4,** to search for; prospect for (deposits of gold, ore, etc.); [*pfv. only*] to find; discover (same).

развезти́ [*infl. like* везти́] *v., pfv. of* развози́ть.

разве́ивать *v.impfv.* [*pfv.* разве́ять] **1,** (*of the wind*) to scatter; disperse. **2,** *fig.* to dispel.

развенча́ть *v.impfv.* [*pfv.* развенча́ть] to discredit; debunk.

развёрнутый *adj.* **1,** unfolded; unfurled. **2,** *mil.* deployed; extended. **3,** all-out; full-scale. **4,** detailed; comprehensive.

разверну́ть *v., pfv. of* развёртывать *and* развора́чивать (*in senses #1 & #2*). —**разверну́ться,** *refl., pfv. of* развёртываться *and* развора́чиваться.

разве́рстка *n.* **1,** apportionment; allotment. **2,** assessment (*of a tax*).

развёртка [*gen. pl.* -ток] *n.* reamer.

развёртывание *n.* **1,** unfolding; unwrapping; unrolling. **2,** *mil.* deployment. **3,** *fig.* development.

развёртывать *v.impfv.* [*pfv.* разверну́ть] **1,** to unfold; unwrap. **2,** to unroll; unfurl. **3,** *mil.* to deploy. **4,** to launch (a campaign, movement, etc.). **5,** to develop; expand. **6,** *fig.* to develop; display; realize (one's abilities, talent, etc.). —**развёртываться,** *refl.* **1,** to come unfolded; come unrolled; come undone. **2,** *mil.* to deploy. **3,** *fig.* to develop.

развесели́ть *v.pfv.* to cheer up; gladden. —**развесели́ться,** *refl.* to cheer up; become cheerful.

развесёлый *adj., colloq.* gay; merry; jolly.

разве́систый *adj.* (*of a tree*) spreading.

разве́сить [*infl.* -шу, -сишь] *v., pfv. of* разве́шивать.

разве́ска *n.* weighing.

развесно́й *adj.* sold by weight.

развести́ [*infl. like* вести́] *v., pfv. of* разводи́ть. —**развести́сь,** *refl., pfv. of* разводи́ться.

разветви́ться *v.r., pfv. of* разветвля́ться.

разветвле́ние *n.* fork (*in a road*).

разветвлённый *adj.* extensive; far-flung.

разветвля́ться *v.r. impfv.* [*pfv.* разветви́ться] **1,** (*of a tree or bush*) to form branches. **2,** (*of a road*) to fork; divide.

разве́шивать *v.impfv.* [*pfv.* разве́сить] **1,** to weigh out. **2,** [*pfv. also* разве́шать] to hang out (a number of objects). **3,** (*of a tree*) to spread (its branches).

разве́ять [*infl.* -ве́ю, -ве́ешь] *v., pfv. of* разве́ивать.

развива́ть *v.impfv.* [*pfv.* разви́ть] **1,** to develop. **2,** to gather; pick up (speed). **3,** to unwind; unravel. —**развива́ть бу́рную де́ятельность,** to get busy; swing into action —**развива́ть наступле́ние,** to step up an offensive. —**развива́ть успе́х,** to follow up one's success.

развива́ться *v.r.impfv.* [*pfv.* разви́ться] **1,** to develop. **2,** to come unwound. —**развива́ющиеся стра́ны,** developing countries.

разви́лина *n.* fork (*in a road or branches of a tree*).

разви́листый *adj.* forked.

разви́лка [*gen. pl.* -лок] *n.* fork (*in a road*).

развинти́ть [*infl.* -чу́, -ти́шь] *v., pfv. of* разви́нчивать. —**развинти́ться,** *refl., pfv. of* разви́нчиваться.

разви́нченный *adj.* **1,** unscrewed. **2,** (*of a person's gait*) unsteady. **3,** *colloq.* unnerved.

разви́нчивать *v.impfv.* [*pfv.* развинти́ть] to unscrew. —**разви́нчиваться,** *refl.* **1,** to come unscrewed. **2,** *colloq.* to go to pieces. **3,** *colloq.* (*of one's nerves*) to be shot.

разви́тие *n.* development. —**разви́тие собы́тий,** course of events.

развито́й *adj.* [*short form* ра́звит, развита́, ра́звито, ра́звиты] **1,** developed; well-developed. **2,** mature.

разви́ть [*infl.* разовью́, разовьёшь; *past fem.* развила́] *v., pfv. of* развива́ть. —**разви́ться,** *refl., pfv. of* развива́ться.

развлека́тельный *adj.* produced *or* intended for entertainment; entertainment (*attrib.*).

развлека́ть *v.impfv.* [*pfv.* развле́чь] to entertain; amuse. —**развлека́ться,** *refl.* to amuse oneself; seek diversion.

развлече́ние *n.* amusement; entertainment; diversion; recreation.

развле́чь [*infl. like* влечь] *v., pfv. of* развлека́ть. —**развле́чься,** *refl., pfv. of* развлека́ться.

разво́д *n.* **1,** divorce. Они́ в разво́де, they are divorced. **2,** posting (*of sentries*). **3,** breeding. *See also* разво́ды.

разводи́ть *v.impfv.* [*pfv.* развести́; *pres.* -вожу́, -во́дишь] **1,** to take; conduct (*each to his place*). **2,** *mil.* to post (sentries). **3,** to separate; pull apart. **4,** to grant a divorce to. **5,** to open (a drawbridge). **6,** to dilute; dissolve. **7,** to raise; breed. **8,** to grow; cultivate (plants). **9,** to build; make (a fire). **10,** *in* разводи́ть рука́ми, to throw up one's hands. —**разводи́ться,** *refl.* **1,** (*with* с + *instr.*) to divorce; get a divorce from. **2,** to breed; multiply.

разво́дка *n., colloq.* separating. Разво́дка моста́, opening up of a drawbridge.

разводно́й *adj., in* разводно́й мост, drawbridge; разводно́й (га́ечный) ключ, adjustable wrench.

разво́ды [*gen.* -дов] *n.pl.* **1,** design; pattern. **2,** *colloq.* streaks; stains. В разво́дах, streaked.

развóз *n.* delivery; conveyance; transport.

развози́ть *v.impfv.* [*pfv.* **развезти́**; *pres.* **-вожý, -вóзишь**] **1,** to deliver; convey; transport (*each to his or its destination*). **2,** *impers., colloq.* to become impassable: Дорóгу развезлó, the road became impassable.

развóзка *n., colloq.* delivery; conveyance; transport.

разволновáть *v.pfv.* [*infl.* **-нýю, -нýешь**] to upset; throw into a state. —**разволновáться**, *refl.* to become highly upset.

развора́чивать *v.impfv.* **1,** [*pfv.* **развернýть**] = **развёртывать** (*in all senses*). **2,** [*pfv.* **развернýть**] to turn (a vehicle) around. **3,** [*pfv.* **развороти́ть**] to turn (a place) upside down (*during a search*). **4,** [*pfv.* **развороти́ть**] to smash; shatter. —**развора́чиваться**, *refl.* [*pfv.* **развернýться**] **1,** to turn around (*in a vehicle*). **2,** *fig.* (*of events*) to develop; unfold.

разворовáть [*infl.* **-рýю, -рýешь**] *v., pfv. of* **разворóвывать**.

разворóвывать *v.impfv.* [*pfv.* **разворовáть**] *colloq.* to steal; make off with.

разворóт *n.* **1,** U-turn. **2,** turn (*in a road*). **3,** (*with gen.*) *colloq.* development (of). **4,** inside (*of something that folds over*). **5,** double page; centerfold.

развороти́ть [*infl.* **-рочý, -рóтишь**] *v., pfv. of* **развора́чивать** (*in senses #3 & #4*).

разврáт *n.* debauchery; depravity.

разврати́ть [*infl.* **-щý, -ти́шь**] *v., pfv. of* **развраща́ть**. —**разврати́ться**, *refl., pfv. of* **развраща́ться**.

разврáтник *n.* profligate; lecher; libertine; rake; roué.

разврáтничать *v.impfv.* to lead a dissolute life.

разврáтный *adj.* dissolute; profligate.

развраща́ть *v.impfv.* [*pfv.* **разврати́ть**] to corrupt; deprave; debauch. —**развраща́ться**, *refl.* **1,** to become corrupted. **2,** to give way to debauchery.

развраще́ние *n.* (*with gen.*) corruption (of).

развращённый *adj.* corrupt; depraved; dissolute. —**развращённость**, *n.f.* depravity.

развьючивать *v.impfv.* [*pfv.* **развьючить**] to unload (a pack animal).

развязáть [*infl.* **-вяжý, -вя́жешь**] *v., pfv. of* **развя́зывать**. —**развязáться**, *refl., pfv. of* **развя́зываться**.

развя́зка [*gen. pl.* **-зок**] *n.* **1,** outcome; upshot. **2,** climax; dénouement. **3,** (highway) interchange. Кольцевáя развя́зка, traffic circle.

развя́зный *adj.* overly familiar; forward.

развя́зывать *v.impfv.* [*pfv.* **развязáть**] **1,** to untie. **2,** *fig., colloq.* to free; release. —**развязáть войнý**, to unleash a war. —**развязáть рýки** (+ *dat.*), to untie someone's hands (*fig.*). —**развязáть язы́к**, **1,** (*with dat.*) to loosen someone's tongue. **2,** to start talking.

развя́зываться *v.r.impfv.* [*pfv.* **развязáться**] **1,** to come untied; come loose; come undone. **2,** *fig.* (*with* **с** + *instr.*) *colloq.* to get rid of; finish with.

разгадáть *v., pfv. of* **разгáдывать**.

разгáдка [*gen. pl.* **-док**] *n.* **1,** solving; unraveling. **2,** solution.

разгáдывать *v.impfv.* [*pfv.* **разгадáть**] **1,** to solve; unravel. **2,** to figure out; divine.

разгáр *n.* high point; height: в разгáр (*or* в разгáре) сезóна, at the height of the season. —в (пóлном *or* сáмом) разгáре, at its height; in full swing.

разгерметизáция *n.* loss of pressure.

разгибáть *v.impfv.* [*pfv.* **разогнýть**] to unbend; straighten. —**рабóтать, не разгибáя спины́,** to work without letup.

разгибáться *v.r.impfv.* [*pfv.* **разогнýться**] to straighten up.

разгильдя́й *n., colloq.* slob.

разглагóльствовать *v.impfv.* [*pres.* **-ствую, -ствуешь**] *colloq.* to speak at length; hold forth.

разгла́живать *v.impfv.* [*pfv.* **разгла́дить**] **1,** to smooth out. **2,** to press; iron. —**разгла́живаться**, *refl.* to become smoothed out.

разглашáть *v.impfv.* [*pfv.* **разгласи́ть**] to divulge; disclose; make known.

разглаше́ние *n.* divulging; divulgence; disclosure.

разгляде́ть *v.pfv.* [*infl.* **-жý, -ди́шь**] to discern; make out.

разгля́дывать *v.impfv.* to examine closely; look over.

разгне́ванный *adj.* furious; enraged; incensed.

разгне́вать *v.pfv.* to infuriate; enrage. —**разгне́ваться**, *refl.* to fly into a rage.

разговáривать *v.impfv.* to talk; speak; converse. Разговáривать по-рýсски, to speak Russian. Они́ не разговáривают друг с дрýгом, they don't talk to each other; they are not on speaking terms.

разгове́ться *v.r.pfv.* to break the Lenten fast.

разговóр *n.* **1,** conversation. **2,** talk: Тóлько и разговóру, что об э́том, it's all that people are talking about. **3,** subject: перемени́ть раз-говóр, to change the subject. Э́то другóй разговóр, that's another matter; that's something else again. —**без разговóров!; и никаки́х разговóров!**, and no argument!; I want to hear nothing more about it!

разговори́ть *v.pfv., colloq.* to draw (someone) into conversation. —**разговори́ться**, *refl., colloq.* **1,** to get into a conversation; get to talking. **2,** to warm to one's subject.

разговóрник *n.* phrase book.

разговóрный *adj.* **1,** conversational. **2,** colloquial. —**разговóрная бýдка**, telephone booth. —**разговóрный язы́к**, colloquial *or* spoken language.

разговóрчивый *adj.* talkative; loquacious. —**разговóрчивость**, *n.f.* loquaciousness.

разгóн *n.* **1,** dispersal. **2,** momentum. —**с разгóна**, at top speed; full tilt.

разгоня́ть *v.impfv.* [*pfv.* **разогнáть**] **1,** to disperse; break up. **2,** *fig.* to dispel (a feeling). **3,** to drive (a vehicle) at high speed; race. —**разгоня́ться**, *refl.* to gather momentum.

разгора́живать *v.impfv.* [*pfv.* **разгороди́ть**] to partition; divide into sections by means of partitions.

разгора́ться *v.r.impfv.* [*pfv.* **разгоре́ться**] **1,** to begin to burn properly. **2,** (*of one's cheeks*) to become flushed. **3,** *fig.* (*of passions, an argument, etc.*) to flare (up); erupt.

разгороди́ть [*infl.* **-рожý, -рóдишь** *or* **-роди́шь**] *v., pfv. of* **разгора́живать**.

разгорячи́ть *v., pfv. of* **горячи́ть**. —**разгорячи́ться**, *refl., pfv. of* **горячи́ться**.

разгра́бить v.pfv. [infl. -блю, -бишь] to rob; loot; ransack; plunder.

разграбле́ние n. **1,** delimitation. **2,** differentiation.

разграни́чивать v.impfv. [pfv. **разграни́чить**] **1,** to delimit; demarcate. **2,** to distinguish; differentiate.

разграфи́ть v., pfv. of **графи́ть**.

разгреба́ть v.impfv. [pfv. **разгрести́**] to rake aside; shovel aside. Разгреба́ть снег, to shovel snow.

разгрести́ [infl. like **грести́**] v., pfv. of **разгреба́ть**.

разгро́м n. **1,** crushing defeat; rout. **2,** destruction; devastation. **3,** colloq. havoc; chaos.

разгроми́ть v., pfv. of **громи́ть**.

разгро́мный adj., colloq. scathing; blistering.

разгружа́ть v.impfv. [pfv. **разгрузи́ть**] **1,** to unload (a vehicle, vessel, etc.). **2,** fig., colloq. to relieve (of part of one's work). —**разгружа́ться**, refl. to unload; discharge cargo.

разгрузи́ть [infl. -гружу́, -гру́зишь or -грузи́шь] v., pfv. of **разгружа́ть**. —**разгрузи́ться**, refl., pfv. of **разгружа́ться**.

разгру́зка n. unloading.

разгрыза́ть v.impfv. [pfv. **разгры́зть**] to bite in two; crack with one's teeth.

разгры́зть [infl. like **грызть**] v., pfv. of **разгрыза́ть**.

разгу́л n. **1,** carousing. **2,** fig. (with gen.) wave: разгу́л наси́лия, wave of violence.

разгу́ливать v.impfv. [pfv. **разгуля́ть**] colloq. **1,** [impfv. only] to take a stroll. **2,** to dispel (a feeling). **3,** to amuse in order to keep awake. —**разгу́ливаться**, refl., colloq. **1,** to live it up; let oneself go. **2,** to become wide-awake. **3,** (of the weather) to clear up.

разгу́лье n., colloq. revelry.

разгу́льный adj., colloq. wild; fast; loose.

разгуля́ть v., pfv. of **разгу́ливать**. —**разгуля́ться**, refl., pfv. of **разгу́ливаться**.

раздава́ть v.impfv. [pfv. **разда́ть**; pres. -даю́, -даёшь] to distribute; give out; hand out. —**раздава́ться**, refl. **1,** to be heard; resound; ring out. **2,** to become wider; expand. **3,** to move aside; make way.

раздави́ть v.pfv. [infl. -давлю́, -да́вишь] **1,** pfv. of **дави́ть** (in senses #5 & #6). **2,** to overwhelm; crush.

разда́ривать v.impfv. [pfv. **раздари́ть**] to give away (as gifts).

раздари́ть [infl. -дарю́, -да́ришь] v., pfv. of **разда́ривать**.

разда́точный adj. distributing; distribution (attrib.).

разда́ть [infl. like **дать**; past fem. раздала́] v., pfv. of **раздава́ть**. —**разда́ться**, refl. [past tense stress as in да́ться] pfv. of **раздава́ться**.

разда́ча n. distribution.

раздва́ивать v.impfv. [pfv. **раздвои́ть**] to cut in two; divide in half. —**раздва́иваться**, refl. to divide; be divided.

раздвига́ть v.impfv. [pfv. **раздви́нуть**] **1,** to draw apart; spread apart; pull apart. **2,** to draw aside; move aside. **3,** to push one's way through (a crowd). **4,** to extend (a table). —**раздвига́ться**, refl. **1,** (of a curtain) to part; (of a crowd) to step aside; make way. **2,** to expand. **3,** [impfv. only] (of a table) to expand; open up.

раздвижно́й adj. **1,** expandable: раздвижно́й стол, expandable table. **2,** sliding: раздвижна́я дверь, sliding door. Раздвижно́й за́навес, draw curtain.

раздви́нуть v., pfv. of **раздвига́ть**. —**раздви́нуться**, refl., pfv. of **раздвига́ться**.

раздвое́ние n. division; split. —**раздвое́ние ли́чности**, split personality.

раздво́енный adj. divided; double. —**раздво́енное изображе́ние**, split picture (on TV). —**раздво́енное копы́то**, cloven hoof.

раздвои́ть v., pfv. of **раздва́ивать**. —**раздвои́ться**, refl., pfv. of **раздва́иваться**.

раздева́лка [gen. pl. -лок] n. **1,** cloakroom; checkroom. **2,** dressing room; locker room.

раздева́льня [gen. pl. -лен] n. = **раздева́лка**.

раздева́ние n. undressing.

раздева́ть v.impfv. [pfv. **разде́ть**] to undress (someone). —**раздева́ться**, refl. **1,** to get undressed. **2,** to take off one's coat.

разде́л n. **1,** division; dividing up. **2,** partition(ing). **3,** section; part (of a book, article, etc.). **4,** branch (of medicine, mathematics, etc.).

разде́лать v., pfv. of **разде́лывать**. —**разде́латься**, refl., pfv. of **разде́лываться**.

разделе́ние n. division.

раздели́тельный adj. **1,** dividing: раздели́тельная черта́, dividing line. **2,** gram. partitive; disjunctive. —**раздели́тельный знак**, division sign.

раздели́ть [infl. -делю́, -де́лишь] v., pfv. of **дели́ть** and **разделя́ть**. —**раздели́ться**, refl., pfv. of **дели́ться** (in sense #1) and **разделя́ться**.

разде́лывать v.impfv. [pfv. **разде́лать**] **1,** to dress; prepare (for cooking). **2,** (with под + acc.) to finish (in imitation wood grain, marble, etc.). —**разде́лывать под оре́х**, see **оре́х**.

разде́лываться v.r.impfv. [pfv. **разде́латься**] (with с + instr.) colloq. **1,** to finish off; dispose of. **2,** to settle (debts); settle up with (someone). **3,** to get even with; settle scores with.

разде́льный adj. **1,** separate. **2,** (of speech) clear; distinct.

разделя́ть v.impfv. [pfv. **раздели́ть**] **1,** to divide. **2,** to share. **3,** to separate. —**разделя́ться**, refl. **1,** to divide; be divided. **2,** to split up (into groups). **3,** (of two people) to break up; split up.

разде́ть [infl. -де́ну, -де́нешь] v., pfv. of **раздева́ть**. —**разде́ться**, refl., pfv. of **раздева́ться**.

раздира́ть v.impfv. [pfv. **раздо́рать**] **1,** colloq. to tear to pieces. **2,** [impfv. only] fig. to tear apart: раздира́емый разногла́сиями, torn by dissension. **3,** [impfv. only] to tear at; rend (one's heart). **4,** [impfv. only] to break (the silence); rend (the air). —**раздира́ться**, refl. **1,** colloq. to tear; rip. **2,** [impfv. only] fig. (with instr.) to be torn (by dissension, rivalries, etc.).

раздира́ющий adj. heart-rending; heartbreaking.

раздобре́ть v., pfv. of **добре́ть** (in sense #2).

раздобыва́ть v.impfv. [pfv. **раздобы́ть**] colloq. to obtain; wangle; get hold of.

раздобы́ть [infl. -бу́ду, -бу́дешь; past fem. -была́] v., pfv. of **раздобыва́ть**.

раздо́лье *n.* 1, open space; expanse. 2, *fig.* freedom.

раздо́льный *adj.* 1, vast; spacious; far-flung. 2, free; carefree.

раздо́р *n.*, often *pl.* discord; dissension.

раздоса́довать *v.pfv.* [*infl.* -дую, -дуешь] *colloq.* to vex.

раздража́ть *v.impfv.* [*pfv.* раздражи́ть] 1, to irritate; annoy. 2, to irritate (the skin, eyes, etc.). —раздража́ться, *refl.* to become irritated.

раздраже́ние *n.* irritation.

раздражённый *adj.* irritated. —раздражённо, *adv.* with a sound (*or* look) of irritation.

раздражи́тель *n.m.* irritant.

раздражи́тельный *adj.* irritable. —раздражи́тельность, *n.f.* irritability.

раздражи́ть *v.*, *pfv. of* раздража́ть. —раздражи́ться, *refl.*, *pfv. of* раздража́ться.

раздразни́ть *v.pfv.* [*infl.* -дразню́, -дра́знишь] 1, to tease; provoke. 2, to whet (a desire, one's appetite, etc.).

раздроби́ть [*infl.* -блю́, -би́шь] *v.*, *pfv. of* дроби́ть *and* раздробля́ть. —раздроби́ться, *refl.*, *pfv. of* дроби́ться *and* раздробля́ться.

раздро́бленность *n.f.* disunity; division; fragmentation.

раздробля́ть *v.impfv.* [*pfv.* раздроби́ть] 1, to smash; splinter. 2, *fig.* to fragment; splinter. 3, to reduce; convert (into smaller units). —раздробля́ться, *refl.* to splinter.

раздува́ть *v.impfv.* [*pfv.* разду́ть] 1, to fan (a fire). 2, inflate. 3, *fig.* to stir up; whip up; foment. 4, *colloq.* to exaggerate; blow up. 5, *impers.*, *colloq.* to be puffed up: У него́ разду́ло щёку, his cheek is puffed up. —раздува́ться, *refl.* 1, to swell up; be swollen; be puffed up. 2, to bulge.

разду́мать *v.pfv.* to change one's mind. —разду́маться, *refl.* (with о) *colloq.* to begin to reflect (on).

разду́мчивый *adj.*, *colloq.* pensive; reflective.

разду́мывать *v.impfv.* to ponder; think; deliberate. —не разду́мывая, without a moment's hesitation.

разду́мье *n.* 1, thought; meditation. 2, *usu. pl.* thoughts. 3, second thoughts; doubts.

разду́тый *adj.* 1, swollen; puffed up; bloated. 2, inflated; excessive: разду́тые ци́фры, inflated figures; разду́тые шта́ты, excess of personnel; overstaffing. 3, exaggerated; overblown.

разду́ть [*infl.* -ду́ю, -ду́ешь] *v.*, *pfv. of* раздува́ть. —разду́ться, *refl.*, *pfv. of* раздува́ться.

развева́ть *v.impfv.* [*pfv.* рази́нуть] *colloq.* to open (one's mouth) wide. —рази́нув рот, open-mouthed.

разжа́лобить *v.pfv.* [*infl.* -блю, -бишь] to move to pity; stir.

разжа́лование *n.* demotion.

разжа́ловать *v.pfv.* [*infl.* -лую, -луешь] to demote.

разжа́ть [*infl.* разожму́, разожмёшь] *v.*, *pfv. of* разжима́ть. —разжа́ться, *refl.*, *pfv. of* разжима́ться.

разжева́ть [*infl.* -жую́, -жуёшь] *v.*, *pfv. of* разжёвывать.

разжёвывать *v.impfv.* [*pfv.* разжева́ть] to chew; masticate.

разже́чь [*infl.* разожгу́, разожжёшь, …разожгу́т; *past* разжёг, разожгла́, разожгло́, разожгли́] *v.*,

pfv. of разжига́ть. —разже́чься, *refl.*, *pfv. of* разжига́ться.

разжива́ться *v.r.impfv.* [*pfv.* разжи́ться] *colloq.* to get rich.

разжига́ние *n.* 1, kindling. 2, *fig.* igniting (of conflicts); fomenting (of hatred); unleashing (of war).

разжига́ть *v.impfv.* [*pfv.* разже́чь] 1, to kindle; light. 2, *fig.* to kindle; inflame; foment. 3, *fig.* to unleash (a war). —разжига́ться, *refl.* to catch (fire); start burning.

разжижа́ть *v.impfv.* [*pfv.* разжиди́ть] *colloq.* to dilute; make thinner.

разжиже́ние *n.*, *colloq.* dilution.

разжима́ть *v.impfv.* [*pfv.* разжа́ть] to unclench; relax; release. —разжима́ться, *refl.* to open; part; relax.

разжире́ть *v.*, *pfv. of* жире́ть.

разжи́ться [*infl. like* жи́ться; *past* -жи́лся, -жила́сь, -жило́сь, -жили́сь] *v.r.*, *pfv. of* разжива́ться.

раззадо́ривать *v.impfv.* [*pfv.* раззадо́рить] *colloq.* to excite; get (someone) excited.

рази́нуть *v.*, *pfv. of* развева́ть.

рази́ня *n.m. & f.*, *colloq.* scatterbrain.

рази́тельный *adj.* striking. —рази́тельно, *adv.* strikingly.

рази́ть *v.impfv.* [*pres.* ражу́, рази́шь] 1, to strike. 2, to defeat; crush. 3, *impers.* (with *instr.*) *colloq.* to reek (of): От него́ рази́т во́дкой, he reeks of vodka.

разлага́ть *v.impfv.* [*pfv.* разложи́ть] 1, to separate (*or* break down) into (its) constituent parts. 2, *math.* to expand. 3, *fig.* to corrupt. 4, *fig.* to demoralize. —разлага́ться, *refl.* 1, to decompose; decay. 2, to degenerate.

разла́д *n.* 1, lack of coordination; disorder. 2, discord; dissension.

разла́живать *v.impfv.* [*pfv.* разла́дить] *colloq.* 1, to put out of commission. 2, to disrupt. —разла́живаться, *refl.*, *colloq.* 1, to go out of commission. 2, *fig.* to go bad.

разла́мывать *v.impfv.* 1, [*pfv.* разлома́ть] to tear down. 2, [*pfv.* разлома́ть *or* разломи́ть] to break (*into parts or pieces*). —разла́мываться, *refl.* to break apart.

разлени́ться *v.r.pfv.* [*infl.* -леню́сь, -ле́нишься] *colloq.* to become utterly lazy.

разлета́ться *v.r.impfv.* [*pfv.* разлете́ться] 1, to fly in all directions; scatter into the air. 2, *fig.* (of news) to spread. 3, *colloq.* to be shattered. 4, *fig.* (of hopes, dreams, etc.) to vanish; be shattered; be dashed. 5, (with в + *acc. or* к) *colloq.* to rush; dash (into *or* up to).

разле́чься [*infl. like* лечь] *colloq.* to stretch out.

разли́в *n.* 1, bottling. 2, overflowing. 3, high water; spring flood. —в разли́в, for consumption on the premises.

разлива́ние *n.* pouring.

разлива́тельный *adj.*, *in* разлива́тельная ло́жка, ladle.

разлива́ть *v.impfv.* [*pfv.* разли́ть] 1, to spill. 2, to pour (into many containers): разлива́ть чай, to pour the tea. 3, *fig.* to spread; diffuse. 4, *in* (их) водо́й не разольёшь, the two of them are inseparable. —разлива́ться, *refl.* 1, to spill. 2, (of a river) to overflow its banks. 3, *fig.* to spread. 4, [*impfv. only*] *colloq.* to sing (*melodiously*); say (*with feeling*); sob (*bitterly*).

разливно́й *adj.* (*of beer*) on draft; on tap.

разлинова́ть *v.pfv.* [*infl.* -ну́ю, -ну́ешь] to rule; line.

разли́ть [*infl.* **разолью́, разольёшь**; *past fem.* **разлила́**] *v., pfv. of* **разлива́ть**. —**разли́ться**, *refl.* [*past* разли́лся, разлила́сь, разлило́сь *or* разли́лось, разлили́сь *or* разли́лись] *pfv. of* **разлива́ться**.

различа́ть *v.impfv.* [*pfv.* **различи́ть**] **1**, to distinguish; tell apart. **2**, to discern; make out. —**различа́ться**, *refl.* [*impfv. only*] to differ.

разли́чие *n.* **1**, difference: разли́чие во взгля́дах, difference of opinion. **2**, distinction: де́лать *or* проводи́ть разли́чие, to make *or* draw a distinction. —**зна́ки разли́чия**, insignia.

различи́мый *adj.* **1**, distinguishable. **2**, discernible.

различи́тельный *adj.* distinctive; distinguishing.

различи́ть *v., pfv. of* **различа́ть**.

разли́чно *adv.* differently; in different ways.

разли́чный *adj.* **1**, different; differing. **2**, various; diverse.

разложе́ние *n.* **1**, decomposition. **2**, *fig.* decay; degeneration. **3**, disintegration; breakup.

разложи́ть [*infl.* -ложу́, -ло́жишь] *v., pfv. of* **раскла́дывать** *and* **разлага́ть**. —**разложи́ться**, *refl., pfv. of* **раскла́дываться** *and* **разлага́ться**.

разло́м *n.* **1**, breaking up; breakup. **2**, break.

разлома́ть *v., pfv. of* **разла́мывать**. —**разлома́ться**, *refl., pfv. of* **разла́мываться**.

разломи́ть [*infl.* -ломлю́, -ло́мишь] *v., pfv. of* **разла́мывать** (*in sense #2*). —**разломи́ться**, *refl., pfv. of* **разла́мываться**.

разлу́ка *n.* **1**, separation. Жить в разлу́ке, to be separated. **2**, parting.

разлуча́ть *v.impfv.* [*pfv.* **разлучи́ть**] to separate: разлучи́ть дете́й с роди́телями , to separate the children from their parents. —**разлуча́ться**, *refl.* to part company; separate.

разлюби́ть *v.pfv.* [*pfv.* -люблю́, -лю́бишь] to cease to love; no longer love.

размагни́чивать *v.impfv.* [*pfv.* **размагни́тить**] to demagnetize.

разма́зать [*infl.* -ма́жу, -ма́жешь] *v., pfv. of* **разма́зывать**. —**разма́заться**, *refl., pfv. of* **разма́зываться**.

размазня́ *n., colloq.* **1**, gruel. **2**, wishy-washy person.

разма́зывать *v.impfv.* [*pfv.* **разма́зать**] **1**, to spread; smear. **2**, *colloq.* to pad (a story, report, etc.). —**разма́зываться**, *refl.* to smear; become smeared.

разма́лывать *v.impfv.* [*pfv.* **размоло́ть**] to grind.

разма́тывать *v.impfv.* [*pfv.* **размота́ть**] to unwind; unreel. —**разма́тываться**, *refl.* to unwind; become unwound.

разма́х *n.* **1**, swing; sweep (*of one's arm*). **2**, span: разма́х кры́льев, wingspan. **3**, *fig.* range; scope. —**со всего́ разма́ху**, with all one's might.

разма́хивать *v.impfv.* [*pfv.* **размахну́ть**] **1**, [*impfv. only*] (*with instr.*) to wave; swing; brandish. **2**, (*with instr.*) to draw back (*in order to strike with*). **3**, to open (a door) wide; spread (one's hands) apart. —**разма́хиваться**, *refl.* **1**, to draw back one's arm (*in order to strike someone or something*); haul off. **2**, [*impfv. only*] to sway back and forth.

размахну́ть *v., pfv. of* **разма́хивать**. —**размахну́ться**, *refl., pfv. of* **разма́хиваться**.

разма́чивать *v.impfv.* [*pfv.* **размочи́ть**] to soak; steep.

разма́шистый *adj., colloq.* **1**, (*of a motion*) sweeping. **2**, (*of handwriting*) sprawling. **3**, (*of an expanse of land*) broad.

размежева́ние *n.* division; separation.

размежева́ть [*infl.* -жу́ю, -жу́ешь] *v., pfv. of* **размежёвывать**. —**размежева́ться**, *refl., pfv. of* **размежёвываться**.

размежёвывать *v.impfv.* [*pfv.* **размежева́ть**] **1**, to divide up; establish the boundaries between. **2**, to separate. —**размежёвываться**, *refl.* **1**, (*with* с + *instr.*) to set the boundary line (between oneself and someone else). **2**, *fig.* to split up; (*with* с + *instr.*) break (with).

размельча́ть *v.impfv.* [*pfv.* **размельчи́ть**] to crush; grind; reduce to small particles.

разме́н *n.* exchange. Разме́н де́нег, changing of money.

разме́нивать *v.impfv.* [*pfv.* **разменя́ть**] to change (money). —**разме́ниваться**, *refl.* **1**, *obs.* (*with instr.*) to exchange. **2**, *colloq.* to waste one's energies.

разме́нный *adj.* change (*attrib.*): разме́нная ка́сса, change booth. —**разме́нная моне́та**, small change.

разменя́ть *v., pfv. of* **разме́нивать**. —**разменя́ться**, *refl., pfv. of* **разме́ниваться**.

разме́р *n.* **1**, size: разме́р ко́мнаты, the size of a room. Я ношу́ боти́нки деся́того разме́ра, I wear a size ten shoe. **2**, amount. В двойно́м разме́ре, twice as much. Ссу́да в разме́ре ты́сячи до́лларов, a $1,000 loan. **3**, *often pl.* scale; extent; dimensions; proportions. Разме́ры бе́дствия, the extent of the disaster. **4**, *pros.* meter. **5**, *music* measure.

разме́ренный *adj.* measured.

размеря́ть *v.impfv.* [*pfv.* **разме́рить**] to measure.

размеси́ть [*infl.* -мешу́, -ме́сишь] *v., pfv. of* **разме́шивать** (*in sense #1*).

размести́ [*infl. like* мести́] *v., pfv. of* **размета́ть**[1].

размести́ть [*infl.* -щу́, -сти́шь] *v., pfv. of* **размеща́ть**. —**размести́ться**, *refl., pfv. of* **размеща́ться**.

размета́ть[1] *v.impfv.* [*pfv.* **размести́**] **1**, to sweep; sweep clean. **2**, to sweep away; sweep up.

размета́ть[2] [*infl.* -мечу́, -ме́чешь] *v., pfv. of* **размётывать**. —**размета́ться**, *refl.* **1**, to lie with one's arms and legs outstretched. **2**, (*of one's hair*) to hang loosely. **3**, to stretch; extend.

разме́тить [*infl.* -чу, -тишь] *v., pfv. of* **размеча́ть**.

разме́тка [*gen. pl.* -ток] *n.* **1**, marking. **2**, mark.

размётывать *v.impfv.* [*pfv.* **размета́ть**] **1**, to scatter; disperse. **2**, to destroy; demolish. **3**, to stretch out; spread apart.

размеча́ть *v.impfv.* [*pfv.* **разме́тить**] to mark; mark up; mark out.

разме́шивать *v.impfv.* **1**, [*pfv.* **размеси́ть**] to knead. **2**, [*pfv.* **размеша́ть**] to stir.

размеща́ть *v.impfv.* [*pfv.* **размести́ть**] **1**, to place; arrange; station (many people or items). **2**, *mil.* to station; deploy. **3**, to find lodging for; quarter (troops). **4**, to place (orders); float (a loan). —**размеща́ться**, *refl.* **1**, (*of many people*) to take their places; take seats. **2**, to be housed; be quartered.

размеще́ние *n*. **1,** placement; arrangement; stationing. **2,** *mil.* stationing; deployment. **3,** distribution. **4,** quartering; billeting (*of troops*). **5,** placing (*of orders*); floating (*of a loan*).

размина́ть *v.impfv.* [*pfv.* **размя́ть**] **1,** to mash; knead. **2,** *colloq.* to stretch (one's legs); unlimber (one's muscles). —**размина́ться,** *refl., colloq.* **1,** to stretch one's legs. **2,** to limber up; unlimber.

размини́ровать *v.impfv. & pfv.* [*pres.* **-рую, -руешь**] to clear of mines.

разми́нка *n., colloq.* limbering up; warm-up.

размину́ться *v.r.pfv., colloq.* **1,** to miss each other; fail to meet. **2,** (*of letters*) to cross in the mail. **3,** to pass by each other (*in a narrow place*).

размножа́ть *v.impfv.* [*pfv.* **размно́жить**] **1,** to make copies of. **2,** to raise; breed. —**размножа́ться,** *refl.* to multiply; reproduce; breed; propagate.

размноже́ние *n*. **1,** copying; reproduction. **2,** reproduction; propagation.

размно́жить *v., pfv. of* **размножа́ть.** —**размно́житься,** *refl., pfv. of* **размножа́ться.**

размозжи́ть *v.pfv.* to smash; shatter.

размока́ть *v.impfv.* [*pfv.* **размо́кнуть**] to become soggy.

размо́кнуть [*past* **-мо́к, -мо́кла**] *v., pfv. of* **размока́ть.**

размо́л *n*. **1,** grinding; milling. **2,** *in* кру́пного размо́ла, coarse; ме́лкого размо́ла, finely ground.

размо́лвка [*gen. pl.* **-вок**] *n.* spat; tiff.

размоло́ть [*infl.* **-мелю́, -ме́лешь**] *v., pfv. of* **разма́лывать.**

размора́живать *v.impfv.* [*pfv.* **разморо́зить**] to defrost; unfreeze. —**размора́живаться,** *refl.* to defrost; melt.

размота́ть *v., pfv. of* **разма́тывать.** —**размота́ться,** *refl., pfv. of* **разма́тываться.**

размочи́ть [*infl.* **-мочу́, -мо́чишь**] *v., pfv. of* **разма́чивать.**

размы́в *n.* washing away; erosion.

размыва́ть *v.impfv.* [*pfv.* **размы́ть**] **1,** to wash away; wash out: Вода́ размы́ла доро́гу, the water (*or* floodwaters) washed out the road. **2,** to erode.

размыка́ть *v.impfv.* [*pfv.* **разомкну́ть**] **1,** to open. **2,** to break (a circuit). —**размыка́ться,** *refl.* **1,** to come apart; separate. **2,** (*of a drawbridge*) to open. **3,** *mil.* to open ranks.

размы́ть [*infl.* **-мо́ю, -мо́ешь**] *v., pfv. of* **размыва́ть.**

размышле́ние *n.* **1,** reflection; thought; rumination. **2,** *pl.* thoughts; ruminations. —**пи́ща для размышле́ния,** food for thought. —**по зре́лом размышле́нии,** on second thought.

размышля́ть *v.impfv.* to reflect; ponder.

размягча́ть *v.impfv.* [*pfv.* **размягчи́ть**] to soften. —**размягча́ться,** *refl.* to grow soft.

размягче́ние *n.* softening.

размягчи́ть *v., pfv. of* **размягча́ть.** —**размягчи́ться,** *refl., pfv. of* **размягча́ться.**

размяка́ть *v.impfv.* [*pfv.* **размя́кнуть**] **1,** to become soft. **2,** *colloq.* to go limp. **3,** *colloq.* (*of a person*) to be softened up.

размя́кнуть [*past* **-мя́к, -мя́кла**] *v., pfv. of* **мя́кнуть** *and* **размяка́ть.**

размя́ть [*infl.* **разомну́, разомнёшь**] *v., pfv. of* **мять** (*in sense #1*) *and* **размина́ть.** —**размя́ться,** *refl., pfv. of* **размина́ться.**

разнаря́дка [*gen. pl.* **-док**] *n.* order; voucher.

разна́шивать *v.impfv.* [*pfv.* **разноси́ть**] to break in (shoes).

разнести́ [*infl. like* **нести́**] *v., pfv. of* **разноси́ть**[1]. —**разнести́сь,** *refl., pfv. of* **разноси́ться.**

разнима́ть *v.impfv.* [*pfv.* **разня́ть**] to separate; pull apart.

ра́зниться *v.r.impfv.* to differ.

ра́зница *n.* difference. —**больша́я ра́зница,** it makes a big difference. —**кака́я ра́зница?,** what difference does it make?

разнобо́й *n.* lack of coordination; inconsistency.

разнови́дность *n.f.* a variety.

разновре́менный *adj.* occurring at different times.

разногла́сие *n.* **1,** disagreement; difference. **2,** discrepancy.

разноголо́сица *n., colloq.* **1,** dissonance. **2,** disagreement. **3,** discrepancy.

разноголо́сый *adj.* discordant.

ра́зное *n., decl. as an adj.* **1,** various things. **2,** (*as a heading*) miscellaneous.

разнома́стный *adj.* of different colors.

разнообра́зие *n.* variety; diversity.

разнообра́зить *v.impfv.* [*pres.* **-жу, -зишь**] to vary; diversify.

разнообра́зный *adj.* diverse; varied.

разнорабо́чий *n., decl. as an adj.* unskilled workman; person who does odd jobs.

разноречи́вый *adj.* conflicting; contradictory.

разноро́дный *adj.* heterogeneous. —**разноро́дность,** *n.f.* heterogeneity.

разно́с *n.* **1,** carrying; delivery. **2,** *colloq.* sharp rebuke; dressing-down.

разноси́ть[1] *v.impfv.* [*pfv.* **разнести́**; *pres.* **-ношу́, -но́сишь**] **1,** to carry; deliver (*each to its place*). **2,** to distribute; hand around. **3,** to enter; record. **4,** *colloq.* to scatter; disperse. **5,** to spread. **6,** *colloq.* to shatter; destroy. Разнести́ в ще́пки, to smash/blow to bits. **7,** *colloq.* to berate; upbraid. **8,** *colloq.* to criticize; excoriate; pan. **9,** *impers., colloq.* to swell: У меня́ щёку разнесло́, my cheek is swollen. —**разноси́ться,** *refl.* **1,** (*of news, a rumor, etc.*) to spread; get around. **2,** (*of a sound*) to resound. **3,** (*of an odor*) to spread.

разноси́ть[2] [*infl.* **-ношу́, -но́сишь**] *v., pfv. of* **разна́шивать.**

разно́ска *n., colloq.* distribution; handing out.

разно́сный *adj., colloq.* scathing; blistering.

разносторо́нний *adj.* **1,** *math.* scalene. **2,** multifaceted; versatile. **3,** (*of education*) all-round. —**разносторо́нность,** *n.f.* versatility.

ра́зность *n.f.* **1,** *obs.* difference. **2,** *math.* difference. —**ра́зные ра́зности,** various things; this and that.

разно́счик *n.* **1,** delivery man. **2,** peddler.

разноцве́тный *adj.* of different colors.

разношёрстный *adj.* **1,** (*of animals*) of different colors. **2,** *fig., colloq.* motley.

разноязы́чный *adj.* multilingual; polyglot. *Also,* **разноязы́кий.**

разну́зданный *adj.* **1,** (*of a horse*) unbridled. **2,** *fig.* rowdy; unruly.

разну́здывать *v.impfv.* [*pfv.* **разнузда́ть**] to unbridle.

ра́зный *adj.* **1,** different; differing: ра́зные вку́сы, differing tastes. **2,** different; not the same: говори́ть на ра́зных языка́х, to speak different languages; not speak the same language. **3,** various: ра́зные тео́рии, various theories. **4,** *colloq.* all sorts of: ра́зная ру́хлядь, all sorts of junk. *See also* **ра́зное.**

разню́хивать *v.impfv.* [*pfv.* **разню́хать**] *colloq.* **1,** to sniff out. **2,** *fig.* to smell about; nose about.

разня́ть [*infl.* **-ниму́, -ни́мешь;** *past fem.* **разняла́**] *v., pfv. of* **разнима́ть.**

разоблача́ть *v.impfv.* [*pfv.* **разоблачи́ть**] to expose; unmask.

разоблаче́ние *n.* **1,** exposure. **2,** *usu. pl.* revelations; exposé.

разоблачи́ть *v., pfv. of* **разоблача́ть.**

разобра́ть [*infl.* **разберу́, разберёшь;** *past fem.* **разобрала́**] *v., pfv. of* **разбира́ть.** —**разобра́ться,** *refl.* [*past tense stress as in* **бра́ться**] *pfv. of* **разбира́ться.**

разобща́ть *v.impfv.* [*pfv.* **разобщи́ть**] **1,** to separate; cut off (from each other). **2,** *fig.* to alienate; estrange.

разобщённость *n.f.* **1,** estrangement. **2,** isolation. **3,** disunity.

разобщи́ть *v., pfv. of* **разобща́ть.**

ра́зовый *adj.* one-time; for one-time use only.

разогна́ть [*infl.* **разгоню́, разго́нишь;** *past fem.* **разогнала́**] *v., pfv. of* **разгоня́ть.** —**разогна́ться,** *refl.* [*past tense stress as in* **гна́ться**] *pfv. of* **разгоня́ться.**

разогну́ть *v., pfv. of* **разгиба́ть.** —**разогну́ться,** *refl., pfv. of* **разгиба́ться.**

разогрева́ть *v.impfv.* [*pfv.* **разогре́ть**] **1,** to heat up; warm up. **2,** to reheat; warm over: разогре́тый обе́д, warmed-over dinner. —**разогрева́ться,** *refl.* to get hot; get warm.

разоде́ть *v.pfv.* [*infl.* **-оде́ну, -оде́нешь**] *colloq.* to dress (someone) up. —**разоде́ться,** *refl., colloq.* to dress up; get dressed up.

разодра́ть [*infl.* **раздеру́, раздерёшь;** *past fem.* **разодрала́**] *v., pfv. of* **раздира́ть.** —**разодра́ться,** *refl.* [*past tense stress as in* **дра́ться**] **1,** *pfv. of* **раздира́ться. 2,** *colloq.* to have a fight.

разозли́ть *v., pfv. of* **злить.** —**разозли́ться,** *refl., pfv. of* **зли́ться.**

разойти́сь [*infl.* **разойду́сь, разойдёшься;** *past* **разошёлся, разошла́сь, разошло́сь, разошли́сь**] *v.r., pfv. of* **расходи́ться.**

ра́зом *adv., colloq.* **1,** at once; at the same time. **2,** at once; instantly. **3,** at once; in one gulp; with one stroke.

разомкну́ть *v., pfv. of* **размыка́ть.** —**разомкну́ться,** *refl., pfv. of* **размыка́ться.**

разорва́ть [*infl.* **-рву́, -рвёшь;** *past fem.* **разорвала́**] *v., pfv. of* **разрыва́ть.** —**разорва́ться,** *refl.* [*past tense stress as in* **рва́ться**] *pfv. of* **разрыва́ться.**

разоре́ние *n.* **1,** destruction; devastation. **2,** bankruptcy; ruin.

разори́тельный *adj.* devastating; ruinous.

разори́ть *v., pfv. of* **разоря́ть.** —**разори́ться,** *refl., pfv. of* **разоря́ться.**

разоружа́ть *v.impfv.* [*pfv.* **разоружи́ть**] *v.t.* to disarm. —**разоружа́ться,** *refl.* to disarm.

разоруже́ние *n.* disarmament.

разоружи́ть *v., pfv. of* **разоружа́ть.** —**разоружи́ться,** *refl., pfv. of* **разоружа́ться.**

разоря́ть *v.impfv.* [*pfv.* **разори́ть**] **1,** to ravage; devastate. **2,** to ruin. —**разоря́ться,** *refl.* **1,** to be ruined. **2,** to lose everything; go broke.

разосла́ть [*infl.* **-шлю́, -шлёшь**] *v., pfv. of* **рассыла́ть.**

разоспа́ться *v.r.pfv.* [*infl. like* **спать**] *colloq.* to fall fast asleep.

разостла́ть [*infl.* **расстелю́, рассте́лешь**] *v., pfv. of* **расстила́ть.**

разоткрове́нничаться *v.r.pfv.* (*with* **пе́ред**) *colloq.* to open up one's heart (to); pour out one's thoughts (to).

разохо́титься *v.r.pfv.* [*infl.* **-чусь, -тишься**] (*with inf. or* **на** + *acc.*) *colloq.* to have a sudden desire to *or* for.

разочарова́ние *n.* disappointment; disillusionment; disenchantment.

разочаро́ванный *adj.* disappointed; disillusioned; disenchanted.

разочарова́ть [*infl.* **-ру́ю, -ру́ешь**] *v., pfv. of* **разочаро́вывать.** —**разочарова́ться,** *refl., pfv. of* **разочаро́вываться.**

разочаро́вывать *v.impfv.* [*pfv.* **разочарова́ть**] to disappoint; disillusion. —**разочаро́вываться,** *refl.* (*with* **в** + *prepl.*) to be disappointed (with); become disillusioned (with).

разраба́тывать *v.impfv.* [*pfv.* **разрабо́тать**] **1,** to work out; develop (a plan, theory, etc.). **2,** to develop (a new aircraft, technology, etc.). **3,** to cultivate (land). **4,** [*impfv. only*] to work (a mine); mine (a certain mineral).

разрабо́тка *n.* **1,** development. **2,** cultivation (*of land*). **3,** mining; extraction.

разра́внивать *v.impfv.* [*pfv.* **разровня́ть**] to level.

разража́ться *v.r.impfv.* [*pfv.* **разрази́ться**] **1,** to break out. **2,** (*with instr.*) to burst into (tears, laughter, etc.).

разраста́ться *v.r.impfv.* [*pfv.* **разрасти́сь**] to grow; expand; increase in size.

разрасти́сь [*infl. like* **расти́**] *v.r., pfv. of* **разраста́ться.**

разрежа́ть *v.impfv.* [*pfv.* **разреди́ть**] **1,** to thin out. **2,** to rarefy (the air).

разре́з *n.* **1,** cut; split. **2,** *med.* incision. **3,** section: попере́чный разре́з, cross section. **4,** *fig.* sense; aspect: в друго́м разре́зе, in a different sense (*or* light). —**в разре́зе** (+ *gen.*), in the light of.

разре́зать [*infl.* **-ре́жу, -ре́жешь**] *v., pfv. of* **ре́зать** (*in senses #1 & #2*) *and* **разреза́ть.**

разреза́ть *v.impfv.* [*pfv.* **разре́зать**] **1,** to cut; slit. **2,** to cut open; lance. **3,** to bisect; divide in half.

разреклами́ровать *v.pfv.* [*infl.* **-рую, -руешь**] *colloq.* to advertise; publicize; ballyhoo.

разреша́ть *v.impfv.* [*pfv.* **разреши́ть**] **1,** (*with dat.*) to permit; allow: Разреши́те мне спроси́ть..., *permit/ allow me to ask...* **2,** to solve (a problem). **3,** to settle; resolve (a dispute, conflict, etc.). —**разреша́ющая си́ла,** resolving power.

разреша́ться *v.r.impfv.* [*pfv.* **разреши́ться**] **1,** [*impfv. only*] (*with dat.*) to be permitted; be allowed: Ему́ не разреша́ется (+ *inf.*), he is not permitted/allowed to... **2,** to be solved; be settled. —**разреши́ться от бре́мени** (+ *instr.*), to give birth to; be delivered of.

разреше́ние *n.* **1,** permission: с ва́шего разреше́ния, with your permission. **2,** solution; resolution; settlement. **3,** *colloq.* permit; license.

разреши́ть *v., pfv. of* **разреша́ть.** —**разреши́ться,** *refl., pfv. of* **разреша́ться.**

разрисова́ть *v.pfv.* [*infl.* **-су́ю, -су́ешь**] to draw all over: Сте́ны бы́ли разрисо́ваны цвета́ми, the walls had flowers drawn all over them.

разровня́ть *v., pfv. of* **разра́внивать.**

разро́зненный *adj.* **1,** (*of a set*) incomplete; (*of one of such a set*) odd. **2,** uncoordinated.

разро́знивать *v.impfv.* [*pfv.* **разро́знить**] to break; break up (a set or collection of something).

разруба́ть *v.impfv.* [*pfv.* **разруби́ть**] **1,** to chop up. **2,** to cut up.

разруби́ть [*infl.* **-ру́блю, -ру́бишь**] *v., pfv. of* **разруба́ть.**

разруга́ть *v.pfv., colloq.* **1,** to berate; chastise. **2,** to tear apart; pan (a book, play, etc.). —**разруга́ться,** *refl., colloq.* to quarrel.

разру́ха *n.* (economic) ruin.

разруша́ть *v.impfv.* [*pfv.* **разру́шить**] **1,** to destroy; demolish. Разруша́ть до основа́ния, to raze to the ground. **2,** *fig.* to wreck (one's plans, hopes, etc.); ruin (one's health). —**разруша́ться,** *refl.* **1,** to be destroyed; collapse. **2,** *fig.* to be ruined.

разруше́ние *n.* **1,** destruction (*act of destroying*). **2,** *pl.* destruction (*heavy damage*).

разруши́тель *n.m.* destroyer; wrecker.

разруши́тельный *adj.* destructive.

разру́шить *v., pfv. of* **разруша́ть.** —**разру́шиться,** *refl., pfv. of* **разруша́ться.**

разры́в *n.* **1,** break; rupture. **2,** breaking (*of relations*); breakup. **3,** burst (*of a shell*). **4,** gap. —**разры́в се́рдца,** heart failure.

разрыва́ть *v.impfv.* [*pfv.* **разорва́ть**] **1,** to tear; tear open; tear up. **2,** to blow up. *Also impers.*: Его́ разорва́ло на ча́сти, he was blown to bits. **3,** *impers.* to burst: коте́л разорва́ло, the boiler burst. **4,** *fig.* to break off; sever (relations, ties, etc.). **5,** *v.i.* (*with* с + *instr.*) *colloq.* to break (with someone). **6,** [*pfv.* **разры́ть**] to dig; dig up.

разрыва́ться *v.r.impfv.* [*pfv.* **разорва́ться**] **1,** to tear; be torn. **2,** to break; snap. **3,** to burst; explode; go off. **4,** (*of relations*) to be broken off. **5,** [*impfv. only*] to be torn apart (*emotionally*). **6,** [*impfv. only*] *colloq.* to be everywhere at once. —**у меня́ се́рдце разрыва́ется,** my heart is breaking; it breaks my heart.

разрывно́й *adj.* (*of a bullet, shell, etc.*) explosive.

разрыда́ться *v.r.pfv.* to burst into tears; begin to sob.

разры́ть [*infl.* **-ро́ю, -ро́ешь**] *v., pfv. of* **разрыва́ть** (*in sense #6*).

разрыхля́ть *v.impfv.* [*pfv.* **разрыхли́ть**] to loosen (soil, dirt, etc.).

разря́д *n.* **1,** category. **2,** class; rank: спортсме́н пе́рвого разря́да, top-class athlete: сле́сарь тре́тьего разря́да, metalworker of the third rank. **3,** discharge (*of electricity, a weapon, etc.*).

разряди́ть [*infl.* **-ряжу́, -ря́дишь** *or* **-ряди́шь**] *v., pfv. of* **разряжа́ть.** —**разряди́ться,** *refl., pfv. of* **разряжа́ться.**

разря́дка *n.* **1,** unloading (*of a weapon*); using up (*of a battery*). **2,** *fig.* relaxation; lessening (*of tension*); détente.

разряжа́ть *v.impfv.* [*pfv.* **разряди́ть**] **1,** to unload (a weapon). **2,** to use up; run down (a battery). **3,** *fig.* to relax; ease (tension); defuse (a situation). Разряди́ть атмосфе́ру, to clear the air. **4,** *colloq.* to dress up; deck out. —**разряжа́ться,** *refl.* **1,** (*of a battery*) to run down. **2,** *fig.* to become less tense. **3,** *colloq.* to get dressed up.

разубежда́ть *v.impfv.* [*pfv.* **разубеди́ть**] (*with* в + *prepl.*) to change someone's mind (about); convince to the contrary. —**разубежда́ться,** *refl.* (*with* в + *prepl.*) to change one's mind (about).

разува́ть *v.impfv.* [*pfv.* **разу́ть**] to take off (someone's) shoes. —**разува́ться,** *refl.* to take off one's shoes.

разуверя́ть *v.impfv.* [*pfv.* **разуве́рить**] (*with* в + *prepl.*) to disillusion (about); disabuse (of); change someone's mind (about). —**разуверя́ться,** *refl.* (*with* в + *prepl.*) to lose faith (in); lose hope (of).

разузнава́ть *v.impfv.* [*pfv.* **разузна́ть;** *pres.* **-знаю́, -знаёшь**] *colloq.* **1,** [*impfv. only*] to make inquiries; try to find out. **2,** to find out.

разузна́ть [*infl.* **-зна́ю, -зна́ешь**] *v., pfv. of* **разузнава́ть.**

разукра́шивать *v.impfv.* [*pfv.* **разукра́сить**] *colloq.* to adorn; embellish.

разукрупня́ть *v.impfv.* [*pfv.* **разукрупни́ть**] to break up into smaller units.

ра́зум *n.* reason; intellect. —**у меня́ ум за ра́зум захо́дит,** I am at my wits' end.

разуме́ние *n., obs.* understanding. —**де́йствовать по своему́ разуме́нию,** to do as one sees fit.

разуме́ть *v.impfv.* **1,** to mean. **2,** *obs.* to understand.

разуме́ться *v.r.impfv.* to be understood; be taken to mean. —**разуме́ется,** naturally; of course. —**само́ собо́й разуме́ется,** it goes without saying.

разу́мно *adv.* sensibly; rationally. —*adj., used predicatively,* reasonable: Это вполне́ разу́мно, that is entirely reasonable.

разу́мный *adj.* **1,** intelligent; rational: разу́мное существо́, an intelligent/rational being. **2,** clever. **3,** reasonable; sensible; logical.

разу́ть [*infl.* **разу́ю, разу́ешь**] *v., pfv. of* **разува́ть.** —**разу́ться,** *refl., pfv. of* **разува́ться.**

разу́чивать *v.impfv.* [*pfv.* **разучи́ть**] to learn. —**разу́чиваться,** *refl.* to forget; forget how (to); lose one's ability (to).

разучи́ть [*infl.* **-учу́, -у́чишь**] *v., pfv. of* **разу́чивать.** —**разучи́ться,** *refl., pfv. of* **разу́чиваться.**

разъеда́ть *v.impfv.* [*pfv.* **разъе́сть**] to eat away; corrode.

разъедине́ние *n.* **1,** separation. **2,** disconnecting. **3,** disengagement.

разъединя́ть *v.impfv.* [*pfv.* **разъедини́ть**] **1,** to separate. **2,** to disconnect. **3,** *fig.* to estrange. —**разъедини́ться,** *refl.* **1,** to come apart. **2,** to disengage. **3,** *fig.* to become estranged.

разъе́зд *n.* **1,** departure (*of people in different directions*). **2,** *pl.* travels: в разъе́здах, traveling; on the move. **3,** *mil.* mounted patrol. **4,** *R.R.* short stretch of double track.

разъездно́й *adj.* **1,** traveling. **2,** for traveling.

разъезжа́ть *v.impfv.* to travel. —**разъезжа́ться,** *refl.* [*pfv.* **разъе́хаться**] **1,** to depart (*in various directions*). **2,** to pass by each other; miss each other; fail to meet. **3,** to be able to pass by each other (*on a narrow street, road, etc.*). **4,** (*of a married couple*) to separate; break up. **5,** *colloq.* to fall apart; come apart.

разъе́сть [*infl. like* **есть**] *v., pfv. of* **разъеда́ть.**

разъе́хаться [*infl.* **разъе́дусь, разъе́дешься**] *v.r., pfv. of* **разъезжа́ться.**

разъяря́ть *v.impfv.* [*pfv.* **разъяри́ть**] to enrage; infuriate. —**разъяря́ться,** *refl.* to become enraged; fly into a rage.

разъясне́ние *n.* explanation; clarification.

разъясни́тельный *adj.* explanatory.

разъясни́ть *v.impfv.* [*pfv.* **разъясни́ть**] to explain; elucidate; clarify. —**разъясня́ться,** *refl.* to become clear; be cleared up.

разы́грывать *v.impfv.* [*pfv.* **разыгра́ть**] **1,** to perform; put on. **2,** to play (a certain card, chess opening, etc.). **3,** to raffle (off). **4,** to pose as; play the role of. **5,** to feign (surprise). **6,** *colloq.* to play a trick (*or* joke) on. —**разы́грывать из себя́** (+ *acc.*), *colloq.* to play the role of. —**разыгра́ть (что́-нибудь) как по но́там,** to perform (*or* carry out) with precision.

разы́грываться *v.r.impfv.* [*pfv.* **разыгра́ться**] **1,** to play; frolic. **2,** *colloq.* (*of a performer*) to warm to one's part. **3,** *fig.* to increase in intensity; build up. **4,** to take place; develop.

разыска́ть *v.pfv.* [*infl.* **разыщу́, разы́щешь**] **1,** *pfv. of* **разы́скивать. 2,** to find.

разы́скивать *v.impfv.* [*pfv.* **разыска́ть**] to search for; hunt for; seek.

рай [*2nd loc.* **раю́**] *n.* paradise.

райко́м *n.* district committee (*contr. of* **райо́нный комите́т**).

райо́н *n.* **1,** area; region. **2,** district (*of a city*). **3,** subdivision of an oblast; raion. —**райо́нный,** *adj.* district (*attrib.*).

ра́йский *adj.* heavenly. —**ра́йская пти́ца,** bird of paradise.

рак *n.* **1,** cancer. **2,** crawfish. **3,** *cap., astron.* Cancer: тро́пик Ра́ка, Tropic of Cancer. —**кра́сный как рак,** red as a beet.

ра́ка *n.* shrine (*of a saint*).

раке́та *n.* **1,** rocket. **2,** missile. —**освети́тельная раке́та; сигна́льная раке́та,** flare.

раке́та-носи́тель [*gen.* **раке́ты-носи́теля**] *n.f.* launch vehicle; booster rocket.

раке́тка [*gen. pl.* **-ток**] *n.* (tennis) racket.

раке́тный *adj.* rocket (*attrib.*); missile (*attrib.*).

ракетоноси́тель *n.m.* launch vehicle; booster rocket.

ра́ковина *n.* **1,** shell. **2,** sink. **3,** bandstand. —**ушна́я ра́ковина,** auricle (*of the ear*).

ра́ковый *adj.* **1,** cancer (*attrib.*); cancerous. **2,** of (a) crawfish.

ракообра́зное *n., decl. as an adj.* crustacean.

раку́рс *also,* **ра́курс** *n.* **1,** *art* foreshortening. В раку́рсе, foreshortened. **2,** *fig.* perspective.

раку́шка [*gen. pl.* **-шек**] *n.* shell; seashell.

ра́ма *n.* frame.

ра́мка [*gen. pl.* **ра́мок**] *n.* **1,** small frame. **2,** *pl.* limits; bounds: вы́йти за ра́мки (+ *gen.*), to exceed; go beyond the bounds of. —**в ра́мках** (+ *gen.*), within the framework of.

ра́мочный *adj.* frame (*attrib.*).

ра́мпа *n., theat.* footlights.

ра́на *n.* wound.

ранг *n.* rank.

ранго́ут *n., naut.* masts and spars. —**ранго́утный,** *adj., in* **ранго́утное де́рево,** *naut.* spar.

ра́нее *adv.* earlier; sooner.

ране́ние *n.* **1,** wounding; injuring. **2,** wound; injury: получи́ть ране́ние, to be wounded; be injured.

ра́неный *adj.* wounded; injured. —*n.* wounded man; casualty. Ухо́д за ра́неными, care of the wounded.

ра́нец [*gen.* **ра́нца**] *n.* **1,** knapsack. **2,** satchel.

ранжи́р *n., in* **по ранжи́ру,** in size order.

рани́мый *pres. passive participle of* **ра́нить,** hurt: легко́ рани́мый челове́к, person who is easily hurt.

ра́нить *v.impfv. & pfv.* to wound; injure. Он был ра́нен в но́гу, he was wounded in the leg.

ра́нний *adj.* early.

ра́но *adv.* early. —*adj., used predicatively,* early: Ещё ра́но, it is still early. —**ра́но и́ли по́здно,** sooner or later.

рант [*2nd loc.* **ранту́**] *n.* welt (*of a shoe*).

ра́нчо *n.indecl.* ranch.

рань *n.f., colloq.* early morning hours: в таку́ю рань, at such an ungodly hour.

ра́ньше *adv.* **1,** earlier; sooner. **2,** before. **3,** (*with gen.*) before; ahead of. **4,** before; formerly. —**ра́ньше вре́мени; ра́ньше сро́ка,** ahead of time; ahead of schedule.

рапи́ра *n.* rapier; foil.

ра́порт *n.* report.

рапортова́ть *v.impfv. & pfv.* [*pres.* **-ту́ю, -ту́ешь**] to report.

рапс *n.* rape (*plant*). —**ра́псовый,** *adj.* rape (*attrib.*): ра́псовое ма́сло, rape oil.

рапсо́дия *n.* rhapsody.

рас- *prefix, var. of* **раз-** (*used before voiceless consonants*).

ра́са *n.* race: жёлтая ра́са, the yellow race.

раси́зм *n.* racism. —**раси́ст,** *n.* racist. —**раси́стский,** *adj.* racist.

раска́иваться *v.r.impfv.* [*pfv.* **раска́яться**] to repent; be sorry. Раска́иваться в свои́х посту́пках, to repent one's actions.

раскалённый *adj.* scorching; burning hot; red-hot.

раскали́ть *v., pfv. of* **раскаля́ть.** —**раскали́ться,** *refl., pfv. of* **раскаля́ться.**

раска́лывать *v.impfv.* [*pfv.* **расколо́ть**] **1,** to split; cleave. **2,** to chop (nuts); break (sugar) up into pieces. **3,** *fig.* to split; divide. —**раска́лываться,** *refl.* to split; split up. У меня́ раска́лывается голова́, I have a splitting headache.

раскаля́ть *v.impfv.* [*pfv.* **раскали́ть**] to make red-hot. —**раскаля́ться,** *refl.* to become red-hot.

раска́пывать *v.impfv.* [*pfv.* **раскопа́ть**] **1,** to dig; dig up. **2,** to excavate. **3,** *fig., colloq.* to dig up; unearth.

раска́рмливать *v.impfv.* [*pfv.* **раскорми́ть**] to fatten (up).

раска́т *n.* peal; clap; burst (*of thunder, laughter, etc.*).

раската́ть *v., pfv. of* **раска́тывать**[1].

раска́тистый *adj.* rolling; resounding.

раскати́ть [*infl.* **-качу́, -ка́тишь**] *v., pfv. of* **раска́тывать**[2]. —**раскати́ться,** *refl., pfv. of* **раска́тываться.**

раска́тывать[1] *v.impfv.* [*pfv.* **раската́ть**] **1,** to unroll. **2,** to smooth out; level. **3,** to roll (dough).

раска́тывать[2] *v.impfv.* [*pfv.* **раскати́ть**] **1,** to set in motion by rolling. **2,** [*impfv. only*] *colloq.* to drive (*or* ride) a lot, to one's heart's content, etc. —**раска́тываться,** *refl.* **1,** to gather speed. **2,** to roll around. **3,** to resound.

раска́чивать *v.impfv.* [*pfv.* **раскача́ть**] **1,** to rock. **2,** [*impfv. only*] (*with instr.*) to swing. **3,** *fig., colloq.* to rouse to action. —**раска́чиваться,** *refl.* **1,** to swing back and forth. **2,** [*impfv. only*] *colloq.* to sway (*while walking*). **3,** *fig., colloq.* to bestir oneself; get (oneself) moving.

раска́шляться *v.r.pfv.* to have a fit of coughing.

раска́яние *n.* repentance; remorse.

раска́яться [*infl.* **-ка́юсь, -ка́ешься**] *v.r., pfv. of* **раска́иваться.**

расквартирова́ние *n.* quartering; billeting.

расквартирова́ть *v.pfv.* [*infl.* **-ру́ю, -ру́ешь**] to quarter; billet.

расква́шивать *v.impfv.* [*pfv.* **расква́сить**] *colloq.* to smash in; bloody: расква́сить нос (+ *dat.*), to bloody someone's nose.

расквита́ться *v.r.pfv.* (*with* **с** + *instr.*) *colloq.* **1,** to settle up (with); settle one's debts (with). **2,** *fig.* to settle scores (with); get even (with).

раскида́ть *v., pfv. of* **раски́дывать** (*in sense #4*).

раски́дистый *adj.* (*of a tree*) spreading.

раски́дывать *v.impfv.* [*pfv.* **раски́нуть**] **1,** to spread; spread out. **2,** to pitch (a tent); set up (camp). **3,** *in* раски́дывать умо́м, *colloq.* to ponder. **4,** [*pfv.* **раскида́ть**] to scatter; scatter about. —**раски́дываться,** *refl.* [*pfv.* **раски́нуться**] **1,** to stretch; extend (*over a wide area*). **2,** *colloq.* to stretch out; sprawl.

раски́нуть *v., pfv. of* **раски́дывать.** —**раски́нуться,** *refl., pfv. of* **раски́дываться.**

раскиса́ть *v.impfv.* [*pfv.* **раски́снуть**] *colloq.* **1,** to become soggy; become limp. **2,** *fig.* to become listless; become apathetic. **3,** *fig.* to become very emotional.

раски́снуть [*past* **-ки́с, -ки́сла**] *v., pfv. of* **раскиса́ть.**

раскла́д *n.* **1,** apportionment. **2,** *fig.* breakdown: раскла́д цифр, breakdown of the figures. —**раскла́д сил,** (political) alignment.

раскла́дка *n.* **1,** laying out; spreading. **2,** making (*of a fire, bed, etc.*). **3,** apportionment.

раскладно́й *adj.* folding.

раскладу́шка [*gen. pl.* **-шек**] *n., colloq.* cot.

раскла́дывать *v.impfv.* [*pfv.* **разложи́ть**] **1,** to put (*each in its place*); put away. **2,** to lay out; spread out. **3,** to distribute; apportion. **4,** to make; build (a fire). —**раскла́дываться,** *refl., colloq.* to lay one's things out.

раскла́ниваться *v.r.impfv.* [*pfv.* **раскла́няться**] **1,** to bow. **2,** (*of a performer*) to take a bow. **3,** (*with* **с** + *instr.*) to greet (with a bow).

расклеивать *v.impfv.* [*pfv.* **расклеить**] **1,** to unglue; unseal. **2,** to post (a notice, placard, etc.) in many places. —**расклеиваться,** *refl.* **1,** to come unstuck; come apart. **2,** *fig., colloq.* to fall through. **3,** *fig., colloq.* to feel run-down.

расклейка *n.* posting; hanging up.

раско́ванность *n.f.* lack of inhibition; easygoing manner.

раско́ванный *adj.* uninhibited; unconstrained.

раскова́ть [*infl.* **-кую́, -куёшь**] *v., pfv. of* **раско́вывать.**

раско́вывать *v.impfv.* [*pfv.* **раскова́ть**] **1,** to unshoe (a horse). **2,** to unchain; unshackle.

раско́л *n.* split; schism; cleavage.

раскола́чивать *v.impfv.* [*pfv.* **расколоти́ть**] *colloq.* to break; smash.

расколоти́ть [*infl.* **-лочу́, -ло́тишь**] *v., pfv. of* **раскола́чивать.**

расколо́ть [*infl.* **-колю́, -ко́лешь**] *v., pfv. of* **коло́ть** (*in sense #4*) *and* **раска́лывать.** —**расколо́ться,** *refl., pfv. of* **раска́лываться.**

раско́льник *n.* **1,** religious dissenter. **2,** *fig.* person exercising a divisive influence; splitter.

раско́льнический *adj.* schismatic; divisive.

расконсерви́ровать *v.impfv. & pfv.* [*pres.* **-рую, -руешь**] to reactivate.

раскопа́ть *v., pfv. of* **раска́пывать.**

раско́пки [*gen.* **-пок**] *n.pl.* excavations.

раскорми́ть [*infl.* **-кормлю́, -ко́рмишь**] *v., pfv. of* **раска́рмливать.**

раскоря́ка *n.m. & f., colloq.* bowlegged person.

раско́сый *adj.* (*of someone's eyes*) slanting.

раскоше́ливаться *v.r.impfv.* [*pfv.* **раскоше́литься**] *colloq.* to pay up; loosen one's purse strings.

раскра́дывать *v.impfv.* [*pfv.* **раскра́сть**] to rob; steal.

раскра́ивать *v.impfv.* [*pfv.* **раскрои́ть**] to cut out (material for a garment).

раскра́сить [*infl.* **-шу, -сишь**] *v., pfv. of* **раскра́шивать.**

раскра́ска *n.* **1,** coloring. **2,** coloration.

раскрасне́ться *v.r.pfv.* to blush; become flushed; turn red.

раскра́сть [*infl. like* **красть**] *v., pfv. of* **раскра́дывать.**

раскра́шивание *n.* coloring. —**альбо́м для раскра́шивания,** coloring book.

раскра́шивать *v.impfv.* [*pfv.* **раскра́сить**] **1,** to color (a picture, photograph, etc.). **2,** to paint (with various colors).

раскрепоща́ть *v.impfv.* [*pfv.* **раскрепости́ть**] to emancipate.

раскрепощéние *n.* emancipation.

раскритиковáть *v.pfv.* [*infl.* -ку́ю, -ку́ешь] to criticize severely.

раскричáться *v.r.pfv.* [*infl.* -чу́сь, -чи́шься] *colloq.* **1,** to start shouting. **2,** (*with* на + *acc.*) to start swearing (at); call (someone) a lot of names.

раскрои́ть *v., pfv. of* **крои́ть** (*in sense #1*) *and* **раскрáивать.**

раскроши́ть *v., pfv. of* **кроши́ть.** —**раскроши́ться,** *refl., pfv. of* **кроши́ться.**

раскрути́ть [*infl.* -кручу́, -кру́тишь] *v., pfv. of* **раскру́чивать.** —**раскрути́ться,** *refl., pfv. of* **раскру́чиваться.**

раскру́чивать *v.impfv.* [*pfv.* **раскрути́ть**] to untwist; unwind. —**раскру́чиваться,** *refl.* to come untwisted; come unwound.

раскрывáть *v.impfv.* [*pfv.* **раскры́ть**] **1,** to open. **2,** to uncover; expose; bare. **3,** *fig.* to uncover (a plot); expose (illegal activities); solve (a crime). **4,** to reveal. **5,** to discover. —**раскрывáть свои́ кáрты,** to reveal (*or* tip) one's hand.

раскрывáться *v.r.impfv.* [*pfv.* **раскры́ться**] **1,** to open. **2,** to uncover oneself; expose oneself. **3,** to be uncovered; be exposed. **4,** to come out; come to light. **5,** to reveal one's secrets; tell one's story.

раскры́тие *n.* **1,** opening. **2,** exposure. **3,** revelation; disclosure.

раскры́ть [*infl.* -крó́ю, -крó́ешь] *v., pfv. of* **раскрывáть.** —**раскры́ться,** *refl., pfv. of* **раскрывáться.**

раскупáть *v.impfv.* [*pfv.* **раскупи́ть**] to buy up.

раскупи́ть [*infl.* -куплю́, -ку́пишь] *v., pfv. of* **раскупáть.**

раску́поривать *v.impfv.* [*pfv.* **раску́порить**] to uncork.

раску́ривать *v.impfv.* [*pfv.* **раскури́ть**] **1,** to get (a pipe, cigarette, etc.) lighted. **2,** [*impfv. only*] *colloq.* to pass the time smoking.

раскури́ть [*infl.* -курю́, -ку́ришь] *v., pfv. of* **раску́ривать.**

раскуси́ть *v.pfv.* [*infl.* -кушу́, -ку́сишь] **1,** *pfv. of* **раску́сывать. 2,** *fig., colloq.* to see through (someone).

раску́сывать *v.impfv.* [*pfv.* **раскуси́ть**] to bite; bite into pieces.

раску́тывать *v.impfv.* [*pfv.* **раску́тать**] to unwrap.

рáсовый *adj.* racial; race (*attrib.*).

распáд *n.* **1,** disintegration; breakup. **2,** *chem.; physics* decay.

распадáться *v.r.impfv.* [*pfv.* **распáсться**] **1,** to disintegrate; fall apart. **2,** *fig.* to break up.

распáивать *v.impfv.* [*pfv.* **распая́ть**] to unsolder.

распаковáть [*infl.* -ку́ю, -ку́ешь] *v., pfv. of* **распакó́вывать.** —**распаковáться,** *refl., pfv. of* **распакó́вываться.**

распакó́вка *n.* unpacking.

распакó́вывать *v.impfv.* [*pfv.* **распаковáть**] to unpack. —**распакó́вываться,** *refl., colloq.* to unpack; get unpacked.

распаля́ть *v.impfv.* [*pfv.* **распали́ть**] *colloq.* **1,** to make burning hot. **2,** *fig.* to fire up. —**распаля́ться,** *refl., colloq.* **1,** to become burning hot. **2,** *fig.* to become fired up.

распáривать *v.impfv.* [*pfv.* **распáрить**] **1,** to steam; stew. **2,** *colloq.* to cause to sweat.

распáрывать *v.impfv.* [*pfv.* **распорó́ть**] **1,** to unstitch. **2,** *colloq.* to rip open (the skin). —**распáрываться,** *refl.* to rip; split.

распáсться [*infl. like* пáсть] *v.r., pfv. of* **распадáться.**

распахáть [*infl.* -пашу́, -пáшешь] *v., pfv. of* **распáхивать** (*in sense #1*).

распáхивать *v.impfv.* **1,** [*pfv.* **распахáть**] to plow; plow up. **2,** [*pfv.* **распахну́ть**] to throw open; fling open. —**распáхиваться,** *refl.* [*pfv.* **распахну́ться**] to swing open; fly open.

распахну́ть *v., pfv. of* **распáхивать** (*in sense #2*). —**распахну́ться,** *refl., pfv. of* **распáхиваться.**

распашó́нка [*gen. pl.* -нок] *n.* baby's short-sleeved undershirt that opens down the back.

распая́ть *v., pfv. of* **распáивать.**

распевáть *v.impfv., colloq.* to sing (*loudly or gaily*).

распекáть *v.impfv.* [*pfv.* **распéчь**] *colloq.* to tell off; upbraid.

распереть [*infl.* разопру́, разопрёшь; *past* распёр, распёрла] *v., pfv. of* **распирáть.**

распéться *v.r.pfv.* [*infl.* -поюсь, -поёшься] *colloq.* **1,** (*of a singer*) to warm up. **2,** to sing away.

распечáтывать *v.impfv.* [*pfv.* **распечáтать**] to unseal; break the seal of.

распéчь [*infl. like* пéчь] *v., pfv. of* **распекáть.**

распивáть *v.impfv.* [*pfv.* **распи́ть**] *colloq.* **1,** to drink up (*together with someone else*). **2,** [*impfv. only*] to drink slowly; linger over.

распи́ливать *v.impfv.* [*pfv.* **распили́ть**] to saw up.

распили́ть [*infl.* -пилю́, -пи́лишь] *v., pfv. of* **распи́ливать.**

распинáть *v.impfv.* [*pfv.* **распя́ть**] to crucify. —**распинáться,** *refl.* [*impfv. only*] *colloq.* **1,** (*with* за + *acc.*) to stand up for; vouch for; go to bat for. **2,** (*with* о) to speak with passion (about).

распирáть *v.impfv.* [*pfv.* **распереть**] *colloq.* **1,** to cause to bulge; cause to burst. **2,** *impers.* to bulge; burst: Егó кармáны распирáло от дéнег, his pockets were bulging with money. **3,** [*impfv. only*] (*of a feeling*) to consume (someone).

расписáние *n.* schedule; timetable.

расписáть [*infl.* -пишу́, -пи́шешь] *v., pfv. of* **распи́сывать.** —**расписáться,** *refl., pfv. of* **распи́сываться.**

распи́ска [*gen. pl.* -сок] *n.* (written) receipt. —**под распи́ску,** on condition that the recipient signs for it.

расписнó́й *adj., colloq.* painted with designs.

распи́сывать *v.impfv.* [*pfv.* **расписáть**] **1,** to write down; note down; copy down; enter (a number of items). **2,** to schedule; assign. **3,** to paint; decorate. **4,** *fig., colloq.* to describe in glowing terms. —**распи́сываться,** *refl.* **1,** to sign one's name. **2,** *colloq.* to register one's marriage. **3,** (*with* в + *prepl.*) *colloq.* to openly admit; openly advertise.

распи́ть [*infl.* разопью́, разопьёшь; *past fem.* распилá] *v., pfv. of* **распивáть.**

распи́хивать *v.impfv.* [*pfv.* **распихáть**] *colloq.* **1,** to push aside; force one's way through. **2,** to shove; stuff (*into various places*).

распла́вить [*infl.* -влю, -вишь] *v., pfv. of* **расплавля́ть.** **распла́вленный** *adj.* molten.

расплавля́ть *v.impfv.* [*pfv.* **распла́вить**] to melt; melt down.

распла́каться *v.r.pfv.* [*infl.* -пла́чусь, -пла́чешься] to burst into tears.

распланиро́вать *v.pfv.* [*infl.* -рую, -руешь] to plan out (one's day, work, etc.).

распланирова́ть [*infl.* -ру́ю, -ру́ешь] *v., pfv. of* **плани́ровать.**

распла́стывать *v.impfv.* [*pfv.* **распласта́ть**] **1,** to slice into layers. **2,** to spread; spread out; spread flat. —**распла́стываться,** *refl.* to lie flat.

распла́та *n.* **1,** payment. **2,** *fig.* retribution. —**день** (*or* **час**) **распла́ты,** day of reckoning.

расплати́ться [*infl.* -плачу́сь, -пла́тишься] *v.r., pfv. of* **распла́чиваться.**

распла́чиваться *v.r.impfv.* [*pfv.* **расплати́ться**] **1,** (*with* **с** + *instr.*) to pay off; settle accounts (with). **2,** (*with* **с** + *instr.*) to get even (with). **3,** (*with* **за** + *acc.*) to pay (for); take the punishment (for).

расплеска́ть [*infl.* -плещу́, -пле́щешь] *v., pfv. of* **расплёскивать.** —**расплеска́ться,** *refl., pfv. of* **расплёскиваться.**

расплёскивать *v.impfv.* [*pfv.* **расплеска́ть**] to spill. —**расплёскиваться,** *refl.* (*of a liquid*) to spill.

расплести́ [*infl. like* **плести́**] *v., pfv. of* **расплета́ть.**

расплета́ть *v.impfv.* [*pfv.* **расплести́**] to untwist; unbraid.

расплоди́ть *v., pfv. of* **плоди́ть.** —**расплоди́ться,** *refl., pfv. of* **плоди́ться.**

расплыва́ться *v.r.impfv.* [*pfv.* **расплы́ться**] **1,** (*of a liquid*) to run; (*of something in the air*) to spread. **2,** *fig.* to become indistinct; become blurred. **3,** *fig., colloq.* to grow fat. **4,** *fig.* (*of a smile, look of satisfaction, etc.*) to spread across one's face. —**расплыва́ться в улы́бке,** to break into a broad smile.

расплы́вчатый *adj.* **1,** indistinct. **2,** (*of a photograph*) blurred; blurry. **3,** *fig.* vague.

расплы́ться [*infl. like* **плыть**] *v.r., pfv. of* **расплыва́ться.**

расплю́щивать *v.impfv.* [*pfv.* **расплю́щить**] to flatten; crush; squash. —**расплю́щиваться,** *refl.* to be flattened out.

распознава́ние *n.* **1,** recognition. **2,** diagnosis.

распознава́ть *v.impfv.* [*pfv.* **распозна́ть**; *pres.* -знаю́, -знаёшь] **1,** to recognize; identify. **2,** to diagnose (an illness). **3,** to discern; make out.

разпозна́ть [*infl.* -зна́ю, -зна́ешь] *v., pfv. of* **распознава́ть.**

располага́ть *v.impfv.* **1,** (*with instr.*) to have; have at one's disposal. **2,** (*with instr.*) to make use of; do with. **3,** (*with* **к**) to be conducive to. **4,** *obs.* to intend; plan. **5,** [*pfv.* **расположи́ть**] to arrange; station; post. **6,** [*pfv.* **расположи́ть**] (*often with* **к себе́** *or* **в свою́ по́льзу**) to win over. —**располага́ться,** *refl.* [*pfv.* **расположи́ться**] **1,** to settle down; sit down. **2,** *in* располага́ться ла́герем, to camp; encamp; set up camp. **3,** [*impfv. only*] *obs.* to intend; plan.

располага́ющий *adj.* pleasing; attractive.

располза́ться *v.r.impfv.* [*pfv.* **расползти́сь**] **1,** to crawl; crawl away (*in different directions*). **2,** *colloq.* to unravel; come apart at the seams. **3,** *colloq.* to become blurred; become indistinct.

расползти́сь [*infl. like* **ползти́**] *v.r., pfv. of* **располза́ться.**

расположе́ние *n.* **1,** arrangement; layout; disposition. **2,** location; position. **3,** favor; sympathies. **4,** (*with* **к**) liking (for); fondness (for). **5,** (*with* **к**) inclination (toward); tendency (toward). **6,** *colloq.* mood; desire: У меня́ нет расположе́ния (+ *inf.*), I am not in the mood to... —**расположе́ние ду́ха,** mood; frame of mind.

располо́женный *adj.* **1,** located; situated. **2,** (*with* **к**) fond (of). **3,** (*with* **к**) inclined (to); disposed (toward). **4,** (*with inf.*) of a mood (to); in the mood (for).

расположи́ть [*infl.* -ложу́, -ло́жишь] *v., pfv. of* **располага́ть** (*in senses #5 & #6*). —**расположи́ться,** *refl.* **1,** *pfv. of* **располага́ться. 2,** (*with inf.*) *obs.* to decide (to); make up one's mind (to). **3,** (*with* **к**) *colloq.* to take a liking (to).

распоро́ть [*infl.* -порю́, -по́решь] *v., pfv. of* **поро́ть** (*in sense #2*) *and* **распа́рывать.** —**распоро́ться,** *refl., pfv. of* **распа́рываться.**

распоряди́тель *n.m.* manager; superintendent; person in charge.

распоряди́тельный *adj.* efficient; businesslike.

распоряди́ться [*infl.* -жу́сь, -ди́шься] *v.r., pfv. of* **распоряжа́ться.**

распоря́док [*gen.* -дка] *n.* order; routine.

распоряжа́ться *v.r.impfv.* [*pfv.* **распоряди́ться**] **1,** (*with inf. or* **о**) to order (*that something be done*); (*with* **чтобы**) see (to it) that (*something is done*). **2,** [*impfv. only*] to be in charge; give orders; (*with instr.*) be in charge of; direct; manage. **3,** (*with instr.*) to handle; do with (money, property, etc.).

распоряже́ние *n.* **1,** order: отда́ть распоряже́ние, to give an order. **2,** directive. **3,** (*with instr.*) disposition (of). **4,** disposal: име́ть в своём распоряже́нии, to have at one's disposal; предоста́вить в распоряже́ние (+ *gen.*), to place at the disposal of; make available to.

распоя́сать [*infl.* -поя́шу, -поя́шешь] *v., pfv. of* **распоя́сывать.** —**распоя́саться,** *refl., pfv. of* **распоя́сываться.**

распоя́сывать *v.impfv.* [*pfv.* **распоя́сать**] to ungird. —**распоя́сываться,** *refl.* **1,** to take off one's belt. **2,** *fig., colloq.* to cast off all restraint; let oneself go.

распра́ва *n.* (*with* **с** + *instr.*) harsh treatment (of); savage punishment (of); reprisals (against).

распра́вить [*infl.* -влю, -вишь] *v., pfv. of* **расправля́ть.** —**распра́виться,** *refl., pfv. of* **расправля́ться.**

расправля́ть *v.impfv.* [*pfv.* **распра́вить**] **1,** to smooth out. **2,** to straighten. —**расправля́ть кры́лья,** to spread one's wings (*lit. & fig.*).

расправля́ться *v.r.impfv.* [*pfv.* **распра́виться**] **1,** to get smoothed out. **2,** (*with* **с** + *instr.*) to deal with (*severely or cruelly*). **3,** (*with* **с** + *instr.*) *colloq.* to dispose of; finish off. —**расправля́ться без суда́,** to take the law into one's own hands.

распределе́ние *n.* **1,** distribution. Распределе́ние роле́й, casting. **2,** assignment (*of a recent graduate or young specialist*).

распредели́тель *n.m.* **1,** distributor (*person*). **2,** distribution center. **3,** *mech.* distributor.

распредели́тельный *adj.* distribution (*attrib.*); distributing; distributive. —**распредели́тельный вал,** camshaft. —**распредели́тельный щит,** switchboard.

распределя́ть *v.impfv.* [*pfv.* **распредели́ть**] **1,** to distribute. **2,** to assign (roles, duties, etc.).

распродава́ть *v.impfv.* [*pfv.* **распрода́ть;** *pres.* -даю́, -даёшь] **1,** to sell off. **2,** to sell out: Кни́га распро́дана, the book is sold out.

распрода́жа *n.* sale; clearance sale.

распрода́ть [*infl. like* **прода́ть**] *v., pfv. of* **распродава́ть.**

распростере́ть [*past* -стёр, -стёрла, *not used in future*] *v., pfv. of* **распростира́ть.** —**распростере́ться,** *refl., pfv. of* **распростира́ться.**

распростёртый *adj.* **1,** outstretched. **2,** prostrate. —**с распростёртыми объя́тиями,** with open arms.

распростира́ть *v.impfv.* [*pfv.* **распростере́ть**] to stretch out; spread; extend. —**распростира́ться,** *refl.* **1,** to lie with arms outstretched. **2,** *fig.* to stretch; extend.

распрости́ться *v.r.pfv.* [*infl.* -щу́сь, -сти́шься] (*with* **с** + *instr.*) *colloq.* to say goodbye (to); bid farewell (to); take leave (of).

распростране́ние *n.* **1,** spreading; spread. **2,** dissemination. **3,** proliferation. **4,** expansion; extension. **5,** extent; range. Име́ть большо́е распростране́ние, to be widespread. О́бласть распростране́ния живо́тного, area over which an animal is to be found.

распространённый *adj.* widespread; common; prevalent.

распространя́ть *v.impfv.* [*pfv.* **распространи́ть**] **1,** to spread. **2,** to disseminate; circulate. **3,** to expand. **4,** to extend. **5,** to give off. —**распространя́ться,** *refl.* **1,** to spread. **2,** to extend. **3,** (*with* **о**) *colloq.* to dwell at great length (upon). Распространя́ться на те́му, to enlarge *or* expand on a subject.

ра́спря *n., usu. pl.* discord; contention; strife.

распряга́ть *v.impfv.* [*pfv.* **распря́чь**] to unharness.

распрямля́ть *v.impfv.* [*pfv.* **распрями́ть**] to straighten; unbend. —**распрямля́ться,** *refl.* to straighten up.

распря́чь [*infl.* -прягу́, -пряжёшь, ...-прягу́т; *past* -пря́г, -прягла́, -прягло́, -прягли́] *v., pfv. of* **распряга́ть.**

распу́гивать *v.impfv.* [*pfv.* **распуга́ть**] *colloq.* to frighten away; scare away.

распуска́ть *v.impfv.* [*pfv.* **распусти́ть**] **1,** to dismiss. **2,** to disband; dissolve. **3,** to allow (*e.g.* children) to run all about a place. **4,** to loosen (a rope); let out (reins); let down (one's hair). **5,** to open; spread; unfurl. **6,** *colloq.* to spread (rumors, gossip, etc.). **7,** *colloq.* to dissolve; melt. **8,** *colloq.* to be too lenient with; let get out of hand. —**распуска́ть язы́к,** *colloq.* to speak too freely. —**распуска́ть со́пли, слю́ни, ню́ни,** *see* **со́пли/слю́ни/ню́ни.**

распуска́ться *v.r.impfv.* [*pfv.* **распусти́ться**] **1,** (*of buds*) to open. **2,** (*of fabric, stockings, etc.*) to become unraveled. **3,** *colloq.* to come untied; come undone. **4,** *colloq.* (*of hair*) to hang down. **5,** *colloq.* (*of muscles*) to relax. **6,** *colloq.* to become flabby. **7,** *colloq.* (*of rumors*) to circulate; go around. **8,** *colloq.* to dissolve (*in water*). **9,** *colloq.* to let oneself go. **10,** *colloq.* to get out of hand.

распусти́ть [*infl.* -пущу́, -пу́стишь] *v., pfv. of* **распуска́ть.** —**распусти́ться,** *refl., pfv. of* **распуска́ться.**

распу́тать *v., pfv. of* **распу́тывать.** —**распу́таться,** *refl., pfv. of* **распу́тываться.**

распу́тица *n.* time of the year when roads are impassable.

распу́тник *n.* profligate; lecher; libertine.

распу́тничать *v.impfv.* to lead a dissolute life.

распу́тный *adj.* dissolute; profligate; licentious.

распу́тство *n.* profligacy; licentiousness; dissoluteness.

распу́тывать *v.impfv.* [*pfv.* **распу́тать**] **1,** to untangle; disentangle; unravel. **2,** *fig.* to unravel. —**распу́тываться,** *refl.* **1,** to come untangled. **2,** *fig., colloq.* to disentangle oneself (*from a situation*). **3,** *fig., colloq.* to be cleared up; be settled. **4,** *in* распу́таться с долга́ми, to free oneself of debt.

распу́тье *n.* crossroads. —**на распу́тье,** at the crossroads.

распуха́ть *v.impfv.* [*pfv.* **распу́хнуть**] **1,** to swell; swell up; become swollen. **2,** to bulge.

распу́хнуть [*past* -пу́х, -пу́хла] *v., pfv. of* **распуха́ть.**

распуши́ть *v., pfv. of* **пуши́ть.**

распу́щенность *n.f.* **1,** lack of discipline; laxity. **2,** dissoluteness; dissipation.

распу́щенный *adj.* **1,** (*of one's hair*) loose; hanging down. **2,** *colloq.* undisciplined. **3,** dissolute.

распыли́тель *n.m.* sprayer; atomizer.

распыля́ть *v.impfv.* [*pfv.* **распыли́ть**] **1,** to pulverize. **2,** to spray. **3,** to disperse; scatter.

распя́тие *n.* **1,** crucifixion. **2,** crucifix.

распя́ть [*infl.* -пну́, -пнёшь] *v., pfv. of* **распина́ть.**

расса́да *n.* seedlings.

рассади́ть [*infl.* -сажу́, -са́дишь] *v., pfv. of* **расса́живать.**

расса́дник *n.* **1,** nursery (*for plants*). **2,** *fig.* breeding ground (*of crime, infection, etc.*).

расса́живать *v.impfv.* [*pfv.* **рассади́ть**] **1,** to seat (*each in his place*). **2,** to separate; seat apart. **3,** to plant farther apart. —**расса́живаться,** *refl.* [*pfv.* **рассе́сться**] (*of many people*) to take their (respective) seats.

расса́сываться *v.r.impfv.* [*pfv.* **рассоса́ться**] **1,** (*of a tumor*) to dissolve. **2,** *colloq.* (*of a crowd*) to melt away.

рассвести́ [*infl.* -светёт; *past* -свело́] *v., pfv. of* **рассвета́ть.**

рассве́т *n.* dawn; daybreak.

рассвета́ть *v.impfv.* [*pfv.* **рассвести́**] *impers.* to dawn: Рассвета́ет, it is getting light; day is dawning; day is breaking.

рассвирепе́ть *v., pfv. of* **свирепе́ть.**

расседа́ться *v.r.impfv.* [*pfv.* **рассе́сться**] to crack.

рассёдлывать *v.impfv.* [*pfv.* **расседла́ть**] to unsaddle.

рассе́ивание *n.* scattering; dispersion; dispersal.

рассе́ивать *v.impfv.* [*pfv.* **рассе́ять**] **1,** to scatter (seeds). **2,** to disperse. **3,** to diffuse (light). **4,** *fig.* to dispel (doubts, fears, rumors, etc.). **5,** to distract; take someone's mind off things. —**рассе́иваться,** *refl.* **1,** to scatter; disperse. **2,** (*of fog*) to lift; dissipate; (*of clouds*) to disappear. **3,** *fig.* (*of doubts, fears, etc.*) to be dispelled. **4,** to get one's mind off things; unwind.

рассека́ть *v.impfv.* [*pfv.* **рассе́чь**] **1,** to cleave; split. **2,** to slash; gash. **3,** to cut in two.

рассекре́чивать *v.impfv.* [*pfv.* **рассекре́тить**] to declassify.

рассе́лина *n.* cleft; fissure.

расселя́ть *v.impfv.* [*pfv.* **рассели́ть**] **1,** to settle (many people). **2,** to separate; force to live in separate places. —**расселя́ться,** *refl.* to settle in different places.

рассерди́ть *v., pfv. of* **серди́ть.** —**рассерди́ться,** *refl., pfv. of* **серди́ться.**

рассе́рженный *adj.* angry.

рассе́сться [*infl. like* **сесть**] *v.r., pfv. of* **расса́живаться** *and* **рассада́ться.**

рассече́ние *n.* cutting in two; splitting in two.

рассе́чь [*infl. like* **сечь**; *past* -сёк, -секла́, -секло́, -секли́] *v., pfv. of* **рассека́ть.**

рассе́яние *n.* **1,** dispersion; scattering. **2,** diffusion (*of light*). **3,** dispelling (*of doubts, rumors, etc.*).

рассе́янно *adv.* absent-mindedly; absently.

рассе́янность *n.f.* absent-mindedness. По рассе́янности, absent-mindedly.

рассе́янный *adj.* **1,** scattered; dispersed. **2,** (*of light*) diffused. **3,** absent-minded.

рассе́ять [*infl.* -сею, -сеешь] *v., pfv. of* **рассе́ивать.** —**рассе́яться,** *refl., pfv. of* **рассе́иваться.**

расска́з *n.* **1,** story. **2,** account.

рассказа́ть [*infl.* -скажу́, -ска́жешь] *v., pfv. of* **расска́зывать.**

расска́зчик *n.* narrator; storyteller.

расска́зывание *n.* telling; narration.

расска́зывать *v.impfv.* [*pfv.* **рассказа́ть**] to tell; relate; recount. Рассказа́ть исто́рию, to tell a story. Рассказа́ть кому́-нибудь о случи́вшемся, to tell someone about what happened. —**расска́зываться,** *refl.* [*impfv. only*] to be told. В Би́блии расска́зывается о..., the Bible tells of...

рассла́бить [*infl.* -блю, -бишь] *v., pfv. of* **расслабля́ть.** —**рассла́биться,** *refl., pfv. of* **расслабля́ться.**

расслабле́ние *n.* **1,** weakening. **2,** weakness.

рассла́бленность *n.f.* weakness; loss of energy.

рассла́бленный *adj.* **1,** weak; debilitated. **2,** (*of one's gait*) unsteady; unsure.

расслабля́ть *v.impfv.* [*pfv.* **рассла́бить**] **1,** to weaken; debilitate. **2,** to relax (muscles). **3,** to loosen. —**расслабля́ться,** *refl.* to relax.

рассла́ивать *v.impfv.* [*pfv.* **рассло́ить**] to stratify.

рассле́дование *n.* investigation.

рассле́довать *v.impfv. & pfv.* [*pres.* -дую, -дуешь] to investigate.

рассло́ение *n.* stratification: рассло́ение о́бщества, stratification of society.

рассло́ить *v., pfv. of* **рассла́ивать.**

расслы́шать *v.pfv.* [*infl.* -шу, -шишь] to hear; catch.

рассма́тривать *v.impfv.* [*pfv.* **рассмотре́ть**] **1,** to examine; scrutinize. **2,** to consider; take up; examine. **3,** [*impfv. only*] (*with* как) to regard (as); consider (to be). *See also* **рассмотре́ть.**

рассмеши́ть *v., pfv. of* **смеши́ть.**

рассмея́ться *v.r.pfv.* [*infl.* -смею́сь, -смеёшься] to burst out laughing.

рассмотре́ние *n.* examination; consideration.

рассмотре́ть *v.pfv.* [*infl.* -смотрю́, -смо́тришь] **1,** *pfv. of* **рассма́тривать. 2,** to discern; make out; spot.

рассова́ть [*infl.* -сую́, -суёшь] *v., pfv. of* **рассо́вывать.**

рассо́вывать *v.impfv.* [*pfv.* **рассова́ть**] *colloq.* to stuff (*in various places*).

рассо́л *n.* brine.

рассо́льник *n.* soup with pickled cucumbers.

рассо́рить *v.pfv.* to set to quarreling; cause a quarrel between. —**рассо́риться,** *refl.* (*with* с + *instr.*) to have a falling-out (with).

рассортирова́ть *v., pfv. of* **сортирова́ть.**

рассортиро́вка *n.* sorting out.

рассоса́ться [*infl.* -сосётся] *v.r., pfv. of* **расса́сываться.**

рассо́хнуться [*past* -со́хся, -со́хлась] *v.r., pfv. of* **рассыха́ться.**

расспра́шивать *v.impfv.* [*pfv.* **расспроси́ть**] to question.

расспроси́ть [*infl.* -спрошу́, -спро́сишь] *v., pfv. of* **расспра́шивать.**

расспро́сы [*gen.* -сов] *n.pl.* questions; questioning.

рассредото́чение *n.* dispersal; spreading out.

рассредото́чивать *v.impfv.* [*pfv.* **рассредото́чить**] to disperse; spread out.

рассро́чивать *v.impfv.* [*pfv.* **рассро́чить**] to spread (payments) over a period of time.

рассро́чка *n., usu. in* в рассро́чку, on the installment plan; on time.

расстава́ние *n.* parting; taking leave.

расстава́ться *v.r.impfv.* [*pfv.* **расста́ться**; *pres.* -стаю́сь, -стаёшься] (*with* с + *instr.*) **1,** to part (with). **2,** to leave (a place). **3,** *fig.* to give up; say goodbye to (an idea, dream, etc.). —**расста́ться с жи́знью,** to die.

расста́вить [*infl.* -влю, -вишь] *v., pfv. of* **расставля́ть.**

расставля́ть *v.impfv.* [*pfv.* **расста́вить**] **1,** to place; arrange. **2,** to assign (personnel); post (sentries). **3,** to spread (apart); move apart.

расстано́вка *n.* **1,** placement; arrangement. **2,** placement (*of personnel*). **3,** (political) alignment: расстано́вка сил, alignment of forces. **4,** intermittent pauses. —**говори́ть с расстано́вкой,** to speak in measured tones.

расста́ться [*infl.* -ста́нусь, -ста́нешься] *v.r., pfv. of* **расстава́ться.**

расстёгивать *v.impfv.* [*pfv.* **расстегну́ть**] to unfasten; unbutton; unhook; undo. —**расстёгиваться,** *refl.* **1,** to come undone. **2,** to unbutton one's coat.

расстила́ть *v.impfv.* [*pfv.* **разостла́ть**] to spread (a covering over a surface). —**расстила́ться,** *refl.* **1,** to be spread out. **2,** to stretch; extend.

расстоя́ние *n.* distance. —**держа́ться на расстоя́нии,** to keep one's distance.

расстра́ивать *v.impfv.* [*pfv.* **расстро́ить**] **1,** to throw into disorder; break up. **2,** to impair; damage; ruin. **3,** to disrupt; upset. **4,** to frustrate; thwart; foil. **5,** to upset (*emotionally*); disturb. **6,** to throw out of tune. **7,** *in* расстра́ивать желу́док, to upset one's stomach; cause indigestion. **8,** *in* расстро́ить сва́дьбу, to break off one's engagement. —**расстро́иться,** *refl.* **1,** to be thrown into disorder. **2,** to be disrupted. **3,** (*of one's health*) to be impaired. **4,** to become upset. **5,** to get out of tune.

расстре́л *n.* execution by a firing squad.

расстре́ливать *v.impfv.* [*pfv.* **расстреля́ть**] **1,** to execute by a firing squad. **2,** to shoot up; rake with fire. **3,** to use up; exhaust (one's ammunition).

расстри́га *n.m.* unfrocked monk; unfrocked priest.

расстрига́ть *v.impfv.* [*pfv.* **расстри́чь**] to unfrock; defrock.

расстри́чь [*infl. like* стричь] *v., pfv. of* **расстрига́ть**.

расстро́енный *adj.* **1,** disorganized; thrown into disorder. **2,** upset (*emotionally*). **3,** (*of one's health*) impaired. **4,** out of tune.

расстро́ить *v., pfv. of* **расстра́ивать.** —**расстро́иться,** *refl., pfv. of* **расстра́иваться**.

расстро́йство *n.* **1,** upsetting; disruption. **2,** disorder; disarray. **3,** *med.* disorder. **4,** distress. —**расстро́йство желу́дка,** upset stomach. —**расстро́йство пищеваре́ния,** indigestion.

расступа́ться *v.r.impfv.* [*pfv.* **расступи́ться**] **1,** to step aside; make way. **2,** to part; open.

расступи́ться [*infl.* -ступлю́сь, -сту́пишься] *v.r., pfv. of* **расступа́ться**.

рассуди́тельный *adj.* reasonable; sensible; judicious; prudent. —**рассуди́тельность,** *n.f.* prudence; discretion; good sense.

рассуди́ть *v.pfv.* [*infl.* -сужу́, -су́дишь] **1,** to settle (a dispute); settle a dispute between. **2,** to decide; conclude; judge. **3,** to think; reflect.

рассу́док [*gen.* -дка] *n.* **1,** sanity. **2,** common sense; good sense; reason: го́лос рассу́дка, the voice of reason. —**в по́лном рассу́дке,** in full possession of one's faculties.

рассу́дочный *adj.* rational.

рассужда́ть *v.impfv.* **1,** to reason. **2,** (*with* о) to discuss. **3,** (*with* о) to discourse (on); expound (on).

рассужде́ние *n.* **1,** reasoning. **2,** *pl.* discussion; comments; remarks. **3,** *pl.* objections; arguments: без (вся́ких) рассужде́ний, without any arguments.

рассу́чивать *v.impfv.* [*pfv.* **рассучи́ть**] **1,** to untwist. **2,** to roll down (one's sleeves).

рассучи́ть [*infl.* -сучу́, -су́чишь] *v., pfv. of* **рассу́чивать**.

рассчи́танный *adj.* **1,** calculated; intentional. **2** (*with* на + *acc.*) intended (for); designed (for); meant (for).

рассчи́тывать *v.impfv.* [*pfv.* **рассчита́ть**] **1,** to calculate. **2,** to figure; plan. **3,** to dismiss; discharge; fire. **4,** [*impfv. only*] (*with inf.*) to intend (to); expect (to). **5,** [*impfv. only*] (*with* на + *acc.*) to count on. —**рассчи́тываться,** *refl.* **1,** (*with* с + *instr.*) to settle up with (someone); pay off (one's debts). **2,** (*with* с + *instr.*) to settle scores (with); get even (with). **3,** *colloq.* to lose one's job. **4,** [*impfv. only*] (*with* за + *acc.*) to answer for; pay for.

рассыла́ть *v.impfv.* [*pfv.* **разосла́ть**] to send out; mail out; circulate.

рассы́лка *n.* sending out; mailing out.

рассы́льный *n., decl. as an adj.* delivery boy; errand boy; deliveryman.

рассы́пать [*infl.* -сы́плю, -сы́плешь] *v., pfv. of* **рассыпа́ть.** —**рассы́паться,** *refl., pfv. of* **рассыпа́ться**.

рассыпа́ть *v.impfv.* [*pfv.* **рассы́пать**] to spill; scatter; strew. —**рассыпа́ться,** *refl.* **1,** to spill; be strewn. **2,** to crumble; fall to pieces. **3,** to scatter; disperse. **4,** (*of one's hair*) to hang loosely. **5,** (*with* в + *prepl. pl.*) *colloq.* to be profuse (with): рассыпа́ться в извине́ниях, to apologize profusely. Рассыпа́ться в похвала́х (+ *dat.*), to lavish praise upon; be effusive in one's praise of. Рассыпа́ться кому́-нибудь в комплиме́нтах, to shower someone with compliments.

рассы́пчатый *adj.* friable; crumbly.

рассыха́ться *v.r.impfv.* [*pfv.* **рассо́хнуться**] to crack (*as a result of drying up*).

раста́лкивать *v.impfv.* [*pfv.* **растолка́ть**] *colloq.* **1,** to push (everyone) aside. **2,** to awaken; arouse (*by shaking*).

раста́пливать *v.impfv.* [*pfv.* **растопи́ть**] **1,** to light (a stove). **2,** to melt. —**раста́пливаться,** *refl.* **1,** (*of a stove*) to light. **2,** to melt.

раста́птывать *v.impfv.* [*pfv.* **растопта́ть**] to trample; crush.

растаска́ть *v., pfv. of* **раста́скивать** (*in senses #1 & #2*).

раста́скивать *v.impfv.* [*pfv.* **растащи́ть**] **1,** [*pfv. also* **растаска́ть**] to carry away; remove (*one at a time, bit by bit*). **2,** [*pfv. also* **растаска́ть**] to steal; make off with. **3,** *colloq.* to pull apart; separate.

раста́чивать *v.impfv.* [*pfv.* **расточи́ть**] to chisel out.

растащи́ть [*infl.* -тащу́, -та́щишь] *v., pfv. of* **раста́скивать**.

раста́ять *v., pfv. of* **та́ять**.

раство́р *n.* solution: щелочно́й раство́р, alkaline solution. —**строи́тельный раство́р,** mortar.

растворе́ние *n.* dissolving; dissolution.

раствори́мый *adj.* soluble. —**раствори́мость,** *n.f.* solubility.

раствори́тель *n.m.* solvent.

раствори́ть *v.pfv.* **1,** [*infl.* -творю́, -тво́ришь] *pfv. of* **растворя́ть** (*in sense #1*). **2,** [*pfv.* -творю́, -твори́шь] *pfv. of* **растворя́ть** (*in sense #2*). —**раствори́ться,** *refl.* [*same distinction in stress*] *pfv. of* **растворя́ться**.

растворя́ть *v.impfv.* [*pfv.* **раствори́ть**] **1,** to open. **2,** to dissolve. —**растворя́ться,** *refl.* **1,** (*of a door, window, etc.*) to open; swing open. **2,** (*of a substance*) to dissolve.

растворя́ющий *adj.* solvent.

растека́ться *v.r.impfv.* [*pfv.* **расте́чься**] **1,** (*of liquids*) to run; spread. **2,** (*of a crowd*) to set out (*in various directions*). **3,** (*with* по) (*of a smile, feeling, etc.*) to come over (one's face, body, etc.). **4,** [*impfv. only*] *colloq.* to go into unnecessary detail.

расте́ние *n.* plant.

растениево́дство *n.* plant growing; plant cultivation.

растере́ть [*infl.* разотру́, разотрёшь; *past* растёр, растёрла] *v., pfv. of* **растира́ть**.

расте́рзанный *adj.* **1,** torn to shreds. **2,** *colloq.* disheveled. **3,** *fig.* tormented.

растерза́ть *v.pfv.* **1,** to tear to bits. **2,** *fig.* to torment. Растерза́ть чьё-нибудь се́рдце, to tear at one's heart; tear one's heart out.

растéрянный *adj.* confused; bewildered. —**растéрянно,** *adv.* in bewilderment. —**растéрянность,** *n.f.* confusion; bewilderment.

растеря́ть *v.pfv.* to lose (many things). —**растеря́ться,** *refl.* **1,** (*of many things*) to be lost. **2,** to become confused; be bewildered; become flustered.

растéчься [*infl. like* течь] *v.r., pfv. of* **растека́ться**.

расти́ *v.impfv.* [*pfv.* вы́расти; *pres.* расту́, растёшь; *past* рос, росла́, росло́, росли́] **1,** to grow. **2,** to grow up. **3,** to grow; increase; rise; go up.

растира́ние *n.* **1,** grinding. **2,** rubbing; massaging.

растира́ть *v.impfv.* [*pfv.* растере́ть] **1,** to grind (into small particles). **2,** to rub (onto the surface of something). **3,** to rub; massage.

расти́тельность *n.f.* **1,** vegetation. **2,** *colloq.* hair (*on one's face or body*).

расти́тельный *adj.* plant (*attrib.*); vegetable (*attrib.*). —**расти́тельное ма́сло,** vegetable oil.

расти́ть *v.impfv.* [*pfv.* вы́растить; *pres.* ращу́, расти́шь] **1,** to raise; bring up (children). **2,** to train (personnel). **3,** to raise; grow; cultivate (plants).

растлева́ть *v.impfv.* [*pfv.* растли́ть] **1,** to sexually abuse; molest; violate; ravish (a minor). **2,** *fig.* to corrupt.

растле́ние *n.* **1,** sexual abuse; molestation; violation (*of a minor*). **2,** decay; decadence.

растле́нный *adj.* corrupt; decadent.

растли́ть *v., pfv. of* **растлева́ть**.

растолка́ть *v., pfv. of* **раста́лкивать**.

растолкова́ть [*infl.* -ку́ю, -ку́ешь] *v., pfv. of* **растолко́вывать**.

растолко́вывать *v.impfv.* [*pfv.* растолкова́ть] to explain.

растоло́чь *v., pfv. of* **толо́чь**.

растолсте́ть *v.pfv.* to grow fat; put on a lot of weight.

растопи́ть [*infl.* -топлю́, -то́пишь] *v., pfv. of* **топи́ть** (*in sense #3*) *and* **раста́пливать.** —**растопи́ться,** *refl., pfv. of* **раста́пливаться**.

расто́пка *n.* **1,** lighting (*of a stove*). **2,** *colloq.* kindling wood.

растопта́ть [*infl.* -топчу́, -то́пчешь] *v., pfv. of* **раста́птывать**.

растопы́ривать *v.impfv.* [*pfv.* растопы́рить] *colloq.* to spread apart.

расторга́ть *v.impfv.* [*pfv.* расто́ргнуть] to annul; abrogate.

расто́ргнуть [*past* -то́рг *or* -то́ргнул, -то́ргла] *v., pfv. of* **расторга́ть**.

расторже́ние *n.* annulment; abrogation.

расторо́пный *adj.* capable; competent; efficient. —**расторо́пность,** *n.f.* capability; competence; efficiency.

расточа́ть *v.impfv.* [*pfv.* расточи́ть] **1,** to squander; dissipate. **2,** to lavish; shower: расточа́ть похвалы́ (+ *dat.*), to lavish praise upon.

расточи́тель *n.m.* squanderer; spendthrift.

расточи́тельный *adj.* extravagant; wasteful. —**расточи́тельность,** *n.f.* extravagance; wastefulness.

расточи́тельство *n.* squandering; dissipation.

расточи́ть *v.pfv.* **1,** [*pfv.* -точу́, -точи́шь] *pfv. of* **расточа́ть. 2,** [*pfv.* -точу́, -то́чишь] *pfv. of* **раста́чивать**.

растрави́ть [*infl.* -травлю́, -тра́вишь] *v., pfv. of* **растравля́ть**.

растравля́ть *v.impfv.* [*pfv.* растрави́ть] to irritate; *fig.* rub salt on (a wound).

растранжи́рить *v., pfv. of* **транжи́рить**.

растра́та *n.* **1,** squandering; waste. **2,** embezzlement.

растра́тить [*infl.* -тра́чу, -тра́тишь] *v., pfv. of* **раста́чивать**.

растра́тчик *n.* embezzler.

растра́чивать *v.impfv.* [*pfv.* растра́тить] **1,** to squander; dissipate. **2,** to embezzle.

растрево́жить *v.pfv.* **1,** to alarm; upset. **2,** to stir up; disturb.

растрёпа *n.m. & f., colloq.* slovenly person; slob.

растрёпанный *adj.* **1,** disheveled. **2,** tattered.

растрепа́ть *v.pfv.* [*infl.* -треплю́, -тре́плешь] **1,** to mess up; muss. **2,** to wear out; tatter. —**растрепа́ться,** *refl.* **1,** to become disheveled. **2,** to become tattered.

растре́скаться *v.r.pfv.* to crack all over.

растро́ганный *adj.* deeply touched; deeply moved. —**растро́ганно,** *adv.* with emotion.

растро́гать *v.pfv.* to move; touch; affect deeply. —**растро́гаться,** *refl.* to be (deeply) touched; be (deeply) moved.

растру́б *n.* **1,** flare (*of a garment, bell, etc.*). **2,** bell (*of a musical instrument*).

растряса́ть *v.impfv.* [*pfv.* растрясти́] **1,** to strew; scatter. **2,** *fig., colloq.* to waste; spend needlessly. **3,** *impers.* to be shaken up (*while riding*): Его́ растрясло́, he was shaken up.

растрясти́ [*infl. like* трясти́] *v., pfv. of* **растряса́ть**.

растя́гивать *v.impfv.* [*pfv.* растяну́ть] **1,** to stretch. **2,** to strain; sprain. **3,** to spread out. **4,** to prolong; drag out. **5,** *in* растя́гивать слова́, to drawl. —**растя́гиваться,** *refl.* **1,** to stretch; become stretched. **2,** to extend; stretch. **3,** *colloq.* to stretch out. **4,** *colloq.* to tumble headlong; go sprawling. **5,** to be stretched out; be dragged out (*over a period of time*).

растяже́ние *n.* strain; sprain.

растяжи́мость *n.f.* **1,** stretchability. **2,** tensile strength.

растяжи́мый *adj.* **1,** stretchable. **2,** *fig.* loose; imprecise.

растя́жка *n.* stretching: отда́ть ту́фли на растя́жку, to have one's shoes stretched.

растя́нутый *adj.* **1,** stretched out; extended. **2,** *fig.* (*of a book, novel, etc.*) too long; overlong.

растяну́ть [*infl.* -тяну́, -тя́нешь] *v., pfv. of* **растя́гивать. —растяну́ться,** *refl., pfv. of* **растя́гиваться**.

растя́па *n.m. & f., colloq.* dolt; dope.

расфасова́ть *v., pfv. of* **фасова́ть**.

расфасо́вка *n.* packaging.

расформирова́ть [*infl.* -ру́ю, -ру́ешь] *v., pfv. of* **расформиро́вывать**.

расформиро́вывать *v.impfv.* [*pfv.* расформирова́ть] to disband.

расфранчённый *adj., colloq.* dressed up; dolled up.

расха́живать *v.impfv.* to pace back and forth. Ва́жно расха́живать, to strut.

расхва́ливать *v.impfv.* [*pfv.* **расхвали́ть**] to extol; rave about; praise to the skies.

расхвали́ть [*infl.* -хвалю́, -хва́лишь] *v., pfv. of* **расхва́ливать**.

расхва́рываться *v.r.impfv.* [*pfv.* **расхвора́ться**] *colloq.* to become ill.

расхва́статься *v.r.pfv., colloq.* to brag endlessly.

расхва́тывать *v.impfv.* [*pfv.* **расхвата́ть**] *colloq.* to buy up; snap up; snatch up.

расхвора́ться *v.r., pfv. of* **расхва́рываться**.

расхити́тель *n.m.* embezzler (*of public property*).

расхища́ть *v.impfv.* [*pfv.* **расхи́тить**] to steal; embezzle; misappropriate.

расхище́ние *n.* theft; embezzlement; misappropriation.

расхлёбывать *v.impfv.* [*pfv.* **расхлеба́ть**] *colloq.* to untangle; straighten out. —**расхлёбывать ка́шу**, to work one's way out of it.

расхля́банный *adj., colloq.* **1,** rickety; wobbly. **2,** *fig.* lax; undisciplined. —**расхля́банность**, *n.f., colloq.* laxity.

расхо́д *n.* **1,** *usu. pl.* expenses. **2,** *usu. pl., comm.* costs. **3,** *pl.* expenditures; outlay; spending. **4,** consumption: расхо́д то́плива, fuel consumption. —**вы́вести** *or* **пусти́ть в расхо́д**, *colloq.* to shoot; execute.

расходи́ться *v.r.impfv.* [*pfv.* **разойти́сь**; *pres.* -хожу́сь, -хо́дишься] **1,** to depart (*in different directions*); disperse. **2,** to pass by each other; miss each other; fail to meet. **3,** to be able to pass by each other (*in a narrow place*). **4,** to part company; (*of a married couple*) separate; break up. **5,** to come apart. **6,** to divide; diverge. **7,** to differ; be at variance. Расходи́ться во мне́ниях, to hold different opinions; disagree. **8,** (*of an item*) to sell; be sold out; (*of money*) be spent. **9,** to gather speed. **10,** *fig.* to get worked up.

расхо́дный *adj.* expense (*attrib.*).

расхо́дование *n.* **1,** spending; expenditure. **2,** *colloq.* consumption.

расхо́довать *v.impfv.* [*pfv.* **израсхо́довать**; *pres.* -дую, -дуешь] **1,** to spend; expend. **2,** *colloq.* to use (up); consume.

расхожде́ние *n.* **1,** divergence. **2,** difference: расхожде́ние во мне́ниях, difference of opinion.

расхо́жий *adj., colloq.* **1,** everyday; for everyday use or wear. **2,** in great demand; in great vogue.

расхола́живать *v.impfv.* [*pfv.* **расхолоди́ть**] to dim the enthusiasm of; dampen the ardor of.

расхоте́ть *v.pfv.* [*infl. like* **хоте́ть**] (*with inf. or gen.*) *colloq.* to want no longer; lose all desire (to *or* for). —**расхоте́ться**, *refl., impers.* (*with dat.*) *colloq.* = **расхоте́ть**.

расхохота́ться *v.r.pfv.* [*infl.* -хохочу́сь, -хохо́чешься] to burst out laughing; roar with laughter.

расхрабри́ться *v.r.pfv., colloq.* to summon up one's courage; grow bolder.

расцара́пывать *v.impfv.* [*pfv.* **расцара́пать**] to scratch (severely).

расцвести́ [*infl. like* **цвести́**] *v., pfv. of* **расцвета́ть**.

расцве́т *n.* **1,** flowering; blooming; blossoming. **2,** *fig.* flowering; golden age. **3,** *fig.* peak; prime: в расцве́те сил *or* своего́ тала́нта, at the peak of one's powers; в расцве́те лет, in the prime of life.

расцвета́ть *v.impfv.* [*pfv.* **расцвести́**] **1,** to flower; blossom; bloom. **2,** *fig.* (*of a person*) to blossom. **3,** *fig.* (*of one's face*) to light up. **4,** *fig.* to flourish.

расцвети́ть [*infl.* -цвечу́, -цвети́шь] *v., pfv. of* **расцве́чивать**.

расцве́тка *n.* color scheme; color combination.

расцве́чивать *v.impfv.* [*pfv.* **расцвети́ть**] **1,** to give a bright color to. **2,** to adorn. **3,** *fig.* to embellish.

расцелова́ть *v.pfv.* [*infl.* -лу́ю, -лу́ешь] to kiss fervently; shower with kisses. —**расцелова́ться**, *refl.* to exchange kisses.

расце́нивать *v.impfv.* [*pfv.* **расцени́ть**] **1,** to price; set a price on. **2,** to assess; estimate; rate. **3,** (*with* **как**) to regard (as); consider (to be).

расцени́ть [*infl.* -ценю́, -це́нишь] *v., pfv. of* **расце́нивать**.

расце́нка *n.* **1,** appraisal; valuation. **2,** price; rate.

расцепи́ть [*infl.* -цеплю́, -це́пишь] *v., pfv. of* **расцепля́ть**. —**расцепи́ться**, *refl., pfv. of* **расцепля́ться**.

расцепля́ть *v.impfv.* [*pfv.* **расцепи́ть**] to unhook; unhitch; uncouple. —**расцепля́ться**, *refl.* to come unhitched.

расчеса́ть [*infl.* -чешу́, -че́шешь] *v., pfv. of* **расчёсывать**. —**расчеса́ться**, *refl., pfv. of* **расчёсываться**.

расчёска [*gen. pl.* -сок] *n.* comb.

расче́сть *v.pfv.* [*infl.* разочту́, разочтёшь; *past* расчёл, разочла́, разочло́, разочли́] *colloq.* = **рассчита́ть**. —**расче́сться**, *refl., colloq.* = **рассчита́ться**.

расчёсывать *v.impfv.* [*pfv.* **расчеса́ть**] **1,** to comb. **2,** to scratch (and thus further irritate). —**расчёсываться**, *refl., colloq.* to comb one's hair.

расчёт *n.* **1,** calculation; reckoning: по моему́ расчёту, by my calculations. Это не входи́ло в мои́ расчёты, that did not enter into my calculations; I had not allowed for that. **2,** payment; settlement. Быть в расчёте с, to be all even with. **3,** discharge; dismissal: дать расчёт (+ *dat.*), to dismiss; fire. **4,** *fig.* retribution: С ним бу́дет коро́ткий расчёт, retribution will be swift. **5,** assumption; expectation: в расчёте на (+ *acc.*), on the expectation of. С таки́м расчётом, что..., on the assumption that...; with the idea that... **6,** selfish consideration. Брак по расчёту, marriage for money; marriage of convenience. **7,** *colloq.* benefit; advantage: Нет расчёта (+ *inf.*), there is no point in... **8,** *mil.* crew. —**принима́ть** *or* **брать в расчёт**, *see* **принима́ть**.

расчётливость *n.f.* **1,** thrift. **2,** prudence.

расчётливый *adj.* **1,** thrifty. **2,** prudent; calculating.

расчётный *adj.* **1,** calculation (*attrib.*). **2,** estimated. **3,** of payments; pay (*attrib.*). —**расчётная пала́та**, clearing house.

расчи́стить [*infl.* -чи́щу, -чи́стишь] *v., pfv. of* **расчища́ть**.

расчи́стка *n.* clearing (*of land, roads, etc.*).

расчиха́ться *v.r.pfv., colloq.* to have a fit of sneezing.

расчищáть *v.impfv.* [*pfv.* **расчи́стить**] to clear; rid of obstacles.

расчленéние *n.* 1, division. 2, dismemberment.

расчленя́ть *v.impfv.* [*pfv.* **расчлени́ть**] 1, to divide. 2, to dismember. 3, to break down (*into component parts*).

расчу́вствоваться *v.r.pfv.* [*infl.* **-ствуюсь, -ствуешься**] *colloq.* to be deeply touched.

расша́ркиваться *v.r.impfv.* [*pfv.* **расша́ркаться**] 1, to bow, scraping one's feet. 2, (*with* **пéред**) *colloq.* to bow and scrape (before); kowtow (to).

расша́танный *adj.* 1, wobbly; rickety. 2, (*of one's health*) seriously impaired; (*of one's nerves*) shattered; shot.

расша́тывать *v.impfv.* [*pfv.* **расшата́ть**] 1, to shake loose; knock loose. 2, to make unsteady; make wobbly. 3, *fig.* to undermine; impair. —**расша́тываться**, *refl.* 1, to come loose. 2, to be (*or* become) rickety. 3, *fig.* to break down; collapse; go to pieces. 4, *fig.* (*of one's nerves*) to be shot; be shattered; (*of one's health*) to give way.

расшвы́ривать *v.impfv.* [*pfv.* **расшвыря́ть**] *colloq.* 1, to toss in all directions. 2, *fig.* to toss (money) around.

расшевели́ть *v.pfv., colloq.* to stir; rouse.

расшиба́ть *v.impfv.* [*pfv.* **расшиби́ть**] 1, to hurt; bruise; stub. 2, *colloq.* to smash; shatter. —**расшиба́ться**, *refl.* 1, to hurt oneself (seriously). 2, *colloq.* to be shattered.

расшиби́ть [*infl.* **-бу́, -бёшь;** *past* **-ши́б, -ши́бла**] *v., pfv. of* **расшиба́ть**. —**расшиби́ться**, *refl., pfv. of* **расшиба́ться**.

расшива́ть *v.impfv.* [*pfv.* **расши́ть**] 1, *colloq.* to rip open (*by cutting along the seams or stitches*). 2, to embroider.

расширéние *n.* 1, widening; broadening. 2, expansion. 3, *med.* dilation. —**расширéние вен**, varicose veins.

расширя́ть *v.impfv.* [*pfv.* **расши́рить**] 1, to widen; broaden. 2, to enlarge. 3, *fig.* to broaden; expand. —**расширя́ться**, *refl.* to widen; broaden; expand.

расши́тый *adj.* embroidered.

расши́ть [*infl.* **разошью́, разошьёшь**] *v., pfv. of* **расшива́ть**.

расшифрова́ть [*infl.* **-ру́ю, -ру́ешь**] *v., pfv. of* **расшифро́вывать**.

расшифро́вка *n.* decipherment.

расшифро́вывать *v.impfv.* [*pfv.* **расшифрова́ть**] to decipher; decode.

расшнурова́ть [*infl.* **-ру́ю, -ру́ешь**] *v., pfv. of* **расшнуро́вывать**.

расшнуро́вывать *v.impfv.* [*pfv.* **расшнурова́ть**] to unlace; untie.

расшумéться *v.r.pfv.* [*infl.* **-млю́сь, -ми́шься**] *colloq.* to become noisy; raise a rumpus.

расщéдриться *v.r.pfv., colloq.* to show a little generosity.

расщéлина *n.* cleft; crevice; fissure.

расщепи́ть [*infl.* **-плю́ -пи́шь**] *v., pfv. of* **расщепля́ть**. —**расщепи́ться**, *refl., pfv. of* **расщепля́ться**.

расщеплéние *n.* 1, splitting: расщеплéние а́тома, splitting of the atom. 2, fission: расщеплéние ядра́, nuclear fission.

расщепля́ть *v.impfv.* [*pfv.* **расщепи́ть**] to split. —**расщепля́ться**, *refl.* to split; be split.

ратификацио́нный *adj.* ratification (*attrib.*): ратификацио́нные гра́моты, instruments of ratification.

ратифика́ция *n.* ratification.

ратифици́ровать *v.impfv. & pfv.* [*pres.* **-рую, -руешь**] to ratify.

ра́товать *v.impfv.* [*pres.* **-тую, -туешь**] 1, *obs.* to fight in battle. 2, (*with* **за** + *acc.*) to fight for; advocate; (*with* **про́тив**) inveigh (against).

ра́туша *n.* town hall; city hall.

рать *n.f., archaic* 1, army. 2, battle.

ра́унд *n., boxing* round.

рафина́д *n.* lump sugar.

рафина́дный *adj., in* **рафина́дный заво́д**, sugar refinery.

рафини́ровать *v.impfv. & pfv.* [*pres.* **-рую, -руешь**] to refine.

раха́т-луку́м *n.* Turkish delight.

рахи́т *n.* rickets.

рацио́н *n.* ration.

рационализа́ция *n.* application of modern methods of efficiency; streamlining.

рационализи́ровать *v.impfv. & pfv.* [*pres.* **-рую, -руешь**] to apply modern methods of efficiency to; streamline.

рационали́зм *n.* rationalism.

рационали́ст *n.* 1, rationalist. 2, rational person. —**рационалисти́ческий**, *adj.* rationalistic.

рациона́льный *adj.* 1, rational. 2, efficient. 3, *math.* rational. —**рациона́льность**, *n.f.* rationality.

ра́ция *n.* portable two-way radio; walkie-talkie.

ра́чий [*fem.* **-чья**] *adj.* of (a) crawfish. —**ра́чьи глаза́**, bulging eyes.

рачи́тельный *adj.* zealous; diligent.

ра́шпер *n.* gridiron; grill.

ра́шпиль *n.m.* rasp.

рвану́ть *v.pfv.* 1, to tug; jerk. 2, *colloq.* to dart; dash. 3, *colloq.* to start with a lurch; lurch forward. —**рвану́ться**, *refl.* = **рвану́ть** (*in senses #2 & #3*).

рва́ный *adj.* 1, torn; full of holes. 2, uneven; jagged. 3, *in* **рва́ная ра́на**, laceration.

рвань *n.f., colloq.* 1, tatters; rags. 2, riffraff.

рвать *v.impfv.* [*pres.* **рву, рвёшь;** *past fem.* **рвала́**] 1, [*pfv.* **порва́ть**] to tear; tear up. 2, [*pfv.* **порва́ть**] to break; snap. 3, to pull out; tear out; snatch. 4, to pull off; yank off. 5, to pick; pluck (flowers). 6, [*pfv.* **порва́ть**] to break off; sever (ties, relations, etc.). 7, to blow up. 8, [*pfv.* **вы́рвать**] *impers., colloq.* to vomit; throw up: Его́ рвёт, he is throwing up. —**рвать и мета́ть**, to be in a rage; rant and rave. —**рвать на себé во́лосы**, to tear one's hair. —**рвать на ча́сти**, to harass; harry; beset.

рва́ться *v.r.impfv.* [*pfv.* **порва́ться;** *pres.* **рвусь, рвёшься;** *past* **рва́лся, рвала́сь, рвало́сь** *or* **рвали́сь** *or* **рва́лись**] 1, to be torn. 2, (*of a rope, thread, etc.*) to break; snap. 3, [*impfv. only*] to burst; explode. 4, (*of ties, relations, etc.*) to be broken off. 5, [*impfv. only*] to struggle to free oneself; strain (at): рва́ться с при́вязи, to strain at a leash. 6, [*impfv. only*] (*with various prepositions*) to thirst for; be dying for.

рвач [*gen.* **рвача́**] *n., colloq.* chiseler. —**рва́чество,** *n., colloq.* self-enrichment.

рве́ние *n.* zeal; ardor.

рво́та *n.* vomiting.

рво́тный *adj.* **1,** pert. to vomiting: рво́тная ма́сса, vomit. **2,** inducing vomiting; emetic: рво́тное сре́дство, an emetic. —**рво́тное,** *n.* emetic.

рдест *n.* pondweed.

рдеть *v.impfv.* (*of anything red*) to glow.

ре *n.neut., music* re; D.

реабилита́ция *n.* rehabilitation.

реабилити́ровать *v.impfv. & pfv.* [*pres.* **-рую, -руешь**] to rehabilitate.

реаге́нт *n.* reagent.

реаги́ровать *v.impfv.* [*pres.* **-рую, -руешь**] (*with* на + *acc.*) to react (to).

реакти́в *n.* reagent.

реакти́вный *adj.* **1,** reactive. **2,** jet; jet-propelled. **3,** rocket (*attrib.*): реакти́вная устано́вка, rocket launcher. Реакти́вный снаря́д, missile.

реа́ктор *n.* reactor.

реакционе́р *n.* reactionary.

реакцио́нный *adj.* reactionary.

реа́кция *n.* **1,** reaction (*in various senses*). **2,** *polit.* reaction; extreme conservatism.

реализа́ция *n.* **1,** realization; achievement. **2,** selling; converting to cash.

реали́зм *n.* realism.

реализова́ть *v.impfv. & pfv.* [*pres.* **-зу́ю, -зу́ешь**] **1,** to realize; bring about; see fulfilled. **2,** to sell; convert into cash. —**реализова́ться,** *refl.* to be realized; materialize.

реали́ст *n.* realist. —**реалисти́ческий,** *adj.* realistic.

реа́лия *n., usu. pl.* reality.

реа́льность *n.f.* reality.

реа́льный *adj.* [*short form* **реа́лен, реа́льна**] **1,** real. **2,** realistic; practical. —**реа́льное учи́лище,** *pre-rev.* secondary school stressing scientific subjects (*as opposed to the classics*).

реанима́ция *n.* resuscitation.

ребёнок [*gen.* **-нка;** *pl.* **ребя́та, ребя́т**] *n.* child; baby. *See also* **ребя́та.**

рёберный *adj.* rib (*attrib.*).

ребо́рда *n.* flange (*of a wheel*).

ребри́стый *adj.* **1,** having prominent ribs. **2,** ribbed.

ребро́ [*pl.* **рёбра, рёбер**] *n.* **1,** rib. **2,** edge. —**вопро́с стои́т ребро́м,** the question stands out starkly. —**поста́вить вопро́с ребро́м,** to put a question pointblank.

ре́бус *n.* **1,** rebus. **2,** *fig.* enigma.

ребя́та [*gen.* **ребя́т**] *n.pl.* **1,** *pl. of* **ребёнок. 2,** *colloq.* lads; boys.

ребяти́шки [*gen.* **-шек**] *n.pl., colloq.* children; kids.

ребя́ческий *adj.* **1,** child's; of a child. **2,** childish.

ребя́чество *n.* **1,** *obs.* childhood. **2,** childishness.

ребя́чий [*fem.* **-чья**] *adj., colloq.* **1,** child's; children's. **2,** childish.

ребя́читься *v.r.impfv., colloq.* to behave childishly.

рёв *n.* **1,** roar. **2,** *colloq.* howl (*of a baby*).

рева́нш *n.* revenge (*after a defeat*): взять рева́нш, to gain revenge. — **матч-рева́нш,** return match.

реванши́зм *n.* revanchism.

реванши́ст *n.* revanchist. —**реванши́стский,** *adj.* revanchist.

реве́нь [*gen.* **ревеня́**] *n.m.* rhubarb. —**реве́нный,** *adj.* rhubarb.

ревера́нс *n.* curtsy.

ревербера́ция *n.* reverberation.

реве́ть *v.impfv.* [*pres.* **реву́, ревёшь**] **1,** to roar. **2,** *fig.* (*of a storm, the sea, etc.*) to rage. **3,** *colloq.* to howl; bawl.

ревизиони́зм *n.* revisionism. —**ревизиони́ст,** *n.* revisionist. —**ревизиони́стский,** *adj.* revisionist (*attrib.*).

реви́зия *n.* **1,** inspection. **2,** audit; auditing. **3,** revision. —**ревизио́нный,** *adj.* inspection (*attrib.*); auditing.

ревизова́ть *v.impfv. & pfv.* [*pres.* **-зу́ю, -зу́ешь**] **1,** to inspect. **2,** to audit. **3,** to revise.

ревизо́р *n.* inspector.

ревмати́зм *n.* rheumatism. —**ревма́тиик,** *n., colloq.* rheumatic. —**ревмати́ческий,** *adj.* rheumatic.

ревмя́ *adv., in* **ревмя́ реве́ть,** *colloq.* to howl.

ревни́вец [*gen.* **-вца**] *n., colloq.* jealous person.

ревни́вый *adj.* jealous. —**ревни́во,** *adv.* jealously.

ревни́тель *n.m., obs.* ardent advocate.

ревнова́ть *v.impfv.* [*pres.* **-ну́ю, -ну́ешь**] to be jealous of: Он ревну́ет жену́ к Са́ше, he is jealous of Sasha because his wife likes him; he is jealous over the fact that his wife likes Sasha.

ре́вностный *adj.* ardent; zealous.

ре́вность *n.f.* **1,** jealousy. **2,** *obs.* zeal; ardor.

револьве́р *n.* revolver.

револьве́рный *adj.* revolver (*attrib.*). —**револьве́рный стано́к,** turret lathe.

революционе́р *n.* revolutionary; revolutionist.

революционизи́ровать *v.impfv. & pfv.* [*pres.* **-рую, -руешь**] to revolutionize.

революцио́нный *adj.* revolutionary.

револю́ция *n.* revolution.

реву́н [*gen.* **ревуна́**] *n.* **1,** *colloq.* child who is always crying or yelling. **2,** howling monkey.

ревю́ *n.neut. indecl.* revue.

рега́лии *n.pl.* [*sing.* **рега́лия**] regalia.

рега́та *n.* regatta.

ре́гби (рэ) *n.neut. indecl.* rugby.

регенера́ция *n.* regeneration. —**регенерати́вный,** *adj.* regenerative.

ре́гент *n.* **1,** regent. **2,** director of a church choir. —**ре́гентство,** *n.* regency.

регио́н *n.* region. —**региона́льный,** *adj.* regional.

реги́стр *n.* **1,** register; list. **2,** *music* register. **3,** *music* stop (*of an organ, reed instrument, etc.*).

регистра́тор *n.* registering clerk; registrar. —**регистрату́ра,** *n.* registration office; registry.

регистра́ция *n.* registration. —**регистрацио́нный,** *adj.* registration (*attrib.*).

регистри́ровать *v.impfv.* [*pfv.* **зарегистри́ровать;** *pres.* **-рую, -руешь**] to register; record. —**регистри́роваться,** *refl.* **1,** to register. **2,** to register one's marriage.

регла́мент *n.* **1,** rules; regulations. **2,** order of business; agenda. **3,** speaker's allotted time.

регламента́ция *n.* regulation.

регламенти́ровать *v.impfv. & pfv.* [*pres.* **-ру́ю, -ру́ешь**] to regulate.

регла́н *n.* raglan.

регре́сс *n.* regression; retrogression. **—регресси́вный,** *adj.* regressive; retrogressive.

регресси́ровать *v.impfv.* [*pres.* **-ру́ю, -ру́ешь**] to regress; retrogress.

регули́рование *n.* regulation.

регули́ровать *v.impfv.* [*pres.* **-ру́ю, -ру́ешь**] **1,** to regulate. **2,** [*pfv.* **отрегули́ровать**] to adjust.

регулиро́вка *n.* **1,** regulation. **2,** adjustment.

регуля́рный *adj.* regular. **—регуля́рно,** *adv.* regularly. **—регуля́рность,** *n.f.* regularity.

регуля́тор *n., mech.* regulator; governor.

редакти́рование *n.* editing.

редакти́ровать *v.impfv.* [*pfv.* **отредакти́ровать**; *pres.* **-ру́ю, -ру́ешь**] to edit.

реда́ктор *n.* editor. **—реда́кторский,** *adj.* editorial; editor's.

редакцио́нный *adj.* editorial; editing (*attrib.*). **—редакцио́нная колле́гия,** editorial board. **—редакцио́нная коми́ссия,** drafting committee. **—редакцио́нная статья́,** editorial.

реда́кция *n.* **1,** editing. Под реда́кцией (+ *gen.*), edited by...; under the editorship of... **2,** wording. **3,** version; edition: первонача́льная реда́кция, original version/edition. **4,** editorial staff. **5,** editorial office: письмо́ в реда́кцию, letter to the editor.

реде́ть *v.impfv.* [*pfv.* **пореде́ть**] to thin out.

реди́с *n.* **1,** radish (*plant*). **2,** radishes.

реди́ска [*gen. pl.* **-сок**] *n., colloq.* radish.

ре́дкий *adj.* [*comp.* **ре́же**] **1,** rare. **2,** (*of trains, visits, etc.*) infrequent. **3,** (*of a forest, vegetation, etc.*) sparse. **4,** (*of hair*) thin; (*of teeth*) widely spaced.

ре́дко *adv.* rarely; seldom. **—ре́дко когда́,** very rarely; very seldom.

редколле́гия *n.* editorial board (*contr. of* **редакцио́нная колле́гия**).

ре́дкостный *adj.* rare.

ре́дкость *n.f.* **1,** rarity. **2,** a rarity. **3,** thinness; sparseness. **—на ре́дкость,** exceptionally: Зима́ была́ на ре́дкость холо́дной, the winter was exceptionally cold.

реду́кция *n.* reduction (*in various technical senses*).

реду́т *n.* redoubt.

ре́дька [*gen. pl.* **ре́дек**] *n.* radish.

редюи́т *n.* redoubt.

рее́стр *n.* register; list; log.

ре́же *adj., comp. of* **ре́дкий.** **—***adv., comp. of* **ре́дко.**

режи́м *n.* **1,** regime. **2,** regimen: больни́чный режи́м, hospital regimen. Посте́льный режи́м, bed rest. **3,** procedures: режи́м безопа́сности, safety procedures. **4,** conditions: температу́рный режи́м, temperature conditions.

режиссёр *n., theat., motion pictures* producer; director.

режисси́ровать *v.impfv.* [*pres.* **-ру́ю, -ру́ешь**] to produce; direct (a play or film).

режиссу́ра *n.* **1,** production; direction (*of a play or film*). **2,** producers; directors.

ре́жущий *adj.* **1,** cutting. **2,** (*of a pain*) sharp.

реза́к [*gen.* **-зака́**] *n.* large knife; cutter.

реза́льщик *n.* cutter (*person*).

ре́зание *n.* cutting.

ре́заный *adj.* **1,** cut into pieces. **2,** *sports* sliced.

ре́зать *v.impfv.* [*pres.* **ре́жу, ре́жешь**] **1,** [*pfv.* **разре́зать**] to cut. **2,** [*pfv.* **разре́зать**] to slice. **3,** *colloq.* to cut open (*surgically*). **4,** to carve; engrave. **5,** [*pfv.* **заре́зать**] to kill; slaughter. **6,** [*pfv.* **сре́зать**] *sports* to slice (a ball). **—ре́зать глаз** *or* **глаза́, 1,** (*of bright light*) to hurt one's eyes. **2,** *fig.* to offend the eye. **—ре́зать у́хо** *or* **слух,** to grate on one's ears.

ре́заться *v.r.impfv.* [*pres.* **ре́жусь, ре́жешься**] **1,** to cut; be cut; be able to be cut. **2,** (*of teeth*) to cut through: У ребёнка ре́жутся зу́бы, the child is teething. **3,** *colloq.* to fight (*with swords*).

резви́ться *v.r.impfv.* [*pres.* **-влю́сь, -ви́шься**] to romp; frolic.

ре́звость *n.f.* **1,** playfulness. **2,** speed (*of a horse*).

ре́звый *adj.* **1,** playful; frisky. **2,** (*of a horse*) fast; fast-running.

резеда́ *n.* mignonette.

резе́кция *n., med.* resection.

резе́рв *n.* **1,** reserve: резе́рвы зерна́, reserves of grain. Име́ть в резе́рве, to have in reserve. **2,** *mil.* reserve; reserves.

резерва́ция *n.* (Indian) reservation.

резерви́ровать *v.impfv. & pfv.* [*pfv. also* **зарезерви́ровать**; *pres.* **-ру́ю, -ру́ешь**] to reserve.

резерви́ст *n.* reservist.

резе́рвный *adj.* reserve (*attrib.*).

резервуа́р *n.* **1,** reservoir. **2,** tank.

резе́ц [*gen.* **резца́**] *n.* **1,** cutting tool; cutter. **2,** incisor (*tooth*).

резиде́нт *n.* **1,** resident governor. **2,** resident alien. **3,** chief of a country's intelligence operations in another country.

резиде́нция *n.* residence.

рези́на *n.* rubber.

рези́нка [*gen. pl.* **-нок**] *n.* **1,** eraser. **2,** elastic band. **3,** rubber band. **—жева́тельная рези́нка,** chewing gum.

рези́новый *adj.* rubber.

ре́зка *n.* cutting.

ре́зкий *adj.* [*short form* **ре́зок, резка́, ре́зко, ре́зки** *or* **резки́;** *comp.* **ре́зче**] **1,** (*of one's voice*) shrill; harsh. **2,** (*of an odor*) pungent. **3,** (*of light*) glaring. **4,** (*of cold, wind, etc.*) biting. **5,** (*of a contrast, facial features, etc.*) sharp. **6,** (*of movements*) jerky. **7,** (*of words, criticism, etc.*) harsh. **8,** (*of an increase, decline, etc.*) sharp. **9,** (*of a change*) abrupt; drastic. **10,** (*of a person, manners, etc.*) abrupt; brusque.

ре́зко *adv.* **1,** sharply. **2,** harshly; strongly. **3,** drastically.

ре́зкость *n.f.* **1,** harshness; sharpness; abruptness. **2,** sharpness; clarity; definition. **3,** *pl.* harsh words.

резно́й *adj.* carved.

резня́ *n.* massacre; slaughter.

резолю́ция *n.* resolution.

резо́н *n., colloq.* reason.

резона́нс *n.* **1,** resonance. **2,** *fig.* reaction; response.

резона́тор *n.* resonator.

резонёр *n.* sermonizer; preacher.

резони́ровать *v.impfv.* [*pres.* **-рует**] to resound.

резо́нный *adj., colloq.* reasonable.

результа́т *n.* **1,** result. **2,** *sports* (one's) score; showing: показа́ть лу́чший результа́т, to achieve the best score. —**в результа́те, 1,** as a result. **2,** (*with gen.*) as a result of.

результати́вный *adj.* effective; successful.

ре́зче *adj., comp. of* **ре́зкий.**

ре́зчик *n.* carver; engraver.

резь *n.f.* sharp pain.

резьба́ *n.* **1,** carving. **2,** thread (*of a screw*).

резюме́ (мэ) *n.neut. indecl.* **1,** résumé. **2,** *law* summation.

резюми́ровать *v.impfv. & pfv.* [*pres.* **-рую, -руешь**] to summarize; recapitulate.

рейд *n.* **1,** *naut.* roadstead. **2,** *mil.* raid. **3,** (police) raid.

ре́йка [*gen. pl.* **ре́ек**] *n.* **1,** strip of wood. **2,** measuring rod. —**зубча́тая ре́йка,** rack (*for a pinion*).

рейс *n.* **1,** trip; voyage: пе́рвый рейс, maiden voyage. **2,** flight: рейс сто во́семь, flight 108. —**ре́йсовый,** *adj.* operating on a regular route.

рейсши́на *n.* T square.

ре́йтинг *n.* **1,** rating (*of a chess master*). **2,** approval rating (*of a politician*).

рейту́зы [*gen.* **-ту́з**] *n.pl.* **1,** riding breeches. **2,** tights.

река́ [*acc.* **реку́** *or* **ре́ку;** *pl.* **ре́ки, рек, река́м** *or* **ре́кам**] *n.* river.

ре́квием *n.* requiem.

реквизи́ровать *v.impfv. & pfv.* [*pres.* **-рую, -руешь**] to requisition; commandeer.

реквизи́т *n., theat.* properties; stage props.

реквизи́ция *n.* requisitioning.

рекла́ма *n.* **1,** advertising; publicity. **2,** advertisement; commercial. **3,** sign: нео́новая рекла́ма, neon sign.

реклама́ция *n.* **1,** complaint; grievance. **2,** claim (*for replacement of defective or inferior merchandise*).

реклами́ровать *v.impfv. & pfv.* [*pres.* **-рую, -руешь**] to advertise; publicize.

рекла́мный *adj.* advertising (*attrib.*); publicity (*attrib.*); promotional. —**рекла́мный щит,** billboard.

реклмода́тель *n.m.* advertiser.

рекогносци́ровать *v.impfv. & pfv.* [*pres.* **-рую, -руешь**] to reconnoiter.

рекогносциро́вка *n.* reconnaissance. —**рекогносциро́вочный,** *adj.* reconnaissance (*attrib.*).

рекоменда́тельный *adj.* of recommendation: рекоменда́тельное письмо́, letter of recommendation.

рекоменда́ция *n.* recommendation.

рекомендова́ть *v.impfv. & pfv.* [*pfv. also* **порекомендова́ть;** *pres.* **-ду́ю, -ду́ешь**] to recommend. —**рекомендова́ться,** *refl.* **1,** [*impfv. only*] to be recommended. **2,** [*pfv. also* **отрекомендова́ться**] to introduce oneself.

реконструи́ровать *v.impfv. & pfv.* [*pres.* **-рую, -руешь**] **1,** to redesign. **2,** to reorganize. **3,** to reconstruct.

реконстру́кция *n.* **1,** redesigning. **2,** reorganization. **3,** reconstruction.

реко́рд *n.* record: поста́вить реко́рд, to set a record.

рекорди́ст *n.* **1,** record holder. **2,** (*of an animal*) prizewinner.

реко́рдный *adj.* record (*attrib.*); record-breaking.

рекордсме́н *n.* record holder.

ре́крут *n., pre-rev.* recruit.

ре́ктор *n.* rector (*of a university*).

реле́ (рэ) *n.neut. indecl., electricity* relay.

религио́зный *adj.* religious.

рели́гия *n.* religion.

рели́квия *n.* relic.

рели́кт *n.* relic; ancient artifact.

рельеф *n., art; topog.* relief.

рельефно *adv.* in relief.

рельефный *adj.* **1,** carved in relief. **2,** (*of a surface, design, etc.*) raised; embossed. **3,** *fig.* vivid; graphic. —**рельефная ка́рта,** relief map.

рельс *n., R.R.* rail; track. —**ре́льсовый,** *adj.* rail (*attrib.*).

рема́рка [*gen. pl.* **-рок**] *n.* **1,** note. **2,** *theat.* stage direction.

ремённый *adj.* **1,** of, from, or for a belt. **2,** *mech.* belt (*attrib.*): ремённый приво́д; ремённая переда́ча, belt drive.

реме́нь [*gen.* **ремня́**] *n.m.* **1,** strap. **2,** belt. —**привязно́й реме́нь,** seat belt. —**реме́нь вентиля́тора,** fan belt.

реме́сленник *n.* craftsman; artisan.

реме́сленный *adj.* **1,** craft (*attrib.*). **2,** *fig.* pedestrian; unimaginative. —**реме́сленное учи́лище,** vocational school.

ремесло́ [*pl.* **ремёсла, -сел**] *n.* trade; craft.

ремешо́к [*gen.* **-шка́**] *n.* small strap.

реми́ссия *n., med.* remission.

ремо́нт *n.* repair; repairs. Быть в ремо́нте, to be under (*or* undergoing) repair.

ремонти́ровать *v.impfv. & pfv.* [*pfv. also* **отремонти́ровать;** *pres.* **-рую, -руешь**] to repair; renovate; refurbish; overhaul; recondition.

ремо́нтник *n.* repairman.

ремо́нтный *adj.* repair (*attrib.*).

ренега́т *n.* renegade; turncoat. —**ренега́тство,** *n.* apostasy.

ре́ний *n.* rhenium.

рено́нс *n., cards* revoke.

ре́нта *n., econ.* rent. —**ежего́дная ре́нта,** annuity.

рента́бельный *adj.* profitable; paying. Рента́бельное предприя́тие, going concern. —**рента́бельность,** *n.f.* profitability.

рентге́н *n., colloq.* **1,** X-rays. **2,** X-ray machine.

рентге́нов *adj., in* **рентге́новы лучи́,** X-rays.

рентге́новский *adj.* X-ray (*attrib.*).

рентгеногра́мма *n.* X-ray; X-ray photograph.

рентгеноло́гия *n.* radiology. —**рентгено́лог,** *n.* radiologist.

рентгеноскопи́я *n.* X-raying; X-ray examination.

рентгенотерапи́я *n.* X-ray treatment.

реорганиза́ция *n.* reorganization.

реорганизова́ть *v.impfv. & pfv.* [*pres.* **-зу́ю, -зу́ешь**] to reorganize.

реоста́т *n.* rheostat.

ре́па *n.* turnip.

репара́ции *n.pl.* [*sing.* **-ция**] reparations. —**репарацио́нный,** *adj.* reparations (*attrib.*).

репатриа́нт *n.* repatriate. —**репатриа́ция,** *n.* repatriation.

репатрии́ровать *v.impfv.* & *pfv.* [*pres.* **-рую, -руешь**] to repatriate.

репе́йник *n.* 1, burdock. 2, bur.

репе́р *n.* bench mark.

репертуа́р *n.* repertoire. —**репертуа́рный,** *adj.* repertory (*attrib.*).

репети́ровать *v.impfv.* [*pfv.* **прорепети́ровать**; *pres.* **-рую, -руешь**] 1, to rehearse. 2, [*impfv. only*] to coach; tutor.

репети́тор *n.* tutor; coach. —**репети́торский,** *adj.* tutoring (*attrib.*); tutorial. —**репети́торство,** *n.* tutoring.

репети́ция *n.* rehearsal. —**репетицио́нный,** *adj.* rehearsal (*attrib.*).

ре́плика *n.* 1, retort; rejoinder. 2, *theat.* cue.

репо́лов *n.* linnet.

репорта́ж *n.* 1, report (*in the news media*). 2, reporting.

репортёр *n.* reporter.

репресси́вный *adj.* repressive.

репресси́ровать *v.impfv.* & *pfv.* [*pres.* **-рую, -руешь**] to subject to repression.

репре́ссия *n.* repression.

репри́за *n.* reprise.

репроду́ктор *n.* loudspeaker.

репроду́кция *n.* reproduction; copy.

репута́ция *n.* reputation.

ре́пчатый *adj., in* ре́пчатый лук, onion.

ресни́ца *n.* eyelash.

респекта́бельный *adj.* respectable. —**респекта́бельность,** *n.f.* respectability.

респира́тор *n.* respirator.

респу́блика *n.* republic.

республика́нец [*gen.* **-нца**] *n.* republican.

республика́нский *adj.* 1, republican. 2, of a republic of Russia.

рессо́ра *n.* spring (*on a vehicle*). —**рессо́рный,** *adj.* on springs; having springs.

реставра́тор *n.* restorer (*of works of art*).

реставра́ция *n.* restoration.

реставри́ровать *v.impfv.* & *pfv.* [*pres.* **-рую, -руешь**] to restore.

рестора́н *n.* restaurant. —**рестора́нный,** *adj.* restaurant (*attrib.*).

ресу́рс *n.* 1, *pl.* resources: приро́дные ресу́рсы, natural resources. 2, resort; recourse: после́дний ресу́рс, last resort.

рети́вый *adj.* zealous. —**рети́во,** *adv.* zealously. —**рети́вость,** *n.f.* zeal.

рети́на *n.* retina.

ретирова́ться *v.r.impfv.* & *pfv.* [*pres.* **-ру́юсь, -ру́ешься**] *colloq.* to retire; withdraw.

рето́рта *n.* retort (*vessel*).

ретрогра́д *n.* reactionary.

ретроспекти́вный *adj.* retrospective. —**ретроспекти́вно,** *adv.* in retrospect.

ретроспе́кция *n.* retrospection.

ретушёр *n.* retoucher.

ретуши́ровать *v.impfv.* & *pfv.* [*pres.* **-рую, -руешь**] *photog.* to retouch.

ре́тушь *n.f.* retouching.

рефера́т *n.* 1, synopsis; abstract. 2, paper; essay.

рефере́ндум *n.* referendum.

рефере́нт *n.* 1, reader; reviewer. 2, adviser; consultant.

рефери́ровать *v.impfv.* & *pfv.* [*pres.* **-рую, -руешь**] to abstract; make a synopsis of.

рефле́кс *n.* reflex.

рефлекти́вный *adj.* = **рефлекто́рный.**

рефле́ктор *n.* 1, reflector. 2, reflecting telescope.

рефлекто́рный *adj.* reflex: рефлекто́рная реа́кция, reflex reaction.

рефо́рма *n.* reform. —**реформа́тор,** *n.* reformer.

реформа́тский *adj., in* реформа́тская це́рковь, Reformed Church.

реформа́ция *n., hist.* the Reformation.

реформи́рование *n.* (act of) reforming.

реформи́ровать *v.impfv.* & *pfv.* [*pres.* **-рую, -руешь**] to reform.

реформи́ст *n.* 1, reformist. 2, Reform Jew. —**реформи́стский,** *adj.* Reformist.

рефра́ктор *n.* refracting telescope; refractor.

рефра́кция *n.* refraction.

рефре́н *n.* refrain.

рефрижера́тор *n.* refrigerator.

рехну́ться *v.r.pfv., colloq.* to go mad; go crazy.

рецензе́нт *n.* reviewer; critic.

рецензи́ровать *v.impfv.* [*pfv.* **прорецензи́ровать**; *pres.* **-рую, -руешь**] to review.

реце́нзия *n.* review: реце́нзия на кни́гу (*or* о кни́ге), book review.

реце́пт *n.* 1, prescription. 2, recipe.

рецесси́вный *adj., biol.* recessive.

рециди́в *n.* 1, recurrence. 2, *med.* relapse. 3, *law* second offense.

рецидиви́зм *n.* recidivism. —**рецидиви́ст,** *n.* recidivist.

речево́й *adj.* speech (*attrib.*).

рече́ние *n.* expression; locution.

речи́стый *adj., colloq.* 1, eloquent. 2, talkative.

речитати́в *n., music* recitative. —**говори́ть** *or* **чита́ть речитати́вом,** to intone.

ре́чка [*gen. pl.* **ре́чек**] *n.* small river.

речно́й *adj.* river (*attrib.*).

речь [*pl.* **ре́чи, рече́й, реча́м**] *n.f.* 1, speech: о́рганы ре́чи, organs of speech. 2, a speech: произноси́ть речь, to make a speech. —**речь идёт о,** the question is one of; it is a question of. —**об э́том не мо́жет быть и ре́чи,** that is out of the question.

реша́ть *v.impfv.* [*pfv.* **реши́ть**] 1, (*with inf. or a dependent clause*) to decide (to *or* that). 2, to decide (a question, case, etc.). 3, to decide; determine (the fate, outcome, etc. of something). 4, to solve. Реши́ть зада́чу, to solve a problem; accomplish a task. 5, to settle (an argument, dispute, etc.). —**реша́ться,** *refl.* 1, (*with inf.*) to make up one's mind (to). 2, (*with* на + *acc.*) to decide (on). 3, (*with inf.*) to dare (to); bring oneself (to). 4, to be decided.

реша́ющий *adj.* deciding; decisive; crucial. —**с реша́ющим го́лосом,** voting: член с реша́ющим го́лосом, voting member.

реше́ние *n.* **1,** decision. Измени́ть своё реше́ние, to change one's mind. **2,** ruling; decision; judgment (*of a court*). **3,** solution. Реше́ние зада́чи, the answer to the problem. **4,** resolving; resolution (*of questions, issues, etc.*). **5,** accomplishment (*of tasks*).

решётка [*gen. pl.* **-ток**] *n.* grating; grate; lattice; grille. Ками́нная решётка, fire screen. —**посади́ть за решётку,** to put behind bars. —**сиде́ть за решёткой,** to be behind bars.

решето́ [*pl.* **решёта**] *n.* strainer; sieve.

решётчатый *adj.* lattice (*attrib.*); latticed.

реши́мость *n.f.* determination; resoluteness; resolve.

реши́тельно *adv.* **1,** decisively. **2,** strongly; emphatically; categorically. **3,** absolutely.

реши́тельность *n.f.* **1,** decisiveness. **2,** determination.

реши́тельный *adj.* **1,** (*of a person or action*) decisive; forceful; resolute. **2,** (*of a moment, battle, victory, etc.*) decisive. **3,** (*of an answer*) final; definitive. **4,** (*of a refusal, protest, gesture, etc.*) emphatic.

реши́ть *v., pfv. of* **реша́ть.** —**реши́ться,** *refl., pfv. of* **реша́ться.**

ре́шка *n., in* орёл и́ли ре́шка?, heads or tails?

ре́ять *v.impfv.* [*pres.* **ре́ю, ре́ешь**] **1,** to soar; glide. **2,** to hover. **3,** to flutter.

ржа́веть *v.impfv.* [*pfv.* **заржа́веть**] to rust; become rusty.

ржа́вчина *n.* rust.

ржа́вый *adj.* **1,** rusty. **2,** rust-colored.

ржа́ние *n.* neighing.

ржа́нка [*gen. pl.* **-нок**] *n.* plover.

ржано́й *adj.* rye (*attrib.*): ржано́й хлеб, rye bread.

ржать *v.impfv.* [*pres.* **ржёт**] to neigh.

ри́га *n.* threshing barn.

ри́за *n.* **1,** chasuble. **2,** metal plating on an icon. —**напи́ться до положе́ния риз,** to drink oneself into a stupor.

ри́зница *n.* sacristy; vestry.

рикоше́т *n.* ricochet; rebound. —**рикоше́том,** on the rebound.

рикошети́ровать *v.impfv. & pfv.* [*pres.* **-рует**] to ricochet.

ри́кша [*gen. pl.* **рикш**] *n.* **1,** *n.f.* rickshaw. **2,** *n.m.* rickshaw driver.

ри́млянин [*pl.* **ри́мляне, ри́млян**] *n.m.* [*fem.* **ри́млянка**] Roman.

ри́мский *adj.* Roman.

ринг *n.* boxing ring.

ри́нуться *v.r.pfv.* **1,** to dash; rush: ри́нуться к вы́ходу, to dash/rush for the exit. Ри́нуться помо́чь (+ *dat.*), to rush to help (someone). **2,** *fig.* (*with* в + *acc.*) to plunge into (a task, battle, etc.).

рис *n.* rice.

риск *n.* risk. Идти́ на риск, to take a risk; take a chance. —**на свой страх и риск,** at one's own risk.

рискну́ть *v., pfv. of* **рискова́ть.**

риско́ванный *adj.* **1,** risky. **2,** risqué.

рискова́ть *v.impfv.* [*pfv.* **рискну́ть;** *pres.* **-ку́ю, -ку́ешь**] **1,** to take chances; take chances. **2,** (*with instr.*) to risk. **3,** (*with inf.*) to risk; run the risk (of). **4,** (*with inf.*) to dare (to); venture (to).

рисова́льный *adj.* drawing (*attrib.*).

рисова́льщик *n.* (graphic) artist.

рисова́ние *n.* drawing.

рисова́ть *v.impfv.* [*pfv.* **нарисова́ть;** *pres.* **-су́ю, -су́ешь**] **1,** to draw. **2,** to paint; portray. —**рисова́ться,** *refl.* [*impfv. only*] **1,** to appear; loom; be silhouetted. **2,** *fig.* (*with dat.*) to appear (to); seem (to). **3,** to show off.

рисо́вка *n.* **1,** *obs.* drawing. **2,** showing off.

ри́совый *adj.* rice (*attrib.*).

рису́нок [*gen.* **-нка**] *n.* **1,** a drawing. **2,** design; pattern. **3,** (*when accompanying a scientific article*) figure.

ритм *n.* rhythm.

ри́тмика *n.* rhythmics.

ритми́ческий *adj.* rhythmic; rhythmical.

ритми́чный *adj.* rhythmic; rhythmical. —**ритми́чность,** *n.f.* even rhythm; even pace.

рито́рика *n.* rhetoric. —**ритори́ческий,** *adj.* rhetorical.

ритуа́л *n.* ritual. —**ритуа́льный,** *adj.* ritual.

риф *n.* reef.

рифлёный *adj.* corrugated; fluted.

ри́фма *n.* rhyme.

рифма́ч [*gen.* **-мача́**] *n., colloq.* rhymer; rhymester.

рифмова́ть *v.impfv.* [*pres.* **-му́ю, -му́ешь**] to rhyme; make (something) rhyme. —**рифмова́ться,** *refl.* (*of words, sounds, etc.*) to rhyme.

рифмоплёт *n., colloq.* rhymer; rhymester.

ро́ба *n.* overalls.

ро́ббер *n., cards* rubber.

робе́ть *v.impfv.* to be timid; be shy.

ро́бкий *adj.* [*short form* **ро́бок, робка́, ро́бко, ро́бки**] timid; shy. —**не из ро́бкого деся́тка,** not the timid type.

ро́бко *adv.* timidly.

ро́бость *n.f.* timidity; shyness.

ро́бот *n.* robot. —**робото́техника,** *n.* robotics.

ров [*gen.* **рва;** *2nd loc.* **рву**] *n.* ditch. —**крепостно́й ров,** moat.

рове́сник *n.* person one's own age; contemporary.

ро́вно *adv.* **1,** evenly. **2,** exactly; precisely: ро́вно в де́сять часо́в, at ten o'clock sharp. **3,** *colloq.* absolutely: ро́вно ничего́, absolutely nothing.

ро́вность *n.f.* **1,** evenness. **2,** *fig.* equanimity.

ро́вный *adj.* [*short form* **ро́вен, ровна́, ро́вно, ро́вны** *or* **ровны́**] **1,** even; level. **2,** straight. **3,** steady; equable. **4,** *fig.* even-tempered. —**для ро́вного счёта,** to make it come out even. —**не ровён час,** *colloq.* **1,** you never know. **2,** anything can happen. —**ро́вным счётом, 1,** exactly. **2,** only. —**ро́вным счётом ничего́,** absolutely nothing.

ро́вня *also,* **ровня́** *n.m. & f., colloq.* (one's) equal.

ровня́ть *v.impfv.* [*pfv.* **сровня́ть**] to even; level.

рог [*pl.* **рога́**] *n.* **1,** horn; antler. **2,** horn: труби́ть в рог, to blow a horn. —**брать быка́ за рога́,** to take the bull by the horns. —**наставля́ть рога́** (+ *dat.*), *colloq.* to cuckold.

рога́стый *adj., colloq.* having large horns or antlers.

рога́тка [*gen. pl.* **-ток**] *n.* **1,** bar; barrier. **2,** *fig.* obstacle. **3,** slingshot.

рога́тый *adj.* horned. —**кру́пный/ме́лкий рога́тый скот,** *see* скот.

рога́ч [*gen.* -гача́] *n.* **1,** stag; hart. **2,** stag beetle.

рогови́ца *n.* cornea.

роговой *adj.* **1,** made of horn. **2,** (*of glasses*) horn-rimmed. **3,** horny. **4,** *music* for (the) horn. —**рогова́я обма́нка,** hornblende. —**рогова́я оболо́чка,** cornea.

рого́жа *n.* matting.

рого́з *n.* cattail.

рогоно́сец [*gen.* -сца] *n., colloq.* cuckold.

род *n.* **1,** family. Э́то у него́ в роду́, it runs in his family. **2,** birth; origin; stock. Вести́ свой род от..., to trace one's ancestry back to... **3,** sort; kind. **4,** gender. **5,** genus. **6,** *in* челове́ческий род, the human race. **7,** *in* род заня́тий *or* де́ятельности, line of work; occupation; profession. **8,** *in* род войск, *mil.* arm (*or* branch) of service. —**в не́котором ро́де,** to a certain extent; in a certain sense; in a way. —**в своём ро́де,** in his way; in its way. —**вся́кого ро́да** (+ *nom.*), all sorts of. —**из ро́да в род,** from generation to generation. —**на роду́ напи́сано** (*with dat. & inf.*), destined to. —**от роду,** of age: Ему́ два́дцать лет от роду, he is twenty years of age. —**своего́ ро́да,** a kind of. —**тако́го ро́да** (+ *nom.*), such. —**что́-то в э́том ро́де,** something like that. *See also* ро́дом *and* ро́ды.

роддом *n., colloq.* maternity hospital (*contr. of* роди́льный дом).

ро́дий *n.* rhodium.

роди́льница *n.* woman who has just given birth.

роди́льный *adj.* **1,** maternity (*attrib.*): роди́льный дом, maternity hospital; роди́льное отделе́ние, maternity ward; delivery room. **2,** puerperal: роди́льная горя́чка, puerperal fever.

роди́мый *adj., colloq.* **1,** native. **2,** one's own. —**роди́мое пятно́,** birthmark.

ро́дина *n.* native land; homeland; motherland.

ро́динка [*gen. pl.* -нок] *n.* mole; birthmark.

роди́тели [*gen.* -лей] *n.pl.* parents.

роди́тельный *adj., in* **роди́тельный паде́ж,** genitive case.

роди́тельский *adj.* parental; parents'.

роди́ть *v.pfv.* [*infl.* рожу́, роди́шь; *past fem.* родила́] **1,** *pfv. of* рожа́ть *and* рожда́ть. **2,** to sire; father; beget. —**роди́ться,** *refl.* [*past* роди́лся, родила́сь, роди́ли́сь] *pfv. of* рожда́ться.

родни́к [*gen.* -ника́] *n.* spring (*of water*). —**родни-ко́вый,** *adj.* spring (*attrib.*).

родни́ть *v.impfv.* [*pfv.* сродни́ть *or* породни́ть] to unite; bring together. —**родни́ться,** *refl.* [*pfv.* породни́ться] (*with* с + *instr.*) to become related (to).

родно́й *adj.* **1,** related by blood. Родно́й брат, brother (*as opposed to* двою́родный брат — cousin). **2,** native: родна́я дере́вня, one's native village. Родно́й го́род, home town. **3,** *in direct address,* my dear. —**родны́е,** *n.pl.* relatives.

родня́ *n.* **1,** relatives. **2,** *colloq.* relative.

родови́тый *adj.* of noble birth. —**родови́тость,** *n.f.* noble birth.

родово́й *adj.* **1,** family (*attrib.*). **2,** ancestral. **3,** tribal. **4,** *biol.* generic. **5,** *gram.* gender (*attrib.*). **6,** birth (*attrib.*): родовы́е поту́ги, birth pains; labor pains.

рододе́ндрон (дэ) *n.* rhododendron.

ро́дом *adv.* by birth: Он ро́дом из Фра́нции, he is a native of France; he is a Frenchman by birth.

родонача́льник *n.* **1,** progenitor. **2,** *fig.* father; founder.

родосло́вие *n.* genealogy; pedigree; lineage. *Also,* **родосло́вная.**

родосло́вный *adj.* genealogical. —**родосло́вное де́рево,** family tree.

ро́дственник *n.m.* [*fem.* -ница] relative; relation.

ро́дственный *adj.* **1,** family (*attrib.*): ро́дственные свя́зи, family ties; ties of kinship. **2,** (*of languages, peoples, sciences, etc.*) related. **3,** *fig.* warm; cordial.

родство́ *n.* **1,** relationship; kinship: быть в родстве́ с, to be related to. **2,** *obs.* relatives. **3,** affinity.

ро́ды [*gen.* ро́дов] *n.pl.* birth; childbirth.

ро́жа *n.* **1,** erysipelas (*skin disease*). **2,** *colloq.* ugly face; ugly mug; ugly puss. —**де́лать** *or* **стро́ить** *or* **ко́рчить ро́жи,** to make faces.

рожа́ть *v.impfv.* [*pfv.* роди́ть] **1,** *v.i.* to give birth; have a baby. **2,** *v.t.* to give birth to; bear.

рожда́емость *n.f.* birth rate.

рожда́ть *v.impfv.* [*pfv.* роди́ть] **1,** = рожа́ть. **2,** *fig.* to give rise to; engender. —**рожда́ться,** *refl.* to be born.

рожде́ние *n.* birth. —**день рожде́ния,** birthday.

рождённый *past passive part. of* роди́ть, born: рождённый для сце́ны, born for the stage.

рожде́ственский *adj.* Christmas (*attrib.*).

рождество́ *n.* Christmas.

роже́ница *also,* **рожени́ца** *n.* woman giving birth.

рожо́к [*gen.* рожка́; *pl.* ро́жки, ро́жек *in sense #1;* рожки́, рожко́в *in other senses*] *n.* **1,** small horn (*of an animal*). **2,** *music* horn. **3,** shoehorn. **4,** nursing bottle. —**англи́йский рожо́к,** English horn. —**слухо-во́й рожо́к,** ear trumpet.

рожо́н *n., in* лезть на рожо́н, *colloq.* to ask for trouble.

рожь [*gen., dat. & prep.* ржи; *instr.* ро́жью] *n.f.* rye.

ро́за *n.* **1,** rose. **2,** rosebush.

роза́н *n., obs.* rose.

ро́звальни [*gen.* -ней] *n.pl.* low wide sled.

ро́зга [*gen. pl.* ро́зог] *n.* rod (*for whipping*).

ро́зговенье *n.* first day following a period of fasting.

розе́тка [*gen. pl.* -ток] *n.* **1,** rosette. **2,** small jam dish. **3,** electric outlet.

розмари́н *n.* rosemary.

ро́зница *n., in* в ро́зницу, retail. —**ро́зничный,** *adj.* retail.

ро́зно *adv., obs.* apart; separately.

рознь *n.f.* **1,** dissension; discord; strife. **2,** (*with dat.*) *indicating diversity of similar things:* Челове́к челове́ку — рознь, there are all kinds of people; there are people, and then there are people.

розове́ть *v.impfv.* [*pfv.* порозове́ть] **1,** to turn pink. **2,** [*impfv. only*] (*of anything rose or pink*) to appear; be seen.

розовощёкий *adj.* rosy-cheeked.

ро́зовый *adj.* **1,** rose (*attrib.*). **2,** rose-colored; pink. **3,** *fig.* rosy. —**сквозь ро́зовые очки́,** through rose-colored glasses.

ро́зыгрыш *n.* **1,** drawing (*in a lottery*). **2,** *sports* competition; playoff. **3,** draw; tie; drawn game. **4,** *colloq.* practical joke.

ро́зыск *n.* **1**, search. **2**, investigation. —**уголо́вный ро́зыск**, department of criminal investigation.

рои́ться *v.r.impfv.* to swarm.

рой [*pl.* **рои́**] *n.* swarm.

рок *n.* fate.

рокирова́ть *v.impfv. & pfv.* [*pres.* **-ру́ю, -ру́ешь**] *chess* to castle. *Also,* **рокирова́ться,** *refl.*

рокиро́вка *n., chess* castling: де́лать рокиро́вку, to castle.

роково́й *adj.* fatal.

рококо́ *n.indecl.* rococo.

ро́кот *n.* **1**, roar; rumble. **2**, murmur.

рокота́ть *v.impfv.* [*pres.* **рокочу́, роко́чешь**] to rumble; resound.

ро́лик *n.* **1**, roller; caster. **2**, *pl.* roller skates. **3**, reel (*for movie film*).

ро́ликовый *adj.* roller (*attrib.*). —**ро́ликовые коньки́,** roller skates. —**ро́ликовый подши́пник,** roller bearing.

роль [*pl.* **ро́ли, роле́й, роля́м**] *n.f.* role; part. —**игра́ть роль,** to play a role/part.

ром *n.* rum.

рома́н *n.* **1**, novel. **2**, *colloq.* romance; love affair.

романи́ст *n.* **1**, novelist. **2**, specialist in Romance philology.

рома́нс *n., music* romance.

рома́нский *adj.* **1**, Romance: рома́нские языки́, Romance languages. **2**, Romanesque.

романтизи́ровать *v.impfv. & pfv.* [*pres.* **-ру́ю, -ру́ешь**] to romanticize.

романти́зм *n.* romanticism.

рома́нтик *n.* romanticist.

рома́нтика *n.* **1**, romanticism. **2**, romance; romantic appeal.

романти́ческий *adj.* romantic. *Also,* **романти́чный.**

рома́шка [*gen. pl.* **-шек**] *n.* camomile.

ромб *n.* **1**, rhombus. **2**, diamond (*figure*). —**ромби́ческий,** *adj.* rhombic.

ромбо́ид *n.* rhomboid.

ро́мовый *adj.* rum (*attrib.*).

ромште́кс (тэ) *n.* rump steak.

ро́ндо *n. indecl.* rondo.

роня́ть *v.impfv.* [*pfv.* **урони́ть**] **1**, to drop. **2**, to knock off: урони́ть стака́н со стола́, to knock a glass off the table. **3**, to let (one's head, arms, etc.) drop. **4**, [*impfv. only*] to shed (leaves, tears, etc.). **5**, to utter. **6**, *fig.* to damage; undermine. **7**, *fig.* to demean: роня́ть себя́; роня́ть своё досто́инство, to demean oneself.

ро́пот *n.* **1**, murmur (*of disapproval*); grumbling. **2**, murmuring; rustling; rippling.

ропта́ть *v.impfv.* [*pres.* **ропщу́, ро́пщешь**] **1**, (*with* на + *acc.*) to grumble (about); complain (about). **2**, to murmur; rustle.

роса́ *n.* dew.

роси́нка [*gen. pl.* **-нок**] *n.* dewdrop.

роси́стый *adj.* dewy.

роско́шествовать *v.impfv.* [*pres.* **-ствую, -ствуешь**] to live in luxury; live sumptuously. *Also,* **роско́шничать.**

роско́шный *adj.* **1**, luxurious; sumptuous. **2**, luxurious; lush.

ро́скошь *n.f.* luxury.

ро́слый *adj.* strapping; burly; husky.

ро́сный *adj., in* **ро́сный ла́дан,** benzoin.

росома́ха *n.* wolverine.

ро́спись *n.f.* painting; mural.

ро́спуск *n.* dismissal; dissolution.

росси́йский *adj.* Russian.

россия́нин [*pl.* **-я́не, -я́н**] *n.m.* [*fem.* **-я́нка**] Russian.

ро́ссказни [*gen.* **-ней**] *n.pl., colloq.* tale; yarn; cock-and-bull story.

ро́ссыпь *n.f.* (mineral) deposit.

рост *n.* **1**, growth. **2**, height. Высо́кого ро́ста, tall. Ни́зкого ро́ста, short. Он ро́стом шесть фу́тов, he is six feet tall. Существо́ в рост челове́ка, a creature the height of a man. **3**, rise; increase. **4**, length (*of a garment*): брю́ки сорокового́ разме́ра пе́рвого ро́ста, trousers size forty short. —**во весь рост, 1**, to one's full height. **2**, (*of a portrait*) full-length. **3**, *fig.* in all its magnitude. —**не по ро́сту,** (*of a garment*) not the right size. —**по ро́сту,** according to height; in size order.

ро́стбиф *n.* roast beef.

ростовщи́к [*gen.* **-щика́**] *n.* **1**, moneylender. **2**, usurer. —**ростовщи́ческий,** *adj.* usurious. —**ростовщи́чество,** *n.* usury.

росто́к [*gen.* **-стка́**] *n.* sprout; shoot.

ро́счерк *n.* flourish. —**одни́м ро́счерком пера́,** with a stroke of the pen.

рося́нка *n.* sundew.

росяно́й *adj.* dew (*attrib.*).

рот [*gen.* **рта;** *2nd loc.* **рту**] *n.* mouth. Во рту, in one's mouth. Изо рта, from one's mouth. —**во весь рот, 1**, at the top of one's lungs. **2**, from ear to ear. —**набра́ть воды́ в рот,** to keep silent; keep mum. —**не брать в рот** (+ *gen.*), not to touch (a certain food or drink). —**смотре́ть в рот** (+ *dat.*), to listen spellbound (to someone); hang on every word (that someone says).

ро́та *n., mil.* company.

рота́нг *n.* rattan. —**рота́нговый,** *adj.* rattan.

рота́тор *n.* mimeograph.

ротацио́нный *adj.* rotary. —**ротацио́нная (печа́тная) маши́на,** rotary press.

ро́тный *adj., mil.* company (*attrib.*). —*n.* company commander.

ротово́й *adj.* of the mouth; oral.

ротозе́й *n., colloq.* **1**, idle onlooker. **2**, dimwit; dullard.

ротозе́йство *n., colloq.* extreme absent-mindedness.

рото́нда *n.* rotunda.

ро́тор *n.* rotor.

ро́ща *n.* grove.

рояли́зм *n.* royalism. —**рояли́ст,** *n.* royalist. —**роялистский,** *adj.* royalist.

роя́ль *n.m.* piano.

ртуть *n.f.* mercury. —**рту́тный,** *adj.* mercury (*attrib.*).

руба́нок [*gen.* **-нка**] *n.* plane (*tool*).

руба́ха *n.* shirt.

руба́шка [*gen. pl.* **-шек**] *n.* **1**, shirt. **2**, back (*of a playing card*). —**ночна́я руба́шка, 1**, nightshirt. **2**, nightgown. —**роди́ться в руба́шке,** to be born lucky; be born under a lucky star.

рубе́ж [*gen.* **рубежа́**] *n.* **1,** border; boundary. **2,** *mil.* line: огнево́й рубе́ж, firing line. —**за рубежо́м,** abroad.

рубе́ц [*gen.* **рубца́**] *n.* **1,** scar; welt. **2,** hem. **3,** rumen; paunch (*of an animal*). **4,** tripe.

руби́дий *n.* rubidium.

Рубико́н *n.,* *in* перейти́ Рубико́н, to cross the Rubicon.

руби́н *n.* ruby. —**руби́новый,** *adj.* ruby (*attrib.*).

руби́ть *v.impfv.* [*pres.* **рублю́, ру́бишь**] **1,** to chop. **2,** to chop down; cut down; fell. **3,** to slash. **4,** to build (*out of logs*). —**руби́ться,** *refl.* to fight with swords.

ру́бище *n.* rags; tatters.

ру́бка [*gen. pl.* **ру́бок**] *n.* **1,** chopping; felling. **2,** *naut.* deckhouse. —**боева́я ру́бка,** conning tower. —**рулева́я ру́бка,** pilothouse.

рублёвка [*gen. pl.* **-вок**] *n., colloq.* one-ruble note. —**рублёвый,** *adj.* ruble (*attrib.*); one-ruble (*attrib.*).

ру́бленый *adj.* **1,** chopped. **2,** made of logs.

рубль [*gen.* **рубля́**] *n.m.* ruble.

ру́брика *n.* heading.

рубцева́ться *v.r.impfv.* [*pfv.* **зарубцева́ться;** *pres.* **-цу́ется**] (*of a wound*) to form a scar.

рубцо́вый *adj., in* рубцо́вая ткань, scar tissue.

ру́бчатый *adj.* (*of material*) ribbed.

ру́бчик *n.* **1,** *dim. of* рубе́ц. **2,** rib; ridge (*on material*).

ру́гань *n.f.* swearing; profanity.

руга́тельный *adj.* abusive.

руга́тельство *n.* swearword; expletive.

руга́ть *v.impfv.* [*pfv.* **вы́ругать**] to curse out; swear at. —**руга́ться,** *refl.* [*impfv. only*] **1,** to swear; curse. **2,** to swear at one another.

руда́ [*pl.* **ру́ды**] *n.* ore.

рудиме́нт *n.* rudimentary organ. —**рудимента́рный,** *adj.* rudimentary.

рудни́к [*gen.* **-ника́**] *n.* mine. —**руднико́вый; рудни́чный,** *adj.* mine (*attrib.*).

ру́дный *adj.* ore (*attrib.*); of ore.

рудоко́п *n., obs.* miner.

ружейник *n.* gunsmith.

ружейный *adj.* gun (*attrib.*); rifle (*attrib.*).

ружьё [*pl.* **ру́жья, ру́жей, ру́жьям**] *n.* **1,** gun. **2,** (*in various set expressions*) arms: быть под ружьём, to be under arms; призыва́ть под ружьё, to call to arms.

руи́ны *n.pl.* [*sing.* **руи́на**] ruins.

рука́ [*acc.* **ру́ку;** *pl.* **ру́ки, рук, рука́м**] *n.* **1,** hand. **2,** arm. —**в одни́ ру́ки,** per person; each. —**в рука́х,** in one's hands. —**из пе́рвых рук,** (*of information*) firsthand. —**из рук вон (пло́хо),** atrociously; miserably. —**из рук в ру́ки,** from hand to hand. —**как без рук,** helpless; lost. —**на рука́х, 1,** in one's arms. **2,** *fig.* in one's hands (*i.e.* in one's possession). **3,** *fig.* on one's hands. **4,** (*of a library book*) in use; out. —**на́ руку** (+ *dat.*), to one's liking. —**не с руки́** (+ *dat.*), inconvenient (for); inappropriate (for). —**от рук** (+ *gen.*), at the hands of. —**от руки́,** handwritten; in longhand. —**по рука́м!,** it's a deal! —**по руке́,** the right size. —**под руко́й,** on hand; at hand. —**по́д руку, 1,** by the arm: взять/держа́ть кого́-нибудь по́д руку, to take/hold someone by the arm; take/hold someone's arm. **2,** *in* попа́сть по́д руку, *see* попада́ть. **3,** *in* го-

вори́ть кому́-нибудь под руку, to speak to someone when he (she) is busy. —**рука́ об руку,** hand in hand. Рабо́тать рука́ об руку с, to work hand in hand with. —**ру́ки вверх!,** hands up! —**ру́ки прочь!,** hands off! —**руко́й пода́ть,** a stone's throw. —**с рук,** (*with verbs of buying or selling*) privately.

рука́в [*gen. sing. & nom. pl.* **рукава́**] *n.* **1,** sleeve. **2,** branch (*of a river*). **3,** hose. —**спустя́ рукава́,** carelessly; in a slipshod manner.

рукави́ца *n.* mitten.

руководи́тель *n.m.* **1,** leader. **2,** head.

руководи́ть *v.impfv.* [*pres.* **-вожу́, -води́шь**] (*with instr.*) **1,** to direct; manage; run. **2,** to lead; guide. —**руководи́ться,** *refl.* (*with instr.*) to be guided (by).

руково́дство *n.* **1,** leadership. **2,** (*with instr.*) direction (of); management (of). **3,** guide: руково́дство к де́йствию, a guide to action. **4,** manual; handbook. **5,** leaders.

руково́дствоваться *v.r.impfv.* [*pres.* **-ствуюсь, -ствуешься**] (*with instr.*) to be guided (by).

руководя́щий *adj.* **1,** leading; guiding. **2,** senior; supervisory. —**руководя́щий комите́т,** steering committee.

рукоде́лие *n.* needlework. —**рукоде́льница,** *n.* needleworker.

рукомо́йник *n.* washstand.

рукопа́шный *adj., in* рукопа́шный бой, hand-to-hand fighting/combat.

рукопи́сный *adj.* **1,** manuscript (*attrib.*). **2,** handwritten.

ру́копись *n.f.* manuscript.

рукоплеска́ние *n., usu. pl.* applause.

рукоплеска́ть *v.impfv.* [*pres.* **-плещу́, -пле́щешь**] (*with dat.*) to applaud.

рукопожа́тие *n.* handshake.

рукоположе́ние *n., Orth. Ch.* ordination.

рукоприкла́дство *n., colloq.* beating; physical violence.

рукоя́тка [*gen. pl.* **-ток**] *n.* handle. *Also,* **рукоя́ть,** *n.f.*

рула́да *n., music* roulade.

рулево́й *adj.* rudder (*attrib.*); steering (*attrib.*). —*n.* helmsman. —**рулева́я ру́бка,** pilothouse.

руле́т *n.* meat or potato loaf.

руле́тка [*gen. pl.* **-ток**] *n.* **1,** tape measure. **2,** roulette; roulette wheel.

рули́ть *v.impfv., aero.* to taxi.

руло́н *n.* roll; bolt (*of cloth*); roll (*of wallpaper*).

руль [*gen.* **руля́**] *n.m.* **1,** rudder; helm. **2,** steering wheel. **3,** handlebar(s). —**за рулём,** at (*or* behind) the wheel. —**стать за руль,** to take the helm. —**стоя́ть у руля́,** to be at the helm.

ру́мба *n.* rumba.

румы́н [*gen. pl.* **румы́н**] *n.m.* [*fem.* **румы́нка**] Romanian. —**румы́нский,** *adj.* Romanian.

румя́на [*gen.* **румя́н**] *n.pl.* rouge.

румя́нец [*gen.* **-нца**] *n.* color in one's face; redness in one's cheeks.

румя́нить *v.impfv.* [*pfv.* **наумя́нить**] **1,** to put rouge on; apply rouge to. **2,** [*pfv. also* **зарумя́нить**] to redden; put color in; give a reddish glow to. —**румя́ниться,** *refl.* **1,** [*pfv.* **нарумя́ниться**] to put on rouge. **2,** [*pfv.* **зарумя́ниться**] to turn red; flush.

румя́ный *adj.* ruddy; rosy.

руно́ [*pl.* **ру́на**] *n.* fleece. —**золото́е руно́**, the Golden Fleece.

ру́ны *n.pl.* [*sing.* **ру́на**] runes. —**руни́ческий**, *adj.* runic.

ру́пия *n.* rupee.

ру́пор *n.* **1**, megaphone. **2**, *fig.* mouthpiece.

руса́к [*gen.* **-сака́**] *n.* **1**, European hare. **2**, *colloq.* Russian.

руса́лка [*gen. pl.* **-лок**] *n.* mermaid.

руси́ст *n.* specialist in the Russian language.

русифика́ция *n.* Russification.

русифици́ровать *v.impfv. & pfv.* [*pres.* **-рую, -ру́ешь**] to Russify.

ру́сло *n.* **1**, river bed; channel. **2**, *fig.* course; direction. Входи́ть в норма́льное ру́сло, to return to normal.

русофи́л *n.* Russophile.

русофо́б *n.* Russophobe. —**русофо́бство**, *n.* Russophobia.

ру́сский *adj.* Russian: ру́сский язы́к, the Russian language. —*n.* **1**, Russian (*man*). **2**, *pl.* (the) Russians.

русскоязы́чный *adj.* **1**, Russian-language (*attrib.*). **2**, Russian-speaking.

ру́сый *adj.* **1**, (*of hair*) light brown. **2**, (*of a person*) with light brown hair.

руте́ний *n.* ruthenium.

рути́на *n.* resistance to change; conservatism. —**рутинёр**, *n.* conservative; traditionalist. —**рути́нный**, *adj.* staid; conservative; traditional.

ру́хлядь *n.f., colloq.* junk.

ру́хнуть *v.pfv.* **1**, to collapse; cave in; come tumbling down. **2**, *fig.* (*of hope, plans, etc.*) to collapse; fall through; come to naught.

ручате́льство *n.* guarantee.

руча́ться *v.r.impfv.* [*pfv.* **поручи́ться**] (*with* **за** + *acc.*) to vouch for; guarantee.

ручеёк [*gen.* **-чейка́**] *n., dim. of* **ручей**.

ручей [*gen.* **ручья́**] *n.* brook; stream.

ру́чка [*gen. pl.* **ру́чек**] *n.* **1**, *dim. of* **рука́**. **2**, handle; knob. **3**, arm (*of a chair, sofa, etc.*). **4**, penholder. **5**, pen: ша́риковая ру́чка, ball-point pen. —**доходи́ть до ру́чки**, *colloq.* to reach the breaking point.

ручно́й *adj.* **1**, hand (*attrib.*): ручна́я грана́та, hand grenade. **2**, manual: ручно́й труд, manual labor. **3**, tame; domesticated. Ручна́я обезья́на, pet monkey. —**ручно́й рабо́ты**, handmade. —**ручны́е часы́**, wrist watch.

ру́шить *v.impfv.* to tear down. —**ру́шиться**, *refl.* **1**, to collapse; cave in; come tumbling down. **2**, *fig.* to collapse; fall through.

ры́ба *n.* fish. **2**, *pl., cap.* Pisces. —**ни ры́ба ни мя́со**, neither fish nor fowl.

рыба́к [*gen.* **-бака́**] *n.* (commercial) fisherman.

рыба́лка *n., colloq.* fishing: идти́ на рыба́лку, to go fishing.

рыба́цкий *adj.* fishing (*attrib.*); fisherman's. *Also,* **рыба́чий** [*fem.* **-чья**].

рыба́чить *v.impfv.* to fish.

рыбёшка [*gen. pl.* **-шек**] *n., colloq.* small fish.

ры́бий [*fem.* **-бья**] *adj.* fish (*attrib.*). —**ры́бий жир**, cod-liver oil. —**ры́бий клей**, isinglass.

ры́бка [*gen. pl.* **ры́бок**] *n., dim. of* **ры́ба**. —**золота́я ры́бка**, goldfish.

ры́бный *adj.* fish (*attrib.*). —**ры́бная ло́вля**, fishing.

рыболо́в *n.* fisherman; angler. —**рыболо́вный**, *adj.* fishing (*attrib.*). —**рыболо́вство**, *n.* fishing (*as an economic activity*).

рыво́к [*gen.* **рывка́**] *n.* **1**, jerk; yank. **2**, spurt. **3**, *weightlifting* snatch.

рыга́ть *v.impfv.* [*pfv.* **рыгну́ть**] to belch.

рыда́ние *n.* sobbing.

рыда́ть *v.impfv.* to sob.

рыжеволо́сый *adj.* redheaded.

рыже́ть *v.impfv.* [*pfv.* **порыже́ть**] to become red; turn red.

ры́жий *adj.* **1**, red. **2**, redheaded. **3**, (*of a horse*) chestnut. —*n., colloq.* circus clown.

ры́жик *n.* a variety of edible mushroom.

рык *n.* roar.

рыка́ть *v.impfv.* to roar.

ры́ло *n.* **1**, snout. **2**, *colloq.* mug; puss; kisser.

ры́льце [*gen. pl.* **ры́лец**] *n.* **1**, *dim. of* **ры́ло**. **2**, *bot.* stigma.

ры́нда *n.* ship's bell.

ры́нок [*gen.* **ры́нка**] *n.* market. —**ры́ночный**, *adj.* market (*attrib.*).

рыса́к [*gen.* **-сака́**] *n.* trotter (*horse*).

ры́сий [*fem.* **-сья**] *adj.* **1**, lynx (*attrib.*). **2**, (*of one's eyes*) piercing.

рыси́стый *adj., in* **рыси́стые бега́**, trotting races; **рыси́стая ло́шадь**, trotter.

рыси́ть *v.impfv.* (*of a horse*) to trot.

ры́скать *v.impfv.* [*pres.* **ры́щу, ры́щешь**] **1**, to prowl; be on the prowl. **2**, *colloq.* to wander about; roam.

рысца́ *n.* slow trot; jog trot.

рысь *n.f.* **1**, lynx; bobcat. **2**, trot: ры́сью (*or* на рыся́х), at a trot.

ры́твина *n.* pothole.

рыть *v.impfv.* [*pfv.* **вы́рыть**; *pres.* **ро́ю, ро́ешь**] **1**, to dig. **2**, to dig up.

рытьё *n.* digging.

ры́ться *v.r.impfv.* [*pfv.* **порыться**; *pres.* **ро́юсь, ро́ешься**] (*with* **в** + *prepl.*) **1**, [*impfv. only*] to dig (in the dirt, sand, etc.). **2**, to search; rummage; ransack. —**ры́ться/порыться в па́мяти**, to rack one's brains; try hard to remember.

рыхле́ть *v.impfv.* to become soft; lose its firmness.

рыхли́ть *v.impfv.* [*pfv.* **взрыхли́ть**] to loosen; turn up (soil, dirt, etc.).

ры́хлый *adj.* loose; crumbly; friable.

ры́царский *adj.* **1**, knight's; knights'. **2**, chivalrous.

ры́царство *n.* **1**, knights. **2**, knighthood. **3**, chivalry.

ры́царь *n.m.* knight.

рыча́г [*gen.* **-чага́**] *n.* lever.

рыча́ние *n.* growling; snarling.

рыча́ть *v.impfv.* [*pres.* **рычи́т**] to growl; snarl.

рья́ный *adj.* zealous. —**рья́но**, *adv.* zealously. —**рья́ность**, *n.f.* zeal.

рэ́кет *n.* racket. —**рэкети́р**, *n.* racketeer.

рюкза́к [*gen.* **-зака́**] *n.* knapsack.

рю́мка [*gen. pl.* **рю́мок**] *n.* small liquor glass.

рю́мочка [*gen. pl.* **-чек**] *n., dim. of* **рю́мка**.

ряби́на *n.* **1,** mountain ash; rowan tree. **2,** rowanberries. **3,** pockmark.

ряби́ть *v.impfv.* **1,** to ripple (*trans. & intrans.*). **2,** *impers.* (*usu. with* **в глаза́х**) to see spots before one's eyes; *fig.* be dazzled. В глаза́х ряби́т от..., one is dazzled by...

рябо́й *adj.* **1,** pockmarked. **2,** spotted.

ря́бчик *n.* hazel grouse; hazel hen.

рябь *n.f.* ripples.

ря́вкать *v.impfv.* [*pfv.* **ря́вкнуть**] to roar; bellow.

ряд [*gen.* **ря́да**, *but after 2, 3 & 4*, **ряда́**; *2nd loc.* **ряду́**; *pl.* **ряды́**] *n.* **1,** row: ряд домо́в, row of houses; в пе́рвом ряду́, in the first row. **2,** *mil.* file. **3,** *pl.* ranks: принима́ть в свои́ ряды́, to take into one's ranks. **4,** row of stalls (*in a market*). **5,** [*prepl.* **в ря́де**] series; number: це́лый ряд (+ *gen.*), a whole series (of); в ря́де слу́чаев, in a number of cases. —**в ряд/ряду́**, abreast. —**в ряду́** (+ *gen.*), among. —**из ря́да вон выходя́щий**, *adj.* exceptional; out of the ordinary. —**стоя́ть в одно́м ряду́ с**, to be (*or* rank) on a par with.

ряди́ться *v.r.impfv.* [*pres.* **ряжу́сь, ря́дишься**] *colloq.* **1,** to get dressed up. **2,** (*with instr.*) to dress up (as).

рядово́й *adj.* **1,** ordinary; average; common. **2,** *mil.* of the rank and file: рядово́й соста́в, the rank and file; enlisted personnel. —*n., mil.* private.

ря́дом *adv.* **1,** alongside. **2,** next to each other; side by side. **3,** nearby. **4,** next door. —**ря́дом с** (+ *instr.*), **1,** next to; beside; alongside. **2,** next door to.

ря́са *n.* monk's habit; cassock; frock.

ря́ска *n.* duckweed.

C

C, с *n.neut.* eighteenth letter of the Russian alphabet.

с *also*, **со** *prep.* **A,** *with instr.* **1,** with: Я пойду́ с ва́ми, I'll go with you; чита́ть с трудо́м, to read with difficulty. **2,** and: мы с тобо́й, you and I; хлеб с ма́слом, bread and butter; три с полови́ной, three and a half. **3,** on (*a specified train, plane, etc.*): уе́хать с ра́нним по́ездом, to leave on the early-morning train. **4,** containing: ведро́ с водо́й, a pail of water; мешки́ с песко́м, sandbags. **5,** *used in greetings:* с пра́здником!, happy holiday!; с Но́вым го́дом!, Happy New Year! **B,** *with gen.* **1,** from: с вокза́ла, from the station; с рабо́ты, from work. С са́мого нача́ла, from the very beginning. С утра́ до ве́чера, from morning till night. С головы́ до ног, from head to toe. С ру́сского на англи́йский, from Russian to English. **2,** off; down from; down: сойти́ с ре́льсов, to go off the tracks; упа́сть с ле́стницы, to fall down the stairs; доста́ть кни́гу с по́лки, to take a book from the shelf. **3,** up from; out of: встать со сту́ла, to get up from/ out of/ a chair. Вскочи́ть с посте́ли, to leap out of bed. **4,** *indicating cause:* кати́ться со́ смеху, to roar with laughter; умира́ть с го́лоду, to die of hunger. **5,** (*with certain nouns and verbs*) with: с ва́шего разреше́ния, with your permission; начнём с вас, let's begin with you. **6,** since: с де́тства, since childhood; с тех пор, since then. **C,** *with acc.* about; approximately: с ме́сяц, about a month; величино́й с дом, about the size of a house. —**с тем, что́бы**, *see* **что́бы**.

с- *also*, **со-, съ-,** *prefix* **1,** *indicating motion off or down:* сойти́ с ле́стницы, to go down the stairs; соскользну́ть со стола́, to slip off the table. **2,** *indicating removal from a surface:* соска́бливать, to scrape off. **3,** *indicating bringing or gathering together:* собира́ть, to gather; соединя́ть, to unite. **4,** (*with* **-ся**) *indicating coming together from various places:* съезжа́ться, to gather; assemble (*from various places*). **5,** *indicating joining or fastening together:* свя́зывать, to tie together. **6,** (*with pfv. verbs only*) *indicating motion to a place and back:* сбе́гать, to run (*to a place and return*). **7,** (*with* **-ся**) *indicating harmony in doing something:* спева́ться, to sing in harmony; сраба́тываться, to achieve harmony in work.

саа́м *n.m.* [*fem.* **саа́мка**] Lapp; Laplander. —**саа́мский**, *adj.* Lapp; Lappish.

са́бля [*gen. pl.* **са́бель**] *n.* saber. —**са́бельный**, *adj.* saber (*attrib.*).

сабота́ж *n.* sabotage. —**сабота́жник**, *n.* saboteur.

сабота́жничать *v.impfv., colloq.* = **саботи́ровать** (*in sense #1*).

саботи́ровать *v.impfv. & pfv.* [*pres.* **-рую, -руешь**] **1,** to sabotage. **2,** to engage in acts of sabotage.

са́ван *n.* **1,** shroud. **2,** *fig.* cover; blanket; mantle (*of snow, ice, fog, etc.*).

сава́нна *n.* savanna; savannah.

савра́сый *adj.* (*of a horse*) light brown with a black mane and tail.

са́га *n.* saga.

сагити́ровать *v., pfv. of* **агити́ровать** (*in sense #2*).

сад [*2nd loc.* **саду́**; *pl.* **сады́**] *n.* garden. —**ботани́ческий сад**, botanical gardens. —**де́тский сад**, kindergarten. —**фрукто́вый сад**, orchard. —**я́блоневый сад**, apple orchard.

сади́зм *n.* sadism.

са́дик *n., dim. of* **сад.**

сади́ст *n.* sadist. —**сади́стский,** *adj.* sadistic.

сади́ть *v.impfv.* [*pres.* **сажу́, са́дишь**] *colloq.* = **сажа́ть.**

сади́ться *v.r.impfv.* [*pfv.* **сесть**; *pres.* **сажу́сь, сади́шься**] **1,** to sit; sit down; take a seat. Сади́тесь!, sit down!; have a seat! Сесть за стол/рабо́ту, to sit down at a table; sit (*or* get) down to work. Сесть в посте́ли, to sit up in bed. **2,** (*with* **в** *or* **на** + *acc.*) to board; get on; take (a plane, train, bus, etc.); get into (a car); get on(to); mount (a horse). **3,** (*of a bird, insect, etc.*) to alight; perch. **4,** (*of dust, fog, etc.*) to settle. **5,** (*of an airplane*) to land. **6,** (*of the sun, stars, etc.*) to set. **7,** (*of a building, foundation, etc.*) to sink. **8,** (*of a battery*) to go dead. **9,** (*of material*) to shrink.

са́днить *v.impfv.* **1,** to scratch; abrade. **2,** to smart; sting; burn. В го́рле са́днит, my throat feels scratchy.

садо́вник *n.* gardener.

садово́д *n.* horticulturist; gardener. —**садово́дство,** *n.* horticulture; gardening. —**садово́дческий,** *adj.* horticultural.

садо́вый *adj.* **1,** garden (*attrib.*). **2,** cultivated. —**садо́во-па́рковое иску́сство,** landscape architecture.

садо́к [*gen.* **садка́**] *n.* **1,** fishpond. **2,** pen; coop; warren.

са́жа *n.* soot. В са́же, sooty.

сажа́лка [*gen. pl.* **-лок**] *n.* planter (*machine*).

сажа́ть *v.impfv.* [*pfv.* **посади́ть**] **1,** to plant. **2,** to seat; sit (someone) down. **3,** to place; put. **4,** to set down; land (an aircraft). **5,** to put in prison. **6,** *colloq.* to make (a stain, blot, etc.). —**сажа́ть/посади́ть в кле́тку,** to cage. —**сажа́ть/посади́ть на дие́ту,** to put on a diet. —**сажа́ть/посади́ть на́ кол,** to impale on a stake. —**сажа́ть/посади́ть на цепь,** to chain; chain up. —**сажа́ть/посади́ть под аре́ст,** to place under arrest.

са́женец [*gen.* **-нца**] *n.* seedling.

са́жень *also,* **са́жень** *n.f.* old Russian unit of length equal to approx. 7 feet. —**морска́я са́жень,** fathom.

саза́н *n.* carp (*fish*).

сайга́ *also,* **сайга́к** *n.* a variety of antelope; saiga.

са́йка [*gen. pl.* **са́ек**] *n.* roll (*of bread*)

саквоя́ж *n.* traveling bag.

сакрамента́льный *adj.* **1,** ritual (*attrib.*). **2,** sacred. **3,** traditional.

сакс *n., hist.* Saxon.

саксау́л *n.* tree native to Central Asia; saxaul.

саксо́нский *adj.* Saxon.

саксофо́н *n.* saxophone.

сала́зки [*gen.* **-зок**] *n.pl.* small sled; toboggan.

салама́ндра *n.* salamander.

сала́т *n.* **1,** lettuce. **2,** salad.

сала́тник *n.* salad bowl. *Also,* **сала́тница.**

сала́тный *adj.* **1,** lettuce (*attrib.*); salad (*attrib.*). **2,** light green.

са́лить *v.impfv.* to grease.

са́лки [*gen.* **са́лок**] *n.pl.* tag (*game*).

са́ло *n.* **1,** fat; lard. **2,** tallow. **3,** thin ice.

сало́н *n.* **1,** salon. **2,** lounge (*in a hotel, on a train, ship, etc.*). **3,** passenger section (*of an aircraft*). **4,** showroom. —**сало́н-ваго́н,** parlor car. —**худо́жественный сало́н,** art gallery.

сало́нный *adj.* light; trivial: сало́нный разгово́р, small talk.

салфе́тка [*gen. pl.* **-ток**] *n.* napkin.

са́льдо *n. indecl., bookkeeping* balance.

са́льность *n.f.* profanity; obscenity.

са́льный *adj.* **1,** tallow (*attrib.*). **2,** greasy. **3,** salacious. —**са́льные же́лезы,** sebaceous glands.

са́льто *n. indecl.* somersault. *Also,* **са́льто-морта́ле.**

салю́т *n.* salute.

салютова́ть *v.impfv. & pfv.* [*pres.* **-ту́ю, -ту́ешь**] (*with dat.*) to salute.

саля́ми *n.f. indecl.* salami.

сам *emphatic pronoun* [*fem.* **сама́**; *neut.* **само́**; *pl.* **са́ми**; *gen.* **самого́, само́й, сами́х**; *dat.* **самому́, само́й, сами́м**; *acc. fem.* **саму́** *or* **самое́**; *instr.* **сами́м, само́й, сами́ми**; *prepl.* **само́м, само́й, сами́х**] oneself; myself; yourself; himself; herself; ourselves, etc.: Я сам э́то сде́лаю, I'll do it myself. Письмо́ от самого́ президе́нта, a letter from the President himself. —**быть сами́м собо́й,** to be oneself. Будь сам (сама́) собо́й!, be yourself! —**сам не свой (сама́ на своя́),** not oneself; out of sorts. —**сам по себе́, 1,** oneself; in and of itself; per se. **2,** independently; on one's own. —**сам собо́й,** by itself; of itself. —**сам того́ не** (+ *verbal adv.*), not...; without...: сам того́ не ве́дая, unwittingly; сам того́ не жела́я, unwillingly.

сама́н *n.* adobe. —**сама́нный,** *adj.* adobe.

сама́рий *n.* samarium.

саме́ц [*gen.* **самца́**] *n.* male (*of animals*): саме́ц оле́ня, male deer; buck.

самиздат *n.* underground publication of manuscripts (*in the former Soviet Union*).

са́мка [*gen. pl.* **са́мок**] *n.* female (*of animals*): са́мка оле́ня, female deer.

само- *prefix* self-.

самоана́лиз *n.* self-analysis; introspection.

самобы́тность *n.f.* **1,** originality. **2,** distinctive character.

самобы́тный *adj.* **1,** original. **2,** distinctive.

самова́р *n.* samovar.

самовла́стие *n.* **1,** one-man rule. **2,** *fig.* despotism. —**самовла́стный,** *adj.* despotic.

самовлюблённый *adj.* conceited. —**самовлюблённость,** *n.f.* conceit.

самовнуше́ние *n.* autosuggestion.

самовозгора́ние *n.* spontaneous combustion.

самово́лие *n.* arbitrariness; high-handedness.

самово́льный *adj.* **1,** self-willed; insubordinate. **2,** unauthorized: самово́льная отлу́чка, absence without leave. —**самово́льно,** *adv.* without permission.

самовоспита́ние *n.* self-study.

самовоспламене́ние *n.* spontaneous combustion.

самого́н *n.* homemade liquor, esp. vodka; moonshine. —**самого́нщик,** *n., colloq.* moonshiner.

самодви́жущийся *adj.* self-propelled.

самоде́лка [*gen. pl.* **-лок**] *n., colloq.* homemade article.

самоде́льный *adj.* homemade.

самодержа́вие *n.* autocracy. —**самодержа́вный,** *adj.* autocratic.

самоде́ржец [*gen.* -жца] *n.* autocrat.

самоде́ятельность *n.f.* **1,** individual initiative. **2,** amateur activities; amateur production.

самоде́ятельный *adj.* **1,** independent. **2,** amateur.

самоди́йский *adj.* Samoyed.

самодисципли́на *n.* self-discipline.

самодовле́ющий *adj.* self-contained; independent.

самодово́льный *adj.* self-satisfied; complacent; self-complacent; smug. —самодово́льство, *n.* self-satisfaction; complacency; self-complacency; smugness.

самоду́р *n.* high-handed person. —самоду́рство, *n.* high-handedness.

самозабве́ние *n.* **1,** self-consciousness; reverie. **2,** absorption. **3,** selflessness.

самозабве́нный *adj.* **1,** all-consuming. **2,** selfless.

самозарожде́ние *n.* spontaneous generation.

самозащи́та *n.* self-defense.

самозва́нец [*gen.* -нца] *n.m.* [*fem.* -нка] impostor.

самозва́нный *also* самозва́ный *adj.* pseudo-; false; self-styled.

самока́т *n.* scooter.

самокри́тика *n.* self-criticism. —самокрити́ческий, *adj.* self-critical.

самолёт *n.* plane; airplane; aircraft.

самоли́чно *adv., colloq.* oneself; on one's own; personally.

самолюби́вый *adj.* proud.

самолю́бие *n.* pride; self-respect.

самомне́ние *n.* conceit.

самонаблюде́ние *n.* introspection.

самонаде́янный *adj.* self-assured; presumptuous. —самонаде́янность, *n.f.* self-assurance; presumption.

самоназва́ние *n.* self-designation.

самообеспе́ченный *adj.* self-sufficient. —самообеспе́ченность, *n.f.* self-sufficiency.

самооблада́ние *n.* self-control; equanimity; composure.

самообма́н *n.* self-deception.

самооборо́на *n.* self-defense.

самообразова́ние *n.* self-study.

самообслу́живание *n.* self-service.

самоопределе́ние *n.* self-determination.

самоотверже́ние *n.* = самоотве́рженность.

самоотве́рженный *adj.* selfless. —самоотве́рженность, *n.f.* selflessness.

самоотво́д *n.* (*used with* взять *or* сде́лать) declining of a nomination; withdrawal of one's candidacy.

самоотрече́ние *n.* self-denial.

самоочеви́дный *adj.* self-evident.

самопи́сец [*gen.* -сца] *n.* recorder: бортово́й самопи́сец, flight recorder.

самопи́ска [*gen. pl.* -сок] *n., colloq.* fountain pen.

самопоже́ртвование *n.* self-sacrifice.

самопроизво́льный *adj.* spontaneous. —самопроизво́льность, *n.f.* spontaneity.

самопу́ск *n.* self-starter.

саморо́док [*gen.* -дка] *n.* **1,** nugget. **2,** *fig.* person with exceptional natural talent.

самоса́д *n., colloq.* home-grown tobacco.

самосва́л *n.* dump truck.

самосожже́ние *n.* self-immolation.

самосозна́ние *n.* consciousness.

самосохране́ние *n.* self-preservation.

самостоя́тельный *adj.* independent; self-reliant. —самостоя́тельно, *adv.* independently; on one's own. —самостоя́тельность, *n.f.* independence; self-reliance.

самостре́л *n.* **1,** crossbow. **2,** self-inflicted wound (*made to evade military service*). **3,** *colloq.* soldier with a self-inflicted wound.

самосу́д *n.* mob law; lynching.

самотёк *n.* aimless unplanned progression; drift: пусти́ть де́ло на самотёк, to let matters take their course.

самотёком *adv.* **1,** (*of the movement of liquids*) by gravity. **2,** *fig.* spontaneously; on its own momentum.

самоуби́йство *n.* suicide: поко́нчить жизнь самоуби́йством, to commit suicide. —самоуби́йственный, *adj.* suicidal.

самоуби́йца *n.m. & f.* person who has committed suicide.

самоуваже́ние *n.* self-respect; self-esteem.

самоуве́ренность *n.f.* **1,** cockiness. **2,** self-assuredness.

самоуве́ренный *adj.* **1,** too sure of oneself; cocky. **2,** (*of a look, tone, etc.*) confident; self-assured.

самоуничтоже́ние *n.* self-destruction.

самоуправле́ние *n.* **1,** self-government. **2,** self-management. —самоуправля́ющийся, *adj.* self-governing.

самоупра́вный *adj.* arbitrary. —самоупра́вство, *n.* arbitrariness.

самоучи́тель *n.m.* self-teaching manual.

самоу́чка [*gen. pl.* -чек] *n.m. & f., colloq.* self-taught person; self-educated person. Вы́учиться чему́-нибудь самоу́чкой, to teach oneself something.

самохва́льство *n., colloq.* boasting; self-congratulation.

самохо́дка [*gen. pl.* -док] *n., colloq.* self-propelled gun.

самохо́дный *adj.* self-propelled.

самоцве́т *n.* semiprecious stone. —самоцве́тный, *adj.* semiprecious.

самоце́ль *n.f.* end in itself.

самочи́нный *adj.* **1,** arbitrary. **2,** done on one's own initiative. —самочи́нно, *adv.* on one's own.

самочу́вствие *n.* general physical and mental state: Как ва́ше самочу́вствие?, how are you feeling (in general)?

самура́й *n.* samurai.

самши́т *n.* box tree.

са́мый *adj.* **1,** the very: до са́мого конца́, to the very end. **2,** *in* тот са́мый *or* тот же са́мый, the same: тот са́мый челове́к, кото́рый..., the same person that... **3,** *used in forming superlatives:* са́мый ва́жный вопро́с, the most important question. **4,** *in* са́мое бо́льшее, the most; at (the) most: са́мое по́зднее, at the latest.

сан *n.* rank; title. —посвяща́ть в духо́вный сан, to ordain (*as a clergyman*).

санато́рий *n.* sanitarium; sanatorium.

сангвини́ческий *adj.* excitable; mercurial.

санда́л *n.* sandalwood.

санда́лия *n.* sandal.

санда́ловый *adj.* sandalwood.

са́ни [*gen.* **сане́й**; *dat.* **саня́м**] *n.pl.* sleigh; sled.

санита́р *n.* **1,** hospital attendant. **2,** *mil.* medical orderly. **3,** [*also*, **санита́р-носи́льщик**] stretcher-bearer.

санита́рия *n.* sanitation.

санита́рный *adj.* **1,** sanitary: санита́рное состоя́ние, sanitary conditions. **2,** *mil.* medical: санита́рный батальо́н, medical battalion. —**санита́рное су́дно**, hospital ship. —**санита́рная су́мка**, *mil.* first-aid kit.

са́нки [*gen.* **са́нок**] *n.pl.*, *colloq.* sled; sleigh.

санкциони́ровать *v.impfv. & pfv.* [*pres.* **-рую, -руешь**] to sanction.

са́нкция *n.* **1,** sanction; approval. **2,** *pl.* sanctions.

са́нный *adj.* sled (*attrib.*); sleigh (*attrib.*).

санови́тый *adj.* = **сано́вный.**

сано́вник *n.* dignitary; high official.

сано́вный *adj.* **1,** high-ranking; distinguished. **2,** stately; dignified.

санскри́т *n.* Sanskrit. —**санскри́тский**, *adj.* Sanskrit.

сантигра́мм *n.* centigram.

санти́м *n.* centime.

сантиме́нты [*gen.* **-тов**] *n.pl.*, *colloq.* sentimentality.

сантиме́тр *n.* **1,** centimeter. **2,** tape measure.

сап *n.* glanders.

са́па *n.*, *mil.* trench. —**ти́хой са́пой**, on the sly.

сапёр *n.*, *mil.* sapper. —**сапёрный**, *adj.* of or used by a sapper.

сапо́г [*gen.* **сапога́**; *gen. pl.* **сапо́г**] *n.* boot.

сапо́жник *n.* shoemaker.

сапо́жный *adj.* shoe (*attrib.*).

сапса́н *n.* peregrine falcon.

сапфи́р *n.* sapphire. —**сапфи́рный; сапфи́ровый**, *adj.* sapphire.

сара́й *n.* shed. —**дровяно́й сара́й**, woodshed. —**каре́тный сара́й**, coach house. —**ло́дочный сара́й**, boathouse.

саранча́ *n.* **1,** locusts. **2,** a (single) locust.

сарафа́н *n.* **1,** *pre-rev.* peasant woman's dress. **2,** sleeveless dress.

сарде́лька [*gen. pl.* **-лек**] *n.* small sausage.

сарди́на *n.* sardine. *Also*, **сарди́нка.**

сардони́ческий *adj.* sardonic.

са́ржа *n.* serge. —**са́ржевый**, *adj.* serge.

са́ри *n.neut. indecl.* sari.

сарка́зм *n.* sarcasm.

саркасти́ческий *adj.* sarcastic. —**саркасти́чески**, *adv.* sarcastically.

саркофа́г *n.* sarcophagus.

сары́ч [*gen.* **сарыча́**] *n.* buzzard.

сатана́ *n.* Satan. —**сатани́нский**, *adj.* satanic.

сателли́т *n.* satellite.

сати́н *n.* sateen. —**сати́новый**, *adj.* sateen.

сати́р *n.* satyr.

сати́ра *n.* satire. —**сати́рик**, *n.* satirist. —**сатири́ческий**, *adj.* satirical.

сатра́п *n.* satrap. —**сатра́пия**, *n.* satrapy.

Сату́рн *n.* Saturn.

са́уна *n.* sauna.

сафло́р *n.* safflower.

сафья́н *n.* morocco; morocco leather. —**сафья́нный; сафья́новый**, *adj.* morocco.

са́хар *n.* sugar.

сахари́н *n.* saccharin.

са́харистый *adj.* containing sugar; rich in sugar.

са́харница *n.* sugar bowl.

са́харный *adj.* **1,** sugar (*attrib.*). **2,** *fig.* sugary; honeyed. —**са́харная боле́знь**, diabetes. —**са́харная голова́**, sugar loaf. —**са́харный заво́д**, sugar refinery. —**са́харный песо́к**, granulated sugar. —**са́харная пу́дра**, powdered sugar. —**са́харная свёкла**, sugar beet. —**са́харный тростни́к**, sugar cane.

сахаро́за *n.* sucrose.

сачо́к [*gen.* **сачка́**] *n.* net with a hoop on a long handle.

сба́вить [*infl.* **сба́влю, сба́вишь**] *v.*, *pfv. of* **сбавля́ть.**

сба́вка *n.*, *colloq.* reduction.

сбавля́ть *v.impfv.* [*pfv.* **сба́вить**] **1,** to take off (a certain amount from a price). **2,** to reduce (a price, speed, etc.). —**сбавля́ть вес** *or* **в ве́се**, to lose weight.

сбаланси́рованный *adj.* balanced.

сбаланси́ровать *v.pfv.* [*infl.* **-рую, -руешь**] **1,** *pfv. of* **баланси́ровать**. **2,** to regain one's balance.

сбе́гать *v.pfv.*, *colloq.* **1,** to run (*somewhere and return*). **2,** (*with* за + *instr.*) to run and fetch.

сбега́ть *v.impfv.* [*pfv.* **сбежа́ть**] **1,** (*with* с + *gen. or* по) to run down. Сбежа́ть вниз, to run downstairs; run below. **2,** to run away; escape. **3,** (*of a river, tears, etc.*) to run down; flow down. **4,** to disappear; fade (*from one's face*). **5,** (*with* с + *gen.*) *colloq.* to skip; fail to show up for. —**сбега́ться**, *refl.* (*of many people*) to come running.

сбежа́ть [*infl. like* **бежа́ть**] *v.*, *pfv. of* **сбега́ть.** —**сбежа́ться**, *refl.*, *pfv. of* **сбега́ться.**

сберега́тельный *adj.* savings (*attrib.*). —**сберега́тельный банк**; **сберега́тельная ка́сса**, savings bank. —**сберега́тельная кни́жка**, bankbook; passbook.

сберега́ть *v.impfv.* [*pfv.* **сбере́чь**] **1,** to guard; protect. **2,** to save; conserve. **3,** to put aside (*for future use*).

сбереже́ние *n.* **1,** (*with gen.*) care (of); conservation (of). **2,** *pl.* savings.

сбере́чь [*infl. like* **бере́чь**] *v.*, *pfv. of* **сберега́ть.**

сберка́сса *n.* savings bank (*contr. of* **сберега́тельная ка́сса**).

сберкни́жка [*gen. pl.* **-жек**] *n.* bankbook; passbook (*contr. of* **сберега́тельная кни́жка**).

сбива́ть *v.impfv.* [*pfv.* **сбить**] **1,** to knock off: сбить (кого́-нибудь) с ног, to knock off one's feet; knock down. **2,** to shoot down. **3,** to throw off; disconcert. **4,** to knock together. **5,** to wear down (shoes, heels, etc.). **6,** to reduce; bring down. **7,** to churn (butter); whip (cream, eggs, etc.). —**сбива́ть с пути́**, to lead astray. —**сбива́ть с то́лку**, to confuse.

сбива́ться *v.r.impfv.* [*pfv.* **сби́ться**] **1,** to slip to one side; slip out of position. **2,** to become confused; be disconcerted. **3,** to be off; be wrong. **4,** (*with* с + *gen.*) to lose; be thrown off: сбива́ться со сле́да, to lose the trail; be thrown off the trail. **5,** (*of footwear*) to become worn down. **6,** to crowd together; huddle together. —**сбива́ться с ног,** to be exhausted; be falling off one's feet. —**сбива́ться с ноги́,** to break step. —**сбива́ться с пути́,** to go astray; lose one's way. —**сбива́ться с то́лку,** to become confused.

сби́вчивый *adj.* **1,** confusing; muddled. **2,** inconsistent; contradictory.

сби́тый *adj.* **1,** damaged; battered. **2,** (*of shoes, a road, etc.*) worn down. —**кре́пко сби́тый,** (*of a person*) solidly built.

сбить [*infl.* **собью́, собьёшь**] *v., pfv. of* **сбива́ть.** —**сби́ться,** *refl., pfv. of* **сбива́ться.**

сближа́ть *v.impfv.* [*pfv.* **сбли́зить**] to draw together; bring closer together. —**сближа́ться,** *refl.* **1,** to draw nearer; come closer together. **2,** (*with* **с** + *instr.*) to become close friends (with).

сближе́ние *n.* **1,** coming together; drawing together. **2,** rapprochement. **3,** *mil.* approach; closing in. **4,** *obs.* resemblance.

сбли́зить [*infl.* **-жу, -зишь**] *v., pfv. of* **сближа́ть.** —**сбли́зиться,** *refl., pfv. of* **сближа́ться.**

сбой *n., colloq.* **1,** malfunction: **дава́ть сбо́и,** to malfunction. **2,** *sports* breaking stride.

сбо́ку *adv.* **1,** from the side; from one side. **2,** on the side; on one side. —*prep., with gen.* beside; alongside.

сболтну́ть *v.pfv., colloq.* to blurt out.

сбор *n.* **1,** collection: **сбор по́дписей,** collection of signatures. **Сбор средств,** fund raising. **2,** gathering. **3,** *often pl., theat.* box-office receipts. Де́лать по́лные сбо́ры, to play to packed houses. **4,** duty; toll; levy. **5,** meeting; gathering; assembly. **6,** *mil.* muster. **7,** short course of instruction. **8,** *pl.* preparations (*for a trip*). —**в сбо́ре,** present; on hand.

сбо́рище *n., colloq.* gathering; crowd.

сбо́рка [*gen. pl.* **-рок**] *n.* **1,** assembly; putting together. **2,** gather (*in clothing*).

сбо́рная *n., decl. as an adj.* = **сбо́рная кома́нда.**

сбо́рник *n.* collection; anthology.

сбо́рный *adj.* **1,** gathering (*attrib.*); meeting (*attrib.*); assembly (*attrib.*). **2,** mixed; combined; of various kinds. **3,** prefabricated. —**сбо́рная кома́нда,** combined team; all-star team.

сбо́рочный *adj.* assembly (*attrib.*).

сбо́рщик *n.* **1,** collector (*of taxes, signatures, etc.*). **2,** picker (*of cotton*). **3,** assembler; fitter.

сбра́сывать *v.impfv.* [*pfv.* **сбро́сить**] **1,** to throw off; throw down. **2,** to drop (bombs); dump (waste). **3,** (*with* **в** + *acc.*) *colloq.* to toss (into). **4,** *fig.* to overthrow. **5,** (*of an animal*) to shed. **6,** *fig.* to shake off (apathy, an illness, etc.). **7,** to reduce. **8,** *cards* to discard. **9,** *finance* to dump. —**сбра́сывать со счето́в,** to rule out; count out; discount; write off.

сбрива́ть *v.impfv.* [*pfv.* **сбрить**] to shave off.

сбрить [*infl.* **сбре́ю, сбре́ешь**] *v., pfv. of* **сбрива́ть.**

сброд *n., colloq.* rabble; riffraff.

сбро́сить [*infl.* **сбро́шу, сбро́сишь**] *v., pfv. of* **сбра́сывать.**

сбру́я *n.* harness.

сбыва́ть *v.impfv.* [*pfv.* **сбыть**] **1,** to sell; market. **2,** to get rid of. Сбыва́ть с рук, to get off one's hands. **3,** *v.i.* (*of rising waters*) to recede. —**сбыва́ться,** *refl.* to come true; be realized.

сбыт *n.* sale. Име́ть хоро́ший сбыт, to have a ready market.

сбыть [*infl. like* **быть**] *v., pfv. of* **сбыва́ть.** —**сбы́ться,** *refl.* [*past* **сбы́лся, сбыла́сь, сбыло́сь, сбыли́сь**] *refl., pfv. of* **сбыва́ться.**

сва́дебный *adj.* wedding (*attrib.*).

сва́дьба [*gen. pl.* **-деб**] *n.* wedding.

сва́йный *adj.* built on piles.

сва́ливать *v.impfv.* [*pfv.* **свали́ть**] **1,** to knock down. **2,** to throw down; (*with* **на** + *acc.*) dump (on). **3,** to toss together; toss into a pile. **4,** *colloq.* to overthrow. **5,** *fig.* to throw off; cast off. **6,** (*with* **на** + *acc.*) *colloq.* to shift; dump (work, blame, etc.) on(to) someone else. **7,** (*with* **на** + *acc.*) *colloq.* to blame (something) on. **8,** *colloq.* (*of sleep*) to overcome; (*of an illness*) to strike. **9,** *v.i., colloq.* (*of a large crowd*) to depart. **10,** *v.i., colloq.* to abate. —**сва́ливаться,** *refl.* **1,** to fall. **2,** to collapse; come tumbling down. **3,** *colloq.* to lean; tilt. **4,** *colloq.* to appear from nowhere. **5,** *colloq.* to fall ill. **6,** (*of cattle*) to die.

свали́ть [*infl.* **свалю́, сва́лишь**] *v., pfv. of* **вали́ть**[1] *and* **сва́ливать.** —**свали́ться,** *refl., pfv. of* **вали́ться** *and* **сва́ливаться.**

сва́лка [*gen. pl.* **-лок**] *n.* **1,** dump; dumping ground. **2,** *colloq.* brawl; scuffle.

сваля́ть *v., pfv. of* **валя́ть** (*in sense #3*).

сва́ра *n.* quarrel; row.

сва́ривать *v.impfv.* [*pfv.* **свари́ть**] to weld together.

свари́ть [*infl.* **сварю́, сва́ришь**] *v., pfv. of* **вари́ть** *and* **сва́ривать.** —**свари́ться,** *refl., pfv. of* **вари́ться.**

сва́рка *n.* welding.

сварли́вый *adj.* quarrelsome; cantankerous.

сварно́й *adj.* welded.

сва́рочный *adj.* welding (*attrib.*). —**сва́рочное желе́зо,** wrought iron.

сва́рщик *n.* welder.

сва́стика *n.* swastika.

сват *n.* **1,** matchmaker. **2,** father of one's son-in-law or daughter-in-law.

сва́тать *v.impfv.* [*pfv.* **посва́тать** *or* **сосва́тать**] **1,** to match up; arrange a match for; (*with dat. or* **за** + *acc.*) match (someone) up with. **2,** to propose to; ask for one's hand; request permission to marry. —**сва́таться,** *refl.* [*pfv.* **посва́таться**] (*with* **за** + *acc. or* **к**) to propose to.

сватовство́ *n.* matchmaking.

сва́тья [*gen. pl.* **сва́тий**] *n.* mother of one's son-in-law or daughter-in-law.

сва́ха *n.* matchmaker.

свая́ *n.* pile: **мост на сва́ях,** bridge on piles.

све́дение *n.* **1,** *usu. pl.* information. **2,** *pl.* knowledge. —**доводи́ть до (чьего́-нибудь) све́дения,** to inform; bring to the attention of: Довожу́ до ва́шего све́дения, I beg to inform you. —**доходи́ть до (чьего́-нибудь) све́дения,** to come to the attention of. —**к ва́шему све́дению,** for your information. —**принима́ть к све́дению,** *see* **принима́ть.**

сведе́ние *n.* **1,** leading down; leading away. **2,** joining together; bringing together. **3,** removal (*of stains*). **4,** reduction; squaring; reconciling. Сведе́ние счето́в, settling of scores. **5,** cramp.

све́дущий *adj.* knowledgeable; well-versed.

свеже- *prefix* freshly: свежевы́печенный, freshly baked.

свежева́ть *v.impfv.* [*pfv.* освежева́ть; *pres.* -жу́ю, -жу́ешь] to skin; dress (an animal).

све́жесть *n.f.* **1,** freshness. **2,** cool air. —не пе́рвой све́жести, **1,** not very fresh. **2,** (*of clothes*) not very clean.

свеже́ть *v.impfv.* [*pfv.* посвеже́ть] **1,** to become cool; become chilly; cool off. **2,** (*of a person*) to take on a healthy color.

све́жий *adj.* [*short form* свеж, свежа́, свежо́, све́жи *or* свежи́] **1,** fresh. **2,** cool; chilly. Здесь свежо́, it is chilly in here. **3,** the latest: све́жий но́мер, the latest issue. —на све́жую го́лову, with a fresh mind. —на све́жую па́мять, while (something is) still fresh in one's mind. —со све́жими си́лами, with renewed vigor.

свезти́ *v.pfv.* [*infl. like* везти́] **1,** *pfv. of* свози́ть. **2,** to take; drive (to a certain place). **3,** *colloq.* to take; drive (to and back).

свёкла *n.* **1,** beets. **2,** a (single) beet.

свекло́вица *n.* sugar beet. —свекло́ви́чный, *adj.* beet (*attrib.*); sugar-beet (*attrib.*); beet-sugar (*attrib.*).

свеклоса́харный *adj.* beet-sugar (*attrib.*).

свеко́льник *n.* **1,** beet soup. **2,** beet tops.

свеко́льный *adj.* **1,** beet (*attrib.*). **2,** beet-colored.

свёкор [*gen.* -кра] *n.* father-in-law (*husband's father*).

свекро́вь *n.f.* mother-in-law (*husband's mother*).

сверга́ть *v.impfv.* [*pfv.* све́ргнуть] **1,** *obs.* to throw down. **2,** to overthrow; depose.

све́ргнуть [*past* сверг, све́ргла] *v., pfv. of* сверга́ть.

сверже́ние *n.* overthrow.

све́рить *v., pfv. of* сверя́ть. —све́риться, *refl., pfv. of* сверя́ться.

сверка́ние *n.* **1,** sparkle. **2,** glare.

сверка́ть *v.impfv.* [*pfv.* сверкну́ть] **1,** to sparkle; glitter; shine. **2,** (*of lightning*) to flash.

сверли́льный *adj.* boring (*attrib.*); drilling (*attrib.*).

сверли́ть *v.impfv.* **1,** [*pfv.* просверли́ть] to drill (a hole, tooth, etc.). **2,** [*pfv.* просверли́ть] to drill a hole in; bore through. **3,** *impers.* to cause a gnawing pain: У меня́ сверли́т в у́хе, I have a gnawing pain in my ear. **4,** *fig.* (*of a thought*) to gnaw at; weigh on one's mind. **5,** *in* сверли́ть (кого́-нибудь) глаза́ми *or* взгля́дом, to stare right through (someone).

сверло́ [*pl.* свёрла] *n.* drill (*tool*).

сверля́щий *adj.* **1,** (*of a pain*) gnawing. **2,** (*of a sound*) shrill; piercing.

сверну́ть *v., pfv. of* свёртывать *and* свора́чивать. —сверну́ться, *refl., pfv. of* свёртываться.

сверста́ть *v., pfv. of* верста́ть.

све́рстник *n.* person one's own age; contemporary; peer.

свёрток [*gen.* -тка] *n.* **1,** roll (*of paper, material, etc.*). **2,** package.

свёртывание *n.* **1,** rolling up. **2,** curtailment. **3,** coagulation.

свёртывать *v.impfv.* [*pfv.* сверну́ть] **1,** to roll up. **2,** to curtail; cut back. **3,** *in* сверну́ть ше́ю (+ *dat.*), to wring someone's neck; сверну́ть себе́ ше́ю, to break one's neck; get killed. —свёртываться, *refl.* **1,** to roll up; curl up. **2,** to congeal; curdle; coagulate. **3,** to be reduced; be cut back.

сверх *prep., with gen.* **1,** over. **2,** in addition to; over and above; in excess of. **3,** *fig.* beyond: сверх сил, beyond one's strength; сверх вся́кого ожида́ния, beyond all expectations. —сверх всего́, on top of everything (else). —сверх того́, moreover; furthermore.

сверх- *prefix* super-.

сверхдержа́ва *n.* superpower.

сверхзвуково́й *adj.* supersonic.

сверхпри́быль *n.f.* excess profits.

сверхпроводи́мость *n.f.* superconductivity.

сверхпроводни́к [*gen.* -ника́] *n.* superconductor.

сверхсро́чный *adj.* **1,** additional; extra: сверхсро́чная слу́жба, additional time in service. **2,** *colloq.* extremely urgent.

све́рху *adv.* **1,** from above; from the top. **2,** on top. —све́рху до́низу, from top to bottom.

сверхуро́чный *adj.* overtime (*attrib.*). —сверхуро́чно, *adv.* overtime: рабо́тать сверхуро́чно, to work overtime. —сверхуро́чные, *n.pl.* overtime (pay).

сверхчелове́к *n.* superman. —сверхчелове́ческий, *adj.* superhuman.

сверхчувстви́тельный *adj.* supersensitive.

сверхшта́тный *adj.* supernumerary.

сверхъесте́ственный *adj.* supernatural.

сверчо́к [*gen.* -чка́] *n.* cricket (*insect*).

сверша́ть *v.impfv.* [*pfv.* сверши́ть] = соверша́ть.

сверя́ть *v.impfv.* [*pfv.* све́рить] to check; compare; collate. —сверя́ться, *refl.* (*with* с + *instr. or* по + *dat.*) *colloq.* to check.

све́сить *v.pfv.* [*infl.* све́шу, све́сишь] **1,** *pfv. of* све́шивать. **2,** *colloq.* to weigh. —све́ситься, *refl., pfv. of* све́шиваться.

свести́ [*infl. like* вести́] *v., pfv. of* своди́ть. —свести́сь, *refl., pfv. of* своди́ться.

свет[1] [*2nd loc.* свету́] *n.* light. —в све́те (+ *gen.*), in (the) light of. —при све́те (+ *gen.*), by the light of. —чуть свет, at the crack of dawn.

свет[2] *n.* **1,** world. **2,** society: вы́сший свет, high society. —ни за что на све́те, not for (anything in) the world. —тот свет, the next (*or* other) world. —вы́йти в свет, to come out; be published. —появи́ться на свет, to come into the world; be born. —производи́ть на свет, to bring into the world. —увидеть свет, **1,** to see the light of day; be published. **2,** = появи́ться на свет.

света́ть *v.impfv., impers.* to dawn: Света́ет, day is dawning; day is breaking; it is getting light.

свети́ло *n.* **1,** heavenly body. **2,** *fig.* luminary.

свети́льник *n.* **1,** (electric) lamp. **2,** oil lamp. **3,** candlestick.

свети́ть *v.impfv.* [*pres.* свечу́, све́тишь] **1,** (*of the sun, moon, etc.*) to shine. **2,** [*pfv.* посвети́ть] (*with instr.*) to shine (a light); (*with dat.*) shine a light on; hold up a light for. —**свети́ться**, *refl.* **1**, (*of lights, stars, one's eyes, etc.*) to shine. **2**, *fig.* (*of a person*) to be (all) aglow.

светле́ть *v.impfv.* [*pfv.* **посветле́ть** *or* **просветле́ть**] **1**, to brighten (up); become bright. **2**, [*impfv. only*] (*of anything bright*) to be visible; appear.

светло́ *adj., used predicatively*, light: Уже́ светло́, it is already light.

светло- *prefix, used with colors*, light: светло-зелёный, light green.

светловоло́сый *adj.* light haired; fair-haired.

све́тлость *n.f.* **1**, lightness; brightness. **2**, (*with ва́ша, его́, её, etc.*) lordship; grace: ва́ша све́тлость, your lordship; your grace.

све́тлый *adj.* **1**, light. **2**, bright. **3**, *fig.* lucid: све́тлый ум, lucid mind. **4**, *fig.* (*of memories, moments, etc.*) happy. —**све́тлой па́мяти**, of blessed memory.

светля́к [*gen.* **-ляка́**] *n.* firefly; lightning bug.

светлячо́к [*gen.* **-чка́**] *n.* = **светля́к**.

светово́й *adj.* **1**, light (*attrib.*). **2**, illuminated: свето-вая рекла́ма, illuminated sign; electric sign. —**свето-во́й год**, light year.

светомаскиро́вка *n.* blackout.

светонепроница́емый *adj.* lightproof.

светопреставле́ние *n.* the end of the world.

светофо́р *n.* traffic light.

све́точ *n.* **1**, *obs.* torch. **2**, *fig.* (*with gen.*) torch (of): све́точ и́стины, the torch of truth. **3**, *fig.* luminary; leading light.

светочувстви́тельный *adj., photog.* sensitive to light.

све́тский *adj.* **1**, secular; lay. **2**, worldly. **3**, refined; polite.

светя́щийся *adj.* luminous; luminescent.

свеча́ [*pl.* **све́чи, свече́й, свеча́м**] *n.* **1**, candle. При све́те свечи́; при свеча́х, by candlelight. **2**, (unit of) candlepower. **3**, *in* запа́льная свеча́, spark plug. **4**, suppository. —**игра́ не сто́ит свеч**, the game is not worth the candle.

свече́ние *n.* **1**, luminescence. **2**, fluorescence. **3**, phosphorescence.

све́чка [*gen. pl.* **-чек**] *n.* **1**, candle. **2**, suppository.

свечно́й *adj.* candle (*attrib.*).

све́шать *v., pfv. of* **ве́шать** (*in sense #3*).

све́шивать *v.impfv.* [*pfv.* **све́сить**] **1**, to let hang down; let dangle. **2**, to lower. —**све́шиваться**, *refl.* **1**, to hang down; dangle. **2**, to droop. **3**, *colloq.* (*with* из) to lean out of; (*with* че́рез) to lean over.

свива́льник *n.* swaddling clothes.

свива́ть *v.impfv.* [*pfv.* **свить**] **1**, to twist. **2**, to weave. **3**, to roll; roll up. **4**, to unwind. **5**, [*impfv. only*] to swaddle. —**свива́ться**, *refl.* to roll up.

свида́ние *n.* **1**, appointment; date. **2**, visit (*with a prisoner, patient, etc.*). —**до свида́ния!**, goodbye! —**до ско́рого свида́ния!**, see you soon!

свиде́тель *n.m.* witness.

свиде́тельство *n.* **1**, evidence. **2**, testimony. **3**, certificate; license: свиде́тельство о рожде́нии, birth certificate; бра́чное свиде́тельство, marriage license.

свиде́тельствовать *v.impfv.* [*pres.* **-ствую, -ствуешь**] **1**, to testify; give evidence. **2**, (*with* о) to attest to; be evidence of; bear witness to.

свина́рник *n.* pigpen; pigsty.

свине́ц [*gen.* **-нца́**] *n.* lead.

свини́на *n.* pork.

сви́нка [*gen. pl.* **-нок**] *n.* **1**, little pig. **2**, mumps. —**морска́я сви́нка**, guinea pig.

свино́й *adj.* **1**, pig (*attrib.*). **2**, hog (*attrib.*). **2**, pork (*attrib.*).

свинома́тка [*gen. pl.* **-ток**] *n.* sow (*pig*).

свинопа́с *n.* swineherd.

сви́нский *adj., colloq.* swinish.

сви́нство *n., colloq.* **1**, squalor; filth. **2**, despicable act.

свинти́ть [*infl.* **-чу́, -ти́шь**] *v., pfv. of* **свинчивать**.

свинцо́вый *adj.* **1**, lead (*attrib.*). **2**, leaden; dull gray. —**свинцо́вые бели́ла**, white lead. —**свинцо́вый блеск**, galena. — **свинцо́вый су́рик**, red lead.

сви́нчивать *v.impfv.* [*pfv.* **свинти́ть**] **1**, to screw together. **2**, *colloq.* to unscrew.

свинья́ [*pl.* **сви́ньи, свине́й, сви́ньям**] *n.* **1**, pig; hog; swine. **2**, *in* морска́я свинья́, porpoise. —**под-ложи́ть свинью́** (+ *dat.*), to play a dirty trick on.

свире́ль *n.f.* reed (*primitive musical instrument*).

свирепе́ть *v.impfv.* [*pfv.* **рассвирепе́ть**] to become fierce; become violent.

свире́пость *n.f.* ferocity.

свире́пствовать *v.impfv.* [*pres.* **-ствую, -ствуешь**] **1**, to go on a rampage; wreak havoc. **2**, (*of a storm, fire, etc.*) to rage.

свире́пый *adj.* fierce; ferocious.

свиристе́ль *n.m.* waxwing (*bird*).

свиса́ть *v.impfv.* [*pfv.* **сви́снуть**] to hang down; droop.

сви́снуть [*past* свис, сви́сла] *v., pfv. of* **свиса́ть**.

свист *n.* **1**, whistle; whistling. **2**, hiss; hissing.

свиста́ть *v.impfv.* [*pres.* **свищу́, сви́щешь**] = **свисте́ть**.

свисте́ть *v.impfv.* [*pfv.* **сви́стнуть**; *pres.* **свищу́, свисти́шь**] **1**, to whistle. **2**, to hiss.

свисто́к [*gen.* **-стка́**] *n.* whistle (*instrument or sound*).

свистопля́ска *n., colloq.* bedlam; chaos.

свисту́лька [*gen. pl.* **-лек**] *n., colloq.* whistle; tin whistle.

свисту́н [*gen.* **-туна́**] *n., colloq.* whistler (*one who whistles*).

свистя́щий *adj. & n.* sibilant.

сви́та *n.* suite; retinue.

сви́тер (тэ) *n.* sweater.

сви́ток [*gen.* **-тка**] *n.* **1**, roll. **2**, scroll.

свить [*infl.* **совью́, совьёшь**; *past fem.* свила́] *v., pfv. of* **вить** *and* **свива́ть**. —**сви́ться**, *refl., pfv. of* **свива́ться**.

свихну́ть *v.pfv., colloq.* to dislocate. —**свихну́ться**, *refl., colloq.* **1**, to go mad; go nuts. **2**, to go astray.

свищ [*gen.* свища́] *n.* **1**, knothole. **2**, *med.* fistula.

свия́зь *n.f.* widgeon (*duck*).

свобо́да *n.* freedom; liberty. —**на свобо́де, 1**, at liberty; at large. **2**, at one's leisure. —**выпуска́ть** *or* **отпуска́ть на свобо́ду**, to set free.

свобо́дно *adv.* **1**, freely. **2**, easily. **3**, loosely. **4**, fluently. **5**, in a relaxed manner. —*adj., used predicatively*, unoccupied: Здесь свобо́дно?, is this seat taken?

свобо́дный *adj.* [*short form* **-ден, -дна, -дно, -дны**] **1**, free. **2**, vacant; unoccupied. **3**, loose. **4**, (*of time*) spare; free. **5**, free and easy; relaxed.

свободолюби́вый *adj.* freedom-loving. —**свободолюбие,** *n.* love of freedom.

свободомы́слие *n.* free thought.

свободомы́слящий *adj.* freethinking. —*n.* freethinker.

свод *n.* **1,** code: свод зако́нов, code of laws. **2,** *archit.* arch. **3,** arch (*of the foot*). —**небе́сный свод,** the firmament.

своди́ть[1] *v.impfv.* [*pfv.* **свести́**; *pres.* **свожу́, сво́дишь**] **1,** to lead down; take down; help (someone) down. **2,** to take (a person somewhere on foot). **3,** to lead away. **4,** to join; tie together. **5,** *fig.* to bring together. **6,** to remove (a stain, wart, etc.). **7,** (*with* **на** + *acc. or* **к** *or* **до**) to reduce: своди́ть к ми́нимуму, to reduce to a minimum. **8,** (*with* **в** + *acc.*) to incorporate (into): своди́ть в табли́цу, to tabulate. **9,** to square; settle: своди́ть счёты с, to settle scores with. **10,** *fig.* to turn; switch (a conversation, one's thoughts, etc.). **11,** to cramp. *Also impers.* У меня́ свело́ но́гу, I have a cramp in my leg. —**не своди́ть глаз с** (+ *gen.*), not take one's eyes off... —**своди́ть в моги́лу,** to be the death of. —**своди́ть концы́ с конца́ми,** to make ends meet. —**своди́ть на нет,** to negate; nullify. —**своди́ть с ума́,** to drive mad; drive crazy; drive out of one's mind.

своди́ть[2] *v.pfv.* [*infl.* **свожу́, сво́дишь**] to take to and back; lead to and back.

своди́ться *v.r.impfv.* [*pfv.* **свести́сь**; *pres.* **сво́дится**] to come (down) to: своди́ться на нет *or* к нулю́, to come to naught. Всё де́ло сво́дится к э́тому, the whole thing comes (*or* boils) down to this.

сво́дка [*gen. pl.* **-док**] *n.* summary. Сво́дка пого́ды, weather report; weather forecast.

сво́дник *n.* procurer; pimp.

сво́дничать *v.impfv.* to pander.

сво́дничество *n.* procuring.

сво́дный *adj.* combined; consolidated; composite. —**сво́дный брат, 1,** stepbrother. **2,** half brother. —**сво́дная сестра́, 1,** stepsister. **2,** half sister.

сво́дчатый *adj.* arched; vaulted.

своево́лие *n.* high-handedness.

своево́льный *adj.* strong-willed; headstrong.

своевре́менный *adj.* timely; opportune. —**своевре́менно,** *adv.* in time. —**своевре́менность,** *n.f.* timeliness.

своекоры́стие *n.* self-interest. —**своекоры́стный,** *adj.* self-seeking.

своенра́вие *n.* high-handedness. —**своенра́вный,** *adj.* strong-willed; headstrong.

своеобра́зие *n.* distinctive quality.

своеобра́зный *adj.* distinctive; singular; peculiar.

свози́ть[1] *v.impfv.* [*pfv.* **свезти́**; *pres.* **свожу́, сво́зишь**] **1,** to gather together (*in one place*). **2,** to drive down. **3,** to take away; cart away. *See also* **свезти́.**

свози́ть[2] *v.pfv.* [*infl.* **свожу́, сво́зишь**] to drive; take (someone) to and back.

свой [*infl. like* **мой**] *poss. adj. & pron.,* used when the possessor is the subject of the sentence. **1,** one's; my; his; her; their: снять свою́ шля́пу, to take off one's hat. **2,** one's own: У них своя́ маши́на, they have

their own car. —**свои́,** *n.pl.* one's own people. —**брать своё, 1,** to succeed; prevail. **2,** to take its toll. —**доби́ться своего́,** to gain one's objective; get one's way. —**наста́ивать на своём,** to insist on having one's own way. —**настоя́ть на своём,** to have one's own way. —**оста́ться при свои́х,** to break even (*in gambling*). —**получи́ть своё,** to get one's just reward. —**стоя́ть на своём,** to stand one's ground.

сво́йственник *n.* relative by marriage; in-law.

сво́йственный *adj.* (*with dat.*) characteristic: со сво́йственным ему́ ю́мором, with his characteristic humor. Челове́ку сво́йственно ошиба́ться, to err is human. Исто́рии сво́йственно повторя́ться, history always repeats itself; history is destined to repeat itself.

сво́йство *n.* property; attribute; characteristic.

свойство́ *n.* relationship by marriage. —**быть** *or* **состоя́ть в свойстве́ с** (+ *instr.*), to be related by marriage to.

свола́кивать *v.impfv.* [*pfv.* **своло́чь**] *colloq.* to drag; drag off; drag down.

сво́лочь *n.f., vulg.* **1,** riffraff; rabble. **2,** swine; scoundrel.

своло́чь [*infl. like* **волочь**] *v., pfv. of* **свола́кивать.**

сво́ра *n.* **1,** leash. **2,** pack (*of dogs, wolves, etc.*). **3,** gang.

свора́чивать *v.impfv.* [*pfv.* **сверну́ть**] **1,** *v.i.* to turn: свора́чивать с доро́ги/ в переу́лок/, to turn off the road/ down a side street/. **2,** *v.t., colloq.* to turn: свора́чивать маши́ну нале́во, to turn a car to the left.

своя́к [*gen.* **свояка́**] *n.* brother-in-law (*wife's sister's husband*).

своя́ченица *n.* sister-in-law (*wife's sister*).

свыка́ться *v.r.impfv.* [*pfv.* **свы́кнуться**] (*with* **с** + *instr.*) to get used to.

свы́кнуться [*past* **свы́кся, свы́клась**] *v.r., pfv. of* **свыка́ться.**

свысока́ *adv.* **1,** *obs.* from on high. **2,** with disdain. Смотре́ть на (+ *acc.*) свысока́, to look down on. Говори́ть с (+ *instr.*) свысока́, to talk down to.

свы́ше *adv.* from above; from on high. —*prep., with gen.* **1,** over; more than. **2,** beyond: свы́ше мои́х сил, beyond me; more than I can handle.

свя́занный *adj.* **1,** related; connected. **2,** (*of movements*) awkward; (*of speech*) halting. *See also* **свя́зывать** (*sense #5*).

связа́ть [*infl.* **свяжу́, свя́жешь**] *v., pfv. of* **вяза́ть** *and* **свя́зывать.** —**связа́ться,** *refl., pfv. of* **свя́зываться.**

связи́ст *n.* **1,** *mil.* signalman. **2,** telephone or telegraph worker.

свя́зка [*gen. pl.* **-зок**] *n.* **1,** bunch; bundle. **2,** ligament. —**глаго́л-свя́зка,** linking verb. —**голосовы́е свя́зки,** vocal cords.

связно́й *adj.* liaison (*attrib.*); communications (*attrib.*). —*n.* messenger.

свя́зный *adj.* coherent. —**свя́зность,** *n.f.* coherence.

связу́ющий *adj.* connecting.

свя́зывать *v.impfv.* [*pfv.* **связа́ть**] **1,** to tie; bind; tie up; tie together. **2,** to connect; link; join. **3,** (*with* **с** + *instr.*) to put in touch (with). **4,** *fig.* to bind: свя́зан обеща́нием, bound by a promise; свя́зан расписа́-

нием, bound by (*or* tied to) a schedule. Судьба́ их связа́ла, fate bound them together. **5,** *past passive part. only,* A, to connect; associate: всё, что свя́зано с э́тим, everything connected/associated/having to do/ with it. B, (*with* **с** + *instr.*) to involve; entail: Э́то свя́зано с ри́ском, it involves/entails risk. —**связа́ть свою́ судьбу́ с,** to cast one's lot with. —**связа́ть по рука́м и нога́м, 1,** to bind hand and foot. **2,** *fig.* to tie someone's hands. —**свя́зывать ру́ки** (+ *dat.*), to tie someone's hands.

свя́зываться *v.r.impfv.* [*pfv.* **связа́ться**] (*with* **с** + *instr.*) **1,** to contact; get in touch with. **2,** *colloq.* to get involved (with).

связь *n.f.* **1,** connection. **2,** tie; link: торго́вые свя́зи, trade ties. **3,** contact; touch: потеря́ть связь с, to lose contact/touch with. **4,** (illicit) affair; liaison. **5,** communication(s). Почто́вая/телефо́нная связь, mail/ telephone service. **6,** *pl.* (personal) contacts; connections. **7,** coupling; tie. **8,** *mil.* liaison. —**в связи́ с** (+ *instr.*), **1,** in connection with. **2,** because of; owing to. —**в связи́ с э́тим, 1,** in this connection. **2,** as a result. —**в э́той связи́,** in this connection.

святе́йшество *n.* Holiness: его́ святе́йшество, His Holiness.

святи́лище *n.* **1,** temple; sanctuary. **2,** *fig.* revered place.

свя́тки [*gen.* -**ток**] *n.pl.* Yuletide; the period from Christmas through January 6th.

свя́то *adv.* **1,** as if sacred: свя́то чтить что́-нибудь, to hold something sacred. **2,** scrupulously: свя́то соблюда́ть что́-нибудь, to observe something scrupulously.

свято́й *adj.* holy; sacred. —*n.* saint. —**свята́я и́стина** *or* пра́вда, gospel truth. —**свята́я святы́х,** holy of holies.

свя́тость *n.f.* holiness; sanctity.

святота́тство *n.* sacrilege. —**святота́тственный,** *adj.* sacrilegious.

святота́тствовать *v.impfv.* [*pres.* -**ствую, -ствуешь**] to commit sacrilege.

свя́точный *adj.* Christmas (*attrib.*).

свято́ша *n.m. & f.* pious hypocrite.

свя́тцы [*gen.* -**цев**] *n.pl.* church calendar.

святы́ня *n.* sacred place; holy place.

свяще́нник *n.* **1,** priest. **2,** clergyman.

свяще́ннический *adj.* **1,** priestly; sacerdotal. **2,** clergyman's; clergy's.

свяще́нный *adj.* sacred; holy.

свяще́нство *n.* priesthood.

сгиб *n.* **1,** bend. **2,** crook (*in one's arm*).

сгиба́ть *v.impfv.* [*pfv.* **согну́ть**] to bend. —**сгиба́ться,** *refl.* **1,** (*of an object*) to bend. **2,** (*of a person*) to bend over.

сги́нуть *v.pfv., colloq.* to disappear; vanish.

сгла́дить [*infl.* -**жу, -дишь**] *v., pfv. of* **сгла́живать.**

сгла́живать *v.impfv.* [*pfv.* **сгла́дить**] **1,** to smooth; smooth out. **2,** to smooth out; smooth over; soften.

сгла́зить *v.pfv.* [*infl.* -**жу, -зишь**] to jinx; put a hex on; give (someone) the evil eye.

сглупи́ть *v.pfv.* [*infl.* -**плю́, -пи́шь**] *colloq.* to do or say something foolish.

сгнить *v., pfv. of* **гнить.**

сгнои́ть *v., pfv. of* **гнои́ть.**

сгова́риваться *v.r.impfv.* [*pfv.* **сговори́ться**] **1,** to arrange (to do something). Та́йно сговори́ться (+ *inf.*), to secretly conspire to... **2,** to reach an agreement: С ним тру́дно сговори́ться, it is hard to reach an agreement with him; he is hard to deal with.

сго́вор *n.* **1,** conspiracy. **2,** collusion. **3,** *obs.* agreement; understanding. **4,** *obs.* betrothal.

сговори́ться *v.r., pfv. of* **сгова́риваться.**

сгово́рчивый *adj.* amenable.

сгоня́ть *v.impfv.* [*pfv.* **согна́ть**] **1,** to drive away; drive off; chase away; chase off. **2,** to drive together; round up. **3,** to remove (freckles, wrinkles, etc.). **4,** *colloq.* to take off (weight).

сгора́ние *n.* combustion. —**дви́гатель вну́треннего сгора́ния,** internal-combustion engine.

сгора́ть *v.impfv.* [*pfv.* **сгоре́ть**] **1,** to burn (up); be burned (up); burn down. Сгоре́ть за́живо, to be burned alive; be burned to death. **2,** (*of fuel, firewood, etc.*) to be consumed. **3,** (*of vegetation*) to wither; shrivel. **4,** *fig.* to burn oneself out. **5,** *fig.* (*with* от *or* с + *gen.*) to be dying of (shame, curiosity, etc.).

сго́рбить *v., pfv. of* **го́рбить.** —**сго́рбиться,** *refl., pfv. of* **го́рбиться.**

сго́рбленный *adj.* hunched over.

сгоре́ть [*infl.* сгорю́, сгори́шь] *v., pfv. of* **сгора́ть.**

сгоряча́ *adv.* in the heat of the moment; in a fit of temper.

сгреба́ть *v.impfv.* [*pfv.* **сгрести́**] **1,** to rake together. **2,** to sweep off; brush off; shovel off.

сгрести́ [*infl. like* **грести́**] *v., pfv. of* **сгреба́ть.**

сгруди́ться *also,* **сгру́диться** *v.r.pfv., colloq.* to congregate; cluster.

сгружа́ть *v.impfv.* [*pfv.* **сгрузи́ть**] to unload.

сгрузи́ть [*infl.* сгружу́, сгру́зишь *or* сгрузи́шь] *v., pfv. of* **сгружа́ть.**

сгруппирова́ть *v., pfv. of* **группирова́ть.** —**сгруппирова́ться,** *refl., pfv. of* **группирова́ться.**

сгрыза́ть *v.impfv.* [*pfv.* **сгрызть**] to chew up.

сгрызть [*infl. like* **грызть**] *v., pfv. of* **сгрыза́ть.**

сгуби́ть *v.pfv.* [*infl.* сгублю́, сгу́бишь] *colloq.* to ruin.

сгусти́ть [*infl.* -щу́, -сти́шь] *v., pfv. of* **сгуща́ть.** —**сгусти́ться,** *refl., pfv. of* **сгуща́ться.**

сгу́сток [*gen.* -**стка**] *n.* **1,** clot: сгу́сток кро́ви, blood clot. **2,** *fig.* bundle: сгу́сток эне́ргии, bundle of energy.

сгуща́ть *v.impfv.* [*pfv.* **сгусти́ть**] **1,** to thicken; make thick. **2,** to condense. **3,** to clot; coagulate (blood). —**сгуща́ть кра́ски, 1,** to (grossly) exaggerate. **2,** to make things out to be worse than they are.

сгуща́ться *v.r.impfv.* [*pfv.* **сгусти́ться**] **1,** to thicken; condense. **2,** to clot; coagulate.

сгуще́ние *n.* **1,** thickening. **2,** clotting; coagulation.

сгущённый *adj., in* сгущённое молоко́, condensed milk; evaporated milk.

сда́бривать *v.impfv.* [*pfv.* **сдо́брить**] to season; flavor; spice.

сдава́ть *v.impfv.* [*pfv.* **сдать**; *pres.* сдаю́, сдаёшь] A, *v.t.* **1,** to hand in; turn in. **2,** to hand over; turn over. **3,** to put (in storage); check (in a coatroom, baggage room, etc.). **4,** to return; bring back. **5,** to rent; lease;

let. **6,** to surrender; give up. **7,** *cards* to deal. **8,** *in* сдава́ть экза́мен, to take an examination; сдать экза́мен, to pass an examination. **9,** *in* сдать пози́ции, to yield; give ground. **10,** *in* сдать темп *or* те́мпы, to slacken the pace. **B,** *v.i.* **1,** to weaken. **2,** to decline (*in health*); age. **3,** to break down; give out. **4,** (*of cold, heat, etc.*) to abate.

сдава́ться *v.r.impfv.* [*pfv.* сда́ться; *pres.* сдаю́сь, сдаёшься] **1,** to surrender; give up. **2,** (*in a game, esp. chess*) to resign. **3,** [*impfv. only*] to be for rent. **4,** [*impfv. only*] (*with dat.*) *colloq.* to seem; appear.

сдави́ть [*infl.* сдавлю́, сда́вишь] *v., pfv. of* сда́влвать.

сда́вливать *v.impfv.* [*pfv.* сдави́ть] **1,** to squeeze. **2,** to constrict.

сда́точный *adj.* delivery (*attrib.*).

сдать [*infl. like* дать] *v., pfv. of* сдава́ть. —**сда́ться,** *refl.* [*past tense stress as in* да́ться] *pfv. of* сдава́ться.

сда́ча *n.* **1,** handing over; handing in; turning in. **2,** returning; bringing back. **3,** renting; leasing. **4,** surrender; giving up. **5,** taking (*of an examination*). **6,** *cards* deal; dealing. **7,** change (*money given back*). **8,** *fig., colloq.* riposte. —**дава́ть сда́чи** (*with dat.*), **1,** to hit back; strike back. **2,** to give (someone) tit for tat.

сдва́ивать *v.impfv.* [*pfv.* сдво́ить] to double.

сдвиг *n.* **1,** shift; change. **2,** *fig.* progress; step forward; change for the better. **3,** *geol.* fault.

сдвига́ть *v.impfv.* [*pfv.* сдви́нуть] **1,** to move (*from a certain place*). **2,** to move together; draw together. —**сдви́нуть бро́ви,** to knit one's brows.

сдвига́ться *v.r.impfv.* [*pfv.* сдви́нуться] **1,** to move; budge. **2,** to move closer together. —**сдвига́ться с ме́ста, 1,** to move; budge. **2,** *fig.* to make headway.

сдво́ить *v., pfv. of* сдва́ивать.

сде́лать *v., pfv. of* де́лать. —**сде́латься,** *refl., pfv. of* де́латься (*in senses #3 & #4*).

сде́лка [*gen. pl.* -лок] *n.* transaction; bargain; deal.

сде́льный *adj.* by the piece. —**сде́льная рабо́та,** piecework.

сде́льщик *n.* pieceworker.

сде́льщина *n.* piecework.

сдёргивать *v.impfv.* [*pfv.* сдёрнуть] to pull off.

сде́ржанный *adj.* **1,** restrained. **2,** (*of a person*) reserved. —**сде́ржанно,** *adv.* in a restrained manner; coolly. —**сде́ржанность,** *n.f.* restraint; reserve.

сдержа́ть *v.pfv.* [*infl.* сдержу́, сде́ржишь] **1,** *pfv. of* сде́рживать. **2,** to keep (one's word, a promise, etc.). —**сдержа́ться,** *refl., pfv. of* сде́рживаться.

сде́рживание *n.* deterrence.

сде́рживать *v.impfv.* [*pfv.* сдержа́ть] **1,** to restrain. **2,** to hold back; suppress; repress (tears, laughter, a feeling, etc.). **3,** to deter. **4,** to withstand. **5,** *colloq.* to support (weight). —**сде́рживаться,** *refl.* to restrain oneself.

сдёрнуть *v., pfv. of* сдёргивать.

сдира́ть *v.impfv.* [*pfv.* содра́ть] **1,** to strip; tear off; remove. **2,** [*usu. pfv.*] *colloq.* to cheat; "rip off ".

сдо́ба *n.* **1,** shortening. **2,** sweet rolls; buns.

сдо́бный *adj.* (*of pastry*) rich. —**сдо́бная бу́лка,** bun.

сдо́брить *v., pfv. of* сда́бривать.

сдоброва́ть *v.pfv., in* ему́ (ей) не сдоброва́ть, it will not turn out well for him (her).

сдо́хнуть [*past* сдох, сдо́хла] *v., pfv. of* до́хнуть.

сдре́йфить *v., pfv. of* дре́йфить.

сдружи́ть *v.pfv.* [*infl.* сдружу́, сдру́жишь *or* сдружи́шь] to bring together; make friends of. —**сдружи́ться,** *refl.* to become friends.

сдува́ть *v.impfv.* [*pfv.* сдуть] *v.t.* to blow away; blow off. *Also impers. and intrans.:* У него́ шля́пу сду́ло, his hat blew off. —**как ве́тром сду́ло,** disappeared completely.

сду́ру *adv., colloq.* foolishly; stupidly.

сдуть [*infl.* сду́ю, сду́ешь] *v., pfv. of* сдува́ть.

сё [*dem. pron.* сего́] *used only in certain idiomatic expressions.* —**то-сё; то и сё; то да сё,** this and that: поговори́ть о том, о сём, to talk about this and that. —**ни то ни сё,** ordinary; nondescript. —**ни с того́ ни с сего́,** for no apparent reason; without rhyme or reason.

сеа́нс *n.* **1,** performance; show. **2,** sitting (*for a portrait*). —**сеа́нс одновре́менной игры́,** simultaneous chess exhibition.

себе́ *pron., dat. & prepl. of* себя́.

себесто́имость *n.f.* (prime) cost.

себя́ *refl. pron.* [*dat. & prepl.* себе́; *instr.* собо́й] **1,** oneself (myself, yourself, himself, etc.): недооцени́ть себя́, to underestimate oneself; владе́ть собо́й, control oneself; отвеча́ть за себя́, answer for oneself; ду́мать то́лько о себе́, think only of oneself. **2,** *used in place of the normal pronoun when that person is also the subject of the verb:* Мы взя́ли его́ с собо́й, we took him with us. Возьми́те с собо́й зо́нтик, take along an umbrella. —**быть сами́м собо́й,** *see* сам. —**вне себя́,** beside oneself: вне себя́ от ра́дости, beside oneself with joy. —**к себе́, 1,** to one's home. **2,** (*sign on doors*) "pull". —**ме́жду собо́й,** among oneselves. —**не по себе** (+ *dat.*), **1,** not feeling well. **2,** ill at ease. —**ничего́ себе́,** not bad; pretty good; pretty well. —**от себя́, 1,** for oneself; personally. **2,** (*sign on doors*) "push". —**по себе́,** on one's own; through one's own efforts. —**при себе́,** on one's person. —**про себя́,** to oneself: чита́ть про себя́, to read to oneself. —**сам по себе,** *see* сам. —**сам собо́й,** by itself; of itself. —**так себе,** so-so. —**у себя́,** at home.

себялю́бец [*gen.* -бца] *n.* self-centered person.

себялюби́вый *adj.* selfish; self-centered. —**себялю́бие,** *n.* selfishness; egoism.

сев *n.* sowing.

се́вер *n.* north.

се́верный *adj.* northern; North; northerly.

североамерика́нский *adj.* North American.

се́веро-восто́к *n.* northeast. —**се́веро-восто́чный,** *adj.* northeast; northeastern; northeasterly.

се́веро-за́пад *n.* northwest. —**се́веро-за́падный,** *adj.* northwest; northwestern; northwesterly.

северя́нин [*pl.* -я́не, -я́н] *n.m.* [*fem.* -я́нка] northerner.

севооборо́т *n.* crop rotation.

севрю́га *n.* a variety of sturgeon.

сегме́нт *n., geom.* segment.

сего́ (vo) *pron., gen. of* **сё** *and* **сей.**

сего́дня (vo) *adv.* today. Сего́дня у́тром, this morning. Сего́дня ве́чером, this evening; tonight. **—не сего́дня-за́втра,** any day now.

сего́дняшний (vo) *adj.* today's. Сего́дняшний день, today. **—жить сего́дняшним днём,** to live only for the present.

сегрега́ция *n.* segregation.

седа́лище *n., obs.* seat; place to sit.

седа́лищный *adj.* sciatic: седа́лищный нерв, sciatic nerve.

седе́льник *n.* saddler.

седе́льный *adj.* saddle (*attrib.*).

седе́ть *v.impfv.* [*pfv.* поседе́ть] to turn gray.

седи́ль *n.m.* cedilla.

седина́ [*pl.* седи́ны] *n., often. pl.* gray hair. **—до-жи́ть до седи́н,** to live to be old and gray.

седла́ть *v.impfv.* [*pfv.* оседла́ть] to saddle.

седло́ [*pl.* сёдла, сёдел] *n.* saddle.

седлови́на *n.* depression; dip.

седоволо́сый *adj.* gray-haired; white-haired. *Also,* **седовла́сый.**

седо́й *adj.* **1,** (*of hair*) gray; white. **2,** gray-haired; white-haired. **3,** *in* седа́я дре́вность *or* старина́, hoary antiquity. **—дожи́ть до седы́х воло́с,** to live to be old and gray.

седо́к [*gen.* -дока́] *n.* **1,** rider; horseman. **2,** rider; passenger (*in a carriage*).

седьма́я *n., decl. as an adj.* seventh: одна́ седьма́я, one-seventh.

седьмо́й *ordinal numeral* seventh.

сеза́м *n.* sesame.

сезо́н *n.* season (*for some activity*). **—сезо́нный,** *adj.* season (*attrib.*); seasonal.

сей *dem. pron.* [*fem.* **сия́**; *neut.* **сие́**; *pl.* **сии́**; *gen.* **сего́, сей, сих**; *acc. fem.* **сию́**; *dat.* **сему́, сей, сим**; *instr.* **сим, сей, си́ми**; *prepl.* **сём, сей, сих**] *obs.* this. **—до сих пор,** until now. **—на сей раз,** this time. **—по сей день,** to this day. **—при сём,** hereto; herewith. **—сего́ го́да,** (*with dates — usu. abbr. to* с.г.) of this year. **—сим,** hereby. **—сию́ мину́ту,** this minute; this instant.

сейсми́ческий *adj.* seismic.

сейсмо́граф *n.* seismograph.

сейсмоло́гия *n.* seismology. **—сейсмо́лог,** *n.* seismologist. **—сейсмологи́ческий,** *adj.* seismological.

сейсмосто́йкий *adj.* earthquake-proof.

сейф *n.* safe (*for storing valuables*).

сейча́с *adv.* **1,** now; right now; at present: Он сейча́с за́нят, he is busy right now. **2,** right now; right away; at once; immediately: Я сейча́с верну́сь, I'll be right back. **3,** just; just now: Она́ сейча́с звони́ла, she just called. **—сейча́с же, 1,** right now; immediately; at once. **2,** right away; immediately (*in the past*).

сека́нс *n., trig.* secant.

сека́ч [*gen.* -кача́] *n.* chopper (*tool*).

секве́стр *n.* sequestration.

секвестрова́ть *v.impfv. & pfv.* [*pres.* -ру́ю, -ру́ешь] to sequester.

секво́йя *n.* sequoia; redwood.

секи́ра *n.* poleax.

секре́т *n.* secret. Держа́ть (что́-нибудь) в секре́те, to keep (something) secret. **—по секре́ту,** confidentially; in confidence. **—под больши́м** (*or* по́лным) **секре́том,** in strict confidence.

секретариа́т *n.* secretariat.

секрета́рский *adj.* secretarial.

секрета́рствовать *v.impfv.* [*pres.* -ствую, -ствуешь] to serve as secretary.

секрета́рь [*gen.* -таря́] *n.m.* [*fem.* -та́рша] secretary. **—генера́льный секрета́рь,** *see* **генера́льный.** **—госуда́рственный секрета́рь,** secretary of state.

секрете́р (тэ) *n.* desk; writing table.

секре́тничать *v.impfv., colloq.* **1,** to keep things secret. **2,** to talk confidentially.

секре́тно *adv.* secretly; in secret. **—соверше́нно секре́тно,** top secret.

секре́тность *n.f.* secrecy.

секре́тный *adj.* **1,** secret. **2,** classified.

секре́ция *n.* secretion. **—железа́ вну́тренней секре́ции,** ductless gland; endocrine gland.

секс *n.* sex.

се́кста *n., music* sixth.

секста́нт *n.* sextant.

сексте́т *n.* sextet.

сексуа́льный *adj.* sexual. **—сексуа́льность,** *n.f.* sexuality.

се́кта *n.* sect.

секта́нт *n.* sectarian. **—секта́нтский,** *adj.* sectarian. **—секта́нтство,** *n.* sectarianism.

се́ктор *n.* sector.

секуляриза́ция *n.* secularization.

секуляризи́ровать *v.impfv. & pfv.* [*pres.* -рую, -руешь] to secularize. *Also,* **секуляризова́ть** [*pres.* -зу́ю, -зу́ешь].

секу́нда *n.* **1,** second (*of time or angular measurement*). **2,** *music* second.

секунда́нт *n.* second (*in a duel, chess match, etc.*).

секу́ндный *adj.* **1,** second (*attrib.*): секу́ндная стре́лка, second hand (*on a watch*). **2,** lasting only a second; momentary.

секундоме́р *n.* stopwatch.

секу́щая *n., decl. as an adj., geom.* secant.

секцио́нный *adj.* sectional.

се́кция *n.* section.

селёдка [*gen. pl.* -док] *n.* herring. **—селёдочный,** *adj.* herring (*attrib.*).

селезёнка *n.* spleen. **—селезёночный,** *adj.* splenetic.

се́лезень [*gen.* -зня] *n.m.* drake; male duck.

селе́кция *n.* breeding (*of plants and animals*).

селе́н *n.* selenium.

селе́ние *n.* village; settlement.

селени́т *n.* selenite.

сели́тра *n.* saltpeter; niter. **—аммиа́чная** *or* **аммо́ниевая сели́тра,** ammonium nitrate. **—ка́лиевая** *or* **кали́йная сели́тра,** potassium nitrate. **—на́триевая сели́тра,** sodium nitrate.

сели́тряный *adj.* saltpeter (*attrib.*); nitric.

сели́ть *v.impfv.* to settle. **—сели́ться,** *refl.* to settle; take up residence.

село [*pl.* **сёла**] *n.* village. —**ни к селу́ ни к го́роду,** apropos of nothing; for no apparent reason.

сельдере́й *n.* celery. —**сельдере́йный,** *adj.* celery (*attrib.*).

сельдь [*pl.* **се́льди, -де́й, -дя́м**] *n.f.* herring. —**как се́льди** (*or* **сельде́й**) **в бо́чке,** like sardines.

се́льский *adj.* **1,** rural. **2,** village (*attrib.*). —**се́льское хозя́йство,** agriculture.

сельскохозя́йственный *adj.* agricultural; farm (*attrib.*).

се́льтерский *adj., in* **се́льтерская вода́,** seltzer water.

сема́нтика *n.* semantics. —**семанти́ческий,** *adj.* semantic.

семафо́р *n.* semaphore.

сёмга *n.* smoked salmon; lox.

семе́йный *adj.* family (*attrib.*).

семе́йственность *n.f.* **1,** attachment to family; family spirit. **2,** nepotism.

семе́йственный *adj.* attached to one's family; home-loving.

семе́йство *n.* **1,** = **семья́. 2,** *biol.* family.

семени́ть *v.impfv., colloq., in* **семени́ть нога́ми,** to trip (along); walk with mincing steps.

семенни́к [*gen.* **-ника́**] *n.* **1,** seed plant. **2,** testicle.

семенно́й *adj.* **1,** seed (*attrib.*). **2,** seminal.

семёрка *n.* **1,** the numeral 7. **2,** *colloq.* anything numbered 7. **3,** *cards* seven.

се́меро *collective numeral* seven.

семе́стр *n.* semester.

се́мечко [*gen. pl.* **-чек**] *n.* **1,** *dim. of* **се́мя. 2,** *pl.* sunflower seeds.

семидесятиле́тие *n.* **1,** seventieth anniversary; seventieth birthday. **2,** seventy-year period.

семидесятиле́тний *adj.* **1,** seventy-year (*attrib.*). **2,** seventy-year-old.

семидеся́тый *ordinal numeral* seventieth.

семидне́вный *adj.* seven-day (*attrib.*).

семикра́тный *adj.* sevenfold.

семиле́тие *n.* **1,** seventh anniversary; seventh birthday. **2,** seven-year period.

семиле́тний *adj.* **1,** seven-year (*attrib.*). **2,** seven-year-old.

семина́р *n.* seminar.

семина́рия *n.* seminary. —**семинари́ст,** *n.* seminary student; seminary graduate.

семисо́тый *ordinal numeral* seven-hundredth.

семи́тский *adj.* Semitic. *Also,* **семити́ческий.**

семиуго́льник *n.* heptagon. —**семиуго́льный,** *adj.* heptagonal.

семичасово́й *adj.* seven-hour: **семичасово́й рабо́чий день,** seven-hour workday.

семна́дцать *numeral* seventeen. —**семна́дцатый,** *ordinal numeral* seventeenth.

семь [*gen., dat. & prepl.* **семи́;** *instr.* **семью́**] *numeral* seven.

се́мьдесят [*gen., dat. & prepl.* **семи́десяти;** *instr.* **семью́десятью**] *numeral* seventy.

семьсо́т [*gen.* **семисо́т;** *dat.* **семиста́м;** *instr.* **семьюста́ми;** *prepl.* **семиста́х**] *numeral* seven hundred.

се́мью *adv.* seven times: **се́мью пять — три́дцать пять,** seven times five is 35.

семья́ [*pl.* **се́мьи, семе́й, се́мьям**] *n.* family.

семьяни́н *n.* family man.

се́мя [*gen., dat. & prepl.* **се́мени;** *instr.* **се́менем;** *pl.* **семена́, семя́н, семена́м**] *n.neut.* **1,** seed. **2,** semen. —**пойти́ в семена́,** (*of a plant*) to go to seed.

семядо́ля *n.* cotyledon.

семяизлия́ние *n.* ejaculation.

семяпо́чка [*gen. pl.* **-чек**] *n., bot.* ovule.

сена́т *n.* senate. —**сена́тор,** *n.* senator. —**сена́торский,** *adj.* senator's; senatorial. —**сена́тский,** *adj.* senate (*attrib.*).

сенберна́р (сэ) *n.* Saint Bernard (*dog*).

се́ни [*gen.* **сене́й**] *n.pl.* entrance hall; vestibule.

сенни́к [*gen.* **-ника́**] *n.* straw mattress.

сенно́й *adj.* hay (*attrib.*). —**сенна́я лихора́дка,** hay fever.

се́но *n.* hay. —**соба́ка на се́не,** dog in the manger.

сенова́л *n.* hayloft.

сеноко́с *n.* **1,** haymaking. **2,** hayfield.

сенокоси́лка [*gen. pl.* **-лок**] *n.* machine for mowing hay.

сенсацио́нный *adj.* sensational.

сенса́ция *n.* sensation.

сенсо́рный (сэ) *adj.* sensory.

сентенцио́зный (сэ, тэ) *adj.* sententious.

сенте́нция (сэ, тэ) *n.* maxim; adage.

сентимента́льничать (сэ) *v.impfv.* **1,** to be sentimental. **2,** to be soft; be lenient.

сентимента́льный (сэ) *adj.* sentimental. —**сентимента́льность,** *n.f.* sentimentality.

сентя́брь [*gen.* **-бря́**] *n.m.* September. —**сентя́брьский,** *adj.* September (*attrib.*).

сень [*2nd loc.* **сени́**] *n.f., archaic* canopy. —**под се́нью** (+ *gen.*), under the protection of.

сепарати́зм *n.* separatism. —**сепарати́ст,** *n.* separatist. —**сепарати́стский,** *adj.* separatist.

сепара́тный *adj., polit.* separate: **сепара́тный мир,** separate peace.

сепара́тор *n.* separator.

се́пия (сэ) *n.* **1,** sepia. **2,** cuttlefish.

се́псис (сэ) *n.* sepsis.

се́птима (сэ) *n., music* seventh.

септи́ческий (сэ) *adj.* septic.

се́ра *n.* sulfur. —**ушна́я се́ра,** earwax.

сера́ль *n.m.* seraglio.

серафи́м *n.* seraph.

серб *n.m.* [*fem.* **се́рбка**] Serb.

сербохорва́тский *adj.* Serbo-Croatian.

се́рбский *adj.* Serbian.

сербскохорва́тский *adj.* Serbo-Croatian.

серва́нт *n.* sideboard.

серви́з *n.* set (*of dishes or silverware*): **фарфо́ровый серви́з,** set of china.

сервирова́ть *v.impfv. & pfv.* [*pres.* **-ру́ю, -ру́ешь**] **1,** to set (a table). **2,** to serve (a meal, food, drink, etc.).

сервиро́вка *n.* [*often with* **стола́**] **1,** (act of) setting (a table). **2,** table arrangement.

серде́чник *n.* **1,** *colloq.* person with a heart ailment. **2,** *colloq.* heart specialist. **3,** core (*of a nuclear reactor*).

сердечно *adv.* **1,** cordially; warmly. **2,** sincerely.

сердечно-сосудистый *adj.* cardiovascular.

сердечность *n.f.* warmth; cordiality.

сердечный *adj.* **1,** heart (*attrib.*); cardiac. **2,** hearty; cordial. **3,** warmhearted; kind. **4,** heartfelt; sincere. **5,** of the heart: сердечные тайны, secrets of the heart.

сердитый *adj.* (*with* на + *acc.*) angry (at). —**сердито,** *adv.* angrily.

сердить *v.impfv.* [*pfv.* **рассердить;** *pres.* **сержу́, се́рдишь**] to anger; make angry. —**серди́ться,** *refl.* (*with* на + *acc.*) to be angry (at); become angry (with).

сердоболие *n.* compassion. —**сердобольный,** *adj.* tenderhearted.

сердце [*pl.* **сердца́, серде́ц, сердца́м**] *n.* heart. —всем сердцем, with all one's heart. —в сердцах, *colloq.* in a fit of anger. —от всего сердца, from the bottom of one's heart. —от полноты сердца, in the fullness of one's heart. —от чистого сердца, in all sincerity; from the heart. —по сердцу (+ *dat.*), to one's liking. —положа руку на сердце, in all honesty. —принимать (близко) к сердцу, to take to heart.

сердцебиение *n.* **1,** heartbeat. **2,** heart palpitation.

сердцеви́дка [*gen. pl.* **-док**] *n.* cockle (*mollusk*).

сердцеви́дный *adj.* heart-shaped.

сердцеви́на *n.* **1,** core. **2,** *fig.* core; heart.

сердцеед *n., colloq.* lady-killer.

серебри́стый *adj.* silvery.

серебри́ть *v.impfv.* [*pfv.* **посеребри́ть**] to silver; silver-plate. —**серебри́ться,** *refl.* to become silvery.

серебро́ *n.* silver.

серебряник *n.* silversmith.

серебряный *adj.* silver. —**серебряных дел ма́стер,** silversmith.

середина *n.* middle. —золотая середина, golden mean; happy medium.

середи́нный *adj.* **1,** middle. **2,** *fig.* halfway; compromise (*attrib.*).

серёдка [*gen. pl.* **-док**] *n., colloq.* middle; center.

середня́к [*gen.* **-няка́**] *n.* **1,** middle-class peasant. **2,** person of ordinary ability; mediocrity.

серёжка [*gen. pl.* **-жек**] *n.* **1,** earring. **2,** catkin. **3,** wattle (*on fowl*).

серена́да *n.* serenade.

сере́ть *v.impfv.* [*pfv.* **посере́ть**] to turn gray.

сержа́нт *n.* sergeant. —**сержа́нтский,** *adj.* sergeant's.

серийный *adj.* **1,** serial. **2,** serially produced. —**серийное производство,** serial (*or* series) production.

серия *n.* **1,** series. **2,** set (*of postage stamps*). **3,** part (*of a film*): кинофильм в трёх сериях, three-part film.

сермя́га *n.* **1,** a coarse undyed cloth. **2,** robe made of this cloth.

се́рна *n.* chamois.

серни́стый *adj.* **1,** containing sulfur: серни́стые краси́тели, sulfur dyes. **2,** sulfurous; sulfide (of): серни́стая кислота́, sulfurous acid; серни́стый водоро́д, hydrogen sulfide; серни́стая ртуть, mercuric sulfide.

сернобы́к [*gen.* **-быка́**] *n.* oryx.

серноки́слый *adj.* sulfate (of): серноки́слый аммо́ний/ба́рий/на́трий, ammonium/barium/sodium sulfate. —**серноки́слая соль,** sulfate.

се́рный *adj.* **1,** sulfur (*attrib.*). **2,** sulfuric.

сероводоро́д *n.* hydrogen sulfide.

сероло́гия *n.* serology.

се́рость *n.f.* dullness; drabness.

серп [*gen.* **серпа́**] *n.* sickle. —**серп луны́,** crescent moon.

серпанти́н *n.* **1,** (paper) streamer. **2,** twisting mountain road.

сертифика́т *n.* certificate.

се́рый *adj.* **1,** gray. **2,** *fig.* dull; drab.

серьга́ [*pl.* **се́рьги, серёг, серьга́м**] *n.* earring.

серьёзно *adv.* **1,** seriously. Я говорю́ серьёзно, I'm serious. **2,** (*in direct address*) seriously?; really?

серьёзность *n.f.* seriousness.

серьёзный *adj.* [*short form* **-зен, -зна**] serious.

се́ссия *n.* session.

сестра́ [*pl.* **сёстры, сестёр, сёстрам**] *n.* sister. —**медици́нская сестра́,** (hospital) nurse.

сестрёнка [*gen. pl.* **-нок**] *n.* little sister.

се́стрин *adj.* one's sister's.

сестри́ца *also,* **сестри́чка** *n., dim. of* **сестра́.**

сесть [*infl.* **ся́ду, ся́дешь;** *past* **сел, се́ла**] *v., pfv. of* **сади́ться.**

сет (сэ) *n., tennis* set.

се́тка [*gen. pl.* **се́ток**] *n.* **1,** net. **2,** netting. **3,** window screen. **4,** *colloq.* string bag. **5,** grid.

се́тование *n.* **1,** complaining. **2,** *usu. pl.* complaint.

се́товать *v.impfv.* [*pfv.* **посе́товать;** *pres.* **-тую, -туешь**] (*with* на + *acc. or a dependent clause*) **1,** to complain. **2,** to lament.

се́ттер (сэ, тэ) *n.* setter.

сетча́тка *n.* retina.

се́тчатый *adj.* made of netting or gauze. —**се́тчатая оболо́чка,** retina.

сеть [*2nd loc.* **сети;** *pl.* **се́ти, сете́й, сетя́м**] *n.f.* **1,** net. **2,** network; chain. Доро́жная сеть, highway network; highway system.

сече́ние *n.* section: кони́ческое сече́ние, conic section; попере́чное сече́ние, cross section. —**ке́сарево сече́ние,** Caesarean section.

се́чка [*gen. pl.* **се́чек**] *n.* **1,** chopping knife. **2,** fine-cut straw; chaff.

сечь *v.impfv.* [*pres.* **секу́, сечёшь, ...секу́т;** *past* **сёк, секла́, секло́, секли́**] **1,** to cut to pieces; chop. **2,** slash. **3,** [*pfv.* **вы́сечь**] to whip; flog. **4,** (*of rain, wind, etc.*) to lash. —**се́чься,** *refl.* **1,** (*of hair*) to be brittle; break. **2,** (*of fabric*) to tear; fray.

се́ялка [*gen. pl.* **-лок**] *n.* seeding machine; seeder.

се́янец [*gen.* **-нца**] *n.* seedling.

се́ятель *n.m.* sower.

се́ять *v.impfv.* [*pfv.* **посе́ять;** *pres.* **се́ю, се́ешь**] to sow.

сжа́литься *v.r.pfv.* (*with* над) to take pity on.

сжа́тие *n.* **1,** compression. **2,** (feeling of) constriction. **3,** grip; grasp.

сжа́тость *n.f.* conciseness; terseness.

сжа́тый *adj.* **1,** (*of air*) compressed. **2,** (*of fists*) clenched. **3,** concise; succinct; terse. —**в сжа́тые сро́ки,** in a short space of time.

сжать¹ [*infl.* **сожму́, сожмёшь**] *v., pfv. of* **сжима́ть.** —**сжа́ться,** *refl., pfv. of* **сжима́ться.**

сжать² [*infl.* **сожну́, сожнёшь**] *v., pfv. of* **жать²**.

сжечь [*infl.* **сожгу́, сожжёшь, …сожгу́т**; *past* **сжёг, сожгла́, сожгло́, сожгли́**] *v., pfv. of* **жечь** *and* **сжига́ть**.

сжива́ть *v.impfv.* [*pfv.* **сжить**] **1,** to make (someone) move out (*by making life unbearable*). **2,** in **сжива́ть со све́та** *or* **со́ свету,** to be the death of. —**сжива́ться,** *refl.* (*with* **с** + *instr.*) *colloq.* **1,** to make friends with; become friendly with. **2,** to get used to.

сжига́ть *v.impfv.* [*pfv.* **сжечь**] to burn. —**сжига́ть (свои́) мосты́** *or* **корабли́,** to burn one's bridges.

сжижа́ть *v.impfv.* [*pfv.* **сжиди́ть**] to liquefy.

сжиже́ние *n.* liquefaction.

сжи́женный *adj.* liquefied.

сжима́ть *v.impfv.* [*pfv.* **сжать**] **1,** to squeeze. **2,** to clench (one's fist, teeth, etc.). **3,** to compress. **4,** to constrict. **5,** to hem in. **6,** *fig.* to condense (something written). **7,** *fig.* to reduce (an amount of time allotted). —**сжима́ться,** *refl.* **1,** to be compressed; be clenched. **2,** to shrink; contract. **3,** to tighten; close. **4,** to huddle up.

сжить [*infl. like* **жить**] *v., pfv. of* **сжива́ть**. —**сжи́ться,** *refl.* [*past* **сжи́лся, сжила́сь, сжило́сь** *or* **сжи́лось, сжили́сь** *or* **сжили́сь**] *pfv. of* **сжива́ться**.

сза́ди *adv.* **1,** in back; behind. **2,** from behind; from the rear. —*prep., with gen.* behind.

сзыва́ть *v.* = **созыва́ть**.

си *n.neut., music* si; ti; B.

сиа́мский *adj.* Siamese.

сибари́т *n.* sybarite. —**сибари́тский,** *adj.* sybaritic.

сиби́рский *adj.* Siberian. —**сиби́рская ко́шка,** Persian cat. —**сиби́рская я́зва,** anthrax.

сибиря́к [*gen.* **-яка́**] *n.m.* [*fem.* **-я́чка**] Siberian.

си́вка [*gen. pl.* **си́вок**] *n.m. & f., colloq.* gray horse. —*n.f.* golden plover. —**си́вка глу́пая,** dotterel.

сиву́ха *n.* raw vodka.

си́вый *adj.* **1,** (*of a horse*) gray. **2,** *colloq.* (*of hair*) gray.

сиг [*gen.* **сига́**] *n.* whitefish.

сигану́ть *v., pfv. of* **сига́ть**.

сига́ра *n.* cigar.

сигаре́та *n.* cigarette. —**сигаре́тный,** *adj.* cigarette (*attrib.*).

сига́рный *adj.* cigar (*attrib.*).

сига́ть *v.impfv.* [*pfv.* **сигану́ть**] *colloq.* to jump; leap.

сигна́л *n.* signal.

сигнализа́тор *n.* signaling device.

сигнализа́ция *n.* **1,** signaling. **2,** alarm system. **3,** signaling system.

сигнализи́ровать *v.impfv. & pfv.* [*pres.* **-рую, -руешь**] **1,** to signal. **2,** *fig.* (*with acc. or* **о**) to warn (of).

сигна́льный *adj.* signal (*attrib.*). —**сигна́льный ого́нь,** signal light; beacon. —**сигна́льный экземпля́р,** advance copy (*of a book*).

сигна́льщик *n.* signalman; flagman.

сигнату́ра *n.* label (*on a medicine bottle*).

сиде́лка [*gen. pl.* **-лок**] *n.* nurse.

сиде́ние *n.* sitting.

си́день [*gen.* **-дня**] *n.m., colloq.* stay-at-home. —**си́днем сиде́ть,** to stay home all the time.

сиде́нье *n.* seat.

сиде́ть *v.impfv.* [*pres.* **сижу́, сиди́шь**] **1,** to sit; be sitting: **сиде́ть на полу́,** to be sitting on the floor. **Сиде́ть без де́ла,** to sit around doing nothing. **2,** (*with certain nouns*) to be: **сиде́ть в тюрьме́,** to be in prison; **сиде́ть на дие́те,** to be on a diet. **3,** (*of clothes*) to fit. **4,** *colloq.* to be in prison; spend time in prison. —**сиде́ться,** *refl., used negatively with dat.* to be restless; be unable to sit for long (in a certain place): **Ему́ не сиди́тся на ме́сте,** he can't sit still.

сидр *n.* cider. —**си́дровый,** *adj.* cider (*attrib.*).

сидя́чий *adj.* **1,** sitting. **2,** sedentary. —**сидя́чее ме́сто,** seat. —**сидя́чая забасто́вка,** sit-down strike.

сие́на *n.* sienna.

сиза́ль *n.m.* sisal.

си́зый *adj.* blue-gray.

сикомо́р *n.* sycamore.

сикх *n.* Sikh.

си́ла *n.* **1,** strength. **2,** force: **си́ла уда́ра,** the force of a blow. **Си́лой ору́жия,** by force of arms. **3,** power: **лошади́ная си́ла,** horsepower. **Си́ла печа́тного сло́ва,** the power of the printed word. **4,** effect; force: **вступа́ть в си́лу,** to go into effect/force. **5,** *pl.* (one's) energies: **отдава́ть си́лы** (+ *dat.*), to devote one's energies to. **Про́бовать свои́ си́лы в** (+ *prepl.*), to try one's hand at. **6,** *pl., mil.* forces: **вооружённые си́лы,** armed forces. **7,** *pl.* forces; elements: **реакцио́нные си́лы,** reactionary forces/elements. —**быть (не) в си́лах,** (not) be able to; (not) have the strength (*fig.*). —**в ме́ру сил; по ме́ре сил,** as far as one is able. —**всё, что в чьи́х-нибудь си́лах,** everything in one's power. —**все́ми си́лами,** in every way. —**в си́лу** (+ *gen.*), on the strength of; by virtue of. —**изо всех сил,** with all one's might. —**не под си́лу** (+ *dat.*), too much for; beyond one. —**от си́лы,** at the most. —**че́рез си́лу,** with the utmost difficulty; by forcing oneself. —**что есть сил,** for all one is worth.

сила́ч [*gen.* **-лача́**] *n.* strong man.

силикаге́ль *n.m.* silica gel.

силика́т *n.* silicate.

силико́н *n.* silicone.

си́литься *v.r.impfv.* (*with inf.*) *colloq.* to try (to); make an effort (to)

силко́м *adv., colloq.* by force.

силлоги́зм *n.* syllogism. —**силлогисти́ческий; силлоги́ческий,** *adj.* syllogistic.

силово́й *adj.* **1,** power (*attrib.*): **силова́я ста́нция,** power station; power plant. **2,** of force; using force: **силова́я поли́тика,** policy of force. —**силово́й прие́м, 1,** *sports* body check. **2,** *pl., fig.* strongarm tactics.

сило́к [*gen.* **силка́**] *n.* snare.

силоме́р *n.* dynamometer.

си́лос *n.* silage.

си́лосный *adj.* silage (*attrib.*). —**си́лосная ба́шня,** silo.

силуэ́т *n.* silhouette.

си́льно *adv.* **1,** with great force; hard. **2,** very (much); greatly; strongly: **си́льно оби́деться,** to be very hurt; **си́льно влюблён,** very much in love; **си́льно привя́занный к,** strongly attached to. **Он си́льно пьёт,** he is a heavy drinker.

сильноде́йствующий *adj.* (*of medicine*) potent; powerful.

си́льный *adj.* [*short form* **силён, сильна́, си́льно, сильны́**] **1**, strong; powerful. **2**, severe; heavy; intense; violent. **3**, (*of a student*) good.

сильф *n.* sylph. —**сильфи́да,** *n.* sylphid.

сим *see* **сей**.

симбио́з *n.* symbiosis.

си́мвол *n.* symbol.

символизи́ровать *v.impfv.* & *pfv.* [*pres.* **-рую, -руешь**] to symbolize; be symbolic of.

символи́зм *n.* symbolism.

симво́лика *n.* **1**, symbolism. **2**, symbols.

символи́ческий *adj.* symbolic. *Also,* **символи́чный**.

симме́три́я *n.* symmetry. —**симметри́ческий; симметри́чный,** *adj.* symmetrical.

симпатизи́ровать *v.impfv.* [*pres.* **-рую, -руешь**] (*with dat.*) **1**, to like; be fond of. **2**, to be in sympathy with.

симпати́ческий *adj., anat.; physiol.* sympathetic: симпати́ческая не́рвная систе́ма, sympathetic nervous system. —**симпати́ческие черни́ла,** invisible ink.

симпати́чный *adj.* likable; nice.

симпа́тия *n.* **1**, (*with* **к**) liking (for). **2**, *pl.* sympathies: симпа́тии слу́шателей, the sympathies of the audience.

симпо́зиум *n.* symposium.

симпто́м *m.* symptom. —**симптомати́ческий,** *adj., med.* symptomatic.

симптомати́чный *adj.* **1**, symptomatic; significant; indicative of something. **2**, = **симптомати́ческий**.

симули́ровать *v.impfv.* & *pfv.* [*pres.* **-рую, -руешь**] to simulate; feign.

симуля́нт *n.* faker; malingerer.

симуля́ция *n.* feigning.

симфони́ческий *adj.* **1**, symphony (*attrib.*). **2**, symphonic.

симфо́ния *n.* symphony.

синаго́га *n.* synagogue.

синдика́т *n.* syndicate.

синдро́м *n.* syndrome.

синева́ *n.* **1**, blue color. **2**, blue expanse. —**синева́ под глаза́ми,** blue circles under one's eyes.

синева́тый *adj.* bluish.

синегла́зый *adj.* blue-eyed.

синеку́ра *n.* sinecure.

сине́ль *n.f.* chenille.

сине́ть *v.impfv.* [*pfv.* **посине́ть**] **1**, to turn blue; become blue. **2**, [*impfv. only*] (*of anything blue*) to appear.

си́ний *adj.* (dark) blue.

сини́льный *adj., in* **сини́льная кислота́,** prussic acid.

сини́ть *v.impfv.* [*pfv.* **посини́ть**] **1**, to dye blue. **2**, to rinse in bluing; blue.

сини́ца *n.* titmouse; tomtit.

синко́па *n.* **1**, *music* syncopation. **2**, *gram.* syncope.

синкопи́ровать *v.impfv.* & *pfv.* [*pres.* **-рую, -руешь**] *music* to syncopate.

сино́д *n.* synod. —**синода́льный,** *adj.* synodal.

сино́ним *n.* synonym. —**синоними́ческий; синони́мичный,** *adj.* synonymous.

сино́птика *n.* weather forecasting. —**сино́птик,** *n.* weather forecaster.

синопти́ческий *adj.* pert. to weather forecasting: синопти́ческая ка́рта, weather map.

си́нтаксис *n.* syntax. —**синтакси́ческий,** *adj.* syntactical.

си́нтез (тэ) *n.* **1**, synthesis. **2**, *physics* fusion.

синтеза́тор (тэ) *n., music* synthesizer.

синтези́ровать (тэ) *v.impfv.* & *pfv.* [*pres.* **-рую, -руешь**] to synthesize.

синте́тика (тэ) *n.* synthetic(s).

синтети́ческий (тэ) *adj.* synthetic.

синтои́зм *n.* Shinto; Shintoism.

си́нус *n.* **1**, *math.* sine. **2**, *anat.* sinus. —**синуси́т,** *n.* sinusitis.

синхрониза́ция *n.* synchronization.

синхронизи́ровать *v.impfv.* & *pfv.* [*pres.* **-рую, -руешь**] to synchronize.

синхрони́ческий *adj.* synchronic.

синхро́нный *adj.* synchronous. —**синхро́нный перево́д,** simultaneous translation.

синь *n.f.* blue color.

си́нька *n.* **1**, bluing. **2**, blueprint.

синю́ха *n.* cyanosis.

синю́шность *n.f.* = **синю́ха**.

синя́к [*gen.* **-няка́**] *n.* **1**, bruise; black-and-blue mark. **2**, *in* синяки́ под глаза́ми, dark patches under one's eyes. —**избива́ть до синяко́в,** to beat black-and-blue.

сиони́зм *n.* Zionism. —**сиони́ст,** *n.* Zionist. —**сиони́стский,** *adj.* Zionist.

сип *n.* griffon vulture.

сипе́ть *v.impfv.* [*pres.* **сиплю́, сипи́шь**] **1**, (*of something hot*) to hiss. **2**, to speak in a hoarse voice. **3**, *impers.* to be hoarse: У меня́ в го́рле сипи́т, my throat is hoarse.

си́плый *adj.* hoarse; husky.

си́пнуть *v.impfv.* [*past* **сип** *or* **си́пнул, си́пла**] to become hoarse.

сипу́ха *n.* barn owl.

сире́на *n.* siren.

сире́нь *n.f.* lilac. —**сире́невый,** *adj.* lilac.

си́речь *conj., archaic* that is to say.

сири́ец [*gen.* **-и́йца**] *n.m.* [*fem.* **-и́йка**] Syrian. —**сири́йский,** *adj.* Syrian.

сиро́кко *n.m. indecl.* sirocco.

сиро́п *n.* syrup.

сирота́ [*pl.* **сиро́ты**] *n.m.* & *f.* orphan. —**кру́глый** *or* **кру́глая сирота́,** child who has lost both parents.

сироте́ть *v.impfv.* [*pfv.* **осироте́ть**] **1**, to be orphaned. **2**, *fig.* (*of a place*) to become deserted.

сиротли́вый *adj.* lonely.

сиро́тский *adj.* orphan (*attrib.*); orphan's. —**сиро́тский дом** *or* **прию́т,** orphanage; orphan asylum.

сиро́тство *n.* orphanhood.

систе́ма *n.* system.

систематизи́ровать *v.impfv.* & *pfv.* [*pres.* **-рую, -руешь**] to systematize.

системати́ческий *adj.* systematic. —**системати́чески,** *adv.* systematically.

си́стола *n.* systole. —**систоли́ческий,** *adj.* systolic.

си́тец [*gen.* **си́тца**] *n.* printed cotton fabric; chintz.

си́течко [*gen. pl.* **-чек**] *n.* filter; strainer.

си́тник *n.* **1,** rush (*plant*). **2,** *colloq.* bread made of sifted flour.

си́то *n.* sieve; strainer.

ситуа́ция *n.* situation.

си́тцевый *adj.* made of printed cotton; chintz.

си́филис *n.* syphilis. —**сифили́тик,** *n.,* *colloq.* syphilitic. —**сифилити́ческий,** *adj.* syphilitic.

сифо́н *n.* siphon.

сиюмину́тный *adj.* **1,** of the moment. **2,** immediate; instant.

сия́ние *n.* **1,** glow. **2,** halo. **3,** *fig.* radiance. —**се́верное сия́ние,** northern lights; aurora borealis.

сия́ть *v.impfv.* to shine; beam; glow.

скабрёзный *adj.* indecent; off-color; bawdy; dirty. —**скабрёзность,** *n.f.* dirty word; *pl.* indecent language.

сказ *n.* epic tale.

сказа́ние *n.* legend; tale; story. Библе́йское сказа́ние, Biblical legend; the story in the Bible.

ска́занное *n., decl. as an adj.* what has been said.

сказа́ть [*infl.* **скажу́, ска́жешь**] *v., pfv. of* **говори́ть.** —**как сказа́ть?,** how shall I put it? —**мо́жно сказа́ть,** you might say. —**не́чего сказа́ть,** *see* **не́чего.** —**ничего́ не ска́жешь!,** you must admit! —**ска́зано — сде́лано,** it's as good as done; no sooner said than done. —**сказа́ть своё сло́во, 1,** to have one's say. **2,** to make one's presence felt. —**так сказа́ть,** so to speak; as it were. —**хоте́ть сказа́ть,** to mean. —**чтобы** (*or* **если**) **не сказа́ть...,** if not...; not to say... Тру́дно, чтобы не сказа́ть невозмо́жно, difficult if not impossible. Беста́ктное замеча́ние, е́сли не сказа́ть оскорби́тельное, a tactless remark, not to say insulting. —**чтобы** (*or* **если**) **не сказа́ть бо́льше,** to say the least.

сказа́ться [*infl.* **скажу́сь, ска́жешься**] *v.r., pfv. of* **ска́зываться.**

сказа́тель *n.m.* teller of folk tales.

ска́зка [*gen. pl.* **-зок**] *n.* tale; story.

ска́зочник *n.* storyteller.

ска́зочный *adj.* **1,** fairy-tale (*attrib.*). **2,** fabulous; fantastic.

сказу́емое *n., decl. as an adj., gram.* predicate.

ска́зываться *v.r.impfv.* [*pfv.* **сказа́ться**] **1,** *colloq.* to be told. **2,** (*with* **в** + *prepl.*) to be manifest (in); be seen (in). **3,** to have its effect; (*with* **на** + *prepl.*) have an effect (upon); tell (on *or* upon). **4,** (*with instr.*) *colloq.* to pose as; pretend to be. Сказа́ться больны́м (больно́й), to feign illness. **5,** *obs.* to give warning; give notice.

скак *n., in* **на всём** (*or* **на по́лном**) **скаку́,** at full gallop.

скака́лка [*gen. pl.* **лок**] *n.* jump rope.

скака́ть *v.impfv.* [*pres.* **скачу́, ска́чешь**] **1,** to jump; skip. **2,** to gallop (*on horseback*). **3,** (*of a horse*) to race. **4,** *fig.* to fluctuate sharply. —**скака́ть на одно́й ноге́,** to hop.

скаково́й *adj.* racing (*attrib.*). —**скакова́я доро́жка,** racecourse. —**скакова́я ло́шадь,** racehorse.

скаку́н [*gen.* **-куна́**] *n.* racehorse.

скала́ [*pl.* **ска́лы**] *n.* **1,** rock. **2,** [*often* **отве́сная скала́**] cliff. —**подво́дная скала́,** reef.

скали́стый *adj.* rocky.

ска́лить *v.impfv., in* **ска́лить зу́бы, 1,** to bare one's teeth. **2,** *colloq.* to laugh; smile; grin.

ска́лка [*gen. pl.* **-лок**] *n.* rolling pin.

ска́лывать *v.impfv.* [*pfv.* **сколо́ть**] **1,** to chop away; chip away. **2,** to pin together.

скальки́ровать *v., pfv. of* **кальки́ровать.**

скалькули́ровать *v., pfv. of* **калькули́ровать.**

скальп *n.* scalp (*taken from the head of an enemy*).

ска́льпель *n.m.* scalpel.

скальпи́ровать *v.impfv. & pfv.* [*pres.* **-рую, -руешь**] to scalp.

скаме́ечка [*gen. pl.* **-чек**] *n.* small bench.

скаме́йка [*gen. pl.* **-ме́ек**] *n.* bench. —**скаме́йка для ног,** footstool.

скамья́ [*pl.* **скамьи́** *or* **ска́мьи, скаме́й, скамья́м**] *n.* **1,** bench. **2,** *in* **скамья́ подсуди́мых,** the dock (*in a courtroom*). —**со шко́льной скамьи́, 1,** since one's school days. **2,** right out of school.

сканда́л *n.* **1,** scandal. **2,** row; brawl.

скандализи́ровать *v.impfv. & pfv.* [*pres.* **-рую, -руешь**] to scandalize.

скандали́ст *n.* trouble-maker; rowdy.

сканда́лить *v.impfv.* [*pfv.* **наскандали́ть**] to raise a fuss; kick up a row. **2,** [*impfv. only*] *colloq.* to have an argument. —**сканда́литься,** *refl.* [*pfv.* **оскандали́ться**] *colloq.* to make a fool of oneself.

сканда́льный *adj.* **1,** scandalous. **2,** rowdy; boisterous. **3,** *colloq.* (*of a person*) always making a fuss.

ска́ндий *n.* scandium.

скандина́в *n.m.* [*fem.* **-на́вка**] Scandinavian. —**скандина́вский,** *adj.* Scandinavian.

сканди́ровать *v.impfv. & pfv.* [*pres.* **-рую, -руешь**] **1,** to recite (verse) emphasizing each stressed syllable. **2,** (*of a crowd*) to chant.

ска́пливать *v.impfv.* [*pfv.* **скопи́ть**] to save up; amass. —**ска́пливаться,** *refl.* **1,** to pile up; accumulate. **2,** to gather; congregate.

скарабе́й *n.* scarab.

скарб *n., colloq.* household belongings.

ска́редный *adj., colloq.* miserly; stingy.

скарлати́на *n.* scarlet fever. —**скарлати́нный,** *adj.* of scarlet fever.

ска́рмливать *v.impfv.* [*pfv.* **скорми́ть**] to feed: ска́рмливать се́но лошадя́м, to feed hay to the horses.

скат *n.* **1,** slope; incline. **2,** slide; chute. **3,** *zool.* ray; skate.

ската́ть *v., pfv. of* **ска́тывать** (*in sense #1*).

ска́терть [*pl.* **ска́терти, -те́й, -тя́м**] *n.f.* tablecloth. —**ска́тертью доро́га!,** *colloq.* good riddance!

скати́ть [*infl.* **скачу́, ска́тишь**] *v., pfv. of* **ска́тывать** (*in sense #2*). —**скати́ться,** *refl., pfv. of* **ска́тываться.**

ска́тывать *v.impfv.* **1,** [*pfv.* **ската́ть**] to roll up (*into a ball or bundle*). **2,** [*pfv.* **скати́ть**] to roll down; roll off. —**ска́тываться,** *refl.* [*pfv.* **скати́ться**] **1,** to roll down; roll off; slide down. **2,** to slip off. **3,** *fig.* (*with* **в, на,** *or* **к**) to slip into; drift into (a reactionary political element).

скáут *n.* scout.

скафáндр *n.* **1,** diving suit. **2,** space suit.

скáчка [*gen. pl.* **-чек**] *n.* **1,** horse race. **2,** *pl.* the races. —**скáчки с препя́тствиями,** steeplechase racing (*or* races).

скачкообрáзный *adj.* uneven; spasmodic.

скачóк [*gen.* **-чкá**] *n.* **1,** jump; leap. **2,** *fig.* sudden change. —**скачкáми,** by fits and starts.

скáшивать *v.impfv.* [*pfv.* **скоси́ть**] **1,** to mow; cut. **2,** *fig.* to strike down; cut down. **3,** to twist; tilt. **4,** to cock (one's eye). **5,** to bevel; miter.

скáщивать *v.impfv.* [*pfv.* **скости́ть**] *colloq.* to take off; knock off (a certain amount from a price).

сквáжина *n.* **1,** chink; slit. **2,** hole (*drilled deep into the ground*). —**замóчная сквáжина,** keyhole. —**нефтянáя сквáжина,** oil well.

сквайр *n.* squire.

сквалы́га *n.m. & f., colloq.* cheapskate; skinflint. *Also,* **сквалы́жник,** *n.m.*

сквáттер (тэ) *n.* squatter.

сквер *n.* public garden.

сквéрно *adv.* badly; bad.

сквернослóв *n.* foul-mouthed person. —**сквернослóвие,** *n.* foul language; vile language.

сквернослóвить *v.impfv.* [*pres.* **-влю, -вишь**] to swear; use foul language.

сквéрный *adj.* **1,** foul; nasty. **2,** vulgar; indecent. **3,** *colloq.* bad; awful; lousy.

сквитáть *v.pfv., colloq.* **1,** to pay off (a debt). **2,** *sports* to tie (the score). —**сквитáться,** *refl.* (*with* **с** + *instr.*) *colloq.* **1,** to settle up (with). **2,** to settle scores (with).

сквози́ть *v.impfv.* **1,** *impers.* to be drafty: Здесь сквози́т, there is a draft in here. **2,** (*with* **чéрез**) (*of wind*) to blow through; get through; (*of light*) to pass through; filter through. **3,** to be transparent; admit light. **4,** (*with* **сквозь**) to be seen (through). **5,** *fig.* to creep in: В егó отвéте сквози́ло раздражéние, a trace of irritation crept into his answer.

сквознóй *adj.* **1,** (*of a hole or wound*) going all the way through. **2,** thin; sheer. —**сквознáя вентиля́ция,** cross ventilation. —**сквознóй вéтер,** draft.

сквозня́к [*gen.* **-няка́**] *n.* draft: сидéть на сквозня́ке, to be (*or* sit) in a draft.

сквозь *prep., with acc.* through: пробирáться сквозь толпу́, to make one's way through a crowd.

скворéц [*gen.* **-рца́**] *n.* starling.

скворéчник *n.* bird house (*for starlings*). *Also,* **скворéчня** [*gen. pl.* **-чен**].

скелéт *n.* skeleton. —**скелéтный,** *adj.* skeletal.

скéптик *n.* skeptic. —**скептици́зм,** *n.* skepticism.

скепти́ческий *adj.* skeptical. —**скепти́чески,** *adv.* skeptically; with skepticism.

скéрцо *n. indecl.* scherzo.

скетч *n.* sketch; skit.

ски́дка [*gen. pl.* **-док**] *n.* **1,** discount; reduction. **2,** *fig.* (*with* **на** + *acc.*) allowance (for).

ски́дывать *v.impfv.* [*pfv.* **ски́нуть**] **1,** to throw off; throw down. **2,** *fig., colloq.* to overthrow. **3,** *colloq.* to take off. **4,** *fig.* to shake off (laziness, a feeling, etc.). **5,** to take off; knock off (a certain amount from a price).

ски́ния *n., Bib.* tabernacle.

ски́нуть *v., pfv. of* **ски́дывать.**

ски́петр *n.* scepter.

скипидáр *n.* turpentine. —**скипидáрный,** *adj.* turpentine (*attrib.*).

скирд [*gen.* **скирда́**; *pl.* **скирды́, скирдóв, скирда́м**] *n.* stack (*of hay or straw*). *Also,* **скирда́** [*pl.* **ски́рды, скирд, скирда́м**].

скисáть *v.impfv.* [*pfv.* **ски́снуть**] **1,** to turn sour. **2,** *fig., colloq.* to lose heart; lose interest.

ски́снуть [*past* **скис, ки́сла**] *v., pfv. of* **скисáть.**

скитáлец [*gen.* **-льца**] *n.* wanderer. —**скитáние,** *n.* wandering.

скитáться *v.r.impfv.* to wander; roam.

скиф *n.* **1,** Scythian. **2,** skiff. —**ски́фский,** *adj.* Scythian.

склад *n.* **1,** supply; stock; store. **2,** warehouse; storehouse; depot. **3,** *mil.* dump: склад боеприпáсов, ammunition dump. **4,** way; mode; tenor: склад жи́зни, way of life; склад умá, mentality; turn of mind. **5,** style (*of writing or speaking*). **6,** build; physique. —**ни склáду ни лáду,** no sense whatever. *See also* **склады́.**

склади́ровать *v.impfv. & pfv.* [*pres.* **-рую, -руешь**] to store.

склáдка [*gen. pl.* **-док**] *n.* **1,** fold; crease; pleat. **2,** wrinkle. —**в склáдку,** pleated.

склáдно *adv.* smoothly.

складнóй *adj.* folding; collapsible.

склáдный *adj.* **1,** *colloq.* well-built; well-proportioned. **2,** (*of speech*) smooth; (*of something written*) well phrased. **3,** *colloq.* well-made.

складскóй *adj.* warehouse (*attrib.*); storage (*attrib.*).

склáдчатый *adj.* pleated.

склáдчина *n.* pooling of resources. —**в склáдчину,** jointly.

склады́ [*gen.* **-дóв**] *n.pl., obs.* syllables. —**читáть по складáм,** to read a syllable at a time.

склáдывать *v.impfv.* [*pfv.* **сложи́ть**] **1,** to lay together. **2,** to pile (up). **3,** to put together. **4,** to pack. **5,** to fold. **6,** to compose. **7,** *math.* to add. —**сложá ру́ки,** idly. Сидéть сложá ру́ки, to sit idly by; sit around doing nothing. —**сложи́ть гóлову за** (+ *acc.*), to lay down one's life (for). —**сложи́ть ору́жие,** to lay down one's arms.

склáдываться *v.r.impfv.* [*pfv.* **сложи́ться**] **1,** to be formed. **2,** to take shape. **3,** to develop. Обстоя́тельства склáдывались благоприя́тно, circumstances developed (*or* turned out) favorably. У меня́ сложи́лось впечатлéние, что..., I got the impression that..., **4,** to fold. **5,** *colloq.* to pool one's resources.

склéивать *v.impfv.* [*pfv.* **склéить**] to glue together; paste together. —**склéиваться,** *refl.* to stick together.

склéить *v., pfv. of* **клéить** *and* **склéивать.** —**склéиться,** *refl., pfv. of* **клéиться** *and* **склéиваться.**

склéйка *n.* gluing together.

склеп *n.* burial vault; crypt.

склёпывать *v.impfv.* [*pfv.* **склепáть**] to rivet.

склерóз *n.* sclerosis: рассéянный склерóз, multiple sclerosis. —**склероти́ческий,** *adj.* sclerotic.

склика́ть [*infl.* **скли́чу, скли́чешь**] *v., pfv. of* **скликáть**.

скликáть *v.impfv.* [*pfv.* **склика́ть**] *colloq.* to call together.

скло́ка *n.* squabble; row.

склон *n.* slope; incline. Склон горы́/холма́, side of a mountain/hill. **—на скло́не лет**, in the twilight of one's life.

склоне́ние *n.* 1, inclining. 2, *gram.* declension. 3, *astron.* declination.

склони́ть [*infl.* **склоню́, скло́нишь**] *v., pfv. of* **склоня́ть**. **—склони́ться**, *refl., pfv. of* **склоня́ться**.

скло́нность *n.f.* (*with* **к**) 1, inclination (toward); tendency (toward); disposition (toward). 2, aptitude (for); talent (for); bent (for).

скло́нный *adj.* [*short form* **скло́нен, склонна́, скло́нно, скло́нны**] (*with* **к** *or inf.*) inclined (to); given (to); prone (to).

склоня́емый *adj., gram.* declinable.

склоня́ть *v.impfv.* [*pfv.* **склони́ть**] 1, to incline; bend; bow. 2, *fig.* to persuade. 3, [*pfv.* **просклоня́ть**] *gram.* to decline. 4, [*impfv. only*] *colloq.* to mention constantly; repeat endlessly. *Also,* склоня́ть во всех падежа́х; склоня́ть на все лады́. **—склоня́ть го́лову пе́ред**, to bow to; yield to. **—склоня́ть в свою́ по́льзу**, to win over. **—склоня́ть на свою́ сто́рону**, to win over to one's side.

склоня́ться *v.r.impfv.* [*pfv.* **склони́ться**] 1, to bend over; lean over. 2, (*with* **пе́ред**) to submit (to); yield (to); bow (to). 3, (*with* **на** + *acc. or* **к**) to lean (toward); be inclined (toward). 4, (*with* **на** + *acc. or* **к**) *colloq.* to agree (to). 5, [*impfv. only*] *gram.* to be declined.

скло́чный *adj., colloq.* argumentative; contentious.

скля́нка [*gen. pl.* **-нок**] *n.* 1, small bottle; vial. 2, *naut.* bell: во́семь скля́нок, eight bells.

скоба́ [*pl.* **ско́бы, скоб, скоба́м**] *n.* clamp.

ско́бка [*gen. pl.* **-бок**] *n.* 1, = **скоба́**. 2, *pl.* parentheses. 3, [*also,* **квадра́тные ско́бки**] brackets. **—в ско́бках**, parenthetically.

скобли́ть *v.impfv.* [*pres.* **скоблю́, ско́блишь** *or* **скобли́шь**] to scrape.

скобяно́й *adj.* hardware (*attrib.*): скобяно́й това́р; скобяны́е изде́лия, hardware.

ско́ванность *n.f.* 1, (sense of) awkwardness; inhibition. 2, stiffness (*of movements*).

ско́ванный *adj.* awkward; unnatural. **—ско́ванный льда́ми**, (*of a river*) frozen over; icebound.

скова́ть [*infl.* **скую́, скуёшь**] *v., pfv. of* **ско́вывать**.

сковорода́ [*pl.* **ско́вороды, сковоро́д, -рода́м**] *n.* frying pan.

сковоро́дка [*gen. pl.* **-док**] *n., colloq.* frying pan.

ско́вывать *v.impfv.* [*pfv.* **скова́ть**] 1, to make; forge. 2, to forge together; *fig.* unite. 3, to chain; shackle. 4, to constrain (someone's movements). 5, *fig.* to paralyze: Страх скова́л его́, he was paralyzed by fear. 6, *mil.* to tie down; pin down. 7, to freeze: Лёд скова́л ре́ку, the river was frozen over. *Also impers.* моро́зом скова́ло доро́гу, the road was frozen.

скола́чивать *v.impfv.* [*pfv.* **сколоти́ть**] 1, to nail together. 2, to knock together (*i.e.* build). 3, *fig., colloq.*

to put together; form. 4, *colloq.* to scrape together (money).

ско́лок [*gen.* **-лка**] *n.* (*with gen. or* **с** + *gen.*) exact copy (of); perfect likeness (of).

сколоти́ть [*infl.* **-лочу́, -ло́тишь**] *v., pfv. of* **скола́чивать**.

сколо́ть [*infl.* **сколю́, ско́лешь**] *v., pfv. of* **ска́лывать**.

сколь *adv.* 1, how. 2, as much as.

скольже́ние *n.* sliding; slippage; skid(ding).

скользи́ть *v.impfv.* [*pfv.* **скользну́ть**; *pres.* **-льжу́, -льзи́шь**] 1, to slide. 2, to glide (*along a surface*). 3, to slip. **—скользи́ть по верха́м** *or* **по пове́рхности**, to skim the surface.

ско́льзкий *adj.* [*short form* **ско́льзок, скользка́** *or* **ско́льзка, ско́льзко, ско́льзки**] 1, slippery. 2, *fig.* slippery; treacherous. 3, *fig.* ticklish; delicate.

ско́льзко *adj., used predicatively,* slippery: На у́лицах ско́льзко, the streets are slippery.

скользну́ть *v.pfv.* 1, *pfv. of* **скользи́ть**. 2, (*with* **по**) (*of a bullet*) to graze; glance off. 3, to slip; sneak (into, by, past, etc.).

скользя́щий *adj.* sliding: скользя́щая шкала́, sliding scale. **—скользя́щий уда́р**, glancing blow. **—скользя́щий у́зел**, slipknot.

ско́лько *adv.* how much?; how many?: Ско́лько миль?, how many miles? Ско́лько э́то сто́ит?, how much does this cost? **—во ско́лько?**, *colloq.* (at) what time? **—ско́лько вре́мени**, *see* **вре́мя**. **—ско́лько ни**, however much; as much as. **—ско́лько хоти́те**; **ско́лько уго́дно**, as much as you like.

ско́лько-нибудь *adv.* 1, (*with gen.*) any ... at all. 2, (*with verbs and adjectives*) the least bit.

скома́ндовать *v.pfv.* [*infl.* **-дую, -дуешь**] to order; command.

скомбини́ровать *v., pfv. of* **комбини́ровать**.

ско́мкать *v., pfv. of* **ко́мкать**.

скоморо́х *n., colloq.* buffoon; clown. **—скоморо́шество**, *n., colloq.* buffoonery.

скомпили́ровать *v., pfv. of* **компили́ровать**.

скомпонова́ть *v., pfv. of* **компонова́ть**.

скомпромети́ровать *v., pfv. of* **компромети́ровать**.

сконструи́ровать *v., pfv. of* **конструи́ровать**.

сконфу́женный *adj.* confused; flustered; embarrassed; bewildered.

сконфу́зить *v., pfv. of* **конфу́зить**. **—сконфу́зиться**, *refl., pfv. of* **конфу́зиться**.

сконцентри́ровать *v., pfv. of* **концентри́ровать**. **—сконцентри́роваться**, *refl., pfv. of* **концентри́роваться**.

сконча́ться *v.r.pfv.* to die; pass away.

скопа́ *n.* osprey.

скопе́ц [*gen.* **-пца́**] *n.* 1, castrated man or boy. 2, *hist.* member of the *skoptsy,* a religious sect practicing castration.

скопидо́м *n., colloq.* cheapskate; skinflint. **—скопидо́мство**, *n., colloq.* miserliness.

скопи́ровать *v., pfv. of* **копи́ровать**.

скопи́ть [*infl.* **скоплю́, ско́пишь**] *v., pfv. of* **ска́пливать**. **—скопи́ться**, *refl., pfv. of* **ска́пливаться**.

ско́пище *n.* crowd; throng.

скопле́ние *n.* **1,** accumulating; accumulation. **2,** concentration. **3,** crowd; throng. —**звёздное скопле́ние,** star cluster.

ско́пом *adv., colloq.* in a group; in a crowd; en masse.

скорбе́ть *v.impfv.* [*pres.* **-блю́, -би́шь**] **1,** to grieve; mourn. **2,** (*with* **о**) to mourn the loss of.

ско́рбный *adj.* sorrowful; mournful. —**ско́рбно,** *adv.* sorrowfully; sadly.

скорбь *n.f.* grief; sorrow.

скорбя́щий *adj.* grieving; bereaved. —*n.* mourner.

скоре́е *also,* скоре́й *adj., comp. of* ско́рый. —*adv.* **1,** *comp. of* ско́ро. **2,** hurry up! Иди́ скоре́й!, come quickly! **3,** rather; sooner. **4,** more likely. **5,** more: скоре́е похо́ж на, more like. —**скоре́е всего́,** most probably; most likely.

скорлупа́ [*pl.* **-лу́пы**] *n.* shell (*of an egg, nut, etc.*). —**уйти́ в свою́ скорлупу́,** to withdraw into one's shell.

скорми́ть [*infl.* **скормлю́, ско́рмишь**] *v., pfv. of* ска́рмливать.

скорня́жный *adj.* of furriers; furrier's (*attrib.*).

скорня́к [*gen.* **-няка́**] *n.* furrier.

ско́ро *adv.* **1,** fast; quickly. **2,** soon. —**не ско́ро,** not for some time; not for a long time.

скорогово́рка [*gen. pl.* **-рок**] *n.* **1,** rapid speech; patter. **2,** tongue twister.

скоро́мный *adj.* not to be eaten on fast days. —**скоро́мный день,** non-fast day.

скоропали́тельный *adj., colloq.* hasty; rash.

ско́ропись *n.f.* cursive writing. —**скоропи́сный,** *adj.* cursive.

скороподъёмность *n.f., aero.* rate of climb.

скоропо́ртящийся *adj.* perishable.

скоропости́жный *adj.* (*of death*) sudden.

скороспе́лый *adj.* **1,** early-ripening; fast-maturing. **2,** *fig., colloq.* hasty; premature.

скоростни́к [*gen.* **-ника́**] *n.* high-speed worker.

скоростно́й *adj.* **1,** of speed; speed (*attrib.*). **2,** high-speed. —**скоростно́й бег на конька́х,** speed skating.

скоростре́льный *adj.* (*of a gun*) rapid-firing.

ско́рость [*pl.* **ско́рости, -сте́й, -стя́м**] *n.f.* **1,** speed; velocity. **2,** gear: переключа́ться на пе́рвую ско́рость, to shift into first gear.

скоросшива́тель *n.m.* binder (*for papers*).

скорота́ть *v., pfv. of* корота́ть.

скороте́чный *adj.* transitory; short-lived.

скорохо́д *n.* **1,** *obs.* footman. **2,** *colloq.* fast runner.

скорпио́н *n.* **1,** scorpion. **2,** *cap.* Scorpio.

ско́рчить *v., pfv. of* ко́рчить. —**ско́рчиться,** *refl., pfv. of* ко́рчиться.

ско́рый *adj.* **1,** fast; quick; swift; speedy. **2,** impending; forthcoming. —**в ско́ром бу́дущем,** in the near future. —**в ско́ром вре́мени,** before long; shortly. —**до ско́рой встре́чи!; до ско́рого свида́ния!,** see you soon! —**на ско́рую ру́ку, 1,** in a slapdash manner. **2,** in a hurry; on the run. —**ско́рая по́мощь, 1,** first aid. **2,** *colloq.* ambulance.

скос *n.* **1,** slope; slant. **2,** bevel; miter.

скоси́ть *v.pfv.* **1,** [*pfv.* **скошу́, ско́сишь**] *pfv. of* коси́ть[1] *and* ска́шивать (*in senses #1 & #2*). **2,** [*infl.*

скошу́, скоси́шь] *v., pfv. of* коси́ть[2] *and* ска́шивать (*in senses #3, 4 & 5*).

скости́ть *v., pfv. of* ска́щивать.

скот [*gen.* **скота́**; *acc.* **скот**] *n.* cattle; livestock. —**ме́лкий рога́тый скот,** sheep and goats. —**кру́пный рога́тый скот,** cattle (*cows, oxen, etc.*). —**рабо́чий** *or* **тя́гловый скот,** draft animals.

скоти́на *n.* **1,** cattle; livestock. **2,** *colloq.* brute; beast.

ско́тник *n.* **1,** person who tends cattle. **2,** *colloq.* cattle yard.

ско́тный *adj.* cattle (*attrib.*). —**ско́тный двор, 1,** stockyard. **2,** farmyard.

скотобо́йня [*gen. pl.* **-бо́ен**] *n.* slaughterhouse.

скотово́д *n.* cattle breeder. —**скотово́дство,** *n.* cattle raising; cattle breeding. —**скотово́дческий,** *adj.* cattle-breeding (*attrib.*).

скотоло́жство *n.* sodomy.

скотоприго́нный *adj., in* **скотоприго́нный двор,** stockyard.

ско́тский *adj.* **1,** cattle (*attrib.*). **2,** *colloq.* like that of an animal.

ско́тство *n.* **1,** animal-like existence. **2,** *colloq.* barbarity.

скра́дывать *v.impfv.* to conceal.

скра́шивать *v.impfv.* [*pfv.* **скра́сить**] **1,** to make more attractive. **2,** *fig.* to soften the effect of; tone down; relieve. **3,** *fig.* to brighten up (one's life, existence, etc.).

скребни́ца *n.* currycomb.

скребо́к [*gen.* **-бка́**] *n.* scraper.

скре́жет *n.* **1,** grinding; grating; clanking. **2,** grinding; gnashing (*of teeth*).

скрежета́ть *v.impfv.* [*pres.* **скрежещу́, скреже́щешь**] **1,** *v.i.* to grind; grate; clank. **2,** (*with instr.*) to grind; gnash (one's teeth).

скре́па *n.* **1,** clamp; brace. **2,** *fig.* tie; bond. **3,** *obs.* countersignature.

скрепи́ть [*infl.* **-плю́, -пи́шь**] *v., pfv. of* скрепля́ть.

скре́пка [*gen. pl.* **-пок**] *n.* paper clip.

скрепля́ть *v.impfv.* [*pfv.* **скрепи́ть**] **1,** to fasten together; clamp together. **2,** *fig.* to cement (a friendship, ties, etc.). **3,** to countersign. —**скрепя́ се́рдце,** reluctantly; grudgingly.

скрести́ *v.impfv.* [*pres.* **скребу́, скребёшь;** *past* **скрёб, скребла́, скребло́, скребли́**] to scrape. —**скрести́сь,** *refl.* (*of a cat, mouse, etc.*) to scratch; make a scratching noise.

скрести́ть [*infl.* **-щу́, -сти́шь**] *v., pfv. of* скре́щивать.

скреще́ние *n.* **1,** crossing: скреще́ние шпаг, crossing of swords. **2,** crossing; intersection.

скре́щивание *n.* **1,** crossing. **2,** crossbreeding.

скре́щивать *v.impfv.* [*pfv.* **скрести́ть**] **1,** to cross; place crosswise. **2,** cross; crossbreed. —**скре́щивать шпа́ги** *or* **мечи́,** to cross swords.

скриви́ть *v., pfv. of* криви́ть. —**скриви́ться,** *refl., pfv. of* криви́ться.

скрижа́ль *n.f.* **1,** tablet (*bearing a sacred text*). **2,** *pl.* (*with gen.*) annals (of).

скрип *n.* squeak; creak.

скрипа́ч [*gen.* **-пача́**] *n.m.* [*fem.* **-па́чка**] *n.* violinist.

скрипе́ть *v.impfv.* [*pfv.* **проскрипе́ть;** *pres.* **-плю́, -пи́шь**] to squeak; creak.

скрипи́чный *adj.* violin (*attrib.*). —**скрипи́чный ключ,** treble clef.

скри́пка [*gen. pl.* -**пок**] *n.* violin. —**игра́ть пе́рвую скри́пку,** to play the leading role; be top dog. —**игра́ть втору́ю скри́пку,** to play second fiddle.

скрипу́чий *adj.* squeaky; creaky.

скро́ить *v., pfv. of* **крои́ть** (*in sense #2*).

скро́мник *n.* modest person.

скро́мничать *v.impfv.* to be overly modest.

скро́мный *adj.* modest. —**скро́мно,** *adv.* modestly. —**скро́мность,** *n.f.* modesty.

скрупулёзный *adj.* scrupulous; meticulous.

скрути́ть *v.pfv.* [*infl.* **скручу́, скру́тишь**] **1,** *pfv. of* **крути́ть** (*in sense #2*) *and* **скру́чивать. 2,** *colloq.* to subdue; bend to one's will. **3,** *colloq.* (*of an illness*) to lay (someone) low. —**скрути́ться,** *refl., pfv. of* **скру́чиваться.**

скру́чивать *v.impfv.* [*pfv.* **скрути́ть**] **1,** to twist (cloth, rope, etc.). **2,** to roll (a cigarette). **3,** to tie up; bind securely. **4,** *in* скрути́ть ру́ки кому́-нибудь за спино́й, to twist someone's arms behind his back. —**скру́чиваться,** *refl.* to become twisted.

скрыва́ть *v.impfv.* [*pfv.* **скрыть**] to hide; conceal. —**скрыва́ться,** *refl.* **1,** to hide; be hiding. **2,** to disappear: скрыва́ться и́з виду, to disappear from view; pass out of sight. **3,** [*impfv. only*] to be concealed. **4,** to steal away; steal off.

скры́тие *n.* hiding; concealment.

скры́тничать *v.impfv., colloq.* to be secretive.

скры́тность *n.f.* **1,** secretiveness. **2,** *colloq.* secrecy.

скры́тный *adj.* secretive.

скры́тый *adj.* **1,** hidden; concealed. **2,** (*of threats*) veiled. **3,** latent.

скрыть [*infl.* **скро́ю, скро́ешь**] *v., pfv. of* **скрыва́ть.** —**скры́ться,** *refl., pfv. of* **скрыва́ться.**

скрю́чивать *v.impfv.* [*pfv.* **скрю́чить**] *colloq.* **1,** to bend sharply. Скрю́чить но́ги, to bend/curl/fold up one's legs. Скрю́ченный от тя́жести, bent over from the weight. **2,** *impers.* to be bent; be doubled up: Его́ скрю́чило от бо́ли, he was doubled up in pain. —**скрю́чиваться,** *refl., colloq.* **1,** to huddle up. **2,** to be bent; be doubled up.

скря́га *n.m. & f.* miser; skinflint.

скря́жничать *v.impfv., colloq.* to be a miser.

скуде́ть *v.impfv.* [*pfv.* **оскуде́ть**] to become depleted.

ску́дный *adj.* scanty; meager. —**ску́дность; ску́-дость,** *n.f.* scarcity; paucity.

ску́ка *n.* boredom.

скула́ [*pl.* **ску́лы**] *n.* cheekbone.

скула́стый *adj.* having high cheekbones.

скули́ть *v.impfv.* (*of an animal*) to whine; whimper.

ску́льптор *n.* sculptor.

скульпту́ра *n.* sculpture.

скульпту́рный *adj.* **1,** sculptural; sculptor's. **2,** *fig.* statuesque.

ску́мбрия *n.* mackerel.

скунс *n.* skunk. —**ску́нсовый,** *adj.* skunk (*attrib.*).

скупа́ть *v.impfv.* [*pfv.* **скупи́ть**] to buy up.

скупердя́й *n., colloq.* cheapskate; skinflint; tightwad.

скупе́ц [*gen.* -**пца́**] *n.* miser.

скупи́ть [*infl.* **скуплю́, ску́пишь**] *v., pfv. of* **скупа́ть.**

скупи́ться *v.r.impfv.* [*pfv.* **поскупи́ться;** *pres.* **скуплю́сь, скупи́шься**] **1,** to be stingy. **2,** to scrimp; skimp. **3,** (*with* на + *acc. pl.*) to stint (on); be sparing (with).

ску́пка *n.* buying up.

ску́по *adv.* **1,** stinting oneself; sparingly; frugally. **2,** tersely.

скупо́й *adj.* **1,** stingy. **2,** (*of light, soil, sun, etc.*) poor; weak; (*of rainfall, supplies, rations, etc.*) meager. **3,** (*with* на + *acc. pl.*) sparing (with).

ску́пость *n.f.* stinginess.

ску́пщик *n.* buyer (*of items with the intention of reselling them*).

скуфья́ [*gen. pl.* -**фе́й**] *n.* skullcap. *Also,* **скуфе́йка** [*gen. pl.* -**фе́ек**].

скуча́ть *v.impfv.* **1,** to be bored. **2,** (*with* по + *dat., but prepl. with pers. pronouns*) to miss; long for; yearn for.

скуча́ющий *adj.* bored.

ску́ченный *adj.* congested; overcrowded. —**ску́ченность,** *n.f.* congestion; overcrowding.

ску́чиваться *v.r.impfv.* [*pfv.* **ску́читься**] *colloq.* to crowd together; cluster.

скучне́ть *v.impfv.* [*pfv.* **поскучне́ть**] *colloq.* to look bored; look glum.

ску́чно *adv.* in a boring manner. —*adj., used predicatively* **1,** bored: Мне ску́чно, I am bored. **2,** boring: Ску́чно сиде́ть до́ма одному́, it is boring to sit home alone.

ску́чный *adj.* **1,** boring; tiresome; tedious. **2,** bored.

ску́шать *v.pfv.* to eat; eat up.

слабе́ть *v.impfv.* [*pfv.* **ослабе́ть**] **1,** to weaken; become weak; grow weak. **2,** (*of one's eyesight, health, etc.*) to fail; get worse. **3,** to slacken; subside.

слабина́ *n.* **1,** slack (*in a rope*). **2,** *colloq.* weak spot.

слаби́тельный *adj.* cathartic; purgative. —**слаби́тельное,** *n.* laxative.

сла́бить *v.impfv., impers.* to have diarrhea: Его́ сла́бит, he has diarrhea.

сла́бо *adv.* **1,** weakly; faintly. **2,** poorly.

слабово́лие *n.* weakness of will. —**слабово́льный,** *adj.* weak-willed.

слабора́звитый *adj.* (*of countries*) underdeveloped.

слабоси́лие *n.* weakness; lack of strength.

слабоси́льный *adj.* **1,** weak; feeble. **2,** low-powered.

сла́бость *n.f.* **1,** weakness; debility. **2,** *fig.* weakness: име́ть сла́бость к, to have a weakness for.

слабоу́мие *n.* feeble-mindedness.

слабоу́мный *adj.* feeble-minded. —*n.* feeble-minded person; imbecile; moron.

сла́бый *adj.* **1,** weak. **2,** poor; weak; bad. **3,** (*of light*) dim. **4,** (*of hope*) faint; slight. **5,** loose; lack; slack.

сла́ва *n.* **1,** glory. **2,** fame. **3,** reputation. —**во сла́ву** (+ *gen.*), to the glory of. —**на сла́ву,** marvelously; wonderfully well: уда́ться на сла́ву, to be a great success. —**сла́ва бо́гу,** *see* бог.

слави́ст *n.* Slavicist. —**слави́стика,** *n.* Slavic studies.

сла́вить *v.impfv.* [*pres.* -**влю, -вишь**] **1,** to glorify. **2,** to sing the praises of. —**сла́виться,** *refl.* (*with instr. or* как) to be famous (for *or* as); be renowned (for).

сла́вка [*gen. pl.* **-вок**] *n.* warbler.

сла́вно *adv., colloq.* wonderfully. —*adj., used predicatively, colloq.* nice; wonderful: Как сла́вно!, how nice!; how wonderful!

сла́вный *adj.* **1,** glorious. **2,** famous; renowned. **3,** *colloq.* nice.

славосло́вие *n.* **1,** glorification. **2,** *pl.* paeans of praise.

славосло́вить *v.impfv.* [*pres.* **-влю, -вишь**] to extol; sing the praises of.

славяни́н [*pl.* **-я́не, -я́н**] *n.m.* [*fem.* **-я́нка**] Slav.

славянофи́л *n.* Slavophile.

славя́нский *adj.* Slavic; Slavonic.

слага́емое *n., decl. as an adj.* element; component.

слага́ть *v.impfv.* [*pfv.* **сложи́ть**] **1,** to compose. **2,** (with **с себя́**) to give up; relinquish. —**слага́ться,** *refl.* [*impfv. only*] (with **из**) to be composed of; consist of.

слад *n., colloq., in* сла́ду нет с (+ *instr.*), he (she) is impossible; there is no dealing with him (her).

сла́дить [*infl.* **-жу, -дишь**] *v., pfv. of* сла́живать.

сла́дкий *adj.* [*short form* сла́док, сладка́, сла́дко, сла́дки; *comp.* сла́ще] sweet. —**сла́дкое мя́со,** sweetbread.

сла́дко *adv.* sweetly; sweet.

сла́дкое *n., decl. as an adj.* **1,** sweets. **2,** dessert.

сладкое́жка [*gen. pl.* **-жек**] *n.m. & f., colloq.* person with a sweet tooth.

сладкозву́чный *adj.* sweet-sounding.

сладоречи́вый *adj.* smooth-spoken.

сла́достный *adj.* sweet.

сладостра́стие *n.* sensuality. —**сладостра́стный,** *adj.* sensual.

сла́дость *n.f.* **1,** sweetness. **2,** *pl.* sweets. **3,** *fig., colloq.* delight.

сла́женно *adv.* **1,** in harmony. **2,** harmoniously.

сла́женность *n.f.* harmony.

сла́женный *adj.* harmonious; well-coordinated.

сла́живать *v.impfv.* [*pfv.* **сла́дить**] *colloq.* **1,** to arrange. **2,** (with **с** + *instr.*) to handle; cope (with). —**сла́живаться,** *refl., colloq.* **1,** to be arranged. **2,** to reach an agreement.

сла́зить *v.pfv.* [*infl.* **сла́жу, сла́зишь**] **1,** to climb up (to an attic, onto a roof, etc.). **2,** to go down (to a cellar, basement, etc.). **3,** (with **в** + *acc.*) *colloq.* to reach into (something) and remove something.

сла́лом *n.* slalom.

сла́нец [*gen.* **-нца**] *n.* **1,** slate. **2,** shale. **3,** schist. —**сла́нцевый,** *adj.* slate (*attrib.*); shale (*attrib.*).

сласте́на *n.m. & f., colloq.* person with a sweet tooth.

сла́сти [*gen.* **-сте́й**; *dat.* **-стя́м**] *n.pl.* sweets.

сластолюби́вый *adj.* sensual.

слать *v.impfv.* [*pfv.* **посла́ть**; *pres.* **шлю, шлёшь**] to send.

слаща́вый *adj.* sugary; honeyed.

сла́ще *adj., comp. of* сла́дкий.

сле́ва *adv.* **1,** from the left. **2,** to (*or* on) the left.

слегка́ *adv.* **1,** slightly; a little. **2,** lightly; gently.

след [*gen.* сле́да *or* следа́; *dat.* сле́ду; *2nd loc.* следу́; *pl.* следы́] *n.* **1,** track: све́жие следы́, fresh tracks. **2,** trail: напа́сть на след (+ *gen.*), to come upon the trail of... **3,** trace: От э́того не оста́лось ни следа́, not a

trace of it remains. **4,** footprint; footstep. **5,** mark; scar: следы́ шин, tire marks; следы́ о́спы, smallpox scars. *See also* **сле́дом.**

следи́ть *v.impfv.* [*pres.* **слежу́, следи́шь**] (with **за** + *instr.*) **1,** to follow (*with one's eyes*). **2,** to watch; look after; keep an eye on. **3,** to see that (order, discipline, etc.) is maintained. **4,** *fig.* to follow; keep track of; keep abreast of; keep up with. **5,** to shadow; keep under surveillance. **6,** [*pfv.* **наследи́ть**] *colloq.* to leave footmarks: следи́ть сапога́ми на полу́, to track up the floor.

сле́дование *n.* **1,** following. **2,** movement; travel. По *or* на пути́ сле́дования, along the route. —**по́езд да́льнего сле́дования,** long-distance train.

сле́дователь *n.m.* investigator.

сле́довательно *adv.* consequently.

сле́довать *v.impfv.* [*pfv.* **после́довать**; *pres.* **-дую, -дуешь**] **1,** (with **за** + *instr.*) to follow: сле́довать за проводнико́м, to follow the guide. **2,** (with **за** + *instr.*) to follow; come after: Ле́то сле́дует за весно́й, summer follows spring. Собы́тия сле́довали одно́ за други́м, events followed one upon another. **3,** to follow; come as a result. Отве́та не после́довало, no reply was forthcoming. **4,** (with *dat.*) to follow (rules, advice, an example, etc.). **5,** [*impfv. only*] *impers.* (with **из**) to follow (from): Из э́того сле́дует, что..., from this it follows that... **6,** [*impfv. only*] to proceed: сле́довать в Ки́ев, to proceed to Kiev. **7,** [*impfv. only*] (with **в** *or* **до**) (*of a train or ship*) to be bound for. **8,** [*impfv. only*] *impers.* one should: Сле́дует отме́тить, что..., it should be noted that... Как и сле́довало ожида́ть, as was to be expected. **9,** [*impfv. only*] *impers.* to be owed; be due: Ско́лько с меня́ сле́дует?, how much do I owe? —**как сле́дует,** properly. —**кому́ сле́дует,** to the proper person. —**куда́ сле́дует,** to the proper quarter.

сле́дом *adv.* **1,** close behind; in someone's footsteps. **2,** immediately afterward. —**сле́дом за** (+ *instr.*), **1,** right behind; close behind. **2,** right after; immediately after.

следопы́т *n.* **1,** hunter (who tracks down animals). **2,** *fig.* pioneer; trailblazer.

сле́дственный *adj.* of inquiry; investigatory.

сле́дствие *n.* **1,** consequence; result. **2,** investigation; inquiry. —**причи́на и сле́дствие,** cause and effect.

сле́дуемый *adj.* due: сле́дуемая мне су́мма, the amount due me.

сле́дующий *adj.* **1,** next: на сле́дующий день, the next day; на сле́дующей неде́ле, next week. **2,** following: сле́дующим о́бразом, in the following manner. —**сле́дующее,** *n.* the following.

слежа́ться [*infl.* **-жи́тся**] *v.r., pfv. of* слёживаться.

слеже́ние *n., aerospace* tracking; monitoring. —**ста́нция слеже́ния,** tracking station.

слёживаться *v.r.impfv.* [*pfv.* **слежа́ться**] **1,** to become firmly packed. **2,** to become rumpled (*from lying around a long time*).

слёжка *n.* surveillance: установи́ть слёжку за (+ *instr.*), to place under surveillance.

слеза́ [*pl.* **слёзы, слёз, слеза́м**] *n.* tear: быть в слеза́х, to be in tears.

слеза́ть *v.impfv.* [*pfv.* слезть] (*with* с + *gen.*) **1,** to climb down (from). **2,** to dismount (from). **3,** *colloq.* to get off (a train, bus, etc.). **4,** *colloq.* (*of paint, skin, etc.*) to come off.

слези́нка [*gen. pl.* -нок] *n.* tear; teardrop.

слези́ться *v.r.impfv.* (*of one's eyes*) to water; tear.

слезли́вый *adj.* **1,** easily moved to tears. **2,** tearful. **3,** *fig.* overly sentimental; maudlin.

слёзный *adj.* **1,** tear (*attrib.*); lachrymal: слёзный про́ток, tear duct. **2,** plaintive.

слезоточи́вый *adj.* (*of one's eyes*) teary. —**слезо-точи́вый газ,** tear gas.

слезть [*infl. like* лезть] *v., pfv. of* слеза́ть.

слепе́нь [*gen.* -пня́] *n.m.* horsefly.

слепе́ц [*gen.* -пца́] *n.m.* blind man.

слепи́ть[1] *v.impfv.* [*pres.* слеплю́, слепи́шь] **1,** *obs.* to blind. **2,** to dazzle.

слепи́ть[2] [*infl.* слеплю́, сле́пишь] *v., pfv. of* лепи́ть (*in sense #2*) *and* слепля́ть. —**слепи́ться,** *refl., pfv. of* слепля́ться.

слепля́ть *v.impfv.* [*pfv.* слепи́ть] to glue together; paste together. —**слепля́ться,** *refl.* to stick together; become stuck.

сле́пнуть *v.impfv.* [*pfv.* осле́пнуть; *past* слеп *or* сле́пнул, сле́пла] to go blind; lose one's eyesight.

сле́по *adv.* blindly.

слепо́й *adj.* blind. —*n.* blind man.

слепо́к [*gen.* -пка] *n.* cast; mold.

слепота́ *n.* blindness.

слепы́ш [*gen.* -пыша́] *n.* mole rat.

слеса́рный *adj.* metalworking (*attrib.*); locksmith (*attrib.*). Also, **слеса́рский.**

сле́сарь [*pl.* слесаря́ *or* слеса́ри] *n.m.* **1,** metalworker. **2,** locksmith.

слёт *n.* **1,** flight (*of birds*). **2,** *fig.* gathering; meeting; rally.

слета́ть[1] *v.impfv.* [*pfv.* слете́ть] **1,** (*with* с + *gen.*) to fly down (from). **2,** to fly away. **3,** (*with* с + *gen.*) *colloq.* to slip off; fall off. **4,** *colloq.* to jump down. **5,** *fig.* (*of a feeling*) to pass; disappear. **6,** *in* слета́ть с губ/уст/языка́, to escape one's lips. —**слета́ться,** *refl.* to fly in (*from many places*); come flying in.

слета́ть[2] *v.pfv.* to fly (*to a certain place and return*).

слете́ть [*infl.* -чу́, -ти́шь] *v., pfv. of* слета́ть[1]. —**слете́ться,** *refl., pfv. of* слета́ться.

слечь *v.pfv.* [*infl. like* лечь] to take ill; take to one's bed.

сли́ва *n.* **1,** plum. **2,** plum tree.

слива́ть *v.impfv.* [*pfv.* слить] **1,** to pour off; pour out. **2,** to pour together. **3,** *fig.* to combine; merge. —**слива́ться,** *refl.* **1,** (*of rivers*) to meet; converge. **2,** (*of organizations*) to merge. **3,** (*of sounds, colors, etc.*) to blend. Слива́ться с фо́ном, to melt into the background.

сли́вки [*gen.* -вок] *n.pl.* cream. —**сли́вки о́бщества,** the cream of society.

сли́вовый *adj.* plum (*attrib.*).

сли́вочник *n.* creamer; cream pot.

сли́вочный *adj.* **1,** cream (*attrib.*). **2,** creamy. —**сли́вочное ма́сло,** butter. —**сли́вочное моро́женое,** ice cream. —**сли́вочный сыр,** cream cheese.

сливя́нка *n.* plum brandy.

слиза́ть [*infl.* слижу́, сли́жешь] *v., pfv. of* сли́зывать.

сли́зень [*gen.* -зня] *n.m., zool.* slug.

сли́зистый *adj.* **1,** slimy. **2,** *anat.* mucous: сли́зистая оболо́чка, mucous membrane.

слизня́к [*gen.* -няка́] *n.m., zool.* slug.

сли́зывать *v.impfv.* [*pfv.* слиза́ть] to lick off.

слизь *n.f.* **1,** mucus. **2,** [*also,* расти́тельная слизь] mucilage. **3,** slime.

слиня́лый *adj., colloq.* faded.

слиня́ть *v.pfv., colloq.* to fade.

слипа́ться *v.r.impfv.* [*pfv.* сли́пнуться] **1,** to stick together. **2,** [*impfv. only*] (*of one's eyes*) to be heavy with sleep: У меня́ глаза́ слипа́ются, I can hardly keep my eyes open.

сли́пнуться [*past* сли́пся, сли́плась] *v.r., pfv. of* слипа́ться.

сли́тно *adv.* **1,** together. **2,** (*of a way of spelling*) as one word.

сли́тный *adj.* **1,** continuous; unbroken. **2,** (*of spelling*) as one word.

сли́ток [*gen.* -тка] *n.* **1,** ingot; bar. **2,** *pl.* bullion: зо́лото в сли́тках, gold bullion.

слить [*infl.* солью́, сольёшь; *past fem.* слила́] *v., pfv. of* слива́ть. —**сли́ться,** *refl.* [*past tense stress as in* ли́ться] *pfv. of* слива́ться.

слича́ть *v.impfv.* [*pfv.* сличи́ть] to compare (against each other).

сли́шком *adv.* **1,** too. **2,** (*with certain verbs*) too much; excessively. —**сли́шком мно́го,** too much; too many.

слия́ние *n.* **1,** blending (*of styles, colors, etc.*). **2,** confluence (*of rivers*). **3,** merger; amalgamation. —**слия́ние зву́ков,** *phonet.* liaison.

слобода́ [*pl.* сло́боды, слобо́д, слобода́м] *n., hist.* settlement inhabited by tradesmen or free peasants.

слова́к *n.m.* [*fem.* -ва́чка] *n.* Slovak.

слова́рный *adj.* **1,** dictionary (*attrib.*). **2,** lexical. Слова́рный запа́с, vocabulary.

слова́рь [*gen.* -варя́] *n.m.* **1,** dictionary. **2,** vocabulary.

слова́цкий *adj.* Slovak.

слове́нец [*gen.* -нца] *n.m.* [*fem.* -нка] Slovene. —**слове́нский,** *adj.* Slovenian.

слове́сник *n.* **1,** philologist. **2,** teacher of Russian language and literature.

слове́сный *adj.* verbal; oral.

слове́чко [*pl.* -чки, -чек] *n., dim. of* сло́во. —**замо́лвить** *or* **заки́нуть слове́чко за** (+ *acc.*), to put in a word for.

сло́вник *n.* word list (*for a dictionary*); subject list (*for an encyclopedia*).

сло́вно *conj.* **1,** as if; as though. **2,** like.

сло́во [*pl.* слова́, слов, слова́м] *n.* **1,** word. **2,** one's word: Сдержа́ть (своё) сло́во, to keep one's word. Челове́к сло́ва, a man of his word. **3,** the floor: брать сло́во, to take the floor; проси́ть сло́ва, to ask for the floor. —**в двух слова́х,** in a few words; briefly. —**други́ми слова́ми,** in other words. —**игра́ слов,** play on words. —**к сло́ву (сказа́ть),** by the way. —**на слова́х, 1,** orally. **2,** in words. —**одни́м сло́вом,** in a word. —**от сло́ва до сло́ва,** from beginning to end. —**по слова́м** (+ *gen.*), according to. —**свобо́да сло́ва,** freedom of speech. —**слов нет,** *colloq.* there is no denying; it must be said that... —**сло́во в сло́во,** word for word. —**сло́во за́ слово,** gradually; as the conversation progressed. —**сло́вом,** in a word. —**с пе́рвого сло́ва,** at the outset (of the conversation).

словоохо́тливый *adj.* talkative; loquacious.

словосочета́ние *n.* combination of words. —**усто́йчивое словосочета́ние,** set expression.

словцо́ [*gen. pl.* -**вéц**] *n., colloq.* word. —**кра́сное словцо́,** clever *or* apt expression. Для кра́сного словца́, for effect.

слог [*pl.* **сло́ги, слого́в, слога́м**] *n.* 1, syllable. 2, style.

слогово́й *adj.* syllabic.

слоёный *adj.* puff (*attrib.*); flaky. —**слоёный пиро́г,** puff pastry. —**слоёное тéсто,** puff paste.

сложе́ние *n.* 1, *math.* addition. 2, build; physique.

сложённый *adj.* built: хорошо́ сложённый ю́ноша, well-built young man.

сложи́вшийся *adj.* 1, (*of a person*) fully developed; mature. 2, (*of a situation*) that has developed.

сложи́ть [*infl.* **сложу́, сло́жишь**] *v., pfv. of* **скла́дывать** *and* **слага́ть.** —**сложи́ться,** *refl., pfv. of* **скла́дываться.**

сло́жно *adv.* in a complicated way.

сложноподчинённый *adj., in* **сложноподчинённое предложе́ние,** complex sentence.

сложносочинённый *adj., in* **сложносочинённое предложе́ние,** compound sentence.

сло́жность *n.f.* 1, complexity. 2, *pl.* difficulties. —**в о́бщей сло́жности,** in all; a total of; all told.

сло́жный *adj.* 1, complex; complicated. 2, difficult. 3, intricate. —**сло́жное предложе́ние,** compound *or* complex sentence. —**сло́жные проце́нты,** compound interest. —**сло́жное сло́во,** compound word.

слои́стый *adj.* stratified; laminated. —**слои́стое о́блако,** stratus.

слой [*pl.* **слои́, слоёв**] *n.* 1, layer. 2, coat (*of paint*). 3, *geol.* stratum. 4, (social) stratum: все слои́ населе́ния, all strata of society.

сло́йка [*gen. pl.* **сло́ек**] *n.* puff (*piece of pastry*).

слом *n.* tearing down; dismantling; demolition.

слома́ть *v., pfv. of* **лома́ть.** —**слома́ться,** *refl., pfv. of* **лома́ться** (*in senses #1 & #4*).

сломи́ть *v.pfv.* [*infl.* **сломлю́, сло́мишь**] 1, to break; smash; shatter. 2, to defeat; crush. 3, *fig.* to break (a person, one's spirit, will, resistance, etc.). 4, *in* сломя́ го́лову, at breakneck speed; like mad. —**сломи́ться,** *refl.* to break.

слон [*gen.* **слона́**] *n.* 1, elephant. 2, *chess* bishop. 3, *in* морско́й слон, sea elephant; elephant seal. —**де́лать из му́хи слона́,** to make a mountain out of a molehill. —**слон в посу́дной ла́вке,** bull in a china shop.

слонёнок [*gen.* -**нка;** *pl.* -**ня́та,** -**ня́т**] *n.* baby elephant; young elephant.

слони́ха *n.* she-elephant.

слоно́вость *n.f.* elephantiasis.

слоно́вый *adj.* elephant (*attrib.*). —**слоно́вая боле́знь,** elephantiasis. —**слоно́вая кость,** ivory.

слоня́ться *v.r.impfv., colloq.* to loiter; drift (*from place to place*).

сло́пать *v., pfv. of* **ло́пать.**

слуга́ [*pl.* **слу́ги**] *n.m.* servant; manservant.

служа́нка [*gen. pl.* -**нок**] *n.* servant; maid.

слу́жащий *n., decl. as an adj.* employee; office worker.

слу́жба *n.* 1, service. 2, work; job. Быть на слу́жбе у, be in the employ of. 3, church service. —**срок слу́жбы,** 1, *mech.* service life. 2, *mil.* length of service; tour of duty.

служе́бный *adj.* 1, office (*attrib.*); official. 2, auxiliary; secondary. —**служе́бный вход,** service entrance. —**служе́бное сло́во,** function word.

служе́ние *n.* serving; service.

служи́тель *n.m.* 1, *obs.* servant. 2, attendant. —**служи́тель ку́льта,** clergyman.

служи́ть *v.impfv.* [*pfv.* **послужи́ть;** *pres.* **служу́, слу́жишь**] 1, to serve: служи́ть в а́рмии, to serve in the army. 2, (*with dat.*) to serve; be in the service of. 3, (*with instr.*) to serve (as); function (as). 4, (*of a device*) to work; function; operate. 5, *v.t.* [*impfv. only*] *eccl.* to officiate at; conduct (a service, mass, etc.). 6, [*impfv. only*] (*of a dog*) to beg.

слупи́ть *v., pfv. of* **лупи́ть** (*in senses #2 & #3*).

слух *n.* 1, (sense of) hearing. 2, ear for music: игра́ть по слу́ху, to play by ear. Абсолю́тный слух, absolute/perfect pitch. 3, rumor. —**ни слу́ху ни ду́ху** (*with о or* **от**), there hasn't been a word from... —**превраща́ться в слух,** to be all ears; listen with rapt attention.

слухово́й *adj.* hearing (*attrib.*); auditory. —**слухово́й аппара́т,** hearing aid. —**слухово́е окно́,** dormer window. —**слухово́й рожо́к; слухова́я тру́бка,** ear trumpet.

слу́чай *n.* 1, case: в тако́м слу́чае, in that case. 2, opportunity; chance. 3, incident; occurrence: несча́стный слу́чай, an accident. 4, chance; luck: де́ло слу́чая, a matter of chance/luck. —**во вся́ком слу́чае,** in any case; at any rate. —**в кра́йнем слу́чае,** if worst comes to worst; as a last resort. —**в лу́чшем слу́чае,** at best. —**в проти́вном слу́чае,** otherwise; failing which. —**в слу́чае** (+ *gen.*), in case of; in the event of. —**в слу́чае чего́,** 1, in which case. 2, in the event of trouble. —**в том слу́чае, е́сли...,** in case... —**в ху́дшем слу́чае,** at worse. —**на вся́кий слу́чай,** just in case. —**на слу́чай** (+ *gen.*), in case of; so as to be prepared for. —**на слу́чай, е́сли,** in case...; so as to be prepared when... —**ни в ко́ем слу́чае,** under no circumstances. —**от слу́чая к слу́чаю,** from time to time; on occasion. —**по слу́чаю,** 1, (*with gen.*) on the occasion of. 2, (*with gen.*) on account of; owing to. 3, by chance; by luck. —**при слу́чае,** when the opportunity presents itself.

случа́йно *adv.* 1, by chance; by accident; accidentally. 2, *in questions,* by any chance.

случа́йность *n.f.* 1, (*with gen.*) accidental nature (of something). 2, chance occurrence; accident; happenstance: чи́стая случа́йность, pure accident/happenstance. По счастли́вой случа́йности, by a lucky chance; by good fortune.

случа́йный *adj.* [*short form* **-ча́ен, -ча́йна**] **1,** chance; accidental; random. **2,** (*of earnings, expenses, etc.*) incidental.

случа́ть *v.impfv.* [*pfv.* **случи́ть**] to mate (animals).

случа́ться *v.r.impfv.* [*pfv.* **случи́ться**] **1,** to happen; occur. **2,** (*with* **с** + *instr.*) to happen to: Что случи́лось с ним?, what happened to him? **3,** *impers.* (*with dat. and inf.*) to happen to; have occasion to. **4,** *colloq.* to happen to be (somewhere); turn up (somewhere).

случи́вшееся *participle used as a noun,* what happened; that which happened.

случи́ть *v., pfv. of* **случа́ть.**

случи́ться *v.r., pfv. of* **случа́ться.**

слу́шание *n.* **1,** listening. **2,** attending (*a lecture*); taking (*a course*). **3,** *law* hearing.

слу́шатель *n.m.* **1,** listener. **2,** student. **3,** *pl.* audience.

слу́шать *v.impfv.* **1,** to listen (to). **2,** [*pfv.* **послу́шать**] *fig.* to listen to; heed. **3,** to hear (a case). **4,** [*pfv.* **прослу́шать**] to attend (a lecture); take (a course). —**слу́шаю!, 1,** (*when answering the phone*) hello! **2,** (*on receiving an order*) very well!; I understand!

слу́шаться *v.r.impfv.* [*pfv.* **послу́шаться**] **1,** (*with gen. or acc.*) to obey. **2,** (*with gen.*) to heed (advice). **3,** [*impfv. only*] *law* (*of a case*) to be heard.

слыть *v.impfv.* [*pfv.* **прослы́ть;** *pres.* **слыву́, слывёшь;** *past fem.* **слыла́**] (*with instr.*) to be reputed to be; have a reputation for.

слыха́ть *v.impfv., colloq., used only in the past tense,* to hear.

слы́шать *v.impfv.* [*pfv.* **услы́шать;** *pres.* **слы́шу, слы́шишь**] to hear. Я и слы́шать не хочу́ об э́том, I won't hear of it. —**слы́шаться,** *refl.* [*pfv.* **послы́шаться**] **1,** to be heard. **2,** [*impfv. only*] *fig.* to be felt; be sensed.

слы́шимость *n.f.* **1,** audibility. **2,** (*on radio or TV*) reception. **3,** (*on the telephone*) connection.

слы́шно *adv.* audibly. —*adj., used predicatively* **1,** audible: Его́ не слы́шно, he can't be heard. Мне ничего́ не слы́шно, I can't hear a thing. Слы́шно, как му́ха пролети́т, you could hear a pin drop. **2,** heard; rumored: Что слы́шно?, what's new?

слы́шный *adj.* [*short form* **-шен, -шна**] audible.

слюда́ *n.* mica. —**слюдяно́й,** *adj.* mica (*attrib.*).

слюна́ *n.* saliva.

слю́ни [*gen.* **слюне́й**] *n.pl., colloq.* saliva. —**пуска́ть слю́ни,** to drool; drivel; slobber. —**распуска́ть слю́ни,** *colloq.* **1,** to start crying. **2,** to complain; whine. **3,** to be moved.

слюни́ть *v.impfv.* [*pfv.* **послюни́ть**] to moisten with saliva.

слю́нки [*gen.* **-нок**] *n.pl., colloq.* = **слю́ни.** —у меня́ слю́нки теку́т, my mouth is watering.

слю́нный *adj.* salivary.

слюня́вый *adj.* **1,** covered with saliva. **2,** *colloq.* (*of a child*) slobbering.

сля́коть *n.f.* slush. —**сля́котный,** *adj.* slushy.

сма́зать [*infl.* **сма́жу, сма́жешь**] *v., pfv. of* **сма́зывать.** —**сма́заться,** *refl., pfv. of* **сма́зываться.**

сма́зка *n.* **1,** grease. **2,** greasing; lubrication.

смазли́вый *adj., colloq.* pretty; cute; good-looking.

сма́зочный *adj.* lubrication (*attrib.*); lubricating: сма́зочный материа́л, lubricant.

сма́зчик *n.* grease monkey.

сма́зывание *n.* **1,** oiling; greasing; lubrication. **2,** painting; swabbing. **3,** blurring; slurring over.

сма́зывать *v.impfv.* [*pfv.* **сма́зать**] **1,** to oil; grease; lubricate. **2,** to paint; swab. **3,** to wipe away. **4,** *colloq.* to blur (a picture). **5,** *fig., colloq.* to slur over; gloss over. —**сма́зываться,** *refl.,* **1,** *colloq.* to rub oneself (with something oily). **2,** (*of paint, varnish, etc.*) to be smeared. **3,** *fig., colloq.* to be blurred.

смак *n., colloq.* relish; gusto: есть со сма́ком, to eat with relish/gusto.

смакова́ть *v.impfv.* [*pres.* **-ку́ю, -ку́ешь**] *colloq.* to savor; relish.

сма́нивать *v.impfv.* [*pfv.* **смани́ть**] *colloq.* **1,** to entice. **2,** to lure away.

смани́ть [*infl.* **сманю́, сма́нишь**] *v., pfv. of* **сма́нивать.**

смастери́ть *v., pfv. of* **мастери́ть.**

сма́тывать *v.impfv.* [*pfv.* **смота́ть**] **1,** to wind up; (*with* **в** + *acc.*) wind into. **2,** (*with* **с** + *gen.*) to wind off; unwind (from). **3,** *in* сма́тывать у́дочки, *colloq.* to take off; vamoose. —**сма́тываться,** *refl., colloq.* to take off; vamoose.

сма́хивать *v.impfv.* **1,** [*pfv.* **смахну́ть**] to brush off; brush away. **2,** [*impfv. only*] (*with* **на** + *acc.*) *colloq.* to look like; resemble.

сма́чивать *v.impfv.* [*pfv.* **смочи́ть**] to moisten.

сма́чный *adj., colloq.* tasty. —**сма́чно,** *adv., colloq.* with relish; with gusto.

смежа́ть *v.impfv.* [*pfv.* **смежи́ть**] to close (one's eyes).

сме́жный *adj.* **1,** adjacent; contiguous; adjoining. **2,** allied; related. —**сме́жность,** *n.f.* contiguity.

смека́листый *adj., colloq.* clever; sharp; quick-witted.

смека́лка *n., colloq.* shrewdness; native intelligence.

смека́ть *v.impfv.* [*pfv.* **смекну́ть**] *colloq.* to catch on; get the point.

смеле́ть *v.impfv.* [*pfv.* **осмеле́ть**] to become bolder; grow bolder.

сме́ло *adv.* **1,** boldly. **2,** *colloq.* with full confidence; safely.

сме́лость *n.f.* boldness; daring; audacity; temerity.

сме́лый *adj.* bold; daring; audacious.

смельча́к [*gen.* **-чака́**] *n.* daredevil.

сме́на *n.* **1,** changing; replacement. Сме́на карау́ла, changing of the guard. **2,** alternation (*of the seasons, day and night, etc.*). **3,** shift (*of work or duty*); session (*of school*). **4,** change; set: две сме́ны белья́, two changes/sets of underwear. **5,** a replacement: найти́ сме́ну, to find a replacement. **6,** the rising generation. —**идти́** *or* **приходи́ть на сме́ну** (+ *dat.*), to replace; take the place of.

смени́ть [*infl.* **сменю́, сме́нишь**] *v., pfv. of* **сменя́ть[1]**. —**смени́ться,** *refl., pfv. of* **сменя́ться.**

сме́нный *adj.* **1,** shift (*attrib.*). **2,** removable; replaceable.

сменя́емый *adj.* removable; replaceable.

сменя́ть[1] *v.impfv.* [*pfv.* **смени́ть**] **1,** to change. **2,** to replace; relieve. **3,** to replace; take the place of. —**сменя́ться,** *refl.* **1,** to be replaced. **2,** (*with* **с** + *gen.*) to be relieved from; go off (duty). **3,** (*with instr.*) to turn to; give way to: Ле́то смени́лось о́сенью, summer turned to (*or* gave way to) autumn.

сменя́ть² *v.pfv., colloq.* to exchange; trade.

смерде́ть *v.impfv.* [*pres.* **-ржу́, -рди́шь**] to stink.

смерза́ться *v.r.impfv.* [*pfv.* **смёрзнуться**] to freeze together.

смёрзнуться [*past* **смёрзся, смёрзлась**] *v.r., pfv. of* **смерза́ться**.

сме́рить *v.pfv., colloq.* to measure.—**сме́рить (кого́-нибудь) глаза́ми** *or* **взгля́дом**, to look over (from head to toe).

смерка́ться *v.r.impfv.* [*pfv.* **сме́ркнуться**] *impers.* to get dark: Смерка́ется, it is getting dark; dusk is falling.

смерте́льно *adv.* **1,** mortally; fatally; to death. **2,** terribly: смерте́льно уста́л, terribly tired. Смерте́льно ску́чно, deadly dull.

сме́ртный *adj.* **1,** deadly; mortal; fatal; lethal. **2,** (*of an insult*) grievous. **3,** (*of boredom, exhaustion, etc.*) utter.

сме́ртник *n.* prisoner condemned to death.

сме́ртность *n.f.* death rate; mortality (rate). —**де́тская сме́ртность**, infant mortality.

сме́ртный *adj.* **1,** death (*attrib.*). **2,** mortal. —*n.* mortal: просты́е сме́ртные, mere mortals. —**сме́ртная казнь**, the death penalty; capital punishment.

смертоно́сный *adj.* lethal; fatal; mortal.

смерть [*pl.* **сме́рти, -те́й, -тя́м**] *n.f.* death. —**до сме́рти**, to death: Мне ску́чно до́ смерти, I am bored to death. —**при́ смерти**, near death.

смерч *n.* **1,** whirlwind. **2,** tornado. **3,** waterspout.

смеси́тель *n.m.* mixer; blender.

смести́ [*infl. like* **мести́**] *v., pfv. of* **смета́ть¹**.

смести́ть [*infl.* **-щу́, -сти́шь**] *v., pfv. of* **смеща́ть**. —**смести́ться**, *refl., pfv. of* **смеща́ться**.

смесь *n.f.* mixture; blend.

сме́та *n.* estimate.

смета́на *n.* sour cream.

смета́ть¹ *v.impfv.* [*pfv.* **смести́**] **1,** to sweep away; sweep off. **2,** *fig.* (*of a fire, wind, etc.*) to sweep away.

смета́ть² *v.pfv.* **1,** [*infl.* **-та́ю, -та́ешь**] *pfv. of* **мета́ть²** *and* **смётывать** (*in sense #1*). **2,** [*infl.* **смечу́, сме́чешь**] *pfv. of* **смётывать** (*in sense #2*).

смётка *n., colloq.* quick-wittedness; savvy.

сме́тливый *adj.* bright; clever; quick-witted.

сме́тный *adj.* estimated.

смётывать *v.impfv.* [*pfv.* **смета́ть**] **1,** to baste together. **2,** to stack (hay, straw, etc.).

сметь *v.impfv.* [*pfv.* **посме́ть**] to dare: Никто́ не смел возрази́ть, no one dared raise an objection. —**как вы сме́ете!**, how dare you! —**не сме́йте** (+ *inf.*)!, don't you dare...!

смех *n.* laughter; laugh. —**для** *or* **ра́ди сме́ха**, (just) for fun. —**как** (*or* **сло́вно**) **на́ смех**, as if to mock someone; as if to rub it in. —**не до сме́ху** (+ *dat.*), (one is) in no mood for laughter. —**поднима́ть на́ смех**, to hold up to ridicule. —**умира́ть со́ смеху**, to die laughing.

смехотво́рный *adj.* laughable; ludicrous; ridiculous.

сме́шанный *adj.* **1,** mixed. **2,** hybrid.

смеша́ть *v., pfv. of* **меша́ть** (*in sense #4*) *and* **сме́шивать**. —**смеша́ться**, *refl., pfv. of* **меша́ться** *and* **сме́шиваться**.

смеше́ние *n.* **1,** mixing. **2,** mixture; blend. **3,** confusion. —**смеше́ние языко́в**, babel.

сме́шивание *n.* mixing.

сме́шивать *v.impfv.* [*pfv.* **смеша́ть**] **1,** to mix; blend. **2,** to mix up (*objects previously in order*). **3,** to get (two persons or things) mixed up; confuse with each other. —**сме́шиваться**, *refl.* **1,** (*with* **с** + *instr.*) to mix (with); become mixed (with). **2,** (*with* **с** + *instr.*) to intermingle (with). **3,** (*with* **с** + *instr.*) to blend in (with). Смеша́ться с толпо́й, to melt into the crowd. **4,** to come together; merge; be combined. **5,** to be jumbled up; get mixed up.

смеши́ть *v.impfv.* [*pfv.* **насмеши́ть** *or* **рассмеши́ть**] to make (someone) laugh.

смешли́вый *adj.* easily moved to laughter.

смешно́ *adv.* in a funny way. —*adj., used predicatively,* funny: Э́то не смешно́, that is not funny. Мне не смешно́, I do not find it funny; I am not amused.

смешно́й *adj.* **1,** funny; amusing. **2,** ridiculous; ludicrous. —**до смешно́го**, ridiculously; to the extreme.

смешо́к [*gen.* **-шка́**] *n., colloq.* **1,** chuckle. **2,** *pl.* taunts; digs.

смеща́ть *v.impfv.* [*pfv.* **смести́ть**] **1,** to displace; shift; move. **2,** to remove; dismiss (from office). —**смеща́ться**, *refl.* **1,** to shift. **2,** *fig.* to change.

смеще́ние *n.* **1,** shifting; displacement. **2,** removal; dismissal.

смея́ться *v.r.impfv.* [*pres.* **смею́сь, смеёшься**] **1,** to laugh. **2,** (*with dat.*) to laugh at: смея́ться шу́тке, to laugh at a joke. **3,** (*with* **над**) to make fun of. **4,** (*with* **над**) to laugh off; scoff at. **5,** *colloq.* to joke.

сми́ловаться *v.r.pfv.* [*infl.* **-луюсь, -луешься**] (*with* **над**) to have pity (on); take pity (on); have mercy (on).

смире́ние *n.* **1,** humility. **2,** meekness. **3,** (sense of) resignation.

смире́нный *adj.* humble; meek. —**смире́нно**, *adv.* humbly. —**смире́нность**, *n.f.* humility.

смири́тельный *adj., in* **смири́тельная руба́шка**, strait jacket.

смири́ть *v., pfv. of* **смиря́ть**. —**смири́ться**, *refl., pfv. of* **смиря́ться**.

сми́рно *adv.* quietly; still: сиде́ть сми́рно, to sit still. —*interj., mil.* attention! —**сто́йка сми́рно**, position of attention.

сми́рный *adj.* quiet; mild-mannered.

смиря́ть *v.impfv.* [*pfv.* **смири́ть**] to suppress; repress; curb. —**смиря́ться**, *refl.* **1,** to yield; give in. **2,** (*with* **с** + *instr.*) to reconcile oneself (to); learn to accept.

смо́ква *n.* fig.

смо́кинг *n.* tuxedo; dinner jacket.

смоко́вница *n.* fig tree.

смола́ [*pl.* **смо́лы**] *n.* **1,** resin. **2,** pitch; tar.

смолёный *adj.* tarred.

смоли́стый *adj.* resinous.

смоли́ть *v.impfv.* [*pfv.* **вы́смолить**] **1,** to apply pitch to. **2,** to tar.

смолка́ть *v.impfv.* [*pfv.* **смо́лкнуть**] **1,** to fall silent. **2,** (*of noise, sounds, etc.*) to die away; stop; cease.

смо́лкнуть [*past* **смолк, смо́лкла**] *v., pfv. of* **смолка́ть**.

смо́лоду *adv.*, *colloq.* **1,** since one's youth. **2,** in one's youth.

смолоти́ть *v.*, *pfv. of* молоти́ть.

смоло́ть *v.*, *pfv. of* моло́ть.

смолча́ть *v.pfv.* [*infl.* -чу́, -чи́шь] to be silent; hold one's tongue.

смоль *n.f.*, *in* чёрный как смоль, jet-black.

смоляно́й *adj.* resin (*attrib.*); pitch (*attrib.*); tar (*attrib.*).

смонти́ровать *v.*, *pfv. of* монти́ровать.

сморка́ть *v.impfv.* [*pfv.* вы́сморкать], *in* сморка́ть нос, to blow one's nose. —**сморка́ться,** *refl.* to blow one's nose.

сморо́дина *n.* currants. —**сморо́динный,** *adj.* currant (*attrib.*); made of currants.

сморчо́к [*gen.* -чка́] *n.* morel (*mushroom*).

смо́рщенный *adj.* wrinkled.

смо́рщивать *v.impfv.* [*pfv.* смо́рщить] to wrinkle. —**смо́рщиваться,** *refl.* **1,** to become wrinkled. **2,** to shrivel.

смо́рщить *v.*, *pfv. of* мо́рщить (*in sense #2*) *and* смо́рщивать. —**смо́рщиться,** *refl.*, *pfv. of* мо́рщиться *and* смо́рщиваться.

смота́ть *v.*, *pfv. of* сма́тывать. —**смота́ться,** *refl.*, *pfv. of* сма́тываться.

смотр *n.* **1,** [*2nd loc.* смотру́; *pl.* смотры́] review; parade. Производи́ть смотр войска́м, to review the troops. **2,** [*no 2nd loc.*; *pl.* смо́тры] public showing.

смотре́ть *v.impfv.* [*pfv.* посмотре́ть; *pres.* смотрю́, смо́тришь] **1,** to look. **2,** (*with* на + *acc.*) to look at. **3,** to look over; have a look at; examine. **4,** to watch; see (television, a movie, game, etc.). **5,** *fig.* (*with* на + *acc.*) to regard; look upon. **6,** [*impfv. only*] (*with* в *or* на + *acc.*) to look out on; face. **7,** [*impfv. only*] to appear; peep out. **8,** (*with* за + *instr.*) to look after; keep an eye on. **9,** [*impfv. only*] (*with instr.*) *colloq.* to look like. —**смотри́(те),** **1,** watch out!; take care! **2,** see how!; look how! **3,** (*with* чтобы) see (to it) that... —**смотря́ где,** it depends (on) where. —**смотря́ как,** it depends. —**смотря́ когда́,** it depends (on) when. —**смотря́ по** (+ *dat.*), depending on.

смотре́ться *v.r.impfv.* [*pfv.* посмотре́ться; *pres.* смотрю́сь, смо́тришься] **1,** to look at oneself: смотре́ться в зе́ркало, to look at oneself in the mirror. **2,** [*impfv. only*] to be seen. **3,** *colloq.* (*of a movie, show, etc.*) to be (good, bad, etc.): Фильм хорошо́ смо́трится, it's a good movie. **4,** [*impfv. only*] (*with an adv.*) *colloq.* to look; appear: смотре́ться несура́зно, to look ridiculous.

смотри́тель *n.m.* guard; watchman; keeper.

смотрово́й *adj.* **1,** observation (*attrib.*): смотрова́я вы́шка, observation tower. **2,** *mil.* inspection (*attrib.*); review (*attrib.*).

смочи́ть [*infl.* смочу́, смо́чишь] *v.*, *pfv. of* сма́чивать.

смочь *v.*, *pfv. of* мочь.

смошéнничать *v.*, *pfv. of* моше́нничать.

смрад *n.* stench. —**сма́дный,** *adj.* stinking.

сму́глый *adj.* dark; swarthy; dark-complexioned.

сму́рый *adj.* **1,** dark brown; dark gray. **2,** (*of cloth*) homespun.

сму́та *n.* **1,** *obs.* (civil) strife. **2,** *colloq.* discord. **3,** distress.

смути́ть [*infl.* -щу́, -ти́шь] *v.*, *pfv. of* смуща́ть. —**смути́ться,** *refl.*, *pfv. of* смуща́ться.

сму́тно *adv.* vaguely; dimly.

сму́тный *adj.* **1,** dim; hazy; vague. **2,** troubled. **3,** marked by civil strife. —**сму́тное вре́мя,** *hist.* The Time of Troubles (1605–1613).

смутья́н *n.*, *colloq.* fomenter of civil strife; agitator.

смуща́ть *v.impfv.* [*pfv.* смути́ть] **1,** to embarrass; disconcert. **2,** to trouble; bother; disturb; perturb. —**смуща́ться,** to be embarrassed.

смуще́ние *n.* embarrassment.

смущённый *adj.* **1,** troubled. **2,** embarrassed. —**смущённо,** *adv.* in (*or* with a look of) embarrassment.

смыва́ть *v.impfv.* [*pfv.* смыть] to wash away; wash off. —**смыва́ться,** *refl.* **1,** to wash off; come off. **2,** *colloq.* to disappear; take off.

смыка́ть *v.impfv.* [*pfv.* сомкну́ть] to close (ranks, one's eyes, etc.). —**смыка́ться,** *refl.* **1,** to close. **2,** to close in. **3,** (*with* с + *instr.*) to join; make contact with. **4,** *fig.* to close ranks; unite.

смысл *n.* **1,** sense. **2,** meaning. —**в смы́сле** (+ *gen.*), **1,** in the sense of. **2,** as regards. —**нет смы́сла** (+ *inf.*), there is no sense (*or* point) in...

смы́слить *v.impfv.*, *colloq.* to understand.

смыслово́й *adj.* semantic.

смыть [*infl.* смо́ю, смо́ешь] *v.*, *pfv. of* смыва́ть. —**смы́ться,** *refl.*, *pfv. of* смыва́ться.

смы́чка *n.* **1,** joining; linking; coupling. **2,** *fig.* joining together; unifying.

смычко́вый *adj.* (*of musical instruments*) played with a bow.

смычо́к [*gen.* -чка́] *n.*, *music* bow.

смышлёный *adj.*, *colloq.* bright; clever; smart.

смягча́ть *v.impfv.* [*pfv.* смягчи́ть] **1,** to soften. **2,** to alleviate; mitigate; assuage. **3,** to tone down. —**смягча́ться,** *refl.* **1,** to soften; become soft. **2,** to abate; relent; ease. **3,** (*of the weather*) to become mild.

смягче́ние *n.* **1,** softening. **2,** mitigation.

смягчи́ть *v.*, *pfv. of* смягча́ть. —**смягчи́ться,** *refl.*, *pfv. of* смягча́ться.

смяте́ние *n.* **1,** confusion. **2,** panic.

смяте́нный *adj.* troubled.

смя́тый *adj.* wrinkled; creased.

смять *v.pfv.* [*infl.* сомну́, сомнёшь] **1,** *pfv. of* мять (*in senses #2 & #3*). **2,** to trample upon; trample down. **3,** *mil.* to crush; overrun. **4,** *fig.* to crush; overwhelm. —**смя́ться,** *refl.* **1,** *pfv. of* мя́ться (*in sense #1*). **2,** to be crushed; be smashed in.

снабди́ть [*infl.* -бжу́, -бди́шь] *v.*, *pfv. of* снабжа́ть.

снабжа́ть *v.impfv.* [*pfv.* снабди́ть] (*with instr.*) to supply (with); furnish (with); provide (with).

снабже́ние *n.* supply; supplying; provision.

сна́добье *n.* medicinal herb.

сна́йпер *n.* **1,** sharpshooter. **2,** sniper.

снару́жи *adv.* **1,** from the outside; on the outside. Ждать снару́жи, to wait outside. **2,** outwardly.

снаря́д *n.* **1,** shell; projectile; missile. **2,** apparatus; device; machine. —**гимнасти́ческий снаря́д,** gymnastic apparatus.

снаряди́ть [*infl.* -жу́, -ди́шь] *v., pfv. of* **снаряжа́ть.** —**снаряди́ться,** *refl., pfv. of* **снаряжа́ться.**

снаря́дный *adj.* shell (*attrib.*); ammunition (*attrib.*).

снаряжа́ть *v.impfv.* [*pfv.* **снаряди́ть**] **1,** to equip; outfit. **2,** *colloq.* to send; dispatch. —**снаряжа́ться,** *refl., colloq.* to fit oneself out.

снаряже́ние *n.* **1,** equipping; outfitting. **2,** equipment; outfit.

снасть [*pl.* сна́сти, -сте́й, -стя́м] *n.f.* **1,** equipment; gear. **2,** tackle: рыболо́вная снасть, fishing tackle. **3,** *pl.* rigging.

снача́ла *adv.* **1,** at first; in the beginning. **2,** first (*before doing something else*). **3,** over again; from the beginning.

сна́шивать *v.impfv.* [*pfv.* **сноси́ть**] to wear out (clothes). —**сна́шиваться,** *refl.* (*of clothes*) to wear out.

СНГ *abbr. of* Содру́жество незави́симых госуда́рств, Commonwealth of Independent States.

снег [*2nd loc.* снегу́; *pl.* снега́] *n.* snow. —(свали́ться) как снег на́ голову, like a bolt from the blue; out of a clear blue sky.

снеги́рь [*gen.* -гиря́] *n.m.* bullfinch.

снегово́й *adj.* snow (*attrib.*).

снегоочисти́тель *n.m.* snowplow.

снегопа́д *n.* snowfall.

снегосту́п *n.* snowshoe.

снегохо́д *n.* snowmobile.

снегу́рочка *n.* snow maiden. *Also,* **снегу́рка.**

снеда́ть *v.impfv.* **1,** *obs., colloq.* to eat. **2,** *fig.* to gnaw; consume; torment.

снедь *n.f., obs.* food.

снежи́нка [*gen. pl.* -нок] *n.* snowflake.

снежи́ть *v.impfv., colloq.* to snow.

сне́жный *adj.* **1,** snow (*attrib.*). **2,** snowy. —**сне́жная ба́ба,** snowman. —**сне́жный бара́н,** bighorn sheep. —**сне́жная коза́,** mountain goat.

снежо́к [*gen.* -жка́] *n.* **1,** light snow. **2,** snowball. —**игра́ть в снежки́,** to throw snowballs.

снести́ *v.pfv.* [*infl. like* нести́] **1,** *pfv. of* нести́ (*in sense #11*) *and* сноси́ть[1]. **2,** to take; deliver. —**снести́сь,** *refl., pfv. of* нести́сь (*in sense #5*) *and* сноси́ться[1].

снижа́ть *v.impfv.* [*pfv.* **сни́зить**] **1,** to lower; reduce. **2,** to bring down; land (an airplane). —**снижа́ться,** *refl.* **1,** (*of prices, temperature, etc.*) to go down; come down; drop; fall. **2,** (*of an airplane*) to descend; land.

сниже́ние *n.* **1,** lowering; reduction. **2,** decline; drop. **3,** descent (*of an airplane*).

сни́зить [*infl.* сни́жу, сни́зишь] *v., pfv. of* снижа́ть. —**сни́зиться,** *refl., pfv. of* снижа́ться.

снизойти́ [*infl.* снизойду́, снизойдёшь; *past* снизошёл, снизошла́] *v., pfv. of* снисходи́ть.

сни́зу *adv.* **1,** from below. **2,** from the bottom. —**сни́зу до́верху,** from top to bottom. —**смотре́ть на** (+ *acc.*) сни́зу вверх, to look up to someone.

сни́кнуть *v.pfv.* [*past* сник, сни́кла] **1,** (*of plants*) to droop. **2,** *fig.* to die down. **3,** *fig., colloq.* to feel depressed.

снима́ть *v.impfv.* [*pfv.* **снять**] **1,** to take down; remove. **2,** to take off; remove (clothing, jewelry, make-up, etc.). **3,** to withdraw (a motion, one's candidacy, etc.).

4, to remove; drop (from an agenda, from production, etc.). **5,** to lift (restrictions, a ban, siege, etc.); dismiss (a charge); remit (a punishment). **6,** to dismiss (from a job); remove (from office). **7,** to gather in (a harvest). **8,** to photograph; take a picture of. **9,** to shoot; make (a movie). **10,** to rent. —**снима́ть коло́ду,** to cut the cards. —**снима́ть ко́пию с** (+ *gen.*), to make a copy of. —**снима́ть ме́рку с** (+ *gen.*), to take someone's measurements. —**снима́ть показа́ния** (+ *gen.*), to take evidence from. —**снима́ть с себя́ отве́тственность,** to give up responsibility. —**снима́ть тру́бку,** to pick up the receiver (*of a telephone*).

снима́ться *v.r.impfv.* [*pfv.* **сня́ться**] **1,** (*with* с + *gen.*) to come off (of); come loose (from). **2,** (*with* с + *gen.*) to leave; depart (from). **3,** to be photographed; have one's picture taken. Снима́ться в кино́, to appear in films. —**снима́ться с ла́геря,** to break camp. —**снима́ться с ме́ста,** to pull up stakes. —**снима́ться с я́коря,** to weigh anchor.

сни́мок [*gen.* -мка] *n.* picture; photograph; snapshot.

сниска́ть *v.pfv.* [*infl.* снищу́, сни́щешь] to gain; win.

снисходи́тельность *n.f.* **1,** condescension. **2,** leniency.

снисходи́тельный *adj.* **1,** condescending. **2,** lenient.

снисходи́ть *v.impfv.* [*pfv.* снизойти́; *pres.* -хожу́, -хо́дишь] **1,** (*with* к, до *or inf.*) to condescend (to); deign (to). **2,** (*with* к) to show sympathy (toward); be tolerant (of).

снисхожде́ние *n.* **1,** condescension. **2,** leniency.

сни́ться *v.r.impfv.* [*pfv.* присни́ться] (*with dat.*) to appear in one's dreams: Вы мне сни́лись, I dreamt (*or* had a dream) about you. Мне сни́лось, что..., I dreamt that...

сноб *n.* snob. —**сноби́зм,** *n.* snobbery; snobbishness.

сно́ва *adv.* again; once again; over again; anew.

снова́ть *v.impfv.* [*pres.* сную́, снуёшь] **1,** (*of ships*) to ply back and forth. **2,** to scurry.

сновиде́ние *n.* dream.

сногсшиба́тельный *adj., colloq.* stunning; staggering.

сноп [*gen.* снопа́] *n.* **1,** sheaf. **2,** shaft (*of light*).

снорови́стый *adj., colloq.* clever; smart.

сноро́вка *n.* skill; knack.

снос *n.* **1,** *aero.; naut.* drift. **2,** tearing down; demolition. **3,** *colloq.* wear: Э́тому сно́су нет, you can't wear it out. —**быть на сно́сях,** *colloq.* to be about to give birth.

сноси́ть[1] *v.impfv.* [*pfv.* снести́; *pres.* сношу́, сно́сишь] **1,** to carry down. **2,** to cut off; chop off. **3,** (*of the wind*) to blow off; blow away; (*of water*) to wash away; sweep away. **4,** to tear down (a building). **5,** to endure. **6,** *cards* to discard. —**сноси́ться,** *refl.* (*with* с + *instr.*) to communicate (with); get in touch (with).

сноси́ть[2] *v.pfv.* [*infl.* сношу́, сно́сишь] **1,** *pfv. of* сна́шивать. **2,** *colloq.* to carry (*to a certain place and back*). —**сноси́ться,** *refl., pfv. of* сна́шиваться.

сно́ска [*gen. pl.* -сок] *n.* footnote.

сно́сно *adv., colloq.* **1,** fairly well; tolerably well. **2,** so-so.

сно́сный *adj., colloq.* **1,** tolerable; bearable. **2,** tolerable; passable; fairly good.

снотво́рный *adj.* **1,** taken to induce sleep: снотво́рная табле́тка, sleeping pill. **2,** *fig.* soporific. —**снотво́рное,** *n.* sleeping pill.

снохá [*pl.* снóхи] *n.* daughter-in-law.

сношéние *n., usu. pl.* relations; dealings; intercourse.

снятие *n.* 1, removal. 2, dismissal. 3, gathering in (*of a harvest*). 4, lifting (*of a ban, siege, etc.*). 5, making (*of copies*).

снятóй *adj., in* снятóе молокó, skim milk.

снять [*infl.* сниму́, сни́мешь; *past fem.* сняла́] *v., pfv. of* снима́ть. —сня́ться, *refl.* [*past* сня́лся, сняла́сь, сняло́сь *or* сня́лось, сняли́сь *or* сня́лись] *pfv. of* снима́ться.

со *prep.* = с (*used before certain words beginning with two consonants*): со мной; со стола́; со вре́менем; со все́ми; со слеза́ми на глаза́х.

со- *prefix* 1, = с-. 2, *corresponds to the English prefix* со-: соа́втор, coauthor; сосуществова́ние, coexistence.

соа́втор *n.* coauthor. —соа́вторство, *n.* coauthorship.

соба́ка *n.* 1, dog. 2, *in* морска́я соба́ка, dogfish. —вот где соба́ка зары́та!, so that's what it's all about! —он на э́том соба́ку съел, he knows this subject inside out.

соба́чий [*fem.* -чья] *adj.* 1, of a dog; dog (*attrib.*); canine. 2, *fig., colloq.* a dog's: соба́чья жизнь, a dog's life. —соба́чий хóлод, brutal cold.

соба́чка [*gen. pl.* -чек] *n.* 1, little dog; doggy. 2, trigger. 3, pawl; pallet.

соба́чник *n., colloq.* dog lover.

собесéдник *n.* 1, person to whom one was speaking. 2, (*after an adj.*) person to talk to.

собесéдование *n.* conversation; discussion.

собира́ние *n.* gathering; collecting.

собира́тель *n.m.* collector.

собира́тельный *adj., gram.* collective.

собира́тельство *n.* 1, collecting (*as a hobby*). 2, *anthropology* gathering.

собира́ть *v.impfv.* [*pfv.* собра́ть] 1, to gather (people, firewood, information, etc.). Собира́ть ве́щи с пóла (*or* с пóлу), to gather up one's things from the floor. 2, to collect (books, taxes, signatures, etc.). 3, to pick (fruit); gather in (a harvest). 4, to assemble; put together (a machine, collection, etc.). 5, to convene (a meeting, conference, etc.). 6, to put together; pack: собира́ть ве́щи в я́щик, to pack things into a box. 7, to receive; poll (votes). 8, to take in (a garment). 9, *colloq.* to get (someone) ready to go somewhere: собира́ть детéй в шкóлу, to get the children ready for school. 10, *in* собира́ть на стол, *colloq.* to set the table. 11, to collect (one's thoughts); summon up (one's strength, courage, etc.).

собира́ться *v.r.impfv.* [*pfv.* собра́ться] 1, to gather; assemble. 2, (*of dust, water, etc.*) to collect. 3, to prepare; get ready: собира́ться в дорóгу/óтпуск, to get ready for a trip; get ready to go on vacation. 4, (*of a storm*) to be gathering; be in the offing. 5, [*impfv. only*] (*with inf.*) to intend (to). 6, [*impfv. only*] (*with inf.*) to be about to. 7, [*pfv. only*] (*with inf.*) to make up one's mind (to). 8, (*with* с + *instr.*) to collect (one's thoughts); summon up (one's strength, courage, etc.).

соблаговоли́ть *v.pfv.* (*with inf.*) *obs.* to deign (to).

собла́зн *n.* temptation.

соблазни́тель *n.m.* 1, tempter. 2, seducer.

соблазни́тельный *adj.* 1, tempting. 2, seductive.

соблазня́ть *v.impfv.* [*pfv.* соблазни́ть] 1, to tempt. 2, to seduce. —соблазня́ться, *refl.* to be tempted.

соблюда́ть *v.impfv.* [*pfv.* соблюсти́] to observe; comply with; abide by; honor. Соблюда́ть нейтралитéт, to observe neutrality. Соблюда́ть осторóжность, to exercise caution. Соблюда́ть эконóмию, to be economical.

соблюдéние *n.* observance; compliance.

соблюсти́ [*infl.* -блюду́, -блюдёшь] *v., pfv. of* блюсти́ *and* соблюда́ть.

собóй *also,* собóю *pron., instr. of* себя́.

соболéзнование *n.* condolence; condolences.

соболéзновать *v.impfv.* [*pres.* -ную, -нуешь] (*with dat.*) to commiserate (with).

собóлий [*fem.* -лья] *adj.* sable (*attrib.*).

соболи́ный *adj.* sable (*attrib.*).

сóболь *n.m.* sable.

собóр *n.* 1, cathedral. 2, *hist.* assembly: зéмский собóр, zemski sobor (*legislative assembly in old Russia*). 3, *relig.* council: вселéнский собóр, ecumenical council.

собóрный *adj.* cathedral (*attrib.*).

собóрование *n.* extreme unction.

собóю *pron.* = собóй.

собра́ние *n.* 1, meeting. 2, assembly. 3, collection. —собра́ние сочинéний, collected works.

сóбранный *adj.* 1, tensed up; intense; concentrated. 2, straight; erect. 3, precise; efficient.

собра́т [*pl.* собра́тья, собра́тьев *or* собра́тий] *n.* 1, colleague. 2, *colloq.* counterpart.

собра́ть [*infl.* -беру́, -берёшь; *past fem.* -брала́] *v., pfv. of* собира́ть. —собра́ться, *refl.* [*past tense stress as in* бра́ться] *pfv. of* собира́ться.

сóбственник *n.* owner; proprietor.

сóбственнический *adj.* 1, proprietary. 2, acquisitive; possessive.

сóбственно *particle* 1, actually; in fact. 2, proper: сóбственно гóрод, the city proper. —сóбственно говоря́, strictly speaking.

сóбственнору́чный *adj.* handwritten. Собственнору́чная пóдпись, autograph. —сóбственнору́чно, *adv.* with one's own hands.

сóбственность *n.f.* 1, property. 2, (*with* на + *acc.*) ownership (of).

сóбственный *adj.* one's own. —в сóбственном смы́сле, in the true (*or* literal) sense. —и́мя сóбственное, proper noun. —сóбственной персóной, in person.

собуты́льник *n., colloq.* drinking companion.

собы́тие *n.* event.

сова́ [*pl.* сóвы] *n.* owl.

сова́ть *v.impfv.* [*pfv.* су́нуть; *pres.* сую́, суёшь] to stick; slip; thrust. —сова́ться, *refl.* (*with* в + *acc.*) *colloq.* 1, to plunge (into). 2, to force one's way (into). 3, to butt (into); poke one's nose (into).

соверéн *n.* sovereign (*British coin*).

соверша́ть *v.impfv.* [*pfv.* соверши́ть] 1, to make (a trip, deal, mistake, etc.). 2, to commit (a crime, sin, aggression, etc.). 3, to carry out (a mission, raid, etc.). 4, to accomplish; perform (a feat, miracle, etc.). 5, to perform (a ritual).

совершéние *n.* **1,** accomplishment; completion. **2,** commission; perpetration (*of a crime*).

совершéнно *adv.* completely; entirely; absolutely; perfectly; utterly.

совершеннолéтие *n.* majority; coming of age. —**совершеннолéтний,** *adj. & n.* adult.

совершéнный *adj.* **1,** perfect. **2,** absolute; utter. —**совершéнный вид,** *gram.* perfective aspect.

совершéнство *n.* perfection. —**в совершéнстве,** perfectly; to perfection.

совершéнствование *n.* improvement; perfecting.

совершéнствовать *v.impfv.* [*pfv.* **усовершéнствовать**; *pres.* **-ствую, -ствуешь**] to improve; perfect; refine.

совершúть *v., pfv. of* **совершáть.**

сóвестить *v.impfv.* [*pfv.* **усóвестить**; *pres.* **-щу, -стишь**] *colloq.* to chide; shame. —**сóвеститься,** *refl., colloq.* to be ashamed; feel ashamed.

сóвестливый *adj.* conscientious; scrupulous.

сóвестно *adj., used predicatvely* (*with dat.*) ashamed; embarrassed: Мне бы́ло сóвестно, I was ashamed/ embarrassed.

сóвесть *n.f.* conscience: имéть на сóвести, to have on one's conscience. —**на сóвесть,** conscientiously. —**по сóвести говоря́,** in all conscience; in all honesty; to be honest; to tell the truth.

совéт *n.* **1,** advice; counsel. **2,** council. **3,** soviet: Верхóвный совéт, the Supreme Soviet.

совéтник *n.* adviser.

совéтовать *v.impfv.* [*pfv.* **посовéтовать**; *pres.* **-тую, -туешь**] (*with dat.*) to advise. —**совéтоваться,** *refl.* (*with* **с** *+ instr.*) to consult; seek the advice of.

совéтский *adj.* Soviet. —**Совéтский Сою́з,** the Soviet Union.

совéтчик *n.* adviser.

совещáние *n.* conference.

совещáтельный *adj.* consultative; deliberative. —**прáво совещáтельного гóлоса,** voice but no vote. —**член с совещáтельным гóлосом,** non-voting member.

совещáться *v.r.impfv.* **1,** to deliberate. **2,** (*with* **с** *+ instr.*) to confer (with).

совúный *adj.* **1,** owl's. **2,** owlish.

совладáть *v.pfv.* (*with* **с** *+ instr.*) *colloq.* to cope with; handle; control. —**совладáть с собóй,** to control oneself; get control of oneself.

совладéлец [*gen.* **-льца**] *n.* co-owner; joint owner.

совладéние *n.* joint ownership.

совмести́мый *adj.* compatible. —**совмести́мость,** *n.f.* compatibility.

совмести́тельство *n.* holding of more than one job. Рабóтать по совмести́тельству, to hold another job; hold down two jobs.

совмести́ть [*infl.* **-щý, -сти́шь**] *v., pfv. of* **совмещáть.**

совмéстно *adv.* jointly; together.

совмéстный *adj.* joint; combined. —**совмéстное обучéние,** coeducation.

совмещáть *v.impfv.* [*pfv.* **совмести́ть**] to combine.

совóк [*gen.* **совкá**] *n.* **1,** scoop. **2,** *colloq.* (*since 1989*) A, the Soviet system or society. B, person with a Soviet mentality. —**садóвый совóк,** trowel. —**совóк для мýсора,** dustpan.

совокуплéние *n.* copulation; coition.

совокупля́ться *v.r.impfv.* to copulate.

совокýпно *adv., obs.* jointly.

совокýпность *n.f.* aggregate; sum total.

совокýпный *adj.* joint; combined.

совпадáть *v.impfv.* [*pfv.* **совпáсть**] **1,** to coincide. **2,** to agree; tally.

совпадéние *n.* **1,** coincidence. **2,** identity; concurrence; harmony (*of interests, opinions, etc.*). **3,** combination (*of circumstances*).

совпáсть [*infl. like* **пасть**] *v., pfv. of* **совпадáть.**

соврати́тель *n.m.* seducer.

соврати́ть [*infl.* **-щý, -ти́шь**] *v., pfv. of* **совращáть.**

соврáть *v., pfv. of* **врать.**

совращáть *v.impfv.* [*pfv.* **соврати́ть**] **1,** to pervert. **2,** to seduce.

совращéние *n.* perversion; seduction.

совремéнник *n.* contemporary.

совремéнность *n.f.* **1,** modernity. **2,** the present.

совремéнный *adj.* **1,** contemporary. **2,** modern.

совсéм *adv.* **1,** quite. **2,** completely; entirely. —**не совсéм,** not entirely. —**совсéм не,** not at all; not in the least; not a bit. Вы совсéм не измени́лись, you haven't changed a bit.

совхóз *n.* state farm (*contr. of* **совéтское хозя́йство**).

соглáсие *n.* **1,** consent; assent. **2,** agreement. **3,** harmony.

согласи́тельный *adj.* conciliation (*attrib.*): согла-си́тельная коми́ссия, conciliation committee.

согласи́ться [*infl.* **-шýсь, -си́шься**] *v.r., pfv. of* **соглашáться.**

соглáсно *adv.* in harmony; harmoniously. —*prep., with dat.* according to. —**соглáсно с** (*+ instr.*), in accordance with.

соглáсный *adj.* [*short form* **-сен, -снá**] **1,** (*with* **с** *+ instr.*) in agreement: Я с вáми соглáсен (соглáсна), I agree with you. **2,** (*with* **на** *+ acc.*) agreeable: Он соглáсен на все услóвия, he agrees (*or* is agreeable) to all the conditions. **3,** harmonious. **4,** *phonet.* consonantal: соглáсная бýква, consonant. —*n.* consonant.

согласовáние *n.* **1,** coordination. **2,** *gram.* agreement. Согласовáние времён, sequence of tenses.

согласóванный *adj.* coordinated; concerted. —**со-глáсованность,** *n.f.* coordination.

согласовáть [*infl.* **-сýю, -сýешь**] *v., pfv. of* **со-гласóвывать.**

согласóвываться *v.r.impfv. & pfv.* [*pres.* **-сýется**] (*with* **с** *+ instr.*) **1,** to be consistent (with); be in conformity (with); be in keeping (with). **2,** *gram.* to agree (with).

согласóвывать *v.impfv.* [*pfv.* **согласовáть**] **1,** to coordinate; harmonize. **2,** to clear: согласовáть план с начáльником, to clear the plan with one's supervisor. **3,** *gram.* to make agree.

соглашáтель *n.m.* compromiser; appeaser. —**согла-шáтельский,** *adj.* of compromise; of appeasement. —**соглашáтельство,** *n.* policy of compromise; appeasement.

соглашáться *v.r.impfv.* [*pfv.* **согласи́ться**] **1,** (*with* **с** *+ instr.*) to agree (with). **2,** (*with inf. or* **на** *+ acc.*) to agree (to); consent (to). —**согласи́тесь,** you would agree; you must admit.

соглашéние *n.* agreement.

соглядáтай *n.* detective; sleuth.

согнáть [*infl.* сгоню́, сго́нишь; *past fem.* согнала́] *v., pfv. of* сгоня́ть.

со́гнутый *adj.* **1,** bent. **2,** bent over; stooped.

согну́ть *v., pfv. of* гнуть *and* сгибáть. —**согну́ться,** *refl., pfv. of* гну́ться *and* сгибáться.

согражданúн [*pl.* согрáждане, согрáждан] *n.* fellow citizen.

согревáние *n.* heating; warming.

согревáть *v.impfv.* [*pfv.* согрéть] to warm; heat. —**согревáться,** *refl.* to get warm; warm up.

согревáющий *adj.* warming. —**согревáющий ком-прéсс,** hot compress.

согрешúть *v., pfv. of* грешúть.

со́да *n.* soda: каустúческая со́да, caustic soda. —**питьевáя со́да,** baking soda; bicarbonate of soda.

содéйствие *n.* assistance; help.

содéйствовать *v.impfv. & pfv.* [*pres.* -ствую, -ствуешь] (*with dat.*) **1,** to assist. **2,** to further; promote; contribute to.

содержáние *n.* **1,** support; maintenance; upkeep. Содержáние семьú, support of one's family. Содержáние áрмии, maintaining an army. **2,** confinement: содержáние в тюрьмé, confinement in prison. Содержáние под арéстом, custody; detention. **3,** content: фóрма и содержáние, form and content. **4,** content; amount: содержáние жúра в молокé, the fat content of milk; содержáние белкá в мя́се, the amount of protein in meat. **5,** *colloq.* contents (*of a container*). **6,** contents (*of a book, letter, etc.*); subject matter. **7,** table of contents. **8,** pay; wages; salary.

содержáнка [*gen. pl.* -нок] *n.* kept woman.

содержáтель *n.m., obs.* owner; operator.

содержáтельный *adj.* rich in content; informative; meaty.

содержáть *v.impfv.* [*pres.* -держý, -дéржишь] **1,** to contain. **2,** to support (a family, children, etc.). **3,** to keep (*in a certain state*): содержáть в испрáвности, to keep in working order. **4,** to keep; (forcibly) confine: содержáть под арéстом, to keep under arrest; hold in custody. **5,** *obs.* to own; operate (a business). —**содержáться,** *refl.* **1,** to be kept; be maintained. **2,** to be confined (to an institution). **3,** to be contained: В мя́се содéржатся белкú, meat contains proteins.

содержúмое *n., decl. as an adj.* contents.

со́довый *adj.* soda (*attrib.*).

содóм *n., colloq.* uproar; commotion.

содрáть [*infl.* сдерý, сдерёшь; *past fem.* содралá] *v., pfv. of* драть (*in sense #6*) *and* сдирáть.

содрогáние *n.* shudder.

содрогáться *v.r.impfv.* [*pfv.* содрогну́ться] **1,** to shudder. **2,** (*of the ground*) to shake.

содру́жество *n.* **1,** cooperation; harmony. **2,** association; union. **3,** commonwealth. —**Британское со-дру́жество нáций,** British Commonwealth of Nations. —**Содру́жество незавúсимых госудáрств,** Commonwealth of Independent States.

со́евый *adj.* soybean (*attrib.*). —**со́евые бобы́,** soybeans.

соединéние *n.* **1,** joining; uniting. **2,** linking; connecting. **3,** joint. **4,** *chem.* compound. **5,** *mil.* large unit (*division-size or larger*).

соединённый *adj.* united. —**Соединённые Штáты,** the United States.

соединúтельный *adj.* **1,** connecting. **2,** *gram.* copulative. —**соединúтельная ткань,** connective tissue.

соединя́ть *v.impfv.* [*pfv.* соединúть] **1,** to connect; hook up. **2,** to unite. Соединя́ть сúлы, to join forces. **3,** to link; connect; join. **4,** to combine. —**соединя́ться,** *refl.* **1,** to unite; be united. **2,** to be linked; be connected. **3,** (*with* с + *instr.*) to join; link up (with). **4,** to be combined.

сожалéние *n.* **1,** regret. **2,** pity. —**к сожалéнию,** unfortunately.

сожалéть *v.impfv.* **1,** (*with* о *or a dependent clause*) to regret. **2,** (*with* о) to pity; feel sorry for.

сожжéние *n.* burning.

сожúтель *n.m.* [*fem.* -ница] person (of the opposite sex) with whom one lives. —**сожúтельство,** *n.* cohabitation.

сожúтельствовать *v.impfv.* [*pres.* -ствую, -ствуешь] to live together.

сожрáть *v., pfv. of* жрать.

созвáниваться *v.r.impfv.* [*pfv.* созвонúться] (*with* с + *instr.*) *colloq.* to call (someone) on the telephone; be in touch by phone.

созвáть [*infl. like* звать] *v., pfv. of* созывáть *and* сзывáть.

созвéздие *n.* constellation.

созвонúться *v.r., pfv. of* созвáниваться.

созвýчие *n.* **1,** *music* consonance. **2,** harmony; concord. **3,** assonance.

созвýчный *adj.* **1,** (*of sounds*) harmonious; assonant. **2,** (*with dat.*) in keeping with; in tune with.

создавáть *v.impfv.* [*pfv.* создáть; *pres.* -даю́, -даёшь] **1,** to create. **2,** to build; construct. **3,** to found; establish. **4,** to write; compose. **5,** to develop. **6,** to pose (a threat). **7,** *short form past passive part. only* (*with* для) made (for); cut out (for): со́зданы друг для дру́га, made for each other; не со́здан для э́того, not cut out for this. —**создавáться,** *refl.* to be created; arise; develop. У меня́ создало́сь впечатлéние, что..., I got the impression that...

создáние *n.* **1,** creation (*act of creating*). **2,** founding; establishment. **3,** development. **4,** creation; work. **5,** creature.

создáтель *n.m.* creator; founder.

создáть [*infl. like* дать; *past* со́здал, создала́, со́здало, со́здали] *v., pfv. of* создавáть. —**создáться,** *refl.* [*past tense stress as in* дáться] *pfv. of* создавáться.

созерцáние *n.* contemplation. —**созерцáтельный,** *adj.* contemplative.

созерцáть *v.impfv.* to contemplate.

созидáние *n.* creation. —**созидáтель,** *n.m.* creator. —**созидáтельный,** *adj.* creative.

созидáть *v.impfv.* [*pres.* -дáю, -дáешь] to create.

сознавáть *v.impfv.* [*pfv.* сознáть; *pres.* -знаю́, -знаёшь] to realize; recognize; be conscious of; be aware of. —**сознавáться,** *refl.* (*with* в + *prepl.*) to confess (to).

созна́ние *n.* **1,** consciousness: приходи́ть в созна́ние, to regain consciousness. Без созна́ния, unconscious. **2,** awareness; realization; recognition; consciousness. **3,** confession.

созна́тельно *adv.* consciously; deliberately.

созна́тельность *n.f.* consciousness; awareness: кла́ссовая созна́тельность, class consciousness; полити́ческая созна́тельность, political awareness.

созна́тельный *adj.* **1,** conscious. **2,** deliberate.

созна́ть [*infl.* -зна́ю, -зна́ешь] *v., pfv. of* **сознава́ть.** —**созна́ться,** *refl., pfv. of* **сознава́ться.**

созрева́ние *n.* ripening; maturing.

созрева́ть *v.impfv.* [*pfv.* **созре́ть**] **1,** to ripen; mature. **2,** *fig.* (*of time*) to come: Созре́ло вре́мя (+ *inf.*), the time had come to...

созре́ть *v., pfv. of* **зреть**[1] *and* **созрева́ть.**

созы́в *n.* calling; convening.

созыва́ть *v.impfv.* [*pfv.* **созва́ть**] **1,** to call together; invite; summon. **2,** to call; convene.

соизволя́ть *v.impfv.* [*pfv.* **соизво́лить**] (*with inf.*) *obs.* to deign (to).

соизмери́мый *adj.* commensurable.

соиска́ние *n.* (*with gen.*) competition (*for an award or degree*).

соиска́тель *n.m.* (*with gen.*) **1,** competitor (for). **2,** candidate (for).

со́йка [*gen. pl.* **со́ек**] *n.* jay (*bird*).

сойти́ [*infl.* **сойду́, сойдёшь;** *past* **сошёл, сошла́, сошло́, сошли́**] *v., pfv. of* **сходи́ть.** —**сойти́сь,** *refl., pfv. of* **сходи́ться.**

сок *n.* **1,** juice. **2,** sap. —**в по́лном соку́,** in the prime of life.

сока́мерник *n.* cellmate.

соковыжима́лка [*gen. pl.* **-лок**] *n.* squeezer; juicer.

со́кол *n.* falcon. —**гол как со́кол** (*with different stress*), poor as a church mouse.

соколи́ный *adj.* falcon's. —**соколи́ная охо́та,** falconry.

сократи́ть [*infl.* -щу́, -ти́шь] *v., pfv. of* **сокраща́ть.** —**сократи́ться,** *refl., pfv. of* **сокраща́ться.**

сокраща́ть *v.impfv.* [*pfv.* **сократи́ть**] **1,** to reduce; curtail; pare down. **2,** to shorten. **3,** to abridge; condense. **4,** to abbreviate. **5,** *colloq.* to dismiss; fire. **6,** *math.* to cancel. —**сокраща́ться,** *refl.* **1,** to become *or* grow shorter. **2,** to be shortened. **3,** to be reduced. **4,** *physiol.* to contract.

сокраще́ние *n.* **1,** reduction; curtailment. **2,** shortening. **3,** abridgment; condensation. **4,** cut; deletion. **5,** abbreviation. **6,** contraction (*of muscles*). **7,** *math.* cancellation. **8,** *colloq.* discharge; dismissal.

сокращённо *adv.* for short.

сокрове́нный *adj.* **1,** secret; hidden. **2,** (*of one's thoughts, feelings, etc.*) innermost.

сокро́вище *n.* treasure. —**ни за каки́е сокро́вища,** not for (anything in) the world.

сокро́вищница *n.* treasure house.

сокруша́ть *v.impfv.* [*pfv.* **сокруши́ть**] **1,** to shatter; smash; destroy. **2,** to distress; upset. —**сокруша́ться,** *refl.* [*impfv. only*] **1,** (*with* **о**) to grieve (for *or* over); be distressed (over). **2,** *with a dependent clause,* to regret (that).

сокруше́ние *n.* **1,** smashing; destruction. **2,** distress.

сокрушённый *adj.* grieving; grief-stricken. —**сокрушённо,** *adv.* sorrowfully.

сокруши́тельный *adj.* **1,** (*of a blow*) crushing; crippling; shattering. **2,** (*of a feeling*) overwhelming.

сокруши́ть *v., pfv. of* **сокруша́ть.**

соку́рсник *n.m.* [*fem.* **-ница**] *n.* classmate.

солга́ть *v., pfv. of* **лгать.**

солда́т [*gen. pl.* **-да́т**] *n.* soldier. —**солда́тик,** *n.* toy (*or* tin) soldier. —**солда́тка,** *n.* soldier's wife. —**солда́тский,** *adj.* soldier's.

солева́ренный *adj., in* **солева́ренный заво́д,** saltworks. *Also,* **солева́рный.**

солева́рня [*gen. pl.* **-рен**] *n.* saltworks.

солево́й *adj.* saline.

соле́ние *n.* salting; pickling.

соленои́д *n.* solenoid.

солёность *n.f.* saltiness; salinity.

солёный *adj.* **1,** salt (*attrib.*): солёная вода́, salt water. **2,** salty. **3,** salted; pickled. **4,** *fig., colloq.* spicy; racy; risqué. *See also* **со́лон.**

соле́нье *n., usu. pl.* salted foods.

солеци́зм *n.* solecism.

солидаризи́роваться *v.r.impfv. & pfv.* [*pres.* **-руюсь, -руешься**] (*with* **с** + *instr.*) to express one's solidarity (with); make common cause (with).

солида́рность *n.f.* solidarity.

солида́рный *adj.* [*short form* **-рен, -рна**] **1,** united; as one; of one mind. **2,** (*with* **с** + *instr.*) in full agreement (with); at one (with).

соли́дно *adv.* **1,** solidly. **2,** firmly. **3,** in a sizable amount: соли́дно зараба́тывать, to earn good money.

соли́дный *adj.* [*short form* **-ден, -дна**] **1,** solid; firm. **2,** sound; thorough. **3,** reputable; well-established. **4,** imposing; impressive. **5,** mature; middle-aged. **6,** *colloq.* large; sizable. **7,** *colloq.* sizable; considerable.

соли́ст *n.m.* [*fem.* **-ли́стка**] soloist.

солите́р (тэ) *n.* large diamond; solitaire.

солитёр *n.* tapeworm.

соли́ть *v.impfv.* [*pfv.* **посоли́ть;** *pres.* **солю́, со́лишь** *or* **соли́шь**] **1,** to salt. **2,** to pickle.

со́лка *n.* salting; pickling.

со́лнечно *adv.* like the sun. —*adj., used predicatively,* sunny: Бы́ло со́лнечно и тепло́, it was sunny and warm.

со́лнечный *adj.* **1,** sun (*attrib.*); solar. **2,** sunny. —**со́лнечные очки́,** sunglasses. —**со́лнечное пятно́,** sunspot. —**со́лнечный свет,** sunlight. —**со́лнечное сплете́ние,** solar plexus. —**со́лнечный уда́р,** sunstroke. —**со́лнечные часы́,** sundial.

со́лнце (сонц) *n.* sun: лежа́ть на со́лнце, to lie in the sun.

солнцезащи́тный *adj.* serving as protection against the sun: солнцезащи́тные очки́, sunglasses.

солнцепёк *n.* blazing sun; heat of the sun.

солнцестоя́ние *n.* solstice.

со́ло *n. indecl.* solo.

солове́й [*gen.* **-вья́**] *n.* nightingale.

соловьи́ный *adj.* nightingale (*attrib.*); nightingale's.

со́лод *n.* malt.

солóдка *n.* licorice.

солóдовый *adj.* malt (*attrib.*). —**солóдовый сáхар,** maltose.

солóма *n.* straw.

солóменный *adj.* **1,** straw (*attrib.*). **2,** (*of a roof*) thatched. **3,** straw-colored. —**солóменная вдовá,** grass widow.

солóминка [*gen. pl.* -нок] *n.* a straw. —**хватáться за солóминку,** to grasp at a straw.

сóлон *adj., short form of* **солёный, 1,** salty: У меня во рту сóлоно, I have a salty taste in my mouth. **2,** *fig.* involving misfortune or adversity: Ему сóлоно (*or* сóлон) пришлóсь, he came to grief. —**не сóлоно хлебáвши,** having accomplished nothing.

солонéц [*gen.* -нцá] *n.* dark alkaline soil.

солонúна *n.* corned beef.

солóнка [*gen. pl.* -нок] *n.* salt shaker; saltcellar.

сóлоно *see* сóлон.

солоновáтый *adj.* brackish.

солончáк [*gen.* -чакá] *n.* saline soil; salt marsh.

соль[1] *n.f.* **1,** salt. **2,** (*with gen.*) *colloq.* the point: вся соль рассказа, the whole point of the story.

соль[2] *n.neut. indecl., music* sol; G.

сóльный *adj.* solo.

сольфéджио *n. indecl.* solfeggio.

соля́нка *n.* **1,** saltwort. **2,** a thick soup with meat or fish.

соляной *adj.* salt (*attrib.*); saline.

соля́ный *adj., in* **соля́ная кислотá,** hydrochloric acid.

соля́рий *n.* solarium.

соля́рка *n.* lubricating oil; diesel fuel (*short for* **соля́рное мáсло**).

сом [*gen.* сомá] *n.* sheatfish.

сомалийский *adj.* Somali.

соматический *adj.* somatic.

сóмкнутый *adj.* (*of a formation, order, etc.*) close.

сомкнýть *v., pfv. of* смыкáть. —**сомкнýться,** *refl., pfv. of* смыкáться.

сомневáться *v.r.impfv.* (*with* в + *prepl. or a dependent clause*) to doubt; have doubts; be in doubt: Я в этом не сомневáюсь, I don't doubt that. Вы мóжете не сомневáться в этом, you can be sure of that.

сомнéние *n.* doubt. —**без (всякого) сомнéния,** without a doubt. —**вне (всякого) сомнéния,** beyond (any) doubt. —**подвергáть сомнéнию,** to question; challenge. —**стáвить под сомнéние,** to cast doubt upon; call into question.

сомнительно *adj., used predicatively,* doubtful: Óчень сомнительно, чтóбы..., it is very doubtful whether...

сомнительный *adj.* **1,** doubtful; dubious; questionable. **2,** shady; suspicious.

сомножитель *n.m., math.* factor.

сон [*gen.* снá] *n.* **1,** sleep. **2,** dream. —**вúдеть сон,** to have a dream. —**вúдеть (что- *or* когó-нибудь) во сне,** to have a dream about. —**сквозь сон,** in one's sleep; while half-asleep. —**сон в рýку,** the dream came true. —**со снá,** because one was half-asleep (*or* half-awake): Он со снá ничегó не пóнял, he was too sleepy to understand anything. —**у меня снá ни в однóм глазý,** I am not the least bit sleepy.

сонáта *n.* sonata.

сонéт *n.* sonnet.

сонлúвый *adj.* sleepy; drowsy. —**сонлúвость,** *n.f.* sleepiness; drowsiness.

сонм *n.* **1,** huge throng. **2,** (*with gen.*) multitude (of).

сóнный *adj.* **1,** sleepy; drowsy. **2,** sleeping. —**сóнная артéрия,** carotid artery. —**сóнная болéзнь,** sleeping sickness.

сóня *n.* dormouse. —*n.m. & f., colloq.* sleepyhead.

соображáть *v.impfv.* [*pfv.* **сообразúть**] **1,** to think; ponder. **2,** to figure out. Хорошó соображáть, to be quick to figure things out; be quick-witted. **3,** [*impfv. only*] (*with* в + *prepl.*) *colloq.* to know something about (a subject).

соображéние *n., usu. pl.* **1,** thoughts; views (*on a subject*). **2,** considerations; reasons: по финáнсовым соображéниям, for financial reasons. —**принимáть в соображéние,** to take into consideration.

сообразúтельный *adj.* clever; quick-witted. —**сообразúтельность,** *n.f.* cleverness; quickness of mind.

сообразúть [*infl.* -жý, -зúшь] *v., pfv. of* **соображáть.**

сообрáзно *prep., with dat. or* с + *instr.* in accordance with; in conformity with.

сообрáзность *n.f.* conformity.

сообрáзный *adj.* (*with* с + *instr.*) conforming to; in keeping with. —**ни с чем не сообрáзный,** absurd; ridiculous.

сообразовáть *v.impfv. & pfv.* [*pres.* -зýю, -зýешь] (*with* с + *instr.*) to make (something) conform (to); bring in line with. —**сообразовáться,** *refl.* (*with* с + *instr.*) **1,** to act in accordance with; act in the light of. **2,** to conform (to); correspond (to).

сообщá *adv.* jointly; together; in concert.

сообщáть *v.impfv.* [*pfv.* **сообщúть**] **1,** to report; announce: сообщáть извéстие, to report the news; сообщáть решéние *or* о решéнии, announce a decision. Газéты сообщáют, что..., the newspapers report that... **2,** (*with dat.*) to inform; tell. **3,** to impart; transmit. —**сообщáться,** *refl.* [*impfv. only*] **1,** to be reported. **2,** to be imparted; be transmitted; be communicated. **3,** (*with* с + *instr.*) to communicate (with). **4,** (*with* с + *instr.*) to be linked (to *or* with). **5,** (*of rooms*) to connect.

сообщéние *n.* **1,** report; message; communication. **2,** communication(s). Пути сообщéния, communications (*railways, roads, etc.*). **3,** service: воздýшное/желéзнодорóжное сообщéние, air/rail service.

сообщество *n.* **1,** association. **2,** community: Еврoпéйское сообщество, the European Community. —**в сообществе с,** in the company of.

сообщúть *v., pfv. of* **сообщáть.**

сообщник *n.* accomplice.

соорудúть [*infl.* -жý, -дúшь] *v., pfv. of* **сооружáть.**

сооружáть *v.impfv.* [*pfv.* **соорудúть**] to erect; build.

сооружéние *n.* **1,** erection; construction. **2,** building; structure. **3,** *pl.* installation; *pl.* works.

соотвéтственно *adv.* **1,** accordingly. **2,** respectively. —*prep., with dat. or* с + *instr.* according to; in accordance with.

соотвéтственный *adj.* **1,** (*with dat.*) corresponding (to). **2,** appropriate; proper.

соотве́тствие *n.* accordance; conformity. —**в соотве́тствии с,** in accordance with. —**приводи́ть в соотве́тствие с,** to bring into conformity (*or* into line) with.

соотве́тствовать *v.impfv.* [*pres.* **-ствую, -ствуешь**] (*with dat.*) **1,** to correspond (to); conform (to). Не соотве́тствовать действи́тельности, not be true; not square with the facts. **2,** to answer (the purpose, description, etc.); meet (the requirements); be right for (a position).

соотве́тствующий *adj.* **1,** corresponding. **2,** appropriate; proper; suitable. —**соотве́тствующим о́бразом,** accordingly.

сооте́чественник *n.* compatriot; fellow countryman.

соотнести́ [*infl. like* **нести́**] *v., pfv. of* **соотноси́ть.**

соотноси́тельный *adj.* correlative.

соотноси́ть *v.impfv.* [*pfv.* **соотнести́**; *pres.* **-ношу́, -но́сишь**] to correlate. —**соотноси́ться,** *refl.* [*impfv. only*] (*with* **с** + *instr.*) to correlate (with).

соотноше́ние *n.* **1,** correlation. **2,** ratio. —**соотноше́ние сил,** correlation of forces; balance of forces.

сопе́рник *n.* rival.

сопе́рничать *v.impfv.* (*with* **с** + *instr.*) **1,** to compete (with). **2,** to vie (with). **3,** to compare (with); rival; equal.

сопе́рничество *n.* rivalry.

сопе́ть *v.impfv.* [*pres.* **соплю́, сопи́шь**] to sniffle; wheeze.

со́пка [*gen. pl.* **со́пок**] *n.* **1,** hill or mountain with a rounded summit (*in Asian Russia*). **2,** volcano (*on Kamchatka Peninsula*).

со́пли [*gen.* **сопле́й**] *n.pl., vulgar* snot. —**распуска́ть со́пли,** to be running at the nose.

сопли́вый *adj., colloq.* snotty.

сопло́ [*pl.* **со́пла, со́пел** *or* **сопл**] *n.* nozzle.

сопостави́мый *adj.* comparable.

сопоста́вить [*infl.* **-влю, -вишь**] *v., pfv. of* **сопоставля́ть.**

сопоставле́ние *n.* comparison.

сопоставля́ть *v.impfv.* [*pfv.* **сопоста́вить**] to compare; contrast.

сопра́но *n.neut. indecl.* soprano (*voice*). —*n.f. indecl.* soprano (*singer*). —**сопра́нный; сопра́новый,** *adj.* soprano.

сопреде́льный *adj.* neighboring; adjacent; contiguous.

сопредседа́тель *n.m.* co-chairman.

сопре́ть *v., pfv. of* **преть.**

соприкаса́ться *v.r.impfv.* [*pfv.* **соприкосну́ться**] **1,** to touch; border (each other); be contiguous. **2,** (*with* **с** + *instr.*) to border; adjoin. **3,** (*with instr.*) to touch; bump: соприкосну́ться лба́ми, to touch/bump foreheads.

соприкоснове́ние *n.* **1,** contiguity. **2,** contact. —**то́чки соприкоснове́ния,** things in common; areas of common interest.

соприкосну́ться *v.r., pfv. of* **соприкаса́ться.**

сопроводи́тельный *adj.* accompanying. —**сопроводи́тельное письмо́,** covering letter.

сопроводи́ть [*infl.* **-жу́, -ди́шь**] *v., pfv. of* **сопровожда́ть.**

сопровожда́ть *v.impfv.* [*pfv.* **сопроводи́ть**] **1,** to accompany. **2,** to escort (*for protection*). **3,** to supplement (with additional material). —**сопровожда́ться,** *refl.* [*impfv. only*] (*with instr.*) to be accompanied (by); be escorted (by).

сопровожде́ние *n.* **1,** (act of) accompanying: в сопровожде́нии (+ *gen.*), accompanied by; без сопровожде́ния, unaccompanied. **2,** *music* accompaniment. **3,** *mil.* escort.

сопротивле́ние *n.* resistance.

сопротивля́емость *n.f.* resistance (*ability to resist*).

сопротивля́ться *v.r.impfv.* (*with dat.*) to resist.

сопряга́ть *v.impfv.* to link; connect.

сопряжённый *adj.* [*short form* **-жён, -жена́, -жено́, -жены́**] **1,** (*with* **с** + *instr.*) involving; entailing: Э́то сопряжено́ с больши́ми расхо́дами, it involves/entails great expense. **2,** *mech.* connected.

сопу́тствовать *v.impfv.* [*pres.* **-ствую, -ствуешь**] (*with dat.*) to accompany. Ему́ во всём сопу́тствует уда́ча, he is successful at everything he tries.

сопу́тствующий *adj.* attendant; concomitant.

сор *n.* rubbish; refuse; litter. —**выноси́ть сор из избы́,** to wash one's dirty linen in public; tell tales out of school.

соразме́рить *v., pfv. of* **соразмеря́ть.**

соразме́рно *prep., with dat. or* **с** + *instr.* commensurate with.

соразме́рность *n.f.* proportion; balance.

соразме́рный *adj.* **1,** commensurate; proportionate. **2,** well-proportioned.

соразмеря́ть *v.impfv.* [*pfv.* **соразме́рить**] to make commensurate (with); balance.

сора́тник *n.* comrade in arms.

сорване́ц [*gen.* **-нца́**] *n., colloq.* hoodlum; brat; (*of a girl*) tomboy.

сорва́ть [*infl.* **сорву́, сорвёшь**; *past fem.* **сорвала́**] *v., pfv. of* **срыва́ть.** —**сорва́ться,** *refl.* [*past tense stress as in* **рва́ться**] *pfv. of* **срыва́ться.**

сорвиголова́ [*infl. like* **голова́**] *n.m. & f., colloq.* daredevil.

сorganизова́ть *v.pfv.* [*infl.* **-зу́ю, -зу́ешь**] to organize.

со́рго *n. indecl.* sorghum.

соревнова́ние *n.* **1,** competition. **2,** *pl., sports* competition; contest.

соревнова́ться *v.r.impfv.* [*pres.* **-ну́юсь, -ну́ешься**] to compete.

сориенти́роваться *v.r., pfv. of* **ориенти́роваться** (*in sense #1*).

сори́нка [*gen. pl.* **-нок**] *n.* speck of dust.

сори́ть *v.impfv.* [*pfv.* **насори́ть**] **1,** to litter. **2,** [*impfv. only*] (*with instr.*) to squander. Сори́ть деньга́ми, to toss money around; spend money like water.

со́рный *adj., colloq.* rubbish (*attrib.*); refuse (*attrib.*). —**со́рная трава́,** weed; weeds.

сорня́к [*gen.* **-няка́**] *n.* weed.

соро́дич *n.* **1,** relative. **2,** fellow countryman.

со́рок [*gen., dat., instr. & prepl.* **сорока́**] *numeral* forty.

соро́ка *n.* magpie.

сорокале́тие *n.* **1,** fortieth anniversary; fortieth birthday. **2,** forty-year period.

сорокалéтний *adj.* **1,** forty-year (*attrib.*). **2,** forty-year-old.

сороково́й *ordinal numeral* fortieth.

сороконо́жка [*gen. pl.* **-жек**] *n., colloq.* centipede.

сорокопу́т *n.* shrike.

соро́чка [*gen. pl.* **-чек**] *n.* **1,** shirt. Ночна́я соро́чка, nightshirt; nightgown. **2,** chemise. **3,** back (*of a playing card*). —роди́ться в соро́чке, to be born lucky; be born under a lucky star.

сорт [*pl.* **сорта́**] *n.* **1,** sort; kind. **2,** brand. **3,** quality; grade: пе́рвого со́рта, top-quality; high-grade.

сортирова́ть *v.impfv.* [*pfv.* **рассортирова́ть**; *pres.* **-ру́ю, -ру́ешь**] to sort; assort.

сортирова́ние *n.* sorting.

сортиро́вочный *adj.* sorting (*attrib.*). —**сортиро́вочная ста́нция,** *R.R.* switchyard.

сортиро́вщик *n.* sorter.

сортово́й *adj.* high-quality.

соса́ние *n.* sucking.

соса́тельный *adj.* sucking (*attrib.*).

соса́ть *v.impfv.* [*pres.* **сосу́, сосёшь**] to suck.

сосва́тать *v., pfv. of* **сва́тать.**

сосе́д [*pl.* **сосе́ди, -дей, -дям**] *n.m.* [*fem.* **-се́дка**] neighbor. —**сосе́д по до́му,** next-door neighbor. —**сосе́д по ка́мере,** cellmate. —**сосе́д по ко́мнате,** roommate.

сосе́дний *adj.* neighboring; adjacent; next.

сосе́дский *adj.* the neighbors'.

сосе́дство *n.* **1,** proximity. **2,** *obs.* neighbors. —**по сосе́дству с,** adjacent to; adjoining.

соси́ска [*gen. pl.* **-сок**] *n.* frankfurter.

со́ска [*gen. pl.* **со́сок**] *n.* **1,** nipple (*of a nursing bottle*). **2,** pacifier.

соска́бливать *v.impfv.* [*pfv.* **соскобли́ть**] to scrape off.

соска́кивать *v.impfv.* [*pfv.* **соскочи́ть**] (*with* **с** + *gen.*) **1,** jump off; jump down (from). **2,** to jump out of; leap out of (bed). **3,** to come off.

соска́льзывать *v.impfv.* [*pfv.* **соскользну́ть**] **1,** to slide down. **2,** to slip off.

соскобли́ть [*infl.* **-скоблю́, -ско́блишь** *or* **-скобли́шь**] *v., pfv. of* **соска́бливать.**

соскользну́ть *v., pfv. of* **соска́льзывать.**

соскочи́ть [*infl.* **-скочу́, -ско́чишь**] *v., pfv. of* **соска́кивать.**

соску́читься *v.r.pfv.* **1,** to become bored. **2,** = скуча́ть (*in sense #2*).

сослага́тельный *adj., in* **сослага́тельное накло-не́ние,** subjunctive mood.

сосла́ть [*infl.* **сошлю́, сошлёшь**] *v., pfv. of* **ссыла́ть.** —**сосла́ться,** *refl., pfv. of* **ссыла́ться.**

со́слепа *also,* **со́слепу** *adv., colloq.* because one is unable to see; because of one's poor eyesight.

сосло́вие *n.* estate; class. —**дворя́нское сосло́вие,** the nobility. —**духо́вное сосло́вие,** the clergy. —**крестья́нское сосло́вие,** the peasants. —**купе́ческое сосло́вие,** the merchants.

сосло́вный *adj.* estate (*attrib.*).

сослужи́вец [*gen.* **-вца**] *n.* colleague; fellow worker.

сослужи́ть *v.pfv.* [*infl.* **-служу́, -слу́жишь**], *in* **сослужи́ть слу́жбу** (+ *dat.*), **1,** to do (someone) a favor. **2,** (*with* **хоро́шую**) to serve (someone) well; stand in good stead; (*with* **плоху́ю**) to do (someone) a disservice; serve (someone) poorly; not serve (someone) well.

сосна́ [*pl.* **со́сны, со́сен**] *n.* pine; pine tree. —**сосно́вый,** *adj.* pine (*attrib.*).

сосну́ть *v.pfv., colloq.* to take a nap.

сосня́к [*gen.* **-няка́**] *n.* pine forest.

сосо́к [*gen.* **соска́**] *n.* nipple; teat.

сосредото́чение *n.* (act of) concentration. —**сосредото́ченность,** *n.f.* (degree of) concentration.

сосредото́ченный *adj.* **1,** concentrated. **2,** lost in concentration. **3,** (*of a look*) intent; (*of attention*) rapt.

сосредото́чивать *v.impfv.* [*pfv.* **сосредото́чить**] **1,** to concentrate. **2,** to focus (efforts, attention, etc.). —**сосредото́чиваться,** *refl.* **1,** to be concentrated. **2,** (*with* **на** + *prepl.*) to concentrate (on).

соста́в *n.* **1,** composition; make-up. **2,** staff; personnel. Ли́чный соста́в, personnel. Преподава́тельский соста́в, the faculty. **3,** *in certain expressions,* strength: чи́сленный соста́в, numerical strength. **4,** train; car: пассажи́рский соста́в, passenger train; шесть пассажи́рских соста́вов, six passenger cars. Подвижно́й соста́в, rolling stock. **5,** compound. **6,** *in* соста́в исполни́телей, *theat.* cast. **7,** *in* соста́в преступле́ния, corpus delicti. —**в по́лном соста́ве, 1,** at full strength. **2,** in a group; en masse. —**в соста́ве** (+ *gen.*), consisting of: коми́ссия в соста́ве трёх челове́к, a committee of three. —**включи́ть в соста́в** (+ *gen.*), to incorporate (into). —**входи́ть в соста́в** (+ *gen.*), to form a part of; be a member of. —**выходи́ть из соста́ва** (+ *gen.*), **1,** to withdraw (from). **2,** to secede (from).

состави́тель *n.m.* compiler.

соста́вить [*infl.* **-влю, -вишь**] *v., pfv. of* **составля́ть.** —**соста́виться,** *refl., pfv. of* **составля́ться.**

составле́ние *n.* **1,** compilation. **2,** drawing up; drafting. **3,** formation.

составля́ть *v.impfv.* [*pfv.* **соста́вить**] **1,** to put together (*in one place*). **2,** to form (a group, opinion, etc.). **3,** to put together; build (a collection, library, etc.). **4,** to compile (a list, dictionary, etc.). **5,** to compose; draft; draw up. **6,** to be; represent; constitute. **7,** to total; amount to; come to. **8,** *in* составля́ть компа́нию (+ *dat.*), to keep (someone) company. —**составля́ться,** *refl.* **1,** to be formed. **2,** to be built up; accumulate.

составно́й *adj.* **1,** compound; composite. **2,** component; constituent: составна́я часть, component/constituent part. **3,** sectional. —**составна́я карти́нка,** jigsaw puzzle.

соста́рить *v., pfv. of* **ста́рить.** —**соста́риться,** *refl., pfv. of* **ста́риться.**

состоя́ние *n.* **1,** state; condition: состоя́ние здоро́вья, state of health; в хоро́шем состоя́нии, in good condition. **2,** fortune: нажива́ть состоя́ние, to make a fortune. —**быть в состоя́нии** (+ *inf.*), to be in a position to.

состоя́тельность *n.f.* **1,** wealth. **2,** soundness (*of an argument*).

состоя́тельный *adj.* **1,** well-to-do. **2,** well-founded.

состоя́ть *v.impfv.* [*pres.* **-сто́ю, -стои́шь**] **1,** (*with* из) to consist of: Кварти́ра состои́т из трёх ко́мнат, the apartment consists of three rooms. **2,** (*with instr. or various prepositions*) to be (*with reference to one's status*): состоя́ть па́йщиком, to be a shareholder; состоя́ть в запа́се, to be in the reserves. **3,** (*with* в + *prepl.*) to belong to: состоя́ть в профсою́зе, to belong to a union. **4,** (*with* в + *prepl.*) to be; consist of; lie in: ра́зница состои́т в том, что..., the difference is that... В чём бу́дут состоя́ть мои́ обя́занности?, what will my duties consist of?

состоя́ться *v.r.pfv.* [*infl.* **-сто́ится**] **1,** to take place; be held. **2,** (*of a deal*) to go through.

сострада́ние *n.* compassion. —**сострада́тельный,** *adj.* compassionate.

сострига́ть *v.impfv.* [*pfv.* **состри́чь**] to cut off; clip off.

состри́ть *v.pfv.* to crack; quip; make a wisecrack.

состри́чь [*infl. like* **стричь**] *v., pfv. of* **сострига́ть.**

состро́ить *v.pfv., colloq.* to make (a face).

состря́пать *v., pfv. of* **стря́пать.**

состяза́ние *n.* competition; contest; match.

состяза́ться *v.r.impfv.* to compete.

сосу́д *n.* **1,** vessel; container. **2,** *anat.* vessel: кровено́сный сосу́д, blood vessel.

сосу́дистый *adj.* vascular.

сосу́лька [*gen. pl.* **-лек**] *n.* icicle.

сосу́н [*gen.* **-суна́**] *n.* suckling. *Also,* **сосуно́к** [*gen.* **-нка́**].

сосуществова́ние *n.* coexistence.

сосуществова́ть *v.impfv.* [*pres.* **-ству́ю, -ству́ешь**] to coexist.

сосчита́ть *v., pfv. of* **счита́ть** (*in sense #1*).

сот *n.* **1,** *gen. pl. of* **сто:** не́сколько сот, several hundred. **2,** *see* **со́ты.**

со́тая *n., decl. as an adj.* one-hundredth: одна́ со́тая, one one-hundredth.

сотворе́ние *n.* creation (*of the world*). —**с** *or* **от сотворе́ния ми́ра,** since the world began; since the beginning of time.

сотвори́ть *v., pfv. of* **твори́ть.**

со́тенный *adj., colloq.* hundred-ruble (*attrib.*).

соте́рн (тэ) *n.* sauterne.

сотка́ть *v., pfv. of* **ткать.**

со́тня [*gen. pl.* **со́тен**] *n.* **1,** one hundred. **2,** *pl.* (*with gen.*) hundreds (of): со́тни ты́сяч люде́й, hundreds of thousands of people.

сотова́рищ *n.* associate; colleague.

со́товый *adj.* of or from a honeycomb.

сотру́дник *n.* **1,** collaborator; colleague; associate. **2,** official: сотру́дник посо́льства, embassy official. **3,** (*with gen.*) contributor (*to a newspaper, magazine, etc.*). —**нау́чный сотру́дник,** research associate.

сотру́дничать *v.impfv.* **1,** (*with* с + *instr.*) to cooperate (with); collaborate (with). **2,** (*with* в + *prepl.*) to collaborate on (a book, article, etc.). **3,** (*with* в + *prepl.*) to contribute to; write for (a publication).

сотру́дничество *n.* **1,** cooperation; collaboration. **2,** (*with* в + *prepl.*) contributing (to a publication).

сотряса́ть *v.impfv.* [*pfv.* **сотрясти́**] to shake; rock. Сотряса́ть во́здух, to rend the air. —**сотряса́ться,** *refl.* to shake; tremble.

сотрясе́ние *n.* **1,** shaking; vibration. **2,** shock; impact. —**сотрясе́ние мо́зга,** brain concussion.

сотрясти́ [*infl. like* **трясти́**] *v., pfv. of* **сотряса́ть.** —**сотрясти́сь,** *refl., pfv. of* **сотряса́ться.**

со́ты *n.pl.* [*sing.* **сот**] honeycomb.

со́тый *ordinal numeral* hundredth; one-hundredth.

со́ус *n.* sauce; gravy; dressing. —**со́усник,** *n.* gravy boat.

соуча́стие *n.* complicity. —**соуча́стник,** *n.* accomplice.

соучени́к [*gen.* **-ника́**] *n.m.* [*fem.* **-ни́ца**] fellow classmate.

софа́ [*pl.* **со́фы**] *n.* sofa.

софи́зм *n.* sophism. —**софи́ст,** *n.* sophist. —**софи́стика,** *n.* sophistry. —**софисти́ческий,** *adj.* sophistic.

соха́ [*pl.* **со́хи**] *n.* old wooden plow.

со́хнуть *v.impfv.* [*pfv.* **вы́сохнуть;** *past* сох *or* со́хнул, со́хла] **1,** to dry; become dry. **2,** to dry up. **3,** to wither. **4,** *colloq.* to waste away.

сохране́ние *n.* **1,** keeping; retention. **2,** preservation. **3,** safekeeping: отда́ть на сохране́ние, to turn over for safekeeping.

сохрани́ть *v., pfv. of* **сохраня́ть.** —**сохрани́ться,** *refl., pfv. of* **сохраня́ться.**

сохра́нность *n.f.* **1,** safety. **2,** state of preservation. —**в сохра́нности,** safe; intact.

сохра́нный *adj.* **1,** safe: в сохра́нном ме́сте, in a safe place. **2,** safe; unharmed.

сохраня́ть *v.impfv.* [*pfv.* **сохрани́ть**] **1,** to keep; retain; hold onto. **2,** to keep (a secret, one's balance, etc.). **3,** to maintain; preserve (peace, one's independence, old customs, etc.). **4,** to conserve (one's energy, strength, etc.). **5,** to protect (from damage). —**сохраня́ть за собо́й, 1,** to retain. **2,** to reserve.

сохраня́ться *v.r.impfv.* [*pfv.* **сохрани́ться**] **1,** to be preserved; remain; survive. **2,** (*of food*) to keep; not spoil. **3,** *colloq.* (*of a person*) to be well-preserved.

соцве́тие *n.* raceme.

социализа́ция *n.* socialization.

социализи́ровать *v.impfv. & pfv.* [*pres.* **-рую, -руешь**] to socialize.

социали́зм *n.* socialism. —**социали́ст,** *n.* socialist. —**социалисти́ческий,** *adj.* socialist; socialistic.

социа́льный *adj.* social.

социоло́гия *n.* sociology. —**социо́лог,** *n.* sociologist. —**социологи́ческий,** *adj.* sociological.

соче́льник *n.* **1,** Christmas Eve. **2,** Twelfth Night.

сочета́ние *n.* combination. —**в сочета́нии с,** in conjunction with.

сочета́ть *v.impfv. & pfv.* to combine. —**сочета́ться,** *refl.* **1,** to be combined. **2,** to match; go well together; (*with* с + *instr.*) go well (with).

сочине́ние *n.* **1,** (act of) composing. **2,** (literary) work. **3,** composition (*written for school*).

сочини́тель *n.m.* **1,** *archaic* writer; composer. **2,** *colloq.* liar; storyteller.

сочини́тельный *adj., gram.* coordinate: сочини́тельный сою́з, coordinate conjunction.

сочиня́ть *v.impfv.* [*pfv.* **сочини́ть**] **1,** to compose. **2,** to make up; concoct; invent.

сочи́ть *v.impfv.* to exude. —**сочи́ться,** *refl.* to ooze; trickle.

со́чный *adj.* **1,** juicy; succulent. **2,** *fig.* (*of colors, language, etc.*) rich. —**со́чность,** *n.f.* juiciness; succulence.

сочу́вственный *adj.* sympathetic. —**сочу́вственно,** *adv.* sympathetically.

сочу́вствие *n.* sympathy.

сочу́вствовать *v.impfv.* [*pres.* **-ствую, -ствуешь**] (*with dat.*) **1,** to sympathize (with); feel sorry for; feel for. **2,** to sympathize (with); be in sympathy (with).

со́шка [*gen. pl.* **со́шек**] *n.* prop; support (*for a gun*). —**ме́лкая со́шка,** small fry; pipsqueak.

сошни́к [*gen.* **-ника́**] *n.* plowshare.

сощу́рить *v., pfv. of* **щу́рить.** —**сощу́риться,** *refl., pfv. of* **щу́риться.**

сою́з *n.* **1,** union. **2,** alliance. **3,** *gram.* conjunction. —**в сою́зе с,** in league with.

сою́зник *n.m.* [*fem.* **-ница**] ally. Фра́нция — наш сою́зник (*or* на́ша сою́зница) France is our ally.

сою́знический *adj.* of an ally.

сою́зный *adj.* **1,** union (*attrib.*). **2,** federal. **3,** allied.

со́я *n.* **1,** soybean (*plant*). **2,** *colloq.* soy sauce.

спаге́тти *n.neut. indecl.* spaghetti.

спад *n.* **1,** falling off; decline. **2,** *econ.* recession; slump. **3,** receding (*of water*).

спада́ть *v.impfv.* [*pfv.* **спасть**] **1,** (*with* с + *gen.*) to fall off; fall down from. **2,** (*of water, swelling, etc.*) to go down. **3,** [*impfv. only*] to hang down. **4,** to subside; abate.

спазм *also,* **спа́зма** *n.* spasm. —**спазмати́ческий,** *adj.* spasmodic.

спа́ивать *v.impfv.* **1,** [*pfv.* **спая́ть**] to solder (together); *fig.* unite. **2,** [*pfv.* **спо́ить**] *colloq.* to make drunk; make a drunkard of.

спа́йка *n.* **1,** soldering. **2,** soldered joint. **3,** *fig.* unity; cohesion.

спали́ть *v., pfv. of* **пали́ть** (*in sense #2*).

спа́льный *adj.* sleeping (*attrib.*). —**спа́льное ме́сто,** berth.

спа́льня [*gen. pl.* **-лен**] *n.* bedroom.

спание́ль *n.m.* spaniel.

спанье́ *n., colloq.* sleeping.

спа́ренный *adj.* dual; twin.

спа́ржа *n.* asparagus. —**спа́ржевый,** *adj.* asparagus (*attrib.*).

спа́ривание *n.* mating.

спа́ривать *v.impfv.* [*pfv.* **спа́рить**] **1,** to pair; couple. **2,** to mate. —**спа́риваться,** *refl.* **1,** *colloq.* to pair off. **2,** to mate.

спартакиа́да *n.* Spartacist Games.

спарта́нец [*gen.* **-нца**] *n.m.* [*fem.* **-нка**] Spartan. —**спарта́нский,** *adj.* Spartan.

спа́рывать *v.impfv.* [*pfv.* **спороть**] to remove; take off (*by cutting the stitches*).

спаса́ние *n.* saving; rescuing.

спаса́тель *n.m.* **1,** rescue worker. **2,** lifeguard.

спаса́тельный *adj.* rescue (*attrib.*). —**спаса́тельный жиле́т,** life jacket. —**спаса́тельный круг,** life buoy. —**спаса́тельный люк,** escape hatch. —**спаса́тельная ло́дка** *or* **шлю́пка,** lifeboat. —**спаса́тельный плот,** life raft. —**спаса́тельный по́яс,** life belt; life preserver.

спаса́ть *v.impfv.* [*pfv.* **спасти́**] to save; rescue. —**спаса́ться,** *refl.* **1,** to be saved. **2,** (*with* от) to escape.

спасе́ние *n.* **1,** saving; rescue. **2,** escape. **3,** *fig.* salvation.

спаси́бо *particle* thank you; thanks. Большо́е (вам) спаси́бо!, thank you very much! —**за (одно́) спаси́бо,** without asking for anything in return. —**и на том спаси́бо,** we should be grateful at least for that.

спаси́тель *n.m.* **1,** savior; rescuer. **2,** *relig.* Savior.

спаси́тельный *adj.* that which saves; bringing salvation.

спасова́ть *v., pfv. of* **пасова́ть.**

спасти́ [*infl.* **спасу́, спасёшь;** *past* **спас, спасла́, спасло́, спасли́**] *v., pfv. of* **спаса́ть.** —**спасти́сь,** *refl., pfv. of* **спаса́ться.**

спасти́ческий *adj.* spastic.

спасть [*infl. like* **пасть**] *v., pfv. of* **спада́ть.**

спать *v.impfv.* [*pres.* **сплю, спишь, спит, спим, спи́те, спят;** *past fem.* **спала́**] to sleep. —**спа́ться,** *refl.* [*past* **спало́сь**] *impers.* (*with dat.*) *colloq.* to be able to sleep: Мне не спи́тся, I can't fall asleep; мне пло́хо спало́сь, I did not sleep well.

спа́янный *adj.* united; close-knit. —**спа́янность,** *n.f.* unity; cohesion.

спая́ть *v., pfv. of* **спа́ивать** (*in sense #1*).

спева́ться *v.r.impfv.* [*pfv.* **спе́ться**] **1,** to achieve harmony in singing. **2,** *colloq.* to get along.

спе́вка *n.* choir practice.

спекта́кль *n.m.* show; performance. —**дневно́й спекта́кль,** matinee.

спектр *n.* spectrum. —**спектра́льный,** *adj.* spectral.

спектроско́п *n.* spectroscope. —**спектроскопи́ческий,** *adj.* spectroscopic.

спекули́ровать *v.impfv.* [*pres.* **-рую, -руешь**] (*with instr. or* на + *prepl.*) **1,** *finance* to speculate (in). **2,** *fig.* to exploit; capitalize on; take advantage of.

спекуля́нт *n.* **1,** speculator. **2,** *fig.* exploiter; opportunist.

спекуляти́вный *adj.* **1,** *finance* speculative. **2,** (*of prices*) artificially high. **3,** speculative (*hypothetical*).

спекуля́ция *n.* **1,** speculation; profiteering. **2,** (*with* на + *prepl.*) taking advantage of.

спелена́ть *v., pfv. of* **пелена́ть.**

спе́лый *adj.* ripe. —**спе́лость,** *n.f.* ripeness.

спереди́ *adv.* **1,** in front. **2,** from the front. —*prep., with gen.* in (*or* from) the front of.

спере́ть *v.pfv.* [*infl.* **сопру́, сопрёшь;** *past* **спёр, спёрла**] *colloq.* to steal; swipe.

спе́рма *n.* sperm. —**сперматозо́ид,** *n.* sperm cell.

спёртый *adj., colloq.* (*of air*) close; stuffy.

спеси́вый *adj.* haughty; arrogant; high and mighty.

спесь *n.f.* haughtiness; arrogance. —**сбива́ть спесь с** (+ *gen.*), to take (someone) down a peg.

спеть[1] *v.impfv.* [*pfv.* **поспе́ть;** *pres.* **спе́ет**] to ripen; become ripe.

спеть[2] [*infl.* **спою́, споёшь**] *v., pfv. of* **петь.** —**спе́ться,** *refl., pfv. of* **спева́ться.**

спех *n., colloq.* hurry. —**мне не к спе́ху,** I'm in no hurry.

специализа́ция *n.* specialization.

специализи́роваться *v.r.impfv. & pfv.* [*pres.* **-руюсь, -руешься**] (*with* в + *prepl. or* по) to specialize (in).

специали́ст *n.* specialist; expert.

специа́льно *adv.* **1,** especially: специа́льно для вас, especially for you. **2,** specially: специа́льно подгото́влен, specially trained. **3,** *colloq.* specifically.

специа́льность *n.f.* **1,** specialty; field of specialization: рабо́тать по специа́льности, to work in one's field. **2,** profession: инжене́р по специа́льности, an engineer by profession.

специа́льный *adj.* **1,** special. **2,** specialized.

спе́цифика *n.* specific nature; specific features.

спецификация *n.* specification.

специфи́ческий *adj.* distinctive; peculiar. —**специфи́чность,** *n.f.* distinctive nature.

спе́ция *n.* spice.

спецоде́жда *n.* overalls.

спе́шивать *v.impfv.* [*pfv.* **спе́шить**] to order to dismount. —**спе́шиваться,** *refl.* to dismount.

спе́шить *v., pfv. of* **спе́шивать.** —**спе́шиться,** *refl., pfv. of* **спе́шиваться.**

спеши́ть *v.impfv.* [*pfv.* **поспеши́ть**] **1,** to hurry; rush. **2,** [*impfv. only*] to be in a hurry. **3,** (*with inf.*) to hasten (to). **4,** [*impfv. only*] (*of a timepiece*) to be fast. —**не спеша́,** at a leisurely place; deliberately.

спе́шка *n., colloq.* hurry; rush; haste. —**в спе́шке,** in one's (*or* everyone's) haste.

спе́шно *adv.* in a hurry; hastily.

спе́шность *n.f.* **1,** urgency. **2,** haste.

спе́шный *adj.* **1,** urgent; pressing. **2,** hurried; hasty.

спива́ться *v.r.impfv.* [*pfv.* **спи́ться**] to take to drink; become an alcoholic.

СПИД *n.* AIDS (*contr. of* **синдро́м приобретённого иммунодефици́та**).

спидо́метр *n.* speedometer.

спи́кер *n.* speaker (*of the House of Representatives or of a parliament*).

спи́ливать *v.impfv.* [*pfv.* **спили́ть**] **1,** to saw down. **2,** to saw off.

спили́ть [*infl.* спилю́, спи́лишь] *v., pfv. of* **спи́ливать.**

спина́ [*acc.* спи́ну; *pl.* спи́ны] *n.* back. —**за (чьей-нибудь) спино́й,** behind someone's back. —**спино́й к,** with one's back to.

спи́нка [*gen. pl.* -нок] *n.* **1,** *dim. of* **спина́. 2,** back (*of a garment, piece of furniture, etc.*).

спинно́й *adj.* spinal; dorsal. —**спинно́й мозг,** spinal cord. —**спинно́й хребе́т,** spine; backbone; spinal column.

спинномозгово́й *adj.* spinal.

спира́ль *n.f.* spiral. —**спира́льный,** *adj.* spiral.

спири́т *n.* spiritualist (*one who believes in communication with the dead*). —**спирити́зм,** *n.* spiritualism. —**спирити́ческий,** *adj.* spiritualistic.

спиритуали́зм *n., philos.* spiritualism. —**спиритуали́ст,** *n.* spiritualist.

спирт *n.* **1,** alcohol: древе́сный спирт, wood alcohol. **2,** spirits: камфа́рный спирт, spirits of camphor. —**нашаты́рный спирт,** liquid ammonia.

спиртно́е *n., decl. as an adj., colloq.* alcohol.

спиртно́й *adj.* alcoholic.

спирто́вка [*gen. pl.* -вок] *n.* spirit lamp.

спиртово́й *adj.* spirit (*attrib.*); alcohol (*attrib.*). —**спиртова́я ла́мпа,** spirit lamp.

списа́ть [*infl.* спишу́, спи́шешь] *v., pfv. of* **спи́сывать.** —**списа́ться,** *refl., pfv. of* **спи́сываться.**

спи́сок [*gen.* -ска] *n.* list. —**послужно́й спи́сок,** service record; work record.

спи́сывать *v.impfv.* [*pfv.* **списа́ть**] **1,** to copy. **2,** (*with* с + *gen.*) to base on (*when writing or painting*): спи́сан с живо́го лица́, based on a real-life person. **3,** (*with* у) to copy (from); crib (from). **4,** *finance* to write off. —**спи́сываться,** *refl.* (*with* с + *instr.*) to write to; get in touch with (*by mail*).

спито́й *adj., colloq.* (*of tea or coffee*) weak.

спи́ться [*infl.* спою́сь, сопьёшься; *past* спи́лся, спила́сь, спило́сь *or* спи́лось, спили́сь *or* спи́лись] *v.r., pfv. of* **спива́ться.**

спи́хивать *v.impfv.* [*pfv.* **спихну́ть**] *colloq.* **1,** to push off. **2,** *fig.* to shove aside; kick out.

спи́ца *n.* **1,** spoke. **2,** knitting needle.

спич *n.* (short) speech.

спи́чечница *n.* matchbox holder.

спи́чечный *adj.* match (*attrib.*): спи́чечная коро́бка, matchbox.

спи́чка [*gen. pl.* -чек] *n.* match.

сплав *n.* **1,** alloy. **2,** floating (*of timber*).

спла́вить [*infl.* -влю, -вишь] *v., pfv. of* **сплавля́ть.**

сплавля́ть *v.impfv.* [*pfv.* **спла́вить**] **1,** to fuse; alloy. **2,** *fig.* to bind together; forge together. **3,** to float (something) downstream. **4,** *colloq.* to get rid of; unload.

сплавно́й *adj.* (*of timber*) floating.

сплани́ровать *v., pfv. of* **плани́ровать.**

спла́чивать *v.impfv.* [*pfv.* **сплоти́ть**] **1,** to fasten together; join. **2,** *fig.* to rally; unite. **3,** *in* спла́чивать ряды́, to close ranks. —**спла́чиваться,** *refl.* **1,** to cluster (together). **2,** (*of ranks*) to close. **3,** *fig.* to rally; unite; be united.

сплёвывать *v.impfv.* [*pfv.* **сплю́нуть**] to spit; spit out.

сплести́ [*infl. like* плести́] *v., pfv. of* **плести́** *and* **сплета́ть.** —**сплести́сь,** *refl., pfv. of* **сплета́ться.**

сплета́ть *v.impfv.* [*pfv.* **сплести́**] **1,** to weave. **2,** to entwine; intertwine. —**сплета́ться,** *refl.* **1,** to become entwined; become tangled. **2,** *fig.* to become intertwined.

сплете́ние *n.* **1,** combination: сплете́ние обстоя́тельств, combination of circumstances. **2,** *anat.* plexus: со́лнечное сплете́ние, solar plexus. —**сплете́ние лжи,** web of lies.

спле́тник *n.m.* [*fem.* -ница] gossip (*person*).

спле́тничать *v.impfv.* [*pfv.* **наспле́тничать**] to gossip.

спле́тня [*gen. pl.* -тен] *n.* gossip; item of gossip.

сплеча́ *adv.* **1,** with a full sweep of the arm. **2,** in haste; without thought. —**руби́ть сплеча́,** to shoot straight from the hip.

сплоти́ть [*infl.* -чу́, -ти́шь] *v., pfv. of* **спла́чивать.** —**сплоти́ться,** *refl., pfv. of* **спла́чиваться.**

сплохова́ть *v.pfv.* [*infl.* -ху́ю, -ху́ешь] *colloq.* to make a blunder.

сплоче́ние *n.* rallying; uniting.

сплочённость *n.f.* unity; solidarity; cohesion.

сплочённый *adj.* **1,** pressed close together. **2,** united.

сплошно́й *adj.* **1,** solid; continuous; unbroken. **2,** complete; total. **3,** *colloq.* pure; sheer; utter.

сплошь *adv.* **1,** leaving no space uncovered: Не́бо сплошь заволокло́ облака́ми, the sky was completely covered with clouds. **2,** entirely: сплошь состоя́ть из, to consist entirely of. —сплошь и (*or* да) ря́дом, *colloq.* very often.

сплутова́ть *v., pfv. of* плутова́ть.

сплыва́ть *v.impfv.* [*pfv.* сплыть] *colloq.* **1,** to swim downstream; float downstream. **2,** to overflow. —бы́ло да сплы́ло, it came and it went; it's gone for good.

сплыть [*infl. like* плыть] *v., pfv. of* сплыва́ть.

сплю́нуть *v., pfv. of* сплёвывать.

сплю́снутый *adj.* flat; flattened. *Also,* сплю́щенный.

сплю́щивать *v.impfv.* [*pfv.* сплю́щить] to flatten. —сплю́щиваться, *refl.* to become flat; flatten out.

спляса́ть *v., pfv. of* пляса́ть.

сподви́жник *n.* associate; comrade in arms.

сподру́чный *adj., colloq.* convenient; handy.

спозара́нку *adv., colloq.* early in the morning.

спои́ть [*infl.* спою́, спои́шь *or* споишь] *v., pfv. of* спа́ивать (*in sense #2*).

споко́йно *adv.* calmly; peacefully. —*adj.,* used predicatively, quiet; peaceful: Здесь споко́йно, it is quiet/ peaceful here. —спи́те споко́йно!, sleep well! —у меня́ на душе́ споко́йно, my mind is at ease.

споко́йный *adj.* [*short form* -ко́ен, -ко́йна] **1,** calm; tranquil; quiet; peaceful. **2,** (*of light, color, etc.*) restful. **3,** *colloq.* comfortable. —споко́йной но́чи!, good night!

споко́йствие *n.* **1,** quiet; calm; tranquillity. **2,** public order. **3,** composure; equanimity.

спола́скивать *v.impfv.* [*pfv.* сполосну́ть] *colloq.* to rinse; rinse out.

сполза́ть *v.impfv.* [*pfv.* сползти́] **1,** to climb down; crawl down. **2,** to slip off; slip down. **3,** to trickle down. **4,** to slope down. **5,** (*of an expression, smile, etc.*) to fade (from one's face). **6,** *fig.* to slip; drift.

сползти́ [*infl. like* ползти́] *v., pfv. of* сполза́ть.

сполна́ *adv.* in full.

сполосну́ть *v., pfv. of* спола́скивать.

споло́хи *n.pl.* [*sing.* споло́х] **1,** *obs.* northern lights. **2,** flashes of lightning. **3,** bright flashes of light.

спо́нсор *n.* sponsor.

спонта́нный *adj.* spontaneous.

спор *n.* **1,** argument. **2,** dispute; controversy. —спо́ру нет, there is no question.

спо́ра *n.* spore.

споради́ческий *adj.* sporadic.

спо́рить *v.impfv.* [*pfv.* поспо́рить] **1,** to argue. **2,** [*impfv. only*] to dispute; challenge; question: Никто́ уже́ не спо́рит, что..., no one challenges any longer the fact that..., Не спо́рю, что..., I don't deny that... **3,** *colloq.* to bet. **4,** *fig.* (*with* с + *instr. or* про́тив) to fight; battle. **5,** (*with* с + *instr.*) to compete (with). **6,** (*with* за + *acc.*) to vie for.

спори́ться *v.r.impfv., colloq.* to go well; work out well; turn out well.

спо́рный *adj.* **1,** controversial. **2,** debatable; moot. **3,** unsettled; outstanding. **4,** disputed.

спо́ро *adv., colloq.* smoothly.

споро́ть [*infl.* спорю́, спо́решь] *v., pfv. of* спа́рывать.

спорт *n.* sports.

спортза́л *n.* gymnasium (*contr. of* спорти́вный зал).

спорти́вный *adj.* sports (*attrib.*); sporting; athletic. Спорти́вная площа́дка, athletic field; playing field. Спорти́вный зал, gymnasium. —из спорти́вного интере́са, for the fun of it.

спортсме́н *n.m.* [*fem.* -ме́нка] athlete; sportsman. —спортсме́нский, *adj.* sportsmanlike.

спорхну́ть *v.pfv.* **1,** to fly away; flit away. **2,** to land suddenly.

спо́рщик *n., colloq.* **1,** person involved in an argument. **2,** person who likes to argue.

спо́рый *adj., colloq.* **1,** (*of work, movements, etc.*) smooth. **2,** profitable.

спорынья́ *n.* ergot.

спо́соб *n.* way; method.

спосо́бность *n.f.* **1,** ability. **2,** *usu. pl.* (*with* к) aptitude (for). **3,** *usu. pl.* faculties: у́мственные спосо́бности, mental faculties. **4,** capacity; power: пропускна́я спосо́бность, carrying capacity; покупа́тельная спосо́бность, purchasing power.

спосо́бный *adj.* [*short form* -бен, -бна] **1,** able; bright; talented. **2,** (*with* к) good (at); having a gift (for). **3,** (*with* к, на *or inf.*) capable (of).

спосо́бствовать *v.impfv.* [*pres.* -ствую, -ствуешь] (*with dat.*) to further; promote; contribute to.

спотыка́ться *v.r.impfv.* [*pfv.* споткну́ться] to stumble; trip.

спохвати́ться [*infl.* -хвачу́сь, -хва́тишься] *v.r., pfv. of* спохва́тываться.

спохва́тываться *v.r.impfv.* [*pfv.* спохвати́ться] *colloq.* to suddenly remember.

спра́ва *adv.* **1,** from the right. **2,** to (*or* on) the right.

справедли́во *adv.* fairly; justly.

справедли́вость *n.f.* **1,** justice; fairness. **2,** correctness. —справедли́вости ра́ди, in all fairness. —отда́ть справедли́вость (+ *dat.*), to give credit to; give (someone) his due.

справедли́вый *adj.* **1,** just; fair. **2,** just; justifiable. **3,** correct; valid.

спра́вить [*infl.* -влю, -вишь] *v., pfv. of* справля́ть. —спра́виться, *refl., pfv. of* справля́ться.

спра́вка [*gen. pl.* -вок] *n.* **1,** *usu. pl.* reference: для спра́вок, for reference purposes. **2,** information. **3,** certificate. Спра́вка с ме́ста рабо́ты, (work) reference. —наводи́ть спра́вки о, to make inquiries about.

справля́ть *v.impfv.* [*pfv.* спра́вить] *colloq.* to celebrate (an occasion). Справля́ть сва́дьбу, to hold a wedding. —справля́ться, *refl.* **1,** (*with* о) to inquire (about). **2,** (*with* в + *prepl.*) to consult (a book, dictionary, etc.). **3,** (*with* с + *instr.*) to cope with; handle (a task); handle; control (a child, horse, class, etc.).

спра́вочник *n.* reference book; directory.

спра́вочный *adj.* reference (*attrib.*); information (*attrib.*); inquiry (*attrib.*).

спра́шивать *v.impfv.* [*pfv.* спроси́ть] **1,** (*with acc. or* у) to ask (someone). **2,** (*with acc. or* о) to ask (about); inquire about: спроси́ть доро́гу, to ask the way; спроси́ть о чьём-нибудь здоро́вье, to inquire about someone's health. Мо́жно спроси́ть ва́шу фами́лию?, may I ask your name? 3, (with acc. or gen.) to ask for. 4, to ask for (someone); ask to see. 5, to call on (a pupil). 6, colloq. to ask; charge (a price). 7, (with c + gen.) to hold accountable. —спра́шиваться, refl. 1, (with y) colloq. to ask permission (of). Не спрося́сь (+ gen.), without asking (someone). 2, [impfv. only] impers.: Спра́шивается, one may ask; the question arises.

спрессова́ть v., pfv. of прессова́ть.

спринт n. sprint. —спри́нтер, n. sprinter.

спринцева́ть v.impfv. [pres. -цу́ю, -цу́ешь] to syringe.

спринцо́вка [gen. pl. -вок] n. 1, syringing. 2, syringe.

спрова́живать v.impfv. [pfv. спрова́дить] colloq. to escort out; send on one's way; send packing.

спровоци́ровать v., pfv. of провоци́ровать.

спроекти́ровать v., pfv. of проекти́ровать.

спрос n., econ. demand: спрос и предложе́ние, supply and demand. —без спро́са; без спро́су, without permission.

спроси́ть [infl. спрошу́, спро́сишь] v., pfv. of спра́шивать. —спроси́ться, refl., pfv. of спра́шиваться.

спросо́нок adv., colloq. half-awake; being only half-awake. Also, спросо́нья.

спроста́ adv., colloq. 1, out of naïveté. 2, directly; straight to the point. 3, for no reason; just like that.

спрут n. octopus.

спры́гивать v.impfv. [pfv. спры́гнуть] (with c + gen.) to jump off; jump down (from).

спры́скивать v.impfv. [pfv. спры́снуть] colloq. to sprinkle.

спряга́ть v.impfv. [pfv. проспряга́ть] to conjugate (a verb).

спряже́ние n., gram. conjugation.

спрясть v., pfv. of прясть.

спря́тать v., pfv. of пря́тать. —спря́таться, refl., pfv. of пря́таться.

спу́гивать v.impfv. [pfv. спугну́ть] to frighten off; frighten away.

спуд n., in под спу́дом, hidden; under wraps; из-под спу́да, from hiding; from under wraps.

спуск n. 1, lowering. 2, descent; going down. 3, descent; slope. 4, in спуск на́ воду, launching (of a ship). —не дава́ть спу́ска (+ dat.), colloq. to give someone no quarter.

спуска́ть v.impfv. [pfv. спусти́ть] 1, to lower; let down. 2, to launch (a ship). 3, to send down (an order, directive, etc.). 4, to release; let loose. 5, to let the air out of; let the water out of. 6, v.i. (of a tire) to go flat. 7, colloq. to pardon; forgive. 8, colloq. to sell; unload. 9, colloq. to squander; throw away. 10, in спуска́ть куро́к, to pull the trigger. 11, in спуска́ть пе́тлю, to drop a stitch. —не спуска́ть глаз с (+ gen.), not let out of one's sight. —спуска́ть с ле́стницы, to kick out; give (someone) the boot. —спустя́ рукава́, carelessly; in a slipshod manner.

спуска́ться v.r.impfv. [pfv. спусти́ться] 1, to go down; descend. 2, (of a plane, bird, etc.) to land. 3, to sail

downstream. 4, (of fog, dusk, etc.) to descend; fall. 5, [impfv. only] to hang down. 6, [impfv. only] to slope down.

спускно́й adj. drain (attrib.): спускно́й кран, drain cock; petcock.

спусково́й adj. = спускно́й. —спускова́я кно́пка, photog. shutter release. —спусково́й крючо́к, trigger.

спусти́ть [infl. спущу́, спу́стишь] v., pfv. of спуска́ть. —спусти́ться, refl., pfv. of спуска́ться.

спустя́ prep., with acc. after. —немно́го спустя́, a little (while) later.

спу́танный adj. 1, tangled. 2, confused; muddled; incoherent.

спу́тать v., pfv. of пу́тать. —спу́таться, refl., pfv. of пу́таться.

спу́тник n. 1, traveling companion. 2, satellite.

спьяна́ also, спьяну́ adv., colloq. while drunk.

спя́тить v.pfv. [infl. спя́чу, спя́тишь] colloq. to go crazy; go nuts.

спя́чка n. 1, [usu. зи́мняя спя́чка] hibernation. 2, colloq. drowsiness; lethargy.

сраба́тывать v.impfv. [pfv. срабо́тать] colloq. 1, to make; turn out. 2, (of a device, machine, etc.) to work; operate. —сраба́тываться, refl. 1, (of a machine) to wear out. 2, to work well together; (with c + instr.) work well with.

срабо́танность n.f. 1, harmony in work. 2, wear (and tear).

срабо́тать v., pfv. of сраба́тывать. —срабо́таться, refl., pfv. of сраба́тываться.

сравне́ние n. 1, comparison. 2, simile. —по сравне́нию с; в сравне́нии с, compared to; in comparison with. —не идёт (ни) в (како́е) сравне́ние с, cannot compare to; is in no way comparable to.

сра́внивать v.impfv. 1, [pfv. сравни́ть] to compare. 2, [pfv. сравня́ть] to make equal. Сравня́ть счёт, to tie the score. 3, [pfv. сровня́ть] to even; level. Сровня́ть с землёй, to raze to the ground; level.

сравни́мый adj. comparable. —ни с чем не сравни́мый, incomparable; in a class by itself.

сравни́тельно adv. 1, comparatively. 2, (with c + instr.) compared to.

сравни́тельный adj. comparative.

сравни́ть v., pfv. of сра́внивать (in sense #1). —сравни́ться, refl. (with c + instr.) to compare: Никто́ не мо́жет сравни́ться с ней, no one can compare to her.

сравня́ть v., pfv. of равня́ть and сра́внивать (in sense #2). —сравня́ться, refl. (with c + instr.) to become the equal of; achieve equality with.

сража́ть v.impfv. [pfv. срази́ть] 1, to strike down. 2, fig. (of news) to stagger. —сража́ться, refl. to fight (in battle).

сраже́ние n. battle.

срази́ть [infl. -жу́, -зи́шь] v., pfv. of сража́ть. —срази́ться, refl., pfv. of сража́ться.

сра́зу adv. 1, at once; immediately; right away. 2, all at once. 3, just: сра́зу за (+ instr.), just beyond or behind. —сра́зу по́сле (+ gen.), 1, right after. 2, just past.

срам n., colloq. shame.

срами́ть *v.impfv.* [*pfv.* осрами́ть; *pres.* -млю́, -ми́шь] *colloq.* to shame; disgrace. —**срами́ться**, *refl.*, *colloq.* to disgrace oneself.

срамни́к [*gen.* -ника́] *n.*, *colloq.* shameless person.

срамно́й *adj.*, *colloq.* indecent.

сраста́ние *n.* knitting (*of bones*).

сраста́ться *v.r.impfv.* [*pfv.* срасти́сь] to grow together; (*of bones*) knit.

срасти́сь [*infl. like* расти́] *v.r.*, *pfv. of* сраста́ться.

срасти́ть [*infl.* -щу́, -сти́шь] *v.*, *pfv. of* сра́щивать.

сраще́ние *n.* **1**, joining together. **2**, growing together.

сра́щивание *n.* **1**, setting (*of a bone*). **2**, joining; splicing. **3**, *fig.* merging.

сра́щивать *v.impfv.* [*pfv.* срасти́ть] **1**, to set (a broken bone). **2**, to join together; splice. **3**, to merge; intertwine.

сре́бреник *n.* ancient silver coin; piece of silver.

среда́ *n.* **1**, [*acc.* сре́ду] Wednesday. **2**, [*acc.* среду́] surroundings; environment; milieu; *physics* medium. —**окружа́ющая среда́**, the environment.

среди́ *prep.*, *with gen.* **1**, in the middle of. **2**, among. —**среди́** (*or* **средь**) **бе́ла дня**, in broad daylight.

среди́на *n.* = середи́на. —**среди́нный**, *adj.* = середи́нный.

сре́дне *adv.*, *colloq.* fair; so-so.

средне- *prefix* **1**, central: среднеазиа́тский, Central Asian. **2**, middle: среднеангли́йский язы́к, Middle English.

средневеко́вый *adj.* medieval. —**средневеко́вье**, *n.* the Middle Ages.

среневе́с *n.* middleweight.

сре́днее *n.*, *decl. as an adj.* average: вы́ше/ни́же сре́днего, above/below average. —**в сре́днем**, on the average.

сре́дний *adj.* **1**, middle. **2**, center: сре́дний прохо́д, center aisle. **3**, medium: сре́дний бомбарди́ровщик, medium bomber. **4**, average; mean. **5**, average; mediocre. **6**, *gram.* neuter. **7**, (*of school or education*) secondary. —**сре́дние века́**, the Middle Ages. —**сре́дних лет**, middle-aged. —**сре́дней руки́**, ordinary; of no particular distinction.

средото́чие *n.* focus; focal point; center; hub.

сре́дство *n.* **1**, means; way. **2**, *pl.* means: сре́дства произво́дства, means of production; челове́к со сре́дствами, man of means. **3**, *pl.* funds: сбор средств, fund raising. **4**, medication; remedy: возбужда́ющее сре́дство, stimulant; сре́дство от ка́шля, cough remedy. **5**, agent: отбе́ливающее сре́дство, bleaching agent. Мо́ющее сре́дство, detergent. Сре́дство от насеко́мых, insect repellent. —**сре́дства ма́ссовой информа́ции**, the media.

средь *prep.* = среди́.

срез *n.* **1**, cut; slice; section. **2**, microscopic section.

сре́зать [*infl.* сре́жу, сре́жешь] *v.*, *pfv. of* ре́зать (*in sense #6*) *and* среза́ть. —**сре́заться**, *refl.*, *pfv. of* среза́ться.

среза́ть *v.impfv.* [*pfv.* сре́зать] **1**, to cut off; cut away. Среза́ть цветы́, to cut flowers. **2**, to strike down; cut down. **3**, *fig.* to reduce; cut down. **4**, to cut off (*while speaking*). **5**, *sports* to slice (a ball). **6**, *colloq.* to flunk (a student). **7**, *in* срезать у́гол, to take a shortcut. —**среза́ться**, *refl.* (*with* на + *prepl.*) to flunk (an examination).

сре́зывать *v.impfv.* = среза́ть.

срисова́ть [*infl.* -су́ю, -су́ешь] *v.*, *pfv. of* срисо́вывать.

срисо́вывать *v.impfv.* [*pfv.* срисова́ть] to copy.

сровня́ть *v.*, *pfv. of* ровня́ть *and* сра́внивать (*in sense #3*).

сродни́ *adv.* (*with dat.*) *colloq.* **1**, related (to). **2**, *fig.* akin (to).

сродни́ть *v.*, *pfv. of* родни́ть. —**сродни́ться**, *refl.* (*with* с + *instr.*) **1**, to become close to. **2**, to get used to.

сро́дный *adj.* related.

сродство́ *n.* affinity.

сро́ду *adv.*, *colloq.* **1**, (*fol. by* не) never (in one's whole life). **2**, since one was born; always.

срок *n.* **1**, period of time: в коро́ткий срок, in a short time. Срок ожида́ния, waiting period. **2**, term: избира́ться сро́ком на четы́ре го́да, to be elected for a four-year term. **3**, date: намеча́ть срок, to set the date. **4**, deadline. —**в срок**; **к сро́ку**, in time; on time; on schedule. —**до сро́ка**; **ра́ньше сро́ка**, ahead of time; ahead of schedule. —**кра́йний** *or* **после́дний** *or* **преде́льный срок**, deadline. —**срок де́йствия**, period of time that something is valid. Срок де́йствия ва́шего па́спорта истёк, your passport has expired. —**срок слу́жбы**, **1**, period of service; enlistment; hitch. **2**, life (*of a battery, machine, etc.*).

сро́чно *adv.* **1**, urgently. **2**, immediately; without delay.

сро́чность *n.f.* **1**, urgency. **2**, *colloq.* hurry.

сро́чный *adj.* **1**, urgent; pressing: сро́чное де́ло, urgent matter. Сро́чный зака́з, rush order. **2**, prompt. **3**, for a fixed period: сро́чная слу́жба, service for a fixed period; regular tour of duty.

сруб *n.* **1**, felling (*of timber*): продава́ть на сруб, to sell for timber. **2**, frame; framework. **3**, log cabin.

сруба́ть *v.impfv.* [*pfv.* сруби́ть] to chop down; fell.

сруби́ть *v.pfv.* [*infl.* срублю́, сру́бишь] **1**, *pfv. of* сруба́ть. **2**, to build (*of logs*).

срыв *n.* failure; breakdown; collapse.

срыва́ть *v.impfv.* [*pfv.* сорва́ть] **1**, to tear off; tear away. **2**, to pick; pluck. **3**, to frustrate; disrupt; thwart; foil. **4**, *fig.*, *colloq.* to win (applause); steal (a kiss); wangle (money). **5**, (*with* на + *prepl.*) to vent (one's feelings) on; take out (one's anger) on. **6**, [*pfv.* срыть] to level with the ground; raze to the ground. —**сорва́ть банк**, to break the bank. —**сорва́ть го́лос**, to strain one's voice.

срыва́ться *v.r.impfv.* [*pfv.* сорва́ться] **1**, to come off; come loose. **2**, to fall; slip; tumble. **3**, to break loose. **4**, (*with* с + *gen.*) to jump up (from) and take off. **5**, (*of applause, a storm, etc.*) to break out. **6**, *fig.*, *colloq.* to fail; fall through. **7**, (*of one's voice*) to break. —**срыва́ться с губ** *or* **с языка́**, to escape one's lips.

срыть [*infl.* сро́ю, сро́ешь] *v.*, *pfv. of* срыва́ть (*in sense #6*).

сря́ду *adv.*, *colloq.* in a row; consecutively.

сса́дина *n.* scratch; abrasion.

ссади́ть [*infl.* ссажу́, сса́дишь] *v.*, *pfv. of* сса́живать.

ссáживать *v.impfv.* [*pfv.* **ссади́ть**] **1,** to scratch. **2,** to help down; help (someone) get down. **3,** to put off; make (someone) get off.

ссóра *n.* quarrel. —**быть в ссóре (с),** to have had a falling-out (with).

ссóрить *v.impfv.* [*pfv.* **поссóрить**] to cause a quarrel between. —**ссóриться,** *refl.* to quarrel.

ссóхнуться [*past* **ссóхся, ссóхлась**] *v.r., pfv. of* **ссыхáться.**

ссýда *n.* loan. —**безвозврáтная ссýда,** outright grant.

ссуди́ть [*infl.* **ссужу́, ссýдишь**] *v., pfv. of* **ссужáть.**

ссужáть *v.impfv.* [*pfv.* **ссуди́ть**] to loan; lend.

ссутýлить *v., pfv. of* **сутýлить.** —**ссутýлиться,** *refl., pfv. of* **сутýлиться.**

ссылáть *v.impfv.* [*pfv.* **сослáть**] to banish; exile. —**ссылáться,** *refl.* (*with* **на** + *acc.*) **1,** to cite; quote; refer (to); allude (to). **2,** to cite (*as an excuse*); plead; allege.

ссы́лка [*gen. pl.* **-лок**] *n.* **1,** reference: перекрёстная ссы́лка, cross-reference. **2,** exile; banishment.

ссы́лочный *adj.* reference (*attrib.*).

ссы́льный *adj.* in exile. —*n.* exile.

ссы́пать [*infl.* **ссы́плю, ссы́плешь**] *v., pfv. of* **ссыпáть.**

ссыпáть *v.impfv.* [*pfv.* **ссы́пать**] to pour.

ссыхáться *v.r.impfv.* [*pfv.* **ссóхнуться**] **1,** to warp; become warped. **2,** *fig., colloq.* to become gaunt. **3,** to cake; become caked.

стабилизáтор *n.* stabilizer.

стабилизáция *n.* stabilization.

стабилизи́ровать *v.impfv. & pfv.* [*pres.* **-рую, -руешь**] to stabilize. —**стабилизи́роваться,** *refl.* to stabilize; become stabilized.

стаби́льность *n.f.* stability.

стаби́льный *adj.* stable. —**стаби́льный учéбник,** standard textbook.

стáвень [*gen.* **-вня**] *n.m.* shutter.

стáвить *v.impfv.* [*pfv.* **постáвить;** *pres.* **стáвлю, стáвишь**] **1,** to stand; place; set; put. **2,** to park (a car). **3,** to install. **4,** to apply (*to a part of one's body*). **5,** to affix (a seal, signature, etc.). **6,** to stage; produce; put on (a play); make; produce (a movie). **7,** to erect (a monument). **8,** to post (a sentry). **9,** to bet; stake. **10,** *with various nouns,* to set: стáвить рекóрд, to set a record; стáвить часы́/буди́льник, to set a watch/ alarm clock/; стáвить себé задáчу, to set a task for oneself; стáвить себé цéлью, to set as one's goal. —**ни во что не стáвить,** to take no account of. —**стáвить вопрóс,** to pose a question. —**стáвить (чтó-нибудь) в винý** (+ *dat.*), to accuse (someone of something); hold (someone) to blame: Емý стáвилось в винý, что..., he was accused of... —**стáвить в примéр,** to make an example of; hold up as an example. —**стáвить диáгноз,** to make a diagnosis. —**стáвить задáчу (пéред),** to assign a task (to). —**стáвить (когó-нибудь) нá ноги,** to get someone on his/her feet. —**стáвить óпыт,** to conduct an experiment. —**стáвить отмéтки,** to give grades. —**стáвить услóвия,** to set *or* lay down conditions.

стáвка *n.* **1,** stake; stakes: повышáть стáвку, to raise the stakes. **2,** rate: стáвка процéнта, rate of interest. **3,**

mil. headquarters. —**дéлать стáвку на** (+ *acc.*), to count on. —**на пóлную стáвку,** full-time.

стáвленник *n.* protégé.

стáвня [*gen. pl.* **-вен**] *n.* shutter.

стадиóн *n.* stadium.

стáдия *n.* stage. По стáдиям, in stages.

стáдный *adj.* (*of animals*) living in herds; gregarious. —**стáдный инсти́нкт,** herd instinct.

стáдо [*pl.* **стадá**] *n.* herd; flock.

стаж *n.* length of service. Слýжащий с больши́м стáжем, employee with a long record of service. Надбáвка к зарплáте за стаж, pay increase for length of service.

стажёр *n.* person undergoing on-the-job training.

стажировáться *v.r.impfv.* [*pres.* **-рýюсь, -рýешься**] to undergo on-the-job-training. *Also,* **стажи́роваться** [*pres.* **-руюсь, -руешься**].

стажирóвка *n.* practical training; on-the-job training.

стáивать *v.impfv.* [*pfv.* **стáять**] to melt.

стáйер *n.* long-distance runner.

стáйка [*gen. pl.* **стáек**] *n., dim. of* **стáя,** small flock; small group.

стакáн *n.* glass: стакáн воды́, glass of water.

стаккáто *adv.* staccato.

стáксель *n.m.* staysail.

сталагми́т *n.* stalagmite.

сталакти́т *n.* stalactite.

сталевáр *n.* steelworker.

сталели́тейный *adj.* pert. to the making of steel: сталели́тейный завóд, steel mill.

сталели́тейщик *n.* steelworker.

сталеплави́льный *adj.* pert. to the smelting of steel: сталеплави́льная печь, steel-smelting furnace.

стáлкивать *v.impfv.* [*pfv.* **столкнýть**] **1,** to push off; push away; push down; push into. **2,** to cause (objects) to strike each other. **3,** *colloq.* to bring together. —**стáлкиваться,** *refl.* (*with* **с** + *instr.*) **1,** to collide. **2,** *fig.* to clash. **3,** run into; encounter.

сталь *n.f.* steel.

стальнóй *adj.* **1,** steel; of steel. **2,** *fig.* steely.

стамéска [*gen. pl.* **-сок**] *n.* chisel.

стан *n.* **1,** figure; build. **2,** mill: прокáтный стан, rolling mill. **3,** camp. —**нóтный стан,** *music* staff.

стандáрт *n.* **1,** standard. **2,** *fig.* stereotype.

стандартизáция *n.* standardization.

стандартизи́ровать *v.impfv. & pfv.* [*pres.* **-рую, -ру- ешь**] to standardize. *Also,* **стандартизовáть** [*pres.* **-зýю, -зýешь**].

стандáртный *adj.* **1,** standard; standardized. **2,** *fig.* standard; conventional.

стани́на *n.* mount; base.

станиóль *n.m.* tin foil.

стани́ца *n.* **1,** large Cossack village. **2,** flock (*of birds*).

станкóвый *adj.* machine (*attrib.*). —**станкóвый пулемёт,** heavy *or* medium machine gun.

станови́ться *v.r.impfv.* [*pfv.* **стать;** *pres.* **становлю́сь, станóвишься**] **1,** to stand: Стáньте передо мной, stand in front of me. **2,** (*with instr.*) to become; get. Стать друзья́ми, to become friends. Стáло хóлодно, it has gotten cold. Погóда стáла лýчше, the weather has gotten better. —**стать в о́чередь,** to get on line. —**стать в по́зу,** to strike a pose. —**стать на коле́ни,** to kneel (down); get down on one's knees. —**стать на́ ноги,** to get on one's feet. —**стать на путь** (+ *gen.*), to embark on a path of. —**стать на сто́рону** (+ *gen.*), to side with; take the side of. *See also* **стать.**

становле́ние *n.* (*with gen.*) formation (of): становле́ние хара́ктера, formation of character.

станово́й *adj.,* pre-rev. district (*attrib.*). —**станово́й хребе́т; станова́я жи́ла,** backbone; mainstay.

стано́к [*gen.* **-нка́**] *n.* **1,** machine: фре́зерный стано́к, milling machine. **2,** machine tool. **3,** any of various devices: печа́тный стано́к, printing press; тка́цкий стано́к, loom; тока́рный стано́к, lathe. **4,** gun mount.

стано́чник *n.* machine operator; machine tool operator.

станс *n.* stanza (*of four lines*).

станцио́нный *adj.* station (*attrib.*).

ста́нция *n.* **1,** station: железнодоро́жная/запра́вочная/косми́ческая ста́нция, railroad/filling/space station. **2,** *R.R.* yard: това́рная ста́нция, freight yard; сортиро́вочная ста́нция, switchyard. —**телефо́нная ста́нция,** telephone exchange.

ста́птывать *v.impfv.* [*pfv.* **стопта́ть**] **1,** to wear down (shoes, heels, etc.). **2,** *colloq.* to trample. —**ста́птываться,** *refl.* (*of shoes, heels, etc.*) to wear down; become worn down.

стара́ние *n.* effort: прилага́ть все стара́ния, to exert every effort.

стара́тель *n.m.* prospector for gold; gold digger.

стара́тельный *adj.* diligent; assiduous; painstaking. —**стара́тельно,** *adv.* diligently; painstakingly. —**стара́тельность,** *n.f.* diligence.

стара́ться *v.r.impfv.* [*pfv.* **постара́ться**] to try.

старе́йшина *n.m.* elder.

старе́ние *n.* aging.

старе́ть *v.impfv.* **1,** [*pfv.* **постаре́ть**] to grow old; get old; age. **2,** [*pfv.* **устаре́ть**] to become obsolete; become antiquated.

ста́рец [*gen.* **-рца**] *n.* (venerable) old man.

стари́к [*gen.* **-рика́**] *n.* old man.

старина́ *n.f.* **1,** ancient times; olden times: в старину́, in ancient/olden times. **2,** old ways; old customs: по старине́, the old way; the traditional way. **3,** relic of the past. —*n.m., colloq.* old man!; old boy! —**тряхну́ть старино́й,** to relive one's youth.

стари́нка *n.,* и **по стари́нке,** the old way.

стари́нный *adj.* **1,** old; ancient. **2,** antique.

ста́рить *v.impfv.* [*pfv.* **соста́рить**] to age; make old. —**ста́риться,** *refl.* to age; grow old.

старичо́к [*gen.* **-чка́**] *n.* little old man.

старове́р *n., hist.* Old Believer.

старода́вний *adj.* **1,** (*of times*) olden. **2,** (*of an object, custom, etc.*) very old.

старожи́л *n.* long-time resident.

старозаве́тный *adj.* **1,** old-fashioned. **2,** antiquated.

старомо́дный *adj.* old-fashioned.

старообра́зный *adj.* old-looking.

старообря́дец [*gen.* **-дца**] *n., hist.* Old Believer.

ста́роста *n.m.* **1,** village elder. **2,** monitor (*in school*). —**церко́вный ста́роста,** churchwarden.

ста́рость *n.f.* old age. —**на ста́рости лет,** in one's old age.

старт *n.* **1,** *sports* start. На старт!, on your mark! **2,** starting line. **3,** *aero.* takeoff. **4,** blast-off.

ста́ртер *n., mech. & sports* starter.

стартова́ть *v.impfv. & pfv.* [*pres.* **-ту́ю, -ту́ешь**] **1,** *sports* to start. **2,** *aero.* to take off. **3,** (*of a space vehicle*) to blast off.

ста́ртовый *adj.* **1,** *sports* starting: ста́ртовая ли́ния, starting line. Ста́ртовый пистоле́т, starter's pistol. **2,** for launching: ста́ртовая площа́дка, launch(ing) pad.

стару́ха *n.* old woman.

стару́шка [*gen. pl.* **-шек**] *n.* old woman.

ста́рческий *adj.* **1,** of old age. **2,** senile. —**ста́рческое слабоу́мие,** senility.

ста́рше *adj., comp. of* **ста́рый** *and* **ста́рший.**

старшекла́ссник *n.* pupil in his senior year.

старшеку́рсник *n.* senior (*in college*).

ста́рший *adj., used only as a modifier* **1,** older; elder. **2,** oldest; eldest. **3,** senior; head. —*n.* **1,** chief; superior; man in charge. **2,** *pl.* adults. **3,** *pl.* one's elders. —**ста́рший курс,** senior year. —**ста́рший лейтена́нт,** first lieutenant.

старшина́ [*pl.* **старши́ны**] *n.m.* **1,** *mil.* master sergeant. **2,** *naval* petty officer. **3,** *pre-rev.* foreman (*of a shop, jury, etc.*). —**старшина́ дипломати́ческого ко́рпуса,** dean of the diplomatic corps.

старшинство́ *n.* seniority.

ста́рый *adj.* old. —**ста́рое,** *n.* the old; the past.

старьё *n., colloq.* old things; junk.

старьёвщик *n.* old-clothes dealer; junkman.

ста́скивать *v.impfv.* [*pfv.* **стащи́ть**] **1,** to pull off; drag off. **2,** to pull into; drag into.

стасова́ть *v., pfv. of* **тасова́ть.**

ста́тика *n.* statics.

стати́ст *n., theat.* extra; supernumerary.

стати́стика *n.* statistics. —**стати́стик,** *n.* statistician. —**статисти́ческий,** *adj.* statistical.

стати́ческий *adj., physics; electricity* static.

стати́чный *adj.* static (*not in motion*).

ста́тный *adj.* graceful; shapely.

ста́тус *n.* status.

ста́тус-кво́ *n.m. indecl.* status quo.

стату́т *n.* statute.

стату́этка [*gen. pl.* **-ток**] *n.* statuette; figurine.

ста́туя *n.* statue.

стать[1] *v.pfv.* [*infl.* **ста́ну, ста́нешь**] **1,** *pfv. of* **станови́ться. 2,** (*of a watch, machine, etc.*) to stop; stop running. **3,** (*of a river*) to freeze over. **4,** [*past tense only*] (*with inf.*) to begin (to); start. **5,** [*future tense only*] (*with inf.*) indicates the future: Он не ста́нет есть, he won't eat. **6,** (*with* с + *instr.*) to happen (to); become (of). **7,** *impers.* (*with* не) to die: Его́ не ста́ло, he died; he was no more. **8,** *colloq.* to cost. —**во что бы то ни ста́ло,** at all costs. —**де́ло ста́ло за** (+ *instr.*), the delay (*or* failure) was due to... —**ста́ло быть,** consequently.

стать² [*pl.* ста́ти, -те́й, -тя́м] *n.f.* figure; build. —**под стать** (+ *dat.*), **1,** right (for). **2,** like. **3,** befitting; becoming. —**с како́й ста́ти?,** why?; what for?

ста́ться *v.r.pfv.* [*infl.* ста́нется] *colloq.* **1,** to happen. Óчень мóжет ста́ться, что..., it may very well happen that... **2,** (*with* **с** + *instr.*) to happen (to); become (of).

статья́ [*pl.* статьи́, -те́й, -тья́м] *n.* **1,** article (*in a magazine or newspaper*). **2,** article; clause; paragraph (*of a constitution, treaty, etc.*). **3,** entry (*in a dictionary*). **4,** item: статья́ расхо́да, expense item. —**по всем статья́м,** in all respects.

стациона́р *n.* **1,** permanent establishment. **2,** hospital.

стациона́рный *adj.* **1,** stationary. **2,** permanent. —**стациона́рный больно́й,** hospital patient (*as opposed to an outpatient*).

стача́ть *v., pfv. of* тача́ть.

ста́чечник *n.* striker. —**ста́чечный,** *adj.* strike (*attrib.*).

ста́чивать *v.impfv.* [*pfv.* сточи́ть] to dull (a cutting instrument) through long use: сто́ченная бри́тва, dull razor.

ста́чка [*gen. pl.* -чек] *n.* (labor) strike.

стащи́ть [*infl.* стащу́, ста́щишь] *v., pfv. of* тащи́ть (*in sense #5) and* ста́скивать.

ста́я *n.* flock (*of birds*); school (*of fish*); pack (*of dogs*).

ста́ять [*infl.* ста́ет] *v., pfv. of* ста́ивать.

ствол [*gen.* ствола́] *n.* **1,** trunk (*of a tree*). **2,** barrel (*of a gun*).

ство́р *n.* = ство́рка.

ство́раживать *v.impfv.* [*pfv.* створо́жить] to curdle. —**ство́раживаться,** *refl.* (*of a substance*) to curdle.

ство́рка [*gen. pl.* -рок] *n.* **1,** leaf; fold (*of a door, gate, mirror, etc.*). **2,** valve (*of a mollusk*).

створо́жить *v., pfv. of* ство́раживать. —**створо́житься,** *refl., pfv. of* ство́раживаться.

ство́рчатый *adj.* folding. —**ство́рчатое окно́,** casement window.

стеари́н *n.* stearin.

стеати́т *n.* steatite.

сте́бель [*gen.* -бля; *pl.* сте́бли, -бле́й, -бля́м] *n.m.* stem; stalk.

стёганка [*gen. pl.* -нок] *n., colloq.* quilted jacket.

стёганый *adj.* quilted. —**стёганое одея́ло; стёганое покрыва́ло,** quilt.

стега́ть *v.impfv.* **1,** [*pfv.* вы́стегать] to quilt. **2,** [*pfv.* отстега́ть *or* стегну́ть] to whip; flog.

стежо́к [*gen.* -жка́] *n.* stitch (*in sewing*).

стезя́ *n., obs.* path; way; road.

стека́ть *v.impfv.* [*pfv.* стечь] to flow down. —**стека́ться,** *refl.* **1,** to flow together. **2,** *fig.* to flock together; throng.

стекленéть *v.impfv.* [*pfv.* остекленéть] **1,** to become like glass. **2,** (*of one's eyes*) to become glassy.

стекло́ [*pl.* стёкла, стёкол] *n.* **1,** glass. **2,** *pl.* windowpanes: Стёкла дребезжáли, the windows rattled. —**ветрово́е** *or* **пере́днее стекло́,** windshield. —**око́нное стекло́,** windowpane. —**увеличи́тельное стекло́,** magnifying glass. —**часово́е стекло́,** crystal (*of a watch*).

стеклова́та *n.* glass wool.

стекловолокно́ *n.* fiberglass.

стеклоду́в *n.* glass blower.

стеклоочисти́тель *n.m.* windshield wiper.

стекля́нный *adj.* **1,** glass. **2,** (*of a stare*) glassy.

стекля́рус *n.* bugles; bugle beads.

стеко́льный *adj.* glass (*attrib.*): стеко́льный заво́д, glass factory.

стеко́льщик *n.* glazier.

стели́ть *v.impfv.* [*pres.* стелю́, сте́лешь] *colloq.* = стлать. —**стели́ться,** *refl., colloq.* = стла́ться.

стелла́ж [*gen.* -лажá] *n.* **1,** shelves. **2,** rack.

сте́лька [*gen. pl.* -лек] *n.* insole; inner sole. —**пьян как сте́лька,** пьян в сте́льку, *colloq.* dead drunk.

стемне́ть *v., pfv. of* темне́ть (*in sense #2*).

стена́ [*acc.* сте́ну; *pl.* сте́ны, стен, стена́м] *n.* wall. —**стена́ в сте́ну,** right next door. —**жить** *or* **сиде́ть в четырёх стена́х,** to sit home all the time. —**лезть на́ стену,** *see* лезть.

стена́ть *v.impfv.* to moan; groan.

стенгазе́та *n.* wall newspaper.

стенд (тэ) *n.* stand.

сте́ндовый (тэ) *adj., in* сте́ндовая стрельба́, trapshooting.

сте́нка [*gen. pl.* -нок] *n.* **1,** *dim. of* стена́. **2,** side (*of a container*). **3,** *anat.* wall. —**поста́вить к сте́нке,** *colloq.* to execute; shoot.

стенно́й *adj.* wall (*attrib.*). —**стенно́й шкаф,** built-in closet.

стеноби́тный *adj., hist.* used to batter down walls: стеноби́тный тара́н, battering ram.

стеногра́мма *n.* stenographic transcript.

стено́граф *n.* stenographer.

стенографи́ровать *v.impfv.* [*pfv.* застенографи́ровать; *pres.* -рую, -руешь] **1,** to take down in shorthand. **2,** [*impfv. only*] to take shorthand.

стенографи́ст *n.m.* [*fem.* -фи́стка] stenographer.

стенографи́ческий *adj.* shorthand (*attrib.*); stenographic.

стеногра́фия *n.* shorthand; stenography.

стенокарди́я *n.* angina pectoris.

сте́нопись *n.f.* mural; mural painting.

сте́ньга *n.* topmast.

степе́нный *adj.* sedate; staid.

сте́пень [*pl.* сте́пени, -не́й, -ня́м] *n.f.* **1,** extent; degree: в значи́тельной сте́пени, to a considerable extent. **2,** academic degree. **3,** *gram.* degree. **4,** *math.* power: де́сять в пя́той сте́пени, ten to the fifth power. —**в вы́сшей сте́пени** (+ *adj.*), extraordinarily; most. —**ни в мале́йшей сте́пени,** not in the least.

степно́й *adj.* steppe (*attrib.*).

степь [*2nd loc.* степи́; *pl.* сте́пи, -пе́й, -пя́м] *n.f.* steppe.

сте́рва *n., vulgar* scoundrel; bastard.

стервя́тник *n.* Egyptian vulture.

стереоме́трия *n.* solid geometry.

стереоско́п *n.* stereoscope. —**стереоскопи́ческий,** *adj.* stereoscopic. —**стереоскопи́я,** *n.* stereoscopy.

стереоти́п *n.* stereotype.

стереотипи́ровать *v.impfv. & pfv.* [*pres.* -рую, -руешь] *printing* to stereotype.

стереоти́пный *adj.* stereotyped.

стереофони́ческий *adj.* stereophonic.

стере́ть [*infl.* **сотру́, сотрёшь**; *past* **стёр, стёрла**] *v., pfv. of* **стира́ть**. —**стере́ться,** *refl., pfv. of* **стира́ться**.

стере́чь *v.impfv.* [*pres.* **стерегу́, стережёшь, ...стерегу́т**; *past* **стерёг, стерегла́, стерегло́, стерегли́**] to guard; watch.

сте́ржень [*gen.* **-жня**] *n.m.* **1,** rod; bar. **2,** pivot. **3,** *fig.* (*with gen.*) core (of); heart (of).

стержнево́й *adj.* (*of a question or issue*) key; pivotal.

стерилиза́тор *n.* sterilizer. —**стерилиза́ция,** *n.* sterilization.

стерилизова́ть *v.impfv. & pfv.* [*pres.* **-зу́ю, -зу́ешь**] to sterilize.

стери́льный *adj.* sterile; sterilized. —**стери́льность,** *n.f.* sterility.

сте́рлинг *n.* sterling. Фунт сте́рлингов, the pound sterling. —**сте́рлинговый,** *adj.* sterling (*attrib.*).

сте́рлядь [*pl.* **сте́рляди, -де́й, -дя́м**] *n.f.* sterlet (*fish*).

стерня́ *n.* **1,** harvested field (*with only the stubble remaining*). **2,** stubble. *Also,* **стернь,** *n.f.*

стеро́ид *n.* steroid.

стерпе́ть *v.pfv.* [*infl.* **стерплю́, сте́рпишь**] to bear; endure. Стерпе́ть оби́ду, to swallow an insult. —**стерпе́ться,** *refl.* (*with* **с** + *instr.*) *colloq.* to get used to; come to accept.

стёртый *adj.* **1,** effaced. **2,** worn smooth. **3,** *fig.* trite.

стесне́ние *n.* **1,** uneasiness; inhibition; constraint. **2,** constriction; feeling of tightness. **3,** *usu. pl.* restrictions; constraints.

стеснённый *adj.* **1,** crowded together. **2,** (*of breathing*) labored. **3,** uneasy; inhibited. **4,** straitened: в стеснённых обстоя́тельствах, in straitened circumstances. **5,** (*with* **в** + *prepl.*) short (of); squeezed (for): стеснён(ный) в сре́дствах, squeezed for money.

стесни́тельность *n.f.* shyness; diffidence.

стесни́тельный *adj.* **1,** *obs.* tight-fitting; constricting. **2,** confining; restrictive. **3,** shy; diffident; inhibited.

стесни́ть *v., pfv. of* **тесни́ть** (*in sense #2*) *and* **стесня́ть**. —**стесни́ться,** *refl., pfv. of* **тесни́ться** (*in sense #1*) *and* **стесня́ться** (*in senses #3 & #4*).

стесня́ть *v.impfv.* [*pfv.* **стесни́ть**] **1,** to crowd; cramp. **2,** to hinder; hamper. **3,** to confine; restrict. **4,** to constrain; inhibit. **5,** to constrict. **6,** (*with* **себя́**) to stint: не стесня́ть себя́ в сре́дствах, not stint oneself. —**стесня́ться,** *refl.* **1,** [*impfv. only*] to feel uneasy; feel awkward; feel self-conscious. **2,** [*pfv.* **постесня́ться**] (*with inf.*) to be afraid (to); be ashamed (to); (*with gen.*) to be shy (in the presence of); be afraid (of). **3,** [*pfv.* **стесни́ться**] to crowd; crowd together; be crowded together. **4,** [*pfv.* **стесни́ться**] (*with* **в** + *prepl.*) to spare; use sparingly: не стесня́ться в сре́дствах, not stint oneself; не стесня́ться в выраже́ниях, not mince words.

стетоско́п *n.* stethoscope.

стече́ние *n.* **1,** flowing together. **2,** coming together; gathering (*of people*). **3,** combination (*of circumstances*).

стечь [*infl. like* **течь**] *v., pfv. of* **стека́ть**. —**сте́чься,** *refl., pfv. of* **стека́ться**.

сти́брить *v.pfv., colloq.* to swipe; pilfer; filch.

стиле́т *n.* stiletto.

стилиза́ция *n.* stylization.

стилизова́ть *v.impfv. & pfv.* [*pres.* **-зу́ю, -зу́ешь**] to stylize.

стили́ст *n.* stylist. —**стили́стика,** *n.* stylistics. —**стилисти́ческий,** *adj.* stylistic.

стиль *n.m.* **1,** style. **2,** *swimming* stroke.

сти́льный *adj.* **1,** period (*attrib.*): сти́льная ме́бель, period furniture. **2,** *colloq.* stylish; chic.

сти́мул *n.* stimulus; incentive.

стимули́рование *n.* stimulation.

стимули́ровать *v.impfv. & pfv.* [*pres.* **-рую, -руешь**] to stimulate.

стипе́ндия *n.* scholarship.

стира́льный *adj.* washing (*attrib.*): стира́льная маши́на, washing machine. —**стира́льный порошо́к,** soap powder; detergent.

стира́ть *v.impfv.* [*pfv.* **стере́ть**] **1,** to wipe off. **2,** to erase. **3,** to rub; chafe; irritate. **4,** [*pfv.* **вы́стирать**] to wash; launder. —**стере́ть в порошо́к,** to make mincemeat of. —**стере́ть с лица́ земли́,** to destroy; wipe from the face of the earth.

стира́ться *v.r.impfv.* [*pfv.* **стере́ться**] **1,** to be effaced; be obliterated; wear away. **2,** to become worn down; wear thin. **3,** [*impfv. only*] to wash: Руба́шка не стира́ется, the shirt is not washable. —**стира́ться в** (*or* **из**) **па́мяти,** to fade from memory.

сти́рка *n.* wash; washing; laundering. —**отдава́ть** (**что́-нибудь**) **в сти́рку,** to have (something) washed; send out to be laundered.

стиро́л *n.* styrene.

сти́скивать *v.impfv.* [*pfv.* **сти́снуть**] **1,** to squeeze. **2,** to hem in. **3,** to constrict. **4,** to grit (one's teeth).

стих [*gen.* **стиха́**] *n.* **1,** verse. **2,** *pl.* poetry; poems.

стиха́рь [*gen.* **-харя́**] *n.m.* surplice.

стиха́ть *v.impfv.* [*pfv.* **сти́хнуть**] **1,** to grow still; become silent. **2,** to die down; subside; abate.

стихи́йность *n.f.* spontaneity.

стихи́йный *adj.* **1,** elemental. **2,** spontaneous. —**стихи́йное бе́дствие,** natural disaster.

стихи́я *n.* element. —**быть в свое́й стихи́и,** to be in one's element.

сти́хнуть [*past* **стих, сти́хла**] *v., pfv. of* **стиха́ть**.

стихоплёт *n., colloq.* rhymer; rhymester.

стихосложе́ние *n.* versification.

стихотворе́ние *n.* short poem.

стихотво́рный *adj.* **1,** poetical. **2,** in verse.

стишо́к [*gen.* **-шка́**] *n., dim. of* **стих**.

стлать *v.impfv.* [*pfv.* **постла́ть**; *pres.* **стелю́, сте́лешь**] to lay (a tablecloth, carpet, etc.); make (a bed). —**стла́ться,** *refl.* [*impfv. only*] **1,** to stretch; extend. **2,** (*of a plant*) to creep.

сто [*gen., dat., instr. & prepl.* **ста**] *numeral* hundred; one hundred.

стог [*2nd loc.* **стогу́**; *pl.* **стога́**] *n.* stack: стог се́на, haystack.

сто́ик *n.* stoic.

сто́имость *n.f.* **1,** cost. **2,** *econ.* value: приба́вочная сто́имость, surplus value.

сто́ить *v.impf.* **1,** to cost: сто́ить де́сять до́лларов, to cost ten dollars. Сто́ить до́рого; сто́ить больши́х де́нег, to cost a lot of money. **2,** (*with gen.*) to be worth: сто́ить больши́х де́нег, to be worth a lot of money. Не сто́ит труда́, it's not worth the trouble. **3,** (*with gen.*) to be worthy of. **4,** (*with inf.*) to be worth (while): Кни́гу сто́ит проче́сть, the book is worth (while) reading. Не сто́ит с ним спо́рить, it is not worth arguing with him. **5,** (*with gen.*) to take (a certain amount of effort): Ему́ сто́ило больши́х уси́лий (+ *inf.*), it took great effort on his part to... —**сто́ит то́лько** (+ *inf.*), one has only to...

стоици́зм *n.* stoicism.

стои́ческий *adj.* stoical. —**стои́чески,** *adv.* stoically.

сто́йка [*gen. pl.* **сто́ек**] *n.* **1,** [*also,* **сто́йка сми́рно**] position of attention. **2,** *sports* stance. **3,** handstand. **4,** post; upright; stanchion. **5,** strut; prop. **6,** counter; bar.

сто́йкий *adj.* **1,** durable; hardy; long-lasting. **2,** *chem.* stable. **3,** *fig.* steadfast; staunch.

сто́йко *adv.* **1,** stoically. **2,** firmly. Сто́йко держа́ться, to stand firm; stand fast.

сто́йкость *n.f.* **1,** durability; hardiness. **2,** *fig.* fortitude; steadfastness.

сто́йло *n.* stall.

стоймя́ *adv.* upright.

сток *n.* **1,** flow; runoff. **2,** drain; gutter.

сто́кер *n.* stoker (*machine*).

стокра́т *adv., archaic* a hundred times. —**стокра́тный,** *adj.* hundredfold: в стокра́тном разме́ре, a hundredfold.

стол [*gen.* **стола́**] *n.* **1,** table. **2,** [*also,* **пи́сьменный стол**] desk. **3,** board; meals: кварти́ра и стол, room and board. **4,** food; cooking. **5,** diet. **6,** department; bureau: стол зака́зов, order department; а́дресный стол, address bureau.

столб [*gen.* **столба́**] *n.* **1,** pole; post; pillar. **2,** column (*of air, smoke, etc.*). —**позвоно́чный столб,** spinal column. —**фона́рный столб,** lamppost.

столбене́ть *v.impf.* [*pfv.* **остолбене́ть**] to freeze (*from terror, shock, etc.*).

столбе́ц [*gen.* **-бца́**] *n.* column (*of print, figures, etc.*).

сто́лбик *n.* **1,** small column. **2,** column (*of print, figures, etc.*). **3,** in сто́лбик ртути, column of mercury. **4,** *bot.* style.

столбня́к [*gen.* **-няка́**] *n.* **1,** tetanus. **2,** *colloq.* stupor; trance.

столбово́й *adj.,* in столбова́я доро́га, *obs.* highway.

столе́тие *n.* **1,** century. **2,** centenary; centennial.

столе́тний *adj.* **1,** hundred-year (*attrib.*). Столе́тний юбиле́й, hundredth anniversary. **2,** hundred-year-old. —**столе́тняя война́,** the Hundred Years' War.

столе́тник *n.* century plant.

сто́лик *n.* small table.

столи́ца *n.* capital (*city*). —**столи́чный,** *adj.* of a capital; capital (*attrib.*).

столкнове́ние *n.* **1,** collision. **2,** clash; conflict.

столкну́ть *v., pfv.* of **ста́лкивать.** —**столкну́ться,** *refl., pfv.* of **ста́лкиваться.**

столкова́ться *v.r.pfv.* [*infl.* **-ку́юсь, -ку́ешься**] *colloq.* to agree; reach agreement.

столова́ться *v.r.impf.* [*pres.* **-лу́юсь, -лу́ешься**] to have one's meals.

столо́вая *n., decl. as an adj.* **1,** dining room. **2,** dining hall; mess hall.

столо́вый *adj.* **1,** table (*attrib.*). **2,** dining-room (*attrib.*). —**столо́вая гора́,** tableland; mesa. —**столо́вая ло́жка,** tablespoon; soupspoon. —**столо́вые прибо́ры,** tableware; flatware.

столо́чь *v.pfv.* [*infl. like* **толо́чь**] *colloq.* to pound; crush; pulverize.

столп [*gen.* **столпа́**] *n.* **1,** = *obs.* = **столб. 2,** *fig.* pillar: столпы́ о́бщества, the pillars of society.

столпи́ться *v.r.pfv.* to crowd; congregate.

столпотворе́ние *n., in* вавило́нское столпотворе́ние, **1,** pandemonium. **2,** babel.

столь *adv.* so: Э́то не столь ва́жно, it's not so important. —**столь же** (+ *adj.*), **как...,** as ... as.

сто́лько *adv.* [*oblique cases pl.* **сто́льких; сто́лькими**] so much; so many: сто́лько де́нег, so much money; в сто́льких места́х, in so many places. —**сто́лько (же)..., ско́лько (и),** as much as; as many as. В Ла́твии почти́ сто́лько же ру́сских, ско́лько и латви́йцев, there are nearly as many Russians in Latvia as Latvians. Плати́ть лю́дям сто́лько, ско́лько они́ стоя́т, to pay people what they are worth.

столя́р [*gen.* **-яра́**] *n.* joiner; cabinetmaker.

столя́рничать *v.impf., colloq.* to be a cabinetmaker.

столя́рный *adj.* joiner's.

стоматоло́гия *n.* stomatology; dentistry. —**стомато́лог,** *n.* stomatologist; dentist.

стон *n.* groan; moan.

стона́ть *v.impf.* [*pres.* **стону́, сто́нешь**] to groan; moan.

стоп *interj.* stop!

стопа́ [*pl.* **стопы́** *in sense* #1; **сто́пы** *in other senses*] *n.* **1,** foot. **2,** *pros.* foot: метри́ческая стопа́, metric foot. **3,** pile (*of objects*). **4,** ream (*of paper*). —**идти́ по стопа́м** (+ *gen.*), to follow in the footsteps of. —**направля́ть свои́ стопы́,** to wend one's way.

сто́пка [*gen. pl.* **-пок**] *n.* **1,** pile. **2,** small glass (*for wine or vodka*).

сто́пор *n., mech.* stop; catch.

сто́порить *v.impf.* [*pfv.* **застопорить**] to stop (an engine, machine, etc.). —**сто́пориться,** *refl.* **1,** to stop; jam; become inoperative. **2,** *fig., colloq.* to come to a standstill.

сто́порный *adj., mech.* stop (*attrib.*); arresting; locking.

стопроце́нтный *adj.* one-hundred-percent (*attrib.*).

стоп-сигна́л *n.* stoplight; brake light.

сто́птанный *adj.* (*of shoes*) worn; worn down at the heels.

стопта́ть [*infl.* **стопчу́, сто́пчешь**] *v., pfv.* of **ста́птывать.** —**стопта́ться,** *refl., pfv.* of **ста́птываться.**

сторгова́ться *v.r.pfv.* [*infl.* **-гу́юсь, -гу́ешься**] *colloq.* to agree on a price (*after bargaining*).

стори́цей *also,* **стори́цею** *adv., obs.* many times over: окупа́ться стори́цей, to pay for itself many times over.

сто́рож [*pl.* **сторожа́**] *n.* watchman; guard. —**церко́вный сто́рож,** sexton.

сторожево́й *adj.* watch (*attrib.*); sentry (*attrib.*). —*n.* watchman. —**сторожева́я ба́шня** *or* **вы́шка,** watchtower. —**сторожево́й ка́тер,** patrol boat. —**сторожево́й пост,** guard post; sentry post. —**сторожева́я соба́ка; сторожево́й пёс,** watchdog.

сторожи́ть *v.impfv.* to guard; watch.

сторо́жка [*gen. pl.* **-жек**] *n.* hut; cabin; lodge (*of a watchman, warden, etc.*).

сторона́ [*acc.* **сто́рону;** *pl.* **сто́роны, сторо́н, сторона́м**] *n.* **1,** side. **2,** direction: в ту сто́рону, in that direction; that way. В сто́рону (+ *gen.*), in the direction of. **3,** *fig.* aspect: положи́тельная сторона́, positive aspect. **4,** *law* party: потерпе́вшая сторона́, the injured party. —**в стороне́,** aside. —**в стороне́ (от),** apart (from); aloof (from). —**в сто́рону,** aside. —**на все четы́ре сто́роны,** wherever one wishes to go. —**на стороне́,** elsewhere; in another place. —**на́ сторону,** (*with verbs of selling*) on the side. —**по ту сто́рону** (+ *gen.*), on the other side (of). —**со всех сторо́н, 1,** on all sides; from all sides. **2,** from all aspects. —**с одно́й стороны́..., с друго́й стороны́...,** on the one hand..., on the other hand... —**со стороны́, 1,** from a distance; without being directly involved. **2,** from elsewhere; from another place. —**со стороны́** (+ *gen.*), **1,** from the direction of. **2,** on the part of. Со свое́й стороны́ я..., for my part, I... Óчень ми́ло с ва́шей стороны́, very kind on your part; very kind of you. **3,** (*of relatives*) on the side of. —**стороно́й, 1,** by: проходи́ть стороно́й, to pass by. **2,** around; avoiding: обходи́ть (что́-нибудь) стороно́й, to sidestep; *fig.* bypass. **3,** *fig.* indirectly; secondhand. —**встать** *or* **стать на сто́рону** (+ *gen.*), to side with; take the side of. —**держа́ться** *or* **остава́ться в стороне́,** to remain aloof; remain on the sidelines.

сторони́ться *v.r.impfv.* [*pfv.* **посторони́ться;** *pres.* **сторо́нюсь, сторо́нишься**] **1,** to stand aside; step aside; make way. **2,** [*impfv. only*] (*with gen.*) to avoid; shun.

сторо́нний *adj., obs.* = посторо́нний. —**сторо́нний наблюда́тель,** outside *or* detached observer.

сторо́нник *n.* supporter; advocate; proponent.

сторублёвка [*gen. pl.* **-вок**] *n., colloq.* hundred-ruble note.

сторублёвый *adj.* **1,** hundred-ruble (*attrib.*). **2,** costing *or* worth one hundred rubles.

стоскова́ться *v.r.pfv.* [*infl.* **-ку́юсь, -ку́ешься**] (*with* по + *dat., but prepl. with pers. pronouns*) *colloq.* to miss; long for.

сточи́ть [*infl.* **сточу́, сто́чишь**] *v., pfv. of* **ста́чивать.**

сто́чный *adj.* drainage (*attrib.*). —**сто́чные во́ды,** sewage. —**сто́чная кана́ва,** gutter. —**сто́чная труба́,** sewer.

стошни́ть *v.pfv., impers.* to vomit; throw up: Меня́ стошни́ло, I threw up.

сто́я *adv.* (*used after verbs*) standing up; while on one's feet.

стоя́к [*gen.* **-яка́**] *n.* upright post.

стоя́ние *n.* standing: до́лгое стоя́ние в о́череди, a long stand in line.

стоя́нка [*gen. pl.* **-нок**] *n.* **1,** stop. **2,** stopping place; encampment. **3,** stand (*for taxis, carriages, etc.*). **4,** parking (*of cars*). **5,** parking lot.

стоя́ть *v.impfv.* [*pres.* **стою́, стои́шь**] **1,** to stand; be standing. **2,** to stand; be situated: Дом стои́т на холму́, the house stands (*or* sits) on a hill. **3,** to be: Маши́на стои́т в гараже́, the car is in the garage. Стоя́ть у вла́сти, to be in power. ♦*Also in many other constructions:* Стои́т си́льный моро́з, there is a heavy frost. Пого́да стоя́ла тёплая, the weather was warm. Зима́ стоя́ла холо́дная, it was a cold winter. Стоя́ла тишина́, it was quiet. Стоя́л коне́ц ию́ня, it was late June. **4,** to stop; cease to function: Мои́ часы́ стоя́т, my watch has stopped. Рабо́та стои́т, work has stopped; work is at a standstill. Заво́д стои́т, the factory stands idle. **5,** (*with* за + *acc.*) to stand for; favor; be in favor of. **6,** (*with* пе́ред) to face; confront. —**стой!; сто́йте!, 1,** stop! **2,** wait a minute! —**стоя́ть на своём,** to stand one's ground.

стоя́чий *adj.* **1,** standing; upright; erect. **2,** (*of water*) stagnant.

сто́ящий *adj.* worthwhile.

страви́ть [*infl.* **стравлю́, стра́вишь**] *v., pfv. of* **стра́вливать.**

стра́вливать *v.impfv.* [*pfv.* **страви́ть**] **1,** to set (two animals) against each other. **2,** *colloq.* to provoke a fight or argument between (two people).

страда́ *n.* **1,** extra hard work performed at harvest time. **2,** *fig.* hard work. **3,** season of hard work.

страда́лец [*gen.* **-льца**] *n.* sufferer.

страда́льческий *adj.* of suffering.

страда́ние *n.* suffering.

страда́тельный *adj., gram.* passive: страда́тельный зало́г, passive voice.

страда́ть *v.impfv.* [*pfv.* **пострада́ть**] **1,** to suffer: страда́ть от жары́, to suffer from the heat; страда́ть бессо́нницей, to suffer from insomnia. Страда́ть за свои́ убежде́ния, to suffer for one's beliefs. **2,** [*impfv. only*] (*with* за + *acc.*) to feel for. **3,** [*impfv. only*] *colloq.* to be poor; be deficient: У него́ страда́ет орфогра́фия, his spelling is poor; he is a poor speller. *See also* **пострада́ть.**

стра́дный *adj.* (*of time*) busy; hectic.

страж *n., obs.* guard; watchman.

стра́жа *n.* **1,** *obs.* guard; watch. **2,** (*with* под) custody: быть под стра́жей, to be in custody; брать под стра́жу, take into custody; содержа́ть под стра́жей, hold in custody. Освобожда́ть из-под стра́жи, to release from custody. —**на стра́же, 1,** on guard. Стоя́ть на стра́же, to stand guard. **2,** (*with gen.*) guarding.

страна́ [*pl.* **стра́ны**] *n.* country. —**страна́ све́та,** cardinal point; point of the compass.

страни́ца *n.* page.

страни́чка [*gen. pl.* **-чек**] *n.* small page.

стра́нник *n.* wanderer.

стра́нно *adv.* strangely. —*adj., used predicatively,* strange: как ни стра́нно, strange as it seems.

стра́нность *n.f.* **1,** strangeness. **2,** *usu. pl.* peculiarity; quirk; eccentricity.

стра́нный *adj.* strange; odd. —**стра́нное де́ло,** it's a strange thing; it is strange.

странове́дение *n.* area studies.

стра́нствие *n.* traveling; wandering. *Also,* **стра́нствование.**

стра́нствовать *v.impfv.* [*pres.* -ствую, -ствуешь] to wander; roam.

стра́стно *adv.* **1,** passionately. **2,** ardently.

страстно́й *adj.* pert. to the week before Easter. —**страстна́я неде́ля,** holy week. —**страстно́й четве́рг,** Holy Thursday. —**страстна́я пя́тница,** Good Friday.

стра́стность *n.f.* passion; ardor.

стра́стный *adj.* **1,** passionate; impassioned. **2,** ardent; fervent. **3,** avid; enthusiastic.

страсть [*pl.* **стра́сти, -сте́й, -стя́м**] *n.f.* **1,** passion. **2,** *usu. pl., colloq.* horrors. —*adv.* [*usu. fol. by* **как** *or* **како́й**] *colloq.* awfully (much); terribly (much).

стратаге́ма *n.* stratagem.

страте́гия *n.* strategy. —**страте́г,** *n.* strategist. —**стратеги́ческий,** *adj.* strategic.

стратифика́ция *n.* stratification.

стратосфе́ра *n.* stratosphere.

стра́ус *n.* ostrich. —**стра́усовый,** *adj.* ostrich (*attrib.*).

страх *n.* fear. Страх пе́ред полётами/пресле́дованием, fear of flying/persecution. —**на свой** (*or* **на со́бственный) страх (и риск),** at one's risk. **2,** on one's own. —**на страх** (+ *dat.*), in order to frighten (someone). —**под стра́хом сме́рти,** on pain of death.

страхова́ние *n.* insurance.

страхова́ть *v.impfv.* [*pfv.* **застрахова́ть**; *pres.* -**ху́ю, -ху́ешь**] to insure. —**страхова́ться,** *refl.* to insure oneself; (*with* **от**) take out insurance (against).

страхо́вка *n.* insurance.

страхово́й *adj.* insurance (*attrib.*).

страхо́вщик *n.* insurer.

стра́шилище *n., colloq.* fright; horrible sight.

страши́ть *v.impfv.* to frighten. —**страши́ться,** *refl.* (*with gen.*) to be afraid (of); fear.

стра́шно *adv.* terribly; awfully. —*adj., used predicatively* **1,** terrible; horrible; awful. **2,** (*with dat.*) afraid: Мне стра́шно, I am afraid.

стра́шный *adj.* [*short form* **стра́шен, страшна́, стра́шно, стра́шны** *or* **страшны́**] **1,** terrible; horrible; dreadful; frightful; awful. **2,** (*with dat.*) frightening (to): Зме́и мне не страшны́, snakes do not frighten me. —**стра́шный суд,** Day of Judgment.

стража́ть *v.impfv., colloq.* to frighten.

стре́жень [*gen.* **-жня**] *n.m.* part of a river where the current is the strongest.

стрека́ч *n., in* **дать** *or* **зада́ть стрекача́,** *colloq.* to take to one's heels.

стрекоза́ [*pl.* **-ко́зы**] *n.* dragonfly; darning needle.

стре́кот *n.* chirping. *Also,* **стрекота́ние.**

стрекота́ть *v.impfv.* [*pres.* -**кочу́, -ко́чешь**] to chirp.

стрела́ [*pl.* **стре́лы**] *n.* **1,** arrow. **2,** boom (*of a derrick*). —**стрело́й,** straight (*or* swift) as an arrow.

стреле́ц [*gen.* **-льца́**] *n.* **1,** *hist.* member of a special military corps in the 16th and 17th centuries; strelets. **2,** *cap.* Sagittarius.

стре́лка [*gen. pl.* **-лок**] *n.* **1,** *dim. of* **стрела́. 2,** arrow (*pointing to something*). **3,** hand (*of a clock or watch*): мину́тная стре́лка, minute hand. **4,** needle (*of a com-*

pass). **5,** *R.R.* switch. **6,** spit (*of land*). —**по часово́й стре́лке,** clockwise. —**про́тив часово́й стре́лки,** counterclockwise.

стрелко́вый *adj.* **1,** rifle (*attrib.*); shooting (*attrib.*). **2,** *mil.* rifle (*attrib.*): стрелко́вая ро́та, rifle company. —**стрелко́вое де́ло,** riflery. —**стрелко́вое ору́жие,** small arms. —**стрелко́вый спорт,** shooting.

стрелови́дный *adj.* **1,** arrow-shaped. **2,** *aero.* sweptback.

стрело́к [*gen.* **-лка́**] *n.* **1,** shot; marksman: хоро́ший стрело́к, a good shot. **2,** *mil.* gunner.

стре́лочник *n., R.R.* switchman.

стрельба́ [*pl.* **стре́льбы**] *n.* **1,** shooting; firing. **2,** *pl.* firing practice. —**откры́ть стрельбу́,** to open fire; start shooting.

стре́льбище *n.* firing range.

стрельну́ть *v.pfv.* **1,** *pfv. of* **стреля́ть. 2,** to fire a shot. **3,** *colloq.* to dash; dart (*away or out of sight*).

стре́льчатый *adj.* shaped like a lancet: стре́льчатая а́рка, lancet arch; стре́льчатое окно́, lancet window.

стре́ляный *adj., colloq.* **1,** shot; killed. **2,** (*of a weapon*) having been fired; (*of a shell or cartridge*) spent. **3,** having been under fire. —**стре́ляный воробе́й,** *colloq.* old hand.

стреля́ть *v.impfv.* [*pfv.* **вы́стрелить** *or* **стрельну́ть**] **1,** to shoot; fire: Не стреля́йте!, don't shoot! **2,** (*with* **в** + *acc. or* **по**) to fire at; shoot at. Вы́стрелить кому́-нибудь в но́гу, to shoot someone in the leg. **3,** (*with* **из**) to fire (a weapon); (*with instr.*) fire (bullets, shells, etc.). **4,** [*impfv. only*] to shoot (and kill): стреля́ть у́ток, to shoot ducks. **5,** [*impfv. only*] to crackle. **6,** [*impfv. only*] (*with instr.*) *colloq.* to crack (a whip). **7,** [*impfv. only*] *impers., colloq.* to have a shooting pain: У меня́ стреля́ет в у́хе, I have a shooting pain in my ear. **8,** [*pfv.* **стрельну́ть** *only*] *colloq.* to cadge; mooch; bum. —**стреля́ть глаза́ми, 1,** to cast a quick eye around. **2,** to make eyes.

стремгла́в *adv.* headlong.

стреми́тельный *adj.* **1,** very fast; rapid; headlong. **2,** energetic. —**стреми́тельно,** *adv.* rapidly; headlong.

стреми́ться *v.r.impfv.* [*pres.* **-млю́сь, -ми́шься**] **1,** (*with* **к**) to seek; aim for; strive for; aspire to. **2,** (*with inf.*) to try (to). **3,** (*with* **в** *or* **на** + *acc.*) to try to get to (a place); try to get into (a school or college). **4,** *obs.* to rush.

стремле́ние *n.* **1,** (*with* **к**) striving (for). **2,** aspiration. **3,** longing; yearning; urge.

стремни́на *n.* rapids (*on a river*).

стре́мя [*gen., dat. & prepl.* **стре́мени;** *instr.* **стре́менем;** *pl.* **стремена́, стремя́н, стремена́м**] *n.neut.* stirrup.

стремя́нка [*gen. pl.* **-нок**] *n.* stepladder.

стрено́жить *v., pfv. of* **трено́жить.**

стре́пет *n.* little bustard.

стрептоко́кк *n.* streptococcus.

стрептомици́н *n.* streptomycin.

стресс *n.* (emotional) stress.

стреха́ [*pl.* **стре́хи**] *n.* eaves.

стригу́щий *adj., in* **стригу́щий лиша́й,** ringworm.

стриж [*gen.* **стрижа́**] *n.* swift (*bird*).

стри́женый *adj.* **1,** (*of hair*) short; closely cropped; (*of a person*) with closely cropped hair. **2,** (*of sheep*) shorn. **3,** (*of a lawn, trees, etc.*) trimmed.

стри́жка [*gen. pl.* **-жек**] *n.* **1,** clipping. **2,** shearing. **3,** haircut. —**маши́нка для стри́жки,** clippers.

стрипти́з *n.* striptease.

стрихни́н *n.* strychnine.

стричь *v.impfv.* [*pfv.* **остри́чь**; *pres.* **стригу́, стри- жёшь, ...стригу́т**; *past* **стриг, стри́гла**] **1,** to cut (one's hair, beard, etc.). **2,** to give (someone) a haircut. **3,** to shear; trim; clip. —**стри́чься,** *refl.* **1,** to cut one's hair. **2,** to get a haircut. **3,** to wear one's hair a certain way: стри́чься ко́ротко, to wear one's hair short.

стробоско́п *n.* stroboscope.

строга́льный *adj.* (*of a machine or tool*) planing. —**строга́льщик,** *n.* planer.

строга́ть *v.impfv.* [*pfv.* **вы́строгать**] to plane (wood).

стро́гий *adj.* [*comp.* **стро́же**] **1,** (*of a person, rule, etc.*) strict. **2,** (*of laws, measures, etc.*) stringent. **3,** (*of a look, voice, etc.*) stern. **4,** (*of criticism, a sentence, etc.*) severe.

стро́го *adv.* **1,** strictly: стро́го говоря́, strictly speaking; стро́го воспреща́ется, strictly forbidden. **2,** severely.

стро́гость *n.f.* **1,** strictness. **2,** severity. —**по всей стро́гости зако́на,** to the full extent of the law.

строево́й *adj.* **1,** *mil.* drill (*attrib.*): строево́й расчёт, drill team. **2,** *mil.* frontline: строево́й офице́р, frontline officer. **3,** (*of material*) building. Строево́й лес, lumber; timber. —**строева́я подгото́вка,** drill. —**строева́я сто́йка,** position of attention.

строе́ние *n.* **1,** a building. **2,** (*with gen.*) structure (of).

строи́тель *n.m.* builder.

строи́тельный *adj.* building (*attrib.*); construction (*attrib.*). —**строи́тельная те́хника,** civil engineering.

строи́тельство *n.* **1,** (act of) building; construction. **2,** construction project. **3,** construction site.

стро́ить *v.impfv.* [*pfv.* **постро́ить**] **1,** to build; construct. **2,** (*with* **на** + *prepl.*) to base (on). **3,** to make (plans, assumptions, etc.). **4,** to organize; plan. **5,** to form; line up: стро́ить солда́т в две шере́нги, to line the soldiers up in two columns. **6,** [*impfv. only*] to make (an expression on one's face): стро́ить гла́зки, to make eyes; стро́ить грима́сы, to make faces. **7,** *in* стро́ить себе́ иллю́зии, to create illusions for oneself; delude oneself. **8,** *in* **стро́ить из себя́** (+ *acc.*), to make oneself out to be. —**стро́иться,** *refl.* **1,** to be built. **2,** to build a house for oneself. **3,** (*with* **на** + *prepl.*) to be based (on). **4,** *mil.* to form; line up.

строй *n.* **1,** [*2nd loc.* **строю́**; *pl.* **строи́, строёв**] *mil.* formation. Со́мкнутый строй, close formation; close order. **2,** [*2nd loc.* **строю́**] *mil.* ranks: стать *or* встать в строй, **a.** to form ranks. **b.** to join the ranks. Оста́ться в строю́, to remain in action. **3,** system: обще́ственный строй, social system. **4,** tone; pitch; key (*of a musical instrument*). **5,** *gram.* structure. **6,** pattern: строй мышле́ния, pattern of thinking. —**вво- ди́ть в строй,** to put into service; put into operation. —**вступа́ть в строй,** to go into operation. —**вы- быва́ть из стро́я,** *see* выбыва́ть. —**выводи́ть из стро́я,** to put out of operation/action/commission; dis-

able. —**выходи́ть из стро́я,** to break down; be disabled; go out of commission. —**прогоня́ть кого́- нибудь сквозь строй,** to make someone run the gauntlet. —**проходи́ть сквозь строй** (+ *gen.*), to run the gauntlet (of).

стро́йка [*gen. pl.* **стро́ек**] *n.* **1,** (act of) building; construction. **2,** construction project. **3,** construction site.

стро́йный *adj.* **1,** graceful; slender; trim. **2,** (*of rows or columns*) regular; even. **3,** logical; coherent; consistent. **4,** harmonious.

строка́ [*acc.* **строку́** *or* **стро́ку**; *pl.* **стро́ки, строк, строка́м**] *n.* line (*of writing*). —**чита́ть ме́жду строк,** to read between the lines.

стро́нций *n.* strontium.

стропи́ло *n.* rafter.

стропти́вый *adj.* obstinate; contrary.

строфа́ [*pl.* **стро́фы**] *n.* stanza.

строчи́ть *v.impfv.* [*pres.* **строчу́, стро́чишь** *or* **строчи́шь**] **1,** [*pfv.* **простро́чи́ть**] to stitch. **2,** [*pfv.* **настрочи́ть**] *colloq.* to scribble off; dash off. **3,** [*impfv. only*] *colloq.* to fire (an automatic weapon); (*of a weapon*) fire; blaze away.

стро́чка [*gen. pl.* **-чек**] *n.* **1,** = **строка́**. **2,** stitch: ажу́рная стро́чка, hemstitch.

строчно́й *adj.* (*of a letter of the alphabet*) small; lowercase. *Also,* **стро́чный**.

струг *n.* plane (*tool*).

стру́жка [*gen. pl.* **-жек**] *n.* **1,** *usu. pl.* shavings. **2,** excelsior. —**мы́льная стру́жка,** soap flakes.

струи́ться *v.r.impfv.* to stream; pour.

стру́йка [*gen. pl.* **стру́ек**] *n.* **1,** trickle (*of water, blood, etc.*). **2,** wisp (*of smoke*).

стру́йный *adj.* jet (*attrib.*). —**стру́йное тече́ние,** jet stream.

структу́ра *n.* structure. —**структу́рный,** *adj.* structural.

струна́ [*pl.* **стру́ны**] *n.* **1,** string (*of a musical instrument, tennis racket, etc.*). **2,** *fig.* chord: заде́ть чувстви́тельную струну́, to strike a sensitive chord. —**игра́ть на сла́бых стру́нах (кого́-нибудь),** to play on someone's weaknesses.

стру́нка [*gen. pl.* **-нок**] *n.* = **струна́**. —**вы́тянуться** *or* **стать в стру́нку,** to stand at attention. —**ходи́ть по стру́нке (у),** to toe the line (for).

стру́нный *adj.* **1,** string (*attrib.*): стру́нный кварте́т, string quartet. **2,** (*of a musical instrument*) stringed.

струп [*pl.* **стру́пья, стру́пьев**] *n.* scab.

стру́сить *v., pfv. of* **тру́сить**.

стручко́вый *adj.* leguminous. —**стручко́вый горо́х,** peas in the pod. —**стручко́вый пе́рец,** red pepper. —**стручко́вая фасо́ль,** string beans.

стручо́к [*gen.* **-чка́**] *n.* pod.

струя́ [*pl.* **стру́и**] *n.* spurt; jet; stream; current. —**бить струёй,** to spurt; jet.

стря́пать *v.impfv.* [*pfv.* **состря́пать**] *colloq.* **1,** to cook. **2,** *fig.* to cook up; concoct.

стряпня́ *n., colloq.* **1,** cooking. **2,** *fig.* concoction.

стряса́ть *v.impfv.* [*pfv.* **стрясти́**] to shake off.

стрясти́ [*infl. like* **трясти́**] *v., pfv. of* **стряса́ть**. —**стрясти́сь,** *refl.* (*with* **с** + *instr.*) *colloq.* (*of a misfortune*) to happen to; befall.

стря́хивать *v.impfv.* [*pfv.* **стряхну́ть**] **1**, to shake off. **2**, to shake down (a thermometer).

студе́нт *n.m.* [*fem.* **-де́нтка**] student.

студе́нческий *adj.* student (*attrib.*); students'.

студе́нчество *n.* **1**, students. **2**, student days; student life.

студёный *adj.*, *colloq.* very cold; freezing; icy.

сту́день [*gen.* **-дня**] *n.m.* aspic (*of meat or fish*).

студи́ть *v.impfv.* [*pfv.* **остуди́ть**; *pres.* **стужу́, сту́дишь**] *colloq.* to cool; chill.

сту́дия *n.* **1**, studio. **2**, school (*of drama, art, ballet, etc.*).

сту́жа *n.*, *colloq.* severe cold.

стук *n.* **1**, knock: **стук в дверь**, knock at the door. **2**, clatter.

сту́кать *v.impfv.* [*pfv.* **сту́кнуть**] **1**, to knock; rap. **2**, to hit; strike. **Сту́кнуть кулако́м по́ столу́**, to bang one's fist on the table. —**сту́каться**, *refl.* (*with instr.*) to bang; bump; knock: **сту́кнуться голова́ми**, to bump heads. **Сту́кнуться голово́й о дверь**, to bang one's head on the door. *See also* **сту́кнуть**.

стука́ч [*gen.* **-кача́**] *n.*, *colloq.* informer; stool pigeon.

сту́кнуть *v.pfv.* **1**, *pfv. of* **сту́кать**. **2**, *colloq.* (*of time*) to come. **3**, *impers.* (*with dat.*) *colloq.*, indicating attainment of a certain age: **Ему́ уже́ сту́кнуло се́мьдесят лет**, he is already seventy. —**сту́кнуться**, *refl.*, *pfv. of* **сту́каться**.

стул *n.* **1**, [*pl.* **сту́лья, сту́льев**] chair. **2**, *med.* stool. —**сиде́ть ме́жду двух сту́льев**, to fall between two stools.

стульча́к [*gen.* **-чака́**] *n.* toilet seat.

сту́льчик *n.*, *dim. of* **стул**. —**высо́кий де́тский сту́льчик**, highchair.

сту́па *n.* mortar (*bowl*).

ступа́ть *v.impfv.* [*pfv.* **ступи́ть**] **1**, to step. **2**, [*impfv. only*] to walk. —**нога́ не ступа́ет (куда́-нибудь)**, not set foot in (a certain place). *See also* **ступи́ть**.

ступе́нчатый *adj.* stepped; graded.

ступе́нь *n.f.* **1**, step (*on a staircase*). **2**, *fig.* step; stage. **3**, *fig.* level. **4**, *rocketry* stage.

ступе́нька [*gen. pl.* **-нек**] *n.* **1**, step (*on a staircase*). **2**, rung (*of a ladder*).

ступи́ть *v.pfv.* [*infl.* **ступлю́, сту́пишь**] **1**, *pfv. of* **ступа́ть**. **2**, (*with* **на** + *acc.*) to set foot on.

ступи́ца *n.* hub (*of a wheel*).

сту́пка [*gen. pl.* **-пок**] *n.* = **сту́па**.

ступня́ *n.* **1**, foot. **2**, sole (*of the foot*).

сту́пор *n.* stupor.

стуча́ть *v.impfv.* [*pfv.* **постуча́ть**; *pres.* **-чу́, -чи́шь**] **1**, to knock; rap: **стуча́ть в дверь**, to knock/rap on the door. **2**, (*with instr.*) to bang; pound: **стуча́ть кулака́ми в дверь**, to bang/pound on the door with one's fists. **3**, (*with* **в** + *acc.*) (*of rain*) to beat against. **4**, (*of one's teeth*) to chatter; (*of one's heart*) to throb. **5**, *impers.* to throb: **У меня́ стучи́т в виска́х**, my temples are throbbing. —**стуча́ться**, *refl.* (*with* **в** + *acc.*) to knock (on); rap (on).

стушева́ться *v.r.*, *pfv. of* **тушева́ться** *and* **стушёвываться**.

стушёвываться *v.r.impfv.* [*pfv.* **стушева́ться**] *colloq.* **1**, to become indistinct; fade away. **2**, to withdraw into the background. **3**, (*with* **пе́ред**) to be overshadowed (by). **4**, to become flustered.

стуши́ть *v.*, *pfv. of* **туши́ть** (*in sense #2*).

стыд [*gen.* **стыда́**] *n.* shame.

стыди́ть *v.impfv.* [*pfv.* **пристыди́ть**; *pres.* **-жу́, -ди́шь**] to shame; put to shame. —**стыди́ться**, *refl.* [*pfv.* **постыди́ться**] (*with gen.*) to be ashamed (of).

стыдли́вый *adj.* **1**, easily embarrassed. **2**, (*of a look or expression*) embarrassed. —**стыдли́вость**, *n.f.* feeling of embarrassment.

сты́дно *adj.*, used predicatively, it is a shame. —**сты́дно!**, shame on you! —**мне сты́дно**, I am ashamed. —**как вам не сты́дно!**, aren't you ashamed!

сты́дный *adj.* shameful.

стык *n.* **1**, joint. **2**, junction.

стыкова́ться *v.r.impfv.* [*pres.* **-ку́ется**] (*of space vehicles*) to dock.

стыко́вка *n.* docking (*of space vehicles*).

сты́лый *adj.*, *colloq.* cold.

сты́нуть *v.impfv.* [*past* **стыл, сты́ла**] = **стыть**.

стыть *v.impfv.* [*pres.* **сты́ну, сты́нешь**] **1**, [*pfv.* **осты́ть**] to cool off; get cold. **2**, [*pfv.* **засты́ть**] *colloq.* to freeze; become frozen. **3**, [*pfv.* **осты́ть**] *fig.* (*of an emotion*) to cool. —**кровь сты́нет (застыла) в жи́лах** (*with* **у**), one's blood runs (ran) cold.

сты́чка [*gen. pl.* **-чек**] *n.* **1**, skirmish; clash. **2**, squabble; altercation.

стю́ард *n.* steward (*aboard ship or aloft*). —**стюарде́сса**, (дэ) *n.* stewardess.

стяг *n.* banner; standard.

стя́гивать *v.impfv.* [*pfv.* **стяну́ть**] **1**, to tighten; draw tight. **2**, to tie (tightly): **стя́гивать кни́ги ремешко́м**, to tie the books with a strap. **3**, to pull off; remove. **4**, *mil.* to gather; concentrate (troops). —**стя́гиваться**, *refl.* **1**, to tighten; become tight. **2**, to assemble; congregate.

стяжа́тель *n.m.* money-grubber. —**стяжа́тельство**, *n.* making money.

стяжа́ть *v.impfv. & pfv.* **1**, to amass (wealth). **2**, to win; gain (fame, respect, etc.).

стяну́ть *v.pfv.* [*infl.* **стяну́, стя́нешь**] **1**, *pfv. of* **стя́гивать**. —**стяну́ться**, *refl.*, *pfv. of* **стя́гиваться**.

суахи́ли *n.m. indecl.* Swahili.

субаре́нда *n.* sublease.

суббо́та *n.* **1**, Saturday. **2**, Sabbath.

суббо́тний *adj.* **1**, Saturday (*attrib.*). **2**, Sabbath (*attrib.*).

суббо́тник *n.* voluntary unpaid work performed on days off (*originally on Saturday*).

субконтине́нт *n.* subcontinent.

сублима́т *n.* sublimate. —**сублима́ция**, *n.*, *chem.* sublimation.

сублими́ровать *v.impfv. & pfv.* [*pres.* **-рую, -руешь**] *chem.* to sublimate.

субордина́ция *n.* deference to rank: **соблюда́ть субордина́цию**, to defer to rank.

субподря́д *n.* subcontract. —**субподря́дчик**, *n.* subcontractor.

субсиди́ровать *v.impfv. & pfv.* [*pres.* **-рую, -руешь**] to subsidize.

субси́дия *n.* subsidy.

субста́нция *n.* substance.

субстра́т *n.* substratum.

субти́льный *adj., colloq.* frail; delicate.

субти́тр *n., motion pictures* subtitle.

субтро́пики [*gen.* **-ков**] *n.pl.* subtropics. —**субтро́пи́ческий**, *adj.* subtropical.

субъе́кт *n.* **1,** subject. **2,** *colloq.* fellow; person; character. —**субъе́кты (Росси́йской) Федера́ции**, subdivisions (*or* components) of the (Russian) Federation.

субъективи́зм *n.* **1,** subjectivism. **2,** subjectivity.

субъекти́вный *adj.* subjective. —**субъекти́вность,** *n.f.* subjectivity.

сува́льда *n.* tumbler (*of a lock*).

сувени́р *n.* souvenir.

суваре́н *n.* sovereign. —**суваренитéт,** *n.* sovereignty. —**суваре́нный,** *adj.* sovereign.

сугли́нок [*gen.* **-нка**] *n.* loam. —**сугли́нистый,** *adj.* loamy.

сугро́б *n.* snowdrift.

сугу́бо *adv.* especially; particularly.

сугу́бый *adj.* **1,** *obs.* double. **2,** special; particular.

суд [*gen.* **суда́**] *n.* **1,** court (*of law*). Предста́ть пе́ред судо́м, to appear in court. **2,** trial: суд над..., the trial of... Быть под судо́м, to be on trial. Идти́/пойти́ под суд, to be put on trial. **3,** judgment; verdict. **4,** *in* вое́нный суд, court-martial. —**пока́ суд да де́ло,** in the meantime; while we're waiting.

суда́к [*gen.* **-дака́**] *n.* pike perch.

суда́рыня *n., obs.* madam.

су́дарь *n.m., obs.* sir.

суда́чить *v.impfv., colloq.* to gossip.

суде́бный *adj.* **1,** court (*attrib.*). **2,** legal; judicial. **3,** forensic. —**суде́бная оши́бка,** miscarriage of justice. —**суде́бный проце́сс,** trial.

суде́йский *adj.* **1,** judge's. Суде́йская до́лжность, judgeship. **2,** referee's; umpire's.

суди́лище *n.* (unfair) trial.

суди́мость *n.f., law* previous conviction.

суди́ть *v.impfv.* [*pres.* **сужу́, су́дишь**] **1,** (*often with* **о**) to judge. **2,** to try (*in court*). **3,** *sports* to referee; umpire. **4,** (*of God, fate, etc.*) to will. **5,** *in* су́дя по (+ *dat., but prepl. with pers. pronouns*) judging by. —**суди́ться,** *refl.* **1,** to go to court. **2,** (*with* с + *instr.*) to sue. **3,** to be tried (*in court*). *See also* **суждено́.**

су́дно *n.* **1,** [*pl.* **суда́, судо́в**] vessel; ship. Нефтенали́вно́е су́дно, oil tanker. **2,** [*pl.* **су́дна, су́ден**], *in* подкладно́е су́дно, bedpan.

су́дный *adj., obs.* of a court; judicial. —**су́дный день,** Judgment Day.

судове́рфь *n.f.* shipyard.

судовладе́лец [*gen.* **-льца**] *n.* shipowner.

судово́й *adj.* ship (*attrib.*); ship's.

судо́к [*gen.* **судка́**] *n.* **1,** gravy boat. **2,** cruet stand. **3,** *pl.* set of interlocking pots for carrying food.

судомо́йка [*gen. pl.* **-мо́ек**] *n.* (woman) dishwasher. —**судомо́йня,** *n.* [*gen. pl.* **-мо́ен**] scullery.

судопроизво́дство *n.* legal proceedings.

су́дорога *n.* **1,** cramp. **2,** convulsion.

су́дорожный *adj.* **1,** convulsive. **2,** *fig.* feverish; frantic; hectic.

судостро́ение *n.* shipbuilding. —**судостро́итель,** *n.m.* shipbuilder. —**судостро́ительный,** *adj.* shipbuilding (*attrib.*).

судоустро́йство *n.* judicial system.

судохо́дность *n.f.* navigability.

судохо́дный *adj.* **1,** shipping (*attrib.*). **2,** navigable. —**судохо́дный кана́л,** ship canal.

судохо́дство *n.* shipping; navigation.

судьба́ [*pl.* **су́дьбы, су́деб, су́дьбам**] *n.* **1,** fate; fortune; destiny. **2,** (one's) fate; (one's) lot. —**во́лею суде́б** (*with different stress*), by the will of fate. —**каки́ми судьба́ми?** (*with different stress*), what brings you here? —**не судьба́, 1,** it was not to be; it was not in the cards. **2,** (*with dat. and inf.*) (one was) not fated (*or* destined) to: Ему́ не судьба́ возврати́ться, he was not destined to return.

судьбоно́сный *adj.* fateful; critical; momentous.

судья́ [*pl.* **су́дьи, су́дей, су́дьям**] *n.m.* **1,** judge. **2,** *sports* referee; umpire.

суеве́рие *n.* superstition. —**суеве́рный,** *adj.* superstitious.

суета́ *n.* **1,** fuss; bustle. **2,** trifle; triviality. —**суета́ суе́т,** vanity of vanities.

суети́ться *v.r.impfv.* [*pres.* **-чу́сь, -ти́шься**] to bustle about.

суетли́вый *adj.* **1,** restless; fidgety. **2,** bustling.

сужде́ние *n.* **1,** judgment; opinion. **2,** judgment: выноси́ть сужде́ние о, to make *or* render a judgment on.

суждено́ *short form neut. of past passive part. of* **суди́ть**, fated; destined: Нам не суждено́ бы́ло вы́играть, we were not fated to win.

суже́ние *n.* narrowing; contraction; constriction.

су́живать *v.impfv.* [*pfv.* **су́зить**] **1,** to narrow. **2,** to take in (a garment). —**су́живаться,** to narrow; become narrow; contract.

су́зить [*infl.* **су́жу, су́зишь**] *v., pfv. of* **су́живать**. —**су́зиться,** *refl., pfv. of* **су́живаться.**

сук [*gen.* **сука́**; *2nd loc.* **суку́**; *pl.* **су́чья, су́чьев** *or* **суки́, суко́в**] *n.* **1,** bough. **2,** knot (*in wood*).

су́ка *n.* bitch. —**су́кин,** *adj., in* **су́кин сын,** *vulg.* son of a bitch.

сукно́ [*pl.* **су́кна, су́кон**] *n.* smooth woolen cloth. —**класть под сукно́,** to shelve; pigeonhole.

суко́нка [*gen. pl.* **-нок**] *n.* cloth; rag.

суко́нный *adj.* **1,** cloth (*attrib.*). **2,** (*of language, speech, etc.*) dull; vapid; uninspired.

сулема́ *n.* mercuric chloride; corrosive sublimate.

сули́ть *v.impfv.* [*pfv.* **посули́ть**] **1,** *obs.* to promise. **2,** [*impfv. only*] to portend; augur.

султа́н *n.* **1,** sultan. **2,** plume. **3,** column (*of steam, smoke, etc.*).

султана́т *n.* sultanate.

султа́нка [*gen. pl.* **-нок**] *n.* red mullet.

сульфанилами́дный *adj., in* **сульфанилами́дные препара́ты,** sulfa drugs.

сульфа́т *n.* sulfate.

сульфи́д *n.* sulfide.

сума́ *n., obs.* bag. —**ходи́ть с сумо́й,** to beg for a living.

сумасбро́д *n., colloq.* nut; screwball.

сумасбро́дный *adj.* **1,** crazy; touched; unbalanced. **2,** mad; wild; reckless.

сумасбро́дство *n.* erratic behavior.

сумасше́дший *adj.* mad; crazy; insane. —*n.* madman; insane person; lunatic. —**сумасше́дший дом,** insane asylum.

сумасше́ствие *n.* madness; insanity.

сумато́ха *n.* bustle; tumult; commotion.

сумато́шный *adj., colloq.* **1,** bustling. **2,** tumultuous; hectic. *Also,* **сумато́шливый.**

сума́х *n.* sumac.

сумбу́р *n.* confusion. —**сумбу́рный,** *adj.* confused.

су́меречный *adj.* **1,** twilight (*attrib.*). **2,** (*of light*) dim; dull.

су́мерки [*gen.* **-рек**] *n.pl.* twilight; dusk.

суме́ть *v.pfv.* (*with inf.*) to be able (to); manage (to); succeed (in).

су́мка [*gen. pl.* **су́мок**] *n.* **1,** bag: су́мка для поку́пок, shopping bag. **2,** (lady's) handbag; purse; pocketbook. **3,** *zool.* pouch. **4,** *anat.* bursa. Воспале́ние су́мки, bursitis. —**санита́рная су́мка,** first-aid kit.

су́мма *n.* **1,** sum; total. **2,** sum; amount (*of money*). —**в су́мме** (+ *gen.*); **на су́мму** (+ *gen.*), amounting to; totaling.

сумма́рный *adj.* **1,** total. **2,** general; generalized.

сумми́ровать *v.impfv. & pfv.* [*pres.* **-рую, -руешь**] **1,** to add up; total. **2,** to sum up; summarize.

сумня́шеся *see* **ничто́же.**

су́мочка [*gen. pl.* **-чек**] *n.* handbag; purse; pocketbook.

су́мрак *n.* semidarkness. —**су́мрачный,** *adj.* gloomy.

су́мчатый *adj. & n.* marsupial.

сумя́тица *n., colloq.* **1,** bustle; commotion. **2,** confusion; turmoil.

сунду́к [*gen.* **-дука́**] *n.* trunk; chest.

су́нуть *v., pfv. of* **сова́ть.** —**су́нуться,** *refl., pfv. of* **сова́ться.**

суп [*pl.* **супы́**] *n.* soup.

суперма́ркет *n.* supermarket.

суперобло́жка [*gen. pl.* **-жек**] *n.* dust jacket.

суперта́нкер *n.* supertanker.

су́песь *n.f.* loam. *Also,* **су́песок** [*gen.* **-ска**].

супина́тор *n.* arch support.

супи́ть *v.impfv.* [*pres.* **су́плю, су́пишь**] *colloq.* to knit (one's brows).

су́пник *n.* soup tureen. *Also,* **су́пница.**

супово́й *adj.* soup (*attrib.*). —**супова́я ло́жка,** soup ladle.

супру́г *n.* husband; spouse. —**супру́га,** *n.* wife; spouse. —**супру́ги,** *n.pl.* husband and wife; married couple.

супру́жеский *adj.* marital; matrimonial; married; conjugal.

супру́жество *n.* married life; matrimony.

сургу́ч [*gen.* **-гуча́**] *n.* sealing wax. —**сургу́чный,** *adj.* of sealing wax.

сурди́нка *n., music* mute. —**под сурди́нку,** quietly; secretly; on the sly.

суре́пица *n.* rape (*plant*); colza. —**суре́пный,** *adj.* rape (*attrib.*): суре́пное ма́сло, rape oil.

су́рик *n.* red lead.

суро́во *adv.* **1,** severely. **2,** sternly.

суро́вость *n.f.* severity; harshness.

суро́вый *adj.* **1,** (*of climate, winter, etc.*) harsh; severe; rigorous. **2,** (*of life, truth, measures, etc.*) harsh. **3,** (*of punishment, a sentence, etc.*) harsh; severe. **4,** (*of a person, look, voice, etc.*) stern. **5,** (*of cloth*) unbleached.

суро́к [*gen.* **сурка́**] *n.* marmot; woodchuck; ground hog.

суррога́т *n.* substitute: суррога́т са́хара, sugar substitute. —**суррога́тный,** *adj.* substitute; ersatz.

сурьма́ *n.* antimony.

суса́льный *adj.* **1,** *in* **суса́льное зо́лото,** gold leaf; **суса́льное серебро́,** silver leaf. **2,** *fig.* lacking substance; vapid; insipid.

су́слик *n.* a kind of ground squirrel; suslik.

су́сло *n.* mash. —**виногра́дное су́сло,** new wine.

суспензо́рий *n.* jockstrap.

суста́в *n., anat.* joint.

суставно́й *adj.* of the joints. —**суставно́й ревмати́зм,** rheumatic fever.

сутенёр *n.* gigolo.

су́тки [*gen.* **су́ток**] *n.pl.* twenty-four-hour period; day and night: тро́е су́ток, three days (and nights). В любо́е вре́мя су́ток, at any hour of the day or night. —**кру́глые су́тки,** round the clock.

су́толока *n., colloq.* bustle; commotion.

су́точный *adj.* a day's. —**су́точные,** *n.pl.* per diem.

суту́лить *v.impfv.* [*pfv.* **ссуту́лить**] to hunch: суту́лить спи́ну, to hunch one's back. —**суту́литься,** *refl.* to stoop; slouch.

суту́лый *adj.* round-shouldered; stooped. —**суту́лость,** *n.f.* stoop; slouch.

суть[1] *n.f.* essence. Суть де́ла, the heart (*or* crux) of the matter. —**по су́ти де́ла,** in essence.

суть[2] *v., archaic, 3rd pers. of* **быть:** Таки́е де́йствия суть не́что ино́е, чем..., such actions are something different from... —**не суть ва́жно,** unimportant.

суфле́ *n.neut. indecl.* soufflé.

суфлёр *n., theat.* prompter.

суфли́ровать *v.impfv.* [*pres.* **-рую, -руешь**] *theat.* (*with dat.*) to prompt.

суфражи́стка [*gen. pl.* **-ток**] *n.* suffragette.

су́ффикс *n.* suffix.

суха́рь [*gen.* **-харя́**] *n.m.* zwieback; rusk.

суха́я *n., decl. as an adj., sports, colloq.* shutout.

су́хо *adv.* **1,** dryly: сказа́ть су́хо, to say dryly. **2,** coldly: приня́ть госте́й су́хо, to receive the guests coldly. —*adj., used predicatively,* dry: Бы́ло су́хо, it was dry.

сухове́й *n.* hot dry wind.

сухожи́лие *n.* tendon.

сухо́й *adj.* [*comp.* **су́ше**] **1,** dry. **2,** dried. **3,** dried-up. **4,** arid. **5,** thin; skinny. **6,** cold; aloof. **7,** (*of a reception, tone, etc.*) cold; chilly. **8,** dry; dull. —**вы́йти сухи́м из воды́,** to emerge unscathed. —**держа́ть по́рох сухи́м,** to keep one's powder dry. *See also* **суха́я.**

сухомя́тка *n., colloq.* dry food (*eaten without a beverage*).

сухопа́рый *adj., colloq.* lean; skinny.

сухопу́тный *adj.* land (*attrib.*); ground (*attrib.*); overland.

сухосто́й *n.* dead trees.

су́хость *n.f.* **1,** dryness. **2,** coldness; aloofness.

сухоща́вый *adj.* lean; skinny.

сучёный *adj.* twisted.

сучи́ть *v.impfv.* [*pres.* сучу́, су́чишь] **1,** to spin; twist. **2,** (*with instr.*) *colloq.* to flap.

сучкова́тый *adj.* **1,** knotty. **2,** gnarled.

сучо́к [*gen.* сучка́] *n.* **1,** twig. **2,** knot (*in wood*). —**без сучка́, без задо́ринки,** without a hitch.

су́ша *n.* land; dry land.

су́ше *adj., comp. of* сухо́й.

суше́ние *n.* drying.

сушёный *adj.* dried.

сушёнье *n.* dried fruit.

суши́лка [*gen. pl.* -лок] *n.* **1,** dryer. **2,** drying room.

суши́льный *adj.* drying (*attrib.*).

суши́льня [*gen. pl.* -лен] *n.* drying room.

суши́ть *v.impfv.* [*pfv.* вы́сушить; *pres.* сушу́, су́шишь] **1,** to dry; make dry. **2,** to parch. —**суши́ться,** *refl.* to dry; become dry.

су́шка [*gen. pl.* су́шек] *n.* **1,** drying. **2,** bagel.

сушь *n.f., colloq.* **1,** dry spell. **2,** dry place; dry land. **3,** dry reading matter.

суще́ственно *adv.* substantially.

суще́ственный *adj.* **1,** essential: суще́ственная ра́зница, an essential difference. **2,** substantial: суще́ственные измене́ния, substantial changes. **3,** substantive: суще́ственный вопро́с, substantive issue. —**суще́ственным о́бразом,** substantially.

существи́тельный *adj., in* и́мя существи́тельное, noun. —**существи́тельное,** *n.* noun.

существо́ *n.* **1,** essence; gist. **2,** being; creature. —**по существу́, 1,** in essence; in effect; essentially. **2,** to the point: говори́ть по существу́, to speak to the point.

существова́ние *n.* existence.

существова́ть *v.impfv.* [*pres.* -ству́ю, -ству́ешь] to exist.

су́щий *adj.* **1,** *obs.* existing. **2,** *colloq.* pure; utter; downright; absolute.

су́щность *n.f.* essence. —**в су́щности, 1,** essentially; in essence. **2,** *in* в су́щности говоря́, as a matter of fact; as a practical matter. —**по са́мой свое́й су́щности,** by its (their) very nature.

сфабрико́ванный *adj.* (*of charges*) fabricated; trumped-up.

сфабрикова́ть *v.pfv.* [*infl.* -ку́ю, -ку́ешь] *colloq.* **1,** to forge. **2,** *pfv. of* фабрикова́ть (*in sense #3*).

сфальши́вить *v., pfv. of* фальши́вить.

сфантази́ровать *v., pfv. of* фантази́ровать (*in sense #2*).

сфе́ра *n.* **1,** sphere. **2,** *fig.* sphere; realm; domain. **3,** *pl.* circles: делово́е сфе́ры, business circles. —**сфе́ра влия́ния,** sphere of influence. —**сфе́ра обслу́живания,** service sector.

сфери́ческий *adj.* spherical.

сферо́ид *n.* spheroid. —**сфероида́льный,** *adj.* spheroidal.

сфинкс *n.* sphinx.

сформирова́ть *v., pfv. of* формирова́ть. —**сформирова́ться,** *refl., pfv. of* формирова́ться.

сформова́ть *v., pfv. of* формова́ть.

сформули́ровать *v., pfv. of* формули́ровать.

сфотографи́ровать *v., pfv. of* фотографи́ровать. —**сфотографи́роваться,** *refl., pfv. of* фотографи́роваться.

схвати́ть [*infl.* схвачу́, схва́тишь] *v., pfv. of* хвата́ть (*in sense #1*) *and* схва́тывать. —**схвати́ться,** *refl., pfv. of* хвата́ться (*in sense #1*) *and* схва́тываться.

схва́тка [*gen. pl.* -ток] *n.* **1,** fight; skirmish. **2,** *pl.* cramps; pains.

схва́тывать *v.impfv.* [*pfv.* схвати́ть] **1,** to seize; grab. **2,** *colloq.* to seize; arrest. **3,** *colloq.* to catch (a cold, illness, etc.). **4,** (*of an illness*) to strike: Его́ схвати́ла пода́гра, he was stricken with gout. **5,** *fig., colloq.* to grasp; comprehend. **6,** *fig., colloq.* (*of an artist, portrait, etc.*) to capture. —**схва́тываться,** *refl.* **1,** (*with за + acc.*) to seize; grab; grasp; snatch. **2,** (*with с + instr.*) to fight; battle; *fig.* grapple with; come to grips with.

схе́ма *n.* **1,** diagram; chart. **2,** outline. **3,** *electronics* circuit.

схемати́ческий *adj.* **1,** schematic; diagrammatic. **2,** [*also,* схемати́чный] sketchy.

схи́зма *n.* schism.

схитри́ть *v., pfv. of* хитри́ть.

схлы́нуть *v.pfv.* **1,** (*of water*) to rush back; sweep back. **2,** (*of a crowd*) to retreat. **3,** *fig.* (*of emotions*) to subside.

сход *n.* **1,** going down; descent. **2,** coming off. **3,** *colloq.* descent; slope. **4,** *pre-rev.* meeting; assembly.

сходи́ть[1] *v.impfv.* [*pfv.* сойти́; *pres.* схожу́, схо́дишь] **1,** (*with с + gen.*) go down; come down; descend (stairs, a mountain, etc.). **2,** (*with по*) to go down; walk down (stairs, a path, etc.). **3,** (*with с + gen.*) to get off (a vehicle); dismount (from a horse). **4,** (*with с + gen.*) to step off (a carpet, sidewalk, etc.); go off (a road, tracks, etc.); come off (an assembly line). **5,** (*with на + acc.*) to step onto. Сходи́ть на бе́рег, to go ashore. **6,** (*of paint, dirt, skin, etc.*) to come off; peel off; (*of sunburn*) to fade. **7,** (*with за + acc.*) to pass for; be taken for. **8,** *colloq.* (*usu. with* хорошо́) to come out all right. **9,** *colloq.* to be all right; be adequate; do. —**сходи́ть на нет,** to come to naught. —**сходи́ть с рук,** to go unnoticed; go unpunished; (*with dat.*) get away with: Это сходи́ло ему́ с рук, he got away with it. —**сходи́ть со сце́ны,** *see* сце́на. —**сходи́ть с ума́,** to go out of one's mind; lose one's mind; go mad.

сходи́ть[2] *v.pfv.* [*infl.* схожу́, схо́дишь] **1,** to go (*to a certain place and return*). **2,** (*with за + instr.*) to go for; go get (someone or something).

сходи́ться *v.r.impfv.* [*pfv.* сойти́сь; *pres.* схожу́сь, схо́дишься] **1,** to meet. **2,** to gather; come together. **3,** (*with с + instr.*) to become friends (with); become intimate (with). **4,** to coincide. **5,** to tally. **6,** *colloq.* to agree. **7,** (*often with на + prepl.*) *colloq.* (*of a belt*) to go around; fit around. —**сходи́ться во вку́сах,** to have similar tastes. —**сходи́ться хара́ктерами,** to be compatible. —**не сходи́ться хара́ктерами,** to be incompatible; not get along.

схо́дка [*gen. pl.* -док] *n., pre-rev.* meeting; assembly.

схо́дни [*gen.* **-ней**] *n.pl.* gangplank.

схо́дный *adj.* **1,** similar. **2,** *colloq.* (*of a price*) fair; reasonable.

схо́дство *n.* similarity; likeness; resemblance.

схо́жесть *n.f., colloq.* similarity; resemblance.

схо́жий *adj., colloq.* similar.

сца́пать *v.pfv., colloq.* to grab; grab hold of.

сцара́пывать *v.impfv.* [*pfv.* **сцара́пать**] to scratch off.

сцеди́ть [*infl.* **сцежу́, сце́дишь**] *v., pfv. of* **сце́живать**.

сце́живать *v.impfv.* [*pfv.* **сцеди́ть**] to strain off.

сце́на *n.* **1,** stage: выступа́ть на сце́не, to appear on (the) stage. **2,** scene: фина́льная сце́на, the final scene. **3,** *colloq.* scene: устро́ить сце́ну, to make a scene. —**сойти́ со сце́ны, 1,** to retire from the stage. **2,** (*of a play*) no longer be performed. **3,** *fig.* to pass from the scene. —**уйти́ со сце́ны,** to retire from the stage. —**яви́ться** *or* **появи́ться** *or* **вы́ступить на сце́ну,** to appear on the scene.

сцена́рий *n.* scenario. —**сценари́ст,** *n.* scenario writer.

сцени́ческий *adj.* stage (*attrib.*); scenic.

сцени́чный *adj.* suitable for the stage.

сце́нка [*gen. pl.* **-нок**] *n.* skit.

сцепи́ть [*infl.* **сцеплю́, сце́пишь**] *v., pfv. of* **сцепля́ть.** —**сцепи́ться,** *refl., pfv. of* **сцепля́ться.**

сцепле́ние *n.* **1,** coupling. **2,** clutch. **3,** *fig.* combination (of circumstances).

сцепля́ть *v.impfv.* [*pfv.* **сцепи́ть**] **1,** to couple. **2,** to interlock (fingers, hands, etc.). —**сцепля́ться,** *refl.* **1,** to engage; mesh. **2,** (*with instr.*) to lock (horns, bumpers, etc.). **3,** *colloq.* to grapple; be locked in combat.

сцепно́й *adj.* coupling (*attrib.*).

счастли́вец [*gen.* **-вца**] *n.m.* [*fem.* **-вица**] lucky person.

счастли́во *also,* **сча́стливо** *adv.* **1,** happily. **2,** luckily: счастли́во отде́латься, to get off lucky. —*interj.* good luck!; all the best!

счастли́вчик *n., colloq.* = **счастли́вец.**

счастли́вый *adj.* [*short form* **сча́стлив** *or* **счастли́в**] *adj.* **1,** happy. **2,** lucky; fortunate. —**счастли́вого пути́!,** have a good trip!; bon voyage!

сча́стье *n.* **1,** happiness. **2,** (good) luck; (good) fortune. Ва́ше сча́стье, что..., you are lucky/fortunate that... —**к сча́стью; по сча́стью,** fortunately. —**на сча́стье, 1,** for (good) luck. **2,** (*with gen. or poss. pron.*) luckily for: на моё сча́стье, luckily for me.

счесть [*infl.* **сочту́, сочтёшь;** *past* **счёл, сочла́, сочло́, сочли́**] *v., pfv. of* **счита́ть** (*in sense #3*). —**счёсться,** *refl., pfv. of* **счита́ться** (*in sense #4*).

счёт [*2nd loc.* **счету́;** *pl.* **счета́,** *except in sense #7*] *n.* **1,** counting: вести́ счёт (+ *dat.*), to keep count of. Э́то не в счёт, that doesn't count. **2,** calculation; reckoning. **3,** count; number: счёт уби́тых и ра́неных, the count of dead and wounded. **4,** account. **5,** bill; (*in a restaurant*) check. **6,** *sports* score. **7,** *pl.* accounts; scores: своди́ть счёты с, to settle scores with. —**без счёту,** countless. —**в два счёта,** *colloq.* in a jiffy. —**в коне́чном счёте,** in the final analysis. —**в счёт** (+ *gen.*), against; to be applied against. —**за счёт** (+ *gen.*), **1,** by using; by taking from. **2,** at the expense of.

—**на счёт, 1,** (*with gen.*) at the expense of. **2,** (*with a poss. pronoun*) about; concerning. —**на счету́,** in ка́ждый ... на счету́, every ... counts. —**на хоро́шем счету́ у,** in good standing with; in the good graces of. —**на э́тот счёт,** on this point; on that score. —**по большо́му счёту,** in the overall (*or* infinite) scheme of things. —**счёту нет** (+ *dat.*), more than one knows what to do with.

счётный *adj.* **1,** calculating (*attrib.*): счётная маши́на, adding machine. **2,** accounts (*attrib.*): счётная кни́га, accounts book.

счетово́д *n.* bookkeeper; accountant. —**счетово́дный,** *adj.* bookkeeping (*attrib.*); accounting (*attrib.*). —**счетово́дство,** *n.* bookkeeping; accounting.

счётчик *n.* **1,** meter: га́зовый счётчик, gas meter. **2,** counter (*person*). —**счётчик Ге́йгера,** Geiger counter.

счёты [*gen.* **-тов**] *n.pl.* abacus.

счисле́ние *n.* **1,** *obs.* calculation; computation. **2,** *math.* numbering: десяти́чная систе́ма счисле́ния, decimal system. **3,** *naut.* reckoning: счисле́ние пути́, dead reckoning.

счи́стить [*infl.* **-щу, -стишь**] *v., pfv. of* **счища́ть.**

счи́танный *adj., usu. pl.* only a few. В счи́танные часы́, in a matter of hours.

счита́ть *v.impfv.* **1,** [*pfv.* **сосчита́ть**] to count: счита́ть до десяти́, to count to ten. Не счита́я..., not counting... Счита́ть чей-нибудь пульс, to take someone's pulse. **2,** to do arithmetic: счита́ть в уме́, to do figures in one's head. **3,** [*pfv.* **счесть**] (*with instr. or* **за** + *acc.*) to consider; regard; look upon: счита́ть что́-нибудь ну́жным, to consider something necessary; счита́ть за честь, to consider it an honor. **4,** to believe; think; feel: Я счита́ю, что..., I believe that... —**счита́ться,** *refl.* **1,** [*pfv.* **посчита́ться**] (*with* **с** + *instr.*) to consider; reckon with; take into consideration; take into account. Не счита́ться с, to ignore. **2,** (*with instr.*) to be considered; be regarded. **3,** *passive of* **счита́ть:** Э́то не счита́ется, that does not count. Счита́ется, что..., it is believed that... **4,** [*pfv.* **счёсться**] (*with* **с** + *instr.*) *colloq.* to settle up (with).

счи́тывание *n., computer science* reading; readout.

счища́ть *v.impfv.* [*pfv.* **счи́стить**] to clear away.

США *abbr. of* **Соединённые Шта́ты Аме́рики,** United States of America; U.S.

сшиба́ть *v.impfv.* [*pfv.* **сшиби́ть**] *colloq.* **1,** to knock off. **2,** to knock down. —**сшиба́ться,** *refl., colloq.* **1,** to collide. **2,** to get into a fight.

сшиби́ть [*infl.* **-бу́, -бёшь;** *past* **сшиб, сши́бла**] *v., pfv. of* **сшиба́ть.** —**сшиби́ться,** *refl., pfv. of* **сшиба́ться.**

сшива́ть *v.impfv.* [*pfv.* **сшить**] **1,** to sew together. **2,** *med.* to suture. **3,** to join together; fasten together. **4,** to make (*by fastening together planks*).

сшить [*infl.* **сошью́, сошьёшь**] *v., pfv. of* **шить** *and* **сшива́ть.**

съеда́ть *v.impfv.* [*pfv.* **съесть**] to eat; eat up.

съеде́ние *n.* being eaten alive. —**отдава́ть** *or* **оставля́ть на съеде́ние** (+ *dat.*), **1,** to leave to be eaten alive by. **2,** *fig.* to leave at the mercy of.

съедо́бный *adj.* edible.

съёживаться *v.r.impfv.* [*pfv.* **съёжиться**] **1,** to shrivel; shrink. **2,** to curl up; huddle up; cuddle up. **3,** to cringe. **4,** to become haggard.

съёжиться *v.r., pfv. of* **ёжиться** *and* **съёживаться.**

съезд *n.* convention; congress.

съездить *v.pfv.* [*infl.* **съезжу, съездишь**] to go; drive (*to a certain place and return*); make a trip (to).

съезжать *v.impfv.* [*pfv.* **съехать**] (*with* **с** + *gen.*) **1,** to go down; ride down; drive down; (*with* **по**) slide down. **2,** to turn off; drive off (a road). **3,** *obs.* to leave; drive out (of). **4,** *colloq.* to move out (of). **5,** *colloq.* to slip down; slip off. —**съезжаться,** *refl.* **1,** to meet; run into each other. **2,** to gather; assemble.

съёмка [*gen. pl.* **-мок**] *n.* **1,** taking down; removal. **2,** survey; surveying: воздушная съёмка, aerial survey. **3,** shooting (*of a picture*).

съёмный *adj.* removable; detachable.

съёмочный *adj., motion pictures* shooting (*attrib.*). —**съёмочная группа,** film crew; camera crew. —**съёмочная площадка,** (movie) set.

съёмщик *n.* tenant; renter.

съестной *adj.* food (*attrib.*). —**съестное,** *n.* food; victuals.

съесть [*infl. like* **есть**] *v., pfv. of* **есть** (*in sense #1*) *and* **съедать.**

съехать [*infl.* **съеду, съедешь**] *v., pfv. of* **съезжать.** —**съехаться,** *refl., pfv. of* **съезжаться.**

съязвить *v., pfv. of* **язвить** (*in sense #3*).

сыворотка *n.* **1,** whey. **2,** *med.* serum.

сыгранность *n.f.* coordination; teamwork.

сыграть *v.pfv.* **1,** *pfv. of* **играть. 2,** *in* сыграть шутку с *or* над, to play a joke (*or* trick) on. **3,** *in* сыграть свадьбу, to have (*or* hold) a wedding. —**сыграться,** *refl.* to play well together; develop teamwork.

сызмала *also,* **сызмалу** *adv., colloq.* since childhood.

сызнова *adv., colloq.* all over again; anew; afresh.

сын [*pl.* **сыновья, -вей, -вьям**] *n.* son.

сынишка [*gen. pl.* **-шек**] *n.m., dim. of* **сын.**

сыновний *adj.* filial.

сынок [*gen.* **сынка**] *n., colloq.* **1,** son. **2,** sonny.

сыпать *v.impfv.* [*pres.* **сыплю, сыплешь**] **1,** to pour (a dry substance). **2,** *fig.* (*with acc. or instr.*) to spout (words, information, figures, etc.). **3,** *v.i.* (*of rain, snow, etc.*) to fall; come down. **4,** *in* сыпать деньгами, to toss money around. —**сыпаться,** *refl.* **1,** (*of a dry substance*) to pour; spill. **2,** to flake off; peel off. **3,** to fly about. **4,** (*of rain, snow, etc.*) to fall; come down. **5,** *fig.* to rain down.

сыпной *adj., in* сыпной тиф, typhus.

сыпняк [*gen.* **-няка**] *n., colloq.* typhus.

сыпучий *adj.* friable; crumbly; loose. —**меры сыпучих тел,** dry measures. —**сыпучий песок,** quicksand.

сыпь *n.f.* rash.

сыр [*pl.* **сыры**] *n.* cheese.

сыр-бор *n., colloq., in* **сыр-бор разгорелся,** a small thing got started: Из-за чего разгорелся сыр-бор?, how did the whole thing get started?

сыреть *v.impfv.* [*pfv.* **отсыреть**] to become damp.

сырец [*gen.* **сырца**] *n., used in compounds,* product in its raw state: шёлк-сырец, raw silk. Нефть-сырец, crude oil. Кирпич-сырец, adobe.

сырник *n.* cheese pancake.

сырный *adj.* cheese (*attrib.*).

сыроежка [*gen. pl.* **-жек**] *n.* a variety of mushroom; russula.

сырой *adj.* **1,** damp. **2,** (*of food*) raw; uncooked; (*of water*) unboiled. **3,** not completely cooked or baked; half-done. **4,** (*of oil*) crude. **5,** in rough form; unfinished.

сыромять *n.f.* rawhide. —**сыромятный,** *adj.* rawhide.

сырость *n.f.* dampness.

сырьё *n.* raw material(s).

сыск *n., pre-rev.* criminal investigation.

сыскать *v.pfv.* [*infl.* **сыщу, сыщешь**] *colloq.* to find. —**сыскаться,** *refl., colloq.* to be found.

сыскной *adj., pre-rev.* of criminal investigation.

сытно *adv.* heartily. Сытно поесть, to have a hearty meal.

сытный *adj.* (*of food or a meal*) filling.

сытость *n.f.* satiety.

сытый *adj.* [*short form* **сыт, сыта, сыто, сыты**] full (*from eating*). —**сыт по горло, 1,** stuffed to the gills. **2,** (*with instr.*) sick and tired of; fed up with.

сыч [*gen.* **сыча**] *n.* little owl.

сычуг [*gen.* **-чуга**] *n.* **1,** fourth stomach of a ruminant animal. **2,** rennet.

сычужина *n.* rennin.

сычужный *adj.* rennet (*attrib.*). —**сычужный фермент,** rennin.

сыщик *n.* detective.

сэкономить *v., pfv. of* **экономить.**

сэр *n.* sir.

сэт *n., tennis* set.

сюда *adv., expressing direction,* here; this way.

сюжет *n.* **1,** subject; subject matter. **2,** *lit.* plot. **3,** *colloq.* topic.

сюжетный *adj.* **1,** of a plot: сюжетное развитие, development of a plot. **2,** having a strong plot.

сюзерен *n.* suzerain. —**сюзеренитет,** *n.* suzerainty. —**сюзеренный,** *adj.* suzerain.

сюита *n., music* suite.

сюрприз *n.* a surprise. —**сюрпризный,** *adj.* surprise (*attrib.*).

сюрреализм *n.* surrealism. —**сюрреалист,** *n.* surrealist. —**сюрреалистический,** *adj.* surrealist.

сюртук [*gen.* **-тука**] *n.* frock coat.

сюсюканье *n., colloq.* lisp; lisping.

сюсюкать *v.impfv., colloq.* to lisp.

сяк *adv., in* так и сяк; то так то сяк, **1,** this way or that; one way or the other. **2,** fair; so-so.

сям *adv., in* там и сям; то там то сям, here and there.

Т

Т, т *n.neut.* nineteenth letter of the Russian alphabet.

та *adj., fem. of* **тот**.

табак [*gen.* **-бака́**] *n.* tobacco. —**де́ло таба́к,** *colloq.* things are in a bad way; things are in a sorry state.

табаке́рка [*gen. pl.* **-рок**] *n.* snuffbox.

табаково́д *n.* tobacco grower. —**табаково́дство,** *n.* tobacco growing. —**табаково́дческий,** *adj.* tobacco-growing.

таба́чный *adj.* tobacco (*attrib.*).

та́бель *n.m.* **1,** table; chart. **2,** [*also,* **та́бель успева́емости**] report card. **3,** sign-out board. —**та́бель о ра́нгах,** *hist.* Table of Ranks.

та́бельный *adj.* shown on a table. —**та́бельная доска́,** time board. —**та́бельное ору́жие,** service revolver. —**та́бельные часы́,** time clock.

та́бельщик *n.* one who records the hours worked by employees; timekeeper.

табле́тка [*gen. pl.* **-ток**] *n.* tablet; pill.

табли́ца *n.* table: **табли́ца умноже́ния,** multiplication table.

табли́чка [*gen. pl.* **-чек**] *n.* tablet; plaque; nameplate.

табли́чный *adj.* tabular.

табло́ *n. indecl.* **1,** (electronic) indicator panel. **2,** *sports* scoreboard.

табльдо́т *n.* table d'hôte.

та́бор *n.* **1,** band of gypsies. **2,** gypsy encampment.

табу́ *n.neut. indecl.* taboo.

табуля́тор *n.* tabulating machine; tabulator.

табу́н [*gen.* **-буна́**] *n.* herd; flock. —**табу́нщик,** *n.* herdsman.

табуре́т *n.* stool.

табуре́тка [*gen. pl.* **-ток**] *n.* stool.

таве́рна *n.* tavern.

та́волга *n.* meadowsweet.

таво́т *n.* axle grease; lubricating grease.

таврёный *adj.* branded.

таври́ть *v.impfv.* to brand (cattle).

тавро́ [*pl.* **та́вра, тавр, тавра́м**] *n.* brand (*on cattle*).

тавтоло́гия *n.* tautology. —**тавтологи́ческий,** *adj.* tautological; redundant.

тага́н *n.* trivet.

таджи́к *n.m.* [*fem.* **-жи́чка**] Tajik. —**таджи́кский,** *adj.* Tajik.

таёжный *adj.* of *or* in the taiga.

таз [*2nd loc.* **тазу́**; *pl.* **тазы́**] *n.* **1,** basin. Умыва́льный таз, washbasin. **2,** pelvis.

та́зовый *adj.* pelvic. —**та́зовая кость,** hipbone.

таи́нственно *adv.* mysteriously.

таи́нственность *n.f.* mystery.

таи́нственный *adj.* **1,** mysterious. **2,** secret.

та́инство *n.* **1,** *obs.* secret; mystery. **2,** sacrament.

таи́ть *v.impfv.* **1,** to conceal; hide; not reveal. **2,** to harbor (a thought, feeling, grudge, etc.). **3,** *in* **таи́ть в себе́,** *fig.* to hold; be fraught with. —**таи́ться,** *refl.* **1,** to hide; be hiding. **2,** to lurk. **3,** to withhold information; not tell the whole story.

тайва́ньский *adj.* Taiwanese.

тайга́ *n.* taiga.

тайко́м *adv.* secretly; surreptitiously; on the sly. —**тайко́м от,** without the knowledge of; without telling.

тайм *n.* period (*of a game*).

та́йна *n.* **1,** secret: глубо́кая та́йна, a deep secret. Держа́ть (что́-нибудь) в та́йне, to keep (something) secret. **2,** mystery. **3,** privacy.

тайни́к [*gen.* **-ника́**] *n.* **1,** hiding place; cache. **2,** hideout; hideaway. —**в тайника́х се́рдца,** in the innermost recesses of one's heart.

та́йно *adv.* secretly; in secret.

та́йнопись *n.f.* secret writing.

та́йный *adj.* **1,** secret. **2,** clandestine. —**та́йный сове́т,** Privy Council.

та́йский *adj.* Thai.

тайфу́н *n.* typhoon.

так *adv.* **1,** this way; that way; like this; like that: He говори́те так!, don't talk like that! **2,** (*before short-form adjectives*) so; that: Э́то не так стра́шно, it's not so (*or* that) terrible. **3,** so; true; correct: Э́то не совсе́м так, that is not entirely correct. **4,** then; in that case. —*particle* **1,** so; then. **2,** thus. **3,** for example. **4,** about: де́вочка, так лет восьми́, a girl of about eight. **5,** *when preceded and followed by the same word,* a real: Вот э́то мужчи́на так мужчи́на!, now there's a real man! —**и так и так,** either way. —**не так,** wrong; amiss; not right: Что́-то не так, something is wrong. —**не так ли?,** isn't that so?; don't you think so? —**так же,** (in) the same way. —**так же ... как и,** as ... as. —**так и быть,** so be it. —**так и не** (+ *verb*), never. —**так как,** since; inasmuch as. —**так себе́,** so-so. —**так что,** so; and so.

такела́ж *n., naut.* rigging.

та́кже *adv.* also; too. —**а та́кже,** as well as.

таки́ *particle, sometimes hyphenated to previous word, colloq.* indeed; after all; in the end: Он был-таки́ америка́нским граждани́ном, he was indeed an American citizen.

тако́в *indef. pron.* [*fem.* **такова́;** *neut.* **таково́;** *pl.* **таковы́**] **1,** such/that is; such/those are: Таковы́ фа́кты, such are the facts; those are the facts. Такова́ цена́, кото́рую мы должны́ плати́ть, that is the price we have to pay. **2,** like that; the same; alike: Все моряки́ таковы́, all sailors are like that. —**и был тако́в,** *colloq.* and off he went; and away he went.

таково́й *indef. pron.* **1,** such; the same: за отсу́тствием таково́го, in the absence of the same. **2,** *pl.* such people; such things; ... such as this: е́сли таковы́е име́ются, if any. Таковы́е существу́ют и в на́ше вре́мя, such people/ things exist in our time as well. —**как таково́й,** as such.

тако́й *indef. adj.* such; such a; a ... like that: тако́й челове́к, such a person; a man like that. Таки́е ве́щи, such things; things like that. В таку́ю пого́ду, in such weather. —*indef. pron.* the sort of person who: Он тако́й, что..., he is the sort of person who... —*adv.* (*used before long-form adjectives only*) so; such: Она́ така́я краси́вая, she is so beautiful; така́я краси́вая де́вушка, such a beautiful girl. —**и всё тако́е,** *colloq.* and all that. —**кто тако́й?,** who is it? Кто вы тако́й?, who are you? —**таки́м о́бразом,** *see* **о́браз.** —**тако́е,** such a thing. —**тако́й же,** the same. —**тако́й же** (+ *adj.*) **как,** as ... as. —**что ж (тут) тако́е** (*or* **тако́го**)?, what of it? —**что тако́е?,** what's the matter?; what's going on? —**что тако́е** (+ *nom.*), what is...?; what is a...? —**что э́то тако́е?,** what is this?

тако́й-то *adj.* **1,** so-and-so. **2,** such and such.

та́кса *n.* **1,** (set) rate. **2,** dachshund.

такси́ *n.neut. indecl.* taxi; cab.

таксо́метр *n.* taximeter.

таксомото́р *n.* taxi.

таксоно́мия *n.* taxonomy. —**таксономи́ческий,** *adj.* taxonomic.

такт *n.* **1,** *music* bar; measure. **2,** rhythm; beat; time: в такт му́зыке, in time to the music. Сби́ться с та́кта, to lose the beat. **3,** tact.

та́к-таки *particle, colloq.* **1,** still; anyway. **2,** really. —**та́к-таки всё,** absolutely everything.

та́ктик *n.* tactician.

та́ктика *n.* tactics. —**такти́ческий,** *adj.* tactical.

такти́чный *adj.* tactful. —**такти́чно,** *adv.* tactfully. —**такти́чность,** *n.f.* tactfulness; tact.

тала́нт *n.* talent. —**тала́нтливый,** *adj.* talented.

талды́чить *v.impfv., colloq.* to talk endlessly; repeat endlessly.

талисма́н *n.* talisman.

та́лия *n.* waist. Собра́ть пла́тье в та́лии, to take a dress in at the waist.

та́ллий *n.* thallium.

талму́д *n.* Talmud. —**талмуди́зм,** *n.* dogmatism; fundamentalism; talmudism.

талмуди́ст *n.* **1,** Talmudic scholar. **2,** dogmatist; fundamentalist. —**талмуди́стский,** *adj.* dogmatic; doctrinaire. —**талмуди́ческий,** *adj.* Talmudic.

тало́н *n.* **1,** coupon. **2,** ration card. —**поса́дочный тало́н,** boarding pass.

та́лый *adj.* melting; melted.

тальк *n.* **1,** talc; talcum. **2,** talcum powder. —**та́льковый,** *adj.* talc (*attrib.*); talcum (*attrib.*).

там *adv.* there; in that place. —**там, где,** where; the place there. —**там же, 1,** in that place. **2,** (*in footnotes*) ibid.

тамада́ *n.m.* toastmaster.

тамари́нд *n.* tamarind.

тамари́ск *n.* tamarisk.

та́мбур *n.* **1,** vestibule. **2,** platform (*of a railway car*). **3,** chain stitch.

тамбури́н *n.* tambourine.

та́мбурный *adj., in* **та́мбурный шов; та́мбурная стро́чка,** chain stitch.

тамо́женник *n.* customs official. —**тамо́женный,** *adj.* customs (*attrib.*).

тамо́жня *n.* **1,** customs. **2,** customhouse.

та́мошний *adj., colloq.* of that place; local.

тампо́н *n.* tampon.

тамта́м *n.* tom-tom.

тана́гра *n.* tanager.

та́нгенс *n., trig.* tangent. —**тангенциа́льный,** *adj.* tangential.

та́нго *n. indecl.* tango.

та́ндем *also,* **танде́м** (дэ) *n.* tandem.

та́нец [*gen.* **та́нца**] *n.* **1,** dance. **2,** *pl.* dance (*affair with dancing*): пойти́ на та́нцы, to go to a dance.

тани́н *n.* tannin. —**тани́нный,** *adj.* tannic.

танк *n.* **1,** *mil.* tank. **2,** tank; cistern.

та́нкер *n.* tanker.

танке́тка [*gen. pl.* **-ток**] *n.* **1,** *mil.* light tank. **2,** wedge heel. **3,** *pl.* wedge-heeled shoes.

танки́ст *n.* member of a tank crew.

та́нковый *adj., mil.* tank (*attrib.*).

танта́л *n.* tantalum.

тантье́ма *n.* bonus.

танцева́льный *adj.* dance (*attrib.*); dancing (*attrib.*): танцева́льный ве́чер, dance.

танцева́ть *v.impfv.* [*pres.* **-цу́ю, -цу́ешь**] to dance. —**танцева́ть от пе́чки,** *colloq.* to start with the basics.

танцо́вщик *n.m.* [*fem.* **-щица**] (ballet) dancer.

танцо́р *n.* dancer.

тапёр *n.* pianist engaged for a dance.

тапио́ка *n.* tapioca.

тапи́р *n.* tapir.

та́почки [*gen.* **-чек**] *n.pl.* [*sing.* **та́почка**] *colloq.* **1,** slippers. **2,** sneakers.

та́ра *n.* **1,** container (*for safeguarding and transporting*). **2,** wrapping material; packing material. **3,** *comm.* tare.

тараба́нить *v.impfv., colloq.* to clatter.

тараба́рщина *n., colloq.* gibberish.

тарака́н *n.* cockroach.

тара́н *n.* **1,** battering ram. **2,** *mech.* ram.

тара́нить *v.impfv.* [*pfv.* **протара́нить**] to ram.

таранта́с *n.* large four-wheeled carriage.

тара́нтул *n.* tarantula.

тара́нь *n.f.* roach (*fish*).

тарара́м *n., colloq.* uproar; hubbub; hullabaloo.

тарата́йка [*gen. pl.* -та́ек] *n.* two-wheeled carriage.

тарато́рить *v.impfv., colloq.* to jabber; chatter.

тарахте́ть *v.impfv.* [*pres.* -хчу́, -хти́шь] *colloq.* 1, to clatter. 2, *fig.* to chatter.

тара́щить *v.impfv.* [*pfv.* вы́таращить] *colloq., in* тара́щить глаза́, to stare; gape.

таре́лка [*gen. pl.* -лок] *n.* 1, plate; dish. 2, *pl.* cymbals. —быть в свое́й таре́лке, to be in one's element. —быть не в свое́й таре́лке, 1, to be out of sorts; be not quite oneself. 2, to feel ill at ease; feel uneasy.

таре́лочка [*gen. pl.* -чек] *n.* 1, *dim. of* таре́лка. 2, clay pigeon. —стрельба́ по таре́лочкам, trapshooting.

тари́ф *n.* 1, tariff. 2, rate. —тари́фный, *adj.* tariff (*attrib.*).

та́ры-ба́ры *n.pl. indecl., colloq.* chatter; tittle-tattle.

таска́ть *v.impfv.* 1, *indeterm. of* тащи́ть. 2, to carry. 3, *colloq.* to wear (for a long time). 4, (*with* за + *acc.*) *colloq.* to pull (by): таска́ть кого́-нибудь за́ уши, to pull someone by the ears. —таска́ться, *refl., colloq.* 1, to wander; amble. 2, (*with* по) to make the rounds of. 3, to hang around. 4, (*with* с + *instr.*) to carry around (*on one's person*). 5, (*with* за + *instr.*) to chase after (women). 6, (*with* с + *instr.*) to have an affair with.

тасова́ть *v.impfv.* [*pfv.* стасова́ть; *pres.* -су́ю, -су́ешь] to shuffle (cards).

тасо́вка *n.* shuffling; shuffle (*of cards*).

тата́рин [*pl.* тата́ры, тата́р] *n.m.* [*fem.* тата́рка] Tatar. —тата́рский, *adj.* Tatar.

татуи́ровать *v.impfv. & pfv.* [*pres.* -рую, -руешь] to tattoo.

татуиро́вка *n.* 1, tattooing. 2, tattoo.

тафта́ *n.* taffeta. —тафтяно́й, *adj.* taffeta.

тахо́метр *n.* tachometer.

тахта́ *n.* ottoman; divan.

тача́нка [*gen. pl.* -нок] *n.* 1, light open carriage. 2, machine-gun cart.

тача́ть *v.impfv.* [*pfv.* вы́тачать *or* стача́ть] to stitch.

та́чка [*gen. pl.* та́чек] *n.* wheelbarrow.

тащи́ть *v.impfv.* [*pfv.* потащи́ть; *pres.* тащу́, та́щишь] 1, to pull; draw; tow. 2, to drag; haul; lug. 3, [*pfv.* вы́тащить] to pull out. 4, [*pfv.* вы́тащить] to drag (someone) somewhere against his will. 5, [*pfv.* вы́тащить *or* стащи́ть] *colloq.* to swipe; pilfer. —тащи́ться, *refl.* 1, to drag along; trail along (the ground). 2, *colloq.* to drag oneself along. 3, *colloq.* to go (somewhere) reluctantly; drag oneself. *See also* таска́ть.

та́яние *n.* melting.

та́ять *v.impfv.* [*pfv.* раста́ять; *pres.* та́ю, та́ешь] 1, to melt; thaw. 2, (*of clouds, smoke, etc.*) to dissipate. 3, *fig.* to fade; wane; dwindle; ebb. 4, *fig.* to fade from view. 5, [*impfv. only*] (*of a person*) to waste away.

тварь *n.f., obs.* 1, creature. 2, wretch.

твердеть *v.impfv.* [*pfv.* затверде́ть] to harden; become hard.

тверди́ть *v.impfv.* [*pres.* -жу́, -ди́шь] 1, to repeat (*or* keep saying) over and over again; (*with* о) talk endlessly about. 2, [*pfv.* затверди́ть *or* вы́твердить] *colloq.* to memorize (*through repetition*).

тве́рдо *adv.* firmly; firm. Твёрдо вы́учить, to learn thoroughly. Твёрдо запо́мнить, to remember well.

твердока́менный *adj.* callous; insensitive; hard-boiled.

твердоло́бый *adj., colloq.* diehard; dyed-in-the-wool.

твёрдость *n.f.* 1, hardness; firmness. 2, resoluteness; steadfastness.

твердоте́льный *adj.* solid-state.

твёрдый *adj.* [*comp.* твёрже] 1, hard. 2, solid. 3, firm. 4, fixed; set. 5, *fig.* steadfast; resolute. —твёрдый знак, hard sign (ъ).

тверды́ня *n.* 1, stronghold. 2, *fig.* bulwark.

твёрже *adj., comp. of* твёрдый.

твид *n.* tweed.

твой [*infl. like* мой] *poss. adj. & pron.* your; yours (*familiar*).

творе́ние *n.* 1, *obs.* creation; creating. 2, creation; product; work. 3, *obs.* creature; being.

творе́ц [*gen.* -рца́] *n.* creator; maker.

твори́тельный *adj., in* твори́тельный паде́ж, instrumental case.

твори́ть *v.impfv.* [*pfv.* сотвори́ть] 1, to create. 2, to perform; do. 3, to commit. 4, *in* твори́ть чудеса́, to work miracles. —твори́ться, *refl.* [*impfv. only*] *colloq.* to be going on.

творо́г [*gen.* -рога́] *n.* 1, curds. 2, cottage cheese. *Also,* тво́рог [*gen.* тво́рога].

творо́жник *n.* curd pancake; cottage-cheese pancake.

тво́рческий *adj.* creative.

тво́рчество *n.* 1, creative activity. 2, works (*of an author*).

те *adj., pl. of* тот.

т.е. *abbr. of* то есть, that is; i.e.

теа́тр *n.* 1, theater: идти́ в теа́тр, to go to the theater. 2, *mil.* theater: теа́тр вое́нных де́йствий, theater of (military) operations.

театра́л *n.m.* [*fem.* -тра́лка] theatergoer; playgoer.

театра́льный *adj.* 1, theater (*attrib.*); theatrical. 2, overly dramatic; histrionic. —театра́льность, *n.f.* theatrics; histrionics.

тебе́ *pron., dat. & prepl. of* ты.

тебя́ *pron., gen. & acc. of* ты.

тевто́н *n.* Teuton. —тевто́нский, *adj.* Teutonic.

теза́урус *n.* thesaurus.

те́зис (тэ) *n.* thesis.

тёзка [*gen. pl.* тёзок] *n.m. & f.* namesake.

теи́зм (тэ) *n.* theism. —теи́ст, *n.* theist. —теисти́ческий, *adj.* theistic.

текст *n.* 1, text. 2, script. 3, *music* words; lyrics; libretto.

тексти́ль *n.m.* textiles. —тексти́льный, *adj.* textile (*attrib.*). —тексти́льщик, *n.* textile worker.

текстово́й *adj.* textual.

текстуа́льный *adj.* 1, textual. 2, literal; word-for-word.

теку́честь *n.f.* 1, fluidity. 2, fluctuation. 3, turnover (*of personnel*).

теку́чий *adj.* 1, fluid; flowing; running. 2, fluctuating; constantly changing.

теку́щий *adj.* 1, current; present. 2, routine; everyday. —теку́щий ремо́нт, routine repairs; preventive maintenance. —теку́щий счёт, (liquid) bank account; checking account.

телеви́дение *n.* television. —**телевизио́нный,** *adj.* television (*attrib.*).

телеви́зор *n.* television set.

теле́га *n.* cart; wagon.

телегра́мма *n.* telegram.

телегра́ф *n.* **1,** telegraph. **2,** telegraph office.

телеграфи́ровать *v.impfv. & pfv.* [*pres.* **-ру́ю, -ру́ешь**] to telegraph; wire; cable.

телеграфи́ст *n.* telegraph operator; telegrapher.

телеграфи́я *n.* telegraphy.

телегра́фный *adj.* telegraph (*attrib.*); telegraphic.

теле́жка [*gen. pl.* **-жек**] *n.* light cart. —**ручна́я теле́жка,** handcart.

телезри́тель *n.m.* (television) viewer.

телека́мера *n.* television camera.

телекоммуника́ции *n.pl.* telecommunications.

телеме́тр *n.* telemeter. —**телеметри́я,** *n.* telemetry.

телёнок [*gen.* **-нка;** *pl.* **теля́та, теля́т**] *n.* calf.

телеобъекти́в *n.* telephoto lens.

телеоло́гия *n.* teleology. —**телеологи́ческий,** *adj.* teleological.

телепа́тия *n.* telepathy. —**телепати́ческий,** *adj.* telepathic.

телепереда́ча *n.* **1,** television transmission. **2,** telecast.

телеподска́зчик *n.* teleprompter.

телесвя́зь *n.f.* telecommunications.

телеско́п *n.* telescope. —**телескопи́ческий,** *adj.* telescopic. —**телеско́пный,** *adj.* telescope (*attrib.*).

теле́сный *adj.* **1,** bodily; corporal. **2,** flesh-colored. **3,** corporeal.

телесту́дия *n.* television studio.

телета́йп *n.* teletype.

телефо́н *n.* telephone. —**телефо́н-автома́т,** *n.* public telephone; pay phone.

телефони́ровать *v.impfv. & pfv.* [*pres.* **-ру́ю, -ру́ешь**] (*with dat.*) to telephone; phone; call.

телефони́ст *n.m.* [*fem.* **-ни́стка**] telephone operator.

телефони́я *n.* telephony.

телефо́нный *adj.* **1,** telephone (*attrib.*). **2,** telephonic.

теле́ц [*gen.* **-льца́**] *n.* **1,** *obs.* calf. **2,** *cap.* Taurus.

тели́ться *v.r.impfv.* [*pfv.* **отели́ться;** *pres.* **те́лится**] to calve.

тёлка [*gen. pl.* **тёлок**] *n.* heifer.

теллу́р *n.* tellurium.

те́ло [*pl.* **тела́, тел, тела́м**] *n.* body. —**держа́ть в чёрном те́ле,** to work (someone) to the bone. —**душо́й и те́лом,** utterly; totally; body and soul. —**ни душо́й ни те́лом не винова́т,** completely innocent.

телогре́йка [*gen. pl.* **-гре́ек**] *n.* padded jacket.

телодвиже́ние *n.* body movement; gesture.

телосложе́ние *n.* build; physique.

телохрани́тель *n.m.* bodyguard.

те́льный *adj., colloq.* worn next to the skin.

те́льце *n.* **1,** [*pl.* **те́льца, те́лец**] little body. **2,** [*pl.* **тельца́, теле́ц**] corpuscle.

теля́тина *n.* veal.

теля́чий [*fem.* **-чья**] *adj.* **1,** calf (*attrib.*); calf's. **2,** veal (*attrib.*). —**теля́чий восто́рг,** childish glee.

тем *adj., instr. sing. & dat. pl. of* **тот.** —*adv., used with comp. degree of adjectives* **1,** so much the: тем лу́чше, so much the better. **2,** (*with* **чем**) the ... the: чем ра́ньше, тем лу́чше, the sooner the better. —**тем бо́лее,** *see* **бо́лее.** —**тем не ме́нее,** nevertheless. —**тем са́мым,** thus; thereby. —**тем, что...,** in that...; by the fact that...

те́ма *n.* **1,** subject; topic; theme. **2,** *music* theme: те́ма с вариа́циями, theme with variations.

тема́тика *n.* subject matter. —**темати́ческий,** *adj.* thematic; topical.

тембр *n.* (тэ) *n.* timbre.

те́мень *n.f., colloq.* darkness.

темне́ть *v.impfv.* **1,** [*pfv.* **потемне́ть**] to become dark; darken. **2,** [*pfv.* **стемне́ть**] *impers.* to get dark: Темне́ет, it is getting dark. **3,** [*impfv. only*] (*of anything dark*) to appear; loom.

темни́ть *v.impfv.* **1,** to darken; make darker. **2,** to obscure. **3,** *colloq.* to prevaricate.

темни́ца *n., obs.* prison; dungeon.

темно́ *adj., used predicatively,* dark: В ко́мнате бы́ло темно́, it was dark in the room.

тёмно- *prefix, used with colors,* dark: тёмно-зелёный, dark green.

темноволо́сый *adj.* dark-haired.

темноко́жий *adj.* dark-skinned.

темнота́ *n.* dark; darkness.

тёмный *adj.* **1,** dark. **2,** gloomy; dismal. **3,** obscure; vague. **4,** shady; unsavory; suspicious. **5,** ignorant. —**темны́м-темно́,** pitch-dark.

темп (тэ) *n.* **1,** *music; chess* tempo. Вы́играть темп, to gain a tempo. **2,** rate; pace; tempo. Набира́ть темп, to gain momentum.

те́мпера (тэ) *n.* tempera; distemper.

темпера́мент *n.* **1,** temperament. **2,** zest; verve; vibrancy. Челове́к с темпера́ментом, spirited/vibrant person.

темпера́ментный *adj.* **1,** temperamental. **2,** spirited; vibrant.

температу́ра *n.* temperature.

температу́рить *v.impfv., colloq.* to have a temperature; be running a temperature.

температу́рный *adj.* temperature (*attrib.*).

темь *n.f., colloq.* darkness.

те́мя [*gen., dat. & prepl.* **те́мени;** *instr.* **те́менем**] *n.neut.* top of the head.

тенденцио́зность (тэ, дэ) *n.f.* **1,** tendentiousness. **2,** biased nature; biased approach.

тенденцио́зный (тэ, дэ) *adj.* **1,** tendentious. **2,** biased; slanted.

тенде́нция (тэ, дэ) *n.* **1,** tendency. **2,** trend. **3,** bias.

те́ндер (тэ, дэ) *n.* **1,** *R.R.* tender. **2,** *naut.* cutter.

тенево́й *adj.* shady. —**теневая́ сторона́** (+ *gen.*), **1,** the shady side (of); the dark side (of). **2,** *fig.* the dark side (of); the seamy side (of). —**теневая́ эконо́мика,** *colloq.* shadow economy.

тенёта [*gen.* **тенёт**] *n.pl.* net; snare.

тени́стый *adj.* shady.

те́ннис (тэ) *n.* tennis. —**тенниси́ст,** *n.* tennis player.

те́нниска (тэ) [*gen. pl.* **-сок**] *n., colloq.* sport shirt; polo shirt.

те́ннисный (тэ) *adj.* tennis (*attrib.*).

тéнор [*pl.* тенорá] *n.* tenor. —**теноро́вый**, *adj.* tenor (*attrib.*).

тент (тэ) *n.* awning.

тень [*2nd loc.* тени́; *pl.* тéни, тенéй, теня́м] *n.f.* **1**, shade: в тени́, in the shade. **2**, shadow. **3**, *fig.* trace (of sadness, doubt, etc.) on one's face. **4**, *fig.* grain; particle (of truth); shadow; particle (of doubt). **5**, ghost. —**броса́ть тень на** (+ *acc.*), to cast aspersions on. —**держа́ться в тени́**, to remain in the background. —**от него́ оста́лась одна́ тень**, he is only a shadow of his former self.

теокра́тия (тэ) *n.* theocracy. —**теократи́ческий**, *adj.* theocratic.

теоло́гия (тэ) *n.* theology. —**теологи́ческий**, *adj.* theological.

теоре́ма *n.* theorem.

теоретизи́ровать *v.impfv.* [*pres.* **-рую, -руешь**] to theorize.

теоре́тик *n.* theoretician; theorist.

теорети́ческий *adj.* theoretical. —**теорети́чески**, *adv.* theoretically.

тео́рия *n.* theory. —**в тео́рии**, in theory; theoretically.

теосо́фия (тэ) *n.* theosophy. —**теосо́ф**, *n.* theosophist. —**теосо́фский; теософи́ческий**, *adj.* theosophical.

тепéрешний *adj., colloq.* present; today's; present-day. Тепéрешняя жизнь, life today.

тепéрь *adv.* now.

теплéть *v.impfv.* [*pfv.* **потеплéть**] to become warm; get warm; warm up.

тéплиться *v.r.impfv.* to flicker; glimmer.

теплица *n.* hothouse; greenhouse. —**тепли́чный**, *adj.* hothouse (*attrib.*).

тепло́ *n.* **1**, warmth. **2**, *physics* heat. —*adv.* warmly. —*adj., used predicatively,* warm: Сего́дня тепло́, it is warm today; мне тепло́, I am warm.

теплова́тый *adj.* tepid; lukewarm.

теплово́з *n.* diesel locomotive.

теплово́й *adj.* heat (*attrib.*); thermal; caloric. —**теплово́й уда́р**, heatstroke.

теплокро́вный *adj.* warm-blooded.

тепломéр *n.* calorimeter.

теплопрово́дный *adj.* heat-conducting.

теплосто́йкий *adj.* heat-resistant.

теплота́ *n.* **1**, heat. **2**, warmth.

теплохо́д *n.* motor ship.

теплу́шка [*gen. pl.* **-шек**] *n., colloq.* heated freight car used to carry people.

тёплый *adj.* **1**, warm. **2**, *fig.* warm; cordial. —**тёплое мéсте́чко**, soft job.

теплы́нь *n.f., colloq.* warm weather; mild weather.

терапéвт *n.* internist. —**терапевти́ческий**, *adj.* therapeutic.

терапи́я *n.* **1**, internal medicine. **2**, therapy.

тéрбий *n.* terbium.

тереби́ть *v.impfv.* [*pres.* **-блю́, -би́шь**] **1**, to pull at; tug at. **2**, *fig., colloq.* to pester; nag.

тéрем [*pl.* терема́] *n.* tower in old Russian mansions where women were kept in seclusion.

терéть *v.impfv.* [*pres.* **тру, трёшь**; *past* тёр, тёрла] **1**, to rub (one's eyes, hands, etc.). **2**, to grate; grind (veg-

etables). **3**, to rub; chafe. Но́вые ту́фли трут, the new shoes are rubbing me. Воротни́к тёр шéю, the collar was rubbing (my, his, etc.) neck. —**терéться**, *refl.* [*pfv.* **потерéться**] **1**, *colloq.* to rub oneself. **2**, (*with* о + *acc.*) to rub against. **3**, *fig., colloq.* to hang around.

терза́ние *n.* torment; anguish; agony.

терза́ть *v.impfv.* **1**, to tear apart; tear to pieces; tear to bits. **2**, to torment. —**терза́ться**, *refl.* to suffer; be tormented.

тёрка [*gen. pl.* тёрок] *n.* grater.

тéрмин *n.* term: техни́ческий тéрмин, technical term.

термина́л *n.* computer terminal.

терминоло́гия *n.* terminology.

терми́т *n.* **1**, termite. **2**, Thermit.

терми́ческий *adj.* thermal.

термодина́мика *n.* thermodynamics. —**термодинами́ческий**, *adj.* thermodynamic.

термо́метр *n.* thermometer.

термопа́ра *n.* thermocouple.

тéрмос (тэ) *n.* thermos (bottle).

термоста́т (тэ) *n.* thermostat.

термоя́дерный *adj.* thermonuclear.

тёрн *n.* **1**, blackthorn. **2**, sloe; sloes.

тéрние *n.* **1**, *obs.* thorn. **2**, *usu. pl., fig.* thorns; vicissitudes.

терни́стый *adj.* **1**, *obs.* thorny. **2**, *fig.* thorny; full of pitfalls: терни́стый путь, thorny path.

терно́вник *n.* blackthorn.

терпели́вый *adj.* patient. —**терпели́во**, *adv.* patiently. —**терпели́вость**, *n.f.* patience; forbearance.

терпéние *n.* patience.

терпéть *v.impfv.* [*pres.* **терплю́, тéрпишь**] **1**, to endure; bear; stand. **2**, to tolerate; stand; put up with. **3**, [*pfv.* **потерпéть**] to suffer; sustain (losses, a defeat, etc.). **4**, *in* врéмя тéрпит, there is plenty of time; врéмя не тéрпит, there is no time to be lost. —**терпéться**, *refl.* [*impfv. only*] (*used negatively with the dative case and inf.*) to be impatient (to); be unable to wait (to): Ему́ не терпéлось нача́ть, he couldn't wait to begin.

терпи́мо *adv.* with tolerance: относи́ться терпи́мо к, to be tolerant of. —*adj., used predicatively, colloq.* tolerable; bearable.

терпи́мость *n.f.* tolerance. —**дом терпи́мости**, *obs.* brothel.

терпи́мый *adj.* **1**, tolerant. **2**, tolerable.

тéрпкий *adj.* [*comp.* **тéрпче**] tart; acrid; astringent; acerbic. —**тéрпкость**, *n.f.* astringency; acerbity.

терракóта (тэ) *n.* terra cotta.

терракóтовый (тэ) *adj.* **1**, terra-cotta. **2**, reddish brown.

террáса *n.* terrace. —**террáсный**, *adj.* terraced.

территориа́льный *adj.* territorial.

террито́рия *n.* **1**, territory. **2**, premises; grounds (*of a building, factory, etc.*).

терро́р *n.* terror.

терроризи́ровать *v.impfv. & pfv.* [*pres.* **-рую, -руешь**] to terrorize.

террори́зм *n.* terrorism. —**террори́ст**, *n.* terrorist. —**террористи́ческий**, *adj.* terrorist (*attrib.*).

тёртый *adj.* **1**, grated. **2**, *fig., colloq.* experienced; worldly-wise. —**тёртый кала́ч**, experienced person; old hand.

тéрция (тэ) *n., music* third.

терьéр (тэ) *n.* terrier.

терять *v.impfv.* [*pfv.* **потерять**] **1,** to lose. **2,** to waste (time, words, etc.). **3,** *v.i.* (*with* **в** + *prepl.*) to lose; suffer; be the worse for: терять в вéсе, to lose weight; терять в перевóде, to suffer in translation; терять в чьём-нибудь мнéнии, to go down in someone's estimation. —**терять гóлову,** to lose one's head. Не терять головы́, to keep one's head. —**терять из виду** (*or* из ви́да), **1,** to lose sight of. **2,** to lose track of. —**терять си́лу, 1,** to lose one's vigor. **2,** to expire; become invalid. —**терять управлéние, 1,** (*with instr.*) to lose control (of). **2,** to go out of control.

теряться *v.r.impfv.* [*pfv.* **потеряться**] **1,** to be lost; get lost. **2,** [*impfv. only*] (*of one's eyesight, memory, etc.*) to fail; fade. **3,** to become flustered; panic.

тёс *n.* boards; planks.

тесáк [*gen.* **-сакá**] *n.* cutlass.

тесáние *n.* cutting; hewing.

тёсаный *adj.* cut; hewn.

тесáть *v.impfv.* [*pres.* **тешу́, тéшешь**] to cut; hew.

тесёмка [*gen. pl.* **-мок**] *n., colloq.* braid.

тесина *n.* board; plank.

теслó [*pl.* **тёсла, тёсел**] *n.* adz.

тесни́на *n.* **1,** gorge; ravine. **2,** defile.

тесни́ть *v.impfv.* **1,** [*pfv.* **потесни́ть**] to crowd; cramp. **2,** [*pfv.* **стесни́ть**] to constrict (the throat, chest, etc.). *Also impers.:* Мне тесни́т грудь, I feel a tightness in my chest. **3,** [*impfv. only*] (*of clothes*) to be too tight. —**тесни́ться,** *refl.* **1,** [*pfv.* **стесни́ться**] to crowd; cluster. **2,** [*pfv.* **потесни́ться**] to squeeze together; move closer together. **3,** to be crowded (together). **4,** to jostle each other.

тéсно *adv.* **1,** close together. **2,** closely: тéсно свя́занный, closely connected. —*adj., used predicatively* **1,** crowded: Здесь тéсно, it is crowded here. **2,** tight: Мне тéсно в плечáх, it feels tight in the shoulders.

теснотá *n.* crowded conditions; close quarters.

тéсный *adj.* [*short form* **тéсен, тесна́, тéсно, тесны́** *or* **тéсны**] **1,** crowded; cramped. **2,** tight; compact; close. **3,** *fig.* close; intimate. **4,** (*of clothes*) tight.

тесóвый *adj.* made of boards or planks.

тест (тэ) *n.* (psychological) test.

тéсто *n.* dough. —**из другóго тéста,** of a different breed; made of different stuff.

тесть *n.m.* father-in-law (*wife's father*).

тесьмá *n.* braid.

тётенька *n., colloq.* aunt; aunty.

тéтерев [*pl.* **тетеревá**] *n.* black grouse.

тетеревя́тник *n.* [*often* **я́стреб-тетеревя́тник**] goshawk.

тетёрка [*gen. pl.* **-рок**] *n.* female black grouse; gray hen.

тетéря *n., regional* black grouse. —**лени́вая тетéря,** lazybones. —**сóнная тетéря,** sleepyhead.

тетива́ *n.* bowstring.

тётка [*gen. pl.* **тёток**] *n.* aunt.

тетрáдка [*gen. pl.* **-док**] *n.* notebook.

тетрáдный *adj.* notebook (*attrib.*).

тетрáдь *n.f.* notebook.

тётя [*gen. pl.* **тётей**] *n.* aunt.

тéфтели *also,* **тефтéли** [*gen.* **-лей**] *n.pl.* meatballs.

технéций *n.* technetium.

тéхник *n.* technician.

тéхника *n.* **1,** technology. **2,** engineering: строи́тельная тéхника, civil engineering. **3,** technique. **4,** (technical) equipment. —**тéхника безопáсности,** accident prevention; safety procedures.

тéхникум *n.* technical school.

техни́ческий *adj.* technical. —**техни́чески,** *adv.* technically.

технóлог *n.* **1,** technologist. **2,** production engineer.

технологи́ческий *adj.* **1,** technological. **2,** production (*attrib.*): технологи́ческий потóк, production line. —**технологи́ческая кáрта,** production chart; flow sheet.

технолóгия *n.* **1,** technology. **2,** engineering: хими́ческая технолóгия, chemical engineering.

течéние *n.* **1,** flow; flowing. **2,** current: по течéнию; прóтив течéния, with/against the current (*or* tide). Вверх/вниз по течéнию, upstream/downstream. Пускáть по течéнию, to set adrift. **3,** section (*of a river*): вéрхнее течéние Ни́ла, the upper Nile; ни́жнее течéние Днéстра, the lower reaches of the Dniester. **4,** *fig.* course: измени́ть течéние истóрии, to change the course of history. **5,** *fig.* trend: нóвые течéния в литератýре, new trends in literature. —**в течéние** (+ *gen.*), **1,** in the course of; during. **2,** for; over a period of. **3,** within (a certain amount of time). —**с течéнием врéмени,** with the passage of time; in the course of time.

тéчка *n.* heat (*in animals*).

течь[1] *v.impfv.* [*pres.* **текý, течёшь, ...текýт**; *past* **тёк, теклá, теклó, текли́**] **1,** to flow. **2,** to stream. **3,** to leak. **4,** *fig.* (*of time, life, etc.*) to pass; flow by. —**у меня́ из нóсу течёт,** my nose is running. —**у меня́ кровь течёт из нóсу,** my nose is bleeding.

течь[2] *n.f.* leak: дать течь, to spring a leak.

тéшить *v.impfv.* [*pfv.* **потéшить**] **1,** *colloq.* to amuse; entertain. **2,** to gratify; please. **3,** to flatter (someone's pride). **4,** to console; comfort. —**тéшить себя́ надéждами,** to hold out hope.

тéшиться *v.r.impfv.* [*pfv.* **потéшиться**] **1,** to amuse oneself. **2,** (*with instr.*) to console oneself (in *or* by); take comfort (in); take consolation (in). **3,** *obs.* (*with* **над**) to make fun of; poke fun at.

тёща *n.* mother-in-law (*wife's mother*).

тиáра *n.* tiara.

тибéтский *adj.* Tibetan.

ти́гель [*gen.* **ти́гля**] *n.m.* crucible.

тигр *n.* tiger.

тигрёнок [*gen.* **-нка**; *pl.* **тигря́та, тигря́т**] *n.* tiger cub.

тигри́ца *n.* tigress.

тигрóвый *adj.* tiger (*attrib.*); tiger's.

тик *n.* **1,** (nervous) tic. **2,** teak (*wood*). **3,** ticking (*cloth*).

ти́канье *n.* ticking (*of a clock*).

ти́кать *v.impfv.* (*of a clock*) to tick.

ти́ккер *n.* ticker.

ти́ковый *adj.* **1,** teak (*attrib.*). **2,** made with ticking.

ти́льда *n.* tilde.

тимиа́н *n.* = **тимья́н.**

тимофе́евка *n.* timothy; timothy grass.

тимья́н *also,* **тимиа́н** *n.* thyme.

ти́на *n.* pond scum. —**ти́нистый,** *adj.* filled with pond scum.

тинкту́ра *n.* tincture.

тип *n.* **1,** type. **2,** phylum. **3,** [*acc.* **ти́па**] *colloq.* character; odd person.

типа́ж [*gen.* **-пажа́**] *n.* model; prototype.

типи́ческий *adj.* typical.

типи́чно *adv.* typically. —*adj., used predicatively,* typical: Э́то типи́чно для него́, that's typical of him.

типи́чный *adj.* typical.

типово́й *adj.* **1,** model. **2,** standard; standardized.

типо́граф *n.* printer; typographer. —**типогра́фия,** *n.* printing house. —**типогра́фский,** *adj.* typographic(al); printer's.

типу́н [*gen.* **-пуна́**] *n.* pip (*bird disease*).

тир *n.* shooting gallery.

тира́да *n.* tirade.

тира́ж [*gen.* **-ража́**] *n.* **1,** drawing (*in a lottery*). **2,** circulation (*of a periodical*). **3,** printing (*of a book*); pressrun. —**вы́йти в тира́ж,** to be no longer able to work; be ready for retirement.

тира́н *n.* tyrant.

тира́нить *v.impfv.* **1,** to tyrannize; oppress. **2,** to torment.

тирани́я *n.* tyranny. —**тирани́ческий,** *adj.* tyrannical.

тира́нство *n.* tyranny.

тира́нствовать *v.impfv.* [*pres.* **-ствую, -ствуешь**] to be a tyrant.

тире́ (рэ) *n.neut. indecl.* dash.

тис *n.* yew.

ти́скать *v.impfv.* [*pfv.* **ти́снуть**] *colloq.* to squeeze; press.

тиски́ [*gen.* **-ко́в**] *n.pl.* vise: зажа́ть в тиски́, to grip in a vise. —**в тиска́х** (+ *gen.*), in the grips of.

тисне́ние *n.* **1,** embossing. **2,** imprint; design.

тиснёный *adj.* embossed.

ти́снуть *v., pfv. of* **ти́скать.**

тита́н *n.* **1,** titan. **2,** titanium. **3,** large boiler. —**тита́ни́ческий,** *adj.* titanic.

титр *n., motion pictures* title; subtitle.

ти́тул *n.* title: присво́ить ти́тул (+ *dat.*), to confer a title on (someone).

титуло́ванный *adj.* titled.

титулова́ть *v.impfv. & pfv.* [*pres.* **-лу́ю, -лу́ешь**] to call; address (someone) by his title.

ти́тульный *adj., printing* title (*attrib.*): ти́тульный лист, title page.

тиф *n.* typhus. —**брюшно́й тиф,** typhoid. —**возвра́тный тиф,** relapsing fever. —**сыпно́й тиф,** typhus.

тифо́зный *adj.* typhoid; typhus (*attrib.*).

ти́хий *adj.* [*comp.* **ти́ше**] **1,** soft; low. **2,** quiet; still. **3,** calm; tranquil. **4,** quiet; retiring. **5,** slow.

ти́хо *adv.* **1,** quietly. **2,** softly. **3,** slowly. —*adj., used predicatively,* quiet: Здесь ти́хо, it is quiet here.

тихомо́лком *adv., colloq.* quietly; without making a sound.

тихо́нько *adv., colloq.* quietly; softly.

тихо́ня *n.m. & f., colloq.* timid person; meek person.

ти́ше *adj., comp. of* **ти́хий.** —*adv., comp. of* **ти́хо.** —*interj.* quiet!; please be quiet!

тишина́ *n.* quiet; silence; stillness.

тишь [*2nd loc.* **тиши́**] *n.f.* quiet; stillness. —**тишь да гладь,** peace and quiet.

тка́ный *adj.* woven.

ткань *n.f.* **1,** cloth; fabric. **2,** *anat.* tissue.

тканьё *n.* **1,** weaving. **2,** cloth. **3,** woven design.

ткать *v.impfv.* [*pfv.* **сотка́ть;** *pres.* **тку, ткёшь;** *past fem.* **ткала́** *or* **тка́ла**] **1,** to weave. **2,** *in* ткать паути́ну, to spin a web.

тка́цкий *adj.* weaving (*attrib.*); weaver's. —**тка́цкий стано́к,** loom.

ткач [*gen.* **ткача́**] *n.m.* [*fem.* **-чи́ха**] weaver.

ткнуть *v., pfv. of* **ты́кать.** —**ткну́ться,** *refl., pfv. of* **ты́каться.**

тле́ние *n.* **1,** rotting; decay. **2,** smoldering.

тле́нный *adj.* mortal.

тлетво́рный *adj.* **1,** noxious. **2,** pernicious; deleterious.

тлеть *v.impfv.* **1,** to rot; decay. **2,** to smolder. —**тле́ться,** *refl., colloq.* to smolder.

тля *n.* plant louse.

тмин *n.* caraway. —**тми́нный,** *adj.* caraway (*attrib.*).

то *dem. adj. & pron., neut. of* **тот,** that: в то вре́мя, at that time. То бы́ли незабыва́емые дни, those were unforgettable days. —*conj.* then: Е́сли он не хо́чет, то не угова́ривайте его́, if he doesn't want to, then don't try to persuade him. —**а то;** **не то,** or; or else; otherwise. —**а то и,** or maybe: челове́к две́сти, а то и бо́льше, some 200 people, or maybe more. —**не то..., не то,** half ... half; a combination of... —**не то что; не то чтобы,** it is not (so much) that... —**то есть,** that is; that is to say. —**то ли..., то ли,** either..., or; a combination of... —**то..., то,** now ... now: Он живёт то в го́роде, то в дере́вне, he divides his time between the city and the country. —**то, что...,** **1,** what... **2,** the fact that...

тобо́й *also,* **тобо́ю** *pron., instr. of* **ты.**

това́р *n.* **1,** (*often pl.*) goods; merchandise. **2,** commodity.

това́рищ *n.* **1,** comrade. **2,** friend. **3,** (*with* по) fellow: това́рищ по рабо́те, fellow worker. —**това́рищ по несча́стью,** comrade in distress. —**това́рищ по ору́жию,** comrade in arms.

това́рищеский *adj.* comradely; friendly.

това́рищество *n.* **1,** comradeship; fellowship; camaraderie. **2,** company; society; association.

това́рный *adj.* **1,** goods (*attrib.*); commodity (*attrib.*). **2,** *R.R.* freight (*attrib.*): това́рный по́езд, freight train.

товарообме́н *n.* barter.

товарооборо́т *n.* commodity turnover.

то́га *n.* toga.

тогда́ *adv.* **1,** then; at that time. **2,** then; in that case. —**тогда́ как,** while; whereas. —**тогда́, когда́...,** when.

тогда́шний *adj., colloq.* of that time; at that time.

того́ (во) *adj., gen. of* **тот.**

тожде́ственный *adj.* identical. —**тожде́ственность,** *n.f.* identity; sameness.

то́ждество *n.* identity: то́ждество взгля́дов, identity of views.

тóже *adv.* **1,** also; too. **2,** (*with neg. verbs*) either: Я тóже не знáю, I don't know either.

той *adj., fem. gen., dat., instr. & prepl. of* **тот.**

ток *n.* **1,** *electricity* current: переме́нный ток, alternating current. Меня́ уда́рило тóком, I got a shock. **2,** current; flow; stream. Ток крóви, bloodstream. **3,** [*2nd loc.* токý; *pl.* токá] threshing floor. **4,** mating (*of birds*). **5,** [*2nd loc.* токý; *pl.* токá] mating ground. **6,** *obs.* toque.

тока́рный *adj.* lathe (*attrib.*). —**тока́рный стано́к,** lathe.

тóкарь [*pl.* токаря́ *or* тóкари] *n.m.* lathe operator; turner.

токова́ние *n.* mating call.

токова́ть *v.impfv.* [*pres.* -ку́ет] (*of a bird*) to utter its mating call.

токоприёмник *n.* trolley (*device for conducting current*).

токсеми́я *n.* toxemia.

токсиколо́гия *n.* toxicology. —**токсико́лог,** *n.* toxicologist. —**токсикологи́ческий,** *adj.* toxicological.

токси́н *n.* toxin.

токси́ческий *adj.* toxic.

тол *n.* TNT; trinitrotoluene.

толи́ка *n., obs.* (*with gen.*) small amount (of). —**ма́лую толи́ку,** a little; tiny bit.

толк [*2nd gen.* тóлку] *n.* **1,** sense: Что тóлку (+ *inf.*)?, what's the sense (*or* point) of...? От негó тóлку не добьёшься, you can't get any sense out of him. **2,** *colloq.* good; use: Тóлку от э́того выходи́ло ма́ло, little good came of it. **3,** *pl.* talk; rumors. **4,** (political) persuasion. **5,** *obs.* explanation; interpretation. **6,** *obs.* opinion; view. —**бе́з толку, 1,** without making any sense. **2,** for nothing; to no purpose. —**брать в толк,** to understand; figure out. —**знать толк в** (+ *prepl.*), to know well; be a connoisseur of. —**сбива́ть с тóлку,** to confuse. —**сбива́ться с тóлку,** to become confused. —**с тóлком,** sensibly; intelligently. *See also* **тóлком.**

толка́ние *n.* pushing. —**толка́ние ядра́,** *sports* shotput.

толка́ть *v.impfv.* [*pfv.* **толкну́ть**] **1,** to push; shove. **2,** to poke; prod. Толка́ть (кого́-нибудь) лóктем, to nudge. **3,** *fig.* (*with* на + *acc.*) to incite (to); put up (to). **4,** *in* **толка́ть ядрó,** *sports* to put the shot. —**толка́ться,** *refl.* **1,** [*impfv. only*] to push; shove: Не толка́йтесь!, don't push!; don't shove! **2,** [*impfv. only*] to push; shove; jostle (one another). **3,** (*with* о + *acc.*) *colloq.* to strike (against). **4,** (*with* в + *acc.*) *colloq.* to knock on the door of; try to get into. **5,** [*impfv. only*] *colloq.* to knock about; idle; loaf.

толка́ч [*gen.* -кача́] *n., colloq.* person who cuts through red tape; expediter.

толкну́ть *v., pfv. of* **толка́ть.** —**толкну́ться,** *refl., pfv. of* **толка́ться.**

толкова́ние *n.* **1,** interpretation. **2,** commentary.

толкова́тель *n.m.* interpreter; commentator.

толкова́ть *v.impfv.* [*pres.* -ку́ю, -ку́ешь] **1,** to interpret. **2,** *colloq.* to explain. **3,** *colloq.* to talk; converse.

толкóвый *adj., colloq.* **1,** intelligent; clever. **2,** clear; intelligible. —**толкóвый словáрь,** defining dictionary.

тóлком *adv., colloq.* **1,** plainly; clearly. **2,** in earnest: засе́сть тóлком за урóки, to get down to one's lessons in earnest. **3,** properly. Тóлком всё разгляде́ть, to have a good look around. Никтó тóлком не знал, nobody really knew.

толкотня́ *n., colloq.* crush (*of people*).

толку́чий *adj., in* **толку́чий ры́нок,** *colloq.* flea market. —**толку́чка,** *n., colloq.* flea market.

толокнó *n.* oatmeal.

толóчь *v.impfv.* [*pfv.* **растолóчь**; *pres.* **толку́, толчёшь, ...толку́т**; *past* **толóк, толкла́, толклó, толкли́**] to crush; pound; pulverize. —**толóчь вóду в сту́пе,** to waste one's time; beat the air.

толóчься *v.r.impfv.* [*pres.* **толку́сь, толчёшься, ...толку́тся**; *past* **толóкся, толкла́сь, толклóсь, толкли́сь**] *colloq.* **1,** to move about (*in a small area*). **2,** to crowd; mill about. **3,** to hang around.

толпа́ [*pl.* **тóлпы**] *n.* crowd. —**тóлпами,** in droves.

толпи́ться *v.r.impfv.* to crowd; throng.

толсте́ть *v.impfv.* [*pfv.* **потолсте́ть**] to get fat; put on weight.

толсти́ть *v.impfv., colloq.* to make (someone) look fat.

толстóвка [*gen. pl.* -вок] *n.* long belted blouse (*as worn by Tolstoy*).

толстогу́бый *adj.* thick-lipped.

толстокóжий *adj.* thick-skinned. —**толстокóжее живóтное,** pachyderm.

толстосу́м *n., colloq.* rich man; person of great wealth.

толсту́ха *also,* **толсту́шка** *n., colloq.* fat woman.

тóлстый *adj.* [*comp.* **тóлще**] **1,** thick. **2,** fat; stout. **3,** (*of cloth*) heavy. —**тóлстая кишка́,** large intestine.

толстя́к [*gen.* -стяка́] *n., colloq.* fat man.

толуóл *n.* toluene.

толчёный *adj.* ground: толчёный минда́ль, ground almonds.

толчея́ *n., colloq.* crush (*of people*).

толчóк [*gen.* -чка́] *n.* **1,** push; shove. **2,** jolt; bump. **3,** shock; tremor. **4,** *fig.* stimulus; impetus; spur. **5,** *weightlifting* clean and jerk.

тóлща *n.* **1,** thick mass; layer. **2,** *fig.* the masses.

тóлще *adj., comp. of* **тóлстый.**

толщина́ *n.* **1,** thickness. **2,** corpulence.

толь *n.m.* tarred roofing paper.

тóлько *adv.* **1,** only: тóлько для мужчи́н, for men only. **2,** not until; not till; only: тóлько в послéднюю мину́ту, not until/till the last minute; only at the last minute. **3,** alone: тóлько в э́том году́, this year alone. **4,** just: Он тóлько пришёл, he just arrived. **5,** (*with* **не**) *used in exclamations for emphasis:* Где тóлько он не быва́л!, where *hasn't* he been?; is there anywhere he hasn't been? Когó там тóлько не встрéтишь!, you can meet absolutely anyone there! Чегó тóлько не приду́мывают лю́ди!, what people won't think of next! —*conj.* only: с удовóльствием, тóлько не сегóдня, with pleasure, only not today. —*particle* just: Поду́мать тóлько!, just think! Вы тóлько попрóбуйте э́тот кóфе!, just taste this coffee! —**да и тóлько,** *see* **да.** —**едва́ тóлько,** = **как тóлько.** —**как тóлько,** as soon as. —**лишь тóлько,** = **как тóлько.** —**оди́н тóлько,** *see* **оди́н.** —**тóлько бы, 1,**

if only. **2**, (*with* **не** + *inf.*) one must simply not; the one thing we must not do is... —**то́лько и,** the only thing: Об э́том то́лько и говори́ли, it was all they talked about. —**то́лько что,** just: Я то́лько что пришёл, I've just arrived.

том¹ *adj., prepl. of* **тот.**

том² [*pl.* **тома́**] *n.* volume.

томага́вк *n.* tomahawk.

тома́т *n.* **1**, tomato. **2**, tomato paste. —**тома́тный,** *adj.* tomato (*attrib.*).

то́мик *n., dim. of* **том.**

томи́тельный *adj.* **1**, oppressive; agonizing. **2**, tedious; tiring.

томи́ть *v.impfv.* [*pres.* **томлю́, томи́шь**] **1**, (*of pain, thirst, etc.*) to torment. **2**, *v.i.* (*of heat*) to be oppressive. **3**, to tire; bore. **4**, to confine (in prison). **5**, to exhaust. —**томи́ться,** *refl.* **1**, to suffer. **2**, to languish (in prison, captivity, etc.). **3**, (*with* **по**) to pine (for).

томле́ние *n.* **1**, anguish; suffering. **2**, languor.

то́мность *n.f.* languor.

то́мный *adj.* languid; languorous.

тому́ *adj., dat. of* **тот.** —**тому́ наза́д,** ago.

тон [*pl.* **тона́** *or* **то́ны**] *n.* **1**, (musical) tone. **2**, tone of voice. **3**, tone; shade. **4**, *fig.* tone; tenor: тон письма́, the tone of the letter. **5**, form: Э́то счита́ется дурны́м то́ном, it is considered poor form. Пра́вила хоро́шего то́на, proper form; social graces; the rules of etiquette. —**в тон, 1**, (*with dat.*) to match. **2**, in the same tone of voice; in kind. —**не в тон,** off key. —**попа́сть в тон,** to strike the right note. —**сба́вить тон,** to quiet down.

тона́льность *n.f., music* key: тона́льность до диез, key of C sharp.

тона́льный *adj.* tonal.

то́ненький *adj., colloq.* thin.

тонзилли́т *n.* tonsillitis.

тонзу́ра *n.* tonsure.

тонизи́ровать *v.impfv. & pfv.* [*pres.* **-рую, -руешь**] *physiol.* to tone up. —**тонизи́рующее сре́дство,** tonic.

то́ник *n.* tonic (*for a drink*).

тони́ческий *adj.* tonic.

то́нкий *adj.* [*comp.* **то́ньше;** *superl.* **тонча́йший**] **1**, thin. **2**, (*of thread, linen, etc.*) fine. **3**, (*of the senses*) keen. **4**, (*of food, wines, etc.*) fine. **5**, subtle. **6**, delicate. **7**, astute; keen; perceptive.

то́нко *adv.* **1**, thinly; thin. **2**, finely. **3**, subtly.

тонкоко́жий *adj.* thin-skinned.

то́нкость *n.f.* **1**, thinness. **2**, fineness. **3**, subtlety. **4**, keenness (*of the senses*). **5**, fine point; subtlety; nicety. —**до то́нкостей,** minutely; down to the fine points.

то́нна *n.* ton.

тонна́ж *n.* tonnage.

тонне́ль (нэ) *n.m.* tunnel.

то́нус *n., physiol.* tone: мы́шечный то́нус, muscle tone.

тону́ть *v.impfv.* [*pres.* **тону́, то́нешь**] **1**, [*pfv.* **пото́нуть**] to sink. **2**, [*pfv.* **утону́ть**] to drown.

то́ньше *adj., comp. of* **то́нкий.**

топа́з *n.* topaz. —**топа́зовый,** *adj.* topaz.

то́пать *v.impfv.* [*pfv.* **то́пнуть**] (*with instr.*) to stamp (one's feet).

топи́ть *v.impfv.* [*pres.* **топлю́, то́пишь**] **1**, to keep the fire going in; heat (a stove); stoke (a furnace). **2**, to heat (a building). **3**, [*pfv.* **растопи́ть**] to melt (butter, fat, etc.). **4**, [*pfv.* **потопи́ть**] to sink (a ship). **5**, [*pfv.* **утопи́ть**] to drown (an animal). —**топи́ться,** *refl.* **1**, (*of a stove*) to burn; be lit. **2**, to melt. **3**, [*pfv.* **утопи́ться**] *colloq.* to drown oneself.

то́пка *n.* **1**, heating. **2**, melting. **3**, furnace.

то́пкий *adj.* swampy; marshy.

топлёный *adj.* **1**, melted. **2**, (*of milk*) baked.

то́пливо *n.* fuel. —**то́пливный,** *adj.* fuel (*attrib.*).

то́пнуть *v., pfv. of* **то́пать.**

топогра́фия *n.* topography. —**топо́граф,** *n.* topographer. —**топографи́ческий,** *adj.* topographical.

то́полевый *adj.* poplar (*attrib.*). Also, **тополи́ный.**

тополо́гия *n.* topology.

то́поль [*pl.* **тополя́**] *n.m.* poplar.

топо́р [*gen.* **топора́**] *n.* ax.

топо́рик *n.* hatchet.

топори́ще *n.* ax handle.

топо́рный *adj.* **1**, of an ax; ax (*attrib.*). **2**, (*of a piece of furniture*) crudely made. **3**, (*of workmanship*) crude. **4**, (*of a person*) unpolished; unrefined; uncouth.

топо́рщить *v.impfv.* to make (hair, fur, etc.) stand on end. —**топо́рщиться,** *refl., colloq.* **1**, (*of one's hair*) to bristle. **2**, to stick out; protrude. **3**, (*of material*) to pucker.

то́пот *n.* tramping (*of feet*); clatter (*of hoofs*).

топота́ть *v.impfv.* [*pres.* **топочу́, топо́чешь**] *colloq.* **1**, [*also,* **топота́ть нога́ми**] to stamp one's feet. **2**, to tramp along.

то́псель *n.m.* topsail.

топта́ние *n.* trampling. —**топта́ние на ме́сте,** marking time.

топта́ть *v.impfv.* [*pres.* **топчу́, то́пчешь**] **1**, to trample; trample down. **2**, to stamp out (a fire). **3**, *colloq.* to soil; track dirt on. **4**, *in* **топта́ть в грязь,** to drag through the mud. —**топта́ться,** *refl.* **1**, to shift from foot to foot. **2**, *colloq.* to walk about; hang about. **3**, *in* **топта́ться на ме́сте,** to mark time.

топча́к [*gen.* **-чака́**] *n.* treadmill.

топь *n.f.* swamp; marsh; bog.

то́ра *n.* Torah.

то́рба *n.* feedbag. —**носи́ться с (ке́м-нибудь) как с пи́саной то́рбой,** to make a fuss over (someone).

торг [*2nd loc.* **торгу́;** *pl.* **торги́**] *n.* **1**, trading; buying and selling. **2**, bargaining. Предме́т то́рга, bargaining chip. **3**, deal. **4**, *obs.* market. **5**, *pl.* auction. Продава́ть с торго́в, to sell at auction; auction off.

торгова́ть *v.impfv.* [*pres.* **-гу́ю, -гу́ешь**] **1**, to do business. **2**, (*of a store*) to be open (for business). **3**, (*with instr.*) to deal in; sell. **4**, (*with* **с** + *instr.*) to trade with (another country). —**торгова́ться,** *refl.* to bargain; haggle; dicker.

торго́вец [*gen.* **-вца**] *n.* merchant; tradesman; dealer. —**торго́вец меха́ми,** fur trader. —**ро́зничный торго́вец,** retailer. —**торго́вец нарко́тиками,** drug dealer. —**у́личный торго́вец,** street vendor.

торго́вля *n.* trade; business; commerce.

торго́вый *adj.* **1**, trade (*attrib.*); commercial. **2**, (*of a ship, fleet, etc.*) merchant. —**торго́вая пала́та,** chamber of commerce. —**торго́вый центр,** shopping center.

тореадо́р *n.* toreador.

торе́ц [*gen.* **торца́**] *n.* **1,** butt end. **2,** wooden paving block.

торже́ственно *adv.* **1,** with great solemnity. **2,** solemnly. —**торже́ственность,** *n.f.* solemnity.

торже́ственный *adj.* **1,** solemn. **2,** momentous. **3,** festive; gala; grand. **4,** triumphal.

торжество́ *n.* **1,** celebration; *pl.* festivities; ceremonies. **2,** triumph; victory. **3,** (feeling of) triumph; exultation. —**с торжество́м,** triumphantly.

торжествова́ть *v.impfv.* [*pfv.* **восторжествова́ть**; *pres.* **-ству́ю, -ству́ешь**] **1,** (with **над**) to triumph (over). **2,** [*impfv. only*] to rejoice; exult. **3,** [*impfv. only*] *obs.* to celebrate (a holiday, victory, etc.).

торжеству́ющий *adj.* triumphant; exultant.

то́ри *n.m. indecl.* Tory.

то́рий *n.* thorium.

торма́шки *n.pl.*, *in* **вверх торма́шки** *and* **вверх торма́шками, 1,** head over heels. Полете́ть вверх торма́шками, to go flying head over heels. **2,** upside-down; topsy-turvy.

торможе́ние *n.* **1,** braking. **2,** retardation.

то́рмоз *n.* **1,** [*pl.* **тормоза́**] brake. На тормоза́х, with the brake partly on. **2,** [*pl.* **то́рмозы**] *fig.* brake; drag; obstacle; hindrance. —**спуска́ть (что́-нибудь) на тормоза́х,** to quietly let (*e.g.* a matter) drop.

тормози́ть *v.impfv.* [*pfv.* **затормози́ть**; *pres.* **-жу́, -зи́шь**] **1,** to brake; apply the brakes (to). **2,** *fig.* to hinder; hamper; impede; retard.

тормозно́й *adj.* brake (*attrib.*): тормозно́й башма́к, brake shoe. —**тормозно́й конду́ктор,** brakeman. —**тормозна́я раке́та,** retro-rocket.

тормоши́ть *v.impfv.*, *colloq.* **1,** to pull at; tug at. **2,** *fig.* to bother; pester.

то́рный *adj.* (*of a road*) even; smooth; worn down; well-trodden.

торова́тый *adj., obs.* generous.

торопи́ть *v.impfv.* [*pfv.* **поторопи́ть**; *pres.* **тороплю́, торо́пишь**] **1,** to hurry (up); rush. **2,** to hasten; speed up. —**торопи́ться,** *refl.* **1,** to hurry; rush. **2,** to be in a hurry. **3,** to be (too) hasty.

торопли́вый *adj.* **1,** hasty; hurried. **2,** always in a hurry; bustling. —**торопли́во,** *adv.* hastily; hurriedly. —**торопли́вость,** *n.f.* haste; hurry.

торо́с *n.* hummock (*in an ice field*).

торпе́да *n.* torpedo.

торпеди́ровать *v.impfv. & pfv.* [*pres.* **-рую, -руешь**] to torpedo.

торпе́дный *adj.* torpedo (*attrib.*). —**торпе́дный ка́тер,** PT boat.

торс *n.* torso.

торт *n.* cake. —**фрукто́вый торт,** fruitcake.

торф *n.* peat. —**торфяно́й,** *adj.* peat (*attrib.*).

торча́ть *v.impfv.* [*pres.* **-чу́, -чи́шь**] **1,** to stick out; jut out; protrude. **2,** *colloq.* to hang around. —**торча́ть пе́ред глаза́ми,** to be ever present; never go away.

торчко́м *adv., colloq.* on end; erect; upright.

торше́р *n.* floor lamp.

тоска́ *n.* **1,** melancholy. **2,** boredom; ennui. **3,** (*with* **по**) longing (for); yearning (for); nostalgia (for).

тоскли́вый *adj.* **1,** melancholy. **2,** dreary; dismal; depressing.

тоскова́ть *v.impfv.* [*pres.* **-ку́ю, -ку́ешь**] **1,** to be melancholy; be depressed. **2,** (*with* **по** + *dat.*, *but prepl. for pers. pronouns*) to miss; long for. —**тоскова́ть по дому́,** to be homesick.

тост *n.* toast: предлага́ть тост, to propose a toast.

то́стер (тэ) *n.* toaster.

тот [*fem.* **та**; *neut.* **то**; *pl.* **те**; *gen.* **того́, той, тех**; *dat.* **тому́, той, тем**; *acc. fem.* **ту**; *instr.* **тем, той, те́ми**; *prepl.* **том, той, тех**] *dem. adj.* **1,** that: в тот моме́нт, at that moment; в то вре́мя, at that time. **2,** (*with* **кото́рый**) the ... that: Э́то та кни́га, кото́рую вы иска́ли?, is this the book you were looking for? **3,** the right: Э́то тот дом?, is this the right house? Я набра́л не тот но́мер, I dialed the wrong number. **4,** the other; the far: по ту сто́рону (+ *gen.*), on the other side of. —*dem. pron.* **1,** that one; that. **2,** the latter. **3,** (*fol. by* **кто**) he (who); the one (who). **4,** (*fol. by* **кото́рый**) the one (that). —**и тот и друго́й,** both. —**не тот, как друго́й,** if not one, then the other. —**ни тот, ни друго́й,** neither; neither one. —**тот и́ли ино́й,** some ... or other; one ... or another. —**тот же; тот са́мый; тот же са́мый,** the same. *See also* **то** *and* **тем.**

тотализа́тор *n.* **1,** totalizator; pari-mutuel machine. **2,** pari-mutuel betting.

тоталитари́зм *n.* totalitarianism. —**тоталита́рный,** *adj.* totalitarian.

тота́льный *adj.* total. —**тота́льная война́,** total war.

тоте́м (тэ) *n.* totem. —**тотеми́зм,** *n.* totemism.

то́-то *particle, colloq.* **1,** that's just the point. **2,** aha!; what did I tell you! **3,** that is why; that is how. **4,** how!: То́-то бы́ло краси́во!, how beautiful it was!

то́тчас *adv.* immediately; at once.

точе́ние *n.* sharpening.

точёный *adj.* **1,** sharpened. **2,** shaped in a lathe. **3,** *fig.* (*of features*) chiseled.

точи́лка [*gen. pl.* **-лок**] *n.* **1,** sharpener. **2,** *colloq.* pencil sharpener.

точи́ло *n.* grindstone; whetstone.

точи́льный *adj.* sharpening (*attrib.*). —**точи́льный ка́мень,** grindstone; whetstone. —**точи́льный реме́нь,** strop.

точи́льщик *n.* grinder; knife grinder.

точи́ть *v.impfv.* [*pres.* **точу́, то́чишь**] **1,** [*pfv.* **наточи́ть**] to sharpen; hone. **2,** [*pfv.* **вы́точить**] to make; turn out (*using a lathe*). **3,** (*of insects, rodents, etc.*) to eat away. **4,** (*of water*) to wear away. **5,** *fig.* (*of an illness*) to wear down; (*of oppressive thoughts*) to gnaw at. **6,** *fig.*, *colloq.* to nag. —**точи́ть зу́бы на** (+ *acc.*), to have it in for; bear a grudge against.

то́чка [*gen. pl.* **то́чек**] *n.* **1,** dot. **2,** point (*in space*): са́мая высо́кая то́чка, the highest point. Отправна́я то́чка, starting point. **3,** period. **4,** *in* **две то́чки,** colon; то́чка с запято́й, semicolon. **5,** *in* **то́чка кипе́ния/замерза́ния,** boiling/freezing point. **6,** *in* **то́чка зре́ния,** point of view; viewpoint. **7,** *in* **горя́чая то́чка,** trouble spot; hot spot; flash point. —*interj.*, *colloq.* enough!; that will do! —**бить в одну́ то́чку,** to concentrate on one thing. —**до то́чки,** thoroughly;

down to the last detail. —**доходить до точки,** to reach the breaking point; reach the end of one's rope; be at the end of one's tether. —**мёртвая точка,** *see* **мёртвый.** —**попасть в (самую) точку,** to hit the nail on the head; put one's finger on it. —**ставить точку на** (+ *prepl.*), to finish; close the books on. —**ставить точки над «и»,** to dot the "i's" and cross the "t's". —**точка в точку,** perfectly; to the letter.

точнée *adj., comp. of* **точный.** —*particle* or rather; to be more precise.

точно *adv.* exactly; precisely; accurately. —*conj.* **1,** like; as. **2,** as if; as though. —**так точно!,** *mil.* yes, sir! —**точно так же,** in exactly the same way. —**точно так же, как...,** just as...

точность *n.f.* **1,** exactness; precision. **2,** accuracy. **3,** punctuality. —**в точности,** exactly; precisely; to the letter. —**с точностью до,** within.

точный *adj.* **1,** exact; precise. **2,** accurate. **3,** punctual. —**точные приборы,** precision instruments.

точь-в-точь *adv.* exactly.

тошнить *v.impfv., impers.* to be nauseous; feel nauseous: Меня тошнит, I feel nauseous.

тошно *adj., colloq., used predicatively,* nauseating; sickening: Мне тошно смотреть на это, it sickens me to look at it.

тошнота *n.* nausea. —**тошнотворный,** *adj.* nauseating; sickening.

тошный *adj., colloq.* **1,** nauseating. **2,** tiresome.

тощать *v.impfv.* [*pfv.* **отощать**] *colloq.* to become very thin; become gaunt; waste away.

тощий *adj.* **1,** emaciated; gaunt. **2,** poor; meager. **3,** (*of vegetation*) withered. **4,** *fig., colloq.* (*of a container*) nearly empty. **5,** (*of meat*) lean; (*of milk*) low-fat. —**на тощий желудок,** on an empty stomach.

тпру *interj.* whoa!

трава [*pl.* **травы**] *n.* **1,** grass; herb. —**сорная трава,** weed; weeds.

травинка [*gen. pl.* **-нок**] *n.* blade of grass.

травить *v.impfv.* [*pres.* **травлю, травишь**] **1,** [*pfv.* **вытравить**] to exterminate; poison. **2,** [*pfv.* **потравить**] to trample (down). **3,** [*pfv.* **затравить**] to hunt (down); *fig.* hound; persecute. **4,** [*pfv.* **вытравить**] to etch. **5,** [*pfv.* **вытравить**] *naut.* to let out; pay out (a rope, cable, etc.). —**травиться,** *refl.* [*impfv. only*] *colloq.* to take poison.

травка [*gen. pl.* **-вок**] *n.* (short) grass.

травление *n.* etching.

травленый *adj.* **1,** etched. **2,** (*of an animal*) hunted.

травля *n.* **1,** hunt; hunting. **2,** *fig.* hounding; persecution.

травма *n.* injury; trauma. —**травматизм,** *n.* accidents; injuries. —**травматический,** *adj.* traumatic. —**травматология,** *n.* traumatology.

травмировать *v.impfv. & pfv.* [*pres.* **-рую, -руешь**] **1,** to injure; damage. **2,** to traumatize.

травоядный *adj.* herbivorous.

травянистый *adj.* **1,** herbaceous. **2,** grassy. **3,** *fig., colloq.* tasteless.

травяной *adj.* **1,** grass (*attrib.*). **2,** grassy.

трагедия *n.* tragedy.

трагизм *n.* tragedy; tragic element.

трагик *n.* tragedian.

трагикомедия *n.* tragicomedy. —**трагикомический,** *adj.* tragicomic.

трагический *adj.* tragic. —**трагически,** *adv.* tragically.

трагичный *adj.* tragic. —**трагично,** *adv.* tragically. —**трагичность,** *n.f.* tragedy; tragic nature.

традиция *n.* tradition. —**традиционный,** *adj.* traditional.

траектория *n.* trajectory. —**траектория полёта,** flight path.

тракт *n.* highway. Почтовый тракт, post road. —**желудочно-кишечный тракт,** alimentary canal. —**пищеварительный тракт,** digestive tract.

трактат *n.* **1,** treatise; tract. **2,** *obs.* treaty.

трактир *n., obs.* tavern; inn. —**трактирщик,** *n., obs.* innkeeper.

трактовать *v.impfv.* [*pres.* **-тую, -туешь**] **1,** to interpret. **2,** (*with* **о**) to treat; discuss (a certain subject).

трактовка *n.* treatment; interpretation.

трактор [*pl.* **тракторы** *or* **трактора**] *n.* tractor. —**тракторист,** *n.* tractor driver. —**тракторный,** *adj.* tractor (*attrib.*).

трал *n.* trawl.

тралить *v.impfv.* to trawl.

тральщик *n.* **1,** trawler. **2,** minesweeper.

трамбовать *v.impfv.* [*pfv.* **утрамбовать;** *pres.* **-бую, -буешь**] to beat down; smooth down.

трамвай *n.* streetcar; trolley; tram. —**трамвайный,** *adj.* streetcar (*attrib.*); trolley (*attrib.*); tram (*attrib.*).

трамплин *n.* **1,** diving board; springboard. **2,** *fig.* springboard; starting point. —**лыжный трамплин,** ski jump.

транжир *n., colloq.* spendthrift.

транжирить *v.impfv.* [*pfv.* **растранжирить**] *colloq.* to squander.

транзистор *n.* transistor.

транзит *n.* transit. —**транзитный,** *adj.* transit (*attrib.*).

транквилизатор *n.* tranquilizer.

транс *n.* trance.

трансатлантический *adj.* transatlantic.

трансепт *n.* transept.

трансконтинентальный *adj.* transcontinental.

транскрибировать *v.impfv. & pfv.* [*pres.* **-рую, -руешь**] to transcribe (*represent by phonetic symbols*).

транскрипция *n., ling., music* transcription.

транслировать *v.impfv. & pfv.* [*pres.* **-рую, -руешь**] to transmit; broadcast.

транслитерация *n.* transliteration.

транслитерировать *v.impfv. & pfv.* [*pres.* **-рую, -руешь**] to transliterate.

трансляция *n.* transmission; broadcast. —**трансляционный,** *adj.* transmission (*attrib.*); broadcasting.

трансокеанский *adj.* transoceanic.

транспарант *n.* **1,** lined paper (*placed under unlined paper*). **2,** banner; streamer.

транспонировать *v.impfv. & pfv.* [*pres.* **-рую, -руешь**] *music* to transpose.

транспониро́вка *n., music* transposition.

тра́нспорт *n.* **1,** transport. **2,** transportation. **3,** shipment; consignment. **4,** supply ship; troopship; troop transport.

транспо́рт *n., bookkeeping* carrying forward.

транспорта́бельный *adj.* transportable.

транспортёр *n.* **1,** conveyor. Ле́нточный транспортёр, conveyor belt. **2,** *mil.* transporter; carrier.

транспорти́р *n.* protractor.

транспорти́ровать *v.impfv. & pfv.* [*pres.* **-рую, -руешь**] **1,** to transport. **2,** *bookkeeping* to carry forward.

транспортиро́вка *n.* transporting; transportation.

тра́нспортник *n.* transport worker.

тра́нспортный *adj.* transport (*attrib.*).

транссиби́рский *adj.* trans-Siberian.

трансформа́тор *n.* **1,** *electricity* transformer. **2,** *theat.* quick-change artist.

трансформа́ция *n.* transformation.

трансформи́ровать *v.impfv. & pfv.* [*pres.* **-рую, -руешь**] to transform; convert.

трансцендента́льный *adj.* transcendental.

трансценде́нтный *adj.* **1,** *philos.* transcendent. **2,** *math.* transcendental.

транше́йный *adj.* trench (*attrib.*). —**транше́йная стопа́,** trench foot.

транше́я *n.* trench.

трап *n.* **1,** ship's ladder. **2,** ramp (*for an airplane*).

тра́пеза *also,* **трапе́за** *n.* food; meal (*originally served in a monastery*).

тра́пезная *also,* **трапе́зная** *n., decl. as an adj.* refectory (*in a monastery*).

тра́пезный *also,* **трапе́зный** *adj.* meal (*attrib.*); dining (*attrib.*).

трапе́ция *n.* **1,** *geom.* trapezoid. **2,** trapeze.

тра́сса *n.* **1,** route. **2,** path (*of a bullet, missile, etc.*). **3,** road; highway.

трасса́нт *n., comm.* drawer.

трасси́ровать *v.impfv. & pfv.* [*pres.* **-рую, -руешь**] to trace (*on a map or chart*).

трасси́рующий *adj.* tracer (*attrib.*): трасси́рующая пу́ля, tracer bullet.

тра́та *n.* **1,** (*with gen.*) spending (of); expenditure (of). **2,** (*preceded by an adj.*) waste: пуста́я тра́та вре́мени, waste of time. **3,** (*often pl.*) expenditures; expenses.

тра́тить *v.impfv.* [*pfv.* **истра́тить** *or* **потра́тить**; *pres.* **тра́чу, тра́тишь**] **1,** to spend (money). **2,** to expend (time, energy, etc.). **3,** to use up. **4,** to waste. —**тра́титься,** *refl.* **1,** to spend money. **2,** to be spent.

тра́улер *n.* trawler.

тра́ур *n.* **1,** mourning. **2,** mourning clothes. —**надева́ть тра́ур,** to go into mourning. —**носи́ть тра́ур по** (+ *dat.*), to be in mourning for. —**снима́ть тра́ур,** to cease mourning.

тра́урница *n.* mourning cloak (*butterfly*).

тра́урный *adj.* **1,** mourning (*attrib.*); funeral (*attrib.*). **2,** *fig.* mournful; sorrowful.

трафаре́т *n.* **1,** stencil. **2,** *fig.* stereotype.

трафаре́тный *adj.* **1,** stenciled. **2,** *fig.* conventional; stereotyped.

трах *interj.* bang!

трахе́я *n.* trachea. —**трахе́йный,** *adj.* tracheal. —**трахеотоми́я,** *n.* tracheotomy.

тра́хнуть *v.pfv., colloq.* **1,** to fire; shoot. **2,** (*of a sound, shot, etc.*) to ring out. **3,** to bang; smash; whack. —**тра́хнуться,** *refl., colloq.* **1,** to fall with a crash. **2,** (*with* **о** + *acc.*) to bang (into *or* against).

трахо́ма *n.* trachoma.

тре́бование *n.* **1,** demand. **2,** *pl.* requirements: отвеча́ть тре́бованиям, to meet the requirements. **3,** requisition; order.

тре́бовательный *adj.* demanding; exacting.

тре́бовать *v.impfv.* [*pfv.* **потре́бовать**; *pres.* **-бую, -буешь**] **1,** (*with gen., acc. or* **чтобы**) to demand. **2,** (*with acc.*) to demand to see (a permit, passport, etc.). **3,** (*with gen.*) to require; need; call for. **4,** (*with acc.*) to summon; send for; call in. —**тре́боваться,** *refl.* to be needed; be required.

требуха́ *n.* entrails.

трево́га *n.* **1,** alarm: чу́вство трево́ги, sense of alarm. **2,** alarm signal: бить трево́гу, to sound the alarm. **3,** alert: поднима́ть по трево́ге, to place on alert. —**возду́шная трево́га,** air-raid alert; air-raid warning. Сире́на возду́шной трево́ги, air-raid siren.

трево́жить *v.impfv.* **1,** [*pfv.* **встрево́жить**] to alarm; worry; trouble. **2,** [*pfv.* **потрево́жить**] to disturb; disrupt. —**трево́житься,** *refl.* [*pfv.* **встрево́житься**] to become alarmed; become worried.

трево́жный *adj.* **1,** anxious; uneasy; troubled. **2,** of alarm: трево́жный взгляд, a look of alarm. **3,** alarming. **4,** (*of time, a moment, etc.*) anxious. **5,** alarm (*attrib.*): трево́жный сигна́л, alarm signal.

треволне́ние *n., colloq.* **1,** worry; agitation. **2,** *pl.* vicissitudes.

тре́звенник *n., colloq.* teetotaler.

трезве́ть *v.impfv.* [*pfv.* **отрезве́ть**] to sober up; become sober.

тре́зво *adv.* soberly.

трезво́н *n.* **1,** sound of church bells. **2,** long ringing of a bell. **3,** *fig., colloq.* talk; gossip. **4,** *fig., colloq.* row; ruckus.

трезво́нить *v.impfv.* **1,** to ring; sound; peal. **2,** *fig.* (*with* **о**) *colloq.* to trumpet; proclaim. **3,** *fig.* (*with* **о**) *colloq.* to spread rumors (about).

тре́звость *n.f.* **1,** sobriety. **2,** temperance; abstinence. —**тре́звость ума́,** cool-headedness.

трезву́чие *n., music* triad.

тре́звый *adj.* **1,** sober; not drunk. **2,** *colloq.* who does not drink; teetotaling. **3,** *fig.* sober; realistic.

трезу́бец [*gen.* **-бца**] *n.* trident.

трек *n., sports* track. —**тре́ковый,** *adj.* track (*attrib.*).

трель *n.f.* trill; warble.

трелья́ж *n.* **1,** trellis. **2,** three-leaf mirror.

тре́моло *n. indecl.* tremolo.

тренажёр *n.* trainer; simulator.

тре́нер *n.* trainer; coach.

тре́нзель *n.m.* snaffle.

тре́ние *n.* **1,** rubbing; rubbing together. **2,** friction. **3,** *pl., fig.* friction; conflict.

трениро́ванный *adj.* trained.

тренирова́ть *v.impfv.* [*pfv.* **натренирова́ть**; *pres.* **-ру́ю, -ру́ешь**] to train; coach. —**тренирова́ться**, *refl.* to train; undergo training.

трениро́вка *n.* **1,** training. **2,** practice; workout; drill. —**трениро́вочный**, *adj.* training (*attrib.*).

трено́га *n.* **1,** tripod. **2,** three-legged shackle (*for a horse*).

трено́гий *adj.* three-legged.

трено́жить *v.impfv.* [*pfv.* **стрено́жить**] to hobble (a horse).

трено́жник *n.* tripod.

тре́нькать *v.impfv., colloq.* to strum.

трепа́к [*gen.* **-пака́**] *n.* trepak (*dance*).

трепа́ло *n.* scutch; swingle. *Also,* **трепа́лка**.

трёпаный *adj., colloq.* **1,** torn; tattered; ragged; frayed. **2,** disheveled; unkempt.

трепа́ть *v.impfv.* [*pres.* **треплю́, тре́плешь**] **1,** [*pfv.* **потрепа́ть**] to dishevel (*by pulling or tugging at*). **2,** [*pfv.* **потрепа́ть**] (*of the wind*) to blow about. **3,** [*pfv.* **потрепа́ть**] (*with* **по** + *dat.*) to pat; stroke. **4,** [*pfv.* **истрепа́ть**] *colloq.* to fray; wear out. **5,** [*impfv. only*] (*with* **за** + *acc.*) to pull (someone's hair, ears, etc.). **6,** [*impfv. only*] *colloq.* to whip; whack. **7,** [*impfv. only*] (*of illness, fever, etc.*) to rack. **8,** [*impfv. only*] to scutch. **9,** *in* трепа́ть не́рвы (+ *dat.*), to get (someone) upset. **10,** *in* трепа́ть языко́м, *colloq.* to babble; chatter. —**трепа́ться**, *refl.* **1,** [*impfv. only*] to flutter. **2,** [*pfv.* **истрепа́ться**] to become frayed; wear out.

тре́пет *n.* **1,** quivering; trembling. **2,** tremor; palpitation. **3,** *fig.* trepidation.

трепета́ние *n.* **1,** quivering; trembling. **2,** palpitation.

трепета́ть *v.impfv.* [*pres.* **трепещу́, трепе́щешь**] **1,** to quiver. **2,** (*of one's heart*) to palpitate. **3,** to flicker. **4,** to tremble (*with an emotion*).

тре́петно *adv.* **1,** with a quiver. **2,** with trepidation.

тре́петный *adj.* **1,** quivering; fluttering; flickering. **2,** of trepidation; trembling. **3,** timid; fearful.

трёпка [*gen. pl.* **-пок**] *n., colloq.* **1,** beating; thrashing. **2,** scolding; bawling out; dressing-down. —**трёпка не́рвов**, strain on one's nerves.

трепыха́ть *v.impfv., colloq.* **1,** to flutter. **2,** to thrash about. **3,** (*with instr.*) to flap; shake. *Also,* **трепыха́ться**, *refl.* (*in senses #1 & #2*).

треск *n.* **1,** crack; cracking sound. **2,** crackle; crackling sound. **3,** *colloq.* fuss; hullabaloo. —**провали́ться с тре́ском**, to fail ignominiously; be a complete flop.

треска́ *n.* cod; codfish.

тре́скаться *v.r.impfv.* [*pfv.* **потре́скаться**] **1,** to crack. **2,** to chap; become chapped.

треско́вый *adj.* cod (*attrib.*); codfish (*attrib.*).

трескотня́ *n., colloq.* **1,** crackle; rattle. **2,** chirping (*of insects*). **3,** *fig.* chatter.

треску́чий *adj., colloq.* **1,** crackling. **2,** (*of a sound*) grating; harsh. **3,** (*of frost*) sharp; harsh. **4,** *fig.* high-flown; high-sounding.

тре́снутый *adj., colloq.* cracked.

тре́снуть *v.pfv.* **1,** to crack; burst. **2,** to crackle. **3,** *colloq.* to hit; smack. —**тре́снуться**, *refl., colloq.* to bang: тре́снуться голово́й о перекла́дину, to bang one's head on the crossbar.

трест *n., econ.* trust.

трете́йский *adj.* of arbitration: трете́йский суд, court of arbitration.

тре́тий [*fem.* **-тья**] *ordinal numeral* third. —**тре́тьего дня**, the day before yesterday. *See also* **тре́тье**.

трети́ровать *v.impfv.* [*pres.* **-рую, -руешь**] to slight; snub.

трети́чный *adj.* tertiary.

треть [*pl.* **тре́ти, -те́й, -тя́м**] *n.f.* a third: две тре́ти, two thirds (2/3).

тре́тье *n., decl. as an adj.* third course; dessert.

третьесо́ртный *adj.* third-rate.

третьестепе́нный *adj.* **1,** insignificant. **2,** third-rate.

треуго́лка [*gen. pl.* **-лок**] *n.* cocked hat.

треуго́льник *n.* triangle. —**треуго́льный**, *adj.* triangular.

трефно́й *adj.* (*of food*) non-kosher. —**трефно́е**, *n.* non-kosher food.

трефо́вый *also,* **тре́фовый** *adj., cards* of clubs: тре́фовый туз, ace of clubs.

тре́фы [*gen.* **треф**] *n.pl., cards* clubs.

трёхвале́нтный *adj.* trivalent.

трёхгла́вый *adj.* three-headed. —**трёхгла́вая мы́шца**, triceps.

трёхгоди́чный *adj.* three-year (*attrib.*).

трёхгодова́лый *adj.* three-year-old.

трёхгра́нник *n.* trihedron. —**трёхгра́нный**, *adj.* trihedral.

трёхдне́вный *adj.* three-day (*attrib.*).

трёхколёсный *adj.* three-wheel(ed). —**трёхколёсный велосипе́д**, tricycle.

трёхко́мнатный *adj.* three-room.

трёхкра́тный *adj.* = **троекра́тный**.

трёхле́тие *n.* **1,** third anniversary; third birthday. **2,** three-year period.

трёхле́тний *adj.* **1,** three-year (*attrib.*). **2,** three-year-old.

трёхме́рный *adj.* three-dimensional.

трёхме́сячный *adj.* **1,** three-month (*attrib.*). **2,** three-month-old.

трёхнеде́льный *adj.* **1,** three-week (*attrib.*). **2,** three-week-old.

трёхсло́жный *adj.* three-syllable.

трёхсотле́тие *n.* three-hundredth anniversary; tercentenary. —**трёхсотле́тний**, *adj.* three-hundred-year (*attrib.*); tercentenary.

трёхсо́тый *ordinal numeral* three-hundredth.

трёхсторо́нний *adj.* **1,** three-sided. **2,** trilateral; tripartite; three-way.

трёхцве́тный *adj.* three-colored; tricolored.

трёхчасово́й *adj.* **1,** three-hour (*attrib.*). **2,** *colloq.* three-o'clock (*attrib.*).

трёхчле́н *n.* trinomial. —**трёхчле́нный**, *adj.* trinomial.

трёхэта́жный *adj.* three-story.

треща́ние *n.* **1,** cracking; crackling. **2,** chirping. **3,** chattering.

треща́ть *v.impfv.* [*pres.* **трещу́, трещи́шь**] **1,** to crack. **2,** to crackle. **3,** to chirp. **4,** to ring loudly; make a racket. **5,** *colloq.* to chatter. **6,** *colloq.* (*of one's head*) to be splitting. **7,** *fig.* to be on the verge of collapse.

тре́щина *n.* **1,** crack; split. Дать тре́щину, to crack. **2,** fissure. **3,** *fig.* rift; split; breach.

трещо́тка [*gen. pl.* **-ток**] *n.* **1,** rattle (*for making a noise*). **2,** *colloq.* chatterbox.

три [*gen. & prepl.* **трёх;** *dat.* **трём;** *instr.* **тремя́**] *numeral* three.

триа́да *n.* triad.

триангуля́ция *n.* triangulation.

триа́совый *adj.* Triassic.

трибу́н *n.* tribune.

трибу́на *n.* **1,** speaker's rostrum. **2,** grandstand; stands.

трибуна́л *n.* tribunal.

тривиа́льный *adj.* trite; banal. —**тривиа́льность,** *n.f.* banality.

тригономе́трия *n.* trigonometry. —**тригонометри́ческий,** *adj.* trigonometric.

три́девять *numeral, colloq., in* **за три́девять земе́ль,** at the other end of the world.

тридцатиле́тний *adj.* **1,** thirty-year (*attrib.*). **2,** thirty-year-old.

тридца́тый *ordinal numeral* thirtieth.

три́дцать [*gen., dat. & prepl.* **-цати́;** *instr.* **-цатью́**] *numeral* thirty.

три́жды *adv.* three times; thrice.

тризм *n.* lockjaw.

трико́ *n. indecl.* **1,** tricot. **2,** tights; leotard.

трикота́ж *n.* **1,** knitted fabric. **2,** knitted wear.

трикота́жный *adj.* **1,** knitting (*attrib.*). **2,** knitted.

трикtráк *n.* backgammon.

трили́стник *n.* trefoil; shamrock.

три́ллер *n.* thriller.

триллио́н *n.* trillion (*U.S.*); billion (*Brit.*).

трило́гия *n.* trilogy.

триме́стр *n.* trimester.

трина́дцатый *ordinal numeral* thirteenth.

трина́дцать *numeral* thirteen.

тринитротолуо́л *n.* trinitrotoluene.

три́о *n. indecl.* trio.

трио́д *n.* triode.

трио́ль *n.f., music* triplet.

три́ппер *n.* gonorrhea.

три́птих *n.* triptych.

три́ста [*gen.* **трёхсо́т;** *dat.* **трёмста́м;** *instr.* **тремя́ста́ми;** *prepl.* **трёхста́х**] *numeral* three hundred.

три́тий *n.* tritium.

трито́н *n., zool.* triton; newt.

триумви́р *n.* triumvir. —**триумвира́т,** *n.* triumvirate.

триу́мф *n.* triumph. —**триумфа́льный,** *adj.* triumphal.

трихи́на *n.* trichina.

трихинеллёз *n.* trichinosis.

тро́гательный *adj.* touching; moving; poignant. —**тро́гательность,** *n.f.* poignancy.

тро́гать *v.impfv.* [*pfv.* **тро́нуть**] **1,** to touch. **2,** to bother; disturb. **3,** to touch; move; affect (*emotionally*). **4,** *v.i.* to start moving. —**тро́гаться,** *refl.* **1,** to start moving. **2,** [*often* **тро́нуться в путь**] to set out; start out. **3,** (*of ice*) to begin to break up. **4,** to be touched; be moved (*emotionally*). *See also* **тро́нуть.**

тро́е [*infl. like* **дво́е**] *collective numeral* three.

троекра́тный *adj.* **1,** three-time. **2,** threefold.

тро́ица *n.* **1,** Trinity. **2,** *colloq.* Whitsunday.

тро́ицын *adj., in* **тро́ицын день,** Whitsunday.

тро́йка *n.* **1,** the numeral 3. **2,** *colloq.* anything numbered 3. **3,** troika. **4,** a grade of "three," signifying "satisfactory." **5,** *cards* three. **6,** *colloq.* [*also,* **костю́м-тро́йка**] three-piece suit.

тройно́й *adj.* triple; three-way. —**тройно́й прыжо́к,** *sports* hop, step and jump.

тро́йня [*gen. pl.* **тро́ен**] *n.* triplets.

тро́йственный *adj.* **1,** triple. **2,** tripartite.

тролле́йбус *n.* trolley bus. —**тролле́йбусный,** *adj.* trolley-bus (*attrib.*).

тролль *n.m., folklore* troll.

тромб *n.* blood clot. —**тромбо́з,** *n.* thrombosis.

тромбо́н *n.* trombone. —**тромбони́ст,** *n.* trombonist.

трон *n.* throne. —**тро́нный,** *adj.* throne (*attrib.*).

тро́нутый *adj.* **1,** [*short form only*] touched; moved (*emotionally*). **2,** *colloq.* touched in the head; wacky.

тро́нуть *v.pfv.* **1,** *pfv. of* **тро́гать. 2,** to touch; damage: **тро́нутый моро́зом,** touched (*or* nipped) by the frost. —**тро́нуться,** *refl.* **1,** *pfv. of* **тро́гаться. 2,** *colloq.* to be slightly crazy (*or* wacky).

троп *n.* trope.

тропа́ *n.* [*pl.* **тро́пы**] *n.* path.

тро́пик *n.* **1,** tropic: **тро́пик Ра́ка,** Tropic of Cancer; **тро́пик Козеро́га,** Tropic of Capricorn. **2,** *pl.* tropics.

тропи́нка [*gen. pl.* **-нок**] *n.* path.

тропи́ческий *adj.* tropical. —**тропи́ческая лихора́дка** *or* **маляри́я,** jungle fever. —**тропи́ческий по́яс,** Torrid Zone.

тропосфе́ра *n.* troposphere.

трос *n.* rope; cable.

трости́нка [*gen. pl.* **-нок**] *n.* thin reed.

тростни́к [*gen.* **-ника́**] *n.* reed; rush; cane. —**са́харный тростни́к,** sugar cane.

тростнико́вый *adj.* **1,** reed (*attrib.*); rush (*attrib.*); cane (*attrib.*). **2,** overgrown with reeds; reedy.

тро́сточка [*gen. pl.* **-чек**] *n.* cane; walking stick.

трость [*pl.* **тро́сти, -сте́й, -стя́м**] *n.f.* cane; walking stick.

троти́л *n.* trinitrotoluene; TNT.

тротуа́р *n.* sidewalk; pavement.

трофе́й *n.* **1,** trophy; memento. **2,** *pl.* spoils; booty. —**трофе́йный,** *adj.* captured (*in war*).

трохе́й *n.* trochee. —**трохеи́ческий,** *adj.* trochaic.

трою́родный *adj., denoting relationships of cousins:* **трою́родный брат; трою́родная сестра́,** second cousin.

троя́кий *adj.* triple; threefold.

троя́нский *adj.* Trojan.

труба́ [*pl.* **тру́бы**] *n.* **1,** pipe: **водопрово́дная труба́,** water pipe. **Дымова́я труба́,** chimney; smokestack. **Сто́чная труба́,** sewer. **Аэродинами́ческая труба́,** wind tunnel. **2,** trumpet. **3,** *anat.* tube. —**вы́лететь в трубу́,** *colloq.* to go broke. —**пусти́ть в трубу́,** *colloq.* **1,** to bankrupt; ruin. **2,** to squander; dissipate.

трубаду́р *n.* troubadour.

труба́ч [*gen.* **-бача́**] *n.* trumpet player.

труби́ть *v.impfv.* [*pfv.* **протруби́ть;** *pres.* **-блю́, -би́шь**] **1,** (*with* **в** + *acc.*) to blow (a trumpet). **2,** to sound; signal; announce. **3,** (*of a trumpet or horn*) to sound; blare. **4,** (*with* **о**) *colloq.* to trumpet; crow about.

тру́бка [*gen. pl.* -**бок**] *n.* **1,** tube; pipe. **2,** receiver (*of a telephone*). Возьми́те тру́бку!, pick up the phone! Я переда́м тру́бку (+ *dat.*), I'll put ... on. **3,** pipe (*for smoking*). **4,** fuse. **5,** roll (*of material*).

трубкозу́б *n.* aardvark.

тру́бный *adj.* **1,** pipe (*attrib.*). **2,** trumpet (*attrib.*).

трубопрово́д *n.* conduit; pipeline.

трубочи́ст *n.* chimney sweep.

тру́бочный *adj.* pipe (*attrib.*): трубочный таба́к, pipe tobacco.

тру́бчатый *adj.* tubular.

труд [*gen.* **труда́**] *n.* **1,** labor: ручно́й труд, manual labor. Вкла́дывать *or* класть мно́го труда́ в (+ *acc.*), to put a lot of work into. **2,** effort; trouble: Не сто́ит труда́, it's not worth the trouble. **3,** (written) work (*usually of a scientific nature*). —дать себе́ (*or* взять на себя́) труд, to take the trouble. —без труда́, without difficulty; easily. —с трудо́м, **1,** with difficulty. **2,** hardly; scarcely; barely.

труди́ться *v.r.impfv.* [*pres.* **тружу́сь, тру́дишься**] **1,** to work; labor; toil. **2,** *colloq.* to bother; take the trouble.

тру́дно *adv.* with difficulty. Тру́дно произноси́мое сло́во, a difficult (*or* hard) word to pronounce. —*adj.*, used predicatively, difficult; hard: Тру́дно сказа́ть, it is difficult/hard to say. Мне тру́дно пове́рить э́тому, I find that hard to believe.

тру́дность *n.f.* difficulty.

тру́дный *adj.* [*short form* **тру́ден, трудна́, тру́дно, тру́дны** *or* **трудны́**] difficult; hard.

трудово́й *adj.* **1,** labor (*attrib.*). **2,** working. **3,** earned: трудовы́е дохо́ды, earned income. —**трудова́я кни́жка,** work-record book.

трудоде́нь [*gen.* -**дня́**] *n.m.* workday (*unit of payment on collective farms*).

трудоёмкий *adj.* labor-intensive.

трудолюби́вый *adj.* hard-working; industrious. —**трудолю́бие,** *n.* industriousness.

трудоспосо́бный *adj.* able to work; able-bodied. —**трудоспосо́бность,** *n.f.* ability to work.

трудотерапи́я *n.* occupational therapy.

трудоустра́ивать *v.impfv.* [*pfv.* **трудоустро́ить**] to place in a job.

трудоустро́йство *n.* job placement.

трудя́щийся *adj.* working; laboring. —*n.* worker; laborer.

тру́женик *n.* worker; toiler.

труни́ть *v.impfv.* (*with* над) to make fun of; kid.

труп *n.* dead body; corpse; cadaver.

трупиа́л *n.* oriole.

тру́пный *adj.* **1,** of or like a corpse. **2,** (*of an odor*) putrid. —**тру́пное окочене́ние,** rigor mortis. —**тру́пный яд,** ptomaine.

тру́ппа *n.* company; troupe.

трус *n.m.* [*fem.* -**си́ха**] coward.

тру́сики [*gen.* -**ков**] *n.pl.* **1,** shorts. **2,** undershorts; underpants; panties.

тру́сить *v.impfv.* [*pfv.* **стру́сить;** *pres.* **тру́шу, тру́сишь**] to be a coward; be afraid; get cold feet.

труси́ть *v.impfv.* [*pres.* **трушу́, труси́шь**] *colloq.* to trot.

труси́ха *n.*, *fem. of* **трус.**

трусли́вый *adj.* cowardly.

тру́сость *n.f.* cowardice.

трусца́ *n.*, *colloq.* trot. —**бе́гать трусцо́й,** to jog.

трусы́ [*gen.* -**со́в**] *n.pl.* **1,** shorts. **2,** undershorts; underpants.

трут *n.* tinder.

тру́тень [*gen.* -**тня**] *n.m.* drone.

труха́ *n.* **1,** dust; flakes; bits (*of hay, straw, rotten wood, etc.*). **2,** *fig.* trash; rubbish.

трухля́вый *adj.* moldering; rotten.

трущо́ба *n.* **1,** thicket. **2,** out-of-the-way place. **3,** slum; *pl.* slums.

трын-трава́ *predicate* (*with dat.*) *colloq.* all the same: Ему́ всё трын-трава́, it's all the same to him; he couldn't care less.

трюи́зм *n.* truism.

трюк *n.* trick; stunt. —**трю́ковый,** *adj.* trick (*attrib.*).

трюм *n.* hold (*of a ship*).

трюмо́ *n. indecl.* pier glass.

трю́фель [*pl.* **трю́фели, -ле́й, -ля́м**] *n.m.* **1,** truffle. **2,** *pl.* chocolate truffles.

тряпи́чник *n.* ragman.

тряпи́чный *adj.* rag (*attrib.*). —**тряпи́чная ку́кла,** rag doll.

тря́пка [*gen. pl.* -**пок**] *n.* **1,** rag. **2,** a cloth. **3,** *pl., colloq.* clothes; finery. **4,** *colloq.* milksop; weakling.

тряпьё *n.* rags.

тряси́на *n.* quagmire.

тря́ска *n.* bumpiness; shaking.

тря́ский *adj.* **1,** (*of a vehicle*) that shakes a lot; shaky. **2,** (*of a road*) bumpy.

трясогу́зка [*gen. pl.* -**зок**] *n.* wagtail (*bird*).

трясти́ *v.impfv.* [*pres.* **трясу́, трясёшь;** *past* **тряс, трясла́, трясло́, трясли́**] **1,** [*pfv.* **тряхну́ть**] to shake: трясти́ де́рево, to shake a tree; трясти́ голово́й, to shake one's head. **2,** [*pfv.* **вы́трясти**] to shake out. **3,** [*impfv. only*] *impers.* (*of a person*) to be shaking: Его́ всего́ трясёт, he is shaking all over. **4,** [*pfv.* **тряхну́ть**] *v.i.* (*of a vehicle*) to shake. —**трясти́сь,** *refl.* [*impfv. only*] **1,** to shake. **2,** to tremble. **3,** *colloq.* to bounce along. **4,** [*impfv. only*] (*with* над) *colloq.* to watch; agonize over the spending of: трясти́сь над ка́ждой копе́йкой, to watch every penny.

тряхну́ть *v.*, *pfv. of* **трясти́** (*in senses #1 and #4*).

тсс *interj.* hush!

тсу́га *n.* hemlock (*tree*).

ту *adj., fem. acc. of* **тот.**

туале́т *n.* **1,** dress; attire. **2,** toilet; grooming. **3,** dressing table; vanity. **4,** rest room; washroom.

туале́тный *adj.* toilet (*attrib.*). —**туале́тный сто́лик,** dressing table; vanity.

ту́ба *n.* tuba.

туберкулёз *n.* tuberculosis. —**туберкулёзный,** *adj.* tubercular; tuberculous.

туберо́за *n.* tuberose.

туви́нец [*gen.* -**нца**] *n.m.* [*fem.* -**нка**] Tuvinian (*one of a people inhabiting southern Siberia*). —**туви́нский,** *adj.* Tuvinian.

ту́го *adv.* **1,** tight; tightly. **2,** *colloq.* with difficulty; slowly: Де́ло идёт ту́го, things are moving slowly.

—*adj., used predicatively, colloq.* **1,** difficult: Ему́ приходи́лось ту́го, he was having a hard time of it. **2,** short of: У меня́ с деньга́ми ту́го, I am short of money.

тугоду́м *n., colloq.* dimwit.

туго́й *adj.* [*comp.* ту́же] **1,** tight; taut. **2,** tightly filled; stuffed. **3,** slow to grasp things; dense; dull. —**туго́й на де́ньги,** tight with one's money. —**туго́й на язы́к,** slow of speech; inarticulate. —**туго́й на́ ухо,** hard of hearing.

тугоу́хий *adj.* hard of hearing; partially deaf.

туда́ *adv., expressing direction,* there: Посмотри́те туда́!, look over there! Положи́те э́то туда́, put it (over) there. —**не туда́,** to the wrong place; in the wrong direction. Вы туда́ не попа́ли, you've got the wrong number (*on the telephone*). —**ни туда́ ни сюда́,** neither backward nor forward; unable to move. —**туда́ и обра́тно,** there and back. Биле́т туда́ и обра́тно, round-trip ticket. Пое́здка туда́ и обра́тно, round trip. —**туда́ и сюда́,** back and forth.

туда́-сюда́ *adv., colloq.* **1,** here and there; around and about. **2,** all right; so-so; passable.

ту́же *adj., comp. of* туго́й.

тужи́ть *v.impfv.* [*pres.* тужу́, ту́жишь] *colloq.* to grieve.

ту́житься *v.r.impfv., colloq.* to exert oneself; make a great effort.

тужу́рка [*gen. pl.* -рок] *n.* man's double-breasted jacket.

туз [*gen. & acc.* туза́] *n.* **1,** *cards* ace. **2,** *colloq.* bigwig.

тузе́мец [*gen.* -мца] *n.m.* [*fem.* -мка] *obs.* native. —**тузе́мный,** *adj., obs.* native; indigenous.

тузи́ть *v.impfv.* [*pfv.* оттузи́ть; *pres.* тужу́, тузи́шь] *colloq.* to thrash; pommel.

тука́н *n.* toucan.

ту́кать *v.impfv.* [*pfv.* ту́кнуть] *colloq.* **1,** to slam. **2,** to tap; clack. —**ту́каться,** *refl.* (*with* о + *acc.*) *colloq.* to bang into.

ту́лий *n.* thulium.

ту́ловище *n.* trunk; torso.

тулу́п *n.* sheepskin coat.

тулья́ [*gen. pl.* туле́й] *n.* crown (*of a hat*).

тума́к [*gen.* тумака́; *acc.* тума́к *or* тумака́] *n., colloq.* punch; wallop; clout.

тума́н *n.* fog.

тума́нить *v.impfv.* [*pfv.* затума́нить] to cloud; obscure. —**тума́ниться,** *refl.* **1,** to be obscured by fog. **2,** (*of one's eyes*) to become dim; (*of the senses*) to become muddled.

тума́нность *n.f.* **1,** fog; fogginess. **2,** *pl.* vagueness; obscurity. **3,** *astron.* nebula.

тума́нный *adj.* **1,** foggy; misty. **2,** *fig.* hazy; vague.

ту́мба *n.* **1,** curbside stone or post. **2,** stand; pedestal.

ту́мбочка [*gen. pl.* -чек] *n.* night table.

тунг *n.* tung tree. —**ту́нговый,** *adj.* tung (*atttrib.*): ту́нговое ма́сло, tung oil.

ту́ндра *n.* tundra. —**ту́ндровый,** *adj.* tundra (*attrib.*).

туне́ц [*gen.* тунца́] *n.* tuna.

тунея́дец [*gen.* -дца] *n.* parasite; sponger. —**туне-я́дство,** *n.* parasitism.

туни́ка *n.* tunic (*worn in ancient times*).

тунне́ль (нэ) *n.m.* tunnel.

тупе́ть *v.impfv.* **1,** to become dull. **2,** *fig.* to become dazed. **3,** *fig.* (*of the senses*) to become dulled.

ту́пик *n.* puffin (*bird*).

тупи́к [*gen.* тупика́] *n.* **1,** blind alley; dead-end street. **2,** *fig.* impasse; deadlock. Перегово́ры зашли́ в тупи́к, negotiations have reached an impasse; negotiations are deadlocked/stalemated/stalled/. —**ста́вить в тупи́к,** to put on the spot; throw for a loss; confound. —**стать в тупи́к,** to be on the spot; be at a loss.

тупико́вый *adj.* dead-end.

тупи́ть *v.impfv.* [*pfv.* иступи́ть *or* затупи́ть; *pres.* туплю́, ту́пишь] to blunt; dull; take the edge off. —**тупи́ться,** *refl.* to become dull.

тупи́ца *n.m. & f.* dimwit; dullard; dolt.

ту́по *adv.* with a dull or blank look on one's face.

тупоголо́вый *adj., colloq.* dimwitted; thickheaded.

тупо́й *adj.* **1,** dull; blunt. **2,** (*of pain, sounds, etc.*) dull. **3,** (*of a person*) dull; obtuse. **4,** (*of a look, expression, etc.*) vacant; blank. —**тупо́й у́гол,** obtuse angle. —**тупо́е ударе́ние,** grave accent.

ту́пость *n.f.* **1,** dullness; bluntness. **2,** dullness; obtuseness.

тупоу́мие *n.* dullness; obtuseness. —**тупоу́мный,** *adj.* thickheaded; dimwitted.

тур *n.* **1,** *dancing* turn (*around the room*). **2,** round (*of a tournament, negotiations, etc.*). **3,** stage; phase. **4,** aurochs. **5,** Caucasian wild goat.

тура́ *n., chess* rook; castle.

турба́за *n.* tourist center. —**молодёжная турба́за,** youth hostel.

турби́на *n.* turbine. —**турби́нный,** *adj.* turbine (*attrib.*).

турбовинтово́й *adj.* turboprop (*attrib.*).

турбореакти́вный *adj.* turbojet (*attrib.*).

туре́цкий *adj.* Turkish. —**туре́цкий бараба́н,** bass drum. —**туре́цкий горо́х,** chickpea.

тури́зм *n.* tourism. —**тури́ст,** *n.* tourist.

туристи́ческий *adj.* **1,** tourist (*attrib.*). **2,** walking (*attrib.*); hiking (*attrib.*): туристи́ческий похо́д, walking tour; hiking expedition. —**туристи́ческое бюро́; туристи́ческое аге́нтство,** travel agency.

тури́стский *adj.* tourist (*attrib.*).

туркме́н [*gen. pl.* -ме́н] *n.m.* [*fem.* -ме́нка] Turkmen (*indigenous inhabitant of Turkmenistan*). —**туркме́н-ский,** *adj.* Turkmen.

турмали́н *n.* tourmaline.

ту́рман *n.* tumbler pigeon.

турне́ (нэ) *n.neut. indecl.* tour.

турни́к [*gen.* -ника́] *n., sports* horizontal bar.

турнике́т *n.* turnstile.

турни́р *n.* tournament.

ту́рок [*gen.* ту́рка; *gen. pl.* ту́рок] *n.m.* [*fem.* тур-ча́нка] Turk.

турухта́н *n.* ruff (*bird*).

ту́скло *adv.* dimly.

ту́склость *n.f.* dullness; dimness.

ту́склый *adj.* **1,** (*of light*) dim. **2,** (*of metals*) dull; lackluster. **3,** dreary; overcast. **4,** *fig.* colorless; insipid.

тускне́ть *v.impfv.* [*pfv.* **потускне́ть**] **1,** to grow dim; lose its luster. **2,** *fig.* to fade; wane. **3,** [*impfv. only*] (*with* **пе́ред**) to pale (before).

тусо́вка [*gen. pl.* **-вок**] *n., colloq.* **1,** gathering. **2,** group; clique.

тут *adv., expressing location,* here. —(**быть**) **тут как тут,** *colloq.* to appear like clockwork; be Johnny-on-the-spot. —**не ту́т-то бы́ло,** it was not to be. —**там и тут,** here and there. —**тут же,** then and there; there and then.

ту́товник *n.* mulberry tree.

ту́товый *adj.* mulberry (*attrib.*). —**ту́товый шелкопря́д,** silkworm. —**ту́товая я́года,** mulberry.

ту́фелька [*gen. pl.* **-лек**] *n.* **1,** small shoe; fancy shoe. **2,** paramecium.

ту́фля [*gen. pl.* **ту́фель**] *n.* shoe: ту́фли на высо́ких каблука́х, high-heeled shoes. —**дома́шние ту́фли,** (bedroom) slippers.

ту́хлость *n.f.* rottenness.

ту́хлый *adj.* rotten; spoiled; tainted.

тухля́тина *n., colloq.* **1,** food that has spoiled or become rotten. **2,** foul odor from such food.

ту́хнуть *v.impfv.* [*past* тух *or* ту́хнул, ту́хла] **1,** [*pfv.* **поту́хнуть**] (*of something burning*) to go out. **2,** [*pfv.* **проту́хнуть**] to spoil; rot.

ту́ча *n.* cloud; storm cloud.

тучне́ть *v.impfv.* [*pfv.* **потучне́ть**] to grow fat; put on weight.

ту́чность *n.f.* **1,** obesity; corpulence. **2,** richness; fertility.

ту́чный *adj.* **1,** fat; stout; obese. **2,** (*of soil*) rich; fertile. **3,** (*of grass, grain, a meadow, etc.*) lush.

туш *n.* flourish (*of trumpets*).

ту́ша *n.* carcass.

туше́ *n.neut. indecl.* touch (*when playing a musical instrument*).

тушева́ть *v.impfv.* [*pfv.* **затушева́ть**; *pres.* **-шу́ю, -шу́ешь**] **1,** to shade; add shading to. **2,** *fig.* to soften; tone down. —**тушева́ться,** *refl.* [*pfv.* **стушева́ться**] *colloq.* to become flustered.

тушёвка *n.* shading.

туше́ние *n.* **1,** extinguishing. **2,** stewing.

тушёнка *n., colloq.* canned stew.

тушёный *adj.* stewed; braised.

туши́ть *v.impfv.* [*pres.* **тушу́, ту́шишь**] **1,** [*pfv.* **поту́шить**] to put out; extinguish (a fire, candle, etc.); turn out; turn off (a light). **2,** [*pfv.* **стуши́ть**] to stew; braise.

тушка́нчик *n.* jerboa.

тушь *n.f.* **1,** India ink. **2,** mascara.

тща́тельный *adj.* careful; thorough; painstaking. —**тща́тельно,** *adv.* carefully; thoroughly; painstakingly. —**тща́тельность,** *n.f.* care; thoroughness.

тщеду́шие *n.* frailty. —**тщеду́шный,** *adj.* frail.

тщесла́вие *n.* vanity. —**тщесла́вный,** *adj.* vain.

тще́тный *adj.* vain; futile. —**тще́тно,** *adv.* vainly; in vain. —**тще́тность,** *n.f.* futility.

тщи́ться *v.r.impfv.* (*with inf.*) to try (to); endeavor (to); take pains (to).

ты [*gen. & acc.* тебя́; *dat. & prepl.* тебе́; *instr.* тобо́й *or* тобо́ю] *pers. pron., 2nd person sing.* you (*familiar*). —**быть с** (+ *instr.*) **на ты,** to address each other as "ты" (*as opposed to* "вы").

ты́кать¹ *v.impfv.* [*pfv.* **ткнуть**; *pres.* **ты́чу, ты́чешь**] (*with acc. or instr.*) **1,** *colloq.* to stick; thrust. **2,** to poke; jab. **3,** *in* ты́кать па́льцем на (+ *acc.*), to point one's finger at. —**ты́каться,** *refl., colloq.* **1,** (*with в* + *acc.*) to bang into. **2,** (*with instr.*) to stick; poke (one's nose, head, etc.) into. **3,** to rush about; bustle about.

ты́кать² *v.impfv.* [*pres.* **ты́каю, ты́каешь**] *colloq.* to address someone using the familiar pronoun **ты.**

ты́ква *n.* pumpkin. —**ты́квенный,** *adj.* pumpkin (*attrib.*).

тыл [*2nd loc.* тылу́; *pl.* тылы́] *n., mil.* **1,** rear. **2,** rear services. —**тыл и снабже́ние,** logistics.

тылово́й *adj., mil.* rear.

ты́льный *adj.* rear; back. —**ты́льная сторона́ руки́,** back of the hand.

тын *n.* paling; fence.

ты́сяча *numeral* thousand.

тысячекра́тный *adj.* thousandfold.

тысячеле́тие *n.* **1,** millennium. **2,** thousandth anniversary.

тысячеле́тний *adj.* **1,** thousand-year (*attrib.*). **2,** thousand-year-old.

ты́сячная *n., decl. as an adj.* thousandth: одна́ ты́сячная, one-thousandth.

ты́сячный *ordinal numeral* thousandth. —*adj.* consisting of many thousands: ты́сячная толпа́, a crowd of many thousands.

тычи́нка *n.* stamen.

тычо́к [*gen.* тычка́] *n., colloq.* **1,** poke; jab. **2,** something sticking up in the air.

тьма *n.* **1,** darkness. **2,** (*with gen.*) *colloq.* a host (of); a multitude (of).

тьфу *interj.* bah!; phooey!

тюбете́йка [*gen. pl.* **-те́ек**] *n.* skullcap (*worn in Central Asia*).

тю́бик *n.* tube (*for glue, toothpaste, etc.*).

тю́бинг *n.* tubing.

тюк [*gen.* тюка́] *n.* **1,** bale. **2,** bundle.

тю́кать *v.impfv.* [*pfv.* **тю́кнуть**] *colloq.* to bang.

тю́левый *adj.* tulle.

тюле́невый *adj.* **1,** seal (*attrib.*). **2,** sealskin.

тюле́ний [*fem.* **-нья**] *adj.* seal (*attrib.*).

тюле́нь *n.m.* seal (*sea animal*).

тюль *n.m.* tulle.

тюльпа́н *n.* tulip. —**тюльпа́нный,** *adj.* tulip (*attrib.*).

тюрба́н *n.* turban.

тюрбо́ *n. indecl.* turbot.

тюре́мный *adj.* prison (*attrib.*); jail (*attrib.*). —**тюре́мное заключе́ние,** imprisonment. Приговори́ть к тюре́мному заключе́нию, to sentence to prison.

тюре́мщик *n., colloq.* jailer.

тю́ркский *adj.* Turkic.

тюрьма́ [*pl.* тю́рьмы, тю́рем] *n.* jail; prison.

тюфя́к [*gen.* тюфяка́] *n.* mattress (*filled with straw, horsehair, etc.*).

тя́вкать *v.impfv.* [*pfv.* **тя́вкнуть**] to yelp.

тяг *n., in* **дать тя́гу,** *colloq.* to take to one's heels; make tracks.

тя́га *n.* **1,** pulling; towing. **2,** pulling power; traction. **3,** thrust (*of an engine*). **4,** rod: соедини́тельная тя́га, connecting rod. **5,** draft (*of a chimney*). **6,** *fig.* (*with* к) bent (for); craving (for).

тяга́ться *v.r.impfv.* [*pfv.* **потяга́ться**] (*with* с + *instr.*) *colloq.* to compete (with); contend (with); vie (with).

тяга́ч [*gen.* **-гача́**] *n.* tractor (*for hauling trailers*). —артиллери́йский тяга́ч, artillery mover. —тяга́ч с прице́пом, tractor-trailer.

тя́гло *n.* **1,** *hist.* tax; impost; assessment. **2,** [*also,* **живо́е тя́гло**] draft animals.

тя́гловый *adj.* **1,** *hist.* taxed. **2,** (*of animals*) draft.

тя́глый *adj.* (*of animals*) draft.

тя́говый *adj.* **1,** tractive. **2,** used to haul: тя́говый кана́т, hauling rope.

тя́гостный *adj.* **1,** burdensome; onerous. **2,** painful; distressing.

тя́гость *n.f.* burden: быть в тя́гость (+ *dat.*), to be a burden (to).

тягота́ [*pl.* **тя́готы**] *n.* **1,** burden. **2,** *pl.* (*with gen.*) the rigors (of): тя́готы пути́, the rigors of the trip.

тяготе́ние *n.* **1,** *physics* gravity. **2,** (*with* к) gravitation (toward). **3,** *fig.* (*with* к) bent (for); liking (for).

тяготе́ть *v.impfv.* **1,** (*with* к) to gravitate (toward); be drawn (toward). **2,** (*with* над) to hang over; tower over. **3,** *fig.* (*with* над) to hang over; weigh upon.

тяготи́ть *v.impfv.* [*pres.* **-щу́, -ти́шь**] **1,** to burden; weigh down. **2,** (*of an article of clothing*) to bother; make uncomfortable. —**тяготи́ться,** *refl.* (*with instr.*) to be burdened (by); feel (something) as a burden.

тягу́честь *n.f.* **1,** stretchability. **2,** malleability. **3,** viscosity.

тягу́чий *adj.* **1,** stretchable. **2,** malleable; ductile. **3,** viscous. **4,** *fig.* slow; drawn-out. **5,** *fig.* dull; boring; monotonous.

тягча́йший *adj., superl. of* **тя́жкий,** very grave.

тя́жба *n., obs.* **1,** lawsuit; litigation. **2,** dispute.

тяжелённый *adj., colloq.* very heavy.

тяжеле́ть *v.impfv.* to become heavy; grow heavy.

тяжело́ *adv.* **1,** heavily. **2,** hard: тяжело́ рабо́тать, to work hard. **3,** gravely; seriously; severely. Он умира́л тяжело́, he died a painful death. —*adj., used predicatively (often with dat.)* **1,** hard; difficult. **2,** miserable; wretched. **3,** grievous; painful.

тяжелоатле́т *n.* **1,** wrestler. **2,** weightlifter.

тяжелове́с *n., sports* heavyweight.

тяжелове́сный *adj.* heavy; ponderous.

тяжёлый *adj.* **1,** heavy. **2,** hard; difficult; arduous. **3,** grave; serious; severe. **4,** painful; grievous; distressing. **5,** (*of thoughts, a feeling, odor, etc.*) oppressive. **6,** (*of a style of writing*) ponderous.

тя́жесть *n.f.* **1,** weight. **2,** load. **3,** *pl., sports* weights. **4,** *physics* gravity. **5,** heaviness. **6,** gravity; severity.

тя́жкий *adj.* **1,** *obs.* heavy. **2,** (*of work*) hard; arduous. **3,** grave; severe. **4,** distressing. —пусти́ться во все тя́жкие, **1,** to let oneself go. **2,** to go all out.

тяну́ть *v.impfv.* [*pfv.* **потяну́ть;** *pres.* **тяну́, тя́нешь**] **1,** to pull; tug. **2,** to haul; tow. **3,** to stretch; extend. **4,** to draw; attract. **5,** *colloq.* to drag (someone) somewhere against his will. **6,** *v.i.* (*with* с + *instr.*) to delay: тяну́ть с отве́том, to delay in answering. **7,** [*impfv. only*] to drag out; prolong. Тяну́ть вре́мя, to procrastinate; stall. **8,** [*impfv. only*] to sustain; prolong (a note, song, etc.). **9,** (*of a chimney*) to draw. **10,** *v.i.* to sustain oneself; subsist. **11,** *usu. impers.* to blow gently; waft. **12,** to weigh (so much). **13,** *impers.* to long to: Его́ тя́нет домо́й, he is longing to go home. —**тяну́ться,** *refl.* **1,** [*impfv. only*] to stretch. **2,** [*pfv.* **протяну́ться**] to stretch; extend (*over a distance*). **3,** [*pfv.* **потяну́ться**] (*with* за *or* к) to reach for; reach out for. **4,** [*pfv.* **потяну́ться**] to follow along; follow in succession. **5,** [*pfv.* **протяну́ться**] to move slowly along. **6,** [*impfv. only*] to last; drag on. **7,** [*impfv. only*] (*with* к) to be drawn (toward). **8,** [*impfv. only*] (*of clouds, smoke, etc.*) to drift. **9,** [*impfv. only*] (*with* за + *instr.*) *colloq.* to try to keep up (with).

тяну́чка *n.* taffy.

тя́пка [*gen. pl.* **тя́пок**] *n.* chopping knife; cleaver.

тя́тя *n.m., colloq.* dad; pop.

У

У, у *n.neut.* twentieth letter of the Russian alphabet.

у *prep., with gen.* **1,** by; at; near: стоя́ть у окна́, to stand at/by/near the window. **2,** at the home of: Обе́дать у Петро́вых, to have dinner at (the home of) the Petrovs. Жить у родны́х, to live with relatives. **3,** *indicating possession:* У меня́ три бра́та, I have three brothers. **4,** from: узна́ть что́-нибудь у сосе́да, to find out something from one's neighbor.

у- *prefix* **1,** *indicating movement away:* убега́ть, to run away. **2,** *indicating the imparting of a quality or attribute:* удлиня́ть, to lengthen; углубля́ть, to deepen. **3,** *indicating reduction:* убавля́ть, to reduce; ушива́ть, to take in.

уба́вить [*infl.* -влю, -вишь] *v., pfv. of* **убавля́ть.** —**уба́виться,** *refl., pfv. of* **убавля́ться.**

убавля́ть *v.impfv.* [*pfv.* **уба́вить**] **1,** to reduce; lower. **2,** *in* убавля́ть в ве́се, *colloq.* to lose weight. —**убавля́ться,** *refl.* **1,** to be reduced in size; become smaller. **2,** to decrease; diminish.

убаю́кать *v., pfv. of* **баю́кать** *and* **убаю́кивать.**

убаю́кивать *v.impfv.* [*pfv.* **убаю́кать**] **1,** to lull to sleep. **2,** *fig.* to lull.

убега́ть *v.impfv.* [*pfv.* **убежа́ть**] **1,** to run away; flee. **2,** to escape. **3,** [*impfv. only*] (*of inanimate objects*) to extend; retreat; disappear (into the distance). **4,** *colloq.* to boil over.

убеди́тельно *adv.* **1,** convincingly; persuasively. **2,** earnestly: Убеди́тельно прошу́ вас, I urge you; I beg of you.

убеди́тельность *n.f.* persuasiveness.

убеди́тельный *adj.* **1,** convincing; persuasive. **2,** (*of a request*) urgent; earnest.

убеди́ть [*infl.* -ди́шь, -ди́т; *1st person sing. not used*] *v., pfv. of* **убежда́ть.** —**убеди́ться,** *refl., pfv. of* **убежда́ться.**

убежа́ть [*infl. like* **бежа́ть**] *v., pfv. of* **убега́ть.**

убежда́ть *v.impfv.* [*pfv.* **убеди́ть**] **1,** (*with* в + *prepl.*) to convince (of). **2,** (*with inf.*) to persuade (to). **3,** [*impfv. only*] to try to persuade; urge. —**убежда́ться,** *refl.* (*with* в + *prepl. or a dependent clause*) **1,** to become convinced (of *or* that). **2,** to make sure (of *or* that). **3,** *in* сам убеди́ться, to see for oneself.

убежде́ние *n.* **1,** persuasion. **2,** *usu. pl.* belief; conviction.

убеждённо *adv.* with conviction. —**убеждённость,** *n.f.* conviction; certainty.

убеждённый *adj.* **1,** convinced. **2,** staunch; confirmed.

убе́жище *n.* **1,** refuge. **2,** asylum: пра́во убе́жища, right of asylum. **3,** *mil.* shelter; dugout.

убере́чь *v.pfv.* [*infl. like* **бере́чь**] to protect. —**убере́чься,** *refl.* to protect oneself.

убива́ть *v.impfv.* [*pfv.* **уби́ть**] to kill. —**убива́ться,** *refl., colloq.* **1,** to be killed. **2,** to hurt oneself. **3,** [*impfv. only*] to work oneself to the bone; "kill oneself". **4,** [*impfv. only*] to grieve.

уби́йственный *adj.* **1,** deadly. **2,** murderous; unbearable. **3,** (*of a result or consequence*) disastrous. **4,** (*of news, criticism, a look, etc.*) devastating.

уби́йство *n.* murder; assassination.

уби́йца *n.m. & f.* killer; murderer; assassin.

убира́ть *v.impfv.* [*pfv.* **убра́ть**] **1,** to take away; remove. **2,** to put away. **3,** to delete; take out. **4,** to clean up; tidy up; straighten up. **5,** *in* убра́ть со стола́, to clear the table. **6,** to make (a bed). **7,** *colloq.* to take in (a garment). **8,** to gather in; harvest. **9,** to decorate; adorn. —**убира́ться,** *refl., colloq.* **1,** to clear out; beat it; vamoose. **2,** to clean up; tidy up.

уби́тый *adj.* **1,** killed; murdered. **2,** *fig.* crushed (*in spirit*): уби́тый го́рем, heartbroken; broken-hearted. —*n.* dead man; person who has been killed. —**спать как уби́тый,** to sleep like a log.

уби́ть [*infl.* убью́, убьёшь] *v., pfv. of* **убива́ть.** —**уби́ться,** *refl., pfv. of* **убива́ться.**

ублажа́ть *v.impfv.* [*pfv.* **ублажи́ть**] *colloq.* to indulge; cater to.

ублю́док [*gen.* -дка] *n., colloq.* **1,** cur; mongrel. **2,** cur (*contemptible person*).

убо́гий *adj.* **1,** wretched; squalid. **2,** crippled; disfigured. **3,** *fig.* empty; sterile.

убо́гость *n.f.* **1,** utter poverty; squalor. **2,** *fig.* emptiness; sterility; poverty.

убо́жество *n.* **1,** utter poverty; squalor. **2,** *fig.* emptiness; sterility; poverty. **3,** *obs.* physical disability; deformity.

убо́й *n.* slaughtering; slaughter (*of animals*). —**корми́ть (как) на убо́й,** to stuff to the gills. —**посыла́ть (кого́-нибудь) на убо́й,** to send off to be slaughtered.

убо́йный *adj.* **1,** (*of animals*) to be slaughtered; intended for slaughter; (*of a place*) slaughtering (*attrib.*). **2,** *mil.* (*of power, energy, etc.*) destructive; lethal.

убо́р *n., archaic* attire. —**головно́й убо́р,** headdress.

убо́ристый *adj.* (*of writing, type, etc.*) close.

убо́рка *n.* **1,** cleaning up; tidying up. **2,** gathering in; harvesting.

убо́рная *n., decl. as an adj.* **1,** lavatory; washroom. **2,** *theat.* dressing room.

убо́рочный *adj.* harvesting (*attrib.*). —**убо́рочная маши́на,** harvester.

убо́рщик *n.* janitor; porter. —**убо́рщица,** *n.* cleaning woman; maid.

убра́нство *n.* **1,** furnishings. **2,** dress; attire.

убра́ть [*infl.* уберу́, уберёшь; *past fem.* убрала́] *v., pfv. of* убира́ть. —**убра́ться,** *refl.* [*past tense stress as in* бра́ться] *pfv. of* убира́ться.

убыва́ть *v.impfv.* [*pfv.* убы́ть] **1,** to decrease; wane; recede; subside. **2,** to leave; take leave.

у́быль *n.f.* **1,** decrease. **2,** loss. —**идти́ на у́быль, 1,** (*of floodwaters*) to recede; (*of the moon*) to wane; (*of a season*) to approach its end. **2,** (*of feelings*) to fade; ebb; subside.

убыстря́ть *v.impfv.* [*pfv.* убыстри́ть] *colloq.* to quicken.

убы́ток [*gen.* -тка] *n.* **1,** loss: продава́ть в убы́ток (*or* с убы́тком), to sell at a loss. **2,** *pl.* losses; damages.

убы́точный *adj.* operating at a loss; showing a loss.

убы́ть [*infl.* убу́ду, убу́дешь; *past* у́был, убыла́, у́было, у́были] *v., pfv. of* убыва́ть.

уважа́емый *adj.* **1,** respected; honored. **2,** (*in direct address or salutations*) dear.

уважа́ть *v.impfv.* to respect.

уваже́ние *n.* respect. —**с уваже́нием,** sincerely yours (*in letters*).

уважи́тельный *adj.* **1,** valid; legitimate. **2,** respectful; deferential. —**уважи́тельно,** *adv.* respectfully; with respect.

ува́жить *v.pfv., colloq.* **1,** to consider; take into consideration. **2,** to comply with; grant (a request). **3,** to respect; honor. **4,** to humor; be nice to.

у́валень [*gen.* -льня] *n.m., colloq.* lout; lummox.

ува́риваться *v.r.impfv.* [*pfv.* увари́ться] *colloq.* to be thoroughly cooked.

увари́ться [*infl.* ува́рится] *v.r., pfv. of* ува́риваться.

уве́домить [*infl.* -млю, -мишь] *v., pfv. of* уведомля́ть.

уведомле́ние *n.* notification; notice.

уведомля́ть *v.impfv.* [*pfv.* уве́домить] to notify; inform.

увезти́ [*infl. like* везти́] *v., pfv. of* увози́ть.

увекове́чение *n.* immortalization; perpetuation.

увекове́чивать *v.impfv.* [*pfv.* увекове́чить] **1,** to immortalize. **2,** to perpetuate.

увеличе́ние *n.* **1,** increase. **2,** magnification; *photog.* enlargement.

увели́чивать *v.impfv.* [*pfv.* увели́чить] **1,** to increase. **2,** to magnify; *photog.* enlarge. —**увели́чиваться,** *refl.* to increase; grow.

увеличи́тель *n.m., photog.* enlarger.

увеличи́тельный *adj.* magnifying. —**увеличи́тельный аппара́т,** enlarger. —**увеличи́тельное стекло́,** magnifying glass.

увели́чить *v., pfv. of* увели́чивать. —**увели́читься,** *refl., pfv. of* увели́чиваться.

увенча́ть *v., pfv. of* венча́ть (*in sense #1*) *and* увенчивать. —**увенча́ться,** *refl., pfv. of* венча́ться (*in sense #1*) *and* уве́нчиваться.

уве́нчивать *v.impfv.* [*pfv.* увенча́ть] to crown. —**уве́нчиваться,** *refl.* **1,** *obs.* to be crowned. **2,** *fig.*

(*with instr.*) to be crowned (with): увенча́ться успе́хом, to be successful; be crowned with success.

увере́ние *n.* assurance.

уве́ренно *adv.* with confidence; confidently.

уве́ренность *n.f.* **1,** confidence. **2,** assurance; certainty. —**уве́ренность в себе́,** self-confidence.

уве́ренный *adj.* [*short form* уве́рен, уве́рена] **1,** sure; certain; confident. **2,** [*usu. short form*] (*with* в + *prepl.*) sure (of); certain (of). —**бу́дьте уве́рены!,** believe me!; (you can) count on it! —**уве́ренный в себе́,** self-confident.

уве́рить *v., pfv. of* уверя́ть. —**уве́риться,** *refl., pfv. of* уверя́ться.

уверну́ться *v.r., pfv. of* увёртываться.

уве́ровать *v.pfv.* [*infl.* -рую, -руешь] (*with* в + *acc.*) to come to believe (in).

увёртка [*gen. pl.* -ток] *n.* subterfuge; dodge; ruse; trick.

увёртливый *adj.* shifty; evasive.

увёртываться *v.r.impfv.* [*pfv.* уверну́ться] (*with* от) to evade; dodge.

увертю́ра *n., music* overture.

уверя́ть *v.impfv.* [*pfv.* уве́рить] to assure. —**уверя́ться,** *refl.* to make sure; assure oneself.

увеселе́ние *n.* entertainment; amusement.

увесели́тельный *adj.* amusement (*attrib.*); entertainment (*attrib.*); pleasure (*attrib.*).

увеселя́ть *v.impfv.* to entertain; amuse.

уве́систый *adj.* weighty; heavy.

увести́ [*infl. like* вести́] *v., pfv. of* уводи́ть.

увеча́ть *v.impfv.* [*pfv.* изуве́чить] to mutilate; maim.

уве́чье *n.* serious injury.

уве́шивать *v.impfv.* [*pfv.* уве́шать] to hang; cover with hangings: уве́шать сте́ну карти́нами, to hang a wall with pictures. Го́род уве́шан фла́гами, the city is decked with flags.

увеща́ние *n.* admonition; exhortation; remonstrance.

увещева́ть *v.impfv.* to admonish; exhort; remonstrate. *Also,* увеща́ть.

увива́ть *v.impfv.* [*pfv.* уви́ть] *usu. passive* **1,** to entwine: уви́т плющо́м, entwined with ivy. **2,** to tie: уви́т ле́нтами, tied with ribbons. —**увива́ться,** *refl.* [*impfv. only*] *colloq.* to hang around.

увида́ть *v.pfv., used only in the past tense, colloq.* to see; catch sight of. —**увида́ться,** *refl., colloq.* to see each other.

уви́деть *v.pfv.* [*infl.* уви́жу, уви́дишь] **1,** *pfv. of* ви́деть. **2,** to catch sight of. —**уви́деться,** *refl., pfv. of* ви́деться (*in senses #2 & #3*).

уви́ливать *v.impfv.* [*pfv.* увильну́ть] (*with* от) *colloq.* **1,** to avoid; dodge. **2,** to evade; get out of (*doing something*). **3,** [*impfv. only*] to try to get out of. **4,** (*with no prep.*) to prevaricate.

уви́ть [*infl. like* вить] *v., pfv. of* увива́ть.

увлажне́ние *n.* **1,** moistening. **2,** moisture.

увлажни́тель *n.m.* humidifier.

увлажня́ть *v.impfv.* [*pfv.* увлажни́ть] to moisten; dampen; humidify. —**увлажня́ться,** *refl.* to become moist; become damp.

увлека́тельный *adj.* fascinating; absorbing.

увлека́ть *v.impfv.* [*pfv.* **увле́чь**] **1,** to drag along: Увлека́ть за собо́й, to drag along behind one. **2,** to carry away; sweep away. **3,** *fig.* to carry away; engross; fascinate; enthrall. —**увлека́ться,** *refl.* **1,** (*with instr.*) to develop an enthusiasm (for). **2,** (*with instr.*) to become engrossed (in); be wrapped up (in). **3,** (*with instr.*) to fall for; become infatuated with. **4,** to get carried away.

увлека́ющийся *adj.* easily carried away; easily falling in love.

увлече́ние *n.* **1,** enthusiasm. **2,** (*with instr.*) passion (for); fascination (with). **3,** (*with instr.*) infatuation (with); crush (on).

увлечённый *adj.* enthusiastic. —**увлечённо,** *adv.* with enthusiasm.

увле́чь [*infl. like* **влечь**] *v., pfv. of* **увлека́ть.** —**увле́чься,** *refl., pfv. of* **увлека́ться.**

уво́д *n.* **1,** evacuation; withdrawal. **2,** theft.

уводи́ть *v.impfv.* [*pfv.* **увести́;** *pres.* **увожу́, уво́дишь**] **1,** to lead away; take away. **2,** to carry off. **3,** to steal.

уво́з *n.* **1,** carting away. **2,** abduction.

увози́ть *v.impfv.* [*pfv.* **увезти́;** *pres.* **увожу́, уво́зишь**] **1,** to take away (*by conveyance*). **2,** to take (someone) with one (*e.g.* to another city). **3,** to abduct.

увола́кивать *v.impfv.* [*pfv.* **уволо́чь**] *colloq.* **1,** to drag away. **2,** to carry off; abduct. **3,** to make off with; steal.

уво́лить *v., pfv. of* **увольня́ть.** —**уво́литься,** *refl., pfv. of* **увольня́ться.**

уволо́чь [*infl. like* **воло́чь**] *v., pfv. of* **увола́кивать.**

увольне́ние *n.* discharge; dismissal.

увольни́тельная *n., decl. as an adj.* pass; written leave of absence.

увольни́тельный *adj., in* **увольни́тельная запи́ска; увольни́тельное свиде́тельство,** pass; written leave of absence.

увольня́ть *v.impfv.* [*pfv.* **уво́лить**] **1,** to dismiss; discharge; fire; lay off. **2,** to release; excuse. **3,** (*usu. imperative*) (*with* **от**) to spare (from). —**увольня́ться,** *refl.* **1,** to be discharged; get one's discharge. **2,** to be released; be excused.

увы́ *interj.* alas!

увяда́ть *v.impfv.* [*pfv.* **увя́нуть**] to fade; wither.

увя́дший *adj.* faded; withered.

увяза́ть[1] [*infl.* **увяжу́, увя́жешь**] *v., pfv. of* **увя́зывать.** —**увяза́ться,** *refl., pfv. of* **увя́зываться.**

увяза́ть[2] *v.impfv.* [*pfv.* **увя́знуть;** *pres.* **-за́ю, -за́ешь**] **1,** to get stuck. **2,** to become mired; get bogged down.

увя́зка *n.* **1,** tying up. **2,** *fig.* coordination; tying together.

увя́знуть [*past* **увя́з, увя́зла**] *v., pfv. of* **вя́знуть** *and* **увяза́ть**[2].

увя́зывать *v.impfv.* [*pfv.* **увяза́ть**] *colloq.* **1,** to tie up; pack up. **2,** *fig.* to coordinate; reconcile; square. —**увя́зываться,** *refl.* **1,** (*with* **с** + *instr.*) to be coordinated (with); tie in (with). **2,** (*with* **за** + *instr.*) *colloq.* to follow; haunt; dog.

увя́нуть [*past* **увя́л, увя́ла**] *v., pfv. of* **вя́нуть** *and* **увяда́ть.**

угада́ть *v., pfv. of* **уга́дывать.**

уга́дчик *n., colloq.* guesser.

уга́дывать *v.impfv.* [*pfv.* **угада́ть**] to guess.

уга́дываться *v.r.impfv.* to be sensed; be felt; be seen.

уга́р *n.* **1,** carbon monoxide fumes. **2,** carbon monoxide poisoning. **3,** *fig.* ecstasy; fever; intoxication.

уга́рный *adj.* **1,** carbon monoxide (*attrib.*); containing carbon monoxide. **2,** *fig.* feverish; frenzied. —**уга́рный газ,** carbon monoxide.

угаса́ние *n.* fading; waning; dying out.

угаса́ть *v.impfv.* [*pfv.* **уга́снуть**] **1,** (*of a fire*) to go out; die out. **2,** *fig.* to fade; wane; ebb.

уга́снуть [*past* **уга́с, уга́сла**] *v., pfv. of* **га́снуть** *and* **угаса́ть.**

углево́д *n.* carbohydrate.

углеводоро́д *n.* hydrocarbon.

углекислота́ *n.* carbonic acid.

углеки́слый *adj.* carbonate (of): углеки́слый ка́льций, calcium carbonate; углеки́слый на́трий, sodium carbonate. —**углеки́слый газ,** carbon dioxide. —**углеки́слая соль,** carbonate.

углеко́п *n., obs.* coal miner.

углеро́д *n.* carbon.

углеро́дистый *adj.* **1,** carbon: углеро́дистая сталь, carbon steel. **2,** carbide (of): углеро́дистый ка́льций, calcium carbide.

углова́тый *adj.* **1,** angular. **2,** *fig.* awkward.

углово́й *adj.* **1,** corner (*attrib.*). **2,** angular: углова́я ско́рость, angular velocity.

углуби́ть [*infl.* **-блю́, -би́шь**] *v., pfv. of* **углубля́ть.** —**углуби́ться,** *refl., pfv. of* **углубля́ться.**

углубле́ние *n.* **1,** deepening. **2,** hollow; depression; dip.

углублённый *adj.* **1,** sunken. **2,** *fig.* in-depth. **3,** *fig.* (*with* **в** + *acc.*) engrossed (in).

углубля́ть *v.impfv.* [*pfv.* **углуби́ть**] **1,** to deepen; make deeper. **2,** *fig.* to broaden (one's knowledge). —**углубля́ться,** *refl.* **1,** to deepen; become deeper. **2,** (*with* **в** + *acc.*) to go deep (into); sink (into). **3,** *fig.* (*with* **в** + *acc.*) to go deep (into); delve (into). **4,** *fig.* (*with* **в** + *acc.*) to become absorbed (in). **5,** *in* углубля́ться в себя́, to withdraw into oneself.

угляде́ть *v.pfv.* [*infl.* **-жу́, -ди́шь**] *colloq.* **1,** to see; spot. **2,** (*with* **за** + *instr.*) to look after; keep an eye on.

угна́ть [*infl.* **угоню́, уго́нишь;** *past fem.* **угнала́**] *v., pfv. of* **угоня́ть.** —**угна́ться,** *refl.* [*past tense stress as in* **гна́ться**] (*with* **за** + *instr.*) (*usu. in neg. sentences*) to keep up (with); keep pace (with).

угнезди́ться *v.r.pfv., colloq.* to nestle.

угнета́тель *n.m.* oppressor.

угнета́ть *v.impfv.* **1,** to oppress. **2,** to depress. **3,** to stifle; inhibit.

угнета́ющий *adj.* **1,** oppressive. **2,** depressing.

угнете́ние *n.* **1,** oppression. **2,** depression; dejection.

угнетённый *adj.* **1,** oppressed. **2,** depressed.

угова́ривать *v.impfv.* [*pfv.* **уговори́ть**] **1,** to persuade. **2,** [*impfv. only*] to try to persuade; coax. —**угова́риваться,** *refl.* (*with inf.*) *colloq.* to agree (to); arrange (to).

угово́р *n.* **1,** *often pl.* persuasion; attempt at persuasion: угово́ры на него́ не де́йствуют, attempts to persuade him are useless. **2,** *colloq.* agreement; arrangement; understanding.

уговори́ть *v., pfv. of* **угова́ривать.** —**уговори́ться,** *refl., pfv. of* **угова́риваться.**

уго́да *n., in* в уго́ду (+ *dat.*), (in order) to please.

угоди́ть *v.pfv.* [*infl.* угожу́, угоди́шь] **1**, *pfv. of* **угожда́ть**. **2**, (*with various prepositions*) *colloq.* to fall (into); step (into); land (in); end up (in). **3**, (*with* в + *acc.*) *colloq.* to hit; strike: Пу́ля угоди́ла ему́ в плечо́, the bullet struck him in the shoulder. **4**, (*with instr.*) *colloq.* to bang: угоди́ть голово́й в стекло́, to bang one's head on the glass; bang into the glass with one's head.

уго́дливый *adj.* obsequious. —**уго́дливость,** *n.f.* obsequiousness.

уго́дник *n.* **1**, *colloq.* sycophant. **2**, saint. —**да́мский уго́дник,** ladies' man.

уго́дничать *v.impfv.* (*with* **пе́ред**) *colloq.* to curry favor (with); play up to.

уго́дничество *n.* obsequiousness; servility.

уго́дно *predicate* **1**, any-: что уго́дно, anything; кто уго́дно, anyone; где (*or* куда́) уго́дно, anywhere. **2**, (*with dat.*) as one likes: Что вам уго́дно?, what would you like? Как вам уго́дно, as you wish; just as you like. Где (*or* куда́) вам уго́дно, anywhere/wherever you like. Когда́ вам уго́дно, whenever you like; whenever you wish to. Како́й уго́дно (+ *noun*), any ... you like. Ско́лько душе́ уго́дно, as much as one's heart desires. —**е́сли уго́дно,** perhaps.

уго́дный *adj.* (*with dat.*) pleasing (to).

уго́дье *n., often. pl.* land (*with reference to its use*): травяно́е уго́дье, grassland; лесны́е уго́дья, forests.

угожда́ть *v.impfv.* [*pfv.* **угоди́ть**] (*with dat. or* на + *acc.*) to please. See also **угоди́ть**.

у́гол [*gen.* угла́; *2nd loc.* углу́] *n.* **1**, corner: в углу́, in the corner; на углу́, on the (street) corner. **2**, angle. **3**, place to live: име́ть свой у́гол, to have a place of one's own. **4**, (*with an adj.*) remote place: глухо́й у́гол, out-of-the-way place; медве́жий у́гол, godforsaken place. —**за угло́м,** around the corner. —**из-за угла́, 1**, from around the corner. **2**, from behind; without warning. —**из угла́ в у́гол,** (*with verbs of walking or pacing*) up and down; back and forth. —**под угло́м в** (+ *acc.*), at an angle of. —**по угла́м,** (*with verbs of talking or whispering*) in secret; in the corridors.

уголёк [*gen.* -лька́] *n.* small piece of coal.

уголо́вник *n.* criminal.

уголо́вный *adj.* criminal (*attrib.*): уголо́вное пра́во, criminal law; уголо́вный ко́декс, criminal code. —**уголо́вное преступле́ние,** felony.

уголо́вщина *n., colloq.* **1**, criminal act. **2**, criminals; the underworld.

уголо́к [*gen.* -лка́] *n.* **1**, *dim. of* у́гол. **2**, cozy corner; nook. —**кра́сный уголо́к,** recreation and reading room.

у́голь [*gen.* у́гля *or* угля́; *pl.* у́гли, у́глей *or* угле́й, у́глям *or* угля́м] *n.m.* **1**, coal. **2**, (piece of) coal: горя́чие у́гли, live coals; live embers. —**быть** *or* **сиде́ть как на у́гольях,** to be on tenterhooks.

уго́льник *n.* **1**, try square. **2**, triangle (*drawing instrument*).

у́гольный *adj.* coal (*attrib.*). —**у́гольная кислота́,** carbonic acid.

у́гольщик *n., colloq.* coal miner.

угомони́ть *v.pfv., colloq.* to calm; calm down. —**угомони́ться,** *refl., colloq.* to calm down; become calm.

уго́н *n.* **1**, driving away; sending away. **2**, hijacking (*of an aircraft*).

угоня́ть *v.impfv.* [*pfv.* **угна́ть**] **1**, to drive away. **2**, to steal (cattle). **3**, to hijack (an aircraft).

угора́здить *v.pfv., colloq., impers.* **1**, to make; prompt; possess: Как э́то вас угора́здило сде́лать э́то?, what on earth made you do it? **2**, (*used sarcastically*) to manage to: Его́ угора́здило заболе́ть, he managed to get sick.

угора́ть *v.impfv.* [*pfv.* **угоре́ть**] **1**, to be overcome by fumes; get carbon monoxide poisoning. **2**, *colloq.* to go mad.

угоре́лый *adj., colloq.* mad; crazy. —**бежа́ть как угоре́лый,** to run like mad.

угоре́ть [*infl.* угорю́, угори́шь] *v., pfv. of* **угора́ть**.

у́горь [*gen.* угря́] *n.m.* **1**, eel. **2**, blackhead; *pl.* acne.

угости́ть [*infl.* -щу́, -сти́шь] *v., pfv. of* **угоща́ть**. —**угости́ться,** *refl., pfv. of* **угоща́ться**.

угото́вить *v.pfv.* [*infl.* -влю, -вишь] **1**, *obs.* to prepare. **2**, *fig.* (*with dat.*) to have in store (for).

угоща́ть *v.impfv.* [*pfv.* **угости́ть**] to treat: угоща́ть госте́й обе́дом, to treat one's friends to dinner. —**угоща́ться,** *refl., colloq.* **1**, to partake oneself. Угоща́йтесь, пожа́луйста!, help yourself! **2**, (*with instr.*) to help oneself to.

угоще́ние *n.* **1**, entertaining; treating. **2**, food; refreshments.

угрева́тый *adj.* covered with blackheads; pimply.

угрожа́ть *v.impfv.* (*with dat.*) to threaten: угрожа́ть кому́-нибудь ору́жием, to threaten someone with a gun. Стране́ угрожа́ет го́лод, the country is threatened with (*or* faces) starvation.

угрожа́ющий *adj.* threatening; menacing.

угро́за *n.* threat; menace. —**быть под угро́зой,** to be in danger. —**ста́вить под угро́зу,** to endanger; jeopardize.

угрызе́ние *n., in* угрызе́ния со́вести, pangs of conscience.

угрю́мый *adj.* **1**, sullen; morose; gloomy. **2**, bleak; forbidding. —**угрю́мость,** *n.f.* sullenness; gloominess; moroseness.

уда́в *n.* boa (*snake*).

удава́ться *v.r.impfv.* [*pfv.* **уда́ться**; *pres.* удаётся] **1**, to be successful; be a success; turn out well. О́пыт уда́лся, the experiment was a success. Брак не уда́лся, the marriage didn't work out. **2**, *impers.* (*with dat. and inf.*) to succeed: Ему́ удало́сь доста́ть биле́ты, he succeeded in getting the tickets.

удави́ть *v.pfv.* [*infl.* удавлю́, уда́вишь] *colloq.* to strangle. —**удави́ться,** *refl., colloq.* to hang oneself.

удавле́ние *n., colloq.* strangling; strangulation.

удале́ние *n.* **1**, withdrawal. **2**, removal. **3**, extraction. **4**, distance.

удалённый *adj.* remote. —**удалённость,** *n.f.* remoteness; distance.

удале́ц [*gen.* -льца́] *n., colloq.* daring person.

удали́ть *v., pfv. of* удаля́ть. —**удали́ться,** *refl., pfv. of* **удаля́ться**.

удало́й *also,* **уда́лый** *adj.* **1,** bold; daring. **2,** dashing.

у́даль *n.f.* boldness; daring; bravado.

удальство́ *n., colloq.* = **у́даль.**

удаля́ть *v.impfv.* [*pfv.* **удали́ть**] **1,** to move away; move farther away. **2,** to remove; take away. **3,** to remove; force to leave: удаля́ть ученика́ из кла́сса, to send a pupil out of the room. **4,** to remove; extract (a tooth, splinter, etc.). —**удаля́ться,** *refl.* **1,** to move away. Удаля́ться от те́мы, to wander from the subject. **2,** (*with* **от**) to get away (from); isolate oneself (from). **3,** to withdraw; retire.

уда́р *n.* **1,** blow. **2,** stroke (*of a clock, bell, etc.*). **3,** bolt (*of thunder or lightning*). **4,** *mil.* attack; thrust; strike; blow. **5,** impact. **6,** *sports* shot; stroke. **7,** *med.* stroke. Со́лнечный уда́р, sunstroke. **8,** *in* электри́ческий уда́р, electric shock. **9,** *in* уда́р судьбы́, stroke of bad luck. —**быть в уда́ре,** *colloq.* to be in good form. —**быть под уда́ром,** to be vulnerable; be under the gun. —**ста́вить под уда́р,** to endanger; jeopardize.

ударе́ние *n.* **1,** accent; stress. **2,** accent mark. **3,** *fig.* emphasis: де́лать ударе́ние на (+ *prepl.*), to stress; emphasize.

уда́рить *v., pfv. of* **ударя́ть.** —**уда́риться,** *refl., pfv. of* **ударя́ться.**

уда́рник *n.* **1,** firing pin. **2,** drummer. **3,** shock worker; pace-setting worker.

уда́рный *adj.* **1,** striking (*attrib.*); percussion (*attrib.*). **2,** shock (*attrib.*): уда́рная волна́/брига́да, shock wave/brigade. **3,** urgent. **4,** (*of a syllable*) stressed.

ударя́ть *v.impfv.* [*pfv.* **уда́рить**] **1,** to strike; hit: ударя́ть ло́шадь кнуто́м, to strike the horse with a whip. Уда́рить кого́-нибудь по лицу́, to slap someone in the face. **2,** (*with instr. and* **в** + *acc. or* **по**) to bang; pound: уда́рить кулако́м по́ столу, to bang/pound one's fist on the table. **3,** *fig.* (*of an illness, emotion, etc.*) to strike. **4,** (*with* **на** + *acc. or* **по**) to attack. *Also intrans.:* уда́рить со всех сторо́н, to attack from all sides. **5,** *fig.* (*with* **по**) to strike a blow (against); combat. **6,** (*with* **в** + *acc.*) to beat (a drum); ring (a bell); sound (an alarm). **7,** to ring out. Уда́рил гром, there was a clap of thunder. **8,** (*of a clock*) to strike (a certain hour). —**не уда́рить лицо́м в грязь, 1,** not disgrace oneself. **2,** not be outdone. —**ударя́ть в го́лову** (+ *dat.*), (*of alcoholic beverages*) to go to one's head. —**уда́рить по рука́м,** to strike a bargain.

ударя́ться *v.r.impfv.* [*pfv.* **уда́риться**] **1,** (*with* **о** *or* **в** + *acc.*) to strike; bang (into *or* against); bump (into). Ло́дка уда́рилась о скалу́, the boat struck a rock. Уда́риться голово́й о дверь, to bang one's head on the door. **2,** *fig.* (*with* **в** + *acc.*) *colloq.* to break into; burst into; give way to (tears, panic, etc.). —**уда́риться в кра́йность,** to go to an extreme.

уда́ться [*infl. like* **да́ться**; *past* **уда́лся, удала́сь, удало́сь, удали́сь**] *v.r., pfv. of* **удава́ться.**

уда́ча *n.* **1,** success. **2,** good luck.

уда́чливый *adj.* **1,** lucky. **2,** successful.

уда́чник *n., colloq.* lucky man.

уда́чно *adv.* **1,** successfully. **2,** well. **3,** aptly. —*adj., used predicatively,* fortunate: Уда́чно, что..., it is fortunate that...,

уда́чный *adj.* **1,** successful. **2,** apt; appropriate; felicitous.

удва́ивать *v.impfv.* [*pfv.* **удво́ить**] **1,** to double. **2,** *fig.* to redouble. —**удва́иваться,** *refl.* to double.

удвое́ние *n.* doubling; redoubling.

удво́ить *v., pfv. of* **удва́ивать.** —**удво́иться,** *refl., pfv. of* **удва́иваться.**

уде́л *n.* fate; lot; destiny.

удели́ть [*infl.* **уделю́, уде́лишь**] *v., pfv. of* **уделя́ть.**

уде́льный *adj., physics* specific: уде́льная теплота́, specific heat. —**уде́льный вес, 1,** specific gravity. **2,** relative amount (*as against a total*); proportion; percentage.

уделя́ть *v.impfv.* [*pfv.* **удели́ть**] **1,** to spare (a small amount of something). **2,** to give; devote (time, attention, etc.).

у́держ *n., in* **без у́держу, 1,** without restraint; with abandon. **2,** (*with verbs of laughing or crying*) uncontrollably. —**ему́** (*or* **на него́**) **нет у́держу,** there is nothing to stop him; there is no holding him back. —**не знать у́держу,** to know no restraint.

удержа́ние *n.* **1,** keeping; retention. **2,** holding back; withholding. **3,** deduction; withholding (*of money*).

удержа́ть [*infl.* **удержу́, уде́ржишь**] *v., pfv. of* **уде́рживать.** —**удержа́ться,** *refl., pfv. of* **уде́рживаться.**

уде́рживать *v.impfv.* [*pfv.* **удержа́ть**] **1,** to hold up; keep from falling. **2,** to restrain; hold back. **3,** to deter. **4,** (*often with* **за собо́й**) to keep; retain. **5,** to deduct; withhold. —**уде́рживаться,** *refl.* **1,** to keep one's feet. **2,** to hold out. **3,** to restrain oneself. **4,** (*with* **от**) to refrain from (*e.g.* smoking); resist; withstand (temptation); hold back (tears). **5,** (*with* **от**) to keep (from); help: Я не мог удержа́ться от сме́ха, I couldn't help laughing.

удесятеря́ть *v.impfv.* [*pfv.* **удесятери́ть**] to increase tenfold.

удешевля́ть *v.impfv.* [*pfv.* **удешеви́ть**] to reduce the price of.

удиви́тельно *adv.* **1,** surprisingly; remarkably. **2,** marvelously. **3,** extremely. —*adj., used predicatively,* surprising: Удиви́тельно, что..., it is surprising that... —**и не удиви́тельно!,** and no wonder!

удиви́тельный *adj.* **1,** surprising. **2,** wonderful; marvelous. **3,** remarkable.

удиви́ть [*infl.* **-влю́, -ви́шь**] *v., pfv. of* **удивля́ть.** —**удиви́ться,** *refl., pfv. of* **удивля́ться.**

удивле́ние *n.* surprise: к моему́ удивле́нию, to my surprise. —**на удивле́ние, 1,** first-rate; splendidly. **3,** *fol. by an adj. or adv.* surprisingly. **4,** (*with dat.*) to the surprise of.

удивлённый *adj.* surprised. —**удивлённо,** *adv.* in surprise.

удивля́ть *v.impfv.* [*pfv.* **удиви́ть**] to surprise. —**удивля́ться,** *refl.* (*with dat.*) to be surprised (at).

удила́ [*gen.* **уди́л**] *n.pl.* bit. —**закуси́ть удила́,** to take the bit in one's teeth.

уди́лище *n.* fishing rod.

уди́льщик *n.* angler.

удира́ть *v.impfv.* [*pfv.* **удра́ть**] *colloq.* to take off; run away.

уди́ть *v.impfv.* [*pres.* ужу́, у́дишь] to fish for: уди́ть ры́бу, to fish. —**уди́ться**, *refl.* (*of fish*) to bite.

удлине́ние *n.* 1, lengthening. 2, extension.

удлинённый *adj.* 1, lengthened. 2, oblong; elongated.

удлини́тель *n.m.* extension cord. —**удлини́тельный**, *adj.* extension (*attrib.*): удлини́тельный шнур, extension cord.

удлиня́ть *v.impfv.* [*pfv.* удлини́ть] 1, to lengthen; make longer. 2, to extend; prolong. —**удлиня́ться**, *refl.* to lengthen; become (*or* get) longer.

удму́рт *n.m.* [*fem.* удму́ртка] Udmurt (*one of a people inhabiting central European Russia*). —**удму́ртский**, *adj.* Udmurt.

удо́бно *adv.* comfortably. —*adj., used predicatively* 1, (*with dat.*) comfortable: Вам удо́бно?, are you comfortable? 2, (*with dat.*) convenient: Когда́ вам бу́дет удо́бно?, when will it be convenient for you? 3, all right: Удо́бно ли спроси́ть его́ об э́том?, is it all right to ask him about it?

удо́бный *adj.* [*short form* -бен, -бна] 1, comfortable. 2, convenient: при пе́рвом удо́бном слу́чае, at the first convenient opportunity.

удобо- *prefix* easy to: удобочита́емый, easy to read; удобопоня́тный, easy to understand; easily understood.

удобовари́мый *adj.* digestible. —**удобовари́мость**, *n.f.* digestibility.

удобре́ние *n.* 1, fertilization. 2, fertilizer.

удобря́ть *v.impfv.* [*pfv.* удо́брить] to fertilize (soil).

удо́бство *n.* 1, comfort. 2, convenience. 3, *pl.* conveniences; amenities: со все́ми удо́бствами, with all the conveniences/amenities.

удовлетворе́ние *n.* 1, satisfaction. 2, (act of) satisfying.

удовлетворённый *adj.* satisfied; contented. —**удовлетворённо**, *adv.* with satisfaction. —**удовлетворённость**, *n.f.* satisfaction; contentment.

удовлетвори́тельно *adv.* satisfactorily. —*n. indecl.* "satisfactory" (*school grade*).

удовлетвори́тельный *adj.* satisfactory.

удовлетворя́ть *v.impfv.* [*pfv.* удовлетвори́ть] 1, to satisfy; make (someone) content. 2, to satisfy; assuage (one's hunger, curiosity, etc.). 3, to grant; comply with (a wish, request, etc.). 4, to meet; satisfy: удовлетворя́ть тре́бование, to meet a demand. Удовлетворя́ть тре́бованиям, to meet/satisfy the requirements. 5, (*with instr.*) to supply (with). —**удовлетворя́ться**, *refl.* (*with instr.*) to be satisfied (with).

удово́льствие *n.* pleasure. С удово́льствием!, with pleasure!; I'll be glad to! К о́бщему удово́льствию, to everyone's delight. —**в своё удово́льствие**, to one's heart's content. —**жить в своё удово́льствие**, to enjoy life.

удово́льствоваться *v.r., pfv. of* дово́льствоваться.

удо́д *n.* hoopoe.

удо́й *n.* 1, yield of milk. 2, milking.

удо́йный *adj.* (*of a cow*) giving much milk.

удорожа́ние *n.* rise in cost *or* price.

удорожа́ть *v.impfv.* [*pfv.* удорожи́ть] to raise the price of. —**удорожа́ться**, *refl.* to go up in price; become more expensive.

удоста́ивать *v.impfv.* [*pfv.* удосто́ить] 1, (*with gen.*) to award; confer (a title, prize, etc.): удосто́ить кого́-нибудь (*acc.*) зва́ния, to confer a title on someone. 2, (*with gen. or instr.*) to consider worthy of; deign to give. Удосто́ить кого́-нибудь (*acc.*) отве́том, to deign to answer someone. Удоста́ивать кого́-нибудь внима́нием/похвалы́, to consider someone worthy of attention/praise. —**удоста́иваться**, *refl.* 1, (*with gen.*) to be awarded (a title). 2, (*with gen.*) to be given; be accorded (something). 3, (*with inf.*) to have the honor of; have the good fortune to.

удостовере́ние *n.* 1, certification; attestation. 2, certificate. 3, *in* удостовере́ние ли́чности, (piece of) identification; identity card. —**в удостовере́ние чего́**, in witness whereof.

удостоверя́ть *v.impfv.* [*pfv.* удостове́рить] 1, to certify; attest. 2, to witness (a signature). —**удостоверя́ться**, *refl.* 1, to be certified: Сим удостоверя́ется, что..., this is to certify that..., 2, (*with в + prepl. or a dependent clause*) to make sure (of *or* that).

удосто́ить *v., pfv. of* удоста́ивать. —**удосто́иться**, *refl., pfv. of* удоста́иваться.

удосу́живаться *v.r.impfv.* [*pfv.* удосу́житься] (*with inf.*) *colloq.* to find time (to); get around to.

удочеря́ть *v.impfv.* [*pfv.* удочери́ть] to adopt (a girl).

у́дочка [*gen. pl.* -чек] *n.* fishing rod (*with the line attached*). —**заки́нуть у́дочку**, to drop a hint; put out a feeler. —**пойма́ть на у́дочку**, to trick; hoodwink. —**попа́сться на у́дочку**, to swallow (*or* take) the bait.

удра́ть [*infl.* удеру́, удерёшь; *past fem.* удрала́] *v., pfv. of* удира́ть.

удружи́ть *v.pfv.* (*with dat.*) *colloq.* to do (someone) a favor.

удруча́ть *v.impfv.* [*pfv.* удручи́ть] to depress; dispirit.

удруча́ющий *adj.* depressing.

удручённый *adj.* depressed; dejected; despondent.

удручи́ть *v., pfv. of* удруча́ть.

удуша́ть *v.impfv.* [*pfv.* удуши́ть] 1, to suffocate; smother. 2, *fig.* to stifle.

удуше́ние *n.* suffocation; asphyxiation.

удуши́ть [*infl.* удушу́, уду́шишь] *v., pfv. of* удуша́ть.

уду́шливый *adj.* suffocating; stifling. —**уду́шливый газ**, choking gas.

уду́шье *n.* 1, difficulty in breathing. 2, suffocation.

уедине́ние *n.* solitude; seclusion.

уединённый *adj.* solitary; secluded. —**уединённо**, *adv.* in seclusion; in solitude; in isolation; alone.

уединя́ть *v.impfv.* [*pfv.* уедини́ть] to seclude; isolate. —**уединя́ться**, *refl.* to withdraw; seclude oneself; closet oneself.

уе́зд *n., hist.* district. —**уе́здный**, *adj.* district (*attrib.*).

уезжа́ть *v.impfv.* [*pfv.* уе́хать] to leave; go away; depart (*by conveyance*).

уе́хать [*infl.* уе́ду, уе́дешь] *v., pfv. of* уезжа́ть.

уж[1] *adv.* = уже́. —*particle, used for emphasis:* Это уж про́сто безобра́зие!, it's simply disgraceful. Не так уж хо́лодно сего́дня, it's not all that cold today.

уж[2] [*gen.* ужа́] *n.* grass snake. —**водяно́й уж**, water snake.

ужа́лить *v., pfv. of* жа́лить.

у́жас *n.* **1,** horror; terror. **2,** *pl.* horrors: у́жасы войны́, the horrors of war. **3,** *colloq.* horrible thing; horrible situation: Про́сто у́жас!, it's simply horrible!

ужаса́ть *v.impfv.* [*pfv.* **ужасну́ть**] to terrify; horrify. —**ужаса́ться**, *refl.* to be terrified; be horrified.

ужаса́ющий *adj.* **1,** terrifying; horrifying. **2,** terrible; horrible.

ужа́сно *adv.* terribly; awfully. —*adj., used predicatively,* terrible; awful: Э́то ужа́сно, that's terrible; that's awful.

ужасну́ть *v., pfv. of* **ужаса́ть**. —**ужасну́ться**, *refl., pfv. of* **ужаса́ться**.

ужа́сный *adj.* terrible; horrible; frightful; awful; dreadful.

у́же *adj., comp. of* **у́зкий**.

уже́ *adv.* **1,** already. **2,** (*in interr. sentences*) yet. **3,** as early as. —**уже́ не,** no longer; any longer; anymore.

уже́ние *n.* fishing; angling.

ужесточа́ть *v.impfv.* [*pfv.* **ужесточи́ть**] **1,** to harden; toughen. **2,** to tighten (control).

ужива́ться *v.r.impfv.* [*pfv.* **ужи́ться**] **1,** to adjust; become adjusted (*to new surroundings*). **2,** (*with* **с** + *instr.*) to get along (with); coexist (with).

ужи́вчивый *adj.* easygoing; easy to get along with.

ужи́мка [*gen. pl.* **-мок**] *n., usu. pl.* grimace.

у́жин *n.* supper; dinner (*if taken in the evening*).

у́жинать *v.impfv.* [*pfv.* **поу́жинать**] to have supper; have dinner.

ужи́ться [*infl. like* жить; *past* ужи́лся, ужила́сь, ужило́сь *or* ужи́лось, ужили́сь *or* ужи́лись] *v.r., pfv. of* **ужива́ться**.

узаконе́ние *n.* **1,** legalization. **2,** *obs.* law; statute.

узако́нивать *v.impfv.* [*pfv.* **узако́нить**] to legalize; legitimize. *Also,* **узаконя́ть**.

узбе́к *n.m.* [*fem.* **-бе́чка**] *n.* Uzbek. —**узбе́кский**, *adj.* Uzbek.

узда́ [*pl.* **у́зды**] *n.* **1,** bridle. **2,** *fig.* restraint; check: держа́ть в узде́, to keep in check.

узде́чка [*gen. pl.* **-чек**] *n.* bridle.

у́зел [*gen.* узла́] *n.* **1,** knot. **2,** junction. **3,** *fig.* hub. **4,** bundle; pack. **5,** node. **6,** *naut.* knot (*measure of speed*). **7,** *mech.* parts; assembly. —**не́рвный у́зел,** ganglion.

узело́к [*gen.* **-лка́**] *n.* **1,** small knot. **2,** small bundle. **3,** nodule.

у́зенький *adj., colloq.* narrow.

у́зкий *adj.* [*short form* у́зок, узка́, у́зко, узки́ *or* у́зки; *comp.* у́же] **1,** narrow. **2,** (*of clothes, shoes, etc.*) tight: Ю́бка мне узка́, the skirt is tight on me. **3,** *fig.* narrow-minded. —**у́зкое ме́сто,** bottleneck.

у́зко *adv.* **1,** tightly. **2,** *fig.* from a narrow perspective: смотре́ть на ве́щи у́зко, to take a narrow view of things. —*adj., used predicatively,* narrow; tight: Здесь у́зко, it is narrow/tight in here.

узкоколе́йный *adj., R.R.* narrow-gauge.

узколо́бый *adj.* narrow-minded.

узлова́тый *adj.* (*of a rope, thread, etc.*) full of knots; knotted.

узлово́й *adj.* **1,** junction (*attrib.*). Узлова́я ста́нция, transfer station; junction point. **2,** *fig.* key; pivotal: узлово́й вопро́с, key/pivotal question.

узнава́ние *n.* recognition.

узнава́ть *v.impfv.* [*pfv.* **узна́ть**; *pres.* узнаю́, узнаёшь] **1,** to recognize. **2,** to find out; learn. **3,** to try to find out; inquire. **4,** to experience; know. **5,** to get to know.

узна́ть [*infl.* узна́ю, узна́ешь] *v., pfv. of* **узнава́ть**.

у́зник *n.* prisoner.

узо́р *n.* design; pattern. —**узо́рчатый**, *adj.* having a design; figured.

у́зость *n.f.* narrowness.

узре́ть *v.pfv.* [*infl.* узрю́, узри́шь] **1,** *pfv. of* **зреть**[2]. **2,** to see; perceive.

узурпа́тор *n.* usurper. —**узурпа́ция**, *n.* usurpation.

узурпи́ровать *v.impfv. & pfv.* [*pres.* **-рую, -руешь**] to usurp.

у́зы [*gen.* уз] *n.pl.* bonds; ties: у́зы дру́жбы, bonds/ties of friendship.

уйгу́р *n.m.* [*fem.* **-гу́рка**] Uigur (*one of a people inhabiting Central Asia and China*). —**уйгу́рский**, *adj.* Uigur.

у́йма *n.* (*with gen.*) *colloq.* a lot (of); heaps (of); tons (of).

уйти́ [*infl.* уйду́, уйдёшь; *past* ушёл, ушла́, ушло́, ушли́] *v., pfv. of* **уходи́ть**.

ука́з *n.* decree; edict; ukase. —**не ука́з** (+ *dat.*), not such that it (*or* one) must be obeyed: Никто́ ему́ не ука́з, he doesn't take orders from anyone.

указа́ние *n.* **1,** indicating; pointing out. **2,** indication. **3,** *usu. pl.* instructions; directions.

ука́занный *adj.* indicated: на ука́занном ме́сте, at the place indicated.

указа́тель *n.m.* **1,** indicator; pointer. **2,** index. **3,** directory.

указа́тельный *adj.* serving to indicate. —**указа́тельное местоиме́ние,** demonstrative pronoun. —**указа́тельный па́лец,** index finger. —**указа́тельный столб,** signpost.

указа́ть [*infl.* укажу́, ука́жешь] *v., pfv. of* **ука́зывать**.

ука́зка [*gen. pl.* **-зок**] *n.* **1,** pointer. **2,** *colloq.* orders: по ука́зке (+ *gen.*), on orders from.

ука́зчик *n., colloq.* one who gives orders.

ука́зывать *v.impfv.* [*pfv.* **указа́ть**] **1,** to point (in a certain direction); (*with* **на** + *acc.*) point to; point at. **2,** to point out; indicate (a road, place, etc.). **3,** (*with* **на** + *acc.*) to point out (mistakes, shortcomings, etc.). **4,** to indicate (one's name, certain information, etc.). **5,** (*with* **на** + *acc. or a dependent clause*) to indicate; suggest; point to (the fact that...). —**указа́ть кому́-нибудь на дверь,** to show someone the door (*i.e.* order out).

ука́тать *v., pfv. of* **ука́тывать**[1].

укати́ть [*infl.* укачу́, ука́тишь] *v., pfv. of* **ука́тывать**[2]. —**укати́ться**, *refl., pfv. of* **ука́тываться**.

ука́тывать[1] *v.impfv.* [*pfv.* **ука́тать**] **1,** to roll (a surface). **2,** to wear (a road) smooth.

ука́тывать[2] *v.impfv.* [*pfv.* **укати́ть**] **1,** *v.t.* to roll away; remove by rolling. **2,** *v.i., colloq.* to leave; take off. —**ука́тываться**, *refl.* **1,** to roll away. **2,** *colloq.* (*of a vehicle*) to drive off.

ука́чивать *v.impfv.* [*pfv.* **укача́ть**] **1,** to rock to sleep. **2,** *impers.* to experience motion sickness: Меня́ ука́чало, I became seasick, carsick, etc.

укла́д *n.* **1,** mode; tenor: укла́д жи́зни, way/mode/ tenor of life. **2,** (socio-economic) system.

укла́дка *n.* **1,** laying. **2,** piling; stacking. **3,** arranging; setting (*of one's hair*).

укла́дчик *n.* **1,** packer. **2,** layer (*of floors, tracks, etc.*).

укла́дывать *v.impfv.* [*pfv.* **уложи́ть**] **1,** to lay; lay down (*gently*). **2,** [*also,* **укла́дывать спать**] to put to bed. **3,** to order to bed; (*of an illness*) lay up. **4,** to pile up; stack. **5,** to arrange; set (one's hair). **6,** to pack. **7,** to lay (tracks, concrete, etc.). **8,** to lay; cover (a surface with a certain material). **9,** *colloq.* to kill.

укла́дываться *v.r.impfv.* **1,** [*pfv.* **уложи́ться**] *colloq.* to pack; pack up. **2,** [*pfv.* **уложи́ться**] (*with* **в** + *acc. or prepl.*) to fit (into); go (into). **3,** [*pfv.* **уле́чься**] to lie down (*in a comfortable position*). **4,** [*pfv.* **уле́чься**] (*of objects*) to lie correctly; lie as desired. —**не укла́дываться в голове́**, to be more than the mind can comprehend. *See also* **уле́чься.**

укло́н *n.* **1,** slope; incline. **2,** *fig.* bias; slant. **3,** *fig.* (political) deviation. —**под укло́н**, downhill; downward.

уклоне́ние *n.* **1,** deviation; digression. **2,** evasion; avoidance.

уклони́ться [*infl.* **уклоню́сь, укло́нишься**] *v.r., pfv. of* **уклоня́ться.**

укло́нчивый *adj.* evasive. —**укло́нчивость,** *n.f.* evasiveness.

уклоня́ться *v.r.impfv.* [*pfv.* **уклони́ться**] **1,** to step aside; move out of the way. **2,** (*with* **от**) to dodge; avoid. **3,** *fig.* (*with* **от**) to evade; avoid. Уклоня́ться от отве́та, to evade a question; avoid answering. **4,** to decline; refuse. **5,** (*with* **от**) to deviate (from); digress (from).

уклю́чина *n.* oarlock.

уко́л *n.* **1,** prick. **2,** *med.* injection. **3,** *fig.* gibe; dig.

уколо́ть *v.pfv.* [*infl.* **уколю́, уко́лешь**] **1,** to prick. **2,** *fig.* to wound; pique.

укомплектова́ние *n.* **1,** manning; staffing. **2,** bringing up to full strength.

укомплектова́ть *v., pfv. of* **комплектова́ть.**

уко́р *n.* reproach. —**не в уко́р будь ска́зано**, no criticism implied.

укора́чивать *v.impfv.* [*pfv.* **укороти́ть**] to shorten.

укоре́ние *n.* taking root.

укорени́вшийся *adj.* deep-seated; ingrained.

укореня́ть *v.impfv.* [*pfv.* **укорени́ть**] **1,** to root; implant. **2,** *fig.* to root; ingrain. —**укореня́ться,** *refl.* **1,** to take root. **2,** *fig.* to become ingrained.

укори́зна *n.* reproach. —**укори́зненный,** *adj.* of reproach; reproachful.

укори́ть *v., pfv. of* **укоря́ть.**

укороти́ть [*infl.* **-чу́, -ти́шь**] *v., pfv. of* **укора́чивать.**

укоря́ть *v.impfv.* [*pfv.* **укори́ть**] (*with* **в** + *prepl.*) to reproach (for).

украдко́й *adv.* stealthily; furtively.

украи́нец [*gen.* **-нца**] *n.m.* [*fem.* **-нка**] Ukrainian. —**украи́нский,** *adj.* Ukrainian.

укра́сить [*infl.* **-шу, -сишь**] *v., pfv. of* **украша́ть.**

укра́сть *v., pfv. of* **красть.**

украша́ть *v.impfv.* [*pfv.* **укра́сить**] to decorate; adorn; embellish.

украше́ние *n.* **1,** (act of) decorating; decoration. **2,** decoration; adornment; embellishment; ornament.

укрепи́ть [*infl.* **-плю́, -пи́шь**] *v., pfv. of* **укрепля́ть.** —**укрепи́ться,** *refl., pfv. of* **укрепля́ться.**

укрепле́ние *n.* **1,** strengthening; consolidation; reinforcement. **2,** *mil.* fortification.

укрепля́ть *v.impfv.* [*pfv.* **укрепи́ть**] **1,** to strengthen; reinforce. **2,** to fortify. **3,** to consolidate. **4,** to invigorate. **5,** to build up (one's strength, confidence, etc.). **6,** to tighten (discipline).

укрепля́ться *v.r.impfv.* [*pfv.* **укрепи́ться**] **1,** to become stronger. **2,** to take up a fortified position. **3,** *fig.* to become firmly established. **4,** *fig.* (*with* **в** + *prepl.*) to become firm (in): укрепи́ться в свои́х убежде́ниях, to become firm in one's beliefs. Укрепи́ться в наме́рении (+ *inf.*), to become ever more determined to...

укро́мный *adj.* secluded.

укро́п *n.* dill.

укроти́тель *n.m.* tamer: укроти́тель львов, lion tamer.

укроти́ть [*infl.* **-щу́, -ти́шь**] *v., pfv. of* **укроща́ть.**

укроща́ть *v.impfv.* [*pfv.* **укроти́ть**] **1,** to tame. **2,** to curb; restrain; subdue.

укроще́ние *n.* **1,** taming. **2,** curbing; restraining; subduing.

укрупне́ние *n.* **1,** enlargement. **2,** amalgamation.

укрупня́ть *v.impfv.* [*pfv.* **укрупни́ть**] to combine into larger units.

укрыва́тельство *n.* concealment (*of a crime*); hiding; harboring (*of a criminal*).

укрыва́ть *v.impfv.* [*pfv.* **укры́ть**] **1,** to cover. **2,** to conceal; harbor; shelter. —**укрыва́ться,** *refl.* **1,** to cover oneself up. **2,** to take cover; take shelter; take refuge. **3,** to escape one's notice: От него́ ничто́ не укро́ется, nothing escapes him.

укры́тие *n.* **1,** concealment. **2,** shelter. —**под укры́тием** (+ *gen.*), under cover of.

укры́ть [*infl.* **укро́ю, укро́ешь**] *v., pfv. of* **укрыва́ть.** —**укры́ться,** *refl., pfv. of* **укрыва́ться.**

у́ксус *n.* vinegar. —**у́ксусница,** *n.* vinegar cruet.

уксусноки́слый *adj., in* уксусноки́слая соль, acetate.

у́ксусный *adj.* vinegar (*attrib.*); acetic. —**у́ксусная кислота́,** acetic acid.

уку́поривать *v.impfv.* [*pfv.* **уку́порить**] **1,** to cork up. **2,** *colloq.* to pack.

уку́с *n.* bite; sting.

укуси́ть [*infl.* **укушу́, уку́сишь**] *v., pfv. of* **куса́ть.**

уку́тывать *v.impfv.* [*pfv.* **уку́тать**] (*with* **в** + *acc.*) to wrap (in). —**уку́тываться,** *refl.* to bundle up; dress warmly.

ула́вливать *v.impfv.* [*pfv.* **улови́ть**] **1,** to catch; perceive; detect. **2,** to grasp (the meaning of something). **3,** *colloq.* to seize: улови́ть моме́нт, to seize the moment. **4,** to pick up (a radio signal).

ула́дить [*infl.* **ула́жу, ула́дишь**] *v., pfv. of* **ула́живать.** —**ула́диться,** *refl., pfv. of* **ула́живаться.**

ула́живание *n.* settlement; reconciliation; adjustment.

ула́живать *v.impfv.* [*pfv.* **ула́дить**] **1,** to settle (a matter). **2,** to settle; reconcile; compose; adjust (differences). —**ула́живаться,** *refl.* to be settled.

уламывать *v.impfv.* [*pfv.* **уломать**] *colloq.* **1,** to persuade; induce; prevail upon. **2,** [*impfv. only*] to try to persuade.

улей [*gen.* **улья**] *n.* beehive.

улепётывать *v.impfv.* [*pfv.* **улепетнуть**] *colloq.* to take to one's heels; skedaddle.

улетать *v.impfv.* [*pfv.* **улететь**] to fly away; fly off.

улететь [*infl.* **-чу, -тишь**] *v., pfv. of* **улетать**.

улетучиваться *v.r.impfv.* [*pfv.* **улетучиться**] **1,** to evaporate. **2,** *colloq.* to vanish.

улечься *v.r.pfv.* [*infl. like* **лечь**] **1,** *pfv. of* **укладываться** (*in senses #3 & #4*). **2,** (*of dust*) to settle. **3,** *fig.* to subside; die down.

улизнуть *v.pfv., colloq.* to slip away; sneak away; steal away.

улика *n.* piece of evidence; *pl.* evidence.

улитка [*gen. pl.* **-ток**] *n.* snail.

улица *n.* street. —**на улице; на улицу,** outside; outdoors. —**с улицы,** from outside; from outdoors.

уличать *v.impfv.* [*pfv.* **уличить**] **1,** to convict; prove guilty. **2,** (*with* **в** + *prepl.*) to catch (*in the act of doing something*).

уличка [*gen. pl.* **-чек**] *n., colloq.* small street; narrow street.

уличный *adj.* street (*attrib.*).

улов *n.* catch (*quantity caught*).

уловимый *adj.* perceptible; audible.

уловить [*infl.* **уловлю, уловишь**] *v., pfv. of* **улавливать**.

уловка [*gen. pl.* **-вок**] *n.* trick; ruse.

уложение *n., hist.* code of law.

уложить [*infl.* **уложу, уложишь**] *v., pfv. of* **укладывать.** —**уложиться,** *refl., pfv. of* **укладываться** (*in senses #1 & #2*).

уломать *v., pfv. of* **уламывать**.

улочка [*gen. pl.* **-чек**] *n., colloq.* small street; narrow street.

улучать *v.impfv.* [*pfv.* **улучить**] to find (time); seize (a moment).

улучшать *v.impfv.* [*pfv.* **улучшить**] to improve; better. —**улучшаться,** *refl.* to improve; get better.

улучшение *n.* **1,** improvement; improving. **2,** *pl.* improvements.

улучшить *v., pfv. of* **улучшать.** —**улучшиться,** *refl., pfv. of* **улучшаться**.

улыбаться *v.r.impfv.* [*pfv.* **улыбнуться**] **1,** to smile. **2,** *fig.* (*with dat.*) to smile on: Судьба ему улыбнулась, fortune smiled on him. **3,** [*impfv. only*] (*with dat.*) *colloq.* to appeal to: Мысль мне не улыбается, the idea doesn't appeal to me.

улыбка [*gen. pl.* **-бок**] *n.* smile.

улыбнуться *v.r., pfv. of* **улыбаться**.

улыбчивый *adj., colloq.* smiling.

ультиматум *n.* ultimatum.

ультра- *prefix* ultra-.

ультразвуковой *adj.* ultrasonic.

ультрамарин *n.* ultramarine. —**ультрамариновый,** *adj.* ultramarine.

ультрасовременный *adj.* ultramodern.

ультрафиолетовый *adj., in* **ультрафиолетовые лучи,** ultraviolet rays.

улюлю *interj.* halloo!

улюлюкать *v.impfv.* to halloo.

ум [*gen.* **ума**] *n.* **1,** mind. **2,** intellect. —**без ума,** (*with verbs of loving*) madly. —**без ума от,** crazy about. —**в своём уме,** in one's right mind. —**в уме, 1,** in one's mind. **2,** in one's head: считать в уме, to do figures in one's head. —**из ума вон,** completely slipped one's mind. —**на уме,** on one's mind. —**себе на уме,** shrewd; crafty. —**с умом,** *colloq.* intelligently. —**сходить с ума,** to go out of one's mind; go mad. —**учить** (+ *acc.*) **уму-разуму,** to teach someone what to do (*or* how to act).

умаление *n.* belittling; derogation.

умалить *v., pfv. of* **умалять**.

умалишённый *adj.* mad; insane. —*n.* madman; lunatic. —**дом (для) умалишённых,** insane asylum.

умалчивать *v.impfv.* [*pfv.* **умолчать**] (*with* **о**) to keep silent (about); say nothing (about); fail to mention.

умалять *v.impfv.* [*pfv.* **умалить**] **1,** to belittle; minimize. **2,** to detract from; diminish.

умасливать *v.impfv.* [*pfv.* **умаслить**] *colloq.* to butter up.

умаять *v.pfv.* [*infl.* **умаю, умаешь**] *colloq.* to exhaust; wear out. —**умаяться,** *refl., colloq.* to become exhausted; become worn out.

умбра *n.* umber.

умелец [*gen.* **-льца**] *n.* skilled craftsman.

умелый *adj.* able; skillful. —**умело,** *adv.* ably; skillfully.

умение *n.* ability; skill.

уменьшаемое *n., decl. as an adj.,* math. minuend.

уменьшать *v.impfv.* [*pfv.* **уменьшить**] to reduce; decrease; lessen. —**уменьшаться,** *refl.* to decrease; diminish; decline.

уменьшение *n.* reduction; decrease; decline; diminution.

уменьшительный *adj., gram.* diminutive. —**уменьшительное имя,** familiar first name (*e.g.* Толя *for* Анатолий).

уменьшить *v., pfv. of* **уменьшать.** —**уменьшиться,** *refl., pfv. of* **уменьшаться**.

умеренный *adj.* **1,** moderate. **2,** temperate. —**умеренно,** *adv.* moderately; in moderation. —**умеренность,** *n.f.* moderation.

умереть [*infl.* **умру, умрёшь;** *past* **умер, умерла, умерло, умерли**] *v., pfv. of* **умирать**.

умерить *v., pfv. of* **умерять**.

умертвить [*infl.* **умерщвлю, умертвишь**] *v., pfv. of* **умерщвлять**.

умерший *n., decl. as an adj.* the deceased; *pl.* the dead.

умерщвление *n.* killing. —**умерщвление плоти,** mortification of the flesh.

умерщвлять *v.impfv.* [*pfv.* **умертвить**] **1,** to kill. **2,** to deaden. —**умерщвлять плоть,** to mortify the flesh.

умерять *v.impfv.* [*pfv.* **умерить**] to moderate; temper.

уместить [*infl.* **-щу, -стишь**] *v., pfv. of* **умещать.** —**уместиться,** *refl., pfv. of* **умещаться**.

уместно *adv.* appropriately; aptly. —*adj., used predicatively,* appropriate: Было бы уместно (+ *inf.*), it would be appropriate to...; it would be a good idea to...

уместность *n.f.* timeliness; relevance; pertinence.

уме́стный *adj.* appropriate; timely; relevant; pertinent.

уме́ть *v.impfv.* (*with inf.*) to know how (to); be able (to).

умеща́ть *v.impfv.* [*pfv.* умести́ть] to fit; get: умести́ть всё в чемода́н(е), to fit/get everything into the suitcase. —умеща́ться, *refl.* to fit; go (into *or* onto).

умиле́ние *n.* deep feeling; deep emotion. Слёзы умиле́ния, tears of emotion. —приходи́ть в умиле́ние, to be deeply moved.

умили́тельный *adj.* moving; touching; affecting.

умили́ть *v., pfv. of* умиля́ть. —умили́ться, *refl., pfv. of* умиля́ться.

уми́лостивить *v.pfv.* [*infl.* -влю, -вишь] to placate; mollify; propitiate.

уми́льный *adj.* **1,** tender. **2,** touching. **3,** ingratiating; obsequious.

умиля́ть *v.impfv.* [*pfv.* умили́ть] to move; touch; affect. —умиля́ться, *refl.* to be moved; be touched.

умира́ние *n.* dying.

умира́ть *v.impfv.* [*pfv.* умере́ть] to die.

умира́ющий *adj.* dying. —*n.* dying man.

умиротворе́ние *n.* pacification; appeasement.

умиротворя́ть *v.impfv.* [*pfv.* умиротвори́ть] to pacify; appease.

умля́ут *n.* umlaut.

умне́ть *v.impfv.* [*pfv.* поумне́ть] to become wiser; grow wiser.

у́мник *n., colloq.* **1,** clever man; clever child. **2,** smart aleck; wise guy.

у́мница *n.m. & f., colloq.* clever person.

у́мничать *v.impfv., colloq.* to show off one's intelligence.

умножа́ть *v.impfv.* [*pfv.* умно́жить] **1,** *math.* to multiply. **2,** to increase; augment. —умножа́ться, *refl.* to multiply; increase in number.

умноже́ние *n.* **1,** *math.* multiplication. **2,** increase.

умно́жить *v., pfv. of* мно́жить *and* умножа́ть. —умно́житься, *refl., pfv. of* мно́житься *and* умножа́ться.

у́мный *adj.* [*short form* умён, умна́, у́мно *or* умно́, у́мны *or* умны́] intelligent; clever; smart.

умозаключа́ть *v.impfv.* [*pfv.* умозаключи́ть] to conclude; deduce.

умозаключе́ние *n.* conclusion; deduction.

умозаключи́ть *v., pfv. of* умозаключа́ть.

умозре́ние *n.* speculation; conjecture.

умозри́тельный *adj.* speculative.

умоисступле́ние *n.* frenzy: припа́док умоисступле́ния, fit of frenzy.

умоли́ть *v.pfv.* [*infl.* умолю́, умо́лишь] to persuade; prevail upon.

у́молк *n., in* без у́молку, endlessly; incessantly.

умолка́ть *v.impfv.* [*pfv.* умо́лкнуть] **1,** to fall silent. **2,** (*of noise, sounds, etc.*) to die away; stop; cease.

умо́лкнуть [*past* умо́лк, умо́лкла] *v., pfv. of* умолка́ть.

умолча́ние *n.* **1,** silence; keeping silent. **2,** *pl.* (deliberate) omissions; things left unsaid.

умолча́ть [*infl.* -чу́, -чи́шь] *v., pfv. of* ума́лчивать.

умоля́ть *v.impfv.* to beg; plead with; implore; beseech; entreat.

умоля́ющий *adj.* pleading; suppliant.

умонастрое́ние *n.* frame of mind.

умопомеша́тельство *n.* mental derangement; insanity.

умопомраче́ние *n.* daze; trance; stupor.

умопомрачи́тельный *adj., colloq.* stunning; stupendous; fantastic.

умо́ра *n., colloq.* a scream; a riot: Это умо́ра, it's a scream/riot.

умори́тельный *adj., colloq.* screamingly funny; hilarious.

умори́ть *v.pfv., colloq.* **1,** to kill. **2,** to exhaust; wear out. —умори́ть го́лодом, to starve (someone) to death. —умори́ть со́ смеху, to have (someone) in stitches.

у́мственный *adj.* mental; intellectual. —у́мственно, *adv.* mentally: у́мственно отста́лый, mentally retarded.

умудря́ть *v.impfv.* [*pfv.* умудри́ть] to make wiser. —умудря́ться, *refl.* **1,** to become wiser. **2,** (*with inf.*) *colloq.* to manage (to); contrive (to).

умча́ть *v.pfv.* [*infl.* умчу́, умчи́шь] to whisk away. —умча́ться, *refl.* to dash away; speed away.

умыва́льник *n.* washstand; washbasin; washbowl.

умыва́льный *adj.* wash (*attrib.*); washing (*attrib.*).

умыва́ние *n.* washing.

умыва́ть *v.impfv.* [*pfv.* умы́ть] to wash. —умыва́ться, *refl.* to wash (one's hands and face).

умыка́ть *v.impfv.* [*pfv.* умыкну́ть] *colloq.* to steal.

у́мысел [*gen.* -сла] *n.* design; intention. Злой у́мысел, malicious intent. —с у́мыслом, **1,** on purpose; deliberately. **2,** by design.

умы́ть [*infl.* умо́ю, умо́ешь] *v., pfv. of* умыва́ть. —умы́ться, *refl., pfv. of* умыва́ться.

умы́шленный *adj.* intentional; deliberate; premeditated. —умы́шленно, *adv.* deliberately; intentionally; on purpose.

умягча́ть *v.impfv.* [*pfv.* умягчи́ть] **1,** to soften. **2,** *fig.* to mollify.

унаво́зить *v., pfv. of* наво́зить.

унасле́довать *v.pfv.* [*infl.* -дую, -дуешь] to inherit.

унести́ [*infl. like* нести́] *v., pfv. of* уноси́ть. —унести́сь, *refl., pfv. of* уноси́ться.

униа́т *n.* Uniate. —униа́тский, *adj.* Uniate.

универма́г *n.* department store (*contr. of* универса́льный магази́н).

универса́льность *n.f.* universality.

универса́льный *adj.* **1,** universal. **2,** all-round. **3,** multipurpose; all-purpose. —универса́льный магази́н, department store. —универса́льное сре́дство, panacea.

универса́м *n.* supermarket.

университе́т *n.* university. —университе́тский, *adj.* university (*attrib.*).

унижа́ть *v.impfv.* [*pfv.* уни́зить] **1,** to humiliate. **2,** to degrade; debase. **3,** to humble; abase. —унижа́ться, *refl.* **1,** to humble oneself. **2,** (*with* до) to stoop to.

униже́ние *n.* **1,** humiliation. **2,** degradation; abasement. **3,** indignity.

уни́женный *adj.* **1,** humiliated. **2,** humble; abject.

униза́ть [*infl.* унижу́, уни́жешь] *v., pfv. of* уни́зывать.

унизи́тельный *adj.* humiliating; degrading.

уни́зить [*infl.* уни́жу, уни́зишь] *v., pfv. of* унижа́ть. —уни́зиться, *refl., pfv. of* унижа́ться.

унизывать *v.impfv.* [*pfv.* **унизать**] to stud (*with jewels*).

уникальный *adj.* [*short form* **-лен, -льна**] unique.

уникум *n.* unique person; unique object.

унимать *v.impfv.* [*pfv.* **унять**] **1,** to quiet; calm; pacify. **2,** to stop; suppress. —**униматься,** *refl.* **1,** to quiet down; calm down. **2,** to stop; subside; abate; die down. **3,** *colloq.* to desist; (*with* **не**) persist.

унисон *n.* unison. —**в унисон,** in unison.

унитаз *n.* toilet.

унификация *n.* standardizaton.

унифицировать *v.impfv. & pfv.* [*pres.* **-рую, -руешь**] to standardize.

уничижительный *adj.* pejorative.

уничтожать *v.impfv.* [*pfv.* **уничтожить**] **1,** to destroy; annihilate; obliterate; wipe out. **2,** to eliminate; abolish; do away with.

уничтожающий *adj.* **1,** destructive; devastating. **2,** *fig.* scathing; devastating; withering.

уничтожение *n.* **1,** destruction; annihilation. **2,** elimination; abolition.

уничтожить *v., pfv. of* **уничтожать.**

уния *n.* union (*of countries or churches*).

уносить *v.impfv.* [*pfv.* **унести**; *pres.* **уношу, уносишь**] **1,** to carry away; carry off. **2,** *fig.* to take (lives). **3,** *colloq.* to make off with. **4,** *in* **уносить ноги,** to escape; get away. —**уноситься,** *refl.* **1,** to speed away; dash off. **2,** *fig.* (*of thoughts*) to go back. **3,** *fig.* (*of time*) to fly by.

унтер-офицер *n.* noncommissioned officer.

унция *n.* ounce.

унывать *v.impfv.* (*only used negatively*) to lose heart; be dejected; be discouraged.

унылый *adj.* **1,** downcast; despondent; dejected. **2,** cheerless; dreary; dismal.

уныние *n.* despondency; dejection.

унять [*infl.* **уйму, уймёшь;** *past* **унял, уняла, уняло, уняли**] *v., pfv. of* **унимать.** —**уняться,** *refl.* [*past* **унялся, унялась, унялось, унялись**] *pfv. of* **униматься.**

упад *n., in* **до упаду,** till one is about to drop.

упадок [*gen.* **-дка**] *n.* decline; decay. —**упадок духа,** despondency; depression. —**упадок сил,** weakness; loss of strength.

упадочничество *n.* decadence. —**упадочнический,** *adj.* decadent.

упадочный *adj.* **1,** decadent. **2,** depressed: упадочное настроение, depression.

упаковать [*infl.* **-кую, -куешь**] *v., pfv. of* **паковать** *and* **упаковывать.** —**упаковаться,** *refl., pfv. of* **упаковываться.**

упаковка *n.* **1,** packing. **2,** packing material.

упаковочный *adj.* packing (*attrib.*).

упаковщик *n.* packer.

упаковывать *v.impfv.* [*pfv.* **упаковать**] to pack. —**упаковываться,** *refl.* to pack; get packed; pack one's things.

упасти *v.pfv.* [*infl. like* **спасти**] *archaic* to save. —**упаси бог!; боже упаси!, 1,** God forbid!; heaven forbid! **2,** perish the thought!

упасть [*infl. like* **пасть**] *v., pfv. of* **падать.**

упекать *v.impfv.* [*pfv.* **упечь**] *colloq.* **1,** to bake thoroughly. **2,** to send away; banish. **3,** *in* упекать в тюрьму, to toss into jail.

упереть [*infl. like* **переть**] *v., pfv. of* **упирать.** —**упереться,** *refl., pfv. of* **упираться.**

упечь [*infl. like* **печь**] *v., pfv. of* **упекать.**

упиваться *v.r.impfv.* [*pfv.* **упиться**] **1,** *colloq.* to get drunk. **2,** (*with instr.*) to delight in; revel in.

упирать *v.impfv.* [*pfv.* **упереть**] **1,** to place firmly (on *or* against): упирать лестницу в стену, to place a ladder against the wall. **2,** to fix (one's eyes on something): упирать взгляд в дверь, to fix one's eyes on the door. **3,** *v.i.* (*with* **на** + *acc.*) *colloq.* to emphasize; lay stress on.

упираться *v.r.impfv.* [*pfv.* **упереться**] **1,** (*with instr.*) to give a push with. **2,** (*with instr.*) to plant firmly (on *or* against): упираться ногами в землю, to plant one's feet firmly on the ground. **3,** (*with instr.*) *colloq.* to fix (one's eyes on something): упереться взглядом в дверь, to fix one's eyes on the door. **4,** (*with* **в** + *acc.*) *colloq.* to run into; come up against. **5,** *fig., colloq.* to balk; resist.

уписать [*infl.* **упишу, упишешь**] *v., pfv. of* **уписывать.**

уписывать *v.impfv.* [*pfv.* **уписать**] *colloq.* to eat; gobble up.

упитанный *adj.* well-fed; fat; plump.

упиться [*infl. like* **пить;** *past* **упился, упилась, упилось** *or* **упилось, упились** *or* **упились**] *v.r., pfv. of* **упиваться.**

уплата *n.* payment.

уплатить [*infl.* **уплачу, уплатишь**] *v., pfv. of* **уплачивать.**

уплачивать *v.impfv.* [*pfv.* **уплатить**] to pay.

уплести [*infl. like* **плести**] *v., pfv. of* **уплетать.**

уплетать *v.impfv.* [*pfv.* **уплести**] *colloq.* to eat up; devour.

уплотнение *n.* **1,** packing down; compression. **2,** hard spot. **3,** *in* уплотнение рабочего дня, tightening up the schedule of the workday.

уплотнять *v.impfv.* [*pfv.* **уплотнить**] **1,** to pack down (dirt, sand, etc.). **2,** to make more compact; make more crowded. **3,** *fig.* to crowd more into: уплотнять рабочий день, to crowd more into the workday. —**уплотняться,** *refl.* **1,** to be packed down. **2,** to become more crowded. **3,** to give up part of one's living space.

уплывать *v.impfv.* [*pfv.* **уплыть**] **1,** to swim away. **2,** to sail away; sail off. **3,** to float away. **4,** (*of time*) to slip by.

уплыть [*infl. like* **плыть**] *v., pfv. of* **уплывать.**

упование *n., obs.* hope.

уповать *v.impfv., obs.* **1,** to hope. **2,** (*with* **на** + *acc.*) to hope for. **3,** (*with* **на** + *acc.*) to count on.

уподобить [*infl.* **-блю, -бишь**] *v., pfv. of* **уподоблять.** —**уподобиться,** *refl., pfv. of* **уподобляться.**

уподоблять *v.impfv.* [*pfv.* **уподобить**] to liken: уподоблять политику шахматам, to liken politics to chess. —**уподобляться,** *refl.* (*with dat.*) to become like; come to resemble.

упое́ние *n.* rapture; delight.

упоённый *adj.* ecstatic; rapturous; enraptured.

упои́тельный *adj.* delightful; enchanting.

упоко́й *n., in* **за упоко́й** (+ *gen.*), for the repose of.

уполза́ть *v.impfv.* [*pfv.* **уползти́**] **1,** to crawl away. **2,** to move away (*slowly*); drift away.

уползти́ [*infl. like* **ползти́**] *v., pfv. of* **уполза́ть**.

уполномо́ченный *adj.* authorized. —*n.* authorized agent; representative; plenipotentiary.

уполномо́чивать *v.impfv.* [*pfv.* **уполномо́чить**] to authorize; empower.

уполномо́чие *n., in* **по уполномо́чию** (+ *gen.*), by authority of.

уполномо́чить *v., pfv. of* **уполномо́чивать**.

упомина́ние *n.* mentioning; mention: при (одно́м) упомина́нии (+ *gen. or with* о), at the (very) mention of.

упомина́ть *v.impfv.* [*pfv.* **упомяну́ть**] (*with acc. or* о) to mention.

упо́мнить *v.pfv., colloq.* to remember.

упомяну́ть [*infl.* **-мяну́, -мя́нешь**] *v., pfv. of* **упомина́ть**.

упо́р *n.* **1,** support: для упо́ра, for support. **2,** prop; support. **3,** *fig.* emphasis: де́лать упо́р на (+ *acc. or prepl.*), to emphasize; lay emphasis *or* stress on. —**в упо́р,** pointblank.

упо́рный *adj.* stubborn; persistent.

упо́рство *n.* stubbornness; persistence; perseverance.

упо́рствовать *v.impfv.* [*pres.* **-ствую, -ствуешь**] **1,** to be stubborn. **2,** to persist; persevere.

упорхну́ть *v.pfv.* to fly away; flit away.

упоря́доченный *adj.* orderly; efficient; well organized.

упоря́дочить *v.pfv.* to put in order; put right; normalize.

употреби́тельный *adj.* widely used; in common use.

употреби́ть [*infl.* **-блю́, -би́шь**] *v., pfv. of* **употребля́ть**. —**употреби́ться,** *refl., pfv. of* **употребля́ться**.

употребле́ние *n.* use.

употребля́ть *v.impfv.* [*pfv.* **употреби́ть**] to use. —**употребля́ться,** *refl.* to be used.

упра́ва *n.* **1,** pre-rev. council; board. **2,** *colloq.* justice: иска́ть упра́вы, to seek justice. Найти́ упра́ву на (+ *acc.*), to see justice done in the case of.

управи́тель *n.m., obs.* manager; steward.

упра́виться [*infl.* **-влюсь, -вишься**] *v.r., pfv. of* **управля́ться**.

управле́ние *n.* **1,** (*with instr.*) management (of); administration (of). **2,** (*with instr.*) driving (a car); steering (a ship); conducting (an orchestra). **3,** *mech.* control: дистанцио́нное управле́ние, remote control. Рыча́г управле́ния, control lever. **4,** government: ме́стное управле́ние, local government. **5,** (*governmental*) board; bureau; administration; agency; directorate.

управле́нческий *adj.* administrative.

управля́емый *adj.* guided: управля́емый снаря́д, guided missile.

управля́ть *v.impfv.* (*with instr.*) **1,** to operate (a machine); drive (a car). **2,** to manage; administer; run. **3,** to rule; govern. **4,** to control. **5,** to conduct (an orchestra). **6,** *gram.* to govern. —**управля́ться,** *refl.* [*pfv.* **упра́виться**] *colloq.* **1,** (*with* с + *instr.*) to finish (with). **2,** (*with* с + *instr.*) to cope with; deal with; handle. **3,** [*impfv. only*] (*of a vehicle*) to ride; handle (*a certain way*).

управля́ющий *n., decl. as an adj.* manager.

упражне́ние *n.* exercise.

упражня́ть *v.impfv.* to exercise; train. —**упражня́ться,** *refl.* (*with* в *or* на + *prepl.*) to practice.

упраздне́ние *n.* abolition.

упраздня́ть *v.impfv.* [*pfv.* **упраздни́ть**] to abolish.

упра́шивать *v.impfv.* to beg; entreat.

упрева́ть *v.impfv.* [*pfv.* **упре́ть**] *colloq.* to be well-cooked.

упрежда́ть *v.impfv.* [*pfv.* **упреди́ть**] *obs.* **1,** to warn. **2,** to anticipate. —**упрежда́ющий уда́р,** preemptive strike.

упрёк *n.* reproach; rebuke; reproof. —**ста́вить (что́-нибудь) в упрёк** (+ *dat.*), to hold something against someone; fault someone (for something).

упрека́ть *v.impfv.* [*pfv.* **упрекну́ть**] (*with* в + *prepl.*) to reproach; rebuke: упрека́ть кого́-нибудь в неблагода́рности, to reproach someone for his (her) ingratitude.

упре́ть *v., pfv. of* **упрева́ть**.

упроси́ть *v.pfv.* [*infl.* **упрошу́, упро́сишь**] to persuade; talk into; prevail upon.

упрости́ть *v.pfv.* [*infl.* **-щу́, -сти́шь**] *v., pfv. of* **упроща́ть**. —**упрости́ться,** *refl., pfv. of* **упроща́ться**.

упро́чение *n.* strengthening; consolidation.

упро́чивать *v.impfv.* [*pfv.* **упро́чить**] to strengthen; consolidate. —**упро́чиваться,** *refl.* to become firmly established.

упроща́ть *v.impfv.* [*pfv.* **упрости́ть**] **1,** to simplify. **2,** to oversimplify. —**упроща́ться,** *refl.* to become simpler.

упроще́ние *n.* simplification. —**упрощённый,** *adj.* simplified. —**упроще́нство; упроще́нчество,** *n.* oversimplification. —**упроще́нческий,** *adj.* oversimplified; simplistic.

упру́гий *adj.* elastic; resilient; springy. —**упру́гость,** *n.f.* elasticity; resilience.

упря́жка [*gen. pl.* **-жек**] *n.* **1,** team (*of horses, dogs, etc.*). **2,** harness.

упряжно́й *adj.* harness (*attrib.*). —**упряжна́я ло́шадь,** draft horse.

у́пряжь *n.f.* harness.

упря́мец [*gen.* **-мца**] *n., colloq.* stubborn person.

упря́миться *v.r.impfv.* [*pres.* **-млюсь, -мишься**] to be stubborn; balk.

упря́мство *n.* stubbornness; obstinacy.

упря́мый *adj.* **1,** stubborn; obstinate. **2,** persistent.

упря́тать [*infl.* **упря́чу, упря́чешь**] *v., pfv. of* **упря́тывать**.

упря́тывать *v.impfv.* [*pfv.* **упря́тать**] *colloq.* **1,** to hide; put away. **2,** *in* упря́тывать в тюрьму́, to toss into prison.

упуска́ть *v.impfv.* [*pfv.* **упусти́ть**] **1,** to lose hold of; let slip out of one's hands. **2,** to let slip by; miss; lose (a chance, opportunity, etc.). —**упуска́ть и́з виду, 1,** to let out of one's sight. **2,** to lose sight of; overlook; fail to realize.

упусти́ть [*infl.* **упущу́, упу́стишь**] *v., pfv. of* **упуска́ть**.

упуще́ние *n.* **1,** omission. **2,** oversight.

упы́рь [*gen.* **упыря́**] *n.m.* vampire.

ура́ *interj.* hurrah!; hurray! —**на ура́, 1,** *mil.* by storm. **2,** hoping for the best. **3,** with enthusiasm.

уравне́ние *n.* **1,** equalization. **2,** *math.* equation.

ура́внивать *v.impfv.* **1,** [*pfv.* **уравня́ть**] to equalize; make equal. **2,** [*pfv.* **уровня́ть**] to level; even.

уравни́тельный *adj.* **1,** equalizing. **2,** applied equally to all.

уравнове́сить [*infl.* **-шу, -сишь**] *v., pfv. of* **уравнове́шивать.**

уравнове́шенный *adj.* **1,** balanced. **2,** *fig.* even-tempered; levelheaded. —**уравнове́шенность,** *n.f.* even temper.

уравнове́шивать *v.impfv.* [*pfv.* **уравнове́сить**] **1,** to balance. **2,** *fig.* to counterbalance; offset.

уравня́ть *v., pfv. of* **ура́внивать** (*in sense #1*).

урага́н *n.* hurricane.

уразумева́ть *v.impfv.* [*pfv.* **уразуме́ть**] to understand.

ура́н *n.* **1,** uranium. **2,** *cap.* Uranus.

ура́новый *adj.* uranium (*attrib.*).

урва́ть [*infl.* **урву́, урвёшь;** *past fem.* **урвала́**] *v., pfv. of* **урыва́ть.**

урду́ *n.m. indecl.* Urdu.

урегули́рование *n.* settlement.

урегули́ровать *v.pfv.* [*infl.* **-рую, -руешь**] to settle (an issue, dispute, etc.).

уре́зать [*infl.* **уре́жу, уре́жешь**] *v., pfv. of* **уре́зывать** *and* **уреза́ть.**

уреза́ть *v.impfv.* = **уре́зывать.**

урезо́нивать *v.impfv.* [*pfv.* **урезо́нить**] *colloq.* **1,** to bring to reason. **2,** [*impfv. only*] to reason with; try to persuade.

уре́зывать *v.impfv.* [*pfv.* **уре́зать**] **1,** *colloq.* to shorten (*by cutting off a part*). **2,** to reduce; cut; curtail. **3,** to abridge (someone's rights). *Also,* **уреза́ть.**

уреми́я *n.* uremia. —**уреми́ческий,** *adj.* uremic.

уре́тра *n.* urethra.

у́рна *n.* **1,** urn. **2,** refuse container. —**избира́тельная у́рна,** ballot box.

у́ровень [*gen.* **-вня**] *n.m.* **1,** level: у́ровень мо́ря, sea level. **2,** *fig.* standard: жи́зненный у́ровень, standard of living. **3,** level (*instrument*). —**быть на у́ровне,** *colloq.* to be up to the mark; be up to par. —**идти́ в у́ровень с ве́ком,** to keep up with the times.

уровня́ть *v., pfv. of* **ура́внивать** (*in sense #2*).

уро́д *n.* **1,** freak; monster. **2,** ugly person. **3,** monstrosity.

уроди́ть *v.pfv.* [*infl.* **-жу́, -ди́шь**] to bear; yield. —**уроди́ться,** *refl.* **1,** to come up; grow; ripen. **2,** *colloq.* to be born. **3,** (*with* **в** + *acc.*) *colloq.* to take after; resemble.

уро́дливость *n.f.* **1,** ugliness. **2,** deformity.

уро́дливый *adj.* **1,** deformed; misshapen. **2,** extremely ugly; hideous. **3,** *fig.* improper; distorted; perverted.

уро́довать *v.impfv.* [*pfv.* **изуро́довать;** *pres.* **-дую, -дуешь**] **1,** to disfigure. **2,** to mutilate; maim. **3,** *fig.* to corrupt.

уро́дский *adj., colloq.* ugly; hideous.

уро́дство *n.* **1,** deformity. **2,** ugliness. **3,** abnormality.

урожа́й *n.* harvest; crop.

урожа́йность *n.f.* productivity; yield.

урожа́йный *adj.* **1,** (*of ground, soil, etc.*) productive; fertile. **2,** (*of crops*) high-yield. **3,** (*of a year, season, etc.*) good (*for crops*); productive.

урождённая *adj.* nee.

уроже́нец [*gen.* **-нца**] *n.m.* [*fem.* **-нка**] native.

уро́к *n.* lesson.

уроло́гия *n.* urologist. —**уро́лог,** *n.* urologist. —**урологи́ческий,** *adj.* urological.

уро́н *n.* **1,** damage; harm. **2,** losses; casualties.

урони́ть [*infl.* **уроню́, уро́нишь**] *v., pfv. of* **роня́ть.**

уро́чище *n.* natural boundary.

уро́чный *adj.* **1,** *obs.* fixed; set; agreed-upon. **2,** usual; customary.

урча́ние *n.* rumbling.

урча́ть *v.impfv.* [*pres.* **-чу́, -чи́шь**] to rumble.

урыва́ть *v.impfv.* [*pfv.* **урва́ть**] *colloq.* **1,** to snatch; grab. **2,** *fig.* to find (time).

уры́вками *adv., colloq.* in snatches; by fits and starts.

урю́к *n.* dried apricots.

ус [*pl.* **усы́**] *n.* **1,** whisker (*of an animal*). **2,** *bot.* tendril. **3,** *in* кито́вый ус, whalebone. —**в ус не дуть,** *colloq.* not to give a damn. *See also* **усы́.**

усади́ть [*infl.* **усажу́, уса́дишь**] *v., pfv. of* **уса́живать.**

уса́дка *n.* shrinkage.

уса́дьба [*gen. pl.* **-деб**] *n.* **1,** country estate. **2,** farmstead.

уса́живать *v.impfv.* [*pfv.* **усади́ть**] **1,** to seat; sit; offer a seat to. **2,** (*with* **за** + *acc.*) to sit (someone) down to. **3,** to plant (with). —**уса́живаться,** *refl.* [*pfv.* **усе́сться**] **1,** to sit down; take a seat. **2,** (*with* **за** + *acc. or inf.*) to sit down to; settle down to.

уса́тый *adj.* **1,** with a (big) mustache. **2,** (*of an animal*) having whiskers.

уса́ч [*gen.* **усача́**] *n., colloq.* man with a (big) mustache.

усва́ивать *v.impfv.* [*pfv.* **усво́ить**] **1,** to master. **2,** to acquire (a habit, instinct, etc.). **3,** to adopt (a custom, manner, etc.). **4,** to digest; assimilate.

усвое́ние *n.* **1,** mastering. **2,** acquiring. **3,** assimilation.

усво́ить *v., pfv. of* **усва́ивать.**

усе́ивать *v.impfv.* [*pfv.* **усе́ять**] to dot; stud: Не́бо усе́яно звёздами, the sky is studded with stars.

усека́ть *v.impfv.* [*pfv.* **усе́чь**] to truncate.

усе́рдие *n.* **1,** zeal. **2,** diligence.

усе́рдный *adj.* **1,** zealous. **2,** diligent.

усе́рдствовать *v.impfv.* [*pres.* **-ствую, -ствуешь**] **1,** to show great zeal; work hard. **2,** (*with inf.*) to take pains (to).

усе́сться [*infl. like* **сесть**] *v.r., pfv. of* **уса́живаться.**

усе́чь [*infl. like* **сечь;** *past* усёк, усекла́, усекло́, усекли́] *v., pfv. of* **усека́ть.**

усе́ять [*infl.* **усе́ю, усе́ешь**] *v., pfv. of* **усе́ивать.**

усиде́ть *v.pfv.* [*infl.* **-жу́, -ди́шь**] **1,** to keep one's seat. **2,** to sit; stay (*in one place*). **3,** *colloq.* to keep a job.

уси́дчивый *adj.* assiduous. —**уси́дчивость,** *n.f.* assiduousness.

у́сик *n.* **1,** small mustache. **2,** *zool.* feeler. **3,** *bot.* tendril; runner.

усиле́ние *n.* **1,** strengthening; reinforcement. **2,** intensification. **3,** amplification (*of sound*).

уси́ленно *adv.* **1,** with great force. **2,** hard; diligently; in earnest: уси́ленно гото́виться к экза́менам, to study hard for one's examinations. **3,** *colloq.* with great effort; with great difficulty.

уси́ленный *adj.* **1,** increased; extra. **2,** intense; strenuous. **3,** (*of requests, questions, etc.*) repeated; persistent.

уси́ливать *v.impfv.* [*pfv.* уси́лить] **1,** to strengthen; reinforce. **2,** to increase; intensify; step up. **3,** to amplify (sound). —уси́ливаться, *refl.* **1,** to become stronger. **2,** to increase; become more intense. **3,** (*of rain*) to come down harder. **4,** [*impfv. only*] (*with inf.*) *obs.* to strive (to); endeavor (to).

уси́лие *n.* effort: прилага́ть все уси́лия, to make every effort. —де́лать над собо́й уси́лие, to force oneself.

усили́тель *n.m.* amplifier; booster.

уси́лить *v., pfv. of* уси́ливать. —уси́литься, *refl., pfv. of* уси́ливаться.

ускака́ть *v.pfv.* [*infl.* ускачу́, уска́чешь] **1,** to skip away; hop away. **2,** to gallop off.

ускольза́ть *v.impfv.* [*pfv.* ускользну́ть] **1,** to slip out: ускользну́ть из рук, to slip out of one's hands. **2,** *colloq.* to slip away; sneak away; steal away. **3,** (*with* от) *colloq.* to elude; evade; give (someone) the slip. **4,** (*with* от) *colloq.* to slip away (from); get away (from) (*i.e.* be lost). **5,** *in* ускользну́ть от чьего́-нибудь внима́ния, to escape one's notice. **6,** (*with* от) *colloq.* to avoid giving (an answer, explanation, etc.).

ускоре́ние *n.* acceleration.

ускори́тель *n.m.* **1,** accelerator. **2,** *rocketry* booster.

ускоря́ть *v.impfv.* [*pfv.* уско́рить] **1,** to accelerate; speed up; quicken. **2,** to hasten; bring on sooner. —ускоря́ться, *refl.* **1,** to pick up speed; accelerate. **2,** to be speeded up.

усла́вливаться *v.* = усло́вливаться.

усла́да *n., obs.* pleasure; delight.

услади́ть [*infl.* -жу́, -ди́шь] *v., pfv. of* услажда́ть.

услажда́ть *v.impfv.* [*pfv.* услади́ть] **1,** to delight; bring pleasure to. **2,** *obs.* to brighten up. **3,** *obs.* to relieve; mitigate.

усла́ть [*infl.* ушлю́, ушлёшь] *v., pfv. of* усыла́ть.

уследи́ть *v.pfv.* [*infl.* -жу́, -ди́шь] (*with* за + *instr.*) **1,** to keep an eye on. **2,** to follow; keep track of.

усло́вие *n.* **1,** condition: непреме́нное усло́вие, essential condition. Ста́вить усло́вия, to lay down conditions. Поста́вить усло́вием, что..., to stipulate that...; make it conditional upon. **2,** *pl.* conditions: усло́вия труда́, working conditions. **3,** *pl.* terms; provisions (*of a treaty, contract, etc.*): на льго́тных усло́виях, on favorable terms. **4,** *obs.* agreement: заключи́ть усло́вие, to conclude an agreement. —в усло́виях (+ *gen.*), under conditions of... —ни при каки́х усло́виях, under no circumstances. —при про́чих ра́вных усло́виях, other things being equal. —при таки́х усло́виях, under such conditions. —при усло́вии, что..., on condition that; provided.

усло́виться [*infl.* -влюсь, -вишься] *v.r., pfv. of* усло́вливаться.

усло́вленный *adj.* **1,** agreed-upon. **2,** [*short form only*] agreed: как усло́влено, as agreed.

усло́вливаться *v.r.impfv.* [*pfv.* усло́виться] to agree; arrange: усло́вливаться встре́титься, to agree/arrange to meet; усло́виться о цене́, to agree on the price.

усло́вно *adv.* conditionally; tentatively. Он получи́л год усло́вно, he was given a year on probation; he was given a one-year suspended sentence.

усло́вность *n.f.* convention; conventionality.

усло́вный *adj.* **1,** agreed-upon; prearranged. **2,** conventional. **3,** conditional. **4,** relative. **5,** (*of a line*) imaginary. **6,** *gram.* conditional. —усло́вный пригово́р, suspended sentence. —усло́вный рефле́кс, conditioned reflex.

усложне́ние *n.* complication.

усложня́ть *v.impfv.* [*pfv.* усложни́ть] to complicate. —усложня́ться, *refl.* to be complicated; become complicated.

услу́га *n.* **1,** favor; good turn: оказа́ть услу́гу (+ *dat.*), to do (someone) a favor. Плоха́я услу́га, disservice; ill turn. **2,** *pl.* services: предлага́ть свои́ услу́ги, to offer one's services. **3,** *pl.* facilities. **4,** *in* до́брые услу́ги, *dipl.* good offices. —к ва́шим услу́гам, **1,** at your service. **2,** at your disposal.

услу́живать *v.impfv.* [*pfv.* услужи́ть] (*with dat.*) **1,** to help; oblige; accommodate; do something for. **2,** [*impfv. only*] *obs.* to serve; be a servant to.

услужи́ть [*infl.* услужу́, услу́жишь] *v., pfv. of* услу́живать.

услу́жливый *adj.* obliging; helpful; accommodating.

услыха́ть *v.pfv.* [*infl. like* слы́шать] = услы́шать.

услы́шать *v., pfv. of* слы́шать.

усма́тривать *v.impfv.* [*pfv.* усмотре́ть] **1,** *colloq.* to spot; detect. **2,** (*with* за + *instr.*) *colloq.* to look after; keep an eye on. **3,** (*with* в + *prepl.*) to see (in); see (as): усма́тривать в ко́м-нибудь сопе́рника, to see someone as a rival.

усмеха́ться *v.r.impfv.* [*pfv.* усмехну́ться] to smile; grin.

усме́шка *n.* **1,** smile; grin. **2,** sneer; smirk.

усмире́ние *n.* **1,** suppression. **2,** pacification.

усмиря́ть *v.impfv.* [*pfv.* усмири́ть] **1,** to pacify; quiet. **2,** to suppress; put down.

усмотре́ние *n.* discretion; judgment.

усмотре́ть [*infl.* усмотрю́, усмо́тришь] *v., pfv. of* усма́тривать.

усну́ть *v.pfv.* to fall asleep.

усоверше́нствование *n.* **1,** improvement; refinement. **2,** advanced training: ку́рсы усоверше́нствования, advanced training program.

усоверше́нствовать *v., pfv. of* соверше́нствовать.

усо́вестить *v., pfv. of* со́вестить. —усо́веститься, *refl., pfv. of* со́веститься.

усомни́ться *v.r.pfv.* (*with* в + *prepl.*) to doubt; have doubts about.

усоно́гий *adj., in* усоно́гий рак, barnacle.

усо́пший *adj., obs.* deceased. —*n., obs.* the deceased.

усо́хнуть [*past* усо́х, усо́хла] *v., pfv. of* усыха́ть.

успева́емость *n.f.* progress (*in one's studies*). —та́бель успева́емости, report card.

успева́ть *v.impfv.* [*pfv.* успе́ть] **1,** (*with inf.*) to have time (to). **2,** (*with* на + *acc. or* к) *colloq.* to be in/on time (for). **3,** [*impfv. only*] to do well (*in one's studies*). **4,** (*with* в + *prepl.*) *obs.* to be successful (in).

успе́ние *n., relig.* **1,** death; passing. **2,** Assumption. —успе́нский, *adj.* Assumption (*attrib.*): Успе́нский собо́р, Cathedral of the Assumption.

успе́ть *v., pfv. of* успева́ть. —успе́ется, *impers., colloq.* there's plenty of time!

успéх *n.* **1,** success. **2,** *pl.* progress: дéлать успéхи, to make progress. —**как вáши успéхи?,** how are you getting along? —**с тем же успéхом,** might (just) as well; just as easily.

успéшный *adj.* successful. —**успéшно,** *adv.* successfully. —**успéшность,** *n.f.* success.

успокáивать *v.impfv.* [*pfv.* **успокóить**] **1,** to calm; calm down. **2,** to quiet; quiet down (a child, group, etc.). **3,** to relieve; soothe (pain); calm (one's nerves); settle (one's stomach). **4,** to allay (suspicions, doubts, etc.). —**успокáиваться,** *refl.* **1,** to calm down. **2,** (*of pain, a storm, etc.*) to subside; abate. **3,** *colloq.* to be satisfied.

успокоéние *n.* **1,** calming; quieting; soothing. **2,** peace of mind; tranquillity.

успокоúтельный *adj.* **1,** calming; soothing. **2,** reassuring. —**успокоúтельное срéдство,** sedative; tranquilizer.

успокóить *v., pfv. of* **успокáивать.** —**успокóиться,** *refl., pfv. of* **успокáиваться.**

устá [*gen.* **уст**] *n.pl., obs.* mouth. —**вáшими бы устáми да мёд пить,** if only it were true! —**из пéрвых уст,** firsthand. —**из уст** (+ *gen.*), from the mouth of; from. —**из уст в устá,** by word of mouth. —**у всех на устáх,** on everyone's lips.

устáв *n.* **1,** regulations; rules. **2,** bylaws. **3,** charter: устáв ООН, the U.N. Charter. **4,** *mil.* manual: боевóй устáв, field manual.

уставáть *v.impfv.* [*pfv.* **устáть;** *pres.* устаю́, устаёшь] to tire; get tired. —**не уставáя,** tirelessly.

устáвить [*infl.* **-влю, -вишь**] *v., pfv. of* **уставлять.** —**устáвиться,** *refl., pfv. of* **уставляться.**

уставлять *v.impfv.* [*pfv.* **устáвить**] **1,** to place; arrange. **2,** (*with instr.*) *colloq.* to fill (with); cram (with); stuff (with). **3,** (*with* **в** *or* **на** + *acc.*) to point; direct; aim (something at something). —**уставляться,** *refl., colloq.* **1,** (*with* **в** + *acc.*) to fit (into); go (into). **2,** (*with instr.*) to be crowded (with); be crammed (with). **3,** (*with* **на** + *acc.*) to stare (at).

устáвный *adj.* prescribed.

устáлость *n.f.* fatigue.

устáлый *adj.* tired.

ýсталь *n.f., obs.* = **устáлость.** —**без ýстали,** tirelessly. —**не знать ýстали,** to be tireless; be indefatigable.

устанáвливать *v.impfv.* [*pfv.* **установúть**] **1,** to install. **2,** to establish. **3,** to set; fix. **4,** to determine; ascertain. —**устанáвливаться,** *refl.* **1,** to be established. **2,** to be formed. **3,** to set in.

установúть [*infl.* **-новлю́, -нóвишь**] *v., pfv. of* **устанáвливать.** —**установúться,** *refl., pfv. of* **устанáвливаться.**

устанóвка [*gen. pl.* **-вок**] *n.* **1,** placing; mounting; installation. **2,** plant; unit: силовáя устанóвка, power plant; холодúльная устанóвка, refrigeration unit; буровáя устанóвка, drilling rig; дождевáльная устанóвка, sprinkler system. **3,** mount: орудúйная устанóвка, gun mount. **4,** launcher: ракéтная устанóвка, rocket launcher. **5,** adjustment: тóнкая устанóвка, fine adjustment. **6,** setting: устанóвка высотомéра, altimeter setting. **7,** directive; instructions. **8,** precept; tenet: идеологúческие устанóвки, ideological precepts/tenets.

установлéние *n.* establishment.

устанóвленный *adj.* established; fixed; set.

устанóвочный *adj.* fundamental; definitive.

устаревáть *v.impfv.* [*pfv.* **устарéть**] to become obsolete; become antiquated.

устарéвший *adj.* obsolete; outmoded; outdated; out-of-date; antiquated. *Also,* **устарéлый.**

устарéть *v., pfv. of* **старéть** (*in sense #2*) *and* **устаревáть.**

устáть [*infl.* устáну, устáнешь] *v., pfv. of* **уставáть.**

устерегáть *v.impfv.* [*pfv.* **устерéчь**] to guard.

устерéчь [*infl. like* **стерéчь**] *v., pfv. of* **устерегáть.**

устилáть *v.impfv.* [*pfv.* **устлáть**] to cover; overlay.

ýстный *adj.* oral; verbal. —**ýстно,** *adv.* orally; verbally.

устóй *n.* **1,** support; foundation. **2,** abutment (*of a bridge*). **3,** *pl., fig.* foundations: устóи óбщества, the foundations of society. **4,** *colloq.* cream forming on the surface of a liquid.

устóйчивость *n.f.* **1,** stability. **2,** *med.* resistance.

устóйчивый *adj.* **1,** stable; steady. **2,** *med.* resistant.

устоять *v.pfv.* [*infl.* устою́, устоúшь] **1,** to remain on one's feet; keep one's balance. **2,** to hold; not give way; not fall. **3,** to hold out; stand firm; stand one's ground. **4,** (*with* **пéред** *or* **прóтив**) to withstand; resist. —**устояться,** *refl.* **1,** (*of liquids*) to settle. **2,** *fig.* to become fixed; become firmly established: устоя́вшиеся взгляды, set views.

устрáивать *v.impfv.* [*pfv.* **устрóить**] **1,** to arrange; organize. Устрóить вечерúнку, to give a party. **2,** to arrange; settle; put in order. **3,** to place (in a job, school, etc.). **4,** to put up (in lodgings). **5,** to build; make; construct. **6,** *colloq.* to make; create (a scene, scandal, etc.). **7,** *colloq.* to suit: Это меня вполнé устрáивает, that suits me fine. —**устрáиваться,** *refl.* **1,** to work out: Всё устрóилось, everything worked out. **2,** to settle down (in a comfortable place): устрóиться на дивáне, to settle down on the couch. **3,** to get settled (in a house or apartment). **4,** to get a job. **5,** to manage; make out; get along; get by.

устранéние *n.* removal; elimination.

устранять *v.impfv.* [*pfv.* **устранúть**] to remove; eliminate. —**устраняться,** *refl.* **1,** (*with* **от**) to withdraw (from); retire (from). **2,** to disappear.

устрашáть *v.impfv.* [*pfv.* **устрашúть**] to frighten; scare. —**устрашáться,** *refl.* to be frightened.

устремúть [*infl.* **-млю́, -мúшь**] *v., pfv. of* **устремлять.** —**устремúться,** *refl., pfv. of* **устремляться.**

устремлéние *n.* **1,** surge; onrush. **2,** aspiration.

устремлять *v.impfv.* [*pfv.* **устремúть**] **1,** to direct; fix (one's gaze, attention, etc.). **2,** *mil.* to throw: устремúть все сúлы на борьбý, to throw all one's forces into the battle. —**устремляться,** *refl.* **1,** to rush; dash; (*with* **вниз**) swoop down. **2,** (*with* **на** + *acc. or* **к**) to be directed (toward); (*of one's eyes*) be fixed (on); (*of a person*) concentrate (on).

ýстрица *n.* oyster. —**ýстричный,** *adj.* oyster (*attrib.*).

устроúтель *n.m.* organizer.

устрóить *v., pfv. of* **устрáивать.** —**устрóиться,** *refl., pfv. of* **устрáиваться.**

устро́йство *n.* **1,** arranging; organizing. **2,** arrangement; layout. **3,** device: запи́сывающее устро́йство, recording device. Печа́тающее устро́йство, printer. Вытяжно́е устро́йство, exhaust system. **4,** (political or social) system. —**устро́йство на рабо́ту,** getting a job.

усту́п *n.* ledge.

уступа́ть *v.impfv.* [*pfv.* уступи́ть] **A,** *v.t.* **1,** to yield; give up; let have; cede. **2,** *colloq.* to sell (*at a reduced price*); let go; let have: уступи́ть что́-нибудь за пятьдеся́т до́лларов, to let something go for fifty dollars. **3,** *colloq.* to deduct; knock off (a certain amount from a price): уступи́ть два рубля́, to deduct/ knock off/ two rubles. **B,** *v.i.* (*with dat.*) **1,** to yield (to); succumb (to); give in (to). **2,** to be inferior to; be second (to). —**уступи́ть ме́сто** (+ *dat.*), **1,** to give up one's seat (to). **2,** *fig.* to give way (to).

уступи́тельный *adj., gram.* concessive.

уступи́ть [*infl.* уступлю́, усту́пишь] *v., pfv. of* **уступа́ть.**

усту́пка [*gen. pl.* -пок] *n.* **1,** yielding; giving up. **2,** concession; идти́ на (*or* де́лать) усту́пки, to make concessions. **3,** *colloq.* discount; reduction.

усту́пчивый *adj.* amenable; compliant.

устыди́ть *v.pfv.* [*infl.* -жу́, -ди́шь] to shame; put to shame. —**устыди́ться,** *refl.* (*with gen.*) to feel ashamed (of).

у́стье [*gen. pl.* у́стьев] *n.* **1,** mouth (*of a river*). **2,** opening; mouth.

усугуби́ть [*infl.* -блю́, -би́шь] *v., pfv. of* **усугубля́ть.** —**усугуби́ться,** *refl., pfv. of* **усугубля́ться.**

усугубля́ть *v.impfv.* [*pfv.* усугуби́ть] **1,** to increase; heighten; intensify; redouble. **2,** to (further) aggravate; make (even worse). —**усугубля́ться,** *refl.* to be (further) heightened.

усы́ [*gen.* усо́в] *n.pl.* [*sing.* ус] **1,** mustache. **2,** whiskers (*of an animal*).

усыла́ть *v.impfv.* [*pfv.* усла́ть] to send away.

усынови́ть [*infl.* -влю́, -ви́шь] *v., pfv. of* **усыновля́ть.**

усыновле́ние *n.* adoption (*of a child*).

усыновля́ть *v.impfv.* [*pfv.* усынови́ть] to adopt (a child).

усыпа́льница *n.* burial vault.

усыпа́ть [*infl.* усы́плю, усы́плешь] *v., pfv. of* **усыпа́ть.**

усыпа́ть *v.impfv.* [*pfv.* усы́пать] **1,** to strew; bestrew. **2,** *fig.* to stud: Не́бо усы́пано звёздами, the sky is studded with stars.

усыпи́тельный *adj.* **1,** *med., obs.* soporific. **2,** *fig.* soporific; monotonous.

усыпи́ть [*infl.* -плю́, -пи́шь] *v., pfv. of* **усыпля́ть.**

усыпля́ть *v.impfv.* [*pfv.* усыпи́ть] **1,** to put to sleep; lull to sleep. **2,** to put (a sick animal) to sleep; put to death. **3,** *fig.* to lull (someone's vigilance); allay; put to rest (suspicions).

усыпля́ющий *adj.* soporific.

усыха́ть *v.impfv.* [*pfv.* усо́хнуть] *colloq.* **1,** to wither. **2,** to become wizened.

ута́ивать *v.impfv.* [*pfv.* утаи́ть] **1,** to conceal; hold back; withhold. **2,** to hide. **3,** to steal; appropriate.

ута́йка *n., colloq.* concealment. —**без ута́йки,** without concealing anything; without holding anything back.

ута́птывать *v.impfv.* [*pfv.* утопта́ть] to trample down.

ута́скивать *v.impfv.* [*pfv.* утащи́ть] **1,** to carry away; drag away. **2,** *colloq.* to drag (someone) somewhere against his will. **3,** *colloq.* to make off with; steal.

утащи́ть [*infl.* утащу́, ута́щишь] *v., pfv. of* **ута́скивать.**

у́тварь *n.f.* utensils.

утверди́тельный *adj.* affirmative. —**утверди́тельно,** *adv.* affirmatively; in the affirmative.

утверди́ть [*infl.* -жу́, -ди́шь] *v., pfv. of* **утвержда́ть.** —**утверди́ться,** *refl., pfv. of* **утвержда́ться.**

утвержда́ть *v.impfv.* [*pfv.* утверди́ть] **1,** [*impfv. only*] to maintain; assert; claim; contend. **2,** to approve; confirm. Утверди́ть резолю́цию, to approve a resolution. Утверди́ть кого́-нибудь в до́лжности (+ *gen.*), to approve/confirm someone for the post of... **3,** to establish firmly. **4,** (*with* в + *prepl.*) to reinforce someone's belief (that). Утверди́ть кого́-нибудь в наме́рении (+ *inf.*), to reinforce someone's intention to... —**утвержда́ться,** *refl.* **1,** to become firmly established. **2,** (*with* в + *prepl.*) to become firm in (one's views, intentions, etc.).

утвержде́ние *n.* **1,** assertion; claim; contention. **2,** approval; confirmation. **3,** establishment.

утека́ть *v.impfv.* [*pfv.* уте́чь] **1,** (*of a liquid or gas*) to leak; escape. **2,** (*of time*) to pass; fly by. —**мно́го воды́ утекло́ с тех пор,** a lot of water has flown under the bridge since then.

утёнок [*gen.* -нка; *pl.* утя́та, утя́т] *n.* duckling. —**га́дкий утёнок,** ugly duckling.

утепля́ть *v.impfv.* [*pfv.* утепли́ть] **1,** to warm; heat. **2,** to winterize.

утере́ть [*infl. like* тере́ть] *v., pfv. of* **утира́ть.**

утерпе́ть *v.pfv.* [*infl.* утерплю́, уте́рпишь] to restrain oneself.

уте́ря *n.* loss (*of papers, documents, etc.*).

утеря́ть *v.pfv.* to lose; mislay.

утёс *n.* cliff.

утёсистый *adj.* **1,** rocky; craggy. **2,** steep; precipitous.

уте́ха *n., colloq.* **1,** pleasure; delight; fun. **2,** comfort; consolation.

уте́чка *n.* **1,** leak; leakage. **2,** *fig.* outflow; drain. —**уте́чка мозго́в,** brain drain.

уте́чь [*infl. like* течь] *v., pfv. of* **утека́ть.**

утеша́ть *v.impfv.* [*pfv.* уте́шить] to console; comfort. —**утеша́ться,** *refl.* **1,** to console oneself. **2,** (*with instr.*) to take comfort (in); take consolation (in). **3,** to calm down; pull oneself together.

утеше́ние *n.* consolation; comfort; solace. —**в утеше́ние** (+ *dat.*), in order to console (someone); as a way of consoling (someone).

утеши́тель *n.m.* comforter.

утеши́тельный *adj.* comforting; consoling. —**утеши́тельный приз,** consolation prize.

уте́шить *v., pfv. of* **утеша́ть.** —**уте́шиться,** *refl., pfv. of* **утеша́ться.**

утилиза́ция *n.* utilization.

утилизи́ровать *v.impfv. & pfv.* [*pres.* -рую, -руешь] to utilize.

утилитари́зм *n.* utilitarianism. —**утилита́рный,** *adj.* utilitarian.

ути́ль *n.m.* scrap. —**ути́льный,** *adj.* scrap (*attrib.*).

утильсырьё *n.* = **ути́ль.**

ути́ный *adj.* duck (*attrib.*); duck's.

утира́ть *v.impfv.* [*pfv.* **утере́ть**] **1,** to wipe away (tears, sweat, etc.). **2,** to wipe (one's face, brow, etc.). —**утира́ть нос** (+ *dat.*), *colloq.* to show up; get the better of.

утиха́ть *v.impfv.* [*pfv.* **ути́хнуть**] to subside; abate; die down.

ути́хнуть [*past* **ути́х, ути́хла**] *v., pfv. of* **утиха́ть.**

утихоми́ривать *v.impfv.* [*pfv.* **утихоми́рить**] *colloq.* to calm; pacify; placate. —**утихоми́риваться,** *refl.,* *colloq.* **1,** to calm down. **2,** to abate.

у́тка [*gen. pl.* **у́ток**] *n.* **1,** duck. **2,** *fig.* canard. **3,** *colloq.* bedpan.

уткну́ть *v.pfv., colloq.* **1,** to plant firmly. **2,** to hide; bury. —**уткну́ться,** *refl., colloq.* **1,** (*with* **в** + *acc.*) to bury oneself (in a pillow, book, etc.). **2,** (*with instr. and* **в** + *acc.*) to bury (a part of oneself) in. **3,** (*with* **в** + *acc.*) to bang into; strike.

утконо́с *n.* (duck-billed) platypus.

утле́гарь *n.m.* jib boom; outrigger.

у́тлый *adj.* **1,** (*of a boat*) rickety. **2,** wretched. **3,** *obs.* decrepit.

уто́к [*gen.* **утка́**] *n., textiles* woof; weft; filling.

утоле́ние *n.* (*with gen.*) **1,** appeasing (of hunger); quenching (of thirst). **2,** *fig.* relief (of).

утоли́ть *v., pfv. of* **утоля́ть.**

утолща́ть *v.impfv.* [*pfv.* **утолсти́ть**] to thicken.

утолще́ние *n.* bulge.

утоля́ть *v.impfv.* [*pfv.* **утоли́ть**] **1,** to appease; assuage (one's hunger); quench (one's thirst). **2,** *fig.* to relieve; alleviate.

утоми́тельный *adj.* **1,** tiring; fatiguing. **2,** tiresome; dull.

утоми́ть [*infl.* **-млю́, -ми́шь**] *v., pfv. of* **утомля́ть.** —**утоми́ться,** *refl., pfv. of* **утомля́ться.**

утомле́ние *n.* fatigue.

утомлённый *adj.* tired.

утомля́ть *v.impfv.* [*pfv.* **утоми́ть**] to tire. —**утомля́ться,** *refl.* to tire; become tired; get tired.

утону́ть [*infl.* **утону́, уто́нешь**] *v., pfv. of* **тону́ть** (*in sense #2*) *and* **утопа́ть.**

утонча́ть *v.impfv.* [*pfv.* **утончи́ть**] **1,** to thin; make thinner. **2,** *fig.* to refine.

утончённый *adj.* refined; exquisite. —**утончённость,** *n.f.* refinement.

утончи́ть *v., pfv. of* **утонча́ть.**

утопа́ть *v.impfv.* [*pfv.* **утону́ть**] **1,** to drown. **2,** [*impfv. only*] (*with* **в** + *prepl.*) to be rolling in (money, wealth, etc.); be bathed in (light, verdure, etc.).

утопа́ющий *n., decl. as an adj.* drowning man.

утопи́зм *n.* utopianism.

утопи́ть *v.pfv.* [*infl.* **утоплю́, уто́пишь**] **1,** *pfv. of* **топи́ть** (*in sense #5*). **2,** (*with* **в** + *prepl. or acc.*) to sink (into); embed (in). —**утопи́ться,** *refl., pfv. of* **топи́ться** (*in sense #3*).

уто́пия *n.* utopia. —**утопи́ческий,** *adj.* utopian.

утопле́ние *n.* drowning.

уто́пленник *n.* drowned man.

утопта́ть [*infl.* **утопчу́, уто́пчешь**] *v., pfv. of* **ута́птывать.**

у́точка [*gen. pl.* **-чек**] *n., dim. of* **у́тка.** —**ходи́ть у́точкой,** to waddle.

уточне́ние *n.* **1,** making (something) more precise. **2,** a clarification: внести́ уточне́ния в прое́кт, to make clarifications in the draft; make some things in the draft more precise.

уточня́ть *v.impfv.* [*pfv.* **уточни́ть**] **1,** to make more precise. **2,** to state more precisely. **3,** to find out more about.

утра́ивать *v.impfv.* [*pfv.* **утро́ить**] to triple; treble. —**утра́иваться,** *refl.* to triple; increase threefold.

утрамбова́ть *v., pfv. of* **трамбова́ть.**

утра́та *n.* loss.

утра́тить [*infl.* **-чу, -тишь**] *v., pfv. of* **утра́чивать.**

утра́чивать *v.impfv.* [*pfv.* **утра́тить**] to lose.

у́тренний *adj.* morning (*attrib.*).

у́тренник *n.* **1,** morning performance. **2,** early-morning frost.

у́треня *n.* matin; morning prayer.

утри́ровать *v.impfv. & pfv.* [*pres.* **-рую, -руешь**] to exaggerate.

утриро́вка *n.* exaggeration.

у́тро [*gen.* **у́тра** *but* **утра́** *after* **с, до** *and the time of day; dat.* **у́тру** *but* **утру́** *after* **к**) *n.* morning. Шесть часо́в утра́, six o'clock in the morning. —**к утру́; под у́тро,** toward morning. —**по утра́м,** each morning. —**с утра́ до ве́чера,** from morning till night. *See also* **у́тром.**

утро́ба *n.* belly; womb.

утро́бный *adj.* **1,** uterine. **2,** (*of sounds*) deep; from the belly.

утро́ить *v., pfv. of* **утра́ивать.** —**утро́иться,** *refl., pfv. of* **утра́иваться.**

у́тром *adv.* in the morning. —**вчера́/за́втра/сего́дня у́тром,** yesterday/tomorrow/this morning.

утружда́ть *v.impfv.* **1,** to bother; trouble. **2,** to overburden; tire. **3,** *in* утружда́ть себя́, to extend oneself; take a lot of trouble. —**утружда́ться,** *refl.* = **утружда́ть себя́.** Не утружда́йтесь!, don't trouble yourself!; don't go to a lot of trouble!

утряса́ть *v.impfv.* [*pfv.* **утрясти́**] *colloq.* to settle (a matter). —**утряса́ться,** *refl., colloq.* to get straightened out.

утрясти́ [*infl. like* **трясти́**] *v., pfv. of* **утряса́ть.** —**утрясти́сь,** *refl., pfv. of* **утряса́ться.**

утучня́ть *v.impfv.* [*pfv.* **утучни́ть**] to fatten; fatten up.

утю́г [*gen.* **утюга́**] *n.* iron (*for ironing*).

утю́жить *v.impfv.* [*pfv.* **вы́утюжить**] to iron; press.

утю́жка *n.* ironing; pressing.

утяжеля́ть *v.impfv.* [*pfv.* **утяжели́ть**] to make heavier; increase the weight of.

утяну́ть *v.pfv.* [*infl.* **утяну́, утя́нешь**] *colloq.* **1,** to drag away; drag off. **2,** to drag (someone) somewhere against his will.

уха́ *n.* fish soup.

уха́б *n.* pothole. —**уха́бистый,** *adj.* full of potholes; bumpy.

ухажёр *n., colloq.* **1,** ladies' man; philanderer. **2,** suitor; admirer.

уха́живание *n.* **1,** looking after; caring for; tending. **2,** courting; paying court to. **3,** *pl.* advances.

ухáживать *v.impfv.* (*with* за + *instr.*) **1,** to look after; take care of; care for; tend. **2,** to court; woo. **3,** to play up to.

ýхарь *n.m., colloq.* dashing fellow; gay blade. **—ýхарский,** *adj., colloq.* dashing. **—ýхарство,** *n., colloq.* bravado; bluster.

ýхать *v.impfv.* [*pfv.* **ýхнуть**] *colloq.* **1,** to cry out; gasp. **2,** (*of an owl*) to hoot. **3,** to make a loud noise; ring out; resound. **4,** to fall; tumble. **5,** to squander; fritter away.

ухвáт *n.* oven fork.

ухватúть [*infl.* **ухвачý, ухвáтишь**] *v., pfv. of* **ухвáтывать.** **—ухватúться,** *refl., pfv. of* **ухвáтываться.**

ухвáтка [*gen. pl.* **-ток**] *n., colloq.* **1,** movement of the body. **2,** knack. **3,** manner; way.

ухвáтывать *v.impfv.* [*pfv.* **ухватúть**] to grasp. **—ухвáтываться,** *refl.* (*with* за + *acc.*) **1,** to grasp; grab hold of. **2,** *fig., colloq.* to tackle (a job, task, etc.). **3,** *fig., colloq.* to jump at (an offer, opportunity, etc.).

ухитря́ться *v.r.impfv.* [*pfv.* **ухитрúться**] (*with inf.*) *colloq.* to manage (to); contrive (to).

ухищрéние *n.* device; trick.

ухищря́ться *v.r.impfv.* to contrive; scheme.

ухлóпать *v.pfv., colloq.* **1,** to kill. **2,** to squander.

ухмы́лка [*gen. pl.* **-лок**] *n., colloq.* grin; smirk.

ухмыля́ться *v.r.impfv.* [*pfv.* **ухмыльнýться**] *colloq.* to grin; smirk.

ýхнуть *v., pfv. of* **ýхать.**

ýхо [*pl.* **ýши, ушéй, ушáм**] *n.* ear. **—во все ýши слýшать,** to be all ears. **—в однó ýхо вошлó, в другóе вы́шло,** in one ear and out the other. **—и ýхом не вести́,** not to pay the least attention. **—пó уши в** (+ *prepl.*), up to one's ears; head over heels (*in work, love, debt, etc.*). **—пропускáть ми́мо ушéй,** to ignore; pay no attention to.

ухóд *n.* **1,** leaving; departure. **2,** withdrawal. **3,** quitting: ухóд с рабóты, quitting one's job. **4,** care: ухóд за рáнеными/маши́ной, care of the wounded; care of a car. **—ухóд на пéнсию,** retirement.

уходи́ть *v.impfv.* [*pfv.* **уйти́;** *pres.* **ухожý, ухóдишь**] **1,** to leave; go away: уйти́ из дóма, to leave home; уйти́ от жены́, to leave one's wife; уйти́ в шкóлу, to leave for school; уйти́ в óтпуск, to leave on vacation. Пóезд ужé ушёл, the train has already left. **2,** to leave; quit: уйти́ из шкóлы, to leave/quit school; уйти́ с рабóты, to quit one's job. **3,** to retire: уйти́ со сцéны, to retire from the stage; уйти́ на пéнсию, to retire. **4,** (*with* от) to avoid (giving an answer); evade (responsibility, a question, etc.); elude (pursuers); escape (punishment). **5,** (*of time*) to go by. **6,** *fig.* (*with* на + *acc.*) to go into: Мнóго рабóты ушлó на э́то, a lot of work went into that. **7,** (*with* в + *acc.*) to sink (into). **8,** *fig.* (*with* в + *acc.*) to become absorbed (in). **9,** *colloq.* to boil over. **—уйти́ в себя́,** to withdraw into oneself. **—уйти́ из жи́зни,** to die; depart this world.

ухóженный *adj.* well-cared-for; well-groomed; well maintained; well-kept.

ухудшáть *v.impfv.* [*pfv.* **ухýдшить**] to worsen; make worse. **—ухудшáться,** *refl.* to worsen; become worse; deteriorate.

ухудшéние *n.* worsening; deterioration.

ухýдшить *v., pfv. of* **ухудшáть.** **—ухýдшиться,** *refl., pfv. of* **ухудшáться.**

уцелéвший *n., decl. as an adj.* survivor.

уцелéть *v.pfv.* **1,** to escape injury; escape damage. **2,** to survive.

уцéнивать *v.impfv.* [*pfv.* **уцени́ть**] to reduce the price of; mark down.

уцени́ть [*infl.* **уценю́, уцéнишь**] *v., pfv. of* **уцéнивать.**

уцепи́ть *v.pfv.* [*infl.* **уцеплю́, уцéпишь**] *colloq.* to grab. **—уцепи́ться,** *refl.* (*with* за + *acc.*) **1,** to grab hold of. **2,** *fig., colloq.* to jump at (an idea, offer, etc.).

учáствовать *v.impfv.* [*pres.* **-ствую, -ствуешь**] (*with* в + *prepl.*) **1,** to participate (in); take part (in). **2,** to share (in).

учáстие *n.* **1,** (*with* в + *prepl.*) participation (in). **2,** (*with* в + *prepl.*) sharing (in). **3,** (*with* к) sympathy (for); concern (for). **—принимáть учáстие в** (+ *prepl.*), **1,** to take part in. **2,** to take an interest in (someone); show concern for.

участи́ть [*infl.* **-щý, -сти́шь**] *v., pfv. of* **учащáть.** **—участи́ться,** *refl., pfv. of* **учащáться.**

участкóвый *adj.* district (*attrib.*). **—**_n._, *colloq.* district militia officer.

учáстливый *adj.* sympathetic.

учáстник *n.* participant. Учáстник конферéнции, conferee. Учáстник состязáния, contestant. Учáстник соглашéния, party to an agreement.

учáсток [*gen.* **-стка**] *n.* **1,** plot (*of land*). **2,** section (*of a road, pipeline, etc.*). **3,** area; portion (*of a surface*). **4,** *mil.* sector. **5,** *fig.* area; field; sphere. **6,** district; precinct. **7,** *pre-rev.* police district.

ýчасть *n.f.* fate; lot.

учащáть *v.impfv.* [*pfv.* **участи́ть**] to increase the frequency of; make more frequent. **—учащáться,** *refl.* **1,** to become more frequent. **2,** (*of one's pulse*) to quicken.

учáщийся *n., decl. as an adj.* student; pupil.

учёба *n.* **1,** studies. **2,** training.

учéбник *n.* textbook.

учéбный *adj.* **1,** educational: учéбное заведéние, educational institution. **2,** teaching: учéбные посóбия, teaching aids. **3,** *mil.* training: учéбное пóле, training ground. **—учéбный год,** school year; academic year. **—учéбный план,** curriculum. **—учéбная стрельбá,** firing practice.

учéние *n.* **1,** studies; studying; learning. **2,** apprenticeship. **3,** teaching. **4,** *mil.* exercise. **5,** doctrine. **6,** (*with gen.*) the teachings (of).

учени́к [*gen.* **-никá**] *n.m.* [*fem.* **-ни́ца**] **1,** pupil. **2,** apprentice. **3,** disciple.

учени́ческий *adj.* **1,** pupil's; pupils'. **2,** crude; amateurish.

учени́чество *n.* **1,** time spent as a student. **2,** apprenticeship.

учёность *n.f.* learning; erudition.

учёный *adj.* **1,** learned; erudite; scholarly. **2,** scientific. **3,** academic. **4,** (*of animals*) trained. **—**_n._ **1,** scientist. **2,** scholar. **—учёный секретáрь,** academic secretary. **—учёная стéпень,** (college) degree.

учéсть [*infl.* **учтý, учтёшь;** *past* **учёл, учлá, учлó, учли́**] *v., pfv. of* **учи́тывать.**

учёт *n.* **1,** stock-taking; inventory. **2,** record: учёт осмо́тра, record of inspection. **3,** registration: брать (кого́-нибудь) на учёт, to register (someone). Стать *or* встать на учёт, to register. **4,** consideration; taking into account: с учётом (+ *gen.*), in consideration of; taking into account. —**бухга́лтерский учёт,** book-keeping.

учетверя́ть *v.impfv.* [*pfv.* **учетвери́ть**] to quadruple. —**учетверя́ться,** *refl.* to quadruple; go up four times.

учётный *adj.* **1,** record (*attrib.*); registration (*attrib.*). **2,** *finance* discount (*attrib.*).

учи́лище *n.* (specialized) school: реме́сленное учи́лище, vocational school.

учини́ть [*infl.* **учиню́, учини́шь**] *v., pfv. of* **чини́ть** (*in sense #3) and* **учиня́ть**.

учиня́ть *v.impfv.* [*pfv.* **учини́ть**] **1,** *obs.* to carry out. **2,** *colloq.* to make (a scene); create (a scandal).

учи́тель [*pl.* **учителя́**] *n.m.* [*fem.* **учи́тельница**] teacher.

учи́тельский *adj.* teachers'. —**учи́тельская,** *n.* teachers' room.

учи́тельство *n.* **1,** teaching. **2,** teachers.

учи́тельствовать *v.impfv.* [*pres.* **-ствую, -ствуешь**] to teach; be a teacher.

учи́тывать *v.impfv.* [*pfv.* **уче́сть**] **1,** to consider; take into consideration; take into account; take account of. **2,** to take stock of. **3,** *in* учи́тывать ве́ксель, to discount a note.

учи́ть *v.impfv.* [*pfv.* **вы́учить**; *pres.* **учу́, у́чишь**] **1,** [*pfv. also* **научи́ть**] (*with dat. or inf.*) to teach: учи́ть кого́-нибудь англи́йскому языку́, to teach someone English; учи́ть кого́-нибудь пла́вать, to teach someone how to swim. **2,** (*with acc.*) to study (a subject, foreign language, etc.); study; memorize (a lesson, part, etc.). **3,** (*with acc.*) [*usu. pfv.*] to learn: вы́учить ру́сский язы́к, to learn Russian; вы́учить слова́ наизу́сть, to learn the words by heart. —**учи́ться,** *refl.* **1,** [*impfv. only*] to study (somewhere); be a student. **2,** [*impfv. only*] (*with dat.*) to study (a subject, foreign language, etc.). **3,** [*pfv.* **вы́учиться** *or* **научи́ться**] (*with dat.*) to learn (a subject, foreign language, etc.); (*with inf.*) learn how (to).

учреди́тель *n.m.* founder.

учреди́тельный *adj.* constituent: учреди́тельное собра́ние, constituent assembly.

учрежда́ть *v.impfv.* [*pfv.* **учреди́ть**] to found; establish.

учрежде́ние *n.* **1,** founding; establishment. **2,** institution; establishment: культу́рное учрежде́ние, cultural institution. **3,** (social) institution: отжи́вшее учрежде́ние, outmoded institution.

учти́вый *adj.* polite; courteous. —**учти́вость,** *n.f.* politeness; courteousness.

учу́ять *v.pfv.* [*infl.* **учу́ю, учу́ешь**] *colloq.* **1,** to smell. **2,** *fig.* to sense.

уша́нка [*gen. pl.* **-нок**] *n.* cap with earflaps.

уша́стый *adj., colloq.* with big ears.

уша́т *n.* tub (*carried on a pole inserted through handles*). —**вылива́ть на** (+ *acc.*) **уша́т холо́дной воды́, 1,** to dampen someone's enthusiasm. **2,** to throw cold water on.

у́ши *n., pl. of* **у́хо.**

уши́б *n.* injury; bruise.

ушиба́ть *v.impfv.* [*pfv.* **ушиби́ть**] to hurt; injure; bruise: ушиби́ть себе́ па́лец, to hurt one's finger. —**ушиба́ться,** *refl.* to hurt oneself.

ушиби́ть [*infl.* **ушибу́, ушибёшь**; *past* **уши́б, уши́бла**] *v., pfv. of* **ушиба́ть.** —**ушиби́ться,** *refl., pfv. of* **ушиба́ться.**

уши́бленный *adj.* injured.

ушива́ть *v.impfv.* [*pfv.* **уши́ть**] to take in (a garment).

уши́ть [*infl.* **ушью́, ушьёшь**] *v., pfv. of* **ушива́ть.**

у́шко [*pl.* **у́шки, у́шек**] *n., dim. of* **у́хо.**

ушко́ [*pl.* **ушки́, ушко́в**] *n.* **1,** = **у́шко. 2,** eye (*of a needle*). **3,** tab; hook.

ушни́к [*gen.* **-ника́**] *n., colloq.* ear specialist.

ушно́й *adj.* ear (*attrib.*). —**ушна́я ра́ковина,** auricle (*of the ear*).

уще́лье *n.* gorge; ravine; canyon.

ущеми́ть [*infl.* **-млю́, -ми́шь**] *v., pfv. of* **ущемля́ть.**

ущемле́ние *n.* **1,** jamming; catching. **2,** *fig.* infringement; abridgment (*of freedom, rights, etc.*). **3,** *med.* strangulation.

ущемля́ть *v.impfv.* [*pfv.* **ущеми́ть**] **1,** to jam; catch: ущемля́ть па́лец две́рью, to catch one's finger in the door. **2,** to hurt; offend. **3,** to hurt; wound (someone's pride). **4,** to infringe upon; abridge (someone's freedom, rights, etc.). **5,** to oppress.

уще́рб *n.* harm; damage. —**в уще́рб** (+ *dat.*), to the detriment of. —**на уще́рбе,** on the wane.

уще́рбный *adj.* **1,** (*of the moon*) waning. **2,** *fig.* waning; declining. **3,** *fig.* defective; inferior; flawed.

ущипну́ть *v.pfv.* to pinch.

уэ́льский *adj.* Welsh.

ую́т *n.* comfort.

ую́тный *adj.* cozy; comfortable.

уязви́мый *adj.* vulnerable. —**уязви́мость,** *n.f.* vulnerability.

уязвля́ть *v.impfv.* [*pfv.* **уязви́ть**] **1,** *obs.* to sting; wound. **2,** *fig.* to hurt; pique.

уясня́ть *v.impfv.* [*pfv.* **уясни́ть**] **1,** (*often with* **себе́** *or* **для себя́**) to get a clear idea of. **2,** *obs.* to explain.

Ф, ф *n.neut.* 21st letter of the Russian alphabet.

фа *n.neut., music* fa; F.

фа́брика *n.* factory; mill.

фабрика́нт *n.* factory owner; manufacturer.

фабрика́т *n.* manufactured item; finished product.

фабрика́ция *n.* manufacture; fabrication.

фабрикова́ть *v.impfv.* [*pres.* **-ку́ю, -ку́ешь**] **1,** *obs.* to manufacture. **2,** *colloq.* to turn out; crank out (*in large numbers*). **3,** [*pfv.* **сфабрикова́ть**] *colloq.* to fabricate; make up: сфабрико́ванные обвине́ния, trumped-up charges.

фабри́чный *adj.* **1,** factory (*attrib.*). **2,** factory-made. —*n., obs.* factory worker. —**фабри́чная ма́рка,** trademark.

фа́була *n.* plot (*of a story*).

фавн *n.* faun.

фаво́р *n.* favor: быть в фаво́ре у, to be in someone's favor; be in someone's good graces.

фавори́т *n.* favorite.

фавори́тизм *n.* favoritism.

фаго́т *n.* bassoon. —**фаготи́ст,** *n.* bassoonist.

фагоци́т *n.* phagocyte.

фа́за *n.* phase.

фаза́н *n.* pheasant. —**фаза́ний** *adj.* [*fem.* **-нья**] pheasant (*attrib.*); pheasant's.

фа́зис *n.* phase.

фа́кел *n.* torch.

фа́кельный *adj.* of a torch. —**фа́кельное ше́ствие,** torchlight procession.

фа́кельщик *n.* **1,** torchbearer. **2,** one who puts something to the torch.

факси́миле *n.neut. indecl.* facsimile.

факсими́льный *adj.* facsimile (*attrib.*). —**факси-ми́льный аппара́т,** fax machine.

факт *n.* fact. Факт, что..., it is a fact that... Факт тот, что..., the fact of the matter is... —**поста́вить пе́ред фа́ктом,** to present with a fait accompli.

факти́чески *adv.* **1,** in fact; in actual fact; as a matter of fact; in point of fact. **2,** for all practical purposes; to all intents and purposes.

факти́ческий *adj.* **1,** actual. **2,** factual. **3,** de facto: факти́ческое призна́ние, de facto recognition. —**факти́ческий брак,** common-law marriage.

фа́ктор *n.* factor.

факто́рия *n.* trading post.

факту́ра *n.* **1,** *art* manner of execution. **2,** texture; finish. **3,** *comm.* invoice; bill.

факультати́вный *adj.* optional; elective.

факульте́т *n.* university department; faculty: физи́ческий факульте́т, physics department.

фал *n.* halyard.

фала́нга *n.* phalanx.

фа́лда *n.* tail (*of a coat*); coattail.

фалли́ческий *adj.* phallic.

фалло́пиев *adj., in* **фалло́пиевы тру́бы,** Fallopian tubes.

фа́ллос *n.* phallus.

фальсифика́тор *n.* falsifier.

фальсифика́ция *n.* **1,** falsification. **2,** forgery. **3,** adulteration.

фальсифици́ровать *v.impfv. & pfv.* [*pres.* **-рую, -руешь**] **1,** to falsify. **2,** to distort. **3,** to adulterate.

фальста́рт *n., sports* false start.

фальце́т *n.* falsetto. —**фальце́тный,** *adj.* falsetto.

фальши́вить *v.impfv.* [*pfv.* **сфальши́вить;** *pres.* **-влю, -вишь**] **1,** to be insincere; be hypocritical. **2,** to play or sing off key.

фальши́вка [*gen. pl.* **-вок**] *n., colloq.* forged document; forgery.

фальши́во *adv.* **1,** falsely. **2,** off key.

фальшивомоне́тчик *n.* counterfeiter.

фальши́вый *adj.* **1,** false. **2,** forged; counterfeit. **3,** false; insincere.

фальшь *n.f.* **1,** cheating; dishonesty. **2,** falseness; hypocrisy; insincerity. **3,** *music* false note(s); being off key.

фами́лия *n.* last name; family name; surname.

фами́льный *adj.* family (*attrib.*).

фамилья́рничать *v.impfv.* (*with* **с** + *instr.*) *colloq.* to be overly familiar (with); take liberties (with).

фамилья́рный *adj.* familiar; unceremonious. —**фамилья́рно,** *adv.* unceremoniously —**фамилья́рность,** *n.f.* familiarity.

фанабе́рия *n., colloq.* arrogance; snobbery.

фанати́зм *n.* fanaticism. —**фана́тик,** *n.* fanatic. —**фанати́ческий; фанати́чный,** *adj.* fanatic; fanatical.

фане́ра *n.* **1,** veneer (*thin layer of wood*). **2,** plywood. —**фане́рный,** *adj.* plywood (*attrib.*).

фант *n., usu. pl.* forfeits (*game*).

фантазёр *n.* dreamer; visionary.

фантази́ровать *v.impfv.* [*pres.* **-рую, -руешь**] **1,** to indulge in fantasy. **2,** [*pfv.* **сфантази́ровать**] to make up; dream up. **3,** to make things up. **4,** to improvise.

фанта́зия *n.* **1,** fantasy; fancy. **2,** imagination. **3,** *colloq.* whim; fancy. **4,** *music* fantasy.

фантасмагóрия *n.* phantasmagoria. —**фантасмаго-рѝческий,** *adj.* phantasmagoric.

фантáст *n.* **1,** visionary. **2,** writer or artist treating the fantastic.

фантáстика *n.* fantasy. —**наýчная фантáстика,** science fiction.

фантастѝческий *adj.* **1,** fantastic. **2,** fantasy (*attrib.*). *Also,* **фантастѝчный.**

фантóм *n.* phantom.

фанфáра *n.* **1,** trumpet; bugle. **2,** fanfare; flourish.

фанфарóн *n., colloq.* braggart.

фáра *n.* headlight. —**зáдняя фáра,** taillight.

фараóн *n.* **1,** Pharaoh. **2,** *cards* faro.

фарвáтер (тэ) *n.* waterway; channel.

Фаренгéйт *n.* Fahrenheit: сóрок грáдусов по Фаренгéйту, forty degrees Fahrenheit.

фарисéй *n.* pharisee. —**фарисéйский,** *adj.* pharisaic.

фармаколóгия *n.* pharmacology. —**фармакóлог,** *n.* pharmacologist. —**фармакологѝческий,** *adj.* pharmacological.

фармакопéя *n.* pharmacopoeia.

фармацéвт *n.* pharmacist. —**фармацéвтика,** *n.* pharmaceutics. —**фармацевтѝческий,** *adj.* pharmaceutical.

фармáция *n.* pharmacy (*preparation of drugs*).

фарс *n.* farce.

фáртинг *n.* farthing.

фáртук *n.* apron.

фарфóр *n.* china; porcelain. —**фарфóровый,** *adj.* china; porcelain.

фарцóвщик *n., colloq.* black marketeer (*reselling merchandise and currency acquired from foreigners*).

фарш *n.* stuffing; filling.

фарширóванный *adj.* stuffed.

фаршировáть *v.impfv.* [*pres.* **-рýю, -рýешь**] to stuff.

фас *n.* **1,** front (*of one's face*). **2,** front (*of an object, building, etc.*). —**в фас; фáсом,** full face.

фасáд *n.* **1,** front (*of a building*). **2,** façade.

фасéтка [*gen. pl.* **-ток**] *n.* facet (*of a gem*). *Also,* **фасéт.**

фасовáть *v.impfv.* [*pfv.* **расфасовáть;** *pres.* **-сýю, -сýешь**] to package (food).

фасóвка *n.* packaging. —**фасóвочный,** *adj.* packaging (*attrib.*).

фасóлевый *adj.* of (kidney) beans; bean (*attrib.*): фасóлевый суп, bean soup.

фасóль *n.f.* **1,** kidney beans. **2,** a (single) kidney bean.

фасóн *n.* **1,** cut (*of a garment*). **2,** fashion; style. **3,** *colloq.* style; manner.

фасóнистый *adj., colloq.* **1,** fashionable; stylish. **2,** fancy; elaborate.

фасóнный *adj.* shaped.

фат *n.* fop.

фатá *n.* bridal veil.

фаталѝзм *n.* fatalism. —**фаталѝст,** *n.* fatalist.

фаталистѝческий *adj.* **1,** fatalistic. **2,** fatal; inevitable.

фатáльный *adj.* **1,** fatal. **2,** of resignation: фатáльный вид, air of resignation.

фатовáтый *adj.* foppish.

фатовствó *n.* foppery.

фáуна *n.* fauna.

фашѝзм *n.* fascism. —**фашѝст,** *n.* fascist. —**фашѝстский,** *adj.* fascist.

фаэтóн *n.* phaeton.

фаѝнс *n.* glazed pottery; delftware. —**фаѝнсовый,** *adj.* made of delftware.

феврáль [*gen.* **-ралѝ**] *n.m.* February. —**феврáльский,** *adj.* February (*attrib.*).

федералѝзм *n.* federalism. —**федералѝст,** *n.* federalist.

федерáльный *adj.* federal.

федератѝвный *adj.* federated; federal.

федерáция *n.* federation.

феерѝческий *adj.* **1,** *theat.* based on a fairy tale. **2,** *fig.* magical; fabulous.

феéрия *n.* **1,** *theat.* play or ballet based on a fairy tale. **2,** *fig.* enchanting spectacle.

фейервéрк *n.* fireworks.

фельдмáршал *n.* field marshal.

фéльдшер [*pl.* **фельдшерá**] *n.* medical assistant.

фельетóн *n.* humorous or satirical article. —**фельетонѝст,** *n.* writer of such articles. —**фельетóнный,** *adj.* humorous; satirical.

феминѝзм *n.* feminism. —**феминѝст; феминѝстка,** *n.* feminist. —**феминѝстский; феминистѝческий,** *adj.* feminist (*attrib.*).

фен *n.* hair dryer.

фéникс *n.* phoenix.

фенобарбитáл *n.* phenobarbital.

фенóл *n.* phenol.

фенóмен *n.* phenomenon; marvel; whiz.

феноменáльный *adj.* phenomenal.

фéнхель *n.m.* fennel.

феóд *n.* fief.

феодáл *n.* feudal lord. —**феодалѝзм,** *n.* feudalism. —**феодáльный,** *adj.* feudal.

ферзь [*gen. & acc.* **ферзѝ**] *n.m., chess* queen. —**фéрзевый,** *adj.* queen's.

фéрма *n.* **1,** farm. **2,** girder; truss.

фермéнт *n.* ferment; enzyme.

фéрмер *n.* farmer. —**фéрмерский,** *adj.* farmer's; farmers'.

фéрмерство *n.* **1,** farming. **2,** farmers.

фéрмий *n.* fermium.

фермуáр *n., obs.* **1,** clasp. **2,** necklace.

ферротѝпия *n.* ferrotype; tintype.

ферýла *n.* ferule.

фéска [*gen. pl.* **фéсок**] *n.* fez.

фестивáль *n.m.* festival. —**фестивáльный,** *adj.* festival (*attrib.*).

фестóн *n.* **1,** *pl.* scallops (*on material*). **2,** festoon (*ornamental carving*). —**фестóнный; фестóнчатый,** *adj.* scalloped.

фетѝш *n.* fetish.

фетишизѝровать *v.impfv.* [*pres.* **-рую, -руешь**] to make a fetish of.

фетр *n.* felt. —**фéтровый,** *adj.* felt.

фехтовáние *n., sports* fencing. —**фехтовáльный,** *adj.* fencing (*attrib.*). —**фехтовáльщик,** *n.* fencer.

фехтовáть *v.impfv.* [*pres.* **-тýю, -тýешь**] *sports* to fence.

фешенебельный (нэ) *adj.* fashionable; high-class.

фея *n.* fairy.

фи *interj.* fie!; tut!; pshaw!

фиакр *n.* (hired) carriage.

фиалка [*gen. pl.* -**лок**] *n.* violet (*flower*).

фиаско *n.* fiasco.

фибра *n.* **1**, *obs.* fiber. **2**, *usu. pl., fig.* fiber: всеми фибрами души, with every fiber of one's soul.

фибрин *n.* fibrin.

фибриноген *n.* fibrinogen.

фиброзный *adj.* fiber (*attrib.*); fibrous.

фига *n.* **1**, fig. **2**, fig tree. **3**, *colloq.* fig (*insulting gesture*).

фигляр *n.* **1**, *obs.* (circus) acrobat; performer of tricks. **2**, *colloq.* buffoon.

фиговый *adj.* fig (*attrib.*). —**фиговый листок**, fig leaf.

фигура *n.* **1**, figure. **2**, *chess* piece. **3**, *cards* face card.

фигуральный *adj.* figurative; metaphorical.

фигурировать *v.impfv.* [*pres.* -**рую**, -**руешь**] to figure; appear.

фигурист *n.m.* [*fem.* -**истка**] figure skater.

фигурка [*gen. pl.* -**рок**] *n.* **1**, *dim. of* **фигура**. **2**, figurine.

фигурный *adj.* **1**, figure (*attrib.*): фигурное катание на коньках, figure skating. **2**, (*of a pattern*) figured.

фидер (дэ) *n., electricity* feeder.

физик *n.* physicist.

физика *n.* physics.

физиология *n.* physiology. —**физиолог**, *n.* physiologist. —**физиологический**, *adj.* physiological.

физиономия *n.* **1**, face. **2**, facial expression; look. **3**, physiognomy.

физиотерапия *n.* physiotherapy; physical therapy. —**физиотерапевт**, *n.* (physio)therapist.

физически *adv.* physically.

физический *adj.* **1**, physical. **2**, physics (*attrib.*); of physics. —**физическая культура**, physical training; physical education.

физкультура *n.* = **физическая культура**.

физкультурный *adj.* athletic. —**физкультурный зал**, gymnasium. —**физкультурный костюм**, gym suit.

фиксаж *n., photog.* fixing agent; hypo.

фиксированный *adj.* fixed: фиксированная цена, fixed price.

фиксировать *v.impfv. & pfv.* [*pfv. also* **зафиксировать**; *pres.* -**рую**, -**руешь**] **1**, to fix; set. **2**, to record (*on paper, film, etc.*). **3**, to fix (one's gaze, attention, etc.). **4**, *photog.* to fix.

фиктивный *adj.* **1**, fictitious. **2**, forged. —**фиктивный брак**, pro forma marriage (*carried out to meet a certain legal requirement*).

фикус *n.* rubber plant (*ornamental house plant*). —**бенгальский фикус**, banyan.

фикция *n.* fiction; invention; fabrication.

филактерия *n.* phylactery.

филантропия *n.* philanthropy. —**филантроп**, *n.* philanthropist. —**филантропический**, *adj.* philanthropic.

филармония *n.* philharmonic society. —**филармонический**, *adj.* philharmonic.

филателия (тэ) *n.* philately. —**филателист**, *n.* philatelist. —**филателистический**, *adj.* philatelic.

филе *n.neut. indecl.* **1**, filet; sirloin. **2**, fillet (*of meat, fish, etc.*).

филёнка [*gen. pl.* -**нок**] *n.* panel. —**филёночный**; **филёнчатый**, *adj.* paneled.

филёр *n.* detective; agent.

филиал *n.* branch (*of a store, institution, etc.*). —**филиальный**, *adj.* branch (*attrib.*).

филигранный *adj.* **1**, filigree. **2**, *fig.* meticulous.

филигрань *n.f.* filigree.

филин *n.* eagle owl.

филиппика *n.* philippic.

филиппинский *adj.* Philippine.

филодендрон (дэ) *n.* philodendron.

филология *n.* philology. —**филолог**, *n.* philologist. —**филологический**, *adj.* philological.

философия *n.* philosophy. —**философ**, *n.* philosopher.

философский *adj.* philosophic(al). —**философски**, *adv.* philosophically.

философствовать *v.impfv.* [*pres.* -**ствую**, -**ствуешь**] to philosophize.

фильм *n.* film; movie; motion picture.

фильмотека *n.* film library.

фильтр *n.* filter.

фильтрация *n.* filtration.

фильтровальный *adj.* filter (*attrib.*); filtering.

фильтровать *v.impfv.* [*pres.* -**рую**, -**руешь**] **1**, to filter. **2**, *fig., colloq.* to screen; select.

фимиам *n.* incense. —**курить фимиам** (+ *dat.*), to sing the praises of.

финал *n.* **1**, finale. **2**, *sports* finals; final round. —**финалист**, *n.* finalist. —**финальный**, *adj.* final.

финансирование *n.* financing; funding.

финансировать *v.impfv. & pfv.* [*pres.* -**рую**, -**руешь**] to finance.

финансист *n.* financier.

финансовый *adj.* financial; fiscal.

финансы [*gen.* -**сов**] *n.pl.* finance; finances.

финик *n.* date (*fruit*).

финикиец [*gen.* -**ийца**] *n.* Phoenician. —**финикийский**, *adj.* Phoenician.

финиковый *adj.* date (*attrib.*). —**финиковая пальма**, date palm.

финифть *n.f., obs.* enamel.

финиш *n.* **1**, finish (*of a race*). **2**, finish line.

финишировать *v.impfv. & pfv.* [*pres.* -**рую**, -**руешь**] *sports* to finish.

финишный *adj.* finish (*attrib.*): финишная лента (*or* ленточка), the tape.

финка [*gen. pl.* **финок**] *n.* **1**, *fem. of* **финн**. **2**, *colloq.* knife; dagger.

финн *n.m.* [*fem.* **финка**] Finn.

финно-угорский *adj.* Finno-Ugric.

финский *adj.* Finnish.

финт *n., sports* feint.

финтить *v.impfv.* [*pres.* -**чу**, -**тишь**] *colloq.* to be tricky; resort to deception.

финтифлюшка [*gen. pl.* -**шек**] *n., colloq.* knick-knack.

фиоле́товый *adj.* violet.

фио́рд *n.* fiord.

фи́рма *n.* business firm.

фи́рменный *adj.* company (*attrib.*); house (*attrib.*). —**фи́рменное блю́до**, specialty of the house. —**фи́рменный знак**, trademark.

фисгармо́ния *n.* harmonium.

фиска́л *n.*, *colloq.* tattler; talebearer.

фиска́лить *v.impfv.*, *colloq.* to tattle; tell tales.

фиста́шка *n.* pistachio. —**фиста́шковый**, *adj.* pistachio.

фисту́ла *also,* **фистула́** *n.* 1, *med.* fistula. 2, falsetto.

фити́ль [*gen.* -тиля́] *n.m.* wick.

фи́шка [*gen. pl.* **фи́шек**] *n.* chip (*used in games*).

флаг *n.* flag. —**под фла́гом** (+ *gen.*), 1, (*of a ship*) flying the flag of. 2, *fig.* under the banner of. 3, *fig.* under the guise of.

фла́гман *n.* 1, flag officer. 2, flagship.

фла́гманский *adj.*, *in* **фла́гманский кора́бль**, flagship.

флагшто́к *n.* flagpole.

фла́жный *adj.* flag (*attrib.*).

флажо́к [*gen.* -жка́] *n.* small flag.

флако́н *n.* small bottle.

флама́ндец [*gen.* -дца] *n.m.* [*fem.* -дка] Fleming. —**флама́ндский**, *adj.* Flemish.

флами́нго *n.m. indecl.* flamingo.

фланг *n.*, *mil.* flank. —**фланго́вый**, *adj.* flanking.

фланéль *n.f.* flannel. —**фланéлевый**, *adj.* flannel.

фла́нец [*gen.* -нца] *n.* flange.

флани́ровать *v.impfv.* [*pres.* -**рую**, -**руешь**] *colloq.* to stroll; saunter.

фланки́ровать *v.impfv. & pfv.* [*pres.* -**рую**, -**руешь**] *mil.* to flank.

флебит *n.* phlebitis.

флегма *n.* 1, phlegm; sluggishness; apathy. 2, *colloq.* phlegmatic person.

флегма́тик *n.* phlegmatic person. —**флегмати́ческий**; **флегмати́чный**, *adj.* phlegmatic.

флéйта *n.* flute. —**флейти́ст**, *n.* flutist.

флéксия *n.*, *gram.* inflection. —**флекти́вный**, *adj.* inflected.

флёр *n.* crepe.

фли́гель [*pl.* **флигеля́**] *n.m.* 1, wing (*of a building*). 2, annex.

флирт *n.* flirting; flirtation.

флиртова́ть *v.impfv.* [*pres.* -**ту́ю**, -**ту́ешь**] to flirt.

флокс *n.* phlox.

флома́стер *n.* soft-tip pen.

фло́ра *n.* flora.

флори́н *n.* florin.

флот *n.* 1, fleet. 2, navy. —**военно-морско́й флот**, navy. —**возду́шный флот**, air force. —**торго́вый флот**, merchant fleet; merchant marine.

флоти́лия *n.* 1, flotilla. 2, fleet: **китобо́йная флоти́лия**, whaling fleet.

фло́тский *adj.* naval.

флоэ́ма *n.* phloem.

флуоресце́нция *n.* fluorescence.

флуоресци́ровать *v.impfv.* [*pres.* -**рует**] to fluoresce.

флюга́рка [*gen. pl.* -**рок**] *n.* 1, ship's emblem. 2, *colloq.* weather vane.

флю́гер [*pl.* **флюгера́**] *n.* weather vane.

флюоресце́нция *n.* = флуоресце́нция. —**флюоресци́ровать**, *v.* = флуоресци́ровать.

флюс *n.* 1, gumboil. 2, *metall.* flux.

фля́га *n.* flask; canteen. *Also,* **фля́жка**.

фо́бия *also,* **фоби́я** *n.* phobia.

фойé *n.neut. indecl.* lobby (*of a theater*).

фок *n.* foresail.

фок-ма́чта *n.* foremast.

фокстерьéр (тэ) *n.* fox terrier.

фокстро́т *n.* fox trot.

фо́кус *n.* 1, *physics; photog.* focus. 2, *fig.* focal point; center. 3, trick.

фокуси́ровать *v.impfv. & pfv.* [*pres.* -**рую**, -**руешь**] to focus.

фокусиро́вка *n.* focusing.

фо́кусник *n.* magician; conjurer; prestidigitator.

фо́кусничать *v.impfv.*, *colloq.* to do odd or peculiar things.

фо́кусный *adj.* focal.

фо́кус-по́кус *n.*, *colloq.* hocus-pocus.

фол *n.*, *sports* foul.

фолиа́нт *n.* large book; volume; folio.

фо́лио *n. indecl.* folio.

фолли́кул *n.* follicle.

фо́льга *n.* foil: алюми́неная фо́льга, aluminum foil.

фолькло́р *n.* folklore. —**фольклори́ст**, *n.* specialist in folklore.

фон *n.* background.

фона́рик *n.*, *dim. of* **фона́рь**.

фона́рный *adj.* lamp (*attrib.*); lantern (*attrib.*). —**фона́рный столб**, lamppost.

фона́рщик *n.*, *obs.* lamplighter.

фона́рь [*gen.* **фонаря́**] *n.m.* 1, lantern. 2, (*in combinations*) -light: за́дний/карма́нный/у́личный фона́рь, taillight/ flashlight/ street light/. 3, *in* проекцио́нный фона́рь, projector. 4, bay window; skylight. 5, *colloq.* black eye.

фонд *n.* 1, fund: фонд за́работной пла́ты, wage fund; фонд по́мощи, relief fund. 2, (charitable) foundation. 3, (*in a library*) collection. 4, *pl.* stocks; securities.

фо́ндовый *adj.* stock (*attrib.*). —**фо́ндовая би́ржа**, stock exchange; stock market.

фонéма (нэ) *n.* phoneme. —**фонемати́ческий**, *adj.* phonemic.

фонéтика (нэ) *n.* phonetics. —**фонети́ческий**, *adj.* phonetic.

фоногра́мма *n.* recording.

фоноло́гия *n.* phonology.

фоноте́ка *n.* record library.

фонта́н *n.* fountain. —**бить фонта́ном**, to gush.

фонтани́ровать *v.impfv.* [*pres.* -**рует**] to gush; gush forth.

фонта́нчик *n.* 1, *dim. of* **фонта́н**. 2, water fountain; drinking fountain.

фо́ра *n.* 1, *sports* advantage; head start (*given a weaker player*). 2, *chess* odds: фо́ра коня́, knight odds. —**табли́ца фор**, table of handicaps.

фо́рвард *n.*, *sports* forward.

форе́йтор *n.* postilion.

форе́ль *n.f.* trout.

фо́рзац *n.* flyleaf.

фо́рма *n.* **1**, form. **2**, shape. **3**, mold. **4**, uniform. —в фо́рме, **1**, in good shape *or* condition. **2**, in uniform. —для фо́рмы, for form's sake. —по всей фо́рме, **1**, properly. **2**, really and truly.

формали́зм *n.* formalism. —формали́ст, *n.* formalist. —формалисти́ческий, *adj.* formalistic.

формальдеги́д *n.* formaldehyde.

форма́льно *adv.* formally; officially; legally.

форма́льность *n.f.* formality; technicality.

форма́льный *adj.* formal.

форма́т *n.* format; size.

форма́ция *n.* **1**, structure. **2**, *geol.* formation.

фо́рменный *adj.* **1**, uniform (*attrib.*). **2**, *obs.* formal; official. **3**, *colloq.* real; regular; downright.

формирова́ние *n.* **1**, forming; formation. **2**, *mil.* unit.

формирова́ть *v.impfv.* [*pfv.* сформирова́ть; *pres.* -ру́ю, -ру́ешь] **1**, to form; mold. **2**, to form; organize. —формирова́ться, *refl.* **1**, to form; be formed. **2**, to mature; develop.

формова́ть *v.impfv.* [*pfv.* сформова́ть; *pres.* -му́ю, -му́ешь] to shape; mold; model.

фо́рмула *n.* formula.

формули́ровать *v.impfv. & pfv.* [*pfv. also* сформули́ровать; *pres.* -рую, -руешь] to word; phrase; formulate.

формулиро́вка *n.* **1**, formulation. **2**, formula. **3**, wording.

формуля́р *n.* **1**, *pre-rev.* record of service. **2**, maintenance log. **3**, charge card (*inserted in a library book*).

форпо́ст *n.* outpost.

форс *n.*, *colloq.* show; swank; ostentation. —для фо́рса, for show.

форси́рованный *adj.* accelerated. —форси́рованный марш, *mil.* forced march.

форси́ровать *v.impfv. & pfv.* [*pres.* -рую, -руешь] **1**, to speed up. **2**, *mil.* to make a forced crossing of (*e.g.* a river).

форси́ть *v.impfv.* [*pres.* -шу́, -си́шь] *colloq.* to show off.

форсу́нка [*gen. pl.* -нок] *n.* sprayer; injector.

форт [*2nd loc.* форту́; *pl.* форты́] *n.* fort.

фо́рте (тэ) *adv.*, *music* forte.

фо́ртель *n.m.*, *colloq.* trick.

фортепья́но (тэ) *n. indecl.* piano. —фортепья́нный, *adj.* piano (*attrib.*).

форти́ссимо *adv.* fortissimo.

фортифика́ция *n.* fortification. —фортификацио́нный, *adj.* fortification (*attrib.*).

фо́рточка [*gen. pl.* -чек] *n.* small hinged windowpane.

форту́на *n.* fortune.

фо́рум *n.* forum.

форшла́г *n.*, *music* grace note.

форште́вень (штэ) [*gen.* -вня] *n.m.*, *naut.* stem.

фосге́н *n.* phosgene.

фосфа́т *n.* phosphate. —фосфа́тный; фосфа́товый, *adj.* phosphate.

фо́сфор *n.* phosphorus.

фосфоресце́нция *n.* phosphorescence. —фосфоресци́рующий, *adj.* phosphorescent.

фо́сфорный *adj.* phosphoric; phosphorous.

фо́то *n. indecl.*, *colloq.* photo; photograph.

фотоаппара́т *n.* camera.

фотогени́чный *adj.* photogenic.

фотогравю́ра *n.* photogravure; photoengraving.

фото́граф *n.* photographer.

фотографи́ровать *v.impfv.* [*pfv.* сфотографи́ровать; *pres.* -рую, -руешь] **1**, to photograph; take a picture of. **2**, [*impfv. only*] to take a picture; take pictures. —фотографи́роваться, *refl.* to be photographed; have one's picture taken.

фотографи́ческий *adj.* photographic.

фотогра́фия *n.* **1**, photography. **2**, photograph. **3**, photographer's studio.

фотока́рточка [*gen. pl.* -чек] *n.*, *colloq.* photograph; snapshot.

фотоко́пия *n.* photocopy.

фотолаборато́рия *n.* photo lab.

фотолюби́тель *n.m.* amateur photographer.

фото́метр *n.* photometer.

фото́н *n.* photon.

фотоси́нтез (тэ) *n.* photosynthesis.

фотосни́мок [*gen.* -мка] *n.* photograph; snapshot.

фотоста́т *n.* photostat machine.

фотосфе́ра *n.* photosphere.

фотоэлектри́ческий *adj.* photoelectric.

фотоэлеме́нт *n.* photoelectric cell; electric eye.

фо́фан *n.*, *colloq.* dope; jerk.

фрагме́нт *n.* fragment. —фрагмента́рный, *adj.* fragmentary.

фра́за *n.* **1**, sentence. **2**, phrase.

фразеоло́гия *n.* phraseology. —фразеологи́ческий, *adj.* phraseological.

фразёр *n.* phrasemonger. —фразёрство, *n.* phrasemongering.

фрак *n.* tail coat; tails.

фраки́йский *adj.* Thracian.

фракцио́нный *adj.* **1**, factional. **2**, factious.

фра́кция *n.* (political) faction.

фрамбе́зия *n.* yaws.

фраму́га *n.* transom.

франк *n.* **1**, franc (*monetary unit*). **2**, *hist.* Frank.

франки́ровать *v.impfv. & pfv.* [*pres.* -рую, -руешь] to prepay the postage (on).

франкмасо́н *n.* freemason. —франкмасо́нство, *n.* freemasonry.

франт *n.* dandy; fop.

франти́ть *v.impfv.* [*pres.* -чу́, -ти́шь] *colloq.* to dress like a dandy.

франтова́тый *adj.*, *colloq.* foppish.

фра́нций *n.* francium.

францу́женка [*gen. pl.* -нок] *n.* Frenchwoman; French girl.

францу́з *n.* **1**, Frenchman. **2**, *pl.* the French. —францу́зский, *adj.* French.

фрахт *n.* **1**, freight. **2**, freight charges.

фрахтова́ть *v.impfv.* [*pfv.* зафрахтова́ть; *pres.* -ту́ю, -ту́ешь] to charter.

фра́чный *adj.* of or for a tail coat; worn with a tail coat.

фрега́т *n.* **1,** frigate. **2,** frigate bird.

фре́за *also,* **фреза́** *n.* milling cutter.

фре́зерный *adj.* milling (*attrib.*): фре́зерный стано́к, milling machine.

фрезерова́ние *n.* milling.

фрезерова́ть *v.impfv. & pfv.* [*pres.* **-ру́ю, -ру́ешь**] to cut; mill (metal).

фрейди́стский *adj.* Freudian.

фре́йлина *n.* lady in waiting.

френоло́гия *n.* phrenology.

френч *n.* service jacket.

фрео́н *n.* freon.

фре́ска [*gen. pl.* **-сок**] *n.* fresco. —**фре́сковый,** *adj.* fresco (*attrib.*).

фриво́льный *adj.* ribald.

фриги́дность *n.f., physiol.* frigidity.

фриз *n.* frieze.

фрикаде́лька (дэ) [*gen. pl.* **-лек**] *n.* ball of minced meat or fish cooked in soup.

фрикасе́ (сэ) *n.neut. indecl.* fricassee.

фрикати́вный *adj.* fricative.

фронт [*pl.* **фро́нты, фронто́в, фронта́м**] *n.* **1,** *mil.* front. **2,** *meteorology* front: тёплый фронт, warm front. **3,** *fig.* front: еди́ный фронт, united front. —**стать во фронт,** to stand at attention.

фронта́льный *adj.* frontal.

фронтиспи́с *n.* frontispiece.

фронтови́к [*gen.* **-вика́**] *n.* frontline soldier.

фронтово́й *adj., mil.* front (*attrib.*); frontline.

фронто́н *n.* pediment.

фру́кт *n.* **1,** piece of fruit. **2,** *pl.* fruit.

фрукто́вый *adj.* fruit (*attrib.*). —**фрукто́вый сад,** orchard.

фрукто́за *n.* fructose.

фрустра́ция *n.* frustration.

фтор *n.* fluorine.

фтори́д *n.* fluoride.

фто́ристый *adj.* fluoride (of): фто́ристый на́трий, sodium fluoride.

фтороуглеро́д *n.* fluorocarbon.

фу *interj.* **1,** (*of disgust, contempt, etc.*) ugh! **2,** (*of fatigue, relief, etc.*) whew!

фу́га *n., music* fugue.

фуга́с *n.* land mine.

фуга́ска [*gen. pl.* **-сок**] *n., colloq.* **1,** land mine. **2,** demolition bomb.

фуга́сный *adj.* high-explosive. —**фуга́сная бо́мба,** demolition bomb.

фуже́р *n.* tall wineglass.

фу́кать *v.impfv.* [*pfv.* **фу́кнуть**] *colloq.* **1,** to snort. **2,** to blow. **3,** (*of an engine, locomotive, etc.*) to puff.

фукси́н *n.* fuchsin; magenta.

фу́ксия *n.* fuchsia.

фунда́мент *n.* foundation.

фундаментали́зм *n.* fundamentalism. —**фундаментали́ст,** *n.* fundamentalist.

фундамента́льный *adj.* **1,** solid; sturdy. **2,** (*of knowledge*) thorough; profound. **3,** (*of research, a work, study, etc.*) basic. —**фундамента́льная библиоте́ка,** main library.

фунду́к [*gen.* **-дука́**] *n.* filbert.

фуникулёр *n.* **1,** funicular railway. **2,** cable car.

функциона́льный *adj.* functional.

функциони́ровать *v.impfv.* [*pres.* **-рую, -руешь**] to function.

фу́нкция *n.* function.

фунт *n.* pound (*unit of weight; monetary unit*).

фу́нтик *n., colloq.* cone-shaped paper bag.

фу́ра *n.* **1,** wagon. **2,** van.

фура́ж [*gen.* **-ража́**] *n.* fodder; forage.

фура́жка [*gen. pl.* **-жек**] *n.* service cap.

фура́жный *adj.* forage (*attrib.*); fodder (*attrib.*). —**фура́жное зерно́,** feed grain.

фурго́н *n.* van.

фу́рия *n.* **1,** *myth.* Fury. **2,** *colloq.* shrew; virago.

фуро́р *n.* furor; sensation.

фуру́нкул *n., med.* furuncle; boil.

фут *n.* foot (*12 inches*).

футбо́л *n.* soccer. —**футболи́ст,** *n.* soccer player.

футбо́лка [*gen. pl.* **-лок**] *n.* sport shirt.

футбо́льный *adj.* soccer (*attrib.*).

футля́р *n.* case: футля́р для очко́в, eyeglass case.

фу́товый *adj.* one foot in length; one-foot (*attrib.*).

футури́зм *n.* futurism. —**футристи́ческий,** *adj.* futuristic.

футфа́йка [*gen. pl.* **-фа́ек**] *n.* jersey.

фы́рканье *n.* snorting; snort.

фы́ркать *v.impfv.* [*pfv.* **фы́ркнуть**] **1,** to snort. **2,** (*of an engine, locomotive, etc.*) to puff. **3,** *colloq.* to chuckle. **4,** (*with* на + *acc.*) *colloq.* to grumble (at).

фюзела́ж *n.* fuselage.

X

X, x *n.neut.* 22nd letter of the Russian alphabet.

ха́живать *v.impfv., colloq.* to go (*regularly*).

хака́с *n.m.* [*fem.* **-ка́ска**] Khakass (*one of a people inhabiting southern Siberia*). —**хака́сский,** *adj.* Khakass.

ха́ки *n.neut. indecl. & adj.* khaki.

хала́т *n.* **1,** oriental robe. **2,** bathrobe. **3,** (surgeon's) gown; (artist's) smock. —**рабо́чий хала́т,** overalls.

хала́тность *n.f.* **1,** indifference. **2,** negligence.

хала́тный *adj.* **1,** indifferent; lackadaisical. **2,** negligent.

халва́ *n.* paste made of nuts, sugar and oil; halvah.

хали́ф *n.* caliph. —**халифа́т,** *n.* caliphate.

халту́ра *n., colloq.* **1,** work performed (*or* money earned) on the side. **2,** hackwork. —**халту́рный,** *adj., colloq.* hack. —**халту́рщик,** *n., colloq.* hack worker; hack.

халу́па *n.* **1,** peasant's shack. **2,** *colloq.* shack.

халцедо́н *n.* chalcedony.

хам *n., colloq.* cad; boor.

хамелео́н *n.* chameleon.

хами́тский *adj.* Hamitic.

хами́ть *v.impfv.* [*pres.* **-млю́, -ми́шь**] (*with dat.*) *colloq.* to be rude (to); be disrespectful (to).

ха́мский *adj., colloq.* boorish. —**ха́мство,** *n., colloq.* boorishness.

хан *n.* khan.

хандра́ *n.* melancholy; depression.

хандри́ть *v.impfv.* to be depressed; have the blues; be down in the dumps.

ханжа́ *n.m. & f.* self-righteous person; hypocrite.

ха́нжеский *also,* **ханжеско́й** *adj.* sanctimonious; self-righteous.

ха́нжество *also,* **ханжество́** *n.* sanctimony; self-righteousness.

ханжи́ть *v.impfv., colloq.* to play the hypocrite; put on an act.

ха́нство *n.* khanate.

хао́с *n.* chaos. —**хаоти́ческий,** *adj.* chaotic.

хаоти́чный *adj.* chaotic. —**хаоти́чность,** *n.f.* chaotic state.

ха́пать *v.impfv.* [*pfv.* **ха́пнуть**] *colloq.* **1,** to grab; snatch. **2,** to steal; swipe.

хапу́га *n.m. & f., colloq.* **1,** thief. **2,** bribe taker.

хараки́ри *n.neut. indecl.* hara-kiri.

хара́ктер *n.* **1,** character; personality; disposition. **2,** nature (*of something*): хара́ктер рабо́ты, the nature of the work. **3,** (strength of) character: проявля́ть хара́к-тер, to show *or* demonstrate character. Челове́к с хара́ктером, strong-willed person. **4,** character (*in a story, play, etc.*). —**вы́держать хара́ктер,** to stand firm. —**носи́ть (како́й-нибудь) хара́ктер,** to be ... (in nature): носи́ть вре́менный хара́ктер, to be temporary (in nature).

характеризова́ть *v.impfv. & pfv.* [*pres.* **-зу́ю, -зу́ешь**] **1,** to describe; characterize. **2,** to be characteristic of; be typical of. —**характеризова́ться,** *refl.* [*impfv. only*] (*with instr.*) to be characterized (by); be marked (by).

характери́стика *n.* **1,** description; characterization. **2,** character reference.

хара́ктерно *adv.* in one's own distinctive way. —*adj., used predicatively* **1,** (*with* **для**) characteristic (of). **2,** significant: Хара́ктерно, что..., it is significant that...

хара́ктерный *adj.* **1,** typical; characteristic. **2,** distinctive. **3,** *theat.* character (*attrib.*).

харза́ *n.* yellow-throated marten.

хари́зма *n.* charisma. —**харизмати́ческий,** *adj.* charismatic.

ха́ркать *v.impfv.* [*pfv.* **ха́ркнуть**] *colloq.* to expectorate; spit. Ха́ркать кро́вью, to spit blood.

ха́ртия *n.* charter. —**Вели́кая ха́ртия во́льностей,** Magna Carta.

харче́вня [*gen. pl.* **-вен**] *n., obs.* (cheap) eating place.

харчи́ [*gen.* **-че́й**] *n.pl., colloq.* food; grub.

харчо́ *n. indecl.* mutton soup.

ха́ря *n., colloq.* face; mug; puss.

ха́та *n.* peasant's hut. —**моя́ ха́та с кра́ю,** it has nothing to do with me.

ха́ять *v.impfv.* [*pres.* **ха́ю, ха́ешь**] *colloq.* to find fault with; run down.

хвала́ *n.* praise.

хвале́бный *adj.* **1,** laudatory. **2,** (*of a song, hymn, etc.*) of praise.

хвалёный *adj.* (much) vaunted; famous.

хвали́ть *v.impfv.* [*pfv.* **похвали́ть**; *pres.* **хвалю́, хва́лишь**] to praise. —**хвали́ться,** *refl.* (*with instr.*) to boast (about *or* of); brag (about).

хва́статься *v.r.impfv.* [*pfv.* **похва́статься**] (*with instr.*) to boast (about *or* of); brag (about).

хвастли́вый *adj.* boastful. —**хвастли́вость,** *n.f.* boastfulness.

хвастовство́ *n.* boasting; bragging.

хвасту́н [*gen.* **-стуна́**] *n.m.* [*fem.* **-сту́нья**] *colloq.* braggart.

хват *n., colloq.* dashing fellow; gay blade.

хвата́ть *v.impfv.* **1,** [*pfv.* **схвати́ть**] to seize; grab; grasp; snatch. **2,** [*pfv.* **хвати́ть**] *impers.* (with gen.) to suffice; be enough; last: Вре́мени не хвата́ет, there is not enough time. Э́того нам хва́тит на ме́сяц, that will last us a month. Хва́тит!, enough! На сего́дня хва́тит, that will be enough for today. С меня́ хва́тит, I've had enough! Хва́тит тебе́ пла́кать!, enough of your crying. ♦ (*With* **не** + *dat. and gen.*) to be short of; lack: Им не хвата́ет средств, they are short of funds; ему́ не хвати́ло му́жества, чтобы (+ *inf.*), he lacked the courage to... **3,** [*impfv. only*] (with **не**) *impers.* **A,** to be missing: Не хвата́ет двух страни́ц, two pages are missing. **B,** to miss (someone): Мне вас не хвата́ет, I miss you. —**наско́лько хвата́ет глаз**, as far as the eye can see. *See also* **хвати́ть.**

хвата́ться *v.r.impfv.* (with **за** + *acc.*) **1,** [*pfv.* **схвати́ться**] to grab; grasp. **2,** [*impfv. only*] *fig.* to take up; seize upon; embrace. —**хвата́ться за́ голову**, to clutch one's head (*in horror or despair*). —**хвата́ться за соло́минку**, to grasp at a straw.

хвати́ть *v.pfv.* [*infl.* **хвачу́, хва́тишь**] **1,** *pfv. of* **хвата́ть** (*in sense #2*). **2,** *colloq.* to strike; hit. **3,** *colloq.* to experience; suffer. **4,** *colloq.* to drink; guzzle. **5,** *in* **хвати́ть че́рез край**, to go too far. —**хвати́ться**, *refl.* (with gen.) *colloq.* to miss; notice the absence of.

хва́тка *n.* **1,** grip; grasp. **2,** skill. —**мёртвая хва́тка**, mortal grip; iron grip.

хва́ткий *adj.* **1,** (*of hands*) that grip tightly. **2,** (*of one's eyes*) keen. **3,** (*of a person*) clever; crafty.

хво́йный *adj.* **1,** coniferous. **2,** pine (*attrib.*).

хвора́ть *v.impfv., colloq.* to be ill; be ailing.

хво́рост *n.* **1,** brushwood. **2,** pastry sticks.

хворости́на *n.* switch; stick; rod.

хво́рый *adj., colloq.* sickly; ailing.

хворь *n.f., colloq.* illness; ailment.

хвост [*gen.* **хвоста́**] *n.* **1,** tail. **2,** tail end; tag end: плести́сь в хвосте́, to be at the tail end. **3,** *colloq.* line; queue: стоя́ть в хвосте́, to stand in line.

хвоста́тый *adj.* having a tail.

хво́стик *n.* **1,** *dim. of* **хвост. 2,** pony tail. —**с хво́стиком**, plus a little more: пятьдеся́т лет с хво́стиком, fifty plus (years).

хвостово́й *adj.* tail (*attrib.*).

хвощ [*gen.* **хвоща́**] *n.* horsetail (*plant*).

хвоя́ *n.* **1,** pine needles. **2,** branches of a pine tree.

хек *n.* hake (*fish*).

хе́рес *n.* sherry.

херуви́м *n.* cherub. —**херуви́мский**, *adj.* cherubic.

хе́тты [*gen.* **-тов**] *n.pl.* Hittites. —**хе́ттский**, *adj.* Hittite.

хиба́ра *n.* shanty; hovel.

хиба́рка [*gen. pl.* **-рок**] *n.* = **хиба́ра.**

хи́жина *n.* hut; shack.

хиле́ть *v.impfv., colloq.* to fade; decline; become sickly.

хи́лый *adj.* sickly; feeble.

химе́ра *n.* chimera. —**химери́ческий**, *adj.* chimerical.

хи́мик *n.* chemist.

химика́лии [*gen.* **-лий**] *n.pl.* chemicals. *Also,* **химика́ты** [*gen.* **-тов**].

химиотерапи́я *n.* chemotherapy.

хими́ческий *adj.* chemical. —**хими́ческий каранда́ш**, indelible pencil. —**хими́ческая чи́стка**, dry cleaning.

хи́мия *n.* chemistry.

химчи́стка *n., colloq.* **1,** dry cleaning. **2,** dry cleaning establishment; dry cleaner's (*contr. of* **хими́ческая чи́стка**).

хи́на *n.* quinine.

хи́нди *n.m. indecl.* Hindi.

хини́н *n.* quinine.

хи́нный *adj.* quinine (*attrib.*). —**хи́нное де́рево**, cinchona (*tree*).

хире́ть *v.impfv.* [*pfv.* **захире́ть**] *colloq.* **1,** to decline in health. **2,** (*of plants*) to wither. **3,** to decay; fall into decay.

хирома́нт *n.* palmist; palm reader. —**хирома́нтия**, *n.* palmistry.

хиру́рг *n.* surgeon. —**хирурги́ческий**, *adj.* surgical. —**хирурги́я**, *n.* surgery.

хитре́ц [*gen.* **-треца́**] *n.* cunning person.

хитреца́ *n., colloq.* cunning. *Also,* **хитри́нка.**

хитри́ть *v.impfv.* [*pfv.* **схитри́ть**] **1,** to use cunning; resort to guile. **2,** (with **с** + *instr.*) to try to outwit. **3,** *colloq.* to maneuver; contrive.

хитро́ *also,* **хи́тро** *adv.* **1,** slyly. **2,** *colloq.* cleverly.

хитросплете́ние *n., usu. pl.* **1,** intricacies; complexities. **2,** schemes; stratagems.

хи́трость *n.f.* **1,** cunning; guile. **2,** ingenuity. **3,** ruse; trick. —**не велика́ хи́трость**, it takes no great skill.

хитроу́мие *n.* cleverness.

хитроу́мный *adj.* **1,** clever. **2,** ingenious. **3,** intricate.

хи́трый *adj.* [*short form* **хитёр, хитра́, хитро́** *or* **хи́тро, хитры́** *or* **хи́тры**] **1,** sly; crafty; cunning; wily. **2,** *colloq.* clever; ingenious.

хихи́канье *n.* giggling.

хихи́кать *v.impfv.* to giggle.

хище́ние *n.* theft; embezzlement; misappropriation.

хи́щник *n.* **1,** beast of prey; bird of prey. **2,** *fig.* predator.

хи́щнический *adj.* **1,** (*of instincts, habits, etc.*) predatory. **2,** rapacious. **3,** destructive (*to the environment*).

хи́щничество *n.* **1,** preying on others. **2,** plundering.

хи́щный *adj.* predatory; rapacious. —**хи́щная пти́ца**, bird of prey.

хладнокро́вие *n.* equanimity; composure.

хладнокро́вно *adv.* **1,** calmly. **2,** in cold blood.

хладнокро́вный *adj.* **1,** cool; calm; collected. **2,** (*of an act*) cold-blooded; in cold blood.

хлам *n.* junk; rubbish.

хлеб *n.* **1,** bread. **2,** loaf of bread. **3,** [*pl.* **хлеба́**] grain.

хлеба́ть *v.impfv.* [*pfv.* **хлебну́ть**] *colloq.* to gulp (down). *See also* **хлебну́ть.**

хле́бец [*gen.* **-бца**] *n.* small loaf of bread.

хле́бница *n.* breadbasket.

хлебну́ть *v.pfv., colloq.* **1,** *pfv. of* **хлеба́ть. 2,** to drink; have a drop to drink: хлебну́ть ли́шнего, to have a drop too much to drink. **3,** *fig.* (with gen.) *colloq.* to experience; know: хлебну́ть го́ря, to have known much sorrow.

хле́бный *adj.* **1,** bread (*attrib.*). **2,** of grain; grain (*at-*

trib.): хлéбная би́ржа, grain exchange. **3**, rich in grain. **4**, *colloq.* profitable; lucrative.

хлебопёк *n.* baker.

хлеборóб *n.* farmer.

хлебосóл *n.* hospitable person; good host. —**хлебо-сóльный,** *adj.* hospitable. —**хлебосóльство,** *n.* hospitality.

хлеб-сóль [*gen.* **хлéба-сóли**] *n.m.* **1**, bread and salt (*symbol of hospitality*). **2**, hospitality. —*interj.* hearty appetite!

хлев [*2nd loc.* **хлеву́**; *pl.* **хлева́**] *n.* **1**, barn (*for livestock*). **2**, *colloq.* pigsty.

хлестáть *v.impfv.* [*pfv.* **хлестну́ть**; *pres.* **хлещу́, хлéщешь**] **1**, to whip; lash; flog. **2**, (*of sharp branches, thorns, etc.*) to cut. **3**, (*of rain*) to come down in torrents. **4**, (*of water, blood, etc.*) to gush. **5**, (*with* **в** *or* **o** + *acc.*) to beat against; lash. **6**, (*with instr.*) to lash (one's tail). **7**, *fig.* to flay; castigate; excoriate.

хлёсткий *adj.* [*comp.* **хлёстче**] **1**, (*of a wind*) biting. **2**, *fig., colloq.* biting; scathing; trenchant. **3**, *colloq.* (*of a sound, blow, etc.*) sharp.

хлестну́ть *v., pfv. of* **хлестáть**.

хли́пкий *adj., colloq.* **1**, rickety. **2**, frail. **3**, watery.

хлоп *interj.* bang!

хлóпанье *n.* banging; slamming; clapping.

хлóпать *v.impfv.* [*pfv.* **похлóпать** *or* **хлóпнуть**] **1**, to slap; bang: хлóпать когó-нибудь по спинé, to slap someone on the back; хлóпать кулакóм пó столу, to bang one's fist on the table. **2**, (*with instr.*) to slam (a door); crack (a whip); flap (one's wings). **3**, (*of a cork*) to pop; (*of a shot*) to ring out. **4**, to clap; applaud; (*with dat.*) applaud (someone). —**хлóпать в ладóши,** to clap one's hands. —**хлóпать глазáми** *or* **ушáми,** to look blank.

хлóпаться *v.r.impfv.* [*pfv.* **хлóпнуться**] *colloq.* to fall down; flop.

хлопéц [*gen.* **-пца**] *n., colloq.* boy; lad; youth.

хлопковóд *n.* cotton grower. —**хлопковóдство,** *n.* cotton growing. —**хлопковóдческий,** *adj.* cotton-growing.

хлóпковый *adj.* cotton. —**хлóпковый долгонóсик,** boll weevil. —**хлóпковое мáсло,** cottonseed oil.

хлопкоочисти́тельный *adj., in* **хлопкоочисти́тельная маши́на,** cotton gin.

хлóпнуть *v., pfv. of* **хлóпать**. —**хлóпнуться,** *refl., pfv. of* **хлóпаться**.

хлóпок [*gen.* **-пка**] *n.* cotton.

хлопóк [*gen.* **-пка́**] *n.* **1**, loud noise; bang; sound (*of a shot*); pop (*of a cork*). **2**, slap; pat (*on the back*). **3**, *pl.* clapping; applause.

хлопотáть *v.impfv.* [*pfv.* **похлопотáть**; *pres.* **-почу́, -пóчешь**] **1**, [*impfv. only*] to fuss; bustle about. **2**, (*with* **o**) to seek; try to get. **3**, (*with* **чтóбы**) to make efforts (to); try to see to it that. **4**, (*with* **за** + *acc.*) to make efforts; intercede (on behalf of).

хлопотли́вый *adj.* **1**, busy; bustling. **2**, difficult; demanding; onerous.

хлопóтный *adj., colloq.* = **хлопотли́вый** (*in sense #2*).

хлопотня́ *n., colloq.* bustling about; feverish activity.

хлопоту́н [*gen.* **-туна́**] *n.m.* [*fem.* **-ту́нья**] *colloq.* hustler; busybody.

хлóпоты [*gen.* **хлопóт**; *dat.* **хлóпотам**] *n.pl.* **1**, chores. **2**, efforts. **3**, worries; cares.

хлопу́шка [*gen. pl.* **-шек**] *n.* **1**, fly swatter. **2**, cracker (*party favor*).

хлопчáтник *n.* cotton plant.

хлопчатобумáжный *adj.* cotton.

хлóпья [*gen.* **-пьев**] *n.pl.* flakes: хлóпья снéга, snowflakes; кукуру́зные хлóпья, corn flakes.

хлор *n.* chlorine.

хлори́д *n.* chloride.

хлори́рование *n.* chlorination.

хлори́ровать *v.impfv. & pfv.* [*pres.* **-рую, -руешь**] to chlorinate.

хлóристый *adj.* **1**, chlorous. **2**, *in compounds,* ... chloride: хлóристый аммóний/кáлий/нáтрий, ammonium/potassium/sodium chloride.

хлóрка *n., colloq.* bleaching powder.

хлóрный *adj.* chloric. —**хлóрная и́звесть,** chloride of lime. —**хлóрная кислотá,** perchloric acid.

хлорофи́лл *n.* chlorophyll.

хлорофóрм *n.* chloroform.

хлороформи́ровать *v.impfv. & pfv.* [*pres.* **-рую, -руешь**] to chloroform.

хлы́нуть *v.pfv.* **1**, to stream; gush; pour; rush. **2**, (*of rain*) to come down in torrents. **3**, (*of a crowd*) to stream; surge.

хлыст [*gen.* **хлыстá**] *n.* **1**, whip. **2**, *hist.* member of a religious sect that practiced flagellation; khlyst.

хлыщ [*gen.* **хлыщá**] *n., colloq.* fop; dandy.

хлю́пать *v.impfv., colloq.* to splash; make a splashing sound. —**хлю́пать нóсом,** to sniff.

хлю́пкий *adj., colloq.* **1**, soggy. **2**, rickety. **3**, frail.

хлябь *n.f.* **1**, *archaic* abyss. **2**, *colloq.* mud.

хля́стик *n.* half-belt (*at the back of a coat*).

хмелёк [*gen.* **-лькá**] *n., dim. of* **хмель**. —**под хмелькóм,** tipsy; high.

хмелéть *v.impfv.* [*pfv.* **охмелéть** *or* **захмелéть**] *colloq.* to become tipsy; get high.

хмель *n.m.* **1**, hop (*plant*). **2**, hops. **3**, *colloq.* intoxication: во хмелю́, intoxicated.

хмельнóй *adj.* **1**, intoxicated. **2**, intoxicating. —**хмельнóе,** *n.* alcohol; liquor.

хму́рить *v.impfv.* [*pfv.* **нахму́рить**] **1**, to knit (one's brows). **2**, *in* хму́рить лицó, to frown. —**хму́риться,** *refl.* **1**, to frown. **2**, (*of the sky*) to be overcast.

хму́рый *adj.* **1**, (*of a person*) gloomy; somber; sullen. **2**, (*of the weather, sky, etc.*) gloomy; overcast; dismal.

хна *n.* henna.

хны́канье *n., colloq.* whining; whimpering.

хны́кать *v.impfv.* [*pres.* **хны́чу, хны́чешь** *or* **хны́каю, хны́каешь**] *colloq.* to whine; whimper.

хóбби *n.neut. indecl.* hobby.

хóбот *n.* trunk (*of an elephant*).

ход *n.* **1**, motion: зáдний ход, reverse motion. **2**, speed: замедля́ть ход, to reduce one's speed; slow down. **3**, operation (*of a machine*). **4**, [*pl.* **хóды** *or* **ходы́**] stroke (*of an engine, piston, etc.*). **5**, *fig.* course; progress: ход собы́тий, course of events. Ход мы́слей, train of thought. **6,** [*pl.* **хóды** *or* **ходы́**] move (*in chess*); lead (*in cards*). На сороковóм ходý, on the fortieth move. **7,** [*pl.* **хóды**] *fig.* move; maneuver. **8,** [*pl.* **ходы́**] entrance; door: парáдный/чёрный ход, front/back door. **9,** [*pl.* **ходы́**] passage; passageway. **10,** *fig.* chance of success: Емý хóду нет, he has no chance. **11,** *obs.* procession. —**в большóм ходý,** in great demand. —**в пóлном ходý,** in full swing. —**в хóде** (+ *gen.*), in the course of; during. —**дать ход** (+ *dat.*), to start up; set in motion. —**дать хóду,** *colloq.* to take to one's heels. —**знать все ходы́ и вы́ходы,** to know all the ins and outs. —**идти́ свои́м хóдом, 1,** to proceed under one's own power (*or* steam). **2,** to proceed at one's own pace. —**на пóлном ходý,** while moving at top speed. —**на ходý, 1,** in operation. **2,** quickly; on the run. **3,** while something is in motion. —**не давáть хóду** (+ *dat.*), to give someone no chance. —**пойти́ в ход, 1,** to come into use; come into play. **2,** to become much in demand. —**пóлный ход!,** full speed ahead! —**пóлным хóдом, 1,** apace: идти́ пóлным хóдом, to proceed apace. **2,** at top speed; full tilt. —**пусти́ть в ход, 1,** to start; set in motion. **2,** to use; resort to; bring into play: пусти́ть в ход все срéдства, to move heaven and earth; leave no stone unturned. —**с хóду,** without stopping; while in motion.

ходáтай *n.* intercessor.

ходáтайство *n.* **1,** application; solicitation; petition. **2,** intercession.

ходáтайствовать *v.impfv.* [*pfv.* **походáтайствовать**; *pres.* **-ствую, -ствуешь**] **1,** (*with* **о**) to apply (for); petition (for); solicit. **2,** (*with* **за** + *acc.*) to intercede (on behalf of).

хóдики [*gen.* **-ков**] *n.pl., colloq.* wall clock (*driven by weights*).

ходи́ть *v.impfv.* [*pres.* **хожý, хóдишь**] **1,** *indeterm. of* **идти́. 2,** to walk; be able to walk. **3,** (*of trains, buses, etc.*) to run; operate. **4,** (*of news, rumors, etc.*) to be going around. **5,** (*with* **в** + *prepl.*) to wear: ходи́ть в шýбе, to be wearing a fur coat. Ходи́ть с бородóй, to have a beard. **6,** (*with* **за** + *instr.*) to look after; care for.

хóдкий *adj., colloq.* **1,** agile. **2,** (*of a vehicle, ship, etc.*) fast-moving. **3,** (*of merchandise*) fast-selling. **4,** (*of an expression*) currently popular.

ходовóй *adj.* **1,** *mech.* working; operational. **2,** performance (*attrib.*): ходовы́е испытáния, performance tests. Ходовы́е кáчества маши́ны, performance of a car. **3,** *colloq.* popular; fast-selling. **4,** *colloq.* (*of an expression, anecdote, etc.*) currently popular. —**ходовáя пружи́на,** mainspring (*of a watch*).

ходóк [*gen.* **-докá**] *n.* **1,** walker. **2,** (*with various prepositions*) *colloq.* regular visitor (to). **3,** (*with* **на** + *acc. or* **по**) *colloq.* person who is adroit (with *or* at). **4,** *obs.* envoy; delegate.

ходýли [*gen.* **-лей**] *n.pl.* stilts.

ходýлочник *n.* stilt (*bird*).

ходýльный *adj.* stilted.

ходýн [*gen.* **-дунá**] *n., colloq.* walker. —**ходи́ть ходунóм, 1,** to shake violently. **2,** *fig.* to be in a whirl.

ходьбá *n.* walking; walk: полчасá ходьбы́, half-an-hour's walk.

ходя́чий *adj.* **1,** walking. **2,** (*of a sick person*) able to walk; ambulatory. **3,** *fig.* current; currently popular.

хождéние *n.* **1,** walking; going: хождéние в кинó, going to the movies. **2,** circulation (*of money*). **3,** *fig.* use; currency: имéть широкóе хождéние, to be in wide use; enjoy wide currency.

хозрасчёт *n.* self-supporting basis; financial autonomy; economic accountability (*contr. of* **хозя́йственный расчёт**).

хозя́ин [*pl.* **хозя́ева, хозя́ев**] *n.* **1,** owner. **2,** master. **3,** (*preceded by an adj.*) (good, bad, etc.) administrator. **4,** employer; boss. **5,** landlord. **6,** host. —**хозя́ева пóля,** *sports* the home team.

хозя́йка [*gen. pl.* **-йек**] *n., fem. of* **хозя́ин.** —**домáшняя хозя́йка,** housewife.

хозя́йничать *v.impfv.* **1,** to be in charge; run things. **2,** to keep house. **3,** *colloq.* to throw one's weight around.

хозя́йский *adj.* **1,** master's. **2,** proprietary: хозя́йское отношéние к, proprietary attitude toward. **3,** *fig.* watchful: хозя́йским глáзом, with a watchful eye. **4,** *fig.* imperious. —**дéло хозя́йское,** *colloq.* it's up to you (to decide).

хозя́йственник *n.* administrator; manager.

хозя́йственность *n.f.* efficiency (*in running a household*).

хозя́йственный *adj.* **1,** economic. **2,** household (*attrib.*). **3,** thrifty; economical. —**хозя́йственный магази́н,** store selling household goods. —**хозя́йственное мы́ло,** kitchen soap. —**хозя́йственная сýмка,** shopping bag.

хозя́йство *n.* **1,** economy. **2,** housekeeping. **3,** equipment. **4,** farm. —**домáшнее хозя́йство, 1,** housekeeping. **2,** household. —**сéльское хозя́йство,** agriculture.

хозя́йствование *n.* management.

хозя́йствовать *v.impfv.* [*pres.* **-ствую, -ствуешь**] **1,** to manage; be a manager. **2,** to keep house.

хозя́йчик *n., colloq.* small proprietor.

хоккеи́ст *n.* hockey player.

хоккéй *n.* hockey. —**хоккéйный,** *adj.* hockey (*attrib.*).

хóленый *adj.* well-groomed.

холéра *n.* cholera.

холéрик *n.* temperamental, high-strung person. —**холери́ческий,** *adj.* choleric; temperamental; high-strung.

холéрный *adj.* cholera (*attrib.*).

холестери́н *n.* cholesterol.

хóлить *v.impfv.* to take care of.

хóлка *n.* withers.

холл *n.* **1,** (meeting) hall. **2,** lobby.

холм [*gen.* **холмá**] *n.* hill.

хóлмик *n.* small hill; knoll.

холми́стый *adj.* hilly.

хóлод [*pl.* **холодá**] *n.* **1,** cold. **2,** *pl.* cold weather: пéрвые холодá, the first cold weather.

холодáть *v.impfv.* [*pfv.* **похолодáть**] *impers.* to get cold; turn cold.

холодéть *v.impfv.* [*pfv.* **похолодéть**] **1,** to grow cold. **2,** *fig.* to turn cold (*from fear, horror, etc.*).

холодéц [*gen.* **-дцá**] *n., colloq.* aspic (*of meat or fish*).

холоди́льник *n.* refrigerator; icebox.

холоди́льный *adj.* refrigeration (*attrib.*); refrigerating.

холоди́ть *v.impfv.* [*pres.* **-жу́, -ди́шь**] to cool; chill.

холоднéть *v.impfv., impers.* to get cold; turn cold.

хо́лодно *adv.* coldly. —*adj., used predicatively*, cold: Здесь хо́лодно, it is cold here; мне хо́лодно, I am cold.

холоднова́тый *adj., colloq.* rather cold.

холоднокро́вный *adj., zool.* cold-blooded.

хо́лодность *n.f.* coldness.

холо́дный *adj.* [*short form* **хо́лоден, холодна́, хо́лодно, хо́лодны** *or* **холодны́**] **1,** cold. **2,** unheated. **3,** (*of a garment, blanket, etc.*) light; thin; not providing sufficient warmth. —**холо́дное ору́жие,** plain weapon (*sword, bayonet, etc.*).

холодо́к [*gen.* **-дка́**] *n., colloq.* **1,** coolness; chill. **2,** cool breeze. **3,** cool place. **4,** cool (*of the day, evening, etc.*). **5,** *fig.* chill; coolness (*in relations*).

холо́п *n.* **1,** *hist.* serf; bondsman. **2,** *fig.* lackey; stooge.

холо́пский *adj.* **1,** *hist.* serf's. **2,** *fig.* servile.

холо́пство *n.* **1,** *hist.* serfdom. **2,** *fig.* servility.

холо́пствовать *v.impfv.* [*pres.* **-ствую, -ствуешь**] **1,** to be servile. **2,** (*with* **пéред**) to kowtow (to).

холости́ть *v.impfv.* [*pfv.* **вы́холостить**; *pres.* **-щу́, -сти́шь**] to castrate; geld (an animal).

холосто́й *adj.* **1,** (*of a man*) single; unmarried. **2,** bachelor (*attrib.*). **3,** blank: холосто́й патро́н, blank cartridge. **4,** *mech.* idling: рабо́тать на холосто́м ходу́, to idle.

холостя́к [*gen.* **-стяка́**] *n.* bachelor. —**холостя́цкий,** *adj., colloq.* bachelor (*attrib.*); bachelor's.

холощéние *n.* castration.

холощёный *adj.* castrated; gelded.

холст [*gen.* **холста́**] *n.* **1,** linen. **2,** sackcloth; burlap. **3,** *painting* canvas.

холсти́на *n.* = холст.

холсти́нка *n.* **1,** piece of cloth. **2,** linen or cotton fabric.

холу́й *n., colloq.* flunky; stooge.

холщо́вый *adj.* **1,** linen. **2,** burlap.

хо́ля *n., colloq.* loving care. —**жить в хо́ле,** to be lovingly cared for.

хому́т [*gen.* **-мута́**] *n.* collar (*for a horse*).

хомя́к [*gen.* **-мяка́**] *n.* hamster.

хор [*pl.* **хоры́** *or* **хо́ры**] *n.* **1,** chorus. **2,** choir. —**хо́ром,** in unison; all together. *See also* **хо́ры.**

хора́л *n.* chorale.

хорва́т *n.m.* [*fem.* **-ва́тка**] Croat. —**хорва́тский,** *adj.* Croatian.

хо́рда *n., math.* cord.

хорéй *n.* trochee. —**хореи́ческий,** *adj.* trochaic.

хорёк [*gen.* **хорька́**] *n.* polecat; fitch; ferret.

хореогра́фия *n.* choreography. —**хореóграф,** *n.* choreographer. —**хореографи́ческий,** *adj.* choreographic.

хорéя *n.* chorea.

хори́ст *n.* member of a choir; chorister.

хорме́йстер *n.* choirmaster.

хорово́д *n.* round dance with singing.

хорово́й *adj.* choral.

херони́ть *v.impfv.* [*pfv.* **похорони́ть**; *pres.* **хороню́, хоро́нишь**] to bury; inter.

хорохо́риться *v.r.impfv., colloq.* to swagger; bluster.

хоро́шенький *adj.* **1,** pretty; attractive; cute. **2,** *colloq.* good. **3,** *colloq., ironic* fine; nice; pretty: хоро́шенькая исто́рия, a fine/nice/pretty mess.

хоро́шенько *adv., colloq.* properly; thoroughly. Хоро́шенько отдохну́ть, to have a good rest. Сту́кните хоро́шенько!, give a good knock!

хорошéть *v.impfv.* [*pfv.* **похорошéть**] to get prettier; become more attractive.

хоро́ший *adj.* [*short form* **хоро́ш, хороша́, хорошо́, хороши́**] **1,** good. **2,** nice. **3,** [*short form only, used with* **собо́й**] pretty; attractive; good-looking. —**всегó хоро́шего!,** all the best!

хорошо́ *adv.* well: хорошо́ себя́ чу́вствовать, to feel well. Хорошо́ ска́зано!, well said! Хорошо́ па́хнуть, to smell good. —*adj., used predicatively* **1,** good; fine; nice: Это хорошо́, that's good; that's nice. Хорошо́, что..., it's a good thing that... Пока́ всё хорошо́, so far, so good. **2,** (*with dat.*) satisfied; happy: Вам бу́дет хорошо́ там, you'll be happy there; you'll like it there. —*particle* all right; O.K.; very well. —*n. indecl.* "good" (*school grade*).

хо́ры [*gen.* **хо́ров**] *n.pl.* gallery; balcony.

хорь [*gen.* **хоря́**] *n.m.* = хорёк.

хорько́вый *adj.* fitch (*attrib.*).

хотéние *n., colloq.* desire.

хотéть *v.impfv.* [*pres.* **хочу́, хо́чешь, хо́чет, хоти́м, хоти́те, хотя́т**] **1,** to want: Что вы хоти́те?, what do you want? Она́ хо́чет уйти́, she wants to leave. Я хочу́, чтобы письмо́ пришло́ во́время, I want the letter to arrive on time. **2,** to like; wish: Хоти́те ещё ча́шку ко́фе?, would you like another cup of coffee? Де́лайте, как хоти́те, do as you like/wish/please. —**хо́чешь не хо́чешь,** like it or not.

хотéться *v.r.impfv.* [*pres.* **хо́чется**] *impers.* (*with dat.*) **1,** to want: Мне хо́чется поговори́ть с ним, I want to have a talk with him. **2,** to feel like: Ему́ не хо́чется идти́, he doesn't feel like going.

хоть *conj.* **1,** [*also,* **хоть и**] although; though. **2,** if you like. **3,** at least. **4,** even if. **5,** for example. **6,** any-: хоть что, anything; хоть где, anywhere. **7,** *used with the imperative form of the verb in a number of idiomatic expressions:* хоть убéй, for the life of me; хоть отбавля́й, more than enough; хоть шаро́м покати́, absolutely empty; мо́крый, хоть вы́жми (*or* выжима́й), wringing wet. —**хоть бы, 1,** even if. **2,** only. —**хоть бы и так,** *colloq.* **1,** what of it?; what if it is? **2,** even so. —**хоть бы что** (+ *dat.*), *colloq.* couldn't care less. —**хоть куда́,** *colloq.* first-rate.

хотя́ *conj.* **1,** although. **2,** though. —**хотя́ бы, 1,** if only. **2,** even if. **3,** at least. —**хотя́ и, 1,** although; even though. **2,** albeit.

хохла́тый *adj.* crested.

хохла́ч [*gen.* **-лача́**] *n.* hooded seal.

хо́хлиться *v.r.impfv.* [*pfv.* **нахо́хлиться**] **1,** (*of a bird*) to ruffle its feathers. **2,** *fig., colloq.* to be glum.

хохо́л [*gen.* **хохла́**] *n.* **1,** crest (*of a bird*). **2,** topknot. **3,** *obs., colloq.* Ukrainian.

хохоло́к [*gen.* **-лка́**] *n., dim. of* **хохо́л** (*in senses #1 & #2*).

хо́хот *n.* loud laughter.

хохота́ть *v.impfv.* [*pres.* **хохочу́, хохо́чешь**] to laugh loudly.

хохоту́н [*gen.* **-туна́**] *n.m.* [*fem.* **-ту́нья**] *colloq.* merry fellow; one easily moved to laughter.

храбре́ц [*gen.* **-бреца́**] *n.* brave man.

храбри́ться *v.r.impfv., colloq.* to pretend not to be afraid; keep a stiff upper lip.

хра́брый *adj.* brave. —**хра́бро**, *adv.* bravely. —**хра́брость**, *n.f.* bravery.

храм *n.* temple. —**Храм Васи́лия Блаже́нного**, St. Basil's Cathedral (*on Red Square*).

хране́ние *n.* storage; safekeeping. Сдава́ть бага́ж на хране́ние, to check one's baggage. —**ка́мера хране́ния (багажа́)**, baggage room.

храни́лище *n.* storehouse; depository; repository.

храни́тель *n.m.* 1, keeper; custodian. 2, curator (*of a museum*).

храни́ть *v.impfv.* 1, to keep; save: храни́ть письмо́, to keep/save a letter. Храни́ть та́йну, to keep a secret. 2, to store: храни́ть что́-нибудь в се́йфе/ на скла́де/, to store something in a safe/warehouse. 3, to maintain (silence, a custom, etc.).

храп *n.* 1, snore; snoring. 2, snorting (*of a horse*).

храпе́ть *v.impfv.* [*pres.* **-плю́, -пи́шь**] 1, to snore. 2, (*of a horse*) to snort.

храпови́к [*gen.* **-вика́**] *n.* ratchet. —**храпово́й**, *adj.* ratchet (*attrib.*).

храпу́н [*gen.* **-пуна́**] *n., colloq.* snorer.

хребе́т [*gen.* **-бта́**] *n.* 1, spine; backbone. 2, mountain range.

хрен *n.* horseradish. —**хрен ре́дьки не сла́ще**, it's a choice of two evils; one is as bad as the other.

хрестома́тия *n.* reader (*book*).

хризанте́ма (тэ) *n.* chrysanthemum.

хрип *n.* wheeze. —**предсме́ртный хрип**, death rattle.

хрипе́ть *v.impfv.* [*pres.* **-плю́, -пи́шь**] 1, to wheeze. 2, to be hoarse.

хри́плый *adj.* hoarse. —**хри́пло**, *adv.* hoarsely; in a hoarse voice.

хри́пнуть *v.impfv.* [*past* **хрип** *or* **хри́пнул, хри́пла**] to become hoarse.

хрипота́ *n.* hoarseness.

хрипотца́ *n., colloq.* slight hoarseness.

христиани́н [*pl.* **-тиа́не, -тиа́н**] *n.m.* [*fem.* **-тиа́нка**] Christian. —**христиа́нский**, *adj.* Christian. —**христиа́нство**, *n.* Christianity.

Христо́с [*gen.* **Христа́**] *n.* Christ.

хром *n.* 1, chromium. 2, chrome. 3, chrome leather.

хромати́ческий *adj.* chromatic.

хрома́ть *v.impfv.* 1, to limp. 2, *colloq.* to be deficient. 3, *colloq.* to be weak; be poor (*in a certain school subject*): Он хрома́ет по орфогра́фии (*or* у него́ хрома́ет орфогра́фия), he is poor in spelling. —**хрома́ть на о́бе ноги́**, to flounder.

хроми́рование *n.* chrome plating.

хроми́ровать *v.impfv. & pfv.* [*pres.* **-рую, -руешь**] to plate with chrome; chrome-plate.

хро́мистый *adj.* chrome (*attrib.*): хро́мистая сталь, chrome steel.

хроми́т *n.* chromite.

хро́мовый *adj.* chrome (*attrib.*). —**хро́мовая кислота́**, chromic acid.

хромо́й *adj.* lame. —*n.* lame person.

хромоно́гий *adj.* lame.

хромосо́ма *n.* chromosome.

хромота́ *n.* lameness.

хро́ник *n., colloq.* chronically ill person.

хро́ника *n.* 1, chronicle. 2, news items. 3, newsreel.

хроника́льный *adj.* chronicle (*attrib.*); in chronicle form. —**хроника́льный фильм**, newsreel.

хрони́ческий *adj.* 1, chronic. 2, chronically ill.

хvillage. хроноло́гия *n.* chronology. —**хронологи́ческий**, *adj.* chronological.

хроно́метр *n.* 1, timepiece. 2, chronometer.

хронометра́ж *n.* time (and motion) study. —**хронометражи́ст**, *n.* time-study man.

хронометри́ровать *v.impfv. & pfv.* [*pres.* **-рую, -руешь**] to time; clock.

хронометри́ст *n.* timer; timekeeper.

хру́пкий *adj.* [*short form* **хру́пок, хрупка́, хру́пко, хру́пки**] 1, fragile; brittle. 2, frail; delicate.

хру́пкость *n.f.* 1, fragility. 2, frailty.

хруст *n.* crunch; crunching sound.

хруста́лик *n.* 1, *colloq.* something made of crystal. 2, lens of the eye.

хруста́ль [*gen.* **-сталя́**] *n.m.* 1, crystal. 2, item made of crystal.

хруста́льный *adj.* 1, crystal. 2, like crystal.

хруста́н *n.* dotterel.

хрусте́ть *v.impfv.* [*pfv.* **хру́стнуть**; *pres.* **хрущу́, хрусти́шь**] to crunch.

хрустя́щий *adj.* crisp.

хрущ [*gen.* **хруща́**] *n.* cockchafer.

хрю́канье *n.* grunting (*of a pig*).

хрю́кать *v.impfv.* [*pfv.* **хрю́кнуть**] (*of a pig*) to grunt.

хряк [*gen.* **хряка́**] *n.* male hog.

хрящ [*gen.* **хряща́**] *n.* 1, cartilage. 2, gristle. —**хряще-ва́тый**, *adj.* cartilaginous; gristly. —**хрящево́й**, *adj.* cartilage (*attrib.*).

худе́ть *v.impfv.* [*pfv.* **похуде́ть**] to get thin; lose weight.

ху́до *n., obs., colloq.* harm. —*adv.* badly; poorly: ху́до оде́тый, poorly dressed. —*adj., used predicatively* (*with dat.*) 1, bad; in a bad way. 2, unwell: Ему́ ху́до, he is not feeling well.

худоба́ *n.* thinness; leanness.

худо́жественность *n.f.* artistic value; artistry.

худо́жественный *adj.* 1, art (*attrib.*); of art. 2, artistic. —**худо́жественная литерату́ра**, fiction. —**худо́жественный фильм**, feature film.

худо́жество *n.* 1, *obs.* art. 2, *colloq.* trick; escapade.

худо́жник *n.m.* [*fem.* **-ница**] 1, artist. 2, painter.

худо́й *adj.* 1, [*comp.* **ху́же**] bad. 2, [*comp.* **худе́е**] thin; skinny. 3, [*comp.* **худе́е**] *colloq.* worn; tattered; full of holes. —**на худо́й коне́ц**, *colloq.* if worst comes to worst. *See also* **ху́же**.

худосо́чный *adj.* sickly; haggard.

худоща́вый *adj.* thin; lean; skinny.

ху́дшее *n., decl. as an adj.* 1, the worse: переме́на к ху́дшему, change for the worse. **2,** the worst: пригото́виться к ху́дшему, to prepare for the worst.

ху́дший *adj., used only as a modifier, comp. and superl. of* плохо́й *and* худо́й, worse; worst. —в ху́дшем слу́чае, in the worst case; at worst.

ху́же *adj., comp. of* плохо́й *and* худо́й, worse. —*adv., comp. of* плохо́ *and* ху́до, worse. —тем ху́же, so much the worse. —ху́же всего́, worst of all. —ху́же всего́ то, что..., the worse of it is that...

хук *n., boxing* hook.

хула́ *n.* (verbal) abuse.

хулига́н *n.* hooligan; hoodlum.

хулига́нить *v.impfv.* to behave like a hooligan (*or* hoodlum).

хулига́нский *adj.* like that of a hooligan or hoodlum.

хулига́нство *n.* hooliganism; disorderly conduct.

хули́тель *n.m.* detractor.

хули́ть *v.impfv.* to disparage.

ху́нта *n.* junta.

хурма́ *n.* persimmon.

ху́тор [*pl.* хутора́] *n.* farm. —хуторско́й, *adj.* farm (*attrib.*).

Ц, ц *n.neut.* 23rd letter of the Russian alphabet.

ца́пать *v.impfv.* [*pfv.* ца́пнуть] *colloq.* to grab; snatch.

ца́пля [*gen. pl.* -пель] *n.* heron. —бе́лая ца́пля, egret.

ца́пнуть *v., pfv. of* ца́пать.

цара́пать *v.impfv.* **1,** [*pfv.* цара́пнуть] to scratch. **2,** [*pfv.* нацара́пать] *colloq.* to scribble; scrawl. —цара́паться, *refl.* [*impfv. only*] **1,** to scratch; make scratching sounds; have a tendency to scratch. **2,** to scratch each other.

цара́пина *n.* scratch.

цара́пнуть *v., pfv. of* цара́пать.

царе́вич *n.* tsarevitch.

царе́вна [*gen. pl.* -вен] *n.* tsarevna.

цареуби́йство *n.* regicide.

цари́зм *n.* tsarism.

цари́ть *v.impfv.* **1,** *obs.* (*of a monarch*) to reign. **2,** *fig.* (*of silence*) to reign; (*of conditions*) to prevail.

цари́ца *n.* **1,** tsarina. **2,** *fig.* (*with gen.*) queen (of): цари́ца мод, queen of fashion. —цари́ца ба́ла, belle of the ball.

ца́рский *adj.* **1,** of the tsar; tsar's. **2,** tsarist. **3,** *fig.* regal.

ца́рственный *adj.* regal; majestic.

ца́рство *n.* **1,** kingdom; realm. **2,** reign. **3,** *fig.* kingdom: живо́тное ца́рство, animal kingdom. —венча́ние на ца́рство, coronation.

ца́рствование *n.* reign. —в ца́рствование (+ *gen.*), during the reign of.

ца́рствовать *v.impfv.* [*pres.* -ствую, -ствуешь] to reign.

царь [*gen.* царя́] *n.m.* **1,** tsar. **2,** *fig.* king: царь звере́й, king of beasts.

цвести́ *v.impfv.* [*pres.* цвету́, цветёшь; *past* цвёл, цвела́, цвело́, цвели́] **1,** to bloom; blossom; flower. **2,** *fig.* (*with instr.*) to be the picture (of beauty, health, etc.). **3,** *fig.* to flourish.

цвет *n.* **1,** [*pl.* цвета́] color: цвета́ ра́дуги, the colors of the rainbow. Цвет лица́, complexion. **2,** [*pl.* цветы́] (*sing. rare*) flower. **3,** [*pl.* цветы́] blossom. —во цве́те лет, in one's prime; in the prime of life. —в цвету́, in bloom.

цвете́ние *n.* blossoming; blooming; flowering.

цвети́стый *adj.* **1,** colorful. **2,** *fig.* flowery; florid.

цветко́вый *adj.* (*of plants*) flowering.

цветни́к [*gen.* -ника́] *n.* flower bed; flower garden.

цветно́й *adj.* colored; color (*attrib.*). —цветна́я капу́ста, cauliflower. —цветно́й каранда́ш, crayon. —цветны́е мета́ллы, non-ferrous metals. —цветно́е стекло́, stained glass.

цветово́дство *n.* floriculture.

цветово́й *adj.* color (*attrib.*). —цветова́я слепота́, colorblindness.

цвето́к [*gen.* -тка́; *pl.* цветы́, цвето́в, цвета́м] *n.* flower.

цветоло́же *n., bot.* receptacle.

цветоно́жка [*gen. pl.* -жек] *n., bot.* pedicel.

цвето́чек [*gen.* -чка] *n., dim. of* цвето́к. —э́то то́лько (*or* всё) цвето́чки, that is only the beginning (of the bad news); that is nothing compared with what is to come.

цвето́чница *n.* flower girl.

цвето́чный *adj.* flower (*attrib.*); floral.

цвету́щий *adj.* **1,** flowering; blossoming; blooming. **2,** *fig.* healthy; robust. **3,** *fig.* flourishing; prospering.

цеди́лка [*gen. pl.* -лок] *n., colloq.* strainer.

цеди́ть *v.impfv.* [*pres.* цежу́, це́дишь] **1,** to strain; filter. **2,** to pour slowly (*through a narrow opening*). **3,** to sip. **4,** *colloq.* to utter (*often slowly and with suppressed anger*).

це́дра *n.* dried lemon or orange peel.

це́зий *n.* cesium.

цейтно́т *n., chess* time trouble.

целе́бный *adj.* **1,** medicinal; curative. **2,** healthful; salubrious.

целево́й *adj.* having a specific purpose. —**целева́я устано́вка,** aim; objective.

целенапра́вленный *adj.* purposeful.

целесообра́зный *adj.* advisable; expedient. —**целесообра́зность,** *n.f.* advisability; expediency.

целеустремлённый *adj.* purposeful.

целико́м *adv.* **1,** whole: проглоти́ть целико́м, to swallow whole. **2,** wholly; entirely. —**целико́м и по́лностью,** completely; fully.

целина́ *n.* virgin land; virgin soil.

цели́нный *adj.* virgin: цели́нные зе́мли, virgin lands.

цели́тель *n.m.* healer.

цели́тельный *adj.* healing; curative.

це́лить *v.impfv.* (*with* **в** + *acc.*) to aim (at). *Also,* **це́литься,** *refl.*

целлофа́н *n.* cellophane. —**целлофа́новый,** *adj.* cellophane (*attrib.*).

целлуло́ид *n.* celluloid. —**целлуло́идный,** *adj.* celluloid.

целлюло́за *n.* cellulose. —**целлюло́зный,** *adj.* cellulose.

целова́ть *v.impfv.* [*pfv.* **поцелова́ть**; *pres.* **целу́ю, целу́ешь**] to kiss. —**целова́ться,** *refl.* **1,** (*of two people*) to kiss. **2,** (*with* **с** + *instr.*) to exchange kisses (with).

це́лое *n., decl. as an adj.* **1,** whole; the whole. **2,** *math.* whole number; integer.

целому́дренный *adj.* chaste. —**целому́дрие,** *n.* chastity.

це́лостность *n.f.* unity. —**территориа́льная це́лостность,** territorial integrity.

це́лостный *adj.* unified; integrated.

це́лость *n.f.* **1,** (*with gen.*) the safety (of). **2,** wholeness; unity. —**в це́лости,** intact. —**в це́лости и сохра́нности,** safe and sound.

це́лый *adj.* **1,** whole; entire. **2,** intact; undamaged. **3,** safe; unharmed: цел и невреди́м, safe and sound. —**в це́лом, 1,** on the whole. **2,** as a whole. —**в о́бщем и це́лом,** on the whole; all in all. —**по це́лым дням;** це́лыми дня́ми, for days on end. *See also* **це́лое.**

цель *n.f.* **1,** target; mark: попа́сть в цель, to hit the target/mark. **2,** aim; goal; purpose; objective. —**с це́лью; в це́лях** (+ *gen. or with inf.*), with the aim of; for the purpose of; with a view to. —**с э́той це́лью,** toward this end.

це́льность *n.f.* unity; wholeness.

це́льный *adj.* **1,** whole; of one piece. **2,** single; unified; integrated. **3,** (*of a person, his nature, etc.*) sound; steady; solid. **4,** complete; finished. **5,** (*of milk, blood, etc.*) whole.

Це́льсий *n.* Celsius; Centigrade: де́сять гра́дусов по Це́льсию, ten degrees Celsius/Centigrade.

цеме́нт *n.* cement.

цементи́ровать *v.impfv. & pfv.* [*pres.* **-рую, -руешь**] **1,** to cement. **2,** to caseharden.

цеме́нтный *adj.* cement.

цена́ [*acc.* **це́ну**; *pl.* **це́ны**] *n.* **1,** price. **2,** *fig.* (*with dat.*) worth; value. Знать це́ну (+ *dat.*), to know the worth/value of. Какова́ же цена́ (+ *dat.*), е́сли..., what is the value (*or* good) of..., if...? —**в цене́, 1,** in price. **2,** high-priced. **3,** highly valued. —**цено́й** (+ *gen.*), **1,** at the cost of. **2,** through: цено́й огро́мных уси́лий, through enormous effort. —**цены́ нет** (*with noun in dat.*), priceless.

ценз *n.* requirement: возрастно́й ценз, age requirement.

це́нзор *n.* censor.

цензу́ра *n.* **1,** censorship. **2,** censor's office.

цензу́рный *adj.* **1,** censorship (*attrib.*). **2,** able to pass censorship; printable.

цени́тель *n.m.* judge; connoisseur.

цени́ть *v.impfv.* [*pres.* **ценю́, це́нишь**] **1,** *colloq.* to appraise; evaluate. **2,** to judge. **3,** to appreciate. **4,** to value; prize.

це́нник *n.* price list.

це́нность *n.f.* **1,** value. **2,** *pl.* valuables. **3,** *pl.* values.

це́нный *adj.* **1,** valuable. **2,** (*of a parcel*) having a stated value. —**це́нные бума́ги,** securities.

цент *n.* cent.

це́нтнер *n.* centner (*100 kilograms*).

центр *n.* center.

централиза́ция *n.* centralization.

централизо́ванный *adj.* centralized.

централизова́ть *v.impfv. & pfv.* [*pres.* **-зу́ю, -зу́ешь**] to centralize.

центра́льный *adj.* central.

центри́ст *n.* centrist. —**центри́стский,** *adj.* centrist.

центрифу́га *n.* centrifuge.

центробе́жный *adj.* centrifugal: центробе́жная си́ла, centrifugal force.

центрово́й *adj.* center (*attrib.*); central. —*n.* center (*on a basketball team*).

центростреми́тельный *adj.* centripetal.

цеп [*gen.* **цепа́**] *n.* flail.

цепене́ть *v.impfv.* [*pfv.* **оцепене́ть**] to become numb; become rigid.

це́пкий *adj.* [*short form* **це́пок, цепка́** *or* **це́пка, це́пко, це́пки**] **1,** prehensile; tenacious. **2,** *fig.* keen; perceptive. **3,** (*of one's memory*) retentive. **4,** *fig., colloq.* persistent; dogged.

це́пкость *n.f.* tenacity.

цепля́ться *v.r.impfv.* (*with* **за** + *acc.*) to cling (to).

цепно́й *adj.* chain (*attrib.*). —**цепно́е колесо́,** sprocket wheel. —**цепна́я реа́кция,** chain reaction.

цепо́чка [*gen. pl.* **-чек**] *n.* **1,** small chain: цепо́чка для часо́в, watch chain. **2,** row; line; file: цепо́чкой, in a line.

цеппели́н *n.* zeppelin.

цепь [*2nd loc.* **цепи́**; *pl.* **це́пи, цепе́й, цепя́м**] *n.f.* **1,** chain. **2,** *fig.* (*with gen.*) chain (*of mountains, islands, events, etc.*). **3,** *electricity* circuit.

церебра́льный *adj.* cerebral. —**церебра́льный парали́ч,** cerebral palsy.

церемониа́л *n.* ceremonial; ritual. —**церемониа́льный,** *adj.* ceremonial.

церемо́ниться *v.r.impfv.* to stand on ceremony.

церемо́ния *n.* **1,** ceremony. **2,** *pl., colloq.* ceremonies; formalities. Без дальне́йших церемо́ний, without further ado.

церемо́нный *adj.* ceremonious.

це́рий *n.* cerium.

церковнославя́нский *adj.* Church Slavonic.

церко́вный *adj.* of the church; church (*attrib.*).

це́рковь [*gen., dat. & prepl.* **це́ркви**; *instr.* **це́рковью**; *pl.* **це́ркви, церкве́й, церква́м**] *n.f.* church.

цеса́ревич *n.* crown prince (*in tsarist Russia*).

цеса́рка [*gen. pl.* **-рок**] *n.* guinea fowl; guinea hen.

цех *n.* **1**, shop (*in a factory*). **2**, *hist.* guild.

цехово́й *adj.* shop (*attrib.*). —**цехово́й профсою́з,** shop union.

цеце́ *n.f. indecl.* [*often* **му́ха цеце́**] tsetse fly.

циа́н *n.* cyanogen.

циани́д *n.* cyanide.

циа́нистый *adj.* cyanic. —**циа́нистый ка́лий,** potassium cyanide.

циа́новый *adj.* cyanic.

циано́з *n.* cyanosis.

цивилиза́ция *n.* civilization.

цивилизо́ванный *adj.* civilized.

цивилизова́ть *v.impfv. & pfv.* [*pres.* **-зу́ю, -зу́ешь**] to civilize.

циви́льный *adj., obs.* civilian.

цига́рка [*gen. pl.* **-рок**] *n., colloq.* hand-rolled cigarette.

цика́да *n.* cicada.

цикл *n.* **1**, cycle. **2**, series (*of lectures, concerts, etc.*).

цикламе́н *n.* cyclamen.

цикли́ческий *adj.* cyclical. *Also,* **цикли́чный.**

цикло́н *n.* cyclone. —**циклони́ческий,** *adj.* cyclonic.

циклотро́н *n.* cyclotron.

цико́рий *n.* chicory. —**цико́рный,** *adj.* chicory (*attrib.*).

цику́та *n.* water hemlock.

цили́ндр *n.* **1**, cylinder. **2**, top hat. —**цилиндри́ческий,** *adj.* cylindrical.

цимба́лы [*gen.* **-ба́л**] *n.pl.* dulcimer.

цинга́ *n.* scurvy.

цини́зм *n.* cynicism. —**ци́ник,** *n.* cynic.

цини́ческий *adj.* = **цини́чный.**

цини́чный *adj.* **1**, cynical. **2**, indecent; off-color. —**цини́чность,** *n.f.* cynicism.

цинк *n.* zinc. —**ци́нковый,** *adj.* zinc (*attrib.*).

ци́нния *n.* zinnia.

цино́вка [*gen. pl.* **-вок**] *n.* mat.

цирк *n.* circus.

цирка́ч [*gen.* **-кача́**] *n., colloq.* circus performer.

цирково́й *adj.* circus (*attrib.*).

цирко́н *n.* zircon.

цирко́ний *n.* zirconium.

циркули́ровать *v.impfv.* [*pres.* **-рую, -руешь**] *v.i.* to circulate.

ци́ркуль *n.m.* pair of compasses (*for drawing*).

циркуля́р *n.* circular; directive.

циркуля́ция *n.* circulation.

цирро́з *n.* cirrhosis.

цирю́льник *n., obs.* barber.

цирю́льня [*gen. pl.* **-лен**] *n., obs.* barbershop.

цисте́рна *n.* **1**, cistern; tank. **2**, tank car.

цитаде́ль (дэ) *n.f.* citadel.

цита́та *n.* quotation.

цити́рование *n.* quoting; citing.

цити́ровать *v.impfv.* [*pfv.* **процити́ровать**; *pres.* **-рую, -руешь**] to quote; cite.

цитоло́гия *n.* cytology. —**цитологи́ческий,** *adj.* cytological.

ци́тра *n.* zither.

цитра́т *n.* citrate.

ци́трус *n.* citrus.

ци́трусовый *adj.* citrus. —**ци́трусовые,** *n.pl.* citrus plants.

цифербла́т *n.* dial (*of an instrument*); face (*of a clock*).

ци́фра *n.* number; numeral; figure.

цифрово́й *adj.* numerical. —**цифрова́я вычисли́тельная маши́на,** digital computer.

ци́церо *n.neut. or m. indecl., typog.* pica.

цо́кать *v.impfv.* [*pfv.* **цо́кнуть**] **1**, *v.i.* to clatter; clank. **2**, *v.t.* (*with instr.*) to click: **цо́кать языко́м,** to click one's tongue. **3**, *v.i.* (*of birds and small animals*) to chirp; twitter.

цо́коль *n.m.* socle.

цо́кольный *adj., in* **цо́кольный эта́ж,** ground floor.

цо́кот *n.* clatter; clink.

цуг *n.* team of horses harnessed in tandem or in pairs. —**цу́гом,** *adv.* in tandem.

цука́т *n.* candied fruit; candied peel.

цыга́н [*pl.* **цыга́не, цыга́н, цыга́нам**] *n.m.* [*fem.* **цыга́нка**] Gypsy. —**цыга́нский,** *adj.* Gypsy.

цы́пки [*gen.* **цы́пок**] *n.pl., colloq.* red spots (*on the skin*).

цыплёнок [*gen.* **-нка**; *pl.* **цыпля́та, цыпля́т**] *n.* chicken; chick.

цы́почки *n.pl.* tiptoes. —**стать на цы́почки,** to stand on one's tiptoes. —**ходи́ть на цы́почках,** to tiptoe.

Ч

Ч, ч *n.neut.* 24th letter of the Russian alphabet.

чабáн [*gen.* **-банá**] *n.* shepherd.

чабёр [*gen.* **чабрá**] *n.* savory (*plant*). *Also,* **чáбер** [*gen.* **чáбра**].

чабрéц *also,* **чебрéц** [*gen.* **-рецá**] *n.* thyme.

чáвкать *v.impfv.* **1,** to munch; eat noisily. **2,** to tramp; tread noisily.

чад [*2nd loc.* **чаду́**] *n.* **1,** fumes. **2,** daze: быть (как) в чаду́, to be in a daze.

чади́ть *v.impfv.* [*pfv.* **начади́ть**; *pres.* **чажу́, чади́шь**] **1,** to smoke; emit fumes. **2,** (*with instr.*) to give off (*while smoking, cooking, etc.*).

чáдный *adj.* **1,** smoky. **2,** smoking. **3,** *fig.* dazed. **4,** *fig.* deadening.

чáдо *n., archaic* offspring; child.

чадрá *n.* veil worn by Moslem women.

чаёвничать *v.impfv., colloq.* to leisurely drink tea.

чаевы́е *n.pl., decl. as an adj.* tip; gratuity.

чаепи́тие *n.* drinking of tea.

чаи́нка [*gen. pl.* **-нок**] *n.* tea leaf.

чай [*2nd gen.* **чáю**] *n.* tea. —**дать на чай** (+ *dat.*), to tip (someone).

чáйка [*gen. pl.* **чáек**] *n.* gull; sea gull.

чáйная *n., decl. as an adj.* tearoom.

чáйник *n.* teakettle; teapot.

чáйница *n.* tea caddy.

чáйный *adj.* tea (*attrib.*). —**чáйная лóжка**, teaspoon. —**чáйная чáшка**, teacup.

чал *n.* mooring line.

чáлить *v.impfv.* to moor (a ship).

чáлка [*gen. pl.* **чáлок**] *n.* mooring line.

чалмá *n.* turban.

чáлый *adj.* roan.

чан [*pl.* **чаны́**] *n.* vat.

чáра *n., archaic* goblet.

чáрка [*gen. pl.* **чáрок**] *n., archaic* cup.

чаровáть *v.impfv.* [*pres.* **-ру́ю, -ру́ешь**] to charm; captivate.

чаровни́ца *n.* charming woman; enchantress.

чародéй *n.* **1,** sorcerer; magician. **2,** *fig.* charmer. —**чародéйка**, *n.* sorceress; *fig.* enchantress. —**чародéйство**, *n.* sorcery.

чару́ющий *adj.* charming; captivating; enchanting.

чáры [*gen.* **чар**] *n.pl.* **1,** *obs.* magic charm. **2,** charm; charms.

час [*gen.* **чáса**, *but after 2, 3 & 4* **часá**; *pl.* **часы́,**

часóв] *n.* **1,** hour. **2,** (*in telling time*) o'clock: пять часóв, five o'clock; в семь часóв, at seven o'clock. Час дня, 1 P.M.; час нóчи, 1 A.M. В девя́том часу́ утрá, between 8 and 8:30 in the morning. —**в дóбрый час!**, good luck! —**в котóром часу́?**, (at) what time? —**котóрый (тепéрь) час?**, what time is it? —**расти́ не по дням, а по часáм, 1,** (*of a child*) to grow by the hour; shoot up like a beanstalk. **2,** (*of a city, town, etc.*) to grow by leaps and bounds. —**с чáсу на час**, at any hour; at any moment. —**час óт часу**, by the hour; by the minute: Ему́ станóвится лу́чше час óт часу, he is getting better by the minute; he is improving steadily. Час óт часу не лéгче!, things are getting worse by the minute. —**часáми**, for hours. *See also* **часы́**.

часóвня [*gen. pl.* **-вен**] *n.* chapel.

часовóй *adj.* **1,** lasting an hour; hour-long. **2,** hourly; per hour. **3,** *colloq.* one-o'clock (*attrib.*). **4,** clock (*attrib.*); watch (*attrib.*). —*n.* sentry. —**часовóй механи́зм, 1,** clockwork. **2,** timing device. —**часовóй пóяс**, time zone.

часовщи́к [*gen.* **-щикá**] *n.* watchmaker.

частéнько *adv., colloq.* fairly often.

части́ть *v.impfv.* [*pres.* **чащу́, части́шь**] *colloq.* **1,** to speak (too) rapidly. **2,** to strike rapid blows. **3,** (*of rain*) to beat down steadily.

части́ца *n.* **1,** small part. **2,** particle: части́ца пы́ли, particle of dust. **3,** *gram.* particle.

части́чный *adj.* partial. —**части́чно**, *adv.* partly; partially.

чáстник *n., colloq.* private trader.

чáстное *n., decl. as an adj.* **1,** *math.* quotient. **2,** the particular.

чáстность *n.f.* detail. —**в чáстности**, in particular; specifically.

чáстный *adj.* **1,** private. **2,** particular; special. —**чáстный итóг**, subtotal. —**чáстным óбразом**, privately. *See also* **чáстное**.

чáсто *adv.* **1,** often; frequently. **2,** densely; close together.

частокóл *n.* fence; paling.

частотá *n.* **1,** frequency: частотá слу́чаев, frequency of cases. **2,** [*pl.* **частóты**] *physics; radio* frequency: ультравысóкая частотá, ultrahigh frequency.

частóтный *adj.* frequency (*attrib.*).

часту́шка [*gen. pl.* **-шек**] *n.* jingle; ditty.

чáстый *adj.* [*comp.* **чáще**] **1,** frequent. **2,** quick; rapid;

rapid-fire. **3,** dense; thick. **4,** set close together; close. **5,** (*of a comb, sieve, etc.*) fine. **6,** (*of rain*) steady.

часть [*pl.* ча́сти, частéй, частя́м] *n.f.* **1,** part: рáвные чáсти, equal parts; запасны́е чáсти, spare parts. Чáсти тéла, parts of the body. **2,** *denoting a fraction:* пя́тая часть населéния, one-fifth of the population. **3,** *mil.* unit. **4,** department: учéбная часть, teaching department. **5,** *colloq.* field; sphere: не по моéй чáсти, out of my line. Служи́ть по э́той чáсти, to work in this capacity. —**бóльшая часть** (+ *gen.*), most (of). —**бóльшей чáстью; по бóльшей чáсти,** for the most part. —**по чáсти** (+ *gen.*), *colloq.* in the matter of...; when it comes to... —**по частя́м,** in parts; piecemeal.

чáстью *adv.* partly; in part.

часы́ [*gen.* часóв] *n.pl.* **1,** clock; watch. **2,** *mil.* guard duty; sentry duty: стоя́ть на часáх, to stand guard, **3,** *in* песóчные часы́, hourglass; **сóлнечные часы́,** sundial. —**рабóтать как часы́,** to work like clockwork; perform flawlessly.

чáхлый *adj.* **1,** (*of a person*) sickly. **2,** (*of plants*) wilted; withered.

чáхнуть *v.impfv.* [*pfv.* зачáхнуть; *past* чáх *or* чáхнул, чáхла] **1,** (*of plants*) to wilt; wither. **2,** (*of persons*) to become weak; fade; waste away.

чахóтка *n., med.* consumption; tuberculosis. —**чахóточный,** *adj.* consumptive.

чáша *n.* **1,** drinking bowl (*used in olden times*). Кругова́я чáша, loving cup. **2,** large bowl. —**чáша весóв,** scale: склони́ть чáшу весóв в пóльзу (+ *gen.*), to tip the scales in favor of. —**чáша терпéния,** one's patience. Переполни́ть чáшу терпéния, to be the last straw; be the straw that broke the camel's back.

чашели́стик *n.* sepal.

чáшечка [*gen. pl.* -чек] *n.* **1,** small cup. **2,** *bot.* calyx. —**колéнная чáшечка,** kneecap.

чáшка [*gen. pl.* чáшек] *n.* cup. —**колéнная чáшка,** kneecap.

чáща *n.* dense forest. —**в чáще лéса,** in the thick of the forest.

чáще *adj., comp. of* чáстый. —*adv., comp. of* чáсто. —**чáще всегó,** most often; usually.

чащóба *n., colloq.* = чáща.

чáяние *n., obs.* hope; expectation. —**пáче чáяния,** *see* пáче.

чáять *v.impfv.* [*pres.* чáю, чáешь] *obs.* to expect. —**души́ не чáять в** (+ *prepl.*), to dote upon.

чвáниться *v.r.impfv.* to swagger; boast.

чванли́вый *adj.* conceited; pretentious.

чвáнный *adj.* arrogant; conceited.

чвáнство *n.* arrogance; conceit.

чебрéц [*gen.* -рецá] *n.* = чабрéц.

чебурéк *n.* mutton pie (*Caucasian dish*).

чегó (во) *pron., gen. of* что. —*adv., colloq.* why?; what for?: Чегó я тудá пойду́?, why should I go there? —**до чегó,** how!: До чегó онá краси́ва!, how lovely she is! —**пóсле чегó,** after which; whereupon. —**чегó бы не,** what: Чегó бы он не дал за э́то!, what he wouldn't give for that! —**чегó дóброго,** for all one knows.

чей [*fem.* чья; *neut.* чьё; *pl.* чьи; *gen.* чьегó, чьей, чьих; *acc. fem.* чью; *dat.* чьему́, чьей, чьим; *instr.*

чьим, чьей, чьи́ми; *prepl.* чьём, чьей, чьих] *poss. pron.* **1,** *interr.* whose?: Чья э́то шля́па?, whose hat is this? **2,** *rel.* whose: человéк, чьё и́мя извéстно всем, a man whose name is known to all.

чей-либо [*infl. like* чей] *indef. pron.* = чéй-нибудь.

чéй-нибудь [*infl. like* чей] *indef. pron.* someone's; somebody's; anyone's; anybody's.

чéй-то [*infl. like* чей] *indef. pron.* someone's; somebody's.

чек *n.* **1,** check. **2,** (*in a store*) slip (*to be presented to the cashier when paying*); receipt (*from the cashier used to claim one's purchase*).

чекá *n.* pin; linchpin.

Чекá *n.fem. indecl., contr. of* Чрезвычáйная коми́ссия, Cheka (*Soviet security agency, 1917–22*).

чекáн *n.* stamp; punch; die.

чекáнить *v.impfv.* [*pfv.* отчекáнить] **1,** to mint; coin. **2,** to engrave; emboss. **3,** *fig.* to articulate.

чекáнка *n.* **1,** minting (*of coins*); mintage. **2,** embossed design.

чекáнный *adj.* **1,** used for engraving. **2,** engraved; embossed. **3,** *fig.* precise; crisp.

чеки́ст *n.* member of the Cheka.

чéковый *adj.* check (*attrib.*); checking. —**чéковая кни́жка,** checkbook.

челéста *n.* celesta.

чёлка *n.* bangs (*of hair*): носи́ть чёлку, to wear bangs.

чёлн [*gen.* челнá] *n.* canoe.

челнóк [*gen.* -нокá] *n.* **1,** = чёлн. **2,** shuttle. —**челнóчный,** *adj.* shuttle (*attrib.*).

челó [*pl.* чёла] *n., archaic* forehead; brow. —**бить челóм** (+ *dat.*), **1,** to bow humbly before. **2,** to beseech. **3,** to thank earnestly.

человéк [*gen. pl.* человéк; *other pl. forms rarely used*] *n.* **1,** person; man. **2,** man (*i.e. the human race*): Человéк — разу́мное существó, man is a rational being.

человеконенави́стник *n.* misanthrope. —**человеконенави́стнический,** *adj.* misanthropic. —**человеконенави́стничество,** *n.* misanthropy.

человекообрáзный *adj.* anthropomorphous; anthropoid.

человекоподóбный *adj.* anthropoid; manlike.

человéко-чáс [*pl.* -часы́, -часóв] *n.* man-hour.

человéчек [*gen.* -чка] *n.* little man.

человéческий *adj.* **1,** human. **2,** humane. —**человéческий род,** the human race.

человéчество *n.* mankind; humanity.

человéчный *adj.* humane. —**человéчность,** *n.f.* humaneness; humanity.

чéлюсть *n.f.* **1,** jaw; jawbone. **2,** denture; set of false teeth. —**челюстнóй,** *adj.* jaw (*attrib.*); jawbone (*attrib.*).

чéлядь *n.f.* servants.

чем *pron., instr. of* что. —*conj.* **1,** than: лу́чше пóздно, чем никогдá, better late than never. Бóльше чем когдá-либо рáньше, more than ever before. **2,** (*with* тем) the..., the...: Чéм рáньше, тем лу́чше, the sooner the better. **3,** (*with inf.*) instead of; rather than.

чём *pron., prepl. of* что.

чемери́ца *n.* hellebore.

чемода́н *n.* suitcase. —**чемода́нчик,** *n.* small suitcase.

чемпио́н *n.* champion. —**чемпиона́т,** *n.* championship (*tournament*). —**чемпио́нский,** *adj.* championship (*attrib.*). —**чемпио́нство,** *n.* championship.

чему́ *pron., dat. of* **что.**

чепе́ц [*gen.* **чепца́**] *n.* cap formerly worn by elderly women, usually tied under the chin.

чепуха́ *n., colloq.* **1,** nonsense. **2,** trifling matter. **3,** trifling amount.

че́пчик *n.* **1,** *dim. of* **чепе́ц. 2,** (baby's) bonnet.

червеобра́зный *adj.* vermiform. —**червеобра́зный отро́сток,** vermiform appendix.

че́рви [*gen.* **черве́й**] *n.pl.,* cards hearts.

черви́веть *v.impfv.* [*pfv.* **очерви́веть**] to become wormy.

черви́вый *adj.* worm-eaten; wormy.

черво́нец [*gen.* **-нца**] *n.* **1,** pre-rev. three-ruble gold coin. **2,** ten-ruble note in use from 1922 through 1947.

черво́нный *adj.* **1,** *archaic* red; scarlet. **2,** *cards* of hearts: черво́нный туз, ace of hearts. —**черво́нное зо́лото,** pure gold.

червото́чина *n.* **1,** wormhole. **2,** *fig.* flaw.

че́рвы [*gen.* **черв**] *n.pl.* = **че́рви.**

червь [*gen.* **червя́**; *pl.* **че́рви, черве́й, червя́м**] *n.m.* **1,** worm. **2,** *fig.* a nobody. **3,** *fig.* (*with gen.*) nagging sense (of doubt, regret, etc.).

червя́к [*gen.* **-вяка́**] *n.* = **червь.** —**замори́ть червяка́,** *colloq.* to have a bite to eat.

червя́чный *adj., mech.* worm (*attrib.*): червя́чная шестерня́, worm gear.

червячо́к [*gen.* **-чка́**] *n.* small worm. —**замори́ть червячка́,** *colloq.* to have a bite to eat.

черда́к [*gen.* **-дака́**] *n.* attic. —**черда́чный,** *adj.* attic (*attrib.*).

черёд [*gen.* **череда́**] *n., colloq.* **1,** (one's) turn. **2,** time: Наста́л черёд (+ *inf.*), the time has come to... —**идти́ свои́м чередо́м,** to take its normal course.

череда́ *n.* **1,** *obs.* = **черёд. 2,** column; file. **3,** *fig.* sequence; chain. **4,** bur marigold.

чередова́ние *n.* alternation.

чередова́ть *v.impfv.* [*pres.* **-ду́ю, -ду́ешь**] to alternate. —**чередова́ться,** *refl.* to alternate; take turns.

че́рез *prep., with acc.* **1,** across: перейти́ че́рез у́лицу, to walk across the street; cross the street. **2,** over: перепры́гнуть че́рез забо́р, to jump over the fence. **3,** through: идти́ че́рез лес, to walk through the forest. **4,** via; by way of: е́хать че́рез Минск, to go by way of Minsk. Уходи́ть че́рез чёрный ход, to leave by the back door. **5,** in (*expressing time from the present*): Я приду́ че́рез де́сять мину́т, I'll come in ten minutes. **6,** after (*an interval of*): верну́ться че́рез год, to return after a year; че́рез де́сять лет по́сле войны́, ten years after the war. **7,** with; using: Э́то сло́во пи́шется че́рез чёрточку, this word is spelled with a hyphen. **8,** through; with the aid of: говори́ть че́рез перево́дчика, to speak through an interpreter. **9,** *indicating intervals of two:* че́рез день, every other day. Они́ живу́т че́рез дом от нас, they live two houses away from us. **10,** *indicating a specified interval:* печа́тать че́рез два интерва́ла, to double-space. Они́

живу́т че́рез три до́ма отсю́да, they live three houses away. Взбежа́ть на ле́стницу че́рез три ступе́ньки, to run up the stairs three steps at a time.

черёмуха *n.* a kind of cherry tree.

черено́к [*gen.* **-нка́**] *n.* **1,** handle; haft. **2,** cutting; graft.

че́реп [*pl.* **черепа́**] *n.* skull; cranium.

черепа́ха *n.* **1,** turtle; tortoise. **2,** tortoise shell.

черепа́ховый *adj.* **1,** turtle (*attrib.*). **2,** tortoise-shell (*attrib.*).

черепа́ший [*fem.* **-шья**] *adj.* **1,** turtle's. **2,** *fig.* snail-like: черепа́шьим ша́гом, at a snail's pace.

черепи́ца *n.* (unglazed) tile. —**черепи́чный,** *adj.* tile (*attrib.*); tiled.

черепно́й *adj.* cranial. —**черепна́я коро́бка,** cranium.

черепо́к [*gen.* **-пка́**] *n.* fragment of pottery. —**разби́ться в черепки́,** to be smashed to smithereens.

черессе́дельник *n.* saddle girth.

чересчу́р *adv.* **1,** too. **2,** (*with verbs*) too much. —**чересчу́р мно́го,** too much; too many.

чере́шневый *adj.* cherry (*attrib.*).

чере́шня [*gen. pl.* **-шен**] *n.* **1,** sweet cherries. **2,** a (single) sweet cherry. **3,** cherry tree.

черешо́к [*gen.* **-шка́**] *n.* **1,** petiole. **2,** = **черено́к** (*in sense #1*).

черка́ть *also,* **чёркать** *v.impfv.* [*pfv.* **черкну́ть**] *colloq.* **1,** (*with* по) to scratch; leave a mark on. **2,** [*impfv. only*] to cross out (a word or words); mark up (a page).

черке́с *n.m.* [*fem.* **черке́шенка**] Circassian. —**черке́сский,** *adj.* Circassian.

черкну́ть *v.pfv., colloq.* **1,** *pfv. of* **черка́ть. 2,** to write; dash off: Черкни́те мне не́сколько слов, drop me a line.

черне́ть *v.impfv.* [*pfv.* **почерне́ть**] **1,** to turn black. **2,** [*impfv. only*] (*of anything black*) to appear; loom.

черни́ка *n.* **1,** blueberries; huckleberries; whortleberries. **2,** a single such berry. **3,** a bush yielding any of these berries.

черни́ла [*gen.* **-ни́л**] *n.pl.* ink.

черни́льница *n.* inkwell.

черни́льный *adj.* ink (*attrib.*). —**черни́льный каранда́ш,** indelible pencil. —**черни́льный оре́шек,** gallnut.

черни́ть *v.impfv.* **1,** [*pfv.* **зачерни́ть** *or* **начерни́ть**] to blacken; make black. **2,** [*pfv.* **очерни́ть**] to blacken; slander; defame.

черни́чный *adj.* blueberry (*attrib.*); huckleberry (*attrib.*); whortleberry (*attrib.*).

чёрно-бе́лый *adj.* black-and-white.

черно-бу́рый *adj.* dark brown. —**черно-бу́рая лиси́ца,** silver fox.

чернови́к [*gen.* **-вика́**] *n.* rough draft; rough copy.

черново́й *adj.* (*of something written*) rough; preliminary.

черного́рец [*gen.* **-рца**] *n.m.* [*fem.* **-рка**] Montenegrin. —**черного́рский,** *adj.* Montenegrin.

чернозём *n.* rich black topsoil of central European Russia; chernozem.

чернокожий *adj.* dark-skinned. —*n.* black man; black.

черномазый *adj., colloq.* swarthy; dark-complexioned.

чернорабочий *adj.* unskilled. —*n.* unskilled laborer.

черносли́в *n.* prunes.

чернота́ *n.* blackness; darkness.

чёрный *adj.* **1,** black. **2,** (*of a door, yard, staircase, etc.*) back. **3,** *fig.* dark; somber. —*n.* **1,** black; negro. **2,** *neut.* black (clothes): Она́ была́ вся в чёрном, she was all in black. **3,** *pl., chess* black: игра́ть чёрными, to be black; play the black pieces. —**бере́чь на чёрный день,** to put aside for a rainy day. —**чёрное де́рево,** ebony. —**чёрная доска́,** blackboard. —**чёрный дрозд,** blackbird. —**чёрные мета́ллы,** ferrous metals. —**чёрная рабо́та,** menial work; dirty work. —**чёрный ры́нок,** black market. —**чёрный спи́сок,** blacklist. —**чёрным по бе́лому,** in black and white; in the clearest possible terms.

чернь *n.f., obs.* rabble; riffraff.

черня́вый *adj., colloq.* dark-haired.

черпа́к [*gen.* **-пака́**] *n.* scoop.

черпа́лка [*gen. pl.* **-лок**] *n., colloq.* scoop.

че́рпать *v.impfv.* [*pfv.* **черпну́ть**] **1,** to draw (water); scoop up (dirt, sand, etc.). **2,** [*impfv. only*] *fig.* to draw; derive; cull.

черстве́ть *v.impfv.* **1,** [*pfv.* **зачерстве́ть** *or* **почерстве́ть**] (*of bread*) to become stale. **2,** [*pfv.* **очерстве́ть**] to become callous; become hardhearted.

чёрствый *adj.* **1,** stale. **2,** callous; hardhearted. —**чёрствость,** *n.f.* callousness.

чёрт [*pl.* **че́рти, черте́й, чертя́м**] *n.* devil. —**до чёрта,** *colloq.* **1,** awfully. **2,** (*with gen.*) plenty (of); galore. —**иди́ к чёрту!,** go to hell! —**к чёрту!,** to hell with it! —**како́го чёрта** (+ *subject & verb*), what the hell is/does...? —**на кой чёрт?,** *colloq.* what the hell for? —**ни черта́,** *colloq.* not a thing. —**чёрт возьми́!; чёрт побери́!,** what the hell? —**чёрт (его́) зна́ет!,** God knows! —**чёрт с** (+ *instr.*), to hell with...! —**чёрта с два!,** *colloq.* like hell!; absolutely not!

черта́ *n.* **1,** line. **2,** boundary. В черте́ го́рода, within the city limits. **3,** *pl.* features: черты́ лица́, facial features. **4,** trait; feature; characteristic. —**в о́бщих черта́х,** in general terms; in broad outline.

чертёж [*gen.* **-тежа́**] *n.* drawing; draft; design.

чертёжник *n.* draftsman.

чертёжный *adj.* drawing (*attrib.*).

чертёнок [*gen.* **-нка;** *pl.* **-теня́та, -теня́т**] *n., colloq.* little devil; imp.

черти́ть *v.impfv.* [*pfv.* **начерти́ть;** *pres.* **черчу́, че́ртишь**] to draw (a line, figure, map, diagram, etc.).

чёртов *adj.* of the devil; devil's. —**чёртова дю́жина,** baker's dozen. —**чёртово колесо́,** Ferris wheel.

черто́вски *adv., colloq.* awfully: черто́вски рад, awfully glad. Черто́вски серди́т, mad as hell. Черто́вски го́лоден, famished. Черто́вски далеко́, a hell of a long way.

черто́вский *adj.* **1,** of the devil; devilish. **2,** *colloq.* hellish; damnable.

чертовщи́на *n.* **1,** devils. **2,** *fig., colloq.* something awful or ridiculous.

черто́г *n., obs.* **1,** chamber. **2,** palace.

чертополо́х *n.* thistle.

чёрточка [*gen. pl.* **-чек**] *n.* **1,** line. **2,** hyphen.

чертыха́ться *v.r.impfv.* [*pfv.* **чертыхну́ться**] *colloq.* to swear; curse.

черче́ние *n.* drawing. —**техни́ческое черче́ние,** mechanical drawing. —**черче́ние на компью́тере,** computer-aided design.

чеса́лка [*gen. pl.* **-лок**] *n.* combing machine; carding machine.

чеса́льный *adj.* combing (*attrib.*); carding (*attrib.*).

чеса́ние *n.* combing; carding.

чеса́ть *v.impfv.* [*pfv.* **почеса́ть;** *pres.* **чешу́, че́шешь**] **1,** to scratch (*to relieve an itch*). **2,** [*impfv. only*] to comb (hair). **3,** [*impfv. only*] to comb; card (flax, cotton, etc.). —**чеса́ть заты́лок** (*or* в заты́лке), *colloq.* to scratch one's head (*in puzzlement*). —**чеса́ть язы́к** (*or* языко́м), *colloq.* to babble; prattle.

чеса́ться *v.r.impfv.* [*pres.* **чешу́сь, че́шешься**] **1,** to itch: У меня́ че́шется спина́, my back itches. *Also fig.* У него́ че́шутся ру́ки (+ *inf.*), he is itching to... **2,** [*pfv.* **почеса́ться**] to scratch oneself (*to relieve itching*). **3,** *colloq.* to comb one's hair.

чесно́к [*gen.* **-нока́**] *n.* garlic. —**чесно́чный,** *adj.* garlic (*attrib.*).

чесо́тка *n.* scabies; mange.

че́ствование *n.* **1,** honoring. **2,** celebration (*in honor of someone*).

че́ствовать *v.impfv.* [*pres.* **-ствую, -ствуешь**] to honor; pay tribute to.

чести́ть *v.impfv.* [*pres.* **чещу́, чести́шь**] **1,** *obs.* to honor. **2,** *obs.* to call (by a name or title). **3,** *colloq.* to curse out.

че́стно *adv.* honestly. —**че́стно говоря́,** to be honest...; in all honesty.

честно́й *adj., obs.* honored.

че́стность *n.f.* honesty.

че́стный *adj.* honest. —**че́стное сло́во!,** word of honor!; honest to goodness!

честолю́бец [*gen.* **-бца**] *n.* ambitious person.

честолюби́вый *adj.* ambitious. —**честолю́бие,** *n.* ambition.

честь *n.f.* **1,** honor: в честь (+ *gen.*), in honor of. **2,** credit: де́лать честь (+ *dat.*), to be a credit to. —**отдава́ть честь** (+ *dat.*), to salute. —**пора́ и честь знать, 1,** it's time to stop. **2,** it's time we were going. —**с че́стью,** with distinction; with flying colors. —**честь че́стью,** properly.

чёт *n., colloq.* even number.

чета́ *n.* **1,** pair; couple. **2,** married couple. —**не чета́** (+ *dat.*), **1,** not the equal of; no match for. **2,** too good for; head and shoulders above.

четве́рг [*gen.* **-верга́**] *n.* Thursday. —**по́сле до́ждичка в четве́рг,** *colloq.* who knows when?

четвере́ньки *n.pl.,* in **на четвере́ньках,** on one's hands and knees; on all fours.

четвёрка *n.* **1,** the numeral 4. **2,** *colloq.* anything numbered 4. **3,** team of four horses. **4,** a grade of "four", signifying "good". **5,** *cards* four.

четверно́й *adj.* quadruple; fourfold.

четверня́ *n.* **1,** team of four horses. **2,** *colloq.* quadruplets.

че́тверо [*gen. & prepl.* **-ры́х;** *dat.* **-ры́м;** *instr.* **-ры́ми**] *collective numeral* four.

четвероно́гий *adj.* four-legged. —**четвероно́гое,** *n.* quadruped.

четверости́шие *n.* four-line verse; quatrain.

четверта́к [*gen.* **-така́**] *n., obs.* twenty-five kopecks.

четвёртка [*gen. pl.* **-ток**] *n., obs.* quarter.

четвертно́й *adj.* **1,** *in* **четвертна́я но́та,** *music* quarter note. **2,** (*of a grade*) for a (school) quarter. **3,** *obs.* twenty-five-ruble. —**четвертна́я,** *n., obs.* twenty-five-ruble note.

четвертова́ние *n.* (execution by) quartering.

четвертова́ть *v.impfv. & pfv.* [*pres.* **-ту́ю, -ту́ешь**] to quarter (*as a method of execution*).

четвёртый *ordinal numeral* fourth.

че́тверть *n.f.* quarter; fourth: три че́тверти, three quarters; three fourths (3/4). Че́тверть шесто́го, a quarter past five; без че́тверти семь, a quarter to seven.

четвертьфина́л *n.* quarterfinal; quarterfinals. —**четвертьфина́льный,** *adj.* quarterfinal.

чётки [*gen.* **чёток**] *n.pl.* rosary (*beads*).

чёткий *adj.* [*short form* **чёток, четка́** *or* **чётка́, чётко, чётки;** *comp.* **чётче**] **1,** clear; distinct. **2,** clear-cut. **3,** precise. **4,** efficient.

чётко *adv.* **1,** clearly; distinctly. **2,** smartly: чётко шага́ть, to step smartly.

чёткость *n.f.* **1,** clarity. **2,** precision; efficiency.

чётный *adj.* (*of a number*) even.

четы́ре [*gen. & prepl.* **четырёх;** *dat.* **четырём;** *instr.* **четырьмя́**] *numeral* four.

четы́режды *adv.* four times.

четы́реста [*gen.* **четырёхсот;** *dat.* **четырёмста́м;** *instr.* **четырьмяста́ми;** *prepl.* **четырёхста́х**] *numeral* four hundred.

четырёхгоди́чный *adj.* four-year (*attrib.*).

четырёхголо́сный *adj., music* four-part.

четырёхгра́нник *n.* tetrahedron. —**четырёхгра́нный,** *adj.* tetrahedral.

четырёхдне́вный *adj.* four-day (*attrib.*).

четырёхкла́ссный *adj.* (*of schools or courses*) four-year.

четырёхколёсный *adj.* four-wheel(ed).

четырёхкра́тный *adj.* fourfold; quadruple.

четырёхле́тие *n.* **1,** fourth anniversary; fourth birthday. **2,** four-year period.

четырёхле́тний *adj.* **1,** four-year (*attrib.*). **2,** four-year-old.

четырёхме́сячный *adj.* **1,** four-month (*attrib.*). **2,** four-month-old.

четырёхнеде́льный *adj.* **1,** four-week (*attrib.*). **2,** four-week-old.

четырёхсотле́тие *n.* four-hundredth anniversary. —**четырёхсотле́тний,** *adj.* four-hundred-year (*attrib.*).

четырёхсо́тый *ordinal numeral* four-hundredth.

четырёхсто́пный *adj.* tetrameter. —**четырёхсто́пный стих,** tetrameter. —**четырёхсто́пный ямб,** iambic tetrameter.

четырёхсторо́нний *adj.* four-sided; quadrilateral.

четырёхуго́льник *n.* quadrangle; quadrilateral. —**четырёхуго́льный,** *adj.* quadrangular.

четырёхэта́жный *adj.* four-story.

четы́рнадцатый *ordinal numeral* fourteenth.

четы́рнадцать *numeral* fourteen.

чех *n.m.* [*fem.* **че́шка**] Czech.

чехарда́ *n.* leapfrog.

чехо́л [*gen.* **чехла́**] *n.* **1,** cover; slipcover. **2,** case.

чечеви́ца *n.* **1,** lentil. **2,** *obs.* lens. —**чечеви́чный,** *adj.* lentil (*attrib.*).

чече́нец [*gen.* **-нца**] *n.m.* [*fem.* **-нка**] Chechen (*one of a people inhabiting the Caucasus*. —**чече́нский,** *adj.* Chechen.

чечётка [*gen. pl.* **-ток**] *n.* **1,** tap dance. **2,** redpoll (*bird*).

че́шский *adj.* Czech.

чешу́йчатый *adj.* scaly.

чешуя́ *n.* scales (*of a fish, snake, etc.*).

чи́бис *n.* lapwing; pewit.

чиж [*gen.* **чижа́**] *n.* siskin (*bird*).

чили́ец [*gen.* **-и́йца**] *n.m.* [*fem.* **-и́йка**] Chilean. —**чили́йский,** *adj.* Chilean.

чин [*pl.* **чины́**] *n.* **1,** rank; grade. **2,** official. —**чин чи́ном,** properly.

чина́р *also,* **чина́ра** *n.* Oriental plane tree.

чини́ть *v.impfv.* **1,** [*pfv.* **почини́ть;** *pres.* **чиню́, чи́нишь**] to fix; mend; repair. **2,** [*pfv.* **очини́ть;** *pres.* **чиню́, чи́нишь**] to sharpen (a pencil). **3,** [*pfv.* **учини́ть;** *pres.* **чиню́, чини́шь**] to carry out; create. Чини́ть беспоря́дки, to create a disturbance. Чини́ть препя́тствия (+ *dat.*), to put obstacles in someone's way.

чи́нный *adj.* decorous; sedate. —**чи́нность,** *n.f.* decorum; propriety.

чино́вник *n.* **1,** official; functionary. **2,** bureaucrat.

чино́внический *adj.* **1,** official's; officials'. **2,** bureaucratic.

чино́вничество *n.* **1,** officials; officialdom. **2,** bureaucracy.

чино́вничий [*fem.* **-чья**] *adj.* = **чино́внический.**

чино́вный *adj., obs.* high-ranking.

чину́ша *n.m., colloq.* bureaucrat.

чи́псы [*gen.* **-сов**] *n.pl.* potato chips.

чи́рей [*gen.* **чи́рья**] *n., colloq.* boil; abscess.

чири́канье *n.* chirping; twittering.

чири́кать *v.impfv.* to chirp; twitter.

чи́ркать *v.impfv.* [*pfv.* **чи́ркнуть**] **1,** (*with* **о** + *acc. or* **по**) to rub (something) against. **2,** (*with instr.*) to strike (a match).

чиро́к [*gen.* **чирка́**] *n.* teal.

чи́сленно *adv.* numerically.

чи́сленность *n.f.* number; size; numerical strength. —**чи́сленностью в** (+ *acc.*), numbering.

чи́сленный *adj.* numerical.

числи́тель *n.m.* numerator.

числи́тельное *n., decl. as an adj., gram.* numeral. *Also,* **и́мя числи́тельное.**

чи́слить *v.impfv.* **1,** *obs.* to count; calculate. **2,** to list; put down; record. **3,** (*with instr.*) to consider; regard (as). —**чи́слиться,** *refl.* **1,** to be listed; be put down; be recorded. **2,** (*with* **за** + *instr.*) to be put down under the name of; *fig.* be attributed to. **3,** to number: В го́роде чи́слится сто ты́сяч челове́к, the city has a population of 100,000. **4,** (*with instr.*) to be considered; be regarded (as).

число́ [*pl.* **чи́сла, чи́сел**] *n.* **1,** number: чётное число́, even number. **2,** number; quantity. **3,** date; day (*of the month*): Како́е сего́дня число́?, what is today's date?

В после́дних чи́слах декабря́, in the last days of December. **4,** *gram.* number: еди́нственное число́, singular; мно́жественное число́, plural. **5,** *pl., cap., Bib.* (book of) Numbers. —**в том числе́,** including. —**в числе́** (+ *gen.*), among.

числово́й *adj.* numerical.

чи́стик *n.* guillemot (*bird*).

чисти́лище *n.* purgatory.

чисти́льщик *n.* cleaner. —**чи́стильщик сапо́г,** shoeshine boy; bootblack.

чи́стить *v.impfv.* [*pfv.* **почи́стить** *or* **вы́чистить;** *pres.* **чи́щу, чи́стишь**] **1,** to clean. **2,** to clean out; clear out. **3,** to shine (shoes); brush (one's teeth). **4,** to clear (a road); dredge (a river). **5,** [*pfv.* **очи́стить**] to peel; pare. **6,** *fig., colloq.* to purge.

чи́стка *n.* **1,** cleaning. **2,** purge.

чи́сто *adv.* **1,** cleanly; neatly. **2,** purely. **3,** *colloq.* exactly; just: Она́ рассужда́ет чи́сто по-же́нски, she reasons just like a woman. —*adj., used predicatively,* clean: Здесь чи́сто, it is clean here. —**чи́сто-на́чисто,** spotlessly clean.

чистови́к [*gen.* **-вика́**] *n., colloq.* first draft.

чистово́й *adj.* (*of a copy, manuscript, etc.*) final; clean.

чистога́н *n., colloq.* cash.

чистокро́вный *adj.* thoroughbred.

чистописа́ние *n.* penmanship.

чистопло́тный *adj.* clean; neat; tidy; cleanly.

чистопоро́дный *adj.* thoroughbred.

чистосерде́чие *n.* open-heartedness; sincerity. —**чистосерде́чный,** *adj.* open-hearted; sincere.

чистота́ *n.* **1,** cleanliness. **2,** purity.

чи́стый *adj.* [*comp.* **чи́ще**] **1,** clean. **2,** pure. **3,** clear. **4,** (*of income, weight, etc.*) net. **5,** *colloq.* pure; sheer; utter. —**чи́стой** *or* **чисте́йшей воды́,** of the first water; of the first order. —**чи́стое по́ле,** open country.

чита́льный *adj., in* **чита́льный зал,** reading room.

чита́льня [*gen. pl.* **-лен**] *n.* reading room.

чита́тель *n.m.* reader. —**чита́тельский,** *adj.* reader's; readers'.

чита́ть *v.impfv.* [*pfv.* **прочита́ть** *or* **проче́сть**] **1,** to read. **2,** to recite (a poem, prayer, etc.). **3,** to give; deliver (a lecture, sermon, admonition, etc.); give; teach (a course). —**чита́ться,** *refl.* [*impfv. only*] **1,** to be read. **2,** to be legible. **3,** (*of a book*) to read (easily, quickly, etc.). **4,** (*used negatively with dat.*) not to feel like reading.

чи́тка *n.* reading.

чих *n., colloq.* sneeze.

чиха́нье *n.* sneezing.

чиха́ть *v.impfv.* [*pfv.* **чихну́ть**] to sneeze.

чи́ще *adj., comp. of* **чи́стый.**

член *n.* **1,** member. Вступи́ть в чле́ны (+ *gen.*), to become a member of; join. Принима́ть в чле́ны (+ *gen.*), to admit to membership in. **2,** limb (*of the body*). **3,** part (*of a sentence*). **4,** *gram.* article. **5,** *math.* term. —**член-корреспонде́нт,** corresponding member (*of an academy*).

члени́ть *v.impfv.* to divide into parts.

членовреди́тельство *n.* **1,** (deliberate) mutilation (of someone). **2,** self-mutilation.

членоразде́льный *adj.* articulate.

чле́нский *adj.* membership (*attrib.*); чле́нские взно́сы, membership dues.

чле́нство *n.* membership.

чмо́кать *v.impfv.* [*pfv.* **чмо́кнуть**] **1,** [*also,* **чмо́кать губа́ми**] to smack one's lips. **2,** *colloq.* to give (someone) a loud kiss. **3,** to make a squirting sound.

чо́каться *v.r.impfv.* [*pfv.* **чо́кнуться**] to clink glasses (*when making a toast*).

чо́порный *adj.* strait-laced; prim and proper.

чо́хом *adv., colloq.* all at once; in one fell swoop.

чрева́тый *adj.* (*with instr.*) fraught (with): чрева́тый опа́сными после́дствиями, fraught with dangerous consequences.

чре́во *n., archaic* **1,** stomach. **2,** womb.

чревовеща́ние *n.* ventriloquism. —**чревовеща́тель,** *n.m.* ventriloquist.

чрезвыча́йный *adj.* **1,** extraordinary. **2,** emergency: чрезвыча́йное положе́ние, state of emergency. —**чрезвыча́йно,** *adv.* extremely; extraordinarily.

чрезме́рный *adj.* excessive. —**чрезме́рно,** *adv.* excessively.

чте́ние *n.* reading. Чте́ние ле́кций, lecturing.

чтец [*gen.* **чтеца́**] *n.* reader; reciter.

чти́во *n., colloq.* (piece of) literary trash.

чтить *v.impfv.* [*pres.* **чту, чтишь, ...чтят** *or* **чтут**] **1,** to honor. **2,** to revere.

что [*gen.* **чего́;** *dat.* **чему́;** *instr.* **чем;** *prepl.* **чём**] *pron.* **1,** *interr.* what?: Что э́то зна́чит?, what does this mean? О чём он говори́т?, what is he talking about? **2,** *rel.* what; that; which. Он зна́ет что де́лает, he knows what he is doing. Пе́рвое, что пришло́ мне в го́лову, the first thing that came into my head. За пе́рвую неде́лю, что я был (была́) в Москве́, the first week I was in Moscow. Никто́ не подошёл к телефо́ну, что о́чень необы́чно, no one answered the phone, which is very unusual. **3,** *indef.* (*with* **есть** *or* **бы́ло**) quite a lot; quite a bit; plenty: А́втору есть что рассказа́ть, the author has quite a lot to tell. Расска́зывать бы́ло что, there was plenty to tell. У меня́ есть что пое́сть, I have plenty to eat. Сожале́ть ему́ о чём, he has quite a lot to be sorry about. Выбира́ть бы́ло из чего́, there was quite a lot to choose from. —*conj.* that: Я уве́рен, что он говори́т пра́вду, I am certain that he is telling the truth. Э́то так про́сто, что ка́ждый поймёт, it is so simple that anyone can understand it. —*adv.* why?; how come?: Что вы тако́й весёлый?, why are you (*or* how come you're) so jolly? Что же ты молчи́шь?, why are you (*or* how come you're) so quiet? —**а что же** (+ *nom.*), what about...?; how about...? —**не́ за что!,** don't mention it! —**ни за что, 1,** not for anything. **2,** for nothing; in vain. —**ни за что ни про что,** *colloq.* for no reason. —**ни к чему́, 1,** of no use. **2,** (*with inf.*) there is no need to. **3,** for no reason. —**ни с чем, 1,** empty-handed. **2,** *in* оста́ться ни с чем, to be left with nothing; be left destitute. —**ну и что?,** *colloq.* well, what of it?; so what? —**что (бы) ни,** whatever: что ни де́лаешь; что бы ты ни де́лал, whatever you do. —**что вы!, 1,** how can you say that! **2,** *in* ну, что вы!, oh, go on! **3,** *in* нет, что вы!, not at all! **—что до,** as for. **—что** (+ *dat.*) **до,** what does (he, she, etc.) care about...? Что мне до тогó, что..., what do I care if...? **—что за** (+ *nom.*), **1,** what is?; what are?: Что там за кнúги?, what are those books over there? **2,** what kind of; what sort of: Что он за человéк?, what sort of person is he?; what is he like? **—что к чему,** (*with verbs of knowing, understanding, etc.*) what's what; what's going on. **—что ли,** perhaps. **—что ни** (+ *noun*), every: Что ни абзáц, то шедéвр, every paragraph is a masterpiece; there is not a paragraph that is not a masterpiece. **—что с вáми?,** what's the matter with you? **—что с тогó?,** *colloq.* what of it?; so what? Что с тогó, что...?, so what if...? *See also* **чегó** *and* **чем.**

чтóбы *also,* **чтоб** *conj.* **1,** (*with inf.*) in order to; so as to: чтóбы приходúть вóвремя, in order to be on time; чтóбы не мешáть гостя́м, so as not to disturb the guests. **2,** *used to introduce a dependent clause:* Скажúте емý, чтóбы он ушёл, tell him to go away. Я не вúдел, чтóбы ктó-нибудь входúл, I didn't see anyone enter. Онá любит, чтóбы ей льстúли, she likes to be flattered. Стóить тогó, чтóбы о нём рассказáть, to be worth telling about. **—**particle, *used to express a peremptory command:* Чтóбы э́того бóльше не бы́ло!, this must not happen again! **—для тогó, чтóбы; с тем, чтóбы, 1,** (*with inf.*) in order to; so as to. **2,** (*with a dependent clause*) so that; in order that.

чтó-либо *indef. pron.* = **чтó-нибудь.**

чтó-нибудь *indef. pron.* something; anything.

чтó-то *indef. pron.* something. **—**adv., *colloq.* somehow: Мне чтó-то не спалóсь, I somehow couldn't sleep.

чуб [*pl.* чубы́] *n.* forelock.

чубáрый *adj.* (*of a horse*) dappled.

чувáш *n.m.* [*fem.* **чувáшка**] Chuvash (*one of a people inhabiting central European Russia*). **—чувáшский,** *adj.* Chuvash.

чýвственный *adj.* **1,** sense (*attrib.*): чýвственное восприя́тие, sense perception. **2,** sensual. **—чýвственность,** *n.f.* sensuality.

чувствúтельность *n.f.* sensitivity.

чувствúтельный *adj.* **1,** sensitive. **2,** sentimental. **3,** noticeable; perceptible. **4,** severe; keenly felt. **—чувствúтельный нерв,** sensory nerve.

чýвство *n.* **1,** sense: пять чувств, the five senses. Чýвство ю́мора, sense of humor. **2,** feeling: прия́тное чýвство, a pleasant feeling. **3,** consciousness. **—лишúться чувств,** to lose consciousness. **—привестú в чýвство,** to revive; bring around. **—прийтú в чýвство,** to regain consciousness; come to. **—упáсть без чувств,** to faint away.

чýвствовать *v.impfv.* [*pfv.* **почýвствовать;** *pres.* -ствую, -ствуешь] **1,** to feel (pain, cold, etc.). **2,** to have a feeling or sense of (dread, despair, shame, etc.). **3,** to sense (danger, someone's presence, etc.). **4,** (*with* себя́) to feel (*a certain way*): Как вы себя́ чýвствуете?, how do you feel? Чýвствовать себя́ больны́м, to feel ill. **5,** to have a feel for; have an appreciation of (music, art, etc.). **6,** *in* чýвствовать зáпах (+ *gen.*), to smell (something). **—чýвствоваться,** *refl.* **1,** to be felt. **2,** to be sensed.

чугýн [*gen.* чугунá] *n.* **1,** cast iron. **2,** iron pot. **—чугýнный,** *adj.* cast-iron.

чугунолитéйный *adj.* iron (*attrib.*). **—чугунолитéйный завóд,** iron foundry; ironworks.

чудáк [*gen.* -дакá] *n.m.* [*fem.* -дáчка] strange person; queer bird.

чудаковáтый *adj.* odd; queer; peculiar; eccentric.

чудáческий *adj.* strange; odd; queer; eccentric.

чудáчество *n.* **1,** eccentric nature. **2,** *pl.* shenanigans; monkey business.

чудесá *n.,* *pl. of* **чýдо.**

чудéсно *adv.* **1,** wonderfully; marvelously. **2,** *as an interj.* wonderful!; marvelous!

чудéсный *adj.* **1,** miraculous. **2,** wonderful; marvelous.

чудúть *v.impfv., colloq.* to behave oddly; act up.

чýдиться *v.r.impfv.* [*pfv.* **почýдиться**] *impers.* (*with dat.*) *colloq.* **1,** to seem: Емý чýдилось, что..., it seemed to him that... Ей чýдился крик, she thought she heard a shout. Емý чýдилась мышь, he thought he saw a mouse. **2,** to imagine: Э́то вам тóлько почýдилось, you just imagined it.

чýдище *n., colloq.* monster.

чýдно *adv.* **1,** wonderfully; marvelously. **2,** *as an interj.* wonderful!

чуднó *adv., colloq.* **1,** strangely; oddly. **2,** *as an interj.* (it is) strange!

чуднóй *adj., colloq.* odd; strange; queer.

чýдный *adj.* wonderful; marvelous.

чýдо [*pl.* **чудесá, чудéс, чудесáм**] *n.* **1,** miracle. Чýдом, by a miracle; miraculously. **2,** wonder. **—странá чудéс,** wonderland. **—чýдо прирóды,** freak of nature.

чудóвище *n.* monster.

чудóвищность *n.f.* (*with gen.*) monstrosity (of); enormity (of).

чудóвищный *adj.* monstrous.

чудодéй *n., obs.* miracle worker; magician.

чудодéйственный *adj.* wonder-working; miraculous.

чудотвóрец [*gen.* -рца] *n.* miracle worker. **—чудотвóрный,** *adj.* wonder-working; miraculous.

чужáк [*gen.* -жакá] *n., colloq.* stranger; newcomer.

чужбúна *n.* foreign land; foreign soil.

чуждáться *v.r.impfv.* (*with gen.*) to avoid; shun; keep away from.

чýждый *adj.* [*short form* чужд, чуждá, чýждо, чýжды *or* чужды́] **1,** (*often with dat.*) alien (to); foreign (to). **2,** (*with gen.*) devoid (of); free (from).

чужезéмец [*gen.* -мца] *n., obs.* foreigner. **—чужезéмный,** *adj., obs.* foreign.

чужестрáнец [*gen.* -нца] *n., obs.* foreigner. **—чужестрáнный,** *adj., obs.* foreign.

чужóй *adj.* **1,** someone else's; other people's. **2,** foreign; alien. **3,** strange; unfamiliar. **—**n. **1,** stranger. **2,** *neut.* something belonging to someone else. **—на чужóм пóле,** *sports* away; on the road. **—с чужúх слов,** secondhand.

чýкча [*gen. pl.* -чей] *n.m. & f.* [*fem. also* чукчáнка] Chukchi (*one of a people inhabiting northeasternmost Siberia*). **—чукóтский,** *adj.* Chukchi.

чулáн *n.* storeroom; pantry.

чуло́к [*gen.* чулка́; *gen. pl.* чуло́к] *n.* stocking. —чуло́чный, *adj.* stocking (*attrib.*); hosiery (*attrib.*).

чума́ *n.* plague.

чума́зый *adj., colloq.* dirty.

чумно́й *adj.* **1,** of the plague; plague (*attrib.*). **2,** afflicted with the plague. —*n.* person afflicted with the plague.

чура́ться *v.r.impfv.* (*with gen.*) *colloq.* to avoid.

чурба́н *n.* block (*of wood*).

чу́рка [*gen. pl.* чу́рок] *n.* block (*of wood*); strip (*of metal*).

чу́ткий *adj.* [*short form* чу́ток, чутка́, чу́тко, чу́тки; *comp.* чу́тче] **1,** keen; sensitive. **2,** (*of sleep*) light. **3,** sympathetic; kind.

чу́тко *adv.* **1,** closely; чу́тко прислу́шиваться, to listen closely. **2,** sympathetically. **3,** *in* чу́тко спать, to be a light sleeper.

чу́ткость *n.f.* **1,** keenness; sensitivity. **2,** sympathy.

чу́точка *n., colloq., in* чу́точку, a little; a bit. —ни чу́точки, not a bit; not in the least.

чуть *adv.* **1,** hardly; scarcely; barely. **2,** (just) a little; (very) slightly. —*conj.* as soon as. —чуть ли не, almost; nearly; just about: чуть ли не ка́ждый день, nearly every day. —чуть не; чуть бы́ло не, almost; nearly: Он чуть не упа́л, he almost fell. —чуть свет, at the crack of dawn. —чуть то́лько, as soon as. —чуть что, at the drop of a hat.

чутьё *n.* **1,** scent; sense of smell (*of an animal*). **2,** *fig.* flair; instinct; feel.

чуть-чу́ть *adv.* a tiny bit. —чуть-чу́ть не, = чуть не.

чу́чело *n.* **1,** stuffed animal; stuffed bird. **2,** scarecrow.

чу́шка [*gen. pl.* чу́шек] *n., colloq.* baby pig. —чугу́н в чу́шках, pig iron.

чушь *n.f., colloq.* nonsense.

чу́ять *v.impfv.* [*pfv.* почу́ять; *pres.* чу́ю, чу́ешь] **1,** to smell; scent. **2,** *fig.* to sense. —ног под собо́й не чу́ять, **1,** to be utterly exhausted. **2,** to be walking on air.

чьё *pron., neut. of* чей. —чья, *pron., fem. of* чей.

Ш

Ш, ш *n.neut.* 25th letter of the Russian alphabet.

ша́баш *n.* **1,** sabbath. **2,** *fig.* (*with gen.*) wave (of); orgy (of). —ша́баш ведьм, witches' sabbath.

шаба́шить *v.impfv.* [*pfv.* пошаба́шить] *colloq.* to quit work; knock off work.

ша́бер *n.* scraper.

шабло́н *n.* **1,** mold. **2,** template; stencil. **3,** *fig.* stereotype.

шабло́нный *adj.* **1,** standard. **2,** *fig.* stereotyped; trite.

ша́вка [*gen. pl.* ша́вок] *n., colloq.* small dog.

шаг [*gen.* ша́га, *but after* 2, 3 & 4 шага́; *pl.* шаги́] *n.* **1,** step: сде́лать шаг, to take a step. **2,** pace: отсчита́ть де́сять шаго́в, to mark off ten paces. **3,** *pl.* (sound of) footsteps. **4,** pace (*when walking*): ускóрить шаг; приба́вить ша́гу, to quicken one's pace. **5,** step; action: риско́ванный шаг, risky step. **6,** *pl., fig.* strides: де́лать больши́е шаги́, to make great strides. —два шага́ (от); в двух шага́х (от), a few steps (from); a stone's throw (from). —на ка́ждом шагу́, at every step; at every turn. —ни на шаг, 1, not a step; not one step. **2,** not at all; not a bit. —ни ша́гу, not a step; not one step. —у́зки в шагу́, tight in the crotch; tight in the seat. —шаг за ша́гом, step by step.

шага́ть *v.impfv.* [*pfv.* шагну́ть] **1,** to step. **2,** to stride; pace. **3,** *fig.* to progress; make progress.

ша́гом *adv.* at a walk. —ша́гом марш!, forward march!

шагоме́р *n.* pedometer.

шажо́к [*gen.* шажка́] *n.* small step; short step.

ша́йба *n.* **1,** *mech.* washer. **2,** *sports* puck.

ша́йка [*gen. pl.* ша́ек] *n.* **1,** gang; band. **2,** small washbasin.

шака́л *n.* jackal.

шала́нда *n., naut.* scow.

шала́ш [*gen.* шалаша́] *n.* crude hut (*consisting of stakes covered with branches or straw*).

шале́ (лэ) *n.neut. indecl.* chalet.

шале́ть *v.impfv.* [*pfv.* ошале́ть] *colloq.* to go crazy.

шали́ть *v.impfv.* to act up; misbehave; be naughty.

шаловли́вый *adj.* **1,** playful. **2,** mischievous; naughty. —шаловли́вость, *n.f.* playfulness.

шалопа́й *n., colloq.* playboy; good-for-nothing.

ша́лость *n.f.* prank.

шало́т *n.* shallot.

шалу́н [*gen.* -луна́] *n.* naughty child; mischief-maker.

шалфе́й *n.* sage (*plant*).

ша́лый *adj., colloq.* crazy; nuts.

шаль *n.f.* shawl.

шально́й *adj., colloq.* **1,** crazy; mad. **2,** (*of a bullet, bomb, etc.*) stray; random. —шальны́е де́ньги, easy money.

шама́н *n.* shaman. —шама́нство, *n.* shamanism.

ша́мкать *v.impfv., colloq.* to mumble.

шампа́нское *n., decl. as an adj.* champagne.

шампу́нь *n.m.* shampoo.

шанкр *n.* chancre. —**мя́гкий шанкр,** soft chancre; chancroid. —**твёрдый шанкр,** hard chancre; chancre.

шанс *n.* chance: ша́нсы на успе́х, chances of success. Ша́нсы на ва́шей стороне́, the odds are in your favor.

шансоне́тка [*gen. pl.* -ток] *n.* **1,** light comic song. **2,** cabaret singer.

шанта́ж [*gen.* -тажа́] *n.* blackmail.

шантажи́ровать *v.impfv.* [*pres.* -ру́ю, -ру́ешь] to blackmail.

шантажи́ст *n.* blackmailer.

ша́пка [*gen. pl.* ша́пок] *n.* **1,** cap; hat. **2,** shock (*of hair*). **3,** headline (*applying to several articles below*). **4,** masthead.

ша́почка [*gen. pl.* -чек] *n.*, *dim. of* ша́пка. —**Кра́сная ша́почка,** Little Red Riding Hood.

ша́почник *n.* hatter.

ша́почный *adj.* **1,** hat (*attrib.*). **2,** *in* ша́почное знако́мство, nodding acquaintance. —**прийти́ к ша́почному разбо́ру,** to arrive just when everyone is leaving.

шар [*gen.* ша́ра, *but after* 2, 3 & 4 шара́; *pl.* шары́] *n.* **1,** sphere. **2,** ball: билья́рдный шар, billiard ball. —**возду́шный шар,** balloon. —**земно́й шар,** the earth; the globe. —**про́бный шар,** trial balloon. —**хоть шаро́м покати́,** completely empty.

шараба́н *n.* four-wheeled open carriage.

шара́да *n.* charade.

шара́хать *v.impfv.* [*pfv.* шара́хнуть] *colloq.* **1,** to smack. **2,** to shoot. —**шара́хаться,** *refl.*, *colloq.* **1,** to jump aside (*from fear or surprise*). **2,** to dash. **3,** [*impfv. only*] (*with* от) to shun; keep away from.

шарж *n.* **1,** caricature. **2,** overacting.

шаржи́ровать *v.impfv.* [*pres.* -ру́ю, -ру́ешь] **1,** to caricature. **2,** to overact.

ша́рик *n.* **1,** *dim. of* шар. **2,** marble: игра́ть в ша́рики, to play marbles. —**кровяны́е ша́рики,** blood corpuscles.

ша́риковый *adj.* ball-shaped. —**ша́риковый подши́пник,** ball bearing. —**ша́риковая ру́чка,** ball-point pen.

шарикоподши́пник *n.* ball bearing.

ша́рить *v.impfv.* to feel; fumble; grope; rummage. —**ша́рить глаза́ми** (*with* по), to run one's eyes (over).

ша́рканье *n.* shuffling (*of feet*).

ша́ркать *v.impfv.* [*pfv.* ша́ркнуть] **1,** [*impfv. only*] (*with* по) to shuffle (along). **2,** (*with instr.*) to shuffle (one's feet).

шарлата́н *n.* charlatan; quack. —**шарлата́нский,** *adj.* quack; fraudulent. —**шарлата́нство,** *n.* quackery; charlatanism.

шарма́нка [*gen. pl.* -нок] *n.* barrel organ. —**шарма́нщик,** *n.* organ grinder.

шарни́р *n.* hinge; joint.

шарова́ры [*gen.* -ва́р] *n.pl.* **1,** loose trousers gathered at the ankles (*part of the national costume of certain countries*). **2,** (sports) pants: лы́жные шарова́ры, ski pants.

шарови́дный *adj.* like a ball; round.

шарово́й *adj.* spherical. —**шарово́й шарни́р,** ball-and-socket joint.

шарообра́зный *adj.* spherical.

шарф *n.* scarf.

шасси́ *n.neut. indecl.* **1,** chassis. **2,** *aero.* undercarriage; landing gear.

шата́ние *n.* **1,** swaying; wobbling. **2,** *fig.* wavering; vacillation. **3,** *colloq.* roaming; wandering.

шата́ть *v.impfv.* **1,** to sway; rock; shake. **2,** *impers.* to reel; stagger: Его́ шата́ло, he was reeling. —**шата́ть-ся,** *refl.* **1,** to sway. **2,** to reel; stagger. **3,** to wobble; be unsteady. **4,** (*of a tooth*) to be loose. **5,** *colloq.* to roam about; knock about.

шате́н (тэ) *n.m.* [*fem.* -те́нка] person with brown hair.

шатёр [*gen.* шатра́] *n.* large tent.

ша́ткий *adj.* **1,** shaky; unsteady; rickety; wobbly. **2,** *fig.* shaky; precarious. **3,** *fig.* wavering; vacillating.

ша́тко *adv.* unsteadily. —**ни ша́тко ни ва́лко,** fair to middling.

шату́н [*gen.* шатуна́] *n.* connecting rod.

ша́фер [*pl.* шафера́] *n.* best man (*at a wedding*).

шафра́н *n.* saffron; crocus. —**шафра́нный,** *adj.* saffron (*attrib.*).

шах *n.* **1,** shah. **2,** *chess* check.

шахмати́ст *n.* chess player.

ша́хматный *adj.* **1,** chess (*attrib.*). **2,** like a checkerboard; in checkerboard fashion. **3,** *colloq.* checked; checkered.

ша́хматы [*gen.* -мат] *n.pl.* **1,** chess. **2,** chess set.

ша́хта *n.* **1,** mine; pit. **2,** shaft. **3,** silo (*for a missile*).

шахтёр *n.* miner. —**шахтёрский,** *adj.* miner's; miners'.

ша́хтный *adj.* mine (*attrib.*).

ша́шечница *n.*, *obs.* checkerboard.

ша́шечный *adj.* of or pert. to checkers; checkers (*attrib.*). —**ша́шечная доска́,** checkerboard.

ша́шка [*gen. pl.* ша́шек] *n.* **1,** saber; sword. **2,** checker piece. **3,** *pl.* checkers (*game*). —**дымова́я ша́шка,** smoke pot; smudge pot.

шашлы́к [*gen.* -лыка́] *n.* shashlik; shish kebab.

ша́шни [*gen.* -ней] *n.pl.*, *colloq.* **1,** tricks; pranks. **2,** (love) affairs.

шва́бра *n.* mop.

шваль *n.f.*, *colloq.* **1,** trash; junk. **2,** good-for-nothing. **3,** riffraff; rabble.

шва́ртов *n.* mooring line; *pl.* moorings.

швартова́ть *v.impfv.* [*pfv.* пришвартова́ть; *pres.* -ту́ю, -ту́ешь] to moor (a ship). —**швартова́ться,** *refl.* (*of a ship*) to tie up.

швед *n.m.* [*fem.* шве́дка] Swede.

шве́дский *adj.* Swedish. —**шве́дский стол,** smorgasbord.

шве́йник *n.* worker in a garment factory.

шве́йный *adj.* sewing (*attrib.*). —**шве́йная маши́на,** sewing machine. —**шве́йная фа́брика,** clothing (*or* garment) factory.

швейца́р *n.* doorman.

швейца́рец [*gen.* -рца] *n.m.* [*fem.* -рка] Swiss. —**швейца́рский,** *adj.* Swiss.

швец [*gen.* швеца́] *n.*, *obs.* tailor. —**и швец, и жнец, и в ду́ду игре́ц,** jack-of-all-trades.

швея́ *n.* seamstress.

шво́рень [*gen.* -рня] *n.m.* = шкво́рень.

швырну́ть *v., pfv. of* **швыря́ть**.

швыро́к [*gen.* **-рка́**] *n.* **1**, *colloq.* toss. **2**, logs; firewood. **3**, object tossed in the air for firing practice.

швыря́ние *n.* tossing; flinging; hurling.

швыря́ть *v.impfv.* [*pfv.* **швырну́ть**] **1**, (*with acc. or instr.*) to toss; fling; hurl. **2**, *impers.* to toss: Ло́дку швыря́ло на волна́х, the boat was tossing on the waves. **3**, *in* швыря́ть де́ньги *or* деньга́ми, to toss (*or* throw) money around. —**швыря́ться**, *refl.* [*impfv. only*] (*with instr.*) *colloq.* **1**, to toss; hurl (at one another). **2**, *fig.* to trifle with.

шевели́ть *v.impfv.* [*pfv.* **пошевели́ть** *or* **шевельну́ть**; *pres.* **шевелю́, шеве́лишь** *or* **шевели́шь**] **1**, (*with instr.*) to move; wiggle. **2**, (*with acc.*) to stir. **3**, *in* шевели́ть мозга́ми, to use one's brains. **4**, *in* па́льцем не шевельну́ть, not to lift a finger. —**шевели́ться**, *refl.* **1**, to move; stir. **2**, *fig.* to show signs of life.

шевельну́ть *v., pfv. of* **шевели́ть**. —**шевельну́ться**, *refl., pfv. of* **шевели́ться**.

шевелю́ра *n.* head of hair.

шевио́т *n.* cheviot. —**шевио́товый**, *adj.* cheviot.

шевро́ *n. indecl.* kidskin. —**шевро́вый**, *adj.* kidskin; kid.

шевро́н *n., mil.* chevron; stripe.

шеде́вр (дэ) *n.* masterpiece.

шезло́нг *n.* **1**, chaise longue. **2**, deck chair.

ше́йка [*gen. pl.* **ше́ек**] *n.* **1**, *dim. of* **ше́я**. **2**, neck; narrow part. —**ше́йка ма́тки**, cervix.

ше́йный *adj.* **1**, neck (*attrib.*). **2**, *anat.* cervical. —**ше́йный плато́к**, neckerchief.

шейх *n.* sheik.

ше́лест *n.* rustle; rustling.

шелесте́ть *v.impfv.* [*pres.* **-сти́т**] to rustle.

шёлк [*gen.* **шелка́**] *n.* silk. —**в долгу́ как в шелку́**, up to one's ears in debt.

шелкови́нка [*gen. pl.* **-нок**] *n.* (piece of) silk thread.

шелкови́стый *adj.* silky; silken.

шелкови́ца *n.* mulberry.

шелкови́чный *adj.* mulberry (*attrib.*). —**шелкови́чный червь**, silkworm.

шелково́дство *n.* sericulture.

шёлковый *adj.* **1**, silk. **2**, (*of hair*) silken. **3**, *fig., colloq.* meek; docile.

шелкопря́д *n.* **1**, silkworm. **2**, moth: непа́рный шелкопря́д, gypsy moth.

шелла́к *n.* shellac.

шелохну́ть *v.pfv.* (*with acc. or instr.*) to move (slightly). —**шелохну́ться**, *refl.* to move; stir.

шелуди́вый *adj., colloq.* mangy.

шелуха́ *n.* husk; peel; hull. —**карто́фельная шелуха́**, potato peelings; potato skins.

шелуши́ть *v.impfv.* to shell; peel; husk. —**шелуши́ться**, *refl.* (*of paint, one's skin, etc.*) to peel.

ше́льма *n.m. & f., colloq.* scoundrel; rascal.

шельме́ц [*gen.* **-меца́**] *n., colloq.* = **ше́льма**.

шельмова́ть *v.impfv.* [*pfv.* **ошельмова́ть**; *pres.* **-му́ю, -му́ешь**] *colloq.* to disparage; run down.

шельф *n.* shelf: континента́льный шельф, continental shelf.

шемя́кин *adj., in* **шемя́кин суд**, unfair trial.

шепеля́вить *v.impfv.* [*pres.* **-влю, -вишь**] to lisp; pronounce *s* as *sh* and *z* as *zh*.

шепеля́вый *adj.* lisping. —**шепеля́вость**, *n.f.* lisp.

шепну́ть *v., pfv. of* **шепта́ть**.

шёпот *n.* whisper. —**шёпотом**, *adv.* in a whisper.

шептала́ *n.* dried peaches; dried apricots.

шепта́ние *n.* whispering.

шепта́ть *v.impfv.* [*pfv.* **прошепта́ть** *or* **шепну́ть**; *pres.* **шепчу́, ше́пчешь**] to whisper. —**шепта́ться**, *refl.* [*impfv. only*] to whisper (to each other).

шепту́н [*gen.* **-туна́**] *n., colloq.* **1**, whisperer. **2**, spreader of gossip.

шербе́т *n.* sherbet.

шере́нга *n.* **1**, rank; column; file. **2**, (*with gen.*) row (of); line (of).

шери́ф *n.* sheriff.

шерохова́тость *n.f.* **1**, roughness. **2**, rough edge. **3**, *pl., fig.* disagreements; squabbles.

шерохова́тый *adj.* **1**, rough. **2**, *fig.* crude.

шерсти́нка [*gen. pl.* **-нок**] *n.* strand of wool.

шерсти́стый *adj.* woolly.

шерсти́ть *v.impfv.* (*of rough material*) to irritate the skin; itch.

шерсть *n.f.* **1**, wool. **2**, hair; fur (*of animals*). —**про́тив ше́рсти**, against the grain. —**гла́дить про́тив ше́рсти**, to rub someone the wrong way.

шерстяно́й *adj.* wool; woolen.

шерша́веть *v.impfv.* [*pres.* **-веет**] to become rough.

шерша́вый *adj.* rough.

ше́ршень [*gen.* **-шня**] *n.m.* hornet.

шест [*gen.* **шеста́**] *n.* pole.

шеста́я *n., decl. as an adj.* sixth: одна́ шеста́я, one-sixth.

ше́ствие *n.* procession. —**замыка́ть ше́ствие**, to bring up the rear.

ше́ствовать *v.impfv.* [*pres.* **-ствую, -ствуешь**] to march; parade.

шестёрка *n.* **1**, the numeral 6. **2**, *colloq.* anything numbered 6. **3**, group of six. **4**, team of six horses. **5**, *cards* six.

шестерня́ *n.* **1**, [*gen. pl.* **-рён**] gear; cogwheel; pinion. **2**, [*gen. pl.* **-не́й**] *colloq.* team of six horses.

ше́стеро *collective numeral* six.

шестидеся́тый *ordinal numeral* sixtieth.

шестидне́вный *adj.* six-day (*attrib.*).

шестикра́тный *adj.* sixfold.

шестиме́сячный *adj.* **1**, six-month (*attrib.*). **2**, six-month-old.

шестисо́тый *ordinal numeral* six-hundredth.

шестиуго́льник *n.* hexagon. —**шестиуго́льный**, *adj.* hexagonal.

шестна́дцатый *ordinal numeral* sixteenth.

шестна́дцать *numeral* sixteen.

шесто́й *ordinal numeral* sixth.

шесто́к [*gen.* **-тка́**] *n.* **1**, hearth (*of a Russian stove*). **2**, perch; roost.

шесть [*gen., dat. & prepl.* **шести́**; *instr.* **шестью́**] *numeral* six.

шестьдеся́т [*gen., dat. & prepl.* **шести́десяти**; *instr.* **шестью́десятью**] *numeral* sixty.

шестьсо́т [*gen.* **шестисо́т**; *dat.* **шестиста́м**; *instr.* **шестьюста́ми**; *prepl.* **шестиста́х**] *numeral* six hundred.

ше́стью *adv.* six times: Ше́стью шесть — три́дцать шесть, six times six is 36.

шеф *n.* **1,** *colloq.* boss; chief. **2,** patron; sponsor. —**шеф-по́вар,** chef.

ше́фство *n.* patronage; sponsorship.

ше́фствовать *v.impfv.* [*pres.* -ствую, -ствуешь] (*with* над) to be a patron of; sponsor.

ше́я *n.* neck. —**бро́ситься на ше́ю** (+ *dat.*), to throw one's arms around someone's neck. —**ве́шаться на ше́ю** (+ *dat.*), to throw oneself at. —**гнуть ше́ю пе́ред,** to kowtow to. —**по (са́мую) ше́ю,** up to one's neck (*in work, debt, etc.*). —**получи́ть по ше́е,** to get it in the neck. —**посади́ть (кого́-нибудь) на чью́-нибудь ше́ю,** to thrust upon; dump upon. —**сади́ться на ше́ю** (+ *dat.*); **сиде́ть на ше́е у,** to live off; sponge off; be a burden to. —**слома́ть (себе́) ше́ю, 1,** to break one's neck. **2,** *fig.* to fall on one's face.

ши́бкий *adj., colloq.* fast; swift; quick.

ши́бко *adv., colloq.* **1,** fast. **2,** very; very much.

ши́ворот *n., in* **за ши́ворот,** by the scruff of the neck. —**ши́ворот-навы́ворот,** topsy-turvy.

шизофрени́я *n.* schizophrenia. —**шизофре́ник,** *n.* schizophrenic. —**шизофрени́ческий,** *adj.* schizophrenic.

шии́т *n.* Shiite. —**шии́тский,** *adj.* Shiite.

шик *n.* stylishness: оде́т с ши́ком, stylishly dressed. Счита́ться ши́ком, to be considered chic.

шика́рно *adv.* **1,** smartly. **2,** *as an interj., colloq.* splendid!

шика́рный *adj.* **1,** smart; chic. **2,** *colloq.* fine; grand.

ши́кать *v.impfv.* [*pfv.* **ши́кнуть**] *colloq.* **1,** (*with* на + *acc.*) to shoo away by saying шш. **2,** (*with* на + *acc.*) to hush; say шш to. **3,** (*with dat.*) to hiss (a performer).

ши́ллинг *n.* shilling.

ши́ло [*pl.* **ши́лья, ши́льев**] *n.* awl.

шилоклю́вка [*gen. pl.* -вок] *n.* avocet (*bird*).

шилохво́сть *n.f.* pintail (*duck*).

шимпанзе́ (зэ) *n.m. indecl.* chimpanzee.

ши́на *n.* **1,** tire. **2,** *med.* splint.

шине́ль *n.f.* overcoat.

шинка́рь [*gen.* -каря́] *n.m., obs.* tavern keeper.

шинкова́ть *v.impfv.* [*pres.* -ку́ю, -ку́ешь] to chop; shred (cabbage).

ши́нный *adj.* tire (*attrib.*).

шино́к [*gen.* **шинка́**] *n., obs.* tavern.

шиншилла́ *n.* chinchilla.

шиньо́н *n.* chignon.

шип [*gen.* **шипа́**] *n.* **1,** thorn. **2,** tenon. **3,** spike; cleat.

шипе́ние *n.* hissing; sizzling; fizzing.

шипе́ть *v.impfv.* [*pres.* **шиплю́, шипи́шь**] to hiss; sizzle; fizz.

шипо́вки *n.pl.* [*sing.* **шипо́вка**] *colloq.* spikes; cleats.

шипо́вник *n.* wild rose.

шипу́честь *n.f.* effervescence.

шипу́чий *adj.* sparkling; effervescent. —**шипу́чее,** *n.* sparkling beverage.

шипу́чка *n., colloq.* sparkling beverage.

шипя́щий *adj.* **1,** hissing. **2,** *phonet.* sibilant. —*n., phonet.* sibilant.

ши́ре *adj., comp. of* **широ́кий.**

ширина́ *n.* width; breadth. В три ме́тра ширино́й, three meters wide. Име́ть три ме́тра в ширину́, to be three meters wide.

ши́ринка *n., colloq.* fly (*on trousers*).

ши́рить *v.impfv.* **1,** *colloq.* to widen; make wider; open wider. **2,** *fig.* to expand. —**ши́риться,** *refl.* to expand.

ши́рма *n.* **1,** screen. **2,** *fig.* screen; cover.

широ́кий *adj.* [*short form* **широ́к, широка́, широко́** *or* **широ́ко, широки́** *or* **широ́ки;** *comp.* **ши́ре**] **1,** wide; broad. **2,** loose; loose-fitting. **3,** extensive. **4,** generous. **5,** *in* широ́кая пу́блика, the general public; широ́кий чита́тель, the general/average reader. **6,** *in* това́ры широ́кого потребле́ния, consumer goods. —**жить на широ́кую но́гу,** to live in grand style.

широко́ *adv.* **1,** widely; wide. **2,** broadly. —**жить широко́,** to live in grand style.

широковеща́ние *n.* broadcasting.

широковеща́тельный *adj.* **1,** broadcasting (*attrib.*). **2,** *fig.* high-sounding.

ширококоле́йный *adj., R.R.* broad-gauge.

широкопле́чий *adj.* broad-shouldered.

широкоуго́льный *adj.* wide-angle.

широта́ [*pl.* **широ́ты**] *n.* **1,** *colloq.* width. **2,** breadth; broad scope; wide range. **3,** latitude.

ширпотре́б *n., colloq.* **1,** mass consumption. **2,** consumer goods.

ширь *n.f.* expanse; open space. —**во всю ширь, 1,** to its full extent. **2,** *fig.* to the fullest.

шить *v.impfv.* [*pfv.* **сшить;** *pres.* **шью, шьёшь**] **1,** [*impfv. only*] to sew. **2,** to make (a garment). **3,** [*impfv. only*] to embroider. **4,** [*impfv. only*] *colloq.* to have one's clothes made (somewhere). —**он ни шьёт ни по́рет,** he keeps hemming and hawing.

шитьё *n.* **1,** sewing. **2,** needlework. **3,** embroidery.

ши́фер *n.* slate. —**ши́ферный,** *adj.* slate (*attrib.*).

шифо́н *n.* chiffon. —**шифо́новый,** *adj.* chiffon.

шифонье́рка [*gen. pl.* -рок] *n.* chiffonier.

шифр *n.* **1,** cipher; code. **2,** call number (*of a library book*).

шифрова́льщик *n.* cipher clerk; cryptographer.

шифро́ванный *adj.* in code; coded.

шифрова́ть *v.impfv.* [*pfv.* **зашифрова́ть;** *pres.* -ру́ю, -ру́ешь] to encipher; code; encode.

шифро́вка *n.* **1,** enciphering; encoding. **2,** *colloq.* coded message.

шиш [*gen.* **шиша́**] *n., colloq.* **1,** fig (*insulting gesture*). **2,** nothing; nil.

ши́шка [*gen. pl.* **ши́шек**] *n.* **1,** *bot.* cone. **2,** bump; lump. **3,** *colloq.* big shot.

шишкова́тый *adj.* knobby.

шишкови́дный *adj.* cone-shaped; pineal. —**шишкови́дная железа́,** pineal gland.

шкала́ [*pl.* **шка́лы**] *n.* **1,** scale; dial. **2,** *fig.* scale: шкала́ зарабо́тной пла́ты, wage scale.

шка́лик *n.* **1,** old Russian unit of liquid measure equal to about 1/8 of a pint. **2,** small vodka glass or bottle of this capacity.

шка́нцы [*gen.* -нцев] *n.pl.* quarterdeck.

шкату́лка [*gen. pl.* -лок] *n.* small box.

шкаф [*2nd loc.* шкафу́; *pl.* шкафы́] *n.* closet; cabinet; cupboard. —**кни́жный шкаф**, bookcase. —**несгора́емый шкаф**, safe. —**платяно́й шкаф**, wardrobe.

шка́фик *also,* **шка́фчик** *n.* small closet; small cabinet.

шквал *n.* squall. —**шква́листый**, *adj.* gusty.

шква́рки [*gen.* -рок] *n.pl.* cracklings.

шкво́рень [*gen.* -рня] *n.m.* pivot; kingbolt; kingpin.

шкив [*pl.* шкивы́] *n.* pulley.

шки́пер *n.* skipper; captain.

шко́ла *n.* **1,** school. Шко́ла-интерна́т, boarding school. **2,** schooling; training: пройти́ хоро́шую шко́лу, to receive thorough training. —**суро́вая шко́ла жи́зни**, the bitter experience of life; the school of hard knocks.

шко́лить *v.impfv.* [*pfv.* вы́школить] *colloq.* to school; train; discipline.

шко́льник *n.* schoolboy. —**шко́льница**, *n.* schoolgirl.

шко́льнический *adj.* schoolboy (*attrib.*); typical of a schoolboy.

шко́льничество *n.* schoolboyish behavior; schoolboy pranks.

шко́льный *adj.* school (*attrib.*).

шку́ра *n.* skin; hide; pelt. —**быть в чье́й-нибудь шку́ре**, to be in someone's shoes. —**дели́ть шку́ру неуби́того медве́дя**, to count one's chickens before they are hatched. —**драть шку́ру с** (+ *gen.*), **1,** to tan someone's hide. **2,** to exploit mercilessly; bleed white. —**дрожа́ть за свою́ шку́ру**, to worry about one's own skin. —**испы́тывать (что́-нибудь) на свое́й шку́ре**, to experience (something) personally. —**спасти́ свою́ шку́ру**, to save one's own skin. —**спусти́ть шку́ру с** (+ *gen.*), to tan someone's hide.

шку́рка *n.* **1,** *dim. of* **шку́ра**. **2,** sandpaper.

шку́рник *n.,* *colloq.* self-seeker; one who looks out only for himself.

шку́рный *adj.,* *colloq.* selfish; self-seeking.

шлагба́ум *n.* barrier; gate.

шлак *n.* slag.

шланг *n.* hose.

шлейф *n.* train (*of a dress*).

шлем *n.* **1,** helmet. **2,** *cards* slam.

шлёпанцы *n.pl.* [*sing.* **шлёпанец**] *colloq.* bedroom slippers.

шлёпать *v.impfv.* [*pfv.* **шлёпнуть**] **1,** to smack; slap; spank. **2,** (*with instr.*) to make a noise with. **3,** [*impfv. only*] *colloq.* to tramp. **4,** [*impfv. only*] (*with* по) *colloq.* to tramp; slosh (through water, mud, etc.). —**шлёпаться**, *refl.,* *colloq.* to tumble; flop; plop.

шлёпка *n.,* *colloq.* spanking.

шлёпнуть *v.,* *pfv. of* **шлёпать**. —**шлёпнуться**, *refl.,* *pfv. of* **шлёпаться**.

шлепо́к *n.* [*gen.* -пка́] *n.* slap; smack.

шлифова́льный *adj.* polishing (*attrib.*).

шлифова́льщик *n.* polisher.

шлифо́ванный *adj.* polished.

шлифова́ть *v.impfv.* [*pfv.* отшлифова́ть; *pres.* -фу́ю, -фу́ешь] **1,** to polish. **2,** to grind.

шлифо́вка *n.* polishing. —**шлифо́вщик**, *n.* polisher.

шлюз *n.* **1,** sluice. **2,** lock (*in a canal*). —**шлю́зный**, *adj.* sluice (*attrib.*).

шлюп *n.* sloop.

шлю́пка [*gen. pl.* -пок] *n.* boat. —**спаса́тельная шлю́пка**, lifeboat.

шлю́ха *n.,* *colloq.* slut.

шля́гер *n.* hit song.

шля́па *n.* hat. —**де́ло в шля́пе**, *colloq.* it's in the bag. —**снима́ть шля́пу пе́ред**, to take off one's hat to (*fig.*).

шля́пка [*gen. pl.* -пок] *n.* **1,** *dim. of* **шля́па**. **2,** head (*of a nail*). **3,** cap (*of a mushroom*).

шля́пник *n.* hatter.

шля́пный *adj.* hat (*attrib.*). —**шля́пный ма́стер**, hatter.

шля́ться *v.r.impfv.,* *colloq.* to wander about; gad about.

шмель [*gen.* шмеля́] *n.m.* bumblebee.

шмы́гать *v.impfv.* [*pfv.* **шмыгну́ть**] **1,** *colloq.* to bustle; scurry. **2,** [*impfv. only*] (*with instr.*) to scrape: шмы́гать нога́ми по́ полу, to scrape one's feet on the floor. —**шмы́гать но́сом**, to sniff; sniffle.

шмыгну́ть *v.pfv.* **1,** *pfv. of* **шмы́гать**. **2,** to dart; slip.

шмя́каться *v.r.impfv.* [*pfv.* **шмя́кнуться**] to fall with a thud.

шнитт-лу́к *n.* chive.

шни́цель *n.m.* schnitzel.

шно́ркель *n.m.* snorkel.

шнур [*gen.* шнура́] *n.* **1,** cord; lace. **2,** electric cord. **3,** fuse.

шнурова́ть *v.impfv.* [*pfv.* зашнурова́ть; *pres.* -ру́ю, -ру́ешь] to lace; tie.

шнуро́вка *n.* lacing.

шнуро́к [*gen.* -рка́] *n.* lace: шнуро́к для боти́нок, shoelace.

шныря́ть *v.impfv.,* *colloq.* **1,** to scurry; scamper. **2,** to poke about; prowl about; snoop about. **3,** *in* шныря́ть глаза́ми, to cast one's eyes about.

шов [*gen.* шва] *n.* **1,** seam. **2,** stitch; suture. **3,** *mech.* joint. —**треща́ть по (всем) швам**, to come apart at the seams.

шовини́зм *n.* chauvinism. —**шовини́ст**, *n.* chauvinist. —**шовинисти́ческий**, *adj.* chauvinistic.

шок *n.,* *med.* shock.

шоки́ровать *v.impfv.* [*pres.* -рую, -руешь] to shock.

шо́ковый *adj.* of shock: шо́ковое состоя́ние, state of shock. —**шо́ковая терапи́я**, shock therapy.

шокола́д *n.* **1,** chocolate. **2,** hot chocolate. —**шокола́дный**, *adj.* chocolate.

шо́мпол [*pl.* шомпола́] *n.* ramrod.

шо́рник *n.* saddler; harness maker.

шо́рный *adj.* saddle (*attrib.*); harness (*attrib.*); saddler's.

шо́рох *n.* rustle; rustling.

шо́рты [*gen.* шорт] *n.pl.* shorts.

шо́ры [*gen.* шор] *n.pl.* blinkers; blinders.

шоссе́ (сэ) *n.neut. indecl.* highway.

шоссе́йный (сэ) *adj.* road (*attrib.*); highway (*attrib.*). —**шоссе́йная доро́га**, highway.

шосси́ровать *v.impfv. & pfv.* [*pres.* -рую, -руешь] *obs.* to make into a highway.

шотла́ндец [*gen.* -дца] *n.m.* [*fem.* -дка] Scotchman; Scotsman.

шотла́ндка [*gen. pl.* -док] *n.* **1,** *fem. of* шотла́ндец. **2,** tartan; plaid.

шотла́ндский *adj.* Scottish; Scotch.

шофёр *n.* driver; chauffeur. —**шофёрский,** *adj.* driver's; chauffeur's.

шпа́га *n.* sword.

шпага́т *n.* **1,** string; cord; twine. **2,** *gymnastics* split.

шпа́жный *adj.* of a sword.

шпаклева́ть *v.impfv.* [*pfv.* зашпаклева́ть; *pres.* -лю́ю, -лю́ешь] to putty; fill with putty.

шпаклёвка *n.* **1,** puttying. **2,** putty.

шпа́ла *n.* railroad tie.

шпале́ра *n., usu. pl.* **1,** trellis. **2,** row of trees along a road. **3,** *mil.* rows; columns. **4,** *obs.* wallpaper.

шпана́ *n., colloq.* **1,** hoodlum; punk. **2,** rabble; riffraff.

шпанго́ут *n.* frame (*of a ship, plane, etc.*).

шпа́нка *n.* Spanish fly.

шпа́нский *adj., obs.* Spanish. —**шпа́нская му́шка,** Spanish fly.

шпарга́лка [*gen. pl.* -лок] *n., colloq.* pony; crib (*concealed student's notes*).

шпа́рить *v.impfv.* [*pfv.* ошпа́рить] *colloq.* **1,** to pour boiling water on. **2,** to scald.

шпат *n.* spar (*mineral*). —**алма́зный шпат,** corundum. —**плавико́вый шпат,** fluorspar; fluorite. —**полево́й шпат,** feldspar.

шпа́тель (тэ) *n.m.* **1,** spatula. **2,** palette knife; putty knife.

шпа́ция *n., printing* space.

шпенёк [*gen.* -нька́] *n.* peg; prong.

шпигова́ть *v.impfv.* [*pfv.* нашпигова́ть; *pres.* -гу́ю, -гу́ешь] **1,** to lard. **2,** *fig.* to stuff (with); fill (with).

шпик *n., colloq.* detective; sleuth.

шпиль *n.m.* **1,** spire; steeple. **2,** capstan.

шпи́лька [*gen. pl.* -лек] *n.* **1,** hairpin. **2,** tack; brad (*used in shoemaking*). **3,** *fig.* sarcastic comment; dig. —**подпуска́ть шпи́льки** (+ *dat.*), to needle (someone).

шпина́т *n.* spinach. —**шпина́тный,** *adj.* spinach (*attrib.*).

шпингале́т *n.* latch; catch; bolt.

шпи́ндель (дэ) *n.m.* spindle; shaft.

шпио́н *n.* spy.

шпиона́ж *n.* espionage.

шпио́нить *v.impfv.* to spy.

шпио́нский *adj.* espionage (*attrib.*); spy (*attrib.*).

шпио́нство *n.* spying.

шпиц *n.* **1,** *obs.* spire; steeple. **2,** spitz (*dog*).

шпон *n., printing* lead; slug.

шпо́нка [*gen. pl.* -нок] *n., mech.* key; dowel.

шпо́ра *n.* spur.

шпо́рник *n.* delphinium; larkspur.

шприц *n.* (hypodermic) syringe.

шпро́ты [*sing.* шпро́та] *n.pl.* sprats.

шпу́лька [*gen. pl.* -лек] *n.* spool; bobbin.

шпыня́ть *v.impfv., colloq.* **1,** to poke; jab. **2,** *fig.* to nag; needle.

шрам *n.* scar.

шрапне́ль *n.f.* shrapnel. —**шрапне́льный,** *adj.* shrapnel (*attrib.*).

шрифт [*pl.* шрифты́] *n.* print; type; typeface.

шта́б [*pl.* штабы́] *n., mil.* staff; headquarters.

шта́бель [*pl.* штабеля́] *n.m.* pile; stack.

шта́б-кварти́ра *n.* headquarters (building).

штабно́й *adj., mil.* staff (*attrib.*). —*n.* staff officer.

штаке́тник *n.* **1,** fence. **2,** pickets (*forming a fence*).

штамп *n.* **1,** *mech.* die. **2,** (rubber) stamp. **3,** imprint. **4,** *fig.* stereotype. **5,** *fig.* cliché.

штампова́льный *adj., mech.* punching; stamping. —**штампова́льный пресс,** punch press.

штампо́ванный *adj.* **1,** pressed; shaped. **2,** *fig.* stock; trite.

штампова́ть *v.impfv.* [*pres.* -пу́ю, -пу́ешь] **1,** to stamp. **2,** *mech.* to punch; press; shape. **3,** *fig., colloq.* to grind out; crank out.

штампо́вка *n.* **1,** stamping. **2,** punching; pressing.

штампо́вочный *adj., mech.* punching; stamping. —**штампо́вочный пресс,** punch press.

шта́нга *n.* **1,** rod; bar. **2,** *sports* barbell. **3,** *sports* crossbar (*between goal posts*).

штанги́ст *n.* weightlifter.

штанда́рт *n.* standard; banner.

штани́на *n., colloq.* pants leg; trouser leg.

штани́шки [*gen. pl.* -шек] *n.pl., colloq.* short pants.

штаны́ [*gen.* -но́в] *n.pl., colloq.* trousers; pants.

штат *n.* **1,** state: Соединённые Шта́ты, the United States. **2,** (permanent) staff: сокраще́ние шта́тов, staff reduction; reduction in personnel.

штати́в *n.* **1,** stand; base. **2,** *photog.* tripod.

шта́тный *adj.* staff (*attrib.*); permanent; regular.

шта́тский *adj. & n.* civilian. —**шта́тское,** *n.* civilian clothes.

штевень [*gen.* -вня] *n.m., naut.* sternpost.

штемпелева́ть (тэ) *v.impfv.* [*pfv.* заштемпелева́ть; *pres.* -лю́ю, -лю́ешь] to stamp; postmark.

ште́мпель (тэ) [*pl.* штемпеля́] *n.m.* **1,** rubber stamp. **2,** imprint made with a rubber stamp. —**почто́вый ште́мпель,** postmark.

ште́мпельный (тэ) *adj.* stamp (*attrib.*); stamping (*attrib.*). —**ште́мпельная поду́шка,** stamp pad; ink pad.

ште́псель (тэ) [*pl.* штепселя́] *n.m.* **1,** electric plug. **2,** *colloq.* electric outlet.

ште́псельный (тэ) *adj.* of an electric plug or outlet. —**ште́псельная ви́лка,** electric plug. —**ште́псельная розе́тка,** electric outlet.

штибле́ты *n.pl.* [*sing.* штибле́та] (men's) shoes; boots (*with laces*).

штилево́й *adj., naut.* calm. —**штилевы́е по́лосы,** *naut.* the doldrums.

штиль *n.m., naut.* calm.

штифт [*gen.* штифта́] *n.* pin; peg; dowel.

шток *n., mech.* rod: поршнево́й шток, piston rod.

штокро́за *n.* hollyhock.

што́пальный *adj.* for darning: што́пальная игла́, darning needle.

што́пать *v.impfv.* [*pfv.* зашто́пать] to darn.

што́пка *n.* **1,** darning. **2,** *colloq.* darning thread.

што́пор *n.* **1,** corkscrew. **2,** *aero.* spin. —**што́пор на хвост,** tailspin.

што́ра *n.* **1,** windowshade; blind. **2,** curtain.

шторм *n.* storm; gale (*at sea*).

штормова́ть *v.impfv.* [*pres.* -му́ю, -му́ешь] to weather a storm.

штормово́й *adj.* **1,** storm (*attrib.*). **2,** stormy. —**ве́тер штормово́й си́лы,** wind of gale force.

штоф *n.* **1,** damask. **2,** old Russian unit of liquid measure equal to about 2 1/2 pints. **3,** *obs.* wine bottle of this capacity.

што́фный *adj.* damask.

штраф *n.* **1,** fine. **2,** penalty.

штрафно́й *adj.* **1,** penalty (*attrib.*). **2,** penal. —**штрафно́й бросо́к,** *basketball* free throw. —**штрафно́й уда́р,** *soccer* penalty kick.

штрафова́ть *v.impfv.* [*pfv.* **оштрафова́ть;** *pres.* -фу́ю, -фу́ешь] **1,** to fine. **2,** to penalize.

штрейкбре́хер *n.* strikebreaker.

штри́пка [*gen. pl.* -пок] *n.* strap for fastening trousers to footwear.

штрих [*gen.* **штриха́**] *n.* **1,** stroke (*in drawing*). **2,** *fig.* detail; feature. —**после́дние штрихи́,** the final (*or* finishing) touches.

штрихова́ть *v.impfv.* [*pfv.* **заштрихова́ть;** *pres.* -ху́ю, -ху́ешь] *drawing* to shade; hatch.

штрихо́вка *n.*, *drawing* shading; hatching.

штуди́ровать *v.impfv.* [*pfv.* **проштуди́ровать;** *pres.* -рую, -руешь] to study.

шту́ка *n.* **1,** piece; item; unit: пять штук яи́ц, five eggs. Сто́ить де́сять до́лларов шту́ка, to cost ten dollars apiece. **2,** *colloq.* thing. **3,** *colloq.* trick. —**за шту́ку,** apiece; each. —**в то́м-то и шту́ка; вот в э́том вся шту́ка,** *colloq.* that's just the point!

штука́рь [*gen.* -каря́] *n.m.*, *colloq.* jokester; prankster.

штукату́р *n.* plasterer.

штукату́рить *v.impfv.* [*pfv.* **оштукату́рить**] to plaster.

штукату́рка *n.* **1,** plaster. **2,** plastering. —**штука-ту́рный,** *adj.* plaster (*attrib.*); plastering (*attrib.*).

штурва́л *n.* steering wheel (*of a ship or aircraft*). —**за штурва́лом,** at the helm; at the controls.

штурва́льный *adj.* steering (*attrib.*). —*n.* man at the wheel; helmsman.

штурм *n.*, *mil.* storm; assault; (*with gen.*) storming (of).

шту́рман *n.* navigator.

штурмова́ть *v.impfv.* [*pres.* -му́ю, -му́ешь] *mil.* to storm.

штурмови́к [*gen.* -вика́] *n.* **1,** low-flying attack aircraft. **2,** storm trooper (*in Nazi Germany*).

штурмо́вка *n.* strafing.

штурмово́й *adj.* assault (*attrib.*). —**штурмова́я авиа́ция, 1,** ground-attack aircraft. **2,** ground-attack forces.

шту́чка [*gen. pl.* -чек] *n.*, *dim. of* **шту́ка.**

шту́чный *adj.* by the piece; sold by the piece.

штык [*gen.* **штыка́**] *n.* bayonet. —**встре́тить** *or* **приня́ть в штыки́,** to meet with extreme hostility; be up in arms over.

штыково́й *adj.* bayonet (*attrib.*).

штырь [*gen.* **штыря́**] *n.m.* pin; dowel.

шу́ба *n.* fur coat.

шуга́ *n.* drift ice.

шу́лер [*pl.* **шулера́**] *n.* cardsharp; cheat. —**шу́лер-ский,** *adj.* cheating; dishonest. —**шу́лерство,** *n.* cheating.

шум *n.* **1,** noise. **2,** *fig.* fuss: подня́ть шум, to make (*or* raise) a fuss. **3,** *fig.* stir; sensation: вы́звать шум; наде́лать шу́ма, to cause a sensation; cause quite a stir. **4,** *in* шум в се́рдце, heart murmur; шум в уша́х, buzzing in one's ears. —**мно́го шу́ма из ничего́,** much ado about nothing.

шуме́ть *v.impfv.* [*pres.* -млю́, -ми́шь] **1,** to make (a) noise; be noisy. **2,** *fig.*, *colloq.* to make a fuss. —**у меня́ шуми́т в уша́х,** I have a buzzing in my ears.

шуми́ха *n.*, *colloq.* fuss; uproar; clamor; hullabaloo.

шумли́вый *adj.* **1,** noisy; boisterous. **2,** *colloq.* high-sounding.

шу́мно *adv.* noisily. —*adj.*, *used predicatively*, noisy: Здесь сли́шком шу́мно, it is too noisy in here.

шу́мный *adj.* **1,** noisy. **2,** lively; bustling. **3,** *fig.* causing a sensation: шу́мный успе́х, huge (*or* sensational) success.

шумови́к [*gen.* -вика́] *n.*, *theat.* sound effects man.

шумо́вка [*gen. pl.* -вок] *n.* straining spoon; skimmer.

шумово́й *adj.* sound (*attrib.*). —**шумовы́е эффе́кты,** sound effects.

шумо́к [*gen.* **шумка́**] *n.*, *colloq.* slight noise. —**под шумо́к,** secretly; on the sly.

шу́рин *n.* brother-in-law (*wife's brother*).

шуру́п *n.* screw.

шурша́ние *n.* rustling.

шурша́ть *v.impfv.* [*pres.* -шу́, -ши́шь] to rustle.

шу́стрый *adj.*, *colloq.* bright; smart.

шут [*gen.* шута́] *n.* jester. —**шут горо́ховый,** buffoon.

шути́ть *v.impfv.* [*pfv.* **пошути́ть;** *pres.* шучу́, шу́тишь] **1,** to joke; jest: Вы шу́тите!, you're joking! **2,** (*with* с + *instr.*) to play (with). **3,** (*with* над) to make fun of. **4,** [*impfv. only*] (*with instr.*) to trifle (with). —**шути́ть с огнём,** to play with fire. —**шу́тки шути́ть,** to joke.

шути́ха *n.1*, *fem. of* шут. **2,** rocket (*firework*).

шу́тка [*gen. pl.* шу́ток] *n.* joke. —**в шу́тку,** in jest; as a joke. —**не до шу́ток,** it's no joke; it's no laughing matter. Ему́ не до шу́ток, he is in no mood for jokes. —**не на шу́тку,** really; genuinely; seriously. —**с ним шу́тки пло́хи,** he is not to be trifled with; you don't fool around with him. —**сыгра́ть шу́тку с,** to play a joke (*or* trick) on. —**шу́тки в сто́рону; кро́ме шу́ток,** joking aside.

шутли́вый *adj.* **1,** *colloq.* frequently telling jokes; jocular. **2,** (*of a remark, song, etc.*) humorous; facetious.

шутни́к [*gen.* -ника́] *n.* joker; jokester.

шутовско́й *adj.* **1,** of a jester. Шутовско́й колпа́к, fool's cap. **2,** mischievous; prankish.

шутовство́ *n.* buffoonery.

шу́точный *adj.* **1,** humorous; facetious. **2,** (*usu. neg.*) trifling: Это не шу́точное де́ло, it's no trifling (*or* laughing) matter.

шутя́ *adv.* **1,** in jest; jokingly. **2,** easily; without any difficulty. —**не шутя́,** seriously; in earnest.

шушу́каться *v.r.impfv.*, *colloq.* to whisper (to each other).

шхе́ры [*gen.* **шхер**] *n.pl.* rocky islets along a rugged coast.

шху́на *n.* schooner.

шш *interj.* shh!; hush!

Щ

Щ, щ *n.neut.* 26th letter of the Russian alphabet.

щаве́левый *adj.* sorrel (*attrib.*). —**щаве́левая кислота́,** oxalic acid.

щаве́ль [*gen.* **-веля́**] *n.m.* sorrel.

щади́ть *v.impfv.* [*pfv.* **пощади́ть**; *pres.* **щажу́, щади́шь**] **1,** to spare; spare the life of; have mercy on. **2,** to spare: не щади́ть уси́лий, to spare no effort; щади́ть чьё-нибудь самолю́бие, to spare someone's pride.

щебёнка *n., colloq.* = **щебень.**

щ́ебень [*gen.* **ще́бня**] *n.m.* macadam. —**щебёночный,** *adj.* macadam(ized).

щ́ебет *n.* twitter; chirping. *Also,* **щебета́ние.**

щебета́ть *v.impfv.* [*pres.* **щебечу́, щебе́чешь**] **1,** to twitter; chirp. **2,** *colloq.* to chatter.

щего́л [*gen.* **щегла́**] *n.* goldfinch.

щеголева́тый *adj.* stylish; dapper.

щёголь *n.m.* dandy; fop.

щегольну́ть *v., pfv. of* **щеголя́ть.**

щегольско́й *adj.* **1,** smart; handsome; elegant. **2,** dashing; jaunty.

щегольство́ *n.* **1,** foppery; dandyism. **2,** showing off.

щеголя́ть *v.impfv.* [*pfv.* **щегольну́ть**] **1,** [*impfv. only*] to wear fancy clothes. **2,** (*with* в + *prepl.*) *colloq.* to sport. **3,** (*with instr.*) *colloq.* to show off; flaunt.

щ́едрый *adj.* generous. —**щ́едро,** *adv.* generously. —**щ́едрость,** *n.f.* generosity.

щека́ [*acc.* **щёку**; *pl.* **щёки, щёк, щека́м**] *n.* cheek. —**уплета́ть** *or* **упи́сывать за о́бе щеки́,** to eat ravenously; devour; gobble up.

щеко́лда *n.* door latch.

щекота́ние *n.* tickling sensation.

щекота́ть *v.impfv.* [*pfv.* **пощекота́ть**; *pres.* **щекочу́, щеко́чешь**] to tickle.

щеко́тка *n.* **1,** tickling. **2,** tickling sensation. —**боя́ться щеко́тки,** to be ticklish.

щекотли́вый *adj.* ticklish; delicate. —**щекотли́вость,** *n.f.* ticklishness; delicacy.

щеко́тно *adj., used predicatively,* tickling: Мне щеко́тно, it tickles.

щеко́тный *adj.* causing a tickling sensation.

щели́стый *adj., colloq.* full of cracks.

щ́елка [*gen. pl.* **щёлок**] *n.* crack; slit.

щ́елканье *n.* **1,** snapping; cracking; clicking. **2,** warbling (*of birds*).

щ́елкать *v.impfv.* [*pfv.* **щёлкнуть**] **1,** to flick: щёлкнуть кого́-нибудь по́ носу, to give someone a flick on the nose. **2,** (*of a lock, shutter, etc.*) to click. **3,** (*with instr.*) to crack (a whip); snap (one's fingers, a shutter, etc.); click (one's tongue); turn (a key) with a click. **4,** to crack (nuts). **5,** [*impfv. only*] (*of a bird*) to warble.

щелкопёр *n., obs.* hack writer.

щёлок *n.* lye.

щелочно́й *adj.* alkaline. —**щёлочность,** *n.f.* alkalinity.

щёлочь *n.f.* alkali.

щелчо́к [*gen.* **-чка́**] *n.* **1,** flick; fillip. **2,** click; crack. **3,** snap (*of the fingers*). **4,** *colloq.* slight; snub.

щель [*2nd loc.* **щели́**; *pl.* **щ́ели, щеле́й, щеля́м**] *n.f.* **1,** crack; slit. **2,** slot (*for a coin*). **3,** *mil.* slit trench. —**голосова́я щель,** glottis.

щеми́ть *v.impfv.* **1,** to constrict. **2,** to ache; hurt. **3,** *fig.* to oppress; weigh on.

щемя́щий *adj.* oppressive; nagging.

щени́ться *v.r.impfv.* [*pfv.* **още́ни́ться**] to have pups.

щено́к [*gen.* **щенка́**; *pl.* **щенки́, щенко́в** *or* **щеня́та, щеня́т**] *n.* pup; puppy.

щепа́ [*pl.* **щ́епы, щеп, щепа́м**] *n.* **1,** chip of wood. **2,** chips; kindling. **3,** shingles (*for a roof*).

щепа́ть *v.impfv.* [*pres.* **щеплю́, щ́еплешь**] to chop; cleave.

щепети́льный *adj.* punctilious.

щ́епка [*gen. pl.* **щ́епок**] *n.* chip; sliver. —**худо́й как щ́епка,** thin as a rail.

щепо́тка [*gen. pl.* **-ток**] *n.* = **щепо́ть.**

щепо́ть *also,* **щ́епоть** *n.f.* **1,** three fingers (the thumb, index and middle finger) held together. **2,** pinch: щепо́ть со́ли, pinch of salt.

щерба́тый *adj.* **1,** cracked. **2,** with teeth missing. **3,** *colloq.* pockmarked.

щерби́на *n.* **1,** chip; nick. **2,** place where a tooth is missing. **3,** *colloq.* pockmark.

щети́на *n.* **1,** bristles. **2,** *colloq.* stubble (*of beard*). —**щети́нистый,** *adj.* bristly.

щети́ниться *v.r.impfv.* [*pfv.* **още́ти́ниться**] to bristle.

щётка [*gen. pl.* **щёток**] *n.* **1,** brush: щётка для воло́с, hairbrush; зубна́я щётка, toothbrush. **2,** fetlock. —**щётка для ковра́,** carpet sweeper.

щёточный *adj.* brush (*attrib.*).

щ́ечный *adj.* cheek (*attrib.*).

щи [*gen.* **щей**] *n.pl.* cabbage soup. —**попа́сть как кур во́ щи,** to get into a jam; get into hot water.

щи́колотка [*gen. pl.* **-ток**] *n.* ankle.

щипа́ть *v.impfv.* [*pres.* **щиплю́, щи́плешь**] **1,** [*pfv.*

щипну́ть] to pinch. **2,** [*impfv. only*] to burn; sting. **3,** [*impfv. only*] *impers.* to burn; smart: У меня́ щи́плет глаза́, my eyes are smarting. **4,** [*pfv.* **ощипа́ть** *or* **общипа́ть**] to pluck. **5,** [*impfv. only*] to nibble. —**щипа́ться,** *refl.* [*impfv. only*] **1,** to pinch. **2,** to pinch each other.

щипко́вый *adj., in* **щипко́вые инструме́нты,** instruments played by plucking.

щипко́м *adv.* pizzicato.

щипну́ть *v., pfv. of* **щипа́ть** (*in sense #1*).

щипо́к [*gen.* **щипка́**] *n.* pinch; nip; tweak.

щипцы́ [*gen.* **-цо́в**] *n.pl.* tongs. —**хирурги́ческие щипцы́,** forceps. —**щипцы́ для зави́вки,** curling irons. —**щипцы́ для оре́хов,** nutcracker.

щи́пчики [*gen.* **-ков**] *n.pl.* tweezers.

щит [*gen.* **щита́**] *n.* **1,** shield. **2,** screen; guard: щит от гря́зи, mudguard. **3,** board; panel: распредели́тельный щит, switchboard; рекла́мный щит, billboard; щит управле́ния, control panel. **4,** shell (*of a turtle*).

5, *basketball* backboard. —**верну́ться на щите́,** to return home defeated. —**верну́ться со щито́м,** to return home victorious. —**поднима́ть на щит,** to extol; praise to the skies.

щитови́дный *adj.* thyroid: щитови́дная железа́, thyroid gland.

щито́к [*gen.* **щитка́**] *n.* **1,** *dim. of* щит. **2,** panel. **3,** dashboard. **4,** *sports* shinguard.

щитомо́рдник *n.* copperhead (*snake*).

щу́ка *n.* pike (*fish*).

щуп *n.* **1,** probing device. **2,** dipstick.

щу́пальце [*gen. pl.* **-лец**] *n.* tentacle.

щу́пать *v.impfv.* [*pfv.* **пощу́пать**] to feel; touch. —**щу́пать** (+ *acc.*) **глаза́ми,** to look over; scan.

щу́плый *adj., colloq.* puny; thin; frail.

щу́рить *v.impfv.* [*pfv.* **сощу́рить**], *in* щу́рить глаза́, to squint. —**щу́риться,** *refl.* to squint.

щу́чий [*fem.* **-чья**] *adj.* pike's. —**как по щу́чьему веле́нию,** as if by magic.

Ъ

Ъ, ъ *n.neut., called* **твёрдый знак,** 27th letter of the Russian alphabet.

Ы

Ы, ы *n.neut.* 28th letter of the Russian alphabet.

Ь

Ь, ь *n.neut., called* **мя́гкий знак,** 29th letter of the Russian alphabet.

Э

Э, э *n.neut., also called* **э оборо́тное,** thirtieth letter of the Russian alphabet.

эбе́новый *adj.* ebony. —**эбе́новое де́рево,** ebony.

эбони́т *n.* ebonite; vulcanite.

эвакуа́ция *n.* evacuation. —**эвакуацио́нный,** *adj.* evacuation (*attrib.*).

эвакуи́рованный *n., decl. as an adj.* evacuee.

эвакуи́ровать *v.impfv. & pfv.* [*pres.* **-рую, -руешь**] to evacuate.

эве́н *n.m.* [*fem.* **эве́нка**] Even (*one of a people inhabiting eastern Siberia*).

эве́нк *n.m.* [*fem.* **эвенки́йка**] Evenk (*one of a people inhabiting eastern Siberia*). —**эвенки́йский,** *adj.* Evenki.

эве́нский *adj.* Even: эве́нский язы́к, the Even language (*see* **эве́н**).

эвкали́пт *n.* eucalyptus. —**эвкали́птовый,** *adj.* eucalyptus (*attrib.*).

эвкли́дов *adj.* Euclidean: эвкли́дова геоме́трия, Euclidean geometry.

эволюциони́ровать *v.impfv. & pfv.* [*pres.* **-рую, -руешь**] to evolve.

эволю́ция *n.* evolution. —**эволюцио́нный,** *adj.* evolutionary.

э́врика *interj.* eureka!

эвфеми́зм *n.* euphemism. —**эвфемисти́ческий,** *adj.* euphemistic.

эгалита́рный *adj.* egalitarian.

эги́да *n.* aegis: под эги́дой (+ *gen.*), under the aegis of; under the auspices of.

эгои́зм *n.* egoism; selfishness. —**эгои́ст; эго́истка,** *n.* egoist; egotist. —**эгоисти́ческий; эгоисти́чный,** *adj.* egoistic; egotistical; selfish.

эготи́зм *n.* egotism.

эгоцентри́ческий *adj.* egocentric; self-centered.

эдельве́йс (дэ) *n.* edelweiss.

Эде́м (дэ) *n.* Eden.

эй *interj.* hey!

эйнште́йний (тэ) *n.* einsteinium.

эйфори́я *n.* euphoria.

эква́тор *n.* equator. —**экваториа́льный,** *adj.* equatorial.

эквивале́нт *n.* equivalent. —**эквивале́нтность,** *n.f.* equivalence. —**эквивале́нтный,** *adj.* equivalent.

эквилибри́ст *n.* tightrope walker; high-wire artist. —**эквилибри́стика,** *n.* balancing act; tightrope walking.

экзальта́ция *n.* exaltation; ecstasy. —**экзальтиро́ванный,** *adj.* in a state of exaltation; ecstatic.

экза́мен *n.* examination. —**экзамена́тор,** *n.* examiner. —**экзаменацио́нный,** *adj.* examination (*attrib.*).

экзаменова́ть *v.impfv.* [*pfv.* **проэкзаменова́ть**; *pres.* **-ну́ю, -ну́ешь**] to examine. —**экзаменова́ться,** *refl.* to take an examination.

экзе́ма (зэ) *n.* eczema.

экземпля́р (зэ) *n.* **1,** copy (*one of many*): в трёх экземпля́рах, in three copies; in triplicate. **2,** specimen: ре́дкий экземпля́р, rare specimen.

экзистенциали́зм *n.* existentialism. —**экзистенциали́ст,** *n.* existentialist. —**экзистенциа́льный,** *adj.* existential(ist).

экзо́тика *n.* exotic things; exotic objects. —**экзоти́ческий,** *adj.* exotic.

экиво́к *n., usu. pl.* ambiguity: говори́ть с экиво́ками, to talk in ambiguities; говори́ть без экиво́ков, to talk straight to the point.

э́кий *adj., colloq.* what a...!

экипа́ж *n.* **1,** carriage. **2,** crew.

экипирова́ть *v.impfv. & pfv.* [*pres.* **-ру́ю, -ру́ешь**] to equip.

экипиро́вка *n.* equipping; equipment.

эклекти́зм *n.* eclecticism. —**экле́ктик,** *n.* eclectic. —**эклекти́ческий; эклекти́чный,** *adj.* eclectic.

экле́р *n.* éclair.

экли́птика *n., astron.* ecliptic.

эколо́гия *n.* ecology. —**экологи́ческий,** *adj.* ecological.

эконо́м *n., obs.* **1,** thrifty person. **2,** manager of a household; steward. **3,** economist.

эконо́мика *n.* **1,** economics. **2,** economy (*of a country*).

экономи́ст *n.* economist.

эконо́мить *v.impfv.* [*pfv.* **сэконо́мить**; *pres.* **-млю, -мишь**] **1,** to save: эконо́мить вре́мя, to save time; эконо́мить на материа́лах, to save on materials. **2,** [*impfv. only*] to economize.

экономи́ческий *adj.* economic.

экономи́чный *adj.* (*of a device, method, etc.*) economical.

эконо́мия *n.* **1,** economy; thrift: соблюда́ть эконо́мию, to be economical; economize. **2,** (*with gen.*) saving (of): эконо́мия то́плива, saving of fuel; fuel economy. **3,** savings; amount saved (*by economizing*): Эконо́мия соста́вила..., the savings amounted to...

эконо́мка [*gen. pl.* **-мок**] *n., obs.* housekeeper.

эконо́мничать *v.impfv., colloq.* to economize; scrimp; watch one's pennies.

эконо́мный *adj.* economical; thrifty.

экра́н *n.* **1,** screen. **2,** the screen (*motion pictures*). **3,** shield: тепловой экра́н, heat shield.

экраниза́ция *n.* filming.

экранизи́ровать *v.impfv. & pfv.* [*pres.* **-рую, -руешь**] to make into a movie.

эксгума́ция *n.* exhumation.

эксгуми́ровать *v.impfv. & pfv.* [*pres.* **-рую, -руешь**] to exhume.

экскава́тор *n.* steam shovel.

э́кскурс *n.* digression.

экскурса́нт *n.* person on an excursion; sightseer.

экскурсио́нный *adj.* excursion (*attrib.*).

экску́рсия *n.* **1,** excursion; sightseeing tour. **2,** tourist group; sightseeing party.

экскурсово́д *n.* tour guide.

эксли́брис *n.* bookplate.

экспанси́вный *adj.* expansive; effusive.

экспансиони́зм *n.* expansionism. —**экспансио-ни́стский,** *adj.* expansionist.

экспа́нсия *n.* (territorial) expansion.

экспатриа́ция *n.* expatriation. —**экспатриа́нт,** *n.* expatriate.

экспатрии́ровать *v.impfv. & pfv.* [*pres.* **-рую, -руешь**] to expatriate.

экспеди́ция *n.* expedition. —**экспедицио́нный,** *adj.* expeditionary.

экспериме́нт *n.* experiment. —**эксперимента́ль-ный,** *adj.* experimental. —**эксперименти́рование,** *n.* experimentation.

эксперименти́ровать *v.impfv.* [*pres.* **-рую, -руешь**] to experiment.

экспе́рт *n.* expert.

эксперти́за *n.* **1,** examination by experts. **2,** committee of experts.

экспе́ртный *adj.* **1,** expert. **2,** of experts.

эксплуата́тор *n.* exploiter. —**эксплуата́торский,** *adj.* exploiter (*attrib.*); exploiting.

эксплуатацио́нный *adj.* operating; operational.

эксплуата́ция *n.* **1,** exploitation. **2,** operation.

эксплуати́ровать *v.impfv.* [*pres.* **-рую, -руешь**] **1,** to exploit; take advantage of. **2,** to operate; run.

экспози́метр *n., photog.* exposure meter; light meter.

экспози́ция *n.* **1,** display; exhibit. **2,** *photog.* exposure.

экспона́т *n.* exhibit.

экспоне́нт *n.* **1,** exhibitor. **2,** *math.* exponent. —**экспо-ненциа́льный,** *adj.* exponential.

экспони́ровать *v.impfv. & pfv.* [*pres.* **-рую, -руешь**] **1,** to exhibit. **2,** *photog.* to expose.

экспоно́метр *n., photog.* exposure meter; light meter.

э́кспорт *n.* **1,** export. **2,** exports. —**экспортёр,** *n.* exporter.

экспорти́ровать *v.impfv. & pfv.* [*pres.* **-рую, -руешь**] to export.

э́кспортный *adj.* export (*attrib.*).

экспре́сс *n.* express (*train, ship, bus, etc.*). —**экспре́сс по́чта,** express mail.

экспресси́вный *adj.* expressive.

экспре́ссия *n.* expression; expressiveness.

экспро́мт *n.* something composed on the spur of the moment; something just dashed off. —**экспро́мтом,** *adv.* impromptu; extemporaneously.

экспроприа́ция *n.* expropriation.

экспроприи́ровать *v.impfv. & pfv.* [*pres.* **-рую, -руешь**] to expropriate.

экста́з *n.* ecstasy. —**экстати́ческий,** *adj.* ecstatic.

экстерн (тэ) *n.* student allowed to take examinations without attending classes.

экстерриториа́льный *adj.* extraterritorial.

экстравага́нтный *adj.* eccentric; bizarre; outlandish.

экстраги́ровать *v.impfv. & pfv.* [*pres.* **-рую, -руешь**] to extract.

экстра́кт *n.* extract.

экстра́кция *n.* extraction.

экстраордина́рный *adj.* extraordinary.

экстраполи́ровать *v.impfv. & pfv.* [*pres.* **-рую, -руешь**] to extrapolate.

экстраполя́ция *n.* extrapolation.

экстрема́льный *adj.* extreme.

экстреми́зм *n.* extremism. —**экстреми́ст,** *n.* extremist. —**экстреми́стский,** *adj.* extremist.

э́кстренно *adv.* urgently.

э́кстренный *adj.* **1,** urgent. **2,** special. —**э́кстренный слу́чай,** emergency.

эксце́нтрик *n.* **1,** clown. **2,** *obs.* eccentric (person). **3,** *mech.* cam.

эксцентри́ческий *adj.* **1,** = эксцентри́чный. **2,** *theat.* comical; improbable. **3,** *math.* eccentric.

эксцентри́чный *adj.* eccentric; odd. —**эксцентри́ч-ность,** *n.f.* eccentricity.

эксце́сс *n., usu. pl.* excesses.

эктопла́зма *n.* ectoplasm.

эласти́чный *adj.* **1,** elastic. **2,** supple. —**эласти́ч-ность,** *n.f.* elasticity.

элева́тор *n.* **1,** grain elevator. **2,** lift; hoist.

элега́нтный *adj.* elegant. —**элега́нтно,** *adv.* elegantly. —**элега́нтность,** *n.f.* elegance.

элеги́ческий *adj.* **1,** elegiac. **2,** [*also,* элеги́чный] *fig.* melancholy.

эле́гия *n.* **1,** elegy. **2,** *fig.* melancholy.

электризова́ть *v.impfv. & pfv.* [*pfv. also* наэлектри-зова́ть; *pres.* **-зу́ю, -зу́ешь**] **1,** to electrify; charge with electricity. **2,** *fig.* to electrify; thrill.

эле́ктрик *n.* electrician. —**инжене́р-эле́ктрик,** *n.* electrical engineer.

электри́к *adj. indecl.* grayish blue.

электрифика́ция *n.* electrification.

электрифици́ровать *v.impfv. & pfv.* [*pres.* **-рую, -руешь**] to electrify; provide with electric power.

электри́ческий *adj.* electric. —**электри́ческий стул,** electric chair.

электри́чество *n.* electricity.

электри́чка [*gen. pl.* **-чек**] *n., colloq.* **1,** electric railway. **2,** electric train.

электро- *prefix* electric(al): электропо́езд, electric train; электроте́хник, electrical engineer.

электрово́з *n.* electric locomotive.

электро́д *n.* electrode.

электродви́гатель *n.m.* electric motor.

электрока́р *n.* electric (*i.e.* battery-operated) vehicle for carrying loads or baggage.

электрокардиогра́мма *n.* electrocardiogram.

электрокардио́граф *n.* electrocardiograph.

электро́лиз *n.* electrolysis.

электроли́ния *n.* electric power line.

электроли́т *n.* electrolyte.

электромагнети́зм *n.* electromagnetism. —**электромагни́т**, *n.* electromagnet. —**электромагни́тный**, *adj.* electromagnetic.

электромонтёр *n.* electrician.

электро́н *n.* electron.

электро́ника *n.* electronics.

электро́нный *adj.* **1,** electron (*attrib.*). **2,** electronic. —**электро́нная ла́мпа**, electron tube; vacuum tube.

электропереда́ча *n.* carrying of electricity; power transmission. —**ли́нии электропереда́чи**, electric power lines.

электропита́ние *n.* power supply.

электроста́нция *n.* electric power station; power plant.

электроста́тика *n.* electrostatics. —**электростати́ческий**, *adj.* electrostatic.

электроте́хник *n.* electrical engineer. —**электроте́хника**, *n.* electrical engineering.

электроэне́ргия *n.* electrical energy; electric power.

элеме́нт *n.* **1,** element. **2,** *pl.* (*with gen.*) elements (of); fundamentals (of). **3,** *electricity* cell: сухо́й элеме́нт, dry cell. **4,** *colloq.* individual; character: тёмный элеме́нт, suspicious-looking individual/character.

элемента́рный *adj.* elementary.

элеро́н *n.* aileron.

эликси́р *n.* elixir.

эли́та *n.* elite.

э́ллинский *adj.* Hellenic.

э́ллипс *n.* **1,** ellipse. **2,** = **э́ллипсис**.

э́ллипсис *n.*, *ling.* ellipsis.

эллипсо́ид *n.* ellipsoid.

эллипти́ческий *adj.* elliptical.

эль *n.m.* ale.

э́льф *n.* elf.

эма́левый *adj.* enamel (*attrib.*); enameled.

эмалиро́ванный *adj.* enameled.

эмалирова́ть *v.impfv.* [*pres.* **-ру́ю, -ру́ешь**] to enamel.

эма́ль *n.f.* enamel.

эмана́ция *n.* emanation.

эмансипа́тор *n.* emancipator. —**эмансипа́ция**, *n.* emancipator.

эмансипи́ровать *v.impfv. & pfv.* [*pres.* **-рую, -руешь**] to emancipate.

эмба́рго *n. indecl.* embargo.

эмбле́ма *n.* emblem. —**эмблемати́ческий**, *adj.* emblematic.

эмболи́я *n.* embolism.

эмбриоло́гия *n.* embryology. —**эмбрио́лог**, *n.* embryologist.

эмбрио́н *n.* embryo. —**эмбриона́льный**, *adj.* embryonic.

эмигра́нт *n.* émigré; emigrant. —**эмигра́нтский**, *adj.* émigré (*attrib.*).

эмигра́ция *n.* **1,** emigration. **2,** émigrés. —**в эмигра́ции**, abroad; in a foreign land (*to which one has emigrated*).

эмигри́ровать *v.impfv. & pfv.* [*pres.* **-рую, -руешь**] to emigrate.

эми́р *n.* emir. —**эмира́т**, *n.* emirate.

эмисса́р *n.* emissary.

эми́ссия *n.* **1,** *finance* issuing; issuance. **2,** *physics* emission.

эмоциона́льный *adj.* emotional. —**эмоциона́льно**, *adv.* emotionally; with emotion.

эмо́ция *n.* emotion.

эмпири́зм *n.* empiricism. —**эмпи́рик**, *n.* empiricist. —**эмпири́ческий**, *adj.* empirical.

э́му *n.m. indecl.* emu.

эму́льсия *n.* emulsion.

эмфизе́ма (зэ) *n.* emphysema.

эндеми́ческий *adj.* endemic.

энди́вий *n.* endive.

эндокри́нный *adj.* endocrine.

эндокриноло́гия *n.* endocrinology.

э́ндшпиль *n.m.*, *chess* end game.

энерге́тик (нэ) *n.* energy. —**энергети́ческий**, *adj.* energy (*attrib.*).

энерги́чный (нэ) *adj.* **1,** (*of a person*) energetic. **2,** (*of measures, protests, etc.*) forceful; vigorous; energetic. —**энерги́чно**, *adv.* energetically; vigorously.

эне́ргия (нэ) *n.* **1,** energy. **2,** (electric) power.

энергобло́к (нэ) *n.* power generating unit.

э́нный *adj.* **1,** any; an unspecified; a certain. **2,** *colloq.* unlimited; endless: э́нное коли́чество, an endless amount. —**в э́нной сте́пени**, to the nth degree.

э́нский *adj.* X (*used to designate something that cannot be identified*).

энтери́т *n.* enteritis.

энтомоло́гия *n.* entomology. —**энтомо́лог**, *n.* entomologist. —**энтомологи́ческий**, *adj.* entomological.

энтузиа́зм *n.* enthusiasm. —**энтузиа́ст**, *n.* enthusiast.

энцефали́т *n.* encephalitis.

энци́клика *n.* encyclical.

энциклопе́дия *n.* encyclopedia. —**энциклопеди́ческий**, *adj.* encyclopedic.

эпати́ровать *v.impfv. & pfv.* [*pres.* **-рую, -руешь**] to shock.

эпиго́н *n.* imitator; copier.

эпигра́мма *n.* epigram. —**эпиграммати́ческий**, *adj.* epigrammatic.

эпи́граф *n.* epigraph.

эпидемиоло́гия *n.* epidemiology. —**эпидемио́лог**, *n.* epidemiologist.

эпиде́мия *n.* epidemic. —**эпидеми́ческий**, *adj.* epidemic.

эпиде́рмис (дэ) *n.* epidermis.

эпизо́д *n.* episode.

эпизоди́ческий *adj.* **1,** episodic. **2,** occasional; sporadic.

э́пик *n.* epic poet.

эпикуре́ец [*gen.* **-е́йца**] *n.* epicurean. —**эпикуре́йский**, *adj.* epicurean.

эпиле́псия *n.* epilepsy. —**эпиле́питик**, *n.* epileptic. —**эпилепти́ческий**, *adj.* epileptic.

эпило́г *n.* epilogue.

эпи́стола *n.* epistle. —эпистоля́рный, *adj.* epistolary.

эпита́фия *n.* epitaph.

эпите́лий (тэ) *n.* epithelium. —эпителиа́льный, *adj.* epithelial.

эпи́тет *n.* epithet.

эпице́нтр *n.* epicenter.

эпи́ческий *adj.* epic.

эполе́та *n.* epaulet. *Also,* эполе́т.

эпопе́я *n.* epic; epic work.

эпо́ха *n.* epoch; age; era. —эпоха́льный, *adj.* epochal.

э́ра *n.* era. —до на́шей э́ры, B.C.: в двухсо́том году́ до на́шей э́ры, in 200 B.C. —на́шей э́ры, A.D.: в двухсо́том году́ на́шей э́ры, in 200 A.D.

э́рбий *n.* erbium.

эрг *n.* erg.

эре́кция *n., physiol.* erection.

эрза́ц *n.* substitution; imitation.

э́рика *n.* brier; heath.

Эрмита́ж *n.* the Hermitage Museum (*in St. Petersburg*).

эро́зия *n.* erosion.

эроти́зм *n.* eroticism.

эро́тика *n.* **1,** sensuality. **2,** erotic literature. —эроти́ческий, *adj.* erotic.

эруди́рованный *adj.* erudite.

эруди́т *n.* erudite person.

эруди́ция *n.* erudition.

эрцге́рцог *n.* archduke. —эрцгерцоги́ня, *n.* archduchess. —эрцге́рцогство, *n.* archduchy.

эска́дра *n., naval* squadron.

эска́дренный *adj.* squadron (*attrib.*). —эска́дренный миноно́сец, destroyer.

эскадри́лья [*gen. pl.* -лий] *n.* (air) squadron.

эскадро́н *n.* (cavalry) squadron. —эскадро́нный, *adj.* squadron (*attrib.*).

эскала́тор *n.* escalator.

эскала́ция *n.* escalation.

эска́рп *n., mil.* escarpment.

эсква́йр *n.* esquire.

эски́з *n.* **1,** sketch. **2,** draft; outline. —эски́зный, *adj.* rough; preliminary; in outline form.

эскимо́ *n. indecl.* ice cream on a stick.

эскимо́с *n.m.* [*fem.* -мо́ска] Eskimo. —эскимо́сский, *adj.* Eskimo.

эско́рт *n., mil.* escort.

эскорти́ровать *v.impfv.* [*pres.* -ру́ю, -ру́ешь] *mil.* to escort.

эсми́нец [*gen.* -нца] *n., naval* destroyer (*contr. of* эска́дренный миноно́сец).

эспера́нто *n. indecl.* Esperanto.

эсплана́да *n.* esplanade.

эссе́ *n.neut. indecl.* essay.

эссе́нция *n.* **1,** essence: ро́мовая эссе́нция, essence of rum. **2,** *fig.* essence.

эстака́да *n.* **1,** trestle; overpass. **2,** pier.

эста́мп *n.* print.

эстафе́та *n.* relay race. **2,** baton (*used in a relay race*). —эстафе́тный, *adj.* relay (*attrib.*); used in a relay race.

эсте́тика (тэ) *n.* esthetics. —эсте́т, *n.* esthete. —эстети́ческий, *adj.* esthetic.

эсто́нец [*gen.* -нца] *n.m.* [*fem.* -нка] Estonian. —эсто́нский, *adj.* Estonian.

эстраго́н *n.* tarragon.

эстра́да *n.* **1,** stage; platform. **2,** vaudeville. —эстра́дный, *adj.* vaudeville (*attrib.*).

эстроге́н *n.* estrogen.

эта́ж [*gen.* этажа́] *n.* floor; story.

этаже́рка [*gen. pl.* -рок] *n.* bookcase.

э́так *adv., colloq.* **1,** so; like this; like that. **2,** about; approximately; some. —и так и э́так, **1,** this way and that. **2,** any way you look at it.

э́такий *adj., colloq.* **1,** such; such a... **2,** what a...!

этало́н *n.* **1,** standard (*of measurement*). **2,** *fig.* model.

эта́п *n.* **1,** stage; leg (*of a journey*). **2,** *fig.* stage; phase. **3,** halting place (*for troops, or prisoners going into exile*). **4,** group of prisoners traveling under guard. —по эта́пу, under guard; under escort.

эта́пный *adj.* **1,** of or pert. to prisoners going into exile. **2,** *fig.* (*of an event*) epochal; landmark.

э́тика *n.* ethics.

этике́т *n.* etiquette.

этике́тка [*gen. pl.* -ток] *n.* label.

эти́л *n.* ethyl.

этиле́н *n.* ethylene.

этили́рованный *adj.* (*of gasoline*) leaded.

эти́ловый *adj.* ethyl (*attrib.*).

этимоло́гия *n.* etymology. —этимо́лог, *n.* etymologist. —этимологи́ческий, *adj.* etymological.

эти́ческий *adj.* ethical. *Also,* эти́чный.

этни́ческий *adj.* ethnic.

этногра́фия *n.* ethnography. —этно́граф, *n.* ethnographer. —этнографи́ческий, *adj.* ethnographic.

этноло́гия *n.* ethnology. —этно́лог, *n.* ethnologist. —этнологи́ческий, *adj.* ethnological.

э́то *dem. adj., neut. of* э́тот, this: э́то сло́во, this word. —*dem. pron.* **1,** this; that; it: Что э́то?, what is this? Что э́то зна́чит?, what does this/that mean? Я уже́ знал об э́том, I already knew about it. Что вы хоти́те э́тим сказа́ть?, what do you mean by that? **2,** this is; that is; it is: Э́то дуб, this is an oak tree; э́то ложь, that's/it's a lie. Э́то о́чень про́сто, this (that, it) is very simple. Кака́я э́то у́лица?, what street is this? Чей э́то зо́нтик?, whose umbrella is this? **3,** (*of neuter nouns only*) this one. —*particle* **1,** (the one) who: Кто э́то звони́л?, who was that who called? Э́то он вы́болтал секре́т?, was it *he* who spilled the beans? **2,** *used as an intensifier:* Что э́то с ва́ми?, what's the matter with you?; what is it that's the matter with you? Куда́ э́то он пошёл?, where on earth has he gone?

э́тот [*fem.* э́та; *neut.* э́то; *pl.* э́ти; *gen.* э́того, э́той, э́тих; *dat.* э́тому, э́той, э́тим; *acc. fem.* э́ту; *instr.* э́тим, э́той, э́тими; *prepl.* э́том, э́той, э́тих] *dem. adj.:* э́тот дом, this house; э́та кни́га, this book; э́то сло́во, this word; э́ти лю́ди, these people. —*dem. pron.* this one: Я возьму́ э́тот, I'll take this one.

этру́сский *adj.* Etruscan.

этю́д *n.* **1,** *art* sketch. **2,** essay. **3,** *music* étude. **4,** chess problem.

эфеме́рный *adj.* ephemeral.

эфе́с *n.* hilt (*handle of a sword*).

эфио́п *n.m.* [*fem.* **эфио́пка**] Ethiopian. —**эфио́пский**, *adj.* Ethiopian.

эфи́р *n.* **1,** ether (*upper regions of the atmosphere*). **2,** *chem.* ether: эти́ловый эфи́р, ether; ethyl ether. **3,** *radio; TV* airwaves; air: выходи́ть в эфи́р, to go on the air. Передава́ть в эфи́р, to broadcast. —**прямо́й эфи́р**, live broadcasting.

эфи́рный *adj.* **1,** ether (*attrib.*). **2,** ethereal. —**эфи́рное вре́мя**, *radio; TV* air time. —**эфи́рное ма́сло**, essential oil.

эффе́кт *n.* **1,** effect. **2,** *pl.* шумовы́е эффе́кты, sound effects. —**с эффе́ктом**, with emphasis; with a flourish.

эффекти́вный *adj.* **1,** effective. **2,** efficient. —**эффекти́вно**, *adv.* effectively; efficiently. —**эффекти́вность**, *n.f.* effectiveness; efficiency.

эффе́ктный *adj.* striking; showy; flashy.

э́хо *n.* echo. —**отдава́ться** *or* **откли́каться э́хом**, to echo.

эхоло́т *n.* sonic depth finder.

эшафо́т *n.* scaffold.

эшело́н *n.* **1,** *mil.* echelon. **2,** special train.

Ю

Ю, ю *n.neut.* 31st letter of the Russian alphabet.

юа́нь *n.m.* yuan (*monetary unit of China*).

юбиле́й *n.* anniversary; jubilee. —**юбиле́йный**, *adj.* anniversary (*attrib.*).

юбиля́р *n.* person or institution whose anniversary is being celebrated.

ю́бка [*gen. pl.* **ю́бок**] *n.* skirt. —**ни́жняя ю́бка**, half slip; petticoat. —**ю́бка-клёш**, flared skirt.

ю́бочка [*gen. pl.* **-чек**] *n.* short skirt. —**шотла́ндская ю́бочка**, kilt.

ювели́р *n.* jeweler.

ювели́рный *adj.* **1,** jewelry (*attrib.*); jeweler's (*attrib.*). **2,** *fig.* finely wrought; exquisite.

юг *n.* south.

ю́го-восто́к *n.* southeast. —**ю́го-восто́чный**, *adj.* southeast; southeastern; southeasterly.

ю́го-за́пад *n.* southwest. —**ю́го-за́падный**, *adj.* southwest; southwestern; southwesterly.

югосла́вский *adj.* Yugoslav; Yugoslavian.

южа́нин [*pl.* **южа́не, южа́н**] *n.m.* [*fem.* **южа́нка**] southerner.

южноамерика́нский *adj.* South American.

ю́жный *adj.* southern; South; southerly.

ю́зом *adv.* into a skid: пойти́ ю́зом, to skid.

ю́кка *n.* yucca.

юла́ *n.* **1,** top (*toy*). **2,** *colloq.* fidgety person; fidgety child.

юлиа́нский *adj., in* юлиа́нский календа́рь, Julian calendar.

юли́ть *v.impfv., colloq.* **1,** to keep moving about; fidget. **2,** (*of an insect*) to scurry about; (*of one that flies*) to flit. **3,** *fig.* (*with* пе́ред) to play up to; ingratiate oneself (with). **4,** *fig.* to equivocate.

ю́мор *n.* humor.

юморе́ска *n.* humoresque.

юмори́ст *n.* humorist. —**юмористи́ческий**, *adj.* humorous.

ю́нга *n.* cabin boy.

юне́ц [*gen.* **юнца́**] *n., colloq.* youth; lad.

ю́нкер *n.* **1,** [*pl.* **ю́нкеры**] Junker. **2,** [*pl.* **юнкера́**] *pre-rev.* military cadet.

ю́ность *n.f.* youth.

ю́ноша [*gen. pl.* **-шей**] *n.m.* youth (*young man*).

ю́ношеский *adj.* **1,** youth (*attrib.*). **2,** youthful.

ю́ношество *n.* **1,** youth; young people. **2,** youth (*time when one is young*).

ю́ный *adj.* young; youthful.

Юпи́тер *n.* **1,** Jupiter. **2,** *l.c.* floodlight.

юр *n., in* на (са́мом) юру́, **1,** in an open (*or* exposed) place. **2,** *colloq.* in the midst (*or* center) of everything.

юриди́чески *adv.* legally.

юриди́ческий *adj.* juridical; legal; judicial. —**юриди́ческий факульте́т**, department *or* faculty of law; law school.

юрисди́кция *n.* jurisdiction.

юриско́нсульт *n.* legal adviser (*to a company, institution, etc.*).

юриспруде́нция *n.* jurisprudence.

юри́ст *n.* lawyer.

ю́ркий *adj.* **1,** nimble; agile. **2,** *fig., colloq.* clever; sharp.

юркну́ть *also,* **ю́ркнуть** *v.pfv.* to dart; scamper.

юро́дивый *adj., obs.* touched; crazy; cracked.

юро́дство *n.* **1,** madness; derangement. **2,** irrational act.

юро́дствовать *v.impfv.* [*pres.* **-ствую, -ствуешь**] to act like a madman.

юро́к [*gen.* **юрка́**] *n.* brambling.

ю́рский *adj.* Jurassic.

ю́рта *n.* nomad's tent.

юсти́ция *n.* justice. —**мини́стр юсти́ции,** Minister of Justice; (*U.S.*) Attorney General.

ют *n.* quarterdeck.

юти́ться *v.r.impfv.* [*pres.* **ючу́сь, юти́шься**] **1,** to nestle. **2,** to huddle. **3,** to be cooped up.

юфть *n.f.* Russia leather.

Я

Я, я *n.neut.* 32nd and last letter of the Russian alphabet. —**от А до Я,** from A to Z.

я [*gen. & acc.* **меня́;** *dat. & prepl.* **мне;** *instr.* **мной** *or* **мно́ю**] *pers. pron., 1st pers. sing.* I.

я́беда *n.m. & f., colloq.* **1,** tattler. **2,** spreader of malicious gossip. —*n.f., colloq.* malicious gossip.

я́бедник *n., colloq.* spreader of malicious gossip.

я́бедничать *v.impfv.* [*pfv.* **ная́бедничать**] (*with* **на** + *acc.*) *colloq.* **1,** to tell (on); tattle (on). **2,** to spread malicious gossip (about).

я́бедничество *n., colloq.* spreading of malicious gossip.

я́блоко [*pl.* **я́блоки, я́блок**] *n.* apple. —**в я́блоках,** dappled: се́рый в я́блоках, dapple gray. —**глазно́е я́блоко,** eyeball. —**я́блоко мише́ни,** bull's-eye. —**я́блоко раздо́ра,** apple of discord; bone of contention.

я́блоневый *adj.* of apple trees. Я́блоневый цвет, apple blossom. Я́блоневый сад, apple orchard. *Also,* **я́блонный.**

я́блоня *n.* apple tree.

я́блочко [*pl.* **-чки, -чек**] *n., dim. of* **я́блоко.**

я́блочный *adj.* apple (*attrib.*); of apples.

яви́ть [*infl.* **явлю́, я́вишь**] *v., pfv. of* **явля́ть.** —**яви́ться,** *refl., pfv. of* **явля́ться.**

я́вка [*gen. pl.* **я́вок**] *n.* **1,** appearance; attendance. **2,** secret meeting place; safe house.

явле́ние *n.* **1,** phenomenon. **2,** occurrence. **3,** *theat.* scene.

явля́ть *v.impfv.* [*pfv.* **яви́ть**] **1,** to show; reveal. **2,** *in* **явля́ть собо́й,** *colloq.* to be. —**явля́ться,** *refl.* **1,** (*with instr.*) to be: явля́ться по́лной неожи́данностью, to be a complete surprise. **2,** to appear; report: яви́ться в суд, to appear in court; яви́ться на рабо́ту, to report for work.

я́вный *adj.* **1,** overt; open: я́вная вражда́, overt/open hostility. **2,** obvious: Это я́вное недоразуме́ние, this is an obvious (*or* is obviously a) misunderstanding. **3,** blatant; patent. —**я́вно,** *adv.* obviously.

я́вор *n.* sycamore; Eurasian maple.

я́вочный *adj.* secret. —**я́вочным поря́дком,** without prior permission.

я́вственный *adj.* clear; distinct.

я́вствовать *v.impfv.* [*pres.* **-ствует**] to be clear; be apparent; be obvious.

явь *n.f.* reality.

ягдта́ш *n.* game bag.

я́гель *n.m.* reindeer moss.

ягнёнок [*gen.* **-нка;** *pl.* **ягня́та, ягня́т**] *n.* lamb.

ягни́ться *v.r.impfv.* [*pfv.* **оягни́ться**] (*of a ewe*) to give birth.

ягня́тник *n.* bearded vulture.

я́года *n.* **1,** berry. **2,** *in* **ви́нная я́года,** fig. —**одного́ по́ля я́года,** birds of a feather.

я́годицы *n.pl.* [*sing.* **я́годица**] buttocks.

я́годник *n.* **1,** berry patch. **2,** berry bush. **3,** *colloq.* one who likes to pick berries.

я́годный *adj.* berry (*attrib.*).

ягуа́р *n.* jaguar.

яд *n.* **1,** poison. **2,** *fig.* venom.

я́дерный *adj.* nuclear.

ядови́тый *adj.* **1,** poison; poisonous; venomous; toxic. **2,** *fig.* venomous; vicious; malicious.

ядохимика́т *n.* pesticide.

ядрёный *adj., colloq.* **1,** (*of a plant*) hearty; (*of a fruit*) juicy. **2,** (*of a person*) robust; vigorous; hale and hearty. **3,** bracing; invigorating.

я́дрица *n.* unground buckwheat.

ядро́ [*pl.* **я́дра, я́дер, я́драм**] *n.* **1,** kernel. **2,** core. **3,** nucleus. **4,** *fig.* heart; core. **5,** *mil.* ball: пу́шечное ядро́, cannon ball. **6,** *sports* shot: толка́ть ядро́, to put the shot.

я́зва *n.* **1,** ulcer; sore. **2,** *fig.* curse; plague. —**сиби́рская я́зва,** anthrax.

я́звенный *adj.* ulcerous. —**я́звенная боле́знь,** peptic ulcer.

язви́тельный *adj.* caustic; biting; cutting; sarcastic.

язви́ть *v.impfv.* [*pres.* **язвлю́, язви́шь**] **1,** *obs.* to sting. **2,** *fig.* to taunt. **3,** [*pfv.* **съязви́ть**] to say or remark sarcastically.

язы́к [*gen.* **языка́**] *n.* **1,** tongue: обже́чь себе́ язы́к, to burn one's tongue. Копчёный язы́к, smoked tongue. **2,** language: иностра́нный язы́к, foreign language. На ру́сском языке́, in Russian. **3,** clapper (*of a bell*). **4,** *mil.* prisoner (*to be interrogated*). —**говори́ть на ра́зных языка́х,** to be speaking different languages; be on different wavelengths. —**держа́ть язы́к за зуба́ми,** to hold one's tongue. —**найти́ о́бщий язы́к,** to find common ground. —**срыва́ться с языка́,** to escape one's lips. —**язы́к не повернётся** (*with* **у**), one can't bring oneself to say it.

языка́стый *adj., colloq.* sharp-tongued.

языкове́д *n.* linguist. —**языкове́дение,** *n.* linguistics.

языково́й *adj.* linguistic; language (*attrib.*).

языко́вый *adj.* tongue (*attrib.*).

языкозна́ние *n.* linguistics.

язы́ческий *adj.* heathen; pagan. —**язы́чество,** *n.* paganism.

язычко́вый *adj., phonet.* uvular. —**язычко́вый инструме́нт,** reed instrument.

язы́чник *n.* heathen; pagan.

язычо́к [*gen.* -чка́] *n.* **1,** *dim. of* **язы́к. 2,** tongue (*of a shoe*). **3,** uvula. **4,** *music* reed. **5,** catch; fastener.

язь [*gen.* язя́] *n.m.* a fish of the carp family.

яи́чко [*pl.* яи́чки, яи́чек] *n.* **1,** *dim. of* яйцо́. **2,** testicle.

яи́чник *n., anat.* ovary.

яи́чница *n.* [*also* яи́чница-глазу́нья] fried eggs. —**яи́чница-болту́нья,** scrambled eggs.

яи́чный *adj.* egg (*attrib.*).

яйцеви́дный *adj.* egg-shaped.

яйцево́д *n.* oviduct.

яйцекладу́щий *adj.* oviparous.

яйцекле́тка *n., biol.* ovule.

яйцеро́дный *adj.* oviparous.

яйцо́ [*pl.* я́йца, яи́ц, я́йцам] *n.* egg. —**яйцо́-пашо́т,** poached egg.

як *n.* yak.

я́кобы *conj.* that (*implying skepticism about a statement*): Говоря́т, я́кобы он ско́ро уезжа́ет, they say (that) he is leaving soon. —*particle* supposedly; allegedly: письмо́, я́кобы напи́санное им, a letter allegedly written by him.

я́корный *adj.* of an anchor. —**я́корное ме́сто; я́корная стоя́нка,** (place of) anchorage.

я́корь [*pl.* якоря́] *n.m.* **1,** anchor. **2,** *electricity* armature. —**стать на я́корь,** to anchor. —**стоя́ть на я́коре,** to stand *or* lie at anchor. —**я́корь спасе́ния,** last hope; last means of salvation.

яку́т *n.m.* [*fem.* яку́тка] Yakut (*one of a people inhabiting northeastern Siberia*). —**яку́тский,** *adj.* Yakut.

якша́ться *v.r.impfv.* (*with* с + *instr.*) *colloq.* to hobnob (with); rub elbows (with).

ял *n.* yawl.

я́лик *n.* skiff; dinghy; wherry.

я́ловый *adj.* (*of cows, sheep, etc.*) dry; giving no milk.

я́ма *n.* hole; pit. —**возду́шная я́ма,** air pocket. —**выгребна́я я́ма,** cesspool. —**долгова́я я́ма,** debtors' prison.

яма́ец [*gen.* -а́йца] *n.m.* [*fem.* -а́йка] Jamaican. —**яма́йский,** *adj.* Jamaican.

ямб *n.* iamb. —**четырёхсто́пный ямб,** iambic tetrameter. —**пятисто́пный ямб,** iambic pentameter.

ямби́ческий *adj.* iambic.

я́мка [*gen. pl.* я́мок] *n.* **1,** *dim. of* я́ма. **2,** dimple.

я́мочка [*gen. pl.* -чек] *n.* dimple.

ямс *n.* yam.

ямщи́к [*gen.* -щика́] *n.* stagecoach driver.

янва́рь [*gen.* -варя́] *n.m.* January. —**янва́рский,** *adj.* January (*attrib.*).

я́нки *n.m. indecl.* Yankee.

янта́рь [*gen.* -таря́] *n.m.* amber. —**янта́рный,** *adj.* amber.

япо́нец [*gen.* -нца] *n.m.* [*fem.* -нка] Japanese (man): Он япо́нец, he is Japanese. —**япо́нский,** *adj.* Japanese.

яр [*2nd loc.* яру́] *n.* **1,** cliff. **2,** ravine.

яра́нга *n.* tent made of reindeer hides.

ярд *n.* yard (*36 inches*).

яре́мный *adj., in* **яре́мная ве́на,** jugular vein.

я́ркий *adj.* [*short form* я́рок, ярка́, я́рко, я́рки; *comp.* я́рче] **1,** bright; brilliant. **2,** *fig.* striking; vivid; graphic. **3,** *fig.* brilliant; outstanding.

я́рко *adv.* **1,** brightly; brilliantly. **2,** clearly; distinctly.

я́рко- *prefix, used with colors,* bright: я́рко-кра́сный, bright red.

я́ркость *n.f.* brightness; brilliance.

ярлы́к [*gen.* -лыка́] *n.* label; tag.

ярлычо́к [*gen.* -чка́] *n.,* *dim. of* ярлы́к.

я́рмарка [*gen. pl.* -рок] *n.* (trade) fair. —**я́рмарочный,** *adj.* fair (*attrib.*).

ярмо́ [*pl.* я́рма] *n.* **1,** yoke (*for oxen*). **2,** *fig.* yoke (*of oppression*).

яровиза́ция *n.* vernalization.

яровизи́ровать *v.impfv. & pfv.* [*pres.* -рую, -руешь] to vernalize.

ярово́й *adj.* (*of crops*) spring (*attrib.*): ярова́я пшени́ца, spring wheat.

я́ростный *adj.* **1,** furious. **2,** violent.

я́рость *n.f.* fury; rage.

я́рус *n.* **1,** tier. **2,** deck (*of a bridge*). —**я́русный,** *adj.* tiered.

я́рый *adj.* **1,** furious; violent. **2,** fervent; zealous.

ярь-медя́нка [*gen.* я́ри-медя́нки] *n.* verdigris.

я́сельный *adj.* nursery (*attrib.*).

я́сеневый *adj.* ash (*attrib.*).

я́сень *n.m.* ash (*tree*).

я́сли [*gen.* я́слей] *n.pl.* **1,** manger. **2,** nursery; day nursery.

ясне́ть *v.impfv.* to become clear; clear up.

я́сно *adv.* clearly. —*adj., used predicatively,* clear: Всё я́сно?, is everything clear? Сего́дня я́сно, it is a clear day today. —*particle* **1,** I see; I understand. **2,** *colloq.* of course.

яснови́дение *n.* clairvoyance. —**яснови́дец** [*gen.* -дца] *n.* clairvoyant (person). —**яснови́дящий,** *adj.* clairvoyant.

я́сность *n.f.* clarity.

я́сный *adj.* [*short form* я́сен, ясна́, я́сно, я́сны *or* ясны́] clear. —**я́сное де́ло,** of course; it goes without saying. —**ясне́е я́сного,** as clear as day; crystal-clear.

я́ства *n.pl.* [*sing.* я́ство] food; victuals.

я́стреб [*pl.* ястреба́ *or* я́стребы] *n.* hawk.

ястреби́ный *adj.* **1,** hawk's. **2,** hawklike.

ястребо́к [*gen.* -бка́] *n.* **1,** *dim. of* я́стреб. **2,** *colloq.* fighter plane.

ятага́н *n.* scimitar.

ять *n.m.* name of the old letter Ѣ of the Russian alphabet, replaced in 1918 by the letter е. —**на ять,** *colloq.* **1,** first-rate; perfectly; to a T.

я́хонт *n., obs.* **1,** ruby. **2,** sapphire.

я́хта *n.* yacht.

яхтсме́н *n.* yachtsman.

яче́йка [*gen. pl.* ячее́к] *n.* **1,** tiny opening (*one of* *many*). **2,** socket (*of a tooth*). **3,** cell (*of a communist party*). **4,** foxhole.

ячме́нный *adj.* barley (*attrib.*).

ячме́нь [*gen.* -меня́] *n.m.* **1,** barley. **2,** sty (*on one's eye*).

я́чневый *adj.* made of fine-ground barley.

я́шма *n.* jasper. —**я́шмовый,** *adj.* jasper (*attrib.*).

я́щер *n.* pangolin.

я́щерица *n.* lizard.

я́щик *n.* **1,** box. **2,** [*also,* **я́щик стола́**] drawer. **3,** *in* почто́вый я́щик, mailbox; му́сорный я́щик, garbage can. —**откла́дывать в до́лгий я́щик,** to put off indefinitely. —**сыгра́ть в я́щик,** *colloq.* to die; kick the bucket.

я́щур *n.* foot-and-mouth disease.

A Glossary
of Proper Nouns

CONTINENTS

Africa	Áфрика
America	Амéрика
Antarctica	Антаркти́да (continent)
	Антáрктика (South Polar Region)
Asia	Áзия
Eurasia	Еврáзия
Europe	Еврóпа

COUNTRIES

Afghanistan	Афганистáн
Albania	Албáния
Algeria	Алжи́р
Angola	Ангóла
Argentina	Аргенти́на
Armenia	Армéния
Australia	Австрáлия
Austria	Áвстрия
Azerbaijan	Азербайджáн
Bahrain	Бахрéйн
Bangladesh	Бангладéш
Barbados	Барбáдос
Belarus	Беларýсь (f.)
Belgium	Бéльгия
Belize	Бели́з
Benin	Бени́н
Bhutan	Бутáн
Bolivia	Боли́вия
Bosnia	Бóсния
Botswana	Ботсвáна
Brazil	Брази́лия
Brunei	Брунéй (нэ)
Bulgaria	Болгáрия
Burma	Би́рма
Burundi	Бурýнди
Cambodia	Камбóджа
Cameroon	Камерýн
Canada	Канáда
Chad	Чад
Chile	Чи́ли
China	Китáй
Colombia	Колýмбия
Congo	Кóнго
Costa Rica	Кóста-Ри́ка
Croatia	Хорвáтия
Cuba	Кýба
Cyprus	Кипр
Czech Republic	Чéхия
Denmark	Дáния
Dominican Republic	Доминикáнская респýблика
Ecuador	Эквадóр
Egypt	Еги́пет (*gen.* -пта)
El Salvador	Сальвадóр
Eritrea	Эритрéя
Estonia	Эстóния
Ethiopia	Эфиóпия
Fiji	Фи́джи
Finland	Финлáндия
France	Фрáнция
Gabon	Габóн
Gambia	Гáмбия
Georgia	Грýзия
Germany	Гермáния
Ghana	Гáна
Great Britain	Великобритáния
Greece	Грéция
Grenada	Гренáда
Guatemala	Гватемáла
Guinea	Гвинéя
Guyana	Гайáна

Haiti	Гаи́ти	Paraguay	Парагва́й
Honduras	Гондура́с	Peru	Перу́
Hungary	Ве́нгрия	Philippines	Филиппи́ны
		Poland	По́льша
Iceland	Исла́ндия	Portugal	Португа́лия
India	И́ндия		
Indonesia	Индоне́зия	Qatar	Ка́тар
Iran	Ира́н		
Iraq	Ира́к	Romania	Румы́ния
Ireland	Ирла́ндия	Russia	Росси́я
Israel	Изра́иль (*m.*)	Rwanda	Руа́нда
Italy	Ита́лия		
Ivory Coast	Бе́рег Слоно́вой	Saudi Arabia	Сау́довская Ара́вия
	Ко́сти	Senegal	Сенега́л
		Sierra Leone	Сье́рра-Лео́не
Jamaica	Яма́йка	Singapore	Сингапу́р
Japan	Япо́ния	Slovakia	Слова́кия
Jordan	Иорда́ния	Slovenia	Слове́ния
		Somalia	Сомали́
Kazakhstan	Казахста́н	South Africa	Ю́жно-Африка́нский
Kenya	Ке́ния		Сою́з
Korea	Коре́я	Spain	Испа́ния
Kuwait	Куве́йт	Sri Lanka	Шри Ла́нка
Kyrgyzstan	Кыргызста́н	Sudan	Суда́н
		Surinam	Сурина́м
Laos	Лао́с	Swaziland	Сва́зиленд
Latvia	Ла́твия	Sweden	Шве́ция
Lebanon	Лива́н	Switzerland	Швейца́рия
Lesotho	Лесо́то	Syria	Си́рия
Liberia	Либе́рия		
Libya	Ли́вия	Taiwan	Тайва́нь (*m.*)
Lithuania	Литва́	Tajikistan	Таджикиста́н
Luxembourg	Люксембу́рг	Tanzania	Танза́ния
		Thailand	Таила́нд
Macedonia	Маке́дония	Togo	То́го
Madagascar	Мадагаска́р	Trinidad and Tobago	Тринида́д и Тоба́го
Malawi	Мала́ви	Tunisia	Туни́с
Malaysia	Мала́йзия	Turkey	Ту́рция
Mali	Мали́	Turkmenistan	Туркмениста́н
Malta	Ма́льта		
Mauritania	Маврита́ния	Uganda	Уга́нда
Mauritius	Маври́кий	Ukraine	Украи́на
Mexico	Ме́ксика	United States	Соединённые Шта́ты
Moldova	Молдо́ва	Uruguay	Уругва́й
Mongolia	Монго́лия	Uzbekistan	Узбекиста́н
Morocco	Маро́кко		
Mozambique	Мозамби́к	Venezuela	Венесуэ́ла
		Vietnam	Вьетна́м
Namibia	Нами́бия		
Nepal	Непа́л	Yemen	Й́емен
Netherlands	Нидерла́нды	Yugoslavia	Югосла́вия
New Zealand	Но́вая Зела́ндия		
Nicaragua	Никара́гуа	Zaire	Заи́р
Niger	Ни́гер	Zambia	За́мбия
Nigeria	Ниге́рия	Zimbabwe	Зимба́бве
Norway	Норве́гия		
Oman	Ома́н	### HISTORIC REGIONS, TERRITORIES, PRINCIPALITIES	
Pakistan	Пакиста́н	Alsace	Эльза́с
Panama	Пана́ма	Anatolia	Анато́лия

Andorra	Андо́рра
Aragon	Араго́н
Assyria	Асси́рия
Babylon	Вавило́н
Balkans	Балка́ны
Bavaria	Бава́рия
Bessarabia	Бессара́бия
Birobidzhan	Биробиджа́н
Brittany	Брета́нь (*f.*)
Burgundy	Бургу́ндия
Byzantium	Византи́я
Cape Cod	Кейп-Ко́д
Cape of Good Hope	мыс До́брой Наде́жды
Castile	Касти́лия
Cornwall	Ко́рнуолл
Crimea	Крым
Dalmatia	Далма́ция
England	А́нглия
Flanders	Фла́ндрия
Galicia	Гали́ция
Gibraltar	Гибралта́р
Greenland	Гренла́ндия
Holland	Голла́ндия
Hong Kong	Гонко́нг
Indochina	Индокита́й
Jutland	Ютла́ндия
Kashmir	Кашми́р
Kurdistan	Курдиста́н
Labrador	Лабрадо́р
Liechtenstein	Ли́хтенштейн
Lombardy	Ломба́рдия
Macao	Мака́о
Manchuria	Маньчжу́рия
Melanesia	Мелане́зия
Mesopotamia	Месопота́мия
Micronesia	Микроне́зия
Monaco	Мона́ко
Montenegro	Черного́рия
New England	Но́вая А́нглия
Normandy	Норма́ндия
Oceania	Океа́ния
Palestine	Палести́на
Patagonia	Патаго́ния
Persia	Пе́рсия
Phoenicia	Финики́я
Polynesia	Полине́зия
Provence	Прове́нс
Prussia	Пру́ссия
Punjab	Пенджа́б

Saar	Саа́р
San Marino	Сан-Мари́но
Savoy	Саво́йя
Saxony	Саксо́ния
Scandinavia	Скандина́вия
Schleswig-Holstein	Шле́звиг-Го́льштейн
Scotland	Шотла́ндия
Serbia	Се́рбия
Siam	Сиа́м
Siberia	Сиби́рь (*f.*)
Silesia	Силе́зия
Sinai	Сина́йский полуо́стров
Soviet Union	Сове́тский Сою́з
Thrace	Фра́кия
Tibet	Тибе́т
Transcaucasia	Закавка́зье
Transvaal	Трансваа́ль
Transylvania	Трансильва́ния
Tuscany	Тоска́на
Tyrol	Тиро́ль (*m.*)
Ulster	О́льстер
Wales	Уэ́льс
Yucatan	Юката́н

REPUBLICS OF THE RUSSIAN FEDERATION

Adygeya	Адыге́я
Altay	Алта́й
Bashkortostan	Башкортоста́н
Buryatia	Буря́тия
Chechen	Чече́нская Респу́блика
Chuvash	Чува́шская Респу́блика
Dagestan	Дагеста́н
Gorno-Altay	Го́рный Алта́й
Ingush	Ингу́шская Респу́блка
Kabardino-Balkar	Кабарди́но-Балка́рская Респу́блика
Kalmykia	Калмы́кия
Karachay-Cherkess	Карача́ево-Черке́сская Респу́блика
Karelia	Каре́лия
Khakassia	Хака́сия
Komi	Ко́ми
Mari El	Ма́рий Эл
Mordovia	Мордо́вия

North Ossetia	Се́верная Осе́тия	Crete	Крит
Tatarstan	Татарста́н	Curacao	Кюраса́о
Tuva	Ту́ва	Easter Island	о́стров Па́схи
Udmurt	Удму́ртская	Elba	Э́льба
	Респу́блика	Gotland	Го́тланд
Yakutia	Яку́тия	Guadalcanal	Гуадалкана́л
		Guadeloupe	Гваделу́па
		Guam	Гуам

ISLAND GROUPS

Aleutian Islands	Алеу́тские острова́	Hokkaido	Хокка́йдо
Antilles	Анти́льские острова́	Honshu	Хо́нсю
Azores	Азо́рские острова́	Iwo Jima	Иводзи́ма
Bahamas	Бага́мские острова́	Java	Я́ва
Balaeric Islands	Балеа́рские острова́	Leyte	Ле́йте
Canary Islands	Кана́рские острова́	Long Island	Лонг-А́йленд
Cape Verde Islands	острова́ Зелёного	Luzon	Лусо́н
	Мы́са	Madeira	Маде́йра
Channel Islands	Норма́ндские острова́	Majorca	Мальо́рка, Майо́рка
Falkland Islands	Фолкле́ндские	Man, Isle of	о́стров Мэн
	острова́	Martinique	Мартини́ка
Faroe Islands	Фаре́рские острова́	Mindanao	Миндана́о
Galapagos Islands	острова́ Гала́пагос	New Guinea	Но́вая Гвине́я
Kurile Islands	Кури́льсие острова́	Okinawa	Окина́ва
Leeward Islands	Подве́тренные	Puerto Rico	Пуэ́рто-Ри́ко
	острова́	Réunion	Реюньо́н
Maldive Islands	Мальди́вские острова́	Rhodes	Ро́дос
Mariana Islands	Мариа́нские острова́	Sakhalin	Сахали́н
Marshall Islands	Ма́ршалловы острова́	Sardinia	Сарди́ния
Orkney Islands	Оркне́йские острова́	Sicily	Сици́лия
Ryukyu Islands	острова́ Рюкю́	Sumatra	Сума́тра
Samoa	Само́а	Tahiti	Таи́ти
Seychelles	Сейше́льские острова́	Tasmania	Тасма́ния
Shetland Islands	Шетла́ндские острова́	Timor	Тимо́р
Solomon Islands	Соломо́новы острова́	Vancouver	Ванку́вер
Virgin Islands	Вирги́нские острова́	Zanzibar	Занзиба́р
Windward Islands	Наве́тренные острова́		

STATES OF THE UNION

Alabama	Алаба́ма
Alaska	Аля́ска
Arizona	Аризо́на
Arkansas	Арка́нзас
California	Калифо́рния
Colorado	Колора́до
Connecticut	Конне́ктикут
Delaware	Де́лавэр
Florida	Флори́да
Georgia	Джо́рджия

ISLANDS

Antigua	Анти́гуа
Aruba	Ару́ба
Bali	Ба́ли
Bermuda	Берму́дские острова́
Borneo	Борне́о
Bornholm	Бо́рнхольм
Corfu	Ко́рфу
Corsica	Ко́рсика

Hawaii	Гава́йи
Idaho	А́йдахо
Illinois	Иллино́йс
Indiana	Индиа́на
Iowa	А́йова
Kansas	Ка́нзас
Kentucky	Кенту́кки
Louisiana	Луизиа́на
Maine	Мэн
Maryland	Мэ́риленд
Massachusetts	Массачу́сетс
Michigan	Мичига́н
Minnesota	Миннесо́та
Mississippi	Миссиси́пи
Missouri	Миссу́ри
Montana	Монта́на
Nebraska	Небра́ска
Nevada	Нева́да
New Hampshire	Нью-Хэ́мпшир
New Jersey	Нью-Дже́рси
New Mexico	Нью-Ме́ксико
New York	Нью-Йо́рк
North Carolina	Се́верная Кароли́на
North Dakota	Се́верная Дако́та
Ohio	Ога́йо
Oklahoma	Оклахо́ма
Oregon	Орего́н
Pennsylvania	Пенсильва́ния
Rhode Island	Род-А́йленд
South Carolina	Ю́жная Кароли́на
South Dakota	Ю́жная Дако́та
Tennessee	Теннесси́
Texas	Теха́с
Utah	Ю́та
Vermont	Вермо́нт
Virginia	Вирги́ния
Washington	Вашингто́н
West Virginia	За́падная Вирги́ния
Wisconsin	Виско́нсин
Wyoming	Вайо́минг

CANADIAN PROVINCES

Alberta	Альбе́рта
British Columbia	Брита́нская Колу́мбия
Manitoba	Манито́ба
New Brunswick	Нью-Бра́нсуик
Newfoundland	Ньюфаундле́нд
Nova Scotia	Но́вая Шотла́ндия
Ontario	Онта́рио
Prince Edward Island	о́стров При́нца Эдуарда
Quebec	Квебе́к
Saskatchewan	Саскатчева́н

CITIES

Aberdeen	А́бердин
Abidjan	Абиджа́н
Abu Dhabi	Абу́-Да́би
Acapulco	Акапу́лько
Accra	А́ккра
Aden	А́ден (дэ)
Addis Ababa	Адди́с-Абе́ба
Albany	О́лбани
Aleppo	Але́ппо
Alexandria	Александри́я
Algiers	Алжи́р
Alma-Ata	Алма́-Ата́
Amman	Амма́н
Amsterdam	Амстерда́м
Anchorage	А́нкоридж
Ankara	Анкара́
Annapolis	Ана́полис
Antwerp	Антве́рпен
Archangel	Арха́нгельск
Arles	Арль (m.)
Ashkhabad	Ашхаба́д
Asmara	Асма́ра
Astrakhan	А́страхань (m.)
Asunción	Асунсьо́н
Athens	Афи́ны
Atlanta	Атла́нта
Atlantic City	Атла́нтик-Си́ти
Auckland	О́кленд
Auschwitz	Осве́нцим
Avignon	Авиньо́н
Baghdad	Багда́д
Baku	Баку́
Baltimore	Ба́лтимор
Bangkok	Бангко́к
Barcelona	Барсело́на
Basel	Ба́зель (m.)
Beijing	Пеки́н, Бэйцзи́н
Beirut	Бейру́т
Belfast	Бе́лфаст
Belgrade	Белгра́д
Bergen	Бе́рген
Berlin	Берли́н
Berne	Берн

Bethlehem	Вифлеём	Edinburgh	Эдинбург
Birmingham	Бирмингем	Edmonton	Эдмонтон
Bogotá	Богота́		
Bombay	Бомбе́й	Fairbanks	Фэ́рбенкс
Bonn	Бонн	Florence	Флоре́нция
Bordeaux	Бордо́	Fort Worth	Форт-Уэ́рт
Boston	Бо́стон	Frankfurt	Фра́нкфурт
Brasilia	Брази́лия		
Bratislava	Братисла́ва	Geneva	Жене́ва
Brazzaville	Браззави́ль (m.)	Genoa	Ге́нуя
Bremen	Бре́мен	Glasgow	Гла́зго
Bremerhaven	Бре́мерхафен	Guadalajara	Гвадалаха́ра
Brisbane	Бри́сбен		
Bristol	Бри́столь (m.)	Hague, The	Гаа́га
Bruges	Брю́гге	Haifa	Ха́йфа
Brussels	Брюссе́ль (m.)	Halifax	Га́лифакс
Bucharest	Бухаре́ст	Hamburg	Га́мбург
Budapest	Будапе́шт	Hanoi	Хано́й
Buenos Aires	Буэ́нос-А́йрес	Hanover	Ганно́вер
Buffalo	Бу́ффало	Harare	Хара́ре
Bukhara	Бухара́	Harbin	Харби́н
		Havana	Гава́на
Cairo	Каи́р	Heidelberg	Ге́йдельберг
Calcutta	Кальку́тта	Helsinki	Хе́льсинки
Calgary	Ка́лгари	Hiroshima	Хироси́ма
Cambridge	Ке́мбридж	Honolulu	Гонолу́лу
Canberra	Ка́нберра	Houston	Хью́стон
Cannes	Канн		
Canterbury	Ке́нтербери	Indianapolis	Индиана́полис
Canton	Канто́н	Irkutsk	Ирку́тск
Capetown	Ке́йптаун	Istanbul	Стамбу́л
Caracas	Кара́кас		
Cardiff	Ка́рдифф	Jericho	Иерихо́н
Casablanca	Касабла́нка	Jersey City	Дже́рси-Си́ти
Chicago	Чика́го	Jerusalem	Иерусали́м
Cincinnati	Цинцинна́ти	Johannesburg	Йоха́ннесбург
Cleveland	Кли́вленд		
Cologne	Кёльн	Kabul	Кабу́л
Colombo	Коло́мбо	Kansas City	Ка́нзас-Си́ти
Conakry	Ко́накри	Karachi	Кара́чи
Copenhagen	Копенга́ген	Katmandu	Катманду́
Cracow	Кра́ков	Kazan	Каза́нь (f.)
		Kharkov	Ха́рьков
Dacca	Да́кка	Khartoum	Харту́м
Dakar	Дака́р	Kiev	Ки́ев
Dallas	Да́ллас	Kingston	Ки́нгстон
Damascus	Дама́ск	Kinshasa	Кинша́са
Dar es Salaam	Дар-эс-Сала́м	Kishinev	Кишинёв
Denver	Де́нвер	Kuala Lumpur	Куа́ла-Лу́мпур
Des Moines	Де-Мо́йн	Kyoto	Кио́то
Detroit	Детро́йт		
Djakarta	Джака́рта	Lagos	Ла́гос
Dover	Дувр	Lahore	Лахо́р
Dresden	Дре́зден	Lancaster	Ла́нкастер
Dubai	Диба́й	Las Vegas	Лас-Ве́гас
Dublin	Ду́блин	Leeds	Лидс
Dubrovnik	Дубро́вник	Le Havre	Гавр
Dusseldorf	Дю́ссельдорф	Leicester	Ле́стер
		Leipzig	Ле́йпциг
		Lhasa	Лха́са

Lima	Ли́ма	Ottawa	Отта́ва
Lisbon	Лиссабо́н	Oxford	О́ксфорд
Little Rock	Литл-Ро́к		
Liverpool	Ливерпу́ль (*m.*)	Paris	Пари́ж
Ljubljana	Любля́на	Perth	Перт
London	Ло́ндон	Philadelphia	Филаде́льфия
Los Angeles	Лос-А́нджелес	Phnom Penh	Пномпе́нь (*m.*)
Louisville	Лу́исвилл	Phoenix	Фи́никс
Luanda	Луа́нда	Pisa	Пи́за
Lucerne	Люце́рн	Pittsburgh	Пи́тсбург
Lusaka	Луса́ка	Plymouth	Пли́мут
Lvov	Льво́в	Port-au-Prince	Порт-о-Пре́нс
Lyons	Лио́н	Portland	По́ртленд
		Portsmouth	По́ртсмут
Madrid	Мадри́д	Prague	Пра́га
Managua	Мана́гуа	Pretoria	Прето́рия
Manchester	Ма́нчестер	Providence	Про́виденс
Manila	Мани́ла	Pyongyang	Пхенья́н
Marseilles	Марсе́ль (*m.*)		
Mecca	Ме́кка	Quebec	Квебе́к
Melbourne	Ме́льбурн	Quito	Ки́то
Memphis	Ме́мфис		
Mexico City	Ме́хико	Raleigh	Ро́ли
Miami	Майа́ми	Rangoon	Рангу́н
Milan	Мила́н	Rawalpindi	Раваллпи́нди
Milwaukee	Милуо́ки	Regina	Риджа́йна
Minneapolis	Миннеа́полис	Reno	Ри́но
Minsk	Минск	Reykjavik	Ре́йкьявик
Mobile	Моби́л	Richmond	Ри́чмонд
Mogadishu	Могади́шо	Riga	Ри́га
Mombasa	Момба́са	Rio de Janeiro	Ри́о-де-Жане́йро
Montevideo	Монтевиде́о	Riyadh	Эр-Рия́д
Montreal	Монреа́ль (*m.*)	Rochester	Ро́честер
Moscow	Москва́	Rome	Рим
Munich	Мю́нхен	Rotterdam	Ро́ттердам
Murmansk	Му́рманск		
Mysore	Майсу́р	Saigon	Сайго́н
		St. Louis	Сент-Лу́ис
Nairobi	Найро́би	St. Paul	Сент-По́л
Naples	Неа́поль (*m.*)	St. Petersburg	Санкт-Петербу́рг
Nashville	На́швилл	Salt Lake City	Солт-Лейк-Си́ти
Nassau	На́ссау	Samarkand	Самарка́нд
Nazareth	Назаре́т	San Diego	Сан-Дие́го
Newark	Нью́арк	San Francisco	Сан-Франци́ско
New Delhi	Де́ли	San Juan	Сан-Хуа́н
New Orleans	Но́вый Орлеа́н	Santiago	Сантья́го
New York	Нью-Йо́рк	São Paulo	Сан-Па́улу
Nice	Ни́цца	Sarajevo	Сарае́во
Nicosia	Никоси́я	Seattle	Сиэ́тл
Nizhniy Novgorod	Ни́жний Но́вгород	Seoul	Сеу́л
Nottingham	Но́ттингем	Sevastopol	Севасто́поль (*m.*)
Novosibirsk	Новосиби́рск	Seville	Севи́лья
Nuremburg	Ню́рнберг	Shanghai	Шанха́й
		Skopje	Ско́пье
Oakland	О́кленд	Sofia	Софи́я
Odessa	Оде́сса	Southampton	Саутге́мптон
Omaha	О́маха	Stockholm	Стокго́льм
Osaka	О́сака	Strasbourg	Страсбу́рг
Oslo	О́сло		

Stuttgart	Шту́тгарт
Sydney	Си́дней
Taipei	Тайбэ́й
Tallinn	Та́ллин
Tashkent	Ташке́нт
Tbilisi	Тбили́си
Tegucigalpa	Тегусига́льпа
Teheran	Тегера́н
Tel Aviv	Тель-Ави́в
Tirana	Тира́на
Tokyo	То́кио
Toronto	Торо́нто
Trieste	Трие́ст
Tripoli	Три́поли
Tulsa	Та́лса
Tunis	Туни́с
Turin	Тури́н
Tver	Тверь (*f.*)
Ulan Bator	Ула́н-Ба́тор
Vancouver	Ванку́вер
Venice	Вене́ция
Versailles	Верса́ль (*m.*)
Victoria	Викто́рия
Vienna	Ве́на
Vientiane	Вьентья́н
Vilnius	Ви́льнюс
Vladivostok	Владивосто́к
Volgograd	Волгогра́д
Warsaw	Варша́ва
Washington	Вашингто́н
Wellington	Ве́ллингтон
Wilmington	Уи́лмингтон
Winnipeg	Ви́ннипег
Wroclaw	Вро́цлав
Yekaterinburg	Екатеринбу́рг
Yerevan	Ерева́н
Yokohama	Йокоха́ма
York	Йорк
Zagreb	За́греб
Zurich	Цю́рих

SECTIONS OF CITIES

Brighton Beach	Бра́йтон Би́ч
Bronx	Бронкс
Brooklyn	Бру́клин
Coney Island	Ко́ни-А́йленд
Harlem	Га́рлем
Hollywood	Го́лливуд
Manhattan	Манха́ттан
Montmartre	Монма́ртр
Queens	Квинс

Soho	Со́хо
Westminster	Ве́стминстер

OCEANS

Arctic	Се́верный Ледови́тый океа́н
Atlantic	Атланти́ческий океа́н
Indian	Инди́йский океа́н
Pacific	Ти́хий океа́н

SEAS

Adriatic	Адриати́ческое мо́ре
Aegean	Эге́йское мо́ре
Arabian	Арави́йское мо́ре
Aral	Ара́льское мо́ре
Azov, of	Азо́вское мо́ре
Baltic	Балти́йское мо́ре
Bering	Бе́рингово мо́ре
Black	Чёрное мо́ре
Caribbean	Кари́бское мо́ре
Caspian	Каспи́йское мо́ре
Dead	Мёртвое мо́ре
Irish	Ирла́ндское мо́ре
Japan, of	Япо́нское мо́ре
Mediterranean	Средизе́мное мо́ре
North	Се́верное мо́ре
Okhotsk	Охо́тское мо́ре
Red	Кра́сное мо́ре
South China	Ю́жно-Кита́йское мо́ре
White	Бе́лое мо́ре
Yellow	Жёлтое мо́ре

LAKES

Albert	о́зеро Альбе́рт
Baikal	Байка́л
Chad	о́зеро Чад
Erie	о́зеро Э́ри
Great Bear	Большо́е Медве́жье о́зеро
Great Salt	Большо́е Солёное о́зеро
Great Slave	Большо́е Нево́льничье о́зеро

Huron	о́зеро Гуро́н
Ladoga	Ладо́жское о́зеро
Michigan	о́зеро Мичига́н
Onega	Оне́жское о́зеро
Ontario	о́зеро Онта́рио
Superior	о́зеро Ве́рхнее
Tanganyika	о́зеро Танганьи́ка
Titicaca	о́зеро Титика́ка
Victoria	Викто́рия

RIVERS

Amazon	Амазо́нка
Amur	Аму́р
Angara	Ангара́
Arno	А́рно
Columbia	Колу́мбия
Congo	Ко́нго
Danube	Дуна́й
Delaware	Де́лавэр
Dnieper	Днепр
Dniester	Днестр
Don	Дон
Elbe	Э́льба
Euphrates	Евфра́т
Ganges	Ганг
Hudson	Гудзо́н
Indus	Инд
Irrawaddy	Ирава́ди
Irtysh	Ирты́ш
Jordan	Иорда́н
Lena	Ле́на
Loire	Луа́ра
Mackenzie	Макке́нзи
Mekong	Меко́нг
Mississippi	Миссиси́пи
Missouri	Миссу́ри
Neva	Нева́
Niger	Ни́гер
Nile	Нил
Ob	Обь
Oder	О́дер
Ohio	Ога́йо
Orinoco	Орино́ко
Paraná	Парана́
Po	По
Potomac	Пото́мак

Rhine	Рейн
Rhone	Ро́на
Rio Grande	Ри́о-Гра́нде
St. Lawrence	Свято́го Лавре́нтия
Seine	Се́на
Susquehanna	Саскуэха́нна
Thames	Те́мза
Tigris	Тигр
Vistula	Ви́сла
Volga	Во́лга
Volta	Во́льта
Yangtze	Янцзы́
Yellow	Жёлтая
Yenisei	Енисе́й
Yukon	Ю́кон
Zambezi	Замбе́зи

GULFS, BAYS, STRAITS, CHANNELS, CANALS

Aden, Gulf of	А́денский зали́в
Aqaba, Gulf of	Ака́бский зали́в
Bengal, Bay of	Бенга́льский зали́в
Bering Strait	Бе́рингов проли́в
Biscay, Bay of	Биска́йский зали́в
Bosp(h)oros	Босфо́р
English Channel	Ла-Ма́нш
Gibraltar, Strait of	Гибралта́рский проли́в
Hormuz, Strait of	Хорму́зский проли́в
Hudson Bay	Гудзо́нов зали́в
Kiel Canal	Ки́льский кана́л
Magellan, Strait of	Магелла́нов проли́в
Mexico, Gulf of	Мексика́нский зали́в
Oman, Gulf of	Ома́нский зали́в
Panama Canal	Пана́мский кана́л
Persian Gulf	Перси́дский зали́в
Suez Canal	Суэ́цкий кана́л

MOUNTAIN RANGES

Adirondacks	Адиро́ндак
Alleghenies	Аллега́ны
Alps	А́льпы
Andes	А́нды
Appalachians	Аппала́чи
Carpathians	Карпа́ты
Catskills	го́ры Ка́тскилл
Caucasus	Кавка́з

Himalayas	Гимала́и
Pyrenees	Пирене́и
Rocky Mountains	Скали́стые го́ры
Urals	Ура́л
Vosges	Воге́зы

MOUNTAIN PEAKS

Ararat	Арара́т
Elbrus	Эльбру́с
Etna	Э́тна
Everest	Эвере́ст
Fuji, Fujiyama	Фудзия́ма
Kilimanjaro	Килиманджа́ро
Matterhorn	Ма́ттерхорн
Mauna Loa	Ма́уна-Ло́а
McKinley	Мак-Ки́нли
Mont Blanc	Монбла́н
Pike's Peak	Пайкс-Пик
Popocatepetl	Попокате́петль
Ranier	Рейни́р
Sinai	Сина́й
Vesuvius	Везу́вий
Whitney	Уи́тни

FAMOUS NAMES

Adams	А́дамс
Aeschylus	Эсхи́л
Aesop	Эзо́п
Andersen	А́ндерсен
Archimedes	Архиме́д
Aristophanes	Аристофа́н
Aristotle	Аристо́тель
Atatürk	Ататю́рк
Attila	Атти́ла
Bach	Бах
Bacon	Бэ́кон
Balzac	Бальза́к
Beethoven	Бетхо́вен
Bismarck	Би́смарк
Bizet	Бизе́
Boccaccio	Бокка́ччо
Bolivar	Боли́вар
Borodin	Бороди́н
Botticelli	Боттиче́лли
Brahms	Брамс
Brezhnev	Бре́жнев
Bronte	Бро́нте
Browning	Бра́унинг

Bruegel	Бре́йгель
Buddha	Бу́дда
Burbank	Бе́рбанк
Burns	Бёрнс
Bush	Буш
Byron	Ба́йрон
Caesar	Це́зарь
Calvin	Кальви́н
Caruso	Кару́зо
Cervantes	Серва́нтес
Cézanne	Сеза́нн
Chagall	Шага́л
Chaplin	Ча́плин
Charlemagne	Карл Вели́кий
Chaucer	Чо́сер
Chekhov	Че́хов
Chopin	Шопе́н
Christ	Христо́с
Churchill	Че́рчилль
Cicero	Цицеро́н
Clausewitz	Кла́узевиц
Clemenceau	Клемансо́
Clinton	Кли́нтон
Columbus	Колу́мб
Confucius	Конфу́ций
Copernicus	Копе́рник
Corneille	Корне́ль
Cortés	Корте́с
Cromwell	Кро́мвель
Curie	Кюри́
Dante	Да́нте
Darwin	Да́рвин
da Vinci	да Ви́нчи
Debussy	Дебюсси́
de Gaulle	де Голль
Demosthenes	Демосфе́н
Descartes	Дека́рт
Diaghilev	Дя́гилев
Dickens	Ди́ккенс
Diderot	Дидро́
Diogenes	Диоге́н
Disraeli	Дизра́эли
Dostoyevsky	Достое́вский
Dreiser	Дра́йзер
Dryden	Дра́йден
Dvorak	Дво́ржак
Edison	Э́дисон
Einstein	Эйнште́йн
Eisenhower	Эйзенха́уэр
Emerson	Э́мерсон
Erasmus	Эра́зм
Euripides	Еврипи́д
Faulkner	Фо́лкнер
Flaubert	Флобе́р
Franco	Фра́нко

Franklin	Фра́нклин	Marshall	Ма́ршалл
Freud	Фрейд	Marx	Маркс
		Matisse	Мати́сс
Galileo	Галиле́й	Maugham	Мо́эм
Gandhi	Га́нди	Mayakovsky	Маяко́вский
Garibaldi	Гариба́льди	Melville	Ме́лвилл
Gauguin	Гоге́н	Mendeleyev	Менделе́ев
Genghis Khan	Чингисха́н	Mendelssohn	Ме́ндельсон
Gershwin	Ге́ршвин	Metternich	Ме́ттерних
Goethe	Гёте	Michelangelo	Микела́нджело
Gogol	Го́голь	Milton	Ми́льтон
Gorbachev	Горбачёв	Mohammed	Муха́ммед
Gorki	Го́рький	Molière	Молье́р
Goya	Го́йя	Monet	Моне́
Grieg	Григ	Montesquieu	Монтескьё
Gutenberg	Гу́тенберг	Mozart	Мо́царт
		Mussolini	Муссоли́ни
Hamilton	Га́мильтон		
Hammarskjöld	Ха́ммаршельд	Nabokov	Набо́ков
Handel	Ге́ндель	Napoleon	Наполео́н
Hannibal	Ганниба́л	Newton	Нью́тон
Hawthorne	Хо́торн	Nietzsche	Ни́цше
Haydn	Гайдн	Nijinsky	Нижи́нский
Hegel	Ге́гель	Nixon	Ни́ксон
Hemingway	Хемингуэ́й		
Herodotus	Геродо́т	Paderewski	Падере́вский
Hippocrates	Гиппокра́т	Pasternak	Пастерна́к
Hitler	Ги́тлер	Pasteur	Пасте́р
Homer	Гоме́р	Pericles	Пери́кл
Horace	Гора́ций	Picasso	Пика́ссо
Hugo	Гюго́	Plato	Плато́н
		Poe	По
Jefferson	Джефферсон	Prokofiev	Проко́фьев
Joan of Arc	Жа́нна д'Арк	Proust	Пруст
Johnson	Джо́нсон	Puccini	Пуччи́ни
Joyce	Джойс	Pushkin	Пу́шкин
Kafka	Ка́фка	Rabelais	Рабле́
Keats	Китс	Rachmaninov	Рахма́нинов
Kennedy	Ке́ннеди	Racine	Раси́н
Kerensky	Ке́ренский	Raphael	Рафаэ́ль
Khrushchev	Хрущёв	Rasputin	Распу́тин
King	Кинг	Reagan	Ре́йган
Kipling	Ки́плинг	Rembrandt	Ре́мбрандт
Krylov	Крыло́в	Renoir	Ренуа́р
		Richelieu	Ришелье́
Lenin	Ле́нин	Robespierre	Робеспье́р
Lincoln	Ли́нкольн	Rockefeller	Рокфе́ллер
Linnaeus	Линне́й	Rodin	Роде́н
Liszt	Лист	Roosevelt	Ру́звельт
Lomonosov	Ломоно́сов	Rousseau	Руссо́
Longfellow	Лонгфе́лло	Rubens	Ру́бенс
Luther	Лю́тер		
		Sakharov	Са́харов
MacArthur	Мака́ртур	Sartre	Сартр
Machiavelli	Макиаве́лли	Schumann	Шу́ман
Madison	Ме́дисон	Schweitzer	Шве́йцер
Magellan	Магелла́н	Scott	Скотт
Manet	Мане́	Shakespeare	Шекспи́р
Mao Tse-tung	Ма́о Цзэ-ду́н		

Shaw	Шóу	Tolstoy	Толстóй
Shelley	Шéлли	Trostsky	Трóцкий
Shostakovich	Шостакóвич	Truman	Трýмэн
Sibelius	Сибéлиус	Turgenev	Тургéнев
Socrates	Сокрáт		
Solzhenitsyn	Солженицын	van Gogh	ван Гог
Sophocles	Софóкл	Verdi	Вéрди
Stalin	Стáлин	Virgil	Вергилий
Steinbeck	Стéйнбек	Voltaire	Вольтéр
Stendahl	Стендáль		
Strauss	Штрáус	Wagner	Вáгнер
Stravinsky	Стравинский	Washington	Вáшингтон
		Webster	Уэбстер
Talleyrand	Талейрáн	Whitman	Уитмен
Tamerlane	Тимýр	Wilson	Вильсон
Tchaikovsky	Чайкóвский	Wordsworth	Вóрдсворт
Tennyson	Тéннисон	Wright	Райт
Thackeray	Тéккерей		
Thatcher	Тэтчер	Xenophon	Ксенофóнт
Thoreau	Тóро		
Thucydides	Фукидид	Yeats	Йитс
Tito	Тито	Yeltsin	Éльцин
		Zola	Золя́